# The Form Book®

## Flat Annual for 2005

All the 2004 returns

## The BHB's Official Record

Complete record of all Flat racing
from 9 November 2003 to
6 November 2004

totesport

Published by Raceform Ltd
Compton, Newbury, Berkshire, RG20 6NL
Raceform Limited is a wholly owned subsidiary of MGN Limited



ISBN 1-904317-59-6

Printed by William Clowes Ltd, Beccles, Suffolk.



Cover photo: Attraction (left) wins the Coronation Stakes
at Royal Ascot from Majestic Desert and Red Bloom
(Photo: © Edward Whitaker/Racing Post)

# CONTENTS



Editor: Graham Dench

Head of Analysis Team: Ashley Rumney

Race Analysts & Notebook Writers:
Dave Bellingham, Mark Brown, Steffan Edwards, Walter Glynn,
Keith Hewitt, Richard Lowther, Lee McKenzie, David Orton,
Darren Owen, Neville Ring, Colin Roberts, Ashley Rumney,
Desmond Stoneham, David Toft, Ron Wood, Richard Young.

Production: Ashley Rumney & Richard Lowther

# The Form Book

# Flat Racing Annual 2005

Welcome to the 2005 edition of *The Form Book,* now in A4 format to accommodate the increased fixture list and featuring enhanced editorial.

Race details contain Racing Post Ratings assessing the merit of each individual performance, speed figures for every horse that clocks a worthwhile time, weight-for-age allowances, stall positions for every race and the starting price percentage, in addition to the traditional features.

A race Focus is included after the result and endeavours to combiner the opinions o fthe notebook writer, the handicapper, speed figure expert and, where appropriate, the paddock observer in order to provide a snapshot of the merit of each individual race The extended Notebook comments are printed below each race and cover all horses which are considered worthy of inclusion by our expert race-readers and analysts. The comments provide an analysis of the winning performance and, where applicable, explain possible reasons for improvement or attempt to explain why any horse failed to run to its best. More importantly, our team will also indicate the conditions under which horses are likely to be seen to best advantage.

---

## The official record

**THE FORM BOOK** records comprehensive race details of every domestic race, every major European Group race and every foreign event in which a British-trained runner participated. In the **NOTEBOOK** section, extended interpretation is provided for all runners worthy of a mention, including all placed horses and all favourites. Generally speaking, the higher the class of race, the greater the number of runners noted.

**MEETING BACK REFERENCE NUMBER** is the Raceform number of the last meeting run at the track and is shown to the left of the course name. Abandoned meetings are signified by a dagger.

**THE GOING**, The Official going, shown at the head of each meeting, is recorded as follows: Turf: Hard; Firm; Good to firm; Good; Good to soft; Soft; Heavy.
All-Weather: Fast; Standard; Slow.
There may be variations for non-British meetings

New for 2004, where appropriate, is a section indicating track bias and any differences to the official going indicated by race times.

**THE WEATHER** is shown below to th e date for selected meetings.

**THE WIND** is given as a strength and direction at the Winning Post, classified as follows:
Strength: gale; v.str; str; fresh; mod; slt; almost nil; nil.
Direction: (half) against; (half) bhd; (half) across from or towards stands.

**VISIBILITY** is good unless otherwise stated.

**RACE NUMBERS** for Foreign races carry the suffix 'a' in the race header and in the index.

**RACE TITLE** is the name of the race as shown in the Racing Calendar.

**COMPETITIVE RACING CLASSIFICATIONS** are shown on a scale from Class A to Class H. All Pattern races are Class A.

**THE RACE DISTANCE** is given for all races, and is accompanied by (s) for races run on straight courses and (r) for courses where there is a round track of comparable distance. On some tracks the course is identified by a specific name i.e. (J) for Jubilee . On All-Weather courses (F) for Fibresand or (P) for Polytrack indicates the nature of the artificial surface on which the race is run.

**OFFICIAL RACE TIME** as published in the Racing Calendar is followed in parentheses by the time when the race actually started. This is followed by the race class, age restrictions, handicap restrictions and the official rating of the top weight.

**PRIZE MONEY** shows penalty values down to sixth place (where applicable).

**THE POSITION OF THE STARTING STALLS** is shown against each race, in the form of: High (H), Centre (C) or Low (L). If one stands at the start facing towards the finish, the stalls are numbered from left to right. If the stalls are placed adjacent to the left rail they are described as low, if against the right rail they are described as high. Otherwise they are central.

**IN THE RACE RESULT**, the figures to the far left of each horse (under FORM) shows the most recent form figures. The figure in bold is the finishing position in this race as detailed below.

**1...40** - finishing positions first to fortieth; **b** - brought down;
**c** - carried out; **f** - fell; **p** - pulled up; **r** - refused; **ro** - ran out;
**s** - slipped up; **u** - unseated rider; **v** - void race.

A figure to the left of the Raceform Note-Book comment is the last race in which the horse warranted an extended comment.

**THE OFFICIAL DISTANCES** between the horses are shown on the left-hand side immediately after their position at the finish.

**NUMBER OF DAYS SINCE PREVIOUS RUN** is the superscript figure immediately following the horse name and suffix.

**PREVIOUS RACEFORM RACE NUMBER** is the boxed figure to the right of the horse's name.

**THE HORSE'S AGE** is shown immediately before the weight carried.

**WEIGHTS** shown are actual weights carried.

**OFFICIAL RATING** is the figure in bold type directly after the horse's name in the race result. This figure indicates the Official BHB rating, at entry, after the following adjustments had been made:
(i) Overweight carried by the rider.
(ii) The number of pounds out of the handicap (if applicable).
(iii) Penalties incurred after the publication of the weights.
However, no adjustments have been made for:
(i) Weight-for-age.
(ii) Riders' claims.

**HEADGEAR** is shown immediately befoe the jockey's name and in parentheses and expressed as: **b** (blinkers); **v** (visor); **h** (hood); **e** (eyeshield); **c** (eyecover); **p** (sheepskin cheekpieces).

**THE JOCKEY** is shown for every runner followed, in superscript, by apprentice allowances in parentheses.

**APPRENTICE ALLOWANCES** The holders of apprentice jockeys' licences under the provisions of Rule 60(iii) are permitted to claim the following allowances in Flat races:
7lb until they have won 20 Flat races run under the Rules of any recognised
Turf Authority; thereafter 5lb until they have won 50 such Flat races; thereafter 3lb until they have won 95 such Flat races.
These allowances can be claimed in the Flat races set out below, with the exception of races confined to apprentice jockeys:
(a) All handicap handicaps other than those Rated stakes which are classified as listed races.
(b) All selling and claiming races.
(b) All weight-for-age races classified C, D, E, F, G and H.

**THE DRAW** for places at the start is shown after each jockey's name.

**RACING POST RATINGS**, which record the level of performance attained in this race for each horse, appear in the column under each horse. These are the work of handicappers Simon Turner and Paul Curtis, who head a dedicated team dealing with Flat races for Raceform and sister publication, the *Racing Post*.

**THE TRAINER** is shown for every runner.

**COMMENT-IN-RUNNING** is shown for each horse in an abbreviated form. Details of abbreviations appear later in this section.

**STARTING PRICES** appear below the jockey in the race result. The favourite indicator appears to the right of the Starting Price; 1 for the favourite, 2 for the second-favourite and 3 for third-favourite. Joint favourites share the same number.

**RACE TIMES** in Great Britain are official times which are electronically recorded and shown to 100th of a second. Figures in parentheses following the time show the number of seconds faster or slower than the Raceform Median Time for the course and distance.

**RACEFORM MEDIAN TIMES** are compiled from all races run over the course and distance in the preceding five years. Times equal to the median are shown as (0.00). Times under the median are preceded by minus, for instance, 1.8 seconds under the median would be shown (-1.8). Record times are displayed either referring to the juvenile record (1.2 under 2y best) or to the overall record (1.2 under best).

**GOING CORRECTION** appears against each race to allow for changing conditions of the ground. It is shown to a hundredth of a second and indicates the adjustment per furlong against the median time. The going based on the going correction is shown in parentheses and is recorded in the following stages:
Turf: HD (Hard); F (Firm); GF (Good to firm); G (Good); GS (Good to soft); S (Soft); HVY (Heavy). All-Weather: FST (Fast); STD (Standard); SLW (Slow)

**WEIGHT-FOR-AGE** allowances are given where applicable for mixed-age races.

**STARTING PRICE PERCENTAGE** follows the going correction and weight-for-age details, and gives the total SP percentage of all runners that competed. It precedes the number of runners taking part in the race.

**SELLING DETAILS** (where applicable) and details of any claim are given. Friendly claims are not detailed.

**SPEED RATINGS** appear below the race time and going correction. Raceform Speed Ratings are not directly comparable with BHB and RPR ratings and are an expression of a horse's speed in terms of lengths-per-mile as opposed to pounds in weight. Theoretically, if one horse has a speed figure five points superior to another and both horses run to their best form in a race run over a mile, the first horse should beat the second by five lengths. In a race run over two miles the margin should be ten lengths and so on.

The speed ratings are the work of acknowledged expert Dave Bellingham, and the figues take no account of the effect of weight, either historically or on the day. That component is left completely to the user's discretion. What is shown is the speed rating represented in its purest form, rather than one that is altered for weight using a mathematical formula that treats all types of horses as if they are the same.

Before the speed figures can be calculated, it is necessary to establish a set of standard or median times for every distance at every track. This is achieved by looking at the times recorded by all winners over a particular trip going back several years (in order to get a large enough sample) and producing an average. A distance has to have enough races run over it in order to produce a reliable median time, otherwise no median is calculated and no speed ratings are produced for races over that trip.

Once a meeting has taken place, a 'raw' unadjusted speed rating is calculated for each winner on the card. This is done by working out how many lengths per mile the winning time was faster or slower than the median for the trip. A difference of 0.2 of a second equals one length. The raw speed ratings of all winners on the card are then compared with a 'par' figure for the class of race, which is a rating that should be achievable by the average winner in that class of race. The idea is that the better-class horses should run faster compared with the median time than horses of lesser ability.

The difference between the 'raw' speed rating and the 'par' figure for each race is then noted. The fastest and slowest races compared with the par are then discarded and the rest are averaged to produce the going allowance or track variant. This figure gives an idea of as to how much the elements, of which the going is one, have affected the final times of each race.

The figure representing the going allowance is then used to adjust the raw speed figures and produce the final ratings, which represent how fast the winners would have run on a perfectly good surface with no external influences including the weather. The ratings for beaten horses are worked out by taking the number of lengths they were behind the winner, adjusting that to take into account the distance of the race and deducted from the winner's rating.

**TOTE** prices include £1 stake. Exacta dividends are shown in parentheses. The Computer Straight Forecast dividend is preceded by the letters CSF, Computer Tricast is preceded by CT and Tote Trio dividend is preceded by the word Trio. Jackpot, Placepot and Quadpot details appear at the end of the meeting to which they refer.

**OWNER** is followed by the breeder's name and the trainer's location.

**STEWARDS' INQUIRIES** are included with the result, and any suspensions and/or fines incurred. Objections by jockeys and officials are included, where relevant.

**HISTORICAL FOCUS** details occasional points of historical significance.

**FOCUS** The Focus section has been enhanced to help readers distinguish good races from bad races and reliable form from unreliable form, by drawing together the opinions of handicapper, time expert and paddock watcher and interpreting their views in a punter-friendly manner.

**NOTEBOOK** horses marked with the diamond symbol are those deemed by our racereaders especially worthy of note in future races.

**OFFICIAL EXPLANATIONS,** where the horse is deemed to have run well above or below expectation, are included in the Notebook section.

# Abbreviations and their meanings

## Paddock comments

gd sort - well made, above average on looks
h.d.w - has done well, improved in looks
wl grwn - well grown, has filled to its frame
lengthy - longer than average for its height
tall - tall
rangy - lengthy and tall but in proportion, covers a deal of ground
scope - scope for physical development
str - strong, powerful looking
w'like - workmanlike, ordinary in looks
lt-f - light-framed, not much substance
cmpt - compact
neat - smallish, well put together
leggy - long legs compared with body
angular - unfurnished behind the saddle, not filled to frame
unf - unfurnished in the midriff, not filled to frame
narrow - not as wide as side appearance would suggest
small - lacks any physical scope
nt grwn - not grown
lw - looked fit and well
bkwd - backward in condition
t - tubed
swtg - sweating
b (off fore or nr fore) - bandaged in front
b.hind (off or nr) - bandaged behind

## At the start

stdd s - jockey purposely reins back the horse
dwlt - missed the break and left for a short time
s.s - slow to start, left longer than a horse that dwelt
s.v.s - started very slowly
s.i.s - started on terms but took time to get going
ref to r - either does not jump off, or travels a few yards and then stops
rel to r - tries to pull itself up in mid-race
w.r.s - whipped round start

## Position in the race

led - in lead on its own
disp ld - upsides the leader

w ldr - almost upsides the leader
w ldrs - in a line of three or more disputing the lead
prom - on the heels of the leaders, in the front third of the field
trckd ldr(s) - just in behind the leaders giving impression that it could lead if asked
chsd ldr - horse in second place
chsd clr ldrs - horse heads main body of field behind two clear leaders
chsd ldrs - horse is in the first four or five but making more of an effort to stay close to the pace than if it were tracking the leaders.
clsd - closed
in tch - close enough to have a chance
hdwy - making ground on the leader
gd hdwy - making ground quickly on the leader, could be a deliberate move
sme hdwy - making some ground but no real impact on the race
stdy hdwy - gradually making ground
ev ch - upsides the leaders when the race starts in earnest
rr - at the back of main group but not detached
bhd - detached from the main body of runners
hld up - restrained as a deliberate tactical move
nt rcvr - lost all chance after interference, mistake etc.
wknd - stride shortened as it began to tire
lost tch - had been in the main body but a gap appeared as it tired
lost pl - remains in main body of runners but lost several positions quickly

## Riding

effrt - short-lived effort
pushed along - received urgings with hands only, jockey not using legs
rdn - received urgings from the saddle, including use of the whip
hrd rdn - received maximum assistance from the saddle including use of whip
drvn - received forceful urgings, jockey putting in a lot of effort and using whip
hrd drvn - jockey very animated, plenty of kicking, pushing and reminders

## Finishing comments

jst failed - closing rapidly on the winner and probably would have led a stride after the line
r.o - jockey's efforts usually involved to produce an increase in pace without finding an appreciable turn of speed
r.o wl - jockey's efforts usually involved to produce an obvious increase in pace without finding an appreciable turn of speed
unable qckn - not visibly tiring but does not possess a sufficient change of pace
one pce - not tiring but does not find a turn of speed, from a position further out than unable qckn
nt r.o. - did not consent to respond to pressure
styd on - going on well towards the end, utilising stamina
nvr able to chal - unable to produce sufficient to reach a challenging position
nvr nr to chal - in the opinion of the racereader, the horse was never in a suitable position to challenge.
nrst fin - nearer to the winner in distance beaten than at any time since the race had begun in earnest
nvr nrr - nearer to the winner position-wise than at any time since the race had begun in earnest
rallied - responded to pressure to come back with a chance having lost its place
no ex - unable to sustain its run
bttr for r - likely to improve for the run and experience
rn green - inclined to wander and falter through inexperience
too much to do - left with too much leeway to make up

## Winning comments

v.easily - a great deal in hand
easily - plenty in hand
comf - something in hand, always holding the others
pushed out - kept up to its work with hands and heels without jockey resorting to whip or kicking along and wins fairly comfortably
rdn out - pushed and kicked out to the line, with the whip employed
drvn out - pushed and kicked out to the line, with considerable effort and the whip employed
all out - nothing to spare, could not have found any more
jst hld on - holding on to a rapidly diminishing lead, could not have found any more if passed
unchal - must either make all or a majority of the running and not be challenged from an early stage

# Complete list of abbreviations

a - always
gng - going
qckn - quicken
a.p - always prominent
gp - group
r - race
abt - about
grad - gradually
racd - raced
appr - approaching
grnd - ground
rch - reach
awrdd - awarded
hd - head
rcvr - recover
b.b.v - broke blood-vessel
hdd - headed
rdn - ridden
b.d - brought down
hdwy - headway
rdr - rider
bdly - badly
hld - held
reard - reared
bef - before
hmpd - hampered
ref - refused
bhd - behind
imp - impression
rn - ran
bk - back
ins - inside
rnd - round
blkd - baulked
j.b - jumped badly
r.o - ran on
blnd - blundered
j.w - jumped well
rr - rear
bmpd - bumped

jnd - joined
rspnse - response
bnd - bend
jst - just
rt - right
btn- beaten
kpt - kept
s - start
bttr - better
l - length
sddle - saddle
c - came
ld - lead
shkn - shaken
ch - chance
ldr - leader
slt - slight
chal - challenged
lft - left
sme - some
chse - chase
m - mile
sn - soon
chsd - chased
m.n.s - made no show
spd- speed
chsng - chasing
mde - made

st - straight
circ - circuit
mod - moderate
stmbld - stumbled
cl - close
mid div - mid division
stdd - steadied
clr - clear
mstke - mistake
stdy - steady
clsd - closed
n.d - never dangerous
strly - strongly
comf - comfortably
n.g.t - not go through
styd - stayed
cpld - coupled
n.m.r - not much room
styng - staying
crse - course
nk - neck
s. u - slipped up
ct - caught
no ex - no extra
swtchd - switched
def - definite
nr - near
swvd - swerved

dismntd - dismounted
nrr - nearer
tk - took
disp - disputed
nrst fin - nearest finish
t.k.h - took keen hold
dist - distance
nt - not
t.o - tailed off
div - division
nvr - never
tch - touch
drvn - driven
one pce - one pace
thrght - throughout
dwlt - dwelt
out - from finish
trbld - troubled
edgd - edged
outpcd - outpaced
trckd - tracked
effrt - effort
p.u - pulled up
u.p - under pressure
ent - entering
pce - pace
u.str.p- under strong pressure

ev ch - every chance
pckd - pecked
w - with
ex - extra
pl - place
w.r.s - whipped round start
f - furlong
plcd - placed
wd - wide
fin - finished
plld - pulled
whn - when
fnd - found
press - pressure
wknd - weakened
fnl - final
prog - progress
wl - well
fr - from
prom - prominent
wnr - winner
gd - good
qckly - quickly
wnt - went
fi-wy ß- halfway

# Racing Post Ratings

**Racing Post Ratings for each horse are shown in the right hand column, headed RPR, and indicate the actual level of performance attained in that race. The figure in the back index represents the BEST public form that Raceform's Handicappers still believe the horse capable of reproducing.**

To use the ratings constructively in determining those horses best-in in future events, the following procedure should be followed:

(i) In races where all runners are the same age and are set to carry the same weight, no calculations are necessary. The horse with the highest rating is best-in.

(ii) In races where all runners are the same age but are set to carry different weights, add one point to the Raceform Rating for every pound less than 10 stone to be carried; deduct one point for every pound more than 10 stone.

For example,

| Horse | Age & wt | Adjustment from 10st | Base rating | Adjusted rating |
|---|---|---|---|---|
| Great Sport | 3-10-1 | -1 | 78 | 77 |
| Peter The Hermit | 3-9-13 | +1 | 80 | 81 |
| Let's Fly | 3-9-7 | +7 | 71 | 78 |
| Rossendale | 3-8-11 | +17 | 60 | 77 |

**Therefore Peter The Hermit is top-rated (best-in)**

(iii) In races concerning horses of different ages the procedure in (ii) should again be followed, but reference must also be made to the Official Scale of Weight-For-Age.

For example,

12 furlongs, July 20th

| Horse | Age & wt | Adjustment from 10st | Base rating | Adjusted rating | W-F-A deduct | Final rating |
|---|---|---|---|---|---|---|
| Kwang-Su | 5-10-0 | 0 | 90 | 90 | Nil | 90 |
| Nassorian | 4-9-9 | +5 | 88 | 88 | Nil | 88 |
| Dansellon | 3-9-4 | +10 | 85 | 95 | -12 | 83 |
| Dark Legend | 4-8-7 | +21 | 73 | 94 | Nil | 94 |

**Therefore Dark Legend is top-rated (best-in)**

(A 3-y-o is deemed 12lb less mature than a 4-y-o or older horse on 20th July over 12f. Therefore, the deduction of 12 points is necessary.)

The following symbols are used in conjunction with the ratings:

++: almost certain to prove better
+: likely to prove better
d: disappointing (has run well below best recently)
?: form hard to evaluate
t: tentative rating based on race-time rating may prove unreliable

**Weight adjusted ratings for every race are published daily in Raceform Private Handicap and our new service Raceform Private handicap ONLINE (www.raceform.co.uk).**

**For subscription terms please contact the Subscription Department on (01635) 578080.**

# The Official Scale of Weight, Age & Distance (Flat)

The following scale should only be used in conjunction with the Official ratings published in this book. Use of any other scale will introduce errors into calculations. The allowances are expressed as the number of pounds that is deemed the average horse in each group falls short of maturity at different dates and distances.

| Dist | | Jan | | Feb | | Mar | | Apr | | May | | Jun | | Jul | | Aug | | Sep | | Oct | | Nov | | Dec | |
|---|---|---|---|---|---|---|---|---|---|---|---|---|---|---|---|---|---|---|---|---|---|---|---|---|---|
| (fur) | Age | 1-15 | 16-31 | 1-14 | 15-28 | 1-15 | 16-31 | 1-15 | 16-30 | 1-15 | 16-31 | 1-15 | 16-30 | 1-15 | 16-31 | 1-15 | 16-31 | 1-15 | 16-30 | 1-15 | 16-31 | 1-15 | 16-30 | 1-15 | 16-31 |
| 5 | 2 | - | - | - | - | - | 47 | 44 | 41 | 38 | 36 | 34 | 32 | 30 | 28 | 26 | 24 | 22 | 20 | 19 | 18 | 17 | 17 | 16 | 16 |
| | 3 | 15 | 15 | 14 | 14 | 13 | 12 | 11 | 10 | 9 | 8 | 7 | 6 | 5 | 4 | 3 | 2 | 1 | 1 | - | - | - | - | - | - |
| 6 | 2 | - | - | - | - | - | - | - | - | 44 | 41 | 38 | 36 | 33 | 31 | 28 | 26 | 24 | 22 | 21 | 20 | 19 | 18 | 17 | 17 |
| | 3 | 16 | 16 | 15 | 15 | 14 | 13 | 12 | 11 | 10 | 9 | 8 | 7 | 6 | 5 | 4 | 3 | 2 | 2 | 1 | 1 | - | - | - | - |
| 7 | 2 | - | - | - | - | - | - | - | - | - | - | - | - | 38 | 35 | 32 | 30 | 27 | 25 | 23 | 22 | 21 | 20 | 19 | 19 |
| | 3 | 18 | 18 | 17 | 17 | 16 | 15 | 14 | 13 | 12 | 11 | 10 | 9 | 8 | 7 | 6 | 5 | 4 | 3 | 2 | 2 | 1 | 1 | - | - |
| 8 | 2 | - | - | - | - | - | - | - | - | - | - | - | - | - | - | 37 | 34 | 31 | 28 | 26 | 24 | 23 | 22 | 21 | 20 |
| | 3 | 20 | 20 | 19 | 19 | 18 | 17 | 15 | 14 | 13 | 12 | 11 | 10 | 9 | 8 | 7 | 6 | 5 | 4 | 3 | 3 | 2 | 2 | 1 | 1 |
| 9 | 3 | 22 | 22 | 21 | 21 | 20 | 19 | 17 | 15 | 14 | 13 | 12 | 11 | 10 | 9 | 8 | 7 | 6 | 5 | 4 | 4 | 3 | 3 | 2 | 2 |
| | 4 | 1 | 1 | - | - | - | - | - | - | - | - | - | - | - | - | - | - | - | - | - | - | - | - | - | - |
| 10 | 3 | 23 | 23 | 22 | 22 | 21 | 20 | 19 | 17 | 15 | 14 | 13 | 12 | 11 | 10 | 9 | 8 | 7 | 6 | 5 | 5 | 4 | 4 | 3 | 3 |
| | 4 | 2 | 2 | 1 | 1 | - | - | - | - | - | - | - | - | - | - | - | - | - | - | - | - | - | - | - | - |
| 11 | 3 | 24 | 24 | 23 | 23 | 22 | 21 | 20 | 19 | 17 | 15 | 14 | 13 | 12 | 11 | 10 | 9 | 8 | 7 | 6 | 6 | 5 | 5 | 4 | 4 |
| | 4 | 3 | 3 | 2 | 2 | 1 | 1 | - | - | - | - | - | - | - | - | - | - | - | - | - | - | - | - | - | - |
| 12 | 3 | 25 | 25 | 24 | 24 | 23 | 22 | 21 | 20 | 19 | 17 | 15 | 14 | 13 | 12 | 11 | 10 | 9 | 8 | 7 | 7 | 6 | 6 | 5 | 5 |
| | 4 | 4 | 4 | 3 | 3 | 2 | 2 | 1 | 1 | - | - | - | - | - | - | - | - | - | - | - | - | - | - | - | - |
| 13 | 3 | 26 | 26 | 25 | 25 | 24 | 23 | 22 | 21 | 20 | 19 | 17 | 15 | 14 | 13 | 12 | 11 | 10 | 9 | 8 | 8 | 7 | 7 | 6 | 6 |
| | 4 | 5 | 5 | 4 | 4 | 3 | 3 | 2 | 1 | - | - | - | - | - | - | - | - | - | - | - | - | - | - | - | - |
| 14 | 3 | 27 | 27 | 26 | 26 | 25 | 24 | 23 | 22 | 21 | 20 | 19 | 17 | 15 | 14 | 13 | 12 | 11 | 10 | 9 | 9 | 8 | 8 | 7 | 7 |
| | 4 | 6 | 6 | 5 | 5 | 4 | 4 | 3 | 2 | 1 | - | - | - | - | - | - | - | - | - | - | - | - | - | - | - |
| 15 | 3 | 28 | 28 | 27 | 27 | 26 | 25 | 24 | 23 | 22 | 21 | 20 | 19 | 17 | 15 | 14 | 13 | 12 | 11 | 10 | 9 | 8 | 8 | 7 | 7 |
| | 4 | 6 | 6 | 5 | 5 | 4 | 4 | 3 | 3 | 2 | 1 | - | - | - | - | - | - | - | - | - | - | - | - | - | - |
| 16 | 3 | 29 | 29 | 28 | 28 | 27 | 26 | 25 | 24 | 23 | 22 | 21 | 20 | 19 | 17 | 15 | 14 | 13 | 12 | 11 | 10 | 9 | 9 | 8 | 8 |
| | 4 | 7 | 7 | 6 | 6 | 5 | 5 | 4 | 4 | 3 | 2 | 1 | - | - | - | - | - | - | - | - | - | - | - | - | - |
| 18 | 3 | 31 | 31 | 30 | 30 | 29 | 28 | 27 | 26 | 25 | 24 | 23 | 22 | 21 | 20 | 18 | 16 | 14 | 13 | 12 | 11 | 10 | 10 | 9 | 9 |
| | 4 | 8 | 8 | 7 | 7 | 6 | 6 | 5 | 5 | 4 | 3 | 2 | 1 | - | - | - | - | - | - | - | - | - | - | - | - |
| 20 | 3 | 33 | 33 | 32 | 32 | 31 | 30 | 29 | 28 | 27 | 26 | 25 | 24 | 23 | 22 | 20 | 18 | 16 | 14 | 13 | 12 | 11 | 11 | 10 | 10 |
| | 4 | 9 | 9 | 8 | 8 | 7 | 7 | 6 | 6 | 5 | 4 | 3 | 2 | 1 | - | - | - | - | - | - | - | - | - | - | - |

# Effect of the draw

## (R.H.) denotes right-hand and (L.H.) left-hand courses.

**RULES OF RACING No. 28 (v): The Starter shall check the runners and riders and, for Flat races, assign the horses to the places drawn by lot, all horses taking their place at the Start in the order drawn for them. The rider who has drawn No. 1 must always be placed on the left and the other riders must take their places in consecutive numbers from the left. Presuming the Stands are on the outside of the course, on right-handed courses, low numbers will be towards the stands' rail at the start of the race. On left-handed courses, high numbers will be towards the stands' rail.**

**ASCOT (R-H)** - When the ground rides soft, runners invariably tack over towards the outside rail down the side of the course in races of beyond 1m. This part of the course is partially covered by overhanging trees and the ground is definitely at its quickest there, presumably as it is sheltered, but this seems common knowledge among the jockeys. Prior to the 2000 season, low numbers were often thought to have the advantage on the straight course when fields were at their biggest, irrespective of the ground, but this is no longer the case. At the Royal Meeting two years ago, runners racing widest had an edge, while last season there wasn't a great deal in it bar the odd meeting. The one factor that does lead to one flank dominating is truly heavy/bottomless ground, when it's a case of the nearer to the far rail (high) the better. High numbers also seem to do best in the 2m4f Ascot Stakes at the Royal Meeting, with runners drawn low often forced to use early energy to gain a position.

**AYR (L-H)** - Between 1995 and 1997 and particularly in 1996 and 1997, a high draw proved crucial in both the Gold and Silver Cups on fast ground, with runners drawn low rarely getting a look in, but since then the bias has become less accentuated. Prior to 1995, runners drawn between 5 and 15 had the best of it on soft ground, and that's probably about true again now. On the round course, low numbers enjoy a decent advantage when the fields are big, and runners who normally race prominently are likely to find a high draw a difficult hurdle to overcome.

**BATH (L-H)** - It used to thought that low numbers were favoured in races of up to a mile, as the course turns left most of the way. However, results in recent times suggest that high numbers often do best in big-field sprints, the logic being that those drawn low tend to go too fast early in order to hold a position, and duck away when the rail kinks left about a furlong out, allowing high numbers to fly past.

**BEVERLEY (R-H)** - A high draw is essential on good or fast ground over the straight five furlongs and also on the round course, particularly in races at up to 1m 100y. In sprints, the runners have to negotiate a right-handed jink not long after the start and it seems harder here than at probably any course for runners drawn low to get over to the favoured rail. High numbers are particularly favoured on genuinely firm ground. However, when conditions are testing there is a strip of ground by the stands' rail that is significantly quicker than the middle of the course. Under such conditions those drawn very low hold a decisive advantage. Runners drawn high on the round course, especially in races over 7f 100y, are favoured as the course turns right soon after the start. The course management experimented with moving stalls to the stands' side over five furlongs last season, but that also caused a major bias, this time in favour of those drawn low. Apparently this was down to a compressed strip of ground, caused by vehicles, the same strip that rides faster on soft/heavy going. The plan is to continue with the trial this year, after work has been carried out to even out the surface.

**BRIGHTON (L-H)** - When the ground is soft or worse, runners invariably tack across to the stands' rail in the straight. When this is the case, high numbers enjoy a slight edge, but results are too inconclusive to ever be bullish. On fast ground, low-drawn prominent-racers are best in sprints.

**CARLISLE (R-H)** - It has long been considered that high numbers do best in sprints here, and that was certainly the case throughout the early parts of last season. This was apparently down to those racing nearest the inside fence being on virgin ground uncovered by the removal of hurdle wings, while those racing wider were on the surface used in hurdle races. This advantage disappeared later in the campaign, and a watching brief is advised this time. When the ground rides soft, low numbers, who race widest, enjoy a definite advantage and, while soft ground had rarely been seen here in the past, largely because they do not race after August, it was often in evidence during the wet summer last year.

**CATTERICK (L-H)** - When the ground is testing, the stands' rail is definitely the place to be, which suits high numbers in five-furlong races. However, when the ground is good or firmer, horses drawn on the far side (low) hold the edge. Low numbers are marginally preferred in races run on the round course on all surfaces, particularly so over 5f 212y as runners have to take a left-handed bend into the straight. When the ground is soft, horses switched to race on the stands' rail are benefited.

**CHEPSTOW (L-H)** - High numbers enjoyed a massive advantage in straight-course races (up to 1m 14y) two years ago, but this strip of ground was broken up by machine in the winter of 2001, and last season there wasn't much in the draw.

**CHESTER (L-H)** - Low numbers have an advantage, especially in races at up to 7f 122y, when a slow start from a high draw can be virtually impossible to overcome, given the constantly turning nature of the course. Soft ground seems to accentuate the advantage enjoyed by runners drawn low, until it has been raced on a few times, when a higher draw becomes less of a disadvantage as the ground on the inside becomes chewed up.

**DONCASTER (L-H)** - High numbers are best in sprints, a bias accentuated by softer ground. Low numbers take over on the straight mile, as long as there are enough runners in order for a split (12+), while seven furlongs seems to be the cut-off point, when both rails are favoured over the centre. Low numbers are best in big fields on the round course.

**EPSOM (L-H) -** When the ground is on the soft side, jockeys tack over to the stands' side to look for the better ground. The ground is better here in such conditions as the course cambers away from the stands' rail towards the far side. In five-furlong races, the stalls are invariably placed on the stands' side, so when the going is soft the majority of the runners are on the best ground from the outset. Prominent racers drawn low in round-course races are able to take the shortest route around Tattenham Corner, and on faster ground have a decisive edge over six and seven furlongs, and 1m 114y. Over five furlongs, high numbers used to hold quite an advantage, but the bias is not so great these days.

**FOLKESTONE (R-H) -** Prior to 1998, Folkestone was never thought of as having much of a draw bias, but nowadays it is common to see fields split into two groups in straight-course races, with runners rarely taken down the centre. The far rail usually rides faster than the stands' rail, favouring horses drawn high, and front-runners drawn on that side are always worth consideration.

**GOODWOOD (R-H) & (L-H) -** High numbers are favoured on the round course, particularly over seven furlongs and a mile, except in very wet conditions when jockeys tend to tack over to the stands' side in the straight. The advantage enjoyed by runners drawn by the far rail (high) in the Stewards' Cup has returned the past two years, having disappeared in 1999 as a result of work to break up the surface by machine on that side, but the stands'-side bunch has finished closer than previously each time.

**HAMILTON (R-H) -** It is helpful to be drawn high in sprints if the ground is good to soft or softer, particularly early in the year, and last year it looked a case of the nearer the fence the better (due to the wet summer in Scotland the ground was often soft). A high draw is a definite advantage in races over 1m 65y as there is a tight right-hand loop into the home straight. It is not uncommon for the ground to become too bad for the use of stalls here.

**HAYDOCK (L-H) -** High numbers used to be favoured in sprints when the ground was good or softer, but now there's rarely a great deal in it.

**KEMPTON (R-H) -** On the separate sprint track, when the stalls are on the far side and the ground is on the soft side, a high draw is an advantage. When the stalls are placed on the stands' side, low numbers are clearly favoured, and when the runners stretch right across the track, low numbers now comfortably hold the edge (which was not the case prior to 2000). The advantages become less defined on faster ground.

**LEICESTER (R-H) -** It used to be considered that low numbers had an advantage on the straight course, particularly on soft ground, but in recent seasons the bias has turned full circle, and high numbers (who usually race towards the centre) are now almost always favoured.

**LINGFIELD Turf (L-H) -** The draw advantage is nothing like as defined as it was in years past, and now only the occasional meeting, in favour of high numbers, seems to be affected. The one factor that can have a massive effect on the draw is heavy rainfall on to firm ground. Presumably because of the undulating nature of the track and the fact that the far rail on the straight course is towards the bottom of a slope where it joins the round course, rainfall seems to make the middle and far side of the straight course ride a lot slower. In these conditions, runners drawn right up against the stands' rail, often only the top three or four stalls, have a massive edge. The advantage does not seem to be anything like as great over sprint distances as it is over seven furlongs and 7f 140y under any conditions.

**LINGFIELD All-Weather (L-H) -** Since the Polytrack was laid horses have been able to win from just about anywhere. Front runners do well over the shorter trips, especially 6f, but over any distance beyond a mile they have a desperate time.

**MUSSELBURGH (R-H) -** High numbers are slightly favoured over seven furlongs and a mile. Over five furlongs, low numbers have a considerable advantage on soft ground, irrespective of the size of the field, but high numbers do best in big fields on very firm going. The one place not to be is down the centre.

**NEWBURY (L-H) -** When the ground is genuinely soft, it is not uncommon to see runners race wide down the back straight and the side of the course in events of between 1m 3f 56y and two miles. It is particularly the case in races of 1m 5f 61y, which start on a chute at the far end of the back straight. In such circumstances, a high draw becomes a huge advantage. Many consider a low draw to be an advantage in big-field races over the round 7f 64y and 1m 7y courses, since there is a sharpish left-hand bend into the home straight not long after the starts. While this is pretty much the case when the ground is good or firmer, it is definitely not true when the ground becomes soft. After a few races, the ground on the rail becomes chewed up and horses that are drawn high are able to race on the better ground (often only four or five horse widths off the rail) and swing onto the better ground in the straight, so while they are travelling that bit further, the surface is that much better. In races run on the straight course, a high draw is an advantage on any ground.

**NEWCASTLE (L-H) -** On the straight course, it used to be a case of high numbers being favoured when the ground was good or firmer, and low numbers having an advantage when the ground rode good to soft or softer. However, these days, the far side seems best whatever the going.

**NEWMARKET July Course (R-H) -** The draw often plays a part here, although it varies with some regularity. As a rule of thumb, when they're racing on the stands'-side half of the track, high numbers are best when the ground is good to firm or faster, there's not much in it on good, while runners racing wide of the stands' rail are best on slower. Runners racing nearest the far rail are best on soft ground when they race on the far-side half of the track.

**NEWMARKET Rowley Mile (R-H) -** The far rail definitely has ridden faster than the centre of the course since racing resumed two season ago, favouring high numbers in big fields. When the going is soft, runners right up against the far rail have always held sway when nothing switches up the stands' side (in which case they are favoured) but soft ground is not a common occurrence here. In late season, it has been known for the stands' rail to be moved to unveil virgin ground up against the stands' side. In these circumstances, runners drawn low can have a big advantage.

**NOTTINGHAM (L-H) -** On the straight course, it used to be a case of low numbers being favoured when the stalls were on the far rail and high numbers when they were on the stands' rail, but these days the advantage does not seem to be that great. The occasional meeting will pop up where one side or the other has the edge, normally in early season.

**PONTEFRACT (L-H) -** Low numbers are considered best here for the same reason as at Chester, in that the course has several distinct left-hand turns with a short home straight, but the advantage is not that great. A high draw can be a big setback on fast ground, since it forces runners to race wide or drop in behind and onto the rail. The ground can become so bad that the stalls are moved to the outside of the course, or dispensed with.

**REDCAR (L-H) -** It is not unusual to see fields verging on 30 in straight-course races several times throughout a season but there is rarely much in the draw.

**RIPON (R-H) -** High numbers are slightly favoured on the round course, especially over a mile. However, the draw has a massive effect in sprint races, where any runner drawn in the centre stalls can be completely ignored. The optimum conditions for low numbers seems to be when the ground is good or faster and there are 12 runners or below. When the stalls stretch far enough across the course, there is a fast strip of ground towards the far rail that horses drawn high can utilise.

**SALISBURY (R-H) -** High numbers are best on the straight course on good or faster ground, particularly so last season after a temporary rail was taken down in mid-summer. Low numbers take over on good to soft or slower.

**SANDOWN (R-H) -** High numbers enjoy a decent advantage in double-figure fields over the extended 7f and over a mile. On the separate sprint course, the advantage is even greater. When the going is on the soft side of good and the stalls are placed on the far side (high), high numbers have a massive advantage. When the stalls are placed on the stands' side, low numbers enjoy a slight advantage when all the runners stay towards the stands' rail, but when a few break off and go to the far side high numbers comfortably hold the upper hand again. The far rail is without doubt much faster than the stands' rail, which in turn is much faster than the centre of the course over five furlongs. The softer the ground becomes, the greater the advantage.

**SOUTHWELL All-Weather (R-H) -** A low draw is a major advantage over the straight 5f. Horses can win from most positions from 6f to 1m though a very wide draw is an inconvenience. For some reason, horses drawn low have a spectacular record over 1m 4f and front runners do very well at trips up to 7f. The effect of the draw can often be determined by the existence of a track bias.

**THIRSK (L-H) -** In sprints, high numbers are definitely favoured when the ground is genuinely firm. However, on good to firm ground and softer, the bias does not seem as great as it used to be, and last year the far side often proved best thanks to patchy watering. When the going is on the soft side, low numbers always have the advantage as the far rail becomes the place to be. Low numbers are also favoured over seven furlongs and a mile.

**WARWICK (L-H) -** Low numbers are slightly favoured on fast ground, only because the course turns left-handed at some point over all distances. However, when the ground is genuinely soft, high numbers have the edge, as the outside rail rides much faster.

**WINDSOR (Fig. 8) -** It is not uncommon to see large fields right throughout the summer here, particularly over sprint distances and in 1m 67y events. Over the latter distance, runners drawn high enjoy the edge since the start is set on a chute and the course follows a tight right-handed loop to the point where it joins the sprint track. In sprints, high numbers hold a definite advantage when the ground is good or faster, and a very low draw can become a difficult hurdle to overcome in big fields. Soft ground swings the bias to the opposite, while good to soft levels things out.

**WOLVERHAMPTON All-Weather (L-H) -** There is little advantage in the draw over 5f. From 6f to 1m 4f low numbers are at a disadvantage at most meetings as the inside of the track can get slower than elsewhere, but this can be reversed when the track has been prepared differently following very wet or very cold weather.

**YARMOUTH (L-H) -** High numbers have a big advantage when the ground is firm and the fields are large, but nothing like as much as they had in 1996/97. Part of the reason for high numbers enjoying such an advantage is that the off-shore breeze blows away from the stands' rail, making it difficult for the watering to be even.

**YORK (L-H) -** The draw at York is not as unpredictable in sprints as some would believe, and runners who race just to the far side of centre are usually favoured. This changes on soft/heavy ground, though, when the stands' rail (high) definitely rides best.

# Key to racereaders' initials

JF ......................Jon Freeman
WG ....................Walter Glynn
KH ......................Keith Hewitt
RL ................Richard Lowther
IM ..................Iain MacKenzie
LM....................Lee McKenzie
JN.............Jonathan Neesom
DO ....................Darren Owen
CR ....................Colin Roberts
JR ....................Joe Rowntree
JS........................John Santer
ST ......................Steve Taylor
RY ..................Richard Young

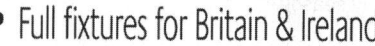

# The Form Book®

## WINTER RACING 2003

## The BHB's Official Record

Complete record of Foreign Turf Racing and All-Weather from November 9th to December 31st 2003

# NOTES

## 5659 COLOGNE (R-H)
Sunday, November 9

**OFFICIAL GOING: Soft**

### 5964a BUCHMACHER SIMON SPRINGER SPRINT-PREIS (LISTED) 6f
3:00 (3:17) 3-Y-O+ £8,442 (£2,597; £1,299; £649)

RPR

1 **Terroir (IRE)**[35] 5399 8-9-0 ........ WMongil 12 —
(NLindgren, Sweden)
2 3 ½ **Konig Shuffle (GER)**[28] 5528 7-9-4 ........ (b) ADeVries 9 —
(MRolke, Germany)
3 nk **Wild Advice (IRE)**[28] 5528 3-9-4 ........ PHeugl 13 —
(UOstmann, Germany)
4 2 **Best Smiling (GER)**[42] 5261 3-8-7 ........ (b) WPanov 2 —
(FrauEMader, Germany)
5 ½ **Just Sing A Song**[42] 5261 4-8-7 ........ BClos 5 —
(JHeidenreich, Germany)
6 hd **Lady Lonsdale (GER)**[35] 5399 4-8-11 ........ NRichter 3 —
(ASchutz, Germany)
7 2 **Minerwa (GER)**[21] 5664 3-8-9 ........ FilipMinarik 15 —
(MarioHofer, Germany)
8 hd **Gold Type (IRE)**[9] 5866 4-9-4 ........ (b) THellier 16 —
(BruceHellier, Germany)
9 shd **Shawdon**[35] 5399 8-9-4 ........ MTimpelan 6 —
(NLindgren, Sweden)
10 nk **Encanto (GER)**[210] 1047 3-8-11 ........ (b) ABoschert 7 —
(PRau, Germany)
11 1 **Night Set (GER)**[28] 5528 4-9-2 ........ JPalik 4 —
(MWeber, Germany)
12 3 ½ **Triton Dance (IRE)**[28] 5524 3-8-7 ........ NGMcCullagh 11 —
(MJGrassick, Ire) *raced in mid-division til weakening over 2f out (208/10)*[2]
13 shd **Avening**[16] 5732 3-8-11 ........ PDobbs 8 —
(RHannon) *always outpaced (58/1)* 3
14 ½ **Olindera (GER)** 3-8-7 ........ ABest 14 —
(PRau, Germany)
15 2 **Aversham**[9] 5854 3-8-11 ........ PRoberts 1 —
(RHannon) *prominent to half-way (44/10)* 1
16 2 **Liandero (IRE)**[133] 8-9-2 ........ PAJohnson 10 —
(FrauMBlasczyk)

1m 13.31s **16** Ran **SP% 24.8**
Speed ratings: .
**Owner** Stall Lambada Ab & Stall Gransater **Bred** Howard Kaskel **Trained** Sweden

**NOTEBOOK**
**Avening**was among the backmarkers from the off.
**Aversham**dropped away quickly having shown speed to halfway.

## 5902 SAN SIRO (R-H)
Sunday, November 9

**OFFICIAL GOING: Soft**

### 5965a PREMIO CASTELLANZA (MAIDEN FILLIES) 1m
3:20 (3:42) 2-Y-0 £6,494 (£2,857; £1,558; £779)

RPR

1 **Japigia (IRE)**[43] 5242 2-8-13 ........ APolli 3 —
(MGQuinlan) *led or disputed lead, definite leader 3f out, ridden out, ran on well (2.79/1F)* 1
2 3 **Night Beauty (GER)** 2-8-10 ........ EBotti 4 —
(HBlume, Germany)
3 3 **Nukleana (GER)** 2-8-10 ........ AGoritz 10 —
(UOstmann, Germany)
4 1 ½ **Dama Di Picche (IRE)** 2-8-10 ........ WGambarota 8 —
(LLedda, Italy)
5 ½ **My Silvia (ITY)** 2-8-10 ........ MDeiana 14 —
(FBeluschi, Italy)
6 3 ½ **Scent Of Ireland (IRE)**[57] 4903 2-8-13 ........ DVargiu 6 —
(LD'Auria, Italy)
7 6 **Charles (ITY)** 2-8-10 ........ DPorcu 15 —
(WCeriotti, Italy)
8 ½ **Barmad Di San Jore (ITY)** 2-8-13 ........ MEsposito 1 —
(JHeloury, Italy)
9 15 **Selling Point (ITY)** 2-8-13 ........ MTellini 12 —
(NataleLaRosa, Italy)
10 6 **La Boheme (ITY)** 2-8-10 ........ DViola 11 —
(G&CCagnoni, Italy)
11 3 ½ **Maschera D'Argento (IRE)** 2-8-10 ........ SMulas 13 —
(BGrizzetti, Italy)
12 hd **Tatagulas (IRE)** 2-8-10 ........ SLandi 9 —
(RFeligioni, Italy)
13 shd **Alianca (GER)** 2-8-10 ........ GBietolini 5 —
(RRohne, Germany)
14 ¾ **Valzafosa** 2-8-13 ........ MMonteriso 7 —
(MCiciarelli, Italy)
15 10 **Queen Of Easter (ITY)** 2-8-13 ........ AParravani 2 —
(RSantini, Italy)

1m 47.4s **15** Ran **SP% 26.4**
Speed ratings: .
**Owner** B Bardi **Bred** Dr Bruno Bardi **Trained** Newmarket, Suffolk

**NOTEBOOK**
**Japigia(IRE)**shared the pacesetting duties until gaining a definite advantage with three furlongs to run and then stayed on strongly all the way to the line. She is entered in the Newmarket December Sales.

## 5876 WOLVERHAMPTON (A.W) (L-H)
Monday, November 10

**OFFICIAL GOING: Standard**
Unusually for a meeting here, there was no great pace or track bias.
Wind: almost nil Weather: overcast

### 5966 LITTLEWOODS BET DIRECT AW JOCKEYS CHAMPIONSHIP NURSERY 6f (F)
12:45 (12:45) (E) (0-75,75) 2-Y-0 £2,093 (£598; £299) Stalls Low

Form RPR

0664 1 **Maunby Raver**[35] 5415 2-7-8 **55** ........ RoryMoore(7) 6 64
(PCHaslam) *hld up: rdn and hdwy on ins 2f out: led over 1f out: drvn out* **12/1**
0256 2 ½ **Bridgewater Boys**[44] 5226 2-8-4 **58** ........ (b) GDuffield 8 65
(KARyan) *sn chsng ldrs: rdn to join ldr 2f out: r.o ins fnl f* **10/1**
0562 3 4 **Emaradia**[37] 5380 2-8-0 **54** ........ JoannaBadger 4 49
(PDEvans) *led 1f: chsd ldrs: rdn over 3f out: kpt on same pce fnl f* **14/1**
4000 4 nk **Little Eye (IRE)**[35] 5421 2-8-11 **65** ........ NPollard 5 59
(JRBest) *stmbld s: bhd tl late hdwy on outside: nvr nrr* **16/1**
2603 5 shd **Piccleyes**[10] 5844 2-8-11 **65** ........ PDobbs 7 59
(RHannon) *prom: hrd rdn and outpcd over 2f out: kpt on ins fnl f* **9/1**
250 6 hd **Green Ridge**[9] 5869 2-9-3 **71** ........ JFEgan 9 64
(PWD'Arcy) *prom: rdn over 2f out: btn whn edgd lft over 1f out* **9/2**[1]
2150 7 shd **Embassy Lord**[34] 5440 2-8-5 **66** ow6 ........ (b) JDO'Reilly(7) 10 59
(JO'Reilly) *led after 1f: rdn over 2f out: hung bdly lft wl over 1f out: sn hdd: wknd ins fnl f* **16/1**
5642 8 1 **Crewes Miss Isle**[38] 5340 2-9-7 **75** ........ SWhitworth 12 65
(AGNewcombe) *hld up: sn bhd: hdwy on outside 3f out: eased whn btn ins fnl f* **14/1**
0000 9 1 **Birikina**[17] 5725 2-8-0 **61** ow4 ........ PPMathers(7) 11 48
(ABerry) *s.i.s: outpcd* **25/1**
0320 10 3 **Bajan Storm**[20] 5686 2-8-7 **61** ........ (b[1]) FNorton 3 39
(MBlanshard) *rdn and bhd fnl 4f* **20/1**
2600 11 nk **Tregarron**[16] 5751 2-8-8 **62** ........ DaneO'Neill 2 39
(RHannon) *outpcd* **5/1**[2]
4130 12 2 **Easily Averted (IRE)**[12] 5829 2-9-6 **74** ........ SWKelly 1 45
(JAOsborne) *prom tl rdn and wknd 2f out* **13/2**[3]
5445 13 6 **Compassion (IRE)**[6] 5916 2-8-6 **63** ........ SHitchcott(3) 13 16
(MissLAPerratt) *chsd ldrs: rdn over 4f out: sn wknd* **10/1**

1m 16.21s (0.51) **Going Correction** -0.075s/f (Stan) **13** Ran **SP% 117.8**
Speed ratings: **93,92,87,86,86 86,86,84,83,79 79,76,68**CSF £125.05 CT £1705.33 TOTE £13.40: £5.80, £4.80, £4.50; EX 178.60.
**Owner** Maunby Investment Management **Bred** A S Leftwich **Trained** Middleham Moor, N Yorks
■ Rory Moore's first winner in Britain.

**FOCUS**
A modest nursery and the winning time was almost a second slower than the maiden later in the afternoon.

**NOTEBOOK**
**Maunby Raver**, making his sand debut, was given a very competent ride. He stuck to the inside rail rounding the home turn, but was fortunate that this was a rare meeting where the usual bias towards those racing wide was not in operation. The yard do very well on this surface, but the winning time was almost a second slower than the maiden later in the afternoon so the form may not add up to much.
**Bridgewater Boys**, who has had plenty of opportunities to get off the mark, ran well under a positive ride despite his rider losing his whip turning for home. His brilliant veteran jockey compromised superbly by slapping the horse with the palm of his hand using the identical style to the one he would have used with his whip.
**Emaradia**, who has plenty of miles on the clock for one so young, has shown her best form over five but did not fail for lack of stamina here. She was just not good enough.
**Little Eye(IRE)**, dropping back from a mile for this sand debut, was down on his nose leaving the stalls and soon out the back. Staying on down the outside in the straight, he was very unfortunate not to finish closer and looks worth another try on this surface.
**Piccleyes**is no great shakes, but may be worth a try over seven.
**Green Ridge**, making her sand and handicap debuts, was disappointing after holding every chance and perhaps this outing came too quick.
**Tregarron**, well backed, never went a yard.

### 5967 BETDIRECT.CO.UK H'CAP (DIV I) 1m 100y(F)
1:15 (1:17) (D) (0-85,85) 3-Y-0+ £3,318 (£948; £474) Stalls Low

Form RPR

2200 1 **Cardinal Venture (IRE)**[9] 5873 5-9-9 **80** ........ RWinston 6 98
(KARyan) *mde all: pushed clr 2f out: rdn and edgd lft over 1f out: unchal* **7/2**[1]
4061 2 7 **Spark Up**[21] 5681 3-8-5 **64** ........ (b) MHenry 10 67
(JWUnett) *a.p: wnt 2nd over 5f out: rdn 3f out: sn btn* **6/1**
5536 3 hd **Countykat (IRE)**[30] 5486 3-9-4 **77** ........ (v) DarrenWilliams 2 80
(KRBurke) *chsd ldrs: rdn over 3f out: one pce fnl 2f* **11/2**[3]
3400 4 4 **Cherished Number**[24] 5618 4-8-10 **67** ........ GDuffield 3 61
(ISemple) *hld up: stdy hdwy 5f out: rdn 4f out: no imp fnl 2f* **5/1**[2]
0654 5 1 **Glory Quest (USA)**[37] 5379 6-8-12 **72** ........ LEnstone(3) 7 64
(MissGayKelleway) *hld up: rdn over 4f out: sme hdwy 2f out: no further prog* **6/1**
60 6 12 **Middleton Grey**[108] 3554 5-10-0 **85** ........ SWhitworth 8 52
(AGNewcombe) *hld up in rr: stdy hdwy over 5f out: rdn over 3f out: sn wknd* **12/1**
6600 7 1 ½ **Ymlaen (IRE)**[21] 5681 3-9-0 **73** ........ MFenton 9 37
(BPalling) *wl bhd fnl 5f* **50/1**
1002 8 2 **Bella Beguine**[9] 5878 4-8-12 **69** ........ (b) CCatlin 4 29
(ABailey) *chsd ldr 3f: rdn 4f out: wknd 3f out* **8/1**
0500 9 17 **Surdoue**[128] 3007 3-9-5 **81** ........ LisaJones(3) 5 5
(PHowling) *t.k.h: prom tl wknd 5f out: t.o* **20/1**

1m 48.32s (-2.68) **Going Correction** -0.075s/f (Stan)
**WFA** 3 from 4yo+ 2lb **9** Ran **SP% 108.4**
Speed ratings: **110,103,102,98,97 85,84,82,65**CSF £21.79 CT £98.45 TOTE £5.10: £1.70, £1.30, £1.70; EX 26.50.
**Owner** Tony Fawcett **Bred** Patrick Gleeson **Trained** Hambleton, N Yorks

**FOCUS**
A very hot pace, the field finished well strung out and the winning time was 1.29 seconds faster than the second division.

**NOTEBOOK**
**Cardinal Venture(IRE)**, last in his only previous try on sand, bounced out of the gates and ran his field into the ground. This was a very impressive victory and he still has scope on this surface but, as with all horses with his style of running, his future prospects will depend on whether he can dominate from the front just like he did here.

**Spark Up**, raised 2lb for her narrow victory here last month and upped in trip, tried to get on terms with the winner in the second half of the race but to no avail and she looked very tired inside the final furlong, only just holding on for second. A return to seven looks needed.
**Countykat(IRE)**, winner of his only previous try on Fibresand and placed a couple of times on sand at Nad Al Sheba last winter, did not run at all badly and on this evidence could do with a longer trip.
**Cherished Number**was not completely disgraced, but is still to match his turf from on this surface.
**Glory Quest(USA)**not surprisingly found this trip far too short and will do better back over farther on this surface.
**Middleton Grey**, making his debut for the yard, almost certainly needed this first start in four months.
**Bella Beguine**was trying this trip for the first time and did not see it out.

## 5968 LITTLEWOODS BET DIRECT AW TRAINERS CHAMPIONSHIP MAIDEN STKS — 6f (F)
1:50 (1:53) (D ) 2-Y-O — £3,020 (£863; £431) Stalls Low

| Form | | | Horse | RPR |
|---|---|---|---|---|
| 2355 | 1 | | **Pompey Blue**[12] 5829 2-8-9 71 .... NCallan 10 (PJMcbride) *a.p: led 2f out: rdn over 1f out: edgd lft ins fnl f: r.o wl* **5/2**[1] | 66+ |
| | 2 | 1¾ | **Colour Code (IRE)** 2-9-0 .... ADaly 2 (MPTregoning) *s.i.s: hdwy over 2f out: r.o ins fnl f: nt trble wnr* **10/1** | 66 |
| 5235 | 3 | nk | **Bond Brooklyn**[13] 5824 2-9-0 67 .... (v[1]) RFfrench 13 (BSmart) *a.p: rdn 3f out: r.o ins fnl f* **6/1**[3] | 65 |
| 004 | 4 | 1½ | **Blue Power (IRE)**[34] 5440 2-9-0 59 .... DarrenWilliams 4 (KRBurke) *led: rdn and hdd 2f out: wknd ins fnl f* **33/1** | 61 |
| 4052 | 5 | hd | **Pick Of The Crop**[20] 5687 2-9-0 73 .... SWKelly 11 (JRJenkins) *hld up: hdwy over 3f out: sn rdn: one pce fnl 2f* **7/1** | 60 |
| | 6 | 6 | **Docklands Blue (IRE)** 2-8-9 .... IMongan 9 (NPLittmoden) *prom tl rdn and wknd over 2f out* **13/2** | 37 |
| | 7 | 2½ | **Vittorioso (IRE)** 2-9-0 .... (p) MFenton 6 (MissGayKelleway) *hld up: rdn and sme hdwy on ins over 3f out: wknd over 2f out* **33/1** | 34 |
| 35 | 8 | ½ | **King Of Music (USA)**[39] 5335 2-9-0 .... DaneO'Neill 3 (GProdromou) *s.i.s: sn swtchd rt: hld up: c v wd st: nvr nr ldrs* **9/2**[2] | 33 |
| 0620 | 9 | ½ | **Intikraft (IRE)**[4] 5930 2-9-0 68 .... (v) CCatlin 1 (MrsStefLiddiard) *prom: rdn 3f out: wknd wl over 1f out* **25/1** | 31 |
| 00 | 10 | ¾ | **Masafi (IRE)**[9] 5876 2-9-0 .... GDuffield 5 (SirMarkPrescott) *prom early: bhd fnl 4f* **25/1** | 29 |
| 0 | 11 | 2½ | **Dial Square**[12] 5825 2-9-0 .... SDrowne 8 (PHowling) *a bhd* **16/1** | 22 |
| 0 | 12 | 10 | **Brave Chief**[137] 2714 2-9-0 .... SWhitworth 12 (JAPickering) *hung bdly rt thrght: a bhd* **66/1** | — |
| 0 | 12 | dht | **Sonne De Loup**[4] 5929 2-8-9 .... FNorton 7 (MrsStefLiddiard) *prom 3f* **100/1** | — |

1m 15.31s (-0.39) **Going Correction** -0.075s/f (Stan) **13** Ran SP% **117.9**
Speed ratings: **99,96,96,94,94 86,82,82,81,80 77,63,63**CSF £26.78 TOTE £3.60: £1.60, £3.80, £1.80; EX 37.10.
**Owner** Mrs Joan Langmead **Bred** Mrs Joan M Langmead **Trained** Newmarket, Suffolk

**FOCUS**
Probably a fair maiden as the winning time was nearly a second faster than the opening nursery.

**NOTEBOOK**
**Pompey Blue**had the best form coming into this, albeit on turf, but took to the Fibresand well and left her field for dead from the home turn. She can make her mark in better company on this surface.
**Colour Code(IRE)**, a half-brother to several winners in Italy, took time to warm up but was finishing in good style. He may be well down the stable's juvenile pecking order, but should win a race on this surface.
**Bond Brooklyn**, with the visor on rather than the usual blinkers, could really do with an extra furlong.
**Blue Power(IRE)**had it to do judged on official figures, but does possess early pace so may be worth dropping to the minimum trip.
**Pick Of The Crop**was unable to confirm Southwell form with Bond Brooklyn and this was probably a better race.
**King Of Music(USA)**missed the break and was all but carried out on the home bend. He should be given another chance.
**Brave Chief** *Official explanation: jockey said colt had hung right-handed and was virtually unsteerable round the bend*

## 5969 LITTLEWOODS BET DIRECT MAIDEN STKS (DIV I) — 7f (F)
2:25 (2:27) (D ) 3-Y-O — £2,310 (£660; £330) Stalls High

| Form | | | Horse | RPR |
|---|---|---|---|---|
| 2022 | 1 | | **Perfect Night**[14] 5799 3-8-9 67 .... SDrowne 7 (RCharlton) *sn w ldr: led over 3f out: clr over 1f out: readily* **8/11**[1] | 76+ |
| 6300 | 2 | 5 | **Zagala**[45] 5203 3-8-9 55 .... (t) RWinston 9 (SLKeightley) *hld up in tch: chsd wnr over 2f out: rdn and swtchd lft wl over 1f out: no imp* **9/1**[3] | 63 |
| 2005 | 3 | 4 | **Danger Bird (IRE)**[62] 4792 3-8-9 53 .... ACulhane 10 (RHollinshead) *hld up: hdwy over 3f out: rdn over 2f out: wknd wl over 1f out* **16/1** | 53 |
| 0524 | 4 | 5 | **Shamwari Fire (IRE)**[19] 5712 3-8-7 52 .... NataliaGemelova[(7)] 6 (IWMcinnes) *hld up in tch: rdn 3f out: wknd over 1f out* **6/1**[2] | 46 |
| 2340 | 5 | 1¾ | **Bahamian Belle**[28] 5538 3-8-9 52 .... (b) JEdmunds 3 (JBalding) *plld hrd: prom tl rdn and wknd wl over 1f out* **20/1** | 36 |
| | 6 | 4 | **Nicholas Nickelby** 3-9-0 .... IMongan 4 (NPLittmoden) *s.i.s: rdn 4f out: a bhd* **11/1** | 31 |
| 0000 | 7 | 3 | **Abaninetoes (IRE)**[14] 5787 3-8-9 44 .... NCallan 2 (PDEvans) *led over 3f: rdn and hdd over 2f out* **100/1** | 19 |
| | 8 | ¾ | **Harry Tu** 3-8-7 .... BFayosMartin[(7)] 5 (MissGayKelleway) *s.i.s: a bhd* **20/1** | 22 |
| 65 | 9 | 23 | **Sweet Talking Girl**[128] 2996 3-8-9 .... PFitzsimons 1 (JMBradley) *chsd ldrs tl wknd over 3f out: t.o* **50/1** | — |
| | 10 | 2½ | **Easy Breeze** 3-8-11 .... LPKeniry[(3)] 8 (JMBradley) *a bhd: rdn 4f out: t.o* **100/1** | — |

1m 28.66s (-1.54) **Going Correction** -0.075s/f (Stan) **10** Ran SP% **109.9**
Speed ratings: **105,99,94,89,87 82,79,78,51,49**CSF £6.52 TOTE £1.80: £1.10, £2.70, £3.70; EX 5.20.
**Owner** Perfect Night Partnership **Bred** S Emmet And Miss R Emmet **Trained** Beckhampton, Wilts

**FOCUS**
An uncompetitive maiden and little to get excited about outside the winner, though the winning time was about a second and a half faster than the second division.

**NOTEBOOK**
**Perfect Night**has hit the crossbar too many times for comfort, but even she could not miss the target here and she was never in the remotest danger of defeat. This will have helped her confidence and she looks worth a try in a three-year-old-only handicap on this surface.
**Zagala**was the only one to try and give the winner a race from the home bend, but was soon put in her place. She is already exposed as modest on this surface and her proximity rather demonstrates the quality of the horses behind her.
**Danger Bird(IRE)**ran as well as her official mark entitled her to, but still posted defeat number 14.
**Shamwari Fire(IRE)**did not improve for the return to Fibresand over this shorter trip, but more positive tactics might be what he needs.
**Bahamian Belle**achieved nothing on this step up in trip.

## 5970 BETDIRECT.CO.UK H'CAP (DIV II) — 1m 100y(F)
3:00 (3:00) (D ) (0-85,80) 3-Y-O+ — £3,307 (£945; £472) Stalls Low

| Form | | | Horse | RPR |
|---|---|---|---|---|
| 0433 | 1 | | **Lakota Brave**[37] 5377 9-9-10 80 .... SDrowne 8 (MrsStefLiddiard) *hld up: rdn and hdwy over 2f out: r.o to ld nr fin* **8/1** | 88 |
| 4144 | 2 | nk | **Shatin Hero**[4] 5933 3-7-13 57 .... (p) RFfrench 2 (MissLAPerratt) *a.p: led 3f out: rdn wl over 1f out: ct nr fin* **7/1**[3] | 64 |
| 4505 | 3 | 1½ | **Just Wiz**[27] 5568 7-8-12 71 .... (b) J-PGuillambert[(3)] 5 (NPLittmoden) *hld up: rdn 4f out: hdwy over 2f out: nt qckn fnl f* **8/1** | 75 |
| 0041 | 4 | 1¼ | **Shotacross The Bow (IRE)**[25] 5596 6-8-10 66 .... FNorton 10 (MBlanshard) *hld up: jnd ldrs 5f out: rdn 2f out: one pce* **5/1**[2] | 67 |
| 1053 | 5 | ¾ | **Crusoe (IRE)**[108] 3580 6-8-8 67 .... LisaJones[(3)] 6 (ASadik) *w ldr: rdn over 2f out: wknd ins fnl f* **7/1**[3] | 67 |
| 3/ | 6 | 5 | **Ulysees (IRE)**[32] 5466 4-9-1 71 .... GDuffield 4 (ISemple) *prom: rdn over 3f out: wknd over 2f out* **12/1** | 60 |
| 3-00 | 7 | ½ | **Zilch**[13] 5820 5-9-9 79 .... IMongan 9 (MLWBell) *hld up: rdn 3f out: no rspnse* **8/1** | 67 |
| 5200 | 8 | 2½ | **Swift Alchemist**[11] 5838 3-9-1 73 .... GBaker 7 (KRBurke) *led: rdn and hdd 3f out: sn wknd* **8/1** | 56 |
| 0003 | 9 | 9 | **Bressbee (USA)**[4] 5937 5-9-8 78 .... (v) DaneO'Neill 3 (JWUnett) *hld up: hdwy over 5f out: rdn over 3f out: wknd over 2f out* **9/2**[1] | 42 |
| 3006 | 10 | 1¾ | **Zarin (IRE)**[37] 5377 5-9-5 75 .... ACulhane 1 (DWChapman) *prom: rdn 4f out: sn wknd* **25/1** | 35 |

1m 49.61s (-1.39) **Going Correction** -0.075s/f (Stan)
**WFA** 3 from 4yo+ 2lb **10** Ran SP% **115.8**
Speed ratings: **103,102,101,99,99 94,93,91,82,80**CSF £62.51 CT £476.19 TOTE £7.80: £2.50, £2.80, £2.40; EX 65.40.
**Owner** Valley Fencing **Bred** Buckram Thoroughbred Enterprises Inc **Trained** Great Shefford, Berks

**FOCUS**
Quite a competitive handicap and the pace was sound.

**NOTEBOOK**
**Lakota Brave**, making his debut for the yard, has lost none of his ability and responded to pressure to get up near the line and further extend his already impressive winning record on sand. He could be in for yet another good winter.
**Shatin Hero**, making his sand debut, did everything right and looked in control racing down the home straight only to have the race snatched from him. He should be able to make amends.
**Just Wiz**, who has a great record here, proved hard work for his rider as he was off the bridle before halfway and dourly stayed on for pressure to finish third. He is better over the extra furlong here and is back on a winning mark.
**Shotacross The Bow(IRE)**, raised 6lb for his Southwell win, is another who is probably better over the extra furlong, but his overall winning record does not inspire confidence.
**Crusoe(IRE)**likes this surface, but he was hammered for his victory here in June and needs a bit more leniency from the Handicapper to give him a chance.
**Bressbee(USA)**is at his best when able to dominate, but he was hopping up and down when the stalls opened and missed the break completely. A mid-race move to try and get back into contention finally bottomed him, though his trainer was of the opinion that this race came too soon after his Nottingham effort. *Official explanation: trainer said race may have come too soon after the gelding's previous run four days before*

## 5971 BET DIRECT FREEPHONE 0800 32 93 93 CLASSIFIED STKS — 1m 4f (F)
3:35 (3:35) (F ) 3-Y-O+ — £2,100 (£600; £300) Stalls Low

| Form | | | Horse | RPR |
|---|---|---|---|---|
| 0166 | 1 | | **Smoothie (IRE)**[4] 5935 5-9-4 60 .... CCatlin 1 (IanWilliams) *hld up: hdwy over 5f out: rdn and wnt 2nd over 2f out: led ins fnl f: all out* **4/1**[1] | 72 |
| 4323 | 2 | ½ | **Easibet Dot Net**[5] 5928 3-8-12 58 .... (p) GDuffield 4 (ISemple) *dwlt: sn rcvrd: hld up: reminder over 6f out: hdwy over 5f out: led 4f out: hrd rdn wl over 1f out: hdd ins fnl f: rn* **5/1**[2] | 71 |
| 6600 | 3 | 14 | **Geri Roulette**[19] 5705 5-9-1 51 .... JCarroll 3 (EJAlston) *chsd ldr: led briefly over 4f out: rdn and wkng whn n.m.r on ins over 2f out* **14/1** | 47 |
| 0251 | 4 | 2 | **Paradise Valley**[28] 5542 3-8-12 54 .... (t) SDrowne 5 (MrsStefLiddiard) *hld up towards rr: nvr nr ldrs* **14/1** | 47 |
| 5004 | 5 | 2½ | **Ipledgeallegiance (USA)**[20] 5692 7-9-4 50 .... ACulhane 9 (DWChapman) *hld up towards rr: n.d* **13/2**[3] | 44 |
| 0054 | 6 | nk | **Pearson Glen (IRE)**[5] 5928 4-9-4 58 .... RWinston 2 (GASwinbank) *prom: rdn 5f out: wknd 3f out* **7/1** | 43 |
| 3302 | 7 | ½ | **Queensberry**[21] 5680 4-8-11 55 .... (v) JDO'Reilly[(7)] 7 (JO'Reilly) *a bhd* **7/1** | 42 |
| 6050 | 8 | ¾ | **Nimbus Twothousand**[13] 5819 3-8-6 48 .... (b) DCorby[(3)] 12 (PRWood) *prom: chsd ldr over 4f out tl over 2f out: sn wknd* **33/1** | 38 |
| 0 | 9 | 3 | **Amanpuri (GER)**[20] 5692 5-8-11 52 .... (e[1]) BFayosMartin[(7)] 8 (MissGayKelleway) *a bhd* **33/1** | 37 |
| 0300 | 10 | 13 | **Interstice**[53] 5012 6-9-4 58 .... SWhitworth 11 (AGNewcombe) *hld up and bhd: short-lived effrt over 3f out* **4/1**[1] | 17 |
| 2000 | 11 | 9 | **Eurolink Artemis**[9] 5881 6-9-1 52 .... (bt) MFenton 10 (MissGayKelleway) *led: hdd over 4f out: sn wknd* **25/1** | — |

2m 39.55s (-1.95) **Going Correction** -0.075s/f (Stan)
**WFA** 3 from 4yo+ 6lb **11** Ran SP% **118.1**
Speed ratings: **103,102,93,92,90 90,89,89,87,78 72**CSF £23.35 TOTE £5.10: £1.50, £2.30, £4.70; EX 29.00.
**Owner** Miss S Howell **Bred** Miss Mary Duckett **Trained** Portway, Warwicks
■ Stewards Enquiry : G Duffield two-day ban: used whip with excessive frequency (Nov 19,21)

**FOCUS**
A tight, if low-grade classified event and the pace was good.

**NOTEBOOK**
**Smoothie(IRE)**, best in on adjusted official ratings, confirmed the promise of his effort on turf last week and came out best after a protracted duel with the runner-up. He is likely to end up over hurdles.
**Easibet Dot Net**ran a very creditable first race on sand and he and the winner had the race to themselves from a long way out. He is still a maiden, but is also lightly raced and has the ability to win a small contest on this surface.
**Geri Roulette**is proven on this surface at a low level, but she had a bit to find on adjusted official ratings and was left behind by the front two from the final bend.
**Paradise Valley**, who finally got off the mark over ten furlongs on turf last time, was presumably ridden to get this longer trip but never got into it. His jockey reported that he had a breathing problem. *Official explanation: jockey said gelding had a breathing problem*
**Ipledgeallegiance(USA)**is still to prove conclusively that he stays this trip on the Flat and never got into it. *Official explanation: jockey said gelding was never moving well*
**Queensberry**, having a second try over this longer trip, never managed to get out of the rear group.
**Interstice**, given a patient ride, threatened to get involved racing down the far side on the second circuit, but his effort came to nothing. He is capable of much better than this.


The Form Book, Raceform Ltd, Compton, RG20 6NL

## 5972 LITTLEWOODSCASINO.COM H'CAP 2m 46y(F)
4:10 (4:10) (E ) (0-70,66) 3-Y-O+ £2,065 (£590; £295) Stalls Low

Form RPR

0551 1 **Vin Du Pays**[21] 5680 3-9-5 **66**.................................................... NCallan 7 77
(MBlanshard) *hld up: hdwy 8f out: led 3f out: sn rdn: drvn out* **11/2**

3200 2 1 1/2 **Digger (IRE)**[96] 3900 4-9-10 **65**........................................(t) LEnstone(3) 12 74
(MissGayKelleway) *hld up and plld hrd: hdwy over 5f out: rdn over 3f out: ev ch over 2f out: styd on one pce fnl f* **14/1**

0500 3 5 **Mysterium**[35] 5417 9-8-2 **40**................................................(v) GGibbons 9 43
(NPLittmoden) *hld up and bhd: hdwy 7f out: rdn over 3f out: one pce fnl 2f* **9/1**

0006 4 7 **Prince Of The Wood (IRE)**[27] 5560 3-7-13 **46**...................... CCatlin 11 41
(ABailey) *hld up in tch: rdn 5f out: wknd over 3f out* **20/1**

1301 5 2 **High Policy (IRE)**[21] 5682 7-9-7 **66**..............(p) StephanieHollinshead(7) 2 58
(RHollinshead) *hld up and bhd: rdn and sme hdwy over 4f out: n.d* **4/1**[1]

0603 6 1 1/2 **Melograno (IRE)**[13] 5819 3-7-13 **46**........................................ JMackay 3 36
(RMBeckett) *chsd ldrs: wnt 2nd 8f out: led over 5f out: rdn and hdd 3f out: wknd 2f out* **14/1**

2024 7 6 **Spitting Image (IRE)**[6] 5920 3-9-3 **64**.................................... ACulhane 4 47
(MrsMReveley) *hld up in tch: rdn and wknd over 4f out* **5/1**[3]

3334 8 3 **Worlaby Dale**[13] 5817 7-8-3 **46**.......................................... RThomas(5) 5 26
(MrsSLamyman) *s.i.s: a bhd* **9/2**[2]

1002 9 dist **Golden Fields (IRE)**[12] 5826 3-8-4 **51** ow6.........................(v) GHannon 8 —
(APJones) *chsd ldr after 3f: led over 8f out tl over 5f out: wknd qckly: t.o* **66/1**

04-0 10 12 **Kebreya (USA)**[45] 5189 4-9-10 **65**...............................(v[1]) SHitchcott(3) 10 —
(RFord) *led: hdd over 8f out: wknd qckly: t.o fnl 6f* **33/1**

-003 11 3 **Groundswell (IRE)**[153] 2248 7-8-4 **42**................................ JFanning 6 —
(FerdyMurphy) *hld up in tch: wknd qckly 7f out: t.o fnl 6f* **14/1**

200 12 1 1/2 **Little Sky**[38] 5343 6-8-5 **46**.......................................... J-PGuillambert(3) 1 —
(DMullarkey) *hld up mid-div: dropped rr over 7f out: t.o fnl 6f* **66/1**

3m 40.14s (-2.16) **Going Correction** -0.075s/f (Stan)
**WFA** 3 from 4yo+ 9lb **12 Ran SP% 110.9**
Speed ratings: **102,101,98,95,94 93,90,89,—,— —,—**CSF £71.59 CT £651.89 TOTE £8.20: £3.00, £3.80, £2.60; EX 94.60.
**Owner** J Oliver,W Garrett,C J Ward & Anne Page **Bred** Bodfari Stud Ltd **Trained** Upper Lambourn, Berks

**FOCUS**
A modest staying handicap in which the leaders went off far too fast.

**NOTEBOOK**
**Vin Du Pays**, raised a stone after winning a 12-furlong classified event here last time, was always travelling well and was brave in holding off the runner-up from the home turn. Another rise in the weights is assured, but staying contests on this surface are not usually that competitive and his proven stamina should enable him to find further opportunities during the winter.
**Digger(IRE)**did his best to get on terms with the winner from the home bend, but was never quite finding enough. If he ever learns to settle there are races waiting for him over this sort of trip on Fibresand.
**Mysterium**is not as good as he was and even over this sort of trip he appears to lack pace these days.
**Prince Of The Wood(IRE)**is still a maiden and looks tripless.
**High Policy(IRE)**, raised 3lb for his win here last month, is a guaranteed stayer and was given his usual patient ride, but failed to pick up the leaders when asked and this was disappointing.
**Spitting Image(IRE)**did not see out the trip on this sand debut.
**Worlaby Dale**is still a maiden under all codes and did not improve for the switch to sand.
**Little Sky** *Official explanation: trainer said mare failed to handle the ground*

## 5973 LITTLEWOODS BET DIRECT MAIDEN STKS (DIV II) 7f (F)
4:40 (4:41) (D ) 3-Y-O £2,310 (£660; £330) Stalls High

Form RPR

5- 1 **Rezzago (USA)**[392] 5239 3-9-0 ............................................... NCallan 3 64+
(PWHarris) *hld up: hdwy over 4f out: led over 1f out: rdn out* **7/4**[1]

40 2 hd **Kingston Town (USA)**[16] 5742 3-8-11 .................(p) J-PGuillambert(3) 1 63
(NPLittmoden) *a.p: rdn to ld over 2f out: hdd over 1f out: rallied ins fnl f: r.o* **7/1**

2000 3 1 1/4 **Victory Flip (IRE)**[37] 5376 3-8-9 55........................................(p) ACulhane 10 55
(RHollinshead) *hld up: hdwy over 2f out: rdn over 1f out: kpt on ins fnl f* **7/2**[2]

5350 4 3 1/2 **Brandywine Bay (IRE)**[47] 5151 3-8-9 41...........................(p) GHannon 8 46
(APJones) *s.i.s: outpcd: rdn and hdwy wl over 1f out: nt rch ldrs* **14/1**

5000 5 12 **Deco Lady**[9] 5879 3-8-9 50.......................................................(v) SWKelly 6 16
(PDEvans) *led: rdn and hdd over 3f out: wknd over 2f out* **14/1**

0300 6 2 **Rich Dancer**[98] 3835 3-8-9 55................................................ JFanning 5 11
(JDBethell) *w ldr: led over 3f out: rdn and hdd over 2f out: sn wknd* **16/1**

05 7 5 **Show Me The Lolly (FR)**[13] 5815 3-8-9 ......................... SWhitworth 2 —
(PJMcbride) *hmpd on ins sn after s: short-lived effrt on outside over 2f out* **5/1**[3]

0000 8 shd **Guard**[24] 5611 3-9-0 44.............................................................. IMongan 7 —
(NPLittmoden) *prom tl rdn and wknd over 2f out* **33/1**

0030 9 5 **Eddies Jewel**[35] 5420 3-8-7 36....................................(v[1]) PPMathers(7) 4 —
(JSWainwright) *outpcd* **50/1**

50 10 4 **Sadie Jane**[55] 4973 3-8-9 ......................................................... CCatlin 9 —
(JMBradley) *prom tl wknd over 4f out* **66/1**

1m 30.13s (-0.07) **Going Correction** -0.075s/f (Stan) **10 Ran SP% 113.4**
Speed ratings: **97,96,95,91,77 75,69,69,63,59**CSF £14.01 TOTE £2.30: £1.30, £2.70, £1.10; EX 14.00 Place 6 £146.15, Place 5 £16.92.
**Owner** Mrs P W Harris **Bred** Lantern Hill Farm Llc **Trained** Ringshall, Bucks

**FOCUS**
A poor maiden run in a time about a second and a half slower than the first division and little promise amongst the beaten horses.

**NOTEBOOK**
**Rezzago(USA)**, not seen since showing promise on his debut more than a year ago, did not break well from his low draw and therefore had to circle the field on the outside. He hit the front going well enough, but did nothing once there and only scrambled home. He might have needed this after such a long absence and his next start will tell us more.
**Kingston Town(USA)**, following a moderate effort on his second start, confirmed the promise shown on his debut and made the favourite fight all the way. Using the third as a guide, he should get a handicap mark in the high 50s and could be interesting off that when returned to a longer trip.
**Victory Flip(IRE)**, a long-standing maiden, had her chance turning for home but was again unable to take it. She is the benchmark to the value of the form.
**Brandywine Bay(IRE)**, a maiden after 14 attempts coming into this, made up a lot of late ground and finished clear of horses rated much higher than her. She may be able to find a very poor race off her proper mark over farther.
**Show Me The Lolly(FR)**had looked as though she needed a longer trip than a mile last time, so this drop back was never going to be in her favour and meeting trouble after the start was the final nail in her coffin. She can at least now be handicapped and she should get a very modest mark.

T/Plt: £191.00 to a £1 stake. Pool: £34,801.45. 132.95 winning tickets. T/Qpdt: £8.60 to a £1 stake. Pool: £4,573.00. 389.80 winning tickets. KH

# 5684 TOULOUSE
Tuesday, November 11

**OFFICIAL GOING: Good to soft**

## 5974a PRIX FILLE DE L'AIR (GROUP 3) (F&M) 1m 2f 110y
2:15 (2:20) 3-Y-O+ £21,429 (£8,571; £6,429; £4,286)

RPR

1 **Walkamia (FR)**[39] 5354 3-8-8 ............................................. CSoumillon 11 110
(AFabre, France) *in rear early, headway to go 5th straight, hard ridden and edged left 1 1/2f out, led 100 yards out, driven out*

2 1 1/2 **Monturani (IRE)**[23] 5667 4-8-11 ............................................... DBonilla 7 105
(GWragg) *mid division on outside, went 3rd entering straight, ridden to lead over 1 1/2f out, headed 100 yards out, no extra*

3 1 1/2 **Handria (FR)**[22] 5684 6-8-11 ...............................................(b) FXBertras 10 102
(FRohaut, France) *held up in rear, 8th straight, ridden and headway 1 1/2f out, took 3rd 100 yards out, stayed on*

4 3/4 **Place Rouge (IRE)**[17] 5752 4-9-4 ........................................... TThulliez 4 108
(JHMGosden) *close up tracking leaders, 2nd straight, every chance over 1 1/2f out, soon ridden and one pace*

5 1 1/2 **Kiltubber (IRE)**[80] 4401 4-8-11 ....................................................(b) TGillet 6 98
(JEHammond, France) *mid division early, 9th straight, stayed on under pressure from over 1f out*

6 2 1/2 **Aynthia (USA)**[38] 5384 3-9-1 ...........................................(b) C-PLemaire 8 103
(H-APantall, France) *raced in 2nd til led 4 1/2f out, headed over 1 1/2f out, weakened*

7 hd **Amathia (IRE)**[16] 5781 4-8-11 ...................................................... TJarnet 1 94
(RGibson, France) *close up on inside, 4th straight, one pace final 2f*

8 3/4 **Red Stella (FR)**[22] 5684 4-8-11 .......................................... MBlancpain 5 92
(CLaffon-Parias, France) *mid division, 6th straight, ridden and one pace final 1 1/2f*

9 4 **Fleurie Domaine**[16] 5781 4-8-11 ....................................... J-PCarvalho 9 85
(MarioHofer, Germany) *soon struggling in last, 10th straight, never a factor*

10 2 1/2 **Bonne Gargotte (FR)**[26] 5605 4-8-11 ................................ PSogorb 2 81
(GHenrot, France) *mid division on inside, hampered and dropped to rear 3 1/2f out, no danger after*

11 **Nashwan Rose**[37] 5403 4-8-11 ..............................................(b) DBoeuf 12 81
(ELibaud, France) *close up on outside, 7th and weakening entering straight*

12 **No Coincidence (IRE)**[30] 3-8-8 ................................................ ELegrix 3 83
(ELibaud, France) *set good paced til headed 4 1/2f out, weakened qucikly, tailed off*

2m 10.6s
**WFA** 3 from 4yo+ 4lb **12 Ran**
Speed ratings: .
**Owner** Lagardere Family **Bred** Snc Lagardere Elevage **Trained** France

**NOTEBOOK**
**Walkamia(FR)**, mid division early on she challenged for the lead early in the straight. The filly hung left one out before being straightened and finally won with plenty in hand. She is in the catalogue at the forthcoming Newmarket sales but could still continue her career or be sent to stud.
**Monturani(IRE)**, never far from the leading group, she took the lead over a furlong out but had nothing in reserve when challenged by the winner. It was another sound effort from this filly.
**Handria(FR)**, held up at the tail of the field she was still last at the entrance to the straight. She began her challenge early in the straight and ran on well to take third place in the dying stages of the race. She now goes to stud.
**Place Rouge(IRE)**, always well placed, she battled well on the far rail throughout the straight and only lost third place close home.

# 5886 LINGFIELD (L-H)
Wednesday, November 12

**OFFICIAL GOING: Standard**
Wind: mod hlf against Weather: mostly sunny

## 5975 LITTLEWOODSCASINO.COM APPRENTICE H'CAP (DIV I) 1m 5f (P)
12:05 (12:06) (F ) (0-75,75) 3-Y-O+ £2,257 (£645; £322) Stalls Low

Form RPR

3604 1 **Maystock**[28] 5576 3-8-8 **62**.................................................(v) LTreadwell 8 73
(GAButler) *lw: close up: trckd ldr wl over 3f out: clr of remainder over 2f out: led narrowly over 1f out: styd on wl fnl f* **3/1**[2]

0P50 2 2 **Astromancer (USA)**[47] 5200 3-7-5 **52** oh2.......................... DFentiman(7) 7 60
(MHTompkins) *lw: w ldr tl led after 3f: clr w wnr fr over 2f out: hdd narrowly over 1f out: unable qck ins fnl f* **20/1**

5030 3 4 **Macaroni Gold (IRE)**[22] 5692 3-8-2 **61** ow4.................... DTudhope(5) 5 64
(WJarvis) *s.s: t.k.h and hld up in last: prog on outer over 4f out: chsd clr ldng pair over 2f out: no imp* **25/1**

5506 4 1 1/2 **Final Dividend (IRE)**[12] 5848 7-7-8 **48**.................... AshleighHorton(7) 6 49
(JMPEustace) *racd in midfield: pushed along and outpcd fr 3f out: kpt on same pce fnl 2f* **8/1**

0555 5 5 **Two Of A Kind (IRE)**[31] 5504 3-8-5 **64**.......................... HGemberlu(5) 10 58
(JWHills) *hld up in rr: in last pair 4f out: effrt on wd outside 3f out: sn outpcd and no ch* **20/1**

0/-0 6 1 **Hello Holly**[37] 5419 6-7-12 **45**............................................ KristinStubbs 4 37
(MrsALMKing) *hld up in rr: outpcd 3f out: nt clr run on inner sn after: no ch* **25/1**

0204 7 nk **Esperance (IRE)**[10] 5891 3-8-3 **62** ow1........................... MCoumbe(5) 1 54
(JAkehurst) *racd in midfield: lost pl and wl in rr 3f out: no ch after* **11/2**[3]

4000 8 2 1/2 **Beyond The Pole (USA)**[35] 5452 5-8-10 **60**........................ WHogg(3) 2 48
(BRJohnson) *trckd ldrs: outpcd 3f out: nt clr run sn after: no ch after* **9/1**

0603 9 3 1/2 **Aveiro (IRE)**[20] 5717 7-7-7 **45** oh11................................(b) LiamJones(5) 9 28
(BGPowell) *lw: trckd ldrs: pushed along 4f out: wknd 3f out* **16/1**

4302 10 8 **Sea Plume**[12] 5855 4-10-0 **75**.................................................... PGallagher 3 47
(LadyHerries) *led for 3f: pressed ldr after: rdn and fnd nil 4f out: sn wknd and bhd* **9/4**[1]

2m 47.57s (-0.51) **Going Correction** +0.05s/f (Slow)
**WFA** 3 from 4yo+ 7lb **10 Ran SP% 115.4**
Speed ratings: **103,101,99,98,95 94,94,92,90,85**CSF £65.20 CT £1239.63 TOTE £4.30: £2.00, £12.00, £7.10; EX 111.70.
**Owner** Stock Hill Racing **Bred** Stock Hill Stud **Trained** Blewbury, Oxon

**FOCUS**
A weak 0-75 run in a fractionally faster time than the median.
**NOTEBOOK**
**Maystock** is not the most straightforward of characters, but she recorded a sound effort at the course last month when just finding the two miles too far and this drop back in trip proved ideal. She could follow up if kept on the go.
**Astromancer(USA)** has come down 14lb in the weights this year as a result of several very poor runs, but she put up a much improved effort on this occasion. She clearly acts well on the surface and, given there was a gap back to the third, should be up to winning a race of this nature.
**Macaroni Gold(IRE)** showed fair form in maidens but a bad run on his handicap debut at Southwell dented confidence with regards to his chance. That was on the Fibresand however, and today's surface clearly suited better. There should be improvement to come from him when stepping up to two miles, as he could not match the front pair for pace.
**Final Dividend(IRE)** is on a winning mark and this effort suggests he could soon be ready to capitalise.
**Two Of A Kind(IRE)** was given too much to do and would have appreciated a stronger-run race.
**Esperance(IRE)** failed to build on his promising All-Weather debut last time.
**Beyond The Pole(USA)** continues out of form.
**Sea Plume** looked far superior to her rivals on form and was fully entitled to win this on her solid second in a much better race at Newmarket last time, but having raced prominently she dropped away tamely once coming under pressure. There was presumably something amiss. *Official explanation: trainer was unable to offer any explanation for the filly's poor running; trainer later said filly had scoped dirty*

## 5976 BETDIRECT.CO.UK H'CAP (DIV I) 1m (P)
12:35 (12:36) (E) (0-75,72) 3-Y-0+ £2,299 (£657; £328) Stalls High

Form RPR
4102 **1** **Didnt Tell My Wife**[6] 5933 4-8-12 **60** LisaJones(3) 8 71
(CFWall) *lw: settled wl in rr: gd prog over 1f out: rdn to ld last 100y: sn in command* **4/1**[2]
0311 **2** *1¼* **Deeper In Debt**[20] 5719 5-9-12 **71** GCarter 11 79
(JAkehurst) *trckd ldrs: rdn and effrt 2f out: led narrowly ent fnl f: hdd and nt qckn last 100y* **7/2**[1]
5003 **3** *nk* **College Delinquent (IRE)**[16] 5796 4-9-7 **66** (t) DaneO'Neill 1 73
(KBell) *b.hind: trckd ldrs: lost pl and rdn over 2f out: effrt and prog over 1f out: ev ch ent fnl f: nt qckn last 100y* **8/1**
2340 **4** *1¼* **Miss Issy (IRE)**[12] 5856 3-8-10 **57** NCallan 5 62
(JGallagher) *settled towards rr: rdn and prog on outer over 2f out: drvn and cl up 1f out: one pce* **50/1**
60-0 **5** *1* **Ember Days**[15] 5821 4-8-12 **57** ADaly 7 59
(JLSpearing) *racd towards rr: pushed along over 2f out: effrt and nt clr run briefly over 1f out: kpt on same pce u.p fnl f* **20/1**
0232 **6** *1* **Dhakhirah (IRE)**[91] 4071 3-9-9 **70** LDettori 12 70
(ACStewart) *racd in midfield: u.p and struggling over 4f out: hrd drvn and sme prog on outer over 2f out: no imp over 1f out* **12/1**
0004 **7** *½* **Foolish Thought (IRE)**[16] 5793 3-8-13 **63** SHitchcott(3) 4 62
(RAFahey) *led for 1f: led again 3f out: hdd ent fnl f: wknd rapidly last 100y* **12/1**
5005 **8** *¾* **Magic Warrior**[13] 5837 3-8-13 **60** PDobbs 10 57
(JCFox) *hld up in last: effrt 2f out: nt clr run over 1f out: one pce after* **14/1**
1050 **9** *½* **Pango**[18] 5756 4-9-12 **71** SDrowne 3 67
(HMorrison) *trckd ldrs: n.m.r 2f out: nt clr run over 1f out: btn after and eased* **5/1**
00-2 **10** *½* **Polar Kingdom**[15] 5820 5-9-13 **72** DMernagh 2 67
(TDBarron) *lw: led after 1f to 3f out: cl up but hld whn bdly hmpd on inner over 1f out: nt rcvr* **9/2**[3]
3000 **11** *6* **Chateau Nicol**[13] 5837 4-8-10 **58** (b) LPKeniry(3) 6 39
(BGPowell) *t.k.h: trckd ldrs: chal over 2f out: ev ch whn hung lft and lost action over 1f out: wknd rapidly* **50/1**
1m 39.09s (-0.42) **Going Correction** +0.05s/f (Slow)
**WFA** 3 from 4yo+ 2lb **11** Ran SP% **118.9**
Speed ratings: **104,102,102,101,100 99,98,97,97,96 90**CSF £18.35 CT £108.47 TOTE £5.80: £2.10, £2.60, £2.30; EX 14.60.
**Owner** G D Newton **Bred** Mrs Frank Campbell **Trained** Newmarket, Suffolk
**FOCUS**
A competitive handicap where the time was again just inside the median.
**NOTEBOOK**
**Didnt Tell My Wife**, who reportedly came out of his race at Nottingham six days ago in good shape, was given a fine ride from the blossoming Lisa Jones, who weaved her mount through the field to take it up in the last half furlong. He is a reliable animal who should continue to give a good account of himself if kept on the go.
**Deeper In Debt** has been on a roll of late but, off a mark 10lb higher than when winning at Bath on his penultimate start, could not complete the hat-trick. *Official explanation: jockey said gelding hung left*
**College Delinquent(IRE)**, who has yet to win in handicap company, was a bit short of room and lost his position turning in, but got himself involved again and ran creditably.
**Miss Issy(IRE)** is exposed as a moderate maiden and her close proximity somewhat weighs the form down.
**Ember Days**, having only her second run of the season, did not receive the clearest of runs through and deserved to finish closer. She is quite lightly raced and may be capable of improvement.
**Dhakhirah(IRE)** did not have the pace to get herself involved and ideally wants a stiffer test.
**Foolish Thought(IRE)** could not repel the late challengers having been in front for most of the way.
**Magic Warrior** can count himself unfortunate not to have finished closer after getting hampered.
**Pango** was still in with a chance when badly tightened up.
**Polar Kingdom**ran a good race but was beaten at the time of getting hampered.
**Chateau Nicol** caused all the trouble when cutting up Pango who went on to do the same to Polar Kingdom.

## 5977 LITTLEWOODS BET DIRECT AW JOCKEYS CHAMPIONSHIP MEDIAN AUCTION MAIDEN STKS 5f (P)
1:10 (1:11) (E) 2-Y-0 £2,299 (£657; £328) Stalls High

Form RPR
33 **1** **Darting (USA)**[15] 5822 2-8-9 LDettori 6 67
(GAButler) *s.i.s: sn trckd ldrs: pressed ldr wl over 1f out: rdn to ld ins fnl f: fnd little in front: jst hld on* **13/8**[1]
4 **2** *shd* **Dandouce**[15] 5812 2-8-9 (v) ACulhane 3 67
(SLKeightley) *b.hind: led: hrd rdn over 1f out: narrowly hdd ins fnl f: kpt on wl: jst failed* **7/1**[3]
66 **3** *shd* **Aperitif**[15] 5812 2-9-0 MHills 8 72
(WJHaggas) *lw: bucking on way to post: racd wd in midfield: shkn up 2f out: gd prog fnl f: gaining fast at fin* **12/1**
442 **4** *1* **Helibel (IRE)**[12] 5844 2-8-9 73 DaneO'Neill 7 63
(MrsAJPerrett) *mounted on crse: s.i.s: settled in last trio: effrt over 1f out: hanging lft but r.o ins fnl f: nt rch ldrs* **2/1**[2]
003 **5** *½* **Laconia (IRE)**[15] 5812 2-8-9 61 JFEgan 5 61
(JSMoore) *lw: scope: taken down early: trckd ldrs: hanging and nt qckn fr 2f out: kpt on same pce fnl f* **16/1**
0 **6** *2* **Averami**[6] 5929 2-8-9 SDrowne 4 54
(AMBalding) *trckd ldrs: rdn 2f out: one pce and no imp fnl f* **25/1**
**7** *½* **Ask The Clerk (IRE)**[46] 5236 2-9-0 GBardwell 1 58
(HJCollingridge) *trckd ldrs: cl up on inner 1f out: wknd ins fnl f* **16/1**
00 **8** *½* **Limit Down (IRE)**[12] 5844 2-8-11 DCorby(3) 9 56
(MJWallace) *racd in last pair: outpcd 1/2-way: one pce and n.d after* **100/1**
60 **9** *¾* **Big Bad Burt**[62] 4847 2-9-0 NCallan 2 53
(MJWallace) *lw: dwlt: racd in last: rdn 3f out: effrt on inner over 1f out: no prog fnl f* **25/1**
06 **10** *3* **Your Just Lovely (IRE)**[30] 5547 2-8-6 LPKeniry(3) 10 38
(AMBalding) *b: sn pressed ldr: ev ch jst over 2f out: wknd rapidly over 1f out* **20/1**
60.62 secs (0.84) **Going Correction** +0.05s/f (Slow) **10** Ran SP% **116.8**
Speed ratings: **95,94,94,93,92 89,88,87,86,81**CSF £13.20 TOTE £2.10: £1.60, £2.30, £2.20; EX 21.90.
**Owner** Raymond Tooth **Bred** Shadwell Farm Llc **Trained** Blewbury, Oxon
**FOCUS**
Not much of a race but it did at least produce an exciting finish with two short heads separating the first three home.
**NOTEBOOK**
**Darting(USA)**, who seemingly found seven furlongs too far last time, appreciated this drop back in trip and only just held on.
**Dandouce**, who again had the visor on, showed plenty of zip before weakening on her debut at the trip. She saw her race out much better on this occasion and was coming back at the winner towards the end.
**Aperitif**, a 70,000gns purchase, has yet to live up to that price tag but this was a better effort. He would have got up in a few more strides and should be winning when upped to six furlongs.
**Helibel(IRE)** had to be mounted on course and hung under pressure. The drop back to five furlongs did not bring about any improvement.
**Laconia(IRE)** finished in front of both Dandouce and Aperitif at Nottingham last month but could not confirm the form.
**Averami** is likely to better once handicapped.
**Limit Down(IRE)** is another likely to stand a better chance in handicaps.
**Big Bad Burt** has shown promise and can now compete at handicap level.

## 5978 LITTLEWOODS BET DIRECT AW TRAINERS CHAMPIONSHIP MAIDEN STKS 1m 4f (P)
1:40 (1:41) (D) 3-Y-0+ £2,415 (£690; £345) Stalls Low

Form RPR
4-23 **1** **Sentry (IRE)**[9] 5907 3-9-0 87 LDettori 15 73
(JHMGosden) *lw: b.hind: sn prom: pushed along over 4f out: effrt to chal over 2f out: drvn and looked reluctant fr over 1f out: forced* **13/8**[1]
0-35 **2** *hd* **Bucks**[15] 5817 6-9-6 64 IMongan 7 73
(DKIvory) *b: trckd ldrs: effrt and squeezed through to ld wl over 2f out: sn hrd pressed: kpt on u.p fnl f: hdd last strides* **10/1**
5020 **3** *1¼* **Remembrance**[10] 5891 3-9-0 66 (t) JTate 6 71
(JMPEustace) *settled towards rr: prog over 3f out: chsd ldng pair over 2f out : clsd and ch ins fnl f: nt qckn last 100y* **6/1**[3]
04-2 **4** *8* **Maxilla (IRE)**[205] 1159 3-8-9 72 DaneO'Neill 9 54
(LMCumani) *lw: hld up in tch: prog on outer 4f out: outpcd by ldrs over 2f out : no imp over 1f out: wknd ins fnl f* **11/2**[2]
6 **5** *2½* **Schooner (GER)**[70] 4653 3-9-0 MTebbutt 1 55
(LadyHerries) *settled wl in rr: sme prog and swtchd to outer over 2f out: nudged along to take modest 5th ins fnl f: nvr nr ldrs* **20/1**
54 **6** *1¾* **Mofeyda (IRE)**[21] 5711 3-8-9 SDrowne 13 48
(ACStewart) *hld up towards rr: prog on outer 3f out: sn outpcd: drvn and btn over 2f out* **6/1**[3]
0/ **7** *7* **Little Bud**[37] 5463 9-9-1 DSweeney 5 37
(MissAMNewton-Smith) *taken down early: a in rr: outpcd and wl btn fnl 3f* **66/1**
0-55 **8** *1¼* **Daisycutter**[21] 5711 3-8-9 60 JFEgan 4 35
(GWragg) *rn in snatches: trckd ldrs: wl outpcd fr 3f out: wknd* **20/1**
5050 **9** *3* **Ladies Day**[11] 5879 3-8-9 70 JPaulielo 14 31
(TGMills) *lw: snatched up sn after s: sn prom but rn in snatches: wknd rapidly over 2f out* **20/1**
**10** *2* **Glesni** 4-8-10 BReilly(5) 8 28
(SCWilliams) *w'like: b.bkwd: weak: s.i.s: a wl in rr: passed wkng rivals fnl 3f* **33/1**
0604 **11** *1¾* **Byinchka**[41] 5329 3-9-0 50 ACulhane 10 30
(SLKeightley) *b.hind: prom: lost pl and pushed along after 4f: styd in tch tl wknd rapidly 3f out* **50/1**
6 **12** *4* **Seejay**[91] 4086 3-8-9 SCarson 12 19
(MAAllen) *lw: sn trckd ldr: led over 3f out to wl over 2f out: wknd rapidly* **100/1**
224 **13** *11* **Musical Gift**[242] 722 3-9-0 GCarter 3 8
(CNAllen) *lw: led to over 3f out: wknd rapidly: t.o* **9/1**
40B **14** *shd* **Repetoire (FR)**[128] 3067 3-8-6 LPKeniry(3) 11 —
(KOCunningham-Brown) *a in rr: detached in last over 3f out: t.o* **40/1**
2m 34.39s (0.41) **Going Correction** +0.05s/f (Slow)
**WFA** 3 from 4yo+ 6lb **14** Ran SP% **125.3**
Speed ratings: **100,99,99,93,92 90,86,85,83,82 80,78,70,70**CSF £18.57 TOTE £2.40: £1.40, £3.20, £2.40; EX 21.00.
**Owner** Highclere Thoroughbred Racing IV **Bred** Mrs G Doyle **Trained** Manton, Wilts
**FOCUS**
A weak maiden, made up of largely frustrating types, and very few managed to get into the argument.
**NOTEBOOK**
**Sentry(IRE)**, clear best in at the weights, finally got off the mark, but only just. He had looked like doing well early in the season, having run second to the smart Westmoreland Road on his reappearance, but was off the track for nearly seven months after that on account of the ground. Disappointing on his return last month, when looking slightly unwilling, he did nothing to suggest otherwise on this occasion, but he clearly has ability and this longer trip was in his favour.
**Bucks**, dropping in trip, was only just denied a first win. He understandably tried to put his proven stamina to good use around three furlongs out when quickening the tempo, and it almost paid off. He is officially rated 23lb lower than the winner, and while it is important not to take that too literally, this was a solid effort. He will be one to watch out for over the coming All-Weather season over this trip and beyond.
**Remembrance** has some fair form at this venue and seemed to get this extra distance well enough. He looks capable of winning a weak race.
**Maxilla(IRE)** was having her first run since April and will come on considerably for the experience. She looks ordinary, though.
**Byinchka** *Official explanation: trainer said gelding hung left*


The Form Book, Raceform Ltd, Compton, RG20 6NL

## 5979 LITTLEWOODS BET DIRECT ON 0800 329393 NURSERY 7f (P)

**2:10** (2:13) (C ) 2-Y-O **£5,133** (£1,947; £973; £442) **Stalls** Low

Form RPR

01 **1** **Bravo Maestro (USA)**[13] 5836 2-9-6 **86** SWhitworth 13 97+
(DWPArbuthnot) *lw: strong: s.i.s: sn rcvrd and wl in tch: trckd ldr over 2f out: led over 1f out and sn clr: pushed out: impressive* **9/4**[1]

5300 **2** 2 ½ **Pregnant Pause (IRE)**[16] 5789 2-7-7 **64** oh2 DFox(5) 11 69
(SKirk) *prom: rdn over 2f out: styd on to take 2nd ent fnl f: no ch w wnr* **10/1**

4001 **3** 1 **Rowan Pursuit**[18] 5745 2-7-9 **64** oh11 (b) FPFerris(3) 8 66
(MHTompkins) *outpcd and pushed along in last trio after 2f: effrt on outer over 2f out: styd on wl fnl f: nrst fin* **50/1**

515 **4** ½ **Celtic Heroine (IRE)**[19] 5734 2-8-8 **74** MHenry 10 75
(MAJarvis) *lw: racd in midfield: rdn over 3f out: prog to chse ldng trio over 2f out: styd on same pce fnl f* **10/1**

1500 **5** 1 **Anuvasteel**[12] 5854 2-8-13 **79** WRyan 6 83+
(NACallaghan) *restrained s and sn in last: outpcd after 2f and pushed along: struggling 3f out: styd on steadily fr over 1f out: no ch* **25/1**

0641 **6** 1 **Cartronageeraghlad (IRE)**[4] 5950 2-8-9 **75** 6ex ow1 (b) LDettori 7 71
(JAOsborne) *lw: led at fast pce: hdd & wknd over 1f out* **5/2**[2]

5141 **7** 1 ¾ **Knight Onthe Tiles (IRE)**[8] 5916 2-8-13 **79** 6ex (b) NPollard 12 71
(JRBest) *s.i.s: towards rr: effrt u.p on outer over 2f out: no imp on ldrs* **16/1**

310 **8** 2 **Binnion Bay (IRE)**[12] 5854 2-9-4 **84** PDobbs 3 71
(RHannon) *racd in midfield: rdn and effrt over 2f out: sn outpcd: no ch after* **20/1**

6000 **9** 3 ½ **Taranai (IRE)**[58] 4936 2-7-9 **64** oh7 LisaJones(3) 1 42
(BWDuke) *s.i.s: outpcd and a wl in rr* **100/1**

1620 **10** ½ **Wavertree Dream**[5] 5944 2-9-6 **86** IMongan 9 63
(NPLittmoden) *outpcd and pushed along in rr after 2f: sme prog u.p 3f out: n.d fnl 2f* **12/1**

3242 **11** 9 **Big Bradford**[16] 5797 2-9-7 **87** (b) SDrowne 4 41
(ELJames) *sn lost pl and rdn: struggling in rr fr halfwaay* **11/2**[3]

5231 **12** 3 **Rise**[76] 4526 2-9-6 **86** (b) SCarson 2 33
(AndrewReid) *b.hind: chsd ldr to 3f out: wknd rapidly* **20/1**

6014 **13** 13 **Scarlet Empress**[16] 5797 2-8-12 **78** (b) DaneO'Neill 5 —
(RHannon) *lw: chsd ldrs tl wknd rapidly over 2f out: eased over 1f out: t.o* **20/1**

1m 25.59s (-0.41) **Going Correction** +0.05s/f (Slow) **13** Ran SP% **127.6**
Speed ratings: **104,101,100,99,98 97,95,92,88,88 78,74,59**CSF £25.50 CT £947.32 TOTE £3.20: £1.50, £4.80, £11.60; EX 71.40.
**Owner** Derrick C Broomfield **Bred** Pacelco S A & Partners **Trained** Upper Lambourn, Berks

**FOCUS**
They went a really good gallop in what was an interesting nursery.

**NOTEBOOK**
**Bravo Maestro(USA)**, who looked a horse of some potential when winning his maiden at the course last time - the fastest of the three run over that trip on the day - travelled strongly on the outer of the field before being unleashed straightening for home and quickening right away. He has plenty more to offer and looks better than an average handicapper. Connections report he may come back here for a £75,000 race in March.
**Pregnant Pause(IRE)** is well exposed but ran well and seemed to show an improvement in form for the switch to Polytrack.
**Rowan Pursuit**, who was racing from 11lb out of the handicap, could not go the early pace but finished with a purpose and was edging nearer with every stride.
**Celtic Heroine(IRE)** won her maiden at this course last month prior to running respectably in a Newbury nursery, and shaped very much as though the step up to a mile will suit.
**Anuvasteel** was being ridden along in rear for most of the race and his jockeys effort paid off as he ran on for a share of the prize-money.
**Cartronageeraghlad(IRE)**, winner of an ultra-competitive nursery at Doncaster on Saturday, went off too fast and did not get home as a result.

## 5980 LITTLEWOODS BET DIRECT EBF FILLIES' H'CAP 1m 2f (P)

**2:45** (2:45) (C ) (0-100,78) 3-Y-O **£7,482** (£2,838; £1,419; £645) **Stalls** Low

Form RPR

1524 **1** **Dance In The Sun**[16] 5795 3-9-7 **78** DaneO'Neill 6 88
(MrsAJPerrett) *lw: hld up in last pair: smooth prog on outer over 2f out: shkn up to ld over 1f out: qcknd clr: rdn out* **3/1**[2]

6010 **2** 2 **Bravo Dancer**[14] 5828 3-9-6 **77** ACulhane 5 83
(MRChannon) *hld up in tch: smmoth prog 3f out: rdn to chal 2f out: ev ch over 1f out: sn outpcd by wnr: r.o* **3/1**[2]

4211 **3** 3 **Estimation**[12] 5856 3-8-11 **68** LDettori 7 69
(RMHCowell) *hld up in last: prog over 2f out: chsd ldrs and rdn over 1f out: sn outpcd* **5/2**[1]

2626 **4** 5 **Estimate**[39] 5360 3-8-7 **64** (v) JFEgan 4 56
(CEBrittain) *cl up: effrt to ld 3f out: hdd & wknd over 1f out* **33/1**

4262 **5** 2 ½ **Wasted Talent (IRE)**[26] 5609 3-9-2 **73** (p) SDrowne 3 60
(JGPortman) *prom: led over 7f out to 3f out: sn hrd rdn: wknd over 1f out* **9/1**

3360 **6** 7 **Nuzzle**[10] 5891 3-8-5 **62** SCarson 1 37
(MQuinn) *led to over 7f out: rdn 5f out: wknd over 2f out* **16/1**

3210 **7** 14 **Miss Pebbles (IRE)**[13] 5838 3-9-0 **71** IMongan 2 20
(BRJohnson) *lw: t.k.h: prom tl wknd wl over 2f out* **5/1**[3]

2m 7.03s (-0.36) **Going Correction** +0.05s/f (Slow) **7** Ran SP% **114.1**
Speed ratings: **103,101,99,95,93 87,76**CSF £12.39 TOTE £4.40: £2.00, £2.20; EX 15.00.
**Owner** Hesmonds Stud **Bred** Hesmonds Stud Ltd **Trained** Pulborough, W Sussex

**FOCUS**
Not the strongest 0-100 you will ever see with top-weight and winner Dance In The Sun being rated 78.

**NOTEBOOK**
**Dance In The Sun**, having found herself a bit tapped for toe half a mile out, was soon pulling double and quickened away up the straight. Her trainer believes a return to a mile four will not inconvenience despite appearing to fail to get it last time, as Perrett put that down to it being the filly's first run since June rather than lack of stamina.
**Bravo Dancer** travelled well but the winner had too much speed for her.
**Estimation** was racing off a 6lb higher mark than when winning at Southwell on his penultimate start and could not complete the hat-trick.
**Estimate** remains a maiden and failed to improve for a switch to the Polytrack.
**Miss Pebbles(IRE)** *Official explanation: jockey said filly hung right*

## 5981 BETDIRECT.CO.UK H'CAP (DIV II) 1m (P)

**3:15** (3:17) (E ) (0-75,72) 3-Y-0+ **£2,289** (£654; £327) **Stalls** High

Form RPR

4365 **1** **Labrett**[18] 5756 6-9-12 **71** (p) MFenton 10 80+
(MissGayKelleway) *lw: b.hind: racd on outer: sn trckd ldrs: shkn up over 1f out: r.o to ld last 150y: sn clr* **10/3**[1]

-040 **2** 1 ¾ **Priors Dale**[103] 3760 3-9-11 **72** DaneO'Neill 8 77
(KBell) *trckd ldng pair: effrt over 1f out: jnd ldr ent fnl f: sn outpcd by wnr* **66/1**

0500 **3** ¾ **My Maite (IRE)**[13] 5839 4-8-9 **54** (t) NDay 2 57
(RIngram) *led at mod pce: rdn and hdd over 2f out: kpt on and ev ch 1f out: one pce fnl f* **10/1**

0400 **4** nk **Quantum Leap**[16] 5796 6-9-1 **60** PaulEddery 6 62
(SDow) *hld up in rr: effrt 2f out: nt clr run thrght fnl f: kpt on* **20/1**

-600 **5** hd **Hadath (IRE)**[3] 5796 6-9-4 **66** (p) LPKeniry(3) 5 68
(BGPowell) *b: pressed ldr: led narrowly over 2f out: hdd & wknd last 150y* **25/1**

2102 **6** hd **Qualitair Wings**[8] 5918 4-9-0 **62** SHitchcott(3) 9 63
(JHetherton) *t.k.h early: hld up bhd ldrs: effrt 2f out: drvn and one pce fnl f* **4/1**[2]

200 **7** shd **Amoras (IRE)**[56] 5001 6-9-13 **72** MHills 1 73
(JWHills) *trckd ldrs: effrt 2f out: hanging lft and nt qckn 1f out* **14/1**

0000 **8** ½ **Feather Boa (IRE)**[10] 5891 3-9-6 **67** NCallan 12 67
(MBlanshard) *settled towards rr: drvn and effrt wl over 1f out: one pce fnl f* **16/1**

1520 **9** ½ **Resonate (IRE)**[14] 5832 5-8-11 **59** FPFerris(3) 3 58
(AGNewcombe) *lw: hld up in rr: effrt on inner 2f out: nowhere to go fr over 1f out: nt rcvr* **9/1**

6000 **10** hd **Coppington Flyer (IRE)**[13] 5838 3-8-8 **58** LisaJones(3) 4 56
(BWDuke) *trckd ldrs: cl up on inner over 1f out: nt clr run after: nt rcvr* **20/1**

0004 **11** shd **Oases**[10] 5892 4-8-12 **57** SWhitworth 7 55
(DShaw) *dwlt: plld hrd and hld up in last pair: drvn and effrt 2f out: no prog fnl f* **8/1**[3]

0022 **12** 1 **Night Kiss (FR)**[13] 5837 3-8-13 **60** RSmith 11 56
(RHannon) *hld up wl in rr: drvn and effrt 2f out: no prog fr over 1f out* **4/1**[2]

1m 41.49s (1.98) **Going Correction** +0.05s/f (Slow)
**WFA** 3 from 4yo+ 2lb **12** Ran SP% **120.7**
Speed ratings: **92,90,89,89,89 88,88,88,87,87 87,86**CSF £260.89 CT £2059.99 TOTE £3.80: £1.20, £13.40, £3.60; EX 179.00.
**Owner** A P Griffin **Bred** Bearstone Stud **Trained** Newmarket, Suffolk

**FOCUS**
The weaker of the two divisions with the time being considerably slower than the first, although the pace was not as fast.

**NOTEBOOK**
**Labrett** is usually restrained in rear but he received a more positive ride on this occasion and stayed on strongly down the straight to record his tenth career victory.
**Priors Dale** left his disappointing Nottingham handicap debut behind and kept on well for second, suggesting he will be winning when returned to a mile and a quarter.
**My Maite(IRE)** set a steady gallop but left himself vulnerable to anything with a finishing kick.
**Quantum Leap** received no luck in running and had to sit and suffer.
**Hadath(IRE)** ran a decent race.
**Qualitair Wings** was slightly disappointing and did not really finish his race.
**Amoras(IRE)** hung left under pressure and failed to pick up.
**Resonate(IRE)** was crying out for somewhere to go but found his luck was out.
**Coppington Flyer(IRE)** was in the same boat as Resonate.

## 5982 LITTLEWOODSCASINO.COM APPRENTICE H'CAP (DIV II) 1m 5f (P)

**3:50** (3:50) (F ) (0-75,68) 3-Y-0+ **£2,257** (£645; £322) **Stalls** Low

Form RPR

0011 **1** **Cold Turkey**[13] 5839 3-9-7 **68** HPoulton(3) 5 83+
(GLMoore) *hld up in last trio and wl off the pce: smooth prog over 3f out: led over 1f out: sprinted clr* **11/4**[2]

0222 **2** 6 **Danehill Lad (IRE)**[13] 5839 3-9-9 **67** LTreadwell 8 74
(TKeddy) *trckd ldrs: prog 5f out: led 3f out: rdn and hdd over 1f out : no ch w wnr after* **3/1**[3]

0206 **3** 1 ¼ **Dame Margaret**[36] 5437 3-7-8 **43** LiamJones(5) 7 48
(MLWBell) *plld hrd: trckd ldng trio: outpcd and rdn over 2f out: effrt again to chse ldng pair wl over 1f out: kpt on same pce* **25/1**

1200 **4** 3 ½ **Forever My Lord**[42] 5312 5-8-12 **56** DFentiman(7) 3 56
(JRBest) *s.s: hld up in last trio and off the pce: rdn and prog 3f out: one pce and no imp fr 2f out* **8/1**

4015 **5** 4 **Classic Millennium**[19] 5727 5-8-7 **49** LauraPike(5) 9 44
(WJMusson) *trckd ldrs: lost pl over 4f out: effrt again over 2f out: sn outpcd and btn* **5/2**[1]

000/ **6** 1 ½ **Charmante Femme**[35] 5456 5-8-13 **50** PGallagher 6 43
(PDEvans) *led to over 4f out: sn rdn: cl up over 2f out: sn wknd* **14/1**

0506 **7** 18 **Zoeanna (IRE)**[134] 2873 3-8-3 **50** WHogg(3) 4 17
(RGuest) *trckd ldr: led over 4f out to 3f out: wknd: t.o* **33/1**

40-0 **8** 7 **Hektikos**[40] 5343 3-8-11 **62** JCoffill-Brown(7) 1 20
(SDow) *lw: hld up in last trio: wknd 5f out: sn t.o* **100/1**

1006 **9** 1 ¼ **Persephone Heights**[26] 5608 3-8-8 **52** DAStamp 2 8
(DJCoakley) *trckd ldng pair to 5f out: sn btn: wknd and eased over 2f out : t.o* **11/1**

2m 47.72s (-0.36) **Going Correction** +0.05s/f (Slow)
**WFA** 3 from 5yo 7lb **9** Ran SP% **114.1**
Speed ratings: **103,99,98,96,93 93,81,77,76**CSF £11.14 CT £163.49 TOTE £4.10: £1.80, £1.50, £3.10; EX 8.50 Place 6 £57.79, Place 5 £13.21.
**Owner** A Grinter **Bred** Worksop Manor Stud **Trained** Woodingdean, E Sussex

**FOCUS**
This was run in a similar time to the first division but Cold Turkey was most impressive and would have won either race.

**NOTEBOOK**
**Cold Turkey** was given a patient ride by Poulton, who does not have a bad wins-to-rides ratio, and came through hard held before taking it up approaching the furlong pole and running right away with it. He has improved this season for stepping up to middle distances and may bid for a four-timer if taking up his engagement in the claimer on Thursday.
**Danehill Lad(IRE)** has developed a habit of finishing second but is not ungenuine. His turn will come.
**Dame Margaret** saw her race out well enough despite pulling hard.
**Forever My Lord** never got into it.
**Classic Millennium** would have preferred a stronger pace.
**Persephone Heights** continues to run poorly and dropped right out.
T/Jkpt: £1,977.40 to a £1 stake. Pool: £13,926.00. 5.00 winning tickets. T/Plt: £58.50 to a £1 stake. Pool: £36,986.70. 460.90 winning tickets. T/Qpdt: £9.90 to a £1 stake. Pool: £4,173.30. 310.00 winning tickets. JN

# 5975 LINGFIELD (L-H)

Thursday, November 13

**OFFICIAL GOING: Standard**

Wind: lt bhd Weather: overcast

## 5984 EBF BET DIRECT ON 0800 32 93 93 MAIDEN STKS (DIV I) 1m (P)

12:20 (12:22) (D ) 2-Y-O £3,094 (£884; £442) Stalls High

Form RPR

1 **Rendezvous Point (USA)** 2-8-9 ........ LDettori 8 71+
(JHMGosden) *unf: scope: lengthy: leggy: lw: sn prom: effrt and rn green over 2f out: chsd ldr over 1f out : styd on to ld last strides* **5/2**[1]

03 2 *hd* **Pergolacha (IRE)**[10] 5905 2-8-9 ........ DaneO'Neill 11 71
(LMCumani) *pressed ldr: led over 2f out: rdn over 1f out: kpt on wl: hdd last strides* **8/1**

04 3 *1* **Pukka (IRE)**[10] 5905 2-9-0 ........ KDalgleish 5 74
(LMCumani) *lw: s.i.s: sn trckd ldrs: pushed along over 3f out: rdn and unable qck 2f out: styd on wl fnl f: nrst fin* **10/1**

0 4 *1 3/4* **Resonance**[14] 5833 2-8-9 ........ WRyan 1 65
(MrsAJPerrett) *s.s: settled wl in rr: pushed along 2f out: prog over 1f out: shkn up and styd on wl fnl f* **33/1**

3 5 *1 1/4* **La Landonne**[41] 5342 2-8-6 ........ J-PGuillambert(3) 6 62
(PMPhelan) *t.k.h: hld up in midfield: effrt over 2f out: sn unable qck: kpt on same pce fnl f* **7/1**

3 6 *2 1/2* **Evaluator (IRE)**[14] 5836 2-9-0 ........ AClark 9 62
(TGMills) *racd freely: led to over 2f out: wknd fnl f* **3/1**[2]

0 7 *1 1/4* **Land Of Nod (IRE)**[19] 5754 2-8-9 ........ SWKelly 4 54
(GAButler) *prom: chal 3f out: rdn and wknd 2f out* **4/1**[3]

8 *1 1/2* **Just Filly (IRE)** 2-8-9 ........ GHannon 3 50
(APJones) *w'like: bit bkwd: s.s: sn rcvrd into midfield: rdn over 3f out: wknd 2f out* **100/1**

9 *1* **Donastrela (IRE)** 2-8-9 ........ MFenton 10 48
(AMBalding) *leggy: unf: s.v.s: a wl in rr: nvr a factor* **33/1**

0 10 *1 1/2* **Wake Up Henry**[6] 5940 2-9-0 ........ SDrowne 7 50
(RCharlton) *pushed along in rr over 5f out: no prog 3f out* **20/1**

04 11 *2* **Burlington Place**[52] 5113 2-9-0 ........ JFEgan 12 46
(SKirk) *racd in midfield: rdn and struggling over 3f out: wknd* **25/1**

12 *17* **Skelthwaite** 2-9-0 ........ JFanning 2 8
(MHTompkins) *w'like: bit bkwd: s.v.s: a detached in last: t.o* **33/1**

1m 40.19s (0.68) **Going Correction** +0.025s/f (Slow) **12** Ran SP% **124.7**
Speed ratings: **97,96,95,94,92 90,89,87,86,85 83,66**CSF £23.07 TOTE £2.80: £2.00, £2.50, £3.30; EX 27.50.
**Owner** George Strawbridge **Bred** B D Mags Stables Et Al **Trained** Manton, Wilts

**FOCUS**
This could prove to be a decent maiden with plenty of promising individuals in the line-up.

**NOTEBOOK**
**Rendezvous Point(USA)**, a $500,000 purchase who is related to dirt performers, showed distinct signs of inexperience but battled well under pressure and got up late on to snatch it. This was a most promising debut and she should be up to winning in a higher grade next season.
**Pergolacha(IRE)** is progressing with racing and makes for a nice prospect for middle-distance races next season.
**Pukka(IRE)**, a stablemate of the second, falls into exactly the same basket and should also continue to progress.
**Resonance**, reportedly beginning to go in her coat, improved on her debut running at the course two weeks ago and should win her maiden with little fuss next season.
**La Landonne**, who made a promising debut over six furlongs at the course last month, looks in need of this trip and may have appreciated being ridden more prominent.
**Evaluator(IRE)** raced freely and did not see out his race. He is worth giving another chance to.
**Land Of Nod(IRE)**, well supported in the market, was beaten with quarter of a mile left to run.

## 5985 BETDIRECT.CO.UK NEW SITE H'CAP (DIV I) 7f (P)

12:50 (12:52) (E ) (0-75,74) 3-Y-O+ £2,404 (£687; £343) Stalls Low

Form RPR

5004 1 **Compton Banker (IRE)**[29] 5574 6-9-10 **70**........(v) SWKelly 5 80
(GAButler) *settled wl in rr: stl plenty to do 2f out: swtchd to outer over 1f out: str run to ld last 75y* **12/1**

-000 2 *1/2* **Sir Laughalot**[180] 1661 3-9-7 **68**........ ACulhane 6 76
(MissECLavelle) *racd on outer: hld up in midfield: effrt 2f out: r.o to chal last 100y: outpcd by wnr after* **50/1**

1305 3 *1/2* **Dorchester**[12] 5875 6-10-0 **74**........ LDettori 3 81
(WJMusson) *settled wl in rr: gd prog on inner wl over 1f out: jnd ldrs last 100y: one pce after* **13/2**

0040 4 *1* **Foolish Thought (IRE)**[1] 5976 3-8-13 **63**........ SHitchcott(3) 7 68
(RAFahey) *pressed ldr: led 3f out: kicked 3l clr over 1f out: wknd and hdd last 75y* **10/1**

0042 5 *2* **Zak Facta (IRE)**[23] 5690 3-8-10 **57**........(v) CCogan 2 57
(MissDAMchale) *b: prom: drvn and cl up 2f out: unable qck and btn whn n.m.r 150y out* **16/1**

0402 6 *nk* **Jagged (IRE)**[11] 5892 3-8-12 **59**........ DarrenWilliams 16 58
(KRBurke) *b: pressed ldrs: hrd rdn over 2f out: stl cl up over 1f out: fdd fnl f* **6/1**[3]

0215 7 *nk* **Duo Leoni**[42] 5326 3-8-13 **60**........ MTebbutt 11 58
(RMBeckett) *wl in rr: detached in last pair over 2f out: rapid prog on inner fnl f: fin wl* **33/1**

-001 8 *nk* **Majhool**[29] 5574 4-9-12 **72**........ IMongan 9 69
(GLMoore) *b: lw: hld up bhd ldrs: effrt and nt clr run 2f out: styng on whn hmpd last 150y: nt rcvr* **4/1**[1]

0411 9 *nk* **Mistral Sky**[14] 5837 4-9-10 **70**........(v) SDrowne 1 67
(MrsStefLiddiard) *lw: hld up in midfield: effrt over 2f out: swtchd rt ent fnl f: one pce* **5/1**[2]

4000 10 *shd* **Peyto Princess**[47] 5224 5-8-12 **61**........ LisaJones(3) 12 57
(MABuckley) *a towards rr: rdn and no prog over 2f out: kpt on fnl f* **20/1**

0351 11 *hd* **Teyaar**[17] 5794 7-9-5 **65**........ PMcCabe 4 61
(MrsNMacauley) *b: lw: racd towards rr: effrt and n.m.r 2f out: no prog over 1f out* **12/1**

4153 12 *1 1/4* **Ripple Effect**[57] 4990 3-9-7 **73**........(t) BReilly(5) 8 66
(CADwyer) *prom: rdn over 2f out: wknd wl over 1f out* **20/1**

1350 13 *4* **Its Ecco Boy**[16] 5811 5-8-9 **55**........ DKinsella 14 38
(PHowling) *prom: drvn to chse ldr wl over 1f out: wkng whn hmpd last 150y: eased* **12/1**

6100 14 *2* **Azreme**[103] 3788 3-9-10 **71**........(v) MFenton 10 49
(PWD'Arcy) *slopwly into stride: a wl in rr: rdn in last pair over 2f out: no prog* **25/1**

0000 15 *1/2* **Toppling**[31] 5553 5-8-11 **57**........ PFitzsimons 13 33
(JMBradley) *led to 3f out: wknd rapidly wl over 1f out* **20/1**

0-34 16 *7* **Fire Dome (IRE)**[106] 3703 11-8-11 **60**........ J-PGuillambert(3) 15 19
(AndrewReid) *b: b.hind: a towards rr: rdn and struggling over 2f out* **25/1**

1m 25.28s (-0.72) **Going Correction** +0.025s/f (Slow)
**WFA** 3 from 4yo+ 1lb **16** Ran SP% **129.2**
Speed ratings: **105,104,103,102,100 100,99,99,99,98 98,97,92,90,89 81**CSF £539.25 CT £2632.96 TOTE £13.10: £2.10, £3.60, £1.70, £4.50; EX 386.90.
**Owner** Erik Penser **Bred** David Jamison Bloodstock **Trained** Blewbury, Oxon

**FOCUS**
This was a real competitive handicap with less than six lengths covering the first eleven home.

**NOTEBOOK**
**Compton Banker(IRE)** is a funny character but had the race run to suit and came flying down the outside up the straight to win his first race for well over a year. He would not be one to bank on for a follow-up due to his nature.
**Sir Laughalot** had shown promise in handicaps prior to this and was sent off a big price. He rewarded any each-way supporters and looked to have it won until Compton Banker came and stole it.
**Dorchester** had a nice run through but the burden of top weight halted any further progress.
**Foolish Thought(IRE)**, seventh at the course yesterday, ran most creditably but may have gone for home too soon.
**Zak Facta(IRE)** was tight for room inside the furlong pole but his winning chance had already gone.
**Jagged(IRE)** had every chance but raced too close to the pace.
**Duo Leoni** was a long way behind turning in but all of a sudden picked up and came home with a rare rattle. She was closing with every stride and can win a race of this nature if continuing in the same form. *Official explanation: jockey said, regarding the running and riding, filly was hanging right-handed and therefore he was unable to get her balanced until reaching the rails in the home straight, where she ran on strongly; trainer added that this was filly's first run on the all-weather*
**Majhool** was unlucky and should have finished much closer.

## 5986 EBF BET DIRECT ON 0800 32 93 93 MAIDEN STKS (DIV II) 1m (P)

1:20 (1:22) (D ) 2-Y-O £3,080 (£880; £440) Stalls High

Form RPR

1 **Red Spell (IRE)** 2-9-0 ........ DaneO'Neill 7 76
(RHannon) *w'like: scope: str: lw: prom: effrt over 2f out: rdn to ld over 1f out: styd on wl* **7/1**

2 *2* **Bienvenue** 2-8-9 ........ ADaly 8 66
(MPTregoning) *unf: scope: settled wl in rr: pushed along 3f out: prog 2f out: shkn up and r.o wl fnl f to take 2nd nr fin* **5/1**[2]

3 *nk* **Impartial** 2-9-0 ........ JFanning 5 71
(PFICole) *w'like: scope: bit bkwd: trckd ldrs: rdn wl over 2f out: kpt on same pce fr over 1f out* **5/1**[2]

46 4 *nk* **Waziri (IRE)**[11] 5887 2-9-0 ........ MFenton 2 70
(HMorrison) *pressed ldr: led wl over 2f out: drvn and hdd over 1f out: wknd ins fnl f* **11/4**[1]

0 5 *2* **Inchpast**[6] 5938 2-9-0 ........ LDettori 3 66
(MHTompkins) *chsd ldrs: drvn wl over 2f out: one pce and no imp fr over 1f out* **25/1**

0 6 *2* **Polar Dancer**[17] 5792 2-8-9 ........ WRyan 4 56
(MrsAJPerrett) *led to wl over 2f out: wknd over 1f out* **20/1**

0 7 *1/2* **Ameyrah (IRE)**[19] 5757 2-8-9 ........ ACulhane 1 55
(MRChannon) *lw: s.i.s: racd in last pair and rn green: pushed along and kpt on one pce fnl 2f: n.d* **6/1**[3]

0 8 *2 1/2* **Cora (IRE)**[15] 5830 2-8-9 ........ SWKelly 10 50
(LMCumani) *racd in midfield: drvn and effrt over 3f out: wknd over 2f out* **20/1**

0 9 *shd* **Nuts For You (IRE)**[12] 5868 2-8-9 ........ SDrowne 6 49
(RCharlton) *t.k.h: prom tl wknd over 2f out* **10/1**

10 *5* **Crackleando** 2-8-11 ........ J-PGuillambert(3) 11 43
(NPLittmoden) *w'like: bit bkwd: a wl in rr: wl bhd fr over 2f out* **14/1**

6 11 *1 1/2* **Solo Sole (ITY)**[11] 5902 2-9-0 ........ KDalgleish 12 40
(LMCumani) *w'like: s.v.s: sn in tch in last pair: pushed along and wknd over 2f out* **14/1**

1m 40.54s (1.03) **Going Correction** +0.025s/f (Slow) **11** Ran SP% **122.6**
Speed ratings: **95,93,92,92,90 88,87,85,85,80 78**CSF £42.60 TOTE £7.20: £2.50, £2.20, £2.40; EX 59.70.
**Owner** Mrs John Lee **Bred** Tom Darcy And Vincent McCarthy **Trained** East Everleigh, Wilts

**FOCUS**
A fair maiden made-up mainly of future handicappers.

**NOTEBOOK**
**Red Spell(IRE)**, who had been unable to get on the track prior to now due to an injured knee, always held a good position and was never going to get caught once going on over a furlong out. This was a promising debut and if progressing the right way, should be up to winning a better race.
**Bienvenue**, whose family tend to improve with time, made a most pleasing debut and is sure to have learned plenty.
**Impartial**, a 70,000gns purchase, could not quicken under pressure but showed more than enough to suggest he will pay his way.
**Waziri(IRE)** is now qualified for handicaps and should do better in that sphere.
**Inchpast**, another likely to do better once qualified for handicaps, kept on well enough and should improve for a step up in trip.
**Polar Dancer** showed up well early and is sure to win races for connections once qualified for a mark.
**Ameyrah(IRE)** still looks in need of experience and it is likely we will see a different filly next season after she has had a chance to develop.

## 5987 BETDIRECT.CO.UK NEW SITE H'CAP (DIV II) 7f (P)

1:50 (1:51) (E ) (0-75,72) 3-Y-O+ £2,404 (£687; £343) Stalls Low

Form RPR

2064 1 **Mr Bountiful (IRE)**[26] 5636 5-8-9 55........ SWKelly 5 64
(MDods) *lw: pressed ldrs: str reminders wl over 2f out: effrt over 1f out: drvn to ld nr fin* **7/1**[3]

214 2 *nk* **Just One Smile (IRE)**[16] 5811 3-9-1 62........ JFEgan 6 70
(TDEasterby) *trckd ldrs: rdn over 2f out: effrt over 1f out: r.o wl fnl f to take 2nd last stride* **5/1**[2]

0321 3 *shd* **Trousers**[36] 5455 4-9-12 72........ LDettori 3 80
(AndrewReid) *b: b.hind: s.i.s: sn cl up: rdn to chse ldr wl over 1f out: drvn to ld last 150y: hdd nr fin* **3/1**[1]

0004 4 *1* **Blakeshall Boy**[17] 5794 5-8-12 58........ DeanMcKeown 4 64
(RLee) *racd in midfield: prog 2f out: styng on and ch whn nt clr run ins fnl f* **14/1**

3230 5 *shd* **George Stubbs (USA)**[24] 5673 5-9-7 70........(b) J-PGuillambert(3) 10 75
(NPLittmoden) *racd in midfield: effrt over 2f out: taken to outer and styd on wl fnl f: nvr able to chal* **10/1**

4060 6 *1/2* **Heidelburg (IRE)**[20] 5729 3-9-2 63........ ACulhane 14 67
(SKirk) *settled wl in rr: effrt over 2f out: styd on wl fr over 1f out: nrst fin* **20/1**

/00- **7** *nk* **Kilmeena Lad**[520] 2042 7-9-9 72 ........ LPKeniry(3) 1 75
(JCFox) *bit bkwd: hld up bhd ldrs: effrt 2f out: bdly hmpd over 1f out: nt rcvr* **50/1**

4000 **8** *nk* **Goodenough Mover**[16] 5811 7-9-8 68 ........ DaneO'Neill 12 71
(JSKing) *mde most: rdn 2f out: hdd & wknd last 150y* **8/1**

1440 **9** *1 1/4* **Fearby Cross (IRE)**[38] 5427 7-9-4 67 ........ LisaJones(3) 2 66
(WJMusson) *s.i.s: racd towards rr: progres on inner 2f out: clsng on ldrs whn bdly hmpd last 75y: no ch after* **11/1**

5026 **10** *nk* **Inistrahull Island (IRE)**[17] 5787 3-8-9 56 ........ JFanning 9 55
(MHTompkins) *hld up in last pair: plenty to do 2f out: pushed along and r.o steadily fr over 1f out: nvr nr ldrs* **20/1**

3003 **11** *1/2* **King David**[11] 5892 4-8-11 57 ........ RPrice 11 54
(DBurchell) *w ldr to 2f out: wknd over 1f out* **10/1**

2464 **12** *2 1/2* **Jonny Ebeneezer**[9] 5918 4-9-10 70 ........ SDrowne 16 61
(RMHCowell) *prom: rdn over 2f out: wkng whn hmpd jst over 1f out* **7/1**[3]

0 **13** *7* **Sestina (FR)**[17] 5793 3-9-4 65 ........ PDoe 7 39
(SDow) *a wl in rr: in last pair and struggling over 2f out* **100/1**

1000 **14** *hd* **Tuscan Treaty**[13] 5849 3-8-8 60 ........ JFMcDonald(5) 13 33
(TTClement) *s.i.s: racd on outer: drvn and effrt fr rr 3f out: wknd 2f out* **40/1**

0000 **15** *3 1/2* **Dunedin Rascal**[57] 4991 6-9-12 72 ........ (b) SCarson 8 36
(EAWheeler) *bit bkwd: a wl in rr* **25/1**

6650 **16** *2* **Fulvio (USA)**[113] 3500 3-9-11 72 ........ IMongan 15 31
(JamiePoulton) *racd towards rr: rdn and effrt 3f out: wknd over 2f out* **25/1**

1m 25.67s (-0.33) **Going Correction** +0.025s/f (Slow)
**WFA** 3 from 4yo+ 1lb **16** Ran SP% **133.6**
Speed ratings: **102,101,101,100,100 99,99,99,97,97 96,93,85,85,81 79**CSF £43.05 CT £127.87 TOTE £10.40: £2.40, £1.30, £2.50, £3.80; EX 44.90 Trifecta £123.70 Pool of £906.44 - 5.20 winning units.
**Owner** Denton Hall Racing Ltd **Bred** Peter McCutcheon **Trained** Piercebridge, Co Durham

**FOCUS**
A rough race with plenty of horses failing to get a run.

**NOTEBOOK**
**Mr Bountiful(IRE)**, back on the All-Weather for the first time since June, he found plenty under pressure and got up late on to to record his fifth career victory.
**Just One Smile(IRE)** had every chance but found the winner too strong.
**Trousers** could not hold off the late challengers under her big weight but ran a brave race and continues in form.
**Blakeshall Boy** was slightly unlucky not to finish closer, but is hard to win with.
**George Stubbs(USA)** ran on up the straight without ever looking likely to win.
**Heidelburg(IRE)** was gaining at the finish and may be worth trying back over further.
**Kilmeena Lad** got badly hampered and had no chance after.
**Fearby Cross(IRE)** ran better than the bare result suggests, being done no favours by getting hampered.

## 5988 BET DIRECT ON ATTHERACES INTERACTIVE MAIDEN STKS 6f (P)
2:20 (2:21) (D) 3-Y-O+ **£2,299** (£657; £328) **Stalls** Low

Form RPR

56 **1** **Phrenologist**[17] 5799 3-9-0 ........ DaneO'Neill 6 71
(JRFanshawe) *trckd ldrs: rdn 2f out: r.o u.p fnl f to ld last strides* **7/1**

023 **2** *nk* **Salon Prive**[17] 5799 3-9-0 68 ........ LDettori 9 70
(CACyzer) *mde most: rdn over 1f out: kpt on fnl f: hdd last strides* **5/2**[1]

4330 **3** *1 1/2* **Monte Mayor Lad (IRE)**[24] 5678 3-9-0 62 ........ (b[1]) SDrowne 1 66
(DHaydnJones) *racd towards rr of main gp: rdn over 2f out: styd on wl fnl f to take 3rd nr fin* **14/1**

5003 **4** *nk* **Mynd**[9] 5919 3-9-0 56 ........ DeanMcKeown 10 65
(RMWhitaker) *w ldr to over 1f out: wknd ins fnl f* **14/1**

5-00 **5** *2* **Tatweer (IRE)**[5] 5953 3-9-0 ........ (v) DarrenWilliams 2 59
(DShaw) *chsd ldrs: hrd rdn over 2f out: one pce fnl 2f* **50/1**

0400 **6** *shd* **Inching**[36] 5451 3-8-9 60 ........ MHenry 3 53
(RMHCowell) *s.i.s: sn wl in tch: rdn to chse ldrs over 2f out : fdd over 1f out* **14/1**

4460 **7** *shd* **Calusa Lady (IRE)**[31] 5553 3-8-9 59 ........ (v[1]) AClark 7 53
(GBBalding) *s.s: rcvrd and in tch in rr 1/2-way: rdn and no prog fnl 2f* **14/1**

2230 **8** *1 1/4* **Montana**[45] 5283 3-9-0 68 ........ RSmith 13 54
(RHannon) *s.s: sn in midfield: rdn 2f out: hanging and fnd nil over 1f out* **8/1**

6533 **9** *nk* **Go Go Girl**[32] 5508 3-8-6 63 ........ LPKeniry(3) 14 48
(LGCottrell) *racd wd: in tch in rr: c v wd bnd 2f out: no ch after* **4/1**[2]

U00 **10** *1/2* **Arran**[17] 5799 3-9-0 ........ MTebbutt 5 52
(HJCollingridge) *b: s.i.s: bhd: detached in last trio 1/2-way: shuffled along and kpt on steadily fr over 1f out* **100/1**

6040 **11** *2 1/2* **Beneking**[14] 5837 3-9-0 62 ........ NCallan 8 44
(JGallagher) *chsd ldrs tl wknd 2f out* **6/1**[3]

00 **12** *nk* **Nathan Detroit**[17] 5799 3-9-0 ........ DSweeney 11 43
(PJMakin) *b: b.hind: racd on outer: chsd ldrs: rdn over 2f out: sn wknd* **20/1**

0 **13** *7* **Easy Breeze**[3] 5969 3-9-0 ........ PFitzsimons 4 22
(JMBradley) *lost pl bef 1/2-way: wl bhd fnl 2f* **200/1**

**14** *4* **Sargents Dream** 3-8-9 ........ ADaly 12 5
(JAGilbert) *unf: s.s: a wl bhd* **300/1**

1m 12.69s (-0.23) **Going Correction** +0.025s/f (Slow) **14** Ran SP% **121.7**
Speed ratings: **102,101,99,99,96 96,96,94,94,93 90,89,80,75**CSF £24.71 TOTE £7.10: £1.90, £1.70, £3.80; EX 25.20.
**Owner** The Leonard Curtis Partnership **Bred** Miss L A Perratt **Trained** Newmarket, Suffolk

**FOCUS**
A weak race but the front pair could do alright handicapping.

**NOTEBOOK**
**Phrenologist** had shown in two starts prior to this that he had ability and reversed form Salon Prive on this drop back in trip. He was always well placed and could be the type to do well in handicaps next season.
**Salon Prive** was bang there throughout but despite trying desperately, could not hold off the winner. He is a consistent type who should pay his way in handicaps.
**Monte Mayor Lad(IRE)**, in the first-time blinkers, finished strongly and was closing with every stride at the line.
**Mynd** ran well but did not see out the trip as well as others.
**Tatweer(IRE)** put up an improved effort and could be the type for a weak race on the All-Weather through the winter.
**Montana** is a very disappointing animal and can afford to be missed if ever he does get his head in front.
**Go Go Girl** is another disappointing sort.
**Beneking** is well exposed but still should have fared better.
**Sargents Dream** *Official explanation: jockey said filly hung right*

## 5989 BET DIRECT ON CHANNEL 4 PAGE 613 CLAIMING STKS 1m 4f (P)
2:50 (2:51) (E) 3-5-Y-O **£2,065** (£590; £295) **Stalls** Low

Form RPR

2640 **1** **Compton Eclaire (IRE)**[14] 5839 3-7-10 57 ........ (v[1]) JFMcDonald(5) 6 50
(GABButler) *dwlt: hld up in rr: progres on outer over 2f out: sn rdn: r.o fnl f to ld last stride* **9/4**[2]

4004 **2** *hd* **Landescent (IRE)**[11] 5890 3-8-5 52 ........ (v) MFenton 10 54
(MQuinn) *hld up in last: stdy prog fr 3f out: drvn over 1f out: styd on to dispute ld nr fin: hdd on post* **8/1**

4000 **3** *shd* **Rasid (USA)**[15] 5827 5-9-3 79 ........ DaneO'Neill 7 60
(CADwyer) *dwlt: hld up in rr: prog on outer 3f out: rdn 2f out: styd on fnl f to ld last 30y: hdd fnl strides* **7/1**[3]

1406 **4** *3/4* **Khuzdar (IRE)**[8] 5928 4-8-10 39 ........ SHitchcott(3) 2 55
(MRChannon) *dwlt: hld up in rr: prog over 3f out: rdn to chse ldr wl over 1f out: kpt on u.p to chal last 50y: nt qckn* **7/1**[3]

0000 **5** *hd* **Water Of Life (IRE)**[23] 5695 4-8-2 49 ow1 ........ RMiles(5) 1 49
(JRBoyle) *trckd ldrs: effrt to ld on inner 2f out: kicked 2l clr over 1f out: wknd and hdd last 30y* **20/1**

2005 **6** *7* **Dark Dolores**[21] 5717 5-8-6 35 ........ DSweeney 11 37
(JRBoyle) *led for 2f: pressed ldr tl led again 3f out: hdd & wknd 2f out* **25/1**

2006 **7** *1 1/4* **Route Barree (FR)**[41] 5344 5-8-10 46 ........ PDoe 8 39
(SDow) *s.s: sn prom: drvn 4f out: wknd u.p over 2f out* **10/1**

4000 **8** *3/4* **Elheba (IRE)**[24] 5680 4-8-12 55 ........ (b) LisaJones(3) 4 43
(MWigham) *dwlt: a in rr: struggling over 2f out* **33/1**

1540 **9** *1 1/2* **Appleacre**[20] 5727 4-9-0 85 ........ IMongan 9 40
(BRJohnson) *b: pushed up to ld after 2f: rdn and hdd 3f out: sn btn* **2/1**[1]

0000 **10** *18* **Onya**[134] 2898 3-8-5 44 ........ JFEgan 5 10
(JWHills) *t.k.h: trckd ldrs: rdn 4f out: sn wknd: t.o* **33/1**

2m 34.18s (0.20) **Going Correction** +0.025s/f (Slow)
**WFA** 3 from 4yo+ 6lb **10** Ran SP% **123.8**
Speed ratings: **100,99,99,99,99 94,93,93,92,80**CSF £21.27 TOTE £2.10: £1.20, £2.80, £2.40; EX 18.80.Landescent was the subject of a friendly claim by M Quinn for £7,000.
**Owner** Erik Penser **Bred** Declan And Catherine Macpartlin **Trained** Blewbury, Oxon

**FOCUS**
A tight finish to what was only a moderate race.

**NOTEBOOK**
**Compton Eclaire(IRE)**, swapping from blinkers to a visor, she travelled well in rear and mowed down the runner-up in the dying strides. This represented a drop in grade and as she was getting all the weight, may be one to take on next time in a better race.
**Landescent(IRE)**, who ran well at this trip last time, confirmed it suits with another solid display. He should have a race of this in him.
**Rasid(USA)** was a very useful horse two seasons ago when trained by Ed Dunlop and owned by Hamdan Al Maktoum, but he has completely lost his way of late. This however, was his best run for a while, albeit in a bad race, and he should be capable of winning a handicap during the winter.
**Khuzdar(IRE)** has been running in better races on turf and did not really achieve much in finishing where he did. He at least proved he handles the surface though.
**Water Of Life(IRE)** did not run badly and improved on her recent form.
**Appleacre** attempted to make all but was beaten a fair way from home. She is not in the best of form at present. *Official explanation: trainer was unable to offer any explanation for the filly's poor running*

## 5990 LITTLEWOODSCASINO.COM (S) STKS 6f (P)
3:20 (3:20) (G) 2-Y-O **£2,093** (£598; £299) **Stalls** Low

Form RPR

3000 **1** **Fools Entire**[17] 5789 2-8-11 65 ........ ACulhane 6 59
(MRChannon) *chsd ldrs: rdn over 2f out: styd on u.p to ld last 100y: drvn out* **7/2**[2]

0050 **2** *1/2* **Lady Predominant**[17] 5785 2-8-3 55 ........ DCorby(3) 3 52
(MRChannon) *towards rr: pushed along bef 1/2-way: prog u.p 2f out: styd on to take 2nd nr fin* **14/1**

4030 **3** *3/4* **Princess Kai (IRE)**[29] 5575 2-8-6 60 ........ (b[1]) NDay 5 50
(RIngram) *pressed ldr: led wl over 2f out: rdn over 1f out: fnd nil in front ins fnl f: hdd last 100y* **5/1**[3]

5623 **4** *nk* **Emaradia**[3] 5966 2-8-11 54 ........ NCallan 4 54
(PDEvans) *led to wl over 2f out: hrd rdn and cl up after: one pce fnl f* **13/2**

4062 **5** *1* **City General (IRE)**[24] 5679 2-8-13 58 ........ (p) LPKeniry(3) 2 56
(JSMoore) *chsd ldrs: rdn over 2f out: one pce fr over 1f out* **16/1**

00 **6** *3/4* **Jaolins**[14] 5835 2-8-6 ........ RSmith 8 44
(RHannon) *t.k.h: prom: hanging rt 2f out: rdn and fnd nil jst over 1f out* **13/2**

0234 **7** *2 1/2* **Joint Destiny (IRE)**[41] 5340 2-8-6 56 ........ SWhitworth 9 36
(GLMoore) *pressed ldrs: rdn over 2f out: nt qckn and btn wl over 1f out: fdd* **5/2**[1]

4206 **8** *1/2* **Costa Del Sol (IRE)**[13] 5844 2-8-6 53 ........ RMiles(5) 7 40
(JJBridger) *racd in rr: outpcd bef 1/2-way: one pce and n.d after* **10/1**

1000 **9** *nk* **Stamford Blue**[7] 5931 2-9-2 53 ........ (p) JDSmith 1 44
(JSMoore) *racd in rr: outpcd bef 1/2-way: one pce and n.d after* **50/1**

3605 **10** *5* **Lady Mo**[21] 5721 2-8-11 55 ........ DKinsella 10 24
(AndrewReid) *rel to r: a wl bhd* **16/1**

**11** *hd* **Introduction** 2-8-11 ........ MFenton 12 23
(WJMusson) *w'like: bit bkwd: s.s: m green and a bhd* **20/1**

6000 **12** *1/2* **He's A Rocket (IRE)**[12] 5876 2-8-6 50 ........ NChalmers(5) 11 22
(MrsCADunnett) *racd wd: pressed ldrs tl wknd rapidly over 2f out* **50/1**

0 **13** *28* **La Fonteyne**[16] 5818 2-8-6 ........ JFanning 13 —
(CBBBooth) *a in rr: wknd 1/2-way: t.o* **25/1**

1m 13.69s (0.77) **Going Correction** +0.025s/f (Slow) **13** Ran SP% **134.2**
Speed ratings: **95,94,93,92,91 90,87,86,86,79 79,78,41**CSF £57.48 TOTE £5.10: £2.20, £10.00, £1.50; EX 48.00.The winner was sold to T Connors for 5,600gns. Lady Predomient was claimed by Andrew Reid for £5,500.
**Owner** Village Racing **Bred** F Adams **Trained** West Ilsley, Berks

**FOCUS**
A poor race dominated by the two Channon trained runners.

**NOTEBOOK**
**Fools Entire** is well exposed and was getting off the mark at the tenth attempt. This was a poor race so it would be unwise to get carried away with the form.
**Lady Predominant**, a stablemate of the winner, ran on from out of the pack to press her more fancied stablemate all the way to the line.
**Princess Kai(IRE)** was up there throughout and looked set to go close turning in but did not find as much under pressure as looked likely.
**Emaradia** had every chance but could not hold off the principals.
**Joint Destiny(IRE)** was slightly disappointing having been there with every chance two out.

## 5991 LITTLEWOODS BET DIRECT APPRENTICE H'CAP 1m 2f (P)
3:50 (3:52) (F ) (0-85,84) 3-Y-O+ £3,094 (£884; £442) Stalls Low

Form RPR

6203 **1** **Dower House**[31] 5537 8-9-8 **77** ........ DCorby 2 86
(AndrewTurnell) *hld up in midfield: effrt over 2f out: rdn and r.o wl fnl f to ld last strides* **10/1**

2421 **2** *hd* **Retirement**[55] 5031 4-8-10 **72** ........ SaleemGolam(7) 1 81
(MHTompkins) *cl up gng wl: trckd ldr 2f out: rdn to ld last 150y: hdd fnl strides* **16/1**

0426 **3** *2 ½* **J R Stevenson (USA)**[6] 5945 7-9-7 **76** ........ LisaJones 9 81
(MWigham) *led: kicked on 2f out: hdd and nt qckn last 150y* **4/1**[1]

0622 **4** *hd* **Alrafid (IRE)**[19] 5756 4-9-11 **83** ........ AQuinn(3) 7 87
(GLMoore) *hld up in midfield: lost pl and in rr over 2f out: no prog tl r.o wl fnl f: unable to chal* **4/1**[1]

2003 **5** *nk* **Most-Saucy**[35] 5463 7-9-0 **72** ........ DNolan(3) 13 76
(IAWood) *settled wl in rr: effrt over 2f out: r.o fnl f: nvr rchd ldrs* **8/1**[3]

1021 **6** *½* **Ofaraby**[24] 5683 3-9-4 **80** ........ DFox(3) 3 83
(MAJarvis) *trckd ldr to 1/2-way: styd cl up: rdn over 2f out: sn outpcd and btn* **5/1**[2]

-040 **7** *1* **Liberty Royal**[19] 5756 4-9-2 **78** ........ LMcVicar(7) 14 79
(PJMakin) *dwlt: hld up in last pair: prog on wd outside to chse ldrs 2f out: lost grnd bnd sn after: kpt on ins fnl f* **20/1**

1000 **8** *1* **Classic Role**[10] 5910 4-9-6 **75** ........ SHitchcott 6 74
(RIngram) *cl up: nt clr run over 2f out: wknd over 1f out* **16/1**

1200 **9** *2 ½* **Night Warrior (IRE)**[19] 5753 3-8-11 **75** ........ PPMathers(5) 4 70
(DFlood) *racd in last: effrt on inner over 2f out: sn no prog and btn* **20/1**

3221 **10** *½* **Cruise Director**[199] 1262 3-9-4 **84** ........ ARutter(7) 10 78
(WJMusson) *a towards rr: wknd 2f out* **16/1**

0145 **11** *5* **Tropical Coral (IRE)**[38] 5425 3-9-0 **76** ........ JFMcDonald(3) 8 61
(AJLidderdale) *prom: chsd ldr 1/2-way to 2f out: wknd rapidly* **20/1**

-000 **12** *5* **The Gaikwar (IRE)**[19] 5756 4-9-3 **77** ........ MSavage(5) 11 53
(NEBerry) *chsd ldrs: rdn and wkng whn hmpd wl over 1f out* **40/1**

5010 **13** *1 ½* **Indian Welcome**[7] 5935 4-9-6 **75** ........(b) LPKeniry 12 48
(HMorrison) *dwlt: in rr: effrt 3f out: sn btn* **9/1**

2m 6.67s (-0.72) **Going Correction** +0.025s/f (Slow)
**WFA** 3 from 4yo+ 4lb **13 Ran SP% 121.2**
Speed ratings: **103,102,100,100,100 100,99,98,96,96 92,88,86**CSF £152.91 CT £755.61 TOTE £11.00: £3.60, £4.60, £2.10; EX 146.40 Place 6 £151.85, Place 5 £61.61.
**Owner** Mrs Claire Hollowood **Bred** Lord Howard De Walden **Trained** Malton, N Yorks

**FOCUS**
A fair handicap that produced a close finish. There was not much distance separating the front six at the line.

**NOTEBOOK**
**Dower House** is not the easiest horse to win with, but under a strong ride from Dean Corby got up on the line. He has been in good form of late and should continue to do well.
**Retirement**, having his first run since winning at Ayr in September, travelled strongly and looked to have done enough when getting to the front, but the winner had other ideas. This was a solid effort back up in grade and proven ability to handle the surface should see he does well in future.
**J R Stevenson(USA)** attempted to make all and was not disgraced. He finds it hard to win but his turn will come again.
**Alrafid(IRE)** picked up again inside the final furlong having hit a flat spot and ran with credit.
**Most-Saucy** never really had a chance to get into it and is worth another chance.
**Ofaraby** is only lightly raced and open to improvement. He was up there throughout but could not muster the pace to go with the principals.
T/Jkpt: Not won. T/Plt: £179.70 to a £1 stake. Pool: £40,841.15. 165.85 winning tickets. T/Qpdt: £23.70 to a £1 stake. Pool: £3,826.50. 119.30 winning tickets. JN

# 5966 WOLVERHAMPTON (A.W) (L-H)
Friday, November 14

**OFFICIAL GOING: Standard**
Wind: str bhd Weather: wet and windy

## 5992 BET DIRECT NO Q H'CAP (DIV I) 7f (F)
12:30 (12:31) (D ) (0-85,83) 3-Y-O+ £3,360 (£960; £480) Stalls High

Form RPR

2240 **1** **Ashtree Belle**[12] 5888 4-8-12 **72** ........ RThomas(5) 1 84
(DHaydnJones) *chsd ldrs: led ins fnl f: rdn out* **4/1**[2]

0020 **2** *1* **Bella Beguine**[4] 5967 4-9-0 **69** ........(v[1]) JFanning 5 78
(ABailey) *w ldr: led 4f out: rdn 2f out: hdd ins fnl f: kpt on* **9/1**

6203 **3** *½* **Cloud Dancer**[20] 5742 4-9-5 **74** ........ DaneO'Neill 4 82
(DJCoakley) *hld up: stdy hdwy over 4f out: rdn over 1f out: ev ch ins fnl f: edgd lft: nt qckn* **9/2**[3]

1102 **4** *nk* **Jan Brueghel (USA)**[24] 5685 4-8-11 **66** ........ NCallan 7 73
(TDBarron) *sn chsng ldrs: rdn over 2f out: ev ch ins fnl f: nt qckn* **9/4**[1]

4040 **5** *9* **Vintage Style**[44] 5300 4-8-7 **62** ........(b) GDuffield 8 47
(HAMcwilliams) *hld up: hdwy 5f out: rdn and wknd 2f out* **20/1**

5400 **6** *3 ½* **Carols Choice**[216] 1030 6-7-9 **53** oh8 ........ LisaJones(3) 3 29
(ASadik) *led 3f: wknd 2f out* **40/1**

4010 **7** *6* **Compton Arrow (IRE)**[23] 5702 7-8-8 **63** ........ JoannaBadger 9 24
(DNicholls) *s.i.s: rdn over 3f out: a bhd* **16/1**

1543 **8** *6* **Million Percent**[11] 5908 4-10-0 **83** ........ DarrenWilliams 2 29
(KRBurke) *sn bhd: rdn 4f out: no rspnse* **6/1**

660 **9** *16* **Mr Stylish**[57] 5025 7-7-12 **53** ........(vt) DKinsella 6 —
(JSMoore) *prom: sn hung bdly rt: lost pl 5f out: t.o* **20/1**

1m 30.57s (0.37) **Going Correction** +0.075s/f (Slow) **9 Ran SP% 111.1**
Speed ratings: **100,98,98,97,87 83,76,69,51**CSF £36.54 CT £161.40 TOTE £6.40: £1.40, £2.50, £1.70; EX 26.50.
**Owner** Mason Gill Racing **Bred** P A Mason **Trained** Efail Isaf, Rhondda C Taff

**FOCUS**
This turned out to be very competitive with four in line in the home straight.

**NOTEBOOK**
**Ashtree Belle**, back up to seven, showed just how she has progressed by defying a mark 12lb higher than when winning over course and distance for the same apprentice back in June.
**Bella Beguine**, switching from blinkers to a visor, ran a lot better than she had done over the stretch mile here four days ago.
**Cloud Dancer** had shown she can handle Fibresand when twice narrowly beaten at Southwell two years ago. She did not help her chances by lugging left in the closing stages.
**Jan Brueghel(USA)**, raised 2lb, would not have been inconvenienced by the return to seven. This was his first visit to Dunstall Park and it could be that Southwell suits him better.
**Mr Stylish** *Official explanation: jockey said gelding had hung both ways throughout*

## 5993 BET DIRECT NO Q DEMO 08000 837 888 CLAIMING STKS 1m 100y(F)
1:00 (1:02) (F ) 2-Y-O £2,086 (£596; £298) Stalls Low

Form RPR

0660 **1** **Myannabanana (IRE)**[17] 5816 2-8-7 52 ........ SWKelly 9 54
(PHowling) *chsd ldrs: reminder over 6f out: hrd rdn to ld 3f out: all out* **14/1**

0 **2** *shd* **Jakarmi**[8] 5929 2-8-9 ........ DKinsella 10 56
(BPalling) *a.p: rdn over 2f out: ev ch and edgd fr over 1f out: r.o* **20/1**

0014 **3** *1* **Armentieres**[14] 5845 2-8-1 59 ........(b) LisaJones(3) 5 49
(JLSpearing) *hld up and bhd: rdn and hdwy over 2f out: styd on wl towards fin* **6/4**[1]

0 **4** *3* **Turks And Caicos (IRE)**[93] 4074 2-8-8 ........ PDineley(7) 7 53
(PCHaslam) *s.i.s: rdn and hdwy over 3f out: r.o one pce fnl 2f* **40/1**

06 **5** *2* **Druid**[113] 3523 2-8-10 ........ LEnstone(3) 11 47
(PCHaslam) *hld up: rdn and hdwy over 3f out: sn edgd lft: eased whn btn ins fnl f* **20/1**

5046 **6** *3* **Yamato Pink**[18] 5785 2-8-8 53 ........ JoannaBadger 13 36
(KRBurke) *s.i.s: hdwy over 4f out: rdn and ev ch 2f out: wknd over 1f out* **16/1**

00 **7** *5* **Mistress Hollie (IRE)**[18] 5798 2-7-11 ........(p) RThomas(5) 6 19
(MrsPNDutfield) *hld up and bhd: hdwy over 4f out: wknd over 2f out:* **50/1**

1000 **8** *hd* **Maggies Choice (IRE)**[66] 4795 2-8-6 56 ow2 ........ IMongan 1 23
(NPLittmoden) *sn bhd* **9/2**[2]

0000 **9** *4* **Little Flute**[42] 5340 2-8-11 52 ........ RSmith 3 20
(CGCox) *prom tl hmpd on ins 3f out: nt rcvr* **8/1**[3]

3400 **10** *27* **Be My Alibi (IRE)**[8] 5931 2-8-3 58 ow1 ........ JFEgan 12 —
(JSMoore) *led: hdd 3f out: sn wknd and eased* **12/1**

006 **11** *20* **Given A Chance**[105] 3764 2-8-10 52 ........ MFenton 8 —
(JGGiven) *w ldr tl rdn 4f out: wkng whn hmpd on ins 3f out: eased fnl 2f* **16/1**

0 **12** *9* **Rosie Maloney (IRE)**[30] 5572 2-8-5 ........ J-PGuillambert(3) 4 —
(NPLittmoden) *a bhd: lost tch 4f out: t.o* **16/1**

1m 52.66s (1.66) **Going Correction** +0.075s/f (Slow) **12 Ran SP% 115.2**
Speed ratings: **94,93,92,89,87 84,79,79,75,48 28,19**CSF £246.70 TOTE £16.20: £2.80, £6.70, £1.10; EX 215.00.The winner was claimed by Gay Kelleway for £5,000.
**Owner** Richard Berenson **Bred** Thomas Kiely **Trained** Newmarket, Suffolk
■ Stewards Enquiry : L Enstone six-day ban: careless riding (Nov 24-26,28,29,Dec 1)
S W Kelly four-day ban: used whip with excessive force (Nov 24, 26-28)

**FOCUS**
A modest claimer.

**NOTEBOOK**
**Myannabanana(IRE)** had a hard race and his rider was handed a four-day ban for using his whip with excessive force. *Official explanation: trainer said, regarding the improved form shown, gelding was slowly away and raced on a slower part on the track at Nottingham last time out*
**Jakarmi** stepped up considerably on his debut over six on his debut at Nottingham last week. He probably would have won this had he not been intent on leaning on the winner in the home straight.
**Armentieres** confirmed just how well she stays on this switch back to Fibresand and simply found top gear too late.
**Turks And Caicos(IRE)** showed a big improvement on his debut over six at Hamilton in August.
**Druid** was another to appreciate a step up to six and was not knocked about when clearly held in the closing stages.
**Yamato Pink**, a half-sister to 12-furlong winner Sungio who later scored over hurdles, had been running over sprint distances on fast ground in the summer.
**Given A Chance** *Official explanation: jockey said gelding had suffered interference in running*

## 5994 BET DIRECT NO Q VOICE AUTOMATED BETTING NURSERY 7f (F)
1:35 (1:36) (E ) (0-75,75) 2-Y-O £2,086 (£596; £298) Stalls High

Form RPR

510 **1** **Ermine Grey**[63] 4865 2-9-7 **75** ........(v) PaulEddery 6 82
(DHaydnJones) *hld up in tch: rdn to ld over 1f out: drvn out* **7/1**[3]

5020 **2** *¾* **Come What July (IRE)**[83] 4395 2-8-9 **63** ........(b) ACulhane 10 68
(RGuest) *hld up: hdwy over 3f out: hrd rdn and r.o ins fianl f: nt rch wnr* **12/1**

15 **3** *1 ¼* **Among Dreams**[52] 5132 2-8-10 **64** ........ SWKelly 4 66
(JAOsborne) *w ldr: rdn to ld 2f out: hdd over 1f out: nt qckn ins fnl f* **9/4**[1]

4345 **4** *4* **Two Of Clubs**[32] 5535 2-8-13 **70** ........ LEnstone(3) 9 62
(PCHaslam) *a.p: rdn over 2f out: edgd lft and wknd ins fnl f* **9/2**[2]

2250 **5** *2 ½* **Nessen Dorma (IRE)**[91] 4162 2-9-2 **70** ........ MFenton 12 56
(JGGiven) *hld up: bhd whn pushed along 3f out: hdwy whn on outside fnl f: n.d* **14/1**

004 **6** *1* **Park Ave Princess (IRE)**[18] 5789 2-8-9 **63** ........ IMongan 8 46
(NPLittmoden) *prom tl rdn and wknd over 2f out* **7/1**[3]

050 **7** *½* **Desert Beau (IRE)**[39] 5422 2-8-10 **64** ........ RHavlin 5 46
(MrsPNDutfield) *bhd tl hdwy on ins wl over 1f out: no further prog fnl f* **50/1**

033 **8** *¾* **Desert Image (IRE)**[55] 5087 2-9-0 **68** ........ SDrowne 11 48
(AJLidderdale) *hld up: rdn 3f out: sn bhd* **8/1**

510 **9** *7* **Chase The Rainbow**[17] 5824 2-8-10 **64** ........ JFanning 2 27
(MJohnston) *led: rdn and hdd 2f out: sn wknd* **8/1**

0504 **10** *2 ½* **Lord Greystoke (IRE)**[24] 5691 2-8-10 **64** ........ SWhitworth 7 20
(CPMorlock) *prom over 3f* **16/1**

0000 **11** *11* **Corylus (USA)**[14] 5845 2-8-10 **64** ........ GDuffield 1 —
(SirMarkPrescott) *sn outpcd and bhd* **20/1**

1m 32.06s (1.86) **Going Correction** +0.075s/f (Slow) **11 Ran SP% 123.1**
Speed ratings: **92,91,89,85,82 81,80,79,71,68 56**CSF £92.22 CT £257.64 TOTE £10.40: £2.80, £4.80, £1.40; EX 152.40.
**Owner** L M Baker **Bred** D Brocklehurst **Trained** Efail Isaf, Rhondda C Taff

**FOCUS**
Ermine Grey had not been disgraced in the St Leger sales race at Doncaster last time.

**NOTEBOOK**
**Ermine Grey** is apparently a much better horse when getting cover and travelled well for much of the race.
**Come What July(IRE)**, like the winner, ran in a valuable sales race last time. He handled the surface and can go one better over a longer trip.
**Among Dreams** had no excuses on this step up to seven and appeared to act on the surface well enough.
**Two Of Clubs** had already been trumped when seeming to get found out by the extra furlong on this sand debut.

## 5995 BET DIRECT NO Q ON 08000 93 66 93 CLAIMING STKS (DIV I) 6f (F)
2:10 (2:11) (F ) 3-5-Y-O £2,093 (£598; £299) Stalls Low

Form RPR

0015 **1** **Queen Of Night**[20] 5742 3-8-10 78 ........ NCallan 2 63
(TDBarron) *s.i.s: sn chsng ldrs: rdn to ld wl over 1f out: r.o* **2/1**[1]

2305 **2** *¾* **Komena**[32] 5546 5-8-8 45 ........ IMongan 11 59
(JWPayne) *hld up: hdwy over 2f out: chsd wnr fnl f: nt qckn* **7/1**

0030 **3** *3* **Caustic Wit (IRE)**$^{98}$ 3968 5-8-10 52 ........................ RMiles$^{(5)}$ 3 57
(MSSaunders) *a.p: led over 3f out: rdn and hdd wl over 1f out: no ex fnl f* **33/1**

-000 **4** *1½* **Legalis (USA)**$^{158}$ 2224 5-9-5 71 ........................ PFessey 10 57
(KARyan) *hld mid-div: rdn and hdwy on outside 2f out: one pce fnl f* **9/2**$^{2}$

0-00 **5** *hd* **Fiennes (USA)**$^{86}$ 4288 5-8-6 42 ........................(p) LisaJones$^{(3)}$ 4 46
(MrsNMacauley) *broke wl: lost pl after 1f: rdn and hdwy over 2f out: no imp fnl f* **33/1**

060 **6** *3* **Patientes Virtis**$^{29}$ 5598 4-8-7 51 ........................(v) J-PGuillambert$^{(3)}$ 13 38
(MissGayKelleway) *prom tl rdn and wknd over 1f out* **6/1**$^{3}$

0600 **7** *4* **Lady Alruna (IRE)**$^{7}$ 5945 4-7-7 53 ........................(v$^{1}$) DFox$^{(5)}$ 6 14
(PTMidgley) *s.i.s: hdwy on ins over 3f out: wknd wl over 1f out* **33/1**

0200 **8** *1* **Nickel Sungirl (IRE)**$^{18}$ 5787 3-7-11 45 ......... StephanieHollinshead$^{(7)}$ 8 17
(RHollinshead) *bhd fnl 4f* **33/1**

-012 **9** *nk* **Westmead Tango**$^{93}$ 4092 3-8-10 53 ........................(v) SWKelly 1 22
(JRJenkins) *prom: rdn over 3f out: wknd wl over 1f out* **7/1**

4030 **10** *2½* **Cloudless (USA)**$^{10}$ 5919 3-7-12 64 ........................ MHenry 5 3
(JWUnett) *led over 2f: wknd 2f out* **9/1**

4460 **11** *9* **Avondale Lad (IRE)**$^{24}$ 5690 3-8-11 48 ........................(v$^{1}$) JFEgan 9 —
(MDods) *prom 3f: eased whn btn fnl 2f* **25/1**

060- **12** *1¼* **Lord Merlin (IRE)**$^{377}$ 5598 4-9-5 78 ........................ JoannaBadger 7 —
(DNicholls) *s.s: a in rr* **16/1**

0000 **13** *4* **Baytown Flyer**$^{20}$ 5742 3-8-4 37 ........................(p) JEdmunds 12 —
(JBalding) *s.i.s: bhd most of way* **66/1**

1m 15.89s (0.19) **Going Correction** +0.075s/f (Slow) **13 Ran SP% 123.8**
Speed ratings: **101,100,96,94,93 89,84,83,82,79 67,65,60**CSF £16.01 TOTE £2.80: £1.30, £2.10, £10.40; EX 20.30.
**Owner** Timothy Cox **Bred** Trevor Calver **Trained** Maunby, N Yorks
■ Stewards Enquiry : P Fessey one-day ban: used whip with excessive frequency and without allowing gelding time to respond (Nov 24)

**FOCUS**
This was over half a second quicker than the second division.

**NOTEBOOK**
**Queen Of Night** was well in on official ratings and appreciated the return to this surface.
**Komena**, a springer in the market on this belated All-Weather debut, would have been no less than 31lb better off with the winner in a handicap. This augurs well for the future.
**Caustic Wit(IRE)**, whose two wins as a juvenile came over this trip, did not find a step up from five the answer.
**Legalis(USA)** landed a handicap over course and distance last December but had not been seen since finishing lame at Pontefract in June.
**Fiennes(USA)** has not won for exactly two years and had a tough task at these weights.
**Avondale Lad(IRE)** *Official explanation: jockey said gelding had hung left-handed*

## 5996 BET DIRECT NO Q H'CAP (DIV II) 7f (F)
**2:45** (2:45) (D) (0-85,77) 3-Y-O+ **£3,360** (£960; £480) **Stalls High**

Form RPR

2002 **1** **Flint River**$^{12}$ 5888 5-9-7 74 ........................ ACulhane 4 87
(HMorrison) *a.p: led over 3f out: rdn over 1f out: comf* **11/10**$^{1}$

0201 **2** *2* **Mufreh (USA)**$^{24}$ 5685 5-9-10 77 ........................ SWhitworth 5 85
(AGNewcombe) *s.i.s: hld up: hdwy over 4f out: chsd wnr 3f out: rdn over 1f out: no imp* **7/2**$^{2}$

3000 **3** *3½* **Danielle's Lad**$^{24}$ 5685 7-9-5 72 ........................(b) MFenton 1 71
(BPalling) *led early: hld up in tch: jnd ldrs 3f out: rdn wl over 1f out: wknd ins fnl f* **8/1**$^{3}$

0000 **4** *2* **Lockstock (IRE)**$^{12}$ 5892 5-8-5 63 ........................ RMiles$^{(5)}$ 8 57
(MSSaunders) *chsd ldrs: lost pl and n.m.r 3f out: hdwy over 1f out: r.o* **20/1**

2203 **5** *¾* **Blonde En Blonde (IRE)**$^{25}$ 5681 3-9-1 69 ........................ IMongan 2 61
(NPLittmoden) *hld up: rdn over 3f out: hdwy over 2f out: wknd fnl f* **8/1**$^{3}$

2260 **6** *1½* **Coronado Forest (USA)**$^{24}$ 5688 4-8-10 63 ........................ DaneO'Neill 9 52
(MRHoad) *sn led: hdd 5f out: rdn over 3f out: wknd over 2f out* **8/1**$^{3}$

0000 **7** *7* **Laggan Minstrel (IRE)**$^{10}$ 5918 5-8-2 55 ........................(p) PFessey 3 26
(PWD'Arcy) *rdn over 3f out: a bhd* **16/1**

3030 **8** *1½* **Ellamyte**$^{18}$ 5794 3-7-6 53 ........................(v) BSwarbrick$^{(7)}$ 7 20
(DGBridgwater) *w ldr: led 5f out tl over 3f out: rdn and wknd over 2f out* **40/1**

60/ **9** *½* **Sugar Cube Treat**$^{798}$ 4568 7-7-9 51 oh10 ........................ LisaJones$^{(3)}$ 6 17
(MMullineaux) *a bhd* **66/1**

1m 29.37s (-0.83) **Going Correction** +0.075s/f (Slow)
**WFA** 3 from 4yo+ 1lb **9 Ran SP% 117.8**
Speed ratings: **107,104,100,98,97 95,87,86,85**CSF £4.98 CT £20.81 TOTE £1.60: £1.60, £1.40, £1.90; EX 5.60.
**Owner** The Firm **Bred** P D Savill **Trained** East Ilsley, Berks

**FOCUS**
Flint River maintained his unbeaten record at Dunstall Park.

**NOTEBOOK**
**Flint River**, back up in distance, had little difficulty in making it four out of four at this track with his other victories having come over the stretch mile. He looks set for another successful winter campaign.
**Mufreh(USA)**, raised 6lb, had to be content to play second fiddle to the ready winner.
**Danielle's Lad** was 7lb better off than when beaten a length by Flint River over the extended mile here back in February.
**Lockstock(IRE)**, again without the blinkers, would not mind a return to a mile on this evidence.
**Blonde En Blonde(IRE)** was unable to sustain her effort.

## 5997 BET DIRECT ON ATTHERACES INTERACTIVE MAIDEN AUCTION STKS 5f (F)
**3:20** (3:23) (F) 2-Y-O **£2,205** (£630; £315) **Stalls Low**

Form RPR

420 **1** **Peters Choice**$^{23}$ 5700 2-8-7 67 ........................ NCallan 9 83
(ISemple) *mde all: rdn clr wl over 1f out: unchal* **7/2**$^{1}$

0440 **2** *8* **Scottish Exile (IRE)**$^{29}$ 5590 2-8-8 60 ........................ DarrenWilliams 8 56
(KRBurke) *a.p: rdn over 2f out: wnt 2nd ins fnl f: no ch w wnr* **6/1**$^{2}$

6 **3** *½* **Docklands Blue (IRE)**$^{4}$ 5968 2-7-13 ........................ LisaJones$^{(3)}$ 4 48
(NPLittmoden) *outpcd: hdwy over 1f out: r.o ins fnl f* **6/1**$^{2}$

5335 **4** *1* **Smart Starprincess (IRE)**$^{27}$ 5630 2-7-13 61 ........................(b) FPFerris$^{(3)}$ 6 45
(PABlockley) *w wnr: rdn over 2f out: one pce* **7/2**$^{1}$

0006 **5** *1¼* **Fayr Firenze (IRE)**$^{13}$ 5876 2-8-7 52 ........................(b) SRighton 11 45
(MFHarris) *chsd ldrs: rdn over 3f out: wknd over 2f out* **25/1**

4600 **6** *1¾* **Melaina**$^{24}$ 5689 2-8-2 52 ........................ RSmith 1 34
(MSSaunders) *chsd ldrs tl wknd over 2f out* **33/1**

4466 **7** *1¼* **Designer City (IRE)**$^{24}$ 5686 2-8-3 57 ow1 ........................ JFanning 10 31
(ABerry) *outpcd: wl bhd tl hdwy over 1f out: n.d* **14/1**

6500 **8** *½* **Kumari (IRE)**$^{18}$ 5785 2-7-11 50 ........................ JFMcDonald$^{(5)}$ 7 28
(WMBrisbourne) *hdwy over 3f out: wknd over 2f out* **9/1**

0035 **9** *2½* **Laconia (IRE)**$^{2}$ 5977 2-8-3 61 ow1 ........................ JFEgan 5 20
(JSMoore) *chsd ldrs: rdn 3f out: wknd wl over 1f out* **7/1**$^{3}$

0 **10** *nk* **I Wish I Knew**$^{49}$ 5197 2-8-7 ........................ DSweeney 3 23
(PJMakin) *outpcd* **40/1**

0400 **11** *3½* **Intitnice (IRE)**$^{33}$ 5512 2-8-10 52 ........................(b) GDuffield 13 14
(ABerry) *chsd ldrs: rdn 3f out: sn wknd* **25/1**

500 **12** *7* **Reckless Moment**$^{186}$ 1561 2-8-3 49 ow1 ........................ PDoe 12 —
(WGMTurner) *a bhd* **33/1**

61.53 secs (-1.07) **Going Correction** +0.075s/f (Slow) **12 Ran SP% 118.2**
Speed ratings: **111,98,97,95,93 91,89,88,84,83 78,66**CSF £21.97 TOTE £4.10: £1.60, £2.30, £2.50; EX 35.10.
**Owner** Peter Tsim **Bred** G And Mrs A Young **Trained** Carluke, S Lanarks

**FOCUS**
Peters Choice clocked the fastest time of the day compared with standard.

**NOTEBOOK**
**Peters Choice** ran this field ragged on this switch to the All-Weather having pulled hard under restraint last time. He can score again.
**Scottish Exile(IRE)**, another making her sand debut, was 6lb worse off than when four lengths behind the winner at Musselburgh in September.
**Docklands Blue(IRE)**, a half-sister to a seven-furlong juvenile winner in Ireland, showed why she had made her debut over six here earlier in the week.
**Smart Starprincess(IRE)** got run out of the money after trying to go with the winner.

## 5998 BET DIRECT NO Q ON 08000 93 66 93 CLAIMING STKS (DIV II) 6f (F)
**3:50** (3:50) (F) 3-5-Y-O **£2,086** (£596; £298) **Stalls Low**

Form RPR

5300 **1** **Ally Makbul**$^{14}$ 5856 3-7-13 55 ........................ DFentiman$^{(7)}$ 8 65
(JRBest) *broke wl: hld up and sn lost pl: nt clr run 3f out: rdn and hdwy to ld 1f out: r.o wl* **8/1**$^{3}$

0124 **2** *3½* **Empress Josephine**$^{29}$ 5598 3-8-10 55 ........................(v) SWKelly 1 58
(JRJenkins) *sn prom: led over 4f out: rdn clr 2f out: hdd 1f out: sn btn* **9/2**$^{2}$

0000 **3** *1* **Attorney**$^{57}$ 5025 5-8-7 45 ........................(e$^{1}$) LisaJones$^{(3)}$ 13 55
(DShaw) *broke wl: hld up and sn lost pl: hdwy over 1f out: r.o ins fnl f* **9/1**

0500 **4** *2½* **Travelling Times**$^{31}$ 5561 4-8-12 52 ........................(v) LEnstone$^{(3)}$ 9 53
(JSWainwright) *a.p: rdn over 3f out: one pce fnl 2f* **14/1**

0200 **5** *1½* **Somethingabouther**$^{29}$ 5598 3-8-4 48 ........................ PDoe 5 37
(PWHiatt) *a.p: rdn 3f out: hit on nose by whip wl over 1f out: one pce* **10/1**

5104 **6** *2½* **Amelia (IRE)**$^{109}$ 3647 5-8-4 51 ........................ DKinsella 3 30
(AndrewReid) *a.p: rdn over 2f out: wknd fnl f* **3/1**$^{1}$

-003 **7** *2½* **Giverand**$^{46}$ 5283 4-8-10 44 ........................ RHavlin 10 28
(MissJacquelineSDoyle) *outpcd: nvr nr ldrs* **25/1**

00-0 **8** *2½* **Warlingham (IRE)**$^{12}$ 5892 5-9-5 63 ........................(e$^{1}$) SDrowne 12 30
(MPitman) *outpcd: n.d* **9/2**$^{2}$

0-05 **9** *½* **Bells Boy's**$^{98}$ 3952 4-8-9 40 ........................ GParkin 6 18
(KARyan) *hld up and bhd: hdwy over 3f out: sn rdn: wknd fnl f* **33/1**

646 **10** *1¾* **Lake Eyre (IRE)**$^{105}$ 3766 4-8-6 39 ........................ JEdmunds 11 10
(JBalding) *prom: rdn over 3f out: sn wknd* **16/1**

0600 **11** *3* **Star Lad (IRE)**$^{126}$ 3181 3-9-1 57 ........................(b) GGibbons 7 10
(RBrotherton) *led over 1f: rdn 3f out: wknd over 2f out* **20/1**

6000 **12** *¾* **I T Consultant**$^{9}$ 5924 5-8-7 45 ........................(b) JFanning 2 —
(MissLAPerratt) *s.i.s: hdwy over 4f out: rdn and wknd over 2f out* **11/1**

1m 16.46s (0.76) **Going Correction** +0.075s/f (Slow) **12 Ran SP% 124.0**
Speed ratings: **97,92,91,87,85 82,79,75,75,72 68,67**CSF £45.00 TOTE £11.00: £2.60, £1.80, £2.60; EX 106.50.Amelia (no.12) was claimed by Raymond O'Neill for £5,000.
**Owner** Malcolm Ward **Bred** Mill House Stud **Trained** Hucking, Kent

**FOCUS**
This was over half a second slower than the first division.

**NOTEBOOK**
**Ally Makbul**, supported in the ring, appreciated a return to sprinting having been campaigned at between eight and ten furlongs in the summer.
**Empress Josephine** tried to slip her field on the home turn on this step up from the minimum distance but had no answer to the winner.
**Attorney** wore eyeshields instead of the regular visor for this return to the sand. He had a stiff task at the weights.
**Travelling Times** was another who would have been better off with the first two in a handicap.
**Somethingabouther**, previously trained by Dean Ivory, seems more effective at the minimum trip.
**Amelia(IRE)**, previously trained by John Cullinan, changed hands again after the race having been claimed for £5,000.

## 5999 BETDIRECT.CO.UK AMATEUR RIDERS' H'CAP 1m 6f 166y(F)
**4:20** (4:20) (G) (0-80,79) 3-Y-O+ **£2,247** (£642; £321) **Stalls High**

Form RPR

0502 **1** **Mr Mischief**$^{32}$ 5534 3-11-8 **79** ow1 ........................ MrBHaslam$^{(5)}$ 9 93
(PCHaslam) *hld up: stdy hdwy over 5f out: rdn to ld wl over 1f out: styd on* **11/1**

6545 **2** *1¼* **Glory Quest (USA)**$^{4}$ 5967 6-12-0 **72** ........................ MissEJJones 1 84
(MissGayKelleway) *a.p: led over 4f out: rdn and hdd wl over 1f out: nt qckn fnl f* **5/2**$^{1}$

5003 **3** *17* **Mysterium**$^{4}$ 5972 9-9-7 **40** ........................(v) MrsEmmaLittmoden$^{(3)}$ 7 30
(NPLittmoden) *t.k.h: prom tl wknd over 2f out* **9/2**$^{3}$

2022 **4** *8* **Chaka Zulu**$^{9}$ 5928 6-10-2 **53** ........................ MrSIrving$^{(7)}$ 11 33
(ACWhillans) *hld up: hdwy over 6f out: wknd over 3f out* **9/2**$^{3}$

3160 **5** *½* **Royal Axminster**$^{81}$ 4451 8-9-6 **41** ........................ MissAWallace$^{(5)}$ 6 20
(MrsPNDutfield) *hdwy on ins to ld after 5f: hdd over 4f out: wknd over 3f out* **20/1**

4260 **6** *1¼* **Party Ploy**$^{9}$ 5928 5-11-2 **67** ........................ MissHAClements$^{(7)}$ 8 44
(KRBurke) *led 5f: prom tl wknd over 3f out* **12/1**

35-0 **7** *10* **Dancer Polish (POL)**$^{24}$ 5692 5-9-12 **42** ........................ MissSBrotherton 3 6
(ASadik) *prom: lost pl 8f out: bhd fnl 5f* **25/1**

5040 **8** *1½* **Profiler (USA)**$^{86}$ 4279 8-9-3 **40** ........................ MissZMorgan-Murphy$^{(7)}$ 5 —
(FerdyMurphy) *a bhd* **20/1**

300/ **9** *1½* **Intensity**$^{5}$ 5491 7-11-0 **63** ........................ MissFayeBramley$^{(5)}$ 10 23
(PABlockley) *bhd fnl 4f* **7/1**

2123 **10** *dist* **Hajeer (IRE)**$^{260}$ 630 5-10-4 **53** ........................ MrsMarieKing$^{(5)}$ 12 —
(PWHiatt) *prom 4f: dropped rr 8f out: t.o fnl 6f* **7/2**$^{2}$

3m 21.14s (0.34) **Going Correction** +0.075s/f (Slow)
**WFA** 3 from 5yo+ 8lb **10 Ran SP% 129.1**
Speed ratings: **102,101,92,88,87 87,81,80,80,**—CSF £42.03 CT £154.20 TOTE £10.10: £3.10, £2.10, £2.20; EX 38.90 Place 6 £21.64, Place 5 £7.68.
**Owner** Middleham Park Racing **Bred** Mrs Maureen Barbara Walsh **Trained** Middleham Moor, N Yorks

**FOCUS**
Unusually for an amateurs event, they went no pace for the first circuit.

**NOTEBOOK**
**Mr Mischief**, who changed hands for 6,000 gns at Doncaster Sales last month, was already twice a winner over the stretch mile here. He travelled well and had no problem with this stamina test.

**Glory Quest(USA)**, making a quick reappearance, was more at home over this sort of trip and simply met one too good.
**Mysterium**, another who ran here on Monday, eventually got left for dead by the two principals.
T/Plt: £40.90 to a £1 stake. Pool: £33,605.40. 598.70 winning tickets. T/Qpdt: £6.50 to a £1 stake. Pool: £3,054.80. 346.40 winning tickets. KH

## 5922 MAISONS-LAFFITTE (R-H)

Friday, November 14

**OFFICIAL GOING: Very soft**

### 6000a PRIX ISOLA BELLA (LISTED) (FILLIES) (STRAIGHT) 7f (S)

**2:15** (2:15) 3-Y-O **£13,312** (£5,325; £3,994; £2,662)

| Form | Pos | Dist | Horse / Trainer / Comment | Jockey | RPR |
|---|---|---|---|---|---|
| | 1 | | **Great News (FR)**[45] 5292 3-8-12 (CLaffon-Parias, France) | MBlancpain 3 | — |
| | 2 | 4 | **Blaise Castle (USA)**[13] 5882 3-8-12 (GAButler) *disputed lead til took clear advantage over 2f out, ridden over 1f out, headed final furlong, kept on* | ELegrix 7 | — |
| | 3 | 1 | **Cote Quest (USA)**[33] 3-8-12 (MmeCHead-Maarek, France) **1** | NGuesdon 6 | — |
| | 4 | shd | **Semire (FR)**[89] 4233 3-8-12 (MmeCBarande-Barbe, France) | TJarnet 8 | — |
| | 5 | 1 ½ | **Soierie (FR)**[26] 5628 3-8-12 (HVanDePoele, France) | SPasquier 9 | — |
| | 6 | 1 ½ | **Red Fox (IRE)**[10] 3-8-12 (JEHammond, France) | CSoumillon 1 | — |
| | 7 | 2 | **A La Mer (GER)**[135] 2911 3-8-12 (AndreasLowe, Germany) | ASuborics 4 | — |
| | 8 | snk | **Stormy Larissa (IRE)**[25] 3-8-12 (MmeCHead-Maarek, France) | C-PLemaire 10 | — |
| | 9 | 6 | **Tahirah**[6] 5946 3-8-12 (RGuest) *tracked leaders til weakened over 2f out* | TThulliez 5 | — |
| | 10 | ¾ | **Precious Pearl (IRE)**[19] 5783 3-9-2 (ELellouche, France) | DBoeuf 2 | — |

1m 26.8s **10** Ran SP% **7.7**
Speed ratings: .
**Owner** Mme C Morange **Bred** Mme Patricia Morange **Trained** France

**NOTEBOOK**
**Blaise Castle(USA)**, fourth in a similar race at Saint-Cloud last time, was bang there throughout and went on two out only to get passed inside the final furlong. This was not a bad effort.
**Tahirah** was never in the hunt on ground that would probably have been too soft.

## 5992 WOLVERHAMPTON (A.W) (L-H)

Saturday, November 15

**OFFICIAL GOING: Standard**

### 6001 "CANDY" APPLIANCES AT WATERLINE H'CAP 5f (F)

**7:00** (7:00) (E ) (0-75,74) 3-Y-0+ **£2,051** (£586; £293) **Stalls** Low

| Form | Pos | Dist | Horse / Trainer / Comment | Jockey | RPR |
|---|---|---|---|---|---|
| 2004 | 1 | | **Gone'N'Dunnett (IRE)**[14] 5880 4-9-3 **63** (v) (MrsCADunnett) *hld up: hdwy 2f out: rdn to ld ins fnl f: edgd lft: r.o* **8/1** | DaneO'Neill 3 | 74 |
| 6004 | 2 | 1 ½ | **Frascati**[33] 5538 3-9-3 **70** (ABerry) *prom: sn pushed along: n.m.r and outpcd over 3f out: hdwy over 1f out: r.o* **14/1** | SJDonohoe(7) 8 | 76 |
| 0400 | 3 | 2 ½ | **Sea The World (IRE)**[38] 5451 3-9-3 **63** (DShaw) *chsd ldrs: n.m.r and outpcd over 3f out: hdwy 2f out: styd on same pce fnl f* **40/1** | NCallan 1 | 60 |
| 034 | 4 | 1 | **Roman Quintet (IRE)**[38] 5451 3-9-3 **68** (DWPArbuthnot) *chsd ldrs: rdn to ld over 1f out: hdd & wknd ins fnl f* **7/1**[2] | JFMcDonald(5) 2 | 62 |
| 000 | 5 | 1 ¼ | **Park Star**[12] 5909 3-9-5 **65** (DShaw) *sn pushed along and prom: lost pl over 3f out: styd on ins fnl f* **20/1** | IMongan 6 | 54 |
| 2466 | 6 | 1 ¼ | **Only One Legend (IRE)**[87] 4276 5-10-0 **74** (KARyan) *led: hdd over 3f out: outpcd whn hmpd wl over 1f out: styd on ins fnl f* **25/1** | GParkin 7 | 59 |
| 4002 | 7 | hd | **Roxanne Mill**[26] 5673 5-9-10 **70** (JMBradley) *chsd ldrs: rdn over 1f out: wknd fnl f* **4/1**[1] | SDrowne 4 | 54 |
| 3310 | 8 | 1 | **Daintree Affair (IRE)**[36] 5472 3-9-4 **64** (KRBurke) *w ldrs: led over 3f out: rdn and hdd over 1f out: wknd fnl f* **20/1** | DarrenWilliams 13 | 45 |
| 0000 | 9 | ½ | **Cash**[14] 5880 5-9-2 **62** (PaulJohnson) *sn pushed along and prom: hmpd and lost pl over 3f out: n.d after* **15/2**[3] | KDalgleish 9 | 41 |
| 3241 | 10 | hd | **Prima Stella**[217] 1030 4-9-7 **70** (NPLittmoden) *s.i.s: outpcd: hdwy 1/2-way: sn wknd* **7/1**[2] | J-PGuillambert(3) 11 | 48 |
| 2300 | 11 | 2 | **New Options**[167] 2027 6-9-9 **69** (WJMusson) *s.i.s: outpcd* **20/1** | PaulEddery 10 | 40 |
| 0144 | 12 | ½ | **River Days (IRE)**[214] 1063 5-9-8 **68** (bt) (MissGayKelleway) *chsd ldrs: wkng whn hmpd over 1f out* **4/1**[1] | MFenton 12 | 38 |

62.69 secs (0.09) **Going Correction** -0.075s/f (Stan) **12** Ran SP% **115.1**
Speed ratings: **96,93,89,88,86 84,83,82,81,80 77,76**CSF £100.15 CT £4195.32 TOTE £9.50: £2.70, £3.60, £7.60; EX 109.80.
**Owner** College Farm Thoroughbreds **Bred** Ocal Bloodstock **Trained** Hingham, Norfolk
■ Stewards Enquiry : S Drowne one-day ban: careless riding (Nov 24)

**FOCUS**
A routine sprint handicap for the track.

**NOTEBOOK**
**Gone'N'Dunnett(IRE)**was well handicapped having dropped to a mark 1lb lower than for his last win on sand. Patiently ridden, he was brought with his effort wide and on this occasion the front-runners did come back.
**Frascati**, winner of her last two starts on sand a year ago, both over the straight five at Southwell, came home in good style and is well handicapped at present.
**Sea The World(IRE)**another whose best form so far has been over the Southwell five, ran a decent rails from his rails draw and is worth bearing in mind with his yard beginning to find a bit of form.
**Roman Quintet(IRE)**does not quite seem to get home on this surface and that was again the case. He may be better off back on Polytrack on which he gained his only victory to date.
**Park Star**, a winner three times over the Southwell five, ran her best race since the spring and is worth keeping an eye on with her stable just running into a bit of form.
**Only One Legend(IRE)**is better over six and, even though he managed to get the early lead, found a few of his rivals too speedy at a vital stage.
**Roxanne Mill**has won here and is very well handicapped compared to turf, but her form on sand has dropped below her turf form in recent seasons and this effort was little more than fair.
**Prima Stella**was entitled to need this first run in seven months and she should eventually leave this form well behind.
**River Days(IRE)**has a great record here, but faded rather tamely and the only mitigation is that she probably needed it.

### 6002 "STOVES" COOKING AT WATERLINE MAIDEN STKS 7f (F)

**7:30** (7:31) (D ) 2-Y-O **£3,062** (£875; £437) **Stalls** High

| Form | Pos | Dist | Horse / Trainer / Comment | Jockey | RPR |
|---|---|---|---|---|---|
| 363 | 1 | | **Dumnoni**[16] 5834 2-8-9 73 (JulianPoulton) *chsd ldr: led over 2f out: sn clr* **13/8**[1] | IMongan 6 | 81+ |
| 44 | 2 | 8 | **Titus Salt (USA)**[29] 5620 2-9-0 (TDBarron) *chsd ldrs: rdn over 2f out: sn outpcd* **10/3**[3] | NCallan 5 | 66 |
| 6004 | 3 | 4 | **Redbank (IRE)**[15] 5847 2-9-0 71 (t) (NACallaghan) *chsd ldrs: lost pl 5f out: n.d after* **3/1**[2] | DaneO'Neill 4 | 56 |
| | 4 | nk | **Par Indiana (IRE)** 2-8-9 (ISemple) *dwlt: outpcd: r.o ins fnl f: nvr nrr* **25/1** | MTebbutt 1 | 50 |
| 06 | 5 | ½ | **Unintentional**[9] 5929 2-8-9 (RBrotherton) *prom: sn drvn along: wknd over 2f out* **25/1** | GGibbons 11 | 49 |
| | 6 | 1 ½ | **Vampire Queen (IRE)**[52] 5163 2-8-9 (RPElliott) *led over 4f: wknd over 1f out* **33/1** | DeanMcKeown 2 | 45 |
| 00 | 7 | hd | **Elusive Dream**[9] 5934 2-9-0 (SirMarkPrescott) *sn outpcd* **12/1** | GDuffield 7 | 50 |
| | 8 | 3 ½ | **Quirkie (IRE)** 2-8-9 (KRBurke) *s.i.s: sn prom: wknd over 2f out* **33/1** | DarrenWilliams 9 | 36 |
| 40 | 9 | 2 ½ | **Zonnebeke**[14] 5877 2-8-2 (KRBurke) *chsd ldrs over 4f* **20/1** | RKeogh(7) 8 | 30 |
| | 10 | 16 | **Fred's First** 2-9-0 (BPalling) *s.i.s: outpcd: sme hdwy over 4f out: sn wknd* **33/1** | DKinsella 12 | — |

1m 29.41s (-0.79) **Going Correction** -0.075s/f (Stan) **10** Ran SP% **115.1**
Speed ratings: **101,91,87,86,86 84,84,80,77,59**CSF £6.26 TOTE £2.40: £1.10, £1.80, £1.90; EX 7.20.
**Owner** Meddler Bloodstock **Bred** Southill Stud **Trained** Kentford, Suffolk

**FOCUS**
A modest maiden and the winner proved different class.

**NOTEBOOK**
**Dumnoni**, third in a couple of decent-looking maidens on Polytrack, had no problem with the change in surface and was running all over her rivals from the final bend. She may not have beaten much, but is still improving and should be able to make her mark in handicap company.
**Titus Salt(USA)**was completely outclassed by the winner, but this trip would have been plenty sharp enough. He can be expected to do better now that he can be handicapped and an opportunity should be found.
**Redbank(IRE)**was stepping back three furlongs in trip for this sand debut and it showed as he was completely exposed for toe where it mattered.
**Par Indiana(IRE)**, a half-sister to a couple of juvenile winners, was noted staying on towards in the latter stages. Her stable have been doing well here lately and improvement can be expected, especially if stepped up in trip.
**Unintentional**did not appear to improve for the switch to this surface nor the extra furlong, but at least she can now be handicapped.
**Elusive Dream** finished out of the frame for the third time in three starts and will be a totally different proposition when turning up in handicap company over a much longer distance at three.

### 6003 "BELLING" APPLIANCES AT WATERLINE MAIDEN STKS 1m 1f 79y(F)

**8:00** (8:00) (D ) 2-Y-O **£3,136** (£896; £448) **Stalls** Low

| Form | Pos | Dist | Horse / Trainer / Comment | Jockey | RPR |
|---|---|---|---|---|---|
| 0002 | 1 | | **Clog Dance (USA)**[16] 5834 2-8-9 73 (JHMGosden) *trckd ldrs: led 4f out: rdn out* **11/8**[1] | DaneO'Neill 13 | 73 |
| 6033 | 2 | 1 ½ | **Bill Bennett (FR)**[15] 5847 2-9-0 71 (JJay) *hld up: hdwy u.p over 1f out: r.o: nt rch wnr* **10/1** | KDalgleish 10 | 75 |
| 06 | 3 | 1 ¾ | **Baawrah**[18] 5810 2-8-11 (MRChannon) *chsd ldrs: rdn over 2f out: styd on same pce fnl f* **33/1** | DCorby(3) 7 | 72 |
| 3 | 4 | 2 | **Majestic Vision**[24] 5710 2-9-0 (PWHarris) *chsd ldrs: rdn 1/2-way: hung rt over 1f out: styd on same pce* **7/2**[2] | NCallan 6 | 68 |
| 044 | 5 | 14 | **Dolly Wotnot (IRE)**[74] 4644 2-8-6 67 (NPLittmoden) *chsd ldrs: rdn over 1/2-way: wknd over 3f out* **12/1** | J-PGuillambert(3) 11 | 35 |
| 00 | 6 | 3 | **Ilwadod**[66] 4818 2-8-11 (MRChannon) *mid-div: rn in snatches: wknd over 3f out* **20/1** | SHitchcott(3) 5 | 34 |
| 0650 | 7 | 1 | **Bretton**[46] 5290 2-9-0 45 (p) (RHollinshead) *w ldr: rdn over 3f out: wkng whn n.m.r 2f out* **66/1** | DeanMcKeown 4 | 32 |
| 00 | 8 | hd | **Verasi**[12] 5905 2-9-0 (RCharlton) *chsd ldrs 7f* **10/1** | SDrowne 2 | 31 |
| 0060 | 9 | 1 ¼ | **Platinum Pirate**[39] 5439 2-9-0 55 (b[1]) (KRBurke) *mde most over 5f: wknd over 2f out* **50/1** | DarrenWilliams 8 | 29 |
| 660 | 10 | 12 | **Quarry Island (IRE)**[153] 2394 2-8-9 45 (v[1]) (PDEvans) *sn outpcd* **66/1** | SWKelly 12 | — |
| 0 | 11 | 6 | **Can Can Flyer (IRE)**[8] 5940 2-9-0 (MJohnston) *hld up: bhd fr 1/2-way* **9/1**[3] | JFanning 9 | — |
| 000 | 12 | 1 ¼ | **Sweet Fury (IRE)**[32] 5565 2-9-0 68 (EALDunlop) *s.i.s: hdwy over 6f out: wknd 1/2-way* **33/1** | MFenton 3 | — |
| | 13 | 3 | **Beauchamp Spark** 2-9-0 (APJones) *slowly in to stride: hdwy 6f out: wknd 4f out* **66/1** | GHannon 1 | — |

2m 2.52s (-0.38) **Going Correction** -0.075s/f (Stan) **13** Ran SP% **117.3**
Speed ratings: **98,96,95,93,80 78,77,77,76,65 60,58,56**CSF £15.24 TOTE £2.40: £1.40, £2.70, £11.50; EX 10.80.
**Owner** Maktoum Al Maktoum **Bred** Gainsborough Farm Llc **Trained** Manton, Wilts

**FOCUS**
A moderate maiden and the first four finished miles clear of the rest.

**NOTEBOOK**
**Clog Dance(USA)**appreciated the step up in trip and, after travelling really well, won this by being sent clear rounding the home bend. This will have enhanced her value as a broodmare.
**Bill Bennett(FR)**, whose best previous effort came over a slightly longer trip on easy ground on turf, made up an enormous amount of late ground, but the winner had got first run and he could not peg her back. He is well worth persevering with on this surface and a longer trip should suit.
**Baawrah**is bred to stay and, under a positive ride, ran his best race to date. He can now be handicapped.
**Majestic Vision**, who showed ability on his Nottingham debut last month, was having to be shoved along from a long way out and might have been placed had he not hung right through greenness down the home straight. There still appears to be improvement to come, but he is going to need a greater test of stamina.
**Dolly Wotnot(IRE)**did not improved for the switch to sand nor longer trip and was beaten a long way.

## 6004 "WATERLINE" UK'S NUMBER 1 KITCHEN DISTRIBUTOR FILLIES' H'CAP 1m 1f 79y(F)

**8:30** (8:30) (E ) (0-75,74) 3-Y-0+ **£2,100** (£600; £300) **Stalls** Low

Form RPR

1335 **1** **Strong Hand**[30] 5597 3-9-6 **74**........................................ PMulrennan(5) 4 88
(MWEasterby) *trckd ldrs: led over 1f out: r.o wl* **4/1**[2]

0031 **2** *3 1/2* **Star Of Normandie (USA)**[9] 5935 4-9-9 **74**.......................... BReilly(5) 5 81
(GGMargarson) *chsd ldrs: lost pl over 5f out: hdwy over 2f out: rdn and edgd lft 1f out: no imp* **7/2**[1]

0632 **3** *1 1/2* **Miss Glory Be**[74] 4643 5-9-0 **60**...........................................(p) MFenton 2 64
(MissGayKelleway) *chsd ldrs: rdn and ev ch over 1f out: no ex* **5/1**[3]

0246 **4** *shd* **Jessinca**[67] 4800 7-8-0 **46**........................................................ DKinsella 3 50
(APJones) *led: rdn and hdd over 1f out: no ex* **11/1**

1540 **5** *3* **Top Of The Class (IRE)**[26] 5672 6-8-2 **48**...............(v) JoannaBadger 12 46
(PDEvans) *s.i.s: hld up: hdwy over 3f out: sn rdn: styd on same pce* **12/1**

0005 **6** *shd* **Den'S-Joy**[29] 5622 7-9-4 **64**.........................................(p) DarrenWilliams 7 62
(MissDAMchale) *s.i.s: hdwy 6f out: wkng whn hung lft over 1f out* **13/2**

1400 **7** *3/4* **Vermilion Creek**[5] 5937 4-7-10 **49** ow2........... StephanieHollinshead(7) 8 45
(RHollinshead) *hld up: sme hdwy over 1f out: n.d* **25/1**

6030 **8** *6* **Miss Champers (IRE)**[14] 5878 3-9-3 **66**................................ NCallan 11 50
(PDEvans) *hld up: hdwy over 3f out: wknd over 1f out* **25/1**

0000 **9** *hd* **Eurolink Artemis**[5] 5971 6-8-3 **52**...............................(p) LisaJones(3) 13 36
(MissGayKelleway) *hld up: rdn whn hmpd over 3f out: sn wknd* **25/1**

1000 **10** *1 1/4* **Zahunda (IRE)**[39] 5444 4-7-12 **51**................................. BSwarbrick(7) 10 32
(WMBrisbourne) *hld up: racd keenly: hdwy over 5f out: wknd over 2f out* **25/1**

0461 **11** *hd* **Tanga Dancer**[88] 4261 3-8-1 **50**............................................... PMQuinn 9 31
(BSmart) *prom: lost pl over 6f out: sn bhd* **25/1**

4 **12** *12* **Chiasso (USA)**[18] 5815 3-8-8 **57**............................................ SDrowne 6 14
(HMorrison) *chsd ldrs 7f* **15/2**

4200 **13** *18* **Pooka's Daughter (IRE)**[220] 983 3-8-9 **58**...................... PFitzsimons 1 —
(JMBradley) *w ldr over 5f: wknd over 2f out* **33/1**

2m 1.07s (-1.83) **Going Correction** -0.075s/f (Stan)
**WFA** 3 from 4yo+ 3lb **13** Ran SP% **122.2**
Speed ratings: **105,101,100,100,97 97,97,91,91,90 90,79,63**CSF £17.03 CT £73.87 TOTE £8.70: £2.50, £2.40, £2.10; EX 28.10.
**Owner** Mrs Jean Turpin **Bred** Mrs Jean Turpin **Trained** Sheriff Hutton, N Yorks

**FOCUS**
Quite a competitive fillies' handicap and an impressive winner.

**NOTEBOOK**
**Strong Hand**, well backed on the exchanges, had not set the world alight in two starts over inadequate trips at Southwell but, upped in distance, was a completely different proposition this time and she was cantering all over her rivals from some way out. She can win again.
**Star Of Normandie(USA)**remains in good form and made up a lot ground over the last couple of furlongs. Even though she did not necessarily get the run of the race, being forced widest of all on the home bend, the winner won with so much in hand that it is hard to imagine the result would have been any different.
**Miss Glory Be**, a multiple winner here, ran right up to her best and should find a race or two this winter.
**Jessinca**likes this surface and performed well under a positive ride, but her winning record in recent years is so poor that she can never be supported with any great confidence.
**Top Of The Class(IRE)**, rated 10lb lower on sand compared to turf, stayed on well on this return to Fibresand but may find this trip a little too sharp for her now. This was her first start for 26 days and for her that is a very long holiday.
**Den'S-Joy**, winner of this race last year off a 6lb higher mark, has not shown her best form for some time and this was little better.

## 6005 "FRANKE" SINKS AND TAPS AT WATERLINE MAIDEN STKS 1m 100y(F)

**9:00** (9:03) (D ) 3-Y-0+ **£2,282** (£652; £326) **Stalls** Low

Form RPR

0320 **1** **Merdiff**[9] 5933 4-9-2 64..............................................................(t) SWKelly 2 73
(WMBrisbourne) *chsd ldrs: led over 6f out: rdn clr 2f out: all out* **15/8**[1]

4234 **2** *nk* **Over Rating**[34] 5506 3-8-9 68......................................................... RHavlin 12 67
(JHMGosden) *trckd ldrs: outpcd over 2f out: rallied to chse wnr and hung lft 1f out: r.o wl* **7/2**[2]

0 **3** *5* **Realism (FR)**[205] 1196 3-9-0 ....................................... DarrenWilliams 11 62
(PWHiatt) *prom: chsd wnr over 3f out: rdn over 1f out: styd on same pce* **100/1**

046 **4** *3* **Maid For Life (IRE)**[33] 5554 3-8-9 ............................................ NCallan 4 51
(MJWallace) *chsd ldrs: rdn over 2f out: sn wknd* **8/1**[3]

00 **5** *5* **Felidae (USA)**[32] 5560 3-8-7 ............................................. MLawson(7) 6 45
(MBrittain) *sn outpcd: rdn 1/2-way: nvr nrr* **100/1**

0005 **6** *3/4* **Deco Lady**[5] 5973 3-8-9 50........................................... JoannaBadger 7 38
(PDEvans) *prom: rdn 1/2-way: wknd over 3f out* **50/1**

0-00 **7** *3/4* **Marakash (IRE)**[103] 3843 4-9-2 60......................................... DSweeney 13 42
(MRBosley) *sn outpcd* **25/1**

2505 **8** *4* **Bar Of Silver (IRE)**[34] 5501 3-9-0 55...............................(p) GGibbons 10 34
(RBrotherton) *chsd wnr 5f: wknd over 2f out* **40/1**

060 **9** *17* **Foggieloan**[46] 5289 3-8-9 48.......................................................... RSmith 3 —
(CGCox) *bhd fr 1/2-way* **100/1**

**10** *1/2* **Full English**[17] 4-8-8 ......................................................... LisaJones(3) 5 —
(APJones) *dwlt: outpcd* **100/1**

0 **11** *2* **Kallista's Pride**[26] 5678 3-8-9 .................................................. JFanning 9 —
(JAOsborne) *led: hdd over 6f out: wknd over 3f out* **50/1**

1m 50.67s (-0.33) **Going Correction** -0.075s/f (Stan)
**WFA** 3 from 4yo 2lb **11** Ran SP% **82.3**
Speed ratings: **98,97,92,89,84 83,83,79,62,61 59**CSF £3.43 TOTE £2.20: £1.10, £1.20, £17.90; EX 3.90.
**Owner** Thats Racing Partnership **Bred** Sheikh Ahmed Bin Rashid Al Maktoum **Trained** Great Ness, Shropshire

**FOCUS**
A very modest maiden, weakened further when Jubilee Time and Crystal Choir refused to enter the stalls, and not many winners will come out of it.

**NOTEBOOK**
**Merdiff**, who had at least previously shown ability on Fibresand, did not have much to beat. He was kept tight against the inside rail the whole way, not a problem at recent meetings here, and won this by being ridden into a clear lead on the turn for home. Fortunately for him the advantage he established was just too much for the runner-up to bridge.
**Over Rating**, who almost certainly needs further than this, had a lot of ground to make up on the favourite turning in and, despite trying hard, her late flourish was always going to be a stride too late. It was still disappointing that she could not win a race like this, bearing in mind the opposition, and her name is sadly appropriate.
**Realism(FR)**appeared to run a blinder considering his starting price, though it should be borne in mind that he was well held by the front pair and more than half the field started at 25/1 or bigger. Even so, this was a big improvement from his debut and the yard know how to get winners around here.
**Maid For Life(IRE)**deemed a non-trier by the local stewards in her most recent start though that was overturned on appeal, had every chance and it was disappointing that she ultimately finished behind a 100/1 shot. She may be better suited by the faster Polytrack surface.
**Felidae(USA)**did not achieve much in finishing a remote fifth.

## 6006 "SMEG" APPLIANCES AT WATERLINE H'CAP 1m 100y(F)

**9:30** (9:30) (F ) (0-65,65) 3-Y-0+ **£2,170** (£620; £310) **Stalls** Low

Form RPR

3420 **1** **Pharoah's Gold (IRE)**[13] 5892 5-9-9 **60**....................(e) DarrenWilliams 2 71
(DShaw) *trckd ldrs: led 1f out: r.o* **12/1**

5332 **2** *1 3/4* **Rock Concert**[14] 5881 5-8-10 **54**..................................(v) PPMathers(7) 12 61
(IWMcinnes) *led 6f out: rdn and hdd 1f out: unable qck* **3/1**[1]

3203 **3** *1 1/4* **Mcqueen (IRE)**[13] 5891 3-9-8 **61**.......................................... DSweeney 13 66
(MrsHDalton) *trckd ldrs: rdn over 2f out: hung lft fr over 1f out: no ex ins fnl f* **5/1**[3]

4600 **4** *5* **Gold Guest**[24] 5704 4-8-12 **54**...............................................(v[1]) DNolan(5) 5 48
(PDEvans) *s.i.s: sn prom: rdn and wknd over 1f out* **10/1**

2600 **5** *3* **Kirkby's Treasure**[34] 5516 5-8-11 **55**........................... SJDonohoe(7) 7 43
(ABerry) *hld up: hmpd over 6f out: nvr trbld ldrs* **25/1**

1405 **6** *nk* **Allegrina (IRE)**[105] 3779 3-9-12 **65**............................................... NCallan 6 52
(KARyan) *chsd ldrs: rdn over 2f out: wknd over 1f out* **13/2**

0- **7** *2 1/2* **Ras Tailteann (IRE)**[45] 5318 3-9-7 **60**............................................ SDrowne 1 42
(DavidWachman, Ire) *hld up in tch: rdn over 3f out: wknd over 2f out* **4/1**[2]

2403 **8** *hd* **White Park Bay (IRE)**[56] 5084 3-9-9 **65**.............................. LisaJones(3) 3 47
(JGallagher) *led 1f: wknd wl over 2f out* **8/1**

5500 **9** *7* **Scottish River (USA)**[23] 5720 4-9-9 **65**......................... NChalmers(5) 11 32
(MDIUsher) *s.s: outpcd* **20/1**

0000 **10** *2 1/2* **Phantom Flame (USA)**[9] 5933 3-9-2 **55**.................................. JFanning 9 17
(MJohnston) *hld up: hdwy over 5f out: wknd 3f out* **20/1**

000 **11** *hd* **Open Handed (IRE)**[50] 5202 3-9-4 **57**...................................(t) VHalliday 4 18
(BEllison) *led over 7f out: hdd 6f out: wknd over 2f out* **50/1**

5000 **12** *1 1/2* **Theorist**[22] 5724 3-9-7 **60**..........................................................(p) ADaly 8 18
(JLSpearing) *hld up: rdn over 3f out: a in rr* **25/1**

0000 **13** *9* **Our Paddy (IRE)**[16] 5540 4-9-4 **55**...................................... DaneO'Neill 10 —
(MrsLCJewell) *s.s: outpcd* **33/1**

1m 49.8s (-1.20) **Going Correction** -0.075s/f (Stan)
**WFA** 3 from 4yo+ 2lb **13** Ran SP% **125.0**
Speed ratings: **103,101,100,95,92 91,89,89,82,79 79,77,68**CSF £46.27 CT £222.15 TOTE £15.40: £4.10, £1.20, £2.50; EX 43.40 Place 6 £58.39, Place 5 £2.91.
**Owner** The Whiteman Partnership **Bred** Rathbarry Stud **Trained** Averham, Notts

**FOCUS**
A modest handicap run at a fair pace.

**NOTEBOOK**
**Pharoah's Gold(IRE)**, whose best performances on sand have been over shorter, found this surface less demanding than at Southwell and saw the trip out much better this time. This victory gives his trainer a few more options.
**Rock Concert**, who goes well for an inexperienced rider, was given a positive ride and did little wrong, but the winner had the better turn of foot from the home turn and condemned her to finish runner-up here yet again.
**Mcqueen(IRE)**, five of whose seven previous starts have been on Polytrack, was making his debut here and ran a nice race, but could probably do with a return to further in order to help him get off the mark.
**Gold Guest**, making his debut for his fifth stable and visored for the first time, continues to freefall down the handicap and did not run badly. He is likely to be given plenty of chances to regain the winning thread.
**Kirkby's Treasure**has won over just short of a mile on turf, but has yet to really convince over this sort of trip and never seriously got into the race.
**Allegrina(IRE)**, making her sand debut, may just have needed this after a three-month break.
**Ras Tailteann(IRE)**, a rare Irish challenger making his sand and handicap debuts, had every chance but never really picked up.
T/Plt: £29.80 to a £1 stake. Pool: £46,727.60. 1,144.05 winning tickets. T/Qpdt: £2.60 to a £1 stake. Pool: £1,962.80. 542.20 winning tickets. CR

# 5780 CAPANNELLE (R-H)

Sunday, November 16

**OFFICIAL GOING: Good to soft**

## 6007a PREMIO RIBOT (GROUP 2) 1m

**1:30** (1:36) 3-Y-0+ **£52,622** (£24,369; £13,649; £6,844)

RPR

**1** **Duca D'Atri (IRE)**[564] 4-9-2 ...................................................(b) DVargiu 2 109
(ARenzoni, Italy) *in touch, headway 2f out, quickened to challenge inside final furlong, led close home, driven out*

**2** *1/2* **Romaldo (GER)**[203] 1252 3-9-2 ............................................... TJarnet 5 110
(AMaggi, Italy) *prominent, 3rd on outside straight, effort to challenge & every chance over 1f out, led inside final furlong til headed clo*

**3** *nse* **Marbye (IRE)**[28] 5667 3-8-13 ................................................. MDemuro 6 107
(BGrizzetti, Italy) *led, pushed along when pressed over 2f out, headed inside final furlong but rallied and kept on gamely to line, just missed* 2

**4** *3 1/2* **T E Lawrence (USA)**[203] 1252 3-9-2 .................................. GMarcelli 3 103
(OPessi, Italy) *mid-division, 7th straight, good headway over 1 1/2f out to press leaders, every chance 1f out, no extra final stages*

**5** *1* **Tea Garden (IRE)**[203] 1252 3-9-2 ............................................... LDettori 7 101
(APeraino, Italy) *mid-division, effort and headway 2f out, unable to quicken final furlong*

**6** *1 1/2* **Peppercorn (GER)**[35] 5525 6-9-2 ...................................... ABoschert 13 96
(UOstmann, Germany) *never better than mid-division*

**7** *1/2* **Medici (GER)**[35] 5525 3-9-2 ............................................. J-PCarvalho 14 97
(MarioHofer, Germany) *mid-division, some late headway*

**8** *shd* **Piccolo Boy** 4-9-2 ............................................................... PBorrelli 10 95
(GLigas, Italy) *towards rear, never a factor*

**9** *1/2* **Checkit (IRE)**[15] 5872 3-9-2 ................................................ TEDurcan 8 96
(MRChannon) *in touch towards rear, 9th straight, effort 2f out, unable to quicken*

**10** *1* **Diacada (GER)**[35] 5530 3-8-13 ............................................(b) WMongil 1 91
(HBlume, Germany) *never better than mid-division*

**11** *2* **Salselon**[14] 5904 4-9-2 .................................................... AParravani 11 88
(MCiciarelli, Italy) *held up tracking leaders, came wide entering straight, effort over 2f out, no impression* 1

**12** *5* **Blueberry Forest (IRE)**[21] 5779 5-9-2 .............................. GBietolini 12 78
(PHirschberger, Germany) *always behind*

**13** *3/4* **Caluki**[21] 6-9-2 ..................................................................... DPorcu 4 76
(LCamici, Italy) *never a factor*

14 2 **Giovane Imperatore**364 5740 5-9-2 ........ MPasquale 9 72
(LBrogi, Italy) *close up til weakened approaching straight* 3

1m 37.1s
**WFA** 3 from 4yo+ 2lb **14 Ran SP% 134.4**
Speed ratings: .
**Owner** Scuderia Aterno **Bred** Scuderia Aterno **Trained** Italy

**NOTEBOOK**
**Duca D'Atri(IRE)**appeared no more than a decent handicapper on his previous form but pulled off a massive shock here.
**Checkit(IRE)**was never able to land a blow, but was reportedly unsuited by the false ground, and lost his action a couple of times in the race. He is best forgiven this effort.

## 6008a PREMIO ROMA - SIS (GROUP 1) 1m 2f
**2:00** (2:11) 3-Y-O+ **£93,377** (£49,903; £29,805; £14,903)

RPR
1 **Imperial Dancer**22 5752 5-9-2 ........ TEDurcan 7 119
(MRChannon) *held up in last, 7th straight, headway 3f out, ridden to challenge 2f out, quickened to lead over 1f out, ran on well* **53/10**
2 3 **Altieri**35 5530 5-9-2 ........ MEsposito 5 114
(VCaruso, Italy) *towards rear, 8th straight, pushed along over 3f out, ridden and stayed on from 2f out to take 2nd final 100yds* **77/10**
3 snk **Sunstrach (IRE)**43 5383 5-9-2 ........ LDettori 6 114
(EBorromeo, Italy) *raced in 3rd, pressing leader over 3f out, led over 2 1/2f out, ridden & headed over 1f out, no extra & lost 2nd final 100y* **48/10**
4 3/4 **Trumbaka (IRE)**42 5403 4-8-13 ........ TJarnet 3 109
(MmeCHead-Maarek, France) *held up in mid-division, 5th straight, driven over 2f out, stayed on under pressure to take 4th final strides* **33/10**2
5 hd **Fair Mix (IRE)**28 5662 5-9-2 ........ SPasquier 2 112
(MRolland, France) *in touch, 4th straight, driven 3f out, kept on til lost 4th final strides* **11/4**1
6 1 1/2 **Execute (FR)**15 5884 6-9-2 ........ DBoeuf 10 109
(JEHammond, France) *held up, last on rail straight, driven over 2f out, stayed on at one pace but never threatened* **9/2**3
7 2 1/2 **Quel Del Giaz (IRE)**92 4198 4-9-2 ........ DPorcu 4 105
(FCamici, Italy) *led, pushed along over 3f out, headed over 2 1/2f out, soon ridden and no extra* **56/1**
8 1 **Blu For Life (IRE)**189 1547 6-9-2 ........ MMimmocchi 1 103
(RMimmocchi, Italy) *raced in 2nd, under pressure and 3rd straight, soon beaten* **45/1**
9 3 1/2 **Maktub (ITY)**28 5666 4-9-2 ........ MDemuro 8 97
(BGrizzetti, Italy) *in touch, 6th and soon ridden straight, unable to quicken* **52/10**
10 2 1/2 **Vangelis (USA)**28 5662 4-9-2 ........ FBlondel 9 93
(ADeRoyer-Dupre, France) *held up, 9th straight, pushed along on outside over 3f out, no impression* **20/1**

2m 1.60s **10 Ran SP% 137.5**
Speed ratings: .
**Owner** Imperial Racing **Bred** Launceston Stud **Trained** West Ilsley, Berks

**NOTEBOOK**
**Imperial Dancer**opened his Group 1 account in the best possible style, and this was a fully deserved success. Given a confident hold-up ride, he could be called the winner as soon as he hit the front. He is expected to remain in training.
**Altieri**came from off the pace, and did well to deny Sunstrach second place, though the winner had already flown. This smart performer should continue to make his mark in Group races.
**Sunstrach(IRE)**last year's winner benefitted from a good ride from Dettori, who gave his mount every chance in the race. He lost nothing in defeat here.
**Trumbaka(IRE)**had to be given strong assistance from the saddle to get up for fourth close home, and never challenged the leaders at any stage.

## 6009a PREMIO UMBRIA (GROUP 3) 6f
**2:30** (2:44) 2-Y-O+ **£31,851** (£14,830; £8,328; £4,164)

RPR
1 **Glad To Be Fast (IRE)**14 5904 3-9-8 ........ WMongil 11 —
(MarioHofer, Germany) *in touch, quickened to challenge over 1f out, led inside final furlong, ran on well* 2
2 1 3/4 **Fairy Beauty**490 3060 5-9-8 ........(b) PAgus 3 —
(MMorelli, Italy) *close up on rail, led over 1 1/2f out, ran on til headed inside final furlong, kept on*
3 1 1/2 **Golden Pivotal**28 5665 2-8-5 ........ DVargiu 6 —
(GFratini, Italy) *always in touch, finished well from over 1f out to take 3rd final strides*
4 nse **Mangayoh (IRE)**28 5664 4-9-8 ........(b) MBelli 10 —
(ARenzoni, Italy) *prominent, ran on from over 1f out, just missed 3rd*
5 nse **Royal Millennium (IRE)**8 5953 5-9-8 ........ TEDurcan 8 —
(MRChannon) *behind, progress over 2f out, finished strongly from over 1f out to dispute 3rd, nearest at finish* 1
6 nk **Slap Shot (IRE)**28 5664 4-9-8 ........ PAragoni 17 —
(LRiccardi, Italy) *led narrowly in centre til headed over 1 1/2f out, kept on to line* 3
7 snk **Sopran Foldan (IRE)**14 5904 5-9-8 ........ MDemuro 2 —
(BGrizzetti, Italy) *raced on rail, some late headway*
8 1 **Regina Saura**28 5664 5-9-5 ........(b) MEsposito 16 —
(MCiciarelli, Italy) *prominent til no extra final stages*
9 1/2 **Rychter (ITY)**42 5397 2-8-5 ........ MPasquale 7 —
(LBrogi, Italy) *always mid-division*
10 2 1/4 **Fiepes Shuffle (GER)**35 5528 3-9-11 ........ J-PCarvalho 1 —
(MarioHofer, Germany) *behind early on rail, never a threat* 2
11 nk **Krisman (IRE)**175 1855 4-9-8 ........ AParravani 5 —
(MCiciarelli, Italy) *mid-division, never dangerous*
12 1/2 **King Cheetah (USA)** 4-9-8 ........(b) PBorrelli 4 —
(ARenzoni, Italy) *never a threat*
13 1 1/2 **San Dany (IRE)**126 3258 3-9-8 ........ GMarcelli 15 —
(LAntonacci, Italy) *prominent til 2f out*
14 2 **Dream Chief (USA)**14 5904 7-9-8 ........ DPorcu 12 —
(MGuarnieri, Italy) *speed 3f*
15 6 **Bislacca** 3-9-5 ........ LManiezzi 14 —
(SIbido, Italy) *always towards rear*
16 **Golden Danetime (IRE)**410 5056 3-9-8 ........ CColombi 13 —
(RSantini, Italy) *never a factor*
17 **Mount Abu (IRE)**14 5904 6-9-8 ........ LDettori 18 —
(JHMGosden) *prominent on outside to halfway*

69.20 secs **17 Ran SP% 174.0**
Speed ratings: .
**Owner** Stall Jenny **Bred** Gestut Romerhof **Trained** Germany

**NOTEBOOK**
**Glad To Be Fast(IRE)**runner up to Salselon in a Group 3 last time, he carried on his good form here. Showing good speed once he hit the front, he was still full of running at the line.
**Fairy Beauty**blazed a trail on the rail, and showed good speed throughout. He coped well with the loose ground, and this was a good effort.
**Golden Pivotal**a neat two-year-old, he went over the ground well, and this was a good effort against his elders. He has a very speedy pedigree, yet has raced over as far as a mile this season. It would be no surprise to see him do well in a sprinting campaign next year.
**Royal Millennium(IRE)**was well behind at half-way, but made rapid headway in the final stages to contest a three way photo for third. Like Checkit he wasn't suited by the loose ground, so this admirably tough campaigner did well in the circumstances.
**Mount Abu(IRE)**was prominent to half-way but quickly faded and finished last. Both his recent efforts in Italy have been far removed from his previously smart form.

# 6001 WOLVERHAMPTON (A.W) (L-H)
Monday, November 17

**OFFICIAL GOING: Standard**
Wind: almost nil Weather: raining

## 6010 BET DIRECT NO Q H'CAP (DIV I) 6f (F)
**12:40** (12:40) (D ) (0-85,85) 3-Y-O+ **£3,402** (£972; £486) **Stalls** Low

Form RPR
3305 1 **Canterloupe (IRE)**15 5888 5-9-5 **76** ........ DSweeney 8 88
(PJMakin) *hld up in tch: rdn over 2f out: led over 1f out: drvn out* **11/2**3
0606 2 1 1/4 **Heidelburg (IRE)**4 5987 3-8-6 **63** ........ JFEgan 7 71
(SKirk) *sn bhd: swtchd rt over 2f out: hdwy over 1f out: edgd lft ins fnl f: fin wl* **15/2**
1144 3 1 **Landing Strip (IRE)**15 5888 3-9-3 **77** ........ FPFerris(3) 3 82
(JMPEustace) *led after 1f: rdn over 2f out: hdd over 1f out: nt qckn* **7/2**1
0000 4 shd **Bond Royale**140 2848 3-9-8 **79** ........ IMongan 11 84
(BSmart) *a.p: rdn over 2f out: one pce fnl f* **12/1**
0100 5 hd **Law Breaker (IRE)**9 5953 5-10-0 **85** ........ ADaly 5 89
(JAGilbert) *sn bhd: hdwy wl over 1f out: kpt on one pce fnl f* **4/1**2
6000 6 2 1/2 **Our Chelsea Blue (USA)**198 1334 5-8-3 **60** ........ FNorton 12 57
(AWCarroll) *hld up in tch: rdn over 2f out: wknd 1f out* **25/1**
1060 7 2 1/2 **Indian Maiden (IRE)**15 5888 3-9-2 **73** ........ SWhitworth 10 62
(MSSaunders) *sn bhd: hdwy over 3f out: no further prog fnl 2f* **12/1**
0-00 8 1 1/4 **Turn Around**10 5941 3-9-3 **74** ........ DaneO'Neill 9 59
(BWHills) *nvr nr ldrs* **20/1**
0000 9 1 **Toppling**4 5985 5-8-0 **57** ........ ANicholls 4 39
(JMBradley) *w ldrs: rdn over 3f out: ev ch over 2f out: eased whn btn ins fnl f* **33/1**
1000 10 1 1/2 **Blakeshall Quest**28 5681 3-9-3 **74** ........ GGibbons 1 52
(RBrotherton) *chsd ldrs: rdn 4f out: sn wknd* **33/1**
0000 11 8 **Prince Of Blues (IRE)**14 5909 5-9-9 **80** ........ TWilliams 2 34
(MMullineaux) *led 1f: prom tl rdn and wknd over 2f out* **12/1**
1440 12 3 **River Days (IRE)**2 6001 5-8-4 **68** ........(bt) BFayosMartin(7) 13 13
(MissGayKelleway) *a bhd* **14/1**
6003 13 7 **Pips Song (IRE)**101 3969 8-7-12 **55** oh3 ........ JoannaBadger 6 —
(PWHiatt) *s.i.s: a in rr* **16/1**

1m 15.39s (-0.31) **Going Correction** -0.05s/f (Stan) **13 Ran SP% 119.5**
Speed ratings: **100,98,97,96,96 93,89,88,86,84 74,70,60**CSF £44.33 CT £165.44 TOTE £2.40: £2.80, £4.20, £1.40; EX 36.30.
**Owner** R A Ballin & The Billinomas **Bred** The Lavington Stud **Trained** Ogbourne Maisey, Wilts

**FOCUS**
Probably just an ordinary sprint handicap run in a slower time than the second division.
**NOTEBOOK**
**Canterloupe(IRE)**, making her Fibresand debut, took well to the surface and was gaining her first win in over a year. If kept on the go this winter, she should continue to give a good account of herself.
**Heidelburg(IRE)**, who gained her only previous win round here, was doing her best work late on and looks well worth another try over seven furlongs.
**Landing Strip(IRE)** once again tried to make every yard, but he proved unable to last home and the suspicion that he will be better back over five furlongs remains.
**Bond Royale**, just 3lb higher than when scoring here last season, ran an encouraging race and if able to build on this she could well end her 11-month losing run.
**Law Breaker(IRE)**, lightly-raced since causing a 66/1 shock at Doncaster in March, showed signs of a return to form and should win his share of races on Fibresand this winter.
**Indian Maiden(IRE)** failed to build on the encouragement he showed at Lingfield last time.

## 6011 BET DIRECT ON 0800 32 93 93 MEDIAN AUCTION MAIDEN STKS 6f (F)
**1:10** (1:10) (F ) 2-Y-O **£2,289** (£654; £327) **Stalls** Low

Form RPR
2562 1 **Bridgewater Boys**7 5966 2-9-0 58 ........(b) GDuffield 5 64
(KARyan) *a.p: rdn over 1f out: led wl ins fnl f: r.o* **4/1**2
4322 2 1/2 **Bookiesindexdotcom**16 5876 2-8-9 65 ........(v) SWKelly 6 57
(JRJenkins) *w ldr: led over 3f out: rdn over 2f out: hdd wl ins ins fnl f: no ex* **8/1**
2353 3 1 1/4 **Bond Brooklyn**7 5968 2-9-0 67 ........(v) DarrenWilliams 10 58
(BSmart) *hld up: rdn and hdwy on outside 2f out: kpt on same pce fnl f* **3/1**1
0 4 1 1/2 **Quincannon (USA)**32 5595 2-9-0 ........ SDrowne 9 54
(TDBarron) *s.i.s: sn pushed along and rcvrd after 1f: rdn and hdwy 2f out: no ex fnl f* **5/1**3
0 5 1 **Vittorioso (IRE)**7 5968 2-9-0 ........(p) MFenton 7 51
(MissGayKelleway) *a.p: rdn over 3f out: one pce fnl 2f* **66/1**
6 3 **Sable 'n Silk** 2-8-9 ........ FNorton 1 37
(DHaydnJones) *nvr trbld ldrs* **25/1**
0230 7 1 3/4 **Iphigenia (IRE)**45 5337 2-8-6 63 ........ LisaJones(3) 4 32
(PWHiatt) *chsd ldrs tl wknd 2f out* **10/1**
0620 8 2 **Garrigon**23 5751 2-9-0 66 ........ IMongan 12 31
(NPLittmoden) *hld up and sn bhd: short-lived effrt over 3f out* **11/2**
6443 9 1 3/4 **Faites Vos Jeux**16 5876 2-8-9 58 ........ TWilliams 3 20
(CNKellett) *led over 2f: rdn over 2f out: wknd wl over 1f out* **33/1**
43 10 3 1/2 **Saffron River**121 3427 2-9-0 ........ ACulhane 2 15
(RHollinshead) *s.i.s: a bhd* **25/1**
11 3 **Calculaite** 2-9-0 ........ AngelaHartley 8 6
(MrsGSRees) *s.i.s: outpcd* **40/1**
3 12 2 1/2 **Royal Awakening (IRE)**82 4508 2-9-0 ........ NCallan 11 —
(APJarvis) *chsd ldrs tl wknd over 2f out* **9/1**

1m 16.56s (0.86) **Going Correction** -0.05s/f (Stan) **12 Ran SP% 121.8**
Speed ratings: **92,91,89,87,86 82,80,77,75,70 66,63**CSF £35.26 TOTE £7.50: £2.60, £1.10, £2.00; EX 27.40.
**Owner** Bishopthorpe Racing **Bred** Southill Stud **Trained** Hambleton, N Yorks
■ Stewards Enquiry : S W Kelly one-day ban: used whip with arm above shoulder height (Nov 29)

**FOCUS**
A moderate maiden.
**NOTEBOOK**
**Bridgewater Boys**, a slightly unlucky loser over course and distance last time when Duffield dropped his whip in the straight, made no mistake this time. However, things could be tougher next time as he is sure to take a significant rise in the weights for this success.
**Bookiesindexdotcom** has had plenty of chances and would have been 12lb worse off with the winner had this been a handicap.
**Bond Brooklyn**, who had 9lb in hand of the winner at the figures, ran a respectable race, but will probably have to improve on this to get off the mark.
**Quincannon(USA)** was well backed to improve on his debut effort and did so. He would have been even closer with a better start and, providing he continues to progress, a minor maiden like this one could come his way.
**Vittorioso(IRE)** also appeared to improve on his debut running.
**Garrigon**, second off 68 in a Pontefract nursery last month, was a major disappointment on his first attempt on Fibresand.

## 6012 BET DIRECT ON ATTHERACES INTERACTIVE MAIDEN AUCTION STKS 1m 100y(F)
**1:40** (1:41) (F) 2-Y-O **£2,282** (£652; £326) **Stalls** Low

Form RPR
6036 **1** **Almond Willow (IRE)**[14] 5906 2-8-9 66 SWKelly 7 65
(JNoseda) *a.p: rdn over 2f out: hung lft and flashed tail wl over 1f out: r.o to ld wl ins fnl f* **3/1**[2]
232 **2** 1 1/4 **Hawkit (USA)**[16] 5877 2-9-0 73 DaneO'Neill 1 67
(JAOsborne) *hld up and bhd: hdwy 3f out: sn rdn: led briefly ins fnl f: nt qckn* **6/4**[1]
003 **3** 1 1/2 **Keltic Rainbow (IRE)**[16] 5877 2-8-3 58 ow1 PaulEddery 4 53
(DHaydnJones) *chsd ldrs: rdn over 2f out: kpt on ins fnl f* **10/1**
00 **4** 1/2 **Rood Boy (IRE)**[21] 5798 2-8-7 DKinsella 10 56
(JSKing) *sn w ldr: led 3f out: sn rdn: hdd and no ex ins fnl f* **40/1**
055 **5** 7 **Elitista (FR)**[21] 5798 2-8-2 58 JTate 9 36
(EJO'Neill) *hld up in tch: rdn over 3f out: wknd wl over 1f out* **20/1**
5 **6** 1 3/4 **Beau West**[11] 5934 2-8-3 ow1 JFEgan 6 34
(SKirk) *led: rdn and hdd 3f out: wknd over 1f out: eased whn btn btn fnl f* **10/1**
062 **7** 1 1/4 **Hold The Line**[41] 5439 2-8-2 70 ow2 LTreadwell(7) 12 37
(WGMTurner) *prom: rdn 3f out: sn wknd: hung lft wl over 1f out* **11/2**[3]
00 **8** 2 1/2 **Biscar Two (IRE)**[23] 5744 2-8-7 DeanMcKeown 3 30
(RMWhitaker) *a bhd* **66/1**
00 **9** 1 3/4 **Pattern Man**[16] 5877 2-8-8 ow1 DarrenWilliams 8 27
(JRNorton) *a bhd* **66/1**
00 **10** 5 **Winslow Boy (USA)**[19] 5830 2-8-10 MFenton 5 19
(CFWall) *bhd: n.m.r and snatched up over 3f out: n.d after* **16/1**
000 **11** 4 **Casantella**[117] 3494 2-8-2 50 GDuffield 2 2
(MGQuinlan) *prom: reminder over 5f out: wknd over 3f out* **66/1**
560 **12** 21 **Shalamak**[105] 3844 2-8-2 57 MHenry 13 —
(BRMillman) *hld up and bhd: rdn 4f out: t.o* **50/1**
0 **13** 2 **Weet An Store (IRE)**[16] 5877 2-8-10 (t) ACulhane 11 —
(RHollinshead) *a bhd: rdn 4f out: t.o* **66/1**

1m 51.8s (0.80) **Going Correction** -0.05s/f (Stan) **13 Ran SP% 119.6**
Speed ratings: **94,92,91,90,83 82,80,78,76,71 67,46,44**CSF £7.52 TOTE £4.90: £1.10, £1.50, £2.70; EX 12.80.
**Owner** W L Armitage **Bred** David Allan **Trained** Newmarket, Suffolk
**FOCUS**
A weak maiden that is unlikely to produce too many winners.
**NOTEBOOK**
**Almond Willow(IRE)**, making her Fibresand debut, and switching back into a maiden after a couple of runs in handicap company, got off the mark despite looking a difficult ride. A rise in the weights for this success is likely and she may find things tougher next time.
**Hawkit(USA)** is becoming a very disappointing sort. He is not short of pace and may be worth dropping back to seven furlongs.
**Keltic Rainbow(IRE)** ran her race again for her in-form yard, but things may be a little easier in handicaps.
**Rood Boy(IRE)** appears to be progressing along the right lines, but handicapping looks his game.
**Elitista(FR)** was beaten a long way and this did not offer much hope for the immediate future.
**Hold The Line** had 6lb in hand of the winner on the book, but was beaten a long way and has to be considered a major disappointment.
**Winslow Boy(USA)** *Official explanation: jockey said colt failed to handle the bend*
**Weet An Store(IRE)** *Official explanation: trainer said colt had a breathing problem*

## 6013 BETDIRECT.CO.UK STKS SHOWCASE H'CAP 1m 100y(F)
**2:10** (2:18) (C) (0-95,95) 3-Y-O+ **£5,551** (£1,708; £854; £427) **Stalls** Low

Form RPR
2001 **1** **Cardinal Venture (IRE)**[7] 5967 5-9-5 86 6ex NCallan 5 101
(KARyan) *mde all: rdn clr 2f out: r.o* **3/1**[1]
4331 **2** 3/4 **Lakota Brave**[7] 5970 9-9-5 86 6ex FNorton 1 99
(MrsStefLiddiard) *hld up: smooth hdwy 4f out: sn rdn: wnt 2nd over 1f out: r.o ins fnl f: nt rch wnr* **16/1**
5000 **3** 2 **Ovigo (GER)**[14] 5910 4-7-11 67 FPFerris(3) 2 76
(PABlockley) *bhd tl hdwy over 2f out: edgd lft and kpt on ins fnl f* **33/1**
5060 **4** 3 1/2 **Certain Justice (USA)**[16] 5873 5-9-4 85 SDrowne 3 86
(PFICole) *chsd ldrs: rdn over 3f out: wnt 2nd over 2f out: wknd fnl f* **7/1**[3]
010 **5** nk **Te Quiero**[19] 5827 5-9-12 93 (t) SWKelly 6 94
(MissGayKelleway) *prom: rdn over 4f out: wknd 2f out* **7/1**[3]
3015 **6** hd **Blue Trojan (IRE)**[10] 5945 3-8-4 73 JFEgan 13 73
(SKirk) *nvr nr ldrs* **8/1**
1005 **7** 2 **Diamond Max (IRE)**[9] 5946 5-8-13 85 DNolan(5) 10 81
(PDEvans) *sn bhd: n.d* **9/1**
3001 **8** 1 1/4 **Yorker (USA)**[17] 5846 5-8-2 69 ow1 GDuffield 12 63
(MsDeborahJEvans) *chsd ldrs tl wknd over 3f out* **20/1**
0003 **9** hd **Nashaab (USA)**[16] 5873 6-9-8 89 DaneO'Neill 4 82
(PDEvans) *dwlt: a bhd* **6/1**[2]
5520 **10** 3 1/2 **Lygeton Lad**[44] 5372 5-10-0 95 (t) MFenton 11 81
(MissGayKelleway) *s.i.s: a bhd* **20/1**
0402 **11** 3 1/2 **Vicious Warrior**[23] 5749 4-8-11 78 DeanMcKeown 8 56
(RMWhitaker) *chsd ldrs tl wknd over 3f out* **12/1**
3220 **12** 8 **Del Mar Sunset**[10] 5945 4-9-8 89 ACulhane 9 51
(WJHaggas) *hld up: hdwy whn nt clr run over 3f out: sn bhd* **12/1**
0560 **13** 6 **Nuit Sombre (IRE)**[9] 5952 3-9-1 84 (b) JFanning 7 33
(MJohnston) *prom: rdn over 4f out: wknd over 3f out* **10/1**

1m 49.05s (-1.95) **Going Correction** -0.05s/f (Stan)
**WFA** 3 from 4yo+ 2lb **13 Ran SP% 128.2**
Speed ratings: **107,106,104,100,100 100,98,97,96,93 89,81,75**CSF £59.70 CT £1050.86 TOTE £4.50: £2.20, £3.70, £14.80; EX 42.50 Trifecta £1303.40 Pool of £3,304.51 - 1.80 winning tickets.
**Owner** Tony Fawcett **Bred** Patrick Gleeson **Trained** Hambleton, N Yorks

**FOCUS**
A good handicap run at a fast pace.
**NOTEBOOK**
**Cardinal Venture(IRE)** made it two out of two round here with a fine front-running performance. He was not left alone up front but, under a 6lb penalty for his success over course and distance last time, kept up a relentless gallop and never looked like being caught. He should continue to prove hard to beat round here.
**Lakota Brave**, also carrying a 6lb penalty for a recent success over course and distance, ran a great race, only to be beaten by a better horse. His trainer is proving she can do particularly well with this type of horse.
**Ovigo(GER)**, off a feather weight, ran his best race to date in this country on his Fibresand debut. If he can build on this he should be placed to effect off his current sort of mark.
**Certain Justice(USA)**, whose trainer does well with his runners round here, made a pleasing enough Fibresand debut, but looks just a little too high in the weights.
**Te Quiero**, last season's Lincoln Trial winner, is at his best when able to dominate.
**Blue Trojan(IRE)** was probably just a little bit out of his depth.
**Nashaab(USA)** could never get into it after missing the kick.
**Lygeton Lad** had no easy task off top weight and is a better horse round Lingfield.
**Del Mar Sunset** ran a very lacklustre race.
**Nuit Sombre(IRE)** may have had enough for the time being.

## 6014 BET DIRECT NO Q H'CAP (DIV II) 6f (F)
**2:40** (2:43) (D) (0-85,84) 3-Y-O+ **£3,388** (£968; £484) **Stalls** Low

Form RPR
0000 **1** **Bond Playboy**[14] 5908 3-9-13 84 IMongan 4 94
(BSmart) *w ldr: led over 4f out: rdn over 2f out: all out* **25/1**
6501 **2** nk **Quiet Times (IRE)**[16] 5880 4-9-4 75 (b) NCallan 7 84
(KARyan) *led over 1f: w wnr: rdn over 2f out: ev ch ins fnl f: r.o* **5/1**[2]
3303 **3** shd **Monte Mayor Lad (IRE)**[4] 5988 3-8-5 62 (b) FNorton 13 71
(DHaydnJones) *a.p: rdn over 2f out: sltly outpcd wl over 1f out: rallied ins fnl f* **9/1**
5225 **4** 2 1/2 **Rafters Music (IRE)**[44] 5377 8-8-12 72 LisaJones(3) 3 74
(JulianPoulton) *chsd ldrs: outpcd over 3f out: rallied on ins wl over 1f out: one pce fnl f* **7/1**[3]
5063 **5** 1 1/2 **Esatto**[25] 5718 4-8-10 67 DeanMcKeown 1 64
(PABlockley) *chsd ldrs: rdn over 2f out: one pce* **7/1**[3]
-000 **6** 3/4 **Cashel Mead**[51] 5217 3-9-7 78 ADaly 2 73
(JLSpearing) *sn bhd: hdwy on ins over 1f out: nvr trbld ldrs* **14/1**
6606 **7** nk **Geronimo**[32] 5598 6-7-12 55 DKinsella 6 49
(MissGayKelleway) *s.i.s: bhd tl hdwy over 1f out: r.o* **7/1**[3]
0200 **8** hd **Effective**[32] 5597 3-8-11 68 DarrenWilliams 12 61
(APJarvis) *prom: rdn over 3f out: wknd wl over 1f out* **25/1**
6000 **9** 1 1/2 **Safranine (IRE)**[14] 5909 6-7-10 60 (p) RoryMoore(7) 11 49
(MissAStokell) *chsd ldrs: rdn over 3f out: sn wknd* **14/1**
0660 **10** nk **Currency**[10] 5941 6-9-5 76 PFitzsimons 9 64
(JMBradley) *prom 2f* **14/1**
0140 **11** 5 **Sir Desmond**[51] 5216 5-9-9 80 (p) ACulhane 10 53
(RGuest) *sn bhd* **11/4**[1]
0500 **12** 3/4 **New Foundation (IRE)**[18] 5837 3-7-9 57 (t) JFMcDonald(5) 8 28
(MrsStefLiddiard) *a bhd* **25/1**
0060 **13** 1 3/4 **Semenovskii**[10] 5941 3-9-3 74 JFEgan 5 39
(PWD'Arcy) *a bhd* **14/1**

1m 14.79s (-0.91) **Going Correction** -0.05s/f (Stan) **13 Ran SP% 129.0**
Speed ratings: **104,103,103,100,98 97,96,96,94,94 87,86,84**CSF £154.44 CT £1286.23 TOTE £27.80: £7.10, £2.90, £2.50; EX 203.70.
**Owner** R C Bond **Bred** P A Mason **Trained** Hambleton, N Yorks
**FOCUS**
Not a bad sprint handicap, run in a faster time than the first division.
**NOTEBOOK**
**Bond Playboy** showed little on turf this year, but he goes well on Fibresand and appreciated the return to this surface. He is plenty high enough in the weights and a further rise could be enough to stop him.
**Quiet Times(IRE)** posted a bold effort to follow up his recent course and distance success off a 7lb higher mark. He is probably worth keeping an eye on whilst in this form.
**Monte Mayor Lad(IRE)**, still a maiden, ran a cracker. He has had plenty of chances before now, but there is surely a race to be won with him while his trainer is in such blinding form.
**Rafters Music(IRE)** is not an easy horse to win with but this was a respectable effort.
**Esatto**, 8lb lower than on turf, has a running style not ideally suited to Fibresand racing and probably ran well in the circumstances.
**Sir Desmond** has won on Fibresand so this surface cannot be blamed for this poor showing.

## 6015 BET DIRECT IN RUNNING SKY TEXT 293 (S) STKS (DIV I) 1m 100y(F)
**3:10** (3:10) (G) 3-Y-O+ **£2,065** (£590; £295) **Stalls** Low

Form RPR
3100 **1** **Consignia (IRE)**[17] 5846 4-9-0 48 (v[1]) PaulEddery 5 53
(DHaydnJones) *hld up in tch: rdn over 2f out: r.o u.p to ld cl home* **7/1**
6066 **2** 1/2 **Conchonita**[126] 3269 3-8-7 40 DKinsella 2 47
(BPalling) *prom: led briefly over 5f out: led over 3f out tl over 2f out: hrd rdn to ld wl over 1f out: hdd cl home* **25/1**
0560 **3** hd **Givemethemoonlight**[165] 2132 4-8-9 48 IMongan 11 47
(LGCottrell) *hld up and bhd: smooth hdwy on outside 4f out: led over 2f out: rdn and hdd wl over 1f out: ev ch ins fnl f: rn* **4/1**[2]
0050 **4** 5 **Second Venture (IRE)**[23] 5742 5-8-7 37 (p) DFentiman(7) 9 41
(JRWeymes) *a.p: rdn and ev ch 2f out: wknd ins fnl f* **25/1**
2004 **5** 3 **Air Of Esteem**[41] 5444 7-9-5 50 DeanMcKeown 13 40
(IanEmmerson) *hld up: hdwy on outside over 3f out: sn rdn: wknd 2f out* **6/1**[3]
0606 **6** nk **Neutral Night (IRE)**[27] 5690 3-8-7 45 (v) GGibbons 1 29
(RBrotherton) *led 3f: led again over 4f out tl over 3f out: wknd 2f out* **25/1**
0603 **7** 1 1/4 **Storm Shower (IRE)**[151] 2508 5-8-11 41 (v) LisaJones(3) 8 31
(MrsNMacauley) *s.i.s: bhd tl hdwy on ins over 2f out: wknd over 1f out* **11/1**
0640 **8** 1 3/4 **Distinctlysplendid**[81] 4529 3-8-12 36 GDuffield 7 28
(IAWood) *w ldr: led briefly 5f out: rdn over 3f out: wknd over 2f out* **25/1**
5600 **9** nk **Nite-Owl Fizz**[32] 5596 5-8-12 55 JDO'Reilly(7) 3 32
(JO'Reilly) *a bhd* **10/1**
0200 **10** 1 3/4 **High Diva**[25] 5717 4-8-10 48 ow1 DaneO'Neill 10 19
(BRJohnson) *hld up: rdn 3f out: sn bhd* **5/2**[1]
0050 **11** 9 **Generous Share**[21] 5799 3-8-7 50 SWhitworth 12 —
(MSSaunders) *hld up: rdn over 5f out: bhd fnl 4f* **11/1**
2000 **12** 2 **Threat**[116] 3515 7-9-0 43 PFitzsimons 6 —
(JMBradley) *prom tl rdn and wknd 4f out* **25/1**

0-00 **13** *dist* **Indrapura Star (USA)**[169] 2022 3-8-7 47 ............................ AQuinn(5) 4 —
(MissJFeilden) *hld up: rdn over 4f out: sn bhd: t.o* **25/1**

1m 50.63s (-0.37) **Going Correction** -0.05s/f (Stan)
**WFA** 3 from 4yo+ 2lb **13** Ran SP% **124.2**
Speed ratings: **99,98,98,93,90 90,88,87,86,84 75,73,**—CSF £181.21 TOTE £10.70: £3.70, £12.60, £1.50; EX 259.80.There was no bid for the winner.
**Owner** I Jerrard **Bred** Ardrums House Stud **Trained** Efail Isaf, Rhondda C Taff

**FOCUS**
A weak seller run in a time fractionally faster than the second division.

**NOTEBOOK**
**Consignia(IRE)**, with a visor replacing blinkers, and dropping down in grade from claiming company, kept up his yard's good run of form with a narrow success. This looks to be his level and he should continue to go well if kept to this grade.
**Conchonita**, a lightly-raced maiden dropping three furlongs in trip, posted one of her best efforts to date and now connections appear to have found her trip she could well find a similar race.
**Givemethemoonlight** ran respectably on this return from a break, but remains a maiden.
**Second Venture(IRE)** has not won for over a year and was well held by the front three.
**Air Of Esteem** appeared to have everything to suit and has to be considered disappointing.
**Nite-Owl Fizz** *Official explanation: trainer's representative said gelding had missed the break and resented the kick-back*
**High Diva** is a most disappointing maiden.

## 6016 BET DIRECT IN RUNNING SKY TEXT 293 (S) STKS (DIV II) 1m 100y(F)
**3:40** (3:40) (G) 3-Y-O+ **£2,065** (£590; £295) **Stalls** Low

Form RPR
1600 **1** **Pup's Pride**[72] 4734 6-9-2 52 ............................ (v) LisaJones(3) 5 63
(MrsNMacauley) *broke wl: sn mid-div: rdn and lost pl 4f out: gd hdwy on outside 2f out: r.o to ld cl home* **10/1**
3604 **2** *¾* **Noul (USA)**[44] 5377 4-9-5 72 ............................ PFessey 6 62
(KARyan) *hld up: rdn over 3f out: hdwy on outside over 1f out: r.o wl ins fnl f* **10/11**[1]
0203 **3** *1* **Feast Of Romance**[72] 4734 6-8-11 51 ............................ J-PGuillambert(3) 1 55
(PHowling) *w ldr: led over 6f out: rdn over 2f out: clr wl over 1f out: ct cl home* **5/1**[2]
0000 **4** *¾* **Swynford Welcome**[17] 5848 7-8-9 40 ............................ DNolan(5) 12 53
(IAWood) *a.p: rdn 4f out: chsd wnr 2f out to 1f out: no ex* **10/1**
5000 **5** *1* **Malmand (USA)**[76] 4631 4-9-5 42 ............................ (v) GGibbons 3 56
(RBrotherton) *s.i.s: hdwy 6f out: rdn over 3f out: one pce fnl 2f* **25/1**
003 **6** *7* **Samar Qand**[16] 5879 4-8-9 49 ............................ (p) JFEgan 11 31
(JulianPoulton) *bhd: hdwy over 3f out: sn rdn: wknd over 1f out* **6/1**[3]
0006 **7** *½* **Mutarafaa (USA)**[121] 3396 4-9-0 44 ............................ (e[1]) IMongan 2 35
(DShaw) *hld up in tch: rdn 3f out: sn lost pl* **16/1**
0056 **8** *3 ½* **Deco Lady**[2] 6005 3-8-7 50 ............................ NCallan 4 23
(PDEvans) *led 2f: w ldr tl rdn over 3f out: wknd 2f out* **20/1**
040 **9** *1* **Achilles Rainbow**[116] 3527 4-9-0 39 ............................ DarrenWilliams 13 26
(KRBurke) *hld up: stdy hdwy over 5f out: rdn over 3f out: wknd over 2f out* **25/1**
000 **10** *½* **Tedzar (IRE)**[121] 3398 3-8-7 35 ............................ (b) NChalmers(5) 9 25
(BRJohnson) *hld up in tch: rdn 3f out: sn wknd* **20/1**
00/0 **11** *dist* **Bettergetgone**[135] 3005 4-8-2 35 ............................ BSwarbrick(7) 10 —
(WClay) *a bhd: t.o fnl 4f* **66/1**
020/ **12** *11* **Presidents Lady**[1146] 4677 6-8-9 42 ............................ JoannaBadger 7 —
(PWHiatt) *prom: rdn over 5f out: sn lost pl: t.o fnl 4f* **33/1**

1m 50.91s (-0.09) **Going Correction** -0.05s/f (Stan)
**WFA** 3 from 4yo+ 2lb **12** Ran SP% **129.0**
Speed ratings: **98,97,96,95,94 87,87,83,82,82** —,—CSF £19.83 TOTE £12.10: £2.80, £1.10, £1.80; EX 24.60.There was no bid for the winner.
**Owner** West Indies Capital Company Limited **Bred** Lord Halifax **Trained** Sproxton, Leics

**FOCUS**
Another weak seller run in a time fractionally slower than the first division.

**NOTEBOOK**
**Pup's Pride** appreciated the step up in trip and drop in grade to get back on the scoresheet. He usually wins his share of races on Fibresand over the winter.
**Noul(USA)**, with the blinkers left off this time, had 20lb in hand of the winner on official figures and clearly failed to run to his mark.
**Feast Of Romance**, with the cheekpieces left off and stepping up in trip, ran well enough, but he is not that easy to win with.
**Swynford Welcome** appeared to appreciate the drop in grade and ran well. However, she has never won over a trip this far and seven furlong probably suits better.
**Malmand(USA)** did not run too badly but will need to step up on this to get back to winning ways.

## 6017 LITTLEWOODSCASINO.COM H'CAP 2m 46y(F)
**4:10** (4:10) (E) (0-75,72) 3-Y-O+ **£2,044** (£584; £292) **Stalls** Low

Form RPR
2150 **1** **Snow's Ride**[17] 5855 3-9-5 72 ............................ IMongan 6 88+
(WRMuir) *chsd ldr: led over 6f out: rdn clr over 2f out: eased ins fnl f* **4/1**[2]
0406 **2** *5* **Madhahir (IRE)**[47] 5298 3-8-8 61 ............................ (p) NCallan 3 71
(CADwyer) *a.p: chsd wnr 6f out: rdn 4f out: no imp fnl 2f* **16/1**
0520 **3** *3* **Red Scorpion (USA)**[17] 5855 4-9-11 69 ............................ JFEgan 5 75
(WMBrisbourne) *hld up in rr: hdwy over 3f out: styd on same pce fnl 2f* **9/2**[3]
4061 **4** *3* **Sashay**[58] 5085 5-8-10 61 ............................ StephanieHollinshead(7) 4 64
(RHollinshead) *hld up: hdwy over 4f out: rdn over 3f out: no imp fnl 2f* **9/1**
2002 **5** *3 ½* **Digger (IRE)**[7] 5972 4-9-4 65 ............................ (t) LEnstone(3) 2 64
(MissGayKelleway) *hld up and bhd: hdwy 8f out: rdn 3f out: wknd 2f out* **15/8**[1]
4400 **6** *6* **E Minor (IRE)**[20] 5817 4-9-3 66 ............................ NChalmers(5) 11 57
(TWall) *hld up: hdwy 7f out: rdn and wknd over 4f out* **20/1**
6036 **7** *3* **Melograno (IRE)**[7] 5972 3-7-9 51 oh5 ............................ LisaJones(3) 12 39
(RMBeckett) *hld up in tch: lost pl bnd 7f out: hdwy over 5f out: wknd 4f out* **33/1**
0605 **8** *17* **Lapadar (IRE)**[12] 5927 4-9-0 65 ............................ (p) DFentiman(7) 1 32
(JRWeymes) *set stdy pce: rdn and hdd over 6f out: wknd 5f out* **66/1**
0204 **9** *shd* **Toni Alcala**[54] 5146 4-9-8 66 ............................ JFanning 9 33
(RFFisher) *hld up: hdwy on ins after 6f: wknd over 4f out* **16/1**
0-20 **10** *¾* **Fast Cindy (USA)**[128] 3203 4-9-2 60 ............................ DaneO'Neill 8 26
(JWUnett) *a bhd* **14/1**
2200 **11** *24* **Ulshaw**[94] 4164 6-8-3 54 ............................ PPMathers(7) 10 —
(BJLlewellyn) *prom tl lost pl on outside bnd 7f out: t.o* **12/1**

3m 38.92s (-3.38) **Going Correction** -0.05s/f (Stan)
**WFA** 3 from 4yo+ 9lb **11** Ran SP% **118.3**
Speed ratings: **106,103,102,100,98 95,94,85,85,85 73**CSF £65.09 CT £303.11 TOTE £5.00: £1.80, £5.40, £2.20; EX 180.30 Place 6 £137.67, Place 5 £71.95.
**Owner** The Parkside Partnership **Bred** Biddestone Stud And Partner **Trained** Lambourn, Berks

**FOCUS**
Just an ordinary staying handicap run at a fair enough pace.

**NOTEBOOK**
**Snow's Ride** had never run on this surface, but he confirmed the promise he showed on his only previous starts on an All-Weather surface (Polytrack) and won comfortably. There are more races to be won with him this winter.
**Madhahir(IRE)** confirmed the promise he showed when upped to this trip at Newcastle last time and a minor race may come his way.
**Red Scorpion(USA)**, still a maiden, may just have run a little bit below form on his first attempt on Fibresand.
**Sashay** ran below her best.
**Digger(IRE)** has yet to truly convince that he stays this trip.
T/Jkpt: Not won. T/Plt: £143.20 to a £1 stake. Pool: £46,638.65. 237.70 winning tickets. T/Qpdt: £70.90 to a £1 stake. Pool: £3,451.10. 36.00 winning tickets. KH

# 5984 LINGFIELD (L-H)
### Tuesday, November 18
**OFFICIAL GOING: Standard**

## 6018 BET DIRECT ITV PAGE 367 MAIDEN STKS (DIV I) 6f (P)
**12:20** (12:22) (D) 2-Y-O **£3,080** (£880; £440) **Stalls** Low

Form RPR
05 **1** **Aesculus (USA)**[12] 5930 2-8-9 ............................ WRyan 6 66
(LMCumani) *mde all: rdn out* **13/2**[3]
00 **2** *1 ½* **Muktasb (USA)**[12] 5929 2-9-0 ............................ RHills 7 66
(MPTregoning) *t.k.h: trckd ldrs: rdn to press wnr over 1f out: nt qckn ins fnl f* **4/1**[2]
**3** *nk* **Halabaloo (IRE)** 2-8-9 ............................ JFEgan 2 61
(GWragg) *str: lw: scope: bit bkwd: missed break and hmpd s: hdwy and in tch after 2f: shkn up and wd home turn: r.o wl fnl f: improv* **11/1**
05 **4** *2 ½* **Rockley Bay (IRE)**[12] 5929 2-9-0 ............................ DSweeney 9 58
(PJMakin) *b: b.hind: chsd wnr over 3f: 3rd and one pce whn sltly hmpd by loose horse over 2f out* **8/1**
4000 **5** *3* **Get To The Point**[12] 5931 2-9-0 65 ............................ PaulEddery 8 49
(PWD'Arcy) *s.i.s: gd hdwy 3f out: wknd over 1f out* **3/1**[1]
0 **6** *1 ¼* **Beresford Boy**[21] 5812 2-9-0 ............................ IMongan 10 45
(DKIvory) *b: hdwy over 3f out: wknd over 2f out* **50/1**
0 **7** *5* **Eugenie**[53] 5190 2-8-9 ............................ DaneO'Neill 11 25
(RHannon) *wd: in tch to 1/2-way* **10/1**
50 **U** **Ragged Jack (IRE)**[24] 5757 2-9-0 ............................ SWKelly 5 —
(GABulter) *lw: jinked rt: stmbld and uns rdr leaving stalls* **3/1**[1]

1m 14.54s (1.62) **Going Correction** +0.10s/f (Slow) **8** Ran SP% **113.8**
Speed ratings: **93,91,90,87,83 81,74,**—CSF £32.32 TOTE £10.80: £2.00, £2.60, £2.80; EX 30.20.
**Owner** Lord Hartington **Bred** Lord Hartington **Trained** Newmarket, Suffolk

**FOCUS**
A fair maiden, but run in a time 1.14sec slower than the second division.

**NOTEBOOK**
**Aesculus(USA)**, a half-sister to a ten-furlong seller winner, had shown ability in turf maidens and made all to get off the mark. She should improve further when stepped up in trip.
**Muktasb(USA)**travelled well enough and was possibly distracted by the loose horse, but he had every chance and he looks likely to be better suited by a mile in time.
**Halabaloo(IRE)**looked in need of the run beforehand and, after a low start, was done few favours when Ragged Jack unseated his rider and hampered her. That left her with a lot to do, and it is to her credit that she ran on with such a flourish to finish third. She looks sure to benefit a good deal from this outing and win a race in time.
**Rockley Bay(IRE)**was not helped by being slightly stopped in his run by the loose horse, but he now qualifies for a handicap mark, and it is in that sphere that he should come into his own.
**Get To The Point**, who has a fairly exposed profile, is probably a good guide to the level of the form.

## 6019 BET DIRECT ON CHANNEL 4 PAGE 613 STKS (H'CAP) (DIV I) 7f (P)
**12:50** (12:52) (E ) (0-70,70) 3-Y-O+ **£2,134** (£609; £304) **Stalls** Low

Form RPR
0006 **1** **I Wish**[19] 5837 5-9-3 62 ............................ LPKeniry(3) 10 70
(MMadgwick) *t.k.h: prom: outpcd by runner-up over 2f out: rallied and r.o fnl f: led on line* **12/1**
0641 **2** *shd* **Mr Bountiful (IRE)**[5] 5987 5-9-5 61 6ex ............................ SWKelly 15 69
(MDods) *t.k.h: prom: led 3f out: qcknd 4l ahd 2f out: hrd rdn fnl f: jst ct* **11/2**[3]
6005 **3** *hd* **Hadath (IRE)**[6] 5981 6-9-3 66 ............................ (p) AHindley(7) 11 73
(BGPowell) *b: lw: prom: outpcd by runner-up over 2f out: rallied and r.o fnl f* **14/1**
0260 **4** *nk* **Inistrahull Island (IRE)**[5] 5987 3-8-13 56 ............................ JFanning 9 62
(MHTompkins) *lw: in tch: rdn to chse ldrs over 1f out: styd on wl fnl f* **5/1**[2]
4566 **5** *½* **Icecap**[47] 5326 3-8-12 55 ............................ ADaly 2 60
(PButler) *hld up towards rr: rdn and hdwy over 1f out: nrst fin* **20/1**
2305 **6** *nk* **George Stubbs (USA)**[5] 5987 5-9-11 70 ............................ (b) J-PGuillambert(3) 5 74
(NPLittmoden) *in tch: rdn to chse ldrs over 1f out: kpt on fnl f* **9/2**[1]
-505 **6** *dht* **Taiyo**[63] 4971 3-8-12 55 ............................ IMongan 4 59
(JWPayne) *sn in mid-div: rdn 3f out: styd on wl fnl f* **25/1**
1305 **8** *hd* **Temper Tantrum**[16] 5892 5-9-6 62 ............................ (p) SCarson 7 66
(AndrewReid) *b: b.hind: mid-div: rdn to chse ldrs over 1f out: kpt on fnl f* **7/1**
5550 **9** *½* **Kinsman (IRE)**[159] 2294 6-8-12 54 ............................ (p) PDoe 1 56
(TDMccarthy) *towards rr on rail: rdn and sme hdwy over 1f out: nvr nrr* **16/1**
0040 **10** *hd* **Oases**[6] 5981 4-9-3 59 ............................ SWhitworth 14 61
(DShaw) *s.s: hld up and bhd: rdn and styd on wl fnl 2f: nvr nrr* **15/2**
2240 **11** *1* **Byo (IRE)**[26] 5718 5-9-9 68 ............................ SHitchcott(3) 3 67
(MQuinn) *prom: rdn over 2f out: sn outpcd* **16/1**
0000 **12** *5* **Coppington Flyer (IRE)**[6] 5981 3-8-12 58 ............................ LisaJones(3) 12 44
(BWDuke) *nvr nr to chal* **14/1**
40-0 **13** *3* **Bedazzled**[54] 5178 3-8-13 56 ............................ GCarter 16 33
(JAGlover) *uns rdr bef s: s.i.s: a bhd* **50/1**
-400 **14** *7* **Sharpinch**[16] 5888 5-10-0 70 ............................ DaneO'Neill 6 29
(PRChamings) *led 4f: wknd wl over 1f out* **66/1**
0600 **15** *15* **Brilliant Waters**[50] 5280 3-8-12 55 ............................ SDrowne 8 —
(DWPArbuthnot) *rdn 1/2-way: a towards rr: b.b.v* **50/1**

1m 25.86s (-0.14) **Going Correction** +0.10s/f (Slow)
**WFA** 3 from 4yo+ 1lb **15** Ran SP% **121.3**
Speed ratings: **104,103,103,103,102 102,102,102,101,101 100,94,91,83,65**CSF £73.55 CT £957.09 TOTE £13.60: £4.90, £2.50, £5.60; EX 124.00.
**Owner** Mrs Gail Gaisford **Bred** J M T Gaisford **Trained** Denmead, Hants

**FOCUS**
A tight finish, with the first ten home covered by a length and a half.

**NOTEBOOK**
**I Wish~~~**looked fairly handicapped beforehand and, with the benefit of her recent outing after a two-month break under her belt, found just enough to get the best of a tight finish.
**Mr Bountiful(IRE)**looked to have a nicked it turning into the straight but he hit the wall inside the last and the line came just too late.
**Hadath(IRE)**appreciated the drop back to his best distance and looks on a winning mark.
**Inistrahull Island(IRE)**, who never got into a challenging position on his last outing here, was far more popular in the market on this occasion and was one of those staying on best of all at the finish.
**Icecap**, who is still a maiden, was another staying on well at the finish.
**George Stubbs(USA)**continues to run well but the Handicapper may just have him for the time being.
**Brilliant Waters** *Official explanation: trainer said gelding had bled from the nose*

## 6020 BET DIRECT ITV PAGE 367 MAIDEN STKS (DIV II) 6f (P)
**1:20** (1:20) (D ) 2-Y-O **£3,066** (£876; £438) **Stalls** Low

Form — RPR
553 **1** **Kabreet**[10] [5947] 2-9-0 77 ........ SDrowne 4 — 65
(EALDunlop) *lw: trckd ldrs: led jst ins fnl f: pushed out: readily* **5/4**[1]
040 **2** ½ **Burlington Place**[5] [5984] 2-9-0 ........ JFEgan 11 — 64
(SKirk) *led: hrd rdn 2f out: hdd jst ins fnl f: kpt on: nt pce of wnr* **10/1**
0 **3** ½ **Comeraincomeshine (IRE)**[57] [5119] 2-8-4 ........ RMiles(5) 5 — 57
(TGMills) *chsd ldrs: rdn over 2f out: styd on fnl f* **8/1**
00 **4** 1 **Foot Fault (IRE)**[99] [4040] 2-8-9 ........ WRyan 8 — 54
(NACallaghan) *prom: jnd ldr 1/2-way: one pce appr fnl f* **25/1**
**5** 1¼ **Locator (IRE)** 2-9-0 ........ JTate 1 — 55
(JMPEustace) *leggy: scope: bit bkwd: hld up in tch: outpcd over 2f out: kpt on fnl f* **12/1**
00 **6** ½ **Emilys Dawn**[22] [5798] 2-8-9 ........ ANicholls 3 — 49
(DKIvory) *b: towards rr: rdn over 2f out: styd on fnl f* **33/1**
0 **7** ¾ **Sabrina Brown**[12] [5930] 2-8-9 ........ SCarson 7 — 47
(GBBalding) *bit bkwd: in tch: outpcd over 2f out: no imp* **14/1**
4 **8** 2 **Charlieismydarling**[28] [5686] 2-9-0 ........ JFanning 9 — 46
(JAOsborne) *lw: dwlt: sn chsng ldrs: rdn and btn 2f out* **6/1**[3]
50 **9** shd **Science Academy (USA)**[41] [5449] 2-8-9 ........ DaneO'Neill 6 — 40
(PFICole) *stdd in rr s: brief effrt 1/2-way: wknd over 2f out* **9/2**[2]
0 **10** 14 **Miss Millietant**[18] [5850] 2-8-9 ........ CCogan 10 — —
(LMontagueHall) *outpcd in rr: no ch fr 1/2-way* **50/1**
**11** 2 **Evening Fragrance** 2-9-0 ........ MFenton 2 — —
(GCHChung) *leggy: unf: bit bkwd: dwlt: a bhd: no ch whn carried hd awkwardly over 2f out* **16/1**

1m 13.4s (0.48) **Going Correction** +0.10s/f (Slow) **11 Ran SP% 126.1**
Speed ratings: **100,99,98,97,95 95,94,91,91,72 69**CSF £16.73 TOTE £2.10: £1.10, £2.40, £2.70; EX 18.90.
**Owner** Jumeirah Racing **Bred** Stowell Hill Ltd And S P Tindall **Trained** Newmarket, Suffolk

**FOCUS**
The race was run in a time 1.14sec faster than the first division.

**NOTEBOOK**
**Kabreet**set a decent standard and in the end won with a bit in hand. He should pay his way in handicap company.
**Burlington Place**, who did not get home over a mile last time, appreciated the return to sprinting. He too may now take the handicap route.
**Comeraincomeshine(IRE)**, a half-sister to top-class miler Where Or When and several smart staying types, reportedly pulled a muscle first time out. She was staying on well at the finish and will do better over farther.
**Foot Fault(IRE)**, returning from a three-month absence, ran well and is now eligible for handicaps.
**Locator(IRE)**, a half-brother to a couple of older winners in France, ran a respectable race on his debut and should do better when stepped up in trip.
**Evening Fragrance**lost a shoe and hung left throughout according to his rider. *Official explanation: jockey said gelding had lost a shoe and hung left throughout*

## 6021 BETDIRECT.CO.UK CLAIMING STKS 7f (P)
**1:50** (1:54) (F ) 2-Y-O **£2,243** (£641; £320) **Stalls** Low

Form — RPR
062 **1** **Star Of Light**[19] [5836] 2-9-2 73 ........ PaulEddery 2 — 73
(BJMeehan) *dwlt: sn in tch: effrt 2f out: drvn to ld ins fnl f* **3/1**[1]
0 **2** ¾ **Stonor Lady (USA)**[25] [5735] 2-7-12 ........ DKinsella 1 — 53
(BJMeehan) *lw: w ldrs: led after 1f tl 2f out: lft in ld over 1f out: hdd ins fnl f: kpt on* **20/1**
2200 **3** nk **Mustang Ali (IRE)**[26] [5721] 2-8-9 65 ........ JFEgan 4 — 63
(SKirk) *mid-div: sn outpcd: hdwy over 1f out: nrst fin* **5/1**[3]
0343 **4** 1½ **Ever Cheerful**[28] [5686] 2-8-4 67 ........ LTreadwell(7) 10 — 62
(WGMTurner) *lw: w ldrs: led 2f out: hung rt and hdd over 1f out: one pce* **7/1**
6005 **5** 2½ **Blofeld**[42] [5440] 2-8-3 55 ........ FNorton 11 — 47
(WJarvis) *t.k.h: prom: no ex over 1f out* **25/1**
1410 **6** 1¾ **Knight Onthe Tiles (IRE)**[6] [5979] 2-8-9 77 ........(b) DFentiman(7) 13 — 56
(JRBest) *lw: wd: hdwy 3f out: one pce fnl 2f* **4/1**[2]
0 **7** 1 **Introduction**[5] [5990] 2-8-0 ........ LisaJones(3) 8 — 41
(WJMusson) *outpcd and bhd: styd on fnl 2f* **50/1**
000 **8** nk **Czars Princess (IRE)**[96] [4123] 2-8-6 60 ........ IMongan 12 — 43
(GLMoore) *b: b.hind: in tch: effrt 3f out: outpcd fnl 2f* **8/1**
00 **9** ½ **Sonne De Loup**[8] [5968] 2-7-9 ow2 ........ JFMcDonald(5) 3 — 36
(MrsStefLiddiard) *prom over 2f: sn outpcd and dropped to rr: gng on wl at fin* **100/1**
006 **10** 1¼ **Jaolins**[5] [5990] 2-8-0 ow2 ........ ANicholls 15 — 32
(RHannon) *wd: hdwy 3f out: wknd 2f out* **12/1**
000 **11** 3½ **Nordic Dancer (IRE)**[14] [5913] 2-8-0 60 ........ MHenry 5 — 24
(RMHCowell) *s.i.s: rdn 3f out: nvr nr to chal* **20/1**
0 **12** ½ **Skelthwaite**[5] [5984] 2-8-8 ........ JFanning 6 — 30
(MHTompkins) *rdn 3f out: a towards rr* **66/1**
0020 **13** 1 **Jomus**[66] [4882] 2-8-11 65 ........ CCogan 14 — 31
(LMontagueHall) *bolted to s: chsd ldrs 4f* **20/1**
**14** ½ **Cicatrice** 2-8-7 ........ PGallagher(7) 9 — 33
(ACharlton) *w'like: bit bkwd: s.s: a bhd* **40/1**
0001 **15** 6 **Dee Dee Girl (IRE)**[32] [5621] 2-8-1 58 ........ ADaly 7 — 5
(RHannon) *lw: led 1f: wknd 3f out* **12/1**

1m 27.76s (1.76) **Going Correction** +0.10s/f (Slow) **15 Ran SP% 125.7**
Speed ratings: **93,92,91,90,87 85,84,83,83,81 77,77,76,75,68**CSF £72.48 TOTE £3.90: £1.70, £11.80, £2.30; EX 125.20.Stonor Lady was claimed by Paul Darcy for £7,000
**Owner** J H Widdows **Bred** J H Widdows **Trained** Upper Lambourn, Berks
■ Stewards Enquiry : J F McDonald one-day ban: used whip when out of contention (Nov 28)

**NOTEBOOK**
**Star Of Light**had shown fair form in maiden company and got a good run through on the inside rounding the turn into the straight. He took plenty of driving, though, and not for the first time suggested that farther is going to suit.
**Stonor Lady(USA)**, bred for the dirt, ran much better than she had on her debut in a Newbury maiden, but of course she was taking on much lesser opposition on this occasion.
**Mustang Ali(IRE)**is a half-brother to a stayer in Blue Hawk and the way he was staying on at the end of this contest suggests he might be suited by a step back up to a mile - he had an excuse on the last occasion he tried the distance.
**Ever Cheerful**threw away his chance by hanging badly to his right in the straight. *Official explanation: jockey said gelding hung right in the straight*
**Blofeld**did not get home over this longer trip.
**Knight Onthe Tiles(IRE)**, best in at the weights, lost ground by travelling wide for much of the way.

## 6022 BET DIRECT FREEPHONE 0800 32 93 93 MAIDEN STKS 1m 2f (P)
**2:20** (2:22) (D ) 3-Y-0+ **£2,331** (£666; £333) **Stalls** Low

Form — RPR
30 **1** **Tetou (IRE)**[27] [5711] 3-8-9 ........ SWKelly 8 — 69
(BJMeehan) *prom: hmpd on rail 3f out: eased outside: rallied and r.o wl fnl f: led on line* **6/1**
**2** hd **Seven Year Itch (IRE)** 3-9-0 ........ ADaly 4 — 73
(MPTregoning) *t.k.h: prom: chsd ldr 2f out: drvn to ld ins fnl f: swished tail: jst ct* **6/4**[1]
33 **3** 3½ **Rozanee**[37] [5513] 3-8-9 ........ IMongan 6 — 62
(JWPayne) *prom: led 3f out: qcknd 3l ahd: hrd rdn and hdd ins fnl f: no ex* **5/1**[3]
43 **4** 5 **Saada One (IRE)**[21] [5815] 3-8-9 ........ DaneO'Neill 11 — 53
(LMCumani) *chsd ldrs: outpcd 3f out: sn btn* **11/4**[2]
06 **5** ¾ **Tata Naka**[27] [5711] 3-8-4 ........ NChalmers(5) 12 — 52
(MrsCADunnett) *in tch: hrd rdn 3f out: sn btn* **50/1**
0 **6** nk **Shaamit's All Over**[286] [471] 4-8-8 ........ BReilly(5) 2 — 51
(BAPearce) *mid-div: effrt over 3f out: sn outpcd* **100/1**
**7** 1¼ **Elegant Gracie (IRE)** 3-8-9 ........ SDrowne 5 — 49
(RGuest) *w'like: s.s: hld up in rr: pushed along 6f out: sme hdwy 3f out: n.d* **20/1**
0-6 **8** 1¼ **Wavet**[198] [1374] 3-8-9 ........ RPrice 1 — 47
(MrsLydiaPearce) *led tl 3f out: wknd 2f out* **14/1**
60 **9** nk **Seejay**[6] [5978] 3-8-9 ........ SCarson 14 — 46
(MAAllen) *b: b.hind: prom: led briefly over 3f out: wknd over 2f out* **100/1**
0 **10** 11 **Osorno**[22] [5793] 3-9-0 ........ AClark 13 — 31
(CFWall) *b: b.hind: s.s: wd most of way: plld hrd in rr: no ch fnl 3f* **33/1**
0-0 **11** nk **Maximinus**[43] [5426] 3-8-11 ........ LPKeniry(3) 7 — 31
(MMadgwick) *plld hrd: chsd ldrs 3f: n.d fr 1/2-way* **66/1**
06 **12** 11 **Mrs Boz**[47] [5327] 3-8-9 ........ SWhitworth 9 — 6
(AWCarroll) *dwlt: sn in mid-div: wd 4f out: sn wknd* **50/1**
0 **13** 7 **Harry Tu**[8] [5969] 3-8-7 ........ BFayosMartin(7) 10 — —
(MissGayKelleway) *a bhd* **33/1**
**14** 3½ **Sawah**[6] 3-8-11 ........ LisaJones(3) 3 — —
(DShaw) *b: w'like: s.s: lost 10l: a bhd* **100/1**

2m 8.58s (1.19) **Going Correction** +0.10s/f (Slow)
**WFA** 3 from 4yo 4lb **14 Ran SP% 123.3**
Speed ratings: **99,98,96,92,91 91,90,89,88,80 79,71,65,62**CSF £15.08 TOTE £5.90: £1.70, £1.60, £2.20; EX 32.20.
**Owner** Mrs Susan Roy **Bred** Corbally Stud **Trained** Upper Lambourn, Berks

**FOCUS**
A modest maiden.

**NOTEBOOK**
**Tetou(IRE)**did well to win as she was stopped in her run turning out of the back straight but stayed on strongly down the outside in the straight. She would have been an unlucky loser had she not got up.
**Seven Year Itch(IRE)**, coltish in the preliminaries, is a full-brother to the smart performer Great Dane. Strong in the market for this modest heat, he flashed his tail under pressure and may not be one to trust implicitly.
**Rozanee**tried to steal the race heading towards the final turn but hit the wall approaching the final furlong.
**Saada One(IRE)**did not find the step up in trip bringing about any dramatic approvement.
**Tata Naka**, who has shown only moderate form to date, now qualifies for a mark.

## 6023 LITTLEWOODS BET DIRECT NURSERY STKS (H'CAP) 1m (P)
**2:50** (2:53) (D ) (0-85,78) 2-Y-O **£3,206** (£916; £458) **Stalls** High

Form — RPR
0041 **1** **Freak Occurence (IRE)**[15] [5906] 2-9-6 77 ........(v1) SDrowne 10 — 83
(MissECLavelle) *lw: chsd ldr: rdn over 3f out: styd on to ld wl ins fnl f* **5/2**[1]
0614 **2** 1½ **Chubbes**[10] [5950] 2-9-3 74 ........(v) JFanning 6 — 77
(MCPipe) *led and set gd pce: pushed along 3f out: hdd and one pce ins fnl f* **4/1**[3]
065 **3** 3 **Keep On Movin' (IRE)**[22] [5792] 2-8-13 75 ........ RMiles(5) 9 — 71
(TGMills) *sn bhd: rdn and hdwy over 1f out: nrst fin* **12/1**
5003 **4** nk **Amwell Brave**[20] [5830] 2-9-0 71 ........ MFenton 11 — 66
(JRJenkins) *sn bhd: rdn and hdwy over 1f out: nvr nrr* **33/1**
0002 **5** 1¾ **Bold Joe (IRE)**[18] [5847] 2-9-1 72 ........ GGibbons 1 — 63
(PMitchell) *lw: sn prom in chsng gp: no imp on ldng pair fnl 3f* **25/1**
6052 **6** hd **Wizard Looking**[29] [5677] 2-9-2 73 ........(t) DaneO'Neill 12 — 64
(RHannon) *towards rr: hdwy on outside 3f out: hung lft over 1f out: no ex* **16/1**
3266 **7** nk **Abington Angel**[34] [5571] 2-9-4 78 ........(t) LPKeniry(3) 8 — 68
(BJMeehan) *lw: mid-div: effrt 3f out: nt pce to chal* **20/1**
0261 **8** shd **St Savarin (FR)**[14] [5913] 2-9-3 74 ........(e1) NPollard 4 — 64
(JRBest) *chsd ldrs: rdn and btn 3f out* **7/2**[2]
3645 **9** ½ **Darn Good**[36] [5551] 2-8-8 72 ........ PGallagher(7) 5 — 61
(RHannon) *hld up in rr: hmpd on rail over 2f out and wl over 1f out: styd on fnl f* **20/1**
0434 **10** 2½ **Sachin**[14] [5913] 2-9-1 72 ........(b1) SWKelly 2 — 55
(GAButler) *chsd ldrs: drvn along 3f out: wknd over 1f out* **8/1**
001 **11** 7 **Uncle John**[17] [5877] 2-8-12 69 ........ JFEgan 3 — 36
(SKirk) *mid-div: drvn along over 4f out: n.d fnl 3f: wl btn whn bmpd and eased wl over 1f out* **7/1**

1m 40.48s (0.97) **Going Correction** +0.10s/f (Slow) **11 Ran SP% 124.3**
Speed ratings: **99,97,94,94,92 92,91,91,91,88 81**CSF £12.58 CT £106.70 TOTE £3.80: £1.60, £1.70, £3.10; EX 21.10.
**Owner** Lots Of Luck Gentlemen Syndicate **Bred** St Simon Foundation **Trained** Hatherden, Hants

**NOTEBOOK**
**Freak Occurence(IRE)**, visored for the first time, caught the tiring leader late. He confirmed that he is in fine form and, although happier on easier ground on turf, he handled this surface well.
**Chubbes**, stepping back up to the distance over which he won a Windsor seller last month, made it a real test and had all but the winner in trouble turning in. He did just too much as it happens but should gain compensation in the coming weeks.
**Keep On Movin'(IRE)**stayed on from off the pace and ran well enough given that the track was favouring pace horses.

**Amwell Brave**was another to make good late progress and the step up to a mile certainly seems to have brought about great improvement in his form.
**Bold Joe(IRE)**does not look particularly well handicapped at present.
**St Savarin(FR)**was beaten before stamina became an issue.

## 6024 BET DIRECT ON CHANNEL 4 PAGE 613 STKS (H'CAP) (DIV II) 7f (P)
3:20 (3:23) (E ) (0-70,70) 3-Y-0+ £2,125 (£607; £303) Stalls Low

Form RPR
0000 1 **Chateau Nicol**[6] 5976 4-9-2 58....(v) JFanning 1 71
(BGPowell) *hld up on rail in midfield: hdwy 2f out: drvn to ld nr fin* **40/1**
0411 2 *nk* **Gallery Breeze**[16] 5892 4-9-5 61.... ADaly 7 73
(JLSpearing) *led tl over 3f out: led over 2f out: qcknd 3l ahd: hung rt over 1f out: hdd nr fin* **7/1**
0052 3 *3/4* **Smith N Allan Oils**[22] 5787 4-8-13 55....(p) JFEgan 10 65
(MDods) *lw: bhd: rdn and hdwy over 1f out: fin wl* **12/1**
0000 4 *3/4* **Peyto Princess**[5] 5985 5-9-5 61.... SWKelly 3 69
(MABuckley) *b. nr hind: t.k.h: chsd ldrs: rdn 2f out: kpt on fnl f* **16/1**
0405 5 *1 1/4* **Acorazado (IRE)**[81] 4558 4-8-11 53.... GCarter 9 58
(GLMoore) *mid-div: rdn and hdwy over 2f out: styd on fnl f* **5/1**[2]
5425 6 *nk* **A Woman In Love**[22] 5794 4-9-0 56.... SDrowne 5 60
(MissBSanders) *s.s: plld hrd towards rr: rdn and hdwy over 1f out: kpt on* **13/2**
5032 7 *shd* **Looking For Love (IRE)**[20] 5832 5-9-6 62....(p) RFfrench 6 66
(JGPortman) *a.p: no ex appr fnl f* **13/2**
0240 8 *1/2* **Castaigne (FR)**[33] 5596 4-8-12 54....(t) SCarson 12 56
(BWDuke) *s.i.s: hld up in rr: nt clr run wl over 1f out: nrst fin* **25/1**
4600 9 *1 3/4* **Calusa Lady (IRE)**[5] 5988 3-9-2 59....(v) AClark 2 57
(GBBalding) *prom: rdn over 3f out: wknd over 1f out* **20/1**
4400 10 *shd* **Fearby Cross (IRE)**[5] 5987 7-9-8 67.... LisaJones(3) 15 64
(WJMusson) *wd: bhd tl rdn and styd on fnl 2f* **6/1**[3]
4110 11 *nk* **Mistral Sky**[5] 5985 4-10-0 70....(v) MFenton 8 67
(MrsStefLiddiard) *t.k.h: in tch: outpcd 1/2-way: n.d after* **9/2**[1]
0056 12 *1/2* **Adantino**[22] 5794 4-8-12 54.... MHenry 4 49
(BRMillman) *bhd: hrd rdn and hdwy over 1f out: n.d* **20/1**
5000 13 *1 1/4* **Contrary Mary**[10] 5946 8-9-8 64.... RPrice 13 56
(JAkehurst) *towards rr: sme hdwy 3f out: hrd rdn and no ex fnl 2f* **20/1**
0000 14 *1 3/4* **Laggan Minstrel (IRE)**[4] 5996 5-8-12 54....(t) FNorton 16 41
(PWD'Arcy) *in tch over 4f* **25/1**
0024 15 *3/4* **Badou**[32] 5611 3-8-12 55....(v) CCogan 11 40
(LMontagueHall) *chsd ldrs 5f* **25/1**
0000 16 *3* **Warden Warren**[10] 5946 5-10-0 70....(b) DaneO'Neill 14 47
(MrsCADunnett) *pressed ldr: led over 3f out tl over 2f out: sn wknd* **40/1**

1m 25.9s (-0.10) **Going Correction** +0.10s/f (Slow)
**WFA** 3 from 4yo+ 1lb **16 Ran SP% 132.6**
Speed ratings: **104,103,102,101,100 100,100,99,97,97 97,96,95,93,92 88**CSF £299.93 CT £3785.78 TOTE £54.50: £8.40, £2.30, £3.30, £5.90; EX 1422.70.
**Owner** Basingstoke Commercials **Bred** Aston House Stud **Trained** Morestead, Hants

**NOTEBOOK**
**Chateau Nicol**was undoubtedly well handicapped on his best form, but it needed a leap of faith to believe he could win this following his recent dismal efforts. He travelled well and got a dream run through on the inside, though, and appeared to win on merit.
**Gallery Breeze**is progressing well and looked likely to score the hat-trick when kicking clear into the straight. However, she hung off a straight line in the closing stages and that cost her in the end.
**Smith N Allan Oils**is another who is well handicapped at present, but he is a difficult horse to win with and was only running on when it was all over on this occasion.
**Peyto Princess**is another who is not known for having a winning habit.
**Acorazado(IRE)**is worth keeping in mind for a similar event as he is a well-handicapped animal in the care of a trainer who knows his onions.
**Mistral Sky**has failed to translate the form of his classified stakes win back in handicap company.

## 6025 BET DIRECT IN RUNNING SKY TEXT 372 AMATEUR RIDERS' H'CAP 1m 4f (P)
3:50 (3:50) (F ) (0-80,83) 3-Y-0+ £3,234 (£924; £462) Stalls Low

Form RPR
0111 1 **Cold Turkey**[6] 5982 3-10-4 67.... MrEDehdashti(5) 15 82+
(GLMoore) *s.s: hdwy to ld over 3f out: rdn out* **6/5**[1]
1111 2 *1 1/2* **Mission To Mars**[16] 5890 4-11-4 70.... MrSWalker 7 82
(PRHedger) *b: dwlt: hld up in mid-div: hdwy 4f out: chsd wnr 2f out: no imp fnl f* **3/1**[2]
0345 3 *1 1/2* **Reminiscent (IRE)**[46] 5344 4-10-11 63....(v) MsCWilliams 16 73
(RFJohnsonHoughton) *dwlt: sn in mid-div: hdwy over 3f out: sn outpcd: styd on wl fnl f* **20/1**
0160 4 *1/2* **King Revo (IRE)**[40] 5463 3-11-2 79.... MrBHaslam(5) 1 88
(PCHaslam) *dwlt: jnd ldr after 2f tl over 3f out: no ex over 1f out* **8/1**[3]
0035 5 *3* **Most-Saucy**[5] 5991 7-10-13 72.... GBartley(7) 13 76
(IAWood) *towards rr: hdwy 3f out: one pce fnl 2f* **12/1**
0600 6 *1 1/4* **Gingko**[19] 5839 6-10-6 65.... MrJKing(7) 2 67
(PRWebber) *slt ld tl over 3f out: wknd over 1f out* **12/1**
-563 7 *hd* **Mandoob**[19] 5839 6-10-5 64.... MissFGuillambert(7) 6 66
(BRJohnson) *mid-div: rdn and no imp fnl 3f* **14/1**
0430 8 *1/2* **Silver Prophet (IRE)**[68] 4848 4-11-3 69.... MrsSBosley 3 70
(MRBosley) *chsd ldrs: outpcd over 3f out: sn btn* **25/1**
5200 9 *5* **Starry Mary**[52] 5220 5-9-10 51.... MrsSMoore(3) 14 44
(ELJames) *lw: wd: bhd: pushed along 3f out: nvr trbld ldrs* **25/1**
3035 10 *8* **Chevronne**[22] 5795 3-10-12 70.... MrLJefford 8 50
(LGCottrell) *chsd ldrs to 1/2-way: drvn along and bhd fnl 4f* **12/1**
2400 11 *5* **Paso Doble**[118] 3504 5-10-6 65.... MrJMillman(7) 10 37
(BRMillman) *prom to 1/2-way* **33/1**
4006 12 *15* **Peppershot**[96] 4133 3-9-9 60.... MrJPemberton(7) 12 8
(GPEnright) *s.s: sn chsng ldrs: wknd over 4f out* **66/1**

2m 34.64s (0.66) **Going Correction** +0.10s/f (Slow)
**WFA** 3 from 4yo+ 6lb **12 Ran SP% 128.2**
Speed ratings: **101,100,99,98,96 95,95,95,92,86 83,73**CSF £4.73 CT £53.72 TOTE £2.10: £1.10, £1.70, £6.40; EX 6.40 Place 6 £69.80, Place 5 £18.06.
**Owner** A Grinter **Bred** Worksop Manor Stud **Trained** Woodingdean, E Sussex

**NOTEBOOK**
**Cold Turkey**was able to run off a mark 1lb lower than for his last win and took advantage in a race which lacked strength in depth. He will find things much more difficult once reassessed.
**Mission To Mars**, chasing a five-timer, ran into an equally progressive type for once and just came up short. He still looks capable of winning off this higher mark.
**Reminiscent(IRE)**, who stays farther than this, was doing his best work at the finish.
**King Revo(IRE)**enjoyed a good pitch throughout and ran a solid race against a couple of progressive types.
**Most-Saucy**came with a promising run approaching the turn in but her effort flattened out in the straight.
**Gingko**has shown his best All-Weather form on the Southwell Fibresand.
T/Plt: £83.50 to a £1 stake. Pool: £33,827.45. 295.70 winning tickets. T/Qpdt: £6.50 to a £1 stake. Pool: £2,943.10. 330.70 winning tickets. LM

# 5685 SOUTHWELL (L-H)
## Wednesday, November 19

**OFFICIAL GOING: Standard**
Wind: slt across Weather: overcast

## 6026 PRESS RED TO BET DIRECT H'CAP (DIV I) 1m (F)
12:00 (12:01) (F ) (0-65,65) 3-Y-0+ £2,128 (£608; £304) Stalls Low

Form RPR
0000 1 **Barzak (IRE)**[11] 5946 3-9-12 65....(t) ACulhane 8 74
(SRBowring) *a.p: led over 2f out: rdn out* **16/1**
2154 2 *1* **Second Of May**[20] 5837 3-9-9 62.... FNorton 12 69
(PRChamings) *hld up: hdwy over 2f out: rdn over 1f out: r.o* **5/1**[1]
4000 3 *nk* **Maggie's Pet**[29] 5688 6-8-9 46....(t) SWhitworth 11 52
(KBell) *bhd: hdwy over 2f out: styd on* **25/1**
0650 4 *1 1/4* **Shifty**[33] 5622 4-9-3 54....(b) ANicholls 14 58
(DNicholls) *hld up: hdwy u.p over 1f out: nt rch ldrs* **8/1**
5000 5 *3 1/2* **Rosti**[170] 2045 3-8-4 50.... RoryMoore(7) 1 47
(PCHaslam) *sn led: hdd over 2f out: rdn and wknd ins fnl f* **12/1**
4003 6 *3/4* **Lord Of Methley**[33] 5622 4-8-13 50....(v) VHalliday 6 45
(RMWhitaker) *chsd ldrs: rdn over 2f out: wknd fnl f* **12/1**
0021 7 *hd* **Dangerous Beans**[19] 5848 3-9-1 54.... ADaly 4 49
(SKirk) *sn outpcd: styd on appr fnl f: nt trble ldrs* **6/1**[2]
00 8 *3* **Banutan (IRE)**[25] 5749 3-9-11 64.... DarrenWilliams 3 53
(KRBurke) *hld up in tch: rdn over 2f out: wknd over 1f out* **20/1**
0-00 9 *5* **Spy Gun (USA)**[156] 2436 3-9-2 60.... NChalmers(5) 5 39
(TWall) *prom: rdn over 3f out: wknd over 1f out* **25/1**
6000 10 *2* **Dubai Dreams**[13] 5933 3-8-11 57....(v) PMakin(7) 7 32
(MJPolglase) *chsd ldrs over 5f* **7/1**
0202 11 *3/4* **Titian Lass**[28] 5712 4-8-11 48....(b) DaneO'Neill 10 22
(CEBrittain) *sn outpcd* **13/2**[3]
6000 12 *3* **Lucayan Monarch**[18] 5878 5-9-7 65.... DerekNolan(7) 9 33
(PABlockley) *s.s: hdwy 1/2-way: wknd over 1f out* **20/1**
0005 13 *1 1/4* **Wilderbrook Lahri**[28] 5704 4-8-8 45....(b) RFfrench 2 10
(BSmart) *dwlt: outpcd* **12/1**
0620 14 *6* **The Loose Screw (IRE)**[38] 5516 5-8-11 48.... NPollard 15 1
(GMMoore) *s.i.s: sn chsng ldrs: wknd 3f out* **16/1**

1m 43.77s (-0.83) **Going Correction** 0.0s/f (Stan)
**WFA** 3 from 4yo+ 2lb **14 Ran SP% 120.0**
Speed ratings: **104,103,102,101,97 97,97,94,89,87 86,83,82,76**CSF £88.87 CT £2010.40 TOTE £14.90: £5.80, £1.90, £8.20; EX 111.50.
**Owner** Clark Industrial Services Partnership **Bred** Clarks Industrial Services Partnership **Trained** Edwinstowe, Notts

**FOCUS**
Just a moderate race run in an almost identical time to the second division.

**NOTEBOOK**
**Barzak(IRE)**, having only his second start on this surface, finally returned to the sort of form that saw him make a winning debut. He is on a nice mark and could well add to this. *Official explanation: trainer said, regarding the improved form shown, colt benefited from today's stronger handling*
**Second Of May**, making her debut on this surface, ran her race and can have no real excuses.
**Maggie's Pet** ran one of her better races in the first-time tongue tie and may get a little further.
**Shifty**, with the blinkers on for his Fibresand debut, ran respectably, but will need to step up on this to pick up a similar contest.
**Rosti** showed plenty of pace and seven furlongs may suit better.
**Dangerous Beans** has yet to prove fully effective on Fibresand.

## 6027 ALLWEATHER-RACING.COM (S) STKS (DIV I) 7f (F)
12:30 (12:30) (G ) 3-Y-0+ £2,128 (£608; £304) Stalls Low

Form RPR
3020 1 **Hurricane Coast**[12] 5945 4-9-5 55.... GParkin 5 54
(PABlockley) *trckd ldrs: smooth hdwy 2f out: rdn to ld and hung rt ins last: styd on* **12/1**
4640 2 *1 1/4* **Jonny Ebeneezer**[6] 5987 4-9-5 70....(p) MFenton 8 51
(RMHCowell) *led: rdn: n.m.r and hdd wl over 1f out: drvn ins last: kpt on* **10/11**[1]
-306 3 *shd* **Levantine (IRE)**[69] 4835 6-9-5 41....(p) SWhitworth 9 51
(AGNewcombe) *cl up: rdn to ld and edgd lft wl over 1f out: drvn and hdd ins last: hmpd and lost 2nd nr line* **16/1**
0060 4 *2 1/2* **Proud Victor (IRE)**[19] 5856 3-9-4 45....(v) DarrenWilliams 1 44
(DShaw) *chsd ldrs: rdn over 2f out: kpt on u.p ins last* **40/1**
5010 5 *nk* **Speedfit Free (IRE)**[36] 5561 6-9-11 58....(b) NCallan 16 50
(ISemple) *in tch: hdwy to chse ldrs 2f out: sn rdn and kpt on ins last* **8/1**[2]
0000 6 *1 1/2* **Heathyardsblessing (IRE)**[28] 5706 6-9-5 50.... DeanMcKeown 10 40
(RHollinshead) *towards rr: hdwy over 2f out: rdn and styd on ins last: nrst fin* **40/1**
0004 7 *1/2* **Swynford Welcome**[2] 6016 7-9-1 40.... DNolan(5) 11 40
(IAWood) *midfield: rdn along 1/2-way: styd on fnl 2f: nrst fin* **9/1**[3]
0000 8 *1 3/4* **Thaayer**[142] 2863 8-9-5 40.... GGibbons 3 34
(IAWood) *in tch: hdwy on inner over 2f out: rdn and wknd over 1f out* **25/1**
0605 9 *shd* **Turku**[71] 4806 5-9-2 53....(v) LisaJones(3) 15 34
(DShaw) *in tch on outer: rdn along 3f out: sn no imp* **10/1**
0000 10 *nk* **A One (IRE)**[111] 3712 4-9-5 45.... DSweeney 7 33
(BPalling) *chsd ldrs: rdn 3f out: sn wknd* **20/1**
0600 11 *5* **Eager Angel (IRE)**[137] 2992 5-9-0 37.... IMongan 4 16
(RFMarvin) *s.i.s: a rr* **50/1**
5060 12 *3 1/2* **Zoeanna (IRE)**[7] 5982 3-8-13 50.... ACulhane 14 7
(RGuest) *hmpd s: a rr* **20/1**
0600 13 *1 1/4* **Blue Circle**[30] 5678 3-9-4 34....(b) TWilliams 2 9
(MMullineaux) *prom: rdn along 3f out: wknd 2f out* **66/1**
1500 14 *1 3/4* **Kumakawa**[260] 672 5-9-5 42....(b) SCarson 6 5
(EAWheeler) *bhd fr 1/2-way* **20/1**
0000 15 *nk* **Better Pal**[126] 3300 4-9-2 54.... DCorby(3) 13 4
(PRWood) *a rr* **33/1**


The Form Book, Raceform Ltd, Compton, RG20 6NL

0020 **16** *2* **Margarets Wish**[38] 5507 3-8-6 38 ................. StephanieHollinshead(7) 12 —
(TWall) *slowly to stride: a bhd* **40/1**

1m 31.58s (0.78) **Going Correction** 0.0s/f (Stan)
**WFA** 3 from 4yo+ 1lb **16** Ran SP% **128.0**
Speed ratings: **95,93,93,90,90 88,87,85,85,85 79,75,74,72,72 69**CSF £21.99 TOTE £21.60: £3.90, £1.10, £4.40; EX 34.20.There was no bid for the winner.
**Owner** Mrs Joanna Hughes **Bred** Ian H Wills **Trained** Southwell, Notts

**FOCUS**
This was a competitive race won by a 55 rated performer.

**NOTEBOOK**
**Hurricane Coast**, who had only got his head in front once prior to today, travelled strongly and made a pleasing All-Weather debut. He hung right under pressure and did not find as much as once looked likely but, did enough.
**Jonny Ebeneezer** is not the horse he was but, performs creditably in this type of event. He ran a solid race.
**Levantine(IRE)**, unsuccessful in several attempts on the All-Weather in the past, he handled it perfectly well on this occasion but, looked an awkward ride up the straight and his jockey could not get serious with him. He should have finished closer.
**Proud Victor(IRE)** ran his best race for a while and was edging closer with every stride.
**Speedfit Free(IRE)** ran well on the return to this surface.
**Heathyardsblessing(IRE)** ran betetr than his price suggested and may appreciate a stiffer test.
**Swynford Welcome**, who ran well at Wolverhampton two days prior to this, could not muster the speed to get close.
**Kumakawa** *Official explanation: veterinary gelding bled from the nose*

## 6028 PRESS RED TO BET DIRECT H'CAP (DIV II) 1m (F)
**1:00** (1:00) (F ) (0-65,65) 3-Y-0+ **£2,121** (£606; £303) **Stalls** Low

Form RPR
0405 **1** **Sky Dome (IRE)**[34] 5596 10-9-6 57 ..............................(v) JFanning 12 74
(MHTompkins) *hld up: hdwy over 2f out: rdn to ld ins fnl f: edgd lft: r.o wl* **6/1**[3]
0060 **2** *2 1/2* **Mutarafaa (USA)**[2] 6016 4-8-7 44 ..............................(e[1]) IMongan 14 56
(DShaw) *trckd ldrs: rdn to ld over 1f out: hdd and unable qck ins fnl f* **12/1**
6441 **3** *1* **Scramble (USA)**[28] 5704 5-9-1 52 ..............................(bt) DaneO'Neill 11 62
(BEllison) *trckd ldrs: led on bit over 2f out: rdn and hdd over 1f out: styd on same pce ins fnl f* **9/2**[1]
0600 **4** *8* **Noble Pursuit**[135] 3066 6-9-7 58 ........................ DeanMcKeown 13 52
(PABlockley) *chsd ldrs: rdn over 2f out: wknd over 1f out* **7/1**
5000 **5** *1* **Thesaurus**[14] 5928 4-9-11 62 ........................ KDalgleish 10 54
(ACrook) *dwlt: outpcd: styd on ins fnl f: nvr nrr* **20/1**
2464 **6** *1 1/2* **Jessinca**[4] 6004 7-8-9 46 ........................ DKinsella 1 35
(APJones) *broke wl: sn lost pl and bhd: styd on ins fnl f* **15/2**
4020 **7** *shd* **Ballare (IRE)**[49] 5307 4-8-11 48 ........................ FNorton 3 37
(BobJones) *s.i.s: hld up: hdwy over 3f out: rdn and wknd wl over 1f out* **12/1**
0001 **8** *nk* **Locombe Hill (IRE)**[12] 5945 7-9-13 64 ........................ ANicholls 5 52
(DNicholls) *trckd ldrs: rdn over 2f out: sn wknd* **5/1**[2]
6100 **9** *8* **Blunham**[33] 5626 3-8-9 55 ........................ AndrewWebb(7) 2 27
(MCChapman) *led over 5f: sn wknd* **33/1**
-004 **10** *nk* **Jessie**[112] 3683 4-8-10 47 ........................ KimTinkler 6 19
(DonEnricoIncisa) *mid-div: sn pushed laong: wknd 3f out* **25/1**
403 **11** *3/4* **Alice Brand (IRE)**[112] 3683 5-8-12 49 ........................ NPollard 16 19
(GMMoore) *chsd ldrs: rdn and ev ch over 2f out: sn wknd* **16/1**
5400 **12** *3 1/2* **Red Delirium**[29] 5688 7-9-3 54 ..............................(b) GGibbons 7 17
(RBrotherton) *dwlt: outpcd* **16/1**
5244 **13** *8* **Shamwari Fire (IRE)**[9] 5969 3-8-6 52 ........................ PPMathers(7) 4 —
(IWMcinnes) *s.s: outpcd* **14/1**
0600 **14** *6* **Landofheartsdesire (IRE)**[112] 3683 4-8-8 48 ..............(v) LEnstone(3) 15 —
(JSWainwright) *chsd ldrs: rdn 1/2-way: wknd over 2f out* **40/1**

1m 43.8s (-0.80) **Going Correction** 0.0s/f (Stan)
**WFA** 3 from 4yo+ 2lb **14** Ran SP% **121.2**
Speed ratings: **104,101,100,92,91 90,89,89,81,81 80,77,69,63**CSF £73.40 CT £360.92 TOTE £5.90: £1.70, £6.40, £2.40; EX 45.50.
**Owner** Pollards Stables **Bred** Andrew Bradley **Trained** Newmarket, Suffolk

**FOCUS**
Another moderate handicap.

**NOTEBOOK**
**Sky Dome(IRE)**, whose last win came in this race last year off a 5lb higher mark, is clearly on a good mark and did the job nicely. Like the winner of the first division, he could well follow-up in similar company.
**Mutarafaa(USA)**, without a win since February 2002, bounced back to form the first time eye-shields. He is also on a nice mark and if able to build on this a similar race could come his way.
**Scramble(USA)** probably ran below the form he showed to take a Newcastle claimer last time and he is not easy to win with.
**Noble Pursuit**, with the cheekpieces left off this time, remains on a long losing run.
**Thesaurus** made a reasonable Fibresand debut and may be worth another try over a little further.
**Locombe Hill(IRE)** ran a mile below his best on his Fibresand debut.

## 6029 TIM & KAY SLATER'S BIG DAY CLAIMING STKS 6f (F)
**1:35** (1:35) (F ) 2-Y-0 **£2,058** (£588; £294) **Stalls** Low

Form RPR
1500 **1** **Muy Bien**[13] 5931 2-9-2 75 ..............................(v[1]) SWKelly 4 72
(JRJenkins) *chsd ldr: hdwy over 1f out: rdn and hun g lft ins last: styd on wl* **7/1**
6641 **2** *1 1/2* **Maunby Raver**[9] 5966 2-8-8 55 ........................ RoryMoore(7) 9 66
(PCHaslam) *a.p: effrt and ev ch over 1f out: rdn and nt qckn ins last* **3/1**[1]
5045 **3** *2 1/2* **Tictactoe**[48] 5324 2-8-4 58 ........................ LisaJones(3) 10 51
(DJDaly) *wnt rt s and bhd: hdwy 1/2-way: rdn and edgd rt 2f out styd on u nder press ent last: nrst fin* **6/1**[3]
1650 **4** *nk* **Only If I Laugh**[25] 5751 2-8-13 76 ..............................(b) LPKeniry(3) 7 59
(BJMeehan) *led: rdn 2f out: hdd over 1f out and sn wknd* **11/2**[2]
6610 **5** *2* **Foxies Future (IRE)**[22] 5824 2-8-9 67 ..............................(p) DaneO'Neill 2 46
(JRWeymes) *s.i.s and bhd: wd st: styd on fnl 2f: nrst fin* **8/1**
506 **6** *4* **Sparkling Clear**[34] 5595 2-8-6 50 ..............................(v[1]) MHenry 12 31
(RMHCowell) *chsd ldrs: rdn wl over 2f out: sn wknd* **50/1**
2100 **7** *6* **Wares Home (IRE)**[51] 5273 2-9-2 80 ........................ DarrenWilliams 8 23
(KRBurke) *s.i.s: a rr* **6/1**[3]
5500 **8** *2 1/2* **Shamrock Tea**[54] 5191 2-9-0 65 ........................ RFfrench 5 13
(MESowersby) *chsd ldrs: rdn along 1/2-way: sn wknd* **33/1**
1000 **9** *1 3/4* **Are You There**[26] 5726 2-8-6 64 ow1 ........................ NCallan 6 —
(TDBarron) *chsd ldrs tl wknd 1/2-way* **7/1**
600 **10** *1 1/4* **Miss Judged**[46] 5380 2-8-5 40 ..............................(t) GHannon 13 —
(APJones) *a rr* **100/1**
0000 **11** *2* **Darcie Mia**[15] 5913 2-7-10 42 ..............................(b[1]) DFentiman(7) 3 —
(JRWeymes) *a rr* **66/1**
4500 **12** *5* **Game Flora**[26] 5725 2-8-5 53 ow3 ........................ SHitchcott(3) 11 —
(MESowersby) *bhd fr 1/2-way* **50/1**
**13** *30* **Dandy Jim** 2-8-6 ........................ JFanning 14 —
(DWChapman) *v s.i.s: a wl b ehind* **50/1**

1m 16.72s (-0.08) **Going Correction** 0.0s/f (Stan) **13** Ran SP% **116.4**
Speed ratings: **100,98,94,94,91 86,78,74,72,70 68,61,21**CSF £26.81 TOTE £7.70: £2.70, £1.80, £2.80; EX 28.80.
**Owner** Kevin Reddington **Bred** K J Reddington **Trained** Royston, Herts

**FOCUS**
A reasonable claimer.

**NOTEBOOK**
**Muy Bien**, back on what appears to be his favoured surface with a visor on for the first time, ran a decisive winner without looking too straightforward under pressure. Things will be tough in handicap company off his current sort of mark and he may best off kept to this sort of level.
**Maunby Raver**, off the mark in a Wolverhampton nursery last time, ran well in the face of a stiff task. He is likely to take a rise in the weights for this and his best opportunity of further success is probably if kept to this sort of grade.
**Tictactoe**, still a maiden and beaten in a seller last time, had a bit to find at the weights with some of these, but ran well.
**Only If I Laugh**, without a hood on on this occasion, failed to convince he stayed this trip.
**Foxies Future(IRE)** has to be considered a little disappointing in first time cheekpieces.
**Wares Home(IRE)** was the best off at the weights, but he failed to deliver on his first attempt on this surface. *Official explanation: jockey said colt would not face the kickback*
**Are You There** does not appear to be progressing.

## 6030 LITTLEWOODS BET DIRECT RATED STKS (H'CAP) 5f (F)
**2:05** (2:05) (C ) (0-95,95) 3-Y-0+ **£6,905** (£2,124; £1,062; £531) **Stalls** High

Form RPR
2000 **1** **Trinculo (IRE)**[25] 5743 6-8-11 88 ..............................(p) J-PGuillambert(3) 7 99
(NPLittmoden) *w ldrs: rdn over 1f out: led ins fnl f: r.o* **20/1**
1005 **2** *hd* **Quito (IRE)**[25] 5737 6-9-7 95 ..............................(b) ACulhane 2 105
(DWChapman) *s.i.s: hdwy over 1f out: r.o* **14/1**
5001 **3** *1* **Dancing Mystery**[12] 5941 9-9-1 89 ..............................(b) SCarson 4 96
(EAWheeler) *s.i.s: sn chsng ldrs: led 2f out: hdd and unable qck ins fnl f* **7/1**[3]
1443 **4** *1/2* **Landing Strip (IRE)**[2] 6010 3-8-1 78 oh1 ........................ FPFerris(3) 6 83
(JMPEustace) *dwlt: outpcd: hdwy over 1f out: r.o* **8/1**
6102 **5** *shd* **Zarzu**[15] 5919 4-8-1 80 ........................ RThomas(5) 15 85+
(CRDore) *hld up: hdwy over 1f out: r.o* **20/1**
0403 **6** *1 1/4* **Now Look Here**[12] 5941 7-8-5 79 ........................ GGibbons 9 79
(BAMcmahon) *w ldr: led over 3f out: hdd 2f out: sn hung lft: no ex ins fnl f* **12/1**
200 **7** *3/4* **Bond Boy**[11] 5953 6-9-5 93 ........................ IMongan 1 91
(BSmart) *sn outpcd: styd on u.p fnl f: nvr trbld ldrs* **13/2**[2]
0022 **8** *1/2* **Steel Blue**[12] 5941 3-8-8 82 ..............................(p) FNorton 5 78
(RMWhitaker) *chsd ldrs: rdn 1/2-way: no ex fnl f* **9/1**
600 **9** *hd* **Sundried Tomato**[16] 5908 4-9-4 92 ........................ DarrenWilliams 10 87
(PWHiatt) *chsd ldrs: sn drvn along: styd on same pce appr fnl f* **14/1**
5501 **10** *1/2* **Maktavish**[16] 5909 4-8-7 84 ..............................(p) DMcGaffin(3) 14 78
(ISemple) *w ldrs 3f: eased whn btn ins fnl f* **8/1**
0000 **11** *2 1/2* **Prince Of Blues (IRE)**[2] 6010 5-8-6 80 ........................ SWKelly 8 65
(MMullineaux) *led: hdd over 3f out: hmpd over 1f out: sn wknd* **33/1**
1120 **12** *1/2* **Massey**[210] 1181 7-9-7 95 ........................ DeanMcKeown 16 78
(TDBarron) *sn outpcd* **11/2**[1]
0053 **13** *1/2* **Kathology (IRE)**[30] 5673 6-8-1 78 oh1 ........................ LisaJones(3) 13 59
(DRCElsworth) *s.i.s: outpcd* **10/1**
3000 **14** *2* **No Time (IRE)**[11] 5953 3-9-2 90 ........................ DaneO'Neill 11 64
(MJPolglase) *sn outpcd* **16/1**
0006 **15** *6* **Consensus (IRE)**[16] 5908 4-8-6 80 ........................ TWilliams 3 33
(MBrittain) *chsd ldrs over 3f* **25/1**

58.42 secs (-1.88) **Going Correction** -0.20s/f (Stan) **15** Ran SP% **125.8**
Speed ratings: **107,106,105,104,104 102,100,100,99,99 95,94,93,90,80**CSF £275.44 CT £2179.76 TOTE £25.50: £6.30, £6.00, £4.30; EX 486.80.
**Owner** Miss Vanessa Church **Bred** Humphrey Okeke **Trained** Newmarket, Suffolk

**FOCUS**
A very decent sprint handicap in which those that raced down the centre of the track had an advantage over those drawn high.

**NOTEBOOK**
**Trinculo(IRE)**, racing for the first time at this track since his racecourse debut four and a half years ago, has never been short of early pace and just managed to hold on. A rise in the handicap will leave him with few options on this surface, but he would be hard to beat if turning out again.
**Quito(IRE)**loves this surface and a strongly run race, but has never won over this trip and that proved his downfall as he only just failed to get up.
**Dancing Mystery**, a winner over course and distance several years ago, was not best away and the energy he had to use up to take a prominent position early cost him dear in the last half-furlong.
**Landing Strip(IRE)**was forced to adopt totally different tactics compared to recent starts after missing the break, but did come home in good style.
**Zarzu**made an encouraging start for his new yard, finishing in good style against the stands' rail.
**Now Look Here**, making his sand debut at the age of seven, showed good early pace down the centre of the track. He has not won for a very long time, but is extremely well handicapped and looks worth another try on Fibresand.
**Bond Boy**was taken off his feet and over this straight five that is a major handicap.
**Sundried Tomato**, a smart performer on this surface though yet to win over this trip on sand, has started this winter rated 10lb higher than he started last and that is going to make life awkward.
**Prince Of Blues(IRE)** *Official explanation: jockey said gelding suffered interference in running*
**Massey**, reappearing after a seven-month break, was racing over this trip for the very first time and could never go the pace. He should come on for this and will appreciate a return to further, though options will be few and far between off this mark.

## 6031 BETDIRECT.CO.UK MAIDEN STKS 6f (F)
**2:40** (2:41) (D ) 3-Y-0+ **£2,310** (£660; £330) **Stalls** Low

Form RPR
2506 **1** **Jalouhar**[18] 5878 3-9-0 60 ..............................(p) JFanning 13 60
(BPJBaugh) *a.p: hdwy to ld over 1f out: sn rdn: edgd rt wl ins last: kpt on* **14/1**
4204 **2** *1 1/2* **Beveller**[54] 5203 4-9-0 48 ........................ SWKelly 5 55
(WMBrisbourne) *dwlt: sn in tch: hdwy over 2f out: rdn to chal and hung lft over 1f out: drvn and hld whn sltly hmpd nr fin* **13/2**[3]
-000 **3** *2* **Second Minister**[123] 3418 4-9-0 50 ..............................(b[1]) PDoe 8 49
(DFlood) *led: rdn 2f out: drvn and hdd over 1f out: sn one pce* **8/1**
3234 **4** *shd* **Dark Champion**[28] 5702 3-9-0 61 ........................ IMongan 2 49
(JeddO'Keeffe) *in tch on inner: hdwy 2f out: sn rdn and one pce appr last* **5/1**[1]
-005 **5** *shd* **Tatweer (IRE)**[6] 5988 3-9-0 60 ..............................(v) DarrenWilliams 6 48
(DShaw) *in tch: rdn along and sltly outpcd 1/2-way: styd on u.p appr last: nrst fin* **8/1**

426- **6** *nk* **Shadowfax**[341] 5887 3-9-0 .......... ACulhane 12 48
(MissGayKelleway) *stdd s and bhd: hdwy 2f out: styd on wl fnl f: nrst fin* **7/1**

2250 **7** *hd* **Firecat**[23] 5793 4-9-0 48.......... DSweeney 3 47
(APJones) *squeezed out s and bhd: hdwy on inner over 2f out: rdn wl over 1f out: kpt on same pce* **14/1**

2040 **8** *1 1/2* **Cleveland Way**[136] 3038 3-9-0 52..........(v) RFitzpatrick 14 42
(DCarroll) *chsd ldrs on outer: rdn along wl over 2f out: drvn and kpt on same pce fnl 2f* **50/1**

00 **9** *3 1/2* **Blue Maeve**[16] 5907 3-9-0 .......... GParkin 11 32
(JHetherton) *towards rr: pushed along and hdwy over 2f out: kpt on ins last: nvr a factor* **100/1**

5506 **10** *5* **La Corujera**[74] 4731 3-8-9 62.......... NCallan 4 12
(TDBarron) *chsd ldrs: rdn along 1/2-way: sn wknd* **13/2**[3]

0000 **11** *nk* **Subtle Move (USA)**[19] 5856 3-8-9 49..........(v) FNorton 10 11
(DShaw) *a towards rr* **66/1**

**12** *1 3/4* **White O' Morn** 4-8-9 .......... GGibbons 7 6
(BAMcmahon) *prom: rdn along wl over 2f out: grad wknd* **50/1**

6246 **13** *1 3/4* **Roan Raider (USA)**[19] 5849 3-8-7 44..........(vt) KGhunowa(7) 16 6
(MJPolglase) *a rr* **25/1**

**14** *9* **Natural Grace** 3-8-9 .......... MFenton 15 —
(DJDaly) *dwlt: a rr* **33/1**

36-0 **15** *nk* **Dancing Ridge (IRE)**[56] 5149 6-9-0 45..........(p) DeanMcKeown 1 —
(ASenior) *midfield on inner: rdn along 1/2-way: sn lost pl and bhd* **66/1**

**16** *3/4* **Sierra Nevada (GER)** 3-8-9 .......... DaneO'Neill 9 —
(MAMagnusson) *a rr* **6/1**[2]

1m 17.1s (0.30) **Going Correction** 0.0s/f (Stan) **16** Ran SP% **120.4**
Speed ratings: **98,96,93,93,93 92,92,90,85,79 78,76,74,62,61 60**CSF £97.85 TOTE £18.00: £5.90, £2.00, £3.50; EX 93.20.
**Owner** Miss S M Potts **Bred** Roy Matthews **Trained** Audley, Staffs

**FOCUS**
A modest maiden run in a slower time than the two-year-old claimer.

**NOTEBOOK**
**Jalouhar**has had plenty of chances, but at least he is proven on the surface and was produced at just the right time to gain his first win at the 19th attempt.
**Beveller**seemed to appreciate dropping back a furlong on this slow surface, but was badly in at the weights and may be better off back in handicap company.
**Second Minister**ran with credit under a positive ride especially as he might have just needed this after a four-month break, but is another that may be better off in handicaps.
**Dark Champion**, for whom this trip on a slow surface would have been a stern test, did not seem to lack for stamina and ran with credit, especially as he was racing on the slower inside.
**Tatweer(IRE)**was staying on at the line and might appreciate a step back up to seven.
**Shadowfax**, racing for the first time in 11 months, took a pull at the start and was content to hang about at the back of the field early, but he was noted staying on in fine style down the straight under hands and heels riding to finish right alongside the placed horses. With this outing under his belt, he is well worth watching out for from now on.
**Firecat**ran with some credit considering his handicap mark and that fact that he raced closest to the inside rail. Another furlong probably suits him better.

## 6032 ALLWEATHER-RACING.COM (S) STKS (DIV II) 7f (F)
**3:10** (3:11) (G) 3-Y-0+ **£2,128** (£608; £304) **Stalls** Low

Form RPR

0003 **1** **Repeat (IRE)**[29] 5690 3-9-4 50.......... ACulhane 12 58
(KARyan) *trckd ldrs: led over 1f out: drvn out* **7/1**[3]

0363 **2** *1/2* **Bulawayo**[18] 5878 6-9-11 57.......... GGibbons 10 63
(BAMcmahon) *trckd ldrs: rdn and ev ch over 1f out: r.o* **3/1**[1]

5004 **3** *2* **Travelling Times**[5] 5998 4-9-2 52..........(v) LEnstone(3) 9 52
(JSWainwright) *led over 5f: no ex ins fnl f* **10/1**

600 **4** *1/2* **Mr Stylish**[5] 5992 7-9-5 53..........(vt) JDSmith 2 51
(JSMoore) *s.i.s: hld up: hdwy u.p over 1f out: nt rch ldrs* **12/1**

1U06 **5** *2* **Brilliantrio**[8] 5622 5-9-6 49..........(t) LVickers 14 47
(MCChapman) *sn outpcd: hdwy over 1f out: no imp ins fnl f* **16/1**

400 **6** *3/4* **Achilles Rainbow**[2] 6016 4-9-5 39.......... DarrenWilliams 5 44
(KRBurke) *prom: rdn 1/2-way: wknd fnl f* **40/1**

0003 **7** *1 1/2* **Attorney**[5] 5998 5-9-8 45..........(e) LisaJones(3) 16 46
(DShaw) *hld up: sme hdwy over 1f out: n.d* **11/2**[2]

0050 **8** *1 3/4* **Champagne Rider**[13] 5936 7-9-5 42..........(v) SWhitworth 11 36
(DShaw) *w ldr over 4f: wknd over 1f out* **25/1**

6006 **9** *3/4* **Tayif**[15] 5919 7-9-5 58.......... ANicholls 8 34
(DNicholls) *dwlt: hdwy over 4f out: rdn and wknd over 1f out* **11/2**[2]

6400 **10** *hd* **Distinctlysplendid**[2] 6015 3-8-13 36.......... DNolan(5) 7 33
(IAWood) *mid-div: lost pl over 4f out: hrd rdn over 2f out: no rspnse* **40/1**

6000 **11** *8* **Bold Effort (FR)**[106] 3858 11-9-2 40..........(b) LPKeniry(3) 15 13
(KOCunningham-Brown) *dwlt: outpcd* **50/1**

-460 **12** *1 1/2* **Chesnut Cracker**[107] 3836 3-8-6 40..........(t) PDineley(7) 6 5
(PCHaslam) *hld up in tch: wknd 1/2-way* **16/1**

0000 **13** *3/4* **Bond Solitaire**[29] 5690 3-8-13 46.......... RFfrench 4 3
(BSmart) *chsd ldrs 4f* **33/1**

1420 **14** *3* **Tap**[78] 4643 6-9-4 53.......... LTreadwell(7) 3 6
(IanEmmerson) *sn pushed along: bhd fr 1/2-way* **9/1**

0000 **15** *5* **Sally Traffic**[61] 5047 4-9-0 35..........(p) FNorton 13 —
(RMWhitaker) *chsd ldrs 5f* **40/1**

0000 **16** *3 1/2* **Precious Freedom**[30] 5678 3-9-4 48..........(p) JFanning 1 —
(JBalding) *s.i.s: sn prom: wknd 3f out* **40/1**

1m 31.3s (0.50) **Going Correction** 0.0s/f (Stan)
**WFA** 3 from 4yo+ 1lb **16** Ran SP% **125.3**
Speed ratings: **97,96,94,93,91 90,88,86,85,85 76,74,73,70,64 60**CSF £27.43 TOTE £10.40: £3.70, £2.60, £4.90; EX 52.40.The winner was sold to Mr J T Billson for 3,250gns.
**Owner** Crewe And Nantwich Racing Club **Bred** Philip Hore Jnr **Trained** Hambleton, N Yorks

**FOCUS**
A modest seller run in a fractionally faster time than the first division.

**NOTEBOOK**
**Repeat(IRE)**, from a stable in form, tracked the leading group until produced to lead a furlong out, but drifted left in the closing stages and just managed to hold on with little to spare. This was his first victory at the 21st attempt and this is his grade.
**Bulawayo**, a Wolverhampton regular but appearing at this track for the first time in three and a half years, had the run of the race but, despite holding every chance, could never quite force his head in front. He is not the easiest to win with and tends to pop up when least expected.
**Travelling Times**ran with credit on this drop in class under a positive ride, but is nowhere near as good as he was and finds this trip a furlong too far.
**Mr Stylish**, winner of a division of this contest last year, was brought with his effort wide and late but could never really get on terms. *Official explanation: jockey said gelding had hung both ways throughout*
**Brilliantrio**, who is mixing Flat racing with hurdling these days, not surprisingly found this trip too sharp.

## 6033 BET DIRECT ON 0800 32 93 93 H'CAP 2m (F)
**3:40** (3:42) (F) (0-60,59) 3-Y-0+ **£2,079** (£594; £297) **Stalls** Low

Form RPR

0303 **1** **Macaroni Gold (IRE)**[7] 5975 3-9-3 57.......... MTebbutt 9 77+
(WJarvis) *hld up and bhd: hdwy after 6f: trckd ldrs 6f out: chsd ldr 4f out: led 2f out: sn clr: eased ins last* **6/1**[3]

-501 **2** *3* **Ambitious Annie**[103] 3973 4-8-1 39.......... StephanieHollinshead(7) 13 47
(RHollinshead) *in tch on outer: hdwy to ld 1/2-way: rdn along 3f out: hdd 2f out and kpt on same pce* **10/1**

5620 **3** *1 1/4* **Great As Gold (IRE)**[176] 1509 4-9-10 55..........(p) DaneO'Neill 3 62
(BEllison) *hld up and bhd: hdwy over 6f out: chsd ldrs over 4f out: sn rdn along: drvna nd kpt on same pce fnl 2f* **3/1**[1]

6554 **4** *2* **Fairmorning (IRE)**[67] 3276 4-8-10 41.......... ADaly 8 46
(JWUnett) *bhd: hdwy over 5f out: rdn along 3f out: kpt on u.p fnl 2f: nrst fin* **25/1**

550- **5** *12* **High Jinks**[394] 5383 8-8-5 39.......... LisaJones(3) 6 32
(RNBevis) *chsd ldrs: drvn along 5f out: wknd over 3f out* **20/1**

0040 **6** *2 1/2* **First Pressure**[20] 5839 3-9-4 58.......... TQuinn 15 48
(DRCElsworth) *led 3f: styd prom tld riven along and outpcd 4f out* **7/1**

0-00 **7** *8* **Kagoshima (IRE)**[72] 4775 8-9-1 46..........(v) VHalliday 16 28
(JRNorton) *hld up and bhd: stdy hdwy 6f out: rdn along 4f out and sn no imp* **33/1**

5561 **8** *nk* **Spa Lane**[22] 5817 10-9-4 56.......... PGallagher(7) 5 38
(JFCoupland) *hld up and bhd: sme hdwy on outer 6f out: sn rdn along and nvr a factor* **4/1**[2]

4605 **9** *3/4* **Charnwood Street (IRE)**[6] 5682 4-8-11 42..........(e) DarrenWilliams 4 23
(DShaw) *midfield: rdn along and outpcd 7f out: bhd after* **16/1**

00-0 **10** *7* **Known Maneuver (USA)**[22] 5823 5-10-0 59.......... LVickers 11 33
(MCChapman) *a rr: bhd fr 1/2-way* **66/1**

1230 **11** *3/4* **Hajeer (IRE)**[5] 5999 5-9-8 53.......... ACulhane 2 26
(PWHiatt) *a rr* **13/2**

0000 **12** *2* **Kristal Forest (IRE)**[154] 1794 4-8-9 40.......... IMongan 7 11
(MrsSLamyman) *prom: rdn along over 4f out and sn wknd* **14/1**

-000 **13** *20* **Sweetstock**[28] 5703 5-8-4 38 ow3.......... LPKeniry(3) 14 —
(MrsGSRees) *a rr: bhd fr 1/2-way* **50/1**

0-00 **14** *dist* **A Two (IRE)**[177] 1871 4-9-3 48.......... MFenton 10 —
(BPalling) *chsd ldrs: led after 3f tl hdd 1/2-way: rdn along 6f out and sn wknd: t.o fnl 3f* **50/1**

5500 **15** *3/4* **All On My Own (USA)**[15] 5914 8-8-2 40 ow2.......... PPMathers(7) 12 —
(IWMcinnes) *in tch 6f: sn outpcd and bhd: t.o fnl 3f* **33/1**

3m 45.78s (-6.72) **Going Correction** 0.0s/f (Stan)
**WFA** 3 from 4yo+ 9lb **15** Ran SP% **126.7**
Speed ratings: **101,99,98,97,91 90,86,86,86,82 82,81,71,—,—**CSF £63.91 CT £222.64 TOTE £5.90: £2.60, £3.30, £2.40; EX 74.60 Place 6 £342.63, Place 5 £90.40.
**Owner** Dr J Walker **Bred** Thomas Stacey **Trained** Newmarket, Suffolk

**FOCUS**
A moderate staying handicap in which the field finished spread out all over Nottinghamshire behind the front four.

**NOTEBOOK**
**Macaroni Gold(IRE)**, stepping up in trip again, performed much better than on his Fibresand debut and saw the two miles out really well. He had the advantage of being lightly raced and unexposed compared to his rivals, so there seems no reason why he should not win again.
**Ambitious Annie**, raised just 3lb for her Wolverhampton win, ran another solid race and is well suited by staying trips on this surface. Her basement rating makes her the ideal type for regional racing in the new year.
**Great As Gold(IRE)**, running for the first time since winning over hurdles in May, ran well enough and there should be a similar event for him under these condition this winter.
**Fairmorning(IRE)**, still a maiden and back on sand after a couple of outings over hurdles, ran with credit and finished a long way clear of the rest.
**High Jinks**achieved very little and is without a win in five and a half years, though he was absent for more than three of those.
**First Pressure**did not improve for the step up in trip, but at least gave his rider a workout on his return from a broken arm.
**Spa Lane**, proven under the conditions, seemed likely to play a part when moving up smoothly on the outside leaving the back straight, but went from one extreme to the other in a matter of strides.
**Hajeer(IRE)**ran a stinker for the second time in six days.
T/Plt: £309.70 to a £1 stake. Pool: £34,817.80. 82.05 winning tickets. T/Qpdt: £95.20 to a £1 stake. Pool: £3,629.30. 28.20 winning tickets. CR

# 6000 MAISONS-LAFFITTE (R-H)
Wednesday, November 19

**OFFICIAL GOING: Heavy**

## 6034a PRIX CONTESSINA (LISTED) 6f (S)
**2:00** (1:59) 3-Y-0+ **£13,312** (£5,325; £3,994; £2,662)

RPR

**1** **Soave (GER)**[19] 5866 4-9-7 .......... ABoschert 8 114
(ATrybuhl, Germany)

**2** *1/2* **Charming Groom (FR)**[19] 5866 4-8-12 .......... DBonilla 6 104
(FHead, France)

**3** *2 1/2* **Vasywait (FR)**[37] 4-8-12 .......... DBoeuf 3 96
(J-LGay, France)

**4** *nk* **Halmahera (IRE)**[11] 5953 8-8-12 ..........(b) CSoumillon 5 95
(KARyan) *led or disputed lead til close 2nd half-way, ridden over 1 1/2f out, stayed on steadily under pressure til lost 3rd final s*

**5** *1* **Cheese 'n Biscuits**[20] 5838 3-8-9 .......... GCarter 2 89
(GLMoore) *towards rear, ridden half-way, stayed on steadily to line*

**6** *1 1/2* **Welsh Emperor (IRE)**[19] 5866 4-8-12 ..........(b) DaleGibson 7 88
(TPTate) *led or disputed lead til led narrowly half-way, headed 2f out, ridden and unable to quicken*

**7** *4* **Sweet Name (USA)**[18] 5884 4-8-9 .......... C-PLemaire 4 73
(MmeCHead-Maarek, France)

**8** *8* **Valiantly**[38] 5523 4-8-9 .......... TThulliez 1 49
(NClement, France)

1m 16.4s **8** Ran
Speed ratings: .
**Owner** Stall Happy End **Bred** Gestut Etzean **Trained** Germany

**NOTEBOOK**
**Halmahera(IRE)**shared the lead until challenged by the eventual winner and second one out, he then stayed on one paced and just lost third place in the final strides. Connections reported the ground may have been a little dead for him.
**Cheese 'n Biscuits**stayed on well in the final stages but never threatened to reach the leaders.

**Welsh Emperor(IRE)** shared the lead until coming under pressure and weakening one and a half out. A disappointing show from the favourite on his ideal ground and his last two races may have come a little close together.

## 6035a PRIX BELLE DE NUIT (LISTED) (F&M) 1m 4f

**2:30** (2:35) 3-Y-O+ **£13,312** (£5,325; £3,994; £2,662)

RPR

1 **Sweet Stream (ITY)**20 3-8-9 .......... TGillet 8 108
(JEHammond, France) 1

2 2 ½ **Subtile Bed (FR)**27 3-8-9 .......... SPasquier 12 105
(BSecly, France)

3 1 ½ **Condition**27 3-8-9 .......... TThulliez 15 102
(PBary, France)

4 2 **Violin Time (USA)**78 3-8-9 .......... ACarre 18 99
(AFabre, France)

5 hd **Buenos Aires (IRE)**47 5354 3-8-9 .......... GBenoist 11 99
(ELellouche, France)

6 shd **Vipassana**16 5912 3-8-9 .......... C-PLemaire 16 99
(DSepulchre, France)

7 snk **Trill**24 5783 3-8-9 .......... CSoumillon 10 99
(AFabre, France)

8 ¾ **Vijanti**30 5684 4-9-0 .......... CStefan 1 97
(JEPease, France)

9 shd **Imoya (IRE)**109 3781 4-9-0 .......... PJSmullen 14 96
(BJMeehan) *mid-division towards outside, 5th straight, ridden 2f out, one pace from 1 1/2f out*

10 1 ½ **Mystic Mile (IRE)**12 5942 4-9-0 .......... PRobinson 6 94
(MAJarvis) *prominent, 4th on rail straight, pushed along over 1 1/2f out, unable to quicken*

11 3 **Shamara (IRE)**19 5852 3-8-9 .......... ELegrix 9 91
(CFWall) *mid-division, 7th towards inside straight, ridden over 1 1/2f out, never in contention*

12 1 **Aliyshan (IRE)**184 1731 3-8-9 .......... MJKinane 17 89
(JohnMOxx, Ire) *in touch on outside, led from half-way to 5f out, pushed along well over 3f out, 2nd straight, soon weakened*

13 7 **In Love**19 5852 3-8-9 .......... DBonilla 5 79
(EALDunlop) *mid-division, 11th straight, pushed along 2f out, never dangerous*

14 ½ **Change Partners (IRE)**15 5917 3-8-9 .......... SDrowne 4 78
(RCharlton) *towards rear, pushed along straight, never dangerous*

15 8 **Gold Bar (IRE)**25 5755 3-8-9 .......... RHills 3 66
(MPTregoning) *held up in rear, 12th on outside straight, ridden over 2f out, no impression*

16 2 ½ **High Straits**19 4-9-0 ..........(b) ABadel 2 61
(MmeMBollack-Badel, France)

17 5 **Sovana (IRE)**47 5354 3-8-13 .......... TJarnet 7 59
(MmeCHead-Maarek, France)

18 4 **Blue Icon**61 5056 3-8-9 ..........(b) DBoeuf 13 49
(ELellouche, France)

2m 44.0s
**WFA** 3 from 4yo 6lb **18** Ran SP% **10.2**
Speed ratings: .
**Owner** Team Valor **Bred** Paolo Torrente **Trained** France

**NOTEBOOK**
**Imoya(IRE)** raced on the outside and not far from the leaders rounding the final turn, but the filly was unable to accelerate in the straight
**Mystic Mile(IRE)** on the rail tucked in behind the leading group, but came under pressure one and a half out and could not quicken
**Shamara(IRE)** raced in mid division and was never a threa
**In Love** came under pressure soon after entering the straight and was never in a position to challenge.
**Change Partners(IRE)** was towards the rear of the field throughout this race and found it too hot.
**Gold Bar(IRE)** was ridden along rounding the final turn but could never get on terms.

# 6010 WOLVERHAMPTON (A.W) (L-H)

Friday, November 21

**OFFICIAL GOING: Standard**
Wind: nil Weather: fine but misty for last race

## 6036 BET DIRECT IN RUNNING SKY TEXT 293 H'CAP (DIV I) 7f (F)

**12:50** (12:51) (F) (0-60,60) 3-Y-O+ **£2,107** (£602; £301) **Stalls** High

Form RPR

3002 1 **Zagala**11 5969 3-9-8 **55** ..........(t) ACulhane 10 67
(SLKeightley) *sn prom: wnt 2nd over 3f out: rdn to ld 2f out: edgd lft ins fnl f: r.o wl* **5/1**1

6060 2 1 ¾ **Geronimo**4 6014 6-9-9 **55** ..........(p) DKinsella 6 63
(MissGayKelleway) *hld up mid-div: rdn and hdwy over 3f out: chsd wnr over 1f out: nt qckn ins fnl f* **11/2**2

1300 3 1 ½ **Victory Vee**20 5878 3-9-12 **59** .......... NCallan 2 63
(MBlanshard) *chsd ldrs: rdn over 3f out: kpt on same pce fnl 2f* **8/1**

6004 4 ¾ **Gold Guest**6 6006 4-9-3 **54** ..........(v) DNolan(5) 5 56
(PDEvans) *s.i.s: rdn and hdwy over 2f out: kpt on one pce fnl f* **5/1**1

2250 5 2 ½ **Pawn In Life (IRE)**228 951 5-9-7 **60** .......... Laura-JayneCrawford(7) 1 56
(TDBarron) *prom: lost pl on ins over 3f out: n.d after* **16/1**

4000 6 5 **Red Delirium**2 6028 7-9-8 **54** ..........(b) GGibbons 7 37
(RBrotherton) *outpcd: hdwy over 1f out: nvr nr ldrs* **14/1**

7 2 ½ **Tango Step (IRE)**21 5860 3-9-0 **54** .......... PPMathers(7) 8 30
(BernardLawlor, Ire) *outpcd: sme hdwy over 1f out: n.d* **25/1**

0000 8 1 **Dasar**28 5728 3-9-7 **54** .......... DarrenWilliams 11 27
(MBrittain) *hld up: hdwy on outside over 4f out: sn rdn and wknd* **40/1**

3230 9 ½ **On The Trail**45 5438 6-9-7 **56** .......... LisaJones(3) 3 28
(DWChapman) *chsd ldrs tl wknd 2f out* **11/1**

1001 10 1 ¾ **Consignia (IRE)**4 6015 4-9-8 **54** 6ex ..........(v) PaulEddery 4 22
(DHaydnJones) *chsd ldrs: rdn after 1f: sn bhd* **6/1**3

0423 11 3 **Baby Barry**20 5880 6-10-0 **60** ..........(v) DaneO'Neill 12 20
(MrsGSRees) *s.i.s: sn chsng ldrs: rdn over 4f out: sn wknd* **7/1**

0-00 F **Bedazzled**3 6019 3-9-9 **56** ..........(b1) GCarter 9 —
(JAGlover) *led: hdd and rdn 2f out: wknd 1f out: collapsed wl ins fnl f: dead* **25/1**

1m 30.68s (0.48) **Going Correction** 0.0s/f (Stan)
**WFA** 3 from 4yo+ 1lb **12** Ran SP% **117.6**
Speed ratings: **97,95,93,92,89 83,81,79,79,77 73,**—CSF £31.05 CT £222.12 TOTE £6.20: £2.10, £1.50, £2.60; EX 36.40.
**Owner** Mrs C C Regalado-Gonzalez **Bred** J E Jackson **Trained** Waltham-On-The-Wolds, Leics

**FOCUS**
The winning time was a shade faster tha the other division but slower than the seven furlong maiden.
**NOTEBOOK**
**Zagala** seems to have improved since having her tongue tied and found a switch to handicaps enabling her to lose her maiden tag.
**Geronimo** had the cheekpieces refitted for this step back up to seven. He has slipped to a useful mark but does not win very often.
**Victory Vee** has slipped down the ratings but was still 7lb higher than when successful over course and distance in August.
**Gold Guest** appeared not to have got home over the stretch mile here six days ago, but did not seem suited by this shorter trip.
**Pawn In Life(IRE)** had an inexperienced pilot for this first outing since April. *Official explanation: jockey said gelding had bled from the nose*
**Red Delirium** *Official explanation: jockey said gelding had hung left-handed throughout*

## 6037 BET DIRECT ON 0800 32 93 93 NURSERY 5f (F)

**1:20** (1:33) (E) (0-75,74) 2-Y-O **£2,233** (£638; £319) **Stalls** Low

Form RPR

4201 1 **Peters Choice**7 5997 2-9-11 **74** 7ex .......... NCallan 4 83+
(ISemple) *mde all: pushed clr fnl f: comf* **4/9**1

0044 2 2 ½ **Blue Power (IRE)**11 5968 2-8-10 **59** .......... DarrenWilliams 8 59
(KRBurke) *a.p: rdn 3f out: kpt on ins fnl f: nt trble wnr* **15/2**2

0061 3 nk **Chickado (IRE)**20 5876 2-9-5 **68** .......... PaulEddery 9 67
(DHaydnJones) *chsd ldrs: outpcd 3f out: rallied on outside over 1f out: r.o ins fnl f* **10/1**3

3354 4 ¾ **Smart Starprincess (IRE)**7 5997 2-8-5 **61** ..........(b) SYourston(7) 6 57
(PABlockley) *prom: chsd wnr over 3f out: sn rdn: no ex ins fnl f* **25/1**

6234 5 1 ½ **Emaradia**8 5990 2-8-5 **54** .......... JoannaBadger 7 45
(PDEvans) *chsd ldrs: no hdwy fnl 2f* **20/1**

3454 6 nk **Blue Moon Hitman (IRE)**15 5931 2-8-7 **56** .......... ADaly 10 46
(ABerry) *lost pl 3f out: hdwy over 1f out: n.d* **12/1**

5502 7 9 **Bond Romeo (IRE)**24 5818 2-9-7 **70** .......... RFfrench 1 29
(BSmart) *prom tl wknd wl over 1f out* **12/1**

006 8 6 **Knight To Remember (IRE)**76 4735 2-8-2 **51** .......... PFessey 3 —
(KARyan) *outpcd* **100/1**

5400 9 1 **Finians Gold**113 3725 2-8-10 **59** .......... DSweeney 2 —
(JGMO'Shea) *sn outpcd* **100/1**

000 10 5 **Desert Light (IRE)**31 5686 2-7-9 **47** oh17 ..........(v1) LisaJones(3) 5 —
(DShaw) *sn outpcd* **250/1**

62.32 secs (-0.28) **Going Correction** 0.0s/f (Stan) **10** Ran SP% **116.5**
Speed ratings: **102,98,97,96,93 93,79,69,67,59** CSF £4.11 CT £17.03 TOTE £1.50: £1.10, £1.90, £2.20; EX 5.50.
**Owner** Peter Tsim **Bred** G And Mrs A Young **Trained** Carluke, S Lanarks

**FOCUS**
Peters Choice repeated his win over course and distance a week ago and again clocked the best time of the day.
**NOTEBOOK**
**Peters Choice** would have had another 5lb to carry had his new mark been in force and connections plan to bring him back to Dunstall Park for a hat-trick bid. He has taken to this surface like a duck to water.
**Blue Power(IRE)** has been running as if he would be suited by a drop back to the minimum trip but that did not really turn out to be the case.
**Chickado(IRE)** got caught flat-footed over this shorter distance and definitely needs a return to six.
**Smart Starprincess(IRE)** was 8lb better off than when nearly ten lengths behind the winner here a week ago.
**Emaradia** was reverting to five.

## 6038 BET DIRECT THROUGH ATTHERACES RED BUTTON CLAIMING STKS 5f (F)

**1:50** (1:56) (F) 3-Y-O+ **£2,100** (£600; £300) **Stalls** Low

Form RPR

0001 1 **Sharp Hat**17 5919 9-9-2 66 .......... ACulhane 13 74
(DWChapman) *a chsng ldrs: rdn over 2f out: r.o to ld wl ins fnl f* **5/1**3

2410 2 1 **Prima Stella**6 6001 4-8-12 70 .......... J-PGuillambert(3) 4 70
(NPLittmoden) *rdn and hdwy 2f out: r.o ins fnl f* **4/1**1

5000 3 nk **Henry Tun**36 5598 5-9-2 56 ..........(b) JEdmunds 7 69
(JBalding) *w ldr: led over 3f out: rdn over 1f out: hdd and no ex wl ins fnl f* **14/1**

00-3 4 1 ¾ **Blueberry Rhyme**105 3968 4-8-12 66 ..........(v) DSweeney 10 59
(PJMakin) *hdwy over 2f out: kpt on ins fnl f* **9/2**2

5500 5 1 ½ **Marabar**35 5616 5-8-11 74 .......... DaleGibson 5 53
(DWChapman) *outpcd: hdwy fnl f: nvr nrr* **5/1**3

6000 6 ¾ **Star Lad (IRE)**7 5998 3-8-12 57 ..........(b) GGibbons 6 51
(RBrotherton) *led over 1f: sn rdn: wknd fnl f* **50/1**

5020 7 shd **Catchthebatch**58 5156 7-8-11 53 .......... DCorby(3) 1 53
(MJWallace) *chsd ldrs: rdn over 2f out: wknd ins fnl f* **14/1**

0020 8 nk **Mr Spliffy (IRE)**17 5919 4-8-12 54 .......... DarrenWilliams 8 50
(KRBurke) *bhd fnl 3f* **16/1**

4000 9 2 **Ladies Knight**25 5794 3-9-4 56 .......... NCallan 12 49
(DShaw) *s.i.s: outpcd* **40/1**

1604 10 1 ¼ **Monte Verde (IRE)**108 3858 3-8-7 50 ..........(p) DKinsella 2 34
(BPalling) *chsd ldrs tl wknd over 2f out* **20/1**

00-0 11 2 **Ellens Lad (IRE)**55 5216 9-9-8 78 ..........(b) PaulEddery 3 42
(WJMusson) *chsd ldrs tl wknd over 1f out* **12/1**

0000 12 9 **Vision Of Dreams**34 5634 3-8-9 74 ..........(b) MTebbutt 9 —
(BJMeehan) *outpcd* **7/1**

62.72 secs (0.12) **Going Correction** 0.0s/f (Stan) **12** Ran SP% **120.1**
Speed ratings: **99,97,96,94,91 90,90,89,86,84 81,67** CSF £25.22 TOTE £5.30: £2.20, £1.90, £2.60; EX 13.80. The winner was claimed by A S Reid for £8,000. Prima Stella was claimed by J R Toller for £10,000
**Owner** Miss N F Thesiger **Bred** Littleton Stud **Trained** Stillington, N Yorks

**FOCUS**
This was won in a time nearly half a second slower than the preceding two-year-old event.
**NOTEBOOK**
**Sharp Hat** had won handicaps over course and distance around this time of the year for the last two seasons. He was claimed for £8,000 and now goes to Andrew Reid.
**Prima Stella** did win over course and distance in April but seems better over six. She was claimed by James Toller for £10,000.
**Henry Tun** would have been much better off with the first two in a handicap and showed definite signs of a return to form.
**Blueberry Rhyme** was not disgraced on this first start since August.
**Marabar**, in the same ownership as the winner, was previously trained by John Akehurst. She was totally unsuited by the drop back to five on this All-Weather debut.
**Star Lad(IRE)** failed to get home despite the drop back from six.

## 6039 LITTLEWOODS BET DIRECT MAIDEN STKS 7f (F)
2:25 (2:26) (D) 3-Y-O £2,415 (£690; £345) Stalls High

Form RPR
55 **1** **Roman Maze**$^{20}$ 5879 3-9-0 ........ SWKelly 5 73
(WMBrisbourne) *a.p: rdn to ld wl over 1f out: r.o wl* **5/1**$^{3}$
6 **2** *2 ½* **Nicholas Nickelby**$^{11}$ 5969 3-8-11 ........ J-PGuillambert$^{(3)}$ 1 67
(NPLittmoden) *w ldr tl rdn over 3f out: styd on one pce fnl f* **25/1**
4026 **3** *¾* **Jagged (IRE)**$^{8}$ 5985 3-9-0 61 ........ DarrenWilliams 11 65
(KRBurke) *led: rdn 3f out: hdd wl over 1f out: one pce fnl f* **6/1**
3033 **4** *½* **Monte Mayor Lad (IRE)**$^{4}$ 6014 3-9-0 62 ........ (b) FNorton 12 64
(DHaydnJones) *a.p: rdn over 2f out: one pce fnl f* **5/1**$^{3}$
0523 **5** *nk* **Wainwright (IRE)**$^{21}$ 5849 3-9-0 60 ........ (p) DeanMcKeown 10 63
(PABlockley) *hld up: hdwy over 3f out: rdn over 2f out: no ex ins fnl f* **4/1**$^{2}$
0003 **6** *1 ¼* **Victory Flip (IRE)**$^{11}$ 5973 3-8-2 55 ........ (p) StephanieHollinshead$^{(7)}$ 3 55
(RHollinshead) *hld up: hdwy over 2f out: no imp fnl f* **16/1**
6066 **7** *4* **Neutral Night (IRE)**$^{4}$ 6015 3-8-9 45 ........ (v) GGibbons 4 45
(RBrotherton) *prom: rdn over 2f out: wknd over 1f out* **66/1**
5000 **8** *12* **Bugle Call**$^{25}$ 5793 3-8-11 43 ........ LPKeniry$^{(3)}$ 2 20
(KOCunningham-Brown) *s.i.s: wl bhd fnl 4f* **80/1**
0040 **9** *1 ½* **My Girl Pearl (IRE)**$^{103}$ 4017 3-8-4 48 ........ (b$^{1}$) JFMcDonald$^{(5)}$ 9 11
(MSSaunders) *hld up: rdn over 3f out: sn struggling* **66/1**
3226 **10** *2* **Blaina**$^{83}$ 4587 3-8-9 75 ........ TQuinn 6 6
(DRCElsworth) *prom: rdn over 3f out: sn wknd* **5/2**$^{1}$
**11** *3* **Maggie Maquette** 3-8-9 ........ DSweeney 8 —
(WSKittow) *squeezed out s: hld up: rdn over 3f out: sn bhd* **66/1**
0400 **12** *5* **Ruby Anniversary**$^{73}$ 4792 3-8-9 43 ........ JEdmunds 7 —
(JBalding) *a bhd* **66/1**

1m 29.86s (-0.34) **Going Correction** 0.0s/f (Stan) **12** Ran SP% **113.1**
Speed ratings: **101,98,97,96,96 94,90,76,74,72 69,63**CSF £124.35 TOTE £5.00: £1.80, £4.40, £2.30; EX 65.80.
**Owner** The Jenko and Thomo Partnership **Bred** Juddmonte Farms **Trained** Great Ness, Shropshire
■ Stewards Enquiry : Darren Williams one-day ban: careless riding (Dec 1)

**FOCUS**
This was won in a time significantly faster than the two divisions of the seven furlong handicap.

**NOTEBOOK**
**Roman Maze** was none the worse after finishing lame over the extended nine furlongs here at the start of the month. He is on the upgrade.
**Nicholas Nickelby** showed tremendous improvement on his course and distance debut here last week and shaped as though he will get further.
**Jagged(IRE)** did not find a switch back to a maiden from handicap company the answer.
**Monte Mayor Lad(IRE)** was not suprisingly back up to seven after his good effort in a handicap here on Monday.
**Wainwright(IRE)** was another reverting from six to seven furlongs.

## 6040 BETDIRECT.CO.UK H'CAP (DIV I) 1m 4f (F)
3:00 (3:00) (F) (0-60,64) 3-Y-O+ £2,051 (£586; £293) Stalls Low

Form RPR
3530 **1** **Fight The Feeling**$^{31}$ 5692 5-9-8 **52** ........ (v$^{1}$) ADaly 2 61
(JWUnett) *hld up in tch: rdn to chal wl over 1f out: r.o to ld nr fin* **7/1**$^{3}$
6104 **2** *hd* **Kentucky Bullet (USA)**$^{98}$ 4141 7-9-1 **45** ........ SWhitworth 3 54
(AGNewcombe) *a.p: rdn over 2f out: led wl over 1f out: hdd nr fin* **9/1**
0650 **3** *3 ½* **Ersaal (USA)**$^{24}$ 5817 3-9-5 **55** ........ KDalgleish 6 58
(JJay) *a.p: wnt 2nd 8f out: rdn and ev ch 2f out: one pce* **50/1**
0350 **4** *½* **Sorbiesharry (IRE)**$^{20}$ 5881 4-8-13 **46** ........ LisaJones$^{(3)}$ 11 49
(MrsNMacauley) *hld up: hdwy on ins 2f out: kpt on towards fin* **14/1**
0030 **5** *shd* **Sabreline**$^{73}$ 4800 4-9-1 **45** ........ DaneO'Neill 8 48
(BRFoster) *led: rdn over 2f out: hdd wl over 1f out: wknd towards fin* **33/1**
0045 **6** *½* **Ipledgeallegiance (USA)**$^{11}$ 5971 7-9-6 **50** ........ ACulhane 9 52
(DWChapman) *hld up: rdn and hdwy over 3f out: no imp fnl 2f* **12/1**
460 **7** *½* **Claptrap**$^{31}$ 5692 3-9-1 **54** ........ FPFerris$^{(3)}$ 4 55
(JAOsborne) *hld up and bhd: stdy hdwy fnl f: nvr nr to chal* **9/1**
000- **8** *2* **Phantom Stock**$^{423}$ 4870 3-9-0 **50** ........ TQuinn 10 48
(WJarvis) *a bhd* **10/1**
1661 **9** *3* **Smoothie (IRE)**$^{11}$ 5971 5-10-1 **64** 6ex ........ DNolan$^{(5)}$ 7 58
(IanWilliams) *hld up in tch: rdn over 3f out: wknd wl over 1f out* **5/2**$^{1}$
0002 **10** *¾* **Fairy Wind (GER)**$^{31}$ 5692 6-9-5 **49** ........ SWKelly 5 41
(BJCurley) *prom: lost pl over 6f out: rdn over 5f out: bhd fnl 4f* **4/1**$^{2}$
5001 **11** *shd* **Top Trees**$^{22}$ 4765 5-9-7 **51** ........ FNorton 12 43
(WSKittow) *hld up: rdn over 3f out: a bhd* **12/1**

2m 41.38s (-0.12) **Going Correction** 0.0s/f (Stan) **11** Ran SP% **117.1**
**WFA** 3 from 4yo+ 6lb
Speed ratings: **100,99,97,97,97 96,96,95,93,92 92**CSF £68.28 CT £2904.73 TOTE £8.70: £2.60, £2.30, £5.60; EX 53.00.
**Owner** T Morning **Bred** G W Smith **Trained** Wolverhampton, W Midlands
■ Stewards Enquiry : F P Ferris eight-day ban: failed to all reasonable and permissible measures throughout the race (Dec 1-3,6,8-10,12)

**FOCUS**
This was over a second and a half slower than the other division.

**NOTEBOOK**
**Fight The Feeling**, visored for the first time, was supported in the market having worked well when tried in the headgear. *Official explanation: trainer said, regarding the improved form shown, gelding benefited from being fitted with a visor for the first time*
**Kentucky Bullet(USA)**, three times a winner over course and distance, very nearly pulled it off on his first outing since August. He can soon go one better.
**Ersaal(USA)**, who showed ability for Ed Dunlop as a juvenile, ran by far his best race for his new connections.
**Sorbiesharry(IRE)** has been slipping down the ratings and gave the first indication that he is capable of staying this trip.
**Sabreline** was reverting to a mile and a half having been bought out of David Arbuthnot's stable for 2,200 gns last month.
**Ipledgeallegiance(USA)** was going up and down on the spot from the quarter-mile marker.
**Claptrap** was never put in the race at any stage and Ferris was given an eight-day ban for failing to make sufficient effort.

## 6041 BET DIRECT RUGBY PRICES SKY PAGE 372 (S) STKS 6f (F)
3:35 (3:36) (G) 2-Y-O £2,093 (£598; £299) Stalls Low

Form RPR
6006 **1** **Melaina**$^{7}$ 5997 2-8-1 52 ........ (p) JFMcDonald$^{(5)}$ 1 48
(MSSaunders) *prom: led over 4f out: rdn over 2f out: edgd lft over 1f out: drvn out* **7/1**
0064 **2** *1 ¾* **Fisher's Dream**$^{48}$ 5380 2-8-11 44 ........ (v) DarrenWilliams 13 48
(JRNorton) *led over 1f: chsd ldr tl rdn over 2f out: edgd lft ins fnl f: kpt on* **16/1**
6604 **3** *¾* **Philly Dee**$^{50}$ 5324 2-8-3 47 ........ LisaJones$^{(3)}$ 2 41
(JJay) *a.p: wnt 2nd over 2f out: ev ch 1f out: one pce* **5/1**$^{3}$
4460 **4** *1 ¾* **Whittinghamvillage**$^{24}$ 5818 2-8-6 59 ........ FNorton 7 35
(ABerry) *led early: prom: rdn and sltly outpcd 3f out: kpt on ins fnl f* **11/2**
0625 **5** *nk* **City General (IRE)**$^{8}$ 5990 2-8-13 58 ........ (p) LPKeniry$^{(3)}$ 8 44
(JSMoore) *hld up in tch: outpcd 3f out: rallied 2f out: one pce* **3/1**$^{1}$
0065 **6** *nk* **Fayr Firenze (IRE)**$^{7}$ 5997 2-8-11 52 ........ (b) SRighton 6 38
(MFHarris) *prom: outpcd over 3f out: rallied over 1f out: one pce fnl f* **10/1**
0600 **7** *9* **Dress Pearl**$^{56}$ 5191 2-8-6 54 ........ DeanMcKeown 9 6
(ABerry) *bhd fnl 3f* **20/1**
0000 **8** *½* **He's A Rocket (IRE)**$^{8}$ 5990 2-8-6 50 ........ NChalmers$^{(5)}$ 10 10
(MrsCADunnett) *prom tl wknd 3f out* **33/1**
0000 **9** *1 ½* **Almost Royal (IRE)**$^{48}$ 5380 2-8-6 47 ........ NCallan 11 —
(RMBeckett) *prom early: bhd fnl 3f* **14/1**
0 **10** *5* **Millietom (IRE)**$^{20}$ 5876 2-8-11 ........ (p) GParkin 5 —
(KARyan) *s.i.s: outpcd* **9/2**$^{2}$
0000 **11** *5* **Caplaw Song**$^{27}$ 5745 2-8-0 32 ow1 ........ PPMathers$^{(7)}$ 3 —
(ABerry) *s.i.s: outpcd* **50/1**

1m 15.97s (0.27) **Going Correction** 0.0s/f (Stan) **11** Ran SP% **119.0**
Speed ratings: **98,95,94,92,91 91,79,78,76,70 63**CSF £111.33 TOTE £10.20: £3.30, £4.30, £2.20; EX 95.10.The winner was bought in for 4,000gns
**Owner** Bali Royal Racing **Bred** Barry Minty **Trained** Haydon, Somerset
■ Stewards Enquiry : N Chalmers caution: careless riding

**FOCUS**
Most of these have had plenty of chances.

**NOTEBOOK**
**Melaina**, fitted with cheekpieces, was a springer in the market. She found the combination of six furlongs and selling company doing the trick
**Fisher's Dream** was not inconvenienced by a step up from the minimum distance.
**Philly Dee** looks set to score when coming through on the inside turning for home but she failed to deliver the goods.
**Whittinghamvillage** could not take advantage of a drop in grade on this second run on Fibresand.
**City General(IRE)** may need a return to seven.
**Fayr Firenze(IRE)** was back up to six for this first try in a seller.

## 6042 BET DIRECT IN RUNNING SKY TEXT 293 H'CAP (DIV II) 7f (F)
4:10 (4:10) (F) (0-60,60) 3-Y-O+ £2,100 (£600; £300) Stalls High

Form RPR
0000 **1** **Semper Paratus (USA)**$^{19}$ 5892 4-9-7 53 ........ (b) MTebbutt 6 66
(HJCollingridge) *a.p: rdn over 3f out: wnt 2nd 2f out: led ins fnl f: all out* **6/1**
0001 **2** *hd* **Mon Secret (IRE)**$^{39}$ 5540 5-9-9 55 ........ RFfrench 12 68
(BSmart) *bhd tl hdwy over 2f out: hrd rdn over 1f out: ev ch ins fnl f: r.o* **5/1**$^{3}$
3500 **3** *½* **Its Ecco Boy**$^{8}$ 5985 5-9-4 55 ........ DNolan$^{(5)}$ 1 63
(PHowling) *led: rdn over 2f out: hdd ins fnl f: no ex: fin 4th hd, 1¼l & ½l; plcd 3rd* **12/1**
004 **4** *1* **Mr Stylish**$^{2}$ 6032 7-9-7 53 ........ (vt) JDSmith 10 59
(JSMoore) *hld up and bhd: rdn over 2f out: hdwy over 1f out: nt rch ldrs: fin 5th, plcd 4th* **16/1**
3005 **5** *½* **Fabrian**$^{15}$ 5933 5-9-9 55 ........ (e) DaneO'Neill 3 59
(DWPArbuthnot) *prom: rdn and outpcd over 3f out: kpt on ins fnl f: fin 6th, plcd 5th* **4/1**$^{2}$
5000 **6** *½* **Muqarrar (IRE)**$^{51}$ 5300 4-9-8 54 ........ (e$^{1}$) KDalgleish 7 57
(TJFitzgerald) *bhd tl late hdwy: nrst fin: fin 7th, plcd 6th* **20/1**
0100 **7** *½* **Glenrock**$^{39}$ 5540 6-9-2 53 ........ PBradley$^{(5)}$ 9 55
(ABerry) *prom: rdn over 3f out: sn btn: fin 8th, plcd 7th* **25/1**
1442 **8** *½* **Shatin Hero**$^{11}$ 5970 3-9-5 55 ........ (p) SHitchcott$^{(3)}$ 11 56
(GCHChung) *hld up: rdn over 3f out: no rspnse: fin 9th, plcd 8th* **9/4**$^{1}$
0/ **9** *10* **Vijay (IRE)**$^{55}$ 5235 4-9-11 60 ........ (b) DMcGaffin$^{(3)}$ 2 36
(ISemple) *prom tl wknd wl over 1f out: fin 10th, plcd 9th* **16/1**
3000 **10** *15* **Three Days In May**$^{34}$ 5636 4-9-7 60 ........ TO'Brien$^{(7)}$ 4 —
(MRChannon) *hld up in tch: wknd over 2f out: fin 11th, plcd 10th* **25/1**
**11** *1* **Animal Lover (IRE)**$^{21}$ 5860 3-9-8 55 ........ (t) WMLordan 8 —
(THogan, Ire) *a bhd: fin 12th, plcd 11th* **33/1**
0600 **D** *1 ¼* **Game Guru**$^{228}$ 951 4-9-13 59 ........ (b) DeanMcKeown 5 69
(TDBarron) *chsd ldrs: rdn over 2f out: r.o one pce fnl f: fin 3rd, hd & 1¼l: disqualfied for rdr failing to weigh in* **14/1**

1m 30.92s (0.72) **Going Correction** 0.0s/f (Stan)
**WFA** 3 from 4yo+ 1lb **12** Ran SP% **123.2**
Speed ratings: **95,94,92,91,91 90,89,89,77,60 59,93**CSF £35.87 CT £364.89 TOTE £7.30: £1.80, £2.20, £4.30; EX 57.50.
**Owner** The Tin Man Partnership **Bred** Lantern Hill Farm Llc **Trained** Exning, Suffolk
■ Stewards Enquiry : Dean McKeown seven-day ban: failed to weigh in (Dec 1-3,6,8-10)

**FOCUS**
Semper Paratus returned to form having come in for support on the exchanges.

**NOTEBOOK**
**Semper Paratus(USA)** found the re-application of blinkers instead of cheekpieces and a return to Fibresand enabling him to bounce back to form with a hard-fought win. *Official explanation: trainer said, regarding the improved form shown, gelding benefited from the re-application of blinkers and appeared to be better suited by the Fibresand surface*
**Mon Secret(IRE)** is a real seven-furlong specialist. He could not quite peg back the winner off a mark 8lb higher than when he won at Southwell in March.
**Its Ecco Boy** ran a fine race for one who probably barely gets seven on a surface as demanding as this.
**Mr Stylish** had run a similar race in a Southwell seller two days earlier.
**Fabrian** continues to slip down the ratings.
**Muqarrar(IRE)** was fitted with an eyeshield for this first run on sand. He needs a return to further on this evidence.
**Shatin Hero** had been a model of consistency recently for Linda Perratt, but blotted his copybook on his first start for a new yard.
**Game Guru**, two stone lower in the handicap than this time last year, ran well on this comeback.

## 6043 BETDIRECT.CO.UK H'CAP (DIV II) 1m 4f (F)
4:40 (4:41) (F) (0-60,58) 3-Y-O+ £2,044 (£584; £292) Stalls Low

Form RPR
3232 **1** **Easibet Dot Net**$^{11}$ 5971 3-9-4 57 ........ (p) DMcGaffin$^{(3)}$ 6 71
(ISemple) *a.p: rdn over 5f out: led 4f out: clr over 1f out: r.o* **9/4**$^{1}$
0142 **2** *¾* **Ambersong**$^{32}$ 5682 5-9-3 47 ........ FNorton 7 60
(AWCarroll) *hld up and bhd: swtchd rt 4f out: hdwy 3f out: styd on wl ins fnl f: nt rch wnr* **7/2**$^{3}$
-006 **3** *2 ½* **Vandenberghe**$^{20}$ 5881 4-9-5 49 ........ PaulEddery 4 58
(JAOsborne) *hld up: smooth hdwy 5f out: rdn over 2f out: r.o one pce fnl f* **10/1**
4001 **4** *nk* **To Wit To Woo**$^{20}$ 5879 3-9-6 56 ........ MHills 11 65
(BWHills) *hld up mid-div: hdwy over 6f out: chsd wnr 4f out tl no ex ins fnl f* **10/3**$^{2}$

0003 5 16 **Cantemerle (IRE)**[17] 5914 3-9-4 54....(b) SWKelly 10 39
(WMBrisbourne) *bhd: rdn 8f out: nvr nr ldrs* **16/1**
3330 6 3 ½ **Margold (IRE)**[73] 4793 3-8-12 55.... BSwarbrick(7) 9 35
(RHollinshead) *a bhd* **50/1**
6003 7 16 **Geri Roulette**[11] 5971 5-9-7 51.... ANicholls 3 7
(EJAlston) *prom: rdn over 6f out: led briefly over 4f out: wknd 3f out* **14/1**
5326 8 3 ½ **Tarkwa**[86] 4504 4-9-0 44.... MHenry 12 —
(RMHCowell) *hld up: hdwy over 5f out: wknd 3f out* **25/1**
3000 9 ½ **Little Richard (IRE)**[63] 5048 4-8-11 44....(v) DCorby(3) 5 —
(MWellings) *chsd ldrs: rdn over 6f out: wknd over 4f out* **33/1**
4-00 10 18 **Spring Pursuit**[70] 4874 7-9-2 46.... NCallan 2 —
(RJPrice) *sn bhd: t.o* **16/1**
3000 11 18 **Interstice**[11] 5971 6-10-0 58.... SWhitworth 8 —
(AGNewcombe) *hld up in tch: wknd over 4f out: t.o* **12/1**
-000 12 15 **Rivelli (IRE)**[71] 4838 4-9-11 58....(b) LPKeniry(3) 1 —
(BRFoster) *led: hdd over 4f out: wknd over 3f out* **100/1**

2m 39.76s (-1.74) **Going Correction** 0.0s/f (Stan)
**WFA** 3 from 4yo+ 6lb **12** Ran SP% **121.0**
Speed ratings: **105,104,102,102,91 89,78,76,76,64 52,42**CSF £9.90 CT £67.43 TOTE £3.90: £1.10, £1.90, £3.50; EX 12.40 Place 6 £232.36, Place 5 £118.36.
**Owner** www.easibet dot net **Bred** L A C Ashby Newhall Estate Farm **Trained** Carluke, S Lanarks

**FOCUS**
This was won in a time over 1.6 seconds faster than the first division.

**NOTEBOOK**
**Easibet Dot Net** built on the promise of his second here last time and stole enough of an advantage early in the short home straight to hold on.
**Ambersong**, 10lb higher than when landing a seller over course and distance in September, showed why he had tackled further on his next two starts.
**Vandenberghe** ran his best race since finishing second off a 8lb higher mark here last December.
**To Wit To Woo** may well have got found out by the longer trip.
T/Plt: £584.30 to a £1 stake. Pool: £38,782.70. 48.45 winning tickets. T/Qpdt: £418.30 to a £1 stake. Pool: £2,826.70. 5.00 winning tickets. KH

## 5983 SAINT-CLOUD (L-H)
Friday, November 21

**OFFICIAL GOING: Very soft**

### 6044a PRIX TANTIEME (LISTED) 1m
1:45 (1:47) 3-Y-O+ £13,312 (£5,325; £3,994; £2,662)

RPR
1 **Excelsius (IRE)**[20] 5872 3-8-9 .... DBonilla 13 102
(JLDunlop) *drawn 13, soon disputing 2nd on outside, 2nd straight, brought across to stands rails, driven to lead 2f out, ridden out, r* 1
2 2 ½ **Maxwell (FR)**[20] 5884 3-8-12 .... SPasquier 1 100
(MmeCHead-Maarek, France)
3 hd **Lindholm (GER)**[61] 4-9-1 .... TJarnet 9 101
(WernerGlanz, Germany)
4 1 ½ **Eagle Rise (IRE)**[40] 3-8-9 .... ASuborics 7 94
(ASchutz, Germany)
5 1 **Free Taxe (FR)**[20] 4-8-8 .... C-PLemaire 8 89
(J-MBeguigne, France)
6 2 ½ **Eubea (FR)**[40] 4-8-8 .... TGillet 12 84
(ADeRoyer-Dupre, France)
7 snk **Ryono (USA)**[40] 5526 4-9-1 .... TCastanheira 4 91
(PLautner, Germany)
8 snk **Princess Mix (FR)**[197] 1474 4-8-8 .... CStefan 2 83
(JEPease, France)
9 2 ½ **Zalida (IRE)**[29] 3-8-6 .... ACarre 3 78
(AFabre, France)
10 hd **Berber (GER)**[26] 5779 5-8-11 .... KKerekes 6 81
(WFigge, Germany)
11 **Dionello (FR)**[22] 8-8-11 .... FSpanu 10 81
(MmeCBarande-Barbe, France)
12 **Whim (FR)**[36] 5605 4-8-8 .... CSoumillon 5 78
(CBresson, France)
13 **Lugny (FR)**[36] 5605 5-9-1 .... IMendizabal 11 85
(PVanDePoele, France)
14 **Sensible (FR)**[80] 4651 5-8-11 .... TThulliez 14 81
(PBary, France)

1m 49.1s **Going Correction** +0.25s/f (Good)
**WFA** 3 from 4yo+ 2lb 14 Ran SP% **6.8**
Speed ratings: **109,106,106,104,103 101,101,101,98,98 98,98,98,98.**
**Owner** V Schirone **Bred** Allevamento Annarosa Di Schirone Vitantonio **Trained** Arundel, W Sussex

**NOTEBOOK**
**Excelsius(IRE)**gained a belated first win of the season on his favoured soft ground.

## 6018 LINGFIELD (L-H)
Saturday, November 22

**OFFICIAL GOING: Standard**
There appeared to be a fast strip of ground down the centre of the track in the straight.

### 6045 BIG AL'S 50TH BIRTHDAY MAIDEN STKS 5f (P)
12:00 (12:00) (D) 2-Y-O £3,066 (£876; £438) Stalls High

Form RPR
60 1 **Intriguing Glimpse**[29] 5733 2-8-9 .... SDrowne 5 65
(MissBSanders) *trckd ldrs: shkn up 2f out: effrt on outer over 1f out: led ins fnl f: drvn out* **5/1**[3]
0 2 ¾ **Five Years On (IRE)**[25] 5812 2-9-0 .... PRobinson 2 67
(WJHaggas) *b.hind: lw: trckd ldrs: effrt 2f out: rdn and cl up 1f out: sn nt qckn: kpt on nr fin* **6/1**
4402 3 shd **Scottish Exile (IRE)**[8] 5997 2-8-9 60.... DarrenWilliams 3 62
(KRBurke) *pressed ldr: led narrowly over 3f out: rdn over 1f out: hdd and one pce ins fnl f* **3/1**[2]
0 4 hd **Dont Call Me Derek**[25] 5812 2-8-9 .... BReilly(5) 7 70+
(SCWilliams) *s.i.s: hld up in last pair and detached fr rest: prog 2f out: shuffled along and styd on wl fnl f: improve* **16/1**
023 5 1 **After All (IRE)**[25] 5818 2-8-9 62.... SWKelly 6 58
(GAButler) *s.i.s: sn wl in tch: rdn and unable qck wl over 1f out: one pce after* **5/2**[1]
000 6 ½ **Miss Judgement (IRE)**[25] 5812 2-8-9 49.... FNorton 1 56
(WRMuir) *racd on inner: led to over 3f out: pressed ldr after: ev ch 1f out: wknd last 100y* **20/1**
0000 7 ¾ **Crispin Girl (IRE)**[16] 5931 2-8-9 52.... ADaly 9 53
(JLSpearing) *chsd ldrs: rdn and outpcd 2f out: one pce after* **14/1**
0 8 ½ **Clearing Sky (IRE)**[50] 5342 2-8-9 .... IMongan 4 52
(MissZCDavison) *s.i.s: outpcd and detached in last pair: rdn bef 1/2-way: no prog tl kpt on ins fnl f* **25/1**
0400 9 1 ½ **Maxi's Princess (IRE)**[16] 5931 2-8-9 60....(t) DSweeney 10 46
(PJMakin) *b.hind: racd on wd outside: chsd ldrs tl wknd wl over 1f out* **8/1**

60.14 secs (0.36) **Going Correction** +0.125s/f (Slow) **9** Ran SP% **116.8**
Speed ratings: **102,100,100,100,98 97,96,95,93**CSF £35.46 TOTE £6.70: £1.60, £2.20, £1.50; EX 37.20.
**Owner** Edward Hyde **Bred** Copy Xpress Ltd **Trained** Epsom, Surrey

**FOCUS**
A modest maiden.

**NOTEBOOK**
**Intriguing Glimpse**, a half-sister to another Polytrack scorer Another Glimpse, is bred to appreciate this surface and got off the mark on her All-Weather debut. She should pay her way in handicap company.
**Five Years On(IRE)**, a half-brother to three winners abroad, is bred to do better over farther so there was no disgrace in this performance over the minimum trip.
**Scottish Exile(IRE)**ran well again and should find a modest race on this surface in time.
**Dont Call Me Derek**was the eyecatcher, as he finished well under a tender ride after missing the break and being held up off the pace. He is one to keep an eye on and the market will guide regarding his chance in future races. *Official explanation: jockey said gelding was slowly away and resented the kick-back in the first part of the race; trainer said gelding was found to be lame*
**After All(IRE)**, who was sent off favourite for this despite boasting an official rating of just 62, had her chance.

### 6046 BETDIRECT.CO.UK (S) STKS (DIV I) 1m (P)
12:30 (12:31) (G ) 2-Y-O £2,037 (£582; £291) Stalls High

Form RPR
0400 1 **The Job**[22] 5845 2-8-11 65.... WRyan 7 59
(ADSmith) *s.i.s: hld up in last pair: stdy prog fr over 3f out: rdn over 1f out: r.o fnl f to ld last 100y* **7/1**
0400 2 1 ¼ **Delcienne**[40] 5549 2-8-6 50.... NPollard 3 51
(GGMargarson) *led for 2f: w ldr tl led again wl over 2f out: kicked 3l clr on inner wl over 1f out: worn down last 100y* **16/1**
2300 3 ¾ **Lyrical Girl (USA)**[28] 5751 2-8-3 64.... SHitchcott(3) 6 50
(MRChannon) *lw: settled towards rr: hmpd and snatched up over 3f out: rdn and effrt over 2f out: styd on to take 3rd nr fin* **5/2**[1]
6300 4 1 **Hunting Pink**[25] 5816 2-8-6 48.... JFEgan 10 47
(HMorrison) *cl up: lost pl over 5f out: rapid prog on outer to trck ldrs over 4f out: rdn to chse ldr over 1f out: wknd fnl f* **12/1**
0143 5 1 **Armentieres**[8] 5993 2-8-11 55....(b) ADaly 2 50
(JLSpearing) *trckd ldrs: effrt over 3f out: drvn on outer and outpcd 2f out: kpt on ins fnl f* **5/1**[3]
6350 6 1 **Stanhope Forbes (IRE)**[19] 5906 2-8-11 69.... NCallan 4 48
(NPLittmoden) *free to post: cl up: rdn over 2f out: wknd over 1f out* **7/2**[2]
0456 7 1 ¾ **Look No More**[32] 5698 2-8-4 47.... LTreadwell(7) 1 44
(WGMTurner) *cl up on inner: rdn and lost pl over 2f out: struggling after* **16/1**
0000 8 ¾ **Reedsman (IRE)**[50] 5339 2-8-11 49....(b) PRobinson 9 43
(MHTompkins) *dwlt: rcvrd to ld after 2f: hdd wl over 2f out: wknd wl over 1f out* **16/1**
5006 9 1 ¼ **Allodarlin (IRE)**[32] 5689 2-8-7 56 ow1.... ACulhane 11 36
(PFICole) *lw: towards rr: rdn and effrt over 3f out: no prog and btn 2f out* **7/1**
0 10 ¾ **Oh Frigate**[33] 5679 2-8-11 .... DaneO'Neill 5 38
(HCandy) *a towards rr: rdn and brief effrt over 3f out: wknd over 2f out* **33/1**
606 11 12 **Bouncer**[163] 2293 2-8-11 46.... SDrowne 12 12
(WRMuir) *chsd ldrs tl wknd wl over 3f out: t.o 2f out* **50/1**

1m 42.13s (2.62) **Going Correction** +0.125s/f (Slow) **11** Ran SP% **122.7**
Speed ratings: **91,89,89,88,87 86,84,83,82,81 69**CSF £117.89 TOTE £9.50: £2.60, £7.80, £1.50; EX 118.70.The winner was bought in for 7000gns
**Owner** Pertemps Group Limited **Bred** A Smith **Trained** Westward Ho!, Devon

**FOCUS**
A weak seller.

**NOTEBOOK**
**The Job**, who made his debut in the Brocklesby, has been lightly-raced since and this was his first attempt in a seller. This looks his grade.
**Delcienne** ran one of her best races to date on this Polytrack debut. This was a good effort at the weights and a similar race could come her way if she continues to go the right way.
**Lyrical Girl(USA)**, well in at the weights, was stepping up in trip and making her Polytrack debut. This was her first run for Mick Channon and she showed enough to suggest she can make her mark at this level.
**Hunting Pink** had plenty to find at the weights, but is a disappointing sort whatever the case.
**Armentieres**, a disappointing favourite in this grade at Wolverhampton last time, has still to prove she is fully effective on an All-Weather surface.
**Stanhope Forbes(IRE)**, the highest-rated runner in the field, disappointed.
**Reedsman(IRE)** *Official explanation: jockey said colt was checked at the start*

### 6047 BETDIRECT.CO.UK (S) STKS (DIV II) 1m (P)
1:00 (1:00) (G ) 2-Y-O £2,037 (£582; £291) Stalls High

Form RPR
0013 1 **Rowan Pursuit**[10] 5979 2-8-11 63....(b) PRobinson 8 57
(MHTompkins) *settled towards rr: trapped bhd wall of horses fr 3f out to wl over 1f out: plld out and r.o strly fnl f to ld last 75y* **10/11**[1]
000 2 1 ½ **Good Vibrations**[50] 5340 2-8-7 42 ow1.... ACulhane 11 50
(PFICole) *s.s: t.k.h and hld up: nt clr run 3f out: slipped through on inner to ld wl over 1f out: sn 3l clr: hdd last 75y* **20/1**
400 3 1 ¾ **Must Be So**[16] 5931 2-8-6 60.... NPollard 12 45
(DRCElsworth) *b.hind: hld up towards rr: stdy prog gng easily to trck ldrs 2f out: sn outpcd: hrd rdn and styd on same pce fr over 1f out* **7/1**[2]
6600 4 4 **Quarry Island (IRE)**[7] 6003 2-8-6 40.... JoannaBadger 4 36
(PDEvans) *w ldr: led over 3f out: drvn and hdd over 1f out: wknd fnl f* **50/1**
5400 5 1 ½ **Nothing Matters**[22] 5845 2-8-6 43.... FNorton 10 33
(PRChamings) *hld up in last pair: plenty to do whn nt clr run over 2f out: effrt on inner sn after: no ch whn n.m.r 1f out: one pce* **33/1**

0500 **6** *3* **Desert Beau (IRE)**[8] 5994 2-8-11 57....(v[1]) RHavlin 7 31
(MrsPNDutfield) *cl up: rdn to chse ldr wl over 2f out: hanging lft and wknd over 1f out* **10/1[3]**

0550 **7** *nk* **Ynys**[46] 5443 2-8-11 42.... DKinsella 1 30
(BPalling) *racd in midfield: lost pl on inner and in last pair over 2f out: no ch after* **66/1**

040 **8** *½* **Out Of My Way**[80] 4655 2-8-6 35.... RBrisland 5 24
(TMJones) *pushed along in last after 2f: drvn and prog on wd outside to chse ldrs 2f out: wknd over 1f out* **50/1**

2060 **9** *nk* **Costa Del Sol (IRE)**[9] 5990 2-8-6 50.... JFMcDonald(5) 6 29
(JJBridger) *cl up tl wknd fr over 2f out* **12/1**

0000 **10** *10* **Kinda Cute**[50] 5340 2-8-6 40.... MartinDwyer 3 2
(MQuinn) *led to over 3f out: wknd rapidly over 2f out* **33/1**

0000 **11** *nk* **Maggies Choice (IRE)**[8] 5993 2-8-11 53.... IMongan 2 6
(NPLittmoden) *lw: cl up: pushed along over 4f out: wknd rapidly over 2f out* **20/1**

5406 **12** *1 ½* **David's Girl**[25] 5816 2-8-6 53.... NCallan 9 —
(DMorris) *b: racd on outer in midfield: drvn over 4f out: effrt u.p to chse ldrs over 2f out: wkng rapidly whn n.m.r over 1f out* **7/1[2]**

1m 42.14s (2.63) **Going Correction** +0.125s/f (Slow) **12** Ran SP% **115.0**
Speed ratings: **91,89,87,83,82 79,78,78,78,68 67,66**CSF £25.97 TOTE £1.60: £1.10, £4.60, £2.90; EX 28.70.The winner was sold to Colin Clarke for 9000gns
**Owner** Rowan Stud Partnership **Bred** Rowan Farm Stud **Trained** Newmarket, Suffolk

**FOCUS**
Like the first division, this was moderate stuff.

**NOTEBOOK**
**Rowan Pursuit**, third in a decent nursery over seven furlongs here last time, did not have to run up to that form to take this seller. Sold for 9,000gns, she is likely to join John Akehurst.
**Good Vibrations**, making her debut on this surface with plenty to find at the weights, made her effort tight against the far rail and was running on empty when caught by the winner. Had she raced down the centre she would have been much closer.
**Must Be So**, stepping up in trip and dropping in grade for her Polytrack debut, did not find as much as had looked likely and she may be worth a try over seven furlongs.
**Quarry Island(IRE)**, with the visor left off, had it all to do at the weights and was well beaten.
**Nothing Matters** will need to find improvment to win a race.

## 6048 LEVY BOARD CONDITIONS STKS — 6f (P)
**1:35** (1:36) (C) 2-Y-O — **£4,732** (£1,795; £897; £408) **Stalls** Low

Form — RPR

1230 **1** **Petardias Magic (IRE)**[22] 5865 2-8-11 82.... RFfrench 1 83
(EJO'Neill) *lw: chsd ldng pair: rdn to chse ldr over 1f out: sustained chal fnl f to ld nr fin* **7/4[1]**

3106 **2** *nk* **Mister Saif (USA)**[36] 5613 2-9-0 85.... DaneO'Neill 3 85
(RHannon) *lw: pressed ldr: led wl over 2f out: drvn over 1f out: styd on fnl f: hdd nr fin* **11/4[3]**

**3** *nk* **Mr Lambros** 2-8-8.... MartinDwyer 5 78
(AMBalding) *wlike: str: s.s: racd in last tl prog over 2f out: shkn up over 1f out: styd on wl fnl f: nrst fin* **7/1**

1 **4** *3 ½* **Western Roots**[252] 723 2-9-4.... SDrowne 4 78
(PFICole) *racd in 5th: pushed along 1/2-way: rdn and outpcd on outer 2f out: n.d after* **8/1**

52 **5** *hd* **Elusive Kitty (USA)**[26] 5798 2-8-6.... SWKelly 2 65
(GAButler) *lw: chsd ldng trio: drvn over 2f out: one pce and btn wl over 1f out* **5/2[2]**

0006 **6** *14* **Anatom**[50] 5338 2-8-6 40.... FNorton 6 23
(MQuinn) *led to wl over 2f out: stl upsides ldr 2f out: wknd rapidly over 1f out* **150/1**

1m 12.8s (-0.12) **Going Correction** +0.125s/f (Slow) **6** Ran SP% **115.9**
Speed ratings: **105,104,104,99,99 80**CSF £7.26 TOTE £2.90: £1.10, £1.90; EX 10.80.
**Owner** Miss Sarah Diane Warren **Bred** Mountarmstrong Stud **Trained** Newmarket, Suffolk

**FOCUS**
Just an ordinary affair.

**NOTEBOOK**
**Petardias Magic(IRE)**, out of his depth in a French Group Two last time, found this grade more suitable and ran out a narrow winner. A trip to the States or Dubai has been mentioned.
**Mister Saif(USA)**, beaten in a Newmarket nursery off 87 last time, appeared to run his race and gives a good guide as to the strength of the form.
**Mr Lambros**, an 88,000gns half-brother to two juvenile winners, made a cracking start to his career. A slow start did not help matters, but he finished to good effect and should have little trouble in winning a maiden.
**Western Roots**, not seen since winning the first two-year-old race of the year here in March, was nibbled at in the ring and, although no match for the front three, ran respectably.
**Elusive Kitty(USA)**, dropping back from a mile, was most disappointing and it may be this trip was too short.

## 6049 EUROPEAN BREEDERS FUND LITTLEWOODS BET DIRECT FILLIES' RATED STKS (H'CAP) — 1m (P)
**2:05** (2:05) (C) (0-90,89) 3-Y-O+ — **£7,179** (£2,723; £1,361; £618) **Stalls** High

Form — RPR

0312 **1** **Star Of Normandie (USA)**[7] 6004 4-8-4 75.... BReilly(5) 4 87
(GGMargarson) *taken down early and reluctant to go to post: trckd ldrs: cl up gng easily 2f out: shkn up to ld last 150y: sn clr* **5/1[3]**

000 **2** *1 ½* **Amoras (IRE)**[10] 5981 6-8-4 70.... JFEgan 7 79
(JWHills) *stdd s: hld up in last pair: plenty to do whn prog 2f out: r.o wl to take 2nd wl ins fnl f: nt rch wnr* **14/1**

0040 **3** *1 ¼* **Looking Down**[79] 4690 3-8-4 72.... MartinDwyer 10 78
(RHannon) *lw: led to 5f out: pressed ldr tl led again over 2f out: drvn on inner over 1f out: hdd and one pce last 150y* **14/1**

2211 **4** *hd* **Annishirani**[20] 5891 3-8-6 74.... SWKelly 9 79
(GAButler) *plld hrd: led 5f out to over 2f out: one pce over 1f out* **4/1[1]**

0204 **5** *¾* **Duty Paid (IRE)**[20] 5889 3-9-7 89.... TQuinn 12 92
(DRCElsworth) *b.hind: trckd ldrs: cl up and rdn 2f out: nt qckn over 1f out: one pce after* **11/2**

2432 **6** *hd* **Chetak (IRE)**[50] 5341 3-9-4 86.... MHills 8 89
(BWHills) *racd on outer: hld up in rr: prog over 2f out: shuffled along and one pce fr over 1f out* **9/2[2]**

413 **7** *¾* **Sandenista**[26] 5790 3-8-4 72.... WRyan 6 73
(LMCumani) *dwlt: hld up in last pair: prog on inner over 3f out: rdn and one pce fnl 2f* **10/1**

120 **8** *5* **Perfect Love**[18] 5918 3-8-12 80.... SDrowne 2 70
(GAButler) *settled wl in rr: pushed along 1/2-way: drvn and no prog 2f out* **10/1**

**9** *½* **No Frontier (IRE)**[22] 5863 5-8-5 71....(t) WMLordan 1 60
(THogan, Ire) *chsd ldrs: rdn wl over 2f out: wknd rapidly on inner over 1f out* **20/1**

3056 **10** *1 ½* **Zither**[20] 5889 3-9-2 84.... DaneO'Neill 5 69
(RHannon) *lw: chsd ldrs: pushed along and lost pl 1/2-way: struggling in rr after* **14/1**

31-0 **11** *8* **Just A Glimmer**[20] 5889 3-9-0 82.... IMongan 3 49
(LGCottrell) *racd in midfield: wknd 3f out* **16/1**

1m 39.84s (0.33) **Going Correction** +0.125s/f (Slow)
**WFA** 3 from 4yo+ 2lb **11** Ran SP% **121.5**
Speed ratings: **103,101,100,100,99 99,98,93,92,91 83**CSF £75.54 CT £697.73 TOTE £6.80: £2.00, £5.60, £3.20; EX 67.70.
**Owner** Norcroft Park Stud **Bred** Columbiana Farm **Trained** Newmarket, Suffolk

**FOCUS**
A fair handicap run at no more than a reasonable pace.

**NOTEBOOK**
**Star Of Normandie(USA)**, well held in second over an extended nine furlongs at Wolverhampton last time, was not inconvenienced by this drop in trip or switch to Polytrack and won well.
**Amoras(IRE)**, out of form since finishing second at Epsom in July, is on a winning mark and ran well.
**Looking Down**, returning from a short break, has not won for over a year, but this was pleasing.
**Annishirani**, chasing the hat-trick after wins over seven and ten furlongs here on her last two starts, was too keen for her own good.
**Duty Paid(IRE)**, fourth over course and distance in a fillies' Listed race last time, did not look keen when put under pressure and is beginning to look like one to have reservations about. That said, if you do not want to give up on her just yet, further could suit.
**Chetak(IRE)** continues in reasonable form, but still only has a maiden win to her name.

## 6050 BET DIRECT ON 0800 329393 H'CAP — 7f (P)
**2:40** (2:40) (C) (0-95,95) 3-Y-O+ — **£5,150** (£1,953; £976; £444) **Stalls** Low

Form — RPR

5200 **1** **Lygeton Lad**[5] 6013 5-10-0 95....(t) MFenton 14 105
(MissGayKelleway) *b.hind: hld up wl in rr: plenty to do over 2f out: effrt on wd outside over 1f out: str run fnl f to ld last stride* **14/1**

000 **2** *shd* **Incline (IRE)**[18] 5918 4-8-5 77.... RMiles(5) 6 87
(TGMills) *s.i.s: sn in midfield: prog to trck ldrs 2f out: rdn to ld ins fnl f: edgd rt and hdd fnl stride* **25/1**

0000 **3** *½* **Camp Commander (IRE)**[56] 5210 4-9-12 93....(t) DaneO'Neill 12 102
(CEBrittain) *s.s: racd wl in rr: stdy prog fr 3f out: effrt over 1f out: pressed ldr wl ins fnl f: styd on* **20/1**

0153 **4** *1 ¼* **Marshman (IRE)**[14] 5946 4-9-8 89.... PRobinson 10 95
(MHTompkins) *hld up towards rr: rdn and effrt on outer 2f out: hanging lft over 1f out: styd on ins fnl f: nvr able to chal* **6/1[3]**

0010 **5** *hd* **Just Fly**[169] 2161 3-8-13 81.... JFEgan 8 86
(SKirk) *mostly chsd ldr: drvn to chal and upsides ins fnl f: no ex last 100y* **33/1**

0052 **6** *¾* **Quito (IRE)**[3] 6030 6-10-0 95....(b) ACulhane 15 98
(DWChapman) *stdd s: hld up in last: stl last over 1f out: rapid prog fnl f: hopeless task* **8/1**

2154 **7** *nk* **What-A-Dancer (IRE)**[55] 5260 6-8-11 78.... NPollard 11 81
(GASwinbank) *trckd ldrs: rdn 2f out: one pce and no imp fnl f* **12/1**

0120 **8** *hd* **Border Edge**[21] 5873 5-9-0 86....(v) JFMcDonald(5) 3 88
(JJBridger) *sn led and set str pce: drvn over 2f out: hdd & wknd ins fnl f* **16/1**

6314 **9** *½* **Waterside (IRE)**[23] 5838 4-9-1 82.... MHills 16 83
(JWHills) *b.hind: t.k.h: hld up in rr: prog on outer 1/2-way: rdn to chse ldrs 2f out: no imp fnl f* **12/1**

0604 **10** *1* **Certain Justice (USA)**[5] 6013 5-9-4 85.... SDrowne 7 83
(PFICole) *racd in midfield: rdn over 2f out: one pce and no prog over 1f out* **8/1**

14-0 **11** *1 ¼* **Jummana (FR)**[20] 5889 3-9-10 92.... SWKelly 2 87
(GAButler) *trckd ldrs: rdn 2f out: unable qck over 1f out: wknd fnl f* **8/1**

052 **12** *shd* **Golden Chalice (IRE)**[14] 5946 4-9-9 90.... MartinDwyer 13 85
(AMBalding) *lw: racd on outer in midfield: drvn and effrt over 2f out: fdd over 1f out* **11/2[2]**

4050 **13** *5* **Agilis (IRE)**[41] 5506 3-9-1 83.... SWhitworth 9 65
(JamiePoulton) *lw: chsd ldrs: lost pl and pushed along 1/2-way: in rr and struggling over 2f out* **25/1**

0021 **14** *¾* **Flint River**[8] 5996 5-9-0 81.... JFanning 1 62
(HMorrison) *racd on inner: disp 2nd pl to over 2f out: wknd rapidly fnl f* **9/2[1]**

0164 **15** *4* **Gem Bien (USA)**[25] 5814 5-8-12 82.... DCorby(3) 4 53
(AndrewTurnell) *racd on inner in midfield: struggling whn n.m.r over 2f out: wknd over 1f out* **25/1**

1m 25.38s (-0.62) **Going Correction** +0.125s/f (Slow)
**WFA** 3 from 4yo+ 1lb **15** Ran SP% **128.4**
Speed ratings: **108,107,107,105,105 104,104,104,103,102 101,100,95,94,89**CSF £344.44 CT £6985.40 TOTE £20.90: £7.20, £5.10, £5.50; EX 967.20.
**Owner** J McGonagle & B J McGonagle **Bred** Khalifa Abdulla Dasmal **Trained** Newmarket, Suffolk

**FOCUS**
A really competitive handicap run at a decent enough pace.

**NOTEBOOK**
**Lygeton Lad**, well beaten on Fibresand last time, is a different horse round here and came from well off the pace to gain his sixth course win. It goes without saying he must be respected when racing here.
**Incline(IRE)** looked like ending a year-long losing run until being nailed on the line by course specialist Lygeton Lad. He looks up to winning off this sort of mark.
**Camp Commander(IRE)**, without a win since landing the Victoria Cup at Ascot, and 11lb higher than when last running on this surface, ran a cracker.
**Marshman(IRE)**, who won this very race last year, ran respectably off an 8lb higher mark.
**Just Fly** goes well on this surface and, given every chance, he ran well.
**Quito(IRE)** finished well enough from off the pace, but has still to prove his effectiveness on this track.
**Border Edge** ensured there was a decent pace.
**Golden Chalice(IRE)** was a long way below form on this Polytrack debut.
**Flint River** dropped out very tamely. *Official explanation: jockey said gelding had ran flat*

## 6051 LITTLEWOODS BET DIRECT CHURCHILL STKS (LISTED RACE) — 1m 2f (P)
**3:15** (3:15) (A) 3-Y-O+ — **£14,500** (£5,500; £2,750; £1,250) **Stalls** Low

Form — RPR

1220 **1** **Compton Bolter (IRE)**[28] 5752 6-9-2 103.... MartinDwyer 1 106
(GAButler) *hld up wl in rr: in last trio over 2f out: gd prog sn after: swtchd lft to chal over 1f out: battled on wl to ld last strid* **7/2[1]**

1203 **2** *shd* **Grand Passion (IRE)**[21] 5872 3-8-10 103.... JFEgan 2 104
(GWragg) *hld up in midfield: prog on outer over 2f out: led jst over 1f out: sn jnd: r.o u.p: pipped on post* **8/1[2]**

3131 **3** *1 ½* **Windy Britain**[39] 5568 4-8-9 82.... SWKelly 6 96
(LMCumani) *dwlt: hld up in last trio: prog on wd outside 2f out: hanging lft but r.o wl to take 3rd ins fnl f: nt rch ldng pair* **14/1**

1633 **4** ½ **Blue Sky Thinking (IRE)**[16] 5936 4-9-0 90 ................. DarrenWilliams 5 100
(KRBurke) *b: lw: hld up wl in rr: nt clr run and in last pair 3f out: prog wl over 1f out: styd on fnl f: nrst fin* **50/1**

0335 **5** ¾ **Persian Lass (IRE)**[15] 5943 4-8-9 94 .................................. SDrowne 13 94
(PWHarris) *w ldrs: ev ch fr 3f out to jst over 1f out: one pce fnl f* **12/1**[3]

3166 **6** *shd* **Eastern Breeze (IRE)**[14] 5952 5-9-0 96 ............................ PaulEddery 4 98
(PWD'Arcy) *hld up towards rr: rdn and effrt over 2f out: styd on same pce fr over 1f out* **8/1**[2]

0000 **7** 1½ **Rapscallion (GER)**[70] 4878 4-9-0 85 ......................................(b[1]) JTate 8 96
(JMPEustace) *t.k.h: trckd ldrs: rdn and cl up 2f out: fdd fnl f* **50/1**

4121 **8** 2½ **Tadris (USA)**[20] 5889 3-8-7 103 .......................................... RHills 14 88
(MPTregoning) *hld up in rr: prog on outer over 3f out: rdn over 2f out: fdd wl over 1f out* **7/2**[1]

0421 **9** 1¼ **Babodana**[21] 5872 3-8-12 107 ............................................ PRobinson 12 91
(MHTompkins) *lw: led to over 7f out: lost pl sltly over 4f out: effrt again over 2f out: cl up but looking hld whn hmpd over 1f out: nt* **14/1**

1346 **10** 1¼ **Lundy's Lane (IRE)**[35] 5643 3-8-10 107 ................................ IMongan 3 87
(CEBrittain) *s.i.s: hld up tl prog on outer 7f out: led over 3f out to jst over 1f out: wknd rapidly* **8/1**[2]

2324 **11** 1¼ **Tizzy May (FR)**[22] 5853 3-8-10 96 .................................... DaneO'Neill 10 85
(RHannon) *lw: t.k.h: led over 7f out to over 3f out: wknd 2f out* **14/1**

5104 **12** 1¼ **Czarina Waltz**[24] 5827 4-8-9 86 ............................................... RMullen 7 77
(CFWall) *hld up towards rr: rdn and no prog over 2f out: no ch after* **20/1**

041 **13** 6 **Cornelius**[16] 5936 6-9-0 100 ................................................. ACulhane 9 71
(PFICole) *hld up towaards rr: prog on outer over 4f out: rdn and wknd wl over 2f out* **20/1**

00-0 **14** 13 **Sunny Glenn**[22] 5853 5-9-0 85 ............................................ PMcCabe 11 48
(MrsPNDutfield) *prom tl wknd over 3f out: t.o* **200/1**

2m 6.83s (-0.56) **Going Correction** +0.125s/f (Slow)
**WFA** 3 from 4yo+ 4lb **14** Ran SP% **119.4**
Speed ratings: **107,106,105,105,104 104,103,101,100,99 98,97,92,82**CSF £29.85 TOTE £5.60: £2.20, £2.30, £5.40; EX 37.10.
**Owner** Erik Penser **Bred** Rathasker Stud **Trained** Blewbury, Oxon

**FOCUS**
The ratings of the third and fourth placed horses suggests this was just an ordinary Listed event, but take nothing away from Compton Bolter, who was winning this race for the third time. The early pace was just steady.

**NOTEBOOK**
**Compton Bolter(IRE)**, winner of this race in 2000 and 2001, gained his third win in the event and his fourth Listed success of the campaign with a tough performance. This effort was all the more creditable given the fact he raced against the apparently unfavoured far-rail. A gelding, he is sure to be kept on the go for a little longer yet and could race in Dubai this winter.
**Grand Passion(IRE)**, third in this grade over a mile at Newmarket last time, got every yard of this ten furlong trip and only lost out on a bob of the heads. He goes well round here and should be kept on the right side if turning out for some of the better contests round here.
**Windy Britain**, a prolific winner in much lower grade on turf this year, ran a cracker on her first attempt at Listed level and gained some all-important black type.
**Blue Sky Thinking(IRE)**, stepping up in trip and making his Polytrack debut, had 11lb to find with the winner at the weights so ran a fine race in the circumstances.
**Persian Lass(IRE)**, another Polytrack debutant, ran respectably, but looks to fall just short of this level.
**Eastern Breeze(IRE)** would have preferred a stronger pace, but still ran well.
**Rapscallion(GER)**, out of form since winning the 2001 Horris Hill, failed to prove he gets this trip after racing keenly in the first-time blinkers, but still showed a bit more than he has done of late and may just be one to keep an eye on.
**Tadris(USA)**, stepping back up in trip after her success over a mile here in a fillies' Listed race, ran below form and may now be retired.

## 6052 BET DIRECT IN RUNNING SKY TEXT 293 H'CAP 1m 4f (P)
**3:45** (3:45) (C ) (0-95,93) 3-Y-O+ **£5,785** (£1,780; £890; £445) **Stalls** Low

Form RPR

5000 **1** **High Point (IRE)**[35] 5639 5-8-11 **76** ................................. DaneO'Neill 10 87
(GPEnright) *trckd ldr after 2f: rdn over 3f out: led over 1f out: drvn and kpt on wl fnl f* **16/1**

0006 **2** 1 **Gig Harbor**[28] 5753 4-9-5 **84** .................................................. ACulhane 8 93
(MissECLavelle) *trckd ldrs: gng easily over 2f out: rdn and effrt to chal over 1f out: ev ch ent fnl f: nt qckn* **5/1**[2]

3303 **3** ¾ **Typhoon Tilly**[42] 5490 6-8-10 **75** .............................................. SDrowne 7 83
(CREgerton) *t.k.h: cl up: lost pl sltly and rdn over 2f out: renewed effrt over 1f out: pressed ldrs fnl f: one pce* **14/1**

6041 **4** ½ **Maystock**[10] 5975 3-7-7 **69** oh1 ...............................(v) JFMcDonald[(5)] 9 76
(GAButler) *s.i.s: hld up in midfield: prog on outer to chse ldrs over 2f out: nt qckn over 1f out: r.o ins fnl f* **12/1**

1000 **5** 1½ **Gallant Boy (IRE)**[14] 5952 4-9-1 **80** ...................................(t) NCallan 16 85
(PDEvans) *hld up in rr: rdn 3f out: prog u.p over 2f out: one pce over 1f out* **14/1**

5032 **6** *shd* **Nawow**[26] 5795 3-8-9 **80** .................................................. MartinDwyer 14 85
(PDCundell) *sn led: hrd pressed fr over 2f out: hdd & wknd over 1f out* **13/2**[3]

1025 **7** ¾ **Siena Star (IRE)**[28] 5738 5-8-12 **77** ........................................ MHills 2 81
(PFICole) *hld up in rr: stdy prog on inner gng easily over 2f out: shkn up and one pce over 1f out* **10/1**

0455 **8** ½ **Complete Circle**[16] 5935 3-8-13 **84** ...............................(v) PaulEddery 5 87
(PWD'Arcy) *hld up wl in rr: rdn 3f out: sme prog 2f out: no imp ldrs over 1f out* **20/1**

3244 **9** *hd* **Brilliant Red**[98] 4186 10-9-12 **91** ..........................................(t) IMongan 4 94
(JamiePoulton) *lw: s.s: hld up wl in rr: rdn 3f out: no prog tl styd on fnl f* **16/1**

4311 **10** 1 **Golano**[26] 5795 3-8-4 **75** ......................................................... RMullen 11 76
(CFWall) *trckd ldrs: rdn and cl up 3f out: wknd wl over 1f out* **7/2**[1]

5000 **11** *hd* **High Hope (FR)**[47] 5423 5-9-1 **80** ....................................... SWhitworth 12 81
(GLMoore) *hld up in rr: prog to chse ldrs over 2f out: wknd over 1f out* **14/1**

3-50 **12** 3 **Back In Action**[182] 1825 3-8-8 **79** ...........................................(t) RHills 15 75
(MAMagnusson) *b.hind: lw: dwlt: hld up in last trio: shkn up and no prog 3f out: no ch after* **8/1**

2000 **13** ½ **Linning Wine (IRE)**[64] 5042 7-9-11 **93** ........................... LPKeniry[(3)] 13 89
(BGPowell) *hld up in midfield: smooth prog 3f out: trckd ldrs 2f out: rdn and fnd nil over 1f out: wknd* **10/1**

0040 **14** *nk* **Astrocharm (IRE)**[22] 5852 4-8-10 **75** ................................(b) JFanning 6 70
(MHTompkins) *prom on inner tl wknd u.p fr over 2f out* **16/1**

2m 35.48s (1.50) **Going Correction** +0.125s/f (Slow)
**WFA** 3 from 4yo+ 6lb **14** Ran SP% **131.6**
Speed ratings: **100,99,98,98,97 97,96,96,96,95 95,93,93,93**CSF £102.82 CT £1203.74 TOTE £21.30: £7.80, £3.00, £3.70; EX 227.30 Place 6 £581.04, Place 5 £292.48..
**Owner** The Aedean Partnership **Bred** Ballymacoll Stud Farm Ltd **Trained** Lewes, E Sussex

**FOCUS**
Not a bad handicap dominated by a couple of proven Polytrack performers.

**NOTEBOOK**
**High Point(IRE)** carried on where he left off on this surface last winter with a decisive victory. This was his fifth course success and he must be kept on the right side of round here.
**Gig Harbor** took well to this surface in five attempts last winter and ran another solid race. He may be a little high in the weights, but was not helped by the fact Culhane brought him with his challenge against the far-rail.
**Typhoon Tilly** made a very pleasing Polytrack debut over a trip probably on the short side.
**Maystock** found this tougher than the handicap she won over a furlong further here last time and is another who appears to find this trip just on the short side.
**Gallant Boy(IRE)**, only 1lb higher than when winning here earlier in the year, was a little bit below his best and is not particularly consistent.
**Nawow** tried to make every yard and to be fair, did not drop right out when headed.
**Golano**, chasing the hat-trick after a couple of recent wins round here, ran too bad to be true.
**Linning Wine(IRE)** is fully effective round here, but this was disappointing.
T/Plt: £987.10 to a £1 stake. Pool: £26,368.60. 19.50 winning tickets. T/Qpdt: £122.70 to a £1 stake. Pool: £2,520.60. 15.20 winning tickets. JN

# FONTAINEBLEAU
Saturday, November 22

**OFFICIAL GOING: Very soft**

## 6053a PRIX DENISY (LISTED) 1m 7f
**2:00** (1:59) 3-Y-O+ **£13,312** (£5,325; £3,994; £2,662)

RPR

**1** **Le Carre (USA)**[23] 5843 5-9-4 .......................................... CSoumillon 10 —
(ADeRoyer-Dupre, France)

**2** 4 **Albanov (IRE)**[23] 5843 3-8-7 ................................................(b) TJarnet 11 —
(JLDunlop) *tracked leader til led 4f out, headed over 1f out, kept on same pace (72/10 cpld)*

**3** 3 **Terrazzo (USA)**[19] 5912 8-9-7 ................................................ OPlacais 2 —
(NBranchu, France)

**4** ¾ **Soreze (FR)**[23] 5843 5-9-4 ................................................. SPasquier 7 —
(DSepulchre, France)

**5** ¾ **Capo Rosso (FR)**[30] 4-9-1 .................................................. DBourillon 1 —
(ESotteau, France)

**6** *snk* **Contact Dancer (IRE)**[189] 1676 4-9-1 ...................................... ELegrix 6 —
(JLDunlop) *raced in 4th to straight, one pace final 2f (72/10 cpld)*

**7** 1 **Balthazar (FR)**[23] 5843 5-9-1 .................................................. DBonilla 5 —
(ALyon, France)

**8** **Bailamos (GER)**[20] 3-8-10 ............................................... FilipMinarik 8 —
(PSchiergen, Germany)

**9** **Liquido (GER)**[20] 5903 4-9-4 ....................................... LHammer-Hansen 4 —
(HSteinmetz, Germany)

**10** **Herminoe**[24] 5828 3-8-4 ............................................................ TThulliez 9 —
(WRMuir) *led to 4f out, weakened over 2f out (82/1)*

**11** **Kirschblute (GER)**[34] 5659 4-9-1 ........................................ ABoschert 3 —
(ATrybuhl, Germany)

3m 14.0s
**WFA** 3 from 4yo+ 8lb **11** Ran
Speed ratings: .
**Owner** J-R De Aragao Bozano **Bred** Haras Santa Maria De Araras **Trained** France

**NOTEBOOK**
**Albanov(IRE)** took the advantage two out and hugged the stands rail, but he had nothing in reserve when challenged by the eventual winner.
**Contact Dancer(IRE)** was given every chance in the straight, but faded as the race came to an end.
**Herminoe** led until the straight, but dropped out of contention to finish one but last.

# KYOTO (R-H)
Sunday, November 23

**OFFICIAL GOING: Firm**

## 6054a MILE CHAMPIONSHIP (GRADE 1) 1m
**6:40** (12:00) 3-Y-O+ **£510,637** (£203,938; £128,013; £72,924)

RPR

**1** **Durandal (JPN)**[49] 4-9-0 ............................................... KenichiIkezoe 11 116
(MSakaguchi, Japan)

**2** ¾ **Fine Motion (IRE)**[336] 4-8-10 ................................................. YTake 18 111
(YIto, Japan)

**3** 1¼ **Gallant Arrow (JPN)**[196] 3-8-12 .......................................... HMiyuki 3 112
(HSakiyama, Japan)

**4** *nk* **Balance Of Game (JPN)**[147] 4-9-0 ....................... KatsuharuTanaka 10 112
(YMunakata)

**5** ½ **Millennium Bio (JPN)**[168] 5-9-0 ................................................. HShii 13 111
(MRyoke, Japan)

**6** *nk* **Eagle Cafe (USA)**[21] 6-9-0 ................................................... SFujita 8 110
(FKojima, Japan)

**7** *nse* **Eishin Champ (USA)**[175] 3-8-12 ............................................ KAndo 14 110
(TSetoguchi, Japan)

**8** *nse* **Sidewinder (JPN)** 5-9-0 ................................................. YFukunaga 2 110
(SKitahashi, Japan)

**9** *hd* **Special Kaldoun (IRE)**[50] 5385 4-9-0 ...................................... DBoeuf 5 110
(DSmaga, France)

**10** 1 **Magnaten (USA)**[364] 5789 7-9-0 ............................................ OPeslier 7 108
(KazuoFujisawa, Japan)

**11** ½ **My Sole Sound (JPN)**[147] 4-9-0 ............................................ MHonda 16 107
(KatsuichiNishiura, Japan)

**12** *nk* **Osumi Cosmo (JPN)**[168] 4-8-10 .......................................... KTsuneishi 1 102
(TNakao, Japan)

**13** *nse* **Rosado (JPN)**[21] 7-9-0 ....................................................... KTsunoda 9 106
(KHashiguchi, Japan)

**14** *hd* **Telegnosis (JPN)**[77] 4761 4-9-0 ....................................... MKatsuura 17 105
(HSugiura, Japan)

**15** *nse* **Win Kluger (JPN)**[196] 3-8-12 ................................................... KTake 6 105
(SMatsumoto, Japan)

**16** 1 **Tout Seul (IRE)**[50] 5385 3-8-12 ............................................... KFallon 12 103
(RFJohnsonHoughton)

17 *nse* **T M Sunday (JPN)**[238] 7-9-0 ........ SAkiyama 4 103
(NFukushima)
18 *nk* **Il Bacio (JPN)**[49] 6-8-10 ........ SKawashima 15 99
(SKobiyama, Japan)
1m 33.3s
**WFA** 3 from 4yo+ 2lb 18 Ran
Speed ratings: .
**Owner** T Yoshida **Bred** Shadai Farm **Trained** Japan

# 6026 SOUTHWELL (L-H)
## Monday, November 24

**OFFICIAL GOING: Standard**
A major speed bias was in operation and all eight winners raced close to the pace. It also paid to race away from the inside rail up the straight.
Wind: almost nil Weather: fine

## 6055 BET DIRECT THROUGH ATTHERACES AMATEUR RIDERS' H'CAP (DIV I) 1m (F)
12:05 (12:08) (G) (0-60,63) 3-Y-0+ £2,114 (£604; £302) Stalls Low

Form RPR
3322 1 **Rock Concert**[9] 6006 5-11-5 **55** ........ MissEJJones 11 67
(IWMcinnes) *a.p: chsd ldr over 3f out: rdn 2f out: styd on to ld ins last: sn drvn and jst hld on* **9/2**[2]
0602 2 *shd* **Mutarafaa (USA)**[5] 6028 4-10-8 **44** ........ (e) MsCWilliams 9 56
(DShaw) *in tch: hdwy 3f out: rdn 2f out: drvn ent last: kpt on wl jst hld* **6/1**[3]
4051 3 *1 ¾* **Sky Dome (IRE)**[5] 6028 10-11-6 **63** 6ex ........ (v) MrSWarren(7) 10 72
(MHTompkins) *towards rr: hdwy on outer 3f out: kpt on fnl 2f: nrest fin ish* **6/1**[3]
4413 4 *2* **Scramble (USA)**[5] 6028 5-10-13 **52** ........ (bt) MissLEllison(3) 15 57
(BEllison) *cl up: led after 2f: pushed clr 3f out: rdn wl over 1f out: wknd and hdd ins last* **4/1**[1]
0500 5 *nk* **Our Glenard**[52] 5344 4-10-6 **47** ........ MissALTurner(5) 16 51
(SLKeightley) *s.i.s: sn chsng ldrs: rdn along 3f out: kpt on same pce fnl 2f* **25/1**
0026 6 *3 ½* **Disabuse**[63] 5117 3-10-5 **50** ........ MrADuarte(7) 14 47
(SCWilliams) *towards rr: hdwy on outer over 3f out: rdn and edgd lft 2f out: sn no imp* **9/1**
5405 7 *3 ½* **Top Of The Class (IRE)**[9] 6004 6-10-5 **46** ........ (v) MissHayleyBryan(5) 6 36
(PDEvans) *bhd: hdwy 3f out: sn rdn and kpt on: nvr nr ldrs* **20/1**
6030 8 *3* **Storm Shower (IRE)**[7] 6015 5-10-5 **41** ........ (v) MrsMMorris 8 25
(MrsNMacauley) *in tch: wd st: sn rdn and wknd* **28/1**
4646 9 *¾* **Jessinca**[5] 6028 7-10-4 **45** ........ MrWayneLewis(5) 3 27
(APJones) *in tch: rdn along and wd st: sn btn* **20/1**
0506 10 *11* **Halcyon Magic**[26] 5832 5-9-12 **39** ........ (b) MrSRees(5) 2 —
(MissJFeilden) *led 2f: cl up tl rdn along 3f out and sn wknd* **16/1**
5000 11 *6* **Stand By**[39] 5598 6-10-7 **50** ........ (v) WRich(7) 1 —
(TDMccarthy) *cl up: rdn along 3f out: sn wknd* **33/1**
0000 12 *shd* **Larky's Lob**[102] 4110 4-10-9 **50** ........ (e[1]) MrPEvans(5) 5 —
(PaulJohnson) *m idfield: rdn along 1/2-way: sn outpcd* **40/1**
20/0 13 *6* **Presidents Lady**[7] 6016 6-10-1 **42** ........ MrsMarieKing(5) 4 —
(PWHiatt) *chsd ldrs: wkng whn hmpd over 4f out: bhd after* **100/1**
0000 14 *3* **Better Pal**[5] 6027 4-10-13 **54** ........ MissAWallace(5) 12 —
(PRWood) *s.i.s: sn in tch on outer: rdn along 1/2-way and sn wknd* **50/1**
4006 15 *27* **Achilles Rainbow**[5] 6032 4-10-0 **39** ........ MrSDobson(3) 7 —
(KRBurke) *sn outpcd and bhd* **33/1**
1m 45.01s (0.41) **Going Correction** -0.025s/f (Stan)
**WFA** 3 from 4yo+ 2lb 15 Ran SP% 110.7
Speed ratings: **96,95,94,92,91 88,84,81,81,70 64,64,58,55,28**CSF £24.59 CT £153.75 TOTE £5.70: £1.50, £2.10, £2.90; EX 26.20.
**Owner** Ivy House Racing **Bred** Cheveley Park Stud Ltd **Trained** Catwick, E Yorks

**FOCUS**
A modest contest and, with the track again favouring front runners, very few got into it.

**NOTEBOOK**
**Rock Concert**, who likes this surface, was always up with the pace and battled on resolutely when the runner-up came to challenge. She goes very well for an inexperienced rider and all three of her wins have been under a girl.
**Mutarafaa(USA)**is running well at the moment without much reward and was only beaten on the nod. His sole previous victory came in a maiden over this course and distance.
**Sky Dome(IRE)**stayed on down the middle of the track but could not confirm last week's form with Mutarafaa under his 6lb penalty.
**Scramble(USA)**, winner of a division of this race last year off a 4lb lower mark, looked set to follow up when stretching four lengths clear of his field straightening up for home, but at recent meetings here the inside rail has not been the place to be and that may well have been the reason why he faded so dramatically.
**Our Glenard**has gained both his wins over farther and was found wanting for toe over this trip.
**Disabuse**was having only his sixth ever start and gives the impression that he is not completely devoid of ability, but he may need to drop down in grade to get off the mark.
**Achilles Rainbow** *Official explanation: jockey said gelding bled from the nose*

## 6056 BET DIRECT "RED TO BET" FILLIES' H'CAP (DIV I) 6f (F)
12:35 (12:36) (E) (0-70,67) 3-Y-0+ £2,051 (£586; £293) Stalls Low

Form RPR
0000 1 **Grandma Lily (IRE)**[97] 4273 5-9-13 **67** ........ IMongan 1 80
(MCChapman) *chsd ldrs: rdn over 1f out: led ins fnl f: r.o* **7/2**[2]
0530 2 *¾* **Chispa**[19] 5924 5-9-4 **58** ........ DarrenWilliams 10 69
(KRBurke) *led: rdn over 1f out: hdd ins fnl f: kpt on* **5/2**[1]
4006 3 *4* **Carols Choice**[10] 5992 6-8-2 **47** ow2 ........ NChalmers(5) 12 46
(ASadik) *chsd ldr: rdn and ev ch over 1f out: no ex ins fnl f* **10/1**
60-0 4 *1 ¾* **Najaaba (USA)**[43] 5506 3-8-12 **57** ........ AQuinn(5) 5 51
(MissJFeilden) *sn outpcd: hdwy over 1f out: nrst fin* **20/1**
6040 5 *1 ¾* **Bijan (IRE)**[66] 5047 5-7-5 **38** oh1 ........ BSwarbrick(7) 2 27
(RHollinshead) *sn outpcd: hdwy over 1f out: nvr nrr* **8/1**[3]
0004 6 *2 ½* **Ladystgeorge**[38] 5625 4-7-5 **38** oh3 ........ LiamJones(7) 11 19
(MMullineaux) *chsd ldrs: rdn 1/2-way: wknd wl over 1f out* **66/1**
500 7 *½* **Sweet Coral (FR)**[48] 5433 3-8-3 **43** ........ JoannaBadger 4 23
(BSRothwell) *mid-div: hmpd and lost pl over 4f out: n.d after* **33/1**
0450 8 *1* **Lady Natilda**[18] 5933 3-8-13 **53** ........ (b[1]) PaulEddery 6 30
(DHaydnJones) *rr: hdwy 1/2-way: wknd wl over 1f out* **9/1**
130 9 *¾* **Certa Cito**[34] 5685 3-9-8 **62** ........ KDalgleish 7 36
(TDEasterby) *dwlt and hmpd s: outpcd* **10/1**
0005 10 *nk* **Penny Valentine**[54] 5304 3-7-5 **38** ........ DFentiman(7) 8 11
(JRBest) *sn outpcd* **14/1**
3500 11 *4* **Mabel Riley (IRE)**[25] 5837 3-8-6 **49** ........ LisaJones(3) 3 10
(MABuckley) *chsd ldrs: n.m.r and wknd 1/2-way* **17/2**
500- 12 *5* **Aunt Doris**[415] 5091 6-7-12 **45** ow6 ........ (e[1]) SarahMitchell(7) 9 —
(PaulJohnson) *broke wl: lost pl over 4f out: sn bhd* **66/1**
1m 16.51s (-0.29) **Going Correction** -0.025s/f (Stan) 12 Ran SP% 118.0
Speed ratings: **100,99,93,91,89 85,85,83,82,82 76,70**CSF £12.18 CT £80.00 TOTE £4.90: £1.50, £1.20, £5.40; EX 9.90.
**Owner** David Fravigar,Alan Mann,David Marshall **Bred** G D Waters **Trained** Market Rasen, Lincs

**FOCUS**
A modest handicap and the front three were to the fore throughout.

**NOTEBOOK**
**Grandma Lily(IRE)**, reunited with the last jockey to win on her and racing for the first time in three months, was given a shrewd ride. Despite racing tight to the inside rail on the home turn, she was brought wide once into the straight and was produced at just the right time to score. She has a good record on Fibresand but did show an ungainly head-carriage during the course of this race.
**Chispa**, dropped 4lb since her last run on sand, showed plenty of early speed but was just worn down. She is nothing like as good as she was, but still has enough ability to win a similar contest on this surface.
**Carols Choice**was helped by racing prominently on a speed-favouring track, but is still to win beyond the minimum trip.
**Najaaba(USA)**, who would have needed her outing at Goodwood last month having previously been off the track for a year, showed a bit more here and this was not a bad performance against the track bias.
**Bijan(IRE)**, without a win in two years, ideally needs at least another furlong to show her best.
**Ladystgeorge**is only moderate, but would have been done no favours by racing tight to the inside rail.

## 6057 BET DIRECT THROUGH ATTHERACES AMATEUR RIDERS' H'CAP (DIV II) 1m (F)
1:05 (1:05) (G) (0-60,60) 3-Y-0+ £2,107 (£602; £301) Stalls Low

Form RPR
4000 1 **Mister Benji**[39] 5598 4-10-7 51 ........ (p) MrEDehdashti(5) 14 63
(BPJBaugh) *cl up: led briefly over 2f out: sn ridde: edgd lft and hdd 2f out: rallied u.p to ld ins last: styd on* **33/1**
6504 2 *2* **Shifty**[5] 6026 4-10-10 54 ........ (b) MissKellyHarrison(5) 13 62
(DNicholls) *cl up on outer gng wl: effrt to ld 2f out: rdn and hung bdly rt fr 11/2f out: hdd ins last: one pce* **11/2**[2]
3063 3 *2 ½* **Levantine (IRE)**[5] 6027 6-10-2 41 ........ (p) MissCHannaford 11 44
(AGNewcombe) *led: rdn along 3f out: sn hdd and n.m.r 2f out: drvn and kpt on same pce* **4/1**[1]
0-00 4 *3 ½* **Flambe**[141] 3035 5-11-2 60 ........ MrBHaslam(5) 5 56
(PCHaslam) *midfield: hdwy on inner over 3f out: rdn and kpt on fnl 2f: nrst fin* **13/2**[3]
2460 5 *shd* **Qobtaan (USA)**[164] 2340 4-10-8 47 ........ MrsSBosley 9 43
(MRBosley) *towards rr: hdwy 2f out: rdn and styd on ins last: nrst fin* **16/1**
0003 6 *shd* **Maggie's Pet**[5] 6026 6-10-2 46 ........ (t) MissJoeyEllis(5) 15 42
(KBell) *in tch: rdn along 3f out: kpt on same pce fnl 2f* **7/1**
U065 7 *hd* **Brilliantrio**[5] 6032 5-10-3 49 ........ (t) MissSArnold(7) 1 44
(MCChapman) *trckd ldrs: hdwy on inner 3f out: rdn and ev ch over 2f out: wknd wl over 1f out* **14/1**
0604 8 *1* **Proud Victor (IRE)**[5] 6027 3-10-1 45 ........ (v) MrSDobson(3) 12 38
(DShaw) *towards rr: wd st: hdwy 2f out: sn rdn and styd on ins last: nrst fin* **11/1**
0000 9 *5* **Our Destiny**[35] 5680 5-9-8 40 ........ (v) MissETucker(7) 4 23
(DBurchell) *in tch: rdn along over 3f out: grad wknd* **14/1**
6253 10 *3 ½* **The Gay Fox**[91] 9-9-10 42 ........ (bt) MrsRPowell(7) 10 18
(BGPowell) *nvr nr ldrs* **12/1**
0000 11 *shd* **Abaninetoes (IRE)**[14] 5969 3-9-9 41 ........ MissHayleyBryan(5) 6 17
(PDEvans) *in tch: rdn along after 3f: sn lost pce and bhd* **100/1**
3400 12 *2 ½* **Spanish Star**[238] 880 6-10-6 45 ........ MrsMMorris 2 16
(MrsNMacauley) *a rr* **16/1**
0-00 13 *6* **Torzal**[223] 1071 3-9-8 40 ........ MissALTurner(5) 16 —
(RFMarvin) *a rr* **100/1**
4032 14 *¾* **Scurra**[27] 5819 4-10-7 53 ........ MrEWhillans(7) 3 11
(ACWhillans) *chsd ldrs: rdn along 1/2-way: sn weaken ed* **16/1**
0-00 15 *10* **Waterline Spirit**[181] 1888 3-10-7 48 ........ MissEJJones 8 —
(PDEvans) *prom: rdn along over 3f out: sn wknd* **100/1**
0050 16 *16* **The Gambler**[112] 3835 3-10-11 57 ........ (e[1]) MrPEvans(5) 7 —
(PaulJohnson) *a rr* **25/1**
1m 45.01s (0.41) **Going Correction** -0.025s/f (Stan)
**WFA** 3 from 4yo+ 2lb 16 Ran SP% 118.0
Speed ratings: **96,94,91,88,87 87,87,86,81,78 78,75,69,68,58 42**CSF £198.43 CT £703.88 TOTE £25.60: £6.60, £1.10, £1.70, £2.20; EX 145.60.
**Owner** J H Chrimes And Mr & Mrs G W Hannam **Bred** D J And Mrs K D Smart **Trained** Audley, Staffs
■ Stewards Enquiry : Mr E Dehdashti one-day ban: failed to keep straight from stalls (Dec 26)

**FOCUS**
Another modest contest, run in an identical time to the first division. Again those that raced up with the pace dominated.

**NOTEBOOK**
**Mister Benji**is a light of former days, but is now off a mark 43lb lower than as a juvenile and that was enough for him to score under a positive ride. He was fortunate to do so, however, as his talented amateur managed to keep him straight while the runner-up decided to come home via the Tattersalls lawn.
**Shifty**looked to be travelling best on the outside of the leaders turning in and the race appeared his for the taking halfway down the straight, but he then lived up to his name by starting to hang violently to his right. His rider made no attempt to correct her whip hand and he ended up right against the stands' rail with the result that the combination had the race snatched from them.
**Levantine(IRE)**does not look an ideal mount for an amateur, but was given a positive ride and that enabled him to finish as close as he did.
**Flambe**, racing for the first time in four months, did best of those coming from off the pace.
**Qobtaan(USA)**, off since June, made some late headway but remains a maiden after 15 attempts.
**Maggie's Pet**again looked to need farther.
**Brilliantrio**ultimately did worst of the four leaders who turned for home in a line across the track, but she was racing tight against the inside rail and that would not have done her any favours.

## 6058 BET DIRECT IN RUNNING (S) STKS 7f (F)
1:40 (1:41) (G) 2-Y-O £2,135 (£610; £305) Stalls Low

Form RPR
0350 1 **Could She Be Magic (IRE)**[20] 5913 2-8-6 56 ........ KDalgleish 5 59
(TDEasterby) *w ldrs: led over 4f out: rdn clr over 1f out: styd on* **7/2**[1]
5100 2 *3* **Chase The Rainbow**[10] 5994 2-8-11 59 ........ JFanning 6 56
(MJohnston) *a.p: chsd wnr over 2f out: rdn over 1f out: styd on same pce* **13/2**[3]
6505 3 *¾* **Rare Coincidence**[27] 5816 2-8-11 54 ........ (p) SRighton 16 54
(RFFisher) *s.s: hdwy over 4f out: rdn and hung lft over 1f out: styd on same pce* **10/1**


The Form Book, Raceform Ltd, Compton, RG20 6NL

0000 **4** *2* **Salut Saint Cloud**[21] 5905 2-8-4 45 .....(v) LTreadwell(7) 7 49
(MissVHaigh) *hld up: outpcd over 2f out: styd on ins fnl f* **40/1**

2606 **5** *shd* **Pardon Moi**[33] 5707 2-8-11 49 ..... DaneO'Neill 15 49
(MrsCADunnett) *chsd ldrs: rdn over 2f out: wknd over 1f out* **12/1**

460 **6** *3 1/2* **Comic Genius**[59] 5198 2-8-6 45 ..... PaulEddery 2 35
(DHaydnJones) *hld up: rdn over 2f out: nvr trbld ldrs* **8/1**

0466 **7** *shd* **Yamato Pink**[10] 5993 2-8-6 49 ..... JoannaBadger 4 35
(KRBurke) *s.i.s: hld up: hdwy u.p over 2f out: no imp over 1f out* **14/1**

4040 **8** *5* **Soleil D'Hiver**[83] 4645 2-7-13 45 ..... RoryMoore(7) 9 22
(PCHaslam) *led: hdd over 4f out: wknd 2f out* **12/1**

000 **9** *nk* **Casantella**[7] 6012 2-7-13 50 .....(v[1]) SaleemGolam(7) 10 22
(MGQuinlan) *prom to 1/2-way* **50/1**

0000 **10** *3 1/2* **Reedsman (IRE)**[2] 6046 2-8-11 49 .....(b) NCallan 3 18
(MHTompkins) *chsd ldrs over 4f* **14/1**

4002 **11** *nk* **Delcienne**[2] 6046 2-8-6 50 ..... NPollard 14 12
(GGMargarson) *chsd ldrs over 4f* **11/2**[2]

200 **12** *2* **Jimmy Gee (IRE)**[38] 5621 2-8-11 49 ..... ANicholls 13 12
(DNicholls) *sn outpcd and bhd* **16/1**

00 **13** *shd* **Jocks Boy**[18] 5930 2-8-6 ..... NChalmers(5) 8 12
(PRWood) *prom to 1/2-way* **50/1**

**14** *12* **Posh Sheelagh** 2-8-7 ow1 ..... MFenton 1 —
(JGGiven) *dwlt: outpcd* **16/1**

005 **15** *nk* **Secret Bloom**[35] 5679 2-8-11 43 ..... VHalliday 12 —
(JRNorton) *dwlt: outpcd* **100/1**

1m 31.17s (0.37) **Going Correction** -0.025s/f (Stan) **15 Ran SP% 119.0**
Speed ratings: **96,92,91,89,89 85,85,79,79,75 74,72,72,58,58**CSF £24.11 TOTE £4.80: £1.70, £1.90, £3.00; EX 28.10.The winner was bought in for 7,000gns
**Owner** Malcolm Caine **Bred** Miss Ciara Doyle **Trained** Great Habton, N Yorks

**FOCUS**
A modest seller in which it was crucial to be close to the pace, and very few got into it.

**NOTEBOOK**
**Could She Be Magic(IRE)**, very well backed on this drop into selling company, was always in the ideal position close to the pace and had little difficulty in pulling away from some modest rivals. Connections managed to retain her for 7,000gns at the subsequent auction and she may be able to hold her own in slightly better company on this surface.
**Chase The Rainbow**, whose best form on turf was on fast ground, ran much better than on her Fibresand debut and could find an ordinary seller.
**Rare Coincidence**has developed a habit of starting slowly and on this speed-favouring track that was always going to be a massive handicap. Despite that he managed to throw down a challenge in the straight, but then added to his problems by hanging left into the deeper stuff. All in all this performance was better than it looks and there could be a small race in him when things go right.
**Salut Saint Cloud**did make a little headway, but has nothing in the way of scope.
**Pardon Moi**showed good early pace under a positive ride and that was a big advantage on this track. A drop back to six might help.
**Reedsman(IRE)** *Official explanation: jockey said colt hung right*
**Delcienne**, runner-up in a Polytrack seller just 48 hours earlier, ran a stinker on this switch to Fibresand. *Official explanation: jockey said filly was unsuited by the ground*

## 6059 BETDIRECT.CO.UK NOVICE STKS 1m (F)
**2:10** (2:11) (D ) 2-Y-O **£3,052** (£872; £436) **Stalls** Low

Form RPR

2321 **1** **Countrywide Flyer (IRE)**[39] 5599 2-8-12 82 ..... NCallan 9 84
(TDBarron) *a.p: hdwy to chal over 2f out: sn drvn and hung persistently lft thrght fnl 2f: hrd rdn and led nr line* **13/8**[1]

2441 **2** *nk* **Queenstown (IRE)**[32] 5715 2-8-13 88 .....(b) LPKeniry(3) 12 88
(BJMeehan) *led: rdn along and jnd over 2f out: hrd drvn over 1f out: hdd and no ex nr line* **11/2**

4326 **3** *2 1/2* **Weet A Head (IRE)**[31] 5726 2-9-2 85 ..... ACulhane 8 82
(RHollinshead) *in tch: hdwy to chse ldng pair over 2f out: sn rdn: kpt on ins last* **7/2**[2]

0 **4** *9* **Blue Java**[30] 5757 2-8-12 ..... KDalgleish 4 58
(HMorrison) *bhd: hdwy 3f out: rdn and kpt on appr last: nvr nr ldrs* **20/1**

5000 **5** *hd* **Thevenis**[49] 5421 2-8-12 59 ..... RFfrench 13 58
(JSKing) *in tch on outer: rdn along 3f out: sn one pce* **50/1**

00 **6** *1 1/2* **Wake Up Henry**[11] 5984 2-8-12 ..... DaneO'Neill 5 55
(RCharlton) *chsd ldrs: rdn over 2f out: grad wknd* **25/1**

0 **7** *5* **Queen's Fantasy**[18] 5932 2-8-7 ..... PaulEddery 2 39
(DHaydnJones) *a bhd* **100/1**

5220 **8** *3/4* **Carriacou**[23] 5871 2-8-2 80 ..... BReilly(5) 3 37
(PWD'Arcy) *towards rr: pushed along whn hmpd bnd after 3f: no ch after* **5/1**[3]

2400 **9** *2 1/2* **Cottingham (IRE)**[46] 5459 2-8-5 67 ..... AndrewWebb(7) 1 37
(MCChapman) *a rr* **50/1**

4006 **10** *shd* **First Acorn**[48] 5443 2-8-7 42 .....(p) NPollard 7 31
(GMMoore) *a rr* **100/1**

1 **11** *1 1/2* **Freddie Freccles**[34] 5691 2-9-0 ..... MFenton 6 35
(JGGiven) *towards rr whn hmpd bnd after 3f and no ch after* **12/1**

2060 **12** *3 1/2* **Ceasar (IRE)**[41] 5557 2-8-5 58 ..... PDineley(7) 10 25
(PCHaslam) *towards rr whn hmpd bnd after 3f: no ch after* **66/1**

0 **13** *2 1/2* **Over The Years (USA)**[18] 5932 2-8-12 ..... DaleGibson 14 20
(TPTate) *s.i.s: a rr* **100/1**

5003 **14** *17* **City Affair**[32] 5721 2-8-9 62 .....(b) DCorby(3) 11 —
(MrsLCJewell) *prom: rdn along over 3f out: sn wknd* **25/1**

1m 42.72s (-1.88) **Going Correction** -0.025s/f (Stan) **14 Ran SP% 120.9**
Speed ratings: **108,107,105,96,96 94,89,88,86,86 84,81,78,61**CSF £10.14 TOTE £3.00: £1.20, £2.60, £1.70; EX 14.40.
**Owner** Nigel Shields **Bred** Gay O'Callaghan **Trained** Maunby, N Yorks

**FOCUS**
A decent event of its type, run at a cracking gallop. The winning time was 2.29 seconds faster than both divisions of the amateur riders' contest.

**NOTEBOOK**
**Countrywide Flyer(IRE)**, bought for 19,500gns by current connections after winning over course and distance last month, had to battle very hard to get the better of a prolonged battle with the runner-up and managed to force his head in front on the line. The winning time was very good so the form may be solid and he can continue to gradually recoup his purchase price.
**Queenstown(IRE)**ran a blinder on this sand debut, although it has to be said that his style of running was perfectly suited to the way the track was riding. Even so he should be able to find a race on sand without too much difficulty.
**Weet A Head(IRE)**ran a perfectly acceptable sand debut and pulled a mile clear of the rest. His stable know how to campaign a horse on Fibresand to maximum effect.
**Blue Java**was beaten out of sight by the three market leaders but deserves credit for doing best of those that raced off the pace on only his second racecourse appearance.
**Thevenis**, unplaced in five previous starts, probably did not achieve much here.
**Carriacou**got into a barging match with Freddie Freccles on the home bend which would have done her few favours, but she was already well off the pace at the time. We did not learn anything new about her here.
**Freddie Freccles**got into a barging match with Carriacou on the home bend which made an already difficult task impossible.

## 6060 LITTLEWOODS BET DIRECT MAIDEN STKS 1m 4f (F)
**2:45** (2:47) (D ) 3-Y-O+ **£2,275** (£650; £325) **Stalls** Low

Form RPR

-352 **1** **Bucks**[12] 5978 6-9-4 65 ..... IMongan 2 78+
(DKIvory) *chsd ldrs: led 2f out: rdn clr* **11/4**[1]

3060 **2** *8* **Sea Holly (IRE)**[33] 5709 3-8-12 74 ..... KDalgleish 15 66
(GGMargarson) *chsd ldrs: rdn over 2f out: styd on same pce appr fnl f* **7/2**[2]

2625 **3** *1 3/4* **Wasted Talent (IRE)**[12] 5980 3-8-7 68 .....(p) RHavlin 11 59
(JGPortman) *chsd ldrs: led over 5f out: hdd 2f out: sn outpcd* **4/1**[3]

0 **4** *6* **Fortunes Favourite**[20] 5917 3-8-7 ..... NPollard 13 50
(GMMoore) *hld up: hdwy over 2f out: sn hung lft: n.d* **50/1**

0500 **5** *5* **Calcar (IRE)**[20] 5917 3-8-12 44 ..... SWhitworth 9 47
(MrsSLamyman) *hdwy 8f out: ev ch 3f out: wknd wl over 1f out* **50/1**

-500 **6** *3 1/2* **Berkeley Heights**[139] 3085 3-8-7 66 ..... RFfrench 14 37
(BSmart) *prom: lost pl over 6f out: sn bhd* **16/1**

B362 **7** *1/2* **T K O Gym**[70] 4948 4-9-4 42 ..... JoannaBadger 12 41
(DNicholls) *plld hrd and prom: lost pl after 2f: hdwy 7f out: wknd over 3f out* **14/1**

3005 **8** *1 3/4* **Ashtaroute (USA)**[20] 5914 3-8-0 46 ..... AndrewWebb(7) 5 33
(MCChapman) *sn outpcd* **33/1**

-640 **9** *14* **Desert Heat**[28] 5799 5-9-4 70 ..... DaneO'Neill 4 17
(ISemple) *led 1f: remained handy tl wknd 3f out* **8/1**

6-00 **10** *3* **Sweet Aroma**[59] 5203 4-8-6 26 ..... StevenHarrison(7) 16 8
(MrsNMacauley) *sn outpcd* **100/1**

/060 **11** *5* **My Mate Henry**[16] 5951 4-9-4 45 ..... DeanMcKeown 7 5
(TTClement) *s.i.s: rcvrd to ld after 1f: hdd over 5f out: wknd over 3f out* **66/1**

**12** *15* **Briar (CZE)**[45] 4-9-1 ..... DCorby(3) 1 —
(MPitman) *sn outpcd* **13/2**

0556 **13** *20* **Mon Petit Diamant**[115] 3049 3-8-0 40 ..... MNem(7) 6 —
(MJPolglase) *s.i.s: sn prom: wknd 7f out* **50/1**

0 **14** *6* **Full English**[9] 6005 4-8-10 ..... LisaJones(3) 8 —
(APJones) *chsd ldrs: rdn 8f out: wknd over 6f out* **100/1**

**15** *20* **Tadzio**[11] 4-8-13 ..... BReilly(5) 10 —
(MJGingell) *sn outpcd* **100/1**

2m 39.83s (-2.27) **Going Correction** -0.025s/f (Stan)
**WFA** 3 from 4yo+ 6lb **15 Ran SP% 119.2**
Speed ratings: **106,100,99,95,92 89,89,88,79,77 73,63,50,46,33**CSF £11.54 TOTE £4.50: £1.60, £1.20, £1.90; EX 19.20.
**Owner** M Murphy **Bred** Meon Valley Stud **Trained** Radlett, Herts

**FOCUS**
A fair maiden of its type and a very easy winner.

**NOTEBOOK**
**Bucks**was travelling best from a long way out and treated his younger rivals with contempt. He should have broken his duck before now, though that is not really his fault, and there are more races to be won with him on this surface provided he is professionally ridden.
**Sea Holly(IRE)**had a big chance on official ratings but, despite running with credit, he did look one-paced in the latter stages.
**Wasted Talent(IRE)**ran up to his best under a positive ride but remains a maiden after 21 attempts.
**Fortunes Favourite**was having only her second ever start so was not as streetwise as the front three, and under the circumstances this was not a bad effort.
**Briar(CZE)**, an experienced hurdler running on the Flat for the first time in this country, ran too poorly to be true.

## 6061 BET DIRECT IN RUNNING SKY TEXT 293 H'CAP 1m 6f (F)
**3:15** (3:15) (E ) (0-75,75) 3-Y-O+ **£2,072** (£592; £296) **Stalls** Low

Form RPR

3031 **1** **Macaroni Gold (IRE)**[5] 6033 3-8-8 **63** 6ex ..... MTebbutt 8 73
(WJarvis) *trckd ldrs: smooth hdwy over 4f out: shkn up to ld over 2f out: rdn and hung lft and rt 1 1/2f out: drvn and styd on ins las* **15/8**[1]

5452 **2** *3/4* **Glory Quest (USA)**[10] 5999 6-10-0 **75** ..... ACulhane 9 84
(MissGayKelleway) *hld up: stdy hdwy over 5f out: chal 2f out: sn rdn and ev ch tl drvn and nt qckn wl ins last* **3/1**[2]

2004 **3** *6* **Forever My Lord**[12] 5982 5-8-0 **54** ..... DFentiman(7) 10 55
(JRBest) *led: clr 1/2-way: rdn along over 3f out: hdd over 2 out: kpt on same pce* **20/1**

6500 **4** *13* **Simple Ideals (USA)**[38] 5624 9-7-12 **45** oh18 ..... KimTinkler 6 29
(DonEnricoIncisa) *trckd ldrs: rdn along over 4f out: wknd over 2f out* **20/1**

6050 **5** *6* **Lapadar (IRE)**[7] 6017 4-9-4 **65** .....(p) DaneO'Neill 2 42
(JRWeymes) *c hased ldr: rdn along over 5f out: wknd over 3f out* **100/1**

5511 **6** *2 1/2* **Vin Du Pays**[14] 5972 3-9-4 **73** ..... NCallan 3 46
(MBlanshard) *hld up in tch: pushed along 6f out: rdn over 4f out and no hdwy* **5/1**[3]

1040 **7** *14* **Dash Of Magic**[48] 5442 5-7-12 **45** oh2 ..... DaleGibson 5 —
(JHetherton) *towards rr: hdwy 6f out: sn rdn along and nvr a factor* **33/1**

-000 **8** *11* **Crossed Wire**[24] 5855 5-9-1 **67** ..... AQuinn(5) 4 8
(MissJFeilden) *chsd ldrs: rdn along 6f out: sn wknd* **25/1**

0603 **9** *1 1/4* **In Luck**[20] 5917 5-8-5 **52** ..... RFfrench 7 —
(BSmart) *hld up in rr: effrt and sme hdwy 6f out: sn rdn along and nvr a factor* **5/1**[3]

1361 **10** *9* **Humdinger (IRE)**[83] 4639 3-8-5 **63** ..... LisaJones(3) 1 —
(DShaw) *chsd ldrs: rdn along over 6f out: sn wknd* **16/1**

3m 7.39s (-2.21) **Going Correction** -0.025s/f (Stan)
**WFA** 3 from 4yo+ 8lb **10 Ran SP% 116.3**
Speed ratings: **105,104,101,93,90 88,80,74,73,68**CSF £6.91 CT £82.24 TOTE £2.60: £1.10, £1.40, £4.30; EX 7.50.
**Owner** Dr J Walker **Bred** Thomas Stacey **Trained** Newmarket, Suffolk

**FOCUS**
Very few got into this.

**NOTEBOOK**
**Macaroni Gold(IRE)**looked sure to score easily turning in but he did not find as much under pressure as his rider expected. Hanging left in the straight, he eventually did just enough. He is lightly raced enough to find further improvement and a return to two miles should suit.
**Glory Quest(USA)**, a solid Fibresand performer, once again ran a solid race on his favoured surface. He finished clear of the rest and can soon go one better.
**Forever My Lord**, having his first outing on Fibresand, did not get home having made most of the running. He does stay farther than this but a faster surface is more suitable.
**Simple Ideals(USA)**had little chance from way out of the handicap.
**In Luck**, who is still a maiden, was having her first start for her new stable. She has shown nothing in two starts on Fibresand.

## 6062 BET DIRECT "RED TO BET" FILLIES' H'CAP (DIV II) 6f (F)
3:45 (3:45) (E) (0-70,67) 3-Y-O+ £2,044 (£584; £292) Stalls Low

Form RPR
0221 1 **Perfect Night**[14] 5969 3-9-13 67 .......... DaneO'Neill 5 77
(RCharlton) *chsd ldrs: led 2f out: edgd lft fnl f: rdn out* **1/1**[1]
5006 2 1 1/4 **Eastern Blue (IRE)**[42] 5546 4-8-8 48 .......... (p) IMongan 10 54
(MrsLStubbs) *hld up in tch: outpcd over 2f out: r.o ins fnl f* **8/1**
6460 3 1/2 **Lake Eyre (IRE)**[10] 5998 4-8-0 40 oh1 ow2 .......... ANicholls 4 45
(JBalding) *led 4f: styd on u.p* **16/1**
4006 4 1 1/4 **Inching**[11] 5988 3-9-3 57 .......... (v[1]) MHenry 6 58
(RMHCowell) *dwlt: sn chsng ldrs: rdn over 2f out: styd on same pce fnl f* **14/1**
3350 5 3/4 **Sharoura**[42] 5546 7-8-11 52 ow6 .......... DSwift(7) 7 57
(RAFahey) *chsd ldrs: sn pushed along: no imp fnl f* **13/2**[3]
6000 6 1 1/2 **Eager Angel (IRE)**[5] 6027 5-7-12 38 oh1 ow5 .......... (p) RThomas(5) 8 37
(RFMarvin) *hld up: rdn over 2f out: nvr trbld ldrs* **25/1**
3001 7 nk **Ally Makbul**[10] 5998 3-8-8 55 .......... DFentiman(7) 11 48
(JRBest) *chsd ldrs: rdn over 2f out: styng on same pce whn edgd rt over 1f out* **5/1**[2]
0000 8 2 1/2 **Court Music (IRE)**[13] 5704 4-8-1 41 .......... (v[1]) RFfrench 9 27
(REBarr) *sn outpcd* **20/1**
04-0 9 3 1/2 **Pat's Miracle (IRE)**[24] 5856 3-8-4 44 .......... JoannaBadger 1 19
(JohnBerry) *dwlt: outpcd* **66/1**
0/0 10 3/4 **Sugar Cube Treat**[10] 5996 7-7-12 41 .......... LisaJones(3) 2 14
(MMullineaux) *dwlt: outpcd* **40/1**
0005 11 8 **Tamarella (IRE)**[27] 5811 3-9-5 59 .......... NPollard 3 8
(GGMargarson) *chsd ldrs over 3f* **14/1**

1m 16.6s (-0.20) **Going Correction** -0.025s/f (Stan) **11 Ran SP% 122.9**
Speed ratings: **100,98,97,96,95 93,92,89,84,83 72**CSF £9.98 CT £93.46 TOTE £2.20: £1.40, £3.10, £3.70; EX 13.70 Trifecta £130.60 Pool £1,527.30 - 8.30 winning units; Place 6 £10.63, Place 5 £4.75.
**Owner** Perfect Night Partnership **Bred** S Emmet And Miss R Emmet **Trained** Beckhampton, Wilts

**FOCUS**
Another weak handicap with little worthwhile recent form on offer.

**NOTEBOOK**
**Perfect Night**, whose confidence must have received a boost from her recent maiden win, found a weak handicap on her debut at this track. She coped well enough with the step back in trip and should continue to run well on the surface.
**Eastern Blue(IRE)**is well handicapped on her best form and was staying on well at the end of this contest. She could well find a Fibresand handicap while in this form.
**Lake Eyre(IRE)**, still chasing her first win, ran a decent race from 1lb out of the handicap and with 2lb overweight being put up by her rider. She would not be without hope if able to race off her own mark in the near future.
**Inching**, another who is still a maiden, is happier on the All-Weather than she is on turf, and this was a fair effort in the first-time visor.
**Sharoura**has not won a race on the All-Weather in 11 starts and does look more at home on turf.
**Ally Makbul**was unable to reproduce her Wolverhampton form on this slower surface.
T/Jkpt: £18,647.30 to a £1 stake. Pool: £52,527.76. 2.00 winning tickets. T/Plt: £7.50 to a £1 stake. Pool: £41,395.75. 3,979.90 winning tickets. T/Qpdt: £3.30 to a £1 stake. Pool: £3,587.60. 801.60 winning tickets. CR

# 6055 SOUTHWELL (L-H)
## Tuesday, November 25

**OFFICIAL GOING: Standard**
The bias towards those that raced up with the pace was not as pronounced as the previous day, but the bias against the inside rail certainly was.

## 6063 BET DIRECT NO Q ON 08000 93 66 93 H'CAP (DIV I) 6f (F)
12:10 (12:12) (F) (0-65,65) 3-Y-O+ £2,142 (£612; £306) Stalls Low

Form RPR
1042 1 **Far Note (USA)**[59] 5224 5-9-12 63 .......... (b) ACulhane 2 71
(SRBowring) *trckd ldrs: gd hdwy 2f out: rdn to ld and edgd rt over 1f out: drvn ins last and kpt on* **8/1**[2]
0201 2 1/2 **Hurricane Coast**[6] 6027 4-9-11 62 7ex .......... GParkin 5 69
(PABlockley) *in tch: hdwy on inner 3f out: rdn to chal over 1f out and ev ch tl drvn and no ex wl ins last* **16/1**
0042 3 shd **Majik**[49] 5438 4-9-9 60 .......... TQuinn 15 66+
(DJSFrenchDavis) *outpcd and rdn along in rr 1/2-way: effrt and n.m.r over 2f out: rdn wl over 1f out: styd on strly ins last* **7/2**[1]
4004 4 shd **Doctor Dennis (IRE)**[27] 5832 6-8-12 49 .......... (v) NPollard 3 55
(MrsLydiaPearce) *sn outpcd and bhd: gd hdwy 2f out: rdn to chal ins last: nt qckn nr fin* **11/1**
0560 5 3 **Catch The Cat (IRE)**[18] 5941 4-8-10 52 .......... (v) TEaves(5) 6 49
(JSWainwright) *a.p: effrt to chal 2f out and ev ch tl rdn and n.m.r over 1f out: sn wknd* **10/1**[3]
0005 6 1 **Malahide Express (IRE)**[21] 5919 3-9-11 65 .......... (b) LFletcher(3) 13 59
(MJPolglase) *sn led: rdn 2f out: hdd & wknd over 1f out* **40/1**
3110 7 hd **Mr Pertemps**[224] 1061 5-9-5 56 .......... RFfrench 9 49
(RAFahey) *in tch tl rdn along and outpcd 1/2-way: kpt on u.p fnl 2f* **7/2**[1]
0405 8 3/4 **Vintage Style**[11] 5992 4-9-7 58 .......... (b) IMongan 10 49
(HAMcwilliams) *chsd ldrs on outer: rdn along wl over 2f out: grad wknd* **33/1**
3020 9 1 1/4 **Savile's Delight (IRE)**[24] 5878 4-9-5 56 .......... GGibbons 8 43
(RBrotherton) *chsd ldrs: rdn 2f out: drvn and edgd lft over 1f out: sn wknd* **33/1**
3236 10 2 1/2 **Xaloc Bay (IRE)**[44] 5516 5-9-3 54 .......... (b) MFenton 1 34
(BPJBaugh) *dwlt: sn rdn along in rr: nvr a factor* **10/1**[3]
2224 11 1 1/2 **Blessingindisguise**[20] 5924 10-8-12 49 .......... (b) DaleGibson 4 24
(MWEasterby) *chsd ldrs to 1/2-way: sn outpcd and bhd* **12/1**
0060 12 shd **Boisdale (IRE)**[49] 5438 5-9-4 55 .......... JoannaBadger 11 30
(DNicholls) *in tch: rdn along and outpcd fr 1/2-way* **25/1**
0400 13 1 1/4 **Beneking**[12] 5988 3-9-8 59 .......... NCallan 16 30
(JGallagher) *racd wd: a rr* **25/1**
1000 14 4 **High Esteem**[49] 5438 7-9-9 60 .......... JFanning 7 19
(MABuckley) *cl up: rdn along 1/2-way: sn wknd* **18/1**
3200 15 1 1/4 **Valuable Gift**[110] 3937 6-9-2 53 .......... (p) SWhitworth 12 9
(RCGuest) *racd wd: a towards rr* **40/1**
0/00 16 11 **Levelled**[94] 4381 9-8-13 50 .......... KDalgleish 14 —
(DWChapman) *rrd s: a bhd* **66/1**

1m 16.5s (-0.30) **Going Correction** -0.10s/f (Stan) **16 Ran SP% 120.9**
Speed ratings: **98,97,97,97,93 91,91,90,88,85 83,83,81,76,74 60**CSF £120.00 CT £557.50 TOTE £10.20: £2.00, £2.90, £1.30, £3.10; EX 109.80.
**Owner** Apb Racing **Bred** Juddmonte Farms **Trained** Edwinstowe, Notts

**FOCUS**
A modest handicap in which the whole field were keen to come down the centre of the track after turning in.

**NOTEBOOK**
**Far Note(USA)**, unplaced in three starts on sand last autumn, came into this race in good form on turf and saw the trip out well. He still has some scope on this surface.
**Hurricane Coast**may have been beaten, but almost certainly stepped up on the form of his selling win here last time. He may have been a little unlucky not to win too, as the furlong shorter trip and racing towards the inside of the track down the straight probably did not help him.
**Majik**made good late headway on the wide outside, but could not quite get there. He still looks to need a return to seven furlongs.
**Doctor Dennis(IRE)**continues his long losing run, but emerged with some credit as he was racing on the slowest part of the track.
**Catch The Cat(IRE)**is brilliantly handicapped compared to turf, but there is a good reason for that and he has never won beyond the minimum trip.
**Malahide Express(IRE)**showed plenty of early speed, but did not get home and may need a return to the minimum trip.
**Mr Pertemps**broke well enough, but soon found himself buried in the pack getting all the kickback and could never get in a blow.

## 6064 BET DIRECT IN RUNNING SKY TEXT 293 H'CAP (DIV I) 1m (F)
12:40 (12:40) (E) (0-70,71) 3-Y-O+ £2,086 (£596; £298) Stalls Low

Form RPR
0004 1 **Lockstock (IRE)**[11] 5996 5-9-4 60 .......... (b) JFanning 11 72
(MSSaunders) *chsd ldrs: rdn to ld 1f out: r.o* **8/1**
0311 2 1 1/4 **How's Things**[24] 5881 3-9-2 65 .......... RThomas(5) 7 74
(DHaydnJones) *sn led: rdn and hdd 1f out: styd on same pce ins fnl f* **10/3**[1]
4034 3 1 1/4 **Magic Mamma's Too**[35] 5688 3-8-9 53 .......... DMernagh 4 60
(TDBarron) *chsd ldrs: rdn and ev ch over 1f out: no ex ins fnl f* **16/1**
3210 4 1/2 **Brandy Cove**[55] 5300 6-9-10 66 .......... RFfrench 14 72+
(BSmart) *s.s: hdwy u.p over 1f out: nt rch ldrs* **11/1**
6024 5 2 1/2 **Bond Millennium**[28] 5823 5-9-13 69 .......... IMongan 9 70
(BSmart) *hld up in tch: rdn over 2f out: no ex fnl f* **6/1**
2113 6 1 **Estimation**[13] 5980 3-9-5 68 .......... BReilly(5) 2 67
(RMHCowell) *hld up: hdwy 1/2-way: swtchd lft over 1f out: one pce* **5/1**[2]
0000 7 1 1/2 **Simply The Guest (IRE)**[118] 3680 4-7-12 40 oh6 .......... (t) KimTinkler 15 36
(DonEnricoIncisa) *sn pushed along and prom: outpcd 3f out: n.d after* **66/1**
0000 8 1/2 **Cumbrian Princess**[70] 4962 6-7-12 40 oh2 .......... DaleGibson 13 35
(MBlanshard) *prom over 5f* **66/1**
0500 9 shd **Champagne Rider**[6] 6032 7-7-11 42 .......... (v) LisaJones(3) 8 36
(DShaw) *trckd ldrs: plld hrd: wknd over 1f out* **50/1**
4000 10 1 1/4 **Vermilion Creek**[10] 6004 4-8-5 47 .......... WRyan 12 39
(RHollinshead) *chsd ldrs 6f* **33/1**
6323 11 6 **Miss Glory Be**[10] 6004 5-9-3 59 .......... (p) MFenton 1 39
(MissGayKelleway) *hld up: hdwy 1/2-way: rdn and wknd over 1f out* **10/1**
0001 12 2 **Barzak (IRE)**[6] 6026 3-9-13 71 6ex .......... (t) ACulhane 6 47
(SRBowring) *hld up in tch: lost pl over 5f out: sn bhd* **11/2**[3]
3/6 13 7 **Ulysees (IRE)**[15] 5970 4-9-9 68 .......... DMcGaffin(3) 5 30
(ISemple) *dwlt: outpcd* **25/1**
300 14 2 **Kanz Wood (USA)**[75] 4838 7-9-9 65 .......... SWhitworth 10 23
(AWCarroll) *dwlt: outpcd* **33/1**

1m 43.56s (-1.04) **Going Correction** -0.10s/f (Stan)
**WFA** 3 from 4yo+ 2lb **14 Ran SP% 118.5**
Speed ratings: **101,99,98,98,95 94,93,92,92,91 85,83,76,74**CSF £32.65 CT £435.72 TOTE £8.80: £2.40, £2.40, £4.00; EX 55.30.
**Owner** Chris Scott **Bred** W H Joyce **Trained** Haydon, Somerset

**FOCUS**
A fair handicap of its kind, but one run in a time 1.02sec slower than the second division.

**NOTEBOOK**
**Lockstock(IRE)**, who won his maiden on his last visit here two years ago, appreciated the return to a mile and the refitting of the blinkers also appeared to have a positive effect.
**How's Things**, chasing a hat-trick, made a brave attempt off a 9lb higher mark, and on this evidence he has not finished winning yet.
**Magic Mamma's Too**, who ran well on Fibresand last winter, is continuing that form this time around, but he is one for placepot punters only.
**Brandy Cove**, who had finished in the first three on seven of his previous eight starts over this course and distance, was running against the pace bias and ran well in the circumstances. He will not be long in getting back in the winners' enclosure here.
**Bond Millennium**is another who goes well on this surface, but he is not the easiest to win with and switching towards the far rail in the straight was no help.
**Estimation**was another who was done no favours by being switched to race on the slower ground next to the far rail in the straight.
**Barzak(IRE)**could never get close enough to the front and ran below form as a result.

## 6065 BET DIRECT NO Q ON 08000 93 66 93 H'CAP (DIV II) 6f (F)
1:10 (1:11) (F) (0-65,64) 3-Y-O+ £2,142 (£612; £306) Stalls Low

Form RPR
4055 1 **Acorazado (IRE)**[7] 6024 4-9-2 53 .......... (be) WRyan 14 64
(GLMoore) *racd wd and bhd: hdwy 2f out: str run ent last: led on line* **4/1**[1]
0043 2 hd **Travelling Times**[6] 6032 4-8-8 50 .......... (v) TEaves(5) 11 60
(JSWainwright) *chsd ldrs: rdn along 1/2-way: hdwy un der press to ld ent last: sn drvn: hdd on line* **14/1**
5235 3 3/4 **Wainwright (IRE)**[4] 6039 3-9-2 60 .......... DerekNolan(7) 16 68
(PABlockley) *led after 1f: rdn 2f out: drvn and hdd ent last: no ex last 100 yds* **14/1**
0001 4 3/4 **Semper Paratus (USA)**[4] 6042 4-9-2 60 7ex .......... (b) SaleemGolam(7) 1 66
(HJCollingridge) *in tch on inner: rdn along and outpcd 1/2-way: hdwy over 1f out: kpt on ins last: nrst fin* **11/2**[2]
0055 5 2 **Tatweer (IRE)**[6] 6031 3-9-7 58 .......... (v) DarrenWilliams 10 58
(DShaw) *chsd ldrs: rdn along over 2f out: drvn and one pce appr last* **14/1**
5624 6 1 **Pilgrim Princess (IRE)**[67] 5047 5-8-10 47 .......... ANicholls 7 44
(EJAlston) *chsd ldrs: rdn along over 2f out: drvn and one pce appr last* **9/1**[3]
0000 7 hd **Cash**[10] 6001 5-9-5 59 .......... LisaJones(3) 12 55
(PaulJohnson) *bhd: rdn along 1/2-way: styd on appr last: nrst fin* **16/1**
0060 8 2 1/2 **Polar Force**[25] 5849 3-9-5 63 .......... TO'Brien(7) 13 52
(MRChannon) *racd wd: midfield and rdn along 1/2-way: sn no imp* **16/1**
0006 9 1 1/4 **Dil**[84] 4641 8-9-3 54 .......... KDalgleish 4 39
(MrsNMacauley) *towards rr: rdn along 1/2-way: nvr a factor* **20/1**
0010 10 1 **Ally Makbul**[1] 6062 3-8-11 55 .......... DFentiman(7) 3 37
(JRBest) *towards rr: rdn along and hdwy whn swtchd lft over 1f out: sn no imp* **16/1**
500 11 3/4 **Roman Empire**[19] 5933 3-9-8 59 .......... JFEgan 8 39
(TJEtherington) *racd wd: a rr* **40/1**


The Form Book, Raceform Ltd, Compton, RG20 6NL

0010 **12** *2* **Locombe Hill (IRE)**[6] 6028 7-9-6 64 LTreadwell(7) 6 38
(DNicholls) *s.i.s: a rr* **9/1**[3]
0303 **13** *1* **Caustic Wit (IRE)**[11] 5995 5-8-10 52 MSavage(5) 5 23
(MSSaunders) *cl up: rdn over 2f out and sn wknd* **10/1**
2300 **14** *1 1/4* **On The Trail**[4] 6036 6-9-5 56 ACulhane 9 23
(DWChapman) *led 1f: cl up tl rdn and wknd wl over 1f out* **9/1**[3]
5000 **15** *8* **Mabel Riley (IRE)**[1] 6056 3-8-12 49 JFanning 2 —
(MABuckley) *bhd fr 1/2-way* **40/1**
1000 **16** *2* **Blunham**[6] 6028 3-9-4 55 (b[1]) IMongan 15 —
(MCChapman) *cl up to 1/2-way: sn lost pl and bhd* **25/1**

1m 17.03s (0.23) **Going Correction** -0.10s/f (Stan) 16 Ran SP% **125.6**
Speed ratings: **94,93,92,91,89 87,87,84,82,81 80,77,76,74,63 61**CSF £60.67 CT £535.71 TOTE £5.20: £1.60, £2.50, £2.70, £3.10; EX 66.50.
**Owner** D T L Limited **Bred** Miss Ann Hennessy **Trained** Woodingdean, E Sussex

**FOCUS**
A moderate race, run in a time 0.53sec slower than the first division, and those who raced middle to stands' side proved at an advantage.

**NOTEBOOK**
**Acorazado(IRE)**, who ran with promise last time, took advantage of the faster ground towards the stands' side to finish with a rare rattle and lead on the line. He is versatile as regards All-Weather surface as he also acts on Polytrack, so there could be more to come.
**Travelling Times**, who has never run a bad race on Fibresand, also benefited from racing wide in the straight.
**Wainwright(IRE)**, who is still a maiden, was running without the headgear this time. He threw away his chance by remaining on the slower ground towards the far side.
**Semper Paratus(USA)**found the drop back in trip against him and was doing his best work at the finish. He ran well considering he was being asked to run on nearest to the far-side rail and will do better returned to seven.
**Tatweer(IRE)**, making his handicap debut, needs to drop a few pounds.
**Pilgrim Princess(IRE)**, despite a number of fine efforts, is still a maiden on sand.

## 6066 BET DIRECT NO Q CLAIMING STKS 1m (F)
**1:40** (1:42) (F) 2-Y-O **£2,107** (£602; £301) **Stalls** Low

Form RPR
6601 **1** **Myannabanana (IRE)**[11] 5993 2-9-1 60 (v[1]) MFenton 11 63
(MissGayKelleway) *hld up in tch: led ins fnl f: rdn clr* **5/1**[3]
5102 **2** *2 1/2* **Turf Princess**[31] 5745 2-8-7 59 DFentiman(7) 15 57
(JRBest) *w ldrs: led over 2f out: rdn and hdd ins fnl f: unable to qiucken* **4/1**[2]
3004 **3** *3 1/2* **Katie's Role**[21] 5915 2-8-6 57 ANicholls 14 41
(IanEmmerson) *w ldr: led over 5f out: hdd over 2f out: rdn and ev ch over 1f out: wknd ins fnl f* **10/1**
3000 **4** *3* **Brother Cadfael**[77] 4795 2-8-3 47 RFfrench 16 31
(JohnAHarris) *hld up: hdwy 5f out: wknd over 1f out* **50/1**
0062 **5** *2 1/2* **Frambo (IRE)**[60] 5198 2-8-11 57 LisaJones(3) 2 37
(JGPortman) *chsd ldrs: outpcd 3f out: n.d after* **5/1**[3]
0453 **6** *nk* **Tictactoe**[6] 6029 2-9-0 58 ACulhane 13 36
(DJDaly) *s.s: hdwy over 3f out: rdn and wknd over 1f out* **7/2**[1]
2000 **7** *6* **Jimmy Gee (IRE)**[1] 6058 2-8-5 49 JoannaBadger 12 14
(DNicholls) *s.i.s: hdwy over 3f out: wknd over 2f out* **25/1**
0420 **8** *hd* **The King Of Rock**[60] 5198 2-9-5 63 SWhitworth 3 27
(AGNewcombe) *hld up: effrt 1/2-way: n.d* **20/1**
0004 **9** *1/2* **Nocatee (IRE)**[38] 5633 2-8-9 57 RoryMoore(7) 7 23
(PCHaslam) *trckd ldrs: lost pl 1/2-way: sn bhd* **12/1**
0330 **10** *nk* **Sugarbabe**[77] 4795 2-8-1 48 RThomas(5) 4 13
(MBlanshard) *chsd ldrs over 5f* **16/1**
0060 **11** *1* **Given A Chance**[11] 5993 2-8-11 47 ADaly 10 15
(JGGiven) *led: hdd over 5f out: wknd over 3f out* **40/1**
5 **12** *3/4* **Tamarina (IRE)**[59] 5222 2-8-6 ow3 MSavage(5) 1 14
(NEBerry) *prom: chsd ldr 1/2-way: wknd over 2f out* **14/1**
00 **13** *hd* **Skelthwaite**[7] 6021 2-8-13 JFanning 8 15
(MHTompkins) *a in rr* **50/1**
00 **14** *15* **Confuzion (IRE)**[28] 5816 2-8-4 (p) GHannon 5 —
(APJones) *sn pushed along in rr: bhd fr 1/2-way* **40/1**

1m 44.11s (-0.49) **Going Correction** -0.10s/f (Stan) 14 Ran SP% **122.3**
Speed ratings: **98,95,92,89,86 86,80,80,79,79 78,77,77,62**CSF £24.08 TOTE £6.00: £2.40, £2.10, £4.30; EX 18.70.The winner was claimed by J Weymes for £8,000. Turf Princess was claimed by Ian Emmerson for £10,000.
**Owner** Twilight Racing **Bred** Thomas Kiely **Trained** Newmarket, Suffolk

**FOCUS**
A moderate claimer.

**NOTEBOOK**
**Myannabanana(IRE)**, whose stamina for the trip was proven, followed up his hard-fought Wolverhampton success with an easier win this time. This was his first and only start for Gay Kelleway as he was subsequently claimed by John Weymes.
**Turf Princess**had a stamina doubt against her name coming into the race but saw the trip out well enough. This gives her connections more options.
**Katie's Role**was best in at the weights according to adjusted official ratings but did not quite get home over this longer trip.
**Brother Cadfael**may have needed his first outing in two and a half months but he shaped with some modest promise on his first start since being gelded.
**Frambo(IRE)**was slightly disappointing as she failed to run up to the form of her last outing here. However, she may well come on for this first run in two months.
**Tictactoe**hinders her chance of winning races by starting so slowly. If that can be sorted out she has the ability to win in this grade.

## 6067 LITTLEWOODS BET DIRECT MAIDEN STKS 1m (F)
**2:10** (2:12) (D) 3-Y-O **£2,310** (£660; £330) **Stalls** Low

Form RPR
402 **1** **Kingston Town (USA)**[15] 5973 3-8-11 62 (p) J-PGuillambert(3) 10 67
(NPLittmoden) *in tch: pushed along 1/2-way: gd hdwy whn edgd lft over 2f out: rdn to ld over 1f out: drvn clr ins last* **11/4**[2]
6006 **2** *5* **Sophrano (IRE)**[23] 5891 3-9-0 68 NCallan 9 57
(PWHarris) *a.p: rdn to ld over 2f out: drvn and hdd appr last: kpt on same pce* **9/4**[1]
4030 **3** *1/2* **White Park Bay (IRE)**[10] 6006 3-8-9 62 DaneO'Neill 13 51
(JGallagher) *a.p: rdn 2f out: kpt on u.p fnl f* **5/1**[3]
0306 **4** *1/2* **Silver Crystal (IRE)**[28] 5815 3-8-6 45 LisaJones(3) 8 50
(MrsNMacauley) *chsd ldrs: rdn over 2f out: drvn and kpt on same pce appr last* **33/1**
03 **5** *3* **Realism (FR)**[10] 6005 3-9-0 DarrenWilliams 14 49
(PWHiatt) *cl up on outer: hdwy to chal over 2f out and ev ch tl rdn: hung lft and wknd over 1f out* **7/1**
0500 **6** *3 1/2* **Nimbus Twothousand**[15] 5971 3-8-9 44 (b) CCatlin 4 37
(PRWood) *cl up on inner: rdn along 3f out: wkng whn hmpd over 2f out* **33/1**
4656 **7** *5* **Danum**[150] 2781 3-9-0 65 ACulhane 1 32
(RHollinshead) *nvr nr ldrs* **14/1**
**8** *3 1/2* **Trofana Falcon** 3-9-0 MTebbutt 15 25
(HJCollingridge) *nvr nr ldrs* **20/1**
-000 **9** *4* **Compos Mentis**[29] 5795 3-8-11 67 (b[1]) DMcGaffin(3) 6 17
(DMorris) *in tch on inner: rdn along 1/2-way: sn wknd* **16/1**
0004 **10** *hd* **Matriarchal**[88] 4545 3-8-9 38 KimTinkler 11 12
(DonEnricoIncisa) *a rr* **66/1**
0 **11** *1 1/2* **Moonglade (USA)**[56] 5289 3-8-6 ow2 (t) AQuinn(5) 16 11
(MissJFeilden) *sn led: rdn along 3f out: sn hdd & wknd* **66/1**
0 **12** *10* **Sawah**[7] 6022 3-9-0 SWhitworth 7 —
(DShaw) *s.i.s: a rr* **100/1**
0 **13** *nk* **Recall (IRE)**[28] 5815 3-8-9 MFenton 3 —
(JGGiven) *a bhd* **12/1**
0P00 **14** *3 1/2* **Scrappy Doo**[31] 5742 3-8-7 26 LTreadwell(7) 12 —
(MissVHaigh) *bhd fr 1/2-way* **100/1**
40B0 **15** *18* **Repetoire (FR)**[13] 5978 3-8-9 49 ANicholls 5 —
(KOCunningham-Brown) *s.i.s: a bhd* **50/1**

1m 44.44s (-0.16) **Going Correction** -0.10s/f (Stan) 15 Ran SP% **124.4**
Speed ratings: **96,91,90,90,87 83,78,75,71,70 69,59,59,55,37**CSF £9.11 TOTE £3.90: £1.30, £1.30, £2.00; EX 9.70.
**Owner** Friends of the Turf Racing Limited **Bred** Swettenham Stud And International Horse Brokers **Trained** Newmarket, Suffolk

**FOCUS**
A weak maiden in which the leaders went off too quick.

**NOTEBOOK**
**Kingston Town(USA)**benefited from sitting just off the pace as the leaders appeared to go off too quick, and in the end he picked them up easily enough. He shapes as though he will stay farther.
**Sophrano(IRE)**was one of the leaders who probably went off too fast. He kept on well enough for second, though, and is another for whom a step back up in trip should suit.
**White Park Bay(IRE)**, who likes to be up with the pace, could not get to the lead due to the fast pace. She ran a creditable race in the circumstances, although this is not the first time she has run well without winning.
**Silver Crystal(IRE)**ran a good race on the ratings but will have a better chance of success in selling company.
**Realism(FR)**looked a danger two furlongs out but tired from over a furlong out. He paid for racing up with the pace from the outset.
**Nimbus Twothousand**was going backwards when hampered early in the straight.

## 6068 BETDIRECT.CO.UK H'CAP 1m 3f (F)
**2:40** (2:41) (E) (0-75,75) 3-Y-O+ **£2,135** (£610; £305) **Stalls** Low

Form RPR
5012 **1** **Mi Odds**[49] 5442 7-9-12 **73** ACulhane 1 84
(MrsNMacauley) *hld up: hdwy over 4f out: led over 1f out: drvn out* **3/1**[1]
0025 **2** *3/4* **Digger (IRE)**[8] 6017 4-9-9 **70** (t) NCallan 15 79
(MissGayKelleway) *chsd ldrs: rdn over 1f out: hung lft ins fnl f: r.o* **13/2**
0000 **3** *1 1/2* **Classic Role**[12] 5991 4-9-11 **72** IMongan 9 79
(RIngram) *chsd ldr: led over 4f out: rdn and hdd over 1f out: no ex ins fnl f* **16/1**
0060 **4** *1 1/2* **Stravmour**[34] 5705 7-7-12 **45** oh2 DaleGibson 14 50
(RHollinshead) *hld up: plld hrd: hdwy over 3f out: sn rdn: styd on* **66/1**
6344 **5** *1/2* **East Cape**[49] 5442 6-7-12 **45** oh1 KimTinkler 16 49
(DonEnricoIncisa) *hld up: hdwy over 6f out: n.m.r and lost pl over 4f out: styd on ins fnl f* **14/1**
6006 **6** *hd* **Gingko**[7] 6025 6-9-4 **65** DeanMcKeown 3 68
(PRWebber) *chsd ldrs: rdn over 2f out: wknd ins fnl f* **11/2**[3]
0544 **7** *nk* **Trouble Mountain (USA)**[31] 5738 6-9-3 **69** PMulrennan(5) 11 72
(MWEasterby) *hld up: hdwy 6f out: outpcd over 2f out: styd on ins fnl f* **13/2**
0066 **8** *8* **Vanbrugh (FR)**[23] 5890 3-8-13 **65** (vt) DarrenWilliams 13 55
(MissDAMchale) *dwlt: hld up: styd on u.p ins fnl f: nvr nrr* **66/1**
0535 **9** *8* **Crusoe (IRE)**[15] 5970 6-9-5 **66** DaneO'Neill 7 43
(ASadik) *prom over 7f* **16/1**
1630 **10** *3* **Duc's Dream**[28] 5817 5-8-11 **61** DMcGaffin(3) 12 34
(DMorris) *hld up: rdn over 4f out: n.d: eased wl over 1f out* **5/1**[2]
2000 **11** *2* **Night Warrior (IRE)**[12] 5991 3-9-4 **70** DSweeney 8 39
(DFlood) *hld up: wknd over 5f out* **14/1**
5000 **12** *5* **Surdoue**[15] 5967 3-9-9 **75** PaulEddery 2 36
(PHowling) *sn led: hdd over 4f out: wknd over 2f out* **66/1**
0000 **13** *2* **Toro Bravo (IRE)**[41] 5577 3-9-1 **67** MTebbutt 4 25
(RMBeckett) *chsd ldrs over 7f* **66/1**
006 **14** *hd* **Gracious Air (USA)**[42] 5568 5-7-5 **45** oh5 (p) DFentiman(7) 6 3
(JRWeymes) *hld up: bhd fnl 5f* **50/1**
4064 **15** *8* **Khuzdar (IRE)**[12] 5989 4-7-8 **48** ow1 TO'Brien(7) 5 —
(MRChannon) *hld up: bhd fnl 5f* **10/1**
5130 **16** *dist* **Crunchy (IRE)**[171] 2198 5-9-1 **67** (t) THamilton(5) 10 —
(BEllison) *prom to 1/2-way* **20/1**

2m 26.09s (-2.81) **Going Correction** -0.10s/f (Stan)
**WFA** 3 from 4yo+ 5lb 16 Ran SP% **130.6**
Speed ratings: **106,105,104,103,102 102,102,96,90,88 87,83,82,82,76** —CSF £23.19 CT £284.29 TOTE £3.80: £1.70, £1.90, £4.70, £23.00; EX 31.90 Trifecta £241.50 Pool of £918.50 - 2.70 winning units.
**Owner** Tic-Tac.com **Bred** G Wiltshire **Trained** Sproxton, Leics

**FOCUS**
A good-quality handicap run at a fair pace.

**NOTEBOOK**
**Mi Odds**, a real Fibresand specialist, was held up early but made steady headway through the field as the race progressed and battled on well to score down the straight. He has done connections proud and there seems no reason why another contest or two should not come his way on Fibresand.
**Digger(IRE)**, dropping back in trip, never stopped trying down the straight and perhaps this sort of distance suits him best.
**Classic Role**has experience of Polytrack, but was making his Fibresand debut and ran a cracker under a positive ride. He looks well worth another try on this surface.
**Stravmour**, yet to be placed in seven previous starts including two bumpers, ran by far his best race to date and may not be totally without hope even at the age of seven.
**East Cape**, who finished just over two lengths behind Mi Odds here on his last start, was doing his best work late on and has shown more than enough to suggest he can win a race on this surface.
**Gingko**had every chance turning for home but was easily brushed aside down the straight.
**Trouble Mountain(USA)**was making his sand debut in his 53rd race and only offered limited encouragement.
**Crusoe(IRE)**finds this trip too far.
**Duc's Dream**has a good record over this course and distance and is capable of much better than this.

## 6069 BET DIRECT IN RUNNING MEDIAN AUCTION MAIDEN STKS 7f (F)
3:10 (3:12) (F) 2-Y-O £2,331 (£666; £333) Stalls Low

| Form | | | | RPR |
|---|---|---|---|---|
| 426 | 1 | | **Benny The Ball (USA)**[24] 5871 2-9-0 88 ........ IMongan 8 (NPLittmoden) *cl up: led 1/2-way: shkn up ent last: styd on wl* **10/11**[1] | 81+ |
| 4025 | 2 | 1 | **Fadeela (IRE)**[21] 5913 2-8-4 67 ........ (e) BReilly[(5)] 16 (PWD'Arcy) *a.p: cl up and ev ch 2f out tl drvn and one pce fnl f* **20/1**[3] | 73 |
| 00 | 3 | 5 | **Book Matched**[17] 5947 2-9-0 ........ RFfrench 10 (BSmart) *towards rr: hdwy over 2f out: styd on wl fnl f: nearest fin* **50/1** | 66 |
| 00 | 4 | ½ | **Bold Blade**[35] 5691 2-9-0 48 ........ (b[1]) CCatlin 12 (BSmart) *led to 1/2-way: rdn over 2f out and grad wknd* **66/1** | 64 |
| 0 | 5 | 5 | **African Star**[18] 5939 2-9-0 ........ DaneO'Neill 14 (MrsAJPerrett) *in tch: effrt to chse ldrs over 2f out: sn rdn and btn* **25/1** | 52 |
| 005 | 6 | nk | **Cornish Gold**[17] 5948 2-8-9 67 ........ PaulEddery 6 (DHaydnJones) *in tch: rdn along over 2f out: sn btn* **20/1**[3] | 46 |
| 00 | 7 | 3 | **Jolizero**[18] 5940 2-9-0 ........ NPollard 15 (GGMargarson) *nvr nr ldrs* **50/1** | 44 |
| 0005 | 8 | ½ | **Smart Boy Prince (IRE)**[43] 5544 2-8-7 55 ........ SYourston[(7)] 11 (PABlockley) *in tch: rdn along 1/2-way and sn outpcd* **66/1** | 42 |
| 0 | 9 | ½ | **Dalida**[18] 5939 2-8-2 ........ RoryMoore[(7)] 13 (PCHaslam) *bhd fr 1/2-way* **33/1** | 36 |
| 6 | 10 | 1 | **Vampire Queen (IRE)**[10] 6002 2-8-9 ........ DeanMcKeown 4 (RPElliott) *a rr* **66/1** | 34 |
| 2 | 11 | ¾ | **Colour Code (IRE)**[15] 5968 2-9-0 ........ TQuinn 5 (MPTregoning) *chsd ldrs: rdn 2f out: sn wknd* **2/1**[2] | 37 |
| 6 | 12 | 1 | **Celtic Solitude (IRE)**[20] 5925 2-8-9 ........ JFanning 7 (MJohnston) *s.i.s: a bhd* **25/1** | 29 |
| 05 | 13 | 2 | **Inchpast**[12] 5986 2-8-7 ........ SaleemGolam[(7)] 2 (MHTompkins) *s.i.s: a bhd* **20/1**[3] | 29 |
| 2300 | 14 | dist | **Iphigenia (IRE)**[8] 6011 2-8-9 63 ........ ACulhane 3 (PWHiatt) *a bhd: t.o and virtually p.u over 1f out* **33/1** | — |

1m 29.68s (-1.12) **Going Correction** -0.10s/f (Stan) **14** Ran SP% **122.0**
Speed ratings: **102,100,95,94,88 88,85,84,83,82 81,80,78,**—CSF £26.98 TOTE £2.00: £1.10, £3.80, £29.80; EX 22.00.
**Owner** Miss Vanessa Church **Bred** Mrs Adele Dilschneider **Trained** Newmarket, Suffolk

**FOCUS**
A fair pace, but probably not a great deal of strength in depth.

**NOTEBOOK**
**Benny The Ball(USA)**, who raced in Listed company last time, absolutely dwarfed his rivals, especially the filly in second. Despite his dominance on official ratings he was forced to grind out a result, but did so in resolute style and the longer straight here was more suitable for a horse of his size. He is likely to be put away until next year.
**Fadeela(IRE)**has proved herself on this surface before and ran well again, making sure the favourite could not take things easy. Maidens here will get weaker as the winter progresses so she should find a race and there is always the option of handicap company.
**Book Matched**, making his sand debut, showed his first sign of ability and can now be handicapped. He should get a mile.
**Bold Blade**set the early pace and rallied quite well after looking likely to drop away at halfway. He may be worth trying in handicap company off his basement mark.
**Colour Code(IRE)**ran poorly though the distance he was beaten was exacerbated by racing tight against the inside rail. *Official explanation: jockey had no explanation for the poor form shown*
**Iphigenia(IRE)** *Official explanation: jockey said filly lost her action*

## 6070 BET DIRECT IN RUNNING SKY TEXT 293 H'CAP (DIV II) 1m (F)
3:40 (3:41) (E) (0-70,70) 3-Y-O+ £2,086 (£596; £298) Stalls Low

| Form | | | | RPR |
|---|---|---|---|---|
| 2033 | 1 | | **Mcqueen (IRE)**[10] 6006 3-9-3 61 ........ JFEgan 6 (MrsHDalton) *a.p: chsd ldr over 3f out: rdn to ld and edgd lft over 1f out: sn clr* **7/1** | 85 |
| 1305 | 2 | 8 | **Neven**[31] 5749 4-9-5 61 ........ DMernagh 12 (TDBarron) *chsd ldrs: rdn over 2f out: styd on same pce* **4/1**[2] | 69 |
| 0003 | 3 | 2½ | **Ovigo (GER)**[8] 6013 4-9-11 67 ........ GParkin 5 (PABlockley) *s.s: hld up: hdwy 3f out: sn rdn: styd on same pce fnl 2f* **7/2**[1] | 70 |
| 0425 | 4 | 4 | **Zak Facta (IRE)**[12] 5985 3-8-12 56 ........ (v) CCogan 4 (MissDAMchale) *led: hdd over 6f out: led over 4f out: hdd & wknd over 1f out* **20/1** | 51 |
| 504 | 5 | 1½ | **Captain Darling (IRE)**[23] 5577 3-9-3 66 ........ AQuinn[(5)] 14 (RMHCowell) *hld up: hdwy over 3f out: sn rdn: wkng whn hung lft over 1f out* **20/1** | 58 |
| 0005 | 6 | 2 | **Supreme Salutation**[21] 5918 7-9-12 68 ........ ACulhane 10 (DWChapman) *hld up: effrt over 3f out: sn wknd* **10/1** | 56 |
| 3020 | 7 | 1½ | **Hoh's Back**[44] 5515 4-9-7 66 ........ (p) LisaJones[(3)] 13 (PaulJohnson) *chsd ldrs over 5f* **8/1** | 51 |
| 4201 | 8 | 1 | **Pharoah's Gold (IRE)**[10] 6006 5-9-9 65 ........ (e) DarrenWilliams 2 (DShaw) *hld up in tch: wknd 3f out* **11/2**[3] | 48 |
| 0534 | 9 | nk | **Goodbye Mr Bond**[36] 5683 3-9-0 58 ........ DeanMcKeown 3 (EJAlston) *prom over 4f* **14/1** | 40 |
| 00-0 | 10 | 13 | **Nevinstown (IRE)**[177] 2034 3-8-9 53 ........ (bt[1]) WMLordan 8 (NiallMoran, Ire) *s.s: outpcd* **66/1** | 9 |
| 0414 | 11 | ½ | **Shotacross The Bow (IRE)**[15] 5970 6-9-9 65 ........ NCallan 1 (MBlanshard) *sn outpcd* **7/1** | 20 |
| 0000 | 12 | 5 | **Subtle Move (USA)**[6] 6031 3-8-2 51 ow2 ........ (v) THamilton[(5)] 11 (DShaw) *sn pushed along in rr: bhd fr 1/2-way* **100/1** | — |
| 2200 | 13 | 10 | **Friday's Takings**[141] 3061 4-10-0 70 ........ (b) RFfrench 9 (BSmart) *led over 6f out: hdd over 4f out: wknd 3f out* **16/1** | — |
| 0000 | 14 | 25 | **Bold Effort (FR)**[6] 6032 11-8-0 42 ow2 ........ (b) CCatlin 7 (KOCunningham-Brown) *chsd ldrs over 5f* **100/1** | — |

1m 42.54s (-2.06) **Going Correction** -0.10s/f (Stan)
**WFA** 3 from 4yo+ 2lb **14** Ran SP% **128.4**
Speed ratings: **106,98,95,91,90 88,86,85,85,72 71,66,56,31**CSF £36.31 CT £123.35 TOTE £9.80: £1.90, £2.60, £1.90; EX 65.70 Place 6 £49.80, Place 5 £24.83.
**Owner** R Edwards And W J Swinnerton **Bred** Philip Newton **Trained** Shifnal, Shropshire

**FOCUS**
A modest handicap though an impressive winner and a time more than a second faster than the first division.

**NOTEBOOK**
**Mcqueen(IRE)**, a maiden coming into this, broke his duck in some style and turned Wolverhampton form around with Pharoah's Gold by some 23 lengths despite only being 5lb better off. The slower track was almost certainly the reason for this improved effort and he can win again.
**Neven**ran into one on this return to Fibresand, but this was still a fair effort and he will surely find another race here during the winter.
**Ovigo(GER)**was taking on easier company than at Wolverhampton the previous week, but did not run up to that form and he was not helped by being kept tight to the inside rail down the straight. He should not be written off just yet. *Official explanation: trainer said gelding bled from the nose*
**Zak Facta(IRE)**showed his usual early pace out in front but, not for the first time, found this trip too far.
**Captain Darling(IRE)**, back on Fibresand after a spin over hurdles, likes fast ground and did not seem to appreciate this slower surface.
**Supreme Salutation**never threatened to take a hand, but has such a good record on Fibresand that things will go right for him at some point.
**Pharoah's Gold(IRE)**, raised 5lb for his Wolverhampton win, gets this trip at that venue but still seems to find it too far on this slower surface.
T/Jkpt: Not won. T/Plt: £45.10 to a £1 stake. Pool: £40,016.45. 647.45 winning tickets. T/Qpdt: £10.10 to a £1 stake. Pool: £3,458.20. 251.60 winning tickets. CR

# 6044 SAINT-CLOUD (L-H)
Tuesday, November 25

**OFFICIAL GOING: Holding**

## 6071a PRIX PETITE ETOILE (LISTED) (FILLIES) 1m 2f 110y
1:45 (1:45) 3-Y-O £13,312 (£5,325; £3,994; £2,662)

| | | | RPR |
|---|---|---|---|
| 1 | | **Samando (FR)**[30] 3-8-12 ........ C-PLemaire 14 (FDoumen, France) | 106 |
| 2 | 4 | **Maredsous (FR)**[22] 5912 3-9-2 ........ YBarberot 3 (DSepulchre, France) | 103 |
| 3 | 2 | **Valtar (FR)**[24] 5882 3-9-2 ........ SLadjadj 5 (Y-MPorzier, France) 1 | 99 |
| 4 | shd | **Russian Hill**[25] 3-8-12 ........ ACarre 11 (AFabre, France) | 95 |
| 5 | snk | **Felicity (IRE)**[18] 5943 3-9-2 ........ ELegrix 10 (JHMGosden) *close up, led after 2f, pushed along and ran on when pressed over 1 1/2f out, headed over 1f out, one pace closing stages* | 99 |
| 6 | 1 | **Best Ever (FR)**[42] 3-8-12 ........ DBoeuf 8 (ELellouche, France) | 93 |
| 7 | 3 | **Village D'Eze (FR)**[53] 5354 3-8-12 ........ RMarchelli 16 (MRolland, France) | 88 |
| 8 | 1 | **Bonne Mere (FR)**[33] 3-8-12 ........ IMendizabal 2 (JCNapoli, France) | 86 |
| 9 | 1½ | **Anna Victoria (GER)**[44] 5525 3-8-12 ........ (b) TGillet 13 (GSybrecht, Germany) | 84 |
| 10 | shd | **Epopee (IRE)**[36] 5684 3-8-12 ........ (b) J-BEyquem 6 (FRohaut, France) | 83 |
| 11 | | **Advaline (FR)**[56] 5292 3-8-12 ........ (b) ABadel 9 (MmeMBollack-Badel, France) | 83 |
| 12 | | **Cambiata (FR)**[52] 5387 3-8-12 ........ SPasquier 4 (JDeRoualle, France) | 83 |
| 13 | | **Dance In The Sun**[13] 5980 3-8-12 ........ DBonilla 15 (MrsAJPerrett) *held up towards rear, pushed along 2f out, no impression* | 83 |
| 0 | | **Sea Blue**[117] 3-8-12 ........ TThulliez 7 (PBary, France) | — |
| 0 | | **Four Green (FR)**[64] 3-8-12 ........ NGuesdon 1 (MmeCHead-Maarek, France) | — |
| 0 | | **Anadiyla (IRE)**[105] 3-8-12 ........ CSoumillon 12 (ADeRoyer-Dupre, France) | — |

2m 29.6s **Going Correction** +1.10s/f (Soft) **16** Ran SP% **20.0**
Speed ratings: **112,109,107,107,107 106,104,103,102,102 102,102,102,—,— —.**
**Owner** H Wirth **Bred** Barry Root **Trained** France

**NOTEBOOK**
**Felicity(IRE)**, chasing more valuable black type, is a keen type who has difficulty seeing out her trip.
**Dance In The Sun**, a Polytrack winner last time, had never previously run on ground this soft.

# 6045 LINGFIELD (L-H)
Wednesday, November 26

**OFFICIAL GOING: Standard**
Wind: light across Weather: bright and sunny

## 6072 BET DIRECT ON ATTHERACES INTERACTIVE MAIDEN STKS (DIV I) 1m (P)
11:45 (11:46) (D) 2-Y-O £3,041 (£869; £434) Stalls High

| Form | | | | RPR |
|---|---|---|---|---|
| 0 | 1 | | **Ascertain (IRE)**[19] 5939 2-9-0 ........ IMongan 3 (NPLittmoden) *chsd ldrs: rdn and prog to chse ldr 3f out: led over 2f out : drvn out* **40/1** | 80 |
| | 2 | 1¼ | **Kali** 2-8-9 ........ DSweeney 11 (RCharlton) *lt-f: bit bkwd: settled towards rr: stdy prog fr over 2f out: rdn to chse wnr ins fnl f: r.o: nrst fin* **20/1** | 72 |
| | 3 | nk | **Boxgrove (FR)** 2-9-0 ........ JFEgan 6 (CEBrittain) *str: bit bkwd: s.i.s: rn green but sn in tch in midfield: effrt and rdn 3f out: chsd wnr over 1f out to ins fnl f: kpt on* **25/1** | 77 |
| | 4 | 3½ | **Magical Gift** 2-8-9 ........ SWhitworth 4 (DWPArbuthnot) *leggy: lt-f: s.s: racd in last pair to 1/2-way: gd prog over 2f out: drvn to chse ldrs over 1f out: wknd ins fnl f* **33/1** | 64 |
| 4 | 5 | 4 | **Okoboji (IRE)**[19] 5939 2-9-0 ........ MartinDwyer 7 (MPTregoning) *mde most to over 2f out: wknd fnl f* **11/4**[1] | 60 |
| 5 | 6 | 2½ | **Soviet Sceptre (IRE)**[117] 3750 2-9-0 ........ CCatlin 9 (GAButler) *lw: trckd ldrs: rdn 3f out: unable qck and btn 2f out: fdd* **11/4**[1] | 55 |
| 5 | 7 | ¾ | **Mambina (USA)**[25] 5869 2-8-9 ........ ACulhane 12 (MRChannon) *racd in midfield: shkn up and outpcd over 2f out: no ch after* **4/1**[2] | 48 |
| | 8 | nk | **Secret Place** 2-9-0 ........ WRyan 10 (EALDunlop) *w'like: bit bkwd: settled in rr: shuffled along and no prog over 2f out: nvr nr ldrs* **16/1** | 52 |
| | 9 | ½ | **Irish Blade (IRE)** 2-9-0 ........ DaneO'Neill 1 (HCandy) *w'like: s.i.s: a in rr: struggling in last pair 3f out* **5/1**[3] | 51 |
| 0 | 10 | ½ | **Gliding By**[25] 5877 2-8-9 ........ MFenton 5 (PRChamings) *chsd ldrs: rdn over 4f out: wknd over 2f out* **33/1** | 45 |
| | 11 | 5 | **Self Razin (IRE)** 2-8-6 ........ FPFerris[(3)] 8 (MrsStefLiddiard) *neat: s.i.s: reminder after 1f: a struggling and wl in rr* **100/1** | 34 |



The Form Book, Raceform Ltd, Compton, RG20 6NL

63 **12** *2* **Rendoro (USA)**[30] 5798 2-9-0 .......... TQuinn 2 35
(RHannon) *racd on innr: pressed ldr to over 3f out: wknd rapidly 2f out* **7/1**

1m 40.21s (0.70) **Going Correction** +0.10s/f (Slow) **12** Ran SP% **126.3**
Speed ratings: **100,98,98,94,90 88,87,87,86,86 81,79**CSF £680.83 TOTE £73.10: £10.90, £5.50, £11.70; EX 647.80.
**Owner** Paul J Dixon **Bred** Darley **Trained** Newmarket, Suffolk

**FOCUS**
This may turn out to be a fair maiden for the time of year, as three of the first four home were newcomers.

**NOTEBOOK**
**Ascertain(IRE)**significantly impoved from his debut and sprang something of a suprise in the process. He was well beaten on his debut earlier this month, but looked a different horse this time, making smooth headway to challenge and when hitting the front, stuck to his task well. He will most likely be put away until next year, and the form of this race should have come to light by then, but he may be a fair colt.
**Kali**, reportedly highly-strung, made a pleasing debut and was doing all of her best work late on. This race was very much needed and it would be a suprise if she were not to build on this effort.
**Boxgrove(FR)**ran very green throught the early stages of the contest but, once finding his stride, caught the eye. He looks a big, backward type who will do much better in time, but there was a lot to like about this display.
**Magical Gift**was sluggish at the start and did well to finish where she did. She will improve plenty for this and can find a maiden on this surface during the winter.
**Okoboji(IRE)**may have found forcing the pace and this extra furlong against hime. He may be better than this and, although he failed to build on his promising debut run, it is unwise to write him off.

## 6073 BET DIRECT ON ITV PAGE 367 H'CAP (DIV I) 1m 2f (P)
**12:15** (12:16) (F) (0-60,60) 3-Y-0+ **£2,086** (£596; £298) **Stalls** Low

Form RPR
4004 **1** **Quantum Leap**[14] 5981 6-10-0 **60** .......... PaulEddery 2 70
(SDow) *lw: settled in rr: rdn and prog on outer fr 3f out: styd on u.p to ld nr fin: jst hld on* **6/1**[2]

2400 **2** *shd* **Castaigne (FR)**[8] 6024 4-9-8 **54** .......... (t) MFenton 13 64
(BWDuke) *dwlt: hld up wl in rr: last 3f out: gd prog on outer over 1f out: r.o wl fnl f: jst failed* **20/1**

4615 **3** *½* **True Companion**[23] 5910 4-9-10 **59** .......... J-PGuillambert(3) 8 68
(NPLittmoden) *settled towards rr: rdn and prog 3f out: drvn to ld wl over 1f out: hdd u.p nr fin* **3/1**[1]

040- **4** *hd* **Regal Gallery (IRE)**[462] 4053 5-9-6 **52** .......... TQuinn 6 60
(CAHorgan) *dwlt: settled wl in rr: stdy prog on inner over 2f out: plld out to press ldr ins fnl f: nt run on* **20/1**

0-00 **5** *2½* **Dickie Deadeye**[147] 2889 6-10-0 **60** .......... RHavlin 5 61
(GBBalding) *bit bkwd: racd in midfield: prog on inner 3f out: pressed ldrs 2f out: unable qck fnl f* **25/1**

122- **6** *3* **Sammy's Shuffle**[454] 4277 8-9-12 **58** .......... (b) IMongan 7 51
(JamiePoulton) *b: racd in midfield: prog 3f out: pressed ldrs 2f out: rdn and fnd nil over 1f out: wknd fnl f* **10/1**

006B **7** *1¼* **Another Secret**[20] 5937 5-9-5 **56** .......... AQuinn(5) 3 46
(GLMoore) *prom: rdn and lost pl wl over 2f out: n.d after* **16/1**

4000 **8** *nk* **Harlot**[24] 5891 3-9-6 **59** .......... LisaJones(3) 11 48
(JohnBerry) *racd towards rr: rdn and effrt on outer 3f out: no prog and btn wl over 1f out* **25/1**

1030 **9** *2* **Kyle Of Lochalsh**[65] 5116 3-9-9 **59** .......... DaneO'Neill 14 43
(GGMargarson) *s.v.s: hld up wl in rr: shuffled along and no prog over 2f out: nvr nr ldrs* **12/1**

2200 **10** *½* **Squeaky**[22] 5920 6-10-0 **60** .......... JFEgan 1 42
(MissKMGeorge) *w ldr to 1/2-way: sn rdn and lost pl: no ch over 2f out* **14/1**

0053 **11** *1½* **Balerno**[35] 5705 4-9-7 **53** .......... MTebbutt 12 31
(RIngram) *settled wl in rr: drvn and effrt on outer 3f out: sn no prog and btn* **13/2**[3]

-000 **12** *3* **Marakash (IRE)**[11] 6005 4-9-6 **52** .......... (p) GBaker 10 22
(MRBosley) *wl in tch: smooth prog to chse ldr 3f out: rdn and fnd nil 2f out: wknd rapidly over 1f out* **25/1**

0400 **13** *3* **Premier Cheval (USA)**[24] 5892 4-9-8 **54** .......... MartinDwyer 9 16
(RRowe) *prom: trckd ldr 1/2-way: led over 3f out: hdd & wknd rapidly wl over 1f out* **10/1**

0556 **14** *4* **Anemos (IRE)**[34] 5719 8-9-6 **57** .......... BReilly(5) 4 8
(PWD'Arcy) *mde most to over 3f out: wknd rapidly* **10/1**

2m 8.37s (0.98) **Going Correction** +0.10s/f (Slow)
**WFA** 3 from 4yo+ 4lb **14** Ran SP% **121.2**
Speed ratings: **100,99,99,99,97 94,93,93,92,91 90,88,85,82**CSF £127.81 CT £427.10 TOTE £6.80: £2.30, £3.40, £2.00; EX 147.00.
**Owner** Mrs M E O'Shea **Bred** L C And Mrs A E Sigsworth **Trained** Epsom, Surrey

**FOCUS**
A tight handicap run at a strong early gallop, suiting those held up off the pace.

**NOTEBOOK**
**Quantum Leap**prospered for a hold-up ride to win his first race since July 2001 and his first attempt at this trip. He has been given a chance by the Handicapper recently and should not go up too much for this success, but although he can remain competitive of this mark, his overall record means he is no good thing to follow-up.
**Castaigne(FR)**was only marginally denied a first win at the 31st attempt. She has slipped in the weights of latet and is has improvement in her on this surface, but her maiden tag can be no coincidence.
**True Companion**, on fair-looking mark for All-Weather racing, had every chance but was not good enough on the day. He is not the most straightforward of rides, but has the ability to win a race on this surface.
**Regal Gallery(IRE)**acquitted herself well after a lenghty absence form the racecourse. However, she looks to have her quirks as she seemed to hang around when produced to win her race. She is one to watch.

## 6074 BET DIRECT ON ATTHERACES INTERACTIVE MAIDEN STKS (DIV II) 1m (P)
**12:45** (12:46) (D) 2-Y-0 **£3,041** (£869; £434) **Stalls** High

Form RPR
3 **1** **Messe De Minuit (IRE)**[23] 5911 2-9-0 .......... DaneO'Neill 10 70+
(RCharlton) *lw: trckd ldrs: pushed along 3f out: effrt u.p on outer wl over 1f out: styd on wl fnl f to ld nr fin* **7/2**[3]

62 **2** *½* **Suave Quartet (USA)**[30] 5792 2-9-0 .......... MartinDwyer 1 69
(GAButler) *mde most: set stdy pce tl kicked on fr 1/2-way: drvn over 1f out : worn down nr fin* **5/2**[2]

2 **3** *1* **Bienvenue**[13] 5986 2-8-9 .......... ADaly 4 62
(MPTregoning) *lw: trckd ldrs: pushed along 3f out: unable qck over 1f out: styd on fnl f* **7/4**[1]

**4** *¾* **Music Mix (IRE)** 2-9-0 .......... TQuinn 2 65
(EALDunlop) *neat: bit bkwd: prom: rdn over 2f out: unable qck over 1f out: kpt on* **20/1**

0 **5** *nk* **Daggers Canyon**[19] 5939 2-9-0 .......... NCallan 6 64
(JulianPoulton) *t.k.h: mostly chsd ldr: rdn over 2f out: wknd ins fnl f* **33/1**

**6** *1¼* **Sunny Lady (FR)** 2-8-9 .......... WRyan 5 57
(EALDunlop) *unf: bit bkwd: settled towards rr: outpcd 3f out: shuffled along and styd on steadily fr over 1f out: nrst fin* **25/1**

**7** *½* **Day One** 2-9-0 .......... JFEgan 9 61
(GWragg) *w'like: bit bkwd: racd in midfield: rdn and effrt over 2f out: chsd ldrs over 1f out: rn green and fdd fnl f* **12/1**

**8** *¾* **Prince Valentine** 2-9-0 .......... MTebbutt 7 59
(DBFeek) *unf: bit bkwd: settled in rr: outpcd 3f out: kpt on steadily fnl 2f: n.d* **100/1**

**9** *1¾* **Red Contact (USA)** 2-9-0 .......... RSmith 11 55
(ACharlton) *w'like: bit bkwd: dwlt: wl in rr: outpcd and wl off the pce 3f out: styd on fr over 1f out: nrst fin* **50/1**

**10** *19* **Monte Major (IRE)** 2-9-0 .......... MHenry 8 13
(MAJarvis) *w'like: bit bkwd: prom tl wknd over 3f out: t.o* **20/1**

0 **11** *nk* **Silver Island**[19] 5938 2-9-0 .......... CCatlin 3 13
(GAButler) *s.i.s: sn in midfield: pushed along over 4f out: wknd 3f out: t.o* **20/1**

**12** *5* **Bless 'Em All** 2-8-9 .......... FNorton 12 —
(MBlanshard) *leggy: a in rr: last and struggling over 3f out: t.o* **50/1**

1m 42.6s (3.09) **Going Correction** +0.10s/f (Slow) **12** Ran SP% **120.8**
Speed ratings: **88,87,86,85,85 84,83,82,81,62 61,56**CSF £11.66 TOTE £4.10: £2.10, £1.10, £1.20; EX 12.60.
**Owner** Mountgrange Stud **Bred** Lisieux Stud **Trained** Beckhampton, Wilts

**FOCUS**
This was the weaker of the two divisions and was run in a time over two seconds slower.

**NOTEBOOK**
**Messe De Minuit(IRE)**confirmed the promise of his debut and won going away. He stayed this trip without any fuss and should have no problems getting ten furlongs next year. This form is nothing special, but he looks the type to do well in handicaps as a three-year-old.
**Suave Quartet(USA)**made a bold bid to make all the running, but although he did little wrong, he could do with dropping a furlong. He should find a maiden this winter.
**Bienvenue**, well-backed on the back of her debut over course-and-distance earlier in the month, was unable to find the change of gear to trouble the first two. She will come on again for this and looks the sort to get further as a three-year-old.
**Music Mix(IRE)**ran well for a long way and will come on quite a lot for the experience.
**Daggers Canyon**was free early in the race and as expected was outclassed when the pace got serious.
**Sunny Lady(FR)**was caught out by the lack of pace early on and will do better with a stronger gallop. This was a satisfactory debut.
**Bless 'Em All** *Official explanation: jockey said filly hung right*

## 6075 BET DIRECT ON 0800 32 93 93 CLAIMING STKS 1m 4f (P)
**1:15** (1:17) (F) 3-Y-0+ **£2,128** (£608; £304) **Stalls** Low

Form RPR
3333 **1** **Decelerate**[231] 977 3-8-11 58 .......... NCallan 2 52
(IAWood) *swtg: t.k.h: hld up in rr: prog over 3f out: nt clr run over 2f out: drvn on outer and r.o fnl f to ld last strides* **10/1**

3000 **2** *hd* **Raheel (IRE)**[9] 5795 3-9-5 54 .......... (t) DaneO'Neill 6 60
(PMitchell) *s.s: hld up in rr: prog on outer over 3f out: drvn to dispute ld wl over 1f out: led ins fnl f:hdd last strides* **12/1**

0005 **3** *1¼* **Water Of Life (IRE)**[13] 5989 4-9-4 49 .......... IMongan 9 51
(JRBoyle) *t.k.h: hld up in midfield: prog 3f out: drvn to dispute ld wl over 1f out: hdd ins fnl f: one pce* **9/1**

0210 **4** *shd* **Dangerous Beans**[7] 6026 3-9-5 54 .......... JFEgan 11 58
(SKirk) *chsd ldrs: pushed along over 3f out: nt qckn wl over 1f out: kpt on ins fnl f* **4/1**[2]

2514 **5** *nk* **Paradise Valley**[16] 5971 3-9-1 54 .......... (t) CCatlin 14 54
(MrsStefLiddiard) *settled towards rr: pushed along over 3f out: outpcd wl over 2f out: styd on fr wl over 1f out: nrst fin* **16/1**

0042 **6** *2* **Landescent (IRE)**[13] 5989 3-9-3 55 .......... (v) MFenton 10 53
(MQuinn) *trckd ldrs: effrt to press ldr 3f out: rdn and ev ch wl over 1f out: wknd fnl f* **5/1**[3]

0000 **7** *shd* **Gemma**[58] 5281 3-8-6 40 .......... DSweeney 3 41
(PJMakin) *b: b.hind: t.k.h: led for 1f: styd cl up: rdn over 2f out: fdd over 1f out* **50/1**

3050 **8** *nk* **Leophin Dancer (USA)**[33] 5069 5-8-12 38 .......... LisaJones(3) 5 44
(PWHiatt) *t.k.h: hld up towards rr: riddden and effrt over 2f out: one pce and no imp on ldrs* **25/1**

6401 **9** *½* **Compton Eclaire (IRE)**[13] 5989 3-8-10 52 .......... (v) MartinDwyer 4 44
(GAButler) *hld up wl in rr: effrt on inner over 2f out: one pce and no prog over 1f out* **5/2**[1]

050 **10** *1* **Radiant Bride**[28] 5826 3-7-9 45 .......... JFMcDonald(5) 1 33
(DWPArbuthnot) *t.k.h: hld up in midfield: trckd ldrs fr 3f out: rdn and cl up on inner whn hmpd over 1f out: nt rcvr* **16/1**

1000 **11** *5* **Maureen Ann**[20] 5937 3-8-8 48 .......... AClark 8 33
(MissBSanders) *dwlt: t.k.h: hld up in last: pushed along and lost tch wl over 2f out* **25/1**

0350 **12** *shd* **Cadwallader (USA)**[205] 1417 3-9-1 58 .......... (t) TQuinn 13 40
(PBurgoyne) *led after 1f to wl over 1f out: wknd rapidly* **33/1**

00 **13** *14* **Top Son**[42] 5574 4-9-7 .......... JoannaBadger 16 19
(APJones) *prom tl wknd over 4f out: t.o* **100/1**

004 **14** *2½* **Comanche Woman**[154] 2666 3-8-4 39 .......... SWhitworth 7 4
(KOCunningham-Brown) *dwlt: in rr tl rapid prog to join ldr 5f out: wknd rapidly over 3f out: t.o* **66/1**

2m 39.62s (5.64) **Going Correction** +0.10s/f (Slow)
**WFA** 3 from 4yo+ 6lb **14** Ran SP% **118.9**
Speed ratings: **85,84,84,83,83 82,82,82,81,81 77,77,68,66** CT £17.40 TOTE £4.20: £4.50, £3.40, £; EX217.40 1.The winner was claimed by Tony Charlton for £6,000. Radiant Bride was claimed by Kurl Burke for £3,000. Dangerous Beans
**Owner** John Purcell **Bred** John Purcell **Trained** Upper Lambourn, Berks

**FOCUS**
A blanket finish and traffic problems means this form should be treated warily.

**NOTEBOOK**
**Decelerate**, although running very freely early on, defied an eight-month absence to win under a strong ride. He was clear best at the weights, but was unproven over this far and he did very well to overcome traffic problems in the straight. He should continue to pay his way this winter around this track, which he loves. He was subsequently claimed by Tony Charlton for £6,000.
**Raheel(IRE)**was unfortunate to be reeled in as he gave everything in defeat. He beat the rest fair and square, did very well to overcome a slow start and, although he is a tricky ride, he has a race at this level within his compass.
**Water Of Life(IRE)**held every chance and ran his race with no excuses.

**Dangerous Beans**was well-backed for this despite not having an obvious chance at the weights. He was prominent throughout, but lacked the necessary change of gears to win this. He was not beaten far and is one to keep an eye on.
**Paradise Valley**was done little favours in-running and got badly outpaced turning in. He was finishing well however, and will be of interest if staying in this grade next time.
**Compton Eclaire(IRE)**is a lot better than her finishing position would suggest. She was kept out the back for most of the way and her rider elected to keep to the inside, where she had nowhere to go, and that proved very costly. She is not straightforward, but this is best forgotten. *Official explanation: trainer had no explanation for the poor form shown*
**Cadwallader(USA)** *Official explanation: jockey said gelding had a breathing problem*

## 6076 BET DIRECT ON ITV PAGE 367 H'CAP (DIV II) 1m 2f (P)
1:45 (1:45) (F ) (0-60,60) 3-Y-0+ **£2,079** (£594; £297) **Stalls** Low

Form RPR
5021 **1** **Compton Drake**[21] 5928 4-9-6 52 MartinDwyer 10 69+
(GAButler) *lw: trckd ldr: led after 3f: mde rest: 3l clr and in command 3f out: drvn over 1f out: kpt on* **11/10**[1]
0002 **2** *1 ½* **Lyrical Way**[34] 5717 4-9-5 51 (b) FNorton 7 63
(PRChamings) *prom: chsd wnr 5f out: rdn and no imp 3f out: kpt on ins fnl f: nvr able to chal* **25/1**
0005 **3** *1 ¾* **Man The Gate**[33] 5729 4-9-12 58 TQuinn 3 67
(PDCundell) *lw: prom: rdn over 3f out: chsd ldng pair wl over 2f out: clr of remainder fnl 2f: kpt on* **11/1**
0030 **4** *2* **Welsh Wind (IRE)**[29] 5821 7-9-10 56 (t) IMongan 8 61
(MWigham) *dwlt: settled in last pair: wl off the pce fr 4f out: pushed along and styd on steadily fr over 2f out: nvr nr ldrs* **16/1**
0-05 **5** *1 ½* **Ember Days**[14] 5976 4-9-8 54 ADaly 11 57
(JLSpearing) *racd towards rr: pushed along over 4f out: sme prog to chse clr ldrs over 2f out: hanging lft and no hdwy after* **9/1**
5003 **6** *1 ¼* **My Maite (IRE)**[14] 5981 4-9-7 53 (t) NDay 1 53
(RIngram) *lw: racd in midfield: pushed along and outpcd fr 4f out: n.d fnl 2f* **7/1**[2]
2040 **7** *2* **Esperance (IRE)**[14] 5975 3-9-10 60 DaneO'Neill 5 57
(JAkehurst) *hmpd s: racd in last pair: wl off the pce 4f out: modest late prog* **16/1**
0050 **8** *nk* **Wellington Hall (GER)**[53] 5359 5-9-4 57 (b) PGallagher(7) 4 53
(ACharlton) *led for 3f: chsd wnr to 5f out: steadily wknd fr 3f out* **33/1**
2000 **9** *1 ¼* **Colourful Lady (USA)**[29] 5817 3-9-8 58 NCallan 13 52
(PWHarris) *b.hind: a towards rr: rdn and struggling over 3f out* **33/1**
0300 **10** *shd* **Toledo Sun**[30] 5795 3-9-9 59 MTebbutt 12 53
(HJCollingridge) *a in rr: brief effrt on outer over 3f out: sn no prog* **15/2**[3]
0553 **11** *3 ½* **In Spirit (IRE)**[186] 1833 5-10-0 60 WMLordan 9 47
(BJCurley) *b: a in last trio: pushed along and no prog over 3f out* **50/1**
340B **12** *5* **Indian Blaze**[20] 5937 9-9-6 55 J-PGuillambert(3) 2 33
(AndrewReid) *b: b.hind: racd in midfield: rdn over 4f out: sn wknd* **16/1**
4222 **U** **Fife And Drum (USA)**[49] 5453 6-9-8 59 (p) AQuinn(5) 6 —
(MissJFeilden) *stmbld bdly s and uns rdr* **12/1**

2m 7.95s (0.56) **Going Correction** +0.10s/f (Slow)
**WFA** 3 from 4yo+ 4lb **13** Ran **SP% 127.2**
Speed ratings: **101,99,98,96,95 94,93,92,91,91 88,84,—**CSF £43.73 CT £243.98 TOTE £2.00: £1.40, £5.90, £3.30; EX 53.00.
**Owner** Erik Penser **Bred** Meon Valley Stud **Trained** Blewbury, Oxon

**FOCUS**
A fair handicap run in a time nearly half a second faster than the first division.

**NOTEBOOK**
**Compton Drake**, racing off a 7lb lower mark than on turf, was sent to the front plenty soon enough and made the best of his way home. Front-runners find things tough over this trip, so this was probably a better performance than it looked.
**Lyrical Way**was in vain pursuit of the winner in the second half of the contest, but could never quite narrow the gap. There will be other opportunities for him under these conditions this winter.
**Man The Gate**ran his race and is well handicapped on his best form.
**Welsh Wind(IRE)**, well handicapped on his turf form, stayed on late in the day and may be worth a try over a mile and a half here, but a record of just two wins from 56 starts has to be a concern.
**Ember Days**, rated 13lb lower on sand than on turf, was trying her longest trip to date and did not really convince either way whether she saw it out.
**My Maite(IRE)**never got into it and was disappointing, but he was forced to race tight to the inside rail from his draw and at this meeting that was a big handicap.

## 6077 LITTLEWOODS BET DIRECT NURSERY 6f (P)
2:20 (2:20) (D ) (0-85,71) 2-Y-0 **£2,968** (£848; £424) **Stalls** Low

Form RPR
6412 **1** **Maunby Raver**[7] 6029 2-8-5 **62** RoryMoore(7) 7 63
(PCHaslam) *lw: chsd ldrs: rdn and effrt 2f out: chal fnl f: styd on wl to ld lasst strides* **9/2**
0235 **2** *nk* **After All (IRE)**[4] 6045 2-8-12 **62** MartinDwyer 6 62
(GAButler) *lw: s.i.s: hld up in last pair: prog on outer over 2f out: rdn to ld narrowly ins fnl f: hdd last strides* **4/1**[3]
0001 **3** *hd* **Fools Entire**[13] 5990 2-8-8 **63** BReilly(5) 5 63
(JAGilbert) *dwlt: racd in rr: rdn over 2f out: nt qckn over 1f out: r.o ins fnl f: nrst fin* **8/1**
0402 **4** *½* **Burlington Place**[8] 6020 2-8-13 **63** JFEgan 9 61
(SKirk) *lw: pressed ldr: led over 2f out: narrowly hdd ins fnl f: one pce nr fin* **11/4**[1]
3551 **5** *nk* **Pompey Blue**[16] 5968 2-9-7 **71** NCallan 2 68+
(PJMcbride) *trckd ldrs: nt clr run on inner over 1f out: cl up ent fnl f: unable qck* **7/2**[2]
0000 **6** *¾* **Taranai (IRE)**[14] 5979 2-8-4 **57** LisaJones(3) 1 52
(BWDuke) *in rr: outpcd 2f out: styd on again ins fnl f* **50/1**
6200 **7** *3* **Intikraft (IRE)**[16] 5968 2-8-10 **60** (b[1]) FNorton 4 46
(MrsStefLiddiard) *chsd ldrs: drvn to chal 1/2-way: ev ch wl over 1f out: sn wknd* **25/1**
4060 **8** *4* **Power To Burn**[22] 5916 2-8-10 **60** (t) CCatlin 8 34
(KBell) *racd wd: in tch in rr tl wknd wl over 1f out* **25/1**
4516 **9** *1* **Forzenuff**[45] 5496 2-9-6 **70** DaneO'Neill 3 41
(JRBoyle) *led to over 2f out: wknd rapidly over 1f out* **12/1**

1m 13.77s (0.85) **Going Correction** +0.10s/f (Slow) **9** Ran **SP% 115.5**
Speed ratings: **98,97,97,96,96 95,91,85,84**CSF £22.43 CT £139.56 TOTE £5.40: £2.10, £1.50, £1.70; EX 24.30.
**Owner** Maunby Investment Management **Bred** A S Leftwich **Trained** Middleham Moor, N Yorks

**FOCUS**
A competitive nursery, but with little more than two lengths covering the front six the form is probably only ordinary.

**NOTEBOOK**
**Maunby Raver**, who has been in good form on Fibresand, had questions to answer on this surface off a 7lb higher mark, but proved up to the task and the way he battled back after the runner-up had headed him was especially creditable. Despite this victory, his best chance of further success probably still lies back on Fibresand.
**After All(IRE)**was last to leave the stalls, but still did not lose as much ground as she did here four days ago. Brought with her effort wide and late, she looked to have timed her run to perfection but did not seem to quite go through with her effort and was worried out of it. Either she did not stay or her attitude has to be called into question.
**Fools Entire**, making his debut for the yard after winning a course-and-distance seller last time, took a long time to get into gear and when he did it was a few strides too late. He has been placed over further on turf so looks worth stepping up in trip.
**Burlington Place**ran up to his best under a positive ride, but remains vulnerable to a finisher over this trip.
**Pompey Blue**, winner of a Fibresand maiden last time, would have finished much closer had she enjoyed a clear passage in the home straight.

## 6078 BETDIRECT.CO.UK CLASSIFIED STKS 6f (P)
2:55 (2:55) (D ) 3-Y-0+ **£3,484** (£1,072; £536; £268) **Stalls** Low

Form RPR
3601 **1** **Texas Gold**[24] 5888 5-9-3 85 MartinDwyer 10 99+
(WRMuir) *lw: t.k.h early: hld up in midfield: prog over 2f out: shkn up over 1f out: r.o to ld last 100y: pushed out* **11/10**[1]
1005 **2** *¾* **Law Breaker (IRE)**[9] 6010 5-8-12 85 BReilly(5) 6 95
(JAGilbert) *pressed ldr: rdn 2f out: led 1f out: hdd and unable qck last 100y* **14/1**
1400 **3** *1 ¼* **Sir Desmond**[9] 6014 5-8-12 80 (p) CCatlin 5 86
(RGuest) *chsd ldrs: rdn and sltly outpcd over 2f out: prog on inner over 1f out: nt pce to chal last 100y* **12/1**
1025 **4** *2 ½* **Zarzu**[7] 6030 4-8-7 80 RThomas(5) 8 79
(CRDore) *trckd ldrs: cl enough over 1f out: rdn and nt qckn fnl f* **10/1**[3]
0/-0 **5** *½* **Cretan Gift**[23] 5908 12-9-0 85 (b) J-PGuillambert(3) 4 82
(NPLittmoden) *racd towards rr: outpcd over 2f out: styd on ins fnl f: n.d* **20/1**
0000 **6** *nk* **Prince Of Blues (IRE)**[7] 6030 5-8-12 80 (p) JBramhill 13 76
(MMullineaux) *led: hdd & wknd 1f out* **50/1**
3-00 **7** *2* **Uncle Bernon**[98] 4282 4-8-12 78 RHavlin 14 70
(GBBalding) *b.hind: s.i.s: racd in last trio: outpcd fr 1/2-way: kpt on u.p fnl f: no ch* **50/1**
-600 **8** *1 ¾* **Power Bird (IRE)**[38] 3-8-9 78 PDoe 2 62
(DFlood) *s.i.s: racd in last trio: modest late prog* **66/1**
0220 **9** *shd* **Steel Blue**[7] 6030 3-9-0 82 (p) DeanMcKeown 7 67
(RMWhitaker) *s.i.s: racd in last trio: outpcd and rdn 1/2-way: no ch after* **13/2**[2]
323- **10** *1* **Magic Glade**[410] 5216 4-9-3 85 MFenton 12 67
(CRDore) *bit bkwd: racd towards rr: effrt and sme prog on outer over 2f out: wknd over 1f out* **12/1**
0300 **11** *3* **Emerald Fire**[24] 5888 4-8-6 77 (v[1]) LPKeniry(3) 1 50
(AMBalding) *lw: trckd ldrs: trapped on inner and lost pl bdly 1/2-way: drvn and brief effrt over 1f out: sn wknd* **14/1**
0004 **12** *10* **Bond Royale**[9] 6010 3-8-9 79 IMongan 3 20
(BSmart) *lw: pressed ldrs to over 3f out: wknd rapidly over 2f out: eased fnl f: t.o* **10/1**[3]

1m 11.82s (-1.10) **Going Correction** +0.10s/f (Slow) **12** Ran **SP% 118.0**
Speed ratings: **111,110,108,105,104 103,101,98,98,97 93,80**CSF £17.96 TOTE £1.80: £1.30, £4.90, £3.30; EX 27.90.
**Owner** C L A Edginton **Bred** Coln Valley Stud **Trained** Lambourn, Berks

**FOCUS**
A decent classified event run at a very strong pace.

**NOTEBOOK**
**Texas Gold**, who absolutely loves this track, was given a copybook ride, stalking the pace on the outside of the field and being produced at just the right time. His last nine starts here have yielded five victories and four second places.
**Law Breaker(IRE)**has shown much better form on Fibresand in the past, so this fine effort will hearten connections for a return to that surface.
**Sir Desmond**came with his usual late flourish, but did so tight against the inside rail and at this meeting that probably was not the place to be.
**Zarzu**was not disgraced, but appears to lack the required turn of foot for this surface these days.
**Cretan Gift**, a Pattern-class performer in his time, was also one of the best All-Weather sprinters around a few years ago and this effort suggests there is still some ability there, but he still seems likely to find a few too speedy for him these days off this sort of mark.
**Prince Of Blues(IRE)**showed a lot more sparkle than he has for some time, especially as he made the running against the inside rail. His best form has been at Wolverhampton, so he could still be of interest back there.

## 6079 BET DIRECT IN RUNNING SKY TEXT 293 H'CAP 2m (P)
3:30 (3:30) (E ) (0-75,75) 3-Y-0+ **£2,331** (£666; £333) **Stalls** Low

Form RPR
3313 **1** **Hefin**[42] 5576 6-8-12 **59** NCallan 12 70
(IAWood) *lw: prom: trckd ldr gng easily over 3f out: led over 2f out and kicked on: hld on wl fnl f* **4/1**[2]
0311 **2** *1* **Macaroni Gold (IRE)**[2] 6061 3-8-7 **63** 6ex SWhitworth 8 73
(WJarvis) *b.hind: dwlt: hld up in rr: stdy prog 4f out to chse ldng pair over 2f out: chsd wnr over 1f out: no imp last 100y* **11/4**[1]
5064 **3** *3* **Final Dividend (IRE)**[14] 5975 7-7-10 **46** (p) FPFerris(3) 10 52
(JMPEustace) *racd in midfield: effrt 3f out: outpcd by ldrs over 2f out: styd on to take 3rd ins fnl f* **16/1**
P502 **4** *1* **Astromancer (USA)**[14] 5975 3-7-12 **54** MHenry 5 59
(MHTompkins) *lw: pressed ldr: led over 3f out to over 2f out: wknd fnl f* **10/1**
5203 **5** *¾* **Red Scorpion (USA)**[9] 6017 4-9-8 **69** JFEgan 2 73
(WMBrisbourne) *hld up in midfield: lost pl on inner and last 6f out: swtchd wd 5f out: outpcd over 3f out: styd on fr over 1f out: no ch* **5/1**[3]
/-06 **6** *4* **Hello Holly**[14] 5975 6-7-12 **45** oh4 PMQuinn 6 44
(MrsALMKing) *racd in midfield: effrt and sme prog over 3f out: outpcd over 2f out: fdd over 1f out* **25/1**
2000 **7** *3 ½* **Starry Mary**[8] 6025 5-8-4 **51** FNorton 1 46
(ELJames) *trckd ldng pair to 4f out: hmpd on inner 3f out: no ch after* **66/1**
2024 **8** *1 ¼* **Academy (IRE)**[37] 5675 8-8-11 **58** CCatlin 11 52
(AndrewTurnell) *dwlt: racd towards rr: rdn 4f out: effrt u.p 3f out: sn btn* **14/1**
6453 **9** *hd* **Rome (IRE)**[54] 5343 4-9-11 **72** DaneO'Neill 4 65
(GPEnright) *dwlt: wl in rr: prog on outer to chse ldrs over 4f out: outpcd and btn wl over 2f out* **14/1**
0-06 **10** *1 ½* **Dance Light (IRE)**[21] 5927 4-9-4 **65** DeanMcKeown 7 57
(TTClement) *b: a towards rr: outpcd and btn over 3f out* **33/1**
3020 **11** *½* **Sea Plume**[14] 5975 4-10-0 **75** MartinDwyer 3 66
(LadyHerries) *lw: led to over 3f out: sn wknd* **8/1**
2300 **12** *shd* **Hajeer (IRE)**[7] 6033 5-8-4 **51** JBramhill 13 42
(PWHiatt) *chsd ldrs: rdn and lost pl over 3f out: sn wknd* **25/1**

0406 **13** *hd* **First Pressure**[7] 6033 3-7-13 **58**....(p) LisaJones(3) 9 49
(DRCElsworth) *t.k.h: hld up in tch: lost pl and struggling 4f out* **33/1**
0043 **14** *3* **Forever My Lord**[2] 6061 5-8-0 **54**.... DFentiman(7) 14 41
(JRBest) *dwlt: hld up last: effrt on wd outside 5f out: rdn and struggling 4f out* **16/1**

3m 26.81s (-1.77) **Going Correction** +0.10s/f (Slow)
**WFA** 3 from 4yo+ 9lb **14** Ran SP% **123.7**
Speed ratings: **108,107,106,105,105 103,101,100,100,99 99,99,99,98**CSF £15.01 CT £166.31 TOTE £5.80: £2.10, £2.10, £5.70; EX 19.10 Place 6 £1,330.91, Place 5 £44.38.
**Owner** Christopher Shankland **Bred** Jaffer R Ali **Trained** Upper Lambourn, Berks

**FOCUS**
A fair staying handicap run at a sound pace.

**NOTEBOOK**
**Hefin**, proven under the conditions, was in the ideal position compared with his last outing here and was set alight at just the right time to get first run on the favourite. He was never going to relinquish the advantage after that.
**Macaroni Gold(IRE)**, bidding for an eight-day hat-trick, was off the same mark as when scoring at Southwell 48 hours earlier. Given a patient ride, he was caught out for a bit of pace when the winner went for home off the bend. He could never quite get back on terms and it may be that the slower Fibresand surface suits him better.
**Final Dividend(IRE)**, trying this trip for the first time on the Flat, seemed to see it out well enough and could find an ordinary contest under similar conditions.
**Astromancer(USA)**, another trying this trip for the first time, set the pace and it was only well inside the last furlong that she visibly tired. More patient tactics may help her if she is tried over this distance again.
**Red Scorpion(USA)**may have been unfortunate not to finish closer as he was trapped away on the inside for a circuit and when pulled wide about five furlongs from home, found himself caught out for pace. As a result he had plenty to do, but then got his second wind and was coming home strongly. He goes on Fibresand too, so he still has possibilities in a similar contest on either surface.
**Sea Plume**again failed to sparkle on this surface and was already on the retreat when short of room on the inside three furlongs from home.
T/Plt: £3,861.80 to a £1 stake. Pool: £29,096.40. 5.50 winning tickets. T/Qpdt: £14.00 to a £1 stake. Pool: £4,294.20. 225.40 winning tickets. JN

# 6036 WOLVERHAMPTON (A.W) (L-H)

## Friday, November 28

**OFFICIAL GOING: Standard**
Wind: slt across Weather: fine

## 6080 BET DIRECT ON 0800 32 93 93 H'CAP (DIV I) 5f (F)

**12:50** (12:50) (E) (0-75,73) 3-Y-0+ **£2,037** (£582; £291) **Stalls** Low

Form RPR
0064 **1** **Polish Emperor (USA)**[21] 5941 3-9-10 **70**....(b) JFanning 9 81
(PWHarris) *mde all: rdn wl over 1f out: rdn out* **5/2**[1]
0-34 **2** *1 1/2* **Blueberry Rhyme**[7] 6038 4-9-6 **66**....(v) DSweeney 6 72
(PJMakin) *a.p: rdn 3f out: chsd wnr 2f out: r.o one pce fnl f* **7/1**[3]
6510 **3** *2* **Kiss The Rain**[28] 5849 3-8-4 **50**.... GGibbons 8 49
(RBrotherton) *prom: outpcd and rdn over 3f out: hdwy on outside fnl f: edgd lft: r.o* **16/1**
4000 **4** *1/2* **Cark**[64] 5178 5-8-1 **47**.... ANicholls 10 44
(JBalding) *hld up and bhd: hdwy over 2f out: sn rdn: one pce fnl f* **14/1**
0042 **5** *1 3/4* **Frascati**[13] 6001 3-9-6 **73**.... SJDonohoe(7) 2 64
(ABerry) *mid-div: hdwy wl over 1f out: no imp* **15/2**
0005 **6** *2* **Lone Piper**[42] 5606 8-8-0 **46** ow1.... CCatlin 5 30
(JMBradley) *prom: rdn over 2f out: wknd fnl f* **16/1**
0000 **7** *3/4* **Intellibet One**[31] 5811 3-9-0 **60**.... DaneO'Neill 7 41
(PDEvans) *nvr nr ldrs* **20/1**
4666 **8** *1/2* **Only One Legend (IRE)**[13] 6001 5-9-13 **73**....(b) NCallan 12 53
(KARyan) *prom: rdn over 2f out: wknd wl over 1f out* **7/1**[3]
-524 **9** *hd* **Valazar (USA)**[311] 357 4-9-4 **64**.... ACulhane 11 43
(DWChapman) *w wnr over 2f: rdn and wknd wl over 1f out* **13/2**[2]
2005 **10** *1* **Somethingabouther**[14] 5998 3-7-9 **44**.... LisaJones(3) 13 19
(PWHiatt) *s.i.s: a bhd* **25/1**
4003 **11** *5* **Sea The World (IRE)**[13] 6001 3-9-2 **62**.... DarrenWilliams 1 20
(DShaw) *a bhd* **12/1**
1000 **12** *3 1/2* **Brioso (IRE)**[32] 5794 3-8-11 **57**....(b[1]) JTate 3 3
(JMPEustace) *rdn over 3f out: sn bhd* **12/1**

62.77 secs (0.17) **Going Correction** +0.075s/f (Slow) **12** Ran SP% **121.1**
Speed ratings: **101,98,95,94,91 88,87,86,86,84 76,71**CSF £19.86 CT £240.12 TOTE £2.60: £1.40, £2.30, £5.20; EX 40.00.
**Owner** Mrs P W Harris **Bred** Chevington Stud **Trained** Ringshall, Bucks

**FOCUS**
Polish Emperor appears to be improving and scored with something in hand.

**NOTEBOOK**
**Polish Emperor(USA)** confirmed just how effective he can be over the minimum trip on Fibresand. He might still be ahead of the Handicapper next time.
**Blueberry Rhyme**, back in handicap company, may have come up against a progressive sort in the winner and might now be ready for a return to six.
**Kiss The Rain**, without the visor this time, needs a return to six.
**Cark** does not have a very good strike rate but was coming back after a two-month break.
**Frascati**, raised 3lb, could well benefit for a return to Southwell.
**Sea The World(IRE)** *Official explanation: jockey said gelding hung left-handed*

## 6081 BET DIRECT ON 0800 32 93 93 H'CAP (DIV II) 5f (F)

**1:20** (1:20) (E) (0-75,73) 3-Y-0+ **£2,037** (£582; £291) **Stalls** Low

Form RPR
2100 **1** **Woodland Blaze (IRE)**[180] 2027 4-9-13 73.... IMongan 6 83
(PRChamings) *sn chsng ldrs: wnt 2nd over 3f out: rdn over 2f out: r.o u.p to ld cl home* **6/1**[2]
0644 **2** *hd* **Rellim**[65] 5156 4-8-1 50.... FPFerris(3) 2 59
(PABlockley) *led: hrd rdn fnl f: hdd cl home: r.o* **10/1**
0056 **3** *2* **Malahide Express (IRE)**[3] 6063 3-9-2 65....(b) LFletcher(3) 5 67
(MJPolglase) *hdwy over 3f out: sn rdn: edgd rt jst over 1f out: nt qckn* **10/1**
3405 **4** *3/4* **Time N Time Again**[27] 5880 5-9-4 67.... DAllan(3) 10 66+
(EJAlston) *mid-div: rdn over 3f out: hdwy 2f out: nt clr run jst over 1f out tl ins fnl f: nt rcvr* **5/1**[1]
0003 **5** *1/2* **Henry Tun**[7] 6038 5-8-10 56....(b) JEdmunds 11 54
(JBalding) *a.p: rdn 2f out: one pce fnl f* **13/2**[3]
0002 **6** *1/2* **Sandgate Cygnet**[46] 5538 3-8-12 61.... DMcGaffin(3) 4 57
(ISemple) *s.s: rdn over 2f out: hdwy whn hung lft over 1f out: kpt on towards fin* **5/1**[1]
0200 **7** *3/4* **Catchthebatch**[7] 6038 7-8-4 53.... DCorby(3) 9 46
(MJWallace) *stdd s: hld up in rr: rdn and sme hdwy over 1f out: n.d* **20/1**
0063 **8** *hd* **Carols Choice**[4] 6056 6-7-13 45.... RFfrench 8 38
(ASadik) *prom: rdn over 2f out: wknd ins fnl f* **9/1**
-002 **9** *2 1/2* **Enjoy The Buzz**[42] 5625 4-7-10 45.... LisaJones(3) 12 29
(JMBradley) *s.i.s: a bhd* **50/1**
0041 **10** *2* **Gone'N'Dunnett (IRE)**[13] 6001 4-9-10 70....(v) DaneO'Neill 13 47
(MrsCADunnett) *sn bhd* **5/1**[1]
0300 **11** *3/4* **Sabana (IRE)**[78] 4838 5-8-1 47.... PFitzsimons 3 21
(JMBradley) *s.i.s: a bhd* **25/1**
0164 **12** *6* **Hagley Park**[230] 1030 4-8-4 50.... AClark 1 3
(MQuinn) *sn chsng ldrs: rdn over 3f out: wknd over 2f out* **25/1**
3000 **13** *3 1/2* **Floppie Disk**[49] 5472 3-9-3 63.... CCatlin 7 4
(JAPickering) *prom: lost pl after 1f: sn bhd* **25/1**

62.72 secs (0.12) **Going Correction** +0.075s/f (Slow) **13** Ran SP% **124.1**
Speed ratings: **102,101,98,97,96 95,94,94,90,86 85,76,70**CSF £62.76 CT £606.56 TOTE £7.60: £3.10, £2.90, £6.20; EX 129.70.
**Owner** Patrick Chamings Sprint Club **Bred** The Alpine Sunset Partnership **Trained** Baughurst, Hants

**FOCUS**
Ian Mongan rode a winner on his first ride for trainer Patrick Chamings.

**NOTEBOOK**
**Woodland Blaze(IRE)**, off course for six months, has gone well when fresh in the past and defied a mark 6lb higher than when scoring at Southwell in May.
**Rellim** confirmed her liking for this surface on her first outing for a new stable. She went down with all guns blazing.
**Malahide Express(IRE)** was duly dropped back to five but is at his best when he is able to make the running.
**Time N Time Again**, dropping back to five, had no luck in running in the home straight and was definitely third best on merit.
**Henry Tun** was set to go up 4lb tomorrow after his good effort in a claimer last week. Like the third, he is another who is best when able to dominate.
**Sandgate Cygnet**, whose turf form suggested she would handle Fibresand, could never recover from an indifferent start.

## 6082 BET DIRECT ON ATTHERACES INTERACTIVE MEDIAN AUCTION MAIDEN STKS 1m 100y(F)

**1:50** (1:52) (F) 2-Y-O **£2,317** (£662; £331) **Stalls** Low

Form RPR
05 **1** **Lasting Delight**[55] 5378 2-8-9.... GDuffield 6 67+
(SirMarkPrescott) *mid-div: hdwy 4f out: sn rdn: led jst over 1f out: edgd rt ins fnl f: drvn out* **9/2**[2]
460 **2** *3/4* **Russalka**[21] 5938 2-8-9 63.... NCallan 11 63
(JulianPoulton) *s.i.s: hld up: hdwy 3f out: sn rdn: styd on ins fnl f* **20/1**
6035 **3** *2 1/2* **Piccleyes**[18] 5966 2-9-0 63.... DaneO'Neill 4 63
(RHannon) *w ldr: led over 5f out: rdn and hdd jst over 1f out: no ex ins fnl f* **10/1**
32 **4** *1 1/2* **New York (IRE)**[23] 5923 2-8-9.... ACulhane 5 55
(WJHaggas) *a.p: chsd ldr over 3f out: sn rdn: wknd fnl f* **2/1**[1]
023 **5** *3/4* **Petite Colleen (IRE)**[26] 5886 2-8-9 72.... FNorton 9 53
(DHaydnJones) *hld up in tch: rdn over 3f out: outpcd over 2f out: styd on again towards fin* **9/2**[2]
02 **6** *2* **Jakarmi**[14] 5993 2-9-0.... DKinsella 12 54
(BPalling) *hld up: hdwy on outside over 5f out: wknd over 2f out* **7/1**[3]
0 **7** *12* **Ivory Coast (IRE)**[29] 5833 2-8-9.... IMongan 3 24
(WRMuir) *prom tl rdn and wknd over 3f out* **16/1**
0 **8** *nk* **Vesta Flame**[21] 5940 2-8-9.... JFanning 7 23
(MJohnston) *a bhd* **33/1**
3 **9** *nk* **Drizzle**[42] 5620 2-9-0.... MHenry 13 27
(JWUnett) *s.i.s: a bhd* **10/1**
**10** *nk* **Kilminchy Lady (IRE)**[86] 4668 2-8-9.... KDalgleish 8 22
(WRMuir) *s.i.s: a bhd* **50/1**
0 **11** *8* **Calculaite**[11] 6011 2-9-0.... MFenton 2 10
(MrsGSRees) *led 3f: wknd over 3f out* **100/1**
**12** *2 1/2* **What A Spree** 2-8-6.... LPKeniry(3) 10 —
(WRMuir) *a bhd* **66/1**
00 **13** *1* **Beauchamp Surprise**[20] 5948 2-8-9.... CCatlin 1 —
(GAButler) *bhd fnl 4f* **33/1**

1m 52.59s (1.59) **Going Correction** +0.075s/f (Slow) **13** Ran SP% **121.3**
Speed ratings: **95,94,91,90,89 87,75,75,74,74 66,64,63**CSF £99.29 TOTE £3.90: £1.40, £6.90, £6.10; EX 173.40.
**Owner** Miss K Rausing **Bred** Miss K Rausing **Trained** Newmarket, Suffolk

**FOCUS**
Lasting Delight caught out those who thought she might be on a mission to obtain a handicap mark.

**NOTEBOOK**
**Lasting Delight** justified market support and duly appreciated the step up from six furlongs. She still showed signs of greeness and there is further improvement to come.
**Russalka** made a highly satisfactory switch to the sand and is certanily capable of going one better on this evidence.
**Piccleyes** had previously been campaigned at around six furlongs and it could be that seven is his optimum trip at the moment.
**New York(IRE)**, stepping up from seven, had her stamina limitations exposed on this demanding surface.
**Petite Colleen(IRE)**, out of a mare who won over hurdles, found this trip inadequate even on this testing surface.
**Jakarmi** found this company hotter than when narrowly beaten over course and distance in a claimer a fortnight ago.

## 6083 LITTLEWOODS BET DIRECT NURSERY 7f (F)

**2:20** (2:22) (E) (0-85,81) 2-Y-O **£3,402** (£972; £486) **Stalls** High

Form RPR
0252 **1** **Fadeela (IRE)**[3] 6069 2-8-2 **67**....(e) BReilly(5) 8 75
(PWD'Arcy) *hld up: hdwy over 3f out: rdn over 2f out: led ins fnl f: rdn out* **6/1**[2]
0004 **2** *1* **Little Eye (IRE)**[18] 5966 2-8-3 **63**.... NPollard 6 68
(JRBest) *a.p: rdn to ld 2f out: hdd ins fnl f: kpt on* **7/1**[3]
6142 **3** *8* **Chubbes**[10] 6023 2-9-0 **74**....(v) JFanning 3 59
(MCPipe) *led: rdn 3f out: hdd 2f out: wknd over 1f out* **6/4**[1]
1033 **4** *nk* **Sweet Cando (IRE)**[31] 5824 2-8-5 **65**.... GDuffield 5 49
(MissLAPerratt) *chsd ldrs: rdn over 3f out: wknd over 2f out* **12/1**
0402 **5** *hd* **Bethanys Boy (IRE)**[25] 5906 2-9-2 **76**.... CCatlin 4 60
(BEllison) *w ldr: rdn and ev ch 2f out: wknd wl over 1f out* **9/1**
101 **6** *2* **Ermine Grey**[14] 5994 2-9-7 **81**....(v) PaulEddery 9 60
(DHaydnJones) *bhd: sme hdwy over 1f out: n.d* **8/1**
4553 **7** *3* **Lady Piste (IRE)**[56] 5340 2-8-8 **68** ow1....(t) NCallan 7 39
(PDEvans) *rdn over 4f out: sn bhd* **25/1**
2246 **8** *3/4* **Baker Of Oz**[60] 5278 2-8-12 **72**.... DaneO'Neill 2 41
(RHannon) *sn outpcd* **7/1**[3]

6650 **9** 8 **Garnock Venture (IRE)**[32] 5789 2-8-0 60 DaleGibson 11 9
(ABerry) *a bhd* **66/1**
3533 **10** 6 **Bond Brooklyn**[11] 6011 2-8-10 70 (b) RFfrench 1 —
(BSmart) *prom over 3f* **14/1**
1m 29.63s (-0.57) **Going Correction** +0.075s/f (Slow) **10** Ran SP% **120.1**
Speed ratings: **106,104,95,95,95 92,89,88,79,72**CSF £49.17 CT £97.78 TOTE £7.70: £2.10, £2.10, £1.40; EX 70.40.
**Owner** M Al Salem **Bred** Musaid Abo Salim **Trained** Newmarket, Suffolk
**FOCUS**
This could turn out to be solid form with the first two pulling well clear.
**NOTEBOOK**
**Fadeela(IRE)** justified the decision to run again quickly with her trainer fearing that she may get hammered by the Handicapper after her good second at Southwell on Tuesday.
**Little Eye(IRE)** was not inconvenienced by the return to a longer trip and simply met one too good. His turn is near.
**Chubbes** was set to rise 4lb in future handicaps. He may have gone off too quickly and got found out by this more demanding surface despite a drop back from a mile.
**Sweet Cando(IRE)** was trying a longer trip on her All-Weather bow.
**Bethanys Boy(IRE)**, up 4lb, possibly paid the penalty for going the strong pace on his sand debut.
**Ermine Grey** could never get competitive off a 6lb higher mark.

## 6084 BETDIRECT.CO.UK H'CAP 6f (F)
2:50 (2:50) (D) (0-80,78) 3-Y-O+ £3,052 (£872; £436) Stalls Low

Form RPR
0230 **1** **Port St Charles (IRE)**[151] 2855 6-9-8 74 IMongan 13 82
(PRChamings) *a.p: rdn over 2f out: led wl over 1f out: jst hld on* **10/1**
0006 **2** nk **Cashel Mead**[11] 6014 3-9-12 78 ADaly 7 85
(JLSpearing) *s.i.s: rapid hdwy on outside fnl f: jst failed* **8/1**
2254 **3** hd **Rafters Music (IRE)**[11] 6014 8-9-3 72 LisaJones(3) 4 79
(JulianPoulton) *sn bhd: gd hdwy fnl f: fin wl* **9/2**[2]
0000 **4** 1 1/4 **Dunedin Rascal**[15] 5987 6-9-4 70 (b) SWhitworth 6 73
(EAWheeler) *hld up and bhd: hdwy wl over 1f out: str run ins fnl f: no ex cl* **20/1**
0010 **5** 1 1/4 **If By Chance**[31] 5811 5-9-1 70 (b) SHitchcott(3) 12 69
(RCraggs) *led: rdn over 2f out: hdd wl over 1f out: one pce fnl f* **11/1**
6056 **6** 1/2 **Paddywack (IRE)**[20] 5946 6-9-6 72 (b) ACulhane 9 70
(DWChapman) *hld up: hdwy over 3f out: rdn over 2f out: ev ch wl over 1f out: wknd towards fin* **9/4**[1]
0000 **7** 3/4 **Winning Pleasure (IRE)**[31] 5811 5-9-8 74 JEdmunds 1 69
(JBalding) *prom: lost pl after 2f: rallied on ins over 1f out: no imp fnl f* **12/1**
2000 **8** shd **African Spur (IRE)**[41] 5634 3-9-2 75 DerekNolan(7) 8 70
(PABlockley) *hld up: rdn over 2f out: hdwy wl over 1f out: no ex fnl f* **20/1**
0000 **9** hd **Ronnie From Donny (IRE)**[21] 5941 3-9-8 74 DaneO'Neill 5 68
(BEllison) *prom: rdn and sltly outpcd over 3f out: rallied 2f out: wknd ins fnl f* **10/1**
0004 **10** 1 3/4 **Legalis (USA)**[14] 5995 5-9-3 69 NCallan 3 58
(KARyan) *rdn over 3f out: a bhd* **6/1**[3]
0600 **11** 1/2 **Whippasnapper**[161] 2526 3-9-0 73 DFentiman(7) 10 61
(JRBest) *hld up: short-lived effrt over 2f out* **33/1**
0000 **12** hd **Warden Warren**[10] 6024 5-8-13 70 (p) BReilly(5) 2 57
(MrsCADunnett) *chsd ldrs 2f: sn bhd* **25/1**
0000 **13** 2 **Blakeshall Quest**[11] 6010 3-9-8 74 GGibbons 11 55
(RBrotherton) *prom: rdn over 2f out: wknd wl over 1f out* **50/1**
1m 15.91s (0.21) **Going Correction** +0.075s/f (Slow) **13** Ran SP% **126.8**
Speed ratings: **101,100,100,98,97 96,95,95,94,92 91,91,89**CSF £87.40 CT £435.85 TOTE £10.50: £3.30, £3.60, £1.70; EX 132.40.
**Owner** Twenty Twenty Research **Bred** Michael Collins **Trained** Baughurst, Hants
**FOCUS**
Ian Mongan made it two out of two with a double for Patrick Chamings.
**NOTEBOOK**
**Port St Charles(IRE)**, coming back after a five-month absence, has run well when fresh in the past. Defying a mark 7lb higher than when successful at Southwell back in January, he is a rarity in that he handles all three All-Weather tracks.
**Cashel Mead** must surely have won had she not fluffed the start. She is well handicapped on her turf form.
**Rafters Music(IRE)** finished with a flourish but it has to be said that the runner-up came from behind him.
**Dunedin Rascal** could not sustain his run as well as both the second and third but does seem to be coming to hand.
**If By Chance** was by no means disgraced in this company.
**Paddywack(IRE)** would not mind a drop back to the minimum distance.

## 6085 BET DIRECT ON ITV PAGE 367 (S) STKS 1m 4f (F)
3:20 (3:20) (G) 3-Y-O+ £2,093 (£598; £299) Stalls Low

Form RPR
3013 **1** **Royal Prodigy (USA)**[51] 2765 4-9-11 63 DaneO'Neill 1 61
(RJHodges) *chsd ldrs: rdn over 4f out: led 1f out: r.o wl* **10/11**[1]
0400 **2** 1 1/4 **Al's Alibi**[26] 5890 10-9-6 41 FNorton 2 54
(WRMuir) *hld up mid-div: hdwy over 5f out: rdn over 3f out: ev ch 1f out: nt qckn* **6/1**[2]
345- **3** 9 **Bella Pavlina**[205] 5284 5-9-1 39 KDalgleish 8 36
(WMBrisbourne) *chsd ldr: led over 5f out: rdn over 3f out: hdd 1f out: wknd* **6/1**[2]
6030 **4** 3 1/2 **Aveiro (IRE)**[16] 5975 7-9-3 34 (b) LPKeniry(3) 12 35
(BGPowell) *hld up in tch: rdn over 3f out: wknd 2f out* **10/1**[3]
036 **5** 5 **Samar Qand**[11] 6016 4-9-1 49 (p) NCallan 6 23
(JulianPoulton) *prom: rdn over 3f out: wknd 2f out* **10/1**[3]
0500 **6** 15 **Giust In Temp (IRE)**[29] 4365 4-9-3 37 LFletcher(3) 10 5
(PWHiatt) *hld up towards rr: hdwy over 5f out: rdn over 3f out: wknd over 2f out* **12/1**
0000 **7** 5 **Bugle Call**[7] 6039 3-9-0 43 SWhitworth 4 —
(KOCunningham-Brown) *s.s: bhd tl hdwy over 5f out: wknd over 3f out* **25/1**
50-4 **8** 1 1/2 **Felix Holt (IRE)**[30] 5826 3-9-0 32 (b) NPollard 5 —
(JRBest) *dwlt: hrd rdn over 5f out: a bhd* **66/1**
05 **9** dist **Final View (FR)**[19] 3955 4-9-3 (b[1]) J-PGuillambert(3) 9 —
(NPLittmoden) *s.i.s: a bhd: t.o fnl 4f* **25/1**
6000 **10** dist **Look East**[30] 5832 4-9-6 35 (p) CCatlin 7 —
(MrsCADunnett) *bhd fnl 7f: t.o fnl 5f* **66/1**
106/ **11** 4 **Bathwick Dream**[895] 2184 6-9-1 GBaker 3 —
(BRMillman) *led over 6f: wknd qckly over 4f out: t.o* **16/1**
0005 **12** dist **Malmand (USA)**[11] 6016 4-9-11 42 (v) GGibbons 11 —
(RBrotherton) *s.i.s: bhd: rdn over 5f out: eased 3f out: t.o* **16/1**
2m 41.13s (-0.37) **Going Correction** +0.075s/f (Slow)
**WFA** 3 from 4yo+ 6lb **12** Ran SP% **129.3**
Speed ratings: **104,103,97,94,91 81,78,77,—,— —,—**CSF £7.35 TOTE £1.80: £1.10, £2.30, £3.80; EX 10.10.The winner was bought in for 3,500gns.
**Owner** D Charlesworth **Bred** Bertram N Linder **Trained** Charlton Adam, Somerset
**FOCUS**
An uncompetitive seller.
**NOTEBOOK**
**Royal Prodigy(USA)** has landed two selling hurdles since being bought out of Martin Pipe's stable when winning a similar event here in June.
**Al's Alibi** would have been meeting the winner on no less than 17lb better terms in a handicap.
**Bella Pavlina** had not been seen since pulling up over hurdles in May. She seemed to have her stamina limitations exposed.
**Aveiro(IRE)** does not seem to find much off the bridle these days.
**Samar Qand** has yet to prove she stays this trip.
**Look East** *Official explanation: jockey said gelding lost its action on the final bend*
**Bathwick Dream** *Official explanation: trainer said mare bled from the nose*
**Malmand(USA)** *Official explanation: jockey said gelding lost its action*

## 6086 BET DIRECT IN RUNNING SKY TEXT 293 MAIDEN STKS 1m 1f 79y(F)
3:50 (3:50) (D) 3-Y-O £2,299 (£657; £328) Stalls Low

Form RPR
**1** **Valerian (IRE)**[34] 5764 3-9-0 MFenton 11 72+
(CharlesO'Brien, Ire) *s.i.s: sn prom: rdn 3f out: led ins fnl f: carried hd high: drvn out* **10/1**
62 **2** 2 1/2 **Nicholas Nickelby**[7] 6039 3-8-11 J-PGuillambert(3) 6 67
(NPLittmoden) *a.p: led over 3f out: sn rdn: hdd ins fnl f: nt qckn* **3/1**[2]
3606 **3** 1/2 **Nuzzle**[16] 5980 3-8-9 58 (v) FNorton 9 61
(MQuinn) *a.p: rdn over 3f out: swtchd rt over 1f out: kpt on ins fnl f* **12/1**
00-0 **4** 3 **Suerte**[25] 5907 3-8-9 62 JFanning 8 55
(JGGiven) *hld up: stdy hdwy over 5f out: rdn over 3f out: one pce fnl 2f* **6/1**[3]
3064 **5** 2 **Silver Crystal (IRE)**[3] 6067 3-8-6 45 LisaJones(3) 4 51
(MrsNMacauley) *sn bhd: hdwy over 1f out: n.d* **20/1**
2342 **6** 3/4 **Over Rating**[13] 6005 3-8-9 64 DaneO'Neill 2 50
(JHMGosden) *sn led: rdn and hdd over 3f out: wknd over 1f out* **6/5**[1]
065 **7** 3/4 **Tata Naka**[10] 6022 3-8-4 NChalmers(5) 10 48
(MrsCADunnett) *hld up: hdwy over 3f out: wknd 2f out* **40/1**
6500 **8** 1 1/4 **Red Moor (IRE)**[28] 5856 3-9-0 45 ACulhane 3 51
(RHollinshead) *hld up in tch: rdn over 3f out: wkng whn n.m.r on ins over 2f out* **25/1**
0054 **9** nk **Lovellian**[113] 3939 3-8-9 52 GBaker 12 45
(BRMillman) *s.i.s: sn prom: rdn over 3f out: wknd over 2f out* **20/1**
035 **10** 12 **Realism (FR)**[3] 6067 3-9-0 DarrenWilliams 1 26
(PWHiatt) *led early: prom tl wknd over 3f out* **20/1**
00 **11** 6 **Galley Law**[62] 5227 3-8-11 SHitchcott(3) 5 14
(RCraggs) *s.s: rdn 4f out: a bhd* **100/1**
2m 3.46s (0.56) **Going Correction** +0.075s/f (Slow) **11** Ran SP% **123.1**
Speed ratings: **100,97,97,94,92 92,91,90,90,79 74**CSF £38.87 TOTE £9.10: £2.40, £1.60, £2.70; EX 48.80 Place 6 £155.54, Place 5 £74.06.
**Owner** L V Pearson **Bred** Lars Pearson **Trained** Straffan, Co Kildare
**FOCUS**
A modest maiden.
**NOTEBOOK**
**Valerian(IRE)**, whose trainer ran out of time with him in Ireland, proved good enough in this company despite displaying a high head carriage. He is likely to be sold on.
**Nicholas Nickelby** was stepping up from seven and perhaps the stretch mile here might be the answer.
**Nuzzle** was having her first taste of Fibresand and even on this surface she showed why she has been running over ten furlongs.
**Suerte**, a sister to useful mile and a quarter handicapper Crow Wood, ran respectably on her All-Weather debut.
**Silver Crystal(IRE)** had previously been campaigned exclusively at a mile.
**Over Rating** was disappointing and had not excuses on account of the trip being on the short side this time.
T/Plt: £327.70 to a £1 stake. Pool: £41,210.15. 91.80 winning tickets. T/Qpdt: £29.40 to a £1 stake. Pool: £3,621.60. 91.10 winning tickets. KH

# 6072 LINGFIELD (L-H)
## Saturday, November 29

**OFFICIAL GOING: Standard**
The track appeared to be favouring those that made their runs late down the centre of the course.
Wind: Straight behind Weather: Murky

## 6087 BET DIRECT NO Q MAIDEN STKS (DIV I) 1m 2f (P)
11:55 (11:55) (D) 2-Y-O £3,558 (£1,095; £547; £273) Stalls Low

Form RPR
0653 **1** **Keep On Movin' (IRE)**[11] 6023 2-8-4 74 RMiles(5) 3 59
(TGMills) *lw: prom: lost pl 1/2-way: prog on inner 3f out: chsd ldr 2f out: drvn to ld ins fnl f: edgd rt: jst hld on* **7/2**[2]
4050 **2** shd **Trompe L'Oeil (IRE)**[40] 5671 2-8-9 60 MFenton 12 59
(EALDunlop) *racd in midfield tl prog to ld 5f out: kicked on over 2f out: edgd rt and hdd ins fnl f: kpt on: jst failed* **25/1**
04 **3** 1 1/2 **Resonance**[16] 5984 2-8-9 WRyan 4 56+
(MrsAJPerrett) *lw: hld up in last pair: smooth prog but stl plenty to do 2f out: r.o strly fnl f: hopeless task: sure to do bttr* **5/1**[3]
00 **4** 3/4 **Absolutelythebest (IRE)**[61] 5278 2-9-0 TQuinn 10 60
(EALDunlop) *hld up in last trio: prog on outer over 3f out: rdn and unable qck 2f out: styd on fnl f: nrst fin* **25/1**
33 **5** nk **Master Theo (USA)**[45] 5578 2-9-0 IMongan 8 59
(HJCollingridge) *chsd ldr to 1/2-way: sn chsd new ldr: rdn over 2f out: cl up 1f out: fdd last 100y* **5/2**[1]
05 **6** nk **Semelle De Vent (USA)**[30] 5833 2-8-9 RHavlin 9 54
(JHMGosden) *trckd ldrs: rdn and unable qck over 2f out: n.d after: kpt on* **7/1**
0 **7** 2 **Crackleando**[16] 5986 2-8-11 J-PGuillambert(3) 13 55
(NPLittmoden) *hld up in rr: prog to chse ldrs 3f out: no imp 2f out: wknd fnl f* **33/1**
**8** 3/4 **Wings Of Morning (IRE)**[34] 5776 2-9-0 SWhitworth 5 54
(NACallaghan) *plld hrd early and hld up in last trio: in last pair and no ch 2f out: taken wd in st: shuffled along and styd on fnl f* **40/1**

0332 **9** *1* **Bill Bennett (FR)**[14] 6003 2-9-0 74 KDalgleish 7 52
(JJay) *taken down early: racd wd: led to 1/2-way: prom after: losing pl whn hmpd on inner over 2f out* **5/1**[3]

000 **10** *½* **Almost Welcome**[89] 4610 2-9-0 39 PDoe 11 51
(SDow) *a towards rr: effrt 3f out: no prog 2f out* **100/1**

00 **11** *hd* **Warif (USA)**[46] 5563 2-9-0 RFfrench 6 51
(EJO'Neill) *sn chsd ldrs: rdn over 3f out: wknd 2f out* **8/1**

00 **12** *2½* **Sportula**[31] 5830 2-8-9 DaneO'Neill 2 41
(MrsAJPerrett) *nvr gng wl: in rr and pushed along 1/2-way: struggling over 2f out* **50/1**

2m 13.0s (5.61) **Going Correction** +0.20s/f (Slow) **12** Ran SP% **123.8**
Speed ratings: **85,84,83,83,82 82,81,80,79,79 79,77**CSF £98.04 TOTE £3.50: £2.20, £10.10, £1.10; EX 99.40.
**Owner** J E Harley **Bred** Leslie Tucker **Trained** Headley, Surrey

**FOCUS**

A race run at a dawdle early and eventually became a half-mile sprint.

**NOTEBOOK**

**Keep On Movin'(IRE)**was ridden much closer to the pace this time, which was just as well, as it enabled her to keep tabs on the runner-up when she made her bid for glory off the final bend. She was brave in the finish, but the way the race was run this did not fully test her ability to see out the longer trip.

**Trompe L'Oeil(IRE)**, who had shown very little in four starts on turf, improved greatly on this sand debut but this effort owes a great deal to a fine tactical ride from her jockeyr, who made a sudden burst for victory half a mile from home only to have the race snatched from her. The slow final time does cast a doubt over the precise value of the form however.

**Resonance**was given an awful lot to do, sitting right at the back in a slowly-run race and remained on the bridle for a very long way. When she did try to make headway, she had to take the slalom route through and around horses, but finished with such a flourish that with a more positive ride she would probably have won. She will be a short price to make amends.

**Absolutelythebest(IRE)**appeared to run with credit following two moderate efforts on turf, but the form should be taken with a large pinch of salt. She should get a modest handicap mark though.

**Master Theo(USA)**had looked as though he would benefit from this step up in trip, but would probably have preferred a proper gallop and he was done for foot down the home straight.

**Bill Bennett(FR)**pulled himself to the front early and did far too much too soon. Given a more patient ride in a truly-run race, he will show this form to be all wrong. *Official explanation: jockey said gelding hung right*

## 6088 BET DIRECT NO Q VOICE AUTOMATED BETTING CLASSIFIED STKS (DIV I) 7f (P)

**12:25** (12:28) (F) 3-Y-0+ **£2,114** (£604; £302) **Stalls** Low

Form RPR

4003 **1** **Pants**[33] 5793 4-8-10 52 ANicholls 15 63
(AndrewReid) *b. b.hind: hld up in last pair: stl wl in rr over 2f out: taken to wd outside bnd wl over 1f out: str run fnl f to ld last* **16/1**

2604 **2** *nk* **Inistrahull Island (IRE)**[11] 6019 3-8-12 57 JFanning 13 65
(MHTompkins) *cl up: prog to join ldrs 3f out: led 2f out and kicked on: looked wnr fnl f: tl collared last strides* **5/1**[3]

0021 **3** *½* **Zagala**[8] 6036 3-8-9 61 (t) ACulhane 10 61
(SLKeightley) *racd in midfield: prog on outer to press ldrs over 2f out: sn unable qck: styd on wl u.p fnl f* **10/3**[1]

4256 **4** *nk* **A Woman In Love**[11] 6024 4-8-10 55 TQuinn 12 60
(MissBSanders) *hld up wl in rr: effrt towards outer over 2f out: r.o fnl f: jst outpcd* **9/2**[2]

2365 **5** *½* **Pancakehill**[190] 1799 4-8-10 56 IMongan 7 59
(DKIvory) *t.k.h: prom: effrt 2f out: chsd ldr over 1f out: no imp ins fnl f: lost three pls nr fin* **16/1**

5500 **6** *1* **Kinsman (IRE)**[11] 6019 6-8-13 53 (p) PDoe 9 60
(TDMccarthy) *s.s: hld up wl in rr: stdy prog over 2f out: rdn to chse ldrs over 1f out: nt qckn* **14/1**

0504 **7** *nk* **Mad Mick Meeson**[61] 5283 3-8-12 58 (t) AClark 16 59
(GBBalding) *racd on outer: hld up in rr: prog over 2f out: unable qck over 1f out: kpt on one pce fnl f* **25/1**

3404 **8** *shd* **Miss Issy (IRE)**[17] 5976 3-8-9 55 (v[1]) NCallan 11 56
(JGallagher) *hld up towards rr: effrt whn nt clr run 3f out: kpt on one pce fnl 2f* **9/1**

000 **9** *1* **Roman Empire**[4] 6065 3-8-12 59 JMcAuley 5 56
(TJEtherington) *chsd ldrs: rdn and cl up over 2f out: hanging lft and nt qckn over 1f out* **20/1**

5610 **10** *nk* **A Teen**[27] 5892 5-8-13 55 DKinsella 2 55
(PHowling) *prom: rdn and lost pl on inner over 2f out: n.d after* **25/1**

0523 **11** *hd* **Smith N Allan Oils**[11] 6024 4-8-13 56 (p) MFenton 8 55
(MDods) *racd in midfield: effrt over 2f out: sn squeezed out and lost pl: nt clr run over 1f out: styng on but no ch whn hmpd last* **11/2**

0000 **12** *6* **Tuscan Treaty**[16] 5987 3-8-9 56 JMackay 6 37
(TTClement) *prom: rdn to chse ldr briefly wl over 1f out: wknd rapidly fnl f* **33/1**

2300 **13** *2½* **Montana**[16] 5988 3-8-12 60 DaneO'Neill 3 34
(RHannon) *pressed ldr: led wl over 3f out to 2f out: wknd rapidly over 1f out* **20/1**

3-00 **14** *13* **Sandrone (IRE)**[12] 4837 3-8-9 53 (b[1]) CCatlin 4 —
(PMPhelan) *pressed ldrs 3f: lost pl rapidly u.p: sn wl bhd: t.o* **50/1**

0000 **15** *3½* **Ginger Ice**[56] 5376 3-8-12 55 NPollard 1 —
(GGMargarson) *led to wl over 3f out: sn wknd: t.o* **66/1**

1m 27.2s (1.20) **Going Correction** +0.20s/f (Slow)
**WFA** 3 from 4yo+ 1lb **15** Ran SP% **125.4**
Speed ratings: **101,100,100,99,99 98,97,97,96,96 95,89,86,71,67**CSF £90.58 TOTE £14.30: £3.20, £2.00, £1.80; EX 145.20.
**Owner** A S Reid **Bred** A S Reid **Trained** Mill Hill, London NW7

**FOCUS**

A typically competitive if low-grade race of its type with a few hard luck stories.

**NOTEBOOK**

**Pants**has run well here before and also been placed several times on Fibresand, but she put up an amazing performance this time, finishing with a real flourish down the wide outside to get up near the line and record her first win at the 36th attempt. As impressive as this was, her overall record does not suggest a quick follow-up.

**Inistrahull Island(IRE)**travelled so well that he may have got to the front sooner than his rider had wanted, but he still looked likely to win a furlong out only for a 35-raced maiden to come from out of the clouds and do him near the line. He will surely not remain a maiden for much longer, but is unlikely to get much help from the Handicapper either.

**Zagala**, up 6lb for her Wolverhampton win, kept battling away and was still going forward at the line. She may be better suited by a mile on this faster surface.

**A Woman In Love**, who wins in her turn, produced her usual strong finish but so did several others.

**Pancakehill**is not straightforward, but did not run at all badly on this first start in six months.

**Kinsman(IRE)**continues to drop down the handicap and this effort suggests he has not completely lost all ability.

**Miss Issy(IRE)**did not enjoy the clearest of runs, but has had plenty of chances.

**Smith N Allan Oils**endured a nightmare passage and this effort should be forgotten.

## 6089 PRESS RED TO BET DIRECT MAIDEN STKS 1m 4f (P)

**12:55** (12:56) (D ) 3-Y-O **£2,310** (£660; £330) **Stalls** Low

Form RPR

0602 **1** **Sea Holly (IRE)**[5] 6060 3-9-0 74 KDalgleish 12 70
(GGMargarson) *trckd ldrs: prog 1/2-way: led over 3f out: drvn fnl 2f: hld on* **11/2**[3]

6 **2** *¾* **So Vital**[26] 5907 3-9-0 RPrice 9 69
(MrsLydiaPearce) *bkwd: racd in midfield: prog 1/2-way: chsd wnr 3f out: chal fnl 2f: a jst hld* **12/1**

65 **3** *hd* **Schooner (GER)**[17] 5978 3-9-0 MTebbutt 11 69+
(LadyHerries) *settled in last: sme prog but wl off the pce 3f out: rdn and styd on strly fr over 1f out: gaining fast at fin: will improv* **10/1**

0030 **4** *nk* **Grand Folly (FR)**[54] 5425 3-8-9 65 IMongan 2 63
(AMHales) *trckd ldrs: outpcd whn nt clr run wl over 2f out: styd on wl fr over 1f out: nrst fin* **14/1**

5225 **5** *1* **Hoh Viss**[113] 3960 3-9-0 72 JFEgan 6 67
(SKirk) *trckd ldrs: nt clr run over 3f out: sn outpcd: effrt over 2f out: styd on same pce fr over 1f out* **10/1**

0203 **6** *1* **Remembrance**[17] 5978 3-9-0 63 (tp) JTate 8 65
(JMPEustace) *hld up in midfield: trckd ldrs 3f out: cl up over 1f out: plld out ent fnl f: hung rt and nt run on* **5/2**[1]

32 **7** *5* **Namaste**[25] 5917 3-8-9 TQuinn 13 53
(HRACecil) *lw: disp ld tl over 3f out: 4th and btn whn hmpd on inner wl over 1f out: wknd* **7/2**[2]

**8** *6* **Splendid Touch**[21] 3-8-9 38 SWhitworth 4 44
(JRJenkins) *towards rr: outpcd fr 3f out: no ch after* **66/1**

4000 **9** *1½* **Distinctlysplendid**[10] 6032 3-8-10 34 ow1 DNolan[(5)] 10 48
(IAWood) *racd towards rr: rdn over 4f out: btn 3f out* **100/1**

04 **10** *16* **Nassau Street**[28] 5879 3-9-0 MFenton 5 23
(DJSFfrenchDavis) *a in rr: rdn 6f out: wl bhd over 2f out: t.o* **50/1**

**11** *4* **Dub Dash (USA)** 3-8-9 BReilly[(5)] 1 17
(SCWilliams) *w'like: s.s: a wl in rr: t.o over 2f out* **16/1**

-500 **12** *7* **Back In Action**[7] 6052 3-9-0 75 (bt[1]) CCatlin 7 6
(MAMagnusson) *t.k.h: disp ld to 4f out: wknd rapidly: t.o* **7/1**

0400 **13** *5* **Ella's Wish (IRE)**[27] 5891 3-8-9 60 (b[1]) RHavlin 16 —
(JHMGosden) *cl up tl wknd rapidly over 2f out: t.o* **25/1**

0500 **14** *24* **Prince Ivor**[82] 4766 3-9-0 40 RSmith 3 —
(JCFox) *a in rr: lost tch 1/2-way: t.o 4f out* **66/1**

0 **15** *dist* **Carolina Morning (IRE)**[32] 5815 3-8-9 NCallan 14 —
(HJCollingridge) *hld up in rr: wknd over 5f out: sn t.o: fin v slowly* **33/1**

2m 34.76s (0.78) **Going Correction** +0.20s/f (Slow) **15** Ran SP% **129.8**
Speed ratings: **105,104,104,104,103 102,99,95,94,83 81,76,73,57,—**CSF £72.83 TOTE £7.60: £2.70, £4.90, £3.50; EX 134.20.
**Owner** P E Axon **Bred** Swettenham Stud **Trained** Newmarket, Suffolk

**FOCUS**

Probably not a bad maiden of its type, run at a sound pace, and there should be a winner or two to come out of it.

**NOTEBOOK**

**Sea Holly(IRE)**, a good second over this trip at Southwell five days earlier, made full use of his proven stamina and was sent for home before the home bend. He may be able to make his mark in handicap company on sand at around this trip. cvbg dg xdgxc , a good second over this trip at Southwell five days earlier, made full use of his proven stamina and was sent for home before the home bend. He may be able to make his mark in handicap company on sand at around this trip.\n\x\x , a good second over this trip at Southwell five days earlier, made full use of his proven stamina and was sent for home before the home bend. He may be able to make his mark in handicap company on sand at around this trip.\n

**So Vital**, having only his second start, ran a cracker and should be able to find a middle-distance maiden on sand before too long.

**Schooner(GER)**, given a patient ride, came home as though his tail was on fire and had his effort started just 20 yards earlier he would have won. Performances like this can be misleading as races are run in different ways, but he obviously possesses some ability.

**Grand Folly(FR)**, making her sand debut on her 12th start, was staying on strongly at the line after running into traffic and getting outpaced racing down the hill. She lacks scope, but is not completely without ability and may be better suited by the slower Fibresand surfaces.

**Hoh Viss**, another making his sand debut, did not enjoy the clearest of runs, but his lack of pace was a bigger problem.

**Remembrance**still had a chance of making the frame a furlong from home but, despite the cheekpieces, he hung violently to his right and lost all chance. Unless there was a physical reason for this, he should be treated with a degree of caution.

**Namaste**was already beaten when getting squeezed out on the final bend. Even her great trainer will have to perform miracles to get a win out of her.

**Carolina Morning(IRE)** *Official explanation: jockey said filly lost her action*

## 6090 BETDIRECT.CO.UK NOVICE STKS 7f (P)

**1:25** (1:26) (D) 2-Y-O **£3,248** (£928; £464) **Stalls** Low

Form RPR

0 **1** **Caledonian (IRE)**[28] 5867 2-8-12 TQuinn 1 78+
(DRCElsworth) *settled wl in rr: plenty to do whn effrt over 2f out: str run fnl f: led last strides: cheekily* **16/1**

1062 **2** *hd* **Mister Saif (USA)**[7] 6048 2-9-5 84 DaneO'Neill 11 81
(RHannon) *trckd ldrs: rdn and sltly outpcd over 2f out: styd on to chse ldr ins fnl f: led last 50y: hdd fnl strides* **2/1**[2]

**3** *½* **Skidmark** 2-8-8 PFitzsimons 13 69
(DRCElsworth) *w'like: s.s and lft 6l: hld up in last: stl last but gng easily over 2f out: r.o strly fnl f: promising* **50/1**

2310 **4** *nk* **Rise**[17] 5979 2-8-11 84 (b) IMongan 4 71
(AndrewReid) *led: kicked on over 2f out: 2l clr ins fnl f: hdd last 50y* **10/1**[3]

10 **5** *nk* **Crocodile Dundee (IRE)**[36] 5731 2-9-5 SWhitworth 5 78
(JamiePoulton) *trckd ldrs: rdn fr 3f out: no imp tl styd on wl fnl f: nrst fin* **6/4**[1]

3434 **6** *nk* **Ever Cheerful**[11] 6021 2-8-5 66 LTreadwell[(7)] 2 71?
(WGMTurner) *prom: chsd ldr 3f out: drvn and no imp over 1f out: lost four pls ins fnl f* **20/1**

36 **7** *3* **Scarlett Rose**[28] 5868 2-8-7 CLowther 14 58
(DrJDScargill) *prom: chsd ldr 4f out to 3f out: wknd fnl f* **11/1**

03 **8** *nk* **Comeraincomeshine (IRE)**[11] 6020 2-8-2 RMiles[(5)] 6 57
(TGMills) *trckd ldrs: effrt on inner 3f out: outpcd over 2f out: fdd over 1f out* **10/1**[3]

00 **9** *1¼* **I Wish I Knew**[15] 5997 2-8-12 DSweeney 3 59?
(PJMakin) *racd in midfield: rdn and outpcd over 2f out: no prog after* **100/1**

60 **10** *hd* **Moscow Times**[57] 5345 2-8-12 NPollard 9 59
(DRCElsworth) *hld up in rr: outpcd over 2f out: shuffled along over 1f out: nvr nr ldrs: do bttr* **11/1**

11 *5* **Golden Drift** 2-8-5 ow2 JFEgan 8 39
(GWragg) *bkwd: dwlt: a in rr: outpcd over 2f out: wknd* **25/1**

02 **12** *3* **Stonor Lady (USA)**[11] 6021 2-8-2 BReilly[(5)] 12 34
(PWD'Arcy) *a towards rr: wknd wl over 2f out* **33/1**

6650 **13** *4* **Fox Hollow (IRE)**[87] 4655 2-8-12 35 CCatlin 7 29
(MJHaynes) *chsd ldr to 4f out: wknd: sn bhd* **200/1**

1m 27.37s (1.37) **Going Correction** +0.20s/f (Slow) **13** Ran SP% **129.1**
Speed ratings: **100,99,99,98,98 98,94,94,92,92 87,83,79**CSF £50.47 TOTE £24.30: £3.60, £1.50, £10.10; EX 98.40.
**Owner** The Caledonian Racing Society **Bred** Ballylinch Stud **Trained** Whitsbury, Hants

**FOCUS**
A fascinating contest run at a decent pace.

**NOTEBOOK**
**Caledonian(IRE)**, a Derby entry, was a springer in the market but appeared to have an impossible task turning for home. However, he found an amazing turn of foot to cut down the leaders in the straight and in the end even scored a little comfortably despite the winning margin. He looks an interesting prospect.
**Mister Saif(USA)**is not enjoying much luck at the moment and, despite doing nothing wrong, was nailed on the line again for the second time in seven days. He will not be an easy horse to place.
**Skidmark ◆**, a half brother to several winners including Kastaway, Musally and Rampant, ran a race that was just as eye-catching as his stable companion the winner. Given a patient ride after mising the break, he made up an enormous amount of ground in the closing stages and is bred to appreciate much further than this. Few would want to oppose him in maiden company on this surface.
**Rise**, given a positive ride, performed with a good deal of credit and time will show she was probably up against a couple of very smart rivals. She is handicapped up to her best, but will not always run into such useful unexposed types.
**Crocodile Dundee(IRE)**, proven on the surface, came off the bridle some way out but took too long getting into gear and his late rally was never going to be enough. He probably needs further now.
**Ever Cheerful**had a lot to do on official ratings, especially against some useful and unexposed rivals, but he was not totally disgraced over a trip that is still probably beyond his best.

## 6091 BET DIRECT NO Q MAIDEN STKS (DIV II) 1m 2f (P)
**1:55** (1:56) (D) 2-Y-O **£3,542** (£1,090; £545; £272) **Stalls** Low

Form RPR

043 **1** **Pukka (IRE)**[16] 5984 2-9-0 79 LDettori 5 71+
(LMCumani) *settled in midfield: stdy prog over 3f out: swooped into ld wl over 1f out: sn in command: pushed out* **8/15**[1]

063 **2** *2* **Baawrah**[14] 6003 2-9-0 71 ACulhane 10 67
(MRChannon) *prom in chsng gp: chsd ldr over 4f out to 2f out: drvn to chse wnr 1f out: no imp* **8/1**[2]

06 **3** *nk* **Polar Dancer**[16] 5986 2-8-9 WRyan 12 62
(MrsAJPerrett) *dwlt: settled in rr: stdy prog on outer fr 3f out: rdn and styd on same pce fr over 1f out* **16/1**

40 **4** *1* **Chara**[28] 5869 2-8-9 SWhitworth 2 60
(JRJenkins) *settled wl in rr: prog on outer over 2f out: chsd ldrs over 1f out: kpt on one pce* **10/1**[3]

0620 **5** *3* **Hold The Line**[12] 6012 2-8-7 67 LTreadwell[(7)] 3 60
(WGMTurner) *t.k.h: led for 2f: chsd ldr to 5f out: rdn 3f out: hanging lft and btn over 1f out* **16/1**

00 **6** *nk* **Abbeygate**[28] 5871 2-9-0 MTebbutt 11 59
(TKeddy) *dwlt: hanging rt thrght: hld up in last: stdy prog fr 3f out: nt clr run over 1f out: hung rt and one pce fnl f* **14/1**

0 **7** *½* **Jango Malfoy (IRE)**[29] 5847 2-9-0 MFenton 7 58
(BWDuke) *prom in chsng gp: led over 4f out to wl over 1f out: sn wknd on inner* **100/1**

000 **8** *2½* **Elusive Dream**[14] 6002 2-9-0 JMackay 6 54
(SirMarkPrescott) *settled in rr: lost tch fr 3f out: no ch after* **10/1**[3]

6450 **9** *nk* **Darn Good**[11] 6023 2-9-0 69 DaneO'Neill 4 53
(RHannon) *chsd ldrs: rdn over 3f out: wknd 2f out* **8/1**[2]

0 **10** *½* **Spring Whisper (IRE)**[22] 5939 2-8-9 (v[1]) TQuinn 9 47
(EALDunlop) *hld up in midfield: prog over 3f out: rdn and cl up 2f out: wknd rapidly over 1f out* **20/1**

00 **11** *8* **Flying Patriarch**[29] 5847 2-9-0 (b) RBrisland 1 38
(GLMoore) *chsd ldrs: pushed along and lost pl 6f out: struggling in rr over 3f out* **100/1**

0000 **12** *dist* **Mystic Promise (IRE)**[39] 5691 2-9-0 30 (b[1]) KDalgleish 8 —
(MrsNMacauley) *dwlt: plld way into ld after 2f and sn clr: wknd and hdd over 4f out: sn t.o* **100/1**

2m 9.84s (2.45) **Going Correction** +0.20s/f (Slow) **12** Ran SP% **131.8**
Speed ratings: **98,96,96,95,92 92,92,90,90,89 83,—**CSF £6.81 TOTE £1.70: £1.60, £2.50, £4.60; EX 7.30.
**Owner** Fittocks Stud **Bred** Fittocks Stud **Trained** Newmarket, Suffolk

**FOCUS**
Probably only a fair maiden, despite the winning time being 3.16 seconds faster than the first division, and little to get excited about outside the first four.

**NOTEBOOK**
**Pukka(IRE)**appreciated the extra quarter-mile and needed only to be nudged out to score. He should continue to progress.
**Baawrah**does not looks an easy ride, but the way he ground out second place having been off the bridle some way out suggests he might need even further.
**Polar Dancer** ran a similar race to the stable's representative in the first division, albeit not quite as dramatic, and she too should find a race now that she can be handicapped.
**Chara**saw the longer trip out well and looks as though she would not mind an even greater test of stamina. She too can also be handicapped.
**Hold The Line**does not look an easy ride and did not help his chance by pulling hard early. The form of his Southwell second in October has not worked out at all.
**Mystic Promise(IRE)** *Official explanation: jockey said gelding made a noise*

## 6092 BET DIRECT NO Q DEMO 08000 837 888 H'CAP 6f (P)
**2:30** (2:32) (E) (0-70,70) 3-Y-O+ **£2,149** (£614; £307) **Stalls** Low

Form RPR

1100 **1** **Mistral Sky**[11] 6024 4-9-12 68 (v) MFenton 5 80
(MrsStefLiddiard) *trckd ldrs: pushed along over 2f out: c wdst of all st: drvn to chal fnl f: led last 75y* **9/1**

4100 **2** *nk* **Siraj**[30] 5837 4-9-5 61 (b[1]) LDettori 3 72
(NAGraham) *settled towards rr: prog over 2f out: rdn to ld over 1f out: hdd last 75y: jst hld* **5/1**[1]

0600 **3** *2* **Polar Force**[4] 6065 3-9-4 63 DCorby[(3)] 8 68
(MRChannon) *hld up in rr: stdy prog gng easily over 2f out: nt clr run over 1f out: rdn and one pce fnl f* **10/1**

6500 **4** *½* **Fulvio (USA)**[16] 5987 3-10-0 70 (v) IMongan 1 74
(JamiePoulton) *trckd ldrs: effrt and cl up over 1f out: nt pce to chal fnl f* **25/1**

0004 **5** *nk* **Peyto Princess**[11] 6024 5-9-1 60 LisaJones[(3)] 4 63
(MABuckley) *hld up wl in rr: prog on inner over 2f out: nt clr run over 1f out: nt rcvr* **7/1**

0005 **6** *1* **Park Star**[14] 6001 3-9-7 63 DarrenWilliams 7 63
(DShaw) *hld up in rr: effrt 2f out: one pce and nvr able to chal* **20/1**

5226 **7** *½* **Woodbury**[32] 5811 4-9-2 58 GBaker 2 56
(KRBurke) *hld up in midfield: trckd ldrs fr over 2f out: nowhere to go over 1f out: no prog whn in the clr fnl f* **7/1**

344 **8** *1¼* **Roman Quintet (IRE)**[14] 6001 3-9-10 66 (t) DaneO'Neill 12 60
(DWPArbuthnot) *hld up: last of main gp 2f out but stl gng wl enough: shuffled along and styd on fnl f: nvr nr ldrs* **8/1**

0400 **9** *3* **Captain Cloudy**[29] 5849 3-9-1 60 LPKeniry[(3)] 6 45
(MMadgwick) *disp ld to over 1f out: wknd* **25/1**

3510 **10** *2½* **Teyaar**[16] 5985 7-9-8 64 PMcCabe 14 42
(MrsNMacauley) *w ldrs to 2f out: wknd* **8/1**

0006 **11** *shd* **Legal Set (IRE)**[45] 5574 7-9-10 66 FNorton 10 44
(JRBest) *disp ld to over 1f out: wknd* **11/2**[2]

00-0 **12** *2½* **Kilmeena Lad**[16] 5987 7-10-0 70 JFEgan 13 40
(JCFox) *dwlt: racd wd: prog and in tch 1/2-way: wknd 2f out* **13/2**[3]

0050 **13** *1* **Tamarella (IRE)**[5] 6062 3-9-3 59 NPollard 11 26
(GGMargarson) *w ldrs tl wknd rapidly over 1f out* **20/1**

0060 **14** *15* **Goodwood Prince**[48] 5506 3-10-0 70 TQuinn 9 —
(SDow) *hld up: outpcd after 2f: t.o over 2f out* **20/1**

1m 12.93s (0.01) **Going Correction** +0.20s/f (Slow) **14** Ran SP% **133.7**
Speed ratings: **107,106,103,103,102 101,100,99,95,91 91,88,87,67**CSF £55.28 CT £482.94 TOTE £13.80: £3.10, £2.90, £4.90; EX 105.20.
**Owner** Shefford Valley Stud **Bred** Peter Nelson **Trained** Great Shefford, Berks

**FOCUS**
A competitive handicap run at a decent pace.

**NOTEBOOK**
**Mistral Sky**returned to form after a couple of modest efforts and battled on in resolute style to score. The drop back to six did not appear to bother him at all.
**Siraj**, proven under the conditions and blinkered for the first time, appreciated the drop back to six and only just lost out in the battle to the line. There will be other days for him.
**Polar Force**ran his best race for quite some time, but remains a most disappointing sort.
**Fulvio(USA)**did very well on this surface last winter and this was much more like it. He is dropping back to a reasonable mark.
**Peyto Princess**did not enjoy the clearest of runs and also made her effort tight against the inside rail which appeared to be the slowest part of the track. She has only managed one win from 41 starts, but is running well enough to suggest there may be a small race in her on this surface.
**Park Star**looks better on Fibresand.
**Woodbury**, the gamble of the race, found himself in a pocket turning in but it is unlikely that his chances of winning were affected.
**Roman Quintet(IRE)**did not run as badly as his finishing position would suggest and is worth keeping an eye on.
**Teyaar** *Official explanation: jockey said gelding lost its action*
**Legal Set(IRE)**could never get the lead on his own.
**Kilmeena Lad** *Official explanation: jockey said gelding hung left*
**Goodwood Prince** *Official explanation: jockey said gelding lost its action soon after start*

## 6093 BET DIRECT NO Q ON 08000 93 66 93 H'CAP 1m 2f (P)
**3:05** (3:05) (E) (0-75,75) 3-Y-O+ **£2,404** (£687; £343) **Stalls** Low

Form RPR

1633 **1** **Paragon Of Virtue**[246] 835 6-9-13 74 JFanning 12 84
(PMitchell) *prom: trckd ldr 1/2-way: led over 2f out: pushed out and styd on wl* **12/1**

4132 **2** *1* **Mad Carew (USA)**[29] 5848 4-9-9 70 (be) SWhitworth 6 78
(GLMoore) *trckd ldrs gng wl: effrt 2f out: chsd wnr over 1f out: swtchd lft ins fnl f: nt qckn and a hld* **6/1**[3]

310 **3** *2* **Hip Hop Harry**[47] 5537 3-9-7 72 TQuinn 5 77
(EALDunlop) *hld up in midfield: lost pl bdly over 3f out and wl in rr: effrt on inner 2f out: styd on wl fnl f: nt rch ldrs* **20/1**

4051 **4** *shd* **Ryan's Future (IRE)**[38] 5712 3-9-10 75 CCatlin 13 79
(JAkehurst) *plld hrd: sn led: rdn and hdd over 2f out: one pce* **8/1**

0041 **5** *nk* **Quantum Leap**[3] 6073 6-9-5 66 6ex PaulEddery 14 70
(SDow) *hld up tl wnt prom over 4f out: rdn and ev ch 2f out: one pce after* **10/1**

3150 **6** *hd* **Analyze (FR)**[14] 4848 5-9-8 72 LPKeniry[(3)] 7 76
(BGPowell) *t.k.h: trckd ldrs: rdn and effrt 2f out: one pce over 1f out* **12/1**

0402 **7** *1¾* **Priors Dale**[17] 5981 3-9-7 72 ACulhane 4 72
(KBell) *t.k.h: chsd ldr to 1/2-way: rdn over 2f out: steadily fdd* **14/1**

50S3 **8** *¾* **Climate (IRE)**[47] 5550 4-10-0 75 DSweeney 11 74
(JRBoyle) *hld up in rr: effrt over 2f out: hanging bdly and fnd nil over 1f out* **10/1**

0033 **9** *nk* **College Delinquent (IRE)**[17] 5976 4-9-5 66 (t) DeanMcKeown 9 64
(KBell) *settled in midfield: in tch and gng wl 2f out: rdn and fnd nil over 1f out* **14/1**

4522 **10** *hd* **Carrowdore (IRE)**[27] 5891 3-9-6 71 DaneO'Neill 2 69
(RHannon) *in rr: prog over 3f out: rdn and no hdwy over 2f out* **9/2**[1]

3015 **11** *½* **Burgundy**[27] 5890 6-9-6 67 (v) IMongan 3 64
(PMitchell) *rel to r: drvn thrght and a in rr* **8/1**

0003 **12** *shd* **Rasid (USA)**[16] 5989 5-9-9 70 NCallan 1 67
(CADwyer) *hld up in rr: rdn and no prog wl over 2f out* **14/1**

0026 **13** *nk* **Four Jays (IRE)**[48] 5506 3-9-4 72 J-PGuillambert[(3)] 8 69
(NPLittmoden) *racd towards rr: drvn 3f out: sn struggling* **20/1**

3003 **14** *nk* **Free Option (IRE)**[45] 5573 8-9-13 74 LDettori 10 70
(BHanbury) *a in rr: rdn and no prog 3f out* **11/2**[2]

2m 10.27s (2.88) **Going Correction** +0.20s/f (Slow)
**WFA** 3 from 4yo+ 4lb **14** Ran SP% **133.2**
Speed ratings: **96,95,93,93,93 93,91,91,90,90 90,90,90,89**CSF £91.16 CT £1477.83 TOTE £14.10: £3.80, £2.40, £5.50; EX 107.30.
**Owner** Debbie & Marc Thornton **Bred** Cliveden Stud Ltd **Trained** Epsom, Surrey

**FOCUS**
A competitive handicap, but a slow pace and a winning time nearly half a second slower than the second division of the two-year-old maiden.

**NOTEBOOK**
**Paragon Of Virtue**appeared fit enough after a nine-month break and was in the ideal position in a slowly-run race. He came home in good style and can do at least as well this winter as he did last.
**Mad Carew(USA)**was another that raced close to the pace and made sure the winner did not have it all his own way. He also did well here last winter and on this showing should do so again this time round.
**Hip Hop Harry**, making his sand debut, was much less experienced than those around him but ran very well to make the frame and would probably have been even better suited by a proper all-round gallop.
**Ryan's Future(IRE)**, another making his sand debut and running for a new yard, looked as though he may have done too much early by pulling hard in front. However, he lasted longer than may have been expected and connections will have been heartened by this.
**Quantum Leap**, carrying a 6lb penalty for his course and distance victory three days earlier, found this tougher but was not disgraced.

**Analyze(FR)**, back on sand after four starts over hurdles, took a good grip early and was found wanting for speed where it mattered.
**Carrowdore(IRE)**, once again started favourite, but he is a very difficult horse to win with and never looked like justifying the support.
**Free Option(IRE)**, held up in a slowly-run race, never showed at all and is better than this.

## 6094 BET DIRECT NO Q VOICE AUTOMATED BETTING CLASSIFIED STKS (DIV II) 7f (P)
3:40 (3:42) (F) 3-Y-0+ £2,114 (£604; £302) Stalls Low

Form RPR
0001 1 **Chateau Nicol**[11] 6024 4-8-13 62 ....(v) JFanning 10 78+
(BGPowell) *lw: trckd ldng pair: led gng easily wl over 1f out: sn wl clr: eased last 75y* **5/1**[2]
0515 2 5 **Cold Climate**[31] 5832 8-8-13 56 .... FNorton 5 62
(BobJones) *slowly into stride: sn chsd ldrs: effrt over 2f out: drvn to take 2nd ins fnl f: no imp* **10/1**
6412 3 *nk* **Mr Bountiful (IRE)**[11] 6019 5-8-13 63 .... JFEgan 4 61
(MDods) *led at fast pce: hdd wl over 1f out: kpt on same pce* **9/4**[1]
-430 4 2 **Pirouettes (IRE)**[48] 5508 3-8-9 58 .... MFenton 13 53
(MissGayKelleway) *s.i.s: sn in tch in midfield: rdn and effrt over 2f out: styd on ins fnl f* **12/1**
0005 5 1 **Balmacara**[33] 5787 4-8-10 50 ....(p) ACulhane 7 51
(MissKBBoutflower) *wl in rr: prog on inner over 2f out: drvn and kpt on fr over 1f out: n.d* **33/1**
5004 6 *hd* **Its Ecco Boy**[8] 6042 5-8-13 54 .... DKinsella 12 53
(PHowling) *sn restrained in rr: in last trio over 2f out: gng wl enough but no ch whn nt clr run over 1f out: r.o last 150y: nvr nr ld* **14/1**
4006 7 ½ **Tender (IRE)**[27] 5892 3-8-6 60 .... LisaJones(3) 11 49
(DJDaly) *racd in midfield: rdn 3f out: one pce and nvr rchd ldrs* **7/1**[3]
0005 8 ½ **Gun Salute**[33] 5793 3-8-12 53 .... RBrisland 2 51
(GLMoore) *s.i.s: sn in midfield: prog to chse ldrs over 2f out : nt clr run sn after: fdd* **16/1**
5665 9 1 **Icecap**[11] 6019 3-8-9 55 .... ADaly 15 45
(PButler) *hld up wl in rr: shkn up 2f out: one pce and no ch* **14/1**
0263 10 ½ **Jagged (IRE)**[8] 6039 3-8-12 60 .... GBaker 1 47
(KRBurke) *trckd ldrs: rdn over 2f out: wknd wl over 1f out* **7/1**[3]
000 11 1¾ **Nathan Detroit**[16] 5988 3-8-12 60 ....(b[1]) DSweeney 16 43
(PJMakin) *hld up in midfield: rdn wl over 2f out: sn no prog and btn* **20/1**
0-00 12 2½ **Warlingham (IRE)**[15] 5998 5-8-13 57 .... IMongan 8 36
(MPitman) *w ldr at fast pce to 2f out: wknd* **25/1**
4000 13 2½ **Crafty Politician (USA)**[79] 4852 6-8-13 50 .... WRyan 9 30
(GLMoore) *chsd ldrs: lost pl and struggling wl over 2f out* **25/1**
-065 14 3½ **Unsuited**[68] 5115 4-8-10 60 .... SWhitworth 6 18
(JELong) *s.v.s: a wl in rr* **25/1**
2200 15 2 **Sunset King (USA)**[59] 5308 3-8-12 59 .... RSmith 14 16
(JCFox) *racd in midfield: rdn 1/2-way: sn lost pl and btn* **25/1**
3632 16 10 **Bulawayo**[10] 6032 6-8-10 57 .... J-PGuillambert(3) 3 —
(AndrewReid) *chsd ldrs: rdn 4f out: sn wknd: t.o* **9/1**

1m 25.27s (-0.73) **Going Correction** +0.20s/f (Slow)
**WFA** 3 from 4yo+ 1lb **16** Ran SP% **141.5**
Speed ratings: **112,106,105,103,102 102,101,101,100,99 97,94,91,87,85 74**CSF £58.69 TOTE £8.40: £2.90, £3.30, £1.80; EX 77.50 Place 6 £209.08, Place 5 £86.41..
**Owner** Basingstoke Commercials **Bred** Aston House Stud **Trained** Morestead, Hants

**FOCUS**
A very decent pace and few got into it. The winning time was nearly two seconds faster than the first division.

**NOTEBOOK**
**Chateau Nicol**,a 40/1 winner over course and distance last time, was even more impressive this time and was laughing at his opponents over the last couple of furlongs. The Handicapper is bound to take a very dim view of this
**Cold Climate**is yet to win beyond six, but stays the trip well enough on this surface and battled on well to win the separate race for second.
**Mr Bountiful(IRE)**took the field along at a decent clip and appeared to have most of them in trouble turning in, so it must have been a big shock to his rider when he looked sideways and saw the winner cruising past him as though he had only just joined in.
**Pirouettes(IRE)**, who had a bit of form on Fibresand for John Gosden; ran a creditable debut for the yard and should find an opportunity to break her duck.
**Balmacara**is still a maiden after 27 starts so is probably flattered by this.
**Its Ecco Boy**, given a patient ride, tried to make progress turning for home but ran into heavy traffic and had to be switched. He ran on again towards the finish, but would probably only have been fourth at best with a clear run.
T/Plt: £222.50 to a £1 stake. Pool: £28,185.20. 92.45 winning tickets. T/Qpdt: £35.40 to a £1 stake. Pool: £1,996.60. 41.70 winning tickets. JN

# 6080 WOLVERHAMPTON (A.W) (L-H)
Saturday, November 29

**OFFICIAL GOING: Standard**

## 6095 BET DIRECT FREEPHONE 0800 32 93 93 H'CAP 5f (F)
7:00 (7:01) (F) (0-60,60) 3-Y-0+ £2,100 (£600; £300) Stalls Low

Form RPR
0000 1 **Lady Pekan**[33] 5794 4-9-4 **53** ....(b[1]) FPFerris(3) 6 65
(PSMcentee) *trckd ldr: rdn to ld ins fnl f: drvn out* **28/1**
0014 2 ½ **Strensall**[26] 5909 6-9-10 **56** .... RFitzpatrick 7 67
(REBarr) *nvr far away: rdn 2f out: hrd rdn ent fnl f and wnt 2nd ins* **11/4**[1]
3620 3 1 **Erracht**[43] 5606 5-9-8 **54** .... GBaker 8 61
(KRBurke) *in tch: hdwy and short of room whn swtchd lft ins fnl f: r.o wl* **8/1**
0020 4 *shd* **Laurel Dawn**[28] 5880 5-9-9 **58** .... LFletcher(3) 3 65
(IWMcinnes) *led tl rdn and hdd ins fnl f: no ex* **7/1**[3]
0000 5 1¼ **Cash**[4] 6065 5-9-10 **59** .... LisaJones(3) 10 61
(PaulJohnson) *pushed along in mid-div fr 1/2-way: kpt on fnl f* **7/1**[3]
0006 6 *nk* **Our Chelsea Blue (USA)**[12] 6010 5-9-13 **59** .... SRighton 9 60
(AWCarroll) *slowly away and wl bhd: mde late hdwy: nvr nrr* **9/1**
0003 7 *nk* **King's Ballet (USA)**[38] 5706 5-9-10 **56** .... DaneO'Neill 2 56
(PRChamings) *s.i.s and outpcd: hdwy over 1f out: nvr nr to chal* **9/2**[2]
0006 8 1 **Star Lad (IRE)**[8] 6038 3-9-6 **52** ....(b) GGibbons 5 49
(RBrotherton) *prom tl rdn and wknd over 1f out* **33/1**
2000 9 2½ **Catchthebatch**[1] 6081 7-9-4 **53** .... DCorby(3) 11 41
(MJWallace) *prom on outside for 3f* **12/1**
0000 10 ½ **Rivelli (IRE)**[8] 6043 4-9-4 **55** ....(b) NChalmers(5) 1 41
(BRFoster) *outpce thrght* **66/1**
0040 11 2 **Salerno**[231] 1030 4-9-9 **55** .... MFenton 4 34
(MissGayKelleway) *mid-div: eased whn btn ins fnl f* **12/1**
0000 12 7 **Intellibet One**[1] 6080 3-9-9 **60** .... DNolan(5) 13 15
(PDEvans) *outpcd and dropped wl in rr over 1f out: t.o* **25/1**

63.31 secs (0.71) **Going Correction** +0.15s/f (Slow) **12** Ran SP% **118.1**
Speed ratings: **100,99,97,97,95 94,94,92,88,88 84,73**CSF £101.56 CT £705.90 TOTE £30.80: £4.40, £1.80, £2.90; EX 190.00.
**Owner** P S J Croft **Bred** Jeremy Green And Sons **Trained** Newmarket, Suffolk

**FOCUS**
A moderate sprint where those drawn middle to high seemed at a slight advantage.

**NOTEBOOK**
**Lady Pekan**responded to the application of first-time blinkers to gain her first success since 2001. She has had her problems and has been very inconsistent this year, however, she has fallen in the weights of late and if on her best form, was well in for this. She is no good thing to follow up, but is in good heart and the blinkers certainly helped. *Official explanation: trainer said, regarding the improved form, filly benefited from the fitting of blinkers for the first time, and from the Fibresand surface*
**Strensall**failed to capitalise on a very favourable looking All-Weather mark, yet again did little wrong in defeat. He may be feeling the effects of a very busy turf campaign, but there are still races to be won with him around this circuit.
**Erracht**, another who looks well-treated on her turf form, was the unlucky horse in the race. She suffered traffic problems when mounting her challenge and would have been closer, but would not have won. When she is able to race more prominently, this tough mare should gain compensation.
**Laurel Dawn**ran well for a long way, but again failed to see out his race. He is on a very long losing run and recieves little respite from the Handicapper.
**King's Ballet(USA)**blew it at the start on this All-Weather debut and is capable of better.

## 6096 BET DIRECT ON ATTHERACES INTERACTIVE CLAIMING STKS 1m 6f 166y(F)
7:30 (7:30) (E) 3-Y-0+ £2,065 (£590; £295) Stalls High

Form RPR
4600 1 **Claptrap**[8] 6040 3-8-8 54 .... IMongan 8 64+
(JAOsborne) *slowly away and dropped out in rr: gd hdwy to trck ldrs gng wl fr 1/2-way: led 2f out: sn clr: v easily* **7/4**[1]
5145 2 10 **Paradise Valley**[3] 6075 3-8-10 54 ....(t) CCatlin 6 54
(MrsStefLiddiard) *hld up in mid-div: hdwy 3f out: rdn 2f out: r.o to chse wnr fiins fnl f* **17/2**
0033 3 5 **Mysterium**[15] 5999 9-9-1 40 ....(v) J-PGuillambert(3) 1 48
(NPLittmoden) *hld up towards rr: hdwy over 3f out: styd on ins fnl 2f: nvr nr to chal* **5/1**[2]
3020 4 2 **Queensberry**[19] 5971 4-8-13 52 .... JDO'Reilly(7) 5 48
(JO'Reilly) *racd keenly: trckd ldr: led 7f out: rdn and hdd 2f out: wknd over 1f out* **8/1**[3]
5555 5 2½ **Two Of A Kind (IRE)**[17] 5975 3-9-2 61 .... MHenry 7 49
(JWHills) *chsd ldrs: wnt 2nd 7f out: rdn over 2f out: sn btn* **12/1**
5610 6 3 **Spa Lane**[10] 6033 10-8-5 55 .... PGallagher(7) 11 33
(JFCoupland) *hld up: hdwy 7f out: rdn and wknd 2f out* **5/1**[2]
-064 7 9 **Roppongi Dancer**[18] 4999 4-8-11 30 ....(t) ACulhane 9 21
(MrsNMacauley) *towards rr: rdn over 5f out: sn wl bhd* **20/1**
4336 8 16 **Peggy Lou**[23] 5312 3-8-1 47 .... JoannaBadger 10 —
(BJLlewellyn) *slowly away: sn in tch: rdn over 5f out: wknd over 3f out: t.o* **12/1**
0505 9 17 **Lapadar (IRE)**[5] 6061 4-9-2 60 ....(b[1]) DFentiman(7) 4 —
(JRWeymes) *led tl hdd 7f out: sn wknd: t.o* **20/1**
000- 10 *dist* **Shearwater**[591] 912 6-8-11 22 .... SRighton 3 —
(ASenior) *prom for 5f: wknd qckly: t.o fnl 7f* **80/1**

3m 22.6s (1.80) **Going Correction** +0.15s/f (Slow)
**WFA** 3 from 4yo+ 8lb **10** Ran SP% **117.5**
Speed ratings: **101,95,93,91,90 89,84,75,66,—**CSF £17.36 TOTE £2.30: £1.70, £2.50, £1.50; EX 19.80.The winner was claimed by Nick Littmoden for £6,000.
**Owner** Mountgrange Stud **Bred** M F Kentish **Trained** Upper Lambourn, Berks

**FOCUS**
Claptrap wins this weak contest easily at the 14th attempt.

**NOTEBOOK**
**Claptrap**needed to take a drop in class to lose his maiden tag, but could not scored any easier. He was an eyecatcher last time when given a very tender ride under an apprentice jockey, but with Mongan aboard this time, finally showed his true colours. He proved his stamina and if he can reproduce this effort, he must go very close next time out.
**Paradise Valley**did little to convince he gets this trip and will be better over shorter, when he can be ridden more prominently.
**Mysterium**, dropping in class, again ran his race and is finding some consistency, but is not nearly as good as he used to be.
**Queensberry**is an in-and-out performer and he looked to find this too far.
**Spa Lane**, who looked to have a good chance at the weights, again ran a flat race.

## 6097 BET DIRECT LIVE FOOTBALL IN RUNNING MAIDEN STKS 6f (F)
8:00 (8:00) (D) 2-Y-0 £3,010 (£860; £430) Stalls Low

Form RPR
6 1 **Sable 'n Silk**[12] 6011 2-8-9 .... FNorton 3 51
(DHaydnJones) *s.i.s and sn pushed along to keep in tch: hdwy u.str riding over 1f out: rn to ld last stride* **10/1**
2 *shd* **Anisette** 2-8-9 .... NCallan 8 50
(JulianPoulton) *a.p: led over 1f out: r.o u.p: hdd last stride* **14/1**
444 3 ½ **Turkish Delight**[103] 4236 2-8-9 70 .... MTebbutt 12 49
(DMorris) *a in tch on outside: ev ch ins fnl f: ne ex cl home* **9/2**[2]
50 4 ¾ **United Spirit (IRE)**[21] 5947 2-8-9 .... CCatlin 13 47
(MAMagnusson) *racd wd: hdwy on outside over 1f out: r.o: nvr nrr* **10/1**
40 5 2½ **Charlieismydarling**[11] 6020 2-9-0 .... JFanning 7 44
(JAOsborne) *a.p: led 2f out: hdd over 1f out: wknd ins fnl f* **8/1**[3]
55 6 *nk* **Sir Jasper (IRE)**[39] 5686 2-9-0 ....(v[1]) DMernagh 4 43
(TDBarron) *chsd ldr. lost pl ben 1/2-way: nvr plcd to chal after* **16/1**
4650 7 *nk* **Love In The Mist (USA)**[33] 5789 2-8-9 67 .... DaneO'Neill 10 37
(EALDunlop) *mid-div: rdn over 2f out: nt improve position after* **9/2**[2]
6000 8 *shd* **Miss Judged**[10] 6029 2-8-9 33 .... GHannon 9 37
(APJones) *chsd ldrs to 1/2-way* **66/1**
9 ½ **Roving Vixen (IRE)** 2-8-9 .... ADaly 1 35
(JLSpearing) *sn bhd and styd there* **33/1**
10 2½ **Cornwallis** 2-9-0 .... ACulhane 11 33
(RGuest) *outpcd thrght* **14/1**
11 7 **Monkey Or Me (IRE)** 2-9-0 .... GParkin 6 12
(PTMidgley) *wl bhd fr 1/2-way* **66/1**
12 1 **Shaymee's Girl** 2-8-9 .... GGibbons 5 4
(MsDeborahJEvans) *led tl hdd 2f out: wknd qckly* **66/1**
435 13 5 **Celadon (IRE)**[85] 4699 2-9-0 73 .... IMongan 2 —
(NPLittmoden) *slowly away: a bhd* **10/3**[1]

1m 17.62s (1.92) **Going Correction** +0.15s/f (Slow) **13** Ran SP% **115.4**
Speed ratings: **93,92,92,91,87 87,87,86,86,82 73,72,65** TOTE £12.70: £2.60.
**Owner** Mrs M L Parry **Bred** Mrs M L Parry **Trained** Efail Isaf, Rhondda C Taff

**FOCUS**
A fair maiden for this track, which looks likely to throw up a few winners this winter.

**NOTEBOOK**
**Sable 'n Silk**showed the benefit of her debut run to get up on the line. She was sluggish at the start, ran green and looked an unlikely winner, but really responded well to her rider's urgings and can only improve on this effort.
**Anisette**made a pleasing debut and was only narrowly denied a debut success. She is bred to go on this surface and, as she is entitled to come on plenty for this, it is only a matter of time before she goes one better.
**Turkish Delight**, the yardstick to the form of this contest, had every chance but was unable to quicken where it mattered. She has had excuses since her fine debut effort and is capable of winning a maiden on the sand over this trip.
**United Spirit(IRE)**covered more ground than most on the outside of the field and showed ability without being able to trouble the principals. She now qualifies for handicaps.
**Celadon(IRE)**was never at the races on his debut for his new yard and was bitterly disappointing, but is surely capable of better. *Official explanation: jockey said colt had missed the break and would not face the kickback*

## 6098 BET DIRECT IN RUNNING SKY TEXT 293 H'CAP — 1m 1f 79y(F)
8:30 (8:30) (D ) (0-85,82) 3-Y-0+ — £3,500 (£1,000; £500) Stalls Low

Form — RPR
3351 **1** **Strong Hand**[14] 6004 3-9-9 **82** ........ PMulrennan(5) 7 98+
(MWEasterby) *hld up: gd hdwy 3f out: led wl over 1f out: drvn out* **11/8**[1]
0121 **2** ½ **Mi Odds**[4] 6068 7-10-0 **79** 6ex ........ ACulhane 5 91
(MrsNMacauley) *mid-div: strly rdn and hdwy wl over 1f out: r.o to go 2nd ins fnl f* **13/2**[2]
4504 **3** 2 **Intricate Web (IRE)**[26] 5910 7-9-4 **72** ........ DAllan(3) 11 80+
(EJAlston) *in rr: plent to do 2f out: styd on ins fnl 2f: nvr nrr* **12/1**
0216 **4** 1½ **Ofaraby**[16] 5991 3-9-12 **80** ........ NCallan 6 85
(MAJarvis) *a.p: led over 3f out: hdd wl voer 1f out: no ex fnl f* **15/2**
30/ **5** 1 **Henry Afrika (IRE)**[21] 5958 5-9-11 **76** ........(p) DeanMcKeown 8 79
(DGMcCardle, Ire) *a.p: rdn and wknd ent fnl f* **40/1**
5141 **6** 6 **Nowell House**[46] 5558 7-9-12 **77** ........ DaleGibson 3 68
(MWEasterby) *in tch tl lost pl over 3f out: nvr dangerous after* **33/1**
3651 **7** 4 **Labrett**[17] 5981 6-9-11 **76** ........(p) MFenton 13 59
(MissGayKelleway) *towards rr: effrt on outside over 2f out: wknd over 1f out* **7/1**[3]
3520 **8** 7 **Mister Arjay (USA)**[22] 5945 3-9-10 **78** ........(be) CCatlin 10 47
(BEllison) *a towards rr* **33/1**
5020 **9** ½ **Oldenway**[140] 3204 4-8-12 **70** ........ DSwift(7) 2 38
(RAFahey) *prom tl wknd over 3f out* **25/1**
0030 **10** 2½ **Bressbee (USA)**[19] 5970 5-9-11 **76** ........(b) DaneO'Neill 1 39
(JWUnett) *led tl hde3d 6f out: sn wknd* **12/1**
0000 **11** 1½ **The Gaikwar (IRE)**[16] 5991 4-9-5 **75** ........ MSavage(5) 4 35
(NEBerry) *prom: led 6f out: hdd over 3f out: wknd qckly* **66/1**
02 **12** 17 **Hiawatha (IRE)**[26] 5910 4-9-3 **71** ........ DMcGaffin(3) 12 —
(ISemple) *chsd ldrs: rdn and wknd over 4f out* **10/1**
4100 **13** dist **Todlea (IRE)**[163] 2482 3-9-11 **79** ........ IMongan 9 —
(JAOsborne) *in rr: lost tch over 4f out: t.o* **14/1**

2m 0.97s (-1.93) **Going Correction** +0.15s/f (Slow)
**WFA** 3 from 4yo+ 3lb — **13** Ran SP% **124.5**
Speed ratings: **114,113,111,110,109 104,100,94,94,91 90,75,—**CSF £10.29 CT £84.99 TOTE £2.40: £1.50, £2.20, £4.20; EX 11.90.
**Owner** Mrs Jean Turpin **Bred** Mrs Jean Turpin **Trained** Sheriff Hutton, N Yorks

**FOCUS**
A fair handicap won by a progressive horse in this sphere.

**NOTEBOOK**
**Strong Hand**followed up a recent success over course-and-distance, despite an 8lb rise in the weights, in impressive style. She has really improved for a step up to this trip and the way in which she ran on this occasion indicates she will be very hard to beat when attempting the hat-trick.
**Mi Odds**again ran a brave race under his 6lb penalty and is a very likeable performer, but will find life a lot harder when reassesed for this.
**Intricate Web(IRE)**, dropping in trip, was set a fair bit to do in the circumstances and was running on strongly at the business end of the race. He is becoming an in-and-out performer, but can certainly win a race on the sand on this evidence.
**Ofaraby**looks better on the Fibresand and although there was little disgrace in this defeat, he had every chance and may be a bit too high in the weights for this sort of company.
**Todlea(IRE)** *Official explanation: trainer said gelding had a breathing problem*

## 6099 ALLWEATHER-RACING.COM (S) STKS — 1m 100y(F)
9:00 (9:01) (G ) 3-Y-0+ — £2,107 (£602; £301) Stalls Low

Form — RPR
6001 **1** **Pup's Pride**[12] 6016 6-9-1 55 ........(v) LisaJones(3) 10 59
(MrsNMacauley) *wl in rr tl hdwy on ins over 2f out: led jst ins fnl f: drvn out* **10/3**[2]
0000 **2** 1½ **Forty Forte**[161] 2579 7-9-4 59 ........(p) NCallan 9 56
(MissSJWilton) *led tl hdd jst ins fnl f: hung rt and kpt on one pce* **9/1**
2012 **3** hd **Hurricane Coast**[4] 6063 4-9-4 55 ........ GParkin 1 55
(PABlockley) *hld up: hdwy over 2f out: ev ch 1f out: nt qckn after* **11/4**[1]
0031 **4** 1 **Repeat (IRE)**[10] 6032 3-9-2 52 ........ ACulhane 7 53
(MissGayKelleway) *mid-div: hdwy on outside over 2f out: rdn and nt qckn ins fnl f* **5/1**[3]
6000 **5** ½ **Nite-Owl Fizz**[12] 6015 5-8-11 55 ........ JDO'Reilly(7) 13 52
(JO'Reilly) *a.p: chsd ldr 7f out: wkng whn hmpd ins fnl f* **12/1**
0005 **6** 7 **Jouvert**[46] 5564 3-8-4 49 ........ PGallagher(7) 4 33
(RHannon) *prom: ev ch appproaching fnl f: wknd qckly ins fnl f* **22/1**
3500 **7** 2 **Mehmaas**[23] 5937 7-8-13 51 ........(v) DeanMcKeown 6 28
(REBarr) *mid-div: effrt over 3f out: son wknd* **13/2**
00 **8** 14 **Easy Breeze**[16] 5988 3-8-11 ........ PFitzsimons 2 —
(JMBradley) *a in rr* **100/1**
01-0 **9** 2 **Harry The Hoover (IRE)**[6] 1623 3-8-11 78 ........ DaneO'Neill 3 —
(MJGingell) *slowly away: a bhd: lost tch over 4f out: sddle slipped* **10/1**
0000 **10** shd **Bontadini**[31] 5826 4-8-13 60 ........ MTebbutt 8 —
(DMorris) *a bhd* **16/1**
0 **11** dist **Tadzio**[5] 6060 4-8-8 ........(v[1]) BReilly(5) 5 —
(MJGingell) *v.s.a: t.o fr 1/2-way* **50/1**

1m 52.81s (1.81) **Going Correction** +0.15s/f (Slow)
**WFA** 3 from 4yo+ 2lb — **11** Ran SP% **119.7**
Speed ratings: **96,94,94,93,92 85,83,69,67,67** —CSF £33.88 TOTE £4.30: £1.50, £1.80, £1.80; EX 47.10.There was no bid for the winner
**Owner** West Indies Capital Company Limited **Bred** Lord Halifax **Trained** Sproxton, Leics

**NOTEBOOK**
**Pup's Pride**is in great form and followed up his recent course-and-distance win of a similar contest readily. This is his sort of level, tends to hold his form well and he goes well for today's rider.
**Forty Forte**ran a good race considering he had been absent from the track for five months prior to this. He was unable to maintain his gallop at the head of affairs and understandably blew up close home, but will be sharper next time and may be about to hit top form.
**Hurricane Coast**has been consistent since switching to Fibresand, but after being produced to win his race, could not quicken over a trip that just stretches him. He looks better suited to Southwell on this evidence and should not be written off.
**Repeat(IRE)**ran a solid race for his new yard, but will be better back at seven furlongs.
**Harry The Hoover(IRE)** *Official explanation: jockey said saddle slipped*

## 6100 BET DIRECT FOOTBALL CASHBACKS FILLIES' H'CAP — 7f (F)
9:30 (9:30) (F ) (0-65,65) 3-Y-0+ — £2,072 (£592; £296) Stalls High

Form — RPR
323 **1** **Bint Makbul**[48] 5509 4-9-3 **53** ........ DaneO'Neill 7 67+
(RHannon) *trckd ldrs: led over 2f out: kpt up to work fnl f* **9/4**[1]
2150 **2** 2 **Duo Leoni**[16] 5985 3-9-9 **60** ........ MTebbutt 6 69
(RMBeckett) *mid-div: hdwy 3f out: wnt 2nd 2f out: no imp fnl f* **9/1**
0-04 **3** ¾ **Najaaba (USA)**[5] 6056 3-9-3 **57** ........ LisaJones(3) 8 64
(MissJFeilden) *towards rr: rdn 1/2-way: hdwy 2f out: r.o wl fnl f* **12/1**
3052 **4** 1¾ **Komena**[15] 5995 5-9-0 **50** ........ NCallan 3 53
(JWPayne) *in tch tl outpce3d over 2f out: styd on u.p fnl f* **9/2**[3]
0300 **5** 1½ **Miss Champers (IRE)**[14] 6004 3-9-4 **62** ........ KTMaher(7) 2 61
(PDEvans) *led after 2f: hdd over 2f out: wknd ins fnl f* **12/1**
0612 **6** 2½ **Spark Up**[19] 5967 3-9-13 **64** ........(b) MHenry 9 57
(JWUnett) *towards rr: mde sme late hdwy* **7/2**[2]
4500 **7** 6 **Lady Natilda**[5] 6056 3-9-2 **53** ........ PaulEddery 4 31
(DHaydnJones) *led for 2f: in tch tl wknd wl over 1f out* **16/1**
0303 **8** 3 **Ivy Moon**[33] 5787 3-9-1 **52** ........ RHavlin 11 23
(BJLlewellyn) *prom on outside to 1/2-way* **14/1**
2000 **9** 2 **Lunar Leader (IRE)**[71] 5031 3-9-9 **65** ........(p) BReilly(5) 5 31
(MJGingell) *slowly away: a bhd* **20/1**
0- **10** 3 **Hispaniola (IRE)**[574] 1182 5-9-10 **60** ........ DaleGibson 10 18
(MWEasterby) *a struggling in rr* **40/1**
0400 **11** 9 **Gunnhildr (IRE)**[27] 5891 3-9-9 **60** ........(v) DSweeney 12 —
(PJMakin) *slowly away: a bhd* **22/1**
2000 **12** 4 **Pooka's Daughter (IRE)**[14] 6004 3-9-3 **54** ........ PFitzsimons 1 —
(JMBradley) *prom early: sn pushed along: lost tch 1/2-way* **33/1**

1m 30.17s (-0.03) **Going Correction** +0.15s/f (Slow)
**WFA** 3 from 4yo+ 1lb — **12** Ran SP% **123.6**
Speed ratings: **106,103,102,100,99 96,89,86,83,80 70,65**CSF £23.74 CT £212.48 TOTE £2.90: £1.10, £3.40, £3.50; EX 29.30 Place 6 £39.18, Place 5 £15.54.
**Owner** Malih L Al Basti **Bred** D Lowe **Trained** East Everleigh, Wilts

**FOCUS**
A weak fillies' handicap run at a sound pace.

**NOTEBOOK**
**Bint Makbul**, the unexposed runner in the field, justified favouritism and relished the surface. She is definitely at the right end of the handicap, posted a fair time on this occcasion and may be the type to run up a sequence.
**Duo Leoni**, who caught the eye last time, confirmed her well-being with a creditable performance, but has a habit of finding less than expected off the bridle and is not one to trust.
**Najaaba(USA)**has shown all her best form to date in her last two starts on the sand and improved for the step up to this trip. She is moderate, but lightly-raced and may have more to offer.
**Komena**, who was not certain to get this trip, actually got outpaced and was staying on well at the death. She has been consistent of late, but her form figures may flatter her slightly and she is on a long losing run.
**Spark Up**was disappointing.
**Gunnhildr(IRE)** *Official explanation: trainer said filly had hung left-handed in the home straight*
T/Plt: £51.90 to a £1 stake. Pool: £45,153.10. 634.10 winning tickets. T/Qpdt: £15.60 to a £1 stake. Pool: £1,929.90. 91.40 winning tickets. JS

# 6071 SAINT-CLOUD (L-H)
Saturday, November 29

**OFFICIAL GOING: Holding**

## 6101a PRIX SOLITUDE (LISTED) (FILLIES) — 1m
1:15 (1:14) 3-Y-O — £13,312 (£5,325; £3,994; £2,662)

RPR
**1** **Qui Es Tu (IRE)**[34] 5783 3-9-0 ........ FBlondel 12 100
(J-MSauve, France)
**2** shd **Nicolaia (GER)**[20] 5963 3-9-0 ........ WMongil 6 100
(HSteinmetz, Germany)
**3** shd **Fasayil (IRE)**[109] 3-9-0 ........ FSpanu 7 100
(JEHammond, France) *finished 4th, placed 3rd*
**4** hd **Coremis (FR)**[17] 3-9-0 ........ SPasquier 11 99
(JEPease, France) *finished 3rd, disqualified, placed 4th*
**5** hd **Indian Dancer (FR)**[10] 3-9-0 ........ CStefan 8 99
(JEPease, France)
**6** 2½ **Tashkiyla (FR)**[22] 3-9-0 ........ CSoumillon 10 94
(ADeRoyer-Dupre, France)
**7** 2 **Sarre (FR)**[28] 5882 3-9-0 ........ ACarre 1 90
(PCostes, France)
**8** 3 **Princess Jones**[10] 3-9-0 ........ MBlancpain 13 84
(YDeNicolay, France)
**9** 1 **De Blanc (IRE)**[34] 5781 3-9-0 ........ TThulliez 9 82
(ARenzoni, Italy)
**10** 4 **Vadahilla (FR)**[143] 3-9-0 ........ RMarchelli 4 74
(XNakkachdji, France)
**11** **Richemaur (IRE)**[21] 5952 3-9-0 ........ DBonilla 2 74
(MHTompkins) *mid division til outpaced from 2 1/2f out, eased when beaten inside final f*
**12** **Lady Nadine**[195] 1705 3-9-0 ........ ELegrix 5 74
(RPritchard-Gordon, France)
**13** **La Moraleja (IRE)**[56] 5387 3-9-0 ........ CNora 3 74
(RMartin-Sanchez, Spain)

1m 49.1s **Going Correction** +0.10s/f (Good) — **13** Ran
Speed ratings: **103,102,102,102,102 99,97,94,93,89 89,89,89.**
**Owner** M Jarlan **Bred** J M Jarlan **Trained** France

**NOTEBOOK**
**Richemaur(IRE)**has failed to shine this year.

## TOKYO (L-H)
Sunday, November 30

**OFFICIAL GOING: Yielding**

### 6102a CAPITAL STKS (LISTED) 1m
**5:40** (12:00) 3-Y-O+ **£126,617** (£50,464; £31,482; £18,231)

RPR

1 **Siberian Hawk (USA)** 3-8-10 YShibata 7 107
(TTezuka, Japan)

2 *nk* **Eishin Tsurugizan (JPN)**[203] 3-9-0 NYokoyama 12 110
(HFujiwara, Japan)

3 *½* **Gamble Rose (JPN)** 6-8-7 OPeslier 8 100
(ISamejima, Japan)

4 *1* **Eishin Harima O (JPN)** 5-8-12 MDemuro 1 103
(MSakaguchi, Japan)

5 *¾* **Tout Seul (IRE)**[7] 6054 3-8-10 (b) KFallon 11 102
(RFJohnsonHoughton)

6 *1 ¾* **Royal Cancer (JPN)** 5-8-12 YTake 2 98
(HideyukiMori, Japan)

7 *nk* **Grass World (USA)**[378] 7-9-0 TEda 5 99
(KSuzuki, Japan)

8 *1 ¼* **Meiner Solomon (JPN)**[182] 3-8-10 MEbina 10 95
(SKunieda, Japan)

9 *½* **World Scale (USA)** 3-8-10 KatsuharuTanaka 6 94
(YMunakata)

10 *1* **Trust Fire (JPN)**[399] 5-9-0 HGoto 9 94
(MichifumiKono, Japan)

11 *4* **Green Blitz (IRE)** 9-8-12 KTake 3 84
(KFujioka, Japan)

12 *3* **Hyuma (IRE)**[203] 3-8-10 KAndo 4 78
(KYamauchi, Japan)

1m 37.1s
**WFA** 3 from 5yo+ 2lb **12** Ran
Speed ratings: .
**Owner** Yoshio Fujita **Bred** Bryan Boone & Ashford Stud **Trained** Japan

**NOTEBOOK**
**Tout Seul(IRE)**gave a good account of himself in first time blinkers, but just looked to be feeling the effects of having his second hard race in the space of a week in the final stages. He certainly appears to retain plenty of enthusiasm though, and remains in training.

### 6103a JAPAN CUP (GRADE 1) 1m 4f
**6:25** (12:00) 3-Y-O+ **£1,322,346** (£526,638; £331,034; £197,937)

RPR

1 **Tap Dance City (USA)**[49] 6-9-0 TSato 1 120+
(SSasaki, Japan) *made all, 7 lengths clear 9f out, 5 lengths clear straight, driven 2f out, ran on well, unchallenged* **128/10**[1]

2 *9* **That's The Plenty (JPN)**[35] 3-8-10 KAndo 10 119
(KHashiguchi, Japan) *raced in 2nd, pushed along straight, driven and ran on from 2f out but no impression on winner*

3 *¾* **Symboli Kris S (USA)**[28] 4-9-0 OPeslier 5 116
(KazuoFujisawa, Japan) *raced in 7th, 10th and pushed along in centre straight, ridden over 1 1/2f out, stayed on to take 3rd final strides*

4 *hd* **Neo Universe (JPN)**[35] 3-8-10 MDemuro 8 118
(TSetoguchi, Japan) *towards rear, 8th on inside straight, ridden and ran on from over 1 1/2f out to go 3rd til no extra and lost place final st*

5 *1 ¼* **Active Bio (JPN)**[210] 6-9-0 KTake 11 114
(HSakiyama, Japan) *towards rear, progress from half-way and 3rd straight, under pressure 2f out, ridden and rallied from 1 1/2f out, stayed on*

6 *nk* **Tigertail (FR)**[14] 4-8-10 TGillet 17 110
(RodCollet, France) *towards rear, hard ridden 2f out, finished well from over 1 1/2f out, nearest at finish*

7 *½* **Ange Gabriel (FR)**[56] 5406 5-9-0 TJarnet 9 113
(ELibaud, France) *raced in 3rd, dropped back to mid-division on rail half-way, pushed along and kept on straight but never dangerous*

8 *½* **Denon (USA)**[85] 4748 5-9-0 CNakatani 2 112
(RJFrankel, U.S.A) *disputed 9th, 6th straight, ridden on inside 2f out, ran on til one pace final 100yds*

9 *1 ¼* **Islington (IRE)**[36] 5771 4-8-10 KFallon 14 106
(SirMichaelStoute) *raced in 5th, pushed along straight, ridden over 1 1/2f out, ran on til no extra inside final furlong*

10 *1 ½* **Derby Regno (JPN)**[28] 5-9-0 HMiyuki 12 108
(STakahashi, Japan) *behind, ridden straight, never a threat*

11 *½* **Sunrise Pegasus (JPN)**[28] 5-9-0 YShibata 18 107
(SIshizaka, Japan) *never a factor*

12 *nk* **Ana Marie (FR)**[14] 4-8-10 C-PLemaire 6 103
(PDemercastel, France) *raced in 6th, lost place approaching straight, pushed along straight, no impression*

13 *nse* **Slew Valley (USA)**[64] 5247 6-9-0 JChavez 15 107
(GSciacca, U.S.A) *towards rear, took closer order from half-way, 4th on rail straight, hard ridden 2f out, no extra from 1 1/2f out*

14 *½* **Sakura President (JPN)**[35] 3-8-10 (b) YTake 3 108
(FKojima, Japan) *raced towards rear, never dangerous*

15 *3* **Tsurumaru Boy (JPN)**[28] 5-9-0 NYokoyama 7 102
(KHashiguchi, Japan) *in rear, never dangerous*

16 *dist* **Johar (USA)**[36] 5773 4-9-0 ASolis 13 —
(RichardEMandella, U.S.A) *raced in 8th, 9th straight, effort over 1 1/2f out, no impression*

17 *2* **Sarafan (USA)**[17] 6-9-0 VEspinoza 16 —
(NDrysdale, U.S.A) *disputed 9th, soon under pressure and beaten straight*

18 *dist* **Fields Of Omagh (AUS)**[29] 5885 6-9-0 (b) StevenKing 4 —
(TMcevoy, Australia) *raced in 4th, 7th and under pressure straight, weakened quickly*

2m 28.7s
**WFA** 3 from 4yo+ 6lb **18** Ran SP% **7.2**
Speed ratings: .
**Owner** Yushun Horse **Bred** Echo Valley Horse Farm & Swettenham Stud **Trained** Japan

**NOTEBOOK**
**Tap Dance City(USA)**had won a pair of Grade 2 events and been Grade 1 placed beforehand, and carried on his good form here. Sent immediately into the lead, he was well clear at half-way and none of his rivals were capable of landing a blow in the straight.
**That's The Plenty(JPN)**chased the winner in second place all through the race. A winner over a mile and seven furlongs at Grade 1 level last time out, his guaranteed stamina came in useful as no rivals behind were able to trouble him in the straight.
**Symboli Kris S(USA)**third twelve months ago, he was a good Grade 1 winner last time out and sent off the warm favourite on this occasion. However the way the race was run didn't suit and, although he stayed on strongly to finish third, that was as competitive as he got.
**Neo Universe(JPN)**the Japanese 2,000 Guineas and Derby winner, he finished behind That's the Plenty last time out. He came with a decent effort to take third midway in the straight before getting tired close home. He should have a good season in 2004.
**Islington(IRE)** bowed out of racecourse action with honour maintained, but never threatened to land a blow in the race. Connections reported she lost a shoe and was bumped entering the straight which did not help. A high-class filly in every respect, she was a credit to connections.

## 6095 WOLVERHAMPTON (A.W) (L-H)
Monday, December 1

**6104 Meeting Abandoned** - Waterlogged

## AQUEDUCT (L-H)
Saturday, November 29

**OFFICIAL GOING: Fast**

### 6112a REMSEN STKS (GRADE 2) (DIRT) 1m 1f (D)
**8:10** (8:10) 2-Y-O **£75,000** (£25,000; £13,750; £7,500)

RPR

1 **Read The Footnotes (USA)**[56] 5408 2-8-10 JDBailey 9 108
(RVioletteJr, U.S.A)

2 *3 ¾* **Master David (USA)**[74] 4965 2-8-4 JSantos 8 95
(BJMeehan) *mid-division, effort 3 wide approaching straight, 2nd straight, ran on well tol ine but not press winner final stages SP 12*

3 *10 ¾* **West Virginia (USA)** 2-8-8 SBridgmohan 7 79
(TPletcher, U.S.A)

4 *¾* **Artie Schiller (USA)** 2-8-4 RMigliore 3 74
(AJerkens, U.S.A)

5 *1 ½* **Big Booster (USA)** 2-8-4 NArroyoJr 1 71
(JKimmel, U.S.A)

6 *¾* **El Prado Rob (USA)**[76] 4930 2-8-4 EPrado 5 70
(NZito, U.S.A)

7 *1 ¼* **Mustanfar (USA)** 2-8-4 AGryder 4 67
(KMclaughlin, U.S.A)

8 *nse* **Pa Pa Da (USA)** 2-8-4 JRVelazquez 11 67
(DDonk, U.S.A)

9 *3 ¼* **Who Is Chris G (USA)** 2-8-4 RADominguez 6 61
(RKlesaris, U.S.A)

10 *1 ¼* **Milestone Victory (USA)** 2-8-4 JCastellano 2 59
(NBrennan, U.S.A)

11 *15 ¾* **Tap Day (USA)** 2-8-4 MLuzzi 10 30
(MHennig, U.S.A)

1m 50.62s **11** Ran
Speed ratings: .
**Owner** Klaravich Stables **Bred** Lawrence Goichman **Trained** USA

**NOTEBOOK**
**Read The Footnotes(USA)**, highly regarded by connections, was winning his second successive Grade Two race in good style here. He will now be sent to Florida for a short break, before a 2004 campaign in which the Kentucky Derby will be the early aim.
**Master David(USA)**, whose connections were making bold noises about his prospects beforehand, fully vindicated their confidence with this excellent display. He can certainly win at this level if displaying a similar level of form.

## 6087 LINGFIELD (L-H)
Tuesday, December 2

**OFFICIAL GOING: Standard**
Wind: nil Weather: overcast

### 6113 CHRIS WEATHERLY RETIREMENT CLASSIFIED STKS (DIV I) 6f (P)
**12:00** (12:00) (E ) 3-Y-O+ **£2,016** (£576; £288) **Stalls** Low

Form RPR

0610 1 **Taranaki**[46] 5616 5-8-12 70 SWhitworth 1 70+
(PDCundell) *trckd ldr: led wl over 1f out and eased to centre of crse: sn clr: pushed out* **3/1**[2]

0003 2 *5* **Second Minister**[13] 6031 4-8-12 50 (b) PDoe 2 55
(DFlood) *led: rdn over 2f out: hdd wl over 1f out: drvn out to hold on to 2nd* **16/1**

561 3 *¾* **Phrenologist**[19] 5988 3-8-12 69 DaneO'Neill 5 53
(JRFanshawe) *sn trckd ldrs: rdn over 2f out: sn outpcd: kpt on u.p to take 3rd nr fin* **3/1**[2]

2400 4 *nk* **Byo (IRE)**[14] 6019 5-8-12 67 RWinston 6 52
(MQuinn) *chsd ldr: rdn over 2f out: unable qck and btn over 1f out* **11/1**

2530 5 *1 ¼* **The Gay Fox**[8] 6057 9-8-9 42 (bt) LPKeniry(3) 4 48
(BGPowell) *s.i.s: in rr tl prog into midfield over 2f out: sn outpcd: n.d after* **100/1**

050 6 *shd* **Tickle**[33] 5837 5-8-9 50 (vt[1]) DSweeney 3 45
(PJMakin) *trckd ldrs: rdn and outpcd over 2f out: n.d after* **66/1**

3056 7 *1 ¾* **George Stubbs (USA)**[14] 6019 5-8-9 69 (b) J-PGuillambert(3) 9 43
(NPLittmoden) *sn pushed along in rr: struggling fr 1/2-way: nvr a factor* **6/1**[3]

0604 8 *shd* **Tripti (IRE)**[51] 5497 3-8-4 57 JFMcDonald(5) 7 39
(JJBridger) *s.i.s: a towards rr: rdn and struggling 1/2-way* **25/1**

1001 9 *hd* **Mistral Sky**[3] 6092 4-9-4 68 (v) MFenton 8 48
(MrsStefLiddiard) *a in rr: rdn and struggling 1/2-way* **11/4**[1]

10 *5* **Richie Rich (IRE)**[98] 4489 8-8-12 55 WMLordan 11 27
(JarlathPFahey, Ire) *a in rr: last and struggling over 3f out: wknd 2f out* **50/1**

24 **11** *1 1/4* **Walker Bay (IRE)**[51] 5508 5-8-9 48 (b[1]) RSmith 10 20
(JCFox) *s.i.s: racd on outer: a in rr: wknd 2f out* **66/1**

1m 11.89s (-1.03) **Going Correction** 0.0s/f (Stan) **11** Ran SP% **115.0**
Speed ratings: **106,99,98,97,96 96,93,93,93,86 85**CSF £46.27 TOTE £4.10: £1.30, £6.30, £1.70; EX 92.80.
**Owner** Eric Evers **Bred** E D Evers **Trained** Compton, Berks

**FOCUS**
Few got into this.

**NOTEBOOK**
**Taranaki**, back over six furlongs, was well in at the weights. This comfortable victory proved his effectiveness on this surface.
**Second Minister**looks an improved performer since being fitted with blinkers and adopting front-running tactics.
**Phrenologist**, making his handicap debut and having his first run against older horses, may prove best back over seven.
**Byo(IRE)**found this trip more suitable but is probably best at around five and a half furlongs.
**The Gay Fox**, who had a stiff task at the weights, was keeping on when it was all over.
**Mistral Sky**was never in the hunt and this must have been an off day.

## 6114 ALLWEATHER-RACING.COM H'CAP (DIV I) 1m (P)
**12:30** (12:30) (E ) (0-75,74) 3-Y-O+ **£2,331** (£666; £333) **Stalls** High

Form RPR
4046 **1** *hd* **Sewmore Character**[67] 5195 3-9-10 **72** DSweeney 1 79
(MBlanshard) *settled towards rr: prog over 2f out: swtchd ins and drvn to ld ent fnl f: hdd last strides: fin 2nd, hd: plcd 1st* **25/1**
0330 **2** *1 1/4* **College Delinquent (IRE)**[3] 6093 4-9-5 **66** (t) SWhitworth 5 70
(KBell) *hld up in rr: prog over 2f out: nt clr run wl over 1f out: chsd ldrs ins fnl f: hld whn n.m.r last 75yds: fin 3rd, hd & 1 1/4l* **7/1**
0156 **3** *1 3/4* **Blue Trojan (IRE)**[15] 6013 3-9-8 **70** JFEgan 12 70
(SKirk) *racd on outer in midfield: pushed along over 3f out: effrt on wd outside wl over 1f out: kpt on same pce: fin 4th: plcd 3rd* **11/2**[3]
045 **4** *1* **Captain Darling (IRE)**[7] 6070 3-8-13 **66** BReilly[(5)] 10 64
(RMHCowell) *plld hrd: pressed ldr: pushed along 3f out: drvn and stl ev ch jst over 1f out: wknd and eased fnl f: fin 5th: plcd 4th* **8/1**
3213 **5** *1* **Trousers**[19] 5987 4-9-13 **74** DaneO'Neill 2 69
(AndrewReid) *led: rdn 2f out: hdd & wknd ent fnl f: fin 6th: plcd 5th* **10/3**[1]
0340 **6** *1 3/4* **Captain Ginger**[100] 4413 3-9-7 **72** LFletcher[(3)] 7 63
(HMorrison) *plld hrd early: hld up towards rr: rdn and no rspnse over 2f out: n.d: fin 7th: plcd 6th* **8/1**
2000 **7** *shd* **Superchief**[36] 5796 8-9-4 **65** (bt) EAhern 6 56
(MissBSanders) *t.k.h early: trckd ldrs: rdn and cl up 2f out: fnd nil and btn whn nt clr run jst over 1f out: fin 8th: plcd 7th* **14/1**
000 **8** *1 1/2* **Banutan (IRE)**[13] 6026 3-8-12 **60** JFanning 4 48
(KRBurke) *trckd ldng pair: gng easily over 2f out: sn rdn: wknd rapidly over 1f out: fin 9th: plcd 8th* **25/1**
0053 **9** *5* **Hadath (IRE)**[14] 6019 6-9-4 **68** LPKeniry[(3)] 3 44
(BGPowell) *hld up in last: reminder over 4f out: detached and struggling 3f out: fin 10th: plcd 9th* **10/1**
4660 **10** *1/2* **Leonor De Soto**[118] 3899 3-8-11 **59** NPollard 11 34
(JRBest) *prom tl wknd 3f out: fin 11th: plcd 10th* **40/1**
0010 **D** **Lobos (SWI)**[26] 5933 4-9-1 **62** IMongan 8 69
(GLMoore) *hld up in rr: stdy prog on outer 3f out: rdn to chal ent fnl f: drvn to ld last strides: fin 1st, hd: subsequently disq* **4/1**[2]

1m 38.75s (-0.76) **Going Correction** 0.0s/f (Stan)
**WFA** 3 from 4yo+ 1lb **11** Ran SP% **119.1**
Speed ratings: **102,101,99,98,97 96,95,94,89,88 103**CSF £103.96 CT £701.44 TOTE £6.40: £2.20, £13.30, £1.60; EX 240.70.
**Owner** Aykroyd And Sons Ltd **Bred** Lady Wills **Trained** Upper Lambourn, Berks

**FOCUS**
They went a moderate pace in the early stages. The principals all came from the rear.

**NOTEBOOK**
**Sewmore Character**remains a maiden, but he did nothing wrong in the battle to the line and just missed out.
**College Delinquent(IRE)**, back over a more suitable trip, was a shade unlucky in that he had to wait for a run at a crucial moment.
**Blue Trojan(IRE)**was easy to back. He stayed on late and might be of interest over farther.
**Captain Darling(IRE)**ran well for a long way and was not given a hard time when his measure had been taken.
**Trousers**ran another decent race off a 2lb higher mark.
**Superchief** *Official explanation: trainer said gelding had subsequently scoped badly*
**Lobos(SWI)**got there near the line to land a bit of a gamble. He should remain competitive when he is reassessed. He was subsequently disqualified due to the prohibited substance stanozolol appearing in urine sample.

## 6115 BET DIRECT NO Q ON 08000 93 66 93 NURSERY 1m (P)
**1:00** (1:01) (E ) (0-85,84) 2-Y-O **£2,341** (£669; £334) **Stalls** High

Form RPR
5005 **1** **Anuvasteel**[20] 5979 2-8-13 **76** WRyan 8 83+
(NACallaghan) *settled towards rr: progres on inner whn nt clr run briefly over 2f out: swtchd wd and effrt over 1f out: led last 150yds:* **2/1**[1]
0042 **2** *1 1/2* **Little Eye (IRE)**[4] 6083 2-8-2 **65** ow2 NPollard 5 67
(JRBest) *trckd ldrs: effrt on outer 2f out: rdn to chal 1f out: nt qckn ins fnl f* **5/1**
061 **3** *1* **Mountcharge (IRE)**[100] 4415 2-9-2 **79** GCarter 11 79
(CNAllen) *hld up wl in rr: prog over 2f out: drvn and effrt against rail over 1f out: kpt on same pce* **9/2**[3]
0411 **4** *nk* **Freak Occurence (IRE)**[14] 6023 2-9-2 **84** JFMcDonald[(5)] 1 83
(MissECLavelle) *led: kicked 2l clr 2f out: hdd and one pce last 150yds* **3/1**[2]
0200 **5** *6* **Jomus**[14] 6021 2-8-1 **64** oh1 ow3 CCogan 2 49
(LMontagueHall) *dwlt: in rr tl progres into midfield after 3f: pushed along over 3f out: sn outpcd: n.d after* **66/1**
1000 **6** *1/2* **Wares Home (IRE)**[13] 6029 2-8-7 **70** DSweeney 9 54
(KRBurke) *restrained sn after s and hld up in last: wl off the pce over 2f out: pushed along over 1f out: nvr nr ldrs* **40/1**
0000 **7** *shd* **Turnberry (IRE)**[40] 5721 2-8-2 **65** (b[1]) SWhitworth 6 49
(JWHills) *trckd ldrs: effrt to chse ldr briefly 2f out: wknd rapidly over 1f out* **40/1**
1423 **8** *nk* **Chubbes**[4] 6083 2-9-1 **78** (v) DaneO'Neill 3 61
(MCPipe) *pressed ldr to 2f out: wknd and eased* **7/1**
0046 **9** *3/4* **Park Ave Princess (IRE)**[18] 5994 2-7-12 **61** oh3 JBramhill 4 42
(NPLittmoden) *racd on outer: towards rr: rdn over 3f out: brief effrt over 2f out: sn wknd* **16/1**
000 **10** *3* **Rumour Mill (IRE)**[55] 5448 2-8-5 **68** CCatlin 7 43
(NEBerry) *chsd ldrs tl wknd 3f out* **33/1**

1m 38.79s (-0.72) **Going Correction** 0.0s/f (Stan) **10** Ran SP% **120.9**
Speed ratings: **103,101,100,100,94 93,93,93,92,89**CSF £12.82 CT £42.86 TOTE £2.80: £1.40, £1.30, £2.20; EX 16.00.
**Owner** Tipp-Ex Rapid Racing **Bred** G H Beeby And Viscount Marchwood **Trained** Newmarket, Suffolk

**FOCUS**
The pace was fair.

**NOTEBOOK**
**Anuvasteel**took advantage of a 3lb lower mark. He appreciated the return to a mile and the way he won he will get a bit farther too.
**Little Eye(IRE)**, having his first run on Polytrack, ran a decent race and saw out the mile but appeared to want to hang in behind the winner slightly in the final furlong.
**Mountcharge(IRE)**, making his sand debut, had been off the track for three months. He stayed on the inside in the home straight and made good late headway, if unable to peg back the front two.
**Freak Occurence(IRE)**, without the visor this time, made a bold bid to notch the hat-trick off a 7lb higher mark.
**Jomus**, having his second run since leaving the care of Lynda Ramsden, made a little late headway.

## 6116 CHRIS WEATHERLY RETIREMENT CLASSIFIED STKS (DIV II) 6f (P)
**1:30** (1:30) (E ) 3-Y-O+ **£2,016** (£576; £288) **Stalls** Low

Form RPR
1530 **1** **Ripple Effect**[19] 5985 3-8-4 70 (t) BReilly[(5)] 4 61
(CADwyer) *cl up: chsd ldr 2f out: effrt on outer to ld ent fnl f: sn in command: rdn out* **4/1**[3]
0-30 **2** *2 1/2* **Royal Fashion (IRE)**[227] 1123 3-8-4 65 NChalmers[(5)] 5 53
(MissSheenaWest) *dwlt: rcvrd to chse ldrs after 2f: effrt on outer 2f out: styd on to take 2nd wl ins fnl f* **9/1**
0500 **3** *3/4* **Night Cap (IRE)**[136] 3399 4-8-9 47 J-PGuillambert[(3)] 6 54
(TDMccarthy) *racd freely: led: 3l clr over 2f out: hung rt over 1f out: hdd and nt qckn ent fnl f* **16/1**
0061 **4** *3/4* **I Wish**[14] 6019 5-8-6 65 LPKeniry[(3)] 3 49
(MMadgwick) *chsd ldr to 2f out: sn rdn and nt qckn: wl hld in 4th whn n.m.r 100yds out* **7/2**[2]
0300 **5** *1 1/2* **Aintnecessarilyso**[46] 5606 5-8-8 42 ow1 MSavage[(5)] 8 48
(NEBerry) *chsd ldrs: lost pl u.p 1/2-way: effrt again 2f out: no imp on ldrs* **66/1**
3030 **6** *shd* **Kilmeena Star**[134] 3468 5-8-12 39 DaneO'Neill 10 47?
(JCFox) *racd in last: detached fr rest over 2f out: swtchd to inner and styd on fnl f: no ch* **66/1**
0004 **7** *1/2* **Dunedin Rascal**[4] 6084 6-8-12 70 (b) SWhitworth 2 45
(EAWheeler) *settled in rr: drvn over 2f out: no prog* **7/2**[2]
0060 **8** *shd* **Onefortheboys (IRE)**[51] 5509 4-8-12 36 PDoe 7 45
(DFlood) *dwlt: sn rdn to stay in tch: struggling fr over 2f out* **33/1**
5004 **9** *1/2* **Fulvio (USA)**[3] 6092 3-8-12 70 (v) IMongan 9 43
(JamiePoulton) *racd on outer: trckd ldrs: rdn over 2f out: outpcd and btn sn after* **11/4**[1]
350 **10** *nk* **Calendar Girl (IRE)**[43] 5678 3-8-9 48 DSweeney 1 40
(PJMakin) *chsd ldrs: pushed along over 3f out: wknd over 1f out* **20/1**

1m 12.46s (-0.46) **Going Correction** 0.0s/f (Stan) **10** Ran SP% **117.7**
Speed ratings: **103,99,98,97,95 95,94,94,94,93**CSF £38.64 TOTE £4.40: £1.50, £4.90, £3.10; EX 45.70.
**Owner** Miss Lilo Blum **Bred** Littleton Stud **Trained** Newmarket, Suffolk

**FOCUS**
This looked the weaker of the two divisions and the time was slower.

**NOTEBOOK**
**Ripple Effect**, having her second run since leaving Andrew Balding, won this a shade comfortably. This looks her trip.
**Royal Fashion(IRE)**ran well on this first start since April, keeping on steadily after missing the kick.
**Night Cap(IRE)**was backed at big prices on this first run since July. Hanging when in front, he had refused to enter the stalls on his last intended start and obviously has his own ideas. *Official explanation: jockey said gelding hung right in the straight*
**I Wish**, who became a little warm in the preliminaries, had no excuses othe than that seven furlongs might be her best trip.
**Aintnecessarilyso**was without the cheekpieces on this first run since leaving Milton Bradley.
**Fulvio(USA)**was disappointing following his good run here at the weekend.

## 6117 LITTLEWOODS BET DIRECT RATED STKS SHOWCASE H'CAP 1m 2f (P)
**2:00** (2:00) (C ) (0-95,90) 3-Y-O+ **£6,287** (£2,384; £1,192; £542) **Stalls** Low

Form RPR
3121 **1** **Star Of Normandie (USA)**[10] 6049 4-8-7 **81** BReilly[(5)] 5 92
(GGMargarson) *reluctant to post (as usual): trckd ldrs: effrt 2f out: squeezed through to ld last 100yds: hld on wl* **9/1**
6224 **2** *nk* **Alrafid (IRE)**[19] 5991 4-9-0 **83** SWhitworth 4 93
(GLMoore) *t.k.h: hld up in tch: prog over 3f out: rdn to dispute ld on outer 2f out: hdd last 100yds: jst hld after* **5/1**[1]
0360 **3** *hd* **Zonergem**[21] 5873 5-9-7 **90** (b) MTebbutt 1 100
(LadyHerries) *hld up in midfield: prog on inner 2f out: plld out and effrt over 1f out: cajoled along and r.o ins fnl f: gaining at fin* **16/1**
2040 **4** *nk* **Northside Lodge (IRE)**[53] 5468 5-9-0 **83** JFanning 2 92
(PWHarris) *led at slow pce for 2f: styd cl up: pushed along over 3f out: effrt to press ldrs 1f out: r.o one pce* **11/2**[2]
4263 **5** *3/4* **J R Stevenson (USA)**[19] 5991 7-8-7 **76** SWKelly 14 84
(MWigham) *hld up in last trio: effrt 2f out: weaved through over 1f out: nvr able to chal* **8/1**
0062 **6** *shd* **Gig Harbor**[10] 6052 4-9-2 **85** CCatlin 6 93
(MissECLavelle) *prom: trckd ldr 7f out: upsides and qcknd pce over 3f out: stl disputing ld ins fnl f: one pce last 75yds* **7/1**[3]
2440 **7** *1/2* **Brilliant Red**[10] 6052 10-9-6 **89** (t) IMongan 11 96
(JamiePoulton) *dwlt and drvn first f: racd in last trio: effrt on inner 2f out: prog over 1f out: styd on same pce fnl f* **16/1**
0000 **8** *hd* **Linning Wine (IRE)**[10] 6052 7-9-4 **90** LPKeniry[(3)] 10 97
(BGPowell) *hld up towards rr: prog on outer over 3f out: rdn 2f out: styd on same pce fnl f* **20/1**
4-13 **9** *nk* **Rejuvenate (IRE)**[38] 5756 3-8-13 **85** DaneO'Neill 12 91
(MrsAJPerrett) *led after 2f and set stdy pce: jnd 4f out: qcknd over 3f out: hdd 1f out: lost several pls nr fin* **5/1**[1]
2031 **10** *shd* **Dower House**[19] 5991 8-8-10 **82** DCorby[(3)] 8 88
(AndrewTurnell) *plld hrd: cl up: rdn and effrt 2f out: nt qckn over 1f out: one pce after* **12/1**
0005 **11** *1/2* **Gallant Boy (IRE)**[10] 6052 4-8-10 **79** (t) EAhern 9 84
(PDEvans) *t.k.h: hld up towards rr: nt wl plcd on outer 2f out: kpt on same pce fnl f* **10/1**


The Form Book, Raceform Ltd, Compton, RG20 6NL

4016 **12** *nk* **Blue Patrick**[96] 4534 3-9-2 **88** ........ JTate 13 92
(JMPEustace) *dwlt: hld up in last: stl last and pushed along 2f out: one pce and no prog* **40/1**

0400 **13** *3/4* **Liberty Royal**[19] 5991 4-8-7 **76** ........ DSweeney 3 79
(PJMakin) *t.k.h: hld up in midfield: lost pl and pushed along over 2f out: n.d fnl f* **16/1**

2m 10.12s (2.73) **Going Correction** 0.0s/f (Stan)
**WFA** 3 from 4yo+ 3lb **13 Ran SP% 124.0**
Speed ratings: **89,88,88,88,87 87,87,87,86,86 86,86,85**CSF £55.60 CT £733.52 TOTE £9.70: £2.70, £2.20, £2.90; EX 54.50 Trifecta £1326.60 Part won. Pool of £1,868.46 - 0.20 winning units..
**Owner** Norcroft Park Stud **Bred** Columbiana Farm **Trained** Newmarket, Suffolk

**FOCUS**
A competitive handicap in which just over four lengths covered the whole field at the line, but a sedate early pace had a lot to do with it.

**NOTEBOOK**
**Star Of Normandie(USA)**, back over ten furlongs, remains in top form. She has estabished a good rapport with Reilly.
**Alrafid(IRE)**was ridden more prominently and just missed out. A stronger pace would have suited him.
**Zonergem**did not get the fast pace he could have done with on this All-Weather bow, but he was coming home well if needing more than a little cajoling to do so.
**Northside Lodge(IRE)**was unable to enhance his excellent record over this track and trip but this was a decent effort nonetheless.
**J R Stevenson(USA)**adopted hold-up tactics but the lack of pace was against him.
**Gig Harbor**, who only conceded defeat in the last half-furlong, is best at twelve furlongs.
**Rejuvenate(IRE)**went on with a mile to run and only set a steady pace. A host of rivals were breathing down his neck turning in and he was swallowed up with a furlong to go.

## 6118 BETDIRECT.CO.UK NOVICE STKS 6f (P)
**2:30** (2:31) (D) 2-Y-O **£3,178** (£908; £454) **Stalls** Low

Form RPR

**1** **Missus Links (USA)** 2-8-3 ........ RSmith 13 68+
(RHannon) *w ldr: led narrowly jst over 1f out: shkn up fnl f: a holding rivals* **11/4[1]**

0104 **2** *3/4* **Sweetest Revenge (IRE)**[33] 5835 2-9-0 78 ........ ADaly 9 77
(MDIUsher) *mde most: rdn and hdd jst over 1f out: kpt on wl but readily hld by wnr* **4/1[3]**

42 **3** *nk* **Dandouce**[20] 5977 2-8-7 ........ ACulhane 2 69
(SLKeightley) *chsd ldrs: rdn and outpcd over 2f out: effrt over 1f out: styd on to take 3rd nr fin* **5/1**

6200 **4** *hd* **Imperium**[61] 5334 2-8-12 79 ........ JFEgan 3 74
(BJMeehan) *plld hrd early: trckd ldrs: rdn 2f out: hanging and nt qckn over 1f out: styd on same pce* **7/1**

5001 **5** *1 1/2* **Muy Bien**[13] 6029 2-9-2 75 ........ (v) SWKelly 14 73
(JRJenkins) *racd in midfield: shkn up over 2f out: plld out and rdn over 1f out: hanging and fnd nil* **10/1**

0 **6** *1/2* **Bettalatethannever (IRE)**[96] 4527 2-8-12 ........ DaneO'Neill 6 68
(SDow) *restrained s: hld up wl in rr: pushed along on outer 2f out: no prog tl r.o fnl f: do bttr* **33/1**

0334 **7** *hd* **Oro Verde**[48] 5575 2-8-12 91 ........ PGallagher(7) 4 74
(RHannon) *pressed ldng pair to over 2f out: wknd ins fnl f* **7/2[2]**

50 **8** *1 1/4* **Prenup (IRE)**[26] 5929 2-8-4 ........ DCorby(3) 7 58
(LMCumani) *racd in midfield: pushed along wl over 2f out: sn outpcd and btn* **33/1**

60 **9** *1 1/4* **Solo Sole (ITY)**[19] 5986 2-8-12 ........ CCatlin 8 59
(LMCumani) *racd in midfield: rdn and outpcd over 2f out: no ch after* **40/1**

**10** *1* **Embassy Sweets (USA)** 2-7-12 ........ JFMcDonald(5) 5 47
(PFICole) *settled wl in rr: pushed along over 2f out: one pce and no prog* **14/1**

**11** *1* **Backlash** 2-8-3 ........ SWhitworth 1 44
(AWCarroll) *s.v.s: a last: one pce fnl 2f* **50/1**

1m 13.15s (0.23) **Going Correction** 0.0s/f (Stan) **11 Ran SP% 124.1**
Speed ratings: **98,97,96,96,94 93,93,91,90,88 87**CSF £14.41 TOTE £3.90: £1.70, £1.90, £2.00; EX 41.10.
**Owner** Coriolan Partnership Ii **Bred** L Gallagher, Fred Rosenblum And Ashford Stud **Trained** East Everleigh, Wilts
■ Stewards Enquiry : A Daly three-day ban: careless riding (Dec 12,13,15)

**FOCUS**
The pace was only ordinary in this novice event.

**NOTEBOOK**
**Missus Links(USA)**, who cost 23,000 gns as a yearling, knew her job and did this nicely. She can win again in ordinary company.
**Sweetest Revenge(IRE)**tried to make all and there was no disgarce in this given that she was conceding 11lb to the winner.
**Dandouce**, minus the visor, proved that she stayed the six. She is eligible for handicaps now.
**Imperium**was squeezed out at the first bend on this Polytrack debut. Not blinkered this time, he still looked a less-than-easy ride despite having been gelded since his last run.
**Muy Bien**gave his rider plenty of problems when asked for his effort once in line for home.
**Bettalatethannever(IRE)**was still a bit green, but he finished to good effect and there should be improvement to come.

## 6119 ALLWEATHER-RACING.COM H'CAP (DIV II) 1m (P)
**3:00** (3:01) (E) (0-75,74) 3-Y-O+ **£2,331** (£666; £333) **Stalls** High

Form RPR

5060 **1** **Topton (IRE)**[24] 5946 9-9-5 66 ........ (b) RWinston 1 76
(PHowling) *s.s: sn rcvrd into midfield: effrt over 2f out: rdn to ld last 100yds: kpt on wl* **10/1**

0620 **2** *1* **Tourmalet**[34] 5832 3-9-10 72 ........ ACulhane 8 80
(MRChannon) *cl up: trckd ldr over 2f out: led gng easily over 1f out: shkn up and hanging sn after: hdd and nt qckn last 100yds* **9/2[2]**

6062 **3** *3/4* **Heidelburg (IRE)**[15] 6010 3-9-3 65 ........ JFEgan 11 71
(SKirk) *hld up in rr: prog over 2f out: drvn and r.o to take 3rd ins fnl f: nt rch ldng pair* **11/2[3]**

1450 **4** *1* **Tropical Coral (IRE)**[19] 5991 3-9-12 74 ........ TQuinn 2 78
(CTinkler) *trckd ldrs: lost pl 2f out: nudged along and hanging lft over 1f out: kpt on fnl f: eased nr fin* **8/1**

2000 **5** *1* **Learned Lad (FR)**[81] 4872 5-9-4 65 ........ IMongan 6 67
(JamiePoulton) *mde most to over 1f out: wknd ins fnl f* **7/1**

5200 **6** *nk* **Resonate (IRE)**[20] 5981 5-8-10 57 ........ DaneO'Neill 10 58
(AGNewcombe) *stdd s: hld up in last: stl in last pair over 1f out: eased to outer and r.o fnl f: nvr nr ldrs: do bttr* **7/2[1]**

5000 **7** *shd* **Scottish River (USA)**[17] 6006 4-9-1 62 ........ ADaly 3 63
(MDIUsher) *t.k.h: pressed ldr to over 2f out: sn btn: no ch whn n.m.r nr fin* **20/1**

000 **8** *1* **Kanz Wood (USA)**[7] 6064 7-9-4 65 ........ SWhitworth 12 63
(AWCarroll) *hld up in last pair: nudged along and sme prog on inner over 1f out: nvr nr ldrs and no hdwy fnl f* **40/1**

6402 **9** *1 3/4* **Oh So Rosie (IRE)**[9] 5945 3-8-9 60 ........ (p) LPKeniry(3) 9 54
(JSMoore) *chsd ldrs: rdn 3f out: wknd wl over 1f out* **10/1**

2000 **10** *1/2* **Snuki**[164] 2571 4-9-7 68 ........ RBrisland 5 61
(GLMoore) *racd in midfield: rdn over 2f out: sn btn* **9/1**

0346 **11** *2 1/2* **Maddie's A Jem**[31] 5880 3-9-6 68 ........ SWKelly 7 56
(JRJenkins) *prom: rdn 3f out: wknd rapidly over 2f out* **12/1**

1m 39.91s (0.40) **Going Correction** 0.0s/f (Stan)
**WFA** 3 from 4yo+ 1lb **11 Ran SP% 122.5**
Speed ratings: **98,97,96,95,94 93,93,92,91,90 88**CSF £56.97 CT £287.65 TOTE £9.10: £3.00, £1.30, £2.40; EX 51.30.
**Owner** Liam Sheridan **Bred** George Strawbridge **Trained** Newmarket, Suffolk

**FOCUS**
There was no real pace on.

**NOTEBOOK**
**Topton(IRE)**is well treated on sand compared with turf. This was his first victory on Polytrack, although he was successful here three times on the old Equitrack surface.
**Tourmalet**was travelling easily when moving to the front, but she did not find a great deal. This trip might have stretched her stamina, but she is essentially a frustrating sort.
**Heidelburg(IRE)**ran on well in the latter stages and certainly seemed to see out the mile.
**Tropical Coral(IRE)**, who is not badly handicapped at present, was back over what appears her optimum trip.
**Learned Lad(FR)**, who tried to make all, has recorded all his wins over ten furlongs.
**Resonate(IRE)**, given an eye-catching ride, was dropped in at the start and held up at the back off a moderate pace. Angled inside on the approach to the home turn, he was then switched to the outer in the straight and ran on in good style, but the leaders had flown. He is definitely one to keep an eye on. *Official explanation: jockey said, regarding the running and riding, he missed the kick and then dropped horse in to get it covered up; he added that horse was going well but came off the bridle entering the final bend and was never able to make significant headway thereafter*

## 6120 FRED GIBSON MEMORIAL AMATEUR RIDERS' H'CAP 2m (P)
**3:30** (3:31) (F ) (0-65,74) 3-Y-O+ **£2,093** (£598; £299) **Stalls** Low

Form RPR

0605 **1** **Waverley Road**[68] 5171 6-9-6 41 ........ MrBKing(5) 5 51
(MMadgwick) *trckd clr ldrs: chsd clr ldr wl over 3f out: shkn up to ld ent fnl f: kpt on wl* **10/1**

3521 **2** *1 1/2* **Bucks**[8] 6060 6-11-9 74 5ex ow4 ........ MrMichaelMurphy(7) 13 82
(DKIvory) *hld up wl off the pce: nt clr run 6f out and 4f out: stdy prog 3f out: nudged along and kpt on to take 2nd last strides: to* **9/4[1]**

0333 **3** *nk* **Mysterium**[3] 6096 9-9-7 40 ........ (v) MrsEmmaLittmoden(3) 9 48
(NPLittmoden) *hld up: prog and prom 9f out: led 6f out and sn 8l clr: hdd and one pce ent fnl f* **8/1**

5024 **4** *1 3/4* **Astromancer (USA)**[6] 6079 3-9-9 54 ........ MrSWarren(7) 6 60
(MHTompkins) *chsd ldr after 3f to 7f out: chsd clr ldr briefly 4f out: rdn over 2f out: one pce over 1f out* **5/1[3]**

/26- **5** *11* **Tommy Carson**[582] 633 8-9-3 38 ........ MissKellyHarrison(5) 8 31
(JamiePoulton) *wl in rr: pushed along 7f out: nvr on terms: kpt on u.p fnl 2f* **33/1**

0426 **6** *1* **Landescent (IRE)**[6] 6075 3-9-10 55 ........ (v) GBartley(7) 11 46
(MQuinn) *wl in rr: pushed along 7f out: effrt u.p on outer 3f out: nvr on terms* **16/1**

50-5 **7** *1/2* **High Jinks**[13] 6033 8-9-9 42 ow5 ........ MrSDobson(3) 10 33
(RNBevis) *chsd clr ldrs tl fdd 3f out* **8/1**

0002 **8** *1/2* **Raheel (IRE)**[6] 6075 3-10-2 54 ........ (t) MrSWalker 1 44
(PMitchell) *dwlt: hld up wl in rr: prog over 5f out: effrt to dispute 2nd over 3f out: wknd over 2f out* **4/1[2]**

0060 **9** *3/4* **Peppershot**[14] 6025 3-9-11 56 ........ MrJPemberton(7) 2 45
(GPEnright) *dwlt: a wl in rr: rdn and no prog 6f out* **50/1**

055/ **10** *2 1/2* **Alka International**[288] 733 11-9-5 40 ........ MrsCThompson(5) 3 26
(MrsPTownsley) *chsd ldr for 3f: steadily wknd fr 6f out: bhd fnl 3f* **25/1**

0/6 **11** *12* **Charmante Femme**[20] 5982 5-9-13 46 ........ MissEFolkes(3) 7 18
(PDEvans) *led and sn clr: reluctant bnd 9f out and sn pressed: hdd 6f out: rdr lost iron briefly sn after: wknd: t.o* **10/1**

0000 **12** *1* **Coctail Lady (IRE)**[29] 3467 3-9-2 47 ow2 ........ (t) MrAshleePrice(7) 14 18
(BWDuke) *chsd clr ldrs tl wknd 6f out: t.o* **25/1**

0000 **13** *dist* **Prince Du Soleil (FR)**[19] 5279 7-9-5 42 ........ MrNSoares(7) 12 —
(JRJenkins) *a bhd: t.o fnl 6f* **25/1**

3m 28.84s (0.26) **Going Correction** 0.0s/f (Stan)
**WFA** 3 from 5yo+ 8lb **13 Ran SP% 130.2**
Speed ratings: **99,98,98,97,91 91,90,90,90,89 83,82,—**CSF £34.10 CT £207.46 TOTE £15.50: £6.10, £1.10, £2.00; EX 64.90 Place 6 £175.12, Place 5 £89.47.
**Owner** All Four Corners **Bred** Roger C Denton **Trained** Denmead, Hants

**FOCUS**
They went a decent clip, but the form of this amateurs' race looks rather suspect.

**NOTEBOOK**
**Waverley Road**, having his first run since leaving Alan Jarvis, saw out the two miles to win readily enough but this form is questionable.
**Bucks**, under his penalty, was given a great deal to do by his inexperienced rider. Although he closed to within striking distance, Murphy then proved of little assistance in the latter stages.
**Mysterium**led with three-quarters of a mile to run and quickened clear, but he had done too much too soon and was cut down.
**Astromancer(USA)**was always in the front rank and ran a respectable race over a trip on the far side for her.
T/Plt: £696.70 to a £1 stake. Pool: £40,089.70. 42.00 winning tickets. T/Qpdt: £42.00 to a £1 stake. Pool: £4,890.80. 86.00 winning tickets. JN

# 6063 SOUTHWELL (L-H)
## Wednesday, December 3

**OFFICIAL GOING: Standard**

## 6121 LITTLEWOODSPOKER.COM APPRENTICE H'CAP 1m 4f (F)
**1:00** (1:00) (E) (0-75,71) 3-Y-O+ **£2,023** (£578; £289) **Stalls** Low

Form RPR

0000 **1** **Dubai Dreams**[14] 6026 3-7-10 54 ........ (v) KGhunowa(10) 8 62
(MJPolglase) *mde all: rdn clr wl over 1f out: drvn and kpt on gamely ins last* **16/1**

0500 **2** *nk* **Majlis (IRE)**[146] 3144 6-9-1 58 ........ PMakin 2 65
(RMHCowell) *bhd: rdn along 4f out: wd st: gd hdwy 2f out: str run to chal ent last: sn rdn and kpt on* **10/1**

0252 **3** *3/4* **Digger (IRE)**[8] 6068 4-9-13 70 ........ (t) PPMathers 10 76
(MissGayKelleway) *hld up in tch: hdwy 3f out: effrt over 1f out: sn shkn up and ev ch tl drvn and one pce ins last* **6/5[1]**

6402 **4** *5* **Court Of Appeal**[29] 5920 6-9-13 **70**....(t) RoryMoore 1 69
(BEllison) *trckd ldrs on inner: hdwy 3f out: rdn over 1f out: sn one pce* **9/2**[2]

0355 **5** *nk* **Most-Saucy**[15] 6025 7-9-9 **71**.... SaleemGolam(5) 5 69
(IAWood) *towards rr: hdwy over 2f out: sn rdn and no imp appr last* **7/1**[3]

00-0 **6** *1 1/4* **Phantom Stock**[12] 6040 3-8-1 **54** ow5.... DTudhope(5) 4 50
(WJarvis) *hld up: hdwy on outer half way: chsd ldrs 3f out: sn rdn and wknd fnl 2f* **8/1**

4300 **7** *1 1/2* **Silver Prophet (IRE)**[15] 6025 4-9-9 **66**.... LTreadwell 9 60
(MRBosley) *s.i.s and bhd: gd hdwy 5f out: cl up 3f out: sn rdn and wknd fnl 2f* **16/1**

04-0 **8** *3/4* **Bid Spotter (IRE)**[6] 215 4-7-11 **45**.... SYourston(5) 6 38
(MrsLucindaFeatherstone) *chsd wnr: rdn along over 3f out: sn wknd* **20/1**

00/0 **9** *10* **Intensity**[19] 5999 7-8-7 **60**.... DerekNolan(10) 3 38
(PABlockley) *chsd ldng pair: rdn along 3f out: sn wknd* **33/1**

050 **10** *19* **Show Me The Lolly (FR)**[23] 5973 3-8-1 **54**.... DeanWilliams(5) 7 3
(PJMcbride) *chsd ldrs: rdn along 1/2-way: sn wknd* **40/1**

2m 39.22s (-2.88) **Going Correction** -0.25s/f (Stan)
**WFA** 3 from 4yo+ 5lb **10** Ran SP% **118.2**
Speed ratings: **99,98,98,94,94 93,92,92,85,73**CSF £163.99 CT £341.09 TOTE £12.60: £3.70, £3.60, £1.10; EX 144.00.
**Owner** Apb Racing **Bred** Miss S N Ralphs **Trained** Southwell, Notts
■ This was Kevin Ghunowa's first winner.

**FOCUS**
A steady pace to this apprentice handicap.

**NOTEBOOK**
**Dubai Dreams**dictated the pace at the head of affairs as he prefers and he made all in dogged style. He has fallen in the weights after a winless turf campaign and had looked badly out of form coming into this but, under a well-judged ride, he kept pulling out more in the straight over a trip he was not sure to stay. Now he has found his form, he could well go in again as he looks well treated on his best form.
**Majlis(IRE)**, well backed, came from way off the pace to mount a serious challenge in the straight having been almost tailed off at halfway, but could not reach the eventual winner and remains a maiden on the Flat. This was his first run since July so he is entitled to come on a fair bit for this and, although he may go up in the weights, this former useful hurdler has races in him on this surface.
**Digger(IRE)**, not for the first time, found less than expected off the bridle and is becoming expensive to follow. He was clear of the rest however and no doubt has the ability to win in this sphere, but has something to prove now.
**Court Of Appeal**got outpaced and was staying on at the death, but does not look a natural on sand.
**Most-Saucy**was unable to land a blow form off the pace, but does not look that suited to this track or the Fibresand and will be better back at Lingfield.
**Show Me The Lolly(FR)** *Official explanation: jockey said filly was in season*

## 6122 FREE £25 BONUS @ LITTLEWOODSPOKER.COM (S) STKS 5f (F)
**1:30** (1:30) (G) 2-Y-O **£2,016** (£576; £288) **Stalls** High

Form RPR

0636 **1** **Alizar (IRE)**[57] 5440 2-8-4 45.... LFletcher(3) 7 55
(MJPolglase) *cl up: led wl over 1f out: rdn clr ent last* **8/1**

6043 **2** *3* **Philly Dee**[12] 6041 2-8-8 45 ow1.... ACulhane 8 45
(JJay) *trckd ldrs: pushed along and outpcd 2f out: rdn and styd on ins last* **7/2**[3]

4546 **3** *1 1/2* **Blue Moon Hitman (IRE)**[12] 6037 2-8-12 53.... FNorton 9 44
(ABerry) *chsd ldrs on stands rail: rdn along 2f out: kpt on same pce* **10/3**[2]

2345 **4** *1* **Emaradia**[12] 6037 2-8-12 54.... JoannaBadger 6 40
(PDEvans) *chsd ldrs: rdn along 2f out: sn one pce* **5/1**

000 **5** *1 3/4* **Jocks Boy**[9] 6058 2-8-12.... ANicholls 10 34
(PRWood) *dwlt and outpcd tl styd on fnl 2f: nrst fin* **66/1**

0000 **6** *shd* **Are You There**[14] 6029 2-8-5 57....(v[1]) PMakin(7) 2 34
(TDBarron) *chsd ldrs on outer: pushed along 1/2-way: sn rdn and no hdwy fnl 2f* **9/4**[1]

0000 **7** *1 1/2* **Coleorton Prince (IRE)**[116] 3993 2-8-12.... RWinston 5 29
(KARyan) *led: pushed along 1/2-way: hdd wl over 1f out and grad wknd* **20/1**

0000 **8** *shd* **Desert Light (IRE)**[12] 6037 2-8-12 23.... MFenton 4 28
(DShaw) *spd to 1/2-way: sn rdn along and outpcd* **66/1**

0000 **9** *1/2* **Katz Pyjamas (IRE)**[39] 5746 2-8-7 42.... GDuffield 3 21
(MrsADuffield) *outpcd fr 1/2-way* **20/1**

00P0 **10** *8* **Shamone**[36] 5818 2-8-12 38....(p) JFanning 1 —
(HAMcwilliams) *wnt lft s: chsd ldrs: rdn along 1/2-way: sn wknd* **66/1**

59.98 secs (-0.32) **Going Correction** -0.25s/f (Stan) **10** Ran SP% **117.8**
Speed ratings: **92,87,84,83,80 80,77,77,76,64**CSF £35.05 TOTE £12.20: £3.50, £2.20, £1.70; EX 48.20.There was no bid for the winner.
**Owner** Paul J Dixon **Bred** Epona Bloodstock Ltd **Trained** Southwell, Notts
■ Stewards Enquiry : Joanna Badger caution: used whip with excessive frequency

**FOCUS**
Those drawn middle-to-high had a distinct advantage in this weak juvenile sprint.

**NOTEBOOK**
**Alizar(IRE)**finally got off the mark at the 12th attempt in decisive fashion. Having been up with pace from the start, she burnt off her rivals and stayed on strongly, suggesting she may have more to offer back at six furlongs. Although this was a poor contest, she is well bred and has taken time to come to herself, so may have more to offer this winter. There was no bid at the subsequent auction.
**Philly Dee**stayed on all too late in the day and would have been better suited ridden closer to the pace, as she is proven over six furlongs.
**Blue Moon Hitman(IRE)**held every chance on the stands' side rail, but once again found little under pressure and looks a short runner.
**Emaradia**was never on terms and this must go down as a disappointing effort as she held the winner and the fourth horse on previous form. She may have been better racing more prominently.
**Are You There**, racing in a first-time visor, was unable to get competitive from her low draw. However, she was one of the first beaten and is seemingly going the wrong way.

## 6123 LITTLEWOODSPOKER.COM H'CAP 2m (F)
**2:00** (2:00) (D) (0-85,83) 3-Y-O+ **£3,290** (£940; £470) **Stalls** Low

Form RPR

1501 **1** **Snow's Ride**[16] 6017 3-9-9 **83**.... IMongan 7 99+
(WRMuir) *a.p: disp ld 5f out tl led over 2f out: sn rdn: drvn ins last and styd on gamely* **7/4**[1]

2006 **2** *nk* **Bid For Fame (USA)**[12] 3977 6-10-0 **80**.... TQuinn 2 92+
(NJHenderson) *cl up: disp ld 5f out: pushed along 2f out: rdn over 1f out: kpt on* **7/2**[2]

4522 **3** *12* **Glory Quest (USA)**[9] 6061 6-9-9 **75**.... ACulhane 5 73
(MissGayKelleway) *in tch: hdwy 5f out: rdn along 3f out: sn drvn and outpcd fnl 2f* **9/2**[3]

4550 **4** *6* **Complete Circle**[11] 6052 3-9-8 **82**....(e[1]) PaulEddery 8 72
(PWD'Arcy) *trckd ldrs: effrt 4f out: sn rdn along and outpcd fnl 3f* **14/1**

1416 **5** *7* **Nowell House**[4] 6098 7-9-11 **77**.... DaleGibson 4 59
(MWEasterby) *hld up: effrt 5f out: sn rdn along and wknd 3f out* **14/1**

-000 **6** *3 1/2* **Kagoshima (IRE)**[14] 6033 8-7-8 **51** oh7 ow1....(v) JFMcDonald(5) 3 29
(JRNorton) *hld up: hdwy on outer to chse ldrs 5f out: rdn and wknd over 3f out* **50/1**

5005 **7** *3/4* **Calcar (IRE)**[9] 6060 3-8-0 **60** oh14 ow2.... CCatlin 6 37
(MrsSLamyman) *led: rdn along and hdd over 5f out: sn wknd* **80/1**

2-12 **8** *3* **Rebelle**[327] 276 4-8-11 **63**.... SWhitworth 1 36
(PBowen) *trckd ldrs on inner: rdn along 5f out: drvn 3f out and sn btn* **7/2**[2]

3m 38.36s (-14.14) **Going Correction** -0.25s/f (Stan)
**WFA** 3 from 4yo+ 8lb **8** Ran SP% **115.5**
Speed ratings: **105,104,98,95,92 90,90,88**CSF £8.17 CT £22.98 TOTE £3.10: £1.70, £1.10, £1.80; EX 12.30.
**Owner** The Parkside Partnership **Bred** Biddestone Stud And Partner **Trained** Lambourn, Berks

**FOCUS**
This was fairly competitive and was run at a fair pace, but suprisingly the two horses that forced the pace came right away from the others and very few managed to get into it.

**NOTEBOOK**
**Snow's Ride**confirmed had looked a progressive type when winning easily last time at Wolverhampton over this trip and confirmed that with a battling success. He was 11lb higher for that win and was made to pull out all the stops by the runner-up, but gamely responded to his rider's urgings and always looked like holding on. No doubt he will pay with the Handicapper again for this, but it was a very solid effort and he looks one to follow.
**Bid For Fame(USA)**confirmed had looked a progressive type when winning easily last time on this surface at Wolverhampton over this trip and confirmed that with a battling success. He was 11lb higher for that win and was made to pull out all the stops by the runner-up, but gamely responded to his rider's urgings and always looked like holding on. No doubt he will pay with the Handicapper again for this, but it was a very solid effort and he looks one to follow.
**Glory Quest(USA)**ran well for a long way and is a tough performer, but again did not look to stay this trip too well. He is a trustworthy individual who pays for his consistency with the Handicapper, but he should continue to pay his way this winter.
**Complete Circle**moved well in behind the leaders before lacking the stamina required to get competitive over a trip too far. She has the ability, but her optimum trip is unknown.
**Rebelle**, backed in the ring, was well beaten. This was her first outing since January and first for new connections. She should come on for the run, but she dropped out tamely when push came to shove.

## 6124 LITTLEWOODS BET DIRECT STKS SHOWCASE H'CAP 1m (F)
**2:30** (2:30) (C) (0-95,92) 3-Y-O+ **£5,531** (£1,702; £851; £425) **Stalls** Low

Form RPR

0011 **1** **Cardinal Venture (IRE)**[16] 6013 5-10-0 **92**.... RWinston 5 103
(KARyan) *mde all: rdn clr wl or 1f out: drvn side last: edgd lft and kpt on* **11/4**[1]

105 **2** *1/2* **Te Quiero**[16] 6013 5-10-0 **92**....(t) MFenton 8 102
(MissGayKelleway) *trckd ldrs: hdwy over 2f out: rdn to chse wnr over 1f out: sn drvn and kpt on wl* **8/1**

0140 **3** *1/2* **Cool Temper**[26] 5945 7-8-13 **77**....(t) JFanning 9 86
(PFICole) *sn outpcd in rr: hdwy 3f out: swtchd outside and rdn wl over 1f out: styd on wl fnl f: nrst fin* **8/1**

5350 **4** *2* **Crusoe (IRE)**[8] 6068 6-7-11 **66**....(b) JFMcDonald(5) 10 71
(ASadik) *chsd ldrs: rdn over 2f out: kpt on same pce approachong last* **16/1**

2104 **5** *2* **Brandy Cove**[8] 6064 6-8-2 **66**.... RFfrench 3 67
(BSmart) *hld up: hdwy on inner over 2f out: sn rdn and kpt on same pce appr last* **5/1**[2]

1134 **6** *2* **Penwell Hill (USA)**[279] 631 4-8-5 **69**.... DMernagh 4 66
(TDBarron) *chsd ldrs: rdn along 3f out: sn wknd* **7/1**[3]

2200 **7** *3/4* **Del Mar Sunset**[16] 6013 4-9-8 **86**.... ACulhane 1 82
(WJHaggas) *cl up: rdn over 2f out: swtchd rt and drvn wl over 1f out: sn wknd* **14/1**

0010 **8** *5* **Barzak (IRE)**[8] 6064 3-8-3 **68**....(p) JBramhill 12 54
(SRBowring) *chsd ldrs on outer: rdn along 3f out: wknd fnl 2f* **7/1**[3]

0000 **9** *1/2* **Lucayan Monarch**[14] 6026 5-7-5 **62**....(p) SYourston(7) 7 47
(PABlockley) *dwlt: a rr* **50/1**

6000 **10** *8* **Power Bird (IRE)**[7] 6078 3-8-13 **78**.... PDoe 11 47
(DFlood) *a bhd* **14/1**

5363 **11** *2 1/2* **Countykat (IRE)**[23] 5967 3-8-12 **77**.... IMongan 6 41
(KRBurke) *bhd fr 1/2-way* **11/1**

4050 **12** *9* **Pride Of Kinloch**[167] 2500 3-8-0 **65** oh1 ow2.... CCatlin 2 11
(JHetherton) *chsd ldrs: rdn along 1/2-way: sn wknd* **40/1**

1m 41.5s (-3.10) **Going Correction** -0.25s/f (Stan)
**WFA** 3 from 4yo+ 1lb **12** Ran SP% **122.5**
Speed ratings: **105,104,104,102,100 98,97,92,91,83 81,72**CSF £26.04 CT £164.25 TOTE £3.30: £1.80, £3.40, £3.00; EX 29.90 Trifecta £347.80 Pool of £4,262.26 - 8.70 winning units.
**Owner** Tony Fawcett **Bred** Patrick Gleeson **Trained** Hambleton, N Yorks

**FOCUS**
Once again it proved to be an advantage racing close to the pace and the field were well strung at the finish.

**NOTEBOOK**
**Cardinal Venture(IRE)**completed the hat-trick by making all in grand style. He gained both of his previous wins at Wolverhampton, but adjusted very well to this track and its slower surface and a 6lb rise for his last victory proved no problem. His connections will be hoping the Handicapper does not react too harshly to this and he will now most likely be given a break before returning to this surface next year.
**Te Quiero**was unable to go with the winner early on and is best when allowed to dominate, but ran well in the circumstances. He is best at Wolverhampton and on this evidence, has more races in him this winter.
**Cool Temper**is the one to take out of the race. Having been held off the pace, he was flying late on and had he been produced earlier, he would have finished closer. He has done well for his current connections on turf this year and looks like translating that to the sand if he can reproduce this effort.
**Crusoe(IRE)**, with the blinkers back on, was well held in third but improved on his latest running over this shorter trip.
**Brandy Cove**had every chance of getting closer in the straight but ran out of gas and may have been at a disadvantage in sticking to the far-side rail.
**Penwell Hill(USA)**, having his first run since February, ran very much as though this outing was needed. He will be a lot sharper next time and is one to keep on the right side of when the market speaks in his favour.

## 6125 ROYAL FLUSH JACKPOT @ LITTLEWOODSPOKER.COM CLAIMING STKS 1m 3f (F)
**3:00** (3:00) (F) 3-Y-O+ **£2,044** (£584; £292) **Stalls** Low

Form RPR

5021 **1** **Mr Mischief**[19] 5999 3-9-2 84.... RoryMoore(7) 2 78
(PCHaslam) *trckd ldrs: hdwy to ld 1/2-way: rdn clr wl over 1f out: styd on* **8/13**[1]



The Form Book, Raceform Ltd, Compton, RG20 6NL

4002 **2** *3* **Al's Alibi**[5] 6085 10-8-7 41 FNorton 3 54
(WRMuir) *hld up in tch: pushed along 1/2-way: hdwy over 3f out: rdn to chse wnr over 1f out: sn drvn and no imp fnl f* **7/2**[2]

064/ **3** *4* **Moon Shot**[398] 5587 7-9-13 64 VSlattery 4 68
(AGJuckes) *a.p: ev ch over 3f out: sn rdn and one pce fnl 2f* **16/1**

4000 **4** *4* **Spanish Star**[9] 6057 6-8-13 45 JoannaBadger 5 49
(MrsNMacauley) *hld up: hdwy 3f out: sn rdn and no further prog* **20/1**

0 **5** *3 1/2* **Turftanzer (GER)**[46] 5631 4-9-7 41 KimTinkler 6 52
(DonEnricoIncisa) *led to 1/2-way: sn rdn along and wknd* **66/1**

00/ **6** *nk* **Broughton Melody**[754] 5682 4-8-10 MFenton 1 40
(WJMusson) *in tocuh on inner: rdn along over 4f out: sn wknd* **33/1**

3006 **7** *16* **Behan**[9] 5631 4-8-7 27 (b) VHalliday 7 15
(ACrook) *prom: rdn along 1/2-way: sn wknd* **50/1**

4006 **8** *3/4* **Port Moreno (IRE)**[13] 3541 3-8-6 48 ow1 (v) RHavlin 10 17
(JGMO'Shea) *chsd ldrs: rdn alonga nd wknd 1/2-way* **14/1**

0-0 **9** *1 1/2* **By All Men (IRE)**[319] 332 3-8-12 DerekNolan(7) 8 28
(PABlockley) *hld up: short lived effrt over 3f out: nvr a factor* **10/1**[3]

0000 **10** *4* **Mawhoob (USA)**[43] 5692 5-8-2 47 (v) StevenHarrison(7) 9 8
(MrsNMacauley) *in tch to 1/2-way: sn outpcd and bhd* **66/1**

2m 26.35s (-2.55) **Going Correction** -0.25s/f (Stan)
**WFA** 3 from 4yo+ 4lb **10** Ran SP% **118.4**
Speed ratings: **99,96,93,91,88 88,76,76,74,72**CSF £2.79 TOTE £1.80: £1.02, £1.60, £2.70; EX 3.90.Mr Mischief was claimed by P C Haslam for £14,000 (friendly).
**Owner** Middleham Park Racing **Bred** Mrs Maureen Barbara Walsh **Trained** Middleham Moor, N Yorks

**FOCUS**
A very weak contest mainly consisting of frustrating sorts.

**NOTEBOOK**
**Mr Mischief**had to be kept up to his work in the straight, but always looked like scoring as official figures suggested he should. He has now won all of his four starts on Fibresand and will be better suited by a return to further, but there are not many options for him on the sand.
**Al's Alibi**is a consistent sort in this grade and again ran a sound race as he is rated 43lb lower than the winner but, at the age of ten, he is likely to remain vulnerable to sharper types.
**Moon Shot**ran well for a long way, but understandably tired on this first outing for more than a year. He moves well and handled this surface, so can find a weak race.
**By All Men(IRE)**, unexposed and well backed for this, never looked like troubling the principals at any stage.

## 6126 LITTLEWOODSCASINO.COM MAIDEN STKS 1m (F)
**3:30** (3:30) (D ) 3-Y-O+ **£2,240** (£640; £320) **Stalls** Low

Form RPR

**1** **Trance (IRE)**[147] 3118 3-9-0 75 DMernagh 10 65
(TDBarron) *trckd ldrs: hdwy on ouyer 1/2-way: led over 2f out and sn rdn clr* **11/8**[1]

4066 **2** *6* **Chesnut Ripple**[121] 3837 4-8-10 53 RHavlin 6 48
(DShaw) *trckd ldrs: hdwy 3f out: rdn to chse wnr wl over 1f out: sn no imp* **4/1**[2]

6665 **3** *2 1/2* **Pacific Ocean (ARG)**[68] 5199 4-9-1 46 (t) FNorton 2 48
(MrsStefLiddiard) *trckd ldrs whn hmpd on inner after 2f: swtchd rt and hdwy over 2f out: sn rdn and kpt on same pce* **9/1**

0000 **4** *1* **Petrolero (ARG)**[68] 5203 4-9-1 41 (t) CCatlin 4 46
(MrsStefLiddiard) *keen: chsd ldrs: rdn 2f out: sn one pce* **33/1**

**5** *13* **Devious Paddy (IRE)**[20] 5584 3-9-0 76 KimTinkler 1 20
(NTinkler) *sn outpcd: a rr* **11/1**

3200 **6** *2 1/2* **Middleham Park (IRE)**[121] 3830 3-8-11 65 LEnstone(3) 12 15
(PCHaslam) *prom: led over 3f out: rdn and hdd over 2f out: sn wknd* **4/1**[2]

00 **7** *1 1/2* **Quidditch**[133] 3503 3-8-9 SWhitworth 11 7
(PBowen) *led: rdn along and hdd over 3f out: sn wknd* **50/1**

00 **8** *2 1/2* **Moonglade (USA)**[8] 6067 3-8-9 (t) PaulEddery 3 2
(MissJFeilden) *prom: rdn along over 3f out: wknd over 2f out* **100/1**

40 **9** *4* **Chiasso (USA)**[18] 6004 3-8-6 52 LFletcher(3) 7 —
(HMorrison) *in tch: rdn along and outpcd fr 1/2-way* **13/2**[3]

00 **10** *3 1/2* **Sawah**[8] 6067 3-9-0 JFanning 5 —
(DShaw) *s.i.s: a bhd* **66/1**

1m 41.83s (-2.77) **Going Correction** -0.25s/f (Stan)
**WFA** 3 from 4yo 1lb **10** Ran SP% **121.2**
Speed ratings: **103,97,94,93,80 78,76,74,70,66**CSF £7.30 TOTE £2.80: £1.30, £2.10, £2.40; EX 13.00 Place 6 £10.38, Place 5 £5.89.
**Owner** Nigel Shields **Bred** Forenaghts Stud Co Ltd **Trained** Maunby, N Yorks

**FOCUS**
A poor maiden contest with very little strength in depth.

**NOTEBOOK**
**Trance(IRE)**, last seen in July when trained by Dermot Weld, ran away with this on his British debut for his powerful new connections in this sphere. He was prominent throughout and despite his rider having to get serious with him over two furlongs out, he scored easily in the end. He will improve for further and it would be a surprise if he were not to build on this.
**Chesnut Ripple**had every chance, but was no match for the winner on this debut for his new connections. He seemed to improve for this drop in trip though and he has the ability to lose his maiden tag on this surface when dropped in grade.
**Pacific Ocean(ARG)**improved on previous efforts on this step up in trip, but is only plating-class.
**Petrolero(ARG)**Petrolero ran well enough for most of the race, but was too keen early on and that did not help him get home over this extra furlong.
**Devious Paddy(IRE)**was closely matched with the winner on their Irish form, but was taken off his feet at the start and although he is better than this, he looks flattered by his current rating.
T/Plt: £17.30 to a £1 stake. Pool: £35,916.65. 1,509.25 winning tickets. T/Qpdt: £3.30 to a £1 stake. Pool: £2,876.20. 637.30 winning tickets. JR

# 6113 LINGFIELD (L-H)
## Saturday, December 6

**OFFICIAL GOING: Standard**
There was the usual bias against front runners and those that raced closest to the inside rail.
Wind: mod hlf against Weather: cloudy

## 6127 BET DIRECT IN RUNNING SKY TEXT 293 H'CAP (DIV I) 7f (P)
**11:55** (11:56) (F ) (0-65,74) 3-Y-O+ **£2,100** (£600; £300) **Stalls** Low

Form RPR

5152 **1** **Cold Climate**[7] 6094 8-9-7 **58** FNorton 10 69
(BobJones) *chsd ldrs: led ins fnl f: pushed clr: readily* **10/1**

0101 **2** *1 1/2* **He Who Dares (IRE)**[30] 5937 5-9-4 **55** MFenton 9 62
(AWCarroll) *dwlt: in rr: nt clr run ins fnl 2f: weaved through and fin wl to go 2nd nr fin* **10/1**

6042 **3** *3/4* **Inistrahull Island (IRE)**[7] 6088 3-9-8 **59** JFanning 14 64
(MHTompkins) *cl up: rdn 2f out: chsd wnr wl ins fnl f: lost 2nd nr fin* **7/1**[3]

0046 **4** *1 1/4* **Its Ecco Boy**[7] 6094 5-9-3 **54** RWinston 16 56
(PHowling) *mid-div: outpcd over 2f out: styd on fnl f* **14/1**

0060 **5** *3/4* **Waltzing Wizard**[29] 5945 4-8-10 **52** PBradley(5) 1 52
(ABerry) *led: rdn over 2f out: hdd and no ex ins fnl f* **50/1**

0200 **6** *shd* **Social Contract**[73] 5151 6-9-3 **54** PaulEddery 2 54
(SDow) *w ldrs tl no ex over 1f out* **25/1**

0011 **7** *1/2* **Chateau Nicol**[7] 6094 4-10-2 **74** (v) AHindley(7) 15 73
(BGPowell) *trckd ldrs: outpcd 2f out: kpt on fnl f* **5/1**[1]

4123 **8** *nk* **Mr Bountiful (IRE)**[7] 6094 5-9-12 **63** SWKelly 6 61
(MDods) *dwlt: sn chsng ldrs: wnt 2nd 2f out: wknd 1f out* **8/1**

5006 **9** *1/2* **Kinsman (IRE)**[7] 6088 6-8-13 **53** (p) J-PGuillambert(3) 8 50
(TDMccarthy) *t.k.h in midfield: rdn to chse ldrs 2f out: no ex over 1f out* **20/1**

0623 **10** *nk* **Heidelburg (IRE)**[4] 6119 3-9-9 **65** JFMcDonald(5) 3 61
(SKirk) *sn in rr: rdn 1/2-way: hdwy on rail wl over 1f out: no ex* **13/2**[2]

2564 **11** *3/4* **A Woman In Love**[7] 6088 4-9-4 **55** IMongan 7 49
(MissBSanders) *dwlt: plld hrd in rr: n.d* **9/1**

0056 **12** *1/2* **Park Star**[7] 6092 3-9-10 **61** RHavlin 11 54
(DShaw) *chsd ldrs tl wknd wl over 1f out* **33/1**

0031 **13** *1 3/4* **Pants**[7] 6088 4-9-8 **59** ANicholls 13 48
(AndrewReid) *wd: towards rr: rdn 3f out: n.d* **16/1**

0000 **14** *1* **Roy McAvoy (IRE)**[40] 5796 5-10-0 **65** EAhern 4 51
(MrsGHarvey) *dwlt: sn pushed along in rr: sme hdwy 2f out: sn wknd* **50/1**

5056 **15** *3/4* **Taiyo**[18] 6019 3-9-3 **54** TQuinn 12 38
(JWPayne) *prom: hrd rdn 3f out: wknd 2f out* **16/1**

0404 **16** *nk* **Foolish Thought (IRE)**[23] 5985 3-9-4 **62** DSwift(7) 5 46
(RAFahey) *sn in rr: lost tch 1/2-way* **12/1**

1m 26.8s (-26.00) **Going Correction** +0.175s/f (Slow) **16** Ran SP% **123.4**
Speed ratings: **102,100,99,98,97 97,96,96,95,95 94,93,91,90,89 89**CSF £102.21 CT £758.81 TOTE £9.00: £2.50, £3.60, £3.10, £2.20; EX 114.90.
**Owner** The Cold Climate Partnership **Bred** Juddmonte Farms **Trained** Wickhambrook, Suffolk

**FOCUS**
A typically competitive, if modest, Polytrack handicap run at a good pace and a similar time to the second division.

**NOTEBOOK**
**Cold Climate**, 16lb better off with Chateau Nicol for a five-length beating seven days earlier, was always in the perfect position to strike and did this nicely. He has been around for a while, but this was only his third start on sand and he may be able to win again.
**He Who Dares(IRE)**, in good form on turf during the autumn, ran a good deal better than in his only previous try on this surface, staying on well to the line, and should be able to find a race on it.
**Inistrahull Island(IRE)**had every chance, but again found a couple too good. He has the ability to win on this surface, but is not enjoying much luck at the moment.
**Its Ecco Boy**was coming home in good style and may be worth a try over a mile, but a record of just two wins from 51 starts is a little off-putting.
**Waltzing Wizard**, who has shown little since making his belated reappearance in August, has slipped to a plater's mark and ran his best race for some time under a positive ride.
**Social Contract**did not perform badly and is very well handicapped on his old sand form.
**Chateau Nicol**, raised a massive 16lb after his cakewalk here last week, found things a good deal harder this time, but also did not see a great deal of daylight.
**Mr Bountiful(IRE)**was badly in at the weights with the winner compared to last week.

## 6128 BET DIRECT ON CHANNEL 4 PAGE 613 CLAIMING STKS (DIV I) 1m (P)
**12:25** (12:26) (F ) 3-Y-O+ **£2,058** (£588; £294) **Stalls** High

Form RPR

0150 **1** **Burgundy**[7] 6093 6-8-12 65 KDalgleish 1 63
(PMitchell) *s.s: bhd and cajoled along: swtchd wd over 3f out: str run to ld fnl 50 yds* **2/1**[1]

5603 **2** *1 1/4* **Givemethemoonlight**[19] 6015 4-8-5 46 JFEgan 3 53
(LGCottrell) *prom: hrd rdn over 1f out: ev ch ins fnl f: nt qckn* **8/1**

-004 **3** *1* **Senor Miro**[197] 1778 5-8-6 50 CCatlin 5 52
(JAkehurst) *hdwy over 2f out: led over 1f out: hrd rdn and hdd fnl 50 yds: no ex* **11/1**

0056 **4** *1/2* **Fabrian**[15] 6042 5-9-2 53 (e) DaneO'Neill 12 61
(DWPArbuthnot) *t.k.h: pressed ldr: led 2f out tl over 1f out: one pce* **6/1**[3]

4U05 **5** *2 1/2* **Estrella Levante**[47] 5678 3-8-13 52 (be[1]) RBrisland 2 53
(GLMoore) *dwlt: hld up towards rr: effrt whn hmpd and snatched up over 2f out: rallied and r.o fnl f* **12/1**

3540 **6** *3/4* **Jamestown**[30] 5933 6-9-0 50 JFanning 4 51
(CSmith) *mid-div: rdn 3f out: styd on same pce* **12/1**

0000 **7** *hd* **Ginger Ice**[7] 6088 3-8-3 47 (p) NPollard 6 41
(GGMargarson) *hld up and bhd: hdwy 2f out: hrd rdn and no ex 1f out* **66/1**

0000 **8** *1/2* **Zhitomir**[51] 5596 5-9-4 52 SWKelly 8 53
(MDods) *mid-div: rdn over 4f out: nt pce to chal* **16/1**

6100 **9** *nk* **Espada (IRE)**[212] 1451 7-9-8 81 EAhern 11 57
(JAOsborne) *led tl 2f out: wknd over 1f out* **9/2**[2]

-550 **10** *1 1/2* **Senor Toran (USA)**[219] 1312 3-8-13 52 TQuinn 7 45
(PBurgoyne) *chsd ldrs over 5f* **33/1**

0606 **11** *shd* **Eurolink Zante (IRE)**[30] 5937 7-9-1 49 (p) J-PGuillambert(3) 10 49
(TDMccarthy) *mid-div: rdn to chse ldrs over 2f out: wknd over 1f out* **12/1**

1m 39.88s (0.37) **Going Correction** +0.175s/f (Slow)
**WFA** 3 from 4yo+ 1lb **11** Ran SP% **118.6**
Speed ratings: **105,103,102,102,99 99,98,98,98,96 96** CT £2.90 TOTE £1.50: £1.70, £3.10, £; EX29.90 1.Jamestown was claimed by M J Polglase for £8,000; Givemethemoonlight was claimed by Mrs S Liddiard for £6,000; There was a f
**Owner** Nigel Shields **Bred** Cheveley Park Stud Ltd **Trained** Epsom, Surrey
■ Stewards Enquiry : N Pollard caution: careless riding

**FOCUS**
A modest contest, but the pace was good even though the time was still nearly half a second slower than the second division.

**NOTEBOOK**
**Burgundy**, a real character these days, fluffed the start as usual and had plenty of ground to make up, but he is still a class above these rivals when in the mood and mowed them down with a devastating late run down the wide outside. A repeat is highly unlikely though. *Official explanation: , a real character these days, fluffed the start as usual and had plenty of ground to make up, but he is still a class above these rivals when in the mood and mowed them down with a devastating late run down the wide outside. A repeat is highly unlikely though.*
**Givemethemoonlight**ran about as well as could be expected considering she was 12lb worse in with the winner than she would have been in a handicap. *Official explanation: ran about as well as could be expected considering she was 12lb worse in with the winner than she would have been in a handicap.*
**Senor Miro**, a five-year-old maiden who has been lightly raced in the last couple of seasons, with another to run with credit at the weights and may be able to find a modest seller on the surface, though he may be better back over seven. *Official explanation: , a five-year-old maiden who has been lightly raced in the last couple of seasons, with another to run with credit at the weights and may be able to find a modest seller on the surface, though he may be better back over seven.*

**Fabrian**, another five-year-old maiden, probably ran up to his best and has had plenty of chances. *Official explanation: , another five-year-old maiden, probably ran up to his best and has had plenty of chances.*
**Estrella Levante**was squeezed out when trying to make progress on the home turn but for which he would have finished a few lengths closer. *Official explanation: was squeezed out when trying to make progress on the home turn but for which he would have finished a few lengths closer.*
**Espada(IRE)**, by far the highest rated horse in the field, was returning from injury on this first start since May. He made the early running at a good pace, but always looked to be a sitting duck on this surface and so it proved. *Official explanation: , by far the highest rated horse in the field, was returning from injury on this first start since May. He made the early running at a good pace, but always looked to be a sitting duck on this surface and so it proved.*

## 6129 BET DIRECT NO Q DEMO 08000 837 888 MAIDEN AUCTION STKS 6f (P)
12:55 (12:58) (E) 2-Y-O £2,257 (£645; £322) Stalls Low

Form RPR
35 **1** **La Landonne**23 5984 2-8-2 FNorton 6 57
(PMPhelan) *prom: led over 1f out: rdn out* **2/1**2
00 **2** *nk* **Lady Korrianda**32 5915 2-8-4 ow2 JFanning 9 58
(MJWallace) *mid-div: hdwy on outside over 1f out: edgd lft and r.o wl fnl f* **14/1**
**3** *½* **Starcross Venture** 2-8-2 ow5 THamilton(5) 12 60
(RAFahey) *dwlt: outpcd and bhd: gd hdwy over 1f out: chsd wnr ins fnl f: r.o* **100/1**
05 **4** *1* **Lyrical Lady**47 5677 2-8-5 EAhern 5 55
(MrsAJBowlby) *a.p: one pce appr fnl f* **20/1**
**5** *1 ½* **Ex Mill Lady** 2-7-11 JFMcDonald(5) 1 47
(JohnBerry) *hld up in midfield: shkn up and hdwy over 1f out: styd on same pce* **100/1**
5 **6** *½* **Red Rocky**167 2599 2-8-2 CCatlin 4 46
(JGallagher) *s.s: t.k.h: swtchd wd and hdwy over 3f out: one pce fnl 2f* **8/1**
0 **7** *½* **Vrisaki (IRE)**179 2247 2-8-13 DaneO'Neill 13 55
(MissDMountain) *prom: hrd rdn over 1f out: no ex* **25/1**
3 **8** *¾* **Velvet Touch**30 5930 2-8-2 JMackay 2 42
(JRJenkins) *led tl over 1f out: wknd fnl f* **6/1**3
**9** *nk* **Mugeba** 2-8-3 ow1 PaulEddery 7 42+
(WJMusson) *s.s: hld up and bhd: sme hdwy over 1f out: nvr in chalng position* **50/1**
00 **10** *½* **Marksgold (IRE)**91 4735 2-8-4 LPKeniry(3) 8 44
(KBell) *chsd ldrs over 3f* **33/1**
00 **11** *1* **Introduction**18 6021 2-8-7 MFenton 11 41
(WJMusson) *outpcd in rr: nvr trbld ldrs* **40/1**
**12** *nk* **Chorus Beauty** 2-8-8 JFEgan 3 42
(GWragg) *in tch: rdn to chse ldrs 2f out: hung lft and wknd over 1f out* **15/8**1
**13** *1 ½* **Mystic Moon** 2-8-2 AMackay 14 31
(JRJenkins) *dwlt: wd: hld up towards rr: shkn up 2f out: n.d* **50/1**
**14** *6* **Cape Tia (IRE)** 2-8-5 ANicholls 10 16
(RAFahey) *dwlt: outpcd: a bhd* **25/1**
1m 15.38s (2.46) **Going Correction** +0.175s/f (Slow) **14** Ran SP% **123.9**
Speed ratings: **90,89,88,87,85 84,84,83,82,82 80,80,78,70**CSF £28.06 TOTE £3.20: £2.00, £4.10, £7.60; EX 71.20.
**Owner** Wood Hall Stud Limited **Bred** Wood Hall Stud Limited **Trained** Shenley, Herts

**FOCUS**
A modest maiden and the form may not amount to much.

**NOTEBOOK**
**La Landonne**showed a horrible head carriage, but she had form on the surface and was still good enough to just hold on. This race probably took little winning and she may struggle in handicap company.
**Lady Korrianda**, carrying 2lb overweight which may have made the difference between victory and defeat, left her previous form well behind and finished with quite a rattle. The form is nothing to get carried away with, but her trainer knows how to find the right opportunity and a small race can be found.
**Starcross Venture**, a half-sister to a couple of winners carrying 5lb overweight on this racecourse debut, performed with credit as she had to weave a path through and was forced to make her challenge tight against the inside rail. This was not a great race, but in the long term she is still likely to prove the best of these.
**Lyrical Lady**, who started slowly in both her previous outings, broke on terms this time despite half jumping in the air as the stalls opened and ran much better as a result. She can now be handicapped.
**Ex Mill Lady**, a half-sister to a winning plater, made a creditable enough debut but may not have achieved much.
**Velvet Touch**, placed on her sole turf start, made the early running but this was not a day for front runners.
**Chorus Beauty**, a 16,000gns Royal Applause filly out of a half-sister to Rainbow Ways, never looked like offering a threat.

## 6130 BET DIRECT NO Q ON 08000 93 66 93 H'CAP 1m 5f (P)
1:25 (1:26) (E) (0-75,75) 3-Y-O+ £2,331 (£666; £333) Stalls Low

Form RPR
0564 **1** **Western (IRE)**37 5839 3-9-1 **68** TQuinn 7 78
(JAkehurst) *mid-div: dropped to rr and eased outside 3f out: gd hdwy over 1f out: str run to ld last stride* **16/1**
1111 **2** *hd* **Cold Turkey**18 6025 3-9-1 **75** HPoulton(7) 11 85+
(GLMoore) *s.s: t.k.h towards rr: stdy hdwy 3f out: led ins fnl f: ct last stride* **10/3**1
1662 **3** *1* **Big Bertha**34 5890 5-9-4 **65** JFEgan 4 74
(JohnBerry) *hld up in rr: rdn 3f out: styd on wl fnl 2f: nrst fin* **12/1**
6021 **4** *nk* **Sea Holly (IRE)**7 6089 3-9-6 **73** KDalgleish 5 81
(GGMargarson) *prom: led over 2f out: rdn 3l ahd: hdd and no ex ins fnl f* **7/1**3
3453 **5** *1* **Reminiscent (IRE)**18 6025 4-9-2 **63** (v) DaneO'Neill 2 70
(RFJohnsonHoughton) *wd: hld up in rr: smooth hdwy on outside 3f out: styd on same pce fnl 2f* **7/1**3
4430 **6** *2 ½* **Easter Ogil (IRE)**174 2398 8-9-2 **63** VSlattery 9 66
(JaneSouthcombe) *mid-div: hdwy 3f out: briefly wnt 2nd over 1f out: wknd fnl f* **40/1**
0414 **7** *1* **Maystock**14 6052 3-9-2 **69** (v) EAhern 6 71
(GAButler) *hld up in tch: chsd ldr 2f out tl over 1f out: sn wknd* **4/1**2
3555 **8** *1 ¼* **Most-Saucy**3 6121 7-9-10 **71** SWKelly 10 71
(IAWood) *mid-div: reminder 6f out: no imp fnl 2f* **20/1**
6033 **9** *1 ¾* **Mumbling (IRE)**7 5727 5-9-5 **69** LPKeniry(3) 8 67
(BGPowell) *chsd ldrs: rdn 5f out: wknd 2f out* **14/1**
5630 **10** *¾* **Mandoob**18 6025 6-8-12 **62** J-PGuillambert(3) 1 59
(BRJohnson) *chsd ldrs tl wknd over 3f out* **16/1**
0043 **11** *¾* **Danakil**11 5183 8-9-5 **73** JCoffill-Brown(7) 13 69
(SDow) *in rr: rdn over 2f out: nvr trbld ldrs* **20/1**
3543 **12** *½* **Kristoffersen**40 5795 3-9-8 **75** IMongan 14 70
(RMStronge) *wd: mid-div: effrt 3f out: sn rdn and btn* **8/1**
0133 **13** *½* **Lazzaz**49 5635 5-9-4 **65** RWinston 3 59
(PWHiatt) *led tl over 2f out: wknd over 1f out* **25/1**
0040 **14** *10* **Go Classic**159 2853 3-9-2 **69** MFenton 12 49
(AMHales) *chsd ldr: rdn 5f out: wknd over 3f out* **100/1**
2m 48.38s (0.30) **Going Correction** +0.175s/f (Slow)
**WFA** 3 from 4yo+ 6lb **14** Ran SP% **122.1**
Speed ratings: **106,105,105,105,104 102,102,101,100,100 99,99,98,92**CSF £66.11 CT £693.30 TOTE £14.80: £5.40, £2.00, £3.30; EX 93.00.
**Owner** H R Hunt **Bred** M P B Bloodstock Ltd **Trained** Epsom, Surrey

**FOCUS**
A competitive handicap run at a good pace.

**NOTEBOOK**
**Western(IRE)**, 9lb better off with Cold Turkey for a beating of less than a length here in October, came with a strong late run between horses to snatch the race on the line and record his first win at the tenth attempt. He is still unexposed on the surface and may be capable of even better.
**Cold Turkey**, bidding for a five-timer, was badly in with the winner compared to their running here in October, though he has improved since. He hit the front at just the right time here, but had his rider spent less time looking over his shoulder and concentrating on getting the gelding home the result may have been different. That is far from certain, but it certainly did not make for great viewing.
**Big Bertha**had shown her effectiveness under these conditions and was coming home in good style. He has the ability to win another contest here.
**Sea Holly(IRE)**, stepping up from maiden company, did everything right but was just worn down in the latter stages. Sticking to the inside rail when in front down the home straight was probably a bigger handicap than the extra furlong and he should be given the chance to atone.
**Reminiscent(IRE)**stayed on late, but lacked a turn of foot where it matters and probably needs a greater test of stamina.
**Easter Ogil(IRE)**is back on a winning mark and did not run badly on this first start since June, but the fact remains he is still to win beyond a mile.
**Maystock**, winner of a course-and-distance apprentice contest here last month, found things tougher off a 7lb higher mark in a better race.

## 6131 BET DIRECT NO Q MAIDEN STKS 1m 2f (P)
1:55 (1:58) (D) 3-Y-O+ £2,299 (£657; £328) Stalls Low

Form RPR
4-24 **1** **Maxilla (IRE)**24 5978 3-8-9 63 EAhern 8 68
(LMCumani) *w ldrs: led after 2f and set stdy pce: rdn and hld on wl fnl f* **3/1**2
3-2 **2** *nk* **Margery Daw (IRE)**54 5554 3-8-9 DaneO'Neill 13 67
(MPTregoning) *cl up: rdn to press wnr fnl 2f: nt qckn nr fin* **5/2**1
-025 **3** *1* **Bluegrass Boy**66 5308 3-9-0 63 RHavlin 12 70
(GBBalding) *hdwy 4f out: wnt cl 3rd 2f out: sltly outpcd over 1f out: kpt on fnl 100 yds* **16/1**
00 **4** *1 ¼* **State Of Balance**59 5455 5-8-9 LPKeniry(3) 3 63
(KBell) *stdd in rr s: hld up and bhd: stdy hdwy 2f out: nt clr run and swtchd rt over 1f out: fin wl* **100/1**
54 **5** *¾* **Betterware Boy**151 3081 3-9-0 FNorton 7 67
(PMPhelan) *t.k.h: in tch: effrt over 2f out: carried hd awkwardly: styd on same pce* **14/1**
3442 **6** *hd* **Cayman Sunrise (IRE)**39 5815 3-8-9 65 TQuinn 6 61
(EALDunlop) *t.k.h and restrained in front: led 2f: hrd rdn over 1f out: no ex* **9/2**3
-400 **7** *5* **Blue Rondo (IRE)**215 1417 3-9-0 65 CCatlin 9 57
(IanWilliams) *w ldrs tl wknd 2f out* **20/1**
**8** *1 ¼* **Bold Ridge (IRE)** 3-9-0 JFEgan 4 55
(SKirk) *towards rr: pushed along 4f out: nvr able to chal* **33/1**
33 **9** *1 ¾* **Wood Fern (UAE)**206 1596 3-9-0 RLappin 1 52
(MRChannon) *hld up and bhd: shkn up over 2f out: nvr trbld ldrs* **6/1**
06 **10** *¾* **Shaamit's All Over**18 6022 4-8-7 BReilly(5) 10 45
(BAPearce) *chsd ldrs 7f* **33/1**
00 **11** *5* **Recall (IRE)**11 6067 3-8-9 MFenton 5 36
(JGGiven) *sn stdd bk in midfield: pushed along and lost tch over 3f out* **50/1**
0 **12** *5* **Elegant Gracie (IRE)**18 6022 3-8-9 JMackay 14 27
(RGuest) *s.s: hdwy on outside 6f out: wknd 3f out* **25/1**
64-0 **13** *1 ¼* **Silistra**34 5890 4-9-3 65 (p) IMongan 11 30
(MrsLCJewell) *w ldrs tl wknd qckly over 2f out* **50/1**
2m 10.71s (3.32) **Going Correction** +0.175s/f (Slow)
**WFA** 3 from 4yo+ 3lb **13** Ran SP% **118.0**
Speed ratings: **93,92,91,90,90 90,86,85,83,83 79,75,74**CSF £9.99 TOTE £4.40: £1.80, £1.30, £5.60; EX 10.60.
**Owner** L Marinopoulos **Bred** Michael Dalton **Trained** Newmarket, Suffolk

**FOCUS**
Not a great maiden run a modest pace and few winners are likely to come out of it.

**NOTEBOOK**
**Maxilla(IRE)**looked better suited by this trip rather than the 12 furlongs she was beaten over last month. She deserves extra credit for this win as she probably found herself in front earlier than she wanted and had to do it the hard way. She may be able to make her mark in modest handicap company.
**Margery Daw(IRE)**, stepping up in trip, had every chance but found the winner too determined. She is no great shakes, but judging by the winner and third's handicap marks she should receive a handicap mark which reflects that.
**Bluegrass Boy**ran a creditable sand debut, but is already fairly exposed.
**State Of Balance**, unplaced in four previous starts, two on sand and two in bumpers, but was the real eye-catcher of this race. She made up a lot of late ground from the back of the field and is one to keep an eye on, especially as she can now be handicapped.
**Betterware Boy**, racing for the first time since a couple of outings in the middle of the year, was not totally disgraced on this debut for the yard despite sticking his tongue out at the crowd down the home straight.
**Cayman Sunrise(IRE)**, making her sand debut, pulled far too hard early to give her much chance of getting home.
**Wood Fern(UAE)**, racing for the first time since finishing third in a couple of turf maidens in the spring, never offered much hope.

## 6132 BETDIRECT.CO.UK NEW SITE H'CAP 6f (P)
2:30 (2:30) (D) (0-80,80) 3-Y-O+ £3,178 (£908; £454) Stalls Low

Form RPR
0041 **1** **Compton Banker (IRE)**23 5985 6-9-8 **74** (v) EAhern 6 87
(GAButler) *dwlt: hld up in tch: effrt over 1f out: jnd ldr ins fnl f: rdn to ld last stride* **7/2**1
0660 **2** *shd* **Jayanjay**34 5888 4-9-7 **73** TQuinn 4 86
(MissBSanders) *prom: rdn to ld ins fnl f: kpt on: hdd last stride* **9/1**
6660 **3** *1 ½* **Only One Legend (IRE)**8 6080 5-9-6 **72** (b) RWinston 10 80
(KARyan) *mid-div: effrt whn bdly hmpd over 2f out: rallied and r.o wl to go 3rd nr fin* **7/1**

4003 **4** *nk* **Sir Desmond**[10] 6078 5-9-12 **78**........(p) CCatlin 3 85
(RGuest) *prom: swtchd rt over 1f out: rdn and swtchd lft ins fnl f: one pce* **5/1**[2]

3000 **5** *1* **Emerald Fire**[10] 6078 4-9-2 **73**........(v) NChalmers(5) 7 77
(AMBalding) *mid-div: rdn over 2f out: nrst fin* **20/1**

2200 **6** *½* **Override (IRE)**[186] 2079 3-9-7 **73**........JTate 9 76
(JMPEustace) *towards rr: rdn over 2f out: styd on wl fnl f* **8/1**

0105 **7** *nk* **Just Fly**[14] 6050 3-9-9 **80**........JFMcDonald(5) 5 82
(SKirk) *a.p: no ex over 1f out* **6/1**[3]

0600 **8** *1* **Goodwood Prince**[7] 6092 3-9-2 **68**........PDoe 2 67
(SDow) *led: sn 3l clr: hdd & wknd ins fnl f* **50/1**

4565 **9** *nk* **Awarding**[114] 4129 3-10-0 **80**........DaneO'Neill 8 78
(RFJohnsonHoughton) *stdd s: plld hrd in midfield: rdn to chse ldrs 2f out: cl 6th and hld whn sltly hmpd ins fnl f* **12/1**

-000 **10** *2* **Turn Around**[19] 6010 3-9-3 **69**........FNorton 11 61
(BWHills) *bhd: sme hdwy in midfield whn nt clr run wl over 1f out: nvr able to chal* **40/1**

4102 **11** *½* **Prima Stella**[15] 6038 4-9-2 **68**........SWKelly 14 59
(JARToller) *s.s: hdwy 2f out: in tch and styng on whn bdly hmpd ins fnl f: nt rcvr* **12/1**

0000 **12** *3* **The Fisio**[29] 5941 3-8-13 **72**........RJKilloran(7) 13 54
(AMBalding) *s.s: bhd: rdn over 2f out: nvr trbld ldrs* **33/1**

0000 **13** *4* **Telepathic (IRE)**[47] 5673 3-9-3 **69**........GCarter 1 39
(ABerry) *s.s: sn chsng ldrs: rdn 3f out: hld whn bdly hmpd ins fnl f* **50/1**

0060 **14** *11* **Consensus (IRE)**[17] 6030 4-9-9 **75**........TWilliams 12 12
(MBrittain) *wd: plld hrd in midfield: rdn over 2f out: sn wknd* **25/1**

1m 13.55s (0.63) **Going Correction** +0.175s/f (Slow) **14 Ran SP% 120.1**
Speed ratings: **102,101,99,99,98 97,97,95,95,92 92,88,82,68**CSF £32.82 CT £218.32 TOTE £5.00: £2.10, £2.60, £4.30; EX 46.70.
**Owner** Erik Penser **Bred** David Jamison Bloodstock **Trained** Blewbury, Oxon
■ Stewards Enquiry : C Catlin three-day ban: careless riding (Dec 15-17)

**FOCUS**
A typically competitive Polytrack sprint and a rough race.

**NOTEBOOK**
**Compton Banker(IRE)**, who is in good form just now, had the strong pace he needed on this drop back in trip and came with a strong run on the outside to get up on the line. Despite the 4lb higher mark, he is still well handicapped on his best form.
**Jayanjay**had never quite run up to his turf form in his limited tries on sand, but the Handicapper had given him a chance and he very nearly took advantage of it. He looks worth giving a chance to to make amends.
**Only One Legend(IRE)**got into all sorts of trouble on the home bend and would have finished much closer without it.
**Sir Desmond**, who was done no favours by challenging tight against the inside rail here last time, ended up doing precisely the same thing here after having to be switched to avoid the weakening Goodwood Prince. He is worth another chance to show what he can do when things go his way.
**Emerald Fire**is dropping down the handicap and is now 2lb lower than when winning over course and distance in March. This effort suggests she may be running back into form.
**Override(IRE)**was far from disgraced on this first start since June, but may need another furlong.
**Just Fly**lacked pace down the home straight and is probably better over seven.
**Goodwood Prince**went off like a bat out of hell and merely set it up for the finishers.

## 6133 BET DIRECT ON CHANNEL 4 PAGE 613 CLAIMING STKS (DIV II) 1m (P)
**3:05** (3:05) (F) 3-Y-0+ **£2,051** (£586; £293) **Stalls** High

Form RPR

5230 **1** **Smith N Allan Oils**[7] 6088 4-9-4 56........(p) JFEgan 1 60
(MDods) *trckd ldrs: led over 1f out: drvn out* **11/4**[1]

5350 **2** *hd* **Dispol Evita**[88] 4806 4-8-10 47........HPoulton(7) 2 59
(JamiePoulton) *s.s: sn in tch: hrd rdn over 2f out: styd on wl to go 2nd nr fin* **16/1**

0000 **3** *hd* **Zinging**[73] 5157 4-8-12 48........FNorton 7 54
(JJBridger) *trckd ldrs: ev ch over 1f out: styd on* **16/1**

0055 **4** *½* **Balmacara**[7] 6094 4-8-13 50........(p) IMongan 11 53
(MissKBBoutflower) *mid-div: rdn 4f out: drvn to chse ldrs over 1f out: kpt on* **12/1**

0260 **5** *1 ½* **Four Jays (IRE)**[7] 6093 3-9-4 70........(p) J-PGuillambert(3) 4 59
(NPLittmoden) *w ldrs: led after 2f tl over 1f out: no ex fnl f* **9/2**[3]

0010 **6** *shd* **Consignia (IRE)**[15] 6036 4-8-5 49........(v) PaulEddery 12 42
(DHaydnJones) *towards rr: rdn and styd on fnl 2f: nt pce to chal* **8/1**

0036 **7** *½* **Maggie's Pet**[12] 6057 6-8-5 46........(t) CCatlin 8 41
(KBell) *chsd ldrs: hrd rdn and btn over 1f out* **10/1**

-356 **8** *½* **Paintbrush (IRE)**[106] 4345 3-8-8 47........SWKelly 10 43
(MrsLStubbs) *in rr: hrd rdn 3f out: styd on wl fnl f* **50/1**

0346 **9** *½* **Compton Emerald (IRE)**[39] 5819 3-7-7 65........(b) JFMcDonald(5) 5 32
(GAButler) *towards rr: rdn over 2f out: n.d* **4/1**[2]

0000 **10** *4* **Power Bird (IRE)**[3] 6124 3-9-2 72........PDoe 6 41
(DFlood) *sn led: hdd after 2f: hrd rdn and wknd wl over 1f out* **9/1**

0240 **11** *6* **Badou**[18] 6024 3-8-13 51........(v) EAhern 3 24
(LMontagueHall) *pressed ldrs tl wknd qckly over 1f out* **11/1**

000- **12** *8* **Chocolate Boy (IRE)**[416] 5299 4-9-0 48........JFanning 9 6
(GLMoore) *hld up towards rr: pushed along and lost tch 3f out* **25/1**

1m 39.43s (-0.08) **Going Correction** +0.175s/f (Slow)
**WFA** 3 from 4yo+ 1lb **12 Ran SP% 128.6**
Speed ratings: **107,106,106,106,104 104,104,103,103,99 93,85**CSF £56.15 TOTE £3.90: £1.70, £6.40, £3.50; EX 48.90.Compton Emerald was claimed by M Patel for £3,000
**Owner** Smith & Allan Racing **Bred** A J Holder **Trained** Piercebridge, Co Durham
■ Stewards Enquiry : J F Egan two-day ban: used whip with excessive frequency (Dec 15,16)

**FOCUS**
A modest contest, but run at a decent pace and a time nearly half a second faster than the first division.

**NOTEBOOK**
**Smith N Allan Oils**made up for his luckless effort here last week and was very well backed to do so. His rider was forced to take advantage of the gap that appeared on the inside turning in which meant he ended up on the slowest part of the track, but despite that he battled on in great style to hold off a couple of serious late challenges. He may be better suited by seven.
**Dispol Evita**, a three-time winner here a couple of winters ago, was well backed on this debut for the yard and was closing the winner down fast at the line. She may need a bit further than this these days.
**Zinging**ran his best race since winning on this track in March, but has only managed two victories from 52 starts.
**Balmacara**ran her second reasonable race on this track within a week, but remains a long-standing maiden.
**Four Jays(IRE)**, one of those best in on official figures, is another with a poor strike rate and is not performing much better despite taking on ever-easier competition.
**Consignia(IRE)**probably found eve this company too hot and may be better on Fibresand in any case.
**Compton Emerald(IRE)**was friendless in the market and ran poorly.

## 6134 BET DIRECT IN RUNNING SKY TEXT 293 H'CAP (DIV II) 7f (P)
**3:40** (3:40) (F) (0-65,65) 3-Y-0+ **£2,093** (£598; £299) **Stalls** Low

Form RPR

4040 **1** **Miss Issy (IRE)**[7] 6088 3-9-2 53........(v) IMongan 8 63
(JGallagher) *hdwy over 2f out: led over 1f out: rdn out* **10/1**

3050 **2** *¾* **Temper Tantrum**[18] 6019 5-9-3 61........(p) RoryMoore(7) 11 69
(AndrewReid) *hld up towards rr: smooth hdwy 2f out: chal 1f out: nt qckn fnl 75 yds* **5/1**[2]

1000 **3** *1 ¼* **Cayman Breeze**[38] 5832 3-10-0 65........PDoe 10 70
(SDow) *hld up in rr: hdwy whn rn v wd bnd into st: styd on fnl f* **40/1**

3231 **4** *nk* **Bint Makbul**[7] 6100 4-9-7 58........DaneO'Neill 2 62
(RHannon) *chsd ldrs: one pce appr fnl f* **5/1**[2]

6000 **5** *1* **Calusa Lady (IRE)**[18] 6024 3-9-4 55........AClark 14 57
(GBBalding) *hld up in rr: hdwy 2f out: rdn and no imp over 1f out* **33/1**

0045 **6** *1 ¼* **Peyto Princess**[7] 6092 5-9-8 59........JBramhill 6 58
(MABuckley) *hld up in rr: rdn and styd on fnl 2f: nvr nrr* **8/1**[3]

4254 **7** *1 ½* **Zak Facta (IRE)**[11] 6070 3-9-3 54........(v) CCogan 16 49
(MissDAMchale) *prom: ev ch 2f out: wknd over 1f out* **20/1**

0014 **8** *½* **Semper Paratus (USA)**[11] 6065 4-9-8 59........(b) MTebbutt 7 53
(HJCollingridge) *broke wl and led briefly: hld up in tch: outpcd over 2f out: sn btn* **10/1**

5300 **9** *¾* **Penny Pie (IRE)**[39] 5823 3-9-12 63........TQuinn 5 55
(PWHarris) *sn pushed along in midfield: no hdwy fnl 2f* **8/1**[3]

4112 **10** *1* **Gallery Breeze**[18] 6024 4-9-13 64........ADaly 12 53
(JLSpearing) *mid-div tl wknd over 2f out* **7/2**[1]

0 **11** *1 ¼* **Richie Rich (IRE)**[4] 6113 8-9-4 55........WMLordan 3 41
(JarlathPFahey, Ire) *chsd ldrs 5f* **66/1**

005 **12** *hd* **Spindor (USA)**[35] 5878 4-9-10 61........(b) SWKelly 13 47
(JAOsborne) *sn led: hdd & wknd over 1f out* **14/1**

0555 **13** *2 ½* **Tatweer (IRE)**[11] 6065 3-9-4 55........(v) RWinston 4 34
(DShaw) *in rr: lost tch 3f out: mod hdwy over 1f out: nvr nr ldrs* **20/1**

0120 **14** *¾* **Westmead Tango**[22] 5995 3-9-1 52........AMackay 1 30
(JRJenkins) *a in rr: lost tch 3f out* **50/1**

0000 **15** *2 ½* **Coppington Flyer (IRE)**[18] 6019 3-9-3 54........(b¹) MFenton 15 25
(BWDuke) *chsd ldrs 5f* **16/1**

1m 26.72s (0.72) **Going Correction** +0.175s/f (Slow) **15 Ran SP% 126.9**
Speed ratings: **102,101,99,99,98 96,95,94,93,92 91,90,88,87,84**CSF £58.41 CT £1982.48 TOTE £10.60: £3.60, £2.30, £9.30; EX 65.80 Place 6 £128.69, Place 5 £31.32.
**Owner** C R Marks (banbury) **Bred** Mrs Marian Maguire **Trained** Chastleton, Oxon

**FOCUS**
Another competitive if low-grade handicap run in a similar time to the first division.

**NOTEBOOK**
**Miss Issy(IRE)**, a maiden coming into this, has steadily dropped down the handicap during the autumn and battled on well to get off the mark at the 15th attempt. Now that she has managed to put her head in front, she may be able to add to this.
**Temper Tantrum**, racing over his ideal trip, ran his best race since returning to the Polytrack and an opportunity can be found.
**Cayman Breeze**, making his Polytrack debut, was forced very wide on the home bend and, considering how far he was beaten, he may have been unlucky not to score. He should be able to make amends.
**Bint Makbul**, raised 5lb for her Wolverhampton success in a fillies' handicap, appeared to handle this surface well enough but was just not quite good enough on the day.
**Calusa Lady(IRE)**offered a little encouragement, but is still a maiden.
**Peyto Princess**has only managed one win from 42 starts, but ran another creditable race on this surface and may be worth a try over a mile.
**Penny Pie(IRE)** *Official explanation: jockey said filly lost her action in the home straight*
**Gallery Breeze**played up in the stalls and ran a stinker, even allowing for running very wide on the home bend. *Official explanation: jockey said filly hit her head on the stalls*
**Superchief** *Official explanation: trainer said gelding scoped badly*
T/Plt: £72.80 to a £1 stake. Pool: £25,890.90. 259.50 winning tickets. T/Qpdt: £14.70 to a £1 stake. Pool: £1,887.80. 94.90 winning tickets. LM

# 6095 WOLVERHAMPTON (A.W) (L-H)
Saturday, December 6

**OFFICIAL GOING: Slow**

## 6135 BET DIRECT ON SKY ACTIVE CLASSIFIED STKS 7f (F)
**7:00** (7:02) (E) 3-Y-0+ **£2,079** (£594; £297) **Stalls** High

Form RPR

2300 **1** **Arc El Ciel (ARG)**[192] 1911 5-9-0 66........CCatlin 9 83
(MrsStefLiddiard) *in rr and nt gng pce: rdn and hdwy 2f out: led 2f out: styd on* **20/1**

0060 **2** *2* **Zarin (IRE)**[26] 5970 5-9-0 69........ACulhane 3 78
(DWChapman) *towards rr and nt gng pce: hdwy wl over 1f out: hung lft but styd on to go 2nd ins fnl f* **50/1**

2035 **3** *2* **Blonde En Blonde (IRE)**[22] 5996 3-8-11 69........IMongan 1 70
(NPLittmoden) *in tch but sn rdn and outpcd 1/2-way: styd on past btn horses finhal f* **8/1**[3]

551 **4** *hd* **Roman Maze**[15] 6039 3-9-0 68........SWKelly 4 72+
(WMBrisbourne) *s.i.s: sn in tch: chsng ldrs whn short of room and swtchd rt over 1f out: styd on one pce* **5/2**[2]

0201 **5** *½* **Teehee (IRE)**[35] 5878 5-9-0 70........(b) MFenton 8 71
(BPalling) *a in tch: hung lft over 1f out and no hdwy after* **8/1**[3]

2211 **6** *1 ½* **Perfect Night**[12] 6062 3-8-11 72........DaneO'Neill 11 64
(RCharlton) *trckd ldrs: rdn to ld over 2f out: hdd & wknd 1f out* **2/1**[1]

0000 **7** *2* **Warden Warren**[8] 6084 5-8-9 67........(p) BReilly(5) 7 62
(MrsCADunnett) *mid-div: nvr nr to chal* **16/1**

0003 **8** *4* **Danielle's Lad**[22] 5996 7-9-0 70........(b) FNorton 5 52
(BPalling) *trckd ldr: led 1/2-way: rdn and hdd over 2f out: wknd over 1f out* **9/1**

3/60 **9** *11* **Ulysees (IRE)**[11] 6064 4-9-0 63........RWinston 6 25
(ISemple) *a bhd and hanging rt* **25/1**

0030 **10** *17* **Pips Song (IRE)**[19] 6010 8-9-0 50........PDoe 2 —
(PWHiatt) *set str pce tl hdd 1/2-way: wknd qckly: eased over 1f out: t.o* **50/1**

1m 32.38s (2.18) **Going Correction** +0.275s/f (Slow) **10 Ran SP% 112.5**
Speed ratings: **98,95,93,93,92 90,88,84,71,52**CSF £702.35 TOTE £31.50: £5.10, £7.00, £2.00; EX 769.70.
**Owner** Shefford Valley Stud **Bred** Santa Maria De Araras **Trained** Great Shefford, Berks

**FOCUS**
Slow ground and an ordinary pace but an improved effort from the winner, a real course and distance specialist

**NOTEBOOK**

**Arc El Ciel(ARG)**looked to have a bit to find on official ratings on this first run since May but this course and distance specialist turned in an improved effort and, as Southwell's surface should also suit, looks capable of winning again this winter.

**Zarin(IRE)**has slipped to a much more realistic mark and ran his best race for his very shrewd yard, that will no doubt be placing him to best advantage in due course

**Blonde En Blonde(IRE)**does not look the easiest of rides and is not the most consistent but ran creditably and shaped as though the return to a mile would suit.

**Roman Maze**, facing his stiffest task to date on artificial surfaces, was anything but disgraced and fared the best of those racing up with the pace. He is likely to stay an extra furlong and it will be no surprise to see him win again.

**Teehee(IRE)**looked to have a good chance at the weights and came here in good form but he is not consistent and again looked anything but an easy ride. He remains one to tread carefully with.

**Perfect Night**looked the pick of the weights and came here on the three timer but did not get home in the conditions having raced keenly from her wide draw. Given the way she went through her race, six furlongs may be her optimum trip.

**Warden Warren**was again below his best but is slipping back to a fair mark and will be of interest when it looks as though he will be able to get an uncontested lead.

**Danielle's Lad**has yet to win on sand but had form that gave him claims in this company. However he was below his best having helped to force the issue and he may be best watched on sand till getting his head in front where it matters.

**Pips Song(IRE)** *Official explanation: jockey said gelding ran too freely in the early stages*

## 6136 BET DIRECT PRESS RED TO BET CLAIMING STKS — 6f (F)

**7:30** (7:30) (F) 3-Y-O+ — **£2,079** (£594; £297) **Stalls** Low

Form — RPR

0-00 **1** **Ellens Lad (IRE)**[15] 6038 9-9-6 70..........(b) PaulEddery 9 — 80
(WJMusson) *a.p: hrd rdn over 1f out: kpt on gamely to ld cl home* **25/1**

2543 **2** *hd* **Rafters Music (IRE)**[8] 6084 8-9-6 74.......... IMongan 3 — 79
(JulianPoulton) *outpcd and wl in rr tl rdn and gd hdwy over 1f out: r.o to hold ev ch wl ins fnl f: jst hld* **2/1**[1]

0011 **3** *nk* **Sharp Hat**[15] 6038 9-9-6 69.......... ANicholls 5 — 78
(DNicholls) *a.p: led wl over 1f out: rdn and r.o: hdd cl home* **11/2**[3]

0105 **4** *3 ½* **Speedfit Free (IRE)**[17] 6027 6-8-10 56..........(b) MTebbutt 13 — 58
(ISemple) *mid-div on outside: hdwy over 1f out: r.o: nvr nr to chal* **9/1**

0151 **5** *shd* **Queen Of Night**[22] 5995 3-8-11 78.......... DMernagh 2 — 58
(TDBarron) *slowly away and outpcd: styd on past btn horses ins fnl 2f* **3/1**[2]

0000 **6** *3* **Catchthebatch**[7] 6095 7-8-9 50.......... DCorby(3) 7 — 50
(MJWallace) *chsd ldr tl rdn over 2f out: styd on ins and prom tl wknd fnl f* **20/1**

0400 **7** *1 ¼* **Salerno**[7] 6095 4-8-9 53..........(p) TEaves(5) 12 — 49
(MissGayKelleway) *led tl heeaded wl over 1f out: sn wknd* **25/1**

2000 **8** *nk* **Valuable Gift**[11] 6063 6-8-1 49..........(e[1]) ACooper(7) 6 — 42
(RCGuest) *a towards rr* **33/1**

0040 **9** *shd* **Legalis (USA)**[8] 6084 5-9-10 65..........(p) RWinston 8 — 57
(KARyan) *outpcd: rdn 1/2-way and nvr on terms* **11/1**

0 **10** *6* **Queen Louisa**[180] 2231 3-8-5..........(t) RFfrench 4 — 20
(FWatson) *a outpcd in rr* **100/1**

5240 **11** *7* **Valazar (USA)**[8] 6080 4-8-10 62.......... ACulhane 1 — 4
(DWChapman) *a in rr* **11/1**

1m 17.62s (1.92) **Going Correction** +0.275s/f (Slow) — **11** Ran SP% **116.8**

Speed ratings: **98,97,97,92,92 88,86,86,86,78 69**CSF £71.83 TOTE £22.00: £3.80, £1.30, £2.30; EX 53.50.Sharp Hat was claimed by D Chapman for £10,000

**Owner** Mrs Rita Brown **Bred** Mrs Chris Harrington **Trained** Newmarket, Suffolk

**FOCUS**

A mixed bag but the pace was sound.

**NOTEBOOK**

**Ellens Lad(IRE)**stepped up considerably on his previous all-weather run to reverse the form with Sharp Hat to the tune of around 12 lengths over this longer trip. Given the way he travelled he may well be able to win again in this sphere. *Official explanation: trainer said, regarding the improved form shown, gelding benefited from a step up from 5f to 6f*

**Rafters Music(IRE)**had a decent chance at the weights and ran a typical race. He remains in decent heart for his new yard but, although capable of winning more races on sand, again showed that he does need things to fall perfectly.

**Sharp Hat**, a tough sort having his first run for David Nicholls, could not confirm recent placings with Ellens Lad but that was due to an improved effort from that rival rather than him being below form. He is capable of adding to his tally in this grade.

**Speedfit Free(IRE)**, a most inconsistent sprinter, ran creditably in the face of a stiff task but, given his overall record, would not be one to lump on from back in handicap company next time.

**Queen Of Night**looked the pick of the weights but struggled after another tardy start and, on this evidence, is going to struggle in handicaps on fibresand from her current mark. *Official explanation: jockey said he suffered interference going into the bend leaving the back straight*

**Salerno**faced a stiff task at the weights and did not get home over this trip in these testing conditions. Five furlongs on genuinely standard ground will see him in a better light.

**Legalis(USA)**, a course and distance winner last December, faced another stiff task at the weights but did not show enough to suggest a return to winning ways was imminent.

## 6137 LITTLEWOODS BET DIRECT MAIDEN STKS — 1m 4f (F)

**8:00** (8:01) (D) 3-Y-O+ — **£2,247** (£642; £321) **Stalls** Low

Form — RPR

30- **1** **Alexander Anapolis (IRE)**[42] 5760 3-8-9 80.......... FNorton 7 — 67
(NACallaghan) *slowly away and t.k.h early: sn in tch: led 3f out: rdn wl over 1f out: kpt up to work ins fnl f* **4/5**[1]

6000 **2** *2* **Exit To Heaven**[59] 5455 3-8-9 57.......... MFenton 6 — 64
(MissGayKelleway) *t.k.h: in tch tl rdn and outpcd 3f out: rallied wl over 1f out and styd on to go 2nd ins fnl f* **16/1**

0303 **3** *1* **White Park Bay (IRE)**[11] 6067 3-8-9 59.......... CCatlin 9 — 62
(JGallagher) *trckd ldrs: rdn over 5f out: lost pl over 3f out: rallied 2f out: styd on after* **9/2**[2]

6400 **4** *3* **Desert Heat**[12] 6060 5-9-5 60..........(p) RWinston 5 — 63
(ISemple) *trckd ldr: cl 2nd 3f out: rdn and wknd fnl f* **10/1**[3]

0305 **5** *4* **Sabreline**[15] 6040 4-8-9 45.......... NChalmers(5) 3 — 52
(BRFoster) *led tl hdd 3f out: rdn and wknd over 1f out* **12/1**

6560 **6** *2 ½* **Danum**[11] 6067 3-9-0 60.......... ACulhane 11 — 53
(RHollinshead) *a bhd: passed sme btn horses in fnl 3f* **12/1**

0000 **7** *dist* **Simon The Poacher**[30] 5936 4-9-5 42.......... VSlattery 2 — —
(LPGrassick) *in tch tl rdn and wknd 5f out: t.o* **50/1**

0000 **8** *6* **Bridewell (USA)**[32] 5914 4-9-5 38.......... DMernagh 12 — —
(FWatson) *a bhd: t.o* **50/1**

03-0 **9** *18* **Kamala**[288] 588 4-9-0.......... IMongan 10 — —
(RBrotherton) *in tch tl rdn 5f out: sn bhd: t.o* **16/1**

0 **10** *dist* **Sargents Dream**[23] 5988 3-8-2.......... DeanWilliams(7) 8 — —
(JAGilbert) *in tch for 5f: sn wl bhd: t.o* **50/1**

2m 47.93s (6.43) **Going Correction** +0.275s/f (Slow)

**WFA** 3 from 4yo+ 5lb — **10** Ran SP% **115.9**

Speed ratings: **89,87,87,85,82 80,—,—,—,—**CSF £16.28 TOTE £2.10: £1.10, £2.70, £1.30; EX 15.60.

**Owner** Mrs N O'Callaghan **Bred** T Stack And Mrs Sue Magnier **Trained** Newmarket, Suffolk

**NOTEBOOK**

**Alexander Anapolis(IRE)**, a fair maiden in Ireland, looked the clear pick of the weights on this first run for new connections over this longer trip and, although landing the odds in workmanlike fashion, will struggle to follow up in handicap company on this evidence from her current mark of 80.

**Exit To Heaven**, inconsistent over middle distances for John Dunlop, ran creditably on this fibresand debut and first run for her new yard and shaped as though she would relish a further step up in trip. Connections will be hoping that the handicapper rates her on her proximity to the third horse rather than the winner.

**White Park Bay(IRE)**did not fail through lack of stamina over this much longer trip and, although fully exposed, may be able to pick up an uncompetitive event in this grade. However she does not look one to take a short price about.

**Desert Heat**ran his best race for his current yard but again left the impression that he has stamina limitations. A drop in trip may help but he is no good thing back in handicaps from his current mark.

**Sabreline**faced a very stiff task at the weights and, although allowed her own way in front, was not surprisingly readily brushed aside. She will be seen to better effect back in handicap company.

**Danum**, who has plenty of stamina in his pedigree, could have been expected to fare a bit better than he did in this company.

**Kamala** *Official explanation: jockey said filly lost her action and as a result was never travelling*

**Sargents Dream** *Official explanation: jockey said saddle slipped and the filly hung right throughout*

## 6138 BET DIRECT NO Q ON 08000 93 66 93 H'CAP — 5f (F)

**8:30** (8:30) (D) (0-85,82) 3-Y-O+ — **£3,388** (£968; £484) **Stalls** Low

Form — RPR

0566 **1** **Paddywack (IRE)**[8] 6084 6-8-13 70..........(b) ACulhane 6 — 84+
(DWChapman) *in rr and outpcd: hdwy on outside over 1f out: str burst ins fnl f to ld nr fin: won gng away* **4/1**[2]

4054 **2** *1 ½* **Time N Time Again**[8] 6081 5-8-7 67.......... DAllan(3) 3 — 76
(EJAlston) *a.p: led on ins wl over 1f out: r.o: hdd nr fin* **3/1**[1]

0410 **3** *nk* **Gone'N'Dunnett (IRE)**[8] 6081 4-8-7 69..........(v) BReilly(5) 1 — 77+
(MrsCADunnett) *towards rr and pushed along thrght: r.o strly fnl f: nvr nrr* **16/1**

0001 **4** *hd* **Lady Pekan**[7] 6095 4-7-9 57..........(b) JFMcDonald(5) 8 — 64
(PSMcentee) *chsd ldrs: ev ch ins fnl f: nt qckn fnl 50yds* **12/1**

3100 **5** *1 ¼* **Daintree Affair (IRE)**[21] 6001 3-8-6 63.......... JoannaBadger 2 — 66
(KRBurke) *in rr: tl r.o wl ins fnl f* **33/1**

6442 **6** *½* **Rellim**[8] 6081 4-7-13 56 oh1 ow1..........(p) CCatlin 10 — 57
(PABlockley) *led: hdd wl over 1f out: wknd ins fnl f* **8/1**

5010 **7** *1 ¼* **Maktavish**[17] 6030 4-9-11 82..........(p) IMongan 7 — 79
(ISemple) *a.p: ev ch over 1f out: steadily fdd fnl f* **6/1**[3]

501F **8** *hd* **Raymond's Pride**[29] 5941 3-9-0 71..........(b) RWinston 4 — 67
(KARyan) *mid-div: rdn 1/2-way: wknd ent fnl f* **25/1**

0006 **9** *2* **Prince Of Blues (IRE)**[10] 6078 5-9-2 73..........(p) JBramhill 11 — 62
(MMullineaux) *prom on outside for 3f* **10/1**

2131 **10** *2 ½* **Gilded Cove**[140] 3432 3-8-12 69.......... JMackay 9 — 49
(RHollinshead) *slowly away: a in rr on outside* **15/2**

3266 **11** *20* **Tigress (IRE)**[257] 789 4-8-6 63..........(b) SWKelly 5 — —
(JWUnett) *a bhd: t.o* **14/1**

63.01 secs (0.41) **Going Correction** +0.275s/f (Slow) — **11** Ran SP% **118.3**

Speed ratings: **107,104,104,103,101 101,99,98,95,91 59**CSF £16.50 CT £178.28 TOTE £4.80: £1.60, £1.70, £3.70; EX 13.30.

**Owner** T S Redman **Bred** Colm McEvoy **Trained** Stillington, N Yorks

**FOCUS**

An ordinary handicap but an overly strong pace on testing ground teed the race up for a finisher.

**NOTEBOOK**

**Paddywack(IRE)**, a tough but inconsistent sprinter, ran right up to his best on this surface but, while winning cosily in the end, was helped by a combination of the deep ground, a blistering pace and the drop back to five furlongs. As this result may well flatter him, he may be one to take on at a short price on faster conditions next time.

**Time N Time Again**, who had not had much luck in running on his last two starts, ran another very creditable race and fared the best of those that raced up with the pace. He is one to keep an eye on and this performance also showed that those racing against the inside rail throughout were at no discernable disadvantage.

**Gone'N'Dunnett(IRE)**ran creditably in terms of form but may be slightly flattered by the way the race panned out and, given his record is one of inconsistency, may be one to take on at shortish odds next time.

**Lady Pekan**confirmed her recent return to form in this stronger event from this 4lb higher mark and may well be a little bit better than the bare form as she was up with the strong pace throughout.

**Daintree Affair(IRE)**was not disgraced but is another who may be slightly flattered by his proximity given the way the race unfolded and more will be needed before he becomes a betting proposition again.

**Rellim**, a real speedster, went off far too quickly in the conditions and not surprisingly failed to run up to his best and, while he is capable of better, an overall record of one win from 35 starts, shows the percentage call is usually to take him on.

**Maktavish**, down in grade, was again below his best and he is not an easy horse to catch right.

**Tigress(IRE)** *Official explanation: jockey said filly lost her action*

## 6139 BET DIRECT THROUGH ATTHERACES H'CAP — 2m 46y(F)

**9:00** (9:00) (F) (0-65,63) 3-Y-O+ — **£2,065** (£590; £295) **Stalls** Low

Form — RPR

-060 **1** **Killing Joke**[32] 5920 3-9-5 63.......... MFenton 2 — 81+
(JGGiven) *trckd ldr: led 6f out: clr over 2f out: styd on wl* **12/1**

500 **2** *11* **Radiant Bride**[10] 6075 3-7-9 46 ow1.......... AReilly(7) 5 — 51
(KRBurke) *towards rr: rdn and hdwy 4f out: wnt 2nd over 2f out: flashed tail and no hdwy fnl f* **33/1**

0614 **3** *2 ½* **Sashay**[19] 6017 5-9-3 60.......... StephanieHollinshead(7) 9 — 62
(RHollinshead) *chsd ldrs: wnt 2nd over 5f out tl over 2f out: one pce after* **13/2**[2]

0065 **4** *5* **Cottam Grange**[30] 4385 3-8-2 46.......... DaleGibson 4 — 42
(MWEasterby) *chsd ldrs rdn 5f out: no hdwy ins fnl 4f* **33/1**

1452 **5** *6* **Paradise Valley**[7] 6096 3-8-6 50..........(t) CCatlin 7 — 39
(MrsStefLiddiard) *in rr: rdn 4f out: nvr a danger* **8/1**[3]

4043 **6** *3 ½* **Broughton Knows**[190] 1727 6-7-13 35.......... JMackay 11 — 20
(WJMusson) *towards rr: hdwy 6f out: rdn 4f out: sn btn* **13/2**[2]

-455 **7** *shd* **Ella Falls (IRE)**[12] 3120 8-8-0 36.......... FNorton 12 — 20
(MrsHDalton) *chsd ldrs tl wknd 4f out* **9/1**

0035 **8** *9* **Cantemerle (IRE)**[15] 6043 3-8-7 51..........(b) SWKelly 8 — 25
(WMBrisbourne) *a wl in rr* **33/1**

4062 **9** *9* **Madhahir (IRE)**[19] 6017 3-8-13 **62**.................................(p) BReilly(5) 6 25
(CADwyer) *a struggling in rr* **15/8**[1]
0000 **10** *11* **Rivelli (IRE)**[7] 6095 4-8-9 **50**.................................. NChalmers(5) 3 —
(BRFoster) *a towards rr: rdn 6f out: lost tch 4f out* **80/1**
200 **11** *shd* **Fast Cindy (USA)**[19] 6017 4-9-7 **57**.................................. RWinston 1 7
(JWUnett) *in tch tl rdn and wknd over 4f out* **12/1**
16-2 **12** *dist* **Welcome Back**[317] 372 6-7-13 **35** oh1 ow1.................. RFfrench 13 —
(KARyan) *led tl hdd 6f out: wknd qckly: t.o* **10/1**
3m 43.19s (0.89) **Going Correction** +0.275s/f (Slow)
**WFA** 3 from 4yo+ 8lb **12** Ran SP% **117.1**
Speed ratings: **108,102,101,98,95 94,93,89,84,79 79,**—CSF £357.51 CT £2779.52 TOTE £18.00: £4.60, £10.60, £2.10; EX 866.40.
**Owner** A Clarke **Bred** Ashley House Stud **Trained** Willoughton, Lincs

**FOCUS**
A modest handicap in which the pace was fair but a much improved performance from Killing Joke.

**NOTEBOOK**
**Killing Joke**turned in a much improved performance on this fibresand debut to win with plenty in hand. He is open to improvement but will need to be as he is likely to face a steep rise in the weights from next Saturday.
**Radiant Bride**had no problems with this longer trip and was not disgraced on this first run for Karl Burke but looked anything but an easy ride when put under maximum pressure and may not be one to place too much faith in.
**Sashay**, a Wolverhampton specialist, was again below her best and may well be a few pounds too high in the weights at present.
**Cottam Grange**did not really improve for the step up to this trip on this all-weather debut and will have to improve a fair bit to get off the mark in this sphere.
**Paradise Valley**, who shaped as though stamina would not be a problem at this course last time, did not improve for the step up to two miles and, given he has had breathing problems in the past, may not be one to place too much faith in.
**Broughton Knows**was below his best but should be all the better for this first start since May. Although only modest, it will be no surprise to see him win again from this rating at some stage this winter.
**Madhahir(IRE)**, who ran well when chasing home subsequent winner Snow's Ride over course and distance last time, was nowhere near that level and looks one to have reservations about.
*Official explanation: trainer was unable to offer any explanation for colt's poor running*
**Fast Cindy(USA)** *Official explanation: jockey said filly hung left on the final circuit*
**Welcome Back** *Official explanation: jockey said gelding ran too freely*

## 6140 BET DIRECT "RED TO BET" H'CAP 1m 1f 79y(F)
9:30 (9:30) (E) (0-70,70) 3-Y-0+ £2,135 (£610; £305) Stalls Low

Form RPR
1106 **1** **Buscador (USA)**[63] 5381 4-9-6 **65**.................................. MarkFlynn(5) 1 79+
(WMBrisbourne) *mde all: kpt on wl after chal appr fnl f* **10/3**[1]
5000 **2** *1 1/4* **Hugh The Man (IRE)**[68] 5276 4-9-13 **67**.............................. IMongan 9 76
(NPLittmoden) *mid-div: rdn over 5f out: kpt on u.p to chse wnr 2f out: chal approachinf fnl f: no imp ins* **5/1**[3]
5042 **3** *3 1/2* **Shifty**[12] 6057 4-9-1 **55**..................................................(b) ANicholls 12 57
(DNicholls) *trckd ldrs: chsd wnr 3f out to 2f out: one pce after* **4/1**[2]
3504 **4** *7* **Crusoe (IRE)**[3] 6124 6-9-11 **65**..........................................(b) LVickers 10 53
(ASadik) *chsd wnr to 3f out: wknd 2f out* **10/3**[1]
4254 **5** *6* **Yenaled**[82] 4940 6-9-11 **65**.................................................. RWinston 5 41
(KARyan) *chsd ldrs tl wknd over 3f out* **15/2**
1000 **6** *3/4* **Azreme**[23] 5985 3-9-12 **68**...............................................(e[1]) PaulEddery 8 42
(PWD'Arcy) *chsd wnr to 3f out: wknd 2f out* **20/1**
3322 **7** *7* **Leonora Truce (IRE)**[132] 3829 4-8-2 **49**............................. AElliott(7) 13 9
(RPElliott) *slowly away: a struggling in rr* **20/1**
1156 **8** *5* **Prideway (IRE)**[256] 797 7-9-6 **65**...................................(b) NChalmers(5) 2 15
(WMBrisbourne) *s.i.s and a in rr* **11/1**
2m 3.65s (0.75) **Going Correction** +0.275s/f (Slow)
**WFA** 3 from 4yo+ 2lb **8** Ran SP% **112.4**
Speed ratings: **107,105,102,96,91 90,84,79**CSF £19.51 CT £66.58 TOTE £7.00: £2.00, £2.40, £2.10; EX 52.40 Place 6 £202.16, Place 5 £19.50..
**Owner** Real Soda **Bred** William H Floyd **Trained** Great Ness, Shropshire

**FOCUS**
An ordinary handicap in which the pace was just fair.

**NOTEBOOK**
**Buscador(USA)**was allowed an uncontested lead but showed the right attitude in the closing stages to record his third win over course and distance and should continue to go well when allowed his own way in front.
**Hugh The Man(IRE)**, who is not an easy ride, ran his best race since March returned to this surface after a short break but, while a strongly run race over a mile may be his ideal requirements, he does not look the easiest of rides.
**Shifty**ran creditably on his first run at Wolverhampton and did not really fail through lack of stamina over this longer trip but is not the most straightforward and is not one to take a short price about.
**Crusoe(IRE)**, who ran well with the blinkers back on in a better contest at Southwell earlier this week, was below his best this time but, although he may be better over a mile, he was never travelling well enough to think he would have even gone close over that trip this time. *Official explanation: vet said gelding spread a front plate*
**Yenaled**failed to settle and ran as though this first outing since September and first for his new yard would do him good. However he is the type that needs things to fall just right.
**Azreme**, wearing an eyeshield for the first time, was again below his best and did not seem to get home over this longer trip in the conditions but, although a drop in distance will help, will have to improve to win from his current mark.
T/Plt: £303.10 to a £1 stake. Pool: £46,159.20. 111.15 winning tickets. T/Qpdt: £22.10 to a £1 stake. Pool: £1,929.60. 64.55 winning tickets. JS

# 6121 SOUTHWELL (L-H)
Monday, December 8

**OFFICIAL GOING: Standard**
This meeting was transferred from Wolverhampton where the track was waterlogged. The 1.10 and 3.35 races were originally due to be run over 9f 79y
Wind: almost nil Weather: bright & sunny

## 6141 BET DIRECT ON 0800 32 93 93 NURSERY 7f (F)
12:10 (12:11) (E) (0-75,75) 2-Y-0 £2,324 (£664; £332) Stalls Low

Form RPR
6000 **1** **Weet An Haul**[48] 5689 2-7-12 **52** oh8.................................. JBramhill 6 53
(PABlockley) *chsd ldrs: led over 2f out: rdn out* **66/1**
0015 **2** *1* **Muy Bien**[6] 6118 2-9-6 **74**...........................................(v) SWKelly 13 72
(JRJenkins) *led: hdd over 5f out: rdn and ev ch fr over 2f out: no ex nr fin* **7/1**[3]
6224 **3** *1 1/2* **Phluke**[101] 4553 2-9-7 **75**................................................ DaneO'Neill 2 69
(RFJohnsonHoughton) *hld up in tch: rdn over 1f out: styd on* **8/1**
6500 **4** *1* **Garnock Venture (IRE)**[10] 6083 2-7-13 **53**................(b[1]) DaleGibson 14 45
(ABerry) *led over 5f out: rdn and hdd over 2f out: styd on same pce fnl f* **50/1**
4121 **5** *1 3/4* **Maunby Raver**[12] 6077 2-8-6 **67**................................ RoryMoore(7) 15 54
(PCHaslam) *chsd ldrs: rdn over 1f out: edgd lft: styd on same pce* **11/4**[2]
5006 **6** *2* **Duncanbil (IRE)**[35] 5911 2-8-2 **56**.......................................... SRighton 7 38
(RFFisher) *mid-div: sn drvn along: styd on approaching fnl f: nvr nrr* **25/1**
6105 **7** *nk* **Foxies Future (IRE)**[19] 6029 2-8-4 **65**.......................... DFentiman(7) 1 47
(JRWeymes) *hld up: hdwy 1/2-way: n.m.r wl over 2f out: rdn and wknd over 1f out* **14/1**
000 **8** *1* **Casantella**[14] 6058 2-7-7 **52** oh14............................ JFMcDonald(5) 12 31
(MJPolglase) *mid-div: sn drvn along: n.d* **66/1**
263 **9** *hd* **Dr Cerullo**[36] 5887 2-9-7 **75**................................................ ACulhane 11 54
(CTinkler) *s.i.s: nvr trbld ldrs* **2/1**[1]
000 **10** *2 1/2* **Limit Down (IRE)**[26] 5977 2-8-7 **64**.................................. DCorby(3) 9 36
(MJWallace) *a in rr* **25/1**
3506 **11** *1* **Stanhope Forbes (IRE)**[16] 6046 2-8-4 **58**.......................(p) GGibbons 8 28
(NPLittmoden) *uchsd ldrs over 4f* **14/1**
4200 **12** *nk* **The King Of Rock**[13] 6066 2-8-3 **57**...................................... CCatlin 5 26
(AGNewcombe) *sn outpcd* **25/1**
0304 **13** *4* **Sir Frank Gibson**[71] 5256 2-8-2 **56**...................................... JFanning 3 15
(MJohnston) *sn outpcd* **12/1**
000 **14** *8* **Zolushka (IRE)**[95] 4691 2-7-13 **53**........................................ JMackay 4 —
(BWDuke) *s.i.s: outpcd* **66/1**
1m 32.37s (1.57) **Going Correction** +0.10s/f (Slow) **14** Ran SP% **122.6**
Speed ratings: **95,93,92,91,89 86,86,85,85,82 81,80,76,66**CSF £478.60 CT £4212.70 TOTE £63.60: £11.60, £3.70, £4.20; EX 1047.10.
**Owner** Ed Weetman (haulage & Storage) Ltd **Bred** Kirtlington Stud Ltd **Trained** Southwell, Notts

**FOCUS**
A moderate nursery run at a good pace from the off and those who raced on the speed looked to have an advantage.

**NOTEBOOK**
**Weet An Haul**, beaten at least 13 lengths in all five on his previous starts, including over this course and distance last time, put up a much-improved effort on this handicap debut from 8lb out of the weights. This was his debut for the Paul Blockley yard and, although things will be tougher when reassessed, he has clearly turned the corner. *Official explanation: trainer said, regarding the improved form shown, this was gelding's first run for the yard*
**Muy Bien**, stepping up to seven furlongs for the first time and switching back from Polytrack to Fibresand, showed plenty of pace and stuck to his task well when headed.
**Phluke**, having his first start for 101 days, stepping up from five furlongs and, making his Fibresand debut, raced slightly further off the pace than the front two, but was never too far away and stuck on well.
**Garnock Venture(IRE)** was lit up by the first-time blinkers and showed enough pace to suggest he will be effective over six furlongs.
**Maunby Raver** has been in good form over six furlongs recently, but did not appear to get this extra furlong.
**Dr Cerullo**, quite well supported in the market, was soon in the rear and, in a race dominated by those on the pace, could never get competitive. Polytrack looks to suit him better.

## 6142 LITTLEWOODS BET DIRECT MEDIAN AUCTION MAIDEN STKS (DIV I) 1m (F)
12:40 (12:41) (F) 2-Y-0 £2,219 (£634; £317) Stalls Low

Form RPR
4 **1** **Atlantic Breeze**[48] 5687 2-8-6 .......................................... LEnstone(3) 2 59
(MrsNMacauley) *chsd ldrs: lost pl 5f out: hdwy over 2f out: led ins fnl f: rdn out* **7/1**[3]
554 **2** *1* **Mrs Gee (IRE)**[72] 5221 2-8-9 **63**.......................................... RWinston 3 57
(RHollinshead) *broke wl: lost pl 6f out: pushed along and hmpd over 4f out: hdwy and nt clr run over 1f out: r.o* **7/2**[2]
0202 **3** *shd* **Come What July (IRE)**[24] 5994 2-9-0 67..........................(b) ACulhane 6 62
(RGuest) *hld up: plld hrd: hmpd over 4f out: hdwy over 1f out: r.o* **13/8**[1]
0502 **4** *1 1/2* **Trompe L'Oeil (IRE)**[9] 6087 2-8-9 71................................... MFenton 10 54
(EALDunlop) *chsd ldrs: led over 2f out: hdd and no ex ins fnl f* **7/2**[2]
005 **5** *5* **Dante's Devine (IRE)**[41] 5813 2-9-0 65................................ CCatlin 5 49
(ABailey) *s.i.s: hdwy over 3f out: wknd over 1f out* **16/1**
0 **6** *1 1/2* **Monte Major (IRE)**[12] 6074 2-9-0 .......................................... MHenry 7 46
(MAJarvis) *chsd ldrs: rdn over 1f out: wknd ins fnl f* **25/1**
00 **7** *1* **Calculaite**[10] 6082 2-9-0 .................................................. JFanning 9 44
(MrsGSRees) *hld up in tch: rdn over 1f out: sn wknd* **100/1**
50 **8** *nk* **Tamarina (IRE)**[13] 6066 2-8-9 ............................................ DaneO'Neill 1 38
(NEBerry) *led over 5f: hung lft and wknd over 1f out* **50/1**
**9** *2* **Oktis Morilious (IRE)** 2-9-0 .............................................. SWKelly 4 39
(JAOsborne) *s.i.s: hld up: hdwy 1/2-way: wknd over 1f out* **16/1**
0 **10** *14* **Timbuktu**[32] 5929 2-9-0 ...................................................... MTebbutt 8 11
(CWThornton) *s.i.s: outpcd* **50/1**
0 **11** *24* **Evening Fragrance**[20] 6020 2-9-0 ....................................(b[1]) JMackay 11 —
(GCHChung) *s.i.s: sn prom: wknd over 3f out* **50/1**
1m 47.26s (2.66) **Going Correction** +0.10s/f (Slow) **11** Ran SP% **117.5**
Speed ratings: **90,89,88,87,82 80,79,79,77,63 39**CSF £30.97 TOTE £12.50: £2.50, £1.50, £1.10; EX 27.20.
**Owner** Richard Underwood **Bred** Mrs D B Mulley **Trained** Sproxton, Leics

**FOCUS**
They were quite well bunched up-front early on in this modest maiden, but despite that the first three home came from off the pace. The winning time was over a second and a half slower than the second division.

**NOTEBOOK**
**Atlantic Breeze**, fourth in a similar race on her debut over six furlongs here 48 days earlier, built on that effort to get off the mark. She got a little outpaced, but picked up well for pressure in straight and did the job in workmanlike style. She should continue to progress with time and distance.
**Mrs Gee(IRE)**, returning from a short break and making her Fibresand debut, was involved in a bit of scrimmaging with Come What July leaving the back straight and had to wait for a gap in the home stretch, but kept on when in the clear. She should find a modest maiden.
**Come What July(IRE)**, fourth in a Wolverhampton nursery over seven furlongs off a mark of 70 last time, ran well enough on this step up in trip, but took a long time to pick up in straight. He does not look that straightforward.
**Trompe L'Oeil(IRE)**, runner-up in a Polytrack maiden over a mile two last time, was disappointing on this Fibresand debut. She appeared to handle the surface well enough, but may have preferred a stronger pace.
**Dante's Devine(IRE)** ran below form on this Fibresand debut.

## 6143 LITTLEWOODSPOKER.COM H'CAP (DIV I) 1m (F)
1:10 (1:10) (F) (0-60,59) 3-Y-0+ £2,072 (£592; £296) Stalls Low

Form RPR
0204 **1** **Queensberry**[9] 6096 4-8-12 **49**...................................... JDO'Reilly(7) 10 58
(JO'Reilly) *hld up: hdwy u.p over 2f out: hung lft over 1f out: led ins fnl f: r.o* **9/1**[3]

6022 **2** ½ **Mutarafaa (USA)**[14] 6055 4-8-11 **46**............................(e) THamilton(5) 11 54
(DShaw) *sn pushed along and prom: rdn and ev ch ins fnl f: r.o* **2/1**[1]

4605 **3** ½ **Qobtaan (USA)**[14] 6057 4-9-1 **45**.............................................. GBaker 1 52
(MRBosley) *hld up: hdwy over 3f out: r.o* **14/1**

5340 **4** *shd* **Goodbye Mr Bond**[13] 6070 3-9-7 **55**...................................... DAllan(3) 3 62
(EJAlston) *chsd ldrs: rdn to ld over 1f out: hdd ins fnl f: styd on* **10/1**

4420 **5** 3½ **Shatin Hero**[17] 6042 3-9-13 **58**...........................................(p) RFfrench 12 58
(GCHChung) *chsd ldrs: rdn over 2f out: styd on same pce appr fnl f* **11/2**[2]

0-02 **6** 1¾ **Princess Grace**[294] 558 4-8-2 **39**................................. RoryMoore(7) 4 36
(MLWBell) *chsd ldr: led over 4f out: rdn and hdd over 1f out: wknd fnl f* **11/1**

0050 **7** 2 **Malmand (USA)**[10] 6085 4-9-0 **44**....................................(b[1]) GGibbons 9 37
(RBrotherton) *s.s: sn prom: outpcd over 3f out: n.d after* **40/1**

0000 **8** ½ **Eurolink Artemis**[23] 6004 6-9-3 **47**......................................(p) MFenton 7 39
(MissGayKelleway) *hld up: rdn over 2f out: n.d* **25/1**

6503 **9** ½ **Ersaal (USA)**[17] 6040 3-9-8 **53**........................................... KDalgleish 14 44
(JJay) *trckd ldrs: rdn over 3f out: wknd over 1f out* **12/1**

0000 **10** 4 **Chickasaw Trail**[44] 5742 5-8-4 **34**...................................... DaleGibson 8 17
(RHollinshead) *a in rr* **50/1**

4000 **11** ½ **Sarn**[44] 5749 4-8-13 **43**............................................................. JFanning 5 25
(ABailey) *prom to 1/2-way* **16/1**

0126 **12** 5 **Maunby Rocker**[16] 5534 3-9-11 **59**.................................. LEnstone(3) 13 31
(PCHaslam) *chsd ldrs over 4f* **11/1**

060 **13** 1 **Marengo**[62] 5442 9-8-7 **37**................................................ JoannaBadger 6 7
(PaulJohnson) *s.i.s: a in rr* **22/1**

000 **14** 28 **Goodwood Promise**[14] 5508 4-8-7 **42** ow2...................... MSavage(5) 2 —
(NEBerry) *led over 3f: wknd 3f out* **66/1**

1m 45.45s (0.85) **Going Correction** +0.10s/f (Slow)
**WFA** 3 from 4yo+ 1lb **14** Ran SP% **118.8**
Speed ratings: **99,98,98,97,94 92,90,90,89,85 85,80,79,51**CSF £25.63 CT £267.03 TOTE £10.10: £2.60, £1.10, £6.00; EX 23.60.
**Owner** J Saul **Bred** G Revitt **Trained** Brierley, S Yorks

**FOCUS**
A moderate handicap run at a decent enough pace throughout and the first three home raced off the speed.

**NOTEBOOK**
**Queensberry**, a well-beaten fourth over an extended one mile-six at Wolverhampton last time, is clearly much better suited to this sort of trip. Kept wide for most of the way from stall ten, he came right down the centre of the track in the straight and always looked like getting there. This was his first win in a handicap.
**Mutarafaa(USA)**, runner-up over course and distance on his last two starts, completed a rather unlucky hat-trick. He is in good form, but is clearly proving hard to win with.
**Qobtaan(USA)**, still a maiden, confirmed the promise he showed on his return from a break over course and distance last time, keeping on well having travelled sweetly towards the rear.
**Goodbye Mr Bond**, never too far off the pace, stuck on right the way to the line to post a better effort than he did here last time.
**Shatin Hero**, stepping back up in trip, never posted a serious threat.

## 6144 BET DIRECT PRESS RED TO BET CLAIMING STKS 7f (F)
**1:40** (1:41) (D ) 3-Y-0+ **£2,121** (£606; £303) **Stalls** Low

Form RPR

2033 **1** **Cloud Dancer**[24] 5992 4-9-0 74........................................ DaneO'Neill 15 78
(DJCoakley) *s.i.s: hld up: hdwy over 3f out: led on bit over 1f out: rdn out* **2/1**[1]

1061 **2** *nk* **Nimello (USA)**[93] 4734 7-9-2 78........................................ LPKeniry(3) 12 83
(AGNewcombe) *hld up in tch: chsd wnr over 1f out: edgd lft: styd on* **10/1**

6320 **3** 5 **Bulawayo**[9] 6094 6-8-12 57................................................. ANicholls 16 63
(AndrewReid) *chsd ldrs: rdn over 1f out: styd on same pce* **16/1**

0045 **4** 1¼ **Mr Stylish**[17] 6042 7-8-10 50............................................(vt) JDSmith 6 58
(JSMoore) *hld up: hdwy over 1f out: nt rch ldrs* **25/1**

000/ **5** ½ **Tinian**[43] 5-8-13 65........................................................... DarrenWilliams 5 60
(KRBurke) *hld up: hdwy u.p over 2f out: edgd lft over 1f out: styd on same pce* **25/1**

0560 **6** *hd* **George Stubbs (USA)**[6] 6113 5-9-5 69...........................(p) JFanning 8 65
(NPLittmoden) *chsd ldrs: led over 2f out: rdn and hdd over 1f out: sn wknd* **9/2**[3]

1024 **7** 3½ **Jan Brueghel (USA)**[24] 5992 4-8-8 66.......... Laura-JayneCrawford(7) 2 52
(TDBarron) *dwlt: nvr nrr* **10/3**[2]

0006 **8** 1½ **Red Delirium**[17] 6036 7-8-12 50.........................................(b) GGibbons 11 46
(RBrotherton) *dwlt: nvr trbld ldrs* **33/1**

0000 **9** ½ **Zahunda (IRE)**[23] 6004 4-8-6 49........................................ KDalgleish 7 38
(WMBrisbourne) *prom over 4f* **66/1**

4000 **10** *nk* **Waterline Dancer (IRE)**[110] 4288 3-8-6 48.......................(vt) SWKelly 4 38
(PDEvans) *hld up: a in rr* **66/1**

000 **11** 2½ **Lion's Domane**[110] 4277 6-8-11 47.................................... RWinston 13 36
(ABerry) *sn drvn along: mde most over 4f: wknd over 1f out* **50/1**

0314 **12** 1 **Repeat (IRE)**[9] 6099 3-8-13 55........................................ ACulhane 10 36
(MissGayKelleway) *hld up: n.d* **14/1**

40 **13** 1 **Coolfore Jade (IRE)**[52] 5617 3-8-7 ow1......................... MSavage(5) 14 32
(NEBerry) *prom over 4f* **33/1**

2440 **14** 7 **Shamwari Fire (IRE)**[19] 6028 3-8-8 47....................... NataliaGemelova(7) 3 18
(IWMcinnes) *prom over 4f* **50/1**

0030 **15** 2½ **King David**[25] 5987 4-8-11 56............................................ RPrice 9 8
(DBurchell) *chsd ldrs over 4f* **20/1**

1000 **16** 3 **Better Off**[65] 5377 5-8-10 73............................................(p) LFletcher(3) 1 2
(MrsNMacauley) *a in rr* **20/1**

1m 31.3s (0.50) **Going Correction** +0.10s/f (Slow) **16** Ran SP% **126.2**
Speed ratings: **101,100,94,93,92 92,88,87,86,86 83,82,80,72,70 66**CSF £21.77 TOTE £3.60: £1.10, £2.60, £8.60; EX 18.10.The winner was claimed by Mr Graham Frankland for £14,000
**Owner** Cloud Dancer Racing **Bred** Cheveley Park Stud Ltd **Trained** West Ilsley, Berks

**FOCUS**
Quite a competitive claimer run at a strong pace and the first two home came from off the speed and raced down the centre of the track in the straight.

**NOTEBOOK**
**Cloud Dancer**, without a win for well over a year, was suited by this drop back into claiming company and was well in at the weights. She had to be shuffled along in the early strides to hold a position having missed a beat at the start, but was soon back on the bridle and, having travelled strongly, it was then just a case of what she would find under pressure, and the answer was plenty. She was claimed for £14,000.
**Nimello(USA)**, making his debut for Tony Newcombe off the back of a 93-day break, was not for the first time a noticeable drifter in the betting. However, under a strong ride, he ran his race and was only just held.
**Bulawayo** was never too far off the pace and kept on all the way to the line. This was a good effort at the weights.
**Mr Stylish** looked an awkward ride towards the rear of the field and only kept on when it was all too late.
**Tinian**, a prolific winner in Germany this year, stuck to the inside throughout on his return to Britain, but showed promise.
**George Stubbs(USA)**, up in trip, with cheekpieces on instead of blinkers, and down in grade, was well held.
**Jan Brueghel(USA)** was reported to have bled from the nose. *Official explanation: trainer's representative said gelding had bled from the nose*
**King David** was reportedly never travelling. *Official explanation: jockey said gelding was never travelling*

## 6145 LITTLEWOODS BET DIRECT MEDIAN AUCTION MAIDEN STKS (DIV II) 1m (F)
**2:10** (2:10) (F ) 2-Y-O **£2,212** (£632; £316) **Stalls** Low

Form RPR

2505 **1** **Nessen Dorma (IRE)**[24] 5994 2-9-0 66................................ ACulhane 5 67
(JGGiven) *chsd ldrs: rdn over 1f out: led ins fnl f: r.o* **6/5**[1]

00 **2** 1½ **Nuts For You (IRE)**[25] 5986 2-8-10 ow1.......................... DaneO'Neill 2 60
(RCharlton) *trckd ldrs: led over 1f out: hdd and unable qck ins fnl f* **11/2**[2]

30 **3** 5 **Drizzle**[10] 6082 2-9-0.......................................................... MHenry 8 54
(JWUnett) *prom: rdn over 3f out: styd on same pce appr fnl f* **14/1**

0050 **4** *hd* **Smart Boy Prince (IRE)**[13] 6069 2-8-7 50.................. DerekNolan(7) 4 54
(PABlockley) *led: rdn and hdd over 1f out: wknd ins fnl f* **14/1**

026 **5** 1¾ **Jakarmi**[10] 6082 2-9-0 62..................................................... DKinsella 7 50
(BPalling) *chsd ldrs: rdn over 2f out: styd on same pce* **9/1**

00 **6** 6 **Can Can Flyer (IRE)**[23] 6003 2-9-0.................................. JFanning 1 38
(MJohnston) *chsd ldrs: rdn over 4f out: wknd 3f out* **15/2**

04 **7** ½ **Turks And Caicos (IRE)**[24] 5993 2-8-11 .................. LEnstone(3) 10 37
(PCHaslam) *hld up: rdn over 3f out: sn wknd* **7/1**[3]

00 **8** *shd* **Spring Whisper (IRE)**[9] 6091 2-8-9 .................................. MFenton 3 32
(EALDunlop) *hld up in tch: rdn over 3f out: hung rt and sn wknd* **16/1**

000 **9** *dist* **Belt And Braces**[142] 3415 2-9-0 30.................................... ANicholls 6 —
(CSmith) *s.i.s: outpcd* **100/1**

000 **R** **Sonne De Loup**[20] 6021 2-8-4 42.................................. JFMcDonald(5) 9 —
(MrsStefLiddiard) *chsd ldrs: rdn and hung rt fr over 4f out: rn out over 3f out* **33/1**

1m 45.65s (1.05) **Going Correction** +0.10s/f (Slow) **10** Ran SP% **118.3**
Speed ratings: **98,96,91,91,89 83,83,82,—,—**CSF £8.04 TOTE £1.70: £1.10, £2.00, £4.50; EX 8.90.
**Owner** Hokey Cokey Partnership **Bred** Robinski Bloodstock Limited **Trained** Willoughton, Lincs

**FOCUS**
Like the first division this was pretty modest stuff, but the winning time was over a second and a half faster and the winner came right down the centre of the track.

**NOTEBOOK**
**Nessen Dorma(IRE)**, stepping up a furlong and switching from a nursery back into a maiden, was never far off the pace and kept on right to the line to get off the mark. Beaten off a mark of 70 last time, the Handicapper looks to have given him a chance by dropping him to 66.
**Nuts For You(IRE)** was well beaten in a Polytrack maiden last time, but this was better. There may be a similarly weak race to be won with her.
**Drizzle** ran respectably, but was well held and will find things easier in handicaps.
**Smart Boy Prince(IRE)**, up a furlong in trip, showed pace but was soon put in his place in the straight.
**Jakarmi** may need dropping in grade.
**Sonne De Loup** *Official explanation: jockey said filly cocked her jaw and became unsteerable*

## 6146 BETDIRECT.CO.UK FILLIES' H'CAP 1m (F)
**2:40** (2:40) (E ) (0-75,69) 3-Y-O+ **£2,121** (£606; £303) **Stalls** Low

Form RPR

3005 **1** **Miss Champers (IRE)**[9] 6100 3-9-1 **59**......................... JoannaBadger 3 73
(PDEvans) *trckd ldrs: led over 1f out: rdn clr* **14/1**

2150 **2** 2½ **Ellen Mooney**[31] 5945 4-9-12 **69**....................................(p) RFfrench 2 78
(BSmart) *w ldr: rdn and ev ch over 1f out: sn outpcd* **15/8**[1]

3221 **3** 1¾ **Rock Concert**[14] 6055 5-8-12 **58**..................................... LFletcher(3) 4 64
(IWMcinnes) *chsd ldrs: rdn over 2f out: styd on same pce* **15/8**[1]

0036 **4** 1½ **Victory Flip (IRE)**[17] 6039 3-8-10 **54**.........................(p) ACulhane 7 57
(RHollinshead) *hld up: hdwy over 2f out: sn rdn: styd on same pce appr fnl f* **10/1**[3]

1136 **5** 3 **Estimation**[13] 6064 3-9-4 **67**............................................... BReilly(5) 1 64
(RMHCowell) *racd keenly: mde most over 6f: wknd ins fnl f* **3/1**[2]

0000 **6** 8 **Oriental Moon (IRE)**[47] 5712 4-7-5 **41** oh1.............(p) DeanWilliams(7) 9 22
(GCHChung) *chsd ldrs: rdn over 3f out: sn wknd* **50/1**

0000 **7** 2 **Mabel Riley (IRE)**[13] 6065 3-8-2 **46**...............................(p) JBramhill 8 23
(MABuckley) *chsd ldrs: rdn over 2f out: wknd over 1f out* **25/1**

2000 **8** 5 **Chanteuse**[131] 3701 3-8-10 **54**........................................... RBrisland 5 21
(DWChapman) *s.s: outpcd* **66/1**

00 **9** 12 **Sugar Cube Treat**[14] 6062 7-7-12 **41** oh6........................ SRighton 6 —
(MMullineaux) *hld up in tch: wknd over 3f out* **80/1**

1m 44.49s (-0.11) **Going Correction** +0.10s/f (Slow)
**WFA** 3 from 4yo+ 1lb **9** Ran SP% **118.9**
Speed ratings: **104,101,99,98,95 87,85,80,68**CSF £41.63 CT £76.21 TOTE £13.30: £4.30, £1.30, £1.02.
**Owner** Mrs S J Lawrence **Bred** Mountarmstrong Stud **Trained** Pandy, Gwent
■ Stewards Enquiry : R Ffrench two-day ban: used whip with excessive frequency (Dec 17,19)

**FOCUS**
A modest fillies' handicap run at a pretty ordinary early pace.

**NOTEBOOK**
**Miss Champers(IRE)** has not been in very good form lately but, stepping back up a furlong in trip and 11lb lower than when last successful, she ran out a clear-cut winner. Entered up over this course and distance on Friday, she could well follow-up under a penalty.
**Ellen Mooney**, back on Fibresand for the first time since winning over course and distance, ran well off a 4lb higher mark.
**Rock Concert**, 3lb higher than when winning over course and distance last time, found this tougher.
**Victory Flip(IRE)** is still a maiden and was comfortably held.
**Estimation**, 1lb lower than when held over course and distance last time, was too keen for her own good.

## 6147 BET DIRECT ON ITV PAGE 367 (S) STKS 1m (F)
**3:10** (3:10) (G ) 2-Y-O **£2,100** (£600; £300) **Stalls** Low

Form RPR

3003 **1** **Lyrical Girl (USA)**[16] 6046 2-8-6 57.......................................... CCatlin 2 50
(MRChannon) *hld up: hdwy over 3f out: rdn over 1f out: r.o to ld nr fin* **7/4**[1]

5053 **2** ½ **Rare Coincidence**[14] 6058 2-8-11 54..............................(p) SRighton 10 54
(RFFisher) *sn w ldr: led over 2f out: rdn over 1f out: edgd lft and hdd nr fin* **7/1**

1435 **3** 2 **Armentieres**[16] 6046 2-8-11 54..............................................(b) ADaly 1 50
(JLSpearing) *chsd ldrs: rdn and ev ch over 1f out: styd on same pce* **6/1**[3]

3004 **4** 4 **Hunting Pink**[16] 6046 2-8-3 49 ........ LFletcher(3) 6 37
(HMorrison) *mde most over 5f: wknd fnl f* **4/1**[2]

0004 **5** 1 3/4 **Salut Saint Cloud**[14] 6058 2-8-11 50 ........ (v) MFenton 11 39
(MissVHaigh) *hld up: rdn 1/2-way: styd on u.p fnl 2f: n.d* **16/1**

000 **6** 7 **Red Acer (IRE)**[191] 2001 2-8-11 49 ........ SWKelly 15 25
(PDEvans) *s.i.s: outpcd: styd on ins fnl f: nvr nrr* **33/1**

4060 **7** shd **David's Girl**[16] 6047 2-8-6 49 ........ JFanning 7 19
(DMorris) *prom over 5f* **25/1**

6255 **8** 3/4 **City General (IRE)**[17] 6041 2-8-13 58 ........ (p) LPKeniry(3) 12 28
(JSMoore) *sn outpcd* **14/1**

4000 **9** 1 **Intitnice (IRE)**[24] 5997 2-8-6 45 ........ BReilly(5) 3 21
(MissKMGeorge) *chsd ldrs over 5f* **20/1**

5500 **10** 3 **Ynys**[16] 6047 2-8-11 42 ........ DKinsella 4 15
(BPalling) *sn outpcd* **80/1**

4000 **11** 3 **Be My Alibi (IRE)**[24] 5993 2-8-6 51 ........ KDalgleish 9 4
(JSMoore) *prom over 4f* **33/1**

**12** 5 **Blues Over (IRE)** 2-8-6 ........ PaulEddery 5 —
(WJMusson) *dwlt: outpcd* **33/1**

0000 **13** 3 1/2 **Stamford Blue**[25] 5990 2-9-2 49 ........ JDSmith 8 —
(JSMoore) *chsd ldrs 5f* **50/1**

000 **14** 1 3/4 **The Laverton Lad**[181] 2244 2-8-11 41 ........ MTebbutt 13 —
(CWThornton) *sn outpcd* **100/1**

2040 **15** 17 **Platinum Chief**[41] 5816 2-8-11 53 ........ (b) DarrenWilliams 14 —
(ABerry) *chsd ldrs 5f: eased fnl 2f* **33/1**

00 **16** 25 **Millietom (IRE)**[17] 6041 2-8-11 ........ (b1) RWinston 16 —
(KARyan) *chsd ldrs 5f: eased fnl 2f* **20/1**

1m 46.08s (1.48) **Going Correction** +0.10s/f (Slow) **16** Ran SP% **125.0**
Speed ratings: **96,95,93,89,87 80,80,79,78,75 72,67,64,62,45 20**CSF £12.91 TOTE £3.70: £1.10, £3.30, £1.90; EX 23.00.The winner was bought in for 9,000gns

**Owner** C S G Limited **Bred** Alexander Pereira **Trained** West Ilsley, Berks

■ Stewards Enquiry : C Catlin one-day ban: used whip with excessive frequency (Dec 19)

**FOCUS**
A moderate but competitive enough seller run at a good pace.

**NOTEBOOK**
**Lyrical Girl(USA)**, third in a mile seller on Polytrack last time, was well in at the weights on this Fibresand debut and, having been outpaced early on, she responded gamely to her pilot's urgings and got up close home. This is her sort of level.
**Rare Coincidence**, third in this grade over seven furlongs here last time, posted a good effort at the weights on this step back up in trip.
**Armentieres**, back on Fibresand, was given every chance and ran a respectable race.
**Hunting Pink**, just behind today's winner at Lingfield last time, was unable to reverse those placings on this Fibresand debut. She is a disappointing sort.
**Salut Saint Cloud**, up a furlong in trip, never really threatened.

## 6148 LITTLEWOODSPOKER.COM H'CAP (DIV II) 1m (F)
3:35 (3:36) (F ) (0-60,58) 3-Y-O+ £2,072 (£592; £296) Stalls Low

Form RPR

-000 **1** **Spy Gun (USA)**[19] 6026 3-9-4 54 ........ NChalmers(5) 5 65
(TWall) *chsd ldrs: led 2f out: hung lft ins fnl f: rdn out* **25/1**

3504 **2** 1 **Sorbiesharry (IRE)**[17] 6040 4-8-11 44 ........ LEnstone(3) 4 53
(MrsNMacauley) *hld up: hdwy 3f out: rdn over 1f out: nt clr run ins fnl f: kpt on* **7/2**[2]

-650 **3** 1 1/2 **Kalou (GER)**[252] 885 5-9-4 48 ........ SWKelly 14 54
(BJCurley) *dwlt: hdwy over 4f out: hrd rdn fr over 2f out: hung lft over 1f out: styd on* **4/1**[3]

6004 **4** 1/2 **Noble Pursuit**[19] 6028 6-9-12 56 ........ GParkin 12 61
(PABlockley) *w ldr: rdn and ev ch 2f out: no ex ins fnl f* **3/1**[1]

5006 **5** 3 **Giust In Temp (IRE)**[10] 6085 4-8-3 33 ........ JoannaBadger 2 32
(PWHiatt) *sn outpcd: nt clr run over 3f out: styd on u.p fnl 2f : nvr nrr* **25/1**

45-3 **6** 1/2 **Bella Pavlina**[10] 6085 5-7-12 35 ........ BSwarbrick(7) 6 33
(WMBrisbourne) *mid-div: sn drvn along: styd on appraoching fnl f: nt pce to chal* **9/1**

0000 **7** 1/2 **Dasar**[17] 6036 3-9-3 48 ........ DarrenWilliams 10 45
(MBrittain) *mde most 6f: wknd fnl f* **40/1**

0000 **8** 5 **Sinjaree**[32] 5937 5-9-8 52 ........ CCatlin 9 39
(MrsSLamyman) *chsd ldrs: lost pl 5f out: n.d after* **16/1**

3230 **9** 2 **Miss Glory Be**[13] 6064 5-9-9 58 ........ (p) TEaves(5) 11 41
(MissGayKelleway) *chsd ldrs: rdn 3f out: wknd wl over 1f out* **15/2**

0540 **10** shd **El Pedro**[37] 5881 4-9-1 50 ........ MSavage(5) 13 33
(NEBerry) *s.i.s: sn chsng ldrs: wknd over 2f out* **25/1**

0000 **11** 1/2 **Vermilion Creek**[13] 6064 4-8-5 42 ........ StephanieHollinshead(7) 1 24
(RHollinshead) *sn outpcd* **16/1**

4610 **12** 4 **Tanga Dancer**[23] 6004 3-9-1 46 ........ RFfrench 7 20
(BSmart) *chsd ldrs 5f* **14/1**

2006 **13** 4 **Littleton Valar (IRE)**[56] 5542 3-8-1 39 ........ (p) DFentiman(7) 3 5
(JRWeymes) *chsd ldrs over 4f* **50/1**

0000 **14** 9 **Subtle Move (USA)**[13] 6070 3-8-8 39 ........ (v) GGibbons 8 —
(DShaw) *bhd fr 1/2-way* **66/1**

1m 45.15s (0.55) **Going Correction** +0.10s/f (Slow)
**WFA** 3 from 4yo+ 1lb **14** Ran SP% **124.8**
Speed ratings: **101,100,98,98,95 94,94,89,87,86 86,82,78,69**CSF £110.24 CT £457.70 TOTE £26.50: £3.40, £1.90, £2.30; EX 254.50 TRIFECTA Not won. Place 6 £29.27, Place 5 £4.97..

**Owner** Derek & Mrs Marie Dean **Bred** Braeburn Farm Corp **Trained** Harton, Shropshire

**FOCUS**
Like the first division this was a moderate handicap and the pace was fair.

**NOTEBOOK**
**Spy Gun(USA)**, 5lb lower than when beaten 15 lengths over course and distance last time on his return from a break, was clearly all the better for that run and posted by far and away his best effort to date to get off the mark. He edged left under pressure, but that was probably through inexperience and he was always holding the runner-up. Lightly-raced, there could be more to come. *Official explanation: trainer had no explanation for the improved form shown*
**Sorbiesharry(IRE)**, back over the course and distance of his only previous success having run over a mile and a half last time and 10lb lower than when gaining that win, finished well from off the pace. The winner crossed his path close home, but it made no difference to the result.
**Kalou(GER)**, dropping in trip on his return from a break, ran respectably but was noted hanging left in the straight.
**Noble Pursuit**, well supported in the market, had every chance from the front, but did not get home.
**Giust In Temp(IRE)** was doing his best work late on and may do better back over a little further.
T/Plt: £37.00 to a £1 stake. Pool: £56,622.60. 1,116.40 winning tickets. T/Qpdt: £3.10 to a £1 stake. Pool: £6,922.30. 1,642.90 winning tickets. CR

# 6141 SOUTHWELL (L-H)
Tuesday, December 9

**OFFICIAL GOING: Standard**

## 6149 BET DIRECT ON ATTHERACES INTERACTIVE H'CAP (DIV I) 6f (F)
12:00 (12:01) (F ) (0-60,60) 3-Y-O+ £2,121 (£606; £303) Stalls Low

Form RPR

5302 **1** **Chispa**[15] 6056 5-10-0 60 ........ DarrenWilliams 3 69
(KRBurke) *cl up: shkn up to ld 2f out: drvn over 1f out: kpt on u.p ins last* **11/2**[2]

0062 **2** 1/2 **Eastern Blue (IRE)**[15] 6062 4-9-2 48 ........ (p) IMongan 4 56
(MrsLStubbs) *trckd ldrs: hdwy over 2f out: rdn to chal over 1f out and sn ev ch: drvn ins last and kpt on* **7/1**[3]

6003 **3** shd **Game Guru**[18] 6042 4-9-6 59 ........ (b) Laura-JayneCrawford(7) 7 66
(TDBarron) *a.p: effrt 2f out and sn rdn: kpt on u.p fnl f* **9/1**

0423 **4** 1 1/4 **Shifty**[3] 6140 4-9-9 55 ........ (b) ANicholls 11 58
(DNicholls) *midfield: wd st: hdwy wl over 1f out: sn rdn and kpt on ins last: nrst fin* **9/2**[1]

5061 **5** 2 1/2 **Jalouhar**[20] 6031 3-10-0 60 ........ (p) JFanning 6 56
(BPJBaugh) *towards rr: hdwy 3f out: rdn wl over 1f out: kpt on: nrst fin* **12/1**

0000 **6** 1/2 **Best Lead**[146] 3301 4-9-10 56 ........ (v1) CCatlin 5 50
(IanEmmerson) *led: rdn along 3f out: hdd 2f out and wknd over 1f out* **66/1**

0060 **7** nk **Dil**[14] 6065 8-8-12 51 ........ StevenHarrison(7) 10 45
(MrsNMacauley) *sn outpcd and bhd: wd st: gd hdwy over 1f out: nrst fin* **14/1**

-060 **8** 3/4 **Silver Mascot**[98] 4642 4-8-13 45 ........ ACulhane 2 36
(RHollinshead) *s.i.s and bhd: hdwy and nt clr run 3f out: styng on whn swtchd rt ent last: nrst fin* **10/1**

0400 **9** 1 3/4 **Cleveland Way**[20] 6031 3-9-3 49 ........ (v) RFitzpatrick 1 35
(DCarroll) *chsd ldrs on inner: rdn along 3f out: kpt on same pce fnl 2f* **25/1**

5040 **10** 1 3/4 **Mad Mick Meeson**[10] 6088 3-9-9 55 ........ (t) AClark 15 36
(GBBalding) *hmpd s and bhd tl sme late hdwy* **12/1**

0003 **11** nk **Amanda's Lad (IRE)**[53] 5625 3-8-11 43 ........ GDuffield 16 23
(MCChapman) *chsd ldrs on outer: rdn along 1/2-way and sn outpcd* **25/1**

0000 **12** 1 1/2 **Evangelist (IRE)**[58] 5497 3-8-5 42 ow2 ........ PBradley(5) 9 17
(ABerry) *a towards rr* **50/1**

0000 **13** 1 **Yob (IRE)**[155] 3050 4-8-8 40 ........ (t) SWKelly 13 12
(PDEvans) *bhd fr 1/2-way* **66/1**

0630 **14** shd **Carols Choice**[11] 6081 6-8-6 43 ........ NChalmers(5) 14 15
(ASadik) *wnt rt s: hdwy to chse ldrs 1/2-way: rdn 2f out and sn wknd* **16/1**

6430 **15** hd **Festive Affair**[129] 3797 5-9-7 53 ........ RFfrench 12 25
(BSmart) *bhd fr 1/2-way* **12/1**

0005 **16** 5 **Cash**[10] 6095 5-9-8 57 ........ LisaJones(3) 8 14
(PaulJohnson) *chsd ldrs to 1/2-way: sn wknd* **10/1**

1m 18.94s (2.14) **Going Correction** +0.25s/f (Slow) **16** Ran SP% **122.5**
Speed ratings: **95,94,94,92,89 88,88,87,84,82 82,80,78,78,78 71**CSF £42.30 CT £348.81 TOTE £6.10: £1.60, £2.30, £4.20, £1.20; EX 22.90.

**Owner** Mrs Elaine M Burke **Bred** Mrs H M Trigg **Trained** Middleham Moor, N Yorks

**FOCUS**
The field finished well strung out.

**NOTEBOOK**
**Chispa**duly went one better than her previous run over course-and-distance with a professional display. She looks on a favourable mark at present and if turning out under a penalty, should be followed.
**Eastern Blue(IRE)**had every chance, but lacked the conviction of the winner in a battle. She has been slipping in the weights and since switching to the sand has looked much better, so could well be capable of making amends before too long in this grade.
**Game Guru**looked to duck the issue slightly when his rider asked for maximum effort, but this was still an improvement and he will be one to keep on the right side when the market speaks in his favour.
**Shifty**would have benefited from a more prominent ride on this drop in trip. He definitely has the ability to win a race in this sphere, but that is more likely when stepping back up in distance.
**Silver Mascot**can do better than this. He was very sluggish at the start and suffered traffic problems when moving well as the race was getting serious.

## 6150 BET DIRECT IN RUNNING SKY TEXT 293 (S) STKS (DIV I) 6f (F)
12:30 (12:30) (G ) 3-Y-O+ £2,086 (£596; £298) Stalls Low

Form RPR

3000 **1** **Playful Spirit**[80] 5070 4-8-7 46 ........ (v) JEdmunds 1 50
(JBalding) *w ldrs: led on bit 1/2-way: edgd rt fnl f: rdn out* **20/1**

0006 **2** 1 3/4 **Heathyardsblessing (IRE)**[20] 6027 6-8-12 46 ........ ACulhane 2 50
(RHollinshead) *chsd ldrs: rdn over 1f out: styd on same pce ins fnl f* **12/1**

0006 **3** hd **Eager Angel (IRE)**[15] 6062 5-8-5 36 ow1 ........ (p) LFletcher(3) 4 45
(RFMarvin) *hld up: hdwy u.p over 2f out: styd on* **33/1**

3005 **4** 1 **Aintnecessarilyso**[7] 6116 5-8-7 42 ........ MSavage(5) 5 46
(NEBerry) *sn pushed along in rr: hdwy over 2f out: rdn over 1f out: one pce fnl f* **25/1**

0500 **5** 2 **Bali-Star**[76] 5156 8-8-12 43 ........ CCatlin 6 40
(RJHodges) *w ldrs: rdn and ev ch over 1f out: no ex fnl f* **16/1**

-005 **6** shd **Fiennes (USA)**[25] 5995 5-8-9 42 ........ (v) LisaJones(3) 8 40
(MrsNMacauley) *mde most to 1/2-way: no ex fnl f* **13/2**[3]

5000 **7** nk **Champagne Rider**[14] 6064 7-8-12 36 ........ (e1) DarrenWilliams 14 39
(DShaw) *hld up in tch: n ot much room and outpcd 1/2-way: styd on fnl f* **40/1**

0000 **8** 3 1/2 **Laggan Minstrel (IRE)**[21] 6024 5-8-7 48 ........ BReilly(5) 16 28
(PWD'Arcy) *prom over 3f* **11/1**

0606 **9** 1 3/4 **Patientes Virtis**[25] 5995 4-8-11 49 ........ (v) J-PGuillambert(3) 7 25
(MissGayKelleway) *sn pushed along in rr: sme hdwy over 1f out: n.d* **11/2**[2]

045/ **10** nk **Recadero (GER)**[123] 7-9-5 ........ MFenton 10 29
(THHansen, Germany) *trckd ldrs: hung rt most of way: wknd wl over 1f out* **11/8**[1]

5305 **11** 2 **The Gay Fox**[7] 6113 9-8-12 40 ........ (bt) LPKeniry(3) 12 16
(BGPowell) *sn outpcd* **14/1**

0000 **12** 1/2 **Attila The Hun**[66] 5374 4-8-12 38 ........ DMernagh 9 15
(FWatson) *chsd ldrs over 4f* **66/1**

000 **13** 6 **Lion's Domane**[1] 6144 6-9-5 47 ........ RWinston 11 4
(ABerry) *s.s: hld up: shkn up wl over 1f out: sn wknd and eased* **25/1**

5-00 **14** 9 **Finningley Connor**[33] 5936 3-8-12 65 ........ DSweeney 15 —
(RonaldThompson) *prom over 3f* **33/1**

60-0 **15** *16* **Lord Merlin (IRE)**[25] 5995 4-8-12 70 JoannaBadger 13 —
(DNicholls) *s.s: sn outpcd* **50/1**
1m 18.88s (2.08) **Going Correction** +0.25s/f (Slow) **15** Ran SP% **123.6**
Speed ratings: **96,93,93,92,89 89,88,84,81,81 78,78,70,58,36**CSF £231.84 TOTE £26.00: £5.70, £4.60, £4.30; EX 135.10.There was no bid for the winner.
**Owner** Simon Mapletoft Racing II **Bred** Ahmed M Foustok **Trained** Scrooby, Notts

**FOCUS**
Playful Spirit wins her first race since a juvenile on her first outing for her new stable.

**NOTEBOOK**
**Playful Spirit**showed the benefit of her change of scenery and posted her first victory since her juvenile season. She has gone alarmingly backwards over the last season or so, but if her new connections can rekindle her enthusiasm for racing, she should progress. There was no bid at the subsequent auction.
**Heathyardsblessing(IRE)**showed he can win a similar contest with his best run for some time. That said he is one-paced and a most inconsistent performer, so has to prove he can reproduce this.
**Eager Angel(IRE)**ran a solid race at these weights, was doing all of her best work late on and looks to be finding some form.
**Aintnecessarilyso**ran his race and this looks about as good as he is.
**Recadero(GER)**ran a shocker. On his foreign form he could have been considered a good thing, but he never looked happy at any stage and dropped out alarmingly. *Official explanation: jockey said horse hung right handed*

## 6151 BET DIRECT ON ATTHERACES INTERACTIVE H'CAP (DIV II) 6f (F)
**1:00** (1:01) (F ) (0-60,60) 3-Y-O+ **£2,114** (£604; £302) **Stalls** Low

Form RPR
0423 **1** **Majik**[14] 6063 4-10-0 60 IMongan 7 75
(DJSFfrenchDavis) *in tch: hdwy on inner over 2f out: rdn to ld ent last: styd on* **7/2**[1]
500 **2** *2* **Never Without Me**[42] 5815 3-8-12 44 (v[1]) PJScallan 12 53
(PJMcbride) *trckd ldrs gng wl: smooth hdwy to chal 2f out: ev ch tl rdn and kpt on same pce fnl f* **9/1**
**3** *1* **Miss Wong One (IRE)**[52] 5645 3-9-9 55 SWKelly 8 61
(FJBowles, Ire) *cl up: led 2f out and sn rdn: edgd lft and hdd ent last: kpt on same pce* **25/1**
0044 **4** *1 1/4* **Doctor Dennis (IRE)**[14] 6063 6-9-3 49 (v) NPollard 11 51
(MrsLydiaPearce) *hld up towards rr: hdwy 2f out: shkn up and styd on ins last: nrst fin* **10/1**
0551 **5** *5* **Acorazado (IRE)**[14] 6065 4-9-10 56 (be) GCarter 15 43
(GLMoore) *bhd: wd st: hdwy 2f out: sn rdn and kpt on ins last: nt rch ldrs* **9/2**[2]
000 **6** *nk* **Blue Maeve**[20] 6031 3-8-11 43 GParkin 14 29
(JHetherton) *towards rr: hdwy 2f out: styd on appr last: nt rch ldrs* **80/1**
0432 **7** *3/4* **Travelling Times**[14] 6065 4-9-1 52 (v) TEaves[(5)] 13 36
(JSWainwright) *towards rr: wd st: rdn 2f out: kpt on appr last: nvr a factor* **12/1**
4230 **8** *nk* **Baby Barry**[18] 6036 6-9-13 59 (v) GDuffield 5 42
(MrsGSRees) *cl up: rdn along over 2f out: sn wknd* **11/1**
0602 **9** *hd* **Geronimo**[18] 6036 6-9-8 57 (p) LisaJones[(3)] 1 40
(MissGayKelleway) *chsd ldrs: rdn along over 2f out and sn wknd* **6/1**[3]
3000 **10** *1 3/4* **On The Trail**[14] 6065 6-9-7 53 ACulhane 3 30
(DWChapman) *led: rdn along and hdd 2f out: sn wknd* **8/1**
0030 **11** *1/2* **Attorney**[20] 6032 5-9-1 47 (e) RWinston 4 23
(DShaw) *chsd ldrs: rdn 1/2-way: sn wknd* **14/1**
5000 **12** *6* **Kenny The Truth (IRE)**[42] 5823 4-8-8 40 (t) PMQuinn 16 —
(MrsJCandlish) *racd wd: a rr* **50/1**
1502 **13** *shd* **Duo Leoni**[10] 6100 3-10-0 60 MTebbutt 10 18
(RMBeckett) *chsd ldrs on outer: rdn along 1/2-way: sn wknd* **12/1**
0600 **14** *12* **Fitz The Bill (IRE)**[57] 5540 3-8-6 41 LFletcher[(3)] 9 —
(NBKing) *a bhd* **66/1**
0000 **15** *8* **Formeric**[109] 4346 7-8-8 40 JMcAuley 6 —
(MissLCSiddall) *a bhd* **66/1**
1m 17.9s (1.10) **Going Correction** +0.25s/f (Slow) **15** Ran SP% **125.3**
Speed ratings: **102,99,98,96,89 89,88,87,87,85 84,76,76,60,49**CSF £35.96 CT £712.72 TOTE £4.80: £1.80, £2.50, £13.40; EX 55.20.
**Owner** Andrew Stimpson **Bred** T Newcombe **Trained** Lambourn, Berks

**FOCUS**
Top-weight Majik gains a deserved win under a decent ride.

**NOTEBOOK**
**Majik**gained a deserved win under a well-judged ride form Mongan. He has hit the frame on his last couple of outings on the sand and clearly likes this track. Doing well to defy top-weight, he was well on top at the death and should continue to hit the frame this winter as he is a genuine sort.
**Never Without Me**ran his best race so far on this handicap debut in the first-time visor. He was suited by the drop in trip and moved well throughout on the bridle before showing greeness under pressure and could not match the winner. He should be capable of scoring in this grade and acts well on this surface.
**Miss Wong One(IRE)**showed she acts on this surface and ran respectably. She may benefit from an extra furlong, but this is her grade.
**Doctor Dennis(IRE)**, not for the first time, ran in snatches and looks very tricky.

## 6152 BET DIRECT PRESS RED TO BET NURSERY 5f (F)
**1:30** (1:30) (E ) (0-85,79) 2-Y-O **£2,016** (£576; £288) **Stalls** High

Form RPR
0442 **1** **Blue Power (IRE)**[18] 6037 2-7-11 **61** ow1 AReilly[(7)] 5 67+
(KRBurke) *chsd ldrs: led over 1f out: r.o* **5/2**[1]
3043 **2** *1 1/2* **Hello Roberto**[33] 5931 2-8-12 **77** KGhunowa[(7)] 7 77
(MJPolglase) *chsd ldrs: swtchd lft over 3f out: pushed along 1/2-way: rdn and ev ch ins fnl f: unable qck nr fin* **9/2**[3]
1451 **3** *1* **Fission**[124] 3938 2-9-7 **79** (b) SWKelly 4 76
(JAOsborne) *bmpd s: sn led: hdd over 1f out: styd on same pce ins fnl f* **7/2**[2]
1505 **4** *3* **Demolition Molly**[110] 4317 2-9-2 **77** LFletcher[(3)] 8 63
(RFMarvin) *w ldrs: rdn and ev ch over 1f out: wknd ins fnl f* **8/1**
011 **5** *1* **Back At De Front (IRE)**[132] 3694 2-8-13 **76** MSavage[(5)] 1 59
(NEBerry) *chsd ldrs: rdn over 1f out: wknd fnl f* **11/1**
405 **6** *1 1/2* **Charlieismydarling**[10] 6097 2-8-7 **65** JFanning 3 42
(JAOsborne) *s.i.s: sn prom: wknd fnl f* **11/2**
4000 **7** *2* **Siegfrieds Night (IRE)**[33] 5931 2-7-9 **56** oh4 LisaJones[(3)] 6 26
(MCChapman) *sn outpcd* **25/1**
654 **8** *2* **Ciacole**[134] 3638 2-8-12 **70** JoannaBadger 2 33
(SCWilliams) *sn outpcd* **14/1**
62.30 secs (2.00) **Going Correction** +0.20s/f (Slow) **8** Ran SP% **114.3**
Speed ratings: **92,89,88,83,81 79,76,72**CSF £13.94 CT £38.40 TOTE £3.90: £2.10, £1.80, £1.70; EX 17.90.
**Owner** F Jeffers **Bred** Farrington Bloodstock **Trained** Middleham Moor, N Yorks

**FOCUS**
A fair nursery run at a sound pace.

**NOTEBOOK**
**Blue Power(IRE)**put his proven stamina to good use and scored decisively. He was moving strongly in the straight up the stands' side rail and when his rider pressed the button , the response was immediate. Although the handicapper will react to this success, he looks to have more to come as he is lightly-raced and may now looks ready for a step back up to six furlongs.
**Hello Roberto**, who had arguably shown her best form on this surface in October, ran a solid race on her return. She could not match the winner at the weights inside the last furlong, but will not always run into such a rival and she is well worth looking for next time out.
**Fission**had every chance if good enough but found her lack of a recent run and the weight concession beyond her in the closing stages. She will come on for this outing.
**Demolition Molly**adapted to this surface well on her All-Weather bow, but ran as though the outing was much needed.
**Back At De Front(IRE)**never looked a serious threat on her first run since July. She may be a little high in the weights after winning two weak races in the summer on turf, but will be better suited by six furlongs.

## 6153 BETDIRECT.CO.UK MAIDEN STKS 1m (F)
**2:00** (2:01) (D ) 3-Y-O **£2,212** (£632; £316) **Stalls** Low

Form RPR
-043 **1** **Najaaba (USA)**[10] 6100 3-8-4 56 BReilly[(5)] 3 61
(MissJFeilden) *midfield: hdwy on inner over 3f out: swtchd rt and effrt to chal over 1f out: sn rdn and styd on to ld wl ins last* **3/1**[1]
0343 **2** *1 3/4* **Magic Mamma's Too**[14] 6064 3-9-0 53 DMernagh 8 63
(TDBarron) *cl up: led 2f out and sn rdn: drvn over 1f out: hdd and no ex wl ins last* **9/2**[3]
4304 **3** *6* **Pirouettes (IRE)**[10] 6094 3-8-9 55 MFenton 12 46
(MissGayKelleway) *chsd ldrs on outer: rdn along 2f out: styd on u.p appr last* **8/1**
5242 **4** *2 1/2* **Jarraaf**[66] 5376 3-9-0 62 RWinston 14 46
(JWUnett) *in tch: hdwy to chse ldrs 2f out: sn rdn and kpt on same pce* **5/1**
0053 **5** *3* **Danger Bird (IRE)**[29] 5969 3-8-9 50 ACulhane 7 35
(RHollinshead) *stdd s: in rr whn bmpd after 2f: styd on fnl 2f: nvr a factor* **20/1**
**6** *1 1/2* **Have Some Fun** 3-9-0 IMongan 11 37
(PRChamings) *chsd ldrs: rdn over 2f out: grad wknd* **10/1**
0645 **7** *3 1/2* **Silver Crystal (IRE)**[11] 6086 3-8-6 50 (p) LisaJones[(3)] 13 25
(MrsNMacauley) *in tch: rdn along 3f out: wknd fnl 2f* **25/1**
2- **8** *2* **Blue Mariner**[503] 3277 3-9-0 KDalgleish 4 26
(PWHarris) *dwlt: chsd along and making grnd whn bmpd and hmpd after 2f: bhd after* **4/1**[2]
0 **9** *3* **Gwazi**[132] 3700 3-9-0 (t) SWKelly 1 20
(MissDAMchale) *sn outpcd and a rr* **66/1**
06 **10** *1 3/4* **Fantasmic River (IRE)**[130] 3763 3-8-9 RFfrench 9 11
(BSmart) *bhd fr 1/2-way* **50/1**
0 **11** *1* **Trofana Falcon**[14] 6067 3-9-0 MTebbutt 6 14
(HJCollingridge) *a rr* **40/1**
5402 **12** *1 1/4* **Kustom Kit For Her**[183] 2225 3-8-9 53 (b[1]) JBramhill 5 7
(SRBowring) *led: rdn along 3f out: hdd 2f out and sn wknd* **25/1**
0040 **13** *8* **Matriarchal**[14] 6067 3-8-9 38 KimTinkler 2 —
(DonEnricoIncisa) *a bhd* **100/1**
-000 **14** *17* **Torzal**[15] 6057 3-8-11 35 LFletcher[(3)] 10 —
(RFMarvin) *a bhd* **100/1**
1m 45.6s (1.00) **Going Correction** +0.25s/f (Slow) **14** Ran SP% **120.4**
Speed ratings: **105,103,97,94,91 90,86,84,81,80 79,77,69,52**CSF £15.20 TOTE £4.70: £1.40, £1.90, £2.20; EX 17.60.
**Owner** A K Sparks **Bred** Darley Stud Management, L L C **Trained** Exning, Suffolk
■ Stewards Enquiry : D Mernagh one-day ban: used whip with excessive frequency (Dec 19)

**FOCUS**
Najabaa relishes the step up to a mile and gets off the mark to land a gamble in the process.

**NOTEBOOK**
**Najaaba(USA)**lost her maiden tag at the seventh attempt and landed a gamble in the process. She has looked an improved performer on this surface and this trip looks to be her optimum. A win in handicap company could well now be on the cards this winter.
**Magic Mamma's Too**constantly hits the frame in this sphere and is reliable on that front, but has now gone 21 runs without a win and, although he was well clear of the rest on this occasion, he is one to avoid.
**Pirouettes(IRE)**did not stay this trip too well, but ran another sound race nonetheless.
**Jarraaf**looks a better horse at Wolverhampton.
**Blue Mariner**was beaten a long way out and does not look a natural for this surface. He is surely capable of better than this, but has a lot to prove now.

## 6154 LITTLEWOODS BET DIRECT STKS SHOWCASE H'CAP 5f (F)
**2:30** (2:30) (C ) (0-100,98) 3-Y-O+ **£6,929** (£2,132; £1,066; £533) **Stalls** High

Form RPR
0254 **1** **Zarzu**[13] 6078 4-8-4 **79** RThomas[(5)] 16 92
(CRDore) *hld up: hdwy over 1f out: r.o to ld wl ins fnl f* **14/1**
0001 **2** *1 1/4* **Bond Playboy**[22] 6014 3-9-3 **87** IMongan 5 96
(BSmart) *chsd ldrs: outpcd 3f out: hdwy u.p over 1f out: ev ch ins fnl f: styd on* **14/1**
0013 **3** *1/2* **Dancing Mystery**[20] 6030 9-9-5 **89** (b) SCarson 11 96
(EAWheeler) *w ldr: led over 3f out: hdd and unable qck wl ins fnl f* **10/1**
0526 **4** *nk* **Quito (IRE)**[17] 6050 6-10-0 **98** (b) ACulhane 1 104
(DWChapman) *chsd ldrs: hdwy over 1f out: r.o* **11/2**[1]
0001 **5** *shd* **Grandma Lily (IRE)**[15] 6056 5-8-2 **72** GDuffield 3 77
(MCChapman) *chsd ldrs: rdn over 1f out: ev ch ins fnl f: styd on same pce* **14/1**
0001 **6** *hd* **Trinculo (IRE)**[20] 6030 6-9-5 **92** (p) J-PGuillambert[(3)] 4 97
(NPLittmoden) *chsd ldrs: rdn and ev ch ins fnl f: no ex* **13/2**[2]
23-0 **7** *2* **Magic Glade**[13] 6078 4-8-10 **80** MFenton 14 78
(CRDore) *chsd ldrs: rdn over 1f out: styd on same pce* **66/1**
4434 **8** *nk* **Landing Strip (IRE)**[20] 6030 3-8-7 **77** JTate 6 74
(JMPEustace) *mid-div: hdwy u.p 2f out: no ex fnl f* **9/1**
5012 **9** *hd* **Quiet Times (IRE)**[22] 6014 4-8-7 **77** (b) RWinston 9 73
(KARyan) *sn outpcd: styd on ins fnl f: nrst fin* **12/1**
0641 **10** *1 1/4* **Polish Emperor (USA)**[11] 6080 3-8-7 **77** (b) JFanning 7 69
(PWHarris) *led: hdd over 3f out: wknd over 1f out* **7/1**[3]
6000 **11** *1/2* **Sundried Tomato**[20] 6030 4-9-3 **90** LFletcher[(3)] 12 80
(PWHiatt) *chsd ldrs: rdn 3f out: wknd over 1f out* **16/1**
1000 **12** *1* **Fromsong (IRE)**[46] 5732 5-9-6 **90** GBaker 8 76
(BRMillman) *chsd ldrs to 1/2-way* **20/1**
4036 **13** *hd* **Now Look Here**[20] 6030 7-8-7 **77** (b) GGibbons 10 63
(BAMcmahon) *chsd ldrs over 3f* **12/1**
1200 **14** *1 1/4* **Massey**[20] 6030 7-9-4 **95** PMakin[(7)] 13 76
(TDBarron) *sn outpcd* **25/1**

1001 **15** 2 ½ **Woodland Blaze (IRE)**[11] 6081 4-8-5 **78**........................ LPKeniry(3) 15 51
(PRChamings) *sn outpcd* **20/1**
6000 **16** 3 **Lincoln Dancer (IRE)**[36] 5908 6-9-1 **85**........................ ANicholls 2 47
(DNicholls) *sn outpcd* **25/1**
60.05 secs (-0.25) **Going Correction** +0.20s/f (Slow) **16** Ran SP% **120.3**
Speed ratings: **110,108,107,106,106 106,103,102,102,100 99,97,97,95,91 86**CSF £181.26 CT £2139.75 TOTE £16.80: £3.60, £5.20, £3.30, £1.90; EX 356.80 Trifecta £2764.30.
**Owner** Page, Pickering, Taylor, Ward, Marsh **Bred** Compton Down Stud **Trained** West Pinchbeck, Lincs

**FOCUS**
A valuable and very competitive sprint run at a generous pace.

**NOTEBOOK**
**Zarzu**won this very competitive sprint in grand style. He is always best off a strong pace, which he got, and this was his first-ever win a handicap. There was an awful lot to like about this victory and, providing he does not shoot up in the weights for this, he looks set for further success in this sphere.
**Bond Playboy**was taken off his feet over this trip, but was another to prosper off the strong pace and will be even better back over his preffered six furlongs.
**Dancing Mystery**, despite looking on a stiff mark on the sand, again aquitted himself well under a forceful ride. He paid for helping set the generous pace this time and had no answer to the winner when challenged, but is in great heart and should be gaining compensation soon.
**Quito(IRE)**is a very tough sort and has had a very successful year, but has never convinced over this trip at any stage in his career. He got taken off his feet early and ran well in the circumstances. He can win off this mark over further.
**Grandma Lily(IRE)**confirmed her well-being with a sound effort in this better company and should not be long in winning once more when her sights are lowered.
**Trinculo(IRE)**failed to follow-up his brave course-and-distance win last time, racing off a 4lb higher mark. This was fairly disappointing as he looked to have everything in his favour, but he was not beaten far and should continue to pay his way in these events.

## 6155 BET DIRECT IN RUNNING SKY TEXT 293 (S) STKS (DIV II) 6f (F)
**3:00** (3:02) (G ) 3-Y-O+ **£2,079** (£594; £297) **Stalls** Low

Form RPR
0004 **1** **Polar Haze**[123] 3969 6-8-12 46...............................(v) RPrice 15 57
(MrsLydiaPearce) *in tch: hdwy 2f out: rdn over 1f out: styd on to ld ins last* **14/1**
3030 **2** 1 **Lay Down Sally (IRE)**[119] 4057 5-8-4 47........................ LFletcher(3) 13 49
(JWhite) *towards rr and rdn along 1/2-way: wd st: gd hdwy wl over 1f out: rdna nd edgd lft ent last: kpt on* **8/1**
0006 **3** ½ **Catchthebatch**[3] 6136 7-8-9 50................................ DCorby(3) 16 53
(MJWallace) *cl up: rdn to ld wl over 1f out: drvn and hdd ins last: no ex* **7/1**
0000 **4** 1 ¼ **Headland (USA)**[49] 5685 5-9-5 71...............................(b) ACulhane 11 56
(DWChapman) *towards rr: wd st: hdwy wl over 1f out: sn rdn and kpt on fnl f* **9/2**[1]
-050 **5** 1 **Bells Boy's**[25] 5998 4-8-12 38...............................(p) GParkin 2 46
(KARyan) *hld up: gd hdwy on inner over 2f out: rdn to chse ldrs over 1f out: wknd ent last* **33/1**
0/00 **6** ½ **Ejay**[43] 5799 4-8-4 45........................................ LisaJones(3) 10 39
(JulianPoulton) *towards rr: hdwy 2f out: sn rdn and kpt on ins last: nrst fin* **33/1**
0000 **7** ½ **Bond Domingo**[129] 3797 4-8-5 40...............................(b) MStainton(7) 5 43
(BSmart) *chsd ldrs: rdn 2f out: wknd appr last* **25/1**
0200 **8** 1 **Mr Spliffy (IRE)**[18] 6038 4-8-5 52........................ AReilly(7) 3 40
(KRBurke) *chsd ldrs: rdn 2f out: no imp appr last* **6/1**[3]
0600 **9** 2 **Boisdale (IRE)**[14] 6063 5-9-5 52........................ ANicholls 8 41
(DNicholls) *led: rdn along 2f out: sn hdd & wknd* **7/1**
5000 **10** 8 **Above Board**[312] 424 8-8-5 43........................ KGhunowa(7) 9 10
(RFMarvin) *a rr* **50/1**
2606 **11** nk **Tefi**[167] 2692 5-8-12 43...............................(b) JEdmunds 12 9
(JBalding) *cl: rdn along 3f out: sn wknd* **12/1**
0000 **12** shd **Goodwood Promise**[1] 6143 4-8-7 40........................ MSavage(5) 6 9
(NEBerry) *cl up: rdn over 2f out: sn wknd* **66/1**
600/ **13** 1 **Katali**[773] 5503 6-8-7 35........................ JFanning 1 1
(ABailey) *a bhd* **11/1**
060/ **14** 1 **Second Generation (IRE)**[950] 1072 6-8-12 37........................ CCatlin 4 3
(RJHodges) *a towards rr* **50/1**
**15** 1 ½ **Royal Ovation**[141] 3476 4-8-12 30........................ IMongan 7 —
(NPLittmoden) *sn rdn along and outpce: a b ehind* **5/1**[2]
1m 18.71s (1.91) **Going Correction** +0.25s/f (Slow) **15** Ran SP% **123.1**
Speed ratings: **97,95,95,93,92 91,90,89,86,76 75,75,74,72,70**CSF £118.15 TOTE £13.00: £2.00, £3.40, £3.30; EX 103.00.There was no bid for the winner.
**Owner** M M Foulger **Bred** Miss S E Hall **Trained** Newmarket, Suffolk

**FOCUS**
A poor contest.

**NOTEBOOK**
**Polar Haze**, with the visor back on, hinted at a return to form when dropped to this level last time and outstayed his rivals close home to win his first race since September 2002. This is clearly his level nowadays, but a recent change of yard seems to have had a positive effect and he should improve further for the run.
**Lay Down Sally(IRE)**may have needed this first outing since August, however, she did not look keen when asked to win her race and is untrustworthy.
**Catchthebatch**found this too stiff test, but came through to lead nicely before tiring and will be seen to a better effect when either dropped in trip or racing over a sharper circuit.
**Headland(USA)**failed to capitalise on a drop in grade and this must go down as a most disappointing effort. In his defence however, all of his best form is at Wolverhampton.

## 6156 LITTLEWOODSPOKER.COM H'CAP 1m 6f (F)
**3:30** (3:30) (D ) (0-80,80) 3-Y-O+ **£3,052** (£872; £436) **Stalls** Low

Form RPR
0062 **1** **Bid For Fame (USA)**[6] 6123 6-9-9 **80**........................ PMulrennan(5) 6 98+
(NTinkler) *trckd ldrs: led over 1f out: rdn clr: eased nr fin* **4/5**[1]
0125 **2** 5 **Victory Quest (IRE)**[113] 4244 3-8-4 **63**...............................(v) CCatlin 10 74
(MrsSLamyman) *trckd ldrs: racd keenly: led 10f out: hdd over 2f out: rdn and ev ch over 1f out: styd on same pce* **100/1**
4024 **3** 4 **Court Of Appeal**[6] 6121 6-8-13 **70**...............................(t) THamilton(5) 9 76
(BEllison) *a.p: chsd ldr over 4f out: led over 2f out: hdd & wknd over 1f out* **12/1**
235- **4** 1 ½ **Northern Nymph**[477] 4002 4-9-4 **77**............. StephanieHollinshead(7) 12 81
(RHollinshead) *hld up: hdwy 1/2-way: wknd wl over 1f out* **66/1**
5223 **5** 12 **Glory Quest (USA)**[6] 6123 6-9-11 **77**........................ ACulhane 5 65
(MissGayKelleway) *hld up in tch: pushed along over 5f out: sn outpcd* **12/1**
2523 **6** 7 **Digger (IRE)**[6] 6121 4-9-6 **72**...............................(p) IMongan 1 51
(MissGayKelleway) *plld hrd and prom: wknd over 3f out* **8/1**[3]
0200 **7** 8 **Sea Plume**[13] 6079 4-9-4 **70**........................ GDuffield 3 39
(LadyHerries) *chsd ldrs over 9f* **14/1**
5002 **8** 3 **Majlis (IRE)**[6] 6121 6-7-13 **58**........................ PMakin(7) 8 23
(RMHCowell) *hld up: a bhd* **13/2**[2]
0532 **9** hd **Paula Lane**[162] 2861 3-8-8 **72**........................ JFMcDonald(5) 7 37
(RCurtis) *hld up: hdwy 1/2-way: wknd over 3f out* **50/1**
0-00 **10** ¾ **Known Maneuver (USA)**[20] 6033 5-7-8 **53**........................ RoryMoore(7) 11 17
(MCChapman) *prom 8f* **150/1**
5004 **11** ¾ **Simple Ideals (USA)**[15] 6061 9-7-12 **50** oh23........................ KimTinkler 2 13
(DonEnricoIncisa) *chsd ldrs: lost pl 9f out: bhd fnl 5f* **100/1**
6001 **12** dist **Sudden Flight (IRE)**[74] 5189 6-10-0 **80**........................ RHavlin 4 —
(RIngram) *led 4f: sn lost pl: bhd fnl 5f* **9/1**
3m 8.51s (-1.09) **Going Correction** +0.25s/f (Slow)
**WFA** 3 from 4yo+ 7lb **12** Ran SP% **118.1**
Speed ratings: **113,110,107,107,100 96,91,89,89,89 88,—**CSF £150.87 CT £651.68 TOTE £1.60: £1.10, £13.60, £3.70; EX 102.10 Place 6 £311.96, Place 5 £156.49.
**Owner** Elite Racing Club **Bred** Swifty Farms, Don Myers And Dana Myers **Trained** Langton, N Yorks

**FOCUS**
A fair handicap which should produce winners on this surface during the winter.

**NOTEBOOK**
**Bid For Fame(USA)**looked only to have to repeat his last run at this track last time to score, and so it proved. Making his first start for his new yard, he dug deep in the straight and pulled right away from his rivals under top weight. He is due a break, but will no doubt continue to hit the frame in this type of event when returning over this trip or further.
**Victory Quest(IRE)**stuck to his task well after being headed in the straight and will be all the better for the run. This is his trip and it was a positive All-Weather debut.
**Court Of Appeal**was running a big race until he emptied over a trip that looks to stretch him on the Fibresand. He ran his best race to date on this track though and could score when dropped in trip.
**Northern Nymph**showed up well for most of the way, until understandably tiring having been off the track since August 2002.
**Sudden Flight(IRE)** *Official explanation: trainer said gelding was unable to dominate and subsequently lost interest*
T/Jkpt: Not won. T/Plt: £465.00 to a £1 stake. Pool: £45,451.95. 71.35 winning tickets. T/Qpdt: £12.20 to a £1 stake. Pool: £5,597.00. 338.00 winning tickets. CR

# 6127 LINGFIELD (L-H)
## Wednesday, December 10

**OFFICIAL GOING: Standard**

## 6157 LYNHURST PRESS H'CAP (DIV I) 1m 2f (P)
**11:50** (11:50) (E ) (0-75,75) 3-Y-O+ **£2,299** (£657; £328) **Stalls** Low

Form RPR
0514 **1** **Ryan's Future (IRE)**[11] 6093 3-9-8 **75**........................ NChalmers(5) 6 86+
(JAkehurst) *t.k.h and hld up in rr: str hdwy over 1f out and fin fast to ld nr fin* **11/2**[3]
0022 **2** ¾ **Lyrical Way**[14] 6076 4-8-9 **54**...............................(b) EAhern 12 64
(PRChamings) *lw: racd wd and settled in mid-div: hdwsay over 3f out: ledc 2f out: r.o: hdd nr fin* **9/2**[2]
6153 **3** nk **True Companion**[14] 6073 4-8-12 **60**........................ J-PGuillambert(3) 9 69
(NPLittmoden) *hld up: hdwy on outside over 2f out: r.o strly fnl f: nvr nrr* **3/1**[1]
4306 **4** 2 **Easter Ogil (IRE)**[4] 6130 8-9-4 **63**........................ VSlattery 14 69
(JaneSouthcombe) *racd wd and hld up wl in rr: gd hdwy appr fnl f: nvr nrr* **10/1**
0030 **5** ½ **Rasid (USA)**[11] 6093 5-9-6 **65**........................ DaneO'Neill 10 70
(CADwyer) *tok t.k.h: hld up in rr: rdn and hdwy over 1f out: nvr nrr* **11/1**
0000 **6** ¾ **Street Life (IRE)**[242] 1020 5-9-8 **67**........................ MFenton 11 71
(WJMusson) *hld up: gd hdwy on ins 2f out: werakened ins fnl furloong* **14/1**
22-6 **7** nk **Sammy's Shuffle**[14] 6073 8-8-12 **57**...............................(b) IMongan 5 60
(JamiePoulton) *b: hld up: hdwy 3f out: rdn over 1f out: one pce* **8/1**
40B0 **8** 1 **Indian Blaze**[14] 6076 9-8-0 **52**........................ RoryMoore(7) 3 53
(AndrewReid) *b: b.hind: prom tl fdd over 1f out* **16/1**
2606 **9** 1 ¼ **Coronado Forest (USA)**[26] 5996 4-9-2 **61**........................ ACulhane 13 60
(MRHoad) *a in rr* **16/1**
5560 **10** ¾ **Anemos (IRE)**[14] 6073 8-8-5 **55**...............................(be) BReilly(5) 8 53
(PWD'Arcy) *hld up: effrt 2f out: sn btn* **16/1**
1000 **11** 1 **Todlea (IRE)**[11] 6098 3-9-13 **75**........................ SWKelly 1 71
(JAOsborne) *led tl hdd 2f out: rdn an d sn weaqkened* **25/1**
0406 **12** 8 **Icannshift (IRE)**[118] 4131 3-9-8 **70**........................ PDoe 4 51
(SDow) *chsd ldrs tl wknd qckly 2f out* **33/1**
1050 **13** 11 **Frankskips**[228] 1233 4-9-10 **69**........................ AClark 7 31
(MissBSanders) *prom tl wknd over 2f out* **33/1**
4-00 **14** 1 **Silistra**[4] 6131 4-9-6 **65**...............................(b) CCatlin 2 25
(MrsLCJewell) *trckd ldr tl wknd over 2f out* **50/1**
2m 8.11s (0.72) **Going Correction** +0.05s/f (Slow)
**WFA** 3 from 4yo+ 3lb **14** Ran SP% **123.1**
Speed ratings: **99,98,98,96,96 95,95,94,93,92 92,85,76,76**CSF £30.19 CT £90.98 TOTE £5.40: £2.30, £1.60, £1.90; EX 22.60.
**Owner** Vimal Khosla **Bred** A F O'Callaghan **Trained** Epsom, Surrey

**FOCUS**
An average handicap and there was no pace on early in the race.

**NOTEBOOK**
**Ryan's Future(IRE)** was weak in the market, but he quickened up nicely under a good ride. This was his second run for Akehurst and he settled better than he did on his first start for the trainer, which allowed his jockey to ride a more patient race. He has not been over-raced and should be open to more improvement.
**Lyrical Way** had to settle for the runner-up spot for a third consecutive race. He is in good form at present, but his style of racing will always make him vulnerable to fast finishers.
**True Companion**, who was proven on the surface and at the trip, again ran well and appeared to have no excuses. He should hit the target before long.
**Easter Ogil(IRE)** came from a long way back and was closing all the time. He won five times on this surface early in the year at up to a mile, but seems to need all of this trip now.
**Rasid(USA)** ran better than he did over course and distance last time.
**Street Life(IRE)**, whom the run will bring on, is one to keep an eye on after this most encouraging effort, which was his first start since April.
**Sammy's Shuffle** has had plenty of chances off this sort of mark and may need a little help from the Handicapper.

## 6158 BET DIRECT NO Q MAIDEN STKS 1m (P)
**12:20** (12:21) (D ) 2-Y-O **£3,146** (£899; £449) **Stalls** High

Form RPR
**1** **Jake The Snake (IRE)** 2-9-0 ........................ IMongan 6 76+
(CNAllen) *w'like: scope: lw: trckd ldrs: led over 2f out: kpt up to work: edgd lft ins fnl f: r.o wl* **2/1**[1]

0 **2** *3* **Secret Place**[14] 6072 2-9-0 ........ EAhern 4 69
(EALDunlop) *trckd ldrs: rideen and r.o to chse wnr fnl f* **25/1**

0 **3** *1* **Albinus**[34] 5932 2-9-0 ........ DaneO'Neill 11 67
(AMBalding) *slowly away: hdwy on outside to trck ldrs after 3f: lost pl 2f our: r.o fnl f* **20/1**

63 **4** *nk* **Nantucket Sound (USA)**[43] 5813 2-9-0 ........ PaulEddery 7 66
(MCPipe) *led tl hdd over 2f out: rdn and kpt on fnl f* **20/1**

23 **5** *shd* **Bienvenue**[14] 6074 2-8-9 ........ ADaly 10 61
(MPTregoning) *in tch tl outpcd over 2f out: rallied and r.o fnl f* **4/1**[2]

3 **6** *shd* **Boxgrove (FR)**[14] 6072 2-9-0 ........ JFEgan 8 66
(CEBrittain) *mid-div: rdn 1/2-way: sme hdwy fnl f* **2/1**[1]

0 **7** *½* **Prince Valentine**[14] 6074 2-9-0 ........ MTebbutt 3 65
(DBFeek) *sn in rr: hdwy on ins over 2f out: hmpd ins fnl f: no ex* **25/1**

04 **8** *hd* **Blue Java**[16] 6059 2-8-11 ........ LFletcher(3) 12 64
(HMorrison) *trckd ldrs: rdn over 2f out: a hld after* **10/1**[3]

45 **9** *½* **Okoboji (IRE)**[14] 6072 2-9-0 ........ PFitzsimons 1 63
(MPTregoning) *s.i.s: hld up in rr: nvr nr to chal* **14/1**

**10** *3 ½* **Separated (USA)** 2-8-9 ........ MFenton 2 50
(EALDunlop) *unf: scope: slowly away: sn rdn along: a in rr* **25/1**

0 **11** *shd* **Embassy Sweets (USA)**[8] 6118 2-8-9 ........ ACulhane 5 50
(PFICole) *hld in rr: nvr on terms* **20/1**

00 **12** *dist* **Skater Boy**[43] 5813 2-8-11 ........ DCorby(3) 9 —
(MissSheenaWest) *sn bhd: t.o* **100/1**

1m 39.88s (0.37) **Going Correction** +0.05s/f (Slow) **12** Ran SP% **129.2**
Speed ratings: **100,97,96,95,95 95,95,94,94,90 90,**—CSF £70.44 TOTE £2.80: £1.40, £7.20, £11.00; EX 108.50.
**Owner** T P Ramsden **Bred** J F Tuthill **Trained** Newmarket, Suffolk

**FOCUS**
The early pace was not strong, but the time was respectable.

**NOTEBOOK**
**Jake The Snake(IRE)** was well backed in the morning and the confidence proved well placed as he ran out a nice winner. He hit the front soon enough and, despite running green, never looked like being caught. He will reportedly by put away now, before being prepared for a crack at the 2000 Guineas and the Derby, although those plans look pie in the sky on the back of this.
**Secret Place** stepped up on his debut, reversing form with both Boxgrove and Okoboji on their latest running. He is going the right way and will not always find such a smart opponent.
**Albinus** appears to have a bright future. He was outpaced when the race got serious, but came home well and will have little trouble making an impact over middle distances next year.
**Nantucket Sound(USA)** deserves some credit for the way he stuck to the task down the far rail after leading for much of the way.
**Bienvenue** is now eligible for handicaps.
**Boxgrove(FR)** already looks in need of farther, but does appear to have a future.
**Prince Valentine** may have even been fourth if he had not been hampered inside the final furlong.
**Okoboji(IRE)** does not look high on ability.
**Skater Boy** *Official explanation: trainer said gelding spread a plate*

## 6159 BET DIRECT ON ATTHERACES INTERACTIVE NOVICE STKS 5f (P)
12:50 (12:50) (D ) 2-Y-O £3,136 (£896; £448) Stalls High

Form RPR

**1** **Treasure Cay** 2-8-8 ........(e[1]) PaulEddery 1 74
(PWD'Arcy) *w'like: s.i.s: sn in tch: hdwy 2f out: led jst ins fnl f: rdn out* **20/1**

3340 **2** *½* **Oro Verde**[8] 6118 2-9-5 91 ........ DaneO'Neill 8 83
(RHannon) *trckd ldr: led briefly ent fnl f: nt qckn fnl 100yds* **7/2**[2]

**3** *1* **Pass Go** 2-8-8 ........ EAhern 6 68
(GAButler) *leggy: lw: in tch: hung lft ins fnl 2f: nt qckn ins fnl f* **4/1**[3]

50U **4** *hd* **Ragged Jack (IRE)**[22] 6018 2-8-12 ........ CCatlin 3 71
(GAButler) *slowly away and wl in rr tl rdn and rapid hdwy appr fnl f: fin wl: nvr nrr* **12/1**

06 **5** *1* **Averami**[28] 5977 2-8-4 ........ LPKeniry(3) 4 62
(AMBalding) *in rr: rdn and mde sme late hdwy* **25/1**

0632 **6** *½* **Trotters Bottom**[41] 5835 2-8-13 87 ........ J-PGuillambert(3) 10 69
(AndrewReid) *b: b.hind: racd wd: no hdwy fnl 2f* **5/2**[1]

3104 **7** *nk* **Rise**[11] 6090 2-8-11 81 ........(b) IMongan 2 63
(AndrewReid) *b: b.hind: led tl rdn ands hdd ent fnl f: wknd qckly* **7/2**[2]

**8** *4* **Midmaar (IRE)**[54] 2-9-2 ........ FNorton 5 52
(MWigham) *trckd ldrs: rdn 1/2-way: wknd 2f out* **12/1**

**9** *¾* **Pat's Nemisis (IRE)**[87] 4911 2-8-2 ........ NChalmers(5) 7 40
(BRJohnson) *a struggling in rr* **66/1**

**10** *3* **Dont Let Go** 2-8-3 ........ JBramhill 9 24
(CRDore) *unf: scope: in tch on outside for 3f* **100/1**

60.25 secs (0.47) **Going Correction** +0.05s/f (Slow) **10** Ran SP% **119.5**
Speed ratings: **98,97,95,95,93 92,92,86,84,80**CSF £89.48 TOTE £69.70: £8.80, £1.50, £2.60; EX 112.70.
**Owner** Bigwigs Bloodstock IV **Bred** D R Tucker **Trained** Newmarket, Suffolk

**FOCUS**
With two of the three debutants finishing first and third the form is probably not that strong for this type of event.

**NOTEBOOK**
**Treasure Cay**, wearing an eyeshield for his debut, showed a good attitude and ran out a nice winner. However, beating a horse rated 91, albeit getting 11lb, will hardly encourage the Handicapper to give him a workable mark. *Official explanation: , wearing an eyeshield for his debut, showed a good attitude and ran out a nice winner. However, beating a horse rated 91, albeit getting 11lb, will hardly encourage the Handicapper to give him a workable mark.*
**Oro Verde**, who has some good form in the book, was given an aggressive ride on this drop back to the minimum distance. He is probably better over six furlongs, but is going to be hard to place at three. *Official explanation: , who has some good form in the book, was given an aggressive ride on this drop back to the minimum distance. He is probably better over six furlongs, but is going to be hard to place at three.*
**Pass Go**, a quite athletic colt and half-brother to 1000 Guineas runner-up Princess Ellen, showed an ugly head carriage and, although he has ability, may not be the most straightforward. He should come into his own over farther. *Official explanation: , a quite athletic colt and half-brother to 1000 Guineas runner-up Princess Ellen, showed an ugly head carriage and, although he has ability, may not be the most straightforward. He should come into his own over farther.*
**Ragged Jack(IRE)** is another who will appreciate farther and is one to keep on the right side of. *Official explanation: is another who will appreciate farther and is one to keep on the right side of.*
**Averami** will be better when stepped up in trip. *Official explanation: will be better when stepped up in trip.*
**Trotters Bottom** could not find the necessary acceleration down the straight and is probably better over six furlongs. *Official explanation: could not find the necessary acceleration down the straight and is probably better over six furlongs.*
**Rise** set a good pace, but was, predictably, unable to hold the finishers. She weakened quickly, but that may have as much to do with being tightened up as anything else. *Official explanation: set a good pace, but was, predictably, unable to hold the finishers. She weakened quickly, but that may have as much to do with being tightened up as anything else.*

## 6160 BET DIRECT PRESS RED TO BET NURSERY 7f (P)
1:25 (1:25) (D ) (0-85,82) 2-Y-O £3,150 (£900; £450) Stalls Low

Form RPR

6106 **1** **Off Beat (USA)**[46] 5751 2-9-0 73 ........(b) SCarson 8 78
(RFJohnsonHoughton) *hld up in rr: smooth hdwy on ins 2f out: r.o wl to ld ins fnl f* **33/1**

0013 **2** *1* **Fools Entire**[14] 6077 2-8-5 64 ........ FNorton 6 67
(JAGilbert) *a.p: rdn 2f out: kpt on gamely to go 2nd nr fin* **14/1**

0051 **3** *½* **Anuvasteel**[8] 6115 2-9-2 82 6ex ........ RoryMoore(7) 5 83
(NACallaghan) *lw: hmpd after 2f: sn rcvrd: hdwy on outside over 2f out: rdn and nt qckn ins fnl f* **15/8**[1]

3002 **4** *½* **Pregnant Pause (IRE)**[28] 5979 2-8-6 65 ........ JFEgan 13 65
(SKirk) *led: rdn over 1f out: hdd ins fnl f: no ex cl home* **7/1**

065 **5** *nk* **Lord Of The Sea (IRE)**[56] 5572 2-9-0 73 ........ IMongan 12 72
(JamiePoulton) *hld up in rr: hdwy appr fnl f: r.o: nvr nrr* **33/1**

2004 **6** *hd* **Imperium**[8] 6118 2-9-6 79 ........ RWinston 7 78
(BJMeehan) *chsd ldr tl one pce fnl f* **16/1**

431 **7** *½* **Disengage (USA)**[35] 5923 2-9-4 77 ........ EAhern 9 75
(GAButler) *a.p: ev ch 1f out: fdd ins fnl f* **5/1**[2]

4443 **8** *5* **Turkish Delight**[11] 6097 2-8-9 68 ........ MTebbutt 10 53
(DMorris) *racd mid-div: no hdwy fnl 2f* **25/1**

5531 **9** *shd* **Kabreet**[22] 6020 2-9-1 74 ........ MFenton 4 59
(EALDunlop) *lw: hmpd after 2f but remained in tch tl wknd over 1f out* **11/2**[3]

000 **10** *1* **Miss Julie Jay (IRE)**[104] 4531 2-7-8 58 ........ JFMcDonald(5) 3 40
(NoelTChance) *slowly away and a in rr* **100/1**

2521 **11** *1 ¼* **Fadeela (IRE)**[12] 6083 2-8-10 74 ........(e) BReilly(5) 11 53
(PWD'Arcy) *prom tl wknd over 1f out* **8/1**

0502 **12** *nk* **Lady Predominant**[27] 5990 2-7-12 57 oh2 ........ DKinsella 15 35
(AndrewReid) *b: b.hind: racd wd: a towards rr* **20/1**

5040 **13** *9* **Lord Greystoke (IRE)**[26] 5994 2-8-2 61 ........ JMackay 14 17
(CPMorlock) *mid-vision: rdn 1/2-way: sn bhd* **40/1**

000 **14** *1 ¼* **Magico**[55] 5590 2-8-1 60 ........ CCatlin 16 13
(AMBalding) *slowly away: a stgruggling in rr* **50/1**

14 **15** *dist* **Western Roots**[18] 6048 2-9-7 80 ........ ACulhane 1 —
(PFICole) *swtg: prom on ins whn hmpd after 2f: nt rcvr and virtually p.u 1/2-way: t.o* **14/1**

1m 26.29s (0.29) **Going Correction** +0.05s/f (Slow) **15** Ran SP% **129.5**
Speed ratings: **100,98,98,97,97 97,96,90,90,89 88,87,77,76,**—CSF £448.55 CT £1319.23 TOTE £53.90: £14.60, £4.80, £1.70; EX 785.50.
**Owner** Eden Racing (II) **Bred** Rio Claro Thoroughbreds **Trained** Blewbury, Oxon
■ Stewards Enquiry : R Winston five-day ban (extended from four after an appeal): careless riding (Dec 19-26, Jan 8)

**FOCUS**
A good nursery and the pace was sound, but it was a rough race and there were a few hard-luck stories.

**NOTEBOOK**
**Off Beat(USA)**, making his All-Weather debut, sprung something of a surprise. He was helped by the strong pace, but had to show determination to squeeze through a gap next to the rail up the straight. Connections reported the switch to hold-up tactics have brought improvement and he should continue to give a good account in strongly-run races.
**Fools Entire** did not enjoy a trouble-free passage and was shuffled back three out. He stayed on down the straight, but the winner had gone. This was still a fair effort and he is capable of winning in this grade.
**Anuvasteel** was one of those to suffer from scrimmaging early in the race. He did recover, but found the amount of ground he had to make up in the straight beyond him.
**Pregnant Pause(IRE)** deserves a deal of credit as he set a good pace and was only run out of it inside the final furlong.
**Lord Of The Sea(IRE)**, making his handicap debut, showed enough to suggest he is no lost cause.
**Imperium** was judged to have caused the early trouble and his jockey picked up a four-day ban as a result.
**Disengage(USA)** was another who comes out of this with credit as he was one of those to race prominently.
**Kabreet** suffered badly in the early trouble.
**Western Roots** came off worst in the early trouble and was soon eased with his jockey shaking his head in apparent disgust. *Official explanation: trainer said gelding was found to be suffering from a bruised foot*

## 6161 LYNHURST PRESS H'CAP (DIV II) 1m 2f (P)
1:55 (1:55) (E ) (0-75,72) 3-Y-0+ £2,299 (£657; £328) Stalls Low

Form RPR

3103 **1** **Hip Hop Harry**[11] 6093 3-9-10 72 ........ EAhern 6 83
(EALDunlop) *a in tch gng wl: hdwy on outside 2f out: led 1f out: hdd ins fnl f: rallied to ld post: all out* **5/1**[2]

055 **2** *shd* **Ember Days**[14] 6076 4-8-7 52 ........ SWKelly 3 63
(JLSpearing) *hld up in tch: gd hdwy 2f out: kpt on u.p to ld ins fnl f: hdd post* **10/1**

0415 **3** *2* **Quantum Leap**[11] 6093 6-9-4 63 ........ PaulEddery 14 70
(SDow) *in rr: gd hdwy over 1f out: styd on: nvr nrr* **8/1**

50-0 **4** *nk* **War Owl (USA)**[34] 5933 6-8-8 53 ........ CCatlin 12 60
(IanWilliams) *plld hrd early and wl bhd tl gd hdwy on outside over 2f out: ev ch appr fnlf urlong: kpt on one pce* **14/1**

2100 **5** *hd* **Miss Pebbles (IRE)**[28] 5980 3-9-9 71 ........(p) DaneO'Neill 8 78
(BRJohnson) *hld up in rr: hdwy hdwy 2f out: nt qckn fnl f* **10/1**

0000 **6** *1* **Londoner (USA)**[77] 5152 5-9-6 65 ........ PDoe 11 70
(SDow) *hld up in tch: rdn 2f out: no further hdwy* **25/1**

4100 **7** *nk* **Mister Clinton (IRE)**[89] 4872 6-8-11 56 ........ GCarter 10 60
(DKIvory) *b: a mid-div* **33/1**

0003 **8** *½* **Classic Role**[15] 6068 4-9-13 72 ........ DSweeney 9 75
(RIngram) *led tl rdn and hdd 1f out: wknd qckly* **10/1**

0400 **9** *1 ½* **Esperance (IRE)**[14] 6076 3-8-9 57 ........(p) JMackay 5 58
(JAkehurst) *a towards rr* **14/1**

0005 **10** *nk* **Learned Lad (FR)**[8] 6119 5-9-6 65 ........ IMongan 1 65
(JamiePoulton) *in front rnk tl wknd appr fnl f* **13/2**[3]

1045 **11** *shd* **Gabor**[18] 5720 4-8-9 61 ........(be) HPoulton(7) 4 61
(GLMoore) *lw: chsd ldrs: rdn and wknd 2f out* **14/1**

0053 **12** *4* **Man The Gate**[14] 6076 4-8-13 58 ........ SCarson 2 51
(PDCundell) *t.k.h: chsd ldr wknd over 1f out* **7/2**[1]

0062 **13** *1* **Sophrano (IRE)**[15] 6067 3-9-3 65 ........(v[1]) ACulhane 7 56
(PWHarris) *a in rr* **10/1**

2m 7.98s (0.59) **Going Correction** +0.05s/f (Slow)
**WFA** 3 from 4yo+ 3lb **13** Ran SP% **126.5**
Speed ratings: **99,98,97,97,96 96,95,95,94,94 93,90,89**CSF £58.05 CT £409.95 TOTE £5.10: £2.70, £3.60, £3.00; EX 90.40.
**Owner** Lucayan Stud **Bred** P D Player **Trained** Newmarket, Suffolk


The Form Book, Raceform Ltd, Compton, RG20 6NL

**FOCUS**
An ordinary event run in a time marginally faster than the first division.

**NOTEBOOK**
**Hip Hop Harry**, who had Ryan's Future, winner of the first division, behind him last time, showed a fine attitude to battle back after being headed inside the final furlong. He is only lightly raced, open to improvement and should stay farther, so there should be more races to be won with him.
**Ember Days** has to be praised for the way she battled her way out of a scrum turning in, and she was only headed again on the line. She may be worth another try on Fibresand.
**Quantum Leap** was weighted reverse recent form with the winner, but despite passing a whole host of horses down the straight, never threatened to get to the front two.
**War Owl(USA)** has shown his best form on Fibresand and he looks sure to hit the target on that surface in the near future.
**Miss Pebbles(IRE)**, sporting first-time cheekpieces, flew down the outside without threatening to take a hand in the finish.
**Classic Role**, who stays much farther than this, deserves some credit as he was only swamped inside the final furlong after leading for much of the contest.
**Man The Gate**, the well-backed favourite, was prominent before folding very tamely down the straight and this has to go down as bitterly disappointing.

## 6162 LITTLEWOODS BET DIRECT CONDITIONS STKS — 1m 2f (P)
**2:25** (2:25) (D) 3-Y-O+ — **£3,419** (£1,052; £526; £263) **Stalls** Low

| Form | | | | | RPR |
|---|---|---|---|---|---|
| 1313 | **1** | | **Windy Britain**[18] 6051 4-8-12 92 (LMCumani) *lw: hld up in tch: shkn up ent fnl f: qcknd to ld nr fin: won gng away* **5/6**[1] | EAhern 9 | 95 |
| 0000 | **2** | 1/2 | **Linning Wine (IRE)**[8] 6117 7-9-1 90 (BGPowell) *trakcke ldrs: rdn to ld 1f out: hdd and nt qckn nr fin* **7/1** | SCarson 6 | 97 |
| 4400 | **3** | 3/4 | **Brilliant Red**[8] 6117 10-9-1 89 (JamiePoulton) *hld up in rr: hdwy on outside 2f out: r.o fnl f: nvr nrr* **6/1**[3] | (t) IMongan 2 | 96 |
| 0201 | **4** | 1 3/4 | **Invader**[164] 2816 7-9-1 86 (CEBrittain) *trckd ldr tl one pce ent fnl f* **12/1** | MFenton 8 | 93 |
| 06-3 | **5** | hd | **Jack Of Trumps (IRE)**[79] 5116 3-8-12 62 (GWragg) *set slow pce tl qcknd over 3f out: rdn and hdd 1f out: fdd* **33/1** | JFEgan 7 | 92? |
| 2242 | **6** | 1/2 | **Alrafid (IRE)**[8] 6117 4-8-8 83 (GLMoore) *plld hrd in rr: mde sme late hdwy* **9/2**[2] | HPoulton(7) 1 | 92 |
| 3600 | **7** | 2 1/2 | **Barrantes**[73] 5251 6-8-5 83 (MissSheenaWest) *hld up in mid-div: wknd over 1f out* **33/1** | NChalmers(5) 5 | 82 |
| 5000 | **8** | 1 3/4 | **Sahaat**[42] 5827 5-9-1 97 (JAOsborne) *a bhd* **14/1** | DaneO'Neill 3 | 84 |
| 50-0 | **9** | 5 | **Bright Green**[226] 1261 4-9-1 76 (JABOld) *plld hrd in rr: hdwy over 3f out: wknd 2f out* **66/1** | CCatlin 10 | 75 |
| 000- | **10** | dist | **Welsh Border**[442] 2280 5-9-1 82 (CRDore) *b: slowly away: a bhd: t.o fnl 2f* **50/1** | JBramhill 4 | — |

2m 15.94s (8.55) **Going Correction** +0.05s/f (Slow) **10** Ran SP% **123.2**
**WFA** 3 from 4yo+ 3lb
Speed ratings: **67,66,66,64,64 64,62,60,56,**—CSF £7.98 TOTE £1.60: £1.10, £2.30, £2.20; EX 8.30.
**Owner** Scuderia Giocri **Bred** Scuderia Giocri **Trained** Newmarket, Suffolk

**FOCUS**
A farcical pace made the form of this competitive-looking race very suspect.

**NOTEBOOK**
**Windy Britain** was winning her sixth race of the year. This was her first success on sand, but she had run well on the surface before and is clearly progressing nicely, although she was well in with most of these on official figures.
**Linning Wine(IRE)**, who was 5lb wrong with the winner, appeared to get first run on the field, but could not hold the challenge of the winner. He likes this surface, but his inflated rating will always make life difficult.
**Brilliant Red**, who had 6lb to find with the winner on adjusted figures, is another who likes it at Lingfield and appears to be coming into form. However, he will struggle to get the decent pace he needs in events like this unless the jockeys rethink their tactics.
**Invader** was another not suited by the farcical pace, but this was still a fair effort on his first start since June. This trip suits him well on this surface.
**Jack Of Trumps(IRE)** set the slow gallop and is probably flattered by his proximity.
**Alrafid(IRE)** was another totally unsuited to the slow pace and is better than this.
**Welsh Border** *Official explanation: vet said gelding was lame*

## 6163 BET DIRECT IN RUNNING SKY TEXT 371 (S) STKS — 7f (P)
**2:55** (2:55) (G) 3-Y-O+ — **£2,170** (£620; £310) **Stalls** Low

| Form | | | | | RPR |
|---|---|---|---|---|---|
| 0030 | **1** | | **Free Option (IRE)**[11] 6093 8-9-4 73 (BHanbury) *hld up: hdwy 2f out: hrd rdn over 1f out: str burst to ld last stride* **3/1**[1] | (b[1]) DaneO'Neill 2 | 70 |
| -000 | **2** | hd | **Warlingham (IRE)**[11] 6094 5-8-12 54 (MPitman) *a.p: rdn to ld over 1f out: edgd lft and hdd lst stride* **14/1** | VSlattery 14 | 64 |
| 0043 | **3** | nk | **Senor Miro**[4] 6128 5-8-12 50 (JAkehurst) *a in tch: pressed ldr thrght fnl f tl cl home* **7/2**[2] | CCatlin 5 | 63 |
| 0530 | **4** | 6 | **Hadath (IRE)**[8] 6114 6-8-9 68 (BGPowell) *mid-div tl hmpd and lost pl over 2f out: hrd rdn and rallied appr fnl f: no ch w first 3* **4/1**[3] | (p) LPKeniry(3) 1 | 48 |
| 0500 | **5** | 3/4 | **Dolphinelle (IRE)**[288] 617 7-8-12 49 (JamiePoulton) *mid-div: passed sme btn horses ins fnl 2f* **33/1** | (v) JFEgan 7 | 46 |
| 3140 | **6** | shd | **Repeat (IRE)**[2] 6144 3-9-4 55 (MissGayKelleway) *b: a mid-div* **14/1** | ACulhane 4 | 52 |
| 0000 | **7** | shd | **Cargo**[140] 3509 4-8-12 48 (HJCollingridge) *in tch tl rdn 2f out: no hdwy after* **14/1** | EAhern 12 | 46 |
| 240 | **8** | 1 3/4 | **Walker Bay (IRE)**[8] 6113 5-8-7 48 (JCFox) *slowly away: sme hdwy over 2f out: nvr nr to chal* **33/1** | (b) RSmith 6 | 36 |
| 0000 | **9** | shd | **Al Muallim (USA)**[83] 5025 9-9-1 50 (AndrewReid) *b: b.hind: towards rr: effrt 2f out: sn btn* **25/1** | (t) J-PGuillambert(3) 13 | 47 |
| 0300 | **10** | 1 3/4 | **Xsynna**[92] 4790 7-8-9 47 (PSMcentee) *led after 1f: wknd over 1f out* **33/1** | LFletcher(3) 3 | 37 |
| 0000 | **11** | nk | **Crafty Politician (USA)**[11] 6094 6-9-4 47 (GLMoore) *mid-div: sn rdn and bhd fr 1/2-way* **8/1** | (bt) IMongan 8 | 42 |
| 010 | **12** | nk | **Meelup (IRE)**[50] 5690 3-8-13 64 (AGNewcombe) *chsd ldrs tl wknd wl over 1f out* **20/1** | (p) NChalmers(5) 15 | 41 |
| 0100 | **13** | 1/2 | **Ally Makbul**[15] 6065 3-8-6 53 (JRBest) *a bhd* **12/1** | DFentiman(7) 9 | 35 |
| 0 | **14** | 1/2 | **Buckenham Stone**[44] 5793 4-8-8 ow1 (MrsLydiaPearce) *in tch to 1/2-way* **33/1** | RPrice 10 | 29 |
| 6040 | **15** | 3/4 | **Monte Verde (IRE)**[19] 6038 3-8-13 48 (BPalling) *led for 1f: wknd wl over 1f out* **25/1** | (p) DKinsella 16 | 32 |
| 2004 | **16** | 1 | **Prince Domino**[40] 5846 4-9-4 49 (GLMoore) *w ldrs tl wknd over 2f out* **14/1** | (bt[1]) SWKelly 11 | 34 |

1m 25.7s (-0.30) **Going Correction** +0.05s/f (Slow) **16** Ran SP% **136.9**
Speed ratings: **103,102,102,95,94 94,94,92,92,90 90,89,89,88,87 86**CSF £49.71 TOTE £3.50: £1.90, £6.20, £1.80; EX 89.50.The winner was sold to Nigel Shields for 6,200gns
**Owner** B Hanbury **Bred** Grange Stud (uk) **Trained** Newmarket, Suffolk

**FOCUS**
A run-of-the-mill seller, but it was run at a sound pace and the first three pulled clear.

**NOTEBOOK**
**Free Option(IRE)**, rated 96 in his pomp, had to drop to selling company to gain his first win since landing a handicap off 72 here in January. This surface obviously suits, but he has never been the most resolute and it was a surprise he showed enough determination to go between horses close home. The first-time blinkers may have helped and they are far from certain to work so well again, but he will always be competitive at this level.
**Warlingham(IRE)**, who had 13lb to find with the winner on adjusted official figures, travelled smoothly and showed a good attitude to win the battle for second. This was his best performance since returning from a year off.
**Senor Miro** was another to impress with the way he travelled and, although he may have got there a trifle soon, he would have done well to match the winner's turn of pace down the straight.
**Hadath(IRE)** lost his chance when hampered two out and the principals had gone by the time he recovered. This run should not be taken literally.
**Dolphinelle(IRE)** never really threatened to repeat last year's success in this race.
**Repeat(IRE)** finished in a huge bunch and probably did not achieve any more than he was entitled to do.

## 6164 BETDIRECT.CO.UK H'CAP — 7f (P)
**3:30** (3:30) (D) (0-80,80) 3-Y-O+ — **£2,331** (£666; £333) **Stalls** Low

| Form | | | | | RPR |
|---|---|---|---|---|---|
| 1540 | **1** | | **What-A-Dancer (IRE)**[18] 6050 6-9-11 77 (GASwinbank) *hld up in rr: stdy hdwy fr 1/2-way: led ent fnl f: rdn out* **11/2**[3] | RWinston 1 | 89 |
| 002 | **2** | 1 1/2 | **Incline (IRE)**[18] 6050 4-9-9 80 (TGMills) *trckd ldrs: rdn 2f out: chsd wnr fnl f* **6/4**[1] | RMiles(5) 4 | 88 |
| -000 | **3** | 3/4 | **Zilch**[30] 5970 5-9-9 75 (MLWBell) *a.p: ev ch 1f out: nt qckn fnl f* **33/1** | MFenton 2 | 81 |
| 0000 | **4** | 1 1/2 | **The Gaikwar (IRE)**[11] 6098 4-8-13 70 (NEBerry) *slowly away and rdn to get in tch: hdwy u.p over 1f out: r.o: nvr nrr* **100/1** | (b) MSavage(5) 10 | 73 |
| 0040 | **5** | 1 3/4 | **Grey Pearl**[133] 3696 4-9-7 73 (MissGayKelleway) *trckd ldr: rdn and hdd ent fnl f: fdd* **25/1** | IMongan 3 | 71 |
| 1005 | **6** | nk | **Pheckless**[201] 1781 4-9-4 70 (RFJohnsonHoughton) *hld up in rr: hdwy on ins over 1f out: one pce fnl f* **10/1** | SCarson 5 | 68 |
| 0030 | **7** | 1/2 | **Danielle's Lad**[4] 6135 7-9-4 70 (BPalling) *led tl hdd over 2f out: wknd fnl f* **25/1** | (b) DKinsella 6 | 66 |
| 0500 | **8** | 3/4 | **Agilis (IRE)**[18] 6050 3-9-7 80 (JamiePoulton) *in rr: mde mod late hdwy* **14/1** | HPoulton(7) 15 | 74 |
| -302 | **9** | 1 1/4 | **Royal Fashion (IRE)**[8] 6116 3-8-8 65 (MissSheenaWest) *slowly away: a towards rr* **16/1** | NChalmers(5) 12 | 56 |
| 0040 | **10** | 1 1/2 | **Fulvio (USA)**[8] 6116 3-9-2 68 (JamiePoulton) *chsd ldrs tl wknd 2f out* **16/1** | JFEgan 7 | 56 |
| 0-00 | **11** | nk | **Kilmeena Lad**[11] 6092 7-9-3 69 (JCFox) *prom tl rdn and wknd 2f out* **20/1** | DaneO'Neill 8 | 56 |
| 0003 | **12** | nk | **Cayman Breeze**[4] 6134 3-8-13 65 (SDow) *mid-div: bhd fnl 2f* **12/1** | PDoe 11 | 51 |
| -216 | **13** | hd | **Spanish Gold**[167] 2716 3-9-6 75 (AMBalding) *a bhd* **16/1** | LPKeniry(3) 16 | 61 |
| 000 | **14** | 1/2 | **Uncle Bernon**[14] 6078 4-9-6 72 (GBBalding) *hld up: a in rr* **20/1** | RHavlin 13 | 56 |
| 5301 | **15** | hd | **Ripple Effect**[8] 6116 3-9-5 76 6ex (CADwyer) *in tch to 1/2-way* **12/1** | (t) BReilly(5) 9 | 60 |
| 0002 | **16** | 6 | **Sir Laughalot**[27] 5985 3-9-4 70 (MissECLavelle) *racd wd: in tch tl rdn and wknd 2f out* **5/1**[2] | EAhern 14 | 39 |

1m 24.57s (-1.43) **Going Correction** +0.05s/f (Slow) **16** Ran SP% **142.0**
Speed ratings: **110,108,107,105,103 103,102,101,100,98 98,98,97,97,97 90**CSF £15.34 CT £294.97 TOTE £7.00: £2.30, £1.30, £3.90, £13.90; EX 35.40 Trifecta £1376.50 Pool of £3,489.96 - 1.80 winning units. Place 6 £79.48, Place 5 £54.16.
**Owner** A Barnes **Bred** Miss V Charlton **Trained** Melsonby, N Yorks

**FOCUS**
This was a fair handicap run in a good time and the first two look worth following in similar events.

**NOTEBOOK**
**What-A-Dancer(IRE)** ran some fair races in the summer and landed his first All-Weather race in good style. He did not do an awful lot in front and, given this was only his third race on the surface, may be open to improvement.
**Incline(IRE)** was heavily supported after running course-specialist Lygeton Lad to a short head on his first try on the surface last time. He did little wrong and can gain compensation off this sort of mark.
**Zilch** appeared to find this surface more to his liking than the Fibresand he encountered on his All-Weather debut last time.
**The Gaikwar(IRE)** ran his best race of the year, but is certainly not one to get too excited about even though he has dropped down the handicap since leaving Amanda Perrett.
**Grey Pearl**, another who has tumbled down the weights, ran her best race for some time on her All-Weather debut.
**Sir Laughalot** was caught very wide on the track and, although that is not always a bad thing here, he dropped right away in the straight. This is obviously not his form.
T/Plt: £452.80 to a £1 stake. Pool: £32,566.20. 52.50 winning tickets. T/Qpdt: £59.30 to a £1 stake. Pool: £3,408.90. 42.50 winning tickets. JS

# 6149 SOUTHWELL (L-H)
### Friday, December 12

**OFFICIAL GOING: Standard**
This meeting was transferred from Wolverhampton due to a waterlogged surface at that track.

## 6165 BET DIRECT ON ATTHERACES INTERACTIVE NURSERY — 6f (F)
**12:15** (12:15) (D) (0-85,73) 2-Y-O — **£3,360** (£960; £480) **Stalls** Low

| Form | | | | | RPR |
|---|---|---|---|---|---|
| 0055 | **1** | | **Blofeld**[24] 6021 2-8-0 55 (WJarvis) *trckd ldrs: led over 1f out: wandered and drew clr ins last* **13/2** | LisaJones(3) 2 | 66 |
| 066 | **2** | 4 | **Smokin Joe**[36] 5930 2-9-1 67 (JRBest) *trckd ldrs: effrt and outpcd 2f out: styd on wl ins last* **7/2**[3] | NPollard 7 | 66 |
| 2314 | **3** | 3/4 | **Lizhar (IRE)**[38] 5916 2-9-4 73 (MJPolglase) *led tl over 1f out: nt qckn* **3/1**[2] | LFletcher(3) 3 | 70 |
| 430 | **4** | 3/4 | **Saffron River**[25] 6011 2-8-7 59 (RHollinshead) *sn chsng ldrs: one pce fnl 2f* **20/1** | RFrench 6 | 54 |
| 5621 | **5** | 2 | **Bridgewater Boys**[25] 6011 2-9-3 69 (KARyan) *hld up: drvn along 3f out: sn chsng ldrs: fdd appr fnl f* **5/2**[1] | (b) RWinston 4 | 58 |

4024 **6** *8* **Burlington Place**[16] 6077 2-9-2 **68** ........ JDSmith 1 33
(SKirk) *s.i.s: sn drvn along: hdwy over 2f out: lost pl over 1f out: eased* **4/1**

1m 16.97s (0.17) **Going Correction** 0.0s/f (Stan) **6** Ran SP% **113.9**
Speed ratings: **98,92,91,90,88 77**CSF £29.74 TOTE £7.10: £2.40, £2.10; EX 32.00.
**Owner** Byculla Thoroughbreds **Bred** Simon Dutfield And William Harrison-Allan **Trained** Newmarket, Suffolk

**FOCUS**
A poor 0-85 nursery with the top weight rated just 73.

**NOTEBOOK**
**Blofeld**got off the mark in decisive fashion, capitalising on his light weight having been well placed throughout on the rail. Appreciating the drop back in distance, he put up a career-best display and may be capable of scoring again under a penalty. *Official explanation: trainer said, regarding the improved form shown, gelding had benefited from the return to 6f*
**Smokin Joe**, a full-brother to the smart sprinter Smokin Beau, ran his best race to date on this switch into handicap company. He showed he acts on this surface and although the winner put him firmly in his place, he can be placed to advantage before too long.
**Lizhar(IRE)**held every chance but is on a stiff mark and looks in need of a drop in the weights.
**Bridgewater Boys**lost a shoe at the start and that cost him, but he really never looked happy at any stage after that and can do better.
**Burlington Place**had a good chance on his Polytrack form, but hated this surface and will do better when back at Lingfield.

## 6166 BET DIRECT NO Q DEMO 08000 837 888 H'CAP (DIV I) 5f (F)
**12:50** (12:50) (F) (0-60,67) 3-Y-0+ **£2,086** (£596; £298) **Stalls** High

Form RPR
0050 **1** **Cash**[3] 6149 5-9-11 **57** ........ (p) RFitzpatrick 8 69
(PaulJohnson) *chsd ldrs: led appr fnl f: hld on towards fin* **12/1**
000 **2** *½* **Abraxas**[95] 4774 5-9-4 **50** ........ (p) CCatlin 2 60
(JAkehurst) *in tch: hrd rdn over 2f out: styd on wl fnl f* **40/1**
5103 **3** *nk* **Kiss The Rain**[14] 6080 3-9-0 **49** ........ (v) LFletcher(3) 4 58
(RBrotherton) *chsd ldrs: outpcd over 2f out: kpt on wl fnl f* **12/1**
0026 **4** *1* **Sandgate Cygnet**[14] 6081 3-9-10 **59** ........ (p) DMcGaffin(3) 7 65
(ISemple) *swvd lft s: sn chsng ldrs: kpt on same pce fnl f* **7/1**[3]
4426 **5** *¾* **Rellim**[6] 6138 4-9-3 **54** ........ DNolan(5) 1 57
(PABlockley) *led tl hdd appr fnl f: fdd* **7/1**[3]
0064 **6** *1 ¾* **Inching**[18] 6062 3-9-9 **55** ........ (v) MHenry 14 52
(RMHCowell) *racd stands' side: outpcd over 2f out: kpt on wl ins last* **10/1**
0035 **7** *shd* **Soaked**[51] 5706 10-9-11 **57** ........ (b) ACulhane 3 54
(DWChapman) *chsd ldrs: wknd fnl f* **10/1**
0035 **8** *1 ¼* **Henry Tun**[14] 6081 5-9-12 **58** ........ (b) JEdmunds 9 50
(JBalding) *chsd ldrs: wknd over 1f out* **7/1**[3]
0030 **9** *shd* **King's Ballet (USA)**[13] 6095 5-9-8 **54** ........ IMongan 6 46
(PRChamings) *hmpd s: swtchd lft after 1f and racd far side: chsd ldrs tl wknd over 1f out* **11/2**[1]
3021 **10** *shd* **Chispa**[3] 6149 5-10-7 67 7ex ........ DarrenWilliams 12 59
(KRBurke) *in tch: rdn and outpcd over 2f out: n.d after* **13/2**[2]
0066 **11** *2* **Our Chelsea Blue (USA)**[13] 6095 5-9-12 **58** ........ SRighton 15 43
(AWCarroll) *dwlt: racd stands' side: a in rr* **16/1**
2500 **12** *½* **Firecat**[23] 6031 4-9-3 **49** ........ DSweeney 5 32
(APJones) *mid-div: rdn over 2f out: nvr a threat* **33/1**
0063 **13** *1* **Catchthebatch**[3] 6155 7-9-1 **50** ........ DCorby(3) 11 29
(MJWallace) *racd towards stands' side: outpcd and bhd fnl 2f* **7/1**[3]
2000 **14** *5* **So Sober (IRE)**[182] 2330 5-8-9 **46** ........ THamilton(5) 16 8
(DShaw) *racd stands' side: outpcd and bhd fnl 3f* **25/1**
0500 **15** *1 ½* **Fiamma Royale (IRE)**[46] 5794 5-9-7 **53** ........ (p) JFanning 13 10
(MSSaunders) *racd stands' side: lost pl over 2f out: sn bhd* **20/1**
0000 **16** *17* **Ladies Knight**[21] 6038 3-9-8 **54** ........ RWinston 10 —
(DShaw) *rrd s: virtually ref to r: a t.o last* **50/1**

61.37 secs (1.07) **Going Correction** +0.175s/f (Slow) **16** Ran SP% **134.1**
Speed ratings: **98,97,96,95,93 91,90,88,88,88 85,84,83,75,72 45**CSF £462.45 CT £5833.37 TOTE £15.90: £2.60, £14.80, £3.10, £4.30; EX 2007.90.
**Owner** Insull, White, Pritchard & Johnson **Bred** F C T Wilson **Trained** White-le-Head, Co Durham

**FOCUS**
A typically competitive sprint for the track where most of the runners raced down the middle of the track.

**NOTEBOOK**
**Cash**who has plummeted in the weights having lost his form this season, gamely registered his first success in just under a year. He is evidently a keen sort, but if returning over this trip in the same mood next time, will take some beating. *Official explanation: trainer's representative said, regarding the improved form shown, last time out gelding ran freely to the start and would not face the kick-back early on*
**Abraxas**ran his best race for some time and looks better on the sand, however he remains winless after 20 outings and is a very tricky performer.
**Kiss The Rain**, with the visor back on, confirmed she is in good form with a solid enough display. She looks as though she is worth a try back at six furlongs.
**Sandgate Cygnet**ran better than her previous outing on the Fibresand, but does not look a natural on this surface.
**Rellim**forced the pace for most of the way and only tired out of it late on. She looks high enough in the weights at present and has not won since February 2002.
**Chispa**failed to follow up his win earlier in the week under his big weight and looks a better horse over six furlongs.

## 6167 BET DIRECT MAIDEN STKS 7f (F)
**1:20** (1:21) (D) 2-Y-0 **£3,125** (£893; £446) **Stalls** Low

Form RPR
442 **1** **Titus Salt (USA)**[27] 6002 2-9-0 71 ........ (b[1]) DMernagh 6 78+
(TDBarron) *mde all: unchal* **7/2**[2]
0364 **2** *3 ½* **Kingsmaite**[45] 5818 2-9-0 66 ........ JBramhill 5 69
(SRBowring) *chsd ldrs: wnt 2nd over 1f out: kpt on: no imp* **9/1**
0043 **3** *3* **Redbank (IRE)**[27] 6002 2-9-0 67 ........ (b[1]) DaneO'Neill 4 62
(NACallaghan) *chsd ldrs: one pce fnl 2f* **4/1**[3]
05 **4** *5* **Daggers Canyon**[16] 6074 2-9-0 ........ IMongan 16 49
(JulianPoulton) *chsd ldrs: outpcd over 2f out: n.d after* **9/1**
6500 **5** *2 ½* **Bretton**[27] 6003 2-9-0 45 ........ (p) ACulhane 10 43
(RHollinshead) *outpcd and lost pl over 4f out: n.m.r over 1f out: styd on wl ins last* **33/1**
4 **6** *¾* **Music Mix (IRE)**[16] 6074 2-9-0 ........ WRyan 2 41
(EALDunlop) *sn bhd: hdwy over 2f out: nt clr run and swtchd lft over 1f out: nvr nr ldrs* **11/4**[1]
60 **7** *shd* **Vampire Queen (IRE)**[17] 6069 2-8-9 ........ DeanMcKeown 11 36
(RPElliott) *mid-divsion: edgd lft over 1f out: nvr nrr* **33/1**
05 **8** *nk* **Vittorioso (IRE)**[25] 6011 2-9-0 ........ (p) MFenton 9 40
(MissGayKelleway) *chsd ldrs: rdn and hung lft over 2f out: lost pl over 1f out* **7/1**
**9** *nk* **Chimes Eight** 2-8-4 ........ THamilton(5) 7 34
(RAFahey) *sn outpcd and bhd: sme hdwy over 1f out: nvr a factor* **14/1**
0 **10** *6* **Monkey Or Me (IRE)**[13] 6097 2-9-0 ........ GParkin 15 24
(PTMidgley) *chsd ldrs: edgd lft and lost pl over 1f out* **66/1**
**11** *1 ¾* **Killing Me Softly** 2-9-0 ........ DSweeney 14 20
(JGallagher) *s.s: a bhd* **66/1**
0 **12** *3* **Battle Back (BEL)**[41] 5869 2-8-4 ........ BReilly(5) 8 7
(SCWilliams) *lost pl over 4f out: sn wl bhd* **33/1**
006 **13** *2 ½* **Emilys Dawn**[24] 6020 2-8-9 57 ........ ANicholls 13 —
(DKIvory) *chsd ldrs: lost pl over 2f out* **12/1**
**14** *½* **Maria Maria (IRE)** 2-8-6 ........ LEnstone(3) 12 —
(MrsNMacauley) *s.i.s: t.o 4f out* **50/1**
00 **15** *10* **Evening Fragrance**[4] 6142 2-9-0 ........ (b) JMackay 3 —
(GCHChung) *lost pl over 4f out: bhd whn eased fnl f* **66/1**

1m 30.76s (-0.04) **Going Correction** 0.0s/f (Stan) **15** Ran SP% **131.0**
Speed ratings: **100,96,92,86,84 83,83,82,82,75 73,70,67,66,55**CSF £37.24 TOTE £3.00: £2.00, £2.40, £2.30; EX 46.50.
**Owner** Sporting Occasions Racing No 5 **Bred** R C Wilson Jr, Trustee **Trained** Maunby, N Yorks
■ Stewards Enquiry : Dean McKeownA eight-day ban: failed to take all reasonable and permissible measures throughout the race to ensure that filly was given a full opportunity of obtaining the best possible placing (Apr 10-17) (banned retrospectively after filly went on to win her next race)

**FOCUS**
An average maiden in which the field were well strung out at an early stage.

**NOTEBOOK**
**Titus Salt(USA)**, who hails from a yard which does so well on this surface, made every yard of the running to win comfortably in the end. He was helped by the application of first-time blinkers and confirmed form with the third horse readily. He looks the type to win races this winter and he could well improve when stepped back up to a mile.
**Kingsmaite**put up a pleasing AW debut and got this trip well. Although he had no chance with the winner, he has the ability to win a race or two in this sphere as moved well throughout and was clear of the rest.
**Redbank(IRE)**, like the winner in first-time blinkers, had every chance if good enough but found little under pressure and failed to reverse recent form. He has the ability, but is becoming frustrating and looks tricky.
**Music Mix(IRE)**was the disappointment of the race having lost any chance at the start, and never got competitive. He had shaped well on his debut on the Polytrack last time and is surely capable of better than this.
**Vampire Queen(IRE)** *Official explanation: 40-day ban: Apr 9-May 18*

## 6168 LITTLEWOODS BET DIRECT H'CAP 1m 6f (F)
**1:55** (1:55) (F) (0-65,65) 3-Y-0+ **£2,149** (£614; £307) **Stalls** Low

Form RPR
506 **1** **Vincent**[66] 5435 8-7-12 **35** oh2 ........ JMackay 8 45
(JohnAHarris) *sn bhd: hdwy 6f out: sn chsng ldrs: styd on to ld nr fin* **10/1**
0660 **2** *hd* **Vanbrugh (FR)**[17] 6068 3-9-2 **60** ........ (vt) DarrenWilliams 4 70
(MissDAMchale) *trckd ldrs: led 8f out: hrd rdn 2f out: hdd nr fin* **16/1**
-063 **3** *5* **Mercurious (IRE)**[77] 5200 3-7-12 **42** oh1 ........ DaleGibson 5 45
(JMackie) *chsd ldrs: one pce fnl 2f* **7/1**[3]
526- **4** *6* **Daunted (IRE)**[387] 5756 7-9-3 **59** ........ DNolan(5) 10 54
(PABlockley) *hld up: hdwy 7f out: sn chsng ldrs: fdd over 1f out* **8/1**
001 **5** *7* **Claptrap**[13] 6096 3-9-3 **61** ........ IMongan 2 47
(RBrotherton) *trckd ldrs: rdn over 3f out: wknd over 1f out: heavily eased nr fin* **11/10**[1]
3015 **6** *3 ½* **High Policy (IRE)**[32] 5972 7-9-7 **65** ........ (p) StephanieHollinshead(7) 9 47
(RHollinshead) *mid-div: hdwy u.p 5f out: lost pl over 1f out* **5/1**[2]
00 **7** *11* **Unleaded**[69] 5359 3-7-9 **42** oh12 ........ LisaJones(3) 13 9
(JAkehurst) *chsd ldrs: lost pl 7f out* **40/1**
0400 **8** *2 ½* **Dash Of Magic**[18] 6061 5-8-3 **40** ........ CCatlin 14 4
(JHetherton) *rr-div: hdwy 6f out: sn chsng ldrs: lost pl over 2f out* **20/1**
4-00 **9** *2* **Bid Spotter (IRE)**[9] 6121 4-8-6 **46** ow1 ........ LPKeniry(3) 7 7
(MrsLucindaFeatherstone) *led tl 8f out: lost pl over 4f out* **25/1**
0005 **10** *23* **Fayrway Rhythm (IRE)**[180] 2389 6-8-3 **40** ........ ANicholls 11 —
(IanEmmerson) *chsd ldrs: sn drvn along: lost pl over 7f out* **33/1**
000 **11** *15* **Top Son**[16] 6075 4-7-12 **35** oh10 ........ JoannaBadger 1 —
(APJones) *chsd ldrs: rdn and lost pl 8f out: sn bhd* **50/1**
-060 **12** *¾* **Dance Light (IRE)**[16] 6079 4-9-9 **60** ........ DeanMcKeown 3 —
(TTClement) *chsd ldrs: lost pl over 5f out: sn bhd* **12/1**
3610 **13** *½* **Humdinger (IRE)**[18] 6061 3-8-13 **62** ........ (e[1]) THamilton(5) 12 —
(DShaw) *sn bhd* **16/1**
0000 **14** *17* **Mawhoob (USA)**[9] 6125 5-8-3 **47** ........ (v) StevenHarrison(7) 15 —
(MrsNMacauley) *s.i.s: bhd: t.o 7f out* **50/1**

3m 10.43s (0.83) **Going Correction** 0.0s/f (Stan)
**WFA** 3 from 4yo+ 7lb **14** Ran SP% **134.4**
Speed ratings: **97,96,94,90,86 84,78,76,75,62 54,53,53,43**CSF £166.00 CT £1227.74 TOTE £9.70: £2.90, £4.10, £2.80; EX 137.50.
**Owner** Mrs A E Harris **Bred** R Stern, V Bloom And P Caplan **Trained** Eastwell, Leics

**NOTEBOOK**
**Vincent**came from a long way off the pace to register his first victory since November 2000. He needs every yard of this trip and only just got up on the line, but looked to have a little left in the tank. He was racing from 2lb out of the handicap here and although his overall record suggests he is far from consistent, he will improve again over further.
**Vanbrugh(FR)**can be considered a little unlucky as he only got headed on the line and gave his all in defeat. He was given a very positive ride considering he was far from certain to get this trip and that cost him late on, but he was well clear of the rest and can gain compensation now connections know he stays.
**Mercurious(IRE)**did not look to stay this trip, but acquitted herself creditably from 1lb out of the handicap.
**Daunted(IRE)**was moving well off the pace, but understandably blew up on this first outing for over a year, and this was a satisfactory comeback display.
**Claptrap**, who won easily in a dire contest last time at Wolverhampton, found next to nothing off the bridle and is very tricky.

## 6169 BET DIRECT NO Q ON 08000 93 66 93 H'CAP 1m (F)
**2:30** (2:31) (D) (0-85,77) 3-Y-0+ **£3,430** (£980; £490) **Stalls** Low

Form RPR
6042 **1** **Noul (USA)**[25] 6016 4-9-4 **69** ........ (b) RWinston 6 81
(KARyan) *sn trcking ldrs: styd on against far rail to ld nr fin* **14/1**
3112 **2** *hd* **How's Things**[17] 6064 3-9-1 **67** ........ PaulEddery 7 79
(DHaydnJones) *chsd ldrs: led on far side over 1f out: hdd nr fin* **6/1**[3]
1403 **3** *1 ¾* **Cool Temper**[9] 6124 7-9-12 **77** ........ (t) ACulhane 10 85
(PFICole) *racd wd: lost pl over 4f out: hdwy on stands' side over 2f out: styd on strly ins last* **7/4**[1]
0041 **4** *nk* **Lockstock (IRE)**[17] 6064 5-9-0 **65** ........ (b) JFanning 3 73
(MSSaunders) *chsd ldrs: nt qckn appr fnl f* **5/1**[2]
0033 **5** *shd* **Critical Stage (IRE)**[36] 5935 4-8-7 **61** ........ (e) LisaJones(3) 2 68
(JohnBerry) *styd on ins: trckd ldr: led over 2f out tl over 1f out: kpt on same pce* **10/1**

6510 **6** 1 1/4 **Labrett**[13] 6098 6-9-11 **76**....(p) MFenton 8 81
(MissGayKelleway) *lost pl over 4f out: hdwy on outer 2f out: styd on ins last* **12/1**
5306 **7** 1 1/2 **First Maite**[51] 5705 10-9-6 **71**.... JBramhill 5 73
(SRBowring) *led overall on outer tl over 4f out: sn outpcd: kpt on fnl f* **20/1**
5044 **8** 1/2 **Crusoe (IRE)**[6] 6140 6-9-0 **65**....(b) DaneO'Neill 11 66
(ASadik) *chsd ldr: n.m.r over 2f out: kpt on fnl f* **12/1**
2010 **9** 1 3/4 **Pharoah's Gold (IRE)**[17] 6070 5-9-0 **65**....(e) DarrenWilliams 9 62
(DShaw) *s.i.s: hdwy and nt clr run 3f out: sn rdn: nvr a threat* **20/1**
0200 **10** 3 1/2 **Oldenway**[13] 6098 4-8-10 **68** ow1.... DSwift(7) 12 58
(RAFahey) *sn chsng ldrs: lost pl 4f out* **25/1**
6000 **11** 8 **Whippasnapper**[14] 6084 3-8-10 **69**.... DFentiman(7) 4 43
(JRBest) *racd on ins: led over 4f out tl over 2f out: sn lost pl and bhd* **33/1**

1m 43.94s (-0.66) **Going Correction** 0.0s/f (Stan)
**WFA** 3 from 4yo+ 1lb **11** Ran SP% **114.8**
Speed ratings: **103,102,101,100,100 99,97,97,95,92 84**CSF £88.47 CT £222.18 TOTE £11.20: £3.10, £3.50, £1.10; EX 75.50.
**Owner** John Duddy **Bred** Mathews Breeding And Racing, Ltd **Trained** Hambleton, N Yorks

**FOCUS**
The track was harrowed before the start of this contest and the runners were spread right across the track from the start as a result.

**NOTEBOOK**
**Noul(USA)**, beaten at odds-on in a seller last time, showed his true colours with the blinkers back on this time. He was well placed throughout on the rails and gamely stuck his head out where it mattered to register a hard-fought success, his first since February this year. Officially rated 10lb higher on the AW than on turf, this was by far his best effort for quite some time and he beat some fair rivals on this occasion.
**How's Things**has been in grand form of late on the sand and went down fighting. He should continue to pay his way in this grade during the winter and it is possible his recent rise in the weights has not ruled out further success.
**Cool Temper**, who caught the eye when finishing fast in a better race last time, was again given a fair amount to do and was forced to stay stands' side in the straight, which was not ideal. He was again finishing fast, and when ridden a touch more prominently he should go in.
**Lockstock(IRE)**again showed he appreciates the headgear but failed to confirm the form with the runner-up on 3lb worse terms. He is in fair form at present and will do better when eased in grade.
**Critical Stage(IRE)**ran quite well on this drop in trip but will be better suited by a return to farther.

## 6170 BET DIRECT NO Q DEMO 08000 837 888 H'CAP (DIV II) 5f (F)
**3:05** (3:08) (F) (0-60,60) 3-Y-0+ **£2,086** (£596; £298) **Stalls** High

Form RPR
0204 **1** **Laurel Dawn**[13] 6095 5-9-9 58.... LFletcher(3) 14 68
(IWMcinnes) *sn chsng ldrs centre: styd on wl appr fnl f: led nr fin* **11/2**[3]
0040 **2** 1 **The Leather Wedge (IRE)**[101] 4642 4-8-10 47.... PBradley(5) 3 54
(ABerry) *overall ldr against far side rail: hdd towards fin* **25/1**
2353 **3** 3/4 **Wainwright (IRE)**[17] 6065 3-9-7 60.... DerekNolan(7) 12 64
(PABlockley) *racd centre: chsd ldrs: kpt on wl fnl f* **7/1**
1242 **4** 1 1/2 **Empress Josephine**[28] 5998 3-9-8 54....(v) SWKelly 6 53
(JRJenkins) *chsd ldrs: kpt on same pce appr fnl f* **10/1**
0000 **5** nk **Sergeant Slipper**[114] 4288 6-8-7 46....(v) PMakin(7) 10 44
(CSmith) *sn outpcd and bhd: styd on wl appr fnl f* **33/1**
0040 **6** 1 1/4 **College Hippie**[37] 5924 4-8-10 49.... PGallagher(7) 7 42
(JFCoupland) *s.i.s: hdwy 2f out: nvr rchd ldrs* **16/1**
0142 **7** hd **Strensall**[13] 6095 6-9-12 58.... RFitzpatrick 4 51
(REBarr) *chsd ldrs: rdn over 2f out: fdd fnl f* **9/2**[2]
5605 **8** hd **Catch The Cat (IRE)**[17] 6063 4-8-13 50....(v) TEaves(5) 1 42
(JSWainwright) *racd against far side rail: chsd ldrs: fdd over 1f out* **4/1**[1]
0041 **9** 1/2 **Polar Haze**[3] 6155 6-9-7 53 7ex....(v) RPrice 9 43
(MrsLydiaPearce) *mid-div: nvr nr ldrs* **8/1**
0000 **10** hd **Safranine (IRE)**[25] 6014 6-9-4 57....(p) LTreadwell(7) 2 46
(MissAStokell) *chsd ldrs towards far side: lost pl over 1f out* **16/1**
0030 **11** 2 1/2 **Sea The World (IRE)**[14] 6080 3-10-0 60.... DarrenWilliams 11 41
(DShaw) *racd centre: bhd fnl 3f* **33/1**
1640 **12** 5 **Hagley Park**[14] 6081 4-9-2 48.... RWinston 15 11
(MQuinn) *racd stands' side: chsd ldrs: lost pl over 2f out: eased* **8/1**
6-54 **13** 3 1/2 **Ivory Venture**[252] 929 3-9-11 57.... DSweeney 16 8
(DKIvory) *racd stands' side: sn outpcd and bhd: eased* **25/1**
0600 **14** 2 1/2 **Star Applause**[159] 3038 3-9-0 46.... JEdmunds 5 —
(JBalding) *bhd fnl 2f: eased* **25/1**
0640 **15** 30 **Cressex Katie**[101] 4641 4-9-12 58.... NPollard 13 —
(JRBest) *s.s: a last: t.o* **8/1**

60.76 secs (0.46) **Going Correction** +0.175s/f (Slow) **15** Ran SP% **137.7**
Speed ratings: **103,101,100,97,97 95,95,94,93,93 89,81,75,71,23**CSF £155.95 CT £1038.03 TOTE £9.90: £3.30, £17.30, £2.10; EX 370.40.
**Owner** Ivy House Racing **Bred** Mrs J M Berry **Trained** Catwick, E Yorks

**FOCUS**
The second division of this sprint was run in a faster time than the first and once again saw those racing down the middle-to-far side of the track favoured, so a high draw was not ideal.

**NOTEBOOK**
**Laurel Dawn**, drawn 14, got his head in front where it matters for the first time since May 2002. The form of his second at this track on his last visit gave him every chance, but he has disappointed since and is a very hard horse to win with. He will pay for this with the Handicapper no doubt, and his win record does not inspire confidence for a follow-up bid.
**The Leather Wedge(IRE)**made a bold bid to make nearly all the running on the far-side rail and ran his best race on this surface for some time. He has hinted at a return to form of late but is an in-and-out performer and would not be certain to repeat this run.
**Wainwright(IRE)**was another to acquit himself well from a high draw, but looks better over six furlongs and, although he has the talent, he remains a maiden.
**Empress Josephine**ran a sound race on her return from a short break and likes it at this venue. She has only won once, but is fairly lightly raced and can win again at this level.
**Cressex Katie**was very slowly away and this run is best forgotten.

## 6171 LITTLEWOODSPOKER.COM APPRENTICE CLASSIFIED STKS 1m (F)
**3:35** (3:36) (G) 3-Y-0+ **£2,142** (£612; £306) **Stalls** Low

Form RPR
0051 **1** **Miss Champers (IRE)**[4] 6146 3-8-4 59.... SJDonohoe(7) 9 72
(PDEvans) *bhd: hdwy over 2f out: led over 1f out: kpt on strly: readily* **2/1**[1]
2213 **2** 1 1/2 **Rock Concert**[4] 6146 5-8-1 58....(v) NataliaGemelova(5) 11 63
(IWMcinnes) *chsd ldrs: kpt on fnl f: no imp* **11/4**[2]
4205 **3** 1 3/4 **Shatin Hero**[4] 6143 3-8-1 59....(p) DeanWilliams(7) 7 63
(GCHChung) *trckd ldrs: led over 3f out: edgd lft and hdd over 1f out: wknd nr fin* **7/1**
00-0 **4** 1/2 **Chabibi**[198] 4-8-3 40.... BReilly(3) 4 59
(THHansen, Germany) *chsd ldrs: kpt on same pce appr fnl f* **4/1**[3]
0045 **5** nk **Air Of Esteem**[25] 6015 7-8-9 48.... LPKeniry 13 61
(IanEmmerson) *chsd ldrs: lost pl over 4f out: hdwy over 2f out: kpt on same pce* **33/1**
6600 **6** 3/4 **Leonor De Soto**[10] 6114 3-7-12 59.... DFentiman(7) 14 56
(JRBest) *bhd: hdwy on wd outsider over 3f out: kpt on one pce fnl 2f* **20/1**
-606 **7** 5 **Jungle Lion**[284] 663 5-8-6 55 ow4....(t) DerekNolan(7) 2 53
(JohnAHarris) *chsd ldrs: lost pl over 1f out* **33/1**
0011 **8** 4 **Pup's Pride**[13] 6099 6-8-9 60....(v) LisaJones 10 41
(MrsNMacauley) *sn bhd: sme hdwy over 2f out: nvr a factor* **5/1**
0000 **9** 3 1/2 **College Star**[72] 5306 5-8-5 29 ow1....(b) LTreadwell(5) 6 35
(JFCoupland) *chsd ldrs: lost pl over 2f out* **50/1**
10P0 **10** 5 **Robin Sharp**[41] 5878 5-8-6 55....(p) NChalmers(3) 1 24
(JAkehurst) *chsd ldrs: led 5f out tl over 3f out: lost pl 2f out* **16/1**
4200 **11** 10 **Tap**[23] 6032 6-8-9 51.... DCorby 5 4
(IanEmmerson) *chsd ldrs: n.m.r and lost pl 3f out* **25/1**
1010 **12** 1 1/4 **Answered Promise (FR)**[13] 4730 4-8-6 58 ow2.... PGallagher(5) 3 4
(AWCarroll) *led tl 5f out: lost pl 3f out* **20/1**
0000 **13** 9 **Court Music (IRE)**[18] 6062 4-8-5 36 ow2....(v) TEaves(3) 12 —
(REBarr) *sn bhd and pushed along* **50/1**

1m 44.18s (-0.42) **Going Correction** 0.0s/f (Stan)
**WFA** 3 from 4yo+ 1lb **13** Ran SP% **138.2**
Speed ratings: **102,100,98,98,97 97,92,88,84,79 69,68,59**CSF £8.36 TOTE £3.70: £1.30, £2.00, £2.50; EX 6.50 Place 6 £803.77, Place 5 £191.13.
**Owner** Mrs S J Lawrence **Bred** Mountarmstrong Stud **Trained** Pandy, Gwent
■ Stewards Enquiry : L P Keniry two-day ban: used whip with excessive force (Dec 22,26)

**FOCUS**
This was run at a sound pace and that helped Miss Champers to her second course-and-distance success in five days.

**NOTEBOOK**
**Miss Champers(IRE)**gained her second course-and-distance win in five days. She was ridden right off the pace early and although she took her time to get to the front, she won comfortably in the end. She confirmed the form with the runner-up readily despite being on worse terms and can win again while in this mood.
**Rock Concert**helped force the pace and ran close to recent course form with the winner. She beat the rest fair and square and can win again over a course-and-distance that looks her optimum.
**Shatin Hero**has generally run respectably since switching to the AW but once again had no excuses on this occasion and is a fiendishly hard horse to win with.
**Chabibi**travelled well for most of the race, but found little under pressure when asked to win her race.
**Leonor De Soto**, who has lost her form of late, ran her best race for some time and is worth keeping an eye on during the coming weeks.
T/Plt: £1,520.70 to a £1 stake. Pool: £29,477.35. 14.15 winning tickets. T/Qpdt: £75.80 to a £1 stake. Pool: £3,381.20. 33.00 winning tickets. WG

# 6165 SOUTHWELL (L-H)
Saturday, December 13

**OFFICIAL GOING: Slow**

## 6172 BET DIRECT NO Q ON 08000 93 66 93 NURSERY (DIV I) 1m (F)
**12:00** (12:00) (E) (0-75,74) 2-Y-0 **£2,576** (£736; £368) **Stalls** Low

Form RPR
5154 **1** **Celtic Heroine (IRE)**[31] 5979 2-9-5 **72**.... MHenry 11 80+
(MAJarvis) *chsd ldrs: led 3f out: rdn and hdd over 1f out: styd on to ld post* **9/4**[1]
010 **2** shd **Blue Empire (IRE)**[40] 5906 2-8-5 **65**.... RoryMoore(7) 4 73+
(PCHaslam) *chsd ldrs: rdn to ld over 1f out: hung lft ins fnl f: hdd post* **7/2**[2]
0300 **3** 5 **Abrogate (IRE)**[74] 5290 2-7-6 **52**.... DFentiman(7) 8 49
(PCHaslam) *chsd ldrs: pushed along 1/2-way: hung lft and wknd fnl f* **20/1**
4001 **4** 3 1/2 **The Job**[21] 6046 2-8-9 **62**.... WRyan 7 51
(ADSmith) *led: hdd ov er 6f out: rdn and ev ch 2f out: sn wknd* **13/2**[3]
0010 **5** 2 **Uncle John**[25] 6023 2-9-1 **68**.... JDSmith 2 53
(SKirk) *sn pushed along in rr: nvr trbld ldrs* **11/1**
020 **6** 3 **Buchanan Street (IRE)**[136] 3698 2-8-7 **60**....(bt[1]) FNorton 5 38
(NACallaghan) *in tch: rdn over 3f out: sn wknd* **14/1**
0060 **7** 8 **Knight To Remember (IRE)**[22] 6037 2-7-13 **52** oh4 ow1.... RFfrench 3 12
(KARyan) *chsd ldrs over 4f* **25/1**
000 **8** 9 **Try The Air (IRE)**[61] 5541 2-8-6 **59**.... CCatlin 10 —
(CTinkler) *prom: rdn 1/2-way: wknd 3f out* **25/1**
416 **9** 8 **Cartronageeraghlad (IRE)**[31] 5979 2-9-7 **74**....(b) SWKelly 6 —
(JAOsborne) *chsd ldrs: led over 6f out: hdd 3f out: wknd 2f out* **7/2**[2]
0000 **10** 2 1/2 **Desert Light (IRE)**[10] 6122 2-7-10 **52** oh28 ow1....(e[1]) LisaJones(3) 9 —
(DShaw) *sn outpcd* **50/1**

1m 46.22s (1.62) **Going Correction** +0.225s/f (Slow) **10** Ran SP% **118.0**
Speed ratings: **100,99,94,91,89 86,78,69,61,58**CSF £9.72 CT £128.26 TOTE £3.70: £1.40, £2.10, £6.30; EX 30.70.
**Owner** P D Savill **Bred** P D Savill **Trained** Newmarket, Suffolk

**FOCUS**
After persistent rain the previous day and overnight the surface was reckoned to be very slow.

**NOTEBOOK**
**Celtic Heroine(IRE)**, suited by the step up in trip and the testing surface, showed real battling qualities and in the end that carried the day.
**Blue Empire(IRE)**, happy to be back on the All-Weather, took what looked a winning advantage, but he hung fire in front and in the end was worried out of it.
**Abrogate(IRE)**, who started life in nurseries from what looked a stiff mark, was having his first outing for 10 weeks.
**The Job**didn't get home and will be suited by a return to the Polytrack track at Lingfield.
**Cartronageeraghlad(IRE)** stopped in a matter of strides and was found to be lame afterwards.
*Official explanation: vet said colt finished lame on the left fore*

## 6173 BET DIRECT NO Q ON 08000 93 66 93 NURSERY (DIV II) 1m (F)
**12:30** (12:31) (E) (0-75,72) 2-Y-0 **£2,576** (£736; £368) **Stalls** Low

Form RPR
04 **1** **Bold Blade**[18] 6069 2-8-9 60....(b) RFfrench 9 70
(BSmart) *led over 6f out: hung rt over 2f out: drvn clr* **8/1**
6403 **2** 6 **Chariot (IRE)**[53] 5698 2-8-13 64.... GBaker 10 61
(MRBosley) *hld up: hdwy over 3f out: rdn over 1f out: styd on same pce* **9/1**
6011 **3** 1/2 **Myannabanana (IRE)**[18] 6066 2-9-2 67....(v) MFenton 5 63
(JRWeymes) *chsd ldrs: rdn over 2f out: sn hung rt: styd on same pce* **5/1**[2]
0400 **4** 3 **Yankeedoodledandy (IRE)**[54] 5671 2-7-6 50.... DFentiman(7) 4 39
(PCHaslam) *outpcd: styd on appr fnl f: nvr nrr* **16/1**

2610 **5** *nk* **St Savarin (FR)**[25] 6023 2-9-7 72 ........ NPollard 2 60
(JRBest) *chsd ldrs: rdn over 2f out: wknd fnl f* **8/1**
1022 **6** *shd* **Turf Princess**[18] 6066 2-8-10 61 ........ ANicholls 1 49
(IanEmmerson) *led: hdd over 6f out: wknd fnl f* **12/1**
603 **7** *8* **Restart (IRE)**[53] 5691 2-8-10 68 ........ RoryMoore(7) 7 39
(PCHaslam) *sn outpcd* **11/2**[3]
051 **8** *8* **Lasting Delight**[15] 6082 2-9-5 70 ........ JMackay 8 23
(SirMarkPrescott) *chsd ldrs: sn pushed along: wknd 3f out* **5/2**[1]
000 **9** *18* **Altares**[42] 5870 2-8-3 54 ........ FNorton 6 —
(PHowling) *s.s: outpcd* **16/1**
000 **10** *10* **Samolis (IRE)**[36] 5940 2-7-13 55 oh14 ow6 ........ (b[1]) RThomas(5) 3 —
(RCurtis) *chsd ldrs to 1/2-way* **66/1**

1m 46.68s (2.08) **Going Correction** +0.225s/f (Slow) **10** Ran SP% **113.8**
Speed ratings: **98,92,91,88,88 88,80,72,54,44**CSF £75.82 CT £405.47 TOTE £13.50: £2.60, £2.20, £1.70; EX 102.50.
**Owner** Paul J Dixon **Bred** J W Ford **Trained** Hambleton, N Yorks

**FOCUS**
Fractionally the slower of the two divisions.

**NOTEBOOK**
**Bold Blade** overcame an outside draw and was soon in front against the running rail. He came right away and faces another stiff hike in his rating.
**Chariot(IRE)**, who raced wide in the backstretch, stayed on to snatch a remote second spot. He looks weighted to the hilt.
**Myannabanana(IRE)**, having his first outing for his new stable, has gone up 15lb for his two wins and looks fully exposed now.
**Yankeedoodledandy(IRE)**, absent since October, stayed on when it was all over.
**St Savarin(FR)**, with the headgear left off, didn't get home on this testing surface.
**Turf Princess**, who has changed stables, is a keen type and this stretched her to breaking point.
**Lasting Delight**, soon pushed along, dropped right away turning in. She had plenty on her plate on her nursery bow but this was surely too bad to be true.

## 6174 STEPHANIE SMITH BIRTHDAY CLAIMING STKS — 1m 3f (F)
**1:00** (1:00) (E) 3-4-Y-O — **£2,086** (£596; £298) **Stalls** Low

Form — RPR
0320 **1** **Theatre Tinka (IRE)**[39] 5920 4-9-1 62 ........ (p) ACulhane 4 67
(RHollinshead) *trckd ldrs: led over 4f out: clr over 2f out: rdn out* **5/1**[2]
1502 **2** *2* **Caroubier (IRE)**[15] 3626 3-8-13 83 ........ CCatlin 5 66
(IanWilliams) *sn outpcd: hdwy 6f out: rdn to chse wnr over 3f: styd on same pce ins fnl f* **8/11**[1]
0365 **3** *18* **Samar Qand**[15] 6085 4-7-11 41 ........ (p) JJeffrey(7) 1 26
(JulianPoulton) *led over 4f: wknd over 1f out* **25/1**
0000 **4** *5* **Platinum Charmer (IRE)**[39] 5920 3-8-13 65 ........ RWinston 12 32
(KARyan) *dwlt: outpcd and racd wd: nvr nr to chal* **10/1**[3]
002 **5** *1 3/4* **Radiant Bride**[7] 6139 3-7-9 47 ow2 ........ AReilly(7) 9 18
(KRBurke) *sn outpcd: effrt over 4f out: sn wknd* **14/1**
5400 **6** *15* **Pertemps Bianca**[217] 1507 3-7-9 45 ........ (b[1]) FPFerris(3) 8 —
(ADSmith) *prom over 6f* **33/1**
**7** *3* **Bonjour Directa (GER)**[41] 3-8-3 ........ JMackay 11 —
(THHansen, Germany) *hld up: effrt over 4f out: sn wknd* **10/1**[3]
0000 **8** *2 1/2* **Toro Bravo (IRE)**[18] 6068 3-8-8 64 ........ (b[1]) WRyan 6 —
(RMBeckett) *chsd ldr: led over 6f out: hdd over 4f out: wknd over 3f out* **16/1**
05 **9** *4* **Turftanzer (GER)**[10] 6125 4-9-7 40 ........ (t) KimTinkler 7 —
(DonEnricoIncisa) *chsd ldrs over 6f* **66/1**
-000 **10** *1 1/4* **A Two (IRE)**[24] 6033 4-8-4 44 ........ JFanning 10 —
(BPalling) *prom over 6f* **33/1**
0404 **11** *dist* **Two Steps To Go (USA)**[194] 2048 4-8-9 40 ........ ANicholls 3 —
(IanEmmerson) *chsd ldrs: lost pl over 6f out: sn bhd* **33/1**

2m 31.37s (2.47) **Going Correction** +0.225s/f (Slow)
**WFA** 3 from 4yo 4lb **11** Ran SP% **119.5**
Speed ratings: **100,98,85,81,80 69,67,65,62,61** — CT £13.70 TOTE £2.30: £1.02, £6.30, £; EX21.20 1.Caroubier (no.3) was claimed by Nigel Shields for £10,000. Theatre Tinka (no.2) was the subject of a friendly claim of £9,000
**Owner** Tim Leadbeater **Bred** Ballylinch Stud **Trained** Upper Longdon, Staffs

**FOCUS**
Plenty with no real chance on official figures and they came in well strung out.

**NOTEBOOK**
**Theatre Tinka(IRE)**, making his All-Weather bow, had nearly a stone and a half to find with the favourite but it did not work out like that and in the end he won going away.
**Caroubier(IRE)** wanted nothing to do with the frantic early pace. He went in pursuit of the winner but, after getting to his quarters, he had to give best inside the last. He was claimed by Nigel Shields.
**Samar Qand**, who had plenty to find, set a strong pace. That she kept on to occupy third spot says little for those behind her.
**Platinum Charmer(IRE)** is basically out of form and has yet to prove conclusively that he stays this far.

## 6175 LITTLEWOODS BET DIRECT MAIDEN STKS — 1m (F)
**1:35** (1:37) (D) 2-Y-O — **£2,142** (£612; £153; £153) **Stalls** Low

Form — RPR
4025 **1** **Bethanys Boy (IRE)**[15] 6083 2-9-0 73 ........ RWinston 15 75
(BEllison) *chsd ldrs: led over 3f out: styd on wl* **7/1**[3]
2200 **2** *3 1/2* **Carriacou**[19] 6059 2-8-4 72 ........ (e[1]) BReilly(5) 2 62
(PWD'Arcy) *hld up in tch: rdn over 2f out: styd on pce fnl f* **9/2**[2]
2322 **3** *1 1/2* **Hawkit (USA)**[26] 6012 2-9-0 72 ........ DaneO'Neill 4 64
(JAOsborne) *a.p: rdn over 2f out: styd on same pce fnl f* **3/1**[1]
**3** *dht* **Victory Lap (GER)** 2-8-9 ........ CCatlin 7 59
(MRChannon) *s.i.s: sn pushed along in rr: hdwy over 2f out: r.o: nt rch ldrs* **20/1**
0034 **5** *1/2* **Amwell Brave**[25] 6023 2-9-0 69 ........ SWKelly 16 63
(JRJenkins) *chsd ldrs: rdn over 2f out: wknd ins fnl f* **12/1**
0504 **6** *7* **Smart Boy Prince (IRE)**[5] 6145 2-8-12 50 ow3 ........ DNolan(5) 13 51
(PABlockley) *led over 4f: wknd over 1f out* **25/1**
**7** *3/4* **My Paris** 2-9-0 ........ GParkin 3 46
(KARyan) *s.i.s: sn prom: wknd 3f out* **40/1**
000 **8** *hd* **Cassanos (IRE)**[53] 5689 2-9-0 60 ........ MFenton 11 45
(MissGayKelleway) *chsd ldrs: lost pl 1/2-way: n.d after* **50/1**
6 **9** *6* **Sunny Lady (FR)**[17] 6074 2-8-9 ........ WRyan 10 27
(EALDunlop) *s.i.s: sn prom: wknd 3f out* **7/1**[3]
**10** *7* **Frankies Wings (IRE)** 2-8-9 ........ RMiles(5) 5 17
(TGMills) *s.i.s: a in rr* **9/2**[2]
**11** *nk* **Patricia Ray** 2-8-2 ........ MHalford(7) 6 11
(CDrew) *s.i.s: outpcd* **66/1**
4006 **12** *1* **Knickyknackienoo**[91] 4876 2-9-0 56 ........ MHenry 14 14
(TTClement) *plld hrd and prom: hmpd over 5f out: sn lost pl* **50/1**
0 **13** *5* **Maid The Cut**[37] 5934 2-8-9 ........ JBramhill 8 —
(ADSmith) *s.i.s: outpcd* **66/1**
**14** *3 1/2* **Thara'A (IRE)** 2-8-9 ........ JFanning 12 —
(EALDunlop) *dwlt: plld hrd and sn prom: wknd 3f out* **20/1**
000 **15** *8* **Fubos**[36] 5940 2-9-0 75 ........ IMongan 9 —
(JulianPoulton) *prom to 1/2-way* **12/1**
**16** *dist* **Mikes Mate** 2-8-9 ........ TEaves(5) 1 —
(CJTeague) *s.s: outpcd* **66/1**

1m 47.19s (2.59) **Going Correction** +0.225s/f (Slow) **16** Ran SP% **126.0**
Speed ratings: **96,92,91,91,90 83,82,82,76,69 69,68,63,59,51** —CSF £36.63 TOTE £8.10: £2.60, £1.80; EX 52.90 TRIFECTA Pl: Hawkit 0.70, Victory Lap £2.90.
**Owner** Graeme Redpath **Bred** K And Mrs Cullen **Trained** Norton, N Yorks

**FOCUS**
Plenty of deadwood.

**NOTEBOOK**
**Bethanys Boy(IRE)**, on his tenth career start but only his second on the All-Weather, ran out a decisive winner. Rated 73 here, he faces an uphill task from his revised mark.
**Carriacou** looked a real threat at one stage but in the end was very definitely second best.
**Hawkit(USA)**, rated 72, is starting to look fully exposed.
**Victory Lap(GER)**, a tall newcomer, made a sluggish start. She still had 10 horses in front of her two furlongs out before finishing with quite a flourish. This will have taught her plenty and she should improve and find a race.
**Amwell Brave** has shown improved form now on his last three starts but he looks rated to the hilt.
**Frankies Wings(IRE)**, a tall newcomer, missed the break and never went a yard. He would not face the kickback but must surely be a lot better than he showed here. *Official explanation: jockey said colt resented the kickback*

## 6176 BETDIRECT.CO.UK H'CAP — 7f (F)
**2:05** (2:05) (D) (0-85,76) 3-Y-0+ — **£2,212** (£632; £316) **Stalls** Low

Form — RPR
0012 **1** **Mon Secret (IRE)**[22] 6042 5-8-7 **58** ........ RFfrench 6 70
(BSmart) *chsd ldrs: rdn over 2f out: n.m.r and led over 1f out: all out* **7/2**[2]
0000 **2** *hd* **Warden Warren**[7] 6135 5-8-8 **64** ........ (b) BReilly(5) 5 76
(MrsCADunnett) *s.i.s: sn chsng ldrs: hung lft wl over 1f out: r.o* **16/1**
4231 **3** *shd* **Majik**[4] 6151 4-9-2 **67** 7ex ........ IMongan 1 78
(DJSFfrenchDavis) *trckd ldrs: rdn and ev ch fr over 1f out: r.o* **10/3**[1]
2401 **4** *1 1/4* **Ashtree Belle**[29] 5992 4-9-6 **76** ........ RThomas(5) 4 84
(DHaydnJones) *hld up in tch: nt clr run over 1f out: styd on same pce towards fin* **13/2**
0000 **5** *3* **Winning Pleasure (IRE)**[15] 6084 5-9-7 **72** ........ JEdmunds 8 73
(JBalding) *chsd ldrs: rdn to ld 2f out: sn hdd: wknd ins fnl f* **12/1**
4134 **6** *3 1/2* **Scramble (USA)**[19] 6055 5-7-11 **51** ........ (bt) FPFerris(3) 7 43
(BEllison) *chsd ldrs: rdn and ev ch 2f out: sn hung lft and wknd* **5/1**[3]
0421 **7** *7* **Far Note (USA)**[18] 6063 5-9-0 **65** ........ (b) DarrenWilliams 3 39
(SRBowring) *sn led: hdd 2f out: sn wknd* **8/1**
0056 **8** *1 1/2* **Supreme Salutation**[18] 6070 7-9-1 **66** ........ ACulhane 2 37
(DWChapman) *chsd ldrs: lost pl wl over 3f out: sn bhd* **11/1**
0000 **9** *2* **African Spur (IRE)**[15] 6084 3-9-0 **72** ........ DerekNolan(7) 9 38
(PABlockley) *hmpd 1/2-way: a in rr* **20/1**

1m 31.72s (0.92) **Going Correction** +0.225s/f (Slow) **9** Ran SP% **113.1**
Speed ratings: **103,102,102,101,97 93,85,84,81**CSF £55.93 CT £201.34 TOTE £3.30: £1.20, £2.90, £2.00; EX 73.80.
**Owner** Pinnacle Monash Partnership **Bred** John Hutchinson **Trained** Hambleton, N Yorks

**FOCUS**
In effect a 0-76 handicap.

**NOTEBOOK**
**Mon Secret(IRE)**, a seven-furlong specialist, showed the right attitude and, after being tightened up, he came off just best in a tight three-way finish.
**Warden Warren**, who likes to race alone, was brought to race agsinst the stands'-side rail and in the end just missed out.
**Majik**, under a 7lb penalty, is in the form of his life.
**Ashtree Belle**, tightened up at a crucial stage, has recorded her three All-Weather wins at Wolverhampton.
**Winning Pleasure(IRE)** hasn't won for over two years and seems better suited by six.
**Supreme Salutation** *Official explanation: jockey said gelding was not moving well*

## 6177 LITTLEWOODSPOKER.COM MAIDEN STKS — 1m 4f (F)
**2:40** (2:41) (E) 3-4-Y-O — **£2,254** (£644; £322) **Stalls** Low

Form — RPR
0 **1** **Dub Dash (USA)**[14] 6089 3-8-9 ........ BReilly(5) 8 74
(SCWilliams) *chsd ldrs: led 4f out: sn hrd rdn: clr over 1f out: eased nr fin* **33/1**
0002 **2** *5* **Exit To Heaven**[7] 6137 3-8-9 60 ........ MFenton 7 62
(MissGayKelleway) *chsd ldrs: rdn over 2f out: styd on same pce* **4/1**[3]
6-2 **3** *1/2* **Newtonian (USA)**[253] 928 4-9-5 ........ DeanMcKeown 11 66
(JParkes) *a.p: chsd wnr over 3f out: rdn and hung rt over 1f out: no ex* **13/2**
**4** *18* **Heathyards Pride** 3-9-0 ........ DaleGibson 4 41
(RHollinshead) *s.i.s: sn outpcd and bhd* **33/1**
04 **5** *4* **Fortunes Favourite**[19] 6060 3-8-4 ........ TEaves(5) 14 31
(GMMoore) *sn outpcd and bhd* **7/1**
2036 **6** *4* **Remembrance**[14] 6089 3-9-0 65 ........ (bt[1]) JTate 6 30
(JMPEustace) *trckd ldrs: racd keenly: led over 6f out: hdd 4f out: wknd 3f out* **11/4**[1]
000 **7** *2 1/2* **Galley Law**[15] 6086 3-9-0 25 ........ RFfrench 10 26
(RCraggs) *prom 7f* **66/1**
0500 **8** *14* **Dr Julian (IRE)**[39] 5914 3-8-7 43 ........ (p) PMakin(7) 5 7
(MissAStokell) *chsd ldrs over 6f* **25/1**
**9** *6* **Sean's Memory (USA)** 3-9-0 ........ CCatlin 12 —
(MrsCADunnett) *s.s: outpcd* **20/1**
0000 **10** *9* **Simon The Poacher**[7] 6137 4-9-2 42 ........ LPKeniry(3) 13 —
(LPGrassick) *s.i.s: outpcd* **66/1**
0-00 **11** *11* **By All Men (IRE)**[10] 6125 3-8-7 50 ........ SYourston(7) 2 —
(PABlockley) *sn outpcd and bhd* **25/1**
-005 **12** *3/4* **Senza Scrupoli**[159] 3062 3-9-0 73 ........ ACulhane 15 —
(MDHammond) *s.i.s: outpcd* **11/1**
0 **13** *11* **Pertemps Conection**[43] 5846 3-8-9 ........ WRyan 3 —
(ADSmith) *prom to 1/2-way* **33/1**
0446 **14** *27* **Hartshead**[160] 3039 4-9-5 65 ........ RWinston 16 —
(GASwinbank) *led: hdd over 6f out: wknd 5f out* **7/2**[2]

2m 47.59s (5.49) **Going Correction** +0.225s/f (Slow)
**WFA** 3 from 4yo 5lb **14** Ran SP% **127.3**
Speed ratings: **90,86,86,74,71 69,67,58,54,48 40,40,32,14**CSF £161.04 TOTE £41.90: £12.00, £1.70, £3.00; EX 686.30.
**Owner** Stuart C Williams **Bred** B C Jones **Trained** Newmarket, Suffolk
■ Stewards Enquiry : R Winston one-day ban: failed to keep straight from stalls (Dec 27)

**FOCUS**
A surprise winner but no fluke.

**NOTEBOOK**
**Dub Dash(USA)**, a big type, had been well beaten on his debut two weeks earlier. He apparently shows nothing at home but he came clear and in the end won easing up. He should improve again.
**Exit To Heaven**, rated 60, is the measure of the form.
**Newtonian(USA)** was having only his third career start and his first outing since April.
**Heathyards Pride** stayed on when it was all over on his belated debut.
**Fortunes Favourite** is at least now qualified for a handicap mark.
**Remembrance**, who had finished a long way ahead of the winner at Lingfield two weeks earlier, was far too keen in first-time blinkers.
**Dr Julian(IRE)** *Official explanation: jockey said gelding had lost its action*
**By All Men(IRE)** *Official explanation: jockey said gelding had bled from the nose*
**Pertemps Conection** *Official explanation: jockey said filly had lost her action*
**Hartshead** was far too keen in front and his rider called it a day before the end of the backstretch. The gelding was reported not to have been suited by the slow surface but that was not the real reason for such an abject failure. *Official explanation: trainer said gelding may have been unsuited by the slow surface*

## 6178 BET DIRECT IN RUNNING SKY TEXT 293 H'CAP — 1m (F)
3:15 (3:15) (E) (0-75,74) 3-Y-0+ — **£2,163** (£618; £309) **Stalls** Low

| Form | Pos | Dist | Horse | Jockey | RPR |
|---|---|---|---|---|---|
| 2-30 | 1 | | **Sangiovese**[44] 5837 4-9-1 **63** | LFletcher(3) 3 | 91 |
| | | | (HMorrison) *mde all: pushed clr over 2f out* | **5/1**[3] | |
| 1045 | 2 | 13 | **Brandy Cove**[10] 6124 6-9-6 **65** | RFfrench 6 | 67 |
| | | | (BSmart) *chsd ldrs: outpcd fnl 2f* | **9/2**[2] | |
| 0602 | 3 | 2 | **Zarin (IRE)**[7] 6135 5-9-11 **70** | ACulhane 16 | 68 |
| | | | (DWChapman) *hld up: styd on appr fnl f: nvr nrr* | **8/1** | |
| 3553 | 4 | 1 ¾ | **Faraway Look (USA)**[177] 2505 6-9-2 **61** | RHavlin 15 | 56 |
| | | | (JGMO'Shea) *hld up: sme hdwy over 1f out: n.d* | **25/1** | |
| 4504 | 5 | 1 ½ | **Tropical Coral (IRE)**[11] 6119 3-9-13 **73** | JFanning 10 | 65 |
| | | | (CTinkler) *hld up: outpcd over 3f out: n.d* | **12/1** | |
| 0000 | 6 | 2 ½ | **Lucayan Monarch**[10] 6124 5-8-13 **58** | (p) DeanMcKeown 5 | 45 |
| | | | (PABlockley) *hld up: effrt over 2f out: n.d* | **25/1** | |
| 0331 | 7 | ¾ | **Mcqueen (IRE)**[18] 6070 3-9-9 **74** | PMulrennan(5) 14 | 59 |
| | | | (MrsHDalton) *hld up: effrt and hung lft 2f out: n.d* | **11/8**[1] | |
| 3000 | 8 | hd | **Tropical Son**[60] 5560 4-7-12 **48** oh2 ow5 | (v) RThomas(5) 12 | 33 |
| | | | (DShaw) *outpcd: nvr nrr* | **50/1** | |
| 4056 | 9 | 3 ½ | **Allegrina (IRE)**[28] 6006 3-9-2 **62** | (b1) RWinston 9 | 40 |
| | | | (KARyan) *chsd ldrs: rdn over 3f out: wknd 2f out* | **14/1** | |
| 0040 | 10 | shd | **Jessie**[24] 6028 4-7-13 **44** | KimTinkler 7 | 21 |
| | | | (DonEnricoIncisa) *prom over 4f* | **50/1** | |
| 6040 | 11 | shd | **Proud Victor (IRE)**[19] 6057 3-7-12 **44** oh2 | (v) DKinsella 1 | 21 |
| | | | (DShaw) *prom over 5f* | **25/1** | |
| 1346 | 12 | 6 | **Quiet Reading (USA)**[141] 3580 6-9-10 **69** | (v) GBaker 11 | 34 |
| | | | (MRBosley) *chsd ldrs 6f* | **14/1** | |
| 0000 | 13 | 12 | **Surdoue**[18] 6068 3-9-12 **72** | PaulEddery 4 | 13 |
| | | | (PHowling) *prom over 4f* | **50/1** | |
| 0400 | 14 | 25 | **Lady Of Gdansk (IRE)**[45] 5832 4-8-0 **45** | CCatlin 8 | — |
| | | | (HJCollingridge) *w wnr 3f: wknd 1/2-way* | **50/1** | |

1m 43.69s (-0.91) **Going Correction** +0.225s/f (Slow)
**WFA** 3 from 4yo+ 1lb — **14** Ran SP% **128.5**
Speed ratings: **113,100,98,96,94 92,91,91,87,87 87,81,69,44**CSF £28.24 CT £187.21 TOTE £9.20: £2.20, £1.50, £2.90; EX 36.50 Place 6 £51.22, Place 5 £30.01.
**Owner** Kentisbeare Quartet **Bred** Jeremy Green And Sons **Trained** East Ilsley, Berks

**NOTEBOOK**
**Sangiovese**, who ran really well here two outings ago, disappointed next time and was back here after a seven-week break. A grand type who looked really well, he turned this into a procession. In time he should win much better races than this on turf.
**Brandy Cove**, back in the right grade, finished clear second best but he looks rated to the hilt.
**Zarin(IRE)**, who is slipping to a more realistic mark, had the worst of the draw. He stayed on in encouraging fashion and his trainer is still on a learning curve with him.
**Faraway Look(USA)**, who hasn't tasted success for over three years, was not knocked about on his first outing since June.
**Mcqueen(IRE)**, who needs plenty of driving, was most disappointing from a 13lb higher mark. The much deeper surface was not solely to blame. *Official explanation: jockey said gelding was never travelling*
T/Plt: £16.20 to a £1 stake. Pool: £21,985.60. 990.55 winning tickets. T/Qpdt: £4.60 to a £1 stake. Pool: £1,488.10. 136.90 winning tickets. CR

# 6135 WOLVERHAMPTON (A.W) (L-H)
Saturday, December 13
**6179 Meeting Abandoned** - Waterlogged

# SHA TIN (R-H)
Sunday, December 14
**OFFICIAL GOING: Good to firm**

## 6185a HONG KONG VASE (GROUP 1) — 1m 4f
5:45 (5:49) 3-Y-0+ — **£640,000** (£240,000; £120,000; £64,000)

| Pos | Dist | Horse | Jockey | RPR |
|---|---|---|---|---|
| 1 | | **Vallee Enchantee (IRE)**[56] 5662 3-8-5 | DBoeuf 3 | 115 |
| | | (ELellouche, France) *held up towards rear, 11th straight, headway over 1 1/2f out, soon hard ridden, stayed on to lead last 50 yards* | **11/2**[2] | |
| 2 | ¾ | **Polish Summer**[21] 6-9-0 | CSoumillon 7 | 118 |
| | | (AFabre, France) *mid division, 7th straight, hard ridden to lead over 1f out, edged right, headed and no extra 50 yards out* | **8/1** | |
| 3 | shd | **Warrsan (IRE)**[56] 5666 5-9-0 | PRobinson 1 | 118 |
| | | (CEBrittain) *lw: tracked leader in 3rd, 3rd straight, ridden 1 1/2f out, switched to inside and stayed on well under pressure closing st* | **12/1** | |
| 4 | nk | **Roosevelt (IRE)**[168] 2832 3-8-9 | MJKinane 9 | 117 |
| | | (DOughton, Hong Kong) *lw: held up towards rear, 10th straight, stayed on final 1 1/2f* | **16/1** | |
| 5 | nk | **Fair Mix (IRE)**[28] 6008 5-9-0 | GMosse 11 | 117 |
| | | (MRolland, France) *mid division, dropped back to 12th entering straight, stayed on steadily down outside under pressure from 1 1/2f out* | **8/1** | |
| 6 | ½ | **River Dancer (IRE)**[22] 4-9-0 | SDye 6 | 116 |
| | | (JSize, Hong Kong) *raced in 2nd til led 2f out, headed over 1f out, beaten when slightly hampered inside final f* | **14/1** | |
| 7 | nk | **Imperial Dancer**[28] 6008 5-9-0 | TEDurcan 14 | 116 |
| | | (MRChannon) *lw: in rear, no room and switched left over 1 1/2f out, satyed on from over 1f out* | **4/1**[1] | |
| 8 | hd | **Kalabar**[56] 5662 3-8-9 | TThulliez 10 | 115 |
| | | (PBary, France) *mid division, 8th straight, ridden and one pace final 1 1/2f* | **7/1**[3] | |
| 9 | nk | **Indian Creek**[57] 5641 5-9-0 | TQuinn 8 | 115 |
| | | (DRCElsworth) *held up in last, ridden on outside over 1 1/2f out, stayed on at one pace* | **8/1** | |
| 10 | ¾ | **Red Pepper**[56] 6-9-0 | DWhyte 2 | 114 |
| | | (CHYip, Hong Kong) *in touch on inside, 5th straight, switched left over 1 1/2f out, stayed on at same pace from over 1f out* | **20/1** | |
| 11 | shd | **Fields Of Omagh (AUS)**[14] 6103 6-9-0 | (v) StevenKing 5 | 114 |
| | | (TMcevoy, Australia) *close up, 6th straight, ridden and one pace final 1 1/2f* | **11/1** | |
| 12 | 4 ¼ | **Maktub (ITY)**[28] 6008 4-9-0 | LDettori 13 | 107 |
| | | (BGrizzetti, Italy) *held up in rear, pushed along over 3f out, 13th straight, soon beaten* | **16/1** | |
| 13 | 2 ¼ | **Industrial Success (IRE)**[29] 3-8-9 | JPSpencer 12 | 104 |
| | | (CHYip, Hong Kong) *raced in 4th, pushed along over 2 1/2f out, 4th straight, soon weakened* | **40/1** | |
| 14 | 6 ¾ | **Sabiango (GER)**[56] 5670 5-9-0 | (b) EPedroza 4 | 94 |
| | | (AWohler, Germany) *coltish: swtg: set steady pace headed 2f out, weakened* | **16/1** | |

2m 28.2s
**WFA** 3 from 4yo+ 5lb — **14** Ran SP% **128.8**
Speed ratings: .
**Owner** Ecurie Wildenstein **Bred** Dayton Investments Ltd **Trained** France

**NOTEBOOK**
**Vallee Enchantee(IRE)** is only small but makes up in class and heart what she lacks in stature. Among the backmarkers entering the straight, she got the full treatment from Boeuf, but responded gamely to get up in the final 50 yards.\n\x\x She has shown a preference for soft ground so this was a particularly praiseworthy effort, and she will remain in training.
**Polish Summer**moved up from midfield to hit the front over a furlong out but, lugging in towards the rail, had no answer to the winner's final burst and only just held on for second.
**Warrsan(IRE)** had failed to regain the weight that he lost on the flight but looked tremendously well and ran close to his best. Always in the leading trio, he was switched to race against the inside rail 200 yards out and almost snatched second on the line. The Dubai Sheema Classic will be his first target of 2004.
**Roosevelt(IRE)**looked tremendously well and showed he had acclimatised since running over an inadequate seven furlongs last time by running really well.
**Imperial Dancer**who looked well in the preliminaries, was attempting the impossible in this steadily-run race. Stone last with over three furlongs to run, he went for an ambitious run up the inside on the home turn. Forced to switch, he plugged on but never looked like getting to the leaders and was hanging slightly on ground that was on the fast side for him. Dubai is likely to be his next port of call.
**Indian Creek**, who was never on the bridle, needs a stronger pace for his exaggerated waiting tactics to be effective.
**Maktub(ITY)**, who ducked off the track and ran through a set of rails earlier in the week, failed to show his true form and will now join Michael Jarvis.

## 6186a HONG KONG SPRINT (GROUP 1) — 5f
6:50 (6:53) 3-Y-0+ — **£456,000** (£176,000; £80,000; £45,600)

| Pos | Dist | Horse | Jockey | RPR |
|---|---|---|---|---|
| 1 | | **Silent Witness (AUS)**[22] 4-9-0 | FCoetzee 11 | 127 |
| | | (ACruz, Hong Kong) *broke fast, chased leader in 2nd on outside, led 120 yards out, ran on strongly* | **10/11**[1] | |
| 2 | 1 | **National Currency (SAF)**[64] 4-9-0 | WMawing 6 | 123 |
| | | (MAzzie, South Africa) *soon led, 1 length clear halfway, ridden 1 1/2f out, headed and no extra 120 yards out* | **8/1**[2] | |
| 3 | ½ | **Cape Of Good Hope**[22] 5-9-0 | (v) MJKinane 14 | 121 |
| | | (DOughton, Hong Kong) *in touch on outside, ridden 1 1/2f out, stayed on* | **33/1** | |
| 4 | 1 ¼ | **Firebolt (IRE)**[22] 5-9-0 | (b) AMarcus 2 | 117 |
| | | (IWAllan, Hong Kong) *prominent towards inside, ridden inside final f, stayed on at same pace* | **16/1** | |
| 5 | 1 ¼ | **Acclamation**[70] 5402 4-9-0 | LDettori 7 | 113 |
| | | (LGCottrell) *towards rear, stayed on steadily from 1 1/2f out* | **11/1** | |
| 6 | ¾ | **The Trader (IRE)**[70] 5402 5-9-0 | (b) KFallon 13 | 110 |
| | | (MBlanshard) *slowly into stride, last til stayed on final 1 1/2f* | **20/1** | |
| 7 | ¾ | **The Tatling (IRE)**[58] 5615 6-9-0 | RMoore 12 | 107 |
| | | (JMBradley) *missed break, towards rear til some late headway* | **16/1** | |
| 8 | ½ | **Cheerful Fortune (NZ)**[22] 4-9-0 | CraigWilliams 10 | 106 |
| | | (TWLeung, Hong Kong) *chased winner til outpaced from over 1 1/2f out* | **12/1** | |
| 9 | 1 ¼ | **Into The Night (AUS)**[43] 4-9-0 | DBeadman 4 | 101 |
| | | (KDryden, Australia) *in touch til outpaced from 1 1/2f out* | **16/1** | |
| 10 | hd | **All Thrills Too (AUS)**[22] 6-9-0 | (b) GMosse 5 | 101 |
| | | (DHayes, Hong Kong) *in touch til pushed along and outpaced from 2f out* | **16/1** | |
| 11 | shd | **Grand Delight (AUS)**[22] 6-9-0 | (b) SDye 3 | 100 |
| | | (JSize, Hong Kong) *speed to halfway* | **20/1** | |
| 12 | nse | **Dantana (AUS)**[50] 4-9-0 | (b) DMOliver 1 | 100 |
| | | (RHore-Lacy, Australia) *prominent on inside rail til weakened 1f out* | **20/1** | |
| 13 | hd | **Bomber Bill (AUS)**[43] 8-9-0 | (b) SArnold 8 | 99 |
| | | (RSmerdon, Australia) *in touch til weakened 2f out* | **25/1** | |
| 14 | 5 ¼ | **Deportivo**[105] 4603 3-9-0 | RHughes 9 | 81 |
| | | (RCharlton) *chased winner on outside, pushed along halfway, soon weakened* | **10/1**[3] | |

56.50 secs — **14** Ran SP% **133.2**
Speed ratings: .
**Owner** Arthur Antonio da Silva & Betty da Silva **Bred** I K Smith **Trained** Hong Kong

**NOTEBOOK**
**Silent Witness(AUS)** took his career record to an unblemished eight wins with another superb performance. Racing down the centre of the course from his wide draw, he seemed in trouble for an instant when National Currency was still in front with over a furlong to run, but Coetzee stayed admirably cool and was eventually able to ease down in the last few strides. At least three more Hong Kong starts are planned in an attempt to break the former colony's ten successive win record, but Europe, and Royal Ascot in particular, could be his destination next summer. He stays six furlongs and should get seven.
**National Currency(SAF)**, who had two handlers in the paddock and was very full of himself beforehand, is a real speedball and was unfortunate to come up against such a brilliant winner.
**Cape Of Good Hope**really needs another furlong.
**Acclamation** stayed on stoutly in the closing stages of his final start before retiring to stud, but needed a stiffer test than this.
**The Trader(IRE)** was the slowest away and for a long time trailed the field, but answered a typical Fallon drive to sneak a share of the prizemoney. He is better with some cut in the ground.

**The Tatling(IRE)**, who did not travel over that well but had settled down on arrival, missed the break and was never able to get competitive.
**Deportivo** had not run since August and it showed. He displayed good\n\x\x early speed but came under pressure at halfway and was the first one beaten.

## 6187a HONG KONG MILE (GROUP 1) 1m
7:55 (7:57) 3-Y-0+ **£640,000** (£240,000; £120,000; £64,000)

RPR

1 **Lucky Owners (NZ)**[22] 3-9-0 ........ FCoetzee 7 120
(ACruz, Hong Kong) *always in touch on inside, 5th straight, ridden 1f out, led 100 yards out, driven out* **12/1**

2 1/2 **Bowman's Crossing (IRE)**[22] 4-9-0 ........ MJKinane 13 119
(DOughton, Hong Kong) *held up in rear, headway 3f out, brought wide straight, stayed on strongly down outside final 1 1/2f, not reach winner* **25/1**

3 1/2 **Lohengrin (JPN)**[42] 4-9-0 ........ KDesormeaux 12 117
(MIto, Japan) *raced in 2nd, carried wide and 3rd straight, ridden and every chance over 1 1/2f out til no extra final 100 yards* **9/2**[1]

4 1/2 **Admire Max (JPN)**[70] 4-9-0 ........ YFukunaga 14 116
(MHashida, Japan) *in touch, headway towards inside to go 2nd straight, led narrowly over 1 1/2f out til headed 100 yards out, one pace* **11/2**[3]

5 shd **Firebreak**[138] 3669 4-9-0 ........ LDettori 10 116
(SaeedBinSuroor) *lw: mid division, 7th straight, stayed on at one pace final 2f* **14/1**

6 1 3/4 **Meridian Star (AUS)**[22] 6-9-0 ........(b) GMosse 6 112
(DHayes, Hong Kong) *last early, headway and 8th straight, stayed on at same pace final 2f* **25/1**

7 shd **Telegnosis (JPN)**[21] 6054 4-9-0 ........ MKatsuura 2 112
(HSugiura, Japan) *held up in 12th, 9th straight, some late headway* **8/1**

8 nk **Ho Choi**[22] 4-9-0 ........(b) CSoumillon 8 111
(IWAllan, Hong Kong) *always prominent on inside, led narrowly over 2f out til headed over 1 1/2f out, one pace* **12/1**

9 4 1/4 **Special Kaldoun (IRE)**[21] 6054 4-9-0 ........ DBoeuf 4 101
(DSmaga, France) *towards rear early, 6th straight, soon ridden and beaten* **5/1**[2]

10 2 1/2 **Mister Acpen (CHI)**[140] 5-9-0 ........(b) DFlores 9 96
(KristinMulhall, U.S.A) *towards rear, 13th straight, never a factor* **16/1**

11 3/4 **Passing Glance**[63] 5530 4-9-0 ........ MartinDwyer 11 94
(AMBalding) *mid division on outside, pushed along 3f out, ridden and beaten entering straight* **16/1**

12 2 1/4 **Citizen Kane (ARG)**[22] 7-9-0 ........ RFradd 5 89
(ACruz, Hong Kong) *in touch, 10th straight, soon beaten* **16/1**

13 8 1/2 **Ninetyfive Emperor (AUS)** 4-9-0 ........(b) JSaimee 3 69
(CLeck, Singapore) *set good pace til ran wide and headed entering straight, weakened* **20/1**

P **Olympic Express**[22] 5-9-0 ........ DWhyte 1 —
(IWAllan, Hong Kong) *towards rear til eased and pulled up over 2 1/2f out, lame* **15/2**

1m 34.3s
**WFA** 3 from 4yo+ 1lb **14** Ran SP% **125.3**
Speed ratings: .
**Owner** Mr & Mrs Leung Kai Fai **Bred** Mrs J A & P Hogan **Trained** Hong Kong

**NOTEBOOK**
**Lucky Owners(NZ)** completed a Group One double for his trainer and jockey.
**Firebreak**goes well fresh and ran a solid race, staying on steadily in the home straight to just miss fourth.
**Passing Glance** has been on the go since April and did not get the best of breaks. Unable to dominate as he likes, he was struggling from the outset and ran some way below his best.

## 6188a HONG KONG CUP (GROUP 1) 1m 2f
8:35 (8:36) 3-Y-0+ **£816,000** (£320,000; £144,000; £80,000)

RPR

1 **Falbrav (IRE)**[50] 5773 5-9-0 ........ LDettori 5 129
(LMCumani) *lw: mid division, 8th straight, soon switched right, quickened to lead just over 1f out, ridden clear, ran on strongly* **5/4**[1]

2 2 **Rakti**[57] 5641 4-9-0 ........ PRobinson 4 125
(MAJarvis) *lw: in rear early, headway on inside over 4f out, bumped by winner 2f out, ridden to go 2nd inside final f, stayed on* **4/1**[2]

3 1 1/4 **Elegant Fashion (AUS)**[29] 5-8-10 ........ GMosse 7 119
(DHayes, Hong Kong) *raced in 5th, 3rd straight, every chance 2f out to just over 1f out, one pace* **10/1**

4 1/2 **Bright Sky (IRE)**[50] 5773 4-8-10 ........ DBoeuf 2 118
(ELellouche, France) *held up, 10th straight, stayed on steadily final 1 1/2f* **10/1**

5 3 1/4 **Self Flit (NZ)**[29] 4-9-0 ........(b) WMawing 12 116
(IWAllan, Hong Kong) *raced in 2nd til led narrowly 2f out, headed just over 1f out, weakened* **40/1**

6 1/2 **Dr More (AUS)**[22] 6-9-0 ........ SDye 1 115
(JSize, Hong Kong) *mid division, 6th straight, one pace final 2f* **50/1**

7 nk **Eishin Preston (USA)**[42] 6-9-0 ........ YFukunaga 13 115
(SKitahashi, Japan) *held up towards rear, 11th straight, some late headway* **6/1**[3]

8 4 1/4 **Blue Stitch**[22] 4-9-0 ........(b) DWhyte 10 107
(ATMillard, Hong Kong) *mid division, 5th straight, outpaced final 2f* **66/1**

9 hd **Tigertail (FR)**[14] 6103 4-8-10 ........ TGillet 6 103
(RodCollet, France) *last to over 1 1/2f out, never a factor* **40/1**

10 1 1/4 **Precision (FR)**[22] 5-9-0 ........ MJKinane 8 105
(DOughton, Hong Kong) *always in rear* **25/1**

11 nk **Denon (USA)**[14] 6103 5-9-0 ........ CNakatani 9 104
(RJFrankel, U.S.A) *raced in 9th, 12th straight, never a factor* **20/1**

12 1 1/4 **Weightless**[71] 5383 3-8-11 ........ TThulliez 3 102
(PBary, France) *led to 2f out, weakened* **9/1**

13 1 1/4 **Magnaten (USA)**[21] 6054 7-9-0 ........ KDesormeaux 14 100
(KazuoFujisawa, Japan) *close up til ridden and weakened 2 1/2f out* **28/1**

14 3/4 **Dano-Mast**[57] 5641 7-9-0 ........ CSoumillon 11 99
(FPoulsen, France) *pushed along early to race in 2nd, 4th straight, weakened quickly* **33/1**

2m 0.90s
**WFA** 3 from 4yo+ 3lb **14** Ran SP% **130.2**
Speed ratings: .
**Owner** Scuderia Rencati & T Yoshida **Bred** Azienda Agricola Francesca **Trained** Newmarket, Suffolk

**NOTEBOOK**
**Falbrav(IRE)**, who looked fantastic beforehand, was contesting his tenth Group One race of 2003 and, surging through the field in the home straight, registered his fifth win in imperious style. His many supporters suffered one anxious moment when he was quite far back and short of room just over two furlongs out but, having switched inside and slightly hampered the runner-up, he showed an electrifying turn of foot to lead at the furlong marker and saw out this shorter trip with ease. After such a hectic campaign his place at stud is well deserved.
**Rakti**, who looked superb, allayed doubts by behaving himself in the preliminaries and quickened up well in the closing stages to be a clear second best. The winner did bump him at the top of the straight but, given the eventual winning margin, it made no difference to the result. He will be back for more in 2004 when a drop back to a mile is being mooted.
**Bright Sky(IRE)**sat on Falbrav's tail but, despite running well, was not good enough to quicken up with him.

# PISA (R-H)
Sunday, December 14

**OFFICIAL GOING: Soft**

## 6189a CRITERIUM DI PISA BLANDFORD SERVICES (LISTED) 7f 110y
2:25 (2:35) 2-Y-0 **£22,727** (£10,000; £5,455; £2,727)

RPR

1 **Distant Way (USA)** 2-8-9 ........ MPasquale 13 105
(LBrogi, Italy)

2 2 1/4 **Bravo Tazio (IRE)**[42] 5902 2-8-9 ........ EBotti 7 100
(ABotti, Italy)

3 5 **Melon Rouge (IRE)**[42] 5902 2-8-9 ........ WGambarota 10 90
(BGrizzetti, Italy)

4 2 3/4 **Tebage Delle Vigne (ITY)** 2-8-9 ........ MTellini 12 85
(PPaciello, Italy)

5 3/4 **Cartoceto (IRE)**[119] 4235 2-8-9 ........ PBorrelli 11 83
(ARenzoni, Italy)

6 5 **Petardias Magic (IRE)**[22] 6048 2-8-9 ........ RFfrench 6 73
(EJO'Neill) *always mid division, outpaced by leaders from over 2f out*

7 3 1/2 **Treno Dei Desideri (IRE)**[70] 5398 2-8-9 ........ GCossu 3 66
(AMaggi, Italy)

8 1 1/2 **Andry Boy (IRE)** 2-8-9 ........ FBranca 2 63
(FFerramosca, Italy)

9 1 1/4 **Indian Bridge (IRE)** 2-8-9 ........ SMulas 1 61
(BGrizzetti, Italy)

10 5 **Catalunya** 2-8-6 ........ MEsposito 8 48
(BGrizzetti, Italy)

11 3/4 **Cay Sal (IRE)**[134] 3820 2-8-9 ........ GBietolini 4 49
(LauraGrizzetti, Italy)

12 15 **Kyoto (ITY)** 2-8-6 ........ PAgus 5 16
(CCongiu, Italy)

13 3 **Bod Revolution (IRE)**[119] 4235 2-8-9 ........ CColombi 9 13
(DGodani, Italy)

1m 32.2s **13** Ran
Speed ratings: .
**Owner** Allevamento La Nuova Sbarra **Bred** Grundy Bloodstock Ltd **Trained** Italy

**NOTEBOOK**
**Petardias Magic(IRE)**was unable to go with the leaders when the tempo increased in the last quarter mile. He got caught up in the French dock workers strike on the way over, and this troubled journey may have taken its toll.

# 6172 SOUTHWELL (L-H)
Monday, December 15

**OFFICIAL GOING: Standard**

This meeting was transferred from Wolverhampton due problems with the surface at that track.

## 6190 BET DIRECT ON ATTHERACES INTERACTIVE H'CAP 1m 3f (F)
1:00 (1:00) (E) (0-70,69) 3-Y-0+ **£2,058** (£588; £294) **Stalls** Low

Form RPR

0004 1 **Spanish Star**[12] 6125 6-7-11 **41** ........ LisaJones(3) 13 56
(MrsNMacauley) *hld up: hdwy over 3f out: chsd wnr over 1f out: styd on to ld wl ins fnl f* **15/2**[2]

5440 2 1/2 **Trouble Mountain (USA)**[20] 6068 6-9-9 **69** ........ PMulrennan(5) 5 83
(MWEasterby) *mid-div: r.o appr fnl f: nt rch wnr* **85/40**[1]

5606 3 1 1/2 **George Stubbs (USA)**[7] 6144 5-9-12 **67** ........ SWKelly 1 79
(MJPolglase) *led 10f out: clr over 3f out: wknd and hdd wl ins fnl f* **10/1**

6610 4 5 **Smoothie (IRE)**[24] 6040 5-9-4 **64** ........ DNolan(5) 4 69
(IanWilliams) *s.i.s: hld up: hdwy over 4f out: chsd wnr over 2f out : wknd fnl f* **8/1**[3]

1346 5 3 **Penwell Hill (USA)**[12] 6124 4-9-6 **68** ........ PMakin(7) 15 68
(TDBarron) *mid-div: rdn over 3f out: wknd wl over 1f out* **8/1**[3]

5606 6 3 1/2 **Danum**[9] 6137 3-8-9 **54** ........(p) ACulhane 2 49
(RHollinshead) *chsd ldrs over 8f* **20/1**

0000 7 3/4 **Night Warrior (IRE)**[20] 6068 3-9-8 **67** ........ PDoe 10 61
(DFlood) *nvr nrr* **20/1**

0010 8 8 **Yorker (USA)**[28] 6013 5-9-11 **66** ........ IMongan 7 48
(MsDeborahJEvans) *hld up: effrt over 5f out: wknd over 3f out* **14/1**

0050 9 2 1/2 **Calcar (IRE)**[12] 6123 3-7-13 **49** ow1 ........(v[1]) RThomas(5) 11 27
(MrsSLamyman) *a in rr* **33/1**

0000 10 2 1/2 **Sinjaree**[7] 6148 5-8-11 **52** ........(v[1]) DaneO'Neill 14 26
(MrsSLamyman) *led 1f: remained handy tl wknd over 2f out* **25/1**

5030 11 8 **Ersaal (USA)**[7] 6143 3-8-9 **54** ........ JFanning 3 16
(JJay) *chsd ldrs over 7f* **16/1**

3400 12 5 **Captain Ginger**[13] 6114 3-9-7 **69** ........ LFletcher(3) 6 24
(HMorrison) *chsd ldrs: over 6f* **12/1**

0065 13 8 **Giust In Temp (IRE)**[7] 6148 4-7-12 **39** oh6 ........ JoannaBadger 8 —
(PWHiatt) *hld up: wknd 4f out* **14/1**

005 14 19 **Felidae (USA)**[30] 6005 3-8-1 **46** ........ TWilliams 12 —
(MBrittain) *bhd fr 1/2-way* **33/1**

5000 15 dist **Morning Sun**[163] 3009 3-7-9 **43** oh3 ........ FPFerris(3) 9 —
(KOCunningham-Brown) *t.o fnl 6f* **66/1**

2m 27.65s (-1.25) **Going Correction** -0.10s/f (Stan)
**WFA** 3 from 4yo+ 4lb **15** Ran SP% **122.7**
Speed ratings: **100,99,98,94,92 90,89,83,82,80 74,70,64,51,**—CSF £21.98 CT £169.87 TOTE £9.90: £2.60, £1.10, £2.70; EX 27.80.



The Form Book, Raceform Ltd, Compton, RG20 6NL

**Owner** Mrs N Macauley **Bred** Granham Farm **Trained** Sproxton, Leics

**NOTEBOOK**
**Spanish Star**, racing off his lowest ever mark on sand, enjoyed the decent pace and came from beind to win his first race since February of last year. He should not go up too much for this but is not the type to bank on producing a similar display next time.
**Trouble Mountain(USA)**, who does not win very often but is fairly consistent, only got going when it was too late. His style of running is also suited by a good gallop.
**George Stubbs(USA)**, a winner over ten furlongs as a three-year-old, has been running over much shorter lately. He ran well for a long way on his debut for his new stable, helping to set a decent clip, but did not get home. This performance showed he is in good form, though, and a handicap over shorter, perhaps the extended nine-furlong trip at Wolverhampton, should be within his reach.
**Smoothie(IRE)**struggles to run two races the same.
**Penwell Hill(USA)**found this trip too far but should drop a pound or two for it, which will help things in the future.

## 6191 BET DIRECT ON 0800 32 93 93 MAIDEN AUCTION STKS 5f (F)
**1:30** (1:30) (F) 2-Y-O £2,205 (£630; £315) **Stalls** High

Form RPR
4023 **1** **Scottish Exile (IRE)**$^{23}$ [6045] 2-8-6 64 (v$^{1}$) DarrenWilliams 7 62+
(KRBurke) *mde all: clr fnl f* **11/8$^{1}$**
30 **2** 5 **Velvet Touch**$^{9}$ [6129] 2-8-2 JBramhill 5 40
(JRJenkins) *chsd ldrs: rdn over 1f out: styd on same pce* **9/2$^{2}$**
0 **3** 1/2 **Fayrz Please (IRE)**$^{175}$ [2642] 2-8-2 AndrewWebb$^{(7)}$ 3 45
(MCChapman) *hmpd s: sn chsng wnr: rdn over 1f out: one pce* **50/1**
**4** 3 **Elvina** 2-8-1 FPFerris$^{(3)}$ 10 30
(AGNewcombe) *s.i.s: hdwy 1/2-way: wknd over 1f out* **6/1**
56 **5** 2 **Red Rocky**$^{9}$ [6129] 2-8-2 PDoe 4 21
(JGallagher) *s.i.s: outpcd* **6/1**
054 **6** 5 **Lyrical Lady**$^{9}$ [6129] 2-8-1 65 NChalmers$^{(5)}$ 11 7
(MrsAJBowlby) *dwlt: outpcd* **8/1**
4056 **7** 1/2 **Charlieismydarling**$^{6}$ [6152] 2-8-7 65 JFanning 2 7
(JAOsborne) *s.i.s and edgd rt s: outpcd* **11/2$^{3}$**
0066 **8** 10 **Anatom**$^{23}$ [6048] 2-8-2 40 FNorton 1 —
(MQuinn) *s.s: sn prom: wknd 1/2-way* **40/1**

59.74 secs (-0.56) **Going Correction** -0.25s/f (Stan) 8 Ran SP% **119.8**
Speed ratings: **94,86,85,80,77 69,68,52**CSF £8.37 TOTE £2.10: £1.10, £1.70, £6.90; EX 9.80.
**Owner** Mrs Melba Bryce **Bred** D J And Mrs Deer **Trained** Middleham Moor, N Yorks

**FOCUS**
A weak maiden.

**NOTEBOOK**
**Scottish Exile(IRE)**, visored for the first time, set a decent standard and ran out a clear winner. Her style of running suits this surface and she could well follow up in handicap company.
**Velvet Touch**, who had shown a liking for easy ground on her only turf start, found this surface more to her liking than the Polytrack on which she raced last time. An extra furlong will suit her.
**Fayrz Please(IRE)**ran with promise given that this was his first outing since June and, although this was not a strong race, he at least looks to be going the right way.
**Elvina**, whose dam won four races over sprint trips, was well supported but never really threatened in the race itself.
**Red Rocky**did not find the drop back in trip at all suitable. She now qualifies for a mark.
**Lyrical Lady**might be happier returning to Lingfield.

## 6192 LITTLEWOODS BET DIRECT H'CAP 6f (F)
**2:00** (2:01) (D) (0-85,82) 3-Y-O+ £3,402 (£972; £486) **Stalls** Low

Form RPR
10 **1** **Blakeset**$^{79}$ [5224] 8-9-0 **68** (v$^{1}$) DMernagh 3 80
(TDBarron) *chsd ldr: rdn to ld over 1f out: r.o* **8/1**
0005 **2** 1 1/4 **Winning Pleasure (IRE)**$^{2}$ [6176] 5-9-4 **72** (b) JEdmunds 8 81
(JBalding) *hld up: r.o ins fnl f: nt rch wnr* **6/1$^{3}$**
0062 **3** hd **Cashel Mead**$^{17}$ [6084] 3-9-12 **80** SWKelly 1 88
(JLSpearing) *chsd ldrs: rdn over 1f out: styd on same pce ins fnl f: eased last strides* **6/1$^{3}$**
0123 **4** 1/2 **Hurricane Coast**$^{16}$ [6099] 4-8-8 **62** DeanMcKeown 12 69
(PABlockley) *trckd ldrs: rdn over 1f out: styd on* **16/1**
0563 **5** 3/4 **Malahide Express (IRE)**$^{17}$ [6081] 3-8-7 **64** (b) LFletcher$^{(3)}$ 5 68
(MJPolglase) *sn led: rdn and hdd over 1f out: no ex ins fnl f* **12/1**
3051 **6** nk **Canterloupe (IRE)**$^{28}$ [6010] 5-10-0 **82** DSweeney 10 85
(PJMakin) *trckd ldrs: outpcd 1/2-way: styd on ins fnl f* **5/1$^{2}$**
0331 **7** 3 **Cloud Dancer**$^{7}$ [6144] 4-9-12 **80** 6ex RWinston 2 74
(KARyan) *mid-divsion: hdwy u.p 2f out: eased whn btn ins fnl f* **6/1$^{3}$**
0210 **8** shd **Chispa**$^{3}$ [6166] 5-8-12 **66** 6ex DarrenWilliams 11 60
(KRBurke) *chsd ldrs: rdn over 2f out: wknd fnl f* **12/1**
0015 **9** 2 **Grandma Lily (IRE)**$^{6}$ [6154] 5-9-4 **72** IMongan 7 60
(MCChapman) *sn outpcd* **4/1$^{1}$**
5661 **10** nk **Paddywack (IRE)**$^{9}$ [6138] 6-9-7 **75** (b) ACulhane 9 62
(DWChapman) *sn outpcd* **9/1**
6000 **11** 15 **Blue Circle**$^{26}$ [6027] 3-7-9 **52** oh18 (p) LisaJones$^{(3)}$ 4 —
(MMullineaux) *chsd ldrs: lost pl 4f out: wknd over 2f out* **150/1**

1m 15.62s (-1.18) **Going Correction** -0.10s/f (Stan) 11 Ran SP% **122.6**
Speed ratings: **103,101,101,100,99 99,95,94,92,91 71**CSF £57.91 CT £323.35 TOTE £12.20: £5.40, £2.80, £2.80; EX 118.20 Trifecta £1503.50 Part won. Pool of £2,117.73 - 0.90 winning tickets..
**Owner** Nigel Shields **Bred** Bolton Grange **Trained** Maunby, N Yorks
■ Stewards Enquiry : S W Kelly seven-day ban: dropped hands and lost second place (Dec 26-Jan 2)

**FOCUS**
A competitive event featuring a number of in-form horses.

**NOTEBOOK**
**Blakeset**, visored for the first time on his return from an 11-week break, showed a good attitude to win again at his favourite track. His record here now reads 21126211 and he clearly retains plenty of ability.
**Winning Pleasure(IRE)**appreciated the drop back to six and finished with a rare rattle. The re-application of blinkers clearly had a beneficial effect.
**Cashel Mead**once again showed that there is a race in her on Fibresand, but she does look on a pretty tough mark at present.
**Hurricane Coast**, who carries his head awkwardly, finds six furlongs on the short side.
**Malahide Express(IRE)**who set the pace, did not get home.
**Canterloupe(IRE)**, 6lb higher, found this track less to her liking than Wolverhampton.
**Grandma Lily(IRE)**was slowly away and stuck in the kickback throughout. This was a bitterly disappointing performance.

## 6193 BETDIRECT.CO.UK MAIDEN STKS 1m (F)
**2:30** (2:32) (D) 3-Y-O+ £2,257 (£645; £322) **Stalls** Low

Form RPR
6063 **1** **Nuzzle**$^{17}$ [6086] 3-8-9 58 (v) RWinston 10 51
(MQuinn) *led 7f out: drvn out* **5/1$^{2}$**
3432 **2** 1 **Magic Mamma's Too**$^{6}$ [6153] 3-9-0 53 DMernagh 9 54
(TDBarron) *led: hdd 7f out: remained handy: rdn over 2f out: styd on* **11/10$^{1}$**
0060 **3** 1 3/4 **Santa Catalina (IRE)**$^{128}$ [3987] 4-8-5 35 (t) TEaves$^{(5)}$ 3 46
(MissGayKelleway) *mid-div: hdwy u.p over 2f out: styd on* **25/1**
6653 **4** 3/4 **Pacific Ocean (ARG)**$^{12}$ [6126] 4-9-1 46 (t) FNorton 11 49
(MrsStefLiddiard) *hld up: hdwy on ouside over 3f out: styd on ins fnl f: nt trble ldrs* **7/1$^{3}$**
662 **5** 1/2 **Chesnut Ripple**$^{12}$ [6126] 4-8-10 53 RHavlin 2 43
(DShaw) *prom: chsd wnr over 3f out: rdn over 1f out: no ex* **5/1$^{2}$**
5000 **6** 1 **Red Moor (IRE)**$^{17}$ [6086] 3-9-0 45 (p) ACulhane 6 46
(RHollinshead) *hld up: hdwy over 1f out: nvr trbld ldrs* **20/1**
660 **7** 2 1/2 **Desires Destiny**$^{194}$ [2094] 5-8-4 48 ow1 MLawson$^{(7)}$ 1 37
(MBrittain) *s.i.s: sn chsng ldrs: wknd over 1f out* **66/1**
530- **8** 1 3/4 **Hellbent**$^{419}$ [5427] 4-9-1 50 SWKelly 4 38
(JAOsborne) *s.i.s: hdwy 1/2-way: wknd over 2f out* **8/1**
00 **9** nk **Gwazi**$^{6}$ [6153] 3-9-0 (t) DarrenWilliams 8 37
(MissDAMchale) *hld up: n.d* **66/1**
0004 **10** 13 **Petrolero (ARG)**$^{12}$ [6126] 4-9-1 44 (t) MFenton 7 11
(MrsStefLiddiard) *sn chsng ldrs: wknd over 2f out* **25/1**
0/ **11** 1 1/4 **Mount Logan**$^{1172}$ [4730] 8-9-1 DaleGibson 5 8
(RCurtis) *s.s: outpcd* **66/1**
4000 **12** 3 **Ruby Anniversary**$^{24}$ [6039] 3-8-9 38 JEdmunds 12 —
(JBalding) *w wnr 3f: wknd over 3f out* **50/1**
0/00 **13** 13 **Presidents Lady**$^{21}$ [6055] 6-8-10 30 JoannaBadger 13 —
(PWHiatt) *sn outpcd* **66/1**

1m 44.46s (-0.14) **Going Correction** -0.10s/f (Stan)
**WFA** 3 from 4yo+ 1lb 13 Ran SP% **124.9**
Speed ratings: **96,95,93,92,92 91,88,86,86,73 72,69,56**CSF £10.76 TOTE £6.20: £3.40, £1.70, £13.30; EX 13.50.
**Owner** A Newby **Bred** Side Hill Stud **Trained** Sparsholt, Oxon

**FOCUS**
A race made up mainly of professional losers.

**NOTEBOOK**
**Nuzzle**, the best of these based on official ratings, finally got off the mark at the 23rd attempt under a positive ride. Needless to say it will be a surprise if she follows up.
**Magic Mamma's Too**again found one too good. He will not find many easier opportunities than this and he simply cannot sensibly be backed to win any race.
**Santa Catalina(IRE)**, still a maiden after 15 starts, ran well enough on her first start since August and her first start for her new stable, but her overall record does not inspire.
**Pacific Ocean(ARG)**will struggle to find a maiden.
**Chesnut Ripple**made it 21 starts without a win.

## 6194 ALLWEATHER-RACING.COM (S) STKS 6f (F)
**3:00** (3:01) (G) 2-Y-O £2,044 (£584; £292) **Stalls** Low

Form RPR
6361 **1** **Alizar (IRE)**$^{12}$ [6122] 2-8-9 54 LFletcher$^{(3)}$ 7 55
(MJPolglase) *mde virtually all: pushed clr fnl f: eased nr fin* **6/4$^{1}$**
3454 **2** 6 **Emaradia**$^{12}$ [6122] 2-8-12 52 SWKelly 2 37
(PDEvans) *chsd ldrs: rdn and ev ch over 2f out: styd on same pce appr fnl f* **13/2$^{3}$**
0000 **3** 2 1/2 **He's A Rocket (IRE)**$^{24}$ [6041] 2-8-7 40 (v$^{1}$) NChalmers$^{(5)}$ 11 30
(MrsCADunnett) *hld up: hdwy and hung lft over 1f out: nt trble ldrs* **40/1**
6065 **4** 1 1/2 **Pardon Moi**$^{21}$ [6058] 2-8-12 49 DaneO'Neill 13 25
(MrsCADunnett) *s.i.s: sn prom: lost pl wl over 3f out: hdwy u.p over 1f out: kpt on* **14/1**
0432 **5** hd **Philly Dee**$^{12}$ [6122] 2-8-8 47 ow1 ACulhane 3 20
(JJay) *chsd ldr: rdn and ev ch over 1f out: sn wknd* **5/2$^{2}$**
0642 **6** 1/2 **Fisher's Dream**$^{24}$ [6041] 2-8-12 54 (v) DarrenWilliams 12 23
(JRNorton) *s.i.s: sn prom: hung lft and wknd over 1f out* **10/1**
0006 **7** 2 1/2 **Are You There**$^{12}$ [6122] 2-8-5 52 (b$^{1}$) GemmaAnderson$^{(7)}$ 10 15
(TDBarron) *chsd ldrs over 3f* **12/1**
4604 **8** shd **Whittinghamvillage**$^{24}$ [6041] 2-8-7 50 FNorton 6 10
(ABerry) *sn pushed along in rr: sme hdwy u.p 2f out: eased whn btn fnl f* **9/1**
0000 **9** 1/2 **Miss Judged**$^{16}$ [6097] 2-8-7 50 (t$^{1}$) GHannon 9 9
(APJones) *s.i.s: hld up: outpcd fr 1/2-way* **25/1**
6600 **10** 1 3/4 **Ticklepenny Lock (IRE)**$^{80}$ [5197] 2-8-12 40 DeanMcKeown 1 8
(CSmith) *outpcd fr 1/2-way* **50/1**
0000 **11** 8 **Coleorton Prince (IRE)**$^{12}$ [6122] 2-8-12 40 RWinston 5 —
(KARyan) *hld up in tch: wknd wl over 1f out* **33/1**
0 **12** 10 **Dandy Jim**$^{26}$ [6029] 2-8-12 RBrisland 4 —
(DWChapman) *s.s: outpcd* **66/1**

1m 16.33s (-0.47) **Going Correction** -0.10s/f (Stan) 12 Ran SP% **128.0**
Speed ratings: **99,91,87,85,85 84,81,81,80,78 67,54**CSF £12.89 TOTE £2.10: £1.30, £2.00, £7.80; EX 9.40.The winner was bought in for 8,500gns
**Owner** General Sir Geoffrey Howlett **Bred** Epona Bloodstock Ltd **Trained** Southwell, Notts

**FOCUS**
A poor seller but the winner is certainly going the right way.

**NOTEBOOK**
**Alizar(IRE)**followed up with another decisive victory over this longer trip. Subsequently bought in for 8,500gns, she is one to keep on the right side while she is in such good form.
**Emaradia**remains in good form but found the winner much too strong. She should continue to run well at this level.
**He's A Rocket(IRE)**, visored for the first time, ran his best race for a while but does not appeal as a type likely to score in the near future.
**Pardon Moi**kept on late in the day but was never really a factor.
**Philly Dee**did not get home after chasing the leader for a long way.

## 6195 FREE £25 BONUS @ LITTLEWOODSPOKER.COM H'CAP 1m 6f (F)
**3:30** (3:31) (E) (0-75,75) 3-Y-O+ £2,044 (£584; £292) **Stalls** Low

Form RPR
1252 **1** **Victory Quest (IRE)**$^{6}$ [6156] 3-8-9 63 (v) DaneO'Neill 4 74
(MrsSLamyman) *chsd ldr: led 3f out: styd on wl* **11/2$^{3}$**
4535 **2** 3/4 **Reminiscent (IRE)**$^{9}$ [6130] 4-9-1 62 (v) SCarson 5 72
(RFJohnsonHoughton) *a.p: chsd wnr and ev ch over 1f out: edgd lft and nt qckn ins fnl f* **10/3$^{2}$**
0604 **3** 4 **Stravmour**$^{20}$ [6068] 7-7-12 45 oh2 DaleGibson 1 50
(RHollinshead) *chsd ldrs: rdn over 2f out: styd on same pce* **12/1**
0001 **4** 2 **Dubai Dreams**$^{12}$ [6121] 3-7-13 60 ow1 (v) PMakin$^{(7)}$ 3 62
(MJPolglase) *led: racd keenly: hdd 3f out: wknd fnl f* **14/1**
5212 **5** 1 3/4 **Bucks**$^{13}$ [6120] 6-10-0 75 IMongan 2 75
(DKIvory) *hld up: drvn along over 4f out: outpcd fnl 3f* **8/11$^{1}$**

3m 5.68s (-3.92) **Going Correction** -0.10s/f (Stan)
**WFA** 3 from 4yo+ 7lb 5 Ran SP% **110.7**
Speed ratings: **107,106,104,103,102**CSF £23.54 TOTE £6.20: £2.70, £1.70; EX 35.00 Place 6 £54.92, Place 5 £31.08.

**Owner** P Lamyman **Bred** Miss Veronica Henley **Trained** Louth, Lincs

**NOTEBOOK**

**Victory Quest(IRE)**, off the same mark as when a promising second at 100-1 last time out, found plenty under pressure to score tidily. He benefited from the disappointing performance of the favourite, but there should be more to come from this lightly-raced sort.

**Reminiscent(IRE)**ran well enough. He is very consistent but does not win that often.

**Stravmour**, 2lb out of the handicap, got this longer trip well enough but was never a threat to the principals.

**Dubai Dreams**, who made the running, did not get home over this longer trip.

**Bucks**, whose trainer later reported that the gelding was never travelling, was a big disappointment and never looked like justifying the decent support for him. *Official explanation: trainer said gelding was never travelling*

T/Jkpt: Not won. T/Plt: £67.00 to a £1 stake. Pool: £35,396.95. 385.40 winning tickets. T/Qpdt: £28.50 to a £1 stake. Pool: £2,542.40. 65.90 winning tickets. CR

## 6190 SOUTHWELL (L-H)

Tuesday, December 16

**OFFICIAL GOING: Standard**

Wind: rain Weather: slt, hlf against

### 6196 BET DIRECT IN VISION SKY PAGE 293 H'CAP (DIV I) 7f (F)

**12:25** (12:26) (F ) (0-60,65) 3-Y-O+ **£2,079** (£594; £297) **Stalls** Low

Form RPR

2505 **1** **Pawn In Life (IRE)**[25] [6036] 5-9-12 **58** DMernagh 5 70
(TDBarron) *chsd ldrs: led over 2f out: drvn out* **11/2**[3]

4234 **2** 1 ½ **Shifty**[7] [6149] 4-9-8 **54** (b) ANicholls 1 62
(DNicholls) *s.i.s: hld up: hdwy 3f out: rdn to chse wnr over 1f out: styd on same pce ins fnl f* **5/1**[2]

0511 **3** nk **Miss Champers (IRE)**[4] [6171] 3-9-12 **65** 6ex SJDonohoe(7) 10 73
(PDEvans) *dwlt: hld up: hdwy and nt clr run over 1f out: r.o* **7/2**[1]

0005 **4** ¾ **Rosti**[27] [6026] 3-8-8 **47** RoryMoore(7) 9 53
(PCHaslam) *trckd ldrs: rdn and hung lft fr over 1f out: styd on same pce* **11/1**

0650 **5** 2 **Brilliantrio**[22] [6057] 5-8-7 **46** AndrewWebb(7) 3 47
(MCChapman) *s.i.s: sn chsng ldrs: rdn whn hmpd over 1f out: styd on same pce* **33/1**

0000 **6** 1 ¼ **Dasar**[8] [6148] 3-9-3 **49** DarrenWilliams 8 47
(MBrittain) *disp ld over 2f: remained handy: rdn and edgd lft over 1f out: wknd ins fnl f* **50/1**

2301 **7** 3 **Smith N Allan Oils**[10] [6133] 4-9-10 **56** (p) SWKelly 2 46
(MDods) *chsd ldrs: rdn over 2f out: wknd over 1f out* **10/1**

3203 **8** 3 ½ **Bulawayo**[8] [6144] 6-9-11 **57** DaneO'Neill 15 38
(AndrewReid) *mid-div: rdn over 2f out: sn wknd* **10/1**

1000 **9** ¾ **Glenrock**[25] [6042] 6-8-13 **50** PBradley(5) 4 29
(ABerry) *w ldrs: led over 4f out: rdn and hdd over 2f out: wknd over 1f out* **25/1**

0000 **10** nk **Open Handed (IRE)**[31] [6006] 3-9-5 **51** (t) RWinston 12 30
(BEllison) *disp ld over 2f: wknd over 2f out* **40/1**

4320 **11** 3 **Travelling Times**[7] [6151] 4-9-1 **52** (v) TEaves(5) 6 23
(JSWainwright) *chsd ldrs 4f* **20/1**

050 **12** 6 **Newclose**[46] [5856] 3-9-0 **46** JFanning 13 —
(NTinkler) *s.s: outpcd* **16/1**

0060 **13** ¾ **Red Delirium**[8] [6144] 7-9-1 **50** (b) LFletcher(3) 16 4
(RBrotherton) *s.i.s: sn pushed along: bhd fr 1/2-way* **20/1**

3655 **14** 1 ¼ **Pancakehill**[17] [6088] 4-9-9 **55** GCarter 11 6
(DKIvory) *hld up: a in rr* **10/1**

0500 **15** 2 ½ **Pride Of Kinloch**[13] [6124] 3-10-0 **60** DeanMcKeown 7 5
(JHetherton) *prom to 1/2-way* **33/1**

055 **16** 6 **Balalaika Tune (IRE)**[79] [5259] 4-9-2 **48** JBramhill 14 —
(WStorey) *chsd ldrs to 1/2-way* **50/1**

1m 31.16s (0.36) **Going Correction** -0.05s/f (Stan) **16** Ran SP% **121.4**

Speed ratings: **95,93,92,92,89 88,84,80,80,79 76,69,68,67,64 57**CSF £29.63 CT £116.32 TOTE £5.40: £1.20, £1.80, £1.40, £2.80; EX 23.00.

**Owner** Laurence O'Kane **Bred** Lt-Col W L Newell **Trained** Maunby, N Yorks

■ Stewards Enquiry : L Fletcher three-day ban: used whip when out of contention and with gelding showing no response (Dec 26,27,29)

Darren Williams two-day ban: careless riding (Dec 26,27)

**FOCUS**

A weak handicap run at a steady pace.

**NOTEBOOK**

**Pawn In Life(IRE)**, well backed in the ring, showed the benefit of his recent comeback run and always looked like landing the spoils when taking up the running turning for home. If turning out under a penalty, he would be hard to beat.

**Shifty**blew it at the start, but again ran a solid race in the circumstances. He is becoming a tad frustrating, yet is a perennial frame-maker and should continue to pay his way this winter.

**Miss Champers(IRE)**had no easy task under her big weight and got going all too late on this drop in trip. She is in great heart at present and when upped in trip again to a mile, should go in before long.

**Rosti**was travelling nicely approaching the straight, but did not possess the change of gears to go with the leaders over this trip. He could do with stepping back to a mile.

### 6197 BET DIRECT ON SKY ACTIVE NURSERY 7f (F)

**12:55** (12:55) (E ) (0-75,68) 2-Y-O **£2,457** (£702; £351) **Stalls** Low

Form RPR

0102 **1** **Blue Empire (IRE)**[3] [6172] 2-9-1 **65** LEnstone(3) 7 80+
(PCHaslam) *trckd ldrs: led on bit over 2f out: rdn clr and hung lft over 1f out: eased nr fin* **10/11**[1]

0001 **2** 5 **Weet An Haul**[8] [6141] 2-8-3 **50** 6ex JBramhill 2 50
(PABlockley) *s.i.s: hld up: hdwy 1/2-way: chsd wnr over 1f out: sn outpcd* **7/2**[2]

5004 **3** 1 ½ **Garnock Venture (IRE)**[8] [6141] 2-8-6 **53** (b) DaleGibson 6 49
(ABerry) *led: hdd over 2f out: styd on same pce appr fnl f* **25/1**

0600 **4** 5 **Ceasar (IRE)**[22] [6059] 2-7-12 **52** RoryMoore(7) 9 35
(PCHaslam) *trckd ldrs: outpcd 3f out: n.d after* **33/1**

5205 **5** 1 ½ **Jasmine Pearl (IRE)**[98] [4788] 2-9-4 **68** LPKeniry(3) 1 48
(BJMeehan) *chsd ldrs 5f* **16/1**

6300 **6** ½ **Sonderborg**[61] [5590] 2-9-1 **62** GCarter 3 40
(GLMoore) *sn outpcd* **14/1**

0046 **7** 8 **Romantic Drama (IRE)**[71] [5421] 2-9-4 **65** (b) RWinston 8 23
(BJMeehan) *chsd ldrs over 4f* **13/2**[3]

000 **8** 3 **One Alone**[47] [5834] 2-8-8 **55** JoannaBadger 10 6
(JGGiven) *sn outpcd* **33/1**

050 **9** nk **Gentleman George**[190] [2228] 2-8-0 **50** FPFerris(3) 5 —
(DKIvory) *chsd ldrs: son drvn along: wknd over 2f out* **40/1**

6650 **10** 4 **Savernake Brave (IRE)**[50] [5789] 2-8-2 **52** LisaJones(3) 4 —
(KRBurke) *s.s: a bhd* **40/1**

1m 31.03s (0.23) **Going Correction** -0.05s/f (Stan) **10** Ran SP% **115.1**

Speed ratings: **96,90,88,82,81 80,71,68,67,63**CSF £3.69 CT £41.14 TOTE £1.80: £1.10, £1.70, £3.50; EX 4.20.

**Owner** Blue Lion Racing II **Bred** Yeomanstown Stud **Trained** Middleham Moor, N Yorks

**FOCUS**

Modest nursery run at a modest pace, but won by a progressive type on the sand.

**NOTEBOOK**

**Blue Empire(IRE)**won in decisive fashion on this drop in trip. He was always going smoothly tracking the leaders and when asked to quicken he made his rivals look pedestrian. Despite a slight tendency to hang left, as he did in his previous contest, he obviously has more to offer and will be rested until returning to this sphere early next year, when he should have matured and he should be followed closely.

**Weet An Haul**was put in his place by the winner, but beat the rest fair and square and his shrewd yard can place him to advantage this winter over this trip.

**Garnock Venture(IRE)** *Official explanation: jockey said colt hung right in the closing stages*

### 6198 PRESS INTERACTIVE TO BET DIRECT CLASSIFIED CLAIMING STKS 1m 3f (F)

**1:25** (1:25) (F ) 3-Y-O+ **£2,079** (£594; £297) **Stalls** Low

Form RPR

0304 **1** **Aveiro (IRE)**[18] [6085] 7-8-9 31 (b) KDalgleish 6 53
(BGPowell) *hld up: outpcd 4f out: hdwy u.p over 1f out: styd on to ld post* **8/1**

2041 **2** shd **Queensberry**[8] [6143] 4-8-7 49 JDO'Reilly(7) 10 58
(JO'Reilly) *chsd ldrs: led 3f out: sn rdn: hdd post* **3/1**[1]

3560 **3** 2 **Delta Force**[172] [2761] 4-8-5 41 DerekNolan(7) 9 53
(PABlockley) *hld up: plld hrd: hmpd and rn wd after 1f: hdwy 4f out: rdn over 1f out: hung lft ins fnl f: styd on* **25/1**

0004 **4** 10 **Misty Man (USA)**[101] [4737] 5-8-6 30 BReilly(5) 5 37
(MissJFeilden) *chsd ldrs: ev ch 3f out: wknd fnl f* **33/1**

5006 **5** ¾ **Berkeley Heights**[22] [6060] 3-8-9 48 (b[1]) RFfrench 8 38
(BSmart) *w ldr: ev ch whn hmpd 3f out: sn wknd* **14/1**

0204 **6** shd **Grand Lass (IRE)**[49] [5819] 4-8-11 55 DMernagh 4 36
(TDBarron) *led 8f: wknd over 1f out* **7/2**[2]

0044 **7** 1 ¾ **Noble Pursuit**[8] [6148] 6-8-12 56 (p) DeanMcKeown 1 34
(PABlockley) *chsd ldrs 7f* **3/1**[1]

-464 **8** 7 **Prince Prospect**[45] [5881] 7-8-7 48 KristinStubbs(7) 3 26
(MrsLStubbs) *hld up: bhd fnl 7f* **15/2**[3]

-000 **9** 28 **Ginner Morris**[13] [3576] 8-8-11 27 GParkin 2 —
(JHetherton) *prom 5f* **25/1**

2m 28.07s (-0.83) **Going Correction** -0.05s/f (Stan)

**WFA** 3 from 4yo+ 4lb **9** Ran SP% **112.4**

Speed ratings: **101,100,99,92,91 91,90,85,64**CSF £30.71 TOTE £6.40: £1.60, £1.90, £7.00; EX 27.60.Queensberry was claimed by Miss L J Sheen for £8,000.

**Owner** The Dream Connection **Bred** Saeed Manana **Trained** Morestead, Hants

■ Stewards Enquiry : J D O'Reilly two-day ban: used whip with excessive frequency (Dec 26,27)

**NOTEBOOK**

**Aveiro(IRE)**came from out of the clouds to nail the runner up on the line. He was badly outpaced at the rear of the field, but his rider never gave up and he really stuck to his task well in the closing stages. He is not the performer of old, but has plummeted in the weights and may now be ready to capitalise on that.

**Queensberry**looked to have the race in the bag when hitting the front three out, but dossed about in front and would have benefited from a more patient ride. He can shortly gain compensation for this, but is somewhat of a moody customer.

**Delta Force**was done no favours early on and ran very freely. But as it was his first outing for six months, he is entitled to improve on this and ran well enough in the circumstances.

**Noble Pursuit**ran a shocker and did not appear to have any obvious excuses.

### 6199 LITTLEWOODS BET DIRECT H'CAP 5f (F)

**1:55** (1:56) (D ) (0-85,80) 3-Y-O+ **£3,500** (£1,000; £500) **Stalls** High

Form RPR

0425 **1** **Frascati**[18] [6080] 3-9-6 **72** FNorton 7 82
(ABerry) *chsd ldrs: rdn over 1f out: edgd lft: r.o to ld post* **9/1**[3]

1010 **2** hd **Palawan**[79] [5251] 7-9-6 **79** AmyKathleenParsons(7) 5 88
(AMBalding) *chsd ldrs: led 2f out: hdd post* **10/1**

1005 **3** 1 ¾ **Daintree Affair (IRE)**[10] [6138] 3-8-10 **62** GBaker 2 66
(KRBurke) *chsd ldrs: rdn and ev ch over 1f out: styd on same pce* **11/1**

3000 **4** ½ **New Options**[31] [6001] 6-9-1 **67** PaulEddery 4 69
(WJMusson) *outpcd: r.o ins fnl f: nt rch ldrs* **25/1**

6000 **5** ½ **St Ivian**[45] [5880] 3-8-8 **63** (v) LEnstone(3) 14 64
(MrsNMacauley) *chsd ldrs: rdn over 1f out: styd on same pce* **25/1**

5432 **6** nk **Rafters Music (IRE)**[10] [6136] 8-9-7 **73** NCallan 3 73
(JulianPoulton) *outpcd: rdn over 1f out: styd on ins fnl f* **10/1**

0300 **7** ½ **Sea The World (IRE)**[4] [6170] 3-8-8 **60** (v[1]) DarrenWilliams 8 58
(DShaw) *s.i.s: hdwy 1/2-way: hung lft over 1f out: styd on same pce* **40/1**

054 **8** 1 **Ridicule**[90] [4991] 4-9-2 **68** (b[1]) RHavlin 1 63
(JGPortman) *s.i.s: sn chsg ldrs: rdn over 1f out: wknd ins fnl f* **25/1**

5635 **9** nk **Malahide Express (IRE)**[1] [6192] 3-8-9 **64** (b) LFletcher(3) 15 58
(MJPolglase) *chsd ldrs over 3f* **7/1**[2]

0000 **10** shd **Ronnie From Donny (IRE)**[18] [6084] 3-9-4 **70** (p) DaneO'Neill 6 64
(BEllison) *chsd ldrs: outpcd 3f out: hdwy u.p over 1f out: wknd ins fnl f* **10/1**

0360 **11** shd **Now Look Here**[7] [6154] 7-9-11 **77** KDalgleish 9 71
(BAMcmahon) *s.i.s: sn chsng ldr: outpcd 3f out: n.d after* **11/2**[1]

6001 **12** 1 ½ **Count Cougar (USA)**[61] [5598] 3-8-9 **61** JMcAuley 16 50
(SPGriffiths) *sn outpcd* **12/1**

0350 **13** 1 ¾ **Henry Tun**[4] [6166] 5-8-6 **58** (v) JEdmunds 11 42
(JBalding) *s.i.s: sn outpcd* **10/1**

0240 **14** 1 ½ **Prime Recreation**[39] [5941] 6-9-5 **71** DaleGibson 10 51
(PSFelgate) *plld hrd: sn led: hdd 2f out: sn rdn and wknd* **10/1**

0560 **15** 1 **Park Star**[10] [6127] 3-8-1 **58** (v) JFMcDonald(5) 13 35
(DShaw) *chsd ldrs to 1/2-way* **10/1**

/-05 **16** 1 ¾ **Cretan Gift**[20] [6078] 12-9-11 **80** (v) J-PGuillambert(3) 12 51
(NPLittmoden) *s.i.s: outpcd* **10/1**

60.18 secs (-0.12) **Going Correction** +0.125s/f (Slow) **16** Ran SP% **131.5**

Speed ratings: **105,104,101,101,100 99,99,97,96,96 96,94,91,89,87 84**CSF £99.92 CT £1036.98 TOTE £9.90: £3.60, £3.20, £3.40, £8.60; EX 111.00 Trifecta £1175.50 Part won. Pool of £1,655.64. - 0.60 winning tickets..

**Owner** Lord Crawshaw **Bred** Exors Of The Late Lord Crawshaw **Trained** Cockerham, Lancs

**NOTEBOOK**

**Frascati**won all out having been handy throughout down the middle of the track and has now won four from five starts over course-and-distance. This is her bag and she is yet to win anywhere else.



The Form Book, Raceform Ltd, Compton, RG20 6NL

**Palawan**did nothing wrong and was only just denied. He is higher this season on the sand than when winning races last year, but on this evidence, should be winning over this trip soon.
**Daintree Affair(IRE)**ran a fair race, but found this too hot. He is gradually finding his form having had his problems since winning his only race at this venue in April.
**New Options**has yet to convince at the minimum trip and was doing all of his best work late on. He will come on again for the run and if returning to the Polytrack over further, would be of interest.
**Now Look Here**ran a disappointing race having looked to have a good chance on form and has a lot to prove now.

## 6200 BETDIRECT.CO.UK H'CAP 2m (F)
2:25 (2:27) (F) (0-60,60) 3-Y-O+ £2,065 (£590; £295) Stalls Low

Form RPR
061 **1** **Vincent**[4] 6168 8-8-7 **39** 6ex JMackay 1 54
(JohnAHarris) *a.p: chsd ldr 4f out: led 2f out: rdn out* **5/1**[1]
6602 **2** *1 3/4* **Vanbrugh (FR)**[4] 6168 3-9-6 **60** (vt) DarrenWilliams 6 73
(MissDAMchale) *led after 1f: rdn and hdd 2f out: no ex ins fnl f* **8/1**[3]
4 **3** *10* **Pipssalio (SPA)**[180] 2505 6-8-10 **42** (bt) FNorton 7 45
(JamiePoulton) *hld up: hdwy over 4f out: wknd 2f out* **25/1**
5012 **4** *8* **Ambitious Annie**[27] 6033 4-8-1 **40** StephanieHollinshead(7) 11 35
(RHollinshead) *plld hrd and prom: wknd over 2f out* **5/1**[1]
0063 **5** *11* **Vandenberghe**[25] 6043 4-9-3 **49** PaulEddery 9 33
(JAOsborne) *hld up: n.d* **17/2**
**6** *2 1/2* **Kyalami (IRE)**[477] 4243 4-7-12 **30** oh5 DKinsella 12 12
(MJPolglase) *led 1f: chsd ldr tl wknd 4f out* **10/1**
3000 **7** *2 1/2* **Hajeer (IRE)**[20] 6079 5-9-2 **48** RWinston 4 27
(PWHiatt) *s.i.s: sn chsng ldrs: pushed along 10f out: wknd over 4f out* **12/1**
0006 **8** *1 1/4* **Kagoshima (IRE)**[13] 6123 8-8-6 **43** (v) JFMcDonald(5) 8 21
(JRNorton) *hld up: hdwy 8f out: wknd wl over 3f out* **16/1**
0640 **9** *4* **Roppongi Dancer**[17] 6096 4-7-9 **30** oh5 (vt[1]) LisaJones(3) 3 4
(MrsNMacauley) *s.i.s: hdwy 9f out: wknd over 7f out* **33/1**
0000 **10** *6* **Jonalton (IRE)**[52] 5048 4-7-13 **31** JBramhill 13 —
(CRDore) *mid-div: wknd over 6f out* **14/1**
0-50 **11** *2* **High Jinks**[14] 6120 8-8-5 **40** ow3 (p) LPKeniry(3) 5 6
(RNBevis) *hld up: wknd 6f out* **20/1**
0000 **12** *1* **Iloveturtle (IRE)**[70] 5435 3-7-13 **46** ow1 AndrewWebb(7) 14 11
(MCChapman) *chsd ldrs 11f* **14/1**
0000 **13** *7* **Temple Of Artemis**[37] 5344 4-9-9 **60** DNolan(5) 10 18
(PABlockley) *hld up: rdn 6f out: a bhd* **33/1**
3055 **14** *1 1/2* **Sabreline**[10] 6137 4-8-11 **48** NChalmers(5) 15 5
(BRFoster) *hld up: hdwy over 6f out: sn wknd* **33/1**
3331 **15** *4* **Decelerate**[20] 6075 3-9-4 **58** DaneO'Neill 16 11
(ACharlton) *hld up: bhd fnl 6f* **6/1**[2]
0605 **16** *dist* **Leahstar**[87] 5069 4-7-12 **30** oh1 JMcAuley 2 —
(MissLCSiddall) *chsd ldrs to 1/2-way* **66/1**

3m 42.26s (-10.24) **Going Correction** -0.05s/f (Stan)
**WFA** 3 from 4yo+ 8lb 16 Ran SP% **124.2**
Speed ratings: **101,100,95,91,85 84,83,82,80,77 76,76,72,71,69** —CSF £41.71 CT £939.55 TOTE £5.80: £1.10, £3.70, £5.40, £1.60; EX 24.00.
**Owner** Mrs A E Harris **Bred** R Stern, V Bloom And P Caplan **Trained** Eastwell, Leics

### NOTEBOOK
**Vincent**made it back-to-back wins at this venue and relished the longer trip. Despite seemingly not going as well as the runner-up three out, he outstayed his rival and confirmed the form despite being 4lb worse off. He has had a recent dental problem corrected of late and that has helped bring about a fresh enthusiasm for this game.
**Vanbrugh(FR)**was again ridden a little surprisingly prominently for one who had stamina reservations, but was not beaten far and stayed this trip well enough. He was well clear of the rest and again can be considered a little unlucky to have run into the winner.
**Pipssalio(SPA)**was himself clear of the remainder, but was never a threat to the leading pair.
**Ambitious Annie**spoiled her chance by running very freely and had nothing left when it mattered. When settling, she can do better than this.

## 6201 BET DIRECT FOOTBALL CASHBACKS (S) STKS 7f (F)
2:55 (2:55) (G) 2-Y-O £2,044 (£584; £292) Stalls Low

Form RPR
556 **1** **Sir Jasper (IRE)**[17] 6097 2-8-11 65 (v) DMernagh 10 48
(TDBarron) *disp ld tl led 1/2-way: rdn over 1f out: all out* **4/1**[3]
0 **2** *shd* **Wings Of Morning (IRE)**[17] 6087 2-8-4 RoryMoore(7) 8 48
(NACallaghan) *disp ld to 1/2-way: rdn and ev ch fr over 1f out: hung rt: styd on* **2/1**[1]
000 **3** *3 1/2* **Casantella**[8] 6141 2-8-7 38 ow4 LFletcher(3) 4 38
(MJPolglase) *chsd ldrs: hmpd 1/2-way: sn rdn: styd on same pce appr fnl f* **40/1**
0400 **4** *1/2* **Platinum Chief**[8] 6147 2-8-11 53 DarrenWilliams 6 38
(ABerry) *chsd ldrs: rdn over 2f out: styd on same pce appr fnl f* **25/1**
0004 **5** *nk* **Brother Cadfael**[21] 6066 2-8-11 42 RFfrench 13 37
(JohnAHarris) *sn pushed along in rr: hdwy and hung lft over 2f out: nt rch ldrs* **18/1**
0000 **6** *1/2* **Desert Light (IRE)**[3] 6172 2-8-8 23 (e) LisaJones(3) 7 36
(DShaw) *prom: rdn over 2f out: styd on same pce* **66/1**
6004 **7** *4* **Quarry Island (IRE)**[24] 6047 2-8-6 40 JoannaBadger 2 21
(PDEvans) *s.i.s: outpcd* **25/1**
0532 **8** *1/2* **Rare Coincidence**[8] 6147 2-8-11 54 (p) SRighton 9 25
(RFFisher) *s.i.s: sn prom: rdn and wknd over 1f out* **9/4**[2]
0060 **9** *18* **First Acorn**[22] 6059 2-8-6 42 (p) NPollard 1 —
(GMMoore) *dwlt: outpcd* **25/1**
6000 **10** *1* **Dress Pearl**[25] 6041 2-8-6 47 DeanMcKeown 12 —
(ABerry) *prom to 1/2-way* **50/1**
0053 **11** *10* **Burkees Graw (IRE)**[141] 3639 2-9-2 60 ANicholls 11 —
(DNicholls) *chsd ldrs to 1/2-way* **10/1**

1m 31.59s (0.79) **Going Correction** -0.05s/f (Stan) 11 Ran SP% **115.9**
Speed ratings: **93,92,88,88,87 87,82,82,61,60 49**CSF £11.40 TOTE £4.40: £1.20, £1.50, £9.10; EX 17.00.There was no bid for the winner.
**Owner** Mrs Liz Jones **Bred** Tim Cox And Peter Jones **Trained** Maunby, N Yorks
■ Stewards Enquiry : Rory Moore two-day ban: used whip down the shoulder in the forehand position (Dec 26,27)
D Mernagh three-day ban: used whip with excessive frequency (Dec 26,27,29)

### NOTEBOOK
**Sir Jasper(IRE)**prospered form strong handling and the drop in grade to get off the mark. He stayed this extra furlong well and as he may well be able to build on this battling victory in similar company.
**Wings Of Morning(IRE)**was looking the most likely winner down the straight, but spoilt his chance by hanging slightly and would have most likely scored with stronger handling. This was a considerable drop in class and if he turns up in this grade next time, he is one to be with.
**Casantella**was made to look very one-paced, but ran her best race to date.
**Rare Coincidence**blew it at the start and was unable to reproduce his fair effort last time.
**Burkees Graw(IRE)**was reported by his jockey to have hung left throughout the closing stages.
*Official explanation: jockey said gelding was hanging left*

## 6202 BET DIRECT IN VISION SKY PAGE 293 H'CAP (DIV II) 7f (F)
3:25 (3:25) (F) (0-60,61) 3-Y-O+ £2,072 (£592; £296) Stalls Low

Form RPR
00-5 **1** **Shahm (IRE)**[291] 641 4-9-1 47 SWKelly 10 60
(BJCurley) *hld up: hdwy u.p over 2f out: r.o to ld wl ins fnl f* **10/1**
0605 **2** *1 1/4* **Waltzing Wizard**[10] 6127 4-9-4 50 FNorton 2 60
(ABerry) *mid-div: sn pushed along: hdwy 1/2-way: rdn to ld over 1f out: hdd wl ins fnl f* **16/1**
5515 **3** *1 1/2* **Acorazado (IRE)**[7] 6151 4-9-10 56 GCarter 16 62
(GLMoore) *bhd: hdwy u.p over 1f out: nt rch ldrs* **13/2**[3]
0001 **4** *nk* **Spy Gun (USA)**[8] 6148 3-9-10 61 6ex NChalmers(5) 8 67
(TWall) *mid-div: hdwy over 2f out: hung lft over 1f out: styd on* **5/1**[2]
400 **5** *1* **Mister Mal (IRE)**[61] 5596 7-9-7 58 (be) THamilton(5) 3 61
(BEllison) *chsd ldrs: led over 4f out: rdn and hdd over 1f out: no ex ins fnl f* **14/1**
0444 **6** *1 1/4* **Doctor Dennis (IRE)**[7] 6151 6-9-3 49 (v) NPollard 15 49
(MrsLydiaPearce) *sn outpcd: swtchd lft 6f out: hdwy over 2f out: no imp fnl f* **8/1**
0001 **7** *1/2* **Mister Benji**[22] 6057 4-9-10 56 (p) JFanning 7 55
(BPJBaugh) *prom: chsd ldr over 2f out: wknd fnl f* **11/1**
5000 **8** *nk* **Sudra**[56] 5688 6-9-2 55 JDO'Reilly(7) 4 53
(JO'Reilly) *s.i.s: hld up: hmpd 1/2-way: nt clr run over 1f out: nt rch ldrs* **25/1**
0454 **9** *1 3/4* **Mr Stylish**[8] 6144 7-9-4 50 (vt) JDSmith 13 44
(JSMoore) *sn outpcd: effrt over 2f out: n.d* **10/1**
0033 **10** *nk* **Game Guru**[7] 6149 4-9-13 59 (b) DMernagh 6 52
(TDBarron) *s.i.s: sn chsng ldrs: lost pl 4f out: n.d after* **3/1**[1]
0300 **11** *2 1/2* **Attorney**[7] 6151 5-8-12 47 (e) LisaJones(3) 5 34
(DShaw) *chsd ldrs over 5f* **20/1**
0600 **12** *1 1/4* **Dil**[7] 6149 8-8-12 51 StevenHarrison(7) 11 34
(MrsNMacauley) *s.i.s: carried lft 6f out: a in rr* **25/1**
0000 **13** *3* **Rivelli (IRE)**[10] 6139 4-8-13 45 (b) ANicholls 1 21
(BRFoster) *chsd ldrs over 5f* **100/1**
2006 **14** *nk* **Middleham Park (IRE)**[13] 6126 3-9-8 57 LEnstone(3) 12 32
(PCHaslam) *broke wl: sn outpcd* **25/1**
2540 **15** *1 1/2* **Zak Facta (IRE)**[10] 6134 3-9-6 52 (v) DarrenWilliams 14 23
(MissDAMchale) *led: hdd over 4f out: wknd wl over 1f out* **11/1**
4030 **16** *6* **Alice Brand (IRE)**[27] 6028 5-8-9 46 TEaves(5) 9 2
(GMMoore) *s.i.s: sn chsng ldrs: wknd 1/2-way* **33/1**

1m 30.61s (-0.19) **Going Correction** -0.05s/f (Stan) 16 Ran SP% **133.7**
Speed ratings: **99,97,95,95,94 92,92,92,90,89 86,85,81,81,79 73**CSF £163.16 CT £1197.00 TOTE £20.30: £3.30, £6.50, £2.60, £1.40; EX 494.10 Place 6 £60.29, Place 5 £35.65.
**Owner** Mrs B J Curley **Bred** Shadwell Estate Company Limited **Trained** Newmarket, Suffolk

### NOTEBOOK
**Shahm(IRE)**finally lost his maiden tag in this weak event. He had failed his followers when well-backed on his last run in February, but did well to overcome that absence on this occasion and if remaining in his current form, he looks well-treated on his best form.
**Waltzing Wizard**has slipped in the weights of late and showed the first signs that he is capable of capitalising on that. He acted on the surface this time and can win in this sphere over seven furlongs.
**Acorazado(IRE)**has never totally convinced over this distance. He was staying on all to late in the day.
**Spy Gun(USA)**found the penalty for his last time success, rather than the drop in trip, his undoing.
**Game Guru**was rushed up to race handily after a sluggish start an that cost him. He is somewhat of an enigma.
T/Jkpt: Not won. T/Plt: £35.50 to a £1 stake. Pool: £38,570.20. 792.85 winning tickets. T/Qpdt: £19.50 to a £1 stake. Pool: £2,234.80. 84.40 winning tickets. CR

# 6157 LINGFIELD (L-H)
## Wednesday, December 17

**OFFICIAL GOING: Standard**
Wind: lt bhd Weather: sunny

## 6203 LITTLEWOODS BET DIRECT NOVICE STKS (DIV I) 7f (P)
12:00 (12:01) (D) 2-Y-O £3,024 (£864; £432) Stalls Low

Form RPR
06 **1** **Bettalatethannever (IRE)**[15] 6118 2-8-12 DaneO'Neill 2 75+
(SDow) *plld hrd: prom: drvn to ld 100 yds out: all out* **11/4**[2]
4412 **2** *hd* **Queenstown (IRE)**[23] 6059 2-9-2 85 (b) RWinston 1 79
(BJMeehan) *s.i.s: hdwy to ld after 1f: hrd rdn and hdd 100 yds out: rallied gamely* **4/6**[1]
600 **3** *5* **Solo Sole (ITY)**[15] 6118 2-8-12 EAhern 5 62
(LMCumani) *hrd rdn and hdwy over 2f out: no imp on ldng pair* **14/1**
**4** *5* **Hilltop Fantasy** 2-8-5 ow2 WRyan 11 43
(DJDaly) *w'like: bit bkwd: in tch: effrt over 2f out: wknd over 1f out* **16/1**
0000 **5** *2 1/2* **Limit Down (IRE)**[9] 6141 2-8-9 64 DCorby(3) 7 43
(MJWallace) *towards rr: rdn 3f out: nvr rchd ldrs* **50/1**
4 **6** *nk* **Magical Gift**[21] 6072 2-8-2 JFMcDonald(5) 9 38
(DWPArbuthnot) *wd: prom 5f* **10/1**[3]
**7** *3/4* **It's Blue Chip** 2-8-8 (e[1]) PaulEddery 6 37
(PWD'Arcy) *unf: bit bkwd: b: s.i.s: mid-div: effrt 3f out: sn rdn and btn* **20/1**
**8** *3/4* **Ground Patrol** 2-8-5 LPKeniry(3) 3 35
(AMBalding) *leggy: s.s: bhd: shkn up over 2f out: sme late hdwy* **25/1**
0000 **9** *shd* **Intitnice (IRE)**[9] 6147 2-8-12 45 JoannaBadger 4 39
(MissKMGeorge) *prom 4f* **100/1**
**10** *3* **Opera Star (IRE)** 2-8-3 ADaly 10 22
(BWHills) *unf: s.i.s: wd: hld up and bhd: n.d whn hung lft ins fnl f* **14/1**
**11** *21* **Mr Strowger**[178] 2612 2-8-12 RSmith 8 —
(ACharlton) *led 1f: wknd over 3f out* **100/1**

1m 26.43s (0.43) **Going Correction** +0.15s/f (Slow) 11 Ran SP% **127.5**
Speed ratings: **103,102,97,91,88 88,87,86,86,82 58**CSF £5.20 TOTE £3.90: £1.20, £1.10, £4.10; EX 7.00.
**Owner** J R May **Bred** Mick McGinn **Trained** Epsom, Surrey
■ Stewards Enquiry : Dane O'Neill one-day ban: used whip without giving gelding time to respond (Dec 26)

### FOCUS
The winner landed a tidy gamble in the first division of the novice stakes.

**NOTEBOOK**

**Bettalatethannever(IRE)**, well backed after an eye-catching run over six furlongs last time, was in a good position throughout and showed a fine attitiude to grind down the runner up late on. He travelled well throughout and despite being keen early on, put up a polished display and beat a decent yardstick in the shape of the runner-up. This trip suited well.

**Queenstown(IRE)**once again went down fighting. He was not helped by missing the break, spent a lot of energy in rushing up to lead, as he prefers, and was giving 4lb to the winner. On the face of it, this was another solid display and although he is becoming exposed, he should win more races this winter. He looks best at this trip.

**Solo Sole(ITY)**improved on his last effort, but was well beaten and may need to drop in grade.

**Hilltop Fantasy**put up a satisfactory debut and is entitled to improve, but already looks the type to do better in handicaps.

## 6204 GREENACRE HOMES CLAIMING STKS (DIV I) 7f (P)

**12:30** (12:32) (F ) 3-Y-0+ **£2,086** (£596; £298) **Stalls** Low

Form RPR

0002 **1** **Warlingham (IRE)**[7] 6163 5-8-11 54 VSlattery 12 61
(MPitman) *plld hrd: chsd ldrs: led ins fnl f: drvn out* **5/1**[2]

0000 **2** 1 3/4 **Harbour House**[47] 5846 4-8-5 39 FNorton 3 51
(JJBridger) *t.k.h: led 2f: ev ch ins fnl f: one pce* **20/1**

0301 **3** nk **Free Option (IRE)**[7] 6163 8-9-3 73 (b) NCallan 8 62+
(GLMoore) *chsd ldrs: sn pushed along: cl 5th whn hmpd ins fnl f: swtchd rt and r.o wl nr fin* **13/8**[1]

0200 **4** 1/2 **Savile's Delight (IRE)**[22] 6063 4-9-5 52 (p) IMongan 13 63
(RBrotherton) *prom: led over 1f out tl ins fnl f: no ex* **20/1**

0000 **5** 2 **Mayzin (IRE)**[47] 5848 3-9-7 45 (p) SWhitworth 14 60?
(RMFlower) *prom: led after 2f tl over 1f out: bmpd and no ex ins fnl f* **100/1**

0000 **6** 3 **Ladywell Blaise (IRE)**[131] 3959 6-7-9 41 JFMcDonald(5) 1 31
(JJBridger) *dwlt: sn in mid-div: effrt 3f out: nt pce to chal* **25/1**

2000 **7** 3 **Dancing Forest (IRE)**[63] 5574 3-9-1 68 DaneO'Neill 5 39
(DKIvory) *b: s.s and lost 10l: wl bhd tl styd on fnl 2f* **8/1**

5304 **8** shd **Hadath (IRE)**[7] 6163 6-8-6 67 (p) LPKeniry(3) 9 32
(BGPowell) *towards rr: pushed along 3f out: nvr rchd ldrs* **11/2**[3]

**9** shd **Thai Hi (IRE)**[51] 5803 3-8-12 JFEgan 11 35
(SKirk) *chsd ldrs tl wknd over 1f out* **20/1**

0524 **10** 1 1/4 **Komena**[18] 6100 5-8-8 49 EAhern 15 28
(JWPayne) *in tch tl rdn and btn over 2f out* **8/1**

0056 **11** 2 **Jouvert**[18] 6099 3-8-3 45 RSmith 10 18
(RHannon) *mid-div: hrd rdn and n.d fnl 3f* **20/1**

2400 **12** 5 **Walker Bay (IRE)**[7] 6163 5-8-2 44 (b) JTate 4 5
(JCFox) *dwlt: a bhd* **33/1**

00 **13** 2 1/2 **Sargents Dream**[11] 6137 3-8-3 BReilly(5) 2 4
(JAGilbert) *mid-div: hrd rdn and btn 3f out* **100/1**

2400 **14** nk **Badou**[11] 6133 3-8-13 47 (v) CCogan 6 9
(LMontagueHall) *dwlt: sn rdn along: a bhd* **33/1**

0000 **15** 22 **Subtle Move (USA)**[9] 6148 3-8-10 40 DarrenWilliams 16 —
(DShaw) *in tch 3f: sn drvn along and bhd* **66/1**

0 **16** dist **Recycling Rita**[92] 4971 4-8-5 DCorby(3) 7 —
(PRHedger) *sn wl bhd: t.o fnl 3f* **100/1**

1m 26.03s (0.03) **Going Correction** +0.15s/f (Slow) **16** Ran SP% **125.6**

Speed ratings: **105,103,102,102,99 96,92,92,92,91 89,83,80,80,54** — CT £6.10 TOTE £1.70: £6.70, £1.40, £; EX175.90 1.The winner (No 7) was claimed by D C Patrick for £7,000. Free Option (No 3) was claimed by Mr Lloyd Bennett for £10,000.e

**Owner** Martin Butler **Bred** Paul Hyland **Trained** Upper Lambourn, Berks

**FOCUS**

A weak contest run at a muddling pace.

**NOTEBOOK**

**Warlingham(IRE)**, despite running very free early on, reversed the form with the third horse on the same terms and won this well. He was given a good, simple ride and is clearly in good form at present.

**Harbour House**ran a much improved race on this return to the sand and, although he is a desperately hard horse to catch right, he may be about to find some form in this sphere.

**Free Option(IRE)**was very unlucky in running and would have finished second at the least with a clearer run in the straight. That said, he is far from straightforward and has a habit of doing this.

**Savile's Delight(IRE)**showed a slight improvement for the reapplication of cheekpieces and this was his best effort to date on sand. However, he was at an advantage in racing up with the pace and may be flattered.

**Mayzin(IRE)**ran a better race in the cheekpieces.

**Dancing Forest(IRE)**is best forgiven this run after badly missing the break.

## 6205 BET DIRECT ON ATTHERACES INTERACTIVE FILLIES' H'CAP 1m 2f (P)

**1:00** (1:03) (E ) (0-70,68) 3-Y-0+ **£2,065** (£590; £295) **Stalls** Low

Form RPR

40-4 **1** **Regal Gallery (IRE)**[21] 6073 5-9-2 **53** PaulEddery 2 64
(CAHorgan) *hld up towards rr: hdwy 2f out: led ins fnl f: rdn out* **9/1**

0552 **2** 1 3/4 **Ember Days**[7] 6161 4-9-1 **52** EAhern 13 60
(JLSpearing) *in tch: effrt 3f out: ev ch ins f: nt qckn* **10/3**[1]

0000 **3** nk **Harlot**[21] 6073 3-8-13 **56** (p) LisaJones(3) 5 63
(JohnBerry) *b: led: edgd rt and hdd ins fnl f: one pce* **40/1**

3043 **4** 1 1/4 **Pirouettes (IRE)**[8] 6153 3-9-1 **55** NCallan 7 60
(MissGayKelleway) *cl up: drvn to press ldr over 2f out: no ex over 1f out* **20/1**

3-22 **5** hd **Margery Daw (IRE)**[11] 6131 3-9-10 **64** DaneO'Neill 9 69+
(MPTregoning) *hld up in midfield: rdn and hdwy over 1f out: nt rch ldrs* **9/2**[2]

6006 **6** 2 **Leonor De Soto**[5] 6171 3-8-8 **55** DFentiman(7) 14 56
(JRBest) *wd: hld up in rr: shkn up over 1f out: nrst fin* **25/1**

004 **7** hd **State Of Balance**[11] 6131 5-9-8 **62** LPKeniry(3) 10 63
(KBell) *lw: t.k.h: stdd in rr: promising hdwy in midfield whn hmpd over 1f out: nvr in chalng position* **9/1**

0000 **8** 1 1/2 **Power Bird (IRE)**[11] 6133 3-9-11 **65** PDoe 1 63
(DFlood) *prom: hrd rdn 2f out: wknd over 1f out* **20/1**

0-60 **9** 1/2 **Wavet**[29] 6022 3-9-1 **55** ACulhane 8 52
(MrsLydiaPearce) *mid-div: rdn over 2f out: no imp* **20/1**

4002 **10** 1 1/2 **Castaigne (FR)**[21] 6073 4-9-5 **56** (t) IMongan 12 51
(BWDuke) *s.s: wd: hld up in midfield: rdn over 2f out: no imp* **7/1**

3502 **11** 1/2 **Dispol Evita**[11] 6133 4-8-9 **53** HPoulton(7) 4 47
(JamiePoulton) *lw: s.s: towards rr: effrt over 2f out: n.d* **9/1**

0040 **12** 9 **Boogie Magic**[138] 3753 3-10-0 **68** GCarter 6 45
(CNAllen) *prom tl wknd 2f out: eased whn no ch over 1f out* **13/2**[3]

0-04 **13** 1/2 **Suerte**[19] 6086 3-9-3 **57** MFenton 11 34
(JGGiven) *lw: prom 7f* **10/1**

2m 9.25s (1.86) **Going Correction** +0.15s/f (Slow)

**WFA** 3 from 4yo+ 3lb **13** Ran SP% **126.8**

Speed ratings: **98,96,96,95,95 93,93,92,91,90 90,83,82**CSF £38.57 CT £1202.81 TOTE £14.60: £5.70, £1.60, £7.90; EX 70.10.

**Owner** Mrs B Sumner **Bred** Mrs B Sumner **Trained** Ogbourne Maisey, Wilts

**FOCUS**

A moderate, but competitive fillies' handicap run at a fair pace.

**NOTEBOOK**

**Regal Gallery(IRE)**produced a decent late burst to win going away. She had pleased on her comeback form a lengthy absence last time over course-and-distance, and showed the benefit of that outing and could well go in again. She will be given time to recover from this.

**Ember Days**had every chance and simply found one better on the day. This was her second successive silver medal and she should not be long going one better in this grade, as she is well treated at present.

**Harlot**responded positively to the first-time cheekpieces and put up her best display for a long time, only tiring late on. *Official explanation: jockey said filly hung badly right throughout*

**Pirouettes(IRE)**, who was not guaranteed to get this trip by any means, was not disgraced. She has been a disappointing type on turf this year, but has shown improvement for her current yard, and it would be a surprise if she were not to lose her maiden tag this winter.

**Margery Daw(IRE)**looked on a fair mark for this handicap debut, but never looked like capitalising on that at any stage and has a lot to prove now.

**State Of Balance**, making her handicap bow, had little luck in running and is better than her position would indicate.

**Castaigne(FR)**was forced to use up too much too soon after falling out of the gates and losing many lengths.

**Dispol Evita**was reported to have been struck into. *Official explanation: trainer said filly was struck into*

## 6206 GREENACRE HOMES CLAIMING STKS (DIV II) 7f (P)

**1:30** (1:34) (F ) 3-Y-0+ **£2,079** (£594; £297) **Stalls** Low

Form RPR

0003 **1** **Zinging**[11] 6133 4-8-13 48 FNorton 9 60
(JJBridger) *hld up towards rr: hdwy 2f out: str run to ld fnl 50 yds* **6/1**[3]

1000 **2** 3/4 **Espada (IRE)**[11] 6128 7-9-5 74 SWKelly 2 64
(JAOsborne) *led: rdn over 2f out: kpt on: hdd fnl 50 yds* **10/1**

5005 **3** shd **Dolphinelle (IRE)**[7] 6163 7-8-7 49 (v) JFEgan 10 52
(JamiePoulton) *bhd: rdn and hdwy over 1f out: fin wl* **16/1**

0000 **4** shd **Dilys**[131] 3969 4-8-6 48 EAhern 7 51
(WSKittow) *hld up in tch: rdn to chse ldrs over 1f out: styd on* **33/1**

0560 **5** nk **Adantino**[29] 6024 4-8-11 51 GBaker 5 55
(BRMillman) *lw: hdwy 2f out: ev ch fnl f: nt qckn nr fin* **14/1**

2033 **6** 1 1/2 **Feast Of Romance**[30] 6016 6-8-10 51 (p) J-PGuillambert(3) 14 53
(PHowling) *b: in tch: rdn to chse ldrs over 2f out: no ex fnl f* **16/1**

6000 **7** 3/4 **Definitely Special (IRE)**[84] 5151 5-8-7 40 LPKeniry(3) 1 48
(NEBerry) *cl up: rdn to press ldr 2f out: no ex fnl f* **40/1**

2605 **8** shd **Four Jays (IRE)**[11] 6133 3-9-7 64 (p) IMongan 6 59
(NPLittmoden) *towards rr: hdwy 2f out: no imp appr fnl f* **11/2**[2]

3000 **9** nk **Xsynna**[7] 6163 7-8-3 47 JTate 12 40
(PSMcentee) *wd: towards rr: effrt over 2f out: nt pce to chal* **25/1**

3050 **10** 2 **The Gay Fox**[8] 6150 9-7-12 44 (bt) KarenPeippo(7) 16 37
(BGPowell) *wd: prom tl wknd over 1f out* **25/1**

0000 **11** 2 **Rathmullan**[217] 1578 4-8-7 38 SCarson 8 34
(EAWheeler) *in rr: mod effrt 2f out: hrd rdn: n.d* **66/1**

5000 **12** 1/2 **Prince Ivor**[18] 6089 3-8-3 40 RSmith 3 29
(JCFox) *b.hind: mid-div: sn rdn along: effrt and in tch whn nt clr run jst ins fnl f: eased* **66/1**

0403 **13** shd **Looking Down**[25] 6049 3-9-2 72 DaneO'Neill 15 42
(RHannon) *prom: rdn 1/2-way: n.m.r and wknd over 2f out* **1/1**[1]

3000 **14** 1 1/4 **Good Form (IRE)**[95] 4339 3-7-12 41 JFMcDonald(5) 4 26
(MissKMGeorge) *prom over 4f* **50/1**

000- **15** 5 **Picatrip**[390] 5761 3-7-9 40 FPFerris(3) 13 8
(PRHedger) *s.s: hrd rdn 3f out: a bhd* **100/1**

1m 26.57s (0.57) **Going Correction** +0.15s/f (Slow) **15** Ran SP% **126.2**

Speed ratings: **102,101,101,100,100 98,98,97,97,95 92,92,92,90,85**CSF £63.83 TOTE £8.60: £1.80, £2.50, £3.40; EX 69.30.

**Owner** J Jenner **Bred** M P Bishop **Trained** Liphook, Hants

**FOCUS**

Zinging landed a gamble in the weaker of the two divisions.

**NOTEBOOK**

**Zinging**produced a fair turn of speed in the straight to win this tidily. He has looked an improved performer since switching to this surface the last twice and if he can maintain this current mood he could follow up at this venue.

**Espada(IRE)**made a bold bid to make all and this was an improvement on his last outing. He will come on again for the experience and although he looks flattered by his current mark, he is capable of scoring in this grade.

**Dolphinelle(IRE)**ran an improved race on his last couple of outings, but has a habit of doing this and is a very hard horse to win with.

**Dilys**ran with credit on her return from a break, but is another in-and-out performer.

**Adantino**again looked to dodge the issue having held every chance in the straight.

**Looking Down**ran a shocker. On official ratings she should have gone close, but she dropped out like a light as if something was amiss. *Official explanation: trainer's representative had no explanation for the poor form shown*

## 6207 BET DIRECT ON 0800 32 93 93 NURSERY 5f (P)

**2:00** (2:03) (D ) (0-85,78) 2-Y-O **£2,936** (£839; £419) **Stalls** High

Form RPR

601 **1** **Intriguing Glimpse**[25] 6045 2-8-9 **66** NCallan 3 65+
(MissBSanders) *lw: prom: sn pushed along: led 1f out: drvn out* **2/1**[1]

0662 **2** 3/4 **Smokin Joe**[5] 6165 2-8-10 **67** NPollard 4 63
(JRBest) *b: rdn and hdwy over 1f out: r.o to take 2nd fnl 75 yds* **9/1**

5160 **3** 3/4 **Forzenuff**[21] 6077 2-8-8 **65** EAhern 5 59
(JRBoyle) *broke wl: prom: rdn and kpt on fnl 2f* **14/1**

0432 **4** hd **Hello Roberto**[8] 6152 2-9-3 **77** LFletcher(3) 2 70
(MJPolglase) *lw: hdwy over 1f out: disputing cl 3rd whn nt clr run ins fnl f: r.o nr fin* **7/1**

1042 **5** nk **Sweetest Revenge (IRE)**[15] 6118 2-9-7 **78** ADaly 10 70
(MDIUsher) *trckd ldrs: wd bnd into st: styd on same pce* **13/2**[3]

1300 **6** hd **Easily Averted (IRE)**[37] 5966 2-9-0 **71** SWKelly 6 62
(JAOsborne) *sn led: rdn and hdd 1f out: no ex* **13/2**[3]

0024 **7** shd **Pregnant Pause (IRE)**[7] 6160 2-8-8 **65** JFEgan 8 56
(SKirk) *outpcd towards rr: styd on wl fnl f: nvr nrr* **9/2**[2]

6150 **8** 4 **Ivory Lace**[177] 2626 2-8-9 **66** DaneO'Neill 9 43
(DKIvory) *hmpd sn after s: sn in tch and wd: outpcd 2f out: n.d after* **40/1**

0115 **9** 1 **Back At De Front (IRE)**[8] 6152 2-9-0 **76** MSavage(5) 7 49
(NEBerry) *prom tl wknd over 1f out: eased whn btn* **25/1**

4106 **10** 1 3/4 **Knight Onthe Tiles (IRE)**[29] 6021 2-8-13 **70** IMongan 1 37
(JRBest) *s.i.s: outpcd: sn wl bhd* **8/1**

60.02 secs (0.24) **Going Correction** +0.15s/f (Slow) **10** Ran SP% **124.7**

Speed ratings: **104,102,101,101,100 100,100,93,92,89**CSF £23.39 CT £215.03 TOTE £2.80: £1.40, £3.20, £6.00; EX 24.30.

**Owner** Edward Hyde **Bred** Copy Xpress Ltd **Trained** Epsom, Surrey

**FOCUS**
A fair nursery run at a sound pace.
**NOTEBOOK**
**Intriguing Glimpse**followed up her maiden win over course-and-distance readily and looks at the right end of the handicap. She is still unexposed and will get six furlongs without much fuss on this showing.
**Smokin Joe**found this too sharp and was making up ground on the winner late on. He improved on his previous display and looked suited by this surface, therefore is one to keep a close eye on when reverting to six once more.
**Forzenuff**can have no excuses. He looks in need of a drop in grade to score again.
**Hello Roberto**was mounting her challenge when meeting serious traffic on the inside and would have been a great deal closer, without winning. She proved she can handle this track and connections should place her to advantage before long.
**Sweetest Revenge(IRE)**lacks the pace to dominate over five furlongs and the stamina to last out over six in this grade.

## 6208 BETDIRECT.CO.UK H'CAP 1m 4f (P)
**2:30** (2:30) (D ) (0-80,79) 3-Y-O+ **£3,073** (£878; £439) **Stalls** Low

Form RPR
5501 **1** **Tight Squeeze**[74] 5373 6-9-11 **76** ........ ACulhane 10 84
(PWHiatt) *hld up in rr: rdn and hdwy over 1f out: str run to ld nr fin* **12/1**
3064 **2** ¾ **Easter Ogil (IRE)**[7] 6157 8-8-11 **62** ........ VSlattery 13 69
(JaneSouthcombe) *b: hdwy 2f out: rdn to ld 100 yds out: hdd and nt qckn nr fin* **10/1**
0000 **3** ½ **High Hope (FR)**[25] 6052 5-9-13 **78** ........(be) SWhitworth 2 84
(GLMoore) *hdwy 3f out: led 1f out tl 100 yds out: kpt on same pce* **12/1**
0000 **4** *nk* **Night Warrior (IRE)**[2] 6190 3-8-11 **67** ........ PDoe 12 73
(DFlood) *hld up in rr: hdwy on rail 2f out: styd on* **33/1**
0050 **5** ¾ **Gallant Boy (IRE)**[15] 6117 4-9-5 **77** ........(t) SJDonohoe[(7)] 6 82
(PDEvans) *towards rr: rdn and r.o fnl 2f: nvr nrr* **7/1**[3]
2222 **6** ½ **Danehill Lad (IRE)**[35] 5982 3-8-10 **66** ........ DaneO'Neill 8 70
(TKeddy) *b: b.hind: dwlt: hld up in midfield: stdy hdwy 3f out: n.m.r on rail and lost pl over 1f out: eased outside: r.o nr fin* **13/2**[2]
6331 **7** 2 **Paragon Of Virtue**[18] 6093 6-10-0 **79** ........ JFanning 16 80
(PMitchell) *lw: b: b.bind: wd: chsd ldrs: led over 2f out tl 1f out: no ex* **5/2**[1]
0253 **8** *shd* **Bluegrass Boy**[11] 6131 3-8-6 **67** ........ RThomas[(5)] 1 68
(GBBalding) *a.p: no ex over 1f out* **16/1**
5550 **9** *1* **Most-Saucy**[11] 6130 7-8-12 **68** ........ DNolan[(5)] 4 67
(IAWood) *chsd ldrs: rdn over 3f out: one pce* **14/1**
2255 **10** *5* **Hoh Viss**[18] 6089 3-9-0 **70** ........ JFEgan 5 62
(SKirk) *led 2f: hrd rdn 3f out: sn btn* **16/1**
4000 **11** 1 ½ **Liberty Royal**[15] 6117 4-9-9 **74** ........ DSweeney 3 64
(PJMakin) *led after 2f tl over 2f out: wknd over 1f out* **20/1**
1200 **12** *1* **Perfect Love**[25] 6049 3-9-7 **77** ........(b[1]) EAhern 15 65
(GAButler) *mid-div: effrt over 2f out: wknd wl over 1f out* **10/1**
0450 **13** *shd* **Gabor**[7] 6161 4-8-10 **61** ........(be) IMongan 11 49
(GLMoore) *dwlt: sn chsng ldrs: wkng whn squeezed 2f out* **14/1**
330 **14** 1 ¾ **Wood Fern (UAE)**[11] 6131 3-9-0 **70** ........ RLappin 7 55
(MRChannon) *lw: stdd in rr after 3f and taken wd: rdn and n.d fnl 3f* **25/1**
0000 **15** *3* **Afadan (IRE)**[32] 2142 5-10-0 **79** ........ SWKelly 14 60
(JRJenkins) *s.s: sn in midfield: btn whn hmpd over 2f out* **33/1**
6300 **16** *4* **Duc's Dream**[22] 6068 5-8-8 **59** ........ NCallan 9 34
(DMorris) *prom 9f: wkng whn hmpd 2f out* **20/1**

2m 34.98s (1.00) **Going Correction** +0.15s/f (Slow)
**WFA** 3 from 4yo+ 5lb **16** Ran SP% **132.3**
Speed ratings: **102,101,101,100,100 100,98,98,98,94 93,93,93,91,89 87**CSF £129.06 CT £1509.61 TOTE £11.90: £3.10, £2.80, £4.20, £9.30; EX 310.40.
**Owner** Anthony Harrison **Bred** Anthony Harrison **Trained** Hook Norton, Oxon
■ Stewards Enquiry : V Slattery two-day ban: careless riding (Dec 26,27)

**FOCUS**
A competitive 0-80 handicap run at a generous gallop.
**NOTEBOOK**
**Tight Squeeze**came from out of the clouds to get up where it matters. She was winning this off a 17lb higher mark than when last successful on this surface and was 5lb higher than when last seen in October. She can reserve a bit for herself, but thrives off a fast pace and should be winning again. Tony Culhane is now three from three on her.
**Easter Ogil(IRE)**looked the winner inside the last furlong and was a little unlucky. He is yet to win beyond a mile, but stayed this extra trip well and his recent form suggets a win is not far off.
**High Hope(FR)**responded well to the first-time blinkers and was going well turning for home, but after shaking the favourite, had no more to offer when the late finishers challenged. This was a marked improvement on recent efforts and if the headgear has the same affect next time, he can win off this mark.
**Night Warrior(IRE)**was suited by the way the race unfolded and improved on recent form, but finds this grade too hot.
**Gallant Boy(IRE)**was given a lot to do and finished fast. He has the talent, but is frustrating.
**Danehill Lad(IRE)**suffered traffic problems and is better than the finishing position suggets.
**Paragon Of Virtue**saw a lot of daylight and had to use plenty of energy to get prominent from his wide draw, and ultimately that cost him.

## 6209 BET DIRECT ON CHANNEL 4 PAGE 613 MAIDEN STKS 6f (P)
**3:00** (3:02) (D ) 3-Y-O+ **£2,320** (£663; £331) **Stalls** Low

Form RPR
0050 **1** **Gun Salute**[18] 6094 3-9-0 52........(p) RBrisland 2 59
(GLMoore) *t.k.h: trckd ldrs: led ins fnl f: drvn out* **8/1**
P006 **2** *nk* **Prince Aaron (IRE)**[113] 4483 3-9-0 47........ GCarter 12 58
(CNAllen) *chsd ldrs: drvn to ld briefly 1f out: ev ch fnl f: r.o* **8/1**
04 **3** *2* **Lucius Verrus (USA)**[100] 4774 3-9-0........ DarrenWilliams 3 52
(DShaw) *prom: ev ch over 1f out: nt qckn fnl f* **16/1**
0400 **4** 1 ¼ **Mad Mick Meeson**[8] 6149 3-9-0 55........(t) AClark 7 48
(GBBalding) *in tch: effrt 2f out: kpt on fnl f* **11/2**[3]
4626 **5** *hd* **A Beetoo (IRE)**[298] 597 3-8-9 63........ NPollard 1 43
(JRBest) *b: dwlt: hdwy over 1f out: hrd rdn: styd on* **7/1**
4000 **6** *nk* **Island Star (IRE)**[82] 5202 3-9-0 57........ PDoe 10 47
(SDow) *led tl 1f out: no ex* **25/1**
2344 **7** *1* **Dark Champion**[28] 6031 3-9-0 56........ DaneO'Neill 9 44
(JeddO'Keeffe) *mid-div: outpcd 1/2-way: styd on fnl f* **7/2**[2]
0 **8** *1* **Maggie Maquette**[26] 6039 3-8-9........ DSweeney 14 36
(WSKittow) *wnt rt s: plld hrd in rr: sme hdwy over 1f out: nt rch ldrs* **50/1**
**9** 1 ¾ **Bandini (SAF)** 3-8-8 ow1........ SJDonohoe[(7)] 5 37
(PDEvans) *leggy: prom tl wknd over 1f out* **20/1**
**10** ½ **Midnight Mambo (USA)** 3-8-9........ EAhern 11 29
(RGuest) *leggy: bhd whn rn wd into st: nvr trbld ldrs* **3/1**[1]
5550 **11** 1 ¼ **Tatweer (IRE)**[11] 6134 3-9-0 52........(v) RWinston 13 30
(DShaw) *wd: in tch tl fdd fnl 2f* **8/1**
**12** ½ **Wodhill Be** 3-8-9........ NCallan 8 24
(DMorris) *w'like: bit bkwd: in tch 4f* **40/1**
00 **13** *9* **Preveza**[51] 5799 4-8-4........ NChalmers[(5)] 4 —
(JWhite) *s.s and lost 10l: sme hdwy on rail after 2f: wknd over 2f out* **100/1**

1m 14.31s (1.39) **Going Correction** +0.15s/f (Slow) **13** Ran SP% **128.3**
Speed ratings: **96,95,92,91,91 90,89,87,85,84 83,82,70**CSF £72.96 TOTE £12.00: £3.20, £1.40, £4.40; EX 116.20.
**Owner** R Henderson **Bred** S Crown **Trained** Woodingdean, E Sussex
■ Stewards Enquiry : R WinstonM seven-day ban (reduced from 10 on appeal): failed to take all reasonable and permissible measures to obtain best possible placing (Feb 21-28)

**FOCUS**
A weak maiden full of exposed sorts.
**NOTEBOOK**
**Gun Salute**, who on one piece of turf form had a big shout for this, responded positively to the cheekpieces and ran out a game victor. He put his proven stamina to good use on this drop in trip, but it was a weak maiden and he is no good thing to build on this.
**Prince Aaron(IRE)**, heavily backed in the ring, almost landed a touch on this drop in trip. He settled better this time due to the pace and, as his stable's runners are in good form at present, may be the one to take from the race.
**Lucius Verrus(USA)**, sold out of Aidan O'Brien's yard unraced, put up his best display yet and may improve for another furlong.
**Dark Champion**was never on terms and this was too bad to be true.
**Maggie Maquette** *Official explanation: jockey said filly broke awkwardly and had no steering thereafter*
**Midnight Mambo(USA)**never looked like justifying favouritism at any stage and this was a most disappointing debut.
**Tatweer(IRE)**, who was a big drifter on the betting exchanges, caught the eye of the Stewards and was banned for 40 days, and his trainer and rider were both heavily fined. *Official explanation: 40-day ban (Feb 21-Mar 31)*

## 6210 LITTLEWOODS BET DIRECT NOVICE STKS (DIV II) 7f (P)
**3:30** (3:31) (D ) 2-Y-O **£3,024** (£864; £432) **Stalls** Low

Form RPR
0563 **1** **Whitgift Rock**[97] 4847 2-8-12 71........ PDoe 11 69
(SDow) *hdwy on outside whn rn wd bnd into st: rdn to join ldrs 1f out: got up nr fin* **7/2**[3]
0132 **2** ½ **Fools Entire**[7] 6160 2-8-7 64........(p) BReilly[(5)] 3 68
(JAGilbert) *plld hrd: prom: slt ld 1f out: hrd rdn: hdd nr fin* **2/1**[2]
**3** 1 ¼ **Jumeirah Scarer** 2-8-8........ ACulhane 6 61
(MRChannon) *leggy: scope: chsd ldrs: ev ch ins fnl f: kpt on same pce* **7/4**[1]
**4** *nk* **Star Fern** 2-8-8........ GCarter 7 60
(JAkehurst) *unf: bit bkwd: s.s: hdwy 2f out: rdn and styd on fnl f* **33/1**
00 **5** 2 ½ **Jango Malfoy (IRE)**[18] 6091 2-8-12........ MFenton 2 58
(BWDuke) *led tl 1f out: no ex* **20/1**
00 **6** *hd* **Sabrina Brown**[29] 6020 2-8-7........ SCarson 1 52
(GBBalding) *t.k.h: trckd ldrs: rdn and one pce appr fnl f* **16/1**
0 **7** *nk* **Red Contact (USA)**[21] 6074 2-8-12........ RSmith 4 57
(ACharlton) *prom: nt handle bnd into st: wknd over 1f out* **20/1**
**8** 3 ½ **Saucy Pickle** 2-8-4 ow1........ NPollard 10 40
(MissZCDavison) *neat: in tch tl rdn and btn over 2f out* **66/1**
**9** *6* **Pick A Berry** 2-8-4 ow1........ JFEgan 9 25
(GWragg) *dwlt: rdn along: a bhd* **14/1**
**10** 1 ½ **Lakeside Guy (IRE)** 2-8-5........ FPFerris[(3)] 5 25
(PSMcentee) *w'like: bit bkwd: b.hind: s.s: plld hrd: sn in tch: wknd 2f out* **33/1**
0 **11** *2* **Midmaar (IRE)**[7] 6159 2-9-2........ FNorton 8 28
(MWigham) *hld up towards rr: lost tch 1/2-way* **10/1**

1m 27.84s (1.84) **Going Correction** +0.15s/f (Slow) **11** Ran SP% **130.5**
Speed ratings: **95,94,93,92,89 89,89,85,78,76 74**CSF £11.67 TOTE £4.90: £1.70, £1.50, £1.50; EX 13.40 Place 6 £205.31, Place 5 £174.03.
**Owner** Whitgift Racing **Bred** Mrs D O Joly **Trained** Epsom, Surrey

**FOCUS**
The winner completed a double for his yard who won both divisions of the novice stakes.
**NOTEBOOK**
**Whitgift Rock**, off since running a personal best on turf in September, did well in the circumstances to win as he did. He was restrained off the pace, which was slow, forced to race wide throughout and was still full of running at the line. He looks the type to get a mile and could be better than he has shown to date.
**Fools Entire**, very keen early, ran another sound race and responded well to the first-time cheekpieces. It would be a suprise if he were not to gain compensation for this during the winter.
**Jumeirah Scarer**was well backed for this debut and looked like justifying favouritism for most of the way, until finding little under pressure and running green late on. He is no star, but will come on plenty for this and should lose his maiden tag before too long.
**Star Fern**blew it at the start, but made good progress late on and this was a fair debut effort.
T/Plt: £466.60 to a £1 stake. Pool: £29,277.10. 45.80 winning tickets. T/Qpdt: £289.80 to a £1 stake. Pool: £2,311.30. 5.90 winning tickets. LM

# 6196 SOUTHWELL (L-H)
## Friday, December 19

**OFFICIAL GOING: Standard**
This meeting was transferred from Wolverhampton.
Wind: fresh, hlf across Weather: fine

## 6211 BET DIRECT ON SKY TEXT PAGE 371 H'CAP (DIV I) 1m (F)
**11:40** (11:41) (F ) (0-60,65) 3-Y-O+ **£2,107** (£602; £301) **Stalls** Low

Form RPR
0222 **1** **Mutarafaa (USA)**[11] 6143 4-8-10 **46**........(e) THamilton[(5)] 5 62
(DShaw) *trckd ldrs: hdwy 2f out: rdn and edgd lft 1f out: drvn and styd on wl to ld nr fin* **5/1**[3]
0-04 **2** *shd* **Chabibi**[7] 6171 4-8-9 **40**........ AStarke 6 56
(THHansen, Germany) *led: rdn over 1f out: drvn and hung rt ins last: hdd nr fin* **4/1**[2]
5406 **3** *5* **Jamestown**[13] 6128 6-9-0 **48**........ LFletcher[(3)] 10 54
(MJPolglase) *a.p: effrt 2f out: rdn and one pce appr last* **9/1**
0006 **4** 3 ½ **Lucayan Monarch**[6] 6178 5-9-8 **58**........(p) DNolan[(5)] 2 57
(PABlockley) *towards rr: swtchd rt and hdwy 2f out: styd on appr last: nvr rch ldrs* **8/1**
5113 **5** ½ **Miss Champers (IRE)**[3] 6196 3-9-12 **65** 6ex........ SJDonohoe[(7)] 9 63
(PDEvans) *towards rr: hdwy 2f out: sn rdn and nvr nr ldrs* **10/3**[1]
4322 **6** *hd* **Magic Mamma's Too**[4] 6193 3-9-0 **53**........ PMakin[(7)] 1 51
(TDBarron) *trckd ldrs on inner: pushed along 3f out: rdn 2f out and sn wknd* **5/1**[3]
0000 **7** ½ **Tropical Son**[6] 6178 4-8-10 **41**........(v) DarrenWilliams 8 38
(DShaw) *nvr nr ldrs* **66/1**

0350 **8** 2 1/2 **Route Sixty Six (IRE)**[21] 4542 7-8-7 **45**.................. LeanneKershaw(7) 4 37
(JeddO'Keeffe) *a rr* **25/1**

0106 **9** 5 **Consignia (IRE)**[13] 6133 4-9-4 **49**....................................(v) PaulEddery 3 31
(DHaydnJones) *trckd wnr: shkn up over 2f out: sn rdn and wknd* **14/1**

4000 **10** 1 1/2 **Dancing King (IRE)**[92] 5015 7-8-0 **31**......................... JoannaBadger 11 10
(PWHiatt) *cl up: rdn along over 2f out: sn wknd* **25/1**

4500 **11** 11 **Sennen Cove**[86] 5151 4-8-5 **36**..........................................(t) JMackay 7 —
(RBastiman) *a rr* **33/1**

1165 **12** 2 1/2 **Relative Hero (IRE)**[21] 5626 3-9-10 **56**...............................(p) NCallan 13 8
(MissSJWilton) *sn outpcd and bhd* **25/1**

0000 **13** 7 **Thaayer**[30] 6027 8-8-7 **38**........................................... GGibbons 12 —
(IAWood) *chsd ldrs on outer: rdn along 3f out: sn wknd* **33/1**

1m 45.84s (1.24) **Going Correction** +0.075s/f (Slow)
**WFA** 3 from 4yo+ 1lb **13** Ran SP% **123.1**
Speed ratings: **96,95,90,87,86 86,86,83,78,77 66,63,56**CSF £24.28 CT £182.00 TOTE £5.50: £2.00, £1.70, £3.80; EX 52.20.
**Owner** J C Fretwell **Bred** Shadwell Farm Llc **Trained** Averham, Notts
■ Stewards Enquiry : A Starke two-day ban: used whip without giving sufficient time for response (Dec 30-31); caution: careless riding

**FOCUS**
This was not a strong race and the slower of the two divisions.

**NOTEBOOK**
**Mutarafaa(USA)**, whose only previous victory had been achieved at this track, finished well to get up on the line and strikes as the type to continue performing with credit.
**Chabibi** may well have won but for hanging right under pressure and could be able to gain compensation in the coming weeks.
**Jamestown** kept on for a share of the prize money but did not achieve much.
**Lucayan Monarch** made some good late headway having been in rear early.
**Miss Champers(IRE)**, a disappointing third at the course three days earlier, never looked like getting there on this occasion.
**Magic Mamma's Too** usually runs consistently despite never winning but this was disappointing.

## 6212 BET DIRECT NO Q MAIDEN STKS 5f (F)
**12:10** (12:11) (D) 2-Y-O **£2,898** (£828; £414) **Stalls** High

Form RPR

3544 **1** **Smart Starprincess (IRE)**[28] 6037 2-8-6 58..................(b) FPFerris(3) 1 60
(PABlockley) *mde all: sn clr: rdn ent last: eased nr fin* **10/3**[3]

302 **2** 1 1/4 **Velvet Touch**[4] 6191 2-8-9 ........................................ SWKelly 2 56
(JRJenkins) *sn chsng wnr: rdn along 2f out: styd on u.p ent last* **5/2**[2]

0000 **3** 4 **Siegfrieds Night (IRE)**[10] 6152 2-8-7 52.................. AndrewWebb(7) 4 47
(MCChapman) *sn rdn along and outpcd in rr* **25/1**

02 **4** shd **Five Years On (IRE)**[27] 6045 2-9-0 ....................................... CLowther 3 46
(WJHaggas) *dwlt: sn wl bhd: hdwy over 1f out: nvr a factor* **5/6**[1]

61.16 secs (0.86) **Going Correction** +0.125s/f (Slow) **4** Ran SP% **110.1**
Speed ratings: **98,96,89,89**CSF £11.74 TOTE £5.80; EX 15.90.
**Owner** Brooklands Racing **Bred** Norelands Bloodstock **Trained** Southwell, Notts

**FOCUS**
A poor maiden where the favourite disappointed badly.

**NOTEBOOK**
**Smart Starprincess(IRE)** finally got off the mark at the 12th attempt. It has been a long time coming and she deserved it.
**Velvet Touch**, second at the course earlier in the week, could not match the winner for speed and wants further.
**Siegfrieds Night(IRE)** is well exposed and remains one to leave alone.
**Five Years On(IRE)** proved most disappointing and is surely capable of better. He appeared to be feeling something. *Official explanation: trainer said gelding stumbled and was unsuited by the surface*

## 6213 BET DIRECT ON 0800 32 93 93 NURSERY 6f (F)
**12:40** (12:42) (E) (0-75,65) 2-Y-O **£3,444** (£984; £492) **Stalls** Low

Form RPR

0551 **1** **Blofeld**[7] 6165 2-9-1 **62** 7ex........................................... LisaJones(3) 3 68+
(WJarvis) *mde all: pushed clr over 1fout: rdn ent last and styd on strly* **11/10**[1]

0445 **2** 1 1/2 **Daring Affair**[126] 4162 2-9-4 **62**........................................... NCallan 2 64
(KRBurke) *a.p:hdwy to chse winner 1/2-way: rdn 2f out and kpt on same pce* **14/1**

004 **3** 2 1/2 **Rood Boy (IRE)**[32] 6012 2-9-3 **61**........................................... IMongan 1 55
(JSKing) *dwlt: hdwy 1/2-way: rdn to chse ldrs wl over 1f out: sn drvn and kpt on same pce* **13/2**[3]

1050 **4** 2 **Foxies Future (IRE)**[11] 6141 2-9-7 **65**................................ DaneO'Neill 4 53
(JRWeymes) *s.i.s: in rr tl swtchd rt and hdwy 2f out: sn rdn and no imp approaching last* **20/1**

3611 **5** 1 1/2 **Alizar (IRE)**[4] 6194 2-9-0 **61** 7ex...................................... LFletcher(3) 8 45
(MJPolglase) *chsd ldrs on outer: rdn 2f out: drvn and wknd over 1f out* **5/2**[2]

004 **6** 2 **Foot Fault (IRE)**[31] 6020 2-8-10 **61**................................ RoryMoore(7) 7 39
(NACallaghan) *chsd ldrs: rdn over 2f out: sn wknd* **10/1**

5000 **7** 3 **Kumari (IRE)**[35] 5997 2-7-13 **48**................................ JFMcDonald(5) 5 17
(WMBrisbourne) *cl up: rdn along 1/2-way: sn wknd* **25/1**

0500 **8** 5 **Peace Treaty (IRE)**[64] 5599 2-8-5 **49**................................ JBramhill 6 —
(SRBowring) *outpcd and bhd fr 1/2-way* **50/1**

1m 17.76s (0.96) **Going Correction** +0.075s/f (Slow) **8** Ran SP% **115.9**
Speed ratings: **96,94,90,88,86 83,79,72**CSF £18.79 CT £73.93 TOTE £1.80: £1.60, £2.80, £1.60; EX 18.00.
**Owner** Byculla Thoroughbreds **Bred** Simon Dutfield And William Harrison-Allan **Trained** Newmarket, Suffolk
■ Stewards Enquiry : I Mongan three-day ban: used whip with excessive force on a 2yo (Dec 30-Jan 1)

**FOCUS**
The winner has won well the last twice now and is eveidently on the up.

**NOTEBOOK**
**Blofeld**, still 3lb well in under his penalty, made every yard of the running for a comfy success and nothing is to say he can not complete the hat-trick.
**Daring Affair**, 4lb lower than when making his All-Weather debut, appreciated this step up in trip and has a similar race in her.
**Rood Boy(IRE)**, well supported prior to the race, landed the each-way support and will improve when stepped back up in trip.
**Foxies Future(IRE)** ran well at a price on this drop back in trip.
**Alizar(IRE)**, easy winner of a seller last time, had every chance but was not good enough. A drop back down in grade should see him in the winner's enclosure again.

## 6214 BET DIRECT ON ATTHERACES INTERACTIVE MEDIAN AUCTION MAIDEN STKS 1m 3f (F)
**1:10** (1:10) (F) 3-4-Y-O **£2,205** (£630; £315) **Stalls** Low

Form RPR

6253 **1** **Wasted Talent (IRE)**[25] 6060 3-8-9 60..............................(p) RHavlin 3 45
(JGPortman) *mde all: rdn wl over 1f out: drvn ins last: kpt on* **10/11**[1]

3400 **2** 1/2 **Make My Hay**[31] 5329 4-9-1 30........................................(b[1]) LFletcher(3) 7 49
(JWhite) *trckd ldrs: hdwy 4f out: rdn to chse wnr ent last: sn drvn and edgd rt: kpt on* **10/1**

0000 **3** 1/2 **Next Flight (IRE)**[219] 1585 4-9-4 44................................ RFitzpatrick 10 48
(REBarr) *trckd ldrs: hdwy 4f out: rdn 2f out: drvn and kpt on fnl f* **25/1**

6032 **4** 1 1/2 **Givemethemoonlight**[13] 6128 4-8-13 46.............................. IMongan 11 41
(MrsStefLiddiard) *hld up in rr: stdy hdwy 4f out: rdn along 2f out: styd on u.p fnl f: nrst fin* **4/1**[2]

0006 **5** shd **Red Moor (IRE)**[4] 6193 3-9-0 45..........................................(p) ACulhane 2 46
(RHollinshead) *in tch: smooth hdwy to trck ldrs over 3f out: shkn up wl over 1f out: sn rdn and kpt on same pce ins last* **7/1**[3]

0662 **6** 3/4 **Conchonita**[32] 6015 3-8-9 43................................................ DaneO'Neill 6 40
(BPalling) *s.i.s and bhd: hdwy 3f out:rdn 2f out: swtchd lft over 1f out: kpt on same pce u.p fnl f* **8/1**

0040 **7** 5 **Aljomar**[95] 4951 4-8-13 41....................................................(p) TEaves(5) 4 37
(REBarr) *chsd wnr: rdn along 3f out: wknd 2f out* **50/1**

0000 **8** 28 **Ruby Anniversary**[4] 6193 3-8-6 38.................................... LisaJones(3) 5 —
(JBalding) *rrd s: a bhd* **20/1**

**9** 21 **Velvet Rhythm** 3-8-3 ow1................................................... RKeogh(7) 8 —
(KRBurke) *a rr: outpcd and b ehind fr 1/2-way* **25/1**

2m 30.77s (1.87) **Going Correction** +0.075s/f (Slow)
**WFA** 3 from 4yo 4lb **9** Ran SP% **119.5**
Speed ratings: **96,95,95,94,94 93,89,69,54**CSF £11.35 TOTE £1.60: £1.10, £1.70, £13.10; EX 11.10.
**Owner** Wasted Talent Partnership **Bred** L And D Fox And Oak Lodge Stud **Trained** Compton, Berks
■ Stewards Enquiry : R Havlin one-day ban: used whip with excessive frequency (Dec 30)

**FOCUS**
An abysmal race.

**NOTEBOOK**
**Wasted Talent(IRE)**, the top-rated in the field off 60, could not help but win what was a dire race. This was her 22nd attempt at it and she would be one to take on again back up in grade.
**Make My Hay**, officially rated 30lb inferior to the winner, stayed on well for second but remains a maiden after 19 starts.
**Next Flight(IRE)** left many disappointing efforts behind with a respectable run.
**Givemethemoonlight** was running on at the finish and clearly appreciated the trip.
**Red Moor(IRE)** has a race in him albeit a poor one.

## 6215 LITTLEWOODS BET DIRECT H'CAP 1m 4f (F)
**1:40** (1:41) (C) (0-95,94) 3-Y-O+ **£5,378** (£1,655; £827; £413) **Stalls** Low

Form RPR

1212 **1** **Mi Odds**[20] 6098 7-9-3 **83**........................................................ ACulhane 1 96
(MrsNMacauley) *hld up in tch: hdwy 4f out: rdn wl over 1f out: drvn ins last and styd on to ld nr fin* **11/4**[1]

6063 **2** 1/2 **George Stubbs (USA)**[4] 6190 5-7-10 **67**...................... JFMcDonald(5) 8 79
(MJPolglase) *trckd ldr: led 2f out: sn rdn and clr ent last: sn drvn: hdd and no ex nr fin* **11/1**

052 **3** 2 1/2 **Te Quiero**[16] 6124 5-10-0 **94**...............................................(t) NCallan 3 102
(MissGayKelleway) *led: rdn along over 2f out: sn hdd and one pce u.p appr last* **6/1**

0500 **4** 1 **Kylkenny**[15] 5952 8-9-2 **85**................................................ LFletcher(3) 5 92
(HMorrison) *chsd ldrs: effrt 3f out: rdn 2f out and sn one pce* **7/2**[2]

2235 **5** 4 **Glory Quest (USA)**[10] 6156 6-8-8 **77**..............................(p) LisaJones(3) 7 78
(MissGayKelleway) *in rr: hdwy 3f out: sn rdn along and kpt on fnl 2f: nrst fin* **8/1**

2020 **6** 9 **Royal Cavalier**[41] 5952 6-9-7 **87**............................................ IMongan 4 74
(RHollinshead) *chsd ldrs: rdn along 4f out: wknd over2f ot* **5/1**[3]

0033 **7** 6 **Ovigo (GER)**[24] 6070 4-8-1 **67**............................................ WMLordan 2 45
(PABlockley) *hld up in tch: hdwy 4f out: rdn along over 2f out and sn btn* **12/1**

0214 **8** 13 **Sea Holly (IRE)**[13] 6130 3-8-3 **74**........................................... JMackay 6 33
(GGMargarson) *chsd ldrs: rdn alo ng over 5f out and sn wknd* **8/1**

2m 39.65s (-2.45) **Going Correction** +0.075s/f (Slow)
**WFA** 3 from 4yo+ 5lb **8** Ran SP% **118.1**
Speed ratings: **111,110,109,108,105 99,95,87**CSF £35.17 CT £171.49 TOTE £3.70: £1.40, £3.30, £1.70; EX 40.20.
**Owner** Tic-Tac.com **Bred** G Wiltshire **Trained** Sproxton, Leics
■ Stewards Enquiry : A Culhane one-day ban: used whip with excessive frequency (Dec 30)

**FOCUS**
A competitive race that saw Mi Odds score his 12th career success.

**NOTEBOOK**
**Mi Odds** has been running consistently well of late and came home with a strong late run to record his 12th career win.
**George Stubbs(USA)** ran another solid race, ridden with a bit more restraint on this occasion.
**Te Quiero** performed most creditably under top-weight but is still 8lb higher than when last winning.
**Kylkenny**, a major disappointment over hurdles when last seen, had never been out of the first three at the course until today.
**Royal Cavalier** failed to pick up as expected and has to go down as a disappointment.
**Sea Holly(IRE)** ran no sort of race. *Official explanation: trainer had no explanation for the poor form shown*

## 6216 BETDIRECT.CO.UK MAIDEN STKS 1m (F)
**2:15** (2:16) (D) 2-Y-O **£3,125** (£893; £446) **Stalls** Low

Form RPR

3642 **1** **Kingsmaite**[7] 6167 2-9-0 66................................................... JBramhill 4 77+
(SRBowring) *cl up: shkn up to ld over 1f out: sn clr* **10/3**[1]

**2** 3 **Denver (IRE)**[75] 5395 2-8-11 ............................................ LPKeniry(3) 5 67
(BJMeehan) *trckd ldrs on inner: n.m.r and checked over 3f out: swtchd rt and wd st: sn rdn and styd on fnl 2f: nrst fin* **6/1**[3]

3223 **3** hd **Hawkit (USA)**[6] 6175 2-8-11 72.......................................... LFletcher(3) 11 67
(JAOsborne) *chsd ldrs: hdwy to ld 2f out: sn rdn and hdd over 1f out: one pce* **4/1**[2]

4000 **4** 5 **Cottingham (IRE)**[25] 6059 2-9-0 60...................................... IMongan 10 56
(MCChapman) *cl up: led over 4f out tl rdn and hdd 2f out: grad wknd* **33/1**

404 **5** 3 **Chara**[20] 6091 2-8-9 66.......................................................... SWKelly 1 44
(JRJenkins) *in tch on inner whn hmpd and lost pl over 3f out: hdwy on inner 2f out: sn rdn and kpt on: nrst fin* **11/1**

46 **6** *1 ½* **Music Mix (IRE)**[7] 6167 2-9-0 ... WRyan 13 46
(EALDunlop) *in tch: hdwy 3f out: rdn along 2f out: sn edgd lft and no imp* **8/1**

0005 **7** *1 ¼* **Thevenis**[25] 6059 2-9-0 60 ... NCallan 3 43
(JSKing) *chsd ldrs: rdn along 3f out: wknd over 2f out* **12/1**

5024 **8** *3* **Trompe L'Oeil (IRE)**[11] 6142 2-8-9 71 ... DaneO'Neill 2 32
(EALDunlop) *nvr nr ldrs* **13/2**

0005 **9** *hd* **Get To The Point**[31] 6018 2-8-9 63 ... (e[1]) BReilly(5) 12 36
(PWD'Arcy) *midfield: hdwy on outer to chse ldrs 3f out: sn rdn along and wknd* **8/1**

0040 **10** *½* **Nocatee (IRE)**[24] 6066 2-8-7 49 ... RoryMoore(7) 14 35
(PCHaslam) *racd wd: a rr* **100/1**

0 **11** *6* **Roving Vixen (IRE)**[20] 6097 2-8-9 ... ADaly 9 17
(JLSpearing) *led: hdd over 4f out: sn rdn along and wknd* **50/1**

**12** *2* **Arctic Queen** 2-8-2 ... RJKilloran(7) 8 13
(AMBalding) *s.i.s: sn in tch: rdn along over 3f out and sn wknd* **20/1**

0006 **13** *21* **Red Acer (IRE)**[11] 6147 2-9-0 49 ... JoannaBadger 7 —
(PDEvans) *slowy nto stride: a bhd* **100/1**

**14** *14* **Mind The Time** 2-8-9 ... THamilton(5) 6 —
(JHetherton) *s.i.s: a bhd* **50/1**

1m 44.43s (-0.17) **Going Correction** +0.075s/f (Slow) **14** Ran SP% **122.6**
Speed ratings: **103,100,99,94,91 90,89,86,85,85 79,77,56,42**CSF £22.84 TOTE £3.70: £1.70, £2.50, £2.40; EX 26.00.
**Owner** S R Bowring **Bred** S R Bowring **Trained** Edwinstowe, Notts

**FOCUS**
This was an ordinary maiden but one that should produce winners.

**NOTEBOOK**
**Kingsmaite**, a respectable second at the course last week, was always travelling well and was never going to be caught when going on a furlong out. He is the type to do well in handicaps.
**Denver(IRE)**, formerly trained by Aidan O'Brien, was unlucky not to finish closer but it is doubtful he would have got to the winner in time even if things had gone to plan. He will be winning before long.
**Hawkit(USA)** is exposed but usually runs his race.
**Cottingham(IRE)** ran well for one of his price.
**Chara** lost ground early but finished well and will improve for a stiffer test of stamina.

## 6217 FREE £25 BONUS @ LITTLEWOODSPOKER.COM (S) STKS 6f (F)
2:50 (2:51) (G ) 3-Y-O+ £2,142 (£612; £306) Stalls Low

Form RPR

0004 **1** **Headland (USA)**[10] 6155 5-9-5 71 ... (b) ACulhane 2 58
(DWChapman) *dwlt: sn in tch on inner: hdwy 3f out: rdden to chal over 1f out: drvn ins last: led nr line* **6/1**[2]

0410 **2** *nk* **Polar Haze**[7] 6170 6-9-0 46 ... (v) JFMcDonald(5) 5 57
(MrsLydiaPearce) *towards rr and pushed along 1/2-way: gd hdwy 2f out: rdn over 1f out: styd on strly ins last: jst hld* **7/1**[3]

0062 **3** *shd* **Heathyardsblessing (IRE)**[10] 6150 6-8-12 46 ... NCallan 3 50
(RHollinshead) *cl up: hdwy to ld wl over 1f out: sn rdn: drvn ins last: hdd and no ex nr fin* **10/1**

1234 **4** *hd* **Hurricane Coast**[4] 6192 4-9-0 62 ... DNolan(5) 6 56
(PABlockley) *midfield: wd st: gd hdwy over 1f out: rdn and hung lft ins last: nrst fin* **15/8**[1]

000/ **5** *½* **Magic Grey**[96] 8-8-12 ... AStarke 1 48
(THHansen, Germany) *stdd s and bhd: swtchd outside and v wd st: gd hdwy over 1f out: rdn and hung lft ent last: fin wl* **7/1**[3]

0060 **6** *1 ¾* **Star Lad (IRE)**[20] 6095 3-8-12 49 ... (b) IMongan 16 42
(RBrotherton) *cl up: rdn along 2f out: drvn and one pce appr last* **16/1**

3000 **7** *½* **Attorney**[3] 6202 5-9-2 47 ... (e) LisaJones(3) 4 48
(DShaw) *towards rr: hdwy on inner 2f out: sn rdn and kpt on appr last: nrst fin* **20/1**

0302 **8** *½* **Lay Down Sally (IRE)**[10] 6155 5-8-7 47 ... RFitzpatrick 12 34
(JWhite) *rrd s and s.i.s: bhd and wd st: hdwy wl over 1f out: rdn and edgd lft ent last: kpt on: nrst fin* **6/1**[2]

6300 **9** *½* **Carols Choice**[10] 6149 6-8-2 43 ... NChalmers(5) 10 33
(ASadik) *led: rdn along over 2f out: hdd over 1f out: sn drvn and grad wknd* **25/1**

0300 **10** *nk* **Pips Song (IRE)**[13] 6135 8-8-12 48 ... JTate 9 37
(PWHiatt) *midfield: hdwy whn n.m.r over 1f out: rdn and hmpd ent last: nvr a factor* **25/1**

1046 **11** *1* **Amelia (IRE)**[35] 5998 5-9-0 50 ... SWKelly 14 36
(WMBrisbourne) *midfield: hdwy on outer to chse ldrs 1/2-way: sn rdn and wknd* **16/1**

0004 **12** *1 ¾* **Cark**[21] 6080 5-9-5 45 ... JBramhill 13 36
(JBalding) *plld hrd: cl up: rdn 2f out: sn wknd* **25/1**

0000 **13** *3* **Attila The Hun**[10] 6150 4-8-9 38 ... LPKeniry(3) 15 20
(FWatson) *cl up: rdn along 1/2-way: wknd over 2f out* **66/1**

2400 **14** *½* **Valazar (USA)**[13] 6136 4-8-12 59 ... DaleGibson 7 18
(DWChapman) *chsd ldrs towards inner: rdn along over 2f out and sn wknd* **14/1**

6000 **15** *nk* **Boisdale (IRE)**[10] 6155 5-9-5 52 ... (t) ANicholls 11 24
(DNicholls) *chsd ldrs: rdn along and wknd over 2f out* **16/1**

60-0 **16** *1 ¾* **St Cassien (IRE)**[47] 923 3-8-12 40 ... RBrisland 8 12
(TMJones) *a bhd* **100/1**

1m 17.56s (0.76) **Going Correction** +0.075s/f (Slow) **16** Ran SP% **140.5**
Speed ratings: **97,96,96,96,95 93,92,91,91,90 89,87,83,82,82 79**CSF £52.27 TOTE £7.60: £3.20, £2.90, £3.80; EX 66.90.There was no bid for the winner
**Owner** Harold D White **Bred** O J Martinez **Trained** Stillington, N Yorks

**FOCUS**
A competitive selling stakes that produced a good finish.

**NOTEBOOK**
**Headland(USA)** responded well to pressure to get there on the line. He ran well last time and deserved to get his head in front.
**Polar Haze** left a disappointing effort last time behind and was narrowly denied.
**Heathyardsblessing(IRE)** could not hold off the front pair late on.
**Hurricane Coast** was gaining with every stride at the line but failed to muster the pace to get any closer.
**Magic Grey** would have been closer but for hanging under pressure. *Official explanation: jockey said, regarding the running and riding, he was told to drop horse in and keep off the inner as it does not like running between horses, adding that horse resents the use of the whip; trainer's representative said horse was having first run for stable, has been difficult to keep sweet and would also be suited by a longer trip*

## 6218 BET DIRECT ON SKY TEXT PAGE 371 H'CAP (DIV II) 1m (F)
3:20 (3:20) (F) (0-60,59) 3-Y-O+ £2,107 (£602; £301) Stalls Low

Form RPR

0330 **1** **Game Guru**[3] 6202 4-9-7 59 ... Laura-JayneCrawford(7) 3 73
(TDBarron) *a.p: effrt 2f out: rdn over 1f out: kpt on wl too ld ins last* **4/1**[2]

5042 **2** *shd* **Sorbiesharry (IRE)**[11] 6148 4-8-13 44 ... PMcCabe 6 58
(MrsNMacauley) *midield: hdwy to trck ldrs 1/2-way: effrt to ld wl over 1f out: sn rdn: drvn and hdd ins last: nt qckn* **3/1**[1]

0455 **3** *2 ½* **Air Of Esteem**[7] 6171 7-9-3 48 ... ANicholls 2 57
(IanEmmerson) *in tch: gd hdwy on inner 2f out: rdn and ev ch ent last: drvn and wknd last 100 yds* **6/1**

6053 **4** *3 ½* **Qobtaan (USA)**[11] 6143 4-9-0 45 ... GBaker 4 47
(MRBosley) *bhd: gd hdwy 3f out: rdn 2f out: kpt ons ame pce* **5/1**[3]

0000 **5** *1 ¼* **Cumbrian Princess**[24] 6064 6-8-3 34 ... DaleGibson 11 34
(MBlanshard) *chsd ldrs: rdn along 3f out: one pce fnl 2f* **14/1**

0400 **6** *shd* **Proud Victor (IRE)**[6] 6178 3-8-10 42 ... (v) DarrenWilliams 5 41
(DShaw) *towards rr: hdwy 3f out: rdn 2f out and no imp* **16/1**

0000 **7** *¾* **Sudra**[3] 6202 6-9-3 55 ... (p) JDO'Reilly(7) 13 53
(JO'Reilly) *chsd ldrs: hdwy to ld 3f out: rdn 2f out: sn hdd: drvn and wknd* **9/1**

0000 **8** *2 ½* **College Star**[7] 6171 5-7-5 29 ... (b) DeanWilliams(7) 12 22
(JFCoupland) *chsd ldrs on outer: rdn along over 2f out: grad wknd* **66/1**

0000 **9** *6* **Zahunda (IRE)**[11] 6144 4-9-4 49 ... SWKelly 1 30
(WMBrisbourne) *in tch: rdn along 1/2-way: sn wknd* **25/1**

0000 **10** *8* **Formeric**[10] 6151 7-8-9 40 ... (v) WMLordan 8 5
(MissLCSiddall) *a rr* **50/1**

0002 **11** *¾* **Forty Forte**[20] 6099 7-9-12 57 ... (p) NCallan 10 20
(MissSJWilton) *led: rdn along and hdd 3f out: sn wknd* **6/1**

4-00 **12** *4* **Pat's Miracle (IRE)**[25] 6062 3-8-6 38 ... JoannaBadger 9 —
(JohnBerry) *dwlt: a rr* **33/1**

0000 **13** *dist* **Blunham**[24] 6065 3-9-2 48 ... IMongan 7 —
(MCChapman) *cl up: rdn along over 3f out and sn wknd* **25/1**

1m 44.46s (-0.14) **Going Correction** +0.075s/f (Slow)
**WFA** 3 from 4yo+ 1lb **13** Ran SP% **126.9**
Speed ratings: **103,102,100,96,95 95,94,92,86,78 77,73,—**CSF £16.81 CT £76.08 TOTE £7.70: £2.40, £1.70, £4.70; EX 22.60 Place 6 £87.90, Place 5 £29.91.
**Owner** Kevin Shaw **Bred** P J Makin **Trained** Maunby, N Yorks
■ Stewards Enquiry : J D O'Reilly two-day ban: used whip from above shoulder height and with an element of force (Dec 30,31)

**FOCUS**
Not much of a race but the stronger of the two divisions.

**NOTEBOOK**
**Game Guru** was up there all the way and battled on gamely to deny the favourite by the shortest of margins. This was his first win for a while but he could follow up now evidently back in good form.
**Sorbiesharry(IRE)** tends to need further but is effective at this trip as shown today. He would have won in another stride or two.
**Air Of Esteem** did not quite last out but lost nothing in defeat.
**Qobtaan(USA)** may be better off with a stiffer test.
T/Plt: £81.50 to a £1 stake. Pool: £23,335.90. 208.85 winning tickets. T/Qpdt: £4.70 to a £1 stake. Pool: £3,014.30. 467.25 winning tickets. JR

# 6203 LINGFIELD (L-H)
## Saturday, December 20

**OFFICIAL GOING: Standard**
Wind: gale force; bhd first 5 races, across last 3 races Weather: rain first 5 races

## 6219 BET DIRECT ON ATTHERACES INTERACTIVE NOVICE STKS (DIV I) 1m (P)
11:50 (11:56) (D ) 2-Y-O £3,052 (£872; £436) Stalls High

Form RPR

3 **1** **Skidmark**[21] 6090 2-8-12 ... PFitzsimons 4 77
(DRCElsworth) *lw: s.s: t.k.h and hld up in rr: stdy prog fr 3f out: shkn up over 1f out: led last 150y: hung rt but styd on wl* **7/4**[2]

0513 **2** *1 ¼* **Anuvasteel**[10] 6160 2-9-6 83 ... WRyan 1 82
(NACallaghan) *led: rdn and pressed 2f out: hdd last 150y: hld whn bmpd last 50y* **10/11**[1]

4426 **3** *1 ½* **Marcus Eile (IRE)**[117] 4455 2-9-9 86 ... DarrenWilliams 6 82
(KRBurke) *chsd ldr for 1f: styd cl up: chsd ldng pair over 2f out: drvn to chal 1f out: one pce fnl f* **16/1**

00 **4** *nk* **Red Contact (USA)**[3] 6210 2-8-12 ... RSmith 3 70
(ACharlton) *hld up in midfield: prog to trck ldr over 2f out: chal 2f out: hanging rt bnd sn after: nt qckn fnl f* **25/1**

**5** *10* **Pure Emotion** 2-8-8 ow1 ... IMongan 10 44
(WRMuir) *leggy: s.s: hld up: prog to trck ldrs 3f out: wknd wl over 1f out* **40/1**

0 **6** *½* **Kilminchy Lady (IRE)**[22] 6082 2-8-7 ... PDoe 9 42
(WRMuir) *chsd ldr after 1f to over 2f out: losing pl whn hmpd sn after: hanging and wknd wl over 1f out* **66/1**

1 **7** *1 ½* **Competitor**[64] 5620 2-9-2 ... CCatlin 8 48
(JAkehurst) *lw: chsd ldrs: rdn over 4f out: losing pl and struggling over 3f out* **8/1**[3]

**8** *1 ¾* **Waltzing Beau** 2-8-12 ... JFanning 7 40
(IAWood) *leggy: unf: s.s: rcvrd to chse ldrs after 2f: wknd 3f out* **25/1**

0 **9** *1 ¾* **Atlantic Tern**[44] 5934 2-8-12 ... SRighton 5 36
(NMBabbage) *t.k.h early: hld up: hanging and struggling over 4f out: sn no ch* **66/1**

**10** *8* **Corton Denham** 2-8-12 ... DaneO'Neill 2 19
(GPEnright) *unf: bit bkwd: s.s: a last and sn detached* **50/1**

1m 42.19s (2.68) **Going Correction** +0.10s/f (Slow) **10** Ran SP% **120.8**
Speed ratings: **90,88,87,86,76 76,74,73,71,63**CSF £3.64 TOTE £3.80: £1.50, £1.10, £3.30; EX 4.30.
**Owner** Raymond Tooth **Bred** P D Player **Trained** Whitsbury, Hants

**FOCUS**
A fair event run in a time marginally slower than the second division.

**NOTEBOOK**
**Skidmark**, who ran a race full of promise on his debut on this surface three weeks ago, was given a patient ride by Fitzsimons and was value for more than the winning distance. He looks to have a bright future and could turn out to be very useful.
**Anuvasteel**, who had proven form on this surface, ran another solid race. This was the first time on the All-Weather he has tried to make all and more patient tactics may suit better on this surface.
**Marcus Eile(IRE)** ran well on his first try on this surface and his first run since August. He had looked badly handicapped before this, but appeared to run to his mark.
**Red Contact(USA)** ran his best race so far, but does appear to have a problem with the bend here at Lingfield. He clearly has ability and is now eligible for handicaps, but may only come into his own on a straighter track.
**Pure Emotion** was beaten a long way and probably did not achieve much, although this was her debut.
**Kilminchy Lady(IRE)** was squeezed out a little on the home turn and was soon on the retreat after that.

**Competitor**, winner of a small auction maiden for Amanda Perrett when last seen in October, struggled to make any impact.

## 6220 BET DIRECT ON ITV PAGE 367 H'CAP (DIV I) 1m 2f (P)

**12:20** (12:22) (F) (0-60,60) 3-Y-0+ **£2,079** (£594; £297) **Stalls** Low

Form RPR

0044 **1** **Gold Guest**[29] 6036 4-8-13 **52**............ SJDonohoe(7) 6 66
(PDEvans) *hld up wl in rr: stdy prog fr over 3f out: shaken up to ld 1f out: sn rdn clr* **11/2**[3]

0304 **2** *3* **Welsh Wind (IRE)**[24] 6076 7-9-10 **56**............(t) IMongan 8 65
(MWigham) *swtg: hld up in midfield: effrt over 2f out: rdn and nt qckn wl over 1f out: r.o to chse wnr ins fnl f: no imp* **10/3**[1]

0000 **3** *1/2* **Scottish River (USA)**[18] 6119 4-9-13 **59**............ ADaly 11 67
(MDIUsher) *s.v.s: hld up in last pair: stdy prog over 2f out: swtchd rt and rdn 1f out: r.o wl fnl f: too much to do* **14/1**

400 **4** *2 1/2* **Coolfore Jade (IRE)**[12] 6144 3-9-6 **60**............ MSavage(5) 7 63
(NEBerry) *trckd ldrs: effrt 3f out: rdn to chal 2f out: hanging and nt qckn over 1f out: btn after* **50/1**

0050 **5** *1/2* **Magic Warrior**[38] 5976 3-9-9 **58**............ RSmith 10 60
(JCFox) *t.k.h: prom: trckd ldr over 3f out: rdn to ld over 1f out: hdd & wknd 1f out* **12/1**

0020 **6** *1/2* **Raheel (IRE)**[18] 6120 3-9-4 **53**............(t) JFanning 5 54
(PMitchell) *hld up in last pair: sme prog on inner whn nt clr run over 2f out : effrt wl over 1f out: sn one pce* **7/1**

3000 **7** *1 1/4* **Toledo Sun**[24] 6076 3-9-8 **57**............ MTebbutt 3 56
(HJCollingridge) *led and set gd pce: rdn 3f out: hdd & wknd over 1f out* **5/1**[2]

6650 **8** *2* **Icecap**[21] 6094 3-9-0 **54**............ BReilly(5) 12 50
(PButler) *trckd ldrs: cl up 3f out: wknd 2f out* **20/1**

-005 **9** *7* **Dickie Deadeye**[24] 6073 6-10-0 **60**............ SCarson 2 43
(GBBalding) *lw: chsd ldr to 6f out: styd prom tl wknd u.p over 2f out* **8/1**

0564 **10** *2 1/2* **Fabrian**[14] 6128 5-9-7 **53**............(e) DaneO'Neill 1 31
(DWPArbuthnot) *b: s.i.s: hld up tl plld way up to trck ldr 6f out: wknd over 3f out: eased* **14/1**

0000 **11** *1 3/4* **Yellow River (IRE)**[117] 4439 3-9-11 **60**............ SWKelly 14 35
(RCurtis) *hld up in rr: rdn and no prog over 2f out: sn wknd* **33/1**

005- **12** *3/4* **Sungio**[381] 4896 5-9-7 **60**............ AHindley(7) 9 34
(BGPowell) *racd in midfield: rdn 5f out: sn in rr and struggling* **33/1**

1000 **13** *1* **Mister Clinton (IRE)**[10] 6161 6-9-10 **56**............ GCarter 4 28
(DKIvory) *racd towards rr: struggling over 3f out: wknd* **10/1**

4000 **14** *6* **Premier Cheval (USA)**[24] 6073 4-9-5 **51**............ PDoe 13 12
(RRowe) *racd in rr: sme prog on outer 1/2-way: wknd over 3f out* **20/1**

2m 8.53s (1.14) **Going Correction** +0.10s/f (Slow)
**WFA** 3 from 4yo+ 3lb **14** Ran **SP% 126.2**
Speed ratings: **99,96,96,94,93 93,92,90,85,83 81,81,80,75**CSF £23.85 CT £257.69 TOTE £8.80: £2.60, £1.80, £6.30; EX 21.30.
**Owner** Diamond Racing Ltd **Bred** The Hon D K And Mrs Oliver **Trained** Pandy, Gwent

**FOCUS**
A moderate race full of disappointing types, but run in a faster time than the second division.

**NOTEBOOK**
**Gold Guest**, racing without the visor he had worn the last twice, appeared to appreciate the step up in trip and showed a fine turn of foot. He was rated 94 at the start of last year, but had tumbled to 52 and may well be up to winning again over this distance.
**Welsh Wind(IRE)**, who does look well handicapped, ran his usual race, running on to take a place without threatening to win. He often catches the eye, but is without a win for more than two years.
**Scottish River(USA)** finished best of all and rattled home, but had too much to do. A slow start did not help his cause and connections were obviously worried about this trip as he had been keen on previous tries beyond a mile, but he did settle all right. He is another to have tumbled down the ratings and may have found his right mark over this trip.
**Coolfore Jade(IRE)**, well beaten in claimers the last three times, ran her best race since arriving from Ireland over a more suitable trip, but is clearly nothing special.
**Magic Warrior** took a good grip and pulled his way towards the leaders, which cannot have been ideal.
**Raheel(IRE)**, who was well backed, continues to frustrate. His rider had to sit and wait for a run on the home turn, but it was his lack of gears over this shorter trip that ultimately cost him. *Official explanation: trainer said gelding had a breathing problem*
**Toledo Sun** was a sitting duck from some way out.
**Fabrian** *Official explanation: jockey said gelding ran very keen early on and hung right*

## 6221 BET DIRECT NO Q ON 0800 32 93 93 H'CAP 5f (P)

**12:50** (12:51) (E) (0-70,68) 3-Y-0+ **£2,058** (£588; £294) **Stalls** High

Form RPR

300 **1** **Panjandrum**[49] 5880 5-9-5 **65**............ MSavage(5) 5 73
(NEBerry) *in tch: rdn to chse ldng pair 2f out: styd on u.p fnl f to ld last strides* **16/1**

440 **2** *hd* **Roman Quintet (IRE)**[21] 6092 3-9-8 **63**............(t) DaneO'Neill 7 70
(DWPArbuthnot) *lw: racd towards outer: mde most: def advantage over 1f out: hrd drvn and fnd little fnl f: hdd last strides* **4/1**[2]

5100 **3** *nk* **Teyaar**[21] 6092 7-9-7 **62**............(v[1]) PMcCabe 4 68
(MrsNMacauley) *pressed ldr: drvn 2f out: styd w ev ch fnl f: nt qckn nr fin* **10/1**

4004 **4** *nk* **Byo (IRE)**[18] 6113 5-9-10 **65**............ CCatlin 3 70
(MQuinn) *w ldrs tl outpcd over 2f out: drvn and styd on fnl f : jst unable to chal* **11/2**[3]

1002 **5** *1/2* **Siraj**[21] 6092 4-9-9 **64**............(b) ACulhane 8 67
(NAGraham) *towards rr: effrt over 2f out: drvn and styd on fnl f: nrst fin* **7/2**[1]

6000 **6** *hd* **Goodwood Prince**[14] 6132 3-9-10 **65**............ PDoe 10 67
(SDow) *racd v wd: in rr after 2f: styd on fr over 1f out: nt rch ldrs* **8/1**

5600 **7** *1* **Park Star**[4] 6199 3-9-3 **58**............ DarrenWilliams 1 56
(DShaw) *w ldrs: lost pl and hmpd on inner 1/2-way: hrd drvn and one pce fr over 1f out* **12/1**

1440 **8** *1/2* **Playtime Blue**[113] 4558 3-9-6 **61**............ GBaker 9 57
(KRBurke) *in tch: rdn to chse ldrs 2f out: hanging and nt run on over 1f out* **20/1**

0040 **9** *1 1/2* **Dunedin Rascal**[18] 6116 6-9-13 **68**............(b) SCarson 2 58
(EAWheeler) *sn drvn in rr: nvr on terms* **14/1**

2041 **10** *21* **Laurel Dawn**[8] 6170 5-9-5 **63**............ LFletcher(3) 6 —
(IWMcinnes) *drvn and lost tch over 3f out: t.o* **7/2**[1]

59.87 secs (0.09) **Going Correction** +0.10s/f (Slow) **10** Ran **SP% 125.0**
Speed ratings: **103,102,102,101,100 100,99,98,95,62**CSF £84.83 CT £704.33 TOTE £23.40: £4.50, £2.70, £5.20; EX 91.50.
**Owner** Leeway Group Limited **Bred** John And Susan Davis **Trained** Earlswood, Monmouths
■ Stewards Enquiry : Dane O'Neill two-day ban: careless riding (Dec 31-Jan 1)

**FOCUS**
A run-of-the-mill handicap with many of the runners racing over an unsuitable trip.

**NOTEBOOK**
**Panjandrum**, whose three previous wins had come on Fibresand, is equally effective on Polytrack and stayed on well to land the spoils. All of his victories have come over the minimum distance.
**Roman Quintet(IRE)**, ridden more prominently than in recent starts, reversed recent six-furlong form with Siraj and was a little unfortunate not to hold on. This is obviously his best trip and he should continue to give his running in this type of event.
**Teyaar** is far from consistent, but stuck to his task well in a first-time visor. How he responds next time is anyone's guess, although a step back up to six furlongs should help.
**Byo(IRE)** came home well, but probably finds this trip too sharp.
**Siraj** was well backed, but could never land a blow. He is better over six furlongs.
**Goodwood Prince** cannot have been helped by racing wide.
**Laurel Dawn**, a dual winner here on Equitrack earlier in his career, was most disappointing. Most of his best recent form, including when winning last time out, was on Fibresand and he does not seem to enjoy this surface.

## 6222 BET DIRECT ON ATTHERACES INTERACTIVE NOVICE STKS (DIV II) 1m (P)

**1:20** (1:20) (D) 2-Y-O **£3,052** (£872; £436) **Stalls** High

Form RPR

36 **1** **Boxgrove (FR)**[10] 6158 2-8-12............ ACulhane 4 71
(CEBrittain) *racd in midfield: pushed along over 3f out: rdn to chse ldr over 1f out: styd on wl to ld last stride* **11/2**[3]

4114 **2** *shd* **Freak Occurence (IRE)**[18] 6115 2-9-4 84............ JFMcDonald(5) 5 82
(MissECLavelle) *lw: trckd ldrs: prog to ld 3f out: drvn 3l clr over 1f out: hdd fnl stride* **9/4**[2]

6 **3** *6* **Another Con (IRE)**[54] 5792 2-8-7............ RHavlin 10 53
(MrsPNDutfield) *pressed ldr to over 3f out: sn outpcd: kpt on to take 3rd ins fnl f* **20/1**

00 **4** *4* **Ivory Coast (IRE)**[22] 6082 2-8-7............ EAhern 9 44
(WRMuir) *chsd ldrs: rdn and outpcd wl over 2f out: no ch after* **33/1**

0 **5** *3/4* **Dubaian Mist**[236] 1260 2-8-2............ NChalmers(5) 7 42
(AMBalding) *racd in midfield: outpcd fr 3f out: n.d after* **14/1**

063 **6** *1 1/4* **La Danseuse**[74] 5443 2-8-7 53............ SWhitworth 3 39
(GCBravery) *in tch: rdn and struggling over 3f out: n.d after* **33/1**

60 **7** *nk* **Vendors Mistake (IRE)**[78] 5337 2-8-7............ ANicholls 6 39
(AndrewReid) *b: b.hind: led to 3f out: wknd rapidly over 1f out* **14/1**

00 **8** *1* **Midmaar (IRE)**[3] 6210 2-9-2............ IMongan 2 46
(MWigham) *a in rr: struggling fnl 3f* **33/1**

01 **9** *8* **Caledonian (IRE)**[21] 6090 2-9-5 82............ DaneO'Neill 8 31
(DRCElsworth) *stmbld sn after s: a towards rr: effrt over 3f out: sn btn: eased over 1f out* **11/8**[1]

**10** *23* **The Stafford (IRE)** 2-8-12............ CCatlin 1 —
(LWells) *w'like: bit bkwd: s.i.s: a last: lost tch bef 1/2-way: t.o* **33/1**

1m 41.92s (2.41) **Going Correction** +0.10s/f (Slow) **10** Ran **SP% 118.1**
Speed ratings: **91,90,84,80,80 78,78,77,69,46**CSF £17.56 TOTE £5.60: £1.60, £1.30, £3.70; EX 30.90.
**Owner** A J Richards **Bred** Ewar Stud Farms **Trained** Newmarket, Suffolk

**FOCUS**
A fair event run in a faster time than the first division.

**NOTEBOOK**
**Boxgrove(FR)** looked an unlikely winner until reeling in the leader on the line. He confirmed the feeling that he needs further and looks sure to win more races when stepped up in trip.
**Freak Occurence(IRE)** again tried to pinch the race off the turn and was a trifle unfortunate not to hold on. He had been put in his place by Anuvasteel last time, suggesting the first division of this race was stronger, despite what the clock said.
**Another Con(IRE)** had obviously learnt a lot from her debut, but was still beaten a fair way.
**Ivory Coast(IRE)** is clearly nothing special, but is at least eligible for handicaps now.
**Dubaian Mist**, who made her debut back in April, has presumably had some problems and is entitled to come on for this, although she will certainly have to if she is to make an impact.
**Vendors Mistake(IRE)**, a springer in the market, took them along, but was soon on the retreat when the race got serious and looked to find this stretching her stamina.
**Caledonian(IRE)** stumbled coming out of the stalls and failed to run his race. *Official explanation: trainer said colt had made a noise*

## 6223 BET DIRECT NO Q (S) STKS 6f (P)

**1:50** (1:54) (G) 2-Y-O **£2,037** (£582; £291) **Stalls** Low

Form RPR

003 **1** **Must Be So**[28] 6047 2-8-6 50............ NPollard 2 45
(DRCElsworth) *b.hind: trckd ldrs: rdn and effrt wl over 1f out: styd on to ld last 50y: jst hld on* **5/2**[1]

5060 **2** *shd* **Stanhope Forbes (IRE)**[12] 6141 2-8-11 53............ EAhern 11 50
(NPLittmoden) *pushed along in last early: sme prog on outer over 2f out: rdn and r.o wl fnl f: jst failed* **9/2**[3]

0000 **3** *1 1/4* **Stamford Blue**[12] 6147 2-8-11 45............(b[1]) JDSmith 10 46
(JSMoore) *racd in last trio tl gd prog on outer over 3f out: led 2f out and sn kicked 2l clr: hdd & wknd last 50y* **25/1**

5530 **4** *hd* **Lady Piste (IRE)**[22] 6083 2-8-4 63............(t) SJDonohoe(7) 1 45
(PDEvans) *trckd ldrs: effrt 2f out: rdn and styd on fr over 1f out: nt pce of ldrs last 100y* **11/4**[2]

0600 **5** *5* **Costa Del Sol (IRE)**[28] 6047 2-8-6 47............(v[1]) JFMcDonald(5) 4 30
(JJBridger) *sn pressed ldr: upsides 2f out: sn rdn and fnd nil: wknd over 1f out* **8/1**

0000 **6** *1 3/4* **Lady Ellendune**[49] 5877 2-8-8 42 ow2............(b) IMongan 5 22
(DJSFfrenchDavis) *pushed along in rr early: prog to chse ldrs over 2f out: wknd over 1f out* **25/1**

6053 **7** *8* **Timely Twist**[61] 5679 2-8-6 47............ JFanning 8 —
(SKirk) *in rr and struggling over 3f out: sn bhd* **10/1**

0 **8** *nk* **Dont Let Go**[10] 6159 2-8-6............ JBramhill 3 —
(CRDore) *led to 2f out: wknd rapidly* **20/1**

0000 **9** *1 1/2* **Crispin Girl (IRE)**[28] 6045 2-8-6 54............ CCatlin 6 —
(JLSpearing) *rdn to press ldrs: wknd rapidly over 2f out* **9/2**[3]

0 **10** *1 1/4* **Blues Over (IRE)**[12] 6147 2-7-13............ LauraPike(7) 7 —
(WJMusson) *chsd ldrs: rdn 4f out: wknd 3f out* **33/1**

0000 **11** *24* **Rue De Vertbois (USA)**[93] 5021 2-8-6 49............ RSmith 9 —
(JCFox) *sn bhd: t.o fr 1/2-way* **33/1**

1m 14.04s (1.12) **Going Correction** +0.10s/f (Slow) **11** Ran **SP% 130.1**
Speed ratings: **96,95,94,93,87 84,74,73,71,70 38**CSF £14.99 TOTE £4.60: £2.00, £2.30, £4.80; EX 25.30.The winner was sold for 4,800gns to Connaught Racing.
**Owner** Mrs Irene Clifford **Bred** D R C And Mrs Elsworth **Trained** Whitsbury, Hants

**FOCUS**
A moderate seller.

**NOTEBOOK**
**Must Be So**, dropping back in trip from a mile, travelled really well, but did not find as much as one may have expected. She did well to hold on, but this is clearly her grade. She was later sold for 4,200 gns.
**Stanhope Forbes(IRE)**, another dropping back in trip, rattled home and would have been in front in another stride or two. He is worth another try at seven furlongs on this surface and in this grade.

**Stamford Blue**, who was also dropping back from a mile, appeared to return to form in first-time blinkers. However, he is far from certain to reproduce this effort.
**Lady Piste(IRE)**, who was well backed, stayed on down the straight to finish a close fourth on her Polytrack debut and is worth a try at seven furlongs on this surface.
**Costa Del Sol(IRE)**has not been finishing his races at all well.
**Crispin Girl(IRE)**, dropped into selling company for the first time, failed to show any improvement.

## 6224 BETDIRECT.CO.UK CONDITIONS STKS 1m (P)
**2:25** (2:27) (D ) 3-Y-O+ **£3,477** (£1,070; £535; £267) **Stalls** High

Form RPR
0002 **1** **Linning Wine (IRE)**[10] [6162] 7-8-12 88 SCarson 12 92
(BGPowell) *lw: hld up wl in rr: smooth prog fr 3f out: led wl over 1f out: sn clr: pushed out* **11/2**[3]
3312 **2** *2 1/2* **Lakota Brave**[33] [6013] 9-8-12 90 CCatlin 6 86
(MrsStefLiddiard) *settled in rr: prog on outer fr 3f out: rdn to chal 2f out: sn outpcd by wnr: drvn to hold on for 2nd* **5/2**[1]
2014 **3** *3/4* **Invader**[10] [6162] 7-8-12 86 (b) DaneO'Neill 10 85
(CEBrittain) *settled in last pair: pushed along over 4f out: effrt 2f out: prog on wd outside over 1f out: kpt on* **9/2**[2]
5000 **4** *nk* **Agilis (IRE)**[10] [6164] 3-8-11 80 IMongan 1 84
(JamiePoulton) *racd towards rr: prog 3f out: drvn and unable qck over 2f out: styd on fr over 1f out* **16/1**
0030 **5** *5* **Nashaab (USA)**[33] [6013] 6-8-12 86 (v) NCallan 4 72
(PDEvans) *lw: chsd ldrs: rdn over 3f out: stl cl up 2f out: wknd over 1f out* **13/2**
000- **6** *nk* **Eastborough (IRE)**[449] [4917] 4-8-9 80 LPKeniry(3) 3 72
(BGPowell) *racd in midfield: rdn and lost pl over 2f out: n.d after* **33/1**
0110 **7** *6* **Chateau Nicol**[14] [6127] 4-8-12 72 (b) JFanning 7 58
(BGPowell) *lw: hld up in midfield: prog over 3f out: led 2f out: sn hdd & wknd rapidly* **10/1**
45/0 **8** *7* **Recadero (GER)**[11] [6150] 7-9-1 JMackay 8 45
(THHansen, Germany) *chsd ldr: led wl over 2f out: hdd & wknd rapidly 2f out* **14/1**
**9** *3/4* **Margalita (IRE)**[186] [2456] 3-8-6 EAhern 2 35
(PMitchell) *chsd ldrs: rdn over 3f out: wknd rapidly over 2f out* **10/1**
0160 **10** *3 1/2* **Blue Patrick**[18] [6117] 3-9-2 86 JTate 9 37
(JMPEustace) *led and set str pce: hdd wl over 2f out: sn wknd rapidly* **14/1**
**11** *1 1/2* **Roar Blizzard (IRE)**[42] 5-8-12 59 (t) GCarter 11 29
(THHansen, Germany) *sn struggling in last: wl bhd fr 1/2-way* **66/1**
0000 **12** **Sahaat**[10] [6162] 5-8-9 97 LFletcher(3) 5 29
(JAOsborne) *chsd ldrs: rdn 1/2-way: wknd 3f out* **14/1**

1m 37.94s (-1.57) **Going Correction** +0.10s/f (Slow)
**WFA** 3 from 4yo+ 1lb **12** Ran SP% **124.0**
Speed ratings: **111,108,107,107,102 102,96,89,88,84 83,83**CSF £20.51 TOTE £4.90: £2.50, £1.40, £2.40; EX 16.30.
**Owner** Favourites Racing **Bred** His Highness The Aga Khan's Studs S C **Trained** Morestead, Hants

**FOCUS**
A decent event run at a sound pace.

**NOTEBOOK**
**Linning Wine(IRE)**, a versatile sort, was dropping back to a mile for the first time, but showed a telling turn of foot in the straight to settle the contest. The drop in trip helped him as he must have a fast pace. He likes it here and can win again.
**Lakota Brave**, who won this race last year, had the edge over the winner on adjusted figures, but could not match that one down the straight. A prolific winner here in the past, he should continue to give a good account, but does look a little high in the weights if returning to handicaps.
**Invader**, with the blinkers back on, is better suited to ten furlongs on this surface.
**Agilis(IRE)** ran better than he was entitled to on official ratings and is worth keeping an eye on when returned to handicaps.
**Nashaab(USA)**, having his first run on this surface, tends to run better when ridden more patiently.
**Chateau Nicol** had a lot on at the weights.
**Sahaat** was officially well in, but his handicap mark does look very inflated and he will be hard to place.

## 6225 BET DIRECT ON 0800 329393 RATED STKS (H'CAP) 6f (P)
**3:00** (3:00) (C ) (0-100,100) 3-Y-O+ **£7,429** (£2,818; £1,409; £640) **Stalls** Low

Form RPR
0052 **1** **Law Breaker (IRE)**[24] [6078] 5-8-1 **85** BReilly(5) 5 97
(JAGilbert) *wl in tch: rdn to chse ldng pair over 1f out: led ent fnl f: kpt on* **8/1**
0420 **2** *1 1/4* **Dusty Dazzler (IRE)**[105] [4722] 3-8-10 **94** AQuinn(5) 1 102
(WGMTurner) *chsd ldrs: rdn over 2f out: kpt on u.p fr over 1f out : a hld* **16/1**
6011 **3** *shd* **Texas Gold**[24] [6078] 5-8-9 **88** EAhern 10 96
(WRMuir) *lw: racd in midfield: rdn over 2f out: swtchd rt and drvn over 1f out: styd on fnl f: nt rch wnr* **9/4**[1]
3140 **4** *3/4* **Waterside (IRE)**[28] [6050] 4-8-4 **83** oh2 SWhitworth 13 89
(JWHills) *lw: racd in rr: prog over 2f out: styd on same pce u.p fnl f* **16/1**
5264 **5** *shd* **Quito (IRE)**[11] [6154] 6-9-5 **98** (b) ACulhane 4 103
(DWChapman) *s.i.s: racd in last trio: pushed along over 3f out: prog wl over 1f out: styd on wl fnl f: nvr nrr* **4/1**[2]
1520 **6** *hd* **Justalord**[77] [5374] 5-8-4 **83** oh1 (p) JMackay 2 88
(JBalding) *led: clr w rival after 2f: hung rt bnd wl over 1f out: hdd ent fnl f: wknd nr fin* **25/1**
2001 **7** *shd* **Lygeton Lad**[28] [6050] 5-9-7 **100** (t) IMongan 12 105
(MissGayKelleway) *lw: dwlt: racd in last trio: rdn bef 1/2-way: stl in last pair over 1f out: r.o wl fnl f: nrst fin* **7/1**[3]
0000 **8** *2* **No Time (IRE)**[31] [6030] 3-8-5 **87** ow2 LFletcher(3) 11 86
(MJPolglase) *racd wd in midfield: outpcd 1/2-way: no imp ldrs over 1f out* **10/1**
-050 **9** *1/2* **Cretan Gift**[4] [6199] 12-8-4 **83** oh3 (v) JBramhill 14 80
(NPLittmoden) *racd in rr: rdn and struggling over 3f out: nvr a factor* **40/1**
0016 **10** *3/4* **Trinculo (IRE)**[11] [6154] 6-8-10 **92** (p) LisaJones(3) 7 87
(NPLittmoden) *pressed ldr and clr of rest tl wknd wl over 1f out* **12/1**
0000 **11** *4* **Sundried Tomato**[11] [6154] 4-8-9 **88** GBaker 8 71
(PWHiatt) *chsd ldng pair to over 2f out: wknd* **20/1**
2000 **12** *1 1/4* **Massey**[11] [6154] 7-8-7 **93** PMakin(7) 9 72
(TDBarron) *chsd ldrs tl wknd over 2f out* **25/1**
6-0 **13** *2 1/2* **Action Fighter (GER)**[42] [5953] 3-9-2 **98** J-PGuillambert(3) 6 70
(NPLittmoden) *dwlt: a in rr: rdn over 3f out: sn struggling* **20/1**

1m 11.4s (-1.52) **Going Correction** +0.10s/f (Slow) **13** Ran SP% **122.6**
Speed ratings: **114,112,112,111,111 110,110,108,107,106 101,99,96**CSF £121.41 CT £399.64 TOTE £11.00: £4.00, £7.70, £2.00; EX 248.10.
**Owner** Terry Connors **Bred** T And J Brady **Trained** Hargrave, Suffolk

**FOCUS**
A competitive event run at a sound pace and producing a good time.

**NOTEBOOK**
**Law Breaker(IRE)** was well suited to the decent pace and showed a good attitude to repel the challengers. He had never won off such a high mark before and, given that he has possibly shown his best form on Fibresand, may be able to win again.
**Dusty Dazzler(IRE)**, returning from a three-month break, ran a really promising race. She won twice here over five furlongs last winter and must be fancied to win over the minimum trip in the near future.
**Texas Gold** could not land the hat-trick off a 3lb higher mark. However, he has a superb record here and it would be wrong to assume he cannot win off this mark on this surface.
**Waterside(IRE)** ran another solid race, but he will probably need some help from the Handicapper if he is to get his head back in front.
**Quito(IRE)** has never been at his best at this track, but there looks to be a race in him on Fibresand over the right trip.
**Justalord** set a good pace, but was never going to hold on. *Official explanation: jockey said gelding hung right*
**Lygeton Lad**, a prolific winner here, flew down the outside. He clearly finds this trip too short.

## 6226 BET DIRECT ON ITV PAGE 367 H'CAP (DIV II) 1m 2f (P)
**3:30** (3:30) (F ) (0-60,60) 3-Y-O+ **£2,072** (£592; £296) **Stalls** Low

Form RPR
0222 **1** **Lyrical Way**[10] [6157] 4-9-11 57 (v) IMongan 11 66
(PRChamings) *hld up wl in rr: drvn and prog over 2f out: styd on wl fr over 1f out to ld last 100y: readily* **11/4**[1]
0003 **2** *1/2* **Double Ransom**[44] [5933] 4-9-4 50 (b) SWKelly 8 58
(MrsLStubbs) *sn cl up: trckd ldng pair over 3f out: led gng easily wl over 1f out: drvn fnl f: hdd and nt qckn last 100y* **10/1**
0000 **3** *1 1/4* **Zawrak (IRE)**[87] [5146] 4-9-7 60 NataliaGemelova(7) 3 66
(IWMcinnes) *lw: settled in midfield: prog 3f out: effrt 2f out: pushed along and ch over 1f out: nt qckn fnl f* **4/1**[2]
06B0 **4** *4* **Another Secret**[24] [6073] 5-9-7 53 (be[1]) ACulhane 4 52
(GLMoore) *racd in midfield: rdn and unable qck over 2f out: kpt on same pce fr over 1f out* **14/1**
2-60 **5** *1* **Sammy's Shuffle**[10] [6157] 8-9-3 56 (b) HPoulton(7) 6 53
(JamiePoulton) *b: chsd ldrs: rdn over 2f out: one pce and no imp fr over 1f out* **8/1**
000 **6** *nk* **Legality**[65] [5596] 3-9-5 54 NCallan 9 50
(JulianPoulton) *hld up: prog to chse ldrs 3f out: cl up 2f out: wknd u.p fnl f* **25/1**
0100 **7** *nk* **Answered Promise (FR)**[8] [6171] 4-9-9 55 SWhitworth 13 51
(AWCarroll) *hld up in last: pushed along over 2f out: nvr nr ldrs* **33/1**
0530 **8** *1 3/4* **Man The Gate**[10] [6161] 4-9-12 58 SCarson 1 51
(PDCundell) *led: rdn over 3f out: hdd & wknd wl over 1f out* **7/1**[3]
222U **9** *1 1/4* **Fife And Drum (USA)**[24] [6076] 6-9-8 59 (p) BReilly(5) 10 50
(MissJFeilden) *racd towards rr: rdn and struggling wl over 2f out: one pce after* **8/1**
0300 **10** *hd* **Kyle Of Lochalsh**[24] [6073] 3-9-9 58 JMackay 14 48
(GGMargarson) *racd wd: t.k.h: hld up in rr: rdn and no prog 3f out* **10/1**
0-00 **11** *3 1/2* **Travel Tardia (IRE)**[66] [5574] 5-9-8 54 JFanning 5 38
(IAWood) *chsd ldr to 2f out: wknd* **66/1**
4045 **12** *5* **Escalade**[49] [5881] 6-8-13 50 PMulrennan(5) 2 25
(WMBrisbourne) *t.k.h: prom tl wknd 3f out* **4/1**[2]
5530 **13** *5* **In Spirit (IRE)**[24] [6076] 5-9-10 56 WMLordan 7 22
(BJCurley) *chsd ldrs tl wknd over 3f out* **10/1**
1500 **14** *2 1/2* **Platinum Boy (IRE)**[92] [5049] 3-9-3 55 (p) LFletcher(3) 12 16
(MWellings) *racd in midfield: rdn 4f out: sn btn* **50/1**

2m 9.45s (2.06) **Going Correction** +0.10s/f (Slow)
**WFA** 3 from 4yo+ 3lb **14** Ran SP% **145.6**
Speed ratings: **95,94,93,90,89 89,89,87,86,86 83,79,75,73**CSF £39.44 CT £127.01 TOTE £3.90: £2.10, £7.50, £1.90; EX 55.00 Place 6 £51.68, Place 5 £45.69..
**Owner** Mrs Alexandra J Chandris **Bred** Mrs J Chandris **Trained** Baughurst, Hants

**FOCUS**
A moderate handicap and run in a slower time that the first division.

**NOTEBOOK**
**Lyrical Way** was ridden more patiently than when runner-up on his last two starts on this surface and the change in tactics did the trick. Has been done no favours by the Handicapper recently, but remains in good form.
**Double Ransom** looked sure to score until finding little in the last furlong. He may be worth trying over slightly shorter, but this was still a fair effort on his first try on the surface.
**Zawrak(IRE)**, another trying this surface for the first time, was a massive gamble and landed the each-way money without being good enough to score. He was stepping back markedly in trip, but does not look the easiest of rides.
**Another Secret** ran better than of late with the headgear on for the first time.
**Sammy's Shuffle** appeared to have no excuses.
**Escalade** was keen early on and, despite tumbling down the weights, has not won for a long time.
T/Plt: £86.90 to a £1 stake. Pool: £28,304.95. 237.75 winning tickets. T/Qpdt: £34.20 to a £1 stake. Pool: £1,752.50. 37.90 winning tickets. JN

# 6135 WOLVERHAMPTON (A.W) (L-H)
Monday, December 22

**OFFICIAL GOING: Slow**
The track had been reinstated following extensive remedial drainage work.
Wind: nil Weather: mostly cloudy and cold

## 6227 MERRY CHRISTMAS FROM BET DIRECT NURSERY 5f (F)
**12:40** (12:40) (E ) (0-75,73) 2-Y-O **£2,002** (£572; £286) **Stalls** Low

Form RPR
006 **1** **Head Of State**[79] [5380] 2-7-12 **50** oh10 JMackay 5 47+
(RMBeckett) *w ldrs: led over 3f out: rdn 2f out: r.o wl* **8/1**[3]
0000 **2** *1/2* **Little Flute**[38] [5993] 2-7-9 **50** oh2 LisaJones(3) 6 45
(TKeddy) *hld up: hdwy over 2f out: sn rdn: chsd wnr fnl f: nt qckn* **20/1**
4421 **3** *6* **Blue Power (IRE)**[13] [6152] 2-9-3 **69** DarrenWilliams 7 43
(KRBurke) *s.i.s: jnd wnr over 3f out: rdn wl over 1f out: wknd fnl f* **4/7**[1]
0000 **4** *2* **Suitcase Murphy (IRE)**[55] [5818] 2-7-12 **50** PMQuinn 3 17
(MsDeborahJEvans) *w ldrs: lost pl and rdn 3f out: sn struggling* **25/1**
3143 **5** *nk* **Lizhar (IRE)**[10] [6165] 2-9-3 **72** LFletcher(3) 1 38
(MJPolglase) *led over 1f: rdn and wknd over 2f out* **11/4**[2]

64.98 secs (2.38) **Going Correction** +0.40s/f (Slow) **5** Ran SP% **110.0**
Speed ratings: **96,95,85,82,81**CSF £105.64 TOTE £8.70: £2.20, £5.90; EX 72.00.
**Owner** Pedro Rosas **Bred** P Asquith **Trained** Lambourn, Berks

**FOCUS**
An uncompetitive event especially by nursery standards.

**NOTEBOOK**

**Head Of State** was supported on the exchanges and backed from 20/1 to small money on course despite being 10lb 'wrong'. He had been working well at home and it does seem as if it has taken time for the penny to drop. *Official explanation: trainer said, regarding the improved form shown, gelding had taken time to mature and had been working well since its previous run*

**Little Flute**, 2lb out of the handicap, had tackled the stretch mile when hampered here last time, and perhaps six furlongs is his optimum.

**Blue Power(IRE)** had been raised 8lb but this was still rather disappointing.

## 6228 LITTLEWOODS BET DIRECT MAIDEN STKS (DIV I) 1m 1f 79y(F)

**1:10** (1:10) (D ) 2-Y-0 **£2,926** (£836; £418) **Stalls** Low

Form RPR

2630 **1** **Dr Cerullo**[14] 6141 2-9-0 75 .......... DaneO'Neill 5 76+
(CTinkler) *prom: led over 6f out: rdn over 2f out: clr over 1f out: r.o wl* **7/4**[1]

065 **2** *6* **Unintentional**[37] 6002 2-8-9 57 .......... IMongan 6 59
(RBrotherton) *hld up in tch: chsd wnr over 4f out: rdn over 3f out: wknd over 1f out* **5/1**[2]

0 **3** *8* **Ctesiphon (USA)**[49] 5911 2-8-9 .......... KDalgleish 2 43
(JGGiven) *chsd ldrs: rdn and wknd over 3f out* **5/1**[2]

5005 **4** *7* **Bretton**[10] 6167 2-9-0 45 .......... (p) NCallan 7 34
(RHollinshead) *hld up: hdwy over 5f out: rdn 4f out: sn wknd* **10/1**

0600 **5** *6* **David's Girl**[14] 6147 2-8-9 42 .......... JFanning 1 17
(DMorris) *led 1f: prom: rdn over 5f out: wknd over 3f out* **33/1**

0003 **6** *8* **Casantella**[6] 6201 2-8-6 38 .......... LFletcher(3) 3 1
(MJPolglase) *led after 1f tl over 6f out: rdn and wknd 4f out* **20/1**

**7** *3/4* **Once Around (IRE)** 2-9-0 .......... JPaulielo 9 5
(TGMills) *dwlt: hld up: rdn over 4f out: sn wl bhd* **6/1**[3]

0600 **8** *1* **Platinum Pirate**[37] 6003 2-8-11 48 .......... LisaJones(3) 8 3
(KRBurke) *hld up in rr: lost tch 4f out* **20/1**

000 **9** *17* **It Must Be Speech**[112] 4627 2-9-0 63 .......... CCatlin 4 —
(SLKeightley) *a bhd: rdn over 4f out: sn lost tch: t.o* **9/1**

2m 7.68s (4.78) **Going Correction** +0.40s/f (Slow) **9** Ran SP% **115.5**

Speed ratings: **94,88,81,75,70 62,62,61,46**CSF £10.16 TOTE £2.90: £1.50, £2.40, £2.00; EX 13.80.

**Owner** Doubleprint **Bred** Eurostrait Ltd **Trained** Compton, Berks

**FOCUS**

A weak maiden.

**NOTEBOOK**

**Dr Cerullo** had more use made of him over this longer trip and stamina was certainly not a problem.

**Unintentional** did not appear to get home on this step up in distance.

**Ctesiphon(USA)** should have been suited by this surface judged on her American pedigree.

## 6229 BET DIRECT CLAIMING STKS 1m 1f 79y(F)

**1:40** (1:40) (F ) 3-Y-0+ **£2,065** (£590; £295) **Stalls** Low

Form RPR

020 **1** **Hiawatha (IRE)**[23] 6098 4-9-3 66 .......... NCallan 9 78+
(ISemple) *hld up: hdwy over 5f out: swtchd lft and led over 1f out: shkn up and sn clr: eased towards fin* **2/1**[1]

0000 **2** *7* **Our Destiny**[28] 6057 5-8-5 37 .......... (v) JTate 10 52
(DBurchell) *led: rdn over 3f out: hdd over 1f out: btn whn edgd rt ins fnl f* **7/1**

00/5 **3** *1 1/2* **Tinian**[14] 6144 5-9-7 62 .......... DarrenWilliams 7 65
(KRBurke) *a.p: rdn 3f out: ev ch 2f out: one pce* **4/1**[2]

1406 **4** *nk* **Repeat (IRE)**[12] 6163 3-8-13 53 .......... IMongan 11 58
(MissGayKelleway) *t.k.h: hdwy 5f out: sn hit on nose by whip: rdn and ev ch 2f out: edgd lft wl over 1f out: sn btn* **6/1**[3]

0006 **5** *3 1/2* **Oriental Moon (IRE)**[14] 6146 4-7-7 36 .......... (p) DeanWilliams(7) 6 36
(GCHChung) *bhd tl sme hdwy over 2f out: n.d* **33/1**

0000 **6** *5* **Vermilion Creek**[14] 6148 4-8-2 39 .......... StephanieHollinshead(7) 3 35
(RHollinshead) *a bhd* **7/1**

0000 **7** *8* **Better Off**[14] 6144 5-8-13 70 .......... (v[1]) JoannaBadger 4 23
(MrsNMacauley) *plld hrd: prom: rdn over 5f out: sn lost pl* **10/1**

0 **8** *1 3/4* **Ziggy Dan**[51] 5879 3-8-11 .......... EAhern 5 20
(MsDeborahJEvans) *chsd ldr tl rdn over 4f out: wknd over 3f out* **33/1**

**9** *dist* **Bachelor's Tonic (IRE)**[39] 5-7-13 ow1 .......... PMakin(7) 8 —
(KAMorgan) *s.i.s: sn wl bhd: t.o fnl 5f* **14/1**

2m 7.72s (4.82) **Going Correction** +0.40s/f (Slow)

**WFA** 3 from 4yo+ 2lb **9** Ran SP% **114.3**

Speed ratings: **94,87,86,86,83 78,71,69,—**CSF £16.37 TOTE £3.60: £1.20, £1.90, £2.00; EX 29.90.The winner (No 2) was claimed by Nigel Shields for £9,000.

**Owner** D Irvine **Bred** Kilcarn Stud **Trained** Carluke, S Lanarks

**FOCUS**

Hiawatha benefitted from a change of tactics and was subsequently claimed for £9,000.

**NOTEBOOK**

**Hiawatha(IRE)**, waited with this time, had no trouble taking the scalps of these rivals and can go on to better things. *Official explanation: trainer said, regarding the improved form shown, gelding benefited from a change of tactics, namely being covered up*

**Our Destiny** adopted the same tactics as when successful in a similar event here in March; he would have been no less than 17lb better off with the winner in a handicap.

**Tinian** should not have been inconvenienced by the step up from seven.

**Repeat(IRE)**, who is more at home in selling company, is not the easiest of rides.

**Bachelor's Tonic(IRE)** *Official explanation: trainer said gelding finished lame*

## 6230 LITTLEWOODS BET DIRECT MAIDEN STKS (DIV II) 1m 1f 79y(F)

**2:10** (2:11) (D ) 2-Y-0 **£2,926** (£836; £418) **Stalls** Low

Form RPR

3320 **1** **Bill Bennett (FR)**[23] 6087 2-9-0 73 .......... IMongan 6 71
(JJay) *hld up: hdwy over 6f out: led over 3f out: rdn over 2f out: drew clr fnl f: r.o wl* **2/1**[1]

4602 **2** *4* **Russalka**[24] 6082 2-8-9 66 .......... NCallan 5 59
(JulianPoulton) *a.p: rdn over 3f out: wnt 2nd and hung lft ins fnl f: no ch w wnr* **3/1**[2]

4 **3** *3/4* **Par Indiana (IRE)**[37] 6002 2-8-9 .......... MTebbutt 3 57
(ISemple) *hld up: hdwy on outside over 3f out: styd on fnl f* **9/2**[3]

500 **4** *3 1/2* **Tamarina (IRE)**[14] 6142 2-8-9 50 .......... CCatlin 8 51
(NEBerry) *a.p: led over 5f out: rdn and hdd over 3f out: wknd ins fnl f* **33/1**

0 **5** *2* **Separated (USA)**[12] 6158 2-8-9 .......... EAhern 2 47
(EALDunlop) *hld up: rdn over 4f out: hdwy over 3f out: wknd wl over 1f out* **6/1**

00 **6** *9* **Timbuktu**[14] 6142 2-9-0 .......... DeanMcKeown 9 35
(CWThornton) *prom: rdn over 3f out: wknd over 2f out* **50/1**

00 **7** *14* **Crackleando**[23] 6087 2-8-11 .......... J-PGuillambert(3) 1 9
(NPLittmoden) *led early: sn lost pl: bhd fnl 4f* **15/2**

00 **8** *2 1/2* **Vesta Flame**[24] 6082 2-8-9 .......... JFanning 4 —
(MJohnston) *prom tl rdn and wknd over 3f out* **40/1**

00 **9** *2* **Sky Cove**[62] 5687 2-8-9 .......... PMulrennan(5) 7 1
(MWEasterby) *sn led: hdd over 5f out: rdn over 4f out: wknd over 3f out* **33/1**

2m 7.19s (4.29) **Going Correction** +0.40s/f (Slow) **9** Ran SP% **112.8**

Speed ratings: **96,92,91,88,86 78,66,64,62**CSF £7.60 TOTE £3.60: £1.60, £1.70, £1.50; EX 4.60.

**Owner** Mr & Mrs Jonathan Jay **Bred** J Jay **Trained** Newmarket, Suffolk

**FOCUS**

A modest affair which turned out to be the fastest of the three races run consecutively over this trip.

**NOTEBOOK**

**Bill Bennett(FR)** only began to come to himself in the autumn having suffered problems with his teeth. Settling much better than at Lingfield last time, he seems to have now really got his act together.

**Russalka** had shaped as though she would benefit from this slightly longer trip here last time, but proved no match for the winner.

**Par Indiana(IRE)** again ran encouragingly and seems to have inherited the stamina on her dams' side.

**Tamarina(IRE)**, stepping up from a mile, is going to need more patient tactics to get this trip by the look of it.

**Separated(USA)** is going to need middle distances next year.

## 6231 BETDIRECT.CO.UK H'CAP 7f (F)

**2:40** (2:41) (E ) (0-75,74) 3-Y-0+ **£2,086** (£596; £298) **Stalls** High

Form RPR

0000 **1** **Ronnie From Donny (IRE)**[6] 6199 3-9-10 **70** .......... DaneO'Neill 7 79
(BEllison) *sn prom: wnt 2nd over 3f out: sn rdn: led wl ins fnl f: all out* **9/2**[2]

0100 **2** *hd* **Yorker (USA)**[7] 6190 5-9-3 **66** .......... LisaJones(3) 3 74
(MsDeborahJEvans) *led early: a.p: rdn over 3f out: ev ch wl ins fnl f: r.o* **10/1**

0405 **3** *1/2* **Grey Pearl**[12] 6164 4-9-11 **71** .......... NCallan 4 78
(MissGayKelleway) *sn led: clr over 3f out: rdn over 2f out: hdd wl ins fnl f: no ex* **8/1**

0455 **4** *1* **Captain Darling (IRE)**[20] 6114 3-9-4 **64** .......... EAhern 10 68
(RMHCowell) *hld up: hdwy over 4f out: rdn and outpcd 3f out: styd on fnl f* **13/2**[3]

0100 **5** *6* **Noble Locks (IRE)**[62] 5685 5-8-12 **65** .......... CarloBandiera(7) 5 54
(JWUnett) *hld up and bhd: hdwy 2f out: nvr trbld ldrs* **14/1**

3001 **6** *3* **Arc El Ciel (ARG)**[16] 6135 5-10-0 **74** .......... CCatlin 9 56
(MrsStefLiddiard) *bhd: rdn over 3f out: nvr nr ldrs* **7/2**[1]

000 **7** *3/4* **Kanz Wood (USA)**[20] 6119 7-9-2 **62** .......... SWhitworth 12 42
(AWCarroll) *s.i.s: hld up: hdwy on ins over 4f out: rdn 3f out: sn wknd* **20/1**

0004 **8** *3/4* **The Gaikwar (IRE)**[12] 6164 4-9-4 **69** .......... (b) MSavage(5) 8 47
(NEBerry) *s.i.s: hld up: hdwy on ins over 3f out: sn rdn: wknd wl over 1f out* **7/1**

6230 **9** *5* **Heidelburg (IRE)**[16] 6127 3-9-4 **64** .......... (b[1]) JFanning 6 30
(SKirk) *prom: rdn and wkng whn n.m.r on ins over 3f out* **9/2**[2]

**10** *11* **Rex Romelio (IRE)**[436] 4-9-5 **65** .......... DarrenWilliams 2 3
(KRBurke) *a bhd* **33/1**

030P **11** *1 3/4* **Weet Watchers**[136] 3972 3-10-0 **74** .......... DSweeney 11 8
(RHollinshead) *sn prom: rdn over 3f out: sn wknd* **33/1**

1m 32.25s (2.05) **Going Correction** +0.40s/f (Slow) **11** Ran SP% **121.9**

Speed ratings: **104,103,103,102,95 91,90,90,84,71 69**CSF £49.86 CT £355.06 TOTE £6.50: £2.60, £4.50, £3.10; EX 73.70 Trifecta £547.10 Pool of £1,464.10 - 1.90 winning units.

**Owner** Keith Middleton **Bred** John And Hugh Naughton **Trained** Norton, N Yorks

■ Stewards Enquiry : Dane O'Neill three-day ban: used whip without allowing gelding time to respond, out of stride pattern, and with excessive force (Jan 2-4)

**FOCUS**

No hanging about with Grey Pearl setting a strong pace.

**NOTEBOOK**

**Ronnie From Donny(IRE)**, gelded during the summer, had dropped to a mark 8lb lower than when winning over six at Southwell at the turn of the year. His commitment could not be faulted on only his second attempt at seven furlongs.

**Yorker(USA)**, back down to a more suitable distance, lost nothing in defeat over a trip that is actually on the short side for him these days.

**Grey Pearl** likes to dominate and the tactics nearly paid off on this first start on Fibresand.

**Captain Darling(IRE)** settled a lot better than at Lingfield and gave the impression that another crack at a mile is called for.

**Noble Locks(IRE)**, ridden by an inexperienced apprentice, gave the impression he will do better with stronger handling.

**Arc El Ciel(ARG)** is normally a model of consistency over this course and distance, but ran a stinker having gone up 8lb.

## 6232 BET DIRECT ON 0800 32 93 93 MAIDEN STKS 5f (F)

**3:10** (3:13) (D ) 3-Y-0+ **£2,257** (£645; £322) **Stalls** Low

Form RPR

0300 **1** **Cloudless (USA)**[38] 5995 3-8-9 55 .......... SWhitworth 8 66
(JWUnett) *hld up in tch: rdn wl over 1f out: led and edgd lft ins fnl f: sn clr: r.o wl* **16/1**

0646 **2** *5* **Inching**[10] 6166 3-8-9 53 .......... EAhern 12 49
(RMHCowell) *a.p: rdn 3f out: wnt 2nd 2f out: ev ch 1f out: one pce* **11/2**[3]

-342 **3** *1 1/4* **Blueberry Rhyme**[24] 6080 4-9-0 68 .......... (v) DSweeney 4 49
(PJMakin) *hld up: rdn and hdwy on ins over 2f out: one pce fnl f* **11/8**[1]

0064 **4** *shd* **Diaphanous**[138] 3883 5-8-9 37 .......... (b) SCarson 9 44
(EAWheeler) *led: rdn over 2f out: hdd and no ex ins fnl f* **16/1**

2055 **5** *1/2* **Multahab**[266] 879 4-9-0 55 .......... IMongan 5 47
(MissGayKelleway) *hld up: rdn and hdwy on outside over 2f out: edgd lft ins fnl f: one pce* **4/1**[2]

0364 **6** *1/2* **Victory Flip (IRE)**[14] 6146 3-8-9 52 .......... (p) NCallan 1 40
(RHollinshead) *outpcd: sn wl bhd: hdwy fnl f: nrst fin* **11/1**

0063 **7** *nk* **Eager Angel (IRE)**[13] 6150 5-8-9 41 .......... (p) DeanMcKeown 13 39
(RFMarvin) *outpcd and bhd: hdwy fnl f: nvr nrr* **25/1**

0006 **8** *2* **Lady Protector**[105] 4774 4-8-9 42 .......... JBramhill 6 32
(JBalding) *prom: rdn over 2f out: wknd fnl f* **16/1**

4603 **9** *1* **Lake Eyre (IRE)**[28] 6062 4-8-9 39 .......... JEdmunds 10 29
(JBalding) *prom tl wknd wl over 1f out* **16/1**

5500 **10** *3/4* **Tatweer (IRE)**[5] 6209 3-9-0 52 .......... (v) DarrenWilliams 7 31
(DShaw) *s.i.s: rdn 3f out: a bhd* **25/1**

0000 **11** *7* **Blue Circle**[2] 6192 3-9-0 34 .......... (p) TWilliams 2 7
(MMullineaux) *rdn over 3f out: a bhd* **100/1**

0 **12** *3/4* **White O' Morn**[33] 6031 4-8-9 .......... PMQuinn 3 —
(BAMcmahon) *towards rr: short-lived effrt over 2f out* **33/1**

63.47 secs (0.87) **Going Correction** +0.40s/f (Slow) **12** Ran SP% **121.0**

Speed ratings: **109,101,99,98,98 97,96,93,91,90 79,78**CSF £100.94 TOTE £18.40: £6.20, £1.70, £1.20; EX 72.50.

**Owner** James Unett **Bred** Juddmonte Farms Inc **Trained** Wolverhampton, W Midlands

**FOCUS**

A modest sprint maiden full of horses who had already been given plenty of chances.

**NOTEBOOK**

**Cloudless(USA)** had been working well on this track, and proved she was not a morning glory with the help of a change of tactics. *Official explanation: trainer said, regarding the improved form shown, filly benefited from an enforced rest due to track repairs to Wolverhampton, and also due to a change of tactics, whereby she was kept covered up*

**Inching**, without the visor this time, had no answer to the winner.

**Blueberry Rhyme** seemed to have found a gilt-edged opportunity but let favourite backers down. *Official explanation: jockey said gelding had been struck into*

**Diaphanous** possesses bags of speed but struggles to get home, and this slow surface would not have helped.

**Multahab** was having his first start on Fibresand, having not been out since having a breathing problem at the end of March. *Official explanation: jockey said colt took a very strong hold to post and he was concerned it might bolt, hence late arrival at start*

**Victory Flip(IRE)** has been running over seven furlongs and a mile and got take off her legs.

**Tatweer(IRE)** *Official explanation: jockey said gelding ducked as stalls opened*

## 6233 SEASONS GREETINGS FROM BET DIRECT H'CAP (DIV I) 1m 4f (F)

**3:40** (3:40) (F) (0-60,60) 3-Y-0+ **£2,044** (£584; £292) **Stalls** Low

Form RPR

1330 **1** **Adalpour (IRE)**$^{266}$ 885 5-9-4 **50** ... JTate 3 61
(DBurchell) *plld hrd early: in tch: rdn to ld over 1f out: rdn out* **20/1**

0436 **2** ½ **Broughton Knows**$^{16}$ 6139 6-7-11 **32** ... LisaJones(3) 6 42
(WJMusson) *hld up: hdwy over 3f out: rdn over 2f out: kpt on ins fnl f* **5/1**$^{2}$

4010 **3** 1 ¾ **Compton Eclaire (IRE)**$^{26}$ 6075 3-9-1 **52** ... (b) EAhern 10 60
(GAButler) *hld up: hdwy over 6f out: rdn over 3f out: one pce fnl f* **6/1**$^{3}$

0633 **4** ½ **Mercurious (IRE)**$^{10}$ 6168 3-8-4 **41** ... DaleGibson 7 48
(JMackie) *hld up in tch: wnt 2nd 7f out: rdn to ld over 2f out: hdd over 1f out: one pce* **5/1**$^{2}$

0022 **5** 3 **Exit To Heaven**$^{9}$ 6177 3-9-4 **60** ... TEaves(5) 2 62
(MissGayKelleway) *led after 1f: hrd rdn and hdd over 2f out: wknd 1f out* **12/1**

0400 **6** 3 ½ **Makarim (IRE)**$^{53}$ 5839 7-10-0 **60** ... (v$^{1}$) GBaker 1 57
(MRBosley) *prom: rdn 4f out: outpcd 3f out: rallied on ins over 1f out: wknd fnl f* **10/1**

0404 **7** 23 **Shatin Special**$^{48}$ 5914 3-8-5 **49** ... (p) DeanWilliams(7) 5 12
(GCHChung) *plld hrd: led 1f: sddle sn slipped: lost pl 5f out: sn bhd* **25/1**

1422 **8** hd **Ambersong**$^{31}$ 6043 5-9-5 **51** ... IMongan 11 13
(AWCarroll) *s.s: bhd: rdn over 7f out: hdwy over 4f out: wknd 3f out* **11/8**$^{1}$

06-5 **9** ½ **Flamenca (USA)**$^{191}$ 383 4-8-5 **42** ow2 ... PMulrennan(5) 9 4
(MrsLBNormile) *hld up in tch: wknd 6f out* **50/1**

0-00 **10** 5 **Final Lap**$^{26}$ 2339 7-7-9 **30** oh8 ... FPFerris(3) 12 —
(STLewis) *dropped rr 7f out: t.o* **100/1**

2m 46.26s (4.76) **Going Correction** +0.40s/f (Slow)

**WFA** 3 from 4yo+ 5lb **10** Ran SP% **118.1**

Speed ratings: **100,99,98,98,96 93,78,78,78,74**CSF £115.84 CT £690.83 TOTE £22.30: £5.60, £2.10, £2.10; EX 166.10.

**Owner** Lewis Racing **Bred** His Highness The Aga Khan's Studs S C **Trained** Briery Hill, Blaenau Gwent

■ Stewards Enquiry : J Tate two-day ban: used whip with excessive force (Jan 2,3)

**FOCUS**

This was over half a second slower than the strongly-run second division.

**NOTEBOOK**

**Adalpour(IRE)** had been bought as a hurdler but connections have not been able to school him sufficiently because of the dry autumn. He stays further and it would be no surprise to see him stay at this game this winter.

**Broughton Knows** could not peg back the winner over a distance that is very much on the short side for him.

**Compton Eclaire(IRE)** was back in blinkers instead of a visor for this first outing on Fibresand.

**Mercurious(IRE)** seems to be struggling to find the right trip.

**Exit To Heaven** is looking fully exposed.

**Makarim(IRE)**, struggling to find his old form, was tried in a visor and really wants further than this.

**Shatin Special** *Official explanation: jockey said saddle slipped*

**Ambersong** *Official explanation: trainer said gelding had run flat*

## 6234 SEASONS GREETINGS FROM BET DIRECT H'CAP (DIV II) 1m 4f (F)

**4:10** (4:10) (F) (0-60,60) 3-Y-0+ **£2,037** (£582; £291) **Stalls** Low

Form RPR

5-06 **1** **Only For Sue**$^{203}$ 2069 4-9-0 45 ... IMongan 2 61
(WSKittow) *a.p: rdn over 7f out: chsd clr ldr over 5f out: led over 2f out: clr whn edgd rt jst over 1f out: styd on wl* **10/1**

0124 **2** 5 **Ambitious Annie**$^{6}$ 6200 4-8-2 40 ... StephanieHollinshead(7) 6 48
(RHollinshead) *hld up and bhd: plenty to do whn hdwy over 4f out: styd on to take 2nd post: nt trble wnr* **6/1**$^{3}$

0104 **3** hd **Nakwa (IRE)**$^{63}$ 5672 5-8-9 43 ... DAllan(3) 3 51
(EJAlston) *plld hrd early: a.p: rdn over 3f out: one pce fnl 2f* **11/4**$^{1}$

3041 **4** 2 **Aveiro (IRE)**$^{6}$ 6198 7-8-7 38 7ex ... (b) KDalgleish 12 43
(BGPowell) *sn w ldr: led 8f out: clr over 6f out: rdn over 3f out: hdd over 2f out: one pce* **4/1**$^{2}$

1042 **5** 2 ½ **Kentucky Bullet (USA)**$^{31}$ 6040 7-9-4 49 ... SWhitworth 9 50
(AGNewcombe) *hld up and bhd: hdwy 5f out: rdn 3f out: no imp fnl 2f* **4/1**$^{2}$

6100 **6** dist **Humdinger (IRE)**$^{10}$ 6168 3-9-5 60 ... THamilton(5) 7 —
(DShaw) *hld up mid-div: wl bhd fnl 6f: t.o* **25/1**

0006 **7** 2 ½ **Annakita**$^{62}$ 5692 3-9-0 53 ... LisaJones(3) 1 —
(WJMusson) *chsd ldrs: wknd over 6f out: t.o* **22/1**

6 **8** 2 **Kyalami (IRE)**$^{6}$ 6200 4-7-9 29 oh4 ... FPFerris(3) 4 —
(MJPolglase) *plld hrd early: wl bhd fnl 6f: t.o* **8/1**

-060 **9** 17 **Brios Boy**$^{10}$ 4315 3-8-3 39 ... (p) JFanning 5 —
(GAHarker) *led 4f: wknd 5f out: t.o* **50/1**

0-0 **10** shd **Hispaniola (IRE)**$^{23}$ 6100 5-9-5 55 ... PMulrennan(5) 10 —
(MWEasterby) *a bhd: t.o fnl 6f* **16/1**

5000 **11** dist **Nominate (GER)**$^{86}$ 4835 3-9-10 60 ... (t) DaneO'Neill 11 —
(STLewis) *s.i.s: a bhd: t.o fnl 6f* **50/1**

3-00 **P** **Kamala**$^{16}$ 6137 4-9-5 50 ... (v$^{1}$) NCallan 8 —
(RBrotherton) *chsd ldrs: wknd qckly 7f out: t.o whn p.u over 5f out* **33/1**

2m 45.65s (4.15) **Going Correction** +0.40s/f (Slow)

**WFA** 3 from 4yo+ 5lb **12** Ran SP% **122.1**

Speed ratings: **102,98,98,97,95 —,—,—,—,— —,—**CSF £67.65 CT £214.80 TOTE £12.00: £3.20, £1.80, £1.80; EX 45.40 Place 6 £127.39, Place 5 £7.32.

**Owner** Ms Susan Arnesen **Bred** A W Schiff **Trained** Blackborough, Devon

**FOCUS**

Aveiro really picked up the pace with a circuit to go and soon had the field well strung out.

**NOTEBOOK**

**Only For Sue** appeared to relish this strongly-run race and scored in the style of one who could defy a penalty.

**Ambitious Annie** found this distance inadequate despite the searching gallop in the final mile. *Official explanation: trainer's representative said filly had finished very lame*

**Nakwa(IRE)** looks well treated but hails from a stable that has been struggling to find some form.

**Aveiro(IRE)** adopted totally different tactics under his penalty. He really threw down the gauntlet going out on the final circuit and had too much use made of him.

**Kentucky Bullet(USA)** is not one who likes to be bullied along and may not have been suited by the way this race was run.

**Kamala** *Official explanation: jockey said filly had lost her action*

T/Jkpt: Not won. T/Plt: £561.00 to a £1 stake. Pool: £71,520.50. 93.05 winning tickets. T/Qpdt: £11.60 to a £1 stake. Pool: £10,309.20. 652.50 winning tickets. KH

# 6227 WOLVERHAMPTON (A.W) (L-H)

### Friday, December 26

**OFFICIAL GOING: Standard**

## 6235 BET DIRECT NO Q ON 08000 93 66 93 AMATEUR RIDERS' H'CAP (DIV I) 6f (F)

**1:05** (1:05) (E) (0-75,75) 3-Y-0+ **£2,044** (£584; £292) **Stalls** Low

Form RPR

0005 **1** **St Ivian**$^{10}$ 6199 3-11-2 **63** ... (v) MrsMMorris 4 72
(MrsNMacauley) *chsd ldr: hrd rdn to ld nr fin* **8/1**

0000 **2** ½ **Larky's Lob**$^{32}$ 6055 4-9-7 **45** ... MrPEvans(5) 6 52
(PaulJohnson) *sn led: rdn over 1f out: kpt on: hdd cl home* **11/1**

005 **3** 3 **Mister Mal (IRE)**$^{10}$ 6202 7-10-8 **58** ... (be) MissLEllison(3) 2 56
(BEllison) *slowly away: rdn and sn chsd ldrs: hung rt thrght fnl 2f: no hdwy ins last* **7/2**$^{3}$

0353 **4** 1 ¾ **Blonde En Blonde (IRE)**$^{20}$ 6135 3-11-3 **67** ... MrsEmmaLittmoden(3) 3 60
(NPLittmoden) *a in tch: rdn over 2f out: kpt on one pce* **2/1**$^{1}$

0500 **5** shd **The Gay Fox**$^{9}$ 6206 9-9-3 **43** oh1 ... (bt) MrsRPowell(7) 7 35
(BGPowell) *mid-div: styd on ins fnl 2f: nvr nr to chal* **14/1**

000 **6** 3 **Sawah**$^{23}$ 6126 3-9-5 **43** oh23 ... MissKellyHarrison(5) 5 26
(DShaw) *slowly away: rdn 1/2-way: nvr on terms* **80/1**

4540 **7** hd **Mr Stylish**$^{10}$ 6202 7-10-0 **50** ... (vt) MrsSMoore(3) 8 33
(JSMoore) *plld hrd on outside: a towards rr* **9/1**

0000 **8** ¾ **Blakeshall Quest**$^{28}$ 6084 3-11-9 **70** ... MissCHannaford 10 51
(RBrotherton) *broke wl: sn hdd: rdn 2f out: wwknd approachinf fnl f* **20/1**

6610 **9** 10 **Paddywack (IRE)**$^{11}$ 6192 6-11-9 **75** ... (b) MrRClark(5) 9 26
(DWChapman) *mid-div: rdn and effrt hafway: btn 2f out and eased ent fnl f* **10/3**$^{2}$

0000 **10** 5 **Blue Circle**$^{4}$ 6232 3-9-3 **43** oh9 ... MissMMullineaux(7) 1 —
(MMullineaux) *a bhd: t.o wl over 1f out* **50/1**

1m 17.95s (2.25) **Going Correction** +0.275s/f (Slow) **10** Ran SP% **122.7**

Speed ratings: **96,95,91,89,88 84,84,83,70,63**CSF £95.19 CT £371.39 TOTE £14.30: £3.60, £3.90, £2.50; EX 105.30.

**Owner** Godfrey Horsford **Bred** P And Mrs Venner **Trained** Sproxton, Leics

**FOCUS**

A moderate handicap run in a similar time to the second division.

**NOTEBOOK**

**St Ivian** gained only his second-ever career success off a mark 2lb lower than when first successful at Southwell in March. He had to work pretty hard to reel in the runner-up in the straight, but the pair were finished clear and he is clearly in good heart.

**Larky's Lob** has not won since February 2002 but, dropping two furlongs in trip and with the headgear left off, he very nearly ended that miserable run. His current rating qualifies him for regional racing when it starts in the new year.

**Mister Mal(IRE)** has not won since May 2001, or on this surface. He did himself no favours with a slow start and hung right under pressure.

**Blonde En Blonde(IRE)**, one of the more prolific winners in the line-up, was disappointing. Seven furlongs may suit her better these days.

**The Gay Fox** may find things easier when the regional racing starts.

**Paddywack(IRE)** was reported to have been struck into soon after the start and to make matters worse his saddle slipped. *Official explanation: jockey said gelding was struck into shortly after leaving the stalls, and that his saddle slipped*

## 6236 BET DIRECT NO Q ON 08000 93 66 93 AMATEUR RIDERS' H'CAP (DIV II) 6f (F)

**1:40** (1:40) (E) (0-75,72) 3-Y-0+ **£2,037** (£582; £291) **Stalls** Low

Form RPR

1005 **1** **Noble Locks (IRE)**$^{4}$ 6231 5-11-0 65 ... MissJCWilliams(7) 8 81
(JWUnett) *w.w in mid-div: hdwy 1/2-way: led over 1f out: rdn clr* **4/1**$^{1}$

0460 **2** 6 **Amelia (IRE)**$^{7}$ 6217 5-9-13 50 ... MrCDavies(7) 9 48
(WMBrisbourne) *hld up in tch: hdwy over 2f out: styd on to chse wnr over 1f out* **8/1**

6000 **3** 1 **Dil**$^{10}$ 6202 8-10-4 48 ... MrsMMorris 10 43
(MrsNMacauley) *racd wd: rdn and hdwy over 2f out: r.o fnl f: nvr nrr* **13/2**

0000 **4** 1 ¾ **Attorney**$^{7}$ 6217 5-9-10 45 ... (e) MissKellyHarrison(5) 5 35
(DShaw) *mid-div: styd on past beten horses fnl f* **10/1**

0113 **5** 4 **Sharp Hat**$^{20}$ 6136 9-11-9 72 ... MrRClark(5) 6 50
(DWChapman) *trckd ldrs on outside: lede 2f out: hdd over 1f out: wknd ins fnl f* **9/2**$^{2}$

0501 **6** 1 **Cash**$^{14}$ 6166 5-10-12 61 ... (p) MrPEvans(5) 4 36
(PaulJohnson) *w ldrs: rdn and wknd appr fnl f* **5/1**$^{3}$

0000 **7** 2 ½ **Yob (IRE)**$^{17}$ 6149 4-9-7 40 oh7 ... (vt) MissEFolkes(3) 7 7
(PDEvans) *a in rr* **40/1**

0000 **8** 3 ½ **Mutared (IRE)**$^{49}$ 5945 5-11-9 70 ... MrsEmmaLittmoden(3) 2 27
(NPLittmoden) *a struggling wl in rr* **8/1**

0060 **9** 1 **Prince Of Blues (IRE)**$^{20}$ 6138 5-11-5 70 ... MissMMullineaux(7) 1 24
(MMullineaux) *rrd up s: rdn and hdwy over 2f out: wknd over 1f out* **13/2**

3000 **10** 1 **Carols Choice**$^{7}$ 6217 6-9-10 40 oh1 ... MissEJJones 3 —
(ASadik) *led: rdn and hdd 2f out: weazkened over 1f out* **16/1**

1m 17.75s (2.05) **Going Correction** +0.275s/f (Slow) **10** Ran SP% **121.1**

Speed ratings: **97,89,87,85,80 78,75,70,69,68**CSF £37.99 CT £179.96 TOTE £6.10: £2.20, £2.20, £1.90; EX 46.60.

**Owner** James Unett **Bred** Francesco Magliari **Trained** Wolverhampton, W Midlands

**FOCUS**

A moderate handicap won well by Noble Locks, who was providing Jane Williams with her first winner.

**NOTEBOOK**

**Noble Locks(IRE)**, 3lb higher than when successful over course and distance in September, ran right away with this for a most decisive success. James Unett's horses are running well and he could well place this one to further success this winter.

**Amelia(IRE)**, well beaten in a seller at Southwell last time, was supported in the market and ran much better this time. However, the winner was too good.
**Dil** has yet to hit top form, but this was by no means a bad effort.
**Attorney** is very hard to win with.
**Sharp Hat**, claimed out of Dandy Nicholls' yard after his third in a claimer here last time, failed to give his true running on his first starts back for David Chapman.
**Cash** was below form and is probably a better horse over five furlongs.

## 6237 BET DIRECT NO Q ON 08000 93 66 93 CLAIMING STKS 6f (F)
2:15 (2:15) (F) 2-Y-O £2,037 (£582; £291) Stalls Low

Form RPR
4536 **1** **Tictactoe**[31] 6066 2-8-10 54 CCatlin 8 57
(DJDaly) *trckd ldrs: wnt 2nd over 2f out: c into centre of crse st: rdn to ld nr fin* **9/2**[2]
4542 **2** *nk* **Emaradia**[11] 6194 2-8-2 52 (b) JoannaBadger 9 48
(PDEvans) *styd on ins and mde most tl rdn and hdd nr fin* **9/2**[2]
6115 **3** *2 1/2* **Alizar (IRE)**[7] 6213 2-8-9 54 KGhunowa(7) 1 55
(MJPolglase) *mid-div: rdn 2f out: styd on one pce fnl f* **4/1**[1]
1150 **4** *1/2* **Back At De Front (IRE)**[9] 6207 2-8-7 74 MSavage(5) 5 49
(NEBerry) *chsd ldrs: ridde over 2f out: one pce after* **5/1**[3]
0003 **5** *3 1/2* **Stamford Blue**[6] 6223 2-8-0 45 (b) LisaJones(3) 3 30
(JSMoore) *outpcd in rr: styd on past btn horses ins fnl 2f* **8/1**
00 **6** *5* **Dandy Jim**[11] 6194 2-8-4 RBrisland 6 16
(DWChapman) *towards rr: hdwy on outside 1/2-way: wknd wl over 1f out* **50/1**
0 **7** *5* **Nanna (IRE)**[190] 2506 2-8-2 PaulEddery 4 —
(RHollinshead) *prom tl rdn 1/2-way: sn btn* **10/1**
0324 **8** *1 1/2* **Moscow Mary**[123] 4444 2-8-8 65 SWhitworth 2 —
(AGNewcombe) *outpcd thrght* **5/1**[3]
00 **9** *1 1/4* **Adriatic Adventure (IRE)**[183] 2714 2-8-6 ADaly 7 —
(JLSpearing) *a bhd* **20/1**

1m 18.08s (2.38) **Going Correction** +0.275s/f (Slow) **9** Ran SP% **116.6**
Speed ratings: **95,94,91,90,85 79,72,70,68**CSF £25.37 TOTE £6.80: £2.10, £1.70, £2.20; EX 28.80.
**Owner** Stormin Thoroughbreds **Bred** White Horse Bloodstock Ltd **Trained** Newmarket, Suffolk

**FOCUS**
A weak claimer.

**NOTEBOOK**
**Tictactoe** would have been 6lb better off at the weights with the runner-up had this been a handicap, but she was ideally suited by this drop back from a mile and ran out a game winner.
**Emaradia** has been kept pretty busy this season (this was her 20th start of the campaign) but, with the headgear back on, she ran well.
**Alizar(IRE)** has gained both her wins in selling company and had plenty to find at the weights with some of these.
**Back At De Front(IRE)** was the best in on official figures, but this effort suggests she is flattered by her rating of 74.
**Moscow Mary** ran below form on her first attempt on Fibresand.

## 6238 LITTLEWOODS BET DIRECT MAIDEN STKS 1m 100y(F)
2:50 (2:50) (D) 3-Y-O+ £2,236 (£639; £319) Stalls Low

Form RPR
-420 **1** **Forever Phoenix**[125] 4378 3-8-8 74 EAhern 8 58
(RMHCowell) *sn trckd ldr: led over 3f out: clr 2f out: flashed tail u.p ent fnl f: hrd rdn: all out* **2/1**[1]
0324 **2** *shd* **Givemethemoonlight**[7] 6214 4-8-9 46 CCatlin 2 58
(MrsStefLiddiard) *a in tch: chsd wnr over 2f out: hrd rdn and r.o gamely fnl f: jst failed* **7/1**
0535 **3** *5* **Danger Bird (IRE)**[17] 6153 3-8-8 50 IMongan 7 48
(RHollinshead) *in rr: rdn and hdwy on outside 3f out: kpt on: no ch w first 2* **16/1**
2424 **4** *9* **Jarraaf**[17] 6153 3-8-13 62 SWhitworth 3 34
(JWUnett) *hld up in tch: rdn over 3f out: wknd over 1f out* **11/4**[2]
206 **5** *2* **Best Before (IRE)**[128] 4281 3-8-6 68 SJDonohoe(7) 4 29
(PDEvans) *stdd s: rdn 1/2-way: nvr nr to chal* **9/2**[3]
-060 **6** *10* **Iamback**[242] 1266 3-8-4 44 ow1 (p) TEaves(5) 5 —
(MissGayKelleway) *led: hdd over 3f out: wknd over 2f out* **33/1**
00 **7** *5* **Ziggy Dan**[4] 6229 3-8-13 JoannaBadger 6 —
(MsDeborahJEvans) *rdn after 3f: bhd sn after* **50/1**
0434 **8** *27* **Pirouettes (IRE)**[9] 6205 3-8-9 50 ow1 (p) NCallan 1 —
(MissGayKelleway) *prom for 3f* **6/1**

1m 52.0s (1.00) **Going Correction** +0.275s/f (Slow)
**WFA** 3 from 4yo 1lb **8** Ran SP% **115.8**
Speed ratings: **106,105,100,91,89 79,74,47**CSF £17.16 TOTE £2.60: £1.70, £1.70, £2.50; EX 18.90.
**Owner** J M Greetham **Bred** J M Greetham **Trained** Six Mile Bottom, Cambs

**FOCUS**
A weak race in which the 74-rated winner failed to run to her mark, but was still good enough to prevail.

**NOTEBOOK**
**Forever Phoenix**, having her first start for new connections, had 32lb in hand of the runner-up at the weights and clearly failed by some way to run to her turf mark of 74. She is likely to need to improve to get competitive in handicaps, but may do if dropped back to around seven furlongs.
**Givemethemoonlight**, dropping back from a mile three, had plenty of find with the winner at the weights, but that one may not have seen out the trip and as a result she closed right the way to the line and was only just held. She has a minor race in her.
**Danger Bird(IRE)** is not progressing and was readily held by the front two.
**Jarraaf** failed to give his running and is better than he showed on this occasion.
**Best Before(IRE)**, a beaten favourite on his only previous try on Fibresand, once again failed to prove his effectiveness on this surface.
**Pirouettes(IRE)**, in cheekpieces for the first time, ran no sort of race at all. *Official explanation: trainer had no explanation for the poor form shown*

## 6239 BETDIRECT.CO.UK H'CAP 1m 1f 79y(F)
3:20 (3:20) (D) (0-85,71) 3-Y-O+ £3,346 (£956; £478) Stalls Low

Form RPR
0211 **1** **Compton Drake**[30] 6076 4-8-12 59 EAhern 1 76
(GAButler) *hld up in tch: stdy hdwy over 3f out: rdn over 2f out: led ent fnl f: r.o wl* **15/8**[1]
5053 **2** *2 1/2* **Just Wiz**[46] 5970 7-9-6 70 (b) J-PGuillambert(3) 5 82
(NPLittmoden) *t.k.h: hdwy 6f out: rdn over 2f out: styd on to chse wnr ins fnl f* **7/2**[3]
1122 **3** *1 1/2* **How's Things**[14] 6169 3-9-7 70 PaulEddery 4 79
(DHaydnJones) *trckd ldrs: wnt 2nd 5f out: led 2f out: hdd ent fnl f: wknd* **11/4**[2]
4303 **4** *5* **Traveller's Tale**[53] 5910 4-9-10 71 RHavlin 3 70
(PGMurphy) *led tl hdd 2f out: wknd over 1f out* **8/1**
0245 **5** *2 1/2* **Bond Millennium**[31] 6064 5-9-6 67 IMongan 6 61
(BSmart) *in rr: rdn 3f out: nvr on terms* **6/1**
5301 **6** *5* **Fight The Feeling**[35] 6040 5-8-10 57 (v) ADaly 2 41
(JWUnett) *plld hrd: trckd ldr to 5f out: rdn and sn bhd* **7/1**

2m 4.72s (1.82) **Going Correction** +0.275s/f (Slow)
**WFA** 3 from 4yo+ 2lb **6** Ran SP% **121.6**
Speed ratings: **102,99,98,94,91 87**CSF £9.82 TOTE £2.70: £2.00, £1.90; EX 9.80.
**Owner** Erik Penser **Bred** Meon Valley Stud **Trained** Blewbury, Oxon

**FOCUS**
A decent enough handicap won well by Compton Drake who looks one to keep on the right of.

**NOTEBOOK**
**Compton Drake** ◆ continued his progression with a clear-cut success over some reasonable yardsticks. The surface was not a problem and he remains one to keep on the right side of.
**Just Wiz** goes well round here and ran another solid race. The winner is probably just a better handicapped horse.
**How's Things** continues in good form, but is now 14lb higher than when last successful.
**Traveller's Tale**, making his Fibresand debut, ran well enough but was simply no match for the front three.
**Bond Millennium** ran below his best and has to be considered disappointing.

## 6240 BET DIRECT ON ATTHERACES INTERACTIVE (S) STKS 1m 4f (F)
3:50 (3:50) (G) 3-Y-O+ £2,037 (£582; £291) Stalls Low

Form RPR
5603 **1** **Delta Force**[10] 6198 4-8-11 41 DerekNolan(7) 4 51
(PABlockley) *t.k.h: a in tch on ins: edgd lft over 3f out: led over 2f out: drvn clr fnl f* **5/1**[3]
4040 **2** *4* **Shatin Special**[4] 6233 3-8-1 49 (p) DeanWilliams(7) 8 40
(GCHChung) *hld up early: hdwy 6f out: wnt 2nd over 2f out: no imp fnl f* **11/1**
5544 **3** *2* **Fairmorning (IRE)**[22] 6033 4-9-4 40 ADaly 5 42
(JWUnett) *a.p: led 5f out: hdd over 2f out: rdn and one pce appr fnl f* **16/1**
0600 **4** *1 3/4* **Red Delirium**[10] 6196 7-9-8 48 (bt) EAhern 9 43
(RBrotherton) *hld up: hdwy over 3f out: sn rdn: kpt on one pce* **16/1**
5400 **5** *1 1/2* **El Pedro**[18] 6148 4-9-3 47 MSavage(5) 10 41
(NEBerry) *hld up: hdwy 6f out: wknd over 1f out* **16/1**
-145 **6** *7* **Failed To Hit**[315] 536 10-9-8 (b) IMongan 6 31
(NPLittmoden) *led tl hdd 5f out: sn rdn: wkng whn hmpd over 3f out* **11/4**[1]
0414 **7** *1 1/2* **Aveiro (IRE)**[4] 6234 7-9-8 31 (p) CCatlin 3 28
(BGPowell) *trckd early ldr: rdn 5f out: steadily wknd* **10/3**[2]
0456 **8** *5* **Ipledgeallegiance (USA)**[35] 6040 7-9-8 48 RBrisland 2 21
(DWChapman) *a struggling in rr* **5/1**[3]
6620 **9** *14* **La Rose**[8] 4070 3-8-8 38 SWhitworth 7 —
(JWUnett) *s.i.s: a bhd: virtually t.o fnl 4f* **20/1**
0004 **10** *11* **Think Quick (IRE)**[86] 5304 3-8-1 40 (t) StephanieHollinshead(7) 1 —
(RHollinshead) *in tch tl wknd qckly 4f out: t.o* **7/1**

2m 44.07s (2.57) **Going Correction** +0.275s/f (Slow)
**WFA** 3 from 4yo+ 5lb **10** Ran SP% **126.3**
Speed ratings: **102,99,98,96,95 91,90,86,77,70**CSF £64.07 TOTE £8.30: £1.60, £6.90, £5.30; EX 129.20.The winner was bought in for 4,000gns.
**Owner** Miss Emma Shally **Bred** Thomas Shally Jnr **Trained** Southwell, Notts
■ This was Derek Nolan's first winner.

**FOCUS**
A moderate seller.

**NOTEBOOK**
**Delta Force**, third in a claimer at Southwell last time on his first start for six months, had plenty to find with some of these at the weights but, under a good ride from Derek Nolan, he won well and looks capable of further success.
**Shatin Special**, still a maiden, was the best in on official figures and ran well. However, the winner was far too good and she may need to improve to pick up a similar contest.
**Fairmorning(IRE)**, back on the level after an unsuccessful spin over hurdles, looked to have every chance but was simply not good enough.
**Red Delirium**, stepping up five furlongs in trip, and with the tongue-tie fitted for the first time since 2000, has yet to hit top form.
**Failed To Hit** goes well round here, but proved unable to overcome a 315-day absence.
**Aveiro(IRE)** had it all to do at the figures, but was below form in any case.
**Ipledgeallegiance(USA)**, dropping in grade, remains below form.

## 6241 LITTLEWOODSCASINO.COM H'CAP 1m 100y(F)
4:20 (4:21) (E) (0-70,69) 3-Y-O+ £2,170 (£620; £310) Stalls Low

Form RPR
2221 **1** **Mutarafaa (USA)**[7] 6211 4-8-4 53 6ex (e) PMakin(7) 6 64+
(DShaw) *trckd ldr: led 5f out: pushed out fnl f* **8/1**
1135 **2** *1 1/2* **Miss Champers (IRE)**[7] 6211 3-9-2 66 SJDonohoe(7) 2 74
(PDEvans) *rdn s to keep in tch: c u.p 3f out: kpt on to chse wnr fr over 1f out* **6/1**[3]
3460 **3** *1* **Quiet Reading (USA)**[13] 6178 6-9-11 67 (v) GBaker 11 73
(MRBosley) *mid-div: hdwy after 3f: rdn 3f out: kpt on one pce fnl f* **16/1**
1346 **4** *2 1/2* **Scramble (USA)**[13] 6176 5-8-3 50 (tp) THamilton(5) 10 51
(BEllison) *towards rr: rdn and hdwy over 4f out: styd on one pce ins fnl 2f* **7/1**
0300 **5** *1/2* **Danielle's Lad**[16] 6164 7-9-11 67 (b) NCallan 4 67
(BPalling) *a.p: ev ch over 1f out: wknd ins fnl f* **14/1**
2300 **6** *1/2* **Miss Glory Be**[18] 6148 5-8-9 56 (p) TEaves(5) 7 55
(MissGayKelleway) *trckd ldrs: rdn over 3f out: no hdwy fnl 2f* **14/1**
0200 **7** *8* **Hoh's Back**[31] 6070 4-9-8 64 (p) RFitzpatrick 12 46
(PaulJohnson) *in rr: hdwy on outside 6f out: rdn over 3f out: no hdwy fnl 2f* **12/1**
1002 **8** *nk* **Yorker (USA)**[4] 6231 5-9-10 66 EAhern 5 47
(MsDeborahJEvans) *led: hdd 5f out: sn wknd* **11/4**[1]
2000 **9** *hd* **Friday's Takings**[31] 6070 4-9-11 67 (b) RFfrench 8 48
(BSmart) *hld up in tch: rdn 3f out: wknd qckly* **14/1**
0110 **10** *5* **Pup's Pride**[14] 6171 6-9-1 60 (v) LisaJones(3) 9 30
(MrsNMacauley) *a struggling in rr* **10/1**
0100 **11** *3/4* **Pharoah's Gold (IRE)**[14] 6169 5-9-6 62 (e) SWhitworth 13 31
(DShaw) *a bhd* **8/1**
6060 **12** *13* **Jungle Lion**[14] 6171 5-8-10 52 (t) CCatlin 1 —
(JohnAHarris) *a bhd: t.o* **33/1**
0002 **13** *dist* **Hugh The Man (IRE)**[20] 6140 4-9-13 69 (p) IMongan 3 —
(NPLittmoden) *in tch for 2f: sn bhd: t.o* **5/1**[2]

1m 51.64s (0.64) **Going Correction** +0.275s/f (Slow)
**WFA** 3 from 4yo+ 1lb **13** Ran SP% **137.9**
Speed ratings: **107,105,104,102,101 101,93,92,92,87 86,73,—**CSF £64.43 CT £820.35 TOTE £11.10: £3.60, £3.40, £4.80; EX 47.70 Place 6 £158.55, Place 5 £38.73.
**Owner** J C Fretwell **Bred** Shadwell Farm Llc **Trained** Averham, Notts

**FOCUS**
A competitive little handicap run at a decent gallop.


The Form Book, Raceform Ltd, Compton, RG20 6NL

**NOTEBOOK**
**Mutarafaa(USA)** finally got his head back in front at Southwell last time and showed what a win can do for a horse's confidence with a decisive victory. He looks one to keep on the right side of for the time being.
**Miss Champers(IRE)** is holding her form really well and this was another highly-creditable effort. She remains below her highest winning mark of 70 and is one to keep on the right side of. She may also be worth another try over further.
**Quiet Reading(USA)** posted an encouraging effort back in third and, a multiple Fibresand winner, he should pay his way this winter.
**Scramble(USA)**, with the cheekpieces on instead of blinkers and eyeshields, and stepping up in trip and dropping in grade, he ran respectably.
**Danielle's Lad** has never won on this surface.
**Yorker(USA)** failed to build on his encouraging effort over seven furlongs here last time. *Official explanation: trainer said gelding was unable to dictate the pace in front without competition*
**Hugh The Man(IRE)** was as though something was amiss.
T/Plt: £562.30 to a £1 stake. Pool: £26,846.80. 34.85 winning tickets. T/Qpdt: £26.40 to a £1 stake. Pool: £1,660.00. 46.40 winning tickets. JS

## 6211 SOUTHWELL (L-H)
Saturday, December 27

**OFFICIAL GOING: Standard**
Wind: Fresh, hlf' bhd. Weather: Overcast and cold

### 6242 BETDIRECT.CO.UK NURSERY — 1m (F)
12:55 (12:55) (D ) (0-85,84) 2-Y-O — £2,999 (£857; £428) Stalls Low

Form — RPR
5051 **1** **Nessen Dorma (IRE)**[19] 6145 2-8-6 **69** — IMongan 10 — 76
(JGGiven) *racd wd: in rr and pushed along 1/2-way: gd hdwy over 2f out: sn rdn: str run fr over 1f out to ld last 100 yds* **7/1**
6421 **2** *1* **Kingsmaite**[8] 6216 2-8-11 **74** 5ex — JBramhill 3 — 79+
(SRBowring) *trckd ldrs: hdwy on inner over 2f out: led on bit wl over 1f out: rdn ent last: hdd and nt qckn last 100 yds* **3/1**[1]
041 **3** *2 1/2* **Bold Blade**[14] 6173 2-8-7 **70** — (b) RFfrench 9 — 70
(BSmart) *led: rdn along over 2f out: hdd wl over 1f out: sn drvn and one pce* **12/1**
3211 **4** *1/2* **Countrywide Flyer (IRE)**[33] 6059 2-9-5 **82** — NCallan 4 — 80
(TDBarron) *trckd ldr: effrt to chal over 2f out and sn ev ch: rdn wl over 1f out and wknd ent last* **10/3**[2]
0113 **5** *1 1/2* **Myannabanana (IRE)**[14] 6173 2-7-11 **67** — (v) DFentiman(7) 11 — 62
(JRWeymes) *hld up: hdwy over 2f out: styd on appr last: nrst fin* **16/1**
020 **6** *3 1/2* **Stonor Lady (USA)**[28] 6090 2-7-9 **61** oh5 — LisaJones(3) 2 — 48
(PWD'Arcy) *dwlt: sn chsng ldrs: rdn along wl over 2f out and sn one pce* **33/1**
41 **7** *7* **Atlantic Breeze**[19] 6142 2-8-5 **68** ow3 — LEnstone(3) 8 — 43
(MrsNMacauley) *nvr nr ldrs* **20/1**
0004 **8** *5* **Cottingham (IRE)**[8] 6216 2-7-12 **61** oh1 — JoannaBadger 6 — 22
(MCChapman) *chsd ldrs on outer: rdn along 1/2-way: sn wknd* **20/1**
1142 **9** *nk* **Freak Occurence (IRE)**[7] 6222 2-9-7 **84** — SDrowne 5 — 44
(MissECLavelle) *prom: rdn along 3f out: sn wknd* **7/2**[3]
5542 **10** *2 1/2* **Mrs Gee (IRE)**[19] 6142 2-8-2 **65** — CCatlin 1 — 20
(RHollinshead) *a rr: bhd fr 1/2-way* **11/1**
0012 **11** *1 3/4* **Weet An Haul**[11] 6197 2-7-12 **61** oh6 ow5 — RThomas(5) 7 — 17
(PABlockley) *chsd ldrs on outer: rdn along over 3f out: sn wknd* **25/1**

1m 45.15s (0.55) **Going Correction** +0.075s/f (Slow) — **11** Ran SP% **121.0**
Speed ratings: **100,99,96,96,94 91,84,79,78,76 74**CSF £27.72 CT £261.35 TOTE £8.90: £3.10, £1.60, £3.40; EX 52.50.
**Owner** Hokey Cokey Partnership **Bred** Robinski Bloodstock Limited **Trained** Willoughton, Lincs
■ Stewards Enquiry : I Mongan three-day ban: careless riding (Jan 7-9)

**FOCUS**
Probably a fair nursery with the front four home all winners last time.

**NOTEBOOK**
**Nessen Dorma(IRE)**, a winner in maiden company when upped to a mile for the first time, made some good progress around the outside of the field before turning in and stayed on strongly up the straight to win going away. He is clearly on the up and one could not rule out the hat-trick.
**Kingsmaite** had a similar profile to the winner coming into the race but found his finishing kick too much.
**Bold Blade** seems to appreciate this trip and may get further.
**Countrywide Flyer(IRE)**, on a hat-trick coming into the race, had every chance but did not seem good enough on the day.
**Myannabanana(IRE)** kept on from the rear without making any real impression.
**Stonor Lady(USA)** improved on this handicap debut and should progress again when granted a stiffer test.
**Freak Occurence(IRE)** was the disappointment of the race, tiring up the straight having been up there early.

### 6243 BET DIRECT NO Q ON 08000 93 66 93 CLAIMING STKS — 5f (F)
1:30 (1:32) (F) 3-Y-O+ — £2,121 (£606; £303) Stalls High

Form — RPR
0000 **1** **Ladies Knight**[15] 6166 3-8-8 54 — THamilton(5) 11 — 56
(DShaw) *chsd ldrs centre: hdwy 2f out: rdn over 1f out: styd on to ld wl ins last* **20/1**
0010 **2** *1* **River Lark (USA)**[93] 5178 4-8-8 47 — RFfrench 2 — 48
(MABuckley) *cl up: led after 1 1/2f: rdn 2f out: drvn over 1f out: hdd and no ex wl ins last* **11/1**
0056 **3** *1/2* **Fiennes (USA)**[18] 6150 5-7-12 42 — (v) StevenHarrison(7) 10 — 44
(MrsNMacauley) *towards rr: hdwy wl over 1f out: styd on strly ins last: nrst fin* **14/1**
2000 **4** *nk* **Mr Spliffy (IRE)**[18] 6155 4-8-2 49 — (v) AReilly(7) 3 — 47
(KRBurke) *cl up: ev ch 2f out: sn rdn and nt qckn ins last* **11/2**[3]
0006 **5** *shd* **Best Lead**[18] 6149 4-8-10 53 — (b[1]) DFentiman(7) 14 — 54
(IanEmmerson) *racd stands side: in tch: rdn over 1f out: kpt on ins last* **14/1**
0054 **6** *1 1/2* **Aintnecessarilyso**[18] 6150 5-8-12 43 — MSavage(5) 7 — 50
(NEBerry) *slowy into strie and bhd: hdwy over 1f out: sn rdn and kpt on ins last: nrst fin* **16/1**
6350 **7** *1 1/4* **Malahide Express (IRE)**[11] 6199 3-8-12 64 — (b) MNem(7) 1 — 48
(MJPolglase) *dwlt: in tch far side: kpt on same pce fnl 2f* **7/2**[1]
0040 **8** *3/4* **Cark**[8] 6217 5-8-9 45 — JEdmunds 12 — 36
(JBalding) *chsd ldrs centre: rdn wl over 1f out and sn one pce* **5/1**[2]
0406 **9** *3/4* **College Hippie**[15] 6170 4-8-5 45 — SJDonohoe(7) 13 — 37
(JFCoupland) *in tch centre: rdn along 2f out and sn no hdwy* **15/2**
0000 **10** *shd* **Aguila Loco (IRE)**[117] 4628 4-8-0 36 — AndrewWebb(7) 9 — 31
(MCChapman) *chsd ldrs centre: rdn 2f out: grad wknd* **33/1**
3030 **11** *1/2* **New Prospective**[109] 4806 5-8-10 45 — LTreadwell(7) 4 — 40
(DNicholls) *in tch far side: rdn along 1/2-way: sn wknd* **11/1**
0606 **12** *2* **Tuscan Dream**[189] 2589 8-8-7 41 ow3 — PBradley(5) 5 — 29
(ABerry) *led 1 1/2f: prom tl rdn 2f out and sn wknd* **12/1**
0000 **13** *1 3/4* **Above Board**[18] 6155 8-8-9 38 — (p) DeanMcKeown 15 — 21
(RFMarvin) *a bhd stands side* **50/1**
0000 **14** *nk* **Blunham**[8] 6218 3-8-9 48 — IMongan 6 — 20
(MCChapman) *midfield: bhd fr 1/2-way* **33/1**
0000 **15** *3* **Goodwood Promise**[18] 6155 4-8-13 33 — (b[1]) CCatlin 8 — 15
(NEBerry) *chsd ldrs centre to 1/2-way: sn wknd* **66/1**

61.10 secs (0.80) **Going Correction** +0.125s/f (Slow) — **15** Ran SP% **123.7**
Speed ratings: **98,96,95,95,94 92,90,89,88,88 87,84,81,80,75**CSF £222.71 TOTE £25.10: £6.20, £3.40, £4.20; EX 344.40.
**Owner** Swann Racing Ltd **Bred** Mark C Collins And Keith West **Trained** Averham, Notts

**FOCUS**
A competitve claiming stakes that caused a bit of a surprise result.

**NOTEBOOK**
**Ladies Knight**, who all but refused to race at the course last time, was fine on this occasion and showed what he can do when he puts his mind to it, winning with a little in hand. This was his second career success from 22 attempts but does not appeal as one to bank on for a follow-up.
**River Lark(USA)** ran well on this first start since September and is entitled to come on for the outing.
**Fiennes(USA)** ran well on this drop back to five furlongs but has only won twice in 50 starts.
**Mr Spliffy(IRE)** ran well enough but only has one win in 49 starts.
**Best Lead** ran his best race for a while and could be winning when upped back up to six furlongs.
**Aintnecessarilyso** would have been closer but for a sluggish start.
**Malahide Express(IRE)** never got into it.
**Cark** disappointed on this drop back down to a more suitable trip.

### 6244 BET DIRECT NO Q ON 08000 93 66 93 MAIDEN STKS — 6f (F)
2:00 (2:02) (D ) 3-Y-O+ — £2,240 (£640; £320) Stalls Low

Form — RPR
3533 **1** **Wainwright (IRE)**[15] 6170 3-9-0 60 — GParkin 9 — 64
(PABlockley) *hld up in rr: wd st: gd hdwy 2f out: rdn and styd on wl to ld ins last: sn clr* **11/4**[1]
26-6 **2** *1 3/4* **Shadowfax**[38] 6031 3-9-0 67 — NCallan 3 — 59
(MissGayKelleway) *trckd ldrs: hdwy to chse ldr 2f out: rdn to ld over 1f out hdd and nt qckn ins last* **3/1**[2]
6030 **3** *1 1/2* **Lake Eyre (IRE)**[5] 6232 4-8-9 39 — JEdmunds 10 — 49
(JBalding) *prom: rdn along and sltly outpcd 2f out: kpt on u.p ins last* **20/1**
043 **4** *3/4* **Lucius Verrus (USA)**[10] 6209 3-8-9 — THamilton(5) 6 — 52
(DShaw) *hld up: hdwy 2f out: sn rdn and kpt on: nrst fin* **7/1**
3440 **5** *1* **Dark Champion**[10] 6209 3-9-0 56 — IMongan 13 — 49
(JeddO'Keeffe) *chsd ldrs: rdn and n.m.r over 1f out: kpt on same pce* **10/1**
6462 **6** *1 3/4* **Inching**[5] 6232 3-8-9 53 — SDrowne 2 — 39
(RMHCowell) *s.i.s: sn in tch: rdn 2f out and sn one pce* **5/1**[3]
2460 **7** *1/2* **Roan Raider (USA)**[38] 6031 3-8-7 42 — (vt) KGhunowa(7) 1 — 42
(MJPolglase) *in tch: hdwy on inner to chse ldrs 2f out: sn rdn: swtchd rt over 1f out and no imp* **40/1**
3646 **8** *3/4* **Victory Flip (IRE)**[5] 6232 3-8-9 52 — (p) DaneO'Neill 4 — 35
(RHollinshead) *dwlt and snswtchd to r wd: a rr* **8/1**
0050 **9** *1/2* **Somethingabouther**[29] 6080 3-8-9 40 — CCatlin 7 — 34
(PWHiatt) *cl up: ev ch 2f out: sn rdn and wknd ent last* **40/1**
4020 **10** *2 1/2* **Kustom Kit For Her**[18] 6153 3-8-9 53 — (b) JBramhill 8 — 26
(SRBowring) *led: rdn 2f out: hdd & wknd over 1f out* **40/1**
0000 **11** *1 1/2* **Subtle Move (USA)**[10] 6204 3-8-6 35 — LisaJones(3) 5 — 22
(DShaw) *a rr* **80/1**
6003 **12** *9* **Granuaile O'Malley (IRE)**[102] 4971 3-8-9 50 — PaulEddery 12 — —
(PWD'Arcy) *bhd fr 1/2-way* **20/1**
00 **13** *7* **Wentbridge Boy**[54] 5907 3-9-0 — DRMcCabe 11 — —
(JO'Reilly) *a bhd* **50/1**

1m 17.72s (0.92) **Going Correction** +0.075s/f (Slow) — **13** Ran SP% **121.1**
Speed ratings: **96,93,91,90,89 87,86,85,84,81 79,67,58**CSF £10.41 TOTE £4.70: £1.40, £1.70, £7.20; EX 10.80.
**Owner** David Wright **Bred** Tony Lewis **Trained** Southwell, Notts

**FOCUS**
A weak race full of frustrating types.

**NOTEBOOK**
**Wainwright(IRE)** was winning at the 14th attempt and did it nicely. This was a weak race though and he would not be one to bank on in a better event.
**Shadowfax** reversed form with Dark Champion and lost nothing in defeat.
**Lake Eyre(IRE)** remains a maiden after 19 starts.
**Lucius Verrus(USA)** improved on previous form on this handicap debut and will improve when stepped back up in trip.
**Dark Champion** would have been a tad closer but for being short of room over a furlong out.
**Inching** was a one-paced sixth.

### 6245 LITTLEWOODS BET DIRECT H'CAP — 1m (F)
2:35 (2:37) (D ) (0-85,82) 3-Y-O+ — £3,458 (£988; £494) Stalls Low

Form — RPR
1365 **1** **Estimation**[19] 6146 3-8-10 **66** — SDrowne 12 — 75
(RMHCowell) *in tch: wd st: hdwy over 2f out: sn rdn and styd on to ld 1f out: kpt on* **9/1**
3060 **2** *3/4* **First Maite**[15] 6169 10-9-1 **70** — DaneO'Neill 8 — 78
(SRBowring) *hld up: swtchd outside and wd st: gd hdwy wl over 1f out: sn rdn and str run ins last: fin wl* **12/1**
0452 **3** *nk* **Brandy Cove**[14] 6178 6-8-10 **65** — RFfrench 5 — 72
(BSmart) *chsd ldrs on inner: hdwy to chal 2f out: sn led and rdn: drvn and hdd 1f out: kpt on* **3/1**[1]
606 **4** *3 1/2* **Middleton Grey**[47] 5967 5-9-13 **82** — SWhitworth 6 — 82
(AGNewcombe) *dwlt: sn in midfield: sltly outpcd 3f out:gd hdwy 2f out: tenderly rdn and n.m.r over 1f out: kpt on ins last* **10/1**
0100 **5** *3* **Barzak (IRE)**[24] 6124 3-8-12 **68** — (p) JBramhill 11 — 62
(SRBowring) *cl up: rdn over 2f out and grad wknd* **12/1**
2342 **6** *3 1/2* **Shifty**[11] 6196 4-7-13 **54** — (b) JoannaBadger 2 — 41
(DNicholls) *led after 1f: rdn along and hdd 3f out: sn wknd* **4/1**[2]
0-20 **7** *1* **Polar Kingdom**[45] 5976 5-8-10 **72** — PMakin(7) 10 — 57
(TDBarron) *cl up: led 3f out: rdn 2f out: sn hdd & wknd over 1f out* **11/2**[3]
0010 **8** *8* **Riska King**[154] 3611 3-9-0 **75** — THamilton(5) 4 — 44
(RAFahey) *hld up: a bhd* **16/1**
5000 **9** *2 1/2* **Haithem (IRE)**[101] 5001 6-7-9 **53** oh17 — (e) LisaJones(3) 1 — 17
(DShaw) *a b ehind* **66/1**
0000 **10** *3/4* **Lakelands Lady (IRE)**[49] 5946 3-9-7 **77** — JEdmunds 3 — 40
(JBalding) *led 1f: cl up tl rdn along 3f out and sn wknd* **25/1**

6520 **11** *10* **North By Northeast (IRE)**[89] [5276] 5-8-9 **64** ow2................(p) NCallan 9 7
(JWPayne) *a rr* **8/1**

1m 44.58s (-0.02) **Going Correction** +0.075s/f (Slow)
**WFA** 3 from 4yo+ 1lb **11** Ran SP% **117.2**
Speed ratings: **103,102,101,98,95 91,90,82,80,79 69**CSF £111.53 CT £411.13 TOTE £12.30: £2.40, £2.90, £2.10; EX 50.50.
**Owner** Bottisham Heath Stud **Bred** Bottisham Heath Stud **Trained** Six Mile Bottom, Cambs

**FOCUS**
A competitive handicap run at a decent pace and again the centre of the track was the place to be.

**NOTEBOOK**
**Estimation**, no better off with Brandy Cove for a three-and-a-half-length beating here last month, again took a keen grip early but his rider eventually managed to settle him. Once into the straight, he was brought down the centre of the track which was a wise move and almost certainly won him the race.
**First Maite**is on a long losing run, but put up another decent effort and was finishing in good style. He finds this trip the absolute minimum for him these days and would probably be better suited by the extended nine furlongs at Wolverhampton.
**Brandy Cove**should have won this. On a day when it was a big advantage to race down the middle of the track, his rider elected to give the inside rail away to no-one and despite that he was still only worn down well inside the last furlong. He is running well enough to win a race when things go his way, and these are his ideal conditions.
**Middleton Grey**remains 4lb above his highest winning mark, but was by no means knocked about and gave the impression he could have finished much closer under a more vigorous ride. He is one to watch out for when the market speaks in his favour. *Official explanation: jockey said, regarding the running and riding, gelding was having to be pushed along throughout and finished tired, and his saddle had slipped back marginally*
**Barzak(IRE)**, not the most consistent of sorts, was up there from the start but faded tamely over the last quarter-mile despite having the kitchen sink thrown at him.
**Shifty**was given a much more positive ride over this longer trip, but the tactic did not work and he capitulated tamely once headed.
**Polar Kingdom**did not appear to see the trip out on this slow surface and reportedly bled from the nose. *Official explanation: vet said gelding had bled from the nose*

## 6246 BET DIRECT ON ATTHERACES INTERACTIVE (S) STKS 5f (F)
3:10 (3:10) (G ) 2-Y-O £2,002 (£572; £286) Stalls High

Form RPR
5441 **1** **Smart Starprincess (IRE)**[8] [6212] 2-8-12 58......................(b) NCallan 2 58
(PABlockley) *qckly away and mde all: sn clr: rdn appr last and kpt on* **4/5**[1]
00 **2** *1 3/4* **Brave Chief**[47] [5968] 2-8-12 ......................................... DeanMcKeown 6 52
(JAPickering) *dwlt: sn chsng ldrs: rdn along wl over 1f out: kpt on ins last* **40/1**
4325 **3** *1/2* **Philly Dee**[12] [6194] 2-8-7 47....................................................... IMongan 1 45
(JJay) *chsd wnr: rdn wl over 1f out: drvn and edgd lft ins last* **4/1**[2]
6426 **4** *1 3/4* **Fisher's Dream**[12] [6194] 2-8-12 54......................................(v) JBramhill 3 44
(JRNorton) *dwlt: sn chsng ldrs: rdn along 2f out and sn one pce* **12/1**
0003 **5** *2* **Siegfrieds Night (IRE)**[8] [6212] 2-8-5 48..................... AndrewWebb(7) 5 37
(MCChapman) *nvr nrldrs* **25/1**
5463 **6** *shd* **Blue Moon Hitman (IRE)**[24] [6122] 2-8-12 49....................... SDrowne 7 37
(ABerry) *chsd ldrs: rdn wl over 1f out: sn wknd* **9/2**[3]
0530 **7** *7* **Burkees Graw (IRE)**[11] [6201] 2-8-10 60....................(b1) LTreadwell(7) 9 17
(DNicholls) *dwlt and wnt lft s: sn rdn along and bhd fr 1/2-way* **16/1**
0P00 **8** *hd* **Shamone**[24] [6122] 2-8-9 28...............................................(p) LisaJones(3) 4 11
(HAMcwilliams) *chsd ldrs: rdn along and lost pl after 2f: sn bhd* **66/1**
3400 **9** *8* **Quidnet**[76] [5512] 2-8-7 46.................................................(p) RFitzpatrick 8 —
(PaulJohnson) *sn outpcd and a bhd* **33/1**

61.51 secs (1.21) **Going Correction** +0.125s/f (Slow) **9** Ran SP% **118.0**
Speed ratings: **95,92,91,88,85 85,74,73,60**CSF £53.51 TOTE £1.70: £1.10, £4.90, £1.20; EX 42.90.There was no bid for the winner
**Owner** Brooklands Racing **Bred** Norelands Bloodstock **Trained** Southwell, Notts

**FOCUS**
A modest seller unlikely to throw up many future winners.

**NOTEBOOK**
**Smart Starprincess(IRE)**adopted the same tactics that saw her win here last time and virtually won the race at the start. She is nothing special and has been fortunate to find a couple of especially weak contests. Things will be tougher for her now.
**Brave Chief**, who has looked a very hard ride in his previous two starts, was more gathered this time and never stopped trying. He is probably the only one in this race with any potential for improvement and will appreciate a return to six.
**Philly Dee**is an exposed plater and merely ran up to her form.
**Fisher's Dream**is only moderate, but does look to need further.
**Blue Moon Hitman(IRE)**continues to struggle to see out the trip.

## 6247 LITTLEWOODSCASINO.COM H'CAP 1m 4f (F)
3:40 (3:42) (E ) (0-70,72) 3-Y-O+ £2,114 (£604; £302) Stalls Low

Form RPR
6043 **1** **Stravmour**[12] [6195] 7-8-2 **43**............................................. DaleGibson 12 56
(RHollinshead) *midfield: hdwy to chse ldrs over 4f out: rdn and nt clr run 2f out: swtchd rtand drvn over 1f out: kpt on to ld last 100 yd* **14/1**
2521 **2** *3/4* **Victory Quest (IRE)**[12] [6195] 3-9-12 **72** 7ex.....................(v) DaneO'Neill 9 84
(MrsSLamyman) *cl up: led over 4f out: rdn and edgd lft 2f out: sn drvn: hdd and no ex last 100 yds* **6/1**[3]
4402 **3** *3/4* **Trouble Mountain (USA)**[12] [6190] 6-9-9 **69**............... PMulrennan(5) 13 80
(MWEasterby) *hld up and wl bhd: hdwy over 3f out: rdn wl over 1f out: str run ent last: fin wl: too much to do* **5/2**[1]
0243 **4** *nk* **Court Of Appeal**[18] [6156] 6-9-7 **67**.................................(t) THamilton(5) 7 77
(BEllison) *hld up and bhd: stdy hdwy 5f out: rdn to chse ldrs over 1f out: sn drvn and kpt on* **4/1**[2]
0000 **5** *1 1/4* **Surdoue**[14] [6178] 3-9-5 **65**............................................... PaulEddery 6 73
(PHowling) *trckd ldng pair: effrt 3f out: rdn to chal 2f out and ev ch tl drvn: edgd rt and wknd ent last* **66/1**
631- **6** *3* **Marmaduke (IRE)**[526] [3078] 7-9-6 **61**.................................. SDrowne 14 64
(MPitman) *in tch: smooth hdwy to chse ldrs over 4f out: rdn 3f out and grad wknd fnl 2f* **8/1**
5400 **7** *1 1/2* **King Priam (IRE)**[120] [4542] 8-7-5 **39** oh5............................(b) MNem(7) 5 40
(MJPolglase) *towards rr: hdwy on inner 4f out: styd on fnl 2f: nrst fin* **33/1**
3445 **8** *shd* **East Cape**[32] [6068] 6-8-1 **42**............................................... KimTinkler 8 43
(DonEnricoIncisa) *chsd ldrs: rdn along 3f out: one pce fnl 2f* **12/1**
0000 **9** *11* **Interstice**[36] [6043] 6-8-13 **54**.............................................. SWhitworth 15 37
(AGNewcombe) *hld up: hdwy on outer 1/2-way: chsd ldrs 4f out: rdn along 3f out and sn wknd* **12/1**
0300 **10** *11* **Ersaal (USA)**[12] [6190] 3-8-3 **52**.....................................(b1) LisaJones(3) 1 18
(JJay) *s.i.s: a rr* **33/1**
0014 **11** *1/2* **Dubai Dreams**[12] [6195] 3-8-5 **58**.................................(v) KGhunowa(7) 3 23
(MJPolglase) *led: rdn along and hdd over 4f out: wknd 3f out* **7/1**
0000 **12** *4* **Iloveturtle (IRE)**[11] [6200] 3-7-13 **45**............................ JoannaBadger 10 3
(MCChapman) *chsd ldrs: rdn along over 5f out: sn wknd* **25/1**
2445 **13** *dist* **Moyne Pleasure (IRE)**[192] [2468] 5-8-5 **46**......................... RFitzpatrick 4 —
(PaulJohnson) *a rr* **25/1**
1006 **14** *hd* **Humdinger (IRE)**[5] [6234] 3-9-0 **60**...................................... NCallan 2 —
(DShaw) *chsd ldrs on inner: rdn along 1/2-way: sn lost pl and bhd* **40/1**
4000 **15** *5* **Blue Rondo (IRE)**[21] [6131] 3-9-0 **60**...................................... CCatlin 11 —
(IanWilliams) *a bhd* **25/1**

2m 41.57s (-0.53) **Going Correction** +0.075s/f (Slow)
**WFA** 3 from 5yo+ 5lb **15** Ran SP% **129.9**
Speed ratings: **104,103,103,102,101 99,98,98,91,84 83,81,—,—,—**CSF £96.84 CT £292.05 TOTE £20.40: £4.10, £3.40, £2.20; EX 123.70 Place 6 £120.62, Place 5 £49.37..
**Owner** E Bennion **Bred** E Bennion **Trained** Upper Longdon, Staffs

**FOCUS**
A competitive handicap run at a sound pace.

**NOTEBOOK**
**Stravmour**, 13lb better off Victory Quest for a beating of just under five lengths over an extra two furlongs here last time, was off the bridle virtually from the start and Gibson certainly earned his fee. He did not give up even when his run was blocked against the inside rail two furlongs out, and his persistence eventually paid off.
**Victory Quest(IRE)**, carrying a 7lb penalty and stepping back in trip, was rightly given a positive ride and kept on battling down the straight despite racing on the slower ground next to the inside rail.
**Trouble Mountain(USA)**was given an extraordinary ride, giving his rivals a healthy start and his jockey seemed in no hurry to make up the ground. When he did eventually take off, it was much too late and this is not a race his young rider will look back on with any great satisfaction.
**Court Of Appeal**, 19lb better off with Victory Quest for a four-length beating over a quarter-mile further here last time, managed to get closer though his overall Flat record shows that he is a very difficult horse to win with.
**Surdoue**is yet to win beyond seven furlongs, but he is tumbling down the handicap and ran his best race so far over middle distances.
**Marmaduke(IRE)**, racing for the first time in 17 months, had every chance and it was only inside the final furlong that he blew up. Given time to recover, he can win races on this surface and he stays much further than this.
**Humdinger(IRE)** *Official explanation: jockey said filly hung left-handed throughout*
T/Plt: £123.40 to a £1 stake. Pool: £32,278.45. 190.80 winning tickets. T/Qpdt: £4.50 to a £1 stake. Pool: £2,026.30. 326.60 winning tickets. JR

# 6219 LINGFIELD (L-H)
## Monday, December 29

**OFFICIAL GOING: Standard**
Wind: almost nil Weather: murky & drizzly

## 6248 BET DIRECT NO Q ON 08000 93 66 93 MAIDEN STKS (DIV I) 6f (P)
12:00 (12:00) (D ) 2-Y-O £2,982 (£852; £426) Stalls Low

Form RPR
6622 **1** **Smokin Joe**[12] [6207] 2-9-0 69..................................................... NPollard 2 66+
(JRBest) *chsd ldng pair: rdn 2f out: effrt over 1f out: hung fire but drvn to ld last 150y: kpt on* **5/1**[3]
2243 **2** *1 1/4* **Phluke**[21] [6141] 2-9-0 73............................................................... SCarson 1 62
(RFJohnsonHoughton) *w ldr: led on inner over 3f out: rdn 2f out: hdd and fdd last 150y* **6/1**
005 **3** *hd* **Saviours Spirit**[59] [5850] 2-8-9 77............................................ RMiles(5) 6 62
(TGMills) *chsd ldrs: rdn and nt qckn 2f out: kpt on ins fnl f : nvr able to chal* **4/1**[2]
**4** *1/2* **Tony The Tap** 2-9-0 ........................................................... WRyan 9 60
(NACallaghan) *squeezed out s: sn last and 5l bhd remainder: clsd over 2f out: pushed along and styd on wl fr over 1f out: nvr nrr: improv* **25/1**
565 **5** *1* **Red Rocky**[14] [6191] 2-8-9 52............................................................. PDoe 5 52
(JGallagher) *led to over 3f out: styd w ldr: rdn 2f out: flashed tail after and ref to go past: wknd fnl f* **33/1**
2352 **6** *1* **After All (IRE)**[33] [6077] 2-8-9 64..........................................(b1) EAhern 8 49
(GAButler) *hld up in tch: trckd ldrs gng easily over 2f out: rdn and nt run on 2f out: no ch after* **11/2**
63 **7** *2 1/2* **Docklands Blue (IRE)**[45] [5997] 2-8-6 ........................ J-PGuillambert(3) 4 42
(NPLittmoden) *in tch in rr: rdn 3f out: sn outpcd: plodded on* **14/1**
**8** *2 1/2* **Noble Desert (FR)** 2-8-9 ..................................................... SDrowne 3 34
(RGuest) *dwlt: in tch in rr tl wknd 2f out* **33/1**
**9** *2 1/2* **Nossenko (USA)** 2-8-9 ............................................................. DaneO'Neill 7 27
(JNoseda) *trckd ldrs: pushed along 1/2-way: rdn and wknd over 2f out* **9/4**[1]
00 **10** *20* **Tomokim (IRE)**[87] [5342] 2-9-0 ............................................. RWinston 10 —
(MQuinn) *racd on wd outside: chsd ldrs: drvn over 3f out: sn wknd: t.o* **100/1**

1m 14.55s (1.63) **Going Correction** +0.20s/f (Slow) **10** Ran SP% **114.5**
Speed ratings: **97,95,95,94,93 91,88,85,81,55**CSF £33.22 TOTE £5.20: £1.10, £2.30, £2.10; EX 16.10.
**Owner** Pennywise Racing Ltd **Bred** Alan Spargo Ltd **Trained** Hucking, Kent

**FOCUS**
Probably a fair maiden where fourth-placed horse Tony The Tap really caught the eye.

**NOTEBOOK**
**Smokin Joe**, who has run well the last twice, continued his good run of form with his first-ever win. He did it with plenty to spare despite looking a little hesitant and is the type to win back in handicap company.
**Phluke** ideally wants further and ran well considering. *Official explanation: trainer said gelding had lost a shoe behind*
**Saviours Spirit** had shown plenty of promise in better races on the turf during the summer and made a pleasing All-Weather debut. He will be winning when upped to seven furlongs.
**Tony The Tap** made a most promising debut, losing ground at the start having been squeezed for room and racing detached from the main group until picking up strongly down the straight and finishing with a purpose. On this evidence he is the one to take from the race. *Official explanation: jockey said gelding had been badly hampered at the start*
**Red Rocky** has got ability but was always going to face a stiff task in making all.
**After All(IRE)** did not look too keen to get on with the job once coming under pressure in the first-time blinkers.
**Nossenko(USA)** proved most disappointing but is entitled to come on for this debut effort.

## 6249 LITTLEWOODS BET DIRECT AW JOCKEYS CHAMPIONSHIP H'CAP (DIV I) 1m 5f (P)
12:30 (12:30) (F ) (0-65,65) 3-Y-O+ £2,058 (£588; £294) Stalls Low

Form RPR
0131 **1** **Royal Prodigy (USA)**[31] [6085] 4-9-12 **63**.......................... DaneO'Neill 10 71
(RJHodges) *settled towards rr: pushed along 6f out: prog u.p 3f out: chsd clr ldr ins fnl f: styd on to ld last strides* **7/1**[3]
5352 **2** *nk* **Reminiscent (IRE)**[14] [6195] 4-10-0 **65**.................................(b) SCarson 6 73
(RFJohnsonHoughton) *prog to trck ldr 6f out: rdn 4f out: led over 2f out and sn kicked 4l clr on inner: wknd and hdd last strides* **11/2**[2]

4006 **3** 1¾ **Makarim (IRE)**[7] 6233 7-9-4 **60**......(p) HayleyTurner(5) 2 66
(MRBosley) *racd in midfield: rdn and nt qckn over 3f out: no prog tl r.o over 1f out: chsd ldng pair last 100y: clsng at fin* **20/1**

0103 **4** 1¼ **Compton Eclaire (IRE)**[7] 6233 3-8-9 **52**...... EAhern 3 56
(GAButler) *settled in rr: rdn over 3f out: prog u.p 2f out: styd on fr over 1f out: nvr able to chal* **9/2**[1]

4004 **5** 2½ **Coolfore Jade (IRE)**[9] 6220 3-8-10 **58** ow1...... MSavage(5) 4 58
(NEBerry) *t.k.h: trckd ldrs: effrt 3f out: rdn to chse clr ldr over 1f out tl wknd ins fnl f* **14/1**

-625 **6** 2 **Komati River**[188] 2657 4-9-1 **52**...... PDoe 8 50
(JAkehurst) *trckd ldr for 3f: lost pl 6f out: effrt again to chse ldng pair over 3f out tl wknd wl over 1f out* **8/1**

0206 **7** 3 **Raheel (IRE)**[9] 6220 3-8-10 **53**......(t) WRyan 1 46
(PMitchell) *stdd s: hld up in last: stdy prog on wd outside 5f out: rdn and nt qckn over 2f out: n.d after* **9/1**

5040 **8** nk **Madiba**[16] 5343 4-9-6 **57**......(b[1]) RWinston 9 50
(PHowling) *trckd ldr after 3f: led and qcknd over 6f out: hdd & wknd over 2f out* **20/1**

1330 **9** 1¼ **Lazzaz**[23] 6130 5-9-11 **62**...... JoannaBadger 11 53
(PWHiatt) *led to over 6f out: sn rdn: styd wl in tch tl wknd 2f out* **10/1**

0-00 **10** hd **Cool Bathwick (IRE)**[100] 5079 4-9-5 **56**...... GBaker 5 47
(BRMillman) *hld up in last trio: rdn over 3f out: no prog and n.d* **25/1**

0025 **11** 2½ **Radiant Bride**[16] 6174 3-7-9 **45**...... AReilly(7) 13 32
(KRBurke) *a in last trio: rdn and struggling 4f out: no ch* **25/1**

-600 **12** 10 **Wavet**[12] 6205 3-8-8 **51** ow1...... NCallan 12 24
(MrsLydiaPearce) *t.k.h: trckd ldrs: rdn and wknd over 3f out* **14/1**

0430 **13** 7 **Very Exclusive (USA)**[88] 5329 4-8-10 **47**...... IMongan 7 11
(GLMoore) *racd in midfield: rdn and looked reluctant 5f out: sn btn* **9/1**

**14** 14 **Chiru (IRE)**[60] 5840 3-9-5 **65**...... LPKeniry(3) 14 9
(BJMeehan) *t.k.h: trckd ldrs tl wknd 5f out: t.o over 2f out* **14/1**

2m 51.27s (3.19) **Going Correction** +0.20s/f (Slow)
**WFA** 3 from 4yo+ 6lb **14** Ran SP% **123.5**
Speed ratings: **98,97,96,95,94 93,91,91,90,90 88,82,78,69**CSF £43.94 CT £747.54 TOTE £5.90: £3.90, £7.20, £13.70; EX 36.20.
**Owner** D Charlesworth **Bred** Bertram N Linder **Trained** Charlton Adam, Somerset

**FOCUS**
A competitive handicap that produced a good finish.

**NOTEBOOK**
**Royal Prodigy(USA)** was winning for the first time in handicap company and received a very good ride from O'Neill to do so. He got up in the dying strides and is in the form of his life.
**Reminiscent(IRE)** nearly managed to nick the race when kicking on from two out but could not hold the winner's late burst. *Official explanation: trainer said gelding lost one front shoe and one rear shoe*
**Makarim(IRE)** stays further than this and will soon be back winning when granted a stiffer test.
**Compton Eclaire(IRE)** failed to confirm Wolverhampton form with Makarim despite being weighted to do so.
**Coolfore Jade(IRE)**, who ran well at a big price when fourth at the course last time, got a little tired inside the final furlong but had run well up until that point.
**Raheel(IRE)** is a frustrating character and remains a maiden after 15 starts.
**Very Exclusive(USA)** *Official explanation: jockey said gelding had a breathing problem*

## 6250 BET DIRECT NO Q ON 08000 93 66 93 MAIDEN STKS (DIV II) 6f (P)
**1:05** (1:05) (D ) 2-Y-O **£2,982** (£852; £426) **Stalls** Low

Form RPR

0 **1** **Chorus Beauty**[23] 6129 2-8-9 ...... SDrowne 5 62+
(GWragg) *trckd ldrs: effrt over 2f out: rdn to ld jst over 1f out: styd on wl* **6/1**[3]

0 **2** 1½ **Mugeba**[23] 6129 2-8-9 ...... MFenton 1 57
(WJMusson) *pushed along to chse ldrs: effrt over 2f out: squeezed through on inner to chse wnr ins fnl f: no imp* **20/1**

**3** 1¼ **Devious Ayers (IRE)** 2-9-0 ...... EAhern 7 58
(GAButler) *dwlt and sltly hmpd s: in rr: rdn and effrt over 2f out: kpt on fr over 1f out: tk 3rd nr fin* **6/1**[3]

065 **4** nk **Averami**[19] 6159 2-8-9 68...... NCallan 3 53
(AMBalding) *wnt lft s: chsd ldrs: rdn over 2f out: unable qck over 1f out: one pce fnl f* **4/1**[2]

0030 **5** ½ **City Affair**[35] 6059 2-9-0 57...... IMongan 6 56
(MrsLCJewell) *wnt rt s: racd freely: pressed ldr tl led over 3f out: hdd & wknd jst over 1f out* **12/1**

0 **6** 1¼ **Cornwallis**[30] 6097 2-9-0 ...... JMackay 8 52
(RGuest) *pushed along in midfield: effrt over 2f out: one pce and no imp on ldrs* **8/1**

4302 **7** ½ **Tonto (FR)**[105] 4933 2-9-0 76...... DaneO'Neill 4 51
(MissDMountain) *racd freely: led to over 3f out: styd pressing ldr: ev ch over 1f out: wknd fnl f* **5/2**[1]

0 **8** 2½ **Genuine Jay Gee (IRE)**[118] 4647 2-9-0 ...... NPollard 10 43
(GGMargarson) *sn pushed along in rr: outpcd and struggling over 2f out* **14/1**

**9** 5 **Sussex Style (IRE)** 2-9-0 ...... SWhitworth 9 28
(RMFlower) *dwlt: a in last pair: struggling wl over 2f out: wknd over 1f out* **50/1**

0 **10** 14 **Pat's Nemisis (IRE)**[19] 6159 2-8-6 ...... J-PGuillambert(3) 2 —
(BRJohnson) *sltly impeded s: sn last and struggling: t.o over 2f out* **33/1**

1m 14.64s (1.72) **Going Correction** +0.20s/f (Slow) **10** Ran SP% **112.3**
Speed ratings: **96,94,92,91,91 89,88,85,78,60**CSF £114.60 TOTE £9.00: £3.10, £4.20, £1.80; EX 99.40.
**Owner** Mrs Claude Lilley **Bred** B W Hills Southbank Ltd And R A N Bonnycastle **Trained** Newmarket, Suffolk
■ Stewards Enquiry : I Mongan caution: used whip with excessive frequency and without giving gelding time to respond

**FOCUS**
Not a bad little maiden but probably just the weaker of the two divisions.

**NOTEBOOK**
**Chorus Beauty**, down the field over course and distance on her debut, reversed form with Mugeba and won with something to spare. She is entitled to improve again and is the type to do well in handicaps.
**Mugeba**, 5lb worse off with the winner for their debut running, squeezed up the inside to chase the winner home but was never going to get to the winner. She too should pay her way in handicap company.
**Devious Ayers(IRE)** is bred to want much further so it must have been encouraging for connections that he could get so close over this trip. He will be winning when upped in distance, with this run sure to have done him good.
**Averami** wants at least seven furlongs and will not be winning until getting it.
**City Affair** is well exposed and has become disappointing.
**Tonto(FR)** failed to get home having raced freely. He is better than this but remains a maiden after eight starts.

## 6251 BETDIRECT.CO.UK NURSERY 7f (P)
**1:35** (1:37) (D ) (0-85,77) 2-Y-O **£3,066** (£876; £438) **Stalls** Low

Form RPR

6105 **1** **St Savarin (FR)**[16] 6173 2-8-12 **68**...... IMongan 11 70
(JRBest) *led after 1f and crossed to inner: shkn up over 1f out: hrd rdn fnl f: jst hld on* **8/1**

6200 **2** hd **Garrigon**[42] 6011 2-8-1 **60**...... LisaJones(3) 9 62
(NPLittmoden) *trckd wnr over 4f out: shkn up over 1f out and clr of rest: clsd ins fnl f: jst failed* **14/1**

422 **3** 1¼ **Little Eye (IRE)**[27] 6115 2-8-12 **68**...... NPollard 7 66
(JRBest) *prom: pushed along 1/2-way: rdn and unable qck 2f out: kpt on fnl f* **3/1**[1]

0000 **4** ½ **Turnberry (IRE)**[27] 6115 2-8-4 **60** ow1......(b) SWhitworth 3 57
(JWHills) *settled towards rr: effrt on inner over 2f out: prog over 1f out: styd on same pce fnl f* **12/1**

525 **5** ½ **Elusive Kitty (USA)**[37] 6048 2-9-0 **70**...... EAhern 2 66
(GAButler) *trckd ldrs: lost pl 1/2-way: nt clr run over 2f out: swtchd to outer and drvn over 1f out: styd on one pce* **7/2**[2]

4452 **6** nk **Daring Affair**[10] 6213 2-8-8 **64**...... NCallan 4 59
(KRBurke) *pressed ldrs: rdn over 2f out: sn one pce and btn* **9/1**

0433 **7** shd **Redbank (IRE)**[17] 6167 2-8-9 **65**......(b) DaneO'Neill 8 60
(NACallaghan) *settled in last pair: plenty to do over 2f out: swtchd to wd outside and rdn over 1f out: styd on fnl f: no ch* **11/1**

005 **8** 2½ **Jango Malfoy (IRE)**[12] 6210 2-8-7 **63** ow2......(bt[1]) MFenton 6 51
(BWDuke) *racd in midfield: rdn over 2f out: no prog wl over 1f out: wknd fnl f* **20/1**

1061 **9** 2 **Off Beat (USA)**[19] 6160 2-9-7 **77**......(b) SCarson 10 60
(RFJohnsonHoughton) *t.k.h: hld up in last pair: nt clr run over 2f out: no prog over 1f out: wknd* **5/1**[3]

3230 **10** ¾ **Man Crazy (IRE)**[110] 4813 2-9-0 **70**...... MTebbutt 1 51
(RMBeckett) *plld hrd: led for 1f: styd prom tl wknd 2f out* **16/1**

61 **11** 1¼ **Sable 'n Silk**[30] 6097 2-8-12 **68**...... SDrowne 5 46
(DHaydnJones) *reluctant to enter stalls: plld hrd early: in tch: rdn 3f out: sn wknd* **16/1**

1m 27.43s (1.43) **Going Correction** +0.20s/f (Slow) **11** Ran SP% **124.2**
Speed ratings: **99,98,97,96,96 95,95,92,90,89 88**CSF £120.70 CT £420.61 TOTE £9.90: £2.10, £1.90, £2.30; EX 61.40.
**Owner** D S Nevison **Bred** F W Holtkotter **Trained** Hucking, Kent

**FOCUS**
A competitive nursery that produced an exciting finish.

**NOTEBOOK**
**St Savarin(FR)**, who has looked a non-stayer over a mile the last twice, appreciated this drop back in trip and dug deep to hold the closing runner-up. This is his trip and he can defy a rise.
**Garrigon** has threatened to get his head in front on numerous occasions and today was nearly his day. A couple more strides would have seen his head in front and it is quite possible a mile will see him in a better light.
**Little Eye(IRE)** has yet to run a bad race since being switched to the All-Weather and again ran well over a trip a tad on the sharp side.
**Turnberry(IRE)**, who looked a non-stayer over a mile last time, could not reach any closer than fourth and would have benefited from a more prominent ride.
**Elusive Kitty(USA)** would have been closer had she received a clear passage through and has a race of this nature in her.
**Redbank(IRE)** was given too much to do and deserves another chance.
**Off Beat(USA)** should have fared better despite not receiving a clear run.
**Sable 'n Silk** *Official explanation: jockey said filly was forced wide on the first bend and was never travelling thereafter*

## 6252 BET DIRECT FOOTBALL CASHBACKS H'CAP 7f (P)
**2:05** (2:06) (C ) (0-100,100) 3-Y-O+ **£6,078** (£2,305; £1,152; £524) **Stalls** Low

Form RPR

0010 **1** **Lygeton Lad**[9] 6225 5-10-0 **100**......(t) MFenton 10 113
(MissGayKelleway) *settled in last trio: stdy prog on outer over 2f out: effrt to ld jst ins fnl f: hanging lft but hld on wl* **9/2**[3]

6302 **2** hd **The Best Yet**[60] 5838 5-7-11 **72**...... FPFerris(3) 9 84
(AGNewcombe) *hld up in last: prog on inner 2f out: r.o to press wnr ins fnl f: ev ch: jst hld* **15/2**

6000 **3** 1¾ **Hand Chime**[58] 5875 6-9-1 **87**...... SDrowne 7 95
(WJHaggas) *hld up in midfield: gng easily but lost pl over 2f out: swtchd to outer and r.o over 1f out: wnt 3rd last 100y: too much to* **11/1**

0003 **4** 1¾ **Camp Commander (IRE)**[37] 6050 4-9-9 **95**......(t) IMongan 6 98
(CEBrittain) *trckd ldrs: effrt over 2f out: rdn and nt qckn wl over 1f out: one pce after* **5/1**

0411 **5** nk **Compton Banker (IRE)**[23] 6132 6-8-6 **78**...... EAhern 1 81
(GAButler) *trckd ldrs: rdn and nt qckn over 2f out: sn lost pl: kpt on one pce over 1f out* **7/2**[1]

5650 **6** 1¾ **Awarding**[23] 6132 3-8-6 **78**......(t) CCatlin 2 76
(RFJohnsonHoughton) *t.k.h: hld up in rr: prog on inner 3f out: rdn to chal over 1f out: wknd ins fnl f* **16/1**

2111 **7** ½ **Haripur**[60] 5838 4-9-11 **97**...... SCarson 3 94
(AndrewReid) *pressed ldr: led over 3f out: kicked 2l clr 2f out: hdd jst ins fnl f: wknd and heavily eased: fin lame* **4/1**[2]

0000 **8** 5 **Sundried Tomato**[9] 6225 4-8-13 **85**...... GBaker 4 69
(PWHiatt) *free to post: racd freely: led to over 3f out: chsd ldr to wl over 1f out: wknd rapidly and eased* **20/1**

2006 **9** 6 **Override (IRE)**[23] 6132 3-7-13 **71**...... JMackay 8 40
(JMPEustace) *t.k.h: racd wd: hld up in tch: rdn over 3f out: wknd wl over 2f out* **9/1**

6-00 **10** 9 **Action Fighter (GER)**[9] 6225 3-9-4 **93**...... J-PGuillambert(3) 5 40
(NPLittmoden) *chsd ldng pair tl wknd u.p over 3f out: t.o* **33/1**

1m 25.56s (-0.44) **Going Correction** +0.20s/f (Slow) **10** Ran SP% **120.8**
Speed ratings: **110,109,107,105,105 103,102,97,90,80**CSF £39.79 CT £287.88 TOTE £7.10: £1.80, £2.90, £3.10; EX 65.80.
**Owner** J McGonagle & B J McGonagle **Bred** Khalifa Abdulla Dasmal **Trained** Newmarket, Suffolk

**FOCUS**
There was a strong pace on here for what was a decent handicap.

**NOTEBOOK**
**Lygeton Lad**, stepping back up to his favourite trip having found six furlongs too short last time, had the race run to suit and came with a strong run down the outside. He probably got to the front a bit too soon as The Best Yet was coming back at him at the finish, but he held on well. He is a class performer round here and his trainer now plans to send him to race in Dubai.
**The Best Yet**tried for an ambitious run up the inside rounding the turn into the straight and the gap opened up for him beautifully. He threw down a determined challenge inside the final furlong but was just edged out. A strong pace suits him and, granted similar conditions, he should soon be going one better.
**Hand Chime**has not won for a long time but he has run well on each of his starts here and his style of running clearly suits this track.

**Camp Commander(IRE)**does not win as many races as he should, but this is his best trip and he has the ability to win a contest around here if dropped a few pounds.
**Compton Banker(IRE)**, chasing a hat-trick off a 4lb higher mark, was taking on higher quality opponents on this occasion and was missing the visor he had worn to his two previous successes.
**Haripur**, returning from a two-month break and racing off a 5lb higher mark, was harried at the head of affairs throughout which did not suit him at all. He also finished lame so clearly was not at his best on this occasion. *Official explanation: jockey said he felt colt was lame in the closing stages*
**Sundried Tomato**raced very freely and basically set the race up for those held up off the pace.

## 6253 CASHBACKS ON SKY TEXT PAGE 372 MAIDEN STKS 7f (P)
**2:35** (2:38) (D ) 3-Y-0+ £2,352 (£672; £336) **Stalls** Low

Form RPR
3300 **1** **Wood Fern (UAE)**[12] 6208 3-9-0 65 .................... RLappin 4 69
(MRChannon) *wl plcd: prog to trck ldng pair 3f out: effrt to ld wl over 1f out: in command after: rdn out* **5/1[2]**
3242 **2** *1 3/4* **Givemethemoonlight**[3] 6238 4-8-9 44 .................... CCatlin 1 59
(MrsStefLiddiard) *trckd ldng pair to 3f out: rdn and nt qckn over 2f out: styd on u.p fnl f to take 2nd last stride* **7/1**
5605 **3** *shd* **Adantino**[12] 6206 4-9-0 48 .................... GBaker 13 64
(BRMillman) *hld up towards rr: prog over 2f out: rdn to chse wnr ins fnl f: no imp: lost 2nd last stride* **14/1**
0005 **4** *2* **Mayzin (IRE)**[12] 6204 3-9-0 51 .................... (p) SWhitworth 15 59
(RMFlower) *led at fast pce: rdn and hdd wl over 1f out: wknd ins fnl f* **14/1**
0 **5** *3/4* **Midnight Mambo (USA)**[12] 6209 3-8-9 .................... EAhern 3 52
(RGuest) *towards rr: prog on outer 3f out: rdn to chse ldrs 2f out: no imp over 1f out* **4/1[1]**
4426 **6** *2 1/2* **Cayman Sunrise (IRE)**[23] 6131 3-8-9 61 .................... WRyan 9 45
(EALDunlop) *towards rr: effrt over 2f out: one pce and nvr rchd ldrs* **5/1[2]**
6265 **7** *1/2* **A Beetoo (IRE)**[12] 6209 3-8-9 60 .................... NPollard 7 44
(JRBest) *sn drvn and wl in rr: sme prog u.p 2f out: one pce after* **11/2[3]**
4004 **8** *3/4* **Mad Mick Meeson**[12] 6209 3-9-0 50 .................... (vt[1]) RHavlin 10 47
(GBBalding) *pressed ldr to 2f out: wknd rapidly fnl f* **8/1**
0000 **9** *1 3/4* **Definitely Special (IRE)**[12] 6206 5-8-8 40 ow2 .................... LPKeniry(3) 16 40
(NEBerry) *stdd s: t.k.h and hld up towards rr: effrt over 2f out: rdn and fnd nil wl over 1f out* **25/1**
40 **10** *1/2* **Strike Lucky**[148] 3816 3-9-0 .................... DSweeney 14 41
(PJMakin) *chsd ldrs: rdn and lost pl bef 1/2-way: n.d after* **25/1**
0650 **11** *1/2* **Unsuited**[30] 6094 4-8-5 53 ow1 .................... RMiles(5) 2 36
(JELong) *settled in midfield: effrt on inner over 2f out: no prog wl over 1f out: wknd fnl f* **40/1**
0006 **12** *6* **Island Star (IRE)**[12] 6209 3-9-0 52 .................... PDoe 12 24
(SDow) *taken down early: outpcd after 2f: wl bhd 3f out* **16/1**
-000 **13** *nk* **Silistra**[19] 6157 4-9-0 55 .................... (b) DaneO'Neill 11 24
(MrsLCJewell) *bmpd s: a in rr: wl bhd fnl 3f* **50/1**
0000 **14** *4* **Law Maker**[157] 3575 3-9-0 40 .................... RWinston 5 13
(MABuckley) *chsd ldrs 3f: sn wknd u.p* **66/1**
**15** *1 1/4* **Devon Maid**[18] 4-8-9 .................... SDrowne 8 —
(RJHodges) *a wl in rr: wl bhd fr 1/2-way* **100/1**

1m 26.42s (0.42) **Going Correction** +0.20s/f (Slow) **15** Ran SP% **126.1**
Speed ratings: **105,103,102,100,99 96,96,95,93,92 92,85,85,80,79**CSF £39.89 TOTE £7.70: £3.40, £2.20, £5.60; EX 99.60.
**Owner** M Channon **Bred** Darley Dubai **Trained** West Ilsley, Berks
■ Stewards Enquiry : G Baker seven-day ban: dropped hands and lost second place (Jan 9,10,12-16)

**FOCUS**
Another race run at a good pace and the time was very respectable, being only 0.86sec slower than that taken by Lygeton Lad in the preceding race.

**NOTEBOOK**
**Wood Fern(UAE)**had clearly found middle distances too far on his last two starts and this drop back in trip suited him well. The time was respectable and he should be placed to advantage in handicap company.
**Givemethemoonlight**has had plenty of opportunites and is one for Placepot punters only.
**Adantino**, another who remains a maiden, would probably have finished second had his jockey not stopped riding in the final strides. Baker was subsequently suspended for seven days for failing to ride out.
**Mayzin(IRE)**set an unsustainable pace and in the circumstances ran really well to hold on to fourth. He has shown improved form since being switched to Polytrack and he looks capable of winning a minor event.
**Midnight Mambo(USA)**, backed into favouritism again, ran better on this step up in trip and shaped as though even farther would suit. She needs one more run for a mark.
**Cayman Sunrise(IRE)**did not find the drop back in trip providing the answer.
**Island Star(IRE)** *Official explanation: jockey said gelding hung left throughout*

## 6254 LITTLEWOODS BET DIRECT AW JOCKEYS CHAMPIONSHIP H'CAP (DIV II) 1m 5f (P)
**3:10** (3:10) (F ) (0-65,65) 3-Y-0+ £2,051 (£586; £293) **Stalls** Low

Form RPR
0020 **1** **Majlis (IRE)**[20] 6156 6-9-10 61 .................... (b) EAhern 12 73
(RMHCowell) *t.k.h and hld up in rr: prog to trck ldrs 5f out: led gng easily jst over 1f out: shkn up and sn clr* **13/2[3]**
0642 **2** *2 1/2* **Easter Ogil (IRE)**[12] 6208 8-9-12 63 .................... VSlattery 7 72
(JaneSouthcombe) *racd in midfield: n.m.r on inner and dropped to last 5f out: prog but plenty to do over 2f out: r.o to take 2nd last 150y* **5/1[1]**
5115 **3** *3/4* **Gemi Bed (FR)**[13] 1833 8-8-4 41 .................... (b) SWhitworth 10 48
(GLMoore) *hmpd after 1f: hld up: prog to trck ldrs 5f out: led gng easily 2f out: rdn and hdd jst over 1f out: nt qckn* **6/1[2]**
6654 **4** *3* **Lanos (POL)**[258] 1065 5-9-6 60 .................... (t) J-PGuillambert(3) 5 63
(RFord) *s.s: hld up in last: rapid prog fr 3f out to chse ldrs 2f out: no imp after* **7/1**
05-0 **5** *3/4* **Sungio**[9] 6220 5-8-13 57 .................... AHindley(7) 14 59
(BGPowell) *hld up in rr: prog to chse ldrs over 2f out: sn rdn and nt qckn* **40/1**
0000 **6** *1 1/4* **Starry Mary**[33] 6079 5-8-8 48 ow1 .................... LPKeniry(3) 1 48
(ELJames) *prom: rdn 3f out: stl cl up 2f out: fdd over 1f out* **20/1**
6051 **7** *shd* **Waverley Road**[27] 6120 6-8-8 45 .................... IMongan 4 45
(MMadgwick) *cl up: trckd ldr 5f out: led 3f out to 2f out: wknd over 1f out* **5/1[1]**
0600 **8** *1 3/4* **Treasure Trail**[20] 5220 4-10-0 65 .................... CCatlin 11 63
(SKirk) *wl in rr: drvn 5f out: struggling after: kpt on u.p* **7/1**
22U0 **9** *1/2* **Fife And Drum (USA)**[9] 6226 6-9-1 57 .................... (p) BReilly(5) 6 54
(MissJFeilden) *racd in midfield: n.m.r 5f out: effrt to chse ldrs over 2f out: no prog over 1f out* **14/1**
00-0 **10** *24* **Promote**[104] 4976 7-8-13 50 .................... DRMcCabe 3 14
(MsAEEmbiricos) *trckd ldrs: n.m.r and lost pl on inner 5f out: in tch over 2f out: sn wknd rapidly: t.o* **66/1**
4000 **11** *3* **Esperance (IRE)**[19] 6161 3-8-12 55 .................... DaneO'Neill 8 14
(JAkehurst) *chsd ldrs tl wknd over 3f out: t.o* **10/1**
3033 **12** *3* **White Park Bay (IRE)**[23] 6137 3-9-1 58 .................... NCallan 13 13
(JGallagher) *trckd ldr: led 6f out to 3f out: wknd rapidly: t.o* **16/1**
0000 **13** *1 1/2* **Beetle Bug**[126] 4437 3-8-4 47 .................... JMackay 2 —
(AMHales) *led to 6f out: sn rdn: wknd 5f out: t.o* **50/1**
4266 **14** *16* **Cantrip**[128] 4385 3-9-5 62 .................... (t) SDrowne 9 —
(MissBSanders) *chsd ldrs tl wknd 5f out: t.o* **14/1**

2m 50.11s (2.03) **Going Correction** +0.20s/f (Slow)
**WFA** 3 from 4yo+ 6lb **14** Ran SP% **124.9**
Speed ratings: **101,99,99,97,96 95,95,94,94,79 77,76,75,65**CSF £39.53 CT £213.62 TOTE £7.30: £2.40, £2.80, £2.10; EX 64.60.
**Owner** Terry Warner **Bred** Kilcarn Stud **Trained** Six Mile Bottom, Cambs

**FOCUS**
Majlis ran out an easy winner of a race run in a time 1.16sec faster than the first division.

**NOTEBOOK**
**Majlis(IRE)**, who was getting off the mark on the Flat at the 12th attempt, found the switch to Polytrack suiting his style of running much better than Fibresand and ran out a cosy winner, although he did get first run on the eventual second.
**Easter Ogil(IRE)**, stepping back up in trip, let the winner get first run and was always playing catch-up. He has the ability to win a similar race provided he gets a strong pace.
**Gemi Bed(FR)**, who was last seen jumping fences, looked much happier back on the Flat and was going as well as anything on the run down the hill. He found less than the winner under pressure but looks worth persevering with on this surface. *Official explanation: jockey said gelding suffered interference on the home turn*
**Lanos(POL)**ran as though he will come on for this first outing in 258 days. He certainly looks to have a race in him here off this sort of mark.
**Sungio**ran a better race back up in trip.
**Starry Mary**has a poor strike rate.
**Waverley Road**, a winner over two miles last time, was outpaced in the closing stages over this shorter trip.

## 6255 CASHBACKS ON ITV TEXT PAGE 367 APPRENTICE H'CAP 1m 2f (P)
**3:40** (3:40) (F ) (0-80,80) 3-Y-0+ £2,999 (£857; £428) **Stalls** Low

Form RPR
2635 **1** **J R Stevenson (USA)**[27] 6117 7-9-9 **75** .................... MSavage(3) 5 85
(MWigham) *hld up in midfield: smooth prog to trck ldng pair 2f out: led jst over 1f out: edgd lft but r.o wl* **3/1[1]**
5045 **2** *1/2* **Tropical Coral (IRE)**[16] 6178 3-9-5 **71** .................... DNolan 8 80
(CTinkler) *hld up in last pair: prog on inner ovr 2f out: rdn and str chal ent fnl f: nt qckn last 100y* **12/1**
0305 **3** *3/4* **Rasid (USA)**[19] 6157 5-9-0 **63** .................... BReilly 3 71
(CADwyer) *hld up towards rr: nt clr run over 2f out: prog over 1f out: r.o to take 3rd wl ins fnl f* **6/1[3]**
1564 **4** *1/2* **Blue Trojan (IRE)**[27] 6114 3-8-11 **68** .................... LTreadwell(5) 1 75
(SKirk) *led 1f: restrained: styd cl up: shkn up and unable qck over 2f out: styd on again fnl f* **7/1**
5141 **5** *3/4* **Ryan's Future (IRE)**[19] 6157 3-10-0 **80** .................... NChalmers 2 86
(JAkehurst) *hld up towards rr: nt clr run 3f out to 2f out: r.o fnl f: no ch* **5/1[2]**
1005 **6** *1 1/4* **Miss Pebbles (IRE)**[19] 6161 3-9-0 **71** .................... (p) DFentiman(5) 7 74
(BRJohnson) *t.k.h: cl up: effrt to ld 2f out to jst over 1f out: hanging rt and wknd* **7/1**
1501 **7** *2 1/2* **Burgundy**[23] 6128 6-9-2 **65** .................... RMiles 9 64
(PMitchell) *hld up wl in rr: prog on wd outside over 2f out: nt qckn wl over 1f out: one pce after* **10/1**
2530 **8** *hd* **Bluegrass Boy**[12] 6208 3-8-11 **66** .................... RThomas(3) 11 64
(GBBalding) *disp ld at stdy pce after 1f: def advantage over 3f out: hdd 2f out: ev ch jst over 1f out: wknd rapidly* **20/1**
0010 **9** *1 3/4* **Muyassir (IRE)**[78] 5498 8-8-4 **56** .................... HayleyTurner(3) 10 51
(MissBSanders) *cl up: rdn and ch 2f out: wknd over 1f out* **16/1**
5600 **10** *shd* **Anemos (IRE)**[19] 6157 8-7-11 **51** ....................[1] BSwarbrick(5) 14 46
(PWD'Arcy) *hld up in rr: rdn over 2f out: no imp on ldrs* **16/1**
060 **11** *3* **Shaamit's All Over**[23] 6131 4-7-10 **50** .................... DeanWilliams(5) 4 40
(BAPearce) *s.i.s: a towards rr: no ch whn hung lft over 1f out* **40/1**
0530 **12** *1 1/4* **Balerno**[33] 6073 4-7-12 **50** .................... StephanieHollinshead(3) 12 37
(RIngram) *w ldrs: rdn and stl cl up 2f out: sn wknd* **20/1**
0000 **13** *6* **Snuki**[27] 6119 4-9-2 **65** .................... (b) AQuinn 6 42
(GLMoore) *disp ld at stdy pce after 1f to over 3f out: wknd rapidly wl over 1f out* **12/1**
/00- **14** *1 3/4* **Arc En Ciel**[543] 2086 5-8-12 **66** .................... HPoulton(5) 13 39
(GLMoore) *in tch tl wknd 4f out: t.o* **50/1**

2m 9.76s (2.37) **Going Correction** +0.20s/f (Slow)
**WFA** 3 from 4yo+ 3lb **14** Ran SP% **131.1**
Speed ratings: **98,97,97,96,96 95,93,92,91,91 88,87,83,81**CSF £43.89 CT £220.94 TOTE £3.90: £1.20, £3.90, £2.50; EX 47.30 Place £305.05, Place 5 £156.51.
**Owner** Claret & Blue Army **Bred** Mike Jones **Trained** Newmarket, Suffolk
■ Stewards Enquiry : M Savage caution:careless riding

**FOCUS**
A steadily-run affair which resulted in a sprint finish.

**NOTEBOOK**
**J R Stevenson(USA)**had less to do in this company but had to overcome a steady pace which would not have suited him. He did it well enough and, if turned out quickly, will not incur a penalty for this win.
**Tropical Coral(IRE)**, who has run her best races in the past over shorter, was quite possibly suited by the way the race developed.
**Rasid(USA)**is a disappointing sort but is at least dropping to a more realistic mark now.
**Blue Trojan(IRE)**appeared to get the longer trip well enough in this steadily-run affair, but whether he can repeat the trick in a more strongly-run race remains a doubt.
**Ryan's Future(IRE)**found himself in a similar race to last time but, off a 5lb higher mark, could not find the same burst of speed that won him the day on that occasion.
**Miss Pebbles(IRE)**looks on a stiff enough mark at present.
**Burgundy**flattered to deceive on the outside over a trip which is probably farther than ideal nowadays.
T/Plt: £466.20 to a £1 stake. Pool: £26,889.25. 42.10 winning tickets. T/Qpdt: £111.50 to a £1 stake. Pool: £3,121.10. 20.70 winning tickets. JN

# [6248] LINGFIELD (L-H)

## Tuesday, December 30

**OFFICIAL GOING: Standard**

Wind: almost nil Weather: overcast

## 6256 LITTLEWOODS BET DIRECT AW TRAINERS CHAMPIONSHIP H'CAP (DIV I) 7f (P)

12:15 (12:20) (E) (0-70,69) 3-Y-0+ £2,107 (£602; £301) Stalls Low

Form RPR

3010 **1** **Smith N Allan Oils**[14] [6196] 4-9-0 55 (p) RWinston 6 67+
(MDods) *trckd ldrs: smooth prog over 2f out: squeezed through to ld jst over 1f out and sn rdn 2l clr: drvn out nr fin* **11/2[2]**

0000 **2** *½* **Superchief**[28] [6114] 8-9-7 62 (bt) SDrowne 7 72+
(MissBSanders) *lw: hld up towards rr: effrt over 2f out: swtchd rt and drvn over 1f out: r.o to chse wnr ins fnl f: clsng nr fin* **12/1**

4554 **3** *2* **Captain Darling (IRE)**[8] [6231] 3-9-9 64 EAhern 10 69
(RMHCowell) *prom: rdn to chse ldng pair over 2f out: unable qck over 1f out: styd on same pce* **5/1[1]**

0040 **4** *nk* **The Gaikwar (IRE)**[8] [6231] 4-9-9 69 (b) MSavage(5) 2 73
(NEBerry) *dwlt: wl in rr: hrd rdn over 2f out: prog on inner wl over 1f out: squeezed though ins fnl f: styd on* **9/1**

6050 **5** *1 ¼* **Four Jays (IRE)**[13] [6206] 3-9-5 60 (p) MartinDwyer 14 61
(NPLittmoden) *pressed ldr: rdn 2f out: upsides jst over 1f out: sn outpcd and] btn* **20/1**

0614 **6** *nk* **I Wish**[28] [6116] 5-9-6 64 LPKeniry(3) 9 64
(MMadgwick) *trckd ldng pair on inner: rdn 2f out: cl up jst over 1f out: fdd fnl f* **10/1**

0002 **7** *1 ¼* **Harbour House**[13] [6204] 4-8-2 43 JTate 12 40
(JJBridger) *lw: mde most to jst over 1f out: wknd fnl f* **11/1**

0464 **8** *shd* **Its Ecco Boy**[24] [6127] 5-8-9 53 LisaJones(3) 4 50
(PHowling) *settled in midfield: effrt over 2f out: rdn to chse ldrs on inner over 1f out and cl up: wknd fnl f* **7/1[3]**

0401 **9** *¾* **Miss Issy (IRE)**[24] [6134] 3-9-3 58 (v) NCallan 16 53
(JGallagher) *chsd ldrs: rdn wl over 2f out: making no prog whn bmpd over 1f out: kpt on ins fnl f* **11/1**

0400 **10** *2 ½* **Fulvio (USA)**[20] [6164] 3-9-4 66 StephanieHollinshead(7) 3 55
(JamiePoulton) *t.k.h: hld up wl in rr: rdn and no prog over 2f out: n.d after* **25/1**

0000 **11** *½* **Dancing Forest (IRE)**[13] [6204] 3-9-11 66 CCatlin 8 53
(DKIvory) *hld up wl in rr: rdn and no prog over 2f out* **20/1**

0501 **12** *2* **Gun Salute**[13] [6209] 3-9-1 56 (p) RBrisland 5 38
(GLMoore) *t.k.h: hld up in rr: plenty to do whn nt clr run over 2f out: no prog after* **14/1**

4060 **13** *½* **Icannshift (IRE)**[20] [6157] 3-9-11 66 PDoe 1 47
(SDow) *hld up in rr: n.m.r on inner 5f out: brief effrt over 2f out: sn btn* **25/1**

00 **14** *½* **Treetops Hotel (IRE)**[141] [4056] 4-9-7 62 DaneO'Neill 11 42
(BRJohnson) *racd wdst of all: hld up in rr: struggling over 2f out* **12/1**

0060 **15** *¾* **Kinsman (IRE)**[24] [6127] 6-8-7 51 J-PGuillambert(3) 15 29
(TDMccarthy) *pressed ldrs: rdn 3f out: sn wknd* **16/1**

1m 25.52s (-0.48) **Going Correction** +0.10s/f (Slow) **15 Ran SP% 125.5**
Speed ratings: **106,105,103,102,101 101,99,99,98,95 95,92,92,91,90**CSF £68.69 CT £358.30 TOTE £7.90: £2.30, £3.70, £2.50; EX 54.40.
**Owner** Smith & Allan Racing **Bred** A J Holder **Trained** Piercebridge, Co Durham
■ Stewards Enquiry : S Drowne three-day ban: careless riding (Jan 10,12,13)

**FOCUS**
A competitive handicap run at a decent pace.

**NOTEBOOK**
**Smith N Allan Oils**, returning to Polytrack after a poor performance on Fibresand, travelled really well and the only question was whether he would get the split. Fortunately he did and it enabled him to get first run on the runner-up.
**Superchief**did not see much daylight and when he finally did get out to make his effort, the winner had already gone for home and he could not quite peg him back. He gave Miss Issy a hefty bump when pulled out for his run which resulted in a three-day ban for Drowne for careless riding.
**Captain Darling(IRE)**was always in the ideal place, but was just caught out for toe off the final bend before staying on again and is probably better suited by a mile.
**The Gaikwar(IRE)**, held up for much of the way, went for an audacious run up the inside rail down the home straight and was finishing in good style. Both of his wins so far have been over a mile and there is another race in him over that trip.
**Four Jays(IRE)**, wearing a dramatic pair of sheepskin cheekpieces, ran with credit under a positive ride especially as his yard is not quite hitting the target at present.
**Miss Issy(IRE)**was already beaten when getting knocked sideways by the runner-up at the furlong pole.

## 6257 LITTLEWOODSCASINO.COM (S) STKS (DIV I) 1m 2f (P)

12:45 (12:50) (G) 3-Y-0+ £2,051 (£586; £293) Stalls Low

Form RPR

3210 **1** **Absolute Utopia (USA)**[101] [5083] 10-9-6 63 JMackay 3 66
(JLSpearing) *reluctant ldr at slow pce for 2f: styd in tch: prog to ld wl over 2f out and kicked on: hrd pressed fnl f: hld on wl* **2/1[1]**

6500 **2** *½* **Icecap**[10] [6220] 3-8-6 51 ADaly 2 54
(PButler) *tk keene hold: hld up in rr: smooth prog 3f out: chsd wnr 2f out: str chal fnl f: a jst hld* **7/1[3]**

0266 **3** *5* **Blue Savanna**[12] [5507] 3-8-11 48 (b) EAhern 5 50
(JGPortman) *lw: trckd ldrs: cl up over 2f out: sn outpcd: kpt on to take 3rd ins fnl f* **8/1**

0006 **4** *¾* **Ladywell Blaise (IRE)**[13] [6204] 6-8-9 41 JTate 6 44
(JJBridger) *hld up towards rr: prog to chse ldrs over 2f out: sn rdn and outpcd: one pce after* **14/1**

0053 **5** *¾* **Dolphinelle (IRE)**[13] [6206] 7-9-0 49 (v) SDrowne 7 47
(JamiePoulton) *hld up in rr: rdn and effrt over 2f out: kpt on one pce fr over 1f out: n.d* **4/1[2]**

2000 **6** *1 ¼* **High Diva**[14] [6015] 4-8-4 45 (p) NChalmers(5) 1 40
(BRJohnson) *hld up in last: prog 3f out: rdn to chse ldrs over 2f out: sn outpcd and btn* **7/1[3]**

00-0 **7** *2* **Chocolate Boy (IRE)**[24] [6133] 4-9-0 43 SWhitworth 4 41
(GLMoore) *hld up in last trio: sme prog over 2f out: nudged along over 1f out: nvr nr ldrs* **25/1**

0000 **8** *1 ¾* **Toro Bravo (IRE)**[17] [6174] 3-8-11 60 (b) MTebbutt 9 38
(RMBeckett) *prom: chsd ldr 5f out to 3f out: chsd wnr wl over 2f out to 2f out: wknd* **14/1**

000- **9** *2 ½* **Caroline's Rose**[19] [5938] 5-8-6 20 LisaJones(3) 13 29?
(APJones) *plld way into ld and sn clr: hdd & wknd wl over 2f out* **50/1**

0-00 **10** *2* **St Cassien (IRE)**[11] [6217] 3-8-11 35 RBrisland 12 30
(TMJones) *racd in midfield: rdn 3f out: sn btn* **66/1**

0000 **11** *hd* **Distinctlysplendid**[31] [6089] 3-8-11 40 (b[1]) NCallan 10 30
(IAWood) *prom: disp 2nd pl 5f out to 3f out: wknd* **25/1**

000- **12** *1 ½* **Kittylee**[18] [2908] 4-8-9 25 RFrench 11 22
(MABuckley) *chsd ldr after 2f to 5f out: lost pl rapidly u.p and sn bhd* **50/1**

2m 11.36s (3.97) **Going Correction** +0.10s/f (Slow)
**WFA** 3 from 4yo+ 3lb **12 Ran SP% 115.9**
Speed ratings: **88,87,83,83,82 81,79,78,76,74 74,73**CSF £15.09 TOTE £2.20: £1.10, £3.40, £2.80; EX 20.70.No bid for the winner. Ice Cap was claimed by A L Sanders for £5,500.
**Owner** M T Lawrance **Bred** Gainsborough Farm Inc **Trained** Kinnersley, Worcs

**FOCUS**
A poor contest run at a dawdle early and the future does not look bright for most of these.

**NOTEBOOK**
**Absolute Utopia(USA)**, who has a good record under these conditions, would have been pleased to get a lead after finding himself in front early. He had little trouble leading again where it really mattered and was always going to win despite the margin. He is only two days short of his 11th birthday, but who is to say he cannot win another race like this.
**Icecap**is yet to really prove she stays this sort of trip, but did her best to stick to the favourite down the home straight. The fact that she could not take advantage, despite getting a stone and seven years from him, does not suggests she is a winner waiting to happen.
**Blue Savanna**, back on the Flat after three spins over hurdles, probably needs a longer trip or a stronger gallop.
**Ladywell Blaise(IRE)**, from a yard in form, is not the most consistent and her best efforts over the years have been over shorter.
**Dolphinelle(IRE)**gets two miles over hurdles, but has never shown much over this trip on the Flat.
**Chocolate Boy(IRE)** *Official explanation: jockey said gelding lost its action*
**Distinctlysplendid** *Official explanation: jockey said gelding ran too keenly early on*

## 6258 BETDIRECT.CO.UK NURSERY 6f (P)

1:15 (1:20) (D) (0-85,79) 2-Y-0 £3,094 (£884; £442) Stalls Low

Form RPR

5310 **1** **Kabreet**[20] [6160] 2-9-1 73 DaneO'Neill 4 78
(EALDunlop) *lw: hld up in last pair: nt clr run over 2f out: swtchd to outer and effrt over 1f out: edgd lft but r.o to ld last 100y: d* **6/1**

0240 **2** *nk* **Pregnant Pause (IRE)**[13] [6207] 2-8-7 65 MartinDwyer 3 69
(SKirk) *settled in midfield: effrt 2f out: rdn to chal ins fnl f: ev ch nr fin: nt qckn* **10/3[2]**

6011 **3** *1 ½* **Intriguing Glimpse**[13] [6207] 2-8-13 71 SDrowne 1 71
(MissBSanders) *lw: trckd ldng pair: effrt 2f out: drvn to chal and ev ch ent fnl f: one pce last 100y* **11/4[1]**

0425 **4** *1 ¼* **Sweetest Revenge (IRE)**[13] [6207] 2-9-6 78 ADaly 6 74
(MDIUsher) *racd freely: trckd ldr: rdn to ld over 1f out: hdd & wknd last 100y* **7/1**

0602 **5** *¾* **Stanhope Forbes (IRE)**[10] [6223] 2-7-9 56 oh1 (p) LisaJones(3) 9 50
(NPLittmoden) *dwlt: racd in last: rdn and outpcd wl over 1f out: styd on ins fnl f: n.d* **7/1**

6221 **6** *¾* **Smokin Joe**[1] [6248] 2-9-3 75 6ex NPollard 7 66
(JRBest) *chsd ldrs: rdn 2f out: making no prog and btn whn hmpd ins fnl f* **4/1[3]**

1040 **7** *1 ¾* **Rise**[20] [6159] 2-9-0 79 (b) SJDonohoe(7) 8 65
(AndrewReid) *b: b.hind: racd in last trio: rdn over 2f out: outpcd and btn over 1f out* **25/1**

3302 **8** *5* **Kuringai**[99] [5114] 2-9-0 72 MFenton 2 43
(BWDuke) *led: pushed along and hdd over 1f out: wknd rapidly* **20/1**

1m 13.03s (0.11) **Going Correction** +0.10s/f (Slow) **8 Ran SP% 117.6**
Speed ratings: **103,102,100,98,97 96,94,87**CSF £27.15 CT £68.18 TOTE £7.10: £2.00, £1.70, £1.60; EX 54.50 Trifecta £122.40 Pool of £1,121.04 - 6.50 winning units.
**Owner** Jumeirah Racing **Bred** Stowell Hill Ltd And S P Tindall **Trained** Newmarket, Suffolk
■ Stewards Enquiry : Dane O'Neill caution: careless riding

**FOCUS**
A decent nursery run at a very good pace.

**NOTEBOOK**
**Kabreet**, returning to six after a troubled passage over seven last time, found himself in a pocket turning in and had to be pulled wide. He found a smart turn of foot when out in the clear and, despite edging left, got up well inside the last furlong.
**Pregnant Pause(IRE)**ran another fine race over a more suitable trip and was only just denied. It is amazing he is still a maiden after 11 attempts and he should put that right before too long.
**Intriguing Glimpse**, trying this trip for the first time on sand, had every chance and there seemed no real excuses except that the inside of the track where she made her effort may have been riding a touch slower.
**Sweetest Revenge(IRE)**ran another fair race over probably her best trip, but she is probably better when able to dominate.
**Stanhope Forbes(IRE)**is fairly exposed, but may be better suited by another furlong.
**Smokin Joe**, carrying a 6lb penalty for his maiden victory here the previous day, had every chance, but this looked a better contest and the interference he received from the winner made absolutely no difference.

## 6259 BET DIRECT ON 0800 32 93 93 MAIDEN STKS 1m 2f (P)

1:45 (1:54) (D) 3-Y-0 £2,299 (£657; £328) Stalls Low

Form RPR

00 **1** **Grand Wizard**[160] [3503] 3-9-0 MTebbutt 1 71
(WJarvis) *hld up in last: sme prog but plenty to do 3f out: stdy hdwy to chse ldr 1f out: shkn up and fnd jst enough to ld last 75y* **25/1**

-225 **2** *½* **Margery Daw (IRE)**[13] [6205] 3-8-9 64 MartinDwyer 4 65+
(MPTregoning) *led at decent pce and sn 4l clr: rdn 2f out: hdd and one pce last 75y* **2/1[1]**

00 **3** *1 ½* **Elegant Gracie (IRE)**[24] [6131] 3-8-9 SDrowne 3 62
(RGuest) *in tch: prog over 3f out: rdn to chse ldr 2f out to 1f out: one pce fnl f* **25/1**

4330 **4** *3* **Springalong (USA)**[95] [5196] 3-8-7 75 SJDonohoe(7) 6 62+
(PDEvans) *lw: prom: outpcd 3f out: shuffled along and kpt on fnl 2f: n.d* **8/1[2]**

0436 **5** *1* **Golden Dual**[141] [4053] 3-9-0 73 PDoe 8 60
(SDow) *prom: chsd ldr over 3f out to 2f out: wknd rapidly fnl f* **10/1[3]**

0000 **6** *3* **Retail Therapy (IRE)**[38] [5683] 3-8-9 33 RFrench 2 50
(MABuckley) *in tch: outpcd 3f out: no ch after: kpt on fnl f* **50/1**

0 **7** *17* **Bold Ridge (IRE)**[24] [6131] 3-9-0 DaneO'Neill 7 24
(SKirk) *in tch tl wknd u.p over 3f out: t.o* **20/1**

0540 **8** *1 ¾* **Lovellian**[32] [6086] 3-8-9 47 GBaker 9 16
(BRMillman) *chsd ldr to over 3f out: wknd rapidly over 2f out: t.o* **25/1**

2m 9.66s (2.27) **Going Correction** +0.10s/f (Slow) **8 Ran SP% 71.8**
Speed ratings: **94,93,92,90,89 86,73,71**CSF £24.41 TOTE £20.00: £3.70, £1.10, £5.20; EX 41.40.
**Owner** Kelly, Shenfield, Slade & Straker-Smith **Bred** Fittocks Stud **Trained** Newmarket, Suffolk

**FOCUS**
A moderately-run contest lacking strength in depth after the withdrawal of the odds-on Jubilee Time.

**NOTEBOOK**
**Grand Wizard**, returning from a five-month break, was given a lot to do, but with the front runners not getting home he was able to pounce late and win despite still showing signs of greenness. This was a poor race, but he does at least have some scope and should get further.
**Margery Daw(IRE)**found herself in front which may not have been ideal, but still very much enjoyed the run of the race and yet managed to once again snatch defeat from the jaws of victory. She remains one to take on rather than back.
**Elegant Gracie(IRE)**showed a little ability and does at least now qualify for handicaps.
**Springalong(USA)**ran a strange race, as he held a good position early but gradually lost touch with the leaders and by the time his rider decided to do something about the situation, it was far too late. He is almost certainly capable of better. *Official explanation: jockey said, regarding the running and riding, gelding took a hold in the first 2f and did not feel right - gelding has a history of leg problems - when the rest of the field made a move 3 1/2f out, adding that when he got gelding balanced in the home straight he rode on to the line; vet said gelding finished sound, although it was wearing foot pads*
**Golden Dual**, making his debut for the yard, was racing for the first time since August and had every chance, but failed to get home.

## 6260 LITTLEWOODS BET DIRECT AW TRAINERS CHAMPIONSHIP H'CAP (DIV II) 7f (P)
**2:15** (2:22) (E) (0-70,69) 3-Y-O+ **£2,107** (£602; £301) **Stalls** Low

Form RPR
1535 **1** **And Toto Too**[60] 5856 3-9-4 66........(v[1]) SJDonohoe[(7)] 5 77
(PDEvans) *trckd ldrs: prog and cl up 2f out: rdn to ld over 1f out and sn 2l clr: styd on wl* **9/2**[1]
4446 **2** *1 3/4* **Lily Of The Guild (IRE)**[110] 4838 4-8-13 54........ NCallan 8 60
(WSKittow) *bmpd s: sn in midfield: prog to chse ldrs over 2f out: rdn and styd on to chse wnr ins fnl f: no imp* **25/1**
0502 **3** *shd* **Temper Tantrum**[24] 6134 5-9-5 63........(p) J-PGuillambert[(3)] 9 69
(AndrewReid) *b: b.hind: hld up towards rr: prog on inner over 2f out: rdn to chse wnr jst over 1f out: styd on same pce fnl f* **6/1**[3]
0056 **4** *1/2* **Pheckless**[20] 6164 4-10-0 69........ SCarson 14 74
(RFJohnsonHoughton) *b.hind: lw: t.k.h: hld up in last pair tl prog 2f out: shkn up and r.o fnl f: nt rch ldrs* **11/2**[2]
5153 **5** *shd* **Acorazado (IRE)**[14] 6202 4-9-1 56........ GCarter 13 61
(GLMoore) *hld up in rr: prog 2f out: r.o one pce fnl f: nrst fin* **7/1**
3020 **6** *1 1/2* **Royal Fashion (IRE)**[20] 6164 3-9-2 62........ NChalmers[(5)] 12 63
(MissSheenaWest) *s.s: hld up in last pair tl prog 2f out: drvn and styd on fr over 1f out: nrst fin* **20/1**
0031 **7** *shd* **Zinging**[13] 6206 4-8-11 52........ GBaker 3 53
(JJBridger) *cl up: rdn 2f out: one pce u.p 1f out: fdd last 100y* **10/1**
100 **8** *1 1/4* **Meelup (IRE)**[20] 6163 3-9-5 60........(p) SWhitworth 4 57
(AGNewcombe) *led: c wd bnd 2f out: hdd over 1f out: wknd fnl f* **50/1**
2020 **9** *nk* **Titian Lass**[41] 6026 4-7-11 45........(b) DeanWilliams[(7)] 7 42
(CEBrittain) *wnt rt s: hld up in rr: lost pl and c wd bnd 2f out: no ch after: styd on fnl f* **20/1**
2300 **10** *shd* **Heidelburg (IRE)**[8] 6231 3-9-9 64........ MartinDwyer 1 60
(SKirk) *settled in rr: rdn over 2f out: no prog over 1f out: one pce* **14/1**
1230 **11** *nk* **Mr Bountiful (IRE)**[24] 6127 5-9-7 62........ CCatlin 11 58
(MDods) *racd in midfield: rdn to chse ldrs over 2f out: wd bnd sn after: wknd fnl f* **10/1**
0004 **12** *1 3/4* **Blakeseven**[103] 5024 3-8-9 50........ PaulEddery 2 41
(WJMusson) *sn prom: chsd ldr 3f out to wl over 1f out: wknd rapidly ins fnl f* **16/1**
0030 **13** *nk* **Cayman Breeze**[20] 6164 3-9-10 65........ PDoe 10 56
(SDow) *hld up wl in rr: c wdst of all bnd 2f out and hmpd sn after: no ch after: kpt on* **16/1**
0021 **14** *nk* **Warlingham (IRE)**[13] 6204 5-9-0 55........ RWinston 15 45
(PHowling) *sn settled towards rr: shuffled along and no prog 2f out* **7/1**
5000 **15** *hd* **Master Rattle**[229] 1612 4-9-1 56........ VSlattery 6 45
(JaneSouthcombe) *chsd ldr to 3f out: wknd 2f out* **40/1**
6215 **16** *2* **Parker**[124] 4524 6-9-11 66........(b) MFenton 16 50
(BPalling) *racd wdst of all: t.k.h and hld up: effrt over 2f out: sn wknd* **20/1**
1m 26.22s (0.22) **Going Correction** +0.10s/f (Slow) **16** Ran SP% **132.0**
Speed ratings: **102,100,99,99,99 97,97,95,95,95 95,93,92,92,92 89**CSF £133.80 CT £716.61 TOTE £6.80: £2.00, £3.40, £2.20, £1.50; EX 337.40.
**Owner** Mrs S J Lawrence **Bred** Mrs M L Parry And P M Steele-Mortimer **Trained** Pandy, Gwent

**FOCUS**
A competitive handicap and a fair pace, though the winning time was 0.7 seconds slower than the first division.

**NOTEBOOK**
**And Toto Too**, well backed for this return to sand after suffering back trouble, was given a good ride and had the race won when taking over halfway up the straight. She is likely to be turned out quickly under a penalty.
**Lily Of The Guild(IRE)**, off for three months, ran a blinder despite getting a hard bump at the start. She is on a winning mark and looks more than capable of winning on this surface.
**Temper Tantrum**, held up early, enjoyed a dream run up the inside rail rounding the home bend though it is debatable whether that was an advantage or not. His stable look about ready to hit top form and he may be one to play his part.
**Pheckless**, drawn wide, found himself out the back early and was hampered rounding the first bend. He eventually found his stride and finished with a real flourish, though it was always going to be too late. He should soon make amends.
**Acorazado(IRE)**, who has been performing on Fibresand lately, ran well on this return to Polytrack though on this surface he may need an extra furlong.
**Royal Fashion(IRE)**was noted staying on nicely towards the end and is another who may benefit from an extra furlong.
**Zinging**, winner of a claimer over course and distance last time, had every chance, but was found out by this return to handicap company and has never been the most consistent in any case.
**Mr Bountiful(IRE)**is looking held by the Handicapper now.
**Warlingham(IRE)**, claimed by current connections after winning over course and distance last time, pulled far too hard early and paid the penalty.

## 6261 LITTLEWOODSPOKER.COM CLAIMING STKS 6f (P)
**2:45** (2:51) (F) 3-Y-O+ **£2,079** (£594; £297) **Stalls** Low

Form RPR
1432 **1** **Type One (IRE)**[85] 5427 5-8-9 78........ RMiles[(5)] 8 79+
(TGMills) *mde all: pushed clr wl over 1f out: 5l ahd ent fnl f: comf* **10/11**[1]
3010 **2** *2* **Ripple Effect**[20] 6164 3-8-1 70........(t) BReilly[(5)] 13 65
(CADwyer) *lw: racd towards rr: effrt on outer over 2f out: drvn and r.o to take 2nd ins fnl f: no ch w wnr* **5/1**[2]
0060 **3** *1 1/4* **Tayif**[41] 6032 7-8-7 52........(t) SCarson 6 62+
(AndrewReid) *b: b.hind: s.s: hld up in last pair tl prog on inner fr 1/2-way: nt clr run 2f out and over 1f out: styd on same pce fnl f* **20/1**
0044 **4** *1 1/4* **Byo (IRE)**[10] 6221 5-9-0 65........ RWinston 11 65
(MQuinn) *racd in midfield: prog to chse ldrs 2f out: one pce u.p fr over 1f out* **8/1**
0000 **5** *shd* **Cargo**[20] 6163 4-8-5 47........ EAhern 3 56
(HJCollingridge) *dwlt: racd towards rr: stdy prog fr 1/2-way: rdn to chse wnr briefly 1f out: wknd ins fnl f* **25/1**
6040 **6** *2 1/2* **Tripti (IRE)**[28] 6113 3-8-1 53 ow1........ JTate 4 45
(JJBridger) *racd in midfield: rdn over 2f out: one pce and no prog over 1f out : fdd* **25/1**
506 **7** *1 1/4* **Tickle**[28] 6113 5-8-0 50........(vt) CCatlin 2 40
(PJMakin) *chsd wnr to over 2f out: wknd over 1f out* **25/1**
0060 **8** *nk* **Legal Set (IRE)**[31] 6092 7-8-9 64........ DeanMcKeown 5 48
(JRBest) *b.hind: prom: chsd wnr over 2f out to 1f out: nt run on and sn wknd* **7/1**[3]
0000 **9** *3/4* **Janes Valentine**[76] 5574 3-7-12 52........ JoannaBadger 7 35
(JJBridger) *hld up in last pair: outpcd over 2f out: modest late prog* **50/1**
2656 **10** *2 1/2* **Naughty Girl (IRE)**[119] 4646 3-8-3 74 ow1........ SJDonohoe[(7)] 14 39
(PDEvans) *a in rr: rdn and struggling over 2f out* **14/1**
6100 **11** *1 1/2* **A Teen**[31] 6088 5-8-8 52........ LisaJones[(3)] 10 36
(PHowling) *chsd ldrs to 1/2-way: sn lost pl and btn* **16/1**
0 **12** *2* **Thai Hi (IRE)**[13] 6204 3-8-4 56........ MartinDwyer 9 23
(SKirk) *prom tl wknd over 2f out* **33/1**
-540 **13** *6* **Ivory Venture**[18] 6170 3-8-0 54........ RFfrench 12 1
(DKIvory) *racd on outer: rdn over 3f out: sn wknd: wl bhd over 1f out* **40/1**
1m 12.42s (-0.50) **Going Correction** +0.10s/f (Slow) **13** Ran SP% **128.9**
Speed ratings: **107,104,102,101,100 97,95,95,94,91 89,86,78**CSF £5.46 TOTE £1.80: £1.50, £1.90, £5.00; EX 6.90.The winner was the subject of a friendly claim by T G Mills for £15,000.
**Owner** Mrs A K Petersen **Bred** Ralph And Helen O'Brien **Trained** Headley, Surrey

**NOTEBOOK**
**Type One(IRE)**, freshened up by a break, quickened clear on the home turn and scored with the minimum of fuss. He is a useful performer in this grade.
**Ripple Effect**, back over six, ran on late down the outer to take second place, but the winner was well in command by that stage.
**Tayif**made up ground from the rear in smooth fashion but his path on the rail was blocked early in the home straight. When the gap did appear, he was unable to quicken up.
**Byo(IRE)**ran a sound enough race back over the six.
**Cargo**, having his second run after a break, ran his best race since the spring.

## 6262 LITTLEWOODSCASINO.COM (S) STKS (DIV II) 1m 2f (P)
**3:15** (3:21) (G) 3-Y-O+ **£2,044** (£584; £292) **Stalls** Low

Form RPR
0050 **1** **Piquet**[68] 5717 5-8-9 39........ GBaker 12 49
(JJBridger) *dwlt: hld up in last tl prog on inner over 2f out: squeezed through to ld lat 150y: styd on wl* **16/1**
0366 **2** *1 1/4* **Remembrance**[17] 6177 3-8-11 63........(t) JTate 2 52
(JMPEustace) *racd in midfield: n.m.r 7f out: effrt over 2f out: rdn and nt qckn over 1f out: styd on fnl f to take 2nd nr fin* **11/4**[1]
5340 **3** *3/4* **Wilom (GER)**[134] 4238 5-9-0 42........ MFenton 3 50
(MRHoad) *t.k.h: prom: trckd ldr over 4f out: led over 2f out: rdn and hdd last 150y: wknd and lost 2nd nr fin* **20/1**
000- **4** *3/4* **Sir Ninja (IRE)**[392] 5838 6-9-0 80........ MartinDwyer 5 49
(SKirk) *hld up towards rr: dropped to last over 2f out: effrt on wd outside wl over 1f out: kpt on ins fnl f: nret fin* **6/1**
0450 **5** *nk* **Pyrrhic**[94] 5157 4-9-0 31........(b) EAhern 4 49
(RMFlower) *t.k.h: hld up in midfield: nt clr run and lost pl over 2f out: effrt over 1f out: keeping on one pce whn n.m.r nr fin* **33/1**
0000 **6** *nk* **Ginger Ice**[24] 6128 3-8-11 38........ NPollard 11 48
(GGMargarson) *s.s: hld up in rr: progre to trck ldrs 2f out: rdn 1f out: fnd nil: wknd last 100y* **14/1**
0/53 **7** *shd* **Tinian**[8] 6229 5-9-6 62........ DarrenWilliams 7 54
(KRBurke) *led to over 2f out: styd pressing ldr: ev ch jst over 1f out: squeezed out sn after: wknd last 100y* **5/1**[3]
3000 **8** *1 1/4* **Private Seal**[68] 5717 8-9-0 41........(t) NCallan 10 46
(JulianPoulton) *chsd ldrs: rdn over 3f out: sn lost pl and struggling: kpt on again u.p fr over 1f out* **10/1**
4266 **9** *7* **Landescent (IRE)**[28] 6120 3-8-11 53........(v) RWinston 6 33
(MQuinn) *trckd ldrs: rdn over 3f out: wknd over 1f out* **4/1**[2]
0000 **10** *2 1/2* **Crafty Politician (USA)**[20] 6163 6-9-6 42........(b) DaneO'Neill 1 34
(GLMoore) *t.k.h: cl up: rdn 3f out: chsd ldng pair briefly over 2f out: wknd rapidly over 1f out* **20/1**
206- **11** *1 1/2* **Orake Prince**[28] 5500 4-8-7 46........ CHaddon[(7)] 8 26
(WGMTurner) *b.hind: chsd ldr to over 4f out: steadily lost pl under presure: fdd fnl 2f* **50/1**
34-0 **12** *14* **Badrinath (IRE)**[26] 1163 9-9-0 48........ GCarter 9 —
(HJCollingridge) *settled in midfield: effrt on outer 3f out: wknd rapidly 2f out* **16/1**
2m 9.23s (1.84) **Going Correction** +0.10s/f (Slow)
**WFA** 3 from 4yo+ 3lb **12** Ran SP% **119.6**
Speed ratings: **96,95,94,93,93 93,93,92,86,84 83,72**CSF £58.05 TOTE £20.70: £4.10, £1.40, £7.70; EX 90.60.No bid for the winner. Remembrance was claimed by Matthew Gingell for £5,500.
**Owner** J J Bridger **Bred** D E And Mrs J Cash **Trained** Liphook, Hants
■ Stewards Enquiry : R Winston four-day ban: careless riding (Jan 10,12-14)

**FOCUS**
A weak race, run in a time 2.13sec faster than the first division.

**NOTEBOOK**
**Piquet**missed the break and was settled in last place. She improved going into the home turn and Baker threaded her through a gap to take it up inside the last and win fairly comfortably. This was her first victory since October 2001.
**Remembrance**, who was rather keen in blinkers on the Fibresand last time, stayed on late in the day. He was hampered early on but had his chance before failing to pick up.
**Wilom(GER)**, the only one of the principals to have raced prominently, is on a long losing run but this was a decent effort.
**Sir Ninja(IRE)**, having his first run for over a year, looked like the race would bring him on. He has never entirely been one to trust, but this was a promising return to action.
**Pyrrhic**, who had a couple of runs over hurdles in the autumn, is a tricky ride.
**Ginger Ice**was the subject of market support. Without the cheekpieces, he threatened to get involved in the straight but did not see out the trip.

## 6263 LITTLEWOODS BET DIRECT CLASSIFIED STKS 1m (P)
**3:45** (3:49) (D) 3-Y-O+ **£3,510** (£1,080; £540; £270) **Stalls** High

Form RPR
5106 **1** **Labrett**[18] 6169 6-8-13 75........(t) MFenton 6 89
(MissGayKelleway) *trckd ldrs: rdn to chse ldr over 2f out: led 1f out: styd on wl* **5/1**[3]

1211 **2** 1 1/4 **Star Of Normandie (USA)**28 6117 4-8-8 83 .......................... BReilly(5) 5 86+
(GGMargarson) *taken down early and wnt sweetly to post: trckd ldrs: effrt but nt clr run 2f out to ins fnl f: r.o: nt rcvr* **15/8**1

2-04 **3** 1 **Silken Brief (IRE)**208 2141 4-8-10 78 ..........................(t) WRyan 4 81
(DJDaly) *settled in midfield: effrt over 2f out: rdn and styd on fr over 1f out: tk 3rd last stride* **12/1**

0430 **4** nk **Skylarker (USA)**179 2965 5-8-13 79 .......................... NCallan 12 83
(WSKittow) *racd freely: led for 1f: led again over 3f out: hrd drvn over 2f out: hdd 1f out: kpt on* **33/1**

1050 **5** hd **Just Fly**24 6132 3-8-12 79 .......................... MartinDwyer 10 83
(SKirk) *prom in chsng gp: chsd ldr 3f out to over 2f out: cl up 1f out: one pce fnl f* **8/1**

0004 **6** 1/2 **Agilis (IRE)**10 6224 3-8-12 79 .......................... SDrowne 9 82
(JamiePoulton) *settled in midfield: effrt over 2f out: drvn and kpt on same pce fr over 1f out* **4/1**2

3013 **7** 1 1/4 **Free Option (IRE)**13 6204 8-8-13 73 .......................... DeanMcKeown 2 79
(WJMusson) *b: b.hind: hld up in last trio: lost tch w ldng gp over 2f out: nudged along and kpt on steadily fr over 1f out: nvr nr ldr* **14/1**

6105 **8** 1/2 **Ammenayr (IRE)**132 4282 3-8-12 80 .......................... DaneO'Neill 11 78
(TGMills) *racd in midfield: rdn over 2f out: sn one pce and no imp on ldrs* **14/1**

1200 **9** 4 **Border Edge**38 6050 5-9-3 84 ..........................(v) GBaker 3 72
(JJBridger) *b: hld up in last trio: rdn and lost tch over 2f out: n.d after* **8/1**

4035 **10** 2 1/2 **Fellow Ship**66 5158 3-8-9 73 .......................... LPKeniry(3) 8 63
(PButler) *dwlt: hld up in last: lost tch over 2f out: no ch after* **50/1**

0- **11** 7 **Adalar (IRE)**443 5252 3-8-10 85 .......................... SJDonohoe(7) 1 51
(PDEvans) *dwlt: drvn to ld after 1f and set str pce: hdd & wknd over 3f out* **25/1**

1m 38.19s (-1.32) **Going Correction** +0.10s/f (Slow)
**WFA** 3 from 4yo+ 1lb **11** Ran SP% **123.4**
Speed ratings: **110,108,107,107,107 106,105,105,101,98 91**CSF £15.32 TOTE £6.50: £1.60, £1.30, £2.90; EX 19.60 Place 6 £15.73, Place 5 £7.14.
**Owner** A P Griffin **Bred** Bearstone Stud **Trained** Newmarket, Suffolk

**FOCUS**
The pace was sound.

**NOTEBOOK**
**Labrett**, back on his favoured surface, was minus the cheekpieces but had a tongue tie on for the first time in a year. Ridden more handily than usual, he picked off the leader at the furlong pole.
**Star Of Normandie(USA)**was more amenable before the race than usual. She looked somewhat unlucky, as she found her path blocked at a vital stage, allowing the winner to take first run, but she obviously remains in good heart.
**Silken Brief(IRE)**left Sir Michael Stoute's yard following a light turf campaign. With the tongue tie on, she ran another good race on a surface which obviously suits her.
**Skylarker(USA)**, dropped considerably in trip for this first start since July, was minus the headgear. This was a fair run but he remains hard to win with.
**Just Fly**ran respectably without convincing that this trip is what he needs.
**Free Option(IRE)**, who has changed stables again, can pay his way when his new yard finds the key to him.
T/Jkpt: Not won. T/Plt: £11.30 to a £1 stake. Pool: £60,817.90. 3,927.05 winning tickets. T/Qpdt: £3.00 to a £1 stake. Pool: £4,345.50. 1,056.10 winning tickets. JN

# 6235WOLVERHAMPTON (A.W) (L-H)
## Wednesday, December 31

**OFFICIAL GOING: Slow**
There was a significant bias towards those that raced away from the inside rail.

## 6264 BETDIRECT.CO.UK H'CAP (DIV I) 5f (F)
12:40 (12:46) (F) (0-65,63) 3-Y-0+ **£2,023** (£578; £289) **Stalls** Low

Form RPR

0014 **1** **Lady Pekan**25 6138 4-9-5 **57** ..........................(b) FPFerris(3) 4 68
(PSMcentee) *mde all: pushed out fnl f* **5/1**3

5002 **2** 1 **Never Without Me**22 6151 3-8-12 **47** .......................... NCallan 2 55
(PJMcbride) *s.i.s: hdwy 2f out: styd on to chse wnr ins fnl f* **9/2**2

0410 **3** 2 1/2 **Laurel Dawn**11 6221 5-9-11 **63** .......................... DAllan(3) 3 62
(IWMcinnes) *chsd wnr tl one pce appr fnl f* **8/1**

1033 **4** 1 1/4 **Kiss The Rain**19 6166 3-8-13 **51** ..........................(v) LFletcher(3) 9 45
(RBrotherton) *prom on outside: threatened appr fnl f: wknd ins* **12/1**

3001 **5** hd **Cloudless (USA)**9 6232 3-9-12 **61** 6ex .......................... SWhitworth 5 55
(JWUnett) *broke wl: sn lost pl and rdn: nvr on terms after* **9/4**1

002 **6** 2 1/2 **Abraxas**19 6166 5-9-4 **53** ..........................(p) CCatlin 6 38
(JAkehurst) *prom tl rdn 1/2-way: sn btn* **9/1**

0630 **7** 3/4 **Catchthebatch**19 6166 7-9-1 **50** .......................... SCarson 8 32
(EAWheeler) *a outpcd in rr* **20/1**

6203 **8** 3 **Erracht**32 6095 5-9-5 **54** .......................... GBaker 1 26
(KRBurke) *prom on ins tl wknd 1/2-way* **11/2**

63.80 secs (1.20) **Going Correction** +0.30s/f (Slow) **8** Ran SP% **114.6**
Speed ratings: **102,100,96,94,94 90,88,84**CSF £27.77 CT £176.49 TOTE £6.70: £2.10, £1.20, £4.10; EX 41.40.
**Owner** P S J Croft **Bred** Jeremy Green And Sons **Trained** Newmarket, Suffolk

**FOCUS**
A decent pace and much the faster of the two divisions. The field were keen to come as wide as possible down the home straight.

**NOTEBOOK**
**Lady Pekan**utilised her early pace to get to the front soon after the start and, brought wide into the straight, had little difficulty holding her rivals at bay. This surface suits her well.
**Never Without Me**, dropping even further in trip, was well backed and showed why with a decent effort, though he could never quite haul the winner back.
**Laurel Dawn**ran one of his better races, but is so in and out that he cannot be relied upon to perform so well next time.
**Kiss The Rain**held a prominent position early, but the principals had too much speed for her and her efforts to stay with them eventually told.
**Cloudless(USA)**could not make the most of a decent break and gradually became outpaced. She failed to pick up when asked and was a shadow of the horse that was so impressive here last time.

## 6265 BETDIRECT.CO.UK H'CAP (DIV II) 5f (F)
1:15 (1:25) (F) (0-65,61) 3-Y-0+ **£2,023** (£578; £289) **Stalls** Low

Form RPR

0264 **1** **Sandgate Cygnet**19 6166 3-9-9 58 ..........................(p) RWinston 6 69
(ISemple) *t.k.h: chsd ldrs: led appr fnl f: rdn out* **7/2**1

4400 **2** 1/2 **Playtime Blue**11 6221 3-9-10 59 .......................... GBaker 9 68
(KRBurke) *chsd ldrs on outside: rdn to press wnr ins fnl f* **12/1**

0306 **3** 3/4 **Percy Douglas**70 5706 3-9-7 56 ..........................(v) AnnStokell 8 62
(MissAStokell) *in rr on outside: hdwy over 1f out: r.o wl fnl f: nvr nrr* **16/1**

5016 **4** nk **Cash**5 6236 5-9-12 61 ..........................(p) RFitzpatrick 1 66
(PaulJohnson) *mid-div: rdn 1/2-way: hdwy whn checked appr fnl f: r.o ins* **11/2**

0546 **5** 1 1/2 **Aintnecessarilyso**4 6243 5-8-8 43 .......................... CCatlin 3 43
(NEBerry) *outpcd and in rr tl mde gd hdwy ins fnl f: nvr nrr* **8/1**

4265 **6** 1 **Rellim**19 6166 4-8-10 52 .......................... DerekNolan(7) 7 49
(PABlockley) *chsd ldr tl rdn and wknd fnl f* **5/1**3

4000 **7** 1/2 **Salerno**25 6136 4-8-12 50 ..........................(p) LisaJones(3) 2 45
(MissGayKelleway) *outpcd: a in rr* **9/2**2

0000 **8** 3/4 **So Sober (IRE)**19 6166 5-8-4 44 .......................... THamilton(5) 5 36
(DShaw) *mid-div: rdn 1/2-way: n.d* **16/1**

0402 **9** hd **The Leather Wedge (IRE)**19 6170 4-8-9 49 .......................... PBradley(5) 4 41
(ABerry) *led tl rdn and hdd appr fnl f: wknd qckly: eased* **8/1**

64.92 secs (2.32) **Going Correction** +0.30s/f (Slow) **9** Ran SP% **114.1**
Speed ratings: **93,92,91,90,88 86,85,84,84**CSF £45.90 CT £589.60 TOTE £4.60: £1.60, £4.00, £3.40; EX 60.60.
**Owner** Mrs A M Young **Bred** G And Mrs A Young **Trained** Carluke, S Lanarks

**FOCUS**
A slower time than the first division by more than a second and the field did not come so wide, preferring to race down the centre of the track.

**NOTEBOOK**
**Sandgate Cygnet**has been threatening to win a race on this surface and everything went right for her this time. She was all out to win though, and this did not look a great race.
**Playtime Blue**looks better on this surface than on Polytrack and made sure the winner had to be kept right up to her work. There may be a race in him on Fibresand, albeit a modest one.
**Percy Douglas**showed some fair form over this course and distance last winter and ran a better race on this return to Fibresand.
**Cash**was stopped in his tracks when first trying for a gap between Rellim and The Leather Wedge, but persisted and finally got through. Without the interference he would probably have finished third. *Official explanation: trainer said gelding hung right in the home straight*
**Aintnecessarilyso**, whose only previous win was two and a half years ago, can be forgiven to a small degree as he raced closest to the inside rail.
**Rellim**showed his usual early pace but is still failing to get home.
**The Leather Wedge(IRE)**took the field along early, but was swamped at the furlong pole and stopped very quickly.

## 6266 BET DIRECT ON CHANNEL 4 PAGE 613 MAIDEN STKS 7f (F)
1:45 (1:55) (D) 2-Y-O **£3,038** (£868; £434) **Stalls** High

Form RPR

2 **1** **Denver (IRE)**12 6216 2-9-0 ..........................(b1) RWinston 2 73
(BJMeehan) *a.p: rdn to ld over 2f out: kpt up to work ins fnl f* **2/1**2

6 **2** 2 **Bahiano (IRE)**54 5939 2-8-7 .......................... DeanWilliams(7) 4 68
(CEBrittain) *a front rnk: led 1/2-way: hdd over 2f out: edgd lft and no imp ins fnl f* **12/1**

**3** 6 **Anna Panna** 2-8-9 .......................... DSweeney 7 48
(HCandy) *in tch on outside: rdn over 2f out: styd on ins fnl f* **20/1**

223 **4** 1 1/2 **Little Eye (IRE)**2 6251 2-9-0 68 .......................... NPollard 6 49
(JRBest) *in tch: rdn 1/2-way: no hdwy fnl 2f* **7/4**1

**5** 6 **Oboe** 2-8-9 .......................... SDrowne 9 29
(RCharlton) *prom on outside tl outpcd 2f out: no hdwy after* **10/1**

5046 **6** 1 **Smart Boy Prince (IRE)**18 6175 2-9-0 55 .......................... DeanMcKeown 5 32
(PABlockley) *led tl hdd 1/2-way: sn btn* **6/1**3

0 **7** 1 **Chimes Eight**19 6167 2-8-4 .......................... THamilton(5) 3 24
(RAFahey) *s.i.s: outpcd and a in rr* **33/1**

054 **8** 25 **Daggers Canyon**19 6167 2-9-0 65 .......................... NCallan 1 —
(JulianPoulton) *chsd ldrs: rdn 1/2-way: wknd qckly: eased over 1f out: t.o* **16/1**

1m 31.75s (1.55) **Going Correction** +0.30s/f (Slow) **8** Ran SP% **114.4**
Speed ratings: **103,100,93,92,85 84,83,54**CSF £26.19 TOTE £3.70: £1.10, £4.80, £4.90; EX 20.30.
**Owner** Gigginstown House Stud **Bred** Gigginstown House **Trained** Upper Lambourn, Berks

**FOCUS**
Not the strongest of maidens, but the front two finished clear and may be capable of better.

**NOTEBOOK**
**Denver(IRE)**had obviously learned from his sand debut at Southwell and responded well to the first-time blinkers. Always in touch, he pulled right away with the runner-up down the straight despite this trip possibly being on the sharp side. He can win again.
**Bahiano(IRE)**, who showed promise in his only start on turf, found the winner too strong but pulled right away from the rest and it will be a surprise if he cannot find an ordinary maiden on this surface.
**Anna Panna**, a half-sister to a winning hurdler, was done for pace from the final bend and probably needs further.
**Little Eye(IRE)**was on and off the bridle from an early stage and it was soon evident this was not going to be his day. This was very disappointing and perhaps this race came a bit too soon.
**Oboe**, out of a half-sister to several winners, showed up for a while but did not offer any immediate promise for the future.
**Smart Boy Prince(IRE)** was surprisingly well backed considering he was more exposed than his rivals and has yet to make the first three. He took the field along early, but was one of the first beaten.

## 6267 LITTLEWOODS BET DIRECT H'CAP 1m 6f 166y(F)
2:20 (2:25) (E) (0-75,75) 3-Y-0+ **£2,009** (£574; £287) **Stalls** High

Form RPR

0-06 **1** **Phantom Stock**28 6121 3-7-12 **52** oh3 .......................... DMernagh 8 73+
(WJarvis) *t.k.h and hld up: gd hdwy 7f out: led over 3f out: pushed clr over 1f out: v easily* **7/1**

2355 **2** 8 **Glory Quest (USA)**12 6215 6-9-7 **73** ..........................(p) TEaves(5) 7 81
(MissGayKelleway) *hld up: hdwy 5f out: wnt 2nd over 2f out: no ch w wnr fr over 1f out* **4/1**2

4165 **3** 8 **Nowell House**28 6123 7-9-9 **75** .......................... PMulrennan(5) 5 73
(MWEasterby) *in tch: hdwy 5f out: styd on ins fnl 2f: nt rch first 2* **10/1**

6143 **4** 3/4 **Sashay**25 6139 5-8-5 **59** .......................... StephanieHollinshead(7) 3 56
(RHollinshead) *chsd ldrs: rdn 6f out and sn outpcd: n.d after* **13/2**3

2321 **5** 5 **Easibet Dot Net**40 6043 3-8-8 **65** ow2 ..........................(p) DMcGaffin(3) 1 53
(ISemple) *trckd ldr: led over 4f out: hdd over 3f out: sn wknd* **11/4**1

6022 **6** 7 **Vanbrugh (FR)**15 6200 3-8-8 **65** ..........................(vt) LisaJones(3) 6 46
(MissDAMchale) *led tl hdd over 4f out: sn wknd* **4/1**2

0000 **7** 19 **Hajeer (IRE)**15 6200 5-7-12 **45** oh1 ..........................(p) JBramhill 2 1
(PWHiatt) *rdn and dropped rr 1/2-way: t.o* **12/1**

000 **8** dist **Fast Cindy (USA)**25 6139 4-8-8 **55** .......................... RWinston 4 —
(JWUnett) *chsd ldrs tl wknd rapidly over 5f out: virtually p.u over 2f out* **20/1**

3m 25.41s (4.61) **Going Correction** +0.30s/f (Slow)
**WFA** 3 from 4yo+ 7lb **8** Ran SP% **114.0**
Speed ratings: **99,94,90,90,87 83,73,—**CSF £34.88 CT £279.84 TOTE £5.50: £2.10, £1.80, £3.00; EX 30.90.
**Owner** The L E H Partnership **Bred** Brook Stud Ltd **Trained** Newmarket, Suffolk

**FOCUS**
A modest staying handicap and ultimately a one-horse race.
**NOTEBOOK**
**Phantom Stock**, who had finished no closer than sixth in five previous outings, improved dramatically over this longer trip and absolutely bolted up. The Handicapper will not be impressed so the temptation must be to bring him out under a penalty, but he is unexposed over this sort of trip and may be able to cope with the inevitable big rise in any case.
**Glory Quest(USA)**can consider himself very unlucky as he ran right up to his best and beat the other established stayers hollow, but unfortunately he ran into an unexposed and very well handicapped rival.
**Nowell House**ran with a little credit, but has never performed as well on this surface as he has on turf or over hurdles.
**Sashay**is an established stayer around here, but may have found this a bit too competitive.
**Easibet Dot Net**travelled well for a long way, but patently failed to stay this longer trip.
**Vanbrugh(FR)**made much of the running, but also gave the inside rail away to no-one and that may have sapped his stamina faster than otherwise would have been the case.
**Fast Cindy(USA)** *Official explanation: trainer said filly was struck into*

## 6268 BET DIRECT ON 0800 32 93 93 H'CAP — 1m 1f 79y(F)
2:55 (3:00) (C ) (0-100,100) 3-Y-0+ — **£6,734** (£2,072; £1,036; £518) **Stalls** Low

| Form | | | | RPR |
|---|---|---|---|---|
| 0612 | **1** | | **Nimello (USA)**[23] 6144 7-8-8 **78** ... SWhitworth 10<br>(AGNewcombe) *hld up: gd hdwy over 4f out: led over 1f out: pushed out: comf* **10/1** | 93 |
| 2121 | **2** | 2 ½ | **Mi Odds**[12] 6215 7-9-5 **89** ... PMcCabe 3<br>(MrsNMacauley) *a.p: r.o gamely to chse wnr fnl f* **10/1** | 99 |
| 2000 | **3** | 2 ½ | **Del Mar Sunset**[28] 6124 4-8-10 **83** ... LisaJones(3) 6<br>(WJHaggas) *chsd ldr: led 3f out: hdd over 1f out: one pce* **16/1** | 88 |
| 5022 | **4** | 4 | **Caroubier (IRE)**[18] 6174 3-8-8 **80** ... DMernagh 5<br>(TDBarron) *in rr: rdn wl over 2f out: styd on past btn horses ins fnl 2f* **25/1** | 77 |
| 3122 | **5** | 2 ½ | **Lakota Brave**[11] 6224 9-9-6 **90** ... SDrowne 4<br>(MrsStefLiddiard) *mid-div: rdn 3f out: no hdwy after* **12/1** | 82 |
| 4033 | **6** | 6 | **Cool Temper**[19] 6169 7-8-8 **78** ... (t) CCatlin 8<br>(PFICole) *a in rr* **9/1**[3] | 58 |
| 3460 | **7** | shd | **Lundy's Lane (IRE)**[39] 6051 3-10-0 **100** ... MFenton 9<br>(CEBrittain) *in tch: rdn 3f out: n.d after* **10/1** | 80 |
| 3511 | **8** | 1 | **Strong Hand**[32] 6098 3-8-11 **88** ... PMulrennan(5) 7<br>(MWEasterby) *mid-div: rdn over 4f out: sn bhd* **2/1**[1] | 66 |
| 0523 | **9** | 6 | **Te Quiero**[12] 6215 5-9-10 **94** ... (t) NCallan 1<br>(MissGayKelleway) *led tl hdd 3f out: rdn and wknd qckly* **7/2**[2] | 60 |
| 0505 | **10** | 30 | **Gallant Boy (IRE)**[14] 6208 4-8-4 **77** ... (t) FPFerris(3) 2<br>(PDEvans) *in rr: lost tch 1/2-way: t.o* **11/1** | — |

2m 2.18s (-0.72) **Going Correction** +0.30s/f (Slow)
**WFA** 3 from 4yo+ 2lb — **10** Ran SP% **118.6**
Speed ratings: **115,112,110,107,104 99,99,98,93,66**CSF £107.25 CT £1595.96 TOTE £12.10: £2.70, £2.50, £4.90; EX 55.50.
**Owner** Ms Gerardine P O'Reilly **Bred** Glencrest Farm **Trained** Yarnscombe, Devon
**FOCUS**
As competitive a handicap as there has ever been on sand and a scorching pace.
**NOTEBOOK**
**Nimello(USA)**, having only his second outing for his current yard, was back to his absolute best and was well supported in the market to do so. The strong gallop was perfect as it enabled him to come from off the pace, which he likes to do, and this was the longest trip he has ever won over. It will be interesting to see where he goes now.
**Mi Odds**is consistency personified and again ran his socks off even though in theory this trip is short of his best.
**Del Mar Sunset**ran with plenty of credit considering there was so much pace on and his chances of getting the lead on his own were slim. He managed to hang in there until the furlong pole and proved he is no back number yet.
**Caroubier(IRE)**, beaten at odds-on in a claimer last time, was making his debut for the yard and ran on to finish a remote fourth. This was still not a bad effort in this company.
**Lakota Brave**should have been suited by the way the race was run, but he has never won off a mark this high and could make no impression down the straight.
**Cool Temper**never got into the race and may be a better horse at Southwell.
**Lundy's Lane(IRE)**is talented, but still faced a stiff task under top weight against these rivals and was making his Fibresand debut.
**Strong Hand**is shooting up the handicap, but was one of the first beaten and she was nothing like the same filly that was so impressive in her two previous starts here. Something was surely amiss. *Official explanation: jockey said filly was never travelling*
**Te Quiero**went off at a rate of knots, but had run himself into the ground rounding the home turn.
**Gallant Boy(IRE)**has won on this track, but never looked happy and did not give his true running at all.

## 6269 BET DIRECT ON ITV PAGE 367 (S) STKS — 1m 100y(F)
3:25 (3:30) (G ) 2-Y-0 — **£2,009** (£574; £287) **Stalls** Low

| Form | | | | RPR |
|---|---|---|---|---|
| 0 | **1** | | **Killing Me Softly**[19] 6167 2-8-12 ... DSweeney 11<br>(JGallagher) *chsd ldrs: led over 2f out: rdn out fnl f* **25/1** | 53 |
| 4606 | **2** | 1 ¾ | **Comic Genius**[37] 6058 2-8-7 42 ... (v) PaulEddery 3<br>(DHaydnJones) *hld up: hdwy on outside 3f out: edgd lft over 2f out: styd on to chse wnr fnl f* **13/2**[3] | 45 |
| 2050 | **3** | 1 ½ | **Marita**[96] 5198 2-8-7 51 ... MFenton 5<br>(JGGiven) *led fo 1f: rdn and lost pl over 3f out: c wd and styd on wl ins fnl 2f* **8/1** | 42 |
| 0054 | **4** | nk | **Bretton**[9] 6228 2-8-12 45 ... (b[1]) DaleGibson 10<br>(RHollinshead) *hld up: t.k.h: rdn and hdwy whn bmpd over 2f out: kpt on ins fnl f* **11/1** | 46 |
| 4004 | **5** | shd | **Platinum Chief**[15] 6201 2-8-12 47 ... GParkin 8<br>(ABerry) *chsd ldr to 3f out: styd prom u.p: wknd ins fnl f* **12/1** | 46 |
| 0045 | **6** | ½ | **Brother Cadfael**[15] 6201 2-8-12 45 ... RFfrench 9<br>(JohnAHarris) *led after 1f: hdd over 2f out: one pce after* **10/1** | 45 |
| 0265 | **7** | 3 ½ | **Jakarmi**[23] 6145 2-8-12 60 ... NCallan 6<br>(BPalling) *prom: rdn over 3f out: wknd over 2f out* **6/4**[1] | 37 |
| 4560 | **8** | 3 | **Look No More**[39] 6046 2-8-5 47 ... CHaddon(7) 7<br>(WGMTurner) *prom early: sn rdn: wknd over 2f out* **20/1** | 31 |
| 4353 | **9** | 3 | **Armentieres**[23] 6147 2-8-13 53 ... (b) ADaly 1<br>(JLSpearing) *a outpcd in rr* **9/2**[2] | 26 |
| 0006 | **10** | 20 | **Desert Light (IRE)**[15] 6201 2-8-9 35 ... (e) LisaJones(3) 2<br>(DShaw) *a wl in rr* **33/1** | — |
| 000 | **11** | 1 ¼ | **Evening Fragrance**[19] 6167 2-8-12 19 ... (b) JMackay 4<br>(GCHChung) *s.i.s and a struggling in rr* **66/1** | — |

1m 55.56s (4.56) **Going Correction** +0.30s/f (Slow) — **11** Ran SP% **120.8**
Speed ratings: **89,87,85,85,85 84,81,78,75,55 54**CSF £179.24 TOTE £38.00: £6.60, £3.90, £1.60; EX 1768.00.No bid for the winner
**Owner** Stuart Prior **Bred** S R Prior **Trained** Chastleton, Oxon
**FOCUS**
A poor seller and a shock winner.
**NOTEBOOK**
**Killing Me Softly**, beaten 23 lengths on his Southwell debut, was at least taking a big drop in class and did have some scope. Given a positive ride and kept well away from the inside rail, he found plenty when asked but, even if progressing again, will find life tough outside selling company.
**Comic Genius**, who has shown a modicum of ability, was kept wide of her field and that as much as anything enabled her to grab the runner's-up spot. A spot of argy-bargy with Bretton on the home bend made little difference.
**Marita**, returning from a three-month break, hit a flat spot mid-race but, brought widest of all down the straight, stayed on to snatch third.
**Bretton**, dropped in class, raced wide and got involved in a bumping match with the runner-up on the home bend before responding to his rider's urgings to reach his final position.
**Platinum Chief**, already well exposed at this level, had every chance but did not see the trip out.
**Brother Cadfael**set the pace, but was in trouble as soon as he was challenged turning for home. He raced closer to the inside rail than those who beat him.
**Jakarmi**, beaten a short head in a claimer over course and distance last month and in a seller for the first time, never looked that happy and racing close to the inside rail probably did him few favours either.
**Armentieres**, the only previous winner in the line up, was never seen with a chance.

## 6270 HAPPY NEW YEAR FROM BET DIRECT H'CAP — 7f (F)
3:55 (4:00) (D ) (0-80,74) 3-Y-0+ — **£3,024** (£864; £432) **Stalls** High

| Form | | | | RPR |
|---|---|---|---|---|
| 0002 | **1** | | **Warden Warren**[18] 6176 5-8-13 **66** ... (b) BReilly(5) 8<br>(MrsCADunnett) *hld up in tch: hdwy 4f out: wnt 2nd 3f out: led over 1f out: r.o wl* **6/1**[3] | 78 |
| 0016 | **2** | ½ | **Arc El Ciel (ARG)**[9] 6231 5-9-12 **74** ... (v) SDrowne 6<br>(MrsStefLiddiard) *hld up: rdn and hdwy over 3f out: wnt 2nd over 1f out: r.o* **13/2** | 85 |
| 0121 | **3** | 6 | **Mon Secret (IRE)**[18] 6176 5-8-13 **61** ... RFfrench 4<br>(BSmart) *chsd ldr to 3f out: wknd appr fnl f* **3/1**[1] | 57 |
| 4053 | **4** | 1 ¾ | **Grey Pearl**[9] 6231 4-9-9 **71** ... NCallan 7<br>(MissGayKelleway) *led tl hdd over 1f out: wknd* **3/1**[1] | 62 |
| 5351 | **5** | ¾ | **And Toto Too**[1] 6260 3-9-4 **73** ... (v) SJDonohoe(7) 2<br>(PDEvans) *rdn and in rr: kpt on past btn horses fnl f* **7/2**[2] | 63 |
| 6126 | **6** | hd | **Spark Up**[32] 6100 3-9-2 **64** ... (b) SWhitworth 3<br>(JWUnett) *a in rr* **12/1** | 53 |
| 2015 | **7** | 7 | **Teehee (IRE)**[25] 6135 5-9-8 **70** ... (b) MFenton 5<br>(BPalling) *in tch tl rdn 3f out: sn btn* **14/1** | 42 |
| 0P00 | **8** | dist | **Robin Sharp**[19] 6171 5-8-5 **53** ow1 ... (v[1]) PDoe 1<br>(JAkehurst) *prom for 2f: sn rdn and wl bhd: t.o* **20/1** | — |

1m 31.34s (1.14) **Going Correction** +0.30s/f (Slow) — **8** Ran SP% **119.0**
Speed ratings: **105,104,97,95,94 94,86,**—CSF £46.22 CT £142.81 TOTE £6.70: £2.20, £1.70, £2.00; EX 26.40 Place 6 £1,081.98, Place 5 £508.53.
**Owner** Annwell Inn Syndicate **Bred** R G Percival **Trained** Hingham, Norfolk
**FOCUS**
A fair race run at a sound pace.
**NOTEBOOK**
**Warden Warren**, 6lb better off with Mon Secret for a narrow defeat at Southwell, does not like being crowded so this small field was a big help, and he was always going to win after taking it up a furlong from home.
**Arc El Ciel(ARG)**ran much better after a rare poor performance on this track last time, and was closing all the way to the line.
**Mon Secret(IRE)**rather confirmed the opinion that he is much better suited by the longer straight at Southwell than here.
**Grey Pearl**adopted her usual trailblazing tactics but, as in her previous start, failed to get home.
**And Toto Too**, carrying a 7lb penalty for her victory at Lingfield the previous day, has also won here in the past but was off the bridle from a long way out and never got into it.
**Robin Sharp**continues to run as though something is amiss.
T/Plt: £8,268.60 to a £1 stake. Pool: £44,174.80. 3.90 winning tickets. T/Qpdt: £375.00 to a £1 stake. Pool: £3,649.50. 7.20 winning tickets. JS

# The Form Book®

## TURF AND ALL-WEATHER FLAT RACING 2004

Complete record of Turf and All-Weather Racing from January 1st to November 6th 2004

# SOUTHWELL (L-H)

Thursday, January 1

**400 Meeting Abandoned** - Waterlogged

RACES 1-399 VOID (numbers exclusive to Computer Raceform)

# WOLVERHAMPTON (A.W) (L-H)

Friday, January 2

**OFFICIAL GOING: Standard**

The going appeared to be riding deeper on the inside of the track and racing on the rail seemed a disadvantage.

Wind: nil Weather: overcast and cold

## 406 BET DIRECT NO Q VOICE AUTOMATED BETTING H'CAP (DIV I) 1m 1f 79y(F)

12:50 (12:57) (F) (0-60,60) 4-Y-O+ £2,926 (£836; £418) Stalls Low

Form RPR

540- **1** **Jair Ohmsford (IRE)**[57] 5935 5-9-11 **57** ................ MFenton 2 70
(WJMusson) *hld up: hdwy on ins over 3f out: rdn to ld over 1f out: r.o wl* **9/2**[1]

353- **2** *4* **Danger Bird (IRE)**[7] 6238 4-9-3 **50** ................ ACulhane 8 55
(RHollinshead) *plld hrd early: led after 1f: rdn over 2f out: hdd over 1f out: one pce* **16/1**

046- **3** *2* **Grand Lass (IRE)**[17] 6198 5-9-6 **52** ................ (b[1]) DMernagh 12 53
(TDBarron) *s.i.s: sn mid-div: rdn and hdwy on outside over 2f out: hung lft fr over 1f out: one pce* **16/1**

534- **4** *2* **Faraway Look (USA)**[20] 6178 7-10-0 **60** ................ RHavlin 7 57
(JGMO'Shea) *prom: pushed along over 4f out: rdn and outpcd over 2f out: styd on fnl f* **6/1**[2]

404- **5** *3/4* **Goodbye Mr Bond**[25] 6143 4-9-6 **56** ................ DAllan(3) 1 52
(EJAlston) *led 1f: prom: rdn and wnt 2nd 3f out: ev ch over 1f out: wknd fnl f* **7/1**[3]

534- **6** *nk* **Qobtaan (USA)**[14] 6218 5-8-13 **45** ................ GBaker 10 40
(MRBosley) *prom: rdn over 2f out: wknd fnl f* **6/1**[2]

426- **7** *2* **Over Rating**[35] 6086 4-9-13 **60** ................ NCallan 5 51
(KARyan) *hld up in tch: rdn over 3f out: wknd wl over 1f out* **7/1**[3]

460- **8** *4* **Jessinca**[39] 6055 8-8-8 **43** ................ LPKeniry(3) 9 26
(APJones) *prom: chsd ldr over 5f out to 3f out: wknd 2f out* **20/1**

450- **9** *2* **Escalade**[13] 6226 7-8-11 **48** ................ PMulrennan(5) 6 27
(WMBrisbourne) *hld up and plld hrd: bhd fnl 4f* **8/1**

050- **10** *1/2* **Top Of The Class (IRE)**[39] 6055 7-8-5 **44** ................ (v) SJDonohoe(7) 4 22
(PDEvans) *dwlt: rdn over 3f out: a bhd* **10/1**

060- **11** *8* **Consignia (IRE)**[14] 6211 5-9-2 **48** ................ (b) PaulEddery 3 10
(DHaydnJones) *plld hrd early: a bhd* **14/1**

032- **12** *13* **First Eagle**[62] 5879 5-9-4 **50** ................ (v) PMcCabe 13 —
(MrsNMacauley) *hld up: stdy hdwy over 5f out: rdn over 3f out: sn wknd* **16/1**

105- **13** *4* **Red Storm**[17] 1566 5-9-5 **51** ................ IMongan 11 —
(JRBoyle) *hld up: hdwy on outside over 4f out: sn rdn: wknd over 3f out* **9/1**

2m 3.76s (0.86) **Going Correction** +0.025s/f (Slow)
**WFA** 4 from 5yo+ 1lb **13** Ran SP% **131.0**
Speed ratings: **97,93,91,89,89 88,87,83,81,81 74,62,59**CSF £88.48 CT £1111.25 TOTE £6.50: £2.40, £4.30, £5.80; EX 132.60.
**Owner** K A Cosby **Bred** Stuart Weld **Trained** Newmarket, Suffolk

**FOCUS**
The pace was very steady in the first part of the race, the overall time being 2.64 seconds slower than the second division, and it developed into something of a sprint. Nevertheless, the form looks above average for the grade.

**NOTEBOOK**
**Jair Ohmsford(IRE)**, who has edged down the handicap, landed a gamble in decisive fashion in the end. He won as if he needs this trip and more, and now that he has got his head in front he should pay to follow on this surface.
**Danger Bird(IRE)**, who was very keen to post, made most of the running but was no match for the winner in the end. She stayed this longer trip.
**Grand Lass(IRE)** ran a better race in the first-time blinkers and over a shorter trip, but she hung in the home straight and could not quicken up. She has slipped to a decent mark, but still does not look like a winner waiting to happen. *Official explanation: jockey said mare hung left in the home straight*
**Faraway Look(USA)**, returning to a more suitable trip, stayed on again in the latter stages, having lost his pitch, but was hanging and not really helping his rider.
**Goodbye Mr Bond**, upped in trip, was always in the front rank but was not helped by racing on the deepest part of the track once in line for home.
**Qobtaan(USA)** did not shape as if this longer trip was the answer.

## 407 BET DIRECT NO Q FILLIES' H'CAP 6f (F)

1:20 (1:25) (E) (0-75,70) 4-Y-O+ £3,283 (£938; £469) Stalls Low

Form RPR

641- **1** **Sandgate Cygnet**[2] 6265 4-9-7 **64** 6ex ................ (p) RWinston 8 75
(ISemple) *t.k.h: mde all: rdn wl over 1f out: drvn out* **9/2**[2]

213- **2** *1* **Zagala**[34] 6088 4-9-4 **61** ................ (t) ACulhane 9 69
(SLKeightley) *hld up: hdwy over 3f out: edgd lft ins fnl f: kpt on: nt trble wnr* **9/2**[2]

246- **3** *1* **Pilgrim Princess (IRE)**[38] 6065 6-8-2 **45** ................ ANicholls 4 50
(EJAlston) *w wnr: rdn over 2f out: ev ch over 1f out: nt qckn* **6/1**[3]

020- **4** *shd* **Prima Stella**[27] 6132 5-9-7 **67** ................ LisaJones(3) 2 72
(JARToller) *a.p: rdn over 2f out: ev ch over 1f out: nt qckn* **10/3**[1]

602- **5** *1/2* **Amelia (IRE)**[7] 6236 6-7-12 **48** ................ BSwarbrick(7) 1 51
(WMBrisbourne) *hld up: hdwy on outside over 2f out: r.o one pce fnl f* **6/1**[3]

660- **6** *1 3/4* **Tigress (IRE)**[27] 6138 5-9-4 **61** ................ (b) MartinDwyer 7 59
(JWUnett) *hld up: rdn and hdwy on outside over 2f out: wknd over 1f out* **16/1**

001- **7** *2 1/2* **Playful Spirit**[24] 6150 5-8-3 **46** ................ (v) JEdmunds 6 36
(JBalding) *prom: rdn over 2f out: wknd over 1f out* **10/1**

405- **8** *1 1/2* **Bijan (IRE)**[39] 6056 6-7-13 **42** oh6 ow1 ................ DaleGibson 3 28
(RHollinshead) *chsd ldrs: pushed along over 5f out: rdn and wknd over 2f out* **25/1**

06F- **9** *1 1/4* **Indian Shores**[57] 5937 5-9-1 **58** ................ PJScallan 10 40
(MMullineaux) *prom tl rdn and wknd 3f out* **25/1**

000- **10** *12* **Chanteuse**[25] 6146 4-8-6 **49** ................ RBrisland 11 —
(DWChapman) *rdn 3f out: a bhd* **40/1**

1m 16.2s (0.50) **Going Correction** +0.025s/f (Slow) **10** Ran SP% **113.1**
Speed ratings: **97,95,94,94,93 91,87,85,84,68**CSF £23.70 CT £120.54 TOTE £5.20: £2.00, £2.10, £1.90; EX 27.40.
**Owner** Mrs A M Young **Bred** G And Mrs A Young **Trained** Carluke, S Lanarks

**FOCUS**
An ordinary fillies' handicap, run in a respectable time. The form looks solid.

**NOTEBOOK**
**Sandgate Cygnet**, a progressive filly, supplemented her win here on New Year's Eve under a penalty. A keen sort, she has learnt to break better and her trainer believes that this trip is her best as her jockey is able to sit longer, while over five more use needs to be made of her. She looks the type who does no more than is necessary and should continue on the upgrade.
**Zagala** has looked an improved filly since being fitted with a tongue tie and this was another decent run, even if the drop back from seven furlongs did not look ideal.
**Pilgrim Princess(IRE)** matched strides with the winner for a long way and should come on for this first run after a break, but her losing run stretches to 23 now.
**Prima Stella**, back over six furlongs for her second run for this yard, was not helped by racing up the inside rail in the straight where the ground was deeper.
**Amelia(IRE)** conceded ground when being dropped out at the start. She began a promising forward move on the wide outside in the straight but the effort fizzled out inside the last.
**Tigress(IRE)** is best over five, but she does stay this trip and she made a little late progress.

## 408 BET DIRECT NO Q ON 08000 93 66 93 CLAIMING STKS 7f (F)

1:50 (1:55) (F) 3-Y-O £2,877 (£822; £411) Stalls High

Form RPR

226- **1** **Turf Princess**[20] 6173 3-8-7 61 ................ DFentiman(7) 4 56
(IanEmmerson) *a.p: rdn 3f out: led ins fnl f: jst hld on* **9/4**[1]

346- **2** *shd* **Ever Cheerful**[34] 6090 3-8-12 73 ................ LTreadwell(7) 3 61
(WGMTurner) *t.k.h: led: rdn and edgd rt over 1f out: hdd ins fnl f: r.o wl* **9/4**[1]

654- **3** *1 1/4* **Pardon Moi**[18] 6194 3-7-13 49 ................ HayleyTurner(5) 5 43
(MrsCADunnett) *hld up: rdn 3f out: hdwy over 1f out: ev ch ins fnl f: no ex towards fin* **4/1**[2]

050- **4** *nk* **Secret Bloom**[39] 6058 3-8-7 38 ................ (v[1]) DarrenWilliams 2 45?
(JRNorton) *s.i.s: hld up: rdn 3f out: hdwy over 1f out: nt qckn fnl f* **33/1**

500- **5** *5* **Savernake Brave (IRE)**[17] 6197 3-8-11 48 ................ (b[1]) GBaker 1 37
(KRBurke) *prom: rdn 3f out: wknd 1f out* **14/1**

040- **6** *2* **Whittinghamvillage**[18] 6194 3-8-0 44 ................ DaleGibson 6 21
(ABerry) *hld up in tch: rdn over 3f out: wknd wl over 1f out* **9/2**[3]

1m 31.76s (1.56) **Going Correction** +0.025s/f (Slow) **6** Ran SP% **109.3**
Speed ratings: **92,91,90,90,84 82**CSF £6.98 TOTE £3.10: £1.40, £1.50; EX 8.30.
**Owner** Ian Emmerson **Bred** Valley Paddocks Racing Limited **Trained** Holmside, Co Durham

**FOCUS**
A weakly-contested claimer and the form is typically moderate.

**NOTEBOOK**
**Turf Princess** was having her first run at the track, but she is a winner at Southwell and is proven over this trip. Her young rider did well to put her head in front, but he became slightly unbalanced a few strides from the line and the runner-up almost snatched the race back out of the fire.
**Ever Cheerful** was able to dictate the pace and kicked a couple of lengths to the good turning in, but he was worn down. A keen sort, he does not really see out this trip despite his late rally.
**Pardon Moi**, last but going well enough turning in, came to have her chance but was held in the last half-furlong. Six furlongs is probably her best trip.
**Secret Bloom**, in a first-time visor, missed the break as usual. While he kept on under pressure, he did not want to put his head down and battle.
**Savernake Brave(IRE)** showed no improvement in the first-time blinkers.
**Whittinghamvillage**, a regressive sort, did not stay this longer trip.

## 409 BETDIRECT.CO.UK MAIDEN STKS 7f (F)

2:20 (2:25) (D) 3-Y-O £3,435 (£1,057; £528; £264) Stalls High

Form RPR

02- **1** **Secret Place**[23] 6158 3-9-0 ................ WRyan 6 65+
(EALDunlop) *a gng wl: led on bit over 2f out: pushed clr wl over 1f out: eased cl home* **4/6**[1]

00- **2** *4* **Vrisaki (IRE)**[27] 6129 3-9-0 ................ CCatlin 3 55
(MissDMountain) *led: rdn over 3f out: hdd over 2f out: sn no ch w wnr* **9/1**

043- **3** *3/4* **Katie's Role**[38] 6066 3-8-9 52 ................ ANicholls 2 48
(IanEmmerson) *a.p: rdn and n.m.r over 3f out: one pce fnl 2f* **7/1**[2]

400- **4** *3* **Zonnebeke**[48] 6002 3-8-9 52 ................ DarrenWilliams 5 41
(KRBurke) *hld up: rdn and outpcd 3f out: sme hdwy appr fnl f: n.d* **25/1**

050- **5** *1/2* **Vittorioso (IRE)**[21] 6167 3-9-0 57 ................ (b[1]) MFenton 7 44
(MissGayKelleway) *t.k.h: prom: rdn over 2f out: c wd st: wknd over 1f out: edgd lft towards fin* **8/1**[3]

**6** *2 1/2* **Royaltea** 3-8-9 ................ IMongan 1 33
(MsDeborahJEvans) *s.i.s: a in rr* **20/1**

**7** *1 1/2* **Silver Emperor (IRE)** 3-8-9 ................ (b[1]) DNolan(5) 4 34
(PABlockley) *s.s: hdwy on ins over 4f out: rdn over 2f out: wknd over 1f out* **16/1**

1m 31.02s (0.82) **Going Correction** +0.025s/f (Slow) **7** Ran SP% **108.1**
Speed ratings: **96,91,90,87,86 83,82**CSF £6.38 TOTE £1.40: £1.30, £2.30; EX 5.50.
**Owner** Khalifa Sultan **Bred** Whitsbury Manor Stud **Trained** Newmarket, Suffolk

**FOCUS**
No strength in depth to this maiden, run less than a second faster than the claimer half an hour earlier. Although the form is modest, the winner should do better.

**NOTEBOOK**
**Secret Place** had run up against the potentially smart Jake The Snake on the Polytrack last time but faced nothing of that calibre on this occasion. Not inconvenienced by the drop in trip, he was value for perhaps twice the margin of victory. His fate lies largely in the hands of the handicapper.
**Vrisaki(IRE)** is eligible for a mark now. Handling this longer trip, he won the separate battle for second place but the winner was in a different class.
**Katie's Role**, who is exposed, lost momentum when tightened up at the three-furlong pole but was not good enough in any case.
**Zonnebeke** ran as if she will get a bit farther than this.
**Vittorioso(IRE)**, tried in blinkers instead of cheekpieces, again looked a less than straightforward ride. He will be suited by a drop back to six furlongs.
**Royaltea** is out of a mare who won over seven furlongs but whose only winning offspring has been a point-to-pointer.
**Silver Emperor(IRE)**, blinkered for this debut, fell out of the stalls and found himself well adrift. He recovered to have his chance turning for home before fading.

## 410 LITTLEWOODS BET DIRECT H'CAP 7f (F)

2:50 (2:55) (D) (0-85,85) 4-Y-O+ £4,075 (£1,254; £627; £313) Stalls High

Form RPR

101- **1** **Blakeset**[18] 6192 9-9-1 **72** ................ (v) DMernagh 4 84
(TDBarron) *led: rdn over 2f out: hdd over 1f out: edgd lft and led again ins fnl f: r.o* **5/2**[1]

014- **2** 1 ½ **Ashtree Belle**[20] [6176] 5-9-5 **76**.......... PaulEddery 3 84
(DHaydnJones) *hld up in tch: rdn to ld wl over 1f out: hdd ins fnl f: nt qckn* **9/2**[3]

/00- **3** 1 ¾ **Just A Glimmer**[41] [6049] 4-9-8 **79**.......... MartinDwyer 9 83
(LGCottrell) *sn w ldr: chal 2f out: sn rdn: no ex fnl f* **12/1**

001- **4** 5 **Ronnie From Donny (IRE)**[11] [6231] 4-9-2 **73** 6ex.......... RWinston 7 64
(BEllison) *prom: rdn 3f out: wknd wl over 1f out* **3/1**[2]

500- **5** 1 **Cretan Gift**[13] [6225] 13-9-2 **76**..........(v) J-PGuillambert[(3)] 6 65
(NPLittmoden) *hld up: rdn and hdwy over 3f out: wknd 2f out* **16/1**

534- **6** hd **Blonde En Blonde (IRE)**[7] [6235] 4-8-10 **67**.......... IMongan 2 55
(NPLittmoden) *s.i.s: outpcd: sme hdwy over 2f out: n.d* **8/1**

143- **7** 1 ¾ **Invader**[13] [6224] 8-10-0 **85**..........(b) MFenton 5 69
(CEBrittain) *s.i.s: rdn over 4f out: a bhd* **11/2**

646- **8** 9 **Tally (IRE)**[130] [4460] 4-9-1 **72**.......... NCallan 8 33
(ABerry) *hld up in tch: rdn 3f out: sn wknd* **40/1**

1m 29.19s (-1.01) **Going Correction** +0.025s/f (Slow) **8** Ran SP% **114.3**
Speed ratings: **106,104,102,96,95 95,93,82**CSF £14.06 CT £111.49 TOTE £3.00: £1.80, £1.30, £3.10; EX 18.60 Trifecta £184.40 Pool of £1,480.90 - 5.70 winning units.
**Owner** Nigel Shields **Bred** Bolton Grange **Trained** Maunby, N Yorks

**FOCUS**
A decent handicap run at a sound pace. This looks solid form, with the winner well in on old form

**NOTEBOOK**
**Blakeset**, 4lb higher, enhanced his fine record on this surface. He is effective at either six or seven furlongs and will still be on a fair mark after the handicapper has had his say.
**Ashtree Belle** threw down a strong challenge to the winner, but having briefly nosed ahead she could not hold on. This was a good effort nonetheless and she remains in top form.
**Just A Glimmer** ran well, appreciating the return to this trip following a couple of runs over a mile on the Polytrack.
**Ronnie From Donny(IRE)**, penalised for his course win last time and effectively only 3lb higher on this occasion, had no excuses. He has never been the most consistent of individuals.
**Cretan Gift** has yet to convince over this trip.
**Blonde En Blonde(IRE)**, back over her best trip, failed to get into it after a slow start.
**Invader**, who has been running creditably on Polytrack of late over farther, found this too sharp.

## 411 BET DIRECT NO Q DEMO 08000 837 888 CLAIMING STKS 5f (F)
**3:20** (3:25) (F) 4-Y-0+ **£2,905** (£830; £415) **Stalls** Low

Form RPR

065- **1** **Best Lead**[6] [6243] 5-8-10 53..........(b) DFentiman[(7)] 1 71
(IanEmmerson) *a.p: rdn over 2f out: led ins fnl f: drvn clr* **33/1**

400- **2** 3 ½ **Hagley Park**[21] [6170] 5-8-4 46.......... MartinDwyer 2 46
(MQuinn) *led 1f: w ldrs: rdn to ld wl over 1f out: hdd ins fnl f: sn btn* **7/1**[3]

500- **3** ¾ **Henry Tun**[17] [6199] 6-8-9 55..........(v) JEdmunds 5 48
(JBalding) *a.p: rdn over 2f out: kpt on same pce fnl f* **7/2**[2]

000- **4** ½ **Allerton Boy**[100] [5156] 5-8-3 37.......... DaleGibson 3 40
(RJHodges) *hld up: hdwy over 2f out: rdn wl over 1f out: r.o one pce fnl f* **40/1**

135- **5** ½ **Sharp Hat**[7] [6236] 10-9-3 72.......... ACulhane 6 53
(DWChapman) *s.i.s: hdwy over 2f out: kpt on towards fin* **13/8**[1]

020- **6** 1 **The Leather Wedge (IRE)**[2] [6265] 5-8-10 49.......... PBradley[(5)] 12 47
(ABerry) *led after 1f: hdd wl over 1f out: sn rdn: wknd fnl f* **20/1**

004- **7** 4 **Mr Spliffy (IRE)**[6] [6243] 5-8-11 49..........(v) DarrenWilliams 11 29
(KRBurke) *sn chsng ldrs: wknd over 2f out* **11/1**

000- **8** 3 **Salerno**[2] [6265] 5-8-6 50..........(p) TEaves[(5)] 10 19
(MissGayKelleway) *chsd ldrs tl rdn and wknd 2f out* **12/1**

563- **9** hd **Fiennes (USA)**[6] [6243] 6-8-2 42..........(v) LisaJones[(3)] 4 12
(MrsNMacauley) *chsd ldrs 2f: b.b.v* **8/1**

005- **10** 1 **Bali-Star**[24] [6150] 9-8-3 43.......... CCatlin 9 6
(RJHodges) *hld up: rdn over 3f out: sn bhd* **14/1**

61.88 secs (-0.72) **Going Correction** +0.025s/f (Slow) **10** Ran SP% **116.8**
Speed ratings: **106,100,99,98,97 96,89,84,84,82**CSF £245.63 TOTE £40.70: £6.80, £2.60, £2.00; EX 263.60.
**Owner** Ian Emmerson **Bred** M Berger **Trained** Holmside, Co Durham
■ Stewards Enquiry : D Fentiman caution: raised whip arm above shoulder height

**FOCUS**
An ordinary claimer contested by the usual suspects, many below form, but the winning time was very decent for the class of contest.

**NOTEBOOK**
**Best Lead** defied a disadvantageous draw, coming right away inside the last for a clear-cut victory. This was his first win since his two-year-old days, but his yard has only just returned to form and there seemed no fluke about it.
**Hagley Park** improved on her third in this event twelve months ago, although she was left behind by the winner in the closing stages after edging ahead early in the straight. She responds well to a positive ride.
**Henry Tun** was never able to dominate. A quirky character, he looked set to finish out of the money after finding nothing early in the home straight but was keeping on in the latter stages.
**Allerton Boy** was making a belated debut on the All-Weather and he appeared to act on the surface. He does most of his racing over this trip, but he stays farther and on the evidence of this run a step up to six could prove beneficial.
**Sharp Hat** was the clear pick on official but could never get into the hunt after a slow start, although he was making ground at the finish.
**The Leather Wedge(IRE)** showed his customary dash but did not get home again.
**Fiennes(USA)** *Official explanation: trainer said gelding bled from the nose*

## 412 BET DIRECT NO Q VOICE AUTOMATED BETTING H'CAP (DIV II) 1m 1f 79y(F)
**3:50** (3:57) (F) (0-60,60) 4-Y-0+ **£2,926** (£836; £418) **Stalls** Low

Form RPR

132- **1** **Rock Concert**[21] [6171] 6-9-3 56.......... NataliaGemelova[(7)] 2 70
(IWMcinnes) *led early: chsd ldr: led again over 3f out: rdn over 2f out: edgd rt ins fnl f: r.o* **5/1**[1]

422- **2** 1 **Givemethemoonlight**[4] [6253] 5-8-12 44.......... CCatlin 6 56
(MrsStefLiddiard) *hld up: hdwy over 4f out: rdn and ev ch over 2f out: nt qckn towards fin* **5/1**[1]

003- **3** 1 ¼ **Scottish River (USA)**[13] [6220] 5-9-13 59.......... ADaly 4 69
(MDIUsher) *hld up: smooth hdwy over 3f out: chal 2f out: sn rdn: no ex fnl f* **9/1**

200- **4** 9 **Titian Lass**[3] [6260] 5-8-6 45.......... DeanWilliams[(7)] 12 37
(CEBrittain) *prom tl rdn and wknd over 2f out* **6/1**[3]

422- **5** 2 **Sorbiesharry (IRE)**[14] [6218] 5-9-0 49..........(p) LEnstone[(3)] 1 37
(MrsNMacauley) *prom: rdn over 4f out: wknd over 3f out* **5/1**[1]

**6** 1 **Free Style (GER)**[62] 4-9-3 49.......... GBaker 10 36
(KRBurke) *nvr nr ldrs* **25/1**

640- **7** ½ **Prince Prospect**[17] [6198] 8-8-7 46.......... KristinStubbs[(7)] 3 31
(MrsLStubbs) *sn mid-div: rdn over 4f out: dropped rr 3f out: n.d after* **14/1**

500- **8** nk **Route Sixty Six (IRE)**[14] [6211] 8-8-3 42.......... LeanneKershaw[(7)] 5 26
(JeddO'Keeffe) *hld up towards rr: short-lived effrt over 3f out* **20/1**

050- **9** 1 ¼ **Bar Of Silver (IRE)**[48] [6005] 4-9-2 49.......... IMongan 11 30
(RBrotherton) *hld up and bhd: rdn over 4f out: hdwy over 3f out: wknd over 2f out* **16/1**

030- **10** hd **Phoenix Nights (IRE)**[77] [5626] 4-8-12 52.......... PPMathers[(7)] 8 33
(ABerry) *a towards rr* **33/1**

020- **11** 4 **Forty Forte**[14] [6218] 8-9-9 55..........(p) NCallan 9 28
(MissSJWilton) *sn led: clr 7f out: rdn and hdd over 3f out: sn lost pl* **20/1**

000- **12** 5 **Polka Princess**[130] [4465] 4-8-12 52.......... LTreadwell[(7)] 7 15
(MWellings) *a bhd* **50/1**

004- **13** 23 **Desert Heat**[27] [6137] 6-10-0 60..........(p) RWinston 13 —
(ISemple) *chsd ldrs: rdn 6f out: lost pl 5f out: t.o* **11/2**[2]

2m 1.12s (-1.78) **Going Correction** +0.025s/f (Slow)
**WFA** 4 from 5yo+ 1lb **13** Ran SP% **120.5**
Speed ratings: **108,107,106,98,96 95,94,94,93,93 89,85,64**CSF £27.70 CT £224.19 TOTE £7.10: £2.20, £1.60, £3.30; EX 23.90 Place 6 £52.98, Place 5 £13.97.
**Owner** Ivy House Racing **Bred** Cheveley Park Stud Ltd **Trained** Catwick, E Yorks

**FOCUS**
This was run at a strong pace thanks to the trailblazing Forty Forte, resulting in a time which was 2.64 seconds faster than the first division. The first three finished well clear and the form looks solid for the grade.

**NOTEBOOK**
**Rock Concert**, who went without the visor, is admirably consistent and she deserved this first win at Dunstall Park. She is brave too, digging deep to hold on despite edging to her right.
**Givemethemoonlight** is a longstanding maiden, but she is running creditably at the moment and there should be a small race for her. This longer trip was not a problem.
**Scottish River(USA)** broke on terms this time and looked a big threat turning in, but after the winner had just edged across him inside the last he was forced to concede defeat. He remains on an attractive mark.
**Titian Lass**, an inconsistent filly, was merely the best of the rest.
**Sorbiesharry(IRE)**, back in the cheekpieces after a couple of decent runs without them, remains one to take on.
**Free Style(GER)**, an ex-German filly, a winner at around a mile in her home country, did not shape badly on this British debut.
T/Jkpt: Not won. T/Plt: £173.80 to a £1 stake. Pool: £62,914.75. 264.25 winning tickets. T/Qpdt: £11.30 to a £1 stake. Pool: £5,133.90. 333.90 winning tickets. KH

# LINGFIELD (L-H)
## Saturday, January 3

**OFFICIAL GOING: Standard**
Wind: almost nil Weather: fine becoming cloudy, cold

## 413 BET ALL WEATHER: BET DIRECT APPRENTICE H'CAP 2m (P)
**11:40** (11:45) (F) (0-85,76) 4-Y-0+ **£2,891** (£826; £413) **Stalls** Low

Form RPR

035- **1** **Red Scorpion (USA)**[38] [6079] 5-8-10 **67**.......... BSwarbrick[(7)] 4 77
(WMBrisbourne) *lw: hld up in last trio: prog on outer 4f out: led wl over 2f out: rdn and hrd pressed over 1f out: hld on wl* **9/4**[1]

641- **2** nk **Western (IRE)**[28] [6130] 4-8-11 **71**.......... NChalmers[(3)] 3 81
(JAkehurst) *lw: dwlt: t.k.h and hld up in last trio: progs 4f out: chsd wnr over 2f out: rdn to chal over 1f out: styd on: jst hld* **11/4**[2]

502- **3** 18 **Redspin (IRE)**[21] [5305] 4-9-4 **75**.......... LPKeniry 7 63
(JSMoore) *trckd ldrs: rdn over 4f out: outpcd fr 3f out: plodded on to take poor 3rd fnl f* **14/1**

0/0- **4** ½ **Arc En Ciel**[5] [6255] 6-8-13 **66**.......... AQuinn[(3)] 5 53
(GLMoore) *chsd ldr: led over 3f out to wl over 2f out: sn wknd* **25/1**

000- **5** 2 ½ **Treasure Trail**[5] [6254] 5-8-10 **65**.......... LTreadwell[(5)] 8 49
(SKirk) *racd in midfield: rdn 5f out: outpcd 3f out: no ch after* **11/2**[3]

206- **6** 1 ½ **Harik**[53] [2360] 10-9-7 **76**.......... HPoulton[(5)] 1 59
(GLMoore) *t.k.h: hld up in last trio: rdn and no rspnse over 3f out: ssn wknd* **10/1**

632- **7** 1 ½ **George Stubbs (USA)**[15] [6215] 6-9-7 **71**.......... LFletcher 6 52
(MJPolglase) *racd freely: led to over 3f out: wknd rapidly over 2f out* **7/1**

660- **8** hd **Cantrip**[5] [6254] 4-8-5 **62**..........(t) LisaJones 9 43
(MissBSanders) *prom: lost plcd 6f out: rdn over 4f out: sn struggling* **25/1**

3m 30.77s (2.19) **Going Correction** +0.15s/f (Slow)
**WFA** 4 from 5yo+ 7lb **8** Ran SP% **108.8**
Speed ratings: **100,99,90,90,89 88,87,87**CSF £7.59 CT £56.67 TOTE £3.50: £1.10, £1.20, £3.20; EX 9.60.
**Owner** Mrs E M Coquelin **Bred** Gainsborough Farm Llc **Trained** Great Ness, Shropshire

**FOCUS**
A modest staying handicap, run at only an ordinary pace, and the race only concerned the front pair from a long way out. The form of the first two looks solid, and they may be ahead of the handicapper. The winning time was unexceptional.

**NOTEBOOK**
**Red Scorpion(USA)**, given a patient ride, had the run of the race this time and cruised to the front running to the final bend. He faced a determined challenge from the runner-up all the way down the straight, but showed all the right qualities to deservedly hold on.
**Western(IRE)**, trying this trip for the first time, certainly saw it out. He just found the winner too determined, but still finished a mile clear of the others.
**Redspin(IRE)**, returning to the Flat after a spell of hurdling, was trying this trip for the first time on the level and was made to look very one-paced over the last half-mile.
**Arc En Ciel**achieved nothing on his second start back following a layoff of almost 18 months.
**Treasure Trail**looks very much on the downgrade on the Flat these days.
**Harik**, who boasts a great record here on both Equitrack and Polytrack, failed to pick up and age may be catching up with him in races like this.
**George Stubbs(USA)**, racing over a trip half a mile further than he has ever tried before, attempted to make all the running over a distance which front runners have a terrible record, so it was little surprise he ended up well and truly beaten.

## 414 BET DIRECT NO Q ON 08000 93 66 93 MAIDEN STKS 5f (P)
**12:10** (12:15) (D) 3-Y-O **£3,682** (£1,133; £566; £283) **Stalls** High

Form RPR

303- **1** **Princess Kai (IRE)**[51] [5990] 3-8-6 55..........(b) FPFerris[(3)] 2 56
(RIngram) *lw: mde all: rdn and hrd pressed fr over 1f out: hld on* **12/1**

630- **2** nk **Docklands Blue (IRE)**[5] [6248] 3-8-6 .......... J-PGuillambert[(3)] 5 55
(NPLittmoden) *outpcd in last: prog over 2f out: styd on to chse wnr fnl 75y: gaining at fin* **25/1**

526- **3** ¾ **After All (IRE)**[5] [6248] 3-8-9 64.......... EAhern 1 52
(GABulter) *chsd wnr: rdn to chal over 1f out: fnd nil and nt go past: lost 2nd last 75y* **9/2**[3]

402- **4** 1 ½ **Pregnant Pause (IRE)**[4] [6258] 3-9-0 65.......... MartinDwyer 3 51
(SKirk) *lw: prom: rdn 2f out: fnd nil and sn btn* **13/8**[2]

04- **5** *1 1/2* **Dont Call Me Derek**[42] 6045 3-9-0 ........ MFenton 4 45
(SCWilliams) *b.hind: hanging rt thrght: chsd ldng trio: dropped to last and rn v wd bnd 2f out: styng on but no ch whn eased last 100y* **6/4**[1]

61.18 secs (1.40) **Going Correction** +0.15s/f (Slow) **5** Ran SP% **107.8**
Speed ratings: **94,93,92,89,87**CSF £166.31 TOTE £15.40: £3.70, £6.60; EX 117.40.
**Owner** Brannigan Bros **Bred** L Wright **Trained** Epsom, Surrey

**FOCUS**
A poor contest consisting mainly of exposed maidens and a modest winning time.

**NOTEBOOK**
**Princess Kai(IRE)**at last managed to find a weak race in which to break her duck and made every yard. She was inclined to hang into the whip in the latter stages and did not have much to spare at the line, suggesting she will struggle outside this company.
**Docklands Blue(IRE)**was completely taken off her feet early, but got going in the second part of the contest and almost pulled the race out of the fire. She is nothing special though and will need to find another contest as weak as this if she is to get off the mark.
**After All(IRE)**again flattered to deceive after holding every chance and even her talented trainer will do well to win a race with her.
**Pregnant Pause(IRE)**was disappointing after his decent effort here earlier in the week and the drop back in trip was not the answer.
**Dont Call Me Derek**, an eye-catcher in his most recent start here, did nothing but continuously hang to his right and looked virtually unrideable. He should be given another chance on a straight or right-handed track, though obviously that will not be on sand in the foreseeable future. *Official explanation: trainer had no explanation for the poor form shown*

## 415 BET DIRECT INTERACTIVE MAIDEN STKS 7f (P)
**12:40** (12:49) (D ) 3-Y-0+ **£3,552** (£1,093; £546; £273) **Stalls** Low

Form RPR
3- **1** **Mr Lambros**[42] 6048 3-8-7 ........ MartinDwyer 8 86+
(AMBalding) *h.d.w: l.w: rel to enter stalls: dwlt: rcvrd rapidly to ld after 2f: mde rest: drew clr fnl 2f: pushed out* **4/6**[1]

020- **2** *4* **Sir Laughalot**[24] 6164 4-9-8 70 ........ LPKeniry(3) 12 71
(MissECLavelle) *plld hrd: hld up bhd ldrs: prog over 2f out: chsd wnr 1f out: styd on but no ch* **6/1**[2]

06- **3** *3 1/2* **Monte Major (IRE)**[26] 6142 3-8-7 ........ NCallan 13 62
(MAJarvis) *t.k.h: trckd ldrs: effrt over 2f out: chsd wnr briefly over 1f out: one pce fnl f* **9/1**[3]

40- **4** *1 1/4* **Dusk Dancer (FR)**[280] 849 4-9-11 ........ RWinston 1 59
(BJMeehan) *lw: towards rr: pushed along over 4f out: prog 2f out: kpt on one pce fnl f* **9/1**[3]

000- **5** *shd* **Fubos**[21] 6175 3-8-8 61 ow1 ........ (v[1]) IMongan 11 60
(JulianPoulton) *chsd ldrs: rdn 1/2-way: c wd bnd 2f out and outpcd: kpt on u.p fnl f* **25/1**

05- **6** *nk* **African Star**[39] 6069 3-8-7 ........ EAhern 14 58
(MrsAJPerrett) *lw: prom: chsd wnr wl over 2f out to over 1f out: fdd* **12/1**

0- **7** *5* **Jackie Kiely**[114] 4847 3-8-7 ........ JPaulielo 15 46
(TGMills) *lw: led for 2f: wkng whn n.m.r on inner 2f out* **16/1**

040- **8** *1 1/4* **Queen Excalibur**[64] 5846 5-9-6 47 ........ (p) SDrowne 4 38
(JMBradley) *racd in last pair: pushed along 1/2-way: modest late prog* **66/1**

**9** *3/4* **Sofistication (IRE)** 3-8-2 ........ CCatlin 10 36
(TGMills) *leggy: bit bkwd: dwlt: rapid prog on outer to chse wnr over 4f out to wl over 2f out: wknd* **16/1**

000- **10** *2 1/2* **Onya**[51] 5989 4-9-6 39 ........ (t) SWhitworth 7 29
(JWHills) *bkwd: hld up wl in rr: struggling fnl 3f* **66/1**

600- **11** *nk* **Roan Raider (USA)**[7] 6244 4-9-8 42 ........ (bt[1]) LFletcher(3) 3 34
(MJPolglase) *racd in midfield: rdn wl over 2f out: wknd sn after* **66/1**

00- **12** *3/4* **Battle Back (BEL)**[22] 6167 3-8-2 ........ RFfrench 5 27
(SCWilliams) *taken v early to post: a in rr: struggling wl over 2f out* **50/1**

**13** *13* **Think It Over (IRE)** 5-9-6 ........ DSweeney 16 —
(APJones) *neat: chsd ldrs to 1/2-way: wknd u.p: t.o* **66/1**

- **14** *2 1/2* **Spiders Web**[420] 4-9-11 ........ MFenton 9 —
(TKeddy) *bkwd: restrained s: a in rr: t.o fnl 2f* **50/1**

0- **15** *1/2* **Lakeside Guy (IRE)**[17] 6210 3-8-4 ........ FPFerris(3) 6 —
(PSMcentee) *a towards rr: wknd 3f out: t.o* **66/1**

060- **16** *3* **Viva Atlas Espana**[156] 3713 4-9-6 52 ........ AClark 2 —
(MissBSanders) *restrained s: a in last pair: t.o* **50/1**

1m 26.0s **Going Correction** +0.15s/f (Slow)
**WFA** 3 from 4yo+ 18lb **16** Ran SP% **130.9**
Speed ratings: **106,101,97,96,95 95,89,88,87,84 84,83,68,65,65 61**CSF £5.20 TOTE £1.70: £1.10, £2.20, £2.50; EX 7.90.
**Owner** Winterbeck Manor Stud **Bred** Witney And Warren Enterprises Ltd **Trained** Kingsclere, Hants
■ Stewards Enquiry : L P Keniry one-day ban: failed to keep straight from stalls (Jan 14)

**FOCUS**
Basically a routine maiden in which the winner proved different class. The winning time was decent for the standard of race and the front two produced an above-average level of form.

**NOTEBOOK**
**Mr Lambros** ◆ was awkward at the stalls and rather jumped in the air when they opened, but he quickly scythed through the field to lead and was never in any danger from that point. He still has scope and can go on to better things.
**Sir Laughalot**, much more exposed than the winner, did his best to get on terms with him in the straight, but could not do so though finishing a clear second best. He is the benchmark to the value of the form.
**Monte Major(IRE)**, though no match for the front pair, ran his best race to date and can now be handicapped.
**Dusk Dancer(FR)** did not appear suited by the drop back in trip and may be capable of better when tried beyond a mile. He can also now be handicapped.
**Fubos** ran by far his best race so far in the first-time visor and is on the sort of handicap mark that could be exploited.
**African Star** raced prominently for a long way before dropping out and is beginning to look very disappointing. His best hope now is that handicapping may bring about some improvement.

## 416 BET DIRECT ON ITV PAGE 367 CLAIMING STKS 1m 2f (P)
**1:15** (1:20) (F ) 3-Y-0 **£2,905** (£830; £415) **Stalls** Low

Form RPR
031- **1** **Lyrical Girl (USA)**[26] 6147 3-8-9 55 ........ SHitchcott(3) 8 56
(MRChannon) *hw: hld up in rr: prog over 3f out to chse ldr over 2f out: rdn to ld over 1f out: edgd rt ins fnl f: hld on* **7/4**[1]

000- **2** *1* **Platinum Pirate**[12] 6228 3-8-11 40 ........ (b) DSweeney 9 53
(KRBurke) *lw: hld up in rr: prog 3f out: chsd ldng pair 2f out: hung fire over 1f out: chsd wnr and clsd fnl f: nt qckn* **12/1**

000- **3** *3 1/2* **Crackleando**[12] 6230 3-9-2 62 ........ J-PGuillambert(3) 6 55
(NPLittmoden) *hld up in rr: prog 3f out: outpcd over 2f out: styd on to take 3rd ins fnl f* **11/1**

020- **4** *2* **Lady Predominant**[24] 6160 3-8-4 52 ........ SCarson 7 36
(AndrewReid) *b: b.hind: trckd ldrs: prog to ld over 3f out: hdd & wknd over 1f out* **5/1**[3]

040- **5** *1 1/2* **Quarry Island (IRE)**[18] 6201 3-7-11 40 ........ FPFerris(3) 5 30
(PDEvans) *prom: led over 7f out to over 3f out: wknd 2f out* **12/1**

530- **6** *6* **Armentieres**[3] 6269 3-8-2 53 ........ (b) ADaly 10 21
(JLSpearing) *racd in midfield: prog to press ldrs over 3f out: sn rdn and fnd nil: wknd 2f out* **4/1**[2]

530- **7** *4* **Timely Twist**[14] 6223 3-8-4 47 ........ MartinDwyer 2 16
(SKirk) *racd freely: led to over 7f out: wknd 3f out* **12/1**

00- **8** *8* **Blues Over (IRE)**[14] 6223 3-8-4 ........ PaulEddery 4 1
(WJMusson) *racd in detached last: nvr on terms: no ch over 2f out* **25/1**

060- **9** *5* **Red Acer (IRE)**[15] 6216 3-8-5 35 ........ CCatlin 1 —
(PDEvans) *chsd ldrs: rdn over 4f out: wknd 3f out* **25/1**

000- **10** *2* **Altares**[21] 6173 3-9-1 48 ........ RWinston 3 —
(PHowling) *dwlt: pushed up to go prom: wknd u.p over 3f out* **16/1**

2m 11.23s (3.84) **Going Correction** +0.15s/f (Slow) **10** Ran SP% **118.0**
Speed ratings: **90,89,86,84,83 78,75,69,65,63**CSF £25.58 TOTE £2.60: £1.20, £3.80, £3.10; EX 48.30.The winner was claimed by Mr H J Manners for £11,000.
**Owner** C S G Limited **Bred** Alexander Pereira **Trained** West Ilsley, Berks

**FOCUS**
A poor contest, run at a modest pace, and a moderate winning time.

**NOTEBOOK**
**Lyrical Girl(USA)** is nothing special, but she at least knows how to win and swept to the front turning for home. She was always holding the runner-up in the closing stages, but gave the impression this was as far as she wanted to go. This is very much her level.
**Platinum Pirate**, racing on Polytrack for the first time, put up an improved effort and was snapping at the winner's heels at the line. However, the fact that he had failed to finish closer than sixth in seven previous outings, together with his handicap mark, drags the form right down.
**Crackleando** ran his best race so far, having been given a patient ride and, even if that is not saying much, he does give the impression he would appreciate a greater test of stamina.
**Lady Predominant** was racing beyond a mile for the first time and did not see out the trip.
**Quarry Island(IRE)**, an exposed maiden, achieved very little.
**Armentieres** ran disappointingly for the second time in four days.

## 417 BET DIRECT NO Q H'CAP 6f (P)
**1:50** (1:55) (D ) (0-85,84) 3-Y-0+ **£4,485** (£1,380; £690; £345) **Stalls** Low

Form RPR
100- **1** **Chateau Nicol**[14] 6224 5-9-3 72 ........ (v) JFanning 6 83
(BGPowell) *lw: settled towards rr: prog fr 1/2-way: hanging lft over 1f out: coaxed along and r.o to ld last 150y: in command after* **14/1**

505- **2** *1 1/4* **Just Fly**[4] 6263 4-9-10 79 ........ MartinDwyer 10 86
(SKirk) *squeezed out after 1f and wl in rr: effrt and nt clr run over 2f out: gd prog over 1f out: r.o wl to take 2nd last strides* **14/1**

034- **3** *nk* **Sir Desmond**[28] 6132 6-9-8 77 ........ (p) CCatlin 3 83
(RGuest) *pushed along in midfield: u.p and outpcd over 2f out: prog on inner over 1f out: staayed on ins fnl f* **10/1**

410- **4** *hd* **Polish Emperor (USA)**[25] 6154 4-9-7 76 ........ (b) NCallan 11 81
(PWHarris) *t.k.h: w ldr: led over 3f out: drvn and hdd last 150y: no ex* **16/1**

623- **5** *1/2* **Cashel Mead**[19] 6192 4-9-11 80 ........ ADaly 2 84
(JLSpearing) *chsd ldrs: rdn 2f out: hanging lft over 1f out: one pce ins fnl f* **16/1**

000- **6** *1* **No Time (IRE)**[14] 6225 4-9-11 83 ........ LFletcher(3) 4 84
(MJPolglase) *led to over 3f out: styd prom tl fdd fnl f* **8/1**

6/0- **7** *shd* **Cormorant Wharf (IRE)**[192] 2679 4-9-6 80 ........ AQuinn(5) 7 81
(TEPowell) *h.d.w: lw: s.i.s: racd in last pair: sme prog on inner 2f out: shuffled along over 1f out: swtchd rt ins fnl f: r.o* **50/1**

101- **8** *2* **Taranaki**[32] 6113 6-9-6 75 ........ SWhitworth 1 70
(PDCundell) *chsd ldng pair: rdn over 2f out: lost pl over 1f out: wknd ins fnl f* **10/3**[1]

603- **9** *nk* **Only One Legend (IRE)**[28] 6132 6-9-3 72 ........ (b) RWinston 9 66
(KARyan) *racd in midfield: rdn whn nt clr run briefly over 2f out: no prog after* **11/2**[3]

040- **10** *1 1/4* **Juwwi**[110] 4938 10-9-0 72 ........ LisaJones(3) 8 62
(JMBradley) *s.i.s: last and outpcd: styd on fnl 2f: nrst fin* **33/1**

321- **11** *1 3/4* **Type One (IRE)**[4] 6261 6-9-12 84 6ex ........ RMiles(3) 5 69
(TGMills) *lw: chsd ldrs: rdn over 2f out: no prog over 1f out: wknd ins fnl f* **4/1**[2]

600- **12** *1/2* **Currency**[47] 6014 7-9-4 73 ........ EAhern 13 56
(JMBradley) *racd wd towards rr: struggling over 2f out* **20/1**

602- **13** *1 1/4* **Jayanjay**[28] 6132 5-9-7 76 ........ SDrowne 14 55
(MissBSanders) *a towards rr: u.p and struggling over 2f out* **14/1**

305- **14** *9* **Hawk**[80] 5574 6-9-3 72 ........ IMongan 12 24
(PRChamings) *lw: racd in midfield tl wknd fr 1/2-way* **20/1**

1m 12.25s (-0.67) **Going Correction** +0.15s/f (Slow) **14** Ran SP% **124.9**
Speed ratings: **110,108,107,107,107 105,105,102,102,100 98,97,96,84**CSF £195.42 CT £2117.54 TOTE £14.60: £5.50, £5.00, £3.10; EX 256.90.
**Owner** Basingstoke Commercials **Bred** Aston House Stud **Trained** Morestead, Hants

**FOCUS**
A competitive handicap run at a rapid pace and a very smart winning time. The form is solid for the grade.

**NOTEBOOK**
**Chateau Nicol** was racing over a trip this short for the first time since May 2002, but the breakneck pace played right into his hands as it enabled him to be played late. This was a decent effort off a 10lb higher mark than for his last win.
**Just Fly**, another whose best form has been over further, did not enjoy the clearest of passages and was forced to come from further back than the winner. He finished with quite a rattle down the outside and may have been unlucky not to have finished even closer.
**Sir Desmond**, for the third consecutive race over this course and distance and with Catlin aboard, came with his trademark late flourish tight against the inside rail. In each case a low draw has probably made that unavoidable, but it would be fascinating to see how he performs if brought wider.
**Polish Emperor(USA)** may be better suited by Fibresand, but at least he ultimately did best of those that helped set the fierce pace.
**Cashel Mead**, making her Polytrack debut, did not run badly but is another that may be better suited by Fibresand.
**No Time(IRE)** is starting to become attractively handicapped, but he got involved in a speed duel with Polish Emperor and eventually paid for it.
**Cormorant Wharf(IRE)**, making his handicap debut and racing for the first time since June, looked to have started on a stiff mark but nonetheless ran a most encouraging race and was by no means knocked about.
**Taranaki** tried to stay in touch with the early pacesetters from his rails draw, but his efforts to do so finally burst him.
**Type One(IRE)**had a lot to do under a 6lb penalty for winning a claimer here earlier in the week in this much better contest, and so it proved. He does seem to go best when fresh.

## 418 LITTLEWOODS BET DIRECT H'CAP — 1m 4f (P)

2:25 (2:30) (C) (0-100,98) 4-Y-0+ £12,296 (£4,664; £2,332; £1,060) Stalls Low

Form RPR

626- 1 **Gig Harbor**[32] 6117 5-9-1 **85** ........ LPKeniry(3) 3 97
(MissECLavelle) *wl plcd: effrt to trck ldr wl over 2f out: rdn to ld wl over 1f out: styd on wl* **7/1**[2]

430- 2 1 1/4 **Flight Of Esteem**[79] 5588 4-9-6 **91** ........ NCallan 1 101
(PWHarris) *lw: cl up: rdn to chse ldng pair over 2f out but sn outpcd: styd on fnl f to take 2nd nr fin* **12/1**

210- 3 nk **Cruise Director**[51] 5991 4-8-9 **83** ........ LisaJones(3) 4 93
(WJMusson) *lw: settled in midfield: rdn and prog over 2f out: outpcd by ldrs wl over 1f out: styd on fnl f to snatch 3rd on line* **7/1**[2]

666- 4 shd **Eastern Breeze (IRE)**[42] 6051 6-10-0 **95** ........ (e) PaulEddery 6 104
(PWD'Arcy) *trckd ldr: led over 3f out and kicked on: drvn and hdd wl over 1f out: one pce fnl f: lost 2 pls nr fin* **13/2**[1]

506- 5 4 **Santando**[112] 4880 4-9-13 **98** ........ (v) MFenton 8 101
(CEBrittain) *jockey stl removing blind as stalls opened and slowly away: hld up last trio: rdn and prog over 2f out: hung lft over 1f ou* **10/1**

011- 6 1 **Tight Squeeze**[17] 6208 7-8-12 **79** ........ RWinston 14 81
(PWHiatt) *hld up in last trio: sme prog fnl 2f: one pce and n.d* **9/1**[3]

003- 7 3/4 **High Hope (FR)**[17] 6208 6-8-11 **78** ........ (be) SWhitworth 2 79
(GLMoore) *hld up towards rr: rdn and prog 3f out: outpcd and btn wl over 1f out* **12/1**

050- 8 nk **Gallant Boy (IRE)**[3] 6268 5-8-3 **77** ........ (t) SJDonohoe(7) 7 77
(PDEvans) *b: settled in rr: effrt 3f out: one pce and no imp ldrs fnl 2f* **14/1**

010- 9 3/4 **Sudden Flight (IRE)**[25] 6156 7-8-13 **80** ........ RHavlin 5 79
(RIngram) *racd in midfield: outpcd over 2f out: one pce after* **50/1**

324- 10 3 **Briareus**[119] 4725 4-8-9 **80** ........ MartinDwyer 12 75
(AMBalding) *lw: sn led and set modest pce: rdn and hdd over 3f out: sn outpcd and btn* **10/1**

360- 11 3/4 **Internationalguest (IRE)**[56] 5952 5-8-9 **81** ........ (v) BReilly(5) 11 75
(GGMargarson) *racd in midfield: outpcd wl over 2f out: no ch after* **20/1**

206- 12 4 **Royal Cavalier**[15] 6215 7-9-4 **85** ........ EAhern 10 73
(RHollinshead) *trckd ldrs tl wknd 2f out* **16/1**

220/ 13 nk **Dusty Carpet**[632] 5279 6-8-9 **76** ........ SDrowne 16 63
(MJWeeden) *hld up in last: outpcd wl over 2f out: no ch* **100/1**

0/6- 14 3 **Eastborough (IRE)**[14] 6224 5-8-11 **78** ........ JFanning 9 61
(BGPowell) *t.k.h: hld up in rr: outpcd wl over 2f out: no ch after* **33/1**

001- 15 nk **High Point (IRE)**[42] 6052 6-8-13 **80** ........ CCatlin 13 62
(GPEnright) *chsd ldrs tl wknd u.p 3f out* **13/2**[1]

003- 16 4 **Brilliant Red**[24] 6162 11-9-6 **87** ........ (t) IMongan 15 63
(JamiePoulton) *lw: s.s: sn chsd ldrs: rdn and wknd wl over 2f out: sn bhd* **10/1**

2m 33.03s (-0.95) **Going Correction** +0.15s/f (Slow)
**WFA** 4 from 5yo+ 4lb **16** Ran SP% **127.5**
Speed ratings: **109,108,107,107,105 104,104,103,103,101 100,98,98,96,95 93**CSF £90.32 CT £629.74 TOTE £8.40: £2.00, £2.90, £2.20, £2.40; EX 157.00.

**Owner** Fraser Miller Racing **Bred** Robert Charles Key **Trained** Hatherden, Hants

### FOCUS

A very competitive handicap with the pace quickening up substantially over the last half-mile. The winning time was good for the class of race and this looks solid, decent form.

### NOTEBOOK

**Gig Harbor**, returning to his ideal trip, had the run of the race as he was able to pounce at the ideal time and established enough of a lead to hold off the late finishers. There will be plenty more opportunities for him here this winter.

**Flight Of Esteem** has won over this trip on turf, but most of his form until now has been over ten furlongs. He was always just off the pace on this occasion and the way he came home strongly suggests he is worth persevering with over this trip during the winter, though he has not always looked the easiest of rides.

**Cruise Director**, well backed and from the same yard that landed a gamble at Wolverhampton the previous day, was tucked away on the fence and took a while to get into top gear after being pulled out turning for home. He finished in good style and looks capable of winning a similar contest, though the cat is rather out of the bag.

**Eastern Breeze(IRE)** travelled really well, but may have found himself in front sooner than he wanted when the leader dropped out quickly running to the final bend. His rider had little choice but to commit him at that point, but he edged to the inside rail after turning for home and was swamped for foot by the winner soon after.

**Santando**, racing for the first time since finishing sixth in the Doncaster St Leger, was handicapped by fluffing the start as his blindfold was still being removed. He tried to get into the race rounding the home bend, but could never land a blow and tended to hang. He may need a slightly greater test of stamina now, but is also not an easy ride.

**Tight Squeeze**, up 3lb from her course-and-distance victory last month, could never get competitive this time.

**Gallant Boy(IRE)** has the ability, but continues to disappoint.

**Briareus**, making his sand debut, set the pace but was a sitting duck and stopped very quickly approaching the final bend.

**High Point(IRE)**, 4lb higher than for his victory over course and distance in November, was close enough for much of the way but dropped out tamely over the last three furlongs.

## 419 BETDIRECT.CO.UK CLASSIFIED STKS — 1m 2f (P)

3:00 (3:06) (E) 4-Y-0+ £3,376 (£1,039; £519; £259) Stalls Low

Form RPR

066- 1 **Gingko**[14] 6068 7-9-2 62 ........ WRyan 5 76
(PRWebber) *lw: hld up in last pair: outpcd and drvn 3f out: c wd bnd 2f out: gd prog u.p over 1f out: led lst 100y: kpt on wl* **7/1**

644- 2 1/2 **Blue Trojan (IRE)**[5] 6255 4-9-0 68 ........ EAhern 6 75
(SKirk) *lw: sn settled in midfield: smooth prog over 3f out: chsd ldr over 2f out: rdn to ld on outer over 1f out: hdd last 100y: s* **5/2**[1]

201- 3 shd **Perfidious (USA)**[78] 5610 6-9-2 70 ........ IMongan 2 75
(JRBoyle) *led at decent pce: rdn and kicked on again 3f out: c wd bnd 2f out: hdd over 1f out: kpt on wl fnl f* **10/3**[2]

601- 4 3 1/2 **Topton (IRE)**[32] 6119 10-9-2 69 ........ (b) RWinston 1 69
(PHowling) *s.i.s: hld up in last pair: effrt over 2f out: one pce on inner fr over 1f out* **8/1**

422- 5 1/2 **Easter Ogil (IRE)**[5] 6254 9-9-2 63 ........ VSlattery 8 68
(JaneSouthcombe) *hld up in tch: rdn 3f out: effrt towards inner and cl up over 1f out: sn btn* **4/1**[3]

000- 6 2 **Todlea (IRE)**[24] 6157 4-9-0 70 ........ (t) MartinDwyer 4 64
(JAOsborne) *mostly chsd ldr to 6f out: styd prom: rdn over 2f out: cl up on inner over 1f out: sn wknd* **11/1**

006- 7 nk **Londoner (USA)**[24] 6161 6-9-2 65 ........ PDoe 7 64
(SDow) *prom: chsd ldr 6f out to over 2f out: wknd tamely over 1f out* **14/1**

/00- 8 18 **Stunning Magic**[99] 5203 4-8-11 33 ........ LisaJones(3) 3 31
(MrsBarbaraWaring) *lw: in tch tl rdn and wknd over 4f out: t.o* **100/1**

2m 7.85s (0.46) **Going Correction** +0.15s/f (Slow)
**WFA** 4 from 6yo+ 2lb **8** Ran SP% **111.3**
Speed ratings: **104,103,103,100,100 98,98,84**CSF £23.51 TOTE £7.00: £1.60, £1.40, £1.80; EX 30.80.

**Owner** Olympic Group Of Partners **Bred** Lord Rothschild **Trained** Cropredy, Oxon

### FOCUS

A competitive classified event run at a solid pace, producing average form for the grade.

### NOTEBOOK

**Gingko**, who was well beaten in a moderate hurdle last time out, appreciated this return to Polytrack and was produced with a well-timed run to score. He had no easy task at the weights and may be worth persevering with on this surface.

**Blue Trojan(IRE)** who ran well on his first attempt over the trip at the beginning of the week, was backed down to favourite. He got to the front halfway up the straight, but had no answer to the winner's challenge and his stamina appeared to be ebbing close home. The extended nine furlongs at Wolverhampton may be his optimum trip.

**Perfidious(USA)**, who drifted out from favouritism, as is often the case set the pace, but preferred to lead with his off fore when not taking the turns and tended to lug right, as he has done in several recent races. Nevertheless, he was coming back at the finish. It is unfortunate there are no right-handed All-Weather tracks in Britain so, unless connections are prepared to take him to Deauville's sand track, his chances of future success may be compromised if the tendency continues.

**Topton(IRE)** was trying this trip for the first time in two years and, although he appeared to get it, never got into a challenging position.

**Easter Ogil(IRE)** has been running well of late, but had a few pounds to find on official ratings and ran as well as could be expected. He may be ready to win back in handicap company.

## 420 BET DIRECT NO Q DEMO 08000 837 888 FILLIES' H'CAP — 7f (P)

3:30 (3:36) (F) (0-65,63) 3-Y-O £2,968 (£848; £424) Stalls Low

Form RPR

131- 1 **Rowan Pursuit**[42] 6047 3-9-7 **63** ........ (b) JFanning 15 66
(JAkehurst) *lw: hld up in midfield: prog to chse ldrs 2f out: edgd lft but rdn to ld 1f out: sn in command* **4/1**[1]

460- 2 1 1/2 **Park Ave Princess (IRE)**[32] 6115 3-8-10 **52** ........ IMongan 2 51
(NPLittmoden) *lw: hld up: hmpd in rr over 4f out: gd prog to chse ldrs over 2f out: styd on to chse wnr ins fnl f: no imp* **10/1**

002- 3 1/2 **Good Vibrations**[42] 6047 3-8-10 **52** ........ CCatlin 3 50
(PFICole) *plld hrd: hld up in midfield: prog to chse ldrs over 2f out: c wd bnd sn after: styd on to take 3rd nr fin* **9/2**[2]

006- 4 3/4 **Taranai (IRE)**[38] 6077 3-8-10 **55** ........ LisaJones(3) 9 51
(BWDuke) *w ldrs: led 4f out: drvn and hdd 1f out: one pce* **12/1**

031- 5 1 3/4 **Must Be So**[14] 6223 3-8-8 **50** ........ NPollard 6 42
(JJBridger) *pressed ldrs: rdn over 2f out: cl up over 1f out: fdd ins fnl f* **7/1**[3]

006- 6 1/2 **Sonderborg**[18] 6197 3-9-1 **57** ........ (p) GCarter 12 47
(GLMoore) *dwlt: wl in rr: prog on inner 2f out: kpt on fnl f: nvr able to chal* **8/1**

060- 7 1/2 **Emilys Dawn**[22] 6167 3-8-13 **55** ........ DSweeney 13 44
(DKIvory) *settled wl in rr: plenty to do over 2f out: prog whn nt clr run over 1f out: pushed along and kpt on: nvr nr ldrs* **20/1**

600- 8 3/4 **Vendors Mistake (IRE)**[14] 6222 3-8-12 **54** ........ SCarson 4 41
(AndrewReid) *lw: sn restrained in midfield: prog on inner whn hmpd over 2f out: renewed effrt to chse ldrs over 1f out: wknd fnl f* **12/1**

153- 9 3/4 **Alizar (IRE)**[8] 6237 3-8-13 **58** ........ LFletcher(3) 14 43
(MJPolglase) *w ldrs: rdn wl over 2f out: wknd jst over 1f out* **9/1**

500- 10 2 **Love In The Mist (USA)**[35] 6097 3-9-6 **62** ........ SDrowne 7 42
(EALDunlop) *chsd ldrs: rdn over 3f out: sn struggling and btn* **9/1**

000- 11 1 1/4 **Chica (IRE)**[181] 3029 3-8-3 **45** ........ RFitzpatrick 5 22
(JAOsborne) *s.s: last whn hmpd on inner after 2f: n.d after* **25/1**

304- 12 1 1/2 **Lady Piste (IRE)**[14] 6223 3-8-6 **55** ........ (b[1]) SJDonohoe(7) 16 28
(PDEvans) *prom: pressed ldr 4f out to 2f out: wknd rapidly* **10/1**

000- 13 2 1/2 **Miss Judged**[19] 6194 3-8-8 **50** ........ (t) GHannon 10 17
(APJones) *prom: bmpd along fr over 2f out: wknd wl over 1f out* **50/1**

400- 14 3 **Out Of My Way**[42] 6047 3-7-12 **40** oh9 ........ RBrisland 8 —
(TMJones) *a towards rr: rdn 1/2-way: sn btn* **66/1**

046- 15 3 1/2 **Foot Fault (IRE)**[15] 6213 3-9-4 **60** ........ WRyan 11 11
(NACallaghan) *led to 4f out: lost pl rapidly: wl in rr over 2f out* **14/1**

1m 27.65s (1.65) **Going Correction** +0.15s/f (Slow) **15** Ran SP% **134.1**
Speed ratings: **96,94,93,92,90 90,89,88,88,85 84,82,79,76,72**CSF £48.22 CT £204.65 TOTE £4.30: £2.10, £4.00, £2.00; EX 78.40 Place 6 £1,333.71, Place 5 £901.71.

**Owner** C C Clarke **Bred** Rowan Farm Stud **Trained** Epsom, Surrey

### FOCUS

A big field but a modest contest run at only a fair pace. The winning time was reasonable for the class of contest, suggesting the form is decent for grade, though still 1.65 slower than Mr Lambros took to win the earlier maiden.

### NOTEBOOK

**Rowan Pursuit**, winner of a seller here last time, is little more than plating class but she has already demonstrated a smart turn of foot on this surface and did so again to make a winning debut for her new yard.

**Park Ave Princess(IRE)**, who has been out of form since August, has plummeted in the handicap as a result and ran much better. She is worth watching out for next time.

**Good Vibrations**, a maiden after four starts, was 7lb better off with the winner compared with their running here in November, but that may have been a little misleading and she seemed the more inconvenienced of the pair by this furlong-shorter trip.

**Taranai(IRE)**, still a maiden, was given a more positive ride but was swamped for foot down the home straight.

**Must Be So**, third behind Rowan Pursuit and Good Vibrations here in November, had won a seller in the meantime and was making her debut for the yard. This effort suggests she needs to return to six.

**Sonderborg** gave herself a bit to do by starting slowly. She never really landed a blow, but gives the impression she may be capable of better.

T/Plt: £936.10 to a £1 stake. Pool: £42,960.75. 33.50 winning tickets. T/Qpdt: £18.60 to a £1 stake. Pool: £4,611.50. 182.80 winning tickets. JN

## [406]WOLVERHAMPTON (A.W) (L-H)

Saturday, January 3

**OFFICIAL GOING: Standard**

(REGIONAL MEETING) This was the first of the new 'regional' race meetings, geared principally to horses rated 45 or lower.

Wind: slt bhd Weather: dull and damp, light rain last two races

### 421 BET DIRECT ON SKY ACTIVE BANDED STKS (DIV I) 6f (F)

12:55 (12:56) (H ) 3-Y-0+ £1,631 (£466; £233) Stalls Low

Form RPR

000- **1** **Cleveland Way**[25] 6149 4-9-3 45 (v) DNolan(5) 12 51
(DCarroll) *w ldrs: led over 4f out: rdn clr over 2f out: drvn out* **6/1**[3]

035- **2** *1* **Lord Melbourne (IRE)**[123] 4631 5-9-8 44 SWKelly 3 48
(JAOsborne) *hld up: pushed along whn nt clr run on ins over 2f out: rdn and hdwy wl over 1f out: r.o ins fnl f: nt rch wnr* **11/2**[2]

004- **3** *2* **Attorney**[8] 6236 6-9-3 43 (e) THamilton(5) 2 42
(DShaw) *sn outpcd and bhd: hdwy whn hung lft 1f out: sn nt clr run: kpt on ins fnl f* **5/1**[1]

020- **4** *½* **Enjoy The Buzz**[36] 6081 5-9-8 42 PFitzsimons 11 41
(JMBradley) *sn chsng ldrs: rdn over 2f out: kpt on same pce* **12/1**

000/ **5** *3* **Magic Eagle**[389] 5870 7-9-8 45 GParkin 5 32
(PTMidgley) *led 1f: prom: rdn over 2f out: wknd ins fnl f* **14/1**

000- **6** *1 ¼* **Carols Choice**[8] 6236 7-9-8 36 GBaker 10 28
(ASadik) *led briefly after 1f: prom: rdn over 2f out: wknd wl over 1f out* **14/1**

000- **7** *shd* **Pips Song (IRE)**[15] 6217 9-9-8 45 DarrenWilliams 6 27
(PWHiatt) *hld up: hdwy 3f out: sn rdn: wknd fnl f* **11/2**[2]

000- **8** *1 ½* **Flying Faisal (USA)**[164] 3501 6-9-8 44 DeanMcKeown 8 23
(JMBradley) *chsd ldrs: rdn 3f out: sn wknd* **8/1**

000- **9** *2 ½* **Threat**[47] 6015 8-9-5 40 LEnstone(3) 4 15
(JMBradley) *mid-div: rdn over 3f out: sn bhd* **16/1**

00U- **10** *14* **Countrywide Girl (IRE)**[148] 3952 5-9-3 32 PBradley(5) 1 —
(ABerry) *chsd ldrs 2f: wl bhd fnl 3f* **33/1**

046- **11** *2 ½* **Ladystgeorge**[40] 6056 5-9-8 34 JBramhill 7 —
(MMullineaux) *s.i.s: rdn and short-lived effrt on outside over 3f out: wl bhd fnl 2f* **33/1**

1m 16.47s (0.77) **Going Correction** +0.025s/f (Slow)
**WFA** 3 from 4yo+ 16lb **11** Ran SP% **105.6**
Speed ratings: **95,93,91,90,86 84,84,82,79,60 57**CSF £33.21 TOTE £6.00: £1.80, £1.30, £2.40; EX 56.40.
**Owner** The Boot & Shoe Ackworth Partnership **Bred** Miss L Pearson **Trained** Warthill, N Yorks
■ The first-ever banded event, a new-style contest for the new regional race meetings.

**FOCUS**
Run in a time fractionally slower than the second division, and the form is poor.

**NOTEBOOK**
**Cleveland Way** was enterprisingly ridden and stole a big enough lead to last home.
**Lord Melbourne(IRE)** may have been a shade unlucky but he really needs seven furlongs.
**Attorney** caused his own trouble by hanging entering the final furlong.
**Enjoy The Buzz** appears to be worth another try at seven.
**Magic Eagle** was not disgraced on his first start for just over a year.

### 422 BET DIRECT ON SKY ACTIVE BANDED STKS (DIV II) 6f (F)

1:30 (1:31) (H ) 3-Y-0+ £1,631 (£466; £233) Stalls Low

Form RPR

050- **1** **Italian Mist (FR)**[109] 4971 5-9-8 39 (e) GFaulkner 9 53
(JulianPoulton) *led over 1f: chsd ldr: rdn over 2f out: swtchd rt and rallied to ld wl ins fnl f: r.o wl* **10/1**

002- **2** *1 ¾* **Larky's Lob**[8] 6235 5-9-5 48 LEnstone(3) 11 48
(PaulJohnson) *prom: led over 4f out: rdn over 2f out: edgd lft over 1f out: hdd and no ex wl ins fnl f* **6/4**[1]

660- **3** *3 ½* **Neutral Night (IRE)**[43] 6039 4-9-8 44 (v) ACulhane 5 37
(RBrotherton) *a.p: rdn 4f out: one pce fnl 2f* **11/2**[2]

000- **4** *3 ½* **Sabana (IRE)**[36] 6081 6-9-8 44 PFitzsimons 8 27
(JMBradley) *a.p: rdn over 3f out: wknd fnl f* **8/1**[3]

006- **5** *nk* **Sawah**[8] 6235 4-9-8 30 DarrenWilliams 10 26
(DShaw) *s.i.s: rdn and hdwy over 3f out: no further prog fnl 2f* **25/1**

/00- **6** *½* **Rivendell**[150] 3880 8-9-8 20 (t) DRMcCabe 1 25
(MWigham) *hld up and bhd: hmpd on ins over 3f out: sn rdn: hdwy wl over 1f out: n.d* **12/1**

006- **7** *1 ¾* **Vlasta Weiner**[109] 4973 4-9-8 38 (b) DeanMcKeown 7 19
(JMBradley) *s.i.s: nvr nr ldrs* **20/1**

000- **8** *1 ¾* **Paris Dreamer**[57] 5939 3-8-7 42 ow6 PMulrennan(5) 3 20
(MWEasterby) *s.i.s: nvr nr ldrs* **14/1**

000- **9** *½* **Lion's Domane**[25] 6150 7-9-3 44 PBradley(5) 2 13
(ABerry) *prom tl rdn and wknd over 2f out* **10/1**

000- **10** *¾* **Sugar Cube Treat**[26] 6146 8-9-8 35 JBramhill 12 10
(MMullineaux) *sn outpcd* **12/1**

000- **11** *6* **Blue Circle**[8] 6235 4-9-8 30 (b) SWKelly 6 —
(MMullineaux) *chsd ldrs: rdn 4f out: sn struggling* **33/1**

500- **12** *2 ½* **Geespot**[72] 5719 5-9-8 44 PJScallan 4 —
(DJSFrenchDavis) *sn outpcd: edgd lft over 3f out: a bhd* **9/1**

1m 16.32s (0.62) **Going Correction** +0.025s/f (Slow)
**WFA** 3 from 4yo+ 16lb **12** Ran SP% **128.3**
Speed ratings: **96,93,89,84,83 83,80,78,77,76 68,65**CSF £26.86 TOTE £14.70: £4.50, £1.20, £2.20; EX 36.30.
**Owner** S P Shore **Bred** Mrs Hilary Trigg & Mr John Veil **Trained** Kentford, Suffolk
■ Stewards Enquiry : P J Scallan caution: careless riding

**FOCUS**
This was marginally quicker than the first division, again the form is poor.

**NOTEBOOK**
**Italian Mist(FR)**, making his Fibresand debut, fought back well after the runner-up went across him in the home straight.
**Larky's Lob** would not have been in the field had his new rating of 48 been in force. He could not hold the winner's renewed effort after forcing his rival to switch.
**Neutral Night(IRE)** did not find this shorter distance the answer, despite having run well at six on turf last year.
**Sabana(IRE)** should have been suited by the step up from the minimum distance.
**Rivendell**, the subject of small office money, was backed down from 66/1. She could never get into it after her rider was forced to snatch up before halfway.

### 423 BET DIRECT INTERACTIVE (S) STKS 7f (F)

2:05 (2:06) (H ) 3-Y-0+ £1,319 (£377; £188) Stalls High

Form RPR

064- **1** **Repeat (IRE)**[12] 6229 4-9-9 51 TEaves(5) 8 63
(MissGayKelleway) *chsd ldrs: rdn to ld 2f out: hung lft over 1f out: drvn out* **5/1**[3]

064- **2** *3 ½* **Lucayan Monarch**[15] 6211 6-9-9 55 (p) DeanMcKeown 9 49
(PABlockley) *s.i.s: sn chsng ldrs: rdn over 3f out: sltly outpcd over 2f out: styd on ins fnl f: nt trble wnr* **6/4**[1]

606- **3** *hd* **Star Lad (IRE)**[15] 6217 4-9-9 47 (b) ACulhane 10 49
(RBrotherton) *led 2f: chsd ldr tl rdn over 2f out: sn sltly outpcd: kpt on ins fnl f* **9/1**

200- **4** *hd* **Arogant Prince**[60] 5919 7-9-6 60 (p) DMcGaffin(3) 7 48
(ISemple) *w ldr: led 5f out: rdn and hdd 2f out: swtchd rt over 1f out: no ex fnl f* **7/2**[2]

000- **5** *3* **Better Off**[12] 6229 6-9-9 65 (p) JoannaBadger 3 41
(MrsNMacauley) *s.i.s: hdwy over 2f out: nvr trbld ldrs* **11/1**

600- **6** *4* **Glenviews Polly (IRE)**[202] 2391 4-9-4 42 ANicholls 5 26
(IanEmmerson) *w ldrs tl rdn 5f out: wknd over 3f out* **14/1**

000- **7** *½* **Almond Beach**[136] 4290 4-9-9 65 DRMcCabe 4 30
(BJMeehan) *chsd ldrs tl lost pl over 5f out: n.d after* **14/1**

000- **8** *6* **Lady Alruna (IRE)**[50] 5995 5-9-4 40 GParkin 2 10
(PTMidgley) *outpcd* **25/1**

006- **9** *5* **Present 'n Correct**[136] 4288 11-9-2 30 (b) SimonJones(7) 6 2
(JMBradley) *s.i.s: a bhd* **25/1**

000- **10** *3 ½* **Chantilly Gold (USA)**[142] 4114 5-9-4 30 (p) PFitzsimons 1 —
(JMBradley) *mid-div: rdn and bhd fnl 3f* **40/1**

1m 31.69s (1.49) **Going Correction** +0.025s/f (Slow) **10** Ran SP% **120.7**
Speed ratings: **92,88,87,87,84 79,78,72,66,62**CSF £13.12 TOTE £8.50: £1.90, £1.10, £3.90; EX 18.90.There was no bid for the winner.
**Owner** J T Billson **Bred** Philip Hore Jnr **Trained** Newmarket, Suffolk

**FOCUS**
There were question marks hanging over most of these coming into this average seller, and the race produced a modest winning time, even for a contest like this. Just fair form for the grade.

**NOTEBOOK**
**Repeat(IRE)**, back in the right grade, seemed to have a tough task at the weights but proved good enough despite hanging into the whip.
**Lucayan Monarch**, dropped in class, showed why he has been tackling a mile lately.
**Star Lad(IRE)** was not beaten for a lack of stamina on only his second attempt at seven furlongs.
**Arogant Prince** does seem to find this trip beyond his best.
**Lady Alruna(IRE)** *Official explanation: trainer's representative said mare was found to be in season*

### 424 PRESS INTERACTIVE TO BET DIRECT MEDIAN AUCTION MAIDEN STKS 1m 1f 79y(F)

2:40 (2:41) (H ) 3-5-Y-0 £1,438 (£411; £205) Stalls Low

Form RPR

4- **1** **Heathyards Pride**[21] 6177 4-9-10 DeanMcKeown 4 52
(RHollinshead) *a.p: rdn and wnt 2nd 3f out: hrd rdn and edgd lft ins fnl f: led last strides* **7/1**

606- **2** *nk* **Iamback**[8] 6238 4-9-0 44 (p) THamilton(5) 7 46
(MissGayKelleway) *led after 1f: rdn over 2f out: edgd rt ent st: edgd lft ins fnl f: hdd last strides* **9/1**

0- **3** *1 ½* **Angelo's Pride**[63] 5876 3-8-6 ow3 SWKelly 1 51
(JAOsborne) *in tch: rdn over 5f out: outpcd over 3f out: hdwy on outside whn edgd rt over 1f out: edgd lft ins fnl f: styd on* **2/1**[1]

400- **4** *13* **Shamwari Fire (IRE)**[26] 6144 4-9-3 45 NataliaGemelova(7) 2 22
(IWMcinnes) *led 1f: chsd ldr tl rdn 3f out: sn wknd* **9/2**[3]

000- **5** *5* **Good Form (IRE)**[17] 6206 4-9-3 36 DerekNolan(7) 5 12
(MissKMGeorge) *plld hrd early: mid-div: rdn 4f out: sn struggling* **14/1**

022- **6** *15* **Lilian**[82] 5542 4-9-0 46 (tp) TEaves(5) 3 —
(MissGayKelleway) *hld up in tch: rdn over 5f out: sn struggling: t.o* **3/1**[2]

00- **7** *9* **Cayman Mischief**[60] 5919 4-9-5 ANicholls 8 —
(JamesMoffatt) *hld up in rr: rdn over 4f out: sn wl bhd: t.o* **25/1**

**8** *14* **Dances In Time** 4-9-5 TWilliams 6 —
(CNKellett) *s.i.s: hung rt most of way: a bhd: t.o fnl 3f* **25/1**

2m 3.17s (0.27) **Going Correction** +0.025s/f (Slow)
**WFA** 3 from 4yo 22lb **8** Ran SP% **113.4**
Speed ratings: **99,98,97,85,81 68,60,47**CSF £65.92 TOTE £7.90: £2.60, £3.20, £1.10; EX 81.40.
**Owner** L A Morgan **Bred** L A Morgan **Trained** Upper Longdon, Staffs

**FOCUS**
This did not take much winning and the form is poor.

**NOTEBOOK**
**Heathyards Pride** needed every yard of this trip to give his trainer a winner on his 80th birthday.
**Iamback** has been beaten in sellers and kept drifting away from the whip.
**Angelo's Pride** was running over a more suitable trip having made his debut here over six. He was another who kept going away from the whip.

### 425 £10 FREE BET @ BET DIRECT SKY ACTIVE BANDED STKS 1m 100y(F)

3:15 (3:15) (H ) 3-Y-0+ £1,680 (£480; £240) Stalls Low

Form RPR

34-6 **1** **Qobtaan (USA)**[1] 406 5-9-8 45 GBaker 3 59
(MRBosley) *hld up: hdwy over 3f out: led on bit over 2f out: rdn and edgd lft wl over 1f out: sn clr: eased towards fin* **11/4**[1]

360- **2** *6* **Maggie's Pet**[28] 6133 7-9-8 44 (t) DRMcCabe 2 46
(KBell) *hld up: hdwy 6f out: rdn over 3f out: kpt on ins fnl f: no ch w wnr* **6/1**[2]

500- **3** *1 ¼* **Newclose**[18] 6196 4-9-8 41 (t) ACulhane 13 44
(NTinkler) *s.i.s: hdwy 6f out: led over 3f out: rdn and hdd over 2f out: sn btn: edgd rt ins fnl f* **9/1**

006- **4** *¾* **Proud Victor (IRE)**[15] 6218 4-9-8 39 DarrenWilliams 7 42
(DShaw) *hld up: rdn over 3f out: hdwy on outside over 1f out: r.o* **9/1**

000- **5** *1 ¼* **Mabel Riley (IRE)**[26] 6146 4-9-8 41 (p) SWKelly 6 40
(MABuckley) *hld up: hdwy 6f out: n.m.r over 3f out: sn rdn: no imp fnl 2f* **14/1**

000- **6** *1 ½* **Wilson Bluebottle (IRE)**[133] 4384 5-9-8 42 (b) DaleGibson 11 36
(MWEasterby) *prom: rdn over 4f out: wknd over 3f out* **10/1**

000- **7** *2* **Courant D'Air (IRE)**[121] 4676 3-7-9 45 RoryMoore(7) 8 32
(PCHaslam) *prom: rdn over 3f out: wknd 2f out* **8/1**[3]

220- **8** *¾* **Leonora Truce (IRE)**[28] 6140 5-9-8 44 DeanMcKeown 9 31
(RPElliott) *led: rdn and hdd over 3f out: wknd wl over 1f out* **10/1**

0/0- **9** *1 ¾* **Sophomore**[15] 5540 10-9-8 42 JMackay 5 27
(JohnAHarris) *a bhd* **16/1**

300- **10** *14* **Pageant**[64] 5846 7-9-5 34 LEnstone(3) 10 —
(JMBradley) *w ldr: rdn over 4f out: wknd over 3f out* **14/1**

00/- **11** *10* **Keltic Flute**[461] [4642] 5-9-1 43.........................................(v[1]) SYourston(7) 4 —
(MrsLucindaFeatherstone) *plld hrd in tch: hmpd on ins bnd over 6f out: bhd fnl 4f* **40/1**

000- **12** *2 ½* **Intitnice (IRE)**[17] [6203] 3-8-2 39.................................... JoannaBadger 12 —
(MissKMGeorge) *prom: rdn over 4f out: wknd over 3f out* **16/1**

000- **13** *dist* **Eurolink Artemis**[26] [6143] 7-9-3 43.........................................(p) TEaves(5) 1 —
(MissGayKelleway) *hld up: stdy hdwy over 5f out: rdn and wknd 3f out: virtually p.u ins fnl f* **11/1**

1m 50.91s (-0.09) **Going Correction** +0.025s/f (Slow)
**WFA** 3 from 4yo+ 20lb **13** Ran SP% **126.1**
Speed ratings: **101,95,93,93,91 90,88,87,85,71 61,59,**—CSF £19.12 TOTE £2.70: £1.50, £2.60, £4.40; EX 16.70.
**Owner** Inca Financial Services **Bred** Darley Stud Management, L L C **Trained** Kingston Lisle, Oxon

**FOCUS**
A good time for the standard of contest, but while the winner looks up to holding his own in better grade, the rest are poor.

**NOTEBOOK**
**Qobtaan(USA)** had failed to get home over slightly further here the previous day, but different tactics enabled him to turn the race into a procession.
**Maggie's Pet** did nothing more than come through to finish best of the rest.
**Newclose**, fitted with a tongue strap for this drop in class, was swiftly brushed aside by the winner.
**Proud Victor(IRE)** got going too late.

## 426 LITTLEWOODS BET DIRECT BANDED STKS 1m 6f 166y(F)
**3:45** (3:46) (H ) 4-Y-O+ **£1,256** (£359; £179) **Stalls** High

Form RPR

506- **1** **Citrus Magic**[298] [699] 7-8-11 33...................(p) StephanieHollinshead(7) 3 46
(KBell) *mde all: rdn clr over 2f out: styd on wl* **7/1**

000- **2** *7* **Unleaded**[22] [6168] 4-8-12 30.................................................... MTebbutt 7 37
(JAkehurst) *hld up: rdn and hdwy over 4f out: styd on to take 2nd ins fnl f: no ch w wnr* **12/1**

/20- **3** *2* **Welcome Back**[28] [6139] 7-9-4 33.............................................. ACulhane 9 34
(KARyan) *hld up: hdwy over 6f out: chsd wnr over 5f out: rdn over 3f out: sn btn: collapsed and died after post* **2/1[1]**

/50- **4** *4* **The Last Mohican**[7] [3276] 5-8-13 31.................................(p) DNolan(5) 8 29
(PHowling) *a.p: rdn over 4f out: no hdwy fnl 3f* **13/2[3]**

400- **5** *2* **Roppongi Dancer**[18] [6200] 5-9-4 25...............................(bt[1]) JoannaBadger 5 27
(MrsNMacauley) *hld up: pushed along 8f out: no hdwy fnl 4f* **10/1**

6- **6** *½* **Gaelic Probe (IRE)**[8] [3973] 10-9-4 34............................(p) PFitzsimons 2 26
(RMHCowell) *bhd: rdn 7f out: nvr nr ldrs* **6/1[2]**

040- **7** *8* **Inglewood**[140] [3461] 4-8-12 35........................................ DeanMcKeown 4 16
(CWThornton) *chsd wnr 8f: rdn and lost pl over 4f out* **7/1**

000- **8** *27* **All On My Own (USA)**[15] [6033] 9-8-11 35..........(b) NataliaGemelova(7) 1 —
(IWMcinnes) *prom: chsd wnr 7f out tl over 5f out: wknd over 4f out: t.o* **9/1**

040- **9** *28* **Comanche Woman**[38] [6075] 4-8-12 35................................(t) JMackay 6 —
(KOCunningham-Brown) *a bhd: rdn 5f out: t.o* **33/1**

3m 23.71s (2.91) **Going Correction** +0.025s/f (Slow)
**WFA** 4 from 5yo+ 6lb **9** Ran SP% **115.7**
Speed ratings: **93,89,88,86,85 84,80,66,51**CSF £86.63 TOTE £11.40: £3.00, £5.10, £1.50; EX 150.30.
**Owner** Mines A Double Club **Bred** Donald Duke **Trained** Letcombe Regis, Oxon

**FOCUS**
A moderate time even for this dire event, and the form is weak.

**NOTEBOOK**
**Citrus Magic** had already shown he stays this trip and this long-standing maiden was ridden accordingly.
**Unleaded** is not going to find many easier opportunities than this.
**Welcome Back** was thought to have probably suffered a heart attack shortly after the finish.

## 427 BET DIRECT FOOTBALL CASHBACKS BANDED STKS 1m 1f 79y(F)
**4:15** (4:15) (H ) 3-Y-O+ **£1,463** (£418; £209) **Stalls** Low

Form RPR

000/ **1** **Ndola**[431] [5530] 5-9-9 35.................................................... PJScallan 12 48
(BJCurley) *a.p: rdn to ld 3f out: rdn out* **11/4[1]**

000- **2** *1 ¼* **Tropical Son**[15] [6211] 5-9-9 38....................................(v) DarrenWilliams 6 46
(DShaw) *hld up: hdwy 4f out: sn rdn: wnt 2nd and edgd lft over 1f out: nt qckn* **8/1**

000- **3** *1 ¾* **Seraph**[16] [5611] 4-9-8 36.........................................................(p) JMackay 1 42
(JohnAHarris) *bhd tl rdn and hdwy over 3f out: r.o one pce fnl f* **20/1**

306- **4** *½* **Dancing Tilly**[23] [4948] 6-9-4 38...................................(p) THamilton(5) 4 41
(RAFahey) *bhd tl hdwy on outside over 1f out: r.o ins fnl f* **10/1**

653- **5** *1 ¾* **Samar Qand**[21] [6174] 5-9-9 38...........................................(p) MTebbutt 13 38
(JulianPoulton) *s.i.s: sn prom: led over 4f out: rdn and hdd 3f out: wknd fnl f* **3/1[2]**

/64- **6** *4* **Fraternity**[148] [3973] 7-9-9 38........................................ DeanMcKeown 3 30
(JAPickering) *hld up in tch: wknd over 3f out* **8/1**

400- **7** *1 ¾* **Soleil D'Hiver**[40] [6058] 3-7-8 40.................................... RoryMoore(7) 5 26
(PCHaslam) *prom tl wknd over 3f out* **10/1**

500- **8** *8* **Malmand (USA)**[26] [6143] 5-9-9 40........................................(v) ACulhane 2 10
(RBrotherton) *hld up in tch: hdwy on ins 5f out: rdn 4f out: wknd 2f out* **11/2[3]**

000- **9** *¾* **Chickasaw Trail**[26] [6143] 6-9-2 30................(p) StephanieHollinshead(7) 9 9
(RHollinshead) *led: rdn and hdd over 4f out: wknd 3f out* **20/1**

B00- **10** *7* **Repetoire (FR)**[39] [6067] 4-9-8 40...........................................(be[1]) ANicholls 7 —
(KOCunningham-Brown) *s.i.s: a bhd* **40/1**

000- **11** *3* **The Laverton Lad**[26] [6147] 3-8-1 35.................................. TWilliams 10 —
(CWThornton) *rdn over 6f out: a bhd* **25/1**

000- **12** *11* **Darcie Mia**[45] [6029] 3-7-8 38.........................................(b) DFentiman(7) 11 —
(JRWeymes) *w ldr tl rdn over 4f out: sn wknd* **25/1**

2m 3.29s (0.39) **Going Correction** +0.025s/f (Slow)
**WFA** 3 from 4yo 22lb 4 from 5yo+ 1lb **12** Ran SP% **127.1**
Speed ratings: **99,97,96,95,94 90,89,82,81,75 72,62**CSF £25.48 TOTE £4.90: £2.20, £3.20, £7.20; EX 72.40 Place 6 £11.38, Place 5 £7.90.
**Owner** Mrs B J Curley **Bred** Loan And Development Corporation **Trained** Newmarket, Suffolk

**FOCUS**
A weak banded contest, run fractionally slower than the earlier maiden auction event, but the form is poor.

**NOTEBOOK**
**Ndola** could hardly have found a softer race on his All-Weather debut, having been off course since October 2002. *Official explanation: trainer's representative said, regarding the improved form shown, gelding had been off the track for over a year and had benefited from the drop in class today*
**Tropical Son** did not help his cause by being inclined to drift in behind the winner.
**Seraph** never appeared likely to overhaul the first two.
**Dancing Tilly** got going too late on her All-Weather debut.
**Samar Qand** did not quite last home despite reverting to a shorter distance.
**Malmand(USA)** *Official explanation: jockey said gelding had lost its action*
T/Plt: £17.50 to a £1 stake. Pool: £43,118.00. 1,792.40 winning tickets. T/Qpdt: £7.90 to a £1 stake. Pool: £2,525.70. 234.80 winning tickets. KH

# SOUTHWELL (L-H)
Sunday, January 4

**OFFICIAL GOING: Standard**
(REGIONAL MEETING)
Wind: slt hlf behind Weather: overcast

## 428 BET DIRECT ON 0800 32 93 93 APPRENTICE BANDED STKS (DIV I) 7f (F)
**12:30** (12:31) (H ) 3-Y-O+ **£1,641** (£469; £234) **Stalls** Low

Form RPR

054- **1** **Rosti**[19] [6196] 4-9-3 45......................................................... RoryMoore(5) 4 53
(PCHaslam) *sn chsng ldrs: effrt 3f out: hung lft: styd on to ld 1f out: kpt on wl* **6/5[1]**

505- **2** *2* **Brilliantrio**[19] [6196] 6-9-3 44......................................... AndrewWebb(5) 7 48
(MCChapman) *w ldrs: led over 2f out: hdd 1f out: nt qckn* **13/2[3]**

000- **3** *1 ¼* **Champagne Rider**[26] [6150] 8-9-8 36...................................(e) THamilton 2 45
(DShaw) *w ldrs: led 4f out tl over 2f out: kpt on same pce* **9/1**

300- **4** *nk* **Storm Shower (IRE)**[41] [6055] 6-9-3 39...................(v) StevenHarrison(5) 1 44
(MrsNMacauley) *s.i.s: hdwy to chse ldrs over 4f out: one pce fnl 2f* **14/1**

400- **5** *shd* **Jessie**[22] [6178] 5-9-1 41.............................................. JaniceWebster(7) 3 44
(DonEnricoIncisa) *sn outpcd and pushed along: hdwy over 2f out: keeping on one pce whn n.m.r last 75yds* **22/1**

006- **6** *nk* **Dasar**[19] [6196] 4-9-5 45.............................................................. MLawson(3) 9 43
(MBrittain) *led tl 4f out: one pce fnl 2f* **8/1**

620- **7** *2* **T K O Gym**[41] [6060] 5-9-3 42................................................(v[1]) LTreadwell(5) 5 38
(DNicholls) *s.i.s: sn pushed along in rr: kpt on fnl f* **6/1[2]**

550- **8** *1 ¼* **Balalaika Tune (IRE)**[19] [6196] 5-9-5 43.......... StephanieHollinshead(3) 8 35
(WStorey) *s.i.s: outpcd and bhd over 2f out: sme late hdwy* **25/1**

400- **9** *2* **Aljomar**[16] [6214] 5-9-8 39................................................................(p) TEaves 6 30
(REBarr) *chsd ldrs: drvn along and lost pl over 4f out: nvr a factor after* **28/1**

1m 31.58s (0.78) **Going Correction** -0.10s/f (Stan) **9** Ran SP% **112.5**
Speed ratings: **91,88,87,86,86 86,84,82,80**CSF £8.58 TOTE £1.40: £1.30, £1.20, £2.00; EX 9.00.
**Owner** Exors of late B M Hawkins/Lord Downshire **Bred** W C Tincknell And Mrs A Tincknell **Trained** Middleham Moor, N Yorks

**FOCUS**
A very modest winning time, but the form is fair and the winner can do better.

**NOTEBOOK**
**Rosti**, top-rated by RPR, was outstanding in the paddock and in the end won readily despite a tendency to hang. A mile will suit him even better.
**Brilliantrio**, led down to the start, did nothing at all wrong on the way back but it was simply a case of meeting one better.
**Champagne Rider**, who has not tasted success for over two years, showed a certain reluctance to go down to the start.
**Storm Shower(IRE)**, absent since November, found this trip on the sharp side.
**Jessie** ran better than of late but it is hard to know what is her best trip.
**Dasar**, closely matched with the runner-up on their running here last time, had no obvious excuse.
**T K O Gym**, in a first-time visor, was warm beforehand on quite a cold day. He is still a maiden after 20 starts now.

## 429 BET DIRECT ON 0800 32 93 93 APPRENTICE BANDED STKS (DIV II) 7f (F)
**1:00** (1:00) (H ) 3-Y-O+ **£1,641** (£469; £234) **Stalls** Low

Form RPR

02-2 **1** **Larky's Lob**[1] [422] 5-9-8 48.................................................... NChalmers 4 57
(PaulJohnson) *hld up: hdwy 4f out: led over 1f out: drew clr* **6/5[1]**

00-1 **2** *5* **Cleveland Way**[1] [421] 4-9-9 45........................................(v) DTudhope(5) 7 51
(DCarroll) *w ldrs: led over 2f out tl over 1f out: kpt on same pce* **6/1[3]**

000- **3** *½* **Sandorra**[158] [3683] 6-9-5 43...................................................... MLawson(3) 6 43
(MBrittain) *chsd ldrs: drvn along over 4f out: one pce fnl 2f* **33/1**

05-0 **4** *½* **Bijan (IRE)**[2] [407] 6-9-5 35.............................. StephanieHollinshead(3) 2 42
(RHollinshead) *hld up in rr: hdwy over 2f out: kpt on: nvr nr ldrs* **8/1**

0/6- **5** *4* **Proprius**[320] [568] 4-9-3 43.................................................... MStainton(5) 8 32
(BSmart) *dwlt: sme hdwy over 2f out: nvr nr ldrs* **16/1**

000- **6** *5* **Landofheartsdesire (IRE)**[46] [6028] 5-9-8 43........................(v) TEaves 9 20
(JSWainwright) *trckd ldrs: outpcd over 3f out: hung lft and n.d after* **12/1**

000- **7** *6* **Court Music (IRE)**[23] [6171] 5-9-8 32.................................(v) THamilton 1 5
(REBarr) *chsd ldr: led over 4f out tl over 2f out: lost pl over 1f out* **33/1**

6P0/ **8** *5* **Mujagem (IRE)**[810] [5287] 8-9-8 45........................................(b) PMulrennan 3 —
(MWEasterby) *sn pushed along and outpcd: a in rr* **11/1**

060- **9** *3 ½* **Tefi**[26] [6155] 6-9-3 41....................................................................(b) PMakin(5) 5 —
(JBalding) *led tl over 4f out: edgd rt and lost pl over 2f out: sn bhd* **11/2[2]**

1m 31.68s (0.88) **Going Correction** -0.10s/f (Stan) **9** Ran SP% **114.0**
Speed ratings: **90,84,83,83,78 72,66,60,56**CSF £8.46 TOTE £1.60: £1.50, £1.60, £6.80; EX 5.70.
**Owner** P And Mrs D M Johnson **Bred** P Balding **Trained** White-le-Head, Co Durham

**FOCUS**
A very modest winning time, the form is only fair.

**NOTEBOOK**
**Larky's Lob**, having his second outing in two days, benefited from a more patient ride and fully appreciated the slightly extended trip. In the end he came right away.
**Cleveland Way**, bidding for his second win in two days, in the end did not see out the extra furlong anywhere near as well as the winner.
**Sandorra**, having her first outing since July and her first run on the Fibresand, had 16lb to find with the winner on RPR.
**Bijan(IRE)**, who has not hit the target for over two years, had a fair bit to find and seemed suited by the return to seven.
**Proprius**, fitted with a cross noseband on his first outing for 11 months, had plenty to find. On the plus side he has very few miles on the clock.
**Tefi** *Official explanation: jockey said gelding had a breathing problem*

## 430 BET DIRECT PRESS RED TO BET BANDED STKS 1m 4f (F)
**1:30** (1:30) (H ) 4-Y-O+ **£1,291** (£369; £184) **Stalls** Low

Form RPR

000- **1** **Dash Of Magic**[23] [6168] 6-9-4 36............................................... CCatlin 6 50
(JHetherton) *chsd ldrs: led over 2f out: kpt on wl* **5/1[2]**


The Form Book, Raceform Ltd, Compton, RG20 6NL

| | | | | |
|---|---|---|---|---|
| 626- | **2** | 2 | **Paddy Mul**[34] 4481 7-9-4 35..........(t) DRMcCabe 4<br>(WStorey) *sn bhd: hdwy over 2f out: swtchd rt over 1f out: styd on to take 2nd nr fin* **11/1** | 47 |
| 044- | **3** | ¾ | **Misty Man (USA)**[19] 6198 6-8-13 30..........(b[1]) BReilly(5) 10<br>(MissJFeilden) *dwlt: t.k.h: hdwy on outer over 4f out: wnt 2nd 1f out: edgd rt and kpt on same pce* **12/1** | 46 |
| 040- | **4** | 2 | **Two Steps To Go (USA)**[22] 6174 5-9-4 36..........(v) ANicholls 3<br>(IanEmmerson) *led tl over 2f out: one pce appr fnl f* **14/1** | 43 |
| 050- | **5** | hd | **Turftanzer (GER)**[22] 6174 5-9-4 36..........(t) KimTinkler 11<br>(DonEnricoIncisa) *chsd ldrs: one pce fnl 2f* **20/1** | 43 |
| 500- | **6** | hd | **Leophin Dancer (USA)**[24] 6075 6-9-1 38.......... LisaJones(3) 7<br>(PWHiatt) *hld up in rr: hdwy 3f out: styd on same pce* **13/2**[3] | 42 |
| 016/ | **7** | nk | **Oulton Broad**[437] 3315 8-9-1 37..........(p) J-PGuillambert(3) 9<br>(RFord) *hld up in mid-div: effrt 3f out: kpt on same pce* **10/1** | 42 |
| 000- | **8** | 3 | **King Priam (IRE)**[8] 6247 9-9-1 34..........(b) LFletcher(3) 5<br>(MJPolglase) *chsd ldrs: drvn along 9f out: lost pl 5f out: kpt on on wd outside fnl 2f* **9/2**[1] | 37 |
| 060- | **9** | 2 ½ | **Behan**[32] 6125 5-9-4 24..........(b) VHalliday 1<br>(ACrook) *sn chsng ldrs: lost pl over 1f out* **20/1** | 34 |
| 105- | **10** | 9 | **Magic Charm**[65] 5848 6-9-4 39.......... SWhitworth 8<br>(AGNewcombe) *mid-div: effrt over 3f out: lost pl 2f out* **13/2**[3] | 20 |
| 600- | **11** | 4 | **Marengo**[27] 6143 10-9-4 34.......... JoannaBadger 2<br>(PaulJohnson) *s.i.s: plld hrd: effrt 4f out: sn wknd and bhd* **16/1** | 14 |
| 0/0- | **12** | 13 | **Kittylee**[5] 6257 5-9-4 25.......... RFfrench 13<br>(MABuckley) *mid-div: lost pl 5f out: sn bhd* **12/1** | — |
| 000- | **13** | 2 ½ | **Ten Past Six**[119] 4751 12-8-11 23..........(be) ACooper(7) 12<br>(RCGuest) *bhd and drvn along 7f out: t.o 3f out* **33/1** | — |
| 000- | **14** | 11 | **Sea Ya Maite**[144] 4066 10-9-4 30.......... JBramhill 14<br>(SRBowring) *s.i.s: hdwy to chse ldrs 8f out: lost pl over 2f out: sn bhd and eased* **22/1** | — |

2m 42.62s (0.52) **Going Correction** -0.10s/f (Stan) **14** Ran SP% **123.7**
Speed ratings: **94,92,92,90,90 90,90,88,86,80 78,69,67,60**CSF £57.59 TOTE £6.50: £2.10, £2.70, £3.50; EX 53.10.
**Owner** 21st Century Racing **Bred** Miss Trudy Huggett **Trained** Malton, N Yorks

**FOCUS**
A modest winning time, just fair form for the grade.

**NOTEBOOK**
**Dash Of Magic**, who won three times last year, is from a stable back in form and, top-rated by RPR, made no mistake. *Official explanation: trainer said, regarding the improved form shown, mare was possibly suited by the drop in trip, adding that his stable had been out of form until recently*
**Paddy Mul**, last seen out over hurdles, stayed on after being switched to snatch second spot near the line. This trip is his bare minimum.
**Misty Man(USA)**, in first-time blinkers, would not settle early on and under pressure wanted to do nothing but hang right. *Official explanation: jockey said gelding hung badly right-handed*
**Two Steps To Go(USA)**, from a stable on a high at present, made this a true test but at the end that really counts his stamina looked at a low ebb.
**Turftanzer(GER)**, a winner in the past in Italy, seemed to run his best race so far here.
**Leophin Dancer(USA)**, more effective over hurdles, has now drawn a blank in no less than 40 starts on the level.
**Oulton Broad**, successful over hurdles when last seen out in October 2002, will improve for the outing.
**King Priam(IRE)**, an old monkey, lost interest when amongst horses on the turn away from the stands. Eventually making his way to the wide outside, he consented to stay on late in the day.
**Sea Ya Maite** *Official explanation: jockey said gelding gurgled*

## 431 BETDIRECT.CO.UK MEDIAN AUCTION MAIDEN STKS — 1m 3f (F)
**2:00** (2:00) (H) 4-6-Y-O — **£1,452** (£415; £207) **Stalls** Low

| Form | | | | RPR |
|---|---|---|---|---|
| 400- | **1** | | **Madiba**[6] 6249 5-9-3 57..........(b) RWinston 3<br>(PHowling) *led: shkn up and qcknd over 2f out: clr over 1f out: readily* **4/1** | 60 |
| 0/5- | **2** | 6 | **Mr Smithers Jones**[323] 550 4-8-9 50.......... BReilly(5) 4<br>(SCWilliams) *trckd ldrs: t.k.h: chal 3f out: sn rdn: one pce* **7/1** | 50 |
| 002- | **3** | 5 | **Make My Hay**[16] 6214 5-9-0 45..........(b) LFletcher(3) 5<br>(JWhite) *rn in snatches: sn in rr and drvn along: hdwy 7f out: rdn 2f out: one pce* **5/2**[1] | 42 |
| 066- | **4** | 13 | **Danum**[20] 6190 4-9-0 49..........(p) ACulhane 2<br>(RHollinshead) *chsd ldrs: rdn 5f out: lost pl 2f out* **3/1**[2] | 22 |
| 330- | **5** | 23 | **White Park Bay (IRE)**[6] 6254 4-8-9 58.......... NCallan 6<br>(JGallagher) *hdwy 7f out: sn chsng ldrs: lost pl over 3f out: sn bhd* **7/2**[3] | — |
| F00/ | **6** | 4 | **Red Crystal**[96] 84 6-8-9..........(p) LEnstone(3) 1<br>(CRWilson) *chsd ldrs: rdn and lost pl over 5f out: t.o 3f out* **33/1** | — |

2m 27.77s (-1.13) **Going Correction** -0.10s/f (Stan)
**WFA** 4 from 5yo+ 3lb **6** Ran SP% **111.2**
Speed ratings: **100,95,92,82,65 62**CSF £29.99 TOTE £5.50: £3.20, £2.60; EX 66.50.
**Owner** Eastwell Manor Racing Ltd **Bred** M L Roberts **Trained** Newmarket, Suffolk
■ Stewards Enquiry : L Enstone one-day ban: used whip with excessive force (Jan 15)

**FOCUS**
A fair winning time for the standard of contest, but the form is modest.

**NOTEBOOK**
**Madiba**, a frustrating type, was due to go hurdling but he wanted no part of it. His rider was keen to get him to the front and, sent for home early in the straight, in the end he ran out a most convincing winner at the 22nd attempt. This will at least have given him some confidence.
**Mr Smithers Jones**, having his first outing for 11 months and taking a big step up in trip, had 22lb to find with the winner on RPR ratings.
**Make My Hay** ran in snatches and has now tried 20 times to break his duck.
**Danum** looked really well but does not see to be fully at home on the All-Weather.
**White Park Bay(IRE)**, having her second outing in less than a week, was again well below par.

## 432 LITTLEWOODS BET DIRECT BANDED STKS — 2m (F)
**2:30** (2:31) (H) 4-Y-0+ — **£1,645** (£470; £235) **Stalls** Low

| Form | | | | RPR |
|---|---|---|---|---|
| 031- | **1** | | **Delta Force**[9] 6240 5-9-0 51.......... DerekNolan(7) 6<br>(PABlockley) *trckd ldrs: t.k.h: led over 3f out: styd on strly to go clr ins last* **7/2**[2] | 50 |
| 060- | **2** | 5 | **Kagoshima (IRE)**[19] 6200 9-9-7 39..........(v) VHalliday 9<br>(JRNorton) *trckd ldrs: styd on to go 2nd over 1f out: no ch w wnr* **4/1** | 44 |
| 60- | **3** | 3 ½ | **Kyalami (IRE)**[13] 6234 5-9-4 24.......... LFletcher(3) 5<br>(MJPolglase) *chsd ldrs: pushed along 8f out: hung lft and one pce fnl 2f* **14/1** | 40 |
| 340- | **4** | 1 ¾ | **Worlaby Dale**[55] 5972 8-9-7 45.......... JQuinn 10<br>(MrsSLamyman) *settled in last pl: hdwy 5f out: effrt on inner and n.m.r 3f out: kpt on same pce* **11/4**[1] | 38 |
| 030/ | **5** | ½ | **Maraud**[43] 3844 10-9-0 25.......... StephanieHollinshead(7) 7<br>(RHollinshead) *led tl over 3f out: lost pl over 1f out* **10/1** | 37 |
| 050- | **6** | 1 ½ | **Ashtaroute (USA)**[41] 6060 4-8-7 40.......... AndrewWebb(7) 2<br>(MCChapman) *in tch: sn pushed along: lost pl 7f out: hung rt: kpt on fnl 2f* **14/1** | 35 |
| 640- | **7** | 15 | **Khuzdar (IRE)**[40] 6068 5-9-0 43.......... BO'Neill(7) 1<br>(ABailey) *t.k.h towards rr: hdwy 8f out: sn chsng ldrs: hung lft 3f out: sn lost pl* **4/1**[3] | 17 |
| 000/ | **8** | 7 | **Niciara (IRE)**[643] 647 7-9-7 32.......... LVickers 8<br>(MCChapman) *mid-div: pushed along 9f out: lost pl over 5f out* **33/1** | 9 |
| 050- | **9** | 21 | **Fayrway Rhythm (IRE)**[23] 6168 7-9-7 39..........(v) ANicholls 3<br>(IanEmmerson) *hld up in rr: hdwy 10f out: sn chsng ldrs: lost pl over 4f out: sn bhd* **20/1** | — |
| 463- | **10** | nk | **Rousing Thunder**[54] 5631 7-9-4 41..........(p) DMcGaffin(3) 4<br>(WStorey) *in tch: lost pl 6f out: sn bhd* **15/2** | — |

3m 45.98s (-6.52) **Going Correction** -0.10s/f (Stan)
**WFA** 4 from 5yo+ 7lb **10** Ran SP% **118.5**
Speed ratings: **97,94,92,91,91 90,83,79,69,69**CSF £45.99 TOTE £2.20: £1.60, £2.40, £3.10; EX 83.00.
**Owner** Miss Emma Shally **Bred** Thomas Shally Jnr **Trained** Southwell, Notts

**FOCUS**
Another weak contest form-wise.

**NOTEBOOK**
**Delta Force**, on his toes beforehand, had two handlers in the paddock and his back legs are best avoided. He took a fierce grip in a race run at a very modest pace but, his stamina untested, he shot clear just inside the last. His young rider should go far.
**Kagoshima(IRE)**, who last won over two years ago, shaped a lot better than he had done on his three most recent starts here.
**Kyalami(IRE)**, last on four starts in Ireland, was having just his third outing here.
**Worlaby Dale**, well supported on only his second start on Fibresand, was dropped right in but he was already struggling when left short of room on the inner at the three furlongs from home marker.
**Maraud**, winner of six hurdle races, was returning to the Flat after an absence of over three years. He enjoys himself in front, but like us all he is not getting any younger.
**Khuzdar(IRE)** would not settle on his first outing for his new trainer and gave himself little prospect of seeing out the trip.
**Rousing Thunder** *Official explanation: jockey said gelding had a breathing problem*

## 433 BET DIRECT ON ITV PAGE 367 (S) STKS — 6f (F)
**3:00** (3:00) (H) 3-Y-0+ — **£1,291** (£369; £184) **Stalls** Low

| Form | | | | RPR |
|---|---|---|---|---|
| 344- | **1** | | **Hurricane Coast**[16] 6217 5-9-7 61.......... DNolan(5) 1<br>(PABlockley) *trckd ldrs: shkn up to ld jst ins fnl f: cheekily* **2/1**[1] | 65 |
| 054- | **2** | ¾ | **Speedfit Free (IRE)**[29] 6136 7-9-7 55..........(b) RWinston 2<br>(ISemple) *mid-div: hdwy on ins 3f out: styd on to go 2nd ins last* **9/4**[2] | 58 |
| 000- | **3** | ¾ | **Aguila Loco (IRE)**[8] 6243 5-9-0 36.......... AndrewWebb(7) 6<br>(MCChapman) *led tl hdd jst ins fnl f: no ex* **40/1** | 56 |
| 600- | **4** | 5 | **Donegal Shore (IRE)**[76] 5682 5-9-2 66..........(t) NChalmers(5) 3<br>(MrsJCandlish) *s.i.s: bhd stl styd on fnl f* **20/1** | 41 |
| 200- | **5** | ½ | **Travelling Times**[19] 6196 5-9-2 51..........(v) TEaves(5) 7<br>(JSWainwright) *w ldrs: edgd rt and wknd over 1f out* **5/1**[3] | 39 |
| 020- | **6** | 2 ½ | **Lay Down Sally (IRE)**[16] 6217 6-8-13 45..........(b) LFletcher(3) 8<br>(JWhite) *chsd ldrs: edgd lft and lost pl over 2f out* **7/1** | 27 |
| 264- | **7** | 1 | **Fisher's Dream**[8] 6246 3-8-5 48..........(v) JBramhill 10<br>(JRNorton) *racd on outer: sn drvn along: chsd ldrs: outpcd over 3f out: n.d after* **14/1** | 29 |
| 000- | **8** | ½ | **Valuable Gift**[29] 6136 7-9-0 45..........(be) ACooper(7) 5<br>(RCGuest) *chsd ldrs: lost pl over 1f out* **16/1** | 27 |
| / | **9** | 7 | **The Block Monster (IRE)**[110] 4979 5-8-9 .......... DerekNolan(7) 4<br>(PABlockley) *s.s: a in rr* **14/1** | 1 |
| 000- | **10** | 4 | **Precious Freedom**[46] 6032 4-9-7 43..........(v[1]) JEdmunds 9<br>(JBalding) *chsd ldrs: ev ch over 2f out: wknd rapidly over 1f out* **28/1** | — |

1m 16.45s (-0.35) **Going Correction** -0.10s/f (Stan)
**WFA** 3 from 4yo+ 16lb **10** Ran SP% **123.1**
Speed ratings: **98,97,96,89,88 85,84,83,74,68**CSF £6.97 TOTE £3.10: £1.60, £1.10, £14.60; EX 8.70.The winner was bought in for 3,800gns.
**Owner** Mrs Joanna Hughes **Bred** Ian H Wills **Trained** Southwell, Notts

**FOCUS**
The form looks solid for the grade.

**NOTEBOOK**
**Hurricane Coast**, tucked away on the inner, behaved himself impeccably on this occasion and won in cheeky fashion.
**Speedfit Free(IRE)**, three times a winner on Fibresand, probably ran close to his best but he is flattered by his proximity to the winner at the line. An eighth career win is surely just around the corner.
**Aguila Loco(IRE)**, who had 24lb to find with the first two on RPR ratings, made this a true test and seemed to see out the sixth furlong alright.
**Donegal Shore(IRE)**, last seen out in October over a mile seven, found this much too sharp.
**Travelling Times** has now been below par in three starts since finishing runner-up here in November.
**Lay Down Sally(IRE)**, warm beforehand, seemed reluctant to go forward in a straight line.

## 434 BET DIRECT IN VISION SKY PAGE 293 BANDED STKS — 1m (F)
**3:30** (3:31) (H) 3-Y-0+ — **£1,491** (£426; £213) **Stalls** Low

| Form | | | | RPR |
|---|---|---|---|---|
| 005- | **1** | | **Printsmith (IRE)**[158] 3683 7-9-8 32.......... JBramhill 4<br>(JRNorton) *chsd ldrs: led over 2f out: clr over 1f out: drvn out* **16/1** | 49 |
| 000- | **2** | 1 ½ | **Simply The Guest (IRE)**[40] 6064 5-9-8 34..........(t) KimTinkler 9<br>(DonEnricoIncisa) *chsd ldrs: outpcd over 3f out: styd on to take 2nd last 75yds* **13/2**[3] | 46 |
| 000- | **3** | 1 ½ | **Kenny The Truth (IRE)**[26] 6151 5-9-3 40..........(t) NChalmers(5) 6<br>(MrsJCandlish) *in tch: outpcd 3f out: styd on to go 2nd 1f out: one pce* **6/1**[2] | 43 |
| 600- | **4** | 8 | **Given A Chance**[40] 6066 3-8-3 40 ow1.......... JFanning 12<br>(JGGiven) *chsd ldrs: wknd over 1f out* **6/1**[2] | 28 |
| 000- | **5** | 1 | **Dancing King (IRE)**[16] 6211 8-9-1 26.......... PMakin(7) 2<br>(PWHiatt) *led tl over 2f out: wknd over 1f out* **10/1** | 25 |
| 000- | **6** | ¾ | **Haithem (IRE)**[8] 6245 7-9-5 36..........(e) LisaJones(3) 8<br>(DShaw) *in tch: outpcd over 4f out: hdwy over 2f out: nvr a factor* **8/1** | 24 |
| 600- | **7** | 5 | **Onefortheboys (IRE)**[33] 6116 5-9-8 36.......... PDoe 11<br>(DFlood) *chsd ldrs: lost pl over 1f out* **9/2**[1] | 14 |
| 000- | **8** | 1 ¾ | **Formeric**[16] 6218 8-9-8 33..........(v) JMcAuley 3<br>(MissLCSiddall) *s.i.s: a bhd* **33/1** | 10 |
| 460- | **9** | ¾ | **Miss Wizz**[51] 5418 4-9-8 37.......... JQuinn 7<br>(WStorey) *chsd ldrs: lost pl over 1f out* **10/1** | 9 |
| 550- | **10** | 5 | **Western Command (GER)**[124] 4639 8-9-8 20.......... JoannaBadger 5<br>(MrsNMacauley) *reluctant to go to s: s.i.s: a bhd* **12/1** | — |
| 000- | **11** | 3 | **Nickel Sungirl (IRE)**[51] 5995 4-9-8 40.......... NCallan 1<br>(RHollinshead) *chsd ldrs: lost pl 3f out* **7/1** | — |

000- **12** 5 **Countess Elton (IRE)**32 [5819] 4-9-3 35............................ TEaves(5) 10 —
(REBarr) *dwlt: sn trcking ldrs: hung lft and lost pl 3f out: sn bhd* **33/1**

1m 44.2s (-0.40) **Going Correction** -0.10s/f (Stan)
**WFA** 3 from 4yo+ 20lb **12** Ran SP% **121.3**
Speed ratings: **98,96,95,87,86 85,80,78,77,72 69,64**CSF £119.31 TOTE £19.00: £4.60, £3.30, £2.50; EX 111.40 Place 6 £196.94, Place 5 £141.98..
**Owner** Mrs Hazel Tattersall **Bred** Joseph O'Callaghan **Trained** High Hoyland, S Yorks

**FOCUS**
Poor but solid form by the front three.

**NOTEBOOK**
**Printsmith(IRE)**, absent since July, recorded her first win for over three years.
**Simply The Guest(IRE)**, out of sorts for some time, ran a lot better.
**Kenny The Truth(IRE)**, happy stepping up in trip, finished clear third best.
**Given A Chance** may be better suited by a drop back to seven.
**Dancing King(IRE)** looked as fit as a flea on his second start in two weeks after a three-month break.
**Haithem(IRE)** had to be walked down to the start.
**Onefortheboys(IRE)**, who is with his third trainer, had finished unplaced in 11 previous starts. The step up from six did not work at all.
**Nickel Sungirl(IRE)** *Official explanation: jockey said filly hung right-handed into the straight*
T/Plt: £27.70 to a £1 stake. Pool: £33,607.35. 884.15 winning tickets. T/Qpdt: £17.90 to a £1 stake. Pool: £2,281.90. 93.90 winning tickets. WG

# 428SOUTHWELL (L-H)

## Monday, January 5

**OFFICIAL GOING: Standard**

## 435 BET DIRECT ON ATTHERACES INTERACTIVE H'CAP 6f (F)

**1:15** (1:15) (E ) (0-70,64) 3-Y-O **£3,290** (£940; £470) **Stalls** Low

Form RPR

035- **1** **Siegfrieds Night (IRE)**9 [6246] 3-8-2 **45**...................... JoannaBadger 1 47
(MCChapman) *chsd ldrs on inner: swtchd rt and hdwy 2f out: rdn over 1f out: styd on to ld ins last* **12/1**

061- **2** 2 **Melaina**45 [6041] 3-8-10 **53**..........................................(p) JQuinn 2 49
(MSSaunders) *led: rdn wl over 1f out: wandered and hdd ins last: one pce* **9/2**3

526- **3** nk **Daring Affair**7 [6251] 3-9-7 **64**...................................(v1) NCallan 5 59
(KRBurke) *trckd ldrs: swtchd ins and hdwy to chal over 1f out: sn rdn and one pce ins last* **13/8**1

043- **4** 7 **Garnock Venture (IRE)**20 [6197] 3-8-7 **50**.....................(b) DaleGibson 3 24
(ABerry) *dwlt: sn cl up: rdn along 2f out: drvn wl over 1f out and sn wknd* **5/2**2

000- **5** 1¾ **Numpty (IRE)**102 [5177] 3-8-6 **49**..................................(t) KimTinkler 4 18
(NTinkler) *outpcd and bhd fr 1/2-way* **10/1**

000- **6** 1¼ **Birikina**56 [5966] 3-8-9 **57**........................................ PBradley(5) 6 22
(ABerry) *in tch on outer: rdn along 1/2-way: sn wknd* **16/1**

1m 16.62s (-0.18) **Going Correction** -0.15s/f (Stan) **6** Ran SP% **107.5**
Speed ratings: **95,92,91,82,80 78**CSF £58.21 TOTE £18.90: £6.70, £1.10; EX 55.50.
**Owner** K D Blanch **Bred** Barronstown Stud And Orpendale **Trained** Market Rasen, Lincs

**FOCUS**
A moderate handicap run at an ordinary pace, and the form looks no better than plating-class.

**NOTEBOOK**
**Siegfrieds Night(IRE)**, an exposed maiden going into this, was off the bridle and going nowhere until halfway, but once he was switched out to the centre of the track on turning in he stayed on dourly to catch the flagging leaders and get off the mark at the 14th attempt. This form probably does not amount to much.
**Melaina**was stepping up from selling company, but in truth this was little better and she ran her race under a positive ride.
**Daring Affair**, visored for the first time, had every chance but found disappointingly little under pressure, and the only excuse may be that she was racing closest to the inside rail, where the ground might have been slower.
**Garnock Venture(IRE)**, who has done all his racing over seven since his racecourse debut, handicapped himself with a tardy start, but soon got himself into a challenging position and was simply not good enough. *Official explanation: jockey said gelding hung right*
**Numpty(IRE)**received quite a buffeting after a furlong but it probably made no difference to his finishing position.

## 436 BET DIRECT PRESS RED TO BET CLAIMING STKS 6f (F)

**1:45** (1:45) (F ) 4-Y-O+ **£2,891** (£826; £413) **Stalls** Low

Form RPR

44-1 **1** **Hurricane Coast**1 [433] 5-8-5 61................................ DeanMcKeown 4 69
(PABlockley) *chsd ldrs tl squeezed out after 1f: hdwy on inner 1/2-way: rdn to chal and edgd lft over 1f out: led jst ins last: kpt on* **7/4**2

35-5 **2** 2 **Sharp Hat**3 [411] 10-9-1 71........................................... ACulhane 1 73
(DWChapman) *cl up on inner: led after 2f: rdn wl over 1f out: hdd and nt qckn ins last* **6/1**3

400- **3** 3 **Legalis (USA)**30 [6136] 6-8-9 60.......................................(b1) NCallan 3 58
(KARyan) *a.p: rdn and ev ch over 1f out: drvn and wknd appr last* **20/1**

000- **4** 5 **High Esteem**41 [6063] 8-8-13 58........................................(p) RFrench 2 47
(MABuckley) *led 2f: cl up tl rdn along over 2f out and sn wknd* **28/1**

615- **5** 2 **Jalouhar**27 [6149] 4-8-9 59...........................................(p) JFanning 7 37
(BPJBaugh) *outpcd and drvn along 1/2-way: nvr a factor* **9/1**

00-5 **6** nk **Travelling Times**1 [433] 5-8-5 51..................................(v) DRMcCabe 6 32
(JSWainwright) *chsd ldrs: rdn along and outpcd 1/2-way: bhd after* **33/1**

515- **7** 7 **Queen Of Night**30 [6136] 4-8-2 76..................................... DMernagh 5 8
(TDBarron) *chsd ldrs: rdn along and v wd st: sn bhd and eased* **13/8**1

1m 15.41s (-1.39) **Going Correction** -0.15s/f (Stan) **7** Ran SP% **109.9**
Speed ratings: **103,100,96,89,87 86,77**CSF £11.35 TOTE £2.30: £1.50, £3.40; EX 12.00.The winner was claimed by David Flood for £6,000.
**Owner** Mrs Joanna Hughes **Bred** Ian H Wills **Trained** Southwell, Notts
■ Stewards Enquiry : R Ffrench caution: careless riding

**FOCUS**
A moderate contest, and the pace was only fair, but decent form for the grade.

**NOTEBOOK**
**Hurricane Coast**, reappearing quickly after having won a seller over course and distance the previous day, did carry his head high and looks quirky, but he had something to chase and the man on board was probably ideal for a horse like him. With McKeown's elbows working overtime, he was cajoled past the leader and, by the time he was given a tap with the whip, the race was already in the bag.
**Sharp Hat**was given a positive ride and tried to expose any chinks in the resolve of the winner, but unfortunately that rival was on his best behaviour. He stays this trip, but is probably better over five.
**Legalis(USA)**has been very disappointing since winning at Wolverhampton 13 months ago. A bout of lameness has not helped and this was another ordinary performance.
**High Esteem**does not lack early speed, but he is a short runner and is not getting home in his races at present.
**Jalouhar**, a winner of only one of his 20 starts going into this, was never seen with a chance.
**Queen Of Night**disappointed for a second time and the way she hung badly right on the home turn must be a cause for concern. *Official explanation: trainer had no explanation for the poor form shown*

## 437 BETDIRECT.CO.UK H'CAP 1m (F)

**2:15** (2:15) (D ) (0-80,73) 4-Y-O+ **£4,046** (£1,245; £622; £311) **Stalls** Low

Form RPR

465- **1** **Penwell Hill (USA)**21 [6190] 5-9-3 **66**................................ DMernagh 3 77
(TDBarron) *trckd ldrs: hdwy to chse clr ldr wl over 1f out: sn rdn: drvn ent last: styd on to ld last 50 yds* **9/4**1

000- **2** ½ **Pharoah's Gold (IRE)**10 [6241] 6-8-12 **61**..................(e) DarrenWilliams 4 71
(DShaw) *in rr: hdwy on inner 3f out: swtchd rt and rdn 2f out: styd on wl ent last: nrst fin* **16/1**

603- **3** 1 **Quiet Reading (USA)**10 [6241] 7-8-13 **67**................(v) HayleyTurner(5) 6 75
(MRBosley) *midfield: hdwy to chse ldrs 3f out: rdn 2f out: kpt on u.p fnl f* **5/1**2

004- **4** ½ **Flambe**42 [6057] 6-8-6 **58**.............................................(b1) LEnstone(3) 2 65
(PCHaslam) *cl up: led over 4f out: rdn clr over 2f out: hung lft o ver 1f out: drvn ins last: hdd & wknd last 50 yds* **6/1**3

063- **5** ½ **Jamestown**17 [6211] 7-7-12 **47**........................................ JoannaBadger 8 53
(MJPolglase) *tracked ldrs: rdn along and outpcd 1/2-way: swtchd wd 2f out: sn rdn and kpt on appr last: nrst fin* **7/1**

602- **6** 8 **First Maite**9 [6245] 11-9-8 **71**.......................................(b) JBramhill 1 61
(SRBowring) *chsd ldrs on inner: rdn along 3f out: sn outpcd* **9/1**

100- **7** 7 **Riska King**9 [6245] 4-9-5 **73**......................................... THamilton(5) 11 49
(RAFahey) *a bhd* **25/1**

015- **8** 1¼ **Mount Royale (IRE)**156 [3797] 6-8-9 **58**.............................. KimTinkler 9 32
(NTinkler) *chsd ldrs: rdn along 1/2-way: sn wknd* **20/1**

000- **9** nk **Friday's Takings**10 [6241] 5-9-1 **64**.................................(b) RFrench 10 37
(BSmart) *sn led: hdd over 4f out: rdn along 3f out and grad wknd* **10/1**

000- **10** 16 **Sinjaree**21 [6190] 6-8-1 **50**.........................................(v) JQuinn 5 —
(MrsSLamyman) *prom: rdn along ov er 3f out and sn wknd* **28/1**

1m 42.69s (-1.91) **Going Correction** -0.15s/f (Stan) **10** Ran SP% **111.3**
Speed ratings: **103,102,101,101,100 92,85,84,83,67**CSF £38.49 CT £157.53 TOTE £2.10: £1.60, £3.00, £1.40; EX 41.10 Trifecta £120.60 Pool of £1,170.66 - 6.89 winning units.
**Owner** Mrs Liz Jones **Bred** Costello, O'Rourke & Simon **Trained** Maunby, N Yorks
■ Stewards Enquiry : D Mernagh two-day ban: used whip with excessive frequency (Jan 16-17)

**FOCUS**
A competitive little handicap run at a sound pace. The form looks solid, and the winner well-treated.

**NOTEBOOK**
**Penwell Hill(USA)**, returning to his ideal trip, did not look like winning until the last 50 yards as the clear leader capitulated. He has been steadily returning to form since his layoff and may be able to defy a rise in the handicap.
**Pharoah's Gold(IRE)**, returning to a more reasonable mark, saw the trip out here better than he has been doing and his yard appear to have hit a bit of form.
**Quiet Reading(USA)**is another returning to a fair mark and was never closer than at the line.
**Flambe**, supported in the market, was given a positive ride and the tactic looked certain to work turning for home as he held a five-length lead and his rivals were all off the bridle. However, his rider became anxious passing the two-furlong pole as the gelding began to falter, and he was eventually swamped by the front three. About 20 yards from the line he went wrong and sadly had to be put down.
**Jamestown**is brilliantly handicapped on his form of a couple of years ago and ran with credit. He may be worth a try back over further.
**First Maite**was taken off his old legs and never got into it.

## 438 LITTLEWOODS BET DIRECT MAIDEN STKS 6f (F)

**2:45** (2:46) (D ) 3-Y-O+ **£3,425** (£1,054; £527; £263) **Stalls** Low

Form RPR

53- **1** **Classic Vision**206 [2337] 4-9-5 ........................................ ACulhane 6 56
(WJHaggas) *dwlt: sn trcking ldrs: hdwy 2f out: led over 1f out: pushed out* **3/1**1

**2** ¾ **Ile Facile (IRE)** 3-8-8 ................................................ NCallan 10 58
(NPLittmoden) *in tch on inner: hdwy 2f out: rdn over 1f out: kpt on ins last* **14/1**

0- **3** 1¼ **Dispol Veleta**180 [3089] 3-8-3 ........................................ JFanning 11 50
(TDBarron) *dwlt: towards rr: hdwy on outer 2f out: rdn over 1f out: kpt on ins last: nrst fin* **33/1**

/62- **4** shd **Shadowfax**9 [6244] 4-9-10 60...........................................(b1) MFenton 2 54
(MissGayKelleway) *chsd ldrs: effrt 2f out: sn rdn and nt qckn ent last* **7/2**3

303- **5** shd **Lake Eyre (IRE)**9 [6244] 5-9-5 45...................................... JEdmunds 3 49
(JBalding) *cl up: led 1/2-way: rdn along 2f out: drvn and hdd over 1f out: wknd ins last* **11/1**

04- **6** ½ **Quincannon (USA)**49 [6011] 3-8-8 ...................................... DMernagh 5 53
(TDBarron) *s.i.s: hdwy over 3f out: rdn to chse ldrs 2f out: drvn and one pce appr last* **10/3**2

002- **7** 1¾ **Brave Chief**9 [6246] 3-8-8 53.......................................... DeanMcKeown 13 47
(JAPickering) *midfield: hdwy to chse ldrs 3f out: rdn 2f out and grad wknd* **12/1**

3- **8** 1¼ **Starcross Venture**30 [6129] 3-8-1 ow3.............................. THamilton(5) 1 42
(RAFahey) *chsd leaders on inner: rdn along 2f out: sn wknd* **8/1**

**9** 2½ **Harbour Princess** 3-8-3 ................................................ ANicholls 14 31
(MFHarris) *a rr* **50/1**

000- **10** 2 **Sennen Cove**17 [6211] 5-9-10 35.......................................(t) KDalgleish 12 30
(RBastiman) *a rr* **50/1**

000- **11** 1¼ **Law Maker**7 [6253] 4-9-10 40............................................ RFrench 7 26
(MABuckley) *led to 1/2-way: rdn along 3f out and sn wknd* **66/1**

0- **12** 11 **Svenson**136 [4348] 3-8-5 ow2.......................................... PBradley(5) 9 —
(ABerry) *towards rr: wd st and sn bhd* **33/1**

660- **13** 4 **Bishop To Actress**76 [5687] 3-7-10 52.......................... SarahMitchell(7) 8 —
(MJPolglase) *chsd ldrs on outer: rdn along over 3f out: sn wknd* **50/1**

1m 16.54s (-0.26) **Going Correction** -0.15s/f (Stan)
**WFA** 3 from 4yo+ 16lb **13** Ran SP% **117.4**
Speed ratings: **95,94,92,92,92 91,89,87,84,81 79,65,59**CSF £43.40 TOTE £3.00: £1.50, £4.90, £13.80; EX 50.10.
**Owner** The Chosen Few Partnership **Bred** R T And Mrs Watson **Trained** Newmarket, Suffolk

**FOCUS**
A slow winning time for the class of contest, being more than a second slower than the earlier claimer, and the form is held down by the fifth.

**NOTEBOOK**
**Classic Vision**, a half-sister to useful sprinter Orientor, did not look sure to be suited by the drop in trip from a mile on her first start since June, but did it nicely in the end. She has probably just been a bit slow to mature and should progress. It is also worth remembering that another of her close relations, the stable's Royal Hunt Cup winner Yeast, did not win until he was four.

**Ile Facile(IRE)**, a half-brother to the useful juvenile Grand, posted a most pleasing debut performance. He managed to get himself hemmed in on the deeper ground on the rail turning in, but still managed to throw down a strong challenge in the straight. On this evidence he will have little trouble finding a similar race.
**Dispol Veleta** was another to catch the eye. This half-sister to Dispol Jazz and Dispol Foxtrot came home well down the outside and showed bags more than when beaten a long way on her debut in a seller back in July. When she manages to break on terms she will be hard to beat in this grade.
**Shadowfax**, sporting first-time blinkers, has become disappointing. His previous efforts over course and distance entitled him to a major chance, but he did not find enough to trouble the principals. He is one to tread carefully with.
**Lake Eyre(IRE)** finished closer to Shadowfax than she had last time, but is fully exposed and will probably have more chance of winning at regional meetings.
**Quincannon(USA)** again needed plenty of driving to get going and, from that slow start, was always playing catch up. He is now eligible for handicaps and will be interesting when he manages to start on terms.

## 439 LITTLEWOODSCASINO.COM (S) STKS 7f (F)
**3:15** (3:15) (G) 3-Y-O+ £2,597 (£742; £371) Stalls Low

Form RPR
64-2 1 **Lucayan Monarch**[2] [423] 6-9-7 55....(p) DeanMcKeown 1 67
(PABlockley) *trckd ldrs: swtchd rt and wd st: hdwy 2f out: sn rdn and led appr last: kpt on* 9/2[2]
360- 2 ½ **Xaloc Bay (IRE)**[41] [6063] 6-9-7 52.... JFanning 3 66
(BPJBaugh) *cl up on inner: led over 4f out: rdn along wl over 1f out: hdd appr last and n ot qckn* 8/1
240- 3 6 **Jan Brueghel (USA)**[28] [6144] 5-9-7 65.... DMernagh 7 51
(TDBarron) *prom: effrt and ev ch 2f out: sn rdn and wknd over 1f out* 6/5[1]
041- 4 2 **Headland (USA)**[17] [6217] 6-9-12 68....(b) ACulhane 5 51
(DWChapman) *cl up: rdn along over 2f out: drvn and wknd wl over 1f out* 5/1[3]
030- 5 4 **Bulawayo**[20] [6196] 7-9-7 55.... ANicholls 8 36
(AndrewReid) *chsd ldrs: rdn over 2f out and sn wknd* 7/1
500- 6 5 **Generous Share**[49] [6015] 4-9-2 47.... JQuinn 6 19
(MSSaunders) *a rr* 33/1
0/0- 7 2 ½ **Meticulous**[128] [4138] 6-9-0 30.... AndrewWebb(7) 4 17
(MCChapman) *led: hdd over 4f out and sn wknd* 100/1
0- 8 10 **Velvet Rhythm**[17] [6214] 4-8-9.... RKeogh(7) 2 —
(KRBurke) *a b ehind* 66/1
1m 29.53s (-1.27) **Going Correction** -0.15s/f (Stan) 8 Ran SP% **109.3**
Speed ratings: **101,100,93,91,86 81,78,66**CSF £35.62 TOTE £3.10: £1.10, £3.20, £1.10; EX 16.00.There was no bid for the winner.
**Owner** A C Kirkham **Bred** Southcourt Stud **Trained** Southwell, Notts

**FOCUS**
Arguably not as uncompetitive a seller as first impressions suggested, and rated, provisionally at least, as above average of its type.

**NOTEBOOK**
**Lucayan Monarch**, who stays further than this, came home well to land his first win since April. However, with the runner-up finding little off the bridle and the favourite dropping away, what he actually achieved is open to question.
**Xaloc Bay(IRE)** was still on the bridle two furlongs out, but found precious little when shaken up. This looks the right trip for him, but he has not won for an awful long time.
**Jan Brueghel(USA)**, dropped into selling company for the first time, was proven over course and distance, but dropped away very tamely. He has clearly got his problems after bleeding last time.
**Headland(USA)**, winner of a seller over six furlongs here last time, was fighting a losing battle from a fair way out.

## 440 BET DIRECT IN RUNNING SKY TEXT 371 H'CAP 1m 4f (F)
**3:45** (3:45) (F) (0-65,63) 4-Y-O+ £2,926 (£836; £418) Stalls Low

Form RPR
362- 1 **Broughton Knows**[14] [6233] 7-8-1 **35**....(b) LisaJones(3) 1 55
(WJMusson) *hld up: hdwy and rdn along 3f out: wd st: styd on to ld over 1f out: sn clr* 5/1[3]
140- 2 8 **Aveiro (IRE)**[10] [6240] 8-9-0 **45**....(b) KDalgleish 5 53
(BGPowell) *trckd ldr: led 1/2-way: clr over 2f out: rdn and hdd over 1f out: sn one pce* 12/1
6/4- 3 5 **Daunted (IRE)**[24] [6168] 8-9-8 **58**.... DNolan(5) 10 59
(PABlockley) *hld up in rr: hdwy 5f out: rdn and hung lft wl over 1f out: sn drvn and no imp* 4/1[1]
00-0 4 hd **King Priam (IRE)**[1] [430] 9-8-4 **35**....(b) DeanMcKeown 6 35
(MJPolglase) *hld up and bhd: swtchd outside and wd st: sn rdn and kpt on appr last: nrst fin* 14/1
450- 5 2 **East Cape**[9] [6247] 7-8-9 **40**.... KimTinkler 2 37
(DonEnricoIncisa) *trckd ldrs: hdwy on inner 3f out: sn rdn and wknd 2f out* 6/1
00-1 6 7 **Dash Of Magic**[1] [430] 6-8-10 **46** 6ex.... THamilton(5) 3 33
(JHetherton) *midfield: hdwy to chse ldrs 5f out: rdn along 3f out and sn wknd* 9/2[2]
225- 7 1 ½ **Exit To Heaven**[14] [6233] 4-9-4 **58**.... TEaves(5) 4 42
(MissGayKelleway) *led to 1/2-way: rdn along 4f out and wknd 3f out* 14/1
005- 8 2 **Surdoue**[9] [6247] 4-10-0 **63**....(p) PaulEddery 8 44
(PHowling) *trckd ldrs: smooth hdwy 5f out: rdn over 2f out and sn wknd* 9/2[2]
500- 9 23 **Calcar (IRE)**[21] [6190] 4-8-10 **45**.... JQuinn 7 —
(MrsSLamyman) *chsd ldrs: rdn along over 4f out and sn wknd* 50/1
26-0 10 ¾ **Over Rating**[3] [406] 4-8-11 **60**.... NCallan 9 6
(KARyan) *chsd ldrs on outer: rdn along over 4f out and sn wknd* 16/1
2m 37.8s (-4.30) **Going Correction** -0.15s/f (Stan) 10 Ran SP% **116.2**
**WFA** 4 from 6yo+ 4lb
Speed ratings: **108,102,99,99,97 93,92,90,75,75**CSF £63.10 CT £263.77 TOTE £6.40: £1.20, £4.30, £2.20; EX 56.00 Place 6 £217.78, Place 5 £20.19.
**Owner** Broughton Thermal Insulation **Bred** Broughton Bloodstock **Trained** Newmarket, Suffolk

**FOCUS**
A very decent winning time, but the leaders probably went off too fast in this poor handicap, and the winner looks opposable after re-assessment.

**NOTEBOOK**
**Broughton Knows**, wearing blinkers for the first time in a while, was suited by the fast gallop and came right away in the straight under another fine hold-up ride from Jones. The leaders probably went off too quickly, which clearly played to his strengths, and the Handicapper is sure to have something to say about this.
**Aveiro(IRE)** was going clear on the bridle turning in, but found less than anticipated when asked for his effort. He was soon left behind by the winner, but he still pulled clear of the third horse so it would be wrong to crab this performance too much.
**Daunted(IRE)**, having his second outing after a long lay-off, did not help his chances by hanging into the rail down the straight.
**King Priam(IRE)**, well beaten behind Dash Of Magic the previous day, reversed the form, but had the race run to suit and does not impress as a future winner.
**East Cape** got stuck on the unfavoured rail for much of the race and deserves more credit than his bare finishing position. He has shown promise on this surface in recent starts and looks more than capable of winning off this mark.
**Dash Of Magic**, a winner of a course and distance banded stakes the previous day, failed to repeat the peformance.
T/Jkpt: Not won. T/Plt: £141.10 to a £1 stake. Pool: £48,204.50. 249.35 winning tickets. T/Qpdt: £12.30 to a £1 stake. Pool: £4,373.70. 261.60 winning tickets. JR

# 421 WOLVERHAMPTON (A.W) (L-H)
## Monday, January 5

**OFFICIAL GOING: Standard**
(REGIONAL MEETING) There were numerous cases of horses who had been kept on the sidelines apparently waiting for the start of Regional Racing.
Wind: slt bhd Weather: overcast and damp

## 441 BET DIRECT ON SKY ACTIVE BANDED STKS 7f (F)
**1:30** (1:30) (H) 3-Y-O+ £1,470 (£420; £210) Stalls High

Form RPR
025- 1 **Indian Warrior**[138] [4288] 8-9-7 40....(b) IMongan 6 51
(JJay) *prom: led wl over 5f out: rdn wl over 1f out: rdn out* 7/4[1]
06-0 2 2 ½ **Vlasta Weiner**[2] [422] 4-9-4 40....(b) LFletcher(3) 7 45
(JMBradley) *a.p: chsd wnr over 5f out: rdn over 3f out: no imp fnl 2f* 14/1
000- 3 4 **Lemarate (USA)**[129] [4546] 7-9-7 40.... RBrisland 8 35
(DWChapman) *a.p: rdn over 3f out: wknd wl over 1f out* 16/1
006- 4 ½ **Blue Maeve**[27] [6151] 4-9-7 40.... GParkin 10 34
(JHetherton) *hld up: swtchd lft 5f out: sn outpcd and rdn: hdwy wl over 1f out: kpt on ins fnl f* 7/2[2]
006- 5 1 ¾ **Vermilion Creek**[14] [6229] 5-9-0 40.... StephanieHollinshead(7) 3 29
(RHollinshead) *outpcd and bhd: hdwy on outside over 1f out: n.d* 9/2[3]
00-0 6 1 ¾ **Pageant**[2] [425] 7-9-7 35.... CCatlin 4 25
(JMBradley) *led over 1f: rdn and lost pl over 4f out: n.d after* 12/1
660- 7 5 **Manikato (USA)**[104] [4507] 10-9-7 30.... VSlattery 2 12
(KGWingrove) *rdn over 5f out: sn bhd* 16/1
06-0 8 3 ½ **Present 'n Correct**[2] [423] 11-9-4 30....(b) FPFerris(3) 5 4
(JMBradley) *prom: rdn over 4f out: wknd over 2f out* 16/1
000- 9 9 **Bold Effort (FR)**[41] [6070] 12-9-7 30....(be) SWhitworth 11 —
(KOCunningham-Brown) *outpcd: a in rr* 20/1
1m 30.5s (0.30) **Going Correction** -0.075s/f (Stan) 9 Ran SP% **113.5**
Speed ratings: **95,92,87,87,85 83,77,73,63**CSF £28.47 TOTE £2.40: £1.20, £4.30, £6.70; EX 39.70.
**Owner** Mr & Mrs Jonathan Jay **Bred** Lady Halifax **Trained** Newmarket, Suffolk
■ Stewards Enquiry : F P Ferris one-day ban: allowed gelding to coast home in its own time (Jan 16)

**FOCUS**
A weak event, although the winner looks capable of better.

**NOTEBOOK**
**Indian Warrior** was having his first outing since last August and took full advantage of a golden opportunity.
**Vlasta Weiner** ran a lot better than he had done in a similar event over six here two days earlier.
**Lemarate(USA)**, who like the winner had not been seen since August, could not take advantage of the introduction of these low-grade events.
**Blue Maeve** was stepping up from six but needs even further on this evidence.

## 442 PRESS INTERACTIVE TO BET DIRECT CLAIMING STKS 1m 100y(F)
**2:00** (2:00) (H) 3-Y-O+ £1,316 (£376; £188) Stalls Low

Form RPR
000- 1 **Ally Makbul**[26] [6163] 4-9-9 51.... NPollard 9 65
(JRBest) *led early: a.p: led 2f out: hung rt and rdn over 1f out: drew clr ins fnl f: r.o wl* 5/1[2]
450- 2 7 **Lord Chamberlain**[80] [5622] 11-9-8 49 ow1....(b) CJDavies(7) 5 56
(JMBradley) *s.i.s: hdwy over 4f out: wnt 2nd and edgd lft ins fnl f: no ch w wnr* 12/1
000- 3 2 **Sudra**[17] [6218] 7-9-11 53....(p) DAllan(3) 12 51
(JO'Reilly) *prom: led over 4f out: rdn over 3f out: hdd 2f out: wknd ins fnl f* 7/2[1]
005- 4 shd **Nite-Owl Fizz**[37] [6099] 6-9-7 55.... JDO'Reilly(7) 6 51
(JO'Reilly) *w ldrs: rdn over 4f out: wknd over 2f out* 5/1[2]
553- 5 5 **Air Of Esteem**[17] [6218] 8-9-7 48.... DFentiman(7) 4 40
(IanEmmerson) *hld up: hdwy 5f out: sn rdn: wknd 2f out* 7/2[1]
004- 6 3 ½ **Red Delirium**[10] [6240] 8-10-0 45....(bt) IMongan 3 33
(RBrotherton) *s.i.s: nvr nr ldrs* 11/2[3]
0- 7 1 ¾ **Welsh Whisper**[65] [5879] 5-9-6.... LPKeniry(3) 8 24
(SABrookshaw) *sn led: hdd and rdn over 4f out: wknd over 2f out* 50/1
600/ 8 12 **Craigmor**[18] [4200] 4-10-0 52.... SRighton 1 4
(MFHarris) *chsd ldrs tl rdn and wknd over 4f out* 33/1
40-0 9 ½ **Queen Excalibur**[2] [415] 5-9-9 47....(p) PFitzsimons 2 —
(JMBradley) *bhd fnl 5f* 16/1
0- 10 26 **Royal Ovation**[27] [6155] 5-9-11 30.... J-PGuillambert(3) 10 —
(NPLittmoden) *chsd ldrs: rdn over 5f out: sn struggling: t.o* 25/1
1m 49.84s (-1.16) **Going Correction** -0.075s/f (Stan) 10 Ran SP% **115.5**
**WFA** 3 from 4yo+ 20lb
Speed ratings: **102,95,93,92,87 84,82,70,70,44**CSF £61.13 TOTE £6.70: £2.20, £5.00, £1.10; EX 82.70.The winner was the subject of a friendly claim by J R Best for £5,000.
**Owner** Malcolm Ward **Bred** Mill House Stud **Trained** Hucking, Kent

**FOCUS**
A very reasonable time for such a poor contest, but the form looks unreliable.

**NOTEBOOK**
**Ally Makbul**, dropped back to six when winning a similar event here in November, was suited by a return to a longer trip acccording to her trainer.
**Lord Chamberlain** came through to finish best of the rest on his first outing on sand since November 2001.
**Sudra** could not take advantage of a drop in grade.
**Nite-Owl Fizz**, a stable companion of the third, was the second string judged on riding arrangements.
**Queen Excalibur** *Official explanation: jockey said mare had a breathing problem*

## 443 LITTLEWOODS BET DIRECT BANDED STKS 5f (F)
**2:30** (2:30) (H) 3-Y-O+ £1,638 (£468; £234) Stalls Low

Form RPR
000- 1 **So Sober (IRE)**[5] [6265] 6-9-7 45.... RWinston 8 54
(DShaw) *a.p: rdn whn nt clr run 2f out: squeezed through to ld jst over 1f out: edgd rt ins fnl f: r.o* 13/2[3]

060- **2** ½ **Torrent**[83] 5561 9-9-7 45........(b) RBrisland 11 52
(DWChapman) *hld up: stdy hdwy over 2f out: rdn and kpt on towards fin* **8/1**

600- **3** 3 **Mangus (IRE)**[166] 3501 10-9-7 40........(be[1]) SWhitworth 6 42
(KOCunningham-Brown) *outpcd in rr: hdwy over 1f out: nrst fin* **25/1**

20-4 **4** nk **Enjoy The Buzz**[2] 421 5-9-7 45........ PFitzsimons 2 41
(JMBradley) *bhd tl hdwy over 1f out: nvr nrr* **9/1**

00-6 **5** ½ **Carols Choice**[2] 421 7-9-7 40........ IMongan 13 39
(ASadik) *a.p: rdn 2f out: ev ch over 1f out: wknd ins fnl f* **7/1**

400- **6** ½ **Cark**[9] 6243 6-9-4 45........(p) LFletcher(3) 3 37
(JBalding) *chsd ldrs: rdn and ev ch over 1f out: wknd ins fnl f* **11/2**[2]

000- **7** 3 **Milly's Lass**[119] 4769 6-9-4 40........(b[1]) FPFerris(3) 9 27
(JMBradley) *prom: rdn and ev ch 2f out: hmpd jst over 1f out: wknd ins f* **33/1**

644- **8** ½ **Diaphanous**[14] 6232 6-9-7 45........(b) SCarson 7 25
(EAWheeler) *led after 1f tl over 2f out: rdn whn bmpd jst over 1f out: wknd ins fnl frulong* **5/1**[1]

255- **9** ¾ **On The Level**[80] 5625 5-9-7 45........ PMcCabe 1 22
(MrsNMacauley) *chsd ldrs: rdn over 3f out: sn btn* **12/1**

500- **10** ¾ **Calendar Girl (IRE)**[34] 6116 4-9-7 45........ DSweeney 10 20
(PJMakin) *chsd ldrs: rdn over 3f out: wknd over 2f out* **10/1**

000- **11** hd **Star Applause**[24] 6170 4-9-4 45........ DAllan(3) 12 19
(JBalding) *chsd ldrs: rdn over 3f out: wknd 2f out* **14/1**

056- **12** ½ **Lone Piper**[38] 6080 9-9-7 45........ CCatlin 5 17
(JMBradley) *led 1f: led again over 2f out: hdd jst over 1f out: wknd qckly* **14/1**

000- **13** 2½ **Mesmerised**[76] 5690 4-9-7 45........ AnnStokell 4 9
(MissAStokell) *sn outpcd* **25/1**

62.87 secs (0.27) **Going Correction** -0.075s/f (Stan) **13** Ran SP% **119.7**
Speed ratings: **94,93,88,87,87 86,81,80,79,78 78,77,73**CSF £56.66 TOTE £7.90: £1.70, £2.00, £12.40; EX 50.40.
**Owner** Averham Park Racing **Bred** W And P Scott And N Ahamad **Trained** Averham, Notts

**FOCUS**
Modest form, but the first two look better than this grade.

**NOTEBOOK**
**So Sober(IRE)** did not get the best of passages but managed to wriggle through a narrow gap and then keep the runner-up at bay. This was his first win for two and a half years with his three previous successes having come over six furlongs.
**Torrent** is not easy to win with and his rider did not put him under pressure until as late as possible.
**Mangus(IRE)** was fitted with headgear for the first time for this return after a five-month break. He got going too late after being taken off his legs early on.
**Enjoy The Buzz** had also shaped as though he wants further when running over six here a couple of days ago.
**Carols Choice** got run out of it despite being back at her best trip.
**Cark** has yet to win on sand.

## 444 BETDIRECT.CO.UK MEDIAN AUCTION MAIDEN STKS 6f (F)
**3:00** (3:00) (H) 3-5-Y-O **£1,438** (£411; £205) **Stalls** Low

Form RPR

400- **1** **Strike Lucky**[7] 6253 4-9-7........ DSweeney 2 56
(PJMakin) *chsd ldr over 4f out: rdn to chal 2f out: edgd lft over 1f out: led ins fnl f: drvn out* **4/1**[3]

405- **2** nk **Dark Champion**[9] 6244 4-9-7 50........ IMongan 5 55
(JeddO'Keeffe) *sn led: rdn 2f out: hdd ins fnl f: r.o* **2/1**[2]

2- **3** 3 **Anisette**[37] 6097 3-8-0........ JTate 7 41
(JulianPoulton) *hld up in tch: rdn and outpcd over 2f out: kpt on fnl f* **11/10**[1]

500- **4** 5 **Somethingabouther**[9] 6244 4-9-2 40........ CCatlin 1 26
(PWHiatt) *led early: prom: rdn over 3f out: wknd 2f out* **12/1**

00-0 **5** 2 **Chantilly Gold (USA)**[2] 423 5-9-2 30........(p) PFitzsimons 3 20
(JMBradley) *hld up and plld hrd: rdn 3f out: short-lived effrt wl over 1f out* **33/1**

00-0 **6** 4 **Chanteuse**[3] 407 4-9-2 49........(b[1]) RBrisland 6 8
(DWChapman) *hld up and plld hrd: rdn 3f out: sn struggling* **25/1**

1m 15.78s (0.08) **Going Correction** -0.075s/f (Stan)
**WFA** 3 from 4yo+ 16lb **6** Ran SP% **115.4**
Speed ratings: **96,95,91,84,82 76**CSF £12.95 TOTE £6.00: £2.10, £1.10; EX 7.90.
**Owner** Mrs P J Makin **Bred** R G Percival And Miss S M Rhodes **Trained** Ogbourne Maisey, Wilts

**FOCUS**
A poor maiden, with the runner-up indicating the level of the form.

**NOTEBOOK**
**Strike Lucky**, dropping back in trip, was inclined to lean towards the runner-up in the home straight and took a while to get his head in front. He is likely to be kept sprinting.
**Dark Champion** did nothing wrong but has had plenty of chances and could not repel a rival who kept edging towards him.
**Anisette** was just touched off over course and distance at the end of November but now needs further by the look of it.

## 445 BET DIRECT IN RUNNING SKY TEXT 293 BANDED STKS 1m 1f 79y(F)
**3:30** (3:31) (H) 3-Y-O+ **£1,473** (£421; £210) **Stalls** Low

Form RPR

00-0 **1** **Malmand (USA)**[2] 427 5-9-9 40........(v) IMongan 6 41
(RBrotherton) *s.i.s: sn mid-div: rdn and plld out wl over 2f out: hdwy over 1f out: edgd lft wl ins fnl f: led nr fin* **5/1**

0/0- **2** hd **Good Timing**[10] 308 6-9-9 45........ GParkin 9 41
(JHetherton) *a.p: wnt 2nd over 5f out: rdn over 4f out: ev ch wl ins fnl f: r.o* **20/1**

400- **3** ½ **Nocatee (IRE)**[17] 6216 3-7-8 45........(v[1]) RoryMoore(7) 4 40
(PCHaslam) *dwlt: reminders over 6f out: rdn over 3f out: hdwy over 1f out: edgd lft wl ins fnl f: styd on* **9/2**[3]

650- **4** ¾ **Giust In Temp (IRE)**[21] 6190 5-9-6 30........ LFletcher(3) 5 39
(PWHiatt) *a.p: rdn 3f out: led jst over 1f out: hdd nr fin* **7/2**[2]

/00- **5** 2½ **Lucky Romance**[168] 3468 5-9-9 45........ RWinston 7 34
(BJMeehan) *led: rdn 3f out: hdd jst over 1f out: eased whn btn towards fin* **6/1**

260- **6** hd **Tarkwa**[45] 6043 5-9-9 45........ MHenry 8 33
(RMHCowell) *a.p: rdn over 4f out: one pce fnl 2f* **5/2**[1]

006- **7** 15 **Timbuktu**[14] 6230 3-8-1 45........ TWilliams 1 3
(CWThornton) *rdn over 6f out: a bhd* **20/1**

060- **8** 16 **Littleton Valar (IRE)**[28] 6148 4-9-1 40........(b[1]) DFentiman(7) 3 —
(JRWeymes) *t.k.h early: bhd fnl 5f: t.o* **20/1**

000- **9** 5 **Morning Sun**[21] 6190 4-9-8 40........(be[1]) CCatlin 2 —
(KOCunningham-Brown) *a bhd: t.o fnl 4f* **33/1**

2m 4.01s (1.11) **Going Correction** -0.075s/f (Stan)
**WFA** 3 from 4yo 22lb 4 from 5yo+ 1lb **9** Ran SP% **117.2**
Speed ratings: **92,91,91,90,88 88,74,60,56**CSF £100.21 TOTE £5.80: £1.90, £8.50, £2.20; EX 46.40.
**Owner** Carpe Diem Racing **Bred** Drumkenny Farm & David Romanik **Trained** Elmley Castle, Worcs
■ Stewards Enquiry : G Parkin one-day ban: used whip with excessive frequency (Jan 16)
I Mongan one-day ban: used whip with excessive frequency (Jan 16)

**FOCUS**
A moderate winning time, even for such a dire contest.

**NOTEBOOK**
**Malmand(USA)** was fitted with an Australian tongue-tie having swallowed his tongue when well beaten in a similar event here two days earlier.
**Good Timing**, fit from hurdling, stuck on well without ever being able to quite force his head in front.
**Nocatee(IRE)** raced lazily despite the first-time visior. He will stay further on this evidence.
**Giust In Temp(IRE)** seems to reserve his best efforts for this course and distance.
**Lucky Romance**, coming back after a six-month break, had never previously tackled beyond seven furlongs.
**Tarkwa** ran a lot better than she had done when attempting a mile and a half on her first visit here in November.
**Morning Sun** *Official explanation: jockey said filly had a breathing problem*

## 446 LITTLEWOODSPOKER.COM BANDED STKS 1m 4f (F)
**4:00** (4:00) (H) 4-Y-O+ **£1,442** (£412; £206) **Stalls** Low

Form RPR

043- **1** **Nakwa (IRE)**[14] 6234 6-9-1 45........ DAllan(3) 8 57
(EJAlston) *prom: lost pl 7f out: hdwy 5f out: led over 2f out: sn rdn clr: eased towards fin* **6/5**[1]

443- **2** 8 **Fairmorning (IRE)**[10] 6240 5-9-4 40........ ADaly 3 45
(JWUnett) *hld up: hdwy over 6f out: rdn over 3f out: tk 2nd ins fnl f: no ch w wnr* **6/1**[3]

030- **3** 1½ **Lampos (USA)**[96] 5298 4-9-0 45........ RWinston 5 43
(MissJACamacho) *hld up and bhd: rdn and hdwy over 4f out: styd on same pce fnl f* **8/1**

065- **4** ¾ **Berkeley Heights**[20] 6198 4-9-0 45........(b) CCatlin 4 42
(BSmart) *bhd tl hdwy over 8f out: wnt 2nd over 7f out: led over 3f out: rdn and hdd over 2f out: sn btn: lost 2nd ins fnl f* **25/1**

000- **5** ½ **Husky (POL)**[43] 4507 6-9-4 45........(p) IMongan 7 41
(RMHCowell) *led: rdn and hdd over 3f out: one pce fnl 2f* **8/1**

450- **6** 10 **Xixita**[101] 5200 4-9-0 45........ SWKelly 6 26
(DrJDScargill) *hld up and bhd: hdwy over 5f out: rdn over 4f out: sn wknd* **33/1**

00-6 **7** 2 **Leophin Dancer (USA)**[1] 430 6-9-4 40........ GBaker 1 23
(PWHiatt) *hld up and bhd: hdwy 5f out: rdn and wknd over 3f out* **8/1**

000- **8** hd **Little Richard (IRE)**[45] 6043 5-9-4 40........ VSlattery 10 23
(MWellings) *prom: rdn over 6f out: wknd over 4f out* **25/1**

050- **9** 8 **Felidae (USA)**[21] 6190 4-8-7 45........ MLawson(7) 2 11
(MBrittain) *prom: rdn over 6f out: wknd 4f out* **33/1**

654- **10** 2 **Cottam Grange**[30] 6139 4-9-0 45........ DaleGibson 9 8
(MWEasterby) *prom: lost pl 7f out: n.d after* **11/2**[2]

2m 39.7s (-1.80) **Going Correction** -0.075s/f (Stan)
**WFA** 4 from 5yo+ 4lb **10** Ran SP% **122.0**
Speed ratings: **103,97,96,96,95 89,87,87,82,81**CSF £8.90 TOTE £2.30: £1.30, £1.30, £3.10; EX 10.90 Place 6 £142.67, Place 5 £64.68.
**Owner** Alan Dick **Bred** Teviot Stud **Trained** Longton, Lancs

**FOCUS**
A good winning time for the grade of contest, and the winner is clearly better than this level.

**NOTEBOOK**
**Nakwa(IRE)** proved much too good for this moderate lot and was well in command in the final quarter-mile.
**Fairmorning(IRE)** had been well beaten in a seller over course and distance on Boxing Day.
**Lampos(USA)** confirmed the opinion that he has been blessed with stamina rather than speed.
**Berkeley Heights** may need more patient tactics if she is going to really get this trip.
**Husky(POL)**, twice a runner-up over hurdles, had never previously attempted beyond ten furlongs on the Flat.
T/Plt: £536.30 to a £1 stake. Pool: £41,218.00. 56.10 winning tickets. T/Qpdt: £59.30 to a £1 stake. Pool: £3,766.60. 47.00 winning tickets. KH

# 413 LINGFIELD (L-H)
### Tuesday, January 6

**OFFICIAL GOING: Standard**
Wind: mod bhd Weather: fine

## 447 BET DIRECT ON SKY ACTIVE MAIDEN STKS 1m (P)
**12:00** (12:03) (D) 3-Y-O **£4,114** (£1,266; £633; £316) **Stalls** High

Form RPR

**1** **Chasing The Dream (IRE)** 3-8-9........ MartinDwyer 3 70
(AMBalding) *racd in mifield: prog over 2f out: shkn up to ld 1f out: styd on wl* **7/1**[3]

3- **2** 1¾ **Jumeirah Scarer**[20] 6210 3-9-0........ CCatlin 5 71
(MRChannon) *pressed ldr: led on inner over 2f out: drvn and hdd 1f out: one pce* **7/4**[1]

**3** 1¼ **Webbswood Lad (IRE)** 3-9-0........ MFenton 6 68
(MrsStefLiddiard) *s.i.s: sn trckd ldrs: rdn and outpcd 2f out: styd on again fnl f* **25/1**

04- **4** 2 **Ashstanza**[68] 5836 3-9-0........ MHenry 9 64
(MAJarvis) *led to over 2f out: wknd fnl f* **8/1**

**5** 1½ **On The Waterfront** 3-9-0........ SDrowne 2 60
(JWHills) *chsd ldrs: cl up and rdn 2f out: wknd fnl f* **33/1**

**6** 1¾ **Sunset Dreamer (USA)** 3-8-9........ EAhern 1 51
(PMitchell) *s.v.s: sn in tch: effrt on inner over 2f out: no imp over 1f out: wknd fnl f* **14/1**

**7** hd **Our Little Rosie** 3-8-9........ DSweeney 8 51
(MBlanshard) *a in rr: rdn and struggling 3f out: n.d after* **33/1**

**8** 1½ **Champagne Shadow (IRE)**[91] 5445 3-9-0........ RBrisland 12 52
(GLMoore) *pressed ldrs tl wknd 2f out* **16/1**

**9** ½ **Devine Command** 3-9-0........ NDay 7 51
(RIngram) *chsd ldrs and lost pl wl over 2f out: no ch after* **33/1**

**10** nk **Silver Cache (USA)** 3-8-9........ SWKelly 11 45
(JNoseda) *s.s: in rr: prog on outer 1/2-way to press ldrs 3f out: sn wknd* **7/1**[3]



The Form Book, Raceform Ltd, Compton, RG20 6NL

11 *21* **Alfridini** 3-9-0 ........................................................(b[1]) DaneO'Neill 4 —
(DRCElsworth) *rel to r: a bhd: rdn and nt keen 1/2-way: t.o* **5/1**[2]
1m 42.37s (2.86) **Going Correction** +0.20s/f (Slow) **11** Ran SP% **114.4**
Speed ratings: **93,91,90,88,86 84,84,83,82,82 61**CSF £18.33 TOTE £13.00: £3.70, £1.30, £6.30; EX 27.00.
**Owner** Mrs L R Lovell **Bred** Mrs Eileen Moran And Daughters **Trained** Kingsclere, Hants

**FOCUS**
A fair-looking maiden full of inexperienced horses, but the time was only a fifth of a second quicker than the seller later in the day.

**NOTEBOOK**
**Chasing The Dream(IRE)**, a half-sister to the stayer Jack Dawson, picked up really nicely when asked, and should be able to win more races especially when tried over further.
**Jumeirah Scarer**, a drifter in the betting, was always close to the pace and, despite kicking for home off the bend, could not respond to the winner's challenge. He should be able to pick up a little race, although his future may lie in handicaps.
**Webbswood Lad(IRE)**, who looked as if he has some maturing to do, ran well on this racecourse debut and clearly possesses the ability to win a race or two.
**Ashstanza**did not settle then tended to hang under pressure. He now qualifies for a handicap mark and on breeding this should be his optimum trip.
**On The Waterfront**made quite an encouraging debut without looking likely to win, and should be better for the experience.
**Sunset Dreamer(USA)**was another who did not run badly, especially as she badly missed the break.
**Silver Cache(USA)** missed the break and then ran green. She can do better with this behind her.
**Alfridini**, a half-brother to the talented but ill-fated Alfini, was blinkered for this debut but stood still when the gates opened and had no chance afterwards. He looks to have his quirks and a watching brief is advised for the present.

## 448 BETDIRECT.CO.UK H'CAP 7f (P)
**12:30** (12:30) (E ) (0-70,70) 4-Y-O+ **£3,465** (£990; £495) **Stalls** Low

Form RPR
101- **1** **Smith N Allan Oils**[7] 6256 5-9-5 **61** 6ex.................................(p) EAhern 2 70
(MDods) *trckd ldrs gng wl: effrt over 2f out: chsd ldr over 1f out: drvn and styd on to ld last strides* **4/1**[1]
000- **2** *hd* **Kilmeena Lad**[27] 6164 8-9-11 **67**................................................ PDobbs 4 75
(JCFox) *prom and gng easily: trckd ldr 3f out: led 2f out: kicked 2l clr over 1f out: worn down last strides* **25/1**
423- **3** *hd* **Spinning Dove**[192] 2790 4-9-6 **62**.............................. MartinDwyer 6 70
(NAGraham) *wl in rr: gd prog fr 2f out: str run fnl f: gaining at fin* **25/1**
150- **4** *1 3/4* **Parker**[7] 6260 7-9-10 **66**............................................(b) MFenton 5 69
(BPalling) *prom: drvn and cl up over 2f out: nt qckn over 1f out: one pce after* **20/1**
023- **5** *3/4* **Temper Tantrum**[7] 6260 6-9-0 **63**..............................(p) RoryMoore[(7)] 13 64
(AndrewReid) *settled wl in rr: last over 2f out: gd prog on inner over 1f out: styd on one pce fnl f* **8/1**
404- **6** *3/4* **The Gaikwar (IRE)**[7] 6256 5-9-6 **67**...............................(b) MSavage[(5)] 9 66
(NEBerry) *dwlt: racd wl in rr: prog on outer over 1f out: kpt on same pce fnl f* **8/1**
20-2 **7** *3/4* **Sir Laughalot**[3] 415 4-9-11 **70**.......................................... LPKeniry[(3)] 12 68
(MissECLavelle) *trckd ldrs: rdn and unable qck 2f out: one pce after* **7/1**
002- **8** *1 1/4* **Espada (IRE)**[20] 6206 8-9-13 **69**.......................................... SWKelly 8 63
(JAOsborne) *led to 2f out: wknd fnl f* **11/1**
505- **9** *shd* **Four Jays (IRE)**[7] 6256 4-9-4 **60**...................................(p) JBramhill 10 54
(NPLittmoden) *racd wl in rr: no prog whn bmpd over 2f out: one pce after* **25/1**
600- **10** *1* **Icannshift (IRE)**[7] 6256 4-9-3 **66**............................... JCoffill-Brown[(7)] 3 58
(SDow) *racd towards rr: shuffled along and no prog wl over 1f out* **50/1**
500- **11** *1/2* **Frankskips**[27] 6157 5-9-10 **66**.................................................. AClark 11 56
(MissBSanders) *racd wd in rr: struggling fnl 2f* **40/1**
300- **12** *1* **Cayman Breeze**[7] 6260 4-9-9 **65**............................................... PDoe 16 53
(SDow) *prog on wd outside to press ldrs 3f out: sn rdn: wknd 2f out* **33/1**
613- **13** *1 1/4* **Phrenologist**[35] 6113 4-9-11 **67**............................................ DaneO'Neill 14 52
(JRFanshawe) *trckd ldrs: rdn 2f out: wknd over 1f out* **13/2**[3]
002- **14** *1 1/4* **Superchief**[7] 6256 9-9-6 **62**...............................................(bt) SDrowne 7 44
(MissBSanders) *t.k.h: trckd ldrs: rdn and nt qckn 2f out: wknd over 1f out: eased* **9/2**[2]
400- **15** *15* **Dunedin Rascal**[17] 6221 7-9-3 **66**...............................(b) LiamJones[(7)] 15 10
(EAWheeler) *chsd ldrs on outer to 3f out: sn wknd: t.o* **50/1**
000- **16** *dist* **Sharpinch**[49] 6019 6-9-9 **65**.................................................. IMongan 1 —
(PRChamings) *pressed ldr to 3f out: wknd rapidly: t.o whn virtually p.u over 1f out* **50/1**
1m 26.78s (0.78) **Going Correction** +0.20s/f (Slow) **16** Ran SP% **122.1**
Speed ratings: **103,102,102,100,99 98,97,96,96,95 94,93,92,90,73** —CSF £112.32 CT £1487.86 TOTE £4.40: £1.30, £5.30, £5.90, £4.50; EX 221.40.
**Owner** Smith & Allan Racing **Bred** A J Holder **Trained** Piercebridge, Co Durham
■ Stewards Enquiry : Rory Moore one-day ban: failed to keep straight from stalls (Jan 17)
L P Keniry one-day ban: failed to keep straight from stalls (Jan 17)

**FOCUS**
A competitive handicap run at a fair pace and producing a close finish. The form looks solid.

**NOTEBOOK**
**Smith N Allan Oils**gained his third course win in successive visits, but had to really battle. He never scores by far, but is well suited by this track, is clearly improving and the Handicapper may not have got his measure yet.
**Kilmeena Lad**, who has been lightly raced of late, is a dual winner here on Equitrack. He travelled well throughout and, if able to build on this effort, is on a good mark on his old form.
**Spinning Dove** was having her first outing for over six months and finished with a wet sail. This was only her eighth race and, if she can repeat this effort, she should have no difficulty losing her maiden tag.
**Parker** showed his first form on this surface without having the speed at the business end
**Temper Tantrum** had traffic problems coming from the back of the field and can be rated a little better than his finishing position.
**The Gaikwar(IRE)**, like the fifth, did not appear on the scene until late having not found the best of runs.
**Phrenologist**, stepping back up in trip, was disappointing on this occasion, and was beaten too soon for the trip to be to blame.
**Superchief**was hampered soon after the start and failed to get into it afterwards. *Official explanation: jockey said gelding disappointed following interference soon after the start*
**Sharpinch** *Official explanation: trainer said gelding had bled from the nose*

## 449 BET DIRECT ALL WEATHER ON 0800 32 93 93 MEDIAN AUCTION MAIDEN STKS 1m 4f (P)
**1:00** (1:01) (E ) 4-6-Y-O **£3,265** (£933; £466) **Stalls** Low

Form RPR
555- **1** **Two Of A Kind (IRE)**[38] 6096 4-9-0 56....................................... EAhern 6 47
(JWHills) *trckd ldrs: rdn to chal 3f out: drvn to ld 1f out: kpt on* **9/2**[2]
0- **2** *1 1/2* **Fleeting Moon**[272] 973 4-8-9 ........................................ MartinDwyer 5 39
(AMBalding) *racd in last pair: pushed along 5f out: prog to chse ldrs whn rn wd bnd 2f out: styd on fnl f to take 2nd last stride* **7/2**[1]
500/ **3** *hd* **Trouble Next Door (IRE)**[292] 4614 6-9-1 35............ J-PGuillambert[(3)] 4 44
(NPLittmoden) *t.k.h: sn trckd ldr: rdn to ld over 3f out: hdd 1f out: nt qckn fnl f* **11/1**
004- **4** *nk* **Morvern (IRE)**[139] 4297 4-9-0 51........................................(v) MFenton 9 44
(JGGiven) *racd in midfield: rdn and prog to chse ldng trio wl over 2f out: cl up 1f out: nt qckn fnl f* **10/1**
405- **5** *1/2* **Vanilla Moon**[86] 5507 4-8-9 48...........................................(v) SWKelly 3 38
(JRJenkins) *prom: rdn to chal 3f out: stl ev ch 1f out: nt qckn* **8/1**
060- **6** *24* **Aitana**[197] 2643 4-8-9 58.......................................................... SDrowne 2 2
(SCWilliams) *chsd ldrs: rdn 5f out: wknd over 3f out: t.o* **7/1**[3]
600- **7** *4* **Shaamit's All Over**[8] 6255 5-8-13 50.......................................(p) GBaker 1 —
(BAPearce) *s.s: hld up in last: lost tch over 3f out: t.o* **20/1**
030- **8** *5* **Amnesty**[76] 5712 5-9-4 60.......................................................... IMongan 7 —
(GLMoore) *in tch tl wknd u.p 4f out: t.o* **7/2**[1]
300- **9** *18* **Bowsprit**[39] 1481 4-8-11 60............................................ LPKeniry[(3)] 8 —
(BGPowell) *led to over 3f out: sn wknd: t.o* **20/1**
2m 37.29s (3.31) **Going Correction** +0.20s/f (Slow)
**WFA** 4 from 5yo+ 4lb **9** Ran SP% **113.2**
Speed ratings: **96,95,94,94,94 78,75,72,60**CSF £20.18 TOTE £6.10: £1.90, £1.30, £5.00; EX 25.60.
**Owner** J W Hills **Bred** Bryan Ryan **Trained** Upper Lambourn, Berks

**FOCUS**
A very modest maiden, run at a steady gallop. The form is held down by the third and looks distinctly ordinary.

**NOTEBOOK**
**Two Of A Kind(IRE)**, a market drifter, carries his head high and took a fair amount of persuasion to put it in front. He has only had seven races, so may have some improvement in him, but will need to find it to win again.
**Fleeting Moon**, another lightly-raced individual, looked short of pace but at least kept galloping and she may find a race, possibly against her own sex. A trip to one of the Fibresand tracks may suit her.
**Trouble Next Door(IRE)**, who is better known as a winning hurdler, ran well despite being very keen on this return from nearly ten months off. With this pipe-opener under his belt, he should be ready for a return to jumping.
**Morvern(IRE)** was unable to pick up after being settled off the pace then having to be switched. He may have needed this after a 20-week break and will be sharper next time.
**Vanilla Moon** is well exposed, and her proximity at the finish adds to the impression that the form is moderate.
**Amnesty**was up in trip on his first outing for new connections, but disappointed and will be scoped to see if he has picked up an infection. *Official explanation: trainer had no explanation for the poor form shown*

## 450 LITTLEWOODS BET DIRECT STKS SHOWCASE H'CAP 1m 2f (P)
**1:35** (1:36) (C ) (0-90,88) 3-Y-O **£8,092** (£2,490; £1,245; £622) **Stalls** Low

Form RPR
060- **1** **Forthright**[66] 5871 3-9-7 **88**.................................................. EAhern 3 84
(CEBrittain) *sn trckd ldr: led over 3f out: rdn over 1f out: styd on* **5/2**[1]
345- **2** *1 1/4* **Amwell Brave**[24] 6175 3-8-2 **69**...................................... JBramhill 7 63
(JRJenkins) *hld up in last pair: pushed along 3f out: c wd bnd 2f out: prog over 1f out: urged along and kpt on to take 2nd nr fin* **14/1**
213- **3** *1/2* **Maybe Someday**[67] 5845 3-8-6 **73**.................................. DSweeney 2 66
(IAWood) *cl up: chsd wnr wl over 2f out: drvn and hld fnl f: lost 2nd nr fin* **7/1**
511- **4** *2 1/2* **Nessen Dorma (IRE)**[10] 6242 3-8-9 **76**.................................. MFenton 6 65
(JGGiven) *trckd ldrs: rdn over 4f out: effrt u.p 3f out: one pce and btn fnl 2f* **7/2**[2]
135- **5** *3/4* **Myannabanana (IRE)**[10] 6242 3-7-6 **66**......................(v) DFentiman[(7)] 1 53
(JRWeymes) *racd in last pair: pushed along and no prog over 3f out: one pce fr over 1f out* **14/1**
201- **6** *6* **Bill Bennett (FR)**[15] 6230 3-8-7 **74**.................................. MartinDwyer 5 50
(JJay) *led to over 3f out: wknd 2f out* **6/1**[3]
2m 12.94s (5.55) **Going Correction** +0.20s/f (Slow) **6** Ran SP% **90.9**
Speed ratings: **85,84,83,81,81 76**CSF £22.44 CT £93.66 TOTE £2.50: £1.70, £3.80; EX 22.80
Trifecta £133.80 Pool £452.35, 2.40 w/u.
**Owner** Wyck Hall Stud **Bred** Wyck Hall Stud Ltd **Trained** Newmarket, Suffolk

**FOCUS**
A fair handicap, although somewhat weakened by withdrawals, and run at a slow pace, resulting in an extremely slow time.

**NOTEBOOK**
**Forthright**, the best looker in the line-up, was always in the right place in a slowly-run contest and picked up well to win with something in hand. He has been gelded since his last run, which has apparently settled him. However, he will find opportunities limited on this surface once re-assessed, and may have to step up in grade.
**Amwell Brave** continued his recent improvement with another good effort. He acts on both All-Weather surfaces and should have no difficulty winning races off his current mark.
**Maybe Someday**, a Fibresand selling winner, ran well on this return from a break, having been gelded, and will find easier opportunities than this, possibly over a shorter trip back on Fibresand.
**Nessen Dorma(IRE)**, raised 10lb for two Fibresand wins, looked somewhat one paced on his debut on this surface, although she may not have stayed the longer trip.
**Myannabanana(IRE)**, another Fibresand performer, was another who may not have got home.

## 451 BET DIRECT ON 0800 32 93 93 (S) STKS 1m (P)
**2:10** (2:10) (G ) 3-Y-O **£2,548** (£728; £364) **Stalls** High

Form RPR
405- **1** **Princess Ismene**[67] 5845 3-8-11 54..........................................(b) IMongan 5 52
(JJay) *hld up in last pair: prog over 3f out: rdn to ld 1f out: hld on wl* **7/2**[2]
330- **2** *3/4* **Redbank (IRE)**[8] 6251 3-8-11 65.......................................(b) DaneO'Neill 2 50
(NACallaghan) *dwlt: sn in tch: trckd ldng pair 3f out: rdn to chal 1f out: fnd nil and hld after* **1/1**[1]
000- **3** *4* **Zolushka (IRE)**[29] 6141 3-8-6 45............................................... EAhern 7 36
(BWDuke) *s.i.s: sn in tch: prog to trck ldrs 3f out: rdn and hanging lft over 1f out: one pce after* **20/1**
20-4 **4** *2 1/2* **Lady Predominant**[3] 416 3-7-13 52........................... RoryMoore[(7)] 3 30
(AndrewReid) *trckd ldr after 2f: led over 2f out: hdd & wknd 1f out* **7/2**[2]
653- **5** *1 1/4* **Defana**[185] 2986 3-8-11 54......................................................... SWKelly 6 32
(MDods) *hld up in last: rdn and outpcd 3f out: sn bhd: styd on fr over 1f out* **16/1**[3]
005- **6** *1 3/4* **Nothing Matters**[45] 6047 3-8-6 40............................................... PDoe 4 23
(PRChamings) *led to over 2f out: wknd over 1f out* **20/1**
500- **7** *16* **Fox Hollow (IRE)**[38] 6090 3-8-11 35........................................ CCatlin 8 —
(MJHaynes) *chsd ldrs tl wknd u.p over 3f out: t.o* **33/1**

500- **8** *11* **Gentleman George**[21] 6197 3-8-8 45 RMiles(3) 1 —
(DKIvory) *t.k.h: chsd ldr for 2f: wknd over 3f out: t.o* **25/1**

1m 42.57s (3.06) **Going Correction** +0.20s/f (Slow) 8 Ran SP% **116.6**
Speed ratings: **92,91,87,84,83 81,65,54**CSF £7.20 TOTE £4.60: £1.20, £1.10, £5.40; EX 12.30.The winner was bought in for 3,200gns. No5 Redbank was bought by Simon Dow for £6,000
**Owner** Aftab Ali **Bred** Bearstone Stud **Trained** Newmarket, Suffolk

**FOCUS**
A poor seller, but the first two came away in the closing stages.

**NOTEBOOK**
**Princess Ismene**, the only previous winner in the field, was backed against the favourite and produced the better turn of foot in the closing stages. A firm-ground winner on turf, she took well to this surface and, having been retained by connections, should find further opportunities here for her in-form trainer.
**Redbank(IRE)**, dropping to this grade for the first time, had 11lb in hand based on official ratings, but was an uneasy favourite and could not match the winner's pace. New connections will have no easy task to find the key to him.
**Zolushka(IRE)**, another dropping in grade, appeared to handle the track better than the Fibresand she encountered last time, and kept on as if a slightly longer trip may be in her favour.
**Lady Predominant**, another backed against the favourite, was dropping back from ten furlongs but folded tamely after looking sure to figure on the turn in, and may need to return to sprint trips.

## 452 BET DIRECT IN RUNNING SKY TEXT 293 CLASSIFIED CLAIMING STKS 6f (P)
**2:45** (2:47) (F) 3-Y-O **£2,884** (£824; £412) **Stalls** Low

Form RPR
060- **1** **Desert Light (IRE)**[6] 6269 3-7-13 35 (v) JFMcDonald(5) 4 52
(DShaw) *prom: trckd ldr over 3f out: led wl over 2f out: kicked clr wl over 1f out: 5l ahd fnl f: unchal* **50/1**
035- **2** *1 ½* **Stamford Blue**[11] 6237 3-8-4 50 (b) MartinDwyer 1 47
(JSMoore) *sn pushed along in last: prog over 2f out: rdn to chse wnr jst over 1f out: r.o but nvr able to chal* **4/1**[2]
025- **3** *5* **Stanhope Forbes (IRE)**[7] 6258 3-8-12 55 EAhern 9 40
(NPLittmoden) *chsd ldrs: rdn after 2f: kpt on one pce fnl 2f: no ch* **6/4**[1]
54-3 **4** *3 ½* **Pardon Moi**[4] 408 3-8-0 49 HayleyTurner(5) 3 23
(MrsCADunnett) *sn chsd ldrs: rdn 3f out: effrt to dispute 2nd over 1f out: sn wknd* **11/2**[3]
050- **5** *¾* **Lady Mo**[54] 5990 3-7-10 50 RoryMoore(7) 10 18
(AndrewReid) *led after 1f to wl over 2f out: wknd over 1f out* **11/1**
003- **6** *6* **He's A Rocket (IRE)**[22] 6194 3-8-3 40 (v) NChalmers(5) 5 5
(MrsCADunnett) *in tch tl wknd over 2f out* **25/1**
655- **7** *½* **Red Rocky**[8] 6248 3-8-3 52 PDoe 7 —
(JGallagher) *hld up and sn swtchd to outer: nvr on terms: no ch whn sltly hmpd wl over 1f out: wknd* **11/2**[3]
006- **8** *2 ½* **Aragon Dancer**[118] 4821 3-8-10 40 RBrisland 2 —
(TMJones) *reluctant to enter stalls: led for 1f: wknd 3f out* **25/1**
005- **9** *½* **Costa Del Sol (IRE)**[17] 6223 3-8-4 45 JTate 8 —
(JJBridger) *in rr and rdn over 3f out: sn bhd* **12/1**

1m 13.12s (0.20) **Going Correction** +0.20s/f (Slow) 9 Ran SP% **116.4**
Speed ratings: **106,104,97,92,91 83,83,79,79**CSF £239.83 TOTE £126.20: £9.00, £1.50, £1.10; EX 720.50.The winner was subject to a friendly claim
**Owner** Swann Racing Ltd **Bred** Anthony M Cahill **Trained** Averham, Notts

**FOCUS**
A moderate claimer producing a shock winner. The time was incredibly quick for a race of this type, being fractionally faster than the following all-aged handicap.

**NOTEBOOK**
**Desert Light(IRE)**, an exposed Fibresand performer, was a totally different proposition on this surface, opening up a clear lead turning in and never being in danger from that point. There appeared no fluke about it and, as he is sure to go up considerably from his current mark of 35, he is likely to be under a penalty out before he is re-assessed. *Official explanation: trainer's representative had no explanation for the improved form shown*
**Stamford Blue**, 8lb better off having been beaten a length and a half by today's favourite over course and distance last month, reversed the placings emphatically but merely followed the winner home.
**Stanhope Forbes(IRE)** was well backed despite having something to find with one or two of his rivals, but turned in a below-par effort.
**Pardon Moi**, dropping in trip, lacks a turn of foot and looks more at home over seven.
**Red Rocky**, an on-course drifter, ran no sort of race.

## 453 LITTLEWOODSPOKER.COM H'CAP 6f (P)
**3:20** (3:21) (G ) (0-55,54) 3-Y-O+ **£2,961** (£846; £423) **Stalls** Low

Form RPR
062- **1** **Prince Aaron (IRE)**[20] 6209 4-9-13 54 GCarter 10 68+
(CNAllen) *chsd ldrs: lost pl 1/2-way: in rr whn hmpd over 2f out: gd prog wl over 1f out: drvn and r.o to ld last 50y: jst hld on* **6/1**[2]
603- **2** *nk* **Tayif**[7] 6261 8-9-11 52 (t) SCarson 12 65+
(AndrewReid) *dwlt: hld up in last: stl in last trio over 2f out: gd prog over 1f out: r.o fnl f: jst failed* **7/1**
004- **3** *¾* **Savile's Delight (IRE)**[20] 6204 5-9-13 54 (p) IMongan 7 65
(RBrotherton) *prom: drvn over 2f out: led over 1f out: hdd u.p last 50y* **6/1**[2]
640- **4** *hd* **Its Ecco Boy**[7] 6256 6-9-12 53 RWinston 8 63
(PHowling) *settled in rr: prog over 3f out to chse ldrs: drvn to chal 1f out and ev ch: fnd nil and btn last 100y* **7/2**[1]
310- **5** *2* **Zinging**[7] 6260 5-9-11 52 GBaker 4 56
(JJBridger) *hld up in rr: prog on outer over 2f out: nt qckn over 1f out: one pce after* **13/2**[3]
003- **6** *½* **Night Cap (IRE)**[35] 6116 5-9-7 51 J-PGuillambert(3) 13 54
(TDMccarthy) *sn chsd ldr: led over 2f out: rdn and hdd over 1f out: wknd fnl f* **10/1**
000- **7** *1* **Loch Laird**[178] 3216 9-9-7 51 LPKeniry(3) 1 51
(MMadgwick) *in rr whn n.m.r after 1f: prog on inner 2f out: chsd ldrs over 1f out: fdd fnl f* **20/1**
300- **8** *1* **King's Ballet (USA)**[25] 6166 6-9-11 52 (p) SDrowne 6 49
(PRChamings) *trckd ldrs: rdn and nt qckn wl over 1f out: wknd ins fnl f* **12/1**
300- **9** *¾* **Patandon Girl (IRE)**[67] 5849 4-9-7 51 SHitchcott(3) 2 45
(ABailey) *chsd ldrs: rdn bef 1/2-way: wknd jst over 1f out* **20/1**
003- **10** *hd* **Flying Tackle**[103] 5178 6-9-10 51 (p) SWKelly 9 45
(MDods) *dwlt: wl in rr: rdn and no prog over 2f out: modest late hdwy* **14/1**
000- **11** *3 ½* **Safranine (IRE)**[25] 6170 7-9-11 52 (p) AnnStokell 5 35
(MissAStokell) *chsd ldrs: rdn over 2f out: wknd over 1f out* **16/1**
000- **12** *3* **Toppling**[50] 6010 6-9-11 52 DaneO'Neill 11 26
(JMBradley) *led to over 2f out: cl up over 1f out: wknd rapidly* **25/1**
400- **13** *3* **Ivory Venture**[7] 6261 4-9-10 54 RMiles(3) 3 19
(DKIvory) *a in rr: wknd over 2f out* **40/1**
006- **14** *1 ¾* **Waraqa (USA)**[193] 2743 5-9-11 52 CCatlin 14 12
(TMJones) *chsd ldrs tl wknd rapidly over 2f out* **20/1**

1m 13.3s (0.38) **Going Correction** +0.20s/f (Slow) 14 Ran SP% **126.5**
Speed ratings: **105,104,103,103,100 100,98,97,96,96 91,87,83,81**CSF £46.44 CT £273.81 TOTE £4.30: £2.80, £2.00, £2.50; EX 61.40.
**Owner** Black Star Racing **Bred** Peter Charles And J R Bamforth **Trained** Newmarket, Suffolk

**FOCUS**
An ordinary handicap, run at a decent pace and a good time despite being slower than the preceding claimer.

**NOTEBOOK**
**Prince Aaron(IRE)**, narrowly beaten in a course and distance maiden last time, travelled well, but he still had a fair amount to do turning in after meeting with trouble. Coming with a strong run to lead, he is obviously in fine heart and the narrow margin of victory means he will not go up too much. His trainer reported he had only just strengthened into his frame, and he should have a fair chance of following up back here next week.
**Tayif**ran a similar race to last time, but on this occasion he came with his run on the outside and nearly got there. He is on a very handy mark these days and, in good heart at present, is well capable of taking advantage.
**Savile's Delight(IRE)**, dropped in trip, struck the front before the furlong pole but edged left under pressure and was collared inside the last. He has taken well to this surface and, nicely treated compared with his turf mark, has a race in him.
**Its Ecco Boy**, whose wins have come over a straight six furlongs, has been running over seven of late. He was well placed in the stretch but could not get by, and it looks as if he needs the extra furlong.
**Zinging** has won twice here over an extra furlong and he was another who found this too sharp.
**Night Cap(IRE)**, who ran well in the face of a stiff task last time, led on the home turn but was on the retreat inside the last. Nevertheless, he ran close to his current handicap mark.

## 454 PRESS INTERACTIVE TO BET DIRECT H'CAP 5f (P)
**3:55** (3:55) (E ) (0-75,73) 3-Y-O+ **£3,360** (£960; £480) **Stalls** High

Form RPR
000- **1** **The Fisio**[31] 6132 4-9-7 66 MartinDwyer 5 78
(AMBalding) *pressed ldr: rdn to ld narrowly 2f out: drvn and styd on wl fnl f* **8/1**
021- **2** *1* **Madrasee**[75] 5718 6-9-5 67 RMiles(3) 1 75
(LMontagueHall) *chsd ldng pair: rdn 2f out: chsd wnr 1f out: kpt on but a hld* **5/2**[1]
00-0 **3** *nk* **Currency**[3] 417 7-10-0 73 SDrowne 10 80
(JMBradley) *in rr and pushed along 3f out: hrd drvn and r.o over 1f out: tk 3rd ins fnl f: unable to chal* **25/1**
40-0 **4** *1 ¼* **Juwwi**[3] 417 10-9-7 73 ow1 CJDavies(7) 8 75
(JMBradley) *s.s: racd in last tl prog on inner wl over 1f out: r.o ins fnl f: nrst fin* **16/1**
006- **5** *½* **Goodwood Prince**[17] 6221 4-9-5 64 PDoe 2 64
(SDow) *hld up in rr: sme prog over 1f out: one pce and nvr able to chal* **9/1**
306- **6** *hd* **Our Fred**[104] 5156 7-9-11 70 (b) JPaulielo 4 69
(TGMills) *led to 2f out: wknd ins fnl f* **20/1**
444- **7** *shd* **Byo (IRE)**[7] 6261 6-9-6 65 RWinston 6 64
(MQuinn) *chsd ldrs: hrd rdn and nt qckn wl over 1f out: one pce after* **4/1**[2]
001- **8** *¾* **Panjandrum**[17] 6221 6-9-4 68 MSavage(5) 3 64
(NEBerry) *s.i.s: drvn up to chse ldrs 3f out: no imp over 1f out: fdd* **11/2**[3]
000- **9** *nk* **Taboor (IRE)**[167] 3509 6-9-10 69 (b) IMongan 9 64
(JWPayne) *racd on outer: in tch: nt qckn 2f out: one pce after* **14/1**
103- **10** *2* **Gone'N'Dunnett (IRE)**[31] 6138 5-9-10 69 (v) DaneO'Neill 7 56
(MrsCADunnett) *dropped to rr and rdn 3f out: sn struggling* **8/1**

59.92 secs (0.14) **Going Correction** +0.20s/f (Slow) 10 Ran SP% **117.3**
Speed ratings: **106,104,103,101,101 100,100,99,98,95**CSF £28.48 CT £502.00 TOTE £8.50: £1.90, £1.50, £3.50; EX 24.80 Place 6 £25.95, Place 5 £14.97.
**Owner** D H Caslon **Bred** E Duggan And D Churchman **Trained** Kingsclere, Hants

**FOCUS**
A tight little sprint, with just 9lb between top and bottom weights, and run in a good time. The winner was well in on two-year-old form.

**NOTEBOOK**
**The Fisio**, who had dropped 24lb in the last 11 months, had taken time to recover from a knee operation. He was the subject of late market support that always looked likely to be justified. He was always holding the favourite, looks on a decent mark, and is capable of following up. *Official explanation: trainer said, regarding the improved form shown, gelding missed the break on its previous run, when ridden by an inexperienced rider over a longer trip*
**Madrasee**, who appreciates a really sharp track, did nothing wrong in defeat on this return from a break. She is on a good mark compared with her turf rating, and can gain compensation before long.
**Currency**improved on his efforts here at the weekend, finishing late and fast, and may benefit from another furlong around this track.
**Juwwi**ran his usual race finishing strongly just behind his stable companion. He has never won on this surface and may be better returning to Fibresand.
**Goodwood Prince** was another supported in the market, ran quite well and is dropping to a fair mark.
**Our Fred**showed plenty of speed on his return from a 15-week break. He should come on for the run and is not badly treated at present.
**Panjandrum** *Official explanation: trainer said gelding had lost both front shoes*
T/Plt: £68.00 to a £1 stake. Pool: £24,714.00. 265.10 winning tickets. T/Qpdt: £9.50 to a £1 stake. Pool: £2,478.10. 192.50 winning tickets. JN

# 435 SOUTHWELL (L-H)
### Tuesday, January 6

**OFFICIAL GOING: Standard**
The track again rode deeper on the inside rail, and the centre of the track was the place to be.

## 455 BET DIRECT ON ATTHERACES INTERACTIVE AMATEUR RIDERS' H'CAP (DIV I) 1m 3f (F)
**12:20** (12:20) (G ) (0-65,76) 4-Y-O+ **£2,891** (£826; £413) **Stalls** Low

Form RPR
/4-3 **1** **Daunted (IRE)**[1] 440 8-10-7 58 StaceyRenwick(7) 4 70
(PABlockley) *a.p: led over 1f out: r.o* **7/2**[2]
005- **2** *3* **Our Glenard**[43] 6055 5-9-10 45 MissALTurner(5) 3 53
(SLKeightley) *s.i.s: hld up: hdwy over 4f out: outpcd over 2f out: r.o ins fnl f* **11/2**[3]
000- **3** *hd* **Interstice**[10] 6247 7-10-7 51 MissCHannaford 2 58
(AGNewcombe) *hld up in tch: rdn and ev ch over 1f out: styd on same pce* **3/1**[1]



The Form Book, Raceform Ltd, Compton, RG20 6NL

300- **4** *hd* **Lazzaz**[8] 6249 6-10-13 62........ MrsMarieKing(5) 1 69
(PWHiatt) *sn led: rdn and hdd over 1f out: styd on same pce* **11/2**[3]
402- **5** *1 1/2* **Shatin Special**[11] 6240 4-9-0 40........(p) MrTThomas(7) 10 45
(GCHChung) *chsd ldrs: rdn and ev ch over 1f out: styd on same pce* **6/1**
600- **6** *8* **Noble Cyrano**[150] 3987 9-8-12 35........ MissJWaring(7) 7 28
(JeddO'Keeffe) *s.s: hld up: effrt over 2f out: sn wknd* **12/1**
605- **7** *8* **Royal Axminster**[53] 5999 9-9-5 40........ MissAWallace(5) 5 21
(MrsPNDutfield) *hdwy over 8f out: wknd over 2f out* **12/1**
50-0 **8** *4* **Western Command (GER)**[2] 434 8-9-3 33 oh3........ MrsMMorris 6 8
(MrsNMacauley) *s.i.s: hdwy over 4f out: wknd over 3f out* **20/1**
600- **9** *3/4* **Goodenough Star**[40] 5497 4-9-2 40........ MrWayneLewis(5) 9 14
(APJones) *chsd ldrs over 7f* **50/1**
000- **10** *24* **Christmas Truce (IRE)**[44] 5344 5-11-11 76 ow11(p)
MrMichaelMurphy(7) 8 14
(IanWilliams) *bhd fnl 8f* **25/1**

2m 31.1s (2.20) **Going Correction** +0.05s/f (Slow) **10** Ran SP% **118.2**
**WFA** 4 from 5yo+ 3lb
Speed ratings: **94,91,91,91,90 84,78,75,75,57**CSF £23.01 CT £64.78 TOTE £4.70: £1.50, £1.40, £1.70; EX 61.10.
**Owner** Mrs Joanna Hughes **Bred** Mrs G Doyle **Trained** Southwell, Notts
■ Stacey Renwick's first winner.

**FOCUS**
They went no great gallop in this weakly contested amateurs' race.

**NOTEBOOK**
**Daunted(IRE)**, brought out quickly, stuck to the inside once in line for home and needed only to be nudged out for a fairly comfortable victory. This is weak form.
**Our Glenard**, back over a more suitable trip, took time to pick up and was only fifth passing the furlong pole, but he ran on well inside the last.
**Interstice**, who has dropped to a mark 7lb lower than he last won off, had no real excuse.
**Lazzaz**reserves his best for Wolverhampton and runs here infrequently.
**Shatin Special**ran well up to a point but remains a maiden.

## 456 BET DIRECT ON ATTHERACES INTERACTIVE AMATEUR RIDERS' H'CAP (DIV II) 1m 3f (F)
**12:50** (12:51) (G) (0-65,65) 4-Y-0+ **£2,884** (£824; £412) **Stalls** Low

Form RPR
503- **1** **Squirtle Turtle**[86] 5507 4-11-0 65........(b) MrOCole(7) 7 77
(PFICole) *sn led: rdn and hdd over 1f out: rallied to ld wl ins fnl f* **11/1**
31-1 **2** *nk* **Delta Force**[2] 432 5-10-10 56 5ex........ MrMScales(5) 3 68
(PABlockley) *chsd wnr: rdn over 3f out: ev ch fr over 1f out: sn hung lft: kpt on* **7/4**[1]
425- **3** *hd* **Kentucky Bullet (USA)**[15] 6234 8-10-7 48........ MissCHannaford 4 59
(AGNewcombe) *chsd ldrs: rdn to ld over 1f out: hdd wl ins fnl f* **4/1**[3]
041- **4** *1 1/2* **Spanish Star**[22] 6190 7-10-2 46........ MrsSMoore(3) 1 55
(MrsNMacauley) *s.i.s: hld up: hdwy over 5f out: outpcd 4f out: r.o ins fnl f* **7/2**[2]
000- **5** *1* **Paso Doble**[49] 6025 6-11-0 62........ MrJMillman(7) 8 70
(BRMillman) *chsd ldrs: rdn over 4f out: styd on same pce fnl f* **14/1**
4U0- **6** *3 1/2* **Night Mail**[34] 5437 4-9-3 40........ MrCCollins(7) 9 42
(MWEasterby) *s.s: hld up: styd on u.p appr fnl f: nvr trbld ldrs* **16/1**
000- **7** *6* **Briery Mec**[169] 3474 9-9-5 37 ow2........(p) MissALHutchinson(5) 2 30
(HJCollingridge) *chsd ldrs 7f* **20/1**
000- **8** *9* **Abracadabjar**[96] 5329 6-9-12 46 ow16........ MissGDGracey-Davison(7) 6 26
(MissZCDavison) *prom to 1/2-way* **50/1**
450- **9** *15* **Silver Crystal (IRE)**[28] 6153 4-10-3 47........(v[1]) MrsMMorris 5 4
(MrsNMacauley) *hld up: wknd over 4f out* **16/1**

2m 32.54s (3.64) **Going Correction** +0.05s/f (Slow) **9** Ran SP% **112.1**
**WFA** 4 from 5yo+ 3lb
Speed ratings: **88,87,87,86,85 83,78,72,61**CSF £29.47 CT £91.80 TOTE £11.10: £2.40, £1.10, £1.70; EX 27.80.
**Owner** Mrs P F I Cole **Bred** Sir Eric Parker **Trained** Whatcombe, Oxon
■ The first winner for Oliver Cole, son of winning trainer Paul Cole.

**FOCUS**
A slow-motion finish to this weak affair, run in a time 1.44sec slower than the first divison.

**NOTEBOOK**
**Squirtle Turtle**, having his first run on sand, was two lengths to the good turning for home, but his stride began to shorten and he was narrowly headed. With the rail proving a big help, he plugged on to stick his head back in front close home.
**Delta Force**, under a penalty for his banded stakes win two days earlier, had every chance but could not force his head in front. He found this trip on the short side.
**Kentucky Bullet(USA)**responded to pressure to edge ahead down the centre of the track, but he did not do much in front and could not hold on.
**Spanish Star**, from a 5lb higher mark, could never get to the leaders.
**Paso Doble**, who raced a little wide of his rivals, did not really see out the trip.
**Night Mail**, who has been hurdling, made a little late progress having been slow to stride.

## 457 BET DIRECT PRESS RED TO BET FILLIES' STKS (H'CAP) 1m (F)
**1:25** (1:26) (E) (0-75,70) 4-Y-0+ **£3,367** (£1,036; £518; £259) **Stalls** Low

Form RPR
431- **1** **Najaaba (USA)**[28] 6153 4-8-7 56........ BReilly(5) 6 75
(MissJFeilden) *hld up: hdwy over 2f out: led over 1f out: sn clr* **2/1**[2]
502- **2** *6* **Ellen Mooney**[29] 6146 5-9-12 70........(p) RFfrench 7 77
(BSmart) *chsd ldrs: rdn over 2f out: ev ch over 1f out: sn outpcd* **15/8**[1]
651- **3** *nk* **Estimation**[10] 6245 4-9-11 69........ NCallan 1 75
(RMHCowell) *hld up: hdwy over 3f out: rdn and ev ch over 1f out: styd on same pce* **5/1**[3]
424- **4** *8* **Inchcoonan**[276] 937 6-9-4 62........ DarrenWilliams 3 52
(KRBurke) *trckd ldrs tl wknd 2f out* **10/1**
000- **5** *2* **Pooka's Daughter (IRE)**[38] 6100 4-8-2 49........ LisaJones(3) 2 35
(JMBradley) *led after 1f: hdd & wknd over 1f out* **33/1**
**6** *1* **Soft Mist (IRE)**[114] 4917 4-8-12 61........ TEaves(5) 4 45
(JJQuinn) *chsd ldrs: rdn 1/2-way: wknd over 3f out* **20/1**
631- **7** *5* **Nuzzle**[22] 6193 4-9-0 58........(v) ACulhane 5 32
(MQuinn) *led 1f: remained handy tl wknd over 2f out* **10/1**

1m 43.83s (-0.77) **Going Correction** +0.05s/f (Slow) **7** Ran SP% **110.7**
Speed ratings: **105,99,98,90,88 87,82**CSF £5.70 TOTE £3.30: £1.60, £1.90; EX 6.60.
**Owner** A K Sparks **Bred** Darley Stud Management, L L C **Trained** Exning, Suffolk

**FOCUS**
This was run at a fair pace, and the winner is improving fast.

**NOTEBOOK**
**Najaaba(USA)**, a progressive filly, was tucked away at the back of the field. Switched to the outside once in line for home, she burst clear for an impressive victory. The Handicapper will take a dim view and connections will be keen to turn her out under a penalty.
**Ellen Mooney**, runner-up in a race that has worked out well last time, stuck on to win the separate tussle for second place, confirming the form with Estimation in the progress.
**Estimation**was left with a rear view of the winner up the home straight and lost out in the battle for second.
**Inchcoonan**, a quirky mare who gave trouble at the stalls, went without headgear on this first run since April.
**Pooka's Daughter(IRE)**has been dropped 18lb in the last year. She was given an uncontested lead and eventually faded with over a furlong to run.

## 458 LITTLEWOODS BET DIRECT H'CAP 6f (F)
**2:00** (2:01) (C) (0-90,79) 3-Y-0 **£8,027** (£2,470; £1,235; £617) **Stalls** Low

Form RPR
511- **1** **Blofeld**[18] 6213 3-8-8 69........ LisaJones(3) 6 75
(WJarvis) *trckd ldrs: styd on to ld wl ins fnl f* **13/8**[1]
152- **2** *1/2* **Muy Bien**[29] 6141 3-8-12 75........(v) BReilly(5) 2 79
(JRJenkins) *chsd ldrs: led 2f out: sn rdn and hung lft: hdd wl ins fnl f* **7/2**[2]
504- **3** *5* **Foxies Future (IRE)**[18] 6213 3-8-2 60........ JQuinn 1 49
(JRWeymes) *sed lsolwy: sn pushed along in rr: hdwy over 2f out: styd on same pce appr fnl f* **18/1**
215- **4** *3* **Bridgewater Boys**[25] 6165 3-8-11 69........(b) NCallan 4 49
(KARyan) *led 4f: sn wknd* **14/1**
515- **5** *4* **Pompey Blue**[41] 6077 3-8-13 71........ PJScallan 3 39
(PJMcbride) *w ldr 4f: sn wknd* **5/1**[3]
231- **6** *17* **Scottish Exile (IRE)**[22] 6191 3-8-12 70........(v) DarrenWilliams 7 —
(KRBurke) *chsd ldrs over 3f* **7/1**

1m 16.35s (-0.45) **Going Correction** +0.05s/f (Slow) **6** Ran SP% **101.4**
Speed ratings: **105,104,97,93,88 65**CSF £5.83 TOTE £2.00: £1.10, £2.00; EX 4.10.
**Owner** Byculla Thoroughbreds **Bred** Simon Dutfield And William Harrison-Allan **Trained** Newmarket, Suffolk

**FOCUS**
Not the strongest of 0-90 handicaps with the topweight Fission, who was withdrawn at the start, racing off 79. However, it was run at a good pace, the time was decent and the form horses dominated.

**NOTEBOOK**
**Blofeld**completed the hat-trick from a stone higher mark than for the first of those course-and-distance wins. Adopting different tactics on this occasion, he stayed on down the centre of the track to get on top in the final 50 yards under a well-judged ride. He should continue to progress.
**Muy Bien**hung to the left when holding a narrow lead and, with his rider persisting in using his whip in his right hand, bumped the rail a couple of times, and the winner got to him in the last 50 yards. This was a decent run at the weights.
**Foxies Future(IRE)**could not take advantage of a big weight pull with Blofeld on their running here last month. She probably needs a bit farther.
**Bridgewater Boys**, who was taken on for the lead, looks high enough in the weights now.
**Pompey Blue**eventually paid the price for helping set a strong pace.
**Scottish Exile(IRE)** *Official explanation: jockey said filly reared in the stalls and never travelled in the race*

## 459 BETDIRECT.CO.UK MAIDEN STKS 1m (F)
**2:35** (2:35) (D) 4-Y-0+ **£3,406** (£1,048; £524; £262) **Stalls** Low

Form RPR
324- **1** **Allied Victory (USA)**[64] 5907 4-9-0 73........ JQuinn 3 64
(EJAlston) *hld up: nt clr run over 3f out: hdwy over 2f out: r.o u.p to ld wl ins fnl f* **4/6**[1]
226- **2** *nk* **Magic Mamma's Too**[18] 6211 4-9-0 53........ DMernagh 2 63
(TDBarron) *led: clr over 2f out: hdd wl ins fnl f* **7/2**[2]
**3** *8* **Now And Again**[11] 5-9-0........ DaleGibson 6 47
(MWEasterby) *s.i.s: sn chsng ldrs: outpcd over 3f out: styd on ins fnl f* **33/1**
625- **4** *hd* **Chesnut Ripple**[22] 6193 5-8-9 48........ RHavlin 5 42
(DShaw) *chsd ldrs: rdn over 2f out: hung lft and wknd over 1f out: fin lame* **9/1**[3]
000- **5** *1 1/2* **Ming The Merciless**[214] 2177 4-9-0 63........ ACulhane 1 44
(JGGiven) *chsd ldrs over 6f* **14/1**
0- **6** *11* **Briar (CZE)**[43] 6060 5-9-0........(p) VSlattery 4 22
(MPitman) *sn outpcd and bhd* **40/1**
306- **7** *8* **Margold (IRE)**[46] 6043 4-8-9 55........ NCallan 7 1
(RHollinshead) *chsd ldr: rdn 1/2-way: wknd over 2f out* **20/1**

1m 44.08s (-0.52) **Going Correction** +0.05s/f (Slow) **7** Ran SP% **109.0**
Speed ratings: **104,103,95,95,94 83,75**CSF £2.71 TOTE £1.40: £1.10, £1.20; EX 3.10.
**Owner** Honest Traders **Bred** Gaines-Gentry Thoroughbreds Llc & William Condren **Trained** Longton, Lancs
■ Stewards Enquiry : J Quinn one-day ban: used whip with excessive frequency (Jan 17)

**FOCUS**
A weak maiden in which the two market leaders finished well clear. The pace was moderate and the winner looks worth taking on in future.

**NOTEBOOK**
**Allied Victory(USA)**, making his sand debut, was held up under a confident ride. That confidence looked misplaced as he took time to pick up the leader, but he eventually responded to his rider's urgings to get there near the finish. This half-brother to Classic winners Pennekamp and Black Minnaloushe was hardly scoring out of turn, having been placed on nine previous occasions.
**Magic Mamma's Too**tried to kick clear off the home turn and stuck on willingly under pressure, but was eventually gunned down. This was a good effort considering he would have received 20lb from the favourite in a handicap.
**Now And Again**missed the kick on this Flat debut but was soon in touch. He stayed on past toiling rivals to snatch third and will be suited by farther.
**Chesnut Ripple**would have finished third but for going lame. *Official explanation: jockey said mare finished foot sore*
**Ming The Merciless**was down in trip for this first run since June.

## 460 BET DIRECT ON 0800 32 93 93 (S) STKS 5f (F)
**3:10** (3:10) (G) 3-Y-0+ **£2,569** (£734; £367) **Stalls** High

Form RPR
00-6 **1** **Cark**[1] 443 6-9-3 45........(p) LFletcher(3) 9 56
(JBalding) *chsd ldrs: led over 1f out: rdn out* **13/2**
350- **2** *1/2* **Soaked**[25] 6166 11-9-6 55........(b) ACulhane 1 55
(DWChapman) *w ldr: led 1/2-way: hdd over 1f out: r.o* **5/2**[1]
300- **3** *1/2* **Festive Affair**[28] 6149 6-9-6 51........ RFfrench 6 53
(BSmart) *chsd ldrs: rdn 1/2-way: r.o* **4/1**[2]
060- **4** *2* **Lady Protector**[15] 6232 5-8-8 40........ PMakin(7) 8 42
(JBalding) *s.i.s: sn chsng ldrs: rdn over 1f out: styd on same pce* **20/1**
04-0 **5** *1 1/2* **Mr Spliffy (IRE)**[4] 411 5-8-13 47........(v) AReilly(7) 10 43
(KRBurke) *prom: jnd ldrs 1/2-way: outpcd over 1f out* **7/1**
001- **6** *1/2* **Ladies Knight**[10] 6243 4-9-7 56........ THamilton(5) 7 47
(DShaw) *s.i.s: outpcd whn stmbld over 3f out: r.o ins fnl f: nvr nrr* **9/2**[3]
63-0 **7** *1/2* **Fiennes (USA)**[4] 411 6-8-13 45........(v) StevenHarrison(7) 4 40
(MrsNMacauley) *sn outpcd: hdwy 1/2-way: no ex fnl f* **14/1**
56-0 **8** *2 1/2* **Lone Piper**[1] 443 9-9-1 45........ BReilly(5) 5 32
(JMBradley) *s.s: outpcd: hdwy 1/2-way: eased whn btn ins fnl f* **25/1**

00-0 **9** *5* **Salerno**[4] 411 5-9-1 50..........(b) TEaves(5) 2 17
(MissGayKelleway) *led to 1/2-way: sn wknd* **14/1**
60.46 secs (0.16) **Going Correction** +0.05s/f (Slow)
**WFA** 3 from 4yo+ 15lb **9** Ran SP% **114.5**
Speed ratings: **100,99,98,95,92 92,91,87,79**CSF £22.91 TOTE £8.90: £3.20, £1.30, £2.50; EX 27.70.There was no bid for the winner
**Owner** J E Abbey **Bred** P G Airey And R R Whitton **Trained** Scrooby, Notts
**FOCUS**
A poor seller.
**NOTEBOOK**
**Cark**, who ran the previous day, had work to do at these weights. This was only the second time he has got his head in front since his racecourse debut.
**Soaked**ran a sound race on this second appearance following a bit of a break.
**Festive Affair**will be suited by a return to six furlongs.
**Lady Protector**, a stablemate of the winner, ran respectably in the face of a stiff task at the weights.
**Mr Spliffy(IRE)**raced on the stands' side a little way apart from his rivals.
**Ladies Knight**, had three of these behind, including today's winner Cark, when scoring over course-and-distance last time, but he was back to his old tricks at the start on this occasion.

## 461 LITTLEWOODSCASINO.COM H'CAP 2m (F)
3:45 (3:45) (F) (0-65,65) 4-Y-0+ £2,905 (£830; £415) Stalls Low

Form RPR
226- **1** **Vanbrugh (FR)**[6] 6267 4-9-8 65..........(vt) DarrenWilliams 2 78
(MissDAMchale) *s.i.s: sn chsng ldrs: led 6f out: rdn over 2f out: r.o* **7/1**[3]
061- **2** *7* **Phantom Stock**[6] 6267 4-8-12 55 6ex.......... MTebbutt 1 61
(WJarvis) *hld up: hdwy 9f out: chsd wnr over 4f out: rdn over 2f out: edgd lft and styd on same pce fnl f* **4/6**[1]
450- **3** *9* **Jamaican Flight (USA)**[80] 5417 11-9-2 52.......... JQuinn 3 49
(MrsSLamyman) *led 10f: wknd over 3f out* **22/1**
611- **4** *1* **Vincent**[21] 6200 9-8-10 46.......... RFfrench 10 42
(JohnAHarris) *hld up: drvn along over 5f out: n.d* **9/2**[2]
000- **5** *12* **Hajeer (IRE)**[6] 6267 6-8-6 45.......... LisaJones(3) 7 29
(PWHiatt) *prom: lost pl 10f out: bhd fr 1/2-way* **25/1**
050- **6** *26* **Lapadar (IRE)**[11] 6096 5-8-13 54..........(b) THamilton(5) 9 12
(JRWeymes) *hld up: rdn 10f out: bhd fr 1/2-way* **80/1**
054- **7** *½* **Minivet**[38] 5069 9-9-5 58.......... DAllan(3) 5 16
(TDEasterby) *s.i.s: sn prom: wknd 7f out* **33/1**
620- **8** *12* **Madhahir (IRE)**[31] 6139 4-9-5 62..........(v¹) NCallan 8 8
(CADwyer) *prom: rdn 9f out: wknd over 4f out* **20/1**
045- **9** *dist* **Fortunes Favourite**[24] 6177 4-8-5 48.......... NPollard 4 —
(GMMoore) *chsd ldrs over 10f* **18/1**
3m 40.48s (-12.02) **Going Correction** +0.05s/f (Slow)
**WFA** 4 from 5yo+ 7lb **9** Ran SP% **113.1**
Speed ratings: **101,97,93,92,86 73,73,67,—**CSF £11.27 CT £97.86 TOTE £9.80: £2.00, £1.10, £4.40; EX 40.30 Place 6 £2.82, Place 5 £2.00.
**Owner** N Bashir **Bred** Breeding Horse Inc **Trained** Newmarket, Suffolk
**FOCUS**
The pace was fair, and this developed into a two-horse race from in the final half-mile. The runner-up looks well handicapped on his old form.
**NOTEBOOK**
**Vanbrugh(FR)**, twice runner-up here last month, was 5lb higher on this occasion. In front a long way out, he was joined by the favourite with three furlongs to run but stayed on the stronger. This track suits him better than Wolverhampton.
**Phantom Stock**was effectively only 3lb higher despite the penalty for his Wolverhampton win. He had every chance once in line for home, but his rival would not be denied and he had to accept defeat inside the last.
**Jamaican Flight(USA)**, last seen over hurdles in October, made a satisfactory return to action.
**Vincent**, who beat today's winner Vanbrugh each time when scoring twice here last month, was another 7lb higher now and could never get into the action.
**Madhahir(IRE)**was very hard work for his rider, the visor not having the desired effect, and eventually cried enough after turning for home in fifth place.
**Fortunes Favourite**, making her handicap debut, did not stay.
T/Plt: £6.70 to a £1 stake. Pool: £26,125.20. 2,816.10 winning tickets. T/Qpdt: £2.30 to a £1 stake. Pool: £2,577.70. 805.10 winning tickets. CR

# 447 LINGFIELD (L-H)
Wednesday, January 7
**OFFICIAL GOING: Standard**
Race times suggest the ground was riding on the slow side.
Wind: fresh bhd Weather: mostly sunny

## 462 LITTLEWOODS BET DIRECT H'CAP 7f (P)
12:20 (12:20) (E) (0-75,73) 3-Y-O £3,474 (£1,069; £534; £267) Stalls Low

Form RPR
330- **1** **Desert Image (IRE)**[54] 5994 3-9-2 68.......... EAhern 4 70
(CTinkler) *racd in midfield on inner: prog over 2f out: r.o wl fnl f to ld last 75y* **14/1**
322- **2** *¾* **Fools Entire**[21] 6210 3-8-11 68.......... BReilly(5) 5 68
(JAGilbert) *prom in chsng gp: rdn to chse clr ldr wl over 1f out: clsd fnl f: jst outpcd nr fin* **7/1**[2]
040- **3** *nk* **Resplendent King (USA)**[96] 5339 3-9-5 71.......... DaneO'Neill 1 70
(TGMills) *prom in chsng gp: rdn over 2f out: clsd fnl f: styd on wl* **8/1**[3]
510- **4** *½* **Head Boy**[76] 5721 3-8-7 59.......... PDoe 8 57
(SDow) *towards rr: pushed along 4f out: prog on inner over 2f out: swtchd rt and r.o wl fr over 1f out: nrst fin* **25/1**
432- **5** *1* **Phluke**[9] 6248 3-9-7 73.......... SCarson 6 69
(RFJohnsonHoughton) *pressed ldr: led 1/2-way: drvn 5l clr 2f out: wknd and hdd last 75y* **7/1**[2]
014- **6** *4* **The Job**[25] 6172 3-8-10 62.......... WRyan 11 48
(ADSmith) *s.i.s: hld up in last trio: rdn over 2f out: styd on fnl f: no ch w ldrs* **10/1**
215- **7** *1* **Maunby Raver**[30] 6141 3-8-7 66.......... RoryMoore(7) 13 49
(PCHaslam) *racd towards rr: effrt over 2f out: one pce and nvr rchd ldrs* **8/1**[3]
536- **8** *1* **Gayle Storm (IRE)**[97] 5323 3-8-11 63.......... JQuinn 14 44
(CTinkler) *s.i.s: hld up in last trio: stl gng wl over 2f out: nudged along whn nt clr run over 1f out: r.o nr fin* **33/1**
050- **9** *nk* **Jango Malfoy (IRE)**[9] 6251 3-8-9 61.......... MFenton 15 41
(BWDuke) *racd in last trio: rdn over 3f out: nvr on terms* **25/1**
02-4 **10** *¾* **Pregnant Pause (IRE)**[4] 414 3-8-13 65.......... ACulhane 7 43
(SKirk) *chsd ldrs: rdn over 3f out: struggling over 2f out: wknd over 1f out* **9/2**[1]
060- **11** *hd* **Knight Onthe Tiles (IRE)**[21] 6207 3-8-10 69..........(b) DFentiman(7) 2 46
(JRBest) *plld hrd early: prom in chsng gp: rdn 3f out: wknd wl over 1f out* **14/1**
0- **12** *¾* **Ask The Clerk (IRE)**[56] 5977 3-9-6 72..........(p) MTebbutt 10 48
(HJCollingridge) *t.k.h: hld up towards rr: shuffled along on outer 3f out: no prog* **8/1**[3]
030- **13** *¾* **Lord Baskerville**[160] 3728 3-9-1 67.......... VSlattery 16 41
(MGQuinlan) *racd in midfield: outpcd and lost pl over 2f out: sn struggling* **50/1**
056- **14** *½* **Trevian**[106] 5141 3-9-4 70.......... MartinDwyer 3 42
(SCWilliams) *led to 1/2-way: wknd 2f out* **16/1**
153- **15** *¾* **Among Dreams**[54] 5994 3-9-0 66.......... SWKelly 12 37
(JAOsborne) *racd towards rr: rdn 3f out: sn btn* **8/1**[3]
1m 27.54s (1.54) **Going Correction** +0.225s/f (Slow) **15** Ran SP% **128.5**
Speed ratings: **100,99,98,98,97 92,91,90,89,89 88,87,87,86,85**CSF £111.94 CT £609.71 TOTE £20.50: £8.60, £3.20, £3.10; EX 208.00.
**Owner** George Ward **Bred** Philip Hore Jnr **Trained** Compton, Berks
**FOCUS**
A competitive handicap, and the form should work out. Phluke set a decent pace but the final time confirmed that the ground was riding on the slow side.
**NOTEBOOK**
**Desert Image(IRE)**, suited by the way the race was run, came through to lead in the closing stages. Yet another example of the tremendous form in which Colin Tinkler's stable is in (7 wins from 24 starts since he returned from Spain), the colt may well have appreciated the switch from Fibresand to this kinder surface.
**Fools Entire**has been running consistently on this surface and once again ran a solid race in defeat, this time off a 4lb higher mark.
**Resplendent King(USA)**had every chance and did not perform too badly on his return from a three-month absence. He should come on for the run.
**Head Boy**was running on well at the end of the race. Having his first outing since October, unfancied in the betting and by a sire whose stock do much better on Fibresand than Polytrack, he ran a most promising race, and he will be an interesting proposition if turning up at Wolverhampton or Southwell in the next few weeks.
**Phluke**, who helped force a decent pace, swept into a clear lead rounding the home bend but fell in a hole inside the last.
**The Job**will be happier when stepping back up to a mile.
**Gayle Storm(IRE)**, a stable-mate of the winner and in the same ownership, caught the eye running on at the finish, without being unduly knocked about.

## 463 BET DIRECT ON 0800 32 93 93 MAIDEN STKS 1m 2f (P)
12:50 (12:50) (D) 4-Y-0+ £3,523 (£1,084; £542; £271) Stalls Low

Form RPR
/35- **1** **Jack Of Trumps (IRE)**[28] 6162 4-9-0 80.......... SDrowne 2 64
(GWragg) *trckd ldrs: lost pl and pushed along 3f out: prog over 2f out: drvn and r.o to ld last 100y: in command nr fin* **6/4**[1]
060- **2** *1 ¼* **Coronado Forest (USA)**[28] 6157 5-9-2 58.......... DaneO'Neill 12 62
(MRHoad) *hld up in rr: prog on outer fr wl over 2f out: drvn to ld narrowly ins fnl f: hdd and outpcd last 100y* **14/1**
000- **3** *1 ¼* **My Lilli (IRE)**[175] 3316 4-8-9 48.......... JQuinn 8 55
(PMitchell) *prom: chsd ldr over 5f out: rdn to ld 3f out: hdd ins fnl f: one pce* **33/1**
030- **4** *1 ½* **Blazing The Trail (IRE)**[159] 3757 4-9-0 70.......... SWhitworth 9 57
(JWHills) *racd in midfield: rdn and prog over 3f out: chsd ldr over 2f out to 1f out: one pce fnl f* **12/1**
22-2 **5** *hd* **Givemethemoonlight**[5] 412 5-8-11 51.......... CCatlin 7 52
(MrsStefLiddiard) *racd in midfield: rdn and outpcd over 2f out: styd on again fnl f* **9/2**[2]
5/3- **6** *½* **Wizard Of Edge**[132] 4532 4-9-0 70.......... SCarson 3 56
(GBBalding) *settled towards rr: outpcd 3f out: pushed along and styd on steadily fr over 1f out: nvr nrr* **6/1**[3]
365- **7** *shd* **Golden Dual**[8] 6259 4-9-0 73.......... PDoe 5 56
(SDow) *racd in midfield: rdn over 2f out: prog on outer over 1f out: one pce fnl f* **14/1**
600- **8** *2 ½* **Operashaan (IRE)**[234] 1695 4-9-0 56.......... ACulhane 10 51
(GLMoore) *prom: rdn over 3f out: wknd wl over 1f out* **16/1**
0- **9** *5* **Curzon Lodge (IRE)**[243] 1495 4-9-0.......... EAhern 1 42
(CTinkler) *hld up in last pair: lost tch 3f out: shuffled along over 1f out: nvr nr ldrs: veered rt nr fin* **8/1**
500- **10** *3* **Unsuited**[9] 6253 5-8-8 53.......... RMiles(3) 4 32
(JELong) *lost pl and in rr after 3f: rdn and no prog wl over 2f out: wknd* **66/1**
0/0- **11** *7* **Mount Logan**[23] 6193 9-9-2.......... MartinDwyer 6 24
(RCurtis) *led for 1f: chsd ldr to over 5f out: wknd over 3f out* **66/1**
06/ **12** *7* **Show Me Heaven**[1628] 3111 7-8-11.......... MTebbutt 14 7
(TTClement) *s.s: racd in last pair: lost tch 4f out: bhd after* **66/1**
**13** *½* **Bennanabaa**[77] 5-9-2..........(t) WRyan 11 11
(SCBurrough) *led after 1f to 3f out: wknd and eased* **20/1**
2m 10.08s (2.69) **Going Correction** +0.225s/f (Slow)
**WFA** 4 from 5yo+ 2lb **13** Ran SP% **122.7**
Speed ratings: **98,97,96,94,94 94,94,92,88,85 80,74,74**CSF £25.99 TOTE £2.10: £1.60, £7.90, £12.50; EX 26.90.
**Owner** Mollers Racing **Bred** Miss Susan Bates **Trained** Newmarket, Suffolk
**FOCUS**
While the winner remains a horse with some potential, the proximity of lowly-rated rivals in second and third confirms this was a poor maiden.
**NOTEBOOK**
**Jack Of Trumps(IRE)**, fifth, although flattered, in a conditions race here last time, won with a bit in hand. Hopefully he can go on from here, but as it stands the form does not amount to anything. Both the second and third are moderate performers and he looks flattered by his current mark of 80.
**Coronado Forest(USA)**, having his 18th start on the level, is thoroughly exposed and not one to trust.
**My Lilli(IRE)**was having her first start since July and ran a promising race. She would have a chance in a minor handicap, provided the handicapper does not over react.
**Blazing The Trail(IRE)**, another having his first run since the summer, came into the straight with every chance but weakened in the manner of a horse who needed the run.
**Givemethemoonlight**is a long-standing maiden and once again ran her usual race.
**Wizard Of Edge**may well have needed the run and will be of more interest in handicap company.
**Curzon Lodge(IRE)**might well have done better had his jockey been more positive on him.
**Bennanabaa** *Official explanation: vet said gelding finished lame on the left fore leg*

## 464 BET DIRECT PRESS RED TO BET H'CAP 1m 2f (P)
1:20 (1:20) (F) (0-60,60) 4-Y-0+ £3,059 (£874; £437) Stalls Low

Form RPR
441- **1** **Gold Guest**[18] 6220 5-9-7 60.......... SJDonohoe(7) 10 72
(PDEvans) *hld up towards rr: stdy prog over 2f out: rdn to ld 1f out: sn clr* **6/1**[1]

012- **2** 2 ½ **He Who Dares (IRE)**[32] 6127 6-9-11 **57**........................ SWhitworth 14 65
(AWCarroll) *s.i.s: plld hrd and hld up in last pair: effrt on wd outside over 2f out: drvn and r.o fr over 1f out: tk 2nd on line* **15/2**[3]

042- **3** *hd* **Welsh Wind (IRE)**[18] 6220 8-9-10 **56**........................(t) DRMcCabe 2 63
(MWigham) *trckd ldrs: rdn and cl up 2f out: nt qckn over 1f out: styd on same pce* **6/1**[1]

352- **4** *shd* **Stolen Song**[32] 5692 4-9-10 **58**........................(p) MartinDwyer 6 65
(MJRyan) *chsd ldr: rdn to ld 3f out: hdd and nt qckn 1f out* **7/1**[2]

522- **5** ½ **Ember Days**[21] 6205 5-9-9 **55**........................ EAhern 5 61
(JLSpearing) *racd in mifield: rdn and prog to chse ldrs over 2f out: kpt on same pce fr voer 1f out* **8/1**

030- **6** *1* **Archirondel**[87] 5500 6-9-9 **55**........................ ACulhane 3 59
(MDHammond) *racd towards rr: hrd rdn and effrt over 2f out: no imp tl styd on ins fnl f* **11/1**

020- **7** 1 ½ **Castaigne (FR)**[21] 6205 5-9-8 **54**........................(t) MFenton 13 56
(BWDuke) *dwlt: settled in rr: pushed along whn nt clr run briefly over 2f out : styd on fnl f: no ch* **14/1**

100- **8** ¾ **Muyassir (IRE)**[9] 6255 9-9-10 **56**........................ SDrowne 4 56
(MissBSanders) *hld up in rr: effrt on inner and nt clr run briefly over 2f out: prog and cl up jst over 1f out: wknd fnl f* **16/1**

045- **9** ¾ **Coolfore Jade (IRE)**[9] 6249 4-9-4 **57**........................ MSavage[(5)] 12 56
(NEBerry) *prom: rdn to press ldr 3f out: ev ch over 1f out: fnd nil and wknd* **16/1**

03-3 **10** *nk* **Scottish River (USA)**[5] 412 5-9-13 **59**........................ ADaly 11 57
(MDIUsher) *racd wd: hld up towards rr: effrt and swtchd ins 2f out: one pce and no ch* **6/1**[1]

006- **11** *5* **Miss Glory Be**[12] 6241 6-9-3 **54**........................(p) TEaves[(5)] 9 43
(MissGayKelleway) *trckd ldrs: effrt and cl up over 2f out: wknd u.p wl over 1f out* **12/1**

003- **12** 1 ¾ **Harlot**[21] 6205 4-9-7 **58**........................(p) LisaJones[(3)] 8 44
(JohnBerry) *racd freely: led to 3f out: wknd 2f out* **25/1**

000- **13** ¾ **Penny Pie (IRE)**[32] 6134 4-9-12 **60**........................(v[1]) NCallan 7 45
(PWHarris) *racd towards rr: losing pl and struggling whn nt clr run over 2f out: sn bhd* **16/1**

260- **14** 3 ½ **Maunby Rocker**[30] 6143 4-9-2 **57**........................ RoryMoore[(7)] 1 36
(PCHaslam) *in tch tl wknd u.p 4f out: sn bhd* **33/1**

2m 9.24s (1.85) **Going Correction** +0.225s/f (Slow)
**WFA** 4 from 5yo+ 2lb **14** Ran SP% **125.4**
Speed ratings: **101,99,98,98,98 97,96,95,95,94 90,89,88,86**CSF £51.82 CT £291.99 TOTE £6.90: £2.30, £3.80, £2.30; EX 54.50.
**Owner** Diamond Racing Ltd **Bred** The Hon D K And Mrs Oliver **Trained** Pandy, Gwent

**FOCUS**
An open-looking handicap in which they went 6-1 the field. The winner has yet to run bad race on the surface.

**NOTEBOOK**
**Gold Guest**ran out an authoritative winner, despite having been raised 8lb for his recent course and distance win. Clearly progressing well, his style of running is ideally suited to the way races tend to be run at this track.
**He Who Dares(IRE)**, another hold-up performer, had the race run to suit and finished well on the outside. He looks handicapped to win a similar contest.
**Welsh Wind(IRE)**, whose losing run stretches back over two years, continues to frustrate despite looking on an attractive mark.
**Stolen Song**, backed in from 12-1, was the gamble of the race. He had shown improved form of late over hurdles, but the fact remains that he has still to get his head in front in 20 starts.
**Ember Days**was slightly disappointing given her recent form but, on the plus side, the Handicapper may drop her slightly for this.
**Scottish River(USA)**threw away his chance by failing to settle.

## 465 BET ON ALL WEATHER CLASSIFIED CLAIMING STKS 6f (P)
**1:50** (1:50) (F) 3-Y-O+ **£2,940** (£840; £420) **Stalls** Low

Form RPR

03-2 **1** **Tayif**[1] 453 8-9-9 52........................(t) SCarson 10 67
(AndrewReid) *settled in rr: prog fr 1/2-way: chsd ldng pair over 1f out: led last 150y: drvn clr* **6/4**[1]

406- **2** *3* **Tripti (IRE)**[8] 6261 4-9-2 53........................ NPollard 12 51
(JJBridger) *pressed ldr: drvn to ld over 2f out: hdd last 150y: no ch w wnr after* **14/1**

000- **3** 1 ¼ **Xsynna**[21] 6206 8-9-0 45........................(v) FPFerris[(3)] 8 48
(PSMcentee) *led to over 2f out: stl ev ch over 1f out: fdd ins fnl f* **40/1**

102- **4** ½ **Polar Haze**[19] 6217 7-9-2 53........................(v) JFMcDonald[(5)] 2 51
(MrsLydiaPearce) *chsd ldng pair to over 1f out: hanging lft and nt qckn after* **8/1**

000- **5** *nk* **A Teen**[8] 6261 6-9-11 52........................ RWinston 7 54
(PHowling) *racd in rr: effrt u.p wl over 2f out: kpt on one pce fnl f: no ch* **16/1**

053- **6** ½ **Adantino**[9] 6253 5-9-13 48........................ GBaker 11 54
(BRMillman) *racd wd: hld up in rr: effrt over 2f out: hanging and c wd bnd sn after: styd on ins fnl f* **7/1**

020- **7** ½ **Harbour House**[8] 6256 5-9-7 45........................ JTate 1 47
(JJBridger) *restless stalls and dwlt: rchd midfield 1/2-way: outpcd over 2f out: no ch after* **6/1**[3]

000- **8** *hd* **Definitely Special (IRE)**[9] 6253 6-8-13 40........................ MSavage[(5)] 5 43
(NEBerry) *racd in midfield: outpcd u.p over 2f out: no ch after* **20/1**

00-0 **9** 2 ½ **Flying Faisal (USA)**[4] 421 6-9-3 45........................ PFitzsimons 4 35
(JMBradley) *chsd ldrs: rdn 1/2-way: wknd 2f out* **25/1**

306- **10** *4* **Kilmeena Star**[36] 6116 6-9-3 40........................ PDobbs 13 23
(JCFox) *hld up in last trio: no prog and btn over 2f out: wknd* **25/1**

005- **11** *1* **Cargo**[8] 6261 5-9-5 47........................ EAhern 9 22
(HJCollingridge) *racd towards outer in midfield: rdn wl over 2f out: wknd wl over 1f out* **11/2**[2]

000- **12** *1* **Rathmullan**[21] 6206 5-8-10 40........................(p) LiamJones[(7)] 3 17
(EAWheeler) *restless stalls and dwlt: a bhd* **50/1**

000- **13** *nk* **Gentle Response**[127] 4632 4-9-2 45........................ SWhitworth 6 15
(CADwyer) *prom tl wknd rapidly over 2f out* **25/1**

1m 13.37s (0.45) **Going Correction** +0.225s/f (Slow) **13** Ran SP% **126.5**
Speed ratings: **106,102,100,99,99 98,97,97,94,89 87,86,85**CSF £25.35 TOTE £2.10: £1.30, £4.10, £11.00; EX 32.60.The winner was the subject of a friendly claim for £8,000 Mr.A.S.Reid.
**Owner** A S Reid **Bred** Theakston Stud **Trained** Mill Hill, London NW7

**FOCUS**
A moderate heat but a decent winning time for the class of contest and the winner can do well in handicaps off current mark.

**NOTEBOOK**
**Tayif**had run two good races over this course and distance since leaving David Nicholls and this looked an easier task than either of those heats. He has never been easy to win with, though, and that ensured his supporters got a price. A comfortable winner in the end, he should continue to be a force at this level.
**Tripti(IRE)**, meeting the winner on similar terms, got slightly closer to him this time than when they both finished behind Type One here eight days previously.
**Xsynna**ran a fair race, given how difficult it is to make the running round here.
**Polar Haze**was not disgraced, given that he is far happier on the Fibresand surface at Southwell.
**A Teen**ran a better race than of late, but that is not saying much given the quality of the opposition.
**Cargo** *Official explanation: trainer said gelding banged its head in the stalls and cut its mouth*

## 466 BETDIRECT.CO.UK H'CAP 1m (P)
**2:20** (2:20) (D ) (0-85,81) 3-Y-O **£4,433** (£1,364; £682; £341) **Stalls** High

Form RPR

631- **1** **Whitgift Rock**[21] 6210 3-8-11 **71**........................ PDoe 1 76
(SDow) *trckd ldrs: effrt to ld wl over 1f out: hrd rdn fnl f : jst hld on* **5/1**[3]

31- **2** *hd* **Skidmark**[18] 6219 3-9-5 **79**........................ PFitzsimons 7 83
(DRCElsworth) *dwlt: hld up in last pair: effrt 2f out: shkn up ent fnl f: r.o wl last 100y: jst failed: too much to do* **6/4**[1]

310- **3** *hd* **Royal Warrant**[109] 5080 3-9-6 **80**........................ MartinDwyer 3 84
(AMBalding) *settled in last trio: effrt 2f out: rdn fnl f: r.o wl nr fin: jst hld* **7/1**

021- **4** *nk* **Blue Empire (IRE)**[22] 6197 3-8-12 **75**........................ LEnstone[(3)] 5 78
(PCHaslam) *t.k.h: hld up in tch: prog to press wnr wl over 1f out : hanging lft and nt qckn fnl f: lost 2 pls nr fin* **9/2**[2]

114- **5** *9* **Countrywide Flyer (IRE)**[11] 6242 3-9-7 **81**........................(b[1]) NCallan 4 63
(TDBarron) *plld hrd: trckd ldr: led wl over 3f out: hdd & wknd wl over 1f out* **8/1**

10- **6** *9* **Freddie Freccles**[44] 6059 3-8-10 **70**........................ MFenton 2 32
(JGGiven) *led to wl over 3f out: wknd u.p: t.o* **40/1**

361- **7** ¾ **Boxgrove (FR)**[18] 6222 3-9-6 **80**........................ ACulhane 6 40
(CEBrittain) *cl up: rdn to chse ldr over 3f out to over 2f out: wknd rapidly: t.o* **6/1**

1m 41.85s (2.34) **Going Correction** +0.225s/f (Slow) **7** Ran SP% **115.2**
Speed ratings: **97,96,96,96,87 78,77**CSF £13.16 TOTE £8.50: £2.50, £1.50; EX 15.00.
**Owner** Whitgift Racing **Bred** Mrs D O Joly **Trained** Epsom, Surrey

**FOCUS**
A fair little handicap, but the final time was poor. The runner-up should improve on this effort.

**NOTEBOOK**
**Whitgift Rock**, whose supporters would have been buoyed by Fools Entire's creditable run in the first off 68, looked to hold every chance here off 71. His challengers may well have been closing at the line, but he always looked like holding on, and connections are convinced that he will be even better when he gets back on the turf.
**Skidmark**, whose challenge came just too late, shapes as though a little farther will suit.
**Royal Warrant**, having been held up, got into a challenging position only to find himself short of room in the straight. This was a good effort on his Polytrack debut and first run for three and a half months, and he should be placed to win.
**Blue Empire(IRE)**was found out on this very different surface by the 10lb rise for his Southwell stroll.
**Countrywide Flyer(IRE)**, another Fibresand performer trying his hand on Polytrack for the first time, ran much too freely in the first-time headgear. *Official explanation: jockey said gelding had run too free*
**Boxgrove(FR)**may have had something amiss with him as this performance looked too bad to be true.

## 467 BET DIRECT FREEPHONE 0800 32 93 93 H'CAP 1m 5f (P)
**2:50** (2:51) (E ) (0-70,70) 4-Y-O+ **£3,381** (£966; £483) **Stalls** Low

Form RPR

140- **1** **Maystock**[32] 6130 4-9-0 **68**........................(v) LTreadwell[(7)] 8 83
(GAButler) *t.k.h: hld up in midfield: prog 4f out: led over 2f out: sn kicked wl clr: unchal* **8/1**

400- **2** *5* **Jadeeron**[84] 5576 5-8-8 **53**........................(p) LisaJones[(3)] 4 61
(MissDAMchale) *prom: lost pl over 4f out: rdn 3f out: styd on again to take 2nd ins fnl f: no ch w wnr* **11/1**

220- **3** ½ **Ambersong**[16] 6233 6-8-9 **51**........................ ACulhane 14 58
(AWCarroll) *t.k.h: hld up in midfield: prog on outer over 2f out: styd on fr over 1f out: no ch w wnr* **8/1**

623- **4** 1 ¼ **Big Bertha**[32] 6130 6-9-10 **66**........................ GBaker 3 72
(JohnBerry) *hld up in midfield: outpcd wl over 2f out: effrt on outer wl over 1f out: kpt on same pce* **7/2**[1]

060- **5** *5* **Raheel (IRE)**[9] 6249 4-8-6 **53**........................(t) WRyan 2 52
(PMitchell) *t.k.h: hld up in last: stl last over 2f out: sme prog but no ch whn nt clr run over 1f out: kpt on ins fnl f* **20/1**

003- **6** 1 ¼ **Zawrak (IRE)**[18] 6226 5-8-12 **61**........................ NataliaGemelova[(7)] 12 58
(IWMcinnes) *prom on outer: led 4f out: bmpd along and hdd over 2f out: wknd rapidly 1f out* **16/1**

660- **7** *1* **Landescent (IRE)**[8] 6262 4-8-6 **53**........................ JQuinn 5 48
(MQuinn) *led: set v stdy pce: hdd 4f out: sn lost pl: no ch whn nt clr run over 1f out* **25/1**

431- **8** *nk* **Beechy Bank (IRE)**[179] 3210 6-10-0 **70**........................ VSlattery 6 65
(MrsMaryHambro) *t.k.h: cl up: outpcd fr wl over 2f out: wknd over 1f out* **16/1**

311- **9** *nk* **Royal Prodigy (USA)**[9] 6249 5-9-13 **69** 6ex........................ DaneO'Neill 11 64
(RJHodges) *hld up in last pair: rdn over 4f out: struggling after* **5/1**[3]

063- **10** *hd* **Makarim (IRE)**[9] 6249 8-8-10 **57**........................(p) HayleyTurner[(5)] 13 51
(MRBosley) *prom: w ldr 4f out: wknd over 2f out* **12/1**

250- **11** 1 ¼ **Radiant Bride**[9] 6249 4-7-13 **46** ow1........................(p) CCatlin 9 39
(KRBurke) *hld up in rr: rdn 4f out: sn struggling* **50/1**

020- **12** *4* **Fairy Wind (GER)**[47] 6040 7-8-6 **48**........................ WMLordan 7 35
(BJCurley) *trckd ldr to 5f out: sn lost pl and btn* **14/1**

226- **P** **Danehill Lad (IRE)**[21] 6208 4-9-5 **66**........................ SDrowne 1 —
(TKeddy) *dwlt: hld up towards rr: p.u over 4f out: lame* **4/1**[2]

2m 54.12s (6.04) **Going Correction** +0.225s/f (Slow)
**WFA** 4 from 5yo+ 5lb **13** Ran SP% **126.1**
Speed ratings: **90,86,86,85,82 82,81,81,81,80 80,77,—**CSF £96.48 CT £747.06 TOTE £9.40: £2.60, £4.60, £3.10; EX 193.00.
**Owner** Stock Hill Racing **Bred** Stock Hill Stud **Trained** Blewbury, Oxon

**FOCUS**
A race run at a dawdle, resulting in a very slow time. The form looks dubious.

**NOTEBOOK**
**Maystock**settled well just off the pace and shot clear on the turn to come home at her leisure. She has won both times Liam Treadwell has ridden her, and they clearly get on well together. Unfortunately the Handicapper is likely to take a dim view of this effort.
**Jadeeron**kept on steadily, but gets farther and would have preferred a stronger pace at this trip.
**Ambersong**was the subject of market support but seems more effective on Wolverhampton's Fibresand.
**Big Bertha**usually runs well here, but is another that would have been suited by a stronger gallop.
**Raheel(IRE)**did not have the race run to suit but, worryingly, he is still a maiden.
**Royal Prodigy(USA)**, bidding for a hat-trick, was always struggling under his penalty in this better grade.

## 468 BET DIRECT IN RUNNING SKY TEXT 293 (S) STKS — 1m (P)

3:20 (3:20) (G ) 4-Y-0+ £2,639 (£754; £377) Stalls High

Form RPR

000- **1** **French Horn**$^{22}$ [5832] 7-9-0 50........................................(p) MartinDwyer 4 53
(MJRyan) *hld up in rr: smooth prog over 2f out: nt clr run briefly over 1f out: urged along and r.o to ld last 75y* **13/2**

403- **2** ¾ **Wilom (GER)**$^{8}$ [6262] 6-9-0 45................................................ MFenton 9 51
(MRHoad) *hld up in rr: smooth prog over 2f out: led over 1f out: drvn and hdd last 75y* **8/1**

336- **3** 2 **Feast Of Romance**$^{21}$ [6206] 7-9-0 50..............................(p) RWinston 10 46
(PHowling) *hld up in rr: prog wl over 2f out: rdn to chal and ev ch over 1f out: nt qckn: wknd nr fin* **6/1**$^{3}$

050- **4** hd **Diliza**$^{105}$ [5157] 5-8-4 49.................................................. RThomas(5) 2 41
(GBBalding) *trckd ldrs: nt qckn and outpcd 2f out: r.o again ins fnl f* **5/1**$^{2}$

530- **5** 5 **Tinian**$^{8}$ [6262] 6-9-5 57..............................................(p) DarrenWilliams 5 39
(KRBurke) *t.k.h: led for 1f: led again over 3f out to over 1f out: wknd* **7/1**

006- **6** 5 **Pertemps Bianca**$^{25}$ [6174] 4-8-9 45...............................(b) PFitzsimons 7 18
(ADSmith) *s.i.s: hld up in rr: rdn and effrt over 2f out: sn outpcd and btn: wknd fnl f* **66/1**

064- **7** 1¼ **Ladywell Blaise (IRE)**$^{8}$ [6257] 7-8-9 45..................................... JTate 12 15
(JJBridger) *trckd ldrs tl wknd rapidly 2f out* **14/1**

060- **8** ½ **Island Star (IRE)**$^{9}$ [6253] 4-9-0 52................................................ PDoe 3 19
(SDow) *t.k.h: prom: led 5f out to over 3f out: wknd rapidly 2f out* **14/1**

000- **9** 3½ **Dancing Forest (IRE)**$^{8}$ [6256] 4-9-0 66............................. DaneO'Neill 6 11
(DKIvory) *dwlt: rcvrd and chsd ldrs on outer 5f out: rdn and wknd over 2f out* **9/4**$^{1}$

00-0 **10** 3 **Almond Beach**$^{4}$ [423] 4-9-0 65.......................................(b) DRMcCabe 8 4
(BJMeehan) *led after 1f to 5f out: ev ch 3f out: sn wknd* **50/1**

**11** 21 **Nod 'N' A Wink**$^{27}$ 6-9-0 ........................................................ NCallan 1 —
(CADwyer) *s.s: rcvrd to chse ldrs after 2f: wknd over 4f out: t.o* **40/1**

1m 41.84s (2.33) **Going Correction** +0.225s/f (Slow) **11** Ran SP% **117.9**
Speed ratings: **97,96,94,94,89 84,82,82,78,75 54**CSF £57.36 TOTE £7.10: £3.00, £3.00, £3.80; EX 44.70.The winner was sold to Michael Wigham for 3,000gns.
**Owner** M J Ryan **Bred** F E Sutherland **Trained** Newmarket, Suffolk

**FOCUS**
A weak race featuring only two horses who had managed to win in the previous 12 months. The runner-up indicates the level of the form.

**NOTEBOOK**
**French Horn**last won in May 2000 and has been generally out of form since then, although he did run well at Newmarket last spring. This drop in grade was needed and he won well enough under a good ride from Dwyer. Needless to say, though, he does not look an obvious one to follow up for his new connections.
**Wilom(GER)**tried his best to cut off the winner's run but in the end Dwyer's mount proved just too strong.
**Feast Of Romance**is much better on Fibresand and reserves his best for Wolverhampton.
**Diliza**, having her first outing since September, could not cope with the increase in tempo rounding the bend into the straight but stayed on again late on.
**Tinian**, who was wearing cheekpieces for the first time, has failed to translate his German form to sand racing in this country.
**Dancing Forest(IRE)**apparently ran flat according to his trainer. *Official explanation: trainer said gelding ran flat*

## 469 BET DIRECT FOOTBALL CASHBACKS H'CAP — 7f (P)

3:50 (3:50) (G ) (0-55,55) 3-Y-0+ £3,045 (£870; £435) Stalls Low

Form RPR

353- **1** **Nearly A Fool**$^{100}$ [5279] 6-9-12 53..........................................(v) NPollard 1 65
(GGMargarson) *mde virtually all: hrd pressed fr 2f out: hld on gamely nr fin* **4/1**$^{1}$

600- **2** shd **Kinsman (IRE)**$^{8}$ [6256] 7-9-7 51...............................(b) J-PGuillambert(3) 4 63
(TDMccarthy) *dwlt: hld up in last trio: gd prog on inner wl over 1f out: pressed wnr fnl f: jst failed* **16/1**

054- **3** hd **Mayzin (IRE)**$^{9}$ [6253] 4-9-10 51................................................(p) EAhern 6 62
(RMFlower) *plld hrd early: chsd ldng pair: rdn and nt qckn over 1f out: r.o again last 150y: jst hld* **4/1**$^{1}$

040- **4** nk **Alafzar (IRE)**$^{61}$ [5945] 6-9-4 52..................................(v) SJDonohoe(7) 15 62
(PDEvans) *hld up in rr: rdn and prog 2f out: styd on u.p fnl f: nrst fin* **13/2**$^{2}$

240- **5** 1 **Lucid Dreams (IRE)**$^{125}$ [4677] 5-9-11 52.......................... DRMcCabe 16 59
(MWigham) *pressed wnr tl nt qckn u.p 1f out: fdd last 100y* **8/1**

560- **6** 1¼ **Taiyo**$^{32}$ [6127] 4-9-11 52............................................................ NCallan 13 56
(JWPayne) *settled towards rr: prog on inner over 2f out: cl up over 1f out: one pce after* **25/1**

550- **7** hd **Pancakehill**$^{22}$ [6196] 5-9-9 53................................................ RMiles(3) 10 57
(DKIvory) *trckd ldrs: rdn over 2f out: unable qck over 1f out: one pce after* **10/1**

340- **8** shd **Scarrottoo**$^{132}$ [4536] 6-9-8 54................................................ BReilly(5) 3 57
(SCWilliams) *cl up: rdn 2f out: ch ent fnl f: nt qckn: eased last 50y* **12/1**

340- **9** ½ **Pirouettes (IRE)**$^{12}$ [6238] 4-9-9 55............................................ TEaves(5) 12 57
(MissGayKelleway) *cl up: rdn over 2f out: fdd u.str.p fnl f* **14/1**

000- **10** hd **Angelica Garnett**$^{127}$ [4632] 4-9-11 52............................................ MFenton 8 53
(TEPowell) *hld up wl in rr: effrt on inner wl over 1f out: one pce and nvr rchd ldrs* **66/1**

000- **11** nk **Mister Clinton (IRE)**$^{18}$ [6220] 7-9-12 53.............................. DaneO'Neill 7 54
(DKIvory) *hld up in last trio: rdn 2f out: one pce and no prog over 1f out* **7/1**$^{3}$

540- **12** ½ **Vizulize**$^{21}$ [4835] 5-9-12 53................................................ SWhitworth 11 52
(AWCarroll) *t.k.h: hld up in last trio: effrt on wd outside over 2f out: no prog over 1f out* **33/1**

006- **13** ¾ **Social Contract**$^{32}$ [6127] 7-9-11 52..................................... PaulEddery 14 49
(SDow) *s.i.s: sn in midfield: rdn 3f out: btn wl over 1f out* **12/1**

000- **14** 7 **Tuscan Treaty**$^{39}$ [6088] 4-9-10 51................................................ JMackay 2 29
(TTClement) *dwlt: racd in midfield tl wknd over 2f out* **40/1**

1m 27.05s (1.05) **Going Correction** +0.225s/f (Slow) **14** Ran SP% **124.7**
Speed ratings: **103,102,102,102,101 99,99,99,98,98 98,97,96,88**CSF £74.53 CT £243.37 TOTE £3.90: £2.20, £5.10, £1.10; EX 85.30 Place 6 £209.20, Place 5 £41.21.
**Owner** J Burns **Bred** Mrs S Shaw **Trained** Newmarket, Suffolk

**FOCUS**
A fair handicap. It looked an open race on paper and, with half a length covering the first four home, that was borne out.

**NOTEBOOK**
**Nearly A Fool**is at his best over seven furlongs and likes to make the running, but that is not a very easy thing to do around here. Setting just an easy pace, though, he had the race run to suit, and in the end just held on. Things fell right this time but one would not like to bet that he gets away with it again.
**Kinsman(IRE)**missed the break and could have done with a stronger pace, but this was still a welcome return to form for this course specialist.
**Mayzin(IRE)**was another to benefit from racing handily off a steady pace.
**Alafzar(IRE)**weaved his way through the field to get into contention late on and he will have chances off his current mark in a more strongly-run race round here.
**Lucid Dreams(IRE)**may well have been flattered by racing prominently off the modest pace.
**Scarrottoo**was beaten when his rider began to ease him down inside the final furlong. However, had he ridden him out he would probably have finished upsides Lucid Dreams.
T/Plt: £371.90 to a £1 stake. Pool: £30,600.65. 60.05 winning tickets. T/Qpdt: £31.90 to a £1 stake. Pool: £2,721.30. 63.00 winning tickets. JN

# 455 SOUTHWELL (L-H)

Thursday, January 8

**OFFICIAL GOING: Standard**
(REGIONAL MEETING)

## 470 BET DIRECT ON SKY ACTIVE AMATEUR RIDERS' BANDED STKS — 6f (F)

1:20 (1:24) (H ) 4-Y-0+ £1,277 (£365; £182) Stalls Low

Form RPR

/66- **1** **Mount Superior (USA)**$^{154}$ [3921] 8-10-7 40..............(b) MissRD'Arcy(7) 1 45
(PWD'Arcy) *in rr: hdwy 1/2-way: str run over 1f out: led last 100 yds* **10/1**

00-3 **2** 1¼ **Aguila Loco (IRE)**$^{4}$ [433] 5-10-9 40.......................................... MrBKing(5) 4 41
(MCChapman) *chsd ldng pair: hdwy 3f out: led wl over 1f out: sn rdn: hdd and nt qckn last 100 yds* **6/4**$^{1}$

00-3 **3** ½ **Lemarate (USA)**$^{3}$ [441] 7-10-9 40.....................(b) MissKellyHarrison(5) 6 40
(DWChapman) *dwlt: sn chsng ldrs: hdwy to chal wl over 1f out: sn rdn and ev ch tl drvn and nt qckn last 100 yds* **8/1**$^{3}$

00-0 **4** 1¼ **Threat**$^{5}$ [421] 8-11-0 40...................................................... MissEJJones 2 36
(JMBradley) *chsd ldrs: outpcd 1/2-way: hdwy 2f out: swtchd lft and rdn ent last:nt qckn last 100 ydss* **9/1**

000- **5** 1 **Above Board**$^{12}$ [6243] 9-10-9 35.................................. MissALTurner(5) 5 33
(RFMarvin) *chsd ldrs: pushed along and outpcd 1/2-way: styd on appr last* **20/1**

000- **6** 1¾ **Home Coming**$^{104}$ [5199] 6-10-9 35...........................(v$^{1}$) MrMMackley(5) 7 28
(PSFelgate) *led: rdn: hung lft and hit rail over 2f out: sn hdd and grad wknd* **20/1**

00-4 **7** 3 **Allerton Boy**$^{6}$ [411] 5-10-7 40.................................... MrJamesWhite(7) 9 19
(RJHodges) *dwlt: sn cl up: led over 2f out: sn rdn and hdd wl over 1f out: sn wknd* **9/2**$^{2}$

500- **8** 1¾ **Moon Royale**$^{124}$ [4730] 6-11-0 30.......................................... MrsMMorris 10 14
(MrsNMacauley) *a rr* **9/1**

000- **9** nk **Batchworth Breeze**$^{168}$ [3515] 6-10-7 30.................... MrCWitheford(7) 11 13
(EAWheeler) *chsd ldrs on outer to 1/2-way: sn wknd* **40/1**

0/0- **10** 5 **Aunt Doris**$^{45}$ [6056] 7-10-9 35.........................................(p) MrPEvans(5) 3 —
(PaulJohnson) *s.i.s: a bhd* **25/1**

1m 20.11s (3.31) **Going Correction** +0.075s/f (Slow) **10** Ran SP% **114.2**
Speed ratings: **80,78,77,76,74 72,68,66,65,58**CSF £23.72 TOTE £10.90: £2.30, £1.20, £1.80; EX 49.20.
**Owner** Paul D'Arcy **Bred** Dr Steve Kramer **Trained** Newmarket, Suffolk
■ A first winner for 16-year-old Rachel D'Arcy, daughter of trainer Paul.

**FOCUS**
An extremely poor contest and a pedestrian time, even for a race of this quality.

**NOTEBOOK**
**Mount Superior(USA)**, for whom this race had been on the map for a while, was accordingly well backed. Given a patient ride on his first outing since August, he was brought wide to pick off the flagging leaders well inside the last furlong.
**Aguila Loco(IRE)**became very fractious in the stalls, a situation not helped by the delay caused by a rival breaking loose. He started well enough though and managed to get to the front in the home straight, but despite a couple of beefy cracks behind the saddle, could do nothing to hold the winner's final burst.
**Lemarate(USA)**is more at home at this new Regional level and held every chance, but was still found wanting and is now without a win in 37 starts.
**Threat**did his best, but he has never shown a great deal on sand in his long career and is a light of former days in any case.
**Above Board**, whose only previous win came over this course and distance, never threatened on this occasion.
**Allerton Boy**should have done much better judged on his recent encouraging sand debut at Wolverhampton.

## 471 PRESS INTERACTIVE TO BET DIRECT CLAIMING STKS — 1m 4f (F)

1:50 (1:51) (H ) 4-Y-0+ £1,270 (£363; £181) Stalls Low

Form RPR

0-04 **1** **King Priam (IRE)**$^{3}$ [440] 9-9-4 35.................................(b) LFletcher(3) 2 49
(MJPolglase) *mde all: rdn over 2f out: drvn ent last and styd on wl* **10/3**$^{2}$

560- **2** 3½ **Ipledgeallegiance (USA)**$^{13}$ [6240] 8-9-3 46.......................... ACulhane 1 40
(DWChapman) *trckd ldrs: hdwy to chse wnr 4f out: rdn to chal 2f out and ev chd tl drvn and one pce ent last* **7/2**$^{3}$

00-5 **3** 16 **Roppongi Dancer**$^{5}$ [426] 5-8-5 30............(bt) StephanieHollinshead(7) 4 11
(MrsNMacauley) *chsd ldrs: pushed along and outpcd 5f out: sn drvn and plugged on fnl 2f* **14/1**

0/ **4** 9 **First Class Girl**$^{595}$ [1584] 5-9-2 ...................................... MHNaughton 8 1
(CBBBooth) *towards rr: sme hdwy 1/2-way: sn rdn along and nvr a factor* **50/1**

00-0 **5** ½ **Sea Ya Maite**$^{4}$ [430] 10-9-0 30.......................................(t) LEnstone(3) 5 2
(SRBowring) *trckd ldrs: hdwy to chse ldng pair over 4f out: rdn along 3f out and sn wknd* **25/1**

110/ **6** 9 **Polish Baron (IRE)**$^{35}$ [5553] 7-9-7 70....................................... RFitzpatrick 7 —
(JWhite) *v.s.a and lost 15 l at s: a bhd* **2/1**$^{1}$

565- **7** 11 **Copplestone (IRE)**$^{22}$ [5435] 8-9-5 30..................................(p) JBramhill 6 —
(WStorey) *a rr: outpcd and bhd fr 1/2-way* **6/1**

0- **8** 26 **Oos And Ahs**$^{36}$ [5420] 4-8-6 ...................................................... TWilliams 3 —
(CWFairhurst) *cl up: rdn along over 5f out: sn wknd* **25/1**

000- **9** dist **Mawhoob (USA)**$^{27}$ [6168] 6-8-10 45.......................(v) StevenHarrison(7) 9 —
(MrsNMacauley) *a rr: wl bhd fr 1/2-way* **16/1**

2m 43.72s (1.62) **Going Correction** +0.075s/f (Slow)
**WFA** 4 from 5yo+ 4lb **9** Ran SP% **115.1**
Speed ratings: **97,94,84,78,77 71,64,47,—**CSF £15.09 TOTE £4.10: £1.40, £1.90, £3.20; EX 10.50.Polish Baron (no.2) was claimed by John Cornwall for £5,000.
**Owner** M J Polglase **Bred** Knocktoran Stud **Trained** Southwell, Notts

**FOCUS**
A dire contest and the race only concerned the front two all the way down the home straight.

**NOTEBOOK**
**King Priam(IRE)**at last found another race he could win and his rider made sure there was no messing about from the start. He only had the runner-up to worry about over the last half-mile and he proved much the more resolute.
**Ipledgeallegiance(USA)**still has to conclusively prove himself over this trip, but he had every chance to pass the winner down the home straight and either could not, or would not, go past.

**Roppongi Dancer**achieved little and has gone the wrong way since a couple of reasonable efforts over hurdles in the autumn.
**Polish Baron(IRE)**, unbeaten in three outings on Fibresand in 2002, had shown nothing over hurdles last month on his first outing for well over a year. He was standing very awkwardly in the stalls well before the race started and, despite all of his rider's urgings, when the gates opened he rooted himself to the spot and gave the field 15 lengths. He plodded around in his own time, so he at least got some exercise, and was subsequently claimed for £5,000. *Official explanation: jockey said gelding sat down in the stalls and was reluctant to race, losing many lengths*

## 472 LITTLEWOODS BET DIRECT BANDED STKS — 1m (F)

**2:20** (2:20) (H ) 3-Y-O+ — **£1,669** (£477; £238) **Stalls** Low

Form — RPR

54-1 **1** — **Rosti**[4] 428 4-9-1 45 — RoryMoore(7) 6 — 50
(PCHaslam) *trckd ldrs: hdwy to ld 2f out: rdn over 1f out: drvn ins last and hld on wl* **5/4**[1]

00-2 **2** ¾ **Simply The Guest (IRE)**[4] 434 5-9-8 35 — (t) KimTinkler 2 — 48
(DonEnricoIncisa) *dwlt and bhd: hdwy on inner 3f out: rdn over 1f out: drvn and ev ch ins last: no ex nr fin* **8/1**

062- **3** 1¼ **Diamond Orchid (IRE)**[21] 5559 4-9-1 45 — SJDonohoe(7) 3 — 46
(PDEvans) *chsd ldrs: rdn along over 2f out: drvn over 1f out and ev ch ins last tl wknd nr fin* **11/2**[2]

05-1 **4** 1¼ **Printsmith (IRE)**[4] 434 7-10-0 35 — JBramhill 11 — 49
(JRNorton) *midfield: hdwy over 3f out: chsd ldrs 2f out: sn rdn and one pce ent last* **7/1**[3]

00-2 **5** 1¼ **Tropical Son**[5] 427 5-9-8 40 — (v) DarrenWilliams 1 — 41
(DShaw) *hld up in rr: hdwy over 3f out: swtchd outside and chsd ldrs 2f out: sn rdn and one pce appr last* **16/1**

600- **6** 1¼ **Desires Destiny**[24] 6193 6-9-1 45 — MLawson(7) 10 — 38
(MBrittain) *cl up: led 3f out tl rdn and hdd 2f out: grad wknd* **25/1**

603- **7** 9 **Santa Catalina (IRE)**[24] 6193 5-9-3 45 — (t) TEaves(5) 12 — 20
(MissGayKelleway) *a rr* **12/1**

600- **8** 1¾ **Regency Malaya**[69] 5845 3-8-2 45 — (bt[1]) SRighton 13 — 17
(MFHarris) *racd wd: sn rdn along and bhd fr 1/2-way* **40/1**

040- **9** hd **Byinchka**[57] 5978 4-9-8 45 — (v[1]) ANicholls 5 — 16
(SLKeightley) *led: rdn along and hdd 3f out: sn wknd* **33/1**

000- **10** 6 **Peace Treaty (IRE)**[20] 6213 3-8-4 45 ow2 — NPollard 15 — 6
(SRBowring) *a bhd* **50/1**

000- **11** 9 **Peartree House (IRE)**[78] 5704 10-9-8 45 — ACulhane 7 — —
(DWChapman) *hld up: a rr* **14/1**

000- **12** 3 **Dr Julian (IRE)**[26] 6177 4-9-8 45 — (v) AnnStokell 9 — —
(MissAStokell) *dwlt: a rr* **50/1**

00-6 **13** 8 **Haithem (IRE)**[4] 434 7-9-8 40 — (e) TWilliams 8 — —
(DShaw) *a bhd* **25/1**

000- **14** 20 **Better Pal**[45] 6055 5-9-5 45 — LPKeniry(3) 14 — —
(PRWood) *chsd ldrs to 1/2-way: sn lost pl and bhd* **66/1**

1m 45.53s (0.93) **Going Correction** +0.075s/f (Slow) — **14** Ran SP% **122.2**
**WFA** 3 from 4yo+ 20lb
Speed ratings: **98,97,96,94,93 92,83,81,81,75 66,63,55,35**CSF £11.02 TOTE £2.00: £1.10, £2.00, £2.10; EX 15.60.
**Owner** Exors of late B M Hawkins/Lord Downshire **Bred** W C Tincknell And Mrs A Tincknell **Trained** Middleham Moor, N Yorks

**FOCUS**
Quite a competitive race of its type, and the form looks solid with the winner likely to do better.

**NOTEBOOK**
**Rosti**is progressive and that was a big advantage in a race like this. Despite facing several challengers, he was always finding plenty in front and won with a bit in hand. He has started the year off in good form and can hold his own in better company.
**Simply The Guest(IRE)**was the last to challenge and managed to reverse recent course form with Printsmith, but the winner was always comfortably holding him.
**Diamond Orchid(IRE)**needed plenty of urging along and responded to get herself into a challenging position, but there was nothing left well inside the last furlong. She probably needs a bit further.
**Printsmith(IRE)**ran a solid race under her penalty in an above-average contest of its type.
**Tropical Son**, from a yard in form, did not perform badly and should do even better in a routine contest of this class.
**Haithem(IRE)** *Official explanation: jockey said gelding lost its action*

## 473 BETDIRECT.CO.UK MEDIAN AUCTION MAIDEN STKS — 1m (F)

**2:50** (2:50) (H ) 3-5-Y-O — **£1,477** (£422; £211) **Stalls** Low

Form — RPR

040- **1** — **Cottingham (IRE)**[12] 6242 3-7-12 58 ow1 — StephanieHollinshead(7) 2 — 63
(MCChapman) *trckd ldrs: smooth hdwy 3f out: led 2f out: rdn clr appr last: styd on* **11/4**[2]

040- **2** 4 **Turks And Caicos (IRE)**[31] 6145 3-7-11 58 — RoryMoore(7) 8 — 54
(PCHaslam) *trckd ldrs: smooth hdwy on outer to ld briefly over 2f out: sn hdd and rdn: drvn: hung lft and one pce appr last* **9/4**[1]

**3** 7 **Galloway Mac** 4-9-10 — MTebbutt 5 — 40
(WAO'Gorman) *s.i.s and wl bhd: hdwy over 3f out: styd on to chse ldng pair wl over 1f out: sn rdn and one pce* **12/1**

500- **4** 15 **Pappy (IRE)**[111] 5044 3-7-13 52 — JBramhill 3 — 5
(JGGiven) *cl up: ev ch over 2f out: sn rdn and wknd* **5/1**[3]

22-6 **5** ½ **Lilian**[5] 424 4-9-0 46 — (v) TEaves(5) 6 — 4
(MissGayKelleway) *led: rdn along 3f out: sn hdd & wknd* **8/1**

030- **6** 9 **Amanda's Lad (IRE)**[30] 6149 4-9-3 40 — AndrewWebb(7) 1 — —
(MCChapman) *trckd ldrs on inner: rdn along 3f out and sn wknd* **14/1**

00- **7** 2 **Manashin**[160] 3763 4-9-5 — RFfrench 4 — —
(BSmart) *chsd ldrs to 1/2-way: sn wknd* **33/1**

036- **8** 5 **Casantella**[17] 6228 3-8-1 47 ow2 — (v) ANicholls 7 — —
(MJPolglase) *chsd ldrs: pushed along whn n.m.r 4f out: sn wknd* **9/1**

1m 45.32s (0.72) **Going Correction** +0.075s/f (Slow) — **8** Ran SP% **112.5**
**WFA** 3 from 4yo 20lb
Speed ratings: **99,95,88,73,72 63,61,56**CSF £9.03 TOTE £4.00: £1.70, £1.10, £3.60; EX 8.40.
**Owner** Twinacre Nurseries Ltd **Bred** B Kennedy **Trained** Market Rasen, Lincs

**FOCUS**
A modest maiden, yet most of the runners were rated higher than 45, and would thus be too good for most 'regional' races.

**NOTEBOOK**
**Cottingham(IRE)**ran poorly here last time but his previous form gave him every chance in what was a weak contest. He did it well enough but will find things tougher in handicap company.
**Turks And Caicos(IRE)**, another who disappointed last time having run with some promise on his sand debut at Wolverhampton, ran well enough but might be happier returning to Dunstall Park.
**Galloway Mac**shaped with promise on his belated racecourse debut for, having missed the break and given the rest four or five lengths head start, he stayed on well to finish a clear third. One would hope that there is improvement to come from him.
**Pappy(IRE)**, stepping up in trip on her sand debut, may well have needed this first run since September, but the suspicion is that she did not stay this longer trip.
**Lilian**ran her best races on turf in selling grade.
**Casantella** *Official explanation: jockey said filly hung right from halfway*

## 474 BET DIRECT FOOTBALL CASHBACKS BANDED STKS — 7f (F)

**3:20** (3:21) (H ) 3-Y-O+ — **£1,662** (£475; £237) **Stalls** Low

Form — RPR

00-3 **1** — **Sandorra**[4] 429 6-9-1 45 — MLawson(7) 1 — 53
(MBrittain) *mde virtually all: rdn clr wl over 1f out: styd on* **14/1**

630- **2** 1¾ **Eager Angel (IRE)**[17] 6232 6-9-5 45 — (p) LFletcher(3) 12 — 49
(RFMarvin) *hld up in rr: hdwy on inner 3f out: swtchd rt 2f out and sn rdn: styd on wl appr last: nt rch wnr* **16/1**

00-3 **3** 3½ **Newclose**[5] 425 4-9-8 45 — (t) ACulhane 5 — 40
(NTinkler) *hld up towards rr: hdwy 3f out: rdn to chse ldrs 2f out: sn drvn and no imp* **2/1**[1]

05-2 **4** ¾ **Brilliantrio**[4] 428 6-9-1 45 — AndrewWebb(7) 10 — 38
(MCChapman) *midfield: pushed along over 3f out: kpt on fnl 2f: nrst fin* **10/3**[2]

00-3 **5** 1½ **Champagne Rider**[4] 428 8-9-8 40 — (e) DarrenWilliams 2 — 34
(DShaw) *trckd ldrs on inner: hdwy to chse wnr 3f out: rdn and wknd 2f out* **13/2**[3]

00-5 **6** 11 **Jessie**[4] 428 5-9-8 45 — KimTinkler 3 — 7
(DonEnricoIncisa) *s.i.s and bhd: hdwy on inner to chse ldrs over 2f out: sn rdn and btn* **12/1**

00-6 **7** 6 **Landofheartsdesire (IRE)**[4] 429 5-9-3 45 — (v) TEaves(5) 9 — —
(JSWainwright) *chsd ldrs: rdn along 3f out: sn wknd* **25/1**

00-6 **8** 1¾ **Glenviews Polly (IRE)**[5] 423 4-9-5 45 — LPKeniry(3) 13 — —
(IanEmmerson) *s.i.s: a rr* **20/1**

00-0 **9** ½ **Formeric**[4] 434 8-9-8 35 — (v) JMcAuley 8 — —
(MissLCSiddall) *in tch: rdn along 1/2-way: sn wknd* **66/1**

600- **10** 13 **Caronte (IRE)**[137] 4402 4-9-8 40 — (b) JBramhill 4 — —
(SRBowring) *cl up: rdn along 3f out: wknd 2f out* **33/1**

/00- **11** 8 **Startled**[69] 5846 5-9-8 45 — MTebbutt 6 — —
(JJay) *a rr* **20/1**

300- **12** 1½ **New Prospective**[12] 6243 6-9-8 45 — ANicholls 7 — —
(DNicholls) *cl up: rdn along 3f out: sn wknd and eased over 1f out: dismntd after line* **12/1**

030- **13** 27 **Granuaile O'Malley (IRE)**[12] 6244 4-9-8 45 — SWKelly 11 — —
(PWD'Arcy) *s.i.s: hdwy and in tch 3f out: sn rdn and wknd* **10/1**

1m 31.2s (0.40) **Going Correction** +0.075s/f (Slow) — **13** Ran SP% **124.6**
Speed ratings: **100,98,94,93,91 78,72,70,69,54 45,43,12**CSF £212.83 TOTE £33.70: £8.10, £4.70, £1.40; EX 462.70.
**Owner** Mel Brittain **Bred** Theobalds Stud **Trained** Warthill, N Yorks
■ The first winner in Britain for Mark Lawson, following 16 in Canada.

**FOCUS**
A poor race but, although the form is of dubious value, the principals all had something to show recently.

**NOTEBOOK**
**Sandorra**, with the benefit of a run behind her following a five-month break, set out to make all and always held the call, for as close as her pursuers got, she never looked like being headed. This was a bad race but she has the right style of running for this track.
**Eager Angel(IRE)**has been a maiden for an eternity and, while she stayed on well from out of the pack to finish second, had she had a chance to go past the winner, one suspects that she would have declined the offer.
**Newclose**ran another fair race without improving noticeably on his previous form.
**Brilliantrio**lost her position when crowded on the first bend and was always playing catch-up thereafter.
**Champagne Rider**looked the main danger to the winner turning in, as he was still travelling well enough, but he found disappointingly little under pressure. His losing run continues.
**New Prospective** *Official explanation: jockey said gelding lost its action behind*

## 475 BET DIRECT IN VISION SKY PAGE 293 BANDED STKS — 1m 6f (F)

**3:50** (3:50) (H ) 4-Y-O+ — **£1,452** (£415; £207) **Stalls** Low

Form — RPR

26-2 **1** — **Paddy Mul**[4] 430 7-9-4 35 — (t) DRMcCabe 4 — 47
(WStorey) *hld up in tch: smooth hdwy 5f out: rdn to ld jst over 1f out: kpt on* **9/4**[1]

60-2 **2** hd **Kagoshima (IRE)**[4] 432 9-9-4 40 — (v) VHalliday 3 — 47
(JRNorton) *a.p: led 1/2-way: rdn along 2f out: drvn and hdd jst over 1f out: rallied wl under preessure ins last: jst hld* **7/2**[2]

0/0- **3** 9 **Ireland's Eye (IRE)**[250] 1051 9-9-4 30 — JBramhill 1 — 38
(JRNorton) *hld up in tch: hdwy to chse ldng pair 3f out: rdn and kpt on same pce fnl 2f* **9/1**[3]

60-3 **4** 17 **Kyalami (IRE)**[4] 432 5-9-1 30 — (e[1]) LFletcher(3) 7 — 21
(MJPolglase) *prom tl pushed along and lost pl after 5f: hdwy to chse ldrs 5f out: rdn and wknd 3f out* **7/2**[2]

050- **5** 17 **Charnwood Street (IRE)**[39] 6033 5-9-4 40 — (v) DarrenWilliams 5 — 4
(DShaw) *led 4f: styd prom tl rdn along over 5f out and sn wknd* **7/2**[2]

/0-0 **6** 3 **Kittylee**[4] 430 5-9-4 30 — (p) RFfrench 6 — 1
(MABuckley) *a bhd* **40/1**

00-0 **7** 18 **Marengo**[4] 430 10-8-11 35 — LTreadwell(7) 8 — —
(PaulJohnson) *keen: trckd ldrs tl led after 4f: pushed along and hdd 1/2-way: sn rdn and wknd over 5f out: bhd fnl 3f* **25/1**

3m 13.44s (3.84) **Going Correction** +0.075s/f (Slow) — **7** Ran SP% **113.7**
Speed ratings: **92,91,86,77,67 65,55**CSF £10.28 TOTE £2.60: £1.90, £3.30; EX 11.00 Place 6 £16.23, Place 5 £10.16.
**Owner** Gremlin Racing **Bred** G Piper **Trained** Muggleswick, Co Durham

**FOCUS**
A proper test at the trip, but a modest winning time and the form is poor.

**NOTEBOOK**
**Paddy Mul**appreciated the step up in trip and just came out on top after a long battle up the straight. This was only the second success of his career but the fact that he stays well stands him in good stead in this sort of company.
**Kagoshima(IRE)**, who stays beyond two miles, made sure this was a true stamina test and had most of his rivals in trouble turning into the straight. He battled back well after being headed but was just denied at the line. He should continue to run well in marathon contests in banded stakes grade.
**Ireland's Eye(IRE)**had been off the track since winning over hurdles in May and is nowhere near as good on the level. He ran well enough considering he probably needed the run, and he will presumably be back over timber soon.
**Kyalami(IRE)**, wearing an eyeshield for the first time, was beaten as they turned into the straight, and heading for the slower ground next to the far-side rail did not help his cause.
**Charnwood Street(IRE)**ran a disappointing race. He was receiving sharp reminders with a circuit to go, and when the tempo quickened with half a mile to run he soon began to flounder.
T/Plt: £28.50 to a £1 stake. Pool: £31,778.85. 811.80 winning tickets. T/Qpdt: £6.10 to a £1 stake. Pool: £2,519.10. 305.50 winning tickets. JR

# 441 WOLVERHAMPTON (A.W) (L-H)

Thursday, January 8

**OFFICIAL GOING: Slow**

Following 3mm of overnight rain, the meeting only passed an inspection at 12.15.

## 476 BETDIRECT.CO.UK H'CAP (DIV I) 6f (F)

1:10 (1:11) (E) (0-75,73) 4-Y-O+ £3,386 (£1,042; £521; £260) Stalls High

| Form | | | | RPR |
|---|---|---|---|---|
| 331- | 1 | | **Wainwright (IRE)**[12] 6244 4-8-12 **62** DNolan(5) 5 (PABlockley) *a.p: rdn to ld over 1f out: all out* 5/1[2] | 71 |
| 020- | 2 | *shd* | **Geronimo**[30] 6151 7-8-12 **57** (p) JQuinn 6 (MissGayKelleway) *hld up: hdwy over 2f out: swtchd rt 1f out: r.o* 8/1 | 66 |
| 100- | 3 | *nk* | **Mr Pertemps**[44] 6063 6-8-5 **55** THamilton(5) 4 (RAFahey) *sn chsng ldrs: led over 3f out: rdn and hdd over 1f out: r.o* 9/2[1] | 63 |
| 051- | 4 | *2 ½* | **St Ivian**[13] 6235 4-9-9 **68** (v) PMcCabe 3 (MrsNMacauley) *chsd ldrs: rdn over 3f out: ev ch over 1f out: no ex ins fnl f* 12/1 | 69 |
| 542- | 5 | *½* | **Time N Time Again**[33] 6138 6-9-6 **68** DAllan(3) 8 (EJAlston) *chsd ldrs: n.m.r and lost pl over 3f out: hdwy u.p over 1f out: no imp fnl f* 5/1[2] | 67 |
| 022- | 6 | *¾* | **Never Without Me**[8] 6264 4-8-2 **47** DaleGibson 9 (PJMcbride) *miud-div: hdwy over 2f out: wknd ins fnl f* 9/2[1] | 44 |
| 000- | 7 | *1 ¼* | **Turn Around**[33] 6132 4-9-7 **66** EAhern 7 (BWHills) *sn outpcd: hdwy over 2f out: wknd over 1f out* 7/1[3] | 59 |
| 051- | 8 | *10* | **Noble Locks (IRE)**[13] 6236 6-9-7 **73** CarloBandiera(7) 2 (JWUnett) *mid-div: wknd 1/2-way* 9/1 | 36 |
| 600- | 9 | *½* | **Prince Of Blues (IRE)**[13] 6236 6-9-5 **67** LisaJones(3) 1 (MMullineaux) *chsd ldrs over 3f* 20/1 | 29 |
| 000- | 10 | *nk* | **Telepathic (IRE)**[33] 6132 4-9-2 **66** PBradley(5) 10 (ABerry) *led: hdd over 3f out: wknd over 1f out* 40/1 | 27 |

1m 18.8s (3.10) **Going Correction** +0.35s/f (Slow) **10** Ran SP% **118.2**
Speed ratings: **93,92,92,89,88 87,85,72,71,71**CSF £45.39 CT £195.03 TOTE £5.10: £1.60, £3.60, £1.50; EX 49.60.
**Owner** David Wright **Bred** Tony Lewis **Trained** Southwell, Notts
■ Stewards Enquiry : J Quinn three-day ban: used whip with excessive frequency, without giving gelding time to respond and down the shoulder in the forehand position (Jan 19-21)

**FOCUS**
A moderate winning time for the class of race (over two seconds slower than the second division), but competitive enough stuff in any case and the front three pulled clear, so the form should work out.

**NOTEBOOK**
**Wainwright(IRE)** took 14 attempts to get off the mark but now he has got the hang of things he followed-up his recent Southwell maiden success. It took all of Nolan's strength from the saddle to hold off the runner-up and a rise in the weights will make the hat-trick bid quite tough, but his yard remain in great form.
**Geronimo**, 5lb lower than when last successful, had to be switched right to get a clear run and would have won this in another stride or two. That said, he is basically a very hard horse to win with and is not guaranteed to confirm this promise next time.
**Mr Pertemps**, 6lb higher than when winning at Southwell in March, ran his race and can have no excuses. He looks capable of winning a similar event whilst in the form, possibly back at Southwell where he is three from seven.
**St Ivian**, up 5lb for his recent course and distance success, had every chance and can have no excuses.
**Time N Time Again** got shuffled back with about three furlongs to go and was never out of the kickback thereafter.
**Never Without Me** looked to have every chance.

## 477 BET DIRECT ON SKY ACTIVE APPRENTICE H'CAP 1m 100y(F)

1:40 (1:40) (G) (0-70,65) 3-Y-O+ £2,604 (£744; £372) Stalls High

| Form | | | | RPR |
|---|---|---|---|---|
| 330- | 1 | | **Ovigo (GER)**[20] 6215 5-9-6 **65** DerekNolan(5) 3 (PABlockley) *hld up and bhd: hdwy and hung lft fr over 2f out: led ins fnl f: comf* 11/4[2] | 78 |
| 32-1 | 2 | *1 ¼* | **Rock Concert**[6] 412 6-9-5 **62** 6ex NataliaGemelova(3) 4 (IWMcinnes) *set stdy pce: rdn over 2f out: edgd rt over 1f out: hdd and unable qck ins fnl f* 2/1[1] | 72 |
| 014- | 3 | *2 ½* | **Spy Gun (USA)**[23] 6202 4-9-6 **60** NChalmers 5 (TWall) *a.p: rdn and hung lft over 1f out: no ex fnl f* 4/1[3] | 65 |
| 211- | 4 | *5* | **Mutarafaa (USA)**[13] 6241 5-9-4 **58** (e) THamilton 2 (DShaw) *chsd ldr 6f: wknd over 1f out* 11/4[2] | 52 |
| 20-0 | 5 | *10* | **T K O Gym**[4] 428 5-8-5 **45** JFMcDonald 1 (DNicholls) *chsd ldrs 5f* 14/1 | 18 |

1m 54.74s (3.74) **Going Correction** +0.35s/f (Slow) **5** Ran SP% **113.3**
Speed ratings: **95,93,91,86,76**CSF £8.98 TOTE £4.50: £1.80, £1.20; EX 7.70.
**Owner** The Dilum Partnership **Bred** Gestut Franken **Trained** Southwell, Notts

**FOCUS**
A moderate winning time, but good form for the grade and an impressive performance from Ovigo.

**NOTEBOOK**
**Ovigo(GER)**, back at Wolverhampton for the first time since finishing third in a much better race in November, was held up off just a moderate gallop but quickened up in good style and ran out a comfortable winner, despite hanging left under a hands and heels ride. This track seems to suit best and he could well follow-up round here.
**Rock Concert**, under a 6lb penalty for her recent course success over an extended nine furlongs, had every chance but found the winner too good.
**Spy Gun(USA)**, 6lb higher than when winning at Southwell two starts back, was a little disappointing on this step back up in trip.
**Mutarafaa(USA)**, chasing the hat-trick, was below form and may have preferred a stronger pace. *Official explanation: jockey said gelding pulled up lame*
**T K O Gym**, up in trip with the visor left off, dropped out very tamely.

## 478 BET DIRECT ON 0800 32 93 93 CLAIMING STKS 1m 4f (F)

2:10 (2:10) (F) 4-Y-O+ £2,919 (£834; £417) Stalls High

| Form | | | | RPR |
|---|---|---|---|---|
| 525- | 1 | | **Paradise Valley**[33] 6139 4-8-7 45 (t) CCatlin 7 (MrsStefLiddiard) *hld up: hdwy over 3f out: styd on to ld wl ins fnl f* 11/2 | 57 |
| 015- | 2 | *1* | **Claptrap**[27] 6168 4-8-6 59 FPFerris(3) 4 (RBrotherton) *hld up: hdwy over 5f out: rdn to ld ins fnl f: sn hdd and unable qck* 7/2[3] | 57 |
| 521- | 3 | *1 ½* | **Dancing Phantom**[22] 5819 9-9-4 77 SHitchcott(3) 6 (JamesMoffatt) *w ldr: led 6f out: rdn over 3f out: hdd and no ex ins fnl f* 9/4[2] | 63 |
| 005- | 4 | *6* | **El Pedro**[13] 6240 5-8-12 45 MSavage(5) 1 (NEBerry) *hld up: hdwy over 6f out: rdn and ev ch over 1f out: sn wknd* 40/1 | 50 |
| 200- | 5 | *8* | **Young Owen**[20] 2048 6-8-7 70 JQuinn 3 (MrsLBNormile) *prom: jnd ldrs over 4f out: wknd over 2f out* 14/1 | 28 |
| 200- | 6 | *1 ¾* | **La Rose**[13] 6240 4-7-9 35 (v) LisaJones(3) 8 (JWUnett) *hld up: a bhd* 66/1 | 20 |
| 601- | 7 | *18* | **Inver Gold**[216] 2178 7-9-7 74 SWhitworth 5 (AGNewcombe) *led to 1/2-way: wknd wl over 3f out* 2/1[1] | 12 |
| 350- | 8 | *23* | **Love's Design (IRE)**[255] 1271 7-8-9 52 JTate 2 (MissSJWilton) *plld hrd and prom: wknd over 3f out* 33/1 | — |

2m 47.14s (5.64) **Going Correction** +0.35s/f (Slow)
**WFA** 4 from 5yo+ 4lb **8** Ran SP% **115.2**
Speed ratings: **95,94,93,89,84 82,70,55**CSF £25.03 TOTE £5.00: £1.70, £1.80, £1.10; EX 20.00.
**Owner** Valley Fencing **Bred** Brook Stud Ltd **Trained** Great Shefford, Berks

**FOCUS**
A weak claimer, but run at a good pace from the off, thanks mainly to the favourite Inver Gold, who does not usually make the running but was sent to the front early by Whitworth.

**NOTEBOOK**
**Paradise Valley** had plenty to find at the weights but, held up off the decent gallop on this drop back from two miles, he responded well to strong pressure to get on top close home. The Handicapper is likely to take a dim view of this, but he should continue to go well for his shrewd yard if kept to this sort of grade.
**Claptrap**, a beaten favourite over a mile six at Southwell last time, posted a better effort this time over a trip shorter of his optimum. He is not very easy to win with but is worth respecting at this sort of level.
**Dancing Phantom**, back on the level after a couple of unsuccessful spins over hurdles, likes his own way out in front but was taken on for the lead by Inver Gold. However, he still posted a creditable enough effort.
**El Pedro**, fifth in a seller over course and distance last time, had every chance.
**Young Owen**, back on the level after a few spins over hurdles, had very little offer on the run to the line.
**Inver Gold**, returning from a 216-day break, does not usually make the running but was sent into an early lead by Whitworth. He gradually dropped out when the pace quickened and was eventually well beaten, but he can do better with more patient tactics with this run under his belt. *Official explanation: jockey said horse had a breathing problem*

## 479 LITTLEWOODS BET DIRECT MAIDEN STKS 5f (F)

2:40 (2:41) (D) 4-Y-O+ £3,227 (£922; £461) Stalls High

| Form | | | | RPR |
|---|---|---|---|---|
| 034- | 1 | | **Mynd**[56] 5988 4-9-0 58 DeanMcKeown 3 (RMWhitaker) *led over 3f: rallied to ld wl ins fnl f* 3/1[2] | 65 |
| 423- | 2 | *nk* | **Blueberry Rhyme**[17] 6232 5-9-0 68 (v) DSweeney 6 (PJMakin) *trckd ldr: led over 1f out: sn rdn: edgd rt and hdd wl ins fnl f* 1/1[1] | 64 |
| 434- | 3 | *3 ½* | **Lucius Verrus (USA)**[12] 6244 4-8-9 50 THamilton(5) 8 (DShaw) *sn pushed along in rr: hdwy u.p over 1f out: nt rch ldrs* 8/1 | 52 |
| 626- | 4 | *nk* | **Inching**[12] 6244 4-8-9 51 EAhern 2 (RMHCowell) *chsd ldrs: rdn 1/2-way: styd on same pce fnl 2f* 7/2[3] | 46 |
| 00-4 | 5 | *8* | **Somethingabouther**[3] 444 4-8-9 40 CCatlin 5 (PWHiatt) *chsd ldrs 3f* 20/1 | 18 |
| 0- | 6 | *7* | **Eternal Beauty (USA)**[124] 4731 4-8-9 SDrowne 1 (MJWallace) *sn outpcd and bhd* 12/1 | — |
| 060- | 7 | *hd* | **Velocitys Image (IRE)**[94] 5420 4-8-6 40 DAllan(3) 4 (EJAlston) *sn outpcd* 40/1 | — |

63.27 secs (0.67) **Going Correction** +0.35s/f (Slow) **7** Ran SP% **123.2**
Speed ratings: **108,107,101,101,88 77,77**CSF £7.07 TOTE £4.80: £1.90, £1.50; EX 8.50.
**Owner** Derek And Jean Clee **Bred** John Rose **Trained** Scarcroft, W Yorks
■ Stewards Enquiry : D Sweeney two-day ban: used whip with excessive frequency and without giving gelding time to respond (Jan 19,20)

**FOCUS**
A decent enough time, but a moderate maiden, with the runner-up well below form.

**NOTEBOOK**
**Mynd**, dropping back to five furlongs and switching from Polytrack to Fibresand, got off the mark under a positive ride from McKeown, who kept things simple from the gate. He could well follow up under a penalty.
**Blueberry Rhyme**, reportedly struck into when a beaten favourite over course and distance last time, had every chance this time but was beaten by the better horse. His time will come, but he is expensive to follow.
**Lucius Verrus(USA)**, dropped back to five furlongs, found the trip too short and should appreciate a step up in trip.
**Inching** has had plenty of chances.
**Eternal Beauty(USA)** should do better over further.

## 480 BETDIRECT.CO.UK H'CAP (DIV II) 6f (F)

3:10 (3:10) (E) (0-75,72) 4-Y-O+ £3,386 (£1,042; £521; £260) Stalls High

| Form | | | | RPR |
|---|---|---|---|---|
| 052- | 1 | | **Soba Jones**[66] 5909 7-9-7 66 JEdmunds 2 (JBalding) *chsd ldr: led 2f out: rdn clr fnl f* 6/1[2] | 85 |
| 002- | 2 | *5* | **Playtime Blue**[8] 6265 4-9-0 59 GBaker 1 (KRBurke) *chsd ldrs: rdn 1/2-way: styd on same pce appr fnl f* 12/1 | 63 |
| 326- | 3 | *nk* | **Rafters Music (IRE)**[23] 6199 9-9-13 72 NCallan 5 (JulianPoulton) *outpcd: hdwy over 1f out: edgd lft ins fnl f: nt rch ldrs* 7/1[3] | 75 |
| 000- | 4 | *½* | **Lady Natilda**[40] 6100 4-8-3 48 PaulEddery 6 (DHaydnJones) *outpcd: hdwy u.p over 1f out: nrst fin* 33/1 | 50 |
| 004- | 5 | *¾* | **New Options**[23] 6199 7-9-8 67 (b) MFenton 4 (WJMusson) *chsd ldrs: rdn over 2f out: btn whn n.m.r ins fnl f* 13/8[1] | 66 |
| 141- | 6 | *nk* | **Lady Pekan**[8] 6264 5-9-1 63 6ex (b) FPFerris(3) 7 (PSMcentee) *led 4f: wknd fnl f* 8/1 | 61 |
| 660- | 7 | *1 ¾* | **Our Chelsea Blue (USA)**[27] 6166 6-8-11 56 SWhitworth 3 (AWCarroll) *s.s: hdwy over 3f out: ev ch 2f out: wknd fnl f* 10/1 | 49 |
| 03-0 | 8 | *1* | **Gone'N'Dunnett (IRE)**[2] 454 5-9-5 69 (v) NChalmers(5) 10 (MrsCADunnett) *chsd ldrs over 4f* 8/1 | 59 |
| 000- | 9 | *1 ¾* | **Blakeshall Quest**[13] 6235 4-9-7 66 CCatlin 8 (RBrotherton) *chsd ldrs over 3f* 33/1 | 51 |
| 105- | 10 | *1* | **If By Chance**[41] 6084 6-9-6 68 SHitchcott(3) 9 (RCraggs) *chsd ldrs 4f* 7/1[3] | 50 |

1m 16.52s (0.82) **Going Correction** +0.35s/f (Slow) **10** Ran SP% **122.3**
Speed ratings: **108,101,100,100,99 98,96,95,92,91**CSF £79.26 CT £521.66 TOTE £6.90: £2.10, £3.40, £1.70; EX 68.40.
**Owner** R L Crowe **Bred** Mrs M J Hills **Trained** Scrooby, Notts

**FOCUS**
An impressive performance from Soba Jones, who recorded a time 2.28 seconds faster than the first division.

**NOTEBOOK**
**Soba Jones**, 4lb higher than when winning at Southwell in February, ran out an impressive winner on his first start for 66 days. He could well follow up.
**Playtime Blue**, runner-up over five furlongs here last time, ran another solid race but the winner was far too good.
**Rafters Music(IRE)** tends to run well without winning these days and that was again the case. He was outpaced early on and may be worth another try over seven furlongs.
**Lady Natilda** could not go the pace early and was brought very wide in the straight. She stuck on well for pressure, but simply had too much ground to make up.
**New Options**, up a furlong in trip and with the blinkers back on, was a little bit disappointing. He is still looking for his first win in this country.

## 481 ALLWEATHER-RACING.COM (S) STKS 7f (F)
3:40 (3:40) (G) 4-Y-0+ £2,597 (£742; £371) Stalls High

Form RPR
06-3 **1** **Star Lad (IRE)**[5] 423 4-8-8 47 (v) FPFerris(3) 1 57
(RBrotherton) *led over 5f: lft clr 1f out* **14/1**[3]
64-1 **2** 3 ½ **Repeat (IRE)**[5] 423 4-8-11 51 MFenton 2 48
(MissGayKelleway) *chsd ldrs: rdn over 2f out: btn over 1f out: lft 2nd ins fnl f* **10/11**[1]
60-0 **3** 3 **Tefi**[4] 429 6-8-11 45 (bt) JEdmunds 4 41
(JBalding) *chsd wnr: rdn over 2f out: wknd over 1f out: lft 3rd ins fnl f* **33/1**
433- **P** **Senor Miro**[29] 6163 6-8-11 54 CCatlin 3 —
(JAkehurst) *hld up in tch: led on bit over 1f out: sn p.u and hdd: dead* **6/5**[2]

1m 32.72s (2.52) **Going Correction** +0.35s/f (Slow) **4** Ran SP% **107.4**
Speed ratings: **99,95,91,—**CSF £27.67 TOTE £19.90; EX 50.50.There was no bid for the winner.
**Owner** R Austin & Mrs P Austin **Bred** R N Auld **Trained** Elmley Castle, Worcs

**FOCUS**
A poor turnout for this seller which would have been won by Senor Miro had that one not broken a leg. The form looks unreliable.

**NOTEBOOK**
**Star Lad(IRE)**, just over three and a half lengths behind Repeat in a Class H seller over course and distance last time, reversed that placing on 5lb better terms, but would have been second had Senor Miro not broken a leg in the straight.
**Repeat(IRE)** had Star Lad just over three and a half lengths behind him when winning a Class H seller over course and distance last time but, on 5lb worse terms, he was unable to confirm those placings.
**Tefi** can have no excuses.
**Senor Miro** would have won this but for sadly breaking a leg in the straight.

## 482 FREE £25 BONUS @ LITTLEWOODSPOKER.COM H'CAP 1m 1f 79y(F)
4:10 (4:10) (F) (0-65,64) 3-Y-O £3,290 (£940; £470) Stalls High

Form RPR
004- **1** **Yankeedoodledandy (IRE)**[26] 6173 3-7-9 45 DFentiman(7) 4 63
(PCHaslam) *chsd ldrs: rdn to ld 1f out: sn clr* **5/2**[1]
544- **2** 7 **Bretton**[8] 6269 3-8-2 45 (b) DaleGibson 9 49
(RHollinshead) *led over 7f out: rdn and hdd 1f out: nt run on* **6/1**
000- **3** 8 **Cassanos (IRE)**[26] 6175 3-9-0 57 MFenton 2 45
(MissGayKelleway) *led 1f: sn lost pl: n.d after* **4/1**[3]
033- **4** 4 **Keltic Rainbow (IRE)**[52] 6012 3-9-1 58 PaulEddery 7 38
(DHaydnJones) *hld up: effrt over 4f out: sn rdn and wknd: bhd whn hung lft over 1f out* **3/1**[2]
000- **5** 2 ½ **Rumour Mill (IRE)**[37] 6115 3-9-0 62 (p) MSavage(5) 5 37
(NEBerry) *chsd ldrs: hung lft and wknd over 1f out* **33/1**
005- **6** shd **Limit Down (IRE)**[22] 6203 3-9-0 57 SDrowne 8 32
(MJWallace) *prom: rdn over 4f out: wknd over 2f out* **13/2**
240- **7** 6 **Lady Bahia (IRE)**[80] 5677 3-9-7 64 TWoodley 6 27
(RPElliott) *s.s: rcvrd to ld after 1f: sn hdd: wknd over 2f out* **14/1**
000- **8** 2 ½ **One Alone**[23] 6197 3-8-6 49 JoannaBadger 3 7
(JGGiven) *sn outpcd* **20/1**
000- **9** ½ **Tortuette**[69] 5845 3-7-13 45 LisaJones(3) 1 2
(Jean-ReneAuvray) *hld up: wknd 4f out* **33/1**

2m 4.51s (1.61) **Going Correction** +0.35s/f (Slow) **9** Ran SP% **118.5**
Speed ratings: **106,99,92,89,86 86,81,79,78**CSF £18.22 CT £58.01 TOTE £4.50: £1.10, £1.90, £1.50; EX 25.70 Place 6 £316.70, Place 5 £155.79.
**Owner** K Tyre **Bred** B Kennedy **Trained** Middleham Moor, N Yorks

**FOCUS**
This was just a modest race, but Yankeedoodledandy ran out a very impressive winner and posted a smart time for the class of race in the process. He looks progressive.

**NOTEBOOK**
**Yankeedoodledandy(IRE)**, stepping up from a mile, ran out a most impressive winner. He readily brushed aside Bretton, who got his own way out in front, and finished 15 lengths clear of the third. He should be able to follow up.
**Bretton**, fourth in a seller over an extended mile here last time, got his own way out in front but had no answer to the winner's turn of foot.
**Cassanos(IRE)**, making his handicap debut, never really threatened.
**Keltic Rainbow(IRE)**, racing for the first time since the middle of November, failed to build on the promise she showed in maiden company. *Official explanation: jockey said filly had hung left*
**Rumour Mill(IRE)** never threatened in first time cheekpieces.
T/Plt: £193.10 to a £1 stake. Pool: £30,969.35. 117.05 winning tickets. T/Qpdt: £19.50 to a £1 stake. Pool: £2,527.50. 95.50 winning tickets. CR

# 476 WOLVERHAMPTON (A.W) (L-H)
Friday, January 9

**OFFICIAL GOING: Standard**
Wind: slt bhd Weather: fine

## 483 BET DIRECT ON SKY ACTIVE AMATEUR RIDERS' H'CAP 2m 46y(F)
1:10 (1:10) (F) (0-65,74) 4-Y-O+ £2,919 (£834; £417) Stalls Low

Form RPR
61-2 **1** **Phantom Stock**[3] 461 4-9-11 **55** 6ex MrNPearce(7) 6 70
(WJarvis) *hld up: hdwy on ins over 4f out: rdn to ld over 2f out: clr fnl f: styd on wl* **6/4**[1]
1/6- **2** 5 **Marmaduke (IRE)**[13] 6247 8-11-3 **61** MrsSBosley 2 70
(MPitman) *led after 1f: rdn and hdd over 2f out: one pce* **11/2**[2]
11-4 **3** 2 ½ **Vincent**[3] 461 9-10-2 **46** MrsMMorris 11 52
(JohnAHarris) *hld up: hdwy over 5f out: rdn 3f out: one pce fnl 2f* **7/1**
560- **4** 1 ½ **Bustling Rio (IRE)**[47] 3120 8-11-5 **63** MsCWilliams 10 67
(PCHaslam) *hld up: hdwy over 5f out: rdn 3f out: one pce fnl 2f* **7/1**
435- **5** 2 ½ **Joely Green**[126] 4710 7-10-12 **59** (b) MrsEmmaLittmoden(3) 7 60
(NPLittmoden) *s.i.s: hld up: stdy hdwy over 6f out: rdn and no imp fnl 3f* **14/1**
43-2 **6** 19 **Fairmorning (IRE)**[4] 446 5-9-5 **40** MissJCWilliams(5) 8 18
(JWUnett) *hld up in tch: chsd ldr over 5f out tl over 4f out: sn wknd* **7/1**
301- **7** 12 **Adalpour (IRE)**[18] 6233 6-10-1 **52** MissETucker(7) 1 16
(DBurchell) *s.v.s: sn in tch: wknd 4f out* **13/2**[3]
450- **8** 26 **Moyne Pleasure (IRE)**[13] 6247 6-9-10 **45** MrPEvans(5) 3 —
(PaulJohnson) *prom 8f: t.o fnl 5f* **20/1**
00-0 **9** 3 ½ **Christmas Truce (IRE)**[3] 455 5-11-9 **74** ow9(p) MrMichaelMurphy(7) 5 —
(IanWilliams) *led 1f: w ldr tl rdn over 5f out: sn lost pl: t.o fnl 4f* **33/1**
064/ **10** 26 **Mighty Max**[247] 3944 6-9-5 **42** ow2 (t) MrGDenvir(7) 9 —
(GAHam) *t.k.h in tch: lost pl after 6f: t.o fnl 6f* **50/1**

3m 44.09s (1.79) **Going Correction** +0.05s/f (Slow)
**WFA** 4 from 5yo+ 7lb **10** Ran SP% **122.5**
Speed ratings: **97,94,93,92,91 81,75,62,61,48**CSF £10.39 CT £47.99 TOTE £2.50: £1.40, £1.20, £2.40; EX 21.50.
**Owner** The L E H Partnership **Bred** Brook Stud Ltd **Trained** Newmarket, Suffolk

**FOCUS**
A good opportunity for the well-handicapped Phantom Stock to get back on the winning trail after a disappointing defeat at Southwell recently. This looks fair form, and the runner-up will still be well-treated when reassessed.

**NOTEBOOK**
**Phantom Stock**did not handle the surface at Southwell when sent off at odds-on there three days earlier, but he bounced right back to his best on his return to this track. Always travelling well, he moved smoothly into the lead rounding the turn into the straight and drew clear for an easy win. As the staying division is so weak on the All-Weather there is every chance he will be able to defy the Handicapper's inevitable vengeance.
**Marmaduke(IRE)**did nothing wrong but just met a very well-handicapped rival. He should soon be winning again, and it is worth noting that he acts on all three All-Weather tracks.
**Vincent**is a thorough stayer, but he has his limitations and they were exposed on this occasion.
**Bustling Rio(IRE)**, having his first outing since being well beaten over hurdles at Aintree in November, looks handicapped near his best at present.
**Joely Green**, having his first outing since September, hails from a stable struggling for winners.

## 484 PRESS INTERACTIVE TO BET DIRECT MAIDEN STKS 1m 4f (F)
1:40 (1:40) (D) 4-Y-O+ £3,425 (£1,054; £527; £263) Stalls Low

Form RPR
000- **1** **Cool Bathwick (IRE)**[11] 6249 5-9-4 56 MartinDwyer 3 65
(BRMillman) *led 1f: w ldr: led again over 3f out: rdn over 2f out: r.o wl* **11/1**
006- **2** 3 ½ **Retail Therapy (IRE)**[10] 6259 4-8-9 35 RFfrench 8 55
(MABuckley) *hld up: sn bhd: hdwy 4f out: sn rdn: edgd lft over 1f out: styd on ins fnl f: nt trble wnr* **25/1**
**3** ½ **Munfarid (IRE)**[189] 2974 4-9-0 75 (t) SDrowne 12 59
(PGMurphy) *hld up: hdwy over 4f out: rdn over 2f out: sn chsng wnr: no imp* **7/2**[2]
0- **4** 2 **Bestseller**[185] 3078 4-8-9 RHavlin 10 51
(JGMO'Shea) *a.p: rdn over 2f out: wknd fnl f* **20/1**
2/6- **5** 2 ½ **Luxi River (USA)**[95] 5431 4-8-9 66 DNolan(5) 1 52
(PABlockley) *t.k.h in tch: jnd ldrs: rdn over 3f out: wknd wl over 1f out* **3/1**[1]
25-0 **6** 2 **Exit To Heaven**[4] 440 4-8-9 58 MFenton 4 44
(MissGayKelleway) *hld up and plld hrd: hdwy over 4f out: rdn over 3f out: wknd over 2f out* **4/1**[3]
264- **7** 3 ½ **Estimate**[58] 5980 4-8-9 60 SWhitworth 6 39
(JohnAHarris) *hld up: hdwy over 5f out: wknd 3f out* **9/2**
0- **8** 1 ½ **Sean's Memory (USA)**[27] 6177 4-9-0 CCatlin 2 42
(MrsCADunnett) *a bhd* **40/1**
00-5 **9** 20 **Young Owen**[1] 478 6-9-4 70 EAhern 9 12
(MrsLBNormile) *s.s: led after 1f: rdn and hdd over 3f out: wknd qckly: t.o* **7/1**
50- **10** 2 **Just Red**[69] 5879 6-9-4 ACulhane 5 9
(RHollinshead) *hld up: hdwy over 6f out: rdn over 4f out: sn wknd: t.o* **25/1**

2m 42.51s (1.01) **Going Correction** +0.05s/f (Slow)
**WFA** 4 from 5yo+ 4lb **10** Ran SP% **121.1**
Speed ratings: **98,95,95,94,92 91,88,87,74,73**CSF £258.30 TOTE £17.00: £3.80, £9.90, £1.50; EX 168.70.
**Owner** W Clifford **Bred** Gaucho Ltd **Trained** Kentisbeare, Devon

**FOCUS**
A weak maiden, although the runner-up looks an improved performer.

**NOTEBOOK**
**Cool Bathwick(IRE)**had not shown enough on his previous All-Weather starts to suggest that he could win even this modest contest, but the combination of a switch to Wolverhampton for the first time and adoption of front-running tactics did the trick.
**Retail Therapy(IRE)**had no chance on official ratings, being rated only 35, but she ran on strongly towards the end of the race and this two-mile hurdles winner shapes as though she will get farther.
**Munfarid(IRE)**, a Hamdan Al Maktoum cast-off, formerly trained in Ireland by Kevin Prendergast, was having his first start for his new stable and his first experience of the All-Weather. On this evidence he looks flattered by his official rating of 75.
**Bestseller**, well beaten in a Newmarket maiden on her only previous start, six months previously, has changed stables and should come on for the run.
**Luxi River(USA)**, who has had only six runs in his career but has been with three different trainers during that time, was beaten on the turn into the straight. Connections will be hoping the Handicapper drops him a few pounds for this.
**Exit To Heaven**did not help herself by taking quite a hold in the early stages.

## 485 LITTLEWOODS BET DIRECT CONDITIONS STKS 1m 100y(F)
2:10 (2:11) (C) 4-Y-O+ £7,186 (£2,725; £1,362; £619) Stalls Low

Form RPR
0/0- **1** **Hail The Chief**[62] 5946 7-9-0 100 ANicholls 7 106
(DNicholls) *a.p: led over 2f out: sn rdn: r.o wl* **11/2**
225- **2** 4 **Lakota Brave**[9] 6268 10-9-0 90 SDrowne 8 98
(MrsStefLiddiard) *hld up in tch: rdn over 3f out: wnt 2nd over 1f out: no ch w wnr* **5/2**[2]
000- **3** 1 ¾ **Action Fighter (GER)**[11] 6252 4-8-11 93 (p) J-PGuillambert(3) 5 94
(NPLittmoden) *led: rdn and hdd over 2f out: edgd rt and wknd over 1f out* **20/1**
600- **4** 3 **Lundy's Lane (IRE)**[9] 6268 4-9-10 100 (b[1]) EAhern 9 98
(CEBrittain) *hld up: stdy hdwy 6f out: rdn over 3f out: wknd over 2f out* **5/1**[3]
520- **5** 2 ½ **Golden Chalice (IRE)**[48] 6050 5-9-0 88 MartinDwyer 1 83
(AMBalding) *chsd ldr tl rdn 3f out: sn wknd* **15/8**[1]
02-6 **6** 2 ½ **First Maite**[4] 437 11-9-0 71 JBramhill 4 78
(SRBowring) *dropped rr and rdn over 6f out: n.d after* **14/1**
0/0- **7** 7 **Midshipman**[338] 468 6-9-0 92 PJScallan 6 63
(AWCarroll) *rdn over 4f out: a bhd* **12/1**

650- **8** *dist* **Muqtadi (IRE)**[83] 5279 6-9-0 51 RWinston 3 —
(MQuinn) *bhd: rdn over 4f out: sn lost tch: t.o* **100/1**

1m 49.64s (-1.36) **Going Correction** +0.05s/f (Slow) **8** Ran SP% **115.5**

Speed ratings: **108,104,102,99,96 94,87,—**CSF £19.90 TOTE £5.40: £1.20, £1.20, £8.40; EX 28.20.

**Owner** Peter M Crane **Bred** Green Meadow Stud And P Crane **Trained** Sessay, N Yorks

**FOCUS**

This was a decent contest for the track, run in a good time, and the winner looked back to form for his new stable.

**NOTEBOOK**

**Hail The Chief**had an outing on turf in November but this was his first start on his favourite surface since returning from the US, where he won three races on dirt, two of which were Graded handicaps. Successful in four of his previous five starts here, his chance depended on whether he still retained the brilliance of old. He won in style but, shamefully, due to the lack of opportunities for horses of his calibre, he may not be seen at Dunstall Park again this season.

**Lakota Brave**did as much as he could and beat the rest fair and square, but he was up against one of the best round here and had to settle for second.

**Action Fighter(GER)**, three times a winner in Germany, did not enjoy the Polytrack at Lingfield much, but the step up in trip, application of cheekpieces and switch to Fibresand brought about a much improved display.

**Lundy's Lane(IRE)**had quite a task on, conceding 10lb all round, and he did not disgrace himself in the circumstances.

**Golden Chalice(IRE)**was travelling best of all turning out of the back straight, but he soon dropped away once pressure was applied. There remains a question mark over him with regards to All-Weather racing.

**First Maite**had it all to do in this grade and never got competitive.

**Midshipman**, a useful tool around here in the past, has clearly had his problems and was having only his second outing in the best part of two years, and his first since February 2003. He has a long way to go to prove he retains his ability.

## 486 BET DIRECT ON 0800 32 93 93 STKS SHOWCASE H'CAP 6f (F)

**2:40** (2:40) (C ) (0-100,98) 3-Y-0+ **£10,192** (£3,136; £1,568; £784) **Stalls** Low

Form RPR

000- **1** **Massey**[20] 6225 8-9-6 **90** DMernagh 3 102
(TDBarron) *mde all: rdn over 2f out: edgd rt over 1f out: drvn out* **6/1**[2]

210- **2** *1 ¼* **Flint River**[48] 6050 6-8-8 **81** LFletcher[(3)] 6 89
(HMorrison) *chsd ldrs: lost pl 4f out: rdn and hdwy over 1f out: r.o to take 2nd post* **5/2**[1]

541- **3** *shd* **Zarzu**[31] 6154 5-8-10 **85** RThomas[(5)] 7 93
(CRDore) *hld up in rr: hdwy over 2f out: rdn wl over 1f out: r.o one pce fnl f* **13/2**[3]

000- **4** *nk* **Bond Boy**[51] 6030 7-9-6 **90** CCatlin 2 97
(BSmart) *a.p: rdn over 2f out: kpt on same pce fnl f* **12/1**

012- **5** *2* **Bond Playboy**[31] 6154 4-9-5 **89** RFfrench 12 90
(BSmart) *a.p: rdn over 2f out: wknd ins fnl f* **6/1**[2]

00-6 **6** *3 ½* **No Time (IRE)**[6] 417 4-8-13 **83** EAhern 13 74
(MJPolglase) *chsd ldrs: rdn over 3f out: wknd over 1f out* **7/1**

160- **7** *1 ½* **Trinculo (IRE)**[20] 6225 7-9-5 **92** (p) J-PGuillambert[(3)] 8 78
(NPLittmoden) *bhd tl hdwy on outside 3f out: no further prog fnl 2f* **16/1**

516- **8** *½* **Canterloupe (IRE)**[25] 6192 6-8-12 **82** DSweeney 10 67
(PJMakin) *prom: rdn 3f out: wknd over 1f out* **9/1**

003- **9** *shd* **Hand Chime**[11] 6252 7-8-10 **87** DanielleDeverson[(7)] 5 71
(WJHaggas) *s.i.s: sme hdwy over 1f out: n.d* **12/1**

000- **10** *1* **Sundried Tomato**[11] 6252 5-8-12 **85** LisaJones[(3)] 4 66
(PWHiatt) *prom over 2f* **11/1**

040- **11** *5* **Flying Treaty (USA)**[91] 5469 7-9-4 **88** AnnStokell 1 54
(MissAStokell) *chsd ldrs: rdn over 3f out: wknd over 1f out* **50/1**

000- **12** *11* **Beauvrai**[188] 2990 4-9-6 **90** RWinston 9 23
(JJQuinn) *hld up: rdn over 2f out: bhd fnl 2f* **25/1**

1m 13.87s (-1.83) **Going Correction** +0.05s/f (Slow) **12** Ran SP% **128.4**

Speed ratings: **114,112,112,111,109 104,102,101,101,100 93,79**CSF £23.19 CT £108.75 TOTE £8.10: £2.70, £1.20, £2.90; EX 44.60 Trifecta £329.80 Pool £836.26, 1.80 w/u.

**Owner** J Edward Boynton **Bred** Sheikh Mohammed Bin Rashid Al Maktoum **Trained** Maunby, N Yorks

■ Stewards Enquiry : R Winston caution: careless riding

**FOCUS**

A classy handicap, run in a very good time. The form looks strong and should throw up plenty of future winners.

**NOTEBOOK**

**Massey**has seen his mark drop 5lb this winter and found himself running off a rating 1lb lower than his last winning mark. With trip and track to suit, he bounced back to form, making every yard of the running, but if he is to win another handicap in the near future it will be off a mark higher than he has ever won off in the past.

**Flint River**came in for a lot of support in the market, even though most of his best form last year was over seven furlongs and a mile. Sure enough, he found himself outpaced before running on really well in the closing stages. He is primed to win, but it will surely be over seven furlongs or farther, not over six.

**Zarzu**ran a cracker off a career-high mark and justified the Handicapper's decision to put him up 6lb for his latest win.

**Bond Boy**, back down to his last winning mark, on turf at least, appreciated the return to six furlongs and gave hope for the future.

**Bond Playboy**did nothing to challenge the impression that he is handicapped up to the hilt at present.

**No Time(IRE)**has yet to win on the All-Weather but continues to drop in the handicap and will at some stage become an interesting proposition.

**Canterloupe(IRE)**was slightly disappointing on her return to the scene of her win in November, but this was a tougher race and she is currently 6lb higher.

## 487 BET DIRECT ON SKY TEXT PAGE 371 (S) STKS 1m 100y(F)

**3:10** (3:12) (G ) 4-Y-0+ **£2,947** (£842; £421) **Stalls** Low

Form RPR

000- **1** **Daimajin (IRE)**[81] 5672 5-9-0 55 (t) MFenton 3 65
(MissGayKelleway) *s.i.s: rdn and hdwy 3f out: r.o u.p to ld cl home* **5/1**[2]

41-4 **2** *1 ¼* **Headland (USA)**[4] 439 6-9-5 68 (b) ACulhane 8 67
(DWChapman) *t.k.h: a.p: led over 4f out: clr 2f out: rdn over 1f out: hung lft ins fnl f: hdd and no ex cl home* **11/2**[3]

00-3 **3** *2 ½* **Sudra**[4] 442 7-8-7 53 (b[1]) JDO'Reilly[(7)] 10 57
(JO'Reilly) *hld up in tch: jnd ldrs over 5f out: chsd ldr over 4f out: rdn over 3f out: one pce fnl 2f* **7/1**

00-1 **4** *¾* **Ally Makbul**[4] 442 4-9-0 51 NPollard 9 56
(JRBest) *chsd ldrs: rdn 5f out: outpcd over 2f out: rallied ins fnl f* **10/11**[1]

000- **5** *1 ¼* **Toro Bravo (IRE)**[10] 6257 4-9-0 60 (b) MTebbutt 2 53
(RMBeckett) *hld up and bhd: rdn 4f out: hdwy over 1f out: nvr trbld ldrs* **16/1**

600- **6** *hd* **Jungle Lion**[14] 6241 6-9-0 47 (t) SWhitworth 7 53
(JohnAHarris) *hld up: sn bhd: hung lft fr 4f out: n.d* **33/1**

00-5 **7** *shd* **Mabel Riley (IRE)**[6] 425 4-8-9 45 (v[1]) SWKelly 1 47
(MABuckley) *prom: rdn over 4f out: wknd over 2f out* **20/1**

20-0 **8** *6* **Forty Forte**[7] 412 8-9-0 55 (p) JTate 6 40
(MissSJWilton) *led: rdn and hdd over 4f out: sn wknd* **7/1**

1m 51.35s (0.35) **Going Correction** +0.05s/f (Slow) **8** Ran SP% **123.0**

Speed ratings: **100,98,96,95,94 94,93,87**CSF £35.19 TOTE £4.40: £1.10, £2.30, £1.30; EX 31.80.The winner was bought in for 8,500gns

**Owner** Simon Mapletoft Racing I **Bred** Harry Sweeney **Trained** Newmarket, Suffolk

**FOCUS**

Not too bad a seller, although Ally Makbul's below-par effort devalues the form somewhat.

**NOTEBOOK**

**Daimajin(IRE)**, dropping into selling grade for the first time on his debut for his new stable, had a tongue-tie on for the first time. Successful in the past over ten furlongs, he needed every yard of this trip.

**Headland(USA)**, a capable performer in this sort of grade, was tackling a trip which in the past has proved too far for him. Once again he shaped as a non-stayer, tiring noticeably in the closing stages.

**Sudra**, blinkered for the first time, reversed recent placings with Ally Makbul but, having looked a threat turning out of the back straight, he found little in the straight.

**Ally Makbul**looked to hold an outstanding chance based on her win here four days previously, but her poor effort suggests that that race had taken more out of her than connections thought.

**Toro Bravo(IRE)**won his maiden over this course and distance as a two-year-old, but he has not been in that sort of form for a while now.

**Jungle Lion** *Official explanation: jockey said gelding had hung badly left-handed throughout*

## 488 BET DIRECT IN VISION SKY PAGE 293 H'CAP 7f (F)

**3:40** (3:41) (E ) (0-75,73) 4-Y-0+ **£3,454** (£1,063; £531; £265) **Stalls** High

Form RPR

162- **1** **Arc El Ciel (ARG)**[9] 6270 6-10-0 **73** (v) SDrowne 2 83
(MrsStefLiddiard) *a.p: rdn over 2f out: r.o u.p to ld last strides* **5/2**[1]

020- **2** *hd* **Yorker (USA)**[14] 6241 6-9-6 **68** LisaJones[(3)] 9 78
(MsDeborahJEvans) *chsd ldrs: lost pl over 4f out: rdn and hdwy on ins over 2f out: r.o ins fnl f* **10/1**

021- **3** *shd* **Warden Warren**[9] 6270 6-9-8 **72** 6ex (b) BReilly[(5)] 1 81
(MrsCADunnett) *t.k.h: w ldr: rdn over 2f out: led jst over 1f out: hdd last strides* **8/1**

005- **4** *1* **Danielle's Lad**[14] 6241 8-9-6 **65** (b) MFenton 8 72
(BPalling) *hld up: hdwy over 5f out: rdn 3f out: kpt on ins fnl f* **11/2**[3]

534- **5** *nk* **Grey Pearl**[9] 6270 5-9-8 **72** TEaves[(5)] 3 78
(MissGayKelleway) *led: rdn 3f out: hdd jst over 1f out: no ex towards fin* **11/2**[3]

34-6 **6** *3 ½* **Blonde En Blonde (IRE)**[7] 410 4-9-3 **65** J-PGuillambert[(3)] 5 62
(NPLittmoden) *mid-div: lost pl and swtchd rt over 4f out: hdwy over 2f out: nvr able to chal* **8/1**

266- **7** *3* **Spark Up**[9] 6270 4-9-5 **64** (b) MHenry 7 54
(JWUnett) *hld up: n.m.r 4f out: dropped rr and nt clr run 3f out: n.d* **16/1**

005- **8** *shd* **Barzak (IRE)**[13] 6245 4-9-7 **66** (b[1]) JBramhill 6 56
(SRBowring) *hld up: hdwy 4f out: wknd wl over 1f out* **16/1**

051- **9** *¾* **Pawn In Life (IRE)**[24] 6196 6-9-3 **62** DMernagh 10 50
(TDBarron) *jnd ldrs 5f out: rdn 3f out: sn wknd* **4/1**[2]

000- **10** *¾* **Whippasnapper**[28] 6169 4-9-6 **65** NPollard 4 51
(JRBest) *plld hrd: prom: rdn 3f out: sn wknd* **20/1**

005- **11** *14* **Marabar**[49] 6038 6-9-11 **70** ACulhane 11 21
(DWChapman) *rdn 4f out: a in rr* **16/1**

1m 29.55s (-0.65) **Going Correction** +0.05s/f (Slow) **11** Ran SP% **133.1**

Speed ratings: **105,104,104,103,103 99,95,95,94,93 77**CSF £34.02 CT £197.18 TOTE £2.90: £1.10, £4.00, £3.10; EX 46.50 Place 6 £130.21, Place 5 £86.62.

**Owner** Shefford Valley Stud **Bred** Santa Maria De Araras **Trained** Great Shefford, Berks

**FOCUS**

A competitive handicap, run at a good clip, and the tightest finish of the day. The form should prove reliable.

**NOTEBOOK**

**Arc El Ciel(ARG)**got up in the final strides to win off a mark in the 70s for the first time in his career. He has improved the best part of 20lb since moving to his current stable a year ago and is clearly at his best over this course and distance.

**Yorker(USA)**is ideally suited by farther than this and it was to his credit that he finished so well next to the far-side rail.

**Warden Warren**, who has yet to win a handicap on turf or sand off a higher mark than 69, had a 6lb penalty yet was collared only in the dying strides. He is clearly at the top of his game at present.

**Danielle's Lad**, who remains a maiden on the All-Weather after 20 attempts, continues to drop in the handicap, and at some point he must surely deliver.

**Grey Pearl**continues to go too fast for her own good and was a sitting duck.

**Blonde En Blonde(IRE)**may well appreciate being dropped back into claiming grade.

**Pawn In Life(IRE)**has run his best races at Southwell and Lingfield.

T/Plt: £158.70 to a £1 stake. Pool: £42,677.85. 196.25 winning tickets. T/Qpdt: £26.70 to a £1 stake. Pool: £3,307.70. 91.50 winning tickets. KH

# [462]LINGFIELD (L-H)

Saturday, January 10

**OFFICIAL GOING: Standard**

Wind: mod bhd Weather: fine but cloudy

## 489 BET DIRECT NO Q MAIDEN STKS 6f (P)

**12:10** (12:12) (D ) 3-Y-0 **£3,799** (£1,169; £584; £292) **Stalls** Low

Form RPR

46-2 **1** **Ever Cheerful**[8] 408 3-8-7 67 (p) LTreadwell[(7)] 6 71
(WGMTurner) *t.k.h: trckd ldr: led over 1f out: hung fire tl drvn clr ins fnl f* **11/2**

053- **2** *1 ¾* **Saviours Spirit**[12] 6248 3-9-0 72 IMongan 7 66
(TGMills) *chsd ldng pair: rdn and nt qckn over 2f out: styd on fnl f to take 2nd nr fin* **6/4**[1]

0- **3** *nk* **Royal Pavillion (IRE)**[86] 5587 3-9-0 PaulEddery 10 65
(WJMusson) *lw: sn led: rdn and hdd over 1f out: one pce after* **5/1**[3]

**4** *2 ½* **Siera Spirit (IRE)** 3-8-2 NicolPolli[(7)] 5 52
(MGQuinlan) *w'like: settled in midfield: nt wl plcd over 2f out: effrt over 1f out and sn swtchd rt: r.o fnl f: should improve* **9/2**[2]

**5** *¾* **Noble Mount** 3-9-0 JMackay 2 55
(RGuest) *leggy: unf: dwlt: rcvrd into midfield 1/2-way: outpcd over 2f out: rdn and kpt on fnl f* **33/1**

\- **6** *1 ¼* **Luchi** 3-8-9 RSmith 3 46
(ACharlton) *leggy: dwlt: rcvrd into midfield after 2f: effrt on inner 2f out: no hdwy fnl f* **50/1**



The Form Book, Raceform Ltd, Compton, RG20 6NL

020- **7** *1 1/4* **Tonto (FR)**[12] 6250 3-9-0 70 ..........(p) CCatlin 14 48
(MissDMountain) *racd in rr and drvn bef 1/2-way: one pce and nvr rchd ldrs* **12/1**

0- **8** *3/4* **Backlash**[39] 6118 3-8-9 .......... SWhitworth 9 40
(AWCarroll) *s.i.s: snatched up after 1f and racd in last trio: shuffled along briefly over 1f out: kpt on: do bttr* **50/1**

063- **9** *3/4* **Son Of Rembrandt (IRE)**[99] 5338 3-9-0 66 .......... JQuinn 12 43
(DKIvory) *chsd ldrs tl wknd wl over 1f out* **16/1**

0- **10** *shd* **Sussex Style (IRE)**[12] 6250 3-9-0 .......... EAhern 8 43
(RMFlower) *prom tl wknd 2f out* **50/1**

**11** *18* **Jaycee Star (IRE)** 3-8-9 .......... PDoe 13 —
(DFlood) *w'like: bit bkwd: dwlt: rn green and struggling in last after 2f: t.o* **40/1**

0- **12** *nk* **Tale Of The Tiger**[264] 1146 3-9-0 ..........(v[1]) NCallan 11 —
(JulianPoulton) *b: sn drvn in rr: t.o over 1f out* **100/1**

00- **13** *1 1/4* **Eugenie**[53] 6018 3-8-9 .......... PDobbs 1 —
(RHannon) *rdn in midfield over 3f out: struggling whn hmpd over 2f out: wknd rapidly: t.o* **50/1**

1m 13.56s (0.64) **Going Correction** +0.125s/f (Slow) **13** Ran SP% **118.0**
Speed ratings: **100,97,97,93,92 91,89,88,87,87 63,63,61**CSF £13.47 TOTE £6.60: £1.40, £1.50, £1.30; EX 10.70.
**Owner** E Goody **Bred** Southill Stud **Trained** Sigwells, Somerset
■ Stewards Enquiry : Paul Eddery two-day ban: careless riding (Jan 21,22)

**FOCUS**
A modest maiden and the early pace was just ordinary. The winner Ever Cheerful was beaten in a Wolverhampton claimer on his previous start and the overall form is not strong, but that said, newcomers Siera Spirit and Noble Mount both shaped with promise.

**NOTEBOOK**
**Ever Cheerful**, a beaten favourite in a Wolverhampton claimer over seven furlongs last time, appreciated this drop in trip and switch to Polytrack to get off the mark at the thirteenth attempt in first-time cheekpieces. This will have boosted his confidence, but he is likely to take a rise in the weights and will find things tougher next time.
**Saviours Spirit**, who had 5lb in hand of the winner on official figures, had every chance but proved one paced in the straight. He should win in his turn and looks likely to get another furlong.
**Royal Pavillion(IRE)**, supported in the market, ran a pleasing enough race on his first start in 86 days. He was nicely clear of the remainder and, given normal improvement, should find a small race.
**Siera Spirit(IRE)**, an 8,500euros yearling, out of a quite useful Irish sprinter, took a while to get the hang of things when coming under pressure and got going too late. She looks sure to improve on this.
**Noble Mount** is bred to need a lot further than this six furlong trip, but shaped with promise.

## 490 BETDIRECT.CO.UK H'CAP — 1m 2f (P)
**12:40** (12:41) (E) (0-75,75) 3-Y-O — **£3,412** (£975; £487) **Stalls** Low

Form — RPR

055- **1** **Keepers Knight (IRE)**[134] 4548 3-8-7 **61** ow1 .......... IMongan 5 67
(PFICole) *pressed ldr: rdn over 4f out: led over 3f out: drvn 3l clr wl over 1f out: hld on u.p* **8/1**

10- **2** *1 1/2* **Competitor**[21] 6219 3-9-2 **70** .......... CCatlin 2 73
(JAkehurst) *led: rdn and hdd over 3f out: chsd wnr after: unable qck over 2f out: kpt on u.p fnl f* **12/1**

301- **3** *1 1/2* **Dr Cerullo**[19] 6228 3-9-7 **75** .......... MartinDwyer 7 75
(CTinkler) *lw: restless stalls: dwlt: hld up tl prog 6f out: chsd ldng pair 3f out: rdn and nt qckn over 2f out: one pce after* **6/4**[1]

004- **4** *1/2* **Ivory Coast (IRE)**[21] 6222 3-8-3 **57** .......... PDoe 4 56
(WRMuir) *lw: sn in last pair: n.m.r on inner 5f out: sn rdn: struggling 3f out: kpt on fr over 1f out: nrst fin* **20/1**

636- **5** *3/4* **La Danseuse**[21] 6222 3-7-9 **52** oh1 .......... LisaJones[(3)] 1 50
(GCBravery) *b.hind: reluctant to enter stalls: sn trckd ldrs: rdn over 3f out: outpcd over 2f out: one pce after* **25/1**

255- **6** *2 1/2* **Elusive Kitty (USA)**[12] 6251 3-9-1 **69** .......... EAhern 8 63
(GAButler) *lw: hld up in last: prog on outer to trck ldrs 3f out: rdn and outpcd over 2f out: no imp after* **5/2**[2]

000- **7** *3* **Spring Whisper (IRE)**[33] 6145 3-8-1 **55** ..........(v) JQuinn 6 43
(EALDunlop) *trckd ldrs: pushed along 4f out: nt qckn and struggling wl over 2f out: hanging rt ins fnl f* **16/1**

240- **8** *20* **Trompe L'Oeil (IRE)**[22] 6216 3-8-12 **66** .......... WRyan 9 18
(EALDunlop) *t.k.h: prom tl wknd over 3f out: eased over 1f out: t.o* **6/1**[3]

400- **9** *4* **Lord Greystoke (IRE)**[31] 6160 3-8-2 **56** .......... JMackay 3 1
(CPMorlock) *prom to over 4f out: sn wknd: t.o* **25/1**

2m 11.08s (3.69) **Going Correction** +0.125s/f (Slow) **9** Ran SP% **120.0**
Speed ratings: **90,88,87,87,86 84,82,66,63**CSF £97.98 CT £221.56 TOTE £11.80: £2.40, £2.70, £1.10; EX 41.30.
**Owner** P F I Cole Ltd **Bred** Tullamaine Castle Stud **Trained** Whatcombe, Oxon

**FOCUS**
Just an ordinary handicap and the winning time was extremely modest. The pace was pretty steady until Mongan kicked for home over three out on the eventual winner Keepers Knight. The first two finishers were in the first two throughout and some of those held up could be a little better than the bare form suggests.

**NOTEBOOK**
**Keepers Knight(IRE)**, beaten in a claimer over seven furlongs when last seen in August, benefited from a positive ride from Mongan on this step up in trip to make a successful handicap debut. He is lightly raced and open to further improvement. *Official explanation: trainer's representative said, regarding the improved form shown, colt had matured and strengthened up in recent weeks*
**Competitor**, stepping up two furlongs in trip, led the eventual winner for much of the way, but let that one get first run over three out and could never peg him back thereafter. This was still a very encouraging effort.
**Dr Cerullo**, off the mark in a weak Wolverhampton maiden last time, was a little bit disappointing. He may be better suited by more positive tactics.
**Ivory Coast(IRE)**, stepping up in trip for her handicap debut, ran respectably but never really posted a serious threat.
**La Danseuse**, another stepping up in trip for her handicap debut, failed to quicken under pressure and may have preferred a stronger pace.
**Elusive Kitty(USA)**, trying this trip for the first time, was held up off the modest pace and never got in a serious challenge.
**Lord Greystoke(IRE)** *Official explanation: jockey said colt had lost its action coming down the hill*

## 491 BET DIRECT NO Q ON 08000 93 66 93 CLASSIFIED STKS — 7f (P)
**1:15** (1:17) (F) 4-Y-0+ — **£3,003** (£858; £429) **Stalls** Low

Form — RPR

050- **1** **Zafarshah (IRE)**[64] 5945 5-8-7 58 .......... SJDonohoe[(7)] 1 68
(PDEvans) *prom: chsd ldr over 2f out: drvn to chal fnl f: edgd ahd last 50y* **11/2**[3]

54-3 **2** *nk* **Mayzin (IRE)**[3] 469 4-9-0 51 ..........(p) JQuinn 16 67
(RMFlower) *lw: led and crossed towards inner after 1f: rdn 2f out: hdd last 50y: jst hld* **8/1**

010- **3** *1/2* **Miss Issy (IRE)**[11] 6256 4-8-11 58 ..........(v) IMongan 5 63
(JGallagher) *settled in midfield: prog 3f out: chsd ldng pair wl over 1f out: no imp tl styd on last 100y: nrst fin* **11/2**[3]

000- **4** *3/4* **Double M**[85] 5606 7-9-0 49 ..........(v) NCallan 8 64
(MrsLRichards) *settled in rr: stdy prog on inner fr 3f out: rdn to dispute 3rd fnl f: nt qckn* **66/1**

000- **5** *2 1/2* **Captain Cloudy**[42] 6092 4-8-11 57 .......... LPKeniry[(3)] 10 58
(MMadgwick) *hld up wl in rr: nt wl plcd over 2f out: nt clr run over 1f out: swtchd rt 1f out: r.o fnl f: too much to do* **50/1**

040- **6** *2* **Foolish Thought (IRE)**[35] 6127 4-9-0 60 ..........(v[1]) EAhern 4 53
(RAFahey) *racd in midfield: rdn over 4f out: no imp u.p 2f out: one pce after* **9/2**[2]

535- **7** *hd* **Acorazado (IRE)**[11] 6260 5-9-0 56 .......... GCarter 7 52
(GLMoore) *lw: settled in rr: rdn 3f out: effrt u.p 2f out: no imp ldrs 1f out* **7/2**[1]

310- **8** *1 1/2* **Pants**[35] 6127 5-8-11 57 .......... ANicholls 6 46
(AndrewReid) *hld up wl in rr: effrt on inner over 2f out: no imp 1f out: fdd* **8/1**

05-0 **9** *nk* **Four Jays (IRE)**[4] 448 4-8-11 58 ..........(p) LisaJones[(3)] 14 48
(NPLittmoden) *chsd ldrs: rdn over 2f out: wknd over 1f out* **14/1**

000- **10** *2* **Master Rattle**[11] 6260 5-9-0 53 .......... VSlattery 2 43
(JaneSouthcombe) *chsd ldrs: rdn 3f out: losing pl and struggling over 2f out* **33/1**

100- **11** *3/4* **Locombe Hill (IRE)**[46] 6065 8-8-7 60 .......... LTreadwell[(7)] 3 41
(DNicholls) *dwlt: racd freely and sn trckd ldr: wknd over 2f out* **12/1**

00- **12** *3* **Amanpuri (GER)**[61] 5971 6-9-0 46 .......... MFenton 12 33
(MissGayKelleway) *a in rr: drvn and struggling fr 1/2-way* **33/1**

000- **13** *2* **Kumakawa**[52] 6027 6-8-7 45 ..........(b) LiamJones[(7)] 15 28
(EAWheeler) *restrained s: t.o after 2f* **100/1**

0/0- **14** *3 1/2* **Magic Stone**[280] 936 4-9-0 45 .......... RSmith 9 20
(ACharlton) *b: b.hind: chsd ldrs tl wknd rapidly 3f out* **100/1**

000- **15** *2 1/2* **Kanz Wood (USA)**[19] 6231 8-9-0 59 .......... SWhitworth 11 13
(AWCarroll) *racd on outer in midfield: pushed along and no prog over 2f out: wknd wl over 1f out: heavily eased* **14/1**

1m 25.94s (-0.06) **Going Correction** +0.125s/f (Slow) **15** Ran SP% **125.7**
Speed ratings: **105,104,104,103,100 98,97,96,95,93 92,89,86,82,80**CSF £49.87 TOTE £9.70: £3.90, £3.00, £2.60; EX 151.60.
**Owner** Waterline Racing Club **Bred** His Highness The Aga Khan's Studs S C **Trained** Pandy, Gwent

**FOCUS**
A decent enough pace, and a fair time for the class of contest.

**NOTEBOOK**
**Zafarshah(IRE)**, returning from a 64-day break, ran out a narrow winner under a good, strong ride from Donohoe. He had little to spare at the line and a rise in the weights will make things tougher, but his yard are at least in good form.
**Mayzin(IRE)**, still a maiden, ran a cracking race from the front. He would have been 7lb better off with the winner had this been a handicap and looks sure to take a rise in the weights for this.
**Miss Issy(IRE)**, well in at the weights, got going a little bit too late. She goes well round here.
**Double M**, on a long losing run, had it all to do at the weights but ran above himself.
**Captain Cloudy**, up a furlong in trip, did not get much luck in running and should probably have finished a bit closer. He is, however, still a maiden.
**Foolish Thought(IRE)**, still a maiden, was well held in the first-time visor.
**Acorazado(IRE)** again shaped as though he may need another furlong on this surface.

## 492 BET DIRECT NO Q DEMO 08000 837 888 MAIDEN STKS — 1m 2f (P)
**1:45** (1:47) (D) 3-Y-O — **£4,114** (£1,266; £633; £316) **Stalls** Low

Form — RPR

004- **1** **Absolutelythebest (IRE)**[42] 6087 3-9-0 71 .......... EAhern 4 75
(EALDunlop) *lw: wl plcd: shkn up to trck ldr over 2f out: drvn fnl f: r.o to ld last strides* **9/2**[3]

632- **2** *nk* **Baawrah**[42] 6091 3-9-0 72 .......... CCatlin 6 74
(MRChannon) *chsd ldr: rdn to ld over 3f out: hrd drvn and kpt on fnl 2f : hdd last strides* **7/2**[2]

0- **3** *1* **Fiddlers Ford (IRE)**[155] 3965 3-9-0 .......... SWKelly 10 72
(JNoseda) *lw: racd in midfield: prog to trck ldrs 3f out: shkn up and effrt 2f out: chsd ldng pair fnl f: styd on: nvr nrr* **12/1**

**4** *5* **Alexander Ambition (IRE)**[157] 3908 3-8-9 75 .......... IMongan 9 58
(SKirk) *trckd ldrs: drvn to chse ldng pair wl over 1f out: cl up ent fnl f: sn wknd* **14/1**

025- **5** *1 1/2* **Night Storm**[161] 3792 3-8-9 72 .......... PDoe 12 56
(SDow) *racd in tch at rr of main gp: rdn and effrt on outer 3f out: effrt to chse ldrs over 1f out: wknd fnl f* **12/1**

00- **6** *3* **Atlantic Tern**[21] 6219 3-9-0 .......... VSlattery 8 55
(NMBabbage) *settled wl in rr: lost tch w main gp over 5f out: rdn and clsd up 3f out: in tch 2f out: wknd over 1f out* **66/1**

0- **7** *1 1/4* **Once Around (IRE)**[19] 6228 3-9-0 .......... JPaulielo 2 53
(TGMills) *prom: rdn wl over 2f out: wknd wl over 1f out* **50/1**

52- **8** *1 1/4* **Princess Alina (IRE)**[72] 5833 3-8-9 .......... MartinDwyer 3 46
(AMBalding) *led to over 3f out: u.p whn n.m.r on inner over 2f out: sn wknd* **5/2**[1]

500- **9** *1 1/2* **Darn Good**[42] 6091 3-9-0 65 .......... PDobbs 13 48
(RHannon) *chsd ldng pair to 1/2-way: sn rdn and lost pl: no ch fnl 3f* **16/1**

022- **10** *nk* **Russalka**[19] 6230 3-8-9 65 ..........(p) NCallan 14 42
(JulianPoulton) *racd on outer: in tch: rdn over 4f out: wknd over 2f out* **8/1**

0- **11** *23* **Desert Tommy**[115] 4997 3-9-0 .......... AClark 1 6
(TGMills) *dwlt: rn green and a struggling: t.o over 4f out* **33/1**

0- **12** *5* **It's A Blessing**[64] 5940 3-8-6 .......... J-PGuillambert[(3)] 11 —
(NPLittmoden) *rdn in rr after 2f: t.o fr 1/2-way* **66/1**

**13** *dist* **Charlies Profit** 3-8-9 .......... JTate 7 —
(JJBridger) *w'like: bit bkwd: s.s: rn green and sn bhd: wl t.o fnl 4f* **66/1**

**14** *1 1/2* **Red Silk** 3-8-9 .......... MHills 5 —
(MrsAJPerrett) *w'like: bit bkwd: rdn and reluctant in rr after 3f: wl t.o fr 1/2-way* **12/1**

2m 10.08s (2.69) **Going Correction** +0.125s/f (Slow) **14** Ran SP% **125.1**
Speed ratings: **94,93,92,88,87 85,84,83,82,81 63,59,—,—**CSF £21.13 TOTE £6.00: £1.40, £1.40, £5.00; EX 21.00.
**Owner** Saeed Suhail **Bred** P D Savill **Trained** Newmarket, Suffolk

**FOCUS**
Just an ordinary maiden and a modest time, but the front three pulled nicely clear.

**NOTEBOOK**
**Absolutelythebest(IRE)**, fourth in a similar race over course and distance last time, needed all of Ahern's strength from the saddle to get off the mark. He could go well in slightly better company if not treated too harshly by the Handicapper.
**Baawrah**, runner-up in this grade over course and distance last time, again had to settle for second. He did little wrong and should win in his turn.
**Fiddlers Ford(IRE)**, well beaten over seven furlongs in a Newmarket maiden on his only previous start, shaped with promise on his return from a break. He should be placed to win a similar contest before too long.

**Alexander Ambition(IRE)**, well held in three starts over seven furlongs in Ireland for Dermot Weld, including in a tongue-tie, was well beaten by the front three and will need to improve to justify her rating of 75.

**Night Storm**, stepping up from seven furlongs and with the tongue-tie left off this time, was comfortably held and is another who will need to improve.

**Princess Alina(IRE)**, runner-up in a seven furlong maiden here 72 days previously, ran below form on this step up in trip.

## 493 BETDIRECT.CO.UK H'CAP 7f (P)

2:15 (2:16) (C) (0-100,82) 3-Y-O £8,932 (£3,388; £1,694; £770) Stalls Low

| Form | | | | RPR |
|---|---|---|---|---|
| 061- | 1 | | **Bettalatethannever (IRE)**[24] 6203 3-9-7 **82** PFitzsimons 6 (SDow) *t.k.h: hld up in 5th: pushed along and effrt on outer over 2f out: swept into ld last 150y: sn clr: impressive* **5/2**[2] | 87 |
| 051- | 2 | 2 | **St Savarin (FR)**[12] 6251 3-8-10 **71** NPollard 5 (JRBest) *led: kicked on over 2f out: hdd and outpcd by wnr last 150y* **6/1** | 71 |
| 101- | 3 | nk | **Kabreet**[11] 6258 3-9-3 **78** EAhern 3 (EALDunlop) *lw: trckd ldng pair: effrt 2f out: rdn to chal 1f out: outpcd whn n.m.r sn after: kpt on* **7/2**[3] | 77 |
| 004- | 4 | ¾ | **Turnberry (IRE)**[12] 6251 3-7-13 **60** ow1 (b) JQuinn 2 (JWHills) *chsd ldng trio: drvn and unable qck over 2f out: kpt on ins fnl f* **14/1** | 57 |
| 21-4 | 5 | shd | **Blue Empire (IRE)**[3] 466 3-8-11 **75** LEnstone(3) 1 (PCHaslam) *lw: trckd ldr: effrt to chal over 1f out: hanging lft and fnd nil fnl f* **9/4**[1] | 72 |
| 610- | 6 | 1 | **Off Beat (USA)**[12] 6251 3-9-2 **77** (b) SCarson 4 (RFJohnsonHoughton) *t.k.h: hld up in 6th: rdn over 2f out: kpt on same pce and nvr able to chal* **12/1** | 71 |
| 324- | 7 | 9 | **Hello Roberto**[24] 6207 3-9-1 **79** LFletcher(3) 7 (MJPolglase) *a in last: rdn over 2f out: wknd wl over 1f out* **12/1** | 49 |

1m 26.42s (0.42) **Going Correction** +0.125s/f (Slow) 7 Ran SP% **117.9**
Speed ratings: **102,99,99,98,98 97,86**CSF £18.77 TOTE £3.30: £2.00, £3.80; EX 34.70.
**Owner** J R May **Bred** Mick McGinn **Trained** Epsom, Surrey

**FOCUS**
A decent little handicap won in impressive fashion by the progressive Betterlatethannever.

**NOTEBOOK**
**Bettalatethannever(IRE)**, off the mark over course and distance last time, was well backed again and followed up in great style. He is progressing fast and could well complete the hat-trick.
**St Savarin(FR)**, up 3lb for his recent course and distance success, had every chance and ran well, simply finding the winner far too good.
**Kabreet**, 5lb higher than when successful over six furlongs here last time, may have been second with a clearer run but was never able to match the winner's turn of foot.
**Turnberry(IRE)**is still a maiden but ran a pleasing race and can be found easier opportunities.
**Blue Empire(IRE)**, a very close fourth in a decent race over a mile here last time, was short of room around a furlong out and never threatened thereafter. He has gained both his wins on Fibresand.

## 494 LITTLEWOODS BET DIRECT H'CAP 1m (P)

2:50 (2:50) (D ) (0-85,83) 4-Y-O+ £4,784 (£1,472; £736; £368) Stalls High

| Form | | | | RPR |
|---|---|---|---|---|
| 320- | 1 | | **Dance On The Top**[90] 5498 6-9-11 **80** (t) MartinDwyer 5 (JRBoyle) *trckd ldr: led wl over 3f out and sn qcknd: in n.d fr over 1f out: rdn out* **9/1** | 96 |
| 351- | 2 | 3½ | **J R Stevenson (USA)**[12] 6255 8-9-5 **79** MSavage(5) 6 (MWigham) *trckd ldrs: prog to chse wnr 3f out: clr of rest over 2f out : no imp fr over 1f out* **11/2**[3] | 87 |
| 061- | 3 | 1¼ | **Labrett**[11] 6263 7-10-0 **83** (t) MFenton 12 (MissGayKelleway) *b: b.hind: lw: racd on outer: in tch: rdn 3f out: sn outpcd: effrt 2f out: kpt on fr over 1f out: nvr able to chal* **9/2**[2] | 88 |
| 462- | 4 | hd | **Sewmore Character**[39] 6114 4-9-5 **74** NCallan 4 (MBlanshard) *t.k.h: hld up in midfield: prog 3f out: sn outpcd: rdn and kpt on same pce fnl 2f* **10/1** | 79 |
| 130- | 5 | shd | **Free Option (IRE)**[11] 6263 9-9-4 **73** DeanMcKeown 1 (WJMusson) *s.i.s: hld up in rr: outpcd fr 3f out: rdn and effrt 2f out: kpt on same pce* **4/1**[1] | 77 |
| /0-0 | 6 | 1½ | **Cormorant Wharf (IRE)**[7] 417 4-9-5 **79** AQuinn(5) 2 (TEPowell) *t.k.h: trckd ldrs: outpcd 3f out: rdn 2f out: one pce fr over 1f out* **13/2** | 80 |
| 500- | 7 | 1 | **Boundless Prospect (USA)**[161] 3785 5-9-6 **75** MHills 3 (JWHills) *hld up in last trio: outpcd 3f out: rdn and prog 2f out: kpt on one pce* **33/1** | 74 |
| 050- | 8 | 1¼ | **Mamore Gap (IRE)**[115] 4995 6-9-4 **73** PDobbs 10 (RHannon) *hld up in last trio: outpcd 3f out: nudged along and kpt on same pce fnl 2f* **25/1** | 69 |
| 050- | 9 | hd | **Ammenayr (IRE)**[11] 6263 4-9-8 **77** IMongan 9 (TGMills) *hld up in last: outpcd 3f out: sme prog 2f out: nvr on terms* **8/1** | 72 |
| 416- | 10 | 9 | **Terraquin (IRE)**[147] 4177 4-9-10 **79** JTate 7 (JJBridger) *racd on outer: hld up: outpcd 3f out: wknd 2f out* **33/1** | 54 |
| /00- | 11 | 1 | **Kingham**[147] 4188 4-9-9 **78** VSlattery 11 (MrsMaryHambro) *led to wl over 3f out: wknd over 2f out* **100/1** | 50 |
| 114- | 12 | 9 | **Annishirani**[49] 6049 4-9-5 **74** EAhern 8 (GAButler) *lw: plld hrd: trckd ldng pair to over 3f out: wknd rapidly* **6/1** | 26 |

1m 38.8s (-0.71) **Going Correction** +0.125s/f (Slow) 12 Ran SP% **122.1**
Speed ratings: **108,104,103,103,102 101,100,99,99,90 89,80**CSF £58.23 CT £263.23 TOTE £14.10: £3.20, £2.90, £3.20; EX 58.80.
**Owner** John Hopkins (t/a South Hatch Racing) **Bred** Fittocks Stud **Trained** Epsom, Surrey

**FOCUS**
This looked quite a competitive handicap on paper, but Dance On Top ran out a most decisive winner in a good time.

**NOTEBOOK**
**Dance On The Top** made it two from three over this course and distance with a most decisive victory. He is sure to take a significant rise in the weights for this, but demands plenty of respect round here.
**J R Stevenson(USA)**, 4lb higher than when winning over ten furlongs here last time, ran well on this drop in trip but proved unable to match the winner's pace. He is probably worth keeping on the right side of whilst in this form.
**Labrett**, up 8lb for his latest win in a classified event over this course and distance, never looked like getting to the winner and may be better ridden slightly closer to the pace.
**Sewmore Character**, runner-up in a weaker race over course and distance last time, ran respectably but remains a maiden.
**Free Option(IRE)** failed to run up to his best.
**Annishirani** ran as though something was amiss. *Official explanation: jockey said filly ran too freely in the early stages*

## 495 BET ALL WEATHER ON 0800 32 93 93 (S) STKS 1m 2f (P)

3:20 (3:22) (G ) 4-Y-0+ £2,639 (£754; £377) Stalls Low

| Form | | | | RPR |
|---|---|---|---|---|
| 000- | 1 | | **Bank On Him**[190] 2954 9-9-2 56 JQuinn 2 (CWeedon) *mde all: set stdy pce tl 3f out: kicked 3l clr 2f out: drvn out and hld on nr fin* **6/1**[3] | 57 |
| 630- | 2 | nk | **Sterling Guarantee (USA)**[98] 5359 6-9-2 69 ANicholls 7 (DNicholls) *b: reluctant to enter stalls: hld up: prog 3f out: effrt on inner and nt clr run briefly over 1f out: chsd wnr last 150y: c* **7/1** | 57 |
| 505- | 3 | 1 | **Pyrrhic**[11] 6262 5-9-2 40 (b) EAhern 11 (RMFlower) *s.s: sn in midfield: effrt on inner over 2f out: chsd wnr over 1f out to last 150y: kpt on* **8/1** | 55 |
| 003- | 4 | 4 | **Cherokee Bay**[103] 5281 4-8-9 51 GCarter 1 (GLMoore) *chsd wnr to over 1f out: wknd ins fnl f* **7/2**[2] | 43 |
| 000- | 5 | nk | **Walker Bay (IRE)**[24] 6204 6-8-11 40 RSmith 12 (JCFox) *hld up in last: effrt over 2f out: sn outpcd: kpt on one pce fr over 1f out: n.d* **33/1** | 42 |
| 000- | 6 | 1 | **Private Seal**[11] 6262 9-9-2 40 (t) NCallan 3 (JulianPoulton) *prom: rdn over 3f out: wknd u.p jst over 1f out* **12/1** | 45 |
| 101- | 7 | 2½ | **Absolute Utopia (USA)**[11] 6257 11-9-7 63 JMackay 9 (JLSpearing) *racd on outer: trckd ldrs: effrt over 2f out: c wd bnd wl over 1f out: fdd* **13/8**[1] | 46 |
| 560- | 8 | 1½ | **Birth Of The Blues**[52] 3918 8-8-9 40 DonnaBashton(7) 14 (ACharlton) *settled in rr: outpcd over 2f out: n.d after* **25/1** | 38 |
| 000- | 9 | 5 | **Mr Whizz**[97] 4633 7-8-13 40 LPKeniry(3) 10 (APJones) *hld up in rr: outpcd wl over 2f out: wknd over 1f out* **33/1** | 29 |
| 560- | 10 | 4 | **Original Sin (IRE)**[86] 5596 4-9-0 52 PDoe 8 (SDow) *chsd ldrs tl wknd over 2f out* **25/1** | 22 |

2m 9.90s (2.51) **Going Correction** +0.125s/f (Slow)
**WFA** 4 from 5yo+ 2lb 10 Ran SP% **119.5**
Speed ratings: **94,93,92,89,89 88,86,85,81,78**CSF £46.53 TOTE £7.10: £2.90, £2.40, £2.30; EX 45.00.The winner was bought in for 6,200gns.
**Owner** Vetlab Supplies Ltd **Bred** Brook Stud Ltd **Trained** Wormley, Surrey

**FOCUS**
A typically moderate seller and the early pace was slow, resulting in a modest final time.

**NOTEBOOK**
**Bank On Him**, back in this grade for the first time since winning over course and distance last February, got back to winning ways with an all-the-way success. It would be no surprise to see him add to this if kept to this level.
**Sterling Guarantee(USA)**did not run anywhere near his official rating but would probably have won with a clear run on the home turn. He should make amends if kept to this level.
**Pyrrhic** had it all to do at the weights, but ran a cracker. There ought to be opportunities for him within the regional racing programme.
**Cherokee Bay** has not won since making a successful debut as a two-year-old and was well held on this occasion.
**Absolute Utopia(USA)** raced widest of all for most of the way, but still held every chance until flatttening out when it mattered. He is better than this and can be given another chance.

## 496 BET DIRECT NO Q VOICE AUTOMATED BETTING H'CAP 5f (P)

3:50 (3:50) (F ) (0-65,65) 3-Y-O £2,905 (£830; £415) Stalls High

| Form | | | | RPR |
|---|---|---|---|---|
| 411- | 1 | | **Smart Starprincess (IRE)**[14] 6246 3-9-0 **58** (b) NCallan 4 (PABlockley) *b: mde all and sn clr: drvn 2f out: 4l ahd 1f out: jst hld on* **3/1**[2] | 62 |
| 53-0 | 2 | nk | **Alizar (IRE)**[7] 420 3-8-9 **56** LFletcher(3) 8 (MJPolglase) *racd on outer: outpcd and pushed along over 3f out: prog over 1f out : chsd wnr ins fnl f: clsng wl at fin: jst failed* **14/1** | 59 |
| 50-5 | 3 | 1½ | **Vittorioso (IRE)**[8] 409 3-8-5 **54** (b) TEaves(5) 10 (MissGayKelleway) *prog and prom in chsng gp over 3f out: drvn and hanging lft over 1f out: kpt on same pce ins fnl f* **20/1** | 51 |
| 002- | 4 | 1½ | **Little Flute**[19] 6227 3-8-5 **52** LisaJones(3) 3 (TKeddy) *b: racd in rr: outpcd over 3f out: styd on one pce on inner fnl f: n.d* **11/2**[3] | 43 |
| 603- | 5 | hd | **Forzenuff**[24] 6207 3-9-7 **65** EAhern 2 (JRBoyle) *racd in midfield: rdn bef 1/2-way: one pce and nvr able to chal* **5/2**[1] | 55 |
| 500- | 5 | dht | **Ivory Lace**[24] 6207 3-9-2 **60** IMongan 9 (DKIvory) *prom in chsng gp: chsd wnr 1/2-way: no imp: wknd ins fnl f* **33/1** | 50 |
| 550- | 7 | ½ | **Rehia**[103] 5277 3-9-2 **60** MHills 5 (JWHills) *racd on outer: outpcd and rdn over 3f out: one pce and n.d fr over 1f out* **10/1** | 48 |
| 061- | 8 | 1¼ | **Head Of State**[19] 6227 3-8-10 **54** JMackay 1 (RMBeckett) *a in rr: last and struggling whn n.m.r on inner over 2f out : no ch* **6/1** | 37 |
| 03-1 | 9 | nk | **Princess Kai (IRE)**[7] 414 3-9-0 **61** (b) FPFerris(3) 7 (RIngram) *dwlt: last whn hmpd after 100y: racd wd after: nvr a factor* **7/1** | 43 |
| 305- | 10 | 1½ | **City Affair**[12] 6250 3-9-1 **62** (p) LPKeniry(3) 6 (MrsLCJewell) *chsd wnr to 1/2-way: wknd wl over 1f out* **16/1** | 38 |

60.49 secs (0.71) **Going Correction** +0.125s/f (Slow) 10 Ran SP% **125.1**
Speed ratings: **99,98,96,93,93 93,92,90,90,87**CSF £48.56 CT £764.49 TOTE £2.60: £1.30, £6.90, £7.70; EX 36.80 Place 6 £60.07, Place 5 £44.15..
**Owner** Brooklands Racing **Bred** Norelands Bloodstock **Trained** Southwell, Notts

**FOCUS**
A moderate handicap.

**NOTEBOOK**
**Smart Starprincess(IRE)** took an age to get off the mark but she has really got the hang of things now and completed the hat-trick with a good front-running performance on this switch from Fibresand to Polytrack. She was all out at the finish, but is dangerous to oppose whilst in this sort of form.
**Alizar(IRE)** failed to show much on her first try on this surface last time, but that was over seven furlongs and this sort of trip suits better - she would have won in a few more strides.
**Vittorioso(IRE)**, making his Polytrack debut and dropping back from seven furlongs, was noted hanging left under pressure but still ran respectably.
**Little Flute** never had the pace to threatened and again shaped as though worth a try over six furlongs.
**Forzenuff**, third in a better race over course and distance last time, was below that form and was disappointing.
T/Plt: £89.70 to a £1 stake. Pool: £29,619.55. 241.00 winning tickets. T/Qpdt: £41.40 to a £1 stake. Pool: £1,709.70. 30.50 winning tickets. JN

# [470]SOUTHWELL (L-H)

Monday, January 12

**OFFICIAL GOING: Standard**

(REGIONAL RACING) The centre of the track was again riding faster than the inside rail.

## 497 BET DIRECT ON SKY ACTIVE AMATEUR RIDERS' BANDED STKS 1m (F)

1:20 (1:21) (H) 4-Y-0+ £1,375 (£393; £196) Stalls Low

Form RPR

060- 1 **Smart Scot**[13] 4005 5-11-2 30 (p) MrEDehdashti(5) 7 36
(BPJBaugh) *a.p: effrt to ld over 2f out and sn pushed clr: rdn and edgd lft 1f out: kpt on* **9/2**[1]

0-05 2 *1* **Sea Ya Maite**[4] 471 10-11-2 30 (t) MissKellyHarrison(5) 6 34
(SRBowring) *in tch: hdwy on outer 3f out: chsd wnr wl over 1f out: sn rdn: kpt on fnl f: nt rch wnr* **5/1**[2]

0U-0 3 *5* **Countrywide Girl (IRE)**[9] 421 5-11-2 30 StaceyRenwick(5) 1 24
(ABerry) *in tch: hdwy over 2f out: rdn to chse ldng pair over 1f out: kpt on same pce* **25/1**

0-00 4 *3/4* **Western Command (GER)**[6] 455 8-11-7 30 MrsMMorris 3 23
(MrsNMacauley) *towards rr: wd st: hdwy over 1f out: styd on wl fnl f: nrst fin* **8/1**

0-06 5 *6* **Pageant**[7] 441 7-11-7 35 MissEJJones 8 11
(JMBradley) *chsd ldrs: rdn along 3f out: sn wknd* **6/1**[3]

000- 6 *1 1/2* **Ginner Morris**[27] 6198 9-11-4 30 (b) MissLEllison(3) 9 8
(JHetherton) *chsd ldrs: rdn 2f out: sn wknd* **9/1**

/0-0 7 *hd* **Meticulous**[7] 439 6-11-2 30 MrMScales(5) 4 7
(MCChapman) *nvr a factor* **25/1**

000- 8 *1 1/2* **College Star**[24] 6218 6-11-7 30 (b) MsCWilliams 2 4
(JFCoupland) *cl up: led 1/2-way: rdn along and hdd over 2f out: sn wknd* **5/1**[2]

500/ 9 *14* **Touch Of Spirit**[38] 5-11-0 35 MrNSoares(7) 10 —
(JRJenkins) *racd wd: bhd fr 1/2-way* **25/1**

0-05 10 *2 1/2* **Chantilly Gold (USA)**[7] 444 5-11-4 30 (b[1]) MrSDobson(3) 11 —
(JMBradley) *s.i.s and bhd: hdwy to chse ldrs over 3f out: sn rdn and wknd* **20/1**

/0-0 11 *3/4* **Aunt Doris**[4] 470 7-11-2 35 (p) MrPEvans(5) 5 —
(PaulJohnson) *sn led: rdn along and hdd 1/2-way: sn wknd* **8/1**

1m 47.92s (3.32) **Going Correction** +0.075s/f (Slow) **11 Ran SP% 114.3**
Speed ratings: **86,85,80,79,73 71,71,70,56,53 52**CSF £24.38 TOTE £9.80: £3.20, £2.70, £3.70; EX 27.30.
**Owner** S Day **Bred** Lord Halifax **Trained** Audley, Staffs

■ Stewards Enquiry : Mr N Soares three-day ban: used whip when out of contention (Jan 23,24,26)

**FOCUS**
As bad a contest as it gets and a slow time even for such a modest contest.

**NOTEBOOK**
**Smart Scot**, who had never previously finished in the places in 14 starts on the Flat and four starts over hurdles, proved good enough to win what was a truly awful race. Connections will be hopeful he can continue to race in this band of contest.
**Sea Ya Maite**, who has not won a race for over two and a half years, appreciated the drop in grade and clearly these sort of races are his future.
**Countrywide Girl(IRE)**, who has been on a steady decline since winning a claimer and seller in heavy ground at Lingfield back in October 2001, at least made the frame on this step up in trip.
**Western Command(GER)**ran a fair race compared with recent efforts but a better pace would have suited.
**Pageant**, who is a better horse on turf, remains a maiden on sand after 26 starts.

## 498 PRESS INTERACTIVE TO BET DIRECT CLAIMING STKS 7f (F)

1:50 (1:50) (H) 3-Y-0+ £1,477 (£422; £211) Stalls Low

Form RPR

4-21 1 **Lucayan Monarch**[7] 439 6-9-12 53 (p) DeanMcKeown 4 60+
(PABlockley) *chsd ldrs: hdwy over 2f out: led wl over 1f out: sn rdn and kpt on fnl f* **8/11**[1]

00-4 2 *2 1/2* **Donegal Shore (IRE)**[8] 433 5-9-12 66 (vt[1]) CCatlin 5 53
(MrsJCandlish) *cl up: rdn along and sltly outpcd over 2f out: drvn and styd on appr last* **14/1**

000- 3 *2 1/2* **Evangelist (IRE)**[34] 6149 4-9-7 40 FLynch 3 42
(ABerry) *trckd ldrs: lost pl 1/2-way: gd hdwy on inner over 2f out: sn rdn and chsd wnr over 1f out: sn drvn and one pce* **40/1**

0-33 4 *1* **Sudra**[3] 487 7-9-5 53 (b) JDO'Reilly(7) 6 45
(JO'Reilly) *prom: hdwy on outer to ld over 3f out: rdn 2f out and sn hdd: drvn and wknd appr last* **9/2**[2]

0-03 5 *3 1/2* **Tefi**[4] 481 6-9-2 45 (bt) PMakin(7) 7 33
(JBalding) *sn led: rdn along and hdd over 3f out: grad wknd* **20/1**

400- 6 *3* **Mr Stylish**[17] 6235 8-9-10 47 (vt) JDSmith 2 26
(JSMoore) *hld up in rr: hdwy 3f out: swtchd outside and rdn along 2f out: no imp* **9/1**

040- 7 *7* **Frank's Quest (IRE)**[140] 4464 4-9-12 58 JMackay 8 11
(JohnAHarris) *racd wd: a rr* **8/1**[3]

000- 8 *6* **Thats All Jazz**[77] 5790 6-9-5 45 JBramhill 1 —
(CRDore) *stdd s and swtchd wd: a rr* **25/1**

1m 31.62s (0.82) **Going Correction** +0.075s/f (Slow) **8 Ran SP% 114.9**
Speed ratings: **98,95,92,91,87 83,75,68**CSF £12.63 TOTE £1.40: £1.10, £1.70, £7.00; EX 9.40.No7 Evangelist was claimed by A Liddiard for £5,000
**Owner** A C Kirkham **Bred** Southcourt Stud **Trained** Southwell, Notts

**FOCUS**
Poor form behind the winner and just an average time.

**NOTEBOOK**
**Lucayan Monarch**had a bit to do strictly at the weights, but he had proved himself an in-form animal on his starts this year and that makes a big difference at this level.
**Donegal Shore(IRE)**, best in at the weights judged on official ratings, appreciated the step up to a more suitable trip. He ran well enough but his rating does need to be revised on the evidence of his recent efforts.
**Evangelist(IRE)**last won when she was a two-year-old. Banded races await.
**Sudra**, beaten in a seller last time, was not suited by the drop back from a mile.
**Tefi**, a winner of one race from 52 starts, is always worth opposing.
**Frank's Quest(IRE)** *Official explanation: vet said gelding was suffering from a back problem*

## 499 BET DIRECT ON 0800 93 66 93 BANDED STKS 5f (F)

2:20 (2:22) (H) 3-Y-0+ £1,470 (£420; £210) Stalls High

Form RPR

60-4 1 **Lady Protector**[6] 460 5-9-0 40 PMakin(7) 9 50
(JBalding) *racd centre: mde virtually all: rdn clr wl over 1f out: styd on strly* **5/1**[2]

05-0 2 *4* **Bali-Star**[10] 411 9-9-7 40 CCatlin 3 38
(RJHodges) *prom far side: chsd wnr fr 1/2-way: rdn along wl over 1f out: kpt on: no ch w wnr* **10/1**

505- 3 *3* **Bells Boy's**[34] 6155 5-9-7 40 (p) GParkin 1 29
(KARyan) *chsd ldrs far side: rdn along 2f out: drvn and styd on appr last* **7/1**[3]

000- 4 *1/2* **Blunham**[16] 6243 4-9-7 40 KDalgleish 8 27
(MCChapman) *bmpd s: sn outpcd and bhd centre: swtchd to far side 2f out: styd on wl u.p appr last: nrst fin* **40/1**

000- 5 *shd* **Sotonian (HOL)**[133] 4628 11-9-4 40 LisaJones(3) 5 27
(PSFelgate) *racd centre: midfield and rdn along 1/2-way: swtchd lft and styd on ins last: nrst fin* **14/1**

0-32 6 *hd* **Aguila Loco (IRE)**[4] 470 5-9-0 40 AndrewWebb(7) 16 26
(MCChapman) *prom stands side: rdn along 2f out: kpt on same pce* **9/4**[1]

0-04 7 *3/4* **Threat**[4] 470 8-9-7 40 JoannaBadger 14 24
(JMBradley) *towards rr and rdn along after 2f: hdwy u.p over 1f out: styd on ins last: nrst fin* **9/1**

006/ 8 *nk* **Our Old Boy (IRE)**[480] 4730 4-9-7 35 DRMcCabe 2 23
(JAGilbert) *chsd ldrs far side: rdn along over 2f out: grad wknd* **33/1**

00-0 9 *shd* **Law Maker**[7] 438 4-9-7 35 DeanMcKeown 15 23
(MABuckley) *spd stands side 3f: sn rdn along and wknd* **33/1**

0-65 10 *1* **Carols Choice**[7] 443 7-9-4 35 J-PGuillambert(3) 7 20
(ASadik) *chsd wnr centre: rdn along 1/2-way: grad wknd* **8/1**

060- 11 *1/2* **Tuscan Dream**[16] 6243 9-9-2 40 PBradley(5) 12 18
(ABerry) *prom: rdn along 2f out: grad wknd* **20/1**

00-0 12 *nk* **Caronte (IRE)**[4] 474 4-9-7 40 (b) JBramhill 6 17
(SRBowring) *chsd ldrs centre: rdn along 1/2-way: grad wknd* **20/1**

520- 13 *2 1/2* **Wittily**[143] 4358 4-9-7 40 (b) FLynch 11 10
(ABerry) *in tch: rdn along 1/2-way: sn wknd* **20/1**

000- 14 *2 1/2* **Subtle Move (USA)**[16] 6244 4-9-7 30 JFanning 10 2
(DShaw) *hmpd s: a rr* **25/1**

000- 15 *3* **Diamond Racket**[118] 4969 4-9-7 40 (b) RBrisland 13 —
(DWChapman) *a rr* **50/1**

59.95 secs (-0.35) **Going Correction** -0.125s/f (Stan) **15 Ran SP% 125.2**
Speed ratings: **97,90,85,85,84 84,83,82,82,81 80,79,75,71,67**CSF £49.91 TOTE £6.80: £2.50, £2.90, £2.20; EX 78.90.
**Owner** Simon Mapletoft Racing II **Bred** P J Wightman **Trained** Scrooby, Notts

**FOCUS**
Poor form, the time was about right for the grade although the winner did show better form on turf.

**NOTEBOOK**
**Lady Protector**was not disgraced in a seller last time and this drop in grade proved just what she needed. Her good draw helped but she should be able to cope with a rise into Band A races.
**Bali-Star**, whose only success to date came from a good draw at Windsor, was another who looks to have been given a chance of another win with the introduction of banded races.
**Bells Boy's**, back down to his best trip, did not have the best of draws and ran a fair race in the circumstances, although he is still a maiden.
**Blunham**was running over a trip well short of his best. He will be happier when returned to seven fulrongs.
**Sotonian(HOL)**, who has always been happier at Wolverhampton, probably needed this first outing since September.
**Aguila Loco(IRE)**finished best of those drawn in double figures and would probably have fared better had he been berthed in a lower stall.
**Carols Choice** *Official explanation: jockey said mare hung right*
**Wittily** *Official explanation: jockey said filly had a breathing problem*

## 500 BET DIRECT ON SKY TEXT PAGE 372 BANDED STKS 1m 3f (F)

2:50 (2:50) (H) 4-Y-0+ £1,624 (£464; £232) Stalls Low

Form RPR

00-3 1 **Seraph**[9] 427 4-8-12 40 (p) JMackay 9 43
(JohnAHarris) *hld up in tch: hdwy to trck ldrs 1/2-way: effrt to chse ldr over 1f out: sn rdn and styd on wl to ld last 100 yds* **8/1**

06-4 2 *hd* **Dancing Tilly**[9] 427 6-9-1 40 (p) CCatlin 3 43
(RAFahey) *pushed along towards rr: hdwy 1/2-way: gd run on outer to ld 2f out: rdn over 1f out: drvn ins last: hdd last 100 yds* **8/1**

50-5 3 *6* **East Cape**[7] 440 7-9-1 40 KimTinkler 1 34
(DonEnricoIncisa) *hld up: sltly hmpd bnd after 2f and sn bhd: hdwy 4f out: styng on whn hmpd over 1f out: swtchd lft: rdn and kpt on* **11/4**[1]

40-4 4 *1 1/2* **Two Steps To Go (USA)**[8] 430 5-8-8 40 (b) DFentiman(7) 4 32
(IanEmmerson) *cl up: led 1/2-way: rdn along and hdd 2f out: sn drvn and wknd appr last* **9/2**[3]

400- 5 *1 3/4* **Antony Ebeneezer**[86] 4420 5-9-1 40 (t) JBramhill 8 29
(CRDore) *trckd ldrs gng wl: smooth hdwy 3f out and ev ch tl rdn and wknd wl over 1f out* **4/1**[2]

00-0 6 *shd* **Aljomar**[8] 428 5-9-1 40 (p) RFitzpatrick 7 29
(REBarr) *cl up: rdn along over 3f out: sn wknd* **50/1**

64-6 7 *7* **Fraternity**[9] 427 7-9-1 40 DeanMcKeown 5 18
(JAPickering) *led to 1/2-way: rdn along and wknd 3f out* **8/1**

000- 8 *2 1/2* **The Recruiter**[23] 4111 4-8-9 40 (v) LisaJones(3) 10 15
(JGMO'Shea) *midfield: hdwy to chse ldrs over 4f out: sn rdn along and wknd* **20/1**

000- 9 *3 1/2* **Morris Dancing (USA)**[257] 1295 5-9-1 40 (p) JFanning 2 9
(BPJBaugh) *trckd ldrs on inner: rdn along 4f out and sn wknd* **50/1**

0- 10 *1 3/4* **Splendid Touch**[39] 6089 4-8-12 40 KDalgleish 6 7
(JRJenkins) *slowly into stgride: a rr* **16/1**

2m 28.95s (0.05) **Going Correction** +0.075s/f (Slow)
**WFA** 4 from 5yo+ 3lb **10 Ran SP% 112.7**
Speed ratings: **102,101,97,96,95 95,89,88,85,84**CSF £66.62 TOTE £7.50: £3.20, £2.00, £1.40; EX 56.60.
**Owner** M F Schofield **Bred** T R Lock **Trained** Eastwell, Leics

■ Stewards Enquiry : C Catlin one-day ban: used whip with excessive force (Jan 23)
D Fentiman caution: careless riding

**FOCUS**
A poor race with the first two clear, but a decent time for the class of contest.

**NOTEBOOK**
**Seraph**had his stamina to prove over this longer trip coming into the race, but on this evidence he is not deficient in that department. His trainer is planning to return him to hurdling soon.
**Dancing Tilly**, who finished just behind Seraph at Wolverhampton on her last start, found that rival just too strong again over this longer trip. Her Fibresand efforts so far suggest she is quite capable of winning at this level.

**East Cape**did not enjoy the smoothest of runs but it is becoming more difficult to keep making excuses for him.
**Two Steps To Go(USA)**, wearing blinkers instead of a visor this time, once again failed to see out the trip.
**Antony Ebeneezer**blew up in the manner of a horse who needed this first run since October.
**Splendid Touch** *Official explanation: jockey said filly hung right handed*

## 501 BET DIRECT MEDIAN AUCTION MAIDEN STKS 1m 6f (F)
**3:20** (3:20) (H ) 4-6-Y-O **£1,431** (£409; £204) **Stalls** Low

Form RPR
/5-2 **1** **Mr Smithers Jones**[8] 431 4-9-0 50 CCatlin 4 53+
(SCWilliams) *keen: hld up in rr: smooth hdwy on outer over 2f out: led wl over 1f out and sn clr: easily* **9/4**[1]
000- **2** *5* **Colonnade**[42] 5635 5-9-1 45 KDalgleish 6 42
(CGrant) *trckd ldng pair: pushed along over 4f out: rdn and outpcd 2f out: sn drvn and styd on ent last: no ch w wnr* **9/2**[3]
0/6- **3** *1 1/4* **Broughton Melody**[40] 6125 5-9-1 46 DeanMcKeown 7 40
(WJMusson) *hld up in rr: hdwy 3f out: pushed along 2f out: sn rdn and kpt on appr last* **5/1**
50-6 **4** *1* **Xixita**[7] 446 4-8-9 45 JBramhill 1 39
(DrJDScargill) *trckd ldr: led 3f out and sn rdn: hdd wl over 1f out: sn drvn and wknd* **20/1**
00-0 **5** *7* **Dr Julian (IRE)**[4] 472 4-9-0 45 (p) AnnStokell 2 35
(MissAStokell) *keen: led: pushed along over 4f out: hdd 3f out and sn wknd* **25/1**
064- **5** *dht* **Penalty Clause (IRE)**[17] 2847 4-8-11 45 (p) LisaJones(3) 5 35
(KAMorgan) *trckd ldrs: pushed along 1/2-way: rdn 4f out and sn wknd* **9/2**[3]
P60- **7** *11* **Theme Park**[160] 3859 4-9-0 60 JMackay 3 20
(JohnAHarris) *in tch: rdn along 3f out: sn wknd* **4/1**[2]
3m 13.52s (3.92) **Going Correction** +0.075s/f (Slow)
**WFA** 4 from 5yo 6lb **7** Ran SP% **112.4**
Speed ratings: **91,88,87,86,82 82,76**CSF £12.20 TOTE £2.70: £1.10, £1.90; EX 18.80.
**Owner** The Lager Khan **Bred** Old Mill Stud **Trained** Newmarket, Suffolk

**FOCUS**
A clear-cut success by the unexposed winner, but a slow time.

**NOTEBOOK**
**Mr Smithers Jones**, who was out for 11 months having caught a virus, had run well on his reappearance but had his stamina to prove over this longer trip. To be honest his stamina was not truly tested in this steadily-run affair, but he did win in style, coming clear inside the final quarter mile to score easily, and he can surely hold his own in better company.
**Colonnade**, returning to the Flat after a couple of outings over hurdles, found the winner in a different league, but kept on well enough to take the second prize.
**Broughton Melody**, ridden to get the trip, kept on well enough on her second run back after a long absence.
**Xixita**did not find the step up in trip bringing about any improvement.
**Dr Julian(IRE)**proved he gets this far at Catterick in September, but he is a long-standing maiden and was beaten a long way out on this occasion.
**Theme Park** *Official explanation: jockey said gelding had lost its action*

## 502 LITTLEWOODSPOKER.COM BANDED STKS 6f (F)
**3:50** (3:52) (H ) 3-Y-O+ **£1,379** (£394; £197) **Stalls** Low

Form RPR
000- **1** **Eternal Bloom**[235] 1774 6-9-0 35 MLawson(7) 2 49
(MBrittain) *cl up on inner: led 3f out: rdn clr over 1f out: wandered ent last: kpt on* **9/2**[2]
00-0 **2** *5* **Court Music (IRE)**[8] 429 5-9-7 35 (v) RFitzpatrick 9 34
(REBarr) *chsd ldrs: hdwy 2f out: sn rdn and edgd lft ent last: sn drvn and kpt on* **12/1**
60-1 **3** *1 1/2* **Desert Light (IRE)**[6] 452 3-8-8 35 (v) LisaJones(3) 12 36
(DShaw) *in tch: hdwy on outer 3f out: rdn to chse wnr and hung lft over 1f out: sn drvn and one pce ins last* **13/8**[1]
006- **4** *hd* **Zara Louise**[112] 5126 4-9-0 30 AElliott(7) 7 29
(RPElliott) *in rr: hdwy 1/2-way: rdn 2f out: drvn and edgd lft ent last: kpt on* **16/1**
046- **5** *1 1/4* **Mimas Girl**[217] 2230 5-9-7 35 (t) JBramhill 6 25
(SRBowring) *in tch: rdn along and hanging lft 2f out: n.m.r ent last no imp* **8/1**
600- **6** *1 1/4* **Redoubtable (USA)**[136] 4546 13-9-7 35 RBrisland 11 21
(DWChapman) *dwlt and bhd: hdwy 2f out: rdn wl over 1f out and sn no imp* **7/1**
000- **7** *3/4* **Sally Traffic**[54] 6032 5-9-7 30 VHalliday 4 19
(RMWhitaker) *cl up: rdn along over 2f out: grad wknd* **20/1**
00-5 **8** *shd* **Above Board**[4] 470 9-9-7 35 (b) DeanMcKeown 10 19
(RFMarvin) *led: rdn and hdd 3f out: drvn and wknd wl over 1f out* **6/1**[3]
00-0 **9** *15* **Blue Circle**[9] 422 4-9-7 30 (p) KDalgleish 3 —
(MMullineaux) *a rr* **40/1**
000- **10** *1 1/4* **Sargents Dream**[26] 6204 4-9-7 30 DRMcCabe 1 —
(JAGilbert) *a rr* **40/1**
/00- **11** *9* **Cool Bart**[251] 1429 4-9-7 30 JFanning 8 —
(BPJBaugh) *chsd ldrs to 1/2-way: sn wknd* **40/1**
1m 16.79s (-0.01) **Going Correction** +0.075s/f (Slow)
**WFA** 3 from 4yo+ 16lb **11** Ran SP% **119.8**
Speed ratings: **103,96,94,94,92 90,89,89,69,67 55**CSF £56.03 TOTE £7.40: £1.50, £4.10, £1.30; EX 74.60 Place 6 £30.44, Place 5 £14.21.
**Owner** Mel Brittain **Bred** Mrs L Abbott **Trained** Warthill, N Yorks

**FOCUS**
A good time considering the class of contest, and a fair performance by the winner.

**NOTEBOOK**
**Eternal Bloom**, having her first outing for almost eight months, came home a clear winner despite carrying her head awkwardly. She looks capable of holding her own in Band B races.
**Court Music(IRE)**, back to her winning trip, hung left under pressure but did run on, and she appears to have found her level.
**Desert Light(IRE)**showed much improved form last time out when winning a claimer on the Polytrack. The switch back to Fibresand, even in this lowly grade, did not suit and he will be happier when returning to Lingfield.
**Zara Louise**, who was having her first run since September, has shown much better form on turf than on Fibresand so far.
**Mimas Girl**, returning from a seven-month absence, did not help her rider by hanging under pressure. *Official explanation: jockey said mare stumbled leaving the starting stalls and lost a shoe*
**Redoubtable(USA)**, returning from a 136-day absence, is now in the twilight of his career.
T/Plt: £45.40 to a £1 stake. Pool: £28,570.40. 458.75 winning tickets. T/Qpdt: £11.60 to a £1 stake. Pool: £2,413.40. 153.40 winning tickets. JR

# 483 WOLVERHAMPTON (A.W) (L-H)
Monday, January 12

**OFFICIAL GOING: Standard**
The middle of the track continues to be the quickest.
Wind: nil Weather: fine

## 503 BET DIRECT NO Q 08000 93 66 93 APPRENTICE H'CAP (DIV I) 7f (F)
**1:10** (1:10) (G ) (0-60,59) 3-Y-O+ **£2,576** (£736; £368) **Stalls** High

Form RPR
000- **1** **Mount Hillaby (IRE)**[88] 5598 4-9-2 51 PMulrennan(3) 8 66+
(MWEasterby) *a.p: led 2f out: sn rdn: r.o wl* **15/8**[1]
050- **2** *3* **Spindor (USA)**[37] 6134 5-9-7 58 (b) SCrawford(5) 1 66
(JAOsborne) *w ldr: led 3f out: rdn and hdd 2f out: no ex fnl f* **16/1**
36-3 **3** *4* **Feast Of Romance**[5] 468 7-9-1 50 (p) DNolan(3) 9 48
(PHowling) *hld up in tch: ev ch 3f out: sn rdn: wknd 2f out* **4/1**[2]
2-21 **4** *1* **Larky's Lob**[8] 429 5-9-5 54 6ex NChalmers(3) 11 49
(PaulJohnson) *hld up: hdwy 4f out: rdn and ev ch 2f out: wknd over 1f out* **5/1**[3]
000- **5** *2* **Phantom Flame (USA)**[58] 6006 4-9-3 49 LEnstone 5 39
(MJohnston) *prom: rdn 4f out: wknd over 2f out* **20/1**
600- **6** *shd* **Karaoke King**[71] 5892 6-9-8 57 RMiles(3) 3 47
(JELong) *prom: losing pl whn n.m.r and dropped rr 4f out: n.d after* **16/1**
306- **7** *1* **Littleton Zephir (USA)**[214] 2290 5-8-8 47 DerekNolan(7) 7 34
(MrsPTownsley) *prom: rdn over 3f out: wknd over 2f out* **20/1**
400- **8** *1/2* **Beauteous (IRE)**[86] 5636 5-8-11 48 PPMathers(5) 2 34
(ABerry) *led: rdn and hdd 3f out: sn wknd* **5/1**[3]
5-04 **9** *shd* **Bijan (IRE)**[8] 429 6-7-12 35 (p) StephanieHollinshead(5) 10 21
(RHollinshead) *bhd: short-lived effrt on outside 3f out* **16/1**
60-0 **10** *1/2* **Jessinca**[10] 406 8-8-5 40 (v) BReilly(3) 4 25
(APJones) *s.i.s: a bhd* **14/1**
300- **11** *14* **Mizhar (USA)**[150] 4153 8-9-13 59 (v) LPKeniry 6 9
(JJQuinn) *hld up: hdwy over 3f out: rdn and wknd over 2f out: eased fnl f* **33/1**
1m 30.37s (0.17) **Going Correction** -0.10s/f (Stan) **11** Ran SP% **124.9**
Speed ratings: **95,91,87,85,83 83,82,81,81,81 65**CSF £38.61 CT £120.29 TOTE £2.90: £2.00, £5.30, £1.80; EX 80.90.
**Owner** D F Spence & J Southway **Bred** Lodge Park Stud **Trained** Sheriff Hutton, N Yorks

**FOCUS**
Probably the better of the two divisions given that the winner is capable of further improvement, and the first three look nicely treated. However, the time was moderate for the class of contest.

**NOTEBOOK**
**Mount Hillaby(IRE)** ◆ had appeared to lose her way after winning a Catterick maiden in 2002 for Barry Hills but, returning from a break and stepping back up in trip, she landed a gamble in good style. If turned out again soon she would escape a penalty.
**Spindor(USA)**, who raced against the inside throughout, held every chance but simply found the winner too good. He was clear of the remainder.
**Feast Of Romance**, on a long losing run and beaten in a seller last time, looked to have every chance but was simply not good enough.
**Larky's Lob**, under a 6lb penalty for his recent banded stakes success, raced wide for most of the way but appeared to be beaten fair and square.
**Phantom Flame(USA)**, still a maiden, ran better than he has done of late.

## 504 BET DIRECT NO Q 08000 93 66 93 APPRENTICE H'CAP (DIV II) 7f (F)
**1:40** (1:41) (G ) (0-60,59) 3-Y-O+ **£2,576** (£736; £368) **Stalls** High

Form RPR
50-2 **1** **Lord Chamberlain**[7] 442 11-9-3 49 (b) FPFerris 7 58
(JMBradley) *outpcd and bhd: rdn and hdwy on outside 3f out: led jst over 1f out: edgd lft fnl f: r.o* **10/1**
640- **2** *1 1/4* **Up Tempo (IRE)**[107] 5224 6-9-6 59 (p) AMullen(7) 9 65
(TDEasterby) *hld up: hdwy over 2f out: rdn whn nt clr run jst over 1f out: sn swtchd lft: r.o ins fnl f: nt trble wnr* **11/2**[3]
052- **3** *1 1/2* **Waltzing Wizard**[27] 6202 5-9-1 52 PPMathers(5) 3 54
(ABerry) *outpcd and bhd: hdwy over 1f out: styd on wl towards fin* **7/2**[1]
40-4 **4** *1/2* **Its Ecco Boy**[6] 453 6-9-2 51 DNolan(3) 5 52
(PHowling) *a.p: led 3f out: sn hrd rdn: edgd rt and hdd jst over 1f out: wknd ins fnl f* **4/1**[2]
465- **5** *nk* **Aintnecessarilyso**[12] 6265 6-8-8 45 MSavage(5) 2 45
(NEBerry) *chsd ldrs: rdn and no hdwy fnl 2f* **12/1**
000- **6** *1/2* **Muqarrar (IRE)**[52] 6042 5-9-1 52 (e) SJDonohoe(5) 10 51
(TJFitzgerald) *hld up: hdwy whn stmbld over 3f out: sn rdn: one pce fnl 2f* **10/1**
500/ **7** *2 1/2* **Port Natal (IRE)**[39] 5842 6-8-8 43 ow3 (b) RMiles(3) 8 36
(PatrickMorris, Ire) *prom: led 4f out to 3f out: sn rdn: wknd over 1f out* **7/1**
0/0- **8** *2* **Hellbent**[28] 6193 5-8-13 50 ow2 SCrawford(5) 4 38
(JAOsborne) *led 3f: rdn and ev ch over 2f out: wknd over 1f out* **14/1**
406- **9** *5* **Chorus**[128] 4738 7-9-2 55 MSaunders(7) 6 30
(BRMillman) *prom tl wknd 3f out* **11/1**
4-12 **10** *1 1/2* **Repeat (IRE)**[4] 481 4-9-9 58 (p) TEaves(3) 1 29
(MissGayKelleway) *prom: rdn over 3f out: wknd over 2f out* **10/1**
1m 30.62s (0.42) **Going Correction** -0.10s/f (Stan) **10** Ran SP% **120.1**
Speed ratings: **93,91,89,89,88 88,85,83,77,75**CSF £66.12 CT £242.01 TOTE £14.60: £5.30, £2.40, £1.50; EX 81.00.
**Owner** W C Harries **Bred** Dragon's Stud **Trained** Sedbury, Gloucs

**FOCUS**
Probably just the weaker of the two divisions and once again the winning time was moderate and the form is modest. The first three home all raced off the pace early on.

**NOTEBOOK**
**Lord Chamberlain**, runner-up in a claimer last time on first run since October, showed the benefit of that run to gain his first win since June 2002. He would escape a penalty for this success if turning out again soon, but does not have a great wins-to-run record and may be worth taking on.
**Up Tempo(IRE)** was supported in the market to end a losing run stretching back to May 2000. He had to be switched left in the straight to get a clear run, but cannot really be considered unlucky and is quite simply just very hard to win with.
**Waltzing Wizard**, runner-up in a similar event at Southwell last time, had to be switched left in the straight to get a clear run but was not unlucky.
**Its Ecco Boy** fared best of those who raced up with the pace.
**Aintnecessarilyso**, stepping up from five furlongs, continues on his long losing run.
**Muqarrar(IRE)** nearly came down when clipping heels turning out of the back straight.
**Port Natal(IRE)** was reported to have finished distressed. *Official explanation: trainer said gelding was found to be distressed post race*

## 505 BET DIRECT NO Q DEMO ON 08000 837 888 H'CAP 1m 4f (F)
2:10 (2:11) (F) (0-55,57) 4-Y-0+ £2,933 (£838; £419) Stalls Low

Form RPR
600- 1 **Sendintank**[179] 3338 4-9-0 **50** BReilly(5) 4 75+
(SCWilliams) *hld up mid-div: swtchd rt and hdwy on outside 3f out: shkn up to ld wl over 1f out: sn clr: easily* **4/1**[2]
00-1 2 *11* **Cool Bathwick (IRE)**[3] 484 5-10-2 **57** 6ex JQuinn 12 59
(BRMillman) *a.p: led over 5f out: rdn over 3f out: hdd wl over 1f out: sn no ch w wnr* **3/1**[1]
20-3 3 *2 ½* **Ambersong**[5] 467 6-9-10 **51** ACulhane 9 49
(AWCarroll) *s.i.s: hdwy over 5f out: rdn over 4f out: wknd over 1f out* **4/1**[2]
016- 4 *½* **Fight The Feeling**[17] 6239 6-10-0 **55** (v) MartinDwyer 10 53
(JWUnett) *hld up and bhd: hdwy over 4f out: wnt 2nd over 3f out tl rdn over 2f out: wknd over 1f out* **7/1**[3]
000- 5 *15* **Colourful Lady (USA)**[47] 6076 4-9-10 **55** NCallan 6 30
(PWHarris) *hld up in tch: rdn over 3f out: sn wknd* **11/1**
05-0 6 *3* **Red Storm**[10] 406 5-9-4 **48** RMiles(3) 7 19
(JRBoyle) *hld up in tch: hdwy over 5f out: rdn over 3f out: wknd over 2f out* **25/1**
030- 7 *2 ½* **In Luck**[49] 6061 6-9-6 **47** RFfrench 3 14
(BSmart) *hld up in tch: lost pl on ins bnd over 6f out: rdn 4f out: no rspnse* **14/1**
061- 8 *3* **Only For Sue**[21] 6234 5-9-12 **53** IMongan 5 15
(WSKittow) *prom: pushed along over 7f out: wknd over 2f out* **4/1**[2]
300- 9 *14* **In Spirit (IRE)**[23] 6226 6-9-12 **53** WMLordan 8 —
(BJCurley) *a bhd: t.o* **14/1**
000- 10 *14* **Platinum Boy (IRE)**[23] 6226 4-9-6 **51** (b) VSlattery 2 —
(MWellings) *led: rdn and hdd 5f out: sn lost pl: t.o* **50/1**
060- 11 *14* **Humdinger (IRE)**[16] 6247 4-9-0 **50** (v[1]) THamilton(5) 11 —
(DShaw) *prom tl rdn and wknd over 4f out: t.o* **33/1**

2m 37.95s (-3.55) **Going Correction** -0.10s/f (Stan)
**WFA** 4 from 5yo+ 4lb **11** Ran SP% **127.9**
Speed ratings: **107,99,98,97,87 85,84,82,72,63 54**CSF £17.84 CT £54.68 TOTE £4.20: £1.50, £1.50, £1.80; EX 15.80.
**Owner** Steve Jones And Phil McGovern **Bred** K G Powter **Trained** Newmarket, Suffolk

**FOCUS**
Just a moderate handicap, but the well-backed Sendintank could hardly have been more impressive and looks well ahead of the Handicapper. He also recorded a decent time.

**NOTEBOOK**
**Sendintank**, racing for the first time in 179 days and stepping up four furlongs in trip, justified considerable market support with a mightily impressive success. He had to be switched wide to get a clear run but, once in the clear, he quickened right away. He looks capable of following up. *Official explanation: trainer's representative said, regarding the improved form shown, gelding benefited from the step up in trip*
**Cool Bathwick(IRE)**, off the mark in a weak course and distance maiden on his previous start, was kept wide early on from his outside stall, but he soon had a good position and can have no excuses - he was simply beaten by a better handicapped horse.
**Ambersong** needed plenty of encouragment from the saddle and never really looked like giving the winner a race. He could be worth a try over two miles.
**Fight The Feeling**, stepped back up to a more suitable trip, could offer little close home.
**Only For Sue**, up 8lb for his recent course and distance success, dropped out tamely and was below form.

## 506 LITTLEWOODS BET DIRECT MAIDEN STKS 7f (F)
2:40 (2:41) (D) 3-Y-0 £3,318 (£948; £474) Stalls High

Form RPR
02- 1 **Honest Injun**[70] 5905 3-9-0 MartinDwyer 4 77
(BWHills) *hld up: hdwy over 4f out: rdn to ld wl over 1f out: r.o wl* **4/9**[1]
2 *¾* **Play Master (IRE)** 3-9-0 PaulEddery 8 75
(DHaydnJones) *s.i.s: hdwy over 5f out: rdn over 2f out: ev ch 1f out: nt qckn* **20/1**
0- 3 *3 ½* **My Paris**[30] 6175 3-9-0 JQuinn 7 66
(KARyan) *s.i.s: stdy hdwy over 5f out: rdn 3f out: wknd fnl f* **33/1**
4 *1 ½* **Heversham (IRE)** 3-9-0 ACulhane 2 63
(WJHaggas) *hld up in tch: rdn whn n.m.r 3f out: wknd fnl f* **12/1**
02- 5 *4* **Mugeba**[14] 6250 3-8-9 MFenton 3 48
(WJMusson) *led: rdn over 2f out: hdd wl over 1f out: wknd 1f out* **11/2**[2]
6 6 *1* **Royaltea**[10] 409 3-8-6 FPFerris(3) 6 45
(MsDeborahJEvans) *prom: rdn over 3f out: wknd over 2f out* **20/1**
2-3 7 *6* **Anisette**[7] 444 3-8-9 NCallan 9 30
(JulianPoulton) *prom: rdn over 3f out: wknd over 2f out* **7/1**[3]
00- 8 *4* **Monkey Or Me (IRE)**[31] 6167 3-9-0 DMernagh 5 25
(PTMidgley) *t.k.h: stdd after 1f: rdn over 3f out: sn bhd* **66/1**
0- 9 *¾* **Posh Sheelagh**[49] 6058 3-8-9 SWKelly 1 18
(JGGiven) *s.i.s: rdn 4f out: a in rr* **50/1**

1m 29.67s (-0.53) **Going Correction** -0.10s/f (Stan) **9** Ran SP% **120.7**
Speed ratings: **99,98,94,92,87 86,79,75,74**CSF £17.92 TOTE £1.60: £1.10, £5.00, £6.50; EX 15.00.
**Owner** Guy Reed **Bred** G Reed **Trained** Lambourn, Berks

**FOCUS**
Just a weak maiden and the form way be worth treating with caution.

**NOTEBOOK**
**Honest Injun**, runner-up in a Redcar maiden when last seen 70 days previously, had to work pretty hard to confirm that promise and probably failed to run to that form on this Fibresand debut. He may be worth a try on Polytrack, but his future now lies in the hands of the Handicapper.
**Play Master(IRE)**, a 15,000gns yearling, out of a modest maiden, made a very pleasing debut. He soon recovered from a slow start and held every chance when it mattered - just finding the more experienced Honest Injun too strong. He looks sure to improve on this and is capable of picking up a similar race.
**My Paris** showed signs of inexperience but still stepped up on his debut effort and, going the right way, he should find things easier in handicaps.
**Heversham(IRE)** was easy to back, but made a respectable debut.
**Mugeba** failed to confirm the promise she showed on Polytrack on this her first start on Fibresand.
**Anisette** ran disappointingly below form.

## 507 BETDIRECT.CO.UK H'CAP 1m 1f 79y(F)
3:10 (3:11) (D) (0-85,84) 4-Y-0+ £4,085 (£1,257; £628; £314) Stalls Low

Form RPR
043- 1 **Intricate Web (IRE)**[44] 6098 8-9-0 **72** DAllan(3) 3 82
(EJAlston) *a.p: rdn 5f out: c wd st: led ins fnl f: r.o* **9/2**[2]
304- 2 *1* **Skylarker (USA)**[13] 6263 6-9-6 **78** LPKeniry(3) 6 86
(WSKittow) *a.p: led 5f out to 4f out: rdn to ld again 2f out: hdd and nt qckn ins fnl f* **9/2**[2]
335- 3 *1 ¾* **Critical Stage (IRE)**[31] 6169 5-8-6 **61** (e) MFenton 1 66
(JohnBerry) *bhd: rdn over 3f out: hdwy on ins over 2f out: kpt on ins fnl f* **12/1**
003- 4 *1 ¾* **Del Mar Sunset**[12] 6268 5-9-13 **82** ACulhane 9 83
(WJHaggas) *a.p: led 4f out: rdn 3f out: hdd 2f out: wknd ins fnl f* **7/2**[1]
224- 5 *¾* **Caroubier (IRE)**[12] 6268 4-9-8 **78** (b) DMernagh 8 78
(TDBarron) *s.i.s: plld hrd: sn mid-div: hdwy over 4f out: rdn over 3f out: one pce fnl 2f* **12/1**
452- 6 *2* **Tropical Coral (IRE)**[14] 6255 4-8-11 **72** DNolan(5) 11 68
(CTinkler) *bhd: rdn 3f out: hdwy over 2f out: no imp fnl f* **9/1**
064- 7 *1 ¾* **Middleton Grey**[16] 6245 6-9-13 **82** SWhitworth 10 74
(AGNewcombe) *hld up and bhd: hdwy over 5f out: rdn over 3f out: wknd over 2f out* **20/1**
061- 8 *5* **Buscador (USA)**[37] 6140 5-8-8 **70** BSwarbrick(7) 5 52
(WMBrisbourne) *led after 1f to 5f out: sn rdn: wknd 2f out* **6/1**[3]
421- 9 *1 ¼* **Noul (USA)**[31] 6169 5-9-4 **73** (b) NCallan 4 53
(KARyan) *hld up: pushed along over 5f out: bhd fnl 4f* **10/1**
610- 10 *12* **East Flares**[91] 5543 4-8-11 **67** SWKelly 12 23
(JWUnett) *bhd tl hdwy 6f out: rdn 5f out: sn wknd* **33/1**
540- 11 *7* **Hov**[88] 5597 4-9-11 **84** LFletcher(3) 2 26
(JJQuinn) *led 1f: prom: rdn over 4f out: sn struggling* **33/1**
160- 12 *6* **Spanish Gold**[33] 6164 4-9-2 **72** MartinDwyer 7 2
(AMBalding) *t.k.h: prom tl rdn and wknd over 3f out* **8/1**

2m 0.66s (-2.24) **Going Correction** -0.10s/f (Stan)
**WFA** 4 from 5yo+ 1lb **12** Ran SP% **129.1**
Speed ratings: **105,104,102,101,100 98,97,92,91,80 74,69**CSF £27.08 CT £239.33 TOTE £6.00: £1.50, £2.50, £4.60; EX 30.70 Trifecta £1361.30 Pool £5,752.18, 3.00 w/u.
**Owner** Morris, Oliver, Pierce **Bred** Moyglare Stud Farm Ltd **Trained** Longton, Lancs

**FOCUS**
A decent, competitive handicap and they went a good pace from the start. However, nothing looks particularly well treated at present.

**NOTEBOOK**
**Intricate Web(IRE)** failed to score throughout last year but has dropped to a reasonable mark as a result. Never too far off the decent pace, he was brought wide in the straight and kept on right the way to the line. He has followed up in the past and, despite not having that much in hand at the finish, he could well do so again.
**Skylarker(USA)**, fourth over a mile at Lingfield last time on his return from nearly six months off, ran another solid race on this return to Fibresand and demands plenty of respect in this sort of contest.
**Critical Stage(IRE)** ran well over a trip short of his best and will be interesting when stepped back up.
**Del Mar Sunset**, a good third over course and distance last time, was unable to build on that and is becoming a little frustrating.
**Caroubier(IRE)** needed plenty of driving as soon as the stalls opened and never gave the winner too much to worry about.
**Buscador(USA)**, 5lb higher than when winning over course and distance on his previous start, ran below form.

## 508 LITTLEWOODSCASINO.COM (S) STKS 1m 100y(F)
3:40 (3:42) (G) 3-Y-0 £2,520 (£720; £360) Stalls Low

Form RPR
650- 1 **Jakarmi**[12] 6269 3-8-11 55 MartinDwyer 3 53
(BPalling) *w ldr: led over 4f out: rdn over 2f out: clr over 1f out: r.o wl* **11/4**[1]
01- 2 *3* **Killing Me Softly**[12] 6269 3-8-11 53 NCallan 1 47
(JGallagher) *led: hdd over 4f out: rdn over 3f out: btn whn edgd rt over 1f out* **7/2**[2]
456- 3 *½* **Brother Cadfael**[12] 6269 3-8-11 45 SWhitworth 8 46
(JohnAHarris) *hld up: rdn over 3f out: hdwy over 2f out: one pce fnl f* **4/1**[3]
50-4 4 *2* **Secret Bloom**[10] 408 3-8-11 47 (v) DarrenWilliams 6 41
(JRNorton) *s.i.s: t.k.h: sn in tch: rdn and sltly outpcd 3f out: hdwy wl over 1f out: one pce fnl f* **8/1**
503- 5 *1 ¾* **Marita**[12] 6269 3-8-6 45 MFenton 7 33
(JGGiven) *hld up in tch: rdn over 4f out: c wd st: no hdwy* **4/1**[3]
045- 6 *nk* **Platinum Chief**[12] 6269 3-8-11 47 ACulhane 2 37
(ABerry) *prom: rdn over 3f out: wknd wl over 1f out* **10/1**
00-0 7 *9* **Miss Judged**[9] 420 3-8-3 45 (bt[1]) FPFerris(3) 4 13
(APJones) *t.k.h: prom: rdn over 2f out: sn wknd* **40/1**
8 *13* **Rejoyce (IRE)** 3-8-6 JQuinn 5 —
(JJay) *sn in rr: lost tch 3f out* **20/1**

1m 51.31s (0.31) **Going Correction** -0.10s/f (Stan) **8** Ran SP% **116.3**
Speed ratings: **94,91,90,88,86 86,77,64**CSF £12.80 TOTE £6.50: £2.60, £1.40, £1.10; EX 13.80.There was no bid for the winner.
**Owner** Mrs M M Palling **Bred** Llety Stud **Trained** Tredodridge, Vale Of Glamorgan

**FOCUS**
A weak seller.

**NOTEBOOK**
**Jakarmi**, well beaten behind Killing Me Softly in this grade on his previous start, left that form well behind to reverse those placings. Connections said he did not like being crowded on the inside rail last time and therefore changed the tactics on this occasion. *Official explanation: trainer said, regarding the improved form shown, gelding was ridden just behind the pace last time and seemed not to like being crowded on the inside rail whereas here it benefited from having space to run when ridden more prominently on the outside*
**Killing Me Softly** proved unable to confirm recent placings with the winner, but ran well and should continue to do so if kept to this grade.
**Brother Cadfael** is still a maiden and may be worth a try in a regional race.
**Secret Bloom** did not appear suited by this step up in trip.
**Marita** is not progressing.

## 509 BET DIRECT IN VISION SKY PAGE 293 H'CAP (DIV I) 6f (F)
4:10 (4:13) (F) (0-60,59) 3-Y-0+ £2,975 (£850; £425) Stalls Low

Form RPR
030- 1 **Caustic Wit (IRE)**[48] 6065 6-9-1 **50** RMiles(3) 1 67
(MSSaunders) *chsd ldrs: rdn to ld wl over 1f out: rdn out* **25/1**
04-3 2 *hd* **Savile's Delight (IRE)**[6] 453 5-9-5 **54** (p) FPFerris(3) 2 70
(RBrotherton) *w ldrs: led over 3f out: rdn and hdd wl over 1f out: ev ch ins fnl f: r.o* **7/2**[2]
50-1 3 *4* **Italian Mist (FR)**[9] 422 5-9-4 **50** (e) GFaulkner 11 54
(JulianPoulton) *led over 2f: rdn and sltly outpcd 2f out: kpt on same pce fnl f* **8/1**
00-4 4 *hd* **Arogant Prince**[9] 423 7-9-6 **55** (v[1]) DMcGaffin(3) 12 58
(ISemple) *a.p: rdn over 2f out: wknd fnl f* **10/1**
60-6 5 *1 ½* **Tigress (IRE)**[10] 407 5-9-13 **59** (b) MartinDwyer 3 58
(JWUnett) *hld up: rdn and hdwy on ins over 2f out: no imp appr fnl f* **20/1**
0-12 6 *½* **Cleveland Way**[8] 429 4-8-11 **48** (v) DNolan(5) 10 45
(DCarroll) *prom: rdn over 3f out: wknd over 2f out* **13/2**[3]
04-3 7 *1* **Attorney**[9] 421 6-8-8 **45** (e) THamilton(5) 13 39
(DShaw) *chsd ldrs: rdn over 3f out: wknd wl over 1f out* **9/1**
20-2 8 *shd* **Geronimo**[4] 476 7-9-11 **57** (p) JQuinn 8 51
(MissGayKelleway) *sn bhd: n.d* **11/4**[1]

03-5 **9** *nk* **Lake Eyre (IRE)**[7] [438] 5-8-13 **45**... JEdmunds 4 38
(JBalding) *hld up and bhd: hdwy over 3f out: wknd over 2f out* **12/1**
210- **10** *3/4* **Warlingham (IRE)**[13] [6260] 6-9-8 **54**... VSlattery 6 45
(PHowling) *rdn over 3f out: a bhd* **9/1**
0-44 **11** *1 1/2* **Enjoy The Buzz**[7] [443] 5-8-8 **40**... PFitzsimons 9 26
(JMBradley) *prom tl wknd over 2f out* **20/1**
160- **12** *3/4* **Flying Edge (IRE)**[87] [5626] 4-9-10 **56**... ANicholls 7 40
(EJAlston) *hld up: rdn 3f out: sn bhd* **12/1**
460- **13** *7* **Victory Flip (IRE)**[16] [6244] 4-9-3 **49**...(p) NCallan 5 12
(RHollinshead) *outpcd: bhd most of way* **28/1**
1m 14.64s (-1.06) **Going Correction** -0.10s/f (Stan) **13** Ran SP% **134.6**
Speed ratings: **103,102,97,97,95 94,93,93,92,91 89,88,79**CSF £119.53 CT £848.04 TOTE £47.70: £10.40, £2.20, £3.00; EX 272.50.
**Owner** Mrs Sandra Jones **Bred** Gainsborough Stud Management Ltd **Trained** Haydon, Somerset

**FOCUS**
Just a moderate handicap run in a slightly faster time than the second division.

**NOTEBOOK**
**Caustic Wit(IRE)**, whose last win came off a mark of 92 in September 2000, ended that losing run with a narrow success. He had little to spare at the finish and, although this will have boosted his confidence, things will be tougher next time.
**Savile's Delight(IRE)** had never previously shown his best form on Fibresand but, supported in the ring, he ran well. Connections have more options for him now he has proven his effectiveness on this surface.
**Italian Mist(FR)** found this harder than the banded stakes he won here last time and was no match for the front two.
**Arogant Prince**, with a visor replacing cheekpieces and dropping a furlong in trip, did not appear to have any excuses.
**Tigress(IRE)** ran an encouraging enough race and may be about to hit form.
**Geronimo** is very hard to win with and never got in a blow. *Official explanation: trainer said race had come too soon for the gelding after his previous run*

## 510 BET DIRECT IN VISION SKY PAGE 293 H'CAP (DIV II) 6f (F)
**4:40** (4:40) (F) (0-60,60) 3-Y-O+ **£2,968** (£848; £424) **Stalls** Low

Form RPR
00-3 **1** **Mr Pertemps**[4] [476] 6-9-4 55...(p) THamilton(5) 10 67
(RAFahey) *a.p: led 1f out: rdn out* **7/4**[1]
02-5 **2** *1* **Amelia (IRE)**[10] [407] 6-8-9 48... BSwarbrick(7) 13 57
(WMBrisbourne) *hld up: rdn and hdwy on outside over 2f out: r.o ins fnl f: nt rch wnr* **9/1**
00-4 **3** *1 1/4* **Lady Natilda**[4] [480] 4-9-2 48... PaulEddery 5 53
(DHaydnJones) *hld up mid-div: hdwy on ins over 2f out: sn rdn: kpt on ins fnl f* **13/2**
000- **4** *nk* **Fiamma Royale (IRE)**[31] [6166] 6-9-0 49... RMiles(3) 6 53
(MSSaunders) *w ldrs: led over 2f out: rdn and hdd 1f out: no ex towards fin* **11/1**
54-2 **5** *3/4* **Speedfit Free (IRE)**[8] [433] 7-9-9 55...(b) ACulhane 12 57
(ISemple) *hld up: hdwy over 3f out: rdn over 2f out: no imp fnl f* **6/1**[3]
334- **6** *3 1/2* **Kiss The Rain**[12] [6264] 4-9-1 50...(v) FPFerris(3) 7 42
(RBrotherton) *prom: rdn and lost pl over 3f out: n.d after* **11/2**[2]
000- **7** *3/4* **Pride Of Kinloch**[27] [6196] 4-9-8 54... MFenton 11 43
(JHetherton) *hld up mid-div: rdn and lost pl 3f out: sme late prog* **33/1**
500- **8** *nk* **Piccolo Prince**[125] [4795] 3-8-7 58... DAllan(3) 9 46
(EJAlston) *led early: chsd ldrs tl rdn and wknd over 2f out* **33/1**
6F-0 **9** *3/4* **Indian Shores**[10] [407] 5-9-7 53... PJScallan 3 39
(MMullineaux) *s.i.s: a bhd* **40/1**
/00- **10** *nk* **Back In Spirit**[166] [3682] 4-8-13 45...(t) PMQuinn 8 30
(BAMcmahon) *plld hrd: sn led: rdn and hdd over 2f out: sn wknd* **20/1**
62-4 **11** *1* **Shadowfax**[7] [438] 4-9-9 60...(b) TEaves(5) 2 42
(MissGayKelleway) *s.i.s: short-lived effrt on ins wl over 1f out* **9/1**
160- **P** **Docduckout**[333] [528] 4-9-11 57... MartinDwyer 4 —
(JWUnett) *outpcd: last whn p.u lame 3f out* **20/1**
1m 15.32s (-0.38) **Going Correction** -0.10s/f (Stan)
**WFA** 3 from 4yo+ 16lb **12** Ran SP% **125.5**
Speed ratings: **98,96,95,94,93 88,87,87,86,86 84,—**CSF £18.67 CT £93.40 TOTE £2.40: £2.00, £1.70, £2.00; EX 32.30 Place 6 £15.48, Place 5 £8.97.
**Owner** Monohydrate Developments **Bred** Bearstone Stud **Trained** Musley Bank, N Yorks

**FOCUS**
Another moderate handicap and the winning time was 0.68 seconds slower than the first division. The fourth looks nicely weighted at present.

**NOTEBOOK**
**Mr Pertemps** has a good record on Fibresand and confirmed the promise of his third over this course and distance last time with a decisive victory. He should continue to go well in this sort of grade.
**Amelia(IRE)**, below form over course and distance on her previous start, ran better this time but was readily held by the winner.
**Lady Natilda** is in decent enough form without looking likely to end a losing run stretching back to October 2002.
**Fiamma Royale(IRE)**, with the cheekpieces left off this time, showed real signs of a return to form and is one to keep an eye on for a similar contest.
**Speedfit Free(IRE)** found this tougher than the seller he finished second in last time.
**Docduckout** *Official explanation: jockey said gelding had pulled up lame*
T/Jkpt: Not won. T/Plt: £55.00 to a £1 stake. Pool: £36,979.35. 490.50 winning tickets. T/Qpdt: £11.80 to a £1 stake. Pool: £2,625.60. 164.30 winning tickets. KH

# 497 SOUTHWELL (L-H)
## Tuesday, January 13

**OFFICIAL GOING: Standard**
As is usual, the inside appeared to ride deeper and slower than the middle of the track.

## 511 LITTLEWOODS BET DIRECT H'CAP (DIV I) 6f (F)
**12:20** (12:21) (D) (0-80,80) 4-Y-O+ **£4,046** (£1,245; £622; £311) **Stalls** Low

Form RPR
20-4 **1** **Prima Stella**[11] [407] 5-8-12 **67**... LisaJones(3) 2 79
(JARToller) *trckd ldrs: effrt 2f out: rdn and qcknd to ld jst ins last: r.o* **10/1**
52-1 **2** *1 1/2* **Soba Jones**[5] [480] 7-9-6 **72** 6ex... JEdmunds 1 80
(JBalding) *led: qcknd 2f out: rdn over 1f out: hdd jst ins last: kpt on same pce* **5/1**[2]
200- **3** *hd* **Polar Kingdom**[17] [6245] 6-9-4 **70**... DMernagh 9 77
(TDBarron) *chsd ldrs: n.m.r and sltly outpcd 1/2-way: hdwy on outer over 1f out: ev ch tl rdn and nt qckn ins last* **5/2**[1]
131- **4** *1 1/2* **Ellens Academy (IRE)**[95] [5473] 9-10-0 **80**... DeanMcKeown 5 82
(EJAlston) *towards rr: hdwy 2f out: rdn and ch on inner ent last: sn drvn and no ex* **8/1**
301- **5** *1/2* **Port St Charles (IRE)**[46] [6084] 7-9-4 **77**... SJDonohoe(7) 3 78
(PRChamings) *dwlt: gd hdwy 1/2-way: chsd ldrs whn n.m.r wl over 1f out: swtchd rt: rdn and no imp ent last* **10/1**
210- **6** *6* **Far Note (USA)**[31] [6176] 6-8-13 **65**...(b) JBramhill 4 48
(SRBowring) *cl up: ev ch 2f out: sn rdn and wknd* **9/1**
313- **7** *1 1/4* **Majik**[31] [6176] 5-9-3 **69**... IMongan 8 48
(DJSFfrenchDavis) *in tch: effrt 2f out: sn rdn and no imp* **7/1**[3]
/00- **8** *hd* **Magic Glade**[35] [6154] 5-9-5 **76**... RThomas(5) 11 55
(CRDore) *cl up on outer: ev ch 2f outr: sn rdn and wkng whn hung rt over 1f out* **16/1**
23-5 **9** *6* **Cashel Mead**[10] [417] 4-10-0 **80**... ACulhane 6 41
(JLSpearing) *unruly stalls: a rr* **15/2**
200- **10** *shd* **Greenwood**[94] [5487] 6-9-12 **78**... SWKelly 7 38
(PGMurphy) *cl up: rdn along 1/2-way: sn weaken ed* **20/1**
01-4 **11** *20* **Ronnie From Donny (IRE)**[11] [410] 4-9-7 **73**... NCallan 10 —
(BEllison) *chsd ldrs: rdn along 1/2-way: sn wknd* **16/1**
1m 14.58s (-2.22) **Going Correction** -0.225s/f (Stan) **11** Ran SP% **125.3**
Speed ratings: **105,103,102,100,100 92,90,90,82,82 55**CSF £63.45 CT £172.57 TOTE £18.60: £3.80, £1.60, £1.90.
**Owner** John Drew **Bred** Normandy Developments Ltd **Trained** Newmarket, Suffolk

**FOCUS**
A competitive race run at a sound pace. The form looks solid, the first three are interesting off their current marks, and there are sure to be a few winners come out of this.

**NOTEBOOK**
**Prima Stella**, a winner on her only previous try over course and distance, quickened up nicely to land her first handicap since her three-year-old days. Although she has done most of her winning at Wolverhampton, there is every chance this track suits better and, as she is unexposed here, there should be more to come.
**Soba Jones** did little wrong under a 6lb penalty for his win at Wolverhampton five days previously. He has winning form over this course and distance, but may be better suited to Dunstall Park.
**Polar Kingdom**, a useful sort in his pomp, was dropping in trip from a mile and ran his best race to date on sand. A major gamble, he found himself short of room on the turn, but could not match the winner's turn of pace. A step up to seven furlongs looks sure to suit.
**Ellens Academy(IRE)**, whose sole All-Weather appearance came when successful over this course and distance nearly three years before, ran well on his first start since October. Although he is not the force of old, he is still well enough handicapped to win a good prize on the sand this winter.
**Port St Charles(IRE)** ran much better than his finishing position suggests. Considering he likes to race up with the pace, missing the break was the first nail in the coffin, but he also had to be switched down the straight. He looks capable of winning off this mark.
**Far Note(USA)** stays this trip well, but found this tougher than the race he won over course and distance in November.

## 512 BET DIRECT IN VISION SKY PAGE 293 H'CAP (DIV I) 1m (F)
**12:50** (12:51) (F) (0-65,65) 4-Y-O+ **£2,947** (£842; £421) **Stalls** Low

Form RPR
4-61 **1** **Qobtaan (USA)**[10] [425] 5-9-0 **51**... JoannaBadger 2 64
(MRBosley) *fly-leapt s and in rr: stdy hdwy 1/2-way: swtchd lft and effrt to ld wl over 1f out: sn rdn and styd on* **4/1**[2]
22-5 **2** *1 3/4* **Sorbiesharry (IRE)**[11] [412] 5-8-11 **48**...(p) PMcCabe 5 57
(MrsNMacauley) *in tch: gd hdwy on outer over 2f out and sn ev ch: rdn over 1f out and kpt on same pce* **6/1**[3]
040- **3** *1/2* **Blakeseven**[14] [6260] 4-8-11 **48**... PaulEddery 6 56
(WJMusson) *dwlt and in rr: gd hdwy 3f out: rdn to chse ldrs over 1f out: kpt on same pce* **10/1**
523- **4** *3* **Brandy Cove**[17] [6245] 7-9-7 **65**... MStainton(7) 1 67
(BSmart) *trckd ldrs: gd hdwy on inner 3f out and ev ch tl rdn wl over 1f out and grad wknd* **4/1**[2]
34-4 **5** *2 1/2* **Faraway Look (USA)**[11] [406] 7-9-7 **58**... DeanMcKeown 7 55
(DShaw) *towards rr: rdn along over 3f out: sme hdwy fnl 2f: nvr a factor* **15/2**
04-5 **6** *1/2* **Goodbye Mr Bond**[11] [406] 4-9-1 **55**...(v[1]) DAllan(3) 4 51
(EJAlston) *t.k.h: cl up: rdn along over 2f out: sn wknd* **8/1**
15-0 **7** *2* **Mount Royale (IRE)**[8] [437] 6-9-7 **58**...(v) KimTinkler 10 50
(NTinkler) *led: rdn along 21/2f out: hdd & wknd wl over 1f out* **25/1**
001- **8** *5* **Duelling Banjos**[68] [5933] 5-10-0 **65**... IMongan 3 47
(JAkehurst) *chsd ldrs: rdn along 1/2-way: sn btn* **9/4**[1]
000- **9** *2* **Hoh's Back**[18] [6241] 5-9-6 **62**...(p) NChalmers(5) 9 40
(PaulJohnson) *chsd ldrs on outer: rdn along 3f out: sn wknd* **16/1**
0- **10** *25* **Rex Romelio (IRE)**[22] [6231] 5-9-9 **60**... DarrenWilliams 8 —
(KRBurke) *sn outpcd and bhd fr 1/2-way* **50/1**
1m 43.9s (-0.70) **Going Correction** -0.225s/f (Stan) **10** Ran SP% **128.7**
Speed ratings: **94,92,91,88,86 85,83,78,76,51**CSF £31.74 CT £238.31 TOTE £5.40: £3.10, £2.40, £3.40; EX 29.70.
**Owner** Inca Financial Services **Bred** Darley Stud Management, L L C **Trained** Kingston Lisle, Oxon

**FOCUS**
Only a moderate handicap. The race produced a slow time, being 2.8 seconds slower than the second division, and the overall form looks poor.

**NOTEBOOK**
**Qobtaan(USA)** came out of the stalls awkwardly, but the slow pace enabled him to get back into the race quite quickly. He had been soundly beaten off lower marks than this in the past, but a win at a Wolverhampton regional meeting ten days previously seems to have done wonders for his confidence. He could well complete the hat-trick while in this form.
**Sorbiesharry(IRE)** tends to run better here than at Wolverhampton and finished second for his third consecutive race at this track. That should give him every chance of finding a suitable opportunity, but a record of one win from 37 starts does not inspire confidence.
**Blakeseven**, a springer in the market, was trying this surface for the first time and was far from disgraced. He may be able to find a small contest on this surface and is at least at the right end of the handicap.
**Brandy Cove**, not for the first time, gave the unfavoured far rail to no-one. He is more than capable of winning in the near future when he is allowed to race on the quicker part of the track.
**Faraway Look(USA)**having his first run for his new stable, never got into the race. Despite being regularly placed, he has not won for more than three years.
**Duelling Banjos**, who was heavily backed, was a big disappointment. He was the first under pressure and may not be suited by this surface.

## 513 BET DIRECT NO Q 08000 93 66 93 APPRENTICE H'CAP 1m 4f (F)
**1:20** (1:20) (F) (0-80,77) 4-Y-O+ **£2,884** (£824; £412) **Stalls** Low

Form RPR
113- **1** **Amir Zaman**[72] [5890] 6-10-0 **77**... BReilly 1 84
(JRJenkins) *keen early: chsd ldr: hdwy to ld over 2f out: rdn over 1f out: kpt on fnl f* **11/4**[2]

552- **2** *nk* **Glory Quest (USA)**[13] [6267] 7-9-8 **71**....................................(p) TEaves 4 78
(MissGayKelleway) *hld up in tch: shkn up and hdwy 3f out: rdn to chse ldrs 2f out: hrd drvn and styd on ins last: no ex nr fin* **15/8**[1]

/23- **3** *2 ½* **Newtonian (USA)**[31] [6177] 5-9-2 **70**................................ DerekNolan(5) 6 73
(JParkes) *trckd ldrs: hdwy 4f out and sn cl up: ev ch tl rdn and hung bdly lft over 1f out: sn one pce* **14/1**

140- **4** *shd* **Dubai Dreams**[17] [6247] 4-7-12 **56**...................................... KGhunowa(5) 5 59
(MJPolglase) *t.k.h: led: pushed along 3f out: hdd over 2f out: rdn and hdd appr last* **9/1**

544- **5** *9* **Lanos (POL)**[15] [6254] 6-8-6 **60**.........................................(t) DFentiman(5) 2 49
(RFord) *dwlt and bhd: tk clsr order 1/2-way: pushed along and carried wd st: sn wknd* **8/1**

653- **6** *6* **Nowell House**[13] [6267] 8-9-7 **70**.......................................... PMulrennan 3 50
(MWEasterby) *t.k.h: chsd ldng pair: pushed along over 4f out: rdn and outpcd whn wd st: sn bhd* **7/2**[3]

2m 41.77s (-0.33) **Going Correction** -0.225s/f (Stan)
**WFA** 4 from 5yo+ 4lb **6** Ran SP% **111.4**
Speed ratings: **92,91,90,90,84 80**CSF £8.21 TOTE £5.10: £2.40, £1.40; EX 11.10.
**Owner** The B C W Partnership **Bred** Meon Valley Stud **Trained** Royston, Herts
■ Stewards Enquiry : T Eaves two-day ban: used whip without allowing gelding time to respond (Jan 24, Feb 17)

**FOCUS**
A fair, but uncompetitive event run at a steady early pace. This led to the race being run in a time which was more than three seconds slower than the seller and the form looks unreliable.

**NOTEBOOK**
**Amir Zaman**, weak in the market, is becoming a bit of a specialist over this course and distance and is now unbeaten in three starts on this surface at this track. He probably won a shade more easily than the winning distance suggests, and there should be more to come for him at this course. He will get no penalty for this win if he is turned out quickly.
**Glory Quest(USA)**, well supported in the betting ring, was a trifle flattered by the beaten distance, but this was still a fair effort. However, he is finding it hard to win at the moment and may need some help from the Handicapper.
**Newtonian(USA)**, making his handicap debut, has not been done any favours with his official rating.
**Dubai Dreams** took a fierce grip out in front, but kept on well enough down the straight.
**Lanos(POL)** again showed he is far from straightforward.
**Nowell House** would have been suited by a stronger gallop, but was beaten a long way. *Official explanation: jockey said gelding ran free early on and then hung right handed*

## 514 BET DIRECT NO Q DEMO 08000 837 888 CLAIMING STKS 7f (F)
**1:50** (1:51) (F) 3-Y-O **£2,933** (£838; £419) **Stalls** Low

Form RPR

561- **1** **Sir Jasper (IRE)**[28] [6201] 3-8-7 59......................................(v) DMernagh 4 62
(TDBarron) *mde all: clr whn rdn over 1f out: easily* **2/1**[1]

26-1 **2** *10* **Turf Princess**[11] [408] 3-8-7 62.......................................... DFentiman(7) 1 44
(IanEmmerson) *in tch: hdwy on inner 3f out: rdn and edgd lft over 1f out: kpt on u.p: no ch w wnr* **4/1**[3]

055- **3** *2 ½* **Jasmine Pearl (IRE)**[28] [6197] 3-8-4 62 ow1...................... LPKeniry(3) 8 30
(BJMeehan) *chsd ldrs: rdn along over 2f out: sn drvn and one pce* **7/1**

36-0 **4** *shd* **Casantella**[5] [473] 3-8-0 47............................................... JMackay 2 23
(MJPolglase) *hld up in rr: hdwy wl over 1f out: kpt on ins last: nvr a factor* **25/1**

00- **5** *6* **Nanna (IRE)**[18] [6237] 3-8-4 ................................................. DaleGibson 6 12
(RHollinshead) *chsd wnr: rdn along 3f out: sn wknd* **40/1**

361- **6** *5* **Tictactoe**[18] [6237] 3-8-8 57................................................ CCatlin 7 4
(DJDaly) *chsd ldrs on outer: rdn along 3f out: wknd over 2f out* **7/2**[2]

446- **7** *12* **Mrs Cee (IRE)**[92] [5544] 3-8-7 76..........................................(b[1]) SWKelly 3 —
(MGQuinlan) *s.i.s: a bhd* **9/1**

050- **8** *1* **Get To The Point**[25] [6216] 3-8-11 59.....................................(v[1]) JQuinn 5 —
(PWD'Arcy) *chsd ldrs: rdn along 3f out: sn wknd* **9/2**

1m 29.56s (-1.24) **Going Correction** -0.225s/f (Stan) **8** Ran SP% **122.5**
Speed ratings: **98,86,83,83,76 71,57,56**CSF £11.25 TOTE £3.30: £1.50, £1.60, £3.50; EX 13.80.The winner was claimed by M Harris for £6,000
**Owner** Mrs Liz Jones **Bred** Tim Cox And Peter Jones **Trained** Maunby, N Yorks

**FOCUS**
Quite a competitive event on paper judged by official ratings, but that was not the case on the track, and the winner faces a big rise for this.

**NOTEBOOK**
**Sir Jasper(IRE)** was always in control and drew right away to score as he pleased. This was a hugely impressive performance and it would be a surprise if he cannot add to this victory in better company for his new connections. *Official explanation: was always in control and drew right away to score as he pleased. This was a hugely impressive performance and it would be a surprise if he cannot add to this victory in better company for his new connections.*
**Turf Princess**, a winner at Wolverhampton on her previous start, came through to take second without ever threatening to get near the winner. She was officially 3lb well in with the winner, but those figures were clearly misleading and this run should not be held against her. *Official explanation: , a winner at Wolverhampton on her previous start, came through to take second without ever threatening to get near the winner. She was officially 3lb well in with the winner, but those figures were clearly misleading and this run should not be held against her.*
**Jasmine Pearl(IRE)**, dropped into claiming company for the first time, has tumbled down the weights since starting her handicap life on 75. She is beginning to look exposed. *Official explanation: , dropped into claiming company for the first time, has tumbled down the weights since starting her handicap life on 75. She is beginning to look exposed.*
**Casantella** never threatened to take a hand and may be a little flattered by her proximity to the placed horses. *Official explanation: never threatened to take a hand and may be a little flattered by her proximity to the placed horses.*
**Tictactoe** may be better at six furlongs, but this was still disappointing. *Official explanation: may be better at six furlongs, but this was still disappointing.*
**Mrs Cee(IRE)**, best in on adjusted official figures, did not appear to take to the blinkers. This was her first run on sand, but she cannot be followed until showing more than this. *Official explanation: , best in on adjusted official figures, did not appear to take to the blinkers. This was her first run on sand, but she cannot be followed until showing more than this.*
**Get To The Point**, dropped in grade and tried in a visor, appears to be going the wrong way. *Official explanation: , dropped in grade and tried in a visor, appears to be going the wrong way.*

## 515 LITTLEWOODS BET DIRECT H'CAP (DIV II) 6f (F)
**2:20** (2:20) (D ) (0-80,80) 4-Y-0+ **£4,046** (£1,245; £622; £311) **Stalls** Low

Form RPR

120- **1** **Quiet Times (IRE)**[35] [6154] 5-9-11 77......................................(b) NCallan 9 93
(KARyan) *chsd ldrs on outer: hdwy to ld 2f out: sn qcknd c lear and styd on wl* **6/1**[3]

040- **2** *4* **Bond Royale**[48] [6078] 4-9-6 79.......................................... MStainton(7) 3 83
(BSmart) *hmpd s: sn trcking ldrs: hdwy 2f out: rdn to chse wnr over 1f out: kpt on* **16/1**

312- **3** *1 ¼* **Royal Grand**[223] [2108] 4-8-13 72.......................................... PMakin(7) 2 72
(TDBarron) *wnt rt s: cl up: ev ch 2f out: sn rdn and one pce appr last* **8/1**

00-0 **4** *nk* **Blakeshall Quest**[5] [480] 4-8-11 66.......................................(v[1]) FPFerris(3) 8 65
(RBrotherton) *towards rr: hdwy on outer 2f out: sn rdn and styd on ins last: nrst fin* **33/1**

506- **5** *1 ½* **Awarding**[15] [6252] 4-9-9 75.......................................................(t) CCatlin 5 70
(RFJohnsonHoughton) *hmpd s and bhd: hdwy on inner 2f out: kpt on u.p appr last: nt rch ldrs* **9/1**

052- **6** *nk* **Winning Pleasure (IRE)**[29] [6192] 6-9-6 72................................ JEdmunds 4 66
(JBalding) *hmpd s: in tch: effrt 2f out: sn rdn and wknd wl over 1f out* **7/2**[2]

310- **7** *¾* **Gilded Cove**[38] [6138] 4-9-3 69............................................. ACulhane 10 61
(RHollinshead) *bhd: wd st: sme late hdwy* **9/1**

101- **8** *½* **Johnston's Diamond (IRE)**[111] [5149] 6-9-11 77......... DeanMcKeown 6 67
(EJAlston) *wnt lft s: trckd ldrs: shkn up 3f out: sn rdn and btn 2f out* **2/1**[1]

000- **9** *1 ¼* **African Spur (IRE)**[31] [6176] 4-8-10 69................................. DNolan(7) 7 55
(PABlockley) *a rr* **12/1**

100- **10** *2* **Winthorpe (IRE)**[136] [4586] 4-9-11 80..................................... LFletcher(3) 1 60
(JJQuinn) *led: rdn along 3f out: hdd 2f out and sn wknd* **25/1**

1m 14.59s (-2.21) **Going Correction** -0.225s/f (Stan) **10** Ran SP% **121.3**
Speed ratings: **105,99,98,97,95 95,94,93,91,89**CSF £100.64 CT £806.74 TOTE £9.80: £3.30, £5.90, £2.20; EX 153.90 Trifecta £639.60 Pool £1,081.16, 1.20 w/u.
**Owner** Yorkshire Racing Club and Francis Moll **Bred** Times Of Wigan Ltd **Trained** Hambleton, N Yorks

**FOCUS**
A fair handicap run in a time similar to the first division, and although not as interesting as that contest, the winner is improved of late.

**NOTEBOOK**
**Quiet Times(IRE)** was a most impressive winner and quickened right away in the closing stages. He can ruin his chance coming out of the stalls, but jumped on terms here and would certainly be interesting if turned out under a penalty.
**Bond Royale** was done no favours coming out of the stalls, but did recover to run her best race for some time. She has done all her winning at Wolverhampton and would be of interest back there in the near future.
**Royal Grand**, a springer in the market, was having his first start since June. He is entitled to come on for this run and does not look badly handicapped at present.
**Blakeshall Quest**, a winner on her only previous run at this track, stepped up on recent efforts in a first-time visor and is worth keeping an eye on when returned to this course.
**Awarding** deserves plenty of credit for this first try on the surface. He was squeezed out at the start and did not appear to enjoy the kickback. However, he stuck on well despite being on the far rail and looks more than capable of winning a good prize.
**Winning Pleasure(IRE)** was another to suffer trouble coming out of the stalls.
**Johnston's Diamond(IRE)**, who tends to run well here, was most disappointing on his first start since September. This was surely too bad to be true.

## 516 BETDIRECT.CO.UK H'CAP 1m 3f (F)
**2:50** (2:50) (D ) (0-80,76) 4-Y-0+ **£4,075** (£1,254; £627; £313) **Stalls** Low

Form RPR

236- **1** **Digger (IRE)**[35] [6156] 5-9-8 **71**.......................................... MFenton 9 81
(MissGayKelleway) *a.p: wd st: led wl over 1f out: sn rdn: drvn ins last and kpt on wl* **4/1**[3]

006- **2** *½* **Street Life (IRE)**[34] [6157] 6-9-1 **67**................................. LisaJones(3) 8 76
(WJMusson) *trckd ldrs: wd st: effrt 2f out: sn rdn and styd on to have ev ch ins last: drvn and no ex nr fin* **7/2**[2]

023- **3** *1 ¼* **Trouble Mountain (USA)**[17] [6247] 7-9-9 **72**..................... DaleGibson 7 79
(MWEasterby) *trckd ldrs: wd st: rdn 2f out and ev ch tl drvn and one pce ins last* **3/1**[1]

201- **4** *6* **Hiawatha (IRE)**[22] [6229] 5-9-3 **66**...................................... DMernagh 2 64
(TDBarron) *trckd ldrs: hdwy on inner 3f out: rdn and ch 2f out: drvn and wknd appr last* **7/1**

201- **5** *3* **Theatre Tinka (IRE)**[31] [6174] 5-9-7 **70**...............................(p) NCallan 4 64
(RHollinshead) *chsd ldr: led 3f out: rdn over 2f out: hdd & wknd wl over 1f out* **14/1**

360- **6** *2 ½* **Fiddlers Creek (IRE)**[69] [5926] 5-9-12 **75**.............................. ACulhane 5 65
(RAllan) *hld up: hdwy over 3f out: rdn along 2f out and sn wknd* **7/1**

0/0- **7** *5* **Environment Audit**[317] [497] 5-9-12 **75**............................... SWKelly 6 57
(JRJenkins) *a rr* **50/1**

031- **8** *3 ½* **Hip Hop Harry**[34] [6161] 4-9-10 **76**........................................ WRyan 3 53
(EALDunlop) *a rr* **13/2**

63-5 **9** *13* **Jamestown**[8] [437] 7-7-12 **47**.................................................. JMackay 1 5
(MJPolglase) *led: rdn along over 4f out: hdd 3f out and sn wknd* **20/1**

2m 24.67s (-4.23) **Going Correction** -0.225s/f (Stan)
**WFA** 4 from 5yo+ 3lb **9** Ran SP% **118.9**
Speed ratings: **106,105,104,100,98 96,92,90,80**CSF £19.08 CT £48.29 TOTE £4.80: £1.40, £2.20, £1.50; EX 36.40.
**Owner** The Inside Rail **Bred** J A Porteous & C B B Booth **Trained** Newmarket, Suffolk

**FOCUS**
A fair handicap run at a sound pace.

**NOTEBOOK**
**Digger(IRE)** does not find much off the bridle, but managed to grind out this win despite hanging right-handed under pressure. This was his first win on sand since his All-Weather debut back in October 2002, and a rise in the weights will make a follow-up very difficult.
**Street Life(IRE)**, trying this surface for the first time, did little wrong and should be up to winning his first race on sand in the near future.
**Trouble Mountain(USA)** was helped by the sound pace and was still ridden more prominently than usual. He is proving hard to win with, but is consistently placed.
**Hiawatha(IRE)**, having his first run for his new trainer, was far from disgraced over a trip that stretched his stamina.
**Theatre Tinka(IRE)** won a course and distance claimer on his previous start, but found this much tougher.
**Fiddlers Creek(IRE)** has yet to rediscover the form he showed last winter.
**Hip Hop Harry** appeared not to run to form on this surface after winning on Polytrack on his previous start.
**Jamestown** *Official explanation: jockey said gelding had lost its action in the latter stages*

## 517 LITTLEWOODSCASINO.COM (S) STKS 1m 4f (F)
**3:20** (3:20) (G ) 4-6-Y-0 **£2,520** (£720; £360) **Stalls** Low

Form RPR

45-0 **1** **Coolfore Jade (IRE)**[6] [464] 4-8-8 55........................................ CCatlin 6 62
(NEBerry) *a.p: rdn to ld wl over 1f out: drvn ins last and kpt on gamely* **7/1**

004- **2** *hd* **Platinum Charmer (IRE)**[31] [6174] 4-8-13 65.......................... NCallan 2 67
(KARyan) *hld up: hdwy 3f out: rdn to chal on outer over 1f out and ev ch tl drvn and no ex nr fin* **12/1**

663- **3** *3* **Eight Woods (IRE)**[318] [653] 6-9-3 65................................... DMernagh 3 62
(TDBarron) *hld up: hdwy on inner 3f out: rdn and hung lft over 1f out: drvn and one pce ins last* **5/4**[1]

46-3 **4** *2 ½* **Grand Lass (IRE)**[11] [406] 5-8-5 50.......................................(v) PMakin(7) 1 53
(TDBarron) *trckd ldng pair: hdwy to ld over 4f out: rdn over 2f out: hdd & wknd wl over 1f out* **4/1**[3]

/6-5 **5** *3* **Luxi River (USA)**[4] 484 4-8-13 66 .......... GParkin 5 54
(PABlockley) *trckd ldrs: hdwy and cl up over 4f out: rdn along over 2f out and sn wknd* **2/1**[2]

00P- **6** *dist* **Kamala**[22] 6234 5-8-9 50 .......... FPFerris(3) 4 —
(RBrotherton) *led: rdn along and hdd over 4f out: sn wknd and bhd* **50/1**

2m 38.73s (-3.37) **Going Correction** -0.225s/f (Stan)
**WFA** 4 from 5yo+ 4lb **6** Ran SP% **119.9**
Speed ratings: **102,101,99,98,96** —CSF £82.78 TOTE £7.50: £3.20, £4.00; EX 76.20.There was no bid for the winner
**Owner** Leeway Group Limited **Bred** Des De Vere Hunt **Trained** Earlswood, Monmouths

**FOCUS**
An average seller full of disappointing types. The time was reasonable and the form looks fair for the grade.

**NOTEBOOK**
**Coolfore Jade(IRE)**, a big gamble, appeared to have everything under control turning in, but she had to show a gritty attitude to fend off the challenge of the runner-up. This was not a good race and there must be a feeling this was the day for her.
**Platinum Charmer(IRE)**, 5lb well in with the winner on official figures, was dropping into selling class for the first time. His only win came on this surface and he may be able to find a race in this grade.
**Eight Woods(IRE)** did himself no favours by hanging into the unfavoured far rail. For a horse who struggles to see this trip out, racing on the deeper ground was far from ideal. *Official explanation: jockey said gelding hung left handed*
**Grand Lass(IRE)**, wearing a visor again instead of blinkers, did little to inspire confidence for the future.
**Luxi River(USA)**, from a stable in great form, had the highest official rating, but that does flatter him. He has been lightly raced and his problems have clearly taken their toll.
**Kamala** had to be given a few cracks to get going and is clearly one to avoid.

## 518 BET DIRECT IN VISION SKY PAGE 293 H'CAP (DIV II) 1m (F)
**3:50** (3:51) (F ) (0-65,65) 4-Y-0+ **£2,947** (£842; £421) **Stalls** Low

Form RPR

31-1 **1** **Najaaba (USA)**[7] 457 4-9-6 62 6ex .......... BReilly(5) 1 78+
(MissJFeilden) *dwlt: hld up in rr: hdwy 3f out: led on bit over 1f out: comf* **4/5**[1]

/04- **2** *3/4* **War Owl (USA)**[34] 6161 7-8-13 53 .......... LisaJones(3) 7 67
(IanWilliams) *cl up: led over 2f out: sn rdn: hdd over 1f out: drvn ins last and kpt on* **12/1**

11-4 **3** *6* **Mutarafaa (USA)**[5] 477 5-9-2 58 .......... (e) THamilton(5) 6 60
(DShaw) *hld up towards rr: hdwy 3f out: rdn 2f out: kpt on same pce* **13/2**[3]

213- **4** *nk* **Mon Secret (IRE)**[13] 6270 6-9-10 61 .......... RFfrench 2 62
(BSmart) *chsd ldrs on inner: rdn over 2f out: sn outpcd* **11/1**

14-3 **5** *1 1/2* **Spy Gun (USA)**[5] 477 4-9-4 60 .......... NChalmers(5) 4 58
(TWall) *cl up: led 1/2-way: rdn along and hdd over 2f out: sn wknd* **6/1**[2]

302- **6** *6* **Goldbricker**[119] 4970 4-8-7 51 .......... BSwarbrick(7) 9 37
(WMBrisbourne) *cl up on outer: rdn along 3f out: sn wknd* **20/1**

301- **7** *2* **Game Guru**[25] 6218 5-9-7 65 .......... Laura-JayneCrawford(7) 5 47
(TDBarron) *led to 1/2-way: sn rdn along and wknd* **6/1**[2]

50-0 **8** *15* **Silver Crystal (IRE)**[7] 456 4-8-11 48 ow1 .......... (v) PMcCabe 8 —
(MrsNMacauley) *dwlt: a rr* **80/1**

1m 41.1s (-63.50) **Going Correction** -0.225s/f (Stan) **8** Ran SP% **119.5**
Speed ratings: **108,107,101,100,99 93,91,76**CSF £13.36 CT £44.63 TOTE £1.90: £1.10, £1.80, £1.60; EX 12.40 Place 6 £53.63, Place 5 £30.16.
**Owner** A K Sparks **Bred** Darley Stud Management, L L C **Trained** Exning, Suffolk

**FOCUS**
This was run in a very decent time, being 2.8 seconds faster than the first division. The first two pulled clear and the form looks solid.

**NOTEBOOK**
**Najaaba(USA)** was given a most confident ride after missing the kick and won with a bit in hand in a quick time. Considering the front two pulled well clear and she was still able to win cosily this was a fair effort. She is progressing nicely and is now unbeaten in three starts over course and distance. Her winning run is unlikely to have come to an end.
**War Owl(USA)** lost nothing in defeat and, although he did not really trouble the winner, he pulled clear of the rest of the field. This was his first run on Fibresand for 20 months and he looks primed to score in an ordinary handicap.
**Mutarafaa(USA)** has paid for his two wins in December and appears to be in the grip of the Handicapper now.
**Mon Secret(IRE)** was soon left behind by the front two. He is better over seven furlongs.
**Spy Gun(USA)** was still there two out, but racing on the slower far rail did not help his cause.
**Game Guru** *Official explanation: jockey said gelding lost its action on the final bend*
T/Jkpt: Not won. T/Plt: £144.50 to a £1 stake. Pool: £32,792.80. 165.65 winning tickets. T/Qpdt: £18.10 to a £1 stake. Pool: £2,952.70. 120.20 winning tickets. JR

# 489 LINGFIELD (L-H)
## Wednesday, January 14

**OFFICIAL GOING: Standard**
Wind: mod bhd Weather: fine races 1 to 4, rain races 5 to 8

## 519 BET DIRECT AT LINGFIELD PARK APPRENTICE CLAIMING STKS 6f (P)
**12:10** (12:14) (F ) 4-Y-0+ **£2,947** (£842; £421) **Stalls** Low

Form RPR

4-11 **1** **Hurricane Coast**[9] 436 5-9-0 61 .......... (b[1]) RMiles(3) 2 81
(DFlood) *chsd ldr and sn clr of remainder: squeezed through on inner to ld over 2f out: sn wl clr: 7l up 1f out: rdn out: unchal* **5/1**[2]

102- **2** *5* **Ripple Effect**[15] 6261 4-8-9 67 .......... (t) BReilly(3) 9 61
(CADwyer) *racd in midfield and sn wl off the pce: prog over 2f out: chsd wnr jst over 1f out: styd on but no ch* **7/4**[1]

50-0 **3** *1 1/4* **Muqtadi (IRE)**[5] 485 6-8-9 51 .......... LEnstone 1 54
(MQuinn) *dwlt: wl in rr and long way off the pce: prog 2f out: swtchd rt over 1f out: r.o: nvr nrr* **20/1**

00-5 **4** *1 1/4* **Cretan Gift**[12] 410 13-9-3 73 .......... (v) J-PGuillambert 7 59
(NPLittmoden) *racd in midfield and wl off the pce: rdn 1/2-way: styd on fnl f: no ch* **5/1**[2]

240- **5** *3* **Komena**[28] 6204 6-8-4 47 .......... LisaJones 6 37
(JWPayne) *chsd clr ldng pair to wl over 1f out: wknd fnl f* **25/1**

200- **6** *3* **Westmead Tango**[39] 6134 4-8-7 55 ow6 .......... PBradley(3) 5 34
(JRJenkins) *dwlt: reminder and sn plld hrd: chsd clr ldng trio to over 2f out: hrd rdn and wknd over 1f out* **25/1**

05-0 **7** *1* **Hawk**[11] 417 6-8-6 69 .......... NChalmers(3) 13 30
(PRChamings) *led: crossed to inner and set str pce: hdd and bmpd over 2f out: wknd over 1f out* **10/1**

00-0 **8** *nk* **Dunedin Rascal**[6] 448 7-7-10 66 .......... (b) LiamJones(7) 10 23
(EAWheeler) *taken steadily to post: hld up in last trio and sn long way off the pce : no ch fr 1/2-way* **10/1**

0 **9** *1 1/4* **Think It Over (IRE)**[11] 415 5-7-8 ow1 .......... HayleyTurner(5) 8 15
(APJones) *racd wd: a outpcd and wl bhd* **66/1**

60-0 **10** *2* **Island Star (IRE)**[7] 468 4-8-7 53 ow5 .......... (v[1]) SJDonohoe(5) 11 22
(SDow) *racd in midfield and wl off the pce: struggling fr 1/2-way: wknd* **25/1**

110/ **11** *7* **Happy Camper (IRE)**[150] 4-8-2 .......... RoryMoore(5) 12 —
(CVonDerRecke, Germany) *bolted to post: chsd clr ldrs to over 3f out: losing pl whn hmpd sn after: wknd* **8/1**[3]

000- **12** *4* **Zeitlos**[89] 5606 5-8-3 40 .......... (b) FPFerris 4 —
(RMFlower) *free to post: hld up wl in rr: eased fr over 2f out* **33/1**

1m 11.43s (-1.49) **Going Correction** +0.05s/f (Slow) **12** Ran SP% **119.7**
Speed ratings: **111,104,102,101,97 93,91,91,89,86 77,72**CSF £13.08 TOTE £8.10: £2.50, £1.10, £6.00; EX 13.60.
**Owner** Mrs Ruth M Serrell **Bred** Ian H Wills **Trained** Upper Lambourn, Berks
■ Stewards Enquiry : S J Donohoe caution: careless riding

**FOCUS**
Some modest performers, but an impressive winner (a good performance at the weights), and a very fast time.

**NOTEBOOK**
**Hurricane Coast**, making his debut for the yard and blinkered for the first time, had no problems with the change of surface and, after travelling really well behind the pacemaker, ultimately bolted up to complete the hat trick. He is considered more than just a plater by his current trainer and will now step up in grade.
**Ripple Effect**, as last time, came from way off the pace but too late to trouble the winner. Her best efforts on sand have been under these conditions.
**Muqtadi(IRE)**, who had a hopeless task last time, performed better at this more realistic level and may prefer a return to further.
**Cretan Gift**stayed on to finish fourth, but never looked like winning at any stage and finding an opportunity at his age is going to be very difficult.
**Komena**aran with some credit, but is without a win in three and a half years.
**Hawk**, who went off at a rate of knots, got into a bit of a barging match with the winner as that rival sneaked through on his inside turning for home, but the petrol was already running out.
**Happy Camper(IRE)**, formerly with David Barron, has been racing in Spain of late. He ruined his chances here by bolting before the start.
**Zeitlos** *Official explanation: jockey said gelding lost its action*

## 520 BET DIRECT ON SKY ACTIVE MAIDEN STKS 1m (P)
**12:40** (12:40) (D ) 4-Y-0+ **£3,513** (£1,081; £540; £270) **Stalls** High

Form RPR

32- **1** **Dawn Piper (USA)**[254] 1394 4-9-0 .......... JPSpencer 8 87+
(DRLoder) *hld up bhd ldrs: smooth prog over 2f out: led wl over 1f out: sn clr: v easily* **1/3**[1]

063- **2** *5* **Ballinger Ridge**[93] 5552 5-9-0 65 .......... MartinDwyer 1 68
(AMBalding) *led: drvn and hdd wl over 1f out: no ch w wnr after but kpt on to hold on for 2nd* **10/1**[3]

6- **3** *nk* **Have Some Fun**[36] 6153 4-9-0 .......... JQuinn 2 67
(PRChamings) *dwlt: sn cl up: rdn over 2f out: sn outpcd: chsd ldng pair over 1f out: kpt on* **50/1**

**4** *1 1/2* **Skip Of Colour**[216] 4-8-9 83 .......... DNolan(5) 4 64
(PABlockley) *trckd ldr: rdn and ev ch 2f out: fdd u.p* **12/1**

252- **5** *shd* **Margery Daw (IRE)**[15] 6259 4-8-9 64 .......... EAhern 6 59
(MPTregoning) *trckd ldrs: rdn and outpcd over 2f out: plodded on fnl f* **11/2**[2]

00-0 **6** *5* **Angelica Garnett**[7] 469 4-8-9 52 .......... MFenton 11 47
(TEPowell) *t.k.h: hld up in rr: outpcd fr 3f out: no ch after: kpt on fnl f* **40/1**

554- **7** *1/2* **Balmacara**[39] 6133 5-8-9 48 .......... (p) IMongan 9 46
(MissKBBoutflower) *racd in midfield: drvn over 2f out: sn btn* **16/1**

**8** *3/4* **Alisa (IRE)**[35] 4-8-6 .......... LisaJones(3) 3 44
(BICase) *s.s: t.k.h early: rdn in midfield over 4f out: struggling fr 3f out* **50/1**

600- **9** *1 1/2* **Lucretius**[250] 1497 5-9-0 47 .......... NCallan 7 46
(DKIvory) *racd towards rr: drvn and effrt over 4f out: sn no prog and btn* **66/1**

**10** *10* **Saleen (IRE)**[63] 4-8-9 .......... SWhitworth 5 18
(PDCundell) *s.s: a wl in rr: bhd fr over 2f out* **100/1**

060- **11** *7* **Miss Celerity**[107] 5283 4-8-9 30 .......... CCatlin 10 2
(MJHaynes) *chsd ldrs tl wknd rapidly over 2f out* **66/1**

-0 **12** *14* **Spiders Web**[11] 415 4-9-0 .......... SCarson 12 —
(TKeddy) *taken down early: racd wd in rr: t.o fnl 3f* **50/1**

1m 39.41s (-0.10) **Going Correction** +0.05s/f (Slow) **12** Ran SP% **125.4**
Speed ratings: **102,97,96,95,95 90,89,88,87,77 70,56**CSF £5.43 TOTE £1.60: £1.10, £2.90, £15.00; EX 7.00.
**Owner** Jumeirah Racing **Bred** Wentworth Racing **Trained** Newmarket, Suffolk
■ A successful first ride of the year for Jamie Spencer and the perfect start for David Loder on his return as a public trainer

**FOCUS**
A fair maiden run at an ordinary pace, but the winner looks interesting if given a mark of around 80.

**NOTEBOOK**
**Dawn Piper(USA)**, gelded since making the frame in a couple of decent maidens last spring, was always travelling well and cruised right away from his rivals. He may not have beaten much, but there is likely to be more to come from him.
**Ballinger Ridge**made the running and saw his race out, but the winner was far too classy. This was his seventh placing from 16 starts and he will continue to prove hard to place.
**Have Some Fun**improved a good deal from his Southwell debut and an opportunity should be found.
**Skip Of Colour**, who raced three times for Pascal Bary in France last year, showed plenty of ability on this debut for his new yard on his first start for seven months. His talented trainer should place him to advantage.
**Margery Daw(IRE)**continues to frustrate and the drop back in trip did her few favours.

## 521 BET DIRECT ON SKY TEXT PAGE 372 H'CAP 1m (P)
**1:10** (1:11) (F ) (0-60,60) 3-Y-0 **£2,961** (£846; £423) **Stalls** High

Form RPR

000- **1** **Diamond Way (USA)**[103] 5342 3-9-7 **59** .......... (v[1]) JPSpencer 9 69
(DRLoder) *racd in rr and nt gng wl: u.p over 3f out: gd prog on outer over 2f out: drvn to ld 1f out: styd on* **2/1**[1]

60-2 **2** *3/4* **Park Ave Princess (IRE)**[11] 420 3-9-2 **54** .......... IMongan 3 62
(NPLittmoden) *chsd ldrs: rdn and effrt to ld jst over 2f out: hdd 1f out: kpt on fnl f but a hld* **9/1**

50-5 **3** *1 1/2* **Lady Mo**[8] 452 3-8-9 **50** .......... J-PGuillambert(3) 6 55
(AndrewReid) *hld up in last pair: sme prog over 2f out: sn rdn: nt clr run over 1f out: r.o wl to chse ldng pair last 100y: gaining at f* **50/1**

06-6 **4** *3* **Sonderborg**[11] 420 3-9-2 **54** .......... (p) GCarter 11 52
(GLMoore) *trckd ldrs: rdn and prog to chal 2f out: nt qckn over 1f out: sn btn* **9/2**[3]

05-1 **5** 2½ **Princess Ismene**[8] [451] 3-9-8 **60** 6ex.................................(b) NCallan 2 52
(JJay) *dwlt: racd wl in rr: rdn over 4f out: nt clr run on inner wl over 2f out: styd on fr over 1f out: n.d* **11/1**

006- **6** 1½ **El Magnifico**[90] [5594] 3-9-4 **56**........................................ SWhitworth 10 44
(PDCundell) *racd in midfield: rdn 4f out: struggling wl over 2f out: kpt on ins fnl f* **20/1**

000- **7** 1½ **Magico**[35] [6160] 3-9-1 **53**..............................................(v[1]) MartinDwyer 8 38
(AMBalding) *restless in stalls: mde most to jst over 2f out: wknd over 1f out* **33/1**

31-5 **8** 3½ **Must Be So**[11] [420] 3-8-10 **48**............................................ NPollard 5 25
(JJBridger) *s.i.s: sn in midfield: effrt over 2f out: no prog wl over 1f out: sn wknd* **14/1**

065- **9** 2½ **Druid**[61] [5993] 3-8-7 **52**.................................................... RoryMoore[(7)] 1 23
(PCHaslam) *restless in stalls: s.i.s: pushed up to press ldr: wknd over 2f out* **33/1**

10-4 **10** hd **Head Boy**[7] [462] 3-9-7 **59**.................................................... PDoe 4 30
(SDow) *racd in midfield: rdn over 2f out: sn lost pl and btn: eased fnl f* **10/3**[2]

000- **11** 4 **Try The Air (IRE)**[32] [6172] 3-9-2 **54**.......................................... EAhern 7 16
(CTinkler) *chsd ldrs: rdn and struggling wl over 3f out: sn wknd* **16/1**

003- **12** 1¼ **Abrogate (IRE)**[32] [6172] 3-8-9 **50**....................................... LEnstone[(3)] 12 9
(PCHaslam) *chsd ldrs tl wknd rapidly wl over 2f out* **9/1**

1m 40.38s (0.87) **Going Correction** +0.05s/f (Slow) **12** Ran SP% **128.1**
Speed ratings: **97,96,94,91,89 87,86,82,80,80 76,74**CSF £22.81 CT £752.82 TOTE £3.10: £2.20, £2.80, £12.10; EX 27.50.
**Owner** Kevin Murphy **Bred** Barry R Ostrager **Trained** Newmarket, Suffolk
■ Stewards Enquiry : J P Spencer one-day ban: used whip with excessive frequency (Jan 26)

**FOCUS**
A modest handicap run at an ordinary pace.

**NOTEBOOK**
**Diamond Way(USA)**, unplaced in three starts at two, looked a very hard ride despite the application of the first-time visor and it was only his rider's persistence that enabled him to score. This looked a modest field and he will do very well to follow up. *Official explanation: trainer said, regarding the improved form shown, colt may have benefited from the fitting of a visor*
**Park Ave Princess(IRE)**again ran up to her best and was unfortunate to come up against an unexposed sort. The problem is that she may continue to edge back up the handicap despite not winning.
**Lady Mo**came from way back and was finishing in great style. This was a much better performance than in her only previous try at the trip and her yard are likely to find an opportunity for her.
**Sonderborg**, well supported in the market, had every chance turning for home but there was nothing more to come. The step up in trip did not bring about any improvement.
**Princess Ismene**, winner of a seller here last week, stayed on as though a longer trip might suit.
**El Magnifico**, making his handicap debut, made a little late headway and gave the impression he is capable of better.
**Head Boy**was very disappointing following his recent encouraging effort here and is surely capable of better. *Official explanation: jockey said gelding ran flat*

## 522 BETDIRECT.CO.UK H'CAP 1m 2f (P)
**1:40** (1:40) (D ) (0-85,85) 3-Y-O **£4,322** (£1,330; £665; £332) **Stalls** Low

Form RPR

01- **1** **Ascertain (IRE)**[49] [6072] 3-9-7 **85**.............................................. IMongan 6 91
(NPLittmoden) *trckd ldrs: effrt to chal over 2f out: drvn to ld over 1f out: clr whn hung rt nr fin* **3/1**[3]

45-2 **2** 2 **Amwell Brave**[8] [450] 3-8-5 **69**................................................ SWKelly 3 71
(JRJenkins) *trckd ldr: upsides fr 1/2-way tl narrow ld wl over 3f out: drvn and hdd over 1f out: one pce* **11/4**[2]

01-3 **3** 1 **Dr Cerullo**[4] [490] 3-8-11 **75**.................................................... EAhern 4 75
(CTinkler) *led to wl over 3f out: styd pressing ldr: rdn and ev ch 2f out: sn one pce* **5/2**[1]

263- **4** 13 **Marcus Eile (IRE)**[25] [6219] 3-9-5 **83**.............................. DarrenWilliams 5 60
(KRBurke) *cl up: rdn over 4f out: nt qckn and btn wl over 2f out: wknd* **7/1**

31-1 **5** 5 **Lyrical Girl (USA)**[11] [416] 3-8-0 **64** oh3 ow2........................... CCatlin 1 32
(HJManners) *racd in last pair: pushed along 1/2-way: struggling over 3f out: sn no ch* **6/1**

40-0 **6** 6 **Lady Bahia (IRE)**[6] [482] 3-8-0 **64**.............................................. JQuinn 2 21
(RPElliott) *cl up: rdn over 4f out: struggling over 3f out: sn wknd* **25/1**

2m 9.05s (1.66) **Going Correction** +0.05s/f (Slow) **6** Ran SP% **110.9**
Speed ratings: **95,93,92,82,78 73**CSF £11.35 TOTE £4.40: £1.30, £3.10; EX 12.20.
**Owner** Paul J Dixon **Bred** Darley **Trained** Newmarket, Suffolk

**FOCUS**
A decent race but run at a steady pace and producing a modest final time.

**NOTEBOOK**
**Ascertain(IRE)**, a surprise winner of his maiden here last time, travelled well and found enough to see off his two main rivals. He did not suggest that he would want much further than this, but has only raced three times so is entitled to go on improving.
**Amwell Brave**, still a maiden, again ran into a progressive sort and would probably have preferred a stronger gallop.
**Dr Cerullo**soon found himself in front and was found wanting for foot over the last couple of furlongs. He would probably have preferred getting a lead in a truly-run race.
**Marcus Eile(IRE)**did not see out the longer trip.
**Lyrical Girl(USA)**, making her debut for the yard, was stepping up in grade and found it all too much.

## 523 BET DIRECT ON 0800 32 93 93 STKS SHOWCASE H'CAP 1m 4f (P)
**2:10** (2:11) (C ) (0-90,89) 4-Y-O+ **£7,293** (£2,766; £1,383; £628) **Stalls** Low

Form RPR

112- **1** **Cold Turkey**[39] [6130] 4-9-0 **79**............................................... SWhitworth 8 89+
(GLMoore) *dwlt: hld up in last: prog over 2f out: nt clr run over 1f out: got through to chse ldr last 150y: r.o wl to ld fnl strides* **6/1**[1]

60-0 **2** nk **Internationalguest (IRE)**[11] [418] 5-9-3 **78**.........................(v) NPollard 7 88
(GGMargarson) *trckd ldrs: effrt over 2f out: rdn to ld jst over 1f out: hdd last strides* **25/1**

211- **3** 1 **Mr Mischief**[42] [6125] 4-9-3 **85**.............................................. LEnstone[(3)] 10 93
(PCHaslam) *hld up wl in rr: effrt on outer over 2f out: hanging lft but r.o fr over 1f out to take 3rd nr fin* **14/1**

030- **4** ¾ **Classic Role**[35] [6161] 5-8-11 **72**................................................ IMongan 4 79
(RIngram) *t.k.h: hld up in midfield: effrt over 2f out: prog to press ldrs whn nowhere to go 1f out: r.o nr fin: nt rcvr* **16/1**

11-6 **5** ¾ **Tight Squeeze**[11] [418] 7-9-3 **78**............................................. ACulhane 3 84
(PWHiatt) *hld up towards rr: rdn wl over 2f out: effrt whn nt clr run over 1f out: swtchd rt and r.o ins fnl f: nrst fin* **13/2**[2]

033- **6** nk **Typhoon Tilly**[53] [6052] 7-9-0 **75**............................................. MFenton 14 80
(CREgerton) *t.k.h: hld up in midfield: trckd ldrs 3f out: cl up over 1f out: sn rdn and nt qckn* **10/1**

01-0 **7** nk **High Point (IRE)**[11] [418] 6-9-5 **80**........................................ JPSpencer 5 85
(GPEnright) *trckd ldrs: lost pl and rdn over 2f out: nt clr run over 1f out: kpt on same pce fnl f* **8/1**

254- **8** hd **Border Tale**[25] [3740] 4-8-10 **80**.................................... HayleyTurner[(5)] 15 85
(CWeedon) *t.k.h: hld up: effrt 4f out: rdn to dispute ld 3f out: narrow ld over 1f out: sn hdd & wknd* **33/1**

22-5 **9** ¾ **Easter Ogil (IRE)**[11] [419] 9-8-0 **64**.................................... LisaJones[(3)] 2 67
(JaneSouthcombe) *hld up wl in rr: effrt on inner over 2f out: n.m.r over 1f out: one pce after* **10/1**

24-0 **10** hd **Briareus**[11] [418] 4-9-1 **80**.................................................. MartinDwyer 9 83
(AMBalding) *t.k.h: pressed ldr: rdn to dispute ld 3f out to over 1f out: hld whn squeezed out ent fnl f: wknd* **11/1**

500- **11** ½ **Moon Emperor**[158] [3977] 7-10-0 **89**.............................................. EAhern 1 91
(JRJenkins) *rrd s: hld up in last trio: prog on wd outside over 3f out: rdn over 2f out: sn no hdwy and btn* **7/1**[3]

20/0 **12** nk **Dusty Carpet**[11] [418] 6-9-0 **75**................................................. NCallan 12 77
(MJWeeden) *hld up in midfield: effrt and n.m.r over 2f out: nt clr run over 1f out: no ch after* **66/1**

50-0 **13** ¾ **Gallant Boy (IRE)**[11] [418] 5-8-8 **76**............................(t) SJDonohoe[(7)] 13 77
(PDEvans) *chsd ldrs: rdn 4f out: struggling and btn on outer over 2f out* **8/1**

41-2 **14** nk **Western (IRE)**[11] [413] 4-8-13 **78**.............................................. CCatlin 11 78
(JAkehurst) *s.i.s: hld up in last trio: rdn on outer wl over 2f out: no prog* **10/1**

326- **15** 2½ **Nawow**[11] [6052] 4-9-0 **79**.......................................................... SCarson 6 76
(PDCundell) *led at mod pce: rdn 4f out: hdd 3f out: cl up whn n.m.r on inner 2f out and over 1f out: wknd rapidly* **16/1**

212- **16** 15 **Victory Quest (IRE)**[18] [6247] 4-8-8 **73**...................................(v) JQuinn 16 47
(MrsSLamyman) *t.k.h: trckd ldrs: rdn over 4f out: wknd 3f out: t.o* **14/1**

2m 35.26s (1.28) **Going Correction** +0.05s/f (Slow)
**WFA** 4 from 5yo+ 4lb **16** Ran SP% **131.3**
Speed ratings: **97,96,96,95,95 94,94,94,94,93 93,93,92,92,91 81**CSF £167.07 CT £2073.94 TOTE £4.80: £1.60, £4.90, £4.30, £7.10; EX 391.20 Trifecta £987.20 Part won. Pool of £1,390.50 - 0.30 winning tickets..
**Owner** A Grinter **Bred** Worksop Manor Stud **Trained** Woodingdean, E Sussex

**FOCUS**
A decent, competitive handicap, but a very steady pace and a slow final time. There was also plenty of trouble over the last couple of furlongs. Despite this, the form may prove solid and the winner is still progressing.

**NOTEBOOK**
**Cold Turkey**, unlucky not to come into this bidding for a six-timer, put up a remarkable effort to come from just about last, find a path through almost the whole field, and get up almost on the line. He keeps on defying the Handicapper and there is no reason to think he has finished yet.
**Internationalguest(IRE)**improved a good deal on his debut effort on this surface earlier this month and looked likely to win a furlong from home. He hung over to the inside rail once in front though, causing problems in behind, and had the race snatched from him almost on the line. This was a decent effort considering his best turf form has been on soft ground and he could be very interesting on Fibresand. *Official explanation: jockey said gelding had hung badly left handed throughout*
**Mr Mischief**, a four-time Fibresand winner at up to 14 furlongs, came with a strong run on the outside in the straight but could not quite get on terms. This was a good effort on this switch to Polytrack, especially as the race may not have necessarily been run to suit.
**Classic Role**still had a chance when hampered by the runner-up a furlong out and he would have gone very close otherwise. He deserves compensation.
**Tight Squeeze**got into all sort of trouble when trying to improve in the home straight and had to be switched to the outside. She finished strongly once out in the clear and was unlucky not to have been placed at least.
**Typhoon Tilly**, who stays further than this, had every chance but was found wanting for pace where it mattered.
**High Point(IRE)**ran better than in his last start here and was still battling away when caught up in the traffic problems a furlong out.
**Briareus**, up there from the start, was already going backwards when hampered a furlong out.
**Moon Emperor**, fly-jumped leaving the stalls and raced at the back. He moved up on the outside racing down the false straight but never managed to offer a threat.
**Dusty Carpet**was ultimately well beaten, but he had met plenty of trouble in running over the last couple of furlongs. This was his second start back after a very long layoff and he may not be totally without hope.
**Victory Quest(IRE)** *Official explanation: jockey said gelding lost its action*

## 524 BET DIRECT (S) STKS 5f (P)
**2:45** (2:47) (G ) 3-Y-O **£2,562** (£732; £366) **Stalls** High

Form RPR

11-1 **1** **Smart Starprincess (IRE)**[4] [496] 3-8-13 58......................(v[1]) NCallan 5 65
(PABlockley) *mde all and sn clr: 6l ahd 2f out: rdn over 1f out: kpt on: unchal* **1/1**[1]

00-5 **2** 3 **Ivory Lace**[4] [496] 3-8-13 60.................................................... IMongan 2 53
(DKIvory) *chsd wnr: rdn 2f out: no imp fnl f: eased nr fin* **6/1**

422- **3** 1½ **Emaradia**[19] [6237] 3-8-13 48.........................................(b) JoannaBadger 3 47
(PDEvans) *disp 2nd pl to over 3f out: sn rdn: kpt on again fnl f to take 3rd last strides* **14/1**

35-2 **4** nk **Stamford Blue**[8] [452] 3-9-4 50.....................................(b) MartinDwyer 9 51
(JSMoore) *outpcd in last and wl bhd: r.o fr over 1f out: nrst fin* **11/2**[3]

006- **5** hd **Easily Averted (IRE)**[28] [6207] 3-9-4 70.................................. SWKelly 10 50
(JAOsborne) *chsd ldng pair 3f out: hrd rdn and no imp wl over 1f out: one pce and lost 2 pls nr fin* **7/2**[2]

0 **6** ¾ **Harbour Princess**[9] [438] 3-8-7 .................................................. PDoe 4 36
(MFHarris) *outpcd towards rr and sn rdn: styd on fnl f: nrst fin* **66/1**

030- **7** 1¾ **Lavish Times**[82] [5725] 3-9-4 52..............................................(b) FLynch 6 40
(ABerry) *outpcd in midfield: shuffled along fr 1/2-way: no prog* **20/1**

000- **8** 1¾ **A Bid In Time (IRE)**[77] [5829] 3-8-13 48......................... DarrenWilliams 7 28
(DShaw) *racd wd: hld up and sn outpcd: struggling fr 1/2-way* **33/1**

00-0 **9** 5 **Gentleman George**[8] [451] 3-8-12 45.......................................... JQuinn 1 7
(DKIvory) *outpcd and a wl in rr* **50/1**

59.74 secs (-0.04) **Going Correction** +0.05s/f (Slow) **9** Ran SP% **119.7**
Speed ratings: **102,97,94,94,94 92,90,87,79**CSF £7.84 TOTE £2.00: £1.10, £1.20, £3.20; EX 10.10.The winner was bought in for 11,400gns. Easily Averted (no.1) was claimed by Christopher Wilson for £6,000.
**Owner** Brooklands Racing **Bred** Norelands Bloodstock **Trained** Southwell, Notts

**FOCUS**
A very fast time for the class of contest, and good form for the grade, although the winner had little to beat.

**NOTEBOOK**
**Smart Starprincess(IRE)**adopted her usual trailblazing tactics and the race was effectively over by halfway. She has taken to this surface like a duck to water and she is likely to bid for the nap hand in an amateur riders' contest over the same trip here on Saturday.
**Ivory Lace**finished only marginally closer to the winner than she did here four days earlier, but has the ability to win a similar contest in her own right.

**Emaradia**is normally a trailblazer, but even she was made to look pedestrian by the winner early and her final placing was probably the best she could have hope for. She is a very hard filly to win with.
**Stamford Blue**was done no favours by the drop in trip, but has the ability to win a similar contest back over further.
**Easily Averted(IRE)**, best in on adjusted official ratings, was dropping in class but had the coffin box and never really had a chance. He is better than he showed here.
**Lavish Times** *Official explanation: jockey said colt hung left*

## 525 PRESS INTERACTIVE TO BET DIRECT H'CAP 1m (P)
**3:20** (3:20) (F ) (0-55,55) 3-Y-0+ £2,982 (£852; £213; £213) **Stalls** High

Form RPR
00-0 **1** **Muyassir (IRE)**[7] 464 9-9-12 **53**................................ JQuinn 2 61
(MissBSanders) *prom in chsng gp: clsd over 2f out: urged along to chal 1f out: led last 100y: drvn out* **6/1**[1]
032- **2** *nk* **Double Ransom**[25] 6226 5-9-12 **53**..........................(b) SWKelly 1 60
(MrsLStubbs) *dwlt: hld up in last: prog 1/2-way: clsd on ldrs 2f out: drvn and nt qckn over 1f out: styd on ins fnl f: nrst fin* **6/1**[1]
000- **3** *hd* **Kyle Of Lochalsh**[25] 6226 4-10-0 **55**..........................(p) NPollard 4 62
(GGMargarson) *t.k.h: prom in chsng gp: clsd over 2f out: rdn to chal over 1f out: nt qckn and jst hld ins fnl f* **8/1**
505- **3** *dht* **Magic Warrior**[25] 6220 4-10-0 **55**................................ RSmith 5 62
(JCFox) *t.k.h: chsd clr ldr: clsd over 2f out: rdn to ld over 1f out: hdd and one pce last 100y* **6/1**[1]
60-6 **5** *1 ½* **Taiyo**[7] 469 4-9-11 **52**................................ NCallan 3 56
(JWPayne) *settled towards rr: effrt 3f out: rdn to chse ldrs wl over 1f out: one pce fnl f* **9/1**
40-0 **6** *1* **Vizulize**[7] 469 5-9-12 **53**................................ ACulhane 8 54
(AWCarroll) *settled towards rr: effrt 3f out: rdn to chse ldrs 2f out: one pce over 1f out* **25/1**
U00- **7** *1* **Fife And Drum (USA)**[16] 6254 7-9-8 **54**..........................(b) BReilly[(5)] 12 53
(MissJFeilden) *led and sn clr: drvn fr 1/2-way: c bk to field over 2f out: hdd over 1f out: wknd fnl f* **7/1**[3]
640- **8** *shd* **Fabrian**[25] 6220 6-9-12 **53**................................ GCarter 10 52
(DWPArbuthnot) *plld hrd: racd wd: hld up in rr: last and detached over 2f out: c wd bnd wl over 1f out: styd on fnl f:nvr nr ldrs* **12/1**
000- **9** *½* **Answered Promise (FR)**[25] 6226 5-9-13 **54**.................. SWhitworth 7 52
(AWCarroll) *racd in midfield: effrt 3f out: no prog and btn wl over 1f out* **9/1**
00-0 **10** *1 ¼* **Mister Clinton (IRE)**[7] 469 7-9-12 **53**..........................(p) IMongan 6 48
(DKIvory) *settled towards rr: rdn over 2f out: no imp ldrs wl over 1f out* **12/1**
50-0 **11** *3* **Pancakehill**[7] 469 5-9-12 **53**..........................(p) EAhern 11 41
(DKIvory) *sn lost pl and in rr: shkn up over 2f out: wknd over 1f out* **13/2**[2]
000- **12** *17* **Senna (IRE)**[100] 5426 4-9-11 **52**................................ SCarson 9 1
(PDCundell) *prom to 1/2-way: wknd rapidly: t.o over 1f out* **33/1**

1m 40.71s (1.20) **Going Correction** +0.05s/f (Slow) **12** Ran SP% **122.0**
Speed ratings: **96,95,95,95,94 93,92,91,91,90 87,70**CSF £42.49 TOTE £9.00: £3.10, £1.90; EX 40.60 Place 3: Kyle of Lochalsh £1.00, M Warrior £1.30; Tricast: Muyassir/D Ransom/Kyle of Lochalsh £120.46, Muyassir/D Ransom/M Warrior £115.84.
**Owner** J M Quinn **Bred** Barronstown Stud And Katom **Trained** Epsom, Surrey

**FOCUS**
A low-grade handicap and a modest final time, which sums up the level of form.

**NOTEBOOK**
**Muyassir(IRE)**was suited by the drop back to a mile, but needed every yard of the trip to get on top. This looked a modest race though and, bearing in mind his winning record in recent years, is likely to struggle if raised in the handicap for this victory.
**Double Ransom**looked the likely winner turning for home, but he took an age to respond when asked for his effort and by the time he did it was too late. He does not look an easy ride and cannot be supported with any great confidence.
**Magic Warrior**, dropping back in trip, ran his race and was only just denied.
**Kyle Of Lochalsh**reversed recent form here with a couple of rivals and only just went down, but he is not the most consistent.
**Taiyo**, still a maiden, ran well enough without suggesting she improved for the longer trip.
**Vizulize**was not totally disgraced as she did not enjoy the clearest of runs on the home turn.
**Fife And Drum(USA)**went off far too fast.
**Fabrian**, who raced wide of the others and took a good grip, seemed likely to finish tailed off coming to the home bend before making some late progress. He is a longstanding maiden, but is not totally devoid of ability.
**Answered Promise(FR)**, a springer in the market, was by no means knocked about.

## 526 LITTLEWOODSPOKER.COM H'CAP 6f (P)
**3:50** (3:51) (E ) (0-70,70) 4-Y-0+ £3,332 (£952; £476) **Stalls** Low

Form RPR
3-21 **1** **Tayif**[7] 465 8-9-5 **61** 6ex..........................(t) SCarson 3 71
(AndrewReid) *dwlt: racd in rr: nt clr run over 2f out: gd prog over 1f out: squeezed through to dispute ld last 100y: won on the nod* **4/1**[1]
0-03 **2** *shd* **Currency**[8] 454 7-10-0 **70**................................ EAhern 1 80
(JMBradley) *settled in midfield: prog wl over 1f out: drvn to dispute ld last 100y: pipped on the post* **5/1**[2]
02-2 **3** *1 ½* **Playtime Blue**[6] 480 4-9-5 **61**................................ DarrenWilliams 8 67
(KRBurke) *mde most: drvn 2f out: hdd and unable qck last 100y* **20/1**
003- **4** *½* **Polar Force**[46] 6092 4-8-13 **62**................................ TO'Brien[(7)] 4 66
(MRChannon) *prom: effrt wl over 1f out: ch ent fnl f: bmpd along and nt qckn last 100y* **8/1**
00-2 **5** *1 ½* **Kilmeena Lad**[8] 448 8-9-11 **67**................................ PDobbs 12 67
(JCFox) *dwlt: racd wl in rr: sme prog over 2f out: rdn wl over 1f out: styd on same pce fnl f* **8/1**
005- **6** *shd* **Emerald Fire**[39] 6132 5-9-9 **70**..........................(v) NChalmers[(5)] 6 69
(AMBalding) *racd in last pair: struggling over 2f out: gd prog on outer fnl f: fin wl* **5/1**[2]
555- **7** *nk* **Hard To Catch (IRE)**[140] 4505 6-10-0 **70**................................ IMongan 14 68
(DKIvory) *w ldr over 3f: losing pl whn hmpd over 2f out: no ch after: kpt on ins fnl f* **25/1**
00-0 **8** *½* **Taboor (IRE)**[8] 454 6-9-13 **69**..........................(b) NCallan 2 66
(JWPayne) *prom: chsd ldr over 2f out: chal and ev ch 1f out: fnd nil and sn wknd* **33/1**
31-1 **9** *¾* **Wainwright (IRE)**[6] 476 4-9-7 **68** 6ex................................ DNolan[(5)] 9 63
(PABlockley) *cl up: rdn over 2f out: fdd wl over 1f out* **13/2**[3]
540- **10** *1* **Sounds Lucky**[201] 2766 8-9-9 **68**..........................(b) J-PGuillambert[(3)] 10 60
(NPLittmoden) *racd in midfield: prog to trck ldrs over 2f out: cl up on inner over 1f out: wknd fnl f* **16/1**
0-04 **11** *nk* **Juwwi**[8] 454 10-9-7 **70**................................ CJDavies[(7)] 7 61
(JMBradley) *s.s: drvn in last: nvr a factor: kpt on fnl f* **12/1**
06-5 **12** *½* **Goodwood Prince**[8] 454 4-9-8 **64**................................ PDoe 5 53
(SDow) *a towards rr: struggling whn squeezed out over 2f out: no ch after* **12/1**
46-0 **13** *½* **Tally (IRE)**[12] 410 4-10-0 **70**................................ FLynch 11 58
(ABerry) *prom: rdn over 2f out: wknd over 1f out* **50/1**
003- **14** *5* **Teyaar**[25] 6221 8-9-7 **63**..........................(b) PMcCabe 13 36
(MrsNMacauley) *racd wd: in tch: rdn over 2f out: c wd bnd sn after and sn wknd* **20/1**

1m 12.57s (-0.35) **Going Correction** +0.05s/f (Slow) **14** Ran SP% **128.4**
Speed ratings: **104,103,101,101,99 99,98,98,97,95 95,94,93,87**CSF £23.42 CT £389.04 TOTE £4.30: £2.60, £1.80, £6.10; EX 23.70 Place 6 £37.98, Place 5 £23.42.
**Owner** A S Reid **Bred** Theakston Stud **Trained** Mill Hill, London NW7
■ Stewards Enquiry : N Chalmers one-day ban: careless riding (Jan 26)

**FOCUS**
A competitive handicap and a decent pace, and the form should work out.

**NOTEBOOK**
**Tayif**, carrying a 6lb penalty for his win here last week, had to weave a path through from the back of the field and, though things got tight at one stage, came with a strong late run to win by a whisker.
**Currency**was delivered with his effort at just the right time and first impressions were that he had prevailed in a bobbing finish, but the evidence of the camera proved otherwise. He at least confirmed that he is back in form and is well enough handicapped, even though he is due to go up 3lb for his good effort here last time.
**Playtime Blue**made the running and kept on battling all the way to the line. He has form on Fibresand, but this was by far his best effort so far on this surface.
**Polar Force**continues to slide down the handicap and ran with credit, but he has not managed to win since his juvenile debut.
**Kilmeena Lad**ran with credit, but is probably better over further these days.
**Emerald Fire**has become brilliantly handicapped and was finishing in good style. She is well worth keeping in mind for a similar event.
**Hard To Catch(IRE)**, drawn widest of all and racing for the first time in five months, ran with plenty of credit especially as he met trouble on the home bend. He was also minus his usual blinkers, so this was an encouraging effort.
**Goodwood Prince**was hampered on the turn for home and may have finished a bit closer otherwise.
T/Plt: £41.80 to a £1 stake. Pool: £27,797.20. 484.65 winning tickets. T/Qpdt: £26.10 to a £1 stake. Pool: £2,439.80. 69.10 winning tickets. JN

# 503 WOLVERHAMPTON (A.W) (L-H)
## Wednesday, January 14

**OFFICIAL GOING: Standard**
(REGIONAL MEETING) The centre of the track was again the place to be.
Wind: slt hlf bhd Weather: mainly fine but cold after a wet morning

## 527 BET DIRECT NO Q 08000 93 66 93 BANDED STKS 7f (F)
**1:30** (1:30) (H ) 3-Y-0+ £1,424 (£407; £203) **Stalls** High

Form RPR
050/ **1** **Dafa**[464] 5124 8-9-7 30................................ PJScallan 9 42
(BJCurley) *s.i.s: rdn and hdwy over 3f out: r.o u.p to ld wl ins fnl f* **9/4**[2]
00-1 **2** *½* **Eternal Bloom**[2] 502 6-9-6 35................................ MLawson[(7)] 4 46
(MBrittain) *a.p: rdn over 2f out: edgd lft over 1f out: ev ch wl ins fnl f: r.o* **2/1**[1]
000- **3** *2 ½* **Packin Em In**[209] 2508 6-9-7 35................................ MHenry 12 34
(JRBoyle) *sn prom: rdn over 2f out: edgd lft and led over 1f out: wandered u.p and hdd wl ins fnl f: no ex* **10/1**
0/-0 **4** *hd* **Keltic Flute**[11] 425 5-9-0 35..........................(v) SYourston[(7)] 2 34
(MrsLucindaFeatherstone) *w ldr: led over 4f out: rdn and hdd over 1f out: one pce* **50/1**
U-03 **5** *¾* **Countrywide Girl (IRE)**[2] 497 5-9-0 30.................. DonnaCaldwell[(7)] 1 32
(ABerry) *led over 2f: prom: rdn and one pce fnl 2f* **16/1**
00-5 **6** *7* **Good Form (IRE)**[11] 424 4-9-0 35................................ DerekNolan[(7)] 11 14
(MissKMGeorge) *hld up and bhd: rdn 3f out: nvr nr ldrs* **10/1**
00-0 **7** *2* **Sennen Cove**[9] 438 5-9-7 35..........................(t) KDalgleish 3 9
(RBastiman) *mid-div: rdn over 3f out: sn struggling* **4/1**[3]
00-6 **8** *10* **Home Coming**[6] 470 6-9-7 35................................ DeanMcKeown 6 —
(PSFelgate) *mid-div: hung lft over 3f out: sn bhd* **10/1**
000/ **9** *29* **Deal In Facts**[725] 240 5-9-0 35................................ SusannahWileman[(7)] 8 —
(CNKellett) *s.i.s: a bhd: t.o* **50/1**
/00- **10** *2* **Single Track Mind**[196] 2902 6-9-7 35................................ JFanning 5 —
(JRBoyle) *s.i.s: a bhd: t.o* **14/1**

1m 31.46s (1.26) **Going Correction** -0.075s/f (Stan) **10** Ran SP% **127.8**
Speed ratings: **89,88,85,85,84 76,74,62,29,27**CSF £8.06 TOTE £2.80: £1.40, £1.30, £3.10; EX 8.10.
**Owner** Mrs B J Curley **Bred** D H Jones **Trained** Newmarket, Suffolk

**FOCUS**
A very slow time for this poor event.

**NOTEBOOK**
**Dafa** is lightly-raced, having apparently broken down on no less than four occasions. Previously campaigned at between a mile and 12 furlongs, this trip is certainly the bare minimum for him. *Official explanation: trainer's representative said, regarding the improved form shown, gelding had benefited from the drop in class*
**Eternal Bloom** won a similar event over six at Southwell two days earlier. She again looked a tricky ride but Lawson does seem to get on well with her.
**Packin Em In**, returning after a seven month lay off, continually drifted away from the whip in the home straight.
**Keltic Flute** had run too freely in the first-time visor over a mile here earlier in the month.
**Countrywide Girl(IRE)** did not find that dropping back from a mile was the answer.
**Home Coming** *Official explanation: jockey said gelding had hung left-handed from three furlongs out*
**Single Track Mind** *Official explanation: jockey said gelding had tired badly and lost its action down the home straight*

## 528 BET DIRECT NO Q DEMO 08000 837 888 BANDED STKS 2m 46y(F)
**2:00** (2:00) (H ) 4-Y-0+ £1,361 (£389; £194) **Stalls** Low

Form RPR
00-2 **1** **Unleaded**[11] 426 4-8-11 35................................ JMackay 7 38
(JAkehurst) *hld up: stdy hdwy over 8f out: jnd ldr over 6f out: led 5f out: rdn 3f out: styd on wl* **9/4**[1]
50-4 **2** *1 ½* **The Last Mohican**[11] 426 5-9-4 30..........................(p) KDalgleish 4 36
(PHowling) *hld up: hdwy over 5f out: chsd wnr over 4f out: rdn over 3f out: no imp fnl f* **3/1**[2]
30/5 **3** *18* **Maraud**[10] 432 10-8-11 30................................ StephanieHollinshead[(7)] 6 14
(RHollinshead) *led: hdd 5f out: sn rdn: wknd over 3f out* **3/1**[2]
/0-3 **4** *8* **Ireland's Eye (IRE)**[6] 475 9-9-4 30................................ JBramhill 5 5
(JRNorton) *s.i.s: hld up: rdn and hdwy over 5f out: wknd 4f out* **3/1**[2]
000- **5** *dist* **Aliabad (IRE)**[7] 5048 9-9-4 30..........................(v) DeanMcKeown 2 —
(JGMO'Shea) *hld up: rdn over 6f out: sn struggling: t.o fnl 5f* **11/1**[3]

00-0 **6** *27* **Repetoire (FR)**[11] 427 4-8-11 30 ...... DRMcCabe 1 —
(KOCunningham-Brown) *w ldr tl rdn over 6f out: wknd over 5f out: eased and t.o fnl 4f* **40/1**

3m 42.39s (0.09) **Going Correction** -0.075s/f (Stan)
**WFA** 4 from 5yo+ 7lb **6** Ran SP% **116.5**
Speed ratings: **96,95,86,82,—** —CSF £9.87 TOTE £3.00: £1.50, £2.20; EX 5.30.
**Owner** Canisbay Bloodstock **Bred** Canisbay Bloodstock Ltd **Trained** Epsom, Surrey
■ Stewards Enquiry : D R McCabe one-day ban: careless riding (Jan 24)

**FOCUS**
A dire affair with the emphasis predictably on stamina.

**NOTEBOOK**
**Unleaded**, suited by this slightly longer trip, had a bit more left in the tank when the runner-up tried to mount a challenge.
**The Last Mohican** had finished six lengths behind Unleaded on 6lb worse terms over the extended 14 furlongs here last time. He tried hard to make a race of it but could never quite manage to take the winner's scalp.
**Ireland's Eye(IRE)** *Official explanation: jockey said gelding had hung left-handed throughout*

## 529 LITTLEWOODS BET DIRECT MEDIAN AUCTION MAIDEN STKS 7f (F)
2:35 (2:37) (H) 3-5-Y-0 **£1,463** (£418; £209) **Stalls** High

Form RPR

00- **1** **Modesty Blaise (SWE)**[260] 1284 4-9-0 ...... TEaves(5) 4 69
(MissGayKelleway) *hld up: hdwy on ins over 4f out: rdn to ld 2f out: clr over 1f out: r.o wl* **9/1**[3]

0- **2** *6* **Weakest Link**[67] 5948 3-8-3 ...... DAllan(3) 6 59
(WJarvis) *a.p: rdn over 3f out: wnt 2nd ins fnl f: no ch w wnr* **16/1**

454- **3** *1 1/4* **Two Of Clubs**[61] 5994 3-7-13 66 ...... DFentiman(7) 10 56
(PCHaslam) *hld up: hdwy over 3f out: sn rdn: kpt on same pce fnl f* **9/4**[2]

2 **4** *shd* **Ile Facile (IRE)**[9] 438 3-8-6 ...... KDalgleish 7 56
(NPLittmoden) *s.i.s: outpcd and bhd: hdwy over 2f out: styd on fnl f* **11/8**[1]

0 **5** *1/2* **Dances In Time**[11] 424 4-9-5 ...... TWilliams 3 50
(CNKellett) *led 1f: w ldr: rdn to ld again briefly over 2f out: wknd fnl f* **100/1**

06-2 **6** *4* **Iamback**[11] 424 4-9-0 47 ......(b) THamilton(5) 1 40
(MissGayKelleway) *led after 1f: rdn and hdd over 2f out: wknd over 1f out* **11/1**

0-3 **7** *5* **Angelo's Pride**[11] 424 3-8-6 ...... PaulEddery 8 32
(JAOsborne) *dwlt: outpcd and bhd: c wd and sme hdwy wl over 1f out: n.d* **10/1**

004- **8** *2 1/2* **Another Expletive**[86] 5679 3-7-11 47 ow1 ...... RThomas(5) 2 22
(JWhite) *prom tl rdn and wknd over 3f out* **33/1**

00- **9** *2* **Dial Square**[65] 5968 3-8-6 ...... JFanning 5 21
(PHowling) *chsd ldrs: lost pl over 5f out: rdn over 4f out: sn bhd* **10/1**

0-0 **10** *3* **Svenson**[9] 438 3-8-6 ...... DRMcCabe 11 14
(JSWainwright) *sn outpcd* **66/1**

000- **11** *24* **Firecat**[33] 6166 5-9-10 45 ......(p) ANicholls 9 —
(APJones) *rdn after 1f: a bhd: t.o* **25/1**

1m 29.89s (-0.31) **Going Correction** -0.075s/f (Stan)
**WFA** 3 from 4yo+ 18lb **11** Ran SP% **124.5**
Speed ratings: **98,91,89,89,89 84,78,75,73,70 42**CSF £145.60 TOTE £9.60: £2.50, £4.20, £1.20; EX 190.80.
**Owner** Twilight Racing **Bred** Marianne And Sven Jonsson **Trained** Newmarket, Suffolk

**FOCUS**
A weak maiden, with the form horses below their best.

**NOTEBOOK**
**Modesty Blaise(SWE)** had a couple of outings on the turf in April last year for James Given. Trained at this track over the winter, she had no trouble justifying some market support and may be capable of better things.
**Weakest Link**, previously trained by Sally Hall, may have plenty of speed in his pedigree but did not seem to mind this step up from six.
**Two Of Clubs**, dropped in class, appeared to get the seven a shade better on this occasion.
**Ile Facile(IRE)**, trying a longer trip, was the subject of office support and ran as if he requires even further.
**Dances In Time** had hung right when tailed off over the extended nine here on her debut. She might be worth a try back at six.

## 530 BETDIRECT.CO.UK BANDED STKS 6f (F)
3:10 (3:10) (H) 3-Y-0+ **£1,652** (£472; £236) **Stalls** Low

Form RPR

4-30 **1** **Attorney**[2] 509 6-9-1 45 ......(e) THamilton(5) 4 48
(DShaw) *sn outpcd: rdn and hdwy on ins over 3f out: led over 1f out: r.o* **5/1**[2]

00/0 **2** *nk* **Port Natal (IRE)**[2] 504 6-8-13 40 ......(b) LTreadwell(7) 3 47
(PatrickMorris, Ire) *a.p: rdn over 3f out: wnt 2nd briefly 2f out: r.o ins fnl f* **5/1**[2]

00-4 **3** *3* **Sabana (IRE)**[11] 422 6-9-6 45 ...... PFitzsimons 5 38
(JMBradley) *outpcd: rdn over 3f out: hdwy 2f out: kpt on same pce fnl f* **14/1**

600- **4** *3/4* **Silver Mascot**[36] 6149 5-9-6 45 ...... DaleGibson 8 36
(RHollinshead) *chsd ldrs: rdn 3f out: sn sltly outpcd: rallied ins fnl f* **8/1**[3]

46-3 **5** *nk* **Pilgrim Princess (IRE)**[12] 407 6-9-6 45 ...... ANicholls 10 35
(EJAlston) *a.p: rdn over 2f out: one pce* **13/8**[1]

01-0 **6** *nk* **Playful Spirit**[12] 407 5-9-6 45 ......(v) JEdmunds 2 34
(JBalding) *w ldr: led 3f out: sn rdn: hdd over 1f out: wknd ins fnl f* **8/1**[3]

460- **7** *3 1/2* **Long Weekend (IRE)**[166] 3754 6-8-13 45 ......(e) PMakin(7) 1 24
(DShaw) *s.i.s: short-lived effrt wl over 1f out* **14/1**

00-0 **8** *1 1/4* **Pips Song (IRE)**[11] 421 9-9-6 45 ...... JTate 13 20
(PWHiatt) *broke wl: lost pl after 1f: n.d after* **12/1**

00-0 **9** *hd* **Mesmerised**[9] 443 4-9-6 45 ...... AnnStokell 6 19
(MissAStokell) *sn bhd: hdwy on ins over 2f out: wknd over 1f out* **33/1**

00-0 **10** *5* **Star Applause**[9] 443 4-9-3 45 ......(v[1]) DAllan(3) 7 4
(JBalding) *led: rdn and hdd 3f out: wknd wl over 1f out* **25/1**

500- **11** *1 1/2* **Garnock Belle (IRE)**[121] 4939 3-8-4 45 ...... JFanning 12 —
(ABerry) *outpcd* **25/1**

000- **12** *1 1/4* **Salonika Sky**[94] 5512 3-8-4 45 ...... JMcAuley 9 —
(CWThornton) *prom: rdn over 3f out: sn wknd* **40/1**

006- **13** *23* **Lady Ellendune**[25] 6223 3-8-4 40 ...... JMackay 11 —
(DJSFfrenchDavis) *s.v.s: a t.o* **33/1**

1m 15.36s (-0.34) **Going Correction** -0.075s/f (Stan)
**WFA** 3 from 4yo+ 16lb **13** Ran SP% **130.7**
Speed ratings: **99,98,94,93,93 92,88,86,86,79 77,75,45**CSF £31.73 TOTE £6.60: £2.40, £1.90, £3.40; EX 45.30.
**Owner** K Nicholls **Bred** J R And Mrs P Good **Trained** Averham, Notts

**FOCUS**
A poor event, not better than a seller.

**NOTEBOOK**
**Attorney**, who ran in better company here two days previously, appears to be suited by having to come from behind.
**Port Natal(IRE)**, a mile winner at Thurles, will be suited by a return to further.
**Sabana(IRE)**, who surprisingly faded over course and distance last time, may be worth a try at seven.
**Silver Mascot** has not won for over two years but has been lightly raced of late.
**Pilgrim Princess(IRE)** was rather disappointing on this drop in grade.
**Playful Spirit** may be more at home at Southwell.
**Lady Ellendune** *Official explanation: jockey said filly was reluctant to race*

## 531 LITTLEWOODSCASINO.COM (S) STKS 1m 100y(F)
3:40 (3:40) (H) 3-Y-0+ **£1,491** (£426; £213) **Stalls** Low

Form RPR

10/ **1** **Consonant (IRE)**[1608] 3807 7-9-9 ...... SRighton 11 73+
(DGBridgwater) *prom: jnd ldr over 5f out: led on bit over 2f out: clr whn rdn over 1f out: eased cl home* **9/2**[3]

05-4 **2** *9* **Nite-Owl Fizz**[9] 442 6-9-6 55 ...... DAllan(3) 1 54
(JO'Reilly) *chsd ldrs: rdn over 4f out: styd on to take 2nd ins fnl f: no ch w wnr* **3/1**[1]

030- **3** *3/4* **Ivy Moon**[46] 6100 4-8-13 47 ...... RThomas(5) 9 47
(BJLlewellyn) *stdd s: plld hrd: hdwy 6f out: rdn 3f out: chsd wnr over 1f out tl ins fnl f: one pce* **14/1**

00-1 **4** *1* **French Horn**[7] 468 7-10-0 50 ...... JMackay 4 55
(MWigham) *hld up and bhd: rdn over 3f out: hdwy over 2f out: one pce fnl f* **7/2**[2]

06-4 **5** *1 1/4* **Proud Victor (IRE)**[11] 425 4-9-4 40 ......(v) THamilton(5) 10 48
(DShaw) *hld up and bhd: hdwy over 4f out: rdn over 3f out: c wd st: no imp fnl f* **10/1**

50-0 **6** *3 1/2* **Love's Design (IRE)**[6] 478 7-9-9 52 ......(p) JTate 6 40
(MissSJWilton) *prom: led over 5f out: rdn and hdd over 2f out: sn btn: wknd fnl f* **9/1**

040- **7** *1 1/2* **Sir Frank Gibson**[37] 6141 3-8-3 50 ...... JFanning 5 37
(MJohnston) *rdn after 1f: bhd fnl 5f* **7/1**

504- **8** *1 1/2* **Second Venture (IRE)**[58] 6015 6-9-9 40 ......(p) KDalgleish 3 34
(PHowling) *prom: rdn over 5f out: sn lost pl* **12/1**

00-5 **9** *1 1/4* **Lucky Romance**[9] 445 5-9-4 45 ......(b[1]) DRMcCabe 8 26
(BJMeehan) *led: hdd 3f out: wknd over 2f out* **9/1**

0-60 **10** *1/2* **Haithem (IRE)**[6] 472 7-9-9 40 ......(e) RFitzpatrick 2 30
(DShaw) *a bhd* **40/1**

1m 48.69s (-2.31) **Going Correction** -0.075s/f (Stan)
**WFA** 3 from 4yo+ 20lb **10** Ran SP% **123.8**
Speed ratings: **108,99,98,97,96 92,91,89,88,87**CSF £19.70 TOTE £4.80: £1.80, £1.20, £5.20; EX 15.10.The winner was bought in for 7,500gns.
**Owner** The Rule Racing Syndicate **Bred** Kilfrush Stud Ltd **Trained** Winchcombe, Gloucs

**FOCUS**
A very fast time for the class of contest, and the winner looks far better than the grade.

**NOTEBOOK**
**Consonant(IRE)** has been plagued by leg trouble since starting favourite for Godolphin in the 1999 Solario Stakes. Retained for 7,500 guineas, he seems sure to make up for lost time in better company.
**Nite-Owl Fizz** found he had caught a tartar for this grade.
**Ivy Moon** was back in the right sort of grade but did not readily accept restraint.
**French Horn** , a recent Polytrack winner having his first run at the track, would have been expected to act on the surface, having handled the mud on turf.
**Proud Victor(IRE)** had the visor back on.
**Lucky Romance** *Official explanation: jockey said mare ran too keen early on in first time blinkers*

## 532 BET DIRECT IN VISION SKY PAGE 293 APPRENTICE BANDED STKS 1m 1f 79y(F)
4:10 (4:10) (H) 3-Y-0+ **£1,368** (£391; £195) **Stalls** Low

Form RPR

/36- **1** **Bella Pavlina**[37] 6148 6-9-4 35 ...... BSwarbrick(5) 4 41
(WMBrisbourne) *prom: rdn and outpcd over 4f out: rallied over 2f out: styd on to ld ins fnl f* **15/8**[1]

50-4 **2** *1 1/2* **Giust In Temp (IRE)**[9] 445 5-9-6 30 ...... PMakin(3) 3 38
(PWHiatt) *prom: led over 6f out tl over 5f out: led again 3f out: rdn 2f out: hdd and nt qckn ins fnl f* **9/2**[3]

000- **3** *1/2* **Vesta Flame**[23] 6230 3-8-1 35 ...... RThomas 6 37
(MJohnston) *led 2f: lost pl over 5f out: styd on wl fnl f* **20/1**

00-0 **4** *1/2* **All On My Own (USA)**[11] 426 9-9-9 35 ......(b) NataliaGemelova 7 36
(IWMcinnes) *s.i.s: hdwy 5f out: rdn and one pce fnl 2f* **33/1**

44-3 **5** *3/4* **Misty Man (USA)**[10] 430 6-9-6 30 ......(b) PGallagher(3) 8 35
(MissJFeilden) *s.i.s: sn rcvrd: led over 5f out to 3f out: no ex fnl f* **5/2**[2]

000- **6** *1* **Middleham Rose**[89] 5621 3-7-10 35 ...... DFentiman(5) 1 33
(PCHaslam) *bhd tl styd on fnl f: nrst fin* **9/2**[3]

60-0 **7** *5* **Manikato (USA)**[9] 441 10-9-9 30 ...... LTreadwell 9 23
(KGWingrove) *prom: rdn 4f out: wknd 3f out* **20/1**

000- **8** *14* **By Definition (IRE)**[19] 4114 6-9-9 30 ...... MSavage 5 —
(JCTuck) *w ldrs tl rdn and wknd over 4f out* **50/1**

00-0 **9** *8* **Battle Back (BEL)**[11] 415 3-8-0 30 ow4 ......(be[1]) DerekNolan(5) 2 —
(SCWilliams) *hld up: rdn over 4f out: sn bhd* **12/1**

2m 3.72s (0.82) **Going Correction** -0.075s/f (Stan)
**WFA** 3 from 5yo+ 22lb **9** Ran SP% **121.8**
Speed ratings: **93,91,91,90,90 89,84,72,65**CSF £11.04 TOTE £3.40: £1.60, £2.10, £3.90; EX 10.50 Place 6 £60.98, Place 5 £40.95.
**Owner** The Cartmel Syndicate **Bred** C Papaioannou **Trained** Great Ness, Shropshire

**FOCUS**
A poor race and a modest winning time after they went no pace to halfway.

**NOTEBOOK**
**Bella Pavlina** appreciated the return to a slightly longer trip.
**Giust In Temp(IRE)** gave another good account of himself over his favourite course and distance.
**Vesta Flame** stepped up on his previous efforts and finished with a real flourish. Significant improvement can be expected over a longer trip.
**All On My Own(USA)** lacked the required acceleration on this return to a more realistic distance.
**Misty Man(USA)** did not find a drop back in distance the answer.
**Middleham Rose**, making her All-Weather debut, is one to keep an eye on when stepped up in distance.
KH

# [519]LINGFIELD (L-H)

Thursday, January 15

**OFFICIAL GOING: Standard**
(REGIONAL MEETING)
Wind: mod bhd Weather: overcast, drizzle

## 533 PRESS INTERACTIVE TO BET DIRECT BANDED STKS (DIV I) 1m (P)
**1:10** (1:10) (H) 3-Y-0+ **£1,645** (£470; £235) **Stalls** High

Form RPR

300- **1** **Balerno**[17] 6255 5-9-8 45 GCarter 2 56
(RIngram) *hld up in midfield: prog on inner to trck ldr over 2f out: led over 1f out and sn clr: 4l ahd ins fnl f: rdn out* **11/4**[2]

/00- **2** ¾ **Miss Peaches**[352] 401 6-9-1 45 KristinStubbs(7) 5 54
(GGMargarson) *cl up: pushed along and outpcd over 2f out: effrt over 1f out: chsd wnr ent fnl f: r.o nr fin: too much to do* **20/1**

4-11 **3** 6 **Rosti**[7] 472 4-9-7 45 RoryMoore(7) 8 46
(PCHaslam) *hld up in midfield: smooth prog on outer to trck ldrs 3f out: nt qckn and outpcd over 2f out: hanging lft and kpt on one pc* **5/4**[1]

-065 **4** 1 ¾ **Pageant**[3] 497 7-9-8 35 CCatlin 10 36
(JMBradley) *w ldr: led halfwaay to 3f out: sn rdn and outpcd: one pce after* **14/1**

6-02 **5** nk **Vlasta Weiner**[10] 441 4-9-8 40 (b) PFitzsimons 1 35
(JMBradley) *s.i.s: pushed up to go prom: led on inner 3f out: rdn and hdd over 1f out: wknd rapidly* **12/1**

000- **6** 1 ½ **Zahunda (IRE)**[27] 6218 5-9-1 45 BSwarbrick(7) 7 32
(WMBrisbourne) *racd towards rr: outpcd over 2f out: no ch after* **10/1**[3]

000- **7** hd **Ro Eridani**[71] 5928 4-9-8 45 JMcAuley 11 32
(TJEtherington) *settled in rr: outpcd wl over 2f out: one pce after* **25/1**

000- **8** 1 **Tedzar (IRE)**[59] 6016 4-9-3 35 NChalmers(5) 6 29
(BRJohnson) *racd towards rr: rdn and outpcd over 2f out: no ch after* **25/1**

05-6 **9** nk **Nothing Matters**[9] 451 3-8-4 42 ow2 PDoe 3 31
(PRChamings) *pressed ldrs: losing pl whn stmbld over 2f out: no ch after* **10/1**[3]

00-0 **10** 6 **Tortuette**[7] 482 3-7-13 45 (v1) LisaJones(3) 9 15
(Jean-ReneAuvray) *last and pushed along bef 1/2-way: wknd over 2f out* **33/1**

00-5 **11** 10 **Dancing King (IRE)**[11] 434 8-9-8 30 JoannaBadger 4 —
(PWHiatt) *led to 1/2-way: wknd v rapidly wl over 2f out: t.o* **20/1**

1m 41.0s (1.49) **Going Correction** +0.05s/f (Slow)
**WFA** 3 from 4yo+ 20lb **11** Ran SP% **123.8**
Speed ratings: **94,93,87,85,85 83,83,82,82,76 66**CSF £64.86 TOTE £3.50: £1.10, £8.10, £1.10; EX 84.10.
**Owner** The Three Amigos **Bred** Juddmonte Farms **Trained** Epsom, Surrey
■ Stewards Enquiry : Rory Moore caution: used whip with arm raised above shoulder height

**FOCUS**
A modest winning time, and the form looks standard for the grade.

**NOTEBOOK**
**Balerno**got first run on the eventual second and won with a bit up his sleeve. He appreciated the drop in trip and grade.
**Miss Peaches**let the winner get first run on her and was finishing all too late. She had not run for almost a year so is entitled to come on for this, and Polytrack clearly suits.
**Rosti**, a capable performer at this level on Fibresand, could not translate his form to Polytrack.
**Pageant**, who is difficult to win with, has shown her best form on Fibresand.
**Vlasta Weiner**did not get home over this longer trip.
**Zahunda(IRE)**was another with Fibresand form attempting the Polytrack for the first time.

## 534 BET DIRECT ON SKY TEXT PAGE 372 MEDIAN AUCTION MAIDEN STKS 1m 2f (P)
**1:40** (1:40) (H) 4-6-Y-0 **£1,291** (£369; £184) **Stalls** Low

Form RPR

406- **1** **Itsonlyagame**[46] 5282 4-9-0 60 IMongan 5 56
(RIngram) *hld up: prog over 2f out: chsd ldr wl over 1f out: rdn to ld ent fnl f: styd on* **6/4**[1]

05-5 **2** ¾ **Vanilla Moon**[9] 449 4-8-9 48 (v) SWKelly 4 50
(JRJenkins) *led to over 7f out: trckd ldr tl led again 2f out: hdd ent fnl f: nt qckn u.p* **15/8**[2]

006- **3** 2 ½ **Ginger Ice**[16] 6262 4-9-0 40 (p) NPollard 1 51?
(GGMargarson) *hld up: prog to trck ldrs 2f out: sn shkn up and looked reluctant: chsd ldng pair over 1f out: no imp* **5/1**[3]

000- **4** 6 **Janes Valentine**[16] 6261 4-8-9 47 NCallan 6 35
(JJBridger) *hld up: effrt to chse ldrs over 2f out: nt qckn and btn wl over 1f out* **10/1**

**5** 1 ¾ **Solmorin**[134] 6-8-11 VSlattery 3 32
(RJBaker) *plld hrd: led over 7f out and sn clr: hdd & wknd 2f out* **20/1**

**6** 11 **Globe Beauty (IRE)**[292] 6-8-11 CCatlin 2 12
(ADWPinder) *chsd ldrs tl wknd u.p over 3f out: t.o* **20/1**

2m 11.01s (3.62) **Going Correction** +0.05s/f (Slow)
**WFA** 4 from 6yo 2lb **6** Ran SP% **110.1**
Speed ratings: **87,86,84,79,78 69**CSF £4.34 TOTE £2.10: £1.30, £2.40; EX 5.90.
**Owner** Mrs Gina Brown **Bred** S Gollogly **Trained** Epsom, Surrey

**FOCUS**
A poor maiden and a very slow time.

**NOTEBOOK**
**Itsonlyagame**had the highest official rating of these and little to beat in a very weak maiden. The time of the race only adds to the impression that he will struggle in handicap company off his current mark.
**Vanilla Moon**is fully exposed and had a bit to find with the winner on ratings, but she has form around here and appeared to run her race.
**Ginger Ice**, whose attitude is questionable, will be more at home in banded races.
**Janes Valentine**faced big stamina doubts coming into the race and failed to dispel them.
**Solmorin**, debuting on the Flat having had one start in a bumper, pulled much too hard for her own good.

## 535 PRESS INTERACTIVE TO BET DIRECT BANDED STKS (DIV II) 1m (P)
**2:10** (2:11) (H) 3-Y-0+ **£1,641** (£469; £234) **Stalls** High

Form RPR

00-4 **1** **Titian Lass**[13] 412 5-9-1 45 (b) DeanWilliams(7) 7 54
(CEBrittain) *prom: pushed along and effrt 2f out: led and edgd rt over 1f out: in command ins fnl f* **9/2**[3]

04-1 **2** 2 **Yankeedoodledandy (IRE)**[7] 482 3-8-1 45 DFentiman(7) 2 55+
(PCHaslam) *lft 12l s: sn in tch in last trio: prog 2f out: nt clr run over 1f out and swtchd rt: r.o wl to take 2nd nr fin* **13/8**[1]

64-0 **3** nk **Ladywell Blaise (IRE)**[8] 468 7-9-8 45 NPollard 9 49
(JJBridger) *settled in midfield: prog over 2f out: chsd wnr ins fnl f: no imp: lost 2nd nr fin* **14/1**

060- **4** ¾ **Colne Valley Amy**[7] 1780 7-9-3 40 (b) AQuinn(5) 8 47
(GLMoore) *settled in rr: rdn and prog over 2f out: chsd ldrs over 1f out: one pce after* **20/1**

03-2 **5** 1 ¼ **Wilom (GER)**[8] 468 6-9-8 45 CCatlin 10 44
(MRHoad) *t.k.h: sn restrained in last pair: prog on wd outside over 2f out: chsd ldrs 1f out: fnd nil u.p* **7/2**[2]

000- **6** nk **Badou**[29] 6204 4-9-5 45 RMiles(3) 6 43
(LMontagueHall) *mde most to over 1f out: wknd fnl f* **10/1**

0-00 **7** 3 **Queen Excalibur**[10] 442 5-9-8 45 (b) PFitzsimons 5 37
(JMBradley) *t.k.h: chsd ldr to wl over 1f out: wknd rapidly fnl f* **25/1**

000- **8** hd **Fitz The Bill (IRE)**[37] 6151 4-9-8 35 PJScallan 3 36
(NBKing) *chsd ldrs: pushed along over 4f out: lost pl and struggling 3f out: n.d fnl 2f* **33/1**

300- **9** nk **Westmead Etoile**[136] 4614 4-9-8 45 SWKelly 1 35
(JRJenkins) *settled in last trio: hrd rdn and no prog 2f out* **16/1**

60-3 **10** 9 **Neutral Night (IRE)**[12] 422 4-9-8 45 (v) IMongan 4 15
(RBrotherton) *t.k.h: prom: rdn over 3f out: wknd over 2f out* **10/1**

1m 41.2s (1.69) **Going Correction** +0.05s/f (Slow)
**WFA** 3 from 4yo+ 20lb **10** Ran SP% **120.8**
Speed ratings: **93,91,90,89,88 88,85,85,84,75**CSF £12.38 TOTE £4.80: £1.10, £1.40, £5.20; EX 15.80.
**Owner** Michael Clarke **Bred** Roldvale Ltd **Trained** Newmarket, Suffolk

**FOCUS**
A steady early pace and modest winning time. The form is just standard for the grade.

**NOTEBOOK**
**Titian Lass**, an inconsistent sort, can probably be considered a lucky winner given the problems the favourite had at the start. That said, she was given the perfect ride, the way the race was run, and beat everything else well enough. This is her level.
**Yankeedoodledandy(IRE)**was the moral winner as with a clean break he would have won easily. Due to go up to a rating of 57 now, this was an opportunity missed.
**Ladywell Blaise(IRE)**, another inconsistent mare, looks to have found her grade having found sellers too tough recently.
**Colne Valley Amy**, who has not shown much aptitude for hurdling, had the blinkers back on for this return to the Flat. She is on a very long losing run.
**Wilom(GER)**, who found nothing under pressure, should have done better given his recent form in sellers at the track.
**Neutral Night(IRE)** *Official explanation: trainer said filly had run too free*

## 536 BET DIRECT ON 0800 93 66 93 BANDED STKS 7f (P)
**2:40** (2:41) (H) 3-Y-0+ **£1,683** (£481; £240) **Stalls** Low

Form RPR

35-2 **1** **Lord Melbourne (IRE)**[12] 421 5-9-7 45 SWKelly 8 56+
(JAOsborne) *hld up in midfield: smooth prog on outer over 2f out: shkn up to ld 1f out: rdn clr* **5/1**[1]

005- **2** 2 ½ **The Gay Fox**[20] 6235 10-9-4 40 (bt) LPKeniry(3) 15 48
(BGPowell) *hld up in last trio: plenty to do over 2f out: rdn and prog on outer over 1f out: styd on wl to take 2nd last strides* **16/1**

500- **3** ½ **Abuelos**[53] 5719 5-9-7 40 PDoe 7 47
(SDow) *hld up in rr: nt clr run over 2f out: prog on outer jst over 1f out: styd on wl to take 3rd nr fin* **14/1**[3]

00-0 **4** nk **Geespot**[12] 422 5-9-4 40 RMiles(3) 1 46
(DJSFfrenchDavis) *prom: nt qckn and lost pl over 2f out: effrt again over 1f out : kpt on same pce fnl f* **20/1**

65-5 **5** nk **Aintnecessarilyso**[3] 504 6-9-2 45 (p) MSavage(5) 11 45
(NEBerry) *sn trckd ldrs: effrt 2f out: drvn to chse wnr ins fnl f: no imp: wknd and lost 3 pls nr fin* **5/1**[1]

00-4 **6** 2 **Shamwari Fire (IRE)**[12] 424 4-9-0 45 NataliaGemelova(7) 6 40
(IWMcinnes) *cl up: rdn over 2f out: pressing ldrs over 1f out: fdd fnl f* **10/1**[2]

00-0 **7** 1 **Definitely Special (IRE)**[8] 465 6-9-0 40 RoryMoore(7) 10 38
(NEBerry) *trckd ldrs: nt clr run over 2f out and again wl over 1f out: hanging and nt qckn after* **16/1**

004- **8** nk **Dilys**[17] 6206 5-9-7 45 IMongan 5 37
(WSKittow) *racd in midfield: pushed along whn n.m.r and snatched up over 2f out: effrt over 1f out: one pce and no ch whn no run fnl f* **5/1**[1]

25-1 **9** nk **Indian Warrior**[10] 441 8-9-13 40 (b) NCallan 13 42
(JJay) *prom: led over 2f out and kicked on: hdd & wknd 1f out* **5/1**[1]

00-0 **10** ½ **Thats All Jazz**[3] 498 6-9-2 45 RThomas(5) 12 35
(CRDore) *racd on outer towards rr: rdn 3f out: one pce and no prog over 1f out* **33/1**

05-0 **11** hd **Costa Del Sol (IRE)**[9] 452 3-8-3 45 NPollard 14 35
(JJBridger) *restrained in last: rdn 3f out: no prog tl styd on ins fnl f* **25/1**

000- **12** 1 ½ **Shirley Oaks (IRE)**[84] 5719 6-9-4 40 LisaJones(3) 9 31
(MissZCDavison) *trckd ldrs: losing pl whn hmpd over 2f out: eased fnl f: sddle slipped* **33/1**

0/0- **13** 1 **Misbehaviour**[13] 1664 5-9-0 45 (p) SJDonohoe(7) 4 28
(PButler) *pushed along in rr over 4f out: no prog and btn over 2f out* **10/1**[2]

00-3 **14** 3 ½ **Xsynna**[8] 465 8-9-7 45 (v) JTate 2 20
(TTClement) *led to over 2f out: wknd rapidly wl over 1f out* **10/1**[2]

000- **15** ½ **Almara**[95] 5497 4-9-7 40 (tp) CCatlin 16 18
(MissKBBoutflower) *racd on outer: in rr and rdn over 4f out: brief effrt 3f out: sn wknd* **50/1**

1m 26.67s (0.67) **Going Correction** +0.05s/f (Slow)
**WFA** 3 from 4yo+ 18lb **15** Ran SP% **128.8**
Speed ratings: **98,95,94,94,93 91,90,90,89,89 88,87,86,82,81**CSF £94.70 TOTE £3.90: £2.30, £2.50, £3.60; EX 60.40.
**Owner** Paul J Dixon **Bred** Fin A Co **Trained** Upper Lambourn, Berks

**FOCUS**
Standard form for the grade, although the winner looks well in on his old form.

**NOTEBOOK**
**Lord Melbourne(IRE)**, back up to his ideal trip, travelled very well throughout and quickened when the button was pressed. He looks one to keep on side at this level.
**The Gay Fox**, dropping into banded grade for the first time, finished well from off the pace, but he is far from sure to repeat this effort next time if his previous form is anything to go by.
**Abuelos** did not get the best of runs but was another pointer to the wellbeing of his trainer's string at the moment.
**Geespot**, a course and distance winner, appears to be coming back to form after a few months' absence.
**Aintnecessarilyso**has yet to convince over this trip.
**Dilys**is worth rating a bit better than her finishing position as she was short of room from the turn into the straight and, once switched to the inside, found her path once again blocked in the straight.
**Shirley Oaks(IRE)** *Official explanation: jockey said saddle slipped*

## 537 BET DIRECT ON SKY ACTIVE BANDED STKS 1m 2f (P)
3:10 (3:11) (H ) 4-Y-0+ £1,662 (£475; £237) Stalls Low

Form RPR
0-25 1 **Tropical Son**[7] 472 5-9-0 40...(v) NCallan 10 52
(DShaw) *chsd ldrs: lost pl 1/2-way: rdn and prog over 3f out: drvn to chal fnl f: hung fire tl urged ahd last stride* **11/2**[2]
05-2 2 *shd* **Our Glenard**[9] 455 5-8-11 45... LPKeniry[(3)] 4 52
(SLKeightley) *dwlt: sn wl in tch: trckd ldng pair over 3f out: led and kicked on over 2f out: drvn fnl f: hdd last stride* **7/4**[1]
501- 3 *1 1/4* **Piquet**[16] 6262 6-9-0 45... NPollard 14 50
(JJBridger) *hld up wl in rr: stdy prog fr 4f out: rdn to take 3rd over 1f out: styd on wl fnl f: nt rch ldng pair* **10/1**
050- 4 *1 3/4* **Essay Baby (FR)**[76] 5856 4-8-12 45... CCatlin 5 47
(PDCundell) *chsd ldrs: rdn and effrt 3f out: kpt on same pce fnl 2f* **20/1**
560- 5 *4* **Paintbrush (IRE)**[40] 6133 4-8-12 45... SWKelly 7 39
(MrsLStubbs) *s.s: rchd midfield after 4f: rdn over 4f out: struggling 3f out: kpt on u.p fnl 2f: n.d* **7/1**[3]
006- 6 *hd* **High Diva**[16] 6257 5-8-9 45...(p) NChalmers[(5)] 13 39
(BRJohnson) *dwlt: racd wd: hld up in rr: rdn 3f out: no prog 2f out: kpt on fnl f* **10/1**
05-3 7 *7* **Pyrrhic**[5] 495 5-9-0 40...(b) PDoe 9 26
(RMFlower) *t.k.h: prom: lost pl 6f out: prog to press ldrs 3f out: nt qckn 2f out: wknd rapidly over 1f out* **9/1**
000- 8 *2* **Monduru**[162] 3880 7-8-7 35...(b) HPoulton[(7)] 2 23
(GLMoore) *t.k.h: disp ld to over 2f out: wknd rapidly* **33/1**
200- 9 *hd* **Ballare (IRE)**[57] 6028 5-9-0 45... DKinsella 1 22
(BobJones) *disp ld to over 2f out: wknd rapidly and eased* **7/1**[3]
0-01 10 *1 1/4* **Malmand (USA)**[10] 445 5-9-6 40...(v) IMongan 8 26
(RBrotherton) *racd in midfield: drvn 1/2-way: struggling 3f out: wknd* **12/1**
000- 11 *16* **Gemma**[50] 6075 4-8-12 40... WRyan 6 —
(PJMakin) *t.k.h: cl up to 1/2-way: wknd 4f out: t.o* **25/1**
000- 12 *11* **Emarati's Image**[53] 2504 6-9-0 45... VSlattery 12 —
(RMStronge) *plld hrd: prom to 1/2-way: sn wknd: t.o* **33/1**
60-6 13 *1* **Tarkwa**[10] 445 5-9-0 45... MHenry 11 —
(RMHCowell) *prom tl wknd over 4f out: t.o* **9/1**

2m 8.64s (1.25) **Going Correction** +0.05s/f (Slow)
**WFA** 4 from 5yo+ 2lb **13** Ran SP% **137.1**
Speed ratings: **97,96,95,94,91 91,85,83,83,82 70,61,60**CSF £17.29 TOTE £5.60: £1.60, £1.20, £4.60; EX 21.50.
**Owner** Swann Racing Ltd **Bred** Natton House Thoroughbreds **Trained** Averham, Notts

**FOCUS**
They only went a fair pace and the form looks average for the grade.

**NOTEBOOK**
**Tropical Son**did not travel anywhere near as well as the runner-up but, under a strong ride from Callan, he found enough to deny the favourite on the line. The step back up in trip suited, but it has taken him a long time to get his head in front and one would not be rushing to back him to follow up.
**Our Glenard**travelled smoothly and kicked clear turning into the straight, but sticking next to the far-side rail probably did not help as he was caught on the very last stride. He deserves to get his head in front again and will have other opportunities at this level.
**Piquet**, who broke a long losing run last time, is suited by a strongly-run race as she likes to come from well off the pace.
**Essay Baby(FR)**ran as though she would come on for this first run since October, and surely she can be found a race at this level.
**Paintbrush(IRE)**, whose jockey booking caught the eye beforehand, was a springer in the market but was always struggling after a slow start. She is probably capable of a bit better.
**High Diva**is still chasing that elusive first win.

## 538 LITTLEWOODSPOKER.COM CLAIMING STKS 5f (P)
3:40 (3:42) (H ) 3-Y-0+ £1,281 (£366; £183) Stalls High

Form RPR
4-05 1 **Mr Spliffy (IRE)**[9] 460 5-9-1 47...(v) RKeogh[(7)] 7 53
(KRBurke) *racd in midfield: stdy prog fr 1/2-way: pressed ldr fnl f: nudged along to ld last 75y* **12/1**
0-61 2 *nk* **Cark**[9] 460 6-9-4 45...(p) MSavage[(5)] 4 53
(JBalding) *trckd ldng pair: rdn to ld over 1f out: hdd and hld last 75y* **11/2**[3]
253- 3 *3* **Philly Dee**[19] 6246 3-7-11 47...(b) LisaJones[(3)] 8 33
(JJay) *hld up in rr and sn outpcd: pushed along over 2f out: prog and hanging lft over 1f out: r.o to take 3rd nr fin* **8/1**
060- 4 *hd* **Tickle**[16] 6261 6-9-4 48...(vt) CCatlin 9 35
(PJMakin) *racd on outer: chsd ldrs: rdn over 2f out: nt qckn wl over 1f out: styd on ins fnl f* **11/4**[2]
00-3 5 *1/2* **Henry Tun**[13] 411 6-9-9 52...(b) IMongan 2 38
(JBalding) *led to 3f out: styd pressing ldr: ev ch over 1f out: wknd ins fnl f* **5/2**[1]
00-6 6 *nk* **Westmead Tango**[1] 519 4-9-4 49...(v) SWKelly 1 32
(JRJenkins) *s.i.s: sn pressed ldrs: rdn whn n.m.r on inner over 2f out: fdd fnl f* **11/2**[3]
44-0 7 *2* **Diaphanous**[10] 443 6-8-11 45...(b) LiamJones[(7)] 3 24
(EAWheeler) *drvn to press ldr: led 3f out to over 1f out: wknd* **11/1**
00-0 8 *1 1/2* **Ivory Venture**[9] 453 4-9-1 50... RMiles[(3)] 5 18
(DKIvory) *outpcd and rdn after 1f: a struggling* **16/1**
00-0 9 *nk* **Gentle Response**[8] 465 4-9-4 45... PJScallan 6 17
(CADwyer) *dwlt: outpcd in last trio: effrt 2f out: no prog over 1f out* **50/1**

59.75 secs (-0.03) **Going Correction** +0.05s/f (Slow)
**WFA** 3 from 4yo+ 15lb **9** Ran SP% **121.0**
Speed ratings: **102,101,96,96,95 95,91,89,89**CSF £80.12 TOTE £6.50: £1.10, £2.60, £2.40; EX 100.50.Cark (no.1) was claimed by Jonathan Jay for £5,000. Philly Dee (no.10) was claimed by D N Carey for £2,000.
**Owner** Mrs Elaine M Burke **Bred** Mrs Maureen O'Meara **Trained** Middleham Moor, N Yorks
■ Apprentice Ronan Keogh's first winner.

**FOCUS**
A decent winning time for the grade of contest, although the form is modest.

**NOTEBOOK**
**Mr Spliffy(IRE)**, who had only had one previous outing on Polytrack, found the switch back to this surface bringing about an improved display. He travelled nicely and his inexperienced rider, winning his first race, only had to push him out to score tidily. There could be more to come from him.
**Cark**, a winner on Fibresand last time, was having his first start on Polytrack and translated his form well. He may have been unlucky to run into the winner and he came clear of the rest, so he could be worth persevering with.
**Philly Dee**always finds one or two too good and the re-application of blinkers and switch to Polytrack made little difference.
**Tickle**, who was supported in the market, found the drop back in trip unsuitable.
**Henry Tun**, a regular on Fibresand, was having his first start on Polytrack. The other surface suits his style of running better.

## 539 LITTLEWOODS BET DIRECT BANDED STKS 1m 4f (P)
4:10 (4:10) (H ) 4-Y-0+ £1,267 (£362; £181) Stalls Low

Form RPR
62-1 1 **Broughton Knows**[10] 440 7-9-7 35...(b) LisaJones[(3)] 2 50
(WJMusson) *dwlt: hld up: prog to trck ldr over 4f out: rdn over 2f out: nt qckn tl urged into ld last 150y: sn clr* **11/10**[1]
00/3 2 *2* **Trouble Next Door (IRE)**[9] 449 6-9-4 35... IMongan 3 41
(NPLittmoden) *chsd clr ldr: led wl over 4f out: sn rdn: hdd and btn last 150y* **5/2**[2]
046- 3 *nk* **Buz Kiri (USA)**[34] 5329 6-9-4 35... NCallan 5 41
(AWCarroll) *racd in midfield: rdn fr 1/2-way: prog u.p to chse ldng pair over 2f out: kpt on: nrst fin* **6/1**[3]
000/ 4 *8* **Doctor John**[19] 2040 7-9-4 35... CCatlin 8 29
(AndrewTurnell) *chsd ldrs: rdn over 4f out: in tch over 3f out: sn btn* **33/1**
0/0- 5 *1 1/2* **Ripcord (IRE)**[65] 2524 6-9-1 35... LPKeniry[(3)] 1 26
(LadyHerries) *prom in chsng gp: chsd ldng pair over 4f out to over 2f out: wknd* **7/1**
00-0 6 *3/4* **Briery Mec**[9] 456 9-9-4 35...(p) GCarter 9 25
(HJCollingridge) *hld up in rr: rdn 4f out: sn no prog and struggling* **25/1**
000/ 7 *14* **April Ace**[488] 2808 8-9-4 35... VSlattery 7 4
(RJBaker) *hld up in last: lost tch w ldrs wl over 3f out: sn bhd* **50/1**
000- 8 *29* **Pat's Miracle (IRE)**[27] 6218 4-9-0 35...(b[1]) WMLordan 10 —
(JohnBerry) *in tch: rdn over 5f out: sn wknd: t.o 3f out* **50/1**
00-0 9 *23* **Stunning Magic**[12] 419 4-9-0 35...(b[1]) DKinsella 4 —
(MrsBarbaraWaring) *racd freely: led and sn clr: wknd and hdd wl over 4f out: sn t.o* **50/1**

2m 34.81s (0.83) **Going Correction** +0.05s/f (Slow)
**WFA** 4 from 6yo+ 4lb **9** Ran SP% **115.6**
Speed ratings: **99,97,97,92,91 90,81,61,46**CSF £3.77 TOTE £2.30: £1.10, £2.10, £1.10; EX 4.00 Place 6 £47.23, Place 5 £34.97.
**Owner** Broughton Thermal Insulation **Bred** Broughton Bloodstock **Trained** Newmarket, Suffolk

**FOCUS**
The pace was nothing special, but the form looks good for the grade.

**NOTEBOOK**
**Broughton Knows**, a good winner at Southwell last time, had it prove on this very different surface. Although he took a while to get into top gear, he won comfortably in the end and will merit plenty of respect in similar company while he remains in this sort of form.
**Trouble Next Door(IRE)**ran a decent race in a maiden here last time and once again ran a respectable race, just finding a rival in top form too good. If kept to Flat racing he has the ability to win a race of this type.
**Buz Kiri(USA)**a maiden after nine starts over hurdles and 28 starts on the Flat, was staying on all too late.
**Doctor John**, who has had an unsuccessful time of it over fences of late, was probably here to have a confidence-boosting run.
**Ripcord(IRE)**, having his first run on the Flat since June, is of little ability and was seen off running down the hill.
T/Plt: £14.70 to a £1 stake. Pool: £30,115.85. 1,493.65 winning tickets. T/Qpdt: £11.40 to a £1 stake. Pool: £2,270.40. 146.60 winning tickets. JN

# 511 SOUTHWELL (L-H)
### Thursday, January 15

**OFFICIAL GOING: Standard**
The track was once again slower on the inside rail.
Wind: fresh across Weather: raining

## 540 BETDIRECT.CO.UK H'CAP (DIV I) 5f (F)
1:00 (1:01) (D ) (0-85,82) 3-Y-0+ £2,645 (£2,645; £622; £311) Stalls High

Form RPR
00-1 1 *dht* **The Fisio**[9] 454 4-9-4 72 6ex... MartinDwyer 6 83
(AMBalding) *chsd ldrs: pushed along 1/2-way: led over 1f out: rdn out* **11/10**[1]
500- 1 **Hout Bay**[93] 5561 7-7-9 52 oh1... FPFerris[(3)] 4 63
(RAFahey) *s.i.s: sn chsng ldrs: outpcd 3f out: hdwy and n.m.r over 1f out: r.o to join wnr post* **11/1**
150- 3 *nk* **Grandma Lily (IRE)**[31] 6192 6-8-13 72... THamilton[(5)] 3 82
(MCChapman) *sn outpcd: hdwy over 1f out: rdn and ev ch ins fnl f: styd on* **10/1**[3]
500- 4 *3/4* **Malahide Express (IRE)**[19] 6243 4-8-6 63 ow3...(b) LFletcher[(3)] 8 71
(MJPolglase) *chsd ldrs: rdn and ev ch over 1f out: unable qck ins fnl f* **20/1**
000- 5 *1* **Sea The World (IRE)**[30] 6199 4-8-4 58...(v) JFanning 9 63
(DShaw) *s.i.s: outpcd: hdwy over 1f out: nt rch ldrs* **33/1**
400- 6 *shd* **Prime Recreation**[30] 6199 7-9-0 68... DaleGibson 2 73
(PSFelgate) *chsd ldrs: drvn along 1/2-way: styd on same pce fnl f* **16/1**
103- 7 *3/4* **Laurel Dawn**[15] 6264 6-8-5 62... DAllan[(3)] 10 64
(IWMcinnes) *chsd ldrs: rdn 1/2-way: no ex fnl f* **10/1**[3]
206- 8 *1* **Justalord**[26] 6225 6-10-0 82...(p) JEdmunds 5 81
(JBalding) *mde most over 3f: wknd ins fnl f* **10/3**[2]
65-1 9 *1/2* **Best Lead**[13] 411 5-8-11 65...(b) DeanMcKeown 11 63
(IanEmmerson) *w ldr 3f: wknd fnl f* **16/1**

60.69 secs (0.39) **Going Correction** +0.225s/f (Slow) **9** Ran SP% **116.7**
Speed ratings: **105,105,104,103,101 101,100,98,97** TRIFECTA W:TF 0.90,HB 6.60; Pl:TF 1.40,HB 3.60, 2.60; Ex:TF/HB, 11.00,HB/TF 24.20; CSF:TF/HB 7.65,HB/TF 11.90;Tri:TF/HB/GL 42.69,HB/TF/GL 66.
**Owner** Northumbria Leisure Ltd **Bred** Mrs Mary Taylor **Trained** Musley Bank, N Yorks

**FOCUS**
This was run at a decent pace throughout which produced a cracking finish between Hout Bay and The Fisio and, after studying the photo finish, the judge was unable to spilt the pair. The form looks solid.

**NOTEBOOK**
**Hout Bay**, in contrast to The Fisio, came into this out of form and had been off since finishing unplaced last October. Suited by the strong early pace, he finished well and this was an excellent first effort for his new stable, as he was racing from 1lb out of the handicap. It is possible that he may build on this as he is at the right end of the handicap for a follow-up bid.
**The Fisio**, came into this on the back of a decent win at Lingfield latest, and confirmed he is well weighted at present with a battling display under his 6lb penalty. He was handy throughout and really put his head down late on so, despite an inevitable rise in the handicap, he is in great heart and could well add to this on either of the All-Weather surfaces.
**Grandma Lily(IRE)** was tapped for toe at the start and looked to have it all to do at halfway, but picked up strongly and was not beaten at all far. She was another to be suited by the early gallop but does appear a bit high in the weights at present.

**Malahide Express(IRE)**held every chance but was not good enough, that said, this was his best effort for sometime.
**Prime Recreation** *Official explanation: jockey said gelding hung right in the closing stages*
**Justalord**dropped out like a light under top weight having set the pace early on, and does look a touch high in the weights.

## 541 BET DIRECT NO Q 08000 93 66 93 MEDIAN AUCTION MAIDEN STKS 7f (F)
**1:30** (1:31) (F) 4-6-Y-0 **£2,905** (£830; £415) **Stalls** Low

Form RPR
0/ **1** **Kennington**[414] 5801 4-8-9 ........................................ HayleyTurner(5) 13 58
(MrsCADunnett) *led 6f out: rdn and edgd lft over 1f out: r.o* **10/1**
266- **2** *nk* **Disabuse**[52] 6055 4-8-9 48........................................ BReilly(5) 3 57
(SCWilliams) *s.i.s: sn pushed along and prom: rdn to chse wnr over 1f out: r.o* **5/2**[2]
53-6 **3** *2 ½* **Adantino**[8] 465 5-9-0 52........................................ MartinDwyer 8 51
(BRMillman) *hld up: hdwy u.p over 1f out: nt rch ldrs* **9/2**[3]
3 **4** *½* **Now And Again**[9] 459 5-9-0 ........................................ DaleGibson 5 50
(MWEasterby) *chsd ldrs: outpcd 1/2-way: r.o ins fnl f* **10/1**
26-2 **5** *nk* **Magic Mamma's Too**[9] 459 4-9-0 53........................................ DMernagh 6 49
(TDBarron) *hmpd 6f out: sn pushed along in rr: sme hdwy over 1f out: n.d* **7/4**[1]
200- **6** *nk* **Kustom Kit For Her**[19] 6244 4-8-9 50........................................ JBramhill 2 43
(SRBowring) *s.i.s: hld up: hdwy 1/2-way: styd on same pce appr fnl f* **25/1**
000- **7** *2* **Sweet Coral (FR)**[52] 6056 4-8-9 40........................................ RWinston 4 38
(BSRothwell) *led 1f: rdn and ev ch 2f out: nt clr run and wknd over 1f out* **50/1**
/40- **8** *8* **Zanjeer**[122] 4951 4-9-0 58........................................ ANicholls 11 23
(DNicholls) *chsd ldrs over 5f* **16/1**
006- **9** *6* **Ejay**[37] 6155 5-8-2 40........................................ MHalford(7) 7 —
(JulianPoulton) *chsd ldrs 4f* **50/1**
006/ **10** *nk* **Dalriath**[121] 4979 5-8-2 45........................................ AndrewWebb(7) 12 —
(MCChapman) *bhd fnl 3f* **40/1**
00- **11** *shd* **White O' Morn**[24] 6232 5-8-9 ........................................ GGibbons 10 —
(BAMcmahon) *mid-div: rdn 1/2-way: sn wknd* **66/1**
\- **12** *dist* **Heyward Place** 4-8-7 ow1........................................ J-PGuillambert(3) 9 —
(TKeddy) *s.s: outpcd* **66/1**

1m 29.83s (-0.97) **Going Correction** -0.25s/f (Stan) **12** Ran SP% **120.4**
Speed ratings: **95,94,91,91,90 90,88,79,72,71 71**,—CSF £34.82 TOTE £18.20: £3.60, £1.40, £2.40; EX 124.60.
**Owner** Andy Middleton **Bred** C J R Trotter **Trained** Hingham, Norfolk
■ Stewards Enquiry : Hayley Turner caution: careless riding; one-day ban: failed to keep straight from stalls (Jan 26)

**FOCUS**
A very moderate maiden, run in a modest time, in which few managed to get into the argument and the field were strung out at the finish. The winner, a Sheikh Mohammed cast off, wins on his debut for new connections.

**NOTEBOOK**
**Kennington**, a Sheikh Mohammed cast-off, got the better of a battle with the runner up in game style having raced handily throughout. His only previous outing was on the Polytrack for John Gosden in a fair maiden in November 2002 in which he was only beaten by three lengths. This was a decent effort for his new connections, who have brought him along quietly, and he is entitled to improve plenty on this.
**Disabuse**held every chance in the closing stages, but could not get past the eventual winner in the final furlong. He was backed for this and may be gain compensation while his yard remains in good form.
**Adantino**, making his Fibresand debut, ran in snatches and is one to lay, rather than play.
**Magic Mamma's Too**was hampered in the first furlong and lost his chance thereafter. This run is best ignored, as he prefers to be racing on the pace.

## 542 BET DIRECT NO Q APPRENTICE CLAIMING STKS 1m (F)
**2:00** (2:00) (F) 4-Y-0+ **£2,884** (£824; £412) **Stalls** Low

Form RPR
01-0 **1** **Game Guru**[2] 518 5-9-2 65........................................ Laura-JayneCrawford(5) 4 71
(TDBarron) *mde all: rdn 2f out: styd on* **6/5**[1]
00-0 **2** *½* **Locombe Hill (IRE)**[5] 491 8-9-1 60........................................ LTreadwell(3) 2 67
(DNicholls) *chsd wnr 6f out: rdn over 1f out: hung lft ins fnl f: styd on* **5/2**[2]
30-5 **3** *2* **Tinian**[8] 468 6-8-7 54........................................ AReilly(5) 1 57
(KRBurke) *chsd wnr 2f: remained handy: rdn over 1f out: kpt on* **5/1**[3]
-041 **4** *7* **King Priam (IRE)**[7] 471 9-8-1 35........................................(b) KGhunowa(5) 3 37
(MJPolglase) *sn outpcd* **5/1**[3]

1m 43.63s (-0.97) **Going Correction** -0.25s/f (Stan) **4** Ran SP% **107.4**
Speed ratings: **94,93,91,84**CSF £4.37 TOTE £1.90; EX 3.40.
**Owner** Kevin Shaw **Bred** P J Makin **Trained** Maunby, N Yorks

**FOCUS**
A modest winning time to this uncompetitive claiming stakes and, although the form is of a fair standard, it may be unreliable.

**NOTEBOOK**
**Game Guru**quickly bagged the lead and, despite looking vulnerable at the top of the straight, found plenty under pressure to gain a fairly straightforward victory. He can be moody, but goes well for today's rider, loves this course-and-distance and can win again in this grade.
**Locombe Hill(IRE)**, 9lb badly off with the winner on adjusted official ratings, looked to be going the better turning for home, yet wandered about when under maximum pressure and looks tricky. This was, however, his best effort since winning on the turf last year at Doncaster.
**Tinian**once again found little off the bridle and is now fully exposed.
**King Priam(IRE)**lacks the pace for this trip and needs further.

## 543 BETDIRECT.CO.UK H'CAP (DIV II) 5f (F)
**2:30** (2:30) (D) (0-85,78) 3-Y-0+ **£4,036** (£1,242; £621; £310) **Stalls** High

Form RPR
42-5 **1** **Time N Time Again**[7] 476 6-9-0 68........................................(p) ANicholls 11 81
(EJAlston) *chsd ldrs: rdn 1/2-way: hung lft over 1f out: r.o to ld nr fin* **8/1**
10-6 **2** *nk* **Far Note (USA)**[2] 511 6-8-11 65........................................(b) JBramhill 2 77
(SRBowring) *chsd ldrs: rdn to ld over 1f out: hdd nr fin* **7/1**
010- **3** *2* **Count Cougar (USA)**[30] 6199 4-8-7 61........................................ RLappin 3 67
(SPGriffiths) *w ldr: led 3f out: rdn and hdd over 1f out: one pce ins fnl f* **20/1**
2-12 **4** *nk* **Soba Jones**[2] 511 7-9-4 72 6ex........................................ JEdmunds 5 77
(JBalding) *w ldrs: rdn and ev ch over 1f out: no ex ins fnl f* **2/1**[1]
026- **5** *nk* **Abraxas**[15] 6264 6-7-13 53 ow1........................................(p) JQuinn 1 57
(JAkehurst) *s.i.s: sn chsng ldrs: rdn over 1f out: no ex ins fnl f* **11/1**
51-4 **6** *shd* **St Ivian**[7] 476 4-9-0 68........................................(v) PMcCabe 10 72
(MrsNMacauley) *chsd ldrs: rdn 1/2-way: hmpd 1f out: no ex* **16/1**
001- **7** *nk* **Ellens Lad (IRE)**[40] 6136 10-9-5 73........................................(b) PaulEddery 7 76
(WJMusson) *edgd rt s: chsd ldrs: rdn and edgd lft over 1f out: no imp fnl f* **13/2**[3]
251- **8** *2* **Frascati**[30] 6199 4-9-10 78........................................ FLynch 6 75
(ABerry) *led 2f: wknd fnl f* **7/2**[2]
000/ **9** *3* **Izzet Muzzy (FR)**[411] 5818 6-8-11 65........................................ RFitzpatrick 9 53
(DShaw) *s.i.s: outpcd* **50/1**
500- **10** *8* **Sahara Silk (IRE)**[100] 5441 3-7-8 68........................................(v) HayleyTurner(5) 4 32
(DShaw) *chsd ldrs: sn drvn along: outpcd fnl 3f* **16/1**
526- **11** *nk* **Sheapys Lass**[181] 3357 3-7-12 67 oh7........................................ JMackay 8 30
(ACrook) *s.i.s and hmpd s: outpcd* **66/1**

60.73 secs (0.43) **Going Correction** +0.225s/f (Slow)
**WFA** 3 from 4yo+ 15lb **11** Ran SP% **120.8**
Speed ratings: **105,104,101,100,100 100,99,96,91,78 78**CSF £63.92 CT £1126.56 TOTE £11.80: £3.50, £2.50, £4.30; EX 76.90.
**Owner** Springs Equestrian Ltd **Bred** Anthony Scholes **Trained** Longton, Lancs

**FOCUS**
This second division of the sprint looked more competitive, but was run in a marginally slower time. The form looks solid and should work out.

**NOTEBOOK**
**Time N Time Again**stayed on well up the stands' side to win this all out on his first run at the track. He is lightly-raced on the sand, so can improve and the application of cheekpieces had a positive effect.
**Far Note(USA)**, well backed when unplaced over six furlongs at the track two days previously, almost made amends over this minimum trip. He looked to lose his concentration late on, but showed enough to suggest he can take a similar event.
**Count Cougar(USA)**ran a sound race and hinted he may be about to hit form once more.
**Soba Jones**looks better over another furlong.
**Frascati**dropped away tamely having helped set the pace for a long way, and it is possible that her latest rise in the weights has found her out.

## 544 LITTLEWOODS BET DIRECT H'CAP 7f (F)
**3:00** (3:01) (C) (0-95,93) 4-Y-0+ **£8,229** (£2,532; £1,266; £633) **Stalls** Low

Form RPR
012- **1** **Mufreh (USA)**[62] 5996 6-8-13 **78**........................................ SWhitworth 8 93
(AGNewcombe) *hld up: hdwy 1/2-way: rdn to ld 1f out: r.o* **11/2**[1]
05-2 **2** *¾* **Just Fly**[12] 417 4-9-1 **80**........................................ ACulhane 2 94
(SKirk) *chsd ldrs: rdn to ld over 1f out: sn hdd: styd on* **13/2**[3]
13-0 **3** *3* **Majik**[2] 511 5-8-4 **69**........................................ JQuinn 1 75
(DJSFfrenchDavis) *chsd ldrs: rdn and ev ch over 1f out: wknd towards fin* **16/1**
30-1 **4** *1 ¼* **Ovigo (GER)**[7] 477 5-7-11 **65**........................................ FPFerris(3) 5 68
(PABlockley) *s.i.s: outpcd: r.o u.p fnl f: nrst fin* **6/1**[2]
201- **5** *3* **Forever Phoenix**[20] 6238 4-8-5 **70**........................................ EAhern 6 65
(RMHCowell) *w ldrs: led on bit 2f out: sn hdd: wknd fnl f* **16/1**
00-0 **6** *1 ¼* **Sundried Tomato**[6] 486 5-9-0 **82**........................................ LFletcher(3) 13 74
(PWHiatt) *led: hdd over 4f out: rdn and ev ch over 1f out: wknd fnl f* **25/1**
00-3 **7** *1* **Just A Glimmer**[13] 410 4-8-13 **78**........................................ MartinDwyer 14 68
(LGCottrell) *hld up: shkn up over 1f out: nvr nr to chal* **25/1**
40-0 **8** *1 ¼* **Flying Treaty (USA)**[6] 486 7-9-9 **88**........................................ AnnStokell 10 75
(MissAStokell) *chsd ldrs: lost pl 4f out: n.d afterwards* **66/1**
230- **9** *hd* **Te Quiero**[15] 6268 6-10-0 **93**........................................(t) MFenton 15 79
(MissGayKelleway) *hld up: rdn 1/2-way: nvr nrr* **12/1**
000- **10** *shd* **Lincoln Dancer (IRE)**[37] 6154 7-8-13 **78**........................................ ANicholls 9 64
(DNicholls) *hld up: hdwy 1/2-way: wknd over 1f out* **28/1**
000- **11** *½* **No Grouse**[173] 3594 4-8-6 **76**........................................ THamilton(5) 12 61
(RAFahey) *hmpd and dropped rr after 1f: n.d after* **20/1**
200- **12** *shd* **York Cliff**[94] 5550 6-9-1 **80**........................................ RWinston 3 64
(WMBrisbourne) *s.i.s: outpcd* **25/1**
03-0 **13** *2* **Hand Chime**[6] 486 7-9-8 **87**........................................ JFanning 7 66
(WJHaggas) *chsd ldrs over 4f* **6/1**[2]
00-3 **14** *1 ¼* **Action Fighter (GER)**[6] 485 4-9-6 **88**........................................(p) J-PGuillambert(3) 4 64
(NPLittmoden) *chsd ldrs: led over 4f out: hdd & wknd 2f out* **20/1**
564- **15** *shd* **Pheckless**[16] 6260 5-8-4 **69**........................................ SCarson 11 45
(RFJohnsonHoughton) *s.i.s: a in rr* **11/1**
01-1 **16** *26* **Blakeset**[13] 410 9-8-13 **78**........................................(v) DMernagh 16 —
(TDBarron) *chsd ldrs to 1/2-way: eased fnl 2f* **13/2**[3]

1m 27.63s (-3.17) **Going Correction** -0.25s/f (Stan) **16** Ran SP% **124.4**
Speed ratings: **108,107,103,102,98 97,96,94,94,94 93,93,91,90,90 60**CSF £37.24 CT £579.12 TOTE £7.00: £2.00, £2.40, £4.40, £2.50; EX 47.80 Trifecta £680.30 Pool of £5,115.50 - 2.20 winning units.
**Owner** M K F Seymour **Bred** Shadwell Farm Inc **Trained** Yarnscombe, Devon

**FOCUS**
A competitive handicap, run in a good time and sure to throw up plenty of winners in the coming weeks, with the first two looking ahead of the Handicapper.

**NOTEBOOK**
**Mufreh(USA)**, absent since November, proved he goes well fresh and won this readily over a trip he is best at. He was given a well-judged ride and, on this evidence, can remain on the up.
**Just Fly**relished this extra furlong and, if he can maintain his current mood, he looks a winner waiting to happen.
**Majik**proved his latest poor effort to be all wrong and returned to the form that had seen him progress into a consistent performer in this sphere. There are still prizes to be won with him.
**Ovigo(GER)**, ran a remarkable race, as he was almost tailed off early on and stayed on strongly in the straight to finish best of all. He showed he can make it at this grade and, although he has a bit to prove next time, should be hitting the net again soon.
**Just A Glimmer**looked to run in snatches, but really caught the eye when staying on late and is one to watch out for.
**Te Quiero**was unable to get to the front from his wide draw, and his chance diminished thereafter. He would ideally be suited to further.
**Hand Chime** *Official explanation: trainer said gelding was found to have bled through both nostrils*
**Blakeset** *Official explanation: jockey said gelding lost its action and was therefore eased in the straight*

## 545 LITTLEWOODSCASINO.COM (S) STKS 1m 3f (F)
**3:30** (3:30) (G) 4-Y-0+ **£2,548** (£728; £364) **Stalls** Low

Form RPR
004- **1** **Orinocovsky (IRE)**[7] 5220 5-9-2 64........................................ MartinDwyer 7 65
(CREgerton) *mde all: clr fnl 3f* **5/2**[2]
00-6 **2** *8* **Jungle Lion**[6] 487 6-9-2 47........................................(e[1]) SWhitworth 8 53
(JohnAHarris) *hld up: hdwy over 3f out: no imp fnl 2f* **20/1**
6 **3** *nk* **Free Style (GER)**[13] 412 4-8-8 47........................................ DarrenWilliams 5 48
(KRBurke) *chsd ldrs: rdn over 3f out: sn outpcd* **11/1**
6-42 **4** *1 ½* **Dancing Tilly**[3] 500 6-8-11 40........................................ JQuinn 3 45
(RAFahey) *chsd ldrs: rdn over 5f out: wknd over 1f out* **9/4**[1]
60-2 **5** *8* **Ipledgeallegiance (USA)**[7] 471 8-9-2 46........................................ ACulhane 2 38
(DWChapman) *chsd ldr: rdn 4f out: wknd over 2f out* **7/2**[3]
00-5 **6** *6* **Ming The Merciless**[9] 459 4-8-13 63........................................ MFenton 1 29
(JGGiven) *prom: rdn 1/2-way: sn wknd* **11/1**
00-6 **7** *11* **Noble Cyrano**[9] 455 9-9-2 35........................................ DaleGibson 4 13
(JeddO'Keeffe) *hld up: wknd over 4f out* **20/1**

8 16 **Diamond Dazzler**[16] 6-9-2 ....................(b) EAhern 6 —
(DPKeane) *s.i.s: sn chsng ldrs: wknd over 4f out* **16/1**

2m 25.03s (-3.87) **Going Correction** -0.25s/f (Stan)
**WFA** 4 from 5yo+ 3lb **8** Ran SP% **113.6**
Speed ratings: **104,98,97,96,91 86,78,67**CSF £48.82 TOTE £5.30: £1.20, £10.00, £4.70; EX 47.80.Orinocovsky (no.5) was sold to Nigel Shields for 9,500gns.
**Owner** Andy J Smith **Bred** N Chatzigrigoriou **Trained** Chaddleworth, Berks
■ Stewards Enquiry : J Quinn one-day ban: used whip with excessive force (Jan 23)

**FOCUS**
A very good time for the class of contest, but apart from the winner the form looks poor.

**NOTEBOOK**
**Orinocovsky(IRE)**, who quickly bagged the lead from his wide draw, made all easily and posted a fast time. He was pulled up on his latest run over hurdles and looks better on the level, but while he confirmed his obvious ability, he beat very little on this occasion.
**Jungle Lion**improved for the application of the eyeshield for the first time, but had no chance with the winner the these weights.
**Free Style(GER)**managed to improve slightly for the step up in trip, but has shown very little in two starts since joining her current yard from Germany.
**Dancing Tilly**had no excuses and was bitterly disappointing.

## 546 BET DIRECT IN VISION SKY PAGE 293 H'CAP — 1m 4f (F)
4:00 (4:00) (E) (0-75,71) 4-Y-0+ £3,423 (£978; £489) Stalls Low

| Form | | | Horse | Jockey | RPR |
|---|---|---|---|---|---|
| 00-1 | 1 | | **Sendintank**[3] [505] 4-8-3 **56** 6ex ....... BReilly(5) 8<br>(SCWilliams) *sn pushed along in rr: hdwy 1/2-way: led over 2f out: hung rt over 1f out: hung lft ins fnl f: comf* **8/13**[1] | | 78+ |
| 43-1 | 2 | 1 3/4 | **Nakwa (IRE)**[10] [446] 6-8-4 **51** 6ex ....... DAllan(3) 5<br>(EJAlston) *hld up: hdwy over 3f out: rdn to chse wnr over 1f out: no ex ins fnl f* **11/2**[2] | | 64 |
| 00-4 | 3 | 6 | **Lazzaz**[9] [455] 6-9-2 **60** ....... MartinDwyer 2<br>(PWHiatt) *chsd ldrs tl wknd over 1f out* **22/1** | | 64 |
| 6/0- | 4 | nk | **Ela Re**[102] [667] 5-8-3 **47** ....... JBramhill 4<br>(CRDore) *prom: rdn and ev ch over 2f out: wknd over 1f out* **50/1** | | 51 |
| 426- | 5 | 3 1/2 | **Shifty**[19] [6245] 5-8-10 **54** ....... ANicholls 3<br>(DNicholls) *hld up: hdwy over 5f out: wknd over 2f out* **40/1** | | 52 |
| 00-1 | 6 | 2 | **Madiba**[11] [431] 5-9-2 **60** 6ex ....... (b) RWinston 10<br>(PHowling) *chsd ldrs tl rdn and wknd over 2f out* **14/1** | | 55 |
| 431- | 7 | 5 | **Stravmour**[19] [6247] 8-8-2 **46** ....... DaleGibson 9<br>(RHollinshead) *hld up: rdn 1/2-way: a in rr* **7/1**[3] | | 34 |
| 346- | 8 | 2 | **Call Of The Wild**[167] [3743] 4-8-2 **55** ....... THamilton(5) 7<br>(RAFahey) *hld up: wknd over 4f out* **33/1** | | 40 |
| 060- | 9 | 6 | **Finger Of Fate**[201] [2793] 4-8-12 **63** ....... LFletcher(3) 11<br>(MJPolglase) *sn led: hdd & wknd over 2f out* **50/1** | | 39 |
| 600- | 10 | dist | **Cote Soleil**[103] [5381] 7-8-5 **49** ....... EAhern 1<br>(CREgerton) *chsd ldrs 7f* **50/1** | | — |

2m 38.09s (-4.01) **Going Correction** -0.25s/f (Stan)
**WFA** 4 from 5yo+ 4lb **10** Ran SP% **112.1**
Speed ratings: **103,101,97,97,95 93,90,89,85,—**CSF £3.49 CT £33.47 TOTE £1.60: £1.10, £2.30, £2.50; EX 6.10 Place 6 £189.96, Place 5 £118.30.
**Owner** Steve Jones And Phil McGovern **Bred** K G Powter **Trained** Newmarket, Suffolk
■ Stewards Enquiry : R Winston 18-day ban (takes into account previous offences; four days deferred): careless riding (Jan 31-Feb 14)

**FOCUS**
A fair time to this poor handicap, in which the winner is value for more than the official winning margin. The first two look well treated at present.

**NOTEBOOK**
**Sendintank**followed up his bloodless victory at Wolverhampton three days previously in similar fashion. However, despite the fact he looked to hae a penalty kick under his 6lb penalty, he had to be kept right up to his work in the straight as he wandered about when in front. He will be better for headgear and despite an forthcoming hefty rise in the weights, he can continue to improve.
**Nakwa(IRE)**, a clear-cut winner of a banded stakes last time, took his time to get to the leaders, but improved under his penalty. He will go up in the weights, but is in fair form at present.
**Lazzaz**looks better at Wolverhampton.
**Ela Re**, a fair winning hurdler, does not look to stay this trip. He got a nice sharpener for another crack at jumping however.
T/Jkpt: Not won. T/Plt: £720.10 to a £1 stake. Pool: £33,986.60. 34.45 winning tickets. T/Qpdt: £181.90 to a £1 stake. Pool: £2,262.50. 9.20 winning tickets. CR

# 527 WOLVERHAMPTON (A.W) (L-H)
## Friday, January 16

**OFFICIAL GOING: Standard**
The track bias favouring the middle of the track remains unchanged.
Wind: almost nil Weather: sunny periods with and odd light shower

## 547 PRESS INTERACTIVE TO BET DIRECT H'CAP — 6f (F)
1:20 (1:20) (E) (0-75,75) 3-Y-O £3,290 (£940; £470) Stalls Low

| Form | | | Horse | RPR |
|---|---|---|---|---|
| 504- | 1 | | **Back At De Front (IRE)**[21] [6237] 3-8-6 **60** ....... CCatlin 3<br>(NEBerry) *a.p: led over 2f out: sn rdn: all out* **20/1** | 65 |
| 52-2 | 2 | 1/2 | **Muy Bien**[10] [458] 3-9-2 **75** ....... (v) BReilly(5) 8<br>(JRJenkins) *hld up: hdwy 3f out: rdn and hung lft fr wl over 1f out: r.o towards fin* **13/8**[1] | 78+ |
| 613- | 3 | 1 | **Chickado (IRE)**[56] [6037] 3-8-13 **67** ....... PaulEddery 4<br>(DHaydnJones) *w ldr: rdn over 2f out: hung lft over 1f out: ev ch whn hung lft again ins fnl f: nt qckn* **9/2**[3] | 67 |
| 435- | 4 | 3 | **Lizhar (IRE)**[25] [6227] 3-9-4 **72** ....... JPSpencer 2<br>(MJPolglase) *led: rdn and hdd over 2f out: edgd lft over 1f out: wknd fnl f* **11/1** | 63 |
| 266- | 5 | shd | **Diamond George (IRE)**[131] [4755] 3-8-7 **61** ....... WMLordan 1<br>(JohnBerry) *hld up: rdn 3f out: no hdwy fnl 2f* **40/1** | 52 |
| 11-1 | 6 | 1 3/4 | **Blofeld**[10] [458] 3-9-4 **75** 6ex ....... LisaJones(3) 9<br>(WJarvis) *outpcd: rdn and hung rt wl over 2f out: n.d* **9/4**[2] | 60 |
| 00-6 | 7 | 13 | **Birikina**[11] [435] 3-7-10 **57** ....... DonnaCaldwell(7) 5<br>(ABerry) *s.i.s: rdn 3f out: a bhd* **100/1** | 3 |
| 321- | 8 | 1 3/4 | **Barras (IRE)**[191] [3089] 3-8-3 **57** ....... (p) MartinDwyer 7<br>(MissGayKelleway) *prom: rdn over 3f out: sn wknd* **16/1** | — |

1m 15.2s (-0.50) **Going Correction** -0.075s/f (Stan) **8** Ran SP% **109.5**
Speed ratings: **100,99,98,94,93 91,74,71**CSF £48.67 CT £166.19 TOTE £16.10: £3.40, £1.10, £1.50; EX 71.60.
**Owner** Leeway Group Limited **Bred** Bold Fashion Partnership **Trained** Earlswood, Monmouths

**FOCUS**
A modest handicap and fair form for the grade.

**NOTEBOOK**
**Back At De Front(IRE)** took advantage of being 6lb lower than when in a handicap two outings ago. She managed to keep a straight line, which was more than could be said for her closest pursuers.
**Muy Bien**, set to go up 4lb tomorrow, yet again shot himself in the foot by hanging left.
**Chickado(IRE)**, back up to six, was another who proved to be a difficult ride and kept hanging towards the inside rail.
**Lizhar(IRE)** should have been suited by the return to an extra furlong.
**Blofeld** *Official explanation: jockey said gelding would not face the kick-back*

## 548 BET DIRECT THROUGH ATTHERACES CLAIMING STKS — 1m 1f 79y(F)
1:50 (1:51) (F) 4-Y-O+ £2,898 (£828; £414) Stalls Low

| Form | | | Horse | RPR |
|---|---|---|---|---|
| 01-4 | 1 | | **Hiawatha (IRE)**[3] [516] 5-9-6 66 ....... EAhern 7<br>(TDBarron) *hld up: stdy hdwy 6f out: led on bit over 2f out: sn rdn clr: r.o wl* **4/7**[1] | 83+ |
| 21-0 | 2 | 5 | **Noul (USA)**[4] [507] 5-9-8 73 ....... (b) NCallan 2<br>(KARyan) *hld up in tch: rdn over 3f out: wnt 2nd 1f out: kpt on: no ch w wnr* **4/1**[2] | 72 |
| 00-5 | 3 | 4 | **Toro Bravo (IRE)**[7] [487] 4-8-7 55 ....... (b) JQuinn 4<br>(RMBeckett) *hld up: rdn and hdwy over 1f out: wknd ins fnl f* **20/1** | 50 |
| 5-01 | 4 | nk | **Coolfore Jade (IRE)**[3] [517] 4-8-6 55 ....... CCatlin 6<br>(NEBerry) *sn w ldr: led over 5f out: rdn and hdd over 2f out: wknd ins fnl f* **11/2**[3] | 48 |
| 30-0 | 5 | 16 | **Phoenix Nights (IRE)**[14] [412] 4-9-3 47 ....... FLynch 5<br>(ABerry) *sn led: hdd over 5f out: rdn and wknd 3f out* **50/1** | 27 |
| 100- | 6 | 1 | **Pup's Pride**[21] [6241] 7-8-7 58 ....... (v) LisaJones(3) 1<br>(MrsNMacauley) *led early: lost pl 6f out: bhd fnl 3f* **16/1** | 17 |

2m 1.19s (-1.71) **Going Correction** -0.075s/f (Stan)
**WFA** 4 from 5yo+ 1lb **6** Ran SP% **111.6**
Speed ratings: **104,99,96,95,81 80**CSF £3.15 TOTE £1.60: £1.10, £1.90; EX 4.40.Hiawatha was claimed by Mrs J Hughes for £12,000.
**Owner** Nigel Shields **Bred** Kilcarn Stud **Trained** Maunby, N Yorks

**FOCUS**
A decent time for this class of contest in an uncompetitive claimer, but the winner is likely to be interesting in handicaps.

**NOTEBOOK**
**Hiawatha(IRE)**, making a quick reappearance, was back down in both trip and grade and proved much too good for this opposition.
**Noul(USA)** has yet to win beyond a mile but appeared to get the trip well enough.
**Toro Bravo(IRE)** seems more effective at a mile.
**Coolfore Jade(IRE)** was dropping back in distance but up in grade after winning at Southwell earlier in the week.

## 549 LITTLEWOODS BET DIRECT FILLIES' H'CAP — 1m 4f (F)
2:20 (2:20) (E) (0-70,67) 4-Y-O+ £3,241 (£926; £463) Stalls Low

| Form | | | Horse | RPR |
|---|---|---|---|---|
| 300- | 1 | | **Molly's Secret**[96] [5500] 6-8-6 **45** ....... (p) JQuinn 4<br>(CGCox) *hld up in tch: led over 2f out: rdn clr wl over 1f out: rdn out* **16/1** | 56 |
| 23-4 | 2 | 3 1/2 | **Big Bertha**[9] [467] 6-10-0 **67** ....... (e1) JPSpencer 2<br>(JohnBerry) *hld up and bhd: rdn and hdwy over 2f out: nt clr run briefly over 1f out: chsd wnr fnl f: no imp* **3/1**[2] | 73 |
| 034- | 3 | 4 | **Compton Eclaire (IRE)**[18] [6249] 4-8-9 **52** ....... (v) EAhern 1<br>(GAButler) *hld up and bhd: rdn and hdwy on outside over 2f out: c wd st: styd on same pce fnl f* **5/2**[1] | 52 |
| 005- | 4 | 2 | **Cumbrian Princess**[28] [6218] 7-7-12 **37** oh2 ....... DaleGibson 9<br>(MBlanshard) *hld up and bhd: hdwy over 3f out: rdn over 2f out: wknd ins fnl f* **33/1** | 34 |
| 006- | 5 | 1 3/4 | **E Minor (IRE)**[60] [6017] 5-9-9 **62** ....... ACulhane 8<br>(TWall) *hld up in tch: rdn over 3f out: wknd over 1f out* **9/1** | 56 |
| 06-2 | 6 | 1/2 | **Retail Therapy (IRE)**[7] [484] 4-7-13 **42** oh6 ....... RFfrench(1) 3<br>(MABuckley) *hld up: stdy hdwy on ins 6f out: rdn and wknd over 3f out* **10/3**[3] | 36 |
| 5-06 | 7 | 1 1/2 | **Exit To Heaven**[7] [484] 4-8-10 **58** ....... (p) TEaves(5) 6<br>(MissGayKelleway) *led: rdn over 3f out: hdd over 2f out: wknd jst over 1f out* **20/1** | 49 |
| 205- | 8 | 15 | **Ela D'Argent (IRE)**[20] [1708] 5-9-6 **59** ....... (t) VSlattery 7<br>(MissKMarks) *prom: rdn and lost pl over 6f out: bhd fnl 5f* **16/1** | 28 |
| 64-0 | 9 | 1 3/4 | **Estimate**[7] [484] 4-9-3 **60** ....... (v) SWhitworth 5<br>(JohnAHarris) *chsd ldr to 3f out: wknd qckly* **20/1** | 26 |

2m 39.4s (-2.10) **Going Correction** -0.075s/f (Stan)
**WFA** 4 from 5yo+ 4lb **9** Ran SP% **110.9**
Speed ratings: **104,101,99,97,96 96,95,85,84**CSF £59.74 CT £157.70 TOTE £16.60: £3.20, £1.10, £1.40; EX 58.20.
**Owner** The Two M's Partnership **Bred** A P Jones **Trained** Lambourn, Berks

**FOCUS**
A weak handicap and the form looks distinctly modest.

**NOTEBOOK**
**Molly's Secret** had been given three months rest after getting jarred up. The fact her trainer thinks she has probably strengthened up since last year would have helped over this trip.
**Big Bertha**, tried in an eyeshield, should not be considered unlucky on her first try on Fibresand.
**Compton Eclaire(IRE)**, with the headgear refitted, could never make her presence felt but did take the scenic route.
**Cumbrian Princess** again had her stamina limitations exposed, having previously tried this trip here nearly two years ago.
**E Minor(IRE)** did not find a drop back from two miles the key to her.
**Retail Therapy(IRE)**, 6lb 'wrong', looks flattered by her second in a maiden over course and distance a week ago on this evidence.
**Estimate** *Official explanation: jockey said filly had breathing problems*

## 550 BETDIRECT.CO.UK MAIDEN STKS — 7f (F)
2:50 (2:51) (D) 3-Y-O+ £3,454 (£1,063; £531; £265) Stalls High

| Form | | | Horse | RPR |
|---|---|---|---|---|
| 0- | 1 | | **Rio Branco**[69] [5947] 3-8-2 ....... MartinDwyer 3<br>(BWHills) *mde all: clr over 2f out: rdn wl over 1f out: drvn out* **7/4**[2] | 68 |
| | 2 | 1 3/4 | **Sabbaag (USA)** 3-8-7 ....... JPSpencer 5<br>(DRLoder) *racd wd: hld up: rdn and hdwy over 2f out: sn chsng wnr: styd on towards fin* **4/7**[1] | 68 |
| | 3 | 3 1/2 | **Mrs Brown** 3-8-2 ....... JMackay 1<br>(SirMarkPrescott) *slowly in to stride: sn chsng wnr: rdn 3f out: lost 2nd 2f out: wknd fnl f* **25/1**[3] | 55 |
| 56- | 4 | 11 | **Scorch**[182] [3363] 3-8-0 ....... SaleemGolam(7) 2<br>(HJCollingridge) *chsd ldrs: rdn 3f out: sn wknd* **40/1** | 32 |

0- **5** *3* **Wodhill Be**[30] [6209] 4-9-6 ........ NCallan 4 20
(DMorris) *t.k.h: prom: rdn over 3f out: sn struggling* **66/1**

1m 30.44s (0.24) **Going Correction** -0.075s/f (Stan)
**WFA** 3 from 4yo 18lb **5** Ran SP% **107.8**
Speed ratings: **95,93,89,76,73**CSF £2.96 TOTE £3.40: £1.60, £1.02; EX 4.70.
**Owner** Guy Reed **Bred** G Reed **Trained** Lambourn, Berks

**FOCUS**
A slowly-run race led to quite a modest time for this maiden, and the form is difficult to weigh up.

**NOTEBOOK**
**Rio Branco** dictated matters from the front and was always holding the odds-on newcomer.
**Sabbaag(USA)** is a half-brother to seven furlong and mile-winner Jazmeer. He probably wants a bit further and would not have been suited by the way things panned out.
**Mrs Brown**, a half-sister to the dual mile winner Cal Mac, is out of a mare who stayed a mile and three-quarters.

## 551 LITTLEWOODSCASINO.COM (S) STKS 1m 6f 166y(F)
**3:20** (3:20) (G ) 4-Y-0+ **£2,520** (£720; £360) **Stalls** High

Form RPR
1-43 **1** **Vincent**[7] [483] 9-9-9 46 ........ JMackay 4 56
(JohnAHarris) *w ldr: led on bit over 2f out: pushed clr over 1f out: eased towards fin* **11/8**[1]
00-5 **2** *3* **Hajeer (IRE)**[10] [461] 6-9-0 40 ........ LisaJones(3) 2 46
(PWHiatt) *hld up: rdn and lost pl over 5f out: sn bhd: rallied over 1f out: styd on to take 2nd nr post* **5/1**
333- **3** *nk* **Mysterium**[45] [6120] 10-9-0 40 ........(v) J-PGuillambert(3) 1 46
(NPLittmoden) *trckd ldrs: rdn over 3f out: chsd wnr fnl f: no imp* **5/2**[2]
60-0 **4** *7* **Landescent (IRE)**[9] [467] 4-8-11 50 ........ MartinDwyer 3 37
(MQuinn) *led: rdn and hdd over 2f out: wknd and eased ins fnl f* **4/1**[3]

3m 22.44s (1.64) **Going Correction** -0.075s/f (Stan)
**WFA** 4 from 6yo+ 6lb **4** Ran SP% **107.3**
Speed ratings: **92,90,90,86**CSF £8.04 TOTE £2.30; EX 9.90.There was no bid for the winner
**Owner** Mrs A E Harris **Bred** R Stern, V Bloom And P Caplan **Trained** Eastwell, Leics

**FOCUS**
A slow winning time in this fair seller.

**NOTEBOOK**
**Vincent** only had to reproduce the sort of form that saw him land back-to-back handicaps at Southwell last month to readily take this event.
**Hajeer(IRE)** rewarded his rider's perseverance by finding a second wind to snatch the runner-up spot.
**Mysterium** stays two miles on turf but has yet to score beyond 12 furlongs at Dunstall Park.

## 552 BET DIRECT IN VISION SKY PAGE 293 FILLIES' H'CAP 1m 1f 79y(F)
**3:50** (3:50) (F ) (0-65,62) 4-Y-0+ **£2,982** (£852; £426) **Stalls** Low

Form RPR
1-11 **1** **Najaaba (USA)**[3] [518] 4-9-9 62 6ex ........ BReilly(5) 11 73+
(MissJFeilden) *hld up in rr: rdn and hdwy on outside over 2f out: led jst over 1f out: r.o wl* **4/7**[1]
2-25 **2** *3/4* **Givemethemoonlight**[9] [463] 5-9-0 47 ........(v[1]) JQuinn 12 57
(MrsStefLiddiard) *hld up: hdwy over 4f out: rdn to ld briefly over 1f out: r.o one pce* **7/1**[2]
53-2 **3** *3/4* **Danger Bird (IRE)**[14] [406] 4-9-0 48 ........ ACulhane 6 56
(RHollinshead) *sn chsng ldr: led 6f out: rdn and hdd over 2f out: kpt on same pce fnl f* **20/1**
500- **4** *1/2* **Wodhill Folly**[88] [5672] 7-8-12 45 ........(v) NCallan 13 52
(DMorris) *hld up and bhd: hdwy 4f out: rdn over 3f out: one pce fnl f* **50/1**
60-2 **5** *1/2* **Maggie's Pet**[13] [425] 7-8-12 45 ........(t) DRMcCabe 8 51
(KBell) *a.p: rdn over 2f out: one pce* **50/1**
501- **6** *3/4* **Mythical Charm**[116] [5122] 5-9-3 50 ........ NPollard 9 55
(JJBridger) *hld up: hdwy over 3f out: sn rdn: no further prog fnl 2f* **25/1**
133- **7** *2 1/2* **Debbie**[107] [5308] 5-8-12 45 ........ SWhitworth 4 45
(BDLeavy) *hld up: lost pl over 3f out: no real prog fnl 2f* **8/1**[3]
266- **8** *nk* **Cayman Sunrise (IRE)**[18] [6253] 4-9-10 58 ........ WRyan 1 57
(EALDunlop) *prom: lost pl 4f out: no imp fnl 2f* **33/1**
60-0 **9** *2 1/2* **Consignia (IRE)**[14] [406] 5-8-12 45 ........(p) PaulEddery 7 39
(DHaydnJones) *prom: rdn over 2f out: wknd over 1f out* **25/1**
040- **10** *3 1/2* **Suerte**[30] [6205] 4-9-9 57 ........ MFenton 5 44
(JGGiven) *a bhd* **66/1**
032- **11** *11* **Cooden Beach (IRE)**[109] [5270] 4-8-9 48 ........ HayleyTurner(5) 10 13
(MLWBell) *a bhd* **10/1**
31-0 **12** *12* **Nuzzle**[10] [457] 4-9-10 58 ........(v) MartinDwyer 3 —
(MQuinn) *led: hdd 6f out: rdn over 4f out: wknd over 3f out* **33/1**

2m 1.49s (-1.41) **Going Correction** -0.075s/f (Stan)
**WFA** 4 from 5yo+ 1lb **12** Ran SP% **120.1**
Speed ratings: **103,102,101,101,100 100,97,97,95,92 82,71**CSF £4.27 CT £45.42 TOTE £1.50: £1.10, £1.10, £4.00; EX 8.30 Place 6 £3.72, Place 5 £2.36.
**Owner** A K Sparks **Bred** Darley Stud Management, L L C **Trained** Exning, Suffolk

**FOCUS**
A pretty good winning time for the class of contest, but the value of form is held down by the presence of long-standing maidens in the places.

**NOTEBOOK**
**Najaaba(USA)** supplemented her hat-trick over a mile at Southwell and continues on the crest of a wave. She won with a shade more in hand than the margin suggests, but it would come as no surprise to see her given a short break.
**Givemethemoonlight** came up against a filly on a roll and deserves a change of fortune.
**Danger Bird(IRE)** was again a shade keen early on but could hardly be accused of caving in once headed.
**Wodhill Folly** was certainly not disgraced on her first start for three months.
**Maggie's Pet** did not appear to be inconvenienced by the slightly longer trip.
**Mythical Charm** had not been seen since causing a shock off effectively the same mark when 4lb 'wrong' at Kempton last September.
T/Plt: £7.40 to a £1 stake. Pool: £31,771.20. 3,118.50 winning tickets. T/Qpdt: £4.00 to a £1 stake. Pool: £1,874.60. 345.90 winning tickets. KH

# 533 LINGFIELD (L-H)
Saturday, January 17

**OFFICIAL GOING: Standard**

## 553 BET DIRECT NO Q 08000 93 66 93 MEDIAN AUCTION MAIDEN STKS 1m (P)
**12:15** (12:17) (E ) 3-Y-0 **£3,339** (£954; £477) **Stalls** High

Form RPR
**1** **Grouville** 3-9-0 ........ PaulEddery 4 74
(BJMeehan) *unf: bit bkwd: trckd ldr: rdn and styd on to ld fnl 75yds* **33/1**
3-2 **2** *1 1/4* **Jumeirah Scarer**[11] [447] 3-9-0 ........ CCatlin 2 71
(MRChannon) *led: rdn over 1f out: hdd fnl 75yds* **7/2**[2]
0- **3** *1/2* **Ground Patrol**[31] [6203] 3-9-0 ........ MartinDwyer 9 70
(AMBalding) *slowly away: rdn and hdwy 2f out: styd on wl fnl f to snatch 3rd on line* **12/1**
54- **4** *shd* **Fizzy Lady**[72] [5930] 3-8-9 ........ MHills 3 65
(BWHills) *b.hind: in tch: hdwy to chse ldrs over 2f out: rdn and nt qckn fnl f* **7/4**[1]
4- **5** *5* **Star Fern**[31] [6210] 3-9-0 ........ IMongan 5 58
(JAkehurst) *lw: in tch tl wknd ins fnl f* **4/1**[3]
**6** *2 1/2* **Never Cried Wolf** 3-9-0 ........ NCallan 8 52
(DRCElsworth) *w'like: bit bkwd: s.s: nvr bttr than mid-div* **25/1**
**7** *3/4* **Fresh Connection** 3-8-9 ........ MFenton 1 46
(GGMargarson) *leggy: bit bkwd: s.i.s: sn chsd ldrs: wknd wl over 1f out* **66/1**
**8** *2 1/2* **La Concha (IRE)** 3-9-0 ........ KDalgleish 12 45
(MrsLCJewell) *w'like: a towards rr: rdn over 2f out: nvr on terms* **50/1**
**9** *1* **Elzees** 3-9-0 ........ SCarson 11 43
(DRCElsworth) *w'like: bit bkwd: b.hind: a struggling in rr* **20/1**
0- **10** *4* **Saucy Pickle**[31] [6210] 3-8-9 ........ NPollard 6 28
(MissZCDavison) *in tch tl rdn and wknd 2f out* **66/1**
**11** *11* **Second User** 3-9-0 ........ SWKelly 10 8
(JRJenkins) *w'like: bit bkwd: a struggling in rr* **33/1**
**12** *hd* **Till There Was You** 3-8-9 ........ RWinston 7 3
(BJMeehan) *leggy: bit bkwd: mid-div: hdwy to chse ldrs 1/2-way: wknd qckly over 2f out* **10/1**

1m 41.44s (1.93) **Going Correction** +0.125s/f (Slow) **12** Ran SP% **114.8**
Speed ratings: **95,93,93,88 85,84,82,81,77 66,66**CSF £136.48 TOTE £68.20: £16.20, £1.20, £3.10; EX 271.30.
**Owner** F T Wilson **Bred** R J Turner **Trained** Upper Lambourn, Berks

**FOCUS**
An ordinary pace and quite a modest winning time. The field was well strung out and the form may prove fair.

**NOTEBOOK**
**Grouville**, a half-brother to three winners including a winner on this surface, was never far away and showed a good attitude at the business end. The form as it stands is not great, but at least he is entitled to improve.
**Jumeirah Scarer** tried to make every yard this time, but again found one to beat him. He can now be handicapped, but is proving expensive to follow and things will not get any easier unless he is dropped in grade.
**Ground Patrol** came from off the pace and was finishing in good style. This was an improvement on his debut and, with his stable going well, an opportunity should be found for him.
**Fizzy Lady** started favourite on account of her stable and a hint of ability in a couple of six-furlong turf maidens last year, but she had every chance and does not appear to be progressing
**Star Fern** finished much further behind Jumeirah Scarer than he had on his debut here.
**Never Cried Wolf**, out of a dam who won three times over distances ranging from six to ten furlongs, was a springer in the market but never managed to get into the contest.

## 554 BET DIRECT NO Q CLAIMING STKS 1m 2f (P)
**12:45** (12:45) (F ) 4-Y-0+ **£2,954** (£844; £422) **Stalls** Low

Form RPR
604- **1** **Barry Island**[49] [5617] 5-9-9 75 ........ NPollard 1 72
(DRCElsworth) *held up in rr: hdwy over 2f out: str burst to ld wl ins fnl f: won gng away* **10/3**[2]
5-30 **2** *1 3/4* **Pyrrhic**[2] [537] 5-8-11 48 ........(b) EAhern 8 57
(RMFlower) *swtg: mid-div: hdwy over 1f out: r.o wl to go 2nd cl home* **14/1**
/6-0 **3** *nk* **Eastborough (IRE)**[14] [418] 5-9-1 75 ........ JFanning 2 60
(BGPowell) *mid-div: hdwy over 1f out: ev ch ins fnl f: nt pce of wnr* **3/1**[1]
40- **4** *hd* **Fortune Point (IRE)**[33] [4872] 6-8-8 63 ........ LTreadwell(7) 12 60
(AWCarroll) *a in tch: ev ch 1f out: nt qckn ins fnl f* **14/1**
000- **5** *nk* **Bontadini**[49] [6099] 5-8-9 48 ........(v) RWinston 6 54
(DMorris) *a.p: trckd ldr 4f out: ev ch over 1f out: nt qckn ins fnl f* **25/1**
00-1 **6** *3/4* **Bank On Him**[7] [495] 9-8-11 56 ........ IMongan 5 54
(CWeedon) *trckd ldr: led 5f out: rdn and hdd ins fnl f: no ex* **5/1**[3]
053- **7** *5* **Water Of Life (IRE)**[52] [6075] 5-8-7 51 ........ RMiles(3) 10 44
(JRBoyle) *b: s.i.s: nvr bttr than mid-div* **8/1**
50-4 **8** *1/2* **Diliza**[10] [468] 5-7-13 47 ........ RThomas(5) 3 37
(GBBalding) *in tch: hmpd after 2f: wknd 2f out* **16/1**
00-0 **9** *3* **Icannshift (IRE)**[11] [448] 4-8-10 60 ........ JCoffill-Brown(7) 4 47
(SDow) *a bhd* **33/1**
000- **10** *6* **Twentytwosilver (IRE)**[13] [5553] 4-8-9 70 ........ MartinDwyer 9 28
(OSherwood) *b: led for 5f: wknd over 2f out* **20/1**
000- **11** *8* **Summer Stock (USA)**[36] [1780] 6-8-4 52 ........(t) TEaves(3) 11 12
(JASupple) *a in rr: rdn 1/2-way: eased fnl f* **16/1**
000- **12** *10* **Don Fayruz (IRE)**[18] [3163] 12-8-6 54 ow1 ........ WRyan 13 —
(BNDoran) *racd wd: a in rr* **33/1**
000- **13** *2 1/2* **Travel Tardia (IRE)**[28] [6226] 6-8-6 51 ow1 ........ SWKelly 14 —
(IAWood) *trckd ldrs tl wknd over 3f out* **50/1**

2m 7.25s (-0.14) **Going Correction** +0.125s/f (Slow)
**WFA** 4 from 5yo+ 2lb **13** Ran SP% **117.4**
Speed ratings: **105,103,103,103,102 102,98,97,95,90 84,76,74**CSF £45.11 TOTE £5.00: £2.00, £4.30, £1.50; EX 61.90.
**Owner** Matthew Green **Bred** The Lavington Stud **Trained** Whitsbury, Hants

**FOCUS**
A range of abilities, but some fair sorts amongst the line-up resulting in a decent winning time for the grade of contest, although the presence of the runner-up anchors the form.

**NOTEBOOK**
**Barry Island**, who showed some fair form when last seen on this surface a couple of years ago, carried on where he left off under a very confident ride. He can certainly win another one of these, but is well handicapped on the best of his form should connections decide to take that route.
**Pyrrhic**ran a cracker to split a couple of horses with whom he was badly in at the weights, and reversed recent running here with Bank On Him. The problem is that he is a long-standing maiden and his handicap mark has crept just too high for him still to be eligible for banded events.
**Eastborough(IRE)**, best in on adjusted official ratings, was ridden in a similar way to the winner in that they both travelled well off the pace before being brought with their efforts, but his turn of foot was nothing like as potent.
**Fortune Point(IRE)**, pulled up in soft ground over hurdles last time, appreciated the return to a sound surface on the Flat and ran about as well as the weights entitled him to.
**Bontadini**ran by far his best race since his last appearance on this track when short-headed over this trip 11 months ago.
**Bank On Him**found these rivals a completely different kettle of fish to those he dominated in a seller over course and distance last week. Taking over at halfway, he was still in front a furlong from home, but was then swamped on all sides.

## 555 BETDIRECT.CO.UK MAIDEN STKS — 1m 2f (P)
1:20 (1:21) (D) 4-Y-O+ £3,828 (£1,178; £589; £294) Stalls Low

Form RPR

1 **Millville** 4-9-0 ........ NCallan 9 77
(MAJarvis) *w'like: slowly away: hld up towards rr: rdn and hdwy to go 2nd 2f out: qckndd to ld ins fnl f: r.o wl* **6/1**$^{3}$

020- 2 3 1/2 **Priors Dale**$^{49}$ [6093] 4-9-0 72 ........ IMongan 5 70
(KBell) *trckd ldrs: wnt 2nd 5f out: led 3f out: rdn over 1f out: hdd ins fnl f: nt pce of wnr* **9/2**$^{2}$

600- 3 1 1/4 **Zalkani (IRE)**$^{208}$ [2647] 4-8-7 51 ........ AHindley$^{(7)}$ 3 68?
(BGPowell) *in rr: hdwy over 1f out: styd on fnl f: nvr nrr* **50/1**

60-2 4 4 **Coronado Forest (USA)**$^{10}$ [463] 5-9-2 59 ........ JFanning 6 61
(MRHoad) *hld up: rdn and hdwy over 2f out: styd on on pce ins fnl 2f* **8/1**

0/ 5 1 1/2 **Andaad**$^{483}$ [4797] 4-8-9 ........ WRyan 12 53
(DJDaly) *bit bkwd: slowly away: towards rr tl mde late hdwy ins fnl 2f* **66/1**

62-4 6 1 1/4 **Sewmore Character**$^{7}$ [494] 4-9-0 74 ........ DSweeney 11 56
(MBlanshard) *mid-div: hdwy to chse ldrs over 3f out: wknd fnl f* **2/1**$^{1}$

304- 7 3/4 **Springalong (USA)**$^{18}$ [6259] 4-8-8 75 ow1 ........ SJDonohoe$^{(7)}$ 14 56
(PDEvans) *in tch tl wknd 2f out* **7/1**

30-4 8 2 1/2 **Blazing The Trail (IRE)**$^{10}$ [463] 4-9-0 63 ........ (b) SWhitworth 8 50
(JWHills) *hld up in tch: hdwy to chse ldrs over 2f out: wknd over 1f out* **10/1**

9 3 **Alimiste (IRE)** 4-8-9 ........ SWKelly 7 40
(IAWood) *small: in rr: lost tch 3f out* **66/1**

65-0 10 2 1/2 **Golden Dual**$^{10}$ [463] 4-9-0 65 ........ PDoe 13 40
(SDow) *slowly away: rdn to trck ldr: led after 3f: hdd 3f out: wknd 2f out* **33/1**

0/4- 11 3/4 **Passando**$^{263}$ [1284] 4-8-9 ........ MartinDwyer 10 34
(AMBalding) *b: b.hind: a struggling in rr* **12/1**

4P- 12 12 **Mysterlover (IRE)**$^{299}$ [790] 4-8-11 ........ J-PGuillambert$^{(3)}$ 1 17
(NPLittmoden) *mid-div whn hmpd 5f out: no ch after* **25/1**

55- 13 nk **Muraqeb**$^{117}$ [5124] 4-8-11 ........ LisaJones$^{(3)}$ 2 17
(MrsBarbaraWaring) *bit bkwd: mid-div: hmpd 5f out: nt rcvr* **25/1**

604/ 14 5 **Prague**$^{563}$ [2661] 6-9-2 62 ........ EAhern 4 8
(JRBoyle) *b: bit bkwd: led for 3f: wknd over 3f out* **33/1**

2m 7.99s (0.60) **Going Correction** +0.125s/f (Slow)
**WFA** 4 from 5yo+ 2lb **14** Ran SP% **124.7**
Speed ratings: **102,99,98,95,93 92,92,90,87,85 85,75,75,71**CSF £32.69 TOTE £9.10: £3.50, £3.10, £30.80; EX 40.80.
**Owner** T G Warner **Bred** Red House Stud **Trained** Newmarket, Suffolk
■ Stewards Enquiry : S J Donohoe two-day ban: careless riding (Jan 28,29)

**FOCUS**
A routine maiden run at only a fair pace, but one or two interesting performances.

**NOTEBOOK**
**Millville**, a half-brother to Wilcuma and Welville, gave the field a start but still proved far too good for them. He is in good hands and looks likely to go on to better things.
**Priors Dale**settled better this time and looked likely to score when sent into a clear lead on the home bend, but the winner picked him off and there was little he could do about it. There is a small race in him over this trip.
**Zalkani(IRE)**, racing for the first time since June, was the real eye-catcher of the contest, staying on nicely over the last couple of furlongs with his rider never getting busy. He looks well handicapped judged on this performance and is definitely one to watch. *Official explanation: jockey said gelding made a noise; jockey said, regarding the running and riding, gelding was reappearing after a six-month break for a wind operation and his orders were to settle gelding, who pulls hard; jockey added that gelding ran keenly early on and, once settled, met with interference turning out of the back straight*
**Coronado Forest(USA)**ran a fair race and had some higher-rated rivals behind him, but this was defeat number 19.
**Andaad**was by no means disgraced on this first start since his racecourse debut 16 months ago.
**Sewmore Character**had the form to win this, but after travelling well did not see out the quarter-mile longer trip.
**Springalong(USA)**, best in on adjusted official ratings and an eye-catcher here last time, was disappointing and there seemed no real excuse.
**Mysterlover(IRE)** *Official explanation: jockey said gelding lost its action after suffering interference turning out of back straight*

## 556 BET DIRECT ON 0800 32 93 93 CONDITIONS STKS — 6f (P)
1:55 (1:55) (C) 3-Y-O+ £7,163 (£2,717; £988; £988) Stalls Low

Form RPR

202- 1 **Dusty Dazzler (IRE)**$^{28}$ [6225] 4-8-9 95 ........ AQuinn$^{(5)}$ 4 88
(WGMTurner) *b: chsd ldrs: rdn and r.o to ld ins fnl f: drvn out* **11/4**$^{2}$

150- 2 1 **Queens Rhapsody**$^{75}$ [5908] 4-9-5 90 ........ EAhern 6 90
(ABailey) *s.i.s: rdn and hdwy over 1f out: rn to chse wnr ins fnl f* **14/1**

00-1 3 2 1/2 **Chateau Nicol**$^{14}$ [417] 5-9-5 77 ........ (v) JFanning 1 83
(BGPowell) *bmpd s: sn trckd ldrs: wnt 2nd over 2f out: rdn and wknd ins fnl f* **9/2**$^{3}$

-111 3 dht **Hurricane Coast**$^{3}$ [519] 5-9-5 61 ........ (b) PDoe 2 83
(DFlood) *led: rdn appr fnl f: hdd & wknd ins* **6/1**

521- 5 4 **Law Breaker (IRE)**$^{28}$ [6225] 6-9-0 90 ........ BReilly$^{(5)}$ 8 71
(JAGilbert) *racd wd: rdn 1/2-way: no hdwy ins fnl 2f* **9/4**$^{1}$

20-5 6 7 **Golden Chalice (IRE)**$^{8}$ [485] 5-9-5 85 ........ (v$^{1}$) MartinDwyer 3 50
(AMBalding) *lw: w ldr: wknd over 2f out* **9/2**$^{3}$

00-0 7 1/2 **Kingham**$^{7}$ [494] 4-9-5 73 ........ VSlattery 5 48
(MrsMaryHambro) *in rr: lost tch 1/2-way* **66/1**

1m 11.62s (-1.30) **Going Correction** +0.125s/f (Slow)
**WFA** 3 from 4yo+ 16lb **7** Ran SP% **116.2**
Speed ratings: **113,111,108,108,103 93,93**CSF £40.03 TOTE £2.80: £1.80, £2.50; EX 23.40.
**Owner** TOCS Ltd **Bred** Newlands House Stud **Trained** Sigwells, Somerset

**FOCUS**
A decent conditions event and a very impressive winning time.

**NOTEBOOK**
**Dusty Dazzler(IRE)**a stone better off with Law Breaker for a beating of just over a length here last month, reversed the form in emphatic terms and is seeing this trip out much better these days. She loves it here.
**Queens Rhapsody**, patiently ridden, was produced with a dangerous-looking effort on reaching the home straight, but the winner had the better finishing speed. He has done all his winning over an extra furlong.
**Chateau Nicol**received a real broadside from Hurricane Coast on leaving the stalls, but still had every chance and was not quite good enough against a couple of classy rivals.
**Hurricane Coast**, in brilliant form of late, ran a blinder on this massive step up in class and has improved out of all recognition since the start of the year. The problem is that he has probably shattered his handicap mark with this effort, when he may well have been able to win a handicap or two with a more gradual rise in class.
**Law Breaker(IRE)**, very well backed to confirm last month's form with Dusty Dazzler despite being a stone worse off, never appeared to be travelling that well and found little off the bridle. *Official explanation: jockey said gelding hung right*
**Golden Chalice(IRE)**, visored for the first time, was trying the shortest trip he has ever attempted and was up against specialist sand sprinters. He showed up for a while, but had blown himself out on reaching the final bend.

## 557 BET DIRECT NO Q VOICE AUTOMATED BETTING H'CAP — 7f (P)
2:25 (2:26) (D) (0-85,80) 3-Y-O £4,390 (£1,351; £675; £337) Stalls Low

Form RPR

02-1 1 **Secret Place**$^{15}$ [409] 3-9-4 77 ........ EAhern 4 88+
(EALDunlop) *t.k.h: hld up in tch: qcknd to ld over 1f out: sn clr* **4/1**$^{2}$

140- 2 2 1/2 **Western Roots**$^{38}$ [6160] 3-9-7 80 ........ SDrowne 8 85
(PFICole) *towards rr: hdwy 2f out: r.o to chse wnr wl ins fnl f* **12/1**

31-1 3 1 **Rowan Pursuit**$^{14}$ [420] 3-8-11 70 ........ (b) JFanning 3 72+
(JAkehurst) *mid-div: rdn 2f out: challoenging whn n.m.r over 1f out: kpt on one pce* **9/2**$^{3}$

06-3 4 1 1/4 **Monte Major (IRE)**$^{14}$ [415] 3-8-4 63 ........ MHenry 5 62
(MAJarvis) *led tl hdd approaching fnl f: fdd ins* **11/2**

002- 5 1 1/2 **Garrigon**$^{19}$ [6251] 3-8-0 62 ........ LisaJones$^{(3)}$ 2 57
(NPLittmoden) *hld up in rr: hdwy on ins whn hmpd ent fnl f: nt rcvr* **10/1**

10-3 6 shd **Royal Warrant**$^{10}$ [466] 3-9-7 80 ........ MartinDwyer 1 75
(AMBalding) *trckd ldr: rdn over 2f out: wknd ent fnl f* **10/3**$^{1}$

006- 7 1 3/4 **Wares Home (IRE)**$^{46}$ [6115] 3-8-8 67 ........ DarrenWilliams 6 58
(KRBurke) *in tch: rdn 2f out: c wd into st: one pce after* **16/1**

126- 8 1 1/4 **Even Easier**$^{184}$ [3348] 3-8-3 62 ........ SWhitworth 9 49
(GLMoore) *a in rr* **50/1**

22-2 9 1 1/2 **Fools Entire**$^{10}$ [462] 3-8-6 70 ........ BReilly$^{(5)}$ 10 54
(JAGilbert) *b: b.hind: lw: plld hrd: in tch tl wknd over 2f out* **11/1**

6-21 10 1/2 **Ever Cheerful**$^{7}$ [489] 3-8-9 75 ........ (p) LTreadwell$^{(7)}$ 7 57
(WGMTurner) *lw: t.k.h: rdn over 2f out: sn wknd* **20/1**

1m 25.99s (-0.01) **Going Correction** +0.125s/f (Slow) **10** Ran SP% **114.4**
Speed ratings: **105,102,101,99,97 97,95,94,92,92**CSF £50.12 CT £228.46 TOTE £6.10: £2.10, £2.00, £2.50; EX 63.80.
**Owner** Khalifa Sultan **Bred** Whitsbury Manor Stud **Trained** Newmarket, Suffolk

**FOCUS**
A very good winning time for the class of contest, but something of a rough race also. Howeer, the form should work out.

**NOTEBOOK**
**Secret Place**maintained his progress and showed a smart turn of foot to score. He enjoyed an uninterrupted run whilst others did not, but was still the winner on merit. He can win again.
**Western Roots**, backed at long odds, had a trouble-free passage this time and stayed on down the straight to finish clear second-best.
**Rowan Pursuit**, bidding for a hat-trick off a 7lb higher mark, was trying to make progress when the door was slammed in her face over a furlong from home. But for that she would probably have finished second.
**Monte Major(IRE)**was given a positive ride, but had no answer to the winner's turn of speed. His style of running may be better suited to Fibresand.
**Garrigon**, patiently ridden, was trying to make progress when murdered against the inside rail a furlong from home.
**Royal Warrant**, third in a very slowly-run race over a mile here last time, was ridden much more positively over this shorter trip, but faded disappointingly. This is as good as he is.

## 558 LITTLEWOODS BET DIRECT H'CAP — 1m 2f (P)
3:00 (3:02) (B) (0-105,105) 4-Y-O+ £12,151 (£4,609; £2,304; £1,047) Stalls Low

Form RPR

66-4 1 **Eastern Breeze (IRE)**$^{14}$ [418] 6-9-4 95 ........ PaulEddery 6 108
(PWD'Arcy) *trckd ldr: led over 2f out: r.o wl* **13/2**$^{2}$

032- 2 1 1/2 **Grand Passion (IRE)**$^{56}$ [6051] 4-9-7 100 ........ SDrowne 2 110
(GWragg) *trckd ldr: rdn to chse wnr appr fnl f: no imp ins* **6/4**$^{1}$

06-5 3 2 1/2 **Santando**$^{14}$ [418] 4-9-4 97 ........ (v) EAhern 5 103
(CEBrittain) *s.i.s: sn mid-div: hdwy over 2f out: styd on* **12/1**

25-2 4 1 1/4 **Lakota Brave**$^{8}$ [485] 10-8-11 88 ........ IMongan 4 92
(MrsStefLiddiard) *t.k.h: mid-div: styd on ins fnl 2f: nvr nrr* **25/1**

101- 5 1/2 **Lygeton Lad**$^{19}$ [6252] 6-10-0 105 ........ (t) MFenton 12 108
(MissGayKelleway) *b: b.hind: hld up: mde sme late hdwy ins fnl 2f* **16/1**

410- 6 1/2 **Dance In The Sun**$^{53}$ [6071] 4-8-6 85 ........ MartinDwyer 11 87
(MrsAJPerrett) *lw: a.p: rdn and no ex appr fnl f* **11/1**

603- 7 2 **Zonergem**$^{46}$ [6117] 6-9-0 91 ........ (p) MTebbutt 3 89
(LadyHerries) *led tl hdd appr fnl f: wknd ins* **10/1**$^{3}$

112- 8 1/2 **Star Of Normandie (USA)**$^{18}$ [6263] 5-8-1 83 ........ BReilly$^{(5)}$ 7 80
(GGMargarson) *towards rr: effrt 2f out: nvr nr to chal* **13/2**$^{2}$

121- 9 hd **Nimello (USA)**$^{17}$ [6268] 8-8-8 85 ........ SWhitworth 10 82
(AGNewcombe) *b.hind: hld up: effrt 2f out: nvr on terms* **16/1**

000- 10 3/4 **Ulundi**$^{22}$ [2964] 9-10-0 105 ........ DaneO'Neill 8 101
(PRWebber) *towards rr: rdn over 3f out: nvr on terms* **16/1**

000- 11 1 1/4 **Compton Commander**$^{22}$ [1438] 6-8-7 87 ........ LisaJones$^{(3)}$ 9 80
(IanWilliams) *a in rr* **50/1**

305- 12 3/4 **Nashaab (USA)**$^{28}$ [6224] 7-8-6 83 ........ SWKelly 14 75
(PDEvans) *slowly away: a towards rr* **20/1**

021- 13 1/2 **Linning Wine (IRE)**$^{28}$ [6224] 8-9-3 94 ........ SCarson 13 85
(BGPowell) *mid-div: gd hdwy 4f out: c wd into st: rdn and wknd qckly over 1f out* **12/1**

2m 7.02s (-0.37) **Going Correction** +0.125s/f (Slow)
**WFA** 4 from 5yo+ 2lb **13** Ran SP% **127.7**
Speed ratings: **106,104,102,101,101 101,99,99,98,98 97,96,96**CSF £17.37 CT £127.07 TOTE £12.10: £2.80, £1.60, £4.30; EX 30.90.
**Owner** Colin Cage and Peter Lupson **Bred** Limestone Stud **Trained** Newmarket, Suffolk

**FOCUS**
A very competitive handicap that should work out form-wise, though as with most races over this trip, the pace was only fair

**NOTEBOOK**
**Eastern Breeze(IRE)**, who found himself in front too soon over 12 furlongs here last time, appreciated both the shorter trip and getting a lead for that much longer. Hitting the front at just the right time, he had more than enough in reserve to hold off the favourite.
**Grand Passion(IRE)**was always in a good position and very much had the run of the race but, although he quickened up well when asked for his effort, the winner was finding just as much.
**Santando**was found wanting for a turn of foot where it mattered, but still ran with plenty of credit considering the drop in trip did him few favours. He needs at least 12 furlongs on a fast surface like this.
**Lakota Brave**does not know how to run badly on sand and again ran his race over a trip probably beyond his best.
**Lygeton Lad**, again on a career-high mark and over a trip beyond his best, tried to deliver his trademark late flourish but over this trip it was nothing like as effective.
**Dance In The Sun**was 7lb higher than when winning a fillies' handicap over this trip in November and found this too competitive.
**Zonergem**, real old character, tried front-running for a change but all that did was to make him a sitting duck.
**Nimello(USA)**, up 7lb, was trying this surface for the first time over a trip beyond his best and he was not at all suited by it.

**Nashaab(USA)**basically lost his race at the start.
**Linning Wine(IRE)**moved up smoothly on the outside running to the final bend, but did not look that happy and then stopped very quickly as though something was amiss.

## 559 BET DIRECT IN VISION SKY PAGE 293 H'CAP — 1m 2f (P)
3:35 (3:35) (E) (0-70,70) 4-Y-0+ — £3,465 (£990; £495) Stalls Low

Form — RPR

053- **1** **Rasid (USA)**[19] 6255 6-9-7 **63** NCallan 9 — 74
(CADwyer) *b.hind: lw: a.p: rdn to go 2nd 2f out: r.o u.p to ld nr fin: all out* **7/1**[3]

44-2 **2** ½ **Blue Trojan (IRE)**[14] 419 4-9-9 **67** MartinDwyer 5 — 77
(SKirk) *trckd ldr: led 4f out: ridden over 1f out: kpt on: hdd cl home* **9/2**[2]

2-50 **3** 1½ **Easter Ogil (IRE)**[3] 523 9-9-5 **64** LisaJones(3) 12 — 71
(JaneSouthcombe) *b: slowly away: in rr whn rdn 4f out: styd on fnl 2f to go 3rd ins fnl f* **14/1**

221- **4** 1¾ **Lyrical Way**[28] 6226 5-9-6 **62** (v) IMongan 6 — 66
(PRChamings) *a.p: rdn over 1f out: kpt on one pce* **14/1**

66-1 **5** nk **Gingko**[14] 419 7-10-0 **70** WRyan 4 — 74
(PRWebber) *led: hdd 4f out: styd on one pce ins fnl 2f* **14/1**

010- **6** shd **Burgundy**[19] 6255 7-9-4 **60** KDalgleish 13 — 63
(PMitchell) *in rr: rdn and hdwy over 1f out: nvr nrr* **33/1**

41-1 **7** nk **Gold Guest**[10] 464 5-9-3 **66** SJDonohoe(7) 1 — 69
(PDEvans) *b.hind: mid-div: hdwy on ins over 2f out: one pce ins fnl 2f* **5/2**[1]

533- **8** 2 **True Companion**[38] 6157 5-9-7 **63** EAhern 14 — 62
(NPLittmoden) *lw: a towards rr: sme late hdwy* **12/1**

021- **9** shd **Kingston Town (USA)**[53] 6067 4-9-9 **70** (p) J-PGuillambert(3) 2 — 69
(NPLittmoden) *a towards rr* **10/1**

004- **10** ¾ **Night Warrior (IRE)**[31] 6208 4-9-9 **67** PDoe 10 — 65
(DFlood) *mid-div: rdn 2f out: no hdwy after* **20/1**

153- **11** ¾ **Quantum Leap**[38] 6161 7-9-7 **63** PaulEddery 8 — 59
(SDow) *sn in rr: nvr on terms* **14/1**

40-4 **12** ¾ **Dusk Dancer (FR)**[14] 415 4-9-7 **65** RWinston 3 — 60
(BJMeehan) *lw: chsd ldrs: rdn over 3f out: wknd over 1f out* **12/1**

034- **13** 3 **Traveller's Tale**[22] 6239 5-10-0 **70** DKinsella 7 — 60
(PGMurphy) *plld hrd: chsd ldrs tl wknd wl over 1f out* **25/1**

000- **14** 2½ **Figura**[129] 4825 6-9-8 **64** DaneO'Neill 11 — 49
(RIngram) *bit bkwd: stdd s: t.k.h: effrt 4f out: wknd over 2f out* **16/1**

2m 9.30s (1.91) **Going Correction** +0.125s/f (Slow)
**WFA** 4 from 5yo+ 2lb — **14** Ran SP% **127.8**
Speed ratings: **97,96,95,94,93 93,93,91,91,91 90,89,87,85**CSF £40.07 CT £451.61 TOTE £8.30: £2.60, £2.60, £3.50; EX 87.00.
**Owner** David L Bowkett **Bred** Shadwell Farm Inc **Trained** Newmarket, Suffolk

**FOCUS**
A dawdle until well past halfway and by far the slowest of the four races run over this trip on the card.

**NOTEBOOK**
**Rasid(USA)**, brilliantly handicapped on the best of his form, had been hinting at a return to form lately and did so, having been in a good position throughout.
**Blue Trojan(IRE)**, closely matched with the winner on their running over course and distance last month, ran almost to the pound with him and looked like winning until not quite getting home.
**Easter Ogil(IRE)**needs to be ridden patiently, but in a falsely-run contest like this the field stays intact for that much longer and he had a real problem steering a path through. By the time he did it was all too late, but he is running well enough to end what is becoming a long losing run for him.
**Lyrical Way**, up 5lb for his win here last month, could never land a blow on this occasion.
**Gingko**, who had both the second and third behind him when winning here last time, was worse off at the weights but it was finding himself in front from the stalls that scuppered his chances as much as anything.
**Burgundy**, a funny customer these days, ran on through beaten horses late on but can never be supported with any confidence.
**Gold Guest**looked a real threat when moving up against the inside rail turning for home, but did not find as much as had looked likely.

## 560 PLOUGH INN (A420) AMATEUR RIDERS' H'CAP — 5f (P)
4:05 (4:06) (F) (0-60,69) 3-Y-0+ — £2,947 (£842; £421) Stalls High

Form — RPR

00-4 **1** **Double M**[7] 491 7-11-3 **51** (v) MrsSBosley 9 — 62
(MrsLRichards) *towards rr: hdwy on ins 2f out: led over 1f out: hld on wl* **11/4**[1]

555- **2** nk **Multahab**[26] 6232 5-10-12 **53** MrDSimms(7) 4 — 63
(MissGayKelleway) *mid-div: c wd into st: rdn to press wnr fnl f* **7/1**

01-6 **3** ½ **Ladies Knight**[11] 460 4-11-7 **55** MsCWilliams 1 — 63
(DShaw) *outpcd in rr: gd hdwy on ins fr 1/2-way: edgd rt ins fnl f: kpt on* **8/1**

300- **4** 2½ **Catchthebatch**[17] 6264 8-10-7 **48** MrCWitheford(7) 5 — 46
(EAWheeler) *mid-div: outpcd 2f out: r.o ins fnl f* **25/1**

656- **5** 1¾ **Rellim**[17] 6265 5-10-11 **50** MrMScales(5) 7 — 41
(PABlockley) *led: hdd 2f out: wknd ent fnl f* **8/1**

50-2 **6** 1¼ **Soaked**[11] 460 11-11-0 **53** (b) MissKellyHarrison(5) 6 — 39
(DWChapman) *prom: led 2f out: hdd & wknd appr fnl f* **4/1**[2]

03-6 **7** ½ **Night Cap (IRE)**[11] 453 5-10-8 **49** WRich(7) 8 — 33
(TDMccarthy) *chsd ldr to 1/2-way: c wd into st: sn btn* **6/1**[3]

050- **8** 1 **Blessed Place**[160] 4021 4-11-0 **55** MrSJEdwards(7) 2 — 35
(Jean-ReneAuvray) *chsd ldrs tl rdn and wknd appr fnl f* **8/1**

26-5 **9** 4 **Abraxas**[2] 543 6-10-11 **52** (p) MrSGascoyne(7) 10 — 16
(JAkehurst) *slowly away: a struggling in rr* **7/1**

60.95 secs (1.17) **Going Correction** +0.125s/f (Slow)
**WFA** 3 from 4yo+ 15lb — **9** Ran SP% **123.1**
Speed ratings: **95,94,93,89,86 84,84,82,76**CSF £24.42 CT £144.79 TOTE £3.60: £1.90, £3.00, £3.00; EX 58.00 Place 6 £133.22, Place 5 343.68.
**Owner** Bryan Mathieson **Bred** M G Tebbitt **Trained** Funtington, W Sussex

**FOCUS**
A very modest handicap, but run at a fair clip and the first three were clear.

**NOTEBOOK**
**Double M**was very well backed and, sticking like a limpet to the inside rail, swept to the front on reaching the straight and just managed to keep his rivals at bay.
**Multahab**, still a maiden, was making progress when taken very wide into the straight, but even though he stayed on and was beaten just a neck at the line, it would be pushing things to say he was unlucky. He does not look an ideal ride for an inexperienced rider, especially on a tricky track like this.
**Ladies Knight**, who often handicaps himself at the start, again found himself with a lot to do, but made up so much ground in the second half of the race that he would have been in front in another half-furlong. *Official explanation: jockey said gelding did not face the kickback*
**Catchthebatch**made a little late headway, but was never a threat and has not won a race for two years.
**Rellim**, a short runner, ran her usual sort of race. If she is not getting the trip here she will not get it anywhere.
**Soaked**could not get his nose in front until past halfway, but then had nothing left.
**Night Cap(IRE)**was still in with a shout when running extremely wide on the home bend, and that soon ended his chances.
**Abraxas**had no chance from his draw, especially after missing the break.
T/Plt: £290.30 to a £1 stake. Pool: £37,174.35. 93.45 winning tickets. T/Qpdt: £48.30 to a £1 stake. Pool: £2,665.10. 40.75 winning tickets. JS

# 547 WOLVERHAMPTON (A.W) (L-H)
### Monday, January 19

**OFFICIAL GOING: Standard**
There was no significant track bias at this meeting.
Wind: slt across Weather: drizzle

## 561 BET DIRECT ON SKY ACTIVE H'CAP — 6f (F)
1:40 (1:40) (F) (0-55,61) 3-Y-0 — £2,947 (£842; £421) Stalls Low

Form — RPR

600- **1** **Vampire Queen (IRE)**[38] 6167 3-8-12 **49** DeanMcKeown 7 — 56
(RPElliott) *chsd ldrs: rdn over 2f out: edgd lft and led ins fnl f: r.o wl* **12/1**

022- **2** 1½ **Velvet Touch**[31] 6212 3-9-3 **54** SWKelly 8 — 56
(JRJenkins) *led after 1f: rdn over 2f out: edgd rt and hdd ins fnl f: nt qckn* **7/2**[2]

600- **3** 1½ **Power To Burn**[54] 6077 3-9-4 **55** (v[1]) DRMcCabe 5 — 53
(KBell) *sn prom: rdn over 2f out: one pce fnl f* **20/1**

4-34 **4** ¾ **Pardon Moi**[13] 452 3-8-7 **49** HayleyTurner(5) 10 — 44
(MrsCADunnett) *chsd ldrs: rdn over 2f out: one pce fnl f* **14/1**

05-6 **5** hd **Limit Down (IRE)**[11] 482 3-9-1 **55** (v[1]) J-PGuillambert(3) 12 — 50
(MJWallace) *sn w ldrs: rdn and ev ch over 2f out: no ex fnl f* **14/1**

00-0 **6** 2½ **Vendors Mistake (IRE)**[16] 420 3-9-0 **51** NCallan 4 — 38
(AndrewReid) *prom: lost pl and hmpd on ins over 3f out: rdn and hdwy 2f out: no imp fnl f* **16/1**

61-2 **7** 1¾ **Melaina**[14] 435 3-8-13 **53** (p) RMiles(3) 13 — 35
(MSSaunders) *led 1f: prom tl rdn and wknd 2f out* **4/1**[3]

000- **8** ½ **The King Of Rock**[42] 6141 3-8-13 **50** (b[1]) SWhitworth 9 — 30
(AGNewcombe) *outpcd: nvr nr ldrs* **14/1**

61-1 **9** shd **Sir Jasper (IRE)**[6] 514 3-9-10 **61** 6ex (v) SRighton 11 — 41
(MFHarris) *broke wl: sn rdn and outpcd* **3/1**[1]

004- **10** 2 **Suitcase Murphy (IRE)**[28] 6227 3-8-10 **47** IMongan 2 — 21
(MsDeborahJEvans) *s.i.s: hld up: bhd fnl 3f* **25/1**

000- **11** hd **Kumari (IRE)**[31] 6213 3-8-4 **46** oh1 NChalmers(5) 6 — 20
(WMBrisbourne) *a bhd* **14/1**

000- **12** 3 **Poacher's Paradise**[115] 5197 3-8-12 **49** DaleGibson 1 — 14
(MWEasterby) *prom: lost pl and hung lft over 3f out: sn bhd* **13/2**

560- **13** 5 **Indrani**[87] 5725 3-8-13 **50** JMackay 3 — —
(JohnAHarris) *s.i.s: a bhd* **33/1**

1m 15.39s (-0.31) **Going Correction** -0.125s/f (Stan) — **13** Ran SP% **132.3**
Speed ratings: **97,95,93,92,91 88,86,85,85,82 82,78,71**CSF £58.46 CT £891.66 TOTE £25.10: £7.10, £2.20, £5.00; EX 128.20.
**Owner** Mrs Sarah Grayson **Bred** Ronnie Boland **Trained** Formby, Lancs
■ A first winner for ex-jockey Bobby Elliott, now training in his own right having previously been assistant to Mark Johnston.

**FOCUS**
A moderate handicap run at an ordinary pace.

**NOTEBOOK**
**Vampire Queen(IRE)**appreciated the step down in trip, having been running over seven, and won a shade readily in the end. She is probably capable of a little more improvement.
**Velvet Touch**, runner-up in a race at Southwell that has worked out well, ran well over this longer trip and there should be a sprint maiden for her.
**Power To Burn**, who has been slipping down the handicap, was visored for the first time.
**Pardon Moi**had her chance in the home straight but did not really want to go past. She is thoroughly exposed.
**Limit Down(IRE)**, who ran over an extended nine furlongs last time, wore a first-time visor. When push came to shove he did not look over-keen to exert himself.
**Sir Jasper(IRE)**, successful in two seven-furlong sellers for David Barron at Southwell, was never going on this first start for the Harris yard. He was reported to have lost his action in the early stages. *Official explanation: jockey said gelding lost its action in the early stages of the race*

## 562 PRESS INTERACTIVE TO BET DIRECT CLAIMING STKS — 1m 100y(F)
2:15 (2:15) (F) 4-Y-0+ — £2,898 (£828; £414) Stalls Low

Form — RPR

-252 **1** **Givemethemoonlight**[3] 552 5-8-10 48 (v) IMongan 2 — 58
(MrsStefLiddiard) *w ldr over 2f: prom: swtchd rt 4f out: led over 3f out: rdn over 2f out: r.o wl* **2/1**[2]

1-43 **2** 1¾ **Mutarafaa (USA)**[6] 518 5-8-10 58 (e) THamilton(5) 5 — 59
(DShaw) *hld up: stdy hdwy 5f out: w wnr 3f out: sn rdn: hung lft fr over 1f out: no imp* **13/8**[1]

002- **3** 7 **Our Destiny**[28] 6229 6-8-5 45 (v) JBramhill 9 — 35
(DBurchell) *prom: jnd ldr 6f out: led 5f out: rdn and hdd over 3f out: wknd over 2f out* **16/1**

0-50 **4** 1¾ **Dancing King (IRE)**[4] 533 8-8-2 30 LisaJones(3) 6 — 31
(PWHiatt) *led: hdd 5f out: rdn 3f out: sn wknd* **40/1**

0-00 **5** 10 **Consignia (IRE)**[3] 552 5-8-4 45 PaulEddery 4 — 9
(DHaydnJones) *bhd tl rdn and hdwy over 3f out: wknd wl over 1f out* **11/1**

504/ **6** ½ **Wekiwa Springs (FR)**[18] 5823 7-8-5 (t) RFfrench 7 — 9
(ThomasCarberry, Ire) *rdn over 4f out: a bhd* **8/1**

0-0 **7** nk **Welsh Whisper**[14] 442 5-7-7 DFentiman(7) 1 — 3
(SABrookshaw) *jinked rt s: hld up: rdn over 4f out: a bhd* **66/1**

00/0 **8** 1½ **Craigmor**[14] 442 4-8-5 45 (b[1]) SRighton 8 — 5
(MFHarris) *prom: rdn over 5f out: wknd over 4f out* **66/1**

00-1 **9** 5 **Daimajin (IRE)**[10] 487 5-9-5 58 (t) MFenton 3 — 9
(MissGayKelleway) *s.i.s: rdn over 4f out: a in rr* **6/1**[3]

1m 49.85s (-1.15) **Going Correction** -0.125s/f (Stan) — **9** Ran SP% **116.5**
Speed ratings: **100,98,91,89,79 79,78,77,72**CSF £5.65 TOTE £3.50: £1.10, £1.60, £5.40; EX 6.20.
**Owner** Valley Fencing **Bred** Mrs P A Reditt And M J Reditt **Trained** Great Shefford, Berks

**FOCUS**
A weak claimer, although the pace was strong and few got into it. The form looks modest despite the first two being well clear.

**NOTEBOOK**
**Givemethemoonlight**had been runner-up five times in her last seven starts and thoroughly deserved this victory. Although this was a particularly weak event, now she has got her head in front it would not be a surprise to see her follow up.
**Mutarafaa(USA)**had a clear chance on official figures but could not cash in. He closed with the eventual winner past the leading pair with three furlongs to run, but once into the home straight he wanted to hang in behind and was never going to go past the mare. He is one to treat with caution.


The Form Book, Raceform Ltd, Compton, RG20 6NL

**Our Destiny**was unable to dominate this time, with Dancing King in opposition, and had nothing to offer once headed at the end of the back straight.
**Dancing King(IRE)**, who had a stiff task on official figures, was also taken on for the lead by the eventual third.
**Daimajin(IRE)**, winner of a seller here on his latest appearance, was always struggling after a sluggish start. *Official explanation: trainer had no explanation for the poor form shown other than that transport problems delayed gelding's arrival on course*

## 563 BET DIRECT ON 0800 93 66 93 MAIDEN STKS — 1m 1f 79y(F)
**2:45** (2:45) (D ) 3-Y-O — **£3,373** (£1,038; £519; £259) **Stalls** Low

Form — RPR
355- **1** **Always Flying (USA)**[79] 5877 3-9-0 64 — JFanning 6 — 67
(MJohnston) *mde all: rdn clr over 2f out: rdn out* **6/4**[1]
0- **2** *5* **Waltzing Beau**[30] 6219 3-9-0 — NCallan 11 — 57
(IAWood) *bhd: hdwy over 5f out: rdn over 3f out: wnt 2nd over 1f out: no ch w wnr* **16/1**
0- **3** *¾* **It's Blue Chip**[33] 6203 3-9-0 — (e) IMongan 2 — 56
(PWD'Arcy) *dwlt: hdwy on outside over 4f out: rdn over 3f out: kpt on same pce fnl 2f* **5/1**[2]
\- **4** *4* **Vivre Sa Vie** 3-8-9 — JMackay 10 — 43
(SirMarkPrescott) *hld up in tch: rdn over 3f out: chsd wnr over 2f out tl over 1f out: wknd fnl f* **13/2**[3]
000- **5** *3½* **Lola's Destiny**[166] 3875 3-8-9 52 — DeanMcKeown 7 — 36
(PABlockley) *sn chsng wnr: rdn over 3f out: lost 2nd over 2f out: wknd over 1f out* **11/1**
06- **6** *hd* **Pepe (IRE)**[76] 5913 3-8-9 — (p) DaleGibson 1 — 35
(RHollinshead) *prom: rdn over 3f out: sn wknd* **16/1**
004- **7** *1¼* **Tamarina (IRE)**[28] 6230 3-8-9 55 — (p) CCatlin 8 — 33
(NEBerry) *prom: rdn over 4f out: sn wknd* **10/1**
00- **8** *½* **Chimes Eight**[19] 6266 3-8-4 — THamilton(5) 5 — 32
(RAFahey) *a bhd* **25/1**
0 **9** *shd* **Silver Cache (USA)**[13] 447 3-8-9 — SWKelly 3 — 31
(JNoseda) *s.s: a bhd* **8/1**
00- **10** *8* **Queen's Fantasy**[56] 6059 3-8-9 — PaulEddery 4 — 15
(DHaydnJones) *hld up mid-divison: pushed along over 6f out: sn bhd* **25/1**
0- **11** *13* **Maria Maria (IRE)**[38] 6167 3-8-11 ow2 — (p) PMcCabe 9 — —
(MrsNMacauley) *dwlt: a bhd* **66/1**

2m 2.29s (-0.61) **Going Correction** -0.125s/f (Stan) **11** Ran SP% **119.5**
Speed ratings: **97,92,91,88,85 85,83,83,83,76 64**CSF £29.70 TOTE £2.00: £1.10, £5.10, £2.00; EX 31.10.
**Owner** The Always Trying Partnership **Bred** Mark Johnston Racing Ltd **Trained** Middleham Moor, N Yorks

**FOCUS**
Always Flying got his own way out in front and controlled the pace to suit himself. The form behind him looks moderate. Interestingly, the only three geldings in the race filled the first three places.

**NOTEBOOK**
**Always Flying(USA)** was becoming a little bit disappointing when last seen in November but, given a break and stepped up in trip, he was well supported in the market and ran out a clear-cut winner. His future lies in the hands of the Handicapper.
**Waltzing Beau**, well held on his debut over a mile on Polytrack, improved on that effort on this step up in trip and switch to Fibresand. A half-brother to the stable's winning stayer Rebelle, he looks the sort to improve over time and distance.
**It's Blue Chip**, well held on his debut over seven furlongs on Polytrack, improved on that form on this switch to Fibresand and step up in trip.
**Vivre Sa Vie**, a half-sister to winning Flat performer, hurdler and chaser Bow Strada, was very easy to back and is likely to be better over further when handicapped.
**Lola's Destiny** raced up with the early pace on this first start for Blockley, but dropped out tamely and failed to progress she gets the trip.
**Silver Cache(USA)** again showed little, but she is one to keep an eye on if her connections persevere with her.

## 564 BET DIRECT H'CAP — 1m 100y(F)
**3:20** (3:20) (D ) (0-80,78) 3-Y-O+ — **£4,065** (£1,251; £625; £312) **Stalls** Low

Form — RPR
160- **1** **Vortex**[148] 4413 5-9-9 73 — (t) MFenton 12 — 84
(MissGayKelleway) *hld up towards rr: hdwy over 3f out: rdn over 2f out: edgd lft 1f out: r.o u.p to ld last strides* **10/1**
05-4 **2** *nk* **Danielle's Lad**[10] 488 8-8-12 65 — (b) RMiles(3) 13 — 75
(BPalling) *led: rdn wl over 1f out: edgd lft and hdd last strides* **20/1**
62-1 **3** *½* **Arc El Ciel (ARG)**[10] 488 6-10-0 78 — (v) IMongan 11 — 87
(MrsStefLiddiard) *hld and bhd: hdwy over 5f out: rdn 3f out: swtchd rt jst ins fnl f: r.o wl towards fin* **9/1**
03-3 **4** *½* **Quiet Reading (USA)**[14] 437 7-8-12 67 — (v) HayleyTurner(5) 8 — 75
(MRBosley) *a.p: rdn over 2f out: kpt on ins fnl f* **11/1**
20-2 **5** *½* **Yorker (USA)**[10] 488 6-9-2 69 — LisaJones(3) 1 — 76
(MsDeborahJEvans) *w ldr: rdn wl over 1f out: no ex towards fin* **13/2**[3]
0-14 **6** *nk* **Ovigo (GER)**[4] 544 5-9-5 69 — NCallan 6 — 75
(PABlockley) *hld up and bhd: hdwy 3f out: sn rdn: c wd st: kpt on fnl f* **9/4**[1]
0/5- **7** *nk* **Henry Afrika (IRE)**[36] 6098 6-9-9 73 — (p) SWKelly 5 — 79
(DGMcCardle, Ire) *hld up mid-div: rdn and hdwy 3f out: no ex ins fnl f* **11/2**[2]
300- **8** *3* **Bressbee (USA)**[51] 6098 6-9-8 72 — (v) RWinston 9 — 71
(JWUnett) *chsd ldrs: rdn 4f out: wknd 3f out* **20/1**
352- **9** *nk* **Miss Champers (IRE)**[24] 6241 4-8-10 67 — SJDonohoe(7) 10 — 66
(PDEvans) *hld up: dropped rr 5f out: n.d after* **8/1**
00-2 **10** *7* **Pharoah's Gold (IRE)**[14] 437 6-8-13 63 — (e) DarrenWilliams 2 — 47
(DShaw) *hld up in tch: wknd over 3f out* **14/1**
24-1 **11** *nk* **Allied Victory (USA)**[13] 459 4-9-9 73 — DeanMcKeown 3 — 56
(EJAlston) *stmbld and rdr lost iron briefly sn after s: sme hdwy on ins over 6f out: wknd over 4f out* **16/1**
30-5 **12** *4* **Free Option (IRE)**[9] 494 9-9-9 73 — DMernagh 4 — 48
(WJMusson) *a bhd* **20/1**
423- **13** *9* **Bowing**[158] 4132 4-9-11 75 — DKinsella 7 — 31
(PGMurphy) *prom 4f* **20/1**

1m 48.81s (-2.19) **Going Correction** -0.125s/f (Stan) **13** Ran SP% **129.6**
Speed ratings: **105,104,104,103,103 102,102,99,99,92 92,88,79**CSF £208.66 CT £1212.23 TOTE £14.10: £5.10, £7.30, £2.60; EX 222.30.
**Owner** Coriolis Partnership **Bred** Juddmonte Farms **Trained** Newmarket, Suffolk
■ Stewards Enquiry : M Fenton caution: careless riding

**FOCUS**
A well-contested handicap in which the pace was fair and the form looks solid.

**NOTEBOOK**
**Vortex**, having his first run since August, came with his challenge off the home turn. Edging left, like the leader, inside the last, he got there on the line. His trainer reckons he will prove even more effective on the Lingfield Polytrack.
**Danielle's Lad**was still travelling well in front turning in and it looked like he would hold on, but he edged over to the far rail under pressure inside the last and was just caught. This trip is a little beyond his best.
**Arc El Ciel(ARG)**was perhaps a slightly unlucky loser, as he was momentarily short of room on the home turn and then had to switch past the eventual winner entering the last. He was running on strongly close home and this was a good effort from a career-high mark.
**Quiet Reading(USA)**is running creditably at present but is taking a long time to come down the handicap as a consequence.
**Yorker(USA)**, who was well supported on this return to a mile, only conceded defeat well inside the final furlong.
**Ovigo(GER)**, back over a more suitable trip, stayed on down the near side in the home straight without quite getting to the leaders. He is obviously quirky but is in good form at present.
**Henry Afrika(IRE)**raced up the slowest ground on the inside rail up the home straight and this was a decent run over a trip which is on the short side for him. *Official explanation: jockey said gelding hung left from halfway down the back straight*

## 565 BET DIRECT ON SKY TEXT PAGE 372 (S) STKS — 7f (F)
**3:50** (3:50) (G ) 4-Y-O+ — **£2,618** (£748; £374) **Stalls** High

Form — RPR
6-33 **1** **Feast Of Romance**[7] 503 7-8-12 49 — (p) SWKelly 6 — 60
(PHowling) *bhd: swtchd rt 4f out: rdn and hdwy 3f out: led ins fnl f: drvn out* **7/1**
-211 **2** *1¾* **Lucayan Monarch**[7] 498 6-9-3 56 — (p) DeanMcKeown 7 — 61
(PABlockley) *hld up: hdwy 3f out: sn rdn: r.o one pce fnl f* **11/4**[2]
30-5 **3** *¾* **Bulawayo**[14] 439 7-8-12 53 — (v) ANicholls 3 — 54
(AndrewReid) *led: rdn 3f out: hdd and no ex ins fnl f* **8/1**
40-3 **4** *4* **Jan Brueghel (USA)**[14] 439 5-8-5 63 — PMakin(7) 1 — 44
(TDBarron) *hld up and bhd: hdwy on ins over 3f out: rdn over 2f out: wknd ins fnl f* **9/4**[1]
060- **5** *1* **Chandelier**[35] 2665 4-8-9 58 — RMiles(3) 8 — 41
(MSSaunders) *s.i.s: stdy hdwy on outside over 5f out: hung lft fr over 1f out: no imp* **25/1**
000- **6** *1½* **Open Handed (IRE)**[34] 6196 4-8-7 45 — (t) THamilton(5) 2 — 38
(BEllison) *bhd: rdn over 3f out: hdwy on ins wl over 1f out: no imp fnl f* **33/1**
00-5 **7** *hd* **Pooka's Daughter (IRE)**[13] 457 4-8-7 45 — CCatlin 4 — 32
(JMBradley) *w ldr: rdn over 2f out: wknd over 1f out* **16/1**
60-2 **8** *7* **Xaloc Bay (IRE)**[14] 439 6-8-12 55 — (p) JFanning 10 — 20
(BPJBaugh) *w ldrs tl wknd 3f out* **9/2**[3]
6-31 **9** *nk* **Star Lad (IRE)**[11] 481 4-9-3 47 — (v) IMongan 11 — 24
(RBrotherton) *prom: rdn over 3f out: wknd 2f out* **14/1**
040 **10** *10* **Threat**[7] 499 8-8-12 40 — (p) PFitzsimons 9 — —
(JMBradley) *prom tl wknd over 4f out* **25/1**
0-60 **11** *10* **Glenviews Polly (IRE)**[11] 474 4-8-7 35 — (v) JBramhill 5 — —
(IanEmmerson) *s.i.s: outpcd* **50/1**

1m 30.29s (0.09) **Going Correction** -0.125s/f (Stan) **11** Ran SP% **124.4**
Speed ratings: **94,92,91,86,85 83,83,75,75,63 52**CSF £27.35 TOTE £8.70: £1.80, £2.60, £2.60; EX 30.50.The winner was bought in for 5,500gns
**Owner** D C Patrick **Bred** Aramstone Stud **Trained** Newmarket, Suffolk

**FOCUS**
A moderate time, even by selling-race standards. The first two in the market ran below form, and the principals came from off the pace.

**NOTEBOOK**
**Feast Of Romance** gained his first win in over a year with a decisive enough success. This is his grade, but he does not win that often and may be one to take on next time.
**Lucayan Monarch**, chasing the hat-trick after a couple of wins at similar level at Southwell, was a little below his recent form, without apparent excuse.
**Bulawayo**, with the visor back on, fared best of those who raced up with the pace, but is quite simply hard to win with.
**Jan Brueghel(USA)**, a beaten favourite in a similar event at Southwell on his previous start, travelled well enough but could only find the one pace under pressure and looks flattered by his current rating. *Official explanation: jockey said gelding had bled from the nose*
**Chandelier**, back on the level for the first time in 208 days after a couple of unsuccessful spins over hurdles, did not help his chances with a slow start and never really threatened when it mattered.
**Xaloc Bay(IRE)**, with the cheekpieces on, dropped out very quickly.

## 566 LITTLEWOODSPOKER.COM H'CAP — 1m 1f 79y(F)
**4:20** (4:20) (E ) (0-75,74) 3-Y-O — **£3,269** (£934; £467) **Stalls** Low

Form — RPR
400- **1** **Gavroche (IRE)**[157] 4160 3-8-7 63 — J-PGuillambert(3) 4 — 70
(MJWallace) *hld up: hdwy over 4f out: rdn over 3f out: led wl over 1f out: edged rt wl ins fnl f: ran on wl* **7/2**[3]
413- **2** *2½* **Bold Blade**[23] 6242 3-9-3 70 — (b) RFfrench 2 — 72
(BSmart) *led: rdn 3f out: hdd wl over 1f out: one pce fnl f* **3/1**[1]
35-5 **3** *5* **Myannabanana (IRE)**[13] 450 3-8-5 65 — (v) DFentiman(7) 6 — 57
(JRWeymes) *prom: pushed along over 6f out: chsd ldr over 5f out: rdn over 3f out: lost 2nd jst over 2f out: wknd over 1f out* **12/1**
13-3 **4** *3½* **Maybe Someday**[13] 450 3-9-7 74 — NCallan 9 — 59
(IAWood) *hld up: stdy hdwy over 5f out: rdn over 3f out: wknd wl over 1f out* **6/1**
340- **5** *9* **Joint Destiny (IRE)**[67] 5990 3-7-11 53 — LisaJones(3) 8 — 20
(EJO'Neill) *nvr nr ldrs* **16/1**
44-2 **6** *3* **Bretton**[11] 482 3-7-12 51 oh4 — (b) DaleGibson 3 — 12
(RHollinshead) *sn chsng ldr: lost 2nd over 5f out: wknd over 3f out* **13/2**
410- **7** *8* **Atlantic Breeze**[23] 6242 3-8-13 66 — (v[1]) PMcCabe 5 — 11
(MrsNMacauley) *a bhd* **25/1**
055- **8** *13* **Dante's Devine (IRE)**[42] 6142 3-8-7 60 — CCatlin 7 — —
(ABailey) *hld up and bhd: rdn 6f out: sn struggling* **12/1**
01-6 **9** *2½* **Bill Bennett (FR)**[13] 450 3-9-7 74 — IMongan 1 — —
(JJay) *chsd ldrs tl wknd over 4f out* **10/3**[2]

2m 0.36s (-2.54) **Going Correction** -0.125s/f (Stan) **9** Ran SP% **123.0**
Speed ratings: **106,103,99,96,88 85,78,66,64**CSF £15.58 CT £118.09 TOTE £4.50: £2.10, £2.00, £2.20; EX 16.60 Place 6 £179.97, Place 5 £47.88.
**Owner** J L Guillambert **Bred** John O'Connor **Trained** Newmarket, Suffolk

**FOCUS**
Not a bad little handicap and a smart time for the grade of contest. The first two are progressive and were clear of a good yardstick.

**NOTEBOOK**
**Gavroche(IRE)**, who hinted at ability in three runs at up to seven furlongs at two, was well backed on this first start for 157 days and duly justified the support on this handicap debut. He had to work pretty hard to get on top, but is lightly-raced and open to further improvement. The local Stewards considered the colt's improved form before rightly referring the case to Portman Square for further investigation. *Official explanation: trainer said, regarding the improved form shown, gelding had strengthened up considerably over the winter since his last run and appears to have been better suited by today's longer trip*

**Bold Blade**, in good form at up to a mile at Southwell recently, posted another solid effort despite racing keenly. He was just unfortunate to bump into such a well handicapped horse.
**Myannabanana(IRE)**, switching back from Polytrack to Fibresand, has still to convince he truly gets this sort of trip.
**Maybe Someday**, third in a steadily-run race over ten furlongs at Lingfield last time, did not appear to get home in this stronger-run contest. His only win to date came over seven furlongs so he may do better back over shorter.
**Joint Destiny(IRE)** never threatened on this step up in trip and class.
**Atlantic Breeze** *Official explanation: jockey said filly had hung badly right-handed*
**Bill Bennett(FR)** *Official explanation: jockey said gelding had hung badly into the rail*
T/Plt: £105.80 to a £1 stake. Pool: £37,782.55. 260.65 winning tickets. T/Qpdt: £50.70 to a £1 stake. Pool: £3,218.40. 46.90 winning tickets. KH

# 540 SOUTHWELL (L-H)
## Tuesday, January 20

**OFFICIAL GOING: Standard**
(REGIONAL MEETING) The track bias appeared negligible for this meeting.

## 567 PRESS INTERACTIVE TO BET DIRECT BANDED STKS 1m (F)
**1:20** (1:20) (H) 3-Y-O+ **£1,480** (£423; £211) **Stalls** Low

Form RPR
00-0 **1** **Mr Whizz**[10] 495 7-9-1 35........................................(be[1]) DerekNolan[(7)] 12 44
(APJones) *cl up: effrt to ld over 2f out: sn rdn: drvn over 1f out: kpt on wl fnl f: jst hld on* **40/1**
00-3 **2** *shd* **Kenny The Truth (IRE)**[16] 434 5-9-3 40......................(t) NChalmers[(5)] 2 44
(MrsJCandlish) *hld up towards rr: hdwy over 3f out: rdn to chse ldrs over 1f out: drvn and styd on ins last: jst failed* **9/2**[2]
04-0 **3** *1 ½* **Second Venture (IRE)**[6] 531 6-9-8 40........................(bt[1]) RWinston 11 41
(PHowling) *cl up: rdn 2f out and ev ch tl drvn and no ex ent last* **11/1**
00-0 **4** *shd* **Sweet Coral (FR)**[5] 541 4-9-8 40................................(p) JoannaBadger 5 41
(BSRothwell) *chsd ldrs: rdn along 2f out: drvn and nt qckn ent last* **25/1**
/00- **5** *¾* **Aboustar**[87] 5742 4-9-1 40.................................................. MLawson[(7)] 14 39
(MBrittain) *t.k.h: led: pushed along and hdd over 2f out: sn rdn and one pce appr last* **16/1**
6-45 **6** *3* **Proud Victor (IRE)**[6] 531 4-9-8 40.............................(v) DarrenWilliams 7 33
(DShaw) *hld up in rr: pushed along 3f out: hdwy 2f out: styd on appr last: nrest fin ish* **8/1**[3]
50-0 **7** *3* **Balalaika Tune (IRE)**[16] 428 5-9-8 40.............................. DRMcCabe 3 27
(WStorey) *in tch on inner: hdwy over 2f out: sn rdn and wknd over 1f out* **25/1**
0-33 **8** *1 ¼* **Lemarate (USA)**[12] 470 7-9-8 40........................................(b) ACulhane 4 25
(DWChapman) *s.i.s: hdwy 3f out: rdn alonga nd kpt on fnl 2f: nvr a factor* **12/1**
5-24 **9** *nk* **Brilliantrio**[12] 474 6-9-8 40.......................................................... IMongan 6 24
(MCChapman) *dwlt: sn midfield: hdwy to chse ldrs 2f out: sn rdn and btn* **7/4**[1]
-025 **10** *5* **Vlasta Weiner**[5] 533 4-9-8 40.......................................(b) PFitzsimons 8 14
(JMBradley) *a rr* **25/1**
200- **11** *5* **Margarets Wish**[33] 6027 4-9-1 40.......... StephanieHollinshead[(7)] 9 4
(TWall) *bhd fr 1/2-way* **33/1**
000- **12** *3* **Ynys**[43] 6147 3-8-2 40........................................................... DKinsella 10 —
(BPalling) *racd wd: rdn along 1/2-way: a rr* **33/1**
000- **13** *½* **Sky Cove**[29] 6230 3-8-2 40............................................... DaleGibson 13 —
(MWEasterby) *a rr* **28/1**
000- **14** *2 ½* **She's A Diamond**[95] 5627 7-9-8 40................................... VSlattery 16 —
(TTClement) *chsd ldrs to 1/2-way: sn wknd* **66/1**
/00- **15** *2 ½* **Diva Dancer**[84] 5815 4-9-8 40............................................ CCatlin 15 —
(JHetherton) *sn outpcd and b ehind* **50/1**
/6-5 **16** *5* **Proprius**[16] 429 4-9-8 40................................................... RFfrench 1 —
(BSmart) *a rr* **12/1**

1m 44.69s (0.09) **Going Correction** -0.125s/f (Stan)
**WFA** 3 from 4yo+ 20lb **16** Ran SP% **122.0**
Speed ratings: **94,93,92,92,91 88,85,84,84,79 74,71,70,68,65 60**CSF £198.43 TOTE £49.50: £11.90, £1.20, £4.40; EX 652.70.
**Owner** The Milk Sheiks **Bred** K D Linsley **Trained** Eastbury, Berks

**FOCUS**
A low-grade contest representing a poor level of form.

**NOTEBOOK**
**Mr Whizz**, who wore the combination of blinkers and an eyeshield for the first time, had 5lb to find with the rest of the field on official ratings. Responding to a positive ride, he just held off the runner-up's challenge.
**Kenny The Truth(IRE)**, clear of the remainder when third last time in a race that is working out well, needed a couple more strides.
**Second Venture(IRE)**, who is not the most consistent, wore blinkers instead of the usual cheekpieces and a tongue tie was employed too.
**Sweet Coral(FR)**, wearing first-time cheekpieces, appeared to see out this longer trip.
**Aboustar**, a keen sort, became warm in the preliminaries. Making his Fibresand debut and having only his fourth run in all, he did not really get home over this longer trip.
**Brilliantrio**, who was taken to post early, reared up in the stalls and was a bit slow to go. She closed on the leaders early in the home straight but the effort soon petered out.

## 568 BET DIRECT ON SKY ACTIVE BANDED STKS 1m 6f (F)
**1:50** (1:51) (H) 4-Y-O+ **£1,484** (£424; £212) **Stalls** Low

Form RPR
30-3 **1** **Lampos (USA)**[15] 446 4-9-0 45............................................ RWinston 8 58+
(MissJACamacho) *hld up in midfield: smooth hdwy to trck ldrs 4f out: led 11/2f out and sn clr: easily* **11/2**[3]
06-1 **2** *8* **Citrus Magic**[17] 426 7-9-6 45......................................(p) JoannaBadger 7 47
(KBell) *led: rdn along over 3f out: hdd 11/2f out: sn drvn and kpt on: no ch w wnr* **10/1**
0-22 **3** *hd* **Kagoshima (IRE)**[12] 475 9-9-6 40..........................................(v) VHalliday 4 47
(JRNorton) *a.p: effrt 3f out and sn ev ch: rdn 2f out and kpt on same pce* **9/2**[2]
40-4 **4** *2* **Worlaby Dale**[16] 432 8-9-6 35............................................ JFanning 5 44
(MrsSLamyman) *trckd ldrs: hdwy 4f out: rdn along over 2f out: sn no imp* **7/2**[1]
50-5 **5** *9* **Charnwood Street (IRE)**[12] 475 5-9-6 35..............(e) DarrenWilliams 2 33
(DShaw) *hld up: rdn along and outpcd in rr 1/2-way: styd on fnl 3f: nvr a factor* **25/1**
300- **6** *1 ½* **Michaels Dream (IRE)**[25] 5624 5-9-6 40................................(v) CCatlin 3 31
(JHetherton) *hld up in rr: effrt and sme hdwy fnl 3f: nvr a factor* **7/2**[1]
50-5 **7** *1 ½* **Turftanzer (GER)**[16] 430 5-9-6 35..........................................(t) KimTinkler 9 29
(DonEnricoIncisa) *cl up: ev ch 3f out: sn rdn along and wknd 2f out* **16/1**
0-05 **8** *14* **Dr Julian (IRE)**[8] 501 4-9-0 40............................................(p) AnnStokell 10 11
(MissAStokell) *in tch: rdn along over 4f out and sn outpcd* **50/1**
00-0 **9** *2* **Little Richard (IRE)**[15] 446 5-9-6 35................................(p) VSlattery 11 8
(MWellings) *chsd ldrs: rdn along 5f out and sn wknd* **50/1**
401/ **10** *dist* **Rodiak**[16] 5425 5-9-6 45................................................................ IMongan 12 —
(PRHedger) *hld up towards rr: bhd fr 1/2-way: t.o fnl 3f* **8/1**
06-0 **11** *1* **Margold (IRE)**[14] 459 4-9-0 45.............................................. ACulhane 13 —
(RHollinshead) *in tch: rdn along and outpcd fr 1/2-way: t.o fnl 3f* **16/1**
000/ **12** *dist* **Mill Emerald**[64] 1425 7-9-6 40.................................................. MHenry 1 —
(MrsGHarvey) *a bhd: t.o fnl 4f: virtually p.u fnl f* **25/1**

3m 8.55s (-1.05) **Going Correction** -0.125s/f (Stan)
**WFA** 4 from 5yo+ 6lb **12** Ran SP% **121.6**
Speed ratings: **98,93,93,92,87 86,85,77,76,— —,—**CSF £59.09 TOTE £8.80: £2.40, £4.40, £1.70; EX 65.40.
**Owner** L A Bolingbroke **Bred** Carolyn L Nicewonder **Trained** Norton, N Yorks

**FOCUS**
A poor contest but a fair performance by the impressive winner, who was returning to something like his form of early 2003.

**NOTEBOOK**
**Lampos(USA)**was an impressive winner in the context of a race of this nature. The step up in trip suited him and he will have no problem staying two miles.
**Citrus Magic**, who seems suited by front-running tactics, ran his race but was no match for the easy winner.
**Kagoshima(IRE)**put in another decent run and a return to two miles will suit him.
**Worlaby Dale**was ridden closer to the pace than usual on this step down in trip.
**Michaels Dream(IRE)**, runner-up on all three starts over hurdles this winter, had the visor back in place on this return to the Flat but was never in the hunt.
**Turftanzer(GER)**looked a non-stayer over this longer trip.

## 569 LITTLEWOODS BET DIRECT MEDIAN AUCTION MAIDEN STKS 6f (F)
**2:20** (2:23) (H) 3-5-Y-O **£1,473** (£421; £210) **Stalls** Low

Form RPR
525- **1** **Pick Of The Crop**[71] 5968 3-8-7 73........................................... SWKelly 2 65
(JRJenkins) *s.i.s and bhd: gd hdwy on inner 2f out: rdn over 1f out: drvn and styd on to ld last 100 yds* **11/4**[1]
26-3 **2** *½* **Daring Affair**[15] 435 3-8-2 63.............................................. JFanning 11 58
(KRBurke) *in tch: hdwy 2f out: rdn to ld briefly ins last: hdd and no ex last 100 yds* **4/1**[2]
0-2 **3** *1 ¾* **Weakest Link**[6] 529 3-8-4 ................................................... DAllan[(3)] 12 58
(WJarvis) *cl up: rdn 2f out and ev ch tl drvn and nt qckn ins last* **6/1**
03- **4** *nk* **Fayrz Please (IRE)**[36] 6191 3-8-0 ............................... AndrewWebb[(7)] 4 57
(MCChapman) *wnt rt s: towards rr: gd hdwy on inner 2f out: rdn and kpt on ins last* **14/1**
400- **5** *½* **Zak Facta (IRE)**[35] 6202 4-9-9 50.........................................(v) CCogan 7 55
(MissDAMchale) *wnt lft s: trckd ldrs: nt clr run and swtchd rt over 2f out: sn rdn and ev ch tl drvn and no ex ins last* **11/2**
0-00 **6** *1 ½* **Miss Judged**[8] 508 3-7-11 45.................................(be) JFMcDonald[(5)] 1 46
(APJones) *chsd ldrs: hdwy on inner to ld wl over 2f out: sn rdn: drvn and hdd ins last: wknd* **100/1**
0-3 **7** *½* **Dispol Veleta**[15] 438 3-8-2 .................................................. DMernagh 13 44
(TDBarron) *bhd and wd st: rdn along wl over 1f out: styd on wl fnl f: nrst fin* **9/2**[3]
00-6 **8** *nk* **Kustom Kit For Her**[5] 541 4-9-4 50..................................... JBramhill 8 43
(SRBowring) *towards rr: wd st: rdn 2f out: kpt on u.p appr last: nrst fin* **33/1**
0- **9** *9* **Mind The Time**[32] 6216 3-8-7 .................................................... CCatlin 10 21
(JHetherton) *cl up: rdn along 1/2-way: sn wknd* **66/1**
0-00 **10** *hd* **Law Maker**[8] 499 4-9-9 35..................................................(b) RFfrench 3 21
(MABuckley) *led: rdn along 1/2-way: sn hdd & wknd* **50/1**
26-0 **11** *4* **Sheapys Lass**[5] 543 3-8-2 60........................................(v[1]) DaleGibson 9 4
(ACrook) *cl up: led briefly 1/2-way: sn rdn and hdd: wknd fnl 2f* **20/1**
05 **12** *5* **Dances In Time**[6] 529 4-9-4 ........................................... TWilliams 5 —
(CNKellett) *hmpd s: a rr* **20/1**
00- **13** *1 ¼* **Limited Magician**[102] 5470 3-8-3 ow1................................ RFitzpatrick 6 —
(CSmith) *hamperd s: a bhd* **100/1**

1m 16.19s (-0.61) **Going Correction** -0.125s/f (Stan)
**WFA** 3 from 4yo 16lb **13** Ran SP% **119.1**
Speed ratings: **99,98,96,95,94 92,92,91,79,79 74,67,65**CSF £12.67 TOTE £3.80: £1.70, £2.30, £2.60; EX 14.40.
**Owner** Buy And Sell Partnership **Bred** The Buy And Sell Partnership **Trained** Royston, Herts

**FOCUS**
Plenty were in with a chance up the home straight in this weak maiden, and neither of the first two ran up to their best,

**NOTEBOOK**
**Pick Of The Crop**was slow to stride and was still last of all turning for home, but he made good progress along the far rail and forged to the front in the last half-furlong.
**Daring Affair**, minus the visor this time, stayed on in the straight to put her head in front, but her lead proved short-lived as she could not withstand the favourite's challenge.
**Weakest Link**ran a good race on this drop in trip but a return to seven furlongs may suit him.
**Fayrz Please(IRE)**found himself at the back of the field after being buffeted quite badly in the first furlong, which was partly his own fault. Taking the shortest route in the straight, he was keeping on at the end and looks the sort to improve as he gains experience.
**Zak Facta(IRE)**ran a sound race, although he was unable to get to the front over this shorter trip.
**Miss Judged**, who had the tongue tie left off, took a slight lead early in the home straight but was unable to hold on inside the final furlong.
**Dispol Veleta**showed promise in staying on from off the pace and there should be a race for her now she is eligible for a handicap mark.

## 570 BET DIRECT INTERACTIVE BANDED STKS 1m 3f (F)
**2:50** (2:50) (H) 4-Y-O+ **£1,666** (£476; £238) **Stalls** Low

Form RPR
40-2 **1** **Aveiro (IRE)**[15] 440 8-9-3 45............................................(b) KDalgleish 1 65
(BGPowell) *mde all: qcknd clr over 3f out: rdn over 1f out and kpt on wl* **11/4**[1]
0-16 **2** *13* **Dash Of Magic**[15] 440 6-9-3 40................................................ CCatlin 2 46
(JHetherton) *a.p: rdn along o ver 3f out: drvn and kpt on same pce fnl 2f* **9/1**
0-33 **3** *¾* **Newclose**[12] 474 4-9-0 40.....................................................(t) ACulhane 4 44
(NTinkler) *hld up and bhd: hdwy over 3f out: rdn and kpt on fnl 2f: nrst fin* **6/1**
04-6 **4** *shd* **Red Delirium**[15] 442 8-9-3 45.............................................(b) IMongan 16 44
(RBrotherton) *m idfield: hdwy to chse ldrs 4f out: wd st: rdn 2f out: sn drvn and one pce* **20/1**
0414 **5** *shd* **King Priam (IRE)**[5] 542 9-9-3 45................................(b) DeanMcKeown 7 44
(MJPolglase) *racd wd and bhd: hdwy and wd st: sn rdn: styd on strly fnl f: nrst fin* **10/1**

003- **6** *1 1/4* **Next Flight (IRE)**[32] 6214 5-8-12 45 TEaves[(5)] 11 42
(REBarr) *towards rr: hdwy 4f out: rdn along wl over 2f out: kpt on appr last: nrst fin* **25/1**

00-6 **7** *hd* **Desires Destiny**[12] 472 6-8-10 40 MLawson[(7)] 8 42
(MBrittain) *prom: chsd wnr 1/2-way: rdn along 3f out: drvn and wknd fnl 2f* **20/1**

06-5 **8** *nk* **Vermilion Creek**[15] 441 5-8-10 35 (p) StephanieHollinshead[(7)] 10 41
(RHollinshead) *in tch on inner: rdn along over 3f out: sn wknd* **40/1**

33-0 **9** *1/2* **Debbie**[4] 552 5-9-3 45 SWhitworth 13 41
(BDLeavy) *hld up and bhd: hdwy 4f out: wd st and sn rdn: drvn over 1f out and plugged on same pce* **7/2**[2]

65-4 **10** *3* **Berkeley Heights**[15] 446 4-9-0 40 (b) RFfrench 15 36
(BSmart) *bhd fr 1/2-way* **25/1**

000- **11** *5* **Gwazi**[36] 6193 4-9-0 45 (tp) DarrenWilliams 12 29
(MissDAMchale) *a rr* **40/1**

00/1 **12** *1 1/2* **Ndola**[17] 427 5-9-3 45 SWKelly 14 26
(BJCurley) *a bhd* **11/2**[3]

00-0 **13** *nk* **Polka Princess**[18] 412 4-8-8 45 ow1 LTreadwell[(7)] 3 27
(MWellings) *chsd ldrs: pushed along 1/2-way: sn lost pl and bhd* **100/1**

040- **14** *1 1/2* **Think Quick (IRE)**[25] 6240 4-9-0 40 DaleGibson 6 24
(RHollinshead) *chsd ldrs: rdn along 5f out: sn wknd* **66/1**

/0-2 **15** *5* **Good Timing**[15] 445 6-9-3 45 GParkin 9 16
(JHetherton) *in tch: rdn along over 5f out and sn wknd* **33/1**

63-0 **16** *9* **Rousing Thunder**[16] 432 7-9-3 45 (tp) DRMcCabe 5 3
(WStorey) *a bhd* **25/1**

2m 26.48s (-2.42) **Going Correction** -0.125s/f (Stan)
**WFA** 4 from 5yo+ 3lb **16** Ran SP% **129.0**
Speed ratings: **103,93,93,92,92 91,91,91,91,89 85,84,84,83,79 72**CSF £26.95 TOTE £3.50: £1.60, £3.00, £2.70; EX 28.40.
**Owner** The Dream Connection **Bred** Saeed Manana **Trained** Morestead, Hants

**FOCUS**
The winner dictated the pace and turned this into a procession, winning in a decent time for a race of this grade.

**NOTEBOOK**
**Aveiro(IRE)**was rushed up to secure the early lead before dictating a moderate pace. Quickening the tempo nearing the end of the back straight, he was clear turning in and, kept up to his work, scored unchallenged. The ease of this victory means similar races will be out in the immediate future, but he could be interesting in handicaps if not punished too severely.
**Dash Of Magic**bounced back from a poor run here last time to finish best of the rest.
**Newclose**was taking a big step up in trip and appeared to see it out.
**Red Delirium**, who raced up the stands' side in the home straight, shaped as if ten furlongs could prove the answer.
**King Priam(IRE)**ran on well up the near side in the final furlong but the effort came too late.
**Desires Destiny**, who has been running over a mile, did not stay.
**Debbie**was tackling a longer trip on this second run since leaving the Ian Wood yard.
**Ndola**, upped in trip, was a bit keen in the early stages and was always in the rear division.
**Rousing Thunder** *Official explanation: jockey said gelding finished lame*

## 571 BET DIRECT THROUGH SKY ACTIVE (S) STKS 1m 4f (F)
**3:20** (3:20) (H) 4-Y-0+ **£1,263** (£361; £180) **Stalls** Low

Form RPR

04-2 **1** **Platinum Charmer (IRE)**[7] 517 4-9-0 65 (p) NCallan 3 56
(KARyan) *hld up: smooth hdwy over 3f out: shkn up to chal and swtchd rt wl over 1f out: sn rdn: styd on to ld ins last* **4/9**[1]

02-5 **2** *1/2* **Shatin Special**[14] 455 4-8-9 40 (p) RFfrench 2 50
(GCHChung) *trckd ldr: led over 4f out: rdn along 3f out: drvn over 1f out: hdd ins last: kpt on wl u.p* **7/1**[3]

0-25 **3** *11* **Ipledgeallegiance (USA)**[5] 545 8-9-4 45 ACulhane 5 39
(DWChapman) *trckd ldrs: smooth hdwy to chse ldr 3f out: rdn over 2f out and sn one pce* **9/2**[2]

50-6 **4** *6* **Lapadar (IRE)**[7] 461 5-8-6 50 (p) DFentiman[(7)] 1 25
(JRWeymes) *led: rdn along 1/2-way: hdd over 4f out and sn wknd* **12/1**

60-0 **5** *5* **Behan**[16] 430 5-9-4 30 (v) VHalliday 4 22
(ACrook) *chsd ldng pair: rdn along 1/2-way: wknd 4f out* **40/1**

2m 41.8s (-0.30) **Going Correction** -0.125s/f (Stan)
**WFA** 4 from 5yo+ 4lb **5** Ran SP% **110.1**
Speed ratings: **96,95,88,84,81**CSF £4.21 TOTE £1.50: £1.10, £2.80; EX 2.70.The winner was bought in for 5,000gns.
**Owner** Platinum Racing Club Limited **Bred** F Hinojosa **Trained** Hambleton, N Yorks

**FOCUS**
Not a bad pace for the size of the field. The winner held an outstanding chance on official figures and the overall form looks weak.

**NOTEBOOK**
**Platinum Charmer(IRE)**, in sheepskin cheekpieces for the first time, won a little more easily than the margin suggests. He looks the type who does just enough.
**Shatin Special**tried to kick clear entering the home straight, and plugged on once the favourite took her measure inside the last. She did well considering the tough task she faced at the weights
**Ipledgeallegiance(USA)**has had plenty of experience over this trip without convincing that he really stays.

## 572 LITTLEWOODSCASINO.COM BANDED STKS 6f (F)
**3:50** (3:50) (H) 3-Y-0+ **£1,480** (£423; £211) **Stalls** Low

Form RPR

0-35 **1** **Champagne Rider**[12] 474 8-9-7 40 (e) DarrenWilliams 9 46
(DShaw) *towards rr: gd hdwy 2f out: rdn over 1f out: styd on u.p ins last to ld last 75 yds* **13/2**[3]

-440 **2** *3/4* **Enjoy The Buzz**[8] 509 5-9-7 40 PFitzsimons 11 44
(JMBradley) *midfield: hdwy 2f out: sn rdn and styd on ent last* **16/1**

05-3 **3** *nk* **Bells Boy's**[8] 499 5-9-7 40 (p) GParkin 4 43
(KARyan) *sn led: riden c lear over 1f out: drvn ins last: hdd and no ex last 75 yds* **5/1**[2]

000- **4** *1* **Lively Felix**[123] 5049 7-9-0 40 BSwarbrick[(7)] 6 40
(DGBridgwater) *chsd ldrs: rdn along and outpcd over 2f out: styd on u.p fnl f* **33/1**

00-4 **5** *nk* **Blunham**[8] 499 4-9-7 40 IMongan 16 39
(MCChapman) *chsd ldrs on outer: rdn along over 2f out: kpt on u.p appr last* **16/1**

040- **6** *hd* **Bells Beach (IRE)**[198] 3034 6-9-7 40 RWinston 3 39
(PHowling) *hld up towards rr: nt clr run 3fd out: gd hdwy 2f out: rdn and kpt on appr last: nrst fin* **13/2**[3]

00/5 **7** *3* **Magic Eagle**[17] 421 7-9-2 40 DNolan[(5)] 15 30
(PTMidgley) *cl up: rdn over 2f out: grad wknd* **10/1**

00/- **8** *1/2* **Speedy James (IRE)**[384] 205 8-9-0 40 LTreadwell[(7)] 12 28
(DNicholls) *dwlt: towards rr: hdwy on outer over 2f out: sn rdn and edgd lft over 1f out: kpt on ins last* **9/1**

46-5 **9** *shd* **Mimas Girl**[8] 502 5-9-7 35 (t) JBramhill 10 28
(SRBowring) *dwlt: a rr* **20/1**

0-00 **10** *shd* **Flying Faisal (USA)**[13] 465 6-9-2 40 (b) BReilly[(5)] 14 28
(JMBradley) *towards rr: hdwy on outer 2f out rdn to chse ldrs over 1f out: drvn and no imp ins last* **14/1**

20-0 **11** *2 1/2* **Leonora Truce (IRE)**[17] 425 5-9-7 40 VSlattery 2 20
(RPElliott) *a rr* **9/1**

000- **12** *1 1/2* **Mister Rushby**[152] 4315 4-9-7 40 ACulhane 8 16
(DWChapman) *chsd ldrs: rdn along 1/2-way: sn wknd* **33/1**

0-12 **13** *1 1/2* **Eternal Bloom**[6] 527 6-9-6 35 MLawson[(7)] 13 17
(MBrittain) *dwlt: a rr* **7/2**[1]

0-00 **14** *2* **Mesmerised**[6] 530 4-9-7 40 AnnStokell 7 5
(MissAStokell) *a bhd* **66/1**

00-0 **15** *2* **Precious Freedom**[16] 433 4-9-7 40 (b[1]) JEdmunds 5 —
(JBalding) *cl up: rdn 2f out: wknd qckly appr last* **28/1**

00/0 **16** *dist* **Deal In Facts**[6] 527 5-9-7 35 TWilliams 1 —
(CNKellett) *chsd ldrs to 1/2-way: sn wknd* **50/1**

1m 17.27s (0.47) **Going Correction** -0.125s/f (Stan) **16** Ran SP% **130.6**
Speed ratings: **91,90,89,88,87 87,83,82,82,82 79,77,75,72,70** —CSF £107.07 TOTE £6.80: £2.30, £4.80, £1.80; EX 105.30 Place 6 £106.96, Place 5 £32.98.
**Owner** The Whiteman Partnership **Bred** Ridgebarn Farm Stud, Mrs L Jenkins And Mrs T She
**Trained** Averham, Notts
■ Stewards Enquiry : B Reilly three-day ban: careless riding (Jan 31, Feb 2-3)

**FOCUS**
This looked competitive for such a low-grade event, but the winning time was pedestrian, even for a contest like this. The form is poor.

**NOTEBOOK**
**Champagne Rider**comes from a yard in fine form at present. Having a rare run at six furlongs, he stayed on to come out top in something of a bunch finish, giving the impression he would not mind a return to seven.
**Enjoy The Buzz**, who remains a maiden, is another who would appreciate a seventh furlong.
**Bells Boy's**ran a fair race over a trip a little beyond his best.
**Lively Felix**, formerly trained by David Arbuthnot, was having his first run since September. That was over ten furlongs, and he found this too sharp.
**Blunham**had tackled the minimum trip on his last two starts but shaped on this occasion as if seven furlongs might be ideal.
**Bells Beach(IRE)**, never nearer on this first run since July, was formerly trained by Tony Newcombe.
**Magic Eagle**used up too much energy in the early stages when taking up a prominent position from his outside berth.
**Eternal Bloom**was involved in some early scrimmaging and could never get into the race from her wide draw.
**Precious Freedom**was still in second spot at the furlong pole before weakening rapidly. He has shown a little more on his last two starts and could be worth trying over five furlongs.
JR

# 553 LINGFIELD (L-H)
### Wednesday, January 21

**OFFICIAL GOING: Standard**

## 573 LITTLEWOODS BET DIRECT H'CAP (DIV I) 6f (P)
**12:40** (12:41) (F) (0-60,65) 3-Y-0+ **£2,968** (£848; £424) **Stalls** Low

Form RPR

53-1 **1** **Nearly A Fool**[14] 469 6-9-9 **55** (v) NPollard 2 68
(GGMargarson) *chsd ldng pair: led over 1f out: rdn out* **9/2**[3]

-211 **2** *1 1/4* **Tayif**[7] 526 8-9-12 **65** 6ex (t) SJDonohoe[(7)] 10 74
(AndrewReid) *hld up in tch: stdy hdwy 1/2-way: styd on to chse wnr fnl f* **5/2**[1]

0-41 **3** *3/4* **Double M**[4] 560 7-9-11 **57** 6ex (v) NCallan 4 64
(MrsLRichards) *hld up: hdwy 1/2-way: r.o fnl f: nvr nrr* **8/1**

4-32 **4** *1* **Mayzin (IRE)**[11] 491 4-9-8 **54** (p) EAhern 7 58
(RMFlower) *led after 1f: rdna and hdd over 1f out: one pce* **4/1**[2]

0-43 **5** *1/2* **Sabana (IRE)**[7] 530 6-8-13 **45** (b) PFitzsimons 3 48
(JMBradley) *s.i.s: hdwy over 1f out: r.o: nvr nrr* **12/1**

60-2 **6** *2* **Torrent**[16] 443 9-8-13 **45** (b) ACulhane 13 42
(DWChapman) *in rr: hdwy over 1f out: r.o wl fnl f* **16/1**

00-4 **7** *3 1/2* **Silver Mascot**[7] 530 5-8-13 **45** DaleGibson 9 31
(RHollinshead) *mid-div: hung rt and wknd over 1f out* **25/1**

00-0 **8** *1/2* **Loch Laird**[15] 453 9-9-0 **49** LPKeniry[(3)] 11 34
(MMadgwick) *outpcd in rr: mde sme late hdwy* **12/1**

40-5 **9** *1 3/4* **Komena**[7] 519 6-8-12 **47** LisaJones[(3)] 6 26
(JWPayne) *outpcd and a bhd* **25/1**

-301 **10** *1 1/2* **Attorney**[7] 530 6-9-0 **51** 6ex (v) THamilton[(5)] 12 26
(DShaw) *mid-div: effrt on outside over 2f out: sn btn* **20/1**

00-0 **11** *1/2* **Master Rattle**[11] 491 5-9-4 **50** VSlattery 1 23
(JaneSouthcombe) *led for 1f: clr w ldr tl wknd qckly appr fnl f* **50/1**

300- **12** *2* **Ellamyte**[68] 5996 4-9-2 **48** (v) SRighton 8 15
(DGBridgwater) *chsd ldrs: sn rdn: wknd 1/2-way* **66/1**

005- **13** *3* **Regal Song (IRE)**[79] 5909 8-9-12 **58** (b) JFanning 14 16
(TJEtherington) *slowly away: a struggling in rr* **20/1**

1m 12.58s (-0.34) **Going Correction** +0.025s/f (Slow) **13** Ran SP% **119.8**
Speed ratings: **103,101,100,99,98 95,91,90,88,86 85,82,78**CSF £14.74 CT £92.36 TOTE £8.10: £2.50, £1.30, £2.90; EX 12.90.
**Owner** J Burns **Bred** Mrs S Shaw **Trained** Newmarket, Suffolk

**FOCUS**
Just a moderate handicap in which both Mayzin and Master Rattle went off at a very fast pace. The form looks solid, and the first two well handicapped on previous form.

**NOTEBOOK**
**Nearly A Fool** had never previously won over six furlongs, but he showed himself at the top of his game by following up his recent success over seven furlongs. He goes well for Neil Pollard and could well complete the hat-trick whilst in this form.
**Tayif**, who has been in cracking form since joining Andrew Reid, was given every chance on this hat-trick bid and ran well.
**Double M**, 3lb wrong at the weights under the 6lb penalty for his success over five furlongs on his previous start, continues in good form but just found a couple too good.
**Mayzin(IRE)**, dropping back a furlong in trip, showed bags, but probably ended up going too fast. He showed enough pace to suggest he will be effective over five furlongs.
**Sabana(IRE)**, racing on Polytrack for the first time, and with the blinkers back on, continues on a long losing run.
**Silver Mascot** *Official explanation: jockey said gelding had hung right-handed*

## 574 PRESS INTERACTIVE TO BET DIRECT MAIDEN STKS 6f (P)
**1:10** (1:11) (D) 3-Y-0+ **£3,779** (£1,163; £581; £290) **Stalls** Low

Form RPR

\- **1** **Aleutian** 4-9-10 JPSpencer 3 76+
(DRLoder) *mde virtually all: shkn up to go clr over 1f out: eased fnl 100yds: promising* **1/3**[1]

0- **2** 3 ½ **Nossenko (USA)**[23] 6248 3-8-3 ............ EAhern 8 50
(JNoseda) *trckd ldrs: kpt on to go 2nd ins fnl f* **8/1**[2]
**3** ¾ **Pickle** 3-8-3 ............ RFfrench 11 48
(SCWilliams) *mid-div: hdwy 2f out: r.o to go 3rd wl ins fnl f* **33/1**
06- **4** ½ **Heartbeat**[205] 2860 3-8-3 ............ DaleGibson 1 46
(PJMcbride) *chsd ldrs: pushed along 1/2-way: styd on ins fnl f* **50/1**
00- **5** hd **Maggie Maquette**[35] 6209 4-9-5 ............ DSweeney 10 45
(WSKittow) *w ldrs: chsd wnr 2f out: tl wknd ins fnl f* **33/1**
5- **6** 2 ½ **Horizontal (USA)**[235] 2002 4-9-10 ............ MTebbutt 6 43
(HJCollingridge) *towards rr: mde sme late hdwy: will do bttr* **16/1**
**7** ¾ **Reckless Fred** 5-9-3 ............ DerekNolan(7) 4 41
(MissKMGeorge) *a towards rr: sme late hdwy* **100/1**
3-0 **8** hd **Starcross Venture**[16] 438 3-8-2 ow4 ............ THamilton(5) 7 39
(RAFahey) *mid-div: rdn 1/2-way: outpcd 2f out* **10/1**[3]
5- **9** 2 ½ **Oboe**[21] 6266 3-8-3 ............ JFanning 13 28
(RCharlton) *sn chsd ldrs: wknd approachinf fnl f* **12/1**
**10** 1 **Imperial Wizard** 3-8-8 ............ ADaly 5 30
(MDIUsher) *a in rr* **25/1**
00- **11** 1 **Hazewind**[120] 5139 3-8-8 ............(t) JoannaBadger 14 27
(PDEvans) *racd wd: bhd fr 1/2-way* **33/1**
/56- **12** 2 ½ **Tanaffus**[165] 3992 4-9-10 70 ............ ACulhane 2 19
(DWChapman) *a outpcd in rr* **33/1**
0-0 **13** hd **Backlash**[11] 489 3-8-4 ow1 ............ SWhitworth 9 14
(AWCarroll) *slowly away: a bhd* **20/1**
0 **14** 5 **Jaycee Star (IRE)**[11] 489 3-8-3 ............ PDoe 12 —
(DFlood) *plld hrd: w ldrs: wknd over 2f out* **50/1**

1m 13.96s (1.04) **Going Correction** +0.025s/f (Slow)
**WFA** 3 from 4yo+ 16lb **14** Ran SP% **134.1**
Speed ratings: **94,89,88,87,87 84,83,82,79,78 76,73,73,66**CSF £3.97 TOTE £1.30: £1.10, £1.70, £9.60; EX 4.40.
**Owner** Jumeirah Racing **Bred** Cliveden Stud Ltd **Trained** Newmarket, Suffolk

**FOCUS**
A modest winning time and the race itself was not strong, but Aleutian made a highly-impressive debut and should be capable of going on to better things.

**NOTEBOOK**
**Aleutian** is a 200,000gns Sheikh Mohammed cast-off, half-brother to a ten furlong winner in Italy, out of a six furlong juvenile winner. His debut had been delayed by a stalls problem, but he gave little trouble and justified strong market support in style. He was eased down close home, and looked value for at least double the winning margin. He should hold his own in a higher grade.
**Nossenko(USA)**, very disappointing when sent off the 9/4 favourite for her racecourse debut over course and distance, ran better this time but will need to improve again to win a maiden.
**Pickle**, who had her racecourse debut delayed by a hip injury, shaped well enough in third, but is probably going to come into her own when handicapped.
**Heartbeat**, racing for the first time since June, ran respectably and will find easier opportunities now she qualifies for a handicap mark.
**Maggie Maquette** should also find easier opportunities now she qualifies for a handicap mark.
**Horizontal(USA)**ran a most eye-catching race, making late headway without being at all knocked about. It transpired he had torn a shoe off and finished lame. *Official explanation: vet said gelding tore off a left fore shoe and finished lame*

## 575 BET DIRECT ON SKY ACTIVE CLAIMING STKS 7f (P)
**1:40** (1:41) (F) 4-Y-0+ **£2,982** (£852; £426) **Stalls** Low

Form RPR
02-2 **1** **Ripple Effect**[7] 519 4-8-7 67 ............(t) BReilly(5) 5 71
(CADwyer) *a.p and gng wl: led jst ins fnl f: sn clr: comf* **6/1**[3]
000- **2** 1 ¾ **Power Bird (IRE)**[35] 6205 4-8-0 62 ............ JMackay 2 55
(DFlood) *in tch: hdwy on ins over 1f out: edgd rt but r.o to go 2nd ins fnl f* **14/1**
64-0 **3** 1 **Pheckless**[6] 544 5-8-13 69 ............ SCarson 3 65
(RFJohnsonHoughton) *s.i.s: hld up towards rr: nt clr run 2f out: hdwy over 1f out: r.o wl fnl f* **7/2**[1]
04-6 **4** ½ **The Gaikwar (IRE)**[15] 448 5-8-9 66 ............(b) CCatlin 6 60
(NEBerry) *hld up: n.m.r over 2f out: hdwy over 1f out: r.o fnl f* **4/1**[2]
40-6 **5** hd **Foolish Thought (IRE)**[11] 491 4-8-2 58 ow4 ............ THamilton(5) 13 57
(RAFahey) *a.p: led 3f out: hdd jst ins fnl f: wknd* **8/1**
02-0 **6** hd **Superchief**[15] 448 9-9-7 65 ............(bt) EAhern 15 71
(MissBSanders) *hld up: hdwy on outside 1/2-way: chsd ldr 2f out tl one pce fnl f* **7/1**
02-0 **7** nk **Espada (IRE)**[15] 448 8-8-9 65 ............ SWKelly 1 58
(JAOsborne) *led for 4f: wknd fnl f* **6/1**[3]
10-0 **8** 1 ¾ **Warlingham (IRE)**[9] 509 6-8-9 54 ............ VSlattery 9 54
(PHowling) *t.k.h: prom tl wknd 2f out* **14/1**
0-03 **9** hd **Muqtadi (IRE)**[7] 519 6-8-6 51 ............ LEnstone(3) 16 53
(MQuinn) *slowly away: rdn 1/2-way: nvr on terms* **20/1**
0-00 **10** 3 **Dunedin Rascal**[7] 519 7-7-12 62 ............(b) LiamJones(7) 4 42
(EAWheeler) *hld up: a in rr* **33/1**
560- **11** ¾ **Naughty Girl (IRE)**[22] 6261 4-8-9 70 ............ SJDonohoe(7) 7 51
(PDEvans) *mid-div: rdn 3f out: sn btn* **33/1**
60-0 **12** ½ **Original Sin (IRE)**[11] 495 4-8-4 46 ............ LisaJones(3) 12 41
(SDow) *in tch: hrd rdn 2f out: wknd sn after* **66/1**
000- **13** ¾ **Squeaky**[56] 6073 7-8-3 56 ............(p) DerekNolan(7) 14 42
(MissKMGeorge) *sn outpcd in rr* **100/1**
0-00 **14** shd **Island Star (IRE)**[7] 519 4-8-3 45 ............ PDoe 8 35
(SDow) *chsd ldr tl wknd qckly 2f out* **100/1**

1m 25.65s (-0.35) **Going Correction** +0.025s/f (Slow) **14** Ran SP% **121.9**
Speed ratings: **103,101,99,99,99 98,98,96,96,92 91,91,90,90**CSF £83.66 TOTE £6.60: £2.40, £3.10, £1.60; EX 153.00.Pheckless was claimed by Elizabeth Batchelor for £10,000; Power Bird was claimed by Mr B.R. Johnson for £6,000.
**Owner** Miss Lilo Blum **Bred** Littleton Stud **Trained** Newmarket, Suffolk

**FOCUS**
A modest claimer in which the result was pretty much in line with previous form. The time was fair for the grade.

**NOTEBOOK**
**Ripple Effect**, a beaten favourite at 7/4 behind Hurricane Coast in a similar race over six furlongs here on her previous start, did not have to face such a progressive rival this time and won in good style. The Handicapper is likely to make her pay for this, but further claiming races will remain an option.
**Power Bird(IRE)**, best in at the weights, ran well on this drop back from ten furlongs but was always being held by the winner.
**Pheckless**, taking a significant drop in grade, finished well from off the pace, but didn't enjoy the best of runs and appeared to get going just a little bit too late.
**The Gaikwar(IRE)** has not won since August 2002, but he ran respectably on this drop in grade.
**Foolish Thought(IRE)**, dropped in grade and with the visor left off this time, needed an early reminder from the saddle. Still a maiden, he does not look easy to win with and probably got to the front too soon on this occasion.

## 576 LITTLEWOODS BET DIRECT H'CAP (DIV II) 6f (P)
**2:10** (2:10) (F) (0-60,58) 3-Y-0+ **£2,961** (£846; £423) **Stalls** Low

Form RPR
62-1 **1** **Prince Aaron (IRE)**[15] 453 4-9-12 58 ............ GCarter 11 79+
(CNAllen) *hld up in rr: hdwy after 2f: led gng wl over 1f out: pushed clr comf* **9/4**[1]
00-5 **2** 2 **A Teen**[14] 465 6-9-3 49 ............ JPSpencer 13 58
(PHowling) *hld up in rr: hdwy on outside 2f out: edgerd rt appr fnl f: r.o wl to go 2nd ins fnl f* **9/1**
00-1 **3** ¾ **Hout Bay**[6] 540 7-9-6 57 6ex ............ THamilton(5) 10 64
(RAFahey) *hld up in tch: rdn over 1f out: r.o wl fnl f* **11/2**[3]
5-21 **4** 1 **Lord Melbourne (IRE)**[6] 536 5-9-5 51 6ex ............ SWKelly 1 55
(JAOsborne) *a.p: rdn and ev ch appr fnl f: kpt on one pce* **7/2**[2]
0-13 **5** hd **Italian Mist (FR)**[9] 509 5-9-4 50 ............(e) GFaulkner 9 53
(JulianPoulton) *trckd ldr: led over 2f out: hdd over 1f out: nt qckn* **25/1**
60-0 **6** ¾ **Long Weekend (IRE)**[7] 530 6-8-13 45 ............(v) DarrenWilliams 2 46
(DShaw) *hld up: rdn over 2f out: hmpd ins fnl f: r.o nr fin* **25/1**
0-26 **7** nk **Soaked**[4] 560 11-9-7 53 ............(b) ACulhane 7 53
(DWChapman) *hld up: effrt over 1f out: one pce fnl f* **14/1**
623- **8** hd **Heathyardsblessing (IRE)**[33] 6217 7-9-0 46 ............ NCallan 4 45
(RHollinshead) *in tch whn hmpd over 2f out: hdwy whn short of room appr fnl f: kpt on ins* **33/1**
500- **9** 1 ¼ **Tamarella (IRE)**[53] 6092 4-9-8 54 ............ MartinDwyer 12 50
(GGMargarson) *prom tl wknd ins fnl f* **16/1**
06-2 **10** ¾ **Tripti (IRE)**[14] 465 4-9-2 48 ............ NPollard 8 41
(JJBridger) *in tch: effrt 2f out: wknd ins fnl f* **11/1**
00-0 **11** hd **Patandon Girl (IRE)**[15] 453 4-9-2 48 ............ RLappin 14 41
(ABailey) *a in rr* **25/1**
000- **12** 1 ¼ **Lydia's Look (IRE)**[168] 3895 7-8-13 45 ............ JFanning 3 34
(TJEtherington) *prom on ins: rdn 2f out: wknd appr fnl f* **20/1**
200- **13** 5 **Illustrious Duke**[159] 4165 6-9-0 49 ............ LisaJones(3) 5 23
(MMullineaux) *led: hdd over 2f out: wknd qckly* **25/1**

1m 13.31s (0.39) **Going Correction** +0.025s/f (Slow) **13** Ran SP% **122.3**
Speed ratings: **98,95,94,93,92 91,91,91,89,88 88,86,79**CSF £21.46 CT £101.50 TOTE £3.50: £2.20, £2.90, £2.00; EX 41.70.
**Owner** Black Star Racing **Bred** Peter Charles And J R Bamforth **Trained** Newmarket, Suffolk
■ Stewards Enquiry : G Faulkner one-day ban: careless riding (Feb 2)

**FOCUS**
The winning time was 0.73 seconds slower than the first division and this was just a moderate race. However, the form looks solid for the grade and the winner is improving.

**NOTEBOOK**
**Prince Aaron(IRE)** has really found his form since being dropped back to six furlongs and he made it two from three over this course and distance with a very comfortable success. He must be kept on the right side of whilst in this form.
**A Teen** finished well from off the pace, but the winner was long gone by the time he hit full stride. He is on a nice mark compared to his turf rating.
**Hout Bay**, 3lb wrong under the 6lb penalty for his success over five furlongs at Southwell last time, ran well enough and can have no real excuses.
**Lord Melbourne(IRE)**, with a 6lb penalty for his win in a regional race, found this much tougher.
**Italian Mist(FR)** can have no real excuses.
**Long Weekend(IRE)** may have finished closer with better luck in running in the straight.
**Patandon Girl(IRE)** *Official explanation: jockey said filly was never travelling*

## 577 BET DIRECT INTERACTIVE H'CAP 1m 2f (P)
**2:40** (2:40) (D) (0-85,83) 4-Y-0+ **£4,550** (£1,400; £700; £350) **Stalls** Low

Form RPR
623- **1** **Swift Tango (IRE)**[91] 5709 4-9-11 **82** ............ EAhern 8 93
(EALDunlop) *hld up in tch: shkn up over 1f out: r.o wl fnl f to ld last 50yds* **14/1**
404- **2** nk **Northside Lodge (IRE)**[50] 6117 6-10-0 **83** ............ PDoe 5 94
(PWHarris) *a.p: led over 2f out: clr over 1f out: r.o fnl f: hdd fnl 50yds* **6/1**[1]
310- **3** 1 ½ **Paragon Of Virtue**[35] 6208 7-9-10 **79** ............ JFanning 10 87
(PMitchell) *in tch: rdn and kpt on fnl f* **10/1**
310- **4** ½ **Dower House**[50] 6117 9-9-12 **81** ............ FLynch 6 88
(AndrewTurnell) *hld up: hdwy on ins whn short of room and swtchd rt over 1f out: r.o wl fnl f: nvr nrr* **16/1**
415- **5** hd **Ryan's Future (IRE)**[23] 6255 4-9-4 **80** ............ NChalmers(5) 4 87
(JAkehurst) *slowly away: rdn and hdwy 3f out: nt qckn ins fnl f* **7/1**[2]
043- **6** 1 ½ **Silken Brief (IRE)**[22] 6263 5-9-8 **77** ............(t) WRyan 1 81
(DJDaly) *trckd ldr: rdn over 1f out: one pce fnl f* **10/1**
000- **7** ¾ **Scotty's Future (IRE)**[123] 5059 6-10-0 **83** ............ JPSpencer 12 86
(DRLoder) *in rr: pushed along 4f out: effrt over 1f out: nvr on terms* **15/2**[3]
43-0 **8** 1 **Invader**[19] 410 8-9-13 **82** ............(b) IMongan 3 83
(CEBrittain) *led tl hdd over 2f out: wknd ent fnl f* **10/1**
61-3 **9** 2 **Labrett**[11] 494 7-10-0 **83** ............(t) MFenton 13 80
(MissGayKelleway) *hld up in midid-ivision: nvr on terms* **16/1**
301- **10** 2 ½ **Sangiovese**[39] 6178 5-9-8 **80** ............ LFletcher(3) 7 73
(HMorrison) *trckd ldr tl over 2f out: wknd over 1f out* **6/1**[1]
35-1 **11** 1 **Jack Of Trumps (IRE)**[14] 463 4-9-7 **78** ............ MartinDwyer 11 69
(GWragg) *prom: rdn over 2f out: wknd wl over 1f out* **7/1**[2]
51-2 **12** shd **J R Stevenson (USA)**[11] 494 8-9-6 **80** ............ MSavage(5) 9 71
(MWigham) *in tch: rdn 3f out: sn btn* **7/1**[2]
024- **13** ½ **Travelling Band (IRE)**[26] 2917 6-9-6 **78** ............ LPKeniry(3) 14 68
(AMBalding) *a in rr* **33/1**
/06- **14** 7 **Tanaji**[53] 1908 5-9-9 **78** ............ CCatlin 2 55
(PRWebber) *in tch tl rdn and wknd wl over 1f out* **66/1**

2m 6.38s (-1.01) **Going Correction** +0.025s/f (Slow)
**WFA** 4 from 5yo+ 2lb **14** Ran SP% **128.0**
Speed ratings: **105,104,103,103,103 101,101,100,98,96 96,95,95,89**CSF £101.78 CT £911.50 TOTE £12.40: £4.50, £3.60, £3.70; EX 180.70.
**Owner** Khalifa Sultan **Bred** Killeen Castle Stud **Trained** Newmarket, Suffolk

**FOCUS**
A decent, competitive handicap, run at a fair pace. The form looks solid.

**NOTEBOOK**
**Swift Tango(IRE)**, returning from a 91-day break, and with the visor left off, took advantage of an All-Weather mark 6lb lower than that of his turf rating. He quickened up nicely when asked and, although he only had a neck to spare at the line, he did what he had to and looks capable of holding his own in better company over this course and distance.
**Northside Lodge(IRE)** goes well round here and ran his race once again under a good, enterprising ride from Doe, who took a couple of lengths out of the field when kicking on over two out. He is always one to respect at Lingfield.
**Paragon Of Virtue** can have no excuses, he was simply unable to match the winner's turn of foot.
**Dower House** did not get the clearest of runs when looking to make his move and he may have grabbed a place with better luck in running.
**Ryan's Future(IRE)** did not appear to have any excuses.
**Scotty's Future(IRE)**was having his first race for a new stable and making his all weather debut.

**Sangiovese**, 17lb higher than when bolting up over a mile at Southwell last time, appeared to have every chance. This does not seem his ideal surface.

## 578 BETDIRECT.CO.UK H'CAP 5f (P)
3:10 (3:10) (E) (0-75,76) 3-Y-O+ £3,370 (£963; £481) Stalls High

Form RPR

1113 1 **Hurricane Coast**$^{4}$ [556] 5-9-6 65 ....................(b) PDoe 10 81
(DFlood) *s.i.s: gd hdwy 2f out: led jst ins fnl f: edgd lft: r.o wl* 15/8$^{1}$

00-0 2 1 3/4 **Prince Of Blues (IRE)**$^{13}$ [476] 6-9-5 64 ....................(p) SWKelly 1 73
(MMullineaux) *led tl rdn: edgd lft and hdd jst ins fnl f: nt pce of wnr* 20/1

41-6 3 nk **Lady Pekan**$^{13}$ [480] 5-9-1 63 ....................(b) FPFerris(3) 8 71
(PSMcentee) *trckd ldr: short of room and swtchd rt appr fnl f: r.o u.p* 16/1

-032 4 1/2 **Currency**$^{7}$ [526] 7-10-0 73 .................... EAhern 2 79
(JMBradley) *s.i.s: hdwy whn short of room appr fnl f: swtchd rt: r.o wl* 5/2$^{2}$

0-11 5 hd **The Fisio**$^{6}$ [540] 4-9-12 76 6ex .................... NChalmers(5) 7 81
(AMBalding) *in tch tl outpcd 1/2-way: r.o ins fnl f* 11/2$^{3}$

2-23 6 3/4 **Playtime Blue**$^{7}$ [526] 4-9-2 61 .................... GBaker 5 63
(KRBurke) *chsd ldrs: rdn 2f out: one pce fnl f* 7/1

06-6 7 3/4 **Our Fred**$^{15}$ [454] 7-9-9 68 ....................(b) IMongan 9 67
(TGMills) *prom: sn rdn: wknd ins fnl f* 16/1

0-00 8 hd **Taboor (IRE)**$^{7}$ [526] 6-9-8 67 ....................(b) NCallan 6 65
(JWPayne) *in rr: c wd into st: nvr on terms* 14/1

03-0 9 shd **Teyaar**$^{7}$ [526] 8-9-4 63 ....................(b) PMcCabe 3 61
(MrsNMacauley) *in rr whn hmpd over 1f out: nvr on terms* 33/1

10-3 10 1/2 **Count Cougar (USA)**$^{6}$ [543] 4-9-2 61 .................... RLappin 4 57
(SPGriffiths) *in tch: rdn 1/2-way: wknd qckly ins fnl f* 25/1

59.42 secs (-0.36) **Going Correction** +0.025s/f (Slow) 10 Ran SP% 121.2
Speed ratings: **103,100,99,98,98 97,96,95,95,94**CSF £47.15 CT £501.82 TOTE £3.30: £1.90, £5.60, £3.20; EX 90.40.
**Owner** Mrs Ruth M Serrell **Bred** Ian H Wills **Trained** Upper Lambourn, Berks
■ Stewards Enquiry : S W Kelly 16-day ban (takes into account previous offences, 4 days deferred): careless riding (Feb 13-25)

**FOCUS**
Just a modest handicap, but several in-form sprinters, and a good pace from the off.

**NOTEBOOK**
**Hurricane Coast**, 10lb well in at the weights, continued his terrific run of form and confirmed that his third in a conditions race over course and distance on his previous start was no fluke with a smooth success. He appears well suited by this track and surface.
**Prince Of Blues(IRE)**, with the cheekpieces back on, absolutely burst out of the gates and showed real signs of a return to form. He had no chance with the well-handicapped winner but stuck to his task and, not so badly weighted himself these days, he could be one to keep an eye on for a similar race.
**Lady Pekan** showed herself just as effective on this surface as Fibresand and ran well. She was squeezed up a furlong out, but it did not appear to effect her finishing position.
**Currency** had to wait for a run and would have been closer with a clearer passage. He is in good form.
**The Fisio**, 2lb wrong at the weights under his penalty, had no obvious excuse.

## 579 BET DIRECT THROUGH SKY ACTIVE (S) STKS 2m (P)
3:40 (3:40) (G) 4-Y-O+ £2,548 (£728; £364) Stalls Low

Form RPR

/05- 1 **Sungio**$^{23}$ [6254] 6-9-4 53 .................... DaleGibson 2 54
(BGPowell) *in tch: hdwy to go 2nd 5f out: led over 2f out: pushed out fnl f* 4/1$^{3}$

50-0 2 2 **Radiant Bride**$^{14}$ [467] 4-8-6 40 ....................(p) DarrenWilliams 4 47
(KRBurke) *hld up in tch: hdwy 4f out: rdn to go 2nd over 1f out: no imp fnl f* 11/1

40-0 3 2 1/2 **Khuzdar (IRE)**$^{17}$ [432] 5-9-2 40 .................... BO'Neill(5) 5 54
(ABailey) *slowly away: wl in rr tl hdwy over 2f out: hung lft appr fnl f: wnt 3rd ins fnl f* 7/1

33-3 4 3/4 **Mysterium**$^{5}$ [551] 10-9-4 40 ....................(v) IMongan 1 48
(NPLittmoden) *mde most tl rdn and hdd over 2f out: wknd ins fnl f* 3/1$^{2}$

500/ 5 shd **Neptune**$^{309}$ [5756] 8-9-4 40 .................... RSmith 6 48
(JCFox) *t.k.h: hld up: hdwy over 5f out: one pce ins fnl 2f* 20/1

663- 6 11 **Blue Savanna**$^{22}$ [6257] 4-8-11 48 ....................(b) EAhern 10 34
(JGPortman) *trckd ldrs tl wknd qckly over 2f out* 11/2

000/ 7 11 **Philosophic**$^{553}$ [3078] 10-9-4 40 .................... SCarson 9 21
(MrsLCJewell) *disp ld early: trckd ldr to 5f out: wknd sn after* 50/1

0-53 8 4 **Roppongi Dancer**$^{13}$ [471] 5-8-6 30 ....................(bt) StephanieHollinshead(7) 8 11
(MrsNMacauley) *t.k.h: in tch tl rdn 6f out: sn bhd* 50/1

0/ 9 1/2 **Bamford Castle (IRE)**$^{453}$ [5458] 9-9-1 75 ....................(p) J-PGuillambert(3) 3 16
(RFord) *in rr: rdn over 4f out: nvr on terms* 9/4$^{1}$

3m 30.89s (2.31) **Going Correction** +0.025s/f (Slow) 9 Ran SP% 120.7
**WFA** 4 from 5yo+ 7lb
Speed ratings: **95,94,92,92,92 86,81,79,79**CSF £48.04 TOTE £5.90: £1.50, £3.80, £2.30; EX 53.80.There was no bid for the winner.
**Owner** Mrs Rachel A Powell **Bred** Baldernock Bloodstock Ltd **Trained** Morestead, Hants

**FOCUS**
A modest winning time, even for a seller, and the form is poor.

**NOTEBOOK**
**Sungio**, the second best in on official figures, just about got this two mile trip and was basically too good for his rivals. Connections will be doing well to find a race as weak next time.
**Radiant Bride** was the only one to chase the winner, but was readily held.
**Khuzdar(IRE)** looked a very hard ride, carrying his head to one side when put under pressure. He did not give his followers a run for their money and is not one to follow.
**Mysterium** did not appear to like being out in front for so long, but that leaves connections with a dilemma as he no longer has a turn of foot.
**Bamford Castle(IRE)**, well clear on the figures, had a long absence to overcome and has not shown anything for a long time. *Official explanation: jockey said gelding was never travelling*

## 580 FREE £25 BONUS @ LITTLEWOODSCASINO.COM APPRENTICE H'CAP 1m (P)
4:10 (4:10) (E) (0-75,72) 3-Y-O £3,262 (£932; £466) Stalls High

Form RPR

56-0 1 **Trevian**$^{14}$ [462] 3-8-11 65 .................... SJDonohoe(3) 2 71+
(SCWilliams) *mid-div: hdwy over 2f out: led over 1f out: r.o wl* 8/1

055- 2 1/2 **Archerfield (IRE)**$^{77}$ [5923] 3-8-11 67 .................... HGemberlu(5) 5 72+
(JWHills) *a in tch: wnt 2nd over 1f out: r.o but no imp ins fnl f* 20/1

40-3 3 2 **Resplendent King (USA)**$^{14}$ [462] 3-9-7 72 .................... MSavage 9 72
(TGMills) *mid-div: rdn and hdwy over 2f out: kpt on one pce fnl f* 5/2$^{1}$

600- 4 3 1/2 **Big Bad Burt**$^{70}$ [5977] 3-8-6 64 ....................(v$^{1}$) KBowman(7) 3 56
(MJWallace) *slowly away: hld up wl in rr: flashed tail u.p over 1f out: r.o ins fnl f: nvr nrr* 7/2$^{3}$

51-2 5 1/2 **St Savarin (FR)**$^{11}$ [493] 3-9-2 72 .................... DFentiman(5) 4 63
(JRBest) *led after 1f: hdd over 1f out: wknd fnl f* 3/1$^{2}$

00-5 6 1 1/2 **Fubos**$^{18}$ [415] 3-8-5 61 ....................(v) MHalford(5) 1 48
(JulianPoulton) *w ldr: hung rt and bmpd over 2f out: werakened over 1f out* 10/1

000- 7 3/4 **Morning Hawk (USA)**$^{82}$ [5845] 3-8-1 52 .................... RThomas 6 38
(JSMoore) *outpcd in rr: rdn 1/2-way: nvr on terms* 50/1

36-0 8 3 **Gayle Storm (IRE)**$^{14}$ [462] 3-8-4 58 .................... RoryMoore(3) 7 37
(CTinkler) *slowly away: a bhd* 7/1

000- 9 5 **Parallel Lines (IRE)**$^{111}$ [5323] 3-8-5 56 .................... HayleyTurner 10 23
(PDEvans) *led for 1f: rdn anwknd over 2f out* 25/1

064- 10 20 **Ricky Martan**$^{236}$ [1964] 3-9-0 70 .................... DerekNolan(5) 8 —
(GCBravery) *chsd ldrs tl rdn and wknd 1/2-way: virtually p.u ins fnl f* 25/1

1m 40.21s (0.70) **Going Correction** +0.025s/f (Slow) 10 Ran SP% 122.9
Speed ratings: **97,96,94,91,90 89,88,85,80,60**CSF £159.50 CT £530.65 TOTE £12.40: £3.30, £4.10, £1.60; EX 168.50 Place 6 £29.32, Place 5 £18.91.
**Owner** The Little Trev Partnership **Bred** L A C Ashby **Trained** Newmarket, Suffolk

**FOCUS**
Just a modest handicap, although the front two are unexposed and finished clear of a fair yardstick in Resplendent King.

**NOTEBOOK**
**Trevian**, 5lb lower than when second last on his handicap debut here on his previous start, was ridden differently and landed a bit of a touch. He was always holding the runner-up, but may need to improve to defy a rise in the weights. *Official explanation: trainer said, regarding the improved form shown, gelding had benefited from the step up in trip and may have benefited from being held up on this occasion*
**Archerfield(IRE)**, stepping up to a mile on her handicap debut, was pushed wide on the home turn but pulled clear of all bar the winner, who was always just holding her. This was a good effort and there may be a similar race in her.
**Resplendent King(USA)**, third over seven furlongs here last time, failed to build on that effort on this trip up in trip.
**Big Bad Burt**, stepping up in trip in the first time visor for this handicap debut, was supported in the market but was given plenty to do and never looked like justifying the confidence.
**St Savarin(FR)** was disappointing and may not truly get a mile.
T/Plt: £29.00 to a £1 stake. Pool: £35,301.00. 886.75 winning tickets. T/Qpdt: £16.60 to a £1 stake. Pool: £2,811.00. 124.60 winning tickets. JS

# 567 SOUTHWELL (L-H)
Thursday, January 22

**OFFICIAL GOING: Standard**
There appeared to be no significant track bias at this meeting, and the ground was riding faster than the official description.
Wind: fresh across Weather: raining

## 581 PRESS INTERACTIVE TO BET DIRECT AMATEUR RIDERS' H'CAP (DIV I) 1m 4f (F)
12:40 (12:40) (G) (0-60,60) 4-Y-O+ £2,576 (£736; £368) Stalls Low

Form RPR

1-12 1 **Delta Force**$^{16}$ [456] 5-11-2 58 .................... StaceyRenwick(5) 2 70
(PABlockley) *s.i.s: plld hrd and sn prom: led 10f out: styd on wl* 10/3$^{2}$

16-4 2 1 3/4 **Fight The Feeling**$^{10}$ [505] 6-10-13 55 ....................(v) MissJCWilliams(5) 6 64
(JWUnett) *sn pushed along and prom: outpcd 3f out: rallied over 1f out: kpt on* 5/1

5-21 3 1/2 **Mr Smithers Jones**$^{10}$ [501] 4-11-0 55 5ex .................... MrSWalker 9 63
(SCWilliams) *hld up: hdwy over 4f out: rdn and ev ch over 1f out: styd on same pce* 11/4$^{1}$

325- 4 5 **Jade Star (USA)**$^{155}$ [4284] 4-10-7 48 .................... MissEJJones 8 49
(MissGayKelleway) *chsd ldrs: rdn and ev ch over 1f out: wknd ins fnl f* 20/1

-004 5 3 1/2 **Western Command (GER)**$^{10}$ [497] 8-9-7 30 .................... MrsMMorris 7 26
(MrsNMacauley) *hld up: hdwy 6f out: outpcd over 4f out: styd on ins fnl f* 20/1

00-3 6 1 1/2 **Interstice**$^{16}$ [455] 7-11-0 51 ....................(p) MissCHannaford 10 44
(AGNewcombe) *hld up in tch: plld hrd: rdn and ev ch over 1f out: sn wknd* 6/1

6-12 7 5 **Citrus Magic**$^{2}$ [568] 7-10-3 45 ....................(p) MissJoeyEllis(5) 11 31
(KBell) *chsd ldrs 7f* 4/1$^{3}$

440- 8 28 **Cryptogam**$^{50}$ [5815] 4-10-6 52 .................... MrNPearce(5) 5 —
(MESowersby) *hld up: rdn 7f out: wknd over 5f out* 50/1

200- 9 5 **Magenta Rising (IRE)**$^{34}$ [5683] 4-10-12 60 ....................(v$^{1}$) MissETucker(7) 4 —
(DBurchell) *chsd ldrs over 7f* 50/1

2m 41.83s (-0.27) **Going Correction** -0.325s/f (Stan) 9 Ran SP% 114.1
**WFA** 4 from 5yo+ 4lb
Speed ratings: **87,85,85,82,79 78,75,56,53**CSF £19.12 CT £50.00 TOTE £5.10: £2.60, £1.60, £1.90; EX 27.20.
**Owner** Miss Emma Shally **Bred** Thomas Shally Jnr **Trained** Southwell, Notts

**FOCUS**
A steady pace and a time nearly three seconds slower than the second division, but fair form for the grade and the winner improved again.

**NOTEBOOK**
**Delta Force** has not looked back since stepping up in trip and deserves plenty of credit for this success, as he was always doing a little too much in front. There looks more to come from him.
**Fight The Feeling** did not appear to do much wrong, but he is not an easy ride for an amateur.
**Mr Smithers Jones** could have done with a stronger pace over this trip and should do better when he faces a stiffer test.
**Jade Star(USA)**, tackling her longest trip to date, did not quite get home, but that may have been down to lack of a recent run, rather than lack of stamina.
**Interstice** was far too free to do himself justice and this run is best forgotten.

## 582 BETDIRECT.CO.UK H'CAP (DIV I) 1m (F)
1:10 (1:10) (F) (0-65,64) 4-Y-O+ £2,919 (£834; £417) Stalls Low

Form RPR

0-22 1 **Simply The Guest (IRE)**$^{14}$ [472] 5-8-8 45 ....................(t) KimTinkler 5 55
(DonEnricoIncisa) *sn pushed along and prom: rdn to ld over 1f out: r.o wl* 6/1$^{2}$

000- 2 4 **Robin Sharp**$^{22}$ [6270] 6-8-11 48 ....................(vt) JQuinn 10 50
(JAkehurst) *led: rdn 3f out: hdd over 1f out: sn outpcd* 40/1

545- 3 1 3/4 **Yenaled**$^{47}$ [6140] 7-9-11 62 .................... NCallan 11 61
(KARyan) *hld up: hdwy over 1f out: no ex ins fnl f* 7/1$^{3}$

0-21 4 nk **Lord Chamberlain**$^{10}$ [504] 11-8-12 49 ....................(b) PFitzsimons 2 47
(JMBradley) *hld up: hdwy and hung lft fr over 1f out: nt rch ldrs* 10/1

05-0 5 2 1/2 **Barzak (IRE)**$^{13}$ [488] 4-9-13 64 ....................(bt) RWinston 9 57
(SRBowring) *chsd ldr 6f out: rdn over 1f out: wknd ins fnl f* 6/1$^{2}$

00-6 6 2 1/2 **Muqarrar (IRE)**$^{10}$ [504] 5-9-1 52 ....................(be$^{1}$) DMernagh 7 40
(TJFitzgerald) *s.i.s: hdwy over 3f out: rdn over 1f out: wknd ins fnl f* 25/1

-611 **7** *nk* **Qobtaan (USA)**[9] 512 5-9-6 57 6ex.......................................... GBaker 6 44
(MRBosley) *hld up: hdwy over 3f out: rdn over 1f out: wkng whn hmpd ins fnl f* **13/8**[1]

00-0 **8** *nk* **Friday's Takings**[17] 437 5-9-8 59..................................(v[1]) PJScallan 4 46
(BSmart) *chsd ldrs: rdn over 2fr out: wknd over 1f out* **20/1**

0-00 **9** *4* **Pancakehill**[8] 525 5-9-0 51..............................................(p) IMongan 8 30
(DKIvory) *hld up: hdwy 1/2-way: wknd over 1f out* **14/1**

3-50 **10** *7* **Jamestown**[9] 516 7-8-9 46.................................................... JMackay 3 11
(MJPolglase) *chsd ldrs: lost pl over 5f out: sn bhd* **15/2**

000- **11** *1 3/4* **Caterham Common**[146] 4546 5-7-12 35 oh5...................... RBrisland 12 —
(DWChapman) *chsd ldrs over 5f* **66/1**

1m 41.19s (-3.41) **Going Correction** -0.325s/f (Stan) **11** Ran SP% **119.2**
Speed ratings: **104,100,98,97,95 92,92,92,88,81 79**CSF £232.36 CT £1759.68 TOTE £6.10: £2.40, £10.60, £2.20; EX 145.00.
**Owner** Don Enrico Incisa **Bred** Rathasker Stud **Trained** Middleham Moor, N Yorks

**FOCUS**
An ordinary contest, full of exposed sorts, and the winner had been beaten twice in regional races lately. However, the time was the best of the three races run over the trip. Those racing close to the pace appeared favoured.

**NOTEBOOK**
**Simply The Guest(IRE)** deserved this after a couple of near misses over course and distance recently, but the Handicapper is hardly likely to forget this in a hurry.
**Robin Sharp** showed a bit more sparkle than of late and is worth keeping in mind if returning to his favoured Wolverhampton.
**Yenaled** may well have just needed this outing to put an edge on him. He is not badly treated at present, and should be able to find a small race before too long.
**Lord Chamberlain** looked to have enough to do turning for home and seemed to battle on well enough despite hanging in.
**Barzak(IRE)** had no excuses and has become disappointing.
**Qobtaan(USA)**, the winner of a couple of minor races recently, now looks to be high enough in the weights for the time being.
**Jamestown** *Official explanation: trainer said gelding bolted on the way to post*

## 583 PRESS INTERACTIVE TO BET DIRECT AMATEUR RIDERS' H'CAP (DIV II) 1m 4f (F)

**1:40** (1:40) (G ) (0-60,60) 4-Y-0+ **£2,569** (£734; £367) **Stalls** Low

Form RPR

0-11 **1** **Sendintank**[7] 546 4-11-0 55 5ex........................................ MrSWalker 5 74
(SCWilliams) *hld up: hdwy 4f out: hung lft fr over 2f out: led over 1f out: styd on wl* **2/5**[1]

36-1 **2** *1 1/4* **Bella Pavlina**[8] 532 6-9-5 35........................................ MrCDavies[(7)] 2 52
(WMBrisbourne) *hld up: hdwy over 4f out: rdn and ev ch over 1f out: styd on* **14/1**

00-5 **3** *7* **Antony Ebeneezer**[10] 500 5-10-3 40..........................(t) MissEJJones 9 47
(CRDore) *plld hrd and prom: led over 2f out: hdd over 1f out: wknd ins fnl f* **22/1**

06-6 **4** *5* **High Diva**[7] 537 5-10-1 45................................................ MrsKHills[(7)] 8 44
(JRBest) *chsd ldrs: led over 3f out: hdd over 2f out: wknd over 1f out* **50/1**

053- **5** *12* **Danny Leahy (FR)**[98] 5596 4-11-0 60............................ MrNPearce[(5)] 6 41
(MDHammond) *hld up: pushed along 5f out: wknd over 2f out* **25/1**

41-4 **6** *4* **Spanish Star**[16] 456 7-10-9 46............................................ MrsMMorris 3 21
(MrsNMacauley) *hld up: hmpd over 4f out: n.d* **14/1**

25-3 **7** *5* **Kentucky Bullet (USA)**[16] 456 8-10-13 50........... MissCHannaford 11 18
(AGNewcombe) *s.i.s: sn chsng ldrs: wknd over 3f out* **8/1**[2]

256- **8** *1* **Komati River**[24] 6249 5-10-7 51................................... MrSGascoyne[(7)] 1 17
(JAkehurst) *chsd ldrs over 8f* **12/1**[3]

0-00 **9** *7* **Meticulous**[10] 497 6-9-2 30................................ MissKellyHarrison[(5)] 7 —
(MCChapman) *hld up: plld hrd: hdwy over 5f out: wknd 4f out* **100/1**

4-45 **10** *5* **Faraway Look (USA)**[9] 512 7-11-7 58.............................. MsCWilliams 4 6
(DShaw) *hld up: hmpd over 4f out: a in rr* **16/1**

000- **11** *6* **Sugar Snap**[162] 4092 4-9-6 40........................................ MissPDrew[(7)] 10 —
(CDrew) *plld hrd: led and sn clr: hdd & wknd over 3f out* **100/1**

2m 38.91s (-3.19) **Going Correction** -0.325s/f (Stan)
**WFA** 4 from 5yo+ 4lb **11** Ran SP% **121.6**
Speed ratings: **97,96,91,88,80 77,74,73,68,65 61**CSF £7.82 CT £69.38 TOTE £1.30: £1.02, £2.90, £4.10; EX 17.10.
**Owner** Steve Jones And Phil McGovern **Bred** K G Powter **Trained** Newmarket, Suffolk
■ Stewards Enquiry : Mr N Pearce one-day ban: careless riding (Feb 3)

**FOCUS**
A soundly run contest, nearly three seconds faster than the first division, and a highly progressive winner.

**NOTEBOOK**
**Sendintank** was able to race off a 1lb lower mark than when successful here seven days previously and was theoretically 10lb well in compared to his future mark. He again looked a far from easy ride, but has plenty of ability and should continue to progress.
**Bella Pavlina** was the only one to give the well-treated winner a race and did well to finish clear, but she may have blown her handicap mark as a result.
**Antony Ebeneezer**, who gained his only success in a division of this race last year, is not one to rely on.
**High Diva**, a long-standing maiden, was travelling as well as any turning for home, but her stamina gave way. She is a frustrating animal, but she does have ability.
**Spanish Star**, messed about leaving the back straight, could never get competitive.
**Kentucky Bullet(USA)** turned in a below-par effort and this can safely be ignored.

## 584 BET DIRECT ON SKY ACTIVE CLASSIFIED STKS 6f (F)

**2:10** (2:10) (F) 4-Y-0+ **£2,912** (£832; £416) **Stalls** Low

Form RPR

40-2 **1** **Up Tempo (IRE)**[10] 504 6-8-4 59..........................................(p) AMullen[(7)] 5 62
(TDEasterby) *hld up: hdwy over 1f out: r.o to ld wl ins fnl f* **10/3**[2]

00-3 **2** *1* **Legalis (USA)**[17] 436 6-8-11 58..........................................(b) NCallan 10 59
(KARyan) *chsd ldr: led over 2f out: hdd wl ins fnl f* **11/1**

1-06 **3** *nk* **Playful Spirit**[8] 530 5-8-8 45..........................................(v) JEdmunds 3 55
(JBalding) *prom: pushed along 1/2-way: styd on ins fnl f* **33/1**

140- **4** *1 1/4* **Semper Paratus (USA)**[47] 6134 5-8-11 59..........................(b) MTebbutt 6 54
(HJCollingridge) *hld up: r.o ins fnl f: nvr nrr* **10/1**

50-2 **5** *1* **Spindor (USA)**[10] 503 5-8-11 58..........................................(b) SWKelly 4 51
(JAOsborne) *s.i.s: hld up: hdwy over 2f out: rdn over 1f out: styd on same pce* **5/1**[3]

5-00 **6** *nk* **Mount Royale (IRE)**[9] 512 6-8-11 54..........................(v) KimTinkler 8 50
(NTinkler) *led over 3f: wknd ins fnl f* **20/1**

1-42 **7** *nk* **Headland (USA)**[13] 487 6-8-11 60..........................................(b) ACulhane 2 49
(DWChapman) *chsd ldrs: rdn over 1f out: wknd ins fnl f* **15/2**

3-50 **8** *5* **Lake Eyre (IRE)**[10] 509 5-8-8 47.............................................. GGibbons 9 31
(JBalding) *chsd ldrs over 3f* **33/1**

53-1 **9** *3 1/2* **Classic Vision**[17] 438 4-8-8 60................................................ JFanning 7 21
(WJHaggas) *s.i.s: sn prom: rdn 1/2-way: wknd over 2f out* **6/4**[1]

1m 14.64s (-2.16) **Going Correction** -0.325s/f (Stan) **9** Ran SP% **119.6**
Speed ratings: **101,99,99,97,96 95,95,88,84**CSF £39.81 TOTE £4.30: £1.80, £4.80, £5.90; EX 75.00.
**Owner** T D Easterby **Bred** T Burns **Trained** Great Habton, N Yorks

**FOCUS**
This was run at a sound pace, but with the exception of the disappointing favourite they were pretty exposed. The form is held down by the third.

**NOTEBOOK**
**Up Tempo(IRE)**, over a trip which could well be on the sharp side for him nowadays, showed a nice turn of foot in the latter stages to win with a little in hand. While his win record doesn't exactly inspire, he is clearly on good terms with himself at present and may be capable of defying a penalty in this mood.
**Legalis(USA)** did nothing wrong and still looks to have what it takes.
**Playful Spirit** appeared to run a cracking race at the weights and would be one to note if turned out in a handicap or regional race before re-assessed.
**Semper Paratus(USA)** was doing his best work in the closing stages and needs to return to seven furlongs.
**Spindor(USA)** did himself no favours by missing the break.
**Mount Royale(IRE)** probably did a little too much too soon from his wide draw.
**Classic Vision**, whose maiden win over course and distance has failed to yield even a placed horse from nine runners, was beaten turning for home. From the same family as the useful miler Yeast, she may well need further than this six furlongs. *Official explanation: trainer's representative had no explanation for the poor form shown*

## 585 BET DIRECT INTERACTIVE MAIDEN STKS 1m (F)

**2:40** (2:41) (D ) 3-Y-0+ **£3,474** (£1,069; £534; £267) **Stalls** Low

Form RPR

2 **1** **Sabbaag (USA)**[6] 550 3-8-6 ............................................ JPSpencer 11 75
(DRLoder) *chsd ldrs: rdn to ld over 1f out: styd on u.p* **2/5**[1]

**2** *1 3/4* **Marinaite** 3-8-1 ........................................................... JBramhill 2 67
(SRBowring) *sn chsng ldrs: led over 4f out: hung rt over 2f out: rdn and hdd over 1f out: no ex towards fin* **12/1**

4 **3** *1* **Alexander Ambition (IRE)**[12] 492 3-7-10 67.......................... DFox[(5)] 8 65
(SKirk) *led 1f: remained handy: rdn over 1f out: styd on* **11/1**[3]

0- **4** *nk* **Ylang Ylang (IRE)**[75] 5959 3-8-1 ............................................ JQuinn 12 64
(WJarvis) *hld up: hdwy 1/2-way: rdn over 2f out: kpt on ins fnl f* **9/2**[2]

6-04 **5** *10* **Casantella**[9] 514 3-8-1 45.............................................. JMackay 10 44
(MJPolglase) *hld up in tch: outpcd over 3f out* **50/1**

000- **6** *4* **Homeric Trojan**[275] 1172 4-9-5 56.................................. MLawson[(7)] 9 41
(MBrittain) *prom to 1/2-way* **100/1**

0 **7** *2 1/2* **Silver Emperor (IRE)**[20] 409 3-8-6 ........................(b) DeanMcKeown 5 36
(PABlockley) *s.i.s: hld up: wknd 1/2-way* **33/1**

0- **8** *22* **Anacapri**[102] 5513 4-9-4 ............................................................ DAllan[(3)] 7 —
(WSCunningham) *n.d* **150/1**

00- **9** *3/4* **Harry Tu**[65] 6022 4-9-12 ........................................................ PJScallan 3 —
(MissGayKelleway) *sn pushed along and prom: wknd 1/2-way* **150/1**

**10** *3 1/2* **Mr Lehman**[37] 7-9-12 ........................................................ ACulhane 6 —
(MrsMReveley) *s.s: hld up: plld hrd: wknd 1/2-way* **50/1**

- **11** *14* **Campbell's Tale (IRE)** 5-9-12 .............................................. DMernagh 4 —
(TJFitzgerald) *led 7f out: hdd over 4f out: wknd over 3f out* **150/1**

00- **12** *5* **Loaded Gun**[60] 5891 4-9-12 62.............................................. MTebbutt 1 —
(MissJFeilden) *bhd fnl 5f* **66/1**

1m 41.55s (-3.05) **Going Correction** -0.325s/f (Stan)
**WFA** 3 from 4yo+ 20lb **12** Ran SP% **117.0**
Speed ratings: **102,100,99,98,88 84,82,60,59,56 42,37**CSF £6.56 TOTE £1.20: £1.02, £3.20, £1.90; EX 10.60.
**Owner** Sheikh Ahmed Al Maktoum **Bred** Darley **Trained** Newmarket, Suffolk

**FOCUS**
A fair maiden, although the third and fourth were a bit below their Irish form.

**NOTEBOOK**
**Sabbaag(USA)** proved well suited by this stiffer test but made hard work of what looked an easy opening for him. He is clearly nothing special on this effort, but may be capable of better when he runs on turf.
**Marinaite**, from the same family as useful Fibresand performers Sailormaite and First Maite and evidently well regarded, gave favourite backers quite a scare. She is sure to have learnt plenty from this and an ordinary maiden should come her way.
**Alexander Ambition(IRE)** looks short of pace and may be worth another try at ten furlongs.
**Ylang Ylang(IRE)** is another who looks to have a touch of the slows and should appreciate a stiffer test.

## 586 LITTLEWOODS BET DIRECT STKS SHOWCASE H'CAP 5f (F)

**3:10** (3:10) (C ) (0-95,90) 4-Y-0+ **£8,112** (£2,496; £1,248; £624) **Stalls** High

Form RPR

133- **1** **Dancing Mystery**[44] 6154 10-10-0 **90**..................................(b) SCarson 10 101
(EAWheeler) *chsd ldrs: rdn to ld towards fin* **14/1**

06-0 **2** *nk* **Justalord**[7] 540 6-9-6 **82**..................................................(p) JEdmunds 11 92
(JBalding) *chsd ldrs: led over 1f out: hdd towards fin* **40/1**

1131 **3** *hd* **Hurricane Coast**[1] 578 5-8-9 **71** 6ex..................................(b) PDoe 13 80
(DFlood) *hld up: hdwy over 1f out: r.o wl* **11/4**[1]

20-1 **4** *1/2* **Quiet Times (IRE)**[9] 515 5-9-7 **83** 6ex..................................(b) NCallan 5 91
(KARyan) *chsd ldrs: rdn over 1f out: r.o* **8/1**[3]

41-3 **5** *1 1/2* **Zarzu**[13] 486 5-9-5 **86**.......................................................... RThomas[(5)] 15 88
(CRDore) *chsd ldrs: rdn over 1f out: no ex ins fnl f* **5/1**[2]

12-5 **6** *shd* **Bond Playboy**[13] 486 4-9-13 **89**............................................ FLynch 6 91
(BSmart) *sn outpcd: hdwy over 1f out: nt rch ldrs* **10/1**

00-0 **7** *nk* **African Spur (IRE)**[9] 515 4-8-0 **69**.............................. SYourston[(7)] 16 70
(PABlockley) *mid-div: rdn 1/2-way: styd on* **50/1**

2-51 **8** *3/4* **Time N Time Again**[7] 543 6-8-12 **74** 6ex..........................(p) ANicholls 8 72
(EJAlston) *s.i.s: hdwy over 3f out: rdn over 1f out: styd on same pce* **16/1**

0-62 **9** *shd* **Far Note (USA)**[7] 543 6-8-3 **65**..........................................(b) JBramhill 14 63
(SRBowring) *hmpd and lost pl over 3f out: r.o ins fnl f: nrst fin* **14/1**

60-0 **10** *hd* **Trinculo (IRE)**[13] 486 7-9-11 **90**..............................(e) J-PGuillambert[(3)] 1 87
(NPLittmoden) *chsd ldrs: outpcd over 3f out: n.d after* **12/1**

102- **11** *hd* **Palawan**[37] 6199 8-9-1 **84**.............................................................. TBlock[(7)] 3 81
(AMBalding) *led over 3f: wknd ins fnl f* **10/1**

03-0 **12** *1 1/2* **Only One Legend (IRE)**[19] 417 6-8-10 **72**..........................(p) RWinston 2 63
(KARyan) *w ldr 2f: wknd ins fnl f* **40/1**

50-3 **13** *1 1/4* **Grandma Lily (IRE)**[7] 540 6-8-10 **72**.......................................... IMongan 9 59
(MCChapman) *hmpd sn after s: outpcd* **14/1**

51-0 **14** *1 1/4* **Frascati**[7] 543 4-8-11 **78**.................................................... PBradley[(5)] 7 61
(ABerry) *chsd ldrs: outpcd fr 1/2-way* **33/1**

115- **15** *1 1/4* **Compton Banker (IRE)**[24] 6252 7-9-2 **78**..........................(v) EAhern 4 56
(GAButler) *s.s: outpcd* **16/1**

00-6 **16** *hd* **Prime Recreation**[7] 540 7-8-6 **68**.................................. DaleGibson 12 45
(PSFelgate) *s.i.s: outpcd* **40/1**

58.95 secs (-1.35) **Going Correction** -0.075s/f (Stan) **16** Ran SP% **124.3**
Speed ratings: **107,106,106,105,103 102,102,101,101,100 100,97,95,93,91 91**CSF £512.76 CT £2004.73 TOTE £11.20: £2.20, £8.50, £1.50, £2.10; EX 1087.10 Trifecta £1091.90 Part won. Pool of £1,538.00 - 0.20 winning tickets..
**Owner** Astrod TA Austin Stroud & Co **Bred** Mrs D Price **Trained** Whitchurch-on-Thames, Oxon
■ Stewards Enquiry : N Callan two-day ban: careless riding (Feb 2,3)

**FOCUS**
A classy sprint, run a decent clip, and the form looks solid. The first three had double figure draws.

**NOTEBOOK**
**Dancing Mystery** retains his enthusiasm remarkably well and, although only a narrow winner, he always looked like getting there. Although he is not as good as he once was, he is still pretty useful at this level.
**Justalord** again showed plenty of pace. This was his best effort for a while, but he may be more at home on a turning track.
**Hurricane Coast**was having his sixth race in three weeks and his second in 24 hours. He is taking his racing well and, despite having been given plenty to do, ran very close to his best again. He is still on the upgrade.
**Quiet Times(IRE)**, carrying a penalty and back down to a trip which is sharp enough for him, was close to a personal best.
**Zarzu** turned in another sound effort in defeat, but he could well be in the grip of the Handicapper for the time being.
**Bond Playboy** is screaming out for a return to six furlongs.
**African Spur(IRE)** was not disgraced in this better contest and can be found an opening before long.
**Time N Time Again** did not do himself any favours by missing a beat at the start.
**Far Note(USA)** ran much better than his final position suggests, for he was always facing an uphill battle after getting squeezed out going to the three-furlong pole.

## 587 BET DIRECT THROUGH SKY ACTIVE (S) STKS 7f (F)
3:40 (3:41) (G) 3-Y-O £2,590 (£740; £370) Stalls Low

Form RPR
466- **1** **Smart Boy Prince (IRE)**[22] 6266 3-8-5 55...................... DerekNolan(7) 6 60
(PABlockley) *chsd ldrs: led over 4f out: pushed out* **7/2**[2]
044- **2** *1 ½* **Hunting Pink**[45] 6147 3-8-4 49...................................... LFletcher(3) 3 51
(HMorrison) *hld up: hdwy over 2f out: rdn to chse wnr over 1f out: styd on same pce* **10/3**[1]
600- **3** *2 ½* **Knight To Remember (IRE)**[40] 6172 3-8-12 45.................... NCallan 1 50
(KARyan) *hld up: hdwy over 3f out: rdn over 1f out: styd on same pce* **25/1**
43-3 **4** *½* **Katie's Role**[20] 409 3-8-7 53................................................ ANicholls 4 44
(IanEmmerson) *chsd ldrs: rdn and edgd rt over 2f out: styd on same pce fnl f* **7/2**[2]
00-4 **5** *3 ½* **Zonnebeke**[20] 409 3-8-7 47.......................................... DarrenWilliams 9 35
(KRBurke) *chsd ldrs: rdn over 2f out: wknd over 1f out* **16/1**
65-0 **6** *nk* **Druid**[8] 521 3-8-5 52.................................................. DWakenshaw(7) 10 39
(PCHaslam) *led: hdd over 4f out: rdn and hmpd over 2f out: hung lft and wknd over 1f out* **25/1**
0- **7** *3* **Heathyards Joy**[113] 5302 3-8-7 .................................... DeanMcKeown 5 27
(RHollinshead) *hld up: hdwy over 3f out: wknd 2f out* **33/1**
0- **8** *1 ¾* **Oktis Morilious (IRE)**[45] 6142 3-8-12 ................................ SWKelly 13 27
(JAOsborne) *outpcd: nvr nrr* **16/1**
060- **9** *¾* **Are You There**[38] 6194 3-8-6 47.......................... GemmaAnderson(7) 2 26
(TDBarron) *sn outpcd* **20/1**
5-60 **10** *¾* **Nothing Matters**[7] 533 3-8-7 40................................................ PDoe 8 18
(PRChamings) *chsd ldrs over 4f* **25/1**
43-4 **11** *½* **Garnock Venture (IRE)**[17] 435 3-8-12 49..........................(b) FLynch 7 22
(ABerry) *chsd ldrs over 4f* **9/1**[3]
000- **12** *shd* **Ticklepenny Lock (IRE)**[38] 6194 3-8-12 35.......................... IMongan 12 22
(CSmith) *prom 3f* **50/1**
00-0 **13** *½* **Eugenie**[12] 489 3-8-7 45.......................................................... RSmith 15 16
(RHannon) *sn outpcd* **33/1**
500- **14** *1 ½* **Far For Lulu**[154] 4309 3-8-7 40.............................................. JQuinn 14 12
(WRMuir) *s.i.s: outpcd* **50/1**
04-0 **15** *13* **Tamarina (IRE)**[3] 563 3-8-7 55..............................................(b[1]) CCatlin 11 —
(NEBerry) *s.i.s: outpcd* **12/1**

1m 29.27s (-1.53) **Going Correction** -0.325s/f (Stan) **15** Ran SP% **123.1**
Speed ratings: **95,93,90,89,85 85,82,80,79,78 77,77,77,75,60**CSF £14.16 TOTE £5.00: £2.60, £1.80, £6.30; EX 11.60.There was no bid for the winner.
**Owner** Brooklands Racing **Bred** J Kennedy **Trained** Southwell, Notts

**FOCUS**
The 15 runners had only one win to their name from 85 appearances, which speaks volumes for the quality of the contest. However, the winner was unexposed at this level and is possibly a cut above average.

**NOTEBOOK**
**Smart Boy Prince(IRE)** took advantage of the drop in class and proved more resolute than some of his rivals. Retained without a bid, he may be capable of following up in a similar contest.
**Hunting Pink** does not look like one to place too much faith in.
**Knight To Remember(IRE)** showed a bit more on this drop in class, but it will have to be a poor contest if he is to get his head in front.
**Katie's Role**, under pressure some way out, lacks a change of gear, but to her credit kept plugging away.
**Tamarina(IRE)** *Official explanation: jockey said filly would not face the kick back*

## 588 BETDIRECT.CO.UK H'CAP (DIV II) 1m (F)
4:10 (4:10) (F) (0-65,62) 4-Y-O+ £2,919 (£834; £417) Stalls Low

Form RPR
66-2 **1** **Disabuse**[7] 541 4-8-11 48...................................................... JPSpencer 10 58+
(SCWilliams) *hld up: pushed along 1/2-way: hdwy u.p over 2f out: hung lft over 1f out: led ins fnl f: styd on u.p* **5/2**[2]
40-4 **2** *1 ¾* **Dubai Dreams**[9] 513 4-9-2 56.......................................(b) LFletcher(3) 1 62
(MJPolglase) *chsd ldrs: led 5f out: hdd over 1f out: sn hmpd and lft in ld again: hdd and unable qck ins fnl f* **20/1**
2-52 **3** *2* **Sorbiesharry (IRE)**[9] 512 5-8-11 48................................(p) PMcCabe 2 50
(MrsNMacauley) *chsd ldrs: rdn over 2f out: styd on same pce appr fnl f* **8/1**
350- **4** *3* **Realism (FR)**[55] 6086 4-9-4 55.............................................. ACulhane 7 51
(PWHiatt) *hld up: effrt over 2f out: nvr trbld ldrs* **66/1**
52-3 **5** *¾* **Waltzing Wizard**[10] 504 5-9-1 52............................................ FLynch 8 47
(ABerry) *chsd ldrs: rdn over 2f out: wknd wl over 1f out* **10/1**
0-31 **6** *½* **Sandorra**[14] 474 6-8-3 47 ow1.......................................... MLawson(7) 4 41
(MBrittain) *led 3f: remained handy tl wknd wl over 1f out* **10/1**
66-0 **7** *1 ¾* **Spark Up**[13] 488 4-9-11 62...............................................(b) MHenry 5 52
(JWUnett) *prom 6f* **7/1**[3]
00-0 **8** *6* **Peartree House (IRE)**[14] 472 10-8-3 40................................ RBrisland 11 18
(DWChapman) *hld up: a in rr* **66/1**
00-1 **9** *3 ½* **Mount Hillaby (IRE)**[10] 503 4-9-0 51.................................. DaleGibson 9 67+
(MWEasterby) *chsd ldrs: lost pl 6f out: hdwy over 2f out: led over 1f out: sn slipped and hdd: virtually p.u* **5/4**[1]
0-50 **10** *21* **Pooka's Daughter (IRE)**[3] 565 4-8-8 45.......................(b[1]) PFitzsimons 6 —
(JMBradley) *chsd ldrs over 5f* **66/1**

1m 41.97s (-2.63) **Going Correction** -0.325s/f (Stan) **10** Ran SP% **124.0**
Speed ratings: **100,98,96,93,92 92,90,84,80,59**CSF £56.73 CT £372.03 TOTE £3.00: £1.10, £3.90, £2.10; EX 67.40 Place 6 £68.62, Place 5 £44.71.
**Owner** J R and T J Allenby **Bred** The Lavington Stud **Trained** Newmarket, Suffolk

**FOCUS**
This was run slightly slower than the first division, but the time would have been comparable had the favourite not lost his action.

**NOTEBOOK**
**Disabuse** was a lucky winner, but on the plus side he should not go up much for this.
**Dubai Dreams** was not disgraced over what looks an inadequate trip for him.
**Sorbiesharry(IRE)** turned in a sound enough effort, but he is thoroughly exposed.
**Realism(FR)**, tackling handicappers for the first time, shaped as though he may benefit from a step up in trip.
**Mount Hillaby(IRE)** looked to be well in control when he found a false patch just over a furlong from home, causing him to lose his action. He was a most unlucky loser. *Official explanation: jockey said filly lost its action*

T/Plt: £114.40 to a £1 stake. Pool: £31,814.70. 202.85 winning tickets. T/Qpdt: £13.00 to a £1 stake. Pool: £2,544.20. 143.80 winning tickets. CR

# 561 WOLVERHAMPTON (A.W) (L-H)
### Friday, January 23

**OFFICIAL GOING: Standard**
There appeared no significant track bias for this meeting.
Wind: mod hlf bhd Weather: raining last 3 races

## 589 PRESS INTERACTIVE TO BET DIRECT AMATEUR RIDERS' H'CAP (DIV I) 1m 1f 79y(F)
12:50 (12:50) (G) (0-70,69) 4-Y-O+ £2,569 (£734; £367) Stalls Low

Form RPR
060- **1** **Sting Like A Bee (IRE)**[16] 5705 5-9-10 **49**.......... MissKellyHarrison(5) 6 62
(JSGoldie) *a.p: edgd lft over 3f out: sn chsng ldr: led ins fnl f: pushed out* **8/1**
06-0 **2** *3 ½* **Littleton Zephir (USA)**[11] 503 5-9-8 **47**.............(b) MrsCThompson(5) 7 53
(MrsPTownsley) *led: clr over 2f out: rdn wl over 1f out: hdd ins fnl f: no ex* **33/1**
-146 **3** *2* **Ovigo (GER)**[4] 564 5-11-2 **69**............................................ MrMScales(5) 5 71
(PABlockley) *s.s: bhd tl rdn and hdwy over 3f out: kpt on same pce fnl f* **7/4**[1]
000- **4** *1 ½* **Yellow River (IRE)**[34] 6220 4-10-5 **57**........................ MrEDehdashti(3) 3 56
(RCurtis) *hld up: hdwy whn nt clr run over 3f out: hrd rdn jst over 1f out: one pce* **33/1**
06-2 **5** *2 ½* **Street Life (IRE)**[10] 516 6-10-12 **67**............................ MissJPledge(7) 4 61
(WJMusson) *s.i.s: bhd tl hdwy over 1f out: nt rch ldrs* **5/2**[2]
0045 **6** *hd* **Western Command (GER)**[1] 581 8-9-3 **37** oh7.......... MrsMMorris 11 31
(MrsNMacauley) *hld up and bhd: hdwy on outside over 3f out: wknd 2f out* **25/1**
00-0 **7** *½* **Morris Dancing (USA)**[11] 500 5-9-5 **51** ow6.....(p) MrJPemberton(7) 10 44
(BPJBaugh) *chsd ldr to 3f out: sn wknd* **66/1**
00-5 **8** *1* **Paso Doble**[17] 456 6-10-7 **62**.......................................... MrJMillman(7) 12 53
(BRMillman) *hld up mid-div: hdwy 4f out: wknd wl over 1f out* **11/1**
-251 **9** *5* **Tropical Son**[8] 537 5-9-11 **45** 5ex................................(v) MsCWilliams 2 26
(DShaw) *prom: hmpd on ins over 3f out: sn wknd* **11/2**[3]
620- **10** *9* **Florenzar (IRE)**[60] 5312 6-10-3 **54**................................ MissEFolkes(3) 9 17
(PDEvans) *hld up mid-divison: stdy hdwy over 5f out: rdn and wknd 3f out* **25/1**
600/ **11** *1 ¼* **Cliquey**[50] 5441 5-10-7 **62**.......................................................... MissAFrieze(7) 8 22
(BJLlewellyn) *dwlt: a bhd* **25/1**
000- **12** *24* **Mutared (IRE)**[28] 6236 6-11-0 **65**........................ MrsEmmaLittmoden(3) 1 —
(NPLittmoden) *prom 3f: t.o fnl 4f* **14/1**

2m 3.75s (0.85) **Going Correction** -0.075s/f (Stan)
**WFA** 4 from 5yo+ 1lb **12** Ran SP% **125.3**
Speed ratings: **93,89,88,86,84 84,83,83,78,70 69,48**CSF £258.43 CT £679.20 TOTE £8.00: £3.50, £8.10, £1.20; EX 132.50.
**Owner** Mrs C Brown **Bred** C H Wacker Iii **Trained** Uplawmoor, E Renfrews
■ Stewards Enquiry : Miss A Frieze one-day ban: used whip when out of contention (Feb 3)
Miss Kelly Harrison one-day ban: careless riding (Feb 3)
Mrs C Thompson one-day ban: used whip without giving mare time to respond (Feb 3)

**FOCUS**
A modest time, about a second slower than the second division. The winner had been given a big chance by the Handicapper.

**NOTEBOOK**
**Sting Like A Bee(IRE)**, who won a two and a half-mile selling hurdle at Hexham in November, had run well over course and distance on his sand debut nearly a year previously. He only had to reproduce that sort of form to score off this mark.
**Littleton Zephir(USA)**, back up to the right sort of trip, was unlucky to come up against a well handicapped sort.
**Ovigo(GER)** gave away several lengths when playing up as the gates opened. He could have burst himself trying to get into it over this slightly longer trip.
**Yellow River(IRE)** was under strong pressure entering the final furlong and should not be considered unlucky.
**Street Life(IRE)** was not helped by a sluggish start and really wants a shade further.

## 590 PRESS INTERACTIVE TO BET DIRECT AMATEUR RIDERS' H'CAP (DIV II) 1m 1f 79y(F)
1:25 (1:25) (G) (0-70,70) 4-Y-O+ £2,569 (£734; £367) Stalls Low

Form RPR
3-30 **1** **Scottish River (USA)**[16] 464 5-10-5 58.......................... MrLNewnes(5) 8 71
(MDIUsher) *s.s: t.k.h: hdwy on ins 7f out: rdn to ld wl over 1f out: hrd rdn ins fnl f: jst hld on* **5/1**[3]
02-3 **2** *shd* **Our Destiny**[4] 562 6-9-8 49 ow4.................................(v) MissETucker(7) 1 62
(DBurchell) *led: rdn over 2f out: hdd wl over 1f out: rallying whn edgd lft ins fnl f: jst failed* **25/1**
2-12 **3** *4* **Rock Concert**[15] 477 6-11-0 62........................................ MissEJJones 6 67
(IWMcinnes) *chsd ldr tl rdn over 2f out: one pce* **7/2**[2]
40-1 **4** *1* **Jair Ohmsford (IRE)**[21] 406 5-10-9 64.............................. MissJPledge(7) 9 67
(WJMusson) *t.k.h: dropped rr 6f out: hdwy on outside over 2f out: r.o fnl f* **6/1**

-523 **5** *3* **Sorbiesharry (IRE)**[1] 588 5-10-0 48..........(p) MrsMMorris 5 45
(MrsNMacauley) *hld up and bhd: hdwy on ins 3f out: no further prog fnl 2f* **6/1**

50-0 **6** *¾* **Top Of The Class (IRE)**[21] 406 7-9-8 45..........(v) MissEFolkes(3) 2 40
(PDEvans) *prom tl wknd 3f out* **33/1**

21-0 **7** *1¼* **Kingston Town (USA)**[6] 559 4-11-4 70......(p) MrsEmmaLittmoden(3) 4 63
(NPLittmoden) *plld hrd: mid-div: short-lived effrt 3f out: btn whn edgd lft over 1f out* **10/1**

0-06 **8** *1¾* **Love's Design (IRE)**[9] 531 7-9-9 50.......... MrASwinswood(7) 7 39
(MissSJWilton) *plld hrd: bhd most of way* **33/1**

0-42 **9** *1½* **Giust In Temp (IRE)**[9] 532 5-9-1 40.......... MrsMarieKing(5) 11 26
(PWHiatt) *plld hrd: prom tl wknd 2f out* **12/1**

100- **10** *1½* **Spitfire Bob (USA)**[127] 5013 5-11-4 66.......... MrSWalker 10 49
(TDBarron) *hld up: rdn 4f out: no rspnse* **15/8[1]**

6 **11** *1½* **Soft Mist (IRE)**[17] 457 4-10-5 57.......... KJMercer(3) 3 37
(JJQuinn) *hld up mid-div: rdn over 5f out: bhd fnl 3f* **50/1**

2m 2.74s (-0.16) **Going Correction** -0.075s/f (Stan)
**WFA** 4 from 5yo+ 1lb **11** Ran SP% **130.7**
Speed ratings: **97,96,93,92,89 89,88,86,85,83 82**CSF £134.92 CT £515.21 TOTE £8.50: £2.50, £4.40, £1.50; EX 180.70.
**Owner** M D I Usher **Bred** The Thoroughbred Corporation **Trained** Upper Lambourn, Berks

**FOCUS**
This race was run about a second faster than the first division, though the time was still unexceptional for the type of contest.

**NOTEBOOK**
**Scottish River(USA)** was again a shade headstrong and soon recovered from a tardy start. Reported to have idled badly in front, he just held the runner-up's renewed challenge.
**Our Destiny** was not taken on for the lead this time and fought back well at the death. The fact his rider could only claim 3lb of her 7lb allowance may have proved vital.
**Rock Concert** was again 6lb higher than when successful over course and distance at the turn of the year.
**Jair Ohmsford(IRE)** ran better than his finishing position suggests under an inexperienced rider.
**Sorbiesharry(IRE)** may have found this coming too soon after his exertions at Southwell the previous day.
**Spitfire Bob(USA)** *Official explanation: trainer had no explanation for the poor form shown*

## 591 BET DIRECT ON SKY ACTIVE CLAIMING STKS 6f (F)

**2:00** (2:03) (F) 3-Y-O **£2,933** (£838; £419) **Stalls** Low

Form RPR

22-3 **1** **Emaradia**[9] 524 3-7-12 48..........(b) JoannaBadger 3 57
(PDEvans) *sn led: rdn over 2f out: r.o wl* **8/1**

00-5 **2** *1¾* **Nanna (IRE)**[10] 514 3-7-13 ow1.......... JQuinn 5 53
(RHollinshead) *a.p: rdn over 3f out: chsd wnr fnl f: no imp* **25/1**

3-02 **3** *nk* **Alizar (IRE)**[13] 496 3-8-8 59.......... JPSpencer 1 61
(MJPolglase) *led early: w ldr: ev ch 2f out: sn rdn: one pce* **5/2[1]**

420- **4** *½* **Crewes Miss Isle**[74] 5966 3-8-8 70.......... SWhitworth 7 59
(AGNewcombe) *sn bhd: hdwy 3f out: swtchd lft ins fnl f: kpt on* **6/1**

04-1 **5** *3* **Back At De Front (IRE)**[7] 547 3-8-13 60.......... MSavage(5) 4 60
(NEBerry) *a.p: rdn and wknd over 1f out* **11/4[2]**

513- **6** *2* **Fission**[45] 6152 3-9-4 79..........(b) SWKelly 8 54
(JAOsborne) *sn chsng ldrs: rdn 3f out: wknd 2f out* **7/2[3]**

**7** *1¼* **Fora Smile** 3-8-9.......... ADaly 11 42
(MDIUsher) *broke wl: sn stdd and outpcd* **25/1**

**8** *1¼* **Fairly Glorious** 3-8-8.......... TEaves(5) 2 42
(THCaldwell) *s.i.s: outpcd* **50/1**

040- **9** *2* **Bish Bash Bosh (IRE)**[95] 5677 3-8-4 45.......... SRighton 9 27
(MFHarris) *sn rdn along: bhd fnl 3f* **33/1**

000- **10** *2½* **Adriatic Adventure (IRE)**[28] 6237 3-8-0 45.......... JMackay 6 15
(JLSpearing) *mid-div: rdn over 3f out: bhd fnl 2f* **50/1**

000- **11** *3½* **Mystic Promise (IRE)**[55] 6091 3-8-6 30..........(b) StevenHarrison(7) 10 18
(MrsNMacauley) *s.s: outpcd* **100/1**

1m 15.96s (0.26) **Going Correction** -0.075s/f (Stan) **11** Ran SP% **118.4**
Speed ratings: **95,92,92,91,87 84,83,81,78,75 70**CSF £188.21 TOTE £9.00: £1.80, £2.70, £1.30; EX 69.70.Emaradia was claimed for £5,000 by Dennis Deacon. Nanna was the subject of a friendly claim of £5,000.
**Owner** Treble Chance Partnership **Bred** Treble Chance Partnership **Trained** Pandy, Gwent
■ Stewards Enquiry : Steven Harrison one-day ban: used whip when out of contention (Feb 3)

**FOCUS**
A moderate claimer with a pace to match.

**NOTEBOOK**
**Emaradia** had four of these rivals behind her when a creditable second in a similar event here on Boxing Day. She was able to dictate matters back on this surface and answered Badger's every call.
**Nanna(IRE)** stepped up on her previous efforts, having finished almost 16 lengths behind the winner over course and distance on Boxing Day.
**Alizar(IRE)** was 4lb better off than when three lengths behind the winner here on Boxing Day.
**Crewes Miss Isle** was a drifter in the market and gave the impression she may be capable of better things.
**Back At De Front(IRE)** may have won a handicap over course and distance a week previously, but had a bit to find in this claimer at these weights.
**Fission** had more to do than when landing a similar event here last August.

## 592 LITTLEWOODS BET DIRECT H'CAP 1m 4f (F)

**2:35** (2:35) (D) (0-80,76) 4-Y-0+ **£4,114** (£1,266; £633; £316) **Stalls** Low

Form RPR

-111 **1** **Sendintank**[1] 583 4-8-3 56 6ex.......... RFfrench 5 72+
(SCWilliams) *hld up: hdwy over 3f out: rdn and edgd lft ins fnl f: qcknd to ld towards fin* **4/6[1]**

00-2 **2** *1* **Jadeeron**[16] 467 5-8-2 54..........(p) LisaJones(3) 7 68
(MissDAMchale) *a.p: led over 2f out: rdn over 1f out: hdd towards fin* **10/1**

132- **3** *6* **Dick The Taxi**[78] 5935 10-9-8 74.......... RMiles(3) 9 79
(RJSmith) *a.p: rdn over 2f out: wknd ins fnl f* **8/1[3]**

04-0 **4** *1* **Night Warrior (IRE)**[6] 559 4-9-0 67.......... PDoe 1 71
(DFlood) *hld up and bhd: hdwy over 2f out: rdn and wknd over 1f out* **14/1**

0-43 **5** *½* **Lazzaz**[8] 546 6-8-13 62.......... ACulhane 2 65
(PWHiatt) *led: rdn and hdd over 2f out: wknd ins fnl f* **20/1**

630- **6** *½* **Countykat (IRE)**[34] 6124 4-9-9 76..........(p) DarrenWilliams 6 78
(KRBurke) *hld up and bhd: hdwy over 2f out: sn rdn: wknd wl over 1f out* **25/1**

52-2 **7** *½* **Glory Quest (USA)**[10] 513 7-9-3 71..........(p) TEaves(5) 8 72
(MissGayKelleway) *hld up: rdn and hdwy over 3f out: wknd 2f out* **4/1[2]**

320- **8** *17* **Paula Lane**[34] 6156 4-9-0 72.......... JFMcDonald(5) 4 48
(RCurtis) *prom: rdn 4f out: sn wknd: t.o* **50/1**

0/0- **9** *26* **Spainkris**[8] 5926 5-9-7 70.......... IMongan 3 7
(ACrook) *chsd ldr tl rdn over 4f out: sn wknd: t.o* **33/1**

2m 38.39s (-3.11) **Going Correction** -0.075s/f (Stan)
**WFA** 4 from 5yo+ 4lb **9** Ran SP% **120.4**
Speed ratings: **107,106,102,101,101 101,100,89,72**CSF £8.81 CT £35.26 TOTE £1.70: £1.10, £3.30, £2.00; EX 11.30.
**Owner** Steve Jones And Phil McGovern **Bred** K G Powter **Trained** Newmarket, Suffolk

**FOCUS**
A decent time was clocked by a horse on the crest of a wave. This is solid form.

**NOTEBOOK**
**Sendintank** would have had another 9lb to carry had his new mark been in force and registered a four-timer by quickening between horses to take it up late and supplement his victory at Southwell the previous day. He may still be ahead of the Handicapper when reassessed.
**Jadeeron** came up against a well handicapped horse and did well to finish clear of the rest.
**Dick The Taxi** was 7lb higher than when winning a weaker event over course and distance nearly a year ago. He is not getting any younger and it would have taken a personal best for him to win this.
**Night Warrior(IRE)** could well have found a mile and a half beyond him on this demanding surface.
**Lazzaz** was 2lb worse off than when nearly eight lengths behind Sendintank at Southwell.

## 593 BET DIRECT INTERACTIVE MAIDEN STKS 1m 100y(F)

**3:10** (3:10) (D) 3-Y-O **£3,386** (£1,042; £521; £260) **Stalls** Low

Form RPR

2 **1** **Play Master (IRE)**[11] 506 3-9-0.......... PaulEddery 7 69
(DHaydnJones) *sn led: hdd over 6f out: w ldr: rdn to ld 2f out: edgd rt 1f out: all out* **5/2[3]**

62- **2** *nk* **Bahiano (IRE)**[23] 6266 3-9-0.......... ACulhane 2 68
(CEBrittain) *a.p: rdn over 2f out: ev ch ins fnl f: r.o* **11/8[1]**

**3** *8* **Global Achiever** 3-9-0.......... RFfrench 6 51
(GCHChung) *t.k.h: led over 6f out: rdn and hdd 2f out: wknd ins fnl f* **40/1**

66 **4** *¾* **Royaltea**[11] 506 3-8-9.......... JoannaBadger 1 45
(MsDeborahJEvans) *hld up in rr: rdn 4f out: hdwy on ins 2f out: nvr trbld ldrs* **100/1**

**5** *½* **Norwegian** 3-9-0.......... JPSpencer 3 49
(DRLoder) *s.i.s: sn pushed along: rdn and hdwy over 4f out: wknd over 2f out* **15/8[2]**

652- **6** *10* **Unintentional**[32] 6228 3-8-9 60.......... IMongan 5 23
(RBrotherton) *led early: prom: rdn over 3f out: wknd over 2f out* **22/1**

1m 50.86s (-0.14) **Going Correction** -0.075s/f (Stan) **6** Ran SP% **113.2**
Speed ratings: **97,96,88,87,87 77**CSF £6.42 TOTE £3.40: £1.20, £1.70; EX 6.00.
**Owner** Jason Weston **Bred** R N Auld **Trained** Efail Isaf, Rhondda C Taff
■ Stewards Enquiry : A Culhane caution: used whip down colt's shoulder in the forehand position

**FOCUS**
This was probably a fair maiden for Dunstall Park, although the two principals did not have much to beat.

**NOTEBOOK**
**Play Master(IRE)** fulfilled the promise of his debut here 11 days previously and was not inconvenienced by the longer trip.
**Bahiano(IRE)**, a half-brother to the useful miler Cadeaux Tryst, was another who did not mind the step up from seven. He is knocking on the door and looks sure to win a similar race.
**Global Achiever** is out of a maiden who was at her best over six. It remains to be seen if he will stay this sort of trip on such a demanding surface.
**Royaltea** had finished a similar distance behind the winner over seven here last time.
**Norwegian**, a half-brother to a couple of winners over five and six furlongs, represented a stable that has made a cracking start to the new season, but there was no confidence behind him in the betting and he was never really travelling at any stage.

## 594 BET DIRECT THROUGH SKY ACTIVE (S) H'CAP 1m 4f (F)

**3:45** (3:45) (G) (0-60,55) 4-Y-0+ **£2,632** (£752; £376) **Stalls** Low

Form RPR

4-35 **1** **Misty Man (USA)**[9] 532 6-8-7 35..........(b) SWhitworth 7 46
(MissJFeilden) *plld hrd early: a.p: rdn to ld 2f out: r.o wl* **10/1**

0-03 **2** *1¾* **Khuzdar (IRE)**[2] 579 5-8-12 40.......... SWKelly 2 48
(ABailey) *hld up and bhd: hdwy 4f out: rdn and ev ch wl over 1f out: sn edgd lft: no ex fnl f* **4/1[2]**

456- **3** *3* **Failed To Hit**[28] 6240 11-9-10 52..........(v) IMongan 6 56
(NPLittmoden) *led: rdn over 4f out: hdd 3f out: one pce fnl 2f* **12/1**

0-14 **4** *2* **Ally Makbul**[14] 487 4-9-9 55.......... NPollard 11 56
(JRBest) *hld up: stdy hdwy 8f out: led 3f out: rdn and hdd 2f out: wknd 1f out* **10/1**

15-2 **5** *7* **Claptrap**[15] 478 4-9-4 53.......... FPFerris(3) 10 43
(RBrotherton) *hld up: hdwy over 5f out: rdn and wknd 3f out* **3/1[1]**

-456 **6** *1¾* **Proud Victor (IRE)**[3] 567 4-8-8 40..........(v) DarrenWilliams 4 28
(DShaw) *hld up mid-div: lost pl 6f out: n.d after* **20/1**

-600 **7** *3½* **Haithem (IRE)**[9] 531 7-7-13 30..........(e) LisaJones(3) 9 13
(DShaw) *t.k.h in rr: nvr nr ldrs* **28/1**

01-0 **8** *6* **Adalpour (IRE)**[14] 483 6-9-5 52.......... AQuinn(5) 1 26
(DBurchell) *s.i.s: sme hdwy on ins over 5f out: wknd 3f out* **4/1[2]**

-050 **9** *1¼* **Dr Julian (IRE)**[3] 568 4-8-8 40..........(p) AnnStokell 3 12
(MissAStokell) *chsd ldr 6f: prom tl rdn and wknd over 3f out* **66/1**

203- **10** *nk* **Knockdoo (IRE)**[160] 3722 11-8-7 35.......... RFitzpatrick 8 6
(JSGoldie) *prom: wnt 2nd 6f out: sn rdn: wknd 4f out* **14/1**

006- **11** *7* **Toberoe Commotion (IRE)**[57] 4615 6-9-4 46.......... RHavlin 12 7
(BJLlewellyn) *hld up: hdwy over 5f out: rdn and wknd over 3f out* **16/1**

06-6 **12** *7* **Pertemps Bianca**[16] 468 4-8-8 40..........(b) JQuinn 5 —
(ADSmith) *t.k.h: prom tl wknd over 3f out* **7/1[3]**

2m 40.6s (-0.90) **Going Correction** -0.075s/f (Stan)
**WFA** 4 from 5yo+ 4lb **12** Ran SP% **125.6**
Speed ratings: **100,98,96,95,90 89,87,83,82,82 77,72**CSF £52.03 CT £508.52 TOTE £16.90: £4.20, £2.00, £3.60; EX 74.80.There was no bid for the winner
**Owner** R J Creese **Bred** Calogo Bloodstock And Newbyth Stud **Trained** Exning, Suffolk
■ Stewards Enquiry : S W Kelly caution: used whip with arm above shoulder height

**FOCUS**
This was fairly competitive by selling standards, although the level of form is obviously low.

**NOTEBOOK**
**Misty Man(USA)** found the combination of a return to both this trip and selling company enabling him to lose his maiden tag.
**Khuzdar(IRE)**, dropping back from two miles, was inclined to duck in behind the winner and again looked a tricky customer.
**Failed To Hit**, 11lb lower than when last in a handicap, kept plugging away in the home straight.
**Ally Makbul**, a winner over the stretched mile here earlier in the month, eventually had her stamina limitations exposed.
**Claptrap** is something of an in-and-out performer.
**Pertemps Bianca** *Official explanation: jockey said filly finished unsound*

**595** **BETDIRECT.CO.UK H'CAP** **1m 100y(F)**
4:15 (4:15) (D ) (0-85,83) 3-Y-O **£4,017** (£1,236; £618; £309) **Stalls** Low

Form RPR
14-5 **1** **Countrywide Flyer (IRE)**[16] [466] 3-9-4 80 JPSpencer 5 92+
(TDBarron) *hld up in tch: slipped through on ins to ld over 2f out: rdn wl over 1f out: drew clr fnl f: eased cl home* **9/2**[3]
00-1 **2** *5* **Gavroche (IRE)**[4] [566] 3-8-4 69 6ex J-PGuillambert(3) 2 71
(MJWallace) *a.p: led over 3f out: rdn and hdd over 2f out: no ch w wnr fnl f* **8/13**[1]
1-10 **3** *5* **Sir Jasper (IRE)**[4] [561] 3-7-13 61 6ex (v) SRighton 1 52
(MFHarris) *led: hdd over 3f out: sn rdn: wknd 2f out* **14/1**
63-4 **4** *2* **Marcus Eile (IRE)**[9] [522] 3-9-7 83 DarrenWilliams 7 70
(KRBurke) *sn outpcd: hdwy 6f out: rdn 3f out: wknd 2f out* **25/1**
13-2 **5** *18* **Bold Blade**[4] [566] 3-8-8 70 (b) RFfrench 4 19
(BSmart) *sn w ldr: rdn over 3f out: sn wknd* **7/2**[2]
61-0 **6** *21* **Boxgrove (FR)**[16] [466] 3-9-3 79 ACulhane 6 —
(CEBrittain) *bhd: outpcd 7f out: lost tch 4f out: t.o* **16/1**

1m 48.56s (-2.44) **Going Correction** -0.075s/f (Stan) **6** Ran SP% **118.7**
Speed ratings: **109,104,99,97,79 58**CSF £8.28 TOTE £3.60: £3.00, £1.10; EX 10.70 Place 6 £72.23, Place 5 £37.88.
**Owner** Nigel Shields **Bred** Gay O'Callaghan **Trained** Maunby, N Yorks

**FOCUS**
A decent little handicap, run in an outstanding time for a race of this type.

**NOTEBOOK**
**Countrywide Flyer(IRE)**, without the blinkers this time, is probably better on Fibresand and there was a lot to like about this performance. He is one to keep on the right side of.
**Gavroche(IRE)** landed a gamble here earlier in the week but proved no match for the winner over this slightly shorter trip with a penalty.
**Sir Jasper(IRE)** seems to be being experimented with by his new trainer with regards to his best trip.
**Bold Blade** probably found this coming too soon.
T/Jkpt: Not won. T/Plt: £86.20 to a £1 stake. Pool: £37,542.45. 317.80 winning tickets. T/Qpdt: £13.10 to a £1 stake. Pool: £3,126.80. 175.60 winning tickets. KH

## 573 LINGFIELD (L-H)
### Saturday, January 24

**OFFICIAL GOING: Standard**
Wind: almost nil Weather: sunny

**596** **BET DIRECT NO Q 08000 93 66 93 AMATEUR RIDERS' H'CAP** **6f (P)**
12:35 (12:35) (F ) (0-70,68) 4-Y-0+ **£2,961** (£846; £423) **Stalls** Low

Form RPR
00-0 **1** **Whippasnapper**[15] [488] 4-10-10 **60** MrEDehdashti(3) 7 71
(JRBest) *s.i.s: in rr tl prog over 2f out: plld out and effrt 1f out: led last 75y: styd on wl* **8/1**
1-63 **2** *1 1/4* **Ladies Knight**[7] [560] 4-10-8 **55** MsCWilliams 4 63
(DShaw) *trckd ldrs on inner: effrt over 1f out: led ins fnl f: hdd and outpcd last 75y* **7/1**[3]
423- **3** *1/2* **Inistrahull Island (IRE)**[49] [6127] 4-10-5 **59** (v[1]) MrSWarren(7) 5 65
(MHTompkins) *sn pressed ldr: led 3f out: hdd and one pce ins fnl f* **6/1**[2]
2-06 **4** *1 1/4* **Superchief**[3] [575] 9-10-11 **65** (bt) MrCDoran(7) 10 67
(MissBSanders) *dwlt: swtchd to r on inner and wl in rr: nt clr run over 2f out: gd prog over 1f out: styd on u.p fnl f* **20/1**
40-0 **5** *3* **Sounds Lucky**[10] [526] 8-11-2 **66** (b) MrsEmmaLittmoden(3) 11 59
(NPLittmoden) *racd in midfield: rdn over 2f out: kpt on same pce fr over 1f out: n.d* **8/1**
01-5 **6** *1/2* **Forever Phoenix**[9] [544] 4-11-4 **68** MrSDobson(3) 6 60
(RMHCowell) *pressed ldrs: rdn and cl up over 1f out: wknd fnl f* **7/1**[3]
065- **7** *1* **Best Before (IRE)**[29] [6238] 4-10-10 **60** MissEFolkes(3) 1 49
(PDEvans) *led to 1/2-way: wknd jst over 1f out* **14/1**
010- **8** *1/2* **Gun Salute**[25] [6256] 4-10-8 **55** (p) MrsSBosley 13 42
(GLMoore) *lw: dwlt: wl in rr: sme prog over 1f out: no imp fnl f* **10/1**
006- **9** *3/4* **Steely Dan**[163] [4128] 5-10-3 **57** MrsLABest(7) 12 42
(JRBest) *wl in rr: last and struggling over 2f out: no ch* **33/1**
000- **10** *2 1/2* **Effective**[68] [6014] 4-11-4 **65** MrSWalker 9 43
(APJarvis) *a towards rr: drvn and no prog over 2f out* **14/1**
1-46 **11** *3/4* **St Ivian**[9] [543] 4-11-6 **67** (v) MrsMMorris 8 42
(MrsNMacauley) *racd wd: a in rr: struggling over 2f out* **14/1**
432- **12** *1/2* **Illusive (IRE)**[343] [546] 7-11-6 **67** MissEJJones 3 41
(MWigham) *chsd ldrs tl wknd 2f out* **12/1**
0-32 **13** *1 1/2* **Legalis (USA)**[2] [584] 6-10-6 **58** (b) MSeston(5) 2 27
(KARyan) *restless in stalls: drvn up to chse ldrs: wknd over 2f out* **9/2**[1]

1m 12.9s (-0.02) **Going Correction** +0.10s/f (Slow) **13** Ran SP% **124.2**
Speed ratings: **104,102,101,100,96 95,94,93,92,89 88,87,85**CSF £65.68 CT £371.05 TOTE £10.40: £4.10, £2.70, £2.30; EX 72.90.
**Owner** Miss Vanessa Church **Bred** Acrum Lodge Stud **Trained** Hucking, Kent

**FOCUS**
They went a good pace, and the form looks solid by amateur riders' standards.

**NOTEBOOK**
**Whippasnapper**, below form on Fibresand in recent starts, appreciated this return to Polytrack to end a year-long losing run in clear-cut fashion. He is one to keep on the right side of if kept to this course.
**Ladies Knight** has gained his only two wins to date over five furlongs, but he gets this trip and ran well.
**Inistrahull Island(IRE)**, dropped a furlong in trip, with the visor on for the first time, ran respectably and showed enough pace to suggest he will be effective over five furlongs.
**Superchief** ran well over a trip on the short side, but he is proving hard to win with.
**Sounds Lucky** did not run a bad race and is one to bear in mind when his trainer hits top form.
**Steely Dan**, a stablemate of the winner, had been off the track since August and ran better than his finishing position suggests. He is one to keep an eye on when he steps up in trip.
**Legalis(USA)**, making his Polytrack debut, ran too badly to be true.

**597** **BET DIRECT NO Q DEMO 08000 837 888 MAIDEN STKS** **7f (P)**
1:05 (1:07) (D ) 3-Y-O **£3,838** (£1,181; £590; £295) **Stalls** Low

Form RPR
0 **1** **Sofistication (IRE)**[21] [415] 3-8-6 RMiles(3) 1 71+
(TGMills) *cl up: chsd ldr over 2f out: rdn to ld on inner last 150y: edgd rt but hld on wl* **12/1**
24 **2** *1/2* **Ile Facile (IRE)**[10] [529] 3-9-0 IMongan 12 73
(NPLittmoden) *pressed ldr: led over 4f out: kicked 2l clr over 2f out: hdd last 150y: kpt on wl but a jst hld* **7/1**[3]
0- **3** *6* **First Of May**[84] [5868] 3-8-9 MHenry 2 52
(MAJarvis) *racd in midfield: outpcd over 2f out: kpt on fnl f to take 3rd nr fin* **13/2**[2]
**4** *3/4* **Stage Right** 3-9-0 NPollard 16 55
(DRCElsworth) *unf: scope: bit bkwd: s.s: rn green and wl in rr: gd prog over 1f out: styd on fnl f: nrst fin* **16/1**
5- **5** *3/4* **Pure Emotion**[35] [6219] 3-8-9 JQuinn 4 48
(WRMuir) *pressed ldng pair: outpcd over 2f out: wknd fnl f: lost 3rd nr fin* **20/1**
**6** *1/2* **Claranete Princess (IRE)** 3-8-9 NCallan 7 47
(MJWallace) *unf: fit: s.i.s: drvn to chse ldrs: outpcd u.p fr 3f out: n.d after* **2/1**[1]
**7** *nk* **Air Of Supremacy (IRE)** 3-9-0 SWKelly 6 51
(JNoseda) *w'like: bit bkwd: s.i.s: racd towards rr: rdn over 4f out: modest late prog* **13/2**[2]
0 **8** *1/2* **Alfridini**[18] [447] 3-8-11 LPKeniry(3) 8 49
(DRCElsworth) *racd in midfield: outpcd fr 3f out: no ch after* **25/1**
0- **9** *hd* **Mystic Moon**[49] [6129] 3-8-9 SWhitworth 3 44
(JRJenkins) *led to over 4f out: wknd over 2f out* **66/1**
**10** *1/2* **Livia (IRE)** 3-8-9 RHavlin 9 43
(JGPortman) *leggy: dwlt: rcvrd into midfield 5f out: outpcd 3f out: no ch after* **66/1**
6 **11** *1 1/2* **Sunset Dreamer (USA)**[18] [447] 3-8-9 EAhern 11 39
(PMitchell) *stdd s: a wl in rr: shuffled along and no prog over 1f out* **16/1**
05- **12** *nk* **Dubaian Mist**[35] [6222] 3-8-9 WRyan 14 38
(AMBalding) *chsd ldrs: outpcd over 3f out: wknd over 1f out* **20/1**
**13** *hd* **Green Falcon** 3-9-0 MHills 15 42
(JWHills) *w'like: bit bkwd: dwlt: racd wd: wl in rr: prog into midfield 1/2-way: wknd 2f out* **8/1**
**14** *5* **Joy And Pain** 3-9-0 JPSpencer 13 29
(GLMoore) *w'like: bit bkwd: sn struggling in rr: wknd 2f out* **33/1**
00 **15** *15* **Jaycee Star (IRE)**[3] [574] 3-8-2 MCoumbe(7) 10 —
(DFlood) *a in rr: t.o 3f out* **150/1**

1m 26.04s (0.04) **Going Correction** +0.10s/f (Slow) **15** Ran SP% **123.0**
Speed ratings: **103,102,95,94,93 93,92,92,92,91 89,89,89,83,66**CSF £89.69 TOTE £25.50: £5.80, £1.90, £2.40; EX 109.00.
**Owner** Mrs L M Askew **Bred** Jockey Hall And Russell Farm Syndicate **Trained** Headley, Surrey

**FOCUS**
They went a decent enough gallop, so the form should be reliable, and the time was decent for a race if its type. Although the bare form is nothing special, there were a few who shaped with promise who should be capable of winning in similar company. The front two pulled nicely clear and it is probably significant that they raced right up with the pace throughout.

**NOTEBOOK**
**Sofistication(IRE)** ◆ stepped up significantly on her debut running over this course and distance with a narrow victory. There should be more to come and, providing the Handicapper is not too hard on her, she should be able to hold her own in a better grade.
**Ile Facile(IRE)** shaped with promise on his first two starts on Fibresand, but he appeared to step up on those efforts on this switch to Polytrack under a positive ride from Mongan. He was well clear of third and should be capable of winning a similar race on this surface.
**First Of May** shaped with promise on her debut in an ordinary Newmarket maiden and, returning from a break, again shaped nicely. She got going all too late and never threatened the leaders, but is likely to get further and is one to keep an eye on.
**Stage Right**, a half-brother to four winners, including at Listed winner, was not keen to go in the stalls and missed the break. However, despite running green, he kept on and is sure to improve a bundle on this.
**Pure Emotion** is likely to find things easier when handicapped.
**Claranete Princess(IRE)**, a 4,900euros half-sister to two middle-distance winners, was strongly supported in the market and was clearly expected to make a winning debut. However, Callan never looked at ease and followers of the gamble soon knew their fate. She should stay further and is clearly thought capable of better.
**Green Falcon** was supported in the ring, but did not show much.
**Joy And Pain** *Official explanation: jockey said gelding hung right throughout*

**598** **LITTLEWOODS BET DIRECT MAIDEN STKS** **1m 2f (P)**
1:40 (1:42) (D ) 3-Y-O **£4,134** (£1,272; £636; £318) **Stalls** Low

Form RPR
32-2 **1** *shd* **Baawrah**[14] [492] 3-9-0 71 CCatlin 1 74
(MRChannon) *led: rdn 3f out: hrd pressed fnl f: hdd and bmpd last stride: fin 2nd: awrdd r* **7/2**[2]
0-3 **2** **Fiddlers Ford (IRE)**[14] [492] 3-9-0 JPSpencer 12 74
(JNoseda) *t.k.h: hld up in rr: prog 3f out: rdn to chal 1f out: edgd lft and last last stride: fin 1st: disqualified:plcd 2nd* **9/4**[1]
5-22 **3** *2 1/2* **Amwell Brave**[10] [522] 3-9-0 71 SWKelly 3 70
(JRJenkins) *lw: hld up in midfield: prog to chse ldng pair over 2f out: drvn to chal on inner 1f out: nt qckn fnl f* **7/2**[2]
63- **4** *2 1/2* **Another Con (IRE)**[35] [6222] 3-8-9 RHavlin 5 60
(MrsPNDutfield) *chsd ldr: rdn over 3f out: rn wd bnd 2f out and sn lost 2nd: one pce after* **25/1**
5 **5** *3* **On The Waterfront**[18] [447] 3-9-0 MHills 4 60
(JWHills) *t.k.h: trckd ldrs: outpcd over 2f out: wknd fnl f* **20/1**
0-0 **6** *nk* **Jackie Kiely**[21] [415] 3-9-0 AClark 6 59
(TGMills) *racd in midfield: rdn over 3f out: no prog over 2f out: one pce after* **25/1**
6- **7** *1 1/4* **Wild Pitch**[245] [1820] 3-9-0 EAhern 13 57
(PMitchell) *t.k.h early: trckd ldrs: effrt and rdn 3f out: sn outpcd: wknd over 1f out* **10/1**
**8** *nk* **Heron's Wing** 3-9-0 JQuinn 10 56
(LadyHerries) *w'like: bit bkwd: s.s: hld up in rr: nudged along 2f out: nvr nr ldrs* **50/1**
0-2 **9** *shd* **Waltzing Beau**[5] [563] 3-9-0 IMongan 11 56
(IAWood) *rrd s: racd in rr: pushed along 4f out: outpcd 3f out: one pce after* **25/1**
00- **10** *19* **Prince Valentine**[45] [6158] 3-9-0 MTebbutt 8 22
(DBFeek) *racd in midfield: rdn and effrt 3f out: wknd rapidly over 1f out: eased: t.o* **14/1**
60- **11** *1* **Athboy**[109] [5439] 3-9-0 NCallan 7 20
(MJWallace) *racd in midfield: rdn and struggling 3f out: sn wknd: t.o* **5/1**[3]
0- **12** *3* **Corton Denham**[35] [6219] 3-9-0 RBrisland 2 15
(GPEnright) *a in rr: rdn and struggling 4f out: t.o* **250/1**
00- **13** *nk* **Miss Millietant**[67] [6020] 3-8-6 RMiles(3) 14 9
(LMontagueHall) *chsd ldrs tl wknd rapidly 3f out: t.o* **100/1**
0 **14** *1 1/2* **Devine Command**[18] [447] 3-9-0 NDay 9 11
(RIngram) *prog to chse ldrs 7f out: wknd over 3f out: t.o* **100/1**

2m 8.97s (1.58) **Going Correction** +0.10s/f (Slow) **14** Ran SP% **128.3**
Speed ratings: **96,97,94,92,90 90,89,89,88,73 72,70,70,69**CSF £11.89 TOTE £5.10: £1.80, £2.10, £2.50; EX 9.70.
**Owner** Sheikh Ahmed Al Maktoum **Bred** Darley **Trained** West Ilsley, Berks
■ Stewards Enquiry : J P Spencer two-day ban: careless riding (Feb 4,5)

**FOCUS**
A fair maiden in which Baawrah was awarded the race in the Stewards room, having been bumped just before the line by first past the post Fiddlers Ford. The form should work out.
**NOTEBOOK**
**Baawrah**, a length in front of Fiddlers Ford over course and distance on his previous start, may have won this outright had Fiddlers Ford not bumped into him just before the line. He was awarded the race in the Stewards room, but things will be tougher next time.
**Fiddlers Ford(IRE)**, third over course and distance in a similar race on his previous start, was disqualified after bumping the second past the post Baawrah, who finished a length in front of him last time. He should have little trouble in making amends.
**Amwell Brave** continues in decent enough form, but is quite simply proving hard to win with. He will surely, however, find a similar race before some of the better horses come out.
**Another Con(IRE)** ran respectably and is now qualified for a handicap mark.
**On The Waterfront** is probably going to come into his own when handicapped.
**Athboy**, making his debut for the Wallace yard, was quite well supported but ran a lacklustre race. The market move suggests he is thought capable of better and, now he is qualified for a handicap mark, he could be one to keep an eye on.

## 599 CHARLIE AND DAN FILLIES' H'CAP — 7f (P)
**2:10** (2:10) (E) (0-75,74) 3-Y-0+ — **£3,353** (£958; £479) **Stalls** Low

Form — RPR
34-5 **1** **Grey Pearl**[15] [488] 5-9-11 **71**........ MFenton 3 — 86
(MissGayKelleway) *prom: effrt on inner to ld wl over 1f out: drvn clr fnl f* **9/1**
2-21 **2** *1½* **Ripple Effect**[3] [575] 4-9-6 **71** 6ex........ BReilly(5) 10 — 82
(CADwyer) *pressed ldr: rdn to chal and w wnr wl over 1f out: nt qckn and hld fnl f* **7/2**[1]
310- **3** *1* **Cloud Dancer**[40] [6192] 5-10-0 **74**........ NCallan 2 — 82
(KARyan) *hld up in rr: prog over 2f out: rdn and styd on fr over 1f out: unable to chal* **10/1**
000- **4** *1¼* **Coppington Flyer (IRE)**[49] [6134] 4-8-1 **50**........ LisaJones(3) 1 — 55
(BWDuke) *racd in midfield: effrt on inner 2f out: pressed ldrs over 1f out: nt qckn fnl f* **50/1**
1-13 **5** *½* **Rowan Pursuit**[7] [557] 3-8-6 **70**........(b) JFanning 4 — 74
(JAkehurst) *s.i.s: racd towards rr: rdn and effrt 2f out: one pce and no imp ldrs* **4/1**[2]
14-0 **6** *shd* **Annishirani**[14] [494] 4-10-0 **74**........ EAhern 12 — 77
(GAButler) *t.k.h: hld up in last trio: sme prog 2f out: pushed along and styd on same pce fnl f* **12/1**
10-0 **7** *½* **Pants**[14] [491] 5-8-9 **55**........ ANicholls 11 — 57
(AndrewReid) *b: b.hind: dwlt: racd in last trio: prog on inner wl over 1f out: no hdwy fnl f* **25/1**
4-66 **8** *¾* **Blonde En Blonde (IRE)**[15] [488] 4-9-3 **63**........ IMongan 9 — 63
(NPLittmoden) *racd on outer in midfield: rdn over 2f out: fdd over 1f out* **25/1**
146- **9** *nk* **I Wish**[25] [6256] 6-9-0 **63**........ LPKeniry(3) 7 — 62
(MMadgwick) *chsd ldrs: rdn over 2f out: fdd over 1f out* **12/1**
05-6 **10** *hd* **Emerald Fire**[10] [526] 5-9-4 **69**........ NChalmers(5) 6 — 67
(AMBalding) *lw: racd in rr: rdn over 4f out: effrt u.p 3f out: rn wd bnd 2f out: sn btn* **11/2**[3]
462- **10** *dht* **Lily Of The Guild (IRE)**[25] [6260] 5-8-8 **54**........ JQuinn 13 — 52
(WSKittow) *t.k.h: hld up in last trio: stl gng wl enough but no ch whn nt clr run 1f out: nvr near ldrs* **10/1**
0-04 **12** *1¼* **Geespot**[9] [536] 5-7-8 **45**........ JFMcDonald(5) 8 — 40
(DJSFfrenchDavis) *prom tl wknd 2f out* **20/1**
540- **13** *6* **Ciacole**[46] [6152] 3-8-6 **70**........ MHenry 5 — 48
(SCWilliams) *led to wl over 1f out: wknd rapidly and eased* **40/1**

1m 25.83s (-0.17) **Going Correction** +0.10s/f (Slow)
**WFA** 3 from 4yo+ 18lb — **13** Ran SP% **118.0**
Speed ratings: **104,102,101,99,99 99,98,97,97,97 97,95,88**CSF £37.64 CT £339.57 TOTE £12.40: £4.70, £2.60, £4.10; EX 70.90.
**Owner** Andrea Wilkinson Gay Kelleway **Bred** Miss J Chaplin **Trained** Newmarket, Suffolk
**FOCUS**
A good race for the grade. They went a decent clip and the form looks solid.
**NOTEBOOK**
**Grey Pearl** has not been getting home after going off too fast at Wolverhampton recently but, switching to Polytrack and ridden with more restraint, she ran out a ready winner. This was her first win since landing a maiden in 2002, but she was rated in the low 90s at one time and, now connections know how to ride her, is one to keep on the right side of.
**Ripple Effect**, comfortable winner of a claimer over course and distance earlier in the week, found this tougher but still ran well under her 6lb penalty.
**Cloud Dancer**, racing on Polytrack for just the second time, came from well off the pace to take third. She could well find a race round here if things fall right for her.
**Coppington Flyer(IRE)** has been bang out of form lately but, with the blinkers left off, this was better. She appeared to flash her tail when hit by the whip and may do better under a more considerate ride.
**Rowan Pursuit** ran respectably against older horses, but never really looked like winning.
**Annishirani** got going too late and ran better than her finishing position suggests. She is one to keep an eye on when stepped back up in trip.
**Lily Of The Guild(IRE)** got no luck in running.

## 600 BETDIRECT.CO.UK H'CAP — 1m 4f (P)
**2:45** (2:46) (C) (0-95,92) 4-Y-0+ — **£10,637** (£4,034; £2,017; £917) **Stalls** Low

Form — RPR
12-1 **1** **Cold Turkey**[10] [523] 4-9-2 **84**........ SWhitworth 4 — 98+
(GLMoore) *s.s: hld up in last: stdy prog 5f out to trck ldrs 2f out: rdn to ld jst over 1f out: styd on wl* **6/1**[3]
30-2 **2** *1½* **Flight Of Esteem**[21] [418] 4-9-10 **92**........ NCallan 7 — 100
(PWHarris) *prom: led over 3f out: drvn and hdd jst over 1f out: one pce fnl f* **5/1**[1]
1-65 **3** *nk* **Tight Squeeze**[10] [523] 7-9-0 **78**........ ACulhane 15 — 86
(PWHiatt) *hld up towards rr: prog 4f out: pressed ldrs 2f out: rdn and styd on same pce fr over 1f out* **12/1**
10-6 **4** *¾* **Dance In The Sun**[7] [558] 4-9-3 **85**........ JPSpencer 5 — 91
(MrsAJPerrett) *sn in midfield: prog to press ldrs over 2f out: hrd rdn and styd on same pce fnl 2f* **12/1**
04-1 **5** *3* **Barry Island**[7] [554] 5-8-8 **75**........ LisaJones(3) 6 — 77
(DRCElsworth) *lw: s.s: plld hrd and hld up in last pair: stdy prog fr 4f out: no imp on ldrs fnl 2f* **11/2**[2]
00-0 **6** *11* **Moon Emperor**[10] [523] 7-9-9 **87**........ EAhern 10 — 72
(JRJenkins) *racd in midfield: lost pl over 5f out: wl in rr and struggling over 4f out: kpt on past wkng rivals fr over 2f out* **20/1**
1-00 **7** *½* **High Point (IRE)**[10] [523] 6-9-1 **79**........ IMongan 14 — 64
(GPEnright) *sn rdn in rr: last and struggling 5f out: kpt on past wkng rivals fnl 3f* **16/1**
30-0 **8** *5* **Te Quiero**[9] [544] 6-10-0 **92**........(t) MFenton 2 — 69
(MissGayKelleway) *b: b.hind: hld up towards rr: prog to trck ldrs over 4f out: cl up over 2f out: sn wknd* **40/1**
0/0- **9** *1* **Adalar (IRE)**[25] [6263] 4-8-5 **80**........ SJDonohoe(7) 1 — 56
(PDEvans) *pressed ldr: led over 5f out to over 3f out: wknd and eased 2f out* **66/1**
600- **10** *7* **Blue Patrick**[35] [6224] 4-9-0 **82**........ JMackay 16 — 47
(JMPEustace) *hld up in rr: prog on outer over 4f out: chsd ldrs over 2f out: sn wknd* **40/1**
26-1 **11** *2½* **Gig Harbor**[21] [418] 5-9-8 **89**........ LPKeniry(3) 9 — 50
(MissECLavelle) *chsd ldrs: lost pl and rdn over 4f out: sn struggling* **13/2**
11-3 **12** *4* **Mr Mischief**[10] [523] 4-8-11 **86**........ RoryMoore(7) 8 — 41
(PCHaslam) *dwlt: hld up in rr: wknd and bhd fnl 3f* **8/1**
10-3 **13** *2½* **Cruise Director**[21] [418] 4-9-1 **83**........ PaulEddery 3 — 35
(WJMusson) *sn in midfield: outpcd over 3f out: wknd over 2f out* **7/1**
0-02 **14** *10* **Internationalguest (IRE)**[10] [523] 5-9-3 **81**........(v) NPollard 13 — 18
(GGMargarson) *prom tl wknd over 4f out: t.o* **20/1**
/00- **15** *23* **Blue Leader (IRE)**[92] [1632] 5-8-13 **77**........(p) JoannaBadger 11 — —
(GBrown) *led to over 5f out: sn wknd: t.o fnl 3f* **100/1**
/0-0 **16** *18* **Midshipman**[15] [485] 6-9-8 **86**........ PJScallan 12 — —
(AWCarroll) *chsd ldrs to 1/2-way: sn wknd: t.o over 3f out* **66/1**

2m 32.11s (-1.87) **Going Correction** +0.10s/f (Slow)
**WFA** 4 from 5yo+ 4lb — **16** Ran SP% **122.9**
Speed ratings: **110,109,108,108,106 98,98,95,94,89 88,85,83,77,61 49**CSF £34.32 CT £360.49 TOTE £5.10: £1.30, £1.40, £2.70, £3.30; EX 36.00.
**Owner** A Grinter **Bred** Worksop Manor Stud **Trained** Woodingdean, E Sussex
**FOCUS**
With the likes of Moon Emperor, High Point and Gig Harbour failing to run up to their best, this was maybe not quite as strong a handicap as you would have expected for the money, but take nothing away from Cold Turkey, who was winning for fifth time on Polytrack and still has more to offer. The pace was better than for many races run over this trip, and the final time was good.
**NOTEBOOK**
**Cold Turkey** made it six wins from his last seven starts with quite a comfortable victory. As usual he missed the kick and was given time to find his stride, but he came there cantering on the turn and quickened away stylishly when asked. He will face tougher opposition in future, and a rise in the weights will also make things difficult, but he just cannot be opposed round here.
**Flight Of Esteem**, runner-up to Gig Harbour over course and distance on his previous start, had every chance and ran another cracker. He is not doing his handicap mark any good.
**Tight Squeeze** is running well in these valuable handicaps round here and, with some of the principals running below form, was able to grab some place money. Culhane gets on well with her.
**Dance In The Sun** ran respectably, but failed to convince that this trip really suits.
**Barry Island** found this harder than the claimer he won over ten furlongs here on his previous outing, and did not help his cause by racing keenly.
**Gig Harbor** is better than he showed here. *Official explanation: jockey said gelding was never travelling and lost its action*
**Mr Mischief** ran a long way below form.
**Cruise Director** *Official explanation: trainer had no explanation for the poor form shown*

## 601 BET DIRECT MAIDEN STKS — 1m 2f (P)
**3:15** (3:18) (D) 4-Y-0+ — **£3,740** (£1,151; £575; £287) **Stalls** Low

Form — RPR
0-24 **1** **Coronado Forest (USA)**[7] [555] 5-9-2 59........ ACulhane 6 — 62
(MRHoad) *mde all: kicked on over 2f out: drvn and kpt on wl fr over 1f out* **5/1**[3]
6-3 **2** *1¾* **Have Some Fun**[10] [520] 4-9-0........ JQuinn 10 — 59
(PRChamings) *trckd wnr: clr of rest fr over 2f out: drvn and nt qckn over 1f out: hld after* **7/1**
00-3 **3** *2* **Zalkani (IRE)**[7] [555] 4-9-0 67........ JPSpencer 11 — 55
(BGPowell) *hld up in rr: prog into midfield gng easily 3f out: sn outpcd: chsd clr ldng pair over 1f out: kpt on: too much to do* **5/2**[1]
60-5 **4** *2½* **Raheel (IRE)**[17] [467] 4-9-0 46........(t) JFanning 3 — 51
(PMitchell) *hld up in midfield: lost pl and in rr 1/2-way: effrt 3f out: sn outpcd: kpt on same pce fnl 2f* **11/1**
232- **5** *2* **Skibereen (IRE)**[163] [4115] 4-8-11 74........ DAllan(3) 8 — 47
(IWMcinnes) *racd in midfield: prog 4f out: rdn to chse ldng pair over 2f out to over 1f out: wknd* **11/4**[2]
6-00 **6** *5* **Over Rating**[19] [440] 4-8-9 56........(p) NCallan 4 — 33
(KARyan) *prom: chsd ldng pair 6f out: drvn 4f out: wknd over 2f out* **25/1**
0- **7** *3* **Glesni**[73] [5978] 5-8-6........ BReilly(5) 1 — 28
(SCWilliams) *bolted bef s: a in rr: pushed along and struggling over 4f out* **11/2**
00/ **8** *½* **Pedler's Profiles**[456] [5466] 4-8-7........ DerekNolan(7) 5 — 32
(MissKMGeorge) *b: t.k.h early: chsd ldng pair to 6f out: losing pl and struggling 4f out* **100/1**
**9** *¾* **Bruzella** 5-8-11........ EAhern 7 — 26
(AJLidderdale) *b: bit bkwd: a in rr: rdn and struggling 4f out* **25/1**

2m 9.05s (1.66) **Going Correction** +0.10s/f (Slow)
**WFA** 4 from 5yo 2lb — **9** Ran SP% **116.8**
Speed ratings: **97,95,94,92,90 86,84,83,83**CSF £39.41 TOTE £6.50: £1.20, £2.30, £1.60; EX 39.30.
**Owner** Ken Webb **Bred** Kent & Kathy Wiechert **Trained** Lewes, E Sussex
**FOCUS**
Lots of disappointing types, and a modest time. The first two raced in the first two throughout and the winner was given a very easy time of things up front.
**NOTEBOOK**
**Coronado Forest(USA)** was left alone up front and Culhane dictated the pace to suit his mount. Things will be a lot harder next time.
**Have Some Fun** tracked the winner throughout, but was always being held. He is now qualified for a handicap mark and, given that he has been beaten by a 59-rated performer, the assessor should not be too harsh.
**Zalkani(IRE)** had no chance given the way the race was run, and the only consolation is he did best of those held up. He is better than this, but probably not by much.
**Raheel(IRE)** would have preferred a stronger pace, but is basically a frustrating sort.
**Skibereen(IRE)**, returning from a break and running for new connections, failed to justify his rating of 74 with the removal of the tongue-tie and blinkers.

## 602 BET DIRECT CLASSIFIED STKS — 1m 2f (P)
**3:45** (3:48) (F) 4-Y-0+ — **£3,017** (£862; £431) **Stalls** Low

Form — RPR
/41- **1** **Regal Gallery (IRE)**[38] [6205] 6-8-13 58........ PaulEddery 2 — 71+
(CAHorgan) *hld up in midfield: prog fr 3f out: swept into ld jst over 1f out: pushed clr* **4/1**[1]
42-3 **2** *2½* **Welsh Wind (IRE)**[17] [464] 8-9-2 56........(t) JFanning 4 — 65
(MWigham) *lw: trckd ldrs: cl up 2f out: nt clr run over 1f out and swtchd rt: r.o to take 2nd ins fnl f: no ch w wnr* **9/2**[2]



The Form Book, Raceform Ltd, Compton, RG20 6NL

03-6 **3** *1 ½* **Zawrak (IRE)**[17] 467 5-8-9 60 NataliaGemelova(7) 1 62
(IWMcinnes) *dwlt: hld up towards rr: prog to chse ldrs over 2f out: unable qck over 1f out: styd on ins fnl f* **7/1**

30-0 **4** *¾* **Amnesty**[18] 449 5-9-2 60 (be1) SWhitworth 6 61
(GLMoore) *hld up towards rr: prog on inner 2f out: styd on fnl f: no ch w ldrs* **20/1**

00-0 **5** *1* **Dancing Forest (IRE)**[17] 468 4-9-0 60 NCallan 5 59
(DKIvory) *trckd ldrs: cl up 2f out: nt clr run 1f out: styd on last 100y* **20/1**

0-00 **6** *hd* **Icannshift (IRE)**[7] 554 4-9-0 57 CCatlin 12 58
(SDow) *s.i.s: plld way up to join ldr after 2f: rdn and ev ch jst over 1f out: sn btn* **50/1**

010- **7** *½* **Mezereon**[84] 5116 4-8-11 58 RFitzpatrick 9 55
(DCarroll) *mde most to jst over 1f out: wknd ins fnl f* **6/1**3

06-1 **8** *1* **Itsonlyagame**[9] 534 4-9-0 60 IMongan 11 56
(RIngram) *sn trckd ldrs: rdn over 2f out: outpcd and btn over 1f out* **14/1**

140- **9** *2 ½* **Anyhow (IRE)**[79] 5935 7-8-13 60 JPSpencer 13 48
(MissKMGeorge) *hld up towards rr: rdn 3f out: sme prog 2f out: no hdwy and btn over 1f out* **4/1**1

006- **10** *1 ¾* **Noble Calling (FR)**[16] 5308 7-9-2 60 EAhern 3 48
(RJHodges) *towards rr: u.p 4f out: struggling and btn 3f out* **16/1**

0-00 **11** *3 ½* **Mister Clinton (IRE)**[10] 525 7-8-13 50 RMiles(3) 8 42
(DKIvory) *plld hrd early: restrained bhd ldrs: lost pl 4f out: wknd 3f out* **25/1**

000- **12** *6* **Master T (USA)**[65] 1927 5-8-11 60 AQuinn(5) 7 31
(GLMoore) *hld up in last trio: rdn and struggling over 3f out: sn bhd* **11/1**

**13** *¾* **Sekwana (POL)**[16] 5-8-13 60 (p) DSweeney 10 27
(MissAMNewton-Smith) *b: a in rr: hrd rdn and wknd 3f out* **100/1**

006- **14** *3* **Legality**[35] 6226 4-8-6 51 BReilly(5) 14 21
(JulianPoulton) *a in rr: rdn and bhd 3f out* **33/1**

2m 9.38s (1.99) **Going Correction** +0.10s/f (Slow)
**WFA** 4 from 5yo+ 2lb **14** Ran SP% **125.1**
Speed ratings: **96,94,92,92,91 91,90,90,88,86 83,79,78,76**CSF £20.97 TOTE £7.20: £2.20, £1.70, £5.00; EX 24.70.
**Owner** Mrs B Sumner **Bred** Mrs B Sumner **Trained** Ogbourne Maisey, Wilts

**FOCUS**
A modest time, but fair form for the grade and Regal Gallery improved again.

**NOTEBOOK**
**Regal Gallery(IRE)** followed up her recent course and distance success in good style and could well go on to complete the hat-trick whilst in this form.
**Welsh Wind(IRE)**, 5lb wrong with the winner at the weights, is in good form and may have been closer with better luck in running. That said, he is very hard to win with.
**Zawrak(IRE)** got going all too late and never threatened.
**Amnesty**, with headgear on for the first time, posted a respectable effort under top weight, but is still a maiden.
**Dancing Forest(IRE)** did not fail through lack of stamina and was running on again after being checked.
**Anyhow(IRE)**, well in at the weights, was below form on his return from a break. *Official explanation: jockey said mare was unsuited by the slow early pace*
**Legality** *Official explanation: trainer said filly had been struck into during the race*

## 603 BET DIRECT ON SKY ACTIVE H'CAP 2m (P)
**4:20** (4:21) (E ) (0-75,75) 4-Y-0+ **£3,402** (£972; £486) **Stalls** Low

Form RPR

500- **1** **Land Of Fantasy**[171] 3903 5-8-9 56 JQuinn 8 66
(LadyHerries) *hld up in midfield: lost pl and last over 4f out: prog 3f out: hrd rdn 2f out: r.o to ld last strides* **50/1**

050- **2** *hd* **Ezz Elkheil**[122] 5152 5-9-13 74 EAhern 3 84
(JRJenkins) *plld hrd early: trckd ldr to 10f out: styd prom: rdn and effrt 2f out: styd on to ld last 75y: hdd fnl strides* **14/1**

440- **3** *½* **Boumahou (IRE)**[92] 5724 4-9-2 70 NCallan 6 79
(APJarvis) *hld up in rr: prog to press ldr 3f out: rdn to ld 2f out: hdd and unable qck last 75y* **40/1**

33-6 **4** *hd* **Typhoon Tilly**[10] 523 7-9-13 74 MFenton 9 83
(CREgerton) *t.k.h: hld up in last trio: prog to trck ldr 4f out to 3f out: styd cl up: drvn to chal fnl f: no ex last 75y* **4/1**2

/6-2 **5** *½* **Marmaduke (IRE)**[15] 483 8-9-2 63 VSlattery 1 72
(MPitman) *lw: led at stdy pce: kicked on 4f out: rdn and hdd 2f out: styd cl up: one pce ins fnl f* **7/1**

35-1 **6** *2 ½* **Red Scorpion (USA)**[21] 413 5-9-7 75 BSwarbrick(7) 11 81
(WMBrisbourne) *hld up in rr: prog over 2f out: rdn and kpt on same pce fr over 1f out* **7/1**

60-4 **7** *2* **Bustling Rio (IRE)**[15] 483 8-8-7 61 RoryMoore(7) 2 64
(PCHaslam) *trckd ldrs: lost pl 3f out: hrd rdn and one pce fnl 2f* **9/1**

0-33 **8** *6* **Ambersong**[12] 505 6-8-1 51 LisaJones(3) 13 47
(AWCarroll) *t.k.h: hld up in rr: prog 6f out: lost pl over 4f out: n.d fnl 2f* **12/1**

112- **9** *½* **Macaroni Gold (IRE)**[59] 6079 4-8-12 66 MTebbutt 7 61
(WJarvis) *b.hind: trckd ldrs: lost pl and in rr over 4f out: drvn and prog 3f out: btn over 1f out: eased* **2/1**1

600- **10** *shd* **Dance Light (IRE)**[43] 6168 5-8-8 55 JMackay 5 50
(TTClement) *hld up towards rr: in tch tl wknd over 2f out* **20/1**

63-0 **11** *13* **Makarim (IRE)**[17] 467 8-8-5 57 (p) HayleyTurner(5) 12 37
(MRBosley) *prog to chse ldr 10f to 4f out: wknd rapidly 3f out* **25/1**

123- **12** *dist* **Top Tenor (IRE)**[116] 5287 4-9-5 73 PDoe 10 —
(BRJohnson) *dwlt: sn prom: wknd rapidly 4f out: t.o* **6/1**3

3m 30.85s (2.27) **Going Correction** +0.10s/f (Slow)
**WFA** 4 from 5yo+ 7lb **12** Ran SP% **130.0**
Speed ratings: **98,97,97,97,97 96,95,92,91,91 85,**—CSF £669.73 CT £24619.48 TOTE £52.30: £14.00, £4.70, £9.90; EX 816.90 Place 6 £87.44, Place 5 £25.30.
**Owner** Lady Herries **Bred** Angmering Park Stud **Trained** Angmering, W Sussex

**FOCUS**
Form that wants treating with caution, as they went no pace early on, resulting in something of a sprint to the line and a moderate winning time.

**NOTEBOOK**
**Land Of Fantasy**, beaten in a seller over a mile for Dean Ivory when last seen 171 days previously, appreciated the removal of the blinkers and step up in trip and ran out a game winner. A truly-run two miles will provide him with more of a test, but this will have done his confidence the world of good.
**Ezz Elkheil**, another returning from a break, ran well on this step up in trip and switch to Polytrack and was just denied.
**Boumahou(IRE)**, a lightly-raced maiden, ran pleasingly and may have a similar race in him, possibly over a little shorter.
**Typhoon Tilly** is unproven over this trip, and a stronger pace would have given a better indication as to whether it suits.
**Marmaduke(IRE)** had every chance.
**Macaroni Gold(IRE)**, returning from a 59-day break, was below his best, even allowing for him being unsuited by the way the race was run.

T/Plt: £54.20 to a £1 stake. Pool: £41,141.35. 554.10 winning tickets. T/Qpdt: £5.50 to a £1 stake. Pool: £2,682.40. 358.70 winning tickets. JN

# 589 WOLVERHAMPTON (A.W) (L-H)
## Monday, January 26

**OFFICIAL GOING: Standard**

## 604 PRESS INTERACTIVE TO BET DIRECT AMATEUR RIDERS' H'CAP 1m 100y(F)
**1:45** (1:46) (G ) (0-75,70) 4-Y-0+ **£2,625** (£750; £375) **Stalls** Low

Form RPR

10/1 **1** **Consonant (IRE)**[12] 531 7-11-2 70 MrLNewnes(5) 7 83+
(DGBridgwater) *chsd ldrs: led on bit over 2f out: drew clr fnl f: readily* **9/4**1

0-50 **2** *4* **Paso Doble**[3] 589 6-10-6 62 MrJMillman(7) 11 67
(BRMillman) *chsd ldrs: pushed along 6f out: rdn over 3f out: kpt on ins fnl f: no ch w wnr* **10/1**3

364- **3** *1 ¼* **Pas De Surprise**[100] 5498 6-10-6 58 MissEFolkes(3) 4 60
(PDEvans) *hld up: hdwy over 5f out: chsd wnr 2f out tl no ex ins fnl f* **12/1**

0-01 **4** *1 ¾* **Mr Whizz**[6] 567 7-9-4 44 5ex ow4 (be) MrAshleePrice(5) 5 42
(APJones) *sn rdn along in rr: hdwy on ins 4f out: one pce fnl 2f* **16/1**

00-0 **5** *½* **Frankskips**[20] 448 5-10-6 62 MrCDoran(7) 6 59
(MissBSanders) *hld up: hdwy on outside over 2f out: no imp fnl f* **16/1**

3-34 **6** *2* **Quiet Reading (USA)**[7] 564 7-11-4 67 (v) MrsSBosley 9 60
(MRBosley) *hld up: hdwy over 3f out: sn rdn: wknd fnl f* **3/1**2

5-42 **7** *1 ¼* **Nite-Owl Fizz**[12] 531 6-9-8 50 MissTO'Brien(7) 10 40
(JO'Reilly) *s.i.s: bhd tl sme hdwy over 1f out: n.d* **14/1**

6-02 **8** *6* **Littleton Zephir (USA)**[3] 589 5-9-6 46 (b) MrsCThompson(5) 8 24
(MrsPTownsley) *prom: led over 3f out tl over 2f out: sn wknd* **12/1**

010- **9** *1 ¾* **Mister Benji**[41] 6202 5-10-4 56 (p) MrEDehdashti(3) 3 30
(BPJBaugh) *prom: led over 4f out tl over 3f out: wknd over 2f out* **12/1**

0-53 **10** *2* **Tinian**[11] 542 6-9-11 49 MrSDobson(3) 12 19
(KRBurke) *a bhd* **12/1**

-504 **11** *20* **Dancing King (IRE)**[7] 562 8-9-1 41 oh8 ow3 MrsMarieKing(5) 1 —
(PWHiatt) *w ldr 3f: wknd over 4f out: t.o* **40/1**

60-0 **12** *10* **Finger Of Fate**[11] 546 4-11-0 63 MrSWalker 2 —
(MJPolglase) *led 4f: sn rdn and wknd: t.o* **20/1**

1m 53.53s (2.53) **Going Correction** 0.0s/f (Stan) **12** Ran SP% **121.3**
Speed ratings: **87,83,81,80,79 77,76,70,68,66 46,36**CSF £26.64 CT £236.09 TOTE £2.40: £1.10, £3.10, £3.70; EX 29.50.
**Owner** The Rule Racing Syndicate **Bred** Kilfrush Stud Ltd **Trained** Winchcombe, Gloucs

**FOCUS**
A very easy winner, who totally dominated, but a slow winning time, and the form is still below his juvenile efforts.

**NOTEBOOK**
**Consonant(IRE)** comfortably followed up his recent comeback win over course-and-distance. Although the winning time was only moderate and he again beat little, he was value for more than the official winning margin. Now he seems to be taking his racing much better he looks the type to win under a penalty, before the Handicapper takes his revenge.
**Paso Doble** ran much his best race for some time. An extra furlong would be in his favour.
**Pas De Surprise**, returning form a three-month break, ran with credit. He is a versatile sort who will come on for the outing and has a race in him on this surface.
**Mr Whizz**, who improved for today's headgear when winning a dire contest last time at Southwell, ran well enough under his penalty. However, he may be better suited by racing over further at this venue..
**Frankskips** *Official explanation: trainer said gelding was later found to have bled from the nose*
**Quiet Reading(USA)** looked to have a fair chance on paper, but ran a flat race and the Handicapper would appear to have his measure at present.

## 605 BET DIRECT THROUGH SKY ACTIVE CLAIMING STKS 1m 1f 79y(F)
**2:20** (2:21) (F ) 4-Y-0+ **£2,912** (£832; £416) **Stalls** Low

Form RPR

6-03 **1** **Eastborough (IRE)**[9] 554 5-9-2 67 JQuinn 4 65
(BGPowell) *hld up: hdwy on ins over 3f out: rdn to ld over 1f out: drvn out* **11/2**3

24-5 **2** *1 ½* **Caroubier (IRE)**[14] 507 4-9-11 75 (v1) NCallan 9 72
(TDBarron) *hld up: hdwy over 3f out: rdn and ev ch wl over 1f out: r.o one pce fnl f* **7/4**1

2521 **3** *½* **Givemethemoonlight**[7] 562 5-9-3 48 (v) IMongan 6 62
(MrsStefLiddiard) *hld up in tch: rdn to ld jst over 2f out: hdd over 1f out: no ex ins fnl f* **5/2**2

0-65 **4** *9* **Foolish Thought (IRE)**[5] 575 4-8-3 58 ow3 (p) THamilton(5) 3 38
(RAFahey) *led: hdd over 5f out: led again over 3f out tl jst over 2f out: sn wknd* **13/2**

0-44 **5** *4* **Two Steps To Go (USA)**[14] 500 5-8-6 35 (b) ANicholls 7 28
(IanEmmerson) *w ldr: led over 5f out: rdn over 4f out: hdd over 3f out: wknd 2f out* **50/1**

066- **6** *1 ¼* **Chapel Royale (IRE)**[98] 3744 7-8-8 47 (t) JoannaBadger 5 27
(MrsNSSharpe) *hld up in rr: pushed along over 6f out: a bhd* **40/1**

00-0 **7** *5* **Answered Promise (FR)**[12] 525 5-8-9 51 RMiles(3) 10 22
(AWCarroll) *prom tl wknd 3f out* **25/1**

3-23 **8** *2* **Danger Bird (IRE)**[10] 552 4-8-12 48 ACulhane 8 20
(RHollinshead) *prom: rdn over 3f out: wknd over 2f out* **8/1**

626- **9** *10* **Conchonita**[38] 6214 4-8-2 45 DKinsella 2 —
(BPalling) *prom: rdn over 5f out: sn lost pl* **20/1**

2m 2.49s (-0.41) **Going Correction** 0.0s/f (Stan)
**WFA** 4 from 5yo+ 1lb **9** Ran SP% **117.8**
Speed ratings: **101,99,99,91,87 86,82,80,71**CSF £15.39 TOTE £7.00: £2.30, £1.10, £1.10; EX 19.50.
**Owner** Christopher Shankland **Bred** Ballyhane Stud **Trained** Morestead, Hants

**FOCUS**
A fair claimer run at a sound pace and the form looks solid.

**NOTEBOOK**
**Eastborough(IRE)** won this tidily, providing the stable with its first winner at the venue. Travelling well off the pace throughout, he showed a fair turn of pace up the inside to join the leaders turning for home. He was given a well-judged ride and looked to have a bit left in the tank at the finish.
**Caroubier(IRE)**, with his usual blinkers swapped for the visor on this occasion, had every chance. This represented a drop in grade and he looked a tricky ride on this occasion.
**Givemethemoonlight** was up against it at the weights, but ran better than her current rating suggests she was entitled to. She is not easy to win with and will take a hike in the weights, but is in good heart at present.
**Foolish Thought(IRE)** did not get home over this extra furlong, but was in the process of running an improved race until he tired.

## 606 BETDIRECT.CO.UK MAIDEN STKS 6f (F)
2:55 (2:56) (D ) 3-Y-O £3,367 (£1,036; £518; £259) Stalls Low

Form RPR

5- **1** **Mount Vettore**[90] 5812 3-9-0 PFitzsimons 5 73+
(MrsJRRamsden) *broke wl: stdd sn after s: hdwy over 1f out: r.o wl to ld towards fin: cleverly* **14/1**

206- **2** ¾ **Toronto Heights (USA)**[111] 5441 3-9-0 76 JQuinn 8 67
(PWChapple-Hyam) *t.k.h in tch: nt clr run over 2f out: rdn wl over 1f out: ev ch wl ins fnl f: nt qckn* **2/1**[2]

0-0 **3** ¾ **Ask The Clerk (IRE)**[19] 462 3-9-0 67 MTebbutt 7 65
(HJCollingridge) *a.p: led 2f out: rdn over 1f out: hdd and no ex towards fin* **16/1**

54-4 **4** 1¼ **Fizzy Lady**[9] 553 3-8-9 67 MHills 9 56
(BWHills) *chsd ldrs: rdn 3f out: ev ch 2f out: kpt on same pce fnl f* **15/8**[1]

525- **5** 1 **Soul Provider (IRE)**[235] 2127 3-8-6 64 FPFerris(3) 1 53
(PABlockley) *s.i.s: hdwy over 2f out: no real imp fnl f* **14/1**

00- **6** nk **Brown Dragon**[122] 5192 3-9-0 PaulEddery 12 57
(DHaydnJones) *led early: prom: rdn and ev ch 2f out: wknd fnl f* **50/1**

5 **7** ½ **Noble Mount**[16] 489 3-9-0 JMackay 3 56
(RGuest) *sn prom: rdn over 2f out: wknd ins fnl f* **16/1**

30-2 **8** 5 **Docklands Blue (IRE)**[23] 414 3-8-6 60 J-PGuillambert(3) 11 36
(NPLittmoden) *prom tl rdn and wknd 2f out* **5/1**[3]

05-0 **9** hd **City Affair**[16] 496 3-8-8 60 ow1 (p) SJDonohoe(7) 10 41
(MrsLCJewell) *hld up: rdn 3f out: bhd fnl 2f* **33/1**

**10** 3 **Dane Rhapsody (IRE)** 3-8-9 MFenton 2 26
(BPalling) *sn led: rdn and hdd 2f out: wknd over 1f out* **50/1**

0 **11** ½ **Fairly Glorious**[3] 591 3-8-9 TEaves(5) 6 30
(THCaldwell) *outpcd* **66/1**

1m 16.38s (0.68) **Going Correction** 0.0s/f (Stan) **11** Ran SP% **118.2**
Speed ratings: **95,94,93,91,90 89,88,82,82,78 77**CSF £42.08 TOTE £21.30: £2.90, £2.20, £3.30; EX 53.90.
**Owner** J David Abell **Bred** Jose Bonifacio C Nogueira **Trained** Sandhutton, N Yorks

**FOCUS**
A fairly modest time for the class of contest, but the winner looks above average for this time of year and those close behind all look capable of losing their maiden tags.

**NOTEBOOK**
**Mount Vettore**, who refused to enter the stalls at this track in November, showed his true colours by travelling well and quickening up late to win with plenty in hand. He ran distinctly green on his debut on turf last year, but this display shows he has done well since and he looks one to progress to a fair level over further.
**Toronto Heights(USA)**, his trainer's first runner since his return from Hong Kong, ran freely in the early stages. Once he settled he had to sit and wait for the gaps to appear, but when an opening came he went through and held every chance. Although he had no answer to the winner when challenged, he can be found easier opportunities.
**Ask The Clerk(IRE)**, a fair maiden on turf in Ireland last year, was switched to Fibresand after two runs on Polytrack and ran by far his best race to date for his current connections. This is his trip and he can win a maiden on this surface.
**Fizzy Lady** shaped as though an extra furlong is now required, but handled the surface and was slightly disappointing.
**Dane Rhapsody(IRE)** *Official explanation: vet said filly had bled from the nose*

## 607 BET DIRECT ON 0800 32 93 93 STKS SHOWCASE H'CAP 6f (F)
3:30 (3:30) (C ) (0-95,95) 3-Y-O+ £8,170 (£2,514; £1,257; £628) Stalls Low

Form RPR

140- **1** **Celtic Mill**[93] 5747 6-9-1 **85** LEnstone(3) 1 94
(DWBarker) *mde all: rdn over 2f out: clr over 1f out: r.o* **20/1**

1313 **2** ¾ **Hurricane Coast**[4] 586 5-9-0 **81** 6ex (b) PDoe 13 88
(DFlood) *hdwy on outside 2f out: rdn over 1f out: hung lft ins fnl f: r.o: nt rch wnr* **8/1**

-124 **3** hd **Soba Jones**[11] 543 7-8-8 **75** JEdmunds 4 81
(JBalding) *a.p: chsd wnr over 3f out to 2f out: kpt on ins fnl f* **16/1**

02-0 **4** 1¼ **Jayanjay**[23] 417 5-8-9 **76** JQuinn 10 78
(MissBSanders) *hld up: hdwy over 3f out: chsd wnr 2f out tl no ex ins fnl f* **25/1**

0-06 **4** dht **Sundried Tomato**[11] 544 5-8-9 **79** LFletcher(3) 7 81
(PWHiatt) *chsd ldrs: rdn over 2f out: hmpd ins fnl f: nt qckn* **12/1**

31-4 **6** 1 **Ellens Academy (IRE)**[13] 511 9-8-9 **79** DAllan(3) 11 78
(EJAlston) *bhd tl hdwy over 1f out: styng on whn hmpd ins fnl fnl f* **10/1**

10-2 **7** 1¼ **Flint River**[17] 486 6-9-1 **82** ACulhane 12 78
(HMorrison) *hld up mid-div: rdn 3f out: no hdwy fnl 2f* **3/1**[1]

34-3 **8** 1 **Sir Desmond**[23] 417 6-8-10 **77** (p) CCatlin 5 70
(RGuest) *sn bhd: nvr nrr* **7/1**[3]

0-14 **9** 1¾ **Quiet Times (IRE)**[4] 586 5-9-5 **86** (b) NCallan 8 73
(KARyan) *s.i.s: n.d* **5/1**[2]

00-0 **10** ¾ **Winthorpe (IRE)**[13] 515 4-8-10 **77** DarrenWilliams 9 62
(JJQuinn) *a bhd* **66/1**

01-5 **11** ¾ **Port St Charles (IRE)**[13] 511 7-8-10 **77** IMongan 6 60
(PRChamings) *sn chsng ldrs: rdn 3f out: sn wknd* **16/1**

00-1 **12** 2 **Massey**[17] 486 8-10-0 **95** DMernagh 2 72
(TDBarron) *prom: rdn over 3f out: wknd over 2f out* **5/1**[2]

40-2 **13** 2½ **Bond Royale**[13] 515 4-8-12 **79** FLynch 3 48
(BSmart) *chsd wnr over 2f: sn rdn: wknd 2f out* **16/1**

1m 14.39s (-1.31) **Going Correction** 0.0s/f (Stan) **13** Ran SP% **126.5**
Speed ratings: **108,107,106,105,105 103,102,100,98,97 96,93,90**CSF £179.33 CT £2747.53 TOTE £13.60: £8.90, £2.40, £3.60; EX 638.50 TRIFECTA Not won..
**Owner** P Asquith **Bred** P Asquith **Trained** Scorton, N Yorks
■ Stewards Enquiry : P Doe caution: careless riding

**FOCUS**
A competitive sprint run at a solid pace, and the form is rock-solid.

**NOTEBOOK**
**Celtic Mill** quickly won the battle for the lead and never looked back from there on. He is hard to go with early on in his races and, putting his proven stamina to good use late on, he added to his impressive record at this venue. Most of his winning has come over an extra furlong, but this was a personal best on the sand, and his style of running should see him add to this success at the trip.
**Hurricane Coast** has been in grand form of late during a busy period, and put in another solid display this time from the widest draw. He has a tendency to hang fire in the closing stages and he will no doubt go up again in the weights for this.
**Soba Jones** ran a blinder back up in class and trip. He finds this company a bit too hot, but proved he is best at six furlongs and on this evidence is in great heart.
**Jayanjay** ran a well enough on his first outing at this venue. He may have benefitted from a more prominent ride.
**Sundried Tomato** has shown a bit more on his last two outings and will no doubt go close before long, as he looks well treated on his best efforts. *Official explanation: jockey said he eased gelding close home to avoid clipping heels*
**Flint River** is better over seven furlongs and will be worth following when returning to that trip.
**Bond Royale** reportedly hung left thoughout the final three furlongs. *Official explanation: jockey said filly had hung left-handed from the final 3f*

## 608 BET DIRECT IN RUNNING SKY PAGE 293 (S) STKS 6f (F)
4:05 (4:06) (G ) 4-Y-O+ £2,590 (£740; £370) Stalls Low

Form RPR

0-00 **1** **Pips Song (IRE)**[12] 530 9-8-13 40 ACulhane 7 57
(PWHiatt) *mid-div: rdn and hdwy 2f out: led ins fnl f: r.o wl* **33/1**

02-4 **2** 1½ **Polar Haze**[19] 465 7-9-5 53 (v) JQuinn 4 58
(MrsLydiaPearce) *rdn and hdwy over 2f out: swtchd lft and led jst over 1f out: hdd ins fnl f: nt qckn* **5/1**[2]

06-0 **3** nk **Chorus**[14] 504 7-8-9 54 ow1 (v) GBaker 9 47
(BRMillman) *s.i.s: bhd tl hdwy on outside fnl f: nrst fin* **13/2**[3]

5-10 **4** hd **Best Lead**[11] 540 5-8-12 62 (b) DFentiman(7) 3 57
(IanEmmerson) *sn led: rdn 2f out: hdd jst over 1f out: no ex ins fnl f* **8/1**

00-0 **5** shd **Mizhar (USA)**[14] 503 8-8-13 55 RWinston 6 50
(JJQuinn) *outpcd and bhd: hdwy fnl f: nvr nrr* **20/1**

23-0 **6** 3½ **Heathyardsblessing (IRE)**[5] 576 7-8-13 46 NCallan 13 40
(RHollinshead) *led early: prom: rdn over 2f out: ev ch over 1f out: wknd ins fnl f* **14/1**

0-44 **7** ½ **Arogant Prince**[14] 509 7-8-6 53 DerekNolan(7) 2 38
(AWCarroll) *prom: rdn over 2f out: wkng whn slty hmpd on ins over 1f out* **13/2**[3]

130- **8** 1¼ **Czar Wars**[97] 5685 9-8-10 66 (b) LFletcher(3) 1 34
(JBalding) *chsd ldrs: rdn 3f out: sn wknd* **4/1**[1]

00-3 **9** hd **Evangelist (IRE)**[14] 498 4-8-8 40 MFenton 10 29
(MrsStefLiddiard) *sn outpcd* **16/1**

5-00 **10** 5 **Hawk**[12] 519 6-8-13 65 IMongan 8 19
(PRChamings) *w ldr: rdn and ev ch over 2f out: wknd over 1f out* **7/1**

015- **11** nk **Cloudless (USA)**[26] 6264 4-9-0 60 SWhitworth 12 19
(JWUnett) *sn bhd* **9/1**

000- **12** 1¼ **Blakeshall Girl**[224] 2428 4-8-8 53 DeanMcKeown 5 9
(JLSpearing) *a bhd* **50/1**

-000 **13** 3½ **Mesmerised**[6] 572 4-8-8 35 AnnStokell 11 —
(MissAStokell) *a bhd* **66/1**

1m 15.76s (0.06) **Going Correction** 0.0s/f (Stan) **13** Ran SP% **120.6**
Speed ratings: **99,97,96,96,96 91,90,89,88,82 81,80,75**CSF £189.78 TOTE £48.90: £7.80, £2.40, £2.40; EX 138.60.There was no bid for the winner
**Owner** Mrs Lucia Stockley & Ken Read **Bred** Gay O'Callaghan **Trained** Hook Norton, Oxon

**FOCUS**
A typically poor seller, lacking strength in depth, but run at a sound pace.

**NOTEBOOK**
**Pips Song(IRE)** stayed on strongly in the straight to win going away. His last win came back in 2002 and he has plummeted in the weights as a result, but ran above his rating on this occasion.
**Polar Haze** looked like scoring when joining the leaders up the far side rail, but hit the front plenty quick enough and had nothing left when challenged. This was not a bad effort at the weights.
**Chorus**, with the visor back on, was fighting a losing battle having blundered the start. However, she stuck to her task well late on and is better then this.
**Best Lead** confirmed he is best over the minimum trip, having moved well until he faded inside the last furlong.
**Mizhar(USA)** could not got the pace early, but stayed on fairly well and will again come on for the run. He could do with the re-application of cheekpieces.
**Czar Wars** was never going and disappointed.

## 609 BET DIRECT INTERACTIVE H'CAP 1m 4f (F)
4:35 (4:37) (E ) (0-70,68) 4-Y-O+ £3,283 (£938; £469) Stalls Low

Form RPR

343- **1** **Fall In Line**[122] 5201 4-9-0 60 JMackay 4 85+
(SirMarkPrescott) *ld 2f: with ldr: ld agn ovr 5f out: rdn ovr 3f out: clr fnl 2f: esd towrds fin* **3/1**[2]

3-12 **2** 8 **Nakwa (IRE)**[11] 546 6-8-9 54 DAllan(3) 11 64
(EJAlston) *hld up in tch: wnt 2nd ovr 4f out: rdn ovr 3f out: no chnce wth wnr fnl 2f* **9/4**[1]

-435 **3** 3½ **Lazzaz**[3] 592 6-9-4 60 ACulhane 5 65
(PWHiatt) *hld up and bhd: plnty to do whn rdn and hdwy 3f out: styd on fnl f* **11/1**

300- **4** nk **Mandoob**[42] 6130 7-9-1 60 (p) J-PGuillambert(3) 8 64
(BRJohnson) *hld up and bhd: stdy hdwy over 5f out: rdn over 3f out: wknd over 2f out* **12/1**

01-5 **5** 7 **Theatre Tinka (IRE)**[13] 516 5-9-12 68 (p) NCallan 9 62
(RHollinshead) *hld up: hdwy 5f out: sn rdn: wknd 4f out* **33/1**

0-12 **6** 6 **Cool Bathwick (IRE)**[14] 505 5-9-5 61 JQuinn 1 46
(BRMillman) *prom tl rdn and wknd over 3f out* **7/1**[3]

04-1 **7** nk **Orinocovsky (IRE)**[11] 545 5-9-8 64 IMongan 7 48
(NPLittmoden) *hld up: stdy hdwy over 5f out: rdn and wknd over 3f out* **7/1**[3]

00-1 **8** 1½ **Molly's Secret**[10] 549 6-8-2 51 (p) AshleighHorton(7) 3 33
(CGCox) *bhd fnl 4f* **11/1**

61-0 **9** ½ **Only For Sue**[14] 505 5-8-11 53 (p) MFenton 10 34
(WSKittow) *prom tl wknd over 4f out* **12/1**

4-31 **10** 2½ **Daunted (IRE)**[20] 455 8-8-13 62 DerekNolan(7) 6 40
(PABlockley) *a bhd* **14/1**

355- **11** 5 **Lord Gizzmo**[157] 4340 7-8-3 45 JBramhill 12 15
(PWHiatt) *prom tl rdn and wknd over 4f out* **50/1**

005/ **12** dist **Chater Flair**[13] 5860 7-8-9 51 ow1 VHalliday 2 —
(DBurchell) *hdwy on ins 9f out: dropped rr over 6f out: sn lost tch: t.o* **100/1**

2m 37.34s (-4.16) **Going Correction** 0.0s/f (Stan)
**WFA** 4 from 5yo+ 4lb **12** Ran SP% **125.4**
Speed ratings: **113,107,105,105,100 96,96,95,94,93 89,—**CSF £10.78 CT £69.33 TOTE £3.60: £2.80, £1.80, £3.30; EX 11.20 Place 6 £203.31, Place 5 £98.33.
**Owner** Neil Greig - Osborne House Ii **Bred** P D Player **Trained** Newmarket, Suffolk

**FOCUS**
An impressive winner and an extremely quick time. An outstanding form performance and the winner should be competitive off much higher marks.

**NOTEBOOK**
**Fall In Line**, making his handicap debut, won by a wide margin despite being eased down, posting a very good winning time. He looks a typical improver for his ultra-shrewd yard, is well-related and should run up a sequence before the Handicapper can get his measure.
**Nakwa(IRE)** has been unlucky to run into two progressive rivals since he won three runs ago over course-and-distance, but has held his form well. He can gain deserved compensation off this mark.
**Lazzaz**, an habitual front-runner, was unusually held up in last place. He was set a fair bit to do, but responded well and seemed to improve for these new tactics.
**Mandoob** could not get into it early on, but made good headway to get involved down the back straight, until he paid for his earlier exertions. He is a 1lb below his last winning mark, has a good record over course-and-distance and will be worth following when his yard show better form.


The Form Book, Raceform Ltd, Compton, RG20 6NL

T/Jkpt: Not won. T/Plt: £558.80 to a £1 stake. Pool: £44,821.25. 58.55 winning tickets. T/Qpdt: £185.30 to a £1 stake. Pool: £3,331.50. 13.30 winning tickets. KH

# 581 SOUTHWELL (L-H)

## Tuesday, January 27

**OFFICIAL GOING: Standard**

Times suggested the surface was riding standard and it proved very difficult to challenge from off the pace.

### 610 BET DIRECT NO Q 08000 93 66 93 H'CAP — 5f (F)

1:20 (1:21) (E) (0-75,73) 3-Y-O — £3,318 (£948; £474) Stalls High

Form — RPR

00-0 **1** **Piccolo Prince**[15] [510] 3-8-1 **53** ... JQuinn 4 — 59
(EJAlston) *chsd ldrs: hdwy 2f out: rdn to ld ins last: kpt on* **11/1**

1-11 **2** *nk* **Smart Starprincess (IRE)**[13] [524] 3-8-11 **63** ... (v) NCallan 6 — 68
(PABlockley) *sn led: rdn wl over 1f out: drvn and hdd ins last: no ex nr fin ish* **3/1**[1]

000- **3** *2 1/2* **Bella Boy Zee (IRE)**[82] [5931] 3-8-2 **57** ... FPFerris(3) 2 — 53
(PABlockley) *wnt rt s: midfield tl hdwy wl over 1f out: styd on ins last: nrst fin* **33/1**

31-6 **4** *1* **Scottish Exile (IRE)**[21] [458] 3-9-2 **68** ... (v) DarrenWilliams 13 — 61
(KRBurke) *chsd ldrs: rdn along 2f out: drvn and kpt on same pce appr last* **8/1**[3]

35-1 **4** *dht* **Siegfrieds Night (IRE)**[22] [435] 3-7-12 **50** ... JoannaBadger 1 — 43
(MCChapman) *sn pushed along in rr: hdwy 2f out: styd on u.p appr last: nrst fin* **16/1**

35-4 **6** *1/2* **Lizhar (IRE)**[11] [547] 3-8-10 **69** ... KGhunowa(7) 12 — 60
(MJPolglase) *in tch stands rails: rdn along 1/2-way: kpt on same pce* **20/1**

02-4 **7** *nk* **Little Flute**[17] [496] 3-8-0 **52** ow2 ... CCatlin 8 — 42
(TKeddy) *sn outpcd and pushed along in rr: hdwy 2f out: sn rdn and kpt fnl f: nrst fin* **8/1**[3]

21-0 **8** *1 1/4* **Barras (IRE)**[11] [547] 3-8-2 **57** ... (v[1]) LisaJones(3) 10 — 43
(MissGayKelleway) *chsd ldrs: rdn along over 2f out: grad wknd* **20/1**

054- **9** *1/2* **Demolition Molly**[49] [6152] 3-9-7 **73** ... (p) DeanMcKeown 3 — 57
(RFMarvin) *bmpd s: sn chsng ldr: rdn along 1/2-way: wknd wl over 1f out* **10/1**

213- **10** *3/4* **Blue Power (IRE)**[36] [6227] 3-8-7 **66** ... AReilly(7) 11 — 47
(KRBurke) *in tch tl rdn along and lost pl after 11/2f: n.d after* **7/1**[2]

0-52 **11** *1 1/2* **Ivory Lace**[13] [524] 3-8-3 **55** ... RFfrench 9 — 31
(DKIvory) *sn outpcd and rdn along in rr: a bhd* **16/1**

61-0 **12** *1 3/4* **Head Of State**[17] [496] 3-8-0 **52** ... JMackay 7 — 22
(RMBeckett) *a rr* **7/1**[2]

63-0 **13** *1 1/4* **Son Of Rembrandt (IRE)**[17] [489] 3-8-10 **62** ... (b[1]) MTebbutt 5 — 27
(DKIvory) *hmpd s: swtchd lft after 1f: a rr* **20/1**

00-0 **14** *25* **Sahara Silk (IRE)**[12] [543] 3-8-8 **65** ... (v) THamilton(5) 14 — —
(DShaw) *s.i.s: a bhd* **16/1**

60.57 secs (0.27) **Going Correction** 0.0s/f (Stan) — **14** Ran SP% **124.5**
Speed ratings: **97,96,92,90,90 90,89,87,86,85 83,80,78,38**CSF £43.08 CT £1109.68 TOTE £8.40: £2.80, £1.30, £18.80; EX 51.60.

**Owner** The Burlington Partnership **Bred** Theobalds Stud **Trained** Longton, Lancs

■ Stewards Enquiry : J Quinn one-day ban: used whip without allowing gelding time to respond and down the shoulder in the forehand position (Feb 7)

**FOCUS**

With Smart Starprincess setting off at her usual strong pace, very few got into it, although those drawn in the centre seemed to have an advantage. The form is fair for the grade.

**NOTEBOOK**

**Piccolo Prince** is bred for this trip, being by Piccolo out of a dual five-furlong winner, and the drop back to the minimum trip on his second start for his new stable proved a good move. Both he and the runner-up finished nicely clear of the rest and connections already have him pencilled in for a 0-75 for three-year-olds here on February 15th.

**Smart Starprincess(IRE)** was chasing a five-timer but, having shown such blinding speed at Lingfield on her last two starts, this slower surface was always going to blunt that pace somewhat. She ran a cracker from the front and, although eventually collared by the lightly-weighted winner, finished clear of the third. Further success looks assured.

**Bella Boy Zee(IRE)**, like the first two, raced down the centre of the track and brought home the main field. This was a promising first outing for her new trainer and can be placed to advantage off her current mark.

**Scottish Exile(IRE)** was not as well drawn and ran a solid race in the circumstances.

**Siegfrieds Night(IRE)** was found out by the drop back in trip. He will appreciate stepping back up to six.

**Lizhar(IRE)** was another whose chance was compromised by her high draw.

**Sahara Silk(IRE)** *Official explanation: jockey said filly sat down in the stalls and was slowly away*

### 611 BET DIRECT NO Q VOICE AUTOMATED BETTING (S) H'CAP (DIV I) — 1m (F)

1:50 (1:50) (G ) (0-60,61) 3-Y-O — £2,548 (£728; £364) Stalls Low

Form — RPR

66-1 **1** **Smart Boy Prince (IRE)**[5] [587] 3-9-6 **61** 6ex ... DerekNolan(7) 2 — 62
(PABlockley) *mde all: rdn over 2f out: drvn ent last and styd on gamely* **13/8**[1]

004- **2** *nk* **Ceasar (IRE)**[42] [6197] 3-8-13 **47** ... GFaulkner 7 — 48
(PCHaslam) *chsd ldrs: pushed along and hdwy over 2f out: rdn to chal over 1f out: drvn and ev ch ins last: no ex nr fin* **11/1**

00-0 **3** *3* **Courant D'Air (IRE)**[24] [425] 3-7-13 **40** ... RoryMoore(7) 9 — 34
(PCHaslam) *a.p: ev ch over 2f out: sn rdn and kpt on same pce appr last* **14/1**

40-0 **4** *nk* **Sir Frank Gibson**[13] [531] 3-8-11 **45** ... JFanning 3 — 38
(MJohnston) *in tch and sn pushed along on inner: swtchd outside and hdwy 2f out: rdn and wandered over 1f out: sn one pce* **11/2**[2]

00-4 **5** *10* **Given A Chance**[23] [434] 3-8-1 **35** ... JQuinn 4 — 6
(JGGiven) *dwlt: a towards rr* **15/2**

00-6 **6** *2* **Middleham Rose**[13] [532] 3-7-8 **35** ... DFentiman(7) 8 — —
(PCHaslam) *in tch: pushed along and outpcd after 3f: bhd after* **6/1**[3]

-045 **7** *nk* **Casantella**[5] [585] 3-8-11 **45** ... JMackay 5 — 11
(MJPolglase) *a rr* **12/1**

56-3 **8** *10* **Brother Cadfael**[15] [508] 3-9-1 **49** ... SWhitworth 6 — —
(JohnAHarris) *s.i.s: a bhd* **10/1**

00-0 **9** *1/2* **Ticklepenny Lock (IRE)**[5] [587] 3-8-2 **36** ow1 ... ANicholls 1 — —
(CSmith) *prom:rdn along 1/2-way: sn wknd* **66/1**

1m 44.97s (0.37) **Going Correction** -0.05s/f (Stan) — **9** Ran SP% **112.8**
Speed ratings: **97,96,93,93,83 81,81,71,70**CSF £20.54 CT £184.93 TOTE £1.80: £1.10, £2.00, £6.60; EX 19.20.The winner was bought in for 4,750gns.

**Owner** Brooklands Racing **Bred** J Kennedy **Trained** Southwell, Notts

**FOCUS**

A fair time for the class of contest, being 0.28 seconds faster than the second division. The form is average for the grade.

**NOTEBOOK**

**Smart Boy Prince(IRE)** was the only previous winner in the race and that experience proved critical as he battled on well to keep his head in front inside the final furlong. His trainer has a phenomenal strike-rate in sellers on the All-Weather, this being his 10th success from 18 starters, and he was keen to retain the gelding at the subsequent auction.

**Ceasar(IRE)** was taking on lesser opposition this time and threw down a determined challenge inside the last. He looks to have found his level.

**Courant D'Air(IRE)** looked the main danger to the eventual winner turning into the straight, but he had no more to give in the latter stages. He will be more at home back in regional contests.

**Sir Frank Gibson** was the only other to get into the picture. He may come from a big stable but he was making only modest headway at the finish and looks decidedly slow.

**Given A Chance** was never seen with a chance.

**Middleham Rose**, who had looked in need of a greater test of stamina when beaten over the extended nine furlongs at Wolverhampton on her All-Weather debut, could not cope with the pace on this drop back in trip.

**Ticklepenny Lock(IRE)** *Official explanation: jockey said colt lost its action*

### 612 BET DIRECT NO Q CLAIMING STKS — 6f (F)

2:20 (2:21) (F) 4-Y-O+ — £2,919 (£834; £417) Stalls Low

Form — RPR

1-10 **1** **Blakeset**[12] [544] 9-9-1 78 ... (v) NCallan 4 — 64
(TDBarron) *dwlt: sn pushed along to join ldr: led wl over 2f out: rdn clr over 1f out: edgd rt ins last: rdn out* **5/6**[1]

0-50 **2** *1 3/4* **Above Board**[15] [502] 9-8-5 35 ... (t) DeanMcKeown 1 — 48
(RFMarvin) *towards rr: gd hdwy 1/2-way: swtchd outside 2f out and sn rdn styd on to chse wnr ins last: kpt on* **100/1**

30-6 **3** *3/4* **Amanda's Lad (IRE)**[19] [473] 4-8-2 40 ... DFox(5) 3 — 48
(MCChapman) *chsd ldrs: rdn 2f out: kpt on u.p fnl f* **100/1**

04-5 **4** *1* **New Options**[19] [480] 7-9-1 66 ... PaulEddery 9 — 53
(WJMusson) *hld up: hdwy on outer over 2f out: sn rdn and kpt on same pce* **6/1**[3]

202- **5** *2* **Bella Beguine**[74] [5992] 5-8-7 70 ow1 ... (v) MFenton 8 — 39
(ABailey) *in tch: effrt over 2f out: sn rdn along and no imp* **11/4**[2]

102- **6** *2* **River Lark (USA)**[31] [6243] 5-8-10 47 ... RFfrench 2 — 36
(MABuckley) *led: rdn along 1/2-way: sn hdd and grad wknd* **16/1**

003- **7** *4* **Dil**[32] [6236] 9-8-5 45 ... (v) JoannaBadger 7 — 19
(MrsNMacauley) *slowly into stgride: a rr* **16/1**

00-4 **8** *4* **High Esteem**[22] [436] 8-8-9 56 ... (p) JFanning 6 — 11
(MABuckley) *cl up to 1/2-way: sn wknd* **20/1**

0-45 **9** *1 1/2* **Blunham**[7] [572] 4-7-12 40 ... RoryMoore(7) 5 — 3
(MCChapman) *cl up: rdn along 1/2-way: sn wknd* **40/1**

1m 16.64s (-0.16) **Going Correction** -0.05s/f (Stan) — **9** Ran SP% **116.5**
Speed ratings: **100,97,96,95,92 90,84,79,77**CSF £153.12 TOTE £1.80: £1.10, £13.40, £13.40; EX 118.80.

**Owner** Nigel Shields **Bred** Bolton Grange **Trained** Maunby, N Yorks

**FOCUS**

An uncompetitive claimer and the form looks unreliable.

**NOTEBOOK**

**Blakeset** brought to the table a career record of 2112211 over this course and distance, a record which suggested that, despite a poor effort last time, he held strong claims in this weak contest. He was only workmanlike in victory in the end and, on this evidence, is likely to struggle off his current mark of 78 back in handicap company.

**Above Board** ran well and his performance in finishing second holds the form down. Had this been a handicap, theoretically he would have been receiving another 33lb from the winner.

**Amanda's Lad(IRE)**, a long-standing maiden, flashed his tail under pressure and showed little inclination to battle for more than minor honours.

**New Options** has still to win a race in this country.

**Bella Beguine**, who had a decent chance at the weights and had won on her previous two starts over the course and distance, failed to fire on her first start for ten weeks.

### 613 LITTLEWOODS BET DIRECT MEDIAN AUCTION MAIDEN STKS — 7f (F)

2:50 (2:50) (F) 3-5-Y-O — £2,989 (£854; £427) Stalls Low

Form — RPR

02- **1** **Wings Of Morning (IRE)**[42] [6201] 3-8-7 ow1 ... NCallan 5 — 74
(PABlockley) *sn led: rdn wl over 1f out: styd on wl* **7/2**[1]

450- **2** *1 3/4* **Regulated (IRE)**[96] [5721] 3-8-6 73 ... RWinston 11 — 69
(JAOsborne) *in tch: hdwy 2f out: rdn to chse wnr ins last: kpt on* **9/2**[3]

3 **3** *1/2* **Galloway Mac**[19] [473] 4-9-10 ... MTebbutt 1 — 67
(WAO'Gorman) *dwlt: sn pushed along to trck ldrs on inner: hdwy to chse wnr over 2f out: sn rdn and one pce appr last* **4/1**[2]

20-0 **4** *5* **Tonto (FR)**[17] [489] 3-8-1 65 ... DFox(5) 8 — 55
(MissDMountain) *towards rr: hdwy on outer over 2f out: rdn and kpt on appr last: nrst fin* **4/1**[2]

0-06 **5** *3/4* **Vizulize**[13] [525] 5-9-5 50 ... ACulhane 10 — 48
(AWCarroll) *hld up towards rr: stdy hdwy on outer over 2f out: sn rdn and one pce wl over 1f out* **6/1**

00-0 **6** *10* **Pride Of Kinloch**[15] [510] 4-9-5 50 ... CCatlin 9 — 23
(JHetherton) *chsd ldrs: rdn over 2f out: sn wknd* **16/1**

**7** *1 1/4* **Midnight Promise** 3-8-6 ... DeanMcKeown 6 — 25
(JAGlover) *midfield: effrt over 2f out: nvr a factor* **12/1**

0-0 **8** *2* **Velvet Rhythm**[22] [439] 4-9-5 ... DarrenWilliams 2 — 15
(KRBurke) *sn in rr: drvn along 1/2-way: nvr a factor* **100/1**

600- **9** *1* **Copperfields Lass**[96] [5719] 5-8-12 40 ... (b[1]) CHaddon(7) 3 — 12
(WGMTurner) *chsd ldrs: rdn along over 2f out: sn wknd* **40/1**

000- **10** *nk* **Mikasa (IRE)**[12] [5598] 4-9-7 51 ... LFletcher(3) 7 — 17
(RFFisher) *sn outpcd and bhd* **66/1**

0/ **11** *2 1/2* **Lady Double U**[631] [1232] 4-9-2 ... DAllan(3) 12 — 5
(TDEasterby) *prom: rdn along 1/2-way: sn wknd* **20/1**

1m 31.16s (0.36) **Going Correction** -0.05s/f (Stan)
**WFA** 3 from 4yo+ 18lb — **11** Ran SP% **117.9**
Speed ratings: **96,94,93,87,86 75,74,71,70,70 67**CSF £18.98 TOTE £3.90: £1.10, £1.80, £1.80; EX 17.30.

**Owner** Ed Weetman (haulage & Storage) Ltd **Bred** Limestone Stud **Trained** Southwell, Notts

**FOCUS**

Not much strength in depth, although the form of the front three is fair, but a double on the card for trainer Paul Blockley.

**NOTEBOOK**

**Wings Of Morning(IRE)** had finished a creditable runner-up in a seller on his first start on Fibresand and his prominent style of racing suited the way the track was riding. He has had his training problems, having suffered from a bout of choking and ringworm, and his trainer expects the gelding to improve a fair bit for this.

**Regulated(IRE)**, another who should come on for the run, was having his first start for three months. However, his stable has not been firing as one would expect this winter, having sent out just two winners on the All-Weather from 62 runners since September.
**Galloway Mac** had his chance early in the straight, but found just the one pace under pressure.
**Tonto(FR)** shapes as though he wants farther.
**Vizulize** was another running against the pace bias.

## 614 BETDIRECT.CO.UK FILLIES' H'CAP 1m (F)
3:20 (3:21) (E) (0-75,71) 4-Y-0+ £3,286 (£939; £469) Stalls Low

| Form | | | | RPR |
|---|---|---|---|---|
| -111 | 1 | | **Najaaba (USA)**[11] 552 4-9-9 **71** BReilly(5) 1 (MissJFeilden) *tracked ldrs: swtchd rt and hdwy to ld over 2f out: sn rdn and hung bdly lft: drvn and hung rt fnl f: kpt on* **5/4**[1] | 82+ |
| 0-25 | 2 | 1 | **Maggie's Pet**[11] 552 7-8-2 **45** (t) DRMcCabe 6 (KBell) *sn led: rdn along and hdd over 2f out: rallied u.p ent last: kpt on* **11/1** | 52 |
| 02-2 | 3 | 3/4 | **Ellen Mooney**[21] 457 5-9-13 **70** (p) RFfrench 5 (BSmart) *trckd ldrs: effrt over 2f out: sn rdn and kpt on fnl f* **10/3**[2] | 75 |
| 30-2 | 4 | 1/2 | **Eager Angel (IRE)**[19] 474 6-8-2 **45** (p) JQuinn 2 (RFMarvin) *hld up in rr: hdwy to chse ldrs wl over 1f out:sn rdn and one pce* **14/1** | 49 |
| 0-56 | 5 | 4 | **Jessie**[19] 474 5-7-12 **41** oh1 (t) KimTinkler 7 (DonEnricoIncisa) *chsd ldrs on outer: rdn over 2f out and sn btn* **25/1** | 36 |
| 51-3 | 6 | 2 | **Estimation**[21] 457 4-9-12 **69** NCallan 3 (RMHCowell) *hld up towards rr: hdwy on outer over 2f out: sn rdn and btn* **6/1**[3] | 60 |
| 00-1 | 7 | 1/2 | **Modesty Blaise (SWE)**[13] 529 4-9-13 **70** MFenton 8 (MissGayKelleway) *prom: rdn along over 2f out and sn wknd* **8/1** | 60 |
| 4-00 | 8 | 9 | **Estimate**[11] 549 4-8-12 **55** (v) SWhitworth 4 (JohnAHarris) *prom: rdn along over 3f out and sn wknd* **33/1** | 25 |

1m 44.07s (-0.53) **Going Correction** -0.05s/f (Stan) 8 Ran SP% **114.7**
Speed ratings: **101,100,99,98,94 92,92,83**CSF £17.03 CT £38.99 TOTE £2.00: £1.50, £1.60, £1.10; EX 18.40.
**Owner** A K Sparks **Bred** Darley Stud Management, L L C **Trained** Exning, Suffolk
■ Stewards Enquiry : B Reilly three-day ban: used whip with excessive force and without giving filly time to respond (Feb 7-9)

**FOCUS**
The second race on the card which revolved around a filly chasing a five-timer. The form is muddling but the winner is still progressing.

**NOTEBOOK**
**Najaaba(USA)**, despite racing off a 9lb higher mark, still gave the impression that she won with a bit more in hand than the winning distance suggests. Having taken it up easily early in the straight, she hung left then right as her rider went for the whip. Reilly received a three-day ban for excessive use and, on reflection, would probably have been better off just pushing the filly out. Her trainer now plans to give the filly a rest and bring her back for a fillies only handicap on soft ground in the spring.
**Maggie's Pet** had two and a half lengths to find with the winner on their last meeting and was 9lb better off at the weights this time, but the result was the same. She remains a maiden.
**Ellen Mooney** had an even greater pull at the weights with Najaaba based on their last meeting, but even 15lb was not enough to turn the tables.
**Eager Angel(IRE)** was not disgraced in her performance given that the track was favouring pace horses.
**Jessie** belongs in regional races.
**Estimation** was another trying the impossible in coming from off the pace.
**Modesty Blaise(SWE)**, a drifter on the exchanges, showed pace to the turn into the straight, but was soon beating a retreat.

## 615 BET DIRECT NO Q VOICE AUTOMATED BETTING (S) H'CAP (DIV II) 1m (F)
3:50 (3:51) (G) (0-60,56) 3-Y-0 £2,541 (£726; £363) Stalls Low

| Form | | | | RPR |
|---|---|---|---|---|
| 320- | 1 | | **Rare Coincidence**[42] 6201 3-9-2 56 (p) DNolan(5) 7 (RFFisher) *sn cl up: led 3f out: rdn and edgd lft wl over 1f out: kpt on* **11/4**[2] | 63 |
| 03-0 | 2 | 2 | **Abrogate (IRE)**[13] 521 3-8-6 48 RoryMoore(7) 4 (PCHaslam) *trckd ldrs: hdwy to chse wnr 2f out: sn rdn and kpt on same pce* **10/3**[3] | 51 |
| 44-2 | 3 | 3 | **Hunting Pink**[5] 587 3-8-11 49 LFletcher(3) 5 (HMorrison) *hld up in tch: hdwy over 2f out: rdn and hung lft over 1f out: sn drvn and no imp* **5/2**[1] | 45 |
| 000- | 4 | 1/2 | **Biscar Two (IRE)**[71] 6012 3-8-10 45 DeanMcKeown 1 (RMWhitaker) *s.i.s: hdwy over 2f out: rdn and onepce whn n.m.r appr last* **12/1** | 40 |
| 00-0 | 5 | 5 | **Soleil D'Hiver**[24] 427 3-7-7 35 DFentiman(7) 8 (PCHaslam) *sn led: rdn along and hdd 3f out: grad wknd* **16/1** | 19 |
| 45-6 | 6 | hd | **Platinum Chief**[15] 508 3-8-12 47 FLynch 9 (ABerry) *chsd ldrs on outer: rdn along 3f out: sn wknd* **14/1** | 30 |
| 03-5 | 7 | 1/2 | **Marita**[15] 508 3-8-10 45 (v1) MFenton 6 (JGGiven) *cl up on inner: rdn along 1/2-way and sn wknd* **8/1** | 27 |
| 00-0 | 8 | 8 | **Peace Treaty (IRE)**[19] 472 3-7-12 33 oh3 JBramhill 3 (SRBowring) *in tch: rdn along 1/2-way: sn wknd* **33/1** | — |

1m 45.25s (0.65) **Going Correction** -0.05s/f (Stan) 8 Ran SP% **112.6**
Speed ratings: **95,93,90,89,84 84,83,75**CSF £11.98 CT £24.23 TOTE £3.70: £1.60, £1.10, £1.30; EX 14.90.The winner was bought in for 4,750gns.
**Owner** Great Head House Estates Limited **Bred** D R Tucker **Trained** Ulverston, Cumbria

**FOCUS**
Effectively a maiden seller and a race run in a time marginally slower time than the first division. The form is weak on the whole.

**NOTEBOOK**
**Rare Coincidence** had been placed in selling company before and, getting away on terms this time, benefited from racing prominently on a day when hold-up horses had little chance. He will be lucky to find another handicap as weak as this one.
**Abrogate(IRE)** was dropping in grade and ran creditably on his return to Fibresand having failed to take to the faster Polytrack surface on his last start.
**Hunting Pink**, who is not one to have much faith in, did not make things easy for her rider by hanging under pressure.
**Biscar Two(IRE)** offered little encouragement.
**Soleil D'Hiver** did not get home and needs to be dropped in trip.

## 616 BET DIRECT IN VISION SKY PAGE 293 H'CAP 2m (F)
4:20 (4:21) (F) (0-65,62) 4-Y-0+ £2,961 (£846; £423) Stalls Low

| Form | | | | RPR |
|---|---|---|---|---|
| 52-4 | 1 | | **Stolen Song**[10] 464 4-9-1 **58** (e1) SWhitworth 3 (MJRyan) *hld up: stdy hdwy 1/2-way: effrt 3f out: rdn to ld 11/2f out: drvn: edgd lft and hdd wl ins last: rallied to ld nr line* **15/2** | 65 |
| 0-31 | 2 | shd | **Lampos (USA)**[7] 568 4-8-8 **51** 6ex RWinston 6 (MissJACamacho) *hld up in tch: stdy hdwy 6f out: trckd ldrs 4f out: rdn 2f out: drvn to ld briefly wl ins last: hdd and no ex nr line* **6/4**[1] | 58 |
| 053- | 3 | 6 | **Altitude Dancer (IRE)**[17] 5298 4-9-2 **59** WMLordan 11 (PABlockley) *a.p: effrt to ld 3f out: sn rdn and hdd 11/2f out: sn drvn and kpt on same pce* **14/1** | 59 |
| 50-3 | 4 | 1 1/2 | **Jamaican Flight (USA)**[21] 461 11-9-0 **50** JQuinn 10 (MrsSLamyman) *led: rdn along 4f out: hdd 3f out: drvn and one pce fnl 2f* **8/1** | 48 |
| 060- | 5 | 1/2 | **Ela Jay**[10] 5048 5-8-6 **45** LFletcher(3) 1 (HMorrison) *hld up in tch: hdwy over 5f out: rdn along over 3f out: swtchd outside and drvn over 2f out: kpt on same pce* **13/2**[2] | 42 |
| -431 | 6 | 11 | **Vincent**[11] 551 9-8-13 **49** JMackay 2 (JohnAHarris) *hld up in rr: hdwy 5f out: rdn along 3f out and nvr a factor* **13/2**[2] | 33 |
| 0-44 | 7 | 1 3/4 | **Worlaby Dale**[7] 568 8-7-10 **35** LisaJones(3) 8 (MrsSLamyman) *s.i.s: plld hrd and sn chsng ldrs: rdn along over 4f out and sn wknd* **7/1**[3] | 17 |
| -310 | 8 | 1 | **Daunted (IRE)**[1] 609 8-9-5 **62** DerekNolan(7) 5 (PABlockley) *prom: rdn along 5f out: sn wknd* **14/1** | 43 |
| 4145 | 9 | 14 | **King Priam (IRE)**[7] 570 9-8-9 **45** (p) DeanMcKeown 9 (MJPolglase) *bhd fr 1/2-way* **20/1** | 9 |
| 610/ | 10 | nk | **Terdad (USA)**[14] 3936 11-8-12 **48** (p) MFenton 4 (JGGiven) *in tch to 1/2-way: sn lost pl and bhd* **25/1** | 12 |

3m 41.77s (-10.73) **Going Correction** -0.05s/f (Stan)
**WFA** 4 from 5yo+ 7lb 10 Ran SP% **124.0**
Speed ratings: **101,100,97,97,96 91,90,90,83,82**CSF £20.39 CT £167.96 TOTE £9.10: £2.20, £1.60, £3.40; EX 32.10 Trifecta £372.00 Pool of £5,239.70 - 10 winning units. Place 6 £11.54, Place 5 £4.26..
**Owner** The Aldora Partnership **Bred** Mrs Wendy Jacqueline Muir **Trained** Newmarket, Suffolk

**FOCUS**
A moderate heat but a thrilling climax, and although the form is modest it looks reliable.

**NOTEBOOK**
**Stolen Song**, who did not go unbacked, had been the subject of support when fourth at Lingfield on his last start on the Flat. That race was over ten furlongs, though, and the step up to two miles posed a big question regarding his stamina. He saw it out well, however, and connections now have new options open to them.
**Lampos(USA)** lost nothing in defeat under his penalty, just being beaten in a bob of heads, and he should be able to remain competitive outside of banded grade.
**Altitude Dancer(IRE)** ran his best race on Fibresand to date. He looks worth persevering with on this surface.
**Jamaican Flight(USA)**, who has never won here, had no excuse as the surface was suiting pace horses.
**Ela Jay** remains a maiden on the Flat and has not progressed from her win over hurdles in November.
**Vincent**, whose last win in a handicap came off a mark of 39, had a 10lb higher mark to overcome on this occasion. In addition he was attempting to run against the pace bias.
T/Jkpt: £9,664.50, to a £1 stake. Pool £20,418.00, 1.5 winning tickets T/Plt: £5.10, to a £1 stake. Pool £49,734.10, 7,087.80 winning tickets T/Qpdt: £2.20, to a £1 stake. Pool £3,640.80, 1,210.40 winning tickets JR

# 596 LINGFIELD (L-H)
### Wednesday, January 28

**OFFICIAL GOING: Standard**
Wind: Fresh across Weather: Cold and Overcast

## 617 BET DIRECT NO Q CLAIMING STKS 5f (P)
1:00 (1:00) (F) 3-Y-0+ £2,954 (£844; £422) Stalls High

| Form | | | | RPR |
|---|---|---|---|---|
| 21-0 | 1 | | **Type One (IRE)**[25] 417 6-9-10 78 RMiles(3) 5 (TGMills) *led after 1f: hit rail over 2f out: qcknd clr wl over 1f out: easily* **4/6**[1] | 84 |
| 0-01 | 2 | 5 | **Whippasnapper**[4] 596 4-9-13 60 NPollard 9 (JRBest) *chsd ldrs: styd on to take 2nd ins fnl f: no ch w wnr* **8/1**[3] | 67 |
| 01-0 | 3 | 3/4 | **Panjandrum**[22] 454 6-9-4 68 MSavage(5) 10 (NEBerry) *in tch: rdn 2f out: r.o fnl f* **10/1** | 60 |
| 5-46 | 4 | 1/2 | **Lizhar (IRE)**[1] 610 3-8-6 69 PDoe 6 (MJPolglase) *w ldrs: ev ch over 2f out: sn outpcd* **25/1** | 56 |
| 06-5 | 5 | 3/4 | **Easily Averted (IRE)**[14] 524 3-8-7 67 ow2 (t) LPKeniry(3) 3 (PButler) *dwlt: towards rr: pushed along and kpt on fnl 2f: nvr rchd ldrs* **25/1** | 57 |
| 001- | 6 | nk | **Somerset West (IRE)**[142] 4767 4-8-13 58 KristinStubbs(7) 7 (MrsLStubbs) *led 1f: outpcd 2f out: sn btn* **33/1** | 51 |
| 00- | 7 | 1/2 | **Dulce De Leche**[226] 2433 3-8-7 (be1) BReilly(5) 4 (SCWilliams) *dwlt: in rr: shkn up 2f out: nvr nr to chal* **14/1** | 57 |
| 010- | 8 | hd | **Majhool**[76] 5985 5-9-9 72 IMongan 8 (GLMoore) *s.i.s: chsd ldrs tl wknd over 1f out* **7/1**[2] | 52 |
| -040 | 9 | 2 | **Juwwi**[14] 526 10-9-8 69 ow2 CJDavies(7) 2 (JMBradley) *s.s: rdn along: a bhd: b.b.v* **16/1** | 51 |

58.88 secs (-0.90) **Going Correction** -0.05s/f (Stan)
**WFA** 3 from 4yo+ 15lb 9 Ran SP% **115.9**
Speed ratings: **105,97,95,95,93 93,92,92,89**CSF £6.44 TOTE £1.40: £1.10, £2.30, £1.90; EX 10.60.The winner was claimed for £14,000 by J.J.Quinn.
**Owner** Mrs A K Petersen **Bred** Ralph And Helen O'Brien **Trained** Headley, Surrey

**FOCUS**
Not a particularly competitive claimer, but won in good style by Type One, who was best in at the weights. A decent time for the grade of contest.

**NOTEBOOK**
**Type One(IRE)** was well beaten in a handicap on his previous start and this drop back into claiming company was just what was required. The best in at the weights, he was always well placed before coming right away in the straight \n\x\x for a comfortable victory. He was claimed for £14,000 by John Quinn, a trainer who does particularly well with his sprinters.
**Whippasnapper**, back to form with a win in an amateurs races over six furlongs here on his previous start, had 13lb to find with the winner at the weights, but showed himself in good heart with a decent effort over a trip just short of his optimum.
**Panjandrum**, who had 7lb to find with the winner at the weights, took a long time to pick up in the straight and has to be considered a little disappointing.
**Lizhar(IRE)**, comfortably held at Southwell the previous day, ran well against her elders until getting tired inside the final furlong.
**Easily Averted(IRE)** never really recovered from a slow start.
**Juwwi** *Official explanation: vet said gelding bled from the nose*



The Form Book, Raceform Ltd, Compton, RG20 6NL

## 618 PRESS INTERACTIVE TO BET DIRECT H'CAP — 1m 4f (P)
1:30 (1:31) (E) (0-75,75) 4-Y-0+ £3,412 (£975; £487) Stalls Low

Form RPR
112- **1** **Mission To Mars**[71] 6025 5-9-11 **72**.................................... JPSpencer 4 89+
(PRHedger) *hld up towards rr: smooth hdwy 2f out: led ins fnl f: qcknd clr on bit* **9/4**[1]
01-3 **2** *2 1/2* **Perfidious (USA)**[25] 419 6-9-6 **70**........................................ RMiles(3) 9 79
(JRBoyle) *led after 1f tl ins fnl f: no ch w wnr* **16/1**
-503 **3** *1 1/4* **Easter Ogil (IRE)**[11] 559 9-9-3 **64**........................................ VSlattery 6 71
(JaneSouthcombe) *hdwy over 3f out: ev ch over 1f out: one pce* **12/1**
4-04 **4** *shd* **Night Warrior (IRE)**[5] 592 4-9-1 **66**........................................ PDoe 8 73
(DFlood) *towards rr: rdn and hdwy over 1f out: kpt on fnl f* **11/1**
322- **5** *1* **Mad Carew (USA)**[60] 6093 5-9-11 **72**.........................(be) SWhitworth 10 77
(GLMoore) *plld hrd in midfield: swtchd wd and hdwy over 2f out: hung lft: styd on same pce* **16/1**
5-00 **6** *nk* **Golden Dual**[11] 555 4-8-7 **58**............................................ PaulEddery 2 63
(SDow) *hld up in rr: stdy hdwy fr 3f out: one pce fnl f* **50/1**
0/00 **7** *nk* **Dusty Carpet**[14] 523 6-9-10 **71**........................................ CCatlin 3 76
(MJWeeden) *in tch: effrt 3f out: one pce fnl f* **33/1**
3-42 **8** *shd* **Big Bertha**[12] 549 6-9-7 **68**............................................ GBaker 12 72
(JohnBerry) *bhd: rdn 3f out: nrst fin* **11/1**
201- **9** *1/2* **Majlis (IRE)**[11] 6254 7-9-10 **71**.........................................(b) EAhern 1 75
(RMHCowell) *hdwy 3f out: ev ch over 1f out: no ex* **14/1**
244- **10** *3/4* **Astromancer (USA)**[57] 6120 4-8-2 **53**................................... JFanning 5 56
(MHTompkins) *led 1f: rdn 3f out: wknd fnl f* **11/1**
40-0 **11** *nk* **Anyhow (IRE)**[4] 602 7-8-6 **60**....................................... DerekNolan(7) 13 62
(MissKMGeorge) *towards rr: rdn and hdwy over 1f out: no ex ins fnl f* **16/1**
30-4 **12** *2 1/2* **Classic Role**[14] 523 5-9-11 **72**........................................... IMongan 15 70
(RIngram) *chsd ldrs: ev ch over 2f out: wknd over 1f out* **11/2**[2]
10-0 **13** *1* **Sudden Flight (IRE)**[25] 418 7-10-0 **75**................................... RHavlin 7 72
(RIngram) *w ldrs tl wknd over 1f out* **25/1**
125- **14** *nk* **Bucks**[44] 6195 7-10-0 **75**................................................. MTebbutt 14 71
(DKIvory) *midfield and wd: rdn and btn 3f out* **20/1**
310- **15** *3/4* **Mcqueen (IRE)**[46] 6178 4-9-9 **74**........................................ DSweeney 11 69
(MrsHDalton) *prom 9f* **25/1**
53-1 **16** *dist* **Rasid (USA)**[11] 559 6-9-6 **67**............................................ NCallan 16 —
(CADwyer) *prom 9f: wl bhd whn virtually p.u fnl f: lame* **10/1**[3]

2m 34.24s (0.26) **Going Correction** -0.05s/f (Stan)
**WFA** 4 from 5yo+ 4lb **16** Ran SP% **129.6**
Speed ratings: **97,95,94,94,93 93,93,93,92,92 92,90,89,89,89** —CSF £42.42 CT £392.18 TOTE £3.00: £1.30, £4.20, £3.50, £2.90; EX 52.70.
**Owner** Ian Hutchins **Bred** C A And R M Cyzer **Trained** Eastergate, W Sussex

**FOCUS**
This looked quite a competitive race on paper, although the winning time was moderate after just an ordinary pace, and it was weakened somewhat by the failure of Classic Role and Rasid to show their form. Take nothing away, however, from Mission To Mars, who could have won by three times the winning margin and should win off higher marks.

**NOTEBOOK**
**Mission To Mars**, who met with defeat for the first time in five starts when runner-up to the very useful Cold Turkey on his previous outing, got back to winning form with an embarrassingly easy success. Having travelled particularly well, Spencer was able to take a pull whilst everything around him was flat to the boards. The Handicapper will have his say, but it will be hard to oppose him next time off the back of this effort.
**Perfidious(USA)** ran an honest race from the front, but was never going to hold off Mission To Mars.
**Easter Ogil(IRE)** has never won over a trip this far, but stamina is not the issue, he was simply outclassed.
**Night Warrior(IRE)** did nothing wrong but may need to come down in the handicap.
**Mad Carew(USA)** shaped pleasingly on his return from a break may well be capable of better.
**Classic Role** ran disappointingly below form.
**Rasid(USA)** dropped right out before being pulled up by Callan. He was found to have finished lame. *Official explanation: trainer said gelding was found to have pulled a muscle in its near hind quarters*

## 619 LITTLEWOODS BET DIRECT H'CAP — 6f (P)
2:00 (2:02) (D) (0-85,78) 3-Y-0 £4,693 (£1,444; £722; £361) Stalls Low

Form RPR
01-3 **1** **Kabreet**[18] 493 3-9-7 **78**................................................ EAhern 2 86+
(EALDunlop) *prom: led 3f out: rdn and r.o wl fnl 2f: readily* **1/1**[1]
24-0 **2** *1 3/4* **Hello Roberto**[18] 493 3-9-6 **77**........................................ JPSpencer 3 80
(MJPolglase) *stdd s: plld hrd: hdwy 3f out: drvn to chal over 1f out: nt qckn* **12/1**
1-25 **3** *3/4* **St Savarin (FR)**[7] 580 3-8-12 **72**...................................... RMiles(3) 7 73
(JRBest) *mid-div: dropped to rr 3f out: rdn and rallied over 1f out: r.o* **7/1**[2]
216- **4** *1 1/2* **Smokin Joe**[29] 6258 3-9-3 **74**.......................................... NPollard 1 70
(JRBest) *dwlt: sn in tch: effrt over 2f out: styd on same pce* **10/1**
15-5 **5** *1 1/4* **Pompey Blue**[22] 458 3-8-13 **70**......................................... NCallan 4 63
(PJMcbride) *t.k.h: w ldrs tl wknd over 1f out* **8/1**[3]
5-24 **6** *nk* **Stamford Blue**[14] 524 3-7-12 **55** oh2...............................(b) DKinsella 10 47
(JSMoore) *wd: bhd: mod effrt u.p 2f out: nvr rchd ldrs* **12/1**
03-5 **7** *1 3/4* **Forzenuff**[18] 496 3-8-8 **65**.............................................. DSweeney 8 51
(JRBoyle) *in tch: outpcd over 2f out: sn btn* **16/1**
3-10 **8** *3* **Princess Kai (IRE)**[18] 496 3-8-4 **61**..................................(b) JQuinn 5 38
(RIngram) *led 3f: wknd wl over 1f out* **16/1**
400- **9** *1* **Rise**[29] 6258 3-9-5 **76**.......................................................(b) IMongan 9 50
(AndrewReid) *dwlt: sn in midfield: sme hdwy on ins ent st: sn wknd* **40/1**
020- **10** *5* **Kuringai**[29] 6258 3-8-10 **67**.............................................. MFenton 6 26
(BWDuke) *chsd ldrs to 1/2-way* **14/1**

1m 12.57s (-0.35) **Going Correction** -0.05s/f (Stan) **10** Ran SP% **119.0**
Speed ratings: **100,97,96,94,93 92,90,86,84,78**CSF £15.15 CT £63.39 TOTE £1.80: £1.10, £4.60, £1.50; EX 14.80 Trifecta £76.30 Pool of £1,258 - 11.70 winning units.
**Owner** Jumeirah Racing **Bred** Stowell Hill Ltd And S P Tindall **Trained** Newmarket, Suffolk

**FOCUS**
Kabreet justified his short odds to take this uncompetitive handicap in decisive fashion and can rate higher again.

**NOTEBOOK**
**Kabreet**, third (St Savarin was a neck in front in second) over seven furlongs here on his previous start, appreciated this drop back to six and did what was required. He looks as though he will be capable of even better given a stronger pace and may now be given a break ahead of a turf campaign.
**Hello Roberto** was another to appreciate a drop back in trip. He chased the winner all the way to the line, but was always just being held.
**St Savarin(FR)**, dropping back from a mile, ran respectably but found this too sharp and will be well suited by a return to seven furlongs.
**Smokin Joe** did not appear to do much wrong, but may need a bit of respite from the Handicapper.
**Pompey Blue** would have preferred a stronger pace, as he raced keenly before weakening very tamely inside the final furlong.
**Kuringai** *Official explanation: trainer was unable to offer any explanation for the colt's poor run*

## 620 BET DIRECT THROUGH SKY ACTIVE (S) STKS — 6f (P)
2:30 (2:31) (G) 3-Y-0 £2,569 (£734; £367) Stalls Low

Form RPR
-023 **1** **Alizar (IRE)**[5] 591 3-8-12 59.............................................. JPSpencer 8 57
(MJPolglase) *chsd ldr: led wl over 1f out: drvn clr* **2/1**[1]
000- **2** *2* **Reedsman (IRE)**[65] 6058 3-8-12 45....................................... NCallan 2 51
(MHTompkins) *prom: drvn along over 3f out: one pce appr fnl f* **25/1**
5-65 **3** *nk* **Limit Down (IRE)**[9] 561 3-8-9 55..........................(v) J-PGuillambert(3) 3 50
(MJWallace) *hdwy over 2f out: one pce appr fnl f* **7/1**[3]
04-0 **4** *1/2* **Lady Piste (IRE)**[25] 420 3-8-9 52..........................(vt) LFletcher(3) 10 49
(PDEvans) *chsd ldrs: outpcd 3f out: carried wd home turn: hrd rdn and rallied over 1f out: r.o* **16/1**
25-3 **5** *4* **Stanhope Forbes (IRE)**[22] 452 3-8-12 53................................ EAhern 12 37
(NPLittmoden) *dwlt: sn outpcd in rr: hdwy whn carried lft over 1f out: nvr nrr* **7/2**[2]
50-0 **6** *1 1/2* **Rehia**[18] 496 3-8-6 57 ow1........................................ HGemberlu(7) 14 33
(JWHills) *dwlt: wd: chsd ldrs: edgd lft and wknd over 1f out* **12/1**
00-0 **7** *3/4* **Magico**[14] 521 3-8-9 49.............................................(v) LPKeniry(3) 5 30
(AMBalding) *in tch: outpcd over 2f out: btn in midfield whn hmpd over 1f out* **25/1**
5-0 **8** *hd* **Oboe**[7] 574 3-8-7........................................................ JFanning 6 24
(RCharlton) *rrd s: rdn 3f out: nvr nr to chal* **20/1**
00-0 **9** *2 1/2* **Fox Hollow (IRE)**[22] 451 3-8-9 35.......................................... RMiles(3) 7 22
(MJHaynes) *mid-div: outpcd 3f out: sn btn* **66/1**
53-3 **10** *1/2* **Philly Dee**[13] 538 3-8-7 47............................................(b) CCatlin 1 15
(NEBerry) *led tl wknd wl over 1f out* **14/1**
00-0 **11** *nk* **Intitnice (IRE)**[25] 425 3-8-5 40..........................(b) DerekNolan(7) 9 19
(MissKMGeorge) *sn drvn along in midfield: no imp whn sltly hmpd on rail ins fnl f* **66/1**
30-0 **12** *nk* **Lord Baskerville**[21] 462 3-8-5 60..................................... NicolPolli(7) 11 18
(MGQuinlan) *prom 4f* **12/1**
000- **13** *1 1/2* **Imperial Princess (IRE)**[88] 5877 3-8-9 40 ow2...................... IMongan 4 11
(DKIvory) *outpcd: a bhd* **50/1**
0 **14** *1* **Fresh Connection**[11] 553 3-8-8 ow1.................................... MFenton 13 7
(GGMargarson) *dwlt: bhd fr 1/2-way* **10/1**

1m 13.21s (0.29) **Going Correction** -0.05s/f (Stan) **14** Ran SP% **122.5**
Speed ratings: **96,93,92,86 84,83,83,80,79 79,78,76,75**CSF £67.57 TOTE £2.60: £1.10, £14.70, £1.90; EX 89.40.The winner was sold to Simon Dow for 9,000gns.
**Owner** General Sir Geoffrey Howlett **Bred** Epona Bloodstock Ltd **Trained** Southwell, Notts

**FOCUS**
A weak seller, but run at a decent pace throughout.

**NOTEBOOK**
**Alizar(IRE)** found the drop back into selling company just what was required. She was sold afterwards to join Simon Dow for 9,000gns, but her overall record suggests she may just struggle outside of this grade.
**Reedsman(IRE)** had 14lb to find with the winner at the weights but, dropped in trip on this return from a break, he shaped encouragingly.
**Limit Down(IRE)** appeared to run his race, but is still looking for his first success.
**Lady Piste(IRE)** is not really progressing.
**Stanhope Forbes(IRE)** ran better than his finishing position suggests as he got outpaced and was carried left in the straight when beginning to pick up. Seven furlongs may also suit better.

## 621 BETDIRECT.CO.UK MAIDEN STKS — 1m (P)
3:00 (3:02) (D) 3-Y-0 £4,192 (£1,290; £645; £322) Stalls High

Form RPR
50- **1** **Somewhere My Love**[116] 5369 3-8-6 ................................... RMiles(3) 3 63
(TGMills) *trckd ldrs: led ins fnl f: rdn out* **9/2**[3]
3 **2** *hd* **Webbswood Lad (IRE)**[22] 447 3-9-0 ....................................... MFenton 7 68
(MrsStefLiddiard) *t.k.h: prom: drvn to dispute ld over 1f out tl ins fnl f: kpt on* **5/1**
25-5 **3** *1/2* **Night Storm**[18] 492 3-8-9 65............................................... PDoe 1 62
(SDow) *dwlt: t.k.h: hdwy over 1f out: cl up whn n.m.r ins fnl f: r.o* **9/1**
0-3 **4** *nk* **Ground Patrol**[11] 553 3-9-0 ............................................... JPSpencer 2 66
(AMBalding) *dwlt: sn trcking ldrs: disp ld over 1f out tl ins fnl f: nt qckn* **5/2**[1]
0- **5** *3 1/2* **Opera Star (IRE)**[42] 6203 3-8-9 ............................................. MHills 5 53
(BWHills) *sn led: hdd over 1f out: no ex fnl f* **14/1**
300- **6** *1 1/4* **Dancing Lyra**[202] 3132 3-9-0 86.............................................. EAhern 11 55
(JWHills) *sn bhd: rdn 3f out: sme late hdwy* **3/1**[2]
**7** *1/2* **Shalati Princess** 3-8-9 ...................................................... PDobbs 10 49
(JCFox) *dwlt: sn in midfield: effrt over 2f out: no imp* **100/1**
**8** *1 1/4* **Lookouthereicome** 3-8-6 ............................................... LisaJones(3) 8 46
(TTClement) *dwlt: sn in midfield: mod effrt on ins over 1f out: nt pce to chal* **66/1**
**9** *3* **Greatest By Phar** 3-9-0 ...................................................... CCatlin 4 44
(JAkehurst) *dwlt: sn pushed along and bhd: nvr nr ldrs* **33/1**
6 **10** *1/2* **Never Cried Wolf**[11] 553 3-9-0 ............................................. NPollard 9 43
(DRCElsworth) *drvn along over 4f out: a towards rr* **20/1**
60-0 **11** *18* **Emilys Dawn**[25] 420 3-8-9 51................................................ DSweeney 6 —
(DKIvory) *plld hrd: prom over 4f* **25/1**

1m 40.98s (1.47) **Going Correction** -0.05s/f (Stan) **11** Ran SP% **119.1**
Speed ratings: **90,89,89,89,85 84,83,82,79,79 61**CSF £26.37 TOTE £3.40: £1.50, £1.50, £2.70; EX 40.10.
**Owner** Miss J A Leighs **Bred** T G Mills **Trained** Headley, Surrey

**FOCUS**
A weak maiden and an extremely slow time, which suggests the form may not amount to much..

**NOTEBOOK**
**Somewhere My Love**, well backed on course, was never far away in a steadily run race and showed the right attitude to score, but she had nothing to spare at the line and both a slow time and the first four finishing in a heap cast a big doubt over the merit of the form. Her future lies totally in the hands of the Handicapper.
**Webbswood Lad(IRE)** took a good grip, but managed to hang in there and went down fighting. However, this was the second time he has made the frame in a slowly run race, so his form figures may be flattering.
**Night Storm**, dropping back from ten furlongs, ran her best race to date and this looks to be her best trip, but whether such a slowly run mile is ideal is another matter.
**Ground Patrol**, although holding every chance and not being beaten far, did not build on the promise of his second start and the form of that maiden is beginning to look very suspect.
**Opera Star(IRE)**, given a positive ride this time, set a modest pace but just proved to be a sitting duck.
**Dancing Lyra**, racing for the first time since July and making his sand debut, was given a lot to do and never looked like getting near the leaders. His rider reported that he was never travelling. *Official explanation: jockey said colt was never travelling*

## 622 BET DIRECT IN RUNNING SKY PAGE 293 H'CAP — 1m 2f (P)
3:30 (3:31) (E) (0-75,75) 3-Y-O — £3,391 (£969; £484) Stalls Low

Form — RPR

04-4 **1** — **Ivory Coast (IRE)**[18] [490] 3-8-2 **56** ........ JQuinn 8 — 58
(WRMuir) *chsd ldrs: led over 2f out: hld on wl fnl f* **12/1**

30-1 **2** *nk* **Desert Image (IRE)**[21] [462] 3-9-5 **73** ........ EAhern 3 — 74
(CTinkler) *chsd ldrs: hrd rdn 2f out: drvn to chal ins fnl f: styd on* **6/1**[3]

55-1 **3** *nk* **Keepers Knight (IRE)**[18] [490] 3-8-13 **67** ........ IMongan 2 — 67
(PFICole) *prom: rdn and hung lft fnl 3f: swtchd to rail and chal ins fnl f: kpt on* **7/2**[2]

234- **4** *½* **Little Eye (IRE)**[28] [6266] 3-9-0 **68** ........ NPollard 11 — 68
(JRBest) *towards rr: rdn and hdwy over 1f out: styd on u.p fnl f* **8/1**

11-4 **5** *hd* **Nessen Dorma (IRE)**[22] [450] 3-9-7 **75** ........ MFenton 10 — 74
(JGGiven) *pressed ldr: rdn and ev ch 1f out: one pce* **14/1**

6-01 **6** *nk* **Trevian**[7] [580] 3-8-11 **65** ........ JPSpencer 7 — 64
(SCWilliams) *hld up in rr: hdwy on outside and hung rt ent st: styd on same pce* **5/2**[1]

06-6 **7** *3* **El Magnifico**[14] [521] 3-7-9 **52** oh1 ........ (p) FPFerris(3) 4 — 45
(PDCundell) *mid-div: rdn 4f out: no imp fnl 2f* **33/1**

52-0 **8** *shd* **Princess Alina (IRE)**[18] [492] 3-8-13 **67** ........ SWhitworth 6 — 60
(AMBalding) *hld up in rr: hrd rdn and hdwy over 1f out: no ex ins fnl f* **16/1**

00-2 **9** *1¾* **Platinum Pirate**[25] [416] 3-8-2 **56** ........ (b) CCatlin 5 — 46
(KRBurke) *towards rr: mod effrt over 3f out: n.d fnl 2f* **20/1**

510- **10** *5* **Lasting Delight**[46] [6173] 3-9-0 **68** ........ JMackay 1 — 49
(SirMarkPrescott) *led tl wknd over 2f out* **11/1**

06-4 **11** *12* **Taranai (IRE)**[25] [420] 3-7-11 **54** ........ LisaJones(3) 13 — 13
(BWDuke) *wd and in tch: outpcd 4f out: sn bhd* **25/1**

2m 8.03s (0.64) **Going Correction** -0.05s/f (Stan) — 11 Ran SP% 116.3
Speed ratings: **95,94,94,94,93 93,91,91,89,85 76**CSF £79.51 CT £309.81 TOTE £15.20: £2.80, £2.80, £1.80; EX 82.30.
**Owner** Mrs J M Muir **Bred** Ian Bryant **Trained** Lambourn, Berks

**FOCUS**
An ordinary pace and the front six finished in a heap.

**NOTEBOOK**
**Ivory Coast(IRE)**, confirmed the promise of her recent effort over course and distance and showed real determination. The blanket finiish suggests the form is modest, but she seems to be improving with racing.
**Desert Image(IRE)**, up 5lb and trying his longest trip to date, got it well enough and was only just held. He may be better suited by a stronger pace.
**Keepers Knight(IRE)**, 7lb worse off with the winner compared to their meeting here earlier this month, made a sudden manoeuvre to the inside rail a furlong from home but, although staying on, could never quite get there. Mongan reported he was hanging that way. *Official explanation: jockey said colt hung left-handed in the last 4f*
**Little Eye(IRE)**, who disappointed on his most recent start when turned out again quickly, was trying his longest trip to date. Held up out the back, he crept closer running to the home bend and looked like he might take a hand, but he could not, or would not, go through the gap that presented itself. He has ability, but remains a maiden after 12 attempts and has questions to answer.
**Nessen Dorma(IRE)** was always thereabouts and was not beaten far, but he looks better on Fibresand.
**Trevian**, unpenalised for his win in an apprentice handicap here last week, was another stepping up in trip. He made progress from the back turning for home, but did not take the turn too well and found himself out in the centre of the track. He failed to land a telling blow from that point and his ability to see out the trip remains unproven. *Official explanation: jockey said gelding hung right-handed in the last 4f*

## 623 BET DIRECT IN VISION SKY PAGE 293 H'CAP — 1m 2f (P)
4:00 (4:00) (F) (0-55,55) 4-Y-0+ — £2,989 (£854; £427) Stalls Low

Form — RPR

0-16 **1** — **Bank On Him**[11] [554] 9-9-6 **53** ........ JQuinn 4 — 67
(CWeedon) *hdwy 4f out: chsd clr ldr over 2f out: led ins fnl f: drvn out* **8/1**

036- **2** *1* **My Maite (IRE)**[43] [6076] 5-9-5 **52** ........ (vt) NDay 6 — 64
(RIngram) *led and racd freely: sn clr: hdd ins fnl f: kpt on* **8/1**

32-2 **3** *5* **Double Ransom**[14] [525] 5-9-6 **53** ........ (b) SWKelly 9 — 56
(MrsLStubbs) *hdwy over 3f out: chsd clr ldrs 2f out: styd on same pce* **11/2**[2]

05-3 **4** *2* **Magic Warrior**[14] [525] 4-9-6 **55** ........ PDobbs 11 — 55
(JCFox) *bhd: rdn 3f out: styd on wl fr over 1f out: nrst fin* **11/1**

5213 **5** *1½* **Givemethemoonlight**[2] [605] 5-9-7 **54** 6ex ........ (v) JPSpencer 8 — 51
(MrsStefLiddiard) *chsd clr ldrs: styd on same pce fnl 2f: nvr able to chal* **9/2**[1]

0-00 **6** *shd* **Answered Promise (FR)**[2] [605] 5-9-1 **51** ........ RMiles(3) 14 — 48
(AWCarroll) *chsd clr ldr and clr of remainder: lost 2nd pl over 2f out: no ex* **50/1**

000- **7** *1¼* **Wind Chime (IRE)**[164] [4203] 7-9-4 **51** ........ SWhitworth 1 — 45
(AGNewcombe) *prom in chsng gp: rdn over 3f out: no ex fnl 2f* **10/1**

000- **8** *nk* **In The Stars (IRE)**[43] [5839] 6-9-5 **52** ........ (v[1]) WRyan 2 — 46
(PRWebber) *rdn 3f out: nvr nr to chal* **11/1**

650- **9** *9* **A Beetoo (IRE)**[30] [6253] 4-9-6 **55** ........ NPollard 7 — 33
(JRBest) *rdn 3f out: nvr trbld ldrs* **33/1**

1-00 **10** *4* **Nuzzle**[12] [552] 4-9-4 **53** ........ RWinston 10 — 24
(MQuinn) *prom 6f* **66/1**

00-3 **11** *hd* **Kyle Of Lochalsh**[14] [525] 4-9-6 **55** ........ (p) EAhern 12 — 25
(GGMargarson) *mid-div: rdn over 4f out: sn bhd* **7/1**[3]

53-0 **12** *8* **Water Of Life (IRE)**[11] [554] 5-9-4 **51** ........ IMongan 5 — 7
(JRBoyle) *rrd s: t.k.h: rdn 3f out: n.d* **12/1**

20-0 **13** *1½* **Castaigne (FR)**[21] [464] 5-9-7 **54** ........ MFenton 13 — 7
(BWDuke) *dwlt: a bhd* **20/1**

00-0 **14** *3* **Fife And Drum (USA)**[14] [525] 7-9-5 **52** ........ (p) PDoe 3 — —
(MissJFeilden) *chsd clr ldrs over 5f: bhd and eased fnl 2f* **16/1**

2m 6.75s (-0.64) **Going Correction** -0.05s/f (Stan)
**WFA** 4 from 5yo+ 2lb — 14 Ran SP% 118.8
Speed ratings: **100,99,95,93,92 92,91,91,83,80 80,74,72,70**CSF £67.62 CT £387.35 TOTE £11.70: £3.30, £4.40, £2.30; EX 89.40.
**Owner** Vetlab Supplies Ltd **Bred** Brook Stud Ltd **Trained** Wormley, Surrey

**FOCUS**
My Maite set a good pace, resulting in a time 1.28sec quicker than the previous handicap, and very few got into it.

**NOTEBOOK**
**Bank On Him**, recording his ninth course and distance success, had not won a handicap for almost two years, but he has been in good form of late and, of course, is always dangerous at his favourite track. Very few got into this race and he may be flattered, but he is sure to remain dangerous at a modest level round here.
**My Maite(IRE)**, who runs his best races when racing prominently, made a brave attempt to nick this from the front. He set a strong pace and was still clear entering the final furlong, but in the end the win proved just beyond him.
**Double Ransom** was beaten a fair way back in third but continues to post a consistent level of form.
**Magic Warrior** never got into contention but appeared to see the trip out well enough, staying on all to late.
**Givemethemoonlight** has been sent off at 7-1 or shorter 17 times but has just one win to her name.
**Water Of Life(IRE)** *Official explanation: trainer said mare finished distressed*

## 624 FREE £25 BONUS @ LITTLEWOODSPOKER.COM H'CAP — 7f (P)
4:30 (4:43) (F) (0-65,65) 4-Y-0+ — £2,989 (£854; £427) Stalls Low

Form — RPR

-660 **1** — **Blonde En Blonde (IRE)**[4] [599] 4-9-12 **63** ........ (b[1]) IMongan 2 — 74
(NPLittmoden) *prom: led over 1f out: drvn out* **33/1**

35-0 **2** *½* **Acorazado (IRE)**[18] [491] 5-9-4 **55** ........ (e[1]) GCarter 4 — 65
(GLMoore) *hld up: hdwy 2f out: drvn to chse wnr ins fnl f: r.o* **16/1**

-064 **3** *1* **Superchief**[4] [596] 9-10-0 **65** ........ (bt) JQuinn 9 — 72
(MissBSanders) *dwlt: hld up towards rr: effrt and nt clr run over 1f out: nrst fin* **5/1**[2]

50-1 **4** *1½* **Zafarshah (IRE)**[18] [491] 5-9-7 **58** ........ (v) JoannaBadger 1 — 62
(PDEvans) *prom: led after 2f tl over 1f out: one pce* **12/1**

23-5 **5** *1* **Temper Tantrum**[22] [448] 6-9-4 **62** ........ (p) RoryMoore(7) 14 — 63
(AndrewReid) *hld up in rr: hdwy over 1f out: no imp fnl f* **20/1**

23-3 **6** *shd* **Inistrahull Island (IRE)**[4] [596] 4-9-8 **59** ........ JFanning 5 — 60
(MHTompkins) *trckd ldrs: hrd rdn over 1f out: one pce* **9/1**

-413 **7** *hd* **Double M**[7] [573] 7-9-3 **54** ........ (v) NCallan 15 — 54
(MrsLRichards) *plld hrd: stdd in rr: rdn and hdwy over 1f out: no imp* **16/1**

300- **8** *1* **Mr Bountiful (IRE)**[29] [6260] 6-9-9 **60** ........ (p) SWKelly 3 — 58
(MDods) *t.k.h: chsd ldrs tl wknd over 1f out* **25/1**

5-42 **9** *¾* **Danielle's Lad**[9] [564] 8-9-11 **65** ........ (b) RMiles(3) 16 — 61
(BPalling) *sn led: hdd 5f out: w ldr after tl wknd over 1f out* **20/1**

01-1 **10** *½* **Smith N Allan Oils**[22] [448] 5-10-0 **65** ........ (p) RWinston 6 — 60
(MDods) *in tch: rdn 3f out: no hdwy fnl 2f* **11/2**[3]

000- **11** *5* **Meelup (IRE)**[29] [6260] 4-9-6 **57** ........ (p) SWhitworth 10 — 39
(AGNewcombe) *mid-div: outpcd 3f out: n.d after* **50/1**

3-11 **12** *½* **Nearly A Fool**[7] [573] 6-9-10 **61** 6ex ........ (v) NPollard 7 — 42
(GGMargarson) *chsd ldrs: wd and wknd ent st* **9/2**[1]

001- **13** *¾* **Wood Fern (UAE)**[30] [6253] 4-10-0 **65** ........ RLappin 12 — 44
(MRChannon) *rdn 3f out: nvr nr to chal* **6/1**

0-00 **14** *16* **Pants**[4] [599] 5-9-4 **55** ........ ANicholls 8 — —
(AndrewReid) *s.s: swtchd wd: gd hdwy 4f out: wknd over 2f out* **20/1**

1m 25.16s (-0.84) **Going Correction** -0.05s/f (Stan) — 14 Ran SP% 117.0
Speed ratings: **102,101,100,98,97 97,97,95,95,94 88,88,87,69**CSF £443.46 CT £3176.52 TOTE £22.60: £5.20, £4.70, £2.30; EX 369.60 Place 6 £35.31, Place 5 £28.56.
**Owner** Elliott and Brown Racing **Bred** Martin Francis **Trained** Newmarket, Suffolk

**FOCUS**
They went 9-2 the field in what was a competitive handicap.

**NOTEBOOK**
**Blonde En Blonde(IRE)** has shown her best form on Fibresand in the past but, with the first-time blinkers working the oracle, she sprang a surprise in what was an open handicap.
**Acorazado(IRE)**is a difficult horse to catch right. He had his chance on the inside but was not quite good enough.
**Superchief** ran his usual sort of race, finishing all too late after running into traffic problems.
**Zafarshah(IRE)**, another infrequent winner, had a visor on this time. It did not seem to improve his performance, though, in what was admittedly a more competitive heat than the one he won here on his previous start.
**Temper Tantrum** has never won off a mark in the 60s but continues to run well enough to make it hard for the Handicapper to drop him.
**Inistrahull Island(IRE)**, who had the visor left off this time, remains a maiden.
**Double M** would have had a stronger chance had he consented to settle better.
**Nearly A Fool** *Official explanation: trainer was unable to offer any explanation for the gelding's poor run.*

T/Jkpt: Not won. T/Plt: £44.90 to a £1 stake. Pool: £73,687.45. 1,195.85 winning tickets. T/Qpdt: £15.50 to a £1 stake. Pool: £5,855.30. 279.00 winning tickets. LM

# 610 SOUTHWELL (L-H)
Thursday, January 29

**OFFICIAL GOING: Standard to slow changing to standard after race 5 (3.10)**
This is the first time that the going description of 'standard to slow' has been used.
Wind: fresh hlf bhd Weather: fine

## 625 PRESS INTERACTIVE TO BET DIRECT H'CAP (DIV I) — 6f (F)
1:10 (1:12) (F) (0-55,55) 4-Y-0+ — £2,968 (£848; £424) Stalls Low

Form — RPR

0-44 **1** — **Its Ecco Boy**[17] [504] 6-8-11 **52** ........ RWinston 9 — 63
(PHowling) *chsd ldrs: rdn to ld over 1f out: r.o* **5/1**[1]

-326 **2** *nk* **Aguila Loco (IRE)**[17] [499] 5-8-5 **46** oh1 ........ JoannaBadger 1 — 56
(MCChapman) *chsd ldrs: rdn and ev ch over 1f out: r.o* **9/1**

-063 **3** *3* **Playful Spirit**[7] [584] 5-8-5 **46** oh1 ........ (v) JEdmunds 4 — 47
(JBalding) *hld up in tch: rdn over 1f out: no ex ins fnl f* **5/1**[1]

06-6 **4** *¾* **Dasar**[25] [428] 4-8-2 **50** oh1 ow4 ........ (b[1]) MLawson(7) 7 — 49
(MBrittain) *hld up: hdwy and hung lft over 2f out: sn rdn: styd on* **6/1**[2]

-126 **5** *1½* **Cleveland Way**[17] [509] 4-8-6 **47** ........ (v) RFitzpatrick 10 — 41
(DCarroll) *mde most over 4f: wknd ins fnl f* **16/1**

622- **6** *1¼* **Eastern Blue (IRE)**[51] [6149] 5-8-9 **50** ........ (p) SWKelly 13 — 41
(MrsLStubbs) *mid-div: outpcd over 2f out: styd on u.p ins fnl f* **6/1**[2]

3010 **7** *3½* **Attorney**[8] [573] 6-8-6 **47** ........ (e) JQuinn 12 — 27
(DShaw) *hld up: nvr trbld ldrs* **16/1**

000- **8** *1¾* **On The Trail**[51] [6151] 7-8-9 **50** ........ RBrisland 3 — 25
(DWChapman) *w ldr: rdn and ev ch over 1f out: wknd ins fnl f* **8/1**

0-00 **9** *3½* **Definitely Special (IRE)**[14] [536] 6-8-5 **46** oh6 ........ CCatlin 6 — 10
(NEBerry) *hld up: a in rr* **20/1**

0-60 **10** *½* **Kustom Kit For Her**[9] [569] 4-8-5 **46** oh1 ........ (b) JBramhill 11 — 9
(SRBowring) *dwlt: a in rr* **33/1**

00-3 **11** *¾* **Festive Affair**[23] [460] 6-8-8 **49** ........ RFfrench 5 — 10
(BSmart) *chsd ldrs: rdn over 3f out: wknd 2f out* **13/2**[3]

0-20 **12** *4* **Xaloc Bay (IRE)**[10] [565] 6-9-0 **55** ........ (v) DarrenWilliams 14 — 4
(BPJBaugh) *sn pushed along and prom: rdn and wknd 3f out: eased fnl f* **16/1**

005- **13** *¾* **Sergeant Slipper**[48] [6170] 7-8-1 **49** oh1 ow3 ........ (v) PMakin(7) 2 — —
(CSmith) *s.i.s: effrt 1/2-way: wknd and eased over 1f out* **20/1**

1m 18.05s (1.25) **Going Correction** +0.075s/f (Slow) — 13 Ran SP% 116.0
Speed ratings: **94,93,89,88,86 84,80,77,73,72 71,66,65**CSF £45.33 CT £244.84 TOTE £6.30: £3.20, £2.50, £1.50; EX 38.70.
**Owner** J Hammond **Bred** Mrs D Ellis **Trained** Newmarket, Suffolk



The Form Book, Raceform Ltd, Compton, RG20 6NL

**FOCUS**
Just 9lb covered the field for this humdrum handicap, the winning time was slow for the grade and the form is modest. The main action unfolded down the centre of the home straight.

**NOTEBOOK**
**Its Ecco Boy**, a positive mover on the exchanges, appreciated the return to seven furlongs and ran out a workmanlike winner. His strike rate is nothing special but there are more options open to him now he has proved his liking for this track.
**Aguila Loco(IRE)** travelled best turning for home but came under pressure going to the last. He stuck on well enough and the sixth furlong was not a problem on this occasion.
**Playful Spirit** was 3lb well in, but was unable to take advantage and did not look to be helping her rider in the latter stages.
**Dasar** showed some improvement in the first-time blinkers, staying on down the deepest part of the track. She has tumbled down the weights and a return to farther will benefit her.
**Cleveland Way** managed to secure the early lead, but was always being harried and the effort expended took its toll in the latter stages.
**Eastern Blue(IRE)**, who went up 2lb for her two seconds over course and distance, could never land a blow.
**On The Trail**, who has a good record in the winter months, weakened in a manner which suggested this first start for 51 days was needed.
**Sergeant Slipper** was reported to have lost his action. *Official explanation: jockey said gelding had lost its action*

## 626 PRESS INTERACTIVE TO BET DIRECT H'CAP (DIV II) 6f (F)
**1:40** (1:43) (F) (0-55,54) 4-Y-0+ **£1,908** (£1,908; £424) **Stalls** Low

Form RPR
-135 **1** *dht* **Italian Mist (FR)**[8] 576 5-8-9 49 ...(e) GFaulkner 12 59
(JulianPoulton) *trckd ldrs: led on bit over 1f out: sn rdn: hung lft and hdd ins fnl f: r.o to join wnr post* **20/1**
5-55 **1** **Aintnecessarilyso**[14] 536 6-8-5 45 ... CCatlin 6 55
(NEBerry) *chsd ldrs: rdn to ld ins fnl f: jnd on post* **8/1**
0-26 **3** *5* **Torrent**[8] 573 9-8-5 45 ...(b) RBrisland 10 40
(DWChapman) *hld up: plld hrd: hdwy over 3f out: one pce fnl f* **16/1**
22-6 **4** *2* **Never Without Me**[21] 476 4-8-10 50 ...(v) NCallan 14 39
(PJMcbride) *chsd ldrs: rdn and ev ch over 1f out: sn wknd* **6/1**[3]
2-52 **5** *½* **Amelia (IRE)**[17] 510 6-8-3 50 ... BSwarbrick[(7)] 9 38
(WMBrisbourne) *hld up: hdwy over 2f out: nvr trbld ldrs* **11/2**[2]
2-42 **6** *¾* **Polar Haze**[3] 608 7-8-13 53 ...(v) JQuinn 16 38
(MrsLydiaPearce) *chsd ldrs: rdn and hung lft 2f out: wknd over 1f out* **11/2**[2]
000- **7** *3* **Brioso (IRE)**[62] 6080 4-9-0 54 ... JMackay 2 30
(JMPEustace) *led over 4f: wknd fnl f* **20/1**
/51- **8** *½* **Shahm (IRE)**[44] 6202 5-8-13 53 ... SWKelly 8 28
(BJCurley) *sn outpcd: nvr nrr* **9/2**[1]
000- **9** *1* **Katy O'Hara**[163] 4264 5-8-5 45 ... DeanMcKeown 4 17
(MissSEHall) *stsarted slowly: outpcd* **25/1**
00-0 **10** *1 ¾* **Back In Spirit**[17] 510 4-8-5 45 oh5 ...(t) GGibbons 15 12
(BAMcmahon) *chsd ldrs: ev ch over 2f out: sn rdn and wknd* **40/1**
0-43 **11** *nk* **Lady Natilda**[17] 510 4-8-7 47 ... PaulEddery 1 13
(DHaydnJones) *hld up: rdn over 2f out: n.d* **7/1**
0-00 **12** *2* **Caronte (IRE)**[17] 499 4-8-5 45 oh10 ...(b) JBramhill 7 —
(SRBowring) *chsd ldrs over 4f* **50/1**
-120 **13** *hd* **Eternal Bloom**[9] 572 6-8-2 49 ow4 ...(v[1]) MLawson[(7)] 3 8
(MBrittain) *s.s: outpcd* **10/1**
0/-0 **14** *dist* **Speedy James (IRE)**[9] 572 8-8-5 45 oh5 ...(v) ANicholls 13 —
(DNicholls) *s.s: outpcd* **28/1**

1m 17.5s (0.70) **Going Correction** +0.075s/f (Slow) **14** Ran SP% **123.0**
Speed ratings: **98,98,91,88,88 87,83,82,81,78 78,75,75,—**, £4.80 TRIFECTA W: I 11.7,A 4.2; Pl: I 5.5,A 2.90; Ex: I/A 143.20,A/I 135.90; CSF: I/A 82.55,A/I 83.68;TC: I/A/T 1327.02,A/I/T 1,256.69; TF Not won.
**Owner** S P Shore **Bred** Mrs Hilary Trigg & Mr John Veil **Trained** Kentford, Suffolk

**FOCUS**
Another tightly-knit handicap, run six tenths of a second faster than the first division. Although the first two put up decent efforts, the race lacked strength in depth.

**NOTEBOOK**
**Aintnecessarilyso**, minus the cheekpieces, has proved very difficult to win with but the drop down a furlong helped today. Throwing down a strong challenge, he looked to have nosed ahead close home but had to settle for a share of the spoils on the nod.
**Italian Mist(FR)**, running here for the first time, was swinging off the bridle with his rider looking over both shoulders for dangers approaching the final furlong, but he found less than he promised when brought under pressure and could not see off a tenacious challenger. He is able when in the mood but one to have reservations about.
**Torrent** was nursed through by his rider to claim third without ever promising to break his long losing streak.
**Never Without Me**, with the visor back on, ran with credit but did not quite see out the trip on this slow surface.
**Amelia(IRE)** was again brought wide for a run but the effort fizzled out in the last furlong and a half.
**Polar Haze**, who hung badly over to the inside rail, will be suited by a return to selling company.
**Brioso(IRE)** is edging down the weights and he showed a little more here without signalling that a return to form is imminent.
**Shahm(IRE)**, a winner over seven here last month, found things happening much too quickly over this shorter trip against seasoned sprinters and his supporters quickly knew their fate.
**Eternal Bloom** lost all chance at the start.
**Speedy James(IRE)** was very slowly away and no longer appears to have any enthusiasm for the game.

## 627 BET DIRECT THROUGH SKY ACTIVE APPRENTICE CLAIMING STKS 1m (F)
**2:10** (2:11) (F) 4-Y-0+ **£2,947** (£842; £421) **Stalls** Low

Form RPR
52-0 **1** **Miss Champers (IRE)**[10] 564 4-7-10 67 ... BSwarbrick[(5)] 10 61
(PDEvans) *chsd ldrs: led 2f out: rdn out* **6/5**[1]
440- **2** *½* **Noble Pursuit**[44] 6198 7-8-2 55 ow2 ... DerekNolan[(3)] 4 64
(PABlockley) *a.p: swtchd rt 2f out: chsd wnr over 1f out: r.o* **7/1**[3]
1-01 **3** *5* **Game Guru**[14] 542 5-8-9 64 ... Laura-JayneCrawford[(3)] 2 60
(TDBarron) *sn led: rdn and hdd 2f out: wknd ins fnl f* **11/4**[2]
120 **4** *3* **Repeat (IRE)**[17] 504 4-8-6 56 ...(p) PGallagher 5 47
(MissGayKelleway) *prom: jnd ldr 1/2-way: rdn and ev ch wl over 1f out: sn wknd* **20/1**
00-0 **5** *2* **Kumakawa**[19] 491 6-8-1 45 ...(b) LiamJones[(5)] 6 43
(EAWheeler) *sn outpcd: rdn over 2f out: styd on ins fnl f* **50/1**
2-66 **6** *1 ¼* **First Maite**[20] 485 11-8-13 70 ...(t) BO'Neill[(5)] 8 52
(SRBowring) *sn outpcd: styd on ins fnl f: nvr nrr* **15/2**
-500 **7** *1 ¼* **Jamestown**[7] 582 7-8-13 46 ... KGhunowa[(5)] 7 49
(MJPolglase) *bhd fnl 5f* **40/1**
0-04 **8** *2 ½* **Sweet Coral (FR)**[9] 567 4-7-12 40 ... KristinStubbs 12 24
(BSRothwell) *hung rt thrght: hld up: wknd over 3f out* **33/1**
60-0 **9** *2* **Maunby Rocker**[22] 464 4-8-8 54 ... DWakenshaw[(7)] 3 37
(PCHaslam) *chsd ldrs over 4f* **14/1**
/0 **10** *14* **The Block Monster (IRE)**[25] 433 5-7-7 45 ... SYourston[(5)] 1 —
(PABlockley) *w ldr over 3f: wknd over 3f out* **50/1**

1m 45.44s (0.84) **Going Correction** +0.075s/f (Slow) **10** Ran SP% **117.1**
Speed ratings: **98,97,92,89,87 86,85,82,80,66**CSF £9.95 TOTE £2.30: £1.10, £2.50, £1.40; EX 13.30.The winner was claimed by J T Billson for £6,000. Game Guru was claimed by Mrs.J.Hughes for £8,000.
**Owner** Mrs S J Lawrence **Bred** Mountarmstrong Stud **Trained** Pandy, Gwent

**FOCUS**
A low-grade apprentice claimer run at a moderate pace and dominated by those at the head of the market.

**NOTEBOOK**
**Miss Champers(IRE)**, dropped in class, had almost a stone in hand on official figures but had to work quite hard. She was claimed afterwards for £6,000 to join Paul Blockley, who saddled the runner-up, but while she escapes a penalty, she would not be an obvious candidate to follow up.
**Noble Pursuit** had to switch right at the two-furlong marker, but it did not affect his chance as he never quite looked like getting to the filly. There remains a question mark over his attitude.
**Game Guru**, whose two wins so far have come over course and distance, had no excuses other than that he was taken on for the lead. He was claimed afterwards for £8,000 and joins Paul Blockley.
**Repeat(IRE)**, who is only a plater, was found out by this longer trip, although he is not the sort to find much for pressure in any case.

## 628 LITTLEWOODS BET DIRECT MEDIAN AUCTION MAIDEN STKS 1m (F)
**2:40** (2:40) (E) 3-4-Y-0 **£3,248** (£928; £464) **Stalls** Low

Form RPR
5 **1** **Norwegian**[6] 593 3-8-6 ... NPollard 7 65
(DRLoder) *chsd ldrs: sn drvn along: led 1f out: styd on* **11/4**[2]
6-34 **2** *2* **Monte Major (IRE)**[12] 557 3-8-6 61 ... NCallan 1 61
(MAJarvis) *led: rdn and hdd 1f out: styd on same pce* **4/6**[1]
-4 **3** *6* **Vivre Sa Vie**[10] 563 3-8-1 ... JMackay 5 43
(SirMarkPrescott) *chsd ldrs: sn drvn along: outpcd fnl 2f* **15/2**[3]
05- **4** *20* **Bundaberg**[157] 4470 4-9-12 ... RWinston 4 —
(PWHiatt) *chsd ldr tl wknd over 2f out* **33/1**
0-0 **5** *8* **Tale Of The Tiger**[19] 489 3-8-6 ...(v) RFfrench 2 —
(JulianPoulton) *sn outpcd* **50/1**
00- **U** **Dalida**[65] 6069 3-7-8 ... DFentiman[(7)] 6 —
(PCHaslam) *uns rdr after 1f* **14/1**

1m 46.87s (2.27) **Going Correction** +0.075s/f (Slow)
**WFA** 3 from 4yo 20lb **6** Ran SP% **110.0**
Speed ratings: **91,89,83,63,55** —CSF £4.71 TOTE £4.40: £1.90, £1.10; EX 4.40.
**Owner** Jumeirah Racing **Bred** Darley **Trained** Newmarket, Suffolk

**FOCUS**
A weak maiden and a slow time, run over a second slower than the preceding claimer. The form is modest.

**NOTEBOOK**
**Norwegian** looked far brighter in his coat than he had done on his debut at Dunstall Park and he clearly learnt from the experience, although he still showed signs of greenness. He stayed on willingly to wear down the favourite but, while there is modest improvement in him, he may struggle in handicap company.
**Monte Major(IRE)**, officially rated 61, seemed to have matters under control as he led into the straight with his rivals all rowing along, but his stride began to shorten going to the final furlong and he was worried out of it. It is disappointing that he could not account for this opposition but a return to seven furlongs will help him.
**Vivre Sa Vie** was made to look painfully slow over a trip which is clearly inadequate for her. She is still leggy and weak and will improve as she strengthens.
**Bundaberg** broke on terms on this first run since last August, but he was left trailing once in line for home.

## 629 BETDIRECT.CO.UK H'CAP 1m 4f (F)
**3:10** (3:10) (E) (0-75,74) 4-Y-0+ **£3,349** (£957; £478) **Stalls** Low

Form RPR
43-1 **1** **Fall In Line**[3] 609 4-9-2 **66** 6ex ... JMackay 5 88+
(SirMarkPrescott) *dwlt: sn chsng ldrs: led over 3f out: sn clr* **1/4**[1]
-044 **2** *8* **Night Warrior (IRE)**[1] 618 4-9-2 **66** ... PDoe 3 70
(DFlood) *hld up: hdwy over 4f out: rdn to chse wnr over 2f out: no imp* **25/1**
0-21 **3** *½* **Aveiro (IRE)**[9] 570 8-8-6 **52** 6ex ow1 ...(b) KDalgleish 1 55
(BGPowell) *s.i.s: hld up: hdwy over 3f out: sn rdn and no imp* **9/1**[2]
36-1 **4** *8* **Digger (IRE)**[16] 516 5-10-0 **74** ... MFenton 8 65
(MissGayKelleway) *chsd ldrs: rdn 5f out: wknd over 2f out* **12/1**[3]
31-0 **5** *6* **Stravmour**[14] 546 8-8-0 **46** ... DaleGibson 4 28
(RHollinshead) *chsd ldrs over 8f* **50/1**
32-0 **6** *10* **George Stubbs (USA)**[26] 413 6-9-7 **70** ... LFletcher[(3)] 6 37
(MJPolglase) *led over 8f: wknd over 2f out* **25/1**
12-0 **7** *dist* **Victory Quest (IRE)**[15] 523 4-9-9 **73** ...(v) JQuinn 2 —
(MrsSLamyman) *chsd ldrs over 8f* **25/1**

2m 40.24s (-1.86) **Going Correction** +0.075s/f (Slow)
**WFA** 4 from 5yo+ 4lb **7** Ran SP% **111.2**
Speed ratings: **109,103,103,98,94 87,—**CSF £11.74 CT £21.94 TOTE £1.20: £1.10, £10.50; EX 13.00.
**Owner** Neil Greig - Osborne House Ii **Bred** P D Player **Trained** Newmarket, Suffolk

**FOCUS**
They went a decent pace in this handicap and, as at Wolverhampton earlier in the week, the winner returned a very smart performance against the clock as he turned the race into a procession. He looks thrown in off his current mark.

**NOTEBOOK**
**Fall In Line** looked a good thing under a 6lb penalty for his impressive Wolverhampton victory three days earlier and duly made no mistake. After half-rearing in the stalls, he was settled in touch and, once striking the front going into the home turn, went on to pulverise the opposition, value for a greater margin of victory as he was eased down in the final 100 yards. He still appeared green - he was edgy in the preliminaries and seemed to look about him once in front - and with further improvement guaranteed he should remain a step ahead of the handicapper.
**Night Warrior(IRE)** ran well considering his exertions the previous afternoon and, although not in the same league as the favourite, deserves credit for the way he stuck on to hold second spot.
**Aveiro(IRE)**, penalised for an all-the-way win in a banded stakes here, was ridden differently on this occasion. Never going particularly well, he stayed on from the rear to challenge for second inside the last but that was the best his supporters could ever hope for. He is going to struggle off his revised mark on this evidence.
**Digger(IRE)**, raised 3lb for his win over a furlong less here earlier in the month, was a spent force in the last two furlongs and may benefit from the re-application of headgear.
**Victory Quest(IRE)** was reported to have lost his action. *Official explanation: jockey said gelding had lost its action*

## 630 ALLWEATHER-RACING.COM (S) STKS 1m 3f (F)
3:40 (3:42) (G) 4-Y-0+ £2,604 (£744; £372) Stalls Low

Form RPR

-014 1 **Coolfore Jade (IRE)**[13] 548 4-8-11 57 CCatlin 6 61
(NEBerry) *mde virtually all: rdn clr and edgd lft over 1f out: styd on wl* **11/8**[1]

0-0 2 6 **Rex Romelio (IRE)**[16] 512 5-9-0 50 (v[1]) GFaulkner 7 51
(KRBurke) *prom: chsd wnr 1/2-way: rdn over 2f out: edgd lft over 1f out: styd on same pce* **9/1**

-052 3 5 **Sea Ya Maite**[17] 497 10-9-0 35 (t) JBramhill 9 43
(SRBowring) *chsd ldrs: rdn over 3f out: sn outpcd* **14/1**

6-55 4 1 **Luxi River (USA)**[16] 517 4-8-11 59 DeanMcKeown 11 42
(PABlockley) *hld up: hdwy 3f out: nvr trbld ldrs* **5/1**[2]

004- 5 6 **Gladys Aylward**[68] 5690 4-8-7 55 ow1 VHalliday 5 28
(ACrook) *chsd ldrs over 7f* **25/1**

-253 6 hd **Ipledgeallegiance (USA)**[9] 571 8-9-0 45 RBrisland 10 32
(DWChapman) *hld up: nvr nr to chal* **11/2**[3]

0 7 7 **Mr Lehman**[7] 585 7-9-0 MFenton 12 21
(MrsMReveley) *hld up: hdwy 7f out: wknd over 3f out* **8/1**

040/ 8 dist **Spring Gift**[16] 201 7-8-9 45 RWinston 1 —
(DWThompson) *chsd ldrs: lost pl 9f out: wknd 5f out* **33/1**

0- 9 20 **Dr Raj**[16] 2129 5-9-0 (t) GGibbons 4 —
(BAMcmahon) *chsd ldrs: rdn 1/2-way: sn wknd* **20/1**

2m 28.15s (-0.75) **Going Correction** +0.075s/f (Slow)
**WFA** 4 from 5yo+ 3lb 9 Ran SP% **113.5**
Speed ratings: **105,100,97,96,91 91,86,—,—**CSF £13.97 TOTE £2.20: £1.20, £2.90, £2.20; EX 16.30.The winner was bought in for 5,500gns.
**Owner** Leeway Group Limited **Bred** Des De Vere Hunt **Trained** Earlswood, Monmouths

**FOCUS**
A weak seller, but the all-the-way winner, who only had to be close to his best to score, recorded a decent time for the type of race.

**NOTEBOOK**
**Coolfore Jade(IRE)**, whose task was simplified by the non-participation of old rival Platinum Charmer, took time to assert and hung over to the far rail but was well on top in the final furlong. Suited by the return to this trip, she posted a decent time for a race of this nature.
**Rex Romelio(IRE)**, a dual winner in Germany two seasons ago who had shown little in a couple of runs for his current yard, was well supported. Dropped in grade and fitted with a visor, he was the only challenger to the favourite but was unable to muster a gear change once in line for home. His German wins came over a mile and he may have found this trip a shade far.
**Sea Ya Maite**, whose losing run stretches back to the spring of 2001, was left trailing by the first two on the approach to the home straight.
**Luxi River(USA)** passed a few rivals once in line for home but continues to operate below the level at which he formerly looked capable.
**Mr Lehman** ought to have improved for this step up in trip and is going the wrong way. His rider reported that he had hung left in the latter stages. *Official explanation: jockey said gelding had hung left in the latter stages*

## 631 BET DIRECT ON SKY ACTIVE H'CAP 1m (F)
4:10 (4:10) (E) (0-70,70) 3-Y-0 £3,255 (£930; £465) Stalls Low

Form RPR

4-12 1 **Yankeedoodledandy (IRE)**[14] 535 3-8-1 57 RoryMoore[(7)] 5 64
(PCHaslam) *a.p: rdn over 3f out: led 1f out: r.o* **8/15**[1]

501- 2 3 1/2 **Could She Be Magic (IRE)**[66] 6058 3-8-8 57 KDalgleish 6 56
(TDEasterby) *plld hrd: w ldr: hrd rdn to ld over 1f out: sn hdd: no ex ins fnl f* **7/2**[2]

54-3 3 3/4 **Two Of Clubs**[15] 529 3-8-13 62 GFaulkner 1 60
(PCHaslam) *w ldr tl led over 3f out: rdn and hdd over 1f out: no ex ins fnl f* **12/1**[3]

300- 4 nk **La Puce**[104] 5613 3-9-7 70 MFenton 2 67
(MissGayKelleway) *trckd ldrs: outpcd wl over 1f out: styd on ins fnl f* **20/1**

0-53 5 1 1/4 **Lady Mo**[15] 521 3-8-4 56 ow5 J-PGuillambert[(3)] 3 50
(AndrewReid) *hld up in tch: racd keenly: rdn over 2f out: nt trble ldrs* **20/1**

06-0 6 11 **Wares Home (IRE)**[12] 557 3-8-13 62 DarrenWilliams 4 32
(KRBurke) *led over 4f: rdn and wknd over 1f out* **12/1**[3]

1m 44.83s (0.23) **Going Correction** +0.075s/f (Slow) 6 Ran SP% **112.4**
Speed ratings: **101,97,96,96,95 84**CSF £2.67 TOTE £1.20: £1.10, £2.00; EX 3.60 Place 6 £28.52, Place 5 £14.11.
**Owner** K Tyre **Bred** B Kennedy **Trained** Middleham Moor, N Yorks
■ Stewards Enquiry : Rory Moore one-day ban: used whip with whip arm above shoulder height (Feb 9)

**FOCUS**
A modest event won by a well-treated horse, but a fair winning time for the type of race.

**NOTEBOOK**
**Yankeedoodledandy(IRE)** had to work hard to get his head in front, but once he got there he soon settled the issue and was going away at the finish. He has already won over an extended nine furlongs, and a return to that trip will be in his favour.
**Could She Be Magic(IRE)** won a seven-furlong seller here on her last outing, and ran her race before being outstayed in the last furlong. She will need to settle better to be truly effective at this trip.
**Two Of Clubs**, another stepping up in trip, ran well enough under a positive ride, and similar tactics back at seven may be in his favour.
**La Puce**, returning from 15 weeks off, ran well and gave the impression that this trip is within her compass. She will be better for the outing.
T/Jkpt: £6,546.40 to a £1 stake. Pool: £18,440.80. 2.00 winning tickets. T/Plt: £84.20 to a £1 stake. Pool: £77,029.25. 667.80 winning tickets. T/Qpdt: £2.10 to a £1 stake. Pool: £7,248.30. 2,465.80 winning tickets. CR

# NAD AL SHEBA (L-H)
Thursday, January 29
**OFFICIAL GOING: Dirt course - fast; turf course - good to firm**

## 632a MARJU INTERNATIONAL RATED STKS (SPONSORED BY DERRINSTOWN STUD) (DIRT) 6f (D)
3:45 (3:45) 3-Y-0+ £32,681 (£10,055; £5,027; £2,513) Stalls High

RPR

1 **San Salvador (USA)**[21] 7-9-0 95 (vt) TEDurcan 7 102
(MAlKurdi, UAE) *trckd ldrs: chal and led over 1f out: r.o wl* **7/1**

2 2 1/2 **Rotulo (ARG)**[46] 6-8-10 91 (t) MSantos 6 90
(DiegoLowther, Sweden) *outpcd early: hdwy 1 1/2f out: same pce fr over 110yds out* **20/1**

3 3 **Conceal**[18] 6-9-0 95 GHind 2 85
(RBouresly, Kuwait) *w ldr: led 1/2-way: rdn over 2f out: ev ch: same pce fnl 110yds* **4/1**[2]

4 1 **Elegance Champion (AUS)**[35] 5-8-10 91 (be) LDettori 5 78
(GMoore, Macau) *led 2f: rdn appr 1/2-way: wknd 1f out* **3/1**[1]

5 1 3/4 **Majestic Horizon**[6] 4-8-9 90 (t) RMullen 3 72
(AAlRaihe, UAE) *s.i.s: a chsng ldrs: kpt on fnl f: nrst fin* **14/1**

6 2 1/2 **National Icon (SAF)**[208] 4-8-9 90 WCMarwing 4 64
(MFDeKock, South Africa) *disp ld 2f: rdn appr 1/2-way: ev ch: wknd over 1f out* **9/2**[3]

7 2 1/2 **Raheibb (IRE)**[18] 6-9-5 100 BDoyle 9 67
(AllanSmith, UAE) *w ldr 2f: rdn 3 1/2f out: wknd fr over 1f out* **15/2**

8 3 1/4 **Jacks Estate (IRE)**[82] 5956 9-9-6 101 MJKinane 1 58
(AdrianMcguinness, Ire) *racd centre: rdn and wknd fr 1/2-way* **12/1**

9 2 1/2 **Peruvian Chief (IRE)**[96] 5743 7-9-8 104 (v) RLMoore 8 53
(NPLittmoden) *outpcd in rr thrght: n.d* **7/1**

1m 11.1s 9 Ran SP% **119.1**
Speed ratings: .
**Owner** H E Sheikh Rashid Bin Mohammed **Bred** D Earl Pardue **Trained** United Arab Emirates

**NOTEBOOK**
**Peruvian Chief(IRE)** never went the pace.

## 633a GREEN DESERT INTERNATIONAL RATED STKS (SPONSORED BY SHADWELL) (TURF) 1m 2f (T)
4:15 (4:15) 3-Y-0+ £32,681 (£10,055; £5,027; £2,513) Stalls Low

RPR

1 **Prince Of War (AUS)**[152] 6-8-11 95 WCMarwing 1 103
(MFDeKock, South Africa) *trckd ldrs: 3rd and rdn st: led 2 1/2f out: pushed out fnl 110yds: comf* **16/1**

2 1 3/4 **Lodge Keeper**[13] 4-8-7 92 ow2 GAvranche 5 98
(NDeCroutte, Bahrain) *mid-div: 7th st: hmpd 2f out: hdwy over 1f out: r.o fnl 110yds: nrst fin* **10/1**

3 2 3/4 **Courageous Duke (USA)**[117] 5365 5-8-11 95 MJKinane 12 95
(JNoseda) *settled in rr: 11th st: rdn and hdwy over 2f out: ev ch 1f out: same pce fnl 110yds* **6/1**[2]

4 3 **Shami**[271] 1340 5-9-0 97 (v) JPSpencer 8 93
(DRLoder) *towards rr: 8th st: rdn and gd hdwy over 2f out: same pce fr over 1f out* **6/1**[2]

5 3/4 **Clodion (IRE)**[34] 8-9-6 104 TEDurcan 6 98
(MAlKurdi, UAE) *cl up: 4th st: lost pl over 2f out: no imp fr over 1f out* **14/1**

6 1 3/4 **Aravis (FR)**[123] 7-9-5 102 LDettori 7 94
(ECharpy, UAE) *towards rr: 9th st: rdn and hdwy over 2f out: same pce fnl f* **5/1**[1]

7 7 **Sole (BRZ)**[42] 6-8-7 90 PHanagan 10 69
(PRudkin, UAE) *mid-div: 6th and rdn st: wknd over 3f out* **40/1**

8 1 1/4 **Wilful**[250] 1809 4-9-5 104 GHind 9 81
(IMohammed, UAE) *in tch: cl 5th and rdn st: grad wknd fr over 1 1/2f out* **15/2**[3]

9 3/4 **Jebal Suraaj (USA)**[204] 3109 4-8-6 91 SChin 3 67
(MJohnston) *led: rdn and hdd 2 1/2f out: wknd qckly: eased* **5/1**[1]

10 7 3/4 **Mahroos (USA)**[48] 6-8-7 90 (v[1]) RHills 4 52
(DougWatson, UAE) *trckd ldr: 2nd and rdn st: sn wknd* **6/1**[2]

11 dist **Halfsong (SWE)**[81] 4-8-8 93 RLMoore 2 —
(KPAndersen, Sweden) *mid-div early: 10th st: wknd qckly 2 1/2f out: eased 2f out* **10/1**

12 dist **Chronos (IRE)**[14] 6-8-7 90 RMullen 11 —
(PRudkin, UAE) *pushed along in rr fr 4f out: t.o st* **33/1**

2m 1.52s
**WFA** 4 from 5yo+ 2lb 12 Ran SP% **124.1**
Speed ratings: .
**Owner** L Nestadt & B Kantor **Bred** Srone Lodge Farm P/l **Trained** South Africa

**NOTEBOOK**
**Courageous Duke(USA)** came to challenge from well back, but had nothing more to give inside the last.
**Shami** made good headway to throw down a challenge two furlongs out, but then had nothing in reserve.
**Jebal Suraaj(USA)**set the pace until weakening just inside the two furlong pole.

## 634a ELNADIM INTERNATIONAL RATED STKS (SPONSORED BY DERRINSTOWN STUD) (DIRT) 7f (D)
4:45 (4:45) 3-Y-0+ £32,681 (£10,055; £5,027; £2,513) Stalls Low

RPR

1 **Bold Demand**[14] 10-9-0 95 BDoyle 10 98
(RBouresly, Kuwait) *in towards rr: 9th st: rdn and gd hdwy 2f out: led 110yds out: pushed out* **8/1**

2 2 1/2 **Northern Rock (JPN)**[116] 6-9-10 105 (bt) TEDurcan 9 102
(MAlKurdi, UAE) *cl up: 7th st: rdn to ld over 2f out and same pce fr over 110yds out* **6/1**

3 2 3/4 **Royal Dignitary (USA)**[180] 3782 4-9-5 100 (v) JPSpencer 2 90
(DRLoder) *cl up: 5th st: chal and disp ld 2f out: wknd u.p fr 1f out* **9/2**[2]

4 3/4 **Fardaan (KSA)**[28] 6-9-5 100 SMadrid 5 88
(JBarton,) *in tch: cl 8th st: no imp fr over 2f out* **4/1**[1]

5 2 **Burnt Ember (USA)**[34] 5-9-5 100 (t) WSupple 7 83
(DougWatson, UAE) *disp ld early: 3rd and chal st: grad wknd fr 2f out* **11/2**[3]

6 3 1/4 **Tudor Wood**[20] 5-9-3 98 GAvranche 4 73
(NDeCroutte, Bahrain) *prom: 4th st: wknd fr 2 1/2f out* **10/1**

7 1 1/4 **Energetic (NZ)**[51] 6-8-9 90 (e) RMullen 3 62
(SLeung, Macau) *disp ld: 2nd and rdn st: grad wknd fr 2f out* **16/1**

8 nse **Attache**[124] 5210 6-9-10 105 GHind 6 77
(IMohammed, UAE) *w ldrs 3f: rdn and lost pl: last st: no imp fnl 2f* **13/2**

9 2 **Sarayat**[481] 5090 4-9-7 102 PaulSmith 8 69
(AllanSmith, UAE) *led early: grad lost pl: 8th and wd st: sn wknd* **20/1**

10 11 **Emran (USA)**[204] 3109 4-8-9 90 (b) RHills 1 29
(MAlMuhairi, UAE) *led after 3f: hdd ent st: sn wknd: eased 1f out* **10/1**

1m 25.24s 10 Ran SP% **121.1**
Speed ratings: .
**Owner** Bouresly Racing Syndicate **Bred** Gainsborough Stud Management Ltd **Trained** Kuwait

**NOTEBOOK**
**Royal Dignitary(USA)** ran his race and will be better for the outing.

## 635a NAYEF SH MAKTOUM BIN RASHID AL MAKTOUM CHALLENGE RI (SPONSORED BY SHADWELL) (DIRT) 1m (D)
5:15 (5:15) 3-Y-0+ £54,469 (£16,759; £8,379; £4,189) Stalls Low

RPR

1 **State Shinto (USA)**[124] 5248 8-9-4 110....(b) RLMoore 8 111
(MAlKurdi, UAE) *in tch: 10th st: rdn and hdwy over 2f out: chal 1f out: led fnl 110yds: drvn out* **13/2**[3]

2 hd **Tropical Star (IRE)**[14] 4-9-4 95....(vt) RMullen 6 111
(AAlRaihe, UAE) *trckd ldrs on ins: 3rd and rdn st: chal 2f out: ev ch: same pce fnl f* **16/1**

3 3/4 **Victory Moon (SAF)**[187] 3590 5-9-4 116.... WCMarwing 5 109
(MFDeKock, South Africa) *mid-div: rdn 1/2-way: 7th st: outpcd 2 1/2f out: r.o fnl f: nrst fin* **1/1**[1]

4 2 **Dubai Honor**[34] 5-9-4 105....(t) WSupple 12 105
(DougWatson, UAE) *rdn and cl 8th st: edgd lft over 1 1/2f out: led over 1f out: hdd & wknd 110yds out* **12/1**

5 1 1/4 **Fabria (PER)**[83] 7-9-0 105.... SMadrid 2 99
(JBarton,) *led: hdd briefly ent st: led 2f out: hdd over 1f out: wknd fnl 165yds* **20/1**

6 3 **Curule (USA)**[14] 7-9-4 102....(vt) SSanders 11 97
(DougWatson, UAE) *w ldrs: racd wd: 5th and rdn st: hmpd over 1 1/2f out: same pce fr over 1f out* **20/1**

7 1 3/4 **Change The Grange (AUS)**[23] 6-9-4 93....(ve) LDettori 4 93
(ATam, Macau) *w ldrs early: 6th and rdn st: wknd fr over 1 1/2f out* **40/1**

8 hd **Blatant**[109] 5530 5-9-4 115.... GHind 10 93
(IMohammed, UAE) *a.p: 4th and rdn st: wknd fr 2f out* **4/1**[2]

9 3/4 **Walmooh**[18] 8-9-4 90....(b) PaulSmith 9 91
(AllanSmith, UAE) *s.i.s: in rr: last and rdn st: same pce fr over 1 1/2f out* **40/1**

10 1 1/4 **Al Maali (IRE)**[42] 5-9-4 102.... RHills 7 89
(DougWatson, UAE) *towards rr: rdn 4f out: 11th st: n.d* **33/1**

11 1 1/2 **Conflict (FR)**[42] 8-9-4 110....(vt) TEDurcan 1 86
(MAlKurdi, UAE) *bmpd s: disp ld after 2f: led ent st: hdd u.p 1 1/2f out: sn wknd* **8/1**

1m 37.37s 11 Ran SP% **125.4**
Speed ratings: .
**Owner** H E Sheikh Rashid Bin Mohammed **Bred** Sheikh Mohammed **Trained** United Arab Emirates

## 636a ALHAARTH STKS (SPONSORED BY DERRINSTOWN STUD) (TURF) 1m 1f (T)
5:45 (5:45) 3-Y-0+ £18,156 (£5,586; £2,793; £1,396) Stalls Low

RPR

1 **Crimson Palace (SAF)**[362] 5-8-9 101.... WCMarwing 3 104+
(MFDeKock, South Africa) *5th st: n.m.r 1 1/2f out: rdn to ld over 1f out: qcknd clr: easily* **3/1**[2]

2 4 3/4 **Gateman**[109] 5530 7-9-0 112.... SChin 8 100
(MJohnston) *trckd ldr: 3rd and rdn st: chal and ev ch over 1f out: same pce fnl f* **6/4**[1]

3 1/2 **Hero's Journey**[607] 1786 5-9-0 105....(vt) TEDurcan 5 99
(MAlKurdi, UAE) *cl up: 4th and rdn st: chal over 1f out: nt qckn fnl f* **16/1**

4 1/2 **Landslide (IRE)**[60] 5-9-0 87.... PHanagan 6 98
(PRudkin, UAE) *trckd ldr: 2nd st: rdn over 2f out: same pce fr over 1f out* **50/1**

5 nk **Cat Belling (IRE)**[110] 5494 4-8-9 100.... LDettori 4 94
(RBouresly, Kuwait) *towards rr: 6th st: rdn 2 1/2f out: same pce fr over 1f out* **14/1**

6 1 **Bonecrusher**[117] 5365 5-9-0 105....(v) JPSpencer 1 96
(DRLoder) *led: rdn over 2f out: hdd over 1f out: wknd* **3/1**[2]

7 7 1/2 **Legacy (JPN)**[106] 5585 4-9-0 105.... MJKinane 2 83
(JohnMOxx, Ire) *settled in rr: last and rdn st: no imp* **13/2**[3]

1m 47.48s
**WFA** 4 from 5yo+ 1lb 7 Ran SP% **117.8**
Speed ratings: .
**Owner** Team Valor **Bred** Adv A P Joubert **Trained** South Africa

**NOTEBOOK**
**Gateman** ran his race but found the winner too strong. Time may show there was no disgrace in this defeat.
**Bonecrusher** set the pace before dropping out, and probably went too quickly.

# [604]WOLVERHAMPTON (A.W) (L-H)
Friday, January 30

**OFFICIAL GOING: Standard to slow**
Wind: mod bhd Weather: raining

## 637 BET DIRECT NO Q DEMO 08000 837 888 H'CAP (DIV I) 5f (F)
1:20 (1:20) (F) (0-60,65) 3-Y-0+ £2,919 (£834; £417) Stalls Low

Form RPR

424- 1 **Empress Josephine**[49] 6170 4-9-5 **53**....(v) DCorby(3) 5 62
(JRJenkins) *mde all: rdn wl over 1f out: drvn out* **6/1**[3]

0-65 2 1 **Tigress (IRE)**[18] 509 5-9-11 **56**....(b) JQuinn 2 62
(JWUnett) *dwlt: bhd tl hdwy on ins over 1f out: r.o ins fnl f* **9/2**[2]

00-5 3 hd **Sotonian (HOL)**[18] 499 11-8-6 **40**.... LisaJones(3) 6 45
(PSFelgate) *chsd ldrs: rdn and sltly outpcd over 2f out: rallied over 1f out: kpt on ins fnl f* **25/1**

4-32 4 hd **Savile's Delight (IRE)**[18] 509 5-10-0 **59**....(b) IMongan 8 63
(RBrotherton) *w wnr: rdn and ev ch 2f out: nt qckn ins fnl f* **7/2**[1]

00-1 5 1 **So Sober (IRE)**[25] 443 6-9-2 **47**.... RWinston 12 48
(DShaw) *hld up: rdn over 3f out: hdwy over 1f out: one pce fnl f* **9/1**

0-40 6 1 **Allerton Boy**[22] 470 5-8-9 **40**.... DaleGibson 4 37
(RJHodges) *dwlt: bhd tl hdwy fnl f: nt rch ldrs* **10/1**

0-41 7 nk **Lady Protector**[18] 499 5-8-10 **48**.... PMakin(7) 9 44
(JBalding) *a.p: rdn 3f out: no ex appr fnl f* **10/1**

00-0 8 1 **King's Ballet (USA)**[24] 453 6-9-5 **50**....(p) NCallan 1 43
(PRChamings) *chsd ldrs: rdn over 3f out: wkng whn hmpd towards fin* **8/1**

-260 9 1 1/4 **Soaked**[9] 576 11-9-6 **51**....(b) ACulhane 11 39
(DWChapman) *prom: rdn over 2f out: wknd wl over 1f out* **10/1**

00-0 10 hd **Safranine (IRE)**[24] 453 7-9-3 **48**....(p) AnnStokell 7 35
(MissAStokell) *chsd ldrs: rdn over 3f out: sn wknd* **33/1**

20-6 11 4 **The Leather Wedge (IRE)**[28] 411 5-8-12 **48**.... PBradley(5) 10 21
(ABerry) *s.i.s: sn chsng ldrs: rdn over 3f out: sn wknd* **20/1**

63.47 secs (0.87) **Going Correction** +0.10s/f (Slow)
**WFA** 3 from 4yo+ 15lb 11 Ran SP% **114.6**
Speed ratings: **97,95,95,94,93 91,91,89,87,87 80**CSF £31.42 CT £626.50 TOTE £8.90: £2.50, £2.20, £8.40; EX 30.70.
**Owner** Mrs Olive Meddle **Bred** Keith Martin Ottesen And Mrs Eileen K Tope-Ottese **Trained** Royston, Herts

**FOCUS**
This looked the weaker of the two divisions and it was run in a slower time.

**NOTEBOOK**
**Empress Josephine** was quickly out of the gates and showed guts late on to hold off her challengers. This was only her second-ever win and she is no good thing to follow up, but she was returning from a short break and is entitled to come on again for the run.
**Tigress(IRE)**, winner of this event last year, blew her winning chance at the start. She did run on well in the straight however, and this effort confirmed she is in good heart at present.
**Sotonian(HOL)** ran by far his best race for some time and, if able to maintain this mood, he could go close off this mark in a similar contest.
**Savile's Delight(IRE)** ran his race, but it looks as though the Handicapper has his measure at present.

## 638 BET DIRECT NO Q DEMO 08000 837 888 H'CAP (DIV II) 5f (F)
1:50 (1:52) (F) (0-60,59) 3-Y-0+ £2,919 (£834; £417) Stalls Low

Form RPR

34-1 1 **Mynd**[22] 479 4-10-0 59.... DeanMcKeown 12 71
(RMWhitaker) *a.p: rdn to ld 1f out: r.o wl* **9/4**[1]

400- 2 2 1/2 **Off Hire**[150] 4642 8-9-3 48....(v) RFitzpatrick 2 51
(CSmith) *led 1f: w ldr: rdn to ld over 2f out: hdd 1f out: no ex ins fnl f* **20/1**

60-0 3 1 3/4 **Our Chelsea Blue (USA)**[22] 480 6-9-3 53.... AQuinn(5) 4 50
(AWCarroll) *s.s: hld up and bhd: hdwy and swtchd rt over 1f out: r.o wl ins fnl f* **6/1**

00-0 4 1/2 **White O' Morn**[15] 541 5-8-4 35 ow5....(t) GGibbons 3 30
(BAMcmahon) *chsd ldrs: rdn over 2f out: one pce appr fnl f* **33/1**

-632 5 3/4 **Ladies Knight**[6] 596 4-9-5 55.... THamilton(5) 6 47
(DShaw) *s.i.s: bhd tl hdwy fnl f: r.o* **7/2**[2]

F-00 6 1 3/4 **Indian Shores**[18] 510 5-9-0 48....(p) LisaJones(3) 9 34
(MMullineaux) *bhd tl hdwy on ins 1f out: n.d* **33/1**

0-35 7 2 **Henry Tun**[15] 538 6-9-5 50....(v) JEdmunds 5 29
(JBalding) *prom: rdn over 2f out: hung lft and wknd over 1f out* **9/2**[3]

000- 8 shd **Levelled**[66] 6063 10-9-0 45.... ACulhane 1 24
(DWChapman) *chsd ldrs: rdn over 2f out: wknd fnl f* **50/1**

60-0 9 2 1/2 **Tuscan Dream**[18] 499 9-8-4 40.... PBradley(5) 7 10
(ABerry) *prom: rdn over 3f out: sn rdn and wknd* **33/1**

/60- 10 1 1/2 **Feeling Blue**[118] 5374 5-9-2 47.... JFanning 10 12
(BNPollock) *led after 1f tl over 2f out: rdn and wknd over 1f out* **20/1**

063- 11 hd **Percy Douglas**[30] 6265 4-9-11 56....(v) AnnStokell 8 20
(MissAStokell) *s.i.s: a bhd* **10/1**

63.14 secs (0.54) **Going Correction** +0.10s/f (Slow) 11 Ran SP% **114.9**
Speed ratings: **99,95,92,91,90 87,84,84,80,77 77**CSF £54.19 CT £246.33 TOTE £3.20: £1.30, £6.80, £1.70; EX 58.60.
**Owner** Derek And Jean Clee **Bred** John Rose **Trained** Scarcroft, W Yorks

**FOCUS**
Modest form, but the faster of the two divisions and the winner is on the upgrade.

**NOTEBOOK**
**Mynd** followed up his maiden success over course-and-distance last time readily. This was a fair effort off top-weight and from his wide draw, and he definitely had a bit up his sleeve come the finish. He will have to be upped in grade now, but remains unexposed on this surface.
**Off Hire**, who is plummeting in the weights due to his poor form, put up his best display for some time. Although he had no chance with the winner, he beat the rest fairly and may go one better in this grade soon.
**Our Chelsea Blue(USA)**, not for the first time, was sluggish at the start and was up against it from then on. That said, she finished with real purpose and, if she can lay up with the pace next time, she can return to winning ways.
**White O' Morn**, wearing a tongue tie for the first time, duly improved for the switch to handicaps.
**Ladies Knight** was another who blew his chance at the start and this run is best forgiven..

## 639 BET DIRECT NO Q VOICE AUTOMATED BETTING MAIDEN STKS 1m 1f 79y(F)
2:20 (2:20) (D) 4-Y-0+ £3,341 (£1,028; £514; £257) Stalls Low

Form RPR

240- 1 **Musical Gift**[79] 5978 4-9-0 70.... IMongan 8 65+
(CNAllen) *hld up: stdy hdwy over 5f out: wnt 2nd over 3f out: rdn to ld 1f out: r.o* **15/8**[1]

534- 2 1 **Pacific Ocean (ARG)**[46] 6193 5-9-1 48....(t) JQuinn 1 63
(MrsStefLiddiard) *plld hrd: w ldr: led 6f out: rdn 2f out: hdd 1f out: kpt on* **4/1**[3]

34 3 9 **Now And Again**[15] 541 5-9-1 .... DaleGibson 2 47
(MWEasterby) *led: hdd 6f out: rdn 4f out: wknd 2f out* **12/1**

3-63 4 3 **Adantino**[15] 541 5-9-1 52.... GBaker 3 41
(BRMillman) *prom: hrd rdn and wknd 2f out* **10/1**

4 5 5 **Skip Of Colour**[16] 520 4-9-0 75.... WMLordan 5 32
(PABlockley) *prom: rdn over 3f out: sn wknd* **2/1**[2]

6 7 **Albee (IRE)** 4-9-0 .... MFenton 7 20
(MissGayKelleway) *dwlt: bhd most of way* **25/1**

7 19 **Marino Mou (IRE)** 4-9-0 .... CCatlin 4 —
(MissDMountain) *dwlt: wl bhd 6f out: t.o* **33/1**

2m 3.79s (0.89) **Going Correction** +0.10s/f (Slow)
**WFA** 4 from 5yo 1lb 7 Ran SP% **111.7**
Speed ratings: **100,99,91,88,84 77,60**CSF £9.34 TOTE £3.10: £1.30, £2.40; EX 11.70.
**Owner** T P Ramsden **Bred** Benedikt Fabbender **Trained** Newmarket, Suffolk

**FOCUS**
A very weak maiden.

**NOTEBOOK**
**Musical Gift** proved disappointing on his debut for his new yard at Lingfield on his previous outing, but he found this much easier and was able to confirm the promise he showed for David Loder early last year. He is likely to have one more run before going hurdling.
**Pacific Ocean(ARG)** had 22lb to find with the winner at the weights, but ran a cracker, pushing that one all the way to the line. His handicap mark will suffer as a result of this effort, but his trainer does well with her small string and may well be able to place this one to good effect.
**Now And Again** showed little but may be worth keeping an eye on next time, as he is now qualified for a handicap mark.
**Adantino** did not appear to get the trip.
**Skip Of Colour** failed to confirm the promise of his British debut and has a long way to go to justify a rating in the 70s.

## 640 BET DIRECT NO Q 08000 93 66 93 H'CAP 7f (F)
2:55 (2:55) (E ) (0-70,70) 3-Y-O £3,255 (£930; £465) Stalls High

| Form | | | | RPR |
|---|---|---|---|---|
| 15-4 | 1 | | **Bridgewater Boys**[24] 458 3-9-2 **65**......(p) NCallan 12<br>(KARyan) *a.p: wnt 2nd over 3f out: led 2f out: sn rdn: edgd rt ins fnl f: drvn out* **9/2**[1] | 71 |
| 2-31 | 2 | 2 | **Emaradia**[7] 591 3-8-5 **54** 6ex......(b) JoannaBadger 9<br>(AWCarroll) *led after 1f: rdn and hdd 2f out: hung rt jst over 1f out: nt qckn* **12/1** | 55 |
| 04-4 | 3 | 2 | **Turnberry (IRE)**[20] 493 3-8-10 **59**......(b) SWhitworth 10<br>(JWHills) *hdwy over 5f out: rdn over 2f out: one pce fnl f* **5/1**[2] | 55 |
| 6-12 | 4 | 1 ½ | **Turf Princess**[17] 514 3-8-6 **62**...... DFentiman(7) 11<br>(IanEmmerson) *hld up: hdwy over 4f out: rdn over 2f out: wknd ins fnl f* **8/1** | 54 |
| 02-3 | 5 | 5 | **Good Vibrations**[27] 420 3-8-4 **53**...... JQuinn 3<br>(PFICole) *chsd ldrs: rdn over 3f out: wknd wl over 1f out* **9/2**[1] | 33 |
| 66-5 | 6 | 6 | **Diamond George (IRE)**[14] 547 3-8-8 **57**...... RFitzpatrick 7<br>(JohnBerry) *prom: n.m.r 4f out: sn rdn and wknd* **10/1** | 22 |
| 610- | 7 | 9 | **Sable 'n Silk**[32] 6251 3-8-12 **61**...... ACulhane 1<br>(DHaydnJones) *led 1f: prom: rdn over 3f out: sn wknd* **10/1** | 3 |
| 00-2 | 8 | 1 ½ | **Vrisaki (IRE)**[28] 409 3-8-11 **60**...... CCatlin 8<br>(MissDMountain) *prom tl wknd over 4f out* **7/1**[3] | — |
| 222- | 9 | 2 | **Bookiesindexdotcom**[74] 6011 3-9-0 **63**......(v) SWKelly 4<br>(JRJenkins) *sn rdn along: wl bhd fnl 5f* **9/1** | — |

1m 31.4s (1.20) **Going Correction** +0.10s/f (Slow) **9** Ran SP% **112.5**
Speed ratings: **97,94,92,90,85 78,67,66,63**CSF £56.27 CT £276.70 TOTE £6.10: £1.80, £2.80, £2.20; EX 65.70.
**Owner** Bishopthorpe Racing **Bred** Southill Stud **Trained** Hambleton, N Yorks

**FOCUS**
Solid form for the grade, but the time was ordinary.

**NOTEBOOK**
**Bridgewater Boys**, a winner over six furlongs here in November, had since been competing in higher-grade races at Southwell. Back to a more suitable level and with cheekpieces replacing the blinkers, he won decisively and can score again in this grade.
**Emaradia**, who got off the mark in a claimer here the week before, ran well but may have found this longer trip stretching her stamina. She looks the yardstick by which to judge the form.
**Turnberry(IRE)**, tackling this surface for the first time and dropped in grade, seemed to handle it but his lack of acceleration counted against him. Southwell may suit him better.
**Turf Princess**, a course and distance winner, ran with credit but will be better off back in claimers.
**Good Vibrations** has been running well in lesser company at Lingfield, but she has yet to show in three attempts that this track really suits her.

## 641 LITTLEWOODS BET DIRECT CONDITIONS STKS 1m 100y(F)
3:25 (3:26) (C ) 3-Y-O+ £7,186 (£2,725; £1,362; £619) Stalls Low

| Form | | | | RPR |
|---|---|---|---|---|
| 212- | 1 | | **Mi Odds**[30] 6268 8-9-9 90...... ACulhane 3<br>(MrsNMacauley) *hld up: rdn and hdwy on outside 3f out: led over 1f out: easily* **7/1**[3] | 101 |
| 4-51 | 2 | 4 | **Countrywide Flyer (IRE)**[7] 595 3-8-7 80 ow1...... JPSpencer 9<br>(TDBarron) *hld up: stdy hdwy over 4f out: rdn over 2f out: tk 2nd ins fnl f: no ch w wnr* **2/1**[2] | 96 |
| 330- | 3 | 1 ½ | **Ephesus**[146] 4736 4-9-9 85......(v) MFenton 6<br>(MissGayKelleway) *hld up: stdy hdwy over 4f out: rdn over 2f out: swtchd rt over 1f out: one pce* **50/1** | 89 |
| /0-1 | 4 | 2 | **Hail The Chief**[21] 485 7-10-0 100...... ANicholls 10<br>(DNicholls) *a.p: led 3f out: rdn and hdd over 1f out: wknd ins fnl f* **6/5**[1] | 89 |
| 2-13 | 5 | 2 | **Arc El Ciel (ARG)**[11] 564 6-9-9 78......(v) CCatlin 4<br>(MrsStefLiddiard) *stdd sn after s: rdn 3f out: hdwy over 1f out: n.d* **25/1** | 80 |
| 3-00 | 6 | 2 ½ | **Invader**[9] 577 8-9-9 82......(b) JQuinn 7<br>(CEBrittain) *prom: rdn 5f out: wknd over 3f out* **20/1** | 75 |
| 5-24 | 7 | shd | **Lakota Brave**[13] 558 10-9-9 88...... IMongan 5<br>(MrsStefLiddiard) *a bhd* **14/1** | 75 |
| 500- | 8 | 7 | **Chappel Cresent (IRE)**[83] 5956 4-9-9...... RWinston 8<br>(DNicholls) *led after 1f: hdd 3f out: sn rdn: wknd 2f out* **50/1** | 60 |
| 0-00 | 9 | 5 | **Flying Treaty (USA)**[15] 544 7-9-7 84...... CJDavies(7) 1<br>(MissAStokell) *led 1f: prom: rdn over 4f out: wknd over 2f out* **66/1** | 54 |
| 0-05 | 10 | 17 | **Phoenix Nights (IRE)**[14] 548 4-9-7 45...... PBradley(5) 2<br>(ABerry) *sn bhd: t.o fnl 3f* **200/1** | 15 |

1m 49.61s (-1.39) **Going Correction** +0.10s/f (Slow)
**WFA** 3 from 4yo+ 20lb **10** Ran SP% **112.5**
Speed ratings: **110,106,104,102,100 98,97,90,85,68**CSF £19.85 TOTE £7.70: £1.10, £1.50, £6.70; EX 22.00.
**Owner** Tic-Tac.com **Bred** G Wiltshire **Trained** Sproxton, Leics
■ Stewards Enquiry : I Mongan three-day ban: dropped hands and lost sixth place (Feb 10-12)

**FOCUS**
A high-class contest run in a decent time, and a career-best performance from the winner. The form looks solid.

**NOTEBOOK**
**Mi Odds** had never previously won over a trip this short, but at the age of eight he is clearly improving and the trip proved no problem. A race like the Lincoln Trial back here in March could be something to aim at.
**Countrywide Flyer(IRE)** bolted up over course and distance in handicap company against his own age group on his previous start and, up in grade and racing against his elders for the first time, he ran a cracker. He is going the right way and is one to keep on the right side of.
**Ephesus** had 5lb to find with the winner at the weights and ran a cracker. His yard is really beginning to hit form and he looks worth keeping in mind for similar contests.
**Hail The Chief**, the star of the 2000/01 All-Weather season, looked good when winning a similar race over course and distance on his return from a break but, in this tougher contest, he was below form. At the age of seven it is hard to expect him to be as good as he was (he landed a Grade Two in America in his prime), but he could still be better than he showed here and can be given another chance.
**Arc El Ciel(ARG)** had it all to do at the weights and looked to run as well as could have been expected.

## 642 BET DIRECT NO Q (S) STKS 7f (F)
4:00 (4:01) (G ) 4-Y-O+ £2,604 (£744; £372) Stalls High

| Form | | | | RPR |
|---|---|---|---|---|
| 0-00 | 1 | | **Warlingham (IRE)**[9] 575 6-9-4 52...... JFanning 12<br>(PHowling) *hld up: hdwy on outside 3f out: led jst ins fnl f: r.o wl* **14/1** | 66 |
| 0-05 | 2 | 1 ¼ | **Mizhar (USA)**[4] 608 8-8-12 55...... RWinston 10<br>(JJQuinn) *bhd: hdwy over 2f out: r.o ins fnl f: nt trble wnr* **9/1** | 57 |
| -331 | 3 | 1 ¼ | **Feast Of Romance**[11] 565 7-9-4 48......(p) SWKelly 9<br>(PHowling) *hld up: rdn over 3f out: hdwy over 1f out: r.o ins fnl f* **3/1**[2] | 60 |
| -334 | 4 | ½ | **Sudra**[18] 498 7-8-9 49......(b) DAllan(3) 1<br>(JO'Reilly) *sn bhd: hdwy 4f out: rdn over 2f out: kpt on same pce fnl f* **20/1** | 53 |
| 2112 | 5 | ¾ | **Lucayan Monarch**[11] 565 6-9-4 56......(p) DeanMcKeown 6<br>(PABlockley) *a.p: rdn 3f out: one pce fnl 2f: fin lame* **5/2**[1] | 57 |
| -440 | 6 | ¾ | **Arogant Prince**[4] 608 7-8-12 53......(b) ACulhane 5<br>(AWCarroll) *led: clr over 4f out: rdn wl over 1f out: hdd jst ins fnl f: wkng whn hmpd towards fin* **16/1** | 49 |
| 0-53 | 7 | 2 | **Bulawayo**[11] 565 7-8-12 53......(v) ANicholls 2<br>(AndrewReid) *chsd ldr: rdn 3f out: lost 2nd 2f out: wknd fnl f* **7/1** | 44 |
| 0-34 | 8 | 10 | **Jan Brueghel (USA)**[11] 565 5-8-5 63...... PMakin(7) 4<br>(TDBarron) *hld up: rdn over 2f out: sn bhd: b.b.v* **4/1**[3] | 19 |
| 600- | 9 | 2 | **Always Believe (USA)**[230] 2363 8-8-12 48......(t) RFfrench 7<br>(MrsPFord) *a bhd* **40/1** | 14 |
| -060 | 10 | ½ | **Love's Design (IRE)**[7] 590 7-8-7 48......(p) AQuinn(5) 11<br>(MissSJWilton) *t.k.h: sn in tch: rdn and wknd over 2f out* **25/1** | 13 |
| 040/ | 11 | 5 | **Heathers Girl**[406] 5945 5-8-7 46...... PaulEddery 3<br>(DHaydnJones) *prom over 2f* **40/1** | — |
| 0- | 12 | 5 | **Blue Bijou**[223] 2568 4-8-7...... DFox(5) 8<br>(TTClement) *wl bhd fnl 5f* **20/1** | — |

1m 30.8s (0.60) **Going Correction** +0.10s/f (Slow) **12** Ran SP% **126.9**
Speed ratings: **100,98,97,96,95 94,92,81,78,78 72,66**CSF £134.04 TOTE £19.10: £6.00, £3.70, £1.40; EX 230.20.There was no bid for the winner; Lucayan Monarch was claimed by Joseph Salter for £6,000
**Owner** David Andrew Brown **Bred** Paul Hyland **Trained** Newmarket, Suffolk
■ Stewards Enquiry : R Winston five-day ban (includes four deferred days): careless riding (Feb 15-19)

**FOCUS**
Solid form for the grade, but the time was ordinary.

**NOTEBOOK**
**Warlingham(IRE)**, who had previously looked more effective at Lingfield than at this track, appreciated the drop in grade. He can win more races if kept to this level.
**Mizhar(USA)**, twice a winner over the minimum trip around here, has looked to need a stiff six furlongs more recently. This return to seven furlongs seemed to be in his favour, and he looks well treated if he can find a handicap at this level.
**Feast Of Romance**, who returned to winning form earlier in the month, was a pound lower and, on a line through Lucayan Monarch and Bulawayo, improved on that victory.
**Sudra** reversed recent Southwell form with Lucayan Monarch, and seems more effective on this track. A return to a mile will suit.
**Lucayan Monarch** failed to run up to recent form with both the third and fourth, but had an excuse as he pulled up lame. *Official explanation: trainer said gelding finished lame*
**Jan Brueghel(USA)** disappointed, but was another with an excuse. *Official explanation: jockey said gelding had bled from the nose*

## 643 BET DIRECT THROUGH SKY ACTIVE H'CAP 1m 1f 79y(F)
4:30 (4:30) (D ) (0-80,79) 4-Y-O+ £4,075 (£1,254; £627; £313) Stalls Low

| Form | | | | RPR |
|---|---|---|---|---|
| 43-1 | 1 | | **Intricate Web (IRE)**[18] 507 8-9-8 **76**...... DAllan(3) 10<br>(EJAlston) *hld up and bhd: rdn 5f out: hdwy over 1f out: str run u.p to ld last strides* **9/4**[1] | 85 |
| 014- | 2 | shd | **To Wit To Woo**[70] 6043 4-8-4 **56**...... DeanMcKeown 8<br>(BWHills) *a.p: rdn over 2f out: led wl ins fnl f: hdd last strides* **4/1**[2] | 65 |
| 04-2 | 3 | 1 | **Skylarker (USA)**[18] 507 6-10-0 **79**...... IMongan 1<br>(WSKittow) *w ldr: rdn over 3f out: led over 2f out: edgd rt 1f out: hdd wl ins fnl f* **5/1**[3] | 86 |
| 060- | 4 | 1 ¾ | **Air Mail**[328] 682 7-10-0 **79**...... ACulhane 5<br>(MrsNMacauley) *hld up in tch: rdn over 2f out: one pce fnl f* **33/1** | 83 |
| 0-42 | 5 | 1 ½ | **Dubai Dreams**[8] 588 4-8-7 **59** ow3......(v) JPSpencer 9<br>(MJPolglase) *led: rdn and hdd over 2f out: wknd ins fnl f* **7/1** | 60 |
| 226- | 6 | 4 | **African Sahara (USA)**[97] 5756 5-9-13 **78**......(t) GCarter 12<br>(MissDMountain) *hld up and bhd: hdwy over 4f out: rdn over 2f out: wknd over 1f out* **8/1** | 72 |
| 65-1 | 7 | hd | **Penwell Hill (USA)**[25] 437 5-9-4 **69**...... DMernagh 3<br>(TDBarron) *prom: rdn over 3f out: wknd over 2f out* **11/2** | 62 |
| | 8 | 4 | **Ballyrush (IRE)**[216] 2809 4-8-9 **68**...... RKeogh(7) 11<br>(KRBurke) *hld up: stdy hdwy over 5f out: lost pl over 3f out: bttr for r* **33/1** | 54 |
| 200- | 9 | 2 ½ | **Say What You See (IRE)**[116] 5425 4-9-6 **72**...... SWhitworth 7<br>(JWHills) *a bhd* **25/1** | 53 |
| 00-4 | 10 | 1 ¾ | **Yellow River (IRE)**[7] 589 4-8-6 **58** ow1...... SWKelly 4<br>(RCurtis) *hld up in tch: rdn 3f out: wknd 2f out* **33/1** | 36 |
| | 11 | 18 | **Harry Potter (GER)**[76] 5-9-5 **70**...... DarrenWilliams 6<br>(KRBurke) *hld up: rdn 4f out: bhd fnl 3f: t.o* **33/1** | 15 |
| 0/ | 12 | 2 ½ | **Bought Direct**[110] 5520 5-8-12 **63**...... JoannaBadger 2<br>(RJSmith) *s.v.s: a wl bhd: t.o* **25/1** | 3 |

2m 1.70s (-1.20) **Going Correction** +0.10s/f (Slow)
**WFA** 4 from 5yo+ 1lb **12** Ran SP% **125.9**
Speed ratings: **109,108,108,106,105 101,101,97,95,94 78,75**CSF £10.99 CT £40.70 TOTE £3.70: £1.60, £2.10, £1.90; EX 24.50 Trifecta £180.60 Pool of £4,859.88 - 19.10 winning units. Place 6 £99.84, Place 5 £42.37.
**Owner** Morris, Oliver, Pierce **Bred** Moyglare Stud Farm Ltd **Trained** Longton, Lancs

**FOCUS**
A decent time for the grade of contest and the form looks solid.

**NOTEBOOK**
**Intricate Web(IRE)** repeated his course and distance win of earlier in the month off a 4lb higher mark, confirming that form with the third in the process. He was only able to get up close home, so should not go up much, and the hat-trick is not out of the question.
**To Wit To Woo ◆**, a course and distance winner who failed to stay a mile and a half last time, had to fight hard to get his head in front only to have the race snatched from him on the post. He looks capable of gaining compensation.
**Skylarker(USA)** was 3lb better off with the winner for a length defeat earlier in the month. He ran his race and has been placed in all three attempts at this track.
**Air Mail** was returning from nearly 11 months off and trying his longest trip to date, and if he is given time to recover he could be of interest in similar races.
**Dubai Dreams**, having his first run on the track, tried to make the most of his stamina but was still found out for pace. A return to further will help him.
**Penwell Hill(USA)**, a specialist over a mile at Southwell, was having his first run here. He may have found the sharper track against him, but also looks a little high in the weights.
**Yellow River(IRE)** *Official explanation: jockey said gelding had a breathing problem*
**Bought Direct** *Official explanation: jockey said horse sat down in the stalls and missed the break*

T/Jkpt: Not won. T/Plt: £257.70 to a £1 stake. Pool: £93,430.90. 264.65 winning tickets. T/Qpdt: £83.80 to a £1 stake. Pool: £8,081.70. 71.30 winning tickets. KH

# 617 LINGFIELD (L-H)

Saturday, January 31

**OFFICIAL GOING: Standard**

High winds and rain made conditions difficult. The inside rail appeared to be an advantage early in the day, but in later races runners drifted to the centre.

Wind: gale force bhd Weather: drizzle

## 644 BET DIRECT NO Q 08000 93 66 93 MAIDEN STKS — 1m (P)

12:15 (12:19) (D ) 3-Y-0+ £4,199 (£1,292; £646; £323) Stalls High

Form RPR

1 **Quickstyx** 3-8-2 ........ CCatlin 3 68
(MRChannon) *leggy: unf: s.i.s: hld up in midfield: trckd ldrs 3f out: rdn to chal on inner fnl f: r.o wl to ld nr fin* **5/2[2]**

23-3 2 *nk* **Spinning Dove**[25] 448 4-9-8 65 ........ JPSpencer 11 67
(NAGraham) *s.i.s: hld up in rr: smooth prog 3f out: effrt on outer to ld over 1f out: hrd drvn and r.o: hdd nr fin* **5/2[2]**

655- 3 *4* **Lord Of The Sea (IRE)**[52] 6160 3-8-8 73 ow1 ........ IMongan 1 64
(JamiePoulton) *trckd ldrs: rdn and cl up over 1f out: sn outpcd: kpt on to take 3rd nr fin* **4/1[3]**

4 *nk* **The King's Bishop** 3-8-7 ........ GCarter 5 62
(SCWilliams) *unf: b.bkwd: prom: rdn to dispute ld over 1f out: outpcd and btn fnl f* **25/1**

0 5 *2* **Bennanabaa**[24] 463 5-9-13 ........(t) ANicholls 4 58?
(SCBurrough) *plld hrd: led after 1f: hdd & wknd over 1f out* **66/1**

20-2 6 *1 1/4* **Priors Dale**[14] 555 4-9-13 72 ........ DSweeney 12 55
(KBell) *prom: pressed ldr 3f out: ev ch wl over 1f out: sn nt qckn: wknd fnl f* **2/1[1]**

7 *3/4* **Young Dynasty** 4-9-13 ........ SCarson 6 53?
(EAWheeler) *w'like: b.bkwd: dwlt: hld up wl in rr: prog into midfield 3f out: rdn and no imp 2f out* **50/1**

0 8 *7* **Our Little Rosie**[25] 447 3-8-2 ........ JQuinn 7 32
(MBlanshard) *always towards rr: u.p and struggling over 2f out* **25/1**

56-4 9 *3/4* **Scorch**[15] 550 3-8-7 53 ........ JoannaBadger 2 35
(HJCollingridge) *uns rdr and bolted bef s: dwlt: last and rdn 1/2-way: sn no ch* **50/1**

0 10 *nk* **Reckless Fred**[10] 574 5-9-6 ........ DerekNolan[(7)] 9 34
(MissKMGeorge) *led for 1f: chsd ldr to 3f out: wknd* **50/1**

0- 11 *nk* **Polish Rhapsody (IRE)**[93] 5833 3-8-4 ow2 ........ JFanning 8 31
(JASupple) *racd in midfield tl wknd 3f out* **33/1**

0-0 12 *2 1/2* **Once Around (IRE)**[21] 492 3-8-7 ........ AClark 10 28
(TGMills) *plld hrd: racd wd: chsd ldrs: pushed along 1/2-way: sn lost pl and struggling* **14/1**

1m 42.62s (3.11) **Going Correction** +0.15s/f (Slow)

**WFA** 3 from 4yo+ 20lb — **12** Ran SP% **135.2**

Speed ratings: **90,89,85,85,83 82,81,74,73,73 73,70**CSF £10.37 TOTE £5.20: £2.40, £1.70, £2.10; EX 14.20.

**Owner** John Breslin **Bred** Genesis Green Stud Ltd **Trained** West Ilsley, Berks

■ Once Around was Tony Clark's final ride before retirement.

**FOCUS**

Just an average maiden, and the pace was steady due to the poor weather conditions. The time was understandably slow, but the winner should rate higher in time.

**NOTEBOOK**

**Quickstyx**, an athletic half-sister to Red Carnation and Red Wine, was well backed for this debut and, getting a split at the right time, showed plenty of spirit to prevail. She looks capable of going on from this.

**Spinning Dove**, an exposed maiden, surged to the front halfway up the straight but was just run out of it. She is consistent and deserves to win a race, and is the guide to the level of the form.

**Lord Of The Sea(IRE)**, who showed promise over seven furlongs here before Christmas, appeared to find the extra furlong too far.

**The King's Bishop**, a half-brother to Snuki, whose two wins were gained here, made a promising debut and should be better for the outing.

**Bennanabaa** was again keen, but seemed to run better for this drop in trip. By a sprinter, he may be interesting over even shorter trips when handicapped.

**Priors Dale**, a proven performer on this surface, was dropping in trip and ran disappointingly for no apparent reason.

## 645 BET DIRECT NO Q CLASSIFIED STKS — 1m 5f (P)

12:45 (12:47) (E ) 4-Y-0+ £3,276 (£936; £468) Stalls Low

Form RPR

3-11 1 **Fall In Line**[2] 629 4-9-6 60 ........ JMackay 2 91+
(SirMarkPrescott) *lw: t.k.h: mde virtually all: drvn clr 4f out: heavily eased last 100y* **30/100[1]**

5033 2 *7* **Easter Ogil (IRE)**[3] 618 9-9-5 64 ........ IMongan 5 69
(JaneSouthcombe) *dwlt: hld up in rr: prog u.p fr 4f out: styd on to snatch remote 2nd last strides* **8/1[3]**

4353 3 *shd* **Lazzaz**[5] 609 6-9-5 58 ........ ACulhane 10 68
(PWHiatt) *t.k.h: prom: rdn to chse clr wnr over 3f out: no imp: lost 2nd last strides* **20/1**

1-21 4 *nk* **Phantom Stock**[22] 483 4-9-0 65 ........ MTebbutt 8 68
(WJarvis) *racd in midfield: drvn and effrt to chse ldng pair 3f out: one pce after* **6/1[2]**

00- 5 *5* **Grand Prairie (SWE)**[15] 1410 8-9-5 65 ........ SWhitworth 4 60
(GLMoore) *dwlt: hld up in last: sme prog fr 3f out: kpt on same pce: n.d* **33/1**

B00- 6 *3* **Indian Blaze**[52] 6157 10-8-12 48 ........ SJDonohoe[(7)] 7 56
(AndrewReid) *b.hind: hld up in rr: rdn and prog to chse clr ldrs over 3f out: no hdwy over 2f out: fdd* **66/1**

3 7 *19* **Munfarid (IRE)**[22] 484 4-9-0 62 ........(t) PDoe 3 27
(PGMurphy) *w wnr to 4f out: sn wknd: t.o* **50/1**

/0-4 8 *6* **Arc En Ciel**[28] 413 6-9-5 60 ........ JQuinn 12 18
(GLMoore) *racd in midfield: rdn over 4f out: sn wknd: t.o* **33/1**

6-10 9 *3/4* **Itsonlyagame**[7] 602 4-9-0 55 ........ NCallan 11 17
(RIngram) *rdn first f: a in rr: wknd 4f out: t.o* **66/1**

0 10 *16* **Sekwana (POL)**[7] 602 5-9-2 48 ........(p) DSweeney 6 —
(MissAMNewton-Smith) *racd in midfield: rdn 1/2-way: sn wknd: t.o* **100/1**

0-16 11 *7* **Madiba**[16] 546 5-9-5 58 ........(b) JPSpencer 9 —
(PHowling) *prom tl wknd rapidly u.p 5f out: t.o* **25/1**

2m 47.18s (-0.90) **Going Correction** +0.15s/f (Slow)

**WFA** 4 from 5yo+ 5lb — **11** Ran SP% **122.7**

Speed ratings: **108,103,103,103,100 98,86,83,82,72 68**CSF £3.35 TOTE £1.40: £1.02, £2.30, £5.00; EX 5.30.

**Owner** Neil Greig - Osborne House Ii **Bred** P D Player **Trained** Newmarket, Suffolk

**FOCUS**

A moderate classified contest, but yet another impressive performance by the fast-improving winner, who looks capable of winning off ratings in the mid-80s. The time was decent for the grade.

**NOTEBOOK**

**Fall In Line**, having his third race of the week, looked really well in on the basis of his two impressive wins despite his penalty. He took to the surface and accomplished the difficult task of making all over this trip in runaway fashion. He is improving fast and has further opportunities before he inevitably takes a major hike in the ratings.

**Easter Ogil(IRE)** has been running consistently well in handicaps of late, but never got into a challenging position and just stayed on to grab the runner-up spot. He is a fair yardstick by which to judge the form.

**Lazzaz**, who is better known as a Fibresand performer, had been well beaten by today's winner at Wolverhampton. He went in pursuit of that rival on the run to the straight, a move which ultimately cost him second place. He has been running into fast-improving sorts in recent outings, and if he can avoid them may be able to pick up a small handicap.

**Phantom Stock**, another switching from Fibresand, did not look as effective on this surface, especially over this shorter trip.

## 646 BETDIRECT.CO.UK CLASSIFIED STKS — 6f (P)

1:20 (1:22) (E ) 3-Y-0+ £3,297 (£942; £471) Stalls Low

Form RPR

-012 1 **Whippasnapper**[3] 617 4-9-7 65 ........ NPollard 1 71
(JRBest) *mde all: drvn 2l clr 2f out: hrd rdn fnl f: jst hld on* **9/1[3]**

3-55 2 *nk* **Temper Tantrum**[3] 624 6-9-0 62 ........(p) SJDonohoe[(7)] 8 70
(AndrewReid) *settled in rr: rdn and prog on inner over 2f out: chsd wnr last 100y: clsng fast at fin* **16/1**

600- 3 *1 1/2* **Semenovskii**[75] 6014 4-9-7 70 ........ PaulEddery 5 71+
(PWD'Arcy) *hld up: n.m.r 4f out: rdn and prog on inner 2f out: styd on to take 3rd nr fin* **6/1[2]**

4-03 4 *1/2* **Pheckless**[10] 575 5-9-7 67 ........ CCatlin 2 64
(JMBradley) *b.hind: prom: chsd wnr over 2f out: no imp ent fnl f: one pce last 100y* **14/1**

1-03 5 *1/2* **Panjandrum**[3] 617 6-9-2 67 ........ MSavage[(5)] 4 63
(NEBerry) *s.i.s: sn in midfield: rdn and effrt over 2f out: one pce fr over 1f out* **12/1**

2-11 6 *shd* **Prince Aaron (IRE)**[10] 576 4-9-7 68 ........ GCarter 11 62
(CNAllen) *t.k.h early and hld up: effrt and rdn on outer over 2f out: one pce and nvr rchd ldrs* **11/8[1]**

55-0 7 *1 1/4* **Hard To Catch (IRE)**[17] 526 6-9-7 69 ........ IMongan 12 59
(DKIvory) *chsd ldrs and sn rdn: keeping on one pce whn nt clr run over 1f out* **20/1**

60-4 8 *3/4* **Tickle**[16] 538 6-9-4 47 ........(vt) DSweeney 3 53
(PJMakin) *hld up towards rr: prog on inner over 2f out: sn rdn: no hdwy over 1f out* **100/1**

400- 9 *1 1/2* **River Days (IRE)**[75] 6010 6-9-4 65 ........(bt) MFenton 10 49
(MissGayKelleway) *chsd wnr to over 2f out: wknd over 1f out* **50/1**

-212 10 *nk* **Ripple Effect**[7] 599 4-9-4 73 ........ NCallan 13 48
(CADwyer) *chsd ldrs tl wknd wl over 1f out* **6/1[2]**

600- 11 *2* **Indian Maiden (IRE)**[75] 6010 4-9-4 70 ........ SWhitworth 6 42
(MSSaunders) *racd in last pair: rdn and struggling over 2f out: modest late prog* **20/1**

21-2 12 *3/4* **Madrasee**[25] 454 6-9-1 68 ........ RMiles[(3)] 14 40
(LMontagueHall) *chsd ldrs: rdn 1/2-way: wknd over 2f out* **9/1[3]**

000- 13 *3* **Mulan Princess (IRE)**[91] 5157 4-9-4 52 ........ ANicholls 7 31
(SCBurrough) *a in last pair: wl bhd over 2f out* **100/1**

02-5 14 *3/4* **Bella Beguine**[4] 612 5-8-13 70 ........(v) THamilton[(5)] 9 28
(ABailey) *nvr on terms: wknd 2f out* **25/1**

1m 12.6s (-0.32) **Going Correction** +0.15s/f (Slow) — **14** Ran SP% **128.2**

Speed ratings: **108,107,105,104,104 104,102,101,99,99 96,95,91,90**CSF £143.46 TOTE £12.00: £2.60, £5.00, £1.90; EX 124.50.

**Owner** Miss Vanessa Church **Bred** Acrum Lodge Stud **Trained** Hucking, Kent

**FOCUS**

A competitive classified contest and a game effort from the winner, although the third looked unlucky. A race run at a decent gallop and a very creditable time for the grade.

**NOTEBOOK**

**Whippasnapper** adopted totally different tactics to when scoring here last weekend and, kicking clear off the home turn, stole enough of an advantage to last home. He found the five furlongs too short when beaten in a claimer three days previously, but is clearly in good form and may be able to go in again before he is reassessed.

**Temper Tantrum**, dropping back from seven furlongs, was catching the winner quickly in the last 100 yards. He has been running consistently well all winter and this was another good effort. A return to seven can see him get his head in front.

**Semenovskii ◆**, the subject of a gamble on this Polytrack debut and first outing since November, arrived on the scene late. He is fairly well treated compared with his turf mark and, now he is proven to act on the surface, should not be long in recovering losses for his supporters.

**Pheckless**, who was ridden more prominently on this drop in trip, just got tired in the last furlong. He looks worth another try over this trip with slightly more patient tactics adopted.

**Panjandrum**, who is better over five, did not help his chance with a slow start.

**Prince Aaron(IRE)**, bidding for a course and distance hat-trick, was a stepping up in grade and, after appearing a danger on the home turn, failed to pick up. However, the inside appeared the place to be in this contest and he can be given another chance. *Official explanation: jockey said gelding ran flat*

**Ripple Effect** had finished in front of today's fourth on her previous start, so on the face of it this was disappointing. However, she was another to race on the outside in the straight, so possibly this can be ignored.

## 647 BET DIRECT NO Q DEMO 08000 837 888 H'CAP — 1m (P)

1:55 (1:55) (D ) (0-80,78) 3-Y-0+ £4,199 (£1,292; £646; £323) Stalls High

Form RPR

60-1 1 **Vortex**[12] 564 5-9-11 **75** ........(t) MFenton 4 84
(MissGayKelleway) *b.hind: prom in chsng gp: chsd ldr over 2f out: drvn to ld over 1f out: hrd rdn to hold on nr fin* **7/2[1]**

112- 2 *nk* **Deeper In Debt**[80] 5976 6-9-8 **72** ........ GCarter 10 80
(JAkehurst) *lw: prom in chsng gp: effrt to ld wl over 2f out: drvn and hdd over 1f out: kpt on ins fnl f: jst hld* **4/1[2]**

303- 3 *1/2* **College Delinquent (IRE)**[60] 6114 5-9-2 **66** ........(t) SWhitworth 2 73
(KBell) *hld up in last pair: prog over 2f out: drvn and r.o to chse ldng pair ins fnl f: nrst fin* **10/1**

16-0 4 *1* **Terraquin (IRE)**[21] 494 4-9-12 **76** ........ GBaker 8 81
(JJBridger) *settled in rr: effrt on outer over 2f out: drvn and styd on fr over 1f out: nt rch ldrs* **66/1**

410- 5 *nk* **Rudood (USA)**[129] 5158 4-10-0 **78** ........ JQuinn 6 82
(LadyHerries) *settled in rr: effrt and nt clr run briefly over 2f out and again over 1f out: rdn and r.o fnl f: nrst fin* **10/1**

000- **6** *hd* **Liberty Royal**[45] 6208 5-9-7 **71** ........ DSweeney 9 75
(PJMakin) *t.k.h: hld up in midfield: effrt over 2f out: chsd ldrs over 1f out: kpt on same pce fnl f* **12/1**

05-0 **7** *2 ½* **Nashaab (USA)**[14] 558 7-9-7 **78** ........ (b[1]) SJDonohoe(7) 11 76
(PDEvans) *wl in rr: last and struggling 3f out: r.o fr over 1f out: n.d* **16/1**

013- **8** *1 ¾* **Summer Recluse (USA)**[255] 1754 5-9-8 **77** ........ NChalmers(5) 3 72
(BRJohnson) *dwlt: sn rcvrd into midfield: prog to press ldrs 2f out: wknd over 1f out* **9/2**[3]

060- **9** *hd* **Sir Francis (IRE)**[156] 4528 6-9-8 **72** ........ SWKelly 12 66
(JNoseda) *b.hind: prom in chsng gp: drvn and cl up 2f out: wknd over 1f out* **20/1**

00-0 **10** *1 ½* **Boundless Prospect (USA)**[21] 494 5-9-8 **72** ........ MHills 1 63
(JWHills) *s.i.s: drvn up to chse clr ldr: wknd 3f out* **14/1**

046- **11** *3* **Agilis (IRE)**[32] 6263 4-10-0 **78** ........ IMongan 5 62
(JamiePoulton) *in tch tl wknd wl over 2f out* **11/1**

200- **12** *29* **Concer Eto**[131] 5122 5-9-9 **73** ........ (b[1]) MHenry 7 —
(SCWilliams) *led and tore off into clr ld: wknd and hdd wl over 2f out: t.o* **14/1**

1m 40.5s (0.99) **Going Correction** +0.15s/f (Slow) **12** Ran SP% **120.1**
Speed ratings: **101,100,100,99,98 98,96,94,94,92 89,60**CSF £17.35 CT £132.16 TOTE £3.70: £2.00, £2.60, £3.00; EX 14.30.
**Owner** Coriolis Partnership **Bred** Juddmonte Farms **Trained** Newmarket, Suffolk

**FOCUS**
A fairly competitive handicap, and though the pace looked ordinary the time was more than two seconds faster than the earlier maiden. The form looks solid for the grade.

**NOTEBOOK**
**Vortex**, having his first run on this surface since winning here in December 2002, came into this in good form but had to work hard to justify favouritism. He should not go up much for this narrow victory, and may be the type that just does enough.
**Deeper In Debt** has a good record on this surface and did nothing wrong in defeat. However, he may need to drop a pound or two before he can win again.
**College Delinquent(IRE)**, returning from a break, ran another good race and was cutting down the principals at the line. This is his trip and track and he is capable of winning off this mark
**Terraquin(IRE)** ran better on this second try on the surface. He seemed to get the trip, but has gained both his wins over seven and a more positive ride over that trip may be the answer.
**Rudood(USA)** ◆ was supported in the market on his first run for new connections and performed with credit, particularly as he didn't enjoy the clearest of runs. He will be suited by a return to further, and is still open to improvement.
**Liberty Royal**, who has dropped right down the handicap, was returning to the course and distance over which he made a winning debut in 2001. This was a better effort and a slight drop in grade may help him.
**Summer Recluse(USA)**, having his first outing since May, was well supported but ran as if the race was needed.
**Concer Eto** *Official explanation: jockey said gelding ran too free*

## 648 BET DIRECT ON 0800 32 93 93 H'CAP 7f (P)
2:30 (2:31) (C ) (0-90,90) 4-Y-0+ **£7,293** (£2,766; £1,383; £628) **Stalls** Low

Form RPR

4-51 **1** **Grey Pearl**[7] 599 5-9-1 **77** ........ MFenton 8 88
(MissGayKelleway) *trckd ldrs: effrt 2f out: led on inner 1f out: drvn clr* **14/1**

5-22 **2** *1 ¾* **Just Fly**[16] 544 4-9-9 **85** ........ ACulhane 6 92
(SKirk) *trckd ldrs: effrt 2f out: drvn to press wnr ent fnl f: sn outpcd* **7/1**[3]

00-0 **3** *nk* **Greenwood**[18] 511 6-8-13 **75** ........ DKinsella 1 81
(PGMurphy) *settled in rr: prog on inner wl over 1f out: styd on fnl f: unable to chal* **33/1**

022- **4** *½* **The Best Yet**[33] 6252 6-9-0 **76** ........ SWhitworth 3 81
(AGNewcombe) *plld hrd early: hld up in midfield: prog 2f out: styd on ins fnl f: nt pce to chal* **7/1**[3]

0-06 **5** *½* **Cormorant Wharf (IRE)**[21] 494 4-8-10 **77** ........ AQuinn(5) 9 80
(TEPowell) *s.i.s: hld up wl in rr: pushed along over 2f out: swtchd to outer over 1f out: r.o wl: nvr nr ldrs* **12/1**

0-66 **6** *shd* **No Time (IRE)**[22] 486 4-9-4 **80** ........ IMongan 5 83
(MJPolglase) *led to 1f out: wknd ins fnl f* **20/1**

32-1 **7** *nk* **Dawn Piper (USA)**[17] 520 4-9-9 **85** ........ JPSpencer 10 87
(DRLoder) *lw: hld up in midfield: rdn over 1f out: one pce and too much to do* **6/5**[1]

10-3 **8** *1 ¼* **Cloud Dancer**[7] 599 5-8-12 **74** ........ NCallan 15 73
(KARyan) *settled in rr: rdn over 2f out: unable qck and btn over 1f out: kpt on ins fnl f* **16/1**

50-2 **9** *nk* **Queens Rhapsody**[14] 556 4-9-9 **90** ........ THamilton(5) 14 89
(ABailey) *t.k.h: racd on outer and wl in tch: rdn and effrt 2f out: wknd 1f out* **10/1**

0-41 **10** *nk* **Prima Stella**[18] 511 5-8-8 **73** ........ LisaJones(3) 7 71
(JARToller) *wl in rr: effrt on inner over 1f out: kpt on same pce fnl f* **33/1**

000- **11** *½* **Border Edge**[32] 6263 6-9-6 **82** ........ (v) GBaker 11 79
(JJBridger) *chsd ldr to 3f out: wknd jst over 1f out* **25/1**

3132 **12** *shd* **Hurricane Coast**[5] 607 5-8-13 **75** ........ (b) PDoe 16 71
(DFlood) *racd wd: hld up in rr: shuffled along over 1f out: nvr nr ldrs* **11/2**[2]

0-13 **13** *2* **Chateau Nicol**[14] 556 5-9-1 **77** ........ (v) JFanning 12 68
(BGPowell) *t.k.h: prom: chsd ldr 3f out: rdn and nt qckn over 1f out: wknd fnl f* **10/1**

050/ **14** *6* **Pairing (IRE)**[69] 6-9-2 **78** ........ RBrisland 4 54
(GLMoore) *a last: wl bhd over 2f out* **66/1**

1m 25.03s (-0.97) **Going Correction** +0.15s/f (Slow) **14** Ran SP% **140.2**
Speed ratings: **111,109,108,108,107 107,107,105,105,104 104,104,101,95**CSF £121.46 CT £3379.54 TOTE £20.70: £5.10, £3.60, £11.50; EX 115.70.
**Owner** Andrea Wilkinson Gay Kelleway **Bred** Miss J Chaplin **Trained** Newmarket, Suffolk

**FOCUS**
A decent handicap run at a good pace and producing a decisive winner. The time was very good for the grade of race and the form should work out.

**NOTEBOOK**
**Grey Pearl** completed a double for her trainer in good fashion off a 6lb higher mark than when scoring here a week previously. This was a step up in grade and she gives the impression that she is well capable of completing the hat-trick while in this form..
**Just Fly** was runner-up for the third successive time but did nothing wrong. However, he is creeping up the weights which will not help his chances.
**Greenwood**, stepped up in trip for his first try on this surface, ran an encouraging race and the Handicapper has given him a chance. However, he has a moderate strike-rate and has flattered to deceive in the past.
**The Best Yet** ran yet another good race over this course and distance, but is another who is creeping up the weights without getting his head in front.
**Cormorant Wharf(IRE)**, who was backed at long prices, has had his problems but now appears to be over them, and judged on this is capable of winning a race at a lower level.
**No Time(IRE)**, who is slipping down the weights, may be capable of scoring on this surface if dropped in trip.
**Dawn Piper(USA)**, who won a maiden over a mile here on his Polytrack debut, was dropping in trip and may have found a competitive race like this too much at this stage of his career.
**Hurricane Coast**, who has been in such good form this month, failed to land a blow over this longer trip, and it may be that his busy schedule has caught up with him. *Official explanation: jockey said gelding ran flat*

## 649 LITTLEWOODS BET DIRECT H'CAP 1m 2f (P)
3:05 (3:07) (C ) (0-100,100) 4-Y-0+ **£14,993** (£5,687; £2,843; £1,292) **Stalls** Low

Form RPR

334- **1** **Blue Sky Thinking (IRE)**[70] 6051 5-9-10 **96** ........ DarrenWilliams 1 108
(KRBurke) *t.k.h early: hld up in tch: prog 4f out: rdn and effrt on outer 2f out: led ent fnl f: styd on wl: readily* **16/1**

04-2 **2** *1 ¾* **Northside Lodge (IRE)**[10] 577 6-8-13 **85** ........ PDoe 3 94
(PWHarris) *trckd ldrs: effrt over 2f out: drvn on inner to chse wnr ins fnl f: no imp last 100y* **7/2**[1]

1-41 **3** *1 ¼* **Hiawatha (IRE)**[15] 548 5-8-4 **76** ........ JQuinn 12 83
(PABlockley) *hld up in tch: prog to chse ldrs 3f out: rdn and kpt on same pce fr wl over 1f out* **16/1**

10-3 **4** *1* **Paragon Of Virtue**[10] 577 7-8-7 **79** ........ JFanning 5 84
(PMitchell) *prom: led over 3f out: drvn 2f out: hdd ent fnl f: fdd* **11/2**[3]

00-0 **5** *hd* **York Cliff**[16] 544 6-7-10 **75** ........ BSwarbrick(7) 14 80
(WMBrisbourne) *drvn in last pair after 1f and looked reluctant: in tch: outpcd over 3f out: styd on fr over 2f out: r.o fnl f: nrst fin* **33/1**

10-4 **6** *¾* **Dower House**[10] 577 9-8-6 **81** ........ DCorby(3) 4 84
(AndrewTurnell) *prom: rdn to chal over 3f out: btn over 1f out: fdd* **4/1**[2]

-653 **7** *3* **Tight Squeeze**[7] 600 7-8-9 **81** ow2 ........ ACulhane 10 79
(PWHiatt) *in tch: outpcd wl over 3f out: one pce and n.d to ldrs after* **11/2**[3]

15-5 **8** *2* **Ryan's Future (IRE)**[10] 577 4-8-6 **80** ........ CCatlin 7 74
(JAkehurst) *hld up: rdn over 4f out: outpcd over 3f out: n.d after* **10/1**

03-0 **9** *12* **Brilliant Red**[28] 418 11-8-13 **85** ........ (t) SWhitworth 9 58
(JamiePoulton) *s.s: racd in last: outpcd 4f out: no ch after: wl bhd fnl 2f* **16/1**

110- **10** *6* **Haripur**[33] 6252 5-9-4 **97** ........ SJDonohoe(7) 6 59
(AndrewReid) *b.hind: trckd ldr: led 5f out to over 3f out: sn wknd: t.o* **12/1**

0-00 **11** *1 ¾* **Te Quiero**[7] 600 6-9-4 **90** ........ (t) MFenton 2 49
(MissGayKelleway) *b.hind: led to 5f out: wknd over 3f out: t.o* **25/1**

12-0 **12** *6* **Star Of Normandie (USA)**[14] 558 5-8-11 **83** ........ AMcCarthy 8 31
(GGMargarson) *chsd ldrs: rdn over 4f out: wknd wl over 3f out: t.o* **10/1**

-240 **13** *1 ¼* **Lakota Brave**[1] 641 10-9-2 **88** ........ IMongan 13 34
(MrsStefLiddiard) *racd wd: in tch: rdn and struggling 1/2-way: t.o over 2f out* **20/1**

2m 6.83s (-0.56) **Going Correction** +0.15s/f (Slow)
**WFA** 4 from 5yo+ 2lb **13** Ran SP% **128.1**
Speed ratings: **108,106,105,104,104 104,101,100,90,85 84,79,78**CSF £74.96 CT £964.07 TOTE £18.20: £4.50, £2.00, £5.00; EX 93.10.
**Owner** Triple Trio Partnership **Bred** Thomas J Murphy **Trained** Middleham Moor, N Yorks

**FOCUS**
A good, competitive handicap run at a fair gallop, and solid form which should work out.

**NOTEBOOK**
**Blue Sky Thinking(IRE)**, who ran fourth in the Listed Churchill Stakes on his Polytrack debut, went up 6lb for that but this drop in grade made the difference and he won this in style. He looks likely to prove a force in good races, and the Winter Derby trial is next on the agenda.
**Northside Lodge(IRE)**, 2lb higher than when narrowly beaten here the week before, confirmed that form with today's fourth and sixth. He is fully effective around here, but is creeping up the handicap without winning.
**Hiawatha(IRE)**, making his Polytrack debut after winning in lesser company on Fibresand, was 10lb higher and in the circumstances ran with credit. He is clearly on the upgrade.
**Paragon Of Virtue**, a regular around here, looks to be struggling off his current mark, but is running too well for the assessor to have much scope to drop him. A drop in grade may be the answer.
**York Cliff** was making his Polytrack debut off his lowest mark to date. He ran well and is the type his new stable will place successfully.
**Dower House** was unable to reverse form from earlier in the month with the second and fourth despite being slightly better off at the weights.
**Tight Squeeze** possibly found the shorter trip in this grade not playing to her strengths.

## 650 BET DIRECT IN VISION SKY PAGE 293 H'CAP 1m 2f (P)
3:40 (3:44) (F ) (0-65,65) 4-Y-0+ **£3,017** (£862; £431) **Stalls** Low

Form RPR

33-0 **1** **True Companion**[14] 559 5-9-8 **62** ........ J-PGuillambert(3) 11 70
(NPLittmoden) *a wl plcd: effrt 2f out: shkn up to ld last 150y: pushed out* **7/1**[2]

00- **2** *1 ¼* **Treetops Hotel (IRE)**[32] 6256 5-9-2 **58** ........ (p) NChalmers(5) 7 64
(BRJohnson) *hld up towards rr: prog on outer over 3f out: drvn to ld wl over 1f out: hdd and one pce last 150y* **7/1**[2]

00-0 **3** *1 ¼* **Figura**[14] 559 6-9-9 **60** ........ NCallan 6 64
(RIngram) *s.i.s: hld up in rr: prog over 3f out: rdn to chse ldrs 2f out: styd on same pce* **12/1**

1/4- **4** *½* **Crossways**[188] 3828 6-9-5 **63** ........ SJDonohoe(7) 3 66
(PDEvans) *disp ld tl led over 3f out: drvn and hdd wl over 1f out: one pce* **14/1**

500- **5** *½* **Inchinnan**[23] 4658 7-9-7 **58** ........ JQuinn 5 60
(CWeedon) *trckd ldrs: rdn over 3f out: unable qck over 2f out: kpt on same pce after* **12/1**

53-0 **6** *nk* **Quantum Leap**[14] 559 7-9-11 **62** ........ PaulEddery 1 63
(SDow) *t.k.h: hld up in rr: prog over 2f out: rdn and styd on one pce fr over 1f out* **8/1**[3]

666- **7** *shd* **Kavi (IRE)**[126] 4297 4-9-8 **61** ........ GBaker 4 62
(SimonEarle) *racd in midfield: rdn and unable qckn over 2f out: styd on again fnl f* **25/1**

040- **8** *¾* **State Of Balance**[45] 6205 6-9-8 **62** ........ LPKeniry(3) 14 62
(KBell) *s.s: hld up in last: plenty to do at rr of main gp over 2f out: prog over 1f out: no imp fnl f* **8/1**[3]

000- **9** *5* **Snuki**[33] 6255 5-9-11 **62** ........ SWhitworth 12 53
(GLMoore) *hld up in rr: rdn 3f out: one pce and nvr threatened ldrs* **33/1**

-241 **10** *7* **Coronado Forest (USA)**[7] 601 5-10-0 **65** ........ ACulhane 2 43
(MRHoad) *disp ld to over 3f out: wknd* **7/1**[2]

3-63 **11** *2* **Zawrak (IRE)**[7] 602 5-9-0 **58** ........ NataliaGemelova(7) 8 32
(IWMcinnes) *s.s: racd on outer: in tch: rdn over 4f out: wknd over 3f out* **7/1**[2]

21-4 **12** *3* **Lyrical Way**[14] 559 5-9-11 **62** ........ (v) IMongan 13 31
(PRChamings) *racd in midfield: drvn 5f out: sn lost pl: last and no ch 3f out* **5/1**[1]

200- **13** *9* **Pont Neuf (IRE)**[192] 3502 4-9-8 **61** ........ MHills 10 14
(JWHills) *trckd ldrs tl wknd wl over 3f out: t.o* **33/1**



The Form Book, Raceform Ltd, Compton, RG20 6NL

331- **14** ½ **Karaoke (IRE)**$^{231}$ [2366] 4-9-12 **65**............................................ JDSmith 9 17
(SKirk) *b.bkwd: t.k.h: prom tl wknd over 3f out: t.o* **8/1**$^{3}$

2m 8.74s (1.35) **Going Correction** +0.15s/f (Slow)
**WFA** 4 from 5yo+ 2lb **14** Ran SP% **131.8**
Speed ratings: **100,99,98,97,97 96,96,96,92,86 85,82,75,75**CSF £60.00 CT £603.74 TOTE £9.50: £3.50, £2.60, £5.80; EX 97.80.
**Owner** Novowel Racing **Bred** S J Simmons **Trained** Newmarket, Suffolk

**FOCUS**
A modest handicap, run nearly two seconds slower than the preceding contest over the same trip, but fair form for the grade.

**NOTEBOOK**
**True Companion**, who goes well for today's rider, was ridden closer to the pace this time and proved too strong for the gambled-on runner-up, the pair having the race to themselves in the straight.
**Treetops Hotel(IRE)** ◆, 24lb lower than when making his debut on this surface a year ago and with the cheekpieces re-applied, was supported in the ring and made a bold bid until cut down by the winner. He looks capable of gaining compensation from his current mark.
**Figura**, a triple course and distance winner last year, has dropped down the weights and was returning to something like her old form. If she can repeat this effort she can find an opening.
**Crossways**, who was returning from a break, having raced in Jersey last year, ran with promise and will appreciate being stepped back up to a mile and a half.
**Inchinnan**, who has been running over hurdles of late, has shown her best form here in fillies' races and may be of interest in similar contests.
**Quantum Leap**, who beat today's winner here in November, was marginally worse off but should have finished closer than he did.
**Kavi(IRE)**, another who was last seen over hurdles, was returning from four months off and making his Polytrack debut. This was not a bad effort in the circumstances.
**Lyrical Way** has been running consistently well here this winter, but ran poorly on this occasion. *Official explanation: jockey said gelding was never travelling*
**Karaoke(IRE)** *Official explanation: jockey said gelding lost its action, having been struck into*

## 651 BETDIRECT.CO.UK MAIDEN STKS 1m 4f (P)
**4:15** (4:18) (D) 3-Y-0+ **£3,513** (£1,081; £540; £270) **Stalls** Low

Form RPR

62- **1** **So Vital**$^{63}$ [6089] 4-9-10 ............................................ JQuinn 5 69
(MrsLydiaPearce) *prom: rdn to chse ldr over 4f out and sn clr of rest: led over 2f out to over 1f out: rallied to ld again last 150y: hld on* **7/4**$^{1}$

003- **2** *hd* **Elegant Gracie (IRE)**$^{32}$ [6259] 4-9-5 61.............................. JPSpencer 9 64
(RGuest) *hld up towards rr: nt clr run 4f out and ldng pair wnt clr: rapid prog 3f out: led over 1f out: hdd last 150y: kpt on:jst h* **6/1**$^{3}$

0 **3** *6* **Alisa (IRE)**$^{17}$ [520] 4-9-2 ..........................................(t) LisaJones$^{(3)}$ 8 55
(BICase) *settled towards rr: outpcd fr 4f out: styd on fr over 2f out to take 3rd ins fnl f* **66/1**

00- **4** *1 ¼* **Imperative (USA)**$^{22}$ [5225] 4-9-10 75........................................ MHenry 7 58
(IanWilliams) *hld up in rr: prog on outer over 4f out: sn outpcd by ldng pair: one pce fr wl over 2f out* **14/1**

23-0 **5** *3* **Bowing**$^{12}$ [564] 4-9-10 70......................................................... DKinsella 3 53
(PGMurphy) *hld up in rr: outpcd over 4f out but stl gng wl enough: styd on fnl 2f: no ch* **9/1**

32-5 **6** *3* **Skibereen (IRE)**$^{7}$ [601] 4-9-3 70......................(bt) NataliaGemelova$^{(7)}$ 13 49
(IWMcinnes) *t.k.h: prom: led over 5f out and kicked on: clr w wnr over 3f out: hdd over 2f out: wknd rapidly over 1f out* **10/1**

4P-0 **7** ½ **Mysterlover (IRE)**$^{14}$ [555] 4-9-10 ........................................ IMongan 10 48
(NPLittmoden) *rn in snatches in midfield: outpcd 4f out: n.d after* **25/1**

23-3 **8** *9* **Newtonian (USA)**$^{18}$ [513] 5-10-0 69............................ DeanMcKeown 4 35
(JParkes) *racd in midfield: outpcd and struggling over 4f out: no ch* **5/1**$^{2}$

0 **9** *1 ¼* **La Concha (IRE)**$^{14}$ [553] 3-8-6 ow3........................................ SWKelly 14 36
(MrsLCJewell) *dwlt: sn chsd ldr: carried wd bnd 9f out and lost pl: wknd over 3f out* **12/1**

-302 **10** *nk* **Pyrrhic**$^{14}$ [554] 5-9-7 50.................................................(b) SJDonohoe$^{(7)}$ 6 32
(RMFlower) *a in rr: outpcd over 4f out: bhd after* **9/1**

0/ **11** ½ **Kirat**$^{667}$ [1669] 6-10-0 ........................................................ SWhitworth 12 32
(GLMoore) *dwlt: sn prom: outpcd by ldrs 4f out: sn wknd* **6/1**$^{3}$

**12** *5* **Luteur Des Pictons (FR)**$^{15}$ 5-9-7 ................................ AHindley$^{(7)}$ 11 24
(BGPowell) *prom tl wknd 4f out* **40/1**

0-0 **13** ½ **Desert Tommy**$^{21}$ [492] 3-8-3 ow3..........................................(b$^{1}$) RMiles$^{(3)}$ 15 26
(TGMills) *s.s: drvn to go prom whn carried wd bnd 9f out: wknd over 4f out* **20/1**

4-00 **14** *9* **Tamarina (IRE)**$^{9}$ [587] 3-7-12 55...................................(p) JoannaBadger 1 5
(NEBerry) *led: tried to run out bnd 9f out: hdd & wknd over 5f out* **66/1**

**15** *dist* **Wild Wild Wes** 4-9-10 ................................................................ NDay 2 —
(RIngram) *w'like: s.s: a in rr: t.o* **40/1**

2m 36.34s (2.36) **Going Correction** +0.15s/f (Slow)
**WFA** 3 from 4yo 25lb 4 from 5yo+ 4lb **15** Ran SP% **141.5**
Speed ratings: **98,97,93,93,91 89,88,82,81,81 81,78,77,71,**—CSF £14.14 TOTE £2.70: £1.60, £3.60, £25.10; EX 22.10 Place 6 £273.49, Place 5 £162.52..
**Owner** Jim Furlong **Bred** J R Furlong **Trained** Newmarket, Suffolk

**FOCUS**
Just an ordinary maiden run at a moderate gallop.

**NOTEBOOK**
**So Vital**, whose course and distance second in November had not particularly worked out, nevertheless justified favouritism. He went in pursuit of the clear leader running down to the straight then, after looking likely to be overhauled, battled back gamely to prevail. The form is nothing exceptional, but with his attitude, he is sure to win more races.
**Elegant Gracie(IRE)**, stepping up in trip, swept through to lead halfway up the straight but was run out of it and may not have stayed. She looks capable of winning a handicap on this surface.
**Alisa(IRE)**, stepping up in trip from her Polytrack debut and fitted with a tongue tie, ran better and was keeping on, albeit some way behind the principals. She has experience in bumpers but seems better in Flat races proper.
**Imperative(USA)**, who has been running over hurdles recently, had the highest mark of those with ratings but looks flattered by that figure.
**Bowing**, who had a turf rating in the 80s when with John Gosden, is now rated 70 but has run well below that mark in both outings on the All-Weather.
**Skibereen(IRE)**, who has run well on this surface in the past, seemed to do too much too soon and paid the price.
**Newtonian(USA)**, making his debut on this surface, looks better on Fibresand judged on this performance, and a return to handicaps on that surface may see him in a better light. *Official explanation: jockey said gelding was never travelling*
T/Plt: £193.50 to a £1 stake. Pool: £38,692.55. 145.95 winning tickets. T/Qpdt: £78.40 to a £1 stake. Pool: £2,609.20. 24.60 winning tickets. JN

# $^{637}$WOLVERHAMPTON (A.W) (L-H)
Monday, February 2

**OFFICIAL GOING: Standard changing to standard to slow after race 3 (2.30)**
(REGIONAL RACING)

## 652 BETDIRECT.CO.UK BANDED STKS (DIV I) 1m 1f 79y(F)
**1:30** (1:30) (H) 3-Y-0+ **£1,634** (£467; £233) **Stalls** Low

Form RPR

5-06 **1** **Red Storm**$^{21}$ [505] 5-9-5 45...............................................(v$^{1}$) RMiles$^{(3)}$ 4 55
(JRBoyle) *trckd ldrs: rdn to ld over 2f out: kpt up to work fnl f* **4/1**$^{2}$

-252 **2** *2 ½* **Maggie's Pet**$^{6}$ [614] 7-9-8 45...........................................(t) DRMcCabe 5 50
(KBell) *trckd ldr: led over 6f out: rdn and hdd over 2f out: one pce and no imp fnl f* **13/8**$^{1}$

00-0 **3** *3 ½* **Unsuited**$^{26}$ [463] 5-9-1 40........................................ NataliaGemelova$^{(7)}$ 7 44
(JELong) *in tch: chsd ldrs 1/2-way: one pce ins fnl 2f* **50/1**

00-0 **4** *6* **Amanpuri (GER)**$^{23}$ [491] 6-9-8 45.......................................... MFenton 6 33
(MissGayKelleway) *racd wd and towards rr: kpt on past btn horses ins fnl 2f* **4/1**$^{2}$

040- **5** ½ **Bevier**$^{207}$ [3148] 10-9-3 45................................................... NChalmers$^{(5)}$ 1 32
(TWall) *in rr: rdn 1/2-way: mde sme late hdwy* **7/1**$^{3}$

-420 **6** ¾ **Giust In Temp (IRE)**$^{10}$ [590] 5-9-8 40........................................ ACulhane 3 31
(PWHiatt) *in tch: rdn wl over 1f out: wknd rapidly ins fnl f* **7/1**$^{3}$

00-0 **7** *1 ¼* **Ellamyte**$^{12}$ [573] 4-9-8 45.................................................. SRighton 9 28
(DGBridgwater) *led for 2f: rdn and wknd over 4f out* **33/1**

004- **8** *12* **Arte Et Labore (IRE)**$^{72}$ [4575] 4-9-8 45..................................... PFessey 8 7
(KARyan) *a in rr* **25/1**

000- **9** *1 ¾* **Marshal Bond**$^{67}$ [5819] 6-9-8 45................................................(b) FLynch 2 4
(BSmart) *sn bhd and struggling in rr* **12/1**

2m 6.72s (3.82) **Going Correction** +0.15s/f (Slow) **9** Ran SP% **119.5**
Speed ratings: **89,86,83,78,77 77,76,65,63**CSF £11.18 TOTE £4.40: £1.90, £1.10, £13.40; EX 15.70.
**Owner** Brian McAtavey **Bred** 949 Racing Partnership **Trained** Epsom, Surrey

**FOCUS**
A typically weak race and, although fair form for the grade by the first two, a time 1.53 seconds slower than the second division.

**NOTEBOOK**
**Red Storm**, dropping in trip and class and with the visor on for the first time, ran out a clear-cut winner of a very weak race. She has done all of her winning over this course and distance.
**Maggie's Pet**, still a maiden, lacked a change of pace in the straight and appears to need further.
**Unsuited** was never really a danger on this Fibresand debut.
**Amanpuri(GER)** was soon pushed along in rear and never threatened. His optimum trip has still to be established.
**Bevier** was a long way below form.
**Giust In Temp(IRE)** weakened badly inside the final furlong having lost his action. *Official explanation: jockey said horse had lost its action*

## 653 BET DIRECT NO Q DEMO 08000 837 888 APPRENTICE BANDED STKS 1m 4f (F)
**2:00** (2:01) (H) 4-Y-0+ **£1,288** (£368; £184) **Stalls** Low

Form RPR

6-12 **1** **Bella Pavlina**$^{11}$ [583] 6-8-12 40........................................ BSwarbrick$^{(5)}$ 3 57+
(WMBrisbourne) *in tch: hdwy 7f out: led 4f out: clr over 2f out: v easily* **1/1**$^{1}$

000- **2** *22* **The Beduth Navi**$^{154}$ [4624] 4-9-0 40............................................ DNolan 2 26
(DGBridgwater) *chsd ldrs tl rdn and lost pl over 4f out: styd on ins fnl 2f to go 2nd ins fnl f: no ch w wnr* **66/1**

000- **3** ½ **Galley Law**$^{51}$ [6177] 4-9-0 30.................................................... TEaves 7 26
(RCraggs) *in tch: rdn over 3f out: kpt on one pce ins fnl 2f* **66/1**

-333 **4** *1* **Newclose**$^{13}$ [570] 4-9-0 40..................................................(t) THamilton 10 24
(NTinkler) *hdwy to chse ldrs over 7f out: plugged on one pce fnl 2f* **11/2**$^{3}$

40-0 **5** ½ **Think Quick (IRE)**$^{13}$ [570] 4-8-7 35............................ RKennemore$^{(7)}$ 8 23
(RHollinshead) *hld up: hdwy over 5f out: nvr nr to chal* **50/1**

6-50 **6** *2 ½* **Vermilion Creek**$^{13}$ [570] 5-9-0 30..............(p) StephanieHollinshead$^{(3)}$ 11 20
(RHollinshead) *mid-div: rdn to go 2nd over 2f out: wknd ins fnl f* **25/1**

/00- **7** *7* **Greenborough (IRE)**$^{38}$ [488] 6-8-12 30...................(p) DerekNolan$^{(5)}$ 12 10
(MrsPFord) *trckd ldr: led briefly over 4f out: wknd over 2f out* **66/1**

50-0 **8** *9* **Moyne Pleasure (IRE)**$^{24}$ [483] 6-9-3 40............................ NChalmers 4 —
(PaulJohnson) *hld up: rdn over 4f out: nvr on terms* **9/1**

4-60 **9** *5* **Fraternity**$^{21}$ [500] 7-9-3 35.................................................(v$^{1}$) AQuinn 6 —
(JAPickering) *plld hrd: led tl hdd over 4f out: sn wknd* **20/1**

000- **10** *20* **Kingsdon (IRE)**$^{97}$ [5819] 7-9-3 35...................................(vt) PMulrennan 9 —
(TJFitzgerald) *rdn fr s: a bhd* **20/1**

-032 **11** *2 ½* **Khuzdar (IRE)**$^{10}$ [594] 5-8-12 40...........................................(p) BO'Neill$^{(5)}$ 5 —
(ABailey) *hld up: nvr gng wl: lost tch over 5f out* **10/3**$^{2}$

000- **12** *dist* **Habibti Sara**$^{258}$ [1739] 4-8-11 35.......................................... MSavage$^{(3)}$ 1 —
(AWCarroll) *trckd ldrs tl rdn and lost pl over 6f out: sn t.o* **40/1**

2m 42.28s (0.78) **Going Correction** +0.15s/f (Slow)
**WFA** 4 from 5yo+ 3lb **12** Ran SP% **120.7**
Speed ratings: **103,88,88,87,87 85,80,74,71,58 56,**—CSF £121.95 TOTE £1.80: £1.10, £28.00, £18.90; EX 126.40.
**Owner** The Cartmel Syndicate **Bred** C Papaioannou **Trained** Great Ness, Shropshire

**FOCUS**
A one-horse race and Bella Pavlina recorded a decent time for the class of contest. However, she could suffer at the hands of the Handicapper for this wide-margin victory.

**NOTEBOOK**
**Bella Pavlina**, runner-up behind the progressive Sendintank at Southwell last time, absolutely bolted up on this drop in grade. Her handicap mark will suffer as a result, but she appears to be progressing.
**The Beduth Navi**, a lightly-raced maiden making his Fibresand debut, lost his position in the back straight before staying on for strong pressure to take a distant second. Headgear may sharpen him up, and he should stay further.
**Galley Law**was dropped in class and gaining his first placing. This may be as good as he is.
**Newclose** continues to find a few too good.
**Khuzdar(IRE)** was a poor race in first-time cheekpieces, but is not one to follow whatever the case.

## 654 BET DIRECT NO Q ON 08000 93 66 93 CLAIMING STKS 6f (F)
**2:30** (2:30) (H) 3-Y-0+ **£1,330** (£380; £190) **Stalls** Low

Form RPR

-654 **1** **Foolish Thought (IRE)**$^{7}$ [605] 4-9-2 56..........................(p) THamilton$^{(5)}$ 5 47
(RAFahey) *chsd ldrs: sn rdn: outpcd over 3f out: rallied u.p to ld over 1f out: kpt on to line* **10/3**$^{1}$

40-6 **2** *hd* **Bells Beach (IRE)**[13] [572] 6-9-4 40........................................ SWKelly 9 43
(PHowling) *mid-div: hdwy over 2f out: r.o strly fnl f and clsng on wnr at line* **5/1**[2]

4406 **3** *2* **Arogant Prince**[3] [642] 7-9-3 53....................................(b) RoryMoore(7) 7 43
(AWCarroll) *trckd ldrs led over 2f out: hdd over 1f out: one pce ins fnl f* **11/2**[3]

0100 **4** *1* **Attorney**[4] [625] 6-9-7 47..................................................(e) LisaJones(3) 1 40
(DShaw) *mid-div: hdwy over 2f out: r.o ins fnl f* **8/1**

3-06 **5** *2* **Heathyardsblessing (IRE)**[7] [608] 7-9-10 45..........(p) DeanMcKeown 8 34
(RHollinshead) *chsd ldrs tl wknd ins fnl f* **20/1**

-000 **6** *shd* **Flying Faisal (USA)**[13] [572] 6-9-7 35 ow4........................ CJDavies(7) 6 38
(JMBradley) *in tch: hdwy over 2f out: fdd appr fnl f* **40/1**

0-30 **7** *1/2* **Neutral Night (IRE)**[18] [535] 4-8-11 45........................(v) DerekNolan(7) 4 26
(RBrotherton) *in rr: hdwy over 2f out: kpt on fnl f: nvr nr to chal* **33/1**

0-50 **8** *3 1/2* **Komena**[12] [573] 6-9-5 45........................................................ IMongan 13 17
(JWPayne) *a towards rr* **8/1**

-001 **9** *1 1/4* **Pips Song (IRE)**[7] [608] 9-9-9 40........................................... JFanning 10 17
(PWHiatt) *a outpced in rr* **7/1**

6-00 **10** *5* **Present 'n Correct**[28] [441] 11-9-0 30........................(b) SimonJones(7) 2 —
(JMBradley) *s.i.s: a bhd* **66/1**

00-0 **11** *16* **On The Trail**[4] [625] 7-9-10 50...........................................(b1) ACulhane 3 —
(DWChapman) *plld hrd: led tl hdd over 2f out and rn wd into st: sn wl bhd* **11/2**[3]

-0 **12** *29* **Campbell's Tale (IRE)**[11] [585] 5-9-8 ...............................(t) MFenton 11 —
(TJFitzgerald) *racd wd: a bhd: t.o* **66/1**

1m 18.06s (2.36) **Going Correction** +0.15s/f (Slow)
**WFA** 3 from 4yo+ 15lb **12** Ran SP% **118.4**
Speed ratings: **90,89,87,85,83 82,82,77,75,69 47,9**CSF £18.80 TOTE £4.20: £1.30, £1.60, £2.60; EX 18.00.Foolish Thought was claimed by Ian Wood for £2,000
**Owner** Northumbria Leisure Ltd **Bred** Moyglare Stud Farm Ltd **Trained** Musley Bank, N Yorks

**FOCUS**
Weak form and a moderate winning time for the grade.

**NOTEBOOK**
**Foolish Thought(IRE)** had been proving hard to win with but, dropping back from an extended nine furlongs, he was the best in at the weights and ran out a narrow winner. This trip was just on the short side for him and he should be suited by a return to seven furlongs or a mile. He was claimed by Ian Wood for £2,000.
**Bells Beach(IRE)**, without a win since May 2001, had 13lb to find with the winner at the weights but, on only her second start for Paul Howling, ran an encouraging race.
**Arogant Prince** did not do himself any favours by chasing early leader On The Trail, who appeared to go off too fast.
**Attorney** had it all to do at the weights and probably ran as well as could have been expected.
**Heathyardsblessing(IRE)** did not appear to improve for the fitting of cheekpieces.
**On The Trail** went off too fast and, hanging right, he stopped to nothing in the straight. *Official explanation: jockey said gelding ran too freely in first-time blinkers*
**Campbell's Tale(IRE)** *Official explanation: trainer said gelding had a breathing problem*

## 655 BETDIRECT.CO.UK BANDED STKS (DIV II) 1m 1f 79y(F)
**3:05** (3:06) (H) 3-Y-0+ **£1,631** (£466; £233) **Stalls** Low

Form RPR

40-0 **1** **Prince Prospect**[31] [412] 8-9-1 45........................... KristinStubbs(7) 8 48
(MrsLStubbs) *slowly away: hdwy but plenty to do 2f out: hung lft appr fnl f but r.o to ld jst ins: sn clr* **7/1**[3]

00-5 **2** *3 1/2* **Phantom Flame (USA)**[21] [503] 4-9-8 45.................................. JFanning 3 42
(MJohnston) *mde most tl hdd 2f out: rallied to ld briefly again 1f out: one pce and jst hld on for 2nd* **4/1**[2]

6000 **3** *hd* **Haithem (IRE)**[10] [594] 7-9-5 30.......................................(e) LisaJones(3) 7 41
(DShaw) *mid-div: hdwy over 2f out: styd on fnl f* **40/1**

3-00 **4** *shd* **Debbie**[13] [570] 5-9-8 40........................................................ SWhitworth 9 41
(BDLeavy) *in tch: rdn to ld 2f out: hdd 1f out: kpt on one pce* **4/1**[2]

0523 **5** *5* **Sea Ya Maite**[4] [630] 10-9-8 35.............................................(t) JBramhill 4 32
(SRBowring) *in tch: rdn over 2f out: wknd appr fnl f* **14/1**

00-4 **6** *3/4* **Wodhill Folly**[17] [552] 7-9-8 45.............................................(v) IMongan 2 30
(DMorris) *in tch: rdn over 4f out: wknd over 1f out* **15/8**[1]

00-0 **7** *1 1/4* **Paris Dreamer**[30] [422] 3-8-1 40........................................... DaleGibson 5 28
(MWEasterby) *in tch: lost pl 5f out and nvr on terms after* **16/1**

00-0 **8** *5* **Beauteous (IRE)**[21] [503] 5-9-8 45.......................................... FLynch 6 19
(ABerry) *w ldr to 2f out: sn wknd* **11/1**

550- **9** *26* **Sabreline**[48] [6200] 5-9-8 45.............................................(b1) CCatlin 1 —
(BRFoster) *sn wl bhd: t.o* **14/1**

2m 5.19s (2.29) **Going Correction** +0.15s/f (Slow)
**WFA** 3 from 4yo+ 21lb **9** Ran SP% **117.3**
Speed ratings: **95,91,91,91,87 86,85,80,57**CSF £35.72 TOTE £9.20: £2.10, £1.40, £7.20; EX 43.70.
**Owner** Mrs L Stubbs **Bred** Noel Sweeney **Trained** Malton, N. Yorks

**FOCUS**
A moderate race. Prince Prospect came nicely clear in the straight and the form of the others is weak.

**NOTEBOOK**
**Prince Prospect** ended a losing run stretching back to December 2001 on this drop into banded company. He came nicely clear in the straight and may be able to follow-up. *Official explanation: trainer said, regarding the improved form shown, gelding is an inconsistent sort who benefited from today's drop in class*
**Phantom Flame(USA)** was not left alone up front and proved no match for the winner. He should do better granted an uncontested lead.
**Haithem(IRE)** has not won for a long time, but this was not a bad effort on this drop in trip.
**Debbie** continues below the pick of her turf form and may be worth another try on the faster Polytrack surface.
**Wodhill Folly**, dropped in grade, was never really going and proved disappointing. *Official explanation: trainer had no explanation for the mare's poor running*

## 656 LITTLEWOODS BET DIRECT MEDIAN AUCTION MAIDEN STKS 1m 100y(F)
**3:35** (3:37) (H) 3-5-Y-0 **£1,449** (£414; £207) **Stalls** Low

Form RPR

6-26 **1** **Iamback**[19] [529] 4-9-5 47..................................................(p) MFenton 4 47
(MissGayKelleway) *trckd ldr: led over 4f out: rdn and hung rt appr fnl f: r.o u.p* **5/1**[2]

40-2 **2** *nk* **Turks And Caicos (IRE)**[25] [473] 3-7-12 58.................. RoryMoore(7) 5 51
(PCHaslam) *in tch: wnt 2nd 4f out: sn rdn: sltly outpcd 2f out: r.o u.p fnl f* **4/9**[1]

**3** *6* **Paddy Boy (IRE)** 3-8-3 ow1........................................... RMiles(3) 3 40
(JRBoyle) *v.s.a and wl in rr: tk clsr order over 2f out: r.o wl to go 3rd ins fnl f* **16/1**

63-6 **4** *nk* **Blue Savanna**[12] [579] 4-9-10 46........................................(b) IMongan 6 38
(JGPortman) *in tch tl rdn and wknd over 2f out* **13/2**[3]

6-50 **5** *1* **Mimas Girl**[13] [572] 5-9-5 30...............................................(t) JBramhill 2 31
(SRBowring) *t.k.h: trckd ldrs tl wknd over 2f out* **33/1**

000/ **6** *25* **Danzig Star**[530] [4049] 4-9-5 ......................................................... PDoe 1 —
(PRChamings) *led tl hdd over 4f out: lost pl qckly over 3f out and sn wl bhd* **25/1**

1m 52.08s (1.08) **Going Correction** +0.15s/f (Slow)
**WFA** 3 from 4yo+ 19lb **6** Ran SP% **111.9**
Speed ratings: **100,99,93,93,92 67**CSF £7.61 TOTE £4.90: £1.70, £1.10; EX 11.00.
**Owner** Twilight Racing **Bred** Mrs J M F Dibben **Trained** Newmarket, Suffolk
■ Stewards Enquiry : Rory Moore one-day ban: used whip with arm above shoulder height (Feb 13)

**FOCUS**
A weak maiden and the right level for the winner, but the third may turn out the best in the long term.

**NOTEBOOK**
**Iamback**, stepping back up in trip, proved just good enough to win what was a weak maiden despite hanging right under pressure. She is likely to struggle in all but the weakest of races.
**Turks And Caicos(IRE)**, who took a while to get into top gear, had no real excuse given the low quality of the opposition.
**Paddy Boy(IRE)** lost a few lengths at the start and ran green. His rider was keen not to give him a hard race on his debut, but the gelding still ran on nicely next to the far-side rail in the straight. He can improve on this bare form.
**Blue Savanna**, whose best trip appears to be a mystery to connections, ran over two miles last time.

## 657 BET DIRECT NO Q BANDED STKS 5f (F)
**4:10** (4:10) (H) 3-Y-0+ **£1,631** (£466; £233) **Stalls** Low

Form RPR

-263 **1** **Torrent**[4] [626] 9-9-7 45.................................................(b) ACulhane 5 52
(DWChapman) *a in tch: rdn and squeezed through to ld jst ins fnl f: r.o wl* **5/2**[2]

00-2 **2** *1 1/4* **Hagley Park**[31] [411] 5-9-7 45............................................ JQuinn 2 48
(MQuinn) *chsd ldrs: wnt 2nd wl over 1f out: led briefly 1f out: kpt on* **5/6**[1]

05-0 **3** *1* **Sergeant Slipper**[4] [625] 7-9-7 45.........................................(v) JFanning 3 44
(CSmith) *slowly away: plenty to over 1f out: fin fast fnl f: nvr nrr* **10/1**[3]

000- **4** *1 3/4* **Statoyork**[184] [3797] 11-9-0 45.................................... DawnWatson(7) 4 38
(DShaw) *hld up: hdwy over 1f out: r.o fnl f* **14/1**

055- **5** *1 3/4* **Pleasure Time**[185] [3759] 11-9-7 45..................................(v) RFitzpatrick 10 32
(CSmith) *chsd ldr: led over 3f out: rdn and hdd 1f out: wknd* **12/1**

060- **6** *2* **Danakim**[164] [4346] 7-9-0 35........................................... DFentiman(7) 7 25
(JRWeymes) *racd wd: sn rdn: nvr on terms* **33/1**

0-00 **7** *3 1/2* **Tuscan Dream**[3] [638] 9-9-2 40.......................................... PBradley(5) 1 13
(ABerry) *led for over 1f: wknd over 1f out* **20/1**

/00- **8** *nk* **View The Facts**[98] [5799] 5-9-4 45...................................(e) LisaJones(3) 8 12
(PLGilligan) *slowly away: a bhd* **25/1**

6-00 **9** *hd* **Lone Piper**[27] [460] 9-9-7 40............................................(b1) PFitzsimons 6 11
(JMBradley) *t.k.h: a bhd* **25/1**

000- **10** *1* **Mill End Teaser**[146] [4789] 3-8-7 45.................................. DaleGibson 9 7
(MWEasterby) *outpcd thrght* **25/1**

63.05 secs (0.45) **Going Correction** +0.15s/f (Slow)
**WFA** 3 from 5yo+ 14lb **10** Ran SP% **125.8**
Speed ratings: **102,100,98,95,92 89,84,83,83,81**CSF £4.99 TOTE £4.10: £1.90, £1.10, £1.70; EX 8.80.
**Owner** David W Chapman **Bred** Mrs Mary Taylor **Trained** Stillington, N Yorks

**FOCUS**
A weak race, but fair form from winner and a very creditable time for the grade.

**NOTEBOOK**
**Torrent**, whose only win since September 2000 came at Ripon last summer, was scoring for the first time on Fibresand. A runner-up on his only previous start in banded grade, he is clearly at home at this level.
**Hagley Park**, who is at her best over this course and distance, was having her first start in banded grade and showed that there are races to be won with her at this level.
**Sergeant Slipper** as usual missed the break and, despite his stablemate helping to set a good pace, got going all too late. *Official explanation: jockey said gelding had lost its action*
**Statoyork**, having his first outing since August, is at the veteran stage of his career, but regional racing gives him more opportunites now.
**Pleasure Time** helped set a decent pace which brought his stablemate, who is often slowly away, into the equation late on.

## 658 BET DIRECT ON SKY ACTIVE BANDED STKS 7f (F)
**4:40** (4:41) (H) 3-Y-0+ **£1,463** (£418; £209) **Stalls** High

Form RPR

00-6 **1** **Badou**[18] [535] 4-9-5 40................................................ RMiles(3) 12 47
(LMontagueHall) *nvr far away: rdn to cl ent fnl f: led wl ins: drvn out* **4/1**[1]

0-40 **2** *1/2* **Silver Mascot**[12] [573] 5-9-8 40........................................ DaleGibson 8 45
(RHollinshead) *chsd ldr: ev ch fnl f: jst hld* **9/1**

4402 **3** *1/2* **Enjoy The Buzz**[13] [572] 5-9-8 40..................................... PFitzsimons 7 44
(JMBradley) *mid-div: hdwy over 2f out: c wd into st: fin strly fnl f: nvr nrr* **6/1**[3]

0250 **4** *shd* **Vlasta Weiner**[13] [567] 4-9-5 40..................................(b) LFletcher(3) 4 44
(JMBradley) *in rr: hdwy on outside 2f out: fin wl fnl f: nvr nrr* **20/1**

00-0 **5** *nk* **Lion's Domane**[30] [422] 7-9-8 40.............................................. FLynch 1 43
(ABerry) *led: hrd rdn and hdd ent fnl f: no ex fnl stages* **25/1**

0-06 **6** *2 1/2* **Long Weekend (IRE)**[12] [576] 6-9-8 40..................(e) DarrenWilliams 6 37
(DShaw) *hld up: hdwy over 2f out: r.o fnl f: nvr nr to chal* **5/1**[2]

00-6 **7** *2* **Zahunda (IRE)**[18] [533] 5-9-1 40.................................(p) BSwarbrick(7) 9 32
(WMBrisbourne) *prom tl rdn and wknd 2f out* **6/1**[3]

4-03 **8** *1 1/2* **Second Venture (IRE)**[13] [567] 6-9-8 40..............................(bt) SWKelly 3 28
(PHowling) *in tch for 4f* **5/1**[2]

06-0 **9** *4* **Kilmeena Star**[26] [465] 6-9-8 40.........................................(p) PDobbs 5 18
(JCFox) *in tch tl wknd over 2f out* **16/1**

00-4 **10** *1 3/4* **Lively Felix**[13] [572] 7-9-8 40............................................. SRighton 2 14
(DGBridgwater) *mid-div: rdn and bhd fr 1/2-way* **8/1**

0-06 **11** *2 1/2* **Chanteuse**[28] [444] 4-9-8 40...........................................(b) RBrisland 10 7
(DWChapman) *slowly away: a bhd* **50/1**

-330 **12** *1* **Lemarate (USA)**[13] [567] 7-9-8 40........................................ ACulhane 11 5
(DWChapman) *sn pushed along: a in rr* **12/1**

1m 31.78s (1.58) **Going Correction** +0.15s/f (Slow) **12** Ran SP% **127.2**
Speed ratings: **96,95,94,94,94 91,89,87,82,80 78,76**CSF £43.20 TOTE £4.80: £1.80, £2.40, £1.90; EX 71.60 Place 6 £11.83, Place 5 £7.16.
**Owner** J Daniels **Bred** D J And Mrs Deer **Trained** Headley, Surrey

**FOCUS**
The principals are only shadows of their former selves, and the form and time were typically modest.

**NOTEBOOK**
**Badou** was always travelling well just off the pace and, when asked to pick up the leaders, did so in good style. He did not find a great deal in front, but that will not worry those who backed him down from 7-1.


The Form Book, Raceform Ltd, Compton, RG20 6NL

**Silver Mascot**, running over seven furlongs for only the second time in his career, got the trip well, especially considering he raced with a decent pace throughout.
**Enjoy The Buzz** was once again putting in his best work at the finish, despite this time running over an extra furlong. He remains a maiden.
**Vlasta Weiner** was dropping back to the trip over which he has shown his best recent form.
**Lion's Domane**, who is not really suited to Fibresand, nevertheless ran his best race for a while.
**Long Weekend(IRE)**, who has only one win to his name from 43 starts, could only muster the one pace up the straight.
T/Plt: £77.00 to a £1 stake. Pool: £36,009.50. 340.95 winning tickets. T/Qpdt: £19.90 to a £1 stake. Pool: £2,618.90. 97.30 winning tickets. JS

## 644 LINGFIELD (L-H)

Tuesday, February 3

**OFFICIAL GOING: Standard**
(REGIONAL RACING)

### 659 BET DIRECT NO Q BANDED STKS (DIV I) 1m (P)
1:40 (1:41) (H) 3-Y-0+ **£1,641** (£469; £234) **Stalls** High

Form RPR
00-0 **1** **Dial Square**[20] [529] 3-8-2 40 (b[1]) CCatlin 11 43
(PHowling) *t.k.h early: cl up: effrt to ld 3f out: sn rdn: jnd wl over 1f out: edgd rt fnl f: jst hld on* **5/1**[3]
0-45 **2** *shd* **Zonnebeke**[12] [587] 3-8-2 45 JFanning 3 43
(KRBurke) *pressed ldr: led briefly over 3f out: jnd wnr wl over 1f out: edgd rt fnl f: nt qckn nr fin* **8/1**
03-4 **3** *nk* **Cherokee Bay**[13] [495] 4-9-7 45 (e[1]) GCarter 8 42
(GLMoore) *in tch: prog to press ldrs 2f out: rdn and nt qckn wl over 1f out: kpt on u.p ins fnl f* **4/1**[2]
00-3 **4** *1 1/2* **Abuelos**[19] [536] 5-9-7 45 PDoe 9 39
(SDow) *hld up: prog 3f out: pressed ldng pair 2f out: ev ch 1f out: nt qckn u.p* **7/2**[1]
046- **5** *3 1/2* **First Class Lady**[105] [5696] 4-9-4 45 LisaJones[(3)] 5 31
(PMitchell) *rr: pushed along 1/2-way: last and outpcd over 2f out: plugged on fr over 1f out: no ch* **14/1**
0-40 **6** *3/4* **Diliza**[17] [554] 5-9-2 45 RThomas[(5)] 12 30
(GBBalding) *hld up: effrt on outer 3f out: sn outpcd: c wd st: n.d* **7/2**[1]
000/ **7** *1 1/4* **El Giza (USA)**[617] [1674] 6-9-7 45 SWhitworth 10 27
(JMBradley) *s.i.s: hld up in rr: effrt 3f out: sn outpcd and btn* **50/1**
0-05 **8** *nk* **Kumakawa**[5] [627] 6-9-0 45 (b) LiamJones[(7)] 1 26
(EAWheeler) *chsd ldrs: outpcd wl over 2f out: last and no ch whn nt clr run over 1f out* **20/1**
00/0 **9** *2 1/2* **Pedler's Profiles**[10] [601] 4-9-7 40 VSlattery 4 21
(MissKMGeorge) *chsd ldrs tl wknd wl over 2f out* **66/1**
000- **10** *2* **Lady Liesel**[112] [5564] 4-9-7 45 GBaker 7 16
(JJBridger) *restless stalls: pressed ldrs tl wknd over 2f out* **20/1**
050- **11** *7* **Dreams United**[162] [4434] 3-7-13 45 FPFerris[(3)] 2 1
(AGNewcombe) *led to over 3f out: sn wknd* **33/1**
1m 42.28s (2.77) **Going Correction** +0.15s/f (Slow)
**WFA** 3 from 4yo+ 19lb **11** Ran SP% **114.8**
Speed ratings: **92,91,91,90,86 85,84,84,81,79 72**CSF £40.50 TOTE £7.10: £2.30, £2.60, £1.50; EX 72.50.
**Owner** Rory Murphy **Bred** J And Mrs Bowtell **Trained** Newmarket, Suffolk

**FOCUS**
A very moderate winning time, almost two seconds slower than the second division, and the form is weak.

**NOTEBOOK**
**Dial Square**, who failed to cope with the kickback at Wolverhampton on his latest start, was fitted with blinkers for the first time. Just holding on in a three-way finish, he will do well to find another race as weak as this. *Official explanation: trainer's said, regarding the improved form shown, gelding may have benefitted from the fitting of blinkers.*
**Zonnebeke** improved for this return to a mile and just failed to get past the leader. She has been beaten in selling company and is a very limited performer.
**Cherokee Bay**, beaten over hurdles on her latest start, wore an eyeshield for the first time. She did not look too keen to put her best foot forward at one stage, but she was staying on at the death and a return to ten furlongs will be in her favour.
**Abuelos** was taken to post early. He had his chance but the obvious conclusion is that he failed to stay this longer trip.
**First Class Lady** has done all her racing over farther and found this trip insufficient.
**Diliza** could never land a telling blow.

### 660 BET DIRECT NO Q DEMO 08000 837 888 MEDIAN AUCTION MAIDEN STKS 7f (P)
2:10 (2:13) (H) 3-5-Y-0 **£1,470** (£420; £210) **Stalls** Low

Form RPR
-634 **1** **Adantino**[4] [639] 5-9-6 52 (b) JPSpencer 9 58
(BRMillman) *hld up: prog to trck ldrs over 2f out: slipped through on inner to ld 1f out: rdn clr* **9/2**
00 **2** *1 3/4* **Devine Command**[10] [598] 3-8-3 NDay 2 54
(RIngram) *chsd ldr to 1/2-way: rdn over 2f out: styd on to chse wnr ins fnl f: no imp* **50/1**
63-2 **3** *1 1/4* **Ballinger Ridge**[20] [520] 5-9-1 65 NChalmers[(5)] 6 51
(AMBalding) *led: rdn over 2f out: hdd 1f out: fdd ins fnl f* **5/2**[1]
0- **4** *1* **Bold Trump**[215] [2925] 3-8-4 ow1 SWhitworth 4 49
(Jean-ReneAuvray) *chsd ldrs: rdn and effrt over 2f out: c wd into st: one pce over 1f out* **7/1**
6-64 **5** *shd* **Sonderborg**[20] [521] 3-7-8 52 ow1 (p) JFMcDonald[(5)] 3 44
(GLMoore) *cl up: rdn to press ldrs over 2f out: cl up over 1f out: nt qckn u.p* **4/1**[3]
00-0 **6** *2* **Dulce De Leche**[6] [617] 3-8-3 (be) PDoe 12 43
(SCWilliams) *cl up: jnd ldr 1/2-way: rdn and stl upsides over 1f out: wknd fnl f* **7/2**[2]
00-0 **7** *2* **Prince Valentine**[10] [598] 3-8-3 65 CCatlin 1 38
(DBFeek) *trckd ldrs: effrt and cl up over 2f out: c wdst of all into st: sn btn* **10/1**
00-4 **8** *hd* **Janes Valentine**[19] [534] 4-9-1 45 GBaker 10 32
(JJBridger) *s.i.s: hld up in last: outpcd 3f out: hanging over 1f out: kpt on* **20/1**
0-00 **9** *5* **Ivory Venture**[19] [538] 4-9-1 45 DSweeney 5 20
(DKIvory) *towards rr: rdn 3f out: wknd over 2f out* **50/1**
0-0 **10** *5* **Saucy Pickle**[17] [553] 3-7-12 JoannaBadger 7 7
(MissZCDavison) *a towards rr: rdn and struggling 3f out* **100/1**
060- **11** *3* **The Footballresult**[140] [4958] 3-7-12 63 MHenry 11 —
(MrsGHarvey) *towards rr: rdn 1/2-way: sn outpcd and bhd* **33/1**
00-0 **12** *7* **Far For Lulu**[12] [587] 3-7-9 35 LisaJones[(3)] 8 —
(WRMuir) *prom 3f: sn wknd: t.o* **66/1**
1m 26.22s (0.22) **Going Correction** +0.15s/f (Slow)
**WFA** 3 from 4yo+ 17lb **12** Ran SP% **124.7**
Speed ratings: **104,102,100,99,99 97,94,94,88,83 79,71**CSF £228.55 TOTE £6.30: £2.70, £12.60, £1.10; EX 306.00.
**Owner** Tarka Two Racing **Bred** S D Bevan **Trained** Kentisbeare, Devon

**FOCUS**
Modest maiden form but a decent time for the class of contest.

**NOTEBOOK**
**Adantino** was always going well and did it nicely to finally break his duck at the 27th attempt. Spencer got a decent tune out of him and the refitting of blinkers was a plus too.
**Devine Command** ran his best race so far. He appreciated the drop from ten furlongs but should get a mile.
**Ballinger Ridge** adopted his customary front-running role but was cut down at the furlong pole. His rider reported that he had hung right. *Official explanation: jockey said gelding hung right in the final 2f*
**Bold Trump** showed more in this grade than he had in a Newbury maiden last July on his only previous start. He should come on for the run.
**Sonderborg** was returning to what is probably her best trip. She has had plenty of opportunities and looks hard work for her riders.
**Dulce De Leche** failed to see out this two furlong longer trip.

### 661 BET DIRECT NO Q ON 08000 93 66 93 BANDED STKS 1m 5f (P)
2:40 (2:40) (H) 4-Y-0+ **£1,470** (£420; £210) **Stalls** Low

Form RPR
600- **1** **Montosari**[24] [3126] 5-9-2 40 JFanning 12 47
(PMitchell) *prog and prom 8f out: trckd ldr gng easily 3f out: shkn up to ld over 1f out: rdn clr* **9/2**[2]
46-3 **2** *3* **Buz Kiri (USA)**[19] [539] 6-9-2 35 PDoe 10 43
(AWCarroll) *chsd ldr 8f out: rdn to ld over 3f out: hdd and one pce over 1f out* **11/2**[3]
0-42 **3** *1* **The Last Mohican**[20] [528] 5-9-2 35 (p) JPSpencer 9 41
(PHowling) *chsd ldr to 8f out: pushed along 5f out: cl up u.p 2f out: one pce after* **4/1**[1]
0-00 **4** *3/4* **Little Richard (IRE)**[14] [568] 5-9-2 30 (p) VSlattery 7 40
(MWellings) *chsd ldrs: drvn 5f out: outpcd 3f out: styd on wl again fr over 1f out* **33/1**
0320 **5** *1 1/2* **Khuzdar (IRE)**[1] [653] 5-8-13 40 (p) DCorby[(3)] 6 38
(ABailey) *dwlt: hld up in rr: stdy prog 5f out: pressed ldrs 2f out: sn rdn and fnd nil* **9/2**[2]
0-02 **6** *1* **Radiant Bride**[13] [579] 4-8-12 35 (p) DarrenWilliams 14 37
(KRBurke) *dwlt: hld up in last: sme prog but outpcd 3f out: kpt on one pce fnl 2f* **8/1**
0-00 **7** *1/2* **Polka Princess**[14] [570] 4-8-7 40 ow2 (p) LTreadwell[(7)] 1 38
(MWellings) *t.k.h: hld up midfield: outpcd over 3f out: kpt on one pce fnl 2f: n.d* **25/1**
60-0 **8** *shd* **Birth Of The Blues**[24] [495] 8-9-2 40 RSmith 13 36
(ACharlton) *dwlt: hld up in rr: effrt 4f out: sn outpcd: kpt on one pce and no ch after* **14/1**
00-5 **9** *hd* **Walker Bay (IRE)**[24] [495] 6-9-2 40 PDobbs 2 36
(JCFox) *settled in midfield: effrt but outpcd over 3f out: one pce u.p fr over 2f out* **16/1**
05-0 **10** *7* **Magic Charm**[30] [430] 6-9-2 35 SWhitworth 5 26
(AGNewcombe) *dwlt: hld up in rr: pushed along over 4f out: sn outpcd and btn* **10/1**
200- **11** *1 1/4* **Giko**[125] [5312] 10-9-2 40 CCatlin 11 24
(JaneSouthcombe) *chsd ldrs: drvn 5f out: outpcd over 3f out: wknd wl over 1f out* **12/1**
6/0- **12** *4* **Bathwick Dream**[67] [6085] 7-9-2 40 GBaker 3 19
(BRMillman) *rrd s but led: rdn and hdd over 3f out: wknd* **50/1**
00-0 **13** *3* **Gemma**[19] [537] 4-8-12 35 (p) DSweeney 8 14
(PJMakin) *midfield tl wknd over 3f out* **50/1**
00/0 **14** *3* **Philosophic**[13] [579] 10-8-9 35 (p) SJDonohoe[(7)] 4 10
(MrsLCJewell) *a in rr: last and u.p 5f out: sn bhd* **50/1**
2m 49.17s (1.09) **Going Correction** +0.15s/f (Slow)
**WFA** 4 from 5yo+ 4lb **14** Ran SP% **124.9**
Speed ratings: **102,100,99,99,98 97,97,97,97,92 91,89,87,85**CSF £29.63 TOTE £5.50: £1.80, £2.90, £2.30; EX 50.10.
**Owner** Caterham Racing (jdrp) **Bred** S Gollogly **Trained** Epsom, Surrey

**FOCUS**
A fair winning time for the grade but the form is weak.

**NOTEBOOK**
**Montosari** was fit from hurdling but hitherto had been exposed as a poor maiden on the Flat. He moved up quickly to join the leaders in the back straight and, clearly going best thereafter, scored decisively.
**Buz Kiri(USA)** again found one too good, and on this occasion there appeared no reason to criticise his attitude.
**The Last Mohican** was sampling this surface for the first time but had been running creditably on Fibresand of late. A step back up in trip should help.
**Little Richard(IRE)** was doing his best work late on, having become outpaced. This looks his level and a return to two miles will suit him.
**Khuzdar(IRE)** showed more than he had the previous day but his appetite for a fight is clearly lacking.

### 662 BET DIRECT NO Q BANDED STKS (DIV II) 1m (P)
3:10 (3:11) (H) 3-Y-0+ **£1,638** (£468; £234) **Stalls** High

Form RPR
01-3 **1** **Piquet**[19] [537] 6-9-7 45 GBaker 12 49
(JJBridger) *taken down early: hld up and last to over 4f out: prog on inner over 2f out: led jst over 1f out: sn clr: comf* **11/2**[2]
004- **2** *2* **Wanna Shout**[27] [4439] 6-9-4 45 RMiles[(3)] 3 45
(RDickin) *prom: chsd ldng pair over 2f out: rdn whn nt clr run over 1f out: styd on to take 2nd last 150y: no imp on wnr* **12/1**
504- **3** *2* **Larad (IRE)**[203] [3289] 3-8-2 45 (b[1]) DKinsella 4 40
(JSMoore) *pressed ldr: upsides fr over 3f out: ev ch over 1f out: sn one pce* **25/1**
3-25 **4** *1/2* **Wilom (GER)**[19] [535] 6-9-7 45 MFenton 1 39
(MRHoad) *sn led: jnd over 3f out: hdd jst over 1f out: immediately btn* **7/2**[1]
/00- **5** *shd* **Chocolate Boy (IRE)**[35] [6257] 5-9-7 45 (p) SWhitworth 2 39
(GLMoore) *midfield: snatched up over 4f out: lost pl and plenty to do in rr over 2f out: rdn and r.o fnl f: nvr nr ldrs* **16/1**
4-03 **6** *nk* **Ladywell Blaise (IRE)**[19] [535] 7-9-7 45 NPollard 5 38
(JJBridger) *towards rr: prog 3f out: rdn over 2f out: nt pce to rch ldrs* **6/1**[3]
-040 **7** *shd* **Geespot**[10] [599] 5-9-2 45 (p) JFMcDonald[(5)] 7 38
(DJSFfrenchDavis) *cl up: rdn and outpcd over 2f out: one pce after* **8/1**

00-2 **8** ½ **Miss Peaches**[19] 533 6-9-0 45 KristinStubbs(7) 8 37
(GGMargarson) *prom: lost pl and pushed along over 2f out: one pce and no hdwy after* **7/2**[1]

00-0 **9** 1¾ **Onefortheboys (IRE)**[30] 434 5-9-0 40 RoryMoore(7) 6 33
(DFlood) *prom: outpcd and hrd rdn over 2f out: fdd* **8/1**

00-3 **10** *10* **Zolushka (IRE)**[28] 451 3-7-13 45 FPFerris(3) 11 11
(BWDuke) *racd wd: in tch: rdn 1/2-way: struggling fr wl over 2f out: sn bhd* **16/1**

0-00 **11** *nk* **Original Sin (IRE)**[13] 575 4-9-7 45 PDoe 10 10
(SDow) *hld up in rr: wknd 3f out: sn bhd* **33/1**

00-0 **12** *19* **Adriatic Adventure (IRE)**[11] 591 3-8-2 40 ADaly 9 —
(JLSpearing) *plld hrd early and hld up: last and wkng 1/2-way: sn t.o* **50/1**

1m 40.34s (0.83) **Going Correction** +0.15s/f (Slow)
**WFA** 3 from 4yo+ 19lb **12** Ran SP% **124.5**
Speed ratings: **101,99,97,96,96 96,96,95,93,83 83,64**CSF £72.50 TOTE £6.50: £2.50, £4.20, £8.60; EX 118.90.
**Owner** J J Bridger **Bred** D E And Mrs J Cash **Trained** Liphook, Hants

**FOCUS**
Just a weak race, but a fair time, nearly two seconds faster than the first division.

**NOTEBOOK**
**Piquet**, third in a similar race over ten furlongs here on her previous outing, was not inconvenienced by this drop back to a mile and ran out a comfortable winner. She should continue to go well in similarly weak events whilst in this sort of form.
**Wanna Shout**, with the cheekpieces left off on her return to the level after a couple of unsuccessful spins over hurdles, ran well on her first outing on Polytrack.
**Larad(IRE)**, racing for the first time since July, stepping up two furlongs in trip, and with the blinkers replacing cheekpieces, shaped respectably.
**Wilom(GER)** again failed to find that much under pressure.
**Chocolate Boy(IRE)**, dropped back in trip and with the cheekpieces on, was reported to have lost his action five furlongs out. *Official explanation: jockey said gelding lost its action*
**Miss Peaches** failed to confirm the promise she showed on her return from a break over course and distance.

## 663 LITTLEWOODS BET DIRECT BANDED STKS 1m 2f (P)
**3:40** (3:40) (H) 4-Y-0+ **£1,501** (£429; £214) **Stalls** Low

Form RPR

300- **1** **Theatre Lady (IRE)**[109] 5622 6-8-8 30 SJDonohoe(7) 3 48
(PDEvans) *racd on inner: cl up: effrt 2f out: drvn and r.o fnl f to ld nr fin* **5/1**[2]

60-4 **2** *nk* **Colne Valley Amy**[19] 535 7-8-10 40 (b) AQuinn(5) 4 47
(GLMoore) *pressed ldrs: rdn to ld wl over 1f out: kpt on u.p: hdd nr fin* **5/1**[2]

00-6 **3** ½ **Private Seal**[24] 495 9-8-8 40 (tp) MHalford(7) 8 46
(JulianPoulton) *racd in midfield: pushed along 4f out: effrt u.p 2f out: styd on wl fnl f: nrst fin* **20/1**

060- **4** ¾ **Achilles Rainbow**[71] 6055 5-8-8 40 AReilly(7) 5 45
(KRBurke) *hld up in midfield: prog to press ldrs 2f out: rdn and nt qckn over 1f out: kpt on same pce* **33/1**

06-3 **5** *nk* **Ginger Ice**[19] 534 4-9-0 40 (v[1]) NPollard 12 44
(GGMargarson) *s.s: t.k.h and hld up in last pair: stdy prog gng wl fr 3f out: effrt over 1f out: sn rdn and nt qckn* **8/1**[3]

-424 **6** *shd* **Dancing Tilly**[19] 545 6-8-10 40 THamilton(5) 10 44
(RAFahey) *racd towards rr: rdn wl over 4f out: prog u.p over 2f out: c wdst of all st: styd on one pce fnl f* **4/1**[1]

0-00 **7** ¾ **Thats All Jazz**[19] 536 6-9-1 40 MTebbutt 6 43
(CRDore) *s.s: hld up in last: plenty to do over 2f out: prog over 1f out: styd on: nt rch ldrs* **16/1**

200- **8** 1½ **Boom Or Bust (IRE)**[39] 5048 5-9-1 40 (p) VSlattery 11 40
(MissKMGeorge) *racd in midfield: effrt and rdn over 2f out: no imp ldrs fr over 1f out* **14/1**

000- **9** 1½ **Prince Ivor**[48] 6206 4-9-0 40 PDobbs 1 37
(JCFox) *mde most to wl over 1f out: wknd* **66/1**

060- **10** *3* **Gracious Air (USA)**[70] 6068 6-9-1 40 (v[1]) JFanning 9 32
(JRWeymes) *hld up in rr: prog on wd outside fr 1/2-way: jnd ldr over 3f out: stl ev ch wl over 1f out: wknd rapidly* **20/1**

00-0 **11** *8* **Ro Eridani**[19] 533 4-9-0 40 DKinsella 2 17
(TJEtherington) *racd freely: pressed ldr to over 3f out: wknd rapidly* **33/1**

000/ **12** 3½ **Italian Counsel (IRE)**[184] 5042 7-8-8 30 LTreadwell(7) 13 11
(LADace) *chsd ldrs: pushed along 1/2-way: wknd u.p over 3f out* **5/1**[2]

01/0 **13** *dist* **Rodiak**[14] 568 5-9-1 40 (b) GCarter 7 —
(PRHedger) *prom to 4f out: wknd rapidly: t.o* **12/1**

2m 10.01s (2.62) **Going Correction** +0.15s/f (Slow)
**WFA** 4 from 5yo+ 1lb **13** Ran SP% **118.3**
Speed ratings: **95,94,94,93,93 93,92,91,90,88 81,78,—**CSF £27.93 TOTE £5.80: £2.40, £3.30, £5.80; EX 30.40.
**Owner** Waterline Racing Club **Bred** Terry Keaney **Trained** Pandy, Gwent

**FOCUS**
A blanket finish, but fair form for the level of race by the front two.

**NOTEBOOK**
**Theatre Lady(IRE)** had only managed one win in her previous 51 starts but, dropped in grade on her return from a 109-day break, had the race run to suit and ran out a narrow winner. Given everything fell right for her, combined with her overall win-to-runs record, she may struggle to follow up.
**Colne Valley Amy** has not won for a long time but, up two furlongs in trip, she was only just denied.
**Private Seal**, with the cheekpieces back on, posted a pleasing effort. He has not won for a long time, but there may be a banded stakes in him.
**Achilles Rainbow** is still a maiden, but this was an encouraging effort on this step up in trip and drop in grade.
**Ginger Ice** did not run badly in a first-time visor.
**Dancing Tilly**, a beaten favourite at Southwell last time, again failed to justify market confidence. She remains a maiden.
**Italian Counsel(IRE)**, in good form over hurdles when last seen in August, proved disappointing on his return to the level. He has never won on the Flat.

## 664 BETDIRECT.CO.UK (S) STKS 1m 2f (P)
**4:10** (4:12) (H) 4-Y-0+ **£1,519** (£434; £217) **Stalls** Low

Form RPR

00-0 **1** **Scotty's Future (IRE)**[13] 577 6-9-1 81 JPSpencer 3 49+
(DRLoder) *hld up: prog to trck ldrs over 2f out: nt clr run over 1f out: pushed along to chse ldr ins fnl f: led last strides* **30/100**[1]

01-0 **2** *hd* **Absolute Utopia (USA)**[24] 495 11-9-6 63 ADaly 8 54+
(JLSpearing) *sn trckd ldrs: effrt to ld over 1f out and kicked on: hdd last strides* **6/1**[2]

500- **3** *2* **Senor Toran (USA)**[59] 6128 4-8-11 46 LPKeniry(3) 10 45
(PBurgoyne) *trckd ldrs: led 1/2-way: rdn and hdd over 1f out: one pce* **33/1**

00-0 **4** 1½ **Margarets Wish**[14] 567 4-8-4 30 NChalmers(5) 5 37
(TWall) *hld up in rr: prog over 2f out: rdn and kpt on same pce fr over 1f out* **33/1**

/00- **5** ¾ **Broughtons Mill**[15] 1585 9-9-1 30 JFanning 13 41
(JASupple) *hld up: prog on outer 3f out: chsd ldrs 2f out: one pce after* **40/1**

0/5- **6** *nk* **Lady At Leisure (IRE)**[8] 226 4-8-9 50 MTebbutt 9 35
(JulianPoulton) *hld up: prog over 3f out: pressed ldrs 2f out: one pce after* **33/1**

055- **7** ¾ **Estrella Levante**[59] 6128 4-8-7 52 (e[1]) JemmaMarshall(7) 6 39
(GLMoore) *t.k.h: hld up: lost tch ldrs over 3f out: nudged along and kpt on fnl f: no ch* **12/1**[3]

000- **8** *shd* **Waterline Dancer (IRE)**[57] 6144 4-8-4 45 ow2 (t) SJDonohoe(7) 7 36
(PDEvans) *racd freely: pressed ldr to over 5f out: stl cl up 2f out: wknd over 1f out* **14/1**

0 **9** *5* **Alimiste (IRE)**[17] 555 4-8-9 MFenton 2 25
(IAWood) *prom tl lost pl 4f out: no ch after* **33/1**

005- **P** **Geography (IRE)**[78] 4371 4-8-7 53 (p) RoryMoore(7) 4 —
(PButler) *stmbld s and rdr lost irons: led to 5f out: sn bhd: p.u ins fnl f* **25/1**

2m 12.04s (4.65) **Going Correction** +0.15s/f (Slow)
**WFA** 4 from 6yo+ 1lb **10** Ran SP% **123.6**
Speed ratings: **87,86,85,84,83 83,82,82,78,—**CSF £2.56 TOTE £1.20: £1.02, £1.30, £5.80; EX 2.60.The winner was bought in for 18,000gns
**Owner** Lucayan Stud **Bred** William J Hamilton **Trained** Newmarket, Suffolk

**FOCUS**
An incredibly slow time, more than two seconds slower the the preceding banded stakes. Scotty's Future did not have to run anywhere near his rating of 81 to win, and the third is one of several who anchor the form.

**NOTEBOOK**
**Scotty's Future(IRE)** had 23lb in hand over the runner-up on official ratings, so did not have to run to anywhere near his mark to end a losing run stretching back to May 2002. He is in the Lincoln, but his trainer indicated he has no intention of going there.
**Absolute Utopia(USA)** bounced back to form after a poor effort on his previous outing, but he was flattered to get so close to the winner.
**Senor Toran(USA)** appeared to appreciate this step back up in trip and this is clearly his level.
**Margarets Wish**, up in trip and making her Polytrack debut, had it all to do at the weights and ran as well as could have been expected.
**Broughtons Mill**, back on the Flat after three unsuccessful runs over hurdles, was another who had very little chance at the weights.

## 665 BET DIRECT INTERACTIVE AMATEUR RIDERS' BANDED STKS 6f (P)
**4:40** (4:41) (H) 4-Y-0+ **£1,281** (£366; £183) **Stalls** Low

Form RPR

00-6 **1** **Redoubtable (USA)**[22] 502 13-11-0 35 MrSWalker 8 43
(DWChapman) *dwlt: sn rcvrd to chse ldng pair: chsd clr ldr 1/2-way: clsd to ld wl over 1f out: sn clr* **11/2**[2]

00-3 **2** *3* **Packin Em In**[20] 527 6-10-11 35 MrEDehdashti(3) 11 34
(JRBoyle) *racd in midfield and wl off the pce: prog over 2f out: bmpd along and r.o to take 2nd last 75y: no ch w wnr* **6/1**[3]

400 **3** 1¼ **Threat**[15] 565 8-10-9 35 MissAWallace(5) 2 30
(JMBradley) *led for 100y: chsd ldr to 1/2-way: cl 3rd and clr of rest 2f out: one pce after* **10/1**

050/ **4** ¾ **Tiny Tim (IRE)**[491] 4970 6-10-7 35 MrSGoswell(7) 3 28
(AMBalding) *hld up bhd ldrs: outpcd after 2f: nudged along and nt on terms 2f out: rdn and r.o fnl f: no ch* **10/1**

000- **5** ¾ **Maron**[21] 3610 7-11-0 35 (b) MrPCowley 1 26
(FJordan) *s.s: rcvrd to ld after 100y and sn wl clr: hdd and fdd wl over 1f out* **12/1**

000- **6** 1¼ **Grand View**[158] 4546 8-10-9 35 (p) MrBKing(5) 6 22
(JRWeymes) *hld up in last trio and sn wl bhd: r.o fr 2f out: hopeless task* **5/1**[1]

-500 **7** *nk* **Pooka's Daughter (IRE)**[12] 588 4-10-11 35 MrSDobson(3) 12 21
(JMBradley) *wl in rr and wl off the pce: rdn and effrt over 2f out: nvr rchd ldrs* **14/1**

0006 **8** *1* **Flying Faisal (USA)**[1] 654 6-10-9 35 MissMSowerby(5) 10 18
(JMBradley) *hld up wl in rr and wl off the pce: modest late prog: no ch* **5/1**[1]

000- **9** *5* **Beenaboutabit**[167] 4291 6-10-9 35 (p) MrJJBest(5) 7 3
(MrsLCJewell) *chsd ldrs but sn outpcd: drvn 1/2-way: wknd 2f out* **25/1**

60-0 **10** ½ **Miss Celerity**[20] 520 4-10-9 30 MrLNewnes(5) 9 2
(MJHaynes) *chsd ldrs but sn outpcd: no prog over 2f out: fdd* **10/1**

0/0- **11** 2½ **Katali**[56] 6155 7-10-7 30 GBartley(7) 13 —
(ABailey) *wnt rt s: a wl in rr* **50/1**

0-56 **12** *5* **Good Form (IRE)**[20] 527 4-10-7 30 (b[1]) MrWPKavanagh(7) 5 —
(MissKMGeorge) *racd in midfield and sn outpcd: u.p and no prog 1/2-way : sn wknd* **16/1**

500- **13** *1* **Kafil (USA)**[221] 2743 10-10-7 35 (v) MissDonnaHandley(7) 4 —
(JJBridger) *squeezed out after 1f: stmbld and nrly uns rdr: bhd after* **20/1**

1m 14.5s (1.58) **Going Correction** +0.15s/f (Slow) **13** Ran SP% **121.1**
Speed ratings: **95,91,89,88,87 85,85,83,77,76 73,66,65**CSF £38.24 TOTE £7.80: £2.00, £2.50, £3.50; EX 45.30 Place 6 £107.57, Place 5 £47.91.
**Owner** David W Chapman **Bred** Wooden Horse Inv Inc And Post Syndicate **Trained** Stillington, N Yorks

■ Stewards Enquiry : Mr W P Kavanagh four-day ban: careless riding (Feb 24, 27, Mar 1)

**FOCUS**
Varying standards of jockeyship in this weak sprint. The 13-year-old Redoubtable won in style, which says it all.

**NOTEBOOK**
**Redoubtable(USA)** had the assistance of the best amateur in the race and, at the grand old age of 13, ran out a clear-cut winner. This was a fine training performance to keep the 'old boy' so sweet.
**Packin Em In** stayed on well without ever looking likely to get to the winner and should do better back over another furlong.
**Threat**, on a long losing run, looked to have every chance.
**Tiny Tim(IRE)**, still a maiden, caught the eye on his first start for 491 days.
**Maron**, with the blinkers back on, went off too fast.
**Grand View**, with the cheekpieces replacing blinkers, was given too much to do on his return from a break.
**Flying Faisal(USA)** does not win very often and he never looked like doing so on this occasion.
T/Plt: £83.40 to a £1 stake. Pool: £36,611.80. 320.45 winning tickets. T/Qpdt: £27.30 to a £1 stake. Pool: £2,337.70. 63.15 winning tickets. JN

[625]**SOUTHWELL** (L-H)

Tuesday, February 3

**OFFICIAL GOING: Standard**

## 666 BET DIRECT ON SKY ACTIVE AMATEUR RIDERS' H'CAP 2m (F)
**2:00** (2:02) (F) (0-80,80) 4-Y-0+ **£2,884** (£824; £412) **Stalls** Low

Form RPR

0-40 **1** **Bustling Rio (IRE)**[10] 603 8-10-7 **60** MsCWilliams 3 71
(PCHaslam) *hld up: hdwy 1/2-way: trckd ldrs over 4f out: led 2f out: sn rdn clr* **3/1**[2]

53-3 **2** 2 1/2 **Altitude Dancer (IRE)**[7] 616 4-9-9 **59** StaceyRenwick(5) 7 67
(PABlockley) *chsd ldr: pushed along and sltly outpcd 1/2-way: hdwy and cl up over 4f out: rdn to ld 3f out: hdd 2f out and sn onepce* **15/8**[1]

2-20 **3** 8 **Glory Quest (USA)**[11] 592 7-11-6 **73** MissEJJones 8 71
(MissGayKelleway) *trckd ldrs: hdwy 5f out: ev ch over 3f out tl rdn and outpcd over 2f out* **5/1**[3]

522- **4** 3/4 **Reminiscent (IRE)**[36] 6249 5-11-0 **67** (b) MissEJohnsonHoughton 5 65
(RFJohnsonHoughton) *hld up in tch: swtchd ins and hdwy 1/2-way: led over 5f out tl rdn along and hdd 3f out: sn wknd* **3/1**[2]

20-0 **5** dist **Paula Lane**[11] 592 4-10-6 **70** MrAshleePrice(5) 6 —
(RCurtis) *prom: led 1/2-way: pushed along and hdd 5f out: sn wknd* **40/1**

6-64 **6** 1 1/2 **High Diva**[12] 583 5-8-13 **45** oh2 ow3 MrsKHills(7) 2 —
(JRBest) *keen: led to 1/2-way: sn lost pl and bhd fnl 4f* **33/1**

300- **7** dist **La Muette (IRE)**[13] 5852 4-11-4 **80** ONelmes(3) 1 —
(MAppleby) *a bhd: t.o fnl 6f* **25/1**

3m 50.62s (-1.88) **Going Correction** +0.025s/f (Slow)
**WFA** 4 from 5yo+ 6lb **7** Ran SP% **110.7**
Speed ratings: **105,103,99,99,— —,—**CSF £8.40 CT £23.70 TOTE £3.20: £1.70, £1.50; EX 9.10.
**Owner** Rio Stainless Engineering Limited **Bred** Loualin Bloodstock **Trained** Middleham Moor, N Yorks

**FOCUS**

A decent winning time for a race of its type due to the strong pace, but the leaders probably went off too fast. The winner was returning to near his best and the form looks solid for the grade. The winner raced alone on the inside for much of the race suggesting the usual track bias favouring the middle was not relevant on this occasion.

**NOTEBOOK**

**Bustling Rio(IRE)**, who has a fair record round here, raced alone down the inside for much of the contest and saved valuable ground as a result. The strong pace also helped and he could be called the winner some way out. This was not a good race, but he is a consistent and versatile performer who should continue to pay his way.

**Altitude Dancer(IRE)**, having his second start for Blockley, stays well and was another suited by the strong pace. He may be able to nick a race on this surface, but does not look the ideal ride for an amateur.

**Glory Quest(USA)** has never appeared to stay this far.

**Reminiscent(IRE)**, runner-up in his last four visits to the track, was sent on too far out and was soon on the retreat. He is better than this, but does not win very often.

**Paula Lane** was beaten a long way.

## 667 BET DIRECT INTERACTIVE H'CAP 1m (F)
**2:30** (2:32) (E) (0-70,69) 3-Y-0+ **£3,283** (£938; £469) **Stalls** Low

Form RPR

-221 **1** **Simply The Guest (IRE)**[12] 582 5-8-11 **53** (t) KimTinkler 3 67
(DonEnricoIncisa) *prom tl pushed along and lost pl on inner after 3f: hdwy over 2f out: sn rdn and styd on ent last: drvn to ld last 100yds* **13/2**[3]

5-10 **2** 1 1/4 **Penwell Hill (USA)**[4] 643 5-9-6 **69** PMakin(7) 7 80
(TDBarron) *cl up: led over 2f out: rdn clr over 1f out: hung lft ent last: hdd & wknd last 100 yds* **5/2**[1]

01-4 **3** 5 **Topton (IRE)**[31] 419 10-9-13 **69** (b) KDalgleish 11 69
(PHowling) *s.i.s and bhd: pushed along 1/2-way: hdwy over 2f out: styng on whn bmpd over 1f out: kpt on ins last: nrst fin* **12/1**

1-00 **4** 1 **Kingston Town (USA)**[11] 590 4-9-8 **67** (p) J-PGuillambert(3) 10 65
(NPLittmoden) *midfield: hdwy on outer over 2f out: rdn to chse ldrs and edgd lft over 1f out: sn btn* **10/1**

000- **5** 3/4 **Bramantino (IRE)**[270] 1502 4-8-6 **55** (b) NataliaGemelova(7) 9 51
(RAFahey) *chsd ldrs: rdn 2f out: styng on whn n.m.r and swtchd rt over 1f out: no imp* **50/1**

00-2 **6** 1/2 **Robin Sharp**[12] 582 6-8-6 **48** (vt) JQuinn 1 43
(JAkehurst) *led: rdn along 3f out: hdd & wknd 2f out* **14/1**

414- **7** 1 1/2 **Lockstock (IRE)**[53] 6169 6-9-9 **65** (b) SCarson 12 57
(MSSaunders) *cl up on outer: ev ch over 2f out: sn rdn and wknd wl over 1f out* **5/1**[2]

-113 **8** 3/4 **Rosti**[19] 533 4-8-4 **46** GFaulkner 5 36
(PCHaslam) *cl up: ev ch 3f out: sn rdn and wknd fnl 2f* **8/1**

023- **9** 3/4 **Zarin (IRE)**[52] 6178 6-9-13 **69** ACulhane 4 58
(DWChapman) *in tch: rdn along over 2f out: n o hdwy* **17/2**

455- **10** nk **Bond Millennium**[39] 6239 6-9-8 **64** FLynch 2 52
(BSmart) *a rr* **12/1**

0/0 **11** 6 **Bought Direct**[4] 643 5-9-4 **63** ABeech(3) 6 38
(RJSmith) *in tch: rdn along 3f out: sn wknd* **66/1**

000- **12** 12 **Laggan Minstrel (IRE)**[56] 6150 6-8-4 **45** ow1 DeanMcKeown 8 —
(PABlockley) *hld up: a rr* **25/1**

1m 44.76s (0.16) **Going Correction** +0.025s/f (Slow) **12** Ran SP% **118.7**
Speed ratings: **100,98,93,92,92 91,90,89,88,88 82,70**CSF £22.78 CT £198.63 TOTE £7.30: £2.40, £2.00, £2.70; EX 35.40.
**Owner** Don Enrico Incisa **Bred** Rathasker Stud **Trained** Middleham Moor, N Yorks
■ Stewards Enquiry : Natalia Gemelova one-day ban: careless riding (Feb 14)

**FOCUS**

An average handicap run at an ordinary pace, but the front two did finish clear and their form looks strong. This race again proved it is easier to come from off the pace at present than it was a few weeks ago.

**NOTEBOOK**

**Simply The Guest(IRE)** followed up his recent course and distance win with a dour success off an 8lb higher mark. He looked up against it turning in, but charged home as others faltered. He seems to have found a new lease of life and must be respected here over this trip.

**Penwell Hill(USA)**, who was four from five over this course and distance coming into the race, lost little in defeat and finished clear of the third-placed horse. He has climbed up the weights, but is another who must be respected at this trip and track.

**Topton(IRE)** was hampered when he started to make his run from off the pace and did well to finish third. He does not run on this surface much, but on this evidence is worth persevering with.

**Kingston Town(USA)**, returning to the scene of his sole win last November, ran well enough despite hanging left in the closing stages. However, he does not look particularly well treated.

**Bramantino(IRE)**, making his All-Weather debut on his first run since May, has slipped down the weights and was done no favours down the straight. This was a better effort, but he is not one to place much faith in.

**Robin Sharp**, runner-up to Simply The Guest last time, failed to get any nearer to that rival despite an 8lb pull.

**Lockstock(IRE)** looks to be handicapped up to his best at present.

## 668 £10 FREE BET @ BET DIRECT SKY ACTIVE MAIDEN STKS 7f (F)
**3:00** (3:01) (D) 3-Y-0+ **£3,347** (£1,030; £515; £257) **Stalls** Low

Form RPR

2 **1** **Marinaite**[12] 585 3-8-2 JBramhill 7 77+
(SRBowring) *cl up: led wl over 2f out: rdn clr wl over 1f out: hung lft ins last: styd on* **11/8**[1]

3 **2** 3 1/2 **Global Achiever**[11] 593 3-8-7 RFfrench 3 68
(GCHChung) *led: ridden along 3f out: sn hdd: drvn and kpt on same pce fr over 1f out* **5/1**

32-5 **3** 1 **Phluke**[27] 462 3-8-7 72 SCarson 2 66
(RFJohnsonHoughton) *cl up on inner: rdn along 3f out: drive and kpt on same pce fnl 2f* **9/2**[3]

242 **4** nk **Ile Facile (IRE)**[10] 597 3-8-7 70 IMongan 1 65
(NPLittmoden) *hampered after 1f: in tch: hdwy 3f out: rdn to chse ldrs 2f out: sn drvn and no imp* **2/1**[2]

**5** 8 **Zuloago (USA)** 3-8-2 ANicholls 4 40
(SLKeightley) *dwlt: sn in tch: rdn over 2f out and sn wknd* **100/1**

0-0 **6** 8 **Anacapri**[12] 585 4-9-2 DAllan(3) 5 20
(WSCunningham) *chsd ldrs: rdn along 1/2-way: sn wknd* **150/1**

**7** dist **Utah Flats (IRE)** 3-8-7 (p) PFitzsimons 6 —
(MrsJRRamsden) *sn outpcd and bhd* **28/1**

1m 31.3s (0.50) **Going Correction** +0.025s/f (Slow)
**WFA** 3 from 4yo 17lb **7** Ran SP% **115.4**
Speed ratings: **98,94,92,92,83 74,—**CSF £9.15 TOTE £2.70: £1.80, £2.10; EX 13.90.
**Owner** S R Bowring **Bred** S R Bowring **Trained** Edwinstowe, Notts

**FOCUS**

Just an average maiden for the time of year, and the pace was only ordinary. However, the winner is promising and has been rated as value for more than the bare margin.

**NOTEBOOK**

**Marinaite**, runner-up over a mile at this course on her debut, showed plenty of speed and had this won a long way out. She is from a family full of good Fibresand performers and looks sure to progress on this surface.

**Global Achiever**, well supported in the betting, took them along early on, but it was soon clear he was no match for the winner. This trip was more to his liking but, judged on the horses directly behind him, he will hardly get a favourable mark when handicapped.

**Phluke** is beginning to look exposed.

**Ile Facile(IRE)** looks in need of farther, but does not look the easiest of rides.

## 669 LITTLEWOODS BET DIRECT CONDITIONS STKS 6f (F)
**3:30** (3:32) (C) 3-Y-0+ **£9,117** (£3,458; £1,729; £786) **Stalls** Low

Form RPR

0-10 **1** **Massey**[8] 607 8-9-3 95 PMakin(7) 5 93
(TDBarron) *mde all: rdn over 1f out: styd on gamely ins last* **4/1**[2]

1243 **2** 3/4 **Soba Jones**[8] 607 7-9-4 75 JEdmunds 3 85
(JBalding) *trckd ldrs: hdwy over 2f out: rdn and edgd rt over 1f out: styd on wl fnl f* **11/1**

1-46 **3** 1/2 **Ellens Academy (IRE)**[8] 607 9-9-5 79 DAllan(3) 9 87
(EJAlston) *dwlt: in rr: hdwy over 2f out: rdn over 1f out: kpt on ins last* **7/1**[3]

-140 **4** nk **Quiet Times (IRE)**[8] 607 5-9-4 85 (b) GParkin 1 82
(KARyan) *a.p: effrt over 2f out and sn ev ch: rdn wl over 1f out: drvn and no ex ins last* **9/1**

000- **5** nk **Haydn (USA)**[142] 4914 3-8-9 85 JQuinn 6 87
(PWChapple-Hyam) *bmpd s: sn chsng ldrs: hdwy on outer 2f out: rdn over 1f out: one pce ins last* **4/1**[2]

1/4- **6** 4 **Kentucky King (USA)**[250] 1939 4-9-4 89 ACulhane 8 69
(PWHiatt) *bhd tl styd on fnl 2f: nvr a factor* **25/1**

00-4 **7** 1 **Bond Boy**[25] 486 7-9-4 90 FLynch 2 66
(BSmart) *cl up: effrt over 2f out and ev ch tl rdn and wknd wl over 1f out* **3/1**[1]

4-02 **8** 1 **Hello Roberto**[6] 619 3-7-12 77 JMackay 10 58
(MJPolglase) *dwlt: a rr* **22/1**

1/ **9** 10 **Full Pitch**[1676] 2512 8-9-4 IMongan 4 33
(WJenks) *in tch on inner: rdn along 1/2-way: grad wknd* **50/1**

2-22 **10** 3 **Muy Bien**[18] 547 3-8-3 78 (v) JBramhill 7 24
(JRJenkins) *wnt lft s: sn chsng ldrs: rdn over 2f out and sn wknd* **14/1**

1m 15.95s (-0.85) **Going Correction** +0.025s/f (Slow)
**WFA** 3 from 4yo+ 15lb **10** Ran SP% **112.7**
Speed ratings: **106,105,104,103,103 98,96,95,82,78**CSF £44.32 TOTE £4.60: £2.70, £2.20, £2.10; EX 58.20.
**Owner** J Edward Boynton **Bred** Sheikh Mohammed Bin Rashid Al Maktoum **Trained** Maunby, N Yorks
■ Massey was winning this race for the second successive year.

**FOCUS**

A competitive sprint run at a sound pace. The first five finished in a heap, so the form gives out mixed signals, but the winner is capable of better.

**NOTEBOOK**

**Massey**, who won his only previous start over this course and distance, needs to get to the front and, despite having plenty of challengers, managed to win that battle. He has a good record when in front early on, and showed bags of determination to see off the late finishers. This was a good effort, but he is vulnerable when taken on for the lead.

**Soba Jones** had 14lb to find on adjusted official ratings and does drag the form down somewhat.

**Ellens Academy(IRE)**, another with plenty to find on official figures, again ran his race and, although he is not the force of old, should be up to winning a similar race on this surface.

**Quiet Times(IRE)** got as close to the winner as adjusted official figures suggested he should.

**Haydn(USA)**, the winner of a maiden when with Aidan O'Brien, showed enough on his first start for his new trainer to suggest he has a future in this country.

**Bond Boy** failed to progress from his improved effort at Wolverhampton. He has yet to prove he is as good on artificial surfaces as he is on turf. *Official explanation: jockey said gelding ran too free in the early stages*

**Hello Roberto** *Official explanation: jockey said filly had lost her action*

## 670 PRESS INTERACTIVE TO BET DIRECT (S) STKS 6f (F)
**4:00** (4:00) (G) 3-Y-0+ **£2,618** (£748; £374) **Stalls** Low

Form RPR

-426 **1** **Polar Haze**[5] 626 7-9-13 53 (v) JQuinn 2 66
(JPearce) *hld up in tch on inner: hdwy 2f out: rdn to ld ins last: sn drvn and jst hld on* **4/1**[2]

0-00 **2** *hd* **African Spur (IRE)**[12] [586] 4-9-2 66 DerekNolan(7) 7 61
(PABlockley) *cl up: effrt 2f out: rdn to ld over 1f out: hdd ins last: drvn and rallied wl nr fin: jst failed* **5/4**[1]

-320 **3** *2 ½* **Legalis (USA)**[10] [596] 6-9-9 57 (b) PFessey 1 54
(KARyan) *cl up: led wl over 2f out: sn rdn: hdd over 1f out and one pce ins last* **15/2**

15-5 **4** *1 ¼* **Jalouhar**[29] [436] 4-9-13 57 (p) KDalgleish 3 54
(BPJBaugh) *chsd ldrs on inner: rdn along and outpcd over 2f out: styd on uncder press ins last* **22/1**

040- **5** *3* **Dusty Wugg (IRE)**[136] [5070] 5-9-1 46 (p) ABeech(3) 5 36
(ADickman) *chsd ldrs: rdn over 2f out: wknd o ver 1f out* **40/1**

30-0 **6** *5* **Czar Wars**[8] [608] 9-9-4 66 (b) MSavage(5) 6 26
(JBalding) *cl up: ev ch over 2f out: sn rdn and wknd over 1f out* **11/1**

-464 **7** *½* **Lizhar (IRE)**[6] [617] 3-8-7 69 DeanMcKeown 8 24
(MJPolglase) *s.i.s: a rr* **7/1**[3]

00-0 **8** *1 ½* **Valuable Gift**[30] [433] 7-9-2 45 (be) ACooper(7) 4 20
(RCGuest) *led: rdn along and hdd wl over 2f out: sn wknd* **66/1**

300- **9** *8* **Mystery Mountain**[293] [1079] 4-9-2 60 DEgan(7) 9 —
(MrsJRRamsden) *in tch on outer: rdn along over 2f out and sn wknd* **10/1**

1m 17.14s (0.34) **Going Correction** +0.025s/f (Slow)
**WFA** 3 from 4yo+ 15lb **9** Ran SP% **114.4**
Speed ratings: **98,97,94,92,88 82,81,79,68**CSF £9.13 TOTE £3.80: £1.70, £1.20, £2.00; EX 18.10.There was no bid for the winner. African Spur was claimed for £6,000 by W I Bloomfield
**Owner** M M Foulger **Bred** Miss S E Hall **Trained** Newmarket, Suffolk
■ This was Jeff Pearce's first winner since getting his licence back.

**FOCUS**
An ordinary seller with little strength in depth, but run at a sound pace and fair form from the principals.

**NOTEBOOK**
**Polar Haze** saved valuable ground by sticking to the inside rail, a move which probably won him the race. All four of his wins have come at this track and this is clearly his trip.
**African Spur(IRE)** has been running in much better races than this and only just failed to get up. He travelled noticeably wider than the winner and that probably cost him the race. He is clearly capable of winning a similar contest.
**Legalis(USA)** goes well over this course and distance and ran his race without ever looking likely to hold the challengers. He is consistent, but does not win very often.
**Jalouhar** was possibly a little flattered as, like the winner, he saved ground down the inside.
**Lizhar(IRE)** tends to run well over this course and distance, but posted a most disappointing effort. *Official explanation: jockey said filly missed the break*

## 671 BET DIRECT FOOTBALL CASHBACKS H'CAP 1m 3f (F)
**4:30** (4:30) (E) (0-70,70) 4-Y-0+ **£3,339** (£715; £715) **Stalls** Low

Form RPR
-111 **1** **Fall In Line**[3] [645] 4-9-8 **66** 6ex JMackay 11 92+
(SirMarkPrescott) *in tch: hdwy to join ldrs over 5f out: led wl over 2f out and sn clr* **1/4**[1]

00-0 **2** *9* **Bressbee (USA)**[15] [564] 6-9-9 **70** (v) DNolan(5) 2 77
(JWUnett) *chsd ldrs tl rdn along and lost pl over 4f out: wd st and styd on u.p fnl 2f* **40/1**

05-0 **2** *dht* **Surdoue**[29] [440] 4-9-5 **63** PaulEddery 12 70
(PHowling) *hld up: stdy hdwy 1/2-way: trckd ldrs 4f out: rdn to chse wnr over 2f out: sn one pce: jnd for 2nd on line* **25/1**

-121 **4** *2 ½* **Delta Force**[12] [581] 5-9-0 **63** DerekNolan(7) 7 66
(PABlockley) *sn led: rdn along 4f out: hdd wl over 2f out and grad wknd* **10/1**[2]

156- **5** *6* **Melodian**[98] [5823] 9-8-2 **51** (b) MLawson(7) 5 44
(MBrittain) *bhd: hdwy 4f out: styd on fnl 2f: nvr a factor* **33/1**

06/0 **6** *nk* **Dalriath**[13] [541] 5-7-7 **40** DFox(5) 3 33
(MCChapman) *chsd ldr: rdn along 4f out: wknd 3f out* **150/1**

0-53 **7** *2* **East Cape**[22] [500] 7-7-12 **40** KimTinkler 9 30
(DonEnricoIncisa) *hld up and bhd: sme hdwy over 4f out: nvr a factor* **33/1**

-425 **8** *1* **Dubai Dreams**[4] [643] 4-8-12 **56** ACulhane 8 44
(MJPolglase) *chsd ldrs: rdn along hafway: sn wknd* **12/1**[3]

4-10 **9** *7* **Allied Victory (USA)**[15] [564] 4-9-11 **69** JQuinn 6 46
(EJAlston) *trcking ldrs whn hmpd after 1f: in tch tl rdn along and wknd over 4f out* **50/1**

/0-0 **10** *3* **Environment Audit**[21] [516] 5-9-13 **69** SWKelly 10 41
(JRJenkins) *chsd ldrs to 1/2-way: sn wknd* **50/1**

000- **11** *dist* **Banningham Blaze**[96] [4987] 4-9-8 **66** (v) JBramhill 1 —
(CRDore) *stdd s: a bhd: t.o fnl 4f* **66/1**

2-52 **F** **Shatin Special**[14] [571] 4-8-1 **45** (p) RFfrench 4 —
(GCHChung) *chsd ldrs whn nt much room and fell after 1f* **66/1**

2m 25.09s (-3.81) **Going Correction** +0.025s/f (Slow)
**WFA** 4 from 5yo+ 2lb **12** Ran SP% **116.5**
Speed ratings: **114,107,107,105,101 101,99,98,93,91** —,— TOTE £1.10: £1.02 TRIFECTA Plcs: B 12.60, S 4.30; EX: F-B 18.30, F-S 10.10; CSF F-B 12.38, F-S 7.09; TC: F-B-S 61.07, F-S-B 58.54.
**Owner** Neil Greig - Osborne House Ii **Bred** P D Player **Trained** Newmarket, Suffolk

**FOCUS**
An amazingly fast winning time for the class of contest. Although this was turned into a one-horse race, the winner being different class, the performance should not be underestimated.

**NOTEBOOK**
**Fall In Line** came right away in the straight and merely confirmed he is miles ahead of the handicapper. He was 20lb well in on official figures, but has shown enough so far to suggest he will be competitive when his new mark kicks in.
**Bressbee(USA)** ridden more patiently over this longer trip and making his first appearance here for two-and-a-half years, ran really well and is not badly treated on his form of a few years ago.
**Surdoue** ran his best race for some time, but his overall profile suggests he is one to be careful with.
**Delta Force**, who has been in cracking form of late, found this much tougher. He did not found much when asked for his effort, but stays much further than this and is not one to write off just yet.
**Melodian** never looked likely to take a hand in the finish, but should at least come on for this first start since October.
**Shatin Special** took a horrible fall.
T/Plt: £45.80 to a £1 stake. Pool: £40,079.70. 638.20 winning tickets. T/Qpdt: £19.80 to a £1 stake. Pool: £2,425.80. 90.50 winning tickets. JR

# 659 LINGFIELD (L-H)
## Wednesday, February 4

**OFFICIAL GOING: Standard**
There was a strong tailwind in the straight throughout the day.

## 672 BET DIRECT ON 0800 32 93 93 H'CAP 1m 2f (P)
**1:10** (1:10) (F) (0-52,52) 4-Y-0+ **£3,003** (£858; £429) **Stalls** Low

Form RPR
500- **1** **Brave Dane (IRE)**[25] [5945] 6-9-0 51 WRyan 11 57
(AWCarroll) *hld up in last pair: smooth prog fr over 2f out: swtchd to inner and carried hd awkwardly 1f out: nudged into ld last 150y:* **12/1**

-006 **2** *3* **Answered Promise (FR)**[7] [623] 5-8-11 51 RMiles(3) 2 52
(AWCarroll) *led: drvn and pressed over 2f out: hdd last 150y: no ch w wnr* **10/1**

B04- **3** *½* **Another Secret**[46] [6226] 6-8-13 50 (b) SWhitworth 13 50
(GLMoore) *hld up in last pair: prog 3f out: rdn 2f out: styd on one pce fr over 1f out* **11/1**

00-3 **4** *1 ½* **My Lilli (IRE)**[28] [463] 4-9-0 52 JQuinn 10 49
(PMitchell) *hld up in rr: prog on wd outside 4f out: drvn to chal over 2f out: wknd ins fnl f* **9/2**[2]

600- **5** *shd* **Shaman**[31] [2821] 7-9-1 52 IMongan 5 49
(GLMoore) *cl up: pressed ldr 3f out: hrd rdn and nt qckn over 1f out: wknd fnl f* **4/1**[1]

3020 **6** *1 ¼* **Pyrrhic**[4] [651] 5-8-13 50 (b) SWKelly 9 45
(RMFlower) *dwlt: racd in rr: rdn 3f out: plodded on one pce fnl 2f* **12/1**

10-5 **7** *3 ½* **Zinging**[29] [453] 5-8-13 50 GBaker 1 39
(JJBridger) *cl up: pushed along and effrt over 2f out: no imp on ldrs over 1f out: wknd fnl f* **10/1**

430- **8** *5* **Forever My Lord**[70] [6079] 6-8-13 50 NPollard 7 30
(JRBest) *chsd ldrs: lost pl 1/2-way: rdn and struggling 4f out: no ch over 2f out* **13/2**[3]

20-0 **9** *5* **Florenzar (IRE)**[12] [589] 6-8-6 50 ow1 SJDonohoe(7) 4 21
(PDEvans) *settled in rr: rdn and struggling over 3f out: no ch after* **33/1**

0/0- **10** *2 ½* **Forest Heath (IRE)**[259] [255] 7-8-12 49 (p) MTebbutt 8 15
(HJCollingridge) *chsd ldr to 3f out: sn wknd: eased fnl f* **16/1**

000- **11** *3* **Esperance (IRE)**[37] [6254] 4-8-13 51 CCatlin 14 12
(JAkehurst) *chsd ldrs: rididen and wknd wl over 3f out* **10/1**

0-02 **12** *dist* **Rex Romelio (IRE)**[6] [630] 5-8-13 50 (v) GFaulkner 12 —
(KRBurke) *racd wd: in tch: prog 1/2-way: sn rdn and wknd rapidly: t.o 3f out* **25/1**

2m 6.26s (-1.13) **Going Correction** -0.05s/f (Stan)
**WFA** 4 from 5yo+ 1lb **12** Ran SP% **115.2**
Speed ratings: **102,99,99,98,97 96,94,90,86,84 81,**—CSF £123.09 CT £1359.66 TOTE £15.70: £4.60, £3.90, £2.90; EX 192.70.
**Owner** Mrs E J Righton **Bred** Gainsborough Stud Management Ltd **Trained** Wixford, Warwicks

**FOCUS**
A low grade handicap and modest form, but the winner might hold his own in slightly better company when things drop right for him.

**NOTEBOOK**
**Brave Dane(IRE)**, who recorded his only previous win in the French provinces in 2001, has been running over hurdles. Making his All-Weather debut, he won very readily but is the type who needs everything to fall just right.
**Answered Promise(FR)** tried to make all the running but only succeeded in setting up the race for his stablemate.
**Another Secret**, who has been dropped another 3lb, stayed on to finish two places ahead of the favourite, her stable-companion.
**My Lilli(IRE)**, who made her move out wide, is running better of late.
**Shaman**, a winner over hurdles on his last outing a month ago, had his chance but could not produce a change of gear under pressure.
**Rex Romelio(IRE)** was reported to have lost his action. *Official explanation: jockey said gelding lost its action*

## 673 BETDIRECT.CO.UK MAIDEN STKS 6f (P)
**1:40** (1:40) (D) 3-Y-O **£4,114** (£1,266; £633; £316) **Stalls** Low

Form RPR
06-2 **1** **Toronto Heights (USA)**[9] [606] 3-9-0 76 JQuinn 4 71
(PWChapple-Hyam) *chsd ldng pair: pushed along over 2f out: effrt to ld on inner jst over 1f out: hrd drvn fnl f: hld on* **9/4**[2]

53-2 **2** *hd* **Saviours Spirit**[25] [489] 3-8-11 70 RMiles(3) 5 70
(TGMills) *led: jnd 1/2-way: rdn over 2f out: hdd jst over 1f out: kpt on fnl f: jst hld* **15/8**[1]

4 **3** *5* **Siera Spirit (IRE)**[25] [489] 3-8-9 IMongan 7 50
(MGQuinlan) *pressed ldr: upsides fr 1/2-way: rdn over 2f out: unable qck over 1f out: wknd ins fnl f* **4/1**[3]

26- **4** *1* **Orchestration (IRE)**[175] [4079] 3-9-0 SWhitworth 3 52
(JWUnett) *chsd ldng quartet: rdn over 2f out: no imp after: one pce* **10/1**

005- **5** *1* **Dancing Prince (IRE)**[124] [5338] 3-9-0 46 NCallan 1 49
(APJarvis) *s.i.s: sn in midfield: rdn over 2f out: kpt on one pce fr over 1f out* **50/1**

22-2 **6** *1 ¼* **Velvet Touch**[16] [561] 3-8-9 57 SWKelly 8 40
(JRJenkins) *s.i.s: sn chsd ldng trio: drvn 1/2-way: no imp 2f out: fdd* **16/1**

3 **7** *5* **Pickle**[14] [574] 3-8-9 CCatlin 11 25
(SCWilliams) *racd in last trio and sn wl off the pce: no ch over 2f out* **12/1**

5-5 **8** *1 ½* **Pure Emotion**[11] [597] 3-8-9 MartinDwyer 6 21
(WRMuir) *racd in midfield: rdn 1/2-way: no imp over 2f out: sn wknd* **20/1**

**9** *nk* **Clare Galway** 3-8-6 J-PGuillambert(3) 2 20
(TDMccarthy) *s.v.s: racd in detached last most of way* **100/1**

-6 **10** *1* **Luchi**[25] [489] 3-8-9 RSmith 10 17
(ACharlton) *wl in rr whn hit rail over 4f out: bhd after* **40/1**

06- **11** *1 ¼* **Cornwallis**[37] [6250] 3-9-0 JMackay 9 18
(RGuest) *racd in midfield: rdn 1/2-way: sn wknd* **33/1**

1m 12.92s **Going Correction** -0.05s/f (Stan) **11** Ran SP% **121.3**
Speed ratings: **98,97,91,89,88 86,80,78,77,76 74**CSF £6.83 TOTE £3.60: £1.10, £1.40, £1.50; EX 9.50.
**Owner** Mrs Jane Chapple-Hyam **Bred** Zubieta Ltd **Trained** Newmarket, Suffolk
■ This was Peter Chapple-Hyam's first winner since he returned from Hong Kong.
■ Stewards Enquiry : J-P Guillambert caution: used whip when out of contention

**FOCUS**
Just fair form, even though the first two finished clear.

**NOTEBOOK**
**Toronto Heights(USA)**, given a good lead by the pair duelling up front, came through on the inside in the straight to edge ahead and there did not seem much wrong with his attitude on this occasion.

**Saviours Spirit** tried to make all and stuck to his guns when headed by the winner, again shaping as if he will appreciate a seventh furlong.
**Siera Spirit(IRE)** matched strides for a long way with the eventual runner-up, whom she had finished behind on her debut.
**Orchestration(IRE)** was sold out of Roger Charlton's yard for 24,000 gns in October, having made his debut for Jeremy Noseda. He is now qualified for handicaps.
**Dancing Prince(IRE)**, gelded since his last run in the autumn, had the visor left off. He again failed to break on terms and never got to the leaders.
**Velvet Touch** was a little disappointing and has started to look exposed.

## 674 BET DIRECT INTERACTIVE CLASSIFIED CLAIMING STKS 6f (P)
2:10 (2:14) (F) 4-Y-O+ £2,933 (£838; £419) Stalls Low

Form RPR
10-0 **1** **Gun Salute**[11] [596] 4-8-9 53....(p) SWhitworth 3 59
(GLMoore) *chsd clr ldrs: clsd on outer to chall 2f out: led ent fnl f: drvn and kpt on wl: edgd lft last 50y* **9/1**
4130 **2** *1 1/4* **Double M**[7] [624] 7-9-3 56....(v) NCallan 2 64
(MrsLRichards) *chsd clr ldrs: clsd to ld on inner wl over 1f out: hdd ent fnl f: hld whn n.m.r last 50y* **3/1**[1]
40-0 **3** *2 1/2* **Scarrotto**[28] [469] 6-8-8 52....(be[1]) BReilly(5) 13 52
(SCWilliams) *chsd ldrs but nvr on terms: drvn over 2f out: kpt on fr over 1f out: nvr able to chal* **8/1**
05-0 **4** *hd* **Cargo**[28] [465] 5-7-10 47.... RoryMoore(7) 7 41
(HJCollingridge) *chsd clr ldrs: drvn over 2f out: kpt on one pce fr over 1f out* **9/1**
22-6 **5** *1/2* **Eastern Blue (IRE)**[6] [625] 5-9-0 50.... MFenton 5 51
(MrsLStubbs) *chsd clr ldrs: drvn over 2f out: sn no imp: one pce* **8/1**
-030 **6** *1/2* **Muqtadi (IRE)**[14] [575] 6-8-5 51.... MartinDwyer 6 40
(MQuinn) *wl in rr and wl off the pce: hrd rdn 2f out: kpt on fr over 1f out: no ch* **10/1**
0-52 **7** *1 1/2* **A Teen**[14] [576] 6-8-13 50.... SWKelly 10 44
(PHowling) *wl in rr and wl off the pce: kpt on fr over 1f out: no ch* **6/1**[2]
01-6 **8** *1* **Somerset West (IRE)**[7] [617] 4-8-0 58.... KristinStubbs(7) 14 35
(MrsLStubbs) *stdd s and swtchd to inner: wl in rr and wl off the pce: nvr a factor* **14/1**
243- **9** *1/2* **Boavista (IRE)**[110] [5627] 4-8-7 57.... SJDonohoe(7) 11 40
(PDEvans) *reluctant to go to post: rrd s: a wl in rr and wl off the pce* **20/1**
050 **10** *3/4* **Dances In Time**[15] [569] 4-8-6 55.... TWilliams 4 30
(CNKellett) *chsd ldr and sn wl clr of rest: wknd rapidly 2f out* **100/1**
-000 **11** *2 1/2* **Dunedin Rascal**[14] [575] 7-8-9 57....(b) SCarson 9 26
(EAWheeler) *a wl in rr and wl off the pce: hrd rdn and no rspnse 2f out* **16/1**
-051 **12** *1 3/4* **Mr Spliffy (IRE)**[20] [538] 5-8-7 53....(v) DarrenWilliams 1 18
(KRBurke) *led at blazing gallop and clr w one rival: hdd & wknd rapidly wl over 1f out* **15/2**[3]
000- **13** *5* **Spinning Jenni**[216] [2916] 4-8-0 54.... CCatlin 12 —
(JMBradley) *a wl bhd* **66/1**

1m 12.8s (-0.12) **Going Correction** -0.05s/f (Stan) **13** Ran SP% **122.2**
Speed ratings: **98,96,93,92,92 91,89,88,87,86 83,80,74**CSF £36.52 TOTE £10.70: £3.40, £1.80, £2.90; EX 56.10.Cargo was claimed by D J Flood for £5,000.
**Owner** R Henderson **Bred** S Crown **Trained** Woodingdean, E Sussex
■ Stewards Enquiry : S Whitworth caution: careless riding

**FOCUS**
Ordinary claiming form, but they went a decent gallop.

**NOTEBOOK**
**Gun Salute**, who became worked up at the start last time, was ridden more prominently here. He has two wins in cheekpieces to his name now this winter.
**Double M** was held when tightened up by the winner nearing the finish. A strongly-run five furlongs is probably his ideal trip.
**Scarrottoo** wore blinkers for the first time, although he has been equipped with cheekpieces before. This was only the third time that he has run on the All-Weather and there could be a race for him on this surface.
**Cargo** had an excuse last time and this was a better run.
**Eastern Blue(IRE)** went without the cheekpieces for this first try on Polytrack.
**Mr Spliffy(IRE)** went off far too fast, especially given he has shown his best form over the minimum trip. The vet reported he finished distressed. *Official explanation: vet said gelding finished distressed*

## 675 BET DIRECT ON SKY ACTIVE H'CAP 7f (P)
2:40 (2:41) (E) (0-75,73) 3-Y-O £3,412 (£975; £487) Stalls Low

Form RPR
-253 **1** **St Savarin (FR)**[7] [619] 3-9-6 **72**.... NPollard 12 77
(JRBest) *mde virtually all: kicked 2l clr wl over 1f out: drvn out* **4/1**[3]
00-4 **2** *3/4* **Big Bad Burt**[14] [580] 3-8-10 **62**....(v) KFallon 7 65
(MJWallace) *dwlt: sn rcvrd to chse ldrs: drvn and effrt 2f out: r.o to take 2nd wl ins fnl f: nt rch wnr* **10/3**[1]
2-20 **3** *3/4* **Fools Entire**[18] [557] 3-8-12 **69**....(v[1]) BReilly(5) 13 70
(JAGilbert) *pressed wnr: drvn and unable qck over 1f out: one pce and lost 2nd wl ins fnl f* **10/1**
050- **4** *1* **Iffy**[99] [5812] 3-8-8 **60**.... SWhitworth 10 59
(PDCundell) *wl in rr: rdn and effrt over 2f out: prog on inner over 1f out: nrst fin* **5/1**
005- **5** *1/2* **Jomus**[64] [6115] 3-8-2 **57**.... RMiles(3) 5 54
(LMontagueHall) *s.s: in rr tl prog on wd outside fr over 3f out: pressed ldrs 2f out: c wd st: one pce after* **25/1**
3-34 **6** *1 3/4* **Maybe Someday**[16] [566] 3-9-7 **73**.... NCallan 1 66
(IAWood) *prom: drvn wl over 2f out: lost pl sn after: renewed effrt over 1f out: one pce* **8/1**
02-5 **7** *2 1/2* **Garrigon**[18] [557] 3-8-10 **62**.... IMongan 9 49
(NPLittmoden) *cl up whn hmpd 5f out: sn pressing ldrs again: rdn and cl up 2f out: wknd over 1f out* **7/2**[2]
060- **8** *6* **Lady Stripes**[121] [5424] 3-8-4 **63** ow1.... KBowman(7) 15 35
(MJWallace) *a wl in rr: pushed along and no prog 2f out* **66/1**
30-2 **9** *nk* **Redbank (IRE)**[29] [451] 3-8-11 **63**.... PaulEddery 14 34
(SDow) *racd on outer: chsd ldrs: rdn over 2f out: wknd over 1f out: eased* **12/1**
265- **10** *3/4* **Trishay**[149] [4763] 3-8-7 **59**.... JQuinn 11 28
(APJarvis) *wl in rr: lost tch main gp fr 1/2-way: reminder over 1f out: no ch* **33/1**
600- **11** *1* **Chiqitita (IRE)**[127] [5290] 3-8-2 **61**.... SaleemGolam(7) 3 28
(TTClement) *pressed ldrs for 2f: sn lost pl and struggling* **66/1**
304- **12** *8* **Blade's Edge**[100] [5786] 3-8-13 **65**.... CCatlin 4 12
(ABailey) *a in rr: last and struggling over 3f out: t.o* **50/1**

1m 26.28s (0.28) **Going Correction** -0.05s/f (Stan) **12** Ran SP% **121.6**
Speed ratings: **96,95,94,93,92 90,87,80,80,79 78,69**CSF £17.70 CT £129.55 TOTE £5.90: £1.90, £1.80, £3.20; EX 17.80.
**Owner** D S Nevison **Bred** F W Holtkotter **Trained** Hucking, Kent

**FOCUS**
A fairly strong 3yo handicap for the time of year, and the form should work out.

**NOTEBOOK**
**St Savarin(FR)**, returning to his best trip, made all the running, the decisive move coming when he was kicked clear approaching the home turn. He will be given a break now with a race at Chester's May meeting his target.
**Big Bad Burt**, Kieren Fallon's first ride in Britain this year, again missed the break, which did not help over this shorter trip. Although he ran on to chase home the winner, he gave the impression that he is not wholly straightforward.
**Fools Entire** was back to form in the first-time visor.
**Iffy**, a handicap debutant having his first run since October, was doing his best work late over this more suitable trip.
**Jomus**, racing from a 7lb lower mark, missed the break and was obliged to race wide.
**Maybe Someday** was down in trip, having failed to get home over around ten furlongs on his last two starts.
**Garrigon** was unable to confirm the form with St Savarin on their running here in December.

## 676 £10 FREE BET @ BET DIRECT SKY ACTIVE MEDIAN AUCTION MAIDEN STKS 1m 5f (P)
3:10 (3:11) (F) 4-6-Y-O £2,912 (£832; £416) Stalls Low

Form RPR
055- **1** **Dolzago**[15] [4654] 4-9-0 48....(b[1]) IMongan 3 58
(GLMoore) *trckd ldr: led over 4f out: rdn and hdd over 2f out: drvn to dispute ld again over 1f out: kpt on wl nr fin* **20/1**
0-2 **2** *shd* **Fleeting Moon**[29] [449] 4-8-9.... MartinDwyer 7 53
(AMBalding) *trckd ldng pair tl wnt 2nd 4f out: shkn up to ld over 2f out: jnd wl over 1f out: disp ld after: jst hld nr fin* **7/4**[2]
40-3 **3** *2* **Boumahou (IRE)**[11] [603] 4-9-0 71.... NCallan 2 55
(APJarvis) *reluctant to enter stalls: settled in 5th: effrt to chse ldng pair over 3f out: drvn over 2f out: nt qckn and no imp* **6/5**[1]
5-52 **4** *4* **Vanilla Moon**[20] [534] 4-8-9 48....(v) SWKelly 6 43
(JRJenkins) *trckd ldng pair: drvn over 4f out: no rspnse and struggling 3f out : n.d after* **12/1**
0-04 **5** *3* **Amnesty**[11] [602] 5-9-4 56....(be) SWhitworth 1 43
(GLMoore) *hld up in last pair: prog to chse ldng trio 3f out and gng wl enough: rdn over 2f out: wknd* **10/1**[3]
02-3 **6** *3* **Make My Hay**[31] [431] 5-9-1 45.... LFletcher(3) 4 39
(JWhite) *racd in last pair: pushed along 7f out: u.p and struggling 5f out: sn no ch* **33/1**
00/ **7** *23* **Joey The Schnoze**[427] [4857] 6-9-4.... NPollard 5 2
(GGMargarson) *led to over 4f out: sn wknd: t.o* **66/1**

2m 47.8s (-0.28) **Going Correction** -0.05s/f (Stan)
**WFA** 4 from 5yo+ 4lb **7** Ran SP% **107.8**
Speed ratings: **98,97,96,94,92 90,76**CSF £49.41 TOTE £25.50: £7.80, £1.40; EX 67.80.
**Owner** R Kiernan, Paul Chapman **Bred** Cheveley Park Stud Ltd **Trained** Woodingdean, E Sussex

**FOCUS**
A weak race, and the form is only selling class.

**NOTEBOOK**
**Dolzago** had a recent run over hurdles on his debut for the yard. In first-time blinkers, he battled well to regain the outright lead near the finish.
**Fleeting Moon**, stepping up a furlong, nosed ahead in the home straight but was just worried out of it. She has no pretensions to a change of gear.
**Boumahou(IRE)** had a clear chance on official ratings, but was unable to quicken up over this shorter trip. This was an opportunity missed.
**Vanilla Moon** was found wanting back over this longer trip. *Official explanation: jockey said filly hung left*
**Amnesty** did not appear to stay the extra three furlongs.

## 677 LITTLEWOODS BET DIRECT STKS SHOWCASE H'CAP 1m (P)
3:40 (3:40) (C) (0-95,93) 4-Y-O+ £7,273 (£2,758; £1,379; £627) Stalls High

Form RPR
20-1 **1** **Dance On The Top**[25] [494] 6-9-8 **87**....(t) DSweeney 1 101
(JRBoyle) *pressed ldr: led over 3f out: kicked clr 2f out: shkn up and in n.d fnl f* **9/4**[1]
21-0 **2** *1 3/4* **Linning Wine (IRE)**[18] [558] 8-10-0 **93**.... SCarson 9 103
(BGPowell) *hld up in last pair: prog 2f out: squeezed through 1f out: sn chsd wnr: styd on but no imp* **8/1**
3-06 **3** *1 1/4* **Quantum Leap**[4] [650] 7-7-9 **63** oh1.... LisaJones(3) 8 70
(SDow) *in tch: effrt on outer to chse ldrs over 2f out: rdn and styd on one pce fr over 1f out* **20/1**
000- **4** *hd* **Our Teddy (IRE)**[145] [4866] 4-10-0 **93**.... MartinDwyer 3 100
(AMBalding) *trckd ldrs: nt clr run on inner 2f out to over 1f out: styd on same pce fnl f* **5/1**[2]
1-30 **5** *1/2* **Labrett**[14] [577] 7-9-3 **82**....(p) MFenton 4 88
(MissGayKelleway) *cl up: rdn 3f out: effrt u.p to chse wnr briefly over 1f out: one pce* **8/1**
46-0 **6** *3* **Agilis (IRE)**[4] [647] 4-8-13 **78**....(b[1]) DKinsella 6 77
(JamiePoulton) *hld up towards rr: effrt whn nt clr run 2f out to over 1f out: no prog after* **25/1**
350- **7** *3/4* **Jewel Of India**[107] [749] 5-9-3 **85**.... DCorby(3) 7 83
(MrsALMKing) *s.i.s: hld up in rr: nt clr run over 2f out to wl over 1f out: no prog after* **16/1**
-020 **8** *1/2* **Internationalguest (IRE)**[11] [600] 5-9-1 **80**....(v) NPollard 10 77
(GGMargarson) *hld up in last pair: rdn 3f out: no prog* **20/1**
-135 **9** *nk* **Arc El Ciel (ARG)**[5] [641] 6-8-13 **78**....(v) IMongan 2 74
(MrsStefLiddiard) *led: rdn and hdd over 3f out: chsd wnr to over 1f out: wknd* **9/1**
300- **10** *nk* **Serieux**[147] [4823] 5-9-13 **92**.... ACulhane 5 87
(MrsAJPerrett) *t.k.h: prom: rdn 2f out: fnd nil: sn wknd and eased* **11/2**[3]
515- **11** *7* **And Toto Too**[35] [6270] 4-7-12 **70**....(v) BSwarbrick(7) 11 50
(PDEvans) *racd on outer: in tch: wknd over 2f out: sn bhd* **16/1**

1m 38.45s (-1.06) **Going Correction** -0.05s/f (Stan) **11** Ran SP% **120.2**
Speed ratings: **103,101,100,99,99 96,95,95,94,94 87**CSF £20.64 CT £301.88 TOTE £3.20: £1.60, £2.40, £4.30; EX 21.30 Trifecta £219.10 Pool of £1,821.26 - 5.90 winning units.
**Owner** John Hopkins (t/a South Hatch Racing) **Bred** Fittocks Stud **Trained** Epsom, Surrey

**FOCUS**
A competitive handicap featuring several Lincoln entries. Although the winning time was nothing out of the ordinary for a race of this grade, the form looks rock solid.

**NOTEBOOK**
**Dance On The Top** followed up his recent course and distance victory in style, again kicking away from his rivals some way out. This was career best form, but he will find opportunities on sand drying up now as his rating moves into the 90s.
**Linning Wine(IRE)**, suited by the strong pace over this trip, came through for second but the winner had flown.
**Quantum Leap** has been running over ten furlongs and is probably more effective at that trip.
**Our Teddy(IRE)**, formerly with George Margarson, ran an encouraging race on his debut for his new yard, particulalry as he was short of room early in the home straight.

**Labrett**, with the cheekpieces on but without the tongue tie, seems held by the handicapper at present.
**Serieux**, making his debut on sand, was rather free and found little when asked for his effort.

## 678 LITTLEWOODS BET DIRECT (S) STKS 5f (P)
4:10 (4:10) (G ) 3-Y-O £2,562 (£732; £366) Stalls High

Form RPR
-520 **1** **Ivory Lace**[8] [610] 3-9-0 55 DSweeney 4 59
(DKIvory) *racd in last pair tl prog fr 3f out: r.o to ld last 150y: rdn out* **8/1**
4-04 **2** ¾ **Lady Piste (IRE)**[7] [620] 3-8-7 52 (vt) SJDonohoe(7) 1 57
(PDEvans) *chsd ldrs: rdn 1/2-way: effrt on inner and ev ch 1f out: one pce ins fnl f* **7/1**
-100 **3** 1 **Princess Kai (IRE)**[7] [619] 3-9-0 61 (b) JQuinn 6 53
(RIngram) *pressed ldr: drvn to ld over 1f out: hdd and no ex last 150y* **9/2**[3]
4640 **4** 1 **Lizhar (IRE)**[1] [670] 3-9-0 69 IMongan 2 50
(MJPolglase) *chsd ldrs: rdn 1/2-way: one pce fr wl over 1f out* **4/1**[2]
0-06 **5** 1 ¼ **Rehia**[7] [620] 3-8-7 57 HGemberlu(7) 5 45
(JWHills) *racd in last pair: outpcd bef 1/2-way: kpt on fnl f: no ch* **16/1**
-653 **6** 1 ½ **Limit Down (IRE)**[7] [620] 3-8-12 53 KFallon 3 38
(MJWallace) *chsd ldrs: rdn 3f out: effrt on outer 2f out: fdd fnl f* **5/2**[1]
0- **7** 1 ¼ **Top Place**[303] [955] 3-8-2 (p) BReilly(5) 8 29
(CADwyer) *a towards rr: outpcd 1/2-way: shkn up and no prog after* **33/1**
50- **8** 1 **Indian Oak (IRE)**[148] [4801] 3-8-5 ow1 LPKeniry(3) 7 26
(MPMuggeridge) *led to over 1f out: wknd* **66/1**
13-0 **9** 2 **Blue Power (IRE)**[8] [610] 3-9-5 66 DarrenWilliams 9 30
(KRBurke) *racd on outer: nvr on terms and sn rdn: struggling fr 1/2-way* **11/2**
3-30 **10** 1 ¼ **Philly Dee**[7] [620] 3-8-7 47 (b) CCatlin 10 14
(NEBerry) *racd wd and nvr on terms: no ch 2f out* **20/1**

59.61 secs (-0.17) **Going Correction** -0.05s/f (Stan) **10 Ran SP% 120.8**
Speed ratings: **99,97,96,94,92 90,88,86,83,81**CSF £64.08 TOTE £11.30: £2.00, £2.30, £2.10; EX 67.40.The winner was bought in for 3,200gns.
**Owner** K T Ivory **Bred** D R Tucker **Trained** Radlett, Herts

**FOCUS**
Fair selling form, and not a bad time for the grade.

**NOTEBOOK**
**Ivory Lace**, happier here than at Southwell, came from off the pace to cut down the leader inside the last.
**Lady Piste(IRE)** ran a better race without finding the drop to the minimum trip ideal.
**Princess Kai(IRE)**, down in grade, got to the front on the home turn but was run down inside the last.
**Lizhar(IRE)** ran a respectable race on this second outing in 24 hours.
**Limit Down(IRE)**, with the visor left off, did not shape as if the drop to five furlongs was the answer.

## 679 BET DIRECT FOOTBALL CASHBACKS H'CAP 1m 4f (P)
4:40 (4:42) (D ) (0-80,80) 4-Y-O+ £4,134 (£1,272; £636; £318) Stalls Low

Form RPR
1111 **1** **Fall In Line**[1] [671] 4-8-11 66 6ex JMackay 13 85+
(SirMarkPrescott) *sn settled to trck ldrs: prog to ld over 3f out: pressed and rdn over 2f out: drew clr 1f out* **2/5**[1]
31-0 **2** 5 **Hip Hop Harry**[22] [516] 4-9-6 75 KFallon 11 89+
(EALDunlop) *settled towards rr: prog over 4f out: rdn to press wnr wl over 2f out: stl cl up 1f out: eased whn btn last 150y* **6/1**[2]
0-40 **3** 1 **Classic Role**[7] [618] 5-9-6 72 IMongan 12 79
(RIngram) *hld up in midfield: n.m.r 5f out: prog 3f out: chsd clr ldng pair over 1f out: kpt on* **25/1**
0-00 **4** 2 ½ **Gallant Boy (IRE)**[21] [523] 5-9-0 73 (t) SJDonohoe(7) 14 76
(PDEvans) *racd in rr: rdn wl over 4f out: sn struggling: kpt on u.p fnl 2f: n.d* **16/1**
1-32 **5** ½ **Perfidious (USA)**[7] [618] 6-9-1 70 RMiles(3) 15 73
(JRBoyle) *drvn up and sn led: rdn and hdd over 3f out: grad wknd fnl 2f* **14/1**[3]
532- **6** ½ **Just Wiz**[40] [6239] 8-9-1 70 (b) J-PGuillambert(3) 3 72
(NPLittmoden) *chsd ldrs: rdn over 3f out: sn outpcd: n.d fnl 2f* **25/1**
0442 **7** 7 **Night Warrior (IRE)**[6] [629] 4-8-3 65 RoryMoore(7) 5 56
(DFlood) *hld up in last: stl wl in rr but gng wl enough 3f out: sme prog but no ch whn nt clr run 2f out: kpt on* **20/1**
0-00 **8** 1 ½ **Sudden Flight (IRE)**[7] [618] 7-9-9 75 RHavlin 6 64
(RIngram) *pressed ldr to 7f out: wknd 3f out* **50/1**
6-14 **9** nk **Digger (IRE)**[6] [629] 5-9-8 74 (p) MFenton 9 63
(MissGayKelleway) *prom: pressed ldr 7f out to over 3f out: wknd rapidly wl over 1f out* **20/1**
60-6 **10** 1 ¼ **Fiddlers Creek (IRE)**[22] [516] 5-9-6 72 (v[1]) JQuinn 4 59
(RAllan) *t.k.h: chsd ldrs: drvn over 3f out: wknd rapidly wl over 1f out* **16/1**
23-0 **11** 1 ½ **Top Tenor (IRE)**[11] [603] 4-8-12 72 NChalmers(5) 10 56
(BRJohnson) *dwlt: a in rr: no prog fnl 2f* **50/1**
/40- **12** 6 **Rolex Free (ARG)**[35] [343] 6-10-0 80 (p) SWhitworth 7 55
(MrsLCTaylor) *a towards rr: rdn and struggling 4f out: wknd* **50/1**
30-6 **13** 6 **Countykat (IRE)**[12] [592] 4-9-6 75 (v) DarrenWilliams 2 41
(KRBurke) *prom tl wknd u.p 4f out* **66/1**
0/ **14** 3 **Trusted Instinct (IRE)**[88] [5520] 4-9-8 77 NCallan 1 39
(CADwyer) *a in rr: wknd over 3f out* **33/1**
116/ **15** 11 **Reviewer (IRE)**[319] [3461] 6-9-8 74 DSweeney 16 19
(MMeade) *racd wd: in tch to 5f out: sn wknd: t.o* **50/1**

2m 31.14s (-2.84) **Going Correction** -0.05s/f (Stan)
**WFA** 4 from 5yo+ 3lb **15 Ran SP% 133.6**
Speed ratings: **107,103,103,101,101 100,96,95,94,93 92,88,84,82,75**CSF £3.17 CT £42.53 TOTE £1.50: £1.20, £2.00, £5.20; EX 6.10 Place 6 £123.33, Place 5 £15.00.
**Owner** Neil Greig - Osborne House Ii **Bred** P D Player **Trained** Newmarket, Suffolk

**FOCUS**
Very strong form from the first two, both of whom have been rated two lengths better than the bare result.

**NOTEBOOK**
**Fall In Line** made it a scarcely believable five wins in the space of ten days, a credit to his trainer's mastery of the programme book and grasp of the penalty system. Remarkably, he was only 6lb higher than when the winning streak began and there is still one more opportunity left for him before his new rating of 86 comes into effect. The way he won this suggests he will remain competitive once his new mark kicks in, although he gives the impression that he would not want a drop back in trip.
**Hip Hop Harry** appreciated the return to this venue having not handled the Southwell Fibresand. He gave the winner a race, but had a thankless task at the weights and this run will not help his handicap mark.
**Classic Role** is largely consistent and enjoys no respite from the handicapper as a consequence.
**Gallant Boy(IRE)** is edging down the weights and this was a better run.
**Perfidious(USA)** made the running as usual but had no answers when headed by the favourite.

T/Jkpt: Not won. T/Plt: £147.40 to a £1 stake. Pool: £55,338.90. 273.95 winning tickets. T/Qpdt: £24.10 to a £1 stake. Pool: £6,080.40. 186.35 winning tickets. JN

# 666 SOUTHWELL (L-H)
### Thursday, February 5

**OFFICIAL GOING: Standard**
Spanish Star was the only winner on the seven-race card to come from off the pace.

## 680 BET DIRECT ON SKY ACTIVE H'CAP (DIV I) 6f (F)
1:30 (1:30) (E ) (0-75,75) 3-Y-O+ £3,283 (£938; £469) Stalls Low

Form RPR
00-3 **1** **Polar Kingdom**[23] [511] 6-9-11 72 DMernagh 9 85
(TDBarron) *cl up: led wl over 2f out: rdn clr appr last: kpt on* **2/1**[1]
-460 **2** 2 ½ **St Ivian**[12] [596] 4-9-5 66 (v) PMcCabe 5 72
(MrsNMacauley) *trckd ldrs: hdwy to chse wnr 2f out: rdn wl over 1f out and kpt on same pce* **33/1**
00-0 **3** 2 **Effective**[12] [596] 4-9-1 62 JQuinn 1 62
(APJarvis) *dwlt: midfield and rdn along on inner 1/2-way: hdwy 2f out: rdn and kpt on appr last* **11/1**
0-04 **4** ½ **Blakeshall Quest**[23] [515] 4-9-1 62 (v) IMongan 14 60
(RBrotherton) *stdd and swtchd lft s: bhd tl hdwy over 2f out: sn rdn and kpt on appr last: nrst fin* **14/1**
00-4 **5** 3 **Malahide Express (IRE)**[21] [540] 4-8-12 62 (p) LFletcher(3) 6 51
(MJPolglase) *led: rdn along 1/2-way: sn hdd and grad wknd* **14/1**
0-13 **6** nk **Hout Bay**[15] [576] 7-8-4 56 THamilton(5) 10 44
(RAFahey) *in tch on outer: hdwy 2f out: sn rdn and kpt on same pce* **9/1**[3]
10-0 **7** nk **Gilded Cove**[23] [515] 4-9-6 67 DaleGibson 2 54
(RHollinshead) *bhd: wd st: hdwy whn hmpd wl over 1f out: sn rdn and kpt on ins last: nrst fin* **12/1**
-502 **8** 2 **Above Board**[9] [612] 9-7-12 45 oh10 (t) RBrisland 7 26
(RFMarvin) *stdd s: sn outpcd and bhd: hdwy on inner 2f out: kpt on appr last: nrst fin* **50/1**
-620 **9** 1 ¼ **Far Note (USA)**[14] [586] 6-9-7 68 (b) ACulhane 12 45
(SRBowring) *racd wd: bhd and rdn whn edgd lft wl over 1f out: kpt on u.p: nvr a factor* **8/1**[2]
0-30 **10** 1 **Grandma Lily (IRE)**[14] [586] 6-9-7 73 BReilly(5) 4 47
(MCChapman) *midfield: effrt over 2f out: sn no imp* **12/1**
3-00 **11** 1 **Only One Legend (IRE)**[14] [586] 6-9-9 70 (p) NCallan 3 41
(KARyan) *a rr* **12/1**
01-0 **12** ¾ **Johnston's Diamond (IRE)**[23] [515] 6-10-0 75 DeanMcKeown 15 44
(EJAlston) *cl up on outer: rdn along over 2f out and sn wknd* **9/1**[3]
000- **13** ¾ **Lakelands Lady (IRE)**[40] [6245] 4-9-11 72 JEdmunds 13 39
(JBalding) *cl up: rdn along over 2f out and sn wknd* **66/1**
51-0 **14** shd **Noble Locks (IRE)**[28] [476] 6-9-6 72 DNolan(5) 11 39
(JWUnett) *a rr* **25/1**
32-0 **15** 1 **Illusive (IRE)**[12] [596] 7-9-3 64 GCarter 8 28
(MWigham) *in tch: rdn along 1/2-way: sn wknd* **33/1**

1m 16.21s (-0.59) **Going Correction** +0.05s/f (Slow) **15 Ran SP% 122.4**
Speed ratings: **105,101,99,98,94 93,93,90,89,87 86,85,84,84,83**CSF £91.62 CT £639.47 TOTE £3.20: £1.30, £8.10, £3.50; EX 115.00.
**Owner** Millie and Poppy Squire **Bred** Mrs Mary Taylor **Trained** Maunby, N Yorks

**FOCUS**
Just a modest handicap, but strong form from Polar Kingdom, who won most decisively. The first two home raced on the pace throughout and the winning time was 0.63 seconds faster than the second division.

**NOTEBOOK**
**Polar Kingdom** had not won since May 2001 and was racing off a mark only 8lb lower than when gaining that last success but, well backed to end that losing run, he ran out a most decisive winner. He should be able to follow up.
**St Ivian**, well beaten on the Polytrack last time, appreciated the return to Fibresand but was simply no match for the winner. He does not have a great wins-to-run record.
**Effective** has come down 10lb in the weighs since winning his maiden in February 2003 and shaped encouragingly.
**Blakeshall Quest** did not have things go her way, but still emerged with credit. She may be worth a try over seven furlongs.
**Malahide Express(IRE)**, with the cheekpieces on instead of blinkers, and stepping up a furlong in trip, had every chance. He has not won for a long time.

## 681 BET DIRECT ON SKY ACTIVE H'CAP (DIV II) 6f (F)
2:00 (2:01) (E ) (0-75,75) 3-Y-O+ £3,283 (£938; £469) Stalls Low

Form RPR
-510 **1** **Time N Time Again**[14] [586] 6-9-12 73 (p) JQuinn 2 82
(EJAlston) *cl up: led wl over 2f out: drvn over 1f out: kpt on wl fnl f* **8/1**[3]
0-31 **2** 1 **Mr Pertemps**[24] [510] 6-8-9 61 (p) THamilton(5) 9 67
(RAFahey) *in tch: wd st and hdwy 2f out: sn rdn and ev ch tl drvn and one pce ins last* **9/4**[1]
5-05 **3** 1 ½ **Barzak (IRE)**[14] [582] 4-9-1 62 (bt) JBramhill 6 64
(SRBowring) *sn outpaced and bhd: rdn along 1/2-way: hdwy over 2f out: sn drvn: styd on wl u.p ins last: nrst fin* **6/1**[2]
0-63 **4** ½ **Amanda's Lad (IRE)**[9] [612] 4-7-7 45 oh5 DFox(5) 1 45
(MCChapman) *prom on inner: effrt 2f out: sn rdn and kpt on same pce ent last* **33/1**
01-0 **5** 3 ½ **Ellens Lad (IRE)**[21] [543] 10-9-11 72 (b) PaulEddery 3 62
(WJMusson) *trac ked ldrs: hdwy 2f out and sn ev ch: rdn appr last and sn btn* **9/1**
3-00 **6** 5 **Teyaar**[15] [578] 8-9-1 62 (b) PMcCabe 10 37
(MrsNMacauley) *outpcd and bhd: wd st: styd on u.p fnl 2f: nrst fin* **14/1**
164- **7** nk **Cash**[36] [6265] 6-8-11 61 (p) LFletcher(3) 7 35
(PaulJohnson) *prom: rdn along over 2f out: grad wknd* **12/1**
60-0 **8** 2 **Naughty Girl (IRE)**[15] [575] 4-8-8 62 SJDonohoe(7) 5 30
(PDEvans) *midfield: effrt over 2f out: sn rdn and no imp* **28/1**
1F0- **9** nk **Raymond's Pride**[61] [6138] 4-9-7 68 (b) NCallan 14 35
(KARyan) *bhd: hld up: hdwy 2f out: sn rdn and no imp* **20/1**
540- **10** 1 ¼ **Ridicule**[51] [6199] 5-9-5 66 (b) RHavlin 4 29
(JGPortman) *led: rdn along 1/2-way: sn wknd* **12/1**
12-3 **11** 1 **Royal Grand**[23] [515] 4-9-3 71 PMakin(7) 13 31
(TDBarron) *racd wd: in tch: rdn along 1/2-way: sn wknd* **6/1**[2]
200- **12** 11 **Scary Night (IRE)**[237] [2336] 4-10-0 75 JEdmunds 12 2
(JBalding) *in tch to 1/2-way: sn wknd* **25/1**

5-52 **13** *8* **Sharp Hat**[31] 436 10-9-9 70 ........ ACulhane 11 —
(DWChapman) *i n tch: rdn along 1/2-way: sn wknd* **12/1**

1m 16.84s (0.04) **Going Correction** +0.05s/f (Slow) **13** Ran SP% **125.2**
Speed ratings: **101,99,97,97,92 85,85,82,82,80 79,64,53**CSF £26.37 CT £128.76 TOTE £11.10: £3.70, £1.30, £1.60; EX 24.60.
**Owner** Springs Equestrian Ltd **Bred** Anthony Scholes **Trained** Longton, Lancs

**FOCUS**
A modest handicap run in a time 0.63 seconds slower than the first division, but decent enough form for the grade. Once again the first two home were never too far off the pace.

**NOTEBOOK**
**Time N Time Again** had never won beyond five furlongs, but he showed he gets this trip under a positive ride from Quinn. He is two from three at this course, and two from three with cheekpieces fitted.
**Mr Pertemps**, 6lb higher than when winning at Wolverhampton on his previous outing, appeared to have every chance. He has a decent record on Fibresand.
**Barzak(IRE)** had never run over a trip this short on his three previous outings and it was easy to see why as he was soon badly outpaced. He finished better than anything and will be one to keep an eye on when he is stepped back up in trip.
**Amanda's Lad(IRE)** was racing from 5lb out of the handicap and was not disgraced.
**Ellens Lad(IRE)** has not won a handicap since September 2000.
**Royal Grand**, third on his first start since June here last time, did not help his chance by racing very wide throughout, although he may have bounced in any case.

## 682 BET DIRECT INTERACTIVE CLAIMING STKS 1m 4f (F)
**2:30** (2:30) (F) 4-Y-O+ **£2,905** (£830; £415) **Stalls** Low

Form RPR

1-46 **1** **Spanish Star**[14] 583 7-8-12 45 ........ ACulhane 4 56
(MrsNMacauley) *dwlt: sn wl bhnd: hdwy 5f out: rdn along to chse ldrs 2f out: styd on u.p to ld ent last* **11/1**

21-3 **2** *3* **Dancing Phantom**[28] 478 9-9-0 70 ........ JFanning 6 54
(JamesMoffatt) *tracked ldrs: hdwy 4f out: led 2f out: sn rdn: hung lft and hdd ent last: one pce: fin lame* **13/8**[1]

4-10 **3** *hd* **Orinocovsky (IRE)**[10] 609 5-9-8 64 ........ IMongan 2 61
(NPLittmoden) *sn led: rdn along over 3f out: sn hdd: drvn and styd on ins last* **7/2**[2]

0141 **4** *1 1/4* **Coolfore Jade (IRE)**[7] 630 4-8-9 57 ........ MSavage(5) 5 54
(NEBerry) *cl up: rdn to ld wl over 2f out: hdd 2f out and sn drvn: swtchd rt ent last and kpt on same pce* **6/1**

1-55 **5** *nk* **Theatre Tinka (IRE)**[10] 609 5-9-4 68 ........(p) NCallan 10 55
(RHollinshead) *in tch: hdwy to chse ldrs 1/2-way: rdn along and outpcd over 3f out: kpt on u.p fnl 2f* **5/1**[3]

1450 **6** *8* **King Priam (IRE)**[9] 616 9-8-10 45 ........(v) DeanMcKeown 3 35
(MJPolglase) *cl up: rdn along 5f out: wknd 4f out* **16/1**

04-5 **7** *26* **Gladys Aylward**[7] 630 4-8-0 54 ........(p) JQuinn 1 —
(ACrook) *a rr* **50/1**

000- **8** *2 1/2* **Pure Speculation**[131] 5215 4-8-2 71 ........ HayleyTurner(5) 8 —
(MLWBell) *in tch: hdwy to chse ldrs 1/2-way: rdn along over 4f out and sn wknd* **12/1**

00-0 **9** *shd* **Platinum Boy (IRE)**[24] 505 4-9-1 48 ........(v) VSlattery 9 —
(MWellings) *a bhd* **100/1**

-000 **10** *3* **Meticulous**[14] 583 6-8-3 30 ........ DFox(5) 7 —
(MCChapman) *prom: rdn along and lost pl after 5f: sn bhd* **100/1**

2m 44.19s (2.09) **Going Correction** +0.05s/f (Slow)
**WFA** 4 from 5yo+ 3lb **10** Ran SP% **117.1**
Speed ratings: **95,93,92,92,91 86,69,67,67,65**CSF £29.46 TOTE £12.60: £2.70, £1.10, £1.80; EX 41.40.
**Owner** Mrs N Macauley **Bred** Granham Farm **Trained** Sproxton, Leics

**FOCUS**
Misleading form, with 70-rated Dancing Phantom a long way off his mark. The winning time was modest.

**NOTEBOOK**
**Spanish Star** had it all to do at the weights and looked like being tailed off when coming under pressure down the back straight, but under a never-say-die ride from Culhane he stuck to his task to get on top inside the final furlong. A rise in the weights for this success is likely and things will be a lot harder next time if he siwtches back to handicap company, but he may just improve for a step up in trip.
**Dancing Phantom** had 23lb in hand over the winner at the weights and the looked the winner on turning in, but he proved unable to resist Spanish Star's challenge and was found to have finished lame. *Official explanation: vet said gelding finished lame*
**Orinocovsky(IRE)** had 14lb to find with the runner-up at the weights, but at the same time was well clear of the winner on the figures. He did not look to have any excuses.
**Coolfore Jade(IRE)** has gained her only two wins in this country in sellers, but this was not a bad effort.
**Theatre Tinka(IRE)** came under pressure a long way from home and proved very one paced. He would be of interest in a change of headgear, or possibly even up in trip.

## 683 £10 FREE BET @ BET DIRECT SKY ACTIVE MAIDEN STKS 1m (F)
**3:00** (3:02) (D) 3-Y-O **£3,386** (£1,042; £521; £260) **Stalls** Low

Form RPR

340- **1** **Vengerov**[119] 5459 3-9-0 71 ........ MFenton 4 72+
(MLWBell) *mde most: rdn 2f out: clr over 1f out: kpt on* **7/2**[3]

530- **2** *5* **Kings Rock**[114] 5557 3-9-0 69 ........ NCallan 7 61
(KARyan) *keen: cl up: ev ch 2f out tl rdn and one pce appr last* **5/2**[2]

0-04 **3** *1 1/2* **Tonto (FR)**[9] 613 3-8-9 65 ........ DFox(5) 12 58
(MissDMountain) *cl up: rdn along over 2f out: kpt on same pce* **8/1**

00- **4** *1* **Maid The Cut**[54] 6175 3-8-9 ........ JQuinn 3 51
(ADSmith) *chsd ldrs: hdwy 2f out: sn rdn and kpt on same pce* **66/1**

3 **5** *2* **Mrs Brown**[20] 550 3-8-9 ........ JMackay 13 46
(SirMarkPrescott) *s.i.s: sn in tch: hdwy and wd st: chsd ldrs 2f out: sn rdn and no imp* **7/4**[1]

00-5 **6** *1/2* **Lola's Destiny**[17] 563 3-8-2 52 ........ DerekNolan(7) 1 45
(PABlockley) *in tch: rdn along 1/2-way: sn drvn and no hdwy* **12/1**

0- **7** *2* **Almanac (IRE)**[91] 5930 3-9-0 ........ JFanning 9 46
(BPJBaugh) *s.i.s: a rr* **66/1**

**8** *1 1/4* **Go Green** 3-8-5 ow3 ........ SJDonohoe(7) 8 41
(PDEvans) *s.i.s and bhd: sme hdwy 2f out: nvr a factor* **50/1**

00- **9** *1* **Bienheureux**[163] 4476 3-9-0 ........ PaulEddery 5 41
(WJMusson) *chsd ldrs: rdn along over 2f out: sn wknd* **33/1**

**10** *10* **This Way That Way** 3-9-0 ........ SWhitworth 10 19
(GCBravery) *s.i.s: a rr* **25/1**

**11** *17* **Divina** 3-8-9 ........ ANicholls 2 —
(SLKeightley) *s.i.s: a bhd* **20/1**

6-00 **12** *5* **Sheapys Lass**[16] 569 3-8-9 50 ........ VHalliday 14 —
(ACrook) *chsd ldrs: rdn along 1/2-way: sn wknd* **66/1**

**13** *7* **Captain Fearless** 3-9-0 ........ GFaulkner 11 —
(MrsCADunnett) *sn outpcd and bhd* **40/1**

1m 45.66s (1.06) **Going Correction** +0.05s/f (Slow) **13** Ran SP% **126.4**
Speed ratings: **96,91,89,88,86 86,84,82,81,71 54,49,42**CSF £12.72 TOTE £5.00: £1.90, £1.50, £2.00; EX 14.10.
**Owner** R A Pegum **Bred** Mrs A Yearley **Trained** Newmarket, Suffolk

**FOCUS**
This was just an ordinary maiden, but there could be one or two to keep an eye on. The pace was just steady and nothing really finished from off the pace.

**NOTEBOOK**
**Vengerov** confirmed the promise he showed in maiden company as a two-year-old with a clear-cut success. He handled the surface well and will be of worthy of respect if kept to Fibresand next time.
**Kings Rock**, returning from a 114-day break, ruined his chance by racing too keenly. There is a race in him if he can learn to settle.
**Tonto(FR)** ran respectably on this first attempt at a mile.
**Maid The Cut** improved significantly on her first two efforts. Her future now lies in the hands of the Handicapper.
**Mrs Brown** was the very well-backed favourite, but proved disappointing. She looks the type to do better when handicapped.

## 684 PRESS INTERACTIVE TO BET DIRECT H'CAP 2m (F)
**3:30** (3:30) (E) (0-70,66) 4-Y-O+ **£3,255** (£930; £465) **Stalls** Low

Form RPR

3-32 **1** **Altitude Dancer (IRE)**[2] 666 4-9-3 59 ........ NCallan 7 69
(PABlockley) *cl up: led 1/2-way: kicked clr 3f out: rdn 2f out: styd on wl* **9/4**[2]

00-1 **2** *3 1/2* **Land Of Fantasy**[12] 603 5-9-9 59 ........ JQuinn 10 65
(LadyHerries) *hld up: hdwy to trck ldrs 5f out: rdn along wl over 2f out: drvn and kpt on same pce appr last* **6/1**[3]

6/5- **3** *shd* **Tommy Carson**[65] 6120 9-8-4 40 ........ CCatlin 9 46
(JamiePoulton) *chsd ldng pair: hdwy and cl up over 4f out: rdn along 3f out: drvn and kpt on same pce fnl 2f* **66/1**

156- **4** *2* **High Policy (IRE)**[55] 6168 8-9-7 64 ........(p) StephanieHollinshead(7) 4 67
(RHollinshead) *trckd ldrs: smooth hdwy over 4f out: rdn along over 2f out and sn one pce* **14/1**

-312 **5** *10* **Lampos (USA)**[9] 616 4-8-9 51 ........ ACulhane 1 42
(MissJACamacho) *hld up in tch: pushed along over 6f out: sn rdn and lost pl: bhd fnl 4f* **1/1**[1]

3- **6** *13* **Pipssalio (SPA)**[51] 6200 7-8-9 45 ........(b) MHenry 8 21
(JamiePoulton) *chsd ldrs: rdn along 5f out: sn wknd* **12/1**

0-00 **7** *dist* **Finger Of Fate**[10] 604 4-9-7 63 ........ IMongan 2 —
(MJPolglase) *plld hrd: sn led: pushed along and hdd 1/2-way: wkng whn n.m.r over 4f out: sn wl bhd and eased* **66/1**

40-0 **8** *hd* **Cryptogam**[14] 581 4-8-6 53 ow6 ........ TEaves(5) 6 —
(MESowersby) *sn bhd: t.o fnl 4f* **66/1**

3m 44.54s (-7.96) **Going Correction** +0.05s/f (Slow)
**WFA** 4 from 5yo+ 6lb **8** Ran SP% **113.9**
Speed ratings: **103,101,101,100,95 88,—,—**CSF £15.98 CT £659.36 TOTE £3.50: £1.10, £2.40, £7.50; EX 11.10.
**Owner** J D Cotterill **Bred** M L Page And Orpendale **Trained** Southwell, Notts
■ Stewards Enquiry : C Catlin one-day ban: careless riding (Feb 16)

**FOCUS**
A modest staying handicap run at a reasonable pace and dominated by an in-form winner.

**NOTEBOOK**
**Altitude Dancer(IRE)** ran out a decisive winner, with Callan taking over from an amateur. He could well follow-up whilst his trainer's horses are in such good form.
**Land Of Fantasy**, up 3lb for his win in a slowly-run handicap over this trip at Lingfield last time, ran respectably but never really looked like getting to the winner.
**Tommy Carson** ran well on his first start on Fibresand and should be capable of finding a banded stakes race on this surface.
**High Policy(IRE)** did not find as much as had looked likely.
**Lampos(USA)** had today's winner six lengths behind last time so this run was too bad to be true. *Official explanation: trainer said gelding ran flat*

## 685 LITTLEWOODS BET DIRECT (S) STKS 7f (F)
**4:00** (4:03) (G) 3-Y-O+ **£2,590** (£740; £370) **Stalls** Low

Form RPR

0P0- **1** **Weet Watchers**[45] 6231 4-9-8 71 ........ NCallan 6 60
(PABlockley) *mde all: rdn along 2f out: styd on strly* **6/1**

3313 **2** *1 1/4* **Feast Of Romance**[6] 642 7-9-13 54 ........(b) SWKelly 7 62
(PHowling) *trckd ldrs: hdwy to chse wnr wl over 1f out: sn drvn and kpt on* **5/1**[3]

3344 **3** *2 1/2* **Sudra**[6] 642 7-9-1 49 ........(b) JDO'Reilly(7) 3 51
(JO'Reilly) *sn rdn along in rr: hdwy on outer over 2f out: sn rdn and kpt on ent last: nrst fin* **8/1**

24-4 **4** *5* **Inchcoonan**[30] 457 6-9-3 60 ........ DarrenWilliams 5 34
(KRBurke) *trckd ldrs on inner: effrt over 2f out: sn rdn and btn* **9/4**[1]

-052 **5** *2 1/2* **Mizhar (USA)**[6] 642 8-9-8 55 ........ IMongan 9 32
(JJQuinn) *in tch: pushed along after 2f: rdn over 2f out and no hdwy* **11/4**[2]

05-0 **6** *1* **Marabar**[27] 488 6-9-3 65 ........ ACulhane 2 25
(DWChapman) *a rr* **8/1**

300- **7** *5* **Burkees Graw (IRE)**[40] 6246 3-8-5 45 ........ JQuinn 11 17
(MrsSLamyman) *chsd ldrs: rdn along 3f out: sn wknd* **50/1**

00-0 **8** *2* **College Star**[24] 497 6-9-8 30 ........(b) MFenton 12 12
(JFCoupland) *chsd wnr: rdn along 1/2-way: sn wknd* **66/1**

050- **9** *5* **Illusionist**[196] 3536 6-9-8 40 ........(v) PMcCabe 1 —
(MrsNMacauley) *a rr* **66/1**

1m 30.33s (-0.47) **Going Correction** +0.05s/f (Slow)
**WFA** 3 from 4yo+ 17lb **9** Ran SP% **115.6**
Speed ratings: **104,102,99,94,91 90,84,82,76**CSF £35.85 TOTE £8.70: £2.50, £2.40, £2.10; EX 50.50.There was no bid for the winner.
**Owner** Ed Weetman (haulage & Storage) Ltd **Bred** Ed Weetman (haulage And Storage) Ltd **Trained** Southwell, Notts
■ Stewards Enquiry : S W Kelly one-day ban: used whip from above shoulder height (Feb 16)

**FOCUS**
A decent winning time for this seller, and fair form from the first two, who once again raced up with the pace.

**NOTEBOOK**
**Weet Watchers** has broken blood vessels in the past so was switched to the Blockley yard to be trained on the course - a move that would limit travelling to the races. Dropped in grade, he was given a positive ride and was always holding the runner-up.
**Feast Of Romance** is a fair enough yardstick in this grade and appeared to run his race.
**Sudra** stayed on from the rear without posing a threat to the winner and may do better over another furlong.
**Inchcoonan** proved very disappointing on this drop in grade and remains below his best.

**Mizhar(USA)**, runner-up in this grade at Wolverhampton last time, ran below that form.

## 686 BET DIRECT FOOTBALL CASHBACKS H'CAP 7f (F)
4:30 (4:31) (E) (0-70,69) 4-Y-0+ £3,283 (£938; £469) Stalls Low

Form RPR

-013 **1** **Game Guru**[7] 627 5-9-9 **64**.....(b) DeanMcKeown 2 74
(PABlockley) *cl up: led wl over 2f out: rdn wl over 1f out: kpt on gamely ins last* **11/2**[3]

40-3 **2** ¾ **Blakeseven**[23] 512 4-8-7 **48**..... PaulEddery 10 56
(WJMusson) *in tch: hdwy 2f out: sn rdn: styd on to chal ins last: sn drvn and kpt on* **9/1**

-006 **3** *nk* **Mount Royale (IRE)**[14] 584 6-8-11 **52**.....(vt) KimTinkler 13 59
(NTinkler) *cl up on outer: pushed along and wd st: sn rdn: kpt on wl fnl f* **11/1**

3-03 **4** ¾ **Majik**[21] 544 5-10-0 **69**.....(p) IMongan 8 75
(DJSFfrenchDavis) *midfield: hdwy over 2f out: rdn and edgd lft wl over 1f out: drvn and kpt ons ame pce fnl f* **3/1**[1]

10-0 **5** *shd* **Mister Benji**[10] 604 5-9-1 **56**.....(p) MTebbutt 4 61
(BPJBaugh) *hld up: hdwy hal;fway: rdn to chse ldrs over 1f out: kpt on same pce* **40/1**

-240 **6** 2½ **Brilliantrio**[16] 567 6-7-8 **40**..... DFox(5) 6 39
(MCChapman) *s.i.s and bhd: hdwy on inner over 2f out: hmpd over 1f out: nrest fin ish* **40/1**

06-0 **7** *nk* **Social Contract**[29] 469 7-8-9 **50**..... CCatlin 11 48
(SDow) *towards rr: wd st: rdn and hdwy 2f out: sn drvn and no imp appr last* **20/1**

45-3 **8** *nk* **Yenaled**[14] 582 7-9-5 **60**.....(p) NCallan 1 58
(KARyan) *trckd ldrs: effrt to chse wnr ov er 2f out: sn rdn and wknd wl over 1f out* **9/2**[2]

0-24 **9** *shd* **Eager Angel (IRE)**[9] 614 6-8-4 **45**.....(p) JQuinn 3 42
(RFMarvin) *hld up in rr: gd hdwy on inner over 2f out: chsd ldrs whn hmpd over 1f out: nt rcvr* **16/1**

51-0 **10** 4 **Pawn In Life (IRE)**[27] 488 6-9-7 **62**..... DMernagh 12 49
(TDBarron) *s.i.s: a rr* **8/1**

500- **11** 2 **Dispol Peto**[267] 1587 4-9-7 **62**..... ANicholls 9 44
(IanEmmerson) *led: rdn along 1/2-way: hdd wl over 2f out and sn wknd* **50/1**

560- **12** 1 **Supreme Salutation**[54] 6176 8-9-8 **63**..... ACulhane 5 43
(DWChapman) *a rr* **33/1**

0/1 **13** 9 **Kennington**[21] 541 4-8-13 **59**..... HayleyTurner(5) 7 16
(MrsCADunnett) *cl up: ev ch over 2f out: sn rdn and wknd* **13/2**

1m 30.17s (-0.63) **Going Correction** +0.05s/f (Slow) **13 Ran SP% 121.8**
Speed ratings: **105,104,103,102,102 99,99,99,99,94 92,91,80**CSF £52.71 CT £556.93 TOTE £7.00: £3.00, £2.90, £4.30; EX 143.20 Place 6 £59.92, Place 5 £26.90.
**Owner** Carl Would **Bred** P J Makin **Trained** Southwell, Notts
■ Stewards Enquiry : I Mongan one-day ban: careless riding (Feb 16)

**FOCUS**
A competitive enough race of its type, and run at a decent pace. The form should work out.

**NOTEBOOK**
**Game Guru**, claimed out of David Barron's yard after finishing third over a mile here last time, was dropped in trip and upped in grade on his debut for Blockley and ran out a determined winner. He did not have much to spare at the line, but is worth keeping on the right side of whilst in this form.
**Blakeseven**, still a maiden, kept the winner up to his work in the closing stages and should be able to find a minor race.
**Mount Royale(IRE)**, up a furlong in trip with the tongue-tie back on, was very keen early but looked to hold every chance when it mattered.
**Majik**, third in a better race over course and distance on his previous start, proved unable to build on that in the first-time cheekpieces.
**Mister Benji** showed signs of a return to form.
**Yenaled** was probably found out by this drop back from a mile, but is a hard horse to win with in any case.
T/Plt: £159.40 to a £1 stake. Pool: £54,538.35. 249.70 winning tickets. T/Qpdt: £28.70 to a £1 stake. Pool: £3,897.10. 100.40 winning tickets. JR

# 632 NAD AL SHEBA (L-H)
Thursday, February 5
**OFFICIAL GOING: Dirt course - fast; turf course - good to firm**

## 687a FAMILY & FAVOURITES INTERNATIONAL RATED STKS (DIRT) 1m 1f (D)
3:15 (3:16) 3-Y-0+ £32,681 (£10,055; £5,027; £2,513) Stalls Low

RPR

**1** **Grand Stand (NZ)**[30] 7-9-3 102.....(e) KMcEvoy 2 102
(PLeyshan, Macau) *qckly away: hld up: trckd ldr: 2nd st: qcknd to ld 1 1/2f out: rdn out* **10/1**

**2** ¾ **Elghani**[41] 7-9-3 102..... RHills 1 101
(ECharpy, UAE) *s.i.s: sn led: hdd 1 1/2f out: styd on wl nr fin* **6/1**

**3** 1 **Afghan (USA)**[41] 6-8-8 94.....(b) TEDurcan 5 90
(MAlKurdi, UAE) *s.i.s: in tch in rr: hdwy st: kpt on wl nr fin* **12/1**

**4** 2¼ **Adiemus**[68] 5484 6-9-5 105.....(b) MJKinane 3 97
(JNoseda) *t.k.h: trckd ldrs: outpcd st: kpt on fnl f* **11/4**[1]

**5** ¾ **Surbiton (USA)**[14] 4-8-9 95.....(b) RMullen 7 85
(AAlRaihe, UAE) *in tch: 4th st: effrt 2f out: no ex nr fin* **7/2**[2]

**6** ½ **Camelot**[118] 5469 5-8-5 90..... EAhern 6 81
(GABulter) *hld up: in tch: outpcd st: no ex fnl f* **11/2**

**7** *nk* **Opportunist (IRE)**[35] 5-8-8 94.....(vt) WSupple 4 83
(DougWatson, UAE) *hld up: trckd ldrs: 3rd st: kpt on tl wknd fnl 1 1/2f* **4/1**[3]

1m 51.7s **7 Ran SP% 115.3**
Speed ratings: .
**Owner** Lau Kwok On & Chan Tak Wing **Bred** D A & Mrs N H Bell **Trained** Macau

**NOTEBOOK**
**Adiemus**, disappointing on his only start over hurdles, was the Winter Derby winner two years ago. He may have needed this first outing since November.
**Camelot**, a useful handicapper, was having his first start on dirt.

## 688a FILLIES & FASHION INTERNATIONAL RATED STKS (DIRT) 1m 2f (D)
3:45 (3:45) 3-Y-0+ £27,234 (£8,379; £4,189; £2,094) Stalls Low

RPR

**1** **Litigado (ARG)**[13] 8-8-7 86..... PHanagan 8 87
(PRudkin, UAE) *mde all: clr ldr st: styd on wl u.p fnl f* **11/2**[3]

**2** ¾ **Nooshman (USA)**[13] 7-8-8 87.....(bt) PJSmullen 9 87
(ECharpy, UAE) *in tch: 4th st: styd on wl nr fin* **16/1**

**3** 3¾ **Deodatus (USA)**[21] 6-8-13 91.....(vt) SSanders 10 85
(ECharpy, UAE) *in tch outside: 5th and racd wd st: styd on fnl f* **3/1**[1]

**4** ¾ **Emteyaz**[35] 6-9-2 95.....(b) BDoyle 7 87
(AllanSmith, UAE) *in tch: prog on ins to 2nd st: kpt on tl wknd nr fin* **7/1**

**5** 3½ **Muthaaber**[35] 6-9-0 93.....(t) RHills 4 79
(DougWatson, UAE) *towards rr: prog to 7th st: styd on same pce fnl 2f* **16/1**

**6** *nk* **Mubeen (IRE)**[21] 4-8-13 98..... WJLee(5) 2 83
(ECharpy, UAE) *towards rr: 8th st: styd on fnl 2f: nt rch ldrs* **9/1**

**7** 8½ **Al Ash Hab (USA)**[41] 5-9-5 98.....(v) WSupple 5 68
(DougWatson, UAE) *trckd ldrs: 3rd st: wknd fnl 2f* **12/1**

**8** 1¾ **Jebal Suraaj (USA)**[7] 633 4-8-10 90..... SChin 3 57
(MJohnston) *mid-div: 5th and effrt st: wknd fnl 2f* **16/1**

**9** 1½ **Dubai Down Under (NZ)**[21] 7-8-11 90..... RLMoore 1 54
(SSeemar, UAE) *sn outpcd in rr: 11th and racd wd st: nvr nr to chal* **12/1**

**10** *nk* **Santando**[19] 558 4-9-4 98.....(v) EAhern 6 62
(CEBrittain) *s.i.s: a towards rr: rdn fr 1/2-way: last st: n.d* **14/1**

**11** 1¾ **Crafty Trust (USA)**[14] 4-8-5 85..... RMullen 11 46
(DougWatson, UAE) *hld up: trckd ldrs: wknd qckly 5f out: eased fnl f* **5/1**[2]

**12** ½ **West Order (USA)**[13] 6-8-7 86.....(b) TEDurcan 12 46
(SSeemar, UAE) *mid-div tl wknd 1/2-way* **16/1**

2m 4.00s
**WFA** 4 from 5yo+ 1lb **12 Ran SP% 125.1**
Speed ratings: .
**Owner** R J Arculli **Bred** Vacacion **Trained** United Arab Emirates

**NOTEBOOK**
**Jebal Suraaj(USA)** has yet to recapture the best of his three-year-old form.
**Santando** needs 12 furlongs to be seen at his best.

## 689a AL SHINDAGHA SPRINT (LISTED RACE) (DIRT) 6f (D)
4:15 (4:18) 3-Y-0+ £50,837 (£15,642; £7,821; £3,910) Stalls High

RPR

**1** **National Currency (SAF)**[53] 6186 5-9-7 116..... WCMarwing 6 118
(MAzzie, South Africa) *mde all: rdn clr 2f out: v easily* **1/1**[1]

**2** 6½ **Persuasivo Fitz (ARG)**[27] 10-9-1 104..... SSanders 8 93
(AllanSmith, UAE) *chsd ldrs: kpt on wl fnl 1 1/2f: no ch w wnr* **9/1**[3]

**3** 1¼ **San Salvador (USA)**[7] 632 7-9-1 102.....(vt) TEDurcan 10 89
(MAlKurdi, UAE) *outpcd early: 12th 1/2-way: kpt on wl fnl 2f: nrst fin* **10/1**

**4** 1½ **Conceal**[7] 632 6-9-1 95..... BDoyle 4 85
(RBouresly, Kuwait) *chsd ldrs: kpt on fnl f: nt rch ldrs* **16/1**

**5** *shd* **Tala Ya (USA)**[13] 6-9-1 86.....(vt) GHind 11 84
(MAlKurdi, UAE) *prom tl grad wknd fnl 2f* **66/1**

**6** 3¼ **Aramram (USA)**[55] 5-9-1 112..... PaulSmith 7 74
(AllanSmith, UAE) *swvd bdly s: bhd far side: kpt on wl fnl 2f: nrst fin* **9/1**[3]

**7** *nk* **Rotulo (ARG)**[7] 632 6-9-1 93.....(t) MSantos 13 74
(DiegoLowther, Sweden) *chsd ldrs: kpt on same pce fnl 2f* **25/1**

**8** 3¼ **Three Points**[187] 3777 7-9-1 108.....(t) PHanagan 5 64
(PRudkin, UAE) *prom tl grad wknd fnl 2f* **25/1**

**9** 1¼ **Mahfooth (USA)**[25] 7-9-1 90..... DO'Donohoe 1 60
(RBouresly, Kuwait) *sn outpcd towards rr: n.d* **40/1**

**10** 3¼ **Chaplinesque (USA)**[69] 5-9-1 100..... RLMoore 3 50
(SSeemar, UAE) *chsd wnr tl wknd over 1f out* **6/1**[2]

**11** 4¼ **Membership (USA)**[110] 5638 4-9-3 110..... EAhern 9 40
(CEBrittain) *chsd ldrs tl grad wknd fnl 2f* **10/1**

**12** *shd* **Dantana (AUS)**[53] 6186 5-9-3 107.....(b) RMullen 12 39
(PLeyshan, Macau) *chsd ldrs stands' side: wknd fr 1/2-way* **25/1**

**13** 6 **Monkston Point (IRE)**[159] 4585 8-9-1 97..... JCarroll 2 19
(RBouresly, Kuwait) *sn outpcd and bhd: n.d* **33/1**

1m 10.12s **13 Ran SP% 126.8**
Speed ratings: .
**Owner** Mr & Mrs G J Beck **Bred** Highlands Farms **Trained** South Africa

**NOTEBOOK**
**National Currency(SAF)** ran out an impressive winner despite not being 100 per cent fit according to his trainer. The Golden Shaheen is next on the agenda, with a trip to Royal Ascot definitely on the cards later in the year. His trainer is adamant that he is a better horse on turf and he looks an exciting prospect for the season ahead.
**Membership(USA)** ran well on Lingfield's Polytrack last year but he got stuck in the kickback here and was never going.

## 690a PICNICS & PADDOCKS INTERNATIONAL RATED STKS (TURF) 1m (T)
4:45 (4:46) 3-Y-0+ £32,681 (£10,055; £5,027; £2,513) Stalls Low

RPR

**1** **Seihali (IRE)**[49] 5-9-4 98..... MJKinane 9 104
(AllanSmith, UAE) *mid-div: 11th st: rdn and gd hdwy over 2f out: led 1f out: drvn out* **6/1**[3]

**2** 1½ **Wizard Of Noz**[194] 3589 4-9-10 104..... LDettori 14 107
(JNoseda) *towards rr: 12th st: stdy hdwy fnl 2f: nrst fin* **9/2**[1]

**3** 1 **Boston Lodge**[122] 5418 4-8-10 90..... EAhern 16 91
(GABulter) *trckd ldrs: cl up 5th st: qcknd to ld 1 1/2f out: hdd fnl f: no ex nr fin* **14/1**

**4** *hd* **Londonnetdotcom (IRE)**[109] 5667 4-9-2 96..... TEDurcan 6 97
(MRChannon) *trckd ldrs: 2nd st: rdn to chal over 1f out: no ex nr fin* **16/1**

**5** *nk* **Majestic Horizon**[7] 632 4-8-10 90.....(t) RMullen 13 90
(AAlRaihe, UAE) *missed break: towards rr: styd on wl fnl 2f: nrst fin* **14/1**

**6** 1¼ **Pacino**[21] 7-8-10 90.....(t) SSanders 88
(ECharpy, UAE) *mid-div: 6th st: kpt on same pce fnl 2f* **10/1**

**7** 1½ **Sole (BRZ)**[7] 633 6-8-10 90..... PHanagan 2 85
(PRudkin, UAE) *mid-div: prog on ins fnl 2f: kpt on nr fin* **50/1**

**8** ½ **Cat Belling (IRE)**[7] 636 4-9-6 100..... JCarroll 1 94
(RBouresly, Kuwait) *v.s.a: in rr: 15th st: styd on fnl 2f: nrst fin* **12/1**

**9** *nse* **Hazelhatch**[21] 4-8-10 90.....(t) GHind 11 83
(MAlKurdi, UAE) *mid-div: effrt fnl 2f: no ex nr fin* **22/1**

**10** *nk* **Hero's Journey**[7] 636 5-9-5 104.....(vt) WJLee(5) 4 97
(MAlKurdi, UAE) *mid-div: hdwy on ins to 4th st: wknd over 1f out* **11/2**[2]

**11** 3¼ **Wilful**[7] 633 4-9-6 100..... KMcEvoy 3 86
(IMohammed, UAE) *mid-div: grad wknd fnl 3f* **25/1**

**12** 1¾ **St Expedit**[301] 7-9-11 105..... BDoyle 7 88
(RBouresly, Kuwait) *led: kpt on u.p tl hdd fnl 1 1/2f: sn wknd* **20/1**

**13** 1¼ **Red Crescent (SAF)**[27] 6-8-13 93.....(t) RLMoore 15 73
(SSeemar, UAE) *towards rr: 14th st: n.d* **50/1**

**14** ½ **Special Parade (SAF)**[105] 6-9-7 101.....(t) PStrydom 12 80
(GeoffWoodruff, South Africa) *a towards rr: last and racd wd st: n.d* **11/2**[2]

**15** *nk* **A Touch Of Frost**[20] 9-9-1 95.....(b) GAvranche 8 74
(NDeCroutte, Bahrain) *trckd ldr: 3rd st: wknd qckly fnl 2f* **10/1**



The Form Book, Raceform Ltd, Compton, RG20 6NL

16 2¾ **Muwassi**$^{19}$ 5-8-10 90............................................(tp) RHills 10 63
(ECharpy, UAE) *mid-div on outside: 7th st: wknd qckly 2f out* **12/1**

1m 36.0s **16** Ran SP% **132.9**
Speed ratings: .
**Owner** Sheikh Ahmed Al Maktoum **Bred** Rathbarry Stud **Trained** UAE

**NOTEBOOK**
**Wizard Of Noz** stayed on well from the rear and had no trouble with this longer trip.
**Boston Lodge**, who has left Paul Cole, won a claimer on his last outing. He looked as though he was set to score until tiring inside the last.
**Londonnetdotcom(IRE)** did not run badly given that she runs her best races from ther front.

## 691a UAE 2000 GUINEAS (GROUP 3) (DIRT) 1m (D)
5:15 (5:19) 3-Y-O **£90,782** (£27,932; £13,966; £6,983) **Stalls** Low

RPR
1 **Little Jim (ARG)**$^{166}$ 3-9-4 100............................................TEDurcan 6 109
(SSeemar, UAE) *trckd ldrs: 2nd st: led 2 1/2f out: kpt on wl: drvn out* **7/1**
2 2½ **Jack Sullivan (USA)**$^{104}$ [5731] 3-8-9 97............................EAhern 12 104
(GAButler) *s.i.s: towards rr: 13th st: styd on wl fnl 2f: nrst fin* **12/1**
3 ½ **Rosencrans (USA)**$^{193}$ 3-8-9 85..............................(vt$^{1}$) LDettori 3 103
(SaeedBinSuroor) *led until hdd fnl 2 1/2f: no ex nr fin* **7/2$^{1}$**
4 ¾ **Lundy's Liability (BRZ)**$^{239}$ 3-9-4 90............................WCMarwing 2 102
(MFDeKock, South Africa) *trckd ldrs: 3rd st: kpt on same pce* **6/1$^{3}$**
5 1½ **Petit Paris (CHI)**$^{281}$ 3-9-4 90..............................(t) MJKinane 14 99
(JBarton,) *mid-div: styd on fnl 2f: nt rch ldrs* **18/1**
6 1½ **Carte Sauvage (USA)**$^{96}$ [5871] 3-8-9 100............................SChin 8 96
(MJohnston) *mid-div: kpt on fnl 1 1/2f: nvr trbld ldrs* **12/1**
7 12 **Ras Hafa (USA)**$^{21}$ 3-8-9 80............................................BDoyle 9 72
(AllanSmith, UAE) *towards rr: 13th st: styd on fnl 2f* **16/1**
8 1¾ **Forthright**$^{30}$ [450] 3-8-9 93............................................SSanders 11 68
(CEBrittain) *mid-div: effrt over 2f out: no ex nr fin* **16/1**
9 hd **Ice Cube (SAF)**$^{194}$ 3-9-4 98..............................(t) PStrydom 4 68
(GeoffWoodruff, South Africa) *in rr: sn bhd: racd wd st: kpt on nr fin: n.d* **9/2$^{2}$**
10 ¾ **Sutter's Fort (IRE)**$^{117}$ [5485] 3-8-9 99..............................(t) KMcEvoy 13 66
(SaeedBinSuroor) *a towards rr: effrt st: n.d* **10/1**
11 nk **Storm Of Tara (USA)**$^{49}$ 3-8-9 80..............................(t) GHind 1 66
(MAlKurdi, UAE) *s.i.s: sn chsd ldrs: 4th st: wknd over 2f out* **25/1**
12 3 **Cupola**$^{41}$ 3-8-9 85............................................WSupple 5 60
(MAlKurdi, UAE) *mid-div on ins: wknd over 2f out* **28/1**
13 7 **Prince Of Denmark (IRE)**$^{49}$ 3-8-9 98..............................(t) RMullen 10 46
(MAlKurdi, UAE) *trckd ldrs: wknd 4f out: eased fnl f* **10/1**
14 2¾ **Clifden (IRE)**$^{187}$ [3804] 3-8-9 105..............................(b) RLMoore 7 40
(MAlKurdi, UAE) *in tch: 5th st: sn wknd: eased fnl f* **14/1**

1m 37.63s **14** Ran SP% **131.7**
Speed ratings: .
**Owner** H E Sheikh Rashid Bin Mohammed **Bred** Haras Don Yeye **Trained** United Arab Emirates

**NOTEBOOK**
**Little Jim(ARG)**, a top-class horse in his native Argentina, led early in the straight and held on well to score by two and a half lengths. He will now be trained for the UAE Derby, while a summer trip to Britain has not been ruled out at this stage.
**Jack Sullivan(USA)**, fifth in the Horris Hill last season, lost ground with a slow start. The way he finished though, suggests he may well be able to reverse the form with the winner over a longer trip.
**Rosencrans(USA)** ran well for a long way but did not get home. He might prefer a drop back to seven furlongs.
**Carte Sauvage(USA)**, placed in Listed grade at two, never seriously got into it.
**Forthright** won a Lingfield handicap over ten furlongs on his last start and this trip looked on the short side.

## 692a JOCKEYS & JAZZ INTERNATIONAL RATED STKS (TURF) 1m 4f (T)
5:45 (5:45) 3-Y-O+ **£32,681** (£10,055; £5,027; £2,513) **Stalls** Low

RPR
1 **Zaajel (IRE)**$^{28}$ 5-8-7 93............................................RHills 9 97
(ECharpy, UAE) *mid-div: 7th st: qcknd wl to ld 2f out: styd on wl u.p nr fin* **13/2**
2 nk **Kayseri (IRE)**$^{69}$ 5-9-1 100..............................(v$^{1}$) BDoyle 11 105
(AllanSmith, UAE) *in tch towards rr: stdy hdwy to 5th st: styd on wl fnl f* **9/1**
3 6¼ **Clodion (IRE)**$^{7}$ [633] 8-9-3 102............................TEDurcan 12 98
(MAlKurdi, UAE) *towards rr: 10th st: hdwy 2f out: styd on wl nr fin* **9/1**
4 1¼ **Shami**$^{7}$ [633] 5-8-9 95..............................(v) LDettori 3 88
(DRLoder) *towards rr: n.m.r ent st: styd on wl fnl 2f: nrst fin* **7/2$^{1}$**
5 shd **Proven (USA)**$^{41}$ 5-9-5 105..............................(p) PHanagan 8 98
(PRudkin, UAE) *in tch in mid-div: 4th st: chal and ev ch 2f out: wknd fnl f* **9/2$^{2}$**
6 4¾ **Fantastic Horse (ARG)**$^{124}$ 5-9-5 105..............................(t) PStrydom 6 90
(GeoffWoodruff, South Africa) *mid-div: racd wd st: styd on same pce fnl f* **11/2$^{3}$**
7 shd **Al Moulatham**$^{21}$ 5-9-1 100............................................$^{1}$ SSanders 1 86
(ECharpy, UAE) *in tch: 2nd st: wknd qckly fnl 2f* **12/1**
8 1¼ **Mojalid**$^{41}$ 5-8-8 94..............................(t) WSupple 4 77
(DougWatson, UAE) *s.i.s: in rr: effrt over 2f out: n.d* **16/1**
9 ¾ **Impaciente Gg (URU)**$^{21}$ 4-8-9 95..............................(v$^{1}$) PJSmullen 7 80
(ASelvaratnam, UAE) *mid-div: hdwy on ins to 3rd st: wknd over 2f out* **12/1**
10 3¾ **Halfsong (SWE)**$^{7}$ [633] 4-8-5 93............................MSantos 5 71
(KPAndersen, Sweden) *led tl hdd 2f out: sn wknd* **16/1**
11 19 **Arabie**$^{221}$ [2815] 6-9-1 100............................SChin 10 49
(MJohnston) *trckd ldrs tl wknd 4f out* **16/1**
12 dist **Rahn**$^{25}$ 5-8-5 90..............................(v$^{1}$) RLMoore 2 —
(SSeemar, UAE) *trckd ldrs tl wknd fr 1/2-way: eased fnl 2f* **50/1**

2m 29.08s
**WFA** 4 from 5yo+ 3lb **12** Ran SP% **124.1**
Speed ratings: .
**Owner** Hamdan Al Maktoum **Bred** Shadwell Estate Company Limited **Trained** United Arab Emirates

**NOTEBOOK**
**Shami**, despite racing over an extra two furlongs, was again doing his best work at the finish.
**Arabie**probably needed this first outing since June.

# $^{652}$WOLVERHAMPTON (A.W) (L-H)
Friday, February 6

**OFFICIAL GOING: Standard**
Wind: slt across Weather: overcast

## 693 BET DIRECT ON SKY ACTIVE AMATEUR RIDERS' H'CAP 1m 4f (F)
1:30 (1:31) (G ) (0-70,68) 4-Y-0+ **£2,618** (£748; £374) **Stalls** Low

Form RPR
261- 1 **Robbie Can Can**$^{24}$ [5329] 5-10-7 51............................MrsSBosley 6 62
(AWCarroll) *hld up: outpcd over 8f out: hdwy 5f out: led over 1f out: styd on wl* **7/2$^{1}$**
6-42 2 6 **Fight The Feeling**$^{15}$ [581] 6-10-8 57..............................(v) MissJCWilliams$^{(5)}$ 4 59
(JWUnett) *chsd ldrs: led over 2f out: hdd over 1f out: sn outpcd* **9/2$^{2}$**
0-06 3 1 **Top Of The Class (IRE)**$^{14}$ [590] 7-9-12 45..............................(v) MissEFolkes$^{(3)}$ 2 45
(PDEvans) *chsd ldrs: led over 3f out: hdd over 2f out: rdn and ev ch over 1f out: no ex ins fnl f* **12/1**
2-32 4 9 **Our Destiny**$^{14}$ [590] 6-10-1 52..............................(v) MissETucker$^{(7)}$ 9 39
(DBurchell) *led after 1f: hdd over 3f out: wknd over 1f out* **14/1**
216/ 5 3½ **Oro Street (IRE)**$^{15}$ [595] 8-11-0 65............................MrShaunJohnson$^{(7)}$ 7 46
(GFBridgwater) *s.s: outpcd* **33/1**
55-0 6 1½ **Lord Gizzmo**$^{11}$ [609] 7-9-10 45............................MrsMarieKing$^{(5)}$ 1 24
(PWHiatt) *led 1f: remained handy tl wknd over 3f out* **7/1**
06-5 7 nk **E Minor (IRE)**$^{21}$ [549] 5-10-7 58............................MrMHowells$^{(7)}$ 3 37
(TWall) *chsd ldrs tl wknd over 2f out* **11/1**
006- 8 1¼ **Prince Minata (IRE)**$^{303}$ [977] 9-9-11 48............................MissAHockley$^{(7)}$ 8 25
(PWHiatt) *prom 8f* **20/1**
03-1 9 17 **Squirtle Turtle**$^{17}$ [456] 4-11-2 68..............................(b) MrOCole$^{(5)}$ 11 19
(PFICole) *chsd ldrs over 8f* **6/1**
640- 10 2 **Gargoyle Girl**$^{18}$ [5463] 7-10-11 55..............................(p) MsCWilliams 12 3
(JSGoldie) *s.s: outpcd* **11/2$^{3}$**
00/0 11 10 **Cliquey**$^{14}$ [589] 5-10-4 55..............................(b) MissAFrieze$^{(7)}$ 5 —
(BJLlewellyn) *s.s: hdwy 8f out: rdn and wknd 7f out* **40/1**

2m 43.35s (1.85) **Going Correction** +0.05s/f (Slow)
**WFA** 4 from 5yo+ 3lb **11** Ran SP% **115.4**
Speed ratings: **95,91,90,84,82 81,80,79,68,67 60**CSF £18.00 CT £168.75 TOTE £5.00: £1.40, £2.00, £3.50; EX 18.60.
**Owner** K F Coleman **Bred** I Robinson & A W Robinson **Trained** Wixford, Warwicks

**FOCUS**
As in so many of these amateur races, the pace was strong. This is fairly decent form from the winner, who had his rivals well strung out behind.

**NOTEBOOK**
**Robbie Can Can** took a while to get his head in front on the Flat and is making up for lost time. He clearly goes well for an amateur, and is at the right end of the handicap to add to this.
**Fight The Feeling** turned in a sound effort off this higher mark.
**Top Of The Class(IRE)** looked to find this trip stretching her stamina.
**Our Destiny** was always being harried up front and dropped away tamely once in line for home.
**Squirtle Turtle** couldn't dominate and didn't take long to spit the dummy out. *Official explanation: jockey said gelding was unable to dominate*

## 694 PRESS INTERACTIVE TO BET DIRECT H'CAP (DIV I) 7f (F)
2:00 (2:01) (F ) (0-60,60) 4-Y-O+ **£2,968** (£848; £424) **Stalls** High

Form RPR
200- 1 **Iced Diamond (IRE)**$^{181}$ [3998] 5-8-13 52............................BSwarbrick$^{(7)}$ 5 62
(WMBrisbourne) *trckd ldrs: led over 1f out: edgd lft ins fnl f: rdn out* **5/1$^{2}$**
1351 2 2 **Italian Mist (FR)**$^{8}$ [626] 5-9-8 54 6ex..............................(e) GFaulkner 12 59
(JulianPoulton) *trckd ldrs: rdn over 1f out: edgd lft: styd on same pce* **12/1**
0-25 3 ½ **Spindor (USA)**$^{15}$ [584] 5-9-6 59..............................(b) SCrawford$^{(7)}$ 11 63
(JAOsborne) *hld up in tch: rdn over 1f out: styd on* **8/1**
2-35 4 1¼ **Waltzing Wizard**$^{15}$ [588] 5-9-4 50............................FLynch 10 51
(ABerry) *hld up: hdwy u.p over 1f out: nt rch ldrs* **5/1$^{2}$**
-214 5 nk **Larky's Lob**$^{25}$ [503] 5-8-11 48............................NChalmers$^{(5)}$ 1 48+
(PaulJohnson) *chsd ldrs: rdn over 2f out: no ex fnl f* **7/1$^{3}$**
-430 6 1 **Lady Natilda**$^{8}$ [626] 4-9-1 47..............................(p) PaulEddery 2 44
(DHaydnJones) *chsd ldrs: led over 2f out: rdn and hdd over 1f out: wknd ins fnl f* **11/1**
40-5 7 1½ **Lucid Dreams (IRE)**$^{30}$ [469] 5-9-5 51............................GCarter 4 45
(MWigham) *hld up: hmpd over 3f out: sme hdwy over 1f out: nvr trbld ldrs* **4/1$^{1}$**
00-5 8 2½ **Better Off**$^{34}$ [423] 6-9-9 60..............................(p) HayleyTurner$^{(5)}$ 8 47
(MrsNMacauley) *s.s: hdwy over 2f out: wkng whn hung lft ins fnl f* **20/1**
0010 9 ½ **Pips Song (IRE)**$^{4}$ [654] 9-9-0 46 6ex............................ACulhane 7 32
(PWHiatt) *led 1f: led 5f out: rdn and hdd over 2f out: wknd over 1f out* **10/1**
500- 10 nk **Youngs Forth**$^{176}$ [4122] 4-8-13 45............................SWhitworth 3 30
(AWCarroll) *s.s: hdwy over 1f out: hmpd ins fnl f: nvr trbld ldrs* **33/1**
0/0- 11 3 **Compton Bay**$^{374}$ [401] 4-8-10 49............................MLawson$^{(7)}$ 9 27
(MBrittain) *led 6f out: hdd 5f out: wknd over 2f out* **50/1**

1m 30.59s (0.39) **Going Correction** +0.05s/f (Slow) **11** Ran SP% **111.7**
Speed ratings: **99,96,96,94,94 93,91,88,88,87 84**CSF £58.66 CT £471.26 TOTE £5.70: £1.90, £4.10, £2.80; EX 58.40.
**Owner** P J Williams **Bred** Mrs Kathleen McElroy **Trained** Great Ness, Shropshire

**FOCUS**
Just an ordinary contest, but run at a fair pace for its class.

**NOTEBOOK**
**Iced Diamond(IRE)** was tackling this surface for the first time and raced without his customary blinkers. This was his best form since 2002 and he clearly goes well fresh.
**Italian Mist(FR)**, not for the first time, didn't impress with his attitude.
**Spindor(USA)** isn't an easy ride, but he does have ability if he can be persuaded to use it.
**Waltzing Wizard** is well treated on his turf form, but he difficult to catch right and needs treating with caution.
**Lucid Dreams(IRE)** was messed around leaving the back-straight, but that can hardly be used as an excuse.

## 695 BET DIRECT FOOTBALL CASHBACKS H'CAP (DIV I) 1m 100y(F)
2:30 (2:31) (F ) (0-60,60) 3-Y-0+ **£2,954** (£844; £422) **Stalls** Low

Form RPR
5235 1 **Sorbiesharry (IRE)**$^{14}$ [590] 5-9-2 48..............................(p) PMcCabe 11 55
(MrsNMacauley) *prom: chsd ldr 1/2-way: outpcd 2f out: rallied to ld nr fin* **12/1**
006- 2 hd **Futuristic**$^{122}$ [5444] 4-9-11 57............................JQuinn 13 64
(JPearce) *a.p: chsd ldr over 2f out: rdn to ld over 1f out: sn hung rt: hdd nr fin* **9/2$^{2}$**

2135 **3** *hd* **Givemethemoonlight**$^{9}$ [623] 5-9-4 **50** (v) IMongan 12 56
(MrsStefLiddiard) *sn led: rdn and hdd over 1f out: ev ch ins fnl f: styd on u.p* **11/4$^{1}$**

-214 **4** *1/2* **Lord Chamberlain**$^{15}$ [582] 11-9-4 **57** ow4 (b) CJDavies(7) 3 62
(JMBradley) *s.i.s: hld up: hdwy over 2f out: rdn and hung lft over 1f out: styd on u.p* **20/1**

02-6 **5** *3/4* **Goldbricker**$^{24}$ [518] 4-8-7 **46** BSwarbrick(7) 6 50
(WMBrisbourne) *hld up: hdwy over 3f out: outpcd over 2f out: styd on ins fnl f* **12/1**

10- **6** *1/2* **Red Lancer**$^{109}$ [5679] 3-8-6 **60** RMiles(3) 10 62
(RJPrice) *mid-div: hdwy 1/2-way: outpcd over 2f out: hung lft over 1f out: r.o ins fnl f* **80/1**

0/0- **7** *nk* **Potsdam**$^{185}$ [3871] 6-9-1 **47** (t) JFanning 9 49
(NiallMoran, Ire) *hld up: hdwy over 3f out: rdn over 1f out: no ex ins fnl f* **9/1**

-144 **8** *1 3/4* **Ally Makbul**$^{14}$ [594] 4-9-9 **55** NPollard 7 53
(JRBest) *chsd ldr to 1/2-way: outpcd fnl 2f* **8/1**

5000 **9** *nk* **Jamestown**$^{8}$ [627] 7-8-10 **45** LFletcher(3) 4 43
(MJPolglase) *prom 5f* **25/1**

0-4 **10** *3/4* **Fortune Point (IRE)**$^{20}$ [554] 6-9-13 **59** ACulhane 8 55
(AWCarroll) *hld up: effrt over 2f out: n.d* **10/1**

50-0 **11** *3 1/2* **Felidae (USA)**$^{32}$ [446] 4-8-1 **40** (bt1) MLawson(7) 5 29
(MBrittain) *s.s: a in rr* **80/1**

64-3 **12** *1 3/4* **Pas De Surprise**$^{11}$ [604] 6-9-5 **58** SJDonohoe(7) 2 43
(PDEvans) *chsd ldrs over 5f* **6/1$^{3}$**

1125 **13** *19* **Lucayan Monarch**$^{7}$ [642] 6-9-6 **55** (b1) FPFerris(3) 1 —
(PSMcentee) *hld up: bhd fr 1/2-way* **14/1**

1m 51.27s (0.27) **Going Correction** +0.05s/f (Slow)
**WFA** 3 from 4yo+ 19lb **13** Ran SP% **122.5**
Speed ratings: **100,99,99,99,98 97,97,95,95,94 91,89,70**CSF £65.28 CT £183.25 TOTE £21.00: £4.80, £2.10, £1.40; EX 112.10.
**Owner** Mrs Liz Nelson **Bred** Mrs R I Nelson **Trained** Sproxton, Leics
■ Stewards Enquiry : I Mongan one-day ban: failed to keep straight from stalls (Feb 17)

**FOCUS**
Quite an exciting finish, but that was due to the reluctance of the some of the runners to pass the post first. The first three home were drawn widest of all.

**NOTEBOOK**
**Sorbiesharry(IRE)** looked as though he was well beaten once in line for home, but with horses stopping in front of him, showed a little more resolution than his rivals.
**Futuristic** having his first outing for present connections, narrowly failed to land a gamble. He didn't look straightforward and may be one to have reservations about.
**Givemethemoonlight** is a consistent mare, but is normally one to take on.
**Lord Chamberlain** again gave the impression that he is saving something for himself.
**Goldbricker** does have ability, but hasn't been one to trust in the past.
**Red Lancer** didn't shape too badly on his first start for current connections, but left the impression he may be better suited to a stiffer test.
**Potsdam** *Official explanation: jockey said gelding had run too freely in the early stages*

## 696 BET DIRECT INTERACTIVE CLAIMING STKS 7f (F)
**3:00** (3:02) (F) 3-Y-O **£2,933** (£838; £419) **Stalls** High

Form RPR

1-45 **1** **Blue Empire (IRE)**$^{27}$ [493] 3-9-7 75 GFaulkner 6 79
(PCHaslam) *chsd ldrs: led over 2f out: rdn out* **7/4$^{1}$**

420- **2** *1 1/4* **Hatch**$^{131}$ [5250] 3-8-13 79 DSweeney 12 68
(RCharlton) *hld up in tch: hung lft and chsd wnr fnl 2f: nt run on* **9/4$^{2}$**

13-6 **3** *1 3/4* **Fission**$^{14}$ [591] 3-9-2 75 (b) SWKelly 4 67
(JAOsborne) *chsd ldr: led 4f out: rdn and hdd over 2f out: styd on same pce fnl f* **11/1**

3-34 **4** *2 1/2* **Katie's Role**$^{15}$ [587] 3-7-11 50 DFox(5) 3 46
(IanEmmerson) *chsd ldrs: outpcd 4f out: r.o ins fnl f* **33/1**

-124 **5** *nk* **Turf Princess**$^{7}$ [640] 3-8-3 62 DFentiman(7) 10 54
(IanEmmerson) *chsd ldrs: rdn over 2f out: styd on same pce* **9/1$^{3}$**

50-1 **6** *nk* **Jakarmi**$^{25}$ [508] 3-8-9 56 NCallan 8 52
(BPalling) *chsd ldrs: rdn whn hmpd 2f out: sn wknd* **14/1**

3-40 **7** *1/2* **Garnock Venture (IRE)**$^{15}$ [587] 3-8-7 47 (b) JFanning 5 49
(ABerry) *mid-div: effrt over 3f out: n.d* **50/1**

-312 **8** *2 1/2* **Emaradia**$^{7}$ [640] 3-8-8 54 (b) JoannaBadger 2 43
(AWCarroll) *led 3f: wknd over 2f out* **10/1**

60-0 **9** *4* **Knight Onthe Tiles (IRE)**$^{30}$ [462] 3-8-9 65 NPollard 1 34+
(JRBest) *n.d* **14/1**

0 **10** *3/4* **Fora Smile**$^{14}$ [591] 3-8-13 ADaly 7 36
(MDIUsher) *hld up: a in rr* **66/1**

0-44 **11** *7* **Secret Bloom**$^{25}$ [508] 3-8-7 47 (v) JBramhill 9 13
(JRNorton) *dwlt: sme hdwy over 3f out: sn wknd* **66/1**

0-0 **12** *1* **Heathyards Joy**$^{15}$ [587] 3-8-2 DaleGibson 11 5
(RHollinshead) *in tch to 1/2-way* **66/1**

1m 30.67s (0.47) **Going Correction** +0.05s/f (Slow) **12** Ran SP% **117.3**
Speed ratings: **99,97,95,92,92 92,91,88,84,83 75,74**CSF £5.41 TOTE £2.00: £1.50, £1.90, £2.00; EX 5.00.The winner was claimed by Nigel Shields for £13,000; Hatch was claimed by Alan Berry for £9,000
**Owner** Blue Lion Racing II **Bred** Yeomanstown Stud **Trained** Middleham Moor, N Yorks

**FOCUS**
The time was reasonable for the grade and this looks very strong claiming form.

**NOTEBOOK**
**Blue Empire(IRE)** took advantage of the drop in class, but was helped by the reluctance of the runner-up to go by. At home over an extra furlong, he should find other opportunities.
**Hatch**, a May foal, has some catching up to do with his rivals. He is one to have reservations about, but he clearly has the ability to win at this level if he puts his best foot forward.
**Fission** is plenty able enough, but she isn't straightforward and again gave trouble at the start.
**Katie's Role** shaped as though a mile should be well within her compass.
**Turf Princess** found this a little more competitive than the claimers she has tackled of late.

## 697 £10 FREE BET @ BET DIRECT SKY ACTIVE MAIDEN STKS 1m 1f 79y(F)
**3:30** (3:30) (D) 4-Y-O+ **£3,315** (£1,020; £510; £255) **Stalls** Low

Form RPR

402- **1** **Call Me Sunshine**$^{216}$ [3009] 4-8-9 70 GFaulkner 6 60
(PCHaslam) *chsd ldrs: rdn over 1f out: r.o to ld post* **5/1$^{3}$**

**2** *shd* **Master Role (IRE)**$^{104}$ [5763] 4-9-0 NCallan 1 65
(MAJarvis) *led 1f: remained handy: led over 2f out: rdn and edgd rt ins fnl f: hdd post* **5/2$^{2}$**

34-2 **3** *3/4* **Pacific Ocean (ARG)**$^{7}$ [639] 5-9-0 48 (t) JQuinn 4 63
(MrsStefLiddiard) *s.i.s: hld up: plld hrd: hdwy to ld 4f out: hdd over 2f out: sn rdn: no ex nr fin* **7/4$^{1}$**

0-65 **4** *2 1/2* **Taiyo**$^{23}$ [525] 4-8-9 50 IMongan 5 54
(JWPayne) *chsd ldrs: rdn over 2f out: styd on same pce fnl f* **6/1**

560- **5** *5* **Dora Corbino**$^{107}$ [5711] 4-8-9 48 ACulhane 3 45
(RHollinshead) *prom over 5f* **33/1**

6 **6** *9* **Albee (IRE)**$^{7}$ [639] 4-9-0 (p) MFenton 2 33
(MissGayKelleway) *dwlt: plld hrd and led after 1f: hdd 4f out: wknd 3f out* **14/1**

0 **7** *18* **Marino Mou (IRE)**$^{7}$ [639] 4-9-0 CCatlin 7 —
(MissDMountain) *sn outpcd* **100/1**

2m 4.90s (2.00) **Going Correction** +0.05s/f (Slow) **7** Ran SP% **106.5**
Speed ratings: **93,92,92,90,85 77,61**CSF £15.40 TOTE £5.70: £1.80, £2.00; EX 12.70.
**Owner** Chelgate Public Relations Ltd **Bred** Brook Stud Ltd **Trained** Middleham Moor, N Yorks

**FOCUS**
A maiden lacking strength in depth and a moderate winning time for the type of race. Neither of the first two ran up to their best.

**NOTEBOOK**
**Call Me Sunshine** is well exposed and didn't have to run anywhere near her current rating to win this first race in seven months.
**Master Role(IRE)**placed in Ireland, looked as if he needed this first run for new connections and was below his best. He will stay further.
**Pacific Ocean(ARG)** rated 22lbs inferior to the winner, pulled far too hard for his own good but confirmed himself an improved performer with another good effort.
**Taiyo** didn't improve for the switch to Fibresand.

## 698 PRESS INTERACTIVE TO BET DIRECT H'CAP (DIV II) 7f (F)
**4:00** (4:01) (F) (0-60,66) 4-Y-0+ **£2,968** (£848; £424) **Stalls** High

Form RPR

-001 **1** **Warlingham (IRE)**$^{7}$ [642] 6-9-12 58 6ex JFanning 4 67
(PHowling) *hld up in tch: rdn to ld 1f out: r.o* **6/1$^{3}$**

6601 **2** *1/2* **Blonde En Blonde (IRE)**$^{9}$ [624] 4-10-6 66 6ex (b) IMongan 12 74
(NPLittmoden) *s.i.s: hld up: hdwy over 2f out: rdn over 1f out: edgd lft ins fnl f: r.o* **7/1**

-214 **3** *3/4* **Lord Melbourne (IRE)**$^{16}$ [576] 5-9-4 50 SWKelly 1 56+
(JAOsborne) *s.i.s: hld up: swtchd lft over 1f out: r.o ins fnl f: nt rch ldrs* **7/2$^{2}$**

6-35 **4** *3/4* **Pilgrim Princess (IRE)**$^{23}$ [530] 6-8-10 45 DAllan(3) 8 49
(EJAlston) *led: rdn and hdd 1f out: no ex* **7/1**

0-03 **5** *2 1/2* **Scarrottoo**$^{2}$ [674] 6-9-1 52 (be1) BReilly(5) 10 50
(SCWilliams) *s.i.s: hdwy 1/2-way: rdn over 1f out: styd on same pce* **3/1$^{1}$**

30-3 **6** *1/2* **Ivy Moon**$^{23}$ [531] 4-8-8 45 RThomas(5) 11 42
(BJLlewellyn) *prom: rdn over 2f out: sn outpcd* **20/1**

-420 **7** *hd* **Headland (USA)**$^{15}$ [584] 6-9-13 59 (b) ACulhane 7 55
(DWChapman) *chsd ldrs: rdn and ev ch over 2f out: wknd ins fnl f* **11/1**

345- **8** *1* **Largs**$^{98}$ [5849] 4-9-2 48 JEdmunds 3 42
(JBalding) *chsd ldrs: lost pl wl over 3f out: n.d after* **33/1**

05-2 **9** *hd* **Dark Champion**$^{32}$ [444] 4-9-4 50 (p) MFenton 6 43
(JeddO'Keeffe) *chsd ldrs: lost pl wl over 3f out: n.d after* **16/1**

00-0 **10** *1/2* **Illustrious Duke**$^{16}$ [576] 6-8-13 48 LisaJones(3) 2 40
(MMullineaux) *chsd ldrs over 4f* **16/1**

0-00 **11** *hd* **Master Rattle**$^{16}$ [573] 5-9-1 47 VSlattery 9 39
(JaneSouthcombe) *chsd ldr: rdn and ev ch over 2f out: wknd over 1f out* **66/1**

1m 30.32s (0.12) **Going Correction** +0.05s/f (Slow) **11** Ran SP% **115.8**
Speed ratings: **101,100,99,98,95 95,95,93,93,93 92**CSF £46.01 CT £172.51 TOTE £10.60: £2.40, £2.10, £2.00; EX 32.00.
**Owner** David Andrew Brown **Bred** Paul Hyland **Trained** Newmarket, Suffolk

**FOCUS**
A low-grade handicap, but the quickest of the three races to be run over seven furlongs.

**NOTEBOOK**
**Warlingham(IRE)**, from a stable in much better form now, had little difficulty following up his victory in a seller here last week. He is still well treated on the best of his form and may be capable of scoring again.
**Blonde En Blonde(IRE)** turned in a sound effort under her welter-burden, and the blinkers have certainly had the desired effect.
**Lord Melbourne(IRE)** was doing his best work in the closing stages and is one to keep an eye on in a similar contest.
**Pilgrim Princess(IRE)** was far from disgraced, but this trip does appear to stretch her.
**Scarrottoo**, a winner here on his only previous visit, is difficult to catch right.

## 699 LITTLEWOODS BET DIRECT (S) H'CAP 2m 46y(F)
**4:30** (4:30) (G) (0-60,53) 4-Y-0+ **£2,534** (£724; £362) **Stalls** Low

Form RPR

U05/ **1** **Reflex Blue**$^{15}$ [4481] 7-8-9 **40** (v) RMiles(3) 5 48+
(RJPrice) *hld up: hdwy 1/2-way: chsd ldr over 5f out: led over 2f out: styd on wl* **9/2**

-423 **2** *11* **The Last Mohican**$^{3}$ [661] 5-8-7 **35** (p) SWKelly 2 36+
(PHowling) *led 2f: remained handy: led over 9f out: rdn and hdd over 2f out: eased whn btn ins fnl f* **5/2$^{1}$**

03-0 **3** *17* **Knockdoo (IRE)**$^{14}$ [594] 11-8-2 **30** CCatlin 1 —
(JSGoldie) *sn drvn along in rr: n.d* **9/1**

56-3 **4** *3 1/2* **Failed To Hit**$^{14}$ [594] 11-9-10 **52** (v) IMongan 6 22
(NPLittmoden) *led after 2f: rdn and hdd over 9f out: wknd 4f out* **4/1$^{3}$**

-530 **5** *4* **Roppongi Dancer**$^{16}$ [579] 5-7-11 **32** ow2..(bt) StephanieHollinshead(7) 8 —
(MrsNMacauley) *prom: chsd ldr 1/2-way: wknd 4f out* **25/1**

5-25 **6** *2 1/2* **Claptrap**$^{14}$ [594] 4-9-5 **53** ACulhane 7 15
(RBrotherton) *prom over 11f* **11/4$^{2}$**

0-05 **7** *20* **Behan**$^{17}$ [571] 5-8-2 **30** (b) JQuinn 3 —
(ACrook) *hld up: wknd 6f out* **25/1**

**8** *1/2* **Olimp (POL)**$^{17}$ 8-9-7 **49** DSweeney 4 —
(MissAMNewton-Smith) *sn outpcd and bhd* **20/1**

3m 42.33s (0.03) **Going Correction** +0.05s/f (Slow)
**WFA** 4 from 5yo+ 6lb **8** Ran SP% **115.9**
Speed ratings: **101,95,87,85,83 82,72,71**CSF £16.00 CT £93.93 TOTE £7.10: £2.20, £1.20, £1.30; EX 30.20.There was no bid for the winner
**Owner** Fox And Cub Partnership **Bred** Biddestone Stud **Trained** Ullingswick, H'fords

**FOCUS**
Typically weak form for the grade, and while the time was respectable, the times of the last two races suggest the track was riding quicker at the end of the day.

**NOTEBOOK**
**Reflex Blue** is unexposed on this surface and had won two selling hurdles recently. He won with plenty in hand and may be capable of following up in a higher grade.
**The Last Mohican** is a poor performer and will find it difficult to win a race of any description.
**Knockdoo(IRE)** at least picked up some prize money.
**Failed To Hit**, although not as good as he was, may have had a valid excuse for his poor run here, as his jockey gave a good impression of riding a finish a circuit too early.

## 700 BET DIRECT FOOTBALL CASHBACKS H'CAP (DIV II) 1m 100y(F)
**5:00** (5:00) (F) (0-60,62) 3-Y-0+ **£2,954** (£844; £422) **Stalls** Low

Form RPR

20-1 **1** **Rare Coincidence**$^{10}$ [615] 3-8-8 62 6ex (p) LFletcher(3) 3 72
(RFFisher) *w ldrs: led over 5f out: clr 2f out: rdn out* **12/1**

0-60 **2** *2 ½* **Zahunda (IRE)**[4] 658 5-8-1 40 ........ BSwarbrick(7) 1 45
(WMBrisbourne) *a.p: chsd wnr 2f out: sn rdn: no imp fnl f* **14/1**

06-0 **3** *1 ¼* **Miss Glory Be**[30] 464 6-9-5 51 ........ (p) JQuinn 6 53
(MissGayKelleway) *chsd ldrs: rdn over 2f out: styd on same pce fnl f* **5/1**[2]

-432 **4** *nk* **Mutarafaa (USA)**[18] 562 5-9-4 55 ........ (e) THamilton(5) 4 57
(DShaw) *chsd ldrs: lost pl over 4f out: hdwy over 2f out: styd on ins fnl f* **9/2**[1]

53-5 **5** *3* **Air Of Esteem**[32] 442 8-9-1 47 ........ ANicholls 10 42
(IanEmmerson) *chsd ldrs: rdn over 2f out: wknd fnl f* **16/1**

60-0 **6** *1 ½* **Victory Flip (IRE)**[25] 509 4-8-6 45 ........ (p) StephanieHollinshead(7) 9 37
(RHollinshead) *hld up: hmpd 7f out: sme hdwy over 1f out: nrst fin* **33/1**

60-1 **7** *4* **Sting Like A Bee (IRE)**[14] 589 5-9-4 55 ........ TEaves(5) 11 39
(JSGoldie) *s.i.s: hld up: effrt over 3f out: n.d* **8/1**

4-35 **8** *1 ¼* **Spy Gun (USA)**[24] 518 4-9-7 58 ........ NChalmers(5) 7 39
(TWall) *hld up: hdwy over 4f out: wknd over 2f out* **7/1**[3]

00-0 **9** *¾* **Hoh's Back**[24] 512 5-9-10 59 ........ (p) LisaJones(3) 5 39
(PaulJohnson) *hld up: rdn over 3f out: n.d* **12/1**

05-4 **10** *3* **Cumbrian Princess**[21] 549 7-8-3 35 ........ DaleGibson 12 8
(MBlanshard) *plld hrd and prom: wknd over 2f out* **12/1**

-316 **11** *1 ½* **Sandorra**[15] 588 6-8-7 46 ........ MLawson(7) 8 16
(MBrittain) *plld hrd: sn led: hdd over 5f out: wknd 3f out* **25/1**

2-32 **12** *1* **Welsh Wind (IRE)**[13] 602 8-9-10 56 ........ (t) JFanning 2 24
(MWigham) *chsd ldrs 6f* **9/2**[1]

1m 49.91s (-1.09) **Going Correction** +0.05s/f (Slow)
**WFA** 3 from 4yo+ 19lb **12** Ran SP% **119.1**
Speed ratings: **107,104,103,102,99 98,94,93,92,89 87,86**CSF £169.82 CT £971.49 TOTE £20.30: £4.60, £4.20, £2.30; EX 528.40 Place 6 £49.76, Place 5 £26.10.
**Owner** Great Head House Estates Limited **Bred** D R Tucker **Trained** Ulverston, Cumbria

**FOCUS**
An ordinary handicap but a good effort from the winner and a decent time for the grade, 1.36 seconds faster than the first division.

**NOTEBOOK**
**Rare Coincidence**, unlike the majority of his rivals, is relatively unexposed on the All-Weather surfaces. The youngest member of the field, he had no trouble adding to his recent selling victory and is certainly on the upgrade.
**Zahunda(IRE)** had no excuses and just met one too good on the day.
**Miss Glory Be** is easing in the weights and showed a bit more than of late. She seems better here than anywhere else and is one to keep an eye on in the coming weeks.
**Mutarafaa(USA)** has proved a model of consistency lately and ran just as well as ever here.
**Air Of Esteem** has never won a handicap on the All-Weather surfaces.
**Welsh Wind(IRE)** broke too well and was always seeing too much daylight. One note of caution, he has only beaten seven horses home here in three outings. *Official explanation: trainer said gelding ran too freely in the early stages and may have been unsuited by today's surface*
T/Plt: £111.40 to a £1 stake. Pool: £43,203.90. 283.00 winning tickets. T/Qpdt: £10.20 to a £1 stake. Pool: £3,124.30. 225.20 winning tickets. CR

## 672 LINGFIELD (L-H)
### Saturday, February 7

**OFFICIAL GOING: Standard**
There appeared to be a bias favouring those that made their efforts close to the inside rail in the home straight and those challenging wide found it tough.

### 701 MULTIPLE SCLEROSIS TRUST APPRENTICE H'CAP 7f (P)
**12:45** (12:46) (F) (0-70,70) 4-Y-0+ **£3,087** (£882; £441) Stalls Low

Form RPR

0-14 **1** **Zafarshah (IRE)**[10] 624 5-8-10 **57** ........ SJDonohoe(5) 7 66+
(PDEvans) *cl up: effrt on inner 2f out: led ent fnl f: pushed out and in command after* **7/2**[1]

5-00 **2** *1 ½* **Hard To Catch (IRE)**[7] 646 6-9-6 **65** ........ MSavage(3) 5 70
(DKIvory) *cl up: pushed along and lost pl 1/2-way: renewed effrt over 2f out: swtchd rt 1f out: r.o to take 2nd nr fin* **12/1**

0121 **3** *nk* **Whippasnapper**[7] 646 4-9-11 **70** ........ MLawson(3) 16 75
(JRBest) *plld hrd and racd wd early: prom: pressed ldr 1/2-way: rdn and ev ch 1f out: one pce* **15/2**

40-1 **4** *½* **Musical Gift**[8] 639 4-10-0 **70** ........ DFox 14 73
(CNAllen) *t.k.h: led: rdn over 1f out: hdd and one pce ent fnl f* **7/1**[3]

006- **5** *½* **Tiger Tops**[106] 5729 5-9-4 **65** ........ PGallagher(5) 1 67
(JASupple) *t.k.h: hld up in rr: gng easily but nt wl plcd 2f out: rdn and styd on fr over 1f out: nt rch ldrs* **14/1**

1-31 **6** *hd* **Piquet**[4] 662 6-8-6 **51** 6ex ........ HayleyTurner(3) 9 53
(JJBridger) *hld up in last: stl last wl over 1f out: shkn up and r.o fnl f: no ch* **8/1**

5-02 **7** *nk* **Acorazado (IRE)**[10] 624 5-9-2 **58** ........ (e) AQuinn 8 59
(GLMoore) *hld up in rr: nt wl plcd 2f out: taken to outer and effrt over 1f out: kpt on: no ch* **9/2**[2]

000- **8** *½* **Carlton (IRE)**[118] 5515 10-9-3 **62** ........ RThomas(3) 10 62
(CRDore) *pressed ldrs: rdn and effrt 2f out: cl up jst over 1f out: fdd* **33/1**

06-0 **9** *shd* **Steely Dan**[14] 596 5-8-6 **53** ........ RoryMoore(5) 15 52
(JRBest) *sn prom: pressed ldng pair 2f out: wknd 1f out* **16/1**

62-0 **10** *1* **Lily Of The Guild (IRE)**[14] 599 5-8-10 **55** ow1 ........ LTreadwell(3) 11 52
(WSKittow) *in last pair and pushed along 4f out: effrt u.p on outer wl over 1f out: no imp* **10/1**

00-2 **11** *shd* **Power Bird (IRE)**[17] 575 4-9-4 **60** ........ NChalmers 3 57
(BRJohnson) *hld up in rr: nt wl plcd 2f out: rdn wl over 1f out: no prog* **10/1**

0-05 **12** *4* **Frankskips**[12] 604 5-8-11 **60** ........ KarenPeippo(7) 12 47
(MissBSanders) *racd wd: in tch: c wdst of all st: wknd over 1f out* **20/1**

400- **13** *8* **Cressex Katie**[57] 6170 5-8-11 **58** ........ DFentiman(5) 6 25
(JRBest) *chsd ldr to 1/2-way: sn wknd: t.o* **33/1**

1m 26.19s (0.19) **Going Correction** -0.05s/f (Stan) **13** Ran SP% **124.8**
Speed ratings: **96,94,93,93,92 92,92,91,91,90 90,85,76**CSF £48.30 CT £316.12 TOTE £4.60: £1.40, £4.00, £2.60; EX 89.30.
**Owner** Waterline Racing Club **Bred** His Highness The Aga Khan's Studs S C **Trained** Pandy, Gwent

**FOCUS**
Only a modest pace and a winning time 0.89 seconds slower the the following maiden, but the winner won well and there were some encouraging efforts behind him.

**NOTEBOOK**
**Zafarshah(IRE)** was given a fine ride by his apprentice, holding a perfect position just behind the leaders in a moderately run race. When the leaders swung wide turning in, he did not need a second invitation to use the faster strip against the inside rail to make his effort and came through to win with plenty to spare.
**Hard To Catch(IRE)** was alongside the winner when taken back by a weakening rival running to the home bend. As a result he had to use up much more energy that the winner to get into a challenging position and, in view of that, this was a decent effort. There is definitely a race in him on this surface.
**Whippasnapper** has been in fine form over shorter recently, but is a winner over this trip. His did not help his cause by taking a fierce hold in front and did well to stay in the thick of the action for as long as he did.
**Musical Gift**, a winner over an extended nine furlongs on Fibresand last time, set only a moderate pace and that left him vulnerable to rivals with a turn of foot. A return to a slower surface a longer trip should see him winning again.
**Tiger Tops** was a real eye-catcher, travelling well at the back of the field and not being set alight until the furlong pole. Both of his wins have come over a mile here and he is very much one to keep a close eye on.
**Piquet** was not given the most positive of rides, hanging around at the back in a moderately run race and not making her effort until far too late. She was racing over a trip short of her best and stepping up in class, but she was still given very little chance.
**Acorazado(IRE)** did not really have the race run to suit and his effort down the outside was never going to be enough. A step up to a mile may help.
**Frankskips** *Official explanation: trainer said gelding was found to have bled from the nose after the race*

### 702 M S TRUST ON 01462 476700 MAIDEN STKS 7f (P)
**1:15** (1:17) (D) 3-Y-0+ **£4,114** (£1,266; £633; £316) Stalls Low

Form RPR

-324 **1** **Mayzin (IRE)**[17] 573 4-9-10 54 ........ (p) DSweeney 14 67
(RMFlower) *plld hrd: led after 1f and sn clr: 5l ahd over 2f out: rdn over 1f out: unchal* **7/4**[1]

**2** *1 ½* **La Peregrina** 3-8-2 ........ JMackay 6 58
(SirMarkPrescott) *settled in midfield: prog over 2f out: shkn up to chse wnr ins fnl f: r.o: nrst fin* **8/1**

0 **3** *1 ¾* **Green Falcon**[14] 597 3-8-7 ........ MHills 5 58
(JWHills) *s.i.s: rn green but sn chsd ldrs: effrt to chse wnr wl over 2f out: one pce and no imp over 1f out* **11/2**[3]

43 **4** *1 ¾* **Alexander Ambition (IRE)**[16] 585 3-7-11 65 ........ DFox(5) 10 49
(SKirk) *racd wd: in tch: prog to dispute 2nd pl over 2f out: no imp wnr: wknd fnl f* **5/2**[2]

400- **5** *4* **Due To Me**[118] 5509 4-9-5 40 ........ (e[1]) SWhitworth 4 38
(GLMoore) *chsd ldrs: shkn up and nt qckn over 2f out: no prog after* **33/1**

00/ **6** *nk* **Hinchley Wood (IRE)**[848] 5248 5-9-10 ........ NPollard 3 42
(JRBest) *prom: chsd wnr 1/2-way to wl over 2f out: wknd wl over 1f out* **66/1**

000- **7** *2 ½* **Time Flyer**[106] 5732 4-9-10 45 ........ SRighton 2 35
(WDeBest-Turner) *led 1f: chsd wnr to 1/2-way: sn btn* **66/1**

06-4 **8** *½* **Heartbeat**[17] 574 3-8-2 59 ........ DaleGibson 7 29
(PJMcbride) *sn in last trio: wl adrift 1/2-way: modest late prog* **14/1**

0-0 **9** *nk* **Mystic Moon**[14] 597 3-8-2 ........ JBramhill 13 28
(JRJenkins) *racd wd: chsd ldrs: rdn 3f out: nt qckn over 2f out: sn btn* **20/1**

000- **10** *1 ½* **Almost Welcome**[70] 6087 3-8-7 50 ........ PDoe 12 29
(SDow) *a in last trio: wl bhd 3f out* **33/1**

5-00 **11** *2* **Costa Del Sol (IRE)**[23] 536 3-8-4 40 ........ RMiles(3) 1 24
(JJBridger) *chsd ldrs over 2f: sn lost pl and struggling* **33/1**

**12** *11* **Mr Dinglawi (IRE)** 3-8-7 ........ GCarter 11 —
(DBFeek) *dwlt: a wl in rr: t.o* **33/1**

1m 25.3s (-0.70) **Going Correction** -0.05s/f (Stan)
**WFA** 3 from 4yo+ 17lb **12** Ran SP% **117.6**
Speed ratings: **102,100,98,96,91 91,88,87,87,85 83,71**CSF £15.42 TOTE £3.20: £1.30, £2.60, £1.90; EX 28.20.
**Owner** Ms Zoe Watkins **Bred** John McEnery **Trained** Jevington, E Sussex

**FOCUS**
A fair pace, but probably a weak maiden and very few got into it.

**NOTEBOOK**
**Mayzin(IRE)**, a well-backed favourite, had solid form on the board and that was all that was required against these rivals. He had no problem crossing over from his wide draw in front and had established a huge advantage by halfway that his rivals never looked like bridging. This should have helped his confidence, but he will find life much tougher back in handicap company.
**La Peregrina**, first foal of the useful Flawless, was friendless in the market, but she made up a lot of ground in the second half of the race and was never nearer than at the line. She did carry her head a bit high, but that may have been down to greenness and better can be expected with this experience under her belt.
**Green Falcon** ran better than on his debut, but was only playing for places from some way out. He may do better once handicapped.
**Alexander Ambition(IRE)** was prominent in the chasing group, but lacked the pace to bridge the gap to the winner. She is looking exposed and connections seem to be struggling to find her best trip.
**Due To Me** achieved very little and her official rating says it all.

### 703 BET DIRECT H'CAP 5f (P)
**1:45** (1:46) (C) (0-95,94) 3-Y-0+ **£7,168** (£2,719; £1,359; £618) Stalls High

Form RPR

6-02 **1** **Justalord**[16] 586 6-9-5 **85** ........ (p) JEdmunds 6 95
(JBalding) *fast away: led 1f: chsd ldr after: rdn 2f out: styd on to ld last 50y: jst hld on* **7/2**[2]

-666 **2** *hd* **No Time (IRE)**[7] 648 4-8-12 **78** ........ KFallon 2 87
(MJPolglase) *sn pushed along to chse clr ldng pair: shkn up over 1f out: styd on wl fnl f: jst failed* **3/1**[1]

33-1 **3** *¾* **Dancing Mystery**[16] 586 10-10-0 **94** ........ (b) DSweeney 1 100
(EAWheeler) *led after 1f and set str pce: drvn 3l clr over 1f out: wknd and hdd last 50y* **7/1**

1-35 **4** *hd* **Zarzu**[16] 586 5-9-1 **86** ........ RThomas(5) 4 92
(CRDore) *racd in last trio and sn wl off the pce: gd prog on inner over 1f out: fin wl: nt rch ldrs* **13/2**[3]

21-5 **5** *nk* **Law Breaker (IRE)**[21] 556 6-9-10 **90** ........ DRMcCabe 3 95
(JAGilbert) *sn off the pce in midfield: rdn 3f out: hanging rt bnd 2f out: styd on wl fnl f: nrst fin* **9/1**

021- **6** *3* **Turibius**[138] 5129 5-8-13 **79** ........ SWhitworth 5 73
(TEPowell) *racd in last trio and sn wl off the pce: rdn 1/2-way: one pce and nvr on terms* **14/1**

02-0 **7** *shd* **Palawan**[16] 586 8-8-12 **83** ........ NChalmers(5) 9 77
(AMBalding) *racd wd: chsd clr ldrs: effrt over 2f out: no imp and btn over 1f out* **14/1**

0-00 **8** *1 ¼* **Trinculo (IRE)**[16] 586 7-9-6 **89** ........ (p) J-PGuillambert(3) 7 78
(NPLittmoden) *chsd clr ldrs: rdn 1/2-way: no imp: wknd over 1f out* **11/1**

00-0 **9** *8* **Beauvrai**[29] 486 4-9-6 **86** ........ MartinDwyer 10 47
(JJQuinn) *outpcd towards rr: no prog 2f out: wknd* **25/1**

000- **10** *6* **Strathclyde (IRE)**[119] [5479] 5-8-13 **79**.................................... NPollard 8 19
(JRBest) *sn drvn and struggling: wl bhd fr 1/2-way: t.o* **13/2**[3]

58.02 secs (-1.76) **Going Correction** -0.05s/f (Stan) **10** Ran SP% **121.9**

Speed ratings: **112,111,110,110,109 104,104,102,89,80**CSF £15.23 CT £73.75 TOTE £5.10: £1.50, £1.90, £1.90; EX 13.90.

**Owner** T H Heckingbottom **Bred** Mrs M S Teversham **Trained** Scrooby, Notts

**FOCUS**

A cracking pace and a very fast winning time. Solid form.

**NOTEBOOK**

**Justalord**, despite breaking in front, was content to tuck in behind Dancing Mystery and let him do all the work. Once asked for his effort in the straight, he gave his all and, after hitting the front well inside the last furlong, just managed to hang on from the favourite. This was a superb effort to win off a mark 13lb higher than he has won off before.

**No Time(IRE)**, who has not been setting the world alight this winter, was well backed to do much better here and was probably unlucky not to win. The gap between the winner and the third was large when he started his effort in the home straight, but was getting narrower all the way to the line, leaving his rider with little room in which to give maximum assistance in the last 20 yards. He had also lost his off-fore shoe during the contest. *Official explanation: jockey said colt lost its off-fore shoe*

**Dancing Mystery** was able to enjoy an uncontested lead and did his best to run his rivals into the ground, but he got tired inside the last furlong and had nothing left. This was still a fine effort trying to concede weight to some decent sprinters.

**Zarzu** was completely taken off his feet and only had one behind him turning in, but he made up a huge amount of ground in the straight and such was his impetus at the line that he would have won in a few more strides. He seems to find this surface a shade too quick for him over this trip.

**Law Breaker(IRE)** is another who probably finds this sharp five a bit too quick for him now and was doing all his best work late on. An extra furlong here or the minimum trip on Fibresand should see him winning again.

**Turibius** could never get into the race at any stage.

**Trinculo(IRE)** had been shaken off at halfway and is probably better suited by the straight five at Southwell.

## 704 BETDIRECT.CO.UK H'CAP 1m 2f (P)

**2:20** (2:20) (C) (0-95,92) 3-Y-O **£8,053** (£2,478; £1,239; £619) **Stalls** Low

Form RPR

31-2 **1** **Skidmark**[31] [466] 3-8-8 **79**.................................... PFitzsimons 8 92+
(DRCElsworth) *hld up in rr: smooth prog to trck ldr over 2f out: shkn up to chal fnl f: rdn to ld nr fin* **6/4**[1]

01-1 **2** *hd* **Ascertain (IRE)**[24] [522] 3-9-7 **92**.................................... IMongan 1 105
(NPLittmoden) *trckd ldrs: prog to ld wl over 2f out: sn kicked 2l clr: drvn and edgd rt fnl f: hdd nr fin* **7/1**[3]

55-3 **3** *7* **Lord Of The Sea (IRE)**[7] [644] 3-8-0 **71**.................... DKinsella 3 71
(JamiePoulton) *hld up in tch: smooth prog over 3f out: chsd ldng pair 2f out: sn rdn and outpcd* **50/1**

2-22 **4** *6* **Baawrah**[14] [598] 3-8-1 **72**.................................... CCatlin 6 61
(MRChannon) *in tch: outpcd and rdn over 3f out: n.d after* **9/1**

55-1 **5** *nk* **Always Flying (USA)**[19] [563] 3-7-7 **69**.................... DFox(5) 9 58
(MJohnston) *led after 1f: rdn over 4f out: hdd wl over 2f out: wknd wl over 1f out* **7/1**[3]

120- **6** *1/2* **Infidelity (IRE)**[96] [5906] 3-7-10 **70**.................... LisaJones(3) 4 58
(ABailey) *racd in midfield: rdn and outpcd over 3f out: no ch after* **33/1**

21- **7** *6* **Denver (IRE)**[38] [6266] 3-8-6 **77**.................................... PaulEddery 5 54
(BJMeehan) *led 1f: chsd ldr to 3f out: sn wknd u.p* **9/1**

00-4 **8** *3* **La Puce**[9] [631] 3-7-12 **69** oh1.................................... JMackay 7 41
(MissGayKelleway) *hld up in last pair: rdn and struggling over 4f out: sn no ch* **33/1**

34-4 **9** *hd* **Little Eye (IRE)**[10] [622] 3-7-12 **69** oh1.................... DaleGibson 10 40
(JRBest) *prom: rdn and lost pl fr 1/2-way: no ch fnl 3f* **25/1**

21 **10** *22* **Sabbaag (USA)**[16] [585] 3-8-5 **76**....................(t) DRMcCabe 2 —
(DRLoder) *t.k.h: trckd ldrs tl wknd rapidly 3f out: t.o* **5/1**[2]

2m 5.86s (-1.53) **Going Correction** -0.05s/f (Stan) **10** Ran SP% **113.4**

Speed ratings: **104,103,98,93,93 92,88,85,85,67**CSF £11.43 CT £353.99 TOTE £2.30: £1.30, £2.00, £5.80; EX 10.50.

**Owner** Raymond Tooth **Bred** P D Player **Trained** Whitsbury, Hants

**FOCUS**

Plenty of in-form runners and a fair pace. The first two pulled a long way clear of the others and this is smart form for the time of year.

**NOTEBOOK**

**Skidmark**, who many thought should have won here last time, was ridden with supreme confidence on this step up in trip. He was always travelling very well, but had to battle much harder than had seemed likely to get the better of the runner-up. The pair pulled a long way clear of the others though and the form looks decent.

**Ascertain(IRE)** continues to progress and was the only one to make a race of it with the winner. The pair did come close inside the last furlong, but that was due to him edging away from the inside rail and he kept on battling despite that. This was another improved effort, conceding 13lb to a useful sort, and there are more races to be won with him.

**Lord Of The Sea(IRE)**, stepping up in trip, could never get on terms with the front pair but still pulled clear of some fair sorts and he will surely not remain a maiden for too much longer.

**Baawrah** is effective over this course and distance, but found this company much tougher than the maidens he has been contesting.

**Always Flying(USA)**, well backed, set the pace but did not find this surface suiting his style of running as much as Wolverhampton did.

**Denver(IRE)** was another that could not carry his Fibresand form over to this surface.

**Little Eye(IRE)** is becoming very expensive to follow and this trip still does not look suitable.

**Sabbaag(USA)** ran a stinker even allowing for the different surface. *Official explanation: trainer's representative said colt had a breathing problem*

## 705 BET DIRECT FOOTBALL CASHBACKS CLASSIFIED STKS 1m 2f (P)

**2:50** (2:51) (E) 4-Y-0+ **£3,339** (£954; £477) **Stalls** Low

Form RPR

1111 **1** **Fall In Line**[3] [679] 4-9-6 86.................................... JMackay 6 83
(SirMarkPrescott) *fast away: mde all: jnd and rdn 4f out: forged clr u.p fr over 1f out* **1/2**[1]

050- **2** *4* **Learned Lad (FR)**[59] [6161] 6-9-1 62.................................... IMongan 1 70
(JamiePoulton) *t.k.h: prom: chsd wnr 1/2-way: rdn to chal 4f out: upsides after tl no ex fr over 1f out* **16/1**

400- **3** *1 1/2* **Dance Party (IRE)**[126] [5381] 4-8-11 62.................... MartinDwyer 4 64
(AMBalding) *hld up in midfield: outpcd fr 4f out: chsd clr ldng trio over 2f out: styd on to take 3rd nr fin* **33/1**

120- **4** *1 3/4* **Must Be Magic**[161] [4578] 7-9-1 63....................(v) NCallan 12 64
(HJCollingridge) *cl up: rdn to chse clr ldng pair over 3f out: no imp over 2f out: lost 3rd nr fin* **16/1**

-301 **5** *1/2* **Scottish River (USA)**[15] [590] 5-9-1 62.................... ADaly 9 63
(MDIUsher) *s.s: t.k.h and hld up in rr: outpcd 4f out: styd on steadily fr over 2f out: no ch* **9/1**[3]

206- **6** *6* **Royal Fashion (IRE)**[39] [6260] 4-8-6 60.................... NChalmers(5) 8 49
(MissSheenaWest) *s.v.s: hld up in last: outpcd 4f out: passed wkng rivals fnl 2f* **50/1**

112- **7** *1 1/2* **Reap**[102] [5821] 6-9-1 65.................................... DeanMcKeown 13 50
(JPearce) *chsd wnr to 1/2-way: wknd 3f out* **6/1**[2]

002- **8** *6* **My Sharp Grey**[51] [4766] 5-8-12 54.................................... DSweeney 7 36
(JGallagher) *hld up in rr: outpcd 4f out: no ch after* **50/1**

400/ **9** *2* **Prince Slayer**[28] [1322] 8-9-1 65.................................... MFenton 3 35
(TPMcgovern) *hld up in midfield: nt clr run over 4f out: sn outpcd and no ch* **66/1**

0/P- **10** *1* **Beltane**[99] [5848] 6-9-1 40.................................... SRighton 10 33
(WDeBest-Turner) *racd in midfield: outpcd 4f out: wknd 3f out* **100/1**

00-5 **11** *3 1/2* **Bontadini**[21] [554] 5-9-1 48....................(v) SWhitworth 2 27
(DMorris) *plld hrd: prom to 4f out: sn wknd* **33/1**

662- **12** *8* **Remembrance**[21] [6262] 4-8-7 57....................(t) SJDonohoe(7) 5 13
(MJGingell) *hld up in rr: outpcd 4f out: sn bhd* **50/1**

01-6 **13** *nk* **Mythical Charm**[22] [552] 5-8-7 48.................... HayleyTurner(5) 11 9
(JJBridger) *t.k.h: prom tl wknd wl over 3f out* **50/1**

2m 5.17s (-2.22) **Going Correction** -0.05s/f (Stan)

**WFA** 4 from 5yo+ 1lb **13** Ran SP% **118.9**

Speed ratings: **106,102,101,100,99 95,93,89,87,86 83,77,77**CSF £9.96 TOTE £1.50: £1.02, £4.20, £6.20; EX 10.70.

**Owner** Neil Greig - Osborne House Ii **Bred** P D Player **Trained** Newmarket, Suffolk

■ A remarkable sixth win in the space of 13 days for Fall In Line, three at Lingfield, two at Southwell and one at Wolverhampton.

**FOCUS**

A race run at a decent pace, but a mockery of a classified stakes with the winner rated 21lb above the contest's upper ceiling.

**NOTEBOOK**

**Fall In Line** made it an amazing six wins in 13 days despite being forced to make his own running over a trip short of his best. The fact that he was made to work for this and has achieved the six-timer on all three All-Weather tracks makes the feat all the more remarkable. He will be given a break now and it will be fascinating to see how he fares on turf off his new mark of 86.

**Learned Lad(FR)**, meeting the winner on 19lb worse terms than he would have done in a handicap, did his best to spoil the party and hassled Fall In Line from a long way out. He could not maintain the effort, but take the winner out and this was a decent performance. He will be reassessed but is currently 1lb lower than for his last win here a year ago.

**Dance Party(IRE)**, racing for the first time in four months, made up a lot of late ground to snatch third place. She is still a maiden, but does not have many miles on the clock and can still be placed to advantage.

**Must Be Magic** did not perform badly on this first outing since August and is a winner over course and distance.

**Scottish River(USA)** is not an easy ride and took a fierce grip out the back. He did make some late progress, but it was far too little too late.

**Reap** is yet to win beyond a mile and may just have needed this first start in four months. Better can be expected after this.

**Prince Slayer** *Official explanation: jockey said gelding hung right*

## 706 BET DIRECT ON 0800 32 93 93 H'CAP 1m 4f (P)

**3:25** (3:26) (B) (0-105,104) 4-Y-0+ **£14,964** (£5,676; £2,838; £1,290) **Stalls** Low

Form RPR

6-10 **1** **Gig Harbor**[14] [600] 5-8-10 **89**.................................... LPKeniry(3) 6 101
(MissECLavelle) *cl up: trckd ldng pair gng easily over 4f out: led over 2f out and kicked on: drvn and hld on wl fnl f* **13/2**[3]

4-15 **2** *3/4* **Barry Island**[14] [600] 5-7-9 **74** oh1.................... LisaJones(3) 5 85
(DRCElsworth) *t.k.h: hld up in last trio: prog on inner 2f out: chsd wnr 1f out: clsng nr fin: too much to do* **6/1**[2]

2-11 **3** *3* **Cold Turkey**[14] [600] 4-8-9 **88**.................................... SWhitworth 7 94
(GLMoore) *s.i.s: hld up in last pair: prog 3f out: effrt over 1f out: styd on same pce: nvr able to chal* **1/1**[1]

50-2 **4** *1 1/2* **Ezz Elkheil**[14] [603] 5-8-0 **76**.................................... JMackay 2 80
(JRJenkins) *led for 1f: led again 5f out: rdn and hdd over 2f out: fdd over 1f out* **10/1**

01-5 **5** *nk* **Lygeton Lad**[21] [558] 6-10-0 **104**.................................... MFenton 4 108
(MissGayKelleway) *hld up in midfield: rdn and prog to chse ldng pair over 2f out: fdd over 1f out* **14/1**

03-0 **6** *1 3/4* **Zonergem**[21] [558] 6-9-0 **90**....................(b) MTebbutt 8 91
(LadyHerries) *hld up in last pair: effrt on outer over 2f out: chsd ldrs over 1f out: no imp* **12/1**

0200 **7** *hd* **Internationalguest (IRE)**[3] [677] 5-8-4 **80**....................(b) MartinDwyer 3 81
(GGMargarson) *trckd ldrs: rdn to dispute 3rd pl over 2f out: wknd and eased over 1f out* **16/1**

540- **8** *3 1/2* **Team-Mate (IRE)**[124] [5423] 6-8-2 **78**.................... DaleGibson 10 74
(MissJFeilden) *racd in midfield: pushed along over 4f out: struggling and btn 3f out* **33/1**

-004 **9** *nk* **Gallant Boy (IRE)**[3] [679] 5-7-12 **74** oh1....................(vt) JoannaBadger 9 69
(PDEvans) *hld up: prog over 7f out: pressed ldr 5f out to 3f out: wknd* **16/1**

0/4- **10** *19* **Don't Sioux Me (IRE)**[14] [2824] 6-9-0 **90**....................(t) JBramhill 1 57
(CRDore) *led after 1f to 5f out: wknd: t.o* **40/1**

2m 31.71s (-2.27) **Going Correction** -0.05s/f (Stan)

**WFA** 4 from 5yo+ 3lb **10** Ran SP% **118.2**

Speed ratings: **105,104,102,101,101 100,100,97,97,84**CSF £45.95 CT £71.38 TOTE £8.90: £2.60, £2.40, £1.10; EX 53.10.

**Owner** Fraser Miller Racing **Bred** Robert Charles Key **Trained** Hatherden, Hants

**FOCUS**

A competitive handicap and the pace was fair. Rock solid form.

**NOTEBOOK**

**Gig Harbor** put a disappointing performance here last time well and truly behind him. He was always getting a nice tow from the two leaders and he was able to bag the inside rail after taking over in front turning for home. That was probably just as well considering how fast the runner-up was finishing.

**Barry Island** seemed to be ridden as though there was a doubt over his stamina, but after making a move turning for home he followed the winner through against the inside rail down the home straight and finished in great style. Ridden a bit closer to the pace he can win over this trip.

**Cold Turkey**, bidding for his seventh win in eight starts, was held up as usual. He had to weave his way through horses to get into contention, but that is the way he likes it and even though things got tight for him at the furlong pole it made little difference. The Handicapper may have him now.

**Ezz Elkheil**, stepping back from two miles, tried to utilise his stamina but was found wanting when a turn of speed was required.

**Lygeton Lad** is limited as to which races he can run in due to his handicap mark and ran about as well as could be expected over a trip well beyond his best. It may be sometime before the Handicapper forgives him for all his success over shorter trips here.

**Zonergem**, not for the first time, hardly convinced that he was giving it his very best shot.

## 707 BET ALL WEATHER: BET DIRECT (S) STKS — 1m (P)
4:00 (4:01) (G) 4-Y-0+ — £2,660 (£760; £380) Stalls High

Form — RPR

500- **1** **Moayed**[163] 4528 5-8-13 80 ....(bt) IMongan 4 73+
(NPLittmoden) *hld up in rr: smooth prog fr 3f out: led wl over 1f out: pushed wl clr fnl f* **5/4**[1]

4-64 **2** 6 **The Gaikwar (IRE)**[17] 575 5-8-8 65 ....(b) MSavage[(5)] 7 60
(NEBerry) *hld up in midfield: prog to trck ldrs 3f out: effrt 2f out: sn outpcd by wnr: kpt on* **2/1**[2]

60-5 **3** 2 1/2 **Chandelier**[19] 565 4-8-10 54 ....(b[1]) RMiles[(3)] 3 54
(MSSaunders) *t.k.h: cl up: led 4f out: rdn and hdd wl over 1f out: sn outpcd* **16/1**

535- **4** 1 **Dolphinelle (IRE)**[39] 6257 8-8-13 47 ....(v) DKinsella 1 52
(JamiePoulton) *hld up in rr: outpcd fr 3f out: effrt 2f out: styd on one pce: no ch* **16/1**

55-0 **5** 2 1/2 **Estrella Levante**[4] 664 4-8-6 52 .... JemmaMarshall[(7)] 5 47
(GLMoore) *t.k.h: w ldr: led 5f out to 4f out: nudged along and outpcd fr over 2f out* **20/1**

3132 **6** 3/4 **Feast Of Romance**[2] 685 7-9-5 53 ....(p) SWKelly 10 51
(PHowling) *hld up in midfield: effrt 3f out: rdn and fnd nil over 2f out* **8/1**[3]

060- **7** 1 1/2 **Eurolink Zante (IRE)**[63] 6128 8-8-10 45 ....(b[1]) J-PGuillambert[(3)] 12 42
(TDMccarthy) *racd on outer in midfield: outpcd fr 3f out: no ch after* **20/1**

00-0 **8** 4 **Waterline Dancer (IRE)**[4] 664 4-8-8 45 ....(vt) NCallan 2 28
(PDEvans) *t.k.h early: cl up: rdn and lost pl over 3f out: struggling after* **33/1**

050- **9** 4 **Penny Valentine**[75] 6056 4-8-8 35 .... NPollard 9 19
(JRBest) *sn pushed along: last and struggling 1/2-way: passed wkng rivals fnl f* **50/1**

-000 **10** 1 1/4 **Pancakehill**[16] 582 5-8-8 47 ....(b) MartinDwyer 8 16
(DKIvory) *cl up tl wknd over 3f out* **11/1**

0654 **11** 1 1/2 **Pageant**[23] 533 7-8-8 35 .... CCatlin 11 13
(JMBradley) *led to 5f out: wknd u.p 3f out* **66/1**

-000 **12** 1 **Ivory Venture**[4] 660 4-8-8 45 ....(b[1]) DSweeney 6 11
(DKIvory) *racd in midfield: rdn over 3f out: sn wknd* **66/1**

1m 37.88s (-1.63) **Going Correction** -0.05s/f (Stan) — **12** Ran SP% **126.4**
Speed ratings: **106,100,97,96,94 93,91,87,83,82 81,80**CSF £3.79 TOTE £2.40: £1.70, £1.40, £3.30; EX 4.80.The winner was bought in for 25,500gns
**Owner** Nigel Shields **Bred** Sentinal Bloodstock And Wong Chung Mat **Trained** Newmarket, Suffolk
■ Stewards Enquiry : C Catlin caution: allowed mare to coast home with no assistance
Martin Dwyer caution: allowed mare to coast home with no assistance
D Sweeney caution: allowed filly to coast home with no assistance

**FOCUS**
A cracking time for a seller, and an impressive performance from the winner, who is better class when right. Fair selling form behind him.

**NOTEBOOK**
**Moayed** had been lightly raced since completing a hat-trick here early last year, the last of which was a 0 to 80 handicap. He was racing for the first time since August but is much better class than this when right and was very well backed. Supporters never had a moment's worry, and connections went to 25,500gns to buy him back, so they obviously believe he can still make his mark back in better company.
**The Gaikwar(IRE)**, stepping down in grade, was given every chance and can consider himself very unlucky to have run into one. This would have been good enough to win most all weather sellers.
**Chandelier** was given a more positive ride than at Wolverhampton and ran better as a result. There may be a small race in him.
**Dolphinelle(IRE)**, a regular in contests like this around here, probably ran to form.
**Feast Of Romance** does not really show his best form on this surface.

## 708 MSTRUST.ORG.UK MAIDEN STKS — 5f (P)
4:30 (4:32) (D) 3-Y-0+ — £3,721 (£1,145; £572; £286) Stalls High

Form — RPR

0- **1** **Tag Team (IRE)**[144] 4957 3-8-10 .... MartinDwyer 10 67
(AMBalding) *pressed ldr over 3f out: rdn to ld jst over 1f out: kpt on wl* **12/1**

23-2 **2** 3/4 **Blueberry Rhyme**[30] 479 5-9-10 66 ....(v) DSweeney 4 64
(PJMakin) *chsd ldrs: rdn 1/2-way: kpt on u.p fnl f: tk 2nd nr fin* **3/1**[2]

4- **3** nk **Pure Folly (IRE)**[114] 5594 3-8-5 .... JMackay 2 58
(SirMarkPrescott) *led: rdn and pressed fr 1/2-way: hdd jst over 1f out: kpt on one pce* **10/1**

55-2 **4** shd **Multahab**[21] 560 5-9-10 56 .... MFenton 7 63
(MissGayKelleway) *chsd ldr to over 3f out: styd cl up: rdn and effrt over 1f out: fnd nil and hld after* **7/4**[1]

0-03 **5** 1 **Ask The Clerk (IRE)**[12] 606 3-8-10 70 .... MTebbutt 8 59
(HJCollingridge) *chsd ldrs: rdn over 2f out: kpt on same pce: nvr able to chal* **5/1**[3]

04-5 **6** 1 1/4 **Dont Call Me Derek**[35] 414 3-8-10 ....(be[1]) MHenry 5 55
(SCWilliams) *sn restrained bhd ldrs: rdn over 2f out: fnd nil and no imp* **5/1**[3]

0-20 **7** 1 **Docklands Blue (IRE)**[12] 606 3-8-2 57 .... LisaJones[(3)] 9 46
(NPLittmoden) *in tch in rr: rdn 3f out: nt pce to rch ldrs after* **12/1**

000- **8** 11 **Avit (IRE)**[220] 2903 4-9-0 45 ....(b[1]) HayleyTurner[(5)] 1 8
(PLGilligan) *outpcd over 3f out: sn t.o* **50/1**

**9** 2 1/2 **Akiramenai (USA)** 4-8-12 .... KristinStubbs[(7)] 6 —
(MrsLStubbs) *uns rdr bef ent stalls: s.v.s: a t.o* **50/1**

59.53 secs (-0.25) **Going Correction** -0.05s/f (Stan) — **9** Ran SP% **123.1**
**WFA** 3 from 4yo+ 14lb
Speed ratings: **100,98,98,98,96 94,92,75,71**CSF £51.32 TOTE £13.90: £3.10, £1.20, £2.80; EX 74.50 Place 6 £8.17, Place 5 £3.33.
**Owner** Magic Moments **Bred** Miss Sally Hodgins **Trained** Kingsclere, Hants

**FOCUS**
A modest maiden run at only a fair pace.

**NOTEBOOK**
**Tag Team(IRE)**, racing for the first time since his debut in September and stepping back a furlong, showed good pace and rather got first run on the runner-up. The form is not great, but he did well to overcome the outside stall and is entitled to improve.
**Blueberry Rhyme** continues to frustrate and took an age to respond when asked for maximum effort, so that by the time he did, it was too late. He has so much ability and will get it right one day, but remains a maiden after 19 attempts.
**Pure Folly(IRE)** showed good speed on this first start since October, but is bred to stay further than this and may do better once handicapped.
**Multahab** has finished runner-up twice over this course and distance, but may have been flattered by his recent effort in an amateur riders' event. He had every chance here, but found little off the bridle and is beginning to look exposed.
**Ask The Clerk(IRE)** did not appear suited by this shorter trip on a faster surface. He is another that looks completely exposed.
**Dont Call Me Derek** has not built on initial promise.

T/Plt: £11.00 to a £1 stake. Pool: £40,530.45. 2,666.95 winning tickets. T/Qpdt: £2.80 to a £1 stake. Pool: £2,394.80. 625.40 winning tickets. JN

# 687 NAD AL SHEBA (L-H)
Saturday, February 7

**OFFICIAL GOING: Dirt course - fast; turf course - good to firm**

## 709a AL MURAQQABAT MAIDEN (SPONSORED BY BBC WORLD) (C&G) (DIRT) — 7f 110y(D)
3:40 (3:43) 3-Y-0+ — £7,262 (£2,234; £1,117; £558) Stalls Low

RPR

**1** **Mawwal** 4-9-11 .... WSupple 3 —
(DougWatson, UAE) *in tch in 5th pl: qcknd wl to ld 2f out: sn clr: comf* **3/1**[3]

**2** 3 1/4 **Russian Relation (USA)**[86] 4-9-11 .... RBurke 1 —
(RSimpson, UAE) *trckd ldrs: outpcd st: kpt on fnl f: nt pce of wnr* **20/1**

**3** 2 1/2 **Literator (FR)**[16] 4-9-11 ....(vt) TEDurcan 2 —
(SSeemar, UAE) *hld up: in tch: 3rd st: rdn and chal over 2f out: kpt on same pce* **8/1**

**4** 7 1/2 **West Country (UAE)**[106] 5723 3-8-7 79 .... SChin 4 —
(MJohnston) *led tl hdd 2f out: grad wknd fnl f* **9/4**[2]

**5** 3 **Starsailor (GER)**[29] 4-9-11 ....(v) RMullen 5 —
(MAlMuhairi, UAE) *trckd ldr: 2nd st: wknd over 2f out* **25/1**

**6** 6 **Istithmar (FR)**[227] 4-9-11 .... JCarroll 8 —
(JFrazierJr, UAE) *v.s.a: bhd: kpt on nr fin: n.d* **33/1**

**7** 6 **Godalming (USA)** 4-9-11 ....(t) LDettori 7 —
(ECharpy, UAE) *sn rdn along in 6th pl: wknd st: nvr trbld ldrs* **13/8**[1]

1m 34.5s
**WFA** 3 from 4yo 17lb — **7** Ran SP% **116.5**
Speed ratings:
**Owner** Malih L Al Basti **Bred** Milton Park Stud Partnership **Trained** United Arab Emirates

**NOTEBOOK**
**West Country(UAE)**, as usual, set the pace until fading in the last quarter-mile.

## 710a AL FAHIDI FORT STKS (GROUP 3) (SPONSORED BY BBC WORLD) (TURF) — 1m (T)
4:40 (4:41) 3-Y-0+ — £54,469 (£16,759; £8,379; £4,189) Stalls Low

RPR

**1** **D'Anjou**[125] 5396 7-9-0 110 .... MJKinane 6 110
(JohnMOxx, Ire) *in tch towards rr: last st: nt clr run 2f out: hrd rdn and r.o wl to ld fnl 110yds: rdn out* **5/1**[2]

**2** 2 1/4 **One More Round (USA)**[112] 5653 6-9-0 109 .... PJSmullen 9 106
(DKWeld, Ire) *towards rr: hdwy st: chal 2f out: led 1f out: hdd fnl 110yds: nt pce of wnr* **15/2**

**3** shd **Surveyor (SAF)**[217] 4-9-6 106 ....(b) WCMarwing 5 111
(MFDeKock, South Africa) *trckd ldrs: 2nd st: chal and ev ch 2f out: styd on same pce* **2/1**[1]

**4** 1 3/4 **St Expedit**[2] 690 7-9-0 105 .... BDoyle 2 102
(RBouresly, Kuwait) *led tl hdd fnl 2f: no ex nr fin* **40/1**

**5** 3 **Bowman (USA)**[177] 4126 5-9-0 110 .... SSanders 10 96
(ECharpy, UAE) *s.i.s: mid-div: styd on fnl 2f: nt rch ldrs* **5/1**[2]

**6** shd **Gateman**[9] 636 7-9-2 112 .... SChin 3 98
(MJohnston) *trckd ldr: 4th st: grad wknd fnl 2f* **5/1**[2]

**7** 6 1/4 **Northern Rock (JPN)**[9] 634 6-9-0 107 ....(vt) TEDurcan 4 83
(MAlKurdi, UAE) *a in mid-div: effrt 2f out: nt rch ldrs* **13/2**[3]

**8** 1/2 **Skoozi (NZ)**[315] 858 9-9-0 100 .... RBurke 8 82
(MKettle, UAE) *in tch on outside: effrt over 2f out: grad wknd: eased fnl 110yds* **50/1**

**9** 4 1/4 **Cat Belling (IRE)**[2] 690 4-8-11 100 .... RMullen 1 71
(RBouresly, Kuwait) *v.s.a: in rr: racd wd and effrt st: n.d* **16/1**

**10** 3 1/4 **Mahfooth (USA)**[2] 689 7-9-0 100 .... GHind 7 67
(RBouresly, Kuwait) *trckd ldrs: 3rd st: wknd over 2f out: eased fnl 110yds* **40/1**

1m 35.97s — **10** Ran SP% **121.2**
Speed ratings: .
**Owner** Barouche Stud Ireland Ltd **Bred** Barouche Stud Ltd **Trained** Currabeg, Co Kildare

**NOTEBOOK**
**D'Anjou**, under a confident ride, ran out a comfortable winner for the new combination of Oxx and Kinane. It is the first time he has won over this far.
**One More Round(USA)**, who showed form here last winter, ran well but the winner proved too good late on.
**Gateman** failed to run up to last week's form in this slightly stronger race.

## 711a UAE 1000 GUINEAS (FILLIES) (SPONSORED BY BBC WORLD) (DIRT) — 1m (D)
5:10 (5:11) 3-Y-0 — £90,782 (£27,932; £13,966; £6,983) Stalls Low

RPR

**1** **Catstar (USA)**[234] 2458 3-8-9 107 ....(t) LDettori 7 108
(SaeedBinSuroor) *mde all: rdn clr 2f out: pushed out* **6/4**[1]

**2** 1 1/4 **Menhoubah (USA)**[133] 5209 3-8-9 105 ....(p) EAhern 6 105
(CEBrittain) *in tch: 3rd st: outpcd over 2f out: styd on wl nr fin* **15/8**[2]

**3** 1 3/4 **Festive Style (SAF)**[136] 3-9-4 79 .... RLMoore 2 111
(SSeemar, UAE) *iln tch: outpcd 1/2-way: 6th st: styd on wl fnl f* **14/1**

**4** 3 **Ibda Ae (KSA)**[15] 3-8-9 100 .... MJKinane 8 96
(SBinSaud, UAE) *trckd ldr: 2nd st: kpt on tl wknd fnl 110yds* **9/2**[3]

**5** 2 1/4 **Tamarillo**[149] 4840 3-8-9 95 ....(t) TEDurcan 3 91
(MAlKurdi, UAE) *trckd ldrs tl lost pl 1/2-way: 7th st: kpt on nr fin* **13/2**

**6** 3/4 **Pomeranze (IRE)**[23] 3-8-9 72 .... WSupple 5 90
(DougWatson, UAE) *t.k.h: in tch towards rr: prog to 5th st: sn wknd* **33/1**

**7** 4 1/2 **Nabtat Saif**[161] 4569 3-8-9 73 .... RMullen 1 81
(DougWatson, UAE) *in tch tl wknd fr 1/2-way* **40/1**

**8** 6 1/2 **Screaming Shamal (USA)**[138] 5118 3-8-9 .... PJSmullen 4 68
(DougWatson, UAE) *s.i.s: a towards rr: last st: eased fnl 110yds* **66/1**

1m 40.46s — **8** Ran SP% **119.8**
Speed ratings: .
**Owner** Godolphin **Bred** Summer Wind Farm **Trained** Newmarket, Suffolk

**NOTEBOOK**
**Catstar(USA)**, runner-up to Attraction in the Queen Mary at Royal Ascot when last seen, dictated the pace and her stamina just held out. Although she will be entered in the Guineas, connections are concerned about her getting this trip, and she may end up running in seven-furlong races.

**Menhoubah(USA)**, in the frame in Group One fillies' races last season, showed she had trained on and was closing on the winner at the finish. She will no doubt renew rivalry at Newmarket.

## 712a AL SEEF INTERNATIONAL RATED STKS (H'CAP) (SPONSORED BY BBC WORLD) (TURF) 1m 2f (T)

5:40 (5:40) (95-110,110) 3-Y-0+ £36,312 (£11,173; £5,586; £2,793) Stalls Low

RPR

1 **Razkalla (USA)**$^{168}$ [4389] 6-9-6 110 .......... JPSpencer 2 111+
(DRLoder) *in tch towards rr: cl up 6th st: nt clr run 2f out: r.o strly to ld fnl 110yds* **11/2**$^{3}$

2 1 ¼ **Prince Of War (AUS)**$^{9}$ [633] 6-9-0 104 .......... WCMarwing 4 103
(MFDeKock, South Africa) *a.p: 4th st: rdn and ev ch fnl f: nt pce of wnr* **9/4**$^{1}$

3 nk **Clodion (IRE)**$^{2}$ [692] 8-8-13 102 .......... TEDurcan 7 101
(MAlKurdi, UAE) *in tch in rr: last st: r.o fnl f: nrst fin* **12/1**

4 ¾ **Scott's View**$^{91}$ [5951] 5-9-6 110 .......... SChin 5 107
(MJohnston) *Prominent: 3rd st: rdn to ld 1 1/2f out: hdd & wknd fnl 110yds* **9/1**

5 1 ¼ **Courageous Duke (USA)**$^{9}$ [633] 5-8-5 95 .......... EAhern 3 90
(JNoseda) *in tch: 5th st: effrt 2f out: kpt on same pce* **3/1**$^{2}$

6 1 ¾ **Mkuzi**$^{139}$ [5106] 5-9-6 110 .......... MJKinane 6 102
(JohnMOxx, Ire) *prom: led after 2f: hdd 1/2-way: 2nd st: wknd over 1f out* **3/1**$^{2}$

7 3 ½ **Simeon**$^{336}$ [691] 5-9-4 108 .......... (v) RLMoore 8 94
(SSeemar, UAE) *prom: led 1/2-way tl hdd fnl 1 1/2f: sn wknd* **25/1**

2m 3.94s **7** Ran SP% **117.7**
Speed ratings: .
**Owner** Sheikh Mohammed **Bred** S N C Godolphin **Trained** Newmarket, Suffolk

**NOTEBOOK**
**Razkalla(USA)** gave Britain their first winner of the carnival, getting up close home after an interrupted run. Despite his age there are not many miles on the clock, and he can win again.
**Scott's View** ran well on his first outing since November, getting to the front before being run out of it in the final half-furlong. He should be better for the outing and a longer trip will help.
**Courageous Duke(USA)** ran a similar race to last week, fading in the closing stages. Possibly he is a little high in the handicap at present.

# 680 SOUTHWELL (L-H)

Sunday, February 8

**OFFICIAL GOING: Standard**
(REGIONAL RACING)
Wind: fresh bhd Weather: cloudy

## 713 BET DIRECT ON ATTHERACES TEXT PAGE 410 APPRENTICE BANDED STKS 7f (F)

2:00 (2:02) (H) 3-Y-0+ £1,305 (£373; £186) Stalls Low

Form RPR

60-1 1 **Smart Scot**$^{27}$ [497] 5-9-7 35 .......... (p) MSavage 5 50+
(BPJBaugh) *chsd ldrs: led and edgd lft over 2f out: sn clr: eased nr fin* **2/1**$^{1}$

040- 2 1 ½ **Fraamtastic**$^{325}$ [740] 7-9-7 30 .......... LTreadwell 13 46
(BAPearce) *mid-div: hdwy over 3f out: rdn to chse wnr over 1f out: styd on* **28/1**

000/ 3 5 **Grub Street**$^{652}$ [1061] 8-9-7 35 .......... MLawson 7 34
(JParkes) *chsd ldrs: rdn over 2f out: wknd fnl f* **50/1**

60-0 4 6 **Miss Wizz**$^{35}$ [434] 4-9-4 35 .......... (p) RoryMoore$^{(3)}$ 12 19
(WStorey) *chsd ldrs over 5f* **12/1**

5040 5 hd **Dancing King (IRE)**$^{13}$ [604] 8-9-4 30 .......... PGallagher$^{(3)}$ 14 18
(PWHiatt) *prom: rdn over 3f out: sn wknd* **10/1**

00-0 6 2 **Caterham Common**$^{17}$ [582] 5-9-7 30 .......... PMakin 8 13
(DWChapman) *s.i.s: nvr trbld ldrs* **16/1**

60-0 7 shd **Velocitys Image (IRE)**$^{31}$ [479] 4-9-2 35 .......... AMullen$^{(5)}$ 2 13
(EJAlston) *mid-div: rdn 1/2-way: sn wknd* **16/1**

0-45 8 1 ¼ **Given A Chance**$^{12}$ [611] 3-7-13 30 .......... BSwarbrick$^{(5)}$ 4 10
(JGGiven) *chsd ldrs over 4f* **9/1**$^{3}$

00-6 9 ¾ **Rivendell**$^{36}$ [422] 8-9-2 30 .......... (t) CCavanagh$^{(5)}$ 3 8
(MWigham) *s.i.s: bhd fr 1/2-way* **11/1**

06-4 10 3 ½ **Zara Louise**$^{27}$ [502] 4-9-2 30 .......... AReilly$^{(5)}$ 6 —
(RPElliott) *sn outpcd* **8/1**$^{2}$

00-6 11 2 ½ **Grand View**$^{5}$ [665] 8-9-2 35 .......... (p) DFentiman$^{(5)}$ 1 —
(JRWeymes) *in rr whn hmpd over 4f out: son wl bhd* **8/1**$^{2}$

0000 12 nk **Meticulous**$^{3}$ [682] 6-9-2 30 .......... (b$^{1}$) AndrewWebb$^{(5)}$ 10 —
(MCChapman) *sn outpcd* **40/1**

-000 13 7 **Caronte (IRE)**$^{10}$ [626] 4-9-2 35 .......... (b) WHogg$^{(5)}$ 9 —
(SRBowring) *led: hdd & wknd over 2f out* **16/1**

460- 14 hd **Amar (CZE)**$^{151}$ [4817] 3-7-13 35 .......... SYourston$^{(5)}$ 11 —
(PABlockley) *s.s: outpcd* **9/1**$^{3}$

1m 29.85s (-0.95) **Going Correction** -0.15s/f (Stan)
**WFA** 3 from 4yo+ 17lb **14** Ran SP% **126.2**
Speed ratings: **99,97,91,84,84 82,82,80,79,75 72,72,64,64**CSF £76.39 TOTE £2.80: £1.40, £8.90, £28.20; EX 74.00.
**Owner** S Day **Bred** Lord Halifax **Trained** Audley, Staffs
■ Stewards Enquiry : Rory Moore one-day ban: used whip from above shoulder height (Feb 19)

**FOCUS**
A dire contest which was run at a modest pace, and the form is poor.

**NOTEBOOK**
**Smart Scot** comfortably followed up his recent win at this track. The drop in trip suited his racing style and he only had to be shaken up to score. Although this was a poor contest, he was value for much more than the official winning margin and can bag the hat-trick at this level.
**Fraamtastic** ran well enough considering she had been off the track since March last year. She will improve for this, but is flattered to have finished so close to the winner.
**Grub Street**, off since 2002, ran well for a long way until he tired out of it in the straight.

## 714 BET DIRECT ON ATTHERACES TEXT PAGE 411 CLAIMING STKS 1m 3f (F)

2:30 (2:31) (H) 4-Y-0+ £1,473 (£421; £210) Stalls Low

Form RPR

3100 1 **Daunted (IRE)**$^{12}$ [616] 8-8-13 60 .......... LisaJones$^{(3)}$ 6 62
(PABlockley) *chsd ldrs: rdn over 3f out: led and edgd lft over 1f out: styd on wl* **1/1**$^{1}$

40-0 2 5 **Frank's Quest (IRE)**$^{27}$ [498] 4-8-3 55 .......... RoryMoore$^{(7)}$ 4 50
(JohnAHarris) *chsd ldrs: led over 4f out: edgd lft and hdd over 1f out: sn btn* **12/1**$^{3}$

-461 3 hd **Spanish Star**$^{3}$ [682] 7-9-2 45 .......... ACulhane 7 54
(MrsNMacauley) *hld up: rdn over 4f out: styd on appr fnl f: nt trble ldrs* **9/4**$^{2}$

5235 4 4 **Sea Ya Maite**$^{6}$ [655] 10-8-12 40 .......... (t) JBramhill 1 43
(SRBowring) *chsd ldrs: rdn over 3f out: wknd 2f out* **14/1**

4-64 5 1 **Red Delirium**$^{19}$ [570] 8-9-2 40 .......... (b) DeanMcKeown 9 46
(RBrotherton) *s.i.s: sn chsng ldrs: wknd over 2f out* **12/1**$^{3}$

/0-0 6 3 ½ **Sophomore**$^{36}$ [425] 10-8-10 40 .......... JMackay 2 34
(JohnAHarris) *hld up: hdwy over 3f out: wknd over 2f out* **25/1**

000- 7 6 **Trojan Wolf**$^{234}$ [2505] 9-8-10 40 .......... SWKelly 8 24
(PHowling) *led: rdn and hdd over 4f out: wknd over 2f out* **16/1**

/00- 8 dist **Stylish Prince**$^{191}$ [3551] 4-8-12 45 .......... DSweeney 3 —
(JGMO'Shea) *hld up: wknd 5f out* **50/1**

2m 29.12s (0.22) **Going Correction** -0.15s/f (Stan)
**WFA** 4 from 7yo+ 2lb **8** Ran SP% **114.5**
Speed ratings: **93,89,89,86,85 83,78,**—CSF £15.25 TOTE £2.00: £1.10, £1.80, £1.70; EX 16.30.Frank's Quest (no.7) was claimed by P Burgoyne for £7,000.
**Owner** Mrs Joanna Hughes **Bred** Mrs G Doyle **Trained** Southwell, Notts
■ Stewards Enquiry : Rory Moore one-day ban: used whip from above shoulder height (Feb 20)

**FOCUS**
A weak event that was run at a modest pace early on resulting in a modest winning time for the grade, although the winner is different class to his rivals.

**NOTEBOOK**
**Daunted(IRE)** took his time to get to the front, but was well on top at the finish. He was entitled to win this on official ratings and does like this venue, having won his last three races here. He hardly appeals as the type to follow up, but his yard is in great form at present.
**Frank's Quest(IRE)** did not stay this trip too well, but at least proved his last running to be all wrong. He will appreciate a slight drop in trip.
**Spanish Star** again stayed on late in the day, but failed to follow up his recent victory on this drop in trip. He would have preferred a stronger early gallop.

## 715 BET DIRECT ON ATTHERACES TEXT PAGE 412 BANDED STKS 1m 4f (F)

3:00 (3:01) (H) 4-Y-0+ £1,683 (£481; £240) Stalls Low

Form RPR

-121 1 **Bella Pavlina**$^{6}$ [653] 6-8-10 40 .......... BSwarbrick$^{(7)}$ 6 54
(WMBrisbourne) *hld up: nt clr run over 4f out: hdwy and swtchd rt over 2f out: styd on to ld wl ins fnl f* **5/6**$^{1}$

62-3 2 1 **Diamond Orchid (IRE)**$^{31}$ [472] 4-9-0 45 .......... (p) RFitzpatrick 3 53
(PDEvans) *w ldr tl led 8f out: clr 3f out: rdn and hdd wl ins fnl f* **12/1**

05-4 3 2 **El Pedro**$^{31}$ [478] 5-8-12 45 .......... MSavage$^{(5)}$ 12 50
(NEBerry) *hld up: hdwy 5f out: rdn over 1f out: styd on same pce ins fnl f* **33/1**

000- 4 6 **Known Maneuver (USA)**$^{20}$ [6156] 6-8-12 45 .......... DFox$^{(5)}$ 8 41
(MCChapman) *chsd ldrs: rdn over 3f out: wknd over 1f out* **100/1**

-162 5 ½ **Dash Of Magic**$^{19}$ [570] 6-9-3 40 .......... CCatlin 13 40
(JHetherton) *chsd ldrs tl wknd over 1f out* **20/1**

4506 6 1 ½ **King Priam (IRE)**$^{3}$ [682] 9-9-3 40 .......... (b) DeanMcKeown 7 38
(MJPolglase) *outpcd: effrt over 3f out: nvr trbld ldrs* **16/1**

500- 7 nk **Jake Black (IRE)**$^{44}$ [5442] 4-9-0 45 .......... DarrenWilliams 10 37
(JJQuinn) *chsd ldrs: rdn over 3f out: wknd over 2f out* **20/1**

0-31 8 1 ½ **Seraph**$^{27}$ [500] 4-9-0 45 .......... (p) JMackay 4 35
(JohnAHarris) *hld up: nvr trbld ldrs* **16/1**

20-0 9 1 **Fairy Wind (GER)**$^{32}$ [467] 7-9-3 45 .......... SWKelly 9 33
(BJCurley) *hld up: effrt and nt clr run over 3f out: n.d* **5/1**$^{3}$

050- 10 7 **Modem (IRE)**$^{93}$ [953] 7-8-10 40 .......... (e) DawnWatson$^{(7)}$ 1 23
(DShaw) *sn outpcd* **33/1**

5-22 11 hd **Our Glenard**$^{24}$ [537] 5-9-3 45 .......... ACulhane 2 23
(SLKeightley) *sn pushed along in rr: effrt over 3f out: sn wknd* **9/2**$^{2}$

/56- 12 1 **Effie Gray**$^{137}$ [3528] 5-9-3 45 .......... DSweeney 15 21
(JWUnett) *chsd ldrs over 8f* **20/1**

-600 13 dist **Kustom Kit For Her**$^{10}$ [625] 4-9-0 45 .......... JBramhill 14 —
(SRBowring) *sn led: hdd 8f out: wknd over 3f out* **100/1**

2m 41.61s (-0.49) **Going Correction** -0.15s/f (Stan)
**WFA** 4 from 5yo+ 3lb **13** Ran SP% **131.0**
Speed ratings: **95,94,93,89,88 87,87,86,85,81 81,80,**—CSF £13.90 TOTE £1.90: £1.10, £2.70, £8.90; EX 19.20.
**Owner** The Cartmel Syndicate **Bred** C Papaioannou **Trained** Great Ness, Shropshire

**FOCUS**
This lacked any real depth, but the winner looks progressive and can score again, although if rated 55 or higher may find things difficult.

**NOTEBOOK**
**Bella Pavlina** is in great form at present and does look to be ahead of the Handicapper on this evidence. She had a nightmare passage throughout and did very well to stick to her task and pick up the eventual runner-up.
**Diamond Orchid(IRE)** does not quite get home over this trip, but ran a solid race in defeat and should be capable of making amends over ten furlongs.
**El Pedro** again got going too late in the day and is very hard to predict.
**Known Maneuver(USA)**
**Fairy Wind(GER)**
**Our Glenard** was never on terms on this switch to the Fibresand and can do better.
**Kustom Kit For Her** *Official explanation: jockey said filly had lost her action*

## 716 BET DIRECT ON ATTHERACES TEXT PAGE 413 BANDED STKS 2m (F)

3:30 (3:32) (H) 4-Y-0+ £1,631 (£466; £233) Stalls Low

Form RPR

-026 1 **Radiant Bride**$^{5}$ [661] 4-8-12 35 .......... (b$^{1}$) DarrenWilliams 6 49+
(KRBurke) *trckd ldrs: led on bit ins fnl f: comf* **8/1**

0-21 2 ½ **Unleaded**$^{25}$ [528] 4-8-12 40 .......... JMackay 8 48
(JAkehurst) *racd keenly: trckd ldr: led 1/2-way: hdd over 4f out: led over 2f out: sn rdn: hdd ins fnl f: kpt on* **4/1**$^{3}$

-223 3 6 **Kagoshima (IRE)**$^{19}$ [568] 9-9-4 40 .......... (v) VHalliday 5 41
(JRNorton) *led to 1/2-way: led over 4f out: rdn and hdd over 2f out: wknd fnl f* **10/3**$^{1}$

6-21 4 6 **Paddy Mul**$^{31}$ [475] 7-9-4 40 .......... (t) DRMcCabe 4 34
(WStorey) *hld up: rdn 6f out: n.d* **4/1**$^{3}$

060- 5 ¾ **Port Moreno (IRE)**$^{67}$ [6125] 4-8-12 45 .......... (v) DSweeney 1 33
(JGMO'Shea) *hld up: hdwy 7f out: wknd 3f out* **8/1**

005/ 6 ½ **Martha Reilly (IRE)**$^{73}$ [879] 8-9-1 35 .......... LisaJones$^{(3)}$ 2 32
(MrsBarbaraWaring) *hld up: a in rr* **25/1**

220- 7 1 ¾ **Bergamo**$^{44}$ [661] 8-8-13 45 .......... (b) TEaves$^{(5)}$ 7 30
(BEllison) *hld up: rdn 6f out: a in rr* **7/2**$^{2}$

0-64 8 15 **Xixita**$^{27}$ [501] 4-8-12 40 .......... JQuinn 3 12
(DrJDScargill) *chsd ldrs tl wknd over 3f out* **16/1**

00/0 9 nk **Niciara (IRE)**$^{33}$ [432] 7-8-13 30 .......... DFox$^{(5)}$ 9 12
(MCChapman) *s.i.s: sn prom: pushed along 10f out: wknd 5f out* **66/1**

3m 47.02s (-5.48) **Going Correction** -0.15s/f (Stan)
**WFA** 4 from 7yo+ 6lb **9** Ran SP% **112.0**
Speed ratings: **97,96,93,90,90 90,89,81,81**CSF £38.00 TOTE £10.90: £2.90, £1.90, £1.10; EX 40.80.
**Owner** Mrs Y Goodwin **Bred** Limestone Stud **Trained** Middleham Moor, N Yorks



The Form Book, Raceform Ltd, Compton, RG20 6NL

**FOCUS**
A weak staying contest run at a steady early pace and the form is poor.
**NOTEBOOK**
**Radiant Bride**, transformed by the application of the blinkers, lost her maiden tag at the 16th time of asking. Although she has looked very tricky prior to this, she won tidily and all of her best form is over this trip. She should not go up in the weights much for this, and could go in again if the headgear has the same effect next time.
**Unleaded**, who has improved since switching to this trip, had no chance with the winner. She was not helped by racing freely early on and she was clear of the rest, so should be given another chance.
**Kagoshima(IRE)** is a consistent sort, but very one paced and hard to win with.
**Bergamo**

## 717 BET DIRECT DAILY SPECIAL OFFERS (S) STKS — 1m (F)
4:00 (4:01) (H) 3-Y-0+ £1,515 (£433; £216) Stalls Low

Form RPR
-200 **1** **Xaloc Bay (IRE)**[10] [625] 6-9-8 52 ........ DarrenWilliams 7 59
(BPJBaugh) *led 7f out: rdn over 3f out: styd on u.p* **8/1**[3]
40-2 **2** *nk* **Noble Pursuit**[10] [627] 7-9-8 57 ........ DeanMcKeown 3 58
(PABlockley) *hld up: hdwy to chse wnr 1/2-way: rdn over 1f out: styd on* **8/11**[1]
-050 **3** *3/4* **Kumakawa**[5] [659] 6-9-1 45 ........ (b) LiamJones(7) 9 57
(EAWheeler) *outpcd: hdwy over 1f out: r.o* **20/1**
4-23 **4** *hd* **Hunting Pink**[12] [615] 3-7-12 48 ........ JQuinn 8 51
(HMorrison) *hld up: hdwy over 2f out: rdn over 1f out: swtchd lft ins fnl f: nt run on* **4/1**[2]
3262 **5** *3 1/2* **Aguila Loco (IRE)**[10] [625] 5-9-8 50 ........ JoannaBadger 6 49
(MCChapman) *plld hrd: led 1f: remained handy: rdn over 1f out: wknd fnl f* **10/1**
003/ **6** *3 1/2* **Ace-Ma-Vahra**[495] [5010] 6-9-3 45 ........ JBramhill 1 36
(SRBowring) *chsd ldrs: rdn over 3f out: wknd wl over 1f out* **33/1**
000- **7** *1 3/4* **Luke After Me (IRE)**[24] [5564] 4-9-8 48 ........ RLappin 5 37
(GASwinbank) *prom over 5f* **16/1**
500- **8** *12* **Over To You Bert**[232] [2053] 5-9-8 49 ........ CCatlin 4 11
(RJHodges) *chsd ldrs: rdn over 3f out: sn wknd* **22/1**

1m 44.44s (-0.16) **Going Correction** -0.15s/f (Stan)
**WFA** 3 from 4yo+ 19lb 8 Ran SP% **116.0**
Speed ratings: **94,93,92,92,89 85,84,72** CT £11.90 TOTE £2.20: £1.10, £3.60, £; EX23.80
1.There was no bid for the winner. Aguila Loco (no.2) was claimed by Steph Liddiard for £4,000. Kumakawa (no.4) was the subject of a friendl
**Owner** Miss S M Potts **Bred** D J And Mrs Deer **Trained** Audley, Staffs

**FOCUS**
This was run at a sound enough pace and this represents typical plating form, as the top two on official figures fought out the finish.
**NOTEBOOK**
**Xaloc Bay(IRE)**, with the headgear left off, did well to outbattle the runner-up late on over a trip that has stretched him in the past. This was his first win since April 2002 and it has to be a doubt as to whether he can follow up.
**Noble Pursuit**, well backed for this, held every chance and can have no excuses. He would have been giving 5lb to the winner if this had been a handicap, but failed to beat him at level weights, so this must rate as a big disappointment.
**Kumakawa** shaped as though he needs further.
**Hunting Pink** looked as though she may have a say in the finish at the top of the straight but, not for the first time, found nil off the bridle.

## 718 BET DIRECT IN RUNNING SKY TEXT PAGE 293 BANDED STKS — 5f (F)
4:30 (4:32) (H) 3-Y-0+ £1,267 (£362; £181) Stalls High

Form RPR
60-6 **1** **Danakim**[6] [657] 7-9-0 35 ........ (be) DFentiman(7) 1 38
(JRWeymes) *chsd ldrs: rdn to ld wl ins fnl f: r.o* **9/2**[2]
0-04 **2** *1/2* **White O' Morn**[9] [638] 5-9-7 30 ........ (t) GGibbons 2 36
(BAMcmahon) *wnt rt s: chsd ldrs: rdn 1/2-way: led over 1f out: hdd wl ins fnl f* **6/4**[1]
000- **3** *2* **Spy Master**[173] [4264] 6-9-0 35 ........ (bt) MLawson(7) 8 29
(JParkes) *s.s: outpcd: hdwy over 1f out: r.o* **12/1**
00-0 **4** *2* **Almara**[24] [536] 4-9-7 35 ........ (tp) JQuinn 7 22
(MissKBBoutflower) *s.i.s: outpcd: r.o ins fnl f: nvr nrr* **20/1**
0/0- **5** *3/4* **Second Generation (IRE)**[61] [6155] 7-9-7 35 ........ CCatlin 6 19
(RJHodges) *sn outpcd: r.o ins fnl f: nvr nrr* **14/1**
00-0 **6** *1 1/4* **Salonika Sky**[25] [530] 3-8-7 35 ........ JMcAuley 11 15
(CWThornton) *chsd ldrs over 3f* **10/1**
0-00 **7** *1* **Precious Freedom**[19] [572] 4-9-7 35 ........ (b) JEdmunds 5 12
(JBalding) *w ldr over 3f: wknd ins fnl f* **10/1**
06/0 **8** *1/2* **Our Old Boy (IRE)**[27] [499] 4-9-7 35 ........ DRMcCabe 3 10
(JAGilbert) *s.i.s and hmpd s: outpcd* **11/2**[3]
000- **9** *1* **Millietom (IRE)**[62] [6147] 3-8-7 30 ........ (b) PFessey 10 —
(KARyan) *led over 3f: wknd ins fnl f* **16/1**
000- **10** *hd* **Gruff**[144] [4988] 5-9-7 35 ........ GParkin 9 —
(PTMidgley) *sn outpcd* **14/1**
000- **11** *3/4* **Silent Angel**[145] [4967] 4-9-0 30 ........ (v[1]) SYourston(7) 4 —
(MrsLucindaFeatherstone) *hmpd s: sn outpcd* **66/1**

60.86 secs (0.56) **Going Correction** +0.05s/f (Slow)
**WFA** 3 from 4yo+ 14lb 11 Ran SP% **124.9**
Speed ratings: **97,96,93,89,88 86,85,84,82,82 81**CSF £12.37 TOTE £6.20: £2.20, £1.10, £3.80; EX 13.30 Place 6 £8.41, Place 5 £3.49..
**Owner** Miss K Buckle **Bred** R T And Mrs Watson **Trained** Middleham Moor, N Yorks
■ Stewards Enquiry : G Gibbons caution: used whip with excessive frquency

**FOCUS**
A dire sprint full of frustrating types and the form is dreadful.
**NOTEBOOK**
**Danakim**, down in grade, stuck to his task well in the straight to win his first race since May 2002. He showed the benefit of a recent comeback run and, on his old form, looks fairly well treated at present.
**White O' Morn** was clear of the rest, but was comfortably held by the winner. She has improved for the recent application of the tongue tie and has a race in her at this level, perhaps over another furlong.
**Spy Master** was taken off her feet on this return to the minimum trip, but was staying on well enough in the straight.
**Almara** was another who failed to cope with the early pace on this drop back from seven furlongs.
**Our Old Boy(IRE)** was badly hampered at the start by the runner up and lost all chance from that point on. This run is best forgotten.
T/Plt: £9.90 to a £1 stake. Pool: £46,799.05. 3,440.70 winning tickets. T/Qpdt: £6.50 to a £1 stake. Pool: £3,086.50. 346.90 winning tickets. CR

# [713]SOUTHWELL (L-H)
Monday, February 9
**OFFICIAL GOING: Standard**

## 719 BET DIRECT ON SKY ACTIVE H'CAP — 7f (F)
2:10 (2:13) (E) (0-75,77) 4-Y-0+ £3,262 (£932; £466) Stalls Low

Form RPR
0063 **1** **Mount Royale (IRE)**[4] [686] 6-8-5 52 ........ (vt) KimTinkler 4 62
(NTinkler) *dwlt: sn trcking ldrs: nt clr run and swtchd rt over 1f out: hdwy ent last: rdn and styd on to ld last 100 yds* **10/3**[1]
60-0 **2** *1 1/4* **Flying Edge (IRE)**[28] [509] 4-8-4 51 ........ ANicholls 11 58
(EJAlston) *cl up: led wl over 2f out: rdn and hdd wl over 1f out: rallied to ld briefly ins last: hdd and no ex last 100 yds* **28/1**
0-25 **3** *1 3/4* **Yorker (USA)**[21] [564] 6-9-7 68 ........ JPSpencer 5 71
(MsDeborahJEvans) *chsd ldrs: rdn along 3f out: drvn and kpt on same pce appr last* **10/3**[1]
21-3 **4** *shd* **Warden Warren**[31] [488] 6-9-6 72 ........ (b) HayleyTurner(5) 7 74
(MrsCADunnett) *chsd ldrs: hdwy on outer to ld wl over 2f out: sn rdn: hdd & wknd ins last* **11/2**[2]
5-30 **5** *1/2* **Yenaled**[4] [686] 7-8-13 60 ........ (p) NCallan 8 61
(KARyan) *hld up: hdwy whn nt clr run on inner and swtchd rt over 1f out rdn and hdwy ent last: sn drvn and kpt on same pce* **8/1**[3]
P0-1 **6** *4* **Weet Watchers**[4] [685] 4-9-11 77 6ex ........ DNolan(5) 2 68
(PABlockley) *sn led: rdn along and hdd wl over 2f out: wknd fnl 2f* **9/1**
6-00 **7** *nk* **Social Contract**[4] [686] 7-8-3 50 ........ (v) CCatlin 3 40
(SDow) *cl up: rdn along over 3f out: sn wknd* **16/1**
40-4 **8** *2 1/2* **Semper Paratus (USA)**[18] [584] 5-8-11 58 ........ (b) MTebbutt 10 42
(HJCollingridge) *prom on outer: rdn along and lost pl 1/2-way: sn outpcd* **8/1**[3]
1-00 **9** *1 3/4* **Pawn In Life (IRE)**[4] [686] 6-8-8 62 ........ (b) PMakin(7) 9 42
(TDBarron) *s.i.s: sn pushed along to chse ldrs on outer: rdn 1/2-way and sn wknd* **12/1**
000- **10** *11* **Drury Lane (IRE)**[142] [5081] 4-10-0 75 ........ ACulhane 1 27
(DWChapman) *sn outpcd and bhd* **50/1**
2406 **U** **Brilliantrio**[4] [686] 6-7-7 45 oh5 ........ DFox(5) 6 —
(MCChapman) *rrd and uns rdr s* **25/1**

1m 30.69s (-0.11) **Going Correction** +0.025s/f (Slow) 11 Ran SP% **116.6**
Speed ratings: **101,99,97,97,96 92,91,89,87,74** —CSF £108.39 CT £343.72 TOTE £5.30: £1.70, £18.20, £1.50; EX 107.40.
**Owner** Langton Partnership **Bred** Joe Crowley And Mr And Mrs A P O'Brien **Trained** Langton, N Yorks

**FOCUS**
An average handicap run at just a fair pace, but the form looks reliable.
**NOTEBOOK**
**Mount Royale(IRE)**, who was winning for the first time outside of claiming or selling company, would have probably won with a bit more in hand had he got a clear run earlier. All his wins have come at seven furlongs, and his record over the trip at this track now reads 1532211531, which is fairly impressive for one so modest.
**Flying Edge(IRE)** had not made much of an impression in two starts at Wolverhampton, but ran much better on his first start here. There is something to build on now.
**Yorker(USA)** looks better suited by a mile these days.
**Warden Warren**, another specialist at the distance, ran a solid race. However, all his handicap wins have come off marks in the 60s and he looks in the grip of the Handicapper for the time being.
**Yenaled** has not won over a trip as short as this for almost three and a half years.
**Weet Watchers** had enjoyed an easy lead when successful last time on a day when pace horses dominated.

## 720 PRESS INTERACTIVE TO BET DIRECT CLAIMING STKS — 1m (F)
2:40 (2:42) (F) 4-Y-0+ £2,891 (£826; £413) Stalls Low

Form RPR
4-52 **1** **Caroubier (IRE)**[14] [605] 4-9-5 73 ........ JPSpencer 1 72
(TDBarron) *s.i.s and bhd: hdwy 3f out: rdn to ld wl over 1f out: sn drvn clr* **2/9**[1]
0-40 **2** *5* **Fortune Point (IRE)**[3] [695] 6-9-1 59 ........ ACulhane 3 57
(AWCarroll) *trckd ldng pair: effrt and nt clr run 2f out: swtchd rt and sn rdn: styd on ent last: no ch w wnr* **7/1**[2]
-530 **3** *1* **Tinian**[14] [604] 6-8-9 45 ........ DarrenWilliams 7 49
(KRBurke) *cl up: ev ch and rdn whn hung lft 2f out: sn drvn and kpt on same pce* **28/1**
204 **4** *shd* **Repeat (IRE)**[11] [627] 4-8-4 53 ........ (p) DAllan(3) 2 47
(MissGayKelleway) *trckd ldrs on inner: rdn along and outpcd over 2f out: sn drvn and kpt on one pce ent last* **14/1**[3]
4566 **5** *1/2* **Proud Victor (IRE)**[17] [594] 4-8-0 40 ........ (v) HayleyTurner(5) 5 43
(DShaw) *trckd ldrs on outer: hdwy 1/2-way: rdn along to chal 2f out sn drvn and btn* **50/1**
0-00 **6** *3 1/2* **Onefortheboys (IRE)**[6] [662] 5-8-2 40 ........ DeanWilliams(7) 6 40
(DFlood) *ste stdy pce: qcknd 3f out: rdn over 2f out: sn hdd & wknd* **50/1**

1m 44.59s (-0.01) **Going Correction** +0.025s/f (Slow) 6 Ran SP% **108.4**
Speed ratings: **101,96,95,94,94 90**CSF £1.94 TOTE £1.20: £1.10, £2.10; EX 2.10.The winner was claimed by J.Gallagher for £12,000.
**Owner** Nigel Shields **Bred** J K Grimes **Trained** Maunby, N Yorks

**FOCUS**
A poor claimer won by the form choice, who is a decent performer at this level.
**NOTEBOOK**
**Caroubier(IRE)** had plenty in hand on official ratings and won as his form entitled him to. His record over a mile on Fibresand now reads 113111.
**Fortune Point(IRE)**, dropping back into claiming grade, ran as well as could be expected against a horse off whom he would have been receiving another 10lb in a handicap.
**Tinian** had plenty to find on these terms and was not disgraced, but he did not look particularly enthusiastic under the whip.
**Repeat(IRE)** is better over shorter.

## 721 LITTLEWOODS BET DIRECT CLASSIFIED STKS — 5f (F)
3:10 (3:17) (F) 3-Y-0+ £2,898 (£828; £414) Stalls High

Form RPR
00-5 **1** **Sea The World (IRE)**[25] [540] 4-9-5 56 ........ (v) NCallan 7 65
(DShaw) *sn pushed along and outpcd centre: hdwy 2f out: n.m.r and swtchd rt over 1f out: rdn and edgd lft: kpt on to ld nr line* **7/1**[3]
-350 **2** *hd* **Henry Tun**[10] [638] 6-9-2 47 ........ (b) DAllan(3) 6 64?
(JBalding) *cl up centre: led 1/2-way: rdn and hung bdly lft fr over 1f out: drvn and hdd nr fin* **14/1**

-410 **3** *1* **Lady Protector**[10] 637 5-8-9 48 PMakin(7) 1 58
(JBalding) *chsd ldrs: rdn along and ev ch ins last: n.m.r and no ex nr fin* **16/1**

0231 **4** *nk* **Alizar (IRE)**[12] 620 3-8-2 59 JQuinn 4 57
(SDow) *chsd ldrs: nt clr run and swtchd rt over 1f out: sn rdn and kpt on ins last* **11/2**[2]

-312 **5** *nk* **Mr Pertemps**[4] 681 6-9-0 60 (p) THamilton(5) 10 59
(RAFahey) *outpcd and rdn along 1/2-way: hdwy wl over 1f out: drvn and hung lft ent last: nrst fin* **5/6**[1]

000- **6** *2 1/2* **Park Star**[51] 6221 4-9-2 56 DarrenWilliams 3 47
(DShaw) *outpcd and bhd far side 1/2-way: styd on u.p appr last: nrst fin* **16/1**

0633 **7** *1 3/4* **Playful Spirit**[11] 625 5-9-2 49 (v) JEdmunds 2 41
(JBalding) *chsd ldrs: rdn along and wkng whn n.m.r over 1f out* **20/1**

56-5 **8** *nk* **Rellim**[23] 560 5-8-9 48 SYourston(7) 12 40
(PABlockley) *led to 1/2-way: sn rdn along and wknd over 1f out* **20/1**

-634 **9** *nk* **Amanda's Lad (IRE)**[4] 681 4-9-0 45 DNolan(5) 11 42
(MCChapman) *rdn along and outpcd 1/2-way: styd on appr last: nvr a factor* **66/1**

000- **10** *1/2* **Valazar (USA)**[52] 6217 5-9-5 54 ACulhane 9 40
(DWChapman) *chsd ldrs: rdn along 2f out: sn wknd* **28/1**

000- **11** *1 1/2* **Maromito (IRE)**[185] 3968 7-9-5 55 KDalgleish 8 35
(RBastiman) *chsd ldrs: rdn along 2f out: sn wknd* **33/1**

440- **12** *hd* **Vanished (IRE)**[185] 3968 4-9-2 60 (p) VHalliday 5 31
(MJPolglase) *cl up: rdn along and wkng whn n.m.r over 1f out: eased* **25/1**

60.95 secs (0.65) **Going Correction** +0.175s/f (Slow)
**WFA** 3 from 4yo+ 14lb 12 Ran SP% 122.1
Speed ratings: **101,100,99,98,98 94,91,90,90,89 87,86**CSF £91.83 TOTE £10.40: £2.10, £3.80, £5.20; EX 161.70.
**Owner** Swann Racing Ltd **Bred** Tally-Ho Stud **Trained** Averham, Notts

**FOCUS**
Just an average race for the grade with a pace to match.

**NOTEBOOK**
**Sea The World(IRE)**, who had dropped to his lowest-ever mark, is suited by a fast pace and that is what he got on this occasion. He initially looked as though he wanted to duck in behind Henry Tun, but his rider managed to convince him to go past inside the last.
**Henry Tun** was meeting a lot of these on worse terms than in a handicap, and in the circumstances this was a solid effort.
**Lady Protector** ran well back over the course and distance over which she enjoyed her first win.
**Alizar(IRE)**, who has been successful three times in selling grade, has been found out on each occasion she has had to run in higher grade.
**Mr Pertemps**, who was doing all his best work in the closing stages, has won over five furlongs in the past but he is at his best over six.
**Park Star** also shaped as though she will do better back over six.

## 722 BETDIRECT.CO.UK MAIDEN STKS 1m 4f (F)
3:40 (3:42) (D) 4-Y-0+ £3,328 (£1,024; £512; £256) Stalls Low

Form RPR

42- **1** **Harelda**[199] 3558 4-8-6 JQuinn 4 71+
(HMorrison) *keen: trckd ldrs: smooth hdwy over 4f out: led 3f out: sn clr* **2/5**[1]

0-0 **2** *14* **Sean's Memory (USA)**[31] 484 4-8-11 (p) CCatlin 7 55
(MrsCADunnett) *pushed along in rr after 4f: hdwy to chse ldrs 5f out: sn rdn along: drvn over 1f out and kpt on: no ch w wnr* **80/1**

0-4 **3** *3/4* **Bestseller**[31] 484 4-8-6 RHavlin 6 49
(JGMO'Shea) *chsd ldng pair: rdn along over 4f out: drvn and one pce fr over 2f out* **9/1**[3]

-554 **4** *1 1/2* **Luxi River (USA)**[11] 630 4-8-4 55 DerekNolan(7) 2 52
(PABlockley) *chsd ldrs: hdwy to ld over 5f out: rdn along 4f out: hdd 3f out: sn drvn along and one pce* **11/1**

**5** *dist* **Datahill (IRE)**[76] 4-8-6 72 PaulEddery 5 —
(PWD'Arcy) *chsd ldr: effrt to dispute ld 1/2-way: rdn along 5f out and sn wknd* **9/2**[2]

/00- **6** *3* **Leyaaly**[292] 1192 5-8-9 30 PMQuinn 1 —
(BAPearce) *chsd ldrs: rdn along after 5f: sn lost pl and t.o fnl 4f* **150/1**

60-0 **7** *28* **Theme Park**[28] 501 4-8-11 53 (t) JMackay 3 —
(JohnAHarris) *led: rdn along 1/2-way: sn hdd & wknd: t.o fnl 4f* **40/1**

2m 40.77s (-1.33) **Going Correction** +0.025s/f (Slow)
**WFA** 4 from 5yo 3lb 7 Ran SP% 112.3
Speed ratings: **105,95,95,94,— —,—**CSF £51.03 TOTE £1.20: £1.02, £11.70; EX 41.60.
**Owner** Sir Thomas Pilkington **Bred** Sir Thomas Pilkington **Trained** East Ilsley, Berks

**FOCUS**
An uncompetitive maiden, but the time was fair. Harelda won easily but was about a stone below her turf form.

**NOTEBOOK**
**Harelda**, whose turf maiden form put her miles clear of the rest on form, just had to show that she could handle this surface to score. She won with any amount in hand and can go on from this providing she remains sound (she has had leg problems in the past).
**Sean's Memory(USA)**, whose jockey was hard at work from a long way out, repaid the effort with a personal best performance. He is of modest ability though, and should not get too high a rating for what he has achieved to date.
**Bestseller** plugged on at the one pace in the straight and should now get a modest handicap mark.
**Luxi River(USA)** is an exposed gelding who has been beaten in sellers.
**Datahill(IRE)**, whose dam finished third in the Oaks, was formerly trained in France and changed hands for 50,000gns at the sales in December. This was an unpromising start to her racing career in this country.

## 723 BET DIRECT FOOTBALL CASHBACKS (S) STKS 7f (F)
4:10 (4:10) (G) 3-Y-0+ £2,590 (£740; £370) Stalls Low

Form RPR

3203 **1** **Legalis (USA)**[6] 670 6-9-8 57 (b) NCallan 2 57
(KARyan) *trckd ldrs: smooth hdwy 2fout:led over 1f out: rdn and hdd wl ins last: rallied to ld nr line* **3/1**[2]

1326 **2** *hd* **Feast Of Romance**[2] 707 7-9-13 53 (b) JPSpencer 6 62
(PHowling) *hld up in tch: smooth hdwy 2f out: shkn up over 1f out: rdn to ld wl ins last: drvn and hdd nr line* **5/2**[1]

4200 **3** *2 1/2* **Headland (USA)**[3] 698 6-9-13 59 (b) ACulhane 3 55
(DWChapman) *trckd ldrs: effrt on outer 2f out: sn rdn and ev ch ent last: sn drvn and wknd* **5/1**

000- **4** *1 3/4* **Earlston**[107] 5742 4-9-8 64 (t[1]) MFenton 4 46
(MissGayKelleway) *cl up: led 1/2-way: rdn and qckn over 2f out: hdd over 1f out and wknd ent last* **7/2**[3]

00-0 **5** *1 1/4* **Cayman Breeze**[34] 448 4-9-8 62 PaulEddery 5 43
(SDow) *hld up in rr: hdwy 2f out: swtchd rt and rdn over 1f out: sn btn* **7/1**

5-54 **6** *3 1/2* **Jalouhar**[6] 670 4-9-13 57 (p) KDalgleish 1 39
(BPJBaugh) *hld up in tch: hdwy over 2f out and sn ev ch tl rdn and wknd over 1f out* **10/1**

6 **7** *9* **Globe Beauty (IRE)**[25] 534 6-9-3 DSweeney 7 7
(ADWPinder) *sn led and set stdy pce: pushed along and hdd 1/2-way: sn wknd* **100/1**

1m 31.51s (0.71) **Going Correction** +0.025s/f (Slow) 7 Ran SP% 115.0
Speed ratings: **96,95,92,90,89 85,75**CSF £11.11 TOTE £3.80: £3.20, £1.10; EX 16.20.There was no bid for the winner.
**Owner** Sunpak Potatoes **Bred** Darley Stud Management Inc **Trained** Hambleton, N Yorks

**FOCUS**
A modest time, even for a seller, and the form is average.

**NOTEBOOK**
**Legalis(USA)** was not sure to appreciate this longer trip, but he rallied well to get back up on the line after being headed inside the last. This is his grade these days.
**Feast Of Romance** had to wait for a gap to appear, but he looked sure to score when eventually hitting the front inside the final furlong. However, he found the winner tenacious in the finish.
**Headland(USA)** tends to have trouble with the seventh furlong.
**Earlston**, having his first start for his new stable, was best in according to official ratings, but may have needed this first outing since October.
**Cayman Breeze** appears to have lost his way since running a fair race on his return to the sand at Lingfield in December.
**Jalouhar** *Official explanation: jockey said gelding had lost a front plate*

## 724 LITTLEWOODSPOKER.COM H'CAP 1m 6f (F)
4:40 (4:40) (F) (0-65,63) 4-Y-0+ £2,954 (£844; £422) Stalls Low

Form RPR

000- **1** **Sun Hill**[26] 5933 4-8-10 52 DSweeney 10 65
(MBlanshard) *trckd ldrs: hdwy 3f out: rdn to chse ldr 2f out: drvn ent last and styd on wl to ld nr line* **66/1**

-160 **2** *shd* **Madiba**[9] 645 5-9-4 55 KDalgleish 9 68
(PHowling) *a.p: led 1/2-way: rdn over 2f out: drvn ent last: hdd and no ex nr line* **25/1**

3533 **3** *4* **Lazzaz**[9] 645 6-9-6 57 ACulhane 5 65
(PWHiatt) *midfield: hdwy and in tch 1/2-way: rdn to chse ldrs over 2f out: sn drvn and kpt on same pce fnl f* **7/1**

1214 **4** *5* **Delta Force**[6] 671 5-9-7 63 DNolan(5) 11 64
(PABlockley) *chsd ldng pair: rdn along over 2f out: drvn over 1f out: wknd* **9/2**[2]

-122 **5** *1 3/4* **Nakwa (IRE)**[14] 609 6-9-2 56 DAllan(3) 3 55
(EJAlston) *trckd ldrs on inner: lost pl 1/2-way: hdwy and pushed along over 4f out: rdn to chse ldrs over 2f out: sn drvn and no imp* **9/4**[1]

-330 **6** *3/4* **Ambersong**[16] 603 6-8-13 50 NCallan 1 48
(AWCarroll) *in tch: pushed along over 4f out: rdn over 2f out: sn no im pression* **7/1**

/0-4 **7** *3 1/2* **Ela Re**[16] 546 5-8-9 46 ow1 MTebbutt 13 39
(CRDore) *hld up towards rr: hdwy on outer 1/2-way: chsd ldrs over 3f out: sn rdn and wknd fnl 2f* **11/2**[3]

/6-3 **8** *3* **Broughton Melody**[28] 501 5-8-8 45 JPSpencer 12 34
(WJMusson) *hld up: a rr* **12/1**

0-53 **9** *1* **Antony Ebeneezer**[18] 583 5-8-3 40 (t) CCatlin 2 28
(CRDore) *in tch: rdn along 1/2-way: wknd 4f out* **10/1**

0-62 **10** *6* **Jungle Lion**[25] 545 6-8-10 47 (t) JMackay 4 27
(JohnAHarris) *hld up towards rr: rapid hdwy on outer to dispute ld 1/2-way: sn rdn along and wknd over 4f out* **40/1**

404- **11** *1 1/2* **San Marco (IRE)**[27] 4105 6-8-8 45 (p) MFenton 7 23
(MrsPSly) *led to 1/2-way: sn rdn along and wknd* **33/1**

63 **12** *nk* **Free Style (GER)**[25] 545 4-8-3 45 JoannaBadger 6 23
(KRBurke) *chsd ldrs: rdn along 1/2-way: sn wknd* **25/1**

-006 **13** *7* **Golden Dual**[12] 618 4-9-1 57 PaulEddery 8 26
(SDow) *dwlt: a bhd* **16/1**

3m 8.65s (-0.95) **Going Correction** +0.025s/f (Slow)
**WFA** 4 from 5yo+ 5lb 13 Ran SP% 126.6
Speed ratings: **103,102,100,97,96 96,94,92,92,88 87,87,83**CSF £1253.49 CT £12308.14 TOTE £102.70: £37.90, £7.60, £3.10; EX 3146.30 TRIFECTA Not won. Place 6 £149.40, Place 5 £83.43.
**Owner** Stanley Hinton **Bred** London Thoroughbred Services Ltd **Trained** Upper Lambourn, Berks
■ Stewards Enquiry : K Dalgleish three-day ban: used whip with excessive frequency (Feb 20,21,23)
D Sweeney three-day ban: used whip with excessive frequency (Feb 20,21,23)

**FOCUS**
The pace was steady and those held up did not figure. The form has a dubious look to it.

**NOTEBOOK**
**Sun Hill**had not shown much on turf or over hurdles, but he took to this surface well on his first attempt. Always in the right position given the moderate gallop, he ran on well to get his nose in front close home as the leader faltered. *Official explanation: trainer said, regarding the improved form shown, this was gelding's first run on an all-weather track and it had benefitted from the step up in trip on this occasion*
**Madiba**, who had the blinkers left off this time, did everything right until faltering close home.
**Lazzaz** does not win very often but this was another solid effort.
**Delta Force**, who might just be in the grip of the Handicapper now, had every chance given the way the race panned out, as he was prominent throughout.
**Nakwa(IRE)**, for whom the race was not run to suit, was struggling to make up lost ground after halfway.
**Ela Re**, held up at the back of the field off the steady gallop, was another ill-served by the way the race was run.
**Jungle Lion** *Official explanation: jockey said gelding hung throughout*
T/Plt: £415.40 to a £1 stake. Pool: £39,159.15. 68.80 winning tickets. T/Qpdt: £182.50 to a £1 stake. Pool: £2,294.10. 9.30 winning tickets. JR

# 693 WOLVERHAMPTON (A.W) (L-H)
Monday, February 9

**OFFICIAL GOING: Standard to slow**
(REGIONAL RACING)
Wind: nil Weather: fine

## 725 BET DIRECT ON SKY ACTIVE BANDED STKS 7f (F)
2:30 (2:32) (H) 3-Y-0+ £1,652 (£472; £236) Stalls High

Form RPR

-240 **1** **Eager Angel (IRE)**[4] 686 6-9-6 45 (p) DeanMcKeown 6 50
(RFMarvin) *hld up and bhd: hdwy 3f out: sn rdn: r.o to ld last stride* **8/1**

/0-0 **2** *shd* **Potsdam**[3] 695 6-9-6 45 (t) SWKelly 7 50
(NiallMoran, Ire) *hld up: hdwy 4f out: rdn over 2f out: led over 1f out: hdd last stride* **7/2**[1]


The Form Book, Raceform Ltd, Compton, RG20 6NL

633- **3** *3* **Levantine (IRE)**[77] 6057 7-9-6 45........................(b[1]) SWhitworth 9 42
(AGNewcombe) *led: rdn and hdd over 1f out: no ex ins fnl f* **7/2**[1]

5-14 **4** *3/4* **Printsmith (IRE)**[32] 472 7-9-6 45........................ JBramhill 3 40
(JRNorton) *chsd ldrs: rdn over 4f out: outpcd over 3f out: rallied jst over 1f out: kpt on ins fnl f* **5/1**[2]

-300 **5** *1 1/4* **Neutral Night (IRE)**[7] 654 4-9-6 45........................(v) ADaly 8 37
(RBrotherton) *s.i.s: bhd: rdn over 4f out: hdwy fnl f: nvr nrr* **50/1**

00-6 **6** *1/2* **Mr Stylish**[28] 498 8-9-6 45........................(vt) JDSmith 12 36
(JSMoore) *stdd s: hld up in rr: pushed along over 3f out: late hdwy on outside: nrst fin* **20/1**

6-64 **7** *1 1/4* **Dasar**[11] 625 4-8-13 45........................(b) MLawson(7) 4 33
(MBrittain) *prom: rdn over 3f out: wknd over 2f out* **25/1**

-006 **8** *1/2* **Indian Shores**[10] 638 5-9-3 45........................(p) LisaJones(3) 5 32
(MMullineaux) *a bhd* **33/1**

-435 **9** *2* **Sabana (IRE)**[19] 573 6-9-3 45........................(b) FPFerris(3) 11 27
(JMBradley) *sn chsng ldrs: rdn and wknd 3f out* **10/1**

5-10 **10** *2* **Indian Warrior**[25] 536 8-9-6 45........................(b) IMongan 10 22
(JJay) *prom: rdn over 3f out: wknd wl over 1f out* **6/1**[3]

0-52 **11** *6* **Phantom Flame (USA)**[7] 655 4-9-6 45........................ JFanning 2 7
(MJohnston) *prom tl wknd over 3f out* **13/2**

1m 32.39s (2.19) **Going Correction** +0.20s/f (Slow) **11** Ran SP% **122.4**
Speed ratings: **95,94,91,90,89 88,87,86,84,82 75**CSF £36.38 TOTE £10.60: £2.60, £1.80, £3.70; EX 47.10.
**Owner** J F Pitchford **Bred** Patrick O'Dwyer **Trained** Southwell, Notts

**FOCUS**
The fact that nine of the runners wore some sort of headgear summed this race up; the form is weak.

**NOTEBOOK**
**Eager Angel(IRE)**, unlucky at Southwell last week, finally broke her duck and has been faring better since stepping up from sprint distances.
**Potsdam** could not have gone any closer to getting off the mark on this drop back from a mile.
**Levantine(IRE)** goes well when fresh and may have run a shade freely in the first-time blinkers.
**Printsmith(IRE)** wants a return to a mile on this evidence.

## 726 BET DIRECT NO Q DEMO 08000 837 888 CLAIMING STKS 1m 1f 79y(F)
**3:00** (3:01) (H) 3-Y-O+ **£1,470** (£420; £210) **Stalls** Low

Form RPR

6-34 **1** **Grand Lass (IRE)**[27] 517 5-9-8 50........................(p) SWKelly 8 53
(TDBarron) *sn led: rdn clr over 2f out: drvn out* **11/4**[2]

0-01 **2** *1 1/2* **Prince Prospect**[7] 655 8-9-6 45........................ KristinStubbs(7) 2 55
(MrsLStubbs) *bhd tl hdwy over 3f out: wnt 2nd jst over 1f out: r.o: nt rch wnr* **4/1**[3]

0-14 **3** *6* **French Horn**[26] 531 7-9-12 50........................(p) GCarter 5 42
(MWigham) *hld up in tch: rdn over 3f out: wknd over 2f out* **9/4**[1]

-010 **4** *1/2* **Malmand (USA)**[25] 537 5-9-12 46........................(v) IMongan 9 41
(RBrotherton) *s.i.s: plld hrd: hdwy over 6f out: rdn over 3f out: wknd over 2f out* **9/1**

0600 **5** *1/2* **Love's Design (IRE)**[10] 642 7-9-8 45........................ AQuinn(5) 4 41
(MissSJWilton) *stdd s: hld up: smooth hdwy over 4f out: chsd wnr over 3f out: sn rdn: wknd fnl f* **20/1**

0-05 **6** *1 1/4* **Think Quick (IRE)**[7] 653 4-9-1 35........................ HFellows(7) 12 34
(RHollinshead) *racd wd: bhd tl hdwy over 1f out: n.d* **50/1**

0-20 **7** *2 1/2* **Good Timing**[20] 570 6-9-13 45........................ GParkin 11 34
(JHetherton) *prom: rdn over 3f out: wknd over 2f out* **20/1**

0-00 **8** *4* **Peace Treaty (IRE)**[13] 615 3-8-1 30........................(t) JBramhill 10 21
(SRBowring) *hld up mid-div: hdwy over 4f out: rdn over 3f out: sn wknd* **66/1**

0-0 **9** *5* **Oktis Morilious (IRE)**[18] 587 3-8-3........................ JFanning 1 13
(JAOsborne) *led early: stdd and sn lost pl: rdn over 4f out: no rspnse* **16/1**

0003 **10** *1* **Haithem (IRE)**[7] 655 7-9-10 30........................(e) LisaJones(3) 6 15
(DShaw) *prom 4f* **16/1**

0-0 **11** *11* **Dr Raj**[11] 630 5-9-11........................(tp) GGibbons 7 —
(BAMcmahon) *prom: rdn over 5f out: wknd over 3f out* **40/1**

2m 5.69s (2.79) **Going Correction** +0.20s/f (Slow)
**WFA** 3 from 4yo+ 21lb **11** Ran SP% **114.6**
Speed ratings: **95,93,88,87,87 86,84,80,76,75 65**CSF £12.91 TOTE £3.10: £1.10, £1.90, £1.50; EX 18.80.Grand Lass was claimed by A.Sadik for £5,000.
**Owner** Nigel Shields **Bred** David F Byrne **Trained** Maunby, N Yorks

**FOCUS**
An ordinary claimer, and modest form, but the first two finished clear .

**NOTEBOOK**
**Grand Lass(IRE)**, in cheekpieces rather than blinkers or a visor, sensibly had plenty of use made of her over this shorter distance.
**Prince Prospect** is the type who needs things to go his way and he could not peg back the enterprisingly-ridden winner.
**French Horn** had the cheekpieces refitted and it may be that he is better suited to the Polytrack.
**Malmand(USA)** paid the penalty for refusing to settle.
**Love's Design(IRE)** had his stamina limitations exposed.

## 727 BET DIRECT NO Q BANDED STKS 1m 4f (F)
**3:30** (3:30) (H) 4-Y-O+ **£1,277** (£365; £182) **Stalls** Low

Form RPR

6-32 **1** **Buz Kiri (USA)**[6] 661 6-9-3 35........................ PDoe 3 44
(AWCarroll) *hld up and bhd: hdwy over 5f out: rdn wl over 1f out: led ins fnl f: r.o* **7/1**

00-3 **2** *1 3/4* **Galley Law**[7] 653 4-8-10 30 ow1........................ TEaves(5) 9 42
(RCraggs) *a.p: rdn to ld over 3f out: hdd ins fnl f: nt qckn* **25/1**

-004 **3** *12* **Little Richard (IRE)**[6] 661 5-9-3 30........................(p) VSlattery 6 23
(MWellings) *prom: rdn over 4f out: wknd over 2f out* **14/1**

4232 **4** *2* **The Last Mohican**[3] 699 5-9-3 35........................(p) SWKelly 10 20
(PHowling) *led: rdn and hdd over 3f out: wknd over 2f out* **11/4**[2]

2536 **5** *1 1/4* **Ipledgeallegiance (USA)**[11] 630 8-9-3 35........................ RBrisland 1 19
(DWChapman) *bhd: rdn over 6f out: styd on fnl 2f: n.d* **14/1**

0456 **6** *3/4* **Western Command (GER)**[17] 589 8-9-3 35........................ PMcCabe 2 17
(MrsNMacauley) *hld up and bhd: hdwy 6f out: wknd over 4f out* **14/1**

460/ **7** *12* **Kaid (IRE)**[53] 420 9-9-3 35........................ IMongan 5 —
(RLee) *hld up: rdn 8f out: wknd fnl 4f* **10/1**

5-00 **8** *15* **Magic Charm**[6] 661 6-9-3 35........................ SWhitworth 7 —
(AGNewcombe) *wnt prom after 2f: wknd over 4f out: t.o* **7/1**[3]

0-00 **9** *4* **Morris Dancing (USA)**[17] 589 5-9-3 30........................(p) JFanning 4 —
(BPJBaugh) *t.k.h in tch: wknd over 4f out: t.o* **25/1**

000- **10** *3* **Bugle Call**[73] 6085 4-8-11 35........................(bt[1]) LPKeniry(3) 8 —
(KOCunningham-Brown) *t.k.h: hdwy 6f out: rdn and wknd over 4f out: t.o* **66/1**

2m 43.38s (1.88) **Going Correction** +0.20s/f (Slow)
**WFA** 4 from 5yo+ 3lb **10** Ran SP% **112.2**
Speed ratings: **101,99,91,90,89 89,81,71,68,66**CSF £54.54 TOTE £3.30: £1.10, £7.00, £3.00; EX 72.60.
**Owner** Serafino Agodino **Bred** Jamm Ltd And W Lazy T Ltd **Trained** Wixford, Warwicks

**FOCUS**
This took little winning and the form is woeful, but the time was fair for a banded race.

**NOTEBOOK**
**Buz Kiri(USA)** gained due reward for some consistent efforts and is just the sort to benefit from regional racing.
**Galley Law** does seem to be going the right way albeit at a very low level.
**Little Richard(IRE)** is fully exposed.
**The Last Mohican** had finished four lengths behind the winner over an extra furlong at Lingfield last week, and this drop in trip was against him.
**Morris Dancing(USA)** *Official explanation: jockey said gelding was hanging both ways*
**Bugle Call** *Official explanation: jockey said gelding ran too free early on*

## 728 BET DIRECT NO Q DEMO 08000 837 888 BANDED STKS 6f (F)
**4:00** (4:01) (H) 3-Y-O+ **£1,645** (£470; £235) **Stalls** Low

Form RPR

4023 **1** **Enjoy The Buzz**[7] 658 5-9-7 40........................ PFitzsimons 9 49
(JMBradley) *hld up: hdwy over 2f out: sn rdn: led wl ins fnl f: r.o* **15/2**

00-0 **2** *1/2* **Katy O'Hara**[11] 626 5-9-7 45........................ JFanning 13 48
(MissSEHall) *s.i.s: sn mid-div: hdwy 3f out: sn rdn: ev ch ins fnl f: r.o* **25/1**

5020 **3** *1/2* **Above Board**[4] 680 9-9-7 45........................(tp) DeanMcKeown 12 46
(RFMarvin) *a.p: rdn to ld over 1f out: hdd wl ins fnl f: kpt on* **12/1**

05-2 **4** *1* **The Gay Fox**[25] 536 10-9-4 45........................(bt) LPKeniry(3) 11 43
(BGPowell) *sn bhd: hdwy over 2f out: r.o ins fnl f* **8/1**

66-1 **5** *1 1/4* **Mount Superior (USA)**[32] 470 8-9-4 45........................(b) LEnstone(3) 8 39
(PWD'Arcy) *a.p: rdn and one pce fnl 2f* **7/1**[3]

06-0 **6** *hd* **Ejay**[25] 541 5-9-4 40........................ LisaJones(3) 2 39
(JulianPoulton) *a.p: rdn and one pce fnl 2f* **100/1**

-310 **7** *3 1/2* **Star Lad (IRE)**[21] 565 4-9-7 45........................(v) IMongan 7 28
(RBrotherton) *led: rdn and hdd over 1f out: wknd fnl f* **5/1**[2]

0-62 **8** *1 1/4* **Bells Beach (IRE)**[7] 654 6-9-7 40........................ SWKelly 1 24
(PHowling) *bhd: sme hdwy on ins over 2f out: sn no imp* **9/2**[1]

-006 **9** *3* **Miss Judged**[20] 569 3-8-1 45........................(be) JFMcDonald(5) 4 15
(APJones) *s.i.s: plld hrd early: a bhd* **9/1**

5-03 **10** *1/2* **Sergeant Slipper**[7] 657 7-9-7 45........................(v) RFitzpatrick 5 14
(CSmith) *sme hdwy whn bdly hmpd wl over 1f out: nt rcvr* **8/1**

00-4 **11** *2 1/2* **Statoyork**[7] 657 11-9-0 45........................(e) DawnWatson(7) 3 6
(DShaw) *s.i.s: a bhd* **14/1**

/0-0 **12** *1 1/2* **Hellbent**[28] 504 5-9-0 45........................(b[1]) SCrawford(7) 10 2
(JAOsborne) *plld hrd: sn w ldrs: wknd 2f out* **12/1**

600- **13** *28* **Alibongo (CZE)**[171] 4354 3-8-6 40........................ JBramhill 6 —
(PABlockley) *prom: rdn and wknd qckly over 3f out: t.o* **20/1**

1m 16.79s (1.09) **Going Correction** +0.20s/f (Slow)
**WFA** 3 from 4yo+ 15lb **13** Ran SP% **123.0**
Speed ratings: **100,99,98,97,95 95,90,89,85,84 81,79,41**CSF £189.23 TOTE £13.10: £4.40, £13.10, £2.80; EX 215.20.
**Owner** Miss F Fenley **Bred** Southern Seafoods **Trained** Sedbury, Gloucs
■ Stewards Enquiry : L Enstone five-day ban: careless riding (Feb 20,21,23-25)

**FOCUS**
This race, although weak, proved that low-grade events can still be very competitive, and the winning time was fair.

**NOTEBOOK**
**Enjoy The Buzz** has to come from behind and Fitzsimons earned praise from trainer Milton Bradley for following his instructions to the letter.
**Katy O'Hara** could not quite take full advantage of a drop in class from the outside draw.
**Above Board** was another to run well from a high draw after being dropped in grade.
**The Gay Fox** was never going to reach the leaders in time.
**Mount Superior(USA)** was deemed to have caused interference to Sergeant Slipper entering the home straight and his rider was given a five-day ban.
**Star Lad(IRE)** *Official explanation: trainer said gelding had breathing problems*
**Sergeant Slipper** was just trying to improve when nearly brought down and this run is best forgotten.

## 729 LITTLEWOODS BET DIRECT MEDIAN AUCTION MAIDEN STKS 1m 4f (F)
**4:30** (4:30) (H) 4-6-Y-O **£1,435** (£410; £205) **Stalls** Low

Form RPR

400- **1** **Earlsfield Raider**[2] 5839 4-9-0 58........................(e[1]) IMongan 2 56
(GLMoore) *hld up: hdwy over 5f out: led over 2f out: sn rdn: clr ins fnl f: eased cl home* **6/4**[1]

6000 **2** *5* **Kustom Kit For Her**[1] 715 4-8-9 45........................ JBramhill 1 43
(SRBowring) *hld up in rr: hdwy 3f out: rdn and chsd wnr fnl 2f: no imp* **14/1**

540- **3** *7* **Rahjel Sultan**[107] 5742 6-9-3 40........................(t) GGibbons 3 38
(BAMcmahon) *hld up: wnt 2nd over 6f out: rdn over 3f out: wknd 2f out* **16/1**

60-6 **4** *shd* **Aitana**[34] 449 4-8-9 53........................ GCarter 5 32
(SCWilliams) *led: rdn and hdd over 2f out: wknd over 1f out* **2/1**[2]

063- **5** *29* **Dame Margaret**[23] 5982 4-8-9 45........................ VSlattery 4 —
(JABOld) *chsd ldr over 5f: rdn 5f out: bhd fnl 4f: t.o* **10/3**[3]

2m 44.82s (3.32) **Going Correction** +0.20s/f (Slow)
**WFA** 4 from 6yo 3lb **5** Ran SP% **109.0**
Speed ratings: **96,92,88,87,68**CSF £20.16 TOTE £2.80: £1.10, £5.50; EX 25.90.
**Owner** Mrs R J Doorgachurn **Bred** Mrs R J Doorgachurn And C Stedman **Trained** Woodingdean, E Sussex

**FOCUS**
They went no pace in this very weak maiden and the form is no better than selling class.

**NOTEBOOK**
**Earlsfield Raider** has been running well over hurdles recently. He found an easy opening, having been fitted with an eyeshield for this first try on Fibresand.
**Kustom Kit For Her** adopted totally different tactics after being tailed off at Southwell the previous day.

## 730 BET DIRECT INTERACTIVE BANDED STKS 1m 100y(F)
**5:00** (5:04) (H) 3-Y-O+ **£1,295** (£370; £185) **Stalls** Low

Form RPR

00-0 **1** **Monduru**[25] 537 7-9-6 35........................(be) SWhitworth 1 40
(GLMoore) *bhd: rdn and gd hdwy on outside over 2f out: led wl over 1f out: drvn out* **16/1**

0-04 **2** *1* **All On My Own (USA)**[26] 532 9-8-13 35.........(b) NataliaGemelova(7) 12 38
(IWMcinnes) *hld up and bhd: hdwy over 2f out: chsd wnr fnl f: kpt on* **14/1**

00-3 **3** *1 1/4* **Vesta Flame**[26] 532 3-8-1 35.............. RFfrench 11 35
(MJohnston) *hld up: rdn and hdwy over 3f out: one pce fnl f* **5/2**[1]

0-00 **4** *1/2* **Welsh Whisper**[21] 562 5-9-3 30.............. LPKeniry(3) 5 34
(SABrookshaw) *hld up: hdwy over 3f out: rdn over 2f out: one pce fnl f* **100/1**

000- **5** *1 1/4* **A Bit Of Fun**[163] 4576 3-8-1 35.............. JMcAuley 6 32
(JJQuinn) *bhd tl hdwy over 1f out: one pce fnl f* **33/1**

0-60 **6** *hd* **Desires Destiny**[20] 570 6-8-13 35.............. MLawson(7) 10 31
(MBrittain) *prom: outpcd over 3f out: rallied over 1f out: no imp fnl f* **7/2**[2]

0-00 **7** *6* **Peartree House (IRE)**[18] 588 10-9-6 35.............. RBrisland 9 19
(DWChapman) *bhd tl hdwy over 3f out: wknd over 1f out* **14/1**

5000 **8** *4* **Pooka's Daughter (IRE)**[6] 665 4-9-6 35..............(p) PFitzsimons 3 10
(JMBradley) *prom: led over 2f out: rdn and hdd wl over 1f out: sn wknd* **9/1**

6540 **9** *2 1/2* **Pageant**[2] 707 7-9-6 35..............(b1) IMongan 4 5
(JMBradley) *chsd ldrs: rdn over 3f out: hmpd wl over 1f out: sn wknd* **25/1**

/-04 **10** *5* **Keltic Flute**[26] 527 5-9-3 35..............(v) LisaJones(3) 13 —
(MrsLucindaFeatherstone) *prom: led over 6f out: rdn and hdd over 2f out: sn lost pl* **25/1**

06-4 **11** *3/4* **Blue Maeve**[35] 441 4-9-6 35.............. GParkin 2 —
(JHetherton) *led 2f: prom: rdn over 3f out: wknd over 2f out* **6/1**[3]

/00 **12** *3* **The Block Monster (IRE)**[11] 627 5-9-6 35..........(b1) DeanMcKeown 8 —
(PABlockley) *dwlt: sn chsng ldrs: rdn over 3f out: wknd qckly over 2f out* **20/1**

1m 54.26s (3.26) **Going Correction** +0.20s/f (Slow)
**WFA** 3 from 4yo+ 19lb **12** Ran SP% **110.7**
Speed ratings: **91,90,88,88,87 86,80,76,74,69 68,65**CSF £172.80 TOTE £26.20: £5.60, £3.80, £1.40; EX 129.60 Place 6 £100.5, Place 5 £56.78.
**Owner** Pleasure Palace Racing **Bred** D J And Mrs Deer **Trained** Woodingdean, E Sussex

**FOCUS**
A competitive if dire event. The winning time was pedestrian and confirms the form as weak.

**NOTEBOOK**
**Monduru**, fitted with an eyeshield, came with a strong run to strike the front once in line for home and held on well.
**All On My Own(USA)** again gave a good account of himself albeit at a lowly level.
**Vesta Flame** had shaped as though he wanted further over the extended nine furlongs here last time.
**Welsh Whisper** ran by far his best race to date.
**A Bit Of Fun** had three runs on turf over six furlongs last summer for David Barron.
**Desires Destiny** was unable to sustain her renewed effort.
KH

# [719]SOUTHWELL (L-H)
## Tuesday, February 10
**OFFICIAL GOING: Standard to slow**

## 731 BET DIRECT ON SKY ACTIVE H'CAP (DIV I) 6f (F)
**1:30** (1:30) (F) (0-60,60) 3-Y-O **£2,912** (£832; £416) **Stalls** Low

Form RPR

1-00 **1** **Head Of State**[14] 610 3-8-11 **50**..............(v1) JMackay 10 61
(RMBeckett) *led: hdd over 4f out: led over 2f out: rdn clr fnl f* **14/1**

00-3 **2** *5* **Bella Boy Zee (IRE)**[14] 610 3-9-2 **55**.............. KFallon 7 51
(PABlockley) *a.p: rdn to chse wnr over 1f out: styd on same pce* **11/10**[1]

1-00 **3** *nk* **Barras (IRE)**[14] 610 3-9-2 **55**..............(b1) MFenton 5 50
(MissGayKelleway) *sn outpcd: hdwy u.p over 1f out: r.o* **12/1**

00-1 **4** *1/2* **Vampire Queen (IRE)**[22] 561 3-9-3 **56**.............. DeanMcKeown 3 50
(RPElliott) *mid-div: hdwy u.p over 2f out: edgd lft over 1f out: no imp fnl f* **7/2**[2]

00-5 **5** *1 3/4* **Numpty (IRE)**[36] 435 3-8-6 **45**..............(t) KimTinkler 4 33
(NTinkler) *prom: outpcd 4f out: hdwy u.p over 1f out: nvr trbld ldrs* **14/1**

0-00 **6** *1/2* **Sahara Silk (IRE)**[14] 610 3-9-7 **60**..............(v) DarrenWilliams 8 47
(DShaw) *led over 4f out: hdd over 2f out: wknd fnl f* **25/1**

0-00 **7** *3* **Backlash**[20] 574 3-8-12 **51**.............. SWhitworth 9 29
(AWCarroll) *s.i.s: sn outpcd* **12/1**

00-0 **8** *3* **Parallel Lines (IRE)**[20] 580 3-8-9 **48**.............. SWKelly 1 17
(PDEvans) *chsd ldrs: rdn over 2f out: wknd over 1f out* **18/1**

00-0 **9** *3* **Mystic Promise (IRE)**[18] 591 3-7-12 **37** oh7..........(b) JoannaBadger 6 —
(MrsNMacauley) *s.i.s: outpcd* **66/1**

000- **10** *3 1/2* **Joe Charlie**[120] 5533 3-9-0 **53**..............(b1) NCallan 11 2
(KARyan) *s.i.s: sn chsng ldrs: wknd wl over 1f out* **9/1**[3]

000- **11** *23* **Katie's Bath Time**[159] 4675 3-8-6 **45**.............. JBramhill 2 —
(IanEmmerson) *w ldrs: lost pl over 4f out: sn bhd* **50/1**

1m 19.07s (2.27) **Going Correction** +0.15s/f (Slow) **11** Ran SP% **121.1**
Speed ratings: **90,83,82,82,79 79,75,71,67,62 31**CSF £30.44 CT £218.13 TOTE £23.10: £4.50, £1.10, £4.20; EX 46.50.
**Owner** Pedro Rosas **Bred** P Asquith **Trained** Lambourn, Berks

**FOCUS**
They appeared to go a decent enough pace, but the time was extremely slow for the grade, even though the winner, who is useful in the grade, scored in good style.

**NOTEBOOK**
**Head Of State**, below form since landing a gamble at Wolverhampton towards the end of 2003, was back down to the mark he won off and, stepped up to six furlongs with a visor on for the first time, he ran away with this. He is said to have his own ideas about the game, but if the headgear continues to have a positive effect he should be competitive off higher marks. *Official explanation: trainer said, regarding the improved form shown, gelding benefited from the fitting of a visor*
**Bella Boy Zee(IRE)** was the subject of significant market confidence but, after tracking the eventual winner in the early stages, she was left behind in the straight. She has not won since May and it will have to be a weak race if she is to end that losing run - her stable has a good record in selling company.
**Barras(IRE)**, with blinkers replacing a visor, did not appear to face the kickback and only picked up when switched out very wide.
**Vampire Queen(IRE)** did not have the speed to hold a position from her inside stall, but kept on in the straight and is probably a little better than she showed here.
**Numpty(IRE)** was backed at long odds and, although well held, hinted at ability.
**Joe Charlie**, with blinkers on for the first time on his return from a break, showed pace but found nothing under pressure.

## 732 BET DIRECT ON SKY ACTIVE H'CAP (DIV II) 6f (F)
**2:00** (2:00) (F) (0-60,60) 3-Y-O **£2,912** (£832; £416) **Stalls** Low

Form RPR

0-06 **1** **Lady Bahia (IRE)**[27] 522 3-9-1 54.............. DeanMcKeown 5 64
(RPElliott) *s.i.s: sn rcvrd to ld: clr 2f out: hung lft ins fnl f: rdn out* **12/1**

105- **2** *5* **Emperor Cat (IRE)**[115] 5632 3-9-0 58.............. DNolan(5) 8 53
(PABlockley) *hld up: hdwy over 2f out: chsd wnr over 1f out: no imp* **12/1**

5-14 **3** *1 1/4* **Siegfrieds Night (IRE)**[14] 610 3-8-11 50.............. JoannaBadger 6 41
(MCChapman) *outpcd: hdwy u.p over 1f out: nt rch ldrs* **4/1**[1]

0-06 **4** *1 3/4* **Dulce De Leche**[7] 660 3-9-2 60..............(be) BReilly(5) 7 46
(SCWilliams) *chsd ldrs: rdn over 2f out: styd on same pce appr fnl f* **13/2**[3]

00-3 **5** *nk* **Power To Burn**[22] 561 3-9-1 54..............(v) DRMcCabe 10 39
(KBell) *hld up in tch: outpcd 1/2-way: rdn and hung lft over 1f out: no imp* **7/1**

1-20 **6** *3* **Melaina**[22] 561 3-9-0 53..............(p) KFallon 4 29
(MSSaunders) *chsd ldrs over 4f* **6/1**[2]

2-40 **7** *1* **Little Flute**[14] 610 3-8-6 48.............. J-PGuillambert(3) 9 21
(TKeddy) *chsd ldrs: lost pl over 4f out: n.d after* **4/1**[1]

006- **8** *1/2* **Dandy Jim**[46] 6237 3-7-12 37 oh7.............. RBrisland 2 8
(DWChapman) *s.s: a in rr* **25/1**

0-52 **9** *nk* **Nanna (IRE)**[18] 591 3-8-12 51.............. JQuinn 3 21
(RHollinshead) *chsd ldrs over 4f* **7/1**

000- **10** *12* **Samara Sound**[104] 5830 3-8-6 45.............. SWhitworth 1 —
(AGNewcombe) *chsd ldrs 4f* **10/1**

1m 18.98s (2.18) **Going Correction** +0.15s/f (Slow) **10** Ran SP% **120.9**
Speed ratings: **91,84,82,80,79 75,74,73,73,57**CSF £151.85 CT £688.57 TOTE £21.90: £5.50, £5.30, £1.40; EX 196.10.
**Owner** Mrs Sarah Grayson **Bred** Piercetown Stud **Trained** Formby, Lancs

**FOCUS**
Like the first division this was a moderate race, and although they again appeared to go a good pace, the winning time was again slow. The form looks slightly more solid than the first division.

**NOTEBOOK**
**Lady Bahia(IRE)** had shown some reasonable form as a juvenile, but despite that connections did not appear to know her optimum trip. As a result she has come tumbling down the weights and, 10lb lower than when well beaten over ten furlongs at Lingfield on her previous outing, she got an easy lead and came right away in the straight despite hanging slightly under pressure. She should continue to go well now connections know she is a sprinter.
**Emperor Cat(IRE)**, racing for the first time in 115 days, proved unable to get a position on the pace but looked to have every chance when in mattered.
**Siegfrieds Night(IRE)** has won over this course and distance, but he was never going on this occasion and stayed on all too late.
**Dulce De Leche**, dropping back in trip for this Fibresand debut, looked to have every chance.
**Power To Burn** did not look to have any excuses.
**Little Flute**, stepping back up in trip, was always being niggled along just off the pace and could never get on terms.

## 733 BET DIRECT NO Q DEMO 08000 837 888 CLAIMING STKS 7f (F)
**2:30** (2:30) (F) 4-Y-0+ **£2,905** (£830; £415) **Stalls** Low

Form RPR

-101 **1** **Blakeset**[14] 612 9-8-12 78..............(v) JPSpencer 7 70+
(TDBarron) *chsd ldrs: led 2f out: sn rdn and hung lft: styd on* **5/6**[1]

0-30 **2** *1 1/2* **Cloud Dancer**[10] 648 5-9-4 73.............. NCallan 6 73+
(KARyan) *hld up: hdwy over 2f out: chsd wnr over 1f out: sn rdn: styd on same pce* **9/4**[2]

43-0 **3** *5* **Boavista (IRE)**[6] 674 4-8-6 57 ow1..............(t) LFletcher(3) 3 51
(PDEvans) *led 5f: wknd ins fnl f* **16/1**

0131 **4** *2* **Game Guru**[5] 686 5-9-7 62..............(b) DeanMcKeown 2 58
(PABlockley) *chsd ldrs: rdn 1/2-way: wknd over 1f out* **7/2**[3]

00-0 **5** *4* **Dispol Peto**[5] 686 4-8-13 62.............. JBramhill 4 40
(IanEmmerson) *chsd ldrs over 4f* **50/1**

0-00 **6** *2* **Maunby Rocker**[12] 627 4-8-2 48.............. DWakenshaw(7) 1 31
(PCHaslam) *sn pushed along in rr: lost tch fnl 3f* **50/1**

1m 31.02s (0.22) **Going Correction** +0.15s/f (Slow) **6** Ran SP% **117.4**
Speed ratings: **104,102,96,94,89 87**CSF £3.24 TOTE £1.60: £1.10, £2.30; EX 4.00.
**Owner** Nigel Shields **Bred** Bolton Grange **Trained** Maunby, N Yorks

**FOCUS**
Not a bad claimer that went pretty much as expected, with top-rated Blakeset running out a decisive enough winner. The time was also fair for the grade, although the first two did not need to be at their best.

**NOTEBOOK**
**Blakeset** was the best in at the weights and made no mistake. He had to be kept up to his work, but that is because he does little in front and he was always holding the runner-up. He is ten from 16 on Fibresand and will continue to prove hard to beat in this grade.
**Cloud Dancer** was the second best in at the weights, but still had 11lb to find with the winner and ran as well as could have been expected.
**Boavista(IRE)**, joint-third best in at the weights, got her own way out in front and ran respectably on this step up in trip with the tongue tie fitted.
**Game Guru** had it all to do at the weights and never really figured.
**Dispol Peto** has won over course and distance in this grade, but he is out of form.

## 734 BET DIRECT NO Q CLASSIFIED STKS 1m 4f (F)
**3:00** (3:00) (F) 4-Y-0+ **£2,877** (£822; £411) **Stalls** Low

Form RPR

0-14 **1** **Jair Ohmsford (IRE)**[18] 590 5-9-0 64.............. MFenton 3 74+
(WJMusson) *hld up in tch: shkn up to ld ins fnl f: sn clr: comf* **9/2**[3]

2-06 **2** *2 1/2* **George Stubbs (USA)**[12] 629 6-8-11 65.............. LFletcher(3) 6 67
(MJPolglase) *led 1f: remained handy: led over 3f out: rdn over 1f out: hdd and unable qck ins fnl f* **11/2**

1414 **3** *2* **Coolfore Jade (IRE)**[5] 682 4-8-8 57.............. CCatlin 7 61
(NEBerry) *a.p: chsd ldr 3f out: sn ev ch: no etxra fnl f* **16/1**

5-02 **4** *10* **Surdoue**[7] 671 4-8-11 63.............. JPSpencer 2 49
(PHowling) *hld up and bhd: hdwy over 3f out: wknd over 2f out* **9/4**[1]

2144 **5** *5* **Delta Force**[1] 724 5-8-7 63.............. DerekNolan(7) 5 42
(PABlockley) *w ldr: led over 5f out: hdd over 3f out: wknd 2f out* **9/2**[3]

2-41 **6** *8* **Stolen Song**[14] 616 4-8-11 64..............(e) SWhitworth 4 30
(MJRyan) *outpcd: hdwy 7f out: wknd 3f out* **7/2**[2]

000- **7** *dist* **Sacsayhuaman**[31] 2246 5-8-11 57.............. KDalgleish 1 —
(DWThompson) *led after 1f: hdd & wknd over 5f out* **50/1**

2m 40.47s (-1.63) **Going Correction** +0.15s/f (Slow)
**WFA** 4 from 5yo+ 3lb **7** Ran SP% **112.6**
Speed ratings: **111,109,108,101,98 92,—**CSF £28.11 TOTE £5.60: £4.20, £3.20; EX 26.80.
**Owner** K A Cosby **Bred** Stuart Weld **Trained** Newmarket, Suffolk

**FOCUS**
The figures suggested this was quite a competitive classified event, but with Surdoue, Delta Force and Stolen Song running below form it may not have been as strong as it first appeared. Having said that, the time very smart for a race of its type, and the winner can be rated better than the winning margin.

**NOTEBOOK**
**Jair Ohmsford(IRE)**, stepping up in trip with Fenton taking over from an amateur, ran out a very comfortable winner and, eased down close home, he was value for a little more than the winning margin. He is sure to take a significant rise in the weights for this, but is worth keeping on the right side of in any case.
**George Stubbs(USA)** returned to form after a couple of below-par efforts, but he was readily held by the winner and has not won since August 2002, or over a trip this far.
**Coolfore Jade(IRE)**, twice a winner in selling company at Southwell already this year, did not look to have any excuses.
**Surdoue** was unable to build on his encouraging second here last time and is inconsistent.
**Delta Force** ran below form and was probably feeling the effects of his effort over a mile six the previous day.
**Stolen Song**, 6lb higher than when winning over two miles last time, was a long way below his best even allowing for this drop in trip.

## 735 BET DIRECT NO Q DEMO 08000 837 888 H'CAP 1m 3f (F)
3:30 (3:30) (D) (0-85,80) 4-Y-O+ £4,351 (£1,339; £669; £334) Stalls Low

Form RPR
35-3 **1** **Critical Stage (IRE)**[29] 507 5-8-9 **61** (e) JPSpencer 8 71
(JohnBerry) *hld up: pushed along 8f out: hdwy 3f out: led and hung lft over 1f out: drvn out* **7/4**[1]
3-11 **2** ¾ **Intricate Web (IRE)**[11] 643 8-9-10 **79** DAllan(3) 6 88
(EJAlston) *hld up: hdwy over 4f out: n.m.r and lost pl over 3f out: hdwy to chse wnr over 1f out: styd on* **6/1**[3]
000- **3** 6 **Toledo Sun**[52] 6220 4-8-1 **55** JoannaBadger 7 54
(HJCollingridge) *led 9f out: rdn and hdd over 1f out: no ex* **12/1**
0-02 **4** 1 **Bressbee (USA)**[7] 671 6-8-13 **70** (v) DNolan(5) 2 68
(JWUnett) *chsd ldrs: rdn over 3f out: styd on same pce fnl 2f* **15/2**
0-46 **5** 1½ **Dower House**[10] 649 9-9-11 **80** DCorby(3) 4 75
(AndrewTurnell) *hld up: hdwy over 3f out: wknd over 1f out* **10/1**
13-1 **6** 2½ **Amir Zaman**[28] 513 6-10-0 **80** KFallon 3 71
(JRJenkins) *hld up in tch: chsd ldr 3f out: rdn and wknd over 1f out* **3/1**[2]
-004 **7** 9 **Kingston Town (USA)**[7] 667 4-8-10 **67** (p) J-PGuillambert(3) 1 44
(NPLittmoden) *chsd ldrs over 7f* **14/1**
40-0 **8** 13 **Hov**[29] 507 4-9-12 **80** DarrenWilliams 5 36
(JJQuinn) *led 2f: wknd over 2f out* **40/1**
2m 27.82s (-1.08) **Going Correction** +0.15s/f (Slow)
**WFA** 4 from 5yo+ 2lb 8 Ran SP% **113.3**
Speed ratings: **109,108,104,103,102 100,93,84**CSF £12.52 CT £93.95 TOTE £2.60: £1.10, £2.40, £3.30; EX 10.10.
**Owner** The 1997 Partnership **Bred** Park Place International Ltd **Trained** Newmarket, Suffolk
■ Stewards Enquiry : D Nolan one-day ban: used whip down the shoulder in the forehand position (Feb 21)

**FOCUS**
Quite a competitive handicap run at a decent pace. The winning time was decent for the grade of contest, and the winner is capable of scoring again before re-assessment.

**NOTEBOOK**
**Critical Stage(IRE)**, third to Intricate Web over an extended nine furlongs at Wolverhampton on his previous outing, appreciated this step up to a more suitable trip to record a hard-fought success under a good, aggressive ride from Jamie Spencer. This was his first win in a year, but he claimed back-to-back victories this time last season and could well do so again, despite being higher in the weights this time around.
**Intricate Web(IRE)** was unable to confirm recent Wolverhampton placings with the winner on 7lb worse terms over this longer trip, but he did not get the clearest of runs on turning in and may have been closer had the winner not got first run. He remains worth keeping on the right side whilst in this form.
**Toledo Sun** did best of those who raced up with the pace. He is still a maiden, but could be of interest down in grade, possibly over a little shorter.
**Bressbee(USA)**, well beaten behind Fall In Line over course and distance last time, proved very one paced under pressure.
**Dower House** travelled well, but found little when asked.
**Amir Zaman** was running over a trip that would be his bare minimum, but was below form in any case.

## 736 LITTLEWOODS BET DIRECT FILLIES' (S) STKS 1m (F)
4:00 (4:00) (G) 3-Y-O £2,555 (£730; £365) Stalls Low

Form RPR
-535 **1** **Lady Mo**[12] 631 3-9-1 51 J-PGuillambert(3) 10 53
(AndrewReid) *chsd ldrs: led 2f out: rdn out* **9/2**
40-5 **2** 1½ **Quarry Island (IRE)**[38] 416 3-8-6 40 ow1 (v) SJDonohoe(7) 5 45
(PDEvans) *hld up in tch: outpcd 3f out: rallied over 1f out: r.o* **33/1**
062- **3** 2 **Comic Genius**[41] 6269 3-8-12 45 PaulEddery 2 39
(DHaydnJones) *hld up: hdwy over 3f out: rdn over 2f out: no ex ins fnl f* **13/2**
40-0 **4** 1¼ **Ciacole**[17] 599 3-8-12 60 NCallan 1 37
(SCWilliams) *chsd ldrs: led over 3f out: rdn and hdd 2f out: wknd fnl f* **9/4**[1]
0450 **5** 1 **Casantella**[14] 611 3-8-9 45 LFletcher(3) 8 34
(MJPolglase) *chsd ldrs: rdn over 2f out: wknd over 1f out* **25/1**
006- **6** 3½ **Mind Play**[117] 5599 3-8-7 40 (b) TEaves(5) 7 27
(MESowersby) *s.i.s: sn prom: wknd 3f out* **50/1**
-452 **7** ½ **Zonnebeke**[7] 659 3-8-12 45 (p) JFanning 3 26
(KRBurke) *w ldr: led over 4f out: hdd over 3f out: wknd over 1f out* **7/2**[2]
0-56 **8** 23 **Lola's Destiny**[5] 683 3-8-12 52 KFallon 4 —
(PABlockley) *chsd ldrs over 5f: eased* **4/1**[3]
0-00 **9** nk **Tortuette**[26] 533 3-8-9 35 (p) LisaJones(3) 6 —
(Jean-ReneAuvray) *led over 3f: wknd over 3f out* **50/1**
1m 47.3s (2.70) **Going Correction** +0.15s/f (Slow) 9 Ran SP% **115.2**
Speed ratings: **92,90,88,87,86 82,82,59,58**CSF £137.37 TOTE £5.80: £2.30, £6.20, £1.50; EX 84.40.The winner was bought for 5,500gns by P Blockley
**Owner** A S Reid **Bred** Mrs M S Teversham **Trained** Mill Hill, London NW7

**FOCUS**
A very weak seller. The time was slow and the form is ordinary for the grade.

**NOTEBOOK**
**Lady Mo** found this drop back into selling company just what was required. This may not have been a great race, but she was forced to race wide throughout and deserves credit. Bought afterwards by Paul Blockley, she should continue to go well at this level.
**Quarry Island(IRE)** ran well on this drop back in trip and return to Fibresand. She is still a maiden, but there looks to be a minor event in her.
**Comic Genius**, with the visor left off, continues in reasonable heart at this lowly level.
**Ciacole**, the best in at the weights, did not appear to get home on this first attempt at a mile.
**Casantella** did not look to have any excuses.
**Zonnebeke**, runner-up in a banded stakes at Lingfield last time, was below form on this switch back to Fibresand with cheekpieces on for the first time.
**Lola's Destiny** ran as though something was amiss. *Official explanation: vet said gelding had bled from the nose*

## 737 FREE £25 BONUS @ LITTLEWOODSPOKER.COM FILLIES' H'CAP 1m (F)
4:30 (4:30) (E) (0-70,70) 4-Y-O+ £3,234 (£924; £462) Stalls Low

Form RPR
2-01 **1** **Miss Champers (IRE)**[12] 627 4-9-10 66 NCallan 2 75
(PABlockley) *a.p: chsd ldr over 3f out: led over 1f out: rdn out* **6/5**[1]
-565 **2** 3½ **Jessie**[14] 614 5-7-12 40 (t) KimTinkler 7 41
(DonEnricoIncisa) *s.i.s: bhd: hdwy over 2f out: styd on* **14/1**
00-0 **3** 1¼ **Westmead Etoile**[26] 535 4-7-12 40 (v[1]) JMackay 3 39
(JRJenkins) *led: rdn and hdd over 1f out: wknd ins fnl f* **25/1**
2-23 **4** 1¼ **Ellen Mooney**[14] 614 5-10-0 70 RFfrench 4 66
(RPElliott) *chsd ldrs: rdn over 3f out: styd on same pce fnl 2f* **4/1**[3]
6-03 **5** 15 **Miss Glory Be**[4] 700 6-8-9 51 (p) JQuinn 1 14
(MissGayKelleway) *chsd ldrs over 5f* **3/1**[2]
0-00 **6** 2½ **Jessinca**[29] 503 8-7-9 40 FPFerris(3) 5 —
(APJones) *chsd ldrs to 1/2-way* **14/1**
03/6 **7** ½ **Ace-Ma-Vahra**[2] 717 6-8-3 45 JBramhill 8 —
(SRBowring) *plld hrd and prom: wknd over 3f out* **33/1**
0-00 **8** dist **Naughty Girl (IRE)**[5] 681 4-8-13 62 (v[1]) SJDonohoe(7) 6 —
(PDEvans) *chsd ldrs to 1/2-way* **25/1**
1m 45.98s (1.38) **Going Correction** +0.15s/f (Slow) **8** Ran SP% **114.4**
Speed ratings: **99,95,94,93,78 75,75,—**CSF £20.10 CT £284.16 TOTE £2.00: £1.20, £1.70, £6.80; EX 38.70 Place 6 £209.89, Place 5 £120.70.
**Owner** J T Billson **Bred** Mountarmstrong Stud **Trained** Southwell, Notts

**FOCUS**
Not a very competitive handicap, but the winner scored as she was entitled to and they finished well strung out.

**NOTEBOOK**
**Miss Champers(IRE)**, claimed out of David Evans' yard after winning over course and distance on her previous start, made a winning debut for her new connections with a fairly straightforward success. She should continue to go well in similar company, while her trainer's horses continue in good form.
**Jessie** has not scored since winning a maiden in August 2001, but this was an encouraging effort. She recovered from a slow start to chase the winner all the way to the line and may find an opportunity in regional racing.
**Westmead Etoile**, racing off her lowest-ever mark in a first-time visor, got her own way out in front and had every chance. She is another who may be better off in regional racing.
**Ellen Mooney** did not really perform with the cheekpieces left off on her debut for a new trainer.
**Miss Glory Be** attracted support in the market, but ran a long way below her best.
T/Jkpt: Not won. T/Plt: £100.70 to a £1 stake. Pool: £40,190.05. 291.10 winning tickets. T/Qpdt: £22.10 to a £1 stake. Pool: £2,527.80. 84.50 winning tickets. CR

# 701 LINGFIELD (L-H)
Wednesday, February 11

**OFFICIAL GOING: Standard**

## 738 BET DIRECT ON SKY TEXT PAGE 372 H'CAP 7f (P)
12:50 (12:53) (F) (0-55,60) 3-Y-O+ £2,989 (£854; £427) Stalls Low

Form RPR
00-2 **1** **Kinsman (IRE)**[35] 469 7-9-4 52 (b) J-PGuillambert(3) 4 61
(TDMcCarthy) *restraind s: hld up wl in rr: stl in last pair wl over 1f out: threaded through fnl f: r.o wl to ld last stride* **14/1**
3241 **2** shd **Mayzin (IRE)**[4] 702 4-10-1 60 6ex (p) JQuinn 5 69
(RMFlower) *plld hrd: led: hrd rdn over 1f out: kpt on wl fnl f: hdd last stride* **4/1**[1]
6341 **3** hd **Adantino**[8] 660 5-9-9 54 6ex (b) JPSpencer 13 63
(BRMillman) *restrained s: hld up wl in rr: plenty to do whn nt clr run over 1f out: swtchd to outer: str run fnl f: jst failed* **9/1**
0-50 **4** ½ **Lucid Dreams (IRE)**[5] 694 5-9-6 51 GCarter 11 58
(MWigham) *racd towards rr: pushed along 3f out: drvn and prog over 1f out: r.o fnl f: jst hld* **20/1**
00-5 **5** nk **Zak Facta (IRE)**[22] 569 4-9-5 50 (vt) SWhitworth 6 57
(MissDAMchale) *t.k.h: prom: drvn to chal over 1f out: ev ch wl ins fnl f: no ex nr fin* **33/1**
0-50 **6** 1 **Zinging**[7] 672 5-9-5 50 GBaker 3 54
(JJBridger) *hld up in midfield and racd on inner: rdn and effrt whn n.m.r 1f out: kpt on same pce fnl f* **10/1**
40-4 **7** nk **Alafzar (IRE)**[35] 469 6-9-0 52 (vt) SJDonohoe(7) 1 55
(PDEvans) *racd on inner: trckd ldrs: cl up 1f out: nt qckn fnl f* **9/2**[2]
1250 **8** shd **Lucayan Monarch**[5] 695 6-9-9 **54** (p) KFallon 9 57
(PSMcentee) *racd towards rr: reminder after 1f: pushed along 1/2-way: effrt whn nt clr run over 1f out and again 1f out: kpt on: no ch* **16/1**
3512 **9** ½ **Italian Mist (FR)**[5] 694 5-9-9 **54** (e) GFaulkner 16 56
(JulianPoulton) *chsd ldrs: rdn and prog on outer to press ldrs 2f out: nt qckn u.p over 1f out: one pce after* **25/1**
0306 **10** nk **Muqtadi (IRE)**[7] 674 6-9-6 51 MartinDwyer 10 52
(MQuinn) *racd towards rr on outer: rdn and no prog over 2f out: kpt on same pce fnl f over 1f out* **50/1**
2144 **11** nk **Lord Chamberlain**[5] 695 11-9-4 56 ow3 (b) CJDavies(7) 14 56
(JMBradley) *s.s: racd in last and sn reminders: no prog tl styd on fnl f: n.d* **25/1**
6-00 **12** ½ **Steely Dan**[4] 701 5-9-8 53 NPollard 15 52
(JRBest) *prom: rdn to press ldr 2f out: stl ev ch but looking hld whn squeezed out ins fnl f: nt rcvr and eased* **12/1**
2143 **13** ¾ **Lord Melbourne (IRE)**[5] 698 5-9-5 50 SWKelly 8 56+
(JAOsborne) *settled in rr: pushed along 3f out: effrt u.p whn nt clr run 1f out: no ch after* **13/2**[3]
34-3 **14** hd **Lucius Verrus (USA)**[34] 479 4-9-5 50 DarrenWilliams 7 47
(DShaw) *wnt lft s: racd in rr: rdn and no prog fr 2f out* **14/1**
00-6 **15** nk **Karaoke King**[30] 503 6-9-10 55 CCatlin 12 51
(JELong) *pressed ldr to 2f out: losing pl whn hmpd jst over 1f out: nt rcvr* **33/1**
-035 **16** 5 **Scarrottoo**[5] 698 6-9-2 52 BReilly(5) 2 45+
(SCWilliams) *pressed ldrs: rdn over 2f out: stl cl up whn bdly hmpd jst over 1f out: nt rcvr* **9/1**
1m 25.9s (-0.10) **Going Correction** +0.05s/f (Slow) **16** Ran SP% **127.8**
Speed ratings: **102,101,101,101,100 99,99,99,98,98 97,97,96,96,95 90**CSF £67.39 TOTE £14.40: £4.30, £1.80, £3.20, £6.20; EX 114.40.
**Owner** James Etheridge **Bred** Elsdon Farms **Trained** Godstone, Surrey
■ Stewards Enquiry : J-P Guillambert two-day ban: careless riding (Feb 23,24)
G Carter one-day ban: careless riding (Feb 23)
C Catlin two-day ban: careless riding (Feb 23,24)

**FOCUS**
A rough race and plenty of hard-luck stories. The form is average.

**NOTEBOOK**

**Kinsman(IRE)** broke a losing run stretching back three years. Travelling well in rear turning in, he had to weave his way through before putting his head in front right on the line. His trainer described him afterwards as 'very, very quirky.'

**Mayzin(IRE)**, well drawn for a front-runner, ran a fine race under his penalty, only conceding defeat right on the line.

**Adantino**, in theory 6lb well in despite the penalty, like the winner came from off the pace after being switched to get a run. He may struggle off his new mark.

**Lucid Dreams(IRE)**, who is not the most consistent, was another to come from off the pace.

**Zak Facta(IRE)**, who has dropped to a decent mark, ran his best race for some time and the newly-applied tongue-tie might have had something to do with it.

**Zinging** found ten furlongs too far last time and was back at his right trip here.

**Steely Dan** can be rated as having finished a few places closer as he was chopped for room inside the last and his rider called it a day.

## 739 BETDIRECT.CO.UK MAIDEN STKS — 1m 2f (P)

1:20 (1:24) (D) 3-Y-O — £3,848 (£1,184; £592; £296) Stalls Low

Form — RPR

023- **1** **Come What July (IRE)**[65] 6142 3-9-0 67 (b) KFallon 3 — 70
(RGuest) *trckd ldrs: shkne up 3f out: effrt to press ldr wl over 1f out : led 1f out: rdn clr* **2/1**[2]

445- **2** 1¾ **Looks The Business (IRE)**[135] 5267 3-8-7 68 (t) CHaddon(7) 8 — 67
(WGMTurner) *racd in midfield: rdn and prog on outer over 2f out to press ldrs: edgd lft and nt qckn over 1f out: styd on fnl f* **20/1**

-223 **3** ½ **Amwell Brave**[18] 598 3-9-0 70 SWKelly 10 — 66
(JRJenkins) *hld up tl prog to ld over 6f out: rdn over 2f out: hdd and nt qckn 1f out* **5/4**[1]

0 **4** ¾ **Champagne Shadow (IRE)**[36] 447 3-9-0 RBrisland 5 — 65
(GLMoore) *racd towards rr: pushed along 4f out: prog over 2f out: shkn up and styd on fnl f: nrst fin* **25/1**

00 **5** 1½ **Our Little Rosie**[11] 644 3-8-9 DSweeney 2 — 57
(MBlanshard) *cl up: rdn over 2f out: one pce fr over 1f out* **33/1**

0 **6** 3½ **Livia (IRE)**[18] 597 3-8-9 RHavlin 7 — 51
(JGPortman) *prom: rdn and cl up over 2f out: wknd jst over 1f out* **33/1**

**7** hd **Preston Hall** 3-9-0 KDalgleish 6 — 55
(MrsLCJewell) *s.i.s: hld up in rr: prog to chse ldrs 4f out: rdn and outpcd over 2f out: one pce after* **66/1**

0 **8** ¾ **Joy And Pain**[18] 597 3-9-0 DaneO'Neill 13 — 54
(GLMoore) *hld up in last pair: sme prog 3f out: rdn and one pce fnl 2f* **50/1**

0-3 **9** 1 **It's Blue Chip**[23] 563 3-9-0 (e) PaulEddery 4 — 52
(PWD'Arcy) *led at slow pce to over 6f out: chsd ldr to 2f out: sn wknd* **15/2**[3]

**10** 7 **Zaffeu** 3-8-11 J-PGuillambert(3) 12 — 39
(NPLittmoden) *s.i.s: in rr tl prog on wd outside 6f out: rdn 4f out: lost tch wl over 2f out* **10/1**

00 **11** 9 **La Concha (IRE)**[11] 651 3-9-0 DarrenWilliams 11 — 23
(MrsLCJewell) *prog to chse ldrs 7f out: rdn over 4f out: wknd over 3f out* **50/1**

0 **12** 6 **Greatest By Phar**[14] 621 3-9-0 CCatlin 1 — 12
(JAkehurst) *a in rr: wknd 4f out: t.o* **50/1**

0 **13** 2½ **Second User**[25] 553 3-9-0 SWhitworth 9 — 8
(JRJenkins) *s.s: a last: rdn and lost tch 1/2-way: t.o* **66/1**

2m 9.72s (2.33) **Going Correction** +0.05s/f (Slow) **13** Ran SP% **122.0**
Speed ratings: **92,90,90,89,88 85,85,84,84,78 71,66,64**CSF £48.09 TOTE £2.80: £1.60, £4.70, £1.02; EX 43.50.
**Owner** The Storm Again Syndicate **Bred** Pat Beirne **Trained** Newmarket, Suffolk

**FOCUS**

A moderate winning time for the grade, and the form looks ordinary.

**NOTEBOOK**

**Come What July(IRE)**, suited by the step up in trip, took this a shade readily in the end. The form is nothing special and the handicapper will decide his fate.

**Looks The Business(IRE)** ran well on this return from a break, but briefly hung fire going to the furlong pole before keeping on.

**Amwell Brave** went on after half a mile and stepped up the gallop, but he was headed at the furlong pole and could provide no answers. He is proving expensive to follow.

**Champagne Shadow(IRE)**, an ex-Irish colt, kept on in a manner which suggested he will improve over twelve furlongs.

**Our Little Rosie** showed more on this step up in trip and is now eligible for handicaps.

## 740 BET DIRECT THROUGH SKY ACTIVE CLAIMING STKS — 1m 5f (P)

1:55 (1:57) (F) 4-Y-0+ — £2,919 (£834; £417) Stalls Low

Form — RPR

000- **1** **Beyond The Pole (USA)**[23] 5975 6-9-1 55 KFallon 11 — 52
(BRJohnson) *prom: trckd ldr 8f out: rdn to ld over 3f out: clr 2f out: kpt on* **9/2**[1]

2510 **2** 1½ **Tropical Son**[19] 589 5-9-3 46 (v) NCallan 2 — 52
(DShaw) *hld up in rr: prog fr 4f out: rdn over 2f out: styd on to chse wnr ins fnl f: unable to chal* **50/1**

05-1 **3** nk **Sungio**[21] 579 6-8-7 53 DaleGibson 8 — 42
(BGPowell) *rousted along to chse ldrs early: pushed along 4f out: rdn and nt qckn over 2f out: styd on ins fnl f* **8/1**

11-0 **4** ¾ **Royal Prodigy (USA)**[35] 467 5-9-7 66 DaneO'Neill 3 — 55
(RJHodges) *reluctant to enter stalls: racd in midfield: effrt 4f out: rdn to chse ldrs 2f out: disp 2nd pl ins fnl f: one pce* **9/2**[1]

0-04 **5** nk **Landescent (IRE)**[26] 551 4-8-3 46 MartinDwyer 12 — 40
(MQuinn) *led: qcknd 8f out: rdn and hdd over 3f out: chsd wnr tl wknd ent fnl f* **20/1**

153- **6** 3½ **Gemi Bed (FR)**[44] 6254 9-8-11 45 (b) SWhitworth 4 — 39
(GLMoore) *hld up towards rr: effrt but outpcd over 3f out: no imp ldrs after* **11/2**[2]

00-0 **7** hd **Master T (USA)**[18] 602 5-9-1 55 MFenton 7 — 43
(GLMoore) *settled in midfield: effrt over 3f out: sn outpcd: one pce fnl 2f* **16/1**

506- **8** 3 **Sholay (IRE)**[8] 5-8-11 JFanning 5 — 35
(PMitchell) *cl up: rdn over 3f out: wknd over 2f out* **20/1**

664- **9** 2 **Private Benjamin**[106] 5158 4-8-11 56 DKinsella 1 — 36
(JamiePoulton) *dwlt: t.k.h: hld up wl in rr: modest prog but outpcd over 3f out: nvr on terms after* **16/1**

35-5 **10** 1¼ **Joely Green**[33] 483 7-8-10 57 (b) J-PGuillambert(3) 6 — 32
(NPLittmoden) *dwlt: hld up in last trio: rdn 5f out: sn struggling and bhd* **6/1**[3]

/50- **11** ¾ **Fortunate Dave (USA)**[53] 5682 5-8-11 60 CCatlin 13 — 29
(IanWilliams) *chsd ldr to 8f out: sn rdn and lost pl: struggling 4f out* **14/1**

050/ **12** 18 **Knocktopher Abbey**[15] 5297 7-9-3 68 JPSpencer 9 — 10
(BRMillman) *dwlt: hld up in last trio: lost tch and eased 4f out: t.o* **7/1**

0/00 **13** 8 **Philosophic**[8] 661 10-8-9 35 ow9 (p) SJDonohoe(7) 10 — —
(MrsLCJewell) *t.k.h: prom tl rdn and weakeneed 7f out: t.o over 4f out* **200/1**

2m 50.24s (2.16) **Going Correction** +0.05s/f (Slow)
**WFA** 4 from 5yo+ 4lb **13** Ran SP% **120.1**
Speed ratings: **95,94,93,93,93 91,90,89,87,87 86,75,70**CSF £256.83 TOTE £5.70: £1.60, £15.00, £1.60; EX 304.70.Landescent was claimed by Miss K George for £5,000.
**Owner** Tann Racing **Bred** Cavallix Inc **Trained** Epsom, Surrey

**FOCUS**

A slow winning time in this modest claimer.

**NOTEBOOK**

**Beyond The Pole(USA)** was just beaten in this event a year ago. Moving past the front-runner with more than three to run, he soon established a decisive advantage, although his lead was being whittled away towards the finish.

**Tropical Son** ran above himself, considering how badly off at the weights he was, and seemed to stay this longer trip pretty well.

**Sungio** won a seller over two miles last time and this slowly-run 13 furlongs was an insufficient test.

**Royal Prodigy(USA)** was one of four battling for second place inside the last but could not find a change of gear.

**Landescent(IRE)** was claimed after the race to join the Karen George stable.

## 741 BET DIRECT NO Q ON 08000 93 66 93 H'CAP — 1m (P)

2:30 (2:32) (E) (0-70,70) 3-Y-O — £3,346 (£956; £478) Stalls High

Form — RPR

60-0 **1** **Athboy**[18] 598 3-8-8 57 ow2 (v[1]) JPSpencer 11 — 63
(MJWallace) *restrained s: hld up in last: effrt whn nt clr run briefly 2f out : gd prog over 1f out: r.o to ld last 75y: cosily* **12/1**

55-2 **2** 1¼ **Archerfield (IRE)**[21] 580 3-9-6 69 DaneO'Neill 2 — 72
(JWHills) *trckd ldr: gng easily 3f out: effrt to ld over 2f out: hdd and nt qckn over 1f out: kpt on again ins fnl f* **4/1**[2]

5-53 **3** nk **Night Storm**[14] 621 3-9-3 66 PDoe 8 — 68
(SDow) *dwlt: hld up in rr: rdn and prog on outer over 2f out: drvn to ld over 1f out: hdd and one pce last 75y* **13/2**

2-50 **4** 1¼ **Garrigon**[7] 675 3-8-10 62 (p) LisaJones(3) 7 — 61
(NPLittmoden) *s.i.s: t.k.h and hld up in rr: rdn and prog on wd outside over 2f out: cl up 1f out: edgd lft and nt qckn* **11/2**[3]

0-33 **5** ¾ **Resplendent King (USA)**[21] 580 3-9-7 70 MFenton 3 — 67
(TGMills) *trckd ldrs: rdn 3f out: lost pl 2f out: keeping on one pce whn snatched up ins fnl f* **7/2**[1]

-016 **6** hd **Trevian**[14] 622 3-9-0 68 BReilly(5) 12 — 65
(SCWilliams) *hld up towards rr: effrt whn nt clr run briefly 2f out: prog on outer over 1f out: one pce fnl f* **7/1**

26-0 **7** nk **Even Easier**[25] 557 3-8-6 55 (p) SWKelly 10 — 51
(GLMoore) *settled in midfield: effrt and n.m.r 2f out: kpt on same pce after: n.d* **16/1**

6-00 **8** 1½ **Gayle Storm (IRE)**[21] 580 3-8-3 52 JQuinn 1 — 45
(CTinkler) *s.i.s: t.k.h and hld up: lost pl over 2f out: styng on whn nt clr run over 1f out: no ch* **20/1**

64-0 **9** 3 **Ricky Martan**[21] 580 3-9-0 63 (b[1]) SWhitworth 4 — 49
(GCBravery) *plld hrd: trckd ldrs: rdn to chal 2f out: wknd rapidly fnl f* **66/1**

206- **10** 2 **Stonor Lady (USA)**[46] 6242 3-8-7 56 PaulEddery 9 — 37
(PWD'Arcy) *led to over 2f out: wknd over 1f out* **33/1**

50-0 **11** 1¼ **Jango Malfoy (IRE)**[35] 462 3-8-8 57 OUrbina 5 — 35
(BWDuke) *pressed ldr: rdn 3f out: stl cl up 2f out: wknd rapidly over 1f out* **33/1**

0-40 **12** 2 **Head Boy**[28] 521 3-8-9 58 CCatlin 6 — 32
(SDow) *a in rr: last and drvn over 3f out: no ch after: hanging bdly fr over 1f out* **12/1**

1m 41.07s (1.56) **Going Correction** +0.05s/f (Slow) **12** Ran SP% **116.8**
Speed ratings: **94,92,92,91,90 90,89,88,85,83 82,80**CSF £56.85 CT £351.82 TOTE £16.50: £3.90, £2.00, £2.10; EX 127.30.
**Owner** D Mcgovern **Bred** Cheveley Park Stud Ltd **Trained** Newmarket, Suffolk

**FOCUS**

Just an average three-year-old handicap and a modest winning time.

**NOTEBOOK**

**Athboy**, who attracted money last time, was visored for this handicap debut. He responded well when a gap opened up along the rail and came from last to first to win going away. This looks the way to ride him. *Official explanation: trainer said, with regard to improved form shown, colt may have benefitted from the fitting of a visor*

**Archerfield(IRE)**, from a 2lb higher mark, ran another solid race and shaped as if she will get another furlong or two.

**Night Storm** ran well on this handicap bow. After missing the kick, she worked her way to the front early in the home straight but was worn down inside the last.

**Garrigon**, equipped with cheekpieces, was tackling a mile for the first time. He was already due to be dropped a couple of pounds before this.

**Resplendent King(USA)**, who was third to two of today's rivals here last time, would have finished a little nearer had he not had to be briefly snatched up inside the last.

**Trevian** was back at what appears his optimum trip.

**Jango Malfoy(IRE)** *Official explanation: jockey said colt lost its action on the final bend*

## 742 LITTLEWOODS BET DIRECT H'CAP — 7f (P)

3:05 (3:09) (D) (0-80,77) 4-Y-0+ — £4,173 (£1,284; £642; £321) Stalls Low

Form — RPR

-130 **1** **Chateau Nicol**[11] 648 5-9-13 77 (v) JFanning 13 — 88
(BGPowell) *t.k.h: hld up in rr: prog on wd outside 2f out: rdn and wl-timed run to ld last 50y* **14/1**

010- **2** nk **Mistral Sky**[71] 6113 5-9-8 72 (v) JPSpencer 7 — 82
(MrsStefLiddiard) *pressed ldr: rdn to ld over 1f out: edgd rt fnl f: nt qckn and hdd last 50y* **9/1**

0-20 **3** nk **Sir Laughalot**[36] 448 4-9-1 68 LPKeniry(3) 1 — 77
(MissECLavelle) *cl up: rdn on inner over 2f out: nt qckn over 1f out: r.o ins fnl f: gaining at fin* **8/1**[3]

-002 **4** nk **Hard To Catch (IRE)**[4] 701 6-9-1 65 DSweeney 9 — 74
(DKIvory) *hld up towards rr: effrt on outer 2f out: styd on wl fnl f: nrst fin* **16/1**

0643 **5** nk **Superchief**[14] 624 9-9-1 65 (bt) JQuinn 5 — 73
(MissBSanders) *plld hrd: cl up: rdn 2f out: hanging and nt qckn over 1f out: styd on ins fnl f* **8/1**[3]

15-0 **6** nk **And Toto Too**[7] 677 4-8-13 70 (b) SJDonohoe(7) 2 — 77
(PDEvans) *s.i.s: hld up in rr: effrt over 1f out: threaded through fnl f: styng on whn nt clr run last 50y* **20/1**

0324 **7** ½ **Currency**[21] 578 7-9-9 73 SDrowne 3 — 79
(JMBradley) *hld up in midfield: rdn over 2f out: no prog tl styd on ins fnl f: unable to chal* **16/1**

-065 **8** *nk* **Cormorant Wharf (IRE)**$^{11}$ [648] 4-9-12 **76**.................... SWhitworth 12 81
(TEPowell) *s.i.s: hld up in last: stl in last pair over 1f out: styd on fnl f: nvr nrr* **11/2**$^{2}$

1213 **9** *shd* **Whippasnapper**$^{4}$ [701] 4-9-6 **70**.............................. NPollard 11 75
(JRBest) *led: drvn over 2f out: hdd over 1f out: losing pl whn rn out of room and snatched up nr fin* **14/1**

60-0 **10** *nk* **Sir Francis (IRE)**$^{11}$ [647] 6-9-5 **69**.............................. PJScallan 6 73
(JNoseda) *s.i.s: hld up wl in rr: stl in last pair whn nt clr run over 1f out: styd on fnl f: no ch* **10/1**

0-03 **11** *nk* **Greenwood**$^{11}$ [648] 6-9-11 **75**.............................. DKinsella 10 78
(PGMurphy) *pressed ldng pair: drvn over 2f out: fdd fnl f* **8/1**$^{3}$

12-2 **12** *shd* **He Who Dares (IRE)**$^{35}$ [464] 6-8-7 **57**.............................. WRyan 14 60
(AWCarroll) *t.k.h on outer: racd in midfield: prog over 2f out: drvn to press ldrs over 1f out: fdd fnl f* **12/1**

6012 **13** *2* **Blonde En Blonde (IRE)**$^{5}$ [698] 4-9-4 **68**.............................. (b) KFallon 8 65+
(NPLittmoden) *chsd ldrs: rdn over 2f out: no prog and btn whn n.m.r ins fnl f: eased* **5/1**$^{1}$

0-03 **14** *3* **Effective**$^{6}$ [680] 4-8-12 **62**.............................. NCallan 4 51
(APJarvis) *racd in midfield: effrt 2f out: nt clr run over 1f out: one pce whn hmpd ins fnl f: nt rcvr* **20/1**

1m 25.65s (-0.35) **Going Correction** +0.05s/f (Slow) **14** Ran SP% **126.8**
Speed ratings: **104,103,103,102,102 102,101,101,101,100 100,100,98,94**CSF £141.75 CT £1124.28 TOTE £21.30: £7.70, £4.10, £2.70; EX 230.10.
**Owner** Basingstoke Commercials **Bred** Aston House Stud **Trained** Morestead, Hants
■ Stewards Enquiry : J Fanning caution: careless riding

**FOCUS**
A fair handicap run at an average pace for the grade. A triumph for the Handicapper.

**NOTEBOOK**
**Chateau Nicol** came through late to overcome a less than favourable draw. He is having a fine winter and there could be a little more to come.
**Mistral Sky**, freshened up by a break and reunited with Spencer, lost nothing in defeat.
**Sir Laughalot**, a springer in the market, ran as though he would appreciate an extra furlong.
**Hard To Catch(IRE)** was slightly inconvenienced as the winner drifted left once in front, but this was another good run over this longer trip.
**Superchief**, who has a good record under Quinn, was ridden more prominently than of late and this was a respectable effort.
**And Toto Too**, with blinkers back on rather than the visor, was staying on when short of room inside the last.
**Cormorant Wharf(IRE)** , who never got into the race, looks one to keep a close eye on.

## 743 BET DIRECT THROUGH ATR INTERACTIVE H'CAP 2m (P)
3:40 (3:41) (D ) (0-85,83) 4-Y-0+ **£4,823** (£1,484; £742; £371) **Stalls** Low

Form RPR

0-33 **1** **Boumahou (IRE)**$^{7}$ [676] 4-8-8 **71**.............................. NCallan 12 82
(APJarvis) *racd in midfield: prog over 3f out: chsd ldr over 2f out: drvn to ld over 1f out: kpt on u.p* **12/1**

-000 **2** *3/4* **High Point (IRE)**$^{18}$ [600] 6-9-6 **77**.............................. DaneO'Neill 5 87
(GPEnright) *cl up: effrt to chse ldr 3f out to over 2f out: styd on to take 2nd ins fnl f: a hld* **11/2**$^{3}$

3-64 **3** *1 3/4* **Typhoon Tilly**$^{18}$ [603] 7-9-4 **75**.............................. SDrowne 2 83
(CREgerton) *hld up towards rr: stdy prog 3f out: rdn and effrt 2f out: styd on same pce fr over 1f out* **7/1**

236- **4** *hd* **Nawamees (IRE)**$^{47}$ [4693] 6-9-11 **82**.............................. SWhitworth 8 90
(GLMoore) *cl up: effrt to ld over 3f out and kicked on: drvn and hdd over 1f out: one pce* **3/1**$^{1}$

5-16 **5** *5* **Red Scorpion (USA)**$^{18}$ [603] 5-8-9 **73**.............................. BSwarbrick$^{(7)}$ 11 75
(WMBrisbourne) *racd in midfield: rdn 5f out: chsd clr ldrs u.p over 2f out: no imp* **4/1**$^{2}$

3-00 **6** *2 1/2* **Brilliant Red**$^{11}$ [649] 11-9-5 **83** ow1.............................. (t) HPoulton$^{(7)}$ 3 82
(JamiePoulton) *dwlt: hld up in last pair: pushed along over 4f out: sn outpcd: kpt on one pce fnl 2f: hung rt fnl f* **20/1**

500- **7** *3 1/2* **Litzinsky**$^{265}$ [1771] 6-8-2 **59**.............................. JMcAuley 4 54
(CBBBooth) *chsd ldr to 9f out: pushed along and lost pl 6f out: outpcd over 3f out: n.d after* **100/1**

213- **8** *8* **Turn Of Phrase (IRE)**$^{11}$ [2296] 5-7-13 **56**.............................. (b) DaleGibson 1 41
(RAFahey) *settled in last trio: rdn 6f out: last and losing tch 5f out: no ch after: passed three eased rivals nr fin* **7/1**

26-1 **9** *3/4* **Vanbrugh (FR)**$^{36}$ [461] 4-9-0 **77**.............................. (vt) DarrenWilliams 14 61
(MissDAMchale) *prom: chsd ldr 9f out: led 5f out: hdd & wknd over 3f out: eased fnl f* **14/1**

-103 **10** *3/4* **Orinocovsky (IRE)**$^{6}$ [682] 5-8-5 **62**.............................. JQuinn 6 45
(NPLittmoden) *led to 5f out: rdn and wknd over 3f out: eased fnl f* **14/1**

/000 **11** *nk* **Dusty Carpet**$^{14}$ [618] 6-8-13 **70**.............................. CCatlin 10 53
(MJWeeden) *racd in rr: rdn over 4f out: sn btn: eased fnl f* **25/1**

3m 25.54s (-3.04) **Going Correction** +0.05s/f (Slow) **11** Ran SP% **116.0**
**WFA** 4 from 5yo+ 6lb
Speed ratings: **109,108,107,107,105 103,102,98,97,97 97**CSF £74.33 CT £504.59 TOTE £13.20: £3.10, £2.40, £3.60; EX 113.40.
**Owner** Mrs B A Headon **Bred** Brian Miller **Trained** Twyford, Bucks

**FOCUS**
A decent winning time for the grade, and the form is solid.

**NOTEBOOK**
**Boumahou(IRE)** appreciated the return to this trip having been a beaten favourite over shorter last time. The time was good for the grade.
**High Point(IRE)**, who is edging back down the weights, put in an improved effort on this return to two miles. The Queen's Prize at Kempton is reportedly his aim.
**Typhoon Tilly** once again delivered less than he had promised.
**Nawamees(IRE)** came into this in good form in novice hurdles but had had a break since Boxing Day. Tackling this trip for the first time on the Flat, he tried to kick clear once in front but was cut down early in the home straight.
**Red Scorpion(USA)** was 6lb higher than when landing an apprentice race here last month.
**Brilliant Red** was taking a big step up in trip and appeared to get it, although he was never in a position to get involved.
**Turn Of Phrase(IRE)** *Official explanation: jockey said gelding coughed*

## 744 BET DIRECT @ SMARTBET.COM (S) STKS 6f (P)
4:15 (4:16) (G ) 3-Y-0 **£2,569** (£734; £367) **Stalls** Low

Form RPR

060- **1** **Jaolins**$^{85}$ [6021] 3-8-6 52.............................. RSmith 10 49
(RHannon) *dwlt: hld up in last: prog 1/2-way: plenty to do 2f out: drvn and r.o wl to ld last 50y: sn clr* **14/1**

-246 **2** *1 1/4* **Stamford Blue**$^{14}$ [619] 3-8-11 53.............................. (b) DerekNolan$^{(7)}$ 3 57
(JSMoore) *led: shkn up and drew 2l clr wl over 1f out: worn down last 50y* **3/1**$^{2}$

5201 **3** *3/4* **Ivory Lace**$^{7}$ [678] 3-8-13 52.............................. DSweeney 7 50
(DKIvory) *chsd ldrs: rdn 1/2-way: sn outpcd: styd on u.p fr over 1f out* **5/2**$^{1}$

-065 **4** *3/4* **Rehia**$^{7}$ [678] 3-8-13 54.............................. KFallon 6 48
(JWHills) *chsd ldr: rdn to chal over 2f out: btn over 1f out: one pce* **5/1**

-042 **5** *1/2* **Lady Piste (IRE)**$^{7}$ [678] 3-8-7 51 ow1.............................. (vt) SJDonohoe$^{(7)}$ 9 47
(PDEvans) *chsd ldng pair: rdn and outpcd wl over 2f out: effrt over 1f out: one pce* **9/2**$^{3}$

60-0 **6** *1 1/4* **Are You There**$^{20}$ [587] 3-8-10 45.............................. (b) FPFerris$^{(3)}$ 1 42
(PSMcentee) *chsd ldrs: rdn over 3f out: sn outpcd: hung rt but kpt on one pce fnl f* **16/1**

-344 **7** *1 1/4* **Pardon Moi**$^{23}$ [561] 3-8-8 47.............................. HayleyTurner$^{(5)}$ 2 39
(MrsCADunnett) *sn pushed along towards rr: no ch whn nt clr run 2f out: plodded on* **20/1**

30- **8** *2* **Royal Awakening (IRE)**$^{86}$ [6011] 3-8-11.............................. JQuinn 5 31
(APJarvis) *a in rr: last and struggling 1/2-way* **11/1**

**9** *shd* **Master Mahogany** 3-8-11.............................. NPollard 8 30
(RJHodges) *in tch: pushed along 4f out: outpcd and btn wl over 2f out* **25/1**

000- **10** *13* **Coleorton Prince (IRE)**$^{58}$ [6194] 3-8-11 35.............................. NCallan 4 —
(KARyan) *in tch: outpcd over 3f out: no ch whn lost action 2f out: eased* **100/1**

1m 13.27s (0.35) **Going Correction** +0.05s/f (Slow) **10** Ran SP% **118.9**
Speed ratings: **99,97,96,95,94 93,91,88,88,71**CSF £56.22 TOTE £19.40: £5.40, £1.50, £1.80; EX 99.20.The winner was bought in for 6,600gns. Ivory Lace was claimed by Steve Woodman for £6,000.
**Owner** Allen & Associates **Bred** F Hinojosa **Trained** East Everleigh, Wilts

**FOCUS**
A typical three-year-old seller, but a fair winning time for the type of race.

**NOTEBOOK**
**Jaolins**, best in on BHB figures, came from off the pace to win a touch readily. The hold-up tactics helped this keen sort to settle better, and she can win again in lowly company.
**Stamford Blue** adopted different tactics and they looked to have paid off, but he was run out of it well inside the final furlong.
**Ivory Lace** was tackling a sixth furlong for the first time and the trip cannot be put down as an excuse.
**Rehia** shaped as if five furlongs is probably her optimum.

## 745 BET DIRECT ON ATTHERACES TEXT PAGE 410 H'CAP 1m (P)
4:50 (4:51) (F ) (0-65,64) 4-Y-0+ **£2,933** (£838; £419) **Stalls** High

Form RPR

-020 **1** **Acorazado (IRE)**$^{4}$ [701] 5-9-7 **58**.............................. GCarter 7 69
(GLMoore) *trckd ldrs: effrt over 2f out: pressed ldr over 1f out: rdn to ld last 150y: readily* **4/1**$^{1}$

-161 **2** *1 1/4* **Bank On Him**$^{14}$ [623] 9-9-9 **60**.............................. JQuinn 10 68
(CWeedon) *trckd ldr aftr 2f: led over 2f out: drvn and hdd last 150y: kpt on same pce* **7/1**$^{2}$

10-6 **3** *2* **Burgundy**$^{25}$ [559] 7-9-8 **59**.............................. KDalgleish 1 63
(PMitchell) *hld up in rr: stl in last trio wl over 1f out: prog on inner after: styd on to take 3rd nr fin* **8/1**$^{3}$

0332 **4** *3/4* **Easter Ogil (IRE)**$^{11}$ [645] 9-9-13 **64**.............................. VSlattery 4 66
(JaneSouthcombe) *hld up in rr: pushed along 3f out: effrt but no ch whn nt clr run 1f out: styd on: nrst fin* **8/1**$^{3}$

000- **5** *hd* **Fen Gypsy**$^{88}$ [5935] 6-9-4 **62**.............................. SJDonohoe$^{(7)}$ 9 64
(PDEvans) *trckd ldrs: lost pl 1/2-way: drvn and effrt 2f out: styd on one pce over 1f out* **8/1**$^{3}$

00-5 **6** *hd* **Captain Cloudy**$^{32}$ [491] 4-9-3 **57**.............................. LPKeniry$^{(3)}$ 2 58
(MMadgwick) *t.k.h: trckd ldr for 2f: cl up 2f out: rdn and nt qckn wl over 1f out* **12/1**

-050 **7** *1/2* **Frankskips**$^{4}$ [701] 5-9-9 **60**.............................. DSweeney 12 60
(MissBSanders) *reluctant to enter stalls: hld up in last: stl last wl over 1f out: nt clr run jst over 1f out: nudged along: nvr nr ldrs* **33/1**

-063 **8** *3/4* **Quantum Leap**$^{7}$ [677] 7-9-10 **61**.............................. PaulEddery 5 60
(SDow) *hld up towards rr: rdn and prog on outer 3f out: cl up 2f out: nt qckn over 1f out* **7/1**$^{2}$

0-20 **9** *shd* **Power Bird (IRE)**$^{4}$ [701] 4-9-9 **60**.............................. NPollard 8 58
(BRJohnson) *sn led: rdn and hdd over 2f out: fdd over 1f out* **20/1**

06-0 **10** *1* **Londoner (USA)**$^{39}$ [419] 6-9-11 **62**.............................. PDoe 6 58
(SDow) *taken down early: s.i.s: hld up in rr: rdn and effrt over 2f out: no prog over 1f out* **25/1**

3-36 **11** *1 1/4* **Inistrahull Island (IRE)**$^{14}$ [624] 4-9-7 **58**.............................. JFanning 3 51
(MHTompkins) *settled in midfield: rdn over 2f out: no prog and btn wl over 1f out: wknd* **8/1**$^{3}$

0-33 **12** *2* **Zalkani (IRE)**$^{18}$ [601] 4-9-12 **63**.............................. KFallon 11 52
(BGPowell) *trckd ldrs: rdn and ev ch 2f out: nt qckn over 1f out: eased fnl f* **8/1**$^{3}$

1m 38.88s (-0.63) **Going Correction** +0.05s/f (Slow) **12** Ran SP% **119.8**
Speed ratings: **105,103,101,101,100 100,100,99,99,98 97,95**CSF £30.77 CT £221.34 TOTE £4.00: £1.40, £2.10, £2.70; EX 45.80 Place 6 £471.71, Place 5 £146.35.
**Owner** D T L Limited **Bred** Miss Ann Hennessy **Trained** Woodingdean, E Sussex

**FOCUS**
A decent winning time for the class of race, and the form is solid for the grade.

**NOTEBOOK**
**Acorazado(IRE)** was without any headgear this time. He needs things to drop just right, and the extra furlong helped in that respect.
**Bank On Him**, down in trip, ran another good race off this 7lb higher mark.
**Burgundy** was staying on against the rail and did not shape as if the drop in trip was required.
**Easter Ogil(IRE)** won this event 12 months ago, but he has been running over middle distances of late and had not tackled this trip since last summer.
**Fen Gypsy**, last seen over hurdles in November, was having his first run on this surface.
**Frankskips** ran a better race than his finishing position suggests and looks one to bear in mind.
**Inistrahull Island(IRE)** *Official explanation: vet said gelding finished lame*
**Zalkani(IRE)**, who sweated up beforehand, was eased down after being in contention turning in. *Official explanation: jockey said gelding lost its action*
T/Plt: £478.80 to a £1 stake. Pool: £39,328.00. 59.95 winning tickets. T/Qpdt: £213.50 to a £1 stake. Pool: £2,972.80. 10.30 winning tickets. JN

# 731 SOUTHWELL (L-H)
Thursday, February 12

**OFFICIAL GOING: Standard**

## 746 BET DIRECT IN RUNNING SKY TEXT PAGE 293 H'CAP (DIV I) 1m 3f (F)
1:40 (1:40) (F ) (0-65,65) 3-Y-0 **£2,905** (£830; £415) **Stalls** Low

Form RPR

0-6 **1** **Red Lancer**$^{6}$ [695] 3-8-13 **60**.............................. RMiles$^{(3)}$ 8 71+
(RJPrice) *trckd ldrs: smooth hdwy to ld 3f out: pushed clr wl over 1f out: styd on* **9/2**$^{2}$

-121 **2** *5* **Yankeedoodledandy (IRE)**[14] [631] 3-9-7 **65**.................. GFaulkner 10 68
(PCHaslam) *hld up towards rr: pushed along and outpcd 1/2-way: hdwy over 3f out: sn rdn and edgd lft over 1f out: drvn and kpt on ins* **4/6**[1]

00-3 **3** *hd* **Nocatee (IRE)**[38] [445] 3-7-8 **45**.................. RoryMoore(7) 2 48
(PCHaslam) *trckd ldrs: gd hdwy on inner over 4f out and sn ev ch: rdn over 2f out and kpt on same pce* **8/1**

5-53 **4** *15* **Myannabanana (IRE)**[24] [566] 3-8-12 **63**....................(v) DFentiman(7) 7 42
(JRWeymes) *hld up in rr: pushed along after 4f: hdwy on outer over 5f out: sn rdn along and nvr nr ldrs* **7/1**[3]

00-0 **5** *6* **Regency Malaya**[35] [472] 3-7-12 **42** oh7..........................(bt) SRighton 1 11
(MFHarris) *led: rdn along over 4f out: hdd 3f out and sn wknd* **66/1**

06-6 **6** *hd* **Pepe (IRE)**[24] [563] 3-8-7 **51**.................................................(p) JQuinn 9 20
(RHollinshead) *bhd fr 1/2-way* **25/1**

60-0 **7** *hd* **Amar (CZE)**[4] [713] 3-7-13 **43** oh7 ow1.................................. JBramhill 5 11
(PABlockley) *rdn along and bhd fr 1/2-way* **40/1**

0-00 **8** *hd* **Paris Dreamer**[10] [655] 3-7-12 **42** oh2................................ DaleGibson 6 10
(MWEasterby) *dwlt: sn chsng ldrs: rdn along and wknd 1/2-way: sn bhd* **66/1**

625- **9** *7* **Frambo (IRE)**[79] [6066] 3-8-5 **54**.............................................. BReilly(5) 3 11
(JGPortman) *chsd ldrs to 1/2-way: sn wknd* **16/1**

2m 28.25s (-0.65) **Going Correction** 0.0s/f (Stan) **9** Ran SP% **116.9**
Speed ratings: **102,98,98,87,82 82,82,82,77**CSF £7.85 CT £22.44 TOTE £5.70: £1.10, £1.20, £1.70; EX 13.50.
**Owner** Fox And Cub Partnership **Bred** Bishop Wilton Stud **Trained** Ullingswick, H'fords
■ Stewards Enquiry : J Bramhill one-day ban: used whip without allowing gelding time to respond (Feb 23)

**FOCUS**
A none too competitive handicap in which the front three finished well clear. The winner's form is decent for the grade.

**NOTEBOOK**
**Red Lancer**, confirmed the promise he showed on his debut for these connections on this step up in trip. A most decisive winner, he is bound to take a significant rise in the weights for this and things will be much harder next time, but he is clearly progressing along the right lines.
**Yankeedoodledandy(IRE)** had shaped as though this step up in trip would suit when winning over a mile here last time, but he proved unable to hold a position and, despite coming under pressure down the back straight, he could never muster the pace to get to the front. This was disappointing even allowing for the fact he was 20lb higher than when gaining his first success and he may be worth another try on Polytrack.
**Nocatee(IRE)**, stablemate of the disappointing favourite, ran respectably with the visor left off this time and his trainer should find a minor opportunity for him.
**Myannabanana(IRE)** ran a long way below his best and this step up in trip did not appear to suit.
**Regency Malaya** did not improve for this step up in trip.

## 747 BET DIRECT ON ATTHERACES TEXT PAGE 410 H'CAP 5f (F)
**2:10** (2:11) (E ) (0-75,72) 3-Y-O **£3,248** (£928; £464) **Stalls** High

Form RPR

-006 **1** **Sahara Silk (IRE)**[2] [731] 3-8-9 **60**.............................(v) DarrenWilliams 7 70
(DShaw) *cl up: rdn to ld wl over 1f out: drvn and edgd lft ins last: styd on* **20/1**

0-01 **2** *1 1/4* **Piccolo Prince**[16] [610] 3-8-7 **58**........................................ JQuinn 8 64
(EJAlston) *chsd ldrs: hdwy 2f out: sn rdn and nt qckn ins last* **85/40**[2]

112 **3** *2 1/2* **Smart Starprincess (IRE)**[16] [610] 3-9-2 **67**........................(v) KFallon 3 64
(PABlockley) *led: rdn 2f out: sn hdd & wknd ent last* **2/1**[1]

03-4 **4** *shd* **Fayrz Please (IRE)**[23] [569] 3-8-4 **62**.................. AndrewWebb(7) 2 59
(MCChapman) *chsd ldrs: outpcd and swtchd to far rail 1/2-way: sn rdn: kpt on wl fnl f* **20/1**

4-15 **5** *1* **Back At De Front (IRE)**[20] [591] 3-8-8 **64**.................... MSavage(5) 11 58
(NEBerry) *sn outpcd and rdn along 1/2-way: styd on appr last: nrst fin* **14/1**

54-0 **6** *1 1/2* **Demolition Molly**[16] [610] 3-9-3 **68**..................(t) DeanMcKeown 4 56
(RFMarvin) *chsd ldrs: rdn along 2f out: grad wknd* **16/1**

-061 **7** *hd* **Lady Bahia (IRE)**[2] [732] 3-8-4 **60** 6ex.......................... THamilton(5) 9 48
(RPElliott) *rrd s: a rr* **10/1**

00-0 **8** *3 1/2* **A Bid In Time (IRE)**[29] [524] 3-7-7 **49** oh4.................. HayleyTurner(5) 6 24
(DShaw) *chsd ldrs: rdn along 1/2-way: sn wknd* **50/1**

0060 **9** *1/2* **Miss Judged**[3] [728] 3-7-8 **50** oh4 ow1......................(be) JFMcDonald(5) 1 24
(APJones) *chsd ldrs: rdn along 1/2-way: sn wknd* **33/1**

16-4 **10** *2* **Smokin Joe**[15] [619] 3-9-7 **72**............................................ NPollard 5 39
(JRBest) *chsd ldrs: sn rdn along: outpcd and bhd fr 1/2-way* **4/1**[3]

-035 **11** *1/2* **Ask The Clerk (IRE)**[5] [708] 3-9-5 **70**................................ MTebbutt 10 35
(HJCollingridge) *sn outpcd: a rr* **14/1**

60.58 secs (0.28) **Going Correction** 0.0s/f (Stan) **11** Ran SP% **128.1**
Speed ratings: **97,95,91,90,89 86,86,80,80,76 76**CSF £65.99 CT £136.93 TOTE £33.10: £6.70, £2.10, £1.10; EX 72.70.
**Owner** Swann Racing Ltd **Bred** John Cullinan **Trained** Averham, Notts
■ Stewards Enquiry : Andrew Webb one-day ban: used whip with excessive frequency (Feb 23)

**FOCUS**
Quite a competitive handicap, and the form looks reliable.

**NOTEBOOK**
**Sahara Silk(IRE)**, who had gained both her previous wins over this course and distance, was ideally suited by this drop back from six furlongs. She has in the past lost her chance with a slow start, but she pinged the gates this time and kept on right the way to the line. She needs things to fall just right and a follow up is no sure thing.
**Piccolo Prince**, 5lb higher than when winning over course and distance on his previous start, did not look to have any excuses.
**Smart Starprincess(IRE)** was not ridden with the forceful tactics that would usually see her hold a healthy advantage at halfway, and that appeared to be her downfall.
**Fayrz Please(IRE)** was not suited by this drop in trip, but still shaped with promise. He could find a similar race over farther.
**Back At De Front(IRE)** has gained all three of her wins over six furlongs.
**Lady Bahia(IRE)** lost her chance with a slow start. She is better than this.
**Smokin Joe** lacked the speed to hold a position on this drop in trip and did not appear to face the kickback when he got behind.
**Ask The Clerk(IRE)** *Official explanation: jockey said gelding lost its action*

## 748 BET DIRECT ON ATTHERACES TEXT PAGE 411 CLAIMING STKS 6f (F)
**2:40** (2:51) (F ) 4-Y-O+ **£2,954** (£844; £422) **Stalls** Low

Form RPR

-035 **1** **Panjandrum**[12] [646] 6-8-10 **65**........................................ MSavage(5) 14 64
(NEBerry) *chsd ldrs on outer: rdn wl over 1f out: styd on to ld ins last* **20/1**

1011 **2** *3/4* **Blakeset**[2] [733] 9-9-0 **78**.................................................(v) SWKelly 5 70+
(TDBarron) *dwlt and sn pushed along in rr: swtchd lft 4f out: gd hdwy on inner 2f out: sn rdn: drvn to ld briefly ent last: no ex* **5/4**[1]

0-00 **3** *3/4* **Gilded Cove**[7] [680] 4-9-1 **67**............................................ MFenton 2 59
(RHollinshead) *hld up on inner: bdly hmpd 4f out: swtchd outside and gd hdwy 2f out: sn rdn and styd on wl fnl f: nrst fin* **12/1**

-551 **4** *nk* **Aintnecessarilyso**[14] [626] 6-8-11 **50**.................................. CCatlin 10 55
(NEBerry) *in tch: sn pushed along: rdn 1/2-way: styd on u.p appr last: nrst fin* **20/1**

4261 **5** *1 3/4* **Polar Haze**[9] [670] 7-9-1 **52**.................................................(v) JQuinn 9 53
(JPearce) *rdn along and outpcd in rr: hdwy on inner 2f out: styd on appr last: nrst fin* **5/1**[3]

1265 **6** *3/4* **Cleveland Way**[14] [625] 4-8-4 **46**..............................(v) DTudhope(7) 1 47
(DCarroll) *cl up: led 1/2-way: rdn and hung lft over 1f out: sn hdd & wknd* **80/1**

-520 **7** *1 1/4* **Sharp Hat**[7] [681] 10-8-11 **70**........................................ ACulhane 7 43
(DWChapman) *outpcd and bhd tl sme late hdwy* **14/1**

4-54 **8** *1/2* **New Options**[16] [612] 7-8-11 **64**...................................(b) PaulEddery 6 42
(WJMusson) *chsd ldrs: rdn and hdwy whn hmpd over 1f out: sn one pce* **14/1**

1-50 **9** *3 1/2* **Port St Charles (IRE)**[17] [607] 7-9-4 **76**...................... JFMcDonald(5) 3 43
(PRChamings) *led to 1/2-way: cl up tl rdn and wkng nwhn hmpd over 1f out* **10/3**[2]

-000 **10** *3* **Only One Legend (IRE)**[7] [680] 6-9-9 **70**..........................(b) NCallan 8 34
(KARyan) *cl up: rdn over 2f out: sn wknd* **25/1**

00-0 **11** *1 1/4* **Scary Night (IRE)**[7] [681] 4-9-1 **75**..............................(p) JEdmunds 13 23
(JBalding) *cl up: rdn along over 2f out: sn wknd* **25/1**

6-00 **12** *2* **Tally (IRE)**[29] [526] 4-9-1 **67**............................................ FLynch 11 17
(ABerry) *sn outpcd and bhd* **66/1**

1m 16.96s (0.16) **Going Correction** 0.0s/f (Stan) **12** Ran SP% **125.2**
Speed ratings: **98,97,96,95,93 92,90,89,85,81 79,76**CSF £45.55 TOTE £26.50: £4.80, £1.20, £4.00; EX 83.10.
**Owner** Leeway Group Limited **Bred** John And Susan Davis **Trained** Earlswood, Monmouths
■ Stewards Enquiry : Paul Eddery caution: careless riding

**FOCUS**
Quite a competitive claimer, although Blakeset did not run to his mark. They appeared to go a good pace, but the winning time was modest for the grade.

**NOTEBOOK**
**Panjandrum** had never won beyond five furlongs and had 14lb to find with Blakeset at the weights, but under a good rode from Savage, who did not panic from his wide stall, he ran out a narrow winner. He is likely to take a rise in the weights for this and, having never won off a mark above 65, he could struggle to follow up back in a handicap.
**Blakeset** found this tougher than the claimer he won over seven furlongs here just two days previously, despite again being best in at the weights. He struggled to go the early pace and may just be better over seven furlongs these days.
**Gilded Cove** has to be considered an unlucky loser. He was badly hampered on the turn for home and after recovering from that has to be switched wide for a run in the straight. Four times a winner last season, he should pay his way again this term.
**Aintnecessarilyso**, stablemate of the winner, had a massive task at the weights but was not beaten very far at all. He could well take a rise in the handicap for this, but is at least running as well as he has done for a long time.
**Polar Haze** had plenty to find at weights and found this tougher than the seller he won over course and distance on his previous start.
**Port St Charles(IRE)** appeared to hold every chance, but found disappointingly little for pressure.

## 749 LITTLEWOODS BET DIRECT STKS SHOWCASE H'CAP 7f (F)
**3:10** (3:19) (C ) (0-95,89) 3-Y-O+ **£8,248** (£2,538; £1,269; £634) **Stalls** Low

Form RPR

0-31 **1** **Polar Kingdom**[7] [680] 6-8-13 **78** 6ex................................ DMernagh 10 90
(TDBarron) *cl up: effrt out: rdn to ld over 1f out: styd on strly* **7/1**

-410 **2** *2 1/2* **Prima Stella**[12] [648] 5-8-5 **73**........................................ LisaJones(3) 4 79
(JARToller) *led: rdn 2f out: hdd over 1f out: kpt on same pce u.p fnl f* **25/1**

01-0 **3** *3* **Sangiovese**[22] [577] 5-8-10 **78**........................................ LFletcher(3) 5 77
(HMorrison) *cl up: ev ch 2f out: sn rdn: hung lft and one pce appr last* **3/1**[2]

-463 **4** *1* **Ellens Academy (IRE)**[9] [669] 9-8-11 **79**.............................. DAllan(3) 6 75
(EJAlston) *i n tch: hdwy over 2f out: rdn wl over 1f out and no imp* **8/1**

12-1 **5** *3* **Mufreh (USA)**[28] [544] 6-9-7 **86**........................................ SWhitworth 3 75
(AGNewcombe) *trckd ldrs: effrt over 2f out: sn rdn and btn wl over 1f out* **11/4**[1]

1-34 **6** *6* **Warden Warren**[3] [719] 6-8-2 **72**..........................(b) BReilly(5) 8 46
(MrsCADunnett) *chsd ldrs: rdn 2f out: sn wknd* **12/1**

30-3 **7** *1 1/4* **Ephesus**[13] [641] 4-9-6 **85**.................................................(v) MFenton 1 55
(MissGayKelleway) *hld up: hdwy 1/2-way: sn rdn and nvr nr ldrs* **16/1**

60-4 **8** *1 1/2* **Air Mail**[13] [643] 7-9-0 **79**................................................ ACulhane 2 46
(MrsNMacauley) *a rr* **14/1**

400- **9** *10* **Mystic Man (FR)**[251] [2156] 6-9-10 **89**................................ NCallan 7 31
(KARyan) *a rr* **9/2**[3]

00-0 **10** *6* **Lincoln Dancer (IRE)**[28] [544] 7-8-8 **73**..........................(v1) ANicholls 9 —
(DNicholls) *chsd ldrs on outer: rdn along 3f out: sn wknd* **25/1**

1m 28.5s (-2.30) **Going Correction** 0.0s/f (Stan) **10** Ran SP% **121.4**
Speed ratings: **113,110,106,105,102 95,93,92,80,73**CSF £169.67 CT £654.68 TOTE £10.00: £3.60, £5.30, £2.00; EX 77.50 Trifecta £278.50 Pool of £1,490.88 - 3.80 winning tickets.
**Owner** Millie and Poppy Squire **Bred** Mrs Mary Taylor **Trained** Maunby, N Yorks

**FOCUS**
A fair handicap won by the bang in-form Polar Kingdom, who recorded a very fast time considering the grade of contest and looks back to his best.

**NOTEBOOK**
**Polar Kingdom** ended a long losing run when winning a weaker race over six furlongs here on his previous start and, under his 6lb penalty, he had little trouble in following up on this step up in trip and class. He remains one to keep on your side.
**Prima Stella**, who has done all of her winning over sprint trips, held every chance if good enough.
**Sangiovese**, 15lb higher than when winning over a mile here two starts back, appreciated the return to this surface having disappointed at Lingfield on his previous outing and did not look to have any excuses.
**Ellens Academy(IRE)** has only ever won over six furlongs and this step up in trip did not appear to bring around improvement.
**Mufreh(USA)**, 8lb higher than when winning a similar race over course and distance on his previous start, was below his best. He may just be best watched until his trainer hits top form.
**Mystic Man(FR)**, racing for the first time in 251 days, was supported in the market but never really gave his followers a run of their money.

## 750 BET DIRECT ON ATTHERACES TEXT PAGE 412 H'CAP 2m (F)
**3:40** (3:44) (F ) (0-65,58) 4-Y-O+ **£2,919** (£834; £417) **Stalls** Low

Form RPR

006/ **1** **Box Builder**[432] [5840] 7-9-7 **58**........................................ LFletcher(3) 9 73
(HMorrison) *hld up in tch: hdwy over 4f out: chal 2f out: sn rdn: drvn to ld ins last: kpt on wl* **4/1**[3]

00/4 **2** *1* **Doctor John**[16] [539] 7-8-1 **35**............................................(p) CCatlin 7 49
(AndrewTurnell) *trac ked ldrs: hdwy to ld over 3f out: rdn 2f out: drvn and hdd ins last: kpt on* **20/1**

4316 **3** *8* **Vincent**[16] 616 9-8-12 **46** ........ JMackay 1 50
(JohnAHarris) *prom: pushed along and outpcd over 5f out: hdwy 3f out: sn rdn and kpt on same pce* **7/2**[2]

05/1 **4** *1 ¾* **Reflex Blue**[6] 699 7-8-9 **46** 6ex ........ (v) RMiles[(3)] 3 48
(RJPrice) *hld up in tch: hdwy on outer 5f out: rdn to chse ldrs over 2f out: sn drvn and one pce* **7/4**[1]

16/0 **5** *4* **Oulton Broad**[39] 430 8-7-12 **35** ........ (p) LisaJones[(3)] 5 33
(RFord) *keen: hld up: hdwy 5f out: rdn along wl over 2f out: nvr rch ldrs* **10/1**

-440 **6** *1 ¾* **Worlaby Dale**[16] 616 8-8-1 **35** ........ JQuinn 6 30
(MrsSLamyman) *hld up and bhd: sme hdwy ov er 3f out: nvr a factor* **6/1**

00-2 **7** *17* **Colonnade**[31] 501 5-8-11 **45** ........ KDalgleish 8 20
(CGrant) *cl up: led over 6f out: rdn along and hdd over 3f out: sn wknd* **16/1**

0/5- **8** *dist* **Aqua Pura (GER)**[34] 5085 5-9-4 **52** ........ SWKelly 4 —
(BJCurley) *led: rdn along and hdd over 6f out: sn wknd* **12/1**

-060 **9** *20* **Exit To Heaven**[27] 549 4-8-6 **53** ........ PMakin[(7)] 2 —
(MrsLucindaFeatherstone) *chsd ldrs: rdn along over 6f out: sn wknd* **20/1**

3m 45.46s (-7.04) **Going Correction** 0.0s/f (Stan)
**WFA** 4 from 5yo+ 6lb **9** Ran SP% **125.1**
Speed ratings: **101,100,96,95,93 92,84,—,—**CSF £85.34 CT £312.50 TOTE £4.30: £1.60, £6.40, £1.60; EX 135.00.
**Owner** M Hutchinson **Bred** M A Hutchinson **Trained** East Ilsley, Berks

**FOCUS**
A very weak staying handicap. The winner is best fresh and improvement may be limited.

**NOTEBOOK**
**Box Builder**, who was last seen in December 2002 being pulled up in a three mile two furlong novice chase, landed a little touch on his return to the level. His stable can get one ready after a break, so there may not be as much improvement left as you might expect, but he is worthy of respect at this sort of level.
**Doctor John**, back on the level with the cheekpieces fitted, chased the winner all the way to the line. He was clear of the remainder and should find a race whilst in this form.
**Vincent** appeared to run his race, but was unable to go with the front two when it mattered.
**Reflex Blue** is not that consistent and proved unable to add to his recent Wolverhampton success.
**Worlaby Dale** looks to be regressing.

## 751 BET DIRECT ON ATTHERACES TEXT PAGE 413 (S) STKS 7f (F)
**4:10** (4:11) (G) 3-Y-O **£2,520** (£720; £360) **Stalls** Low

Form RPR

4-44 **1** **Fizzy Lady**[17] 606 3-8-6 64 ........ (t) MHills 9 54
(BWHills) *chsd ldrs: hdwy over 2f out: rdn to ld wl over 1f out: drvn ent last: styd on* **8/13**[1]

5-15 **2** *2 ½* **Princess Ismene**[29] 521 3-8-12 59 ........ (b) KFallon 2 54
(JJay) *chsd ldrs: hdwy 2f out: rdn to chse win appr last: one pce* **9/2**[2]

0-00 **3** *1* **Fox Hollow (IRE)**[15] 620 3-8-8 30 ........ RMiles[(3)] 8 51
(MJHaynes) *in tch: hdwy 2f out: sn rdn and kpt on appr last: nrst fin* **100/1**

00-3 **4** *nk* **Knight To Remember (IRE)**[21] 587 3-8-11 48 ........ (p) NCallan 5 50
(KARyan) *dwlt: hdwy and wd st: rdn and ch 2f out: sn drvn and one pce* **8/1**

5-66 **5** *1 ½* **Platinum Chief**[16] 615 3-8-11 45 ........ FLynch 1 46
(ABerry) *bhd and pushed along 1/2-way: rdn over 2f out: drvn and styd on appr last: nrst fin* **25/1**

60-0 **6** *5* **Indrani**[24] 561 3-8-6 45 ow3 ........ LFletcher[(3)] 6 32
(JohnAHarris) *led: rdn along 3f out: hdd wl over 1f out and sn wknd* **33/1**

000- **7** *¾* **Kedross (IRE)**[138] 5218 3-8-6 63 ........ DeanMcKeown 7 27
(RPElliott) *cl up: effrt and ev ch 2f out: sn rdn and wknd* **7/1**[3]

40-0 **8** *5* **Bish Bash Bosh (IRE)**[20] 591 3-8-6 40 ........ (b[1]) SRighton 4 14
(MFHarris) *chsd ldrs to 1/2-way: sn lost pl and b ehind* **80/1**

00-0 **9** *3* **Alibongo (CZE)**[3] 728 3-8-4 40 ........ DerekNolan[(7)] 10 12
(PABlockley) *sn outpcd and bhd fr 1/2-way* **33/1**

1m 32.64s (1.84) **Going Correction** 0.0s/f (Stan) **9** Ran SP% **115.7**
Speed ratings: **89,86,85,84,82 77,76,70,67**CSF £3.48 TOTE £1.70: £1.10, £1.70, £9.60; EX 4.60.The winner was sold to Ron Harris for 8,000gns. Princess Ismene was claimed by J Hughes for £6,000. Kedross was claimed by J Jay for £6,000.
**Owner** Baydon House Stud **Bred** Baydon House Stud **Trained** Lambourn, Berks

**FOCUS**
A weak seller and the time was slow.

**NOTEBOOK**
**Fizzy Lady**, stepping up in trip, dropping in grade, and with the tongue-tie fitted for the first time, justified his short odds with a comfortable victory. She is probably capable of winning outside this grade.
**Princess Ismene** did not appear inconvenienced by this drop in trip, simply finding the winner too good.
**Fox Hollow(IRE)** made a very pleasing Fibresand debut and may be worth a try on this surface in Regional Racing.
**Knight To Remember(IRE)** looked to have every chance in the first-time cheekpieces.
**Platinum Chief** was well held on this drop back in trip.

## 752 BET DIRECT IN RUNNING SKY TEXT PAGE 293 H'CAP (DIV II) 1m 3f (F)
**4:40** (4:40) (F) (0-65,63) 3-Y-O **£2,898** (£828; £414) **Stalls** Low

Form RPR

04-2 **1** **Ceasar (IRE)**[16] 611 3-8-9 51 ........ (p) GFaulkner 4 52
(PCHaslam) *trckd ldng pair: hdwy 4f out and sn cl up: shkn up to ld over 1f out: sn rdn: kpt on u.p ins last* **5/1**[1]

0-04 **2** *1 ¼* **Sir Frank Gibson**[16] 611 3-8-3 45 ........ JFanning 8 44
(MJohnston) *led 2f: cl up tl led again wl over 2f out: sn rdn: hung rt and hdd over 1f out: drvn and kpt on* **3/1**[2]

04-4 **3** *¾* **Ashstanza**[37] 447 3-9-7 63 ........ NCallan 3 61
(MAJarvis) *chsd ldrs: rdn and outpce dover 3f out: styd on u.p fnl 2f: nrest fin* **10/3**[3]

00-0 **4** *¾* **Morning Hawk (USA)**[22] 580 3-8-4 46 ........ DKinsella 6 43
(JSMoore) *hld up in touch: gd hdwy to join ldrs 4f out: rdn over 2f out: edgd lft and kpt on same pce appr last* **10/1**

000- **5** *hd* **It Must Be Speech**[52] 6228 3-9-2 58 ........ ANicholls 2 54
(SLKeightley) *hld up in rr: hdwy over 4f out: rdn along 3 out: styd on u.p fnl 2f: nrst fin* **25/1**

0-03 **6** *4* **Courant D'Air (IRE)**[16] 611 3-7-5 40 ........ DFentiman[(7)] 9 30
(PCHaslam) *cl up: led after 2f tl rdn along and hdd wl over 2f out: sn wknd* **7/1**

10-0 **7** *19* **Atlantic Breeze**[24] 566 3-9-4 60 ........ ACulhane 7 19
(MrsNMacauley) *midfield: rdn along 1/2-way and sn outpcd* **6/1**

500- **8** *dist* **Duggan's Dilemma (IRE)**[189] 3938 3-8-10 52 ........ JBramhill 1 —
(IanEmmerson) *a bhd: t.o whn virtually p.u over 3f out* **80/1**

2m 30.94s (2.04) **Going Correction** 0.0s/f (Stan) **8** Ran SP% **117.6**
Speed ratings: **92,91,90,90,89 86,73,—**CSF £10.59 CT £25.01 TOTE £4.70: £1.30, £1.80, £1.60; EX 19.40 Place 6 £24.01, Place 5 £19.50.
**Owner** Wilson Imports **Bred** Mrs R D Peacock **Trained** Middleham Moor, N Yorks

**FOCUS**
A moderate handicap and a modest winning time, 2.69 seconds slower than the first division and the form is ordinary.

**NOTEBOOK**
**Ceasar(IRE)**, runner-up in a seller over a mile on his previous outing, appreciated this step up in trip and responded well to the first-time cheekpieces to get off the mark at the ninth attempt.
**Sir Frank Gibson**, racing over a trip this far for the first time, did not appear to fail through lack of stamina and should find a small race. *Official explanation: jockey said gelding hung right in the closing stages*
**Ashstanza** was a drifter in the market on this Fibresand and handicap debut and was well held.
**Morning Hawk(USA)** has come tumbling down the weights recently and did not shape badly on this step up in trip.
**It Must Be Speech** was comfortably held on this handicap debut.
T/Plt: £11.60 to a £1 stake. Pool: £40,042.20. 2,512.20 winning tickets. T/Qpdt: £7.10 to a £1 stake. Pool: £2,198.60. 227.80 winning tickets. JR

# 709 NAD AL SHEBA (L-H)
## Thursday, February 12
**OFFICIAL GOING: Turf course - good to firm; dirt course - fast**

## 753a AL ROSTAMANI TROPHY (MAIDEN) (DIRT) 1m
**3:45** (3:46) 3-Y-O **£7,262** (£2,234; £1,117; £558) **Stalls** Low

RPR

**1** **Dildaar (USA)** 3-8-9 ........ (t) BDoyle 4 91
(AllanSmith, UAE) *trckd ldr: 2nd and rdn st: led 2f out: sn wl clr: easily* **13/2**

**2** *5* **Slane Hill (USA)**[48] 3-8-9 82 ........ (vt[1]) TEDurcan 1 81
(MAlKurdi, UAE) *in tch: stdy hdwy on ins to ld st: hdd 2f out: kpt on nr fin: no ch w wnr* **11/10**[1]

**3** *hd* **West Country (UAE)**[5] 709 3-8-9 70 ........ SChin 6 81
(MJohnston) *in tch: cl up 5th st: hdwy over 2f out: kpt on nr fin* **5/1**[3]

**4** *2* **Another Legend (IRE)**[28] 3-8-9 ........ PaulSmith 2 77
(AllanSmith, UAE) *in tch: 4th on ins st: no ex fnl 2f* **11/2**

**5** *3 ¼* **Houbara** 3-8-9 ........ GHind 3 71
(SSeemar, UAE) *led tl hdd st: sn wknd* **9/2**[2]

1m 41.48s **5** Ran SP% **111.2**
Speed ratings: .
**Owner** Sheikh Ahmed Al Maktoum **Bred** T F Vanmeter Ii **Trained** UAE

**NOTEBOOK**
**West Country(UAE)**, who did not make it this time, could not produce a change of pace. A return to fast turf may prove the answer.

## 754a AL ROSTAMANI STKS (H'CAP) (DIRT) 1m
**4:15** (4:16) (90-105,102) 3-Y-O+ **£32,681** (£10,055; £5,027; £2,513) **Stalls** Low

RPR

**1** **Burnt Ember (USA)**[14] 634 5-9-4 98 ........ (t) WSupple 6 101
(DougWatson, UAE) *mid-div: stdy hdwy to 3rd on ins st: r.o wl to ld wl ins fnl f* **8/1**

**2** *1 ½* **Walmooh**[14] 635 8-8-10 90 ........ (b) LDettori 4 90
(AllanSmith, UAE) *trckd ldrs: 4th st: led over 1 1/2f out: kpt on tl hdd wl ins fnl f* **5/1**[3]

**3** *3 ¾* **Self Evident (USA)**[118] 5618 4-9-0 94 ........ (b[1]) EAhern 2 86
(GAButler) *led tl hdd over 1 1/2f out: grad wknd nr fin* **6/1**

**4** *4* **Bold Demand**[14] 634 10-9-8 102 ........ BDoyle 11 86
(RBouresly, Kuwait) *mid-div: 5th st: styd on same pce fnl 2f* **9/2**[2]

**5** *1 ¾* **Ice Cube (SAF)**[7] 691 3-8-4 93 ........ (bt) WCMarwing 10 84
(GeoffWoodruff, South Africa) *trckd ldrs: outpcd 1/2-way: 6th st: styd on nr fin* **11/2**

**6** *hd* **Royal Dignitary (USA)**[14] 634 4-9-5 99 ........ (v) JPSpencer 9 79
(DRLoder) *towards rr: racd wd st: styd on fnl 2f: nvr trbld ldrs* **4/1**[1]

**7** *½* **Al Maali (IRE)**[14] 635 5-9-5 99 ........ (t) RHills 1 78
(DougWatson, UAE) *trckd ldrs: 2nd st: wknd fnl 2f* **10/1**

**8** *4 ¼* **Wilful**[7] 690 4-9-3 97 ........ KMcEvoy 7 68
(IMohammed, UAE) *towards rr: 7th st: n.d* **25/1**

**9** *1* **Classical Act (IND)**[116] 5-9-1 95 ........ (t) RMullen 5 64
(SPadmanabhan, India) *a towards rr: 9th st: n.d* **20/1**

**10** *9* **Halfsong (SWE)**[7] 692 4-8-10 90 ........ MSantos 3 41
(KPAndersen, Sweden) *mid-div tl wknd 1/2-way* **25/1**

**11** *10* **Legacy (JPN)**[14] 636 4-9-8 102 ........ PJSmullen 8 33
(JohnMOxx, Ire) *a in rr: nvr nr to chal: eased fnl f* **14/1**

1m 37.4s
**WFA** 3 from 4yo+ 19lb **11** Ran SP% **123.8**
Speed ratings: .
**Owner** Sheikh Majid Bin Mohammed al Maktoum **Bred** Nutbush Farms **Trained** United Arab Emirates

**NOTEBOOK**
**Self Evident(USA)**, having his first run for four months, appreciated the return to forcing tactics and ran well until tiring late on. He should be better for the outing.
**Royal Dignitary(USA)**, who ran encouragingly in a similar race here last week, had to race wide and was always struggling.
**Legacy(JPN)** has failed to beat a rival in two outings here.

## 755a AL ROSTAMANI CUP (H'CAP) (TURF) 6f 110y
**4:45** (4:46) (90-105,105) 3-Y-O+ **£32,681** (£10,055; £5,027; £2,513) **Stalls** Low

RPR

**1** **Hazelhatch**[7] 690 4-8-10 90 ........ (t) JCarroll 4 91
(MAlKurdi, UAE) *s.i.s: in rr: last st: hdwy over 2f out: r.o strly to ld post* **25/1**

**2** *hd* **Boston Lodge**[7] 690 4-8-10 90 ........ EAhern 2 91
(GAButler) *trckd ldrs: 3rd st: led 2f out: kpt on wl u.p tl hdd post* **6/1**

**3** *1* **Pic Up Sticks**[180] 4191 5-8-10 90 ........ TEDurcan 7 88
(MRChannon) *towards rr: 12th st: gd hdwy 2f out: ev ch fnl f: no ex nr fin* **16/1**

**4** *¾* **National Icon (SAF)**[14] 632 4-8-2 90 ........ WCMarwing 3 78
(MFDeKock, South Africa) *trckd ldrs: 2nd st: chal and ev ch 2f out: no ex fnl f* **5/1**[3]

**5** *½* **Baaridd**[32] 6-9-3 97 ........ LDettori 6 91
(AllanSmith, UAE) *mid-div on ins: 5th st: effrt over 1f out: no ex nr fin* **4/1**[1]

**6** *4* **Conceal**[5] 6-9-10 104 ........ BDoyle 10 86
(RBouresly, Kuwait) *trckd ldrs: 4th st: effrt fnl 2f: wknd nr fin* **9/2**[2]

7 3 **Storm Racer (AUS)**[187] 7-9-11 105 (b) MDuPlessis 11 78
(MThwaites, Macau) *in tch towards rr: kpt on same pce st* **8/1**

8 1 1/4 **Orchestrated (AUS)**[164] 7-9-8 102 (t) GHind 1 71
(MAlKurdi, UAE) *led tl hdd 2f out: sn wknd* **25/1**

9 1/2 **Fruit Of Glory**[111] 5732 5-8-11 91 RLMoore 12 59
(MRChannon) *towards rr outside: effrt fnl 2f: nvr trbld ldrs* **7/1**

10 1 1/2 **Mahfooth (USA)**[5] 710 7-9-1 95 WSupple 9 58
(RBouresly, Kuwait) *mid-div tl wknd fnl 2f* **33/1**

11 3/4 **Aversham**[95] 5964 4-8-10 90 (b[1]) SSanders 13 51
(ECharpy, UAE) *a towards rr: n.d* **9/1**

12 4 **Jacks Estate (IRE)**[14] 632 9-9-7 101 PJSmullen 8 50
(AdrianMcguinness, Ire) *mid-div: effrt st: sn wknd* **16/1**

13 5 3/4 **Sarayat**[14] 634 4-9-8 102 PaulSmith 5 34
(AllanSmith, UAE) *chsd ldrs tl racd wd and wknd st* **25/1**

1m 15.7s **13 Ran SP% 129.0**
Speed ratings: .
**Owner** H E Sheikh Rashid Bin Mohammed **Bred** Robinski Bloodstock Limited **Trained** United Arab Emirates

**NOTEBOOK**
**Boston Lodge**, dropping in trip, ran his second good race in a week and was unlucky to be collared on the post. He can gain compensation before long.
**Pic Up Sticks**, who suffered a broken nose when last seen in August, was stepping up in trip and made a promising reappearance. He did not get the best of runs up the rail, but did not produce much when in the clear and this trip, combined with his absence, may have found him out. He looks capable of winning here, given a shorter trip.
**Fruit Of Glory**, having his first run since October, looks a little high in the handicap at present.

## 756a SHEIKH MAKTOUM AL MAKTOUM CHALLENGE ROUND II (GROUP 3) (DIRT) 1m 1f
5:15 (5:15) 3-Y-O+ £72,625 (£22,346; £11,173; £5,586) Stalls Low

RPR

1 **Victory Moon (SAF)**[14] 635 5-9-0 116 WCMarwing 6 120+
(MFDeKock, South Africa) *in tch: rdn along fr 1/2-way: 3rd st: qcknd to ld 1 1/2f out: sn clr: pushed out* **4/5**[1]

2 3 1/4 **Inamorato (USA)**[106] 4-9-0 105 (vt[1]) LDettori 4 114
(SaeedBinSuroor) *trckd ldr: 2nd st: led 2 1/2f out tl hdd 1 1/2f out: nt pce of wnr* **9/2**[2]

3 3 1/4 **Tropical Star (IRE)**[14] 635 4-9-0 109 (vt) RMullen 3 108
(AAlRaihe, UAE) *in tch in mid-div: 6th st: styd on wl fnl f: nt rch ldrs* **13/2**

4 1 **Dinyeper**[74] 5-9-0 110 HKaratas 5 106
(AyhanKasar, Turkey) *towards rr: 7th st: hdwy and racd wd fnl 2f: nrst fin* **25/1**

5 5 3/4 **Blatant**[14] 635 5-9-0 110 KMcEvoy 2 96
(IMohammed, UAE) *trckd ldrs: 4th st: grad wknd fnl 2f* **25/1**

6 1 **State Shinto (USA)**[14] 635 8-9-0 110 (b) RLMoore 7 94
(MAlKurdi, UAE) *towards rr: 8th st: kpt on nr fin: nvr nr to chal* **11/2**[3]

7 1 **Anani (USA)**[102] 5901 4-9-0 106 JPSpencer 1 92
(EALDunlop) *in tch: 5th st: grad wknd fnl 2f* **25/1**

8 4 1/4 **St Expedit**[5] 710 7-9-0 102 WSupple 9 84
(RBouresly, Kuwait) *led tl hdd 2 1/2f out: sn wknd* **33/1**

9 11 **Dutch Gold (USA)**[165] 4606 4-9-0 110 EAhern 8 64
(CEBrittain) *a towards rr: sn rdn along: t.o st: n.d* **25/1**

1m 49.51s **9 Ran SP% 120.8**
Speed ratings: .
**Owner** Mad Syndicate **Bred** Litchfield Stud Close Corp **Trained** South Africa

**NOTEBOOK**
**Victory Moon(SAF)** reversed recent placings with Tropical Star and State Shinto in decisive fashion, and looks well on course for the Dubai World Cup.
**Inamorato(USA)** was 9lb worse off with the winner compared with their running in the UAE Derby here last year, but to his credit finished the same distance behind.
**Anani(USA)**, having his first try on this surface, was well beaten.
**Dutch Gold(USA)**, a winner on the Lingfield Polytrack, ran no sort of race on this first outing for the best part of six months.

## 757a AL ROSTAMANI PLATE (H'CAP) (DIRT) 1m 2f
5:45 (5:45) (90-105,102) 3-Y-O+ £32,681 (£10,055; £5,027; £2,513) Stalls Low

RPR

1 **Emteyaz**[7] 688 6-8-9 94 (b) KMcEvoy 7 98
(AllanSmith, UAE) *trckd ldr: led st: rdn clr 1 1/2f out: pushed out* **13/2**

2 1 3/4 **Mubeen (IRE)**[7] 688 4-8-9 95 PJSmullen 8 96
(ECharpy, UAE) *in tch: cl up 4th st: hrd rdn 2f out: styd on nr fin: nt pce of wnr* **12/1**

3 4 **Afghan (USA)**[7] 687 6-8-8 93 (b) TEDurcan 10 87
(MAlKurdi, UAE) *mid-div: 6th st: hdwy over 2f out: styd on fnl f: nt rch ldrs* **9/1**

4 3 1/2 **Compton Bolter (IRE)**[82] 6051 7-9-4 102 EAhern 6 91
(GAButler) *mid-div: 7th st: styd on fnl 2f: nvr trbld ldrs* **3/1**[1]

5 nk **Channel Four (USA)**[74] 4-8-5 90 RLMoore 1 78
(SSeemar, UAE) *trckd ldrs: 3rd on ins st: wknd fnl f* **7/1**

6 7 1/4 **Camelot**[7] 687 5-8-6 90 JPSpencer 11 66
(GAButler) *trckd ldrs: cl up 5th st: grad wknd over 2f out* **20/1**

7 4 1/4 **Al Ash Hab (USA)**[7] 688 5-8-10 95 (vt) WSupple 4 62
(DougWatson, UAE) *led tl hdd st: grad wknd* **20/1**

8 3 1/4 **Dubai World (USA)**[48] 6-9-4 102 (t) SSanders 3 65
(ECharpy, UAE) *towards rr: 9th st: kpt on nr fin: n.d* **6/1**[3]

9 1/2 **Change The Grange (AUS)**[14] 635 6-8-10 95 (v) LDettori 5 56
(ATam, Macau) *towards rr: 8th and effrt on ins st: sn wknd* **12/1**

10 3 1/2 **Zurbaran (IND)**[108] 5-8-10 95 RMullen 12 50
(SPadmanabhan, India) *trckd ldrs tl rdn and wknd fr 1/2-way: eased fnl f* **20/1**

11 1 1/4 **Swift Tango (IRE)**[22] 577 4-8-5 90 RHills 9 43
(EALDunlop) *towards rr: 10th and effrt st: sn wknd: eased fnl 110yds* **11/2**[2]

12 dist **Arabie**[7] 692 6-8-13 97 SChin 2 —
(MJohnston) *sn bhd: t.o st: nvr nr to chal* **25/1**

2m 3.12s
**WFA** 4 from 5yo+ 1lb **12 Ran SP% 124.0**
Speed ratings: .
**Owner** Sheikh Ahmed Al Maktoum **Bred** Sheikh Ahmed Bin Rashid Al Maktoum **Trained** UAE

**NOTEBOOK**
**Compton Bolter(IRE)**, who won the Churchill Stakes at Lingfield when last seen in November, was keeping on nicely and will be better for the run.
**Camelot**, beaten in a similar handicap here last week, did not improve on that dirt debut.
**Swift Tango(IRE)**, a Polytrack winner last month, was taking a step up in grade off a higher mark.
**Arabie**, who ran on turf here last week, was well beaten on his debut on this surface.

# [725]WOLVERHAMPTON (A.W) (L-H)
## Friday, February 13

**OFFICIAL GOING: Standard to slow**
Wind: nil Weather: overcast

## 758 BET DIRECT NO Q DEMO 08000 837 888 H'CAP 7f (F)
2:20 (2:20) (D) (0-80,71) 3-Y-O £4,036 (£1,242; £621; £310) Stalls High

Form RPR

01-2 1 **Could She Be Magic (IRE)**[15] 631 3-8-7 57 DaleGibson 1 59
(TDEasterby) *led 3f: led again 3f out: sn rdn: drvn out* **9/2**

25-1 2 nk **Pick Of The Crop**[24] 569 3-9-7 71 IMongan 5 72
(JRJenkins) *s.i.s: hld up: hdwy over 3f out: rdn and chsd wnr 2f out: kpt on towards fin* **10/3**[2]

5-41 3 4 **Bridgewater Boys**[14] 640 3-9-7 71 (p) NCallan 4 62
(KARyan) *a.p: rdn over 2f out: one pce fnl f* **9/4**[1]

-103 4 4 **Sir Jasper (IRE)**[21] 595 3-8-12 62 (v) SRighton 3 43
(MFHarris) *w ldr: slt ld 4f out to 3f out: sn rdn: wknd over 1f out* **10/1**

02-1 5 nk **Wings Of Morning (IRE)**[17] 613 3-8-13 70 DerekNolan[(7)] 2 50
(PABlockley) *prom: rdn over 3f out: wknd fnl f* **7/2**[3]

10-0 6 23 **Sable 'n Silk**[14] 640 3-8-7 57 (b[1]) JQuinn 6 —
(DHaydnJones) *s.i.s: bhd: rdn over 4f out: sn lost tch: t.o* **20/1**

1m 31.42s (1.22) **Going Correction** +0.15s/f (Slow) **6 Ran SP% 108.1**
Speed ratings: **99,98,94,89,89 62**CSF £18.19 TOTE £5.30: £2.00, £2.40; EX 20.50.
**Owner** Malcolm Caine **Bred** Miss Ciara Doyle **Trained** Great Habton, N Yorks

**FOCUS**
A moderate handicap with half the field boasting a last-time-out win and the form is fair.

**NOTEBOOK**
**Could She Be Magic(IRE)** did not get home over a mile last time but, dropping back to the trip over which she was successful in a seller at Southwell back in November, came good again. This was only her eighth start and there could be more improvement to come.
**Pick Of The Crop** had no problem with the extra furlong. In fact, he took plenty of time to get into top gear and, on this evidence, will surely get a mile.
**Bridgewater Boys**, who had won two of his previous three starts at the track, had a 6lb higher mark to overcome on this occasion, and that seemed to find him out.
**Sir Jasper(IRE)**, who was back racing over his winning trip, likes to make the running, but he had to fight the eventual winner for the lead on this occasion and had nothing left in the straight.
**Wings Of Morning(IRE)** did not look on a harsh mark for his handicap debut, but he was under pressure leaving the back straight and perhaps that view will have to be reassessed.

## 759 BET DIRECT NO Q CLAIMING STKS 1m 4f (F)
2:55 (2:56) (F) 4-Y-O+ £2,877 (£822; £411) Stalls Low

Form RPR

00-4 1 **Mandoob**[18] 609 7-9-4 59 (p) DaneO'Neill 6 70
(BRJohnson) *hld up: hdwy on ins 5f out: rdn over 3f out: led over 2f out: clr over 1f out: ran on wl* **13/8**[1]

1-04 2 3 1/2 **Royal Prodigy (USA)**[2] 740 5-9-8 66 MFenton 3 69
(RJHodges) *sn chsng ldr: rdn over 5f out: led over 4f out tl over 2f out: hung rt wl over 1f out: sn btn* **9/4**[2]

32-6 3 4 **Just Wiz**[9] 679 8-8-13 70 (b) J-PGuillambert[(3)] 5 57
(NPLittmoden) *hld up in rr: rdn over 4f out: short-lived effrt over 2f out* **5/2**[3]

-52F 4 1 3/4 **Shatin Special**[10] 671 4-7-8 45 ow1 (p) DeanWilliams[(7)] 2 42
(GCHChung) *led: hdd over 4f out: rdn 3f out: wknd over 1f out* **10/1**

66-6 5 23 **Chapel Royale (IRE)**[18] 605 7-8-10 45 (tp) JoannaBadger 1 14
(MrsNSSharpe) *prom: jnd ldr 7f out: rdn and wknd over 4f out: t.o* **40/1**

2m 42.85s (1.35) **Going Correction** +0.15s/f (Slow)
**WFA** 4 from 5yo+ 3lb **5 Ran SP% 109.0**
Speed ratings: **101,98,96,94,79**CSF £5.46 TOTE £2.20: £1.10, £2.00; EX 5.00.
**Owner** J L Guillambert **Bred** Shadwell Estate Company Limited **Trained** Epsom, Surrey

**FOCUS**
A weak claimer, but the winner is from a stable coming back into form and it was a fair form performance.

**NOTEBOOK**
**Mandoob**, twice successful from four previous starts over this course and distance, won what was admittedly a weak affair in good style and, now that his stable is beginning to fire again, could go on from this.
**Royal Prodigy(USA)** did not appear too keen to get involved in a battle up the straight and soon gave up. He has his own ideas about the game.
**Just Wiz** had plenty going for him at the weights, but he is at his best over the extended nine-furlong trip here. His record over that distance reads 3115215232321192, while his record over all other distances at this track reads 344654533.
**Shatin Special**, still a maiden after 22 starts, had her chance but dropped tamely out of contention once the pressure was on.

## 760 BETDIRECT.CO.UK MAIDEN STKS 7f (F)
3:30 (3:30) (D) 3-Y-O+ £3,373 (£1,038; £519; £259) Stalls High

Form RPR

04- 1 **Alfonso**[105] 5850 3-8-7 MHills 1 81+
(BWHills) *a.p: rdn to ld wl over 1f out: rdn out* **4/6**[1]

32 2 6 **Global Achiever**[10] 668 3-8-7 RFfrench 7 66
(GCHChung) *plld hrd: led after 1f: rdn over 2f out: hdd wl over 1f out: wknd ins fnl f* **7/2**[2]

22-0 3 2 1/2 **Bookiesindexdotcom**[14] 640 3-8-2 63 (v) JQuinn 6 54
(JRJenkins) *hld up: hdwy over 4f out: rdn over 3f out: wknd wl over 1f out* **25/1**

50-4 4 nk **Realism (FR)**[22] 588 4-9-10 53 ACulhane 5 59
(PWHiatt) *wnt lft s: hld up in tch: rdn over 3f out: wknd 2f out* **40/1**

05- 5 3 **Midnight Mambo (USA)**[46] 6253 4-9-5 MartinDwyer 3 46
(RGuest) *chsd ldrs: rdn 5f out: wknd over 3f out* **7/1**[3]

35 6 1 1/4 **Mrs Brown**[8] 683 3-8-2 JMackay 4 43
(SirMarkPrescott) *hmpd s: rdn over 4f out: a bhd* **11/1**

0/0 7 3/4 **Lady Double U**[17] 613 4-9-2 DAllan[(3)] 2 41
(TDEasterby) *led 1f: prom: rdn over 4f out: sn wknd* **100/1**

1m 31.66s (1.46) **Going Correction** +0.15s/f (Slow)
**WFA** 3 from 4yo 17lb **7 Ran SP% 110.3**
Speed ratings: **97,90,87,86,83 82,81**CSF £2.89 TOTE £1.60: £1.10, £2.10; EX 3.20.
**Owner** Guy Reed **Bred** G Reed **Trained** Lambourn, Berks

**FOCUS**
This did not take much winning, but Alfonso put up a strong performance for the grade and looks set to go on to better things.



The Form Book, Raceform Ltd, Compton, RG20 6NL

**NOTEBOOK**
**Alfonso** had no trouble dealing with this lot on his All-Weather debut, and this full-brother to Pablo looks set for success in handicap company when he gets back on the turf and is able to get his toe in.
**Global Achiever** was not disgraced in being beaten by what may turn out to be a decent handicapper in the making. His three runs now make him eligible for a mark, and there are races to be won with him on this surface.
**Bookiesindexdotcom** is an exposed performer and anything with a bit of potential will continue to find her out.
**Realism(FR)** had a lot on against the principals judged on his form to-date, and so it proved. He will be more use in handicaps.
**Midnight Mambo(USA)** has failed to live up to expectations so far but is now eligible for handicaps.

## 761 LITTLEWOODS BET DIRECT H'CAP 6f (F)
4:05 (4:06) (C) (0-100,98) 3-Y-O+ £10,140 (£3,120; £1,560; £780) Stalls Low

| Form | | | | | RPR |
|---|---|---|---|---|---|
| 645- | 1 | | **Quito (IRE)**[55] 6225 7-10-0 98 (b) ACulhane 4 | 114 |
| | | | (DWChapman) *hld up: hdwy 3f out: led ins fnl f: pushed out* 7/1 | |
| 0-20 | 2 | 3 | **Queens Rhapsody**[13] 648 4-9-3 87 JFanning 10 | 94 |
| | | | (ABailey) *a.p: rdn over 2f out: kpt on ins fnl f: nt trble wnr* 15/2 | |
| 5101 | 3 | 3/4 | **Time N Time Again**[8] 681 6-8-9 79 6ex (p) JQuinn 7 | 84 |
| | | | (EJAlston) *a.p: rdn over 3f out: kpt on one pce fnl f* 33/1 | |
| 40-1 | 4 | nk | **Celtic Mill**[18] 607 6-9-2 89 LEnstone(3) 1 | 93 |
| | | | (DWBarker) *led: rdn over 2f out: hdd ins fnl f: no ex* 3/1[1] | |
| 2432 | 5 | 1 1/2 | **Soba Jones**[10] 669 7-8-6 76 JEdmunds 11 | 76 |
| | | | (JBalding) *racd wd: chsd ldrs: rdn 3f out: no hdwy fnl 2f* 12/1 | |
| -064 | 6 | hd | **Sundried Tomato**[18] 607 5-8-5 78 LFletcher(3) 3 | 77 |
| | | | (PWHiatt) *a.p: rdn 3f out: wknd ins fnl f* 13/2[3] | |
| 2-56 | 7 | 1/2 | **Bond Playboy**[22] 586 4-9-4 88 FLynch 12 | 86 |
| | | | (BSmart) *sn bhd: rdn over 3f out: hdwy wl over 1f out: no imp fnl f* 20/1 | |
| 0-40 | 8 | nk | **Bond Boy**[10] 669 7-9-6 90 CCatlin 13 | 87 |
| | | | (BSmart) *sn bhd: rdn over 3f out: nvr nr ldrs* 25/1 | |
| 1320 | 9 | 1/2 | **Hurricane Coast**[13] 648 5-8-5 82 (b) RoryMoore(7) 8 | 77 |
| | | | (DFlood) *prom: rdn over 2f out: wknd over 1f out* 9/1 | |
| -311 | 10 | nk | **Polar Kingdom**[1] 749 6-8-8 78 6ex DMernagh 6 | 72 |
| | | | (TDBarron) *a bhd* 4/1[2] | |
| 030- | 11 | 10 | **Gaelic Princess**[125] 5487 4-9-3 87 DaneO'Neill 9 | 51 |
| | | | (AGNewcombe) *sn bhd* 25/1 | |
| 00-0 | 12 | 2 | **Chappel Cresent (IRE)**[14] 641 4-9-6 90 ANicholls 2 | 48 |
| | | | (DNicholls) *hld up mid-div: hdwy on ins 3f out: sn rdn: wknd over 2f out* 66/1 | |
| 1-01 | 13 | 3 1/2 | **Type One (IRE)**[16] 617 6-8-9 82 RMiles(3) 5 | 30 |
| | | | (JJQuinn) *prom early: rdn over 4f out: sn bhd* 33/1 | |

1m 14.92s (-0.78) **Going Correction** +0.15s/f (Slow) 13 Ran SP% 120.1
Speed ratings: **111,107,106,105,103 103,102,102,101,101 87,85,80**CSF £54.18 CT £1694.76 TOTE £8.90: £2.60, £3.50, £7.30; EX 63.40.
**Owner** Michael Hill **Bred** Sheikh Mohammed Bin Rashid Al Maktoum **Trained** Stillington, N Yorks

**FOCUS**
A quality handicap run in a fast time and the form looks rock solid.

**NOTEBOOK**
**Quito(IRE)** had the race run to suit with Celtic Mill setting such a strong pace, and ran out a ready winner. Although fully effective over six furlongs when conditions are like this, he is probably more at home over farther these days, and apparently the Lincoln Trial is next on the agenda.
**Queens Rhapsody**, successful on his two previous visits here, appreciated the return to his favourite track. He ran as though he would appreciate a step back up to seven furlongs, though.
**Time N Time Again** ran a cracking race off a 6lb higher mark and has not been in as good form as this since his three-year-old days.
**Celtic Mill**, running off a career-high mark, set a furious pace which he was unable to maintain inside the final furlong. It looks like the Handicapper may have him now.
**Soba Jones** was unable to reverse recent course and distance form with Celtic Mill despite being 3lb better off at the weights.
**Sundried Tomato** appears to still be a little too high in the handicap at present.
**Polar Kingdom** gained the second of his two wins at Southwell the previous day, and can be excused this.
**Chappel Cresent(IRE)** *Official explanation: jockey said colt lost its action*

## 762 BET IN RUNNING @ BETDIRECT.CO.UK (S) STKS 5f (F)
4:40 (4:40) (G) 3-Y-O+ £2,590 (£740; £370) Stalls Low

| Form | | | | | RPR |
|---|---|---|---|---|---|
| 4063 | 1 | | **Arogant Prince**[11] 654 7-9-7 51 (b) IMongan 5 | 60 |
| | | | (AWCarroll) *sn led: rdn over 2f out: drvn out* 3/1[2] | |
| 00-0 | 2 | 1 | **River Days (IRE)**[13] 646 6-9-2 62 (bt) MFenton 7 | 52 |
| | | | (MissGayKelleway) *a.p: rdn over 2f out: c wd st: r.o one pce fnl f* 7/2[3] | |
| 00-4 | 3 | 1/2 | **Catchthebatch**[27] 560 8-9-0 47 LiamJones(7) 3 | 55 |
| | | | (EAWheeler) *a.p: rdn over 2f out: kpt on same pce fnl f* 8/1 | |
| 2600 | 4 | 3 | **Soaked**[14] 637 11-9-7 49 (b) ACulhane 2 | 44 |
| | | | (DWChapman) *hld up: hdwy over 2f out: rdn over 1f out: no imp fnl f* 4/1 | |
| 30-0 | 5 | 1 3/4 | **Lavish Times**[30] 524 3-8-4 47 ow2 (b) PBradley(5) 4 | 40 |
| | | | (ABerry) *chsd ldrs: rdn 3f out: wknd over 1f out* 20/1 | |
| 0-22 | 6 | 3 | **Hagley Park**[11] 657 5-9-2 45 MartinDwyer 6 | 23 |
| | | | (MQuinn) *prom: rdn 3f out: wknd over 1f out* 11/4[1] | |
| 00-0 | 7 | 3 1/2 | **Burkees Graw (IRE)**[8] 685 3-8-7 45 JQuinn 8 | 15 |
| | | | (MrsSLamyman) *sn bhd* 40/1 | |
| 0-45 | 8 | 1 3/4 | **Somethingabouther**[36] 479 4-9-2 40 CCatlin 1 | 4 |
| | | | (PWHiatt) *led early: sn bhd* 40/1 | |

63.18 secs (0.58) **Going Correction** +0.15s/f (Slow)
**WFA** 3 from 4yo+ 14lb 8 Ran SP% 114.6
Speed ratings: **101,99,98,93,91 86,80,77**CSF £13.72 TOTE £3.30: £1.10, £1.70, £2.80; EX 19.10.There was no bid for the winner
**Owner** Dennis Deacon **Bred** Miss Julie Self **Trained** Wixford, Warwicks

**FOCUS**
A weak seller - none of the runners had won a race since June of last year, and the form is average for the grade.

**NOTEBOOK**
**Arogant Prince** hails from a stable in good form at present and the drop back to five furlongs proved just the ticket. This was a poor race though, so it is not worth getting carried away.
**River Days(IRE)**, the best of these based on official ratings, has been lightly raced since last spring and has clearly had her problems. This drop in grade helped, and a similarly weak affair could be within her grasp.
**Catchthebatch** has not won a race for over two years. He needs to drop a couple of pounds to qualify for banded races.
**Soaked**, who runs his best races from the front, was surprisingly held up. This is not his favourite All-Weather track either.
**Lavish Times** had it to do against his elders for the first time.
**Hagley Park**, who runs her best races when given an uncontested lead, was unable to dominate on this occasion.

## 763 PRESS INTERACTIVE TO BET DIRECT FILLIES' H'CAP 1m 1f 79y(F)
5:10 (5:10) (E) (0-70,72) 4-Y-O+ £3,248 (£928; £464) Stalls Low

| Form | | | | | RPR |
|---|---|---|---|---|---|
| 25-4 | 1 | | **Jade Star (USA)**[22] 581 4-8-10 48 MFenton 7 | 58 |
| | | | (MissGayKelleway) *led 1f: w ldr: led again 5f out: rdn over 2f out: drvn out* 13/2[3] | |
| -230 | 2 | nk | **Danger Bird (IRE)**[18] 605 4-8-10 48 ACulhane 8 | 57 |
| | | | (RHollinshead) *a.p: wnt 2nd over 3f out: rdn and ev ch 2f out: nt qckn ins fnl f* 12/1 | |
| -063 | 3 | 1 1/4 | **Top Of The Class (IRE)**[7] 693 7-8-7 45 (v) JoannaBadger 4 | 52 |
| | | | (PDEvans) *hld up in rr: rdn 5f out: hdwy over 2f out: kpt on same pce fnl f* 12/1 | |
| -011 | 4 | 5 | **Miss Champers (IRE)**[3] 737 4-10-1 72 6ex DNolan(5) 5 | 70 |
| | | | (PABlockley) *prom: rdn over 3f out: wknd over 2f out* 3/1[1] | |
| -061 | 5 | 4 | **Red Storm**[11] 652 5-8-10 51 6ex (v) RMiles(3) 6 | 42 |
| | | | (JRBoyle) *hld up mid-div: rdn and wknd over 2f out* 9/1 | |
| 1353 | 6 | 2 1/2 | **Givemethemoonlight**[7] 695 5-9-2 54 (v) IMongan 9 | 40 |
| | | | (MrsStefLiddiard) *hld up towards rr: stdy hdwy over 5f out: rdn and wknd over 2f out* 7/2[2] | |
| -602 | 7 | 5 | **Zahunda (IRE)**[7] 700 5-7-9 40 BSwarbrick(7) 3 | 17 |
| | | | (WMBrisbourne) *broke wl: stdd after 1f: sn mid-div: rdn 4f out: sn bhd* 7/2[2] | |
| 0-46 | 8 | 1 1/4 | **Wodhill Folly**[11] 655 7-8-7 45 (v) NCallan 2 | 20 |
| | | | (DMorris) *hld up mid-div: bhd fnl 4f* 25/1 | |
| 0-64 | 9 | 12 | **Aitana**[4] 729 4-9-1 53 (be[1]) MartinDwyer 1 | 6 |
| | | | (SCWilliams) *led after 1f to 5f out: rdn and wknd over 3f out* 14/1 | |

2m 4.08s (1.18) **Going Correction** +0.15s/f (Slow) 9 Ran SP% 118.7
Speed ratings: **100,99,98,94,90 88,83,82,72**CSF £82.84 CT £921.92 TOTE £8.30: £3.00, £5.50, £5.10; EX 47.70 Place 6 £200.58, Place 5 £78.25.
**Owner** Ian Frazer **Bred** Swordlestown Stud **Trained** Newmarket, Suffolk

**FOCUS**
An ordinary fillies' handicap and the form is modest.

**NOTEBOOK**
**Jade Star(USA)** did not get home over a mile and a half last time but that was her first run for five months. With the benefit of the outing to sharpen her up and a drop back in trip, she got the better of some average fillies to score narrowly.
**Danger Bird(IRE)** had plenty of time to go past the winner had she been so inclined. The impression given is that she is keeping a little bit for herself.
**Top Of The Class(IRE)** found this an insufficient test of stamina.
**Miss Champers(IRE)** had plenty on her plate under her big weight, over a trip she has struggled to see out in the past, and only three days after her last outing.
**Red Storm** won a poor banded grade race last time out and found the return to handicap company a little tougher.
**Givemethemoonlight** runs her best races from the front.
KH

# 738 LINGFIELD (L-H)
Saturday, February 14

**OFFICIAL GOING: Standard**

## 764 "MISS JULIE ANDREWS, WILL YOU MARRY ME?" MAIDEN STKS 5f (P)
1:05 (1:05) (D) 3-Y-O £4,043 (£1,244; £622; £311) Stalls High

| Form | | | | | RPR |
|---|---|---|---|---|---|
| 600- | 1 | | **Cut And Dried**[140] 5226 3-9-0 57 MartinDwyer 5 | 67 |
| | | | (DMSimcock) *t.k.h: chsd ldrs: pushed along fr 1/2-way: led appr fnl f: r.o wl* 7/1 | |
| 350- | 2 | 3 | **Celadon (IRE)**[77] 6097 3-9-0 66 JQuinn 8 | 56 |
| | | | (NPLittmoden) *s.i.s: pushed along and stdy hdwy fnl 2f: styd on to go 2nd cl home* 3/1[2] | |
| 0-53 | 3 | shd | **Vittorioso (IRE)**[35] 496 3-9-0 53 (b) MFenton 9 | 56 |
| | | | (MissGayKelleway) *chsd ldrs: wnt 2nd 1f out: lost 2nd cl home* 9/2[3] | |
| 4-3 | 4 | 1 | **Pure Folly (IRE)**[7] 708 3-8-9 JMackay 3 | 48 |
| | | | (SirMarkPrescott) *led after 1f: rdn and hdd appr fnl f: one pce after* 5/2[1] | |
| 056- | 5 | shd | **Beau Jazz**[100] 5931 3-9-0 68 SRighton 7 | 52 |
| | | | (WDeBest-Turner) *prom: rdn and one pce fnl f* 8/1 | |
| | 6 | 2 | **Simpsons Mount (IRE)** 3-9-0 (e[1]) EAhern 2 | 45 |
| | | | (RMFlower) *slowly away: nvr nr to chal* 16/1 | |
| 50-0 | 7 | 5 | **Indian Oak (IRE)**[10] 678 3-8-7 35 ow1 LPKeniry(3) 4 | 24 |
| | | | (MPMuggeridge) *led for 1f: prom tl wknd appr fnl f* 66/1 | |
| | 8 | 9 | **Cobalt Runner (IRE)** 3-9-0 NPollard 10 | — |
| | | | (GGMargarson) *a struggling in rr* 33/1 | |
| | 9 | 30 | **Hello Sid** 3-8-9 (b[1]) AQuinn(5) 6 | — |
| | | | (TEPowell) *v.s.a and a wl detached: t.o* 50/1 | |

60.33 secs (0.55) **Going Correction** +0.10s/f (Slow) 9 Ran SP% 107.6
Speed ratings: **99,94,94,92,92 89,81,66,18**CSF £24.92 TOTE £10.90: £2.70, £1.90, £1.70; EX 39.20.
**Owner** Trillium Place Racing **Bred** Mrs B Skinner **Trained** Newmarket, Suffolk
■ A first winner with his first runner for trainer David Simcock, former assistant to, among others, Luca Cumani.

**FOCUS**
A moderate sprint maiden, but the winner took to the surface, putting up a fair performance, and scored decisively.

**NOTEBOOK**
**Cut And Dried**, who had shown some ability on turf for his previous handler, travelled well and picked up nicely to give his trainer a dream start to his new career. He will return here for a handicap later in the month.
**Celadon(IRE)**, who disappointed on Fibresand on his previous run, did much better on this switch to Polytrack. He does not look that well treated handicap-wise at present, and his chances are not helped by a tendency to miss the break. A six-furlong maiden round here may offer his best chance of getting off the mark.
**Vittorioso(IRE)**, who ran well in an ordinary handicap on his debut on this surface, did so again and provides a line to the level of the form.
**Pure Folly(IRE)**, an uneasy favourite, was up with the pace from the start but did not last home. She now qualifies for a handicap mark, and it will be interesting to see whether this free-running sort will be stepped up in trip, as her pedigree suggests she may stay farther.
**Beau Jazz** showed ability on turf last season, but looks high in the handicap judged on this effort and may be better in claimers or sellers.

## 765 BET DIRECT NO Q DEMO 08000 837 888 H'CAP 1m 2f (P)
1:35 (1:35) (F) (0-65,68) 3-Y-O+ £3,360 (£960; £480) Stalls Low

| Form | | | | | RPR |
|---|---|---|---|---|---|
| 00-1 | 1 | | **Brave Dane (IRE)**[10] 672 6-9-7 58 WRyan 1 | 72 |
| | | | (AWCarroll) *hld up in rr: hdwy but plenty to do 2f out: swtchd rt ent fnl f: sn led: qcknd clr* 9/2[1] | |

0-40 **2** *2* **Blazing The Trail (IRE)**[28] 555 4-9-5 **57** ........ SWhitworth 10 67
(JWHills) *mid-div: hdwy 2f out: ev ch ent fnl f: nt pce of wnr* **50/1**

-320 **3** *1 3/4* **Welsh Wind (IRE)**[8] 700 8-9-5 **56** ........ (t) JFanning 11 63
(MWigham) *chsd ldrs: led 2f out: rdn and hdd jst ins fnl f: nt qckn* **9/1**

36-2 **4** *1/2* **My Maite (IRE)**[17] 623 5-9-6 **57** ........ (t) NDay 9 63
(RIngram) *a in tch: hrd rdn over 1f out: styd on one pce* **7/1**[3]

50-2 **5** *3/4* **Learned Lad (FR)**[7] 705 6-10-3 **68** ........ IMongan 3 73
(JamiePoulton) *prom in chsng gp: led 4f out: hdd 2f out: no ex appr fnl f* **9/2**[1]

5-34 **6** *nk* **Magic Warrior**[17] 623 4-9-2 **54** ........ PMcCabe 2 58
(JCFox) *prom: rdn 2f out: fdd ins fnl f* **6/1**[2]

4324 **7** *3/4* **Mutarafaa (USA)**[8] 700 5-9-3 **54** ........ NCallan 12 57
(DShaw) *in rr: rdn 1/2-way: hdwy over 3f out: one pce ins fnl 2f* **8/1**

66-0 **8** *1* **Kavi (IRE)**[14] 650 4-9-9 **61** ........ (b) GBaker 8 62
(SimonEarle) *hld up: rdn 3f out: sme hdwy after but nvr nr to chal* **25/1**

605- **9** *2 1/2* **Sammy's Shuffle**[56] 6226 9-9-2 **53** ........ (b) DKinsella 6 50
(JamiePoulton) *mid-div: nvr nr to chal* **14/1**

00-0 **10** *7* **Snuki**[14] 650 5-9-8 **59** ........ DaneO'Neill 4 43
(GLMoore) *mid-div: rdn over 3f out: wknd 2f out* **9/1**

10-0 **11** *1 1/2* **East Flares**[33] 507 4-9-8 **60** ........ OUrbina 7 41
(JWUnett) *trckd ldr: wknd wl over 2f out* **66/1**

3324 **12** *5* **Easter Ogil (IRE)**[3] 745 9-9-13 **64** ........ VSlattery 13 36
(JaneSouthcombe) *a in rr* **15/2**

100- **13** *9* **Dark Cut (IRE)**[145] 5117 4-9-3 **55** ........ PFitzsimons 5 11
(HAlexander) *a in rr* **66/1**

-000 **14** *17* **Finger Of Fate**[9] 684 4-9-4 **56** ........ (b1) EAhern 14 —
(MJPolglase) *led: sn clr: wknd and hdd 4f out: sn wl bhd* **33/1**

2m 7.34s (-0.05) **Going Correction** +0.10s/f (Slow)
**WFA** 4 from 5yo+ 1lb **14** Ran SP% **124.4**
Speed ratings: **104,102,101,100,100 99,99,98,96,90 89,85,78,64**CSF £261.94 CT £1980.15 TOTE £5.10: £2.70, £5.80, £2.90; EX 199.10.
**Owner** Mrs E J Righton **Bred** Gainsborough Stud Management Ltd **Trained** Wixford, Warwicks

**FOCUS**
A moderate handicap, but run fastest of the three races over the trip on the day, and the winner looks progressive.

**NOTEBOOK**
**Brave Dane(IRE)**seems an improved performer since switching to this surface, gaining his second course and distance win in taking fashion. He will go up a fair amount for this, but looks one to keep on the right side of, especially if reappearing before his new mark comes into force.
**Blazing The Trail(IRE)**, dropped in grade and in the handicap, ran much better as a result. He seems better without the blinkers that he wore when well beaten last time, and looks up to winning a small handicap on this surface.
**Welsh Wind(IRE)**, who has been performing consistently over course and distance, did so again and is the key to the value of the form.
**My Maite(IRE)**, who ran so well in a visor here last time, had the headgear left off and was 5lb higher. Presumably the visor was dispensed with because he ran too free last time, but he does seem suited by forcing tactics.
**Learned Lad(FR)**, who ran well against Fall In Line here last week, was raised 6lb for that effort and the welter burden appeared to take its toll.
**Magic Warrior**finished a lot closer to My Maite this time on better terms, but is yet to prove he is as effective at this trip as at shorter.

## 766 MICHAEL O'DONOVAN MEMORIAL MAIDEN STKS 1m (P)
**2:05** (2:07) (D) 3-Y-O £4,114 (£1,266; £633; £316) **Stalls** High

Form RPR

4 **1** **Heversham (IRE)**[33] 506 3-9-0 ........ MHills 12 76+
(WJHaggas) *led after 2f: clr over 1f out: r.o strly: promising* **2/1**[1]

**2** *5* **Mystic Lad** 3-9-0 ........ IMongan 2 66
(JamiePoulton) *slowly away: wl in rr: rdn and hdwy wl over 1f out: styd on wl to go 2nd cl home* **14/1**[3]

**3** *hd* **African Dream** 3-9-0 ........ SDrowne 8 65
(PFICole) *rapid hdwy to chse wnr over 5f out: no ch w him whn lost 2nd cl home* **20/1**

0-3 **4** *3 1/2* **First Of May**[21] 597 3-8-9 ........ MHenry 4 53
(MAJarvis) *a.p: rdn 2f out: kpt on one pce after* **4/1**[2]

2 **5** *nk* **La Peregrina**[7] 702 3-8-9 ........ JMackay 11 52
(SirMarkPrescott) *hld up in tch: hdwy to chse ldrs 1/2-way: rdn over 2f out: one pce ins fnl 2f* **2/1**[1]

00 **6** *3* **Joy And Pain**[3] 739 3-9-0 ........ DaneO'Neill 1 51+
(GLMoore) *in tch: making hdwy but hld whn hmpd over 1f out: nt rcvr* **50/1**

**7** *4* **Saint Zita (IRE)** 3-8-4 ........ JFMcDonald(5) 9 38
(BJMeehan) *slowly away: a towards rr* **40/1**

**8** *2* **King Of Meze (IRE)** 3-9-0 ........ OUrbina 7 38
(GProdromou) *chsd ldrs: wkng whn edgd lft appr fnl f* **66/1**

0-0 **9** *3* **Sussex Style (IRE)**[35] 489 3-9-0 ........ EAhern 10 32
(RMFlower) *hld up: rdn over 3f out: sn btn* **100/1**

60-0 **10** *4* **The Footballresult**[11] 660 3-8-9 53 ........ MartinDwyer 5 19
(MrsGHarvey) *a in rr* **66/1**

0 **11** *2 1/2* **Shalati Princess**[17] 621 3-8-9 ........ PDobbs 3 14
(JCFox) *slowly away: a bhd* **66/1**

**12** *3* **Shannkara's Quest (USA)** 3-9-0 ........ JQuinn 6 12
(PFICole) *t.k.h: led for 2f: sn outpcd* **14/1**[3]

1m 39.11s (-0.40) **Going Correction** +0.10s/f (Slow) **12** Ran SP% **114.6**
Speed ratings: **106,101,100,97,97 94,90,88,85,81 78,75**CSF £32.56 TOTE £3.80: £1.80, £3.40, £4.00; EX 64.50.
**Owner** Mr & Mrs G Middlebrook **Bred** G And Mrs Middlebrook **Trained** Newmarket, Suffolk

**FOCUS**
A maiden full of inexperienced sorts, but the winner scored in style, achieving a speed rating well above standard for the grade, so he may prove fairly useful.

**NOTEBOOK**
**Heversham(IRE)** showed the benefit of his debut a month ago at Wolverhampton and, handling this surface, quickened clear before the home turn to win in good style. However, this wide-margin victory will have caught the eye of the Handicapper.
**Mystic Lad** ◆ missed the break badly on this racecourse debut, but ran on really well from halfway to snatch the runner-up spot on the line. He will have learned a lot from this, and looks capable of winning an ordinary maiden.
**African Dream**, a nicely-bred debutant who is already gelded, showed plenty of ability until tiring late on, and is another who should improve for the outing and win at a similar level.
**First Of May**, stepping up in trip, seemed to have every chance but was well held. She now qualifies for a handicap mark, and may have her best chance of success in fillies' handicaps.
**La Peregrina**, who ran so promisingly on her debut here last week, was a market drifter and, after having every chance, had nothing left from the home turn. Like the fourth, she may be seen to best effect in fillies' handicaps.

## 767 BET DIRECT IN RUNNING SKY TEXT PAGE 293 FILLIES' H'CAP 1m 4f (P)
**2:40** (2:40) (E) (0-75,65) 4-Y-0+ £3,297 (£942; £471) **Stalls** Low

Form RPR

41-1 **1** **Regal Gallery (IRE)**[21] 602 6-9-13 **61** ........ PaulEddery 5 71+
(CAHorgan) *hld up: stdy hdwy on outside fr over 3f out: r.o to ld ins f* **9/4**[1]

0-00 **2** *1* **Anyhow (IRE)**[17] 618 7-9-6 **57** ........ J-PGuillambert(3) 6 65
(MissKMGeorge) *mid-div: hdwy 3f out: ev ch 1f out: nt pce of wnr* **6/1**[3]

00-3 **3** *3/4* **Dance Party (IRE)**[7] 705 4-9-11 **62** ........ MartinDwyer 10 69
(AMBalding) *in tch: led appr fnl f: hdd ins: kpt on* **5/1**[2]

0633 **4** *1* **Top Of The Class (IRE)**[1] 763 7-8-11 **45** ........ (v) EAhern 1 50
(PDEvans) *trckd ldrs: outpcd over 2f out: styd on again ins fnl f* **15/2**

0-03 **5** *1 1/2* **Figura**[14] 650 6-9-12 **60** ........ NCallan 12 63
(RIngram) *hld up in rr: rdn and hdwy on ins over 1f out: nt pce to rch ldrs* **6/1**[3]

333- **6** *1/2* **Rozanee**[88] 6022 4-9-11 **62** ........ IMongan 7 64
(JWPayne) *trckd ldr: led over 2f out: hdd over 1f out: wknd ins fnl f* **11/1**

0-34 **7** *shd* **My Lilli (IRE)**[10] 672 4-8-13 **50** ........ JFanning 4 52
(PMitchell) *in tch: rdn and hld whn hmpd over 1f out* **9/1**

00-0 **8** *1* **Pont Neuf (IRE)**[14] 650 4-9-7 **58** ........ (t) MHills 9 58
(JWHills) *hld up: rdn 4f out: n.d after* **33/1**

020- **9** *1 1/4* **Dispol Evita**[59] 6205 5-9-5 **53** ........ DKinsella 11 51
(JamiePoulton) *hld up: rdn over 3f out: nvr on terms* **20/1**

03-0 **10** *nk* **Harlot**[38] 464 4-9-2 **56** ........ LisaJones(3) 3 54
(JohnBerry) *led rdn 3f out: hdd and hung rt over 2f out: continued to hang and weaken* **25/1**

000- **11** *22* **Business Matters (IRE)**[149] 5024 4-9-2 **53** ........ RLappin 8 16
(HAlexander) *mid-div: rdn 5f out: sn wl bhd: t.o* **100/1**

2m 37.7s (3.72) **Going Correction** +0.10s/f (Slow)
**WFA** 4 from 5yo+ 3lb **11** Ran SP% **118.6**
Speed ratings: **91,90,89,89,88 87,87,87,86,86 71**CSF £15.29 CT £62.70 TOTE £3.20: £3.00, £1.90, £2.40; EX 34.10.
**Owner** Mrs B Sumner **Bred** Mrs B Sumner **Trained** Ogbourne Maisey, Wilts

**FOCUS**
A fair fillies' handicap and the form looks solid, even though the pace and winning time were slow.

**NOTEBOOK**
**Regal Gallery(IRE)** loves this track, having gained all her four wins over course and distance. She handled the step up in trip and, already 8lb higher than when scoring before Christmas, should not go up too much more for this.
**Anyhow(IRE)** ran her best race since the autumn, having been dropped 3lb. She possibly needs to come down another pound or two.
**Dance Party(IRE)** has taken well to this surface and seemed to have every chance. She has yet to win a race, but her turn cannot be far away.
**Top Of The Class(IRE)**, who has been racing on Fibresand this winter, seemed to stay the trip better on this surface and would be interesting if running in a banded stakes, which she just qualifies for off her current mark.
**Figura**is in fair form at present, but is better at ten furlongs.
**Rozanee**, having her first run for three months and stepping up in trip, did not get home. This was only her fourth outing and she looks capable of winning races.
**Harlot** *Official explanation: jockey said filly was hanging right; trainer said filly returned home lame on the near fore leg*

## 768 LITTLEWOODS BET DIRECT H'CAP 1m 2f (P)
**3:10** (3:10) (C) (0-100,88) 3-Y-0+ £15,103 (£5,728; £2,864; £1,302) **Stalls** Low

Form RPR

26-6 **1** **African Sahara (USA)**[15] 643 5-9-2 **76** ........ (t) GCarter 13 84
(MissDMountain) *hld up in rr: hdwy on outside 3f out: led ins fnl f: all out* **10/1**

00-1 **2** *nk* **Moayed**[7] 707 5-9-6 **80** ........ (bt) IMongan 4 87+
(NPLittmoden) *slowly away: wl in rr tl hdwy over 2f out: rdn and swtchd lft ins fnl f and r.o strly: jst failed* **10/1**

-325 **3** *nk* **Perfidious (USA)**[10] 679 6-8-9 **72** ........ RMiles(3) 2 79
(JRBoyle) *led tl hdd appr fnl f: hung rt ins fnl f and nt qckn cl home* **7/1**[3]

-465 **4** *3/4* **Dower House**[4] 735 9-9-3 **80** ........ (t) DCorby(3) 6 86
(AndrewTurnell) *t.k.h: hld up: hdwy and squeezed through gap over 1f out: r.o ins fnl f* **12/1**

154- **5** *shd* **Stateroom (USA)**[110] 5790 6-8-8 **71** ........ (b) LisaJones(3) 1 76
(JARToller) *t.k.h: mid-div: styd on fnl f* **33/1**

40- **6** *1/2* **Brooklyn's Gold (USA)**[32] 5753 9-9-5 **79** ........ CCatlin 12 83
(IanWilliams) *in rr: effrt on outside 2f out: nt qckn fnl f* **20/1**

-413 **7** *shd* **Hiawatha (IRE)**[14] 649 5-9-2 **76** ........ NCallan 11 80
(PABlockley) *hld up in tch: led appr fnl f: hdd and no ex whn squeezed out ins fnl f* **9/1**

6530 **8** *1/2* **Tight Squeeze**[14] 649 7-9-5 **79** ........ MartinDwyer 8 82
(PWHiatt) *mid-div: rdn 3f out: no imp ins fnl 2f* **10/1**

/0-0 **9** *1/2* **Adalar (IRE)**[21] 600 4-8-7 **75** ........ SJDonohoe(7) 5 78
(PDEvans) *in tch: rdn 3f out: sn btn* **50/1**

000- **10** *1/2* **Oldenway**[64] 6169 5-8-0 **65** ........ THamilton(5) 10 67
(RAFahey) *trckd ldrs: ev ch over 1f out: wknd ins fnl f* **8/1**

50-0 **11** *nk* **Jewel Of India**[10] 677 5-9-9 **83** ........ SDrowne 9 84
(MrsALMKing) *hld up: rdn 3f out: n.d after* **20/1**

4-22 **12** *shd* **Northside Lodge (IRE)**[14] 649 6-9-13 **87** ........ EAhern 3 88+
(PWHarris) *trckd ldrs: ev ch whn n.m.r over 1f out: nt rcvr* **10/3**[1]

251/ **13** *1 1/4* **Lion Hunter (USA)**[495] 5124 5-9-11 **88** ........ LPKeniry(3) 7 87
(MissECLavelle) *plld hrd: prom tl wknd over 2f out* **6/1**[2]

430- **14** *5* **Aventura (IRE)**[121] 5597 4-9-7 **85** ........ LFletcher(3) 14 75
(MJPolglase) *sn chsd ldr: ev chace 2f out: wknd qckly over 1f out* **50/1**

2m 7.86s (0.47) **Going Correction** +0.10s/f (Slow)
**WFA** 4 from 5yo+ 1lb **14** Ran SP% **122.3**
Speed ratings: **102,101,101,100,100 100,100,99,99,99 98,98,97,93**CSF £102.00 CT £757.13 TOTE £10.50: £3.00, £3.50, £1.30; EX 184.20.
**Owner** Miss Debbie Mountain **Bred** Chris Nolan **Trained** Newmarket, Suffolk
■ Stewards Enquiry : R Miles one-day ban: used whip down the shoulder in the forehand position (Feb 25)

**FOCUS**
A decent handicap run at just an ordinary gallop, resulting in a modest winning time for the grade, and there were one or two hard-luck stories. However, the form looks sound.

**NOTEBOOK**
**African Sahara(USA)**, having his first run on this surface since last spring, travelled well and, despite not finding as much under pressure as looked likely, did enough to hold on. This was his first win at ten furlongs and he should not go up much for scoring here, so should remain reasonably handicapped.
**Moayed**, who ran away with a seller here last week, was another stepping up in trip and looked unlucky. He was short of room halfway up the straight and, once in the open, finished strongly. He deserves to gain compensation.

**Perfidious(USA)** returned to something like his best form and was only run out of it near the finish. His tendency to drift right did cause others to be short of room, and he may be one to keep in mind for a race on a right-handed track early in the coming turf season.
**Dower House** came from plum last turning in, and benefited from Perfidious drifting to the centre of the track to get a clear run towards the inside. He possibly needs to drop another pound or two before being able to score again.
**Stateroom(USA)** ◆, having only his second run on this surface and his first outing since October, came through with the fourth and was finishing as well as anything. He looks one to keep in mind for a similar event.
**Northside Lodge(IRE)** travelled well on the heels of the leaders, but failed to get any run in the straight and was carried back by weakening rivals. This form is best ignored.
**Lion Hunter(USA)**, who had not been seen since winning a maiden for Barry Hills 17 months ago, was supported in the market but, after being too keen, dropped away quickly on the run to the straight. He has clearly been showing something at home and should be more settled next time.

## 769 BETDIRECT.CO.UK CLAIMING STKS 1m 2f (P)
**3:45** (3:45) (D) 3-Y-O **£4,134** (£1,272; £636; £318) **Stalls** Low

Form RPR
0- **1** **Varuni (IRE)**[195] 3811 3-8-6 ........ EAhern 4 60
(JGPortman) *a in tch: led ins fnl f: r.o wl* **33/1**
030- **2** ¾ **Zakfree (IRE)**[98] 5950 3-8-6 66 ........(b) J-PGuillambert[(3)] 6 62
(NPLittmoden) *hld up in rr: sme hdwy whn outpcd over 2f out: styd on wl to go 2nside fnl f* **7/1**[3]
-346 **3** 2 **Maybe Someday**[10] 675 3-8-11 71 ........ IMongan 2 60
(IAWood) *hld up: stdy hdwy fr 1/2-way: led wl over 1f out: rdn and d hdd ins fnl f: no ex* **7/4**[2]
-451 **4** ½ **Blue Empire (IRE)**[8] 696 3-9-0 78 ........ NCallan 5 62
(PABlockley) *t.k.h: hld up: hdwy over 2f out: one pce ins fnl f* **5/4**[1]
04-3 **5** 1 **Larad (IRE)**[11] 662 3-8-7 45 ........(b) DKinsella 3 53
(JSMoore) *trckd ldr: led 3f out: hdd wl over 1f out: wknd ent fnl f* **12/1**
205- **6** 5 **Hold The Line**[77] 6091 3-8-7 67 ........(p) CHaddon[(7)] 7 51
(WGMTurner) *t.k.h: trckd ldrs: wknd 2f out* **14/1**
65-0 **7** 20 **Trishay**[10] 675 3-8-6 56 ........ JQuinn 1 5
(APJarvis) *sn led: hdd 3f out: wknd qckly 2f out* **25/1**
0 **8** 26 **Captain Fearless**[9] 683 3-8-3 ........ HayleyTurner[(5)] 8 —
(MrsCADunnett) *rdn 6f out: wknd 4f out: t.o* **66/1**

2m 9.47s (2.08) **Going Correction** +0.10s/f (Slow) **8** Ran SP% **115.9**
Speed ratings: **95,94,92,92,91 87,71,50**CSF £245.48 TOTE £39.40: £6.10, £3.00, £1.10; EX 302.30.
**Owner** J G B Portman **Bred** Mrs P Grubb **Trained** Compton, Berks

**FOCUS**
An ordinary claimer run at a modest pace and a surprise result. The form is just fair for the grade.

**NOTEBOOK**
**Varuni(IRE)**, who was very slowly away on her only previous run in August, travelled well on this Polytrack debut and picked up nicely to score a little cosily. She looks capable of going on from this.
**Zakfree(IRE)**, also making his Polytrack debut and having his first run for three months, finished well from the rear and was closing in on the winner late on without ever threatening to catch her. He stayed the trip well and can pick up a claimer if repeating this performance.
**Maybe Someday**, running in a claimer for the first time since joining his current yard, was well supported against the favourite and had every chance in the race. However, he could not quicken and maybe does not truly stay this trip.
**Blue Empire(IRE)** was an uneasy favourite, and appeared to have his chance in the race. He is three from four on Fibresand, and has failed to score in three tries on this surface, so is clearly more effective on the former.

## 770 BET IN RUNNING @ BETDIRECT.CO.UK CLASSIFIED STKS 7f (P)
**4:20** (4:21) (D) 3-Y-0+ **£4,082** (£1,256; £628; £314) **Stalls** Low

Form RPR
-1 **1** **Aleutian**[24] 574 4-9-9 85 ........ JPSpencer 8 99+
(DRLoder) *mde all: shkn up appr fnl f to confirm superiority: r.o wl* **5/2**[1]
3-1 **2** 1 **Mr Lambros**[42] 415 3-8-1 80 ........ MartinDwyer 9 91
(AMBalding) *s.i.s but plld hrd and sn pressed wnr: rdn over 1f out and no imp fnl f* **3/1**[2]
-511 **3** 1¼ **Grey Pearl**[14] 648 5-9-3 82 ........ MFenton 4 87
(MissGayKelleway) *mid-div: rdn and hdwy 2f out: r.o wl but no imp on first 2 fnl f* **6/1**
401- **4** ¾ **What-A-Dancer (IRE)**[66] 6164 7-9-7 83 ........ EAhern 10 89
(GASwinbank) *slowly away: hdwy over 1f out: r.o fnl f* **9/2**[3]
3-00 **5** shd **Hand Chime**[30] 544 7-9-2 85 ........ DanielleDeverson[(7)] 1 91
(WJHaggas) *slowly away: t.k.h: r.o fnl f: n.d* **20/1**
022- **6** ½ **Incline (IRE)**[66] 6164 5-9-3 82 ........ RMiles[(3)] 2 87
(TGMills) *hld up in tch: no imp on ldrs ins fnl 2f* **9/1**
13-0 **7** ½ **Summer Recluse (USA)**[14] 647 5-9-4 77 ........(p) DaneO'Neill 3 83
(BRJohnson) *s.i.s: hld up: effrt over 1f out: nvr nr to chal* **16/1**
3-50 **8** 1½ **Cashel Mead**[32] 511 4-9-1 79 ........ ADaly 6 77
(JLSpearing) *chsd ldrs tl wknd wl over 1f out* **50/1**
1 **9** 2 **Millville**[28] 555 4-9-4 80 ........ NCallan 11 75
(MAJarvis) *slowly away: a struggling in rr* **25/1**
00-0 **10** ½ **Border Edge**[14] 648 6-9-4 79 ........(v) GBaker 7 73
(JJBridger) *t.k.h: in tch tl wknd qckly over 1f out* **66/1**
6-06 **11** 1 **Agilis (IRE)**[10] 677 4-9-4 74 ........(b) SDrowne 5 71
(JamiePoulton) *chsd ldrs tiull wknd wl over 1f out* **66/1**

1m 25.31s (-0.69) **Going Correction** +0.10s/f (Slow)
**WFA** 3 from 4yo+ 17lb **11** Ran SP% **115.5**
Speed ratings: **107,105,104,103,103 102,102,100,98,97 96**CSF £9.30 TOTE £3.70: £1.40, £2.40, £2.10; EX 14.50.
**Owner** Jumeirah Racing **Bred** Cliveden Stud Ltd **Trained** Newmarket, Suffolk

**FOCUS**
A decent classified contest run at a good pace, and unusually dominated by the front runners. The winner may be capable of holding his own at a higher level.

**NOTEBOOK**
**Aleutian**, who won a six-furlong maiden here on his debut last month, took on this stronger opposition and won with authority. He looks capable of making his mark in better grade contests.
**Mr Lambros** was again untidy leaving the stalls, but soon pulled his way into contention and did well to keep on in pursuit of his older rival. He is still inexperienced and looks the type to improve with maturity.
**Grey Pearl**has been in fine form of late and seemed to run her race without ever posing a threat to the principals.
**What-A-Dancer(IRE)** confirmed recent form with Incline on 2lb worse terms, but missing the break counted against him on this occasion.
**Hand Chime**, who goes well at this track, did not perform badly for his inexperienced rider and has dropped to a mark which will give him a chance to contest lower-grade handicaps.
**Incline(IRE)** ran virtually to the pound with What-A-Dancer compared with December course and distance running. He is capable of scoring on this surface, but is creeping up the handicap without winning.

## 771 BET DIRECT IN VISION SKY PAGE 293 APPRENTICE H'CAP 6f (P)
**4:55** (4:56) (F) (0-70,70) 3-Y-0+ **£2,940** (£840; £420) **Stalls** Low

Form RPR
0024 **1** **Hard To Catch (IRE)**[3] 742 6-9-6 65 ........ MSavage[(3)] 6 78
(DKIvory) *in tch: led ent fnl f: rdn out* **11/2**[3]
-116 **2** ½ **Prince Aaron (IRE)**[14] 646 4-9-12 68 ........ BReilly 3 79
(CNAllen) *in tch: hdwy 2f out: ev ch 1f out: kpt on fnl f* **3/1**[1]
2-00 **3** 1¼ **Illusive (IRE)**[9] 680 7-9-4 60 ........(b) TEaves 4 67
(MWigham) *chsd ldr: led briefly over 1f out: nt qckn ins* **20/1**
00-0 **4** 1 **Carlton (IRE)**[7] 701 10-9-1 60 ........ RThomas[(3)] 5 64
(CRDore) *in rr: hdwy on outside over 1f out: kpt on one pce* **20/1**
6435 **5** shd **Superchief**[3] 742 9-9-9 65 ........(bt) NChalmers 11 69
(MissBSanders) *slowly away: in rr: rdn and styd on fr over 1f out: nvr nr to chal* **10/1**
2112 **6** 1 **Tayif**[24] 573 8-9-7 66 ........(t) SJDonohoe[(3)] 7 67
(AndrewReid) *in rr: hdwy on ins over 1f out: nvr nr to chal* **10/3**[2]
-006 **7** ½ **Teyaar**[9] 681 8-9-1 60 ........ HayleyTurner[(3)] 12 59
(MrsNMacauley) *sn led: hdd over 1f out: wknd* **20/1**
6325 **8** ½ **Ladies Knight**[15] 638 4-9-0 56 ........ THamilton 10 54
(DShaw) *slowly away: passed btn horses fr over 1f out* **8/1**
03-4 **9** ½ **Polar Force**[31] 526 4-8-12 61 ........ TO'Brien[(7)] 13 57
(MRChannon) *nvr on terms* **7/1**
3-10 **10** nk **Classic Vision**[23] 584 4-9-2 58 ........ JFMcDonald 2 54
(WJHaggas) *s.i.s: sn in tch: rdn and wknd 2f out* **20/1**
420- **11** 2½ **Firework**[131] 5427 6-9-5 66 ........(p) MCoumbe[(5)] 8 54
(JAkehurst) *chsd ldrs tl wknd wl over 1f out* **25/1**
0-05 **12** 1 **Sounds Lucky**[21] 596 8-9-8 64 ........(b) AQuinn 9 49
(NPLittmoden) *mid-div: rdn and wknd 2f out* **16/1**

1m 12.65s (-0.27) **Going Correction** +0.10s/f (Slow) **12** Ran SP% **124.9**
Speed ratings: **105,104,102,101,101 99,99,98,97,97 94,92**CSF £21.55 CT £323.60 TOTE £9.80: £3.30, £1.70, £6.80; EX 50.70 Place 6 £151.67, Place 5 £79.21.
**Owner** Mrs Karen Graham **Bred** Flan Hannon **Trained** Radlett, Herts

**FOCUS**
A modest apprentice handicap, but run at a good pace for the grade and the form is fair.

**NOTEBOOK**
**Hard To Catch(IRE)**, dropping back in trip, has been running well on this surface and finally got his reward. He should not go up too much and can supplement this in similar grade contests.
**Prince Aaron(IRE)**, 10lb higher than when gaining the second of his two course and distance wins in January, ran his race and lost nothing in defeat.
**Illusive(IRE)** showed his best form since returning from an 11-month break and, although he has not won for nearly three years, he has been given a chance by the Handicapper.
**Carlton(IRE)** did not run badly, has dropped to a fair mark, and will be interesting in similar contests back on Fibresand, which suits him.
**Superchief** missed the break and did well to finish where he did. He is knocking at the door, but is without a win for almost two years.
**Tayif** was held up as usual, but never got close enough to land a blow.
T/Plt: £1,187.50 to a £1 stake. Pool: £33,673.90. 20.70 winning tickets. T/Qpdt: £111.70 to a £1 stake. Pool: £1,986.40. 13.15 winning tickets. JS

# [758]WOLVERHAMPTON (A.W) (L-H)
### Saturday, February 14

**OFFICIAL GOING: Standard to slow**
Wind: nil Weather: drizzle last 3 races

## 772 BET IN RUNNING ON SKY TEXT PAGE 293 H'CAP 7f (F)
**7:00** (7:01) (E) (0-70,68) 4-Y-0+ **£3,346** (£956; £478) **Stalls** High

Form RPR
3536 **1** **Givemethemoonlight**[1] 763 5-8-10 50 ........(v) IMongan 2 61
(MrsStefLiddiard) *mde all: rdn over 2f out: clr over 1f out: r.o wl* **7/1**[3]
0-05 **2** 2½ **Dispol Peto**[4] 733 4-9-5 59 ........(p) JBramhill 10 64
(IanEmmerson) *chsd wnr tl rdn 4f out: wnt 2nd again jst over 1f out: no imp* **50/1**
0-20 **3** ¾ **Geronimo**[33] 509 7-9-5 59 ........(p) MFenton 5 62
(MissGayKelleway) *hld up and bhd: rdn and hdwy on ins over 2f out: kpt on same pce fnl f* **7/1**[3]
150- **4** 8 **Teehee (IRE)**[45] 6270 6-10-0 68 ........(b) JQuinn 4 51
(BPalling) *a.p: rdn over 3f out: chsd wnr 2f out tl jst over 1f out: wknd fnl f* **11/1**
0011 **5** 1½ **Warlingham (IRE)**[8] 698 6-9-7 61 ........ JFanning 8 40
(PHowling) *hld up in tch: rdn and wknd over 3f out* **4/1**[2]
6-00 **6** hd **Spark Up**[23] 588 4-9-5 59 ........(b) MHenry 6 38
(JWUnett) *hld up: sme hdwy on outside over 4f out: rdn and wknd over 2f out* **16/1**
0-02 **7** hd **Flying Edge (IRE)**[5] 719 4-8-11 51 ........ ANicholls 7 29
(EJAlston) *t.k.h: sn prom: chsd wnr 4f out tl rdn 2f out: sn wknd* **7/1**[3]
-350 **8** ½ **Spy Gun (USA)**[8] 700 4-8-13 56 ........ DCorby[(3)] 1 33
(TWall) *rdr had trble removing blindfold: s.s: a bhd* **14/1**
00-1 **9** 10 **Iced Diamond (IRE)**[8] 694 5-8-11 58 ........ BSwarbrick[(7)] 3 10
(WMBrisbourne) *s.s: a in rr* **2/1**[1]

1m 30.43s (0.23) **Going Correction** +0.125s/f (Slow) **9** Ran SP% **113.7**
Speed ratings: **103,100,99,90,88 88,87,87,75**CSF £267.20 CT £2519.18 TOTE £6.20: £1.50, £7.90, £2.20; EX 129.10.
**Owner** Valley Fencing **Bred** Mrs P A Reditt And M J Reditt **Trained** Great Shefford, Berks

**FOCUS**
An ordinary handicap and just a fair pace for the grade.

**NOTEBOOK**
**Givemethemoonlight** was obviously none the worse for her exertions here the previous day. She forced the pace over this shorter trip and ran out a decisive winner.
**Dispol Peto**, dropped 3lb, seemed to benefit from having the cheekpieces back on.
**Geronimo** did not find a return to seven the answer after being given a month off.
**Teehee(IRE)** was still 4lb above the highest mark off which he has won.
**Warlingham(IRE)** had gone up 3lb after the second of his back-to-back wins over course and distance in selling company. *Official explanation: trainer said gelding ran too free*
**Spy Gun(USA)**, whose rider took three attempts to remove the blindfold, inevitably still had it on when the stalls opened.
**Iced Diamond(IRE)** lost the same ground at the start as Spy Gun but had no excuses.

## 773 BET DIRECT ON SKY ACTIVE CLASSIFIED CLAIMING STKS 1m 100y(F)
**7:30** (7:30) (F) 3-Y-0+ **£2,926** (£836; £418) **Stalls** Low

Form RPR
0-16 **1** **Jakarmi**[8] 696 3-8-5 56 ........ JQuinn 5 64
(BPalling) *hld up: hdwy over 4f out: rdn to chse ldr 3f out: led ins fnl f: r.o* **3/1**[2]

15-0 **2** 1 1/4 **Cloudless (USA)**[19] 608 4-9-6 57 SWhitworth 7 58
(JWUnett) *led: clr over 3f out: rdn over 1f out: hdd and no ex ins fnl f* **8/1**
0-02 **3** 1 3/4 **Frank's Quest (IRE)**[6] 714 4-9-7 55 LPKeniry(3) 3 58
(PBurgoyne) *hld up: rdn and hdwy 3f out: styd on fnl f* **6/1**[3]
-420 **4** 1 3/4 **Nite-Owl Fizz**[19] 604 6-9-7 48 IMongan 8 51
(JO'Reilly) *chsd ldr: rdn over 4f out: lost 2nd 3f out: sn outpcd: kpt on fnl f* **11/4**[1]
0-10 **5** 12 **Daimajin (IRE)**[26] 562 5-9-3 56 PMakin(7) 1 29
(MrsLucindaFeatherstone) *w ldr 7f out to 5f out: sn rdn: wknd 4f out* **15/2**
060- **6** 2 **Miss Koen (IRE)**[56] 1708 5-9-3 60 LFletcher(3) 6 21
(DLWilliams) *rdn over 4f out: a bhd* **10/1**
00-6 **7** 8 **Pup's Pride**[29] 548 7-9-8 55 (v) PMcCabe 2 6
(MrsNMacauley) *hld up: lost pl over 6f out: dropped rr and rdn over 5f out: wl bhd fnl 3f* **7/1**
00-0 **8** 22 **Blakeshall Girl**[19] 608 4-9-4 45 (b1) DeanMcKeown 4 —
(JLSpearing) *bhd: rdn over 5f out: t.o fnl 3f* **66/1**

1m 52.15s (1.15) **Going Correction** +0.125s/f (Slow)
**WFA** 3 from 4yo+ 19lb **8** Ran SP% **111.9**
Speed ratings: **99,97,96,94,82 80,72,50**CSF £25.84 TOTE £3.90: £1.90, £2.10, £1.50; EX 51.00.
**Owner** Mrs M M Palling **Bred** Llety Stud **Trained** Tredodridge, Vale Of Glamorgan

**FOCUS**
A modest claimer run at a decent pace and a fair time for the grade.

**NOTEBOOK**
**Jakarmi** was certainly not inconvenienced by the return back up to the stretch mile.
**Cloudless(USA)** was probably not helped by being taken on for the lead around the first turn and eventually got worn down over this longer trip.
**Frank's Quest(IRE)** was never going to reach the first two in time and needs at least a mile. *Official explanation: jockey said gelding had hung left*
**Nite-Owl Fizz** would have been better off in a handicap.
**Miss Koen(IRE)** *Official explanation: jockey said mare had hung left*

## 774 TONY COWEN LOSS OF INDEPENDENCE DAY MAIDEN STKS 6f (F)
8:00 (8:00) (D) 3-Y-O **£3,341** (£1,028; £514; £257) **Stalls** Low

Form RPR
0-3 **1** **Royal Pavillion (IRE)**[35] 489 3-9-0 MFenton 6 65
(WJMusson) *sn chsng ldr: led over 3f out: rdn wl over 1f out: drvn out* **10/11**[1]
00-6 **2** 2 1/2 **Brown Dragon**[19] 606 3-9-0 65 PaulEddery 4 58
(DHaydnJones) *a.p: rdn over 3f out: chsd wnr wl over 1f out: no imp* **10/1**
25-5 **3** 5 **Soul Provider (IRE)**[19] 606 3-8-9 63 NCallan 3 38
(PABlockley) *bhd: hrd rdn and hdwy over 2f out: wknd ins fnl f* **9/2**[3]
26-4 **4** 6 **Orchestration (IRE)**[10] 673 3-9-0 67 SWhitworth 5 25
(JWUnett) *sn bhd: rdn over 3f out: nvr nr ldrs* **11/4**[2]
0- **5** 1 **Shaymee's Girl**[77] 6097 3-8-9 JoannaBadger 1 17
(MsDeborahJEvans) *led over 2f: rdn and ev ch 2f out: sn wknd* **66/1**
0-0 **6** 10 **Mind The Time**[25] 569 3-9-0 CCatlin 2 —
(JHetherton) *stdd after s: rr whn swtchd wd over 4f out: sn struggling* **50/1**

1m 16.27s (0.57) **Going Correction** +0.125s/f (Slow) **6** Ran SP% **109.8**
Speed ratings: **101,97,91,83,81 68**CSF £10.86 TOTE £2.10: £1.60, £1.90; EX 11.30.
**Owner** Howard Spooner **Bred** Theo Waddington And Mrs Theo Waddington **Trained** Newmarket, Suffolk

**FOCUS**
A modest maiden with a pace to match.

**NOTEBOOK**
**Royal Pavillion(IRE)** proved too good for some modest rivals on this switch to Fibresand.
**Brown Dragon** ran his best race to date but still had to be content with playing second fiddle.
**Soul Provider(IRE)** had finished half a length in front of Brown Dragon over course and distance last month.

## 775 BETDIRECT.CO.UK H'CAP 1m 100y(F)
8:30 (8:30) (D) (0-85,82) 3-Y-O+ **£4,085** (£1,257; £628; £314) **Stalls** Low

Form RPR
0-11 **1** **Vortex**[14] 647 5-9-7 **78** (t) MFenton 1 88
(MissGayKelleway) *led early: hld up in tch gng wl: rdn to ld ins fnl f: drvn out* **6/1**
-102 **2** 1 3/4 **Penwell Hill (USA)**[11] 667 5-8-9 **73** PMakin(7) 7 79
(TDBarron) *mid-div: rdn over 3f out: hdwy on outside and edgd lft fnl f: tk 2nd post* **12/1**
4-23 **3** shd **Skylarker (USA)**[15] 643 6-9-3 **79** MSavage(5) 4 85
(WSKittow) *lft in ld 7f out: rdn over 3f out: hdd over 2f out: led again over 1f out tl ins fnl f: nt qckn* **11/2**[3]
-253 **4** 1/2 **Yorker (USA)**[5] 719 6-8-8 **68** LisaJones(3) 3 73
(MsDeborahJEvans) *hld up: sn bhd: rdn and hdwy on ins over 2f out: ev ch over 1f out: nt qckn ins fnl f* **12/1**
00-0 **5** 2 1/2 **No Grouse**[30] 544 4-8-11 **73** THamilton(5) 8 72
(RAFahey) *hld up: hdwy over 5f out: rdn 3f out: wknd 1f out* **25/1**
020- **6** nk **My Bayard**[223] 3035 5-8-12 **69** NCallan 9 68
(JO'Reilly) *prom: led over 2f out: sn rdn: hdd over 1f out: wknd ins fnl f* **50/1**
1350 **7** 1/2 **Arc El Ciel (ARG)**[10] 677 6-9-7 **78** (v) IMongan 5 76
(MrsStefLiddiard) *hld up: rdn over 3f out: short-lived effrt over 1f out* **14/1**
0-20 **8** hd **Flint River**[19] 607 6-9-8 **82** LFletcher(3) 6 79
(HMorrison) *trckd ldrs: rdn 3f out: wknd over 1f out* **9/2**[1]
0-40 **9** 4 **Air Mail**[2] 749 7-9-8 **79** ACulhane 11 68
(MrsNMacauley) *hld up: stdy hdwy over 5f out: wknd 2f out* **14/1**
-006 **10** 7 **Invader**[15] 641 8-9-7 **78** (b) JQuinn 12 52
(CEBrittain) *w ldrs: rdn whn n.m.r jst over 2f out: sn wknd* **14/1**
0-01 **11** 6 **Scotty's Future (IRE)**[11] 664 6-9-9 **80** JPSpencer 10 42
(DRLoder) *s.i.s: rdn 4f out: a bhd* **5/1**[2]
1463 **P** **Ovigo (GER)**[22] 589 5-8-12 **69** DeanMcKeown 2 —
(PABlockley) *led tl p.u lame 7f out: broke leg: dead* **10/1**

1m 51.22s (0.22) **Going Correction** +0.125s/f (Slow) **12** Ran SP% **114.8**
Speed ratings: **103,101,101,100,98 97,97,97,93,86 80,**—CSF £73.52 CT £423.79 TOTE £5.70: £2.30, £3.80, £1.70; EX 111.20.
**Owner** Coriolis Partnership **Bred** Juddmonte Farms **Trained** Newmarket, Suffolk

**FOCUS**
A competitive handicap but the time was ordinary.

**NOTEBOOK**
**Vortex** continues on the crest of a wave and completed a hat-trick having gone up a total of 5lb.
**Penwell Hill(USA)**, 7lb higher than when successful at Southwell last month, ran a lot better than on his only previous visit here two outings ago.
**Skylarker(USA)** ran another sound race over this slightly shorter distance.
**Yorker(USA)** was 6lb better off than when beaten two lengths by Vortex over course and distance last month.
**No Grouse** ◆ showed signs of a return to form and it should be remembered that his back-to-back wins on turf last spring came over six and seven furlongs.
**My Bayard** made a highly satisfactory comeback on his first outing since last July.
**Flint River** had no excuses on account of the distance this time.
**Invader** *Official explanation: jockey said horse suffered interference in running*

## 776 BET DIRECT INTERACTIVE (S) STKS 1m 1f 79y(F)
9:00 (9:02) (G) 4-6-Y-O **£2,534** (£724; £362) **Stalls** Low

Form RPR
40/0 **1** **Heathers Girl**[15] 642 5-8-8 40 PaulEddery 3 58
(DHaydnJones) *a.p: rdn and wnt 2nd over 2f out: led ins fnl f: drvn out* **50/1**
04-0 **2** 5 **Desert Heat**[43] 412 6-8-13 57 (v1) NCallan 1 53
(ISemple) *led early: a.p: rdn to ld over 2f out: hdd ins fnl f: sn btn* **14/1**[3]
00-0 **3** 8 **Gwazi**[25] 570 4-8-13 40 (vt) ACulhane 5 37
(MissDAMchale) *hld up: rdn over 5f out: bhd 4f out: sme hdwy wl over 1f out: n.d* **66/1**
63-3 **4** 15 **Eight Woods (IRE)**[32] 517 6-8-13 60 JPSpencer 2 7
(TDBarron) *sn led: lost action and hdd over 3f out: rdn and hung lft 2f out: sn eased: fin lame* **4/9**[1]
50-0 **5** 2 1/2 **Illusionist**[9] 685 6-8-13 35 (v) PMcCabe 4 2
(MrsNMacauley) *rdn over 4f out: a bhd* **100/1**
040- **6** 7 **Dundonald**[65] 3835 5-8-13 45 (vt) SRighton 10 —
(MAppleby) *prom: rdn over 5f out: wknd over 4f out* **50/1**
0-50 **7** 3/4 **Bontadini**[7] 705 5-8-13 45 (v) IMongan 9 —
(DMorris) *prom: led over 3f out: rdn and hdd over 2f out: sn wknd* **9/1**[2]
05-P **8** 2 **Geography (IRE)**[11] 664 4-8-13 53 (p) JQuinn 7 —
(PButler) *a bhd: t.o fnl 5f* **50/1**

2m 4.65s (1.75) **Going Correction** +0.125s/f (Slow) **8** Ran SP% **94.3**
Speed ratings: **97,92,85,72,69 63,63,61**CSF £367.50 TOTE £27.20: £4.00, £1.80, £6.50; EX 75.60.There was no bid for the winner
**Owner** Trio Racing **Bred** Barry Adams **Trained** Efail Isaf, Rhondda C Taff

**FOCUS**
This did not take much winning with the odds-on favourite breaking down.

**NOTEBOOK**
**Heathers Girl** was all the better for a comeback run over an inadequate seven furlongs here last time.
**Desert Heat** had no answer to the winner despite the first-time visor.
**Eight Woods(IRE)** was found to have finished lame in both forelegs. *Official explanation: jockey said gelding finished lame*
**Illusionist** *Official explanation: jockey said gelding lost its action turning for home*
**Geography(IRE)** *Official explanation: jockey said gelding moved badly and hung left*

## 777 BET IN RUNNING @ BETDIRECT.CO.UK H'CAP 1m 4f (F)
9:30 (9:30) (F) (0-60,65) 4-Y-O+ **£2,968** (£848; £424) **Stalls** Low

Form RPR
0-41 **1** **Mandoob**[1] 759 7-10-3 65 6ex (p) J-PGuillambert(3) 9 70
(BRJohnson) *dwlt: hld up in rr: hdwy over 3f out: rdn over 2f out: led jst over 1f out: edgd lft ins fnl f: r.o* **11/2**[3]
0-22 **2** 1/2 **Jadeeron**[22] 592 5-9-10 58 (p) LisaJones(3) 11 68
(MissDAMchale) *a.p: rdn over 2f out: edgd lft ins fnl f: styd on towards fin* **5/1**[2]
61-1 **3** 4 **Robbie Can Can**[8] 693 5-9-8 58 HayleyTurner(5) 8 62
(AWCarroll) *bhd: rdn 5f out: hdwy over 2f out: styd on fnl f* **5/1**[2]
1211 **4** 2 1/2 **Bella Pavlina**[6] 715 6-9-10 62 6ex BSwarbrick(7) 7 62
(WMBrisbourne) *hld up mid-div: hdwy over 5f out: led 3f out: sn rdn: hdd jst over 1f out: wknd ins fnl f* **8/1**
4143 **5** 5 **Coolfore Jade (IRE)**[4] 734 4-9-7 55 CCatlin 12 48
(NEBerry) *t.k.h: prom: wnt 2nd 8f out: led over 5f out to 3f out: sn rdn: wknd over 1f out* **11/1**
6-50 **6** 1 **E Minor (IRE)**[8] 693 5-9-6 56 NChalmers(5) 4 47
(TWall) *hld up: rdn and bhd over 4f out: n.d* **40/1**
5333 **7** nk **Lazzaz**[5] 724 6-9-12 57 ACulhane 2 48
(PWHiatt) *prom: rdn over 3f out: wknd over 2f out* **7/2**[1]
-422 **8** 3 **Fight The Feeling**[8] 693 6-9-7 57 (b1) DNolan(5) 1 43
(JWUnett) *hld up mid-div: hdwy over 4f out: sn rdn: wknd 3f out* **12/1**
0-10 **9** 1 1/2 **Molly's Secret**[19] 609 6-9-5 50 (p) JQuinn 3 34
(CGCox) *hld up mid-div: hdwy over 5f out: rdn over 3f out: sn wknd* **15/2**
5-06 **10** 12 **Lord Gizzmo**[8] 693 7-8-6 40 LFletcher(3) 5 6
(PWHiatt) *led: hdd over 5f out: rdn over 4f out: sn wknd* **33/1**
000- **11** nk **Wigmo Princess**[7] 4766 5-8-9 40 (b1) ANicholls 10 6
(SCBurrough) *s.i.s: rdn 5f out: a bhd* **66/1**
100- **12** dist **Branston Nell**[159] 4781 5-9-1 46 (b1) JBramhill 6 —
(CRDore) *chsd ldr 4f: wknd qckly over 5f out: sn t.o* **50/1**

2m 40.89s (-0.61) **Going Correction** +0.125s/f (Slow) **12** Ran SP% **118.7**
**WFA** 4 from 5yo+ 3lb
Speed ratings: **107,106,104,102,99 98,98,96,95,87 86,**—CSF £32.58 CT £148.58 TOTE £7.50: £2.60, £2.90, £2.60; EX 71.10 Place 6 £636.27, Place 5 £163.89.
**Owner** J L Guillambert **Bred** Shadwell Estate Company Limited **Trained** Epsom, Surrey

**FOCUS**
The top two in the weights were rated above 60 because of their penalties. The winning time was very good for a race of its grade.

**NOTEBOOK**
**Mandoob** does appear to have improved since being fitted with cheekpieces and had more to do than when landing a claimer over course and distance the previous day.
**Jadeeron** finds this trip the bare minimum and is capable of going one better over further.
**Robbie Can Can**, raised 7lb for his course and distance win, got going too late on this occasion.
**Bella Pavlina** was effectively 23lb higher than when registering back-to-back victories in banded stakes.
**Coolfore Jade(IRE)** eventually paid the penalty for running freely.
T/Plt: £1,434.80 to a £1 stake. Pool £41,275.40, 21.00 winning tickets T/Qpdt: £221.60 to a £1 stake. Pool £1,827.50, 6.10 winning tickets KH

# 746 SOUTHWELL (L-H)
Sunday, February 15

**OFFICIAL GOING: Standard**
(REGIONAL RACING)

## 778 BET DIRECT ON SKY ACTIVE APPRENTICE BANDED STKS 1m (F)
2:00 (2:00) (H) 3-Y-O+ **£1,438** (£411; £205) **Stalls** Low

Form RPR
60-0 **1** **Gracious Air (USA)**[12] 663 6-9-3 35 (v) DFentiman(5) 2 40
(JRWeymes) *hld up: hdwy 3f out: rdn to ld 1f out: r.o wl* **10/1**


The Form Book, Raceform Ltd, Compton, RG20 6NL

0405 **2** 4 **Dancing King (IRE)**[7] 713 8-9-3 30 PGallagher(5) 5 31
(PWHiatt) *led: rdn and hdd 1f out: sn outpcd* **16/1**

0-32 **3** 1 1/2 **Kenny The Truth (IRE)**[26] 567 5-9-8 40 (t) NChalmers 1 28
(MrsJCandlish) *chsd ldrs: rdn over 2f out: no ex fnl f* **5/4**[1]

040- **4** 3/4 **Mathmagician**[273] 447 5-9-3 35 (p) KGhunowa(5) 6 26
(RFMarvin) *chsd ldrs: rdn over 3f out: styd on same pce appr fnl f* **40/1**

3300 **5** 3 **Lemarate (USA)**[13] 658 7-9-3 40 RoryMoore(5) 7 19
(DWChapman) *chsd ldr: rdn over 3f out: wknd over 1f out* **8/1**[3]

0030 **6** 5 **Haithem (IRE)**[6] 726 7-9-3 40 (t) DawnWatson(5) 4 8
(DShaw) *hld up in tch: rdn over 3f out: sn wknd* **12/1**

000/ **7** 1/2 **Te Anau**[643] 1367 7-9-3 30 LauraPike(5) 3 7
(WJMusson) *hld up: wknd 3f out* **33/1**

0-42 **8** 6 **Colne Valley Amy**[12] 663 7-9-8 40 (b) AQuinn 8 —
(GLMoore) *stsarted slowly: sn chsng ldrs: rdn and wknd over 2f out* **5/2**[2]

1m 44.03s (-0.57) **Going Correction** -0.225s/f (Stan) **8** Ran SP% **112.2**
Speed ratings: **93,89,87,86,83 78,78,72**CSF £145.18 TOTE £13.50: £3.60, £4.90, £1.10; EX 151.90.
**Owner** Sporting Occasions **Bred** Holly Valley Thoroughbreds **Trained** Middleham Moor, N Yorks

**FOCUS**
A weak race, but they went a decent pace and the form should be reliable at this lowly level. However, the time was moderate.

**NOTEBOOK**
**Gracious Air(USA)** had not won since May 2002 but, dropped in trip and switched back to Fibresand, she kept on well from off the pace to end that losing run. This is her sort of level.
**Dancing King(IRE)**, stepping back up to a mile, got an easy lead and had every chance from the front.
**Kenny The Truth(IRE)** has been in reasonable form at this sort of level over this very course and distance lately, but this was a little bit disappointing.
**Mathmagician**, back on the level, and with cheekpieces fitted, appeared to have every chance.
**Lemarate(USA)** did not appear to have any excuses.
**Colne Valley Amy** is possibly better on Polytrack.

## 779 PRESS INTERACTIVE TO BET DIRECT MEDIAN AUCTION MAIDEN STKS 7f (F)
**2:30** (2:31) (H ) 3-5-Y-0 **£1,470** (£420; £210) **Stalls** Low

Form RPR

6-32 **1** **Daring Affair**[26] 569 3-7-11 63 LisaJones(3) 1 65+
(KRBurke) *chsd ldr: led 3f out: rdn clr over 1f out* **11/8**[1]

05-4 **2** 8 **Bundaberg**[17] 628 4-9-8 40 ACulhane 6 50
(PWHiatt) *chsd ldrs: rdn over 2f out: outpcd over 1f out* **33/1**

0-23 **3** 1 3/4 **Weakest Link**[26] 569 3-8-5 63 JQuinn 4 46
(WJarvis) *hld up in tch: rdn over 2f out: wknd over 1f out* **9/4**[2]

050- **4** hd **Gilly's General (IRE)**[111] 5787 4-9-8 46 MFenton 3 45
(JWUnett) *led 4f: wknd over 1f out* **14/1**

**5** 1 1/2 **Macpursie** 3-8-0 DMernagh 5 36
(TDBarron) *s.s: sn in tch: rdn 4f out: wknd 2f out* **13/2**[3]

300- **6** 5 **Frimley's Mattery**[300] 1151 4-9-8 53 RFitzpatrick 2 29
(REBarr) *sn pushed along in rr: wknd over 2f out* **33/1**

0- **7** 3/4 **Star Welcome**[122] 5587 3-8-0 JoannaBadger 7 22
(WJMusson) *s.s: hdwy 5f out: wknd 2f out* **8/1**

1m 29.61s (-1.19) **Going Correction** -0.225s/f (Stan)
**WFA** 3 from 4yo 17lb **7** Ran SP% **109.9**
Speed ratings: **97,87,85,85,83 78,77**CSF £43.48 TOTE £3.60: £1.30, £6.70; EX 31.60.
**Owner** Nigel Shields **Bred** N R Shields And K R Burke **Trained** Middleham Moor, N Yorks

**FOCUS**
A poor maiden and the form is basically weak, but the winner, Daring Affair, who looked exposed going into this, ran out an impressive winner and is by far and away the one to take out of this.

**NOTEBOOK**
**Daring Affair** looked pretty exposed going into this but she got off the mark in most impressive fashion. She had little to beat but, with this sure to have boosted her confidence, she looks well worth considering in a better grade.
**Bundaberg**, dropped in grade and trip, was no match for the winner and probably failed to achieve a great deal in faring the best of the rest.
**Weakest Link** had just over a length to find with the winner on his previous running but, stepped up in trip, he was most disappointing.
**Gilly's General(IRE)** was well beaten on his return from a break.
**Macpursie** was very easy to back and showed signs of inexperience.

## 780 BET DIRECT FOOTBALL CASHBACKS BANDED STKS 6f (F)
**3:00** (3:02) (H ) 3-Y-0+ **£1,358** (£388; £194) **Stalls** Low

Form RPR

0-04 **1** **Miss Wizz**[7] 713 4-9-0 35 (p) RoryMoore(7) 9 34
(WStorey) *chsd ldrs: led over 2f out: rdn over 1f out: jst hld on* **14/1**

00-3 **2** shd **Spy Master**[7] 718 6-9-0 35 (bt) MLawson(7) 10 34
(JParkes) *s.i.s: hld up: hdwy over 2f out: rdn and hmpd over 1f out: r.o wl* **8/1**

-505 **3** 1 **Mimas Girl**[13] 656 5-9-7 30 (b) JBramhill 13 31
(SRBowring) *a.p: chseed wnr over 2f out: rdn over 1f out: styd on* **16/1**

0-61 **4** 2 **Redoubtable (USA)**[12] 665 13-9-7 45 ACulhane 11 25
(DWChapman) *hmpd sn after s: mid-div: hdwy over 2f out: sn rdn: styd on same pce fnl f* **7/2**[2]

06-0 **5** nk **Dandy Jim**[5] 732 3-8-6 30 RBrisland 5 24
(DWChapman) *dwlt: outpcd: r.o ins fnl f: nrst fin* **50/1**

0-02 **6** 1 1/2 **Court Music (IRE)**[34] 502 5-9-7 35 (v) RFitzpatrick 6 20
(REBarr) *chsd ldrs: rdn over 3f out: styng on same pce whn hmpd over 1f out* **13/2**[3]

0-61 **7** 1 1/4 **Danakim**[7] 718 7-9-6 35 (be) DFentiman(7) 14 22
(JRWeymes) *chsd ldrs: rdn over 2f out: wknd over 1f out* **8/1**

6-40 **8** 3/4 **Zara Louise**[7] 713 4-9-7 30 DeanMcKeown 1 14
(RPElliott) *s.i.s: sn chsng ldrs: wkng whn hmpd over 1f out* **16/1**

0-32 **9** 1 1/2 **Packin Em In**[12] 665 6-9-7 35 MHenry 4 9
(JRBoyle) *mid-div: sn drvn along: hung lft over 1f out: nvr trbld ldrs* **3/1**[1]

000- **10** hd **Moonglade (USA)**[74] 6126 4-9-2 30 (t) AQuinn(5) 7 9
(MissJFeilden) *s.s: nvr nrr* **8/1**

0-04 **11** 3/4 **Almara**[7] 718 4-9-7 35 (tp) JQuinn 12 6
(MissKBBoutflower) *broke wl: sn outpcd* **16/1**

0-06 **12** 1/2 **Salonika Sky**[7] 718 3-8-6 35 (b[1]) JMcAuley 3 5
(CWThornton) *led over 3f: wkng whn hung rt over 1f out* **33/1**

00-0 **13** 4 **Gruff**[7] 718 5-9-7 35 GParkin 2 —
(PTMidgley) *chsd ldrs over 3f* **33/1**

000- **14** 14 **Izza**[116] 5700 3-8-6 30 DRMcCabe 8 —
(WStorey) *outpcd* **66/1**

1m 16.91s (0.11) **Going Correction** -0.225s/f (Stan)
**WFA** 3 from 4yo+ 15lb **14** Ran SP% **127.5**
Speed ratings: **90,89,88,85,85 83,81,80,78,78 77,76,71,52**CSF £126.83 TOTE £19.20: £4.70, £3.20, £6.10; EX 291.20.
**Owner** Tony McCormick **Bred** S Hogg **Trained** Muggleswick, Co Durham

■ Stewards Enquiry : J McAuley four-day ban: careless riding (Feb 26-29)

**FOCUS**
A poor race, but it was competitive enough. They appeared to go a good pace, but the winning time was moderate.

**NOTEBOOK**
**Miss Wizz**, still a maiden going into this, appreciated the drop in trip and ran out a very game winner. She had absolutely nothing to spare at the line and you could not back her with too much confidence to follow up in similar company.
**Spy Master**, third over five furlongs here on his previous outing, was well suited by this step up in trip and was only just denied.
**Mimas Girl** was suited by this drop back from an extended mile and ran her race.
**Redoubtable(USA)**, a comfortable winner on his previous outing at Lingfield, ran respectably on this switch back to Fibresand.
**Dandy Jim** shaped well and will be suited by a step up in trip.
**Packin Em In**, proved unable to build on his second to Redoubtable at Lingfield on his previous outing. *Official explanation: jockey said horse was unsuited by the kick-back*

## 781 BET IN RUNNING @ BETDIRECT.CO.UK BANDED STKS 1m 6f (F)
**3:30** (3:30) (H ) 4-Y-0+ **£1,662** (£475; £237) **Stalls** Low

Form RPR

2-11 **1** **Broughton Knows**[31] 539 7-9-0 45 LisaJones(3) 2 53+
(WJMusson) *hld up: hdwy over 3f out: rdn to ld and hung lft 2f out: clr fnl f: eased towards fin* **30/100**[1]

03-6 **2** 4 **Next Flight (IRE)**[26] 570 5-9-3 45 RFitzpatrick 3 48
(REBarr) *chsd ldr: led 10f out: rdn and hdd 2f out: styd on same pce: eased whn btn ins fnl f* **12/1**[3]

45-0 **3** 9 **Fortunes Favourite**[40] 461 4-8-12 45 JQuinn 7 36
(GMMoore) *chsd ldrs: rdn over 3f out: wknd 2f out* **16/1**

5066 **4** nk **King Priam (IRE)**[7] 715 9-9-0 40 (b) LFletcher(3) 4 36
(MJPolglase) *sn drvn to ld: hdd 10f out: wknd 3f out* **8/1**[2]

2354 **5** 1 3/4 **Sea Ya Maite**[7] 714 10-9-3 35 (t) JBramhill 1 34
(SRBowring) *plld hrd and prom: wknd 2f out* **25/1**

/00- **6** 7 **Blazing Saddles (IRE)**[9] 2082 5-8-12 45 (p) NChalmers(5) 5 25
(MrsJCandlish) *in tch: sn pushed along: rdn and wknd over 3f out* **25/1**

0/0- **7** dist **Lady Arnica**[262] 1636 5-9-3 45 (v[1]) IMongan 6 —
(AWCarroll) *chsd ldrs: rdn 8f out: wknd 6f out* **20/1**

3m 8.09s (-1.51) **Going Correction** -0.225s/f (Stan)
**WFA** 4 from 5yo+ 5lb **7** Ran SP% **114.1**
Speed ratings: **95,92,87,87,86 82,—**CSF £4.85 TOTE £1.30: £1.30, £4.00; EX 3.90.
**Owner** Broughton Thermal Insulation **Bred** Broughton Bloodstock **Trained** Newmarket, Suffolk

**FOCUS**
A dire contest run at a modest pace, but won by an in-form performer who is better class than the rest.

**NOTEBOOK**
**Broughton Knows** landed the hat-trick, but it was hard work. He had won his last two outings with the blinkers on, but they were left off on this occasion and it made a big difference, as he was looking about in the straight and hung badly. He is in great form, albeit at this level, and with the headgear back on next time, can be expected to go close again.
**Next Flight(IRE)** shaped as though this trip would suit last time and duly improved, but was no match for the winner. He has never won a race, but was nicely clear of the rest, and at this level has a race in him.
**Fortunes Favourite** ran as though he needs to drop back in trip.

## 782 BET IN RUNNING ON SKY TEXT PAGE 293 (S) STKS 7f (F)
**4:00** (4:00) (H ) 3-Y-0+ **£1,491** (£426; £213) **Stalls** Low

Form RPR

3443 **1** **Sudra**[10] 685 7-9-0 47 (b) JDO'Reilly(7) 6 63
(JO'Reilly) *chsd ldrs: led over 1f out: r.o wl* **5/1**[3]

0-42 **2** 5 **Donegal Shore (IRE)**[34] 498 5-9-2 51 (vt) NChalmers(5) 7 50
(MrsJCandlish) *hld up: rdn 1/2-way: hdwy over 1f out: nt rch wnr* **5/1**[3]

2145 **3** 3/4 **Larky's Lob**[9] 694 5-9-4 47 LFletcher(3) 4 48
(PaulJohnson) *led over 5f: no ex* **11/4**[1]

000- **4** 1 1/4 **Crafty Politician (USA)**[47] 6262 7-9-7 40 IMongan 5 45
(GLMoore) *chsd ldr: rdn over 2f out: styd on same pce appr fnl f* **9/1**

5-06 **5** nk **Marabar**[10] 685 6-9-2 58 ACulhane 9 39
(DWChapman) *chsd ldrs: rdn over 2f out: styd on same pce* **6/1**

3/60 **6** 3 **Ace-Ma-Vahra**[5] 737 6-9-2 45 JBramhill 2 32
(SRBowring) *chsd ldrs over 4f* **25/1**

0-22 **7** nk **Noble Pursuit**[7] 717 7-9-7 57 DeanMcKeown 8 36
(PABlockley) *s.s: nvr nr to chal* **4/1**[2]

00-0 **8** 10 **Moon Royale**[38] 470 6-8-9 30 (v) SaleemGolam(7) 10 6
(MrsNMacauley) *s.i.s: hld up: wknd over 2f out* **28/1**

/00- **9** 3 1/2 **River Canyon (IRE)**[224] 3035 8-9-7 50 DRMcCabe 3 —
(WStorey) *sn pushed along in rr: wknd 3f out* **16/1**

1m 28.63s (-2.17) **Going Correction** -0.225s/f (Stan) **9** Ran SP% **117.5**
Speed ratings: **103,97,96,95,94 91,90,79,75**CSF £30.78 TOTE £6.20: £2.10, £2.10, £1.40; EX 27.00.There was no bid for the winner.
**Owner** J Morris **Bred** Mohammed Jumah Al Nabouda **Trained** Brierley, S Yorks

**FOCUS**
A decent winning time for a regional seller. The form is average.

**NOTEBOOK**
**Sudra** put his proven stamina to good use over this trip to win well. He has been threatening to win in this grade over the trip all year, and this was a deserved success. Although he may well improve for the step back up to a mile, he is a most infrequent winner.
**Donegal Shore(IRE)** ran on well enough, but the winner had gone beyond recall. He has been runner-up on his last two starts over course and distance, and has responded positively to the visor of late.
**Larky's Lob**, down in grade, ran a fair race, but quickly threw in the towel when challenged, and is hard to catch right.
**Crafty Politician(USA)** was produced to win his race, but could not quicken and is one paced.
**Noble Pursuit** lost all chance at the gates and this is best ignored. *Official explanation: trainer had no explanation for the poor form shown*

## 783 BET DIRECT IN VISION SKY PAGE 293 BANDED STKS 1m 3f (F)
**4:30** (4:30) (H ) 4-Y-0+ **£1,393** (£398; £199) **Stalls** Low

Form RPR

0-32 **1** **Galley Law**[6] 727 4-8-12 30 JQuinn 5 49
(RCraggs) *hld up: hdwy 7f out: led over 2f out: rdn clr over 1f out* **13/2**

-321 **2** 5 **Buz Kiri (USA)**[6] 727 6-9-6 35 PDoe 4 47
(AWCarroll) *hld up: hdwy over 2f out: nt rch wnr* **3/1**[2]

53-5 **3** 2 **Samar Qand**[43] 427 5-9-0 35 MTebbutt 8 38
(JulianPoulton) *hld up: hdwy over 4f out: styd on same pce fnl 2f* **6/1**[3]

40-2 **4** 1 1/2 **Fraamtastic**[7] 713 7-8-8 30 ow1 (p) LTreadwell(7) 6 36
(BAPearce) *plld hrd and prom: led over 4f out: rdn and hdd over 2f out: wknd fnl f* **12/1**

/60- **5** 8 **Cumwhitton**[118] 5675 5-8-9 35 THamilton(5) 2 23
(RAFahey) *hld up: hmpd over 4f out and over 3f out: n.d* **25/1**

0-00 **6** *2* **Marengo**[38] [475] 10-9-0 30 ........ JoannaBadger 10 19
(PaulJohnson) *s.i.s: rcvrd to ld 9f out: hdd over 4f out: wknd 3f out* **33/1**
**7** *5* **Top Style (IRE)**[543] [4085] 6-8-11 30 ........ DCorby(3) 7 11
(MJWallace) *hld up: pushed along 1/2-way: wknd 3f out* **5/4**[1]
4566 **8** *1/2* **Western Command (GER)**[6] [727] 8-9-0 30 ........(p) PMcCabe 11 11
(MrsNMacauley) *sn chsng ldrs: rdn over 4f out: wknd 3f out* **25/1**
0-00 **9** *1/2* **Balalaika Tune (IRE)**[26] [567] 5-9-0 35 ........ DRMcCabe 3 10
(WStorey) *plld hrd and prom: rdn over 4f out: hmpd and wknd over 3f out* **40/1**
00-0 **10** *1 3/4* **Diva Dancer**[26] [567] 4-8-12 30 ........ DeanMcKeown 9 7
(JHetherton) *outpcd* **50/1**
0-06 **11** *20* **Anacapri**[12] [668] 4-8-9 35 ........ LEnstone(3) 1 —
(WSCunningham) *chsd ldrs: rdn: edgd lft and bmpd over 3f out: sn wknd* **50/1**
0-00 **12** *dist* **Velvet Rhythm**[19] [613] 4-8-12 30 ........ DarrenWilliams 12 —
(KRBurke) *led: hdd 9f out: wknd 4f out: eased* **100/1**

2m 26.56s (-2.34) **Going Correction** -0.225s/f (Stan)
**WFA** 4 from 5yo+ 2lb **12** Ran SP% **122.7**
Speed ratings: **99,95,93,92,87 85,81,81,81,79 65,—**CSF £26.10 TOTE £8.80: £2.50, £1.20, £1.40; EX 16.90 Place 6 £73.79, Place 5 £45.70..
**Owner** Ray Craggs **Bred** Deerfield Farm **Trained** Sedgefield, Co Durham
■ Stewards Enquiry : L Enstone five-day ban: careless riding (Feb 26-Mar 1)

**FOCUS**
A dire contest run at a modest pace which produced a comfortable winner who enjoyed the switch to this track and could win a 0-45.

**NOTEBOOK**
**Galley Law** readily reversed recent form with the runner-up on these better terms. He enjoyed this drop in trip and showed a fair turn of foot to easily take up the running and extend in the straight. He was value for more than the official winning margin and can follow up.
**Buz Kiri(USA)** could not repeat his recent success, but that was at Wolverhampton and over another furlong, so when he reverts to that venue he can go one better while his stable are in form.
**Samar Qand** ran a fair race from off the pace, but remains a maiden and could do with a drop in trip.
**Top Style(IRE)**, last seen in 2002 in Ireland, was backed if defeat was out of the question for this All-Weather debut. However, he never looked like landing the odds at any stage and has it all to prove now.
T/Plt: £103.70 to a £1 stake. Pool: £42,484.05. 298.85 winning tickets. T/Qpdt: £17.30 to a £1 stake. Pool: £2,940.60. 125.30 winning tickets. CR

# ST MORITZ (R-H)
Sunday, February 8

**OFFICIAL GOING: Races run on ice**

## 784a GRAND PRIX CHRISTOFFEL BAU TROPHY (ICE) 1m
**1:45** (1:45) 4-Y-0+ **£4,995** (£1,998; £1,499; £999)

RPR
**1** **Supertramp (GER)**[22] 8-9-0 ........ GBocskai 3 —
(RRohne, Germany)
**2** *6* **The Rort (USA)**[7] 7-9-4 ........ RHavlin 6 —
(MWeiss, Switzerland) 2
**3** *9* **Molly Mello (GER)**[16] [5963] 5-9-1 ........ MrRKaderli 1 —
(MFHarris) *midfield: styd on at same pce fnl 2f* 1
**4** *1/2* **Vicchio**[88] 6-9-4 ........ AGoritz 10 —
(USuter, Germany) 3
**5** *7* **Give Back Calais (IRE)**[250] [2081] 6-8-11 ........ DMoffatt 8 —
(MissACasotti, Switzerland)
**6** *6* **Pericles (GER)**[91] 7-9-0 ........ JDHillis 2 —
(WBauermeister, Germany)
**7** *7* **Ruby Queen (GER)**[1323] [2389] 6-9-3 ........ BrigitteRenk 7 —
(KarinSuter, Switzerland)
**U** **Dissident (GER)**[7] 6-9-2 ........ PHeugl 4 —
(HBlume, Germany)

1m 43.92s **8** Ran SP% **144.6**
Speed ratings: .
**Owner** Spellbound Stables **Bred** Frau K-B Thom **Trained** Germany

**NOTEBOOK**
**Molly Mello(GER)** had placed form in Listed grade on the Flat in Germany last summer but has not shone over hurdles in two starts in Britain since changing stables.

# [784]ST MORITZ (R-H)
Sunday, February 15

**OFFICIAL GOING: Races run on ice**

## 785a AMERICAN EXPRESS GROSSER PREIS VON ST MORTIZ (ICE) 1m 2f
**1:15** (1:07) 4-Y-0+ **£24,133** (£9,653; £7,239; £4,826)

RPR
**1** **Termac (CZE)**[29] 9-9-0 ........ WMongil 14 —
(ElfiSchnakenberg, Germany)
**2** *6* **Flower Hill (FR)**[83] 6-9-0 ........ MrRKaderli 1 —
(ATrybuhl, Germany)
**3** *3/4* **Etbash (RUS)**[357] [603] 7-9-4 ........ RHavlin 3 —
(MWeiss, Switzerland)
**4** *1 1/2* **Brother's Valcour (FR)**[1370] 6-9-6 ........ NJeanpierre 7 —
(KSchafflutzel, Switzerland)
**5** *2 1/2* **Serpenta (GER)**[78] 5-9-5 ........ THuet 8 —
(MBoutin, France)
**6** *2 1/2* **Auenteufel (GER)**[483] [5414] 5-9-4 ........ BrigitteRenk 6 —
(KarinSuter, Switzerland)
**7** *1* **Safin (GER)**[245] [2411] 4-8-11 ........ GBocskai 2 —
(CVonDerRecke, Germany)
**8** *2 1/2* **Classic Law**[77] 5-8-11 ........ ADeVries 13 —
(CVonDerRecke, Germany)
**9** *4* **Atahuelpa**[105] [4363] 4-9-4 ........ PRoberts 5 —
(MFHarris) *led 7f: grad wknd fr ent st SP 13-2*
**10** *3/4* **Rain Lily (IRE)**[137] [5319] 4-8-12 ........ SHamel 9 —
(MWeiss, Switzerland)
**11** *3 1/2* **Brigadier Du Pin (FR)**[1029] 6-9-0 ........ BMarchand 15 —
(KSchafflutzel, Switzerland)
**12** *8* **Dream For Ever (FR)**[357] [603] 7-9-2 ........ AGoritz 10 —
(USuter, Germany)
**13** *6* **Cameraman (FR)**[99] 8-9-2 ........ FBlondel 11 —
(MBoutin, France)

2m 12.72s
**WFA** 4 from 5yo+ 1lb **13** Ran
Speed ratings: .
**Owner** Gestut Guthler Hof-Kuchyna **Bred** Gestut Guthler Hof **Trained** Germany

**NOTEBOOK**
**Atahuelpa**, a winner of a Newbury claimer in the summer, had not run since finishing fourth over hurdles back in November. He made the running as usual but faded out of contention in the straight.

## 786a GRAND PRIX WINTERTHUR VERSICHERUNGEN (ICE) 1m 1f
**2:15** (2:43) 4-Y-0+ **£3,258** (£1,303; £977; £652)

RPR
**1** **El Oahid** 8-9-3 ........ MrRKaderli 7 —
(BrigitteStebler, Switzerland)
**2** *nk* **All Blade (GER)**[1456] 10-9-8 ........ AGoritz 1 —
(USuter, Germany)
**3** *1 1/2* **Syndaco (IRE)**[609] 5-9-3 ........ RHavlin 9 —
(MWeiss, Switzerland)
**4** *nk* **Fort Knox (GER)**[251] 11-9-8 ........ DMoffatt 5 —
(MissACasotti, Switzerland)
**5** *5* **Special Envoy**[471] [5569] 4-9-2 ........ BMarchand 3 —
(KSchafflutzel, Switzerland)
**6** *2* **Molly Mello (GER)**[7] [784] 5-9-9 ........(b) PRoberts 10 —
(MFHarris) *led tl hdd and no ex ent st SP 39-10*
**7** *6* **Dubai Tower (USA)**[279] [1554] 4-9-9 ........ WMongil 2 —
(KSchafflutzel, Switzerland)
**8** *6* **Empireneyev (USA)**[1352] 8-9-8 ........ NJeanpierre 4 —
(KSchafflutzel, Switzerland)
**9** *2 1/2* **Karlsson (GER)**[596] [2593] 5-9-8 ........ BrigitteRenk 6 —
(HBlume, Germany)
**10** *9* **Sharp Prince (FR)** 8-8-4 ........ MrBWyss 13 —
(BEberle, France)
**11** *hd* **Lovely Boy (SWI)** 10-8-11 ........ ADeVries 11 —
(MissACasotti, Switzerland)
**12** *2* **Pericles (GER)**[7] [784] 7-9-3 ........(b) JPalik 8 —
(WBauermeister, Germany)

1m 59.83s **12** Ran
Speed ratings: .
**Owner** B & W Kilchenmann **Bred** Mrs G Macrae **Trained** Switzerland

**NOTEBOOK**
**Molly Mello(GER)** made a bold bid to make all but she was cooked entering the straight.

# [764]LINGFIELD (L-H)
Monday, February 16

**OFFICIAL GOING: Standard**

## 787 BETDIRECT.CO.UK BANDED STKS (DIV I) 1m (P)
**1:40** (1:40) (H ) 3-Y-0+ **£1,638** (£468; £234) **Stalls High**

Form RPR
0-20 **1** **Miss Peaches**[13] [662] 6-9-1 45 ........ KristinStubbs(7) 7 54
(GGMargarson) *sn bhd: gd hdwy over 1f out: r.o to ld fnl 100 yds: pushed out* **10/1**
20-0 **2** *1 1/4* **Harbour House**[40] [465] 5-9-8 45 ........ NPollard 3 51
(JJBridger) *led 1f: prom: led 1f out: hdd and nt qckn fnl 100 yds* **10/1**
030- **3** *2* **Jahangir**[86] [5280] 5-9-8 45 ........ DaneO'Neill 8 47
(BRJohnson) *plld hrd: led after 1f and restrained in front: hdd 1f out: one pce* **7/1**
2522 **4** *1/2* **Maggie's Pet**[14] [652] 7-9-8 45 ........(t) DRMcCabe 11 46
(KBell) *prom: hrd rdn and ev ch over 1f out: one pce* **5/1**[2]
-254 **5** *1* **Wilom (GER)**[13] [662] 6-9-8 45 ........ SDrowne 2 43
(MRHoad) *chsd ldrs: hrd rdn and ev ch over 1f out: no ex* **6/1**[3]
0000 **6** *1/2* **Pancakehill**[9] [707] 5-9-8 45 ........(t) MartinDwyer 6 42
(DKIvory) *hdwy 3f out: hrd rdn over 1f out: no ex* **9/1**
0-36 **7** *3/4* **Ivy Moon**[10] [698] 4-9-8 45 ........ DSweeney 4 41
(BJLlewellyn) *dwlt: plld hrd towards rr: sme hdwy 3f out: rdn and no imp fnl 2f* **8/1**
/00- **8** *3/4* **Nevinstown (IRE)**[83] [6070] 4-9-8 45 ........(vt[1]) WMLordan 1 39
(NiallMoran, Ire) *s.s: sn in tch: rdn and btn 2f out* **50/1**
00-0 **9** *nk* **Altares**[44] [416] 3-8-3 45 ........ JFanning 9 38
(PHowling) *sn bhd: rdn after 3f: nvr rchd ldrs* **50/1**
03-0 **10** *1* **Santa Catalina (IRE)**[39] [472] 5-9-5 45 ........(t) LisaJones(3) 12 36
(CADwyer) *rr after 2f: n.d* **10/1**
/5-6 **11** *1* **Lady At Leisure (IRE)**[13] [664] 4-9-8 45 ........ RHavlin 10 34
(JulianPoulton) *chsd ldrs: hrd rdn 3f out: sn wknd* **16/1**
3-43 **12** *3* **Cherokee Bay**[13] [659] 4-9-8 45 ........(e) GCarter 5 27
(GLMoore) *mid-div: rdn 3f out: sn bhd* **5/2**[1]

1m 39.99s (0.48) **Going Correction** 0.0s/f (Stan)
**WFA** 3 from 4yo+ 19lb **12** Ran SP% **130.2**
Speed ratings: **97,95,93,93,92 91,91,90,89,88 87,84**CSF £116.73 TOTE £12.50: £5.60, £3.80, £3.70; EX 167.80.
**Owner** G G Margarson **Bred** Chippenham Lodge Stud **Trained** Newmarket, Suffolk

**FOCUS**
They went a steady gallop for this first division of this mile contest. This is fair banded-class form.

**NOTEBOOK**
**Miss Peaches** had run well over course and distance on her penultimate start and left a slightly disappointing run last time behind, winning cosily having taken it up half a furlong out. She is no great shakes, but capable of winning again in this sort of company.
**Harbour House** was up there with the steady pace throughout and only found the one too good. He has still to truly prove himself at a mile.
**Jahangir** was having his first run since pulling up over hurdles at Ascot in November and was unsuited by the modest gallop.
**Maggie's Pet**, having her second run at the course, has been running consistently well of late and had every chance.
**Wilom(GER)** found nothing, as is the norm.
**Pancakehill**, trying her hand at banded racing for the first time, looked set to pose a threat turning in, but was soon beaten.
**Cherokee Bay** was reportedly never travelling. *Official explanation: jockey said filly was never travelling*

## 788 BETDIRECT.CO.UK BANDED STKS (DIV II) — 1m (P)
2:10 (2:10) (H) 3-Y-0+ — £1,634 (£467; £233) Stalls High

Form — RPR

04-2 **1** **Wanna Shout**$^{13}$ [662] 6-9-5 45 ........ LisaJones$^{(3)}$ 11 — 48
(RDickin) *wd: in tch: effrt over 2f out: led ins fnl f: rdn out* **7/1$^{3}$**

00-5 **2** ½ **Chocolate Boy (IRE)**$^{13}$ [662] 5-9-8 45 ........ (be$^{1}$) SWhitworth 4 — 47
(GLMoore) *s.i.s: bhd: sltly hmpd ins fnl 3f: gd hdwy over 1f out: r.o u.p* **5/1$^{2}$**

00-0 **3** nk **Ballare (IRE)**$^{32}$ [537] 5-9-8 40 ........ OUrbina 7 — 46
(BobJones) *towards rr: wd bnd into st: gd hdwy over 1f out: hrd rdn: r.o* **7/1$^{3}$**

0-61 **4** 1½ **Badou**$^{14}$ [658] 4-9-5 45 ........ RMiles$^{(3)}$ 10 — 43
(LMontagueHall) *chsd ldrs: edgd lft and led over 1f out: hdd and nt qckn ins fnl f* **5/1$^{2}$**

50-0 **5** ½ **Bar Of Silver (IRE)**$^{45}$ [412] 4-9-8 45 ........ (v$^{1}$) ADaly 9 — 42
(RBrotherton) *t.k.h: hdwy 3f out: ev ch whn n.m.r over 1f out: bmpd: one pce fnl f* **25/1**

60-0 **6** shd **Eurolink Zante (IRE)**$^{9}$ [707] 8-9-5 45 ........ (b) J-PGuillambert$^{(3)}$ 12 — 42
(TDMcCarthy) *sn bhd: hdwy 2f out: hrd rdn over 1f out: one pce* **14/1**

1-60 **7** hd **Mythical Charm**$^{9}$ [705] 5-9-8 45 ........ NPollard 3 — 41
(JJBridger) *chsd ldrs: rdn 3f out: styd on same pce* **10/3$^{1}$**

000- **8** 1½ **Malaah (IRE)**$^{184}$ [4183] 8-9-1 45 ........ (b) MHalford$^{(7)}$ 5 — 38
(JulianPoulton) *led: hdd and n.m.r on rail over 1f out: no ex* **20/1**

00-0 **9** ½ **Almost Welcome**$^{9}$ [702] 3-8-3 45 ........ PDoe 1 — 37
(SDow) *chsd ldrs: squeezed out ins fnl 3f: nt rcvr* **14/1**

340- **10** ¾ **Royale Pearl**$^{26}$ [5554] 4-9-8 45 ........ DaneO'Neill 2 — 35
(RIngram) *prom over 5f* **10/1**

0-44 **11** 5 **Lady Predominant**$^{41}$ [451] 3-8-3 45 ........ SCarson 6 — 24
(AndrewReid) *in rr: rdn whn hmpd and snatched up ins fnl 3f: nvr nr ldrs* **12/1**

60-4 **12** dist **Achilles Rainbow**$^{13}$ [663] 5-9-8 40 ........ GFaulkner 8 — —
(KRBurke) *prom tl hrd rdn and wknd 3f out* **20/1**

1m 40.11s (0.60) **Going Correction** 0.0s/f (Stan)
**WFA** 3 from 4yo+ 19lb — **12** Ran SP% **124.9**
Speed ratings: **97,96,96,94,94 94,93,92,91,91 86,**—CSF £43.10 TOTE £7.70: £2.40, £1.80, £4.20; EX 18.60.
**Owner** E R C Beech & B Wilkinson **Bred** C C Bromley And Son **Trained** Atherstone on Stour, Warwicks
■ Stewards Enquiry : A Daly one-day ban: careless riding (Feb 27)

**FOCUS**
A very similar time to the first division, confirming both divisions were much of a muchness and that the form is typical for the grade.

**NOTEBOOK**
**Wanna Shout**, who ran well over course and distance last time, confirmed form with todays runner up despite that one getting closer. She raced wide from her draw, but stayed on strongly to win well.
**Chocolate Boy(IRE)**, sporting eyeshield/blinkers for the first time, improved on his previous form, but still found Wanna Shout too strong. He will win a similar race.
**Ballare(IRE)** came wide turning into the straight, but had every chance.
**Badou**, a winner at Wolverhampton last time, has never won over this trip, but seemed to get it well enough.
**Bar Of Silver(IRE)** was slightly unlucky to be closer.
**Mythical Charm**, expected to be suited by this drop back in trip, proved disappointing and could never muster the speed to throw down a serious challenge.
**Achilles Rainbow** *Official explanation: vet said gelding finished distressed*

## 789 BET DIRECT ON 0800 32 93 93 BANDED STKS — 2m (P)
2:40 (2:41) (H) 4-Y-0+ — £1,463 (£418; £209) Stalls Low

Form — RPR

0043 **1** **Little Richard (IRE)**$^{7}$ [727] 5-9-6 35 ........ (p) ADaly 9 — 40
(MWellings) *cl up: drvn and outpcd 4f out: rallied and wd 2f out: styd on to ld ins fnl f* **20/1**

00-2 **2** ¾ **The Beduth Navi**$^{14}$ [653] 4-8-9 35 ........ DNolan$^{(5)}$ 6 — 40
(DGBridgwater) *led 3f: prom: led over 2f out tl ins fnl f: kpt on* **20/1**

-000 **3** 1¼ **Polka Princess**$^{13}$ [661] 4-8-9 40 ow2 ........ (p) LTreadwell$^{(7)}$ 1 — 40
(MWellings) *t.k.h: hdwy 5f out: pressed ldrs 3f out: styd on same pce fnl 2f* **40/1**

450- **4** hd **Second Paige (IRE)**$^{110}$ [1147] 7-9-6 40 ........ (b) OUrbina 5 — 38
(NAGraham) *hld up in rr: hdwy 3f out: hrd rdn and little rspnse: styd on fnl f* **5/4$^{1}$**

-212 **5** 3½ **Unleaded**$^{8}$ [716] 4-9-0 40 ........ JFanning 10 — 34
(JAkehurst) *prom: led 7f out tl over 2f out: hrd rdn and no ex 1f out* **2/1$^{2}$**

6/05 **6** 1¼ **Oulton Broad**$^{4}$ [750] 8-9-3 35 ........ (p) J-PGuillambert$^{(3)}$ 8 — 32
(RFord) *hld up towards rr: hdwy 6f out: hrd rdn 4f out: outpcd fnl 3f* **12/1**

550/ **7** 14 **Sharvie**$^{58}$ [562] 7-9-6 40 ........ (p) JoannaBadger 4 — 15
(MRBosley) *mid-div: rdn 7f out: n.d fnl 4f* **33/1**

305- **8** 3 **Anniversary Guest (IRE)**$^{119}$ [5675] 5-9-3 35 ........ RMiles$^{(3)}$ 3 — 12
(MrsLucindaFeatherstone) *restrained in stalls and lost 12l: plld hrd early: bhd: mod effrt 4f out: eased whn no imp over 2f out* **25/1**

05/6 **9** 1 **Martha Reilly (IRE)**$^{8}$ [716] 8-9-3 35 ........ LisaJones$^{(3)}$ 7 — 10
(MrsBarbaraWaring) *chsd ldrs to 1/2-way: n.d fnl 6f* **33/1**

6-35 **10** dist **Ginger Ice**$^{13}$ [663] 4-9-0 40 ........ (v) NPollard 2 — —
(GGMargarson) *restrained in stalls and lost 10l: plld hrd: hdwy to ld after 3f: hdd 7f out: wkng whn hmpd on rail 5f out* **10/1$^{3}$**

3m 30.44s (1.86) **Going Correction** 0.0s/f (Stan)
**WFA** 4 from 5yo+ 6lb — **10** Ran SP% **116.3**
Speed ratings: **95,94,94,93,92 91,84,83,82,**—CSF £323.53 TOTE £17.80: £2.50, £5.50, £8.60; EX 236.80.
**Owner** Mark Wellings Racing **Bred** Rathbarry Stud **Trained** Broad Lanes, Shropshire

**FOCUS**
Weak form and the first three places were filled by outsiders.

**NOTEBOOK**
**Little Richard(IRE)** appreciated the step up to this trip and battled on doggedly to get the better of the second in the final furlong. This was a poor race and he may struggle to follow up.
**The Beduth Navi** was bang there throughout and ran a fine race. His second at 66/1 last time was evidently no fluke and he has a chance of winning something similar.
**Polka Princess** has done all her winning over six and seven furlongs, but seemed to be suited by this step up in trip.
**Second Paige(IRE)**was given a lot to do and found little anyhow.
**Unleaded** was disappointing and is clearly better served by the surfaces at Southwell and Wolverhampton.

## 790 PRESS INTERACTIVE TO BET DIRECT MEDIAN AUCTION MAIDEN STKS — 1m (P)
3:10 (3:11) (H) 3-5-Y-0 — £1,463 (£418; £209) Stalls High

Form — RPR

000- **1** **Glendale**$^{105}$ [5906] 3-8-2 68 ........ LisaJones$^{(3)}$ 2 — 65
(CADwyer) *chsd ldrs: drvn to go 2nd over 2f out: led ins fnl f: hung bdly rt: rdn out* **7/4$^{2}$**

3-23 **2** 1½ **Ballinger Ridge**$^{13}$ [660] 5-9-10 60 ........ (p) MartinDwyer 4 — 61
(AMBalding) *led: hrd rdn over 1f out: hdd and nt qckn ins fnl f* **11/10$^{1}$**

5-05 **3** 7 **Estrella Levante**$^{9}$ [707] 4-9-3 49 ........ JemmaMarshall$^{(7)}$ 6 — 46
(GLMoore) *stdd s: hld up in tch: promising effrt 3f out: one pce fnl 2f* **20/1**

-000 **4** 1¾ **Costa Del Sol (IRE)**$^{9}$ [702] 3-8-6 35 ow1 ........ (b) NPollard 1 — 43
(JJBridger) *s.i.s: sn chsng ldr: lost 2nd over 2f out: no ex over 1f out* **33/1**

002 **5** 1¼ **Devine Command**$^{13}$ [660] 3-8-5 56 ........ NDay 5 — 39
(RIngram) *chsd ldrs: rdn over 3f out: wknd 2f out* **5/1$^{3}$**

04-0 **6** 16 **Another Expletive**$^{33}$ [529] 3-7-10 45 ow1 ........ RThomas$^{(5)}$ 3 — —
(JWhite) *bhd fr 1/2-way* **33/1**

1m 40.17s (0.66) **Going Correction** 0.0s/f (Stan)
**WFA** 3 from 4yo+ 19lb — **6** Ran SP% **111.3**
Speed ratings: **96,94,87,85,84 68**CSF £3.92 TOTE £2.70: £1.50, £1.10; EX 10.70.
**Owner** Mrs J A Cornwell **Bred** Mrs J A Cornwell **Trained** Newmarket, Suffolk

**FOCUS**
Poor stuff won by the only really unexposed horse in the race, despite him veering right across the course.

**NOTEBOOK**
**Glendale** showed enough in maiden company last season to suggest he could win a poor race such as this and despite hanging badly right and veering across the course under pressure managed to prevail. It will be harder for him from now on.
**Ballinger Ridge** again had every chance without proving good enough. His turn will come one day.
**Estrella Levante** remains a maiden after 14 starts.
**Devine Command** was entitled to confirm course form with Ballinger Ridge, but failed to run his race.

## 791 FREE £10 BET @ BET DIRECT INTERACTIVE (S) STKS — 6f (P)
3:40 (3:41) (H) 3-Y-0+ — £1,515 (£433; £216) Stalls Low

Form — RPR

-620 **1** **Bells Beach (IRE)**$^{7}$ [728] 6-9-1 45 ........ JFanning 12 — 53
(PHowling) *hld up in rr: hdwy on outside 2f out: led jst ins fnl f: rdn clr: readily* **7/1$^{3}$**

5-24 **2** 2½ **The Gay Fox**$^{7}$ [728] 10-9-3 45 ........ (bt) LPKeniry$^{(3)}$ 10 — 50
(BGPowell) *pushed along towards rr: hrd rdn and hdwy over 1f out: styd on to take 2nd ins fnl f* **5/1$^{2}$**

0-40 **3** nk **Tickle**$^{16}$ [646] 6-9-1 50 ........ (vt) DSweeney 11 — 44
(PJMakin) *mid-div: drvn to chse ldrs 2f out: styd on same pce* **5/1$^{2}$**

0-05 **4** nk **Cayman Breeze**$^{7}$ [723] 4-9-6 62 ........ (v$^{1}$) DaneO'Neill 5 — 48
(SDow) *sn prom: jnd ldrs 1/2-way: ev ch over 1f out: one pce* **9/2$^{1}$**

00-0 **5** ½ **Shirley Oaks (IRE)**$^{32}$ [536] 6-8-10 40 ........ NChalmers$^{(5)}$ 7 — 42
(MissZCDavison) *stdd s: hld up towards rr: effrt whn swtchd rt over 1f out: nrst fin* **50/1**

00-0 **6** nk **Over To You Bert**$^{8}$ [717] 5-9-6 49 ........ SDrowne 8 — 46
(RJHodges) *chsd ldrs: styd on same pce fnl 2f* **33/1**

20-6 **7** hd **Lay Down Sally (IRE)**$^{43}$ [433] 6-8-10 45 ........ RThomas$^{(5)}$ 14 — 40
(JWhite) *dwlt: hld up in rr: rdn and hdwy over 1f out: hung lft: nt rch ldrs* **7/1$^{3}$**

0-0 **8** 1 **Top Place**$^{12}$ [678] 3-7-9 ........ (p) HayleyTurner$^{(5)}$ 4 — 37
(CADwyer) *led tl jst ins fnl f: no ex* **25/1**

0/0- **9** nk **Confuzed**$^{153}$ [4971] 4-9-6 ........ MartinDwyer 2 — 41
(AndrewReid) *chsd ldrs tl wknd over 1f out* **7/1$^{3}$**

0-34 **10** nk **Abuelos**$^{13}$ [659] 5-9-6 45 ........ PDoe 3 — 40
(SDow) *dwlt: towards rr: effrt in midfield whn hmpd over 1f out* **8/1**

00-0 **11** 2 **Avit (IRE)**$^{9}$ [708] 4-9-1 45 ........ GFaulkner 9 — 29
(PLGilligan) *w ldrs 4f: btn in midfield whn edgd lft over 1f out* **50/1**

000- **12** 2 **Albury Heath**$^{111}$ [5815] 4-9-6 40 ........ ADaly 1 — 28
(TMJones) *hld up and bhd: shkn up over 1f out: nvr nr ldrs* **50/1**

3-00 **13** 5 **Fiennes (USA)**$^{41}$ [460] 6-9-3 45 ........ (v) LisaJones$^{(3)}$ 13 — 13
(MrsNMacauley) *wd: chsd ldrs 2f* **14/1**

00-0 **14** ¾ **Lady Liesel**$^{13}$ [659] 4-9-1 40 ........ NPollard 6 — 6
(JJBridger) *w ldrs 4f: btn in midfield whn hmpd and snatched up over 1f out* **12/1**

1m 13.22s (0.30) **Going Correction** 0.0s/f (Stan)
**WFA** 3 from 4yo+ 15lb — **14** Ran SP% **127.2**
Speed ratings: **98,94,94,93,93 92,92,91,90,90 87,85,78,77**CSF £42.97 TOTE £8.50: £3.40, £2.10, £2.70; EX 43.80.The winner was bought in for 5,000gns. Confuzed was claimed by D Flood for £4,000.
**Owner** Richard Berenson **Bred** Philip Mahon **Trained** Newmarket, Suffolk

**FOCUS**
A weak race, and the form is below average for the grade, but Bells Beach burst through to win as she pleased.

**NOTEBOOK**
**Bells Beach(IRE)** turned this pretty competitive selling stakes into her own with a cosy success. She burst through to lead entering the final furlong and never looked back.
**The Gay Fox** kept on for the runner up spot, but has not got his head in front for 21 months.
**Tickle** is a very frustrating sort and is without a win in over three years.
**Cayman Breeze** is not one to be taking a short price about.

## 792 FREE £25 BONUS @ LITTLEWOODSPOKER.COM BANDED STKS — 5f (P)
4:10 (4:11) (H) 3-Y-0+ — £1,449 (£414; £207) Stalls High

Form — RPR

0000 **1** **Ivory Venture**$^{9}$ [707] 4-9-0 35 ........ (b) RMiles$^{(3)}$ 7 — 45
(DKIvory) *outpcd and bhd: swtchd lft over 1f out: str run to ld fnl 75 yds* **25/1**

-006 **2** ½ **Onefortheboys (IRE)**$^{7}$ [720] 5-8-10 35 ........ LTreadwell$^{(7)}$ 6 — 43
(DFlood) *outpcd and bhd: gd hdwy ins fnl f: ev ch fnl 50 yds: r.o* **10/1**

-450 **3** nk **Somethingabouther**$^{3}$ [762] 4-9-0 40 ........ LisaJones$^{(3)}$ 5 — 42
(PWHiatt) *in tch: rdn to press ldrs over 1f out: kpt on* **14/1**

5-02 **4** nk **Bali-Star**$^{35}$ [499] 9-8-12 40 ........ JFMcDonald$^{(5)}$ 8 — 41
(RJHodges) *w ldrs: led 1f out: hdd and nt qckn fnl 75 yds* **5/1$^{2}$**

00-0 **5** hd **Lydia's Look (IRE)**$^{26}$ [576] 7-9-3 40 ........ JFanning 4 — 40
(TJEtherington) *pressed ldrs: hrd rdn over 1f out: kpt on* **3/1$^{1}$**

00-0 **6** nk **Calendar Girl (IRE)**$^{42}$ [443] 4-9-3 40 ........ (b$^{1}$) DSweeney 3 — 39
(PJMakin) *chsd ldrs: effrt 2f out: nt qckn wl ins fnl f* **10/1**

00-3 **7** 1 **Mangus (IRE)**$^{42}$ [443] 10-9-3 40 ........ (be) SWhitworth 2 — 36
(KOCunningham-Brown) *mde most to 1f out: no ex ins fnl f* **7/1**

-406 **8** ½ **Allerton Boy**$^{17}$ [637] 5-9-3 40 ........ SDrowne 10 — 34
(RJHodges) *chsd ldrs: effrt 2f out: one pce appr fnl f* **6/1$^{3}$**

0-00 **9** 1 3/4 **Ellamyte**14 652 4-8-12 40 (t) DNolan(5) 9 28
(DGBridgwater) *in tch: rdn 3f out: btn over 1f out* 5/1 2

55-0 **10** 6 **On The Level**42 443 5-8-12 40 (b1) HayleyTurner(5) 1 7
(MrsNMacauley) *sn pushed along: w ldrs over 3f* 14/1

60.80 secs (1.02) **Going Correction** 0.0s/f (Stan) **10** Ran SP% **120.5**
Speed ratings: **91,90,89,89,88 88,86,86,83,73**CSF £262.03 TOTE £30.10: £5.60, £2.60, £3.80; EX 301.10.
**Owner** Dean Ivory **Bred** D J And Mrs Deer **Trained** Radlett, Herts

**FOCUS**
A particularly moderate time, even for a contest like this, despite the good gallop early. The front six were covered by no more than a length and a half, and the form is weak.

**NOTEBOOK**
**Ivory Venture** was winning her first ever race at the 16th attempt and sprang a real surprise. She ran over a mile last time and this drop back to the minimum clearly suited her well.
**Onefortheboys(IRE)** ran on for second having been outpaced early. He has been racing over a mile of late and may six furlongs will prove ideal.
**Somethingabouther** remains a maiden after 24 starts and is evidently not one to enthuse about.
**Bali-Star** rearely wins, but is capable of a big run on his day.
**Lydia's Look(IRE)** was slightly disappointing as everything looked to be right for a bold show. She was not beaten far however, and is worth giving another chance to. *Official explanation: jockey said mare hung right-handed in the closing stages*

## 793 ALLWEATHER-RACING.COM BANDED STKS 1m 2f (P)
**4:40** (4:40) (H ) 4-Y-0+ **£1,302** (£372; £186) **Stalls** Low

Form RPR

00-0 **1** **Kingsdon (IRE)**14 653 7-9-0 35 (vt) MartinDwyer 5 38
(TJFitzgerald) *chsd ldrs: led over 2f out: hrd rdn over 1f out: hld on gamely* 12/1

0-01 **2** *hd* **Monduru**7 730 7-9-6 35 (b) SWhitworth 8 44
(GLMoore) *s.s: bhd: gd hdwy 3f out: hrd rdn and ev ch fnl f: kpt on* 4/1 2

046/ **3** 7 **Adjiram (IRE)**52 2492 8-9-0 30 GCarter 1 25
(AWCarroll) *chsd ldrs: briefly wnt 2nd over 3f out: no ex over 1f out* 2/1 1

-042 **4** 3 1/2 **All On My Own (USA)**7 730 9-8-7 35 (b) NataliaGemelova(7) 3 19
(IWMcinnes) *dwlt: sn in mid-div: chsd ldrs 4f out: hrd rdn over 2f out: one pce* 8/1

056- **5** 5 **Dark Dolores**62 5989 6-8-11 35 J-PGuillambert(3) 2 10
(JRBoyle) *prom: led over 3f out tl over 2f out: hrd rdn and wknd over 1f out* 5/1 3

50-0 **6** 1 1/4 **Penny Valentine**9 707 4-8-6 35 MLawson(7) 6 8
(JRBest) *towards rr: drvn along 6f out: mod hdwy over 2f out: nt trble ldrs* 12/1

0-04 **7** 1 1/4 **Margarets Wish**13 664 4-8-8 30 NChalmers(5) 9 6
(TWall) *towards rr: mod effrt 4f out: n.d* 9/1

000- **8** 7 **Little Miss Tricky**321 888 5-9-0 35 JFanning 10 —
(PMitchell) *a bhd* 20/1

00-0 **9** 1 1/2 **Harry Tu**25 585 4-8-13 35 (t1) SDrowne 7 —
(MissGayKelleway) *a bhd* 14/1

00-0 **10** 5 **View The Facts**14 657 5-8-11 35 (t) LisaJones(3) 12 —
(PLGilligan) *chsd ldr: led 5f out tl over 3f out: sn wknd* 33/1

0/0- **11** 10 **Stopwatch (IRE)**21 991 9-9-0 35 (p) DaneO'Neill 11 —
(MrsLCJewell) *bhd fnl 6f* 20/1

0-00 **12** 11 **Ro Eridani**13 663 4-8-13 35 (b1) DKinsella 4 —
(TJEtherington) *set fast pce: led 5f: wknd qckly* 33/1

2m 7.43s (0.04) **Going Correction** 0.0s/f (Stan)
**WFA** 4 from 5yo+ 1lb **12** Ran SP% **128.6**
Speed ratings: **99,98,93,90,86 85,84,78,77,73 65,56**CSF £62.12 TOTE £11.20: £2.90, £2.60, £1.40; EX 36.70 Place 6 £9,204.88, Place 5 £1,672.55.
**Owner** Mike Browne **Bred** Barronstown Stud **Trained** Norton, N Yorks

**FOCUS**
Woeful form. They went too fast up front early and the front two pulled clear down the straight.

**NOTEBOOK**
**Kingsdon(IRE)**, unsuccessful on his only two previous attempts on the All-Weather, showed great resolution in winning this event in that he was there to be shot at from turning in and the persistent Monduru could not get by. He may be up to winning another race of this nature. *Official explanation: trainer said, regarding the improved form shown, gelding was better suited by today's Polytrack surface*
**Monduru**, winner of a similar race at Wolverhampton on his latest outing, did nothing wrong in second, but just found the winner too strong. He pulled well clear of the third.
**Adjiram(IRE)** was strongly fancied, but did not prove good enough on this first start since running over hurdles on Boxing day.
**All On My Own(USA)** remains a maiden after 28 starts.
**Dark Dolores** went too fast early and paid the price.
T/Plt: £8,134.60 to a £1 stake. Pool: £32,315.75. 2.90 winning tickets. T/Qpdt: £310.70 to a £1 stake. Pool: £3,149.40. 7.50 winning tickets. LM

# 772 WOLVERHAMPTON (A.W) (L-H)
Monday, February 16

**OFFICIAL GOING: Standard to slow**
There was no great track bias at this meeting.
Wind: nil Weather: sunny

## 794 BET DIRECT ON ATTHERACES TEXT PAGE 411 H'CAP (DIV I) 5f (F)
**1:50** (1:51) (F ) (0-60,60) 3-Y-0+ **£2,912** (£832; £416) **Stalls** Low

Form RPR

64-0 **1** **Cash**11 681 6-9-11 60 (p) LFletcher(3) 1 69
(PaulJohnson) *chsd ldrs: rdn over 2f out: led jst over 1f out: drvn out* 9/1 3

24-1 **2** *nk* **Empress Josephine**17 637 4-9-7 56 (v) DCorby(3) 5 64
(JRJenkins) *led after 1f: rdn and hdd jst over 1f out: r.o* 4/1 1

00-2 **3** 1 1/2 **Off Hire**17 638 8-9-2 48 (v) RFitzpatrick 7 51
(CSmith) *led 1f: remained prom and sn rdn: nt qckn fnl f* 6/1 2

0-15 **4** 1 1/4 **So Sober (IRE)**17 637 6-9-0 46 DarrenWilliams 3 44
(DShaw) *hld up mid-div: rdn and hdwy over 2f out: one pce fnl f* 12/1

2-64 **5** 1/2 **Never Without Me**18 626 4-9-2 48 (v) DaleGibson 2 45
(PJMcbride) *mid-div: rdn and hdwy on ins over 2f out: one pce fnl f* 6/1 2

0-03 **6** 3 **Our Chelsea Blue (USA)**17 638 6-9-7 53 SRighton 4 39
(AWCarroll) *s.i.s: rdn over 2f out: hdwy on ins wl over 1f out: no imp fnl f* 9/1 3

030- **7** 2 1/2 **Erracht**47 6264 6-9-8 54 GBaker 6 31
(KRBurke) *mid-div: short-lived effrt 2f out* 12/1

-612 **8** 3 **Cark**32 538 6-9-6 52 NCallan 12 19
(JJay) *racd wd: prom: rdn over 2f out: wknd wl over 1f out* 6/1 2

00-0 **9** 3/4 **Levelled**17 638 10-8-8 40 RBrisland 9 4
(DWChapman) *s.i.s: a bhd* 40/1

63-0 **10** *nk* **Percy Douglas**17 638 4-9-9 55 (p) AnnStokell 10 18
(MissAStokell) *a bhd* 25/1

-000 **11** 12 **Hawk**21 608 6-10-0 60 (p) JQuinn 8 —
(PRChamings) *prom: rdn over 2f out: sn wknd* 10/1

0500 **12** 7 **Dances In Time**12 674 4-9-4 50 TWilliams 11 —
(CNKellett) *a bhd* 50/1

64.31 secs (1.71) **Going Correction** +0.475s/f (Slow) **12** Ran SP% **115.6**
Speed ratings: **105,104,102,100,99 94,90,85,84,84 64,53**CSF £43.09 CT £240.32 TOTE £11.20: £4.10, £1.10, £2.50; EX 58.20.
**Owner** Insull, White, Pritchard & Johnson **Bred** F C T Wilson **Trained** White-le-Head, Co Durham

**FOCUS**
Despite being slightly slower than the second division, the winning time was still decent for a race of this grade and the form is fair. It was crucial to race close to the pace and very few got into this.

**NOTEBOOK**
**Cash** was never far away in a race where it was crucial to be on the pace and battled on well to score. He is a much better horse over this trip, is proven on the track, and remains well handicapped on his best form.
**Empress Josephine**, raised 3lb for her course and distance victory last time, made another bold bid under a positive ride but just found one too good.
**Off Hire** ran well under a positive ride under his optimum conditions, but has not managed a win on sand for three years despite plummeting in the weights.
**So Sober(IRE)** ran with some credit, but is finding life harder since his banded stakes win on this track.
**Never Without Me** has not been getting home over six recently, but could never get on terms with the pace-setters on this return to the minimum.
**Our Chelsea Blue(USA)** can ill-afford to keep losing ground at the start over this trip on this surface.
**Erracht** has shown her best form when able to dominate from the stalls and had no chance when unable to do that here.

## 795 BET DIRECT ON ATTHERACES TEXT PAGE 410 APPRENTICE H'CAP 1m 4f (F)
**2:20** (2:20) (F ) (0-85,82) 4-Y-0+ **£2,877** (£822; £411) **Stalls** Low

Form RPR

54-0 **1** **Border Tale**16 523 4-9-7 78 WHogg(3) 4 88
(CWeedon) *a.p: wnt 2nd over 3f out: led over 2f out: sn rdn: edgd lft over 1f out: r.o* 4/1 2

-140 **2** 1 1/2 **Digger (IRE)**12 679 5-9-8 73 PGallagher 5 81
(MissGayKelleway) *prom: led 8f out tl over 2f out: sn rdn: swtchd rt over 1f out: nt qckn* 4/1 2

0-30 **3** 4 **Cruise Director**23 600 4-9-9 82 ARutter(5) 6 84
(WJMusson) *hld up: hdwy over 3f out: rdn and one pce fnl 2f* 4/1 2

0-05 **4** 4 **York Cliff**16 649 6-9-10 75 BSwarbrick 3 71
(WMBrisbourne) *set slow pce 4f: chsd ldr tl rdn over 3f out: wknd over 2f out* 7/2 1

5102 **5** *hd* **Tropical Son**5 740 5-7-9 49 oh3 (v) DawnWatson(3) 1 44
(DShaw) *hld up in rr: rdn over 3f out: no rspnse* 6/1 3

-000 **6** 13 **Flying Treaty (USA)**17 641 7-9-9 79 CJDavies(5) 7 55
(MissAStokell) *hld up: hdwy over 4f out: rdn over 3f out: wknd over 2f out* 20/1

02-1 **7** 3 **Call Me Sunshine**10 697 4-8-11 65 RoryMoore 2 36
(PCHaslam) *prom: rdn over 4f out: wknd over 3f out* 7/1

2m 51.22s (9.72) **Going Correction** +0.475s/f (Slow)
**WFA** 4 from 5yo+ 3lb **7** Ran SP% **113.8**
Speed ratings: **86,85,82,79,79 70,68**CSF £20.08 TOTE £6.00: £2.30, £1.70; EX 35.70.
**Owner** Chadwick, Dyer & Flynn **Bred** M L Page **Trained** Wormley, Surrey

**FOCUS**
A muddling race run at a dawdle until well past halfway, and a painfully slow winning time, 2.65 seconds slower than the later maiden. The form looks dubious.

**NOTEBOOK**
**Border Tale**, a winning hurdler who had some good form over this sort of trip on turf last summer, was sent for home off the final bend and, even though he hung and was not doing much in front, still did enough.
**Digger(IRE)** took over at halfway and gradually established a significant lead, but did not press home the advantage and the winner rather caught him flat footed off the final bend. He is not easy to win with, but his rider would probably have been better setting sail for home when he was travelling so well in front leaving the back straight, and trying to run the finish out of his rivals.
**Cruise Director**, who has shown some fair form on Polytrack, was probably more unsuited by the pedestrian gallop than the change in surface.
**York Cliff**, who had shown little in his only previous try on Fibresand, was attempting this trip for the first time but did not see it out despite the moderate early pace.
**Tropical Son** was well backed, but never picked up from the rear and is another that probably needed a stronger gallop.
**Flying Treaty(USA)** is a shadow of his former self.
**Call Me Sunshine** was trying this trip for the first time and, even in a race run at a crawl, did not see it out.

## 796 BET DIRECT ON ATTHERACES TEXT PAGE 411 H'CAP (DIV II) 5f (F)
**2:50** (2:50) (F ) (0-60,60) 3-Y-0+ **£2,905** (£830; £415) **Stalls** Low

Form RPR

-236 **1** **Playtime Blue**26 578 4-10-0 60 GBaker 3 77
(KRBurke) *mde all: rdn wl over 1f out: drew clr fnl f: r.o wl* 7/2 1

0-00 **2** 3 **King's Ballet (USA)**17 637 6-9-1 47 (p) JQuinn 5 53
(PRChamings) *chsd ldrs: rdn over 2f out: edgd lft wl over 1f out: kpt on ins fnl f: no ch w wnr* 6/1 2

-030 **3** 1 3/4 **Sergeant Slipper**7 728 7-8-13 45 (v) RFitzpatrick 11 45
(CSmith) *s.i.s: outpcd and bhd: hdwy fnl f: nrst fin* 16/1

-104 **4** 1/2 **Best Lead**21 608 5-9-7 60 (b) DFentiman(7) 8 59
(IanEmmerson) *a.p: ev ch over 2f out: sn rdn: edgd lft wl over 1f out: no ex fnl f* 13/2 3

2631 **5** *nk* **Torrent**14 657 9-8-13 45 (b) ACulhane 10 43
(DWChapman) *s.i.s: bhd tl hdwy over 1f out: kpt on fnl f* 13/2 3

-652 **6** *hd* **Tigress (IRE)**17 637 5-9-10 56 (b) MHills 7 53
(JWUnett) *prom: rdn and lost pl over 3f out: kpt on again towards fin* 7/2 1

1004 **7** *shd* **Attorney**14 654 6-8-9 46 (e) THamilton(5) 1 43
(DShaw) *bhd tl hdwy on ins wl over 1f out: one pce fnl f* 16/1

050- **8** 1 **Extemporise (IRE)**177 4360 4-9-2 48 DaleGibson 9 41
(PJMcbride) *sn outpcd: n.d* 40/1

4103 **9** *nk* **Lady Protector**7 721 5-9-2 48 JEdmunds 4 40
(JBalding) *sn prom: rdn over 2f out: wknd fnl f* 12/1

0/0- **10** 1 1/2 **Vijay (IRE)**87 6042 5-9-12 58 (b) FLynch 2 45
(ISemple) *hld up: hdwy over 2f out: rdn and wknd over 1f out* 16/1

50-0 **11** 13 **Blessed Place**30 560 4-9-7 53 (b1) EAhern 6 —
(Jean-ReneAuvray) *prom tl rdn and wknd 2f out* 14/1

64.11 secs (1.51) **Going Correction** +0.475s/f (Slow) **11** Ran SP% **119.8**
Speed ratings: **106,101,98,97,97 96,96,95,94,92 71**CSF £24.73 CT £308.82 TOTE £5.80: £2.40, £3.00, £5.90; EX 42.70.
**Owner** P Sweeting **Bred** Capt J H Wilson **Trained** Middleham Moor, N Yorks



The Form Book, Raceform Ltd, Compton, RG20 6NL

**FOCUS**
A slightly faster time than the first division, a decent one for the grade, and improved form for the winner. Again it paid to be right on the pace.
**NOTEBOOK**
**Playtime Blue**, who has been running well over this course and distance during the winter, got the early lead and gradually forged clear in the straight. This is his level and as he goes on turf as well he should continue to pay his way.
**King's Ballet(USA)**, who likes to get his toe in on turf, travelled well just behind the leaders and, though he could never get on terms with the winner, finished a clear second best. This was far his best performance to date on sand and he should be able to pick up a modest contest under these conditions.
**Sergeant Slipper** did incredibly well to snatch third in a race where the front runners enjoyed a huge advantage, and he made up an amazing amount of ground to do so. Unfortunately that is his style of running, and his strike rate in recent years is particularly poor.
**Best Lead** broke well enough and was right on the speed for a fair way, but started to struggle as soon as the winner turned the screw. He has found life tough since the Handicapper hammered him with a 12lb rise for his win in a claimer here last month.
**Torrent** probably ran up to the best form he is capable of these days, but only he knows when he will be ready to win again.
**Tigress(IRE)**, under her optimum conditions, got away on terms this time but could make no impression down the home straight.

## 797 BET DIRECT ON ATTHERACES TEXT PAGE 412 MAIDEN STKS 1m 4f (F)
**3:20** (3:20) (D ) 3-Y-O+ **£3,308** (£1,018; £509; £254) **Stalls** Low

Form RPR
**1** **Royal Atalza (FR)**$^{16}$ 7-9-8 ....(p) BReilly$^{(5)}$ 6 68
(CNAllen) *hld up: reminders 7f out: hdwy 6f out: rdn over 4f out: wnt 2nd wl over 1f out: styd on to ld last stride* **7/2**$^{2}$
-43 **2** *shd* **Vivre Sa Vie**$^{18}$ [628] 3-7-12 .... JMackay 7 63
(SirMarkPrescott) *led 3f: w ldr: led again over 4f out: rdn over 2f out: clr over 1f out: ct last stride* **7/2**$^{2}$
4-23 **3** *5* **Pacific Ocean (ARG)**$^{10}$ [697] 5-9-13 60....(t) JQuinn 2 60
(MrsStefLiddiard) *plld hrd in rr: hdwy 5f out: nt clr on ins over 3f out tl squeezed through over 2f out: sn rdn: wknd ins fnl f* **4/1**$^{3}$
0/5 **4** *5* **Andaad**$^{30}$ [555] 4-9-5 .... WRyan 4 48
(DJDaly) *hld up: hdwy 6f out: rdn over 3f out: chsd ldr over 2f out tl wl over 1f out: eased whn btn ins fnl f* **13/2**
444- **5** *19* **Many Thanks**$^{10}$ [5552] 4-9-5 70.... MFenton 5 19
(BSRothwell) *prom: rdn over 5f out: wknd over 4f out* **8/1**
00-4 **6** *6* **Imperative (USA)**$^{16}$ [651] 4-9-10 70.... MHenry 1 15
(IanWilliams) *w ldr: led 9f out: rdn and hdd over 4f out: wkng whn hmpd over 2f out* **10/3**$^{1}$
**7** *dist* **Foxy Trix**$^{67}$ 5-9-8 .... ANicholls 3 —
(JWUnett) *s.i.s: bhd: rdn over 7f out: t.o fnl 5f* **66/1**
6- **8** *dist* **Gotya**$^{237}$ [2652] 4-8-12 .... DFentiman$^{(7)}$ 8 —
(JRWeymes) *t.k.h in tch: rdn over 6f out: sn lost pl: t.o fnl 5f* **50/1**

2m 48.57s (7.07) **Going Correction** +0.475s/f (Slow)
**WFA** 3 from 4yo 24lb 4 from 5yo+ 3lb **8** Ran SP% **115.4**
Speed ratings: **95,94,91,88,75 71,—,—**CSF £16.39 TOTE £6.00: £1.20, £1.90, £1.40; EX 34.50.
**Owner** T P Ramsden **Bred** Mme Gilbert Gallot **Trained** Newmarket, Suffolk
■ Stewards Enquiry : B Reilly two-day ban: used whip with excessive frequency (Feb 27, 28)

**FOCUS**
This race was run 2.65 seconds faster than the apprentice handicap, but that is of no significance at all and the fact that this was won by an ex-French chaser speaks volumes.
**NOTEBOOK**
**Royal Atalza(FR)**, an ex-French chaser purchased for a crack at the Grand National, was pulled up on his British chasing debut and this unconventional switch to the Flat paid off. He did not look like winning for a long way, but his stamina was all-important and he got up right on the line. He was probably fortunate to have found such a terrible race.
**Vivre Sa Vie**, stepped up to a more suitable trip, tried to make her stamina tell and did everything right, but had the race snatched from her on the line. Connections will be keen to get a win out of her, but she will be lucky to find another race as bad as this.
**Pacific Ocean(ARG)**, an exposed maiden, was patiently ridden and given every chance to get this longer trip, but emptied after holding every chance on the home bend.
**Andaad**, stepping up in trip, had every chance on straightening up but did not get home. At least she has a little scope and can now be handicapped.
**Many Thanks** *Official explanation: jockey said filly hung left*
**Imperative(USA)**, who has been mixing hurdling with racing on the Flat, was well backed and had every chance turning for home, but then stopped as if shot. He has little in the way of scope. *Official explanation: jockey said colt was never travelling*

## 798 BET DIRECT ON ATTHERACES TEXT PAGE 413 H'CAP 1m 100y(F)
**3:50** (3:50) (D ) (0-80,77) 3-Y-O **£3,987** (£1,227; £613; £306) **Stalls** Low

Form RPR
0-40 **1** **La Puce**$^{9}$ [704] 3-8-10 **66**.... FLynch 7 66
(MissGayKelleway) *a.p: rdn 3f out: chal 2f out: led last strides: all out* **12/1**
21 **2** *hd* **Play Master (IRE)**$^{24}$ [593] 3-9-3 **73**.... PaulEddery 1 73
(DHaydnJones) *w ldr: rdn to ld over 3f out: edgd rt ins fnl f: hdd last strides* **10/3**$^{2}$
003- **3** *hd* **Book Matched**$^{83}$ [6069] 3-8-9 **65**.... RFfrench 6 65
(BSmart) *s.i.s: hdwy over 5f out: hrd rdn and ev ch fnl 2f: r.o* **7/1**
-534 **4** *1 1/4* **Myannabanana (IRE)**$^{4}$ [746] 3-8-7 **63**....(b$^{1}$) JQuinn 5 60
(JRWeymes) *a.p: rdn over 3f out: kpt on same pce fnl f* **7/1**
233- **5** *1 1/2* **Hawkit (USA)**$^{59}$ [6216] 3-9-2 **72**.... EAhern 3 66
(JAOsborne) *a.p: rdn 2f out: no ex towards fin* **6/1**$^{3}$
40-1 **6** *11* **Vengerov**$^{11}$ [683] 3-9-3 **73**.... MFenton 4 44
(MLWBell) *led: hdd over 3f out: rdn and wknd over 2f out* **9/4**$^{1}$
6-40 **7** *9* **Heartbeat**$^{9}$ [702] 3-7-13 **55**....(v$^{1}$) DaleGibson 8 7
(PJMcbride) *in rr: rdn over 3f out: sn struggling* **28/1**
3-44 **8** *16* **Marcus Eile (IRE)**$^{24}$ [595] 3-9-7 **77**.... DarrenWilliams 2 —
(KRBurke) *prom: rdn over 3f out: sn wknd: t.o* **10/1**

1m 54.92s (3.92) **Going Correction** +0.475s/f (Slow) **8** Ran SP% **113.4**
Speed ratings: **99,98,98,97,95 84,75,59**CSF £50.99 CT £309.02 TOTE £16.00: £3.10, £1.30, £1.80; EX 78.20.
**Owner** Wetherby Racing Bureau 52 **Bred** R P Williams **Trained** Newmarket, Suffolk

**FOCUS**
A modest but competitive little handicap run at a fair pace.
**NOTEBOOK**
**La Puce**, whose only previous win came here, appeared to go backwards after a promising reappearance last month but came good under a positive ride. She was battling for the lead from a very long way out, and her resolution could no be faulted. *Official explanation: trainer said, regarding the improved form shown, filly was better suited by more positive tactics today, and may also have benefited from the change in surface*
**Play Master(IRE)** was on the speed all the way and kept battling right to the line, despite being just about the first off the bridle. He still has plenty of scope and should stay further.
**Book Matched**, stepping up in trip and making his handicap debut, was brought from off the pace and may have even hit the front for a few strides around a furlong from home, but he just flattened out in the closing stages. There should be a similar contest in him.
**Myannabanana(IRE)**, stepping back to a more suitable trip, is a hard ride and the fact that he was eventually not beaten far is purely down to the persistence of his pilot. He does not have much scope, but strikes as just the type to keep on going on Fibresand for many winters to come.
**Hawkit(USA)**, a frustrating individual, had every chance but never looked like landing a telling blow. He is still to win, but this was the first time he has finished out of the frame in seven starts.
**Vengerov**, put up just 2lb for his Southwell maiden win, set the early pace but dropped out very disappointingly and connections could offer no explanation of why. *Official explanation: trainer had no explanation for the poor form shown*

## 799 BET DIRECT DAILY SPECIAL OFFERS (S) STKS 6f (F)
**4:20** (4:22) (G ) 3-Y-O+ **£2,611** (£746; £373) **Stalls** Low

Form RPR
4350 **1** **Sabana (IRE)**$^{7}$ [725] 6-9-6 45....(b) PFitzsimons 10 59
(JMBradley) *chsd ldrs: rdn over 2f out: hung lft over 1f out: led ins fnl f: r.o wl* **33/1**
1453 **2** *3* **Larky's Lob**$^{1}$ [782] 5-9-3 47.... LFletcher$^{(3)}$ 9 50
(PaulJohnson) *w ldr: led over 4f out: rdn over 2f out: hdd and no ex ins fnl f* **10/1**
2625 **3** *nk* **Aguila Loco (IRE)**$^{8}$ [717] 5-9-6 50.... MFenton 7 49
(MrsStefLiddiard) *led early: a.p: rdn over 2f out: kpt on one pce fnl f* **5/1**$^{2}$
0400 **4** *nk* **Juwwi**$^{19}$ [617] 10-9-3 66 ow4.... CJDavies$^{(7)}$ 11 52
(JMBradley) *s.s: bhd tl swtchd rt and hdwy over 1f out: r.o ins fnl f* **9/1**
-540 **5** *1/2* **New Options**$^{4}$ [748] 7-9-6 64....(b) EAhern 12 47
(WJMusson) *a.p: rdn over 2f out: one pce fnl f* **7/2**$^{1}$
4-25 **6** *hd* **Speedfit Free (IRE)**$^{35}$ [510] 7-9-6 53....(b) NCallan 1 46
(ISemple) *mid-div: rdn over 3f out: hdwy on ins over 2f out: one pce fnl f* **5/1**$^{2}$
2615 **7** *2* **Polar Haze**$^{4}$ [748] 7-9-11 58....(v) JQuinn 5 45
(JPearce) *mid-div: rdn 3f out: no hdwy fnl 2f* **11/2**$^{3}$
0525 **8** *2* **Mizhar (USA)**$^{11}$ [685] 8-9-6 50....(p) DarrenWilliams 2 34
(JJQuinn) *sn bhd: n.d* **12/1**
00-0 **9** *1/2* **Drury Lane (IRE)**$^{7}$ [719] 4-9-6 75....(b) RBrisland 4 33
(DWChapman) *bhd fnl 4f* **16/1**
0631 **10** *2 1/2* **Arogant Prince**$^{3}$ [762] 7-9-4 49....(b) RoryMoore$^{(7)}$ 8 30
(AWCarroll) *sn led: hdd over 4f out: rdn 3f out: wknd wl over 1f out* **9/1**
2003 **11** *1/2* **Headland (USA)**$^{7}$ [723] 6-9-11 57....(b) ACulhane 6 29
(DWChapman) *bhd: short-lived effrt over 2f out* **8/1**
-065 **12** *5* **Heathyardsblessing (IRE)**$^{14}$ [654] 7-9-6 45....(p) DeanMcKeown 3 9
(RHollinshead) *s.i.s: a bhd* **33/1**

1m 18.12s (2.42) **Going Correction** +0.475s/f (Slow) **12** Ran SP% **130.6**
Speed ratings: **102,98,97,97,96 96,93,90,90,86 86,79**CSF £364.64 TOTE £39.10: £9.80, £5.30, £1.20; EX 441.60.There was no bid for the winner.
**Owner** E A Hayward **Bred** Churchtown House Stud **Trained** Sedbury, Gloucs

**FOCUS**
An average contest for the grade, but a decent pace and a reasonable time for a seller.
**NOTEBOOK**
**Sabana(IRE)** at last found a race he could win and, despite hanging markedly to his left down the home straight, finished strongly to record his first win since August 2001. This does look his best trip these days, but given his record a follow-up does not look likely. *Official explanation: trainer said, regarding the improved form, gelding is inconsistent*
**Larky's Lob**, reappearing quickly after finishing third at Southwell the previous day, was given a positive ride and looked to have the race won when kicked a few lengths clear off the final bend, but he is not the heartiest of sorts and folded fairly tamely when the winner swooped past at the furlong pole.
**Aguila Loco(IRE)**, returning to probably his best trip, ran up to his best under a positive ride.
**Juwwi** ran his usual sort of race, giving his rivals a start and then coming home in good style. He will probably time his run right one day, but it is an expensive business backing him to do so every time.
**New Options** was a beaten favourite once again and continues to promise more than he actually delivers.
**Arogant Prince** drifted alarmingly in the market and, after showing up for a while, ran accordingly.
**Headland(USA)**never figured. *Official explanation: jockey said gelding lost its action in the home straight*
**Heathyardsblessing(IRE)** *Official explanation: jockey said moved badly and did not handle the bend*

## 800 BET DIRECT IN RUNNING SKY TEXT PAGE 293 H'CAP 1m 1f 79y(F)
**4:50** (4:50) (F ) (0-60,58) 4-Y-O+ **£2,968** (£848; £424) **Stalls** Low

Form RPR
4-02 **1** **Desert Heat**$^{2}$ [776] 6-9-11 **57**....(v$^{1}$) ACulhane 8 63
(ISemple) *hld up and bhd: hdwy over 4f out: rdn over 3f out: led over 2f out: sn clr: drvn out* **20/1**
5361 **2** *1 3/4* **Givemethemoonlight**$^{2}$ [772] 5-9-10 **56** 6ex....(v) JQuinn 2 59
(MrsStefLiddiard) *hld up: rdn and hdwy over 2f out: chsd wnr over 1f out: styd on ins fnl f: nt trble wnr* **9/2**$^{2}$
00-5 **3** *4* **Bramantino (IRE)**$^{13}$ [667] 4-9-2 **53**....(v$^{1}$) THamilton$^{(5)}$ 4 49
(RAFahey) *prom: rdn and outpcd over 3f out: styd on fnl f* **12/1**
-654 **4** *hd* **Taiyo**$^{10}$ [697] 4-9-4 **50**.... NCallan 5 45
(JWPayne) *w ldr: led 6f out: rdn and hdd over 2f out: sn btn* **25/1**
0-36 **5** *7* **Interstice**$^{25}$ [581] 7-9-4 **50**....(p) DeanMcKeown 7 33
(AGNewcombe) *plld hrd: prom: rdn over 2f out: wknd wl over 1f out* **14/1**
3-55 **6** *5* **Air Of Esteem**$^{10}$ [700] 8-8-6 **45**.... DFentiman$^{(7)}$ 10 19
(IanEmmerson) *prom: rdn 4f out: wknd over 2f out* **9/1**$^{3}$
-324 **7** *8* **Our Destiny**$^{10}$ [693] 6-9-6 **52**....(v) JTate 3 11
(DBurchell) *led: hdd 6f out: sn rdn: wknd 4f out* **16/1**
14-2 **8** *3* **To Wit To Woo**$^{17}$ [643] 4-9-12 **58**.... MHills 6 12
(BWHills) *prom: rdn 5f out: wknd over 3f out* **8/11**$^{1}$
010- **9** *6* **Rocinante (IRE)**$^{107}$ [5881] 4-9-8 **54**.... RFfrench 9 —
(JJQuinn) *prom tl wknd over 5f out* **25/1**

2m 6.98s (4.08) **Going Correction** +0.475s/f (Slow) **9** Ran SP% **118.8**
Speed ratings: **100,98,94,94,88 84,76,74,68**CSF £108.30 CT £1146.38 TOTE £18.90: £4.50, £1.40, £2.40; EX 130.00 Place 6 £173.07, Place 5 £82.14.
**Owner** Gordon McDowall **Bred** Greenfield Stud S A **Trained** Carluke, S Lanarks

**FOCUS**
An ordinary handicap run at just a fair pace. With the hot favourite running so badly it probably did not take much winning, and the form can be regarded as modest.
**NOTEBOOK**
**Desert Heat**, a fair second over course and distance 48 hours earlier, was booted into a clear lead off the final bend and that proved a race-winning move. With the favourite running a stinker the form probably does not mean a lot.
**Givemethemoonlight**, racing for the third time in four days and back over a longer trip, utilised very different tactics when winning over seven furlongs here 48 hours earlier. Despite coming off the bridle half a mile out, she never stopped trying but found the winner had gone beyond recall. She is admirably tough.

**Bramantino(IRE)**, wearing a visor rather than blinkers, never looked like winning and merely stayed on to finish a modest third. He may still have just needed this though.
**Taiyo** is still a maiden and probably did not achieve much.
**Interstice** still pulled hard despite the drop in trip.
**To Wit To Woo** broke well enough, but was then off the bridle and going nowhere from a long way out, eventually trailing home well beaten. This was far too bad to be true. *Official explanation: trainer had no explanation for the poor form shown*
T/Plt: £1,060.60 to a £1 stake. Pool: £37,414.55. 25.75 winning tickets. T/Qpdt: £234.10 to a £1 stake. Pool: £2,594.50. 8.20 winning tickets. KH

# [778]SOUTHWELL (L-H)

## Tuesday, February 17

**OFFICIAL GOING: Standard**
Wind: mod hlf against Weather: overcast with showers

## 801 BET DIRECT ON ATR TEXT PAGE 413 H'CAP (DIV I) 5f (F)
**1:10** (1:10) (D ) (0-80,80) 3-Y-O+ **£4,026** (£1,239; £619; £309) **Stalls** High

Form RPR
100- **1** **Maktavish**[73] 6138 5-10-0 **80**..........(p) NCallan 7 89
(ISemple) *mde all: pushed clr 1/2-way: rdn and hung rt over 1f out: drvn and kpt on* **7/2**[1]
600- **2** *3/4* **Blue Knight (IRE)**[222] 3131 5-9-6 **72**.......... JQuinn 5 78
(APJarvis) *in tch: hdwy 2f out: rdn to chse wnr ent last: kpt on* **16/1**
0-51 **3** *nk* **Sea The World (IRE)**[8] 721 4-8-10 **62** 6ex..........(v) DarrenWilliams 6 67
(DShaw) *sn pushed along towards rr: swtchd rt and hdwy over 2f out: sn rdn: kpt on fnl f: nrst fin* **10/1**[3]
02-6 **4** *3/4* **River Lark (USA)**[21] 612 5-7-7 **50** oh3.......... JFMcDonald(5) 1 53
(MABuckley) *prom: rdn along over 2f out: kpt on wl fnl f* **14/1**
-000 **5** *nk* **Taboor (IRE)**[27] 578 6-8-12 **64**..........(b) MFenton 11 66
(JWPayne) *chsd ldrs: rdn along 2f out: kpt on towards fin* **14/1**
-115 **6** *2* **The Fisio**[27] 578 4-9-8 **74**.......... MartinDwyer 4 69
(AMBalding) *s.i.s: hdwy 1/2-way: sn rdn and kpt on same pce appr last* **7/2**[1]
00-0 **7** *2* **Lakelands Lady (IRE)**[12] 680 4-9-1 **67**.......... JEdmunds 10 55
(JBalding) *in tch: rdn along 1/2-way: sn one pce* **40/1**
1-00 **8** *1/2* **Frascati**[26] 586 4-9-11 **77**.......... FLynch 8 63
(ABerry) *sn outpcd and a towards rr* **12/1**
053- **9** *3/4* **Daintree Affair (IRE)**[63] 6199 4-8-11 **63**.......... GBaker 3 46
(KRBurke) *prom: rdn along 1/2-way: wknd wl over 1f out* **6/1**[2]
3-00 **10** *nk* **Gone'N'Dunnett (IRE)**[40] 480 5-9-1 **67**..........(v) DaneO'Neill 2 49
(MrsCADunnett) *s.i.s: a rr* **12/1**
F0-0 **11** *2 1/2* **Raymond's Pride**[12] 681 4-8-13 **65**..........(b) PFessey 9 38
(KARyan) *s.i.s: a rr* **14/1**
60.06 secs (-0.24) **Going Correction** +0.125s/f (Slow) **11** Ran SP% **111.5**
Speed ratings: **106,104,104,103,102 99,96,95,94,93 89**CSF £60.21 CT £496.74 TOTE £3.50: £1.50, £5.40, £2.40; EX 71.10.
**Owner** D G Savala **Bred** V Robin Lawson **Trained** Carluke, S Lanarks

**FOCUS**
A decent handicap, run at a good clip and the form looks solid.

**NOTEBOOK**
**Maktavish** was quickly away and made every yard. He did not look on a bad mark, given that he had run out a clear winner over course and distance last winter off a 1lb lower mark, and this race represented a slight drop in grade from the contests he had been running in late last year.
**Blue Knight(IRE)** must have had his training problems as this was his first outing since July. In the circumstances he ran a highly encouraging race and, although arguably his best form in the past has been over six furlongs, he had no trouble with the minimum trip on this occasion.
**Sea The World(IRE)** was as usual outpaced in the early stages but came through to grab the minor placing inside the last. This was not a bad performance under his penalty.
**River Lark(USA)** was not disgraced given that she was running from 3lb out of the weights.
**Taboor(IRE)**, who is better known as a Polytrack performer, did not run too badly on this slower surface.
**The Fisio** was weak in the market beforehand and disappointing in the race itself, and his rider later reported that the gelding had been unruly in the stalls. *Official explanation: jockey said gelding attempted to duck under the gates prior to the start*

## 802 LITTLEWOODS BET DIRECT MAIDEN H'CAP (DIV I) 1m (F)
**1:40** (1:40) (F ) (0-60,60) 3-Y-O **£2,933** (£838; £419) **Stalls** Low

Form RPR
060- **1** **Poker**[137] 5337 3-8-6 **45**.......... MartinDwyer 8 51+
(WJHaggas) *in tch: pushed along and outpcd 1/2-way: hdwy on inner 2f out: sn rdn and styd on wl to ld ins last: drvn out* **6/4**[1]
05-5 **2** *1 3/4* **Jomus**[13] 675 3-9-3 **56**.......... FLynch 6 58
(LMontagueHall) *s.i.s: racd wd and plld hrd in rr: hdwy over 2f out rdn over 1f out: kpt on wl fnl f* **13/2**[2]
6-30 **3** *1 1/4* **Brother Cadfael**[21] 611 3-8-5 **47**.......... LFletcher(3) 4 46
(JohnAHarris) *trckd ldrs: hdwy 1/2-way: rdn 2f out: led over 1f out tl drvn: edgd lft and hdd isndie last: kpt on same pce* **28/1**
3-02 **4** *2 1/2* **Abrogate (IRE)**[21] 615 3-8-10 **49**.......... GFaulkner 12 43
(PCHaslam) *towards rr: hdwy 3f out: rdn to chse ldrs 2f out: sn drvn and one pce appr last* **7/1**[3]
-000 **5** *shd* **Gayle Storm (IRE)**[6] 741 3-8-13 **52**.......... EAhern 5 46
(CTinkler) *in tch: hdwy 3f out: sn rdn and one pce wl over 1f out* **9/1**
4-43 **6** *5* **Turnberry (IRE)**[18] 640 3-9-4 **57**..........(b) SWhitworth 2 40
(JWHills) *cl up: led wl over 2f out: sn rdn: hdd & wknd over 1f out* **13/2**[2]
-043 **7** *nk* **Tonto (FR)**[12] 683 3-9-2 **60**.......... DFox(5) 10 42
(MissDMountain) *cl up: led after 2f: rdn along 3fr out: sn hdd: drvn 2f out and grad wknd* **8/1**
0-00 **8** *1/2* **Mystic Promise (IRE)**[7] 731 3-7-7 **37** oh7..........(v[1]) HayleyTurner(5) 3 18
(MrsNMacauley) *chsd ldrs: rdn along over 2f out: sn wknd* **66/1**
0-52 **9** *1* **Quarry Island (IRE)**[7] 736 3-8-1 **40**..........(v) JoannaBadger 9 19
(PDEvans) *a rr* **10/1**
000- **10** *1/2* **Prince Of Perles**[179] 4353 3-7-7 **37** oh2..........(v[1]) JFMcDonald(5) 7 14
(DShaw) *hld up pulling hrd: a rr* **20/1**
600- **11** *12* **Unprecedented (IRE)**[154] 4957 3-9-4 **57**.......... DeanMcKeown 1 8
(TTClement) *chsd ldrs on inner: rdn along over 3f out: sn wknd* **50/1**
00-0 **12** *18* **Garnock Belle (IRE)**[34] 530 3-8-2 **41** oh2 ow4.......... ANicholls 11 —
(ABerry) *led tl rn out bnd after 2f: sn b ehind* **40/1**
1m 45.03s (0.43) **Going Correction** -0.075s/f (Stan) **12** Ran SP% **123.5**
Speed ratings: **94,92,91,88,88 83,83,82,81,81 69,51**CSF £11.45 CT £208.67 TOTE £2.20: £1.20, £4.00, £6.00; EX 20.00.
**Owner** The Poker Partnership **Bred** T Hirschfeld **Trained** Newmarket, Suffolk

**FOCUS**
A moderate handicap, but a successful one for those who gambled the winner into 6-4 favouritism. The form is only fair, but the winner is likely to rate a good deal higher in time.

**NOTEBOOK**
**Poker** was the subject of strong market support despite having failed to make much of an impression in three starts in maiden company over six furlongs. He appreciated the step up in distance on his handicap debut and in fact appeared to find this trip the bare minimum, as he looked in trouble early in the straight before staying on strongly inside the final quarter mile. He was winning off a mark of 45, so should not be difficult to place in a follow-up bid, although connections may wait for the turf season now. *Official explanation: trainer said, regarding the improved form shown, gelding had matured over the winter and had been working well at home*
**Jomus**, making his Fibresand debut, finished his race well despite having taken a keen hold in the early stages. He does not look an easy ride, though.
**Brother Cadfael** is a more exposed performer and has been found out on a regular basis in selling grade.
**Abrogate(IRE)**, another whose form made him look more exposed than some in the race, was weak in the market and did not appear to run up to the level of his two previous outings over course and distance.
**Gayle Storm(IRE)** has yet to match the level she reached on turf on the All-Weather.
**Prince Of Perles** *Official explanation: trainer said gelding ran too freely in the early stages*
**Garnock Belle(IRE)** *Official explanation: jockey said he had steering problems on the bend into the straight*

## 803 BET DIRECT ON ATR TEXT PAGE 410 FILLIES' H'CAP 6f (F)
**2:10** (2:11) (E ) (0-75,71) 3-Y-O+ **£3,262** (£932; £466) **Stalls** Low

Form RPR
1-56 **1** **Forever Phoenix**[24] 596 4-9-8 **65**.......... EAhern 2 72
(RMHCowell) *trckd ldrs gng wl: smooth hdwy 2f out: shkn up to ld ins last: sn rdn and kpt on* **4/1**[1]
3-03 **2** *1/2* **Boavista (IRE)**[7] 733 4-8-7 **53**..........(t) LFletcher(3) 1 58
(PDEvans) *led: jnd 2f out: sn rdn along: drvn and hdd ins last: kpt on gamely* **8/1**
00-6 **3** *1 3/4* **Park Star**[8] 721 4-8-8 **56**.......... JFMcDonald(5) 5 56
(DShaw) *a.p: rdn along 2f out: drvn and one pce approachiong last* **16/1**
-044 **4** *1/2* **Blakeshall Quest**[12] 680 4-9-0 **60**..........(v) FPFerris(3) 7 58
(RBrotherton) *in tch: rdn along 1/2-way: kpt on u.p fnl 2f: nrst fin* **5/1**[2]
2401 **5** *shd* **Eager Angel (IRE)**[8] 725 6-8-8 **51** 6ex..........(p) DeanMcKeown 8 49
(RFMarvin) *towards rr: hdwy over 2f out: sn rdn: kpt on appr last: nrst fin* **16/1**
-354 **6** *1 1/4* **Pilgrim Princess (IRE)**[11] 698 6-8-2 **45**.......... JQuinn 9 39
(EJAlston) *cl up: rdn along over 2f out: grad wknd* **11/2**[3]
6330 **7** *2* **Playful Spirit**[8] 721 5-8-6 **49**..........(v) JEdmunds 4 37
(JBalding) *chsd ldrs: rdn along wl over 2f out: sn one pce* **11/1**
-300 **8** *shd* **Grandma Lily (IRE)**[12] 680 6-9-9 **71**.......... BReilly(5) 10 59
(MCChapman) *a rr* **10/1**
13-2 **9** *1 3/4* **Zagala**[46] 407 4-9-6 **63**..........(t) ANicholls 6 46
(SLKeightley) *s.i.s, a rr* **8/1**
3- **10** *17* **Miss Wong One (IRE)**[70] 6151 4-8-13 **56**.......... JPSpencer 3 —
(FJBowles, Ire) *in tch: rdn along 1/2-way: hdwy to chse ldrs 2f out: sn rdn and wknd qckly over 1f out: eased* **8/1**
1m 16.01s (-0.79) **Going Correction** -0.075s/f (Stan) **10** Ran SP% **114.6**
Speed ratings: **102,101,99,98,98 96,93,93,91,68**CSF £35.40 CT £459.18 TOTE £3.40: £2.10, £2.00, £4.70; EX 50.10.
**Owner** J M Greetham **Bred** J M Greetham **Trained** Six Mile Bottom, Cambs

**FOCUS**
Not a strong race, but a fairly decent effort from the winner, who scored cosily.

**NOTEBOOK**
**Forever Phoenix** found this a much less competitive contest than the one she ran in on her last visit here, and she always looked in control with Ahern back in the saddle. In the perfect position throughout, just tracking the leaders, she travelled strongly and found enough when asked to go and win her race. Her connections believe that the quicker surface at Wolverhampton suits her better, and she is likely to have one more run there before beginning a turf campaign.
**Boavista(IRE)** is a consistent type and ran well in defeat on this drop back in trip.
**Park Star**, whose wins have all come over the minimum trip, got the sixth furlong well on this occasion.
**Blakeshall Quest**, who is well handicapped on his best form, was staying on all too late.
**Eager Angel(IRE)** had it to do under her penalty in a stronger race over a trip shorter than ideal.
**Pilgrim Princess(IRE)** is on a losing run that now stretches back 26 starts.
**Zagala** *Official explanation: trainer said filly was found to be in season the following morning*
**Miss Wong One(IRE)** *Official explanation: trainer said filly was in season*

## 804 BET DIRECT ON ATR TEXT PAGE 411 H'CAP 1m 3f (F)
**2:40** (2:42) (F ) (0-55,54) 3-Y-O **£2,926** (£836; £418) **Stalls** Low

Form RPR
0-22 **1** **Turks And Caicos (IRE)**[15] 656 3-9-4 **54**.......... GFaulkner 4 56
(PCHaslam) *trckd ldrs: hdwy to ld 2f out: sn rdn: drvn ins last and jst hld on* **9/2**[2]
-143 **2** *shd* **Siegfrieds Night (IRE)**[7] 732 3-8-9 **50**.......... BReilly(5) 8 52
(MCChapman) *chsd ldrs: hdwy on outer 3f out: rdn to chal 2f out and hung lft: wandered over 1f out: drvn and hung lft ins last: jsthld* **11/1**
-042 **3** *2 1/2* **Sir Frank Gibson**[5] 752 3-8-9 **45**.......... JFanning 3 43
(MJohnston) *led: pushed along 3f out: hdd 2f out: swtchd rt and rallied over 1f out: sn drvn and one pce* **11/2**[3]
0-33 **4** *2* **Nocatee (IRE)**[5] 746 3-8-2 **45**..........(p) DFentiman(7) 2 40
(PCHaslam) *hld up: hdwy 3f out: sn rdn: kpt on fnl 2f: nvr nrr* **7/2**[1]
-440 **5** *5* **Secret Bloom**[11] 696 3-8-11 **47**..........(v) DarrenWilliams 6 34
(JRNorton) *in tch: rdn along 3f out: sn drvn and wknd* **25/1**
00-4 **6** *1* **Biscar Two (IRE)**[21] 615 3-8-9 **45**.......... DeanMcKeown 10 30
(RMWhitaker) *towards rr: hdwy over 4f out: rdn along wl over 2f out: n.d* **7/2**[1]
25-0 **7** *5* **Frambo (IRE)**[5] 746 3-9-4 **54**..........(p) EAhern 1 31
(JGPortman) *chsd ldrs: rdn along over 3f out: wknd 2f out* **16/1**
01-2 **8** *1 1/2* **Killing Me Softly**[36] 508 3-9-1 **51**.......... DSweeney 9 26
(JGallagher) *trckd ldrs: hdwy over 4f out: rdn along over 2f out and sn wknd* **15/2**
06-6 **9** *nk* **Mind Play**[7] 736 3-8-7 **48** oh5 ow3..........(b) PMulrennan(5) 7 22
(MESowersby) *cl up: rdn along over 3f out: wknd over 2f out* **66/1**
0-00 **10** *12* **Ticklepenny Lock (IRE)**[21] 611 3-8-9 **45** oh15.......... ANicholls 11 —
(CSmith) *a rr: bhd fr 1/2-way* **100/1**
2m 30.15s (1.25) **Going Correction** -0.075s/f (Stan) **10** Ran SP% **110.3**
Speed ratings: **92,91,90,88,85 84,80,79,79,70**CSF £48.81 CT £259.88 TOTE £3.40: £1.20, £3.60, £1.40; EX 54.10.
**Owner** Middleham Park Racing **Bred** R N Auld **Trained** Middleham Moor, N Yorks

**FOCUS**
Not a particularly strong heat but it did produce an exciting finish, and the form looks reliable at a modest level.

**NOTEBOOK**

**Turks And Caicos(IRE)** had twice run creditably on this surface this year in regional maidens, and the extra three furlongs on this handicap debut brought about enough improvement to see him get his head in front. It is unlikely he would have won however, had the eventual runner-up not hung in left on a couple of occasions up the straight. Connections plan to give him one more run over this course and distance before the turf season comes around.

**Siegfrieds Night(IRE)** should really have won and would have done so in another stride or two. All of his racing prior to this had been over seven furlongs or shorter, but he got the trip well and it will be surprising if he cannot find a similar race.

**Sir Frank Gibson**, second in a better event at the course last week, ran his race from the front and had every chance.

**Nocatee(IRE)**, a stablemate of the winner and sporting the owners' first colours, is not the quickest of animals and will ultimately require two miles.

**Secret Bloom** failed to improve for this step up in trip.

**Biscar Two(IRE)** was struggling from a fair way out and was another who failed to improve for the step up in trip.

**Killing Me Softly**looked a blatant non-stayer.

## 805 BET DIRECT ON ATR TEXT PAGE 412 MAIDEN STKS 6f (F)

**3:10** (3:11) (D) 3-Y-O+ **£3,367** (£1,036; £518; £259) **Stalls** Low

Form RPR

45 **1** **Skip Of Colour**[18] [639] 4-9-5 65 DNolan(5) 12 67+
(PABlockley) *qckly away and sn clr: rdn and 12 l up 2f out: eased ins last: unchal* **7/1**[3]

0-55 **2** *3 ½* **Zak Facta (IRE)**[6] [738] 4-9-10 50 (vt) SWhitworth 8 57
(MissDAMchale) *in tch: hdwy 1/2-way: sn rdn: kpt on appr last: no ch w wnr* **5/1**[2]

45-0 **3** *½* **Largs**[11] [698] 4-9-5 46 JEdmunds 2 50
(JBalding) *in tch: rdn along 1/2-way: styd on u.p fnl 2f* **20/1**

5-20 **4** *shd* **Dark Champion**[11] [698] 4-9-10 48 DaneO'Neill 6 55
(JeddO'Keeffe) *prom: chsd wnr over 2f out: sn drvn and no imp* **12/1**

544- **5** *1 ½* **Otylia**[123] [5627] 4-9-5 52 FLynch 11 45
(ABerry) *midfield: rdn along 1/2-way: nvr a factor* **28/1**

6340 **6** *hd* **Amanda's Lad (IRE)**[8] [721] 4-9-5 45 BReilly(5) 5 50
(MCChapman) *chsd ldrs: rdn along over 2f out: sn one pce* **16/1**

433- **7** *3* **Brooklands Time (IRE)**[274] [1725] 3-7-12 63 ow1 PPMathers(7) 9 37
(IWMcinnes) *chsd wnr: rdn along 1/2-way: sn wknd* **10/1**

2-40 **8** *shd* **Shadowfax**[36] [510] 4-9-10 58 (p) MFenton 1 40
(MissGayKelleway) *dwlt: a rr* **5/1**[2]

55- **9** *nk* **Mission Affirmed (USA)**[112] [5822] 3-8-9 DMernagh 10 39
(TPTate) *bhd: wd st: swtchd to stands rail 2f out: sn rdn and nvr a factor* **7/1**[3]

0 **10** *2 ½* **Utah Flats (IRE)**[14] [668] 3-8-9 (b[1]) MartinDwyer 7 32
(MrsJRRamsden) *midfield: rdn along 1/2-way: nvr a factor* **16/1**

00-0 **11** *¾* **Roan Raider (USA)**[45] [415] 4-9-7 45 (bt) LFletcher(3) 3 30
(MJPolglase) *a rr* **40/1**

33 **12** *nk* **Galloway Mac**[21] [613] 4-9-10 MTebbutt 4 29
(WAO'Gorman) *stdd s and bhd: wd st: rdn and swtchd to stands rails 2f out: nvr a factor* **9/2**[1]

**13** *23* **Royal Shepley** 3-8-4 ANicholls 13 —
(JBalding) *s.i.s: a b ehind* **33/1**

1m 15.82s (-0.98) **Going Correction** -0.075s/f (Stan)

**WFA** 3 from 4yo 15lb **13** Ran SP% **118.7**

Speed ratings: **103,98,97,97,95 95,91,91,90,87 86,86,55**CSF £39.89 TOTE £10.30: £4.30, £1.70, £3.60; EX 43.30.

**Owner** Trevor Sleath **Bred** Juddmonte Farms **Trained** Southwell, Notts

**FOCUS**

An open-looking maiden, and fair sprint form overall.

**NOTEBOOK**

**Skip Of Colour** turned this into a procession. Despite a middle-distance pedigree, he has not been getting home over farther and appreciated the drop back to sprinting. Eased down inside the last, he was value for double the winning distance, and looks sure to take plenty of beating if turned out under a penalty.

**Zak Facta(IRE)**, who has been tried over a variety of trips and is fully exposed, brought home the main field.

**Largs**, who was running here for the first time, was suited by the fast pace and managed to secure minor place money.

**Dark Champion** is another exposed performer who invariably finds at least one or two too good.

**Otylia** had been well beaten on her only previous start on Fibresand and was returning from a four-month layoff. In the circumstances she did not run too badly.

**Mission Affirmed(USA)** was the one for money, but he looked to find this trip too short and is likely to be stepped up to a mile when the turf season kicks off. He needed this for a mark and was another trying to overcome an absence since October.

**Galloway Mac** was another who looked to find everything happening too quickly. He was reported by his rider as having hung right-handed throughout, and is another who should appreciate stepping back up to a mile. *Official explanation: jockey said colt hung right throughout*

**Royal Shepley** *Official explanation: jockey said filly hung left*

## 806 BET DIRECT ON ATR TEXT PAGE 413 H'CAP (DIV II) 5f (F)

**3:40** (3:42) (D) (0-80,78) 3-Y-0+ **£4,017** (£1,236; £618; £309) **Stalls** High

Form RPR

00-0 **1** **Magic Glade**[35] [511] 5-9-2 73 RThomas(5) 5 80
(CRDore) *trckd ldrs: hdwy to ld wl over 1f out: rdn and kpt on wl fnl f* **12/1**

10-4 **2** *¾* **Polish Emperor (USA)**[45] [417] 4-9-10 76 (b) EAhern 2 80
(PWHarris) *trckd ldrs: hdwy 2f out: rdn over 1f out: kpt on ins last* **10/3**[1]

1013 **3** *hd* **Time N Time Again**[4] [761] 6-9-12 78 (p) JQuinn 10 82
(EJAlston) *cl up stands rail: rdn along over wl over 1f out: drvn and kpt on ins last* **4/1**[2]

6200 **4** *½* **Far Note (USA)**[12] [680] 6-9-1 67 (b) MFenton 1 69
(SRBowring) *in tch on outer: rdn along 2f out: styd on u.p ins last* **11/2**[3]

1-63 **5** *2 ½* **Lady Pekan**[27] [578] 5-8-11 63 (b) DaneO'Neill 3 56
(PSMcentee) *led: rdn along 2f out: hdd wl over 1f out: wknd ent last* **9/1**

0-60 **6** *2 ½* **Prime Recreation**[26] [586] 7-8-12 64 GDuffield 7 48
(PSFelgate) *cl up: rdn 2f out: wknd appr last* **16/1**

4602 **7** *2 ½* **St Ivian**[12] [680] 4-9-2 68 (v) PMcCabe 4 44
(MrsNMacauley) *dwlt: sn in tch: rdn along over 2f out and sn btn* **10/1**

40-0 **8** *1* **Vanished (IRE)**[8] [721] 4-8-5 60 (b[1]) LFletcher(3) 6 32
(MJPolglase) *in tch: hdwy 1/2-way: rdn and wknd wl over 1f out* **66/1**

402- **9** *1 ¼* **Roman Quintet (IRE)**[59] [6221] 4-8-11 63 (t) SWhitworth 8 31
(DWPArbuthnot) *s.i.s: a rr* **15/2**

0-02 **10** *11* **Prince Of Blues (IRE)**[27] [578] 6-8-13 65 (p) JPSpencer 9 —
(MMullineaux) *chsd ldrs: rdn along after 2f: sn outpcd and bhd* **9/1**

60.39 secs (0.09) **Going Correction** +0.125s/f (Slow) **10** Ran SP% **114.4**

Speed ratings: **104,102,102,101,97 93,89,88,86,68**CSF £50.90 CT £195.48 TOTE £12.30: £2.90, £1.40, £2.20; EX 70.80.

**Owner** P O'Gorman **Bred** Juddmonte Farms **Trained** West Pinchbeck, Lincs

■ Stewards Enquiry : E Ahern two-day ban: used whip with excessive frequency and without giving gelding time to respond (Feb 28-29)

**FOCUS**

The time of the race made this marginally the slower of the two divisions. Nevertheless the form looks reliable.

**NOTEBOOK**

**Magic Glade** was a useful three-year-old handicapper for Roger Charlton back in 2002, but was absent for over a year before having his first start for his current stable back in November. He will still be well handicapped based on his best turf form after being reassessed for this victory, so there could be more to come from him.

**Polish Emperor(USA)**, dropping back to his optimum trip, ran well in defeat but had a hard race in the process.

**Time N Time Again** is being kept busy but is maintaining his form very well. Consequently he is unlikely to get any peace from the Handicapper in the near future.

**Far Note(USA)** was weighted to reverse last month's placings with Time N Time Again but, racing on the outside, he hung right and could never quite get on terms with the leaders. *Official explanation: jockey said gelding hung right*

**Lady Pekan** now looks in the grip of the Handicapper.

**Prime Recreation** has not run up to his best on the All-Weather for two years.

**Prince Of Blues(IRE)** *Official explanation: jockey said gelding struck its head on the stalls*

## 807 BET DIRECT ON 0800 32 93 93 (S) STKS 7f (F)

**4:10** (4:10) (G) 3-Y-0+ **£2,583** (£738; £369) **Stalls** Low

Form RPR

3262 **1** **Feast Of Romance**[8] [723] 7-10-0 56 (b) JPSpencer 6 53+
(PHowling) *hld up: smooth hdwy 3f out: rdn over 1f out: styd on to ld ins last* **6/4**[1]

-402 **2** *1 ¼* **Silver Mascot**[15] [658] 5-9-9 40 FLynch 9 45
(RHollinshead) *led and sn clr: rdn wl over 1f out: wknd and hdd ins last* **7/1**

05-2 **3** *½* **Emperor Cat (IRE)**[7] [732] 3-8-7 58 ow1 DNolan(5) 4 50
(PABlockley) *chsd ldrs: hdwy over 2f out: rdn to chse ldr wl over 1f out: sn drvn and one pce* **5/1**[2]

4532 **4** *4* **Larky's Lob**[1] [799] 5-9-6 47 LFletcher(3) 3 34
(PaulJohnson) *s.i.s and bhd: swtchd rt and hdwy 3f out: rdn 2f out: kpt on same pce* **11/2**[3]

00-0 **5** *8* **Mystery Mountain**[14] [670] 4-9-9 53 MartinDwyer 1 14
(MrsJRRamsden) *trckd ldrs: hdwy on inner to chse wnr 3f out: sn rdn and wknd 2f out* **8/1**

004- **6** *1 ½* **Brillyant Dancer**[27] [3890] 6-9-4 40 GDuffield 2 5
(MrsADuffield) *prom: rdn along 1/2-way: sn wknd* **14/1**

00- **7** *9* **Jacks Delight**[150] [5081] 4-9-9 JFanning 7 —
(BDLeavy) *chsd ldrs: rdn along 3f out: wknd 2f out* **66/1**

03-0 **8** *2* **Dil**[21] [612] 9-9-9 45 JoannaBadger 8 —
(MrsNMacauley) *sn outpcd and bhd* **16/1**

053/ **9** *2 ½* **Willyever**[154] [4979] 10-9-9 (vt) EAhern 5 —
(FJBowles, Ire) *in tch: rdn along 1/2-way: sn wknd* **16/1**

1m 30.19s (-0.61) **Going Correction** -0.075s/f (Stan)

**WFA** 3 from 4yo+ 17lb **9** Ran SP% **115.6**

Speed ratings: **100,98,98,93,84 82,72,70,67**CSF £12.59 TOTE £2.00: £1.30, £2.30, £2.00; EX 15.20.There was no bid for the winner.

**Owner** D C Patrick **Bred** Aramstone Stud **Trained** Newmarket, Suffolk

**FOCUS**

An moderate seller, with the winner not having to run to his best to score.

**NOTEBOOK**

**Feast Of Romance**, on whom Spencer had got to the front too soon last time, was delivered with perfect timing on this occasion to win his first race at this track for over four years. This is his grade.

**Silver Mascot**, who wore a cross-noseband, had every chance and ran a respectable race given that he would have been receiving plenty of weight from the winner had this been a handicap.

**Emperor Cat(IRE)**, the only three-year-old in the line-up, appeared to get the trip well enough and was not disgraced against his elders.

**Larky's Lob**, who was having his third start in the space of three days, missed the break and hung right-handed on the bend according to his rider. *Official explanation: jockey said, regarding the running and riding, his orders were to settle behind leaders - as gelding can be keen - but gelding cocked its jaw as stalls opened and lost ground, then took hold of the bit in the back straight before hanging right around the bend, hung left when asked for an effort early in the home straight and was unable to keep pace with the first three in the closing stages; trainer's representative added that this was the gelding's third run in three days*

**Mystery Mountain** was soon beaten when the race began in earnest.

## 808 LITTLEWOODS BET DIRECT MAIDEN H'CAP (DIV II) 1m (F)

**4:40** (4:41) (F) (0-60,60) 3-Y-O **£2,926** (£836; £418) **Stalls** Low

Form RPR

0-30 **1** **Dispol Veleta**[28] [569] 3-9-0 53 JFanning 11 68+
(TDBarron) *hld up in tch: smooth hdwy to chal 2f out: rdn to ld wl over 1f out: r.o wl* **11/2**

404- **2** *5* **Bond Moonlight**[133] [5443] 3-9-7 60 FLynch 7 64
(BSmart) *cl up: led wl over 2f out: rdn and hdd wl over 1f out: drvn and kpt on same pce fnl f* **4/1**[1]

-645 **3** *2 ½* **Sonderborg**[14] [660] 3-8-10 49 (p) GCarter 4 48
(GLMoore) *chsd ldrs: rdn over 2f out: drvn and kpt on same pce appr last* **5/1**[3]

05-5 **4** *nk* **Dancing Prince (IRE)**[13] [673] 3-8-12 51 NCallan 2 49
(APJarvis) *eld up: gd hdwy and swtchd outside over 2f out: rdn over 1f out: kpt on one pce* **8/1**

-036 **5** *5* **Courant D'Air (IRE)**[5] [752] 3-7-8 40 DFentiman(7) 5 27
(PCHaslam) *led: rdn along 3f out: sn hdd and grad wknd* **5/1**[3]

00-3 **6** *1* **Cassanos (IRE)**[40] [482] 3-9-4 57 (p) MFenton 9 42
(MissGayKelleway) *in tch: rdn along over 3f out: sn wknd* **9/2**[2]

-000 **7** *2 ½* **Peace Treaty (IRE)**[8] [726] 3-7-13 38 oh7 ow1 (bt) JQuinn 10 17
(SRBowring) *towards rr: effrt and sme hdwy over 3f out: sn rdn and no imp* **33/1**

00-0 **8** *3 ½* **Bienheureux**[12] [683] 3-8-8 47 PaulEddery 3 18
(WJMusson) *in tch: hdwy on inner to chse ldng pair 3f outr: sn rdn and wknd 2f out* **12/1**

000- **9** *5* **Major Project (IRE)**[124] [5599] 3-7-6 38 oh2 ow1 DeanWilliams(7) 6 —
(PCHaslam) *s.i.s: a bhd* **33/1**

4505 **10** *6* **Casantella**[7] [736] 3-7-13 45 KGhunowa(7) 8 —
(MJPolglase) *in tch: pushed along after 3f: sn wknd and bhd* **20/1**

1m 43.24s (-1.36) **Going Correction** -0.075s/f (Stan) **10** Ran SP% **116.3**

Speed ratings: **103,98,95,95,90 89,86,83,78,72**CSF £27.12 CT £118.52 TOTE £5.70: £2.10, £2.20, £2.00; EX 28.70 Place 6 £146.46, Place 5 £53.51.

**Owner** W B Imison **Bred** B N And Mrs Toye **Trained** Maunby, N Yorks

**FOCUS**

This was the quicker of the two divisions, and a fine effort from the winner, who should be able to score under a penalty.

**NOTEBOOK**

**Dispol Veleta**, having had the obligatory three runs over sprint trips to get a mark, looked sure to appreciate the step up to a mile on her handicap debut, and so it was a little surprising to see her so weak in the market beforehand. She eventually won in style though, and as her half-sisters Dispol Jazz and Dispol Foxtrot ran well in the mud, she looks one to keep in mind for when she gets those sort of conditions on turf.

**Bond Moonlight**, in contrast to the winner, was well supported in the ring. He was probably unlucky to run into an even better handicapped rival and looks fully capable of winning a race off this mark or a little higher.

**Sonderborg** looked to be running back over her best trip, but she met a couple of well-handicapped rivals this time and did herself no favours by hanging right. *Official explanation: jockey said filly hung right*

**Dancing Prince(IRE)** was another who appeared to improve for the step up in trip and he finished nicely clear of the rest.

**Courant D'Air(IRE)**, whose best trip is proving difficult to establish, made the early running but did not get home.

**Cassanos(IRE)** was another who attracted support in the market, but he disappointed in the first-time cheekpieces.

T/Plt: £464.40 to a £1 stake. Pool: £35,470.10. 55.75 winning tickets. T/Qpdt: £47.10 to a £1 stake. Pool: £3,131.80. 49.20 winning tickets. JR

## 794 WOLVERHAMPTON (A.W) (L-H)

Tuesday, February 17

**OFFICIAL GOING: Standard changing to standard to slow after race 1 and changing to slow after race 3 (3.20)**

Wind: nil Weather: raining last 2 races

### 809 BET DIRECT NO Q 08000 93 66 93 BANDED STKS 7f (F)

2:20 (2:21) (H) 3-Y-0+ **£1,281** (£366; £183) **Stalls** High

Form RPR

4052 1 **Dancing King (IRE)**[2] [778] 8-8-13 30 PMakin(7) 1 52
(PWHiatt) *mde all: rdn clr 2f out: easily* **4/1**[2]

0000 2 *8* **Pooka's Daughter (IRE)**[8] [730] 4-9-6 35 (p) ACulhane 8 32
(JMBradley) *hld up: hdwy over 3f out: rdn and chsd wnr fnl 2f: no imp* **10/3**[1]

-035 3 *1 ½* **Countrywide Girl (IRE)**[34] [527] 5-9-1 30 PBradley(5) 12 28
(ABerry) *prom: chsd wnr over 5f out to 2f out: one pce* **11/1**

6-40 4 *shd* **Blue Maeve**[8] [730] 4-9-6 35 (b[1]) KDalgleish 10 28
(JHetherton) *s.i.s: racd wd: hdwy over 5f out: rdn over 3f out: c v wd st: one pce* **9/1**

5400 5 *nk* **Pageant**[8] [730] 7-9-6 35 (b) CCatlin 11 27
(JMBradley) *hdwy over 5f out: rdn over 4f out: outpcd over 3f out: styd on fnl f* **9/1**

-040 6 *3* **Keltic Flute**[8] [730] 5-9-3 35 (v) LisaJones(3) 3 20
(MrsLucindaFeatherstone) *prom: rdn over 3f out: wknd fnl f* **14/1**

00-0 7 *2* **Copperfields Lass**[21] [613] 5-8-13 35 (p) LTreadwell(7) 9 15
(WGMTurner) *broke wl: sn lost pl: n.d after* **12/1**

0-00 8 *1* **Leonora Truce (IRE)**[28] [572] 5-9-6 35 (b) JTate 5 12
(RPElliott) *hld up: rdn over 4f out: sn bhd* **8/1**[3]

040- 9 *2 ½* **Star Wonder**[21] [5081] 4-9-3 35 (b) DCorby(3) 2 6
(BNDoran) *sn outpcd* **40/1**

00/ 10 *shd* **Tyrrellspass (IRE)**[68] [3725] 7-9-6 35 (t) VSlattery 7 6
(JDFrost) *outpcd* **40/1**

000- 11 *5* **Culminate**[148] [5115] 7-8-13 35 (p) NataliaGemelova(7) 4 —
(JELong) *outpcd* **33/1**

6/00 12 *3* **Our Old Boy (IRE)**[9] [718] 4-9-6 35 DRMcCabe 6 —
(JAGilbert) *prom tl rdn and wknd over 3f out* **8/1**[3]

1m 34.25s (4.05) **Going Correction** +0.425s/f (Slow) **12 Ran SP% 115.8**

Speed ratings: **93,83,82,82,81 78,75,74,71,71 66,62**CSF £16.98 TOTE £3.90: £2.40, £1.10, £2.30; EX 11.40.

**Owner** P W Hiatt **Bred** M O'Leary **Trained** Hook Norton, Oxon

**FOCUS**

Decent effort for the grade from the easy winner, but poor form behind him and a modest winning time even for a contest like this.

**NOTEBOOK**

**Dancing King(IRE)** broke well from his inside draw to get the lead and once he kicked for home off the final bend the race was over. His chances of winning again totally depend on him being able to gain the early lead against poor rivals like these.

**Pooka's Daughter(IRE)** has already been twice well beaten in similar contests to this, so it was a surprise to see her start a well-backed favourite, which rather defines the standard of the contest. She ran better, but was chasing the winner in vain down the home straight.

**Countrywide Girl(IRE)** showed up prominently for the whole contest, but that is not saying a lot. She races as though she needs at least a mile, though it will be a desperate race she wins.

**Blue Maeve ♦**, in a race full of desperately bad horses, was the only one worthy of note. He was right alongside the winner turning for home when hanging so badly right that he ended up on the stands' rail, yet was still only beaten just over a length for second. This trip looks the bare minimum for him too, so if the steering can be sorted he may well show himself to be a bit better than he showed here. *Official explanation: jockey said gelding hung right-handed up the straight*

**Pageant** hit a flat spot mid-race and there was no way back from there. This trip would have been too sharp.

### 810 BET DIRECT NO Q CLAIMING STKS 1m 100y(F)

2:50 (2:50) (H) 3-Y-0+ **£1,477** (£422; £211) **Stalls** Low

Form RPR

1440 1 **Ally Makbul**[11] [695] 4-9-7 53 NPollard 9 53
(JRBest) *hld up: hdwy 5f out: led over 4f out: hdd and rdn over 2f out: led ins fnl f: drvn out* **7/2**[1]

-341 2 *2* **Grand Lass (IRE)**[8] [726] 5-9-2 50 (p) NChalmers(5) 2 49
(ASadik) *a.p: rdn over 3f out: kpt on ins fnl f* **9/2**[2]

-530 3 *½* **Bulawayo**[18] [642] 7-9-5 48 SJDonohoe(7) 6 53
(AndrewReid) *hld up: rdn over 3f out: hdwy on ins wl over 1f out: kpt on ins fnl f* **12/1**

4431 4 *½* **Sudra**[2] [782] 7-9-4 47 (b) JDO'Reilly(7) 1 51
(JO'Reilly) *plld hrd: led early: w ldr: led on bit over 2f out: rdn over 1f out: hdd and no ex ins fnl f* **7/2**[1]

6005 5 *1 ½* **Love's Design (IRE)**[8] [726] 7-9-7 45 AQuinn(5) 5 49
(MissSJWilton) *s.s: hld up in rr: stdy hdwy on ins over 4f out: rdn over 2f out: wknd towards fin* **12/1**

000- 6 *¾* **Indian Music**[225] [3052] 7-9-7 35 (p) PBradley(5) 8 47
(ABerry) *hld up: rdn over 3f out: c wd st: hdwy fnl f: nvr nrr* **33/1**

00-4 7 *5* **Earlston**[8] [723] 4-9-12 64 (t) SDrowne 7 36
(MissGayKelleway) *prom: rdn over 3f out: wknd fnl f* **5/1**[3]

0-60 8 *17* **Rivendell**[9] [713] 8-9-6 30 (t) DaleGibson 4 —
(MWigham) *sn led: rdn and hdd over 4f out: wknd over 3f out: eased whn no ch over 1f out* **11/2**

010- 9 *18* **Hymns And Arias**[123] [5621] 3-8-2 47 TWilliams 11 —
(RonaldThompson) *s.i.s: sn prom: rdn over 4f out: sn wknd: eased whn no ch fnl 2f* **25/1**

1m 56.45s (5.45) **Going Correction** +0.425s/f (Slow)

**WFA** 3 from 4yo+ 19lb **9 Ran SP% 116.8**

Speed ratings: **89,87,86,86,84 83,78,61,43**CSF £19.57 TOTE £6.20: £1.70, £2.80, £5.90; EX 41.50.The winner was claimed by Ian Emmerson for £5,000. Sudra was claimed by Declan Daly for £4,000.

**Owner** Malcolm Ward **Bred** Mill House Stud **Trained** Hucking, Kent

**FOCUS**

A terrible contest and desperately slow winning time. The form is dubious and should be treated with caution.

**NOTEBOOK**

**Ally Makbul** appeared to be going much worse than the leader turning for home, but she was the one who responded to pressure and saw the race out well despite looking around her in the home straight. All three of her wins have been here.

**Grand Lass(IRE)** consented to enter the stalls this time and ran to form, but found another drop in trip against her.

**Bulawayo**, running over a longer trip than usual, stayed on at one pace down the straight but was never going to win.

**Sudra**, weak in the market despite winning well at Southwell 48 hours earlier, travelled well in front and looked to be going much the best turning in, but then the head went up and he soon stopped to nothing. He may have done a little bit too much too soon, but has never been the most straightforward in any case.

**Love's Design(IRE)** put himself at an immediate disadvantage by giving his rivals a four-length lead at the start. He gradually got into contention and had every chance turning for home, but then quickly emptied.

**Rivendell**, not for the first time, was well backed at fancy odds and, not for the first time, despite being given a positive ride, flopped completely. *Official explanation: jockey said mare lost her action 4f out*

### 811 LITTLEWOODS BET DIRECT MEDIAN AUCTION MAIDEN STKS 1m 1f 79y(F)

3:20 (3:22) (H) 3-5-Y-0 **£1,449** (£414; £207) **Stalls** Low

Form RPR

2-65 1 **Goldbricker**[11] [695] 4-9-3 46 BSwarbrick(7) 6 50
(WMBrisbourne) *a.p: led over 4f out tl over 2f out: rdn to ld again wl over 1f out: drvn out: fin lame* **11/10**[1]

0-30 2 *hd* **Angelo's Pride**[34] [529] 3-8-3 57 CCatlin 9 50
(JAOsborne) *a.p: slt ld over 2f out tl wl over 1f out: sustained chal u.p: r.o* **13/2**[2]

0002 3 *15* **Kustom Kit For Her**[8] [729] 4-9-5 45 JBramhill 3 15
(SRBowring) *t.k.h: prom: disp ld over 3f out: rdn and wknd over 2f out* **10/1**

- 4 *1* **Certifiable** 3-8-3 SCarson 4 18
(AndrewReid) *t.k.h: prom: led 5f out: sn hdd: rdn and wknd 3f out* **11/1**

66-4 5 *2 ½* **Danum**[44] [431] 4-9-10 47 (p) ACulhane 7 14
(RHollinshead) *hld up in tch: rdn over 3f out: sn wknd* **9/1**

2-65 6 *2 ½* **Lilian**[40] [473] 4-9-5 40 (e[1]) SDrowne 8 4
(MissGayKelleway) *hld up: sme hdwy on outside over 5f out: wknd wl over 3f out* **7/1**[3]

7 *dist* **Secret Connection** 4-9-5 DaleGibson 2 —
(MWigham) *dwlt: hld up: rdn over 4f out: sn wl bhd: t.o* **14/1**

8 *3 ½* **Radmore Spirit**[14] 4-9-5 VSlattery 5 —
(GAHam) *s.s: a bhd: rdn over 4f out: sn lost tch: t.o* **66/1**

P **Laura Lea** 4-9-10 TWilliams 1 —
(RonaldThompson) *led: rdn and hdd 5f out: wknd qckly: p.u lame 4f out* **33/1**

2m 6.81s (3.91) **Going Correction** +0.425s/f (Slow)

**WFA** 3 from 4yo 21lb **9 Ran SP% 112.0**

Speed ratings: **99,98,85,84,82 80,—,—,—**CSF £8.05 TOTE £1.70: £1.10, £1.70, £2.30; EX 3.90.

**Owner** K Bennett **Bred** C A Cyzer **Trained** Great Ness, Shropshire

**FOCUS**

A fair regional maiden in relative terms, but poor in the wider sense, dominated by two horses and run in a time 0.58 seconds faster than the concluding banded stakes.

**NOTEBOOK**

**Goldbricker**, placed three times on turf, has hinted at ability on sand and showed the right sort of attitude in what became a war of attrition down the straight. Bearing in mind the class of contest, this was a fair performance to beat a much higher-rated rival and the pair were miles clear of the others.

**Angelo's Pride**, back up to a more suitable trip and the highest rated in the field, moved up to press the favourite on the turn for home and kept battling right to the line. His official mark probably means he will have to stick to contests like this if he is to win a race.

**Kustom Kit For Her**, back in trip, was close enough on the home bend but then stopped very quickly. This effort suggests she was grossly flattered by her second place here last time.

**Certifiable**, a full-brother to Violent and a half-brother to Shorts, finally managed to take part in a race after transport problems scuppering his intended debut and then he refused to enter the stalls next time. He showed up for a while before dropping away, though in fairness his stable is not noted for first-time-out winners.

**Laura Lea** *Official explanation: vet said gelding was lame behind*

### 812 BETDIRECT.CO.UK BANDED STKS 1m 4f (F)

3:50 (3:50) (H) 4-Y-0+ **£1,652** (£472; £236) **Stalls** Low

Form RPR

52F4 1 **Shatin Special**[4] [759] 4-9-0 45 (p) RFfrench 6 47
(GCHChung) *a.p: led over 2f out: drvn out* **13/2**[3]

3-6 2 *¾* **Pipssalio (SPA)**[12] [684] 7-9-3 45 (t) CCatlin 2 46
(JamiePoulton) *hld up: rdn over 6f out: hdwy wl over 1f out: styd on wl u.p ins fnl f: nt rch wnr* **6/1**[2]

40-5 3 *nk* **Bevier**[15] [652] 10-8-12 45 NChalmers(5) 9 45
(TWall) *hld up: rdn and hdwy over 3f out: styd on wl u.p ins fnl f* **10/1**

2-32 4 *1* **Diamond Orchid (IRE)**[9] [715] 4-9-0 45 (p) RFitzpatrick 8 44
(PDEvans) *led: rdn and hdd over 2f out: no ex ins fnl f* **7/4**[1]

100- 5 *2 ½* **Vitelucy**[113] [3276] 5-8-12 45 AQuinn(5) 5 40
(MissSJWilton) *mid-div: rdn and hdwy over 5f out: outpcd 3f out: kpt on again fnl f* **12/1**

-056 6 *11* **Think Quick (IRE)**[8] [726] 4-8-7 35 RKennemore(7) 3 24
(RHollinshead) *bhd fnl 3f* **33/1**

04-0 7 *5* **San Marco (IRE)**[8] [724] 6-9-3 45 (b) ACulhane 11 16
(MrsPSly) *s.i.s: hld up: rdn over 3f out: sn bhd* **13/2**[3]

000/ 8 *hd* **Cooling Castle (FR)**[67] [5364] 8-8-10 35 SJDonohoe(7) 1 16
(RonaldThompson) *prom: rdn over 5f out: wknd over 3f out* **25/1**

60-5 9 *nk* **Port Moreno (IRE)**[9] [716] 4-9-0 45 (b[1]) RHavlin 10 15
(JGMO'Shea) *hld up: hdwy 5f out: rdn and wknd over 3f out* **12/1**

0-00 10 *25* **Platinum Boy (IRE)**[12] [682] 4-9-0 45 (p) VSlattery 4 —
(MWellings) *prom: rdn over 5f out: wknd 4f out: t.o* **50/1**

0/ **11** *11* **Angiolini (USA)**[103] 3823 7-9-3 35 ........ SDrowne 7 —
(AEJones) *s.i.s: a bhd: t.o fnl 6f* **11/1**

2m 46.89s (5.39) **Going Correction** +0.425s/f (Slow)
**WFA** 4 from 5yo+ 3lb **11** Ran SP% **118.9**
Speed ratings: **99,98,98,97,95 88,85,85,84,68 60**CSF £45.10 TOTE £6.90: £1.80, £2.40, £4.10; EX 59.80.
**Owner** Peter Tsim **Bred** Loan And Development Corporation **Trained** Newmarket, Suffolk

**FOCUS**
A fair pace and a reasonable time for this banded stakes. The form is typical for the grade.

**NOTEBOOK**
**Shatin Special**, a maiden after 22 starts coming into this, was effectively dropping in class with this being her first appearance in a banded stakes. Never far away, she got the better of the favourite turning in and, although she got tired in the straight, she had established enough of an advantage to hold on.
**Pipssalio(SPA)** was off the bridle and going nowhere with nearly a circuit left to race, but then got his second wind and made up a huge amount of ground to get as close as he did. His proximity may have been exaggerated by the leaders tiring though, and he looks a far from easy ride.
**Bevier**, a winner over nine furlongs here a year ago, finished strongly from off the pace but, like the runner-up, that may have been an illusion caused by the front-runners tiring, so the form should not be taken at face value.
**Diamond Orchid(IRE)**, a quirky sort, was able to establish a comfortable lead, but as soon as the winner loomed alongside on the home turn she was in trouble. This trip may be a bit too far.
**Vitelucy**, a winner over further on Polytrack and over two and a half miles over hurdles, was inclined to run in snatches and in her case this may have been an insufficient test of stamina.

## 813 BET DIRECT ON SKY TEXT PAGE 372 BANDED STKS 6f (F)
4:20 (4:22) (H) 3-Y-O+ **£1,459** (£417; £208) **Stalls** Low

Form RPR
0-30 **1** **Evangelist (IRE)**[22] 608 4-9-7 40 ........ (vt[1]) SDrowne 11 45
(MrsStefLiddiard) *mid-div: rdn over 3f out: hdwy on outside over 2f out: led ins fnl f: r.o* **6/1**
0231 **2** *1 ½* **Enjoy The Buzz**[8] 728 5-9-6 40 ........ CJDavies(7) 2 47
(JMBradley) *s.i.s: rdn and hdwy 3f out: led wl over 1f out tl ins fnl frulong: nt qckn* **5/1**[2]
0-53 **3** *1 ¼* **Sotonian (HOL)**[18] 637 11-9-4 40 ........ LisaJones(3) 7 37
(PSFelgate) *led early: a.p: rdn and ev ch over 1f out: no ex ins fnl f* **9/2**[1]
0060 **4** *2 ½* **Flying Faisal (USA)**[14] 665 6-9-7 40 ........ CCatlin 10 29
(JMBradley) *sn bhd: hdwy over 1f out: nt rch ldrs* **11/1**
5-33 **5** *1 ¼* **Bells Boy's**[28] 572 5-9-7 40 ........ (b[1]) GParkin 3 26
(KARyan) *prom: rdn over 2f out: edgd lft over 1f out: wknd ins fnl f* **11/2**[3]
0-05 **6** *1* **Lion's Domane**[15] 658 7-9-2 40 ........ PBradley(5) 6 23
(ABerry) *prom: led over 4f out: rdn and hdd 2f out: wknd ins fnl f* **13/2**
0-00 **7** *nk* **Levelled**[1] 794 10-9-7 40 ........ ACulhane 4 22
(DWChapman) *prom: led briefly 2f out: wknd ins fnl f* **10/1**
-040 **8** *1 ½* **Sweet Coral (FR)**[19] 627 4-9-7 40 ........ (b[1]) KDalgleish 8 17
(BSRothwell) *a bhd* **8/1**
6-06 **9** *2 ½* **Ejay**[8] 728 5-9-0 40 ........ MHalford(7) 1 10
(JulianPoulton) *s.i.s: a bhd* **16/1**
0/50 **10** *8* **Magic Eagle**[28] 572 7-9-4 40 ........ LEnstone(3) 5 —
(PTMidgley) *sn led: hdd over 2f out: sn wknd* **20/1**

1m 18.1s (2.40) **Going Correction** +0.425s/f (Slow) **10** Ran SP% **117.0**
Speed ratings: **101,99,97,94,92 91,90,88,85,74**CSF £36.25 TOTE £9.90: £2.70, £2.00, £1.80; EX 34.90.
**Owner** Valley Fencing **Bred** Michael And Fiona O'Connor **Trained** Great Shefford, Berks

**FOCUS**
A modest line-up typical of the grade, but a run at a good gallop and a creditable winning time.

**NOTEBOOK**
**Evangelist(IRE)**, challenging widest and latest of all, came through with a strong finish to end a long losing run. The first-time combination of a visor and a tongue tie may have been the key, as was the drop back to six. If the headgear works a second time she has the ability to win again at this level.
**Enjoy The Buzz**, despite a slow start, gradually forged his way back into contention and hit the front in plenty of time, but had no answer to the winner's late thrust. His rider did absolutely nothing wrong.
**Sotonian(HOL)**, has been around the track a few times and probably ran up to his best, but he has never won beyond the minimum trip in his long career.
**Flying Faisal(USA)** stayed on in the closing stages to snatch fourth, but he has never been an easy horse to predict and a record of four wins from 62 starts is not great.
**Bells Boy's** had every chance, but is probably better over the minimum trip and remains a maiden after 20 attempts.

## 814 BET DIRECT IN VISION SKY PAGE 293 BANDED STKS 1m 1f 79y(F)
4:50 (4:50) (H) 3-Y-O+ **£1,452** (£415; £207) **Stalls** Low

Form RPR
00-6 **1** **Wilson Bluebottle (IRE)**[45] 425 5-9-9 40 ........ (b) DaleGibson 11 51
(MWEasterby) *plld hrd: led after 1f: clr whn rdn over 1f out: r.o wl* **6/4**[1]
0-03 **2** *3 ½* **Unsuited**[15] 652 5-9-2 40 ........ NataliaGemelova(7) 8 44
(JELong) *hdwy over 6f out: rdn to chse wnr over 3f out: no imp fnl 2f* **14/1**
040- **3** *2* **Nassau Street**[80] 6089 4-9-9 40 ........ (v[1]) CCatlin 13 40
(DJSFfrenchDavis) *bhd tl rdn and hdwy on outside 3f out: one pce fnl 2f* **16/1**
/20- **4** *3 ½* **Time Marches On**[155] 4948 6-9-9 40 ........ ACulhane 6 33
(MrsMReveley) *bhd tl hdwy over 1f out: nrst fin* **9/1**[3]
-646 **5** *1 ¼* **High Diva**[14] 666 5-9-9 40 ........ NPollard 5 31
(JRBest) *hld up: hdwy over 4f out: sn rdn: wknd over 2f out* **7/1**[2]
-506 **6** *¾* **Vermilion Creek**[15] 653 5-9-2 30 ........ (p) StephanieHollinshead(7) 12 30
(RHollinshead) *bhd tl hdwy over 1f out: n.d* **7/1**[2]
00-0 **7** *9* **Greenborough (IRE)**[11] 653 6-9-9 30 ........ (p) RFfrench 3 12
(MrsPFord) *chsd ldrs: rdn over 5f out: wknd over 4f out* **33/1**
0306 **8** *3 ½* **Haithem (IRE)**[2] 778 7-9-6 40 ........ (e) LisaJones(3) 7 5
(DShaw) *a bhd* **10/1**
0-04 **9** *3* **Amanpuri (GER)**[15] 652 6-9-9 40 ........ SDrowne 2 —
(MissGayKelleway) *led 1f: chsd wnr tl rdn over 4f out: wknd over 3f out* **10/1**
00/6 **10** *½* **Hinchley Wood (IRE)**[10] 702 5-9-6 40 ........ LEnstone(3) 9 —
(JRBest) *prom: rdn to chse wnr over 4f out tl over 3f out: wknd over 2f out* **10/1**
00-0 **11** *1 ½* **Ynys**[28] 567 3-8-2 35 ........ DKinsella 1 —
(BPalling) *a bhd* **25/1**
000- **12** *dist* **Countrywide Star (IRE)**[390] 372 6-9-9 40 ........ KDalgleish 10 —
(CNKellett) *s.i.s: sn prom: wknd over 4f out: t.o* **33/1**

2m 7.39s (4.49) **Going Correction** +0.425s/f (Slow)
**WFA** 3 from 4yo+ 21lb **12** Ran SP% **124.6**
Speed ratings: **97,93,92,89,87 87,79,76,73,73 71,**—CSF £26.64 TOTE £2.70: £1.70, £3.90, £4.00; EX 25.90 Place 6 £29.45, Place 5 £16.55.
**Owner** Bert and Dilys Kelly **Bred** Bernard Colclough **Trained** Sheriff Hutton, N Yorks

**FOCUS**
A modest and rather uncompetitive contest, but fair form for the grade from the winner.

**NOTEBOOK**
**Wilson Bluebottle(IRE)**, very well backed, was able to gain an uncontested lead and, despite pulling very hard in front, had little trouble putting daylight between himself and his rivals. The form means little however, and he will be fortunate to be allowed his own way like this every time.
**Unsuited** was in vain pursuit of the winner from the home bend, and probably ran to a similar level of form to when making her debut on the surface last time. Her chances of finally winning a race depend on her finding an even easier race than this.
**Nassau Street** ♦, whose best effort in three previous starts came over course and distance, was out the back early but picked off rival after rival as the race progressed. He even looked like possibly getting on terms with the winner entering the straight before his effort flattened out. He is the one to take from this poor race as he still has a little scope, and this effort also suggests he is worth another try over further.
**Time Marches On** had only managed one outing in the past ten months and this effort should have put him right for a return to hurdles.
**High Diva** has become incredibly hard to win with and her best trip is still uncertain.
**Vermilion Creek** has become very disappointing.
KH

# [787]LINGFIELD (L-H)
Wednesday, February 18

**OFFICIAL GOING: Standard**
Wind: mod across Weather: fine but cloudy

## 815 LITTLEWOODS BET DIRECT H'CAP 1m (P)
1:20 (1:20) (F) (0-52,58) 4-Y-O+ **£2,947** (£842; £421) **Stalls** High

Form RPR
0-40 **1** **Alafzar (IRE)**[7] 738 6-9-1 52 ........ (bt[1]) KFallon 2 60
(PDEvans) *trckd ldrs: plld out and effrt over 1f out: cajoled along to ld ins fnl f: in command after* **3/1**[1]
-000 **2** *¾* **Steely Dan**[7] 738 5-8-13 50 ........ NPollard 10 56
(JRBest) *pressed ldrs: rdn to ld wl over 1f out: hdd and one pce ins fnl f* **7/1**[3]
00-1 **3** *nk* **Balerno**[34] 533 5-9-0 51 ........ GCarter 11 56
(RIngram) *hld up: last over 2f out: prog on outer over 1f out: styd on ins fnl f: nvr able to chal* **7/1**[3]
100- **4** *nk* **Ranny**[110] 5856 4-8-10 50 ........ RMiles(3) 9 55
(DrJDScargill) *t.k.h: trckd ldrs: effrt on wd outside wl over 1f out: one pce fnl f* **25/1**
0-21 **5** *shd* **Kinsman (IRE)**[7] 738 7-9-4 58 6ex ........ (b) J-PGuillambert(3) 6 62
(TDMccarthy) *stdd s: hld up in rr: effrt over 1f out: shkn up and nt qckn fnl f* **11/2**[2]
-316 **6** *shd* **Piquet**[11] 701 6-8-13 50 ........ GBaker 4 54?
(JJBridger) *hld up in rr: effrt over 1f out: cajoled along and nt qckn fnl f* **11/2**[2]
0-54 **7** *1 ¾* **Raheel (IRE)**[25] 601 4-8-12 49 ........ (t) JFanning 8 49
(PMitchell) *s.i.s: sn trckd ldrs: rdn to ld briefly 2f out: wknd fnl f* **10/1**
000- **8** *½* **Galey River (USA)**[149] 5122 5-8-10 47 ........ NCallan 1 46
(JJSheehan) *led for 1f: styd cl up: rdn and lost pl wl over 2f out: no prog over 1f out* **16/1**
54-0 **9** *nk* **Balmacara**[35] 520 5-8-11 48 ........ (p) IMongan 5 46
(MissKBBoutflower) *w ldrs: led over 3f out to 2f out: wknd u.p* **10/1**
0-06 **10** *3* **Angelica Garnett**[35] 520 4-8-7 49 ........ (e[1]) AQuinn(5) 3 40
(TEPowell) *plld hrd: led after 1f to over 3f out: wknd over 2f out* **25/1**
000 **11** *4* **Mister Clinton (IRE)**[25] 602 7-8-13 50 ........ (tp) DaneO'Neill 7 32
(DKIvory) *dwlt: hld up: effrt on wd outside 3f out: wknd wl over 1f out* **14/1**

1m 40.65s (1.14) **Going Correction** +0.025s/f (Slow) **11** Ran SP% **119.2**
Speed ratings: **95,94,93,93,93 93,91,91,90,87 83**CSF £24.28 CT £137.52 TOTE £3.40: £1.80, £2.60, £3.10; EX 35.50.
**Owner** Waterline Racing Club **Bred** His Highness The Aga Khan's Studs S C **Trained** Pandy, Gwent

**FOCUS**
A steadily run race and a slow winning time for the grade, but the form looks fair and reliable.

**NOTEBOOK**
**Alafzar(IRE)** had a set of blinkers on for the first time rather than the visor which he had worn on his last two starts and, with Fallon replacing a less-experienced rider, he found the necessary improvement. He is often held up way off the pace, but off this steady gallop those tactics would have found him in trouble.
**Steely Dan**, running off a career-low mark, benefited from running up with the pace off a slow gallop. He stole a march on the others early in the straight but could not hold off the winner inside the last.
**Balerno** was done no favours by the way the race was run as he was held up towards the rear off the steady pace. He still looks fairly handicapped and will have chances off his current mark in a more strongly-run race.
**Ranny** did not run too badly on her Polytrack debut and first outing since October. It would not be a surprise if she improved for this run.
**Kinsman(IRE)** was another who did not have the race run to suit. He is difficult to win with at the best of times but off a steady pace things are even more tricky.
**Piquet** was yet another unsuited by the way the race was run.

## 816 BETDIRECT.CO.UK MAIDEN STKS 7f (P)
1:50 (1:52) (D) 3-Y-O **£4,104** (£1,263; £631; £315) **Stalls** Low

Form RPR
**1** **Saint Etienne (IRE)** 3-8-9 ........ MartinDwyer 5 55+
(AMBalding) *mde all: pushed along whn lft wl clr over 1f out: unchal after : rdn out* **5/2**[1]
00 **2** *3* **Alfridini**[25] 597 3-9-0 ........ DaneO'Neill 12 53
(DRCElsworth) *dwlt: rcvrd to midfield over 4f out but nt on terms w ldrs: rdn and effrt 3f out: styd on wl to take 2nd last strides* **16/1**
4-40 **3** *nk* **Little Eye (IRE)**[11] 704 3-9-0 66 ........ NPollard 16 52
(JRBest) *chsd ldrs: rdn and effrt over 2f out: carried bdly rt after bnd wl over 1f out: chsd wnr 1f out: edgd lft: lost 2nd fin* **8/1**
00-0 **4** *1 ¼* **Hazewind**[28] 574 3-8-9 51 ow2 ........ SJDonohoe(7) 11 51
(PDEvans) *racd in midfield and nt on terms w ldrs: rdn and prog wl over 1f out: styd on wl fnl f* **100/1**
0- **5** *3 ½* **Instinct**[172] 4576 3-9-0 ........ PDobbs 2 40+
(RHannon) *trckd ldrs gng easily: hanging rt fr 1/2-way: chsd wnr 2f out: hung bdly rt bnd wl over 1f out: nt rcvr* **11/4**[2]
406- **6** *hd* **La Petite Chinoise**[170] 4612 3-8-9 69 ........ KFallon 7 35+
(RGuest) *sn rdn to chse wnr to 3f out: stl in contention but under presssure whn carried bdly rt over 1f out: wknd* **13/2**
2-53 **7** *1 ¼* **Phluke**[15] 668 3-9-0 70 ........ SCarson 14 37+
(RFJohnsonHoughton) *pressed ldrs: rdn to press wnr 3f out to 2f out: carried bdly rt over 1f out: wknd* **6/1**[3]

0-20 **8** *4* **Redbank (IRE)**[14] [675] 3-9-0 60 ........ PaulEddery 13 27
(SDow) *settled off the pce in midfield: nudged along over 1f out: nvr nr ldrs* **16/1**

**9** *1 3/4* **Forge Lane (IRE)** 3-9-0 ........ JQuinn 3 22
(CWeedon) *s.s: in rr gp and sn wl bhd: no prog tl r.o fnl f* **33/1**

**10** *3* **Fly So High** 3-8-2 ........ DawnWatson(7) 15 —
(DShaw) *s.s: wl bhd in rr gp: modest late prog* **33/1**

00- **11** *1 1/4* **Genuinely (IRE)**[109] [5869] 3-8-9 ........ MFenton 4 —
(WJMusson) *sn struggling and wl bhd in rr gp: nvr a factor* **40/1**

**12** *3* **Accendere** 3-9-0 ........ MTebbutt 1 —
(RMBeckett) *a in rr and off the pce: struggling 4f out* **33/1**

0 **13** *2 1/2* **Midnight Promise**[22] [613] 3-9-0 ........ DeanMcKeown 9 —
(JAGlover) *t.k.h: chsd ldrs for 3f: sn wknd: fin lame* **66/1**

050- **14** *3* **Three Welshmen**[203] [3694] 3-9-0 65 ........ SDrowne 6 —
(BRMillman) *racd in midfield and off the pce: wknd over 2f out* **25/1**

00- **15** *5* **Eunice Choice**[133] [5448] 3-8-11 ........ RMiles(3) 10 —
(MJHaynes) *a in rr gp and wl bhd* **100/1**

1m 25.34s (-0.66) **Going Correction** +0.025s/f (Slow) **15** Ran SP% **124.3**
Speed ratings: **104,100,100,98,94 94,93,88,86,83 81,78,75,72,66**CSF £43.18 TOTE £2.60: £1.10, £5.30, £2.80; EX 53.50.
**Owner** G W Chong **Bred** Robinski Bloodstock Limited **Trained** Kingsclere, Hants

**FOCUS**

A race marred by the trouble caused by Instinct, but Saint Etienne recorded a decent time and is likely to rate a lot higher in due course.

**NOTEBOOK**

**Saint Etienne(IRE)**, although no doubt aided by the fact that her main rivals were effectively taken out by Instinct, still impressed in running out an easy winner on her racecourse debut. She is held in some regard at home and she looks sure to go on to better things despite the fact that the bare form does not amount to much.
**Alfridini** is flattered by his finishing position as he missed all the trouble caused by Instinct. He shapes as though he will be suited by farther in handicap company.
**Little Eye(IRE)**, dropping back in trip, was one of the main sufferers of Instinct's actions early in the straight. He is an exposed performer, though, so the fact that he could still finish third does not say a lot for the value of the form.
**Hazewind**, stuffed in his three previous maidens, ran by far his best race to date, underlining the modest level of the form.
**Instinct**, who drifted right on his debut, hung badly right on this occasion, hampering a number of his rivals in the process. *Official explanation: jockey said gelding hung right in the final straight*
**La Petite Chinoise** was under pressure when hampered. She does not have the scope of some of her rivals.
**Forge Lane(IRE)** needed this race experience-wise and should benefit from the outing.
**Midnight Promise** *Official explanation: jockey said gelding finished lame*

## 817 BET DIRECT CLAIMING STKS 7f (P)
**2:20** (2:22) (F) 3-Y-O **£2,968** (£848; £424) **Stalls** Low

Form RPR

3-63 **1** **Fission**[12] [696] 3-8-10 72 ........(b) EAhern 14 64
(JAOsborne) *wl plcd: trckd ldr over 2f out: led over 1f out: rdn and styd on wl fnl f* **6/1**[3]

60-1 **2** *1 1/4* **Jaolins**[7] [744] 3-8-6 52 ........ RSmith 5 57
(RHannon) *dwlt: hld up towards rr: prog fr 3f out: jnd wnr over 1f out: jockey dropped whip ent fnl f: nt qckn after* **11/2**[2]

0425 **3** *2* **Lady Piste (IRE)**[7] [744] 3-7-9 55 ........(vt) BSwarbrick(7) 15 48
(PDEvans) *racd wd: plld hrd and sn restrained towards rr: prog 2f out: styd on wl u.p fr over 1f out: nrst fin* **14/1**

5-00 **4** *3/4* **City Affair**[23] [606] 3-8-9 55 ow3 ........(p) SJDonohoe(7) 11 60
(MrsLCJewell) *hld up in midfield: rdn and prog over 2f out: chsd ldrs over 1f out: one pce fnl f* **33/1**

-210 **5** *3/4* **Ever Cheerful**[32] [557] 3-8-6 73 ........(p) CHaddon(7) 6 55
(WGMTurner) *t.k.h: w ldr: led 3f out: hdd and no ex over 1f out* **8/1**

2-35 **6** *1 1/4* **Good Vibrations**[19] [640] 3-8-6 51 ........ JQuinn 3 44
(PFICole) *dwlt: plld hrd and sn in tch: rdn and effrt over 2f out: no prog u.p over 1f out* **7/1**

60 **7** *2* **Never Cried Wolf**[21] [621] 3-9-5 ........ DaneO'Neill 4 52
(DRCElsworth) *s.v.s: racd wl in rr: drvn and stl in last trio over 1f out: styd on fnl f* **33/1**

2462 **8** *shd* **Stamford Blue**[7] [744] 3-8-0 53 ........(b) DerekNolan(7) 12 40
(JSMoore) *plld hrd and restrained into midfield: rdn over 2f out: sn no prog and btn* **8/1**

654- **9** *shd* **Averami**[51] [6250] 3-8-10 68 ........ MartinDwyer 7 42
(AMBalding) *hld up towards rr: no ch whn nt clr run over 1f out: one pce after* **8/1**

00 **10** *1/2* **Fora Smile**[12] [696] 3-8-11 ........ ADaly 13 42
(MDIUsher) *plld hrd early: restrained and sn wl in rr: drvn in last trio over 1f out: one pce* **100/1**

06-0 **11** *1/2* **Stonor Lady (USA)**[7] [741] 3-8-4 56 ........(v1) PaulEddery 8 34
(PWD'Arcy) *led to 3f out: wknd rapidly over 2f out* **25/1**

-064 **12** *1* **Dulce De Leche**[8] [732] 3-8-10 57 ........(be) BReilly(5) 2 42
(SCWilliams) *prom tl wknd rapidly over 2f out* **14/1**

1-50 **13** *1 1/4* **Must Be So**[35] [521] 3-8-2 48 ........ NPollard 1 26
(JJBridger) *nvr on terms w ldrs: rdn and no prog 2f out* **25/1**

00-0 **14** *nk* **Out Of My Way**[46] [420] 3-8-0 35 ........ RBrisland 9 23
(TMJones) *a towards rr: struggling 3f out* **100/1**

-504 **15** *1/2* **Garrigon**[7] [741] 3-8-12 60 ........(b1) LisaJones(3) 10 36
(NPLittmoden) *rel to r and lft 15l: rcvrd after 2f: rdn and brief effrt on outer 3f out: sn wknd* **5/1**[1]

1m 26.57s (0.57) **Going Correction** +0.025s/f (Slow) **15** Ran SP% **121.1**
Speed ratings: **97,95,93,92,91 90,87,87,87,87 86,85,83,83,83**CSF £36.83 TOTE £4.70: £1.80, £2.30, £4.80; EX 35.20.Jaolins was claimed by P G Murphy for £8,000.
**Owner** Paul J Dixon **Bred** W N Greig **Trained** Upper Lambourn, Berks

**FOCUS**

Fair claiming form.

**NOTEBOOK**

**Fission** was best in on official ratings but all her previous form was on Fibresand and a question remained of how she would handle this quicker surface. In the event she had little trouble with it, but the form of this race suggests she is greatly flattered by her current rating of 72.
**Jaolins** was a winner of a seller over six last time but got this longer trip well. She had plenty to find with the winner on ratings so this was a good performance, and she may have given her more of a fight had her rider not dropped his whip with a furlong to run.
**Lady Piste(IRE)** got the longer trip well despite refusing to settle in the early stages. She can surely be found a small race.
**City Affair**, dropping into a claimer for the first time, ran a better race than of late, but he might have to drop into a seller to have a chance of getting off the mark.
**Ever Cheerful** had a good chance on the ratings but he did not get home and is happier over six.
**Good Vibrations**, not for the first time, did not help her cause by refusing to settle.
**Garrigon** had blinkers on for the first time but clearly resented them and lost his chance at the start. *Official explanation: jockey said, regarding the running and riding, colt planted in the stalls, lent back, dug its heels in and refused to jump, adding that when it did jump it did so awkwardly; trainer said colt was blinkered for the first time, which may have been a factor*

## 818 LITTLEWOODS BET DIRECT MAIDEN STKS 1m 4f (P)
**2:50** (2:51) (D) 3-Y-O+ **£4,124** (£1,269; £634; £317) **Stalls** Low

Form RPR

64-0 **1** **Private Benjamin**[7] [740] 4-9-10 56 ........ NCallan 4 65
(JamiePoulton) *racd in midfield: prog 4f out: effrt to ld wl over 2f out: 2l clr wl over 1f out: kpt on fnl f: jst hld on* **50/1**

043- **2** *nk* **Resonance**[81] [6087] 3-7-12 70 ........ JoannaBadger 6 60
(NATwiston-Davies) *dwlt: t.k.h and hld up in last pair: prog over 3f out: rdn to chse wnr wl over 1f out: styd on steadily: jst failed* **5/2**[1]

530- **3** *2* **Rome (IRE)**[84] [6079] 5-9-13 70 ........ DaneO'Neill 5 62
(GPEnright) *sn in midfield: prog 3f out: drvn to chse ldng pair over 1f out: styd on one pce* **7/1**

0/0 **4** *8* **Kirat**[18] [651] 6-9-13 ........ SWhitworth 9 50
(GLMoore) *wl in tch: rdn and effrt to press wnr over 2f out: wknd wl over 1f out* **33/1**

03 **5** *3* **Alisa (IRE)**[18] [651] 4-9-2 ........(t) LisaJones(3) 10 41
(BICase) *t.k.h: cl up: chsd ldr 6f out to over 4f out: sn rdn: wknd over 2f out* **10/1**

03-2 **6** *5* **Elegant Gracie (IRE)**[18] [651] 4-9-5 67 ........ KFallon 2 33
(RGuest) *cl up: led over 4f out to wl over 2f out: btn whn hmpd wl over 1f out: eased fnl f* **11/4**[2]

**7** *nk* **Cape Canaveral (IRE)**[11] [2051] 5-9-13 ........ IMongan 8 38
(GLMoore) *drvn to dispute ld first 4f: struggling and losing pl 1/2-way: no ch fnl 3f* **9/2**[3]

000- **8** *1 1/4* **Silistra**[51] [6253] 5-9-13 50 ........(v) VSlattery 7 36
(MrsLCJewell) *racd in midfield: wknd over 3f out* **66/1**

-00 **9** *6* **Spiders Web**[35] [520] 4-9-10 ........ GCarter 1 27
(TKeddy) *t.k.h: hld up in rr: wknd over 3f out* **66/1**

22U- **10** *nk* **Crown Agent (IRE)**[267] [1887] 4-9-10 75 ........ MartinDwyer 3 26
(AMBalding) *mde most to over 4f out: wknd over 3f out* **7/1**

/00- **11** *22* **Hektikos**[98] [5982] 4-9-3 57 ........ JCoffill-Brown(7) 11 —
(SDow) *racd wd: in tch to 1/2-way: t.o whn bmpd along 3f out* **50/1**

2m 35.6s (1.62) **Going Correction** +0.025s/f (Slow)
**WFA** 3 from 4yo 24lb 4 from 5yo+ 3lb **11** Ran SP% **117.4**
Speed ratings: **95,94,93,88,86 82,82,81,77,77 62**CSF £171.89 TOTE £60.60: £7.00, £1.50, £2.10; EX 184.50.
**Owner** Mrs J Wotherspoon **Bred** Mrs J Wotherspoon **Trained** Telscombe, E Sussex

**FOCUS**

A modest winning time and the form is of a similar level.

**NOTEBOOK**

**Private Benjamin** was entitled to come on for his recent outing following a three and a half month break, but he had looked exposed as moderate beforehand and his success in this race says more about the mediocrity of his opponents than it does about him.
**Resonance**, an eyecatcher last time out, has changed stables since. Again held up at the rear, though, she took a good while to get into top gear and looks as though she will be suited by a greater test of stamina
**Rome(IRE)** again looked short of pace.
**Kirat**, who had been off the track for the best part of two years before running here last month, has yet to prove he retains the ability which saw him run fifth to Quazar in a Grade Two hurdle at Aintree. *Official explanation: vet said gelding finished lame*
**Alisa(IRE)** now qualifies for a mark and it would not be a surprise to see her stepped up to two miles in handicap company.
**Elegant Gracie(IRE)** was disappointing as she had solid course form in this sort of grade to her name. She was beaten when hampered.
**Cape Canaveral(IRE)** came in for market support but was also disappointing. His rider attempted to make the running but the gelding was unable to find the necessary pace to do so.
**Crown Agent(IRE)** *Official explanation: jockey said gelding hung badly right*

## 819 BET DIRECT ON 0800 32 93 93 H'CAP 6f (P)
**3:20** (3:21) (D) (0-80,75) 3-Y-O **£3,997** (£1,230; £615; £307) **Stalls** Low

Form RPR

6-21 **1** **Toronto Heights (USA)**[14] [673] 3-9-5 **73** ........ JQuinn 6 81
(PWChapple-Hyam) *hld up bhd ldrs: trckd ldng pair over 2f out: shkn up to ld jst ins fnl f: in command after* **13/8**[1]

-020 **2** *2* **Hello Roberto**[15] [669] 3-9-7 **75** ........ JPSpencer 2 77
(MJPolglase) *hld up in last: prog 2f out: hrd rdn to chse wnr wl ins fnl f: no imp* **9/4**[2]

0061 **3** *shd* **Sahara Silk (IRE)**[6] [747] 3-8-12 **66** 6ex ........(v) DarrenWilliams 5 68
(DShaw) *led: hrd rdn and hdd jst over 1f out: kpt on again ins fnl f* **8/1**

20-0 **4** *1 1/4* **Kuringai**[21] [619] 3-8-13 **67** ........ OUrbina 3 65
(BWDuke) *trckd ldr 4f out: rdn to chal over 2f out: led jst over 1f out to jst ins fnl f: wknd* **20/1**

04-0 **5** *1 1/2* **Blade's Edge**[14] [675] 3-8-4 **58** ........ JFanning 1 51
(ABailey) *s.i.s: a in rr: dropped to last over 2f out: one pce after* **25/1**

3-50 **6** *nk* **Forzenuff**[21] [619] 3-8-8 **62** ........ DSweeney 4 55
(JRBoyle) *t.k.h: trckd ldr to 4f out: wknd 2f out* **11/1**

-400 **7** *1* **Little Flute**[8] [732] 3-7-9 **52** oh4 ........ LisaJones(3) 8 42
(TKeddy) *s.i.s: racd on outer: a towards rr: rdn and no imp 2f out* **20/1**

-001 **8** *3* **Head Of State**[8] [731] 3-8-2 **56** 6ex ........(v) JMackay 7 37
(RMBeckett) *in tch: effrt to chse ldrs over 2f out: wknd over 1f out: eased* **7/1**[3]

1m 13.1s (0.18) **Going Correction** +0.025s/f (Slow) **8** Ran SP% **114.2**
Speed ratings: **99,96,96,94,92 92,90,86**CSF £5.17 CT £20.41 TOTE £1.90: £1.10, £1.10, £3.00; EX 5.00.
**Owner** Mrs Jane Chapple-Hyam **Bred** Zubieta Ltd **Trained** Newmarket, Suffolk

**FOCUS**

Just an ordinary handicap, but a decent performance from Toronto Heights, and the form is a good standard for the time of year.

**NOTEBOOK**

**Toronto Heights(USA)** made it two out of two over this course and distance with a smooth success. He is progressing along the right lines and should be able to defy a rise in the weights.
**Hello Roberto** is well suited by this course and distance and she appeared to give her running. She is a reasonable yardstick for this type of event.
**Sahara Silk(IRE)** has only ever won over five furlongs on Southwell's Fibresand, but this was a respectable effort under very different conditions.
**Kuringai** returned to form after a couple of below-par efforts.
**Blade's Edge** did not appear suited by this drop in trip.
**Head Of State** *Official explanation: trainer said gelding was unsuited by the Lingfield surface*



The Form Book, Raceform Ltd, Compton, RG20 6NL

**820** **BET IN RUNNING @ BETDIRECT.CO.UK H'CAP** **1m 2f (P)**
**3:50** (3:50) (E) (0-75,73) 4-Y-0+ **£3,402** (£972; £486) **Stalls** Low

Form RPR
22-5 **1** **Mad Carew (USA)**[21] [618] 5-10-0 72.............................(be) SWhitworth 3 82
(GLMoore) *wl plcd: trckd ldng pair over 2f out: rdn to ld last 150y: edgd lft but sn clr* **8/1**[3]
1612 **2** *2* **Bank On Him**[7] [745] 9-9-2 60........................................ JQuinn 7 66
(CWeedon) *led: set stdy pce tl kicked on over 2f out: hdd and outpcd last 150y* **8/1**[3]
3-01 **3** *1 1/4* **True Companion**[18] [650] 5-9-5 66.............................. J-PGuillambert(3) 1 70
(NPLittmoden) *hld up in midfield: prog over 2f out: drvn to chse ldrs over 1f out: styd on one pce* **8/1**[3]
00-0 **4** *nk* **Say What You See (IRE)**[19] [643] 4-9-9 68........................... MHills 13 72
(JWHills) *trckd ldr: rdn over 2f out: unable qck wl over 1f out: one pce after* **20/1**
20-4 **5** *2 1/2* **Must Be Magic**[11] [705] 7-9-5 63.........................................(v) NCallan 12 62
(HJCollingridge) *trckd ldrs: rdn and effrt over 2f out: wknd over 1f out* **14/1**
033- **6** *nk* **Silvaline**[133] [5452] 5-9-8 66............................................ GCarter 6 65
(TKeddy) *trckd ldrs: rdn and unable qck over 2f out: fdd over 1f out* **4/1**[1]
-031 **7** *hd* **Eastborough (IRE)**[23] [605] 5-9-9 67.................................. KFallon 11 65
(BGPowell) *hld up towards rr: outpcd over 2f out: nvr nr ldrs after* **12/1**
04-2 **8** *shd* **War Owl (USA)**[36] [518] 7-8-10 57.................................. LisaJones(3) 2 55
(IanWilliams) *dwlt: plld hrd and hld up wl in rr: last over 1f out: styd on fnl f: nvr nr ldrs* **9/1**
0-25 **9** *hd* **Learned Lad (FR)**[4] [765] 6-9-10 68..................................... IMongan 14 66
(JamiePoulton) *chsd ldrs: rdn and no prog over 2f out: wknd over 1f out* **14/1**
6-15 **10** *hd* **Gingko**[32] [559] 7-9-12 70.................................................... WRyan 10 67
(PRWebber) *hld up wl in rr: outpcd over 2f out: effrt over 1f out: nvr nr ldrs* **14/1**
354- **11** *1/2* **Bally Hall (IRE)**[174] [4530] 4-10-0 73..................................... EAhern 4 69
(GABUtler) *dwlt: hld up in last: prog on outer 2f out: no imp over 1f out: hopeless task* **5/1**[2]
430- **12** *1* **Danakil**[74] [6130] 9-9-12 70................................................ CCatlin 5 65
(SDow) *hld up in rr: outpcd over 2f out: nvr nr ldrs after* **25/1**
50-0 **13** *3/4* **Mamore Gap (IRE)**[39] [494] 6-9-12 70.................................. PDobbs 8 63
(RHannon) *hld up in midfield: outpcd over 2f out: nvr nr ldrs after: grad lost pl over 1f out* **12/1**
2410 **14** *7* **Coronado Forest (USA)**[18] [650] 5-9-5 63....................... DaneO'Neill 9 44
(MRHoad) *dwlt: t.k.h: hld up in last trio: prog over 4f out: wknd over 2f out* **66/1**

2m 7.56s (0.17) **Going Correction** +0.025s/f (Slow)
**WFA** 4 from 5yo+ 1lb **14** Ran SP% **125.5**
Speed ratings: **100,98,97,97,95 94,94,94,94,94 93,93,92,86**CSF £72.47 CT £545.41 TOTE £10.20: £4.30, £2.30, £5.40; EX 89.80.
**Owner** David Allen **Bred** Pendley Farm **Trained** Woodingdean, E Sussex

**FOCUS**
A muddling pace, but the winner looks one to keep on your side and the form appears solid.

**NOTEBOOK**
**Mad Carew(USA)** shaped well on his return from a break over a mile and a half on his previous outing and confirmed that promise with a clear-cut success. This was his first win in a handicap and he is likely to be forced to step up in grade next time, but he remains worthy of respect off higher marks.
**Bank On Him** is very exposed, but remains in good heart. He loves it round Lingfield.
**True Companion** was only 4lb higher than when successful over this course and distance on his previous outing and has to be considered a little disappointing. He may be better suited by more positive tactics.
**Say What You See(IRE)** looked to be given every chance and ran better than he did at Wolverhampton on his previous outing.
**Must Be Magic** did not build on the form he showed over course and distance last time.
**Silvaline** again failed to exploit an All-Weather mark lower than that of his turf rating and has now been a beaten favourite on his last two starts.
**Bally Hall(IRE)** was given plenty to do, but found very little for pressure in any case.

**821** **BET DIRECT ON 0800 32 93 93 (S) STKS** **1m (P)**
**4:20** (4:21) (G) 3-Y-0+ **£2,562** (£732; £366) **Stalls** High

Form RPR
2001 **1** **Xaloc Bay (IRE)**[10] [717] 6-9-13 52.............................. DarrenWilliams 2 60
(BPJBaugh) *mde all: shkn up over 1f out: rdn out fnl f and a holding rivals* **8/1**[3]
000- **2** *1* **Marakash (IRE)**[84] [6073] 5-9-8 51..........................................(tp) GBaker 9 53
(MRBosley) *hld up in rr: prog fr over 2f out: rdn to chse wnr fnl f: kpt on but alway hld* **14/1**
35-4 **3** *nk* **Dolphinelle (IRE)**[11] [707] 8-9-8 47.......................................(v) IMongan 5 52
(JamiePoulton) *hld up in midfield: rdn over 2f out: prog on inner over 1f out to dispute 2nd pl fnl f: a hld* **7/1**[2]
3060 **4** *1* **Muqtadi (IRE)**[7] [738] 6-9-8 49...................................... MartinDwyer 6 50
(MQuinn) *hld up wl in rr: plenty to do 2f out: swtchd rt over 1f out: r.o fnl f: nt rch ldrs* **9/2**[1]
-143 **5** *2* **French Horn**[9] [726] 7-9-13 50...........................................(p) GCarter 7 51
(MWigham) *chsd ldrs: rdn over 2f out: nt qckn and btn over 1f out* **9/2**[1]
-000 **6** *1 1/2* **Social Contract**[9] [719] 7-9-8 47.......................................(v) CCatlin 10 42
(SDow) *prom: rdn 3f out: wknd over 1f out* **10/1**
06-0 **7** *nk* **Sholay (IRE)**[7] [740] 5-9-8 ............................................ JFanning 12 42
(PMitchell) *hld up in rr: plenty to do 2f out: sme prog over 1f out: sn btn* **10/1**
000- **8** *nk* **Ryan's Bliss (IRE)**[159] [4872] 4-9-0 55......................... J-PGuillambert(3) 3 36
(TDMccarthy) *chsd wnr: rdn 1/2-way: wknd 1f out* **25/1**
06-6 **9** *1/2* **Royal Fashion (IRE)**[11] [705] 4-8-12 58......................... NChalmers(5) 1 35
(MissSheenaWest) *prom: rdn 3f out: wknd jst over 1f out* **9/2**[1]
0 **10** *5* **Mr Dinglawi (IRE)**[11] [702] 3-8-0 ..................................(b[1]) LisaJones(3) 11 29
(DBFeek) *t.k.h: hld up in rr: rdn 1/2-way: sn struggling* **66/1**
010- **11** *11* **Dee Dee Girl (IRE)**[92] [6021] 3-8-3 53......................................... RSmith 4 5
(RHannon) *chsd ldrs to 1/2-way: sn wknd: t.o* **20/1**
00 **12** *1 3/4* **Think It Over (IRE)**[35] [519] 5-9-3 ..................................... DSweeney 8 —
(APJones) *hld up in rr: wknd rapidly fr over 2f: eased: t.o* **66/1**

1m 39.46s (-0.05) **Going Correction** +0.025s/f (Slow)
**WFA** 3 from 4yo+ 19lb **12** Ran SP% **114.6**
Speed ratings: **101,100,99,98,96 95,94,94,94,89 78,76**CSF £106.17 TOTE £9.30: £3.40, £4.30, £2.50; EX 349.30.There was no bid for the winner.
**Owner** Miss S M Potts **Bred** D J And Mrs Deer **Trained** Audley, Staffs

**FOCUS**
Just average selling form.

**NOTEBOOK**
**Xaloc Bay(IRE)**, who ended a long losing run when winning over a mile in a regional seller at Southwell on his previous outing, followed up under a well-judged ride from the front. He is at the top of his game.
**Marakash(IRE)**, dropped back from ten furlongs, and with a tongue-tie on for the first time, finished well from off the pace but proved unable to reel in the winner.
**Dolphinelle(IRE)** did not look to have any excuses.
**Muqtadi(IRE)**, very hard to win with, not for the first time looked like an unlucky loser. He is unlikely to build on this next time.
**French Horn**, another supported in the market, was a little bit disappointing.
**Royal Fashion(IRE)**, a big drifter in the market on this drop in grade and trip, was well beaten and remains on a long losing run. *Official explanation: trainer said filly was later found to be lame*

**822** **BET DIRECT ON ITV PAGE 367 H'CAP** **1m 2f (P)**
**4:50** (4:50) (E) (0-70,70) 3-Y-O **£3,325** (£950; £475) **Stalls** Low

Form RPR
63-4 **1** **Another Con (IRE)**[25] [598] 3-8-10 **59**................................ RHavlin 4 69
(MrsPNDutfield) *mde all: kicked clr 2f out: wl clr after: rdn out: unchal* **8/1**
0-06 **2** *5* **Jackie Kiely**[25] [598] 3-8-7 **59**............................................ RMiles(3) 5 60
(TGMills) *hld up in midfield: effrt whn nt clr run over 2f out: nt clr run over 1f out and swtchd rt: chsd wnr last 100y: no ch* **8/1**
0-34 **3** *1 1/2* **Ground Patrol**[21] [621] 3-9-7 **70**.................................. MartinDwyer 8 68
(AMBalding) *free to post: hld up last: nt clr run over 2f out: prog over 1f out : r.o fnl f: no ch* **9/2**[3]
51 **4** *shd* **Norwegian**[20] [628] 3-9-2 **65**............................................. JPSpencer 2 63
(DRLoder) *trckd ldrs: effrt to dispute 2nd whn n.m.r over 2f out: drvn to chse wnr 1f out to last 100y: fdd* **7/2**[2]
5-13 **5** *1 1/4* **Keepers Knight (IRE)**[21] [622] 3-9-5 **68**.............................(b[1]) KFallon 11 64
(PFICole) *chsd wnr 7f out: drvn over 3f out: nt qckn over 2f out: wknd 1f out* **5/2**[1]
60-0 **6** *2* **Lady Stripes**[14] [675] 3-8-11 **60**........................................... NCallan 1 52
(MJWallace) *hld up towards rr: effrt and nt clr run over 2f out: no ch after : kpt on* **14/1**
40-0 **7** *3* **Trompe L'Oeil (IRE)**[39] [490] 3-8-7 **63**.............................. SJDonohoe(7) 6 50
(AndrewReid) *dwlt: hld up in rr: outpcd over 2f out: no ch after* **33/1**
20-6 **8** *1* **Infidelity (IRE)**[11] [704] 3-9-4 **67**........................................ EAhern 10 52
(ABailey) *trckd ldrs: rdn over 3f out: outpcd 2f out: wknd over 1f out* **8/1**
00-3 **9** *4* **Crackleando**[46] [416] 3-8-7 **59**.................................... J-PGuillambert(3) 9 37
(NPLittmoden) *chsd wnr to 7f out: grad lost pl: wl bhd over 2f out* **20/1**
650- **10** *shd* **Stagecoach Ruby**[158] [4893] 3-7-12 **47** oh1.............................. RBrisland 7 25
(GLMoore) *hld up in rr: prog on outer over 3f out: wknd 2f out* **33/1**

2m 7.44s (0.05) **Going Correction** +0.025s/f (Slow) **10** Ran SP% **119.6**
Speed ratings: **100,96,94,94,93 92,89,88,85,85**CSF £70.50 CT £325.90 TOTE £15.50: £4.00, £2.30, £1.50; EX 117.10 Place 6 £82.12, Place 5 £46.23.
**Owner** Mrs Jasmine B Chesters **Bred** Matthew Tynan **Trained** Axmouth, Devon
■ Stewards Enquiry : K Fallon caution: careless riding

**FOCUS**
Not a bad handicap and probably a race to keep an eye on as the first four home are all lightly-raced, unexposed sorts. The winning time was also fair for the grade.

**NOTEBOOK**
**Another Con(IRE)**, well backed on her handicap debut, justified the market confidence with an impressive success. She is clearly well handicapped and could defy a rise in the weights. One to keep on your side.
**Jackie Kiely**, making his handicap debut, proved no match for the winner but ran a creditable race. There looks to be a race or two in him at a minor level.
**Ground Patrol**, stepping up from a mile on this handicap debut, did not get the clearest of runs on turning in and would have finished a little closer with better luck.
**Norwegian**, off the mark over a mile at Southwell on his previous outing, did not get a clear run on the home turn but cannot be considered unlucky. This was not a bad effort and he looks capable of improving.
**Keepers Knight(IRE)**, fitted with blinkers for the first time, was a very short price to beat some unexposed sorts and was put in his place. *Official explanation: colt was hanging to the left*
T/Plt: £168.20 to a £1 stake. Pool: £37,235.30. 161.60 winning tickets. T/Qpdt: £24.00 to a £1 stake. Pool: £3,199.20. 98.60 winning tickets. JN

## 801 SOUTHWELL (L-H)
### Thursday, February 19

**OFFICIAL GOING: Standard**
Wind: mod hlf against Weather: fine & sunny, but cold

**823** **BET DIRECT ON SKY ACTIVE APPRENTICE MAIDEN H'CAP (DIV I)** **1m (F)**
**1:40** (1:41) (F) (0-60,60) 4-Y-0+ **£2,905** (£830; £415) **Stalls** Low

Form RPR
/606 **1** **Ace-Ma-Vahra**[4] [782] 6-8-8 **45**........................................ CHaddon(5) 1 50
(SRBowring) *chsd ldrs: lost pl over 4f out: hdwy 2f out: styd on to ld last 75yds* **10/1**
060- **2** *1/2* **Middleham Park (IRE)**[13] [6202] 4-8-13 **52**................. DWakenshaw(7) 6 56
(PCHaslam) *s.i.s: sn chsng ldrs: led jst ins fnl f: hdd and nt qckn last 75yds* **11/2**[2]
6-25 **3** *1* **Magic Mamma's Too**[35] [541] 4-9-4 **53**.......... Laura-JayneCrawford(3) 8 55
(TDBarron) *trckd ldrs: led over 1f out: hdd jst ins fnl f: no ex* **6/5**[1]
060- **4** *1 1/4* **Shotley Dancer**[147] [5179] 5-8-5 **40**........................ SuzanneFrance(3) 5 40
(NBycroft) *hld up: hdwy 2f out: styd on ins last* **8/1**[3]
40-4 **5** *1/2* **Mathmagician**[4] [778] 5-7-10 **35**..............................................(b) MNem(7) 3 34
(RFMarvin) *led after 1f: qcknd clr 4f out: hdd over 1f out: wknd towards fin* **10/1**
00/0 **6** *1 1/2* **Te Anau**[4] [778] 7-7-11 **34** ow4.............................................. LauraPike(5) 4 30
(WJMusson) *trckd ldrs: lost pl 4f out: kpt on appr fnl f* **40/1**
600- **7** *5* **Crown City (USA)**[130] [5516] 4-9-2 **48**.................................... BSwarbrick 9 34
(BPJBaugh) *racd wd: hdwy to chse ldrs over 4f out: lost pl 3f out* **11/1**
0000 **8** *5* **Meticulous**[11] [713] 6-7-10 **31** ow1.............................. DeanWilliams(3) 2 7
(MCChapman) *led 1f: lost pl over 4f out* **66/1**
0/0- **9** *27* **Pertemps Wizard**[12] [562] 4-8-10 **47**.................................... BO'Neill(5) 7 —
(ADSmith) *trckd ldrs: lost pl over 4f out: sn bhd: t.o* **33/1**
56-0 **10** *1 1/2* **Tanaffus**[29] [574] 4-10-0 **60**............................................. DFentiman 10 —
(DWChapman) *unruly gng to s: s.i.s: hmpd over 4f out: sn bhd: t.o* **25/1**

1m 44.4s (-0.20) **Going Correction** -0.05s/f (Stan) **10** Ran SP% **109.2**
Speed ratings: **99,98,97,96,95 94,89,84,57,55**CSF £57.87 CT £106.33 TOTE £11.60: £2.10, £1.90, £1.10; EX 89.10.
**Owner** Stuart Burgan **Bred** S R Bowring **Trained** Edwinstowe, Notts
■ Stewards Enquiry : B O'Neill two-day ban: careless riding (Mar 1-2)

**FOCUS**
A rock bottom event and the slower of the two divisions.

**NOTEBOOK**
**Ace-Ma-Vahra**, unplaced in three starts this time afer a failure at stud, snatched it out of the fire but it was a seller in all but name.
**Middleham Park(IRE)**, last seen out over hurdles two weeks earlier, was just edged out.
**Magic Mamma's Too**, who reserves his best for here, has now been placed 13 times from 26 starts. He lacked nothing in assistance from the saddle.
**Shotley Dancer**, a maiden after 27 starts, was having her first try on the All-Weather. Tightened up leaving the back stretch, she stayed on when it was all over.
**Mathmagician**, making a quick return to action, had the blinkers back on. He tried to steal it from the front but seemed to capitulate rather readily.

## 824 BET DIRECT ON SKY ACTIVE APPRENTICE MAIDEN H'CAP (DIV II) 1m (F)
**2:10** (2:12) (F) (0-60,58) 4-Y-0+ **£2,898** (£828; £414) **Stalls** Low

Form RPR
0-44 **1** **Realism (FR)**[6] 760 4-9-7 53 PGallagher 10 73
(PWHiatt) *trckd ldrs: led 2f out: drew rt away coming to fnl f* **7/1**[3]
0-32 **2** *8* **Blakeseven**[14] 686 4-8-11 48 ARutter(5) 7 50
(WJMusson) *trckd ldrs: effrt over 2f out: kpt on same pce* **15/8**[1]
-323 **3** *hd* **Kenny The Truth (IRE)**[4] 778 5-8-5 40 (t) DawnWatson(3) 4 42
(MrsJCandlish) *chsd ldrs: lost pl over 4f out: hdwy on outer 2f out: hung lft: styd on towards fin* **11/2**[2]
3406 **4** *1* **Amanda's Lad (IRE)**[2] 805 4-8-8 45 AndrewWebb(5) 5 45
(MCChapman) *chsd ldrs: one pce fnl 2f* **25/1**
244- **5** *¾* **Jarraaf**[55] 6238 4-9-12 58 DerekNolan 8 56
(JWUnett) *rr-div: hdwy on outer over 4f out: hrd rdn 2f out: one pce* **9/1**
2504 **6** *nk* **Vlasta Weiner**[17] 658 4-8-8 40 (b) BSwarbrick 9 37
(JMBradley) *trckd ldrs on outer: edgd rt over 1f out: one pce* **10/1**
5053 **7** *3* **Mimas Girl**[4] 780 5-7-7 30 (b) CHaddon(5) 6 21
(SRBowring) *led: clr 4f out: hdd 2f out: wknd appr fnl f* **7/1**[3]
-520 **8** *5* **Phantom Flame (USA)**[10] 725 4-8-5 40 WHogg(3) 3 20
(MJohnston) *s.i.s: sme hdwy over 4f out: lost pl over 2f out* **7/1**[3]
0-00 **9** *14* **Cryptogam**[14] 684 4-8-10 47 AMullen(5) 1 —
(MESowersby) *s.s: a bhd* **66/1**
000- **10** *10* **Midges Pride**[166] 4734 4-9-0 49 DeanWilliams(3) 2 —
(MrsADuffield) *sn in rr: hrd rdn over 4f out: sn bhd* **40/1**

1m 43.16s (-1.44) **Going Correction** -0.05s/f (Stan) **10** Ran SP% **114.5**
Speed ratings: **105,97,96,95,95 94,91,86,72,62**CSF £19.87 CT £79.82 TOTE £7.90: £1.70, £1.20, £2.50; EX 21.90.
**Owner** Miss Maria McKinney **Bred** Darley Stud Management Co Ltd **Trained** Hook Norton, Oxon

**FOCUS**
A decent time for the grade, 1.24 seconds faster than the first division, and an impressive effort from the winner.

**NOTEBOOK**
**Realism(FR)**, who has taken time to get the hang of things, came right away. The form is only plating-class but connections will be hoping this signals the start of something better.
**Blakeseven** travelled nicely, but by the time his rider woke up the winner had flown.
**Kenny The Truth(IRE)** keeps running well to be placed, but the target has eluded him in 20 starts now.
**Amanda's Lad(IRE)**, having his 38th start, finds a mile the very limit of his stamina.
**Jarraaf** was having his first outing since Boxing Day.

## 825 PRESS INTERACTIVE TO BET DIRECT CLAIMING STKS 1m 4f (F)
**2:45** (2:45) (F) 4-Y-0+ **£2,870** (£820; £410) **Stalls** Low

Form RPR
2114 **1** **Bella Pavlina**[5] 777 6-8-12 56 BSwarbrick(7) 6 65
(WMBrisbourne) *trckd ldrs: rdn to ld 2f out: readily* **85/40**[2]
-555 **2** *2½* **Theatre Tinka (IRE)**[14] 682 5-9-2 62 (p) ACulhane 3 58
(RHollinshead) *trckd ldr: led 7f out tl 2f out: edgd rt: one pce* **5/2**[3]
-213 **3** *2½* **Aveiro (IRE)**[21] 629 8-8-12 51 (b) KDalgleish 1 51
(BGPowell) *led tl 7f out: one pce fnl 2f* **2/1**[1]
-666 **4** *6* **First Maite**[21] 627 11-9-2 67 JBramhill 2 46
(SRBowring) *s.i.s: sme hdwy on outer over 4f out: sn rdn: nvr on terms* **8/1**
0664 **5** *nk* **King Priam (IRE)**[4] 781 9-8-6 40 (b) DeanMcKeown 8 35
(MJPolglase) *chsd ldrs: pushed along 9f out: outpcd over 4f out: n.d after* **20/1**
44-5 **6** *23* **Many Thanks**[3] 797 4-8-12 70 (p) MFenton 4 10
(BSRothwell) *chsd ldrs: rdn over 5f out: sn outpcd: lost pl over 3f out* **16/1**
**7** *19* **Again Jane**[29] 4-8-0 PFessey 7 —
(JMJefferson) *hld up: lost pl 7f out: t.o 3f out* **66/1**

2m 41.86s (-0.24) **Going Correction** -0.05s/f (Stan)
**WFA** 4 from 5yo+ 3lb **7** Ran SP% **117.2**
Speed ratings: **98,96,94,90,90 75,62**CSF £8.28 TOTE £3.30: £2.00, £2.80; EX 8.50.Aveiro was claimed by J.T Billson for £8,000.
**Owner** The Cartmel Syndicate **Bred** C Papaioannou **Trained** Great Ness, Shropshire

**FOCUS**
Fair claiming form. The winner, back in her right class, has improved significantly this year, and this was her fourth success.

**NOTEBOOK**
**Bella Pavlina** is not very big, but she is all heart and would have been 9lb better off with the runner-up in handicap company.
**Theatre Tinka(IRE)**, who had the clear beating of the winner on official figures, will continue to struggle in handicap company until his present rating, 62, is slashed.
**Aveiro(IRE)** is fully exposed and rated up to the limit now. Connections will not have been unhappy when he was claimed.
**First Maite**, who had a stone in hand of the winner on official ratings, has yet to prove his stamina for this sort of distance and was hence a big negative on the exchanges.

## 826 BET DIRECT ON 0800 93 66 93 FILLIES' H'CAP 7f (F)
**3:20** (3:23) (E) (0-70,68) 3-Y-0+ **£3,241** (£926; £463) **Stalls** Low

Form RPR
4015 **1** **Eager Angel (IRE)**[2] 803 6-8-11 51 6ex (p) DeanMcKeown 2 60
(RFMarvin) *trckd ldrs: led appr fnl f: r.o strly* **9/2**
5652 **2** *3* **Jessie**[9] 737 5-8-0 40 (t) KimTinkler 1 41
(DonEnricoIncisa) *sn chsng ldrs: outpcd over 2f out: hdwy over 1f out: kpt on: no ch w wnr* **10/3**[2]
1-36 **3** *1¼* **Estimation**[23] 614 4-10-0 68 SDrowne 7 66
(RMHCowell) *chsd ldrs: efort 3f out: nt qckn over 1f out* **11/4**[1]
5-02 **4** *¾* **Cloudless (USA)**[5] 773 4-9-3 57 SWhitworth 3 53
(JWUnett) *led: qcknd over 3f out: hdd appr fnl f: one pce* **4/1**[3]
0-06 **5** *½* **Victory Flip (IRE)**[13] 700 4-7-12 45 (p) StephanieHollinshead(7) 6 40
(RHollinshead) *hld up: swtchd outside after 1f: sn chsng ldrs: one pce fnl 2f* **9/1**
6/06 **6** *4* **Dalriath**[16] 671 5-7-9 40 DFox(5) 5 25
(MCChapman) *chsd ldrs: drvn along over 4f out: lost pl over 1f out* **20/1**
6-60 **7** *17* **Pertemps Bianca**[27] 594 4-8-0 40 (b) JQuinn 4 —
(ADSmith) *s.i.s: a last: lost tch over 1f out* **16/1**

1m 29.43s (-1.37) **Going Correction** -0.05s/f (Stan) **7** Ran SP% **108.6**
Speed ratings: **105,101,100,99,98 94,74**CSF £17.77 TOTE £6.90: £2.00, £2.30; EX 22.50.
**Owner** J F Pitchford **Bred** Patrick O'Dwyer **Trained** Southwell, Notts

**FOCUS**
Moderate form, but a decent winning time for the grade.

**NOTEBOOK**
**Eager Angel(IRE)**, her confidence boosted, found this trip much more suitable and won in good style.
**Jessie**, a positive on the exchanges, stuck on to chase home the winner but really needs a mile.
**Estimation** was in a foul mood beforehand and gave real problems on the way down to the start.
**Cloudless(USA)** stepped up the gallop from the front at halfway but in the end was simply not up to it. The surface at Wolverhampton suits her better.

## 827 BET DIRECT H'CAP 1m 6f (F)
**3:55** (3:55) (D) (0-80,77) 4-Y-0+ **£4,046** (£1,245; £622; £311) **Stalls** Low

Form RPR
2-00 **1** **Victory Quest (IRE)**[21] 629 4-9-6 73 (v) DaneO'Neill 3 83
(MrsSLamyman) *chsd ldr: led over 5f out: hld on gamely* **12/1**
06/1 **2** *½* **Box Builder**[7] 750 7-8-13 64 6ex LFletcher(3) 2 73
(HMorrison) *trckd ldrs: rdn over 4f out: rallied over 1f out: nt qckn towards fin* **3/1**[1]
-062 **3** *1* **George Stubbs (USA)**[9] 734 6-9-3 65 KFallon 4 73
(MJPolglase) *trckd ldrs: chal 3f out: nt qckn ins last* **5/1**[2]
12-0 **4** *1* **Macaroni Gold (IRE)**[26] 603 4-8-13 66 (b[1]) MTebbutt 6 72
(WJarvis) *hld up: hdwy to trck ldrs 9f out: effrt 3f out: nt qckn appr fnl f* **3/1**[1]
-203 **5** *3½* **Glory Quest (USA)**[16] 666 7-9-9 71 MFenton 5 73
(MissGayKelleway) *bhd and drvn along 9f out: hdwy over 4f out: brought wd over 2f out: nvr nr to chal* **6/1**[3]
6-10 **6** *30* **Vanbrugh (FR)**[8] 743 4-9-10 77 (vt) DarrenWilliams 1 40
(MissDAMchale) *led: rdn 6f out: sn hdd: lost pl over 3f out: eased over 2f out: sn bhd* **11/1**
62-1 **7** *22* **So Vital**[19] 651 4-9-6 73 JQuinn 7 7
(JPearce) *chsd ldrs: rdn 9f out: sn lost pl and bhd: t.o 3f out* **5/1**[2]

3m 7.60s (-2.00) **Going Correction** -0.05s/f (Stan)
**WFA** 4 from 6yo+ 5lb **7** Ran SP% **113.6**
Speed ratings: **103,102,102,101,99 82,69**CSF £47.30 TOTE £11.50: £6.10, £1.20; EX 53.80.
**Owner** P Lamyman **Bred** Miss Veronica Henley **Trained** Louth, Lincs

**FOCUS**
Fairly decent form.

**NOTEBOOK**
**Victory Quest(IRE)**, who ran poorly on his two previous starts due to a back problem, was back to his best here and proved most determined.
**Box Builder**, having his second start in a week after a 15-month absence, came again and made the winner pull out all the stops. The full two miles suits him slightly better.
**George Stubbs(USA)**, a big negative on the exchanges, did not fail for lack of stamina.
**Macaroni Gold(IRE)**, in first time blinkers, ran better but now looks weighted to the very limit.
**Glory Quest(USA)** seems to have forgotten how to win for the time being at least and, coming very wide once in line for home, never looked like proving successful.
**Vanbrugh(FR)** dropped right out in a matter of strides. *Official explanation: jockey said gelding lost its action*
**So Vital**, in trouble with a circuit to go, was soon detached in last place and in the end completed in his own time. *Official explanation: jockey said colt would not face the kickback*

## 828 BET DIRECT ON SKY TEXT PAGE 372 (S) STKS 7f (F)
**4:30** (4:30) (G) 3-Y-0 **£2,534** (£724; £362) **Stalls** Low

Form RPR
5351 **1** **Lady Mo**[9] 736 3-8-12 51 NCallan 1 60
(KARyan) *trckd ldrs: led over 2f out: r.o wl: readily* **6/4**[1]
-152 **2** *2* **Princess Ismene**[7] 751 3-8-12 59 (b) KFallon 5 55
(PABlockley) *trckd ldrs: chal over 2f out: styd on same pce* **2/1**[2]
-234 **3** *3* **Hunting Pink**[11] 717 3-8-3 48 (b[1]) LFletcher(3) 3 42
(HMorrison) *hld up in last: effrt 3f out: edgd lft and one pce over 1f out* **5/2**[3]
0-06 **4** *6* **Are You There**[8] 744 3-8-7 45 BReilly(5) 4 33
(PSMcentee) *chsd ldrs: rdn over 3f out: wknd appr fnl f* **20/1**
005- **5** *3½* **Aggi Mac**[122] 5676 3-8-6 45 CCatlin 2 18
(NBycroft) *led: qcknd over 3f out: hdd over 2f out: lost pl over 1f out* **25/1**

1m 30.94s (0.14) **Going Correction** -0.05s/f (Stan) **5** Ran SP% **110.5**
Speed ratings: **97,94,91,84,80**CSF £4.85 TOTE £2.30: £1.10, £2.20; EX 4.60.There was no bid for the winner.
**Owner** Wooster Partnership **Bred** Mrs M S Teversham **Trained** Hambleton, N Yorks

**FOCUS**
A reasonable time for the grade, and fair selling form for 3yo's at this time of year

**NOTEBOOK**
**Lady Mo**, having her first outing for her new yard, found this plain sailing.
**Princess Ismene**, another who has changed stables, never looked like finishing anything but second best.
**Hunting Pink**, tried in blinkers, looks very half hearted.
**Are You There**, who had the headgear left off, looks to have completely lost the plot.
**Aggi Mac**, making her all-weather debut and having her first outing since October, quickened it up from the front but was soon put in her place.

## 829 BET DIRECT INTERACTIVE H'CAP 1m 4f (F)
**5:00** (5:00) (E) (0-75,72) 3-Y-0+ **£3,283** (£938; £469) **Stalls** Low

Form RPR
-141 **1** **Jair Ohmsford (IRE)**[9] 734 5-9-11 70 6ex MFenton 2 78+
(WJMusson) *sn trcking ldrs: wnt 2nd 3f out: led over 1f out: r.o wl* **6/5**[1]
-024 **2** *1¾* **Surdoue**[9] 734 4-9-1 63 KFallon 6 70+
(PHowling) *trckd ldr: led over 5f out: hdd over 1f out: kpt on: no real imp* **6/1**[3]
5-31 **3** *3½* **Critical Stage (IRE)**[9] 735 5-9-8 67 6ex (e) JPSpencer 5 71+
(JohnBerry) *hld up: hdwy over 3f out: ev ch 2f out: sn rdn: kpt on same pce* **6/4**[2]
00-4 **4** *2½* **Known Maneuver (USA)**[11] 715 6-7-9 45 (b[1]) DFox(5) 1 41
(MCChapman) *chsd ldrs: edgd lft and outpcd over 2f out* **66/1**
1-02 **5** *3* **Noul (USA)**[34] 548 5-9-13 72 (b) NCallan 3 64
(KARyan) *hld up in rr: drvn along over 3f out: nvr a factor* **12/1**
1-60 **6** *1* **Bill Bennett (FR)**[31] 566 3-8-2 71 CCatlin 4 61
(JJay) *set mod pce: hdd over 5f out: lost pl 2f out* **33/1**

2m 41.31s (-0.79) **Going Correction** -0.05s/f (Stan)
**WFA** 3 from 4yo 24lb 4 from 5yo+ 3lb **6** Ran SP% **111.9**
Speed ratings: **100,98,96,94,92 92**CSF £9.06 TOTE £1.80: £1.10, £2.50; EX 9.00 Place 6 £30.49, Place 5 £23.40.
**Owner** K A Cosby **Bred** Stuart Weld **Trained** Newmarket, Suffolk



The Form Book, Raceform Ltd, Compton, RG20 6NL

**FOCUS**
Improved form again from the progressive winner. The second and third were both eased and have been rated accordingly

**NOTEBOOK**
**Jair Ohmsford(IRE)** continues on the up and always looked to have the runner-up's measure.
**Surdoue**, even with the champion aboard, could not turn the tables on the winner, but to be fair this was a much more creditable effort.
**Critical Stage(IRE)**, under his penalty, had no excuse.
**Known Maneuver(USA)**, in first time blinkers, seemed to run a fraction better, but his immediate future still looks bleak.
**Noul(USA)** has yet to prove his stamina for this sort of trip, and when driven along on the home turn the response was negligible.
**Bill Bennett(FR)** has now finished last in the three handicaps since his maiden win at Wolverhampton in December.
T/Plt: £42.20 to a £1 stake. Pool: £37,485.20. 648.15 winning tickets. T/Qpdt: £30.10 to a £1 stake. Pool: £1,859.40. 45.60 winning tickets. WG

## 753 NAD AL SHEBA (L-H)
### Thursday, February 19

**OFFICIAL GOING: Dirt course - fast; turf course - good to firm**

### 830a BENTLEY MOTORS CUP INTERNATIONAL RATED STKS (DIRT) 7f
**4:45** (4:46) 3-Y-O+ **£27,234** (£8,379; £4,189; £2,094) **Stalls** Low

RPR
1 **Winisk River (IRE)**[614] 2170 4-9-10 99 ....(t) LDettori 5 100+
(SaeedBinSuroor) *missed break: sn in tch on outside: 4th st: rdn to ld over 1f out: sn clr: easily* **5/2**[1]
2 4 ¾ **Lord Nelson (AUS)**[12] 3-8-13 95 ....(t) MDuPlessis 4 94
(MThwaites, Macau) *led tl hdd over 1f out: kpt on nr fin: nt pce of wnr* **11/4**[2]
3 1 **Raheibb (IRE)**[21] 632 6-9-7 97 .... BDoyle 1 83
(AllanSmith, UAE) *trckd ldrs: 3rd st: rdn to chal 2f out: kpt on same pce fnl f* **9/2**
4 5 **Rotulo (ARG)**[14] 689 6-9-3 93 ....(t) MSantos 2 66
(DiegoLowther, Sweden) *towards rr: 5th st: kpt on nr fin: nvr trbld ldrs* **4/1**[3]
5 2 ¾ **Orchestrated (AUS)**[7] 755 7-9-5 95 ....(t) GHind 7 61
(MAlKurdi, UAE) *trckd ldr: 2nd st: grad wknd fnl 2f* **16/1**
6 7 **Jacks Estate (IRE)**[7] 755 9-9-1 97 .... TANaughton(6) 3 46
(AdrianMcguinness, Ire) *s.i.s: a towards rr: n.d* **40/1**
7 8 ¾ **Jarjoor**[196] 3932 4-8-10 86 .... PaulSmith 6 13
(AllanSmith, UAE) *mid-div tl wknd fnl 4f* **11/2**

1m 24.03s
**WFA** 3 from 4yo+ 17lb **7 Ran SP% 117.1**
Speed ratings: .
**Owner** Godolphin **Bred** P H Betts **Trained** Newmarket, Suffolk

**NOTEBOOK**
**Winisk River(IRE)**, purchased by connections as a juvenile, this was actually his first ever run for them and he has clearly had problems. Despite giving weight to all his rivals, did it quite impressively, quickening up well. What he beat is open to question, but there should be more to come.

### 831a DARLEY CAPE VERDI STKS (CONDITIONS RACE) (TURF) (F&M) 1m
**5:15** (5:15) 3-Y-O+ **£47,206** (£14,525; £7,262; £3,631) **Stalls** Low

RPR
1 **Festive Style (SAF)**[12] 711 3-8-9 101 .... RLMoore 3 111
(SSeemar, UAE) *in tch in mid-div: qcknd wl over 2f out: led over 1f out: rdn out* **3/1**[2]
2 6 ½ **Desert Glow (IRE)**[26] 4-9-3 50 ....(v) KMcEvoy 10 87
(SSeemar, UAE) *mid-div: stdy hdwy to 3rd st: chal and ev ch 1 1/2f out: nt pce of wnr* **66/1**
3 1 ½ **A Touch Of Frost**[14] 690 9-9-3 95 ....(b) ASaffar 4 84
(NDeCroutte, Bahrain) *led tl hdd over 1f out: no ex nr fin* **20/1**
4 hd **Naughty Nell**[35] 5-9-3 77 ....(v) RMullen 12 84
(PBrette, Dubai) *s.i.s: towards rr: 11th and racd wd st: styd on wl fnl 2f: nrst fin* **50/1**
5 nk **Fruit Of Glory**[7] 755 5-9-3 90 .... EAhern 7 83
(MRChannon) *mid-div: styd on wl fnl 2f: nt rch ldrs* **14/1**
6 1 **Cat Belling (IRE)**[12] 710 4-9-5 95 .... GHind 5 83
(RBouresly, Kuwait) *v.s.a: mid-div outside: racd wd and effrt st: kpt on same pce* **16/1**
7 ¾ **Londonnetdotcom (IRE)**[14] 690 4-9-3 96 .... TEDurcan 11 80
(MRChannon) *cl up: 2nd st: grad wknd fnl 2f* **10/3**[3]
8 2 ¼ **Gonfilia (GER)**[125] 5628 4-9-3 98 ....(t) LDettori 6 75
(SaeedBinSuroor) *in tch in mid-div: rdn and effrt st: no ex fnl f* **7/4**[1]
9 11 **Girl Scoud (BRZ)**[26] 5-9-3 60 ....(b) DHayse 9 53
(ASelvaratnam, UAE) *a towards rr: 11th st: nvr nr to chal* **100/1**
10 1 ¾ **Sail With The Tide (IRE)**[315] 4-9-3 80 .... BDoyle 2 50
(RBouresly, Kuwait) *a towards rr: last st: n.d* **66/1**
11 1 ¼ **Fabria (PER)**[21] 635 7-9-3 102 .... WSupple 8 47
(JBarton,) *trckd ldrs tl wknd fr 1/2-way: eased fnl f* **9/2**
12 ½ **Tarfaa Bint Swain (USA)**[33] 4-9-3 50 .... SChin 1 46
(ASelvaratnam, UAE) *trckd ldrs tl wknd fr 1/2-way* **100/1**

1m 36.84s
**WFA** 3 from 4yo+ 19lb **12 Ran SP% 126.9**
Speed ratings: .
**Owner** Fort Knox Syndicate **Bred** M J McGrath & L C Baxter **Trained** United Arab Emirates

**NOTEBOOK**
**Fruit Of Glory** appeared to come on a little for her outing here last week and was not disgraced in fifth.
**Londonnetdotcom(IRE)**, seemingly the Channon first-string, ran a good race when fourth here last time, but was slightly disappointing on this occasion. She is betetr than this and worth another chance.
**Gonfilia(GER)**, having her first run since October, never looked like winning and will be better served by softer ground over further.

### 832a CAPANNELLE RACECOURSE INTERNATIONAL RATED STKS (H'CAP) (DIRT) 1m 1f
**5:45** (5:45) (90-105,105) 3-Y-O+ **£32,681** (£10,055; £5,027; £2,513) **Stalls** Low

RPR
1 **Deodatus (USA)**[14] 688 6-8-7 91 ....(vt) SSanders 11 101
(ECharpy, UAE) *in tch: 3rd st: smooth hdwy to ld 2f out: sn wl clr: easily* **13/2**
2 4 ½ **Curule (USA)**[21] 635 7-9-4 102 ....(v) GBirrer 10 104
(DougWatson, UAE) *trckd ldrs: led st: hdd 2f out: kpt on nr fin: no ch w wnr* **13/2**
3 1 ¾ **Adiemus**[14] 687 6-9-4 102 ....(v) LDettori 2 101
(JNoseda) *trckd ldrs: 4th st: styd on same pce fnl 2f* **4/1**[1]
4 ½ **Afghan (USA)**[7] 757 6-8-8 93 ....(b) GHind 5 90
(MAlKurdi, UAE) *mid-div: 6th st: styd on fnl 2f: nvr trbld ldrs* **11/2**[2]
5 nse **Nooshman (USA)**[14] 688 7-8-6 90 ....(bt) TEDurcan 8 88
(ECharpy, UAE) *mid-div: rdn fr 1/2-way: 8th st: styd on fnl 2f: nt rch ldrs* **6/1**[3]
6 4 ½ **Opportunist (IRE)**[14] 687 5-8-8 93 ....(vt) RMullen 3 81
(DougWatson, UAE) *mid-div: rdn fr 1/2-way: 7th st: styd on same pce* **10/1**
7 3 ¾ **Grand Stand (NZ)**[14] 687 7-9-6 105 ....(e) KMcEvoy 4 86
(PLeyshan, Macau) *towards rr: last st: styd on fnl 2f: n.d* **6/1**[3]
8 1 ¼ **Jebal Suraaj (USA)**[14] 688 4-8-6 90 .... SChin 6 70
(MJohnston) *led tl hdd st: grad wknd fnl 2 1/2f* **33/1**
9 3 ¼ **Mahroos (USA)**[21] 633 6-8-6 90 ....(ve) WSupple 7 64
(DougWatson, UAE) *a towards rr: 9th and racd wd st: n.d* **14/1**
10 3 **St Expedit**[7] 756 7-9-4 102 .... BDoyle 1 71
(RBouresly, Kuwait) *hld up: trckd ldrs: 5th st: wknd qckly fnl 2f* **25/1**
11 3 ¾ **Elghani**[14] 687 7-9-4 102 .... RHills 9 64
(ECharpy, UAE) *rrd s: sn mid-div outside: 10th and wknd st* **11/2**[2]

1m 50.77s **11 Ran SP% 128.6**
Speed ratings: .
**Owner** Sheikh Saeed Bin Mohammed Al Maktoum **Bred** Darley Stud Management Inc **Trained** United Arab Emirates

**NOTEBOOK**
**Adiemus** has not run too badly in two starts here so far this year, but is not getting any better at the age of six.
**Jebal Suraaj(USA)** has run poorly on all three attempts here so far this year.

## 809 WOLVERHAMPTON (A.W) (L-H)
### Friday, February 20

**OFFICIAL GOING: Slow**
Conditions were testing and several jockeys reported that their mounts failed to handle the deep ground.
Wind: fresh against Weather: sunny with a cold wind

### 833 PRESS INTERACTIVE TO BET DIRECT H'CAP (DIV I) 7f (F)
**1:50** (1:54) (F ) (0-65,64) 3-Y-O+ **£2,926** (£836; £418) **Stalls** High

Form RPR
0631 1 **Mount Royale (IRE)**[11] 719 6-9-7 **58** 6ex ....(vt) KimTinkler 5 69
(NTinkler) *mde all: rdn over 2f out: drvn out* **6/1**
-000 2 1 ½ **Pawn In Life (IRE)**[11] 719 6-9-10 **61** .... JFanning 7 68
(TDBarron) *chsd ldrs: rdn over 2f out: wnt 2nd 1f out: nt qckn* **9/1**
0-21 3 ½ **Up Tempo (IRE)**[29] 584 6-9-10 **61** ....(b) NCallan 8 67
(KARyan) *bhd: rdn 4f out: hdwy on outside 3f out: kpt on same pce fnl f* **10/3**[1]
0-04 4 2 ½ **Carlton (IRE)**[6] 771 10-9-4 **60** .... RThomas(5) 9 60
(CRDore) *hld up: rdn 4f out: hdwy over 2f out: one pce fnl f* **10/1**
-354 5 shd **Waltzing Wizard**[14] 694 5-8-12 **49** .... FLynch 2 48
(ABerry) *broke wl: n.m.r and lost pl sn after s: bhd whn nt clr run on ins over 3f out: styd on towards fin* **11/2**[3]
5324 6 3 ½ **Larky's Lob**[3] 807 5-8-7 **47** .... LFletcher(3) 3 38
(PaulJohnson) *chsd ldrs: wnt 2nd over 3f out: rdn over 2f out: ev ch wl over 1f out: wknd fnl f* **7/1**
-441 7 15 **Its Ecco Boy**[22] 625 6-9-6 **57** .... KFallon 10 10
(PHowling) *chsd ldrs: rdn over 3f out: wknd over 2f out* **5/1**[2]
-052 8 ½ **Dispol Peto**[6] 772 4-9-8 **59** ....(b) JBramhill 1 11
(IanEmmerson) *sn w wnr: rdn over 3f out: sn wknd* **11/1**
0-40 P **Earlston**[3] 810 4-9-13 **64** ....(bt[1]) MFenton 6 —
(MissGayKelleway) *s.i.s: a bhd: p.u and dismntd ins fnl f* **16/1**

1m 34.41s (4.21) **Going Correction** +0.675s/f (Slow) **9 Ran SP% 115.2**
Speed ratings: **102,100,99,96,96 92,75,75,**—CSF £58.38 CT £209.57 TOTE £5.60: £1.40, £3.80, £1.40; EX 63.80.
**Owner** Langton Partnership **Bred** Joe Crowley And Mr And Mrs A P O'Brien **Trained** Langton, N Yorks
■ Stewards Enquiry : Kim Tinkler caution: careless riding

**FOCUS**
Modest handicap form. The winning time was fractionally quicker than the second division.

**NOTEBOOK**
**Mount Royale(IRE)** is a real seven furlong Southwell specialist and registered his first win at Dunstall Park with the help of the slow surface.
**Pawn In Life(IRE)**, another Southwell specialist, put up his best performance so far at Wolverhampton and was also probably suited by the deep surface.
**Up Tempo(IRE)**, raised 2lb, had to come the scenic route leaving the back straight and was certainly not disgraced.
**Carlton(IRE)** did not mind going back up to seven for this return to Fibresand.
**Waltzing Wizard** had no luck at all in running and did well to finish so close.
**Larky's Lob** had been very busy of late, and it seems to be catching up with him.
**Its Ecco Boy** *Official explanation: trainer said gelding failed to handle the deep ground*
**Earlston** *Official explanation: jockey said gelding lost its action*

### 834 PRESS INTERACTIVE TO BET DIRECT H'CAP (DIV II) 7f (F)
**2:20** (2:20) (F ) (0-65,63) 3-Y-O+ **£2,919** (£834; £417) **Stalls** High

Form RPR
6253 1 **Aguila Loco (IRE)**[4] 799 5-8-13 50 ....(p) MFenton 2 58
(MrsStefLiddiard) *led: rdn over 3f out: hdd jst ins fnl f: rallied to ld towards fin: drvn out* **11/1**
1440 2 1 ¼ **Lord Chamberlain**[9] 738 11-9-5 56 ....(b) CCatlin 9 61
(JMBradley) *bhd: rdn 4f out: hdwy on ins 3f out: led jst ins fnl f: sn edgd lft: hdd and no ex towards fin* **9/1**
2031 3 2 ½ **Legalis (USA)**[11] 723 6-9-9 60 6ex ....(b) NCallan 7 59
(KARyan) *a.p: rdn 3f out: one pce fnl f* **8/1**

-253 **4** *3* **Spindor (USA)**[14] [694] 5-9-1 59 ........ (b) SCrawford(7) 5 50
(JAOsborne) *hld up in tch: rdn and no hdwy fnl 2f* **7/1**

0444 **5** *3* **Blakeshall Quest**[3] [803] 4-9-9 60 ........ (v) IMongan 3 44
(RBrotherton) *chsd wnr: rdn and ev ch over 2f out: swtchd lft wl over 1f out: sn wknd* **5/1**[2]

543- **6** *6* **Captain Darling (IRE)**[52] [6256] 4-9-12 63 ........ SDrowne 8 32
(RMHCowell) *rdn over 4f out: a bhd* **3/1**[1]

0115 **7** *1 1/4* **Warlingham (IRE)**[6] [772] 6-9-10 61 ........ JFanning 4 27
(PHowling) *hld up in tch: wknd over 3f out* **11/2**[3]

0-40 **8** *1 3/4* **Yellow River (IRE)**[21] [643] 4-9-2 53 ........ DaneO'Neill 6 14
(RCurtis) *hdwy on ins 5f out: rdn over 3f out: wknd over 2f out* **25/1**

003- **9** *19* **Victory Vee**[91] [6036] 4-9-7 58 ........ JQuinn 10 —
(MBlanshard) *rdn over 4f out: a bhd: t.o* **12/1**

3546 **10** *1/2* **Pilgrim Princess (IRE)**[3] [803] 6-8-5 45 ........ DAllan(3) 1 —
(EJAlston) *anticipated s and v.s.a: a t.o* **12/1**

1m 34.49s (4.29) **Going Correction** +0.675s/f (Slow) 10 Ran SP% **118.2**
Speed ratings: **102,100,97,94,90 84,82,80,58,58**CSF £107.28 CT £861.60 TOTE £9.80: £1.50, £3.20, £2.10; EX 82.40.
**Owner** Valley Fencing **Bred** John Grogan **Trained** Great Shefford, Berks

**FOCUS**
Ordinary handicap form. The winning time was very similar to the first division.

**NOTEBOOK**
**Aguila Loco(IRE)** was thought to have benefited from having the cheekpieces fitted and stamina was not a problem on only his second start beyond six furlongs.
**Lord Chamberlain** yet again showed a tendency to go left handed and did not help his cause by drifting to the far rail in the closing stages.
**Legalis(USA)**, penalised for winning a seller, gave a decent account of himself in this company.
**Spindor(USA)** was galloping on the spot in the home straight.
**Blakeshall Quest** probably only just stays this trip and got found out by the demanding surface.
**Captain Darling(IRE)** *Official explanation: trainer had no explanation for the poor form shown*
**Warlingham(IRE)** *Official explanation: trainer said gelding failed to handle the deep ground*
**Pilgrim Princess(IRE)** *Official explanation: jockey said mare anticipated the start and hit the gate*

## 835 BET DIRECT ON SKY ACTIVE MAIDEN STKS 1m 1f 79y(F)
2:55 (2:55) (D) 3-Y-0 £3,373 (£1,038; £519; £259) Stalls Low

Form RPR

0-4 **1** **Ylang Ylang (IRE)**[29] [585] 3-8-9 ........ MTebbutt 12 58+
(WJarvis) *s.i.s and wnt rt: racd wd: hld up: hdwy on outside 3f out: led ins fnl f: r.o* **7/2**[3]

300- **2** *1* **Hsi Wang Mu (IRE)**[122] [5698] 3-8-9 50 ........ IMongan 11 56
(RBrotherton) *hld up: hdwy 5f out: rdn over 3f out: led jst over 1f out: hdd and nt qckn ins fnl f* **33/1**

5 **3** *5* **Zuloago (USA)**[17] [668] 3-8-9 ........ ANicholls 4 47
(SLKeightley) *led after 1f: rdn over 3f out: hdd wl over 1f out: wknd ins fnl f* **33/1**

45-2 **4** *1 1/4* **Looks The Business (IRE)**[9] [739] 3-8-7 68 ........ (t) CHaddon(7) 3 49
(WGMTurner) *w ldr: rdn over 3f out: led wl over 1f out: sn hdd: wknd ins fnl f* **11/2**

**5** *4* **Harry Lad** 3-9-0 ........ JoannaBadger 7 42
(PDEvans) *dwlt: wl bhd 6f out: styd on u.p fnl 2f: nrst fin* **33/1**

30-2 **6** *3* **Kings Rock**[15] [683] 3-9-0 65 ........ PFessey 9 36
(KARyan) *prom tl rdn and wknd 3f out* **10/3**[2]

00- **7** *2 1/2* **Strangely Brown (IRE)**[115] [5812] 3-9-0 ........ JMackay 10 32
(SCWilliams) *bhd: rdn over 3f out: sn struggling* **25/1**

0 **8** *16* **Divina**[15] [683] 3-8-9 ........ RHavlin 1 —
(SLKeightley) *led 1f: lost pl 6f out: t.o fnl 4f* **50/1**

00 **9** *6* **Fairly Glorious**[25] [606] 3-8-9 ........ TEaves(5) 6 —
(THCaldwell) *prom: rdn over 5f out: wknd over 3f out: t.o* **100/1**

**10** *5* **Viagrah (IRE)** 3-9-0 ........ JQuinn 2 —
(MJPolglase) *sn bhd: t.o fnl 4f* **40/1**

50-2 **11** *14* **Regulated (IRE)**[24] [613] 3-9-0 67 ........ KFallon 5 —
(JAOsborne) *hld up in tch: wknd 4f out: t.o* **3/1**[1]

00- **12** *11* **Eternal Dancer (USA)**[115] [5813] 3-9-0 ........ JFanning 8 —
(MJohnston) *prom tl wknd 4f out: t.o* **8/1**

2m 11.72s (8.82) **Going Correction** +0.675s/f (Slow) 12 Ran SP% **114.9**
Speed ratings: **87,86,81,80,77 74,72,57,52,48 35,25**CSF £116.67 TOTE £3.40: £1.30, £9.10, £8.20; EX 85.40.
**Owner** R A Scarborough **Bred** R Scarborough And Pacelco S A **Trained** Newmarket, Suffolk

**FOCUS**
A weak maiden in which the slow surface put the emphasis on stamina. The winning time was extremely slow for the grade.

**NOTEBOOK**
**Ylang Ylang(IRE)**, formerly trained by Aidan O'Brien, had given the impression she would appreciate this stiffer test of stamina on her debut for her new connections over a mile last month.
**Hsi Wang Mu(IRE)**, disappointing on her last two starts for Giles Bravery, gave her new trainer plenty of cause for optimism that she can go one better.
**Zuloago(USA)** stepped up considerably on her debut over seven and just failed to get home on the deep ground over this trip.
**Looks The Business(IRE)** was another who had some stamina limitations exposed in the testing ground, despite having finished second over slightly further on the Polytrack last time.
**Harry Lad** is a half-brother to seven furlong course winner Amber Regent who went on to stay this trip. He took a long time to grasp what was required and may be capable of some improvement.
**Regulated(IRE)** *Official explanation: vet said gelding finished lame on the off-fore*
**Eternal Dancer(USA)** *Official explanation: jockey said gelding stopped in running for no apparent reason*

## 836 BET DIRECT INTERACTIVE H'CAP 6f (F)
3:30 (3:31) (D) (0-80,78) 3-Y-0+ £4,085 (£1,257; £628; £314) Stalls Low

Form RPR

1-00 **1** **Johnston's Diamond (IRE)**[15] [680] 6-9-8 72 ........ KFallon 11 84
(EJAlston) *a.p: rdn over 1f out: led wl ins fnl f: r.o* **8/1**

2361 **2** *nk* **Playtime Blue**[4] [796] 4-9-2 66 6ex ........ GBaker 7 77
(KRBurke) *led: hrd rdn wl over 1f out: hdd wl ins fnl f: r.o* **8/1**

0133 **3** *3/4* **Time N Time Again**[3] [806] 6-10-0 78 ........ (p) JQuinn 6 87
(EJAlston) *a.p: rdn over 2f out: kpt on ins fnl f* **4/1**[1]

532- **4** *3 1/2* **Super Canyon**[111] [5880] 6-9-4 68 ........ (vt) NCallan 5 66
(JPearce) *chsd ldrs: rdn over 3f out: kpt on one pce fnl f* **9/1**

000- **5** *3/4* **Romany Nights (IRE)**[104] [5946] 4-9-11 75 ........ DaneO'Neill 13 71
(JWUnett) *s.i.s: bhd tl hdwy fnl f: nrst fin* **14/1**

4102 **6** *1 1/4* **Prima Stella**[8] [749] 5-9-6 73 ........ LisaJones(3) 12 65
(JARToller) *racd wd: sn chsng ldrs: rdn and wknd over 1f out* **9/2**[2]

0351 **7** *1/2* **Panjandrum**[8] [748] 6-9-2 71 6ex ........ MSavage(5) 9 62
(NEBerry) *chsd ldrs: rdn over 2f out: wknd over 1f out* **16/1**

0-20 **8** *1/2* **Bond Royale**[25] [607] 4-9-6 77 ........ MStainton(7) 1 66
(BSmart) *hdwy on ins over 2f out: wknd fnl f* **20/1**

1-05 **9** *2 1/2* **Ellens Lad (IRE)**[15] [681] 10-9-6 70 ........ (b) PaulEddery 10 52
(WJMusson) *prom: rdn over 2f out: wknd over 1f out* **20/1**

0646 **10** *1/2* **Sundried Tomato**[7] [761] 5-9-11 78 ........ LFletcher(3) 3 58
(PWHiatt) *prom: rdn over 3f out: wknd over 1f out* **5/1**[3]

060- **11** *3/4* **Tidy (IRE)**[14] [2926] 4-10-0 78 ........ ACulhane 2 56
(MDHammond) *outpcd* **40/1**

1/0 **12** *2* **Full Pitch**[17] [669] 8-9-6 70 ........ ANicholls 4 42
(WJenks) *a bhd* **50/1**

-020 **13** *4* **Prince Of Blues (IRE)**[3] [806] 6-8-8 65 ........ PVarley(7) 8 25
(MMullineaux) *prom tl rdn and wknd over 2f out* **25/1**

1m 18.41s (2.71) **Going Correction** +0.675s/f (Slow) 13 Ran SP% **117.4**
Speed ratings: **108,107,106,101,100 99,98,97,94,93 92,90,84**CSF £64.58 CT £296.92 TOTE £9.50: £2.90, £2.70, £1.70; EX 101.40.
**Owner** Mollington Golf Club Boys **Bred** Sos Investments **Trained** Longton, Lancs

**FOCUS**
A competitive sprint handicap run at a good pace, and a smart winning time for the class. Strong form.

**NOTEBOOK**
**Johnston's Diamond(IRE)** bounced back to form after a couple of disappointing outings at Southwell, but he did have the outside draw last time. His trainer told the stewards that he may have been helped by the slow surface. *Official explanation: trainer said, regarding the improved form shown, gelding may have been helped by today's slow surface*
**Playtime Blue**, penalised for his win over the minimum trip here earlier in the week, ensured there would be no hanging about and lost nothing in defeat.
**Time N Time Again** was apparently more fancied by his trainer than the winner, having been in something of a purple patch since the cheekpieces were fitted.
**Super Canyon**, previously trained by Peter Harris, made a satisfactory reappearance for one who is usually campaigned in a lower grade.
**Romany Nights(IRE)** showed some promise for the future on his first try on this surface.
**Prima Stella** was not helped by a high draw.

## 837 BETDIRECT.CO.UK H'CAP 1m 100y(F)
4:00 (4:00) (C) (0-100,88) 3-Y-0+ £8,515 (£2,620; £1,310; £655) Stalls Low

Form RPR

0/11 **1** **Consonant (IRE)**[25] [604] 7-9-2 80 ........ KFallon 6 100
(DGBridgwater) *a.p: rdn over 3f out: led 2f out: edgd rt fnl f: r.o* **3/1**[1]

-000 **2** *nk* **Te Quiero**[20] [649] 6-9-10 88 ........ (t[1]) FLynch 2 107
(MissGayKelleway) *hld up: hdwy on outside 3f out: rdn and ev ch whn edgd rt fnl f: r.o* **8/1**[3]

1-03 **3** *6* **Sangiovese**[8] [749] 5-8-11 78 ........ LFletcher(3) 8 85
(HMorrison) *led: rdn over 3f out: hdd 2f out: wknd ins fnl f* **10/3**[2]

060- **4** *3* **The Bonus King**[118] [5747] 4-9-7 85 ........ JFanning 10 85
(MJohnston) *prom: rdn and outpcd 3f out: btn whn edgd rt ins fnl f* **16/1**

03-4 **5** *6* **Del Mar Sunset**[39] [507] 5-8-13 80 ........ LisaJones(3) 3 68
(WJHaggas) *hld up: rdn over 3f out: no rspnse* **10/3**[2]

/4-6 **6** *1 1/2* **Kentucky King (USA)**[17] [669] 4-9-7 85 ........ ACulhane 12 70
(PWHiatt) *hld up in tch: rdn and wknd over 3f out* **16/1**

0-30 **7** *hd* **Ephesus**[8] [749] 4-9-7 85 ........ (v) MFenton 9 69
(MissGayKelleway) *chsd ldrs tl wknd over 2f out* **11/1**

210- **8** *16* **Ile Michel**[9] [5210] 7-9-8 86 ........ RHavlin 11 37
(JGMO'Shea) *a bhd* **20/1**

30-0 **9** *1 1/2* **Aventura (IRE)**[6] [768] 4-9-7 85 ........ JQuinn 7 33
(MJPolglase) *prom: rdn over 3f out: wknd over 2f out* **20/1**

2400 **10** *2* **Lakota Brave**[20] [649] 10-9-8 86 ........ SDrowne 1 29
(MrsStefLiddiard) *hld up: rdn over 3f out: sn struggling* **16/1**

**11** *8* **Rainbow World (IRE)**[237] [2809] 4-9-3 81 ........ ANicholls 4 8
(AndrewReid) *bhd tl rdn and hdwy on ins over 4f out: wknd over 3f out: t.o* **50/1**

000- **12** *23* **Madalyar (IRE)**[218] [1976] 5-9-1 79 ........ DaneO'Neill 5 —
(JonjoO'Neill) *s.i.s: a wl bhd: t.o* **40/1**

1m 54.29s (3.29) **Going Correction** +0.675s/f (Slow) 12 Ran SP% **122.2**
Speed ratings: **110,109,103,100,94 93,93,77,75,73 65,42**CSF £27.43 CT £88.74 TOTE £3.30: £1.20, £2.70, £2.00; EX 44.30.
**Owner** The Rule Racing Syndicate **Bred** Kilfrush Stud Ltd **Trained** Winchcombe, Gloucs

**FOCUS**
The top weight in this 0-100 event was rated only 88, but the winning time was decent for the grade and the form looks very strong.

**NOTEBOOK**
**Consonant(IRE)** has really taken to this surface and completed a course and distance hat-trick. He had to work harder off a 10lb higher mark, but his trainer hopes there might still be further improvement to come.
**Te Quiero** looked a different horse back on Fibresand and was reverting to the right sort of trip. Tried in an eyeshield, he came up against a progressive sort in the winner.
**Sangiovese**, set to drop 2lb tomorrow, has really paid the penalty for his easy win before Christmas.
**The Bonus King** was making his All-Weather debut, having never previously tackled a distance beyond seven furlongs.
**Rainbow World(IRE)** *Official explanation: jockey said colt lost its action*

## 838 BETDIRECT.CO.UK (S) STKS 1m 4f (F)
4:35 (4:38) (G) 4-Y-0+ £2,527 (£722; £361) Stalls Low

Form RPR

5-13 **1** **Sungio**[9] [740] 6-9-10 53 ........ DaleGibson 7 54
(BGPowell) *chsd ldrs: rdn over 6f out: led ins fnl f: edgd lft: r.o* **5/2**[1]

-012 **2** *1/2* **Prince Prospect**[11] [726] 8-9-3 47 ........ KristinStubbs(7) 4 53
(MrsLStubbs) *hld up and bhd: hdwy over 2f out: swtchd lft over 1f out: ev ch ins fnl f: r.o* **7/2**[2]

0566 **3** *4* **Think Quick (IRE)**[3] [812] 4-8-4 35 ........ HFellows(7) 3 37
(RHollinshead) *hld up and bhd: hdwy 4f out: one pce fnl f* **16/1**

-105 **4** *1/2* **Daimajin (IRE)**[6] [773] 5-9-10 56 ........ ACulhane 2 46
(MrsLucindaFeatherstone) *hld up: hdwy 5f out: led 3f out: sn rdn: hdd ins fnl f: wknd* **10/1**

0-43 **5** *9* **Bestseller**[11] [722] 4-8-11 ........ RHavlin 8 23
(JGMO'Shea) *chsd ldr: led 8f out to 3f out: wknd over 1f out* **7/2**[2]

0-00 **6** *12* **Birth Of The Blues**[17] [661] 8-9-5 35 ........ DaneO'Neill 1 10
(ACharlton) *hld up: hdwy on ins 6f out: rdn over 3f out: wknd 2f out* **10/1**

500- **7** *6* **Bojangles (IRE)**[179] [4465] 5-9-2 55 ........ LFletcher(3) 11 —
(RBrotherton) *hld up mid-div: rdn over 4f out: bhd fnl 3f* **6/1**[3]

40-6 **8** *3/4* **Dundonald**[6] [776] 5-9-5 45 ........ (bt[1]) SRighton 10 —
(MAppleby) *a bhd* **33/1**

600/ **9** *18* **Mr Perry (IRE)**[72] [796] 8-9-5 30 ........ RFfrench 6 —
(MrsPFord) *t.k.h: led 4f: remained prom tl wknd 4f out: t.o* **25/1**

000- **10** *dist* **Rival (IRE)**[9] [4835] 5-9-5 45 ........ CCatlin 9 —
(STLewis) *prom: rdn over 6f out: wknd over 5f out: t.o* **66/1**


The Form Book, Raceform Ltd, Compton, RG20 6NL

000- **11** *dist* **Final Lap**[52] 6233 8-9-5 30 ANicholls 5 —
(STLewis) *dropped rr after 3f: t.o fnl 7f* **50/1**

2m 52.13s (10.63) **Going Correction** +0.675s/f (Slow)
**WFA** 4 from 5yo+ 3lb **11** Ran SP% **121.6**
Speed ratings: **91,90,88,87,81 73,69,69,57,—** —CSF £11.35 TOTE £3.30: £1.50, £1.80, £2.70; EX 12.70.There was no bid for the winner.
**Owner** Mrs Rachel A Powell **Bred** Baldernock Bloodstock Ltd **Trained** Morestead, Hants

**FOCUS**
A weak seller with the emphasis again on stamina. The winning time was modest, even for a contest like this.

**NOTEBOOK**
**Sungio**, on his Fibresand debut, found the slow surface just what the doctor ordered having won over two miles at Lingfield a month ago.
**Prince Prospect**, back up in distance, appeared to be coming with a winning run until strength from the saddle tipped the scale against him.
**Think Quick(IRE)** was in the right grade but could never get on terms with the two principals.
**Daimajin(IRE)** tried to slip the field on the home turn but his stamina limitations were exposed in this deep ground.
**Final Lap** *Official explanation: jockey said, regarding the running and riding, he asked to vet to examine gelding on arrival start believing something to be amiss, adding that when he tried to make the running as instructed gelding was not travelling well and was unable to hold its position, so he allowed it to come home in its own time; vet said gelding finished lame*

## 839 BET DIRECT INTERACTIVE H'CAP 2m 46y(F)
**5:10** (5:10) (F ) (0-60,57) 4-Y-0+ **£2,940** (£840; £420) **Stalls** Low

Form RPR
0/42 **1** **Doctor John**[8] 750 7-8-6 35 (p) CCatlin 8 49
(AndrewTurnell) *hld up: hdwy over 6f out: rdn 3f out: swtchd rt over 1f out: led wl ins fnl f: styd on wl* **5/2**[2]

1602 **2** *3* **Madiba**[11] 724 5-9-12 55 KFallon 7 65
(PHowling) *a.p: led 8f out: rdn over 3f out: edgd rt and hdd wl ins fnl f: no ex* **7/4**[1]

3-00 **3** *3/4* **Makarim (IRE)**[27] 603 8-9-11 54 (p) GBaker 4 64
(MRBosley) *hld up in rr: smooth hdwy over 5f out: chal on bit over 2f out: sn rdn: ev ch ins fnl f: one pce* **7/1**

0/3- **4** *14* **Sportsman (IRE)**[25] 215 5-8-6 40 (b) PMulrennan[(5)] 3 33
(MWEasterby) *prom: rdn 7f out: lost pl 6f out: n.d after* **10/1**

434- **5** *15* **Sashay**[51] 6267 6-9-7 57 StephanieHollinshead[(7)] 1 32
(RHollinshead) *hld up: short-lived effrt over 4f out* **5/1**[3]

2233 **6** *6* **Kagoshima (IRE)**[12] 716 9-8-11 40 (v) VHalliday 2 8
(JRNorton) *hld up in tch: wnt 2nd briefly 6f out: wknd over 4f out* **8/1**

410- **7** *dist* **Sariba**[37] 4659 5-8-11 40 DaneO'Neill 6 —
(ACharlton) *led 8f: rdn and wknd over 5f out: t.o* **14/1**

200- **8** *25* **Spectacular Hope**[25] 5787 4-8-11 46 SDrowne 5 —
(JWMullins) *hld up in tch: rdn and wknd over 5f out: t.o* **50/1**

3m 51.44s (9.14) **Going Correction** +0.675s/f (Slow)
**WFA** 4 from 5yo+ 6lb **8** Ran SP% **122.9**
Speed ratings: **104,102,102,95,87 84,—,—**CSF £7.98 CT £27.88 TOTE £2.90: £2.00, £1.30, £1.60; EX 12.70 Place 6 £281.57, Place 5 £135.94.
**Owner** Dr John Hollowood **Bred** A G Nicholson **Trained** Malton, N Yorks

**FOCUS**
This developed into a three-horse slog in the deep ground. It was a fair effort from the back-to-form winner, whose time was creditable for the class.

**NOTEBOOK**
**Doctor John** built on the promise of his good second at Southwell and won going away.
**Madiba** was again without the headgear and probably finds two miles in this sort of ground stretching him to the limit.
**Makarim(IRE)**, who has slipped to a mark no less than 21lb lower than when he last scored, found disappointingly little after looking set to end his long losing run.
T/Plt: £248.00 to a £1 stake. Pool: £48,995.45. 144.20 winning tickets. T/Qpdt: £16.20 to a £1 stake. Pool: £3,727.90. 169.60 winning tickets. KH

# 815 LINGFIELD (L-H)
Saturday, February 21

**OFFICIAL GOING: Standard**

## 840 BET DIRECT NO Q ON 08000 93 66 93 MAIDEN STKS 6f (P)
**1:00** (1:01) (D ) 3-Y-0 **£4,065** (£1,251; £625; £312) **Stalls** Low

Form RPR
3-22 **1** **Saviours Spirit**[17] 673 3-9-0 70 KFallon 3 63+
(TGMills) *mde all: pushed out fnl f* **1/4**[1]

640- **2** *1 1/4* **Mister Completely (IRE)**[141] 5339 3-9-0 52 NPollard 1 59?
(JRBest) *chsd wnr thrght: rdn over 1f out: no imp fnl f* **25/1**

-200 **3** *1 1/4* **Docklands Blue (IRE)**[14] 708 3-8-6 55 J-PGuillambert[(3)] 8 50
(NPLittmoden) *sn pushed along in rr: r.o to go 3rd ins fnl f* **11/1**[3]

**4** *1 1/4* **Kryssa** 3-8-9 IMongan 2 46
(GLMoore) *a abt same pl: rdn 2f out: one pce after* **16/1**

**5** *1 1/4* **Joans Jewel** 3-8-9 AMcCarthy 5 43
(GGMargarson) *in tch to 1/2-way: sn rdn and n.d after* **33/1**

0 **6** *6* **King Of Meze (IRE)**[7] 766 3-9-0 OUrbina 4 30
(GProdromou) *chsd ldrs tl wknd wl over 1f out* **40/1**

2-03 **7** *3/4* **Bookiesindexdotcom**[8] 760 3-8-9 60 (v) JQuinn 7 22
(JRJenkins) *in tch early sn rdn and bhd* **8/1**[2]

0-0 **8** *4* **Lakeside Guy (IRE)**[49] 415 3-9-0 DaneO'Neill 6 15
(PSMcentee) *slowly away: effrt 1/2-way: sn btn* **100/1**

1m 14.14s (1.22) **Going Correction** +0.10s/f (Slow) **8** Ran SP% **115.5**
Speed ratings: **95,93,91,90,88 80,79,74**CSF £13.90 TOTE £1.10: £1.02, £6.40, £1.80; EX 12.20.
**Owner** J E Harley **Bred** Mrs S Shaw **Trained** Headley, Surrey

**FOCUS**
A modest maiden, run in an unexceptional time, in which Saviours Spirit did not have to run to his mark of 70 to get off the mark. That said, this race may produce some minor winners in time.

**NOTEBOOK**
**Saviours Spirit**, a beaten favourite on his last two starts, had the champion jockey taking over from an apprentice and finally got off the mark. He will face no easy task off his current sort of mark in handicaps.
**Mister Completely(IRE)**, who had 18lb to find with the winner at the weights, kept that one up to his work all the way to the line. He would be of interest in handicap company if turned out off his current mark as he is sure to go up in the weights for this.
**Docklands Blue(IRE)** ran respectably back in third and shapes as though she will stay seven furlongs.
**Kryssa**, out of a winner over a mile and a half, made an encouraging debut. She should stay farther and is likely to do better in time.
**Joans Jewel** is a half-brother to a dual winner over seven furlongs on Fibresand and it would be no surprise if she did better on that surface.

## 841 BET DIRECT ON 0800 32 93 93 H'CAP 5f (P)
**1:30** (1:30) (C ) (0-100,94) 3-Y-0+ **£8,932** (£3,388; £1,694; £770) **Stalls** High

Form RPR
6662 **1** **No Time (IRE)**[14] 703 4-9-0 80 KFallon 2 96+
(MJPolglase) *sn chsd ldr: led over 1f out: drvn out* **7/4**[1]

-021 **2** *1 1/4* **Justalord**[14] 703 6-9-8 88 (p) JEdmunds 1 96
(JBalding) *trckd ldrs: hung rt u.p appr fnl f but r.o to chse wnr ins* **11/2**[2]

-354 **3** *nk* **Zarzu**[14] 703 5-9-1 86 RThomas[(5)] 8 93
(CRDore) *in rr: gd hdwy wl over 1f out: r.o ins fnl f: nvr nrr* **7/1**

3200 **4** *3/4* **Hurricane Coast**[8] 761 5-9-1 81 (b) JPSpencer 7 85
(DFlood) *in tch: edgd lft jst ins fnl f: one pce* **9/1**

3-13 **5** *1 1/2* **Dancing Mystery**[14] 703 10-10-0 94 (b) SCarson 5 92
(EAWheeler) *prom tl wknd ins fnl f* **6/1**[3]

2-00 **6** *1/2* **Palawan**[14] 703 8-8-13 82 LPKeniry[(3)] 10 78
(AMBalding) *led tl hdd appr fnl f: fdd* **25/1**

-010 **7** *3 1/2* **Type One (IRE)**[8] 761 6-9-0 80 IMongan 9 62
(JJQuinn) *rdn thrght: a bhd* **25/1**

015- **8** *nk* **Chico Guapo (IRE)**[182] 4372 4-8-13 79 DeanMcKeown 6 60
(JAGlover) *slowly away: short of room 1/2-way: effrt 2f out: wknd over 1f out* **33/1**

/04- **U** **Ok Pal**[175] 4585 4-9-9 92 RMiles[(3)] 4 —
(TGMills) *bhd after 1f: rdn and sme hdwy whn clipped heels jst ins fnl f: uns rdr* **7/1**

-000 **U** **Trinculo (IRE)**[14] 703 7-9-5 88 (e) J-PGuillambert[(3)] 3 —
(NPLittmoden) *towards rr: stl bhd whn bdly hmpd jst ins fnl f: uns rdr* **20/1**

59.68 secs (-0.10) **Going Correction** +0.10s/f (Slow) **10** Ran SP% **116.4**
Speed ratings: **104,102,101,100,97 97,91,91,—,—**CSF £10.63 CT £55.77 TOTE £2.70: £1.10, £1.80, £3.70; EX 10.20.
**Owner** Paul J Dixon **Bred** Tally-Ho Stud **Trained** Southwell, Notts

**FOCUS**
A really competitive sprint handicap, run at a furious pace. The winner has been rated a little better than the bare form.

**NOTEBOOK**
**No Time(IRE)**, 2lb higher than when an unlucky head second to Justalord over course and distance seven days previously, stepped up on that effort to run out a decisive winner. Rated 104 at his best, he could defy a further rise in the weights.
**Justalord**, 3lb higher than when beating No Time, Dancing Mystery, Zarzu, Palawan and Trinculo over course and distance on his previous outing, ran another cracker and remains at the top of his game.
**Zarzu** is 7lb higher than when last successful, but holding his form well and this another solid effort. He is still looking for his first Polytrack success, but acts on the surface well and will always be worthy of respect on both All-Weather surfaces when a strong pace is guaranteed.
**Hurricane Coast** bounced back to form after a couple of below-par efforts.
**Dancing Mystery** looks weighted up to his current best.
**Palawan** was not good enough to dominate this bunch of sprinters.
**Trinculo(IRE)** was hampered by Ok Pal, which resulted in Guillambert being thrown to the ground for a horrible fall.
**Ok Pal**, racing for the first time since August, was looking for a run when clipping heels with Hurricane Coast.

## 842 LITTLEWOODS BET DIRECT WINTER DERBY TRIAL CONDITIONS STKS 1m 2f (P)
**2:05** (2:14) (B ) 4-Y-0+ **£15,027** (£5,700; £2,850; £1,295) **Stalls** Low

Form RPR
32-2 **1** **Grand Passion (IRE)**[35] 558 4-8-12 104 KFallon 5 107+
(GWragg) *hld up in mid-div: stdy hdwy 2f out: shkn up to ld wl ins fnl f: pushed out* **13/8**[1]

6-41 **2** *nk* **Eastern Breeze (IRE)**[35] 558 6-8-13 102 PaulEddery 9 104
(PWD'Arcy) *a.p: led wl over 1f out: rdn and hdd wl ins fnl f: nt qckn nr fin* **8/1**

263- **3** *1* **Corriolanus (GER)**[216] 3449 4-8-12 JQuinn 1 103
(PMitchell) *prom: rdn 2f out: n.m.r appr fnl f: r.o ins* **66/1**

40-6 **4** *shd* **Bonecrusher**[23] 636 5-9-2 (v) JPSpencer 3 105
(DRLoder) *in rr: hdwy u.p over 1f out: r.o ins fnl f* **5/1**[3]

34-1 **5** *1 3/4* **Blue Sky Thinking (IRE)**[21] 649 5-9-2 102 DarrenWilliams 11 102
(KRBurke) *c over to ins fr wd draw at s: in rr tl sme hdwy over 1f out: nvr nr to chal* **9/1**

1-55 **6** *2* **Lygeton Lad**[14] 706 6-8-13 103 (t) MFenton 10 96
(MissGayKelleway) *hld up towards rr on outside: effrt 2f out: n.d* **10/1**

320- **7** *hd* **Vintage Premium**[7] 3001 7-8-13 104 TQuinn 4 95
(RAFahey) *led tl hdd 5f out: rdn over 3f out: wknd wl over 1f out* **25/1**

026- **8** *nk* **Bourgainville**[171] 4663 6-8-13 109 MartinDwyer 7 95
(AMBalding) *in tch: effrt 2f out: wknd ent fnl f* **4/1**[2]

3240 **9** *1* **Easter Ogil (IRE)**[7] 765 9-8-13 64 VSlattery 2 93?
(JaneSouthcombe) *hld up: bhd: fnl 2f* **200/1**

0-14 **10** *shd* **Hail The Chief**[22] 641 7-9-2 96 ANicholls 6 96
(DNicholls) *trckd ldr: led 5f out: rdn and hdd wl over 1f out: wknd qckly* **20/1**

/P-0 **11** *dist* **Beltane**[14] 705 6-8-13 40 SRighton 8 —
(WDeBest-Turner) *mid-div: outpcd and lost tch 3f out* **500/1**

2m 5.47s (-1.92) **Going Correction** +0.10s/f (Slow)
**WFA** 4 from 5yo+ 1lb **11** Ran SP% **115.8**
Speed ratings: **111,110,109,109,108 106,106,106,105,105** —CSF £14.92 TOTE £2.20: £1.40, £2.20, £7.90; EX 17.40.
**Owner** H H Morriss **Bred** Mr & Mrs H H Morriss **Trained** Newmarket, Suffolk

**FOCUS**
A good quality race and the market got it right with Grand Passion reversing recent form with Eastern Breeze. This was, however, something of a muddling trial for the Winter Derby. Both the third and fifth home would have finished closer with better luck in running, and last year's Derby fourth Bourgainville was below form and only just managed to finish in front of the 64-rated Easter Ogil, whose proximity in ninth has to be a slight concern.

**NOTEBOOK**
**Grand Passion(IRE)**, beaten a length and a half behind Eastern Breeze in a handicap over course and distance on his previous outing, reversed that form on effectively 5lb better terms. He has never finished out of the first two on Polytrack and has to be a serious contender for the Winter Derby itself.
**Eastern Breeze(IRE)**, who had today's winner in second when winning a handicap over course and distance on his previous start, was unable to confirm that placing on revised terms but ran a cracker nonetheless. He is another who should go well in the Winter Derby.
**Corriolanus(GER)**, placed in Group company in Germany, ran a cracker on his British debut on what was his first start in 216 days. He would have been even closer with better luck in running and, as he hails from the same connections as Running Stag, it will be no surprise if he improves on this in the Winter Derby.

**Bonecrusher**, hailing from the stable of last year's winner Parasol (who also landed the Winter Derby), ran well on his return to this country after an unsuccessful spin in Dubai. This was also his first run on Polytrack and he is entitled to improve.
**Blue Sky Thinking(IRE)** goes well over course and distance and ran better than his finishing position suggests. Having been given plenty to do, he was making good headway when he met trouble and would have finished closer with better luck.
**Lygeton Lad** has still to convince this trip is what he wants.
**Bourgainville**, last year's Winter Derby fourth, is hard to win with and was below his best.
**Easter Ogil(IRE)** holds the form down a little in finishing ninth, but is no doubt massively flattered.
**Hail The Chief** is better on Fibresand.

## 843 LITTLEWOODS BET DIRECT H'CAP — 1m (P)
**2:40** (2:42) (D) (0-85,84) 3-Y-O — **£4,771** (£1,468; £734; £367) **Stalls** High

Form — RPR
0-36 **1** **Royal Warrant**[35] 557 3-9-2 **79** ........ MartinDwyer 5 — 86
(AMBalding) *chsd ldng pair: pushed along fr 1/2-way: r.o fnl f to ld cl home: all out* **5/1**[3]
41 **2** ½ **Heversham (IRE)**[7] 766 3-9-2 **79** ........ MHills 6 — 85
(WJHaggas) *led: rdn ent fnl f: kpt on but edgd rt and hdd cl home* **5/4**[1]
2-11 **3** 2½ **Secret Place**[35] 557 3-9-7 **84** ........ KFallon 3 — 85
(EALDunlop) *trckd ldr tl faltered and fnd no ex ins fnl f* **2/1**[2]
40-2 **4** nk **Western Roots**[35] 557 3-9-4 **81** ........ SDrowne 2 — 81
(PFICole) *hld up: rdn and hdwy 2f out: fnd little appr fnl f* **8/1**
02-5 **5** 5 **Mugeba**[40] 506 3-7-12 **64** ........ LisaJones(3) 1 — 53
(WJMusson) *t.k.h: towards rr: bhd fnl 2f* **20/1**

1m 39.6s (0.09) **Going Correction** +0.10s/f (Slow) — **5** Ran SP% **110.3**
Speed ratings: **103,102,100,99,94**CSF £11.85 TOTE £11.20: £4.30, £1.10; EX 25.20.
**Owner** The Queen **Bred** Queen Elizabeth **Trained** Kingsclere, Hants

**FOCUS**
Despite the small field this was quite a competitive handicap. However, they only went an ordinary pace.

**NOTEBOOK**
**Royal Warrant** appreciated this step back up to a mile and ran out a game winner. A rise in the weights will make things tougher, but he has claimed a couple of reasonable scalps in the second and third placed horses.
**Heversham(IRE)**, off the mark with a clear-cut success over course and distance (African Dream, winner of the claimer on this card was third that day) on his previous outing, was allowed his own way out in front and ran well. The way he was keeping on at the finish once headed suggests he should be equally effective ridden with more restraint.
**Secret Place**, chasing the hat-trick after a couple of wins over seven furlongs recently, was given every chance by the in-form Fallon, but he gave way pretty easily inside the final furlong. He may not have enjoyed getting into a battle, but can be given the benefit of the doubt and should do better back over shorter.
**Western Roots** may have preferred a strong-run race, as he lacked a change of pace having been held up.
**Mugeba** was the first beaten and may need her sights lowered.

## 844 BETDIRECT.CO.UK H'CAP — 1m 4f (P)
**3:15** (3:15) (C ) (0-95,90) 4-Y-O+ — **£7,279** (£2,761; £1,380; £627) **Stalls** Low

Form — RPR
12-1 **1** **Mission To Mars**[24] 618 5-9-9 **85** ........ JPSpencer 6 — 97+
(PRHedger) *hld up in tch: stdy hdwy 2f out: qcknd wl to ld jst ins fnl f: styd on wl* **1/1**[1]
36-4 **2** 1¼ **Nawamees (IRE)**[10] 743 6-9-6 **82** ........ IMongan 1 — 90
(GLMoore) *a.p: wnt 2nd 5f out: led 2f out: hdd jst ins fnl f: nt pce of wnr* **9/4**[2]
440- **3** 1½ **Pagan Dance (IRE)**[54] 5349 5-10-0 **90** ........(p) DaneO'Neill 5 — 96
(MrsAJPerrett) *stdd s: hdwy 4f out: chsd ldr 2f out tl no ex ent fnl f* **16/1**
-006 **4** ¾ **Brilliant Red**[10] 743 11-9-4 **80** ........(t) CCatlin 4 — 85
(JamiePoulton) *stdd s: hld up: passed btn horses ins fnl 2f* **14/1**
-054 **5** 3½ **York Cliff**[5] 795 6-8-13 **75** ........ KFallon 2 — 74
(WMBrisbourne) *plld hrd: chsd ldr after 3f: led 6f out: hdd 2f out: sn wknd* **10/1**
-643 **6** 2½ **Typhoon Tilly**[10] 743 7-8-13 **75** ........ SDrowne 3 — 71
(CREgerton) *plld hrd: chsd ldrs 2f out: wknd over 1f out* **7/1**[3]
102- **7** 8 **Gralmano (IRE)**[98] 5727 9-9-12 **88** ........ FLynch 8 — 72
(KARyan) *led: hdd 6f out: sn wknd and wl bhd fnl 2f* **25/1**

2m 37.47s (3.49) **Going Correction** +0.10s/f (Slow)
**WFA** 4 from 5yo+ 3lb — **7** Ran SP% **118.8**
Speed ratings: **92,91,90,89,87 85,80**CSF £3.66 CT £20.46 TOTE £1.60: £1.50, £2.50; EX 5.50.
**Owner** Ian Hutchins **Bred** C A And R M Cyzer **Trained** Eastergate, W Sussex

**FOCUS**
A race that lost much of its competitiveness after the withdrawal of Cold Turkey. That said, take nothing away from Mission To Mars, who continues to improve. The winning time was painfully slow for the grade, however, and the form may not be that reliable.

**NOTEBOOK**
**Mission To Mars**, 13lb higher than when hacking up over course and distance on his previous outing, continued his progression with another comfortable victory. This was his sixth win from his last seven starts and he remains one to have on your side.
**Nawamees(IRE)**, stablemate of Cold Turkey, the only horse to have beaten the winner in that one's last seven starts, attracted strong market support, but was put in his place. This was still a good effort against such an improving type and he could be worth keeping in mind for a similar race.
**Pagan Dance(IRE)**, back on the level after a couple of unsuccessful spins over hurdles, ran well under his big weight.
**Brilliant Red** has taken time to find his form this All-Weather season, but this offered encouragement.
**York Cliff** again failed to prove his stamina for this trip and taking a keen grip did not help matters.
**Gralmano(IRE)** *Official explanation: jockey said gelding had ran flat*

## 845 BETDIRECT.CO.UK CLAIMING STKS — 1m (P)
**3:45** (3:47) (E) 3-Y-O — **£3,493** (£1,075; £537; £268) **Stalls** High

Form — RPR
3 **1** **African Dream**[7] 766 3-9-5 ........ KFallon 1 — 83
(PFICole) *trckd ldrs gng wl: led wl over 1f out: in command after* **3/1**[2]
4514 **2** 1¾ **Blue Empire (IRE)**[7] 769 3-9-3 78 ........ JPSpencer 3 — 77
(PABlockley) *s.i.s and hld up: prog 2f out to chse wnr fnl f* **5/2**[1]
3463 **3** 4 **Maybe Someday**[7] 769 3-8-11 67 ........(p) IMongan 4 — 62
(IAWood) *mid-div: rdn 3f out: no ch w first 2 fnl f* **6/1**[3]
0- **4** 1¼ **Eccentric**[157] 4997 3-9-5 ........ ANicholls 2 — 67
(AndrewReid) *led tl hdd wl over 1f out: no hdwy after* **50/1**
6-00 **5** 3 **Even Easier**[10] 741 3-8-4 53 ........(p) SWhitworth 8 — 46
(GLMoore) *v.s.a: sn in tch: effrt 3f out: wknd over 1f out* **8/1**
000- **6** 3½ **Steppenwolf**[113] 5847 3-8-9 47 ........ SRighton 7 — 43
(WDeBest-Turner) *hld up: rdn over 2f out: nvr nr to chal* **100/1**
-135 **7** nk **Rowan Pursuit**[28] 599 3-9-0 69 ........(b) JFanning 6 — 47
(JAkehurst) *hld up: rdn over 2f out: wknd fnl f* **3/1**[2]
000- **8** hd **Mistress Hollie (IRE)**[99] 5993 3-8-0 35 ........(p) DKinsella 5 — 33
(MrsPNDutfield) *prom tl wknd wl over 2f out* **66/1**
-064 **9** 1½ **Are You There**[2] 828 3-7-8 45 ........ JFMcDonald(5) 11 — 29
(PSMcentee) *in tch on outside for 2f: sn bhd* **33/1**
06 **10** shd **Livia (IRE)**[10] 739 3-9-0 ........ RHavlin 10 — 43
(JGPortman) *plld hrd: chsd ldr tl wknd qckly 2f out* **40/1**
0 **11** 15 **Shannkara's Quest (USA)**[7] 766 3-8-9 ........ JQuinn 9 — 5
(PFICole) *outpcd and a bhd* **20/1**

1m 39.46s (-0.05) **Going Correction** +0.10s/f (Slow) — **11** Ran SP% **118.6**
Speed ratings: **104,102,98,97,94 90,90,90,88,88 73**CSF £10.52 TOTE £5.10: £2.40, £1.40, £2.00; EX 18.70.The winner was claimed by Peter Chapple Hyam for £20,000.
**Owner** P F I Cole Ltd **Bred** E Landi **Trained** Whatcombe, Oxon

**FOCUS**
With a top claiming price of £20,000 this attracted some reasonable types and looked a strong race for the grade. The winning time was smart for a claimer.

**NOTEBOOK**
**African Dream** confirmed the promise he showed when third in a course and distance maiden on his debut to get off the mark in decisive fashion. Claimed afterwards for £20,000 by Peter Chapple-Hyam , he should be capable of holding his own in a higher grade.
**Blue Empire(IRE)** appreciated this drop back from a mile and two, running better than he had done in this grade last time. He was clear of the third and should continue to be a force in this grade. *Official explanation: jockey said gelding hung left in final furlong*
**Maybe Someday**, with cheekpieces on for the first time, proved unable to confirm recent placings with Blue Empire despite being on even better terms with that one on this drop back from ten furlongs. He may be worth another try over farther.
**Eccentric**, whose claiming price of £20,000 suggests he has shown something at home, stepped up on the form he showed on his debut on this return from a 157-day break and should continue to go the right way. One to keep an eye on.
**Even Easier** did not have an easy task at the weights and was well beaten.
**Rowan Pursuit** proved disappointing on this drop in grade, despite holding a reasonable chance at the weights. *Official explanation: jockey said filly had ran flat*
**Livia(IRE)** was in for an eye-catching £20,000 claiming price, but finished well beaten. She may be capable of better.

## 846 LITTLEWOODSCASINO.COM MAIDEN STKS — 1m (P)
**4:20** (4:21) (D) 3-Y-O+ — **£3,799** (£1,169; £584; £292) **Stalls** High

Form — RPR
0- **1** **Tiger Tiger (FR)**[111] 5887 3-8-7 ........ IMongan 2 — 74
(JamiePoulton) *chsd ldrs: hmpd on ins 3f out: rallied wl and r.o to ld wl ins fnl f* **16/1**
2-46 **2** ¾ **Sewmore Character**[35] 555 4-9-12 72 ........ KFallon 10 — 72
(MBlanshard) *hld up: hdwy 2f out to ld jst ins fnl f: nt qckn u.p and hdd wl ins fnl f* **11/4**[2]
03 **3** 2 **Green Falcon**[14] 702 3-8-7 ........ MHills 11 — 68
(JWHills) *chsd ldr after 2f: edgd lft and led 3f out: hdd jst ins fnl f: no ex* **8/1**[3]
/22- **4** 1½ **Lawood (IRE)**[132] 5524 4-9-12 ........(b[1]) NCallan 8 — 64
(KARyan) *hld up: r.o one pce ins fnl 2f* **9/1**
00 **5** 2 **Silver Cache (USA)**[33] 563 3-8-2 ........ CCatlin 3 — 55
(JNoseda) *outpcd in rr: passed btn horses fnl f* **25/1**
0-26 **6** 1¼ **Priors Dale**[21] 644 4-9-12 70 ........ DaneO'Neill 9 — 57
(KBell) *slowly away: stdy hdwy to chse ldr over 2f out: wknd over 1f out* **10/1**
65-0 **7** 1 **Best Before (IRE)**[28] 596 4-9-12 56 ........ SDrowne 1 — 55
(PDEvans) *led for 1f: sn outpcd and bhd whn hmpd 3f out* **16/1**
**8** 1½ **Ballinger Express** 4-9-7 ........ MartinDwyer 4 — 47
(AMBalding) *slowly away: in rr: effrt over 1f out: nvr on terms* **14/1**
**9** shd **Mandahar (IRE)** 5-9-12 ........ MTebbutt 6 — 51
(AWCarroll) *outpcd thrght* **50/1**
00-0 **10** 3 **Time Flyer**[14] 702 4-9-12 40 ........ SRighton 5 — 45
(WDeBest-Turner) *led after 1f: hdd 3f out: sn bhd* **100/1**
3-32 **L** **Spinning Dove**[21] 644 4-9-7 67 ........ JPSpencer 7 — —
(NAGraham) *ref to r* **6/4**[1]

1m 39.42s (-0.09) **Going Correction** +0.10s/f (Slow)
**WFA** 3 from 4yo+ 19lb — **11** Ran SP% **122.1**
Speed ratings: **104,103,101,99,97 96,95,94,93,90** —CSF £61.82 TOTE £14.00: £2.30, £1.30, £2.70; EX 67.80.
**Owner** R W Huggins **Bred** Pierre Talvard And Jean-Claude Seroul **Trained** Telscombe, E Sussex

**FOCUS**
Fair maiden form.

**NOTEBOOK**
**Tiger Tiger(FR)**, last in a course and distance maiden on his debut 111 days previously, improved markedly on that effort and was backed to do so. Things will be harder next time, but he can only improve.
**Sewmore Character** is proving hard to win with, but he can have no excuses. His time will come.
**Green Falcon**, stepped up to a mile for the first time, again showed promise but was left behind by the front two inside the final furlong.
**Lawood(IRE)**, a frustrating maiden when trained in Ireland, ran respectably in the first-time blinkers on his debut for a new trainer and they should find a minor opportunity for him.
**Silver Cache(USA)** was never a danger and will find things easier now she is qualified for a handicap mark.
**Ballinger Express** *Official explanation: jockey said filly had hung right into the final bend*
**Time Flyer** *Official explanation: jockey said colt had hung both ways throughout*
**Spinning Dove** did not want to take any part. *Official explanation: jockey said filly had planted at the start and took no further part*

## 847 LITTLEWOODSPOKER.COM H'CAP — 7f (P)
**4:55** (4:56) (E) (0-75,74) 3-Y-O+ — **£3,464** (£1,066; £533; £266) **Stalls** Low

Form — RPR
230- **1** **Harrison Point (USA)**[138] 5416 4-9-13 **73** ........ JPSpencer 14 — 83
(PWChapple-Hyam) *c over to ins fr wd draw: hld up: hdwy 2f out: short of room over 1f out: led ins fnl f: all out* **9/4**[1]
4355 **2** hd **Superchief**[7] 771 9-9-4 **64** ........(bt) JQuinn 8 — 73
(MissBSanders) *hld up: hdwy whn short of room over 1f out: swtchd rt over 1f out: swtchd rt and r.o strly to press wnr cl home* **12/1**
2412 **3** 1 **Mayzin (IRE)**[10] 738 4-9-2 **62** ........(p) DaneO'Neill 1 — 69
(RMFlower) *led tl rdn and hdd jst ins fnl f: nt qckn fnl 100yds* **8/1**
-141 **4** hd **Zafarshah (IRE)**[14] 701 5-9-2 **62** ........ KFallon 16 — 68
(PDEvans) *hld up: hdwy on outside over 1f out: led v briefly jst ins fnl f: no ex nr fin* **7/1**[3]
-642 **5** ¾ **The Gaikwar (IRE)**[14] 707 5-9-3 **63** ........(b) IMongan 5 — 67
(NPLittmoden) *bhd: hdwy towards outside over 1f out: r.o nvr nrr* **12/1**
000- **6** nk **Fearby Cross (IRE)**[95] 6024 8-9-3 **66** ........ LisaJones(3) 15 — 69
(WJMusson) *hld up on outside wl over 1f out: no imp ins fnl f* **33/1**
1126 **7** shd **Tayif**[7] 771 8-9-6 **66** ........(t) SCarson 6 — 69
(AndrewReid) *t.k.h: hdwy on outside 2f out: no ex fnl f* **20/1**



The Form Book, Raceform Ltd, Compton, RG20 6NL

0-00 **8** *hd* **Sir Francis (IRE)**[10] 742 6-9-8 **68** ........ PJScallan 7 71
(JNoseda) *chsd ldrs: ev ch over 1f out: fdd ins fnl f* **9/2**[2]
521- **9** *3/4* **Cold Climate**[77] 6127 9-9-5 **65** ........ OUrbina 11 66
(BobJones) *in tch: rdn and no ex appr fnl f* **14/1**
00-0 **10** *1/2* **Concer Eto**[21] 647 5-9-11 **71** ........ (p) MartinDwyer 9 71
(SCWilliams) *mid-div: rdn and c wd 2f out: no imp appr fnl f* **33/1**
10-2 **11** *nk* **Mistral Sky**[10] 742 5-10-0 **74** ........ (v) MFenton 12 73
(MrsStefLiddiard) *trckd ldrs: ev ch over 1f out: wknd ins fnl f* **14/1**
3240 **12** *hd* **Currency**[10] 742 7-9-12 **72** ........ SDrowne 3 70
(JMBradley) *chsd ldrs tl wknd appr fnl f* **20/1**
-552 **13** *shd* **Temper Tantrum**[21] 646 6-9-3 **63** ........ (p) ANicholls 10 61
(AndrewReid) *in rr: hdwy on outside 2f out: wknd fnl f* **12/1**
0 **14** *1 1/4* **Harry Potter (GER)**[22] 643 5-9-5 **65** ........ DarrenWilliams 2 60
(KRBurke) *trakce ldr tl rdn and wknd over 1f out* **40/1**
146- **15** *5* **Pagan Storm (USA)**[132] 5497 4-9-4 **71** ........ KristinStubbs(7) 13 53
(MrsLStubbs) *slowly away: a bhd* **100/1**

1m 26.04s (0.04) **Going Correction** +0.10s/f (Slow) **15** Ran SP% **127.8**
Speed ratings: **103,102,101,101,100 100,100,99,99,98 98,97,97,96,90**CSF £30.93 CT £205.71 TOTE £3.60: £1.90, £3.30, £4.30; EX 56.20 Place 6 £4.44, Place 5 £3.85.
**Owner** R E Sangster, M O'Donovan, F Cook **Bred** Creston Farm **Trained** Newmarket, Suffolk

**FOCUS**
A very competitive handicap and, due to the race being run at just a steady early pace, nearly every single runner held some sort of chance a furlong and a half out. Fairly strong form.

**NOTEBOOK**
**Harrison Point(USA)**, a maiden winner for John Gosden last season, had the visor left off for his debut for Peter Chapple-Hyam and justified strong market support. He had to wait for a gap, but so did the runner-up so he may not have been value for much more than the winning margin, but he showed a good attitude and should improve.
**Superchief** had to wait for a run, but so did the winner and he cannot be considered unlucky. He has not won for a long time, but his time should come if he maintains this level form.
**Mayzin(IRE)** had every chance from the front and can have no real excuses.
**Zafarshah(IRE)**, 5lb higher than when winning over course and distance on his previous outing, appeared to have every chance.
**The Gaikwar(IRE)** needed plenty of driving and only hit top stride all too late.
**Sir Francis(IRE)** continues below his best.
**Concer Eto** *Official explanation: trainer said gelding was found to be lame on returning home*
T/Plt: £9.90 to a £1 stake. Pool: £39,644.65. 2,911.55 winning tickets. T/Qpdt: £6.10 to a £1 stake. Pool: £1,866.00. 223.70 winning tickets. JS

## [830]NAD AL SHEBA (L-H)

Saturday, February 21

**OFFICIAL GOING: Dirt course - fast; turf course - good to firm**

### 848a SHADAYID STUD STKS (CONDITIONS RACE) (DIRT) 1m 110y

**3:00** (3:00) 3-Y-O £**9,078** (£2,793; £1,396; £698)

RPR

1 **Prince Of Denmark (IRE)**[16] 691 3-9-0 95 ........ (t) TEDurcan 8 93
(MAlKurdi, UAE) *mde all: clr ldr 1/2-way: chal 2f out: styd on wl u.p nr fin* **4/1**[2]
2 *nk* **Tamarillo**[14] 711 3-8-9 95 ........ (t) JCarroll 7 88
(MAlKurdi, UAE) *s.i.s: in tch outside: 3rd st: r.o wl fnl 165yds: nrst fin* **5/2**[1]
3 *1 1/2* **Ras Hafa (USA)**[16] 691 3-9-0 80 ........ BDoyle 1 90
(AllanSmith, UAE) *settled in 5th pl: hdwy on ins st: chal and ev ch fnl f: no ex nr fin* **4/1**[2]
4 *1/2* **Forthright**[16] 691 3-9-0 93 ........ EAhern 5 89
(CEBrittain) *in tch in mid-div: 6th and racd wd st: styd on wl fnl f: nrst fin* **9/2**[3]
5 *1 1/4* **Storm Of Tara (USA)**[16] 691 3-9-0 80 ........ (t) GHind 2 87
(MAlKurdi, UAE) *trckd ldr: 2nd st: hrd rdn and ev ch 2f out: wkng whn hmpd fnl 110yds* **7/1**
6 *6 3/4* **Cupola**[16] 691 3-9-0 85 ........ (v[1]) PJSmullen 6 74
(MAlKurdi, UAE) *trckd ldrs tl wknd st* **11/1**
7 *6 1/4* **Aviation Falcon (USA)** 3-9-0 ........ RLMoore 3 62
(SSeemar, UAE) *v.s.a: sn bhd: poor 7th st: nvr nr to chal* **14/1**
8 *dist* **Houbara**[9] 753 3-9-0 ........ KMcEvoy 4 —
(SSeemar, UAE) *sn outpcd and bhd: last st: n.d* **33/1**

1m 47.38s **8** Ran SP% **117.2**
Speed ratings: .
**Owner** H E Sheikh Rashid Bin Mohammed **Bred** Tally-Ho Stud **Trained** United Arab Emirates

**NOTEBOOK**
**Forthright** improved on his run at the course earlier in the month and was edging closer with every stride at the line.

### 849a ALJABR STKS (H'CAP) (TURF) 1m 4f

**3:30** (3:31) (95-110,110) 3-Y-O+ £**36,312** (£11,173; £5,586; £2,793)

RPR

1 **Rawyaan**[162] 4861 5-9-6 110 ........ (b) RHills 7 111
(JHMGosden) *in tch towards rr: 7th on ins st: swtchd rt over 2f out: r.o wl to ld fnl 165yds* **6/1**
2 *3/4* **Kayseri (IRE)**[16] 692 5-9-1 105 ........ (v) BDoyle 1 105
(AllanSmith, UAE) *t.k.h: hld up: mid-div: 4th st: chal and ev ch over 1f out: nt pce of wnr* **7/4**[1]
3 *1/2* **Classical Act (IND)**[9] 754 5-8-5 95 ........ (t) MDuPlessis 5 94
(SPadmanabhan, India) *led: trckd ldr after 3f: led st tl hdd fnl 165yds: no ex nr fin* **20/1**
4 *shd* **Shami**[16] 692 5-8-5 95 ........ (v) JCarroll 3 94
(DRLoder) *in tch: racd wd and hdwy st: chal over 1f out: unable qck* **7/2**[2]
5 *2* **Santando**[16] 688 4-8-5 95 ........ (v) EAhern 2 94
(CEBrittain) *trckd ldrs: 3rd st: grad wknd fnl 2f* **10/1**
6 *1 3/4* **Mkuzi**[14] 712 5-9-4 108 ........ RMullen 8 101
(JohnMOxx, Ire) *mid-div: 6th and racd wd st: effrt 2f out: grad wknd* **5/1**[3]
7 *4 1/4* **Monetary (GER)**[118] 5781 4-8-13 105 ........ PJSmullen 4 93
(ECharpy, UAE) *in rr: last st: kpt on same pce* **14/1**
8 *4 1/4* **Dubai World (USA)**[9] 757 6-8-13 102 ........ (t) SSanders 6 84
(ECharpy, UAE) *trckd ldrs: led 9f out tl hdd st: sn wknd* **11/1**

2m 31.17s
**WFA** 4 from 5yo+ 3lb **8** Ran SP% **118.4**
Speed ratings: .
**Owner** Hamdan Al Maktoum **Bred** Shadwell Estate Company Limited **Trained** Manton, Wilts

**NOTEBOOK**
**Rawyaan** defied top weight to make a successful debut in Dubai. Now two from two in blinkers, he looks sure to improve and should continue to go well at this level.
**Shami** continues in good heart, but keeps finding a few too good.
**Santando** ran better on this switch from the dirt and should continue to go the right way.
**Mkuzi** did not improve for this step up in trip.

### 850a NASHWAN STKS (H'CAP) (TURF) 7f 110y

**4:05** (4:07) (95-110,110) 3-Y-O+ £**36,312** (£11,173; £5,586; £2,793)

RPR

1 **Cat Belling (IRE)**[2] 831 4-8-9 95 ........ WSupple 3 101
(RBouresly, Kuwait) *mid-div ins: 7th st: swtchd rt and hdwy 2f out: r.o wl to ld fnl 165yds: rdn out* **14/1**
2 *2 1/4* **Western Diplomat (USA)**[373] 4-9-5 105 ........ (t) LDettori 8 105
(SaeedBinSuroor) *led: rdn 2f out: kpt on tl hdd 165yds out: nt pce of wnr* **5/4**[1]
3 *1 1/4* **Baaridd**[9] 755 6-8-11 97 ........ BDoyle 4 94
(AllanSmith, UAE) *trckd ldrs: rdn 2f out: kpt on nr fin* **5/1**[3]
4 *1/2* **Landslide (IRE)**[23] 636 5-8-11 97 ........ PHanagan 6 93
(PRudkin, UAE) *trckd ldr: 2nd st: rdn to chal 2f out: kpt on same pce* **9/1**
5 *2* **Membership (USA)**[16] 689 4-9-11 110 ........ EAhern 5 102
(CEBrittain) *mid-div: 6th st: rdn and effrt 2f out: wknd nr fin* **13/2**
6 *nk* **Ice Cube (SAF)**[9] 754 3-8-9 98 ........ (bt) WCMarwing 1 104
(GeoffWoodruff, South Africa) *hld up: trckd ldr: rdn and effrt over 2f out: sn wknd* **7/2**[2]
7 *4* **Simeon**[14] 712 5-9-5 105 ........ (v) TEDurcan 9 85
(SSeemar, UAE) *in tch towards rr: racd wd and effrt 400m out: sn wknd* **33/1**
8 *2* **Alunissage (USA)**[338] 6-9-1 100 ........ (t) RMullen 2 76
(MAlMuhairi, UAE) *a towards rr: kpt on st: n.d* **66/1**
9 *12* **Royal Beacon**[14] 4-9-3 102 ........ (b[1]) SSanders 7 48
(ChristianWroe, UAE) *mid-div outside: rdn fr 1/2-way: racd wd st: wknd fnl 2f* **33/1**

1m 29.47s
**WFA** 3 from 4yo+ 17lb **9** Ran SP% **120.7**
Speed ratings: .
**Owner** Bouresly Racing Syndicate **Bred** Mrs M O'Callaghan **Trained** Kuwait

**NOTEBOOK**
**Western Diplomat(USA)** has been very lightly raced as this was just his third ever start, but he is talented as he showed when runner-up in the UAE 2000 Guineas last term. He could not hold on this time, though, after making most of the running.
**Membership(USA)** was expected to appreciate the return to turf racing, but he was once again disappointing.

### 851a ERHAAB STUD STKS (H'CAP) (DIRT) 5f

**4:40** (4:43) (90-105,105) 3-Y-O+ £**32,681** (£10,055; £5,027; £2,513)

RPR

1 **Conceal**[9] 755 6-9-6 101 ........ RHills 3 93
(RBouresly, Kuwait) *disp ld: rdn fr 1/2-way: r.o wl to ld 165yds out: rdn out* **9/4**[1]
2 *1/2* **Elegance Champion (AUS)**[14] 5-8-9 90 ........ (be) SChin 6 80
(GMoore, Macau) *bmpd s: trckd ldrs: rdn and hdwy fr 1/2-way: r.o wl fnl f: nrst fin* **4/1**[3]
3 *2 1/4* **Dantana (AUS)**[16] 689 5-9-10 105 ........ (b) KMcEvoy 4 87
(PLeyshan, Macau) *disp ld: rdn 1 1/2f out: hdd fnl 165yds: no ex nr fin* **25/1**
4 *nk* **Raging Creek (USA)**[14] 5-9-2 97 ........ (t) SSanders 1 78
(AllanSmith, UAE) *disp ld: rdn 1 1/2f out: hdd 165yds out: sn wknd* **15/2**
5 *nk* **Magic Master (SAF)**[14] 5-9-5 100 ........ MDuPlessis 7 80
(BWiid, South Africa) *swvd s: disp ld stands' side: rdn 1 1/2f out: hdd 165yds out: wknd nr fin* **5/2**[2]
6 *3 1/4* **Peruvian Chief (IRE)**[23] 632 7-9-5 100 ........ (v) EAhern 2 69
(NPLittmoden) *chsd ldrs: wknd fnl 2f* **16/1**
7 *1 3/4* **Tala Ya (USA)**[16] 689 6-8-9 90 ........ (vt) GHind 8 53
(MAlKurdi, UAE) *sn outpcd and bhd stands' side: kpt on nr fin: nvr trbld ldrs* **6/1**
8 *1 1/4* **Energetic (NZ)**[23] 634 6-8-9 90 ........ (e) RMullen 5 48
(SLeung, Macau) *disp ld tl rdn and wknd fr 1/2-way* **40/1**

58.43 secs **8** Ran SP% **117.6**
Speed ratings: .
**Owner** Bouresly Racing Syndicate **Bred** Sheikh Mohammed Bin Rashid Al Maktoum **Trained** Kuwait

**NOTEBOOK**
**Peruvian Chief(IRE)** improved on the form he showed on his first start out in Dubai, but still has a long way to go.

### 852a SWAIN STUD STKS (H'CAP) (TURF) 7f 110y

**5:15** (5:15) (95-110,108) 3-Y-O+ £**36,312** (£11,173; £5,586; £2,793)

RPR

1 **Three Graces (GER)**[140] 5370 4-9-3 102 ........ (vt) LDettori 8 110
(SaeedBinSuroor) *sn ld: rdn clr 1f out: pushed out nr fin* **7/4**[1]
2 *3 1/2* **One More Round (USA)**[14] 710 6-9-8 108 ........ PJSmullen 1 106
(DKWeld, Ire) *in tch towards rr: 7th st: hdwy 2f out: r.o fnl f: no ch w wnr* **9/4**[2]
3 *3/4* **Maidaan**[41] 8-9-0 99 ........ PaulSmith 3 97
(AllanSmith, UAE) *qckly away: hld up: trckd wnr: rdn 2f out: kpt on same pce* **25/1**
4 *1* **Hazelhatch**[9] 755 4-8-10 96 ........ (t) GHind 6 90
(MAlKurdi, UAE) *slowly away: sn mid-div: 3rd st: rdn and ev ch over 2f out: grad wknd fnl f* **15/2**
5 *1/2* **Royal Dignitary (USA)**[9] 754 4-8-11 97 ........ (b) RHills 5 90
(DRLoder) *in towards rr: 6th st: rdn and effrt over 2f out: wknd fnl f* **12/1**
6 *1 3/4* **Wizard Of Noz**[16] 690 4-9-5 105 ........ JCarroll 4 93
(JNoseda) *trckd ldrs: rdn and effrt 2f out: wknd fnl f* **9/2**[3]
7 *1 3/4* **Tudor Wood**[23] 634 5-8-9 95 ........ (bt[1]) GAvranche 7 79
(NDeCroutte, Bahrain) *hld up: trckd ldr: 2nd st: wknd fnl 2f* **25/1**
8 *5 1/2* **Attache**[23] 634 6-9-5 105 ........ KMcEvoy 2 75
(IMohammed, UAE) *a in rr: n.d* **14/1**

1m 30.33s **8** Ran SP% **119.1**
Speed ratings: .
**Owner** Godolphin **Bred** Darley Stud **Trained** Newmarket, Suffolk

**NOTEBOOK**
**Three Graces(GER)**, formerly with Marcus Tregoning, made an impressive debut in this country, quickening up well to win as he pleased. He likes this fast ground and can win a better race.
**One More Round(USA)** has run creditably on both starts at the course to date and should continue to pay his way.

**Royal Dignitary(USA)** has not really done enough in three starts so far to suggest he is going to be winning soon.
**Wizard Of Noz**, second at the course earlier in the month, was disappointing, but is capable of much better.

## 853a AL RASHIDIYA UNFUWAIN STKS (LISTED) (TURF) 1m 1f
5:45 (5:45) 4-Y-0+ £50,837 (£15,642; £7,821; £3,910)

RPR

1 **Right Approach**$^{126}$ [5643] 5-9-0 115 KMcEvoy 5 106
(MFDeKock, South Africa) *towards rr: 9th st: rdn and stdy hdwy 2f out: r.o wl to ld fnl 55yds* **9/2**$^{2}$

2 *nk* **Surveyor (SAF)**$^{14}$ [710] 4-9-6 112 (b) WCMarwing 10 111
(MFDeKock, South Africa) *trckd clr ldr: 2nd st: rdn over 2f out: chal and ev ch fnl f: jst failed* **11/4**$^{1}$

3 *nk* **St Expedit**$^{2}$ [832] 7-9-0 102 GHind 1 104
(RBouresly, Kuwait) *qckly away: sn wl clr: rdn over 2f out: styd on gamely tl hdd fnl 55yds* **33/1**

4 *hd* **Checkit (IRE)**$^{97}$ [6007] 4-9-0 110 TEDurcan 6 104
(MRChannon) *mid-div: rdn and hdwy 2f out: chal and ev ch fnl f: no ex nr fin* **7/1**

5 *3/4* **Lodge Keeper**$^{23}$ [633] 4-9-0 96 GAvranche 2 103
(NDeCroutte, Bahrain) *in tch towards rr: 11th st: stdy hdwy fnl 2f: nrst fin* **12/1**

6 *1 3/4* **Zirna (NZ)**$^{104}$ 5-9-2 105 MDuPlessis 7 101
(MThwaites, Macau) *trckd ldrs: 4th st: rdn over 2f out: kpt on same pce* **10/1**

7 *nk* **Trademark (SAF)**$^{140}$ [5410] 7-9-4 116 RLMoore 12 103
(SSeemar, UAE) *trckd ldrs: 3rd st: chal and ev ch fnl 1 1/2f: wknd nr fin* **5/1**$^{3}$

8 *3 1/4* **Seihali (IRE)**$^{16}$ [690] 5-9-0 104 BDoyle 11 93
(AllanSmith, UAE) *mid-div outside: hdwy 2f out: kpt on same pce* **7/1**

9 *5 1/4* **Sole (BRZ)**$^{16}$ [690] 6-9-0 90 JCarroll 4 83
(PRudkin, UAE) *towards rr: 8th st: effrt over 2f out: sn wknd* **66/1**

10 *6 1/2* **Red Crescent (SAF)**$^{16}$ [690] 6-9-0 90 (t) RHills 3 71
(SSeemar, UAE) *a towards rr: last st: nvr nr to chal* **66/1**

11 *11* **Sign Of The Wolf**$^{55}$ 4-9-2 110 (t) SSanders 9 53
(ECharpy, UAE) *mid-div tl wknd 2f out: eased fnl 110yds* **7/1**

12 *1 1/4* **Majestic Horizon**$^{16}$ [690] 4-9-0 90 (t) RMullen 8 48
(AAlRaihe, UAE) *a towards rr: racd wd st: eased fnl 110yds* **33/1**

1m 47.65s **12** Ran SP% **124.7**
Speed ratings: .
**Owner** B Kantor, Mrs M Slack, Messrs Chandler & Westwood **Bred** The Queen **Trained** South Africa

**NOTEBOOK**
**Right Approach**, formerly trained by Sir Michael Stoute, came with a wet sail to take the race in the final moments. He appreciated the fast ground and good pace.
**Checkit(IRE)** was one of a few in with a chance entering the final furlong but ventully failed to make the frame.

## 854a SAHM STUD STKS (H'CAP) (TURF) 1m 4f
6:15 (6:15) (95-110,110) 3-Y-0+ £36,312 (£11,173; £5,586; £2,793)

RPR

1 **Scott's View**$^{14}$ [712] 5-9-5 109 SChin 1 111
(MJohnston) *in tch: 6th st: hdwy over 2f out: nt clr run 1f out: swtchd and r.o wl to ld fnl 55yds* **10/3**$^{3}$

2 *1/2* **Dutch Gold (USA)**$^{9}$ [756] 4-9-4 110 LDettori 5 112
(CEBrittain) *trckd ldrs: 3rd st: qcknd to ld 2f out: kpt on wl tl hdd fnl 55yds* **7/1**

3 *1 1/4* **Prince Of War (AUS)**$^{14}$ [712] 6-9-0 104 WCMarwing 7 103
(MFDeKock, South Africa) *in tch towards rr: racd wd and hdwy st: chal and ev ch 1f out: no ex cl home* **5/2**$^{1}$

4 *3/4* **Fantastic Horse (ARG)**$^{16}$ [692] 5-8-13 102 (bt) KMcEvoy 6 101
(GeoffWoodruff, South Africa) *led tl hdd 2f out: grad wknd nr fin* **14/1**

5 *hd* **Zaajel (IRE)**$^{16}$ [692] 5-8-10 100 (t) RHills 4 98
(ECharpy, UAE) *in tch towards rr: 7th st: hdwy 2f out: no ex fnl f* **3/1**$^{2}$

6 *4 3/4* **Clodion (IRE)**$^{14}$ [712] 8-8-11 101 GHind 2 91
(MAlKurdi, UAE) *in tch tl wknd fnl 2f* **6/1**

7 *2* **Zurbaran (IND)**$^{9}$ [757] 5-8-5 95 TEDurcan 8 82
(SPadmanabhan, India) *trckd ldr: 2nd st: rdn and wknd over 2f out* **33/1**

8 *1/2* **Impaciente Gg (URU)**$^{16}$ [692] 4-8-5 95 (b) MWilliamson 3 85
(ASelvaratnam, UAE) *s.i.s: a in rr: nvr nr to chal* **25/1**

2m 29.67s
**WFA** 4 from 5yo+ 3lb **8** Ran SP% **116.9**
Speed ratings: .
**Owner** Great Escape Partnership **Bred** Cliveden Stud Ltd **Trained** Middleham Moor, N Yorks

**FOCUS**
Scott's View recorded a winning time over a second faster than the time Rawyaan achieved over the same course and distance in an earlier race.

**NOTEBOOK**
**Scott's View** shaped well on his debut in Dubai over ten furlongs on his previous outing and built on that promise to run out a narrow winner. He did not get the clearest of runs, but flew when finally in the clear and is probably value for a little more than the winning margin.
**Dutch Gold(USA)** appreciated this return to turf and ran a cracker. He looks capable of picking up a similar race.

# 840 LINGFIELD (L-H)
Monday, February 23

**OFFICIAL GOING: Standard**
Wind: lt hlf against Weather: fine but cloudy

## 855 BET DIRECT NO Q ON 08000 93 66 93 BANDED STKS 1m 2f (P)
1:55 (1:55) (H) 4-Y-0+ £1,655 (£473; £236) Stalls Low

Form RPR

-045 1 **Landescent (IRE)**$^{12}$ [740] 4-8-6 45 DerekNolan$^{(7)}$ 1 48
(MissKMGeorge) *mde all: kicked on over 2f out: drvn 2l clr over 1f out: edgd rt fnl f: hld on* **12/1**

4-21 2 *nk* **Wanna Shout**$^{7}$ [788] 6-9-3 45 LisaJones$^{(3)}$ 6 54
(RDickin) *hld up and sn in midfield: prog to trck ldrs over 2f out: drvn and hanging fr over 1f out: styd on fnl f: jst hld* **9/1**

650- 3 *1/2* **On Guard**$^{122}$ [5729] 6-9-0 45 (v) DKinsella 4 47
(PGMurphy) *settled in midfield: prog to trck ldrs over 2f out: effrt over 1f out: disp 2nd pl fnl f: one pce last 100y* **8/1**$^{3}$

0-52 4 *1/2* **Chocolate Boy (IRE)**$^{7}$ [788] 5-9-0 45 (be) SWhitworth 13 46
(GLMoore) *s.s: swtchd to inner and hld up last: prog 3f out: effrt and drvn on outer over 1f out: kpt on one pce fnl f* **7/2**$^{2}$

0206 5 *shd* **Pyrrhic**$^{19}$ [672] 5-9-0 45 (b) EAhern 7 46
(RMFlower) *settled towards rr: gng wl enough over 2f out: drvn and nt qckn over 1f out: styd on fnl 150y: nt rch ldrs* **8/1**$^{3}$

00-1 6 *hd* **Montosari**$^{20}$ [661] 5-9-0 45 DHolland 3 46
(PMitchell) *t.k.h: cl up: rdn to chse wnr 2f out: drvn and nt qckn over 1f out: one pce fnl f* **9/4**$^{1}$

0-06 7 *2* **Eurolink Zante (IRE)**$^{7}$ [788] 8-8-11 45 (b) LPKeniry$^{(3)}$ 2 42
(TDMccarthy) *trckd ldrs: cl enough 2f out: shkn up and fnd nil over 1f out* **20/1**

2545 8 *1* **Wilom (GER)**$^{7}$ [787] 6-8-11 45 LFletcher$^{(3)}$ 9 40
(MRHoad) *t.k.h: trckd wnr to 2f out: sn nt qckn and btn* **20/1**

-600 9 *1 1/4* **Mythical Charm**$^{7}$ [788] 5-9-0 45 GBaker 8 38
(JJBridger) *hld up in rr: prog over 2f out: effrt on outer wl over 1f out: wknd fnl f* **12/1**

5-60 10 *6* **Lady At Leisure (IRE)**$^{7}$ [787] 4-8-13 45 MTebbutt 12 27
(JulianPoulton) *a towards rr: last and rdn over 4f out: lost tch w ldrs over 2f out* **33/1**

-000 11 *hd* **Platinum Boy (IRE)**$^{6}$ [812] 4-8-13 45 (p) VSlattery 14 27
(MWellings) *racd wd towards rr: rdn over 4f out: sn struggling and btn* **50/1**

-430 12 *1 1/4* **Cherokee Bay**$^{7}$ [787] 4-8-13 45 (e) PDobbs 10 25
(GLMoore) *chsd ldrs: drvn over 3f out: wknd over 2f out* **14/1**

40-0 13 *7* **Royale Pearl**$^{7}$ [788] 4-8-13 45 DaneO'Neill 11 12
(RIngram) *racd on outer in midfield: rdn over 4f out: sn wknd* **20/1**

/00- 14 *14* **Promote**$^{56}$ [6254] 8-9-0 45 PMcCabe 5 —
(MsAEEmbiricos) *racd towards rr: drvn and effrt on outer over 3f out: wkng whn nrly rn off crse bnd wl over 1f out: t.o* **33/1**

2m 8.61s (1.22) **Going Correction** -0.025s/f (Stan)
**WFA** 4 from 5yo+ 1lb **14** Ran SP% **129.4**
Speed ratings: **94,93,93,92,92 92,91,90,89,84 84,83,77,66**CSF £114.22 TOTE £14.50: £2.80, £2.10, £3.80; EX 172.70.
**Owner** Stableline **Bred** Carrigbeg Stud Co Ltd **Trained** Higher Easington, Devon

**FOCUS**
Typically modest banded form. Just an ordinary pace and a modest winning time.

**NOTEBOOK**
**Landescent(IRE)**, making his debut for the yard after being claimed last time, stays further than this and his rider was rightly positive on him. Gradually winding up the pace rounding the home bend, he kept enough in hand to hold off this modest bunch.
**Wanna Shout** was stepping up a quarter of a mile from her victory here last time, but she does stay this trip. She did not have much room in which to manoeuvre a furlong from home and also tended to hang away from the whip, but despite that she did stay on without ever quite looking like getting to the winner.
**On Guard**, returning from a four-month break, had every chance and went down fighting. Rated higher on turf, he is more than capable of winning a race like this.
**Chocolate Boy(IRE)** was very tardy leaving the stalls and was content to sit right out the back. He had to try and weave a path through in order to get a run, but was certainly close enough if good enough a furlong from home. This was the third race in a row that he has finished behind Wanna Shout.
**Pyrrhic** is capable of running tremendous races against much higher-rated rivals, but when dropped to this sort of grade fails to run to the same level. He had every chance on this occasion, but did not pick up anything like quickly enough.
**Montosari** was in a good position throughout, but lacked a turn of foot where it mattered and the three-furlong drop in trip was not in his favour.
**Promote** *Official explanation: jockey said gelding lost its action turning in*

## 856 BET DIRECT NO Q MEDIAN AUCTION MAIDEN STKS 6f (P)
2:30 (2:30) (H) 3-5-Y-0 £1,274 (£364; £182) Stalls Low

Form RPR

2424 1 **Ile Facile (IRE)**$^{20}$ [668] 3-8-10 70 DHolland 1 58
(NPLittmoden) *in tch: pushed along 1/2-way: prog 2f out: drvn and kpt on to ld wl ins fnl f* **4/5**$^{1}$

2 *nk* **Knead The Dough** 3-8-10 JFEgan 2 58
(DECantillon) *in tch: chsd ldr 2f out: rdn to ld on inner jst over 1f out: kpt on: hdd wl ins fnl f* **10/1**

500- 3 *3 1/2* **Flame Princess**$^{154}$ [5126] 4-9-6 40 NCallan 5 42
(JRBoyle) *sn in rr: rdn wl over 2f out: hrd drvn and kpt on one pce to take 3rd ins fnl f* **50/1**

0062 4 *1 1/4* **Onefortheboys (IRE)**$^{7}$ [792] 5-9-4 35 LTreadwell$^{(7)}$ 4 43
(DFlood) *outpcd in last and sn rdn: wl adrift over 2f out: plugged on fr over 1f out: no ch* **20/1**

26-3 5 *shd* **After All (IRE)**$^{51}$ [414] 3-8-5 61 EAhern 3 38
(GAButler) *trckd ldr tl led over 4f out: gng best 2f out: rdn and fnd nil over 1f out: sn hdd & wknd* **9/4**$^{2}$

-204 6 *2 1/2* **Dark Champion**$^{6}$ [805] 4-9-11 48 DaneO'Neill 7 35
(JeddO'Keeffe) *led to over 4f out: chsd ldr to 2f out: sn wknd* **9/1**$^{3}$

4503 7 *1 1/2* **Somethingabouther**$^{7}$ [792] 4-9-3 35 LisaJones$^{(3)}$ 6 26
(PWHiatt) *chsd ldrs: hanging rt fr over 3f out: wknd 2f out* **20/1**

1m 13.32s (0.40) **Going Correction** -0.025s/f (Stan)
**WFA** 3 from 4yo+ 15lb **7** Ran SP% **116.9**
Speed ratings: **96,95,90,89,89 85,83**CSF £10.53 TOTE £1.80: £1.10, £5.60; EX 20.10.
**Owner** Paul J Dixon **Bred** John Foley **Trained** Newmarket, Suffolk
■ A first winner for Darryll Holland on his first day returning to race-riding.
■ Stewards Enquiry : E Ahern three-day ban: failed to ride out for fourth place (Mar 5,8,9)

**FOCUS**
A poor maiden run at an ordinary pace, and a two-horse race according to the market.

**NOTEBOOK**
**Ile Facile(IRE)** had the form on the board and also plenty in hand on adjusted official ratings, but made rather heavy weather of picking off the runner-up. In his defence, this trip is almost certainly shorter than ideal.
**Knead The Dough**, from the same family as Ridgewood Pearl, ran a fine race on this racecourse debut and looked at one stage as though he might hold off the favourite, but in the end was just denied. He should improve, but will probably need to stay in this sort of grade in order to get off the mark.
**Flame Princess**, never closer than fourth in 13 previous outings, achieved nothing here.
**Onefortheboys(IRE)** did not build on his effort over the minimum trip here the previous week and is still a maiden after 16 attempts.
**After All(IRE)**, whose attitude is very questionable, was given a positive ride, but once the challengers arrived she decided she had done enough.
**Somethingabouther** *Official explanation: trainer said filly hung right throughout*

## 857 BET DIRECT NO Q DEMO 08000 837 888 BANDED STKS 1m 4f (P)
3:05 (3:09) (H ) 4-Y-0+ £1,463 (£418; £209) Stalls Low

Form RPR

630 **1** **Free Style (GER)**[14] 724 4-8-12 40 GBaker 6 48
*(KRBurke) hld up and last to 1/2-way: stl only 10th whn reminder 4f out: rapid prog on outer to ld 3f out: sn clr: rdn out: unchal* **10/1**[3]

0-63 **2** 1 ¼ **Private Seal**[20] 663 9-8-8 40 (t) MHalford(7) 5 46
*(JulianPoulton) settled in midfield: outpcd 3f out: rdn and styd on fr 2f out: chsd wnr last 150y: clsng at fin but nvr able to chal* **10/1**[3]

00-0 **3** 1 ¾ **Giko**[20] 661 10-9-1 35 (b) EAhern 1 44
*(JaneSouthcombe) trckd ldrs: cl up 3f out: sn outpcd: kpt on u.p fnl 2f* **20/1**

0431 **4** ½ **Little Richard (IRE)**[7] 789 5-9-7 30 (p) VSlattery 15 49
*(MWellings) prom: chsd ldr over 5f out: led briefly over 3f out: sn outpcd by wnr: no imp after: fdd ins fnl f* **8/1**[2]

46/3 **5** 2 ½ **Adjiram (IRE)**[7] 793 8-9-1 30 WRyan 7 39
*(AWCarroll) t.k.h: hld up bhd ldrs: cl enough 3f out: sn outpcd: one pce after* **5/1**[1]

00-5 **6** 3 **Broughtons Mill**[20] 664 9-8-8 35 RoryMoore(7) 4 35
*(JASupple) hld up towards rr: prog over 3f out: sn outpcd: one pce after* **25/1**

00-0 **7** 4 **Boom Or Bust (IRE)**[20] 663 5-8-8 40 (p) DerekNolan(7) 3 29
*(MissKMGeorge) t.k.h: hld up in midfield: outpcd fr 3f out: grad fdd* **8/1**[2]

040/ **8** 5 **Dont Worry Bout Me (IRE)**[585] 3098 7-9-1 40 (v) SWhitworth 12 21
*(TGMills) rrd s: led to over 3f out: sn wknd* **5/1**[1]

/0-0 **9** ½ **Stopwatch (IRE)**[7] 793 9-9-1 35 (p) NCallan 2 20
*(MrsLCJewell) s.i.s: hld up in rr: outpcd over 3f out: no ch after* **50/1**

530- **10** 5 **Tojoneski**[58] 4737 5-8-8 40 (v[1]) PPMathers(7) 9 13
*(IWMcinnes) prom tl wknd rapidly 3f out* **16/1**

00/5 **11** 9 **Neptune**[21] 579 8-9-1 35 PDobbs 11 —
*(JCFox) a towards rr: u.p and wkng 4f out: t.o* **10/1**[3]

46-5 **12** ½ **First Class Lady**[20] 659 4-8-9 40 LisaJones(3) 10 —
*(PMitchell) racd in midfield to 1/2-way: sn wknd and bhd: t.o* **10/1**[3]

0003 **13** 21 **Polka Princess**[7] 789 4-8-10 40 ow5 LTreadwell(7) 8 —
*(MWellings) in tch tl wknd 1/2-way: sn wl t.o* **14/1**

63-5 **14** 2 **Dame Margaret**[14] 729 4-8-12 40 DaneO'Neill 13 —
*(JABOld) s.i.s: hld up in rr: wknd 1/2-way: sn wl t.o* **12/1**

0-06 **15** 13 **Penny Valentine**[7] 793 4-8-12 35 NPollard 14 —
*(JRBest) pressed ldr: rdn over 7f out: wknd rapidly over 5f out: sn wl t.o* **33/1**

2m 33.48s (-0.50) **Going Correction** -0.025s/f (Stan)
**WFA** 4 from 5yo+ 3lb **15** Ran SP% **125.7**
Speed ratings: **100,99,98,97,96 94,91,88,87,84 78,78,64,62,54**CSF £106.32 TOTE £16.20: £6.00, £2.80, £10.40; EX 103.00.
**Owner** P Sweeting **Bred** Gestut Hof Ittlingen **Trained** Middleham Moor, N Yorks

**FOCUS**
A decent pace and a fair winning time for the grade, but this was only modest banded form.

**NOTEBOOK**
**Free Style(GER)**, having just her fourth outing in this country, won this under an enterprising ride. Held up out the back early, she was given a crack behind the saddle passing the half-mile pole and quickly took off around the outside of the leading group to hit the front, soon establishing a significant advantage. She did get a bit tired down the straight, but her rivals were not good enough to get back on terms.
**Private Seal**, up in trip, ran on from off the pace and was eating into the winner's advantage without looking like catching her. He has flattered to deceive in the past and has not won for more than three years.
**Giko** ran one of his better races, but his recent record away from Les Landes does not suggest he is one to lump on next time.
**Little Richard(IRE)** is a consistent, if slow, stayer and this trip on a fast surface would have been plenty sharp enough.
**Adjiram(IRE)** again attracted market support, but he compromised his chance by pulling hard and had nothing left where it matters.
**Broughtons Mill** looked as though he might take a hand when moving up on the outside turning for home, but then looked awkward for a few strides and was quickly beaten.
**Dont Worry Bout Me(IRE)**, the lead horse for Where Or When, made the running, but was not given an easy lead and folded tamely before reaching the home bend.
**Polka Princess** *Official explanation: trainer said filly was found to be in season the morning after the race*

## 858 BET DIRECT INTERACTIVE CLAIMING STKS 7f (P)
3:40 (3:41) (H ) 3-Y-0+ £1,312 (£375; £187) Stalls Low

Form RPR

-054 **1** **Cayman Breeze**[7] 791 4-9-10 59 DHolland 1 57
*(SDow) t.k.h: trckd ldrs: rdn and effrt 2f out: r.o to ld last 100y: in command after* **4/1**[2]

00-0 **2** 1 ½ **Single Track Mind**[40] 527 6-9-0 30 KarenPeippo(7) 3 50
*(JRBoyle) dwlt: racd in last to 3f out: rapid prog wl over 1f out: bmpd along and r.o to chse wnr last 50y: gaining nr fin* **50/1**

30-3 **3** 1 ¼ **Jahangir**[7] 787 5-9-10 45 DaneO'Neill 10 50
*(BRJohnson) led after 1f: gng easily 2f out: drew 3l clr over 1f out: rdn and nt run on fnl f: hdd last 100y* **9/2**[3]

0-40 **4** ¾ **Janes Valentine**[20] 660 4-9-4 45 NCallan 4 42
*(JJBridger) s.i.s: hld up in rr: progres 2f out: chsd ldrs ent fnl f: one pce after* **16/1**

1430 **5** shd **Lord Melbourne (IRE)**[12] 738 5-9-3 50 SCrawford(7) 2 47+
*(JAOsborne) hld up wl in rr: gng wl enough but plenty to do whn nt clr run 2f out: prog and nt clr run 1f out: r.o: no ch* **7/2**[1]

00-0 **6** 2 **Emarati's Image**[39] 537 6-9-7 40 ADaly 8 39
*(RMStronge) pressed ldrs: rdn 3f out: fdd u.p over 1f out* **33/1**

0/60 **7** shd **Hinchley Wood (IRE)**[6] 814 5-9-10 40 NPollard 5 42
*(JRBest) chsd ldrs: rdn over 2f out: no imp and btn over 1f out* **20/1**

0006 **8** shd **Social Contract**[5] 821 7-9-10 47 JFEgan 15 41
*(SDow) sn in last pair: rdn 1/2-way: effrt on wd outside over 1f out: no prog fnl f* **7/1**

0-00 **9** hd **Waterline Dancer (IRE)**[16] 707 4-9-1 40 (vt) LFletcher(3) 7 35
*(PDEvans) racd in midfield: rdn and no prog over 2f out: btn after* **25/1**

0-05 **10** ½ **Shirley Oaks (IRE)**[7] 791 6-9-0 40 NChalmers(5) 9 35
*(MissZCDavison) wl in rr and rdn 4f out: nvr on terms w ldrs after* **16/1**

0-00 **11** 1 **Hellbent**[14] 728 5-9-10 40 VSlattery 6 37
*(JAOsborne) hld up towards rr: plenty to do whn rdn over 1f out: fnd nil* **25/1**

6-00 **12** 1 **Kilmeena Star**[21] 658 6-9-8 40 (p) PDobbs 11 32
*(JCFox) led for 1f: pressed ldr to over 1f out: wknd rapidly fnl f* **25/1**

0001 **13** 8 **Ivory Venture**[7] 792 4-8-12 35 (b) MSavage(5) 12 6
*(DKIvory) racd in midfield tl wknd u.p over 2f out: sn bhd* **12/1**

00-0 **14** 1 ¼ **Prince Of Perles**[6] 802 3-8-2 35 (v) LisaJones(3) 14 7
*(DShaw) prom: chsng ldng pair and drvn whn jinked sharply rt bnd 2f out: rdr lost iron: nt rcvr* **33/1**

0604 **15** nk **Flying Faisal (USA)**[6] 813 6-9-6 40 ow3 CJDavies(7) 13 11
*(JMBradley) a towards rr: drvn and brief effrt on outer over 2f out: sn wknd and bhd* **20/1**

1m 26.03s (0.03) **Going Correction** -0.025s/f (Stan)
**WFA** 3 from 4yo+ 17lb **15** Ran SP% **121.3**
Speed ratings: **98,96,94,94,93 91,91,91,91,90 89,88,79,77,77**CSF £205.48 TOTE £4.60: £1.90, £35.40, £1.60; EX 630.50.The winner was claimed by J M Bradley for £5,000. Lord Melbourne was claimed by A G Juckes for £5,000.
**Owner** The Cayman Breezers **Bred** M P B Bloodstock Ltd **Trained** Epsom, Surrey

**FOCUS**
A modest claimer run at just a fair pace.

**NOTEBOOK**
**Cayman Breeze**, who was rated 22lb higher on turf less than a year ago, was still by far the best horse in this contest according to official ratings. He appreciated the step back up to seven furlongs and was produced with precision timing, but does not strike as the type likely to follow up. That will be Milton Bradley's problem now.
**Single Track Mind** gave his rivals a start and was content to race out the back for most the way, but his inexperienced rider got quite a run out of him and he flew home down the straight without being able to bridge the gap with the winner. This was the first time in his last 11 starts that he has finished closer than tenth so it would be unwise to get carried away by this effort.
**Jahangir** seemed to be travelling well in front turning for home, but he emptied fairly tamely well inside the last furlong. He remains a maiden after 25 starts on the Flat.
**Janes Valentine** ran better than of late, but is still a maiden. She has failed to stay ten furlongs in the past, but ran as though a mile may suit her better.
**Lord Melbourne(IRE)** is an effective sort in this grade, but his style of racing requires some luck and he did not get any here. He was subsequently claimed.
**Social Contract**, a winner over course and distance three years ago around which time he was rated 82, rather dropped himself out before staying on again. He is not the most reliable of sorts.
**Prince Of Perles** was a close third and still in with a chance when swerving badly to his right turning for home, causing his rider to lose an iron and with it all chance. *Official explanation: jockey said she lost an iron when gelding jinked turning for home*

## 859 BET IN RUNNING @ BETDIRECT.CO.UK BANDED STKS 6f (P)
4:15 (4:18) (H ) 3-Y-0+ £1,645 (£470; £235) Stalls Low

Form RPR

-614 **1** **Badou**[7] 788 4-9-6 45 DHolland 2 56
*(LMontagueHall) cl up: rdn to chse ldr 2f out: led jst ins fnl f: edgd lft nr fin: hld on* **9/4**[1]

5-04 **2** nk **Cargo**[19] 674 5-8-13 45 (bt[1]) RoryMoore(7) 7 55
*(DFlood) led after 1f: rdn and edgd rt over 1f out: hdd jst ins fnl f: kpt on u.p: jst hld* **11/2**[2]

-242 **3** 1 **The Gay Fox**[7] 791 10-9-3 45 (bt) LPKeniry(3) 4 52
*(BGPowell) hld up in rr: wl off the pce 1/2-way: rdn over 2f out: prog over 1f out: r.o wl fnl f: nrst fin* **13/2**[3]

-100 **4** ½ **Indian Warrior**[14] 725 8-9-6 45 (b) NCallan 1 51
*(JJay) squeezed out after 1f: sn rcvrd to chse ldrs: rdn over 2f out: kpt on same pce over 1f out* **33/1**

-000 **5** shd **Master Rattle**[17] 698 5-9-6 45 VSlattery 3 50
*(JaneSouthcombe) chsd ldrs: rdn over 2f out: chsd ldng pair jst over 1f out: nt qckn and hld after* **16/1**

0-30 **6** 3 ½ **Xsynna**[39] 536 8-8-13 45 SaleemGolam(7) 5 40
*(TTClement) led for 1f: chsd ldr to 2f out: sn outpcd and btn: one pce after* **20/1**

0006 **7** 1 **Pancakehill**[7] 787 5-9-6 45 (b) DaneO'Neill 8 37
*(DKIvory) dwlt: wl in rr: rdn and effrt 2f out: one pce and no imp over 1f out* **16/1**

00-0 **8** 1 ¼ **Youngs Forth**[17] 694 4-9-6 45 SWhitworth 13 33
*(AWCarroll) sn lost pl and in rr: rdn and effrt on outer over 2f out: no imp over 1f out* **33/1**

6201 **9** nk **Bells Beach (IRE)**[7] 791 6-9-12 45 DKinsella 9 38
*(PHowling) dwlt: wl in rr: drvn and effrt on wd outside 2f out: no prog over 1f out* **11/2**[2]

6-20 **10** ½ **Tripti (IRE)**[33] 576 4-9-6 45 NPollard 10 31
*(JJBridger) sn rdn to chse ldrs: struggling over 2f out* **12/1**

0-66 **11** nk **Westmead Tango**[39] 538 4-9-6 45 JFEgan 14 30
*(JRJenkins) restless stalls: wnt rt s: a toiling in rr* **20/1**

0-00 **12** 1 **Parallel Lines (IRE)**[13] 731 3-8-5 45 (b) EAhern 11 27
*(PDEvans) bmpd s: nvr on terms: no prog over 1f out* **20/1**

00-0 **13** nk **Lucretius**[40] 520 5-9-1 45 MSavage(5) 6 26
*(DKIvory) a wl in rr: drvn and bhd 2f out* **14/1**

00-0 **14** 7 **Malaah (IRE)**[7] 788 8-9-6 45 (b) MTebbutt 12 5
*(JulianPoulton) wnt lft s: prom to 1/2-way: sn wknd* **10/1**

1m 12.99s (0.07) **Going Correction** -0.025s/f (Stan)
**WFA** 3 from 4yo+ 15lb **14** Ran SP% **130.3**
Speed ratings: **98,97,96,95,95 90,89,87,87,86 86,85,84,75**CSF £13.92 TOTE £3.40: £2.20, £1.70, £2.10; EX 18.30.
**Owner** J Daniels **Bred** D J And Mrs Deer **Trained** Headley, Surrey

**FOCUS**
Fair banded form, but a race run at just a fair pace.

**NOTEBOOK**
**Badou**, who is running well just now, was stepping back from a mile and very much appreciated it. Always in a good position, he needed all his stamina to get the better of the runner-up.
**Cargo**, dropping to banded company for the first time, ran another fine race under a positive ride. He has not won for a while, but is up to winning one of these.
**The Gay Fox** ran a similar sort of race to recent efforts, finishing strongly against the inside rail, and would have won with a little further to go. The problem is that it is an expensive business backing him every time until he gets it right.
**Indian Warrior** was always in about the same place. He is better over an extra furlong these days and lacked speed where it matters.
**Master Rattle**, badly out of form over the past 12 months, ran a little better on this drop in class.
**Bells Beach(IRE)** *Official explanation: trainer said mare was kicked at the start*
**Tripti(IRE)** *Official explanation: jockey said filly lost her action*

## 860 BETDIRECT.CO.UK AMATEUR RIDERS' BANDED STKS 1m (P)
4:50 (4:50) (H ) 4-Y-0+ £1,463 (£418; £209) Stalls High

Form RPR

P-00 **1** **Beltane**[2] 842 6-11-0 40 MrsIDeBest(7) 12 45
*(WDeBest-Turner) s.s: racd in last: pair: plenty to do over 2f out: rapid prog over 1f out: nudged along and styd on to ld nr fin* **33/1**

00-1 **2** nk **Theatre Lady (IRE)**[20] 663 6-11-4 40 MissEFolkes(3) 9 44
*(PDEvans) disp ld tl def advantage over 2f out: hrd pressed fnl f: hdd nr fin* **3/1**[2]

0-00 **3** *1* **Lady Liesel**[7] [791] 4-11-0 40.............................. MissDonnaHandley(7) 4 42
(JJBridger) *settled wl in rr: plenty to do 2f out: prog on inner fnl f: nrst fin* **25/1**

5046 **4** *1* **Vlasta Weiner**[4] [824] 4-11-7 40......................................(b) MrSWalker 11 40
(JMBradley) *sn cl up: effrt 2f out: rdn to press ldr 1f out: nt qckn ins fnl f* **8/1**

3060 **5** *nk* **Haithem (IRE)**[6] [814] 7-11-7 40......................................(t) MrsSBosley 6 39
(DShaw) *racd wl in rr: plenty to do over 2f out: effrt over 1f out: sn one pce* **12/1**

000- **6** *1 1/4* **Prince Du Soleil (FR)**[83] [6120] 8-11-0 40........................ MrNSoares(7) 2 36
(JRJenkins) *t.k.h: w ldrs 2f: styd cl up: effrt to chal over 1f out: bmpd along and wknd fnl f* **20/1**

/0-0 **7** *1* **Misbehaviour**[39] [536] 5-11-0 40................. MissGDGracey-Davison(7) 3 34
(PButler) *chsd ldrs: rdn 3f out: wknd over 1f out* **33/1**

-420 **8** *1 1/2* **Colne Valley Amy**[8] [778] 7-11-4 40........................(b) MrEDehdashti(3) 8 31
(GLMoore) *chsd ldrs: pushed along 1/2-way: outpcd and bmpd along 3f out: no prog after* **11/4**[1]

0400 **9** *1 1/4* **Geespot**[20] [662] 5-11-2 40..............................................(p) MrJJBest(5) 1 28
(DJSFfrenchDavis) *disp ld to 3f out: wknd over 1f out* **7/1**[3]

6-15 **10** *1* **Mount Superior (USA)**[14] [728] 8-11-2 40.............(b) MissRD'Arcy(5) 10 26
(PWD'Arcy) *t.k.h: hld up: sme prog on outer over 3f out: sn nudged along and outpcd* **7/1**[3]

00-0 **11** *6* **Albury Heath**[7] [791] 4-11-2 40...................................... MGoldstein(5) 7 13
(TMJones) *sn lost pl and in rr: wknd over 2f out* **33/1**

6465 **U** **High Diva**[6] [814] 5-11-0 40................................................ MrsKHills(7) 5 —
(JRBest) *t.k.h: hld up towards rr: stmbld and uns rdr 5f out* **7/1**[3]

1m 41.79s (2.28) **Going Correction** -0.025s/f (Stan) **12** Ran SP% **125.4**
Speed ratings: **87,86,85,84,84 83,82,80,79,78 72,**—CSF £131.81 TOTE £61.50: £10.30, £1.90, £4.40; EX 392.90 Place 6 £453.61, Place 5 £111.98.
**Owner** Mrs Gillian Swanton **Bred** Miss Dominy Robinson, Mrs Gillian Swanton And Mr R **Trained** West Overton, Wilts

**FOCUS**
A poor contest and very modest winning time. The form probably does not amount to much and is dubious, with the runner-up better suited to being ridden with more restraint

**NOTEBOOK**
**Beltane**, tailed off in the Winter Derby Trial here 48 hours earlier, was obviously taking a big drop in class though it would still have needed a crystal ball to visualise him winning this. Held up out the back, he was still last turning in, but fortunately for him the leaders had gone off too quick and, despite his rider doing nothing, picked them off down the straight.
**Theatre Lady(IRE)** was given a positive ride on this drop back in trip and eventually got the better of the other pace-setters, but the winner's surge was too late for her to fight back. She deserves some credit for holding on for as long as she did, having been involved in a battle for the lead from the start.
**Lady Liesel** was making good late progress against the inside rail with her rider doing very little, but she is still a maiden after 31 attempts so this effort probably flatters her.
**Vlasta Weiner** had every chance, but is still to convince over this trip.
**Haithem(IRE)**, without a win in over three years, made a fair amount of late headway but in this contest he was not alone in that.
**Colne Valley Amy** is a modest performer, but probably needs further than this these days.
**Geespot** got involved in a speed duel and it was she who cracked first.
T/Plt: £378.50 to a £1 stake. Pool: £37,546.35. 72.40 winning tickets. T/Qpdt: £47.30 to a £1 stake. Pool: £3,495.10. 54.60 winning tickets. JN

# [833]WOLVERHAMPTON (A.W) (L-H)

Monday, February 23

**OFFICIAL GOING: Slow**
Wind: nil Weather: sunny & cold

## 861 LITTLEWOODS BET DIRECT AMATEUR RIDERS' CLAIMING STKS 1m 100y(F)

**2:05** (2:05) (G) 4-Y-0+ **£2,940** (£840; £420) **Stalls** Low

Form RPR

3015 **1** **Scottish River (USA)**[16] [705] 5-11-0 62.................... MrLNewnes(5) 10 76
(MDIUsher) *s.s: hld up in rr: stdy hdwy over 4f out: led wl over 1f out: rdn and edgd lft ins fnl f: r.o wl* **7/2**[2]

-302 **2** *3* **Cloud Dancer**[13] [733] 5-10-9 73........................................ MSeston(5) 13 65
(KARyan) *a.p: rdn and ev ch 2f out: one pce fnl f* **7/4**[1]

440- **3** *1* **Crusoe (IRE)**[65] [6169] 7-11-1 61.........................................(b) MissEJJones 2 63
(ASadik) *led: rdn over 2f out: hdd wl over 1f out: no ex ins fnl f* **10/1**

6020 **4** *1* **Zahunda (IRE)**[10] [763] 5-9-7 40........................................ MrCDavies(7) 6 46
(WMBrisbourne) *dwlt: wl bhd 6f out: rdn over 3f out: hdwy over 1f out: styd on wl ins fnl f: nrst fin* **10/1**

2621 **5** *1 1/2* **Feast Of Romance**[6] [807] 7-10-2 58.................(b) MissFGuillambert(7) 8 52
(PHowling) *hld up: hdwy over 5f out: rdn over 2f out: one pce* **12/1**

-502 **6** *shd* **Paso Doble**[28] [604] 6-10-6 61........................................ MrJMillman(7) 12 56
(BRMillman) *prom tl lost pl over 6f out: rdn 4f out: rallied 2f out: sn no imp* **6/1**[3]

56-0 **7** *1 3/4* **Effie Gray**[15] [715] 5-9-9 45................................................ MrBKing(5) 1 39
(JWUnett) *mid-div: lost pl on ins 6f out: n.d after* **50/1**

0-60 **8** *5* **Dundonald**[3] [838] 5-9-12 40.......................................(bt) MissFTurner(7) 3 33
(MAppleby) *mid-div whn hmpd and dropped rr over 6f out: n.d after* **66/1**

0-00 **9** *5* **Forty Forte**[45] [487] 8-10-2 50.................................. MrASwinswood(7) 11 27
(MissSJWilton) *hdwy 6f out: wknd over 3f out* **33/1**

00-6 **10** *5* **Open Handed (IRE)**[35] [565] 4-10-12 40.....................(t) MissLEllison(3) 9 22
(BEllison) *mid-div: sme hdwy on ins over 4f out: wknd over 2f out* **50/1**

0-40 **11** *dist* **Dusk Dancer (FR)**[37] [559] 4-10-11 61.........................(b[1]) MissJAllison 4 —
(BJMeehan) *plld hrd: chsd ldr after 1f: rdn and wknd over 2f out: t.o* **14/1**

5- **12** *3* **Devious Paddy (IRE)**[82] [6126] 4-10-8 68.................(t) MissARothery(7) 5 —
(NTinkler) *a bhd: lost tch 5f out: t.o* **33/1**

0/02 **U** **Port Natal (IRE)**[40] [530] 6-11-1 ........................................ MrITAmond 7 —
(PatrickMorris, Ire) *prom: hrd rdn 3f out: sn wknd: bhd whn leather broke and uns rdr ins fnl f* **14/1**

1m 58.08s (7.08) **Going Correction** +0.65s/f (Slow) **13** Ran SP% **123.4**
Speed ratings: **90,87,86,85,83 83,81,76,71,66** —,—,—CSF £10.04 TOTE £4.90: £1.60, £1.30, £3.40; EX 15.50.Feast of Romance was claimed by T P Ramsden for £7,000.
**Owner** M D I Usher **Bred** The Thoroughbred Corporation **Trained** Upper Lambourn, Berks
■ Stewards Enquiry : Mr C Davies three-day ban: used whip with excessive force (Mar 23, Apr 2,5)

**FOCUS**
The surface having been harrowed on account of frost, plus the lack of overnight rain, meant that the track was riding very slow, and that was advertised by the poor time of this opening event. However, the form is fair and the winner got a good ride.

**NOTEBOOK**
**Scottish River(USA)** missed the kick and had to make his way patiently through the pack, before joining the leaders turning for home and comfortably extending to success. This was a decent effort on a track that usually favours those ridden prominently and he was value for more then the official margin of victory as he was eased close home. He is in great form at present and does go well for today's rider who has now won twice on him from as many starts.
**Cloud Dancer** , 16lb better off than she would have been in a handicap, held every chance if good enough. She is consistent in this grade, but this trip looked to stretch her. She can win a similar event when reverting back to seven furlongs.
**Crusoe(IRE)** was given a positive ride in order to avoid the kickback from his low draw and was still in with a shout at the top of the straight, but could not go with the front two when challenged. He had been off since being pulled up over hurdles in December, so this was a fair comeback.
**Zahunda(IRE)** ran a remarkable race as she was almost tailed off at halfway, but really stayed on strongly to grab fourth late on. She is inconsistent and a lazy type, but looks worth a try back over another furlong.
**Paso Doble** was unable to build on the form of his previous run over course-and-distance and is a desperately hard horse to catch right.

## 862 BET DIRECT NO Q DEMO 08000 837 888 H'CAP 1m 100y(F)

**2:40** (2:40) (D ) (0-85,83) 4-Y-0+ **£4,108** (£1,264; £632; £316) **Stalls** Low

Form RPR

-111 **1** **Vortex**[9] [775] 5-9-12 **83**...................................................(t) MFenton 6 93
(MissGayKelleway) *hld up: smooth hdwy to join ldrs over 3f out: rdn to ld over 1f out: drvn out* **9/4**[1]

-521 **2** *1/2* **Caroubier (IRE)**[14] [720] 4-9-2 **73**........................................ JPSpencer 1 82
(JGallagher) *dwlt: rdn and hdwy on outside over 2f out: hrd rdn and ev ch ins fnl f: nt qckn* **5/1**

3500 **3** *2 1/2* **Arc El Ciel (ARG)**[9] [775] 6-9-6 **77**......................................(v) SDrowne 4 80
(MrsStefLiddiard) *led early: w ldr: rdn to ld briefly wl over 1f out: no ex ins fnl f* **9/2**[3]

0-14 **4** *hd* **Musical Gift**[16] [701] 4-8-13 **70**................................................ IMongan 5 73
(CNAllen) *stmbld s: hld up in tch: rdn and ev ch over 1f out: no ex ins fnl f* **3/1**[2]

0 **5** *3* **Ballyrush (IRE)**[24] [643] 4-8-3 **67**........................................... RKeogh(7) 2 64
(KRBurke) *prom: rdn over 2f out: wknd 1f out* **40/1**

223- **6** *1* **How's Things**[59] [6239] 4-8-13 **70**........................................... PaulEddery 7 64
(DHaydnJones) *prom: rdn and sltly outpcd over 2f out: wknd fnl f* **9/2**[3]

1-40 **7** *8* **Ronnie From Donny (IRE)**[41] [511] 4-8-10 **72**..................... TEaves(5) 3 49
(BEllison) *t.k.h: sn led: rdn 3f out: hdd wl over 1f out: sn wknd* **20/1**

1m 55.54s (4.54) **Going Correction** +0.65s/f (Slow) **7** Ran SP% **116.0**
Speed ratings: **103,102,100,99,96 95,87**CSF £14.47 TOTE £2.60: £1.20, £4.50; EX 10.30.
**Owner** Coriolis Partnership **Bred** Juddmonte Farms **Trained** Newmarket, Suffolk
■ Stewards Enquiry : J P Spencer one-day ban: used whip from above shoulder height (Mar 8)

**FOCUS**
This was a fairly competitive handicap, run at a sound pace, and most of the field still looked in with a chance turning for home. The race should throw it's share of future winners and the front two showed particularly solid handicap form.

**NOTEBOOK**
**Vortex** duly landed the four-timer off a 5lb higher mark, but was made to pull out all the stops by the runner-up. Having made smooth headway from off the pace to take up the running at the top of the straight, he showed a good attitude under his big weight to score his fourth win at the track from five outings. He adds to his trainer's already strong hand for the Lincoln Trial back here in March.
**Caroubier(IRE)** , the facile winner of a claimer over course-and-distance last time, ran his best race for some time in defeat. This was an encouraging first run for his new connections and, despite a likely rise in the weights, he can add to his impressive Fibresand record before long.
**Arc El Ciel(ARG)** ran his race, but could not reverse recent form with the winner despite these better terms.
**Musical Gift** has been in fair form for his current connections of late. He improved for the switch back to this surface, but stumbled out of the stalls and was found out by this rise in class. *Official explanation: jockey said colt stumbled at the start*
**Ballyrush(IRE)** improved on his recent comeback run and should come on again for this outing. He is one to look out for when eased in grade.
**How's Things** ran in snatches and may well have needed this outing. His rider later reported that he lost his action in the straight. *Official explanation: jockey said colt was not moving well in the closing stages*
**Ronnie From Donny(IRE)** has been gelded since his last run. He spoilt his chance by pulling too hard over this longer trip.

## 863 BET DIRECT NO Q ON 08000 93 66 93 MAIDEN STKS 1m 4f (F)

**3:15** (3:15) (D ) 3-Y-0+ **£3,315** (£1,020; £510; £255) **Stalls** Low

Form RPR

**1** **Jomacomi** 3-8-3 ........................................................................ JFanning 6 66+
(MJohnston) *led after 1f: rdn over 3f out: clr 2f out: eased ins fnl f* **3/1**[2]

36/ **2** *7* **Calvados (USA)**[5] [4385] 5-9-13 ..........................................(b[1]) JQuinn 1 50
(JohnAQuinn, Ire) *hld up: rdn and hdwy 3f out: wnt 2nd 2f out: no ch w wnr* **7/1**[3]

0-46 **3** *7* **Imperative (USA)**[7] [797] 4-9-10 70........................................(t) MFenton 4 40
(MissGayKelleway) *prom: wnt 2nd over 8f out: jnd wnr over 3f out: sn rdn: wkng whn edgd rt wl over 1f out* **10/1**

0-00 **4** *3* **Pont Neuf (IRE)**[9] [767] 4-9-5 55..............................................(t) MHills 2 30
(JWHills) *prom: rdn over 4f out: wknd 3f out* **11/1**

-432 **5** *9* **Vivre Sa Vie**[7] [797] 3-7-12 ........................................................ JMackay 3 17
(SirMarkPrescott) *t.k.h: led 1f: remained prom: rdn over 4f out: sn struggling* **8/11**[1]

2m 49.74s (8.24) **Going Correction** +0.65s/f (Slow)
**WFA** 3 from 4yo 24lb 4 from 5yo 3lb **5** Ran SP% **112.8**
Speed ratings: **98,93,88,86,80**CSF £22.66 TOTE £3.30: £2.60, £6.60; EX 24.80.
**Owner** T McDonagh **Bred** T P And M McDonagh **Trained** Middleham Moor, N Yorks

**FOCUS**
A weak maiden and a modeat winning time, but the winner, who was making his debut, has a future and is likely to rate higher.

**NOTEBOOK**
**Jomacomi** ◆ veered right from the gates and had to be rushed up to race prominently going into the first bend, but from there on moved sweetly and could have been called the winner a long way out. It is hard to know what to make of this form, with the favourite disappointing and the rest being frustrating sorts, but he looks to have a future and should stay further.
**Calvados(USA)** was doing all of his best work late on but never threatened the winner. He has been running over hurdles in Ireland recently, but seemed to respond positively to the first-time blinkers and may be able to build on this effort.
**Imperative(USA)** , making his debut for his new yard, again flattered to deceive and found less than expected off the bridle. He is one to lay rather than play.
**Vivre Sa Vie** was most disappointing and failed to build on her latest display when only narrowly denied over course-and-distance. That race looked to have taken its toll on this occasion. *Official explanation: trainer had no explanation for the poor form shown*

**864** **BET DIRECT ON ATR TEXT PAGE 410 H'CAP** **1m 1f 79y(F)**
**3:50** (3:50) (D ) (0-85,81) 3-Y-O **£4,007** (£1,233; £616; £308) **Stalls** Low

Form RPR
0-61 **1** **Red Lancer**[11] 746 3-8-1 **68** BSwarbrick(7) 3 75
(RJPrice) *hld up: rdn and hdwy on outside over 2f out: led wl over 1f out: edgd lft 1f out: r.o wl* **14/1**
23-1 **2** *3 ½* **Come What July (IRE)**[12] 739 3-8-13 **73** (b) JPSpencer 5 73
(RGuest) *hld up: hdwy on ins over 6f out: rdn and hung lft over 2f out: chsd wnr jst over 1f out: no imp* **12/1**
0-12 **3** *1* **Gavroche (IRE)**[31] 595 3-8-11 **71** KFallon 1 69
(MJWallace) *led 7f out: rdn over 2f out: hdd wl over 1f out: swtchd rt 1f out: one pce* **5/6**[1]
-301 **4** *1 ½* **Dispol Veleta**[6] 808 3-7-12 **57** 6ex DMernagh 6 53
(TDBarron) *hld up: hdwy over 4f out: rdn and one pce fnl 2f* **3/1**[2]
263- **5** *6* **Weet A Head (IRE)**[91] 6059 3-9-7 **81** ACulhane 2 65
(RHollinshead) *led early: prom: rdn over 5f out: wknd over 3f out* **6/1**[3]
0-12 **6** *nk* **Desert Image (IRE)**[26] 622 3-9-1 **75** JQuinn 7 58
(CTinkler) *sn led: hdd 7f out: rdn over 3f out: wknd over 2f out* **20/1**

2m 7.22s (4.32) **Going Correction** +0.65s/f (Slow) **6** Ran SP% **113.0**
Speed ratings: **106,102,102,100,95 95**CSF £151.40 TOTE £16.40: £4.80, £2.20; EX 98.60.
**Owner** Fox And Cub Partnership **Bred** Bishop Wilton Stud **Trained** Ullingswick, H'fords

**FOCUS**
A very decent winning time for the type of contest and the field were well strung out at the finish.

**NOTEBOOK**
**Red Lancer** readily followed up his win at this venue eleven days previously off an 8lb higher mark. Another rise in the weights is inevitable and that will make life a lot harder, but he has seriously improved for the switch to this surface and remains unexposed over farther.
**Come What July(IRE)** tracked the leaders throughout and had every chance in the straight, but had no answer to the winner off his 6lb higher mark.
**Gavroche(IRE)** was disappointing. That said, he might well now be in the Handicapper's grip and was not suited by making the running.
**Dispol Veleta** , a facile winner at Southwell six days prior to this, ran a flat race. She made a brief effort with half a mile to run, but never looked like getting to the leaders and now has it all to prove.
**Weet A Head(IRE)** ran in snatches and will come on for the outing, but had been dropped 4lb since his last run and could have been expected to do better.
**Desert Image(IRE)** did not look happy on this surface and can do better when reverting to the Polytrack once more.

**865** **BETDIRECT.CO.UK (S) STKS** **5f (F)**
**4:25** (4:25) (G ) 3-Y-O **£2,520** (£720; £360) **Stalls** Low

Form RPR
3120 **1** **Emaradia**[17] 696 3-8-13 **54** (b) IMongan 4 57
(AWCarroll) *led early: w ldr: rdn over 2f out: led and rdr dropped whip wl ins fnl f: r.o* **5/2**[2]
6404 **2** *1* **Lizhar (IRE)**[19] 678 3-8-13 **60** (b1) JPSpencer 1 53
(MJPolglase) *sn led: rdn and edgd lft wl over 1f out: hdd wl ins fnl f: nt qckn* **5/2**[2]
0-05 **3** *2* **Lavish Times**[10] 762 3-9-4 **45** (b) FLynch 3 51
(ABerry) *chsd ldrs: rdn over 2f out: swtchd rt wl over 1f out: one pce fnl f* **20/1**
0654 **4** *1 ¼* **Rehia**[12] 744 3-8-13 **49** MHills 5 42
(JWHills) *prom: rdn and edgd lft wl over 1f out: one pce* **6/1**[3]
0-32 **5** *5* **Bella Boy Zee (IRE)**[13] 731 3-8-8 **54** DNolan(5) 6 24
(PABlockley) *chsd ldrs: rdn 3f out: wknd wl over 1f out* **2/1**[1]
00-0 **6** *8* **Duggan's Dilemma (IRE)**[11] 752 3-8-5 **48** (v1) PMakin(7) 2 —
(IanEmmerson) *outpcd* **40/1**
660- **7** *2* **Anatom**[70] 6191 3-8-7 **35** DRMcCabe 7 —
(MQuinn) *sn outpcd* **66/1**

65.25 secs (2.65) **Going Correction** +0.65s/f (Slow) **7** Ran SP% **113.5**
Speed ratings: **104,102,99,97,89 76,73**CSF £9.00 TOTE £4.20: £2.30, £1.30; EX 10.90.The winner was bought in for 5,500gns.
**Owner** Dennis Deacon **Bred** Treble Chance Partnership **Trained** Wixford, Warwicks

**FOCUS**
Typical selling form, but a solid gallop and a decent winning time for the grade.

**NOTEBOOK**
**Emaradia** gets further and put her stamina to good effect in the closing stages to get the better of her stablemate and score a deserved victory. She has been making the running over farther recently, but always showed the speed for this trip as a juvenile. A consistent sort who can win again at this level, she was bought back in by connections at the subsequent auction.
**Lizhar(IRE)** attempted to make this a true test and was hard ridden from the start to go the gallop, which cost her victory, as she had nothing left when challenged in the closing stages. However, she responded positively to the blinkers and ran an improved race.
**Lavish Times** ran a fair race at these weights and could be about to find some form.
**Bella Boy Zee(IRE)**was taken off her feet from the start and was most disappointing. Her rider later reported that she was unsuited by the track. *Official explanation: jockey said filly ran flat and was unsuited by the course*

**866** **BET DIRECT IN RUNNING ON SKY TEXT PAGE 293 H'CAP** **7f (F)**
**5:00** (5:02) (E ) (0-75,74) 4-Y-O+ **£3,367** (£1,036; £518; £259) **Stalls** High

Form RPR
-346 **1** **Warden Warren**[11] 749 6-9-6 **71** (b) BReilly(5) 10 79
(MrsCADunnett) *hld up: rdn and hdwy over 2f out: led 1f out: r.o* **12/1**
2534 **2** *hd* **Yorker (USA)**[9] 775 6-9-7 **67** SDrowne 9 75
(MsDeborahJEvans) *chsd ldrs: rdn over 3f out: r.o ins fnl f* **7/1**
3612 **3** *½* **Givemethemoonlight**[7] 800 5-8-10 **56** (v) IMongan 8 62
(MrsStefLiddiard) *hld up: rdn and hdwy over 3f out: edgd lft fnl f: r.o* **3/1**[1]
-420 **4** *¾* **Danielle's Lad**[26] 624 8-9-6 **66** (b) MFenton 4 70
(BPalling) *chsd ldrs: rdn over 3f out: n.m.r on ins 2f out: plld to wd outside jst over 1f out: r.o* **6/1**[3]
0/ **5** *4* **Grant (IRE)**[135] 5491 4-9-4 **64** (p) JQuinn 5 58
(PatrickMorris, Ire) *chsd ldrs: rdn to ld over 2f out: hdd 1f out: wknd ins fnl f* **25/1**
053- **6** *½* **Dorchester**[102] 5985 7-10-0 **74** PaulEddery 12 67
(WJMusson) *sn chsng ldrs: rdn over 2f out: wknd fnl f* **12/1**
0002 **7** *¾* **Pawn In Life (IRE)**[3] 833 6-8-7 **60** PMakin(7) 2 51
(TDBarron) *dwlt: hdwy fnl f: nvr nrr* **7/1**
6311 **8** *3* **Mount Royale (IRE)**[3] 833 6-9-3 **63** 6ex (vt) KimTinkler 1 47
(NTinkler) *led: rdn and hdd over 2f out: wknd wl over 1f out* **8/1**
000- **9** *3 ½* **Tantric**[128] 5636 5-8-13 **66** JDO'Reilly(7) 3 41
(JO'Reilly) *prom: rdn and ev ch 2f out: wknd over 1f out* **33/1**
053- **10** *4* **Mister Mal (IRE)**[59] 6235 8-8-5 **56** (be) TEaves(5) 11 21
(BEllison) *s.v.s: a bhd* **20/1**
1-00 **11** *¾* **Noble Locks (IRE)**[18] 680 6-9-7 **70** DCorby(3) 6 33
(JWUnett) *hld up: rdn over 3f out: sn struggling* **33/1**
/5-0 **12** *dist* **Henry Afrika (IRE)**[35] 564 6-9-12 **72** (p) JPSpencer 7 —
(DGMcardle, Ire) *a bhd: rdn over 3f out: eased whn no ch over 1f out: virtually p.u fnl f* **10/3**[2]

1m 33.95s (3.75) **Going Correction** +0.65s/f (Slow) **12** Ran SP% **128.4**
Speed ratings: **104,103,103,102,97 97,96,92,88,84 83,**—CSF £97.43 CT £327.18 TOTE £15.70: £2.60, £2.50, £2.50; EX 106.20 Place 6 £885.80, Place 5 £598.12.
**Owner** Annwell Inn Syndicate **Bred** R G Percival **Trained** Hingham, Norfolk

**FOCUS**
The solid early gallop meant this was a true test, and while plenty still had a shout turning for home the first four finished clear. This is solid form.

**NOTEBOOK**
**Warden Warren** dug deep in the final furlong to win narrowly off a career-high mark. This is his trip and he has been running well of late, but his win record does not inspire confidence for a follow-up bid.
**Yorker(USA)** was forced to race wide for most of the contest and that proved costly as he was only just denied.
**Givemethemoonlight** was another who had to race wide until challenging in the straight and ran a solid race on this drop in trip. She is a much improved, tough mare who can go in again over another furlong.
**Danielle's Lad**, second in this last season, was staying on well enough in the final stages after having to be switched for a run, but is very hard to catch right.
**Henry Afrika(IRE)** was never on terms and virtually pulled up. Something may have been amiss. *Official explanation: trainer had no explanation for the poor form shown*
T/Plt: £477.50 to a £1 stake. Pool: £37,520.65. 57.35 winning tickets. T/Qpdt: £182.30 to a £1 stake. Pool: £2,143.50. 8.70 winning tickets. KH

## [855] LINGFIELD (L-H)
### Tuesday, February 24

**OFFICIAL GOING: Standard**
Wind: mod hlf against Weather: murky; drizzly

**867** **BET DIRECT NO Q ON 08000 93 66 93 AMATEUR RIDERS' H'CAP** **1m 4f (P)**
**1:40** (1:40) (F ) (0-60,60) 4-Y-O+ **£2,996** (£856; £428) **Stalls** Low

Form RPR
1-13 **1** **Robbie Can Can**[10] 777 5-11-5 **57** MrsSBosley 4 67
(AWCarroll) *hld up towards rr: prog 5f out: trckd ldrs and nt clr run briefly over 2f out: effrt to ld jst over 1f out: rdn clr* **4/1**[1]
3330 **2** *2* **Lazzaz**[10] 777 6-11-0 **57** MrsMarieKing(5) 2 64
(PWHiatt) *mde most to 3f out: styd pressing ldr: rdn and ev ch over 1f out: one pce fnl f* **13/2**[3]
/00- **3** *nk* **Intensity**[81] 6121 8-10-12 **55** StaceyRenwick(5) 3 62
(PABlockley) *sn trckd ldrs: effrt to ld 3f out: rdn and hdd jst over 1f out: one pce* **7/1**
30-2 **4** *nk* **Sterling Guarantee (USA)**[45] 495 6-10-10 **53** MrJGee(5) 9 59
(AndrewReid) *hld up towards rr: prog to press ldrs over 2f out: shkn up and nt qckn over 1f out* **10/1**
44-5 **5** *nk* **Lanos (POL)**[42] 513 6-11-2 **59** (t) MrSHughes(5) 16 65
(RFord) *v s.i.s: hld up in last trio: prog 5f out: effrt to press ldrs 2f out: one pce over 1f out* **10/1**
5-50 **6** *6* **Joely Green**[13] 740 7-11-0 **55** MrsEmmaLittmoden(3) 5 52
(NPLittmoden) *hld up towards rr: effrt over 3f out: outpcd wl over 2f out: one pce after* **14/1**
0060 **7** *3* **Golden Dual**[15] 724 4-10-7 **55** MrDHutchison(7) 15 47
(SDow) *dwlt: t.k.h and hld up in rr: nt clr run over 3f out to over 2f out: one pce and no ch after* **16/1**
6334 **8** *2 ½* **Top Of The Class (IRE)**[10] 767 7-10-5 **46** (v) MissEFolkes(3) 14 34
(PDEvans) *t.k.h: hld up in rr: outpcd 3f out: no ch after* **10/1**
0/00 **9** *½* **Cliquey**[18] 693 5-10-6 **51** (t) MissAFrieze(7) 13 39
(BJLlewellyn) *dwlt: hld up and sn in last: wl bhd 4f out: kpt on one pce after : no ch* **100/1**
30-0 **10** *1* **Forever My Lord**[20] 672 6-10-6 **47** MrEDehdashti(3) 11 33
(JRBest) *mostly pressed ldr to over 3f out: wknd over 2f out* **8/1**
6-00 **11** *3 ½* **Kavi (IRE)**[10] 765 4-11-0 **60** MrJJBest(5) 10 41
(SimonEarle) *ssn lost pl and in rr: rdn and dropped to last 3f out: r.o fnl f* **20/1**
00-1 **12** *7* **Beyond The Pole (USA)**[13] 740 6-10-10 **55** MrsLABest(7) 12 25
(BRJohnson) *pressed ldr tl wknd rapidly over 3f out* **6/1**[2]
**13** *3 ½* **Secam (POL)**[128] 5-10-9 **52** (b1) MrsCThompson(5) 8 17
(MrsPTownsley) *pressed ldrs: bmpd along and losing pl 5f out: wl bhd over 2f out* **33/1**
60-0 **14** *5* **Cantrip**[52] 413 4-10-9 **57** (bt1) MrCDoran(7) 6 15
(MissBSanders) *pressed ldrs: lost pl and shuffled along 7f out: struggling 4f out* **40/1**

2m 35.76s (1.78) **Going Correction** 0.0s/f (Stan)
**WFA** 4 from 5yo+ 3lb **14** Ran SP% **122.2**
Speed ratings: **94,92,92,92,92 88,86,84,84,83 81,76,74,70**CSF £28.54 CT £182.32 TOTE £3.00: £1.50, £2.40, £2.60; EX 27.10.
**Owner** K F Coleman **Bred** I Robinson & A W Robinson **Trained** Wixford, Warwicks
■ Stewards Enquiry : Mr J J Best two-day ban: careless riding (Mar 23, Apr 2)
Mr C Doran one-day ban: careless riding (Mar 23)

**FOCUS**
They went a moderate pace in this amateurs' event, but it is respectable form given the grade

**NOTEBOOK**
**Robbie Can Can** was briefly short of room coming down the hill, but he stuck to the inside and got to the front approaching the furlong pole. He goes well for this rider.
**Lazzaz**, who has been dropping in the weights, ran well, especially as he was reportedly struck into. *Official explanation: vet said gelding had been struck into*
**Intensity**, a winner of a three-mile hurdle last time, obviously has plenty of stamina. This was his first try on the Polytrack and his best run on sand so far.
**Sterling Guarantee(USA)** was having his first run since leaving David Nicholls. Returning to this trip, he hit a flat spot early in the straight but kept on in a manner which suggested he stayed.
**Lanos(POL)** was unable to find a change of gear in the straight, but had done well to get competitive given that he had missed the break badly, as he is prone to do.
**Beyond The Pole(USA)** benefited from a canny ride by Kieren Fallon last time and was in trouble a good way out on this occasion.

**868** **BET DIRECT NO Q H'CAP** **5f (P)**
**2:10** (2:11) (E ) (0-70,68) 3-Y-O **£3,262** (£932; £466) **Stalls** High

Form RPR
00-1 **1** **Cut And Dried**[10] 764 3-9-5 **66** MartinDwyer 3 69
(DMSimcock) *hld up in rr and pushed along over 3f out: prog wl over 1f out: drvn and r.o to ld nr fin: hld on* **4/1**[1]
2314 **2** *hd* **Alizar (IRE)**[15] 721 3-8-11 **58** JFEgan 5 61
(SDow) *chsd clr ldrs: rdn and effrt 2f out: n.m.r on inner 1f out: r.o wl nr fin: jst hld* **8/1**[3]

56-5 **3** *hd* **Beau Jazz**[10] [764] 3-9-4 **65** ........ SRighton 1 67
(WDeBest-Turner) *chsd ldr: rdn 2f out: styd on to ld jst ins fnl f: edgd rt and nt qckn: hdd nr fin* **33/1**

0613 **4** *1* **Sahara Silk (IRE)**[6] [819] 3-9-6 **67** ........ (v) DarrenWilliams 2 66
(DShaw) *chsd ldr: rdn 1/2-way: tried to cl over 1f out: hanging lft and nt qckn fnl f* **8/1**[3]

1123 **5** *½* **Smart Starprincess (IRE)**[12] [747] 3-9-6 **67** ........ (v) NCallan 4 64
(PABlockley) *led: drew 4l clr over 2f out: drvn and hdd jst ins fnl f: no ex* **9/2**[2]

4620 **6** *nk* **Stamford Blue**[6] [817] 3-8-4 **58** ........ (b) DerekNolan(7) 9 54
(JSMoore) *sn outpcd in last: wl adrift 1/2-way: drvn and r.o fr over 1f out: nrst fin* **12/1**

5-55 **7** *1¾* **Pompey Blue**[27] [619] 3-9-7 **68** ........ KFallon 7 58
(PJMcbride) *racd in midfield: outpcd 3f out: effrt over 1f out: reminders and nt qckn ent fnl f: eased last 100y* **4/1**[1]

4-06 **8** *2½* **Demolition Molly**[12] [747] 3-9-3 **64** ........ (t) DeanMcKeown 6 45
(RFMarvin) *chsd ldng trio: effrt whn nowhere to go on inner and hmpd over 2f out: nt rcvr: wknd over 1f out* **8/1**[3]

000- **9** *2* **Barbilyrifle (IRE)**[123] [5734] 3-9-6 **67** ........ SDrowne 10 41
(HMorrison) *outpcd in last trio: hanging rt and no prog over 1f out* **9/1**

6-55 **10** *shd* **Easily Averted (IRE)**[27] [617] 3-9-2 **63** ........ (t) IMongan 8 36
(PButler) *in rr whn n.m.r after 1f: outpcd and nvr on terms after* **20/1**

59.22 secs (-0.56) **Going Correction** 0.0s/f (Stan) **10** Ran SP% **116.9**
Speed ratings: **104,103,103,101,100 100,97,93,90,90**CSF £36.43 CT £927.19 TOTE £4.90: £2.20, £1.80, £8.50; EX 41.70.
**Owner** Trillium Place Racing **Bred** Mrs B Skinner **Trained** Newmarket, Suffolk

**FOCUS**
A rapid pace and a very decent time for the grade. Reliable form.

**NOTEBOOK**
**Cut And Dried** followed up his recent course win, coming from off the pace to get up close home. He looks a game sort but it is doubtful if there is much more improvement in him.
**Alizar(IRE)** was having his second run after being sold out of Mark Polglase's yard. The strong pace suited and he just failed to get up after pouncing on the leader at the same time as the eventual winner. He could win a similar event.
**Beau Jazz** looked sure to score when striking the front but was cut down by rivals on either side of him close home.
**Sahara Silk(IRE)** found the return to the minimum trip on this fast track too sharp for him.
**Smart Starprincess(IRE)** showed her customary blistering speed and looked as if she had the race in the bag turning in, but she was coming to the end of her tether when collared.
**Pompey Blue** was unsuited by this return to five furlongs.
**Demolition Molly** *Official explanation: jockey said filly clipped heels turning in and lost her action*
**Barbilyrifle(IRE)** *Official explanation: jockey said his goggles smashed and he was unable to see*

## 869 BET DIRECT NO Q DEMO 08000 837 888 MAIDEN STKS 7f (P)
**2:40** (2:40) (D) 3-Y-O+ **£4,046** (£1,245; £622; £311) **Stalls** Low

Form RPR

62-2 **1** **Bahiano (IRE)**[32] [593] 3-8-9 72 ........ KFallon 2 85+
(CEBrittain) *mde virtually all: pushed clr over 1f out: comf* **5/4**[1]

20-2 **2** *2* **Hatch**[18] [696] 3-8-9 74 ........ EAhern 5 75
(RMHCowell) *dwlt: t.k.h and hld up in last: smooth prog over 2f out: effrt to chse wnr and edgd lft 1f out: no imp* **7/2**[2]

-533 **3** *1* **Night Storm**[13] [741] 3-8-4 66 ........ PDoe 1 67
(SDow) *trckd ldrs: cl up 2f out: easily outpcd over 1f out* **9/1**

-032 **4** *5* **Boavista (IRE)**[7] [803] 3-8-4 54 ........ (t) NCallan 8 55
(PDEvans) *taken down early and free to post: racd freely: w wnr to 2f out: wkng whn sltly hmpd 1f out* **16/1**

-335 **5** *3* **Resplendent King (USA)**[13] [741] 3-8-9 69 ........ (b[1]) DaneO'Neill 7 52
(TGMills) *chsd ldrs: rdn 1/2-way: wknd over 2f out* **5/1**[3]

540- **6** *7* **Penel (IRE)**[255] [2355] 3-8-10 64 ow1 ........ SDrowne 3 36
(BRMillman) *chsd ldrs: rdn 1/2-way: sn wknd* **33/1**

05 **7** *1¾* **Bennanabaa**[24] [644] 5-9-12 ........ (t) ANicholls 9 30
(SCBurrough) *dwlt: prog on outer to chse ldrs 4f out: sn rdn: wknd rapidly over 2f out* **50/1**

05- **8** *10* **Dream Of Dubai (IRE)**[168] [4805] 3-8-4 ........ JFanning 6 —
(PMitchell) *settled in rr: wknd tamely 1/2-way: sn wl bhd* **9/1**

1m 24.69s (-1.31) **Going Correction** 0.0s/f (Stan)
**WFA** 3 from 4yo+ 17lb **8** Ran SP% **114.1**
Speed ratings: **107,104,103,97,94 86,84,73**CSF £5.62 TOTE £1.90: £1.10, £1.40, £1.90; EX 8.00.
**Owner** C E Brittain **Bred** Michel Henochsberg And Sunflower International **Trained** Newmarket, Suffolk

**FOCUS**
A reasonable time for a maiden, and a fairly useful effort from winner, who has been rated 2 lengths better than bare result.

**NOTEBOOK**
**Bahiano(IRE)**, down in trip after a good run over a mile at Dunstall Park, needed only to be shaken up to secure a smooth victory. He should be capable of holding his own in handicap company.
**Hatch** was having his first run for this yard, having previously been with Roger Charlton. Clearly quirky, he half-reared leaving the stalls then took a keen tug in the rear, and when he closed in the straight he carried his head high and went left at the furlong pole, hampering the fourth. He handled the surface however, and has the basic ability to win races.
**Night Storm** travelled quite well, but she found the drop in trip not helping as she does lack a turn of foot at the business end.
**Boavista(IRE)**, a frustrating sort, was held when squeezed out at the furlong pole.
**Resplendent King(USA)** has become exposed and the blinkers had no real effect.
**Dream Of Dubai(IRE)** was most disappointing as she had shown clear signs of ability in two runs on this surface last year.

## 870 BET DIRECT ON SKY ACTIVE H'CAP 1m (P)
**3:10** (3:13) (E) (0-75,75) 3-Y-O+ **£3,445** (£1,060; £530; £265) **Stalls** High

Form RPR

1-43 **1** **Topton (IRE)**[21] [667] 10-9-8 **69** ........ (b) JPSpencer 10 81
(PHowling) *dwlt: hld up in last pair: prog over 2f out: drvn on inner and r.o to ld last 150y: kpt on wl* **12/1**

-203 **2** *½* **Sir Laughalot**[13] [742] 4-9-5 **69** ........ LPKeniry(3) 3 80
(MissECLavelle) *trckd ldng pair: rdn to chse ldr over 1f out: ev ch ent fnl f: styd on but hld last 100y* **6/1**[2]

0310 **3** *¾* **Eastborough (IRE)**[6] [820] 5-9-6 **67** ........ SWhitworth 9 76
(BGPowell) *dwlt: sn in midfield: effrt over 2f out: drvn and r.o fr over 1f out: jst unable to chal* **33/1**

12-2 **4** *nk* **Deeper In Debt**[24] [647] 6-9-12 **73** ........ TQuinn 1 82
(JAkehurst) *led and set gd pce: rdn over 1f out: hdd and fdd last 150y* **5/2**[1]

3552 **5** *3½* **Superchief**[3] [847] 9-9-3 **64** ........ (bt) SDrowne 5 65
(MissBSanders) *dwlt: hld up towards rr: angled out over 2f out: effrt over 1f out: hanging and fnd nil* **7/1**

0201 **6** *1¼* **Acorazado (IRE)**[13] [745] 5-9-3 **64** ........ GCarter 12 62
(GLMoore) *s.i.s: hld up in last pair: effrt 2f out: one pce and no imp ldrs over 1f out* **7/1**

100- **7** *6* **Jools**[136] [5486] 6-9-11 **72** ........ MartinDwyer 7 57
(DKIvory) *chsd ldr: rdn wl over 2f out: wknd wl over 1f out* **20/1**

-013 **8** *4* **True Companion**[6] [820] 5-9-5 **66** ........ EAhern 6 42
(NPLittmoden) *lost pl and in rr over 4f out: rdn and struggling over 3f out: no ch after* **6/1**[2]

06-5 **9** *5* **Tiger Tops**[17] [701] 5-9-4 **65** ........ JFanning 11 30
(JASupple) *hld up towards rr: rdn 3f out: wknd over 2f out* **7/1**

0/0 **10** *5* **Trusted Instinct (IRE)**[20] [679] 4-9-11 **72** ........ NCallan 4 26
(CADwyer) *cl up tl wknd rapidly u.p over 2f out* **16/1**

43-6 **11** *18* **Silken Brief (IRE)**[34] [577] 5-10-0 **75** ........ (t) KFallon 8 —
(DJDaly) *pressed ldrs: rdn and wknd over 2f out: eased over 1f out: virtually p.u nr fin* **13/2**[3]

1m 37.57s (-1.94) **Going Correction** 0.0s/f (Stan) **11** Ran SP% **129.3**
Speed ratings: **109,108,107,107,103 102,96,92,87,82 64**CSF £90.61 CT £2419.95 TOTE £14.30: £2.50, £1.90, £7.30; EX 31.70.
**Owner** Liam Sheridan **Bred** George Strawbridge **Trained** Newmarket, Suffolk

**FOCUS**
They went a fair pace and the winning time was good. Rock solid form

**NOTEBOOK**
**Topton(IRE)** needs things to drop just right and they did here, enabling him to come from last to first up the rail. Doncaster's Spring Mile- the Lincoln consolation race- is his target.
**Sir Laughalot** remains a maiden, but this was a solid effort over a trip which recent runs had suggested he would appreciate.
**Eastborough(IRE)** missed the break, but was keeping on in the latter stages. This trip is in all probability on the short side for him.
**Deeper In Debt** set a decent pace and was a couple of lengths to the good early in the straight, but he was worn down. He did little wrong, but the handicapper could be in control now.
**Superchief** remains on a lengthy losing streak but is at least running creditably at present.
**Acorazado(IRE)**, raised 6lb for his recent course victory, missed the kick and could never land a blow at the leaders.
**Jools** ran well for a long way on this first start since October and there are races to be won with him on this surface.
**Trusted Instinct(IRE)** *Official explanation: jockey said colt was hanging right*

## 871 BETDIRECT.CO.UK MAIDEN STKS 1m 2f (P)
**3:40** (3:42) (D) 3-Y-O+ **£3,779** (£1,163; £581; £290) **Stalls** Low

Form RPR

**1** **Barathea Dreams (IRE)** 3-8-3 ........ MartinDwyer 10 53
(JSMoore) *trckd ldr after 2f: led wl over 2f out: kicked 2l clr wl over 1f out: rn green fnl f: hld on wl* **10/1**

4/ **2** *¾* **Jorobaden (FR)**[487] [5454] 4-9-10 ........ GBaker 6 52
(CFWall) *trckd ldrs: rdn and effrt over 2f out: kpt on to chse wnr wl ins fnl f: a hld* **2/1**[1]

0-00 **3** *¾* **Almost Welcome**[8] [788] 3-8-3 45 ........ PDoe 1 50
(SDow) *trckd ldng pair: rdn over 2f out: chsd wnr wl over 1f out to wl ins fnl f: kpt on* **20/1**

04-0 **4** *shd* **Springalong (USA)**[38] [555] 4-9-10 67 ........ SDrowne 3 50
(PDEvans) *trckd ldrs: rdn and effrt over 2f out: kpt on same pce fr over 1f out* **8/1**

**5** *½* **Rollswood (USA)**[21] 4-9-10 ........ (p) SWhitworth 14 49
(PRHedger) *s.s: racd in last: stl last 4f out: rapid prog 3f out: pressed ldrs and nt clr run over 1f out to last 100y: kpt on* **16/1**

06- **6** *2* **Blue Quiver (IRE)**[120] [5793] 4-9-10 ........ PaulEddery 2 46
(CAHorgan) *dwlt: t.k.h: hld up in rr: rdn and prog wl over 2f out: chsd ldrs over 1f out: no imp: eased last 100y* **5/1**[3]

00-6 **7** *1¼* **Steppenwolf**[3] [845] 3-8-3 47 ........ SRighton 4 43
(WDeBest-Turner) *led to wl over 2f out: fdd wl over 1f out* **20/1**

00-0 **8** *2½* **Darn Good**[45] [492] 3-8-3 62 ........ RSmith 11 39
(RHannon) *a in rr: rdn and struggling 4f out: sn bhd: plodded on fnl 2f out* **12/1**

00 **9** *1* **Alimiste (IRE)**[21] [664] 4-9-0 ........ JFMcDonald(5) 8 32
(IAWood) *racd in midfield: rdn and outpcd wl over 2f out: no ch after* **33/1**

-000 **10** *4* **Spiders Web**[6] [818] 4-9-10 ........ GCarter 9 30
(TKeddy) *s.i.s: a in rr: struggling over 3f out* **50/1**

0-55 **11** *nk* **Numpty (IRE)**[14] [731] 3-7-10 40 ........ (t) NataliaGemelova(7) 7 29
(NTinkler) *racd in midfield: rdn over 4f out: struggling fnl 3f* **16/1**

036- **12** *27* **High Cane (USA)**[134] [5552] 4-9-5 67 ........ KFallon 12 —
(MDHammond) *trckd ldrs: shkn up and wknd 3f out: heavily eased over 1f out* **9/2**[2]

0 **13** *9* **Wild Wild Wes**[24] [651] 4-9-10 ........ NDay 13 —
(RIngram) *racd wd: in tch to 4f out: sn wknd u.p: t.o* **50/1**

2m 9.44s (2.05) **Going Correction** 0.0s/f (Stan)
**WFA** 3 from 4yo 22lb **13** Ran SP% **124.2**
Speed ratings: **91,90,89,89,89 87,86,84,83,80 80,58,51**CSF £29.90 TOTE £10.50: £2.80, £1.80, £5.20; EX 47.70.
**Owner** Mrs Fitri Hay **Bred** Shadwell Estate Company Limited **Trained** East Garston, Berks

**FOCUS**
A weak maiden and it was steadily-run to boot. The winning time was poor and all indications are that this was woeful stuff.

**NOTEBOOK**
**Barathea Dreams(IRE)**, in the front rank throughout, held off several challengers in the straight to make a winning debut. Out of a half-sister to Nashwan, Unfuwain and Nayef, this half-brother to a winner in Dubai should improve but will not be easy to place in the short term.
**Jorobaden(FR)** had not run since his debut in a backend maiden as a two-year-old. His dam won the Prix du Cadran over two and a half miles and he will appreciate a step up in trip.
**Almost Welcome** was well beaten in a banded event last time, albeit after being hampered, and his presence in third does not advertise the form.
**Springalong(USA)**, who has had his problems, shaped as if he could be worth a try over twelve furlongs.
**Rollswood(USA)**, who failed to stay in a couple of bumpers, wore cheekpieces on this Flat bow. He was closing when getting stopped in his run, but for which he would have certainly made the frame.
**Blue Quiver(IRE)**, unsuited by the lack of a true gallop, is now eligible for handicaps.
**High Cane(USA)** *Official explanation: trainer had no explanation for the poor form shown*

## 872 LITTLEWOODS BET DIRECT H'CAP 1m 2f (P)
**4:10** (4:12) (D) (0-85,85) 4-Y-O+ **£4,849** (£1,492; £746; £373) **Stalls** Low

Form RPR

1-02 **1** **Hip Hop Harry**[20] [679] 4-9-5 **77** ........ (v[1]) KFallon 2 88
(EALDunlop) *s.i.s: hld up in rr: rdn and prog fr over 3f out: effrt to ld on outer over 1f out: drvn clr* **2/1**[1]

2000 **2** *1¼* **Internationalguest (IRE)**[17] [706] 5-9-7 **78** ........ (v) NPollard 6 87
(GGMargarson) *trckd ldrs: cl up 2f out: sn rdn and nt qckn: r.o wl again last 150y: tk 2nd fnl stride* **14/1**



The Form Book, Raceform Ltd, Compton, RG20 6NL

164- **3** *shd* **Ofaraby**[87] 6098 4-9-7 **79** MHenry 4 88
(MAJarvis) *trckd ldrs: effrt over 2f out: rdn to dispute ld over 1f out: unable qck fnl f: lost 2nd last stride* **11/1**

-152 **4** *3/4* **Barry Island**[17] 706 5-9-7 **78** TQuinn 9 85
(DRCElsworth) *hld up in rr: plenty to do whn effrt over 2f out: shuffled along and prog over 1f out: nt rch ldrs* **7/2**[2]

0-11 **5** *3/4* **Brave Dane (IRE)**[10] 765 6-8-11 **68** WRyan 11 74
(AWCarroll) *hld up in last: stdy prog on inner whn nt clr run over 2f out: nt qckn and btn wl over 1f out* **7/1**[3]

51/0 **6** *shd* **Lion Hunter (USA)**[10] 768 5-10-0 **85** JPSpencer 8 91
(MissECLavelle) *led at decent pce: rdn and hdd 2f out: one pce* **7/1**[3]

0-34 **7** *1 1/4* **Paragon Of Virtue**[24] 649 7-9-8 **79** JFanning 5 82
(PMitchell) *prom: pressed ldr 1/2-way: led gng wl 2f out: hdd and fnd nil over 1f out* **7/1**[3]

000- **8** *hd* **Rebate**[155] 5122 4-9-0 **72** PDobbs 3 75
(RHannon) *racd in midfield: effrt over 2f out: sn rdn and nt qckn: one pce after* **66/1**

040- **9** *3 1/2* **Krugerrand (USA)**[130] 5618 5-9-11 **82** MFenton 1 79
(WJMusson) *s.i.s and sltly hmpd s: hld up in last pair: rn wd bnd 4f out: effrt 2f out: no imp ldrs* **25/1**

2-63 **10** *9* **Just Wiz**[11] 759 8-8-11 **68** (b) EAhern 7 49
(NPLittmoden) *racd in midfield: rdn and wknd over 3f out: sn bhd* **16/1**

0-00 **11** *dist* **Adalar (IRE)**[10] 768 4-9-1 **73** (v[1]) SDrowne 10 —
(PDEvans) *racd freely: pressed ldr to 1/2-way: wknd rapidly: t.o* **50/1**

2m 4.82s (-2.57) **Going Correction** 0.0s/f (Stan)
**WFA** 4 from 5yo+ 1lb **11** Ran SP% **121.2**
Speed ratings: **110,109,108,108,107 107,106,106,103,96** —CSF £34.25 CT £262.10 TOTE £3.20: £1.90, £3.60, £2.00; EX 112.10.
**Owner** Lucayan Stud **Bred** P D Player **Trained** Newmarket, Suffolk

**FOCUS**
A very decent time for the grade. The form looks rock solid.

**NOTEBOOK**
**Hip Hop Harry**, who gave the remarkable Fall In Line a race here last time, appreciated the drop in trip and won readily in the end. But he has his quirks, and the first-time visor was not merely for decoration.
**Internationalguest(IRE)**, who wore a visor rather than blinkers, had not run over this trip since back in the autumn. After hitting something of a flat spot, he finished to good effect and snatched second place on the line.
**Ofaraby**, who has gone well fresh before, threw down a challenge to the winner in the straight but appeared a shade reluctant to go past. Caught for second on the post, this trip looks slightly too far for him.
**Barry Island**, back over this trip, made good late headway without troubling the leaders. He will get it right again at some point.
**Brave Dane(IRE)**, 17lb higher than for the first of his two wins over course and distance, was found out in this better grade.
**Lion Hunter(USA)** ran a better race on this second run for the Lavelle yard, but may be too high in the weights at present.
**Paragon Of Virtue** found nothing when headed and may be in need of a drop in the handicap.

## 873 BET IN RUNNING @ BETDIRECT.CO.UK (S) STKS 1m (P)
4:40 (4:40) (G) 3-Y-0+ £2,618 (£748; £374) Stalls High

Form RPR

0604 **1** **Muqtadi (IRE)**[6] 821 6-9-8 49 JPSpencer 2 52
(MQuinn) *sltly impeded s: settled in last pair: gd prog over 2f out: drvn to ld 1f out: kpt on* **11/2**[3]

0011 **2** *1* **Xaloc Bay (IRE)**[6] 821 6-10-0 53 DarrenWilliams 5 56
(BPJBaugh) *set gd pce: drvn 3l clr 2f out: tired and hdd 1f out: one pce after* **7/2**[2]

0-50 **3** *1* **Free Option (IRE)**[36] 564 9-10-0 71 (b) KFallon 9 54
(WJMusson) *hld up in last pair: nt clr run over 3f out: sn rdn: prog on outer 2f out: drvn and kpt on fnl f: nt rch ldng pair* **7/4**[1]

0-00 **4** *1 3/4* **Miss Celerity**[21] 665 4-9-3 30 SDrowne 4 39
(MJHaynes) *chsd ldng pair: rdn and unable qck over 2f out: btn whn n.m.r 1f out* **100/1**

000- **5** *1 3/4* **Dark Shah (IRE)**[161] 4973 4-9-8 60 (t) MartinDwyer 3 40
(DMSimcock) *wnt lft s: racd in midfield: effrt over 2f out: chsd ldrs over 1f out: hung rt and found nil after* **7/2**[2]

600 **6** *1/2* **Never Cried Wolf**[6] 817 3-7-12 (p) RThomas[(5)] 1 39
(DRCElsworth) *chsd ldrs: pushed along 1/2-way: unable qck wl over 1f out: one pce after* **33/1**

000- **7** *11* **Roman Empire**[87] 6088 4-9-8 56 (b[1]) JFanning 7 15
(TJEtherington) *t.k.h: chsd ldr: rdn over 2f out: wknd rapidly over 1f out* **20/1**

00-2 **8** *13* **Marakash (IRE)**[6] 821 5-9-8 51 (tp) GBaker 6 —
(MRBosley) *t.k.h: in tch: urged along and fnd nil over 2f out: sn btn: eased over 1f out* **14/1**

4-35 **9** *6* **Larad (IRE)**[10] 769 3-8-3 53 (b) DKinsella 8 —
(JSMoore) *dwlt: t.k.h and sn chsd ldrs: rdn 1/2-way: sn wknd: t.o* **20/1**

1m 39.55s (0.04) **Going Correction** 0.0s/f (Stan)
**WFA** 3 from 4yo+ 19lb **9** Ran SP% **116.3**
Speed ratings: **99,98,97,95,93 93,82,69,63**CSF £24.25 TOTE £8.50: £1.80, £1.20, £1.40; EX 29.30.There was no bid for the winner.
**Owner** Mrs S G Davies **Bred** Shadwell Estate Company Limited **Trained** Sparsholt, Oxon

**FOCUS**
They went a decent clip, but the overall standard of the form is poor.

**NOTEBOOK**
**Muqtadi(IRE)**, who finished behind Xaloc Bay here last time out, was well suited by the fast pace that rival set on this occasion and came from last to first. He has never been easy to catch right, however.
**Xaloc Bay(IRE)**, bidding for a hat-trick, skipped clear on the home turn after setting a sound pace but found one too good for him this time.
**Free Option(IRE)**, down in grade and with the blinkers refitted, had a good chance at the weights on this return to his favourite track but was unable to cash in. He has never been the easiest of rides.
**Miss Celerity** ran her best race to date on this step up in trip. She is qualified for regional racing and that may prove her most sensible option.
**Dark Shah(IRE)**, making his seasonal debut and having his first run for a new yard, refused to put his best foot forward when the pressure was on.

## 874 BET DIRECT FOOTBALL CASHBACKS H'CAP 1m 2f (P)
5:10 (5:11) (F) (0-55,55) 4-Y-0+ £3,010 (£860; £430) Stalls High

Form RPR

-402 **1** **Fortune Point (IRE)**[15] 720 6-9-5 **54** IMongan 1 66
(AWCarroll) *led after 2f: mde rest: kicked on 2f out: drvn and hld on wl fnl f* **8/1**

0002 **2** *nk* **Steely Dan**[6] 815 5-9-1 **50** NPollard 2 61
(JRBest) *hld up in rr: prog over 2f out: effrt to press wnr 1f out: ev ch after: nt go past* **9/2**[2]

-023 **3** *3 1/2* **Frank's Quest (IRE)**[10] 773 4-9-1 **54** LPKeniry[(3)] 11 59
(PBurgoyne) *t.k.h: prom: trckd wnr over 4f out: stl pulling hrd 3f out: rdn to chal 2f out: nt qckn and btn over 1f out* **20/1**

05-0 **4** *3/4* **Sammy's Shuffle**[10] 765 9-9-1 **50** (b) JFEgan 14 54
(JamiePoulton) *trckd ldrs: nt qckn and lost pl over 2f out: effrt again on outer over 1f out: styd on same pce* **10/1**

04-3 **5** *hd* **Another Secret**[20] 672 6-9-0 **49** (be) SWhitworth 9 52
(GLMoore) *chsd ldrs: rdn and effrt over 2f out: kpt on same pce fr over 1f out* **7/2**[1]

5-P0 **6** *2* **Geography (IRE)**[10] 776 4-8-10 **53** (p) CHaddon[(7)] 6 53
(PButler) *t.k.h: cl up: nt qckn and btn 2f out: one pce after* **66/1**

1025 **7** *nk* **Tropical Son**[8] 795 5-9-4 **53** (v) NCallan 13 52
(DShaw) *chsd ldrs: rdn and prog on outer over 2f out: one pce and no imp over 1f out* **16/1**

-045 **8** *nk* **Amnesty**[20] 676 5-9-5 **54** (be) DaneO'Neill 10 53
(GLMoore) *dwlt: hld up in last: stl last 3f out: sn outpcd and rdn: kpt on fnl 2f: no ch* **25/1**

3166 **9** *hd* **Piquet**[6] 815 6-9-1 **50** GBaker 8 48
(JJBridger) *dwlt: t.k.h: hld up in last pair: drvn and prog on wd outside 2f out: no imp over 1f out: fdd* **10/1**

30-6 **10** *3* **Archirondel**[36] 464 6-9-6 **55** EAhern 5 48
(MDHammond) *racd in midfield: rdn and effrt over 2f out: fdd over 1f out* **11/2**[3]

500- **11** *4* **Tintawn Gold (IRE)**[116] 5848 4-9-3 **53** JPSpencer 7 39
(SWoodman) *hld up in last trio: rdn and outpcd over 2f out: no ch after* **12/1**

26-5 **12** *1* **Shifty**[40] 546 5-9-5 **54** ANicholls 12 38
(DNicholls) *t.k.h: hld up towards rr: rdn 3f out: sn no prog and btn* **12/1**

55-0 **13** *2 1/2* **Muraqeb**[38] 555 4-9-2 **52** SDrowne 4 31
(MrsBarbaraWaring) *a in rr: struggling and btn over 3f out* **33/1**

0615 **14** *shd* **Red Storm**[11] 763 5-9-1 **50** MartinDwyer 3 29
(JRBoyle) *led for 2f: chsd wnr to over 4f out: wknd u.p 3f out* **25/1**

2m 9.87s (2.48) **Going Correction** 0.0s/f (Stan)
**WFA** 4 from 5yo+ 1lb **14** Ran SP% **123.2**
Speed ratings: **90,89,86,86,86 84,84,84,83,81 78,77,75,75**CSF £42.38 CT £718.66 TOTE £6.90: £2.60, £1.80, £8.20; EX 61.10 Place 6 £139.09, Place 5 £70.16..
**Owner** The T J Racing Partnership **Bred** Dr A J O'Reilly And Skymarc Farm **Trained** Wixford, Warwicks

**FOCUS**
Fair form, but there was no pace on and the winner was able to dictate things. The winning time was very moderate.

**NOTEBOOK**
**Fortune Point(IRE)**, who has been given a chance by the handicapper, dictated his own pace and was always going to hold on once quickening things up at the two pole. He will not always get his own way like he did here.
**Steely Dan** adopted different tactics on this step up in trip. He had his chance, but was reluctant to go through with his challenge.
**Frank's Quest(IRE)** ran his best race since switching to this yard and this looks to be his optimum trip.
**Sammy's Shuffle**, dropped a further 3lb, was keeping on again and looks in good heartt.
**Another Secret** was unable to capitalise on a career-low mark and appeared to have no real excuse.
T/Plt: £304.40 to a £1 stake. Pool: £44,876.95. 107.60 winning tickets. T/Qpdt: £80.40 to a £1 stake. Pool: £2,902.90. 26.70 winning tickets. JN

# 823 SOUTHWELL (L-H)
Tuesday, February 24

**OFFICIAL GOING: Standard to slow**

## 875 BETDIRECT.CO.UK NEW SITE BANDED STKS 1m (F)
2:30 (2:31) (H) 3-Y-0+ £1,302 (£372; £186) Stalls Low

Form RPR

0-24 **1** **Fraamtastic**[9] 783 7-9-3 35 (p) BReilly[(5)] 5 41
(BAPearce) *chsd ldrs: n.m.r and rdn along 3f out: styd on u.p over 1f out: drvn ent last: led last 100 yds* **11/2**[2]

-321 **2** *hd* **Galley Law**[9] 783 4-10-0 30 JQuinn 4 47
(RCraggs) *midfield: hdwy and edgd lft 3f out: rdn to chal over 1f out: drvn and ev ch ins last: not qckn last 100 yds* **9/4**[1]

0521 **3** *1/2* **Dancing King (IRE)**[7] 809 8-9-7 30 PMakin[(7)] 15 45
(PWHiatt) *prom: hdwy to chal 2f out: rdn to ld over 1f out: drvn ent last: hdd and no ex last 100 yds* **7/1**

00/3 **4** *1 1/4* **Grub Street**[16] 713 8-9-1 30 MLawson[(7)] 14 37
(JParkes) *towards rr: hdwy on outer over 3f out: rdn along and wd st: rdn 2f out: styd on u.p appr last: nrst fin* **12/1**

0-01 **5** *nk* **Gracious Air (USA)**[9] 778 6-9-1 35 (v) DFentiman[(7)] 1 36
(JRWeymes) *towards rr: hdwy on inner over 2f out: sn rdn and styd on appr last: nrst fin* **6/1**[3]

0353 **6** *4* **Countrywide Girl (IRE)**[7] 809 5-9-1 30 PPMathers[(7)] 13 27
(ABerry) *cl up: led 3f out: rdn 2f out: sn hdd and grad wknd* **20/1**

4005 **7** *2* **Pageant**[7] 809 7-9-5 30 (b) LisaJones[(3)] 8 23
(JMBradley) *chsd ldrs: rdn along and n.m.r 3f out: sn wknd* **25/1**

0-06 **8** *3* **Caterham Common**[16] 713 5-9-8 30 ACulhane 11 16
(DWChapman) *a midfield* **40/1**

0530 **9** *3 1/2* **Mimas Girl**[5] 824 5-9-8 30 (tp) JBramhill 9 9
(SRBowring) *a midfield* **20/1**

0-06 **10** *6* **Aljomar**[43] 500 5-9-8 35 RFitzpatrick 3 —
(REBarr) *a towards rr* **25/1**

0-00 **11** *1/2* **Moyne Pleasure (IRE)**[22] 653 6-9-5 35 (p) LFletcher[(3)] 2 —
(PaulJohnson) *bhd fr 1/2-way* **12/1**

00-0 **12** *1/2* **Monkey Or Me (IRE)**[43] 506 3-8-3 30 JMcAuley 6 —
(PTMidgley) *led 1f: cl up tl rdn along 3f out and sn wknd* **40/1**

-404 **13** *10* **Blue Maeve**[7] 809 4-9-8 30 KDalgleish 7 —
(JHetherton) *cl up: led after 1f: rdn along and hdd 3f out: sn wknd* **25/1**

-000 **14** *1 1/4* **Morris Dancing (USA)**[15] 727 5-9-8 30 (p) MTebbutt 16 —
(BPJBaugh) *s.i.s: a bhd* **25/1**

00-0 **15** *7* **By Definition (IRE)**[41] 532 6-9-3 30 (v[1]) MSavage[(5)] 12 —
(JCTuck) *sn drvn along and a rr* **66/1**

16 2 ½ **Havana Rose (IRE)**[132] 5579 4-9-8 30..............................(p) DMernagh 10 —
(PatrickMorris, Ire) *bhd fr 1/2-way* **40/1**

1m 46.63s (2.03) **Going Correction** +0.15s/f (Slow)
**WFA** 3 from 4yo+ 19lb **16 Ran SP% 122.0**
Speed ratings: **95,94,94,93,92 88,86,83,80,74 73,73,63,62,55 52**CSF £15.81 TOTE £8.80: £2.20, £1.60, £2.60; EX 21.40.
**Owner** Richard J Gray **Bred** Bloodhorse International Limited **Trained** Newchapel, Surrey
■ A welcome winner for Brian Pearce, his first in over two years.

**FOCUS**
Typically poor form, but a relatively competitive affair producing a tight finish.

**NOTEBOOK**
**Fraamtastic** reversed recent placings with the staying-on Galley Law. She has been in good form since returning from a long absence, but she did not get home over 11 furlongs here last time and found the drop back to a mile suiting her down to the ground.
**Galley Law**found this an insufficient test of stamina and, although staying on well all the way up the straight, could never quite get his head in front. He will appreciate a step back up in trip.
**Dancing King(IRE)** is another who is running well at present and this was a good effort under his penalty.
**Grub Street** once again shaped with promise on his second run back after a lengthy absence.
**Gracious Air(USA)**, a course and distance winner last time out, got outpaced in the early stages and could only stay on when the race was all over. She has never been the most consistent of animals.
**Countrywide Girl(IRE)** has yet to conclusively prove she gets this trip.
**Blue Maeve** *Official explanation: trainer's representative said gelding had breathing problems*
**Morris Dancing(USA)** *Official explanation: jockey said gelding stumbled leaving the stalls*

## 876 NEW SITE @ BETDIRECT.CO.UK BANDED STKS — 5f (F)
**3:00** (3:03) (H) 3-Y-0+ **£1,652** (£472; £236) **Stalls** High

Form RPR

0303 **1** **Sergeant Slipper**[8] 796 7-9-5 45..............................(v) RFitzpatrick 15 50
(CSmith) *s.i.s and bhd stands side: hdwy 2f out: rdn over 1f out: styd on wl fnl f to ld nr fin* **5/1**[2]

-060 **2** *shd* **Ejay**[7] 813 5-9-2 40.............................. LisaJones(3) 14 50
(JulianPoulton) *in tch stands side: pushed along 1/2-way: hdwy and rdn whn n.m.r over 1f out: drvn and ev ch fnl f:jst hld* **12/1**

6315 **3** *¾* **Torrent**[8] 796 9-9-5 45..............................(b) ACulhane 3 47
(DWChapman) *wnt lft s: in tch far side: hdwy wl over 1f out: rdn to ld wl ins last: hdd and nt qckn nr fin* **9/2**[1]

0-60 **4** *1* **The Leather Wedge (IRE)**[25] 637 5-9-0 45.............. PBradley(5) 5 44
(ABerry) *led: rdn wl over 1f ot: drvn 1f out: hdd and one pce wl ins last* **10/1**[3]

-226 **5** *1* **Hagley Park**[11] 762 5-8-12 45.............................. PGallagher(7) 7 40
(MQuinn) *cl up: rdn 2f out: drvn and ev ch whn rdr dropped whip 1f out: wknd ins last* **9/2**[1]

-000 **6** *1* **Lone Piper**[22] 657 9-9-5 35.............................. JBramhill 4 37
(JMBradley) *in tch centre: hdwy to chse ldrs 2f out: sn rdn and one pce appr last* **25/1**

55-5 **7** *shd* **Pleasure Time**[22] 657 11-8-12 45..............................(v) PMakin(7) 1 36
(CSmith) *bmpd s: chsd ldrs far side: rdn wl over 1f out: grad wknd* **16/1**

-610 **8** *2 ½* **Danakim**[9] 780 7-8-12 40..............................(be) DFentiman(7) 11 27
(JRWeymes) *chsd ldrs: rdn and wandereed over 1f out: sn wknd* **20/1**

0060 **9** *nk* **Indian Shores**[15] 725 5-8-12 40..............................(p) PVarley(7) 12 26
(MMullineaux) *outpcd in rr tl sme late hdwy* **20/1**

030- **10** *½* **Alastair Smellie**[206] 3797 8-9-5 40.............................. PMcCabe 2 25
(SLKeightley) *hmpd s: sn outpcd far side tl sme late hdwy* **20/1**

0-00 **11** *1 ¼* **On The Trail**[22] 654 7-9-5 45..............................(b) KDalgleish 10 20
(DWChapman) *wnt lft s: cl up centre: rdn along 2f out and sn wknd* **16/1**

0-00 **12** *hd* **Safranine (IRE)**[25] 637 7-9-5 45..............................(p) AnnStokell 6 20
(MissAStokell) *in tch: rdn along 1/2-way and sn outpcd* **14/1**

000- **13** *1 ¼* **Mr Uppity**[244] 2692 5-8-12 40.............................. MHalford(7) 13 15
(JulianPoulton) *nvr nr ldrs* **40/1**

-000 **14** *shd* **Sheapys Lass**[19] 683 3-7-12 45.............................. RoryMoore(7) 8 15
(ACrook) *hmpd s: a rr* **50/1**

60-0 **15** *6* **Bishop To Actress**[50] 438 3-7-12 45.............................. KGhunowa(7) 9 —
(MJPolglase) *hmpd s: a rr* **50/1**

60-0 **16** *1* **Feeling Blue**[25] 638 5-9-5 45.............................. JQuinn 16 —
(BNPollock) *in tch: rdn over 2f out: sn wknd* **12/1**

61.28 secs (0.98) **Going Correction** +0.15s/f (Slow)
**WFA** 3 from 5yo+ 14lb **16 Ran SP% 120.4**
Speed ratings: **98,97,96,95,93 91,91,87,87,86 84,84,82,81,72 70**CSF £57.13 TOTE £5.70: £1.50, £3.20, £2.40; EX 75.80.
**Owner** C Smith **Bred** P And Mrs Russell **Trained** Temple Bruer, Lincs

**FOCUS**
Poor form, but there was a good pace on and the first two came from way off the pace.

**NOTEBOOK**
**Sergeant Slipper** is an habitual slow starter and once again trailed the field in the early stages, but with his stablemate Pleasure Time helping to set a fierce pace, he eventually came through to score narrowly. He is at his best over this course and distance, but don't bank on a repeat.
**Ejay**, whose previous best run had been over six at this track, appeared to appreciate returning here. She matched the winner stride for stride in his strong finish, but just lost out in the photo.
**Torrent**, an enigmatic sort, looked set to score for a moment before the first two flew past on the stands' side.
**The Leather Wedge(IRE)** helped set a strong gallop but did not quite get home as a result.
**Hagley Park** is difficult to win with and her rider losing his whip a furlong out probably did not make much difference.
**Lone Piper**, whose challenge came all too late, has not won a race for two and a half years.
**Feeling Blue** *Official explanation: jockey said mare was unruly to post*

## 877 BETDIRECT.CO.UK MEDIAN AUCTION MAIDEN STKS — 1m (F)
**3:30** (3:30) (H) 3-5-Y-0 **£1,438** (£411; £205) **Stalls** Low

Form RPR

330 **1** **Galloway Mac**[7] 805 4-9-9.............................. DHolland 4 56
(WAO'Gorman) *hld up in tch: hdwy 3f out: chsd ldrs 2f out: rdn to ld over 1f out: styd on* **2/1**[2]

0023 **2** *2 ½* **Kustom Kit For Her**[7] 811 4-9-4 45..............................(t) JBramhill 5 45
(SRBowring) *cl up: led after 2f: rdn along 2f out: drvn and hdd over 1f out: kpt on same pce* **12/1**

-302 **3** *4* **Angelo's Pride**[7] 811 3-8-4 57.............................. JQuinn 1 41
(JAOsborne) *s.i.s: sn in tch: hdwy on inner 1/2-way: rdn 2f out: sn drvn and wknd over 1f out* **1/1**[1]

5 **4** *7* **Macpursie**[9] 779 3-7-13.............................. DMernagh 2 21
(TDBarron) *cl up: rdn along 3f out: sn wknd* **6/1**[3]

-000 **5** *18* **Mystic Promise (IRE)**[7] 802 3-7-13 30..............................(v) HayleyTurner(5) 6 —
(MrsNMacauley) *chsd ldrs: rdn along 3f out: sn btn* **50/1**

000- **6** *10* **Indrapura Star (USA)**[99] 6015 4-9-4 40.............................. BReilly(5) 8 —
(MissJFeilden) *sn rdn along to chse ldrs: wknd 1/2-way* **40/1**

00-6 **7** *7* **Frimley's Matterry**[9] 779 4-9-9 53.............................. RFitzpatrick 3 —
(REBarr) *led 2f: sn pushed along: rdn over 4f out: sn wknd* **28/1**

1m 45.61s (1.01) **Going Correction** +0.15s/f (Slow)
**WFA** 3 from 4yo 19lb **7 Ran SP% 113.2**
Speed ratings: **100,97,93,86,68 58,51**CSF £23.88 TOTE £4.10: £1.90, £3.00; EX 23.10.
**Owner** Michael McDonnell **Bred** Stetchworth Park Stud Ltd **Trained** Newmarket, Suffolk

**FOCUS**
Weak maiden form, but a fair time for the grade.

**NOTEBOOK**
**Galloway Mac** looked to have been given a great chance in this poor heat, but plenty of people were happy to oppose him. Six furlongs was far too short for him last time and he looked to need every yard of this mile. He is open to improvement in handicap company as is sure to stay farther.
**Kustom Kit For Her** is a long-standing maiden, but she still managed to overturn a 15-length beating by Angelo's Pride at Wolverhampton last time.
**Angelo's Pride** ran a disappointing race, failing to translate his Dunstall Park form to this slower surface.
**Macpursie** was beaten turning in.

## 878 BETDIRECT.CO.UK BANDED STKS — 1m 3f (F)
**4:00** (4:00) (H) 4-Y-0+ **£1,627** (£465; £232) **Stalls** Low

Form RPR

-111 **1** **Broughton Knows**[9] 781 7-9-3 45..............................(b) LisaJones(3) 2 59
(WJMusson) *hld up in rr: hdwy over 3f out and sn pushed along: rdn over 1f out: edgd lft and styd on u.p to ld ins last* **11/10**[1]

065- **2** *nk* **Red Moor (IRE)**[67] 6214 4-8-12 45.............................. ACulhane 5 53
(RHollinshead) *in tch: hdwy 4f out: effrt over 2f out: rdn to ld wl over 1f out: drvn and hdd ins last: no ex nr fin* **8/1**[3]

3-62 **3** *3* **Next Flight (IRE)**[9] 781 5-9-0 45.............................. RFitzpatrick 4 48
(REBarr) *chsd ldrs: rdn along over 2f out: drvn and ch over 1f out: one pce ins last* **10/1**

0-50 **4** *1* **Turftanzer (GER)**[35] 568 5-9-0 35..............................(t) KimTinkler 6 46
(DonEnricoIncisa) *led 2f: chsd clr ldr: stdd 3f out: swtchd lft and hdwy 2f out: rdn and ch over 1f out: drvn and one pce ent last* **16/1**

-220 **5** *11* **Our Glenard**[16] 715 5-9-0 45.............................. PMcCabe 7 29
(SLKeightley) *dwlt: sn in tch: hdwy to chse ldng pair 1/2-way: rdn along 3f out: sn led: hdd & wknd wl over 1f out* **4/1**[2]

6061 **6** *3* **Ace-Ma-Vahra**[5] 823 6-9-0 40.............................. JBramhill 3 24
(SRBowring) *hld up in rr: hdwy on inner and hmpd over 4f out: rdn along 3f out: sn btn* **12/1**

-006 **7** *6* **Marengo**[9] 783 10-9-0 30.............................. JoannaBadger 8 14
(PaulJohnson) *s.i.s: rapid hdwy to ld after 2f: rdn along 3f out: sn hdd & wknd* **33/1**

0000 **8** *21* **Jamestown**[18] 695 7-8-11 45.............................. LFletcher(3) 1 —
(MJPolglase) *hld up: hdwy over 4f out: rdn along and wknd 3f out* **9/1**

2m 30.65s (1.75) **Going Correction** +0.15s/f (Slow)
**WFA** 4 from 5yo+ 2lb **8 Ran SP% 114.3**
Speed ratings: **99,98,96,95,87 85,81,66**CSF £10.78 TOTE £1.70: £1.40, £2.50, £1.70; EX 13.80.
**Owner** Broughton Thermal Insulation **Bred** Broughton Bloodstock **Trained** Newmarket, Suffolk
■ Stewards Enquiry : P McCabe caution: careless riding

**FOCUS**
Fair form, but not a competitive heat.

**NOTEBOOK**
**Broughton Knows** was recording a fourth win on the bounce. He is not straightforward, but Lisa Jones gets the best out of him and she nursed him home to a narrow but cosy success. He will appreciate a return to a longer trip but will no longer be eligible for banded races and is likely to find things tougher.
**Red Moor(IRE)**, dropping into banded grade for the first time, ran well on his first start for two months. His trainer should find a race for him at this level.
**Next Flight(IRE)** was 6lb better off at the weights with Broughton Knows compared with their last meeting, but the result was the same.
**Turftanzer(GER)** finished clear of the rest but does not appeal as one who is likely to score in the near future. His connections suggested he needs a right-handed track.

## 879 DAILY OFFERS @ BETDIRECT.CO.UK (S) STKS — 1m 4f (F)
**4:30** (4:30) (H) 4-Y-0+ **£1,267** (£362; £181) **Stalls** Low

Form RPR

1001 **1** **Daunted (IRE)**[16] 714 8-9-5 60.............................. LisaJones(3) 3 63+
(PABlockley) *hld up in tch: smooth hdwy over 4f out: led over 3f out and sn clr* **8/13**[1]

0261 **2** *3* **Radiant Bride**[16] 716 4-9-0 45..............................(b) GFaulkner 5 53
(KRBurke) *t.k.h: hld up in rr: hdwy over 3f out: rdn to chse wnr 2f out: sn hung lft and no imp* **5/1**[3]

16/5 **3** *5* **Oro Street (IRE)**[18] 693 8-9-3 61.............................. DHolland 2 46
(GFBridgwater) *trckd ldr: hdwy to ld over 4f out: sn rdn along and hdd over 3f out: drvn and wknd 2f out* **7/2**[2]

500- **4** *16* **Cadwallader (USA)**[90] 6075 4-9-0 58.............................. DSweeney 1 22
(PBurgoyne) *mde most tl rdn along and hdd over 4f out: sn wknd* **16/1**

0-05 **5** *3 ½* **Illusionist**[10] 776 6-9-3 35..............................(v) PMcCabe 4 16
(MrsNMacauley) *hld up: hdwy over 5f out: rdn along and wknd 4f out* **33/1**

2m 44.81s (2.71) **Going Correction** +0.15s/f (Slow)
**WFA** 4 from 6yo+ 3lb **5 Ran SP% 109.6**
Speed ratings: **96,94,90,80,77**CSF £4.12 TOTE £1.30: £1.40, £1.70; EX 2.30.The winner was bought in for 2,600gns.
**Owner** Mrs Joanna Hughes **Bred** Mrs G Doyle **Trained** Southwell, Notts
■ Stewards Enquiry : P McCabe one-day ban: used whip down the shoulder with the forehand (Mar 8)

**FOCUS**
A weak seller won in authoritative style and the winner showed fair form for the grade.

**NOTEBOOK**
**Daunted(IRE)**is a useful tool at this level. He has a good record at this track over 11 or 12 furlongs and his record in F,G or H class races over those distances now reads an impressive 52123111. Connections are also convinced that he performs best with a female rider, an opinion supported by the fact that four of his last five victories have been for women.
**Radiant Bride** was set a lot to do given that she won over two miles last time. She did stay on, but the leader had gone beyond recall by the time she got into gear, and a step back up in trip will not do her any harm. That said, she does not look the most resolute in the world. *Official explanation: jockey said filly was hanging left-handed and never felt right*
**Oro Street(IRE)** was the best in on adjusted official ratings, but he owes his rating to his performances on the Flat four years ago, not to the ability he has now.

**880** **BET IN RUNNING @ BETDIRECT.CO.UK BANDED STKS** **1m 6f (F)**
**5:00** (5:00) (H) 4-Y-0+ **£1,435** (£410; £205) **Stalls** Low

Form RPR
-530 **1** **East Cape**[21] [671] 7-9-5 35 KimTinkler 3 52
(DonEnricoIncisa) *in tch: hdwy to trck ldr 4f out: effrt 2f out: rdn to ld over 1f out and sn clr* **11/2**[3]
3212 **2** *5* **Buz Kiri (USA)**[9] [783] 6-9-5 40 DHolland 7 45
(AWCarroll) *hld up in tch: hdwy 4f out: chal over 2f out and sn rdn: drvn and one pce ent last* **4/6**[1]
-214 **3** *1 ½* **Paddy Mul**[16] [716] 7-9-5 40 (t) DRMcCabe 1 46+
(WStorey) *hld up: hdwy on inner whn hmpd 4f out: effrt to chse ldrs over 2f out: sn rdn and kpt on same pce* **9/2**[2]
00-0 **4** *hd* **Trojan Wolf**[16] [714] 9-9-5 35 ACulhane 6 43
(PHowling) *led: rdn along 3f out: drvn 2f out: hdd & wknd over 1f out* **25/1**
3-26 **5** *5* **Fairmorning (IRE)**[46] [483] 5-9-5 40 ADaly 5 37
(JWUnett) *in tch: effrt to chse ldrs 4f out: sn rdn along: one pce fnl 2f* **10/1**
6645 **6** *15* **King Priam (IRE)**[5] [825] 9-9-2 40 (b) LFletcher(3) 2 —
(MJPolglase) *hld up: a rr* **14/1**
600/ **7** *dist* **Sergeant's Inn**[707] [762] 7-8-12 30 SaleemGolam(7) 4 —
(TTClement) *chsd ldr: rdn along over 5f out: wknd 4f out: sn bhd* **50/1**

3m 14.06s (4.46) **Going Correction** +0.15s/f (Slow) **7** Ran SP% **115.1**
Speed ratings: **93,90,89,89,86 77,**—CSF £9.72 TOTE £9.20: £1.70, £1.60; EX 14.60 Place 6 £14.78, Place 5 £10.21..
**Owner** Don Enrico Incisa **Bred** Sir Eric Parker **Trained** Middleham Moor, N Yorks

**FOCUS**
Weak form producing a modest winning time.

**NOTEBOOK**
**East Cape**, for whom this step up in trip was a gamble, bounded clear for an easy win. Now that connections know he stays, a few more doors should open up for him, and he looks the type who could go in again at this level.
**Buz Kiri(USA)** was a warm order in the market in a race which featured many horses with questions to answer, but despite travelling well for most of the way, he found disappointingly little when asked to go and win his race entering the straight.
**Paddy Mul** had run poorly last time but was expected to do better back in trip. It was only inside the final half furlong that he managed to secure third place, though.
**Trojan Wolf** did not get home after setting the pace.
**Fairmorning(IRE)**, who is still a maiden, has run disappointingly on his last two starts.
T/Plt: £8.20 to a £1 stake. Pool: £34,219.55. 3,017.05 winning tickets. T/Qpdt: £3.40 to a £1 stake. Pool: £2,227.20. 471.10 winning tickets. JR

## 867 LINGFIELD (L-H)
### Wednesday, February 25

**OFFICIAL GOING: Standard**
Wind: Slt against Weather: Fair

**881** **BETDIRECT.CO.UK NEW SITE MAIDEN STKS** **5f (P)**
**1:30** (1:31) (D) 3-Y-0 **£3,997** (£1,230; £615; £307) **Stalls** High

Form RPR
4- **1** **Tony The Tap**[58] [6248] 3-9-0 WRyan 3 65+
(NACallaghan) *dwlt: wnt rt after s: led 1f out: drvn clr* **7/4**[2]
22- **2** *1 ½* **Shrink**[187] [4341] 3-8-9 KFallon 1 54+
(MLWBell) *s.s: t.k.h in rr: hdwy over 1f out: jnd wnr ent fnl f: nt qckn* **4/5**[1]
030- **3** *1 ½* **Comeraincomeshine (IRE)**[88] [6090] 3-8-9 64 IMongan 5 42
(TGMills) *bmpd and pushed wd after s: in tch: effrt 2f out: styd on same pce* **8/1**[3]
0-00 **4** *hd* **Lakeside Guy (IRE)**[4] [840] 3-9-0 JPSpencer 4 46
(PSMcentee) *pressed ldrs: briefly disp ld over 1f out: one pce* **80/1**
3-00 **5** *1* **Son Of Rembrandt (IRE)**[29] [610] 3-8-9 56 MSavage(5) 2 43
(DKIvory) *hung rt thrght: led tl over 1f out: no ex* **25/1**

60.51 secs (0.73) **Going Correction** +0.10s/f (Slow) **5** Ran SP% **108.1**
Speed ratings: **98,95,93,92,91**CSF £3.33 TOTE £2.80: £1.20, £1.10; EX 5.00.
**Owner** K J Mercer **Bred** K J Mercer **Trained** Newmarket, Suffolk

**FOCUS**
An average sprint maiden which was run at a fair pace, but the form looks suspect.

**NOTEBOOK**
**Tony The Tap**, who showed promise on his debut over another furlong at this venue on his debut, got off the mark in workmanlike fashion. He veered right at the start and did no favours to the third horse, but recovered well. He is entitled to improve on this display, but his future looks to lie in handicaps.
**Shrink**, who was slowly away and was very keen at the back of pack throughout the first two furlongs, had nothing left in the tank when asked to win her race. She will come on for this run and showed enough to suggest she can win but has now been second on all of her three outings and looks tricky.
**Comeraincomeshine(IRE)** was done no favours by the winner when bumped going into the first bend, but recovered well enough and held every chance. She has an awkward action and looks in need of more time, but could improve back over further.
**Lakeside Guy(IRE)** ran his race, but his proximity at the finish must raise doubts as to the strength of this form.

**882** **NEW SITE @ BETDIRECT.CO.UK H'CAP** **1m 2f (P)**
**2:00** (2:01) (F) (0-65,65) 3-Y-0+ **£2,975** (£850; £425) **Stalls** Low

Form RPR
4-20 **1** **War Owl (USA)**[7] [820] 7-9-3 57 LisaJones(3) 6 69
(IanWilliams) *t.k.h in midfield: hdwy 2f out: led ins fnl f: rdn out* **7/1**[3]
6122 **2** *3* **Bank On Him**[7] [820] 9-9-11 62 JQuinn 8 69
(CWeedon) *chsd ldr: led over 3f out tl ins fnl f: nt qckn* **9/2**[1]
2-20 **3** *1* **He Who Dares (IRE)**[14] [742] 6-9-6 57 IMongan 11 62
(AWCarroll) *s.s: t.k.h in rr: rapid hdwy 2f out: one pce appr fnl f* **11/2**[2]
00-5 **4** *¾* **Fen Gypsy**[14] [745] 6-9-9 60 KFallon 3 63
(PDEvans) *chsd ldrs: one pce appr fnl f* **7/1**[3]
-402 **5** *shd* **Blazing The Trail (IRE)**[11] [765] 4-9-8 60 SWhitworth 2 63
(JWHills) *dwlt: hld up in midfield: effrt and swtchd wd 2f out: hrd rdn over 1f out: swtchd lft: styd on fnl f* **10/1**
500/ **6** *1 ¾* **Hallings Overture (USA)**[497] [5307] 5-10-0 65 PaulEddery 7 65
(CAHorgan) *a.p: no ex appr fnl f* **50/1**
31-0 **7** *1 ¼* **Karaoke (IRE)**[25] [650] 4-9-13 65 JFEgan 14 63
(SKirk) *mid-div: outpcd 3f out: effrt and wd st: no imp* **25/1**
6-00 **8** *1 ½* **Londoner (USA)**[14] [745] 6-9-8 59 PDoe 4 54
(SDow) *in tch: no hdwy fnl 2f* **40/1**
0-00 **9** *2* **Snuki**[11] [765] 5-9-2 53 (be) JPSpencer 10 45
(GLMoore) *t.k.h: chsd ldrs: hrd rdn over 2f out: wknd over 1f out* **16/1**
6-24 **10** *¾* **My Maite (IRE)**[11] [765] 5-9-6 57 (bt) DHolland 12 47
(RIngram) *led tl over 3f out: wknd over 2f out* **11/2**[2]
0-33 **11** *5* **Dance Party (IRE)**[11] [767] 4-9-11 63 MartinDwyer 9 44
(AMBalding) *mid-div: effrt on outside over 3f out: sn hrd rdn and btn* **8/1**
2400 **12** *4* **Easter Ogil (IRE)**[4] [842] 9-9-12 63 VSlattery 5 37
(JaneSouthcombe) *towards rr: rdn 4f out: sn lost tch* **10/1**
14-0 **13** *13* **Lockstock (IRE)**[22] [667] 6-10-0 65 (p) ACulhane 13 16
(MSSaunders) *rrd s: wd: a bhd: rdn and no ch fnl 4f* **20/1**

2m 6.64s (-0.75) **Going Correction** +0.10s/f (Slow)
**WFA** 4 from 5yo+ 1lb **13** Ran SP% **122.1**
Speed ratings: **107,104,103,103,103 101,100,99,97,97 93,90,79**CSF £37.99 CT £192.09 TOTE £7.30: £2.30, £1.60, £2.50; EX 49.00.
**Owner** Mrs Glennie Braune **Bred** Wertheimer Et Frere **Trained** Portway, Warwicks

**FOCUS**
A smart winning time for the grade, and the form looks reliable.

**NOTEBOOK**
**War Owl(USA)**, who spoilt his chances last time by pulling too hard, settled slightly better this time to register his first victory since winning in France four years ago. He benefited from the generous pace on this occasion and showed a useful turn of foot to cut down his rivals in the straight and win going away. He could add to this success while his yard remains in good form, but must have a strong pace to be seen at his best.
**Bank On Him** had every chance and ran up to form, but had no answer to the finishing kick of the winner. He remains in great heart.
**He Who Dares(IRE)** was again slowly away and pulled his head off in the early stages, but really caught the eye when making his move through the pack, only to pay for his early exertions in the final furlong. If this horse could only learn to settle better, he could get back to winning ways, especially when reverting to a mile.
**Fen Gypsy** had every chance and ran his race. He is handicapped to win a similar race and may well come on again as he has only recently returned from a break.
**Blazing The Trail(IRE)** is better than this as he was slowly away and did not endure the best of passages when making his challenge.

**883** **LITTLEWOODS BET DIRECT CONDITIONS STKS** **1m 2f (P)**
**2:30** (2:30) (D) 3-Y-0 **£4,326** (£1,236; £618) **Stalls** Low

Form RPR
1-21 **1** **Skidmark**[18] [704] 3-9-2 86 KFallon 1 95+
(DRCElsworth) *plld hrd in 3rd: led over 1f out: sn clr: easily* **8/15**[1]
1 **2** *2 ½* **Chasing The Dream (IRE)**[50] [447] 3-8-11 MartinDwyer 4 77
(AMBalding) *trckd ldr: led 2f out tl over 1f out: no ch w wnr* **4/1**[3]
-512 **3** *1* **Countrywide Flyer (IRE)**[26] [641] 3-9-2 92 JPSpencer 2 80
(TDBarron) *hung rt thrght: led at sedate pce: rdn 3f out: hdd 2f out: one pce appr fnl f* **10/3**[2]

2m 10.22s (2.83) **Going Correction** +0.10s/f (Slow) **3** Ran SP% **108.3**
Speed ratings: **92,90,89**CSF £2.95 TOTE £1.50; EX 4.20.
**Owner** Raymond Tooth **Bred** P D Player **Trained** Whitsbury, Hants

**FOCUS**
A very moderate winning time, but that was due to the tactical nature of the race, and all three look to have further prizes within their grasp. The winner has been rated better than the bare result.

**NOTEBOOK**
**Skidmark** was not suited by this tactical affair, as he was very keen early, but still won with with ease. He has a progressive profile and there is no doubt he is one of the better three-year-old prospects that has run this winter, so he deserves to take his chances in a higher grade. However, he may have to wait for the turf season now, as there are not many suitable opportunities left on the All-Weather.
**Chasing The Dream(IRE)** ◆, whose maiden win at this venue last time has not worked out, was another to be unsuited by the way the race was run. She was flattered to finish so close, and did not conclusively prove she stays, but she will not always come up against such a useful rival and can win again.
**Countrywide Flyer(IRE)** was not suited by making the running and was done for speed when the tempo quickened. He hung right throughout on this occasion and is a much better horse on the Fibresand over a mile, so this can be easily forgiven. *Official explanation: jockey said gelding hung right throughout*

**884** **DAILY OFFERS @ BETDIRECT.CO.UK (S) H'CAP** **6f (P)**
**3:05** (3:06) (G) (0-60,60) 3-Y-0+ **£2,674** (£764; £382) **Stalls** Low

Form RPR
2010 **1** **Bells Beach (IRE)**[2] [859] 6-9-5 51 6ex JFanning 14 59
(PHowling) *chsd ldrs: led ins fnl f: rdn out* **8/1**
-200 **2** *½* **Tripti (IRE)**[2] [859] 4-8-13 45 NPollard 3 51
(JJBridger) *led: rdn over 2f out: hdd ins fnl f: kpt on* **14/1**
100- **3** *1* **Bannister**[163] [4952] 6-9-7 60 LTreadwell(7) 7 63
(DNicholls) *s.s: bhd: rdn and hdwy over 1f out: swtchd rt and styd on wl fnl f* **12/1**
600- **4** *nk* **Legal Set (IRE)**[57] [6261] 8-10-0 60 KFallon 10 63
(WJMusson) *hld up in midfield: promising effrt 2f out: rdn to chse ldrs over 1f out: kpt on* **13/2**
-546 **5** *½* **Jalouhar**[16] [723] 4-9-9 55 DarrenWilliams 9 56
(BPJBaugh) *prom: hrd rdn over 1f out: styd on same pce* **20/1**
0-00 **6** *nk* **Gentle Response**[41] [538] 4-8-3 35 (b[1]) SWhitworth 11 35
(BRJohnson) *s.s: bhd: effrt and nt clr run ins fnl f: fin wl* **50/1**
-356 **7** *shd* **Good Vibrations**[7] [817] 3-8-4 51 (p) EAhern 2 51
(PFICole) *chsd ldr over 4f: no ex* **10/1**
-154 **8** *nk* **So Sober (IRE)**[9] [794] 6-9-0 46 NCallan 4 45
(DShaw) *mid-div: rdn over 2f out: styd on same pce* **6/1**[3]
000- **9** *nk* **True Holly**[159] [5047] 4-8-8 40 JFEgan 12 38
(SKirk) *hung lft thrght: hld up towards rr: effrt 2f out: nt pce to chal* **16/1**
5405 **10** *nk* **New Options**[9] [799] 7-9-11 60 LisaJones(3) 8 57
(WJMusson) *hld up towards rr: nt clr run fr over 1f out: unable to chal* **5/1**[2]
-042 **11** *1 ¼* **Cargo**[2] [859] 5-8-13 45 (bt[1]) JPSpencer 13 38
(DFlood) *s.s: bhd: hdwy and wd st: hrd rdn and no ex 1f out* **3/1**[1]

1m 13.14s (0.22) **Going Correction** +0.10s/f (Slow)
**WFA** 3 from 4yo+ 15lb **11** Ran SP% **116.5**
Speed ratings: **102,101,100,99,98 98,98,98,97,97 95**CSF £113.08 CT £1361.29 TOTE £9.30: £2.80, £3.60, £3.30; EX 145.20.There was no bid for the winner. Bannister (no.1) was claimed by S.Liddiard for £6,000.
**Owner** Richard Berenson **Bred** Philip Mahon **Trained** Newmarket, Suffolk

**FOCUS**
A weak contest featuring mainly out-of-form runners. The form must be treated with caution, as many suffered traffic problems in the straight.

**NOTEBOOK**
**Bells Beach(IRE)**, who had excuses for her latest defeat, resumed winning ways under a strong ride. She is inconsistent, but is useful at this level and is now two out of two under today's rider.
**Tripti(IRE)** improved for these front-running tactics, but could find no extra when pressed by the winner. She is another inconsistent individual, but is falling in the weights and looks worth a try in a handicap over course-and-distance.
**Bannister** would have been closer but for a slow start, plus he endured traffic problems when making his challenge. He can improve on this.

**Legal Set(IRE)** ran a fair race on this first start for his new connections. He will come on for this, as he had been off since December, and is on a fair mark at present.
**Jalouhar** had every chance on this Polytrack debut.
**Gentle Response** , another who missed the kick, caught the eye when making her challenge before she found trouble inside the last furlong. She can do better and responded well to the first-time blinkers.
**True Holly** *Official explanation: jockey said filly hung left throughout*
**New Options**, backed in the ring, was another who was stopped in his run late on. He is a hard horse to win with.
**Cargo** was most disappointing. He blew his chance at the start and was forced to race wide around the home turn. *Official explanation: trainer said, regarding the poor form shown, he was hoping gelding would make the running but it was unable to do so after throwing its head up when anticipating the start and therefore breaking badly*

## 885 BET ALL WEATHER: BET DIRECT H'CAP 7f (P)
3:40 (3:42) (E ) (0-75,79) 3-Y-0 £3,464 (£1,066; £533; £266) Stalls Low

Form RPR
0-01 **1** **Athboy**[14] [741] 3-8-9 **63**...(v) JPSpencer 1 71
(MJWallace) *hld up towards rr: rdn and hdwy 2f out: r.o to ld wl ins fnl f* **13/2[3]**
0-04 **2** ¾ **Hazewind**[7] [816] 3-7-12 **52** oh1...(t) JoannaBadger 2 58
(PDEvans) *pressed ldrs: led over 2f out tl wl ins fnl f: kpt on* **6/1[2]**
10-6 **3** 1 ¼ **Off Beat (USA)**[46] [493] 3-9-7 **75**...(b) SCarson 8 78
(RFJohnsonHoughton) *dwlt: sn chsng ldrs: rdn 2f out: nt clr run and swtchd rt ins fnl f: r.o* **12/1**
5040 **4** ½ **Garrigon**[7] [817] 3-8-6 **60**... GCarter 3 62
(NPLittmoden) *s.s: hld up and bhd: effrt on rail whn nt clr run wl over 1f out: swtchd rt: nrst fin* **12/1**
0-22 **5** hd **Park Ave Princess (IRE)**[42] [521] 3-8-4 **58**... EAhern 13 59
(NPLittmoden) *s.s: sn cl up: jnd ldrs over 2f out: one pce fnl f* **20/1**
40-2 **6** 1 **Mister Completely (IRE)**[4] [840] 3-7-12 **52**... JQuinn 9 51
(JRBest) *in tch: rdn to press ldrs over 2f out: ev ch over 1f out: one pce* **10/1**
006 **7** 1 ¼ **Joy And Pain**[11] [766] 3-8-4 **58**... JMackay 12 54
(GLMoore) *t.k.h: wd: towards rr: effrt on outside 2f out: no imp* **40/1**
5-12 **8** nk **Pick Of The Crop**[12] [758] 3-9-6 **74**... DHolland 10 69
(JRJenkins) *in rr: pushed along over 4f out: sme late hdwy* **7/1**
-211 **9** ¾ **Toronto Heights (USA)**[7] [819] 3-9-6 **79** 6ex... DNolan(5) 5 72
(PWChapple-Hyam) *prom: ev ch over 2f out: hrd rdn and wknd over 1f out* **5/2[1]**
0-12 **10** shd **Jaolins**[7] [817] 3-7-12 **52**... DKinsella 4 45
(PGMurphy) *plld hrd: led tl over 2f out: wknd over 1f out* **14/1**
50-1 **11** ¾ **Somewhere My Love**[28] [621] 3-9-0 **68**... KFallon 7 59
(TGMills) *mid-div: effrt whn hmpd and snatched up over 2f out: swtchd wd st: unable to chal* **7/1**
6-40 **12** 1 ½ **Taranai (IRE)**[28] [622] 3-7-9 **52** oh1... LisaJones(3) 6 39
(BWDuke) *w ldrs over 4f* **66/1**
1m 26.39s (0.39) **Going Correction** +0.10s/f (Slow) **12** Ran SP% **121.0**
Speed ratings: **101,100,98,98,97 96,95,95,94,94 93,91**CSF £45.62 CT £474.78 TOTE £8.70: £3.00, £1.50, £5.30; EX 57.80.
**Owner** D Mcgovern **Bred** Cheveley Park Stud Ltd **Trained** Newmarket, Suffolk

**FOCUS**
Fairly strong handicap form from a useful bunch of three-year-olds, and a fair winning time for the grade.

**NOTEBOOK**
**Athboy** followed up his recent win at this track in similar style off a 6lb higher mark. He has looked a reformed character since the application of the visor and this drop in trip proved no barrier. He is the type who needs things to drop right with his hold-up style of racing, but it is hard to say how much progression he las left in him and he will be hard to beat when going for the hat-trick.
**Hazewind** held every chance. He was officially 12lb well in for this after his improved showing in a maiden last week, so could well struggle in the future off his new mark.
**Off Beat(USA)** did not enjoy the best of passages and can be considered a touch unlucky, though he would not have beaten the winner.
**Garrigon** again found trouble, but ran better without the headgear on this occasion. He is a tricky sort.
**Park Ave Princess(IRE)**
**Pick Of The Crop** *Official explanation: jockey said colt ran in snatches*
**Toronto Heights(USA)** disappointed and was well beaten under his penalty. He may need a break after his recent busy period and should not be written off just yet. *Official explanation: jockey said gelding ran flat*

## 886 BET IN RUNNING @ BETDIRECT.CO.UK CLAIMING STKS 7f (P)
4:10 (4:10) (F ) 4-Y-0+ £2,975 (£850; £425) Stalls Low

Form RPR
060- **1** **Override (IRE)**[58] [6252] 4-9-7 68... JTate 1 76
(JMPEustace) *trckd ldrs: effrt over 2f out: edgd rt 1f out: drvn to ld ins fnl f* **11/1**
00-0 **2** nk **Meelup (IRE)**[28] [624] 4-8-3 53...(p) SWhitworth 5 57
(AGNewcombe) *led tl ins fnl f: kpt on wl* **40/1**
0112 **3** 1 ¼ **Blakeset**[13] [748] 9-8-11 76...(v) DHolland 2 62
(TDBarron) *w ldr: hrd rdn over 1f out: one pce* **5/2[2]**
10-0 **4** nk **Majhool**[28] [617] 5-8-9 70... IMongan 6 59
(GLMoore) *plld hrd: hdwy 2f out: hrd rdn over 1f out: one pce* **15/8[1]**
2120 **5** 2 ½ **Ripple Effect**[25] [646] 4-8-11 72... BReilly(5) 3 60
(CADwyer) *chsd ldrs: ev ch over 1f out: 5th and btn whn eased ins fnl f* **3/1[3]**
0060 **6** 2 ½ **Social Contract**[2] [858] 7-8-3 47... PaulEddery 4 41
(SDow) *towards rr: shkn up over 2f out: nt trble ldrs* **25/1**
00-0 **7** hd **Bugle Call**[16] [727] 4-8-9 35...(be) CCatlin 7 46
(KOCunningham-Brown) *hld up in rr: outpcd and lost tch over 2f out: kpt on fnl f* **66/1**
2423 **8** 2 **The Gay Fox**[2] [859] 10-8-3 45...(bt) DaleGibson 8 35
(BGPowell) *in rr: rdn over 2f out: n.d* **10/1**
1m 25.88s (-0.12) **Going Correction** +0.10s/f (Slow) **8** Ran SP% **113.6**
Speed ratings: **104,103,102,101,99 96,95,93**CSF £332.78 TOTE £13.70: £3.60, £10.00, £1.20; EX 236.90.Meelup was claimed by Jane Southcombe for £5,000.
**Owner** Paul Kan **Bred** Mount Coote Stud **Trained** Newmarket, Suffolk

**FOCUS**
The time was not bad for a claimer due to the true gallop set by the runner-up, but the form should be treated with caution because the principals appeared to run below par.

**NOTEBOOK**
**Override(IRE)** swooped late to register his first win since he was successful over this trip on turf at this track in 2002. He appreciated this drop in grade, but still had a fair bit to do at these weights and deserves credit.
**Meelup(IRE)** made a bold bid from the front and was only just denied. He was rated 72 at one point as a juvenile, but has plummeted recently having lost his form, so could be capable of improving on this. However, his finishing position still raises serious doubt as to the form of this contest.
**Blakeset** ran below his best, but is a better horse on Fibresand and he can resume winning ways when reverting to either Southwell or Wolverhampton.
**Majhool** spoilt his chance by running too keen early on and can do better, but is a very tricky ride.
**Ripple Effect** looked the likely winner turning in, but found less than expected off the bridle and ran way below her best, as she had a good chance at these weights.

## 887 BETDIRECT.CO.UK H'CAP 1m 4f (P)
4:45 (4:45) (D ) (0-80,83) 4-Y-0+ £4,160 (£1,280; £640; £320) Stalls Low

Form RPR
10 **1** **Millville**[11] [770] 4-9-9 **77**... NCallan 10 84+
(MAJarvis) *s.s: hld up towards rr: rdn and hdwy over 2f out: styd on to ld fnl 75 yds* **13/2[2]**
-021 **2** ¾ **Hip Hop Harry**[1] [872] 4-10-1 **83** 6ex...(v) KFallon 7 89
(EALDunlop) *prom in chsng gp: effrt over 2f out: drvn to ld ins fnl f: hdd fnl 75 yds: kpt on* **11/10[1]**
0-24 **3** 2 **Ezz Elkheil**[18] [706] 5-9-10 **75**... DHolland 3 78
(JRJenkins) *chsd ldr: led over 2f out tl ins fnl f: one pce* **8/1**
-403 **4** ½ **Classic Role**[21] [679] 5-9-6 **71**... IMongan 8 73
(RIngram) *chsd ldrs: effrt over 2f out: one pce appr fnl f* **7/1[3]**
**5** 1 ½ **Kashimo (GER)**[115] 5-8-7 **58**... SWhitworth 5 58
(GLMoore) *hld up towards rr: shkn up and wd st: nt rch ldrs* **40/1**
-540 **6** nk **Raheel (IRE)**[7] [815] 4-7-12 **52** oh3...(t) JQuinn 6 52
(PMitchell) *s.s: towards rr: wd and hdwy wl over 1f out: hrd rdn: no imp* **33/1**
4-01 **7** ¾ **Private Benjamin**[7] [818] 4-8-4 **58** 6ex... JFEgan 4 56
(JamiePoulton) *chsd ldng pair: hrd rdn over 2f out: no ex over 1f out* **20/1**
-024 **8** nk **Bressbee (USA)**[15] [735] 6-8-12 **68**...(v) DNolan(5) 2 66
(JWUnett) *mid-div: effrt 3f out: hrd rdn and no imp whn edgd rt over 1f out* **33/1**
430- **9** 1 ¼ **Kristoffersen**[13] [6130] 4-9-6 **74**... DSweeney 14 70
(RMStronge) *stdd s: hld up and bhd: rdn 3f out: nvr rchd ldrs* **33/1**
40-1 **10** 1 ½ **Maystock**[49] [467] 4-9-3 **78**...(v) LTreadwell(7) 13 72
(GAButler) *stdd s: towards rr: effrt 3f out: wd and no prog fnl 2f* **10/1**
-000 **11** 7 **Adalar (IRE)**[1] [872] 4-9-5 **73**... JoannaBadger 1 56
(PDEvans) *led tl over 2f out: sn wknd* **100/1**
01-0 **12** 2 **Majlis (IRE)**[28] [618] 7-9-4 **69**...(b) EAhern 11 49
(RMHCowell) *s.s: rdn 3f out: a bhd* **16/1**
0040 **13** 5 **Gallant Boy (IRE)**[18] [706] 5-9-6 **71**...(t) SDrowne 12 44
(PDEvans) *s.s: sn chsng ldrs: drvn along and wknd over 4f out* **14/1**
30-0 **14** ¾ **Danakil**[7] [820] 9-9-5 **70**... CCatlin 9 42
(SDow) *wd: towards rr: rdn 3f out: sn bhd* **33/1**
2m 34.01s (0.03) **Going Correction** +0.10s/f (Slow)
**WFA** 4 from 5yo+ 3lb **14** Ran SP% **126.2**
Speed ratings: **103,102,101,100,99 99,99,98,98,97 92,91,87,87**CSF £13.83 CT £65.51 TOTE £9.30: £2.90, £1.30, £2.30; EX 22.50.
**Owner** T G Warner **Bred** Red House Stud **Trained** Newmarket, Suffolk

**FOCUS**
A fair handicap won by a promising type and it should produce its fair share of winners.

**NOTEBOOK**
**Millville**, who was totally unsuited by the drop in trip latest, showed his true form over this longer trip. He still looked to have plenty in hand at the finish and did well to win this off his high mark, as it was only his third career start. Still unexposed, he could be up to winning off a higher mark over middle distances and looks one to follow in the early part of the turf season.
**Hip Hop Harry**, making a quick reappearance having won at the track the day before, had every chance. He got this extra trip without much fuss, but all of his three wins have come over ten furlongs and he could not give the weight away to the winner. It is unlikely he has finished winning yet in this sphere.
**Ezz Elkheil** ran another solid race and he has found consistency on this surface for his current connections. He is well up to winning a similar event.
**Classic Role**, backed at each-way prices in the ring, looked to be going as well as anything two out, but could only keep on at the one pace.
**Kashimo(GER)** put up a fair display on this British debut and is entitled to improve on this as he had been off since November. *Official explanation: jockey said horse had a breathing problem*

## 888 BET DIRECT FOOTBALL CASHBACKS H'CAP 1m (P)
5:15 (5:16) (F ) (0-55,58) 3-Y-0+ £3,003 (£858; £429) Stalls High

Form RPR
-504 **1** **Lucid Dreams (IRE)**[14] [738] 5-9-9 **52**... JFanning 10 58
(MWigham) *plld hrd: chsd ldrs: rdn over 2f out: str chal fnl f: drvn to ld nr fin* **7/1[3]**
2500 **2** shd **Lucayan Monarch**[14] [738] 6-9-11 **54**...(p) JPSpencer 8 60
(PSMcentee) *sn prom: slt ld ins fnl f: hrd rdn: hdd nr fin* **10/1**
-401 **3** ½ **Alafzar (IRE)**[7] [815] 6-10-1 **58** 6ex...(bt) KFallon 12 63
(PDEvans) *led after 1f and set modest pce: qcknd over 2f out: hrd rdn and hdd ins fnl f: kpt on wl* **9/4[1]**
-506 **4** ¾ **Zinging**[14] [738] 5-9-7 **50**... SDrowne 4 53
(JJBridger) *led 1f: hrd rdn and ev ch over 1f out: kpt on* **8/1**
4-30 **5** 1 **Pas De Surprise**[19] [695] 6-9-12 **55**... JoannaBadger 2 56
(PDEvans) *in tch: hmpd and lost pl after 1f: styd on fnl 2f* **16/1**
0-53 **6** shd **Chandelier**[18] [707] 4-9-11 **54**...(b) ACulhane 1 55
(MSSaunders) *dwlt: plld hrd: sn chsng ldrs: hmpd after 1f: outpcd whn hmpd and swtchd rt over 1f out: styd on* **8/1**
3240 **7** 1 **Mutarafaa (USA)**[11] [765] 5-9-10 **53**...(v) NCallan 7 52
(DShaw) *dwlt: plld hrd in rr: rdn 2f out: nt clr run ins fnl f: nrst fin* **15/2**
00-4 **8** hd **Coppington Flyer (IRE)**[32] [599] 4-9-1 **49**... JFMcDonald(5) 5 47
(BWDuke) *hld up in tch: nt clr run 2f out: effrt and hmpd over 1f out: styd on same pce* **16/1**
000- **9** hd **Marnie**[154] [5151] 7-9-6 **49**... JMackay 3 47
(JAkehurst) *dwlt: hld up in rr: effrt and wd st: nvr able to chal* **16/1**
-053 **10** 2 ½ **Estrella Levante**[9] [790] 4-8-13 **49**...(be) JemmaMarshall(7) 6 41
(GLMoore) *dwlt: plld hrd: sn in tch: effrt 2f out: wknd over 1f out* **40/1**
0-13 **11** 1 ½ **Balerno**[7] [815] 5-9-8 **51**... GCarter 9 40
(RIngram) *plld hrd: chsd ldrs tl wknd over 1f out* **6/1[2]**
1m 42.37s (2.86) **Going Correction** +0.10s/f (Slow) **11** Ran SP% **120.7**
Speed ratings: **89,88,88,87,86 86,85,85,85,82 81**CSF £77.18 CT £195.59 TOTE £10.50: £2.70, £5.20, £1.90; EX 55.80 Place 6 £49.45, Place 5 £42.56.
**Owner** Reds Bar Four Partnership II **Bred** Dr Dean Harron **Trained** Newmarket, Suffolk

**FOCUS**
A painfully slow time for a race of this type due to a sedate early gallop. The form looks untrustworthy as the race suited those racing on the pace.

**NOTEBOOK**
**Lucid Dreams(IRE)**, despite running keen in the early stages, ran on well to collar the runner-up close home. He had not run over a mile since his three-year-old campaign, but it is difficult to say that brought about the impovement, as the pace was so weak.
**Lucayan Monarch** was only narrowly denied. He has been in good form for his current connections despite a busy spell.
**Alafzar(IRE)** was not suited by making the running and did so under sufferance. He can do better when he gets a stronger pace over this trip and is ridden off the pace.
**Zinging** can have no excuses and was suited by racing handily.
**Pas De Surprise** did best of those to be held up and can be considered better than the bare form.
**Balerno** ran a stinker after pulling very hard due to the lack of pace.
T/Plt: £274.90 to a £1 stake. Pool: £46,679.70. 123.95 winning tickets. T/Qpdt: £118.90 to a £1 stake. Pool: £2,797.50. 17.40 winning tickets. LM

# 881 LINGFIELD (L-H)
## Thursday, February 26

**OFFICIAL GOING: Standard**
There was a bias towards those horses that raced towards the inside of the track and those that tried to deliver their efforts wide were mainly struggling.
Wind: fresh hlf against Weather: fine & sunny

## 889 LITTLEWOODSCASINO.COM H'CAP — 2m (P)
**1:40** (1:41) (F) (0-65,63) 4-Y-0+ — **£2,975** (£850; £425) **Stalls** Low

| Form | | | | RPR |
|---|---|---|---|---|
| 53-6 | 1 | | **Gemi Bed (FR)**[15] [740] 9-8-13 **45**...(b) SWhitworth 4<br>(GLMoore) *hld up in last pair: stdy prog 4f out: chsd ldr over 2f out: effrt to ld jst over 1f out: rdn clr* **10/1** | 54 |
| -214 | 2 | 2 | **Phantom Stock**[26] [645] 4-9-11 **63**... MTebbutt 2<br>(WJarvis) *hld up: prog to ld 6f out: kicked 3l clr over 2f out: hdd jst over 1f out: one pce* **11/4**[2] | 70 |
| 0-12 | 3 | 1 ½ | **Land Of Fantasy**[21] [684] 5-9-13 **59**... JQuinn 7<br>(LadyHerries) *prom: chsd ldr 5f out: rdn and no imp over 2f out: sn lost 2nd: one pce after* **2/1**[1] | 64 |
| 44-0 | 4 | 5 | **Astromancer (USA)**[29] [618] 4-9-0 **52**... DHolland 8<br>(MHTompkins) *chsd ldr for 4f: styd in tch: outpcd over 3f out: kpt on one pce fnl 2f: no imp on ldrs* **7/2**[3] | 51 |
| 0-00 | 5 | 2 ½ | **Stopwatch (IRE)**[3] [857] 9-8-3 **35**...(p) JoannaBadger 1<br>(MrsLCJewell) *racd in last pair: pushed along 5f out: outpcd over 3f out: n.d after* **50/1** | 31 |
| 0-02 | 6 | nk | **Sean's Memory (USA)**[17] [722] 4-9-3 **55**... DaneO'Neill 5<br>(MrsCADunnett) *mostly in midfield: rdn and outpcd over 3f out: no prog u.p fnl 2f* **16/1** | 51 |
| 150/ | 7 | 2 ½ | **Broughtons Flush**[656] [1331] 6-9-1 **47**... KFallon 3<br>(WJMusson) *mostly trckd ldr fr 10f out to 5f out: outpcd 3f out: steadily wknd* **7/1** | 40 |
| /0-0 | 8 | dist | **Lady Arnica**[11] [781] 5-8-13 **45**...(v) IMongan 6<br>(AWCarroll) *led to 6f out: sn wknd: t.o* **50/1** | — |

3m 28.56s (-0.02) **Going Correction** 0.0s/f (Stan)
**WFA** 4 from 5yo+ 6lb — **8** Ran SP% **113.6**
Speed ratings: **100,99,98,95,94 94,93,—**CSF £37.27 CT £77.39 TOTE £9.10: £2.40, £1.10, £1.40; EX 18.10.
**Owner** B Lennard **Bred** Michel Le Baron **Trained** Woodingdean, E Sussex

**FOCUS**
Modest form, but an even pace and a fair test.

**NOTEBOOK**
**Gemi Bed(FR)**, who has never totally convinced over this trip on the Flat in the past, was given a good patient ride. Making his ground gradually, he pounced on the leader in the straight and appears to have developed more stamina in his old age.
**Phantom Stock** is a guaranteed stayer and his rider deserves full marks for trying to make full use of his proven stamina, kicking for home fully six furlongs out. Unfortunately, the winner has a turn of foot and it was no contest in the home straight.
**Land Of Fantasy**, winner of a slowly run race over course and distance two outings ago, was being niggled along some way from home but could never make his presence felt.
**Astromancer(USA)** is still a maiden and yet to totally convince over this trip.
**Stopwatch(IRE)** achieved very little.
**Sean's Memory(USA)**, backed at fancy odds, never gave his supporters much hope.
**Broughtons Flush**, a three-time winner over this trip on sand in the spring of 2002, was racing for the first time in 22 months and almost certainly needed it.
**Lady Arnica** *Official explanation: trainer said mare was reluctant to race in the latter stages*

## 890 LITTLEWOODS BET DIRECT MAIDEN STKS — 1m (P)
**2:10** (2:12) (D) 3-Y-0 — **£4,212** (£1,296; £648; £324) **Stalls** High

| Form | | | | RPR |
|---|---|---|---|---|
| -4 | 1 | | **Certifiable**[9] [811] 3-9-0... SCarson 2<br>(AndrewReid) *mde virtually all: rdn 2f out: drew 2l clr ent fnl f: hld on nr fin* **66/1** | 73 |
| 460- | 2 | ½ | **Baker Of Oz**[90] [6083] 3-9-0 67... PDobbs 3<br>(RHannon) *trckd ldng pair: rdn over 2f out: styd on u.p to chse wnr ins fnl f: gaining at fin* **9/2**[3] | 72 |
| 5-22 | 3 | 2 ½ | **Archerfield (IRE)**[15] [741] 3-8-9 70... DaneO'Neill 5<br>(JWHills) *w wnr: rdn and upsides 2f out: nt qckn over 1f out: one pce after* **11/8**[1] | 61 |
| 0- | 4 | 1 ½ | **Keelung (USA)**[116] [5886] 3-9-0... MHenry 6<br>(MAJarvis) *dwlt: plld hrd and hld up wl in rr: outpcd over 2f out: effrt on inner over 1f out: styd on wl fnl f: nrst fin* **8/1** | 63+ |
| 0 | 5 | 2 ½ | **Clare Galway**[22] [673] 3-8-10 ow1... DHolland 1<br>(TDMccarthy) *dwlt: sn in midfield: rdn and outpcd wl over 2f out: one pce afteer* **50/1** | 54? |
| 0 | 6 | ¾ | **Air Of Supremacy (IRE)**[33] [597] 3-9-0... EAhern 11<br>(JNoseda) *dwlt: sn in midfield: rdn over 3f out: struggling u.p over 2f out* **7/2**[2] | 56 |
| -200 | 7 | 1 ¼ | **Redbank (IRE)**[8] [816] 3-9-0 60... PaulEddery 4<br>(SDow) *hld up in midfield: pushed along and outpcd over 2f out: hdwy over 1f out: no imp ldrs: eased* **20/1** | 53 |
| 50- | 8 | 1 | **Mambina (USA)**[92] [6072] 3-8-6... DCorby[(3)] 10<br>(MRChannon) *a in rr: rdn and struggling over 3f out* **10/1** | 46 |
| 0 | 9 | hd | **Forge Lane (IRE)**[8] [816] 3-9-0... JQuinn 12<br>(CWeedon) *dwlt: hld up in last pair: stl last over 2f out: shuffled along and no real prog over 1f out* **50/1** | 51 |
| 006- | 10 | 3 ½ | **Kilcullen Lass (IRE)**[129] [5679] 3-8-9 50... SDrowne 7<br>(PDEvans) *racd towards rr: rdn and struggling 3f out: wknd* **100/1** | 38 |
| 0-0 | 11 | 5 | **Almanac (IRE)**[21] [683] 3-9-0... DarrenWilliams 8<br>(BPJBaugh) *chsd ldng trio: rdn 1/2-way: wknd 3f out* **66/1** | 32 |
| 0 | 12 | 3 ½ | **Lookouthereicome**[29] [621] 3-8-9... VSlattery 9<br>(TTClement) *dwlt: hld up: bmpd after 1f: struggling over 3f out: wknd* **33/1** | 19 |

1m 39.15s (-0.36) **Going Correction** 0.0s/f (Stan) — **12** Ran SP% **118.3**
Speed ratings: **101,100,98,96,94 93,92,91,90,87 82,78**CSF £338.02 TOTE £50.20: £9.50, £1.90, £1.10; EX 333.00.
**Owner** A S Reid **Bred** A S Reid **Trained** Mill Hill, London NW7

**FOCUS**
Not much strength in depth, but the pace was solid and the winner showed fairly useful form.

**NOTEBOOK**
**Certifiable ◆**, was much more organised than on his Wolverhampton debut and had obviously derived great benefit from that experience. Making every yard, he was strongly pressed from the home turn but knuckled down in impressive fashion to hold on. There was no fluke about this success and there should be much more to come from him.
**Baker Of Oz**, returning from a three-month break, was travelling well just behind the leaders turning for home and looked as if he could pick them off when he wanted. He quickened up well once asked, but found the winner had more in reserve than had looked likely.
**Archerfield(IRE)** probably had the best sand form coming into this and had every chance rounding the home bend, but she could never get past the battling winner and had to concede defeat on straightening up. She is starting to look exposed.
**Keelung(USA)**, off since his debut in November, was the real eye-catcher. He was pulling his head off out the back early and then took a while to get organised when the tempo quickened, but he did find his stride on reaching the straight and finished in good style. He is gaining experience all the time and looks interesting.
**Clare Galway** was stepping up two furlongs from her debut and did show a little ability.
**Air Of Supremacy(IRE)** was off the bridle some way out and is beginning to look disappointing.

## 891 NEW SITE @ BETDIRECT.CO.UK H'CAP — 6f (P)
**2:40** (2:41) (E) (0-70,70) 3-Y-0 — **£3,444** (£984; £492) **Stalls** Low

| Form | | | | RPR |
|---|---|---|---|---|
| 0-1 | 1 | | **Tag Team (IRE)**[19] [708] 3-9-4 67... MartinDwyer 7<br>(AMBalding) *mde all: gng much bttr than rivals 2f out: sn 4l clr: pushed out fnl f: unchal* **3/1**[1] | 83+ |
| 0-42 | 2 | 2 ½ | **Big Bad Burt**[22] [675] 3-9-1 64...(v) KFallon 8<br>(MJWallace) *s.i.s: sn in midfield: pushed along 4f out: drvn and effrt 2f out: styd on to take 2nd last 100y: no ch w wnr* **10/3**[2] | 68 |
| 3142 | 3 | ½ | **Alizar (IRE)**[2] [868] 3-8-9 58... DHolland 1<br>(SDow) *chsd ldrs: drvn over 2f out: chsd wnr wl over 1f out: no imp: lost 2nd last 100y* **3/1**[1] | 61 |
| -155 | 4 | 2 | **Back At De Front (IRE)**[14] [747] 3-8-9 63... MSavage[(5)] 3<br>(NEBerry) *chsd ldrs: rdn over 2f out: one pce and no imp over 1f out* **16/1** | 60 |
| 6-40 | 5 | 1 ¼ | **Smokin Joe**[14] [747] 3-9-7 70... EAhern 2<br>(JRBest) *dwlt: sn pushed along in last quartet: struggling 1/2-way: styd on over 1f out: no ch* **5/1**[3] | 63 |
| 55-3 | 6 | 1 ¼ | **Jasmine Pearl (IRE)**[44] [514] 3-8-4 53... JQuinn 12<br>(TMJones) *wnt rt s: sn chsd ldrs: rdn wl over 2f out: no prog after* **50/1** | 42 |
| 340- | 7 | shd | **Sachin**[100] [6023] 3-9-4 67... JPMurtagh 4<br>(JRBoyle) *racd in last pair and sn outpcd: pushed along and no prog over 2f out: modest late hdwy* **14/1** | 56 |
| 4-00 | 8 | 2 ½ | **Ricky Martan**[15] [741] 3-8-8 57...(b) SWhitworth 9<br>(GCBravery) *sn pushed along in midfield: outpcd over 2f out: hanging and wl btn over 1f out* **33/1** | 38 |
| -550 | 9 | nk | **Easily Averted (IRE)**[2] [868] 3-9-0 63... IMongan 10<br>(PButler) *chsd wnr to wl over 1f out: wknd rapidly* **12/1** | 43 |
| 00-0 | 10 | shd | **Chiqitita (IRE)**[22] [675] 3-8-2 58 ow3... SaleemGolam[(7)] 5<br>(TTClement) *sn outpcd in last: a bhd* **66/1** | 38 |
| -500 | 11 | 2 ½ | **Must Be So**[8] [817] 3-7-8 48... JFMcDonald[(5)] 11<br>(JJBridger) *a struggling and wl in rr* **33/1** | 21 |

1m 12.44s (-0.48) **Going Correction** 0.0s/f (Stan) — **11** Ran SP% **119.3**
Speed ratings: **103,99,99,96,94 93,92,89,89,89 85**CSF £13.07 CT £33.41 TOTE £4.10: £2.20, £1.90, £1.30; EX 12.20.
**Owner** Magic Moments **Bred** Miss Sally Hodgins **Trained** Kingsclere, Hants

**FOCUS**
The pace was very decent pace and the time smart for the type of contest. Very few got into it. The impressive winner can rate higher again, and it looks solid form in behind.

**NOTEBOOK**
**Tag Team(IRE)**, stepping up a furlong from his victory here last time, again made every yard of the running and had his rivals stone cold from the two-furlong marker. He is starting to look quite useful and still has scope.
**Big Bad Burt** found things happening too quickly for him over this even shorter trip and when he did find his stride the winner was already home and hosed. He is not an easy ride, but should find a race back over further.
**Alizar(IRE)**, who is being kept very busy, was never far away and tried her hardest but could never get on terms with the winner. She probably ran up to her best.
**Back At De Front(IRE)**, back over probably her best trip, had every chance but did not have the speed to get on terms with the winner.
**Smokin Joe** was always struggling after missing the break and looks the type for whom everything has to fall just right. *Official explanation: jockey said colt dwelt in the stalls*
**Easily Averted(IRE)** paid for trying to match strides with the winner.

## 892 BET IN RUNNING @ BETDIRECT.CO.UK FILLIES' H'CAP — 1m 2f (P)
**3:10** (3:10) (D) (0-80,78) 3-Y-0+ — **£4,095** (£1,260; £630; £315) **Stalls** Low

| Form | | | | RPR |
|---|---|---|---|---|
| 5300 | 1 | | **Tight Squeeze**[12] [768] 7-10-0 78... KFallon 4<br>(PWHiatt) *chsd clr ldng pair to 1/2-way: pushed along over 3f out: effrt to go 3rd again over 1f out: drvn to ld last 150y: styd on w* **9/4**[1] | 86 |
| 153- | 2 | 1 ½ | **Doris Souter (IRE)**[168] [4837] 4-9-8 73... DaneO'Neill 8<br>(RHannon) *led for 2f: chsd clr ldr after: clsd to ld 2f out: sn rdn: hdd and one pce last 150y* **8/1** | 78 |
| 1-11 | 3 | 2 | **Regal Gallery (IRE)**[12] [767] 6-9-2 66... PaulEddery 2<br>(CAHorgan) *hld up in rr: effrt to cl whn nt clr run on inner 2f out: kpt on to chse ldng pair wl ins fnl f: no imp* **3/1**[2] | 68+ |
| 20-0 | 4 | 1 ¼ | **Dispol Evita**[12] [767] 5-8-0 50... DKinsella 3<br>(JamiePoulton) *in tch in rr: drvn over 4f out: struggling over 2f out: kpt on u.p fnl f* **16/1** | 49 |
| 1111 | 5 | 1 | **Najaaba (USA)**[30] [614] 4-9-5 75... BReilly[(5)] 5<br>(MissJFeilden) *hld up in tch: trckd ldng pair 5f out: effrt to chal and ev ch 2f out: nt qckn over 1f out: fdd and eased* **5/1**[3] | 73 |
| -035 | 6 | 1 | **Figura**[12] [767] 6-8-9 59... EAhern 6<br>(RIngram) *s.s: hld up in last: smooth prog 3f out: rdn to chse ldrs over 1f out: fnd nil and sn btn* **11/2** | 55 |

3340 **7** ½ **Top Of The Class (IRE)**[2] [867] 7-7-12 48 oh2..........(v) JoannaBadger 1 43
(PDEvans) *plld hrd: led after 2f and sn clr: 8l ahd 4f out: wknd and hdd 2f out* **16/1**

2m 8.63s (1.24) **Going Correction** 0.0s/f (Stan)
**WFA** 4 from 5yo+ 1lb **7** Ran SP% **110.7**
Speed ratings: **95,93,92,91,90 89,89**CSF £19.38 CT £50.70 TOTE £2.70: £1.90, £2.20; EX 14.30.
**Owner** Anthony Harrison **Bred** Anthony Harrison **Trained** Hook Norton, Oxon

**FOCUS**
The form should work out in fillies races, but a moderate pace for the first couple of furlongs and a very modest time for the grade.

**NOTEBOOK**
**Tight Squeeze**, dropping in class, appreciated the injection of pace by Top Of The Class after a couple of furlongs as up to then the race looked as though it might be run at a dawdle. She was having to be scrubbed along to stay in touch running to the final bend, but the further she went the better she was going and she was produced with perfect timing to extend her already impressive record in fillies'-only handicaps.
**Doris Souter(IRE)**, returning from a five-month break, led early but was then content to get a lead from Top Of The Class. She was back in front turning for home, but found the winner much too good.
**Regal Gallery(IRE)**, who has been in cracking form here lately, was up another 5lb after completing her hat-trick and was therefore taking on much better company. Close enough turning for home, she was taken back by the weakening Top Of The Class at a vital stage and though she ran on again, the damage had been done. She would have been second at worse.
**Dispol Evita** did not perform badly, but she is very inconsistent and her best trip is still something of a mystery.
**Najaaba(USA)**, given a short break since completing her fine Fibresand five-timer earlier in the year, was off a 19lb higher mark than when starting the sequence, making her Polytrack debut, and racing over her longest trip to date. In the event, she had every chance, but was done for foot down the home straight and may not be easy to place from now on. *Official explanation: trainer said filly failed to get the trip*
**Figura** seemed to travel well off the pace for a long way, but found very little when let down.
**Top Of The Class(IRE)** pulled her way to the front after a couple of furlongs and soon had a clear lead, but she expended too much energy and once the cavalry arrived she was well and truly cooked.

## 893 BETDIRECT.CO.UK CLAIMING STKS 5f (P)
**3:40** (3:41) (F ) 3-Y-0+ **£2,870** (£820; £410) **Stalls** High

Form RPR
-050 **1** **Sounds Lucky**[12] [771] 8-9-5 60..........(b) DHolland 2 59
(NPLittmoden) *sn chsd ldr: rdn to chal over 1f out: led last 150y: kpt on u.p* **9/2**[3]
2105 **2** 1 **Ever Cheerful**[8] [817] 3-8-1 73..........(p) CHaddon(7) 9 58
(WGMTurner) *racd wdst of all: chsd ldrs: effrt 2f out: pushed along and kpt on fnl f to take 2nd last 50y: nt rch wnr* **7/2**[2]
/0-0 **3** ½ **Confuzed**[10] [791] 4-9-0..........(e¹) LTreadwell(7) 8 56
(DFlood) *s.i.s: t.k.h and hld up in last: nt clr run 2f out: effrt over 1f out: kpt on fnl f to take 3rd last strides* **10/1**
2265 **4** *hd* **Hagley Park**[2] [876] 5-9-0 45..........(v¹) MartinDwyer 5 48
(MQuinn) *led: rdn 2f out: hdd last 150y: one pce and lost 2 pls nr fin* **10/1**
0324 **5** 1¾ **Boavista (IRE)**[2] [869] 4-9-4 54..........(t) SDrowne 1 46
(PDEvans) *cl up: rdn 2f out: nt qckn over 1f out: fdd fnl f* **5/1**
3510 **6** 1½ **Panjandrum**[6] [836] 6-9-4 66..........MSavage(5) 3 46
(NEBerry) *racd wd: chsd ldrs: lost pl and last 2f out: no prog and btn over 1f out* **3/1**[1]
0510 **7** ¾ **Mr Spliffy (IRE)**[22] [674] 5-9-5 53..........(v) DarrenWilliams 6 39
(KRBurke) *chsd ldrs: rdn and cl up 2f out: wknd jst over 1f out* **7/1**

59.69 secs (-0.09) **Going Correction** 0.0s/f (Stan)
**WFA** 3 from 4yo+ 14lb **7** Ran SP% **112.8**
Speed ratings: **100,98,97,97,94 92,90**CSF £19.97 TOTE £6.40: £1.80, £2.40; EX 21.60.Ever Cheerful was claimed (friendly) by W Turner for £9,000.
**Owner** Paul J Dixon **Bred** T Barratt **Trained** Newmarket, Suffolk

**FOCUS**
Typical claiming form, but a race run at an even pace.

**NOTEBOOK**
**Sounds Lucky** loves it here and this was probably his easiest task on this track for some time. Always in the ideal place, he saw his race out well and now that he is back in form he could nick another.
**Ever Cheerful**, best in on adjusted official ratings, ran very well and deserves extra credit as he covered much more ground than his rivals.
**Confuzed**, ninth in all three of his previous starts, was a springer in the market in the first-time eyeshield, but did not enjoy the clearest of runs. When he did get in the clear, he had too much ground to make up and lacked the speed to do it. Nonetheless, he is one to keep in mind.
**Hagley Park** was positive as usual in the first-time visor and took the field along, but despite giving her all was unable to hold on.
**Boavista(IRE)** showed good speed, but despite that was probably not helped by the drop to the minimum.
**Panjandrum** should have done better and was disappointing.

## 894 BETDIRECT.CO.UK NEW SITE (S) STKS 1m 2f (P)
**4:10** (4:13) (G ) 4-Y-0+ **£2,583** (£738; £369) **Stalls** Low

Form RPR
-010 **1** **Scotty's Future (IRE)**[12] [775] 6-9-6 78..........JPMurtagh 3 54
(DRLoder) *hld up towards rr: stdy prog over 2f out: clsd to chal ent fnl f: drvn to ld last 75y* **4/5**[1]
1-02 **2** *nk* **Absolute Utopia (USA)**[23] [664] 11-9-6 63..........ADaly 8 54
(JLSpearing) *hld up in midfield: prog on outer over 2f out: drvn to chal fnl f: ev ch: jst hld* **10/1**
-503 **3** *hd* **Free Option (IRE)**[2] [873] 9-9-6 71..........(b) KFallon 6 54
(WJMusson) *hld up in midfield: prog to chse ldr 2f out: drvn to chal fnl f: ev ch: jst hld* **5/2**[2]
00-3 **4** *nk* **Senor Toran (USA)**[23] [664] 4-8-11 45..........LPKeniry(3) 9 48
(PBurgoyne) *trckd ldr: led 3f out: drvn 3l clr wl over 1f out: kpt on fnl f: hdd and no ex last 75y* **25/1**
6041 **5** 3 **Muqtadi (IRE)**[2] [873] 6-9-6 49..........MartinDwyer 10 48
(MQuinn) *hld up in last pair: stdy prog over 2f out: nt clr run briefly over 1f out: chsd ldng quartet fnl f: shkn up and r.o* **8/1**[3]
0-40 **6** 2 **Achilles Rainbow**[10] [788] 5-8-8 40..........AReilly(7) 1 39
(KRBurke) *trckd ldrs: cl up 3f out: nt clr run on inner and lost pl over 2f out: drvn and one pce fr over 1f out* **66/1**
0503 **7** 6 **Kumakawa**[18] [717] 6-8-8 45..........(b) LiamJones(7) 2 28
(EAWheeler) *chsd ldng pair: drvn 3f out: wknd jst over 2f out* **16/1**
00-0 **8** 8 **Crown City (USA)**[7] [823] 4-8-9 48..........(t) DarrenWilliams 4 9
(BPJBaugh) *s.i.s: racd in last pair: outpcd wl over 2f out: wknd* **66/1**
/00- **9** 6 **Valdasho**[256] [2393] 5-8-10 30..........JQuinn 5 —
(MissKMGeorge) *racd freely: led to 3f out: chsd ldr to 2f out: wknd rapidly* **66/1**
00 **10** 8 **Reckless Fred**[26] [644] 5-8-8..........DerekNolan(7) 7 —
(MissKMGeorge) *t.k.h early: chsd ldrs: drvn over 4f out: wknd 3f out* **100/1**

2m 8.72s (1.33) **Going Correction** 0.0s/f (Stan)
**WFA** 4 from 5yo+ 1lb **10** Ran SP% **119.5**
Speed ratings: **94,93,93,93,90 89,84,78,73,66**CSF £10.95 TOTE £1.90: £1.10, £2.50, £1.20; EX 9.00.The winner was bought in for 16,000gns.
**Owner** Lucayan Stud **Bred** William J Hamilton **Trained** Newmarket, Suffolk

**FOCUS**
A bunch finish and a very modest winning time, even for a seller. Weak form, with the principals all below par.

**NOTEBOOK**
**Scotty's Future(IRE)**was given an excellent ride by his jockey, who tracked his main danger the whole way and produced him at just the right time to score. Despite the amount he had in hand on adjusted official ratings, it is still hard imagining him winning in better company.
**Absolute Utopia(USA)** continues to belie his age under his ideal conditions and just lost out. This looked a cracking effort considering he split two much-higher rated rivals, though caution is advised as almost certainly neither of them ran up to their marks.
**Free Option(IRE)**, who seemed to throw away a decent chance here 48 hours earlier, had no excuses over this longer trip. He had every chance and failed to go through with it, despite the champion's assistance. *Official explanation: vet said gelding finished lame*
**Senor Toran(USA)** ran up to form and even looked like he may have stolen it when shoved into a clear lead off the final bend. He never gave up, but was just run out of the placings.
**Muqtadi(IRE)**, successful in a similar event over a mile here 48 hours earlier, was trying his longest trip on the Flat but did not fail through lack of stamina.

## 895 BETDIRECT.CO.UK H'CAP 7f (P)
**4:40** (4:41) (F ) (0-55,54) 3-Y-0+ **£3,038** (£868; £434) **Stalls** Low

Form RPR
0022 **1** **Steely Dan**[2] [874] 5-9-6 50..........NPollard 2 61
(JRBest) *hld up in midfield: smooth prog over 2f out: trckd ldr ent fnl f: pushed into ld last 100y: sn clr* **4/1**[1]
0005 **2** 1½ **Master Rattle**[3] [859] 5-9-1 45..........VSlattery 9 52
(JaneSouthcombe) *pressed ldr: led 3f out: drvn 2f out: hdd and outpcd last 100y* **12/1**
5002 **3** 1¾ **Lucayan Monarch**[1] [888] 6-9-10 54..........(p) JPMurtagh 10 57
(PSMcentee) *hld up in last pair: plenty to do whn prog over 2f out: drvn and styd on fr over 1f out: tk 3rd nr fin* **11/2**[3]
2531 **4** ¾ **Aguila Loco (IRE)**[6] [834] 5-9-10 54 6ex..........(p) SDrowne 3 55
(MrsStefLiddiard) *prom: rdn over 2f out: hld whn nt clr run briefly 1f out: kpt on* **8/1**
0-41 **5** 1 **Titian Lass**[42] [535] 5-8-9 46..........(b) DeanWilliams(7) 8 45
(CEBrittain) *cl up: effrt to join ldr over 2f out: ev ch jst over 1f out: fdd* **16/1**
0-56 **6** 1½ **Captain Cloudy**[15] [745] 4-9-10 54..........DaneO'Neill 4 49
(MMadgwick) *t.k.h: hld up in last pair: stl keen over 2f out: shuffled along over 1f out: styd on wl: nvr nr ldrs* **11/2**[3]
5-50 **7** *nk* **Pure Emotion**[22] [673] 3-8-1 48..........JQuinn 1 42
(WRMuir) *hld up wl in rr: sme prog over 2f out: drvn and no imp on ldrs over 1f out* **20/1**
0-02 **8** ½ **Harbour House**[10] [787] 5-8-10 45..........JFMcDonald(5) 6 38
(JJBridger) *racd in midfield: rdn and prog to chse ldrs 2f out: fdd over 1f out* **6/1**
-065 **9** *hd* **Vizulize**[30] [613] 5-9-4 48..........DHolland 7 40
(AWCarroll) *t.k.h: hld up in midfield: rdn 3f out: hanging and no prog fr over 1f out* **10/1**
00-0 **10** *nk* **Galey River (USA)**[8] [815] 5-9-3 47..........(e¹) IMongan 11 39
(JJSheehan) *racd in midfield: rdn over 3f out: no prog and btn wl over 1f out* **50/1**
0350 **11** 6 **Scarrottoo**[15] [738] 6-9-6 50..........KFallon 12 27
(SCWilliams) *hld up towards rr: rdn 2f out: no prog: eased ins fnl f* **5/1**[2]
400- **12** 9 **My Girl Pearl (IRE)**[97] [6039] 4-8-10 45..........(b) MSavage(5) 13 —
(MSSaunders) *s.i.s: racd wd: in tch: rdn 1/2-way: wknd wl over 2f out* **66/1**
0-00 **13** 6 **Indian Oak (IRE)**[12] [764] 3-7-12 45 oh10..........DKinsella 5 —
(MPMuggeridge) *led to 3f out: wknd rapidly over 2f out* **100/1**

1m 25.64s (-0.36) **Going Correction** 0.0s/f (Stan)
**WFA** 3 from 4yo+ 17lb **13** Ran SP% **124.7**
Speed ratings: **102,100,98,97,96 94,94,93,93,93 86,75,69**CSF £55.43 CT £284.12 TOTE £5.40: £1.70, £4.80, £3.00; EX 61.20.
**Owner** Mrs Louise Best **Bred** Mrs S E Barclay And L B Snowden **Trained** Hucking, Kent

**FOCUS**
A sound pace, but only modest form.

**NOTEBOOK**
**Steely Dan**, dropping back three furlongs in trip from 48 hours earlier, was given a peach of a ride. Held up out the back, he ran through his rivals on the bridle and his rider never once picked up his whip. This is the way to ride him, though how often that will be possible is hard to predict.
**Master Rattle** signalled a hint of a return to form here last time and confirmed it with a much improved effort under a positive ride.
**Lucayan Monarch**, runner-up over a mile here 24 hours earlier, came from off the pace to make the frame without ever threatening the front pair. He probably finds this trip on such a fast surface a little too sharp.
**Aguila Loco(IRE)**, making his Polytrack debut, was never far away but lacked a turn of foot where it mattered and would be happier back on Fibresand.
**Titian Lass**, stepping up from a victory at banded level here, moved up strongly on the outside of the leader turning in but had nothing left when the challengers arrived. She looks best over a mile these days.
**Captain Cloudy** ◆ was the eye-catcher of the race. Held up out the back and taking a keen grip, he was still pulling hard in last place a furlong and a half from home before staying on to finish a never-nearer sixth. He is still a maiden, but there is ability there and he is one to keep an eye on. *Official explanation: trainer said gelding finished distressed*
**Vizulize** *Official explanation: jockey said mare hung left in the straight*
**Scarrottoo** *Official explanation: jockey said gelding lost its action*

## 896 BET DIRECT FOOTBALL CASHBACKS H'CAP 6f (P)
**5:10** (5:12) (F ) (0-55,55) 3-Y-0+ **£2,996** (£856; £428) **Stalls** Low

Form RPR
-520 **1** **A Teen**[22] [674] 6-9-3 50..........KFallon 7 58
(PHowling) *racd in midfield: effrt over 2f out: drvn on outer over 1f out: r.o fnl f to ld last stride* **4/1**[1]
0-63 **2** *shd* **Park Star**[9] [803] 4-9-1 53..........JFMcDonald(5) 8 61
(DShaw) *trckd ldr: rdn 2f out: led jst ins fnl f: r.o: hdd last stride* **9/2**[2]
5514 **3** 1 **Aintnecessarilyso**[14] [748] 6-8-13 51..........MSavage(5) 4 56
(NEBerry) *n.m.r after 1f and in rr: effrt and nt clr run on inner over 2f out: drvn and threaded through fnl f: tk 3rd nr fin* **12/1**

26-4 **4** *hd* **Inching**[49] 479 4-9-2 **49** ........ EAhern 10 53
(RMHCowell) *s.i.s: sn chsd ldrs: rdn over 2f out: unable qck over 1f out: kpt on same pce* **10/1**

446- **5** *nk* **Doctor Dennis (IRE)**[72] 6202 7-9-0 **47** ........ (v) NPollard 9 50
(JPearce) *settled towards rr: rdn and effrt on outer 2f out: kpt on fr over 1f out: nvr able to chal* **12/1**

3250 **6** *nk* **Ladies Knight**[12] 771 4-9-8 **55** ........ DarrenWilliams 14 57
(DShaw) *s.s: hld up in last: plenty to do over 2f out: drvn and prog on wd outside over 1f out: kpt on: nt rch ldrs* **12/1**

00-0 **7** *nk* **Tamarella (IRE)**[36] 576 4-9-2 **49** ........ AMcCarthy 13 50
(GGMargarson) *chsd ldr: rdn 2f out: led jst over 1f out to jst ins fnl f: fdd* **16/1**

0-01 **8** *½* **Gun Salute**[22] 674 4-9-6 **53** ........ (p) SWhitworth 6 53
(GLMoore) *hld up in rr: effrt and nt clr run over 2f out: nt clr run repeatedly fr over 1f out: nt rcvr* **5/1**[3]

5/0- **9** *¾* **Luceball (IRE)**[118] 5861 4-8-13 **46** ........ (b) JPMurtagh 1 44
(PatrickMorris, Ire) *racd in midfield: rdn and effrt over 2f out: chsd ldrs over 1f out: one pce fnl f* **16/1**

05-0 **10** *nk* **Regal Song (IRE)**[36] 573 8-9-6 **53** ........ (b) SDrowne 2 50
(TJEtherington) *chsd ldrs: rdn over 2f out: sn lost pl: hanging and btn over 1f out: fdd* **16/1**

0-60 **11** *¾* **Karaoke King**[15] 738 6-9-7 **54** ........ DaneO'Neill 11 49
(JELong) *sn rdn in rr: a struggling: effrt u.p wl over 1f out: no prog* **16/1**

00-4 **12** *¾* **Fiamma Royale (IRE)**[45] 510 6-9-1 **48** ........ JQuinn 5 40
(MSSaunders) *n.m.r on inner after 1f and in rr: last 2f out: no prog* **6/1**

0-00 **13** *1 ¾* **Blessed Place**[10] 796 4-9-6 **53** ........ (t) IMongan 12 40
(Jean-ReneAuvray) *led at fast pce to jst over 1f out: wknd rapidly* **50/1**

1m 12.61s (-0.31) **Going Correction** 0.0s/f (Stan) **13** Ran SP% **126.8**
Speed ratings: **102,101,100,100,99 99,99,98,97,97 96,95,92**CSF £22.93 CT £210.25 TOTE £5.50: £2.40, £2.00, £2.60; EX 37.00 Place 6 £10.42, Place 5 £6.99.
**Owner** Mrs A K Petersen **Bred** C B Petersen **Trained** Newmarket, Suffolk

**FOCUS**
A competitive handicap, but a roughish race and only modest form.

**NOTEBOOK**
**A Teen** has been running quite well of late without managing to get his head in front, but on this occasion the assistance of the champion helped him force his way in front right on the line. This was probably an even better performance than it looked as those horses that tried to make their runs down the centre of the track where he was were mostly struggling at this meeting.
**Park Star**, well handicapped on her best form and subject of a gamble, did nothing wrong and was very unfortunate to have the race snatched from her on the line. She deserves to make amends, though that will no be consolation to her backers.
**Aintnecessarilyso** was unlucky not to finish closer as he got caught in traffic on the home bend and then had nothing like a clear run in the straight.
**Inching** ran with credit considering she has looked better on Fibresand, but despite several placings she remains a maiden after 20 attempts. *Official explanation: jockey said filly hung right*
**Doctor Dennis(IRE)** made some late progress.
**Ladies Knight** again gave his rivals a start and though he travelled well out the back before staying on, he never gave himself much chance of getting into it. Constantly missing the break is a handicap he could really do without, but he breaks on terms from time to time and when he does he will win.
**Gun Salute** endured a nightmare run and never saw any daylight at any stage. This run can be safely ignored.
T/Plt: £12.20 to a £1 stake. Pool: £44,394.10. 2,644.20 winning tickets. T/Qpdt: £6.90 to a £1 stake. Pool: £2,766.50. 296.10 winning tickets. JN

## 875 SOUTHWELL (L-H)
### Thursday, February 26

**OFFICIAL GOING: Standard to slow**
Times suggested the surface was on the slow side, a fact backed up by jockey opinion.

## 897 BETDIRECT.CO.UK NEW SITE H'CAP 6f (F)
**2:20** (2:26) (E) (0-70,71) 3-Y-0+ **£3,318** (£948; £474) **Stalls** Low

Form RPR

-213 **1** **Up Tempo (IRE)**[6] 833 6-9-5 **61** ........ (b) TQuinn 11 68
(KARyan) *sn bhd: hdwy 2f out: rdn over 1f out: styd on to ld last 100 yds* **5/1**[3]

451 **2** *1 ¾* **Skip Of Colour**[9] 805 4-9-10 **71** 6ex ........ DNolan(5) 12 73
(PABlockley) *wnt rt s: sn cl up: led wl over 2f out and sn clr: rdn ent last: wknd and hdd last 100 yds* **7/2**[1]

-003 **3** *2* **Gilded Cove**[14] 748 4-9-9 **65** ........ MFenton 9 61
(RHollinshead) *towards rr: wd st: rdn along and hdwy 2f out: kpt on u.p appr last: nrst fin* **4/1**[2]

0/10 **4** *1* **Kennington**[21] 686 4-8-12 **59** ........ (v[1]) HayleyTurner(5) 5 52
(MrsCADunnett) *sn led: pushed alonga nd hdd wl over 2f out: sn rdn: kpt on same pce* **14/1**

5200 **5** *hd* **Sharp Hat**[14] 748 10-9-10 **66** ........ ACulhane 3 58
(DWChapman) *chsd ldrs: wd st: rdn over 2f out: sn drvn and kpt on same pce* **28/1**

2004 **6** *½* **Far Note (USA)**[9] 806 6-9-11 **67** ........ (b) NCallan 7 58
(SRBowring) *chsd ldrs: wd st: rdn and kpt on same pce fnl 2f* **15/2**

6020 **7** *1 ¼* **St Ivian**[9] 806 4-9-12 **68** ........ (p) PMcCabe 10 55
(MrsNMacauley) *midfield: wd st: rdn and kpt on fnl 2f: nrst fin* **14/1**

0020 **8** *2* **Pawn In Life (IRE)**[3] 866 6-9-4 **60** ........ (p) DMernagh 2 41
(TDBarron) *s.i.s and sn rdn along: hdwy on inner 1/2-way: drvn and no imp fnl 2f* **13/2**

4410 **9** *1 ¼* **Its Ecco Boy**[6] 833 6-9-1 **57** ........ CCatlin 6 34
(PHowling) *a midfield* **12/1**

00-0 **10** *1 ¼* **Maromito (IRE)**[17] 721 7-8-8 **50** ........ DSweeney 4 24
(RBastiman) *cl up: rdn over 2f out: sn wknd* **50/1**

0040 **11** *½* **Attorney**[10] 796 6-8-1 **46** ........ (e) LisaJones(3) 13 18
(DShaw) *a rr* **33/1**

0000 **12** *3 ½* **Finger Of Fate**[12] 765 4-8-1 **50** ........ (b) KGhunowa(7) 1 12
(MJPolglase) *dwlt: sn chsng ldrs: rdn along 1/2-way and sn wknd* **50/1**

0060 **13** *3* **Teyaar**[12] 771 8-9-2 **58** ........ JMackay 8 11
(MrsNMacauley) *bhd fr 1/2-way* **25/1**

1m 19.89s (3.09) **Going Correction** +0.475s/f (Slow) **13** Ran SP% **119.2**
Speed ratings: **98,95,93,91,91 90,89,86,84,83 82,77,73**CSF £21.68 CT £76.54 TOTE £6.10: £1.60, £1.80, £1.70; EX 37.50.
**Owner** Yorkshire Racing Club and Francis Moll **Bred** T Burns **Trained** Hambleton, N Yorks

**FOCUS**
Fair handicap form, with no fewer than nine previous course and distance winners. The leaders may have gone off a little too fast and the winning time was modest, but the form should stand up.

**NOTEBOOK**
**Up Tempo(IRE)**, a respectable third at Wolverhampton on his previous run despite not having things go his way, returned to winning form with his second course and distance success from as many starts. After getting badly outpaced he really found his stride in the straight and picked up well to collar at the favourite and score a cosy victory. He is worth keeping on the right side of round here.
**Skip Of Colour** , bidding to follow up his recent course and distance maiden success, looked all over the winner when clear at the furlong marker, but having gone off at a strong pace his stamina gave way and he had no answer to the winner's late burst. He showed enough pace to suggest he could be better over the minimum trip and can be given another chance.
**Gilded Cove** struggled to go the early pace, but kept on in the straight to grab a place.
**Kennington**, who won his maiden round here over seven furlongs, showed plenty of pace on this drop in trip with a visor on for the first time. His chance was not helped when taken on up front and he should be capable of better granted an uncontested lead.
**Sharp Hat** has not won in a handicap for over a year now but, only 2lb higher than when gaining that success, ran respectably.
**Pawn In Life(IRE)** attracted some eye-catching market support but missed the break and soon received some sharp reminders. *Official explanation: jockey said gelding missed the break*

## 898 NEW SITE @ BETDIRECT.CO.UK MAIDEN STKS 5f (F)
**2:50** (2:56) (D) 3-Y-0+ **£3,341** (£1,028; £514; £257) **Stalls** High

Form RPR

3-22 **1** **Blueberry Rhyme**[19] 708 5-9-11 65 ........ (v) DSweeney 2 60
(PJMakin) *trckd ldrs gng wl: hdwy on bit over 1f out: qcknd to ld ins last: comf* **8/11**[1]

-533 **2** *1 ¼* **Vittorioso (IRE)**[12] 764 3-8-11 54 ........ (b) MFenton 4 56
(MissGayKelleway) *led: rdn along over 1f out: drvn and hdd ins last: nt qckn* **3/1**[2]

\- **3** *4* **Uhuru Peak** 3-8-6 ........ PMulrennan(5) 1 42
(MWEasterby) *wnt lft s and outpcd: hdwy 2f out: styd on ins ins last: promising* **33/1**

-042 **4** *1* **White O' Morn**[18] 718 5-9-6 35 ........ (p) GGibbons 8 34
(BAMcmahon) *cl up: rdn and ev ch over 1f out: wknd ent last* **16/1**

530- **5** *nk* **Tabarka (GER)**[157] 5127 3-8-6 60 ........ NCallan 3 32
(PABlockley) *chsd ldrs: pushed along and outpcd 2f out: swtchd rt and rdn ent last: styd on towards fin* **12/1**

06 **6** *3* **Harbour Princess**[43] 524 3-8-6 ........ SRighton 6 22
(MFHarris) *sn outpcd and bhd* **50/1**

6-50 **7** *6* **Abraxas**[40] 560 6-9-11 51 ........ (p) TQuinn 5 6
(JAkehurst) *cl up: rdn along 1/2-way: sn wknd* **15/2**[3]

540- **8** *2* **Minirina**[206] 3836 4-9-6 45 ........ RFitzpatrick 7 —
(CSmith) *cl up: rdn along 1/2-way: sn wknd* **40/1**

62.43 secs (2.13) **Going Correction** +0.575s/f (Slow)
**WFA** 3 from 4yo+ 14lb **8** Ran SP% **115.6**
Speed ratings: **105,103,96,95,94 89,80,76**CSF £3.05 TOTE £1.80: £1.02, £1.60, £6.60; EX 3.30.
**Owner** Mrs P J Makin **Bred** Red House Stud **Trained** Ogbourne Maisey, Wilts

**FOCUS**
A weak maiden, but Blueberry Rhyme looks capable of holding his own back in handicaps.

**NOTEBOOK**
**Blueberry Rhyme** has been proving hard to win with and was becoming quite frustrating, but he made no mistake this time. Having travelled through the early stages well and truly on the bridle, it was just a case of what he would find under pressure, and the answer was plenty. This is sure to have boosted his confidence and he may be able to build on this back in handicap company.
**Vittorioso(IRE)**, switching from Polytrack to Fibresand, looked to have every chance, but had 11lb to find with the winner at the weights and was no match for that one close home.
**Uhuru Peak**, a half-brother the stable's sprint handicappers Elvington Boy and William's Well, showed signs of inexperience - diving to his left on leaving the stalls and always having to be niggled along - but kept on and is sure to be better for the experience.
**White O' Morn**, with the tongue-tie left off but with cheekpieces fitted, had it all to do at the weights and was very one paced where it mattered.
**Tabarka(GER)**, with the blinkers left off, was very easy to back and was well held.

## 899 LITTLEWOODS BET DIRECT H'CAP 2m (F)
**3:20** (3:25) (D) (0-85,80) 4-Y-0+ **£4,026** (£1,239; £619; £309) **Stalls** Low

Form RPR

-001 **1** **Victory Quest (IRE)**[7] 827 4-9-7 **79** 6ex ........ (v) CCatlin 7 91
(MrsSLamyman) *trckd ldrs: hdwy to ld gng wl over 5f out: rdn 2f out: styd on wl fnl f* **8/1**

5/4- **2** *2* **Northern Nymph**[79] 6156 5-9-10 **76** ........ ACulhane 6 86
(RHollinshead) *hld up in tch: smooth hdwy 1/2-way: chsd wnr over 4f out: rdn to chal 2f out and ev ch tl drvn and no ex ins last* **16/1**

0/0- **3** *18* **Ocean Tide**[364] 520 7-9-2 **75** ........ (v) BSwarbrick(7) 9 63
(RFord) *hld up: hdwy 1/2-way: rdn along over 4f out: drvn 3f out: plugged on: but nvr nr ldrs* **50/1**

-321 **4** *15* **Altitude Dancer (IRE)**[21] 684 4-8-6 **64** ........ NCallan 5 34
(PABlockley) *led 3f: cl up: rdn along over 6f out: drvn over 4f out and sn wknd* **7/4**[1]

1402 **5** *2* **Digger (IRE)**[7] 795 5-9-7 **73** ........ MFenton 3 41
(MissGayKelleway) *hld up in tch: hdwy over 4f out: rdn along 3f out: sn drvn and wknd* **10/1**

40-0 **6** *23* **Rolex Free (ARG)**[22] 679 6-9-4 **70** ........ (p) DeanMcKeown 1 10
(MrsLCTaylor) *prom: rdn along 1/2-way: sn wknd* **66/1**

000/ **7** *½* **Gracilis (IRE)**[580] 3327 7-10-0 **80** ........ FLynch 4 20
(GASwinbank) *a rr: wl bhd fr 1/2-way* **33/1**

1 **8** *3* **Royal Atalza (FR)**[10] 797 7-7-13 **51** 6ex ........ (b) JMackay 10 —
(CNAllen) *cl up: led after 3f: rdn along 1/2-way: drvn and hdd over 5f out: wknd qckly* **15/8**[2]

1-20 **9** *2* **Western (IRE)**[43] 523 4-9-4 **76** ........ TQuinn 8 10
(JAkehurst) *hld up: effrt and sme hdwy hafway: rdn along over 5f out and sn outpcd* **7/1**[3]

050/ **10** *dist* **Perestroika (IRE)**[443] 5876 6-8-8 **65** ........ TEaves(5) 2 —
(BEllison) *a rr: bhd fr 1/2-way* **66/1**

3m 51.67s (-0.83) **Going Correction** +0.475s/f (Slow)
**WFA** 4 from 5yo+ 6lb **10** Ran SP% **117.6**
Speed ratings: **105,104,95,87,86 75,74,73,72,—**CSF £121.84 CT £5852.49 TOTE £12.20: £2.50, £3.70, £15.30; EX 121.70 Trifecta £1714.60 Part won. Pool of £2,414.99 - 0.50 winning tickets..
**Owner** P Lamyman **Bred** Miss Veronica Henley **Trained** Louth, Lincs

**FOCUS**
With the likes of Royal Atalza, Altitude Dancer and Digger running below form this was not a very competitive heat, but probably strong form by the front two, who pulled a long way clear of a well strung-out bunch.

**NOTEBOOK**
**Victory Quest(IRE)**, racing under a 6lb penalty for his success over a mile six here on his previous outing, stayed this longer trip well and ran out a determined winner. He goes particularly well on this surface and his record at the track now reads 212711, with the only flop coming when losing his action.
**Northern Nymph**, racing for the first time in 79 days, was the only one to go with the eventual winner and emerged with real credit. He got a little tired in the closing stages and may prove best at a slightly shorter trip.
**Ocean Tide** was no match for the front two on this return to the level, but he is entitled to improve on this first start in a year.
**Altitude Dancer(IRE)**, 5lb higher than when successful over course and distance on his previous outing, came under pressure a long way from home and this was a very lacklustre effort.
**Digger(IRE)** raced keenly and has yet to convince this trip really suits.
**Royal Atalza(FR)** pulled his way to the front and stopped very quickly when headed.

## 900 BETDIRECT.CO.UK CLASSIFIED STKS — 7f (F)
3:50 (3:55) (E) 3-Y-O+ — £3,227 (£922; £461) Stalls Low

Form — RPR
430- **1** — **Uhoomagoo**[121] [5820] 6-9-8 67............(b) NCallan 5 — 83
(KARyan) *hld up: hdwy wl over 2f out: rdn to chal over 1f out: led ent last and kpt on* **4/1**[2]
20-6 **2** 2 ½ **My Bayard**[12] [775] 5-9-1 69............ JDO'Reilly(7) 8 — 77
(JO'Reilly) *a.p: hdwy to chal over 2f out: shkn up to ld over 1f out: sn rdn and hdd ent last: one pce* **4/1**[2]
23-0 **3** 9 **Zarin (IRE)**[23] [667] 6-9-8 67............ ACulhane 7 — 54
(DWChapman) *hld up: hdwy 2f out: sn rdn and kpt on fnl f* **6/1**
0-16 **4** ½ **Weet Watchers**[17] [719] 4-9-8 70............ DeanMcKeown 6 — 53
(PABlockley) *led: rdn along over 2f out: drvn and hdd over 1f out: sn wknd* **7/2**[1]
0-10 **5** 1 ¾ **Modesty Blaise (SWE)**[30] [614] 4-9-5 68............ MFenton 2 — 46
(MissGayKelleway) *chsd ldrs: rdn along 1/2-way: sn wknd* **10/1**
2-15 **6** 2 **Wings Of Morning (IRE)**[13] [758] 3-8-5 68............ JBramhill 1 — 44
(PABlockley) *stdd s: a bhd* **14/1**
00-0 **7** 1 **Riska King**[52] [437] 4-9-3 69............ THamilton(5) 4 — 41
(RAFahey) *a rr* **12/1**
2-30 **8** 3 ½ **Royal Grand**[21] [681] 4-9-1 69............(v[1]) PMakin(7) 3 — 32
(TDBarron) *cl up: rdn along wl over 2f out: drvn and wknd over 1f out* **5/1**[3]

1m 32.55s (1.75) **Going Correction** +0.475s/f (Slow)
**WFA** 3 from 4yo+ 17lb — **8** Ran SP% **116.6**
Speed ratings: **109,106,95,95,93 91,89,85**CSF £20.87 TOTE £5.00: £1.80, £1.40, £2.00; EX 27.30.
**Owner** John Duddy **Bred** C R Mason And Mrs N T Pope **Trained** Hambleton, N Yorks

**FOCUS**
The field were quite closely matched on the figures, so decent form from the front two, who finished a long way clear. The winning time was smart for the grade.

**NOTEBOOK**
**Uhoomagoo**, last seen running below form after having taken a walk in the betting at Redcar in October of last year, was back in good heart on this return from a break and made the most of an All-Weather mark 15lb lower than that on turf with a cosy victory. He could well defy a rise in the weights if remaining on such good terms with himself.
**My Bayard** showed the benefit of his recent comeback outing with a fine effort in defeat. Although no match for the well-handicapped winner, he kept on under pressure and drew a long way clear of the rest. It has to be a slight concern he has just one win to his name in 19 starts, but he may be capable of doubling his tally in similar company.
**Zarin(IRE)**, without a win since landing his maiden in April 2001, was unable to go with the front two but stayed on best of the rest.
**Weet Watchers**, still looking for his first win in a handicap, looked to hold every chance but found little when asked.
**Modesty Blaise(SWE)** looks high enough in the weights.
**Royal Grand** was a long way below form with no obvious excuse.

## 901 DAILY OFFERS @ BETDIRECT.CO.UK (S) STKS — 1m 4f (F)
4:20 (4:26) (G) 4-Y-O+ — £2,534 (£724; £362) Stalls Low

Form — RPR
0011 **1** — **Daunted (IRE)**[2] [879] 8-9-2 60............(p) LisaJones(3) 6 — 63
(PABlockley) *led 1f: cl up tl led again 7f out: rdn clr over 2f out* **4/6**[1]
1030 **2** 6 **Orinocovsky (IRE)**[15] [743] 5-9-5 58............ NCallan 1 — 54
(NPLittmoden) *cl up: led after 1f: hdd 1/2-way: cl up tl rdn and outpcd over 2f out: drvn and kpt on fnl f* **9/4**[2]
4613 **3** ¾ **Spanish Star**[18] [714] 7-9-5 54............ ACulhane 4 — 53
(MrsNMacauley) *trac ked ldrs: pushed along and outpcd 1/2-way: rdn over 3f out: styd on to chse wnr over 1f out: sn drvn: edgd lft and one* **10/1**[3]
5663 **4** 1 ½ **Think Quick (IRE)**[6] [838] 4-7-13 35............ RKennemore(7) 5 — 41
(RHollinshead) *hld up: hdwy over 4f out: rdn along 3f out and sn no imp* **33/1**
1/0- **5** 5 **Star Seventeen**[7] [382] 6-8-2............ BSwarbrick(7) 2 — 34
(MrsNSSharpe) *trckd ldng pair: rdn along 5f out: drvn and wknd over 4f out* **14/1**

2m 48.58s (6.48) **Going Correction** +0.475s/f (Slow)
**WFA** 4 from 5yo+ 3lb — **5** Ran SP% **109.5**
Speed ratings: **97,93,92,91,88**CSF £2.33 TOTE £1.60: £1.10, £1.90; EX 2.40.There was no bid for the winner.
**Owner** Mrs Joanna Hughes **Bred** Mrs G Doyle **Trained** Southwell, Notts

**FOCUS**
The first three in the betting were separated by just 6lb on adjusted official figures, but Daunted won easily. Probably just typical selling form.

**NOTEBOOK**
**Daunted(IRE)**, with declared cheekpieces on for the first time, completed the hat-trick on the step back outside of Regional Racing with a very comfortable victory. He has a tremendous record at this sort of level and should continue to prove hard to beat.
**Orinocovsky(IRE)** has struggled since winning in this grade last month for Charlie Egerton and, dropped back into a seller for the first time since that success, raced very keenly and was again well held.
**Spanish Star** was unable to confirm recent placings with the runner-up on 10lb worse terms. He remains worth a try over farther.
**Think Quick(IRE)** ran respectably, despite having plenty to do at the weights. Regional Racing may suit better.
**Star Seventeen** was best in on the figures and a market springer, but is clearly not the force of old.

## 902 BET IN RUNNING @ BETDIRECT.CO.UK H'CAP — 1m 3f (F)
4:50 (4:56) (F) (0-55,55) 4-Y-O+ — £2,947 (£842; £421) Stalls Low

Form — RPR
0-53 **1** — **Bramantino (IRE)**[10] [800] 4-8-9 53............(p) THamilton(5) 11 — 62
(RAFahey) *towards rr: rdn along on outer over 3f out: gd hdwy 2f out:rdn to chal and edgd lft ent last: drvn to ld last 75 yds* **7/1**
0-10 **2** hd **Sting Like A Bee (IRE)**[20] [700] 5-9-4 55............ TQuinn 10 — 64
(JSGoldie) *hld up in rr: stdy hdwy over 4f out: swtchd rt and then lft over 1f out: rdn to ld ins last: hung rt and hdd last 75 yds* **4/1**[1]
6-21 **3** 5 **Disabuse**[35] [588] 4-9-1 54............ DaleGibson 2 — 55
(MWEasterby) *trckd ldrs: hdwy 4f out: rdn along and swtchd lft over 1f out drvn and ev ch whn hmpd ins last: sn wknd* **9/2**[2]
101- **4** 3 **So Sure (IRE)**[11] [5304] 4-8-13 52............ DeanMcKeown 4 — 48
(JGMO'Shea) *trckd ldrs: hdwy to ld 1/2-way: rdn 2f out: edgd rt over 1f out: drvn and hdd jst ins last: wknd* **8/1**
2351 **5** shd **Sorbiesharry (IRE)**[20] [695] 5-8-12 49............(p) PMcCabe 6 — 45
(MrsNMacauley) *hld up: hdwy 4f out: rdn to chse ldrs over 2f out: drvn and one pce appr last* **6/1**
2F41 **6** 11 **Shatin Special**[9] [812] 4-8-7 46 6ex............(p) RFfrench 8 — 24
(GCHChung) *in tch on outer: hdwy 4f out: chal over 2f out: sn rdn and wknd* **7/1**
1054 **7** 5 **Daimajin (IRE)**[6] [838] 5-9-2 53............ ACulhane 9 — 23
(MrsLucindaFeatherstone) *in tch: hdwy to chse ldrs over 3f out: sn rdn and wknd* **14/1**
6-45 **8** 9 **Danum**[9] [811] 4-8-8 47............ NCallan 5 — 3
(RHollinshead) *a rr* **40/1**
00-3 **9** nk **Intensity**[2] [867] 8-9-4 55............ GParkin 7 — 11
(PABlockley) *prom: rdn along over 4f out: wknd over 2f out* **11/2**[3]
005- **10** 2 **Ice And Fire**[91] [3699] 5-9-1 52............(b) JFanning 1 — 4
(BDLeavy) *cl up: led after 3f: pushed along and hdd 1/2-way: rdn over 3f out and sn wknd* **20/1**
00-6 **11** 1 ¼ **Homeric Trojan**[35] [585] 4-8-6 52 ow2............ MLawson(7) 3 — —
(MBrittain) *led 3f: rdn along and lost pl 1/2-way: sn bhd* **40/1**

2m 33.03s (4.13) **Going Correction** +0.475s/f (Slow)
**WFA** 4 from 5yo+ 2lb — **11** Ran SP% **120.3**
Speed ratings: **103,102,99,97,96 88,85,78,78,77 76**CSF £35.37 CT £142.35 TOTE £10.20: £3.10, £1.50, £2.30; EX 39.70 Place 6 £56.74, Place 5 £38.43.
**Owner** Mrs Kenyon, A Rhodes Haulage, P Timmins **Bred** Mrs Brid Cosgrove **Trained** Musley Bank, N Yorks
■ Stewards Enquiry : T Quinn caution:careless riding
T Hamilton caution:careless riding

**FOCUS**
Modest form, though the pace was decent.

**NOTEBOOK**
**Bramantino(IRE)** owes this victory to a tremendously determined ride from Tony Hamilton. Racing over a trip this far for the first time, and with cheekpieces replacing a visor, he needed plenty of driving from the saddle, but his jockey did not give up and the pair ran out a narrow winner. A rise in the weights for this will make things harder next time, but he may improve for a further step up in trip.
**Sting Like A Bee(IRE)**, supported into favouritism, had to be switched inside to get a run a furlong out and did not help his chance by hanging right, but he appeared to have every chance and cannot be considered unlucky. A similar race looks within his grasp.
**Disabuse**, 6lb higher than when winning over a mile here for Stuart Williams on his previous start, got squeezed out by the front two around a furlong from home but cannot really be considered unlucky.
**So Sure(IRE)**, racing on the Flat for the first time in 148 days having been running over hurdles in the meantime, did not appear to have any excuses.
**Sorbiesharry(IRE)** has never won beyond an extended mile and was comfortably held.
JR

# 861 WOLVERHAMPTON (A.W) (L-H)
Friday, February 27

**OFFICIAL GOING: Slow**

## 903 BETDIRECT.CO.UK NEW SITE AMATEUR RIDERS' H'CAP — 1m 1f 79y(F)
1:00 (1:00) (G) (0-65,68) 4-Y-O+ — £2,618 (£748; £374) Stalls Low

Form — RPR
0151 **1** — **Scottish River (USA)**[4] [861] 5-11-8 68 6ex............ MrLNewnes(5) 13 — 78
(MDIUsher) *slowly away: stdy hdwy over 6f out: led over 2f out: pushed out: comf* **11/4**[2]
5026 **2** 1 **Paso Doble**[4] [861] 6-10-13 61............ MrJMillman(7) 10 — 69
(BRMillman) *towards rr: hdwy over 3f out: ev ch 2f out: nt pce of wnr* **14/1**
46-0 **3** ½ **Call Of The Wild**[21] [546] 4-10-6 52............(p) MrRStephens(5) 6 — 59
(RAFahey) *racd mid-div: hdwy to chse ldrs 3f out: ev ch 2f out: nt qckn after* **20/1**
0-53 **4** hd **Bevier**[10] [812] 10-9-11 45............ MrMHowells(7) 8 — 52
(TWall) *in rr til hdwy over 2f out: r.o fnl f: nvr nrr* **20/1**
00-0 **5** ½ **Sinjaree**[53] [437] 6-10-4 45............ MrsMMorris 7 — 51
(MrsSLamyman) *in rr: hdwy on inner over 2f out: styd on one pce after* **25/1**
-261 **6** 9 **Iamback**[25] [656] 4-10-9 50............(e[1]) MissEJJones 5 — 40
(MissGayKelleway) *in tch: chsd ldr over 4f out: wknd wl over 1f out* **12/1**
-220 **7** 2 **Noble Pursuit**[12] [782] 7-10-9 55............ StaceyRenwick(5) 12 — 41
(PABlockley) *slowly away: sme hdwy over 3f out: nvr nr to chal* **12/1**
0242 **8** 2 **Surdoue**[8] [829] 4-11-6 61............ MrSWalker 4 — 43
(PHowling) *chsd ldr: led over 4f out: rdn and hdd over 2f out: wknd qckly* **9/4**[1]
-305 **9** 18 **Yenaled**[18] [719] 7-10-12 58............ MSeston(5) 3 — 8
(KARyan) *v.s.a: a wl in rr* **7/1**[3]
0-00 **10** 1 ¼ **Illustrious Duke**[21] [698] 6-9-11 45............ MissMMullineaux(7) 11 — —
(MMullineaux) *prom tl rdn and wknd 1/2-way* **50/1**
40-3 **11** 1 **Crusoe (IRE)**[4] [861] 7-11-3 61............(b) MrEDehdashti(3) 2 — 7
(ASadik) *prom to 1/2-way* **12/1**
-020 **12** 9 **Littleton Zephir (USA)**[32] [604] 5-10-0 46............(b) MrsCThompson(5) 1 — —
(MrsPTownsley) *led tl hdd over 4f out: wknd rapidly* **50/1**

2m 12.98s (10.08) **Going Correction** +0.775s/f (Slow) — **12** Ran SP% **117.0**
Speed ratings: **86,85,84,84,84 76,74,72,56,55 54,46**CSF £37.15 CT £642.79 TOTE £3.70: £1.10, £5.30, £5.30; EX 55.90.
**Owner** M D I Usher **Bred** The Thoroughbred Corporation **Trained** Upper Lambourn, Berks

**FOCUS**
This was respectable form for the type of race, but the winning time was slow.

**NOTEBOOK**
**Scottish River(USA)**, penalised for his win in a claimer here earlier in the week, started slowly again but that was not a problem as he eased to a cosy victory. He has established a good rapport with this rider.
**Paso Doble**, an inconsistent sort, finished closer to Scottish River than he had earlier in the week but did not seem to want to go past when he had the chance.
**Call Of The Wild** had the cheekpieces back on for this return to the Flat. He did not find a great deal once coming under pressure and is essentially rather slow.

**Bevier** has an unorthodox training schedule which includes running loose across the fells in the company of his owner. There was only one behind him leaving the back straight, but he stayed on under minimum assistance from his rider. He needs farther.
**Sinjaree** plugged on despite his rider acting as little more than a passenger.
**Surdoue**, taking a step down in trip, was due to go up 4lb the following day. He dropped out quickly once headed and was reported to have pulled up feelingly. *Official explanation: trainer said gelding was pulled up feelingly; vet said gelding was lame*
**Crusoe(IRE)** *Official explanation: jockey said gelding, which was eased in the final furlong, lost its action*
**Littleton Zephir(USA)** *Official explanation: trainer said mare was disappointing and finished distressed*

## 904 NEW SITE @ BETDIRECT.CO.UK H'CAP (DIV I) 5f (F)
**1:35** (1:35) (E) (0-70,67) 3-Y-0+ **£3,241** (£926; £463) **Stalls** Low

Form RPR
6310 **1** **Arogant Prince**[11] 799 7-8-12 51 (b) JQuinn 3 67
(AWCarroll) *mde all: clr over 1f out: comf* **10/1**[2]
4-11 **2** *3* **Mynd**[28] 638 4-9-13 66 DeanMcKeown 5 71
(RMWhitaker) *sltly outpcd early: hdwy 1/2-way: rdn and kpt on to chse wnr ins fnl f* **6/5**[1]
/0-0 **3** *1* **Vijay (IRE)**[11] 796 5-9-5 58 (p) ACulhane 2 60
(ISemple) *in rr: hdwy ins fnl 2f: nvr nr to chal* **12/1**[3]
2656 **4** *hd* **Cleveland Way**[15] 748 4-8-2 47 ow2 (v) DTudhope(7) 4 49
(DCarroll) *a in tch: kpt on one pce fnl f* **33/1**
30-0 **5** *3* **Erracht**[11] 794 6-9-1 54 GBaker 7 44
(KRBurke) *prom: rdn 2f out: kpt on one pce after* **25/1**
-635 **6** *nk* **Lady Pekan**[10] 806 5-9-10 63 (b) NCallan 10 52
(PSMcentee) *trckd wnr tl rdn and wknd ins fnl f* **10/1**[2]
-533 **7** *½* **Sotonian (HOL)**[10] 813 11-7-12 40 LisaJones(3) 11 28
(PSFelgate) *swtchd over to ins fr wd draw at s: a bhd* **16/1**
-000 **8** *shd* **Gone'N'Dunnett (IRE)**[10] 801 5-10-0 67 (p) DaneO'Neill 8 54
(MrsCADunnett) *a struggling in rr* **16/1**
0-45 **9** *½* **Malahide Express (IRE)**[22] 680 4-9-7 60 (b) DHolland 1 45
(MJPolglase) *prom tl wknd wl over 1f out* **12/1**[3]
0-02 **10** *shd* **River Days (IRE)**[14] 762 6-9-3 56 (bt) MFenton 9 41
(MissGayKelleway) *towards rr: sme hdwy on outside after 2f: rn wd into st and no ch after* **12/1**[3]
0005 **11** *shd* **Taboor (IRE)**[10] 801 6-9-11 64 (b) IMongan 6 49
(JWPayne) *outpcd: a bhd* **10/1**[2]
65.33 secs (2.73) **Going Correction** +0.775s/f (Slow) **11** Ran SP% **114.4**
Speed ratings: **109,104,102,102,97 97,96,96,95,95 94**CSF £21.61 CT £151.40 TOTE £14.20: £2.80, £1.10, £6.00; EX 29.20 Trifecta £463.50 Pool £5,092.21, 7.8 w/u.
**Owner** Dennis Deacon **Bred** Miss Julie Self **Trained** Wixford, Warwicks

**FOCUS**
A very decent time for the grade of contest, about half a second faster than the second division. Not many got into this and the winner came down the centre in the home straight.

**NOTEBOOK**
**Arogant Prince** got away to such a flier that the Stewards checked to see if his stall had opened early. Staying on strongly, he is in good heart at present and this was his first win in handicap company for nearly two years.
**Mynd**, attempting a course hat-trick, was 7lb higher than for his latest win. Chasing the winner entering the last without looking like pegging him back, he will probably get another furlong.
**Vijay(IRE)**, equipped with cheekpieces rather than the blinkers he had worn on his last four starts, ran his best race since coming over from Ireland. On this evidence he needs six furlongs.
**Cleveland Way** is better over six furlongs and this was a fair run in the circumstances.
**Erracht** was again unable to dominate and was a spent force turning into the straight.
**Lady Pekan** showed speed to lie up with the eventual winner but was beaten inside the last. This was a decent effort given her high draw.

## 905 NEW SITE @ BETDIRECT.CO.UK H'CAP (DIV II) 5f (F)
**2:10** (2:12) (E) (0-70,66) 3-Y-0+ **£3,241** (£926; £463) **Stalls** Low

Form RPR
3612 **1** **Playtime Blue**[7] 836 4-9-13 66 6ex GBaker 1 76
(KRBurke) *mde all: rdn ent fnl f: drvn out* **6/5**[1]
6526 **2** *½* **Tigress (IRE)**[11] 796 5-9-3 56 (b) MFenton 4 64
(JWUnett) *a.p: chsd wnr fr 1/2-way: r.o wl u.p fnl f* **6/1**[3]
4-01 **3** *2½* **Cash**[11] 794 6-9-10 66 6ex (p) LFletcher(3) 8 66
(PaulJohnson) *trckd wnr to 1/2-way: c wd into st: r.o fnl f* **8/1**
000- **4** *1* **Stoic Leader (IRE)**[122] 5811 4-9-5 58 SRighton 5 54
(RFFisher) *in tch: sn pushed along: one pce ins fnl 2f* **25/1**
4-12 **5** *1¾* **Empress Josephine**[11] 794 4-9-0 56 (v) DCorby(3) 9 46
(JRJenkins) *chsd ldrs: rdn 1/2-way: wknd appr fnl f* **5/1**[2]
0-30 **6** *1* **Mangus (IRE)**[11] 792 10-8-1 40 (be) JMackay 6 26
(KOCunningham-Brown) *in rr: c wd into st: mde sme late hdwy* **40/1**
00-0 **7** *¾* **Telepathic (IRE)**[50] 476 4-9-9 62 FLynch 2 46
(ABerry) *a towards rr* **66/1**
-606 **8** *1½* **Prime Recreation**[10] 806 7-9-11 64 (p) DaleGibson 7 43
(PSFelgate) *mid-div: wknd wl over 1f out* **14/1**
202- **9** *1¼* **Queen Of Bulgaria (IRE)**[138] 5512 3-8-8 61 JQuinn 3 35
(JPearce) *a struggling in rr* **20/1**
0200 **10** *5* **Prince Of Blues (IRE)**[7] 836 6-9-12 65 (b) SWKelly 10 22
(MMullineaux) *prom to 1/2-way* **25/1**
65.87 secs (3.27) **Going Correction** +0.775s/f (Slow)
**WFA** 3 from 4yo+ 14lb **10** Ran SP% **110.6**
Speed ratings: **104,103,99,97,94 93,92,89,87,79**CSF £7.18 CT £36.80 TOTE £1.90: £1.10, £2.10, £2.90; EX 8.90.
**Owner** P Sweeting **Bred** Capt J H Wilson **Trained** Middleham Moor, N Yorks

**FOCUS**
The winning time was average for the grade and about half a second slower than the first division. The form of the first two looks solid.

**NOTEBOOK**
**Playtime Blue**, quickly away to secure the lead from his inside stall, was clearly going best turning in but the runner-up made him work for victory.
**Tigress(IRE)** ran a solid race and was closing the gap on the favourite near the finish.
**Cash**, penalised for his recent course-and-distance win, showed pace but did not help his chance by coming towards the near side in the home straight.
**Stoic Leader(IRE)**, who was having his first run for four months, races only infrequently on sand.
**Empress Josephine** was unable to get her own way up front from her high draw. She is set to go up 4lb now and could struggle.
**Prime Recreation** *Official explanation: jockey said gelding was hanging right-handed from halfway*

## 906 LITTLEWOODS BET DIRECT MAIDEN STKS 6f (F)
**2:45** (2:47) (D) 3-Y-0+ **£3,354** (£1,032; £516; £258) **Stalls** Low

Form RPR
322 **1** **Global Achiever**[14] 760 3-8-9 67 RFfrench 10 74
(GCHChung) *mde all: clr 2f out: kpt up to work fnl f* **11/8**[1]
050- **2** *1¾* **Fit To Fly (IRE)**[245] 2770 3-8-9 81 JFEgan 9 69
(SKirk) *prom: riddden to chse wnr fnl 2f: kpt on* **5/2**[2]
-520 **3** *6* **Nanna (IRE)**[17] 732 3-8-4 50 JQuinn 5 46
(RHollinshead) *chsd ldrs: outpcd 1/2-way: styd on u.p fnl f* **14/1**
44-5 **4** *nk* **Otylia**[10] 805 4-9-5 52 FLynch 1 45
(ABerry) *trckd wnr to 2f out: rdn and wknd ins fnl f* **10/1**
06- **5** *8* **Bright Fire (IRE)**[218] 3529 3-8-1 LisaJones(3) 7 21
(WJMusson) *s.i.s: nvr on terms* **8/1**[3]
55-0 **6** *2½* **Dante's Devine (IRE)**[39] 566 3-8-9 56 CCatlin 3 18
(ABailey) *outpcd thrght* **33/1**
33-0 **7** *nk* **Brooklands Time (IRE)**[10] 805 3-8-4 63 JBramhill 2 12
(IWMcInnes) *s.i.s: rdn and sn in tch: bhd fr 1/2-way* **20/1**
340- **8** *5* **Jilly Why (IRE)**[156] 5144 3-8-4 63 JoannaBadger 4 —
(MsDeborahJEvans) *a struggling in rr* **12/1**
1m 18.81s (3.11) **Going Correction** +0.775s/f (Slow)
**WFA** 3 from 4yo 15lb **8** Ran SP% **112.9**
Speed ratings: **110,107,99,99,88 85,84,78**CSF £4.67 TOTE £2.10: £1.10, £1.40, £2.20; EX 5.90.
**Owner** Dr Johnny Hon **Bred** Limestone Stud **Trained** Newmarket, Suffolk

**FOCUS**
This looked just a modest maiden, but the time was excellent for the grade and the first two recorded very smart speed ratings.

**NOTEBOOK**
**Global Achiever** was not so keen on this step back from seven furlongs. Making all, he was three lengths clear turning for home but his stride was shortening inside the last. This looks his trip.
**Fit To Fly(IRE)** was having his first run since June and making his All-Weather bow. He kept on as if need of an extra furlong and should strip fitter with this run under his belt.
**Nanna(IRE)**, a limited performer who was runner-up in a claimer here last month, merely finished best of the rest.
**Otylia**, a long-standing maiden, is still without the cheekpieces she wore regularly last term.
**Bright Fire(IRE)**, who has been slowly away on each of her three runs so far, is now eligible for handicaps.

## 907 BETDIRECT.CO.UK MEDIAN AUCTION MAIDEN STKS 1m 100y(F)
**3:20** (3:22) (E) 3-4-Y-0 **£3,297** (£942; £471) **Stalls** Low

Form RPR
03-3 **1** **Book Matched**[11] 798 3-8-6 65 RFfrench 7 65
(BSmart) *in tch: hdwy over 3f out: led wl over 1f out: edgd rt but in command after* **5/4**[1]
33-5 **2** *1¾* **Hawkit (USA)**[11] 798 3-8-9 72 ow3 DHolland 3 64
(JAOsborne) *led tl rdn and hdd wl over 1f out: kpt on but no imp fnl f* **2/1**[2]
0- **3** *8* **Wonky Donkey**[277] 1868 3-8-6 JTate 5 45
(SCWilliams) *chsd ldrs: wknd over 1f out* **25/1**
05 **4** *11* **Ballyrush (IRE)**[4] 862 4-9-4 67 RKeogh(7) 6 21
(KRBurke) *w ldrs: wnt 2nd briefly over 3f out: rdn and sn btn* **7/1**[3]
**5** *1¾* **Sunset Blues (FR)** 4-9-8 (be[1]) DCorby(3) 2 18
(KOCunningham-Brown) *s.i.s: nvr on terms* **50/1**
300- **6** *¾* **Showtime Annie**[136] 5557 3-8-1 65 CCatlin 4 11
(ABailey) *chsd ldrs to 1/2-way: sn bhd* **12/1**
000 **7** *3½* **Fora Smile**[9] 817 3-8-6 DKinsella 9 9
(MDIUsher) *racd wd: a bhd* **66/1**
**8** *8* **Bulberry Hill** 3-8-6 DRMcCabe 8 —
(MGQuinlan) *v.s.a: nvr on terms* **28/1**
**9** *4* **Diverted** 3-7-8 NicolPolli(7) 1 —
(MGQuinlan) *a struggling in rr* **33/1**
1m 56.76s (5.76) **Going Correction** +0.775s/f (Slow)
**WFA** 3 from 4yo 19lb **9** Ran SP% **111.7**
Speed ratings: **102,100,92,81,79 78,75,67,63**CSF £3.45 TOTE £1.80: £1.10, £1.10, £7.90; EX 3.10.
**Owner** Paul Darling **Bred** P A Darling **Trained** Hambleton, N Yorks

**FOCUS**
A modest maiden.

**NOTEBOOK**
**Book Matched** confirmed the form with Hawkit in a handicap last time despite edging over towards the stands' rail once in line for home. He ought to get another furlong.
**Hawkit(USA)** was weighted to reverse recent form with Book Matched, but was unable to do so and there were no real excuses. He is certainly expensive to follow.
**Wonky Donkey**, off the track since finishing last on his debut back in May, finished a clear third despite appearing not to stay. There could be a small race for him over slighty shorter.
**Ballyrush(IRE)**, an ex-Irish gelding, again looked in need of a drop in class.
**Sunset Blues(FR)**, who showed little on this debut, is a half-sister to one-time high-class hurdler Ben Ewar.

## 908 DAILY SPECIAL OFFERS @ BETDIRECT.CO.UK CLASSIFIED STKS 1m 4f (F)
**3:50** (3:50) (E) 4-Y-0+ **£3,213** (£918; £459) **Stalls** Low

Form RPR
4/3- **1** **Moon Shot**[86] 6125 8-9-1 61 VSlattery 3 73
(AGJuckes) *t.k.h: trckd ldng pair: led 2f out: styd on wl fnl f* **14/1**
5342 **2** *3½* **Yorker (USA)**[4] 866 6-9-1 67 NCallan 2 68
(MsDeborahJEvans) *trckd ldr: led briefly over 2f out: styd on but no imp on wnr fnl f* **13/2**[3]
040- **3** *1½* **Toni Alcala**[102] 6017 5-8-12 64 LFletcher(3) 7 66
(RFFisher) *wl in rr: styd on fnl 3f but nvr nr to chal* **12/1**
215- **4** *10* **Easibet Dot Net**[58] 6267 4-8-12 62 (v[1]) ACulhane 4 51
(ISemple) *led tl hdd over 2f out: sn wknd* **11/8**[1]
1141 **5** *5* **Bella Pavlina**[8] 825 6-8-11 56 BSwarbrick(7) 1 46
(WMBrisbourne) *hld up in tch tl rdn over 5f out: sn btn* **11/4**[2]
25-1 **6** *23* **Paradise Valley**[50] 478 4-8-12 53 SDrowne 5 9
(MrsStefLiddiard) *a bhd: lost tch 4f out* **13/2**[3]
2m 50.14s (8.64) **Going Correction** +0.775s/f (Slow)
**WFA** 4 from 5yo+ 3lb **6** Ran SP% **109.8**
Speed ratings: **102,99,98,92,88 73**CSF £92.26 TOTE £17.80: £6.00, £3.60; EX 78.70.
**Owner** Whistlejacket Partnership **Bred** Societe Aland **Trained** Abberley, Worcs

**FOCUS**
This was not the most competitive of races and only three of these ever counted, but the winner showed fair form.

**NOTEBOOK**
**Moon Shot** was having his second run for the yard, having latterly been with Michael Cunningham in Ireland. In command when eased towards the finish, he reportedly blew up so there could be a bit more to come.
**Yorker(USA)** appeared to stay this longer trip but only in the context of this somewhat uncompetitive event.
**Toni Alcala**, having his first run since November, usually runs over farther and found this too sharp.
**Easibet Dot Net**, in a first-time visor rather than cheekpieces, set the pace but was quickly beaten once collared.

**Bella Pavlina** was well below form and never got near the leading trio. Her rider reported that she failed to handle the slow surface, and a busy recent schedule could also have caught up with her. *Official explanation: jockey said mare was unsuited by the slow surface*
**Paradise Valley**, who faced a stiff task at the weights, was not tongue-tied on this occasion and was reported to have had breathing problems. *Official explanation: jockey said gelding had breathing problems*

## 909 BET IN RUNNING @ BETDIRECT.CO.UK H'CAP (DIV I) 1m 100y(F)
4:20 (4:24) (F) (0-60,61) 3-Y-O+ £2,968 (£848; £424) Stalls Low

Form RPR
-203 1 **Geronimo**[13] [772] 7-9-7 58 (p) DeanWilliams(7) 10 66
(MissGayKelleway) *racd wd and towards rr: hdwy 3f out: led jst ins fnl f: jst hld on* **25/1**
-021 2 *nk* **Desert Heat**[11] [800] 6-10-3 61 6ex (b[1]) NCallan 2 68
(ISemple) *hld up: rdn and hdwy over 2f out: pressed wnr ins fnl f* **12/1**
-161 3 *nk* **Jakarmi**[13] [773] 3-8-11 60 DKinsella 4 67
(BPalling) *led after 1f: rdn and hdd jst ins fnl f: rallied wl and kpt on to line* **22/1**
2302 4 *1 ½* **Danger Bird (IRE)**[14] [763] 4-9-7 51 MFenton 7 55
(RHollinshead) *led for 1f: styd cl up: no ex ins fnl f* **16/1**
3412 5 *nk* **Grand Lass (IRE)**[10] [810] 5-9-6 50 (p) DHolland 3 53
(ASadik) *prom early: outpcd over 5f out: rallied over 1f out and r.o ins fnl f* **10/1**
6123 6 *nk* **Givemethemoonlight**[4] [866] 5-9-12 56 (v) IMongan 5 58
(MrsStefLiddiard) *mid-div: effrt over 4f out: wknd over 1f out* **5/1**[2]
0/ 7 *3* **Insignificance**[149] [5320] 4-9-2 46 JPMurtagh 9 42
(JohnAQuinn, Ire) *trckd ldrs: rdn over 3f out: sn btn* **9/1**[3]
-441 8 *hd* **Realism (FR)**[8] [824] 4-9-9 53 ACulhane 6 49
(PWHiatt) *sn pushed along: a in rr* **7/4**[1]
06-2 9 *1 ¼* **Futuristic**[21] [695] 4-9-13 57 (v[1]) JQuinn 1 50
(JPearce) *prom tl rdn over 2f out: sn wknd* **5/1**[2]
0151 10 *shd* **Eager Angel (IRE)**[8] [826] 6-9-8 52 6ex (p) DeanMcKeown 11 45
(RFMarvin) *t.k.h: in tch tl wknd 2f out* **12/1**

1m 58.27s (7.27) **Going Correction** +0.775s/f (Slow)
**WFA** 3 from 4yo+ 19lb 10 Ran SP% **118.2**
Speed ratings: **94,93,93,91,91 91,88,88,86,86**CSF £298.55 CT £6769.21 TOTE £22.60: £4.90, £5.40, £4.50; EX 179.90.
**Owner** A P Griffin **Bred** G Reed **Trained** Newmarket, Suffolk

**FOCUS**
A very moderate winning time for the grade, more than two seconds slower the the second division. This is only modest form.

**NOTEBOOK**
**Geronimo** runs mainly over six or seven furlongs these days and the step up in trip helped him end a lengthy losing sequence.
**Desert Heat**, who went up 4lb for his win over father, was wearing first-time blinkers instead of the customary visor. He ran right up to form but did not find a great deal at the business end.
**Jakarmi** , who has only scored in selling and claiming company, ran a decent race but but this was not a strong event of its type.
**Danger Bird(IRE)** was keeping on at the one pace when running short of room at the furlong pole and having to be switched.
**Grand Lass(IRE)**, having her second run from this yard after being claimed from David Barron, was finishing as well as anything having lost her pitch.
**Givemethemoonlight**, having her twelfth race of the year, was set to be raised 4lb the following day.
**Realism(FR)** was slightly short of room at the first bend and was always trailing thereafter. Unpenalised for his win in an apprentice handicap, he was a stone well in here and this run will have disheartened connections. *Official explanation: trainer was unable to offer any explanation for the gelding's poor running*
**Futuristic** was reported to have been unsuited by the slow surface. *Official explanation: jockey said gelding was unsuited by the slow surface*

## 910 BET IN RUNNING @ BETDIRECT.CO.UK H'CAP (DIV II) 1m 100y(F)
4:50 (4:51) (F) (0-60,58) 3-Y-O+ £2,961 (£846; £423) Stalls Low

Form RPR
5213 1 **Dancing King (IRE)**[3] [875] 8-7-13 36 6ex BSwarbrick(7) 6 51
(PWHiatt) *mde all: rdn out fnl f* **10/3**[2]
4402 2 *3* **Lord Chamberlain**[7] [834] 11-9-12 56 (b) CCatlin 9 65
(JMBradley) *mid-div: hdwy to trck wnr 3f out: kpt on but no imp fnl f* **9/1**
4-56 3 *7* **Goodbye Mr Bond**[45] [512] 4-9-9 53 JQuinn 4 47
(EJAlston) *in tch: hdwy to go 3rd 2f out: no ch w first 2* **3/1**[1]
-422 4 *1* **Donegal Shore (IRE)**[12] [782] 5-9-2 51 (vt) NChalmers(5) 7 43
(MrsJCandlish) *mid-div: effrt over 3f out: nvr nr to chal* **16/1**
3500 5 *2* **Spy Gun (USA)**[13] [772] 4-9-12 56 DHolland 5 44
(TWall) *prom and w wnr early: wknd over 2f out* **13/2**[3]
0/01 6 *2* **Heathers Girl**[13] [776] 5-10-0 58 PaulEddery 2 42
(DHaydnJones) *trckd ldrs: wknd over 2f out* **16/1**
-400 7 *hd* **Shadowfax**[10] [805] 4-9-12 56 (e[1]) MFenton 8 39
(MissGayKelleway) *hld up: nvr on terms* **16/1**
5303 8 *¾* **Bulawayo**[10] [810] 7-8-11 48 SJDonohoe(7) 1 30
(AndrewReid) *in tch: rdn over 4f out: sn wknd* **12/1**
6544 9 *4* **Taiyo**[11] [800] 4-9-6 50 (v[1]) NCallan 10 23
(JWPayne) *in front mk tl wknd 3f out* **10/1**
10 *nk* **Temptation Island (IRE)**[149] [5318] 5-9-1 45 JPMurtagh 3 17
(JohnAQuinn, Ire) *a wl bhd* **10/1**

1m 56.24s (5.24) **Going Correction** +0.775s/f (Slow) 10 Ran SP% **114.9**
Speed ratings: **104,101,94,93,91 89,88,88,84,83**CSF £33.01 CT £101.35 TOTE £2.70: £1.40, £2.20, £2.20; EX 22.40 Place 6 £60.48, Place 5 £15.14.
**Owner** P W Hiatt **Bred** M O'Leary **Trained** Hook Norton, Oxon

**FOCUS**
A respectable time for the class of contest, more than two seconds faster than the first division. Only the first two, who showed strong form for the grade, were ever in it.

**NOTEBOOK**
**Dancing King(IRE)**, due to go up 9lb the next day, made all the running at a decent pace and stayed on to see off his sole challenger.
**Lord Chamberlain** was if anything travelling the better turning in, but was unable to get past. This former point-to-pointer is very hard to catch right.
**Goodbye Mr Bond** travelled quite well in midfield, but was briefly short of room on the home turn and when he got free the first two were beyond recall. *Official explanation: jockey said gelding was unlucky in running 3f out*
**Donegal Shore(IRE)**, upped in trip, turned into the straight in a moderate fourth place and made no impression on the leaders.
**Temptation Island(IRE)** *Official explanation: jockey said mare lost her action in the closing stages*
T/Jkpt: Not won. T/Plt: £49.20 to a £1 stake. Pool: £84,700.85. 1,255.15 winning tickets. T/Qpdt: £9.50 to a £1 stake. Pool: £9,514.00. 735.60 winning tickets. JS

# SAINT-CLOUD (L-H)
Friday, February 27

**OFFICIAL GOING: Soft**

## 911a PRIX VOLANDRY 1m
1:50 (1:52) 4-Y-0+ £10,211 (£4,085; £3,063; £2,042)

RPR
1 **Marshall (FR)**[271] [2043] 4-8-12 MBlancpain 9 109
(CLaffon-Parias, France)
2 *shd* **Night Bokbel (IRE)**[20] 5-9-1 CSoumillon 7 112
(DSmaga, France)
3 *2* **Fabuleux River (FR)**[131] 4-8-12 (b) DBonilla 4 105
(NMadamet, France)
4 *1 ½* **Spainnash (IRE)**[131] [5663] 4-8-12 SPasquier 3 102
(FRohaut, France)
5 *½* **Rashbag**[173] 5-9-1 (b) IMendizabal 8 104
(J-CRouget, France)
6 *2* **Qui Es Tu (IRE)**[90] [6101] 4-9-1 TJarnet 1 100
(J-MSauve, France)
7 *3* **Atahuelpa**[12] [785] 4-9-1 PRoberts 2 94
(MFHarris) *close up in 2nd, 3rd straight, ridden over 2f out, outpaced*
8 *¾* **Northern Shine (FR)**[90] 7-9-1 FSpanu 10 93
(ASpanu, France)
9 *2 ½* **Maia Eria (FR)**[117] 4-8-8 TThulliez 6 81
(Y-MPorzier, France)
10 *nk* **As Des As (FR)**[454] 5-8-12 C-PLemaire 5 84
(MmeLAudon, France)

1m 42.5s 10 Ran
Speed ratings: .
**Owner** Alec Head **Bred** Alec & Mme Ghislaine Head **Trained** France

**NOTEBOOK**
**Atahuelpa** was out of his depth in this grade and is better on a sounder surface anyway.

# 889 LINGFIELD (L-H)
Saturday, February 28

**OFFICIAL GOING: Standard**

## 912 DAILY OFFERS @ BETDIRECT.CO.UK H'CAP 5f (P)
1:30 (1:37) (D) (0-80,77) 3-Y-O+ £4,095 (£1,260; £630; £315) Stalls High

Form RPR
21-6 1 **Turibius**[21] [703] 5-10-0 77 KFallon 10 84
(TEPowell) *lw: chsd ldrs: drvn to ld wl ins fnl f: jst hld on* **8/1**
0-42 2 *hd* **Polish Emperor (USA)**[11] [806] 4-10-0 77 (b) DHolland 1 83
(PWHarris) *lw: flyj. s: towards rr tl hdwy 1/2-way: r.o strly fnl f: jst failed* **5/4**[1]
1156 3 *nk* **The Fisio**[11] [801] 4-9-10 73 MartinDwyer 6 78
(AMBalding) *led: rdn and hdd wl ins final f: kpt on* **6/1**[2]
650- 4 *1 ¼* **Another Glimpse**[220] [3509] 6-9-9 72 (t) TQuinn 4 73
(MissBSanders) *bit bkwd: chsd ldrs on ins: r.o fnl f but nt qckn* **33/1**
15-0 5 *¾* **Chico Guapo (IRE)**[7] [841] 4-10-0 77 DeanMcKeown 5 75
(JAGlover) *t.k.h: a mid-div and no threat fnl f* **16/1**
0/5 6 *nk* **Grant (IRE)**[5] [866] 4-9-1 64 (p) JPMurtagh 9 61
(PatrickMorris, Ire) *s.i.s: sn bhd and nvr threatened ldrs* **25/1**
6356 7 *½* **Lady Pekan**[1] [904] 5-8-13 62 (b) NCallan 7 57
(PSMcentee) *lw: trckd ldr tl rdn and wknd fnl f* **20/1**
06-5 8 *hd* **Awarding**[46] [515] 4-9-9 72 (t) DaneO'Neill 2 66
(RFJohnsonHoughton) *slowly away: effrt on outside wl over 1f out: sn no dnager* **7/1**[3]
1-20 9 *2* **Madrasee**[28] [646] 6-9-5 68 FLynch 8 55
(LMontagueHall) *prom: rdn 1/2-way: wknd appr fnl f* **14/1**
-034 10 *1 ¼* **Pheckless**[28] [646] 5-9-3 66 RHughes 3 49
(JMBradley) *s.i.s: a bhd* **9/1**

59.06 secs (-0.72) **Going Correction** -0.05s/f (Stan) 10 Ran SP% **116.4**
Speed ratings: **103,102,102,100,99 98,97,97,94,92**CSF £17.93 CT £68.53 TOTE £10.30: £2.20, £1.20, £2.00; EX 26.40.
**Owner** Vogue Development Company (kent) Ltd **Bred** Bearstone Stud **Trained** Reigate, Surrey

**FOCUS**
A tight finish to this competitive sprint handicap. Solid form.

**NOTEBOOK**
**Turibius**, taking a drop in grade, came through to lead in the final half furlong and just held on, having been prematurely eased, to his jockey's relief. He is high enough in the weights at the moment and connections will probably begin to concentrate on a turf campaign with him.
**Polish Emperor(USA)** lost his race at the start and did remarkably well to get as close as he did. *Official explanation: jockey said gelding jumped awkwardly leaving the stalls and lost some lengths*
**The Fisio** left a couple of disappointing efforts behind and was not beaten far. He looks handicapped out of winning at present, despite going close.
**Another Glimpse**, having his first start for 220 days, kept on without ever threatening to win the race, but would no doubt have pleased connections.
**Chico Guapo(IRE)** had nothing left when it mattered, having pulled too hard early.
**Awarding** is a frustrating character and lost his chance with a slow start.

## 913 BET DIRECT ON 0800 32 93 93 CONDITIONS STKS 1m (P)
2:00 (2:07) (B) 3-Y-O £12,035 (£4,565; £2,282; £1,037) Stalls High

Form RPR
1-12 1 **Ascertain (IRE)**[21] [704] 3-8-11 98 DHolland 4 94+
(NPLittmoden) *lw: trckd ldrs: a gng wl: led 1f out: r.o wl* **10/11**[1]
2-21 2 *2 ½* **Bahiano (IRE)**[4] [869] 3-8-11 72 KFallon 9 87+
(CEBrittain) *trckd ldr: led over 2f out: rdn and hdd 1f out: eased whn hld nr fin* **7/2**[2]
-361 3 *5* **Royal Warrant**[7] [843] 3-8-11 79 MartinDwyer 6 73
(AMBalding) *lw: hld up: rdn and hdwy 2f out: styd on to 3rd cl home* **4/1**[3]
016- 4 *hd* **Petardias Magic (IRE)**[76] [6189] 3-8-13 84 RFfrench 7 74
(EJO'Neill) *lw: t.k.h: racd wd: hdwy over 2f out: lost 3rd pl cl home* **20/1**
311- 5 *3 ½* **Firebelly**[237] [3044] 3-8-12 95 (v[1]) SDrowne 2 65
(MJWallace) *lw: prom: rdn over 2f out: n.d after* **16/1**
0430 6 *½* **Tonto (FR)**[11] [802] 3-8-11 60 (p) GCarter 10 63?
(MissDMountain) *in rr: nvr nr to chal* **100/1**

7 1 1/4 **Well Knit**[167] 3-8-6 ........ JFEgan 3 56
(PWD'Arcy) *leggy: a struggling in rr* **100/1**
023- 8 4 **Doctored**[135] 5599 3-8-11 54 ........ (p) CCatlin 1 52
(BAPearce) *bit bkwd: ld tl hdd over 2f out: sn btn* **100/1**
1 9 4 **Grouville**[42] 553 3-8-11 ........ PaulEddery 5 43
(BJMeehan) *trckd ldrs: rdn and wknd over 2f out* **20/1**
1m 37.91s (-1.60) **Going Correction** -0.05s/f (Stan) **9** Ran SP% **113.0**
Speed ratings: **106,103,98,98,94 94,93,89,85**CSF £3.91 TOTE £1.70: £1.10, £1.60, £1.40; EX 5.00.
**Owner** Paul J Dixon **Bred** Darley **Trained** Newmarket, Suffolk

**FOCUS**
Ascertain won this as expected and has the look of a real improving gelding. The form overall is governed by the likes of Tonto and Doctored, but the first two look better than the bare evidence and the winning time was smart.

**NOTEBOOK**
**Ascertain(IRE)**, who faced a stiff task giving 13lb to Skidmark latest, was well suited to the conditions of the race as he would have been conceding 26lb to Bahiano in a handicap. He stayed on strongly to win going away and is clearly progressing well. He may now be supplemented for the UAE Derby, but would have nothing more than an outsiders chance.
**Bahiano(IRE)** improved on previous form with a solid second, finishing well clear of the third. He will be of interest back on turf.
**Royal Warrant**, a winner in handicap company last time, found this hotter company too much, but was not disgraced.
**Petardias Magic(IRE)** was always going to struggle under his penalty, but is entitled to come on for the outing.
**Firebelly** had been off the track since July.

## 914 BETDIRECT.CO.UK NEW SITE COMING SOON H'CAP 1m 2f (P)
2:35 (2:41) (F) (0-52,52) 4-Y-O+ £2,961 (£846; £423) Stalls Low

Form RPR
5406 1 **Raheel (IRE)**[3] 887 4-8-11 49 ........ (t) DHolland 2 63
(PMitchell) *hld up in tch: hdwy and swtchd rt over 2f out: led 2f out: sn clr: easily* **10/3**[1]
00-6 2 4 **Indian Blaze**[28] 645 10-8-6 46 oh1 ........ TPQueally[(3)] 1 56+
(AndrewReid) *lw: hld up: hdwy on ins over 3f out: nt clr run over 2f out: r.o strly to go 2nd ins fnl f* **5/1**[3]
1435 3 3/4 **French Horn**[10] 821 7-8-11 48 ........ (p) GCarter 14 53
(MWigham) *lw: swtchd over to ins fr wd draw s: hld up: short of room and swtchd to outside 2f out: r.o fnl f* **14/1**
4-35 4 nk **Another Secret**[4] 874 6-8-12 49 ........ (be) SWhitworth 8 53
(GLMoore) *lw: s.i.s: hld up: hdwy over 2f out to chse wnr over 1f out: nt qckn fnl f* **9/2**[2]
-100 5 1 **Itsonlygame**[28] 645 4-8-12 50 ........ IMongan 9 53
(RIngram) *in rr: hdwy and hmpd over 4f out: rdn and hdwy 2f out: one pce fnl f* **16/1**
01-4 6 5 **So Sure (IRE)**[2] 902 4-9-0 52 ........ DeanMcKeown 11 46
(JGMO'Shea) *a in tch: rdn and wknd over 1f out* **13/2**
0/54 7 3 1/2 **Andaad**[12] 797 4-8-12 50 ........ CCatlin 6 37
(DJDaly) *in rr: passed sme btn horses fnl 2f* **16/1**
5030 8 nk **Kumakawa**[2] 894 6-8-2 46 oh1 ........ (b) LiamJones[(7)] 5 33
(EAWheeler) *a in rr* **20/1**
650- 9 1/2 **Tata Naka**[92] 6086 4-8-7 50 ........ HayleyTurner[(5)] 10 36
(MrsCADunnett) *trckd ldr: led over 2f out: sn hdd & wknd qckly* **33/1**
000- 10 7 **Ersaal (USA)**[63] 6247 4-8-10 48 ........ NCallan 4 21
(JJay) *prom tl rdn and wknd over 2f out* **40/1**
5-41 11 1 **Jade Star (USA)**[15] 763 4-9-0 52 ........ MFenton 7 24
(MissGayKelleway) *lw: led tl hdd over 2f out: wknd qckly* **5/1**[3]
OLL- 12 1/2 **Silver Louie (IRE)**[100] 4017 4-8-13 51 ........ SCarson 3 22
(GBBalding) *hld up in mid-div: rdn and wknd over 2f out* **66/1**
000/ 13 17 **Taca D'Oli (FR)**[509] 5124 5-9-1 52 ........ RFfrench 13 —
(EJO'Neill) *mid-div: wknd 4f out: t.o* **40/1**
00-0 14 dist **Silistra**[10] 818 5-8-13 50 ........ (v) DaneO'Neill 12 —
(MrsLCJewell) *trckd ldrs tl wknd over 4f out: t.o* **100/1**
2m 6.27s (-1.12) **Going Correction** -0.05s/f (Stan)
**WFA** 4 from 5yo+ 1lb **14** Ran SP% **121.4**
Speed ratings: **102,98,98,97,97 93,90,90,89,84 83,82,69,—**CSF £18.79 CT £212.31 TOTE £4.60: £1.70, £2.80, £5.30; EX 26.90.
**Owner** Mrs S Sheldon **Bred** Shadwell Estate Company Limited **Trained** Epsom, Surrey

**FOCUS**
A moderate handicap, in which there was no strength in depth, but they went a good gallop. Raheel had the race run to suit and came right away down the straight to win for the first time in 20 starts. Indian Blaze looks better than the bare result.

**NOTEBOOK**
**Raheel(IRE)** was getting off the mark at the 20th attempt and did it easily. He was always travelling strongly and came through to take it up on the turn for home before running on all the way to the line. He has his quirks and was suited by the decent pace, but this win may do his confidence good.
**Indian Blaze** was slightly unlucky not to get closer to the winner as he was travelling well when short of room as the winner kicked.
**French Horn** kept on without ever threatening.
**Another Secret** is well exposed and not one to follow, having won only one of his 31 starts.
**Jade Star(USA)** went too fast for her own good and should have the run ignored.

## 915 LITTLEWOODS BET DIRECT H'CAP 1m 2f (P)
3:10 (3:16) (C) (0-95,95) 3-Y-O+ £12,151 (£4,609; £2,304; £1,047) Stalls Low

Form RPR
/111 1 **Consonant (IRE)**[8] 837 7-9-5 86 ........ KFallon 3 97
(DGBridgwater) *a gng wl bhd ldrs: led 1f out: drvn out* **5/1**[2]
0-64 2 3/4 **Dance In The Sun**[35] 600 4-9-3 85 ........ DaneO'Neill 1 95
(MrsAJPerrett) *led tl rdn and hdd 1f out: kpt on to line* **7/1**[3]
-220 3 shd **Northside Lodge (IRE)**[14] 768 6-9-6 87 ........ IMongan 6 97
(PWHarris) *hld up: rdn and hdwy over 2f out: swtchd rt appr fnl f: r.o* **9/2**[1]
015- 4 3/4 **Arry Dash**[309] 1206 4-9-2 87 ........ SHitchcott[(3)] 5 95
(MRChannon) *hld up: hdwy on ins wl over 1f out: r.o wl fnl f* **14/1**
-101 5 3/4 **Gig Harbor**[21] 706 5-9-11 95 ........ LPKeniry[(3)] 2 102
(MissECLavelle) *lw: trckd ldr tl no ex appr fnl f* **10/1**
0-12 6 1/2 **Moayed**[14] 768 5-9-1 82 ........ (bt) DHolland 10 88
(NPLittmoden) *hld up in rr: hdwy on ouside 2f out: fdd ins fnl f* **5/1**[2]
7 shd **Qudrah (IRE)**[128] 4-9-3 85 ........ (b[1]) RFfrench 4 91
(EJO'Neill) *w'like: a in tch tl one pce fnl f* **66/1**
4-66 8 1 **Kentucky King (USA)**[8] 837 4-8-12 80 ........ ACulhane 8 84
(PWHiatt) *in tch: rdn over 3f out: outpcd ent fnl f* **66/1**
403- 9 nk **Dumaran (IRE)**[126] 5753 6-9-11 92 ........ MFenton 7 96
(WJMusson) *bit bkwd: slowly away: towards rr and nvr nr to chal* **20/1**
4654 10 3 **Dower House**[14] 768 9-8-10 80 ........ (t) DCorby[(3)] 9 78
(AndrewTurnell) *lw: t.k.h: hld up in rr: nvr on terms* **14/1**
6-61 11 2 **African Sahara (USA)**[14] 768 5-8-12 79 ........ (t) GCarter 13 74
(MissDMountain) *a towards rr* **10/1**
-233 12 1 **Skylarker (USA)**[14] 775 6-8-8 80 ow1 ........ (v[1]) MSavage[(5)] 11 73
(WSKittow) *t.k.h: trckd ldrs: rdn 3f out: wknd wl over 1f out* **20/1**
2-51 13 nk **Mad Carew (USA)**[10] 820 5-8-12 79 ........ (be) SWhitworth 14 71
(GLMoore) *in tch tl wknd over 2f out* **16/1**
021- 14 1 1/2 **Turbo (IRE)**[90] 5952 5-9-13 94 ........ (p) RHavlin 12 84
(GBBalding) *bit bkwd: slowly away: a in rr* **9/1**
2m 5.41s (-1.98) **Going Correction** -0.05s/f (Stan)
**WFA** 4 from 5yo+ 1lb **14** Ran SP% **123.9**
Speed ratings: **105,104,104,103,103 102,102,101,101,99 97,96,96,95**CSF £39.84 CT £173.62 TOTE £4.60: £2.50, £2.50, £2.20; EX 47.40 Trifecta £224.10 Pool £1,262.86 - 4 winning units..
**Owner** The Rule Racing Syndicate **Bred** Kilfrush Stud Ltd **Trained** Winchcombe, Gloucs

**FOCUS**
Strong handicap form in this competitive race. Consonant continues unbeaten since returning from injury, and Dance In The Sun and Arry Dash remain progressive, the last-named in particular appealing as one to take for the future.

**NOTEBOOK**
**Consonant(IRE)** has been a revelation since returning from injury and proved his effectiveness on the surface with a solid display. His three previous wins had been at Wolverhampton, but he clearly acts well on the Polytrack and who is to say he can not make it a five-timer.
**Dance In The Sun** is still not exposed and deserves credit for this effort. She is effective at further and should be winning before long.
**Northside Lodge(IRE)** is exposed and still on a 14lb higher mark than when last winning.
**Arry Dash**, a Lincoln hopeful, made a most pleasing return to the action and is the one to take from the race for the future. To get into the Lincoln however, he will have to win beforehand as he is currently unlikely to get in.
**Gig Harbor** appears to be in the handicapper's grip.
**Moayed**, unlucky not to win at the course last time, had every chance, but seemingly failed to see out the trip.

## 916 BETDIRECT.CO.UK MAIDEN STKS 1m 2f (P)
3:40 (3:47) (D) 3-Y-O £5,174 (£1,592; £796; £398) Stalls Low

Form RPR
00-6 1 **Dancing Lyra**[31] 621 3-9-0 73 ........ MHills 7 75
(JWHills) *trckd ldr: led over 2f out: rdn out fnl f* **8/1**
0-31 2 1 1/4 **Fiddlers Ford (IRE)**[35] 598 3-9-0 72 ........ JPSpencer 5 73
(JNoseda) *hld up in tch: rapid hdwy 2f out: chsd wnr ins fnl f* **8/11**[1]
3 nk **Swainson (USA)** 3-9-0 ........ DHolland 9 72
(PMitchell) *neat: b. bkwd: s.i.s and plld hrd early: sn chsng ldrs: wnt 2nd 2f out tl ins fnl f* **16/1**
4 1 1/4 **Zangeal** 3-9-0 ........ GBaker 14 70
(CFWall) *gd sort: rangy: strong: bit bkwd: slowly away and in rr tl hdwy and rn green over 1f out: r.o ins fnl f: should do bttr* **25/1**
2233 5 1 1/2 **Amwell Brave**[17] 739 3-9-0 68 ........ KFallon 2 68
(JRJenkins) *lw: trckd ldrs: rdn over 3f out: one pce fnl f* **15/2**[3]
0 6 1/2 **Zaffeu**[17] 739 3-8-11 ........ TPQueally[(3)] 4 67
(NPLittmoden) *in tch: rdn 3f out: one pce fnl f* **33/1**
00- 7 4 **Ameyrah (IRE)**[107] 5986 3-8-6 ........ SHitchcott[(3)] 8 54
(MRChannon) *hld up: rdn over 3f out: nvr nr to chal* **16/1**
43-2 8 1 1/4 **Resonance**[10] 818 3-8-9 70 ........ JoannaBadger 10 52
(NATwiston-Davies) *slowly aways: a towards rr* **6/1**[2]
000- 9 hd **Foxilla (IRE)**[176] 4706 3-8-9 63 ........ DaneO'Neill 12 52
(DRCElsworth) *mid-div: rdn 4f out: wknd wl over 1f out* **50/1**
0 10 nk **Saint Zita (IRE)**[14] 766 3-8-4 ........ JFMcDonald[(5)] 3 51
(BJMeehan) *led tl hdd over 2f out. wknd over 1f out* **66/1**
00-6 11 hd **Atlantic Tern**[49] 492 3-9-0 53 ........ NCallan 13 56
(NMBabbage) *a in rr* **100/1**
04 12 5 **Champagne Shadow (IRE)**[17] 739 3-9-0 ........ (b[1]) IMongan 6 47
(GLMoore) *a in rr* **16/1**
13 4 **Highfluting** 3-8-9 ........ DSweeney 1 35
(RMFlower) *small: hld up: a in rr* **100/1**
14 3/4 **Lakaam** 3-8-9 ........ RBrisland 11 33
(GPEnright) *leggy: bit bkwd: racd wd: rdn 4f out: sn bhd* **100/1**
2m 11.86s (4.47) **Going Correction** -0.05s/f (Stan) **14** Ran SP% **125.9**
Speed ratings: **80,79,78,77,76 76,72,71,71,71 71,67,64,63**CSF £14.49 TOTE £8.30: £1.70, £1.10, £4.70; EX 24.70.
**Owner** N N Browne **Bred** Shadwell Estate Company Limited **Trained** Upper Lambourn, Berks
■ Stewards Enquiry : M Hills caution: careless riding

**FOCUS**
They went no more than a modest pace and Dancing Lyra, translating his useful turf form to Polytrack at the second attempt, was ideally placed throughout. Just average maiden form overall and the time was pedestrian, but the first two should pay their way in turf handicaps and the third looks promising.

**NOTEBOOK**
**Dancing Lyra**, who posted some very useful form as a juvenile, namely when seventh in the Chesham Stakes, lost all chance of winning on his seasonal return when losing his pitch and this extra quarter mile suited well. He was always up with the pace and had the race in the bag at the furlong marker. He will be of interest in handicap company back on the turf.
**Fiddlers Ford(IRE)**, disqualified from first place at the course last month, could not match the winner for pace and will appreciate the step up to a mile and a half.
**Swainson(USA)** ◆, an interesting newcomer, was tardy on leaving the stalls, but soon up with the pace travelling strongly. He lost second close home, but connections will take plenty of positives from this and he should be winning before long if going the right way.
**Zangeal** ◆, a half-brother to High Accolade who took the eye in the prliminaries, did ever so well to finish fourth, having been slowly away and run green in rear. He finished well and looks a winner waiting to happen.
**Amwell Brave** is well exposed and was always going to be vulnerable to an improver.
**Resonance** never got competitive

## 917 NEW SITE COMING SOON @ BETDIRECT.CO.UK FILLIES' H'CAP 6f (P)
4:15 (4:21) (E) (0-75,75) 3-Y-O+ £3,386 (£1,042; £521; £260) Stalls Low

Form RPR
-561 1 **Forever Phoenix**[11] 803 4-9-9 70 ........ JPMurtagh 1 83+
(RMHCowell) *lw: a in tch on ins: led ent fnl f: sn clr: easily* **3/1**[1]
5-06 2 3 **And Toto Too**[17] 742 4-9-8 69 ........ (b) KFallon 10 73
(PDEvans) *slowly away: hdwy over 1f out: r.o to go 2nd ins fnl f* **9/2**[3]
0120 3 nk **Blonde En Blonde (IRE)**[17] 742 4-9-7 68 ........ IMongan 9 71
(NPLittmoden) *outpcd: hdwy on outside whn edgd lft appr fnl f: r.o* **8/1**
-100 4 1 **Classic Vision**[14] 771 4-8-9 56 ........ ACulhane 8 56
(WJHaggas) *slowly away in rr: styd on ins fnl f: nvr nrr* **25/1**
0-05 5 1/2 **Lydia's Look (IRE)**[12] 792 7-7-12 45 oh5 ........ DKinsella 2 44
(TJEtherington) *in tch: rdn over 2f out: one pce fnl f* **50/1**
0- 6 nk **Margalita (IRE)**[70] 6224 4-10-0 75 ........ DHolland 3 73
(PMitchell) *led tl rdn and hdd ent fnl f: no ex* **16/1**

260- **7** ¾ **Woodbury**[91] 6092 5-8-9 **56** GBaker 7 51
(KRBurke) *racd wd: trckd ldrs tl wknd appr fnl f* **14/1**
300- **8** ½ **Man Crazy (IRE)**[61] 6251 3-8-3 **65** JMackay 4 59
(RMBeckett) *a outpcd in rr* **20/1**
421- **9** 1 **Miss Poppets**[131] 5678 4-9-6 **67** TQuinn 5 58
(DRCElsworth) *mid-div: effrt on outside wl over 1f out: wkng whn hmpd ent fnl f* **6/1**
-632 **10** ¾ **Park Star**[2] 896 4-8-3 **55** JFMcDonald(5) 6 44
(DShaw) *lw: trckd ldr tl wknd over 1f out* **10/3**[2]
/0-0 **11** 3 **Luceball (IRE)**[2] 896 4-7-13 **46** (b) JQuinn 11 26
(PatrickMorris, Ire) *chsd ldrs tl wknd over 1f out* **16/1**

1m 11.99s (-0.93) **Going Correction** -0.05s/f (Stan)
**WFA** 3 from 4yo+ 15lb **11** Ran SP% **120.7**
Speed ratings: **104,100,99,98,97 97,96,95,94,93 89**CSF £16.77 CT £102.71 TOTE £3.60: £1.50, £2.10, £2.60; EX 17.40.
**Owner** J M Greetham **Bred** J M Greetham **Trained** Six Mile Bottom, Cambs

**FOCUS**
This had looked a tricky race beforehand, but improving filly Forever Phoenix turned the race into her own and the time was good. She will take an awful lot of beating in her bid for a hat-trick.

**NOTEBOOK**
**Forever Phoenix**, 5lb higher than when winning easily last time, had no trouble defying that rise and again won as she pleased. She had proved disappointing at the course last month, but showed she acts well on the Polytrack with this display and has every chance of completing the hat-trick.
**And Toto Too** stayed on to claim second, having been slowly away, and deserves some credit for her effort.
**Blonde En Blonde(IRE)** is 5lb higher than when winning at the course last month. She did nothing wrong but needs a return to seven. *Official explanation: jockey said filly was struck into*
**Classic Vision** left a couple of disappointing efforts behind and stayed on for a share of the prize-money. She shapes as though the step up to seven furlongs will suit.
**Lydia's Look(IRE)** is not getting any better and ran as well as could have been expected.

## 918 BET DIRECT ON 0800 32 93 93 H'CAP 7f (P)
**4:50** (4:56) (F ) (0-52,56) 3-Y-0+ **£3,073** (£878; £439) **Stalls** Low

Form RPR
4013 **1** **Alafzar (IRE)**[3] 888 6-9-11 **56** (bt) KFallon 4 69
(PDEvans) *lw: hld up: hdwy and edgd lft 2f out: led ins fnl f: r.o wl* **13/8**[1]
2-00 **2** 1¼ **Lily Of The Guild (IRE)**[21] 701 5-9-7 **52** NCallan 11 62
(WSKittow) *lw: in rr: rapid hdwy 2f out: chsd wnr ins fnl f* **8/1**
-322 **3** ¾ **Blakeseven**[9] 824 4-9-3 **48** PaulEddery 13 56
(WJMusson) *in rr: hdwy on outside over 1f out: r.o wl* **11/1**
-552 **4** nk **Zak Facta (IRE)**[11] 805 4-9-5 **50** (vt) SWhitworth 7 57
(MissDAMchale) *t.k.h: towards rr prog over 1f out: kpt on: nvr nrr* **6/1**[2]
3500 **5** ¾ **Scarrottoo**[2] 895 6-9-5 **50** MartinDwyer 9 55
(SCWilliams) *trckd ldr: led 2f out: hdd and one pce ins fnl f* **11/1**
000 **6** 2 **Mister Clinton (IRE)**[10] 815 7-8-12 **46** (b) RMiles(3) 1 46
(DKIvory) *plld hrd and in rr: hdwy and nt clr run 2f out: kpt on but nt a danger after* **20/1**
5314 **7** ¾ **Aguila Loco (IRE)**[2] 895 5-9-9 **54** (p) MFenton 8 52
(MrsStefLiddiard) *led: hdd 2f out: wknd appr fnl f* **7/1**[3]
40-5 **8** 2 **Joint Destiny (IRE)**[40] 566 3-8-1 **49** RFfrench 3 42
(EJO'Neill) *s.i.s: nvr on terms* **40/1**
5-54 **9** hd **Dancing Prince (IRE)**[11] 808 3-8-2 **50** CCatlin 2 43
(APJarvis) *chsd ldrs tl wknd over 1f out* **16/1**
4000 **10** nk **Little Flute**[10] 819 3-7-9 **46** oh1 LisaJones(3) 12 38
(TKeddy) *lw: v.s.a: a in rr* **33/1**
0-26 **11** 5 **Robin Sharp**[25] 667 6-9-3 **48** (vt) JQuinn 10 27
(JAkehurst) *racd on outside: chsd ldrs: rdn 1/2-way: sn btn* **20/1**
040- **12** 3½ **Tree Roofer**[185] 4510 5-9-3 **48** DHolland 5 19
(NPLittmoden) *chsd ldrs: short of room over 2f out: little ch after* **16/1**
340- **13** 9 **Fire Dome (IRE)**[107] 5985 12-9-7 **52** (t) IMongan 6 —
(AndrewReid) *b: b.hind: hld up in tch: rdn 1/2-way: sn bhd* **40/1**

1m 25.16s (-0.84) **Going Correction** -0.05s/f (Stan)
**WFA** 3 from 4yo+ 17lb **13** Ran SP% **121.8**
Speed ratings: **102,100,99,99,98 96,95,93,92,92 86,82,72**CSF £13.97 CT £116.95 TOTE £2.10: £1.40, £2.00, £3.50; EX 17.90.
**Owner** Waterline Racing Club **Bred** His Highness The Aga Khan's Studs S C **Trained** Pandy, Gwent
■ Stewards Enquiry : K Fallon caution: careless riding
M Fenton one-day ban: careless riding (Mar 13)

**FOCUS**
Alafzar won this with a bit to spare, but it was no more than a fair race, with six of the thirteen runners still being maidens.

**NOTEBOOK**
**Alafzar(IRE)**, who has run a couple of fine races under Fallon at the course in the last couple of weeks, winning and finishing placed, defied top weight in good style, coming through to take it up entering the final furlong. He won with a little in hand and is well enough handicapped to win again.
**Lily Of The Guild(IRE)** confirmed the promise of her two recent runs at the course with a running on second. She does not win very often and would not be one to take a short price about.
**Blakeseven** ran another good race without winning. He remains a maiden after 18 starts, but his turn should come.
**Zak Facta(IRE)** was edging closer with every stride, but remains a maiden after 23 starts.
**Scarrottoo** is a rather frustrating character and can afford to be missed when winning again.

## 919 MAXIE FANTONI 95TH ANNIVERSARY H'CAP 1m 5f (P)
**5:20** (5:25) (F ) (0-65,63) 4-Y-0+ **£3,038** (£868; £434) **Stalls** Low

Form RPR
/4-4 **1** **Crossways**[28] 650 6-10-0 **63** KFallon 1 70
(PDEvans) *lw: a.p: drvn to ld appr fnl f: all out* **11/4**[1]
55-1 **2** hd **Dolzago**[24] 676 4-9-7 **60** (b) IMongan 3 67
(GLMoore) *lw: trckd ldr: led over 2f out: hdd appr fnl f: rallied gamely: jst failed* **13/2**[3]
-222 **3** 1¼ **Jadeeron**[14] 777 5-9-10 **62** (p) LisaJones(3) 8 67
(MissDAMchale) *in rr tl gd hdwy 2f out: styd on same pce* **3/1**[2]
30 **4** 1¼ **Munfarid (IRE)**[28] 645 4-9-7 **60** (t) SDrowne 6 64
(PGMurphy) *hld up in tch: rdn and no imp appr fnl f* **25/1**
310- **5** 1½ **Turtle Valley (IRE)**[154] 5220 8-9-4 **60** JCoffill-Brown(7) 5 61
(SDow) *bit bkwd: towards rr: hdwy 2f out: rdn appr fnl f: no imp* **25/1**
-506 **6** ½ **Joely Green**[4] 867 7-9-6 **55** DHolland 4 56
(NPLittmoden) *prom: rdn over 3f out: fdd over 1f out* **12/1**
P-00 **7** 1 **Mysterlover (IRE)**[28] 651 4-9-0 **56** (t) TPQueally(3) 2 55
(NPLittmoden) *mid-div: rdn over 3f out: one pce after* **33/1**
2612 **8** 2 **Radiant Bride**[4] 879 4-8-6 **45** (b) DarrenWilliams 7 42
(KRBurke) *slowly away: in rr tl sme hdwy 2f out: nvr nr to chal* **8/1**
0-00 **9** ¾ **Forever My Lord**[4] 867 6-8-12 **47** NPollard 9 42
(JRBest) *led tl hdd over 2f out: wknd over 1f out* **16/1**
-530 **10** 2 **Antony Ebeneezer**[19] 724 5-8-0 **35** (t) JBramhill 11 28
(CRDore) *a in rr* **14/1**
006- **11** 16 **Angels Venture**[100] 2082 8-9-1 **50** PDobbs 12 20
(JRJenkins) *in tch tl wknd 4f out* **14/1**
630- **12** 8 **Murzim**[119] 3923 5-9-10 **59** JPSpencer 10 18
(JGallagher) *slowly away: in tch after 3f: rdn 4f out: wknd over 2f out* **10/1**

2m 46.9s (-1.18) **Going Correction** -0.05s/f (Stan)
**WFA** 4 from 5yo+ 4lb **12** Ran SP% **122.7**
Speed ratings: **101,100,100,99,98 98,97,96,95,94 84,79**CSF £21.41 CT £59.35 TOTE £3.80: £1.40, £2.00, £1.60; EX 27.50 Place 6 £6.77, Place 5 £5.05..
**Owner** Trevor Gallienne **Bred** P And Mrs Venner **Trained** Pandy, Gwent

**FOCUS**
No more than a fair handicap, but a good finish.

**NOTEBOOK**
**Crossways**, who made a decent reappearance over a mile two at the course last month, was up there throughout and needed every ounce of Fallon's strength to hold on. This was a fair performance under top weight.
**Dolzago**, who gave a game performance to lose his maiden tag at the course last month in the first-time blinkers, pushed the favourite all the way to the line and nearly got back up. This was a sound effort given he was back in this company off a 12lb higher mark, and the blinkers clearly help him.
**Jadeeron** ran another sound race without winning, but is not one to take a short price about as his win record reads one from 37.
**Munfarid(IRE)** left a shocking effort behind with this keeping-on fourth.
**Radiant Bride** *Official explanation: jockey said filly hung left*
T/Plt: £12.30 to a £1 stake. Pool: £65,432.40. 3,856.35 winning tickets. T/Qpdt: £11.10 to a £1 stake. Pool: £3,003.70. 200.20 winning tickets. JS

# 848 NAD AL SHEBA (L-H)
Saturday, February 28
**OFFICIAL GOING: Turf course - good to firm; dirt course -fast**

## 920a SKYWARDS STKS (CONDITIONS RACE) (DIRT) 7f 110y
**3:40** (3:41) 3-Y-0 **£9,078** (£2,793; £1,396; £698) **Stalls** Low

RPR
**1** **Rosencrans (USA)**[23] 691 3-8-9 98 (vt) LDettori 4 106
(SaeedBinSuroor) *mde all; drew clr 2f out: eased fnl 110yds: v easily* **1/2**[1]
**2** 9½ **Storm Of Tara (USA)**[7] 848 3-8-9 88 (bt[1]) GHind 2 87
(MAlKurdi, UAE) *in tch: 4th st: kpt on wl fnl 2f: no ch w wnr* **12/1**[3]
**3** 5¾ **Prince Of Denmark (IRE)**[7] 848 3-8-9 95 (t) TEDurcan 7 76
(MAlKurdi, UAE) *trckd ldrs: 3rd st: rdn to chal over 2f out: wknd fnl 1 1/2f* **3/1**[2]
**4** 1¾ **Slane Hill (USA)**[16] 753 3-8-9 80 (vt) RLMoore 3 72
(MAlKurdi, UAE) *chsd ldrs: 6th st: kpt on fnl 2f* **33/1**
**5** 4½ **Dillagi (USA)**[64] 3-8-9 PaulSmith 6 63
(AllanSmith, UAE) *in tch towards rr: 5th st: kpt on same pce fnl 2f* **20/1**
**6** 1¾ **Raisoot (USA)**[114] 3-8-9 (b[1]) BDoyle 5 60
(AllanSmith, UAE) *sn outpcd in rr: last and racd wd st: n.d* **33/1**
**7** 11 **Prim (BRZ)**[197] 3-9-4 90 WSupple 1 47
(ASelvaratnam, UAE) *trckd ldr: w ldr 5f out: 2nd st: sn wknd: eased fnl 110yds* **16/1**

1m 31.42s **7** Ran SP% **115.9**
Speed ratings: .
**Owner** Godolphin **Bred** *unknown **Trained** Newmarket, Suffolk

**NOTEBOOK**
**Rosencrans(USA)** built on his third in the UAE 2000 Guineas to run away with this conditions event. He is likely to be stepped back up in grade next time.

## 921a EMIRATES AIRLINE TROPHY (H'CAP) (TURF) 6f 110y
**4:10** (4:12) (90-110,110) 3-Y-0+ **£36,312** (£11,173; £5,586; £2,793) **Stalls** Low

RPR
**1** 1¾ **Cat Belling (IRE)**[7] 850 4-9-1 100 WSupple 4 99
(RBouresly, Kuwait) *towards rr: hdwy 2f out: chal 1f out: nt pce of wnr: fin 2nd: plcd 1st* **9/2**[2]
**2** 1¼ **Naughty Nell**[9] 831 5-8-9 90 RMullen 1 93
(PBrette, Dubai) *in tch in rr: swtched rt and hdwy over 2f out: kpt on: nrst fin: fin 3rd: plcd 2nd* **9/1**
**3** ½ **Rotulo (ARG)**[9] 830 6-8-9 91 (t) KMcEvoy 5 92
(DiegoLowther, Sweden) *trckd ldrs: nt clr run over 2f out: swtchd rt and hdwy over 1f out: no ex nr fin: fin 4th: plcd 3rd* **10/1**
**4** 1¼ **Fruit Of Glory**[9] 831 5-8-9 90 RLMoore 7 88
(MRChannon) *disp ld: led st: rdn 2 1/2f out: hdd fnl f: sn wknd: fin 5th: plcd 4th* **6/1**
**5** hd **A Touch Of Frost**[9] 831 9-8-9 93 (b) ASaffar 6 87
(NDeCroutte, Bahrain) *in tch towards rr: rdn and effrt 2f out: kpt on same pce: fin 6th: plcd 5th* **5/1**[3]
**6** 1¼ **Royal Beacon**[7] 850 4-9-1 100 (b) GBirrer 2 89
(ChristianWroe, UAE) *towards rr: 8th on ins st: kpt on fnl 2f: nt rch ldrs: fin 7th: plcd 6th* **33/1**
**7** 1¾ **Peruvian Chief (IRE)**[7] 851 7-8-10 96 (v) SChin 10 79
(NPLittmoden) *hld up: trckd ldrs: rdn 2f out: wknd fnl f: fin 8th: plcd 7th* **16/1**
**8** ¾ **Hazelhatch**[7] 852 4-8-9 95 (t) GHind 9 76
(MAlKurdi, UAE) *disp ld tl hdd st: grad wknd: fin 9th: plcd 8th* **5/1**[3]
**9** 8¾ **Night Aurora**[415] 5-8-9 90 BDoyle 8 50
(ASelvaratnam, UAE) *rrd s: sn trckd ldrs: rdn st: wknd fnl 1 1/2f: fin 10th: plcd 9th* **40/1**
**D** **Feet So Fast**[9] 5-9-11 110 TEDurcan 3 114
(SSeemar, UAE) *in tch towards rr: 9th and hdwy st: r.o wl to ld 1f out: drvn out: fin 1st, 1 ¾l: disqualified - jockey weighed in light* **10/3**[1]

1m 17.0s **10** Ran SP% **119.2**
Speed ratings: .
**Owner** Bouresly Racing Syndicate **Bred** Mrs M O'Callaghan **Trained** Kuwait

**NOTEBOOK**
**Cat Belling(IRE)** has really hit form since being dropped back from a mile and followed up her recent success over an extended seven furlongs.
**Fruit Of Glory** showed plenty of pace on this drop back from a mile and ran respectably.
**Peruvian Chief(IRE)** has yet to hit top form.
**Feet So Fast**, without a win for over a year, and switching from dirt to turf, finished first past the post but weighed in light.

## 922a EMIRATES AIRLINE STKS (H'CAP) (TURF) 1m 2f
4:45 (4:46) (90-105,105) 3-Y-O+ £32,681 (£10,055; £5,027; £2,513) Stalls Low

RPR

1 **Adiemus**$^{9}$ 832 6-9-0 98 (v) LDettori 3 106
(JNoseda) *in tch in rr: prog on ins ent st: smooth hdwy to ld over 1f out: rdn out* **3/1**$^{1}$

2 3 **Swift Tango (IRE)**$^{16}$ 757 4-8-6 90 PHanagan 5 94
(EALDunlop) *mid-div: rdn and hdwy 2f out: chal and ev ch 1f out: nt pce of wnr* **9/1**

3 2 3/4 **Anani (USA)**$^{16}$ 756 4-9-6 105 WSupple 7 103
(EALDunlop) *mid-div: rdn and hdwy 2f out: kpt on nr fin: nt rch ldrs* **9/2**$^{3}$

4 3/4 **Clodion (IRE)**$^{7}$ 854 8-9-2 100 TEDurcan 11 97
(MAlKurdi, UAE) *towards rr: rdn st: styd on wl fnl f: nrst fin* **10/1**

5 3/4 **Red Crescent (SAF)**$^{7}$ 853 6-8-6 90 (t) KMcEvoy 9 86
(SSeemar, UAE) *trckd ldrs: led 4f out: rdn 2f out: hdd over 1f out: sn wknd* **50/1**

6 4 3/4 **Camelot**$^{16}$ 757 5-8-6 90 (b$^{1}$) RHills 4 77
(GAButler) *mid-div: rdn and effrt 2f out: kpt on same pce* **16/1**

7 1/2 **Mubeen (IRE)**$^{16}$ 757 4-8-13 97 GHind 1 84
(ECharpy, UAE) *towards rr: racd wd st: effrt 2f out: wknd nr fin* **7/2**$^{2}$

8 3 3/4 **Impaciente Gg (URU)**$^{7}$ 854 4-8-8 93 MWilliamson 8 73
(ASelvaratnam, UAE) *mid-div: prog 4f out: wknd fnl 2f* **28/1**

9 3 1/4 **Surbiton (USA)**$^{23}$ 687 4-9-5 104 (b) RMullen 6 78
(AAlRaihe, UAE) *trckd ldrs: hrd rdn st: wknd 2f out* **12/1**

10 6 3/4 **Genereux (ARG)**$^{190}$ 4-8-10 95 RLMoore 2 57
(SSeemar, UAE) *mid-div tl wknd st* **7/1**

11 12 **Al Moulatham**$^{23}$ 692 5-8-13 97 (bt) SSanders 12 38
(ECharpy, UAE) *led tl hrd rdn and hdd 4f out: sn wknd: eased fnl 110yds* **11/1**

12 6 1/4 **Arabie**$^{16}$ 757 6-8-10 95 (b) SChin 10 24
(MJohnston) *trckd ldr tl wknd fr 1/2-way* **50/1**

2m 3.90s
**WFA** 4 from 5yo+ 1lb **12** Ran SP% **126.3**
Speed ratings: .
**Owner** G Lansbury **Bred** Stanley Estate And Stud Co **Trained** Newmarket, Suffolk

**NOTEBOOK**
**Adiemus** is not ideally suited is by the dirt surface in Dubai so this switch to turf was just what was required.
**Swift Tango(IRE)**, another who did not appear to take to the Dubai dirt, ran much better on this switch to turf but found the winner too good.
**Anani(USA)** was another to appreciate a return to turf.
**Camelot**, switching from the dirt to turf, and with blinkers fitted for the first time, was well beaten.
**Arabie** has beaten just one horse home in three starts in Dubai this year.

## 923a EMIRATES AIRLINE CLASSIC H'CAP (DIRT) 6f
5:15 (5:16) (90-110,105) 3-Y-O+ £36,312 (£11,173; £5,586; £2,793) Stalls High

RPR

1 **Saddad (USA)**$^{92}$ 5-8-9 90 RHills 2 102
(DougWatson, UAE) *a.p: led fr 1/2-way: rdn clr 1 1/2f out: kpt on u.p nr fin: jst hld on* **16/1**

2 shd **Sleeping Weapon (USA)**$^{8}$ 5-8-9 90 (vt) WSupple 1 101
(DougWatson, UAE) *chsd wnr: rdn fr 1/2-way: r.o wl fnl 110yds: jst failed* **5/1**$^{3}$

3 3 3/4 **Bo Bid (USA)**$^{9}$ 4-8-10 91 (vt) RLMoore 4 91
(MAlKurdi, UAE) *prom: rdn fr 1/2-way: kpt on same pce* **10/1**

4 5 **Stormont (IRE)**$^{134}$ 5615 4-9-1 96 LDettori 6 81
(HJCollingridge) *trckd ldrs: rdn 2f out: no ex fnl f* **3/1**$^{2}$

5 1 1/4 **Bold Demand**$^{16}$ 754 10-9-7 102 BDoyle 3 83
(RBouresly, Kuwait) *trckd ldrs: rdn fr 1/2-way: wknd fnl 2f* **11/2**

6 3/4 **Lord Nelson (AUS)**$^{9}$ 830 3-8-9 95 (t) MDuPlessis 9 84
(MThwaites, Macau) *prom early: rdn and grad wknd fr 1/2-way* **9/4**$^{1}$

7 8 **Meshty (IRE)**$^{8}$ 9-8-9 90 GHind 8 45
(MAlKurdi, UAE) *sn outpcd in rr: kpt on nr fin: nvr trbld ldrs* **10/1**

8 1 1/4 **Sarayat**$^{16}$ 755 4-9-3 98 PaulSmith 10 49
(AllanSmith, UAE) *chsd ldrs stands' side: wknd fr 1/2-way* **33/1**

9 1 3/4 **Three Points**$^{9}$ 7-9-0 95 (t) PHanagan 7 41
(PRudkin, UAE) *prom tl rdn and wknd fr 1/2-way* **20/1**

1m 10.94s
**WFA** 3 from 4yo+ 15lb **9** Ran SP% **119.6**
Speed ratings: .
**Owner** Hamdan Al Maktoum **Bred** Foxfield **Trained** United Arab Emirates

**NOTEBOOK**
**Stormont(IRE)**, winner of a German Group Two last autumn, ran well up to a point but probably needed this first run since October.

## 924a EMIRATES AIRLINE CUP (H'CAP) (TURF) 6f 110y
5:45 (5:46) (90-110,102) 3-Y-O+ £36,312 (£11,173; £5,586; £2,793) Stalls Low

RPR

1 **Pic Up Sticks**$^{16}$ 755 5-8-10 91 TEDurcan 3 92
(MRChannon) *mid-div: 5th st: rdn and hdwy over 2f out: led over 1f out: drvn out* **3/1**$^{2}$

2 1 **Super Brand (SAF)**$^{202}$ 5-8-9 90 WCMarwing 4 88
(MFDeKock, South Africa) *in tch in rr: racd wd and hdwy st: rdn 2f out: r.o fnl f: nt pce of wnr* **4/1**$^{3}$

3 1/2 **Boston Lodge**$^{16}$ 755 4-9-0 95 LDettori 10 91
(GAButler) *in tch towards rr: 7th st: rdn and hdwy 2f out: no ex nr fin* **15/8**$^{1}$

4 1 3/4 **Majestic Horizon**$^{7}$ 853 4-8-9 90 (t) RMullen 1 81
(AAlRaihe, UAE) *s.i.s: sn chsd ldrs: 4th st: rdn and effrt 2f out: kpt on same pce* **20/1**

5 1 1/4 **Mugharreb (USA)**$^{48}$ 6-9-2 97 RHills 5 84
(MAlMuhairi, UAE) *mid-div: 6th st: rdn and effrt over 1f out: wknd fnl f* **9/2**

6 1 1/4 **Storm Racer (AUS)**$^{16}$ 755 7-9-7 102 (b) MDuPlessis 7 85
(MThwaites, Macau) *trckd ldr: led 2 1/2f out tl hdd over 1f out: sn wknd* **20/1**

7 1/2 **Clod Ber Junior (BRZ)**$^{9}$ 6-9-0 95 (b) SChin 6 77
(ASelvaratnam, UAE) *a towards rr: 8th st: effrt 2f out: nvr trbld ldrs* **33/1**

8 4 1/4 **Tudor Wood**$^{7}$ 852 5-8-10 91 (bt) GAvranche 2 60
(NDeCroutte, Bahrain) *led tl hdd 2 1/2f out: sn wknd* **33/1**

9 4 **Orchestrated (AUS)**$^{9}$ 830 7-9-5 100 (t) GHind 8 57
(MAlKurdi, UAE) *trckd ldrs: 3rd and rdn st: wknd fnl 2f* **25/1**

1m 17.75s **9** Ran SP% **117.2**
Speed ratings: .
**Owner** A Ball & W Harrison-Allan **Bred** J P Coggan **Trained** West Ilsley, Berks

**NOTEBOOK**
**Pic Up Sticks**, unlucky in running last time, enjoyed a better run this time and made amends in good style.
**Boston Lodge** ran another solid race but is struggling to get his head in front at the moment.

## 925a EMIRATES AIRLINE PLATE (H'CAP) (TURF) 1m
6:15 (6:16) (90-105,105) 3-Y-O+ £32,681 (£10,055; £5,027; £2,513) Stalls Low

RPR

1 **Evolving Tactics (IRE)**$^{196}$ 4201 4-9-5 105 TEDurcan 5 107
(DKWeld, Ire) *s.i.s: hld up: towards rr: last st: rdn and hdwy 2f out: r.o wl to ld fnl 110yds* **11/2**$^{3}$

2 2 3/4 **Kundooz**$^{8}$ 5-8-10 96 BDoyle 4 93
(AllanSmith, UAE) *towards rr: rdn and hdwy on ins st: led 1 1/2f out tl hdd fnl 110yds: nt pce of wnr* **12/1**

3 1 3/4 **Skoozi (NZ)**$^{21}$ 710 9-9-1 100 RBurke 1 94
(MKettle, UAE) *trckd ldrs: rdn to ld over 2f out: hdd 1 1/2f out: no ex nr fin* **33/1**

4 3 1/2 **Walmooh**$^{16}$ 754 8-9-1 100 (b) KMcEvoy 7 87
(AllanSmith, UAE) *mid-div: rdn and hdwy 2f out: edgd rt and kpt on nr fin: nt rch ldrs* **15/2**

5 5 3/4 **Jacks Estate (IRE)**$^{9}$ 830 9-8-4 97 TANaughton$^{(7)}$ 11 72
(AdrianMcguinness, Ire) *in tch towards rr: rdn and effrt over 400m out: nvr trbld ldrs* **66/1**

6 1 1/2 **Maidaan**$^{7}$ 852 8-8-13 98 PaulSmith 8 71
(AllanSmith, UAE) *a mid-div: racd wd and effrt st: wknd fnl 1 1/2f* **12/1**

7 1 **Hero's Journey**$^{8}$ 5-9-2 101 (t) GHind 6 72
(MAlKurdi, UAE) *trckd ldrs: 2nd st: rdn and wknd 2f out* **20/1**

8 2 **Modus Vivendi**$^{216}$ 3632 4-9-0 99 WCMarwing 3 66
(MFDeKock, South Africa) *disp ld: trckd ldrs fr 6f out: wknd over 2f out* **5/2**$^{1}$

9 1 **St Expedit**$^{7}$ 853 7-9-5 105 LDettori 9 69
(RBouresly, Kuwait) *trckd ldrs tl wknd fr 1/2-way* **9/2**$^{2}$

10 1/2 **Wahsheeq**$^{37}$ 4-8-11 97 (t) SSanders 12 60
(ECharpy, UAE) *sn rdn along: a towards rr: n.d* **25/1**

11 9 1/2 **Landslide (IRE)**$^{7}$ 850 5-8-9 95 PHanagan 10 39
(PRudkin, UAE) *mid-div outside: racd wd and wknd st* **10/1**

12 3 3/4 **Self Evident (USA)**$^{16}$ 754 4-8-9 95 (b) RLMoore 2 31
(GAButler) *disp ld: led 6f out tl hdd 2f out: sn wknd* **13/2**

1m 36.49s **12** Ran SP% **124.8**
Speed ratings: .
**Owner** Dr M W J Smurfit & Donald Keough **Bred** Moyglare Stud Farm Ltd **Trained** The Curragh, Co Kildare

**NOTEBOOK**
**Self Evident(USA)**, taken on for the lead, did not get home.

# 912 LINGFIELD (L-H)
Sunday, February 29

**OFFICIAL GOING: Standard**
Wind: slt across Weather: fine

## 926 BET DIRECT IN VISION SKY PAGE 293 H'CAP (DIV I) 1m (P)
1:35 (1:36) (F) (0-60,60) 3-Y-O+ £2,940 (£840; £420) Stalls High

Form RPR

3203 1 **Welsh Wind (IRE)**$^{15}$ 765 8-9-10 56 (tp) JFanning 6 65
(MWigham) *chsd ldrs: effrt 2f out: led 100 yds out: rdn out* **9/2**$^{3}$

0-02 2 3/4 **Meelup (IRE)**$^{4}$ 886 4-9-7 53 (p) VSlattery 7 60
(JaneSouthcombe) *led: hrd rdn over 1f out: hdd 100 yds out: kpt on* **16/1**

0500 3 1 1/2 **Frankskips**$^{18}$ 745 5-9-10 56 TQuinn 9 60
(MissBSanders) *prom: ev ch over 1f out: nt qckn* **7/2**$^{2}$

-203 4 nk **He Who Dares (IRE)**$^{4}$ 882 6-9-11 57 SWhitworth 2 60
(AWCarroll) *s.s: t.k.h and bhd: hdwy on outside and wd st: styd on same pce: too much to do* **6/4**$^{1}$

-305 5 1/2 **Pas De Surprise**$^{4}$ 888 6-9-9 55 JoannaBadger 5 57
(PDEvans) *prom: rdn 2f out: one pce appr fnl f* **10/1**

000- 6 5 **Ehab (IRE)**$^{50}$ 5202 5-9-11 57 DaneO'Neill 4 48
(GLMoore) *s.i.s: t.k.h: sn prom: outpcd fnl 2f* **12/1**

-400 7 nk **Taranai (IRE)**$^{4}$ 885 3-8-0 51 CCatlin 10 42
(BWDuke) *in tch: rdn 3f out: btn whn carried wd into st* **33/1**

10-0 8 1 **Rocinante (IRE)**$^{13}$ 800 4-9-8 54 RWinston 1 42
(JJQuinn) *hld up in tch: effrt 2f out: sn outpcd* **16/1**

600- 9 2 1/2 **Thumamah (IRE)**$^{257}$ 2450 5-9-7 53 IMongan 3 36
(BPJBaugh) *towards rr: rdn and outpcd fnl 2f* **25/1**

1m 39.81s (0.30) **Going Correction** -0.025s/f (Stan)
**WFA** 3 from 4yo+ 19lb **9** Ran SP% **115.7**
Speed ratings: **97,96,94,94,93 88,88,87,85** CSF £72.68 CT £280.64 TOTE £6.30: £1.20, £5.60, £1.20; EX 57.00.
**Owner** Miss R M Spearing **Bred** Mark Salmon **Trained** Newmarket, Suffolk

**FOCUS**
A low-grade handicap run at a steady pace and a moderate winning time. Solid but basically modest form.

**NOTEBOOK**
**Welsh Wind(IRE)**, dropping back to a mile, was always in the ideal position to strike and end a losing run stretching back to October 2001. The fact that he has been beaten several times off this mark recently emphasises the modest nature of the form.
**Meelup(IRE)** showed that his effort here four days earlier was no fluke and, given his own way in the lead, again tried to steal the race from the front and was just overhauled. The form is modest though.
**Frankskips** did not build on his promising effort here last time and there appeared to be no excuses.
**He Who Dares(IRE)** fell out of the stalls and had the whole field in front of him for most of the way. He tried to make his move on the wide outside turning for home, but the leaders were quickening at the same time and he could make no impression. He needs a stronger pace, but is not proving easy to win with.
**Pas De Surprise** did not achieve much, but may be happier back on Fibresand.
**Ehab(IRE)**, back on the Flat after three runs over hurdles, was backed at long odds but was easily left behind over the last couple of furlongs.

## 927 BET DIRECT IN RUNNING SKY TEXT PAGE 293 MAIDEN STKS 7f (P)
2:05 (2:06) (D) 3-Y-O £3,304 (£944; £472) Stalls Low

Form RPR

0-4 1 **Eccentric**$^{8}$ 845 3-9-0 ANicholls 4 71
(AndrewReid) *mde all: rdn 6l clr 2f out: tired fnl f: all out* **14/1**

002 **2** *nk* **Alfridini**[11] 816 3-9-0 65 DaneO'Neill 1 70
(DRCElsworth) *s.s: rdn and hdwy to chse wnr 3f out: styd on fnl f: clsng at fin* **15/8**[1]

404- **3** *1 ¼* **Wavertree Girl (IRE)**[185] 4522 3-8-10 91 ow1 DHolland 8 63
(NPLittmoden) *hdwy over 2f out: hrd rdn over 1f out: styd on fnl f: nvr able to chal* **5/2**[2]

046- **4** *8* **Imperium**[81] 6160 3-9-0 77 (t) SDrowne 9 47
(MrsStefLiddiard) *wd: in tch: effrt 3f out: no imp fnl 2f* **7/1**

4-5 **5** *5* **Star Fern**[43] 553 3-9-0 GCarter 7 35
(JAkehurst) *s.s: bhd and wd: rdn 3f out: nvr rchd ldrs* **20/1**

-440 **6** *1 ¼* **Lady Predominant**[13] 788 3-8-9 45 SCarson 2 27
(AndrewReid) *prom 4f: 5th and wkng whn hmpd over 2f out* **66/1**

0 **7** *1* **Fly So High**[11] 816 3-8-9 RWinston 6 24
(DShaw) *s.s: a bhd* **33/1**

40- **8** *19* **Littleton Liberty**[307] 1260 3-8-9 (b[1]) IMongan 5 —
(AndrewReid) *chsd wnr to 1/2-way: sn wknd* **33/1**

620- **P** **Devil's Bite**[128] 5726 3-9-0 77 MHills 3 —
(BWHills) *chsd ldrs: drvn along 4f out: p.u over 3f out: dismntd: b.b.v* **3/1**[3]

1m 25.92s (-0.08) **Going Correction** -0.025s/f (Stan) **9** Ran SP% **119.7**
Speed ratings: **99,98,97,88,82 80,79,58,**—CSF £41.24 TOTE £22.30: £3.80, £1.10, £2.30; EX 60.00.
**Owner** A S Reid **Bred** A S Reid **Trained** Mill Hill, London NW7

**FOCUS**
A fair maiden for the time of year and grade and run at a sound pace.

**NOTEBOOK**
**Eccentric** confirmed the promise of his recent effort here and owes this victory to the enterprise of his rider, who took the race by the scruff of the neck rounding the home bend and established enough of a lead to just hold on. He is entitled to improve again.
**Alfridini** may have been unlucky. Not for the first time, he was awkward leaving the stalls and was off the bridle a long way from home. He could not respond when the leader quickened into a clear lead running to the final bend, but really found his stride on reaching the straight and was closing fast at the line. He should not be long in winning, but looks to need further.
**Wavertree Girl(IRE)**, rated much higher than her rivals on account of her fourth in last season's Princess Margaret, has failed to match that in her other starts and that was again the case here. Despite this being her first start in seven months and her Polytrack debut, she had every chance and this was disappointing.
**Imperium** is becoming an exposed maiden and achieved little here.
**Star Fern** does not seem to be progressing, but can at least now be handicapped.
**Devil's Bite** was in the middle of the pack when her rider looked anxiously down at her and she was quickly pulled up. She was found to have bled. *Official explanation: vet said colt had bled from the nose*

## 928 BET DIRECT NO Q 08000 93 66 93 CLASSIFIED STKS 7f (P)
**2:35** (2:37) (F) 3-Y-0+ **£2,975** (£850; £425) **Stalls** Low

Form RPR

-042 **1** **Hazewind**[4] 885 3-8-5 64 (t) SCarson 5 69
(PDEvans) *dwlt: bhd: gd hdwy over 1f out: drvn to ld fnl 50 yds* **6/1**

-110 **2** *¾* **Nearly A Fool**[32] 624 6-9-8 60 (v) NPollard 4 67
(GGMargarson) *trckd ldrs: drvn to chal over 1f out: ev ch fnl f: nt qckn nr fin* **4/1**[2]

3413 **3** *1 ¼* **Adantino**[18] 738 5-9-8 57 (b) SDrowne 1 64
(BRMillman) *dwlt: sn in tch: rdn to ld over 1f out: hdd and one pce fnl 50 yds* **9/2**[3]

1302 **4** *1* **Double M**[25] 674 7-9-8 56 (v) NCallan 6 61
(MrsLRichards) *hld up and bhd: hdwy on rail whn briefly nt clr run over 1f out: styd on u.p fnl f* **14/1**

-003 **5** *1 ¾* **Illusive (IRE)**[15] 771 7-9-8 60 (b) GCarter 3 57
(MWigham) *t.k.h: hld up in tch: hmpd and lost pl over 1f out: rallied and r.o fnl f* **8/1**

020- **6** *shd* **Duo Leoni**[82] 6151 4-9-5 60 MFenton 8 54
(MrsStefLiddiard) *towards rr: hdwy and wd st: no ex 1f out* **9/1**

4100 **7** *1 ¼* **Its Ecco Boy**[3] 897 6-9-8 57 RWinston 10 54
(PHowling) *mid-div: drvn to chse ldrs over 1f out: sn wknd* **14/1**

5465 **8** *2* **Jalouhar**[4] 884 4-9-8 55 IMongan 2 49
(BPJBaugh) *chsd ldr: hrd rdn and ev ch wl over 1f out: sn wknd* **25/1**

-600 **9** *1* **Karaoke King**[3] 896 6-9-8 54 DaneO'Neill 9 46
(JELong) *prom: hrd rdn 3f out: wknd wl over 1f out* **33/1**

00-4 **10** *1 ¾* **Legal Set (IRE)**[4] 884 8-9-8 60 KFallon 7 42
(WJMusson) *led tl over 1f out: sn btn and n.m.r: wknd* **11/4**[1]

1m 25.3s (-0.70) **Going Correction** -0.025s/f (Stan)
**WFA** 3 from 4yo+ 17lb **10** Ran SP% **120.4**
Speed ratings: **103,102,100,99,97 97,96,93,92,90**CSF £31.32 TOTE £6.40: £2.00, £1.70, £1.90; EX 34.50.
**Owner** M W Lawrence **Bred** Gainsborough Stud Management Ltd **Trained** Pandy, Gwent

**FOCUS**
Fair form for this classified stakes and the pace was good.

**NOTEBOOK**
**Hazewind**, the only three-year-old in the line-up, has improved with every run on sand and won this in good style having been given a very patient ride. He was beaten off a mark of 52 here four days ago, which shows how much he has progressed, and he probably has not finished yet.
**Nearly A Fool** returned to form after a below-par effort last time and was always there or thereabouts. He is better when able to dominate, but with Legal Set in the line-up that was not possible which makes this effort all the more creditable.
**Adantino** had no excuses as he was in the perfect position just behind the leaders and the gap appeared at the ideal time when Legal Set drifted off the rail. He ran on well once through it, but the front two proved too strong. He has ability, but a record of just one win in 29 starts is a bit offputting.
**Double M** was a little bit held up behind Adantino when that rival was going through the gap between Legal Set and the inside rail soon after turning for home, but it probably did not affect his finishing position. He is still to win over this trip.
**Illusive(IRE)**, on a long losing run, would have finished a good deal closer had he not been hampered by the weakening Legal Set and Jalouhar over a furlong from home.
**Legal Set(IRE)** was soon able to get to the front and set the pace, but folded rather tamely on reaching the home straight.

## 929 BETDIRECT.CO.UK H'CAP (DIV I) 1m (P)
**3:05** (3:06) (F) (0-52,57) 4-Y-0+ **£2,912** (£832; £416) **Stalls** High

Form RPR

0-62 **1** **Indian Blaze**[1] 914 10-8-5 45 TPQueally[(3)] 3 54+
(AndrewReid) *mid-div: effrt 2f out: styd on to ld ins fnl f: drvn out* **6/1**[3]

00-0 **2** *1 ½* **Wind Chime (IRE)**[32] 623 7-8-12 49 SWhitworth 9 55
(AGNewcombe) *pressed ldr: led over 2f out: hdd and nt qckn ins fnl f* **8/1**

0221 **3** *½* **Steely Dan**[3] 895 5-9-6 57 6ex NPollard 8 62
(JRBest) *hld up towards rr: promising hdwy over 1f out: rdn and styd on: nt pce to chal* **11/8**[1]

0-40 **4** *1 ¼* **Coppington Flyer (IRE)**[4] 888 4-8-12 49 KFallon 5 51
(BWDuke) *chsd ldrs: hrd rdn over 1f out: one pce* **11/2**[2]

0-03 **4** *dht* **Ballare (IRE)**[13] 788 5-8-8 45 OUrbina 10 47
(BobJones) *chsd ldrs: hrd rdn over 1f out: one pce* **20/1**

0605 **6** *nk* **Haithem (IRE)**[6] 860 7-8-9 46 oh10 ow1 (t) NCallan 4 47
(DShaw) *bhd: sme hdwy and hrd rdn over 1f out: nt rch ldrs* **50/1**

1660 **7** *½* **Piquet**[5] 874 6-8-13 50 SDrowne 6 50
(JJBridger) *hld up: effrt and hrd rdn over 1f out: nvr able to chal* **14/1**

0-12 **8** *1 ½* **Theatre Lady (IRE)**[6] 860 6-8-5 45 oh5 LFletcher[(3)] 2 42
(PDEvans) *mid-div: rdn fr 1/2-way: wknd over 2f out* **10/1**

0/0 **9** *5* **Insignificance**[2] 909 4-8-9 45 (b[1]) MFenton 7 32
(JohnAQuinn, Ire) *led tl over 2f out: wknd wl over 1f out* **16/1**

4353 **P** **French Horn**[1] 914 7-8-11 48 (b) GCarter 1 —
(MWigham) *hld up towards rr: lost action and p.u over 2f out: dismntd: dead* **10/1**

1m 38.25s (-1.26) **Going Correction** -0.025s/f (Stan) **10** Ran SP% **120.3**
Speed ratings: **105,103,103,101,101 101,100,99,94,**—CSF £55.14 CT £106.17 TOTE £6.90: £2.10, £3.30, £1.10; EX 108.30.
**Owner** Mrs Irene Clifford **Bred** Red House Stud **Trained** Mill Hill, London NW7

**FOCUS**
Fair form, a decent pace and a smart winning time for the grade.

**NOTEBOOK**
**Indian Blaze**, possibly unlucky here the previous day, had no problem with the shorter trip and was brought with a well-timed run to score. He is not getting any younger, but was absolutely thrown in here on the majority of his form.
**Wind Chime(IRE)** ran much better than on his reappearance here last month and can find a similar event.
**Steely Dan**, a notoriously hard ride, tried to adopt the same tactics as when winning here three days earlier, but his late finish was nothing like so effective. Backing him is always going to be a risk.
**Coppington Flyer(IRE)**, 6lb lower than for her last win on sand, is not an easy ride and the champion's style did not really work for her.
**Ballare(IRE)** ran up to his best, but remains a maiden.
**Haithem(IRE)** again ran on later without offering a threat. He is capable of better and when he does click is likely to be a big price.

## 930 LITTLEWOODS BET DIRECT H'CAP 6f (P)
**3:35** (3:36) (F) (0-52,56) 3-Y-0+ **£3,045** (£870; £435) **Stalls** Low

Form RPR

46-5 **1** **Doctor Dennis (IRE)**[3] 896 7-9-0 47 (b) NPollard 9 55
(JPearce) *dwlt: bhd: gd hdwy over 1f out: drvn to ld jst ins fnl f: styd on* **9/1**

-066 **2** *¾* **Long Weekend (IRE)**[27] 658 6-8-13 46 oh6 (v) NCallan 13 52
(DShaw) *stdd s: bhd: gd hdwy 2f out: ev ch ins fnl f: kpt on* **16/1**

2-65 **3** *1 ½* **Eastern Blue (IRE)**[25] 674 5-9-1 48 (p) KFallon 3 50
(MrsLStubbs) *in tch: drvn to chal over 1f out: nt qckn fnl f* **4/1**[2]

-000 **4** *½* **Parallel Lines (IRE)**[6] 859 3-7-8 47 oh1 ow1 (b) JFMcDonald[(5)] 11 47
(PDEvans) *mid-div: drvn to chse ldrs over 1f out: one pce* **50/1**

0101 **5** *½* **Bells Beach (IRE)**[4] 884 6-9-9 56 6ex JFanning 14 55
(PHowling) *hld up towards rr: effrt and nt clr run over 1f out: swtchd rt ins fnl f: nrst fin* **8/1**

3140 **6** *nk* **Aguila Loco (IRE)**[1] 918 5-9-7 54 (p) MFenton 4 52
(MrsStefLiddiard) *chsd tearaway ldr: led wl over 1f out: hdd jst ins fnl f: no ex* **13/2**[3]

6141 **7** *1 ¾* **Badou**[6] 859 4-9-4 51 6ex DHolland 5 43
(LMontagueHall) *bmpd sn after s: sn bhd: rdn and styd on appr fnl f: nvr nrr* **3/1**[1]

0-00 **8** *1 ¼* **Tamarella (IRE)**[3] 896 4-9-2 49 AMcCarthy 10 38
(GGMargarson) *prom: hrd rdn and ev ch over 1f out: no ex fnl f* **8/1**

0-33 **9** *1 ½* **Jahangir**[6] 858 5-8-13 46 oh1 DaneO'Neill 1 30
(BRJohnson) *mid-div: hmpd on rail after 1f: rdn and n.d fnl 2f* **7/1**

5-50 **10** *5* **Pleasure Time**[5] 876 11-8-13 46 oh1 (v) JFEgan 8 15
(CSmith) *hdwy 4f out: hrd rdn and wknd over 1f out* **50/1**

3-60 **11** *¾* **Night Cap (IRE)**[43] 560 5-9-0 47 (b[1]) CCatlin 2 14
(TDMccarthy) *free to post and in r: led and set fast pce: hdd & wknd wl over 1f out* **16/1**

0-40 **12** *nk* **Fiamma Royale (IRE)**[3] 896 6-8-12 48 RMiles[(3)] 6 14
(MSSaunders) *t.k.h: bmpd sn after s: mid-div to 1/2-way: sn bhd* **14/1**

-000 **13** *½* **Law Maker**[40] 569 4-8-13 46 oh11 (b) SCarson 12 10
(MABuckley) *wd: chsd ldrs 4f* **66/1**

1m 13.25s (0.33) **Going Correction** -0.025s/f (Stan)
**WFA** 3 from 4yo+ 15lb **13** Ran SP% **126.9**
Speed ratings: **96,95,93,92,91 91,88,87,85,78 77,77,76**CSF £152.58 CT £701.30 TOTE £11.20: £2.90, £5.00, £2.50; EX 174.50.
**Owner** Mrs Lydia Pearce **Bred** David Allan **Trained** Newmarket, Suffolk

**FOCUS**
Modest form and a moderate winning time for the class.

**NOTEBOOK**
**Doctor Dennis(IRE)** weaved through from the rear along the rail in the home straight to notch his first win since June 2001. He is a bit of a character according to his trainer and appears to need things to fall just right.
**Long Weekend(IRE)**, with a visor back on rather than an eyeshield, did nothing wrong but found one that bit better than him on the day. He is devilishly hard to win with.
**Eastern Blue(IRE)**, back in the cheekpieces, proved her effectiveness on this surface without finding as much as she had threatened to.
**Parallel Lines(IRE)** , showing his first form on sand, might be worth another try at seven furlongs.
**Bells Beach(IRE)**, who encountered trouble in running from her high draw, was held under the penalty.
**Aguila Loco(IRE)** put in a decent run considering he had been in action the previous day.
**Badou** was involved in scrimmaging running to the first bend and could never really get into the race thereafter. Seven furlongs might be his optimum trip.

## 931 BET IN RUNNING @ BETDIRECT.CO.UK H'CAP 1m 4f (P)
**4:05** (4:06) (F) (0-55,60) 4-Y-0+ **£3,010** (£860; £430) **Stalls** Low

Form RPR

0-10 **1** **Beyond The Pole (USA)**[5] 867 6-9-7 55 KFallon 4 64
(BRJohnson) *chsd ldrs: rdn 4f out: styd on to ld ins fnl f* **9/2**[2]

022/ **2** *¾* **Belle Rouge**[488] 5529 6-9-7 55 PaulEddery 12 63
(CAHorgan) *chsd ldr: hrd rdn and ev ch over 1f out: nt qckn ins fnl f* **20/1**

4021 **3** *¾* **Fortune Point (IRE)**[5] 874 6-9-12 60 6ex IMongan 13 67
(AWCarroll) *led: hrd rdn and hdd ins fnl f: one pce* **6/1**[3]

50-4 **4** *¾* **Essay Baby (FR)**[16] 537 4-8-9 46 oh1 CCatlin 9 52
(PDCundell) *chsd ldrs: hrd rdn over 1f out: styd on same pce* **16/1**

0250 **5** *1* **Tropical Son**[5] 874 5-9-1 49 (v) NCallan 8 53
(DShaw) *towards rr: drvn and hdwy 2f out: styd on* **20/1**

-340 **6** *hd* **My Lilli (IRE)**[15] 767 4-8-13 50 JPMurtagh 7 54
(PMitchell) *a.p: one pce fnl 2f* **9/1**

0-24 **7** *nk* **Sterling Guarantee (USA)**[5] 867 6-9-5 53........................ ANicholls 1 57
(AndrewReid) *hdwy to chse ldrs over 2f out: hrd rdn over 1f out: one pce* **4/1**[1]

5-16 **8** *2 1/2* **Paradise Valley**[2] 908 4-9-2 53........................................(t) SDrowne 15 53
(MrsStefLiddiard) *s.s: hld up and bhd: shkn up and r.o appr fnl f: nrst fin* **12/1**

0600 **9** *1* **Golden Dual**[5] 867 4-9-4 55........................................ DHolland 3 53
(SDow) *s.s: in rr: mod hdwy 2f out: n.d* **8/1**

5-00 **10** *3 1/2* **Muraqeb**[5] 874 4-9-1 52................................................ JFEgan 2 45
(MrsBarbaraWaring) *rdn 4f out: n.d* **33/1**

-P06 **11** *nk* **Geography (IRE)**[5] 874 4-8-9 53..................................(p) CHaddon(7) 6 46
(PButler) *mid-div: hrd rdn and wknd 3f out* **50/1**

00-5 **12** *1/2* **Shaman**[25] 672 7-9-2 50................................................ DaneO'Neill 10 42
(GLMoore) *chsd ldrs: hrd rdn and wknd 3f out* **33/1**

2065 **13** *1 1/4* **Pyrrhic**[6] 855 5-8-12 46 oh1................................................(b) SWKelly 5 36
(RMFlower) *t.k.h: mid-div tl wknd over 2f out* **14/1**

3400 **14** *2* **Top Of The Class (IRE)**[3] 892 7-8-9 46......................(v) LFletcher(3) 11 33
(PDEvans) *dwlt: plld hrd in midfield: hrd rdn and wknd over 2f out* **14/1**

2m 33.47s (-0.51) **Going Correction** -0.025s/f (Stan)
**WFA** 4 from 5yo+ 3lb **14** Ran SP% **124.9**
Speed ratings: **100,99,99,98,97 97,97,95,95,92 92,92,91,90**CSF £100.39 CT £562.54 TOTE £4.80: £3.50, £5.00, £3.10; EX 96.60 Trifecta £303.00 Pool £682.86 - 1.60 winning units..
**Owner** Tann Racing **Bred** Cavallix Inc **Trained** Epsom, Surrey
■ Stewards Enquiry : J P Murtagh one-day ban: failed to keep straight from stalls (Mar 13)

**FOCUS**
Modest form.

**NOTEBOOK**
**Beyond The Pole(USA)** , reunited with the Champion after being beaten under an amateur last time, was always well placed and stayed on well to forge ahead inside the last.
**Belle Rouge** was having her first run since October 2002, when trained by Michael Blanshard. She stays farther than this and, provided she does not 'bounce', should pay her way on this surface.
**Fortune Point(IRE)**, under a penalty for his win here last time, was again allowed to dictate things up front but he was worn down inside the last. This longer trip did not help.
**Essay Baby(FR)**, who had a run over hurdles earlier in the month, was doing her best work at the end.
**Tropical Son**, back up in trip, stayed on in the latter stages. Six of the runners were clear turning for home and he was the only one of the stragglers to latch onto that sextet.
**My Lilli(IRE)**, not for the first time, shaped as if this trip is a shade far for her.
**Sterling Guarantee(USA)** was well supported, but by the time he managed to get off the rail two or three had got first run on him. He was unable to quicken in any case.
**Paradise Valley** *Official explanation: jockey said gelding was unlucky in running*
**Pyrrhic** *Official explanation: jockey said gelding hung right throughout*

## 932 BET DIRECT IN VISION SKY PAGE 293 H'CAP (DIV II) 1m (P)
4:35 (4:36) (F ) (0-60,60) 3-Y-0+ **£2,940** (£840; £420) **Stalls** High

Form RPR

5-00 **1** **Best Before (IRE)**[8] 846 4-9-10 56........................................ SDrowne 4 66
(PDEvans) *prom: hrd rdn over 2f out: drvn to ld jst ins fnl f: styd on* **10/1**

0023 **2** *1 1/2* **Lucayan Monarch**[3] 895 6-9-8 54....................................(p) JPMurtagh 3 61
(PSMcentee) *in tch on rail: effrt over 2f out: kpt on take 2nd ins fnl f* **7/2**[3]

0112 **3** *3/4* **Xaloc Bay (IRE)**[5] 873 6-9-10 56........................................ IMongan 5 61
(BPJBaugh) *led: hrd rdn and hdd jst ins fnl f: one pce* **7/1**

0-63 **4** *1 1/2* **Burgundy**[18] 745 7-9-11 57........................................ DHolland 10 59
(PMitchell) *towards rr: hdwy 2f out: hrd rdn over 1f out: one pce* **11/4**[1]

00-0 **5** *3* **Kanz Wood (USA)**[50] 491 8-9-9 55........................................ SWhitworth 1 50
(AWCarroll) *towards rr: sme hdwy 2f out: no imp appr fnl f* **12/1**

0464 **6** *2 1/2* **Vlasta Weiner**[6] 860 4-8-8 40................................................(b) CCatlin 6 30
(JMBradley) *prom: outpcd 2f out: sn btn* **33/1**

-536 **7** *1/2* **Chandelier**[4] 888 4-9-5 54................................................(b) RMiles(3) 2 43
(MSSaunders) *dwlt: rdn to chse ldrs: wknd over 1f out* **9/1**

2400 **8** *4* **Mutarafaa (USA)**[4] 888 5-9-7 53........................................(v) NCallan 7 33
(DShaw) *in tch: hrd rdn 3f out: btn whn hmpd over 2f out* **16/1**

0-00 **9** *12* **By Definition (IRE)**[5] 875 6-7-9 34 ow4.................... KristinStubbs(7) 8 —
(JCTuck) *prom over 3f* **66/1**

0-54 **10** *3 1/2* **Fen Gypsy**[4] 882 6-10-0 60................................................ KFallon 9 6
(PDEvans) *bhd: wd and pushed along 1/2-way: no ch fnl 3f: eased over 1f out* **3/1**[2]

1m 38.6s (-0.91) **Going Correction** -0.025s/f (Stan) **10** Ran SP% **123.5**
Speed ratings: **103,101,100,99,96 93,93,89,77,73**CSF £47.77 CT £273.53 TOTE £16.20: £2.60, £1.90, £3.30; EX 94.10.
**Owner** M W Lawrence **Bred** Joe Rogers **Trained** Pandy, Gwent

**FOCUS**
Modest form.

**NOTEBOOK**
**Best Before(IRE)** did not get the best of runs here last time. He has had his resolution called into question in the past, but stuck his neck out willingly to belatedly break his duck.
**Lucayan Monarch** is running well of late despite a hectic schedule and the return to a mile seemed to suit.
**Xaloc Bay(IRE)** is an honest sort but he again teed up the race for stronger finishers.
**Burgundy** ought to have been suited by the strong gallop but was not really able to pick up and could only keep on at the one pace. *Official explanation: jockey said gelding was never travelling*
**Kanz Wood(USA)** was 10lb lower than when running here before Christmas.
**Fen Gypsy** *Official explanation: trainer had no explanation for the poor form shown*

## 933 BETDIRECT.CO.UK H'CAP (DIV II) 1m (P)
5:05 (5:06) (F ) (0-52,58) 4-Y-0+ **£2,905** (£830; £415) **Stalls** High

Form RPR

2-23 **1** **Double Ransom**[32] 623 5-9-0 52........................................(b) KFallon 8 63
(MrsLStubbs) *hdwy 2f out: drvn to ld 1f out: rdn clr* **6/4**[1]

5041 **2** *4* **Lucid Dreams (IRE)**[4] 888 5-9-6 58 6ex.............................. JFanning 3 60
(MWigham) *prom: led briefly over 1f out: nt pce of wnr* **3/1**[2]

-201 **3** *2 1/2* **Miss Peaches**[13] 787 6-8-2 47........................................ KristinStubbs(7) 10 44
(GGMargarson) *sn outpcd and bhd: gd late hdwy* **6/1**

-130 **4** *hd* **Balerno**[4] 888 5-8-13 51................................................ GCarter 4 47
(RIngram) *sn outpcd in rr: hdwy and wd st: one pce appr fnl f* **10/1**

0-00 **5** *nk* **Galey River (USA)**[3] 895 5-8-8 46 oh1........................ NCallan 7 41
(JJSheehan) *sn outpcd in rr: hrd rdn 3f out: styd on u.p fnl 2f* **25/1**

0530 **6** *1* **Estrella Levante**[4] 888 4-8-6 49........................................(be) AQuinn(5) 5 42
(GLMoore) *mid-div: effrt over 2f out: no ex over 1f out* **25/1**

5064 **7** *3/4* **Zinging**[4] 888 5-8-12 50................................................ SDrowne 1 42
(JJBridger) *led 1f: rdn and ev ch over 1f out: wknd fnl f* **11/2**[3]

500- **8** *1/2* **Gran Clicquot**[129] 5717 9-8-8 46 oh1........................ RBrisland 9 36
(GPEnright) *s.i.s: outpcd and wl bhd: nvr trbld ldrs* **20/1**

0650 **9** *1 1/2* **Vizulize**[3] 895 5-8-10 48................................................(v[1]) IMongan 6 35
(AWCarroll) *led after 1f and set gd pce: hdd & wknd over 1f out* **14/1**

-060 **10** *1/2* **Angelica Garnett**[11] 815 4-8-8 46 oh1........................ JFEgan 2 32
(TEPowell) *s.i.s: t.k.h: sn prom: wknd over 2f out* **33/1**

1m 38.89s (-0.62) **Going Correction** -0.025s/f (Stan) **10** Ran SP% **125.8**
Speed ratings: **102,98,95,95,95 94,93,92,91,90**CSF £6.26 CT £23.43 TOTE £2.60: £1.30, £1.50, £1.90; EX 8.00 Place 6 £64.60, Place 5 £32.78..
**Owner** Tyme Partnership **Bred** Limestone Stud **Trained** Malton, N. Yorks

**FOCUS**
Decent form by the winner in the grade.

**NOTEBOOK**
**Double Ransom** , a pound lower, was suited by the fast pace on this return to a mile and came clear in the final furlong to win decisively.
**Lucid Dreams(IRE)**, under a penalty for his win in a falsely-run race here, moved up going well but was left trailing by the winner in the final furlong.
**Miss Peaches** had a lot to do turning for home, but stayed on once switched to the outer and snatched third place near the line.
**Balerno** could not confirm recent course and distance form with Miss Peaches, who deprived him of third place on the line.
**Galey River(USA)** was without the headgear this time. A step up in trip could be required.
**Vizulize**set a strong pace in the first-time visor but was quickly beaten once headed.
T/Jkpt: Not won. T/Plt: £71.70 to a £1 stake. Pool: £50,004.75. 508.60 winning tickets. T/Qpdt: £14.40 to a £1 stake. Pool: £2,585.70. 132.30 winning tickets. LM

# 897 SOUTHWELL (L-H)
Sunday, February 29

**OFFICIAL GOING: Slow**
Wind: slt across Weather: fine

## 934 NEW SITE @ BETDIRECT.CO.UK BANDED STKS 7f (F)
2:25 (2:26) (H ) 3-Y-0+ **£1,494** (£427; £213) **Stalls** Low

Form RPR

0-11 **1** **Smart Scot**[21] 713 5-9-2 40................................................(p) MSavage(5) 6 46
(BPJBaugh) *chsd ldr: led 3f out: rdn and hung lft 2f out: styd on* **5/4**[1]

6522 **2** *1 1/4* **Jessie**[10] 826 5-9-7 40................................................(t) KimTinkler 12 43
(DonEnricoIncisa) *dwlt: sn pushed along: hdwy 1/2-way: styd on ins fnl f: nt rch wnr* **6/1**[3]

3005 **3** *3/4* **Neutral Night (IRE)**[20] 725 4-9-7 40........................................(v) ADaly 4 41
(RBrotherton) *chsd ldrs: rdn over 2f out: styd on* **25/1**

0-45 **4** *1 1/4* **Mathmagician**[10] 823 5-9-7 35....................................(b) DeanMcKeown 3 38
(RFMarvin) *mid-div: rdn 1/2-way: styd on appr fnl f: nt trble ldrs* **20/1**

4022 **5** *5* **Silver Mascot**[12] 807 5-9-7 45........................................ ACulhane 8 25
(RHollinshead) *chsd ldrs tl rdn and wknd over 1f out* **11/4**[2]

0-00 **6** *4* **Beauteous (IRE)**[27] 655 5-9-7 40........................................ FLynch 1 15
(ABerry) *led 4f: rdn and wknd wl over 1f out* **16/1**

0400 **7** *2 1/2* **Sweet Coral (FR)**[12] 813 4-9-7 40....................................(b) KDalgleish 10 9
(BSRothwell) *prom: hung rt 1/2-way: sn wknd* **33/1**

00-5 **8** *1/2* **Aboustar**[40] 567 4-9-0 40................................................ MLawson(7) 11 8
(MBrittain) *mid-div: rdn 4f out: sn wknd* **20/1**

6-05 **9** *1* **Dandy Jim**[14] 780 3-8-4 30................................................ JQuinn 2 5
(DWChapman) *s.i.s: outpcd* **20/1**

60-4 **10** *4* **Shotley Dancer**[10] 823 5-9-7 40........................................ JBramhill 9 —
(NBycroft) *sn outpcd* **33/1**

04-6 **11** *13* **Brillyant Dancer**[12] 807 6-9-7 35....................................(b[1]) GDuffield 5 —
(MrsADuffield) *dwlt: outpcd* **50/1**

1m 34.24s (3.44) **Going Correction** +0.40s/f (Slow)
**WFA** 3 from 4yo+ 17lb **11** Ran SP% **117.3**
Speed ratings: **96,94,93,92,86 82,79,78,77,72 58**CSF £8.05 TOTE £2.00: £1.20, £1.70, £6.60; EX 10.60.
**Owner** S Day **Bred** Lord Halifax **Trained** Audley, Staffs

**FOCUS**
Poor form though the winner is going the right way, but the same cannot be said about most of the others.

**NOTEBOOK**
**Smart Scot** completed the hat-trick with a clear-cut success. He was being closed down at the finish, but was always going to hold on and could well complete the four-timer, even if he has to be stepped up to a Band A race.
**Jessie** had been running well in a better grade recently, but proved unable to make the most of this drop in class.
**Neutral Night(IRE)** lost her chance with a slow start at Wolverhampton last time, but this was a better effort. However, she remains a maiden after 25 starts.
**Mathmagician**, another long-standing maiden, was well held.
**Silver Mascot** was below form with no obvious excuse.
**Sweet Coral(FR)** *Official explanation: jockey said filly had hung right-handed throughout*

## 935 BETDIRECT.CO.UK MEDIAN AUCTION MAIDEN STKS 1m 3f (F)
2:55 (2:57) (H ) 4-6-Y-0 **£1,445** (£413; £206) **Stalls** Low

Form RPR

0-22 **1** **Fleeting Moon**[25] 676 4-8-6 55........................................ LPKeniry(3) 3 49+
(AMBalding) *a.p: chsd ldr over 5f out: led over 2f out: eased wl ins fnl f* **1/3**[1]

0232 **2** *4* **Kustom Kit For Her**[5] 877 4-8-9 45....................................(t) JBramhill 6 43
(SRBowring) *led over 8f: styd on same pce* **9/2**[2]

60-5 **3** *1 3/4* **Dora Corbino**[23] 697 4-8-9 45........................................ ACulhane 4 40
(RHollinshead) *hld up in tch: pushed along 8f out: outpcd over 4f out: styd on u.p ins fnl f* **12/1**[3]

000/ **4** *dist* **Bettys Valentine**[460] 5790 4-8-5 ow1........................ TEaves(5) 1 —
(DWBarker) *chsd ldrs over 6f* **33/1**

0-0 **5** *28* **Blue Bijou**[30] 642 4-9-0................................................ DeanMcKeown 5 —
(TTClement) *chsd ldr tl hung lft and wknd over 5f out* **50/1**

2m 34.38s (5.48) **Going Correction** +0.40s/f (Slow) **5** Ran SP% **105.8**
Speed ratings: **96,93,91,—,—**CSF £1.87 TOTE £1.20: £1.10, £1.20; EX 1.50.
**Owner** M E Wates **Bred** M E Wates **Trained** Kingsclere, Hants

**FOCUS**
A poor maiden, but Fleeting Moon had nothing to beat and is better than this.

**NOTEBOOK**
**Fleeting Moon** confirmed the promise she showed on Polytrack to get off the mark with an easy success. She beat nothing and things will be harder for her in handicaps, but she is at least on a realistic mark.
**Kustom Kit For Her** did not prove she stays this trip, weakening badly in the straight.
**Dora Corbino** was doing her best work late on, but never once looked like giving the winner a race.
**Bettys Valentine** did not improve for this step up in trip.
**Blue Bijou** *Official explanation: jockey said gelding had hung left-handed*

## 936 BET IN RUNNING @ BETDIRECT.CO.UK BANDED STKS 6f (F)
3:25 (3:28) (H ) 3-Y-0+ **£1,505** (£430; £215) **Stalls** Low

Form RPR

3100 **1** **Star Lad (IRE)**[20] 728 4-9-6 45 (b) ADaly 10 48
(RBrotherton) *mde all: rdn over 1f out: all out* **25/1**

3031 **2** *hd* **Sergeant Slipper**[5] 876 7-9-12 45 (v) RFitzpatrick 14 53
(CSmith) *dwlt: hdwy over 1f out: r.o* **12/1**

3501 **3** *2 ½* **Sabana (IRE)**[13] 799 6-9-3 52 (b) BReilly(3) 5 40
(JMBradley) *hld up in tch: n.m.r and lost pl over 4f out: swtchd rt 2f out: r.o ins fnl f: nt rch ldrs* **9/2[1]**

2312 **4** *hd* **Enjoy The Buzz**[12] 813 5-9-6 45 GDuffield 2 39
(JMBradley) *hld up: hmpd over 4f out: nt clr run over 3f out: hdwy over 1f out: styd on same pce ins fnl f* **9/2[1]**

0-32 **5** *3* **Spy Master**[14] 780 6-9-1 40 (bt) MSavage(5) 4 30
(JParkes) *dwlt: hdwy over 1f out: nt trble ldrs* **7/1[3]**

400- **6** *½* **Wub Cub**[176] 4732 4-9-3 45 ABeech(3) 12 28
(ADickman) *sn chsng wnr: edgd lft over 4f out: rdn over 2f out: wknd fnl f* **40/1**

/02U **7** *4* **Port Natal (IRE)**[6] 861 6-8-13 45 (b) LTreadwell(7) 8 16
(PatrickMorris, Ire) *chsd ldrs: hmpd over 4f out: wknd over 1f out* **12/1**

3153 **8** *1* **Torrent**[5] 876 9-9-6 45 (b) ACulhane 7 13
(DWChapman) *hld up in tch: shkn up over 1f out: sn wknd* **6/1[2]**

/0-0 **9** *nk* **Compton Bay**[23] 694 4-9-1 45 TEaves(5) 3 13
(MBrittain) *prom: hmpd over 4f out: wknd over 1f out* **33/1**

-000 **10** *1 ½* **On The Trail**[5] 876 7-9-6 45 KDalgleish 1 —
(DWChapman) *hld up: sme hdwy whn hmpd 2f out: n.d* **16/1**

000- **11** *1 ½* **Bond Domingo**[82] 6155 5-8-13 40 (b) MStainton(7) 11 —
(BSmart) *chsd ldrs: hmpd over 4f out: hung lft 2f out: sn wknd* **20/1**

1200 **12** *3* **Eternal Bloom**[31] 626 6-8-13 45 MLawson(7) 15 —
(MBrittain) *chsd ldrs: rdn over 3f out: wknd over 2f out* **20/1**

00-0 **13** *hd* **Sugar Cube Treat**[57] 422 8-8-13 30 PVarley(7) 13 —
(MMullineaux) *s.i.s: outpcd* **100/1**

0203 **14** *1 ½* **Above Board**[20] 728 9-9-6 45 (t) DeanMcKeown 9 —
(RFMarvin) *chsd ldrs: hmpd over 4f out: wknd over 2f out* **20/1**

-335 **15** *¾* **Bells Boy's**[12] 813 5-9-6 40 (b) GParkin 6 —
(KARyan) *prom: hmpd over 4f out and 2f out: sn wknd* **8/1**

1m 19.67s (2.87) **Going Correction** +0.40s/f (Slow) **15** Ran SP% **120.0**
Speed ratings: **96,95,92,92,88 87,82,80,80,78 76,72,72,70,69**CSF £279.59 TOTE £50.50: £9.40, £4.10, £1.30; EX 247.90.
**Owner** R Austin & Mrs P Austin **Bred** R N Auld **Trained** Elmley Castle, Worcs
■ Stewards Enquiry : M Stainton caution: careless riding
A Daly one-day ban: careless riding (Mar 13); one-day ban: used whip with excessive frequency (Mar 14)

**FOCUS**
Quite a competitive, but very moderate, sprint and questionable form given how the race panned out.

**NOTEBOOK**
**Star Lad(IRE)**, with the blinkers on instead of a visor, gained his first win outside of a seller with a narrow victory.
**Sergeant Slipper** has done all of his winning over five furlongs, but gets this extra furlong well and was just held.
**Sabana(IRE)**, a 33/1 winner of a Wolverhampton seller on his previous run, did not get the clearest of runs and emerged with credit.
**Enjoy The Buzz** endured a nightmare run and it was no surprise he was unable to sustain his effort when finally in the clear. He is better than this.
**Spy Master** is not very consistent.
**Above Board** *Official explanation: jockey said gelding had finished lame*

## 937 BETDIRECT.CO.UK NEW SITE BANDED STKS 1m 4f (F)
3:55 (3:56) (H ) 4-Y-0+ **£1,634** (£467; £233) **Stalls** Low

Form RPR

-620 **1** **Jungle Lion**[20] 724 6-9-1 45 (t) DeanMcKeown 3 57
(JohnAHarris) *w ldrs: led over 8f out: clr fnl 3f* **20/1**

1111 **2** *7* **Broughton Knows**[5] 878 7-9-4 46 (b) LisaJones(3) 6 53
(WJMusson) *dwlt: hld up: hdwy over 2f out: hung lft and chsd wnr over 1f out: no imp* **8/11[1]**

1-05 **3** *1 ½* **Stravmour**[31] 629 8-9-1 45 DaleGibson 5 44
(RHollinshead) *prom: chsd wnr over 4f out: sn rdn: outpcd fnl 3f* **7/2[2]**

5-03 **4** *7* **Fortunes Favourite**[14] 781 4-8-12 45 JQuinn 8 34
(GMMoore) *chsd ldrs: rdn over 3f out: wknd over 2f out* **20/1**

-006 **5** *3* **Maunby Rocker**[19] 733 4-8-12 45 GFaulkner 1 29
(PCHaslam) *prom over 8f* **14/1**

F416 **6** *7* **Shatin Special**[3] 902 4-8-5 45 (p) DeanWilliams(7) 2 19
(GCHChung) *hld up: hdwy 7f out: wknd over 3f out* **17/2[3]**

060- **7** *17* **Laird Dara Mac**[119] 5195 4-8-5 40 SuzanneFrance(7) 9 —
(NBycroft) *sn led: hdd 9f out: wknd wl over 3f out* **100/1**

050/ **8** *12* **Risky Way**[23] 1987 8-9-1 45 (p) KDalgleish 4 —
(BSRothwell) *w ldrs: led 9f out: sn hdd: wknd 5f out* **66/1**

-050 **9** *13* **Phoenix Nights (IRE)**[30] 641 4-8-7 45 (b[1]) PBradley(5) 7 —
(ABerry) *hld up: rdn and wknd over 4f out* **50/1**

2m 46.57s (4.47) **Going Correction** +0.40s/f (Slow)
**WFA** 4 from 6yo+ 3lb **9** Ran SP% **111.3**
Speed ratings: **101,96,95,90,88 84,72,64,56**CSF £33.36 TOTE £23.50: £4.50, £1.02, £1.10; EX 37.30.
**Owner** Mick Rowley **Bred** Buckram Thoroughbred Enterprises Inc **Trained** Eastwell, Leics
■ Stewards Enquiry : J Quinn one-day ban: careless riding (Mar 13)

**FOCUS**
Fair form for the grade by the winner, but a weak race in which Jungle Lion benefited from a positive ride to turn over the favourite. A fair winning time for the grade.

**NOTEBOOK**
**Jungle Lion** benefited from a positive ride on this drop in trip to gain his first win since landing a maiden in 2000 on his debut. This will have boosted his confidence.
**Broughton Knows**, chasing the five-timer, is not an easy ride and was still in the rear when the winner kicked on rounding the home bend. He kept on in the straight, but was never going to get there.
**Stravmour** did not look to have any real excuses.
**Fortunes Favourite** was well beaten and looks a bit tripless.
**Maunby Rocker** continues out of form.

## 938 BETDIRECT.CO.UK (S) STKS 5f (F)
4:25 (4:26) (H ) 3-Y-0+ **£1,319** (£377; £188) **Stalls** High

Form RPR

3502 **1** **Henry Tun**[20] 721 6-9-2 51 (b) DAllan(3) 3 51
(JBalding) *mde all: rdn clr over 1f out: eased nr fin* **11/4[2]**

002 **2** *2* **African Spur (IRE)**[26] 670 4-9-5 64 DeanMcKeown 4 44
(SLKeightley) *chsd ldrs: outpcd whn n.m.r 2f out: styd on u.p ins fnl f* **15/8[1]**

0650 **3** *½* **Heathyardsblessing (IRE)**[13] 799 7-8-12 45 StephanieHollinshead(7) 7 42
(RHollinshead) *sn pushed along in rr: hdwy to chse wnr and hung rt 2f out: no ex ins fnl f* **20/1**

0006 **4** *nk* **Lone Piper**[5] 876 9-9-2 35 BReilly(3) 8 41
(JMBradley) *hld up: hdwy and hmpd 2f out: rdr dropped whip ins fnl f: kpt on* **22/1**

5100 **5** *nk* **Mr Spliffy (IRE)**[3] 893 5-9-4 51 (v) AReilly(7) 5 46
(KRBurke) *chsd ldrs: rdn 1/2-way: kpt on* **12/1**

0400 **6** *nk* **Attorney**[3] 897 6-9-4 45 (e) PMakin(7) 1 45
(DShaw) *s.i.s: hdwy over 1f out: styd on same pce ins fnl f* **16/1**

6120 **7** *5* **Cark**[13] 794 6-9-11 50 (p) JQuinn 2 27
(JJay) *chsd ldrs over 3f* **9/1[3]**

1540 **8** *4* **So Sober (IRE)**[4] 884 6-9-11 45 DarrenWilliams 11 13
(DShaw) *sn outpcd* **12/1**

00-0 **9** *2* **Valazar (USA)**[20] 721 5-9-5 50 ACulhane 6 —
(DWChapman) *chsd ldrs: rdn 1/2-way: wkng whn hmpd wl over 1f out* **20/1**

-604 **10** *nk* **The Leather Wedge (IRE)**[5] 876 5-9-0 45 PBradley(5) 10 —
(ABerry) *s.i.s: sn chsng ldrs: wknd 2f out* **16/1**

236- **11** *9* **Shady Deal**[209] 3847 8-9-5 30 GDuffield 9 —
(JMBradley) *s.i.s: outpcd* **40/1**

63.44 secs (3.14) **Going Correction** +0.575s/f (Slow) **11** Ran SP% **118.4**
Speed ratings: **97,93,93,92,92 91,83,77,73,73 59** CT £4.00 TOTE £1.80: £1.10, £5.80, £; EX7.50 1.There was no bid for the winner. Cark (no.2) was claimed by Garry Noble for £4,000, Mr Spliffy (no.3) was claimed by Queens Head Racing for £
**Owner** J Bladen **Bred** T Tunstall **Trained** Scrooby, Notts
■ Stewards Enquiry : Stephanie Hollinshead caution: careless riding

**FOCUS**
A very ordinary seller and woeful form in behind the winner. The favourite African Spur failed to run to form.

**NOTEBOOK**
**Henry Tun**, dropped in grade, had 13lb to find with the winner at the weights, but that one did not run to form and he ran out a very convincing winner.
**African Spur(IRE)** was well backed on this debut for new connections, but needed plenty of driving and never looked like getting to the winner.
**Heathyardsblessing(IRE)**, with the cheekpieces left off, and dropped a furlong in trip, was unable to go the early pace but finished to good effect and may do better back up in trip.
**Lone Piper** had it all to do at the weights and is on a long losing run, but this was a respectable effort.
**Mr Spliffy(IRE)** has never won on this surface.

## 939 LITTLEWOODS BET DIRECT BANDED STKS 1m (F)
4:55 (4:55) (H ) 3-Y-0+ **£1,515** (£433; £216) **Stalls** Low

Form RPR

600- **1** **Rust En Vrede**[221] 3491 5-9-1 45 DTudhope(7) 14 56
(DCarroll) *chsd ldr: led over 2f out: rdn out* **28/1**

-645 **2** *1 ¼* **Red Delirium**[21] 714 8-9-3 40 (b) DNolan(5) 5 53
(PABlockley) *s.i.s: outpcd: hdwy over 2f out: styd on* **11/1**

-144 **3** *5* **Printsmith (IRE)**[20] 725 7-9-8 45 JBramhill 9 42
(JRNorton) *mid-div: rdn over 3f out: chsd wnr 2f out: no ex fnl f* **9/1**

-014 **4** *½* **Mr Whizz**[10] 604 7-9-1 45 (be) DerekNolan(7) 12 41
(APJones) *chsd ldrs: rdn 1/2-way: styd on same pce appr fnl f* **20/1**

5224 **5** *1 ½* **Maggie's Pet**[13] 787 7-9-8 45 (t) DRMcCabe 7 38
(KBell) *chsd ldrs: rdn over 3f out: styd on same pce fnl 2f* **6/1[3]**

1130 **6** *shd* **Rosti**[26] 667 4-9-8 45 GFaulkner 11 38
(PCHaslam) *hld up: n.m.r over 4f out: hdwy over 2f out: wknd ins fnl f* **5/1[2]**

-556 **7** *5* **Air Of Esteem**[13] 800 8-9-1 45 DFentiman(7) 3 27
(IanEmmerson) *mid-div: sn drvn along: wknd over 3f out* **8/1**

0-61 **8** *½* **Wilson Bluebottle (IRE)**[12] 814 5-9-8 46 (b) DaleGibson 8 26
(MWEasterby) *led 7f out: rdn and hdd over 2f out: wknd over 1f out* **2/1[1]**

-665 **9** *1 ¼* **Platinum Chief**[17] 751 3-7-13 45 ow3 PPMathers(7) 1 26
(ABerry) *mid-div: sn drvn along: dropped rr 1/2-way: no ch whn hrd rdn and hung lft fnl 2f* **40/1**

3160 **10** *5* **Sandorra**[23] 700 6-9-1 45 MLawson(7) 6 12
(MBrittain) *led 1f: remained handy tl wknd over 3f out* **33/1**

/50- **11** *6* **Samba Beat**[414] 292 5-9-8 45 DeanMcKeown 10 —
(RFMarvin) *s.i.s: outpcd* **100/1**

5303 **12** *18* **Tinian**[20] 720 6-9-8 45 DarrenWilliams 2 —
(KRBurke) *sn pushed along and prom: wknd over 3f out* **11/1**

0 **13** *8* **Temptation Island (IRE)**[2] 910 5-9-8 45 JQuinn 4 —
(JohnAQuinn, Ire) *s.i.s: outpcd* **28/1**

1m 48.0s (3.40) **Going Correction** +0.40s/f (Slow)
**WFA** 3 from 4yo+ 19lb **13** Ran SP% **120.1**
Speed ratings: **99,97,92,92,90 90,85,85,83,78 72,54,46**CSF £294.91 TOTE £53.30: £6.10, £3.50, £2.30; EX 1037.50 Place 6 £61.48, Place 5 £37.79.
**Owner** Alan Mann **Bred** T J Cooper **Trained** Warthill, N Yorks
■ Stewards Enquiry : Derek Nolan three-day ban: used whip with excessive frequency (Mar 13,14,16)

**FOCUS**
A poor race, but the front two were clear and this was strong banded form from the pair.

**NOTEBOOK**
**Rust En Vrede**, with the visor left off for this first run in 221 days, finally got off the mark with a decisive success. This was his first start on Fibresand, but he handled the surface well.
**Red Delirium** ran well on his first start for Paul Blockley and shaped as though he may do even better returned to slightly further.
**Printsmith(IRE)** looked to have very chance, but she proved no match for the front two.
**Mr Whizz**, well beaten in a selling hurdle last time, ran better on this return to the level, but at the same time was comfortably held.
**Maggie's Pet** remains a maiden.
**Wilson Bluebottle(IRE)** was a major disappointment, proving unable to build on his recent Wolverhampton success over this shorter trip. *Official explanation: trainer's representative had no explanation for the poor form shown*
**Temptation Island(IRE)** *Official explanation: jockey said mare lost her action in the closing stages*
T/Plt: £57.10 to a £1 stake. Pool: £39,200.20. 500.30 winning tickets. T/Qpdt: £43.60 to a £1 stake. Pool: £2,160.60. 36.60 winning tickets. CR

# [903]WOLVERHAMPTON (A.W) (L-H)

Monday, March 1

**OFFICIAL GOING: Slow**

The run of meetings on testing ground continued.

Wind: nil Weather: sunny

## 940 BET DIRECT ON ATTHERACES TEXT PAGE 410 AMATEUR RIDERS' BANDED STKS 1m 100y(F)

2:20 (2:26) (H ) 4-Y-0+ £1,449 (£414; £207) Stalls Low

Form RPR

00-0 **1** **Jake Black (IRE)**[22] [715] 4-11-7 40 MrSWalker 6 47
(JJQuinn) *led over 1f: remained prom: rdn over 3f out: led ins fnl f: r.o* **9/4**[1]

605- **2** *1 1/4* **Sadlers Swing (USA)**[199] [4165] 8-11-4 40 MrEDehdashti(3) 8 44
(JJSheehan) *s.s: hdwy over 6f out: rdn over 2f out: led wl over 1f out: hdd and edgd rt ins fnl f: nt qckn* **8/1**

-600 **3** *3/4* **Dundonald**[7] [861] 5-11-2 35 (bt) MrLNewnes(5) 2 42
(MAppleby) *w ldr: led 7f out tl over 5f out: led again 2f out: sn rdn: hdd wl over 1f out: nt qckn fnl f* **20/1**

3233 **4** *1* **Kenny The Truth (IRE)**[11] [824] 5-11-0 40 (t) MrDWeekes(7) 4 40
(MrsJCandlish) *hld up: rdn and hdwy over 2f out: one pce fnl f* **5/1**[3]

00/0 **5** *2 1/2* **Mr Perry (IRE)**[10] [838] 8-11-0 30 MrKFord(7) 11 35
(MrsPFord) *bhd tl hdwy on outside 3f out: sn rdn: no imp fnl f* **20/1**

0204 **6** *1 1/2* **Zahunda (IRE)**[7] [861] 5-11-0 40 MrCDavies(7) 9 32
(WMBrisbourne) *t.k.h: sn mid-div: rdn and hdwy over 2f out: eased whn btn ins fnl f* **4/1**[2]

-000 **7** *2 1/2* **Waterline Dancer (IRE)**[7] [858] 4-11-2 40 (t) MissHayleyBryan(5) 7 27
(PDEvans) *hld up mid-div: rdn and hdwy over 2f out: eased whn btn ins fnl f* **16/1**

0424 **8** *1 3/4* **All On My Own (USA)**[14] [793] 9-11-7 40 (b) MissEJJones 3 23
(IWMcinnes) *stmbld s: sn rcvrd: hdwy over 4f out: hrd rdn and ev ch on ins over 1f out: wknd fnl f* **8/1**

0-00 **9** *3 1/2* **Manikato (USA)**[47] [532] 10-11-0 30 (tp) MrSJGraham(7) 5 16
(KGWingrove) *a bhd* **33/1**

000- **10** *1 1/2* **Tern Intern (IRE)**[257] [1833] 5-11-0 35 MissFionaBrown(7) 13 13
(MissJFeilden) *stdd s: a bhd* **22/1**

000- **11** *12* **Rivelli (IRE)**[76] [6202] 5-11-0 40 MrABrooke(7) 10 —
(BRFoster) *hdwy over 6f out: led over 5f out: hdd 2f out: sn wknd* **25/1**

-060 **12** *11* **Aljomar**[6] [875] 5-11-0 35 MissVBarr(7) 1 —
(REBarr) *prom 3f* **40/1**

2m 3.72s (12.72) **Going Correction** +0.925s/f (Slow) **12 Ran SP% 118.6**

Speed ratings: **73,71,71,70,67 66,63,61,58,56 44,33**CSF £18.55 TOTE £2.90: £1.70, £2.90, £5.40; EX 33.00.

**Owner** G A Lucas **Bred** Yeomanstown Stud **Trained** Settrington, N Yorks

■ Stewards Enquiry : Mr S J Graham caution: used whip when out of contention

Miss E J Jones two-day ban: used whip with excessive force (Mar 23, Apr 1)

**FOCUS**

This poor event turned out to be competitive, but the winning time was painfully slow.

**NOTEBOOK**

**Jake Black(IRE)**, a winner over hurdles at Newcastle in November, was suited by a drop back in distance, having failed to stay a mile and a half last time. *Official explanation: trainer's representative said, regarding the improved form shown, gelding had benefited from the drop in trip*

**Sadlers Swing(USA)**, lightly raced, was dropped in class for this first outing since last August.

**Dundonald** stepped up considerably on his three starts at up to a mile and a half here last month, but only boasts a record of one win in 38 attempts.

**Kenny The Truth(IRE)** continues to run well in this sort of company without winning.

## 941 BET DIRECT ON ATTHERACES TEXT PAGE 411 CLAIMING STKS 6f (F)

2:50 (2:56) (H ) 3-Y-0+ £1,477 (£422; £211) Stalls Low

Form RPR

4305 **1** **Lord Melbourne (IRE)**[7] [858] 5-9-7 50 DHolland 3 56
(AGJuckes) *sn outpcd and bhd: rdn and hdwy over 2f out: r.o to ld wl ins fnl f* **2/1**[1]

4-44 **2** *1/2* **Inchcoonan**[25] [685] 6-9-2 55 (p) DarrenWilliams 8 50
(KRBurke) *chsd ldrs: rdn to ld wl over 1f out: sn edgd rt: hdd and nt qckn wl ins fnl f* **8/1**

3246 **3** *1/2* **Larky's Lob**[10] [833] 5-9-4 45 LFletcher(3) 13 53
(PaulJohnson) *hld up: hdwy 3f out: rdn and carried rt fr over 1f out: ev ch ins fnl f: nt qckn* **10/1**

0-05 **4** *5* **Mystery Mountain**[13] [807] 4-9-5 47 IMongan 9 36
(MrsJRRamsden) *hld up: sn bhd: hrd rdn and hdwy over 2f out: kpt on ins fnl f: nt trble ldrs* **20/1**

33-3 **5** *2 1/2* **Levantine (IRE)**[21] [725] 7-9-7 45 (b) SWhitworth 12 31
(AGNewcombe) *a.p: rdn wl over 1f out: sn btn* **7/1**[3]

-020 **6** *1* **River Days (IRE)**[3] [904] 6-9-2 56 (vt[1]) MFenton 7 23
(MissGayKelleway) *s.i.s: sn chsng ldrs: rdn over 2f out: wknd over 1f out* **9/2**[2]

6004 **7** *1/2* **Soaked**[17] [762] 11-9-7 47 (b) ACulhane 6 26
(DWChapman) *sn led: rdn and hdd wl over 1f out: wknd fnl f* **16/1**

6040 **8** *3/4* **Flying Faisal (USA)**[7] [858] 6-9-7 40 (p) CCatlin 11 24
(JMBradley) *led early: sn mid-div: rdn over 3f out: sn bhd* **16/1**

-026 **9** *8* **Court Music (IRE)**[15] [780] 5-9-2 35 (v) RFitzpatrick 4 —
(REBarr) *prom tl rdn and wknd 2f out* **33/1**

00- **10** *3 1/2* **Queen Louisa**[86] [6136] 4-8-10 TEaves(5) 10 —
(FWatson) *s.i.s: a bhd* **66/1**

0-05 **11** *10* **Bar Of Silver (IRE)**[14] [788] 4-9-7 45 (v) RWinston 2 —
(RBrotherton) *bhd fnl 4f* **9/1**

1m 21.26s (5.56) **Going Correction** +0.925s/f (Slow) **11 Ran SP% 115.2**

Speed ratings: **99,98,97,91,87 86,85,84,74,69 56**CSF £17.61 TOTE £2.40: £1.40, £2.00, £3.60; EX 23.50.Larky's Lob (no.4) was claimed for £5,000 by N Tinkler. Lord Melbourne (no.6) was the subject of a friendly claim of £5,000.

**Owner** Mrs K C Price **Bred** Fin A Co **Trained** Abberley, Worcs

■ Stewards Enquiry : Darren Williams one-day ban: careless riding (Mar 13)

**FOCUS**

A poor claimer that was weakened by a couple of morning withdrawals.

**NOTEBOOK**

**Lord Melbourne(IRE)** came from a seemingly hopeless position to make a winning debut for his new connections. He really wants seven but just got away with it on this demanding surface.

**Inchcoonan** had the cheekpieces back on having also sported a visor in the past. This was a much better effort over a trip short of her best.

**Larky's Lob**, done no favours by the runner-up, is another who is arguably better over another furlong.

**Mystery Mountain** was never a threat to the three principals.

**Levantine(IRE)** did not find a drop back to six the answer.

**River Days(IRE)**, back up to six, was fitted with a visor instead of the usual blinkers.

**Bar Of Silver(IRE)** *Official explanation: trainer said gelding was unsuited by the slow ground*

## 942 BET DIRECT ON ATTHERACES TEXT PAGE 412 MEDIAN AUCTION MAIDEN STKS 7f (F)

3:20 (3:26) (H ) 3-5-Y-0 £1,438 (£411; £205) Stalls High

Form RPR

4-33 **1** **Two Of Clubs**[32] [631] 3-8-5 61 (p) GFaulkner 6 67
(PCHaslam) *led over 1f: w ldr: led again over 2f out: sn rdn: clr over 1f out: r.o wl* **1/2**[1]

6453 **2** *6* **Sonderborg**[13] [808] 3-8-0 49 (p) JQuinn 1 47
(GLMoore) *chsd ldrs: rdn 3f out: wnt 2nd jst over 1f out: no ch w wnr* **7/2**[2]

5000 **3** *5* **Dances In Time**[14] [794] 4-9-2 45 (b[1]) ACulhane 5 35
(CNKellett) *led over 5f out: rdn over 3f out: hdd over 2f out: wknd fnl f* **33/1**

0-00 **4** *1 1/2* **Heathyards Joy**[24] [696] 3-8-0 30 RFfrench 3 31
(RHollinshead) *hld up in tch: rdn over 4f out: sn wknd* **50/1**

**5** *5* **My Little Sophia** 4-9-2 SWKelly 4 18
(MMullineaux) *wl bhd fnl 5f* **40/1**

000- **6** *2 1/2* **I Wish I Knew**[93] [6090] 3-8-5 63 JFEgan 2 17
(DJCoakley) *hld up in tch: rdn over 3f out: wknd over 2f out* **6/1**[3]

1m 37.07s (6.87) **Going Correction** +0.925s/f (Slow)

**WFA** 3 from 4yo 16lb **6 Ran SP% 110.5**

Speed ratings: **97,90,84,82,77 74**CSF £2.42 TOTE £1.40: £1.10, £2.00; EX 1.90.

**Owner** Blue Lion Racing II **Bred** P B T Group **Trained** Middleham Moor, N Yorks

**FOCUS**

A dreadful maiden, but the winner bounced back to his best.

**NOTEBOOK**

**Two Of Clubs** made the most of a golden opportunity in a desperate affair.

**Sonderborg** did nothing more than finish best of the rest.

**Dances In Time** had also found this trip beyond her when running here in January.

**I Wish I Knew** *Official explanation: jockey said gelding moved badly throughout*

## 943 BET DIRECT ON ATTHERACES TEXT PAGE 413 BANDED STKS 1m 4f (F)

3:50 (3:56) (H ) 4-Y-0+ £1,599 (£457; £228) Stalls Low

Form RPR

2122 **1** **Buz Kiri (USA)**[6] [880] 6-8-12 40 PDoe 3 53
(AWCarroll) *hld up: hdwy 5f out: rdn over 3f out: led ins fnl f: r.o* **3/1**[2]

3212 **2** *1/2* **Galley Law**[6] [875] 4-8-5 40 TEaves(5) 8 52
(RCraggs) *a.p: led over 3f out tl ins fnl f: hrd rdn: r.o* **7/4**[1]

-310 **3** *10* **Seraph**[22] [715] 4-8-10 40 (p) JQuinn 4 37
(JohnAHarris) *a.p: rdn over 3f out: wknd over 1f out* **6/1**[3]

6301 **4** *3* **Free Style (GER)**[7] [857] 4-9-2 40 GBaker 9 39
(KRBurke) *hld up: hdwy over 6f out: rdn over 4f out: wknd over 3f out* **15/2**

500/ **5** *5* **Buying A Dream (IRE)**[637] [1823] 7-8-12 35 CCatlin 5 25
(AndrewTurnell) *hld up: lost pl 7f out: rdn over 4f out: sme hdwy over 3f out: wknd 2f out* **50/1**

-000 **6** *1/2* **Moyne Pleasure (IRE)**[6] [875] 6-8-9 35 LFletcher(3) 7 25
(PaulJohnson) *led early: w ldr: led again over 6f out: hdd over 3f out: sn rdn: wknd 2f out* **33/1**

6634 **7** *nk* **Think Quick (IRE)**[4] [901] 4-8-3 35 HFellows(7) 10 24
(RHollinshead) *hld up and bhd: hdwy over 6f out: rdn over 4f out: sn wknd* **25/1**

5365 **8** *8* **Ipledgeallegiance (USA)**[21] [727] 8-8-12 35 ACulhane 2 12
(DWChapman) *a bhd* **22/1**

20-4 **9** *dist* **Time Marches On**[13] [814] 6-8-12 40 JFanning 1 —
(MrsMReveley) *bhd fnl 5f: t.o* **8/1**

060- **10** *dist* **Blue Water**[226] [3391] 4-8-3 40 (p) PVarley(7) 6 —
(MMullineaux) *sn led: hdd over 6f out: wknd qckly over 5f out: t.o* **33/1**

2m 54.02s (12.52) **Going Correction** +0.925s/f (Slow)

**WFA** 4 from 6yo+ 2lb **10 Ran SP% 114.6**

Speed ratings: **95,94,88,86,82 82,82,76,—,—**CSF £7.94 TOTE £4.00: £1.30, £1.10, £2.00; EX 6.80.

**Owner** Serafino Agodino **Bred** Jamm Ltd And W Lazy T Ltd **Trained** Wixford, Warwicks

**FOCUS**

A poor contest where only the first two home got the trip in the stamina-sapping conditions.

**NOTEBOOK**

**Buz Kiri(USA)** had finished second over an extra quarter-mile last time and his stamina stood him in good stead in the closing stages.

**Galley Law**, reverting to a longer trip, was 6lb worse off than when five lengths in front of the winner over a furlong shorter at Southwell last month.

**Seraph** got found out by the demanding surface in the home straight.

**Free Style(GER)** found this deep ground a totally different kettle of fish to the Polytrack at Lingfield.

**Time Marches On** *Official explanation: jockey said gelding hung in the back straight*

## 944 BET DIRECT DAILY SPECIAL OFFERS BANDED STKS 5f (F)

4:20 (4:27) (H ) 3-Y-0+ £1,368 (£391; £195) Stalls Low

Form RPR

0424 **1** **White O' Morn**[4] [898] 5-9-4 35 (tp) GGibbons 8 37
(BAMcmahon) *sn pushed along: rdn over 3f out: gd hdwy on outside over 2f out: led over 1f out: all out* **11/4**[2]

00-5 **2** *nk* **Maron**[27] [665] 7-9-4 35 (b) DKinsella 4 36
(FJordan) *s.i.s: bhd tl hdwy on outside wl over 1f out: r.o wl ins fnl f* **7/1**

0064 **3** *1 1/4* **Lone Piper**[1] [938] 9-9-4 35 CCatlin 2 32
(JMBradley) *hld up: hdwy on ins 2f out: sn rdn: swtchd rt jst over 1f out: kpt on ins fnl f* **9/4**[1]

000- **4** *3 1/2* **Attila The Hun**[73] [6217] 5-9-4 30 (v[1]) RWinston 10 20
(FWatson) *led after 1f: rdn and hdd over 1f out: wknd ins fnl f* **20/1**

600- **5** *1* **Only For Gold**[45] [3952] 9-9-4 35 SWhitworth 7 16
(DrPPritchard) *outpcd and bhd: late hdwy: nrst fin* **11/1**

00-0 **6** *nk* **Diamond Racket**[49] [499] 4-9-4 35 (b) ACulhane 5 15
(DWChapman) *hld up in tch: rdn and wknd wl over 1f out* **20/1**

-000 **7** *nk* **Tuscan Dream**[28] [657] 9-9-4 35 FLynch 3 14
(ABerry) *led 1f: prom: rdn over 2f out: wknd fnl f* **12/1**

0 **8** *1* **Havana Rose (IRE)**[6] [875] 4-8-11 30 (p) DAMcCormack(7) 1 11
(PatrickMorris, Ire) *s.i.s: outpcd* **33/1**

36-0 **9** *3 1/2* **Shady Deal**[1] [938] 8-8-11 30 BSwarbrick(7) 9 —
(JMBradley) *chsd ldrs: rdn over 2f out: wknd wl over 1f out* **9/2**[3]

00-0 **10** *27* **Silent Angel**[22] [718] 4-9-4 30 (p) JQuinn 6 —
(MrsLucindaFeatherstone) *prom tl wknd over 2f out: t.o* **40/1**

67.61 secs (5.01) **Going Correction** +0.925s/f (Slow) **10 Ran SP% 119.0**

Speed ratings: **96,95,93,87,86 85,85,83,78,34**CSF £21.75 TOTE £4.40: £1.70, £2.30, £1.10; EX 19.10.

**Owner** Mrs A H Stokes **Bred** M G T Stokes **Trained** Hopwas, Staffs

■ Stewards Enquiry : D A McCormack three-day ban: use whip with excessive frequency (Mar 13-14, 16)

**FOCUS**
This was really scraping the bottom of the barrel and most of these have been on the downgrade for some time.

**NOTEBOOK**
**White O' Morn**, with the tongue-tie back on, made very hard work of losing her maiden tag.
**Maron** is usually campaigned over further and could not quite peg back the winner.
**Lone Piper** was sent off favourite on the strength of his run in a seller at Southwell the previous day.
**Attila The Hun** was reverting to the minimum trip in the first-time visor.
**Only For Gold** found this trip totally inadequate.
**Silent Angel** *Official explanation: jockey said filly had breathing problems*

## 945 BET DIRECT IN RUNNING SKY TEXT PAGE 293 BANDED STKS 1m 1f 79y(F)
**4:50** (4:57) (H) 3-Y-0+ **£1,389** (£397; £198) **Stalls** Low

Form RPR
060- **1** **Mrs Cube**$^{175}$ [4766] 5-9-8 35 RWinston 10 50
(PHowling) *a.p: led 3f out: faltered and rdn 2f out: clr 1f out: r.o wl* **9/2**$^{2}$
00-5 **2** *9* **A Bit Of Fun**$^{21}$ [730] 3-8-2 35 JBramhill 7 32
(JJQuinn) *plld hrd: led early: prom: rdn over 3f out: chsd wnr fnl 2f: one pce* **6/1**$^{3}$
0-06 **3** *1 ¾* **Sophomore**$^{22}$ [714] 10-9-8 35 SWhitworth 4 29
(JohnAHarris) *hld up in tch: rdn over 4f out: one pce fnl 2f* **8/1**
6/35 **4** *2 ½* **Adjiram (IRE)**$^{7}$ [857] 8-9-8 30 (v$^{1}$) WRyan 12 24
(AWCarroll) *sn chsng ldr: led 5f out to 3f out: sn rdn: wknd 1f out* **13/8**$^{1}$
5660 **5** *3* **Western Command (GER)**$^{15}$ [783] 8-9-8 30 (p) RFitzpatrick 5 18
(MrsNMacauley) *bhd tl rdn and hdwy on ins over 2f out: n.d* **12/1**
-040 **6** *½* **Amanpuri (GER)**$^{11}$ [814] 6-9-8 35 MFenton 9 17
(MissGayKelleway) *sn led: hdd 5f out: rdn over 3f out: wknd over 2f out* **9/1**
0060 **7** *4* **Marengo**$^{6}$ [878] 10-9-8 30 (p) JoannaBadger 3 9
(PaulJohnson) *dwlt: rdn over 4f out: nvr nr ldrs* **20/1**
-004 **8** *½* **Welsh Whisper**$^{21}$ [730] 5-9-5 35 LPKeniry$^{(3)}$ 11 8
(SABrookshaw) *plld hrd: sn bhd: short-lived effrt over 4f out* **9/1**
60-0 **9** *8* **Red Acer (IRE)**$^{58}$ [416] 3-8-2 35 CCatlin 8 —
(PDEvans) *s.i.s: sn mid-div: rdn 6f out: bhd fnl 4f* **25/1**
00-0 **10** *3* **Chickasaw Trail**$^{58}$ [427] 6-9-1 30 StephanieHollinshead$^{(7)}$ 2 —
(RHollinshead) *a bhd* **33/1**
005- **11** *3 ½* **Rileys Rocket**$^{160}$ [5131] 5-9-8 35 DeanMcKeown 1 —
(JAPickering) *a bhd* **11/1**
500- **12** *1 ½* **Un Autre Espere**$^{117}$ [4340] 5-9-8 35 LVickers 6 —
(TWall) *bhd fnl 4f* **33/1**

2m 11.33s (8.43) **Going Correction** +0.925s/f (Slow) **12** Ran **SP% 132.2**
**WFA** 3 from 5yo+ 20lb
Speed ratings: **99,91,89,87,84 84,80,80,73,70 67,65**CSF £34.42 TOTE £6.80: £2.10, £1.80, £2.50; EX 44.70 Place 6 £11.44, Place 5 £5.24..
**Owner** Mrs J E Proctor **Bred** Mrs A L Wood **Trained** Newmarket, Suffolk

**FOCUS**
Another poor contest, but the winner was back to her modest three-year-old best for her new yard.

**NOTEBOOK**
**Mrs Cube** had the blinkers left off for this first outing since September. She tried to spit the dummy out entering the home straight but Winston was having none of it.
**A Bit Of Fun** was put in his place once the winner consented to put her best foot forward.
**Sophomore** could not cope with the runner-up let alone the winner.
**Adjiram(IRE)**, dropping back in distance for this Fibresand debut, may have done too much too soon in the first-time visor.
T/Plt: £31.80 to a £1 stake. Pool £55,936.45 - 1,282.50 winning units. T/Qpdt: £5.40 to a £1 stake. Pool £4,321.90 - 588.60 winning units. KH

# 926 LINGFIELD (L-H)
## Tuesday, March 2

**OFFICIAL GOING: Standard**
Wind: mod across Weather: sunny

## 946 BET DIRECT NO Q DEMO 08000 837 888 BANDED STKS 7f (P)
**2:30** (2:34) (H) 3-Y-0+ **£1,666** (£476; £238) **Stalls** Low

Form RPR
-614 **1** **Redoubtable (USA)**$^{16}$ [780] 13-9-7 45 ACulhane 13 49
(DWChapman) *s.s: hdwy 2f out: led ins fnl f: rdn clr* **12/1**
0606 **2** *1 ¾* **Social Contract**$^{6}$ [886] 7-9-7 45 (v) JFEgan 1 44
(SDow) *in tch: effrt over 2f out: ev ch over 1f out: nt qckn* **7/1**
4520 **3** *1 ½* **Zonnebeke**$^{21}$ [736] 3-8-5 45 JFanning 7 41
(KRBurke) *prom: ev ch over 1f out: one pce* **16/1**
0-00 **4** *1* **Malaah (IRE)**$^{8}$ [859] 8-9-0 45 (b) MHalford$^{(7)}$ 5 38
(JulianPoulton) *led tl ins fnl f: no ex* **50/1**
0-00 **5** *1* **Youngs Forth**$^{8}$ [859] 4-9-7 45 (t) SWhitworth 6 36
(AWCarroll) *in tch: effrt over 2f out: ev ch over 1f out: no ex* **16/1**
0-03 **6** *1 ¼* **Confuzed**$^{5}$ [893] 4-9-7 45 (e) KFallon 2 32
(DFlood) *dwlt: t.k.h in midfield: rdn to chse ldrs 2f out: one pce appr fnl f* **7/2**$^{2}$
1410 **7** *2* **Badou**$^{2}$ [930] 4-9-13 45 DHolland 14 33
(LMontagueHall) *mid-div: hdwy 2f out: one pce appr fnl f* **3/1**$^{1}$
563- **8** *nk* **Ballygriffin Kid**$^{203}$ [4057] 4-9-7 45 DaneO'Neill 12 27
(TPMcgovern) *pressed ldr tl wknd 1f out* **10/1**
4230 **9** *¾* **The Gay Fox**$^{6}$ [886] 10-9-7 45 (tp) DaleGibson 15 25
(BGPowell) *outpcd towards rr: nvr rchd ldrs* **12/1**
50-4 **10** *hd* **Gilly's General (IRE)**$^{16}$ [779] 4-9-7 45 (b$^{1}$) MFenton 4 24
(JWUnett) *chsd ldrs tl wknd over 1f out* **20/1**
0052 **11** *hd* **Master Rattle**$^{5}$ [895] 5-9-7 45 VSlattery 10 24
(JaneSouthcombe) *mid-div: hdwy and wd st: pressed ldrs over 1f out: sn wknd* **11/2**$^{3}$
0-30 **12** *2 ½* **Zolushka (IRE)**$^{28}$ [662] 3-8-5 45 EAhern 8 18
(BWDuke) *dwlt: a bhd* **33/1**
0-00 **13** *½* **Bienheureux**$^{14}$ [808] 3-8-5 45 PaulEddery 3 16
(WJMusson) *dwlt: a bhd* **33/1**
0-00 **14** *9* **Lucretius**$^{8}$ [859] 5-9-2 45 (p) MSavage$^{(5)}$ 16 —
(DKIvory) *wd and drvn along: bhd fnl 3f* **33/1**

1m 25.14s (-0.86) **Going Correction** -0.025s/f (Stan) **14** Ran **SP% 126.9**
**WFA** 3 from 4yo+ 16lb
Speed ratings: **103,101,99,98,97 95,93,92,92,91 91,88,88,77**CSF £94.24 TOTE £14.70: £4.80, £3.30, £3.70; EX 135.90.
**Owner** David W Chapman **Bred** Wooden Horse Inv Inc And Post Syndicate **Trained** Stillington, N Yorks

**FOCUS**
Exposed horses, but a decent winning time for the grade.

**NOTEBOOK**
**Redoubtable(USA)**, back up in trip, did not break as well as he usually does but that did not prevent him running out a decisive winner. He reserves his best for this track these days.
**Social Contract** put in a better run than he has been doing of late but is not one in which to place too much faith.
**Zonnebeke** ran better than she had done in a Southwell seller on her latest start. The experiment with the cheekpieces did not last long.
**Malaah(IRE)** ran his best race for quite some time and was only collared inside the last.
**Youngs Forth** had her tongue tied down for the first time and it appeared to bring about a better performance.
**Confuzed**, who was slowly away again, was short of room in the home straight and this run did not really prove whether he needs seven furlongs or not.
**Badou** showed no improvement for the step back up in trip.

## 947 BET DIRECT NO Q ON 08000 93 66 93 BANDED STKS 1m 2f (P)
**3:00** (3:02) (H) 4-Y-0+ **£1,463** (£418; £209) **Stalls** Low

Form RPR
50/1 **1** **Dafa**$^{48}$ [527] 8-8-12 40 SWKelly 8 49
(BJCurley) *chsd ldr: led over 2f out: hrd rdn over 1f out: hung rt and hld on fnl f* **11/4**$^{2}$
-632 **2** *nk* **Private Seal**$^{8}$ [857] 9-8-5 40 (tp) MHalford$^{(7)}$ 14 48
(JulianPoulton) *hld up towards rr: hdwy on outside 3f out: str chal fnl f: r.o* **8/1**
0000 **3** *6* **Platinum Boy (IRE)**$^{8}$ [855] 4-8-12 40 (p) VSlattery 5 37
(MWellings) *in tch: effrt 2f out: styd on same pce* **50/1**
60-5 **4** *hd* **Paintbrush (IRE)**$^{47}$ [537] 4-8-12 40 RWinston 2 37
(MrsLStubbs) *towards rr: effrt whn hmpd by fallers over 2f out: swtchd wd and hdwy entering st: styd on same pce* **7/2**$^{3}$
0000 **5** *hd* **Morris Dancing (USA)**$^{7}$ [875] 5-8-12 30 MTebbutt 6 36
(BPJBaugh) *led tl over 2f out: hrd rdn and wknd over 1f out* **50/1**
0-56 **6** *nk* **Broughtons Mill**$^{8}$ [857] 9-8-5 35 RoryMoore$^{(7)}$ 1 36
(JASupple) *mid-div: outpcd over 2f out: styd on fnl f* **33/1**
/00- **7** *1* **Honey's Gift**$^{19}$ [798] 5-8-12 40 AMcCarthy 3 34
(GGMargarson) *chsd ldrs: hrd rdn and one pce fnl 2f* **10/1**
0-00 **8** *6* **Misbehaviour**$^{8}$ [860] 5-8-12 40 (p) IMongan 9 23
(PButler) *t.k.h: prom tl wknd wl over 1f out* **33/1**
0-01 **9** *9* **Kingsdon (IRE)**$^{15}$ [793] 7-8-12 40 (vt) KFallon 4 7
(TJFitzgerald) *dwlt: hld up towards rr: hmpd by fallers over 2f out: no ch after* **9/4**$^{1}$
/600 **10** *26* **Hinchley Wood (IRE)**$^{8}$ [858] 5-8-12 40 NPollard 12 —
(JRBest) *wd: t.k.h: prom: rdn and btn whn hmpd by faller over 2f out* **33/1**
0000 **B** **Spiders Web**$^{7}$ [871] 4-8-12 30 (b$^{1}$) GCarter 11 —
(TKeddy) *dwlt: t.k.h in rr: b.d by fallers over 2f out* **40/1**
50-0 **B** **Modem (IRE)**$^{23}$ [715] 7-8-12 40 (v) NCallan 10 —
(DShaw) *hld up towards rr: effrt whn b.d by faller over 2f out: dead* **33/1**
-000 **B** **Thats All Jazz**$^{19}$ [663] 6-8-7 40 RThomas$^{(5)}$ 13 —
(CRDore) *dwlt: hld up in rr: effrt whn b.d by fallers over 2f out* **16/1**
-406 **F** **Achilles Rainbow**$^{5}$ [894] 5-8-5 40 AReilly$^{(7)}$ 7 —
(KRBurke) *in tch: rdn to chse ldrs 3f out: cl 5th whn fell over 2f out: broke leg: dead* **25/1**

2m 9.70s (2.31) **Going Correction** -0.025s/f (Stan) **14** Ran **SP% 127.7**
Speed ratings: **89,88,83,83,83 83,82,77,70,49 —,—,—,—**CSF £24.99 TOTE £4.20: £1.70, £2.20, £18.90; EX 33.40.
**Owner** Mrs B J Curley **Bred** D H Jones **Trained** Newmarket, Suffolk
■ Stewards Enquiry : A ReillyG two-day ban: careless riding (Mar 13-14)

**FOCUS**
A very slow winning time for a race marred by a four-horse pile-up going to the two-furlong pole.

**NOTEBOOK**
**Dafa** was tackling three furlongs farther than he had at Wolverhampton, but he has shown his form over farther than this trip before. Despite not helping his rider by hanging right, he proved just the stronger in the duel to the line.
**Private Seal** is running well of late but remains very hard to win with. He is not the most resolute, although he had an excuse to a certain extent on this occasion in that the favourite was leaning into him slightly.
**Platinum Boy(IRE)** reached the frame for the first time since landing a Wolverhampton seller eleven months ago.
**Paintbrush(IRE)**, done no favours in the melee running downhill, stayed on a little and this run can be writen off. He seems to get this trip.
**Morris Dancing(USA)**, who went without the cheekpieces for this first try on the Polytrack, also adopted unfamiliar front-running tactics.
**Kingsdon(IRE)** was effectively put out of the race in the incident approaching the two pole.

## 948 BETDIRECT.CO.UK MEDIAN AUCTION MAIDEN STKS 1m (P)
**3:30** (3:45) (H) 3-5-Y-O **£1,463** (£418; £209) **Stalls** High

Form
5- **1** **Rye (IRE)**$^{237}$ [3096] 3-7-12 CCatlin 1 54+
(JAOsborne) *chsd clr ldr: rdn over 3f out: styd on fnl f whn ldr stopped riding: led on line* **8/11**$^{1}$
-232 **2** *shd* **Ballinger Ridge**$^{15}$ [790] 5-9-7 60 (b$^{1}$) KFallon 5 59+
(AMBalding) *led: sn 10l clr: shkn up briefly over 1f out: jockey looked rnd and stopped riding: rdn fnl 100 yds: ct on line* **15/8**$^{2}$
0-0 **3** *2* **Star Welcome**$^{16}$ [779] 3-7-9 LisaJones$^{(3)}$ 10 50
(WJMusson) *stdd s: hld up in midfield: shkn up and hdwy over 1f out: nrst fin* **25/1**
/0-0 **4** *5* **Magic Stone**$^{52}$ [491] 4-9-7 40 RSmith 4 43
(ACharlton) *mod 5th tl sme hdwy over 2f out: styd on same pce* **66/1**
0 **5** *3* **Young Dynasty**$^{31}$ [644] 4-9-0 LiamJones$^{(7)}$ 8 36
(EAWheeler) *s.s and lost 7l: outpcd towards rr: sme hdwy over 2f out: no imp over 1f out* **20/1**
00 **6** *2* **Shalati Princess**$^{17}$ [766] 3-7-12 RBrisland 6 27
(JCFox) *outpcd and wl bhd: styd on fnl 2f* **50/1**
050- **7** *2* **Mr Dip**$^{266}$ [2255] 4-9-7 65 ACulhane 7 27
(AWCarroll) *chsd ldrs over 5f* **9/1**$^{3}$
00-0 **8** *1* **Ryan's Bliss (IRE)**$^{13}$ [821] 4-8-13 50 J-PGuillambert$^{(3)}$ 9 20
(TDMccarthy) *chsd ldrs over 5f* **25/1**
**9** *2 ½* **Mantel Mini**$^{92}$ 5-8-13 (b$^{1}$) BReilly$^{(3)}$ 3 14
(BAPearce) *stood in stalls and lost 10l: outpcd: a wl bhd* **66/1**
**10** *27* **Lady Heccles**$^{42}$ 5-9-2 SWhitworth 2 —
(MRHoad) *outpcd and bhd: no ch fnl 3f* **66/1**

1m 40.07s (0.56) **Going Correction** -0.025s/f (Stan) **10** Ran **SP% 121.6**
**WFA** 3 from 4yo+ 18lb
Speed ratings: **96,95,93,88,85 83,81,80,78,51**CSF £2.21 TOTE £1.50: £1.02, £1.10, £4.20; EX 2.40.
**Owner** Danny Durkan **Bred** Liam Cashman **Trained** Upper Lambourn, Berks
■ Stewards Enquiry : K Fallon 21-day ban: dropped hands and lost first place (Mar 16-Apr 8)

**FOCUS**
A poor maiden producing a controversial finish, with Fallon referred to the Jockey Club for his ride on the runner-up and the Stewards at Portman Square looking into 'irregular betting patterns'.
**NOTEBOOK**
**Rye(IRE)** has undergone treatment for a knee chip since making her debut last July. She was ten lengths down and being ridden along pretty vigorously with three to run but, staying on, caught Fallon napping on the leader and snatched the race on the line. A fortunate winner, she may get a little farther.
**Ballinger Ridge** adopted his customary front-running role and had quickly opened up a ten-length advantage. Still travelling easily turning in, he was shaken up over a furlong out and the race looked his, but at the furlong pole Fallon looked over his right shoulder and, appearing not to notice that the favourite was making inroads, briefly eased his mount. Taking another look shortly afterwards, Fallon became aware of the danger but was a shade slow to galvanise the gelding who, his momentum lost, was touched off. This was not Fallon's finest hour.
**Star Welcome** ◆ stayed on pleasingly and is now eligible for a handicap mark. She is one to keep an eye on but may need to break better than she has been doing.
**Magic Stone** will need to stumble upon a very poor race if he is to get off the mark.

## 949 LITTLEWOODS BET DIRECT BANDED STKS 1m (P)
**4:00** (4:15) (H) 3-Y-O+ **£1,466** (£419; £209) **Stalls** High

Form RPR
6056 **1** **Haithem (IRE)**$^{2}$ [929] 7-9-4 35 (t) LisaJones$^{(3)}$ 10 47
(DShaw) *s.s: hld up towards rr: hdwy and hung rt over 1f out: led ins fnl f: pushed out* **7/1**$^{3}$
00-5 **2** *¾* **Due To Me**$^{24}$ [702] 4-9-7 40 (be) SWhitworth 7 45
(GLMoore) *plld hrd in midfield: hdwy 2f out: ev ch over 1f out: kpt on* **11/2**$^{2}$
-120 **3** *½* **Theatre Lady (IRE)**$^{2}$ [929] 6-9-7 40 KFallon 1 44
(PDEvans) *led: rdn over 2f out: hdd ins fnl f: kpt on* **1/1**$^{1}$
50/4 **4** *1 ¼* **Tiny Tim (IRE)**$^{28}$ [665] 6-9-0 35 TBlock$^{(7)}$ 2 41
(AMBalding) *w ldrs: hrd rdn 2f out: nt qckn fnl f* **14/1**
465U **5** *nk* **High Diva**$^{8}$ [860] 5-9-7 35 NPollard 5 40
(JRBest) *s.i.s: hdwy to chse ldrs after 2f: ev ch over 1f out: one pce* **15/2**
00-6 **6** *hd* **Prince Du Soleil (FR)**$^{8}$ [860] 8-9-7 40 (p) EAhern 4 40
(JRJenkins) *mid-div: hdwy on outside ent st: chsd ldrs over 1f out: styd on same pce* **12/1**
30-0 **7** *3 ½* **Tojoneski**$^{8}$ [857] 5-9-0 40 NataliaGemelova$^{(7)}$ 8 32
(IWMcinnes) *hld up in rr: effrt on outside 3f out: wd and no imp over 1f out* **25/1**
00-0 **8** *3 ½* **Travel Tardia (IRE)**$^{45}$ [554] 6-9-7 40 IMongan 11 24
(IAWood) *wd early: hdwy to join ldr after 3f: wknd over 1f out* **25/1**
-000 **9** *5* **Queen Excalibur**$^{47}$ [535] 5-9-7 40 (p) DaneO'Neill 3 12
(CRoberts) *prom to 1/2-way* **20/1**
-004 **10** *2* **Miss Celerity**$^{7}$ [873] 4-9-7 30 ADaly 6 8
(MJHaynes) *prom: hrd rdn 3f out: wknd 2f out* **16/1**
000- **11** *6* **Tomokim (IRE)**$^{64}$ [6248] 3-8-3 30 (v$^{1}$) CCatlin 12 —
(MQuinn) *wd: a towards rr: no ch fnl 2f* **50/1**

1m 39.99s (0.48) **Going Correction** -0.025s/f (Stan)
**WFA** 3 from 4yo+ 18lb **11 Ran SP% 124.3**
Speed ratings: **96,95,94,93,93 93,89,86,81,79 73**CSF £46.05 TOTE £10.20: £2.20, £2.30, £1.10; EX 52.90.
**Owner** Century Racing **Bred** Galadari Sons Stud Company Limited **Trained** Averham, Notts
**FOCUS**
A poor event where the winner just needed to reproduce his latest effort
**NOTEBOOK**
**Haithem(IRE)** made the most of an inviting gap along the rail in the straight and scored cosily, despite hanging to his right. He has been running better since the tongue-strap was put back on and this was his first win since December 2000. *Official explanation: jockey said gelding hung right throughout*
**Due To Me** ran well on this step down in grade and up in trip, and there could be a small race for her on this surface.
**Theatre Lady(IRE)** tried to make all, but was caught inside the last and appeared to have no excuses.
**Tiny Tim(IRE)**, who was stepping up in trip, is a very limited performer but would appear to be a good mount for inexperienced riders.

## 950 BET DIRECT ON SKY ACTIVE CLAIMING STKS 1m 5f (P)
**4:30** (4:43) (H) 4-Y-O+ **£1,270** (£363; £181) **Stalls** Low

Form RPR
6120 **1** **Radiant Bride**$^{3}$ [919] 4-8-9 45 (b) DarrenWilliams 7 46
(KRBurke) *patiently rdn: hdwy over 2f out: swtchd lft and qcknd to ld wl ins fnl f: cheekily* **3/1**$^{2}$
-131 **2** *nk* **Sungio**$^{11}$ [838] 6-9-3 52 (b) DaleGibson 4 50
(BGPowell) *trckd ldrs: rdn to ld over 1f out: hdd and nt qckn wl ins fnl f* **1/1**$^{1}$
60-6 **3** *2* **Miss Koen (IRE)**$^{17}$ [773] 5-8-12 53 (t) DaneO'Neill 6 43
(DLWilliams) *stdd s: hld up in rr: smooth hdwy over 3f out: hrd rdn over 1f out: one pce* **25/1**
2324 **4** *4* **The Last Mohican**$^{22}$ [727] 5-9-3 35 (p) RWinston 5 42
(PHowling) *chsd ldr: led over 2f out tl over 1f out: no ex* **8/1**
00-0 **5** *5* **Branston Nell**$^{17}$ [777] 5-8-7 45 RThomas$^{(5)}$ 3 30
(CRDore) *in tch tl rdn and btn 3f out* **16/1**
6-34 **6** *2* **Failed To Hit**$^{25}$ [699] 11-9-1 51 (v) IMongan 8 30
(NPLittmoden) *led tl over 2f out: sn wknd* **6/1**$^{3}$
000- **7** *16* **Blue Rondo (IRE)**$^{13}$ [6247] 4-9-0 55 (v$^{1}$) CCatlin 1 10
(IanWilliams) *chsd ldrs tl wknd 3f out* **12/1**
**8** *hd* **L'Etang Bleu (FR)**$^{9}$ 6-8-10 (tp) CHaddon$^{(7)}$ 9 10
(PButler) *dwlt: sn chsng ldrs: wknd 4f out* **50/1**
600- **9** *26* **Rayware Boy (IRE)**$^{38}$ [566] 8-8-6 (v) DawnWatson$^{(7)}$ 2 —
(DShaw) *reluctant to s and lft 30l: t.o most of way* **50/1**

2m 48.57s (0.49) **Going Correction** -0.025s/f (Stan)
**WFA** 4 from 5yo+ 3lb **9 Ran SP% 121.7**
Speed ratings: **97,96,95,93,90 88,78,78,62**CSF £6.67 TOTE £4.50: £1.40, £1.10, £3.40; EX 9.40.The winner was claimed (friendly) by K R Burke for £5,000.
**Owner** Mrs Y Goodwin **Bred** Limestone Stud **Trained** Middleham Moor, N Yorks
**FOCUS**
The fourth horse sets the standard, as the first three all ran below their best.
**NOTEBOOK**
**Radiant Bride** was looking for room in the straight, but once switched left she was soon in front and won with a bit up her sleeve. She has her quirks but is running more sweetly in the blinkers.
**Sungio** travelled better with the blinkers back on according to Gibson, but was no match for the winner in the end despite the narrow margin. He could have done with a stronger pace.
**Miss Koen(IRE)**, who was tongue-tied for the first time, ran well for a long way and there could be a small race for her on this surface.
**The Last Mohican** has yet to win in 35 starts, but this was the 17th time he has made the frame.

## 951 BET DIRECT INTERACTIVE BANDED STKS 6f (P)
**5:00** (5:11) (H) 3-Y-O+ **£1,456** (£416; £208) **Stalls** Low

Form RPR
0662 **1** **Long Weekend (IRE)**$^{2}$ [930] 6-9-6 40 (v) DarrenWilliams 13 44
(DShaw) *s.s: hld up towards rr: hdwy over 1f out: led ins fnl f: jst hld on* **13/8**$^{1}$
-050 **2** *shd* **Shirley Oaks (IRE)**$^{8}$ [858] 6-9-1 40 NChalmers$^{(5)}$ 7 44
(MissZCDavison) *chsd ldrs: rdn over 1f out: r.o wl fnl f: jst failed* **16/1**
-006 **3** *½* **Gentle Response**$^{6}$ [884] 4-9-6 35 (b) SWhitworth 11 43+
(BRJohnson) *s.i.s: bhd: rdn and hdwy fnl 2f: fin wl* **11/2**$^{3}$
0-06 **4** *nk* **Emarati's Image**$^{8}$ [858] 6-9-6 40 ADaly 8 42
(RMStronge) *t.k.h: pressed ldr: led wl over 1f out tl ins fnl f: kpt on* **16/1**
5330 **5** *shd* **Sotonian (HOL)**$^{4}$ [904] 11-9-3 40 LisaJones$^{(3)}$ 9 41
(PSFelgate) *hld up in tch: effrt 2f out: ev ch ent fnl f: kpt on* **4/1**$^{2}$
0000 **6** *½* **Law Maker**$^{2}$ [930] 4-9-6 35 (b) JFanning 6 40
(MABuckley) *plld hrd: prom: ev ch over 1f out: one pce* **50/1**
00-0 **7** *1* **True Holly**$^{6}$ [884] 4-9-6 40 (v$^{1}$) JFEgan 5 37
(SKirk) *dwlt: sn chsng ldrs: one pce fnl 2f* **9/1**
0624 **8** *nk* **Onefortheboys (IRE)**$^{8}$ [856] 5-8-13 40 LTreadwell$^{(7)}$ 2 36
(DFlood) *s.i.s: sn in midfield: rdn to chse ldrs over 1f out: one pce* **15/2**
-000 **9** *nk* **Hellbent**$^{8}$ [858] 5-9-1 40 ow2 SCrawford$^{(7)}$ 1 37
(JAOsborne) *dwlt: hld up and bhd: hdwy and wd st: no imp* **20/1**
-000 **10** *6* **Levelled**$^{14}$ [813] 10-9-6 35 ACulhane 4 17
(DWChapman) *led tl wknd wl over 1f out* **16/1**
00-3 **11** *¾* **Flame Princess**$^{8}$ [856] 4-9-6 40 JQuinn 12 15
(JRBoyle) *in tch: hrd rdn 3f out: effrt whn carried wd into st: n.d after* **12/1**
0600 **12** *1* **Indian Shores**$^{7}$ [876] 5-8-13 40 (p) PVarley$^{(7)}$ 3 12
(MMullineaux) *s.s: a bhd* **25/1**
00-0 **13** *1 ¾* **Moonglade (USA)**$^{16}$ [780] 4-9-1 30 (tp) AQuinn$^{(5)}$ 10 7
(MissJFeilden) *s.i.s: mid-div and wd: rdn 3f out: effrt whn carried even wdr into st: n.d after* **66/1**

1m 12.81s (-0.11) **Going Correction** -0.025s/f (Stan) **13 Ran SP% 132.6**
Speed ratings: **99,98,98,97,97 97,95,95,94,86 85,84,82**CSF £36.76 TOTE £2.90: £1.30, £8.50, £2.60; EX 64.70 Place 6 £50.50, Place 5 £5.50.
**Owner** The Marlow Lewin Partnership **Bred** F Hinojosa **Trained** Averham, Notts
**FOCUS**
Poor overall form. The winner was not at his best, while Gentle Response looks back to last summer's handicap form.
**NOTEBOOK**
**Long Weekend(IRE)**, runner-up here two days earlier, overcame a wide draw to go one better, but after striking the front he only held on by the skin of his teeth.
**Shirley Oaks(IRE)** recorded her only win over seven furlongs and on this evidence a return to that trip could be what she needs.
**Gentle Response**, who caught the eye in first-time blinkers on her latest start, finished well against the rail. She is attractively handicapped compared to her turf mark.
**Emarati's Image** ran a decent race but might have found this a bit sharp.
**Sotonian(HOL)** is running creditably at present and could yet add to his career haul of a dozen wins.
T/Jkpt: £21,655.00 to a £1 stake. Pool £45,750.62, 1.5 winning tickets T/Plt: £69.50 to a £1 stake. Pool £69,004.15, 724.50 winning tickets T/Qpdt: £1.90 to a £1 stake. Pool £5,443.50, 2,017.40 winning tickets LM

# 934 SOUTHWELL (L-H)
### Wednesday, March 3

**OFFICIAL GOING: Standard to slow**
Wind: Slt across Weather: overcast, rain from race five onwards

## 952 BETDIRECT.CO.UK APPRENTICE H'CAP (DIV I) 1m (F)
**1:50** (1:56) (F) (0-60,60) 4-Y-O+ **£2,919** (£834; £417) **Stalls** Low

Form RPR
400- **1** **Thunderclap**$^{131}$ [5729] 5-8-13 **49** AMullen$^{(4)}$ 5 63
(JJQuinn) *hld up: hdwy over 2f out: chsd ldr and hung lft over 1f out: styd on to ld wl ins fnl f* **7/4**$^{1}$
0300 **2** *¾* **Kumakawa**$^{4}$ [914] 6-8-9 **45** (b) LiamJones$^{(4)}$ 8 57
(EAWheeler) *hld up: hdwy over 3f out: rdn to ld over 1f out: hdd wl ins fnl f* **7/1**$^{3}$
-065 **3** *5* **Victory Flip (IRE)**$^{13}$ [826] 4-8-2 **40** HFellows$^{(6)}$ 2 42
(RHollinshead) *hld up: hdwy over 2f out: nt clr run and swtchd rt over 1f out: nvr able to chal* **8/1**
/066 **4** *2* **Dalriath**$^{13}$ [826] 5-7-13 **35** CHaddon$^{(4)}$ 1 33
(MCChapman) *chsd ldrs: led over 3f out: hdd over 2f out: rdn and ev ch over 1f out: sn wknd* **25/1**
2131 **5** *1 ¼* **Dancing King (IRE)**$^{5}$ [910] 8-9-5 **51** 6ex WHogg 10 47
(PWHiatt) *led over 4f: led over 2f out: hdd & wknd over 1f out* **10/3**$^{2}$
0/00 **6** *6* **Bought Direct**$^{29}$ [667] 5-9-7 **57** DeanWilliams$^{(4)}$ 6 41
(RJSmith) *chsd ldrs tl wknd over 1f out* **11/1**
000- **7** *3 ½* **King Nicholas (USA)**$^{183}$ [4643] 5-9-10 **56** (t) DFentiman 4 33
(JParkes) *chsd ldrs over 5f* **16/1**
300- **8** *¾* **Blue Venture (IRE)**$^{172}$ [2543] 4-9-8 **60** DWakenshaw$^{(6)}$ 3 35
(PCHaslam) *chsd ldrs: rdn 1/2-way: wknd 3f out* **14/1**
50-0 **9** *19* **Samba Beat**$^{3}$ [939] 5-8-7 **45** MNem$^{(6)}$ 7 —
(RFMarvin) *s.s: outpcd* **50/1**
60-0 **10** *hd* **Humdinger (IRE)**$^{51}$ [505] 4-8-11 **47** DTudhope$^{(4)}$ 9 —
(DShaw) *chsd ldrs to 1/2-way: bhd whn hung rt ent st* **33/1**

1m 49.15s (4.55) **Going Correction** +0.525s/f (Slow) **10 Ran SP% 112.7**
Speed ratings: **98,97,92,90,89 83,79,78,59,59**CSF £13.60 CT £78.29 TOTE £3.10: £1.60, £1.90, £1.60; EX 12.10.
**Owner** The Wednesday Club **Bred** D S W Blacker And Lady Legard **Trained** Settrington, N Yorks
**FOCUS**
A modest time for the grade, but the form looks solid. The riders reported that the surface was stamina-sapping.
**NOTEBOOK**
**Thunderclap** was the subject of good support on his return from a four-month absence and justified that confidence. He did not look badly handicapped, and though he has not been the easiest to win with and did not look over-keen to go past Kumakawa entering the final furlong, his young rider did a good job and got him home. The change of stable looks to have done him some good.
**Kumakawa** enjoyed the return to Fibresand and drop back to a mile having run poorly over ten furlongs at Lingfield on his last two starts.
**Victory Flip(IRE)** did not get the best of runs early in the straight but stayed on quite well. She is well handicapped now but is still not one to go overboard about, as she remains a long-standing maiden.
**Dalriath** ran her best race since joining her current stable, giving Dancing King little peace in front.

**Dancing King(IRE)**, who was sweating and on edge beforehand, drifted badly in the betting and failed to reproduce his recent Wolverhampton form.

## 953 BETDIRECT.CO.UK APPRENTICE H'CAP (DIV II) 1m (F)
**2:25** (2:31) (F ) (0-60,57) 4-Y-0+ **£2,919** (£834; £417) **Stalls** Low

Form RPR

0/34 **1** **Grub Street**[8] 875 8-7-8 30 CHaddon(4) 9 39
(JParkes) *hung rt and outpcd 6f out: hdwy over 1f out: r.o to ld wl ins fnl f* **13/2**

110- **2** *nk* **Nod's Nephew**[123] 5881 7-9-2 48 DerekNolan 5 56
(DECantillon) *trckd ldrs: rdn to ld over 1f out: hdd wl ins fnl f* **7/2**[1]

-015 **3** *2* **Gracious Air (USA)**[8] 875 6-8-13 45 (v) DFentiman 8 49
(JRWeymes) *chsd ldrs: outpcd 3f out: hdwy over 1f out: r.o* **9/1**

-253 **4** *1* **Magic Mamma's Too**[13] 823 4-9-3 53 (p) Laura-JayneCrawford(4) 1 55
(TDBarron) *led over 5f: rdn and ev ch over 1f out: no ex ins fnl f* **15/2**

3-00 **5** *½* **Santa Catalina (IRE)**[16] 787 5-8-9 45 DeanWilliams(4) 7 46
(CADwyer) *chsd ldrs: outpcd 5f out: hdwy over 1f out: nt rch ldrs* **40/1**

-241 **6** *3* **Fraamtastic**[8] 875 7-8-9 41 6ex (p) WHogg 3 36
(BAPearce) *chsd ldr: rdn to ld over 2f out: hdd over 1f out: wknd ins fnl f* **9/1**

5005 **7** *1 ¾* **Spy Gun (USA)**[5] 910 4-9-6 56 DTudhope(4) 6 48
(TWall) *dwlt: hld up: plld hrd: hdwy over 4f out: rdn over 3f out: wknd over 1f out* **12/1**

-454 **8** *nk* **Mathmagician**[3] 934 5-7-13 35 (p) KGhunowa(4) 2 26
(RFMarvin) *broke wl: lost plce over 6f out: sn bhd* **20/1**

4022 **9** *nk* **Lord Chamberlain**[5] 910 11-9-7 57 (b) CJDavies(4) 10 47
(JMBradley) *hld up: hdwy over 3f out: rdn and hung lft fr over 2f out: nt run on* **6/1**[3]

3515 **10** *1* **Sorbiesharry (IRE)**[6] 902 5-8-13 49 (p) SaleemGolam(4) 4 37
(MrsNMacauley) *dwlt: hdwy over 4f out: wknd 3f out* **4/1**[2]

1m 49.87s (5.27) **Going Correction** +0.525s/f (Slow) **10** Ran SP% **116.5**
Speed ratings: **94,93,91,90,90 87,85,85,84,83**CSF £29.48 CT £207.50 TOTE £8.10: £2.20, £2.10, £3.80; EX 38.30.
**Owner** Mrs B Sands **Bred** Burton Agnes Stud Co Ltd **Trained** Upper Helmsley, N Yorks

**FOCUS**
A poor contest run in a very modest time for the grade, being 0.72 seconds slower than the first division.

**NOTEBOOK**
**Grub Street**, who last won a race back in the summer of 2000, has been running well in banded grade since returning from a lengthy absence, but this was a step up in class and he got badly outpaced during the first half of the race. He stayed on well up the straight, though, to get up close home, and on this evidence one can see why he was campaigned over middle distances a couple of years ago.
**Nod's Nephew** looked set to score until getting caught by the bottom-weight close home. He is entitled to come on for this first outing since November and, having won at each of the All-Weather venues, is worth bearing in mind for a modest contest in the near future.
**Gracious Air(USA)** ran a similar race to last week, in that her best work was being done late on once the principals had gone beyond reach.
**Magic Mamma's Too**, on whom front-running tactics were employed again, remains frustrating.
**Santa Catalina(IRE)** stepped up on her recent efforts at banded meetings.
**Fraamtastic** looked to be found out by her penalty in this better race.

## 954 NEW SITE @ BETDIRECT.CO.UK CLAIMING STKS 5f (F)
**3:00** (3:06) (F ) 4-Y-0+ **£2,912** (£832; £416) **Stalls** High

Form RPR

0-00 **1** **Scary Night (IRE)**[20] 748 4-8-9 68 (p) JEdmunds 5 62
(JBalding) *chsd ldrs: hung lft over 1f out: hung rt ins fnl f: r.o to ld nr fin* **20/1**

-450 **2** *nk* **Malahide Express (IRE)**[5] 904 4-9-2 60 (b) LFletcher(3) 7 71
(MJPolglase) *led: hung lft ins fnl f: hdd nr fin* **16/1**

5021 **3** *2 ½* **Henry Tun**[3] 938 6-8-2 51 (b) DAllan(3) 6 50
(JBalding) *w ldr: hung lft over 1f out: rdn and ev ch ins fnl f: nt qckn* **85/40**[1]

4004 **4** *½* **Juwwi**[16] 799 10-8-13 63 (p) DarrenWilliams 8 56
(JMBradley) *dwlt: outpcd: swtchd lft over 3f out: hdwy over 1f out: no imp ins fnl f* **8/1**

2005 **5** *nk* **Sharp Hat**[6] 897 10-8-11 66 ACulhane 2 53
(DWChapman) *chsd ldrs: outpcd 2f out: styd on ins fnl f* **13/2**[3]

4064 **6** *nk* **Amanda's Lad (IRE)**[13] 824 4-8-2 45 DFox(5) 3 48
(MCChapman) *chsd ldrs: outpcd 3f out: swtchd rt over 1f out: r.o ins fnl f* **40/1**

5262 **7** *nk* **Tigress (IRE)**[5] 905 5-8-10 56 (b) JQuinn 4 50
(JWUnett) *chsd ldrs: outpcd 3f out: styd on ins fnl f* **7/2**[2]

5106 **8** *shd* **Panjandrum**[6] 893 6-8-10 66 MSavage(5) 1 55
(NEBerry) *s.i.s: hdwy 3f out: rdn over 1f out: styd on same pce* **13/2**[3]

0-00 **9** *12* **Vanished (IRE)**[15] 806 4-7-11 55 ow2 (b) NMackay(5) 9 6
(MJPolglase) *chsd ldrs: hung lft and wknd 2f out* **11/1**

62.97 secs (2.67) **Going Correction** +0.525s/f (Slow) **9** Ran SP% **113.4**
Speed ratings: **99,98,94,93,93 92,92,92,72**CSF £292.16 TOTE £22.80: £4.80, £4.00, £1.10; EX 343.70.Malahide Express (no.1) was claimed by E J Alston for £12,000. Henry Tun (no.8) was claimed by Norman Berry for £5,000.
**Owner** Derrick Moss **Bred** Selrach Bloodstock **Trained** Scrooby, Notts

**FOCUS**
A modest claimer. The hard-to-win-with runner-up sets the standard.

**NOTEBOOK**
**Scary Night(IRE)**, who had fair form on Fibresand this time last year, has had plenty of leg problems and has taken a long time to get fit. The step back from six furlongs looked to suit and now that he is back in form he could win again at a modest level. *Official explanation: trainer said, regarding the impoved form shown, gelding may have benefited from a drop in distance today down to 5f*
**Malahide Express(IRE)**, who was giving weight to everything else, ran well as he would have been receiving weight from all but one of his rivals had this been a handicap. He made almost every yard before getting caught close home.
**Henry Tun** could not dominate this field in the same way as he had when successful in a regional seller last time.
**Juwwi**, who had the cheekpieces back on, once again shaped as though he is coming to hand.
**Sharp Hat**, who is more at home at Wolverhampton, got going all too late.
**Tigress(IRE)**, another Dunstall Park specialist, could not hold her position in the early stages and soon got caught in the kickback.

## 955 BET IN RUNNING @ BETDIRECT.CO.UK H'CAP 7f (F)
**3:35** (3:42) (D ) (0-85,77) 3-Y-0 **£4,082** (£1,256; £628; £314) **Stalls** Low

Form RPR

55-0 **1** **Mission Affirmed (USA)**[15] 805 3-7-13 55 DMernagh 3 71
(TPTate) *w ldr tl led 1/2-way: styd on wl* **33/1**

21-0 **2** *3* **Denver (IRE)**[25] 704 3-9-7 77 (b) KFallon 7 85
(BJMeehan) *sn pushed along and prom: rdn to chse wnr over 1f out: no ex wl ins fnl f* **11/4**[2]

421- **3** *1 ¼* **Titus Salt (USA)**[82] 6167 3-9-6 76 (b) EAhern 6 81
(TDBarron) *chsd ldrs: rdn over 2f out: no ex fnl f* **9/4**[1]

043- **4** *3* **Rood Boy (IRE)**[75] 6213 3-8-4 60 CCatlin 9 58
(JSKing) *prom: outpcd 3f out: n.d after* **25/1**

-321 **5** *3* **Daring Affair**[17] 779 3-8-4 63 LisaJones(3) 1 53
(KRBurke) *s.s: hdwy over 2f out: wknd fnl f* **8/1**

5142 **6** *3 ½* **Blue Empire (IRE)**[11] 845 3-9-2 77 DNolan(5) 4 58
(PABlockley) *chsd ldrs: rdn and ev ch over 2f out: wknd fnl f* **4/1**[3]

1-21 **7** *6* **Could She Be Magic (IRE)**[19] 758 3-8-5 61 DaleGibson 10 27
(TDEasterby) *sn drvn along and prom: hung lft and wknd over 1f out* **15/2**

00-4 **8** *2 ½* **Maid The Cut**[27] 683 3-7-12 54 oh1 JQuinn 8 14
(ADSmith) *dwlt: outpcd* **40/1**

0-00 **9** *14* **Atlantic Breeze**[20] 752 3-8-0 56 JMackay 5 —
(MrsNMacauley) *dwlt: outpcd* **66/1**

1034 **10** *¾* **Sir Jasper (IRE)**[19] 758 3-8-3 59 (v) SRighton 2 —
(MFHarris) *led: hdd & wknd 1/2-way* **25/1**

1m 33.19s (2.39) **Going Correction** +0.525s/f (Slow) **10** Ran SP% **114.9**
Speed ratings: **107,103,102,98,95 91,84,81,65,64**CSF £117.42 CT £299.46 TOTE £39.30: £6.10, £1.80, £1.80; EX 242.80.
**Owner** T P Tate **Bred** Whisper Hill Farm **Trained** Tadcaster, N Yorks

**FOCUS**
An interesting handicap rated positively through Titus Salt. The winner looks ahead of the handicapper, while the runner-up can win off a similar mark. It produced a very decent time for the class of contest.

**NOTEBOOK**
**Mission Affirmed(USA)** appreciated the step up in trip and stayed on strongly enough to suggest that he will get another furlong. Likely to score again, he did not handle the kickback on his previous start on sand so was ridden more prominently on this occasion. *Official explanation: trainer's representative said gelding benefited from the step up in trip and from being ridden more prominently on this occasion*
**Denver(IRE)** failed to stay ten furlongs last time and had the blinkers back on here. He came through to have his chance but was eased when held in the last hundred yards. A mile could prove his optimum trip.
**Titus Salt(USA)**, making his handicap debut, seemed to have no real excuse, although he might just have needed this first start since before Christmas.
**Rood Boy(IRE)** benefited from the return to this trip on this first outing of the year and would appear to be going the right way.
**Daring Affair**, who missed the break, made up ground early in the straight but could not sustain the effort. Her win came in a weak affair.
**Blue Empire(IRE)** was disappointing in that the track and trip ought to have suited him.

## 956 LITTLEWOODS BET DIRECT MAIDEN STKS 6f (F)
**4:10** (4:16) (D ) 3-Y-0 **£3,438** (£1,058; £529; £264) **Stalls** Low

Form RPR

604- **1** **Generous Gesture (IRE)**[149] 5424 3-8-9 73 JMackay 15 73
(MLWBell) *chsd ldrs: led over 2f out: edgd rt ins fnl f: styd on wl* **3/1**[1]

600- **2** *5* **Time To Relax (IRE)**[116] 5950 3-8-9 64 DarrenWilliams 2 58
(JJQuinn) *a.p: rdn to chse wnr over 1f out: styd on same pce* **3/1**[1]

0-5 **3** *2 ½* **Shaymee's Girl**[18] 774 3-8-9 JoannaBadger 9 51
(MsDeborahJEvans) *led over 3f: no ex fnl f* **66/1**

5-53 **4** *2 ½* **Soul Provider (IRE)**[18] 774 3-8-6 58 LisaJones(3) 8 43
(PABlockley) *mid-div: effrt over 2f out: no imp appr fnl f* **7/2**[2]

355- **5** *3 ½* **Jacob (IRE)**[285] 1777 3-8-7 63 SYourston(7) 4 38
(PABlockley) *s.s: outpcd: styd on appr fnl f: nvr nrr* **33/1**

00- **6** *¾* **Killerby Nicko**[216] 3728 3-8-11 DAllan(3) 16 35
(TDEasterby) *hld up in tch: rdn over 3f out: n.d* **25/1**

6- **7** *nk* **Sir Galahad**[194] 4355 3-8-7 AMullen(7) 11 34
(TDEasterby) *s.s: outpcd: sme hdwy over 1f out: n.d* **20/1**

0- **8** *nk* **Niteowl Express (IRE)**[138] 5623 3-8-9 DRMcCabe 6 28
(JO'Reilly) *nvr trbld ldrs* **66/1**

\- **9** *1* **Red Monarch (IRE)** 3-8-7 DerekNolan(7) 5 30
(PABlockley) *chsd ldrs 4f* **20/1**

**10** *hd* **Adorata (GER)** 3-8-9 CCatlin 3 25
(JJay) *s.s: nvr nrr* **25/1**

06 **11** *1* **King Of Meze (IRE)**[11] 840 3-9-0 OUrbina 10 27
(GProdromou) *hld up: a in rr* **40/1**

3-44 **12** *1 ¼* **Fayrz Please (IRE)**[20] 747 3-8-7 60 AndrewWebb(7) 13 23
(MCChapman) *mid-div: hmpd over 4f out: n.d* **7/1**[3]

50- **13** *5* **Smart Danny**[121] 5911 3-9-0 RWinston 1 8
(JJQuinn) *chsd ldrs 4f: eased fnl f* **33/1**

346- **14** *2 ½* **Blue Emperor (IRE)**[316] 1169 3-8-9 70 DNolan(5) 12 1
(PABlockley) *hld up: a in rr* **14/1**

0 **15** *18* **Royal Shepley**[15] 805 3-8-9 JEdmunds 14 —
(JBalding) *s.i.s: sn prom: wkng whn hung lft over 2f out* **66/1**

1m 20.34s (3.54) **Going Correction** +0.525s/f (Slow) **15** Ran SP% **121.4**
Speed ratings: **97,90,87,83,79 78,77,77,75,75 74,72,65,62,38**CSF £10.45 TOTE £3.90: £1.40, £1.40, £21.90; EX 17.80.
**Owner** Mr & Mrs J & P Ransley **Bred** Bakewell Bloodstock **Trained** Newmarket, Suffolk

**FOCUS**
There was no strength in depth, but the winner showed fair form. However, he already has a handicap mark and is nothing to get excited about from that perspective.

**NOTEBOOK**
**Generous Gesture(IRE)** boosted the stable's strike-rate at this track since 2000 to 30 per cent, and in the process made fools of those who thought that, as her dam is from the family of Cover Up, Golan and Researched, she would not have the pace for six furlongs. That said, the deep ground probably helped her in that respect and she looks sure to improve when stepped up to seven furlongs.
**Time To Relax(IRE)** was another for whom this drop back in trip was a worry. However, there were plenty of people who were willing to take a chance as she was backed in from double-figure odds. She looked to find this trip the bare minimum, though, and is another likely to be seen at her best when stepped up in distance.
**Shaymee's Girl**, who led them into the straight, has shown speed on each of her three starts to date, and is now eligible for a handicap mark.
**Soul Provider(IRE)** came out best of the four Blockley runners and ran a fair race against higher-rated rivals.
**Jacob(IRE)** has presumably had his problems as this was his first start since May, but he ran with a little promise under his inexperienced rider and is one to keep in mind for a modest contest.
**Killerby Nicko** was another having his third run for a mark.
**Adorata(GER)** *Official explanation: jockey said, due to greenness, filly froze at the stalls opened and missed the break*
**Fayrz Please(IRE)** ran poorly but can be excused his bad run as he clipped heels on the first turn and could never get into contention afterwards.



The Form Book, Raceform Ltd, Compton, RG20 6NL

## 957 BET DIRECT ON SKY ACTIVE H'CAP 1m 4f (F)
4:45 (4:52) (E) (0-75,74) 3-Y-O £3,349 (£957; £478) Stalls Low

| Form | | | | RPR |
|---|---|---|---|---|
| 1212 | 1 | | **Yankeedoodledandy (IRE)**[20] 746 3-8-7 **65** ............... RoryMoore(7) 9<br>(PCHaslam) *a.p: chsd ldr 8f out: led over 3f out: sn rdn: styd on* **4/1**[2] | 81 |
| -611 | 2 | 3/4 | **Red Lancer**[9] 864 3-9-2 **74** 6ex ............................ BSwarbrick(7) 1<br>(RJPrice) *a.p: rdn to chse wnr over 2f out: sn hung lft: kpt on* **2/1**[1] | 89 |
| 1432 | 3 | 10 | **Siegfrieds Night (IRE)**[15] 804 3-7-13 **55** ............... DFox(5) 6<br>(MCChapman) *hld up: plld hrd: hdwy 5f out: outpcd fnl 3f* **18/1** | 55 |
| 4-43 | 4 | 1 1/4 | **Ashstanza**[20] 752 3-8-12 **63** ............................(p) EAhern 10<br>(MAJarvis) *sn led: rdn and hdd over 3f out: wknd wl over 1f out* **10/1** | 61 |
| -123 | 5 | 14 | **Gavroche (IRE)**[9] 864 3-9-3 **71** ............(v1) J-PGuillambert(3) 2<br>(MJWallace) *s.i.s: hld up: plld hrd: hdwy over 4f out: hung lft and wknd over 2f out* **11/2**[3] | 48 |
| 0-41 | 6 | 9 | **Ylang Ylang (IRE)**[12] 835 3-9-7 **72** ..................... MTebbutt 7<br>(WJarvis) *s.i.s: hld up: effrt over 3f out: sn wknd* **12/1** | 36 |
| -135 | 7 | 22 | **Keepers Knight (IRE)**[14] 822 3-9-3 **68** .................. KFallon 8<br>(PFICole) *hld up in tch: pushed along over 4f out: sn wknd* **8/1** | — |
| 0423 | 8 | 6 | **Sir Frank Gibson**[15] 804 3-7-12 **49** oh3 .................. JQuinn 4<br>(MJohnston) *chsd ldrs: pushed along 9f out: wknd over 4f out* **20/1** | — |
| 050- | 9 | 2 1/2 | **Thevenis**[75] 6216 3-8-9 **60** ................................ CCatlin 5<br>(JSKing) *chsd ldrs over 8f* **50/1** | — |
| 4-21 | 10 | 1/2 | **Ceasar (IRE)**[20] 752 3-8-4 **55** .....................(p) GFaulkner 3<br>(PCHaslam) *chsd ldrs: lost pl 7f out: sn bhd* **12/1** | — |

2m 46.09s (3.99) **Going Correction** +0.525s/f (Slow) **10** Ran SP% **116.3**
Speed ratings: **107,106,99,99,89 83,69,65,63,63**CSF £12.33 CT £127.71 TOTE £5.80: £1.70, £1.70, £5.10; EX 15.70.
**Owner** K Tyre **Bred** B Kennedy **Trained** Middleham Moor, N Yorks
■ Stewards Enquiry : Rory Moore two-day ban: used whip with excessive frequency and with whip arm above shoulder height (Mar 14,16)

**FOCUS**
A fair handicap. The first two are progressive and should do better yet. A very smart time indeed for a contest of its type.

**NOTEBOOK**
**Yankeedoodledandy(IRE)** reversed recent course form with Red Lancer on 14lb better terms. Clearly travelling best when taking it up, he showed the right attitude to hold on when that rival made him battle. He handles this surface well and in all probability has more improvement in him.
**Red Lancer**, who had no problem with this longer trip, was briefly inconvenienced when his rival edged across him at the two pole, but he rallied after drifting over to the inside.
**Siegfrieds Night(IRE)** was anchored by his 5lb higher mark, but he has plenty of stamina and he plugged on to finish best of the rest.
**Ashstanza** reversed course form with Ceasar and Sir Frank Gibson in the first-time cheekpieces but faded in the straight after making the running.
**Gavroche(IRE)**, visored for the first time, did not do a lot right. He missed the break, failed to settle and hung under pressure.

## 958 BET DIRECT INTERACTIVE H'CAP 6f (F)
5:20 (5:26) (F) (0-60,60) 3-Y-O £2,982 (£852; £426) Stalls Low

| Form | | | | RPR |
|---|---|---|---|---|
| -012 | 1 | | **Piccolo Prince**[20] 747 3-9-7 **60** ............................ JQuinn 9<br>(EJAlston) *mid-div: hdwy over 3f out: rdn to ld and hung lft over 1f out: styd on* **7/4**[1] | 68+ |
| 1201 | 2 | 1 1/4 | **Emaradia**[9] 865 3-9-7 **60** 6ex ......................(b) ACulhane 1<br>(AWCarroll) *w ldr: led 4f out: rdn and hdd over 1f out: n.m.r ins fnl f: kpt on* **9/1** | 64 |
| 0-00 | 3 | 1 | **Prince Of Perles**[9] 858 3-7-9 **37** oh2 ..........(b) LisaJones(3) 8<br>(DShaw) *hld up in tch: rdn over 1f out: n.m.r ins fnl f: kpt on* **40/1** | 38 |
| 0-06 | 4 | hd | **Indrani**[20] 751 3-7-13 **45** ......................... RoryMoore(7) 10<br>(JohnAHarris) *dwlt: hdwy over 2f out: styd on* **80/1** | 45 |
| -003 | 5 | 4 | **Barras (IRE)**[22] 731 3-9-0 **53** ......................(v) MFenton 5<br>(MissGayKelleway) *led 2f: rdn over 2f out: wknd fnl f* **9/1** | 41 |
| -030 | 6 | 3/4 | **Bookiesindexdotcom**[11] 840 3-9-4 **57** .............(b) SWKelly 7<br>(JRJenkins) *chsd ldrs: rdn whn n.m.r and lost pl over 3f out: rallied over 1f out: wknd ins fnl f* **18/1** | 43 |
| 0-14 | 7 | 3 | **Vampire Queen (IRE)**[22] 731 3-8-11 **55** ........... NMackay(5) 12<br>(RPElliott) *hld up: styd on appr fnl f: nt trble ldrs* **9/1** | 32 |
| 00-0 | 8 | 3/4 | **Poacher's Paradise**[44] 561 3-8-8 **47** .................. DaleGibson 4<br>(MWEasterby) *s.i.s: sn chsng ldrs: hung lft and wknd over 1f out* **15/2**[3] | 22 |
| -050 | 9 | shd | **Dandy Jim**[3] 934 3-7-5 **37** oh7 .................... DFentiman(7) 6<br>(DWChapman) *s.s: sme hdwy over 2f out: n.d* **25/1** | 12 |
| 0640 | 10 | 3 | **Dulce De Leche**[14] 817 3-8-12 **54** .................. BReilly(3) 11<br>(SCWilliams) *nvr trbld ldrs* **14/1** | 20 |
| 30-5 | 11 | 2 1/2 | **Tabarka (GER)**[6] 898 3-9-7 **60** ........................ GParkin 13<br>(PABlockley) *s.i.s: a in rr* **33/1** | 18 |
| 5-23 | 12 | 6 | **Emperor Cat (IRE)**[15] 807 3-8-12 **56** ............... DNolan(5) 3<br>(PABlockley) *s.i.s: sn chsng ldrs: wknd over 2f out* **4/1**[2] | — |
| 500- | 13 | 4 | **Time's The Master (IRE)**[123] 5876 3-8-1 **40** ......... SRighton 2<br>(MFHarris) *plld hrd and prom: wknd over 2f out* **100/1** | — |

1m 20.66s (3.86) **Going Correction** +0.525s/f (Slow) **13** Ran SP% **121.5**
Speed ratings: **95,93,92,91,86 85,81,80,80,76 72,64,59**CSF £18.37 CT £500.65 TOTE £2.80: £1.60, £3.50, £6.80; EX 24.80 Place 6 £17.92, Place 5 £11.72.
**Owner** The Burlington Partnership **Bred** Theobalds Stud **Trained** Longton, Lancs

**FOCUS**
A poor handicap lacking strength. The winner travelled well and can be rated higher, but it is doubtful if anything behind the first two will be winning.

**NOTEBOOK**
**Piccolo Prince** has been in terrific form of late, but the question was whether he could translate his five-furlong form to this longer distance in this deep ground. He travelled well for most of the contest and looked sure to score comfortably approaching the furlong marker, but in the end he had to be driven out to make sure. This was not a strong race and he got away with it this time, but one gets the impression that he will be happier back over five.
**Emaradia** has also been in good form this winter and put up another sound effort, this time under a 6lb penalty, at a track where she has not been seen at her best in the past.
**Prince Of Perles** had beaten a total of just six horses in his previous seven starts so this was far and away his best performance to date. Whether he can build on this remains to be seen, though.
**Indrani**, another runner dismissed in the betting, had done little to catch the eye on her recent starts but shaped encouragingly on this occasion.
**Barras(IRE)** , the early pacesetter, avoided the kickback this time but did not get home.
**Emperor Cat(IRE)** has done his winning in sellers but this was still a disappointing effort for he never got competitive after missing the break.
T/Plt: £26.60 to a £1 stake. Pool: £58,321.75. 1,595.25 winning tickets. T/Qpdt: £7.50 to a £1 stake. Pool: £5,125.60. 499.40 winning tickets. CR

# 946 LINGFIELD (L-H)
Thursday, March 4

**OFFICIAL GOING: Standard**
Wind: nil Weather: overcast

## 959 BET DIRECT ON SKY ACTIVE H'CAP 1m (P)
1:40 (1:42) (E) (0-70,70) 3-Y-O £3,370 (£963; £481) Stalls High

| Form | | | | RPR |
|---|---|---|---|---|
| 5-52 | 1 | | **Jomus**[16] 802 3-8-11 **60** ..................................... FLynch 5<br>(LMontagueHall) *s.s: racd on wd outside and in tch in rr: prog 3f out: drvn to ld 1f out: kpt on wl* **8/1** | 67 |
| 434 | 2 | 3/4 | **Alexander Ambition (IRE)**[26] 702 3-9-0 **63** .............. JFEgan 10<br>(SKirk) *racd in midfield: rdn 3f out: effrt u.p over 1f out: kpt on u.str driving to take 2nd wl ins fnl f* **20/1** | 68 |
| 514 | 3 | nk | **Norwegian**[15] 822 3-9-2 **65** ......................(v1) JPMurtagh 11<br>(DRLoder) *sn cl up: effrt to chal gng wl 2f out: rdn and ev ch jst over 1f out: unable qck* **6/1**[2] | 69 |
| 5-33 | 4 | shd | **Lord Of The Sea (IRE)**[26] 704 3-9-7 **70** ................ IMongan 7<br>(JamiePoulton) *trckd ldrs: rdn and effrt over 2f out: styd on same pce fr over 1f out* **7/2**[1] | 74 |
| 0166 | 5 | 1 3/4 | **Trevian**[22] 741 3-9-1 **67** ............................(b1) BReilly(3) 4<br>(SCWilliams) *t.k.h: trckd ldrs: gng wl enough whn nt clr run 2f out: nt clr run over 1f out: kpt on* **9/1** | 67+ |
| 5333 | 6 | 1/2 | **Night Storm**[9] 869 3-9-3 **66** ............................... DHolland 9<br>(SDow) *dwlt: hld up in last trio: effrt over 2f out: drvn and styd on fr over 1f out: nt rch ldrs* **13/2**[3] | 65+ |
| 6-11 | 7 | 1 1/2 | **Smart Boy Prince (IRE)**[37] 611 3-8-10 **66** ......... DerekNolan(7) 1<br>(PABlockley) *racd freely: led: hrd rdn and hdd over 2f out: sn outpcd and btn* **20/1** | 61 |
| -506 | 8 | 1/2 | **Forzenuff**[15] 819 3-8-10 **59** ............................ DSweeney 3<br>(JRBoyle) *pressed ldr: led over 2f out: hdd & wknd 1f out* **40/1** | 53 |
| -011 | 9 | 1/2 | **Athboy**[8] 885 3-9-6 **69** 6ex ............................(v) EAhern 6<br>(MJWallace) *hld up in midfield: gng wl enough on inner whn hmpd wl over 1f out: no ch after* **7/2**[1] | 62 |
| 0-10 | 10 | 3/4 | **Somewhere My Love**[8] 885 3-9-5 **68** ...................... KFallon 12<br>(TGMills) *s.i.s: sn chsd ldrs: rdn and lost pl over 2f out: n.d after* **8/1** | 59 |
| 300- | 11 | 2 1/2 | **Elsinora**[140] 5590 3-8-11 **60** ............................. SDrowne 8<br>(HMorrison) *a in last trio: rdn and struggling wl over 2f out* **50/1** | 46 |
| 303- | 12 | 5 | **Drizzle**[87] 6145 3-8-11 **60** ................................ MHenry 2<br>(IanWilliams) *a in last trio: pushed along 1/2-way: btn whn hmpd 2f out: wknd* **33/1** | 34 |

1m 39.56s (0.05) **Going Correction** 0.0s/f (Stan) **12** Ran SP% **121.2**
Speed ratings: **99,98,97,97,96 95,94,93,93,92 89,84**CSF £163.37 CT £1056.10 TOTE £13.90: £4.20, £6.10, £2.60; EX 308.10.
**Owner** J Daniels **Bred** W And R Barnett Ltd **Trained** Headley, Surrey

**FOCUS**
Fair form that looks solid enough. The winner is progressive, and the 5th and 6th better than the bare form.

**NOTEBOOK**
**Jomus** missed the break as usual but settled better this time. This was a good performance as he had been raised 4lb for finishing second to a well-handicapped beast last time, and perhaps he has turned over a new leaf.
**Alexander Ambition(IRE)**, who has been tried over a variety of distances, looks best over a mile for the time being. She ran a sound race and can win a race of this nature.
**Norwegian** had every chance and his galloping style looks better suited to Fibresand.
**Lord Of The Sea(IRE)**, who ran well in a better race over ten furlongs last time, was going on at the finish and looks sure to be suited by a return to a longer trip.
**Trevian**, blinkered for the first time, found himself behind a wall of horses in the straight and by the time he got clear the principals had gone beyond reach. He deserves rating nearer the front quartet.
**Night Storm** shaped as if worth another try over further.
**Athboy** had to be snatched up on the home bend and lost momentum, but he made little progress in the straight and looks in the grip of the Handicapper for the time being.

## 960 BET DIRECT INTERACTIVE FILLIES' H'CAP 7f (P)
2:10 (2:11) (D) (0-80,76) 3-Y-O+ £4,407 (£1,356; £678; £339) Stalls Low

| Form | | | | RPR |
|---|---|---|---|---|
| 1205 | 1 | | **Ripple Effect**[8] 886 4-9-7 **72** ......................(t) BReilly(3) 5<br>(CADwyer) *t.k.h: cl up: trckd ldr 2f out: shkn up to ld ent fnl f: sn clr* **8/1** | 83+ |
| 00-4 | 2 | 3 | **Ranny**[15] 815 4-8-2 **50** ..................................... JQuinn 2<br>(DrJDScargill) *t.k.h: trckd ldr: led over 2f out: rdn and hdd ent fnl f: no ch w wnr after* **10/1** | 54 |
| 1203 | 3 | hd | **Blonde En Blonde (IRE)**[5] 917 4-9-6 **68** ..........(b) IMongan 7<br>(NPLittmoden) *racd towards rr: pushed along 4f out: hrd rdn and no prog over 2f out: r.o fnl f: nrst fin* **13/2**[3] | 71 |
| -062 | 4 | 3/4 | **And Toto Too**[5] 917 4-9-7 **69** .......................(b) KFallon 8<br>(PDEvans) *hld up: effrt on outer over 2f out: rdn and unable qck over 1f out: kpt on same pce after* **2/1**[1] | 70 |
| 46-0 | 5 | nk | **I Wish**[40] 599 6-8-11 **62** ............................ LPKeniry(3) 1<br>(MMadgwick) *dwlt: t.k.h and sn in midfield: effrt 2f out: hanging and nt qckn over 1f out* **10/1** | 62 |
| 1026 | 6 | 1/2 | **Prima Stella**[13] 836 5-9-8 **73** ...................... LisaJones(3) 4<br>(JARToller) *dwlt: plld hrd and sn in midfield: rdn and effrt 2f out: nt qckn and btn over 1f out* **4/1**[2] | 72 |
| 500- | 7 | 1 1/4 | **Lara Falana**[180] 4719 6-8-12 **60** ......................... DHolland 9<br>(MissBSanders) *trckd ldrs: rdn over 2f out: fdd over 1f out* **16/1** | 56 |
| 655- | 8 | 1/2 | **Michelle Ma Belle (IRE)**[144] 5506 4-10-0 **76** ............. JFEgan 10<br>(SKirk) *hld up in rr: prog on outer 1/2-way: pressed ldrs 2f out: wknd fnl f* **12/1** | 71 |
| 0114 | 9 | 3/4 | **Miss Champers (IRE)**[20] 763 4-9-4 **71** ............... DNolan(5) 6<br>(PABlockley) *s.s: settled in last: nudged along 2f out: no prog* **20/1** | 64 |
| -024 | 10 | 5 | **Cloudless (USA)**[14] 826 4-8-9 **57** ..................... SWhitworth 11<br>(JWUnett) *led to over 2f out: wknd rapidly over 1f out* **20/1** | 37 |

1m 25.46s (-0.54) **Going Correction** 0.0s/f (Stan)
**WFA** 3 from 4yo+ 16lb **10** Ran SP% **119.1**
Speed ratings: **103,99,99,98,98 97,96,95,94,89**CSF £86.87 CT £550.61 TOTE £11.20: £2.40, £3.50, £2.00; EX 124.60.
**Owner** Miss Lilo Blum **Bred** Littleton Stud **Trained** Newmarket, Suffolk

**FOCUS**
A fair race of its type and the winner could well follow up, although she might not be so good as this makes her look

**NOTEBOOK**

**Ripple Effect** ran out an easy winner having been the subject of some shrewd support in the market beforehand. She had the tongue tie back on this time after running two poor races without that aid, and clearly its application makes a big difference to her. She could follow up while in this mood.

**Ranny** was unlucky to run into a well-handicapped rival and ran a solid race in second. She clearly has the ability to win a race off her current mark.

**Blonde En Blonde(IRE)**, despite the fact that she was stepping up in trip, again finished strongly and all too late. Three of her five victories have been gained when racing more prominently than this.

**And Toto Too**, back over her best trip, was forced widest of all rounding the turn into the straight and could never land a blow.

**I Wish** does not have a great strike-rate, but she is now back on the mark she won off over course and distance in November.

**Prima Stella** runs her best races on Fibresand.

**Miss Champers(IRE)** *Official explanation: jockey said filly hung right in the final stages*

## 961 £10 FREE BET @ BET DIRECT SKY ACTIVE CLASSIFIED STKS 1m (P)

**2:40** (2:42) (D ) 3-Y-0+ **£2,703** (£2,703; £636; £318) **Stalls** High

Form RPR

-660 **1** *dht* **Kentucky King (USA)**[5] 915 4-9-10 80 ACulhane 9 89+
(PWHiatt) *racd in last pair: plenty to do whn rdn over 2f out: gd prog over 1f out: str run ins fnl f: got up on line* **14/1**

-610 **1** **African Sahara (USA)**[5] 915 5-9-9 79 (t) OUrbina 7 88
(MissDMountain) *settled in rr: prog on outer over 2f out: drvn and effrt over 1f out: r.o to ld last strides: jnd on line* **7/1**

150- **3** *hd* **Brazilian Terrace**[131] 5756 4-9-3 76 MFenton 3 82
(MLWBell) *trckd ldr to 5f out: styd cl up: effrt on inner 2f out: led 1f out: hdd last strides* **20/1**

0-00 **4** *shd* **Aventura (IRE)**[13] 837 4-9-10 80 KFallon 1 88
(MJPolglase) *hld up in midfield: effrt 2f out: plld out and drvn over 1f out: jnd ldrs wl ins fnl f: jst hld nr fin* **20/1**

3-00 **5** *½* **Summer Recluse (USA)**[19] 770 5-9-7 77 (p) DaneO'Neill 6 84
(BRJohnson) *trckd ldr 5f out: rdn to ld wl over 1f out: hdd 1f out: one pce nr fin* **4/1**[1]

000- **6** *½* **Kareeb (FR)**[117] 5946 7-9-1 78 ARutter(7) 5 84
(WJMusson) *hld up in rr: stdy prog on inner fr 2f out: chsd ldrs 1f out: nudged along and kpt on: nvr nr enough to chal* **20/1**

4130 **7** *2 ½* **Hiawatha (IRE)**[19] 768 5-9-6 76 JQuinn 2 76
(PABlockley) *sn chsd ldrs: rdn over 2f out: fdd jst over 1f out* **6/1**[3]

3-45 **8** *½* **Del Mar Sunset**[13] 837 5-9-8 78 DHolland 10 77
(WJHaggas) *led: rdn and hdd wl over 1f out: wknd fnl f* **9/2**[2]

/00- **9** *5* **Zeis (IRE)**[119] 5936 4-9-8 78 SDrowne 11 66
(HMorrison) *stdd s: hld up in last: lost tch 1/2-way: rdn over 2f out: no ch* **20/1**

0650 **10** *¾* **Cormorant Wharf (IRE)**[22] 742 4-9-5 75 IMongan 8 61
(TEPowell) *sn chsd ldrs: drvn and nt run on over 2f out: wl bhd fnl f* **4/1**[1]

5003 **11** *1 ¼* **Arc El Ciel (ARG)**[10] 862 6-9-7 77 (v) EAhern 4 60
(MrsStefLiddiard) *in tch: drvn 3f out: sn wknd* **20/1**

1m 38.31s (-1.20) **Going Correction** 0.0s/f (Stan) **11** Ran SP% **115.4**

Speed ratings: **106,106,105,105,105 104,102,101,96,95 94**, £5.70 TRIFECTA Win: K K 5.70, A S 3.90; Pl: K K 2.40, A S 2.70; Ex: KK-AS 60.60, AS-KK 55.60; CSF: KK-AS 47.83; AS-KK 42.92.

**Owner** P W Hiatt **Bred** Springwood Llc, Pegasus Stud & Morgans Ford Farm **Trained** Hook Norton, Oxon

**FOCUS**

Solid form with very little between the principals. There was nothing to separate most of these on official ratings and it was no surprise to see a tight finish.

**NOTEBOOK**

**African Sahara(USA)** is a consistent type and clearly his performance here five days ago when very disappointing was an aberration. He will get little respite from the Handicapper for this performance, though.

**Kentucky King(USA)**, dropping back in trip, could not handle the pace in the early stages and trailed most of the field for most of the race, but he really found his stride in the straight and forced a dead-heat on the line. A winner on soft ground for Mark Johnston as a juvenile, he could be worth bearing in mind for the opening weeks of the turf season.

**Brazilian Terrace** had every chance after travelling well into the straight. She was making her seasonal and All-Weather debut here and is entitled to come on a bit for the run.

**Aventura(IRE)** has been struggling of late off his current mark in handicaps, but the champion, who rode him to victory over this course and distance last winter, brought about an improved display.

**Summer Recluse(USA)**, who was up there all the way, kept on well in the straight and hinted that his turn may not be far away.

**Kareeb(FR)** was another making his seasonal reappearance. A difficult horse to catch right, he was nevertheless successful at big prices on two occasions last season, and this performance, under an inexperienced rider, was not without promise.

## 962 LITTLEWOODS BET DIRECT H'CAP 1m 4f (P)

**3:10** (3:11) (F ) (0-65,63) 4-Y-0+ **£2,989** (£854; £427) **Stalls** Low

Form RPR

-002 **1** **Anyhow (IRE)**[19] 767 7-9-8 59 DHolland 3 69+
(MissKMGeorge) *hld up wl in rr: nt clr run 3f out: prog over 2f out: trckd ldrs and nt clr run 1f out: str run fnl f: led nr fin* **5/1**[2]

0-04 **2** *½* **Dispol Evita**[7] 892 5-8-13 **50** IMongan 4 56
(JamiePoulton) *s.i.s: hld up in last trio: prog on outer fr 3f out: drvn to ld jst over 1f out: edgd lft fnl f: hdd nr line* **20/1**

5 **3** *2 ½* **Kashimo (GER)**[8] 887 5-9-7 **58** SWhitworth 7 60
(GLMoore) *hld up in midfield: clsd on ldrs 4f out: rdn to chal 2f out: unable qck 1f out: one pce after* **2/1**[1]

6-25 **4** *shd* **Marmaduke (IRE)**[40] 603 8-9-12 **63** EAhern 1 65
(MPitman) *prom: trckd ldr over 7f out: rdn to chal over 2f out: ev ch 1f out: fdd* **9/1**

035 **5** *½* **Alisa (IRE)**[15] 818 4-9-2 **58** LisaJones(3) 9 59
(BICase) *t.k.h: hld up in rr: sme prog 2f out: swtchd to outer 1f out: styd on: nt pce to chal* **50/1**

113- **6** *hd* **Aoninch**[128] 5823 4-9-9 **62** DSweeney 6 63
(MrsPNDutfield) *plld hrd: hld up in rr: prog 3f out: cl up whn nt clr run 1f out: one pce fnl f: nt rcvr* **10/1**

030- **7** *½* **Masjoor**[159] 5227 4-9-7 **60** JPMurtagh 5 60
(NAGraham) *hld up in midfield: effrt 3f out: chsng ldrs whn nt clr run 1f out: one pce after* **25/1**

1435 **8** *½* **Coolfore Jade (IRE)**[19] 777 4-8-13 **52** CCatlin 11 52
(NEBerry) *led: shkn up 2f out: hdd & wknd jst over 1f out* **20/1**

2031 **9** *1* **Welsh Wind (IRE)**[4] 926 8-9-11 **62** 6ex (tp) JFanning 2 60
(MWigham) *trckd ldrs: nt clr run on inner over 2f out: cl up whn nt clr run jst over 1f out: fnd nil fnl f* **12/1**

4-21 **10** *½* **Platinum Charmer (IRE)**[44] 571 4-9-8 **61** GParkin 10 58
(KARyan) *racd in midfield: rdn and lost pl 7f out: last 1/2-way: n.d after: plugged on fnl 2f* **20/1**

-000 **11** *3* **Londoner (USA)**[8] 882 6-9-8 **59** PDoe 12 52
(SDow) *hld up towards rr: prog to chse ldrs 5f out: wknd over 2f out* **25/1**

-531 **12** *1 ½* **Bramantino (IRE)**[7] 902 4-9-0 **58** 6ex (p) THamilton(5) 8 49
(RAFahey) *prom tl wknd wl over 2f out* **13/2**[3]

510- **13** *6* **Waverley Road**[26] 6254 7-8-6 **46** ow1 LPKeniry(3) 13 28
(MMadgwick) *chsd ldr to over 7f out: prom tl wknd 3f out* **16/1**

4220 **14** *9* **Fight The Feeling**[19] 777 6-9-5 **56** KFallon 14 24
(JWUnett) *a in rr: pushed along and no prog over 4f out: eased 3f out* **14/1**

2m 32.93s (-1.05) **Going Correction** 0.0s/f (Stan)

**WFA** 4 from 5yo+ 2lb **14** Ran SP% **126.6**

Speed ratings: **103,102,101,100,100 100,100,99,99,98 96,95,91,85**CSF £111.65 CT £272.42 TOTE £4.30: £2.40, £4.00, £2.10; EX 118.80.

**Owner** Stableline **Bred** The Duke Of Marlborough **Trained** Higher Easington, Devon

**FOCUS**

Solid form. The winner is a bit better than bare result, but she was suited by strong pace which played into the hands of the hold-up horses.

**NOTEBOOK**

**Anyhow(IRE)** had the race run to suit but had to wait an age to get a run. When the gap eventually appeared, though, she fairly flew home, her rider easing up close home to score with a bit in hand. She is the type who needs everything to fall just right, however, and is no good thing to follow up.

**Dispol Evita**, was another to benefit from the way the race was run, having been held up off the pace. This was the first time she has conclusively proved that she gets a mile and a half.

**Kashimo(GER)** had shaped with promise on his debut in this country eight days earlier, and the money came for him on this occasion. This was another solid effort and he can be found a race in time.

**Marmaduke(IRE)** ran best of those who raced prominently in this strongly-run contest. He will be interesting when he steps back up in trip.

**Alisa(IRE)**, another held up out the back, ran one of her better races on her handicap debut.

**Aoninch** did not enjoy much luck in running as she found her path blocked each time her rider went for a run in the straight. Lightly raced and open to improvement, she is entitled to come on for this first outing since October and is worth bearing in mind.

**Welsh Wind(IRE)** did not find a lot off the bridle, having looked to be travelling well turning in.

## 963 BET DIRECT DAILY SPECIAL OFFERS MAIDEN STKS 5f (P)

**3:40** (3:41) (D ) 3-Y-0+ **£4,056** (£1,248; £624; £312) **Stalls** High

Form RPR

4 **1** **Kryssa**[12] 840 3-8-7 IMongan 4 63+
(GLMoore) *in tch in rr: rdn and effrt 2f out: r.o fr over 1f out: led last 100y: sn clr* **7/1**

5-24 **2** *1 ¼* **Multahab**[26] 708 5-9-11 60 MFenton 8 63
(MissGayKelleway) *w ldrs: led 3f out: hanging rt 2f out: hdd and nt qckn last 100y* **3/1**[2]

032- **3** *½* **Second Minister**[93] 6113 5-9-11 60 (bt) JPMurtagh 2 61
(DFlood) *s.i.s: sn in midfield: swtchd to inner and drvn over 1f out: styd on same pce fnl f* **11/4**[1]

350- **4** *1* **Laconia (IRE)**[111] 5997 3-8-7 65 EAhern 1 52
(JSMoore) *w ldrs: ev ch 2f out: rdn and unable qck over 1f out: one pce after* **9/2**[3]

5 **5** *½* **Joans Jewel**[12] 840 3-8-7 AMcCarthy 6 50
(GGMargarson) *s.i.s: racd in last pair: detached fr main gp 1/2-way: reminder over 1f out: styd on steadily fnl f* **25/1**

00-5 **6** *hd* **Maggie Maquette**[43] 574 4-9-6 55 DSweeney 3 49
(WSKittow) *sn chsd ldrs: rdn 2f out: fdd fnl f* **20/1**

5332 **7** *hd* **Vittorioso (IRE)**[7] 898 3-8-12 54 (v[1]) DHolland 10 53
(MissGayKelleway) *racd on outer: chsd ldrs: rdn over 2f out: nt qckn and btn over 1f out* **5/1**

05- **8** *2 ½* **Valentia (IRE)**[211] 3887 3-8-2 ow2 SaleemGolam(7) 7 40
(MHTompkins) *s.i.s: a in rr: no prog on wd outside over 1f out* **20/1**

40-0 **9** *nk* **Tree Roofer**[5] 918 5-9-8 48 TPQueally(3) 5 42
(NPLittmoden) *led to 3f out: wknd wl over 1f out* **25/1**

**10** *5* **Paris Latino (FR)**[38] 5-9-11 VSlattery 9 22
(CLTizzard) *s.i.s: outpcd* **66/1**

60.06 secs (0.28) **Going Correction** 0.0s/f (Stan)

**WFA** 3 from 4yo+ 13lb **10** Ran SP% **117.7**

Speed ratings: **97,95,94,92,91 91,91,87,86,78**CSF £26.69 TOTE £7.20: £3.10, £1.40, £1.30; EX 35.80.

**Owner** D J Deer **Bred** D J And Mrs Deer **Trained** Woodingdean, E Sussex

**FOCUS**

A modest maiden. The winner could go on but those down the field keep the form down.

**NOTEBOOK**

**Kryssa**, based on her breeding, should not really have the speed to win over this trip, and she did look to be struggling for pace coming down the hill, but she found her stride in the straight and went on to win well. She is likely to benefit from a return to six furlongs and can go on from this.

**Multahab** did nothing wrong but once again had to settle for a minor placing. He has plenty of speed and will find a race soon enough.

**Second Minister**, tongue tied for the first time on his return from a three-month break, found this an insufficient test and will be of more interest back over six.

**Laconia(IRE)** had run a fair race over the course and distance on her last visit, and was supported in the market as a consequence. She is entitled to come on for her first outing since November.

**Joans Jewel** made some eye-catching late headway, having been held up off the pace for most of the way. She looks the type who will do better once she receives a handicap mark.

**Maggie Maquette** would be better employed running in moderate handicaps.

**Vittorioso(IRE)** *Official explanation: jockey said gelding hung right throughout*

## 964 PRESS INTERACTIVE TO BET DIRECT H'CAP 1m 2f (P)

**4:10** (4:12) (E ) (0-70,70) 3-Y-0+ **£3,444** (£984; £492) **Stalls** Low

Form RPR

1-00 **1** **Karaoke (IRE)**[8] 882 4-9-9 **65** JFEgan 5 76
(SKirk) *trckd ldrs: outpcd but gng easily over 2f out: effrt to chse clr ldr over 1f out: drvn and r.o to ld nr fin* **20/1**

0-04 **2** *hd* **Say What You See (IRE)**[15] 820 4-9-12 **68** MHills 7 79
(JWHills) *led: set stdy pce tl qcknd 4l clr over 2f out: drvn and hung rt fnl f: hdd nr fin* **7/1**

-022 **3** *2 ½* **Absolute Utopia (USA)**[7] 894 11-9-7 **63** ADaly 3 69
(JLSpearing) *n.m.r after 2f and dropped towards rr: outpcd 3f out: styd on gamely fr over 1f out: tk 3rd last stride* **16/1**

-113 **4** *nk* **Regal Gallery (IRE)**[7] 892 6-9-10 **66** PaulEddery 1 71
(CAHorgan) *hld up in rr: outpcd 3f out: prog on outer over 2f out: kpt on same pce fr over 1f out* **9/2**[3]

4-04 **5** *½* **Springalong (USA)**[9] 871 4-9-4 **67** SJDonohoe(7) 4 72
(PDEvans) *racd in midfield: outpcd 3f out: effrt and prog to chse ldrs over 1f out: one pce after* **16/1**



The Form Book, Raceform Ltd, Compton, RG20 6NL

-115 **6** ½ **Brave Dane (IRE)**[9] [872] 6-9-12 **68**.......................................... WRyan 6 72+
(AWCarroll) *hld up in last: outpcd 3f out: effrt over 1f out: r.o fnl f: no ch* **7/2**[1]

346- **7** ½ **Katiypour (IRE)**[152] [5359] 7-9-10 **69**.................................. LisaJones(3) 2 72
(MissBSanders) *plld hrd: hld up in midfield: outpcd 3f out: effrt 2f out: btn whn nt clr run 1f out* **16/1**

6425 **8** 1 **The Gaikwar (IRE)**[12] [847] 5-9-7 **63**...............................(b) IMongan 11 64
(NPLittmoden) *s.i.s: sn chsd ldrs: outpcd 3f out: one pce and no prog after* **8/1**

00-0 **9** ¾ **Oldenway**[19] [768] 5-9-2 **63**............................................. THamilton(5) 14 63
(RAFahey) *dwlt: hld up in rr: outpcd 3f out: drvn and effrt on outer 2f out: no prog over 1f out* **10/1**

00-0 **10** ½ **Pure Speculation**[28] [682] 4-9-11 **67**........................................ KFallon 10 66
(MLWBell) *chsd ldr: rdn and outpcd 3f out: wknd over 1f out* **14/1**

33-6 **11** ½ **Silvaline**[15] [820] 5-9-10 **66**................................................ DHolland 13 64
(TKeddy) *trckd ldrs: rdn and outpcd 3f out: steadily lost pl* **4/1**[2]

3/4- **12** 1½ **Murdinga**[66] [2851] 5-9-12 **68**........................................(b[1]) DaneO'Neill 8 63
(AMHales) *prom: drvn and outpcd 3f out: losing pl whn hmpd jst over 1f out* **66/1**

3-05 **13** 1½ **Bowing**[33] [651] 4-9-10 **66**................................................ SDrowne 9 58
(PGMurphy) *hld up in rr: outpcd 3f out: n.d after* **25/1**

/00- **14** 1¼ **Linby Lad (IRE)**[286] [1793] 4-10-0 **70**........................................ MFenton 12 60
(JAGlover) *dwlt: hld up in rr: outpcd 3f out: no ch after* **100/1**

2m 8.56s (1.17) **Going Correction** 0.0s/f (Stan) **14** Ran SP% **128.5**
Speed ratings: **95,94,92,92,92 91,91,90,90,89 89,88,86,85**CSF £161.03 CT £2351.27 TOTE £28.00: £5.70, £3.10, £2.90; EX 110.00.
**Owner** Speedlith Group **Bred** P F Headon **Trained** Upper Lambourn, Berks

**FOCUS**
Say What You See set a very steady gallop and as a result very few got into it. The winning time was understandably modest, and the form might not be reliable.

**NOTEBOOK**
**Karaoke(IRE)**, who is due to be dropped 3lb from Saturday, travelled well in behind the pace. When the leader kicked on he looked to have it to do, but he stayed on well to catch him close home.
**Say What You See(IRE)** was given an almost perfect front-running ride by Hills, who dictated a modest gallop before kicking on running down the hill. In the end he found one too good and whether he will get his own way in front in the same way next time remains to be seen.
**Absolute Utopia(USA)**, who has been in good form this winter, ran well on his return to handicap company, despite the fact that the race was not run to suit.
**Regal Gallery(IRE)** once again did not have the race run to suit her hold-up style of running. She is at her best off an end-to-end gallop.
**Springalong(USA)**, making his handicap debut, ran a fair race but it will be more instructive to see him in a truly-run race.
**Brave Dane(IRE)** was another inconvenienced by the lack of a decent gallop. It may still be the case that he is too high in the handicap, though. *Official explanation: jockey said, regarding the running and riding, he got gelding to settle in rear early on, which is the way gelding normally is ridden, and kept it to the inside rather than going wide around the field; he added that there was no pace in the race and turning into the straight he checked slightly and gaps did not appear until the final furlong, where he stayed on*
**Pure Speculation** *Official explanation: jockey said filly lost her action*
**Silvaline** once again disappointed at a short price.

## 965 NEW SITE @ BETDIRECT.CO.UK CLAIMING STKS 7f (P)
**4:40** (4:46) (F) 3-Y-O £2,954 (£844; £422) Stalls Low

Form RPR

4253 **1** **Lady Piste (IRE)**[15] [817] 3-7-8 53...............................(vt) BSwarbrick(7) 5 55
(PDEvans) *a in ldng trio: effrt 2f out: shkn up to ld 1f out: drvn and hld on* **12/1**

4532 **2** nk **Sonderborg**[3] [942] 3-7-10 49.......................................(be[1]) LisaJones(3) 4 52
(GLMoore) *trckd ldrs: rdn and effrt 2f out: pressed wnr ins fnl f: nt qckn nr fin* **12/1**

-422 **3** 1¾ **Big Bad Burt**[7] [891] 3-9-0 64................................................... KFallon 14 62
(MJWallace) *settled in midfield: prog on inner 3f out: rdn to chse ldrs over 1f out: sn nt qckn: one pce fnl f* **6/4**[1]

1522 **4** ½ **Princess Ismene**[14] [828] 3-8-3 57.........................................(b) JQuinn 8 50
(PABlockley) *dwlt: wl in rr tl prog over 2f out: drvn and kpt on same pce on outer fr over 1f out* **20/1**

54-0 **5** ½ **Averami**[15] [817] 3-8-9 64.................................................(v[1]) SDrowne 13 55
(AMBalding) *led to 1f out: fdd* **33/1**

0404 **6** hd **Garrigon**[7] [885] 3-9-0 60.................................................. DHolland 2 59
(NPLittmoden) *s.v.s: wl in rr: prog whn nt clr run 2f out: drvn and r.o fnl f: no ch* **9/2**[2]

146- **7** 1½ **Foley Prince**[129] [5789] 3-9-10 67......................................... JPMurtagh 11 65
(DFlood) *mostly chsd ldr to 2f out: wknd fnl f* **25/1**

5050 **8** 2½ **Casantella**[16] [808] 3-7-8 40.............................................. JFMcDonald(5) 3 33
(MJPolglase) *wl in rr: shkn up over 2f out: no imp on ldrs* **66/1**

-631 **9** 1¼ **Fission**[15] [817] 3-8-9 72...............................................(b) EAhern 10 40
(JAOsborne) *reluctant to enter stalls and rrd up bef s: chsd ldrs tl wknd over 1f out* **5/1**[3]

-300 **10** 1¾ **Zolushka (IRE)**[2] [946] 3-8-3 45............................................ CCatlin 12 29
(BWDuke) *racd on outer: chsd ldrs: hrd rdn 3f out: wknd 2f out* **66/1**

6206 **11** nk **Stamford Blue**[9] [868] 3-8-4 58..........................................(b) DKinsella 1 29
(JSMoore) *s.s: wl in rr and off the pce: no ch whn nt clr run over 1f out* **25/1**

3511 **12** 1 **Lady Mo**[14] [828] 3-8-2 62.................................................. THamilton(5) 9 30
(KARyan) *dwlt: a wl in rr* **10/1**

00- **13** 2 **Roving Vixen (IRE)**[76] [6216] 3-8-2 ow1........................................ ADaly 7 19
(JLSpearing) *dwlt: a wl in rr* **100/1**

-000 **14** 9 **Indian Oak (IRE)**[7] [895] 3-8-3 35........................................ AMcCarthy 6 —
(MPMuggeridge) *chsd ldrs tl wknd 3f out: t.o* **66/1**

1m 26.0s **Going Correction** 0.0s/f (Stan) **14** Ran SP% **120.2**
Speed ratings: **100,99,97,97,96 96,94,91,90,88 87,86,84,74**CSF £136.71 TOTE £12.60: £2.50, £2.30, £1.60; EX 96.60.Big Bad Burt (no.2) was claimed for £10,000 by Miss Gay Kelleway.
**Owner** Mrs S J Lawrence **Bred** Mrs M Fox **Trained** Pandy, Gwent

**FOCUS**
A modest claimer.

**NOTEBOOK**
**Lady Piste(IRE)** has been running well at this sort of level this winter and no-one will begrudge her this success. She used to struggle to see out seven furlongs but gets the trip well nowadays.
**Sonderborg**, dropping in grade, gave the winner plenty to think about in the closing stages and looks eminently capable of winning a race of this nature.
**Big Bad Burt** looked to have a strong chance dropped in grade, and he certainly came in for plenty of support. However, despite having every chance even the champion was unable to get him home, and he looks one to have reservations about.
**Princess Ismene** ran another sound race and would be one to consider back in selling grade.
**Averami** was ridden differently with the visor fitted for the first time.
**Garrigon** again compromised his chance with a poor start.
**Fission** beat Lady Piste by over three lengths over course and distance last time but threw her race away before the start on this occasion.

## 966 BET DIRECT DAILY SPECIAL OFFERS H'CAP 1m 2f (P)
**5:10** (5:14) (F) (0-55,57) 4-Y-O+ £2,982 (£852; £426) Stalls Low

Form RPR

2213 **1** **Steely Dan**[4] [929] 5-9-7 **57** 6ex.............................................. NPollard 14 67+
(JRBest) *hld up in rr: smooth prog over 2f out: trckd ldr over 1f out: pushed into ld last 150y: sn clr* **11/2**[3]

-621 **2** 2 **Indian Blaze**[4] [929] 10-8-12 **51** 6ex.......................................... TPQueally(3) 6 58
(AndrewReid) *cl up: effrt to ld 2f out and kicked 2l clr: hdd and outpcd last 150y: jst hld on for 2nd* **11/2**[3]

503- **3** nk **Kalou (GER)**[58] [6148] 6-8-12 **48**............................................ SWKelly 4 54
(BJCurley) *settled in midfield: prog over 2f out: hrd rdn and effrt over 1f out: styd on same pce fnl f* **4/1**[2]

4061 **4** hd **Raheel (IRE)**[5] [914] 4-9-5 **55** 6ex.......................................(t) DHolland 9 61
(PMitchell) *hld up wl in rr: prog over 2f out: rdn and nt qckn over 1f out: styd on one pce after* **13/8**[1]

-160 **5** ¾ **Paradise Valley**[4] [931] 4-9-3 **53**.........................................(t) SDrowne 8 57
(MrsStefLiddiard) *hld up towards rr: prog over 2f out: drvn and hanging over 1f out: styd on same pce fnl f* **25/1**

1203 **6** ½ **Theatre Lady (IRE)**[2] [949] 6-8-9 **45** oh5.................................. KFallon 13 48
(PDEvans) *settled in midfield: shkn up 3f out: outpcd 2f out: kpt on one pce u.p fr over 1f out* **10/1**

5-04 **7** ¾ **Sammy's Shuffle**[9] [874] 9-9-0 **50**.......................................(b) IMongan 2 52
(JamiePoulton) *wl in tch: effrt to trck ldrs 2f out: hanging and nt qckn over 1f out: fdd* **10/1**

432- **8** 2½ **Great View (IRE)**[142] [5568] 5-8-9 **48**...................................... DCorby(3) 10 46
(MrsALMKing) *s.s: hld up in last: effrt over 2f out: taken to wd outside over 1f out: one pce and no ch* **14/1**

/00- **9** nk **Arrow**[258] [2543] 5-8-13 **49**..................................................... GFaulkner 3 46
(MrsLBNormile) *led to 2f out: wknd over 1f out* **33/1**

050- **10** 1½ **Storm Clear (IRE)**[13] [4241] 5-9-1 **51**...................................... DaneO'Neill 5 45
(DJWintle) *trckd ldr to 5f out and again briefly over 2f out: wknd over 1f out* **66/1**

0450 **11** shd **Amnesty**[9] [874] 5-9-4 **54**...............................................(be) SWhitworth 11 48
(GLMoore) *dwlt: hld up wl in rr: effrt 2f out: no prog over 1f out* **25/1**

-100 **12** 6 **Molly's Secret**[19] [777] 6-8-12 **48**.........................................(p) JQuinn 12 31
(CGCox) *prom: drvn 3f out: wknd over 2f out* **25/1**

06-0 **13** ½ **Prince Minata (IRE)**[27] [693] 9-8-9 **45**.................................... CCatlin 7 27
(PWHiatt) *prom: chsd ldr 5f out to over 2f out: wknd rapidly* **66/1**

2m 6.55s (-0.84) **Going Correction** 0.0s/f (Stan) **13** Ran SP% **131.2**
Speed ratings: **103,101,101,101,100 100,99,97,97,95 95,91,90**CSF £37.44 CT £141.93 TOTE £7.60: £3.10, £2.10, £1.60; EX 28.50 Place 6 £1,557.46, Place 5 £390.88.
**Owner** E A Condon **Bred** Mrs S E Barclay And L B Snowden **Trained** Hucking, Kent

**FOCUS**
Just a moderate handicap and the pace was ordinary, though the form looks solid. Steely Dan won very easily and is well handicapped on the pick of his form.

**NOTEBOOK**
**Steely Dan**, a disappointing favourite when only third over a mile at Lingfield on his previous outing, is every bit as effective over this trip and ran out an easy winner. A winner off a mark of 75 at his best, there could well be more to come from him. *Official explanation: , a disappointing favourite when only third over a mile at Lingfield on his previous outing, is every bit as effective over this trip and ran out an easy winner. A winner off a mark of 75 at his best, there could well be more to come from him.*
**Indian Blaze** continues in good form and ran his race, but he was simply no match for the winner.
**Kalou(GER)**, who mixes Flat racing with hurdling these days, was supported in the market on this return to the level and ran respectably.
**Raheel(IRE)**, well supported when winning over this course and distance on his previous outing, was backed to follow up that victory under his 6lb penalty but did not appear good enough. He did not get the greatest luck in running, having to be switched in the straight, but he was one-paced when in mattered. *Official explanation: jockey said gelding ran too free in early part of race*
**Paradise Valley** showed a little more than he had been showing of late, but was still well held.
**Molly's Secret** *Official explanation: jockey said mare hung right throughout*
T/Plt: £4,053.50 to a £1 stake. Pool: £48,587.45. 8.75 winning tickets. T/Qpdt: £143.90 to a £1 stake. Pool: £4,939.70. 25.40 winning tickets. JN

# 940 WOLVERHAMPTON (A.W) (L-H)
Friday, March 5

**OFFICIAL GOING: Slow**
The continued lack of rain meant the ground was again deep.
Wind: nil Weather: hazy sunshine

## 967 CASHBACKS @ BETDIRECT.CO.UK H'CAP (DIV I) 1m 100y(F)
**1:50** (1:51) (E) (0-70,69) 3-Y-O+ £3,255 (£930; £465) Stalls Low

Form RPR

4204 **1** **Danielle's Lad**[11] [866] 8-9-10 66............................................ ACulhane 7 79
(BPalling) *led after 1f: rdn over 2f out: edgd rt fnl f: all out* **13/2**

00-1 **2** ½ **Thunderclap**[2] [952] 5-8-1 50 ow1.......................................... AMullen(7) 1 62
(JJQuinn) *a.p: rdn and ev ch on ins fnl 2f: nt qckn towards fin* **4/1**[2]

-346 **3** 9 **Quiet Reading (USA)**[39] [604] 7-9-5 66...................(v) HayleyTurner(5) 10 59
(MRBosley) *hld up: rdn and hdwy on outside 3f out: one pce fnl 2f* **7/1**

-102 **4** 3 **Sting Like A Bee (IRE)**[8] [902] 5-8-13 55.................................. TQuinn 5 42
(JSGoldie) *hld up: sn bhd: rdn and hdwy over 2f out: n.d* **7/2**[1]

0-62 **5** 2 **My Bayard**[8] [900] 5-9-6 69.............................................. JDO'Reilly(7) 9 52
(JO'Reilly) *prom: rdn over 3f out: wknd wl over 1f out* **9/2**[3]

03-0 **6** 3½ **Victory Vee**[14] [834] 4-9-1 57............................................ DSweeney 11 32
(MBlanshard) *led 1f: chsd wnr tl rdn and wknd over 2f out* **33/1**

3422 **7** hd **Yorker (USA)**[7] [908] 6-9-11 67............................................ SDrowne 6 42
(MsDeborahJEvans) *hld up: rdn and wknd over 4f out* **5/1**

0-00 **8** hd **Bugle Call**[9] [886] 4-8-0 42 oh5 ow2........................................(be) JQuinn 8 16
(KOCunningham-Brown) *s.i.s: a bhd* **66/1**

2031 **9** 1 **Geronimo**[7] [909] 7-9-1 64 6ex.....................................(p) DeanWilliams(7) 3 36
(MissGayKelleway) *dwlt: a bhd* **12/1**

000- **10** 3 **Roy McAvoy (IRE)**[90] [6127] 6-9-4 60........................................ GBaker 2 26
(MrsGHarvey) *sn in tch: rdn over 3f out: sn wknd* **66/1**

4000 **11** dist **Easter Ogil (IRE)**[9] [882] 9-9-7 63........................................ VSlattery 4 —
(JaneSouthcombe) *rdn and hdwy on ins over 4f out: wknd 3f out: eased fnl f* **25/1**

1m 56.69s (5.69) **Going Correction** +0.825s/f (Slow) **11** Ran SP% **120.4**
Speed ratings: **104,103,94,91,89 86,85,85,84,81** —CSF £32.83 CT £195.61 TOTE £8.90: £2.10, £2.40, £2.50; EX 85.60.
**Owner** Mrs M M Palling **Bred** W H R John And Partners **Trained** Tredodridge, Vale Of Glamorgan

**FOCUS**
A competitive handicap, but only the first two showed their form and not so good as gap to third might suggest. An average winning time for the grade, but still 1.39 seconds faster than the second division.
**NOTEBOOK**
**Danielle's Lad**, who is usually campaigned over seven furlongs or a mile, registered his first win at beyond sprint distances. He held on well despite drifting over towards the stands' rail.
**Thunderclap** was unpenalised for his win in an apprentice race at Southwell two days earlier. He could not take advantage of the winner coming off a true line, with his rider putting up a pound overweight.
**Quiet Reading(USA)** was never a threat to the two principals and may need a return to longer distances now he is getting older.
**Sting Like A Bee(IRE)**, dropping back in distance, was set to go up 5lb in future handicaps following his narrow defeat at Southwell.
**My Bayard** should not have been inconvenienced by the step up from seven.

## 968 CASHBACKS @ BET DIRECT ON SKY ACTIVE H'CAP — 6f (F)
**2:20** (2:21) (D) (0-80,80) 3-Y-0+ — **£2,664** (£2,664; £627; £313) **Stalls** Low

Form — RPR
2004 **1** *dht* **Hurricane Coast**$^{13}$ [841] 5-10-0 80 ....(b) JPMurtagh 5 — 90
(DFlood) *a.p: rdn over 2f out: hmpd jst over 1f out: edgd lft towards fin: r.o to join ldr post* **11/2**$^{2}$
1333 **1** **Time N Time Again**$^{14}$ [836] 6-9-13 79 ....(p) JQuinn 10 — 89
(EJAlston) *a.p: rdn over 2f out: led over 1f out: all out* **5/1**$^{1}$
64-0 **3** *nk* **Middleton Grey**$^{53}$ [507] 6-9-13 79 ....(b) SWhitworth 9 — 88
(AGNewcombe) *hld up: hdwy 3f out: rdn wl over 1f out: ev ch ins fnl frulong: r.o* **11/2**$^{2}$
00-2 **4** *½* **Blue Knight (IRE)**$^{17}$ [801] 5-9-7 73 .... DHolland 7 — 81
(APJarvis) *chsd ldr tl rdn over 2f out: hmpd jst over 1f out: ev ch ins fnl f: carried lft cl home* **7/1**
0033 **5** *¾* **Gilded Cove**$^{8}$ [897] 4-8-13 65 .... ACulhane 13 — 70
(RHollinshead) *outpcd and bhd: gd hdwy on outside over 1f out: no ex ins ins fnl f* **11/1**
6460 **6** *1* **Sundried Tomato**$^{14}$ [836] 5-9-6 75 .... DAllan(3) 4 — 77
(PWHiatt) *chsd ldrs: sltly outpcd 2f out: eased whn btn ins fnl f* **6/1**$^{3}$
3101 **7** *2½* **Arogant Prince**$^{7}$ [904] 7-8-5 57 6ex ....(b) IMongan 12 — 52
(AWCarroll) *led: rdn over 2f out: hdd over 1f out: sn edgd rt: wknd ins fnl f* **10/1**
26-3 **8** *2* **Rafters Music (IRE)**$^{57}$ [480] 9-9-2 71 .... LisaJones(3) 6 — 60
(JulianPoulton) *sn outpcd: nvr trbld ldrs* **14/1**
00-3 **9** *1¾* **Bannister**$^{9}$ [884] 6-8-9 61 ow1 .... SDrowne 2 — 45
(MrsStefLiddiard) *hld up: rdn over 3f out: a bhd* **20/1**
0-03 **10** *shd* **Vijay (IRE)**$^{7}$ [904] 5-8-3 55 ....(p) CCatlin 3 — 38
(ISemple) *s.i.s: a bhd* **16/1**
00-5 **11** *shd* **Romany Nights (IRE)**$^{14}$ [836] 4-9-8 74 .... DaneO'Neill 8 — 57
(JWUnett) *hld up mid-div: rdn over 3f out: sn struggling* **7/1**
-500 **12** *½* **Port St Charles (IRE)**$^{22}$ [748] 7-9-8 74 .... RWinston 11 — 56
(PRChamings) *sn chsng ldrs: rdn over 2f out: wknd over 1f out* **33/1**
0-20 **13** *2* **Mistral Sky**$^{13}$ [847] 5-9-7 73 ....(v) MFenton 1 — 49
(MrsStefLiddiard) *sn bhd* **28/1**

1m 19.41s (3.71) **Going Correction** +0.825s/f (Slow) **13** Ran SP% **127.8**
Speed ratings: **108,108,107,106,105 104,101,98,96,96 96,95,92** TRIFECTA Win HC 3.90 TA 3.20; Pl HC 3.10 TA 2.30 MG 2.50; Ex HC/TA 15.10 TA/HC 19.40; CSF: HC/TA 17.47 TA/HC 16.83; TC: HC/TA/MG 83.49 TA/HC.
**Owner** Springs Equestrian Ltd **Bred** Anthony Scholes **Trained** Longton, Lancs
■ Stewards Enquiry : J P Murtagh one-day ban: careless riding (Mar 16)

**FOCUS**
A competitive handicap, run in a decent time, and solid form. The third is well-handicapped and interesting now back to form.
**NOTEBOOK**
**Time N Time Again** is a model of consistency at the moment and had the benefit of missing the traffic problems in the home straight.
**Hurricane Coast**, despite having gone up 19lb, has held his form remarkably well since the turn of the year. Bumped twice coming to the furlong pole, he would have been an unlucky loser, although his rider was banned for a day for carrying Blue Knight left close home.
**Middleton Grey**, down 3lb, was fitted with headgear for the first time since he changed hands and ran close to his old form.
**Blue Knight(IRE)**, back up to six, has to be considered a shade unlucky and deserves another chance.
**Gilded Cove** soon got left for dead from his wide draw and could not quite sustain a promising-looking run in the home straight.
**Sundried Tomato** has been given a chance by the Handicapper and ran a shade better than his finishing position suggests.

## 969 BET DIRECT FA CUP CASHBACKS MAIDEN STKS — 1m 4f (F)
**2:50** (2:52) (D) 3-Y-0+ — **£3,386** (£1,042; £521; £260) **Stalls** Low

Form — RPR
0- **1** **Golden Quest**$^{132}$ [5744] 3-8-3 .... JFanning 5 — 78+
(MJohnston) *s.i.s: sn rcvrd: led 8f out: rdn clr over 2f out: styd on wl* **3/1**$^{2}$
04-2 **2** *6* **Bond Moonlight**$^{17}$ [808] 3-8-3 63 .... RFfrench 8 — 65
(BSmart) *a.p: chsd wnr 8f out: rdn over 3f out: sn no imp* **7/1**$^{3}$
-463 **3** *5* **Imperative (USA)**$^{11}$ [863] 4-9-10 68 ....(t) MFenton 2 — 58
(MissGayKelleway) *hld up and bhd: hdwy over 4f out: sn rdn: no further prog fnl 3f* **9/1**
230- **4** *7* **Commander Flip (IRE)**$^{156}$ [5306] 4-9-10 65 .... ACulhane 7 — 47
(RHollinshead) *hld up in rr: hdwy over 6f out: rdn 4f out: wknd 3f out* **33/1**
5 **5** *1* **Harry Lad**$^{14}$ [835] 3-8-3 .... JoannaBadger 9 — 46
(PDEvans) *prom: lost pl over 7f out: sn bhd* **25/1**
2 **6** *27* **Master Role (IRE)**$^{28}$ [697] 4-9-10 .... DHolland 3 — 5
(MAJarvis) *hld up: hdwy over 6f out: rdn over 3f out: wknd over 2f out* **4/5**$^{1}$
**7** *25* **Spot In Time**$^{14}$ 4-9-5 .... JQuinn 4 — —
(JPearce) *hld up: hdwy over 6f out: rdn over 5f out: wknd 4f out* **20/1**
**8** *dist* **Classic Lin (FR)**$^{55}$ 4-9-5 .... FLynch 6 — —
(ABerry) *led 4f: wknd qckly over 6f out: t.o fnl 5f* **100/1**

2m 52.24s (10.74) **Going Correction** +0.825s/f (Slow)
**WFA** 3 from 4yo 23lb 4 from 5yo 2lb **8** Ran SP% **115.6**
Speed ratings: **97,93,89,85,84 66,49,—**CSF £22.85 TOTE £4.60: £1.40, £1.50, £2.20; EX 28.40.
**Owner** Syndicate 2002 **Bred** Fittocks Stud **Trained** Middleham Moor, N Yorks

**FOCUS**
A modest maiden; the winner had little to beat and although likely to prove better than bare form, the Handicapper will take no chances. The lack of pace in the first half a mile led to a modest time for a race of its class.
**NOTEBOOK**
**Golden Quest**, a Derby entry, built on the experience of his outing at Musselburgh last back end. He eventually galloped his rivals into the ground after Fanning was not happy with the fact they went no pace early on.
**Bond Moonlight**, stepping up from a mile, could not go with the winner leaving the back straight.
**Imperative(USA)** was again fitted with a tongue-tie but continues to disappoint.
**Master Role(IRE)** was very disappointing over this longer trip and his trainer could offer no explanation. *Official explanation: trainer had no explanation for the poor form shown*

## 970 CASHBACKS @ BETDIRECT.CO.UK H'CAP (DIV II) — 1m 100y(F)
**3:25** (3:26) (E) (0-70,68) 3-Y-0+ — **£3,255** (£930; £465) **Stalls** Low

Form — RPR
401 **1** **La Puce**$^{18}$ [798] 3-8-8 68 .... FLynch 1 — 77
(MissGayKelleway) *led: hdd over 3f out: rdn to ld again 2f out: hung rt fr jst over 1f out: drvn out* **10/1**$^{3}$
233- **2** *1¼* **Active Account (USA)**$^{260}$ [2502] 7-9-10 66 .... IMongan 2 — 72
(MrsHDalton) *prom: rdn over 3f out: sltly hmpd jst over 1f out: r.o ins fnl f* **14/1**
1236 **3** *½* **Givemethemoonlight**$^{7}$ [909] 5-9-4 60 ....(p) SDrowne 5 — 65
(MrsStefLiddiard) *hld up: rdn over 4f out: hdwy 3f out: kpt on ins fnl f* **11/1**
1315 **4** *½* **Dancing King (IRE)**$^{2}$ [952] 8-8-2 51 6ex .... PMakin(7) 6 — 55
(PWHiatt) *a.p: rdn over 3f out: carried rt jst over 1f out: kpt on same pce* **14/1**
3103 **4** *dht* **Eastborough (IRE)**$^{10}$ [870] 5-9-10 66 .... SWhitworth 7 — 70
(BGPowell) *s.i.s: hld up: rdn and hdwy on ins over 2f out: ev ch fr over 1f out: no ex towards fin* **5/1**$^{2}$
1314 **6** *3½* **Game Guru**$^{24}$ [733] 5-9-5 66 ....(b) DNolan(5) 9 — 63
(PABlockley) *hld up: rdn over 6f out: hdwy on ins over 1f out: nvr trbld ldrs* **20/1**
1511 **7** *2* **Scottish River (USA)**$^{7}$ [903] 5-9-12 68 6ex .... DHolland 8 — 60
(MDIUsher) *hld up and bhd: rdn and sme hdwy over 2f out: sn no imp* **8/11**$^{1}$
0212 **8** *6* **Desert Heat**$^{7}$ [909] 6-9-8 64 ....(v) RWinston 4 — 44
(ISemple) *sn prom: led over 3f out: rdn and hdd 2f out: wknd 1f out* **10/1**$^{3}$
0-30 **9** *9* **Crusoe (IRE)**$^{7}$ [903] 7-9-2 61 ....(b) BReilly(3) 10 — 22
(ASadik) *hld up: hdwy 6f out: rdn 5f out: wknd 4f out* **20/1**

1m 58.08s (7.08) **Going Correction** +0.825s/f (Slow)
**WFA** 3 from 5yo+ 18lb **9** Ran SP% **123.9**
Speed ratings: **97,95,95,94,94 91,89,83,74**CSF £147.96 CT £1575.24 TOTE £11.10: £2.70, £3.20, £3.60; EX 227.50.
**Owner** Wetherby Racing Bureau 52 **Bred** R P Williams **Trained** Newmarket, Suffolk

**FOCUS**
A modest handicap, and a modest winning time, 1.39 seconds slower than the first division. With the form horses failing to show their best form it might not be reliable
**NOTEBOOK**
**La Puce** was 2lb higher than when successful over course and distance when more prominently ridden last time. Making the running this time, she found enough despite proving to be a difficult ride.
**Active Account(USA)**, off course since last June, was forced to check for a stride or two as the winner went across him. He should not be considered unlucky but can soon go one better.
**Givemethemoonlight**, 10lb higher than when winning over seven here last month, is standing up well to a busy winter campaign.
**Dancing King(IRE)**, 15lb higher than when scoring over course and distance last week, rather surprisingly did not make the running but gave a very good account of himself nonetheless.
**Eastborough(IRE)** may have just got found out by the slow surface, despite having won over a shade further here in January.
**Scottish River(USA)** would have had another 5lb to carry had his new mark been in force but was taking on better company. *Official explanation: trainer had no explanation for the poor form shown*

## 971 LITTLEWOODS BET DIRECT STKS (H'CAP) — 1m 4f (F)
**4:00** (4:01) (C) (0-100,95) 3-Y-0+ — **£8,398** (£2,584; £1,292; £646) **Stalls** Low

Form — RPR
1-30 **1** **Mr Mischief**$^{41}$ [600] 4-8-9 **85** .... RoryMoore(7) 7 — 99
(PCHaslam) *hld up in tch: wnt 2nd over 7f out: rdn to ld 2f out: rdn out* **15/2**
2035 **2** *2½* **Glory Quest (USA)**$^{15}$ [827] 7-7-8 **68** ow1 ....(v) DeanWilliams(7) 2 — 78
(MissGayKelleway) *set stdy pce: rdn and hdd 2f out: rallied to retake 2nd cl home* **12/1**
2-11 **3** *½* **Mission To Mars**$^{13}$ [844] 5-10-0 **95** .... JQuinn 3 — 105+
(PRHedger) *hld up: hdwy over 4f out: rdn 2f: chsd wnr fnl f: no ex towards finish* **11/4**$^{1}$
-112 **4** *2½* **Intricate Web (IRE)**$^{24}$ [735] 8-9-1 **85** .... DAllan(3) 1 — 91
(EJAlston) *chsd ldr over 7f out: prom: rdn 4f out: one pce fnl 2f* **13/2**
040- **5** *8* **Red Wine**$^{237}$ [3198] 5-9-13 **94** .... DHolland 5 — 88
(JAOsborne) *hld up: lost pl over 7f out: hdwy over 2f out: sn rdn: no imp* **11/2**$^{3}$
0623 **6** *shd* **George Stubbs (USA)**$^{15}$ [827] 6-7-7 **65** .... JFMcDonald(5) 4 — 59
(MJPolglase) *t.k.h: lost pl over 6f out: rdn 3f out: sn bhd* **9/1**
4-01 **7** *shd* **Border Tale**$^{18}$ [795] 4-8-7 **81** .... HayleyTurner(5) 9 — 74
(CWeedon) *prom: rdn over 3f out: wknd over 2f out* **14/1**
00-0 **8** *15* **Compton Commander**$^{48}$ [558] 6-8-12 **82** ....(v) LisaJones(3) 10 — 53
(IanWilliams) *a bhd* **33/1**
-300 **9** *nk* **Ephesus**$^{14}$ [837] 4-8-13 **82** ....(p) MFenton 6 — 53
(MissGayKelleway) *hld up: rdn 4f out: sn bhd* **20/1**
-411 **10** *1¼* **Mandoob**$^{20}$ [777] 7-8-4 **71** ....(p) CCatlin 8 — 40
(BRJohnson) *t.k.h: hdwy 5f out: rdn 4f out: sn wknd* **4/1**$^{2}$

2m 47.52s (6.02) **Going Correction** +0.825s/f (Slow)
**WFA** 4 from 5yo+ 2lb **10** Ran SP% **119.2**
Speed ratings: **112,110,110,108,103 102,102,92,92,91**CSF £95.52 CT £312.17 TOTE £9.50: £2.30, £2.40, £2.00; EX 122.80.
**Owner** Middleham Park Racing I & Mrs C Barclay **Bred** Mrs Maureen Barbara Walsh **Trained** Middleham Moor, N Yorks

**FOCUS**
Useful form, the winner maintaining a perfect record at Wolverhampton and the third not handicapped out of things back at Lingfield. Also a very smart winning time for the grade.
**NOTEBOOK**
**Mr Mischief** stretched his unbeaten record to five on Fibresand, having flopped at Lingfield last time. The fact that he has scored over further stood him in good stead on the demanding surface. *Official explanation: trainer's representative had no explanation for the improved form shown*
**Glory Quest(USA)**, fitted with headgear for the first time in over two years, stays further and fought back to reclaim the runner-up spot.
**Mission To Mars**, raised another 10lb, was switching from the fast Polytrack surface and did not seem to quite get home in this deep ground.
**Intricate Web(IRE)** was tackling this trip for the first time on the All-Weather and did not seem to be beaten for a lack of stamina.


The Form Book, Raceform Ltd, Compton, RG20 6NL

## 972 CASHBACKS @ ITV TELETEXT PAGE 367 (S) STKS — 1m 100y(F)
4:35 (4:36) (G) 4-Y-0+ — £2,569 (£734; £367) Stalls Low

Form — RPR

420/ **1** **General**[12] [1640] 7-8-12 65 ........ CCatlin 9 — 69
(MrsNSmith) *s.i.s: bhd: rdn over 5f out: gd hdwy over 2f out: led ins fnl f: drvn out* **14/1**

-630 **2** 1 1/4 **Just Wiz**[10] [872] 8-8-12 68 ........ (b) DHolland 8 — 66
(NPLittmoden) *hld up: hdwy over 4f out: rdn over 2f out: led jst over 1f out: hdd ins fnl f: nt qckn* **4/7**[1]

2200 **3** 2 1/2 **Noble Pursuit**[7] [903] 7-8-12 53 ........ DeanMcKeown 5 — 61
(PABlockley) *a.p: led over 2f out: sn rdn: hdd jst over 1f out: wknd wl ins fnl f* **9/1**

6-00 **4** 7 **Effie Gray**[11] [861] 5-8-7 45 ........ (b[1]) DSweeney 1 — 41
(JWUnett) *chsd ldrs: rdn over 4f out: wknd over 2f out* **50/1**

0-06 **5** 8 **Over To You Bert**[18] [791] 5-8-12 45 ........ SDrowne 6 — 30
(RJHodges) *prom: lost pl 5f out: rdn over 3f out: sn bhd* **40/1**

3051 **6** 1 1/2 **Lord Melbourne (IRE)**[4] [941] 5-9-4 50 ........ VSlattery 3 — 32
(AGJuckes) *hld up: hdwy 5f out: rdn 3f out: sn wknd* **6/1**[2]

2616 **7** nk **Iamback**[7] [903] 4-8-13 50 ........ (e) MFenton 4 — 27
(MissGayKelleway) *s.i.s: hld up: rdn over 4f out: bhd fnl 3f* **8/1**[3]

044 **8** 5 **Repeat (IRE)**[25] [720] 4-9-4 47 ........ (p) FLynch 7 — 21
(MissGayKelleway) *led: rdn and hdd over 2f out: sn wknd* **16/1**

00-0 **9** dist **Rival (IRE)**[14] [838] 5-8-12 40 ........ GGibbons 2 — —
(STLewis) *prom: rdn 5f out: sn lost pl: t.o* **100/1**

1m 57.39s (6.39) **Going Correction** +0.825s/f (Slow) — **9** Ran SP% **117.0**

Speed ratings: **101,99,97,90,82 80,80,75,**—CSF £22.86 TOTE £11.80: £1.90, £1.10, £2.40; EX 48.20.The winner was sold to Nigel Shields for 8,500gns.

**Owner** Tony A Hayward **Bred** Sheikh Ahmed Bin Rashid Al Maktoum **Trained** Pulborough, W Sussex.

**FOCUS**

A fair seller, with the winner back to his 2001 form, though the runner-up continues to disappoint. A decent winning time for a race of its type.

**NOTEBOOK**

**General** was having his first outing on the Flat since May 2002 having jumped poorly over hurdles last month. This trip was very much on the short side for him.

**Just Wiz**, five times a winner over nine furlongs at Dunstall Park, has yet to score at this trip.

**Noble Pursuit** probably found the stretch mile in the searching ground just beyond him.

**Repeat(IRE)** *Official explanation: trainer said gelding ran too free and failed to stay the full distance*

## 973 CASHBACKS @ SKY TEXT PAGE 372 H'CAP — 2m 46y(F)
5:10 (5:14) (F) (0-60,60) 4-Y-0+ — £2,961 (£846; £423) Stalls Low

Form — RPR

00-1 **1** **Sun Hill**[25] [724] 4-9-6 57 ........ DSweeney 7 — 77+
(MBlanshard) *a gng wl: led on bit 2f out: pushed clr ins fnl f: readily* **11/4**[1]

6022 **2** 7 **Madiba**[14] [839] 5-10-0 60 ........ RWinston 2 — 67
(PHowling) *hdwy after 4f: wnt 2nd 8f out: rdn to ld 4f out: hdd 2f out: outpcd ins fnl f* **7/2**[3]

33 **3** 1 **Aveiro (IRE)**[15] [825] 8-9-6 52 ........ (v) MFenton 8 — 58
(MissGayKelleway) *chsd ldr: led 9f out: rdn and hdd 4f out: one pce fnl 2f* **3/1**[2]

6-30 **4** 10 **Broughton Melody**[25] [724] 5-8-13 45 ........ DeanMcKeown 5 — 39
(WJMusson) *hld up: hdwy 9f out: rdn over 4f out: wknd over 3f out* **10/1**

-003 **5** 5 **Makarim (IRE)**[14] [839] 8-9-12 58 ........ (p) GBaker 6 — 46
(MRBosley) *hld up and bhd: rdn and hung rt 4f out: nvr nr ldrs* **5/1**

442/ **6** dist **Mantles Prince**[315] [2049] 10-10-0 60 ........ VSlattery 4 — —
(AGJuckes) *a bhd: rdn after 5f: t.o fnl 8f* **14/1**

0- **7** 3 1/2 **Prince Nasseem (GER)**[94] [2586] 7-7-8 40 ........ JQuinn 10 — —
(AGJuckes) *a bhd: t.o fnl 7f* **33/1**

450/ **8** 2 1/2 **Paarl Rock**[1008] [1004] 9-9-2 48 ........ GGibbons 1 — —
(STLewis) *led: hdd 9f out: sn rdn: wknd qckly 7f out: t.o* **25/1**

434- **9** 5 **Prideyev (USA)**[186] [4624] 4-9-6 57 ........ SDrowne 9 — —
(BJLlewellyn) *prom: rdn and lost pl after 6f: t.o fnl 7f* **20/1**

040/ **10** dist **Our Place (IRE)**[594] [3172] 5-8-13 48 ........ LPKeniry[(3)] 3 — —
(BNDoran) *prom: rdn after 6f: sn struggling: t.o fnl 7f* **66/1**

3m 56.53s (14.23) **Going Correction** +0.825s/f (Slow)

**WFA** 4 from 5yo+ 5lb — **10** Ran SP% **119.4**

Speed ratings: **97,93,93,88,85** —,—,—,—,—CSF £12.48 CT £30.95 TOTE £4.40: £1.80, £1.40, £1.70; EX 17.10 Place 6 £196.68, Place 5 £68.61..

**Owner** Stanley Hinton **Bred** London Thoroughbred Services Ltd **Trained** Upper Lambourn, Berks

**FOCUS**

Modest form overall, but the winner is unexposed as stayer and value for more than winning margin; he improved the best part of a stone on his previous defeat of Madiba. A moderate winning time for a race of its class, however.

**NOTEBOOK**

**Sun Hill** ◆ has been a revelation since switching to the All Weather and being given a test of stamina, and he showed his win at Southwell to be no fluke. He had no trouble defying a 5lb hike in the ratings and can complete a hat-trick.

**Madiba** had been beaten a short-head by Sun Hill over 14 furlongs on the same terms at Southwell last month. He found his old rival toying with him in the home straight.

**Aveiro(IRE)**, in a visor instead of blinkers, is a confirmed stayer although he had been kept at around a mile and a half by his old connections this winter.

T/Plt: £580.90 to a £1 stake. Pool: £46,513.40. 58.45 winning tickets. T/Qpdt: £88.70 to a £1 stake. Pool: £3,815.80. 31.80 winning tickets. KH

# [920]NAD AL SHEBA (L-H)
Saturday, March 6

**OFFICIAL GOING: Dirt course - fast; turf course - good to firm**

## 974a BURJUMAN BURJ NAHAAR STKS (LISTED) (DIRT) — 1m
3:45 (3:46) 3-Y-0+ — £47,206 (£14,525; £7,262; £3,631) Stalls Low

RPR

**1** **Cherry Pickings (USA)**[65] 7-8-11 95 ........ (t) RLMoore 1 — 115
(MAlKurdi, UAE) *in tch towards rr: cl up: 7th st: hdwy 2 1/2f out: led 1f out: sn clr: rdn out* **16/1**

**2** 3 1/4 **Tropical Star (IRE)**[23] [756] 4-8-11 109 ........ (vt) RMullen 8 — 108
(AAlRaihe, UAE) *trckd ldrs: rdn to ld 2f out: hdd 1f out: kpt on: nt pce of wnr* **9/4**[1]

**3** 1 1/4 **Divine Task (USA)**[394] 6-8-11 105 ........ LDettori 9 — 106
(SaeedBinSuroor) *in tch: rdn to chal 2 1/2f out: kpt on same pce* **9/2**

**4** 2 1/2 **Burnt Ember (USA)**[23] [754] 5-8-11 102 ........ (t) WSupple 6 — 101
(DougWatson, UAE) *trckd ldr: w ldr st: rdn to chal over 2f out: kpt on same pce* **7/1**

**5** 3/4 **Conflict (FR)**[15] 8-8-11 109 ........ (vt) TEDurcan 3 — 99
(MAlKurdi, UAE) *in tch: rdn and hdwy 2fm out: no ex fnl f* **3/1**[2]

**6** 1 **Estimraar (USA)**[343] [858] 7-9-0 112 ........ (vt) GHind 7 — 100
(MAlKurdi, UAE) *qckly away: led: rdn st: hdd 2f out: grad wknd* **4/1**[3]

**7** 3 **Rotulo (ARG)**[7] [921] 6-8-11 91 ........ (bt) KMcEvoy 2 — 91
(DiegoLowther, Sweden) *in tch: nt clr run st: carried hd high and wknd fnl 2f* **40/1**

**8** 7 3/4 **West Order (USA)**[15] 6-8-11 85 ........ (b) PJSmullen 5 — 76
(SSeemar, UAE) *sn outpcd and bhd: racd wd st: n.d* **100/1**

**9** 4 3/4 **Clod Ber Junior (BRZ)**[7] [924] 6-8-11 85 ........ WCMarwing 4 — 66
(ASelvaratnam, UAE) *sn outpcd and bhd: last st: n.d: eased fnl 110yds* **66/1**

1m 36.64s — **9** Ran SP% **117.3**

Speed ratings: .

**Owner** H E Sheikh Rashid Bin Mohammed **Bred** Bradyleigh Farms **Trained** United Arab Emirates

**NOTEBOOK**

**Cherry Pickings(USA)** took this step up in class in his stride, running out a comfortable winner. He is progressing and could well complete the four-timer.

**Divine Task(USA)** ran respectably on this drop back from ten furlongs.

## 975a BURJUMAN AL BASTIKIYA STKS (CONDITIONS RACE) (DIRT) — 1m 1f (D)
4:20 (4:25) 3-Y-0 — £54,469 (£16,759; £8,379; £4,189) Stalls Low

RPR

**1** **Petit Paris (CHI)**[30] [691] 3-9-8 94 ........ (t) WSupple 2 — 107
(JBarton,) *mde all: set stdy early pce: rdn and qcknd clr st: styd on wl* **12/1**[3]

**2** 2 3/4 **Lundy's Liability (BRZ)**[30] [691] 3-9-6 97 ........ (t) WCMarwing 5 — 100
(MFDeKock, South Africa) *hld up: trckd ldrs: 3rd st: rdn over 2f out: styd on nr fin: nt pce of wnr* **11/4**[2]

**3** 1 3/4 **Little Jim (ARG)**[30] [691] 3-9-11 105 ........ (t) TEDurcan 1 — 102
(SSeemar, UAE) *missed break: sn trckd ldr: 2nd st: rdn and effrt 2f out: no ex fnl f* **4/9**[1]

**4** 9 1/2 **Prince Of Denmark (IRE)**[7] [920] 3-8-9 95 ........ (t) BDoyle 3 — 68
(MAlKurdi, UAE) *hld up: in tch: 4th and outpcd st: no ex fnl 2f* **16/1**

**5** 3 3/4 **Storm Of Tara (USA)**[7] [920] 3-8-9 88 ........ (bt) GHind 4 — 61
(MAlKurdi, UAE) *in tch on outside: outpcd 5f out: 5th st* **25/1**

**6** 16 **Senhor Vencedor (BRZ)**[90] 3-9-4 90 ........ PJSmullen 6 — 41
(ASelvaratnam, UAE) *in tch tl rdn and outpcd 5f out: last and racd wd st: eased fnl 110yds* **50/1**

1m 51.54s — **6** Ran SP% **115.3**

Speed ratings: .

**Owner** Prince Sultan Al Kabeer **Bred** Patricio Baeza Alamos **Trained** Saudi Arabia

**NOTEBOOK**

**Petit Paris(CHI)**, behind Little Jim in the Guineas, reversed that form over this longer trip with a good display from the front.

**Little Jim(ARG)** was below his UAE 2000 Guineas-winning form on this step up in trip. He did not prove his effectiveness over this distance, but looked below his best in any case.

## 976a BURJUMAN DUBAI CITY OF GOLD STKS (GROUP 3) (TURF) — 1m 4f
4:55 (4:57) 4-Y-0+ — £72,625 (£22,346; £11,173; £5,586) Stalls Low

RPR

**1** **Fair Mix (IRE)**[83] [6185] 6-9-4 116 ........ OPeslier 2 — 113
(MRolland, France) *trckd ldrs: 3rd st: qcknd to ld 2f out: sn clr: rdn out* **6/1**[3]

**2** 2 **Prince Of War (AUS)**[14] [854] 6-8-11 102 ........ WCMarwing 12 — 103
(MFDeKock, South Africa) *in tch towards rr: 9th st: rdn and hdwy over 2f out: styd on wl: nt pce of wnr* **11/1**

**3** 1 1/2 **Lunar Sovereign (USA)**[139] [5670] 5-9-4 113 ........ (t) LDettori 6 — 108
(SaeedBinSuroor) *in tch: 4th st: rdn and hdwy 2f out: styd on same pce* **6/1**[3]

**4** nk **Razkalla (USA)**[28] [712] 6-8-11 112 ........ TEDurcan 9 — 100
(DRLoder) *mid-div: 7th st: styd on fnl 2f: nt rch ldrs* **4/1**[1]

**5** 3/4 **Lodge Keeper**[14] [853] 4-8-10 104 ........ GAvranche 7 — 100
(NDeCroutte, Bahrain) *towards rr: last st: r.o fnl 2f: nvr trbld ldrs* **11/1**

**6** 1/2 **Rawyaan**[14] [849] 5-8-11 112 ........ (b) RHills 5 — 98
(JHMGosden) *in tch towards rr: 11th st: hdwy 2f out: styd on: nrst fin* **6/1**[3]

**7** nk **Clodion (IRE)**[7] [922] 8-8-11 100 ........ RLMoore 3 — 98
(MAlKurdi, UAE) *mid-div: outpcd 1/2-way: 10th st: styd on fnl f* **40/1**

**8** 3/4 **Mkuzi**[14] [849] 5-8-11 106 ........ RMullen 1 — 97
(JohnMOxx, Ire) *in tch: 5th st: nt clr run 2f out: no ex nr fin* **33/1**

**9** 1/2 **Dutch Gold (USA)**[14] [854] 4-8-13 110 ........ DHolland 8 — 100
(CEBrittain) *trckd ldrs: 2nd st: wknd fnl 2f* **12/1**

**10** 1/2 **Compton Bolter (IRE)**[23] [757] 7-8-11 112 ........ EAhern 11 — 95
(GAButler) *towards rr: 8th st: hdwy over 2f out: hmpd 1 1/2f out: nt rcvr* **13/2**

**11** 3 1/2 **Scott's View**[14] [854] 5-8-11 112 ........ SChin 10 — 90
(MJohnston) *mid-div outside: 6th st: rdn and wknd 2f out* **11/2**[2]

**12** 2 1/4 **St Expedit**[7] [925] 7-8-11 105 ........ GHind 4 — 87
(RBouresly, Kuwait) *led tl hdd 2f out: sn wknd* **25/1**

2m 29.24s

**WFA** 4 from 5yo+ 2lb — **12** Ran SP% **125.2**

Speed ratings: .

**Owner** Ecurie Week-End **Bred** Snc Lagardere Elevage **Trained** France

**FOCUS**

On paper this looked like a reasonable Group Three contest, but the proximity of the 102-rated Prince of War in second could mean the form wants treating with a little caution. Fair Mix provided France with a first winner at the Carnival.

**NOTEBOOK**

**Fair Mix(IRE)**, a Group One winner in France last season, ran out a clear-cut winner on his first start in Dubai. He looks worth a crack at the Sheema Classic on World Cup day.

**Prince Of War(AUS)**, a beaten favourite in a handicap behind Scott's View on his previous outing, was one of the lowest rated runners in the field but ran above himself to be second. This effort will have blown his handicap mark.

**Lunar Sovereign(USA)**, sixth in the Canadian International on his last start for his previous connections, ran respectably on his debut for the Godolphin operation and they should be capable of placing him to effect.

**Razkalla(USA)**, a winner of a handicap on his debut in this country on his previous outing, ran creditably on this step up in grade.

**Rawyaan**, a winner of a handicap over course and distance on his previous outing, was having only his second start in Group company and was well held.

**Mkuzi** may have been closer with better luck in running.

**Dutch Gold(USA)** had a lot to do on this step back up in grade, but was still disappointing.

**Compton Bolter(IRE)**, back on turf, got no luck in running and is better than this.

**Scott's View** looked at the top of his game when winning a handicap over course and distance on his previous outing and he deserved to take his chance in this higher grade. However, he posted a most lacklustre effort.

## 977a BURJUMAN MAHAB AL SHIMAAL STKS (GROUP 3) (DIRT) — 6f
5:25 (5:30) 3-Y-0+ £72,625 (£22,346; £11,173; £5,586) Stalls High

RPR

1 — **Conroy (USA)**[143] 6-9-6 108 ........ LDettori 7 — 104
(ASelvaratnam, UAE) *a.p: rdn to chal 2f out: led fnl f: drvn out* **4/1**[2]

2 ½ **Sleeping Weapon (USA)**[7] 923 5-9-4 100 ........ (vt) WSupple 13 — 101
(DougWatson, UAE) *chsd ldrs: rdn fr 4f out: r.o wl fnl f: nrst fin* **10/1**

3 2½ **San Salvador (USA)**[16] 7-9-4 105 ........ (vt) GHind 4 — 93
(MAlKurdi, UAE) *trckd ldrs: rdn fr 1/2-way: kpt on fnl f: nt pce of ldrs* **7/2**[1]

4 nk **Dantana (AUS)**[14] 851 5-9-6 104 ........ (b) KMcEvoy 11 — 94
(PLeyshan, Macau) *prom: led 2f out: hdd 1f out: no ex nr fin* **12/1**

5 2 **Conceal**[14] 851 6-9-4 108 ........ RHills 8 — 86
(RBouresly, Kuwait) *prom: rdn fr 1/2-way: kpt on same pce* **5/1**[3]

6 2½ **Persuasivo Fitz (ARG)**[16] 10-9-4 102 ........ SSanders 14 — 79
(AllanSmith, UAE) *chsd ldrs stands' side: effrt 2f out: no ex nr fin* **6/1**

7 ¾ **Elegance Champion (AUS)**[14] 851 5-9-4 95 ........ (be) SChin 5 — 76
(GMoore, Macau) *trckd ldrs: rdn fr 1/2-way: kpt on same pce* **12/1**

8 3½ **Clifden (IRE)**[30] 691 3-8-8 100 ........ (b) TEDurcan 10 — 70
(MAlKurdi, UAE) *prom: rdn fr 1/2-way: wknd 2f out* **25/1**

9 nk **Majestic Horizon**[7] 924 4-9-4 89 ........ (t) RMullen 12 — 65
(AAlRaihe, UAE) *sn outpcd stands' side: kpt on fnl f: nt rch ldrs* **25/1**

10 nk **Peruvian Chief (IRE)**[7] 921 7-9-4 96 ........ (v) EAhern 9 — 64
(NPLittmoden) *chsd ldrs: wknd fr 1/2-way* **33/1**

11 ¾ **Prim (BRZ)**[7] 920 3-9-0 90 ........ WCMarwing 2 — 72
(ASelvaratnam, UAE) *chsd ldrs: rdn and wknd fr 1/2-way* **40/1**

12 4 **Halfsong (SWE)**[23] 754 4-9-0 90 ........ DO'Donohoe 1 — 46
(KPAndersen, Sweden) *sn outpcd and bhd: n.d* **100/1**

13 9¼ **One More Round (USA)**[14] 852 6-9-4 108 ........ (b) PJSmullen 6 — 22
(DKWeld, Ire) *trckd ldrs: rdn and wknd fr 1/2-way* **6/1**

1m 11.04s
**WFA** 3 from 4yo+ 14lb — **13** Ran SP% **126.0**
Speed ratings: .
**Owner** Mohammed Al Jamali **Bred** Darley Stud Management Co Ltd **Trained** United Arab Emirates

**NOTEBOOK**
**Conroy(USA)**, who went into this having won the event for the last two years, gamely made it three consecutive wins. He has been plagued by injuries and had lost his form completely in the US, but on his day he is a smart tool and deserves extra credit, as he did not have the benefit of a previous run this time.
**Peruvian Chief(IRE)** was never on terms and has not shown any sparkle in his four outings since coming over from Britain.

## 978a BURJUMAN JEBEL HATTA STKS (GROUP 3) (TURF) — 1m 195y
5:55 (5:57) 3-Y-0+ £72,625 (£22,346; £11,173; £5,586) Stalls Low

RPR

1 — **Surveyor (SAF)**[14] 853 4-9-4 113 ........ (b) WCMarwing 11 — 119
(MFDeKock, South Africa) *trckd ldrs on outside: rdn to chal 2f out: edgd ahd fnl 110yds: jst hld on* **5/2**[1]

2 shd **Vespone (IRE)**[140] 5641 4-9-4 119 ........ (t) LDettori 7 — 119
(SaeedBinSuroor) *led: rdn 2f out: hdd fnl 110yds: rallied nr fin: jst failed* **5/2**[1]

3 2 **Checkit (IRE)**[14] 853 4-8-11 110 ........ TEDurcan 3 — 108
(MRChannon) *mid-div: rdn and hdwy 2f out: kpt on nr fin: nt rch ldrs* **4/1**[2]

4 nse **Trademark (SAF)**[14] 853 7-9-2 112 ........ RLMoore 4 — 113
(SSeemar, UAE) *mid-div: rdn st: kpt on fnl f: nt pce of ldrs* **12/1**

5 1¼ **Membership (USA)**[14] 850 4-9-0 108 ........ DHolland 12 — 109
(CEBrittain) *in rr: last st: rdn and stdy hdwy fnl 2f: nrst fin* **14/1**

6 2¼ **Cat Belling (IRE)**[7] 921 4-8-9 100 ........ WSupple 10 — 99
(RBouresly, Kuwait) *mid-div on outside: rdn and effrt 2f out: kpt on same pce* **14/1**

7 hd **Bowman (USA)**[15] 5-8-11 107 ........ SSanders 9 — 101
(ECharpy, UAE) *trckd ldr: 2nd st: rdn to chal 2f out: wknd fnl f* **10/1**[3]

8 1¼ **Gateman**[28] 710 7-9-0 109 ........ SChin 1 — 101
(MJohnston) *mid-div on ins: rdn and effrt over 2f out: kpt on same pce* **11/1**

9 5½ **Surbiton (USA)**[7] 922 4-8-11 100 ........ (b) RMullen 2 — 87
(AAlRaihe, UAE) *towards rr: racd wd st: kpt on nr fin: n.d* **40/1**

10 3¼ **Jacks Estate (IRE)**[7] 925 9-8-11 97 ........ DO'Donohoe 8 — 81
(AdrianMcguinness, Ire) *a towards rr: 11th st: nvr nr to chal* **66/1**

11 3 **Sign Of The Wolf**[14] 853 4-9-0 105 ........ (t[1]) PJSmullen 6 — 78
(ECharpy, UAE) *trckd ldrs: rdn st: wknd fnl 2f* **25/1**

12 4¾ **Simeon**[14] 850 5-8-11 100 ........ (v) KMcEvoy 5 — 65
(SSeemar, UAE) *a towards rr: racd wd st: n.d* **50/1**

1m 47.62s — **12** Ran SP% **125.3**
Speed ratings: .
**Owner** P T Dimakogiannis **Bred** Lammerskraal Stud **Trained** South Africa

**NOTEBOOK**
**Surveyor(SAF)**, runner-up to Right Approach last time, held on well when Vespone renewed his challenge close home. He has put up some smart performances here this spring.
**Vespone(IRE)**, having his first outing since disappointing on his Godolphin debut in the Champion Stakes last autumn, wore a tongue tie this time. He battled back well after being headed and looks set for a good season for the boys in blue.
**Checkit(IRE)** was beaten a bit farther by Surveyor this time but this was another solid performance. He is a consistent sort.
**Membership(USA)** ran a better race this time and he appeared to appreciate the longer trip.
**Gateman** once again disappointed.

## 979a SHEIKH MAKTOUM AL MAKTOUM CHALLENGE ROUND III (SPONSORED BY BURJUMAN) (DIRT) — 1m 2f
6:25 (6:27) 3-Y-0+ £108,938 (£33,519; £16,759; £8,379) Stalls Low

RPR

1 — **Victory Moon (SAF)**[23] 756 5-9-0 116 ........ WCMarwing 2 — 120+
(MFDeKock, South Africa) *trckd ldrs: nt clr run 2f out: swtchd lft 1f out: r.o wl to ld fnl 110yds: rdn out* **4/9**[1]

2 2¼ **Dinyeper**[23] 756 5-9-0 108 ........ HKaratas 3 — 116
(AyhanKasar, Turkey) *trckd ldr: w ldr fr 1/2-way: rdn to chal 2 1/2f out: led fnl f tl hdd fnl 110yds* **14/1**

3 3¼ **Naheef (IRE)**[140] 5643 5-9-0 111 ........ (vt) LDettori 1 — 110
(SaeedBinSuroor) *sn led: rdn 2 1/2f out: hdd fnl f: no ex nr fin* **4/1**[2]

4 2 **Anani (USA)**[7] 922 4-9-0 102 ........ EAhern 5 — 107
(EALDunlop) *in tch: 3rd and rdn st: effrt 2f out: kpt on same pce* **28/1**

5 1¼ **State Shinto (USA)**[15] 8-9-0 110 ........ (b) TEDurcan 4 — 104
(MAlKurdi, UAE) *in tch: 6th and racd wd st: styd on same pce* **15/2**[3]

6 nk **Dubai Honor**[15] 5-9-0 104 ........ (t) WSupple 7 — 104
(DougWatson, UAE) *in tch: 5th st: hdwy over 2f out: wknd nr fin* **20/1**

7 17 **Dubai Down Under (NZ)**[30] 688 7-9-0 90 ........ RLMoore 6 — 74
(SSeemar, UAE) *in tch on outside: outpcd and racd wd st: nvr nrr* **100/1**

2m 3.30s — **7** Ran SP% **116.9**
Speed ratings: .
**Owner** Mad Syndicate **Bred** Litchfield Stud Close Corp **Trained** South Africa

**NOTEBOOK**
**Victory Moon(SAF)** followed up his recent success with a workmanlike display. He was not suited by the lack of early pace, but should arguably have won more convincingly at these weights. That said, he should now be spot on for his main target, the Dubai World Cup, and does look one of the main dangers to the fancied American performers as he is now fully acclimatised.
**Dinyeper**
**Naheef(IRE)** made an encouraging comeback, on a surface he is not experienced on. He ran up to his rating and can improve for the switch back to turf in due course.
**Anani(USA)** made a brief effort but was outclassed. This was no disgrace and he is another who will appreciate reverting to turf.

# 911 SAINT-CLOUD (L-H)
### Saturday, March 6

**OFFICIAL GOING: Good to soft**

## 980a PRIX EXBURY (GROUP 3) — 1m 2f
2:50 (2:49) 4-Y-0+ £25,704 (£10,282; £7,711; £5,141)

RPR

1 — **Polish Summer**[83] 6185 7-8-12 ........ CSoumillon 1 — 113
(AFabre, France) *raced in 8th, pushed along 2f out, ran on strongly to challenge inside final furlong, led close home, held on well* 2

2 shd **Bright Sky (IRE)**[83] 6188 5-8-13 ........ DBoeuf 8 — 114
(ELellouche, France) *disputed 6th, pushed along 2f out, ridden & ran on well to challenge 1 1/2f out, led briefly final strides, just failed* 1

3 ¾ **Samando (FR)**[102] 6071 4-8-6 ........ C-PLemaire 5 — 106
(FDoumen, France) *raced in 5th, pushed along & ran on 2f out, quickened well from over 1f out to lead 100yds out, headed close home*

4 2 **Sarrasin (FR)**[142] 5605 5-8-10 ........ TThulliez 9 — 106
(CLaffon-Parias, France) *prominent in 2nd, led approaching 2f out, quickened and ran on from 1 1/2f out til headed 100 yards out, kept on*

5 4 **Nysaean (IRE)**[154] 5383 5-9-0 ........ RHughes 3 — 103
(RHannon) *broke smartly and raced in 4th, 3rd straight, driven to chase leaders 2f out, no extra from 1f out* 3

6 ¾ **Qui Es Tu (IRE)**[8] 911 4-8-6 ........ TJarnet 4 — 94
(J-MSauve, France) *raced in 3rd, 4th straight, effort over 1 1/2f out, no extra final furlong*

7 snk **Valtar (FR)**[102] 6071 4-8-6 ........ ELegrix 7 — 93
(Y-MPorzier, France) *disputed last, last and driven straight, never a factor*

8 6 **Poussin (IRE)**[293] 1701 6-8-10 ........ SCoffigny 6 — 87
(ELellouche, France) *soon led and set good pace til headed approaching 2f out, eased over 1 1/2f out* 1

9 hd **Look Honey (IRE)**[139] 5662 4-9-2 ........ YLerner 2 — 93
(CLerner, France) *disputed 6th, niggled approaching straight, disputing 5th straight, never able to challenge*

10 ½ **Ascetic Silver (FR)**[102] 4-8-10 ........ FBlondel 10 — 86
(DProd'Homme, France) *disputed last, 9th straight, driven over 2f out, unable to quicken*

2m 10.7s **Going Correction** -0.05s/f (Good) — **10** Ran SP% **156.9**
Speed ratings: **116,115,115,113,110 109,109,105,104,104.**
**Owner** K Abdulla **Bred** Juddmonte Farms **Trained** France

**NOTEBOOK**
**Polish Summer**, who looked in excellent physical condition, ran out a narrow winner of this Group Three contest. He now heads for the Sheema Classic in Dubai where he will not be without a chance.
**Bright Sky(IRE)** looked held until rallying close home and would have got up in a couple more strides. This was a good effort, she has clearly trained on and now goes for the Dubai Duty Free.
**Samando(FR)**, settled in behind the leaders early on, she made a forward move from one out and stayed on gamely at the one pace. Improvement can be expected and it would be no surprise to see her run in the Prix d'Harcourt.
**Sarrasin(FR)** took a commanding lead shortly after entering the straight and looked the winner at the furlong marker. However, his stride began to shorten in the dying stages and he gradually dropped back.
**Nysaean(IRE)** looked very well in the paddock and was going easily for much of the race, but he found little when coming under pressure one and a half out. This was a little disappointing.

# 959 LINGFIELD (L-H)
### Monday, March 8

**OFFICIAL GOING: Standard**

## 981 BET DIRECT APPRENTICE H'CAP — 2m (P)
2:00 (2:02) (E) (0-70,66) 4-Y-0+ £2,919 (£834; £417) Stalls Low

Form — RPR

2142 1 — **Phantom Stock**[11] 889 4-8-12 **64** ........ DTudhope[(7)] 5 — 72+
(WJarvis) *t.k.h: prom early: lost pl after 5f: in rr whn stmbld bdly 5f out: prog on outer 2f out: styd on wl to ld last 50y* **7/2**[1]

34-5 2 1 **Sashay**[17] 839 6-8-11 **56** ........ StephanieHollinshead[(5)] 4 — 63
(RHollinshead) *led at stdy pce: rdn and pressed fr over 2f out: kpt on wl fnl f: hdd last 50y* **20/1**

-221 3 hd **Fleeting Moon**[8] 935 4-9-3 **62** 6ex ........ LPKeniry 9 — 69
(AMBalding) *hld up in midfield: smooth prog to chal 2f out: rdn and upsides ldr fnl f: fnd nil and btn nr fin* **7/1**

2-04 4 ½ **Macaroni Gold (IRE)**[18] 827 4-9-6 **65** ........ (b) LisaJones 10 — 71
(WJarvis) *hld up in rr: prog on outer fr 3f out: rdn to chal over 1f out: ev ch fnl f: nt qckn last 100y* **11/2**[3]

3-61 5 ¾ **Gemi Bed (FR)**[11] 889 9-8-7 **50** ........ (b) AQuinn[(3)] 11 — 55
(GLMoore) *hld up in rr: prog on outer 3f out: jnd ldrs 2f out: ev ch u.p over 1f out: fnd nil* **5/1**[2]

5066 6 ½ **Joely Green**[9] 919 7-8-13 **53** ........ TPQueally 7 — 58
(NPLittmoden) *racd in midfield: rdn 3f out: effrt u.p over 1f out: one pce fnl f* **12/1**


The Form Book, Raceform Ltd, Compton, RG20 6NL

400- **7** ¾ **Go Classic**[93] 6130 4-9-6 **65** ........ BReilly 3 69
(AMHales) *t.k.h: trckd ldr for 4f: styd in tch: rdn and effrt 2f out: one pce fr over 1f out* **16/1**

036- **8** ¾ **King Flyer (IRE)**[163] 5214 8-9-9 **66** ........ NMackay(3) 12 69
(MissJFeilden) *racd in midfield: prog to chal and ev ch 2f out: fdd fr over 1f out* **7/1**

10-5 **9** ¾ **Turtle Valley (IRE)**[9] 919 8-8-13 **60** ........ JCoffill-Brown(7) 1 62
(SDow) *hld up in midfield: rdn wl over 2f out: nt qckn and btn over 1f out* **12/1**

/06- **10** *hd* **Our Imperial Bay (USA)**[176] 3406 5-9-7 **66** ........(b) DerekNolan(5) 2 68?
(RMStronge) *s.i.s: t.k.h: hld up in last trio: effrt on outer 2f out: sn no prog and btn* **40/1**

20-0 **11** *nk* **Madhahir (IRE)**[62] 461 4-8-10 **60** ........(e[1]) HayleyTurner(5) 6 61
(CADwyer) *trckd ldr after 4f to 4f out: wknd u.p over 2f out* **33/1**

-000 **12** *6* **Mysterlover (IRE)**[9] 919 4-8-6 **51** ........(t) J-PGuillambert 8 45
(NPLittmoden) *prom: chsd ldr 4f out: hrd rdn 3f out: wknd and eased over 2f out* **16/1**

3m 33.11s (4.53) **Going Correction** -0.025s/f (Stan)
**WFA** 4 from 5yo+ 5lb **12 Ran SP% 116.6**
Speed ratings: **87,86,86,86,85 85,85,84,84,84 84,81**CSF £78.48 CT £469.38 TOTE £5.90: £1.70, £4.00, £1.80; EX 127.80.
**Owner** The L E H Partnership **Bred** Brook Stud Ltd **Trained** Newmarket, Suffolk
■ Stewards Enquiry : A Quinn caution: careless riding

**FOCUS**
A modest staying handicap run at a very sedate early pace, resulting in a pedestrian winning time. The form looks very suspect, but the winner can do better.

**NOTEBOOK**
**Phantom Stock**, who pulled hard early due to the lack of early pace, quickened up readily in the straight to win going away. He was unsuited by the nature of the race and is better than the bare form.
**Sashay** set the sedate pace form the off and had the run of the race. She battled well when challenged two out and is on a fair mark at present, so could be of interest when returing to Wolverhampton, where he has done all of she winning.
**Fleeting Moon** held every chance, but did not appear to stay this trip despite the pedestrian gallop.
**Macaroni Gold(IRE)** was another to be unsuited by the tactics of the race and will do better with a sterner test over this trip.
**Gemi Bed(FR)** failed to build on his smooth course-and-distance success off this 5lb higher mark.

## 982 BET DIRECT NO Q DEMO 08000 837 888 MAIDEN STKS 7f (P)
2:30 (2:37) (D) 3-Y-O+ £3,818 (£1,175; £587; £293) Stalls Low

Form RPR

0-22 **1** **Hatch**[13] 869 3-8-8 74 ow1 ........ DHolland 2 78
(RMHCowell) *reluctant to enter stalls: led after 1f: mde rest: shkn up and drew clr over 1f out: rdn out* **2/1**[1]

253- **2** 3½ **Trench Coat (USA)**[145] 5572 3-8-7 73 ........ MartinDwyer 4 68
(AMBalding) *led for 1f: chsd wnr after: rdn and ev ch wl over 1f out: sn outpcd* **6/1**[3]

**3** *nk* **Emsam Ballou (IRE)** 3-8-2 ........ RSmith 14 62+
(RHannon) *dwlt: hld up in rr: pushed along 3f out: prog over 2f out: styd on wl fr over 1f out to take 3rd wl ins fnl f* **14/1**

55 **4** *nk* **On The Waterfront**[44] 598 3-8-7 ........ MHills 10 66
(JWHills) *t.k.h: hld up in midfield: prog over 2f out: c wdst of all bnd wl over 1f out: rdn and styd on fnl f* **25/1**

50-2 **5** 2½ **Fit To Fly (IRE)**[10] 906 3-8-8 72 ow1 ........ SDrowne 5 60
(SKirk) *trckd ldrs: rdn over 2f out: outpcd and btn wl over 1f out: fdd* **7/2**[2]

0-5 **6** *2* **Wodhill Be**[52] 550 4-9-4 ........ JPMurtagh 8 49
(DMorris) *stdd s: hld up wl in rr: pushed along 2f out: shkn up and kpt on steadily fnl f: nrst fin* **100/1**

0-5 **7** ½ **Instinct**[19] 816 3-8-7 ........ PDobbs 9 52
(RHannon) *plld hrd: hld up bhd ldrs: stl taking t.k.h whn nt clr run over 2f out: rdn over 1f out: sn wknd* **6/1**[3]

503- **8** 2½ **Karathaena (IRE)**[245] 3062 4-8-11 78 ........ HGemberlu(7) 3 41
(JWHills) *trckd ldrs: rdn 3f out: losing pl and btn 2f out* **14/1**

**9** *nk* **Avertaine** 3-8-8 ow6 ........ IMongan 7 46
(GLMoore) *dwlt: rn green and sn pushed along wl in rr: modest late prog* **50/1**

**10** ½ **Saintly Scholar (USA)** 3-8-2 ........ JQuinn 15 39
(EALDunlop) *dwlt: racd on outer: hld up towards rr: effrt and sltly hmpd over 2f out: c wd st: nvr on terms* **14/1**

0-0 **11** *hd* **Polish Rhapsody (IRE)**[37] 644 3-8-2 ........ JFanning 11 38
(JASupple) *trckd ldrs: rdn and no imp over 2f out: wknd wl over 1f out* **66/1**

**12** 1½ **Alianna (FR)** 3-8-2 ........ CCatlin 6 34
(SDow) *hld up towards rr: pushed along and no prog 2f out* **50/1**

4 **13** ½ **The King's Bishop**[37] 644 3-8-7 ........ DaneO'Neill 12 38
(SCWilliams) *t.k.h: racd on outer: wl in tch: rdn over 2f out: wknd wl over 1f out* **12/1**

050- **14** *nk* **Miss Trinity**[279] 2080 4-9-1 64 ........ BReilly(3) 13 32
(CNAllen) *t.k.h: hld up and racd on outer: wknd over 2f out* **12/1**

0 **15** ¾ **Mandahar (IRE)**[16] 846 5-9-9 ........ MTebbutt 16 35
(AWCarroll) *sn outpcd and detached in last: nvr a factor* **66/1**

1m 24.94s (-1.06) **Going Correction** -0.025s/f (Stan)
**WFA** 3 from 4yo+ 16lb **15 Ran SP% 131.3**
Speed ratings: **105,101,100,100,97 95,94,91,91,90 90,88,88,87,87**CSF £15.26 TOTE £3.60: £1.60, £1.80, £7.60; EX 17.60.
**Owner** Blue Metropolis **Bred** Meon Valley Stud **Trained** Six Mile Bottom, Cambs

**FOCUS**
Modest maiden run at a fair pace and the first four finished clear of the rest. The winner only needed to improve slightly on his previous second to Bahiano.

**NOTEBOOK**
**Hatch** enjoyed making most of the running on this occasion and won cosily under a well-judged ride. He has shown a tendency to hang in the past and does not always look the most willing when asked to win his races, and although he is talented and can win again, he is a very quirky type.
**Trench Coat(USA)** ◆ paid for trying to go with the winner on this return form a 145 day absence. He showed enough to suggest he can easily get off the mark on this surface over this trip.
**Emsam Ballou(IRE)**, bred along similar lines to champion sprinter Lake Coniston, made a satisfactory belated debut. She lost ground at the start and was finishing best of all.
**On The Waterfront** again ran freely early on and had to be produced wide into the straight, so could be better than the bare form. This was a big drop in trip and now he qualifies for handicaps, he could be of interest when upped again in distance.
**Fit To Fly(IRE)** ran disappointingly and is stuggling to find his optimum trip. He did not improve on his last run (on Fibresand) and may be flattered by his current rating.
**Instinct** had excuses on this occasion and now qualifies for handicaps.

## 983 BET DIRECT NO Q ON 08000 93 66 93 H'CAP 7f (P)
3:00 (3:04) (F) (0-60,60) 3-Y-O £3,003 (£858; £429) Stalls Low

Form RPR

0060 **1** **Joy And Pain**[12] 885 3-9-2 **55** ........ DaneO'Neill 13 59
(GLMoore) *t.k.h early: trckd ldrs: rdn and effrt 2f out: led jst ins fnl f: drvn and jst hld on nr fin* **6/1**[2]

555- **2** *hd* **Joshua's Gold (IRE)**[170] 5067 3-9-3 **56** ........ RFitzpatrick 5 59
(DCarroll) *trckd ldrs: rdn over 2f out: effrt on inner over 1f out: r.o wl fnl f: jst failed* **25/1**

-225 **3** *nk* **Park Ave Princess (IRE)**[12] 885 3-9-5 **58** ........ DHolland 12 60
(NPLittmoden) *chsd ldrs: rdn over 2f out: effrt over 1f out: styd on wl fnl f: jst hld* **5/2**[1]

060 **4** *1* **Livia (IRE)**[16] 845 3-9-1 **54** ........ RHavlin 9 53
(JGPortman) *prom: rdn 2f out: cl up and ch 1f out: kpt on same pce fnl f* **25/1**

0-26 **5** 1¼ **Mister Completely (IRE)**[12] 885 3-8-13 **52** ........ NPollard 16 48
(JRBest) *pressed ldr: drvn to ld 2f out: hdd & wknd jst ins fnl f* **13/2**[3]

2003 **6** *1* **Docklands Blue (IRE)**[16] 840 3-8-12 **54** ........ J-PGuillambert(3) 15 47
(NPLittmoden) *s.s and swtchd to inner: hld up in last: stl last whn nt clr run 2f out: rdn and styd on wl fr over 1f out: nvr nrr* **8/1**

-233 **7** *1* **Weakest Link**[22] 779 3-9-4 **60** ........ LisaJones(3) 1 51
(WJarvis) *pressed ldrs: rdn over 2f out: fdd over 1f out* **12/1**

-140 **8** *hd* **Vampire Queen (IRE)**[5] 958 3-8-11 **55** ........ NMackay(5) 3 45
(RPElliott) *dwlt: racd towards rr: effrt and nt clr run 2f out: rdn and kpt on one pce fr over 1f out* **10/1**

-000 **9** *1* **Ricky Martan**[11] 891 3-8-13 **52** ........(b) SWhitworth 14 39
(GCBravery) *dwlt: swtchd to inner and hld up in rr: drvn and effrt 2f out: one pce and no imp ldrs* **33/1**

6-00 **10** *nk* **Stonor Lady (USA)**[19] 817 3-8-9 **48** ........(e[1]) PaulEddery 8 35
(PWD'Arcy) *t.k.h: hld up in rr: pushed along and no prog 2f out: btn after* **25/1**

5-36 **11** ½ **Jasmine Pearl (IRE)**[11] 891 3-8-10 **49** ........ JQuinn 10 34
(TMJones) *led to 2f out: sn btn: eased ins fnl f* **33/1**

542- **12** *nk* **She's Our Lass (IRE)**[139] 5691 3-8-11 **57** ........ DTudhope(7) 7 42
(DCarroll) *racd on wd outside: nvr on terms: no prog 2f out* **11/1**

-540 **13** 2½ **Dancing Prince (IRE)**[9] 918 3-8-9 **48** ........ SDrowne 4 26
(APJarvis) *a towards rr: rdn and no prog over 2f out* **10/1**

060- **14** 1¼ **Your Just Lovely (IRE)**[117] 5977 3-9-7 **60** ........ MartinDwyer 2 34
(AMBalding) *settled wl in rr: pushed along and no prog 2f out: wknd fnl f* **12/1**

23-0 **15** *3* **Doctored**[9] 913 3-9-1 **54** ........(p) CCatlin 6 20
(BAPearce) *a towards rr: drvn and struggling 1/2-way* **20/1**

1m 26.54s (0.54) **Going Correction** -0.025s/f (Stan) **15 Ran SP% 131.4**
Speed ratings: **95,94,94,93,91 90,89,89,88,87 87,86,84,82,79**CSF £164.32 CT £493.06 TOTE £8.00: £3.10, £9.40, £1.10; EX 321.30.
**Owner** E Farncombe T/A EWS Shavings **Bred** Jonathan Shack **Trained** Woodingdean, E Sussex
■ Stewards Enquiry : N Pollard two-day ban: careless riding (Mar 19-20)

**FOCUS**
A moderate handicap, run at a steady gallop, which is unlikely to throw up too many winners. This was over two seconds slower than the previous event over the same trip.

**NOTEBOOK**
**Joy And Pain** pulled hard due to the lack of early pace, but really stuck to his task well when asked for maximum effort. He reversed recent form with the third horse on 3lb better terms and seems to be going the right way. *Official explanation: trainer's representative had no explanation for the improved form shown other than that gelding was a weak backward type*
**Joshua's Gold(IRE)** only narrowly missed out on losing his maden tag on this Polytrack debut. He is exposed, but has the abilty to score on the All-Weather.
**Park Ave Princess(IRE)** was not beaten at all far, but failed to improve on her latest effort, which gave her an obvious chance on this occasion. She is consistent, but hard to win with.
**Livia(IRE)** ran her best race to date on this handicap debut, but shaped as though she needs a mile at least.
**Mister Completely(IRE)** ran a fair race, but was not helped by his wide draw.
**Docklands Blue(IRE)** is better than the bare form suggests, as she was switched to the inside from her wide draw and suffered traffic problems in the straight. *Official explanation: jockey said, regarding the running and riding, he dropped filly in and stayed to the inner as instructed but then had nowhere to go until straightening up for home*
**Dancing Prince(IRE)** *Official explanation: jockey said gelding hung right*

## 984 AVOID THE QUEUES WITH BET DIRECT NO Q CLAIMING STKS 1m 4f (P)
3:30 (3:32) (F) 4-Y-O+ £2,884 (£824; £412) Stalls Low

Form RPR

0-63 **1** **Miss Koen (IRE)**[6] 950 5-8-3 53 ........(t) DCorby(3) 3 54
(DLWilliams) *hld up in rr: prog 3f out: pressed ldrs 2f out: drvn to ld ins fnl f: edgd lft: hld on* **33/1**

220- **2** ½ **Carrowdore (IRE)**[100] 6093 4-9-3 71 ........ RHughes 9 66
(RHannon) *trckd ldr 4f: styd cl up: gng wl but lost pl bdly on inner over 2f out: effrt over 1f out: r.o wl to take 2nd nr fin* **5/2**[2]

0 **3** *nk* **Rainbow World (IRE)**[17] 837 4-9-2 77 ........ TPQueally(3) 2 68
(AndrewReid) *t.k.h: hld up in midfield: effrt over 2f out: drvn and styd on to chal ins fnl f: jst hld* **14/1**

-510 **4** ½ **Mad Carew (USA)**[9] 915 5-9-7 79 ........(be) SWhitworth 8 67
(GLMoore) *t.k.h: hld up in midfield: prog to trck ldng pair 2f out: trapped on inner fr over 1f out: kpt on nr fin: nt rcvr* **13/8**[1]

4350 **5** ½ **Coolfore Jade (IRE)**[4] 962 4-8-9 52 ........ MSavage(5) 6 61
(NEBerry) *t.k.h: cl up: led 3f out: drvn over 1f out: hdd and fdd ins fnl f* **16/1**

3-00 **6** 1¾ **Top Tenor (IRE)**[33] 679 4-8-11 70 ........(b[1]) DaneO'Neill 5 55
(BRJohnson) *dwlt: hld up in rr: prog 3f out: jnd ldr 2f out: ev ch 1f out: hld whn no room 150y out and whn squeezed out nr fin* **15/2**

000- **7** ¾ **Duc's Dream**[82] 6208 6-9-1 56 ........ JPMurtagh 1 56
(DMorris) *trckd ldrs: lost pl on inner ovcer 4f out: rdn and outpcd over 2f out: one pce after* **14/1**

30-0 **8** *7* **Kristoffersen**[12] 887 4-9-0 71 ........(b[1]) DSweeney 7 47
(RMStronge) *t.k.h early: hld up in rr: progs 4f out: jnd ldrs wl over 2f out: wknd wl over 1f out* **6/1**[3]

/0-5 **9** *5* **Star Seventeen**[11] 901 6-8-2 60 ........ CCatlin 4 25
(MrsNSSharpe) *led to 3f out: wkng whn hmpd on inner over 2f out* **33/1**

**10** *nk* **Sink Or Swim (IRE)**[110] 6-7-9 ........ JFMcDonald(5) 10 23
(JJBridger) *s.s: hld up in rr: effrt on outer over 3f out: wknd wl over 2f out* **50/1**

0 **11** 1¼ **Bruzella**[44] 601 5-8-10 ........ RHavlin 11 31
(AJLidderdale) *s.s: sn rcvrd: trckd ldr after 4f to 3f out: sn wknd* **100/1**

2m 34.88s (0.90) **Going Correction** -0.025s/f (Stan)
**WFA** 4 from 5yo+ 2lb **11 Ran SP% 120.8**
Speed ratings: **96,95,95,95,94 93,93,88,85,84 84**CSF £116.76 TOTE £34.80: £2.60, £1.30, £3.60; EX 127.90.Carrowdore was claimed by T P Ramsden for £12,000.

**Owner** D L Williams **Bred** G Berger **Trained** Chilton, Oxon
■ Stewards Enquiry : D Corby caution: careless riding
T P Queally one-day ban: careless riding (Mar 19)

**FOCUS**
A very messy claimer where once again many runners suffered trouble in running. The winning time was modest and it is unlikely to have much bearing on future results.

**NOTEBOOK**
**Miss Koen(IRE)** showed a neat turn of foot in the straight to score. She has badly lost her form since running well off a higher mark in Ireland in 2002, but ran her best race for some time latest and is in great heart at present. Unfortunately, she is likely to be hit by the Handicapper for this, as she looked to have it all to do at these weights.
**Carrowdore(IRE)** lost his place approaching the final bend, having travelled kindly up to that point, but recovered well and was flying at the death. He is a most frustrating performer who is very hard to catch right, but he does go well over this trip.
**Rainbow World(IRE)** showed the benefit of his recent comeback effort and was not beaten at all far. He has regressed since winning his maiden in Ireland last year, but showed enough to suggest he can bounce back in this grade on the sand.
**Mad Carew(USA)** ◆ was the unlucky horse. Stopped several in his run several times when full of running, he would have gone very close to winning with a clear run and is worth another chance at this trip.
**Coolfore Jade(IRE)** ran a fair race at the weights and only tired out of it late. This race may have come a touch too quick for her.
**Top Tenor(IRE)** appears to be going badly backwards on this evidence.
**Bruzella** *Official explanation: trainer said mare was found to have bled internally*

## 985 BET DIRECT NO Q H'CAP — 1m 2f (P)
4:00 (4:03) (D ) (0-80,80) 3-Y-O — £4,394 (£1,352; £676; £338) Stalls Low

Form — RPR
0022 **1** **Alfridini**[8] 927 3-8-6 **65** DaneO'Neill 1 — 72
(DRCElsworth) *rn in snatches: chsd ldng pair: rdn over 4f out: chsd ldr over 2f out: led jst over 1f out: drvn and hld on nr fin* **7/2**[2]
330- **2** *nk* **Vantage (IRE)**[179] 4843 3-9-4 **77** DHolland 3 — 84
(NPLittmoden) *hld up bhd ldrs: effrt over 2f out: drvn to chal 1f out: nt qckn and jst hld nr fin* **10/1**
030- **3** *1* **Charlie Tango (IRE)**[179] 4843 3-8-8 **70** SHitchcott(3) 7 — 75
(MRChannon) *t.k.h: hld up in last pair: gd prog on inner over 2f out: rdn to chal 1f out: hung rt and nt qckn fnl f* **25/1**
3-41 **4** *1* **Another Con (IRE)**[19] 822 3-8-7 **66** RHavlin 6 — 69
(MrsPNDutfield) *led at decent pce: rdn 2f out: hdd and no ex jst over 1f out* **4/1**[3]
3-12 **5** *½* **Come What July (IRE)**[14] 864 3-9-0 **73** (b) MartinDwyer 8 — 75
(RGuest) *trckd ldrs: effrt and cl up over 2f out: shkn up and nt qckn over 1f out: one pce after* **7/1**
-312 **6** *shd* **Fiddlers Ford (IRE)**[9] 916 3-8-13 **72** SWKelly 10 — 74
(JNoseda) *hld up in last pair: outpcd wl over 2f out: sn pushed along: effrt and nt clr run 2f out: r.o fr over 1f out: hopeless task* **3/1**[1]
0-1 **7** *4* **Varuni (IRE)**[23] 769 3-8-7 **66** RFfrench 4 — 61
(JGPortman) *hld up towards rr: effrt 3f out: rdn and wknd 2f out* **20/1**
0-24 **8** *2½* **Western Roots**[16] 843 3-9-7 **80** SDrowne 5 — 70
(PFICole) *hld up in rr: effrt 3f out: sn no prog and btn* **8/1**
0-26 **9** *2* **Kings Rock**[17] 835 3-8-4 **63** JFanning 9 — 50
(KARyan) *chsd ldr to over 2f out: wknd* **33/1**
4633 **10** *6* **Maybe Someday**[16] 845 3-8-8 **67** (p) JQuinn 2 — 43
(IAWood) *in tch in rr tl wknd 3f out: sn bhd* **25/1**

2m 6.20s (-1.19) **Going Correction** -0.025s/f (Stan) **10** Ran SP% **115.3**
Speed ratings: **103,102,101,101,100 100,97,95,93,89**CSF £35.36 CT £754.58 TOTE £4.10: £2.10, £4.60, £3.00; EX 44.30 Trifecta £906.80 Pool of £1,277.30 - 1 winning ticket.
**Owner** A Heaney **Bred** Miss K Rausing **Trained** Whitsbury, Hants

**FOCUS**
A decent race for the grade won by a progressive sort and the form looks sound. The first two look progressive and the fourth can do better in a less competitive event. The winning time was also decent.

**NOTEBOOK**
**Alfridini**, an unlucky loser last time, made amends over this longer trip on this handicap debut. He is clearly progressive, but it would not be a suprise were his optimum trip to be slightly shorter than this.
**Vantage(IRE)**, who had some fair maiden form as a juvenile, showed he has wintered well with a solid run and was only just denied. He was giving weight away to the winner and, with this run under his belt, looks a shoe in for a maiden at this trip.
**Charlie Tango(IRE)**, who pulled hard early, showed a neat turn of foot when making headway on the inside rail over two out and ran a solid comeback race. He can lose his maiden tag before long in this sphere.
**Another Con(IRE)** probably ran up to the form of her recent success over course and distance off this 5lb higher mark. She lost little in defeat and will find easier opportunities than this.
**Come What July(IRE)**
**Fiddlers Ford(IRE)** was outpaced at the back of the pack as the tempo quickened and is capable of better.

## 986 BETDIRECT.CO.UK H'CAP — 5f (P)
4:30 (4:35) (D ) (0-85,84) 3-Y-O — £4,719 (£1,452; £726; £363) Stalls High

Form — RPR
401- **1** **Peruvian Style (IRE)**[214] 3924 3-8-13 **76** DHolland 2 — 83+
(NPLittmoden) *sn chsd ldng pair: rdn 2f out: styd on to ld fnl 100y: hld on nr fin* **14/1**
200- **2** *nk* **Trick Cyclist**[152] 5450 3-8-10 **80** TBlock(7) 4 — 86
(AMBalding) *hld up in midfield: outpcd over 2f out: rdn and effrt over 1f out: r.o to take 2nd nr fin: nt rch wnr* **25/1**
0-11 **3** *1* **Tag Team (IRE)**[11] 891 3-9-0 **77** MartinDwyer 1 — 79+
(AMBalding) *led: narrowly hdd 2f out: n.m.r on inner and bmpd over 1f out: ev ch ins fnl f: unable qck nr fin* **4/5**[1]
551- **4** *hd* **Green Manalishi**[157] 5338 3-9-0 **77** SWhitworth 3 — 78+
(DWPArbuthnot) *pressed ldr: led narrowly 2f out: bmpd rival over 1f out: hdd and one pce last 100y* **4/1**[2]
0202 **5** *½* **Hello Roberto**[19] 819 3-8-12 **75** DeanMcKeown 9 — 74
(MJPolglase) *settled in last pair: outpcd over 2f out: styd on fnl f: nt rch ldrs* **8/1**[3]
0-11 **6** *1¼* **Cut And Dried**[13] 868 3-8-6 **69** DaneO'Neill 10 — 63
(DMSimcock) *settled in last: outpcd over 2f out: n.d after: kpt on fnl f* **8/1**[3]
6-53 **7** *1½* **Beau Jazz**[13] 868 3-8-3 **66** SRighton 7 — 54
(WDeBest-Turner) *chsd ldrs: outpcd over 2f out: fdd fnl f* **20/1**
243- **8** *2* **Shielaligh**[182] 4778 3-9-7 **84** JQuinn 5 — 64
(MissGayKelleway) *racd in midfield: lost action over 2f out and dropped to rr: no ch after* **16/1**

59.70 secs (-0.08) **Going Correction** -0.025s/f (Stan) **8** Ran SP% **118.9**
Speed ratings: **99,98,96,96,95 93,91,88**CSF £299.57 CT £603.11 TOTE £18.70: £3.30, £5.30, £1.10; EX 232.30.
**Owner** M C S D Racing Ltd **Bred** Forenaghts Stud **Trained** Newmarket, Suffolk
■ Stewards Enquiry : S Whitworth caution: improper riding
Martin Dwyer caution: improper riding

**FOCUS**
A fair sprint in which the leaders set a decent clip, but their barging match in the straight allowed those tracking the pace to capitalise and the form may be suspect. However, the winner should prove a fair bit better than this and the third and fourth will be hard to beat next time if getting an easy lead.

**NOTEBOOK**
**Peruvian Style(IRE)**, who suffered a bad tendon injury when winning last time, showed he has fully recovered with a resolute comeback effort. He had been off for 214 days prior to this, should come on plenty for the outing and is the type his stable do well with.
**Trick Cyclist**, who lost his form dramatically after winning last May as a juvenile, rallied well from off the pace and was only just denied. He looks to have wintered well anjd could be worth chancing back over another furlong.
**Tag Team(IRE)**, up 10lb for his ready win last time, was done no favours by Green Manalishi in the straight when that rival challenged for the lead and bumped him several times. He would have finished closer but for that, however, he was all out at the time and the Handicapper may have him about right at present.
**Green Manalishi** paid for trying to go with the leader early on and was very tired when he hampered Tag Team against the rail approaching the final furlong. He is fairly well regarded by connections and has a lot of natural speed, but looks a touch high in the weights.

## 987 BET DIRECT IN RUNNING (S) STKS — 6f (P)
5:00 (5:04) (G ) 3-Y-O+ — £2,646 (£756; £378) Stalls Low

Form — RPR
200- **1** **Yorkie**[160] 4361 5-9-7 58 RFitzpatrick 13 — 54
(DCarroll) *racd in last trio tl prog on outer wl over 2f out: drvn to chal 1f out: edgd lft but kpt on to ld last 75y* **10/1**
0501 **2** *nk* **Sounds Lucky**[11] 893 8-9-12 60 (b) DHolland 11 — 58
(NPLittmoden) *t.k.h: trckd ldrs: effrt 2f out: rdn to chal and ev ch ins fnl f: jst hld nr fin* **6/1**[3]
100 **3** *hd* **Pips Song (IRE)**[31] 694 9-9-9 48 LisaJones(3) 2 — 58
(PWHiatt) *mde most: rdn and hrd pressed fr 2f out: hdd last 75y* **33/1**
00-0 **4** *½* **Roman Empire**[13] 873 4-9-7 52 (v[1]) JPMurtagh 12 — 51
(TJEtherington) *s.i.s: in rr tl prog on outer over 2f out: styd on u.p fnl f: jst unable to chal* **20/1**
0-40 **5** *shd* **Legal Set (IRE)**[8] 928 8-9-0 59 SJDonohoe(7) 14 — 51
(WJMusson) *hld up wl in rr: effrt and prog 2f out: styd on fr over 1f out: nrst fin* **8/1**
1015 **6** *¾* **Bells Beach (IRE)**[8] 930 6-9-7 55 JFanning 10 — 48
(PHowling) *sn trckd ldrs: rdn and effrt 2f out: one pce fr over 1f out* **5/1**[2]
0000 **7** *hd* **Only One Legend (IRE)**[25] 748 6-9-7 65 (b) TQuinn 4 — 48
(KARyan) *trckd ldrs: effrt on inner wl over 2f out: ev ch ent fnl f: wknd last 100y* **11/4**[1]
0-00 **8** *¾* **Tree Roofer**[4] 963 5-9-4 45 TPQueally(3) 3 — 46
(NPLittmoden) *hld up in last: rdn over 2f out: styd on u.p fr over 1f out: nt rch ldrs* **40/1**
6240 **9** *nk* **Onefortheboys (IRE)**[6] 951 5-9-7 45 RHughes 7 — 45
(DFlood) *racd wl in rr: effrt on wd outside 2f out: rdn 1f out: one pce and nvr rchd ldrs* **25/1**
330 **10** *nk* **Jahangir**[8] 930 5-9-7 45 DaneO'Neill 8 — 44
(BRJohnson) *prom: pressed ldr 2f out: ev ch wl over 1f out: sn fnd nil and btn* **16/1**
20-0 **11** *1¾* **Firework**[23] 771 6-9-7 63 (p) JQuinn 6 — 39
(JAkehurst) *w ldr to 2f out: wknd over 1f out* **7/1**
006- **12** *1* **Arabian Knight (IRE)**[228] 3514 4-9-7 62 VSlattery 9 — 36
(RJHodges) *chsd ldrs: lost pl 1/2-way: rdn and no prog 2f out: fdd* **33/1**
1-60 **13** *hd* **Somerset West (IRE)**[33] 674 4-9-0 52 KristinStubbs(7) 5 — 35
(MrsLStubbs) *s.i.s: sn in midfield: snatched up and dropped to rr over 2f out: no ch after* **20/1**
-036 **14** *2½* **Confuzed**[6] 946 4-9-7 52 (e) RSmith 1 — 27
(DFlood) *w ldr to 1/2-way: sn lost pl and btn* **14/1**

1m 13.0s (0.08) **Going Correction** -0.025s/f (Stan) **14** Ran SP% **124.6**
Speed ratings: **98,97,97,96,96 95,95,94,93,93 91,89,89,86**CSF £65.48 TOTE £15.10: £3.70, £2.10, £4.20; EX 160.60.The winner was sold to M Polglase (for Paul Blockley) for 8,400gns. Sounds Lucky was claimed by Andrew Reid for £6,000.
**Owner** C H Stephenson & Partners **Bred** C Stephenson **Trained** Warthill, N Yorks

**FOCUS**
A weak contest run at a modest pace and once again the runners finished in a heap. The third and fourth anchor the form.

**NOTEBOOK**
**Yorkie** stayed on strongly form off the pace to get up late on, despite having been kept wide entering the straight. This was his first run for 160 days and he is entitled to improve, but is not the soundest of horses. He was claimed by Mark Polglase at the subsequent auction.
**Sounds Lucky**, winner of a claimer at this venue last time, was only just denied a follow up win over this extra furlong. He is consistent in this grade.
**Pips Song(IRE)** ran a blinder at these weights. He is inconsistent, but is in fair heat at present and could gain compensation in this grade when returning to his favoured Wolverhampton.
**Roman Empire** ran his best race for sometime in the first-time blinkers, and would have been closer, but for missing the kick.

## 988 NEW SITE @ BETDIRECT.CO.UK H'CAP — 1m (P)
5:30 (5:35) (F ) (0-55,58) 3-Y-O+ — £3,031 (£866; £433) Stalls High

Form — RPR
-022 **1** **Meelup (IRE)**[8] 926 4-9-11 **55** (p) VSlattery 3 — 64
(JaneSouthcombe) *mde all: rdn and hrd pressed fr over 1f out: hld on wl* **14/1**
06-6 **2** *nk* **Blue Quiver (IRE)**[13] 871 4-9-9 **53** PaulEddery 8 — 61
(CAHorgan) *a chsng wnr: rdn to chal over 1f out: ev ch wl ins fnl f: nt qckn nr fin* **12/1**
0412 **3** *1¾* **Lucid Dreams (IRE)**[8] 933 5-9-10 **54** (p) JFanning 7 — 59
(MWigham) *hld up in rr: shkn up and prog over 2f out: drvn and kpt on fr over 1f out to take 3rd nr fin* **11/2**[3]
-231 **4** *½* **Double Ransom**[8] 933 5-10-0 **58** 6ex (b) DHolland 5 — 62
(MrsLStubbs) *t.k.h early: chsd ldrs: rdn 3f out: effrt u.p over 1f out: one pce* **11/8**[1]
1304 **5** *nk* **Balerno**[8] 933 5-9-7 **51** KDarley 1 — 54
(RIngram) *trckd ldng pair: rdn over 2f out: swtchd rt and effrt over 1f out: nt qckn fnl f: wknd nr fin* **12/1**
0233 **6** *4* **Frank's Quest (IRE)**[13] 874 4-9-7 **54** LPKeniry(3) 4 — 50
(PBurgoyne) *t.k.h: trckd ldrs: rdn over 2f out: sn nt qckn and outpcd: n.d fnl f* **14/1**
51-0 **7** *¾* **Shahm (IRE)**[39] 626 5-9-9 **53** SWKelly 6 — 48
(BJCurley) *s.i.s: hld up in last trio: rdn and effrt over 2f out: hanging rt and no prog over 1f out* **8/1**
0415 **8** *hd* **Muqtadi (IRE)**[11] 894 6-9-8 **52** MartinDwyer 10 — 47
(MQuinn) *hld up in last trio: effrt over 2f out: sn nt qckn and no prog* **14/1**

0-05 **9** 4 **Kanz Wood (USA)**[8] 932 8-9-11 **55**.................................... RHughes 2 42
(AWCarroll) *hld up in midfield: gng wl enough 3f out: rdn and no rspnse over 2f out: wknd and eased fnl f* **12/1**

6212 **10** 1 ¾ **Indian Blaze**[4] 966 10-9-6 **53** 6ex.................................. TPQueally[(3)] 11 37
(AndrewReid) *racd wd: hld up in rr: rdn wl over 2f out: sn struggling and btn* **4/1**[2]

00-0 **11** 11 **Thumamah (IRE)**[8] 926 5-9-9 **53**............................... DeanMcKeown 9 17
(BPJBaugh) *racd in midfield: wknd 3f out: sn bhd* **50/1**

1m 38.37s (-1.14) **Going Correction** -0.025s/f (Stan) **11** Ran SP% **133.6**
Speed ratings: **104,103,101,101,101 97,96,96,92,90 79**CSF £193.22 CT £1092.45 TOTE £22.50: £7.10, £2.90, £2.10; EX 205.00 Place 6 £145.22, Place 5 £55.22.
**Owner** Mark Savill **Bred** Thurloe Breeding **Trained** Combe St Nicholas, Somerset

**FOCUS**
A poor contest which produced decent winning time for the grade and the front four were nicley clear. The runner-up is unexposed and showed improved form on his handicap debut.

**NOTEBOOK**
**Meelup(IRE)** posted a game win from the front. He has hit the frame of all of his last three outings and, as he was once rated 72 as a juvenile, he could be an improver over this trip.
**Blue Quiver(IRE)** ◆ was the only horse to go with the winner and paid late on for running too keen in the early stages, but was still only just denied. He is lightly raced and on this handicap debut he produced his best effort to date, over a trip that could prove to be his optimum.
**Lucid Dreams(IRE)** did best of those to be held up off the pace, but never looked like getting to the leaders. He did however, reverse recent form with the fourth horse on these better terms.
**Double Ransom** was very keen in the early stages and could not find the change of gears required to get to the leaders in the straight, under his 6lb penalty. He looks weighted to his best at present.
**Balerno** ran his race, but on this evidence, looks in the Handicapper's grip.
**Indian Blaze** was disappointing, but would have been better suited by a more prominent ride.
T/Jkpt: Not won. T/Plt: £81.20 to a £1 stake. Pool: £51,505.35. 462.90 winning tickets. T/Qpdt: £25.30 to a £1 stake. Pool: £3,071.60. 89.70 winning tickets. JN

# 967 WOLVERHAMPTON (A.W) (L-H)
Monday, March 8

**OFFICIAL GOING: Slow**
Despite morning watering the surface remained slow
Wind: nil Weather: overcast

## 989 BET DIRECT ON SKY ACTIVE APPRENTICE BANDED STKS 1m 1f 79y(F)
**2:20** (2:21) (H ) 3-Y-0+ **£1,463** (£418; £209) **Stalls** Low

Form RPR

0-05 **1** **Sinjaree**[10] 903 6-9-5 45.................................................. RThomas[(3)] 5 53
(MrsSLamyman) *a.p: wnt 2nd and rdn over 2f out: led 1f out: jst hld on* **11/4**[1]

-534 **2** nk **Bevier**[10] 903 10-9-8 45...................................................... NChalmers 2 52
(TWall) *stmbld s: sn led: hdd 4f out: sn rdn: sltly outpcd wl over 1f out: rallied fnl f: tk 2nd post* **4/1**[2]

0153 **3** shd **Gracious Air (USA)**[5] 953 6-9-3 45..........................(b[1]) DFentiman[(5)] 6 52
(JRWeymes) *t.k.h: a.p: led 4f out: rdn 3f out: hdd 1f out: r.o* **9/2**[3]

05-2 **4** 3 ½ **Sadlers Swing (USA)**[7] 940 8-9-5 40................................ PMakin[(3)] 7 45
(JJSheehan) *hld up in tch: rdn over 3f out: one pce fnl 2f* **11/2**

2334 **5** 1 **Kenny The Truth (IRE)**[7] 940 5-9-3 40..................(t) DawnWatson[(5)] 3 43
(MrsJCandlish) *t.k.h in rr: rdn 5f out: hdwy over 1f out: nt trble ldrs* **10/1**

-032 **6** 3 ½ **Unsuited**[20] 814 5-9-5 40......................................... NataliaGemelova[(3)] 8 36
(JELong) *hld up in tch: rdn over 4f out: sn btn* **9/1**

0104 **7** 2 **Malmand (USA)**[28] 726 5-9-8 45..................................(v) THamilton 4 32
(RBrotherton) *bhd: reminders 6f out: rdn 5f out: no rspnse* **10/1**

000- **8** 3 **Diagon Alley (IRE)**[207] 4122 4-9-5 35............................ BSwarbrick[(3)] 9 26
(KWHogg) *prom: rdn over 4f out: wknd over 3f out* **40/1**

00-0 **9** 18 **Always Believe (USA)**[38] 642 8-9-5 45............................ LTreadwell[(3)] 1 —
(MrsPFord) *led early: hld up and sn lost pl: rdn 4f out: sn struggling: eased over 1f out* **40/1**

2m 9.70s (6.80) **Going Correction** +0.65s/f (Slow) **9** Ran SP% **113.3**
Speed ratings: **95,94,94,91,90 87,85,83,67**CSF £13.33 TOTE £4.30: £1.60, £1.40, £1.10; EX 11.50.
**Owner** P Lamyman **Bred** Wyck Hall Stud Ltd **Trained** Louth, Lincs

**FOCUS**
A competitive little race and probably reasonable form in the context of this lowly grade. The pace was just ordinary and the front four were never too far off the speed.

**NOTEBOOK**
**Sinjaree**, successful in both Germany and Holland, gained his first win in this country on this first start in a banded stakes. Rated 68 at his best, there could be a little more to come now he has finally got his head in front.
**Bevier** ran a solid race, but again shaped as though he can do better when stepped back up in trip. He got outpaced on turning out of the back straight, but kept on inside the final two furlongs and is clearly in good heart.
**Gracious Air(USA)**, with the blinkers replacing the visor and stepping back up in trip, did not have any excuses.
**Sadlers Swing(USA)** appeared to travel well enough, but he did not find as much as had looked likely and lacks a change of pace over this distance. Still a maiden, he has been tried over as far at two miles and his optimum trip remains unclear.
**Kenny The Truth(IRE)** was racing for the 22nd time without success and did not shape as though about to end that losing run.

## 990 BET DIRECT INTERACTIVE BANDED STKS 6f (F)
**2:50** (2:51) (H ) 3-Y-0+ **£1,634** (£467; £233) **Stalls** Low

Form RPR

0000 **1** **On The Trail**[8] 936 7-9-6 45.................................................. ACulhane 5 51
(DWChapman) *w ldr: led over 3f out: hrd rdn ins fnl f: jst hld on* **10/1**

3124 **2** shd **Enjoy The Buzz**[8] 936 5-9-6 45........................................ PFitzsimons 4 51
(JMBradley) *chsd ldrs: rdn and wnt 2nd 2f out: r.o ins fnl f: jst failed* **7/2**[1]

50-0 **3** 3 **Extemporise (IRE)**[21] 796 4-9-6 45..............................(t) DaleGibson 3 42
(PJMcbride) *chsd ldrs: rdn over 3f out: sltly outpcd 2f out: kpt on ins fnl f* **4/1**[2]

1001 **4** 1 **Star Lad (IRE)**[8] 936 4-9-12 45....................................(b) ADaly 2 45
(RBrotherton) *led over 2f: rdn and lost 2nd 2f out: wknd ins fnl f* **10/1**

4006 **5** 4 **Attorney**[8] 938 6-9-1 45.........................................(e) THamilton[(5)] 6 27
(DShaw) *in tch: rdn over 4f out: lost pl over 3f out: sltly hmpd over 2f out: sme hdwy fnl f* **8/1**

0-02 **6** 1 **Katy O'Hara**[28] 728 5-8-13 45.......................................... DFentiman[(7)] 7 24
(MissSEHall) *s.i.s: hdwy over 2f out: wknd over 1f out* **5/1**[3]

-301 **7** 1 **Evangelist (IRE)**[20] 813 4-9-6 45..................................(vt) MFenton 1 21
(MrsStefLiddiard) *chsd ldrs: rdn over 3f out: wknd fnl f* **5/1**[3]

1004 **8** 1 ½ **Indian Warrior**[14] 859 8-8-13 45.........................(b) BSwarbrick[(7)] 8 17
(JJay) *a bhd* **15/2**

/00- **9** 12 **Dancing Ridge (IRE)**[110] 6031 7-9-6 40................................ DKinsella 9 —
(ASenior) *prom tl rdn and wknd over 3f out* **66/1**

00-0 **10** dist **Bold Effort (FR)**[63] 441 12-9-6 30.....................................(be) JMackay 10 —
(KOCunningham-Brown) *s.v.s: a t.o* **66/1**

1m 19.01s (3.31) **Going Correction** +0.65s/f (Slow) **10** Ran SP% **119.6**
Speed ratings: **103,102,98,97,92 90,89,87,71,—**CSF £46.21 TOTE £13.60: £3.00, £1.70, £1.50; EX 47.80.
**Owner** J M Chapman **Bred** Ian Bellamy **Trained** Stillington, N Yorks
■ Stewards Enquiry : A Culhane two-day ban: used with excessive use of the whip and without giving gelding time to respond (Mar 19,20)

**FOCUS**
Just an ordinary banded stakes, but the winning time was good and the front two pulled clear. On The Trail could be one to follow.

**NOTEBOOK**
**On The Trail** had gained all of his previous wins in either December or January and has clearly taken a little longer to come to hand this time around. He had little to spare at the line, but has a good record after ending a losing run of at least eight straight defeats - he has never finished out of the first four on his next start in those circumstances and has also added to the win within his next three outings.
**Enjoy The Buzz**, unlucky at Southwell on his previous outing, returned to form with a solid effort, pulling right away from the remainder.
**Extemporise(IRE)**, making his banded stakes debut, and with a tongue-tie fitted for the first time, struggled to go the pace on this step up from five furlongs and was unable to go with the front two. He should stay farther.
**Star Lad(IRE)** can be a bit hit and miss and this was not one of his better efforts.
**Attorney** never really got in a blow.
**Katy O'Hara** lost his race with a slow start.
**Bold Effort(FR)** *Official explanation: jockey said gelding refused to jump off*

## 991 £10 FREE BET @ BET DIRECT SKY ACTIVE MEDIAN AUCTION MAIDEN STKS 1m 4f (F)
**3:20** (3:23) (H ) 4-6-Y-0 **£1,417** (£405; £202) **Stalls** Low

Form RPR

0-22 **1** **The Beduth Navi**[21] 789 4-8-10 35.............................. BSwarbrick[(7)] 4 56+
(DGBridgwater) *led 1f: led again over 8f out: rdn clr over 3f out: eased ins fnl f* **8/11**[1]

0-53 **2** 10 **Dora Corbino**[8] 935 4-8-12 45.................................................. ACulhane 5 36
(RHollinshead) *hld up: chsd wnr over 6f out: rdn over 5f out: no imp fnl 3f* **7/2**[2]

6340 **3** 9 **Think Quick (IRE)**[7] 943 4-8-5 35.............................. RKennemore[(7)] 1 23
(RHollinshead) *hld up: hdwy 6f out: wknd over 4f out* **7/2**[2]

00-0 **4** 27 **Manashin**[60] 473 4-8-12 35................................................... TWoodley 2 —
(RPElliott) *led after 1f tl over 8f out: wknd over 5f out: t.o* **33/1**

000- **5** 18 **Ziggy Dan**[73] 6238 4-9-3 30.............................................. JoannaBadger 3 —
(MsDeborahJEvans) *plld hrd: prom tl hung rt over 6f out: t.o* **20/1**[3]

2m 50.15s (8.65) **Going Correction** +0.65s/f (Slow) **5** Ran SP% **110.1**
Speed ratings: **97,90,84,66,54**CSF £3.61 TOTE £1.90: £1.10, £1.10; EX 2.40.
**Owner** R W Neale **Bred** R W And Mrs B D Neale **Trained** Winchcombe, Gloucs
■ Stewards Enquiry : B Swarbrick one-day ban: used whip with excessive force (Mar 19)

**FOCUS**
A very weak maiden and is hard to say anything positive about the four horses who chased the 35-rated winner home. The winner was a class above and is likely to be weighted out of banded races after this.

**NOTEBOOK**
**The Beduth Navi**, looked to need two miles when beaten 22 lengths behind Bella Pavlina in a banded stakes over this course and distance two starts back and confirmed the suspicion when narrowly denied over that trip at Lingfield on his previous outing. However, dropped back in trip, he showed just how bad a race this was with an easy victory.
**Dora Corbino** did not offer much promise in second.
**Think Quick(IRE)** is still a maiden after 20 starts.
**Manashin** did not improve for this step up from a mile.

## 992 PRESS INTERACTIVE TO BET DIRECT BANDED STKS 2m 46y(F)
**3:50** (3:51) (H ) 4-Y-0+ **£1,620** (£463; £231) **Stalls** Low

Form RPR

3-34 **1** **Mysterium**[47] 579 10-9-3 40..............................................(v) GGibbons 1 48
(NPLittmoden) *hld up: stdy hdwy over 4f out: rdn over 2f out: edgd lft and led ins fnl f: styd on* **11/2**

1221 **2** 2 ½ **Buz Kiri (USA)**[7] 943 6-9-9 40.................................................. PDoe 6 51
(AWCarroll) *hld up: stdy hdwy 8f out: led over 5f out tl over 3f out: sn rdn: led wl over 1f out: hdd and no ex ins fnl f* **9/4**[2]

-053 **3** 2 ½ **Stravmour**[8] 937 8-9-3 45.............................................. DaleGibson 3 42
(RHollinshead) *prom: wnt 2nd 7f out: led over 3f out: rdn over 2f out: hdd wl over 1f out: one pce* **7/2**[3]

1201 **4** 6 **Radiant Bride**[6] 950 4-9-4 45.............................(b) DarrenWilliams 5 41
(KRBurke) *hld up: stdy hdwy over 4f out: rdn over 2f out: wknd wl over 1f out* **2/1**[1]

50/0 **5** dist **Sharvie**[21] 789 7-9-3 35....................................(v[1]) JoannaBadger 4 —
(MRBosley) *chsd ldr tl rdn 7f out: wknd 6f out: t.o* **25/1**

043- **6** 2 **Ton-Chee**[210] 4049 5-9-3 30.................................................. JBramhill 2 —
(KWHogg) *led: rdn and hdd over 5f out: wknd over 4f out: t.o* **16/1**

3m 55.42s (13.12) **Going Correction** +0.65s/f (Slow)
**WFA** 4 from 5yo+ 5lb **6** Ran SP% **111.4**
Speed ratings: **93,91,90,87,— —**CSF £18.01 TOTE £3.60: £3.00, £1.70; EX 14.60.
**Owner** Alcester Associates **Bred** Stetchworth Park Stud Ltd **Trained** Newmarket, Suffolk

**FOCUS**
A weak race and the winning time was modest. The form may not be worth a great deal as both the second and third horses have yet to prove ideally suited by two miles, while the fourth, Radiant Bride, finds little off the bridle. The first two home raced off the pace.

**NOTEBOOK**
**Mysterium**, without a win since July 2002, and on a losing run on this surface stretching back to November 2000, gained a deserved success on this first attempt in banded company after some consistent efforts in similar company.
**Buz Kiri(USA)** was simply outstayed by the winner. He has gained both his previous wins round here, but those wins were over a mile and a half and he may be better over that sort of trip.
**Stravmour** ran respectably on this step up in trip, but got tired close home and may not have quite got the two miles.
**Radiant Bride** likes to do her work on the bridle and she found little when asked to go and pick up the leaders.

## 993 LITTLEWOODS BET DIRECT (S) STKS 7f (F)
**4:20** (4:22) (H ) 3-Y-0+ **£1,298** (£371; £185) **Stalls** High

Form RPR

0225 **1** **Silver Mascot**[8] 934 5-9-7 45.............................................. DaleGibson 9 59
(RHollinshead) *mde all: clr wl over 1f out: pushed out* **11/2**[3]

-442 **2** 9 **Inchcoonan**[7] 941 6-9-2 55....................................(p) DarrenWilliams 5 32
(KRBurke) *a.p: rdn 3f out: wnt 2nd ins fnl f: no ch w wnr* **7/2**[2]

2300 **3** 1 ¼ **The Gay Fox**[6] 946 10-9-0 45..................................(bt) KarenPeippo[(7)] 8 33
(BGPowell) *outpcd and bhd: hdwy over 1f out: kpt on ins fnl f* **11/1**

0-00 **4** *1* **Travel Tardia (IRE)**[6] 949 6-9-2 40 ........ THamilton(5) 3 31
(IAWood) *chsd ldrs: rdn over 3f out: one pce fnl 2f* **12/1**

6541 **5** *hd* **Foolish Thought (IRE)**[35] 654 4-9-12 54 ........ GGibbons 1 35
(IAWood) *prom: rdn over 3f out: chsd wnr 2f out tl no ex ins fnl f* **6/1**

0313 **6** *2* **Legalis (USA)**[17] 834 6-9-12 56 ........ (b) PFessey 2 30
(KARyan) *s.i.s: outpcd: hdwy over 1f out: n.d* **3/1**[1]

440 **7** *2 ½* **Repeat (IRE)**[3] 972 4-9-12 47 ........ (p) MFenton 7 24
(MissGayKelleway) *chsd wnr: rdn over 3f out: lost 2nd 2f out: wknd over 1f out* **8/1**

-056 **8** *7* **Lion's Domane**[20] 813 7-9-7 40 ........ FLynch 4 2
(ABerry) *hld up in tch: rdn 3f out: wknd 2f out* **16/1**

060/ **9** *29* **Lastofthewhalleys**[616] 2569 6-9-2 35 ........ JBramhill 6 —
(KWHogg) *sn outpcd: t.o* **66/1**

1m 34.01s (3.81) **Going Correction** +0.65s/f (Slow) **9** Ran SP% **111.4**
Speed ratings: **104,93,92,91,90 88,85,77,44**CSF £23.76 TOTE £7.00: £2.20, £1.20, £2.00; EX 43.20.The winner was bought in for 6,500gns.

**Owner** R Hollinshead **Bred** R M West **Trained** Upper Longdon, Staffs

**FOCUS**
This looked a reasonably competitive seller, but Silver Mascot got an easy lead in front and came right away from a largely disappointing bunch. The winning time was very good for the grade.

**NOTEBOOK**
**Silver Mascot** gained his first win since landing a five-furlong maiden at Southwell back in December 2001. Given an easy lead, he travelled well and came well clear in the straight for a cosy success. Everything went his way and the winning margin surely flatters him, but he is clearly on good terms with himself and connections went to 6,500gns to buy him back.

**Inchcoonan** had 15lb in hand of the winner at the weights, but she is not as good as she was and proved unable to go with that one in the straight.

**The Gay Fox** emerges with credit. He was unable to go the early pace under his inexperienced rider, but kept on in the closing stages and was finishing as well as anything in the chasing bunch. That said, he will need to start showing a bit more dash in the early stages of his races if he is to end a losing run stretching back to May 2002.

**Travel Tardia(IRE)** ran respectably on this drop in trip and return to Fibresand, showing a little bit more than he has done in recent months.

**Foolish Thought(IRE)**, claimed for £2,000 after winning a claimer over six furlongs here on his previous outing, was below form on this step up in trip.

**Legalis(USA)**, the second best in at the weights, was along way below form. This slow ground may not have suited.

## 994 NEW SITE @ BETDIRECT.CO.UK BANDED STKS 1m 100y(F)
4:50 (4:51) (H) 3-Y-0+ £1,291 (£369; £184) Stalls Low

Form RPR

60-1 **1** **Mrs Cube**[7] 945 5-9-13 35 ........ RWinston 1 46+
(PHowling) *a.p: rdn to ld over 1f out: r.o wl* **5/6**[1]

000B **2** *3* **Spiders Web**[6] 947 4-9-7 30 ........ (b) PDoe 13 33
(TKeddy) *hld up mid-div: rdn and hdwy over 3f out: r.o ins fnl f: nt trble wnr* **80/1**

00-0 **3** *2 ½* **Final Lap**[17] 838 8-9-7 30 ........ GGibbons 6 28
(STLewis) *chsd ldrs: outpcd 4f out: styd on fnl f* **100/1**

6003 **4** *hd* **Dundonald**[7] 940 5-9-0 35 ........ (bt) DFentiman(7) 5 28
(MAppleby) *s.i.s: hld up: hdwy on outside whn bmpd over 4f out: kpt on ins fnl f* **13/2**[2]

0-00 **5** *hd* **Garnock Belle (IRE)**[20] 802 3-8-3 35 ........ DaleGibson 12 27
(ABerry) *hld up and bhd: rdn over 2f out: hdwy on outside fnl f: nvr nrr* **50/1**

00-0 **6** *½* **Un Autre Espere**[7] 945 5-9-7 35 ........ LVickers 8 26
(TWall) *chsd ldrs: rdn over 3f out: no hdwy fnl 2f* **80/1**

0040 **7** *½* **Welsh Whisper**[7] 945 5-9-2 35 ........ NChalmers(5) 9 25
(SABrookshaw) *s.i.s: hld up: hdwy 5f out: rdn over 3f out: led over 2f out tl over 1f out: wknd ins fnl f* **10/1**

-566 **8** *4* **Broughtons Mill**[6] 947 9-9-0 35 ........ RoryMoore(7) 3 17
(JASupple) *hld up: hdwy on ins over 5f out: rdn over 3f out: wknd over 1f out* **14/1**

0-00 **9** *3* **Chickasaw Trail**[7] 945 6-9-7 30 ........ ACulhane 10 10
(RHollinshead) *mid-div: rdn and bhd fnl 3f* **14/1**

-060 **10** *½* **Caterham Common**[13] 875 5-9-7 30 ........ (b) DarrenWilliams 4 9
(DWChapman) *set str pce: rdn and hdd over 2f out: wknd wl over 1f out* **16/1**

/00- **11** *11* **Forest Queen**[196] 4454 7-9-7 30 ........ JBramhill 2 —
(KWHogg) *s.i.s: a bhd* **100/1**

-040 **12** *3 ½* **Margarets Wish**[21] 793 4-9-7 30 ........ MFenton 7 —
(TWall) *chsd ldrs tl rdn and wknd over 4f out* **14/1**

-000 **13** *26* **Bugle Call**[3] 967 4-9-7 35 ........ (be) JMackay 11 —
(KOCunningham-Brown) *s.s: hld up: hdwy on outside whn hung lft over 4f out: sn lost pl: t.o* **8/1**[3]

1m 58.07s (7.07) **Going Correction** +0.65s/f (Slow)
**WFA** 3 from 4yo+ 18lb **13** Ran SP% **120.4**
Speed ratings: **90,87,84,84,84 83,83,79,76,75 64,61,35**CSF £124.92 TOTE £1.80: £1.10, £29.40, £17.80; EX 108.50 Place 6 £27.19, Place 5 £20.11.

**Owner** Mrs J E Proctor **Bred** Mrs A L Wood **Trained** Newmarket, Suffolk

**FOCUS**
This was not a very competitive race. They went a good pace early, but the final time was slow. Mrs Cube is at the top of her game and won with something to spare, but she beat nothing, and will find things tougher in higher grade.

**NOTEBOOK**
**Mrs Cube** has really hit form since moving to Paul Howling and being dropped into banded racing. After travelling strong into the straight, she found plenty for pressure and looked to win with a little in hand.

**Spiders Web** showed himself none the worse for being brought down at Lingfield on his previous outing, simply finding the winner too good.

**Final Lap** tailed off in a seller over a mile and a half on his previous outing, appeared better suited by this sort of trip.

**Dundonald** ran another solid race, but dimply does not win very often.

**Garnock Belle(IRE)** was doing her best work late on.

**Bugle Call** *Official explanation: jockey said gelding lost its action in the back straight*

T/Plt: £17.50 to a £1 stake. Pool: £31,926.90. 1,328.95 winning tickets. T/Qpdt: £4.50 to a £1 stake. Pool: £2,333.90. 379.60 winning tickets. KH

# 981 LINGFIELD (L-H)
Tuesday, March 9

**OFFICIAL GOING: Standard**

## 995 CASHBACKS @ BET DIRECT ON SKY ACTIVE BANDED STKS 1m 4f (P)
2:20 (2:22) (H) 4-Y-0+ £1,662 (£475; £237) Stalls Low

Form RPR

0600 **1** **Angelica Garnett**[9] 933 4-8-12 45 ........ JFEgan 1 53
(TEPowell) *slowly away and wl bhd tl rapid hdwy 2f out: kpt on u.p to ld wl ins fnl f* **40/1**

-324 **2** *½* **Diamond Orchid (IRE)**[21] 812 4-8-12 45 ........ (p) JPMurtagh 7 52
(PDEvans) *trckd ldr: led 5f out: hrd rdn ent fnl f: kpt on: hdd wl ins* **5/1**[2]

0-16 **3** *1* **Montosari**[15] 855 5-9-0 45 ........ DHolland 14 51
(PMitchell) *s.i.s: sn trckd ldrs: nt qckn whn short of room ins fnl f: styd on cl home* **9/4**[1]

-524 **4** *½* **Chocolate Boy (IRE)**[15] 855 5-9-0 45 ........ (be) IMongan 4 50
(GLMoore) *hld up in rr: hrd rdn and hdwy wl over 1f out: styd on fnl f* **7/1**

3014 **5** *½* **Free Style (GER)**[8] 943 4-8-12 45 ........ GBaker 2 49
(KRBurke) *in mid-div: rdn 2f out: kpt on one pce appr fnl f* **7/1**

50-3 **6** *1 ½* **On Guard**[15] 855 6-9-0 45 ........ (v) DKinsella 15 47
(PGMurphy) *racd wd in tch: one pce ins fnl 2f* **8/1**

3650 **7** *½* **Ipledgeallegiance (USA)**[8] 943 8-9-0 35 ........ ACulhane 5 46
(DWChapman) *hld up in rr: styd on fnl f: nvr nrr* **25/1**

4314 **8** *1 ½* **Little Richard (IRE)**[15] 857 5-9-0 40 ........ (p) VSlattery 11 44
(MWellings) *in tch: rdn and lost pl 4f out: swtchd rt: kpt on but nt nr to chal* **16/1**

6322 **9** *4* **Private Seal**[7] 947 9-8-7 40 ........ (t) MHalford(7) 12 38
(JulianPoulton) *in tch: swtchd rt over 3f out: effrt 2f out: sn btn* **10/1**

0030 **10** *hd* **Polka Princess**[15] 857 4-8-12 40 ........ (p) ADaly 10 38
(MWellings) *t.k.h: prom tl wknd over 2f out* **40/1**

0005 **11** *6* **Morris Dancing (USA)**[7] 947 5-9-0 30 ........ MTebbutt 13 29
(BPJBaugh) *chsd ldrs: rdn and wknd wl over 1f out* **66/1**

0-03 **12** *3* **Giko**[15] 857 10-9-0 35 ........ (b) DaneO'Neill 6 24
(JaneSouthcombe) *hld up:: weakening whn rdn over 2f out* **25/1**

0-44 **13** *nk* **Essay Baby (FR)**[9] 931 4-8-12 45 ........ CCatlin 9 24
(PDCundell) *racd wd: prom tl wknd over 3f out* **13/2**[3]

/0-0 **14** *14* **Forest Heath (IRE)**[34] 672 7-9-0 45 ........ (p) JQuinn 8 3
(HJCollingridge) *led: hdd 5f out: wknd over 2f out* **20/1**

2m 34.69s (0.71) **Going Correction** -0.025s/f (Stan)
**WFA** 4 from 5yo+ 2lb **14** Ran SP% **130.7**
Speed ratings: **96,95,95,94,94 93,93,92,89,89 85,83,83,73**CSF £238.15 TOTE £95.30: £15.70, £2.10, £1.50; EX 555.30.

**Owner** Three Lost Souls Partnership **Bred** Miss K Rausing **Trained** Reigate, Surrey

**FOCUS**
A modest contest run at only an average pace, and a surprise winner.

**NOTEBOOK**
**Angelica Garnett** was the last to leave the stalls and held up out the back, but she made relentless progress around the final bend and ran on well to score despite edging left in the closing stages. This was a poor race, but she was racing over half a mile further than she had ever tried before so is at least unexposed over the trip. *Official explanation: trainer said filly had benefited from the step up in trip*

**Diamond Orchid(IRE)**, again given a positive ride, saw the trip out much better than she did on the slow Wolverhampton Fibresand last time and was only just denied.

**Montosari** ran better on this step back up in trip, but could probably do with even further as he was briefly caught for toe on the home bend which was a bigger problem than the winner crossing him in the closing stages.

**Chocolate Boy(IRE)**, taking another step up in trip, finished well from off the pace and looks to need even further, but is proving very hard to win with.

**Free Style(GER)** was close enough if good enough turning for home, but then proved very one paced. *Official explanation: jockey said filly was hanging right in the closing stages*

**On Guard** raced wide the whole way and had every chance, but is probably better over ten furlongs.

## 996 BET DIRECT CHAMPS LEAGUE CASHBACKS BANDED STKS 1m 2f (P)
2:50 (2:52) (H) 4-Y-0+ £1,666 (£476; £238) Stalls Low

Form RPR

0451 **1** **Landescent (IRE)**[15] 855 4-8-12 45 ........ DHolland 13 55
(MissKMGeorge) *mde all: shkn up appr fnl f: rdn out* **4/1**[1]

-012 **2** *1 ½* **Monduru**[22] 793 7-8-12 45 ........ (be) SWhitworth 12 53+
(GLMoore) *slowly away: wl in rr: hdwy over 1f out and r.o wl to go clr 2nd ins fnl f* **9/2**[2]

4000 **3** *2 ½* **Top Of The Class (IRE)**[9] 931 7-8-7 45 ........ (v) JFMcDonald(5) 3 48
(PDEvans) *plld hrd: a.p: rdn and outpcd appr fnl f* **8/1**

32-0 **4** *¾* **Cooden Beach (IRE)**[53] 552 4-8-7 45 ........ HayleyTurner(5) 7 47
(MLWBell) *slowly away: sn int tch: r.o one pce fnl 2f* **7/1**[3]

05-5 **5** *shd* **Midnight Mambo (USA)**[25] 760 4-8-12 45 ........ MartinDwyer 4 46
(RGuest) *a.p: rdn over 3f out: edgd lft and one pce appr fnl f* **9/2**[2]

0650 **6** *¾* **Pyrrhic**[9] 931 5-8-12 45 ........ (b) JQuinn 8 45
(RMFlower) *t.k.h: towards rr tl hdwy 2f out: effrt and short of room over 1f out: swtchd rt: kpt on* **14/1**

-005 **7** *1 ½* **Galey River (USA)**[9] 933 5-8-12 45 ........ IMongan 6 42
(JJSheehan) *trckd ldrs: rdn over 3f out: wnt 2nd over 2f out: wknd ent fnl f* **14/1**

00-0 **8** *2* **Gran Clicquot**[9] 933 9-8-12 45 ........ RBrisland 14 39
(GPEnright) *racd wd throughout: nvr nr to chal* **25/1**

000- **9** *hd* **Sweet Reflection (IRE)**[216] 3886 4-8-9 45 ........ (t) LisaJones(3) 2 38
(WJMusson) *slowly away: a in rr* **25/1**

000B **10** *1 ½* **Thats All Jazz**[7] 947 6-8-7 40 ........ RThomas(5) 1 36
(CRDore) *hld up: rdn over 2f out: sn btn* **25/1**

0/0- **11** *3 ½* **Elle Royal (IRE)**[265] 1580 5-8-12 45 ........ DaneO'Neill 9 29
(TPMcgovern) *trckd wnr tl wknd 3f out* **40/1**

0/10 **12** *1 ½* **Ndola**[49] 570 5-8-12 45 ........ SWKelly 5 27
(BJCurley) *held up in mid-div: wknd over 3f out* **10/1**

/06- **13** *¾* **Count On Us**[247] 3030 4-8-9 45 ........ LPKeniry(3) 10 25
(PBurgoyne) *slowly away: a in rr* **50/1**

0060 **14** *nk* **Pancakehill**[15] 859 5-8-12 45 ........ CCatlin 11 25
(DKIvory) *in tch tl wknd over 2f out* **14/1**

2m 7.62s (0.23) **Going Correction** -0.025s/f (Stan) **14** Ran SP% **125.0**
Speed ratings: **98,96,94,94,94 93,92,90,90,89 86,85,84,84**CSF £21.23 TOTE £3.60: £1.40, £3.10, £3.30; EX 15.10.

**Owner** Stableline **Bred** Carrigbeg Stud Co Ltd **Trained** Higher Easington, Devon

■ Stewards Enquiry : Martin Dwyer caution: careless riding

**FOCUS**
A modest contest, run at just a fair pace, and not many got into it.

**NOTEBOOK**
**Landescent(IRE)** maintained his perfect record for his new yard and the method of his victory was the same as when winning an identical contest over course and distance last month. It will be interesting to see if he can carry this form outside banded company, but at least his best trip has been found.
**Monduru**, patiently ridden as usual, finished with a flourish but the winner was already home and hosed.
**Top Of The Class(IRE)**, making her debut in banded company, took quite a hold just behind the leaders and the fact that she managed to stay in touch for so long is testament to the mediocrity of the race.
**Cooden Beach(IRE)**, dropping in class, started slowly as usual but, over this longer trip and with the pace only modest, it did not matter too much. She had every chance, but was just found wanting where it matters.
**Midnight Mambo(USA)** ◆, stepping up three furlongs in trip, had every chance but tended to run about in the home straight and could not make much impression. She still has some scope and may be capable of better.
**Pyrrhic**, patiently ridden, tried to get closer in the home straight but was twice interfered with by Midnight Mambo. He may have finished third otherwise, but is still a maiden after 34 attempts which hardly makes him one for the notebook.
**Galey River(USA)** *Official explanation: jockey said gelding hung left*
**Ndola** again showed just what a bad race it must have been that he won at Wolverhampton.

## 997 CASHBACKS @ BET DIRECT INTERACTIVE MEDIAN AUCTION MAIDEN STKS — 1m 2f (P)
**3:20** (3:22) (H) 4-6-Y-O — **£1,438** (£411; £205) **Stalls** Low

| Form | | | | RPR |
|---|---|---|---|---|
| 2322 | **1** | | **Ballinger Ridge**[7] 948 5-9-0 60 (v[1]) MartinDwyer 10<br>(AMBalding) *mde all: rdn out fnl f* **4/5**[1] | 56 |
| 3-64 | **2** | *3 ½* | **Blue Savanna**[36] 656 4-9-0 45 (b) ACulhane 8<br>(JGPortman) *chsd wnr after 2f: rdn 3f out: no imp ins fnl 2f* **10/3**[2] | 50 |
| 044- | **3** | *6* | **Mr Fleming**[140] 5696 5-9-0 45 (b) JQuinn 4<br>(DrJDScargill) *hld up in tch: chsd ldng pair fr 1/2-way: no imp fr over 2f out* **12/1** | 39 |
| 2322 | **4** | *23* | **Kustom Kit For Her**[9] 935 4-8-9 45 (t) JBramhill 5<br>(SRBowring) *chsd ldng pair tl rdn and wknd 1/2-way* **7/1**[3] | — |
| 05 | **5** | *1 ¼* | **Young Dynasty**[7] 948 4-8-7 LiamJones(7) 1<br>(EAWheeler) *v.s.a: a bhd: lost tch 1/2-way* **14/1** | — |
| /00- | **6** | *5* | **Portichol Princess**[22] 387 4-8-9 (t) DSweeney 3<br>(RMStronge) *slowly away: a bhd* **66/1** | — |
| 00-6 | **7** | *nk* | **Indrapura Star (USA)**[14] 877 4-9-0 35 JMcAuley 7<br>(MissJFeilden) *chsd wnr for 2f: sn struggling in rr* **50/1** | — |
| 0-00 | **8** | *5* | **Silver Crystal (IRE)**[56] 518 4-8-6 45 LisaJones(3) 9<br>(MrsNMacauley) *slowly away: a in rr* **16/1** | — |

2m 7.70s (0.31) **Going Correction** -0.025s/f (Stan) **8** Ran SP% **114.8**
Speed ratings: **97,94,89,71,70 66,65,61**CSF £3.62 TOTE £1.90: £1.02, £1.60, £4.20; EX 3.90.
**Owner** Mrs Hazel Barber **Bred** Mrs H V Barber **Trained** Kingsclere, Hants

**FOCUS**
A poor maiden that attracted more interest from both inside and outside the racing industry than would normally have been the case because of what happened to the winner here the previous week. The order changed little during the contest, and very few got it.

**NOTEBOOK**
**Ballinger Ridge**, with a visor on rather than blinkers or cheekpieces, finally managed to get off the mark at the 20th attempt. Ridden as if there was no doubt about him over the trip, he made every yard and, even though he was down to a canter towards the end, his two nearest pursuers were walking.
**Blue Savanna** , who had a lot to do with the winner on official ratings, kept him company for much of the way but was made to look very leg-weary from the home bend and he could not take advantage of the winner's fatigue.
**Mr Fleming**, racing for the first time since October, held a good position just behind the two leaders but when asked to pick up, the response was limited and he was virtually galloping on the spot in the last furlong. He is very moderate, but was entitled to need this.
**Kustom Kit For Her**, placed in her last four starts, all on Fibresand, was in touch early but came off the bridle at halfway and stopped to nothing. Her first try on Polytrack did not appear to suit her at all.

## 998 CASHBACKS @ BETDIRECT.CO.UK BANDED STKS — 7f (P)
**3:50** (3:56) (H) 3-Y-O+ — **£1,295** (£370; £185) **Stalls** Low

| Form | | | | RPR |
|---|---|---|---|---|
| 0063 | **1** | | **Gentle Response**[7] 951 4-9-7 35 (b) SWhitworth 8<br>(BRJohnson) *hld up in tch: swtchd rt over 2f out and rapid hdwy to ld wl over 1f out: sn clr* **6/4**[1] | 52+ |
| 0/44 | **2** | *3 ½* | **Tiny Tim (IRE)**[7] 949 6-9-0 35 RJKilloran(7) 15<br>(AMBalding) *a.p: sltly outpcd over 2f out: styd on to chse wnr ent fnl f* **9/1** | 43 |
| 0-00 | **3** | *1* | **Tojoneski**[7] 949 5-9-0 35 (p) NataliaGemelova(7) 6<br>(IWMcinnes) *racd wd in mid-div: hdwy over 1f out: styd on* **8/1** | 40 |
| -000 | **4** | *shd* | **Kilmeena Star**[15] 858 6-9-7 35 (p) PDobbs 4<br>(JCFox) *hld up: hdwy 3f out: rdn over 1f out: kpt on* **16/1** | 40 |
| 6000 | **5** | *1 ¼* | **Hinchley Wood (IRE)**[7] 947 5-9-7 35 NPollard 9<br>(JRBest) *chsd ldrs: lost pl 1/2-way: rdn over 1f out: kpt on* **6/1**[2] | 37 |
| 00-0 | **6** | *1 ½* | **Miss Millietant**[45] 598 3-8-5 30 (v[1]) JQuinn 13<br>(LMontagueHall) *chsd ldrs: rdn and wknd ent fnl f* **66/1** | 33 |
| 0406 | **7** | *hd* | **Keltic Flute**[21] 809 5-9-0 30 (v) SYourston(7) 2<br>(MrsLucindaFeatherstone) *led: rdn and hdd wl over 1f out: sn btn* **20/1** | 32 |
| 000- | **8** | *¾* | **La Vigna (IRE)**[140] 5686 3-8-5 35 (p) CCatlin 5<br>(MrsLucindaFeatherstone) *trckd ldr tl rdn and wknd wl over 1f out* **66/1** | 30 |
| -003 | **9** | *shd* | **Prince Of Perles**[6] 958 3-8-2 35 (b) LisaJones(3) 3<br>(DShaw) *s.i.s: effrt 1/2-way: one pce fnl 2f* **7/1**[3] | 30 |
| 0000 | **10** | *hd* | **Caronte (IRE)**[30] 713 4-9-7 30 [1] JoannaBadger 11<br>(SRBowring) *a in rr* **50/1** | 29 |
| 00-0 | **11** | *nk* | **Tern Intern (IRE)**[8] 940 5-9-7 35 JMcAuley 7<br>(MissJFeilden) *s.i.s: a bhd* **33/1** | 28 |
| 0/00 | **12** | *4* | **Pedler's Profiles**[35] 659 4-9-0 35 (b[1]) DerekNolan(7) 14<br>(MissKMGeorge) *a struggling in rr* **66/1** | 18 |
| 5300 | **13** | *5* | **Mimas Girl**[14] 875 5-9-7 35 (bt) JBramhill 10<br>(SRBowring) *a bhd* **20/1** | 4 |
| 0002 | **14** | *3* | **Pooka's Daughter (IRE)**[21] 809 4-9-7 30 (p) PFitzsimons 12<br>(JMBradley) *prom for 2f: sn wl bhd* **10/1** | — |
| 000/ | **15** | *6* | **Quarter To**[572] 3899 5-9-7 35 SRighton 1<br>(WDeBest-Turner) *a bhd* **100/1** | — |

1m 26.28s (0.28) **Going Correction** -0.025s/f (Stan)
**WFA** 3 from 4yo+ 16lb **15** Ran SP% **122.8**
Speed ratings: **97,93,91,91,90 88,88,87,87,87 86,82,76,73,66**CSF £14.76 TOTE £1.90: £1.10, £2.40, £3.90; EX 17.20.
**Owner** Coretech Systems Ltd **Bred** S D Bevan **Trained** Epsom, Surrey

**FOCUS**
As low a grade of race as you can get and not very competitive, despite the size of the field. The pace was only fair. The overall form is poor, but the winner had form 10lb better than this last summer and appears revitalised. She could certainly cope with a step up to 0-45 races.

**NOTEBOOK**
**Gentle Response**, up a furlong, was held up early but sliced her way through the field at halfway and swept past the leaders on outside on the home bend before bounding clear. The opposition probably made her look better than she is, but she should be able to follow up in a similar event if one can be found.
**Tiny Tim(IRE)**, always up there, ran well from his wide draw and continues to educate the stable's apprentices, but remains a maiden after 25 attempts.
**Tojoneski**, rated 73 on sand just 18 months ago, made some late progress over a trip that would have been too sharp.
**Kilmeena Star** put up one of his better recent efforts, but that is not saying much and he remains a maiden after 33 starts on the Flat.
**Hinchley Wood(IRE)** ran with a little credit, but connections seem to be having trouble working out his best trip.
**Prince Of Perles** *Official explanation: jockey said gelding hung left*

## 999 CASHBACKS @ ATTHERACES TEXT PAGE 410 (S) STKS — 1m (P)
**4:20** (4:24) (H) 3-Y-O+ — **£1,326** (£379; £189) **Stalls** High

| Form | | | | RPR |
|---|---|---|---|---|
| -065 | **1** | | **Over To You Bert**[4] 972 5-9-7 45 VSlattery 11<br>(RJHodges) *t.k.h: sn trckd ldr: led 3f out: rdn out* **12/1** | 49 |
| 0-05 | **2** | *¾* | **Regency Malaya**[26] 746 3-7-12 35 (bt) SRighton 4<br>(MFHarris) *plld hrd: prom tl outpcd over 2f out: r.o ins to go 2nd ins fnl f* **20/1** | 42 |
| 4000 | **3** | *1 ¼* | **Geespot**[15] 860 5-8-11 40 JFMcDonald(5) 6<br>(DJSFfrenchDavis) *hld up: hdwy over 2f out: chsd wnr over 1f out tl ins fnl f* **11/2**[3] | 39 |
| 0-00 | **4** | *½* | **Oktis Morilious (IRE)**[29] 726 3-8-3 45 JQuinn 7<br>(AWCarroll) *hld up in mid-div: rdn over 4f out: sn outpcd: r.o fnl f* **14/1** | 43 |
| 0-02 | **5** | *1* | **Single Track Mind**[15] 858 6-9-0 40 KarenPeippo(7) 8<br>(JRBoyle) *in rr: mde sme hdwy fnl f* **6/1** | 41 |
| 0-20 | **6** | *1 ½* | **Marakash (IRE)**[14] 873 5-9-7 48 (tp) GBaker 1<br>(MRBosley) *wl bhd tl rapid hdwy 2f out: wknd appr fnl f* **7/2**[2] | 38 |
| 3300 | **7** | *nk* | **Jahangir**[1] 987 5-9-7 45 DaneO'Neill 5<br>(BRJohnson) *t.k.h: led tl hdd 3f out: sn rdn and wknd over 1f out* **3/1**[1] | 37 |
| 0-30 | **8** | *1 ½* | **Flame Princess**[7] 951 4-9-2 45 DSweeney 9<br>(JRBoyle) *in mid-div: wknd wl over 1f out* **10/1** | 28 |
| 0- | **9** | *3* | **Diamond Ribby (IRE)**[169] 5112 3-7-12 JoannaBadger 12<br>(PDEvans) *trckd ldrs: rdn and wknd wl over 2f out* **16/1** | 21 |
| | **10** | *dist* | **Golden Oldie (IRE)**[10] 6-9-7 (b[1]) PDoe 2<br>(DFlood) *slowly away: t.o fr 1/2-way* **25/1** | — |

1m 39.59s (0.08) **Going Correction** -0.025s/f (Stan)
**WFA** 3 from 4yo+ 18lb **10** Ran SP% **114.8**
Speed ratings: **98,97,96,95,94 93,92,91,88,**—CSF £221.49 TOTE £13.70: £2.50, £6.40, £2.00; EX 121.30.There was no bid for the winner.
**Owner** Unity Farm Holiday Centre Ltd **Bred** J K S Cresswell **Trained** Charlton Adam, Somerset

**FOCUS**
A poor seller, made even less competitive by the withdrawal of the front two in the betting forecast. However, the pace was solid.

**NOTEBOOK**
**Over To You Bert**, who had finished unplaced in all 12 of his previous starts, was always on the shoulder of the leader and stayed on well to score, but he would need to find another race as bad as this to win again.
**Regency Malaya**, never closer than fifth in eight previous attempts, was back to a mile after failing to see out an extra three furlongs on Fibresand last time. After pulling hard just behind the early leader, he looked like dropping out on the home bend but was staying on again at the line.
**Geespot** had every chance, but her effort flattened out in the last furlong and she has not been at the top of her game for quite a while now.
**Oktis Morilious(IRE)**, ridden with more restraint this time, was probably not helped by the drop back in trip on a faster surface and, after not seeing a great deal of daylight, was then doing his best work late. He may not be a totally lost cause and does at least have a bit more scope than most of these.
**Single Track Mind** never really got into the race and his recent second place over a furlong shorter here almost certainly flatters him.
**Marakash(IRE)**, held up out the back, looked sure to get involved when moving up on the outside on the home bend, but his effort ended as quickly as it had begun. *Official explanation: trainer said gelding had a breathing problem*
**Jahangir** had the run of the race, but pulled hard in front and folded very tamely in the home straight. He is definitely one to avoid.

## 1000 CASHBACKS @ SKY TEXT PAGE 372 BANDED STKS — 5f (P)
**4:50** (4:52) (H) 3-Y-O+ — **£1,452** (£415; £207) **Stalls** High

| Form | | | | RPR |
|---|---|---|---|---|
| 6621 | **1** | | **Long Weekend (IRE)**[7] 951 6-9-12 40 (v) DarrenWilliams 10<br>(DShaw) *taken over to ins fr wd draw s: in rr tl hdwy 2f out: led ins fnl f: drvn out* **5/1**[3] | 55 |
| 0-00 | **2** | *hd* | **Avit (IRE)**[22] 791 4-9-6 40 JFEgan 6<br>(PLGilligan) *chsd ldrs: led briefly ent fnl f: kpt on* **33/1** | 48 |
| 3305 | **3** | *1 ¾* | **Sotonian (HOL)**[7] 951 11-9-3 40 LisaJones(3) 9<br>(PSFelgate) *hld up: hdwy 2f out: sn rdn: kpt on one pce fnl f* **11/2** | 41 |
| 0000 | **4** | *nk* | **Levelled**[7] 951 10-9-6 35 (b[1]) ACulhane 2<br>(DWChapman) *hld up: rdn and hdwy 2f out: swtchd rt over 1f out: r.o one pce* **16/1** | 40 |
| 030 | **5** | *nk* | **Somethingabouther**[15] 856 4-9-6 40 JQuinn 8<br>(PWHiatt) *hld up in rr: r.o ins fnl f: nvr nr to chal* **10/1** | 39 |
| -064 | **6** | *½* | **Emarati's Image**[7] 958 6-9-6 40 ADaly 1<br>(RMStronge) *mde most tl hdd & wknd ent fnl f* **7/2**[1] | 37 |
| -024 | **7** | *shd* | **Bali-Star**[22] 792 9-9-6 40 CCatlin 3<br>(RJHodges) *disp ld tl wknd over 1f out* **6/1** | 36 |
| 0004 | **8** | *4* | **Parallel Lines (IRE)**[9] 930 3-8-2 40 (v[1]) JFMcDonald(5) 7<br>(PDEvans) *sn pushed along in rr and styd there* **4/1**[2] | 20 |
| 4-00 | **9** | *6* | **Diaphanous**[54] 538 6-9-6 40 (t) SCarson 5<br>(EAWheeler) *disp ld tl rdn and wknd 2f out* **14/1** | — |
| -000 | **10** | *1 ½* | **Definitely Special (IRE)**[40] 625 6-9-1 40 MSavage(5) 4<br>(NEBerry) *slowly away: sn pushed along and a outpcd* **16/1** | — |

60.90 secs (1.12) **Going Correction** -0.025s/f (Stan)
**WFA** 3 from 4yo+ 13lb **10** Ran SP% **119.0**
Speed ratings: **90,89,86,86,85 85,84,78,68,66**CSF £153.61 TOTE £4.70: £1.30, £5.20, £2.30; EX 288.30 Place 6 £76.95, Place 5 £45.19.
**Owner** The Marlow Lewin Partnership **Bred** F Hinojosa **Trained** Averham, Notts
■ Stewards Enquiry : J F Egan two-day ban: used whip from above shoulder height and without giving filly time to respond (Mar 20,22)

**FOCUS**
A modest winning time for the grade, but the winner could handle a step up in class.

**NOTEBOOK**
**Long Weekend(IRE)** was given a very good ride to take this. Drawn widest of all, he was soon dropped in and raced in last until halfway, but picked up well when asked and the gaps appeared at just the right time. This was the second time he has defied the widest draw here, so these last two victories have been even better than they look.
**Avit(IRE)**, never closer than fifth in eight previous starts, seemed to improve a lot here but the modest winning time casts a doubt over a literal interpretation of the form.
**Sotonian(HOL)** ran another creditable race, but this is as good as he is these days.
**Levelled** had every chance, but could not quicken where it matters. He was rated 63lb higher than this at his peak, but this perfectly demonstrates his ability this days.
**Somethingabouther** made a little late headway, but remains a maiden after 26 attempts.
**Emarati's Image** was given his head on this drop back to the minimum trip and set the pace against the inside rail, but folded tamely once the challenges arrived. A longer trip on a slower surface seems to suit him best.
JS

## [974] NAD AL SHEBA (L-H)
Thursday, March 11
**OFFICIAL GOING: Turf course - firm; dirt course - fast**

### 1001a CROWN TOWERS MELBOURNE TROPHY (H'CAP) (TURF) — 1m
3:35 (3:38) (95-112,112) 3-Y-0+ **£54,469** (£16,759; £8,379; £4,189) **Stalls** Low

RPR
1 **Winisk River (IRE)**[21] [830] 4-9-7 109 ....(t) LDettori 2 109
(SaeedBinSuroor) *led early: trckd ldr fr 6f out: 3rd st: rdn and hdwy 2f out: r.o to ld fnl 55yds* **11/10**[1]
2 nk **Trademark (SAF)**[5] [978] 7-9-11 112 .... RLMoore 3 113
(SSeemar, UAE) *trckd ldrs: cl up 5th st: rdn to ld 1 1/2f out: kpt on wl tl hdd fnl 55yds* **6/1**[3]
3 1 ¼ **Checkit (IRE)**[5] [978] 4-9-6 108 ....(v) TEDurcan 10 105
(MRChannon) *in tch towards rr: 9th st: rdn and hdwy fr 2f out: r.o wl fnl f: nrst fin* **5/1**[2]
4 hd **Al Maali (IRE)**[20] 5-8-9 95 .... RHills 1 94
(DougWatson, UAE) *mid-div on ins: 6th st: rdn and effrt 2f out: styd on fnl 110yds* **12/1**
5 ½ **Zirna (NZ)**[19] [853] 5-9-3 105 .... MDuPlessis 8 101
(MThwaites, Macau) *in tch in rr: last and racd wd st: rdn and stdy hdwy 2f out: styd on wl: nrst fin* **8/1**
6 5 ¼ **Royal Beacon**[12] [921] 4-8-13 100 ....(b) GBirrer 5 86
(ChristianWroe, UAE) *towards rr on ins: rdn and outpcd st: styd on fnl f: nt rch ldrs* **33/1**
7 1 **Classical Act (IND)**[19] [849] 5-8-9 95 ....(t) WSupple 4 80
(SPadmanabhan, India) *trckd ldrs: 2nd st: rdn to ld 2f out: hdd 1 1/2f out: hmpd fnl f: nt rcvr* **25/1**
8 3 ¼ **Baaridd**[19] [850] 6-8-9 96 .... MJKinane 9 74
(AllanSmith, UAE) *mid-div: rdn and effrt st: wknd fnl f* **7/1**
9 1 ¾ **St Expedit**[5] [976] 7-9-3 105 ....(bt[1]) BDoyle 6 78
(RBouresly, Kuwait) *trckd ldr: led fr 6f out tl hdd 2f out: sn wknd* **16/1**
10 ¾ **Hero's Journey**[12] [925] 5-8-13 100 ....(t) GHind 7 73
(MAlKurdi, UAE) *in tch: 4th st: wknd fnl 2f* **33/1**
1m 37.65s — 10 Ran SP% **125.5**
Speed ratings: .
**Owner** Godolphin **Bred** P H Betts **Trained** Newmarket, Suffolk

**NOTEBOOK**
**Winisk River(IRE)**, impressive when scoring on his comeback run at the course last time, had to battle hard for the follow up, but showed a good attitude and avoided the 'bounce'. He can only continue to improve.
**Checkit(IRE)** did nothing wrong in third and this tough colt should be winning before long.

### 1002a DARLEY BALANCHINE STKS (CONDITIONS RACE) (F&M) (TURF) — 1m 1f
4:10 (4:14) 3-Y-0+ **£47,206** (£14,525; £7,262; £3,631) **Stalls** Low

RPR
1 **Gonfilia (GER)**[21] [831] 4-9-4 98 ....(t) LDettori 8 104
(SaeedBinSuroor) *mde all: rdn clr 1 1/2f out: easily* **2/1**[1]
2 6 **Desert Glow (IRE)**[21] [831] 4-9-4 94 ....(v) KMcEvoy 5 93
(SSeemar, UAE) *in tch: 5th st: hdwy over 2f out: styd on nr fin: no ch w wnr* **8/1**
3 ½ **Special Parade (SAF)**[35] [690] 6-9-8 98 ....(t) GHind 10 96
(GeoffWoodruff, South Africa) *trckd ldr: 2nd st: rdn over 2f out: kpt on same pce* **6/1**[3]
4 1 ½ **Cat Belling (IRE)**[5] [978] 4-9-6 100 .... RHills 7 91
(RBouresly, Kuwait) *in tch: 4th st: rdn and hdwy 2f out: wknd nr fin* **2/1**[1]
5 5 **Quite Lovely (USA)**[18] 4-9-4 65 .... RLMoore 3 80
(SSeemar, UAE) *trckd ldrs: rdn fr 1/2-way: 3rd on ins st: wknd fnl 2f* **100/1**
6 ¾ **Naughty Nell**[12] [921] 5-9-4 93 .... RMullen 2 79
(PBrette, Dubai) *in tch towards rr: racd wd st: hdwy fnl 2f: no ex nr fin* **7/1**
7 2 ¾ **After The Ball (SAF)**[6] 4-9-4 67 ....(v[1]) TEDurcan 4 73
(SSeemar, UAE) *mid-div: 7th st: wknd fnl 2f* **50/1**
8 9 **Sail With The Tide (IRE)**[21] [831] 4-9-4 77 .... DO'Donohoe 1 57
(RBouresly, Kuwait) *a towards rr: 9th st: nvr nr to chal* **150/1**
9 11 **Monetary (GER)**[19] [849] 4-9-4 102 .... SSanders 6 36
(ECharpy, UAE) *mid-div tl wknd st: eased fnl f* **11/2**[2]
10 17 **Girl Scoud (BRZ)**[21] [831] 5-9-4 60 .... WSupple 9 5
(ASelvaratnam, UAE) *a towards rr: last st: eased fnl f* **100/1**
1m 48.7s — 10 Ran SP% **124.6**
Speed ratings: .
**Owner** Godolphin **Bred** Gestut Auenquelle **Trained** Newmarket, Suffolk

**NOTEBOOK**
**Gonfilia(GER)** won this impressively despite suspicions that the ground would again be riding too fast for her. She pulled right away, winning by a cosy six lengths in the end and should be up to winning back in pattern company.

### 1003a VISIT VICTORIA - THE PLACE TO BE STKS (H'CAP) (TURF) — 1m 4f
4:45 (4:47) (95-112,112) 3-Y-0+ **£54,469** (£16,759; £8,379; £4,189) **Stalls** Low

RPR
1 **Scott's View**[5] [976] 5-9-6 112 .... SChin 3 113
(MJohnston) *in tch in mid-div: 5th st: rdn over 2f out: r.o wl to ld fnl 55yds* **9/2**[3]
2 1 ½ **Simeon**[5] [978] 5-8-5 95 ....(v) RLMoore 5 96
(SSeemar, UAE) *in tch: 3rd st: rdn to chal 2f out: led fnl f: styd on tl hdd fnl 55yds* **66/1**
3 ½ **Clodion (IRE)**[5] [976] 8-8-8 100 .... TEDurcan 6 98
(MAlKurdi, UAE) *towards rr: 8th st: hdwy 2f out: styd on wl: nrst fin* **14/1**
4 1 ¾ **Kayseri (IRE)**[19] [849] 5-8-13 105 ....(v) MJKinane 4 100
(AllanSmith, UAE) *in rr: 9th and racd wd st: styd on wl fnl f: nt rch ldrs* **3/1**[1]
5 nk **Compton Bolter (IRE)**[5] [976] 7-9-4 110 .... EAhern 10 105
(GABulter) *hld up: trckd ldr: 2nd st: rdn to ld over 2f out: hdd fnl f: wknd nr fin* **5/1**
6 ½ **Zaajel (IRE)**[19] [854] 5-8-8 100 ....(t) RHills 2 94
(ECharpy, UAE) *mid-div: 6th st: effrt 1 1/2f out: no ex nr fin* **7/1**
7 5 **Zurbaran (IND)**[19] [854] 5-8-5 95 .... GHind 9 84
(SPadmanabhan, India) *led tl hdd over 2f out: grad wknd* **40/1**
8 2 **Fantastic Horse (ARG)**[19] [854] 5-8-8 100 ....(bt) KMcEvoy 8 84
(GeoffWoodruff, South Africa) *in tch: 4th st: wknd over 2f out* **9/1**
9 8 ¾ **Dubai Honor**[5] [979] 5-8-11 104 ....(t) WSupple 7 74
(DougWatson, UAE) *mid-div: wknd over 2f out* **14/1**
P **Adiemus**[12] [922] 6-9-0 106 ....(v) LDettori 1 —
(JNoseda) *in tch towards rr: broke down and p.u 3 1/2f out: dead* **7/2**[2]
2m 30.59s — 10 Ran SP% **121.8**
Speed ratings: .
**Owner** Great Escape Partnership **Bred** Cliveden Stud Ltd **Trained** Middleham Moor, N Yorks

**NOTEBOOK**
**Scott's View**, a good winner on his penultimate outing, disappointed last time, albeit in group company, but bounced right back to his best. He was always travelling well and stayed on best of all to deny former stablemate Simeon. He is very useful on his day and looks up to winning back in a better grade.
**Compton Bolter(IRE)** had every chance on this drop back into handicap company, but was not good enough.
**Adiemus** sadly broke down and was pulled up with fatal injuries.

### 1004a EMIRATES AIRLINE CUP (H'CAP) (TURF) — 6f 110y
5:20 (5:24) (95-112,112) 3-Y-0+ **£54,469** (£16,759; £8,379; £4,189) **Stalls** Low

RPR
1 **Feet So Fast**[12] [921] 5-9-11 112 .... TEDurcan 7 113+
(SSeemar, UAE) *mid-div: 6th st: hdwy over 2f out: r.o wl to ld fnl f: pushed out* **9/4**[1]
2 2 ¼ **Boston Lodge**[12] [924] 4-8-9 95 ....(b[1]) EAhern 4 91
(GAButler) *trckd ldrs: 3rd st: rdn to ld 1 1/2f out: hdd fnl f: nt pce of wnr* **9/2**[3]
3 1 **Magic Master (SAF)**[19] [851] 5-8-13 100 .... MJKinane 1 92
(BWiid, South Africa) *in tch towards rr: 8th st: hdwy over 2f out: nt clr run and swtchd fnl f: r.o: nrst fin* **14/1**
4 1 ¾ **Conceal**[5] [977] 6-9-2 104 .... RHills 5 90
(RBouresly, Kuwait) *trckd ldr: 2nd st: rdn to ld 2f out: hdd 1 1/2f out: grad wknd* **12/1**
5 nk **Storm Racer (AUS)**[12] [924] 7-8-13 100 ....(b) MDuPlessis 9 86
(MThwaites, Macau) *trckd ldrs: 4th st: effrt over 1f out: no ex nr fin* **20/1**
6 3 ¼ **Pic Up Sticks**[12] [924] 5-8-9 96 .... RLMoore 6 73
(MRChannon) *mid-div: 7th st: kpt on same pce* **5/1**
7 hd **Three Graces (GER)**[19] [852] 4-9-8 110 ....(vt) LDettori 8 85
(SaeedBinSuroor) *mid-div: 5th st: rdn over 2f out: no ex fnl f* **11/4**[2]
8 3 **Orchestrated (AUS)**[12] [924] 7-8-9 96 ....(t) GHind 64
(MAlKurdi, UAE) *led tl hdd 2f out: sn wknd* **66/1**
9 1 ½ **Glad Master (GER)**[740] 7-8-13 100 ....(b) RMullen 2 63
(MAlMuhairi, UAE) *a towards rr: last st: n.d* **40/1**
10 12 **Stormont (IRE)**[12] [923] 4-9-7 109 .... WSupple 10 37
(HJCollingridge) *a towards rr: nvr nr to chal* **16/1**
10 Ran SP% **121.2**
Speed ratings: .
**Owner** H E Sheikh Rashid Bin Mohammed **Bred** Cheveley Park Stud Ltd **Trained** United Arab Emirates

**NOTEBOOK**
**Feet So Fast** made up for the mishap last time out when disqualified after his rider weighed in light. He is staying one step ahead of the Handicapper at present.
**Boston Lodge** gave a slightly improved performance in the first-time blinkers and was not at all disgraced in being beaten by the formerly very classy Feet So Fast.
**Pic Up Sticks** struggled in this better race than the one he won last week off a 5lb higher mark.
**Three Graces(GER)** was fairly impressive when scoring at the course last time, so this has to go down as a disappointing effort.
**Stormont(IRE)** was never in the hunt.

### 1005a MELBOURNE RACING CLUB U.A.E. OAKS (FILLIES) (CONDITIONS RACE) (DIRT) — 1m 1f
5:50 (5:52) 3-Y-0 **£90,782** (£27,932; £13,966; £6,983) **Stalls** Low

RPR
1 **Tamarillo**[19] [848] 3-8-9 95 .... TEDurcan 3 105
(MAlKurdi, UAE) *trckd ldr: led st: styd on wl u.p fnl 1 1/2f: rdn out nr fin* **12/1**
2 1 ½ **Festive Style (SAF)**[21] [831] 3-9-4 106 .... RLMoore 8 111
(SSeemar, UAE) *in tch towards rr: prog to 4th st: chal and ev ch 1 1/2f out: styd on same pce* **6/4**[2]
3 8 ¼ **Menhoubah (USA)**[33] [711] 3-8-9 105 .... LDettori 7 87
(CEBrittain) *mid-div: racd wd st: styd on fnl 2f: nt rch ldrs* **4/6**[1]
4 2 ¾ **Screaming Shamal (USA)**[21] 3-8-9 74 .... RMullen 5 82
(DougWatson, UAE) *mid-div: effrt on ins st: wknd fnl f* **66/1**
5 3 ¼ **Pomeranze (IRE)**[21] 3-8-9 80 .... WSupple 6 76
(DougWatson, UAE) *in tch early: 7th and outpcd st: kpt on nr fin* **50/1**
6 nk **Ibda Ae (KSA)**[33] [711] 3-8-9 96 .... MJKinane 2 75
(SBinSaud, UAE) *led tl hdd st: grad wknd* **11/1**[3]
7 3 **Nabtat Saif**[21] 3-8-9 73 ....(vt[1]) SSanders 1 70
(DougWatson, UAE) *trckd ldrs: 3rd st: wknd fnl 2f* **66/1**
8 14 **Bastikiya (SAF)**[21] 3-9-4 ....(b[1]) KMcEvoy 4 53
(SSeemar, UAE) *sn outpcd and bhd: nvr nr to chal* **150/1**
1m 51.51s — 8 Ran SP% **121.6**
Speed ratings: .
**Owner** H E Sheikh Rashid Bin Mohammed **Bred** P D And Mrs Player **Trained** United Arab Emirates

**NOTEBOOK**
**Tamarillo** turned around recent form with Menhoubah in no uncertain style and is now bound for the UAE Derby after running out an authoritative winner.
**Menhoubah(USA)** was very disappointing especially as this longer trip ought to have suited.

## 1006a MELBOURNE RACING CLUB TROPHY (H'CAP) (TURF) 1m

6:20 (6:22) (95-112,112) 3-Y-0+ **£54,469** (£16,759; £8,379; £4,189) **Stalls** Low

RPR

1 **Walmooh**[12] 925 8-8-13 100 (b) PaulSmith 2 110
(AllanSmith, UAE) *mid-div: 5th on ins st: rdn and hdwy over 2f out: led 1 1/2f out: sn clr: rdn out* **12/1**

2 6 **Membership (USA)**[5] 978 4-9-6 108 LDettori 4 105
(CEBrittain) *in tch in rr: last st: rdn and hdwy 2f out: r.o wl nr fin: no ch w wnr* **11/2**[2]

3 nk **Kundooz**[12] 925 5-8-9 96 BDoyle 3 93
(AllanSmith, UAE) *mid-div: 6th st: rdn and hdwy 2f out: styd on nr fin* **7/1**[3]

4 hd **Mugharreb (USA)**[12] 924 6-8-9 95 WSupple 1 93
(MAlMuhairi, UAE) *trckd ldrs: 3rd st: chal and ev ch 2fm out: styd on same pce* **14/1**

5 1 1/2 **Skoozi (NZ)**[12] 925 9-8-13 100 RBurke 8 94
(MKettle, UAE) *trckd ldrs: 4th st: rdn to chal 2f out: no ex fnl f* **10/1**

6 1/2 **D'Anjou**[33] 710 7-9-11 112 MJKinane 6 105
(JohnMOxx, Ire) *in tch towards rr: hdwy and nt clr run 1 1/2f out: swtchd and r.o nr fin: nt rch ldrs* **11/10**[1]

7 11 **Three Points**[12] 923 7-9-6 108 (t) JCarroll 7 78
(PRudkin, UAE) *led tl hdd 1 1/2f out: sn wknd* **33/1**

8 2 3/4 **Bianconi (SAF)**[250] 4-9-3 105 (v) TEDurcan 10 69
(SSeemar, UAE) *towards rr: rdn 2f out: sn wknd* **12/1**

9 5 3/4 **Al Jadeed (USA)**[145] 5643 4-9-3 105 (b) RHills 5 58
(JHMGosden) *trckd ldr: 2nd st: sn wknd* **8/1**

10 1 **Attache**[19] 852 6-8-13 100 KMcEvoy 9 52
(IMohammed, UAE) *a towards rr: n.d* **25/1**

1m 36.98s **10** Ran **SP%** 124.5
Speed ratings: .
**Owner** Sheikh Ahmed Al Maktoum **Bred** Sheikh Ahmed Bin Rashid Al Maktoum **Trained** UAE

**NOTEBOOK**
**Membership(USA)** put up a solid effort on his return to handicap company. The stronger the pace the better it is for him.
**Al Jadeed(USA)**, having his first outing of the season, was wearing blinkers for the first time.

# 989 WOLVERHAMPTON (A.W) (L-H)

Saturday, March 13

**OFFICIAL GOING: Standard to slow**

Following snow and rain in the previous 48 hours, the surface was quicker than of late.

Wind: mod hlf bhd Weather: an odd shower just prior to racing.

## 1007 BET DIRECT ON 0800 32 93 93 H'CAP 6f (F)

1:50 (1:52) (C) (0-100,96) 3-Y-0+ **£10,244** (£3,152; £1,576; £788) **Stalls** Low

Form RPR

1404 1 **Quiet Times (IRE)**[39] 669 5-9-0 **83** (b) NCallan 4 95
(KARyan) *a.p: rdn over 2f out: led wl over 1f out: rdn out* **10/1**

2-15 2 1 **Mufreh (USA)**[30] 749 6-9-2 **85** SWhitworth 2 94+
(AGNewcombe) *s.i.s: nt clr run over 3f out: rdn and hdwy wl over 1f out: r.o ins fnl f: nt rch wnr* **6/1**[3]

04-U 3 2 **Ok Pal**[21] 841 4-9-7 **90** KDarley 6 93
(TGMills) *led 2f: rdn over 2f out: one pce fnl f* **14/1**

-400 4 1 1/2 **Bond Boy**[29] 761 7-9-4 **87** CCatlin 3 86
(BSmart) *bhd: rdn 3f out: hdwy fnl f: nrst fin* **11/1**

3331 5 1 **Time N Time Again**[8] 968 6-8-12 **81** (p) IMongan 9 77
(EJAlston) *prom: rdn over 3f out: no hdwy fnl 2f* **11/2**[2]

-560 6 1 3/4 **Bond Playboy**[29] 761 4-9-3 **86** FLynch 7 76
(BSmart) *prom: rdn over 3f out: wknd fnl f* **10/1**

-001 7 nk **Johnston's Diamond (IRE)**[22] 836 6-8-9 **78** EAhern 5 67
(EJAlston) *prom: rdn 3f out: wknd over 1f out* **4/1**[1]

000- 8 1 1/4 **Piccled**[131] 5909 6-9-13 **96** DHolland 1 82
(EJAlston) *hdwy to ld 4f out: rdn and hdd wl over 1f out: sn hung rt: wknd ins fnl f* **20/1**

0041 9 4 **Hurricane Coast**[8] 968 5-8-13 **82** (b) RHughes 10 56
(DFlood) *prom tl rdn and wknd wl over 1f out* **4/1**[1]

006- 10 9 **Abbajabba**[126] 5953 8-8-13 **82** JBramhill 11 29
(CWFairhurst) *outpcd* **14/1**

1m 16.97s (1.27) **Going Correction** +0.45s/f (Slow) **10** Ran **SP%** 114.3
Speed ratings: **109,107,105,103,101 99,98,97,91,79**CSF £67.46 CT £842.65 TOTE £12.50: £3.00, £2.30, £2.80; EX 77.30.
**Owner** Yorkshire Racing Club and Francis Moll **Bred** Times Of Wigan Ltd **Trained** Hambleton, N Yorks

■ Stewards Enquiry : R Hughes caution: careless riding

**FOCUS**
A decent sprint handicap, run in a decent time, and good solid form.

**NOTEBOOK**
**Quiet Times(IRE)** had improved during the winter and achieved a personal best by holding the shade unlucky second. His trainer thinks he might be well handicapped when returning to turf.
**Mufreh(USA)** often loses ground at the start and did not get the best of runs leaving the back straight. All his Dunstall Park victories have come over seven.
**Ok Pal** handles soft ground on turf and appeared to stay the six furlongs well enough on this Fibresand debut.
**Bond Boy** was back down to a mark only 4lb higher than when he landed the 2002 Stewards' Cup.
**Time N Time Again** was taking on better company off a 2lb higher mark.
**Bond Playboy** was 6lb better off than when beating the winner by a neck here last November.
**Hurricane Coast** *Official explanation: trainer said gelding finished distressed*

## 1008 BET DIRECT ON SKY ACTIVE CLAIMING STKS 5f (F)

2:25 (2:25) (F) 3-Y-0 **£2,891** (£826; £413) **Stalls** Low

Form RPR

0610 1 **Lady Bahia (IRE)**[30] 747 3-8-7 64 THamilton[(5)] 3 64
(RPElliott) *led after 1f: rdn wl over 1f out: r.o* **9/1**

2012 2 1 1/2 **Emaradia**[10] 958 3-8-7 60 (b) IMongan 1 53
(AWCarroll) *led 1f: chsd wnr: hrd rdn over 2f out: nt qckn ins fnl f* **3/1**[2]

-220 3 shd **Muy Bien**[39] 669 3-9-3 77 (b[1]) DHolland 5 63
(JRJenkins) *bhd: nt clr run after 1f: swtchd lft and bmpd over 3f out: rdn and hdwy over 2f out: kpt on towards fin* **13/8**[1]

0035 4 1 1/2 **Barras (IRE)**[10] 958 3-8-10 51 (v) PGallagher[(7)] 2 57?
(MissGayKelleway) *a.p: rdn over 2f out: one pce fnl f* **25/1**

1554 5 1 1/4 **Back At De Front (IRE)**[16] 891 3-8-8 60 ow1 MSavage[(5)] 9 48
(NEBerry) *prom: rdn over 2f out: wknd ins fnl f* **14/1**

1052 6 2 1/2 **Ever Cheerful**[16] 893 3-8-9 70 (p) AQuinn[(5)] 6 39
(WGMTurner) *sn rdn along: nvr nr to chal* **6/1**[3]

330- 7 1 **Wendy's Girl (IRE)**[166] 5273 3-8-2 64 NMackay[(5)] 7 28
(RPElliott) *bhd fnl 3f* **20/1**

4042 8 1 **Lizhar (IRE)**[19] 865 3-8-2 57 (b) KGhunowa[(7)] 4 26
(MJPolglase) *s.i.s: bmpd over 3f out: sme hdwy on ins over 2f out: wknd over 1f out* **14/1**

020- 9 14 **Amber Legend**[193] 4645 3-8-5 60 JFEgan 8 —
(MsDeborahJEvans) *chsd ldrs tl wknd over 3f out* **25/1**

64.97 secs (2.37) **Going Correction** +0.45s/f (Slow) **9** Ran **SP%** 113.2
Speed ratings: **99,96,96,94,92 88,86,84,62**CSF £34.54 TOTE £8.90: £1.40, £1.90, £1.30; EX 41.90.
**Owner** Mrs Sarah Grayson **Bred** Piercetown Stud **Trained** Formby, Lancs

**FOCUS**
A modest claimer, but several of these had a decent chance on official ratings. The form horses were below form, and the fourth is the best guide to the form.

**NOTEBOOK**
**Lady Bahia(IRE)** got away well enough this time and was soon at the head of affairs. She seems equally effective over five or six on this surface providing she gets a decent break.
**Emaradia** was back down in both distance and grade and had no excuses.
**Muy Bien**, switching to blinkers instead of a visor, is not an easy ride but had a nightmare passage to the first turn. *Official explanation: jockey said colt was hanging left*
**Barras(IRE)** would have been better off in a handicap and there was not disgrace in this performance.
**Back At De Front(IRE)** is another who had something to find at these weights.
**Amber Legend** *Official explanation: jockey said filly was never travelling*

## 1009 LITTLEWOODS BET DIRECT LINCOLN TRIAL (H'CAP) 1m 100y(F)

3:00 (3:01) (B) (0-105,105) 4-Y-0+ **£20,300** (£7,700; £3,850; £1,750) **Stalls** Low

Form RPR

1111 1 **Vortex**[19] 862 5-8-12 **89** (t) IMongan 13 104
(MissGayKelleway) *hld up towards rr: hdwy over 4f out: wnt 2nd over 3f out: rdn over 2f out: led ins fnl f: all out* **7/1**

0002 2 shd **Te Quiero**[22] 837 6-9-2 **93** (t) SDrowne 3 108
(MissGayKelleway) *led: rdn over 2f out: hdd ins fnl f: r.o* **7/2**[1]

100- 3 6 **Creskeld (IRE)**[130] 5918 5-8-10 **87** FLynch 4 89
(BSmart) *chsd ldr tl rdn over 3f out: one pce fnl 2f* **16/1**

220- 4 hd **Danelor (IRE)**[245] 3222 6-8-10 **87** PHanagan 12 89
(RAFahey) *hld up in tch: rdn over 3f out: one pce fnl 2f* **16/1**

12-1 5 shd **Mi Odds**[43] 641 8-9-8 **99** DHolland 7 101
(MrsNMacauley) *bhd tl hdwy on outside over 1f out: r.o* **13/2**[3]

20-0 6 2 1/2 **Vintage Premium**[21] 842 7-9-4 **100** THamilton[(5)] 6 97
(RAFahey) *prom: lost pl over 6f out: rdn over 5f out: n.d after* **25/1**

000- 7 1 3/4 **Sahaat**[84] 6224 6-8-12 **89** SWKelly 9 82
(JAOsborne) *bhd: rdn 4f out: nvr nr ldrs* **25/1**

0-64 8 2 **Bonecrusher**[21] 842 5-9-13 **104** (v) RHughes 11 93
(DRLoder) *rdn 4f out: a bhd* **6/1**[2]

21-0 9 hd **Nimello (USA)**[56] 558 8-8-8 **85** SWhitworth 10 73
(AGNewcombe) *bhd: rdn over 4f out: short-lived effrt on ins over 2f out* **8/1**

45-1 10 1 1/4 **Quito (IRE)**[29] 761 7-10-0 **105** (b) ACulhane 1 91
(DWChapman) *prom tl rdn and wknd 3f out* **7/1**

00-0 11 9 **Mystic Man (FR)**[30] 749 6-8-10 **87** NCallan 5 54
(KARyan) *hld up in tch: rdn over 3f out: wknd over 1f out* **14/1**

410- 12 5 **Cornelius**[112] 6051 7-9-9 **100** KDarley 8 56
(PFICole) *chsd ldrs: rdn over 3f out: sn wknd* **16/1**

1m 51.55s (0.55) **Going Correction** +0.45s/f (Slow) **12** Ran **SP%** 118.0
Speed ratings: **115,114,108,108,108 106,104,102,102,100 91,86**CSF £31.45 CT £382.99 TOTE £6.80: £3.50, £1.90, £6.20; EX 22.40.
**Owner** Coriolis Partnership **Bred** Juddmonte Farms **Trained** Newmarket, Suffolk

**FOCUS**
A top All-Weather handicap, and a good renewal with the runner-up 7lb higher than when taking this race last year. Career bests from first two. The winning time was very smart indeed.

**NOTEBOOK**
**Vortex** has not stopped improving during the winter and just managed to maintain his winning run despite having gone up a total of 16lb. He is not entered in the Lincoln but will be aimed at the Royal Hunt Cup at Ascot in June.
**Te Quiero** loves it round here and made a valiant attempt to repeat last year's victory in this event but just got touched off by his stablemate.
**Creskeld(IRE)** was meeting Te Quiero on 4lb better terms than when beaten a length and three-quarters in this race last year. He did not have the benefit of having run during the winter this time.
**Danelor(IRE)**, on his All-Weather debut, made a promising comeback after finishing lame in the John Smith's Cup at York last June.
**Mi Odds**, 10lb higher than when in a handicap two outings ago, got away with it over this trip here last time but really does want further against this sort of opposition.
**Mystic Man(FR)** *Official explanation: trainer said gelding finished distressed*

## 1010 NEW SITE @ BETDIRECT.CO.UK H'CAP 2m 46y(F)

3:30 (3:31) (D) (0-85,85) 4-Y-0+ **£5,057** (£1,556; £778; £389) **Stalls** Low

Form RPR

0-11 1 **Sun Hill**[8] 973 4-8-5 **66** DSweeney 3 86+
(MBlanshard) *a gng wl: jnd ldr over 4f out: led on bit ins fnl f: v easily* **11/4**[2]

0352 2 3 1/2 **Glory Quest (USA)**[8] 971 7-8-12 **68** (v) IMongan 6 73
(MissGayKelleway) *a.p: led over 4f out: rdn over 3f out: hdd ins fnl f: no ch w wnr* **10/1**

/4-2 3 7 **Northern Nymph**[16] 899 5-9-10 **80** ACulhane 7 77
(RHollinshead) *hld up: rdn and hdwy over 5f out: one pce fnl 3f* **16/1**

0011 4 10 **Victory Quest (IRE)**[16] 899 4-9-10 85 (v) DaneO'Neill 5 70
(MrsSLamyman) *w ldr: led after 2f: rdn and hdd over 4f out: sn btn* **10/1**

-044 5 2 1/2 **Macaroni Gold (IRE)**[5] 981 4-8-4 **65** (b) SWhitworth 1 47
(WJarvis) *s.i.s: hdwy after 6f: rdn and wknd over 4f out* **8/1**

010- 6 12 **Teorban (POL)**[7] 1920 5-9-0 **70** EAhern 2 37
(MPitman) *led 2f: rdn and lost pl 8f out: sn bhd* **15/2**

1421 7 4 **Phantom Stock**[5] 981 4-8-3 **64** DMernagh 4 26
(WJarvis) *hld up: rdn over 6f out: hdwy over 5f out: wknd over 3f out* **5/2**[1]

8 10 **Szeroki Bor (POL)**[12] 5-8-11 **67** DHolland 8 17
(MPitman) *hld up and bhd: rdn over 3f out: sn struggling* **13/2**[3]

3m 49.59s (7.29) **Going Correction** +0.45s/f (Slow)
**WFA** 4 from 5yo+ 5lb **8** Ran **SP%** 115.5
Speed ratings: **99,97,93,88,87 81,79,74**CSF £30.49 CT £371.89 TOTE £3.40: £1.20, £4.00, £3.80; EX 26.00.
**Owner** Stanley Hinton **Bred** London Thoroughbred Services Ltd **Trained** Upper Lambourn, Berks

**FOCUS**
The task of the winner was made easier by the fact that the favourite flopped, but another much-improved effort from winner, and value a lot more than winning margin; further improvement possible. The winning time was modest.

**NOTEBOOK**
**Sun Hill** won hard held despite having gone up another 9lb. He seems to need some cut in the ground and is going to be interesting when reverting back to turf.
**Glory Quest(USA)** found the winner laughing at him in the last three furlongs and is flattered by the margin of defeat.
**Northern Nymph** seemed to be going up and down on the spot from the three-furlong pole.
**Phantom Stock** was most disappointing after his win at Lingfield earlier in the week. *Official explanation: jockey said gelding ran flat*

## 1011 BETDIRECT.CO.UK CONDITIONS STKS 7f (F)
**4:05** (4:10) (C) 4-Y-O+ **£7,360** (£2,791; £1,395; £634) **Stalls High**

Form RPR
-11 **1** **Aleutian**[28] 770 4-9-8 NPollard 7 105
(DRLoder) *w ldr: rdn over 2f out: chalng whn bmpd over 1f out: led wl ins fnl f: r.o* **5/2**[1]
111- **2** *shd* **Cardinal Venture (IRE)**[101] 6124 6-9-0 95 NCallan 3 97
(KARyan) *led: rdn over 2f out: edgd rt over 1f out: hdd wl ins fnl f: r.o* **11/4**[2]
400- **3** *1* **Rockets 'n Rollers (IRE)**[294] 1822 4-9-0 108 DaneO'Neill 6 94
(RHannon) *s.i.s: sn prom: rdn over 2f out: edgd lft wl over 1f out: nt qckn ins fnl f* **6/1**[3]
-202 **4** *½* **Queens Rhapsody**[29] 761 4-9-0 87 JFanning 5 93
(ABailey) *hld up: hdwy over 3f out: rdn over 2f out: cl 4th whn nt clr run and snatched up ins fnl f: nt rcvr* **5/2**[1]
0/0- **5** *4* **Silver Seeker (USA)**[345] 915 4-9-0 96 (p) RWinston 2 83
(ISemple) *s.i.s: sn rcvrd: rdn over 3f out: wknd over 2f out* **25/1**
4000 **6** *5* **Lakota Brave**[22] 837 10-9-0 83 (t) SDrowne 4 71
(MrsStefLiddiard) *bhd fnl 4f* **33/1**
0312 **7** *5* **Sergeant Slipper**[13] 936 7-9-0 47 (v) RFitzpatrick 8 58?
(CSmith) *s.s: outpcd* **100/1**

1m 32.45s (2.25) **Going Correction** +0.45s/f (Slow) **7** Ran SP% **105.9**
Speed ratings: **105,104,103,103,98 92,87**CSF £8.20 TOTE £2.80: £1.50, £2.70; EX 8.70.
**Owner** Jumeirah Racing **Bred** Cliveden Stud Ltd **Trained** Newmarket, Suffolk
■ Stewards Enquiry : N Pollard caution: careless riding

**FOCUS**
This looked a decent contest and the form could well stand the test of time, with a fine effort on paper from winner under a penalty.

**NOTEBOOK**
**Aleutian** just managed to maintain his unbeaten record on this switch to Fibresand. He did meet with some interference and was conceding 8lb to his rivals. His trainer thinks that the Polytrack suits him better.
**Cardinal Venture(IRE)**, returning after a three-month absence, was only beaten on the nod in his bid for a four-timer. He is one to consider when put back on turf.
**Rockets 'n Rollers(IRE)**, making his sand debut, was highly tried last year. The fact that he has not been seen after May on his first two seasons suggests he has been difficult to train.
**Queens Rhapsody** was not inconvenienced by the extra furlong but found himself hemmed in by the rider of the winner in the home straight.

## 1012 BET DIRECT NO Q ON 08000 93 66 93 MAIDEN STKS 1m 100y(F)
**4:40** (4:42) (D) 3-Y-O **£3,373** (£1,038; £519; £259) **Stalls Low**

Form RPR
3-52 **1** **Hawkit (USA)**[15] 907 3-9-0 69 DHolland 3 67
(JAOsborne) *prom: n.m.r and snatched up after 1f: rdn over 1f out: led ins fnl f: r.o wl* **2/1**[2]
53 **2** *2 ½* **Zuloago (USA)**[22] 835 3-8-9 ANicholls 10 57
(SLKeightley) *hdwy over 6f out: rdn to ld 2f out: hdd and no ex ins fnl f* **33/1**
4-22 **3** *5* **Bond Moonlight**[8] 969 3-9-0 64 FLynch 5 51
(BSmart) *prom: lost pl 6f out: rdn over 3f out: hdwy on outside over 2f out: wknd over 1f out* **9/2**[3]
0-3 **4** *2 ½* **Wonky Donkey**[15] 907 3-9-0 DaneO'Neill 6 46
(SCWilliams) *prom: led over 6f out: rdn and hdd 2f out: wknd over 1f out* **14/1**
00-2 **5** *hd* **Hsi Wang Mu (IRE)**[22] 835 3-8-9 68 IMongan 2 41
(RBrotherton) *prom: rdn over 3f out: wknd wl over 1f out* **12/1**
60-2 **6** *9* **Baker Of Oz**[16] 890 3-9-0 68 RHughes 1 27
(RHannon) *led: hdd over 6f out: rdn 3f out: wknd 2f out* **6/4**[1]
664 **7** *10* **Royaltea**[50] 593 3-8-9 51 JoannaBadger 7 1
(MsDeborahJEvans) *a bhd* **33/1**
00- **8** *1 ¾* **Royal Nite Owl**[131] 5911 3-8-7 JDO'Reilly(7) 8 2
(JO'Reilly) *plld hrd: prom tl wknd over 3f out* **50/1**
**9** *3* **Justice Jones** 3-8-11 LisaJones(3) 9 —
(JLSpearing) *s.i.s: a bhd* **16/1**
**10** *27* **Harford Bridge** 3-9-0 VSlattery 4 —
(RJBaker) *s.i.s: a bhd: t.o* **66/1**

1m 56.62s (5.62) **Going Correction** +0.45s/f (Slow) **10** Ran SP% **121.1**
Speed ratings: **89,86,81,79,78 69,59,58,55,28**CSF £75.21 TOTE £3.00: £1.10, £6.20, £2.50; EX 72.00.
**Owner** Paul J Dixon **Bred** Hargus Sexton And Sandra Sexton **Trained** Upper Lambourn, Berks

**FOCUS**
A weak maiden and a very moderate winning time, the winner providing the best guide to form.

**NOTEBOOK**
**Hawkit(USA)** finally broke his duck and being messed about going to the first turn could have been a blessing in disguise.
**Zuloago(USA)** was probably better suited to the extended mile but could not cope with the winner.
**Bond Moonlight** was presumably considered not to have stayed when catching a tartar over a mile and a have last time.
**Wonky Donkey** has yet to prove he gets this trip.
**Hsi Wang Mu(IRE)** had finished six lengths ahead of Zuloago over slightly further here last time.

## 1013 PRESS INTERACTIVE TO BET DIRECT H'CAP 7f (F)
**5:10** (5:11) (D) (0-80,80) 3-Y-O+ **£4,114** (£1,266; £633; £316) **Stalls High**

Form RPR
0-30 **1** **Just A Glimmer**[58] 544 4-9-10 **76** RHughes 6 91
(LGCottrell) *a.p: led on bit over 3f out: rdn 2f out: jst hld on* **11/1**
4-03 **2** *shd* **Middleton Grey**[8] 968 6-10-0 **80** (b) SWhitworth 5 95
(AGNewcombe) *s.i.s: hld up: hdwy over 4f out: hrd rdn and chsd wnr over 1f out: jst failed* **7/2**[1]
50-4 **3** *5* **Parker**[67] 448 7-8-13 **65** KDarley 7 68
(BPalling) *chsd ldrs: rdn over 3f out: one pce fnl 2f* **16/1**
042- **4** *¾* **Sarraaf (IRE)**[147] 5636 8-9-2 **68** RWinston 9 69
(ISemple) *led: rdn and hdd 3f out: wknd ins fnl f* **20/1**
504- **5** *¾* **Branston Tiger**[103] 5685 5-9-7 **73** DHolland 2 72
(JGGiven) *hld up mid-div: rdn and hdwy over 2f out: wknd ins fnl f* **10/1**
0030 **6** *2* **Arc El Ciel (ARG)**[9] 961 6-9-10 **76** (v) SDrowne 12 70
(MrsStefLiddiard) *hld up mid-div: no real prog fnl 2f* **10/1**
3461 **7** *1* **Warden Warren**[19] 866 6-9-5 **74** (b) BReilly(3) 11 65
(MrsCADunnett) *nvr trbld ldrs* **10/1**
22-4 **8** *shd* **Lawood (IRE)**[21] 846 4-9-4 **70** (b) NCallan 4 61
(KARyan) *s.i.s: hld up: hdwy on ins over 3f out: wknd fnl f* **12/1**
0-05 **9** *¾* **No Grouse**[28] 775 4-9-5 **71** PHanagan 8 60
(RAFahey) *hld up mid-div: rdn 3f out: no rspnse* **4/1**[2]
4220 **10** *1* **Yorker (USA)**[8] 967 6-9-1 **67** IMongan 3 54
(MsDeborahJEvans) *a bhd* **9/1**
1123 **11** *5* **Blakeset**[17] 886 9-9-8 **74** (v) EAhern 10 48
(TDBarron) *chsd ldr: rdn and wknd over 2f out: eased over 1f out* **7/1**[3]
-400 **12** *6* **Air Mail**[28] 775 7-9-10 **76** (p) ACulhane 1 35
(MrsNMacauley) *a bhd* **16/1**

1m 32.4s (2.20) **Going Correction** +0.45s/f (Slow) **12** Ran SP% **124.5**
Speed ratings: **105,104,99,98,97 95,94,93,93,91 86,79**CSF £51.87 CT £644.59 TOTE £20.10: £5.70, £1.70, £6.20; EX 100.60 Place 6 £139.92, Place 5 £27.93..
**Owner** Manor Farm Packers Ltd **Bred** Mrs P A Reditt And M J Reditt **Trained** Dulford, Devon

**FOCUS**
An ordinary handicap, but the runner-up is well-handicapped and first two did well to pull clear; and are likely to go up a fair bit for this, but both have good records over course and distance.

**NOTEBOOK**
**Just A Glimmer**, dropped 2lb, seems to save her best for this course and distance.
**Middleton Grey**, back up in distance, looked to have nicked it on the post but the photograph showed otherwise.
**Parker** stuck on to go past a couple of fading rivals in the closing stages.
**Sarraaf(IRE)** probably found a lack of a recent run beginning to tell in the closing stages.
**Branston Tiger** has yet to score beyond six and the fact the ground was on the slow side would not have helped.
**Blakeset** *Official explanation: jockey said gelding lost its action*
T/Plt: £191.30 to a £1 stake. Pool: £51,206.35. 195.40 winning tickets. T/Qpdt: £14.90 to a £1 stake. Pool: £3,445.50. 171.10 winning tickets. KH

# 995 LINGFIELD (L-H)
Sunday, March 14

**OFFICIAL GOING: Standard**
Wind: strong behind. Weather: rain

## 1015 LITTLEWOODS BET DIRECT MAIDEN STKS 1m (P)
**2:10** (2:11) (D) 3-Y-O **£3,311** (£946; £473) **Stalls High**

Form RPR
020- **1** **Count Dracula**[136] 5836 3-9-0 72 MartinDwyer 1 59+
(AMBalding) *prom: rdn 3f out: led 1f out: drvn out* **8/1**
363- **2** *½* **Catalini**[128] 5938 3-8-11 75 DCorby(3) 8 58+
(MRChannon) *hld up towards rr: rdn and hdwy 2f out: r.o fnl f: clsng at fin* **5/2**[2]
-534 **3** *1 ½* **Soul Provider (IRE)**[11] 956 3-8-9 56 DeanMcKeown 4 49
(PABlockley) *led: hrd rdn and hdd 1f out: one pce* **20/1**
3-00 **4** *shd* **Doctored**[6] 983 3-8-11 54 (b) BReilly(3) 6 54
(BAPearce) *a.p: hrd rdn and styd on same pce fnl 2f* **66/1**
**5** *1 ½* **Farnborough (USA)**[222] 3-9-0 NPollard 3 51
(DRCElsworth) *t.k.h in midfield: rdn to chse ldrs over 2f out: one pce appr fnl f* **25/1**
00- **6** *shd* **Moments I Treasure (USA)**[133] 5887 3-8-9 EAhern 5 45
(EALDunlop) *hld up in midfield: effrt 3f out: styd on same pce* **6/1**[3]
**7** *1* **Appolonious** 3-9-0 DaneO'Neill 2 48
(DRCElsworth) *s.s and lost 10l: bhd tl hdwy 2f out: shkn up and styd on: nvr nrr* **25/1**
04-3 **8** *7* **Wavertree Girl (IRE)**[14] 927 3-8-9 82 DHolland 10 27
(NPLittmoden) *plld hrd: chsd ldrs: hung rt 4f out: hrd rdn and btn 3f out* **5/4**[1]
05- **9** *nk* **Munaawesh (USA)**[183] 4883 3-9-0 ACulhane 7 31
(DWChapman) *chsd ldrs: squeezed out and dropped towards rr over 6f out: rdn and nt trble ldrs fnl 4f* **20/1**
06- **10** *1* **Artisticimpression (IRE)**[179] 4997 3-9-0 SDrowne 9 29
(EALDunlop) *dwlt: hdwy and prom after 2f: wknd 3f out* **14/1**
**11** *6* **Princess Bankes**[168] 3-8-9 68 MFenton 11 10
(MissGayKelleway) *mid-div: rdn 4f out: sn bhd* **20/1**

1m 42.1s (2.59) **Going Correction** +0.15s/f (Slow) **11** Ran SP% **128.5**
Speed ratings: **93,92,91,90,89 89,88,81,81,80 74**CSF £28.57 TOTE £13.20: £3.40, £1.40, £6.10; EX 37.20.
**Owner** Kennet Valley Thoroughbreds Iv **Bred** Mrs G Slater **Trained** Kingsclere, Hants

**FOCUS**
A poor maiden run at a moderate pace and the winning time was slow. The form is held down by the second and fourth.

**NOTEBOOK**
**Count Dracula**, off since October, appears to have improved in the meantime and saw the extra furlong out well. He may improve again, but the proximity of much lower-rated horses in third and fourth does not suggest his official mark is lenient.
**Catalini**, making his sand debut, was staying on well at the line and may benefit from a longer trip, but on the other hand with a couple of horses rated in the mid-50s uncomfortably close behind he almost certainly did not run to his official mark.
**Soul Provider(IRE)** appeared to run well using the official ratings of the front two as a guide, but she lacks scope and it is probably best to assess the merit of this performance through the fourth horse.
**Doctored** has made the frame a few times, but he is an exposed maiden who finished last of 15 off his official mark in a handicap last time. That demonstrates how ordinary this form is.
**Farnborough(USA)**, who ran just once for Andre Fabre last season, looks nothing out of the ordinary judged on this effort.
**Wavertree Girl(IRE)** again ran poorly and there were no excuses. She does not appear to have trained on, but it was possible to pick holes in her juvenile form anyway. *Official explanation: jockey said filly hung right*

## 1016 BET DIRECT ON SKY ACTIVE H'CAP 1m 4f (P)
**2:40** (2:42) (F) (0-55,55) 4-Y-O+ **£2,870** (£820; £410) **Stalls Low**

Form RPR
5244 **1** **Chocolate Boy (IRE)**[5] 995 5-8-10 46 oh1 (be) RLMoore 4 57
(GLMoore) *hld up in tch: led over 2f out: pushed clr: comf* **7/2**[1]
33 **2** *6* **Aveiro (IRE)**[9] 973 8-9-2 52 (v) MFenton 3 54
(MissGayKelleway) *prom: led 5f out: hdd and short of room over 2f out: swtchd rt over 1f out: kpt on to regain 2nd ins fnl f* **5/1**[3]
0302 **3** *1 ¼* **Orinocovsky (IRE)**[17] 901 5-9-5 55 DHolland 5 54
(NPLittmoden) *chsd ldrs: ev ch over 2f out: one pce* **7/2**[1]
-240 **4** *4* **Sterling Guarantee (USA)**[14] 931 6-9-3 53 (v[1]) ANicholls 6 46
(AndrewReid) *mid-div: effrt 3f out: nt pce to chal* **4/1**[2]
2003 **5** *5* **Noble Pursuit**[9] 972 7-9-3 53 DeanMcKeown 1 39
(PABlockley) *led tl 5f out: wknd over 2f out* **12/1**


The Form Book, Raceform Ltd, Compton, RG20 6NL

00-4 **6** *7* **Cadwallader (USA)**[19] 879 4-8-11 52 LPKeniry(3) 2 27
(PBurgoyne) *chsd ldrs: rdn 1/2-way: wknd 3f out* **25/1**
1005 **7** *1* **Itsonlyagame**[15] 914 4-8-10 48 (v[1]) JQuinn 8 22
(RIngram) *mid-div: hrd rdn 4f out: sn wknd* **11/2**
0-00 **8** *5* **Humdinger (IRE)**[11] 952 4-8-8 46 oh6 DarrenWilliams 7 12
(DShaw) *a bhd* **33/1**
6-00 **9** *dist* **Sholay (IRE)**[25] 821 5-9-2 52 KDarley 9 —
(PMitchell) *a bhd: no ch and eased 4f out* **14/1**

2m 33.5s (-0.48) **Going Correction** +0.15s/f (Slow) **9** Ran SP% **117.6**
**WFA** 4 from 5yo+ 2lb
Speed ratings: **107,103,101,99,95 91,90,87,**—CSF £21.73 CT £65.96 TOTE £4.00: £1.50, £1.60, £1.10; EX 17.20.
**Owner** Sigma Estates **Bred** Golden Vale Stud **Trained** Woodingdean, E Sussex

**FOCUS**
This was run at a decent pace and resulted in a smart winning time for the grade, with the winner unexposed at the trip.

**NOTEBOOK**
**Chocolate Boy(IRE)** was ridden with more confidence now that connections know he gets the trip and fairly bolted up. Given his trainer's record here it would be no surprise to see him win a few more under similar conditions.
**Aveiro(IRE)** is better known as a Fibresand performer and his rider rightly tried to make full use of his stamina by sending him on a fair way from home, but he had no answer to the finishing pace of the winner.
**Orinocovsky(IRE)** performed creditably, but does look better on Fibresand. *Official explanation: jockey said gelding hung left from three out*
**Sterling Guarantee(USA)** has not progressed from a promising return and again his lack of pace was a problem.
**Noble Pursuit**, on a long losing run, did not find being ridden positively over a much longer trip changing his fortunes.
**Sholay(IRE)** *Official explanation: jockey said gelding bled from the nose*

## 1017 NEW SITE @ BETDIRECT.CO.UK CLASSIFIED STKS 1m 2f (P)
3:10 (3:10) (F) 3-Y-O £2,898 (£828; £414) Stalls Low

Form RPR
1 **1** **Barathea Dreams (IRE)**[19] 871 3-8-12 60 MartinDwyer 1 68+
(JSMoore) *mde all: qcknd clr over 3f out: easily* **5/1**[3]
4046 **2** *7* **Garrigon**[10] 965 3-8-12 60 DHolland 6 52+
(NPLittmoden) *s.s: hld up and bhd: effrt over 2f out: r.o to take 2nd ins fnl f: nt rch wnr* **5/2**[2]
5224 **3** *3/4* **Princess Ismene**[10] 965 3-8-9 55 (b) DeanMcKeown 9 48
(PABlockley) *chsd ldrs: wnt 2nd 3f out tl ins fnl f: no ch w wnr* **10/1**
46-0 **4** *3/4* **Foot Fault (IRE)**[71] 420 3-8-9 57 WRyan 7 46
(NACallaghan) *hld up in rr: shkn up and styd on fnl 2f: nvr nrr* **25/1**
-003 **5** *3/4* **Almost Welcome**[19] 871 3-8-12 50 PDoe 5 48
(SDow) *chsd wnr tl 3f out: one pce* **20/1**
0-00 **6** *1/2* **Trompe L'Oeil (IRE)**[25] 822 3-8-6 60 TPQueally(3) 3 44
(AndrewReid) *in tch: hrd rdn 3f out: one pce* **20/1**
00-0 **7** *7* **Foxilla (IRE)**[15] 916 3-8-9 57 DaneO'Neill 2 32
(DRCElsworth) *prom 7f* **16/1**
-062 **8** *1 3/4* **Jackie Kiely**[25] 822 3-8-12 59 KDarley 10 31
(TGMills) *in tch: rdn over 4f out: drvn to chse ldrs 3f out: wknd 2f out* **7/4**[1]
0500 **9** *1* **Casantella**[10] 965 3-8-9 40 ACulhane 4 27
(MJPolglase) *bhd fnl 3f* **66/1**
4306 **10** *5* **Tonto (FR)**[15] 913 3-8-12 58 (p) OUrbina 8 21
(MissDMountain) *a towards rr: rdn and n.d fnl 3f* **12/1**

2m 10.13s (2.74) **Going Correction** +0.15s/f (Slow) **10** Ran SP% **119.1**
Speed ratings: **95,89,88,88,87 87,81,80,79,75**CSF £17.53 TOTE £3.50: £2.70, £2.10, £3.30; EX 12.10.
**Owner** Mrs Fitri Hay **Bred** Shadwell Estate Company Limited **Trained** East Garston, Berks

**FOCUS**
An impressive all-the-way winner and an improved form performance, although he was allowed to dictate and the winning time was modest, so the form may be misleading.

**NOTEBOOK**
**Barathea Dreams(IRE)**, as when making a winning debut over course and distance last month, was given a positive ride and won this in great style. Obviously the Handicapper had little to go on and this result suggests a mark of 60 was extremely lenient. He is beginning to look quite an interesting prospect.
**Garrigon**, stepping up in trip to help offset his habitual slow starting, stayed on to win the separate race for second and seemed to see out the distance, but he is still to win after 16 attempts.
**Princess Ismene** is basically a plater, but ran with credit over the longest trip she has tried.
**Foot Fault(IRE)**, stepping up three furlongs in trip, ran as though another step up would not hurt.
**Almost Welcome**, beaten just over two lengths by Barathea Dreams here last time, tried to keep tabs on him for much of the way, but was quickly left behind which just goes to show how much the winner has improved.
**Jackie Kiely** admittedly had the worst of the draw, but bearing in mind his progressive profile before today this was disappointing.

## 1018 £10 FREE BET @ BET DIRECT H'CAP 6f (P)
3:40 (3:42) (F) (0-52,54) 3-Y-O+ £2,926 (£836; £418) Stalls Low

Form RPR
0004 **1** **Kilmeena Star**[5] 998 6-9-0 46 oh11 (b[1]) RLMoore 10 56
(JCFox) *prom: led 1f out: drvn out* **25/1**
-000 **2** *hd* **Tree Roofer**[6] 987 5-8-11 46 oh1 TPQueally(3) 3 55
(NPLittmoden) *hld up towards rr: hdwy over 1f out: ev ch ins fnl f: r.o* **14/1**
0065 **3** *nk* **Attorney**[6] 990 6-9-0 46 oh1 (v) DHolland 11 54
(DShaw) *mid-div: effrt over 2f out: ev ch ins fnl f: r.o* **11/1**
6211 **4** *1* **Long Weekend (IRE)**[5] 1000 6-9-8 54 6ex (v) DarrenWilliams 2 59
(DShaw) *s.s: hld up and bhd: edgd rt and effrt over 2f out: gd hdwy to press ldrs over 1f out: kpt on* **5/1**[2]
0206 **5** *2 1/2* **River Days (IRE)**[13] 941 6-9-3 49 (vt) MFenton 5 47
(MissGayKelleway) *led tl 1f out: no ex* **14/1**
6-51 **6** *3/4* **Doctor Dennis (IRE)**[14] 930 7-9-5 51 (b) NPollard 8 46
(JPearce) *hmpd and dropped to rr sn after s: effrt whn hmpd 3f out and bmpd over 2f out: nvr rchd ldrs* **9/2**[1]
-065 **7** *1* **Marabar**[28] 782 6-9-6 52 (b[1]) ACulhane 4 44
(DWChapman) *chsd ldrs: rdn over 2f out: sn outpcd* **12/1**
2002 **8** *1 1/4* **Tripti (IRE)**[18] 884 4-9-1 47 MartinDwyer 12 36
(JJBridger) *w ldrs tl wknd over 1f out* **8/1**
6-44 **9** *2* **Inching**[17] 896 4-9-3 49 (p) EAhern 7 32
(RMHCowell) *dwlt: towards rr: brief effrt 2f out: n.d* **5/1**[2]
003 **10** *2* **Pips Song (IRE)**[6] 987 9-8-13 48 LisaJones(3) 13 25
(PWHiatt) *prom 4f* **15/2**[3]
5013 **11** *3* **Sabana (IRE)**[14] 936 6-9-4 50 (b) PFitzsimons 6 18
(JMBradley) *mid-div: wknd 3f out: rr gp and btn whn bmpd over 2f out* **9/1**

0000 **12** *2 1/2* **Finger Of Fate**[17] 897 4-9-0 46 oh1 (b) DeanMcKeown 9 6
(MJPolglase) *s.i.s: towards rr: brief effrt on outside 3f out: wkng whn bmpd over 2f out* **25/1**

1m 12.64s (-0.28) **Going Correction** +0.15s/f (Slow) **12** Ran SP% **121.4**
Speed ratings: **107,106,106,105,101 100,99,97,95,92 88,85**CSF £346.31 CT £4099.18 TOTE £39.30: £9.90, £4.70, £3.00; EX 243.10.
**Owner** Mrs J A Cleary **Bred** Mrs J A Cleary **Trained** Collingbourne Ducis, Wilts
■ Stewards Enquiry : N Pollard one-day ban: careless riding (Mar 25)
R L Moore one-day ban: failed to keep straight from stalls (Mar 25); further one-day ban: careless riding (Mar 26)
Darren Williams one-day ban: careless riding (Mar 25)

**FOCUS**
A poor race run at a good pace in which, the winner apart, the principals came from behind. However, the form is unlikely to work out.

**NOTEBOOK**
**Kilmeena Star**, who showed signs of a return to form last time, was helped by the first-time blinkers and, given a fine ride, gained his first win on the Flat. This was a modest contest and it remains to be seen if the blinkers have the same effect next time. *Official explanation: jockey said horse hung left*
**Tree Roofer** looked slightly unlucky, as his rider had to sit still for a couple of strides halfway up the straight and, once in the clear, he was closing all the way to the line. Off his current mark he could well gain compensation.
**Attorney**, who has never won on this surface, was always in the right place but could not find an extra gear late on. A return to Fibresand with the eyeshield refitted may be the answer.
**Long Weekend(IRE)** missed the break and then made a lot of ground to challenge before flattening out. Nevertheless this was a fair effort in better company under a penalty.
**River Days(IRE)** set a good gallop until unsurprisingly tiring in the closing stages. She has slipped to a decent mark and a return to the minimum trip on Fibresand will be in her favour.
**Doctor Dennis(IRE)** was better off with the fourth having beaten him over course and distance two weeks previously, but he did not get the best of runs and never figured.

## 1019 PRESS INTERACTIVE TO BET DIRECT H'CAP 1m (P)
4:10 (4:12) (F) (0-52,52) 3-Y-O+ £2,919 (£834; £417) Stalls High

Form RPR
00-0 **1** **Marnie**[18] 888 7-9-3 47 JQuinn 9 55
(JAkehurst) *hdwy 2f out: jnd ldr 1f out: drvn to ld on line* **10/1**
000- **2** *shd* **Masafi (IRE)**[125] 5968 3-8-4 52 JMackay 10 60
(SirMarkPrescott) *chsd ldrs: slt ld over 1f out: hrd rdn and rn green fnl f: r.o: hdd on line* **7/4**[1]
2120 **3** *3/4* **Indian Blaze**[6] 988 10-9-5 52 TPQueally(3) 5 58
(AndrewReid) *hld up: hdwy to press ldrs 3f out: n.m.r and swtchd rt over 1f out: r.o* **9/1**
3406 **4** *hd* **My Lilli (IRE)**[14] 931 4-9-5 49 DHolland 6 55
(PMitchell) *led 1f: prom: hrd rdn over 1f out: kpt on* **8/1**[3]
2013 **5** *2 1/2* **Miss Peaches**[14] 933 6-8-10 47 KristinStubbs(7) 3 47
(GGMargarson) *hld up in midfield: sme hdwy over 1f out: nvr in chalng position* **10/1**
3002 **6** *5* **Kumakawa**[11] 952 6-8-12 49 (b) LiamJones(7) 7 38
(EAWheeler) *outpcd and bhd: nvr rchd ldrs* **20/1**
-350 **7** *1/2* **Larad (IRE)**[19] 873 3-8-2 50 (b) DKinsella 2 38
(JSMoore) *disp ld after 1f: led 2f out tl wknd over 1f out* **25/1**
3154 **8** *3/4* **Dancing King (IRE)**[9] 970 8-8-12 49 PMakin(7) 1 35
(PWHiatt) *disp ld after 1f tl 2f out: wknd over 1f out* **20/1**
000- **9** *1/2* **Introduction**[99] 6129 3-7-10 47 LisaJones(3) 8 32
(WJMusson) *outpcd and bhd: nvr trbld ldrs* **25/1**
-404 **10** *shd* **Coppington Flyer (IRE)**[14] 929 4-9-3 47 OUrbina 11 31
(BWDuke) *wd: t.k.h: hdwy 2f out: wknd over 1f out* **12/1**
0-02 **11** *hd* **Wind Chime (IRE)**[14] 929 7-9-7 51 SWhitworth 12 35
(AGNewcombe) *chsd ldrs to 1/2-way* **3/1**[2]
6006 **12** *3/4* **Never Cried Wolf**[19] 873 3-8-4 52 (p) MartinDwyer 4 34
(DRCElsworth) *bhd fnl 3f* **25/1**

1m 41.56s (2.05) **Going Correction** +0.15s/f (Slow) **12** Ran SP% **129.4**
**WFA** 3 from 4yo+ 18lb
Speed ratings: **95,94,94,93,91 86,85,85,84,84 84,83**CSF £28.40 CT £177.24 TOTE £10.30: £3.20, £1.60, £2.70; EX 45.00.
**Owner** The Grass Is Greener Partnership **Bred** Mrs Wendy Jacqueline Muir **Trained** Epsom, Surrey

**FOCUS**
A moderate handicap run at a steady pace. The winner was well in on old form, so all credit to the runner-up.

**NOTEBOOK**
**Marnie**, who acts on this track, has dropped to a reasonable mark having not won since June 2002. She was given a good ride but only got there on the nod.
**Masafi(IRE)**, making his Polytrack debut, was made favourite on the strength of his connections' record with similar types. He was a little keen early and then showed signs of immaturity, but looked unlucky to get touched off and should have few problems winning races.
**Indian Blaze** travelled well on the heels of the leaders but did not get the best of runs in the straight and was finishing best of all. He is running well at present.
**My Lilli(IRE)**, dropping back in trip, ran well but did not have the pace in the closing stages. She is capable of winning in banded grade, but this performance will not help her rating to fall to that level.
**Wind Chime(IRE)** was prominent early but dropped out tamely.

## 1020 BET DIRECT DAILY SPECIAL OFFERS H'CAP 7f (P)
4:40 (4:42) (F) (0-52,51) 3-Y-O+ £2,954 (£844; £422) Stalls Low

Form RPR
0-00 **1** **Loch Laird**[53] 573 9-9-3 47 GBaker 3 53
(MMadgwick) *towards rr: drvn along over 2f out: hdwy over 1f out: styd on to ld nr fin* **14/1**
5322 **2** *shd* **Sonderborg**[10] 965 3-8-2 51 (be) LisaJones(3) 11 57
(GLMoore) *mid-div: hdwy over 1f out: ev ch fnl 100 yds: kpt on* **11/2**[2]
0-01 **3** *nk* **Dial Square**[40] 659 3-7-13 45 (b) CCatlin 10 50
(PHowling) *chsd ldrs: led over 2f out: hrd rdn fnl f: hdd nr fin* **10/1**
-025 **4** *nk* **Single Track Mind**[5] 999 6-9-0 44 oh4 MartinDwyer 2 48+
(JRBoyle) *dwlt: bhd: gd hdwy to chse ldrs whn nt clr run and snatched up 1f out: gng on at fin* **10/1**
-260 **5** *1/2* **Robin Sharp**[15] 918 6-9-2 46 (v) JQuinn 8 49
(JAkehurst) *drvn to ld: hrd rdn and hdd over 2f out: styd on same pce fnl f* **25/1**
-034 **6** *shd* **Ballare (IRE)**[14] 929 5-9-1 45 (v[1]) OUrbina 12 47
(BobJones) *dwlt: hld up in midfield: hdwy over 2f out: nt qckn fnl f* **12/1**
3223 **7** *nk* **Blakeseven**[15] 918 4-9-4 48 MFenton 4 50
(WJMusson) *towards rr: wd and hdwy over 1f out: hrd rdn: kpt on* **4/1**[1]
3045 **8** *3/4* **Balerno**[6] 988 5-9-6 50 KDarley 1 50
(RIngram) *mid-div whn hmpd on rail after 2f: rdn and rallied over 1f out: nt pce to chal* **7/1**
656- **9** *nk* **Fayr Firenze (IRE)**[114] 6041 3-8-3 49 (b) SRighton 5 48
(MFHarris) *plld hrd: in tch: rdn 2f out: no imp* **25/1**

6062 **10** *1* **Social Contract**[12] 946 7-9-1 45 (v) JFEgan 13 41
(SDow) *chsd ldrs 5f* **7/1**

3003 **11** *nk* **The Gay Fox**[6] 993 10-9-1 45 (bt) SCarson 14 40
(BGPowell) *dwlt: hld up and bhd: rdn over 2f out: nvr rchd ldrs* **6/1**[3]

0003 **12** *½* **Geespot**[5] 999 5-8-9 44 oh4 JFMcDonald(5) 7 38
(DJSFfrenchDavis) *in tch: rdn and btn over 2f out* **16/1**

6141 **13** *1* **Redoubtable (USA)**[12] 946 13-9-5 49 ACulhane 9 40
(DWChapman) *chsd ldrs tl wknd over 1f out* **8/1**

-300 **14** *¾* **Flame Princess**[5] 999 4-8-7 44 oh4 KarenPeippo(7) 15 33
(JRBoyle) *a towards rr: n.d fnl 3f* **50/1**

2416 **15** *nk* **Fraamtastic**[11] 953 7-8-11 44 oh4 (b[1]) BReilly(3) 6 32
(BAPearce) *prom tl wknd over 1f out* **20/1**

1m 26.76s (0.76) **Going Correction** +0.15s/f (Slow)
**WFA** 3 from 4yo+ 16lb **15** Ran SP% **138.6**
Speed ratings: **101,100,100,100,99 99,99,98,97,96 96,95,94,93,93**CSF £98.58 CT £868.85 TOTE £14.30: £7.10, £1.80, £5.50; EX 320.60 Place 6 £594.79, Place 5 £216.75.
**Owner** Miss E M L Coller **Bred** Miss E M L Coller **Trained** Denmead, Hants

**FOCUS**
A moderate handicap, little better than a seller, producing a blanket finish and a few hard-luck stories.

**NOTEBOOK**
**Loch Laird** gained his first win on this surface at only the fifth attempt. He found a big gap opening up on the inside and did just enough to take advantage.
**Sonderborg**, who has responded well to the fitting of the eyeshield and blinkers, came with a strong late run and only just failed. She is running well at present and should be able to get off the mark.
**Dial Square**, another who has improved for the fitting of headgear, probably did too much too soon and was collared late on. His best chance of victory may be if he reappears in banded company before he is reassessed.
**Single Track Mind** has been running well in plating company, and was another who was unlucky in running in this slightly better-class race. He looks one to kep in mind when returned to sellers.
**Robin Sharp** had to work hard to get to the front, and in the circumstances did well to finish where he did.
**Ballare(IRE)**, in a visor for the first time, was ridden to challenge turning in but failed to pick up.
**Blakeseven**, well backed, ran on from well back but never landed a blow.
**Fraamtastic** *Official explanation: jockey said mare hung right*
T/Plt: £1,382.80 to a £1 stake. Pool: £43,284.85. 22.85 winning tickets. T/Qpdt: £197.50 to a £1 stake. Pool: £2,589.90. 9.70 winning tickets. LM

# 952 SOUTHWELL (L-H)

Sunday, March 14

**OFFICIAL GOING: Standard to slow**
The going was described as slow and the bias favoured the horses coming up the centre in the home straight.
Wind: str hlf against Weather: changeable, hvy shower between races 2 and 3

## 1021 NEW SITE AT BETDIRECT.CO.UK BANDED STKS 7f (F)
**2:20** (2:20) (H) 3-Y-0+ **£1,459** (£417; £208) **Stalls** Low

Form RPR

-111 **1** **Smart Scot**[14] 934 5-9-2 45 (p) MSavage(5) 7 57
(BPJBaugh) *trckd ldrs: led 2f out: hung bdly lft: rdn wl clr 1f out: eased towards fin* **10/11**[1]

0053 **2** *8* **Neutral Night (IRE)**[14] 934 4-9-7 40 (v) IMongan 6 37
(RBrotherton) *chsd ldrs: kpt on fnl 2f: no ch w wnr* **13/2**[3]

406U **3** *1¼* **Brilliantrio**[34] 719 6-9-7 40 LVickers 1 34
(MCChapman) *chsd ldrs: led 4f out tl 2f out: one pce* **14/1**

5222 **4** *hd* **Jessie**[14] 934 5-9-7 40 (t) KimTinkler 8 33
(DonEnricoIncisa) *s.i.s: sme hdwy on outside over 4f out: rdn and outpcd over 2f out: kpt on fnl f* **7/2**[2]

0-00 **5** *1¼* **True Holly**[12] 951 4-9-7 35 JDSmith 4 30
(SKirk) *chsd ldrs: outpcd over 2f out: hung lft and kpt on fnl f* **25/1**

0-40 **6** *12* **Lively Felix**[41] 658 7-9-0 40 BSwarbrick(7) 5 —
(DGBridgwater) *lost pl over 4f out: sn bhd* **25/1**

-306 **7** *2* **Xsynna**[20] 859 8-9-7 40 (p) JTate 3 —
(TTClement) *led tl 4f out: lost pl over 2f out: sn bhd* **16/1**

30-0 **8** *½* **Alastair Smellie**[19] 876 8-9-7 40 PMcCabe 2 —
(SLKeightley) *lost pl over 4f out: sn bhd* **14/1**

1m 33.7s (2.90) **Going Correction** +0.275s/f (Slow) **8** Ran SP% **114.8**
Speed ratings: **94,84,83,83,81 68,65,65**CSF £7.51 TOTE £1.60: £1.10, £2.60, £3.30; EX 6.80.
**Owner** S Day **Bred** Lord Halifax **Trained** Audley, Staffs

**FOCUS**
An above-average effort from the winner who looks bettrer than banded grade.

**NOTEBOOK**
**Smart Scot**, who got into this 0-40 race through the back door, made it four from four this year despite again hanging violently. There may be one more chance for him here before he is rated out of it.
**Neutral Night(IRE)**, who had something to find with both the winner and Jessie on their running here last time, has now been placed four times from 26 starts.
**Brilliantrio**, as usual mounted on the track and taken early to post, behaved herself at the start this time.
**Jessie**, meeting the winner on the same terms, missed the break slightly and never looked happy faced with a strong, almost head-on wind.

## 1022 BETDIRECT.CO.UK MEDIAN AUCTION MAIDEN STKS 1m (F)
**2:50** (2:51) (H) 3-5-Y-0 **£1,463** (£418; £209) **Stalls** Low

Form RPR

05-6 **1** **Hold The Line**[29] 769 3-8-7 65 (p) GDuffield 5 62
(WGMTurner) *chsd ldrs: led 2f out: drew clr ins last* **4/1**[3]

406- **2** *3* **Caspian Dusk**[264] 2654 3-8-0 53 CHaddon(7) 10 56
(WGMTurner) *chsd ldrs: outpcd over 4f out: styd on fnl 2f: tk 2nd last 75yds* **33/1**

3023 **3** *1½* **Angelo's Pride**[19] 877 3-8-7 59 SWKelly 3 53
(JAOsborne) *led 1f: chsd ldrs: hung lft and led over 2f out: sn hdd: kpt on same pce* **7/2**[2]

55-5 **4** *11* **Jacob (IRE)**[11] 956 3-8-7 60 NCallan 11 31
(PABlockley) *chsd ldrs: outpcd over 2f out: n.d after* **4/1**[3]

0 **5** *2½* **Bulberry Hill**[16] 907 3-8-7 DRMcCabe 1 26
(MGQuinlan) *w ldr: led after 1f tl over 2f out: wknd over 1f out* **20/1**

50-0 **6** *9* **Mr Dip**[12] 948 4-9-11 57 IMongan 4 8
(AWCarroll) *s.i.s: nvr a factor* **16/1**

**7** *shd* **Mitzi Caspar** 3-8-2 AMackay 7 3
(PLGilligan) *s.s: sme hdwy over 4f out: wknd over 2f out* **33/1**

3224 **8** *5* **Kustom Kit For Her**[5] 997 4-9-6 45 JBramhill 9 —
(SRBowring) *chsd ldrs: lost pl over 2f out* **14/1**

032- **9** *3½* **Chariot (IRE)**[92] 6173 3-8-7 64 DSweeney 2 —
(MRBosley) *chsd ldrs: sn drvn along: outpcd and lost pl over 4f out* **10/3**[1]

**10** *5* **Baroque** 3-8-7 RFitzpatrick 12 —
(CSmith) *s.i.s: t.o 4f out* **33/1**

**11** *9* **Golnessa** 3-8-2 JoannaBadger 6 —
(MrsNMacauley) *s.i.s: t.o 4f out* **28/1**

0- **12** *2* **Billy Whistler**[138] 5818 3-8-7 (b[1]) JEdmunds 8 —
(JBalding) *sn bhd: wl t.o 4f out* **50/1**

1m 49.64s (5.04) **Going Correction** +0.275s/f (Slow)
**WFA** 3 from 4yo 18lb **12** Ran SP% **116.8**
Speed ratings: **85,82,80,69,67 58,57,52,49,44 35,33**CSF £138.85 TOTE £5.50: £1.80, £12.80, £2.00; EX 85.70.
**Owner** Dermot Gascoyne and Gary Dawkins **Bred** Joseph Hogan **Trained** Sigwells, Somerset

**FOCUS**
A very moderate time, even for this grade, and the winner is the best guide to the form.

**NOTEBOOK**
**Hold The Line**, dropped back in trip, settled better and, after looking to hang fire in front, was persuaded to pull clear inside the last. 'Gentleman George', 57, now needs 65 more winners to overtake Edward Hide's 2,593 British wins.
**Caspian Dusk**, stablemate of the winner, was last seen out in a claimer at Brighton in June. He ran as if likely to appreciate a stiffer test.
**Angelo's Pride** looked somewhat reluctant in front and in the end was even run out of second spot.
**Jacob(IRE)**, having his second outing in just over a week after being absent since last May, ran as if this trip was much too sharp.
**Bulberry Hill**, having only his second start, knew his job this time but in the end was beaten a total of 18 lengths.
**Chariot(IRE)**, having his first outing for three months, never went a yard. *Official explanation: trainer said colt was never travelling*

## 1023 BET IN RUNNING @ BETDIRECT.CO.UK BANDED STKS 1m 6f (F)
**3:20** (3:21) (H) 4-Y-0+ **£1,645** (£470; £235) **Stalls** Low

Form RPR

0533 **1** **Stravmour**[6] 992 8-9-2 45 DaleGibson 8 52
(RHollinshead) *t.k.h: hdwy to chse ldrs 9f out: led over 1f out: kpt on wl* **10/3**[2]

-623 **2** *1¼* **Next Flight (IRE)**[19] 878 5-9-2 40 RFitzpatrick 6 50
(REBarr) *chsd ldrs: effrt over 4f out: nt qckn fnl f* **9/1**[3]

0-20 **3** *nk* **Colonnade**[31] 750 5-9-2 40 KDalgleish 5 50
(CGrant) *s.i.s: hdwy over 4f out: sn chsng ldrs: edgd lft 1f out: kpt on same pce* **16/1**

2143 **4** *4* **Paddy Mul**[19] 880 7-9-2 40 (t) DRMcCabe 9 45
(WStorey) *sn chsng ldrs: led 3f out: hdd over 1f out: wknd towards fin* **10/1**

-000 **5** *9* **Muraqeb**[14] 931 4-8-12 45 IMongan 4 33
(MrsBarbaraWaring) *t.k.h: trckd ldrs: drvn along 6f out: wknd 1f out: eased nr fin* **28/1**

5-40 **6** *8* **Berkeley Heights**[54] 570 4-8-12 40 NCallan 3 23
(MrsJCandlish) *trckd ldr: led over 5f out tl 3f out: lost pl over 1f out* **16/1**

20-0 **7** *5* **Bergamo**[4] 716 8-9-2 45 (b) RWinston 2 16
(BEllison) *in rr: sn drvn along: nvr a factor* **9/1**[3]

5301 **8** *6* **East Cape**[19] 880 7-9-2 45 KimTinkler 7 8
(DonEnricoIncisa) *chsd ldrs: drvn along 6f out: sn lost pl* **13/8**[1]

0-44 **9** *21* **Known Maneuver (USA)**[24] 829 6-9-2 40 GDuffield 1 —
(MCChapman) *led tl over 5f out: sn lost pl and bhd: virtually p.u* **11/1**

3m 14.0s (4.40) **Going Correction** +0.275s/f (Slow)
**WFA** 4 from 5yo+ 4lb **9** Ran SP% **113.8**
Speed ratings: **98,97,97,94,89 85,82,78,66**CSF £32.80 TOTE £4.20: £1.80, £2.30, £3.50; EX 26.90.
**Owner** E Bennion **Bred** E Bennion **Trained** Upper Longdon, Staffs

**FOCUS**
An average race for the grade and the time was moderate.

**NOTEBOOK**
**Stravmour** pulled like a train for the first half of the contest. He then had to be vigorously rousted along but in the end was firmly in command. His rider deserves full marks.
**Next Flight(IRE)** keeps running well but the fact remains that he has yet to get his head in front from 19 starts now.
**Colonnade**, dropping back slightly in trip, ran a lot better.
**Paddy Mul** took it up travelling best but in the end he did not truly see it out.
**East Cape** had an off-day, possibly resenting the strong wind and the wet track after a downpour, and this is best overlooked. *Official explanation: trainer's representative had no explanation for the poor form shown*

## 1024 BETDIRECT.CO.UK NEW SITE BANDED STKS 1m (F)
**3:50** (3:50) (H) 3-Y-0+ **£1,645** (£470; £235) **Stalls** Low

Form RPR

3345 **1** **Kenny The Truth (IRE)**[6] 989 5-9-7 40 (t) IMongan 9 50
(MrsJCandlish) *trckd ldrs on outer: led over 2f out: kpt on wl: eased nr fin* **10/1**

1443 **2** *3½* **Printsmith (IRE)**[14] 939 7-9-7 45 JBramhill 10 43
(JRNorton) *chsd ldrs: hrd rdn and wnt 2nd over 2f out: kpt on: no imp* **8/1**

0-11 **3** *5* **Mrs Cube**[6] 994 5-9-13 45 RWinston 1 39
(PHowling) *chsd ldrs: rdn over 4f out: edgd lftover 1f out: one pce* **5/2**[1]

-005 **4** *1½* **Santa Catalina (IRE)**[11] 953 5-9-2 45 TEaves(5) 11 30
(CADwyer) *chsd ldrs: one pce fnl 2f* **18/1**

6452 **5** *hd* **Red Delirium**[14] 939 8-9-2 50 (b) DNolan(5) 5 30
(PABlockley) *chsd ldrs: rdn over 4f out: one pce fnl 2f* **3/1**[2]

-504 **6** *8* **Turftanzer (GER)**[19] 878 5-9-7 40 (t) KimTinkler 6 14
(DonEnricoIncisa) *led tl over 2f out: wknd over 1f out* **10/1**

063- **7** *7* **The Mog**[240] 563 5-9-7 45 (bt) JoannaBadger 3 —
(MissMERowland) *s.i.s: lost pl over 4f out: sn bhd* **40/1**

200- **8** *1½* **Wilheheckaslike**[141] 5746 3-8-4 45 ow1 (v) DRMcCabe 7 —
(WStorey) *trckd ldrs: lost pl over 4f out: sn bhd* **25/1**

00-0 **9** *dist* **Eternal Dancer (USA)**[23] 835 3-8-3 45 (b[1]) JFanning 2 —
(MJohnston) *s.i.s: lost pl over 4f out: sn bhd: t.o* **16/1**

1533 **10** *10* **Gracious Air (USA)**[6] 989 6-9-0 45 (b) DFentiman(7) 8 —
(JRWeymes) *trckd ldrs on outer: lost pl over 4f out: sn bhd: t.o* **6/1**[3]

1m 46.94s (2.34) **Going Correction** +0.275s/f (Slow)
**WFA** 3 from 4yo+ 18lb **10** Ran SP% **114.6**
Speed ratings: **99,95,90,89,88 80,73,72,—,—**CSF £85.86 TOTE £11.70: £3.10, £2.90, £1.10; EX 36.90.
**Owner** S A Mace & A P Simmill **Bred** P J Fortune **Trained** Basford, Staffs

**FOCUS**
This was probably an average race despite the extended distances.

**NOTEBOOK**
**Kenny The Truth(IRE)**, with Ian Mongan in the saddle this time, settled better and in the end won easing down, giving his trainer her first Flat success.

**Printsmith(IRE)** is in good form so far this year but, despite a punishing ride, she was never going to finish better than second best.
**Mrs Cube**, with a 6lb penalty, found this much too tough and she seems better suited by Wolverhampton than else where.
**Santa Catalina(IRE)** is in better form for her new yard but she is still a maiden after 19 attempts now.
**Red Delirium**, having his second outing for his new trainer, was the first to come under serious pressure.

## 1025 BETDIRECT.CO.UK (S) STKS 6f (F)
4:20 (4:21) (H) 3-Y-O+ **£1,305** (£373; £186) **Stalls** Low

Form RPR
00-0 **1** **King Nicholas (USA)**[11] [952] 5-8-12 51....................(tp) MLawson(7) 7 63
(JParkes) *chsd ldrs: outpcd over 4f out: hdwy 2f out: led jst ins fnl f: r.o* **20/1**
-256 **2** *2* **Speedfit Free (IRE)**[27] [799] 7-9-5 51..............................(v) RWinston 5 57
(ISemple) *trckd ldrs: led over 2f out: edgd lft and hdd jst ins fnl f: no ex* **2/1**[1]
40-5 **3** *3 1/2* **Dusty Wugg (IRE)**[40] [670] 5-8-11 45..............................(p) ABeech(3) 4 42
(ADickman) *in rr: hdwy 3f out: styd on same pce fnl 2f* **14/1**
3136 **4** *hd* **Legalis (USA)**[6] [993] 6-9-10 56..............................(b) NCallan 9 51
(KARyan) *chsd ldrs: one pce fnl 2f* **5/2**[2]
4650 **5** *6* **Jalouhar**[14] [928] 4-9-5 52.............................. MSavage(5) 8 33
(BPJBaugh) *w ldrs: wknd over 1f out* **8/1**
0646 **6** *2 1/2* **Amanda's Lad (IRE)**[11] [954] 4-8-12 45.................... AndrewWebb(7) 3 20
(MCChapman) *led tl over 2f out: lost pl over 1f out* **14/1**
-325 **7** *1* **Spy Master**[14] [936] 6-9-5 40..............................(bt) GDuffield 2 17
(JParkes) *s.i.s: sn chsng ldrs: lost pl over 1f out* **8/1**
-230 **8** *2* **Emperor Cat (IRE)**[11] [958] 3-8-9 54 ow4....................(v[1]) DNolan(5) 10 20
(PABlockley) *chsd ldrs on wd outside: lost pl over 1f out* **7/1**[3]
-300 **9** *6* **Philly Dee**[39] [678] 3-7-9 45.............................. DFox(5) 1 —
(NEBerry) *in rr: lost pl over 3f out: sn bhd* **20/1**
00 **10** *12* **Royal Shepley**[11] [956] 3-8-0 .............................. JBramhill 6 —
(JBalding) *w ldrs: wknd 2f out: sn bhd* **66/1**

1m 18.57s (1.77) **Going Correction** +0.275s/f (Slow)
**WFA** 3 from 4yo+ 14lb **10** Ran SP% **121.0**
Speed ratings: **99,96,91,91,83 80,78,76,68,52**CSF £61.40 TOTE £9.90: £2.20, £1.40, £4.00; EX 235.70.There was no bid for the winner.
**Owner** M Wormald **Bred** Calumet Farm **Trained** Upper Helmsley, N Yorks

**FOCUS**
A poor seller, with the runner-up the key to the form, although it remains to be seen if they form is reliable.

**NOTEBOOK**
**King Nicholas(USA)**, having his second outing in a just over a week after six months on the sidelines, sported cheekpieces for the first time. Sticking on after getting outpaced, in the end he won going away. Seven furlongs will suit him even better.
**Speedfit Free(IRE)**, in a visor this time, went for home but in the end he was readily run down by the winner. He seems to prefer Wolverhampton.
**Dusty Wugg(IRE)**, having her first outing for six weeks, stayed on from an unpromising position to make it four places from 21 starts.
**Legalis(USA)**, who is on the downgrade, found himself rather marooned on the outer and he didn't look to be putting it all in.
**Jalouhar** again had the cheekpieces left off and was well below his best.

## 1026 LITTLEWOODS BET DIRECT BANDED STKS 1m 3f (F)
4:50 (4:51) (H) 4-Y-0+ **£1,309** (£374; £187) **Stalls** Low

Form RPR
1625 **1** **Dash Of Magic**[35] [715] 6-9-1 35.............................. MTebbutt 13 45
(JHetherton) *hdwy on wd outside 7f out: sn chsng ldrs: led over 1f out: all out* **5/1**[2]
-221 **2** *hd* **The Beduth Navi**[6] [991] 4-9-1 35.............................. DNolan(5) 6 51
(DGBridgwater) *chsd ldrs: led over 4f out: hdd over 1f out: hrd rdn and rallied ins last: jst hld* **11/4**[1]
3-53 **3** *2 1/2* **Samar Qand**[28] [783] 5-8-8 35..............................(t) MHalford(7) 7 41
(JulianPoulton) *sn chsng ldrs: sn drvn along: kpt on wl fnl f* **8/1**
4540 **4** *3/4* **Mathmagician**[11] [953] 5-8-12 35..............................(b) LFletcher(3) 2 39
(RFMarvin) *bhd: drvn along 6f out: c v wd over 2f out: styd on wl fnl f* **22/1**
6456 **5** *1/2* **King Priam (IRE)**[19] [880] 9-9-1 35..............................(b) NCallan 8 39
(MJPolglase) *hdwy on outside 7f out: sn chsng ldrs: brought v wd over 2f out: kpt on fnl f* **10/1**
-000 **6** *2* **Balalaika Tune (IRE)**[28] [783] 5-9-1 30.............................. DRMcCabe 14 35
(WStorey) *sn chsng ldrs: hung lft over 2f out: fdd fnl f* **28/1**
/341 **7** *3/4* **Grub Street**[11] [953] 8-8-8 35.............................. MLawson(7) 4 34
(JParkes) *rr-div: hdwy on ins over 3f out: nvr rchd ldrs* **6/1**[3]
0006 **8** *3/4* **Moyne Pleasure (IRE)**[13] [943] 6-9-1 35.............................. IMongan 15 33
(PaulJohnson) *sn trcking ldrs: one pce fnl 2f* **22/1**
60-5 **9** *1 1/2* **Cumwhitton**[28] [783] 5-8-10 30.............................. THamilton(5) 5 31
(RAFahey) *s.i.s: sme hdwy on inner 3f out: nvr nr ldrs* **16/1**
3545 **10** *2* **Sea Ya Maite**[28] [781] 10-9-1 35..............................(t) JBramhill 10 27
(SRBowring) *chsd ldrs: wknd fnl f* **20/1**
6605 **11** *3 1/2* **Western Command (GER)**[13] [945] 8-9-1 30................(p) RFitzpatrick 1 22
(MrsNMacauley) *bhd: drvn along 5f out: nvr a factor* **40/1**
3403 **12** *nk* **Think Quick (IRE)**[6] [991] 4-8-7 35.............................. HFellows(7) 3 21
(RHollinshead) *a bhd* **25/1**
00/5 **13** *14* **Buying A Dream (IRE)**[13] [943] 7-9-1 35.............................. DMernagh 11 —
(AndrewTurnell) *chsd ldrs: lost pl over 2f out: eased* **22/1**
-063 **14** *7* **Sophomore**[13] [945] 10-9-1 30.............................. GDuffield 9 —
(JohnAHarris) *chsd ldrs: reminders 6f out: lost pl over 4f out: eased* **18/1**
000- **15** *dist* **Bridewell (USA)**[99] [6137] 5-9-1 35.............................. JFanning 16 —
(FWatson) *s.i.s: a bhd: t.o 4f out* **28/1**
0-04 **16** *20* **Trojan Wolf**[19] [880] 9-9-1 35.............................. RWinston 12 —
(PHowling) *led: hdd over 4f out: hung rt and virtually p.u 3f out: t.o* **12/1**

2m 32.93s (4.03) **Going Correction** +0.275s/f (Slow)
**WFA** 4 from 5yo+ 1lb **16** Ran SP% **127.6**
Speed ratings: **96,95,94,93,93 91,91,90,89,88 85,85,75,70,— —**CSF £17.51 TOTE £7.60: £2.50, £1.30, £3.60; EX 19.60 Place 6 £70.48, Place 5 £49.89.
**Owner** 21st Century Racing **Bred** Miss Trudy Huggett **Trained** Malton, N Yorks
■ Stewards Enquiry : D NolanD four-day ban: used whip with excessive frequency and without allowing gelding time to respond (Mar 26,27,29,30)

**FOCUS**
A poor race, as befits the grade.

**NOTEBOOK**
**Dash Of Magic**, freshened up by a five-week break, recorded her fifth career win, three of them on this surface here.
**The Beduth Navi**, who looked really well, went on and stepped up the gallop. He never flinched under a very hard ride but in the end just missed out.
**Samar Qand**, fitted with a tongue-strap for the first time, gave a problem or two in the stalls. Driven along from start to finish, she has now been placed five times from 15 starts.
**Mathmagician**, in blinkers rather than cheekpieces, has two ways of running. Stepping up in trip, he put his best foot foward on the wide outside when it was all over.
**King Priam(IRE)** is a cunning old rogue and runs his own race.
**Balalaika Tune(IRE)**, an edgy type, tends to do a fraction too much and this trip on a slow surface stretches her to the very limit.
**Grub Street** seemed to be ridden with one eye on staying the extended trip and the waiting was rather overdone.
**Sophomore** *Official explanation: jockey said gelding was lame*
**Bridewell(USA)** *Official explanation: jockey said gelding was never travelling*
**Trojan Wolf** *Official explanation: jockey said gelding lost its action*
T/Plt: £63.80 to a £1 stake. Pool: £35,603.40. 407.10 winning tickets. T/Qpdt: £17.00 to a £1 stake. Pool: £2,324.30. 100.60 winning tickets. WG

# 1021 SOUTHWELL (L-H)
Tuesday, March 16

**OFFICIAL GOING: Standard to slow**

## 1027 £10 FREE BET @ BETDIRECT.CO.UK H'CAP (DIV I) 5f (F)
1:50 (1:51) (E) (0-70,68) 3-Y-O+ **£3,248** (£928; £464) **Stalls** High

Form RPR
5120 **1** **Italian Mist (FR)**[34] [738] 5-9-0 **54**..............................(e) GFaulkner 2 73
(JulianPoulton) *chsd ldrs: led over 1f out: rdn clr* **8/1**
-645 **2** *3* **Never Without Me**[29] [794] 4-7-13 **46**.............................. KJackson(7) 5 55
(PJMcbride) *mde most over 3f: no ex ins fnl f* **9/1**
2506 **3** *1 1/2* **Ladies Knight**[19] [896] 4-9-1 **55**.............................. DarrenWilliams 4 58
(DShaw) *s.i.s: sn prom: outpcd 1/2-way: hdwy u.p over 1f out: r.o* **9/1**
0-23 **4** *3/4* **Off Hire**[29] [794] 8-8-8 **48**..............................(v) RFitzpatrick 3 49
(CSmith) *s.i.s: sn w ldrs: rdn over 1f out: no ex* **10/1**
-013 **5** *1 1/4* **Cash**[18] [905] 6-9-8 **65**..............................(p) LFletcher(3) 7 61
(PaulJohnson) *w ldrs: rdn over 1f out: sn btn* **5/1**[2]
-001 **6** *2 1/2* **Scary Night (IRE)**[13] [954] 4-10-0 **68**..............................(p) JEdmunds 9 56
(JBalding) *chsd ldrs: rdn 1/2-way: wknd over 1f out* **7/1**[3]
0213 **7** *2* **Henry Tun**[13] [954] 6-8-7 **52** ow1..............................(b) MSavage(5) 10 32
(NEBerry) *chasaed ldrs: rdn 1/2-way: wknd over 1f out: hung lft ins fnl f* **9/2**[1]
0055 **8** *1/2* **Sharp Hat**[13] [954] 10-9-10 **64**.............................. ACulhane 6 43
(DWChapman) *sn outpcd* **10/1**
600- **9** *1* **Pays D'Amour (IRE)**[248] [3220] 7-9-9 **63**.............................. ANicholls 11 38
(DNicholls) *sn outpcd* **20/1**
50-0 **10** *1 1/2* **Miss Trinity**[8] [982] 4-9-7 **64**.............................. BReilly(3) 12 34
(CNAllen) *sn outpcd* **25/1**
0-43 **11** *1* **Catchthebatch**[32] [762] 8-8-7 **47**.............................. SCarson 8 14
(EAWheeler) *chsd ldrs: hmpd over 3f out: sn lost pl* **7/1**[3]
050- **12** *6* **Cellino**[189] [4789] 3-8-2 **54**.............................. DMernagh 1 —
(AndrewTurnell) *s.i.s: outpcd* **50/1**

60.35 secs (0.05) **Going Correction** +0.175s/f (Slow)
**WFA** 3 from 4yo+ 12lb **12** Ran SP% **119.7**
Speed ratings: **106,101,98,97,95 91,88,87,86,83 82,72**CSF £77.22 CT £670.48 TOTE £13.10: £2.70, £5.00, £1.90; EX 112.90.
**Owner** S P Shore **Bred** Mrs Hilary Trigg & Mr John Veil **Trained** Kentford, Suffolk

**FOCUS**
A decent time for the grade, 1.19 seconds faster than the second division, and the form looks solid.

**NOTEBOOK**
**Italian Mist(FR)** has been in good form since the start of the year and gained his third win on Fibresand during that period, but it was the first time he had run over the minimum trip since August. That proved no problem at all and he can win again under similar conditions.
**Never Without Me**, with the visor left off, ran well under a positive ride and reversed last month's Wolverhampton running with both Cash and Off Hire. This is his trip, but he remains a maiden after nine attempts.
**Ladies Knight** was slowly away, though not to the same extent as in some of his previous starts. Even so, over this straight five furlongs it was still a handicap he could have done without and he was never going to get there. He may be worth another try over an extra furlong here.
**Off Hire** showed his usual early toe, but is a very difficult horse to win with these days.
**Cash** appeared to run to form and there seemed no excuses.
**Scary Night(IRE)** never got into it, but with the first four home coming from the five lowest stalls he may not have been drawn to advantage.

## 1028 £10 FREE BET @ BET DIRECT SKY ACTIVE CLASSIFIED CLAIMING STKS 1m 6f (F)
2:25 (2:26) (F) 4-Y-0+ **£2,877** (£822; £411) **Stalls** Low

Form RPR
0111 **1** **Daunted (IRE)**[19] [901] 8-8-10 60.............................. LisaJones(3) 2 67+
(PABlockley) *a.p: chsd ldr 11f out: led over 4f out: clr fnl 2f* **5/6**[1]
3023 **2** *6* **Orinocovsky (IRE)**[2] [1016] 5-9-1 55.............................. DHolland 4 61+
(NPLittmoden) *led after 2f: rdn and hdd over 4f out: outpcd fnl 2f* **10/3**[3]
-213 **3** *14* **Mr Smithers Jones**[54] [581] 4-8-13 56.............................. CCatlin 1 45
(SCWilliams) *sn led: hdd 12f out: rdn 7f out: wknd 5f out* **9/4**[2]
4565 **4** *13* **King Priam (IRE)**[2] [1026] 9-8-9 35..............................(b) NCallan 3 20
(MJPolglase) *sn pushed along and prom: wknd over 5f out* **25/1**

3m 12.66s (3.06) **Going Correction** +0.175s/f (Slow)
**WFA** 4 from 5yo+ 4lb **4** Ran SP% **112.2**
Speed ratings: **98,94,86,79**CSF £4.22 TOTE £1.60; EX 3.10.
**Owner** Mrs Joanna Hughes **Bred** Mrs G Doyle **Trained** Southwell, Notts

**FOCUS**
A poor contest and an uneventful race with a predictable outcome. The winning time was also modest and the winner did not need to improve.

**NOTEBOOK**
**Daunted(IRE)**, with his stamina proven and best in on adjusted official figures, picked off Orinocovsky turning for home and had little difficulty pulling clear to record his fifth win of the year at this track.
**Orinocovsky(IRE)**, 2lb worse off with the winner for a 6l beating over 12 furlongs here last month, was soon able to establish an uncontested lead but had no response when the winner ranged alongside on the home bend. He is still to conclusively prove he stays this trip on the Flat.
**Mr Smithers Jones**, winner of a slowly run race over course and distance, was beaten a long way out and this was too bad to be true.
**King Priam(IRE)** finds even this level too hot for him these days.

## 1029 GREAT VALUE OFFERS @ BETDIRECT.CO.UK H'CAP — 1m (F)
3:00 (3:01) (D ) (0-80,80) 3-Y-O — £4,069 (£1,252; £626; £313) Stalls Low

Form — RPR

1-02 **1** **Denver (IRE)**[13] 955 3-9-2 **80**....(b) JFMcDonald(5) 6 — 89
(BJMeehan) *a.p: rdn to ld over 1f out: jst hld on* — 9/2[2]

-521 **2** *shd* **Jomus**[12] 959 3-8-4 **63**.... GDuffield 2 — 72+
(LMontagueHall) *s.s: hld up: hdwy u.p over 1f out: r.o* — 9/2[2]

0-11 **3** *1 ½* **Rare Coincidence**[39] 700 3-8-8 **70** ow2....(p) LFletcher(3) 9 — 76
(RFFisher) *chsd ldr: led 3f out: rdn and hdd over 1f out: unable qck ins fnl f* — 7/1[3]

3-31 **4** *5* **Book Matched**[18] 907 3-8-11 **70**.... RFfrench 4 — 66
(BSmart) *chsd ldrs: rdn over 3f out: styd on same pce fnl 2f* — 9/2[2]

5-01 **5** *1 ¼* **Mission Affirmed (USA)**[13] 955 3-8-4 **63**.... DMernagh 7 — 56
(TPTate) *sn led: rdn and hdd 3f out: wknd over 1f out* — 7/4[1]

400- **6** *2 ½* **Senor Bond (USA)**[129] 5950 3-9-0 **73**.... FLynch 3 — 61
(BSmart) *s.i.s: hdwy to join ldrs over 5f out: hung lft over 2f out: wknd over 1f out* — 25/1

5344 **7** *28* **Myannabanana (IRE)**[29] 798 3-8-3 **62**....(b) JQuinn 1 — —
(JRWeymes) *chsd ldrs: lost pl over 4f out: sn bhd* — 14/1

1m 45.87s (1.27) **Going Correction** +0.175s/f (Slow) — **7** Ran SP% **113.9**
Speed ratings: **100,99,98,93,92 89,61**CSF £24.66 CT £138.40 TOTE £5.40: £3.40, £2.60; EX 39.00.

**Owner** Gigginstown House Stud **Bred** Gigginstown House **Trained** Upper Lambourn, Berks

**FOCUS**
A decent three-year-old handicap and a very tight finish. An improved effort from the winner and also the runner-up, who will be interesting back on Polytrack

**NOTEBOOK**
**Denver(IRE)** ◆, who had finished runner-up in his two previous tries on this track, proved well suited by the return to a mile. He may have been in front longer than ideal and could be a bit better than the winning margin suggests.
**Jomus**, 3lb higher for his Lingfield win over this trip, was forced to make his effort tight against the inside rail and given the way this track has been riding in recent months, that may not have been to his advantage.
**Rare Coincidence** was taking a big step up in class in his hat-trick bid, but earned plenty of credit off an 8lb higher mark including his rider's 2lb overweight. He was not beaten far and there will be other opportunities for him at this track.
**Book Matched** was done for foot over the last couple of furlongs. His victory over Hawkit at Wolverhampton adds up to little despite that horse's win at Wolverhampton three days earlier.
**Mission Affirmed(USA)**, 5lb worse off with Denver after beating him by three lengths over seven furlongs here last time, made the early running but came off the bridle turning for home and was one of the first beaten. This was very disappointing and he is much better than this.

## 1030 BETDIRECT.CO.UK H'CAP — 1m 4f (F)
3:40 (3:42) (C ) (0-95,95) 3-Y-O+ — £8,112 (£2,496; £1,248; £624) Stalls Low

Form — RPR

1415 **1** **Bella Pavlina**[18] 908 6-7-6 **66**.... BSwarbrick(7) 7 — 79
(WMBrisbourne) *a.p: chsd ldr 8f out: led over 3f out: sn rdn: styd on* — 14/1

20/1 **2** *¾* **General**[11] 972 7-7-13 **66** ow1.... CCatlin 10 — 77
(NPLittmoden) *s.i.s: hld up: hdwy 6f out: rdn over 4f out: chsd wnr fnl f: styd on u.p* — 16/1

004- **3** *8* **Kylkenny**[88] 6215 9-9-3 **84**....(t) SDrowne 3 — 84
(HMorrison) *hld up in tch: rdn over 3f out: wknd wl over 1f out* — 9/4[2]

6236 **4** *1 ½* **George Stubbs (USA)**[11] 971 6-7-9 **65**.... LisaJones(3) 6 — 63
(MJPolglase) *sn led: rdn and hdd over 3f out: wknd fnl f* — 9/2[3]

511- **5** *16* **Tempsford (USA)**[164] 5379 4-9-6 **89**.... GDuffield 1 — 63
(SirMarkPrescott) *chsd ldrs: pushed along over 8f out: wknd over 4f out* — 2/1[1]

465/ **6** *nk* **Maniatis**[27] 5481 7-10-0 **95**.... LVickers 4 — 68
(MrsJCandlish) *chsd ldr 4f: wknd 5f out* — 40/1

-303 **7** *6* **Cruise Director**[29] 795 4-8-12 **81**.... MFenton 8 — 45
(WJMusson) *hld up: hmpd 5f out: a bhd* — 5/1

0 **8** *8* **Qudrah (IRE)**[17] 915 4-9-1 **84**....(b) RFfrench 9 — 36
(EJO'Neill) *mid-div: hdwy 8f out: sn rdn and hung rt: wknd 5f out* — 12/1

0-00 **9** *10* **Midshipman**[52] 600 6-9-6 **87** ow1.... PJScallan 5 — 23
(AWCarroll) *chsd ldrs: lost pl 9f out: wkng whn hmpd 5f out* — 33/1

2m 39.9s (-2.20) **Going Correction** +0.175s/f (Slow)
**WFA** 4 from 6yo+ 2lb — **9** Ran SP% **124.6**
Speed ratings: **114,113,108,107,96 96,92,86,80**CSF £227.37 CT £703.36 TOTE £20.10: £2.80, £4.10, £1.10; EX 207.90.

**Owner** The Cartmel Syndicate **Bred** C Papaioannou **Trained** Great Ness, Shropshire

**FOCUS**
A competitive handicap run at a decent pace and won in a very good time. A somewhat surprise result and it may be advisable not to take the form too literally.

**NOTEBOOK**
**Bella Pavlina** was gaining her fifth victory of the year off a 10lb higher mark than when disappointing at Wolverhampton last time, but connections were inclined to blame the very deep ground there and she had been given a little break since. Considering she started off winning banded stakes' this was a remarkable performance.
**General** ran a blinder on this half-mile step up in trip after winning a Wolverhampton seller last time. Now with top All Weather connections, he should be able to find another race under similar conditions.
**Kylkenny**, with the tongue-tie back on, ran well on this first run since December but is not getting any younger and may continue to find a few too good at this level.
**George Stubbs(USA)** was given his usual positive ride and ran a fair race until left behind by the front pair.
**Tempsford(USA)**, an on-course drifter, was off the bridle very early and never figured. *Official explanation: trainer's representative had no explanation for the poor form shown*
**Cruise Director** never figured and is perhaps better on Polytrack.

## 1031 SPECIAL OFFERS @ BETDIRECT.CO.UK (S) STKS — 1m 3f (F)
4:20 (4:20) (G ) 3-6-Y-O — £2,548 (£728; £364) Stalls Low

Form — RPR

3146 **1** **Game Guru**[11] 970 5-10-0 66....(p) DeanMcKeown 6 — 73
(PABlockley) *chsd ldrs: rdn to ld over 1f out: all out* — 5/2[2]

3-26 **2** *nk* **Elegant Gracie (IRE)**[27] 818 4-9-4 67.... DHolland 5 — 64
(RGuest) *hld up in tch: nt clr run and outpcd over 3f out: rallied u.p over 1f out: r.o* — 7/4[1]

023/ **3** *2 ½* **Captain Crusoe**[601] 3285 6-9-10.... RWinston 7 — 65
(PHowling) *hld up: hdwy to ld over 2f out: rdn and hdd over 1f out: no edgd lft and no ex ins fnl f* — 7/2[3]

10-0 **4** *11* **Hymns And Arias**[28] 810 3-8-0 47 ow2.... JQuinn 1 — 44
(RonaldThompson) *chsd ldrs: rdn 4f out: wknd over 2f out* — 16/1

054 **5** *hd* **Ballyrush (IRE)**[18] 907 4-9-9 60.... DarrenWilliams 3 — 47
(KRBurke) *dwlt: plld hrd and sn prom: wkng whn hmpd wl over 1f out* — 13/2

000/ **6** *1 ¾* **Galaxy Fallon**[11] 1764 6-9-2 30.... LEnstone(3) 4 — 39?
(MDods) *chsd ldr 8f: sn rdn and wknd* — 33/1

5-0 **7** *hd* **Devious Paddy (IRE)**[22] 861 4-9-9 60....(t) KimTinkler 2 — 43
(NTinkler) *led: rdn over 4f out: hdd over 2f out: wkng whn hung lft wl over 1f out* — 20/1

0-00 **8** *dist* **Moon Royale**[30] 782 6-9-5 30.... FLynch 8 — —
(MrsNMacauley) *hld up: bhd fnl 5f* — 40/1

2m 32.65s (3.75) **Going Correction** +0.175s/f (Slow)
**WFA** 3 from 4yo 21lb 4 from 5yo+ 1lb — **8** Ran SP% **116.5**
Speed ratings: **93,92,90,82,82 81,81,**—CSF £7.30 TOTE £2.70: £1.40, £1.10, £2.10; EX 9.20.The winner was bought in for 7,500gns

**Owner** Carl Would **Bred** P J Makin **Trained** Southwell, Notts

**FOCUS**
A bad race and a modest winning time, even for a seller, with the winner stepping up in trip.

**NOTEBOOK**
**Game Guru** was racing over this sort of trip for the first time and only just managed to hold on to gain his eighth course victory. This win was very much down to the enterprise of his rider, who suddenly injected a turn of speed straightening up for home and caught his rivals flat-footed. He now heads for the Doncaster Sales next week.
**Elegant Gracie(IRE)**, dropping slightly in trip, was making her Fibresand debut and dropping significantly in class, but was in a bad position turning for home and when eventually in the clear took too long to get into top gear. Her late flourish was always going to be a couple of strides too late and she does not have too many options left open to her now.
**Captain Crusoe**, best in on adjusted official figures, was returning from a layoff of 20 months. He looked dangerous when moving up on the outside turning for home, but did not find as much as had looked likely and probably needed this.
**Hymns And Arias** has done nothing to suggest she was going to appreciate this big step up in trip.
**Ballyrush(IRE)** probably did too much early to give him a chance of seeing out this longer trip.

## 1032 NEW SITE @ BETDIRECT.CO.UK CLASSIFIED STKS — 7f (F)
5:00 (5:01) (F ) 3-Y-O+ — £2,940 (£840; £420) Stalls Low

Form — RPR

1102 **1** **Nearly A Fool**[16] 928 6-9-6 60....(v) NPollard 12 — 73
(GGMargarson) *mid-div: drvn along 1/2-way: hdwy over 2f out: led over 1f out: r.o wl* — 4/1[2]

3301 **2** *3 ½* **Galloway Mac**[21] 877 4-9-6 60.... DHolland 4 — 64
(WAO'Gorman) *sn outpcd and bhd: hmpd 2f out: hdwy over 1f out: nt rch wnr* — 7/2[1]

5-03 **3** *nk* **Largs**[28] 805 4-9-3 45.... JEdmunds 7 — 60?
(JBalding) *chsd ldrs: rdn to ld 2f out: sn hdd: no ex fnl f* — 16/1

2211 **4** *1 ½* **Simply The Guest (IRE)**[42] 667 5-9-6 60....(t) KimTinkler 11 — 59
(DonEnricoIncisa) *sn outpcd: r.o ins fnl f: nvr nrr* — 7/1[3]

-030 **5** *¾* **Effective**[34] 742 4-9-6 60.... JQuinn 3 — 57
(APJarvis) *prom: rdn 1/2-way: wknd fnl f* — 9/1

1123 **6** *hd* **Xaloc Bay (IRE)**[16] 932 6-9-6 56.... DarrenWilliams 6 — 57
(BPJBaugh) *led 5f: wknd fnl f* — 7/1[3]

13-4 **7** *1 ¾* **Mon Secret (IRE)**[63] 518 6-8-13 60.... MStainton(7) 13 — 53
(BSmart) *s.i.s: sn chsng ldrs: rdn and wknd over 1f out* — 7/2[1]

00-4 **8** *6* **Stoic Leader (IRE)**[18] 905 4-9-3 55.... LFletcher(3) 1 — 38
(RFFisher) *hld up: hdwy over 1f out: eased whn btn ins fnl f* — 16/1

/104 **9** *10* **Kennington**[19] 897 4-9-6 56....(v) DaneO'Neill 10 — 13
(MrsCADunnett) *s.i.s: sn chsng ldrs: wknd 3f out: hung lft 2f out* — 7/1[3]

000- **10** *1 ½* **Finningley Connor**[98] 6150 4-9-6 50.... DeanMcKeown 8 — 9
(RonaldThompson) *n.d* — 100/1

0-00 **11** *shd* **Drury Lane (IRE)**[29] 799 4-9-6 60....(b) ACulhane 5 — 9
(DWChapman) *chsd ldrs over 4f: in rr whn hmpd 2f out* — 33/1

6-00 **12** *nk* **Tanaffus**[26] 823 4-9-6 60.... KDalgleish 9 — 8
(DWChapman) *chsd ldrs: lost pl 4f out: bhd fnl 3f* — 66/1

003/ **13** *10* **Prime Offer**[654] 1790 8-9-6 55.... NCallan 2 — —
(JJay) *sn drvn along in rr: bhd fr 1/2-way* — 25/1

1m 31.33s (0.53) **Going Correction** +0.175s/f (Slow) — **13** Ran SP% **133.0**
Speed ratings: **103,99,98,96,96 95,93,87,75,73 73,73,61**CSF £20.45 TOTE £5.10: £2.10, £3.60, £4.40; EX 25.60.

**Owner** J Burns **Bred** Mrs S Shaw **Trained** Newmarket, Suffolk

**FOCUS**
A tight classified stakes judged on official ratings, with more than half the field bang on the ratings ceiling of 60. Despite the proximity of the 45-rated third, the form looks fairly solid.

**NOTEBOOK**
**Nearly A Fool** has been showing his best recent form on Polytrack and connections were concerned about this deeper surface, but he did have winning form here at the beginning of last year and the switch did not bother him in the slightest.
**Galloway Mac** found this drop back from a mile completely against him and was outpaced out the back for a very long way after breaking slowly. He made up a lot of ground in the home straight to snatch second place, but was never going to get anywhere near the winner and did not look at all an easy ride.
**Largs** had every chance and put up one of her better efforts, but is still a maiden after 19 attempts.
**Simply The Guest(IRE)**, on a hat-trick after a couple of wins over a mile here, was another not suited by the shorter trip and was doing all his best work late.
**Effective** did not appear to find this trip on this deeper surface an aid to his chances and is a very difficult horse to win with.
**Mon Secret(IRE)** is at this best under these conditions so this was a bit disappointing.
**Prime Offer** *Official explanation: jockey said gelding was unsuited by today's going (standard to slow)*

## 1033 £10 FREE BET @ BETDIRECT.CO.UK H'CAP (DIV II) — 5f (F)
5:40 (5:40) (E ) (0-70,67) 3-Y-O+ — £3,248 (£928; £464) Stalls High

Form — RPR

0046 **1** **Far Note (USA)**[19] 897 6-9-13 67....(b) JBramhill 2 — 77
(SRBowring) *led: hdd over 3f out: rdn to ld over 1f out: edgd rt: r.o* — 13/2

-513 **2** *½* **Sea The World (IRE)**[28] 801 4-9-7 61....(v) DarrenWilliams 7 — 69
(DShaw) *s.i.s: outpcd: hdwy u.p over 1f out: ev ch ins fnl f: r.o* — 5/1[3]

660- **3** *hd* **Dunn Deal (IRE)**[185] 4889 4-8-11 58.... BSwarbrick(7) 8 — 66
(WMBrisbourne) *chsd ldrs: rdn and ev ch fr over 1f out: edgd lft ins fnl f: kpt on* — 20/1

2-64 **4** *1 ¼* **River Lark (USA)**[28] 801 5-8-8 48.... RFfrench 6 — 51
(MABuckley) *chsd ldrs: rdn and ev ch over 1f out: unable qck ins fnl f* — 16/1

6564 **5** *¾* **Cleveland Way**[18] 904 4-8-6 46....(v) RFitzpatrick 11 — 47
(DCarroll) *sn pushed along in rr: styd on ins fnl f: nvr able to chal* — 12/1

5143 **6** *nk* **Aintnecessarilyso**[19] 896 6-8-12 52.... CCatlin 5 — 52
(NEBerry) *sn pushed along and prom: outpcd over 3f out: rdn over 1f out: kpt on* — 14/1

1530 **7** *½* **Torrent**[16] 936 9-8-2 45....(b) LisaJones(3) 1 — 43
(DWChapman) *w ldr: led over 3f out: hdd over 1f out: wknd ins fnl f* — 16/1

-221 **8** *nk* **Blueberry Rhyme**[19] 898 5-9-11 65....(v) DSweeney 9 — 62
(PJMakin) *hld up: hdwy over 1f out: rdn and hmpd ins fnl f: sn btn* — 3/1[1]



The Form Book, Raceform Ltd, Compton, RG20 6NL

-002 **9** *2* **King's Ballet (USA)**[29] [796] 6-8-7 47..............(p) JQuinn 3 37
(PRChamings) *chsd ldrs: rdn 1/2-way: wknd fnl f* **7/2**[2]

00-1 **10** *1 3/4* **Yorkie**[8] [987] 5-9-10 64 6ex.............. DeanMcKeown 10 48
(PABlockley) *sn outpcd* **10/1**

0-00 **11** *2 1/2* **Lakelands Lady (IRE)**[28] [801] 4-9-10 64..............(p) JEdmunds 4 39
(JBalding) *chsd ldrs: wkng whn stmbld over 2f out* **14/1**

61.54 secs (1.24) **Going Correction** +0.175s/f (Slow) **11** Ran SP% **123.9**
Speed ratings: **97,96,95,93,92 92,91,90,87,84 80**CSF £41.27 CT £646.88 TOTE £9.30: £3.00, £1.50, £5.60; EX 37.30 Place 6 £154.49, Place 5 £32.57.
**Owner** Mrs A Potts **Bred** Juddmonte Farms **Trained** Edwinstowe, Notts

**FOCUS**
A moderate winning time, 1.19 seconds slower than the first division. The principals may struggle off higher marks.

**NOTEBOOK**
**Far Note(USA)**, drawn out in the centre, was given a positive ride and despite hanging across the track and ending up on the stands' side, something he has done here before, saw this race out well. This did not look the strongest of contests though.
**Sea The World(IRE)**, under his ideal conditions, had the race run to suit and arrived there in plenty of time before finding the winner just too strong.
**Dunn Deal(IRE)**, gelded since his last outing six months ago, ran a very creditable sand debut and a race can be found on this surface.
**River Lark(USA)**, racing off her proper mark this time, appeared to run to form.
**Blueberry Rhyme** travelled well as he often does, but racing towards the stands' side was a bigger problem than getting short of room a furlong out.
**King's Ballet(USA)** did not confirm the promise of his recent Wolverhampton effort.
T/Plt: £447.50 to a £1 stake. Pool: £33,807.85. 55.15 winning tickets. T/Qpdt: £17.00 to a £1 stake. Pool: £2,933.00. 127.55 winning tickets. CR

## 1007 WOLVERHAMPTON (A.W) (L-H)
Wednesday, March 17

**OFFICIAL GOING: Standard to slow**
Wind: fine Weather: almost nil

### 1035 BET DIRECT NO Q ON 08000 93 66 93 H'CAP (DIV I) 7f (F)
**1:40** (1:42) (E) (0-70,68) 3-Y-O+ **£4,046** (£1,245; £622; £311) **Stalls** High

Form RPR

0-40 **1** **Stoic Leader (IRE)**[1] [1032] 4-8-12 55.............. LFletcher(3) 9 73+
(RFFisher) *a.p: rdn to ld over 2f out: clr over 1f out: eased wl ins fnl f* **4/1**[2]

32-4 **2** *6* **Super Canyon**[26] [836] 6-10-0 68.............. NCallan 3 66
(JPearce) *prom: outpcd after 1f: hdwy over 3f out: sn rdn: tk 2nd ins fnl f: no ch w wnr* **5/2**[1]

0-00 **3** *3 1/2* **Maromito (IRE)**[20] [897] 7-8-5 45.............. JFanning 10 34
(RBastiman) *w ldr: led over 5f out tl over 2f out: sn rdn: wknd over 1f out* **16/1**

0310 **4** *2* **Geronimo**[12] [967] 7-9-8 62.............. MFenton 5 46
(MissGayKelleway) *hld up: hdwy over 3f out: sn rdn: wknd wl over 1f out* **9/2**[3]

0/0- **5** *nk* **El Hamra (IRE)**[357] [811] 6-9-0 54.............. ACulhane 11 37
(MJHaynes) *sn outpcd and bhd: styd on fnl f: nvr nrr* **16/1**

0-50 **6** *4* **Better Off**[40] [694] 6-9-3 57.............. JoannaBadger 4 30
(MrsNMacauley) *s.i.s: a bhd* **9/1**

402- **7** *1/2* **Jonny Ebeneezer**[119] [6027] 5-9-9 63.............. EAhern 1 35
(RMHCowell) *led over 1f: remained prom: rdn over 3f out: wknd over 2f out* **5/2**[1]

1m 33.81s (3.61) **Going Correction** +0.55s/f (Slow) **7** Ran SP% **117.1**
**WFA** 3 from 4yo+ 15lb
Speed ratings: **101,94,90,87,87 82,82**CSF £15.05 CT £144.29 TOTE £6.70: £3.30, £2.10; EX 24.70.
**Owner** Great Head House Estates Limited **Bred** P J Higgins **Trained** Ulverston, Cumbria

**FOCUS**
This did not take much winning and the time was slightly slower than the other division. The winner was well in on his turf form.

**NOTEBOOK**
**Stoic Leader(IRE)** was 3lb lower than when last in a handicap. He bounced back after being eased when beaten when stepped up to this trip at Southwell the previous day.
**Super Canyon**, a six-furlong specialist, was rather surprisingly caught flat-footed quite early on.
**Maromito(IRE)** had his stamina limitations exposed on this first attempt beyond six furlongs.
**Geronimo** was dropping back from the stretch mile.
**Jonny Ebeneezer** was unsuited by the surface, according to his trainer. *Official explanation: trainer said gelding was unsuited by the fibresand surface*

### 1036 AVOID THE QUEUES WITH BET DIRECT NO Q FILLIES' H'CAP 1m 100y(F)
**2:15** (2:16) (E) (0-75,75) 3-Y-O+ **£3,248** (£928; £464) **Stalls** Low

Form RPR

1115 **1** **Najaaba (USA)**[20] [892] 4-9-11 75.............. BReilly(3) 5 85+
(MissJFeilden) *hld up: hdwy 3f out: sn rdn: led ins fnl f: r.o wl* **7/4**[1]

-006 **2** *1 1/2* **Spark Up**[32] [772] 4-8-10 57.............. SWKelly 4 61
(JWUnett) *hld up: pushed along 5f out: rdn and outpcd 3f out: rallied over 1f out: kpt on ins fnl f: tk 2nd post* **14/1**

2046 **3** *shd* **Zahunda (IRE)**[16] [940] 5-7-5 45 oh5.............. BSwarbrick(7) 6 49
(WMBrisbourne) *prom: rdn over 3f out: led over 2f out tl ins fnl f: nt qckn* **5/1**[3]

011 **4** *6* **La Puce**[12] [970] 3-8-7 71.............. MFenton 3 62
(MissGayKelleway) *w ldr: led over 4f out: rdn over 3f out: hdd over 2f out: wknd ins fnl f* **7/4**[1]

-363 **5** *1* **Estimation**[27] [826] 4-9-7 68.............. EAhern 2 57
(RMHCowell) *led 4f: rdn and wknd over 2f out* **4/1**[2]

1m 54.81s (3.81) **Going Correction** +0.55s/f (Slow) **5** Ran SP% **116.1**
**WFA** 3 from 4yo+ 17lb
Speed ratings: **102,100,100,94,93**CSF £26.06 TOTE £2.90: £1.10, £8.40; EX 60.60.
**Owner** A K Sparks **Bred** Darley Stud Management, L L C **Trained** Exning, Suffolk
■ Brian Reilly was unable to weigh in as the filly kicked him in the knee after the race. The result stood.

**FOCUS**
The two pacesetters seemed to cut each other's throats, and although this was an improved effort from the winner, she could struggle in a higher grade.

**NOTEBOOK**
**Najaaba(USA)** resumed her winning ways back on her favourite surface on this return to a shorter trip. She produced a personal best to defy top weight.
**Spark Up**, who had been blinkered for each of her last eight starts, gave the first indication that she can be effective at a mile.
**Zahunda(IRE)** gave a good account of herself considering she was 5lb 'wrong'.
**La Puce**, raised another 3lb, did not get home after being taken on for the lead.
**Estimation** probably had too much use made of her.

### 1037 BET DIRECT NO Q DEMO 08000 837 888 CLAIMING STKS 1m 1f 79y(F)
**2:50** (2:51) (F) 4-Y-O+ **£2,898** (£828; £414) **Stalls** Low

Form RPR

0240 **1** **Bressbee (USA)**[21] [887] 6-9-7 66.............. (v) SWKelly 7 76
(JWUnett) *led after 1f: clr whn rdn 3f out: drvn out* **5/2**[2]

/016 **2** *2* **Heathers Girl**[19] [910] 5-8-4 58.............. PaulEddery 2 55
(DHaydnJones) *chsd wnr 7f out: rdn over 3f out: kpt on same pce fnl f* **11/1**

6302 **3** *5* **Just Wiz**[12] [972] 8-8-11 62..............(b) CCatlin 3 52
(NPLittmoden) *rdn over 4f out: hdwy on ins over 2f out: swtchd rt wl over 1f out: one pce* **4/5**[1]

4125 **4** *1/2* **Grand Lass (IRE)**[19] [909] 5-8-8 51 ow2..............(p) KDarley 5 48
(ASadik) *prom: lost cheekpiece 7f out: rdn 5f out: wknd fnl f* **4/1**[3]

360- **5** *13* **Blushing Prince (IRE)**[114] [5381] 6-9-7 61..............(t) RWinston 8 35
(MrsLStubbs) *bhd: rdn over 4f out: hdwy on outside over 2f out: wknd wl over 1f out* **11/1**

-000 **6** *2 1/2* **Chickasaw Trail**[9] [994] 6-8-2 30.............. DaleGibson 1 11
(RHollinshead) *led 1f: rdn and wknd over 5f out* **50/1**

0034 **7** *nk* **Dundonald**[9] [994] 5-8-7 40..............(bt) SRighton 6 15
(MAppleby) *rdn over 4f out: a bhd* **33/1**

2m 6.88s (3.98) **Going Correction** +0.55s/f (Slow) **7** Ran SP% **125.7**
Speed ratings: **104,102,97,97,85 83,83**CSF £33.02 TOTE £4.40: £2.10, £4.20; EX 19.50.The winner was claimed by Nigel Shields for £12,000.
**Owner** Team Racing **Bred** Janus Bloodstock Inc And Kan Wong Tam **Trained** Wolverhampton, W Midlands

**FOCUS**
A modest claimer but a fair winning time for the grade.

**NOTEBOOK**
**Bressbee(USA)** found a drop in class and returning to front-running tactics doing the trick. He was claimed for £12,000.
**Heathers Girl**, back in the right sort of grade, stuck to her task without being able to bustle up the winner.
**Just Wiz** was reverting to his optimum distance.
**Grand Lass(IRE)** was under pressure a long way from home after losing one of her cheekpieces on the first turn.

### 1038 BET DIRECT NO Q MAIDEN STKS 6f (F)
**3:30** (3:33) (D) 3-Y-O **£3,367** (£1,036; £518; £259) **Stalls** Low

Form RPR

00-6 **1** **Showtime Annie**[19] [907] 3-8-9 59.............. JFanning 4 62
(ABailey) *a.p: rdn 2f out: led ins fnl f: r.o* **11/2**[3]

0-62 **2** *3/4* **Brown Dragon**[32] [774] 3-9-0 63.............. PaulEddery 6 65
(DHaydnJones) *chsd ldr: rdn 2f out: ev ch 1f out: nt qckn* **6/5**[1]

0-53 **3** *3/4* **Shaymee's Girl**[14] [956] 3-8-9 58.............. JoannaBadger 5 58
(MsDeborahJEvans) *led: rdn 2f out: edgd rt over 1f out: hdd ins fnl f: no ex* **9/1**

303- **4** *2 1/2* **Graceful Air (IRE)**[133] [5923] 3-8-9 64.............. RWinston 8 50
(JRWeymes) *chsd ldrs: rdn over 3f out: outpcd over 2f out: kpt on again ins fnl f* **3/1**[2]

00- **5** *2 1/2* **Flying Spud**[215] [4160] 3-9-0.............. ADaly 9 48
(JLSpearing) *bhd: rdn 4f out: nvr trbld ldrs* **16/1**

0-0 **6** *1 1/2* **Niteowl Express (IRE)**[14] [956] 3-8-9.............. DRMcCabe 3 38
(JO'Reilly) *s.i.s: outpcd* **16/1**

0-06 **7** *4* **Lady Stripes**[28] [822] 3-8-6 58.............. DCorby(3) 2 26
(MJWallace) *hld up: rdn and short-lived effrt on ins over 2f out: eased fnl f* **6/1**

1m 18.73s (3.03) **Going Correction** +0.55s/f (Slow) **7** Ran SP% **121.9**
Speed ratings: **101,100,99,95,92 90,85**CSF £13.67 TOTE £5.30: £3.10, £1.10; EX 13.80.
**Owner** Showtime Ice Cream Concessionaire **Bred** S And R Ewart **Trained** Little Budworth, Cheshire

**FOCUS**
A modest maiden, but solid form for the level.

**NOTEBOOK**
**Showtime Annie** improved considerably on her All-Weather debut over the stretch mile here late last month.
**Brown Dragon** did not help his rider by lugging left in the home straight. *Official explanation: jockey said gelding hung left-handed in the home straight*
**Shaymee's Girl**, who started at 66/1 on her three previous starts, had finished no less than 12 lengths behind the runner-up here last month.
**Graceful Air(IRE)** ran as if she needs a return to seven on this first outing since November.

### 1039 BET DIRECT NO Q ON 08000 93 66 93 H'CAP (DIV II) 7f (F)
**4:10** (4:11) (E) (0-70,66) 3-Y-O+ **£4,036** (£1,242; £621; £310) **Stalls** High

Form RPR

20-6 **1** **Duo Leoni**[17] [928] 4-9-4 58.............. MFenton 6 68
(MrsStefLiddiard) *a.p: led on bit 3f out: rdn 2f out: drvn out* **5/1**[3]

0200 **2** *nk* **St Ivian**[20] [897] 4-9-12 66..............(v) PMcCabe 3 75
(MrsNMacauley) *hld up: hdwy over 3f out: rdn wl over 1f out: ev ch 1f out: nt qckn* **11/1**

0240 **3** *3/4* **Cloudless (USA)**[13] [960] 4-9-1 55.............. SWKelly 4 62
(JWUnett) *hld up: hdwy over 3f out: rdn and ev ch 2f out: nt qckn fnl f* **10/1**

0050 **4** *1 1/2* **Spy Gun (USA)**[14] [953] 4-9-0 54.............. RFfrench 8 58
(TWall) *hld up: rdn and hdwy 2f out: one pce fnl f* **16/1**

0-03 **5** *1 1/2* **Extemporise (IRE)**[9] [990] 4-8-5 45..............(t) DaleGibson 7 45
(PJMcbride) *hld up: rdn and hdwy 2f out: no imp fnl f* **5/1**[3]

0-43 **6** *3/4* **Parker**[4] [1013] 7-9-11 65.............. KDarley 9 63
(BPalling) *hld up: hdwy on outside over 4f out: rdn over 2f out: wknd over 1f out* **3/1**[1]

3110 **7** *9* **Mount Royale (IRE)**[23] [866] 6-9-8 62..............(vt) KimTinkler 10 38
(NTinkler) *t.k.h: hdwy over 5f out: wknd 2f out* **7/2**[2]

1540 **8** *1* **Dancing King (IRE)**[3] [1019] 8-8-2 49.............. PMakin(7) 1 22
(PWHiatt) *led: rdn and hdd over 4f out: wkng whn n.m.r on ins 3f out* **11/1**

5460 **9** *1 1/4* **Pilgrim Princess (IRE)**[26] [834] 6-8-5 45.............. JQuinn 5 15
(EJAlston) *prom: rdn over 3f out: wknd over 2f out* **11/1**

00-0 **10** *10* **Tantric**[23] [866] 5-9-2 63.............. JDO'Reilly(7) 2 8
(JO'Reilly) *prom: hrd rdn over 2f out: wknd wl over 1f out* **10/1**

1m 33.72s (3.52) **Going Correction** +0.55s/f (Slow) **10** Ran SP% **129.6**
Speed ratings: **101,100,99,98,96 95,85,84,82,71**CSF £65.86 CT £555.57 TOTE £9.20: £2.70, £6.00, £2.20; EX 47.60.
**Owner** Mrs Stef Liddiard **Bred** P K Gardner **Trained** Great Shefford, Berks

**FOCUS**
The winning time was fractionally quicker than the less competitive first division. The form looks solid enough without offering much for the future.

**NOTEBOOK**
**Duo Leoni** held on under pressure after going smoothly to the front and the feeling was she would have preferred a stronger pace.
**St Ivian** had the visor back on after reverting to cheekpieces last time. This was the first time he had shown he gets this trip.
**Cloudless(USA)** adopted different tactics, having made the running recently.
**Spy Gun(USA)** showed signs of a return to form but is probably better at a mile.
**Extemporise(IRE)** was up in both class and distance.
**Parker**, again without the blinkers, was obliged to race wide throughout.

## 1040 BETDIRECT.CO.UK (S) STKS — 1m 100y(F)
4:45 (4:45) (G) 3-Y-O — £2,583 (£738; £369) Stalls Low

Form — RPR
-000 **1** **Stonor Lady (USA)**[9] [983] 3-8-7 48 ....... (e) EAhern 8 — 48
(PWD'Arcy) *a.p: led over 3f out: rdn over 2f out: drvn out* **8/1**
-003 **2** *1* **Fox Hollow (IRE)**[34] [751] 3-8-12 48 ....... RWinston 2 — 51
(MJHaynes) *led 1f: prom: rdn over 2f out: r.o one pce fnl f* **14/1**
-344 **3** *1* **Katie's Role**[40] [696] 3-8-7 50 ....... DeanMcKeown 9 — 44
(IanEmmerson) *a.p: rdn and ev ch over 2f out: nt qckn fnl f* **11/4**[1]
4405 **4** *½* **Secret Bloom**[29] [804] 3-8-12 45 ....... (v) DarrenWilliams 12 — 48
(JRNorton) *s.i.s: hld up: rdn and hdwy over 3f out: one pce fnl f* **20/1**
62-3 **5** *9* **Comic Genius**[36] [736] 3-8-7 45 ....... (b[1]) PaulEddery 1 — 24
(DHaydnJones) *led after 1f: rdn and hdd over 3f out: wknd 1f out* **4/1**[2]
4-26 **6** *6* **Bretton**[58] [566] 3-8-12 47 ....... (b) ACulhane 7 — 16
(RHollinshead) *hld up in tch: rdn and wkng whn n.m.r over 3f out* **9/2**[3]
-500 **7** *7* **Pure Emotion**[20] [895] 3-8-7 45 ....... JQuinn 11 — —
(WRMuir) *hld up in tch: rdn and wknd 2f out* **6/1**
50-0 **8** *3* **Three Welshmen**[28] [816] 3-8-12 60 ....... SDrowne 3 — —
(BRMillman) *bhd fnl 3f* **7/1**
0-34 **9** *14* **Knight To Remember (IRE)**[34] [751] 3-8-12 48 ....... NCallan 5 — —
(KARyan) *hld up: rdn 4f out: bhd fnl 3f* **6/1**

1m 56.16s (5.16) **Going Correction** +0.55s/f (Slow) — 9 Ran SP% **128.5**
Speed ratings: **96,95,94,93,84 78,71,68,54**CSF £124.06 TOTE £11.90: £3.60, £3.60, £1.50; EX 144.30.There was no bid for the winner.
**Owner** Mrs J Harris **Bred** T Hyde Jr **Trained** Newmarket, Suffolk

**FOCUS**
A weak seller and a moderate pace.

**NOTEBOOK**
**Stonor Lady(USA)** was down in grade for this return to the Fibresand surface.
**Fox Hollow(IRE)** was not inconvenienced by the longer distance.
**Katie's Role** was beaten for speed rather than stamina.
**Secret Bloom** was reverting to selling company.

## 1041 NEW SITE @ BETDIRECT.CO.UK H'CAP — 2m 46y(F)
5:20 (5:21) (F) (0-65,64) 4-Y-O+ — £2,968 (£848; £424) Stalls Low

Form — RPR
332 **1** **Aveiro (IRE)**[3] [1016] 8-9-2 52 ....... MFenton 8 — 65
(MissGayKelleway) *mde all: rdn over 3f out: clr over 1f out: styd on wl* **15/8**[1]
-210 **2** *15* **Platinum Charmer (IRE)**[13] [962] 4-9-5 60 ....... NCallan 6 — 55
(KARyan) *hld up: stdy hdwy 7f out: chsd wnr 6f out: rdn over 3f out: wknd over 1f out* **6/1**
1312 **3** *10* **Sungio**[15] [950] 6-9-2 52 ....... (b) DaleGibson 10 — 35
(BGPowell) *prom: rdn over 6f out: wknd over 3f out* **9/2**[2]
100/ **4** *1 ¼* **Swing West (USA)**[100] [1383] 10-7-12 34 oh4 ....... (b) SRighton 3 — 16
(AEJones) *hld up: reminders 10f out: rdn 8f out: sn struggling* **20/1**
40-3 **5** *2* **Toni Alcala**[19] [908] 5-9-11 64 ....... LFletcher[(3)] 1 — 43
(RFFisher) *hld up: rdn over 6f out: bhd fnl 4f* **5/1**[3]
-506 **6** *3* **E Minor (IRE)**[32] [777] 5-9-0 50 ....... RFfrench 9 — 26
(TWall) *chsd wnr: lost 2nd 6f out: rdn 5f out: wknd over 3f out* **11/2**
1605 **7** *29* **Paradise Valley**[13] [966] 4-8-11 52 ....... (t) SDrowne 2 — —
(MrsStefLiddiard) *hld up: pushed along over 4f out: sn bhd: eased whn no ch fnl 3f* **9/2**[2]

3m 50.86s (8.56) **Going Correction** +0.55s/f (Slow)
**WFA** 4 from 5yo+ 5lb — 7 Ran SP% **122.2**
Speed ratings: **100,92,87,86,85 84,69**CSF £15.31 CT £47.40 TOTE £1.60: £1.10, £5.70; EX 19.80 Place 6 £212.83, Place 5 £117.65..
**Owner** J T Billson **Bred** Saeed Manana **Trained** Newmarket, Suffolk

**FOCUS**
This took little winning. Aveiro came right away, but it is doubtful if this was an improved performance.

**NOTEBOOK**
**Aveiro(IRE)** dictated matters from the front and ran his field ragged after winding up the pace once in the back straight for the final time.
**Platinum Charmer(IRE)** had his stamina limitations ruthlessly exposed by the winner.
**Sungio** is twice a winner over two miles, but not on this demanding surface.
**Paradise Valley** was reported to have gurgled. *Official explanation: jockey said gelding had a breathing problem*
T/Plt: £111.60 to a £1 stake. Pool: £36,927.10. 241.50 winning tickets. T/Qpdt: £39.40 to a £1 stake. Pool: £2,251.80. 42.20 winning tickets. KH

# [1027] SOUTHWELL (L-H)
Thursday, March 18

**OFFICIAL GOING: Standard**
The going was reckoned to be Slow rather than the official Standard.

## 1042 NEW SITE @ BETDIRECT.CO.UK APPRENTICE H'CAP — 1m 4f (F)
2:25 (2:27) (F) (0-60,66) 3-Y-O+ — £2,996 (£856; £428) Stalls Low

Form — RPR
5300 **1** **Antony Ebeneezer**[12] [919] 5-8-0 35 ....... (t) RThomas[(3)] 16 — 43
(CRDore) *in tch: hdwy 4f out: rdn wl over 1f out: styd on to ld ent last: drvn out* **7/1**[3]
00-5 **2** *1* **It Must Be Speech**[35] [752] 3-8-5 64 ow6 ....... DerekNolan[(5)] 13 — 71
(SLKeightley) *midfield: gd hdwy over 3f out: led 2f out: sn rdn and hdd ent last: kpt on same pce* **16/1**
3103 **3** *hd* **Seraph**[17] [943] 4-8-3 40 ....... (p) RoryMoore[(3)] 10 — 46
(JohnAHarris) *hld up in midfield: gd hdwy over 4f out: effrt and ev ch 2f out tl rdn and one pce ins last* **12/1**
-213 **4** *nk* **Disabuse**[21] [902] 4-9-3 54 ....... PMakin[(3)] 12 — 60
(MWEasterby) *trckd ldrs: gd hdwy to ld 5f out: rdn over 2f out: sn hdd and drvn: kpt on same pce* **4/1**[1]
0003 **5** *4* **Top Of The Class (IRE)**[9] [996] 7-9-1 50 ow5 ....... (v) SJDonohoe[(3)] 6 — 50
(PDEvans) *chsd ldrs: rdn along 4f out: drvn over 2f out: grad wknd* **20/1**
5-30 **6** *7* **Kentucky Bullet (USA)**[56] [583] 8-9-0 49 ....... PGallagher[(3)] 7 — 38
(AGNewcombe) *prom: lost pl and midfield after 4f: effrt and sme hdwy 4f out: sn drvn along and no imp* **9/1**
**7** *4* **Berrywhite (IRE)**[36] 6-8-13 45 ....... THamilton 4 — 28
(CGrant) *cl up: rdn along over 4f out: wknd 3f out* **50/1**
6133 **8** *3 ½* **Spanish Star**[21] [901] 7-9-2 51 ....... LTreadwell[(3)] 1 — 29
(MrsNMacauley) *hld up towards rr. pushed along over 6f out: sn rdn and nvr a factor* **11/1**
6050 **9** *5* **Western Command (GER)**[4] [1026] 8-7-7 30 ....... CHaddon[(5)] 3 — 1
(MrsNMacauley) *a rr* **33/1**
6500 **10** *¾* **Ipledgeallegiance (USA)**[9] [995] 8-7-7 30 ....... DFentiman[(5)] 5 — —
(DWChapman) *a rr* **14/1**
304 **11** *½* **Munfarid (IRE)**[19] [919] 4-9-12 60 ....... (t) JFMcDonald 14 — 29
(PGMurphy) *hld up: a rr* **10/1**
3505 **12** *2 ½* **Coolfore Jade (IRE)**[10] [984] 4-9-4 52 ....... MSavage 2 — 17
(NEBerry) *led 4f: cl up tl rdn along over 5f out and sn wknd* **11/2**[2]
6201 **13** *7* **Jungle Lion**[18] [937] 6-9-10 56 ....... (t) NMackay 11 — 10
(JohnAHarris) *cl up: led after 4f: pushed along and hdd 5f out: drvn and wknd over 3f out* **15/2**
000- **14** *24* **Court One**[206] [4471] 6-8-0 35 ....... BSwarbrick[(3)] 9 — —
(RJPrice) *a bhd* **10/1**
165- **15** *20* **Piste Bleu (FR)**[161] [5079] 4-9-5 58 ....... DTudhope[(5)] 8 — —
(RFord) *a bhd* **25/1**

2m 42.8s **Going Correction** +0.175s/f (Slow)
**WFA** 3 from 4yo 22lb 4 from 5yo+ 2lb — 15 Ran SP% **129.9**
Speed ratings: **104,103,103,103,100 95,93,90,87,86 86,84,80,64,50**CSF £118.08 CT £1362.10 TOTE £8.10: £2.60, £5.60, £4.80; EX 281.00.
**Owner** Castles UK **Bred** John Purcell **Trained** West Pinchbeck, Lincs

**FOCUS**
There was a camera failure and the distances had to be estimated. A poor handicap, and while it was a good effort at the weights from the runner-up, the Handicapper is sure to react.

**NOTEBOOK**
**Antony Ebeneezer**, last seen over hurdles two weeks earlier, had the worst draw to overcome. This trip here brings out the best in him.
**It Must Be Speech**, stepping up in trip, ran his best race to date in achieving his first placing.
**Seraph**, whose only career success was here in January, ran better here than on his two starts since that win.
**Disabuse** set sail for home and it was not lack of stamina that failed to see him last it out.
**Top Of The Class(IRE)**, an in-and-out performer, has not won on the All-Weather since August 2001.
**Court One** *Official explanation: jockey said gelding hung left-handed throughout*

## 1043 £10 FREE BET @ BETDIRECT.CO.UK CLASSIFIED CLAIMING STKS — 1m (F)
3:00 (3:01) (F) 3-Y-O+ — £2,898 (£828; £414) Stalls Low

Form — RPR
60-0 **1** **Supreme Salutation**[42] [686] 8-9-7 60 ....... ACulhane 6 — 67
(DWChapman) *hld up: hdwy 1/2-way: trckd ldrs 2f out: rdn to ld appr last: sn clr* **10/3**[2]
4000 **2** *6* **Mutarafaa (USA)**[18] [932] 5-9-9 51 ....... (v) NCallan 7 — 57
(DShaw) *hld up: hdwy 1/2-way: wd st: led 2f out: sn rdn and hdd appr last: kpt on same pce* **5/1**
6-03 **3** *1 ¼* **Call Of The Wild**[20] [903] 4-9-7 51 ....... (p) PHanagan 10 — 53
(RAFahey) *led 3f: cl up: rdn 3f out: drvn 2f out: sn one pce* **7/1**
-300 **4** *2* **Crusoe (IRE)**[13] [970] 7-9-10 57 ....... DHolland 5 — 52
(ASadik) *sn outpcd and losing pl whn hmpd and bhd after 1f: swtchd wd: hdwy over 2f out: kpt on: nt rch ldrs* **9/2**[3]
0035 **5** *3* **Noble Pursuit**[4] [1016] 7-9-3 53 ....... LisaJones[(3)] 4 — 42
(PABlockley) *chsd ldrs: rdn along over 3f out: sn outpcd* **13/2**
3030 **6** *3* **Bulawayo**[20] [910] 7-9-6 49 ....... (v) ANicholls 9 — 36
(AndrewReid) *racd wd: cl up tl led after 3f: rdn along and hdd 2f out: sn drvn and wknd over 1f out* **16/1**
10-2 **7** *7* **Nod's Nephew**[15] [953] 7-9-4 52 ....... DerekNolan[(7)] 2 — 27
(DECantillon) *cl up: led after 3f: rdn along and hdd 3f out: sn wknd* **3/1**[1]
0-00 **8** *½* **Rocinante (IRE)**[18] [926] 4-9-9 51 ....... RFfrench 8 — 24
(JJQuinn) *chsd ldrs: rdn along 3f out: sn wknd* **16/1**
/00- **9** *17* **Havoc**[371] [710] 5-9-11 50 ....... DeanMcKeown 3 — —
(RonaldThompson) *a bhd* **66/1**
0600 **10** *½* **Pancakehill**[9] [996] 5-9-0 45 ow2 ....... MSavage[(5)] 1 — —
(DKIvory) *chsd ldrs 3f: sn lost pl and bhd* **25/1**

1m 45.05s (0.45) **Going Correction** +0.175s/f (Slow) — 10 Ran SP% **125.9**
Speed ratings: **104,98,96,94,91 88,81,81,64,63**CSF £22.45 TOTE £4.60: £1.50, £1.90, £1.80; EX 30.70.
**Owner** David W Chapman **Bred** M I Marsh **Trained** Stillington, N Yorks

**FOCUS**
A poor claimer but run at a fair pace. The winner was back to form after a break and shouldn't go up too much

**NOTEBOOK**
**Supreme Salutation**, clear top on official ratings and RPR, regained winning form with a vengeance and this will have done his confidence a power of good.
**Mutarafaa(USA)** had 11lb to find with the winner on official figures. Fibresand seems to suit him best.
**Call Of The Wild**, who has yet to win a race of any discription, finds this trip his bare minimum.
**Crusoe(IRE)** seemed to make his own trouble, but the impression was that he was second best on the day.
**Noble Pursuit** continues to disappoint.
**Nod's Nephew**, having his second outing in two weeks after a four-month break, seemed to do too much far too soon and dropped right away on the turn in.

## 1044 BETDIRECT.CO.UK MAIDEN STKS — 6f (F)
3:40 (3:43) (D) 3-Y-O+ — £3,328 (£1,024; £512; £256) Stalls Low

Form — RPR
0-25 **1** **Fit To Fly (IRE)**[10] [982] 3-8-11 72 ....... DHolland 8 — 64
(SKirk) *in tch: rdn along 3f out and sn outpcd: hdwy wl over 1f out: styd on wl under pessure to ld last 75 yds* **13/8**[1]
4000 **2** *1 ½* **Shadowfax**[20] [910] 4-9-10 52 ....... (b) MFenton 10 — 59
(MissGayKelleway) *dwlt: sn cl up on outer: effrt to ld ent last: sn rdn: hdd and nt qckn last 75yds* **20/1**
3245 **3** *¾* **Boavista (IRE)**[21] [893] 4-9-2 60 ow4 ....... SJDonohoe[(7)] 11 — 56
(PDEvans) *cl up: led after 2f: rdn wl over 1f out: drvn and hdd ent last: kpt on same pce* **9/1**
00-2 **4** *½* **Time To Relax (IRE)**[15] [956] 3-8-6 64 ....... DarrenWilliams 9 — 50
(JJQuinn) *chsd ldrs: rdn 2f out: kpt on u.p fnl f* **7/2**[2]
2046 **5** *¾* **Dark Champion**[24] [856] 4-9-10 48 ....... IMongan 7 — 53
(JeddO'Keeffe) *led 2f: cl up tl rdn and one pce fnl 2f* **25/1**
5524 **6** *1 ¾* **Zak Facta (IRE)**[19] [918] 4-9-10 50 ....... (vt) SWKelly 1 — 48
(MissDAMchale) *chsd ldrs: rdn along over 2f out: grad wknd* **13/2**



The Form Book, Raceform Ltd, Compton, RG20 6NL

6-0 **7** *2 ½* **Sir Galahad**[15] 956 3-8-4 ........ AMullen(7) 4 40
(TDEasterby) *a midfield* **50/1**

32-3 **8** *1* **Second Minister**[14] 963 5-9-10 60 ........ (bt) JPMurtagh 6 37
(DFlood) *towards rr: hdwy to chse ldrs over 2f out: sn rdn and no imp* **4/1**[3]

4/ **9** *1 ¾* **Miss Fleurie**[596] 3480 4-9-0 ........ TEaves(5) 3 27
(RCraggs) *s.i.s: a rr* **50/1**

-3 **10** *nk* **Uhuru Peak**[21] 898 3-8-11 ........ DaleGibson 5 31
(MWEasterby) *dwlt: sn rdn along and outpcd fr 1/2-way* **16/1**

3-00 **11** *1 ½* **Brooklands Time (IRE)**[20] 906 3-7-13 52 ........ GEdwards(7) 2 22
(IWMcinnes) *a rr* **50/1**

1m 19.02s (2.22) **Going Correction** +0.175s/f (Slow) **11** Ran SP% **124.0**
**WFA** 3 from 4yo+ 13lb
Speed ratings: **92,90,89,88,87 85,81,80,78,77 75**CSF £44.64 TOTE £2.70: £1.10, £4.50, £2.70; EX 25.70.
**Owner** M Magowan **Bred** Michael Greany **Trained** Upper Lambourn, Berks

**FOCUS**
A modest maiden. The winner is better than the bare form, but he will need to be win from his current mark

**NOTEBOOK**
**Fit To Fly(IRE)** made very hard work of it and will surely be happier back over seven. However unless his official rating is cut he will struggle in handicap company.
**Shadowfax**, out of sorts of late, bounced back and was only just worn down but he seems a habitual maiden.
**Boavista(IRE)** again ran well, but that first win is proving elusive.
**Time To Relax(IRE)** again ran well but this trip looks her bare minimum.
**Dark Champion** had plenty to find and this must go down as one of his better efforts on the All-Weather.
**Zak Facta(IRE)** *Official explanation: jockey said gelding hung left turning for home*

## 1045 NEW SITE @ BETDIRECT.CO.UK H'CAP 1m 4f (F)
**4:20** (4:21) (D) (0-85,81) 3-Y-O+ **£4,046** (£1,245; £622; £311) **Stalls** Low

Form RPR

3522 **1** **Glory Quest (USA)**[5] 1010 7-8-13 68 ........ (v) IMongan 4 78
(MissGayKelleway) *cl up: led after 5f: rdn along 3f out: drvn wl over 1f out: styd on strly ent last* **7/4**[2]

/3-1 **2** *5* **Moon Shot**[20] 908 8-9-3 72 ........ VSlattery 3 75
(AGJuckes) *hld up: smooth hdwy out: jnd wnr on bit 2f out and ev ch tl shkn up appr last and fnd nil* **7/1**[3]

-000 **3** *¾* **Sudden Flight (IRE)**[43] 679 7-9-1 70 ........ RHavlin 1 71
(PDEvans) *tra cked ldrs: smooth hdwy 5f out: cl up 3f out: rdn 2f out and kpt on same pce* **7/1**[3]

0-34 **4** *18* **Jamaican Flight (USA)**[51] 616 11-7-12 58 oh5 ow5 ...... RThomas(5) 6 32
(MrsSLamyman) *led: pushed along and hdd after 5f: rdn along and wknd 4f out* **20/1**

2-10 **5** *25* **Call Me Sunshine**[31] 795 4-8-6 63 ........ GFaulkner 2 —
(PCHaslam) *cl up: rdn along 1/2-way: wknd over 4f out* **11/1**

42-1 **6** *16* **Harelda**[38] 722 4-9-10 81 ........ JQuinn 5 —
(HMorrison) *hld up in rr: pushed along over 5f out: rdn along 4f out and sn btn* **11/8**[1]

2m 41.85s (-0.25) **Going Correction** +0.175s/f (Slow) **6** Ran SP% **116.6**
**WFA** 4 from 7yo+ 2lb
Speed ratings: **107,103,103,91,74 63**CSF £15.02 TOTE £2.40: £1.30, £6.00; EX 25.20.
**Owner** W R B Racing 40 (wrbracing.com) **Bred** Adelphian Ltd And Gainesway Farm **Trained** Newmarket, Suffolk

**FOCUS**
No real strength in depth, and with the favourite running poorly the winner probably merely reproduced recent placed efforts.

**NOTEBOOK**
**Glory Quest(USA)**, suited by the drop back in trip, was not winning out of turn.
**Moon Shot**, hoisted 11lb, came there travelling supremely well, but when asked a question it was a case of 'after you'.
**Sudden Flight(IRE)**, who has changed stables, ran better but is at his very best when able to dominate.
**Jamaican Flight(USA)** has now failed in 18 starts here but was running from out of the handicap over a trip some way short of his best.
**Call Me Sunshine** has to prove he stays this sort of trip.
**Harelda** was in trouble some way out and is clearly a delicate sort. *Official explanation: trainer had no explanation for the poor form shown*

## 1046 BET DIRECT ON SKY ACTIVE (S) STKS 7f (F)
**4:55** (4:57) (G) 3-Y-O **£2,604** (£744; £372) **Stalls** Low

Form RPR

-400 **1** **Garnock Venture (IRE)**[41] 696 3-8-12 47 ........ (b) FLynch 4 52
(ABerry) *cl up: led 2f out: sn rdn clr: edgd lft ent last: drvn out* **20/1**

6330 **2** *¾* **Maybe Someday**[10] 985 3-9-4 67 ........ (b[1]) DHolland 8 56
(IAWood) *led: rdn along and hdd 2f out: drvn and rallied ins last: kpt on* **2/1**[2]

-005 **3** *shd* **Son Of Rembrandt (IRE)**[22] 881 3-8-12 56 ........ IMongan 6 50
(DKIvory) *bmpd s: chsd ldrs on outer: effrt and ch over 2f out: sn rdn and edgd lft: kpt on u.p appr last* **14/1**

060- **4** *1 ¼* **Knickyknackienoo**[96] 6175 3-8-12 51 ........ SWhitworth 7 47
(AGNewcombe) *bmpd s: t.k.h and in tch: hdwy to chse ldrs over 2f out: sn rdn and kpt on same pce appr last* **14/1**

-110 **5** *1 ¾* **Smart Boy Prince (IRE)**[14] 959 3-9-4 66 ........ GDuffield 3 48
(PABlockley) *cl up on inner: rdn along over 2f out: sn drvn and wknd over 1f out* **6/4**[1]

0306 **6** *28* **Bookiesindexdotcom**[15] 958 3-8-7 54 ........ (b) SWKelly 9 —
(JRJenkins) *chsd ldrs and sn rdn along: drvn over 2f out and sn wknd* **13/2**[3]

-520 **7** *1 ½* **Quarry Island (IRE)**[30] 802 3-8-7 45 ........ DarrenWilliams 1 —
(PDEvans) *a rr* **12/1**

5400 **8** *2 ½* **Dancing Prince (IRE)**[10] 983 3-8-12 48 ........ (v) JQuinn 2 —
(APJarvis) *in tch: rdn along 1/2-way: sn wknd* **9/1**

00- **9** *20* **Eminent Aura (USA)**[330] 1182 3-8-7 ........ (v[1]) RFitzpatrick 5 —
(ADickman) *chsd ldrs: rdn along 3f out: sn wknd* **50/1**

1m 33.58s (2.78) **Going Correction** +0.175s/f (Slow) **9** Ran SP% **124.4**
Speed ratings: **91,90,90,88,86 54,52,50,27**CSF £65.01 TOTE £29.50: £5.60, £1.30, £3.10; EX 213.60.There was no bid for the winner. Maybe Someday was claimed by John Balding for £6,000.
**Owner** Robert Aird **Bred** Liam Queally **Trained** Cockerham, Lancs

**FOCUS**
A poor seller in which the form horses were way below their best.

**NOTEBOOK**
**Garnock Venture(IRE)**, who had a fair bit to find, shot clear and in the end did just enough to give his stable a change of fortune.
**Maybe Someday**, tried in blinkers, did not go down without a battle and was claimed by John Balding.
**Son Of Rembrandt(IRE)** ran much better than of late, and this longer trip seemed to suit him.
**Knickyknackienoo** gave his new connections some hope.
**Smart Boy Prince(IRE)**, drawn on the inner, was top-rated on RPR but he was not at his best for the second time running.

## 1047 £10 FREE BET @ BET DIRECT SKY ACTIVE H'CAP 6f (F)
**5:30** (5:31) (E) (0-75,67) 3-Y-O **£3,416** (£976; £488) **Stalls** Low

Form RPR

6134 **1** **Sahara Silk (IRE)**[23] 868 3-9-6 66 ........ (v) DarrenWilliams 5 74
(DShaw) *led 2f: cl up tl led again 3f out: rdn 2f out: drvn and hdd 1f out: rallied to ld again last 100 yds: gamely* **5/1**[2]

0121 **2** *nk* **Piccolo Prince**[15] 958 3-9-4 64 ........ JQuinn 8 71
(EJAlston) *hld up: hdwy 1/2-way: rdn to ld 1f out: sn drvn and edgd lft: hdd and nt qckn last 100 yds* **11/10**[1]

0010 **3** *½* **Head Of State**[29] 819 3-9-0 60 ........ (v) JMackay 11 66
(RMBeckett) *chsd ldrs: effrt and ev ch 2f out: sn rdn and kpt on fnl f* **10/1**[3]

0420 **4** *hd* **Lizhar (IRE)**[5] 1008 3-8-11 57 ........ GDuffield 10 62
(MJPolglase) *cl up: wd st and ev ch 2f out: sn rdn and one pce ent last* **12/1**

230- **5** *1 ¾* **Megabond**[131] 5950 3-9-2 62 ........ FLynch 3 62
(BSmart) *bhd and rdn along 1/2-way: gd hdwy wl over 1f out: styng on whn nt clr run and swtchd rt ins last: kpt on: nrst fin* **14/1**

5545 **6** *1* **Back At De Front (IRE)**[5] 1008 3-8-9 60 ........ MSavage(5) 4 57
(NEBerry) *chsd ldrs: effrt and ch 2f out: sn rdn and wknd appr last* **10/1**[3]

0-13 **7** *1* **Desert Light (IRE)**[66] 502 3-8-5 54 ........ (v) LisaJones(3) 7 48
(DShaw) *chsd ldrs: rdn 2f out: grad wknd* **14/1**

-064 **8** *2* **Indrani**[15] 958 3-7-6 45 ........ DFentiman(7) 2 33
(JohnAHarris) *bmpd s: hdwy to chse ldrs 2f out: sn rdn and wknd* **12/1**

066- **9** *7* **Sparkling Clear**[120] 6029 3-8-1 47 ........ MHenry 6 14
(RMHCowell) *in tch: hdwy to chse ldrs 2f out: swtchd rt and sn wknd* **33/1**

-120 **10** *2* **Jaolins**[22] 885 3-8-10 56 ........ RHavlin 9 17
(PGMurphy) *s.i.s: a rr* **14/1**

00-0 **11** *5* **Barbilyrifle (IRE)**[23] 868 3-9-4 67 ........ (b[1]) LFletcher(3) 1 13
(HMorrison) *wnt lft s: sn cl: up: led after 2f: rdn and hdd 3f out: sn wknd* **14/1**

1m 18.33s (1.53) **Going Correction** +0.175s/f (Slow) **11** Ran SP% **127.5**
Speed ratings: **96,95,94,94,92 91,89,87,77,75 68**CSF £11.79 CT £60.56 TOTE £8.10: £1.60, £1.30, £4.00; EX 13.40 Place 6 £164.64, Place 5 £38.27.
**Owner** Swann Racing Ltd **Bred** John Cullinan **Trained** Averham, Notts

**FOCUS**
A modest handicap, but the runner-up again travelled well and continues to progress.

**NOTEBOOK**
**Sahara Silk(IRE)**, whose three previous wins were over the minimum trip, is happiest here. She showed a willing attitude in a tight four-way finish.
**Piccolo Prince**, who is creeping up the ratings, worked hard to get his head in front but in the end just missed out.
**Head Of State**, an in-and-out performer, was 10lb higher than for his last success.
**Lizhar(IRE)**, slipping down the ratings, had the headgear left off.
**Megabond**, absent since November, was making his All-Weather bow and was unlucky not to have played a hand in the finish.

1048 - 1049a (Foreign Racing) - See Raceform Interactive

# 1015 LINGFIELD (L-H)
Friday, March 19

**OFFICIAL GOING: Standard**

## 1050 NEW SITE @ BETDIRECT.CO.UK MAIDEN STKS 1m 4f (P)
**2:00** (2:03) (D) 3-Y-O **£4,153** (£1,278; £639; £319) **Stalls** Low

Form RPR

2- **1** **Settlement Craic (IRE)**[185] 4958 3-9-0 ........ KDarley 12 69+
(TGMills) *a in tch: led 3f out: clr 1f out: pushed out* **6/4**[1]

**2** *1 ¼* **Muzio Scevola (IRE)** 3-8-11 ........ SHitchcott(3) 2 67+
(MRChannon) *w'like: bit bkwd: trckd ldrs: rdn and styd on to chse wnr fnl f* **10/1**[3]

**3** *1* **Border Saint** 3-9-0 ........ IMongan 4 66+
(MLWBell) *w'like: bit bkwd: hld up: hdwy on outside over 2f out: styd on u.p fnl f* **12/1**

3126 **4** *1 ½* **Fiddlers Ford (IRE)**[11] 985 3-9-0 72 ........ EAhern 3 63+
(JNoseda) *b.hind: trckd ldr to over 2f out: kpt on one pce fnl 2f* **5/2**[2]

00 **5** *1 ¼* **Mr Dinglawi (IRE)**[30] 821 3-9-0 ........ MTebbutt 9 62
(DBFeek) *in tch: chsd wnr over 2f out tl wknd ent fnl f* **100/1**

06 **6** *¾* **Zaffeu**[20] 916 3-9-0 ........ DHolland 1 60
(NPLittmoden) *trckd ldrs tl outpcd ins fnl 2f* **20/1**

0- **7** *1 ¼* **Ocean Rock**[139] 5867 3-9-0 ........ PaulEddery 11 59
(CAHorgan) *hld up in rr: hdwy on outside 3f out: eased whn hld ins fnl f* **50/1**

0 **8** *3* **Lakaam**[20] 916 3-8-9 ........ RBrisland 8 49
(GPEnright) *plld hrd: hld up in rr: a bhd* **100/1**

**9** *8* **Starmix** 3-9-0 ........ SDrowne 10 42
(PFICole) *w'like: bit bkwd: in tch: rdn over 4f out: wknd 3f out* **10/1**[3]

**10** *11* **Harry Came Home** 3-9-0 ........ PFitzsimons 13 26
(JCFox) *unf: bit bkwd: v.s.a: a bhd* **100/1**

00 **11** *3* **Divina**[28] 835 3-8-9 ........ ANicholls 5 16
(SLKeightley) *mde most tl hdd 3f out: wknd qckly* **66/1**

**12** *2 ½* **Stage Two (IRE)** 3-9-0 ........ KDalgleish 15 17
(MJohnston) *str: bit bkwd: rn green: wnt 2nd 6f out: wknd over 3f out* **12/1**

0- **13** *dist* **Pertemps Red**[281] 2311 3-9-0 ........ MFenton 6 —
(ADSmith) *trckd ldrs: rdn 1/2-way: wknd over 2f out: t.o* **100/1**

2m 36.83s (2.85) **Going Correction** 0.0s/f (Stan) **13** Ran SP% **114.3**
Speed ratings: **90,89,88,87,86 86,85,83,78,70 68,67,—**CSF £16.68 TOTE £1.90: £1.10, £5.50, £2.70; EX 36.40.
**Owner** Buxted Partnership **Bred** Pollards Stables **Trained** Headley, Surrey

**FOCUS**
A race contested by some nicely bred types, but the pace did not quicken until the run down to the straight and the time was slow. While the form overall is no more than modest, the first four are probably better than the result suggests

**NOTEBOOK**
**Settlement Craic(IRE)**, who showed promise in his sole juvenile outing over seven furlongs, appreciated the step up to a trip more in keeping with his stout pedigree and got off the mark with the minimum of fuss. A Derby entry looks optimistic at this stage, but he looks to have more good races in him.

**Muzio Scevola(IRE)** is by a sprinter but has clearly inherited the attributes of his dam, who won over this trip. He made a pleasing debut, keeping on nicely having been close to the pace throughout, and he will know much more next time.
**Border Saint**, another debutant, is from a good family who were mostly milers. He was another staying on steadily at the end and should have races in him.
**Fiddlers Ford(IRE)**, a market drifter, was stepping up in trip but does not have much in the way of acceleration and would have preferred a stronger gallop. Nevertheless, he gives a line to the level of the form.
**Mr Dinglawi(IRE)**, who had struggled in his two outings over much shorter trips, clearly appreciated the step up in distance. He is now qualified for handicaps.
**Zaffeu** finished closer to Fiddlers Ford than on their last meeting. He is another who now qualifies for handicaps and looks the sort to make his mark in that sphere.
**Stage Two(IRE)**, a half-brother to some good winners in the USA, showed up for a long way but dropped away quickly in the closing stages. Better can be expected in time.

## 1051 £10 FREE BET @ BETDIRECT.CO.UK H'CAP (DIV I) 6f (P)
**2:30** (2:33) (D ) (0-80,80) 3-Y-0+ **£5,083** (£1,564; £782; £391) **Stalls** Low

Form RPR
1162 **1** **Prince Aaron (IRE)**[34] 771 4-9-5 **71** GCarter 2 91+
(CNAllen) *b.hind: a gng wl bhd ldrs: led jst ins fnl f: sn clr: easily* **11/2**[2]
5611 **2** 2 ½ **Forever Phoenix**[20] 917 4-10-0 **80** EAhern 1 93+
(RMHCowell) *trckd ldr: led 2f out: rdn and hdd jst ins fnl f: nt pce of wnr* **7/2**[1]
1436 **3** 1 ½ **Aintnecessarilyso**[3] 1033 6-8-0 **52** CCatlin 4 60
(NEBerry) *a.p: r.o one pce fnl f* **25/1**
-010 **4** ¾ **Gun Salute**[22] 896 4-8-1 **53** (p) JQuinn 14 59
(GLMoore) *rcd wd: mid-div tl hdwy 2f out: one pce fnl f* **7/1**[3]
6500 **5** hd **Cormorant Wharf (IRE)**[15] 961 4-9-8 **74** JFEgan 5 79
(TEPowell) *in tch: outpcd ins fnl 2f* **8/1**
5012 **6** 1 ¼ **Sounds Lucky**[11] 987 8-8-8 **60** (b) ANicholls 9 61
(AndrewReid) *b: b.hind: t.k.h: effrt on outside 2f out: nt qckn appr fnl f* **20/1**
3-40 **7** nk **Polar Force**[34] 771 4-8-4 **59** DCorby(3) 6 60
(MRChannon) *in rr: mde sme late hdwy but n.d* **10/1**
1563 **8** shd **The Fisio**[20] 912 4-9-9 **75** MartinDwyer 3 75
(AMBalding) *led: hdd 2f out: rdn and wknd ins fnl f* **12/1**
050- **9** 1 ½ **Silver Chime**[155] 5597 4-9-2 **68** SDrowne 7 64
(DMSimcock) *in tch: rdn 1/2-way: wknd wl over 1f out* **14/1**
02-0 **10** shd **Roman Quintet (IRE)**[31] 806 4-8-10 **62** (tp) DaneO'Neill 12 57
(DWPArbuthnot) *trckd ldrs tl wknd over 1f out* **16/1**
0-10 **11** shd **Yorkie**[3] 1033 5-8-12 **64** 6ex NCallan 10 59
(PABlockley) *hld up: hdwy 1/2-way: wknd appr fnl f* **33/1**
0266 **12** 2 **Prima Stella**[15] 960 5-9-2 **71** LisaJones(3) 13 60
(JARToller) *hld up in rr: no hdwy fnl 2f* **16/1**
0020 **13** 1 ¼ **Tripti (IRE)**[5] 1018 4-7-8 **51** oh3 ow1 JFMcDonald(5) 11 36
(JJBridger) *b. hind: in tch tl rdn and wknd 2f out* **66/1**
6-50 **14** 5 **Awarding**[20] 912 4-9-4 **70** (t) KDarley 8 40
(RFJohnsonHoughton) *slowly away: plld hrd: a in rr* **10/1**

1m 10.9s (-2.02) **Going Correction** 0.0s/f (Stan) **14** Ran SP% **118.6**
Speed ratings: **113,109,107,106,106 104,104,104,102,102 101,99,97,90**CSF £23.55 CT £369.12 TOTE £5.90: £1.80, £2.10, £5.70; EX 18.50.
**Owner** Black Star Racing **Bred** Peter Charles And J R Bamforth **Trained** Newmarket, Suffolk

**FOCUS**
A decent sprint run 0.4sec faster than the second division. The principals are progressive and beat several rivals who have been in good form. The race has a solid look to it.

**NOTEBOOK**
**Prince Aaron(IRE)** ◆ has been progressing steadily this winter, and took this off a mark 17lb high than when scoring here in January. He did get the run of the race as the winner drifted off the rail, but there was no doubting the manner of his victory and, although he will go up again, he may not have finished winning yet.
**Forever Phoenix**, another progressive sort, was trying to complete the hat-trick off a mark 15lb higher than when initiating the sequence here a month ago. She did drift off the rail and let the winner through, but otherwise did little wrong and beat the rest well enough. Having taken such a stiff rise in the weights, the Handicapper may be prepared to drop her a pound or two.
**Aintnecessarilyso** is in a good run of form and performed with credit in this better company. In this form he may be able to find another lower-grade race, possibly back on Fibresand.
**Gun Salute**, seemingly helped by the fitting of cheekpieces this winter, gave Prince Aaron 5lb and a beating here in December. He appears to be holding his form, and that gives an indication of how much the winner has progressed.
**Cormorant Wharf(IRE)**, dropping back to the trip over which he scored on his juvenile debut, ran another decent race. He is gradually dropping down the weights and a win may not be too far away.
**Sounds Lucky**, who has been contesting claimers and sellers, ran well enough in this much better grade and is clearly in good heart.

## 1052 BET DIRECT ON SKY ACTIVE MAIDEN STKS 7f (P)
**3:00** (3:03) (D ) 3-Y-0 **£5,200** (£1,600; £800; £400) **Stalls** Low

Form RPR
-342 **1** **Monte Major (IRE)**[50] 628 3-9-0 61 NCallan 4 74
(MAJarvis) *mde all: rdn out fnl f* **9/1**
320- **2** 1 ¼ **Finders Keepers**[212] 4303 3-9-0 87 JPMurtagh 6 71
(EALDunlop) *lw: plld hrd: a.p: wnt 2nd 2f out: no imp ins fnl f* **5/6**[1]
**3** shd **Instant Recall (IRE)** 3-9-0 MHills 2 71
(BJMeehan) *w'like: leggy: prom tl rdn and outpcd over 2f out: styd on wl ins fnl f* **6/1**[2]
**4** 2 ½ **Cheeky Chi (IRE)** 3-8-6 BReilly(3) 7 59
(PSMcentee) *w'like: b.nr hind: plld hrd: trckd ldr tl rdn 2f out: kpt on one pce after* **66/1**
000- **5** ¾ **Desert Reign**[154] 5612 3-9-0 67 JQuinn 12 62
(APJarvis) *bit bkwd: chsd ldrs tl wknd appr fnl f* **33/1**
**6** 3 ½ **Suvari** 3-8-9 DHolland 8 48
(GCBravery) *leggy: bit bkwd: in tch: rdn and no hdwy appr fnl f* **13/2**[3]
55- **7** 1 ¼ **Simonovski (USA)**[138] 5887 3-9-0 EAhern 5 49
(JAOsborne) *t.k.h: in tch tl wknd over 1f out* **12/1**
43 **8** nk **Siera Spirit (IRE)**[44] 673 3-8-2 NicolPolli(7) 3 43
(MGQuinlan) *b. hind: slowly away: in rr: nvr nr to chal* **33/1**
0 **9** shd **Saintly Scholar (USA)**[11] 982 3-8-9 KDarley 13 43
(EALDunlop) *in rr: effrt on outside 2f out: wknd over 1f out* **25/1**
030- **10** hd **Hana Dee**[149] 5701 3-8-9 72 CCatlin 11 43
(MRChannon) *in tch tl wknd wl over 1f out* **16/1**
**11** ¾ **Cool Clear Water (USA)** 3-8-4 JFMcDonald(5) 15 41
(BJMeehan) *w'like: slowly away fr wd draw: swtchd to ins: a in rr* **33/1**
0 **12** ½ **Avertaine**[11] 982 3-8-9 IMongan 9 39
(GLMoore) *a towards rr* **40/1**
0 **13** 1 ¾ **Diverted**[21] 907 3-8-9 SWKelly 10 34
(MGQuinlan) *in tch tl wknd 2f out* **50/1**
0 **14** 2 **Accendere**[30] 816 3-9-0 MTebbutt 16 34
(RMBeckett) *a struggling in rr* **100/1**
0- **15** 2 ½ **Pick A Berry**[93] 6210 3-8-9 SDrowne 14 22
(GWragg) *a bhd* **50/1**

1m 26.25s (0.25) **Going Correction** 0.0s/f (Stan) **15** Ran SP% **127.3**
Speed ratings: **98,96,96,93,92 88,87,86,86,86 85,85,83,80,78**CSF £16.73 TOTE £11.50: £2.10, £1.30, £3.20; EX 18.60.
**Owner** The C H F Partnership **Bred** B Kennedy **Trained** Newmarket, Suffolk

**FOCUS**
An ordinary maiden run over a second and a half slower than the later handicap. Doubtful if the winner improved anything like as much as the line through the disappointing runner-up suggests.

**NOTEBOOK**
**Monte Major(IRE)**, who may have not lasted home when beaten over a mile on Fibresand last time, was given a fine waiting-in-front ride back at this shorter trip and ran on too strongly for the reluctant favourite. The form does not look anything special though.
**Finders Keepers** looked somewhat regressive as a juvenile, but this looked a good opportunity for him. However, he once again refused to settle and, after appearing to have every chance, did not look too keen to go past the leader. He may settle better racing from the front, but looks one to be wary of at present.
**Instant Recall(IRE)**, a quite attractive colt that cost 140,000gns and is from the family of Topanoora. He showed a good deal of promise on this racecourse debut, finishing strongly, and looks capable of winning an ordinary maiden.
**Cheeky Chi(IRE)**, a cheaply-bought filly, was very keen on this racecourse debut and ran well for a long way. She should be capable of picking up a fillies' maiden at around this trip.
**Desert Reign**, dropping back in trip on this Polytrack debut, looks more of a galloper and is bred to get middle distances. He will be interesting in handicaps if stepped up in trip.
**Suvari** was the subject of market support on this racecourse debut, but never really figured. However, the experience should not be lost on her.

## 1053 BET DIRECT ON 0800 32 93 93 FILLIES' H'CAP 1m 2f (P)
**3:30** (3:31) (D ) (0-85,85) 3-Y-0+ **£8,398** (£2,584; £1,292; £646) **Stalls** Low

Form RPR
-642 **1** **Dance In The Sun**[20] 915 4-10-0 **85** DaneO'Neill 2 93
(MrsAJPerrett) *lw: trckd ldrs: wnt 2nd 3f out: led ins fnl f: r.o wl* **7/4**[1]
00-0 **2** ¾ **Lara Falana**[15] 960 6-8-0 **60** LisaJones(3) 1 67
(MissBSanders) *in tch: hdwy over 2f out: rn on to go 2nd cl home* **15/2**
0-10 **3** nk **Maystock**[23] 887 4-9-6 **77** JPMurtagh 8 83
(GAButler) *trckd ldr: led over 3f out: rdn and hdd ins fnl f: no ex and lost 2nd cl home* **11/1**
0021 **4** 1 **Anyhow (IRE)**[15] 962 7-8-8 **64** ow1 DHolland 9 69
(MissKMGeorge) *hld up in rr: hdwy on outside ins fnl 2f: kpt on nvr nrr* **4/1**[2]
00 **5** 1 **Qudrah (IRE)**[3] 1030 4-9-13 **84** EAhern 7 87
(EJO'Neill) *hld up: rdn 3f out: kpt on one pce ins fnl 2f* **20/1**
0356 **6** shd **Figura**[22] 892 6-8-1 **58** JQuinn 6 60
(RIngram) *lw: hld up: hdwy whn n.m.r over 2f out: rdn and one pce after* **10/1**
450- **7** 1 ¼ **Cuddles (FR)**[137] 5910 5-9-6 **77** (p) IMongan 5 77
(CEBrittain) *in tch: rdn 4f out: wknd appr fnl f* **12/1**
-631 **8** ¾ **Miss Koen (IRE)**[11] 984 5-8-0 **55** 6ex ow2 (t) CCatlin 4 56
(DLWilliams) *hld up in rr: rdn over 3f out: nvr nr to chal* **20/1**
53-2 **9** 2 **Doris Souter (IRE)**[22] 892 4-9-2 **73** RSmith 3 68
(RHannon) *led tl hdd over 3f out: wknd over 1f out: eased whn hld* **7/1**[3]

2m 7.72s (0.33) **Going Correction** 0.0s/f (Stan) **9** Ran SP% **115.3**
Speed ratings: **98,97,97,96,95 95,94,93,92**CSF £15.47 CT £108.00 TOTE £1.80: £1.10, £1.60, £5.20; EX 16.00.
**Owner** Hesmonds Stud **Bred** Hesmonds Stud Ltd **Trained** Pulborough, W Sussex
■ Stewards Enquiry : Lisa Jones caution: used whip with excessive frequency

**FOCUS**
A fair fillies' handicap, but run at a modest pace. The winner is better class and was entitled to score.

**NOTEBOOK**
**Dance In The Sun**, who ran well in a better race over course and distance last month, stalked the leaders instead of making the running this time. She had to work hard to get to the front, but this was a decent effort considering she was giving weight all round. She may be up to winning in a higher grade now.
**Lara Falana**, who was well backed against the favourite, is well treated on this surface compared with her turf rating. Having had a warm-up over seven furlongs earlier in the month, she was back to form and was cutting down the winner near the finish. She can certainly win a similar race on this surface before returning to turf.
**Maystock** needs further than this and tried to make the most of her stamina. She did not give best until inside the last and a return to a longer trip with the visor re-applied will be in her favour.
**Anyhow(IRE)** needs a longer trip and a stronger gallop. In the circumstances she did well to finish where she did, particularly as she was stepping up in grade.
**Doris Souter(IRE)** was keen to get the early lead, but dropped out tamely when taken on and this has to go down as a disappointing effort.

## 1054 BETDIRECT.CO.UK H'CAP 1m 5f (P)
**4:00** (4:01) (C ) (0-95,95) 4-Y-0+ **£12,383** (£4,697; £2,348; £1,067) **Stalls** Low

Form RPR
101 **1** **Millville**[23] 887 4-8-12 **82** NCallan 10 90+
(MAJarvis) *hld up in tch: hdwy and squeezed thrugh to ld ins fnl f: sn in command* **2/1**[1]
-113 **2** 1 ¼ **Cold Turkey**[41] 706 4-9-4 **88** SWhitworth 12 95
(GLMoore) *hld up wl in rr: gd hdwy on outside 2f out: ev ch ent fnl f: nt pce of wnr* **4/1**[2]
5-12 **3** shd **Dolzago**[20] 919 4-7-9 **68** oh4 (b) LisaJones(3) 6 74
(GLMoore) *lw: hld up in tch: swtchd rt over 1f out: r.o wl fnl f* **12/1**
210- **4** nk **Flotta**[132] 5952 5-9-0 **84** SHitchcott(3) 2 90
(MRChannon) *chsd ldrs: nt clr run appr fnl f: r.o wl ins* **16/1**
1-00 **5** ¾ **Majlis (IRE)**[23] 887 7-8-1 **68** JQuinn 3 73
(RMHCowell) *mid-div: hdwy and ev ch whn edgd lft appr fnl f: nt qckn* **50/1**
1015 **6** hd **Gig Harbor**[20] 915 5-9-11 **95** LPKeniry(3) 4 100
(MissECLavelle) *lw: in tch: led 2f out: hdd & wknd ins fnl f* **11/1**
0064 **7** nk **Brilliant Red**[27] 844 11-8-12 **79** (t) IMongan 5 83
(JamiePoulton) *hld up in rr: sme hdwy over 1f out: nt pce to chal* **20/1**
3001 **8** 2 **Tight Squeeze**[22] 892 7-9-0 **81** JPMurtagh 7 82
(PWHiatt) *hld up in tch: rdn over 2f out: wknd over 1f out* **16/1**
460- **9** 1 **Anticipating**[181] 5071 4-9-0 **84** MartinDwyer 9 84
(AMBalding) *t.k.h: led over 6f out: hdd 2f out: sn wknd* **6/1**[3]
-243 **10** ¾ **Ezz Elkheil**[12] 887 5-8-8 **75** DHolland 8 74
(JRJenkins) *in front rnk: rdn over 3f out: wknd 2f out* **10/1**
411- **11** 11 **Coup De Chance (IRE)**[148] 5720 4-9-1 **85** (b) DeanMcKeown 11 69
(PABlockley) *a bhd* **20/1**


The Form Book, Raceform Ltd, Compton, RG20 6NL

405/ **12** 7 **Salford Flyer**[48] 2932 8-8-3 **70** ........ ANicholls 1 44
(JaneSouthcombe) *b: led tl hdd over 6f out: wknd over 3f out* **66/1**

2m 46.23s (-1.85) **Going Correction** 0.0s/f (Stan)
**WFA** 4 from 5yo+ 3lb **12** Ran SP% **117.5**
Speed ratings: **105,104,104,103,103 103,103,101,101,100 94,89**CSF £8.81 CT £76.25 TOTE £2.60: £1.10, £2.00, £2.20; EX 12.90 Trifecta £260.50 Pool £84,925.82, 231.40 w/u.
**Owner** T G Warner **Bred** Red House Stud **Trained** Newmarket, Suffolk

**FOCUS**
A decent handicap run at a fair pace and a fine effort from the progressive winner, who is better than the bare form.

**NOTEBOOK**
**Millville ◆**, is making up for lost time, having made a belated debut only in January this year. He was well backed for this step up into a competitive handicap, and showed the right attitude to get through a narrow gap and cut down the runner-up inside the final furlong. He is the sort to go on progressing and can make his mark on turf.
**Cold Turkey ◆** has been really progressive this winter, winning five times and being placed in his other three starts and rising 22lb in the handicap. He made his ground quickly on the run down to the straight and looked likely to prevail halfway up the straight, but was run out of it by a fast-improving sort. There was no disgrace in this and, already proven on turf, can take advantage of a lower handicap mark on that surface.
**Dolzago ◆**, who has been improved for the fitting of blinkers, was taking a big step up in grade and racing off an 8lb higher mark. He was finishing really well and now connections may have to run again before he is reassessed.
**Flotta ◆**, who was unlucky in this race last year, suffered a similar fate this time. He went for the same gap as the winner, but got there a fraction later and was squeezed out. He did well to finish fourth and looks capable of gaining compensation when returned to turf.
**Majlis(IRE)** ran much better with the blinkers left off and, suited by cut in the ground and a flat right-handed track, may be the sort for a race like the Queen's Prize at Kempton over Easter.
**Gig Harbor**, stepping back up in trip, had to fight hard to get past Anticipating on the run to the straight, and this appeared to leave him with nothing in reserve for the finish. He is also high enugh in the weights now.
**Brilliant Red** has dropped 12lb this winter and is running better as a result. He has never won at this trip but seems to need it nowadays. A slight drop in grade may be the answer.
**Anticipating** was very keen and took over at halfway. A protracted battle with Gig Harbour on the run to the turn in appeared to leave both of them vulnerable in the straight.

## 1055 TERRY SMART'S 60TH BIRTHDAY CLAIMING STKS 1m (P)
4:30 (4:32) (D ) 4-6-Y-O **£4,124** (£1,269; £634; £317) **Stalls** High

Form RPR
4250 **1** **The Gaikwar (IRE)**[15] 964 5-8-12 62 ........(b) EAhern 6 73
(NPLittmoden) *trckd ldrs: led wl over 1f out: sn clr* **9/1**
2016 **2** 2 **Acorazado (IRE)**[24] 870 5-8-8 64 ........(be) LisaJones(3) 7 67
(GLMoore) *hld up in rr: stdy hdwy over 2f out: styd on to go 2nd last strides* **8/1**
00 **3** shd **Harry Potter (GER)**[27] 847 5-9-2 61 ........(v[1]) DarrenWilliams 5 72
(KRBurke) *a in tch: chsd wnr fnl f tl lost 2nd last strides* **50/1**
50-3 **4** 3 ½ **Brazilian Terrace**[15] 961 4-8-7 74 ........ HayleyTurner(5) 3 60
(MLWBell) *trckd ldrs: rdn over 2f out: kpt on one pce after* **5/2**[1]
S30- **5** shd **Climate (IRE)**[111] 6093 5-9-2 72 ........ DSweeney 9 64
(JRBoyle) *hld up in rr: effrt on outside over 1f out: nvr nr to chal* **9/1**
3221 **6** ½ **Ballinger Ridge**[10] 997 5-9-0 67 ........(v) MartinDwyer 11 61
(AMBalding) *led after 1f: rdn and hdd 2f out: sn btn* **10/1**
-540 **7** ¾ **Fen Gypsy**[19] 932 6-8-11 59 ........(b) SWKelly 12 56
(PDEvans) *led for 1f: led briefly again 2f out: wknd fnl f* **7/1**[3]
-030 **8** 1 ½ **Greenwood**[37] 742 6-9-7 75 ........ DKinsella 1 63
(PGMurphy) *sn in rr: nvr on terms* **12/1**
0340 **9** 1 ¼ **Pheckless**[20] 912 5-9-3 66 ........ PFitzsimons 4 56
(JMBradley) *s.s: plld hrd: a bhd* **20/1**
2033 **10** 1 ½ **Blonde En Blonde (IRE)**[15] 960 4-8-11 68 ........(b) DHolland 8 46
(NPLittmoden) *towards rr: rdn 1/2-way: nvr on terms* **5/1**[2]
0 **11** 10 **Sink Or Swim (IRE)**[11] 984 6-7-11 ........ JFMcDonald(5) 2 14
(JJBridger) *b: in tch to 1/2-way* **66/1**
03-0 **12** 10 **Karathaena (IRE)**[11] 982 4-8-11 78 ........ MHills 10 —
(JWHills) *slowly away: rdn 1/2-way: a wl in rr* **16/1**

1m 37.57s (-1.94) **Going Correction** 0.0s/f (Stan) **12** Ran SP% **119.7**
Speed ratings: **109,107,106,103,103 102,102,100,99,97 87,77**CSF £78.89 TOTE £14.00: £5.10, £3.00, £9.40; EX 104.30.The winner was claimed by Norman Berry for £11,000.
**Owner** Nigel Shields **Bred** Burton Agnes Stud Co Ltd **Trained** Newmarket, Suffolk

**FOCUS**
Just a modest claimer, but run at decent pace. With the favourite below form The Gaikwar had little to beat.

**NOTEBOOK**
**The Gaikwar(IRE)** is a quirky sort but seemed to get the run of the race and scored decisively. He was claimed afterwards by Norman Berry, who trained him earlier in the season.
**Acorazado(IRE)**, a course winner running in a claimer for the first time, came from well back to snatch second. He was ridden closer to the pace when scoring here last month, and a return to those tactics around here should help.
**Harry Potter(GER)**, a winner over seven furlongs in Germany, ran much better for the fitting of a visor and was only just caught for second. He looks capable of finding a similar race, possible over a furlong shorter.
**Brazilian Terrace**, narrowly beaten last time on her debut on this surface, seemed to have every chance but could not improve on that effort despite having a big chance on official ratings.
**Climate(IRE) ◆** ran a nice race on this return from a break. He has form on the track and on a sound surface on turf, and this should bring him on.
**Ballinger Ridge** was again keen in front and had nothing left for the business end.
**Fen Gypsy** forced his way past the leader on the turn in, but could not sustain the effort.
**Blonde En Blonde(IRE)**, put up a rare lacklustre effort. She has had ten races since Christmas and may need a break.
**Karathaena(IRE)** *Official explanation: jockey said filly lost her action*

## 1056 £10 FREE BET @ BET DIRECT SKY ACTIVE CLASSIFIED STKS 7f (P)
5:00 (5:02) (D ) 3-Y-O+ **£4,400** (£1,354; £677; £338) **Stalls** Low

Form RPR
130- **1** **Miss George**[209] 4374 6-9-3 83 ........ DaneO'Neill 3 91
(DKIvory) *b: b.hind: hld up in rr: hdwy 2f out: str run fnl f to ld fnl 50 yds* **14/1**
2-10 **2** nk **Dawn Piper (USA)**[48] 648 4-9-6 83 ........(v[1]) JPMurtagh 2 93
(DRLoder) *led: rdn over 1f out: kpt on: hdd fnl 50yds* **2/1**[1]
01-4 **3** 1 ¼ **What-A-Dancer (IRE)**[34] 770 7-9-6 83 ........ RWinston 1 90
(GASwinbank) *trckd ldrs: rdn over 1f out: kpt on one pce* **4/1**[2]
1301 **4** ½ **Chateau Nicol**[37] 742 5-9-3 80 ........(b) JFanning 4 86
(BGPowell) *b.hind: lw: plld hrd: in tch tl fdd ins fnl f* **8/1**[3]
60-4 **5** ¾ **The Bonus King**[28] 837 4-9-6 83 ........ KDalgleish 7 87
(MJohnston) *lw: trckd ldr tl rdn 2f out: wknd appr fnl f* **12/1**
5113 **6** nk **Grey Pearl**[34] 770 5-9-2 82 ........ MFenton 8 82+
(MissGayKelleway) *trckd ldrs: rapid hdwy to go 2nd 2f out: wknd appr fnl f: eased* **4/1**[2]
361- **7** ½ **Border Music**[138] 5886 3-8-3 81 ........ MartinDwyer 6 83
(AMBalding) *lw: hld up: effrt on outside 2f out: sn btn* **8/1**[3]
000- **8** 1 **Compton Dragon (USA)**[146] 5747 5-9-3 80 ........ ANicholls 5 80
(DNicholls) *s.i.s: a bhd* **20/1**

1m 24.69s (-1.31) **Going Correction** 0.0s/f (Stan)
**WFA** 3 from 4yo+ 15lb **8** Ran SP% **114.7**
Speed ratings: **107,106,105,104,103 103,102,101**CSF £42.60 TOTE £22.10: £3.50, £1.70, £1.60; EX 85.40.
**Owner** Mrs A Shone **Bred** Mrs C S Knowles **Trained** Radlett, Herts

**FOCUS**
A tight classified event on paper, run at a sound pace and producing a close finish.

**NOTEBOOK**
**Miss George**, having her first race for seven months, repeated last year's victory in this race. She has now won her last four races over course and distance and her sprinter's speed is a useful asset. She is one to keep on the right side.
**Dawn Piper(USA) ◆**, visored for the first time, was keen in front and was only run down late on. He lost nothing in defeat and is one to bear in mind for an early success back on turf.
**What-A-Dancer(IRE)**, a specialist at this trip, is another to keep in mind when returning to turf, as he is rated 5lb lower.
**Chateau Nicol**, who has been in fine form, again was keen in the race and, after coming with an effort on the outside, seemed to flatten out inside the last. He had no easy task on official ratings and remains in good heart.
**The Bonus King** ran better in this lower grade, and now he is slipping in the weights, may be able to recapture his good juvenile form back on turf.
**Grey Pearl** has crept up the weights after two wins in January and the Handicapper appears to have her once again.

## 1057 £10 FREE BET @ BETDIRECT.CO.UK H'CAP (DIV II) 6f (P)
5:30 (5:33) (D ) (0-80,79) 3-Y-O+ **£5,083** (£1,564; £782; £391) **Stalls** Low

Form RPR
50-4 **1** **Another Glimpse**[20] 912 6-9-5 71 ........(t) TQuinn 7 81
(MissBSanders) *hld up: gd hdwy 2f out: led jst ins fnl f: jst hld on* **9/2**[1]
3024 **2** hd **Double M**[19] 928 7-8-4 56 ........(v) ADaly 9 65
(MrsLRichards) *hld up in rr: gd hdwy appr appr fnl f: r.o strly: jst failed* **14/1**
4123 **3** nk **Mayzin (IRE)**[27] 847 4-8-10 62 ........(p) DSweeney 6 71
(RMFlower) *lw: sn trckd ldr: led briefly 1f out: r.o: nt qckn nr fin* **8/1**
-200 **4** ½ **Madrasee**[20] 912 6-8-13 65 ........ DHolland 1 72
(LMontagueHall) *trckd ldrs: n.m.r and swtchd lft appr fnl f: r.o* **10/1**
2051 **5** ½ **Ripple Effect**[15] 960 4-9-10 79 ........(t) BReilly(3) 5 85
(CADwyer) *a in tch: ev ch ent fnl f: fdd* **8/1**
405- **6** nk **Bahamian Belle**[130] 5969 4-7-9 50 ........ LisaJones(3) 2 55
(PSMcentee) *slowly away: sn in tch: hung rt on bnd over 1f out: one pce after* **50/1**
0-24 **7** ½ **Blue Knight (IRE)**[14] 968 5-9-7 73 ........ JQuinn 3 76
(APJarvis) *a in tch: n.m.r whn wkng ins fnl f* **11/2**[2]
4-56 **8** ¾ **Dont Call Me Derek**[41] 708 3-8-1 66 ........ RFfrench 8 67
(SCWilliams) *b: b.hind: outpcd in rr: effrt over 1f out: nvr on terms* **16/1**
0241 **9** ¾ **Hard To Catch (IRE)**[34] 771 6-9-1 70 ........ RMiles(3) 11 69
(DKIvory) *b: b.hind: in rr: effrt on outside 2f out: nvr rchd ldrs* **15/2**[3]
4512 **10** 1 **Skip Of Colour**[22] 897 4-9-8 74 ........ DeanMcKeown 4 70
(PABlockley) *b: led tl hdd & wknd 1f out* **11/2**[2]
0035 **11** ½ **Illusive (IRE)**[19] 928 7-8-8 60 ........(b) GCarter 12 54
(MWigham) *hld up in rr: nvr gng pce* **12/1**
1060 **12** 9 **Panjandrum**[16] 954 6-8-11 63 ........ CCatlin 13 30
(NEBerry) *racd wd in rr: no ch fnl 2f* **33/1**

1m 11.3s (-1.62) **Going Correction** 0.0s/f (Stan)
**WFA** 3 from 4yo+ 13lb **12** Ran SP% **117.2**
Speed ratings: **110,109,109,108,108 107,106,105,104,103 102,90**CSF £68.12 CT £493.27 TOTE £5.10: £2.00, £4.80, £2.50; EX 92.20 Place 6 £49.72, Place 5 £27.74.
**Owner** Edward Hyde **Bred** Copyforce Ltd **Trained** Epsom, Surrey
■ Stewards Enquiry : A Daly one-day ban: used whip with excessive frequency and without giving horse time to respond (Mar 30)

**FOCUS**
A fair sprint handicap, but not as strong as the first division, which was run 0.4sec quicker. The leaders went quick early on and the principals came from off the pace.

**NOTEBOOK**
**Another Glimpse**, who ran well over an inadequate five furlongs last time after a seven-month break, confirmed that promise under a good ride, narrowly holding the runner-up's late surge. He seems most effective at seven furlongs on turf, and if going on from this, might score again.
**Double M** looked unlucky in running, and his strong late run only narrowly failed to catch the winner. He remains in good form and deserves compensation.
**Mayzin(IRE)**, who stays seven furlongs, did best of those to race up with the pace. He deserves plenty of credit for this effort, and it would be no surprise to see him hit the target again before long.
**Madrasee** ran well enough, but is more effective on downhill tracks on turf. She will have to race off a higher mark, but is fit and will be one to watch out for at Brighton or Epsom this spring.
**Ripple Effect** had no easy task, having been raised 7lb for her win in a fillies' race over seven furlongs earlier in the month. This was still a creditable effort, and a return to the longer trip will be in her favour.
**Bahamian Belle**, having her first run since November and only her second on this surface, showed enough to suggest that a lower-grade handicap is within her scope off her current mark.
**Blue Knight(IRE)** seems more effective on the Fibresand tracks.
**Skip Of Colour** probably went too fast on his return to this surface. He seems more effective on the Southwell Fibresand. *Official explanation: trainer said gelding lost both front shoes*
**Illusive(IRE)** *Official explanation: trainer said gelding lost a shoe*
T/Jkpt: Not won. T/Plt: £77.40 to a £1 stake. Pool: £56,194.10. 529.50 winning tickets. T/Qpdt: £23.60 to a £1 stake. Pool: £3,087.20. 96.60 winning tickets. JS

1058 - (Foreign Racing) - See Raceform Interactive

# [1050]LINGFIELD (L-H)
Saturday, March 20

**OFFICIAL GOING: Standard**
It proved an advantage today to be drawn low and race prominently, and so those who ran well from off the pace should be given extra credit.
Wind: str, half bhd Weather: dull & wet

## 1059 ARENA LEISURE MAIDEN STKS 1m (P)
1:05 (1:06) (D ) 3-Y-O+ **£5,096** (£1,568; £784; £392) **Stalls** High

Form RPR
2/ **1** **Wake (USA)**[519] 5336 4-9-11 ........ PJSmullen 6 81+
(BJMeehan) *plld hrd: prom: rdn over 2f out: led ins fnl f: r.o wl* **3/1**[2]
0-4 **2** 1 ¼ **Keelung (USA)**[23] 890 3-8-8 ........ PRobinson 8 78+
(MAJarvis) *hdwy to ld after 2f: hrd rdn and hdd ins fnl f: nt qckn* **11/4**[1]

3 **3** *3* **Emsam Ballou (IRE)**[12] 982 3-8-3 ........ RSmith 1 66+
(RHannon) *set slow pce 2f: prom: one pce appr fnl f* **8/1**

43- **4** *½* **Miss Adelaide (IRE)**[148] 5733 3-8-3 ........ EAhern 11 65+
(BWHills) *t.k.h: prom: one pce appr fnl f* **7/2**[3]

0 **5** *½* **Ballinger Express**[28] 846 4-9-6 ........ MartinDwyer 2 64
(AMBalding) *chsd ldrs: rdn over 2f out: styd on same pce* **20/1**

\- **6** *hd* **Lebenstanz** 4-9-1 ........ NMackay(5) 4 63
(LMCumani) *leggy: s.s: sn in mid-div: pushed along 3f out: styd on fnl f* **20/1**

**7** *3* **Suspicious Minds** 3-8-4 ow1 ........ SWhitworth 5 57
(GCBravery) *neat: s.s: in rr tl rdn and styd on fnl 2f* **33/1**

6- **8** *½* **Mutassem (FR)**[148] 5723 3-8-8 ........ RHills 9 60
(EALDunlop) *b: t.k.h: in tch: rdn over 2f out: sn outpcd* **10/1**

\- **9** *7* **Imperial Dragon (USA)** 4-9-11 ........ DHolland 12 44
(WAO'Gorman) *w'like: scope: s.s: rdn 3f out: a towards rr* **40/1**

5 **10** *1½* **Sunset Blues (FR)**[22] 907 4-9-11 ........(be) NCallan 3 41
(KOCunningham-Brown) *in tch: rdn 1/2-way: wknd 3f out* **100/1**

0 **11** *5* **Alianna (FR)**[12] 982 3-8-3 ........ CCatlin 10 24
(SDow) *a bhd* **100/1**

0 **12** *shd* **Paris Latino (FR)**[16] 963 5-9-11 ........(t) VSlattery 7 29
(CLTizzard) *bhd fnl 4f* **100/1**

1m 39.35s (-0.16) **Going Correction** -0.05s/f (Stan)
**WFA** 3 from 4yo+ 17lb **12** Ran SP% **112.0**
Speed ratings: **98,96,93,93,92 92,89,89,82,80 75,75**CSF £10.18 TOTE £3.30: £1.70, £1.60, £2.50; EX 18.50.
**Owner** Joe L Allbritton **Bred** Lazy Lane Stables Inc **Trained** Upper Lambourn, Berks

**FOCUS**
The pace was not hot, but this was a fair maiden and the first three look interesting for the future.

**NOTEBOOK**
**Wake(USA)**, who looked fit despite his long absence, raced prominently in a steadily-run race and kept on well under pressure. He was considered a potential pattern-grade horse last year and, now that he is sound again, can hopefully build on this.
**Keelung(USA)**, who had the benefit of race fitness, soon got to the front and dictated a steady pace. He may have met a decent rival in the winner and there was no disgrace in this performance as he finished nicely clear of the rest. He is now eligible for a handicap mark.
**Emsam Ballou(IRE)** stayed on well over seven furlongs on her debut but is bred to be a sprinter and this trip looked to stretch her stamina.
**Miss Adelaide(IRE)**, who looked fit for her reappearance, was stepping up to a more suitable trip, but she was slightly disappointing. She is clearly not as good as was once thought by connections.
**Ballinger Express**, whose dam is from the family of high-class sprinter Branston Abby, improved on her debut effort four weeks earlier.
**Lebenstanz**, a quite attractice filly who is closely related to Boreas, was slowly away, not given a hard time and is bred to improve when granted a greater test of stamina.
**Suspicious Minds**, a half-sister to Triumph Hurdle winner Spectroscope, looked in need of the experience but, after giving away a fair amount of ground at the start, was doing her best work at the finish. She should improve when stepped up in trip.

## 1060 AXMINSTER CARPETS JUVENILE CONDITIONS STKS 5f (P)
**1:35** (1:40) (C ) 2-Y-O **£12,180** (£4,620; £2,310; £1,050) **Stalls** High

Form RPR

**1** **Bunditten (IRE)** 2-8-7 ........ SCarson 4 73
(AndrewReid) *b: b.hind: w'like: hung rt thrght: mde all: hrd rdn 1f out: hld on wl* **9/2**[2]

**2** *½* **I'm Aimee** 2-8-7 ........ SDrowne 6 71
(PDEvans) *w'like: prom: rdn to press wnr fnl f: r.o* **33/1**

**3** *2½* **Windy Prospect** 2-8-12 ........ DeanMcKeown 8 66
(PABlockley) *leggy: s.i.s: hdwy to chse wnr over 3f out tl 1f out: one pce* **4/1**[1]

**4** *3½* **Cubic Confessions (IRE)** 2-8-7 ........ SWKelly 7 47
(JAOsborne) *leggy: prom tl wknd over 1f out* **13/2**[3]

**5** *1¾* **Joe Ninety (IRE)** 2-8-12 ........ JDSmith 2 45
(JSMoore) *w'like: bit bkwd: mid-div: no hdwy fnl 2f* **14/1**

**6** *nk* **Bamboozled** 2-8-7 ........ NCallan 3 39
(PDEvans) *leggy: chsd ldrs 2f* **20/1**

**7** *½* **Grand Option** 2-8-12 ........ RLMoore 9 42
(BWDuke) *unf: outpcd: nvr rchd ldrs* **9/2**[2]

**8** *3* **Im Spartacus** 2-8-12 ........ JFanning 10 30
(IAWood) *w'like: cl cpld: mid-div: outpcd fr 1/2-way* **20/1**

**9** *hd* **Itsa Monkey (IRE)** 2-8-9 ........ TPQueally(3) 1 29
(NPLittmoden) *unf: outpcd: a bhd* **25/1**

**10** *15* **His Majesty** 2-8-12 ........ DHolland 5 —
(NPLittmoden) *w'like: cl cpld: outpcd: a wl bhd* **4/1**[1]

59.61 secs (-0.17) **Going Correction** -0.05s/f (Stan) **10** Ran SP% **112.7**
Speed ratings: **99,98,94,88,85 85,84,79,79,55**CSF £145.40 TOTE £5.70: £2.10, £5.10, £2.00; EX 223.60.
**Owner** A S Reid **Bred** Lodge Park Stud **Trained** Mill Hill, London NW7

**FOCUS**
The first two-year-old race of the season, and one dominated by the fillies. One can only guess, but they were nicely stretched at the finish and it is probably reasonable early form.

**NOTEBOOK**
**Bunditten(IRE)**, a February foal and the most expensive runner in the field, was quickly into her stride, had the rail throughout, and held off her rivals in tenacious style despite hanging. She is a speedy filly, but talk of Royal Ascot is premature to say the least. Indeed, it would be unwise to assume the form is as good as the race's conditions title suggests, for last year's event did not work out at all well.
**I'm Aimee**, an April foal and half-sister to Brocklesby second Lord Bankes, showed good speed throughout and ran well despite being unfancied in the ring. She looks a likely type for a minor maiden in the next few weeks.
**Windy Prospect**, an April foal who is certainly bred to be precocious, had his chance but could not match the pace of the fillies in the closing stages. The fact that he now has experience of racing, though, means that he should enjoy a significant advantage over his opposition in the next few weeks.
**Cubic Confessions(IRE)** also showed pace but, unlike some, is bred to improve when eventually stepped up in trip.
**Joe Ninety(IRE)**, a March foal, kept on well enough but found this opposition a bit too strong. He is likely to have to take a drop in grade to get off the mark.
**Bamboozled** was struggling from some way out.
**Grand Option**, the oldest runner in the field, foaled in February, looked a nice type beforehand and was the gamble of the race. The punt never looked like being landed, but we probably did not see the best of him and the experience should bring him on.

## 1061 LADBROKES.COM SPRINT CONDITIONS STKS 5f (P)
**2:05** (2:07) (B ) 4-Y-O+ **£17,400** (£6,600; £3,300; £1,500) **Stalls** High

Form RPR

6621 **1** **No Time (IRE)**[28] 841 4-9-5 85 ........ LDettori 2 106
(MJPolglase) *b.hind: lw: led after 1f: hrd rdn 1f out: slt ld fnl 100 yds: hld on wl* **12/1**

410- **2** *shd* **Speed Cop**[156] 5593 4-8-7 100 ........ MartinDwyer 7 94
(AMBalding) *lw: pressed ldng pair: str chal ins fnl f: jst hld* **9/2**[2]

0212 **3** *¾* **Justalord**[28] 841 6-8-12 89 ........(p) JEdmunds 8 96
(JBalding) *in tch: effrt and hung rt 2f out: drvn to press ldrs 1f out: kpt on* **12/1**

300- **4** *¾* **Dragon Flyer (IRE)**[156] 5591 5-8-7 95 ........ SDrowne 9 88
(MQuinn) *mid-div and wd: rdn and styd on fnl 2f: nvr nrr* **14/1**

225- **5** *½* **Little Edward**[174] 5251 6-9-4 99 ........ LPKeniry 6 97
(BGPowell) *b: led 1f: w wnr tl no ex ins fnl f* **12/1**

02-1 **6** *½* **Dusty Dazzler (IRE)**[63] 556 4-8-10 95 ........ AQuinn 10 87
(WGMTurner) *in rr: effrt and swtchd wd over 1f out: nt rch ldrs* **7/1**

023- **7** *hd* **Fire Up The Band**[182] 5060 5-8-12 106 ........ ANicholls 5 88
(DNicholls) *bit bkwd: in rr: effrt 2f out: nvr able to chal* **3/1**[1]

0600 **8** *1¼* **Peruvian Chief (IRE)**[14] 977 7-9-10 ........(v) EAhern 4 95
(NPLittmoden) *lw: in tch: effrt 2f out: hrd rdn over 1f out: no imp* **12/1**

000- **9** *nk* **Striking Ambition**[167] 5402 4-9-10 105 ........ DHolland 1 94
(GCBravery) *bit bkwd: lw: prom 3f* **11/2**[3]

400- **10** *½* **Ikan (IRE)**[161] 5479 4-8-7 89 ........ KDarley 3 75
(NPLittmoden) *s.i.s: outpcd: a last* **33/1**

57.39 secs (-2.39) **Going Correction** -0.05s/f (Stan) course record **10** Ran SP% **111.4**
Speed ratings: **117,116,115,114,113 112,112,110,110,109**CSF £62.32 TOTE £12.80: £2.90, £2.70, £2.80; EX 99.60.
**Owner** Paul J Dixon **Bred** Tally-Ho Stud **Trained** Southwell, Notts

**FOCUS**
A strongly run race, and useful form. The winner had a stiff task on All-Weather form but, with other factors in his favour, reproduced his turf best form.

**NOTEBOOK**
**No Time(IRE)** had plenty to find with all of his rivals at these weights, but he was match-fit, had good course form, was well drawn and ridden by the right man to exploit the bias towards front runners. One would not be rushing to back him to confirm this form back on turf.
**Speed Cop** ran well on her reappearance and Polytrack debut, only going down narrowly. She was favoured by the weights on this occasion, though, and also benefited from racing prominently on a day when those who raced up with the pace held a big advantage.
**Justalord**, who had crossed swords with the winner on his last two starts here, was weighted to come out on top this time, but his moderate draw did not help his cause and he was forced wide into the straight. He also finished third in this last year.
**Dragon Flyer(IRE)** ◆, who was never at the front end, was forced to race wide throughout and, given the bias towards the front runners, did not perform badly in the circumstances. She traditionally needs her first run of the season, and with an outing under her belt could be one to look out for next time.
**Little Edward**, another making his Polytrack debut as well as his reappearance, showed speed but weakened inside the last in the manner of a horse who needed this outing. He should come on for the run.
**Dusty Dazzler(IRE)** was unable to get to a prominent position from her poor draw and struggled throughout.
**Fire Up The Band**, successful on his only previous visit here on his debut at three, was best in at the weights for his seasonal reappearance but, given that the track was favouring front runners, the tactic of holding him up was never going to prove fruitful. This run should set him up nicely for the start of the turf campaign, though.
**Peruvian Chief(IRE)** was fit from four races in Dubai but seems out of form at present.

## 1062 LITTLEWOODS BET DIRECT WINTER DERBY (LISTED RACE) 1m 2f (P)
**2:35** (2:38) (A ) 4-Y-O+ **£43,500** (£16,500; £8,250; £3,750) **Stalls** Low

Form RPR

/40- **1** **Caluki**[20] 7-9-1 ........ LDettori 2 112
(LCamici, Italy) *str: prom: hrd rdn over 1f out: r.o to ld nr fin* **14/1**

-034 **2** *nk* **Anani (USA)**[14] 979 4-9-1 104 ........ EAhern 3 111
(EALDunlop) *lw: led and set mod pce: qcknd 3f out: hrd rdn fnl f: hdd nr fin* **12/1**

442- **3** *hd* **Bustan (IRE)**[141] 5853 5-8-12 107 ........ RHills 12 108
(MPTregoning) *lw: prom: pressed ldr after 4f: rdr dropped whip 1f out: ev ch fnl f: nt qckn fnl 50 yds* **9/1**[3]

26-0 **4** *nk* **Bourgainville**[28] 842 6-8-12 102 ........ MartinDwyer 1 107
(AMBalding) *lw: in tch: drvn to press ldrs over 1f out: kpt on* **14/1**

060- **5** *½* **Pugin (IRE)**[146] 5782 6-8-12 105 ........ JPMurtagh 9 106+
(DRLoder) *b.hind: towards rr: hrd rdn 3f out: nrst fin* **20/1**

4-15 **6** *¾* **Blue Sky Thinking (IRE)**[28] 842 5-8-12 102 ........ DarrenWilliams 8 105
(KRBurke) *lw: hld up towards rr: hdwy and wd st: kpt on* **10/1**

-412 **7** *½* **Eastern Breeze (IRE)**[28] 842 6-8-12 102 ........ PaulEddery 7 104
(PWD'Arcy) *prom: rdn over 3f out: no ex over 1f out* **10/1**

0-06 **8** *1* **Vintage Premium**[7] 1009 7-8-12 98 ........ PJSmullen 5 102
(RAFahey) *in tch: rdn and lost pl over 2f out: styd on same pce* **66/1**

2-21 **9** *shd* **Grand Passion (IRE)**[28] 842 4-8-12 104 ........ DHolland 14 102
(GWragg) *wd early: chsd ldrs: no ex over 1f out* **7/2**[1]

025- **10** *1¼* **Pawn Broker**[85] 5853 7-8-12 99 ........ DaneO'Neill 4 100
(DRCElsworth) *dwlt: bhd: rdn 2f out: nvr rchd ldrs* **14/1**

63-3 **11** *nk* **Corriolanus (GER)**[28] 842 4-8-12 ........ JQuinn 6 99
(PMitchell) *dwlt: sn in midfield: rdn and btn over 2f out* **14/1**

1111 **12** *2½* **Vortex**[7] 1009 5-8-12 97 ........(t) MFenton 10 95
(MissGayKelleway) *b: b.hind: lw: hld up in rr: effrt and wd st: nt trble ldrs* **14/1**

645- **13** *5* **Private Charter**[223] 4026 4-8-12 110 ........ MHills 11 86
(BWHills) *bit bkwd: mid-div: rdn over 3f out: btn over 2f out* **5/1**[2]

2-15 **14** *18* **Mi Odds**[7] 1009 8-8-12 99 ........ PMcCabe 13 53
(MrsNMacauley) *b: wd: hrd rdn over 2f out: a in rr* **66/1**

2m 5.85s (-1.54) **Going Correction** -0.05s/f (Stan) **14** Ran SP% **115.8**
Speed ratings: **104,103,103,103,102 102,101,101,101,100 99,97,93,79**CSF £163.92 TOTE £9.90: £3.50, £3.80, £3.60; EX 92.30.
**Owner** Scuderia L3c **Bred** Azienda Agricola Rosati Colarieti **Trained** Italy
■ A first winner in Britain for Luigi Camici, who won the Arc in 1988 with Tony Bin.
■ Stewards Enquiry : L Dettori one-day ban: used whip without giving horse time to respond (Mar 31)

**FOCUS**
A quality contest but the pace was not hot and once again the advantage of being drawn low and racing prominently was clear for all to see.

**NOTEBOOK**
**Caluki**, an Italian raider who had 19 wins from 49 previous starts to his name coming into this, including a success on dirt at Cagnes last month, raced keenly just behind the leader in the early stages. He looked in trouble turning in but kept on strongly for Dettori, and this was a good effort under his penalty. His trainer is now reportedly considering targets in Italy and Sweden, so it remains to be seen if he will run again in this country later in the year.
**Anani(USA)**, who finished fourth behind the smart Victory Moon in Dubai a fortnight earlier, was given a terrific front-running ride by Ahern. He had the track bias in his favour and made full use of it, and was only narrowly denied.

**Bustan(IRE)**, making his All-Weather debut, again flattered to deceive. He got himself into a prominent position early on, despite a wide draw, but having appeared to have every chance in the straight he did not really go through with his effort. His chance may have been compromised by his rider dropping his whip a furlong out, but he remains one to have doubts about.
**Bourgainville** was well drawn and, with a run under his belt, ran his usual honest race. He usually finds one or two too good at this sort of level, though, and today was no exception.
**Pugin(IRE)** looks one to take out of the race, as he was not only running over a trip short of his best, but also running against the track bias towards front runners. This was his first start for Loder following a disappointing season with Godolphin last year and he should come on a bundle for the run. He is certainly one to keep in mind for the early-season staying contests back on turf.
**Blue Sky Thinking(IRE)** is another who deserves a mention, as he too was asked the impossible in trying to win his race from the back of the field. He was forced to challenge wide in the straight but kept on well, and there could be a decent race to be won with him back on turf this spring.
**Eastern Breeze(IRE)** was fairly placed throughout and had no excuse.
**Vintage Premium** has not really taken to the All-Weather.
**Grand Passion(IRE)** had a tough draw to overcome but was fairly positioned turning into the straight. He could not muster the pace to remain competitive, though, and this was clearly a sterner test than the trial he won here four weeks earlier. Indeed, not one of the first three home that day could even finish in the first six of this contest.
**Pawn Broker**, last seen over hurdles on Boxing Day, appeared to be ridden with another day in mind.
**Vortex**, chasing a six-timer, has shown his most recent improvement on the slower surface at Wolverhampton. This was also a step up in grade and the decision to hold him up at the back of the field did not help his chance.
**Private Charter**, a course and distance winner and the one to beat on official ratings, ran a long way below his best form and now has questions to answer.

## 1063 LADBROKES.COM SPRING CUP (LISTED RACE) 7f (P)

3:10 (3:12) (A) 3-Y-O £43,500 (£16,500; £8,250; £3,750) Stalls Low

| Form | | | | RPR |
|---|---|---|---|---|
| 31 | 1 | | **Rosencrans (USA)**[21] 920 3-8-11 (vt) LDettori 7 *(SaeedBinSuroor) lw: w ldr: led ins fnl f: rdn out* 6/4[1] | 104 |
| 620- | 2 | 1/2 | **Fokine (USA)**[169] 5348 3-8-11 114 MHills 15 *(BWHills) in tch: effrt over 2f out: ev ch ins fnl f: kpt on* 3/1[2] | 103 |
| -212 | 3 | 1 1/2 | **Bahiano (IRE)**[21] 913 3-8-11 92 DHolland 14 *(CEBrittain) lw: chsd ldrs: sltly outpcd 2f out: styd on fnl f* 12/1 | 99 |
| 61-1 | 4 | hd | **Bettalatethannever (IRE)**[70] 493 3-8-11 88 DaneO'Neill 10 *(SDow) lw: hdwy on outside 3f out: rdn to chse ldrs over 1f out: styd on same pce* 14/1 | 98 |
| 140- | 5 | shd | **Venables (USA)**[213] 4301 3-8-13 106 RHughes 3 *(RHannon) lw: led tl ins fnl f: no ex* 14/1 | 100 |
| 011- | 6 | 1 | **Bravo Maestro (USA)**[129] 5979 3-8-11 96 SWhitworth 9 *(DWPArbuthnot) bit bkwd: in tch: n.m.r over 4f out: effrt and hung lft over 1f out: kpt on fnl f* 6/1[3] | 95 |
| 105- | 7 | hd | **Crocodile Dundee (IRE)**[112] 6090 3-8-11 88 IMongan 1 *(JamiePoulton) towards rr: drvn along over 4f out: hdwy and swtchd wd 2f out: no imp over 1f out* 50/1 | 94 |
| 210- | 8 | 1 | **Treasure House (IRE)**[183] 5038 3-8-11 96 PJSmullen 4 *(BJMeehan) prom: hrd rdn over 1f out: no ex* 66/1 | 92 |
| 031- | 9 | 3 | **Valjarv (IRE)**[168] 5367 3-8-6 96 EAhern 6 *(NPLittmoden) hld up in midfield: nt clr run over 1f out: no hdwy* 20/1 | 79 |
| 631- | 10 | 1 1/2 | **Dumnoni**[126] 6002 3-8-7 81 ow1 NCallan 2 *(JulianPoulton) chsd ldrs: rdn 3f out: wknd wl over 1f out* 100/1 | 76 |
| 013- | 11 | shd | **Glaramara**[183] 5032 3-8-11 94 (b[1]) JFanning 8 *(ABailey) plld hrd: in tch: rdn over 2f out: squeezed out wl over 1f out: n.d after* 33/1 | 79 |
| 243- | 12 | 1 1/4 | **Makfool (FR)**[134] 5944 3-8-11 96 CCatlin 12 *(MRChannon) sn towards rr: rdn over 2f out: n.d* 50/1 | 76 |
| 221- | 13 | 1 1/2 | **Rydal (USA)**[136] 5925 3-8-11 89 (b) KDarley 16 *(GAButler) b.hind: bit bkwd: w ldrs 5f* 50/1 | 72 |
| 260- | 14 | 5 | **Spanish Ace**[234] 3686 3-8-11 103 MartinDwyer 13 *(AMBalding) b: s.i.s: a bhd* 25/1 | 58 |
| 0 | 15 | 2 1/2 | **Well Knit**[21] 913 3-8-6 PaulEddery 5 *(PWD'Arcy) a bhd* 200/1 | 47 |

1m 23.64s (-2.36) **Going Correction** -0.05s/f (Stan) **15** Ran SP% **120.7**
Speed ratings: **111,110,108,108,108 107,107,105,102,100 100,99,97,91,88**CSF £5.14 TOTE £2.40: £1.60, £1.80, £3.50; EX 9.30.
**Owner** Godolphin **Bred** *unknown **Trained** Newmarket, Suffolk
■ Rosencrans was Godolphin's first runner on the All-Weather in Britain.

**FOCUS**
A race which looked well up to its Listed status, and useful form from some progressive 3yos. The first two were entitled to beat the rest more comprehensively than they did, and the fifth and sixth look the best best guide to the form.

**NOTEBOOK**
**Rosencrans(USA)**, the UAE 2000 Guineas third, is an attractive, athletic sort that likes to race prominently and was soon in the van on his first start in this country. That proved the right place to be on this day and he kept on well to win a shade cosily. He is probably not a first division Godolphin inmate, but certainly looks capable of holding his own in Group Three company.
**Fokine(USA)**, who has not grown much, had the highest official rating of these coming into the race and was the one to beat on his two-year-old form, which included a second in the Gimcrack. Bred for this surface, he nevertheless had a horrible draw to overcome, and was forced to race wide all the way. He looked the moral winner in the end and looks to have trained on well.
**Bahiano(IRE)** was taking another big step up in class but throwing his horses in at the deep end has never worried Clive Brittain and the colt certainly came out of the race with plenty of credit. He looks equally effective over seven furlongs as a mile.
**Bettalatethannever(IRE)**, taking a significant step up in grade, had plenty to do against this class of opposition and was not helped by a moderate draw which forced him to race wide. He ran a cracker, though, on his return from a ten-week layoff, and fully justified his trainer's decision to run him here.
**Venables(USA)**, giving weight to the rest, was the second-highest rated of these on official marks and had an ideal draw to exploit the bias towards front runners. He was given a good ride from the front, but there was a stamina doubt hanging over him coming into the race and those fears were not allayed by this performance.
**Bravo Maestro(USA)**, a nice type who has been aimed at this race since November and was strong in the market beforehand, raced keenly and was squeezed up in the early stages before settling in behind the leaders. On a day when those at the head of affairs dominated, he was not in the right place, and it is probably best to forgive him this slightly disappointing run.
**Crocodile Dundee(IRE)** ran better than his finishing position suggests as he was asked a lot by his rider to win from where he was, given the track bias towards front runners. Once again he shaped as though a step up in trip will suit him.

## 1064 LINGFIELD PARK MAIDEN STKS 1m 2f (P)

3:40 (3:42) (D) 3-Y-O £6,938 (£1,601; £1,601; £533) Stalls Low

| Form | | | | RPR |
|---|---|---|---|---|
| 230- | 1 | | **Over The Rainbow (IRE)**[175] 5208 3-9-0 89 MHills 2 *(BWHills) prom: rdn over 2f out: squeezed through ins fnl f: r.o to ld nr fin* 5/2[1] | 80+ |
| 342- | 2 | nk | **Gjovic**[189] 4883 3-9-0 75 PJSmullen 11 *(BJMeehan) led: hrd rdn fnl f: kpt on: hdd nr fin* 4/1[2] | 79 |
| 30-2 | 2 | dht | **Vantage (IRE)**[12] 985 3-9-0 80 DHolland 8 *(NPLittmoden) lw: chsd ldrs: hrd rdn and edgd lft fr over 1f out: ev ch ins fnl f: r.o* 5/2[1] | 79 |
| 602- | 4 | 1 1/2 | **Just Tim (IRE)**[139] 5887 3-9-0 78 DaneO'Neill 7 *(RHannon) chsd ldr: hrd rdn and ev ch over 1f out: nt qckn fnl f* 10/1 | 76 |
| 5-24 | 5 | 2 1/2 | **Looks The Business (IRE)**[29] 835 3-8-7 69 (t) CHaddon(7) 6 *(WGMTurner) hld up towards rr: rdn and hdwy 3f out: no imp appr fnl f* 25/1 | 72 |
| 0- | 6 | 7 | **Scriptorium**[143] 5831 3-8-9 NMackay(5) 4 *(LMCumani) hld up in rr: rdn over 2f out: nvr nr to chal* 14/1 | 59 |
| 3 | 7 | 6 | **Paddy Boy (IRE)**[47] 656 3-8-11 RMiles(3) 1 *(JRBoyle) in rr: rdn over 3f out: nvr trbld ldrs* 100/1 | 48 |
| 0 | 8 | 1 3/4 | **Preston Hall**[38] 739 3-9-0 SWKelly 3 *(MrsLCJewell) stdd s: bhd fnl 3f* 100/1 | 45 |
| 05 | 9 | 25 | **Clare Galway**[23] 890 3-8-9 EAhern 10 *(TDMccarthy) hmpd 1st bnd: swtchd wd and sn chsng ldrs: wknd over 4f out* 50/1 | — |
| -334 | 10 | dist | **Lord Of The Sea (IRE)**[16] 959 3-9-0 70 IMongan 12 *(JamiePoulton) prom: wknd qckly over 2f out: 6th and btn whn virtually p.u over 1f out* 8/1[3] | — |

2m 6.37s (-1.02) **Going Correction** -0.05s/f (Stan) **10** Ran SP% **111.8**
Speed ratings: **102,101,101,100,98 92,88,86,66,—**CSF £5.90 TOTE £3.20; EX 8.40 TRIFECTA Pl: 1.40, G 2.10, V 1.4; Ex: OTR/G 8.4, OTR/V 3.5; CSF: OTR/G 5.90, OTR/V 3.98.
**Owner** Harrison, Jamieson, Parker, Snowden **Bred** Sir Eric Parker **Trained** Lambourn, Berks
■ Stewards Enquiry : I Mongan two-day ban: careless riding (Mar 31, Apr 1)

**FOCUS**
Not a strong pace, but a maiden which should produce a winner or two.

**NOTEBOOK**
**Over The Rainbow(IRE)**, who looked fit for this seasonal reappearance, was the one to beat on his form at two and is bred for middle distances. He tracked the pace next to the rail for most of the race but struggled to get a run in the straight and it was only in the final stages that he squeezed through between horses to edge ahead close home. He deserves rating better than the bare form.
**Vantage(IRE)** had the benefit of race fitness and track experience over his main rivals and enjoyed a fine trip, tracking the leader for most of the race. He had little excuse.
**Gjovic**, rushed up to take the lead despite his wide draw, appreciated the step up to ten furlongs, as his breeding suggested he would. He may be slightly flatterred by his proximity to the winner but looks a likely type for a handicap on turf this spring off what should be a mark around 80.
**Just Tim(IRE)**, who grabbed the favoured inside rail, battled on well under pressure but there were doubts about him staying this trip beforehand and his performance suggested that a drop back to a mile would probably suit.
**Looks The Business(IRE)**, who was held up off the pace, had it to do off a steady pace given the way the track was favouring those who raced prominently. In the circumstances he was not disgraced against superior opposition.
**Scriptorium ◆**, held up at the back on a day when the place to be was at the head of affairs, never got into the race. It is probably fair to say that the best will not be seen of him until he has received a handicap mark.
**Lord Of The Sea(IRE)** *Official explanation: jockey said colt lost his action three furlongs out.*

## 1065 NEW SITE @ BETDIRECT.CO.UK H'CAP 7f (P)

4:15 (4:16) (B) (0-105,105) 3-Y-O+ £15,080 (£5,720; £2,860; £1,300) Stalls Low

| Form | | | | RPR |
|---|---|---|---|---|
| 1-43 | 1 | | **What-A-Dancer (IRE)**[1] 1056 7-8-6 **83** RWinston 3 *(GASwinbank) dwlt: gd hdwy over 1f out: r.o to ld nr fin* 12/1 | 94 |
| 000- | 2 | shd | **Hidden Dragon (USA)**[148] 5732 5-9-6 **97** DeanMcKeown 5 *(PABlockley) b.hind: hld up in tch: n.m.r over 1f out: drvn to chal ins fnl f: r.o* 33/1 | 107 |
| -126 | 3 | 1/2 | **Moayed**[21] 915 5-8-5 **82** (bt) EAhern 7 *(NPLittmoden) s.i.s: plld hrd in midfield: hdwy 2f out: led 1f out: hrd rdn: hdd and nt qckn nr fin* 10/1 | 91 |
| 300- | 4 | 2 | **Fiveoclock Express (IRE)**[155] 5618 4-8-13 **90** (p) IMongan 6 *(MissGayKelleway) b: b.hind: t.k.h in midfield: outpcd 2f out: styd on fnl f* 16/1 | 94 |
| -556 | 5 | nk | **Lygeton Lad**[28] 842 6-9-11 **102** (t) MFenton 15 *(MissGayKelleway) in rr: effrt and wd ent st: nrst fin* 6/1[3] | 105 |
| 5-10 | 6 | shd | **Quito (IRE)**[7] 1009 7-10-0 **105** (b) TQuinn 2 *(DWChapman) b: b.hind: in rr: rdn and styd on fnl 2f: nvr nrr* 14/1 | 108 |
| 2024 | 7 | hd | **Queens Rhapsody**[7] 1011 4-8-13 **90** JFanning 1 *(ABailey) mid-div to rr: outpcd over 2f out: eased outside over 1f out: styd on* 10/1 | 92 |
| 0/ | 8 | nk | **Fast Gate (USA)**[29] 5-9-1 **92** (bt[1]) LDettori 10 *(LPantuosco, Italy) w'like: leggy: a.p: no ex appr fnl f* 4/1[1] | 93 |
| 0-11 | 9 | hd | **Dance On The Top**[45] 677 6-9-3 **94** (t) DSweeney 13 *(JRBoyle) prom: led briefly over 1f out: no ex fnl f* 7/1 | 95 |
| 002- | 10 | shd | **Digital**[147] 5737 7-8-13 **93** SHitchcott(3) 8 *(MRChannon) hld up in rr: effrt and nt clr run wl over 1f out: swtchd rt: styng on whn nt clr run ins fnl f* 33/1 | 93 |
| 023- | 11 | nk | **Yakimov (USA)**[195] 4751 5-8-9 **86** ow1 DaneO'Neill 14 *(DJWintle) sn w ldr: led 2f out tl over 1f out: no ex* 33/1 | 86 |
| -200 | 12 | 3/4 | **Flint River**[35] 775 6-8-3 **80** RLMoore 12 *(HMorrison) t.k.h: in tch: effrt over 2f out: no ex over 1f out* 16/1 | 78 |
| 352- | 13 | 3/4 | **Arctic Desert**[161] 5488 4-8-13 **90** MartinDwyer 11 *(AMBalding) b: lw: wd: t.k.h: in tch: drvn to chse ldrs 2f out: wknd 1f out* 9/2[2] | 86 |
| 30-0 | 14 | shd | **Gaelic Princess**[36] 761 4-8-8 **85** SWhitworth 4 *(AGNewcombe) in tch: outpcd over 2f out: n.d after* 66/1 | 80 |
| -365 | 15 | 5 | **Royal Dignitary (USA)**[28] 852 4-9-5 **96** (v) JPMurtagh 9 *(DRLoder) b: b.hind: led tl 2f out: wknd over 1f out* 16/1 | 78 |

1m 24.31s (-1.69) **Going Correction** -0.05s/f (Stan) **15** Ran SP% **125.5**
Speed ratings: **107,106,106,104,103 103,103,103,102,102 102,101,100,100,94**CSF £378.84 CT £4086.87 TOTE £16.00: £3.50, £9.30, £4.20; EX 441.30.
**Owner** A Barnes **Bred** Miss V Charlton **Trained** Melsonby, N Yorks

**FOCUS**
A decent and competitive handicap, run at a good pace. The form is solid.

**NOTEBOOK**
**What-A-Dancer(IRE)**, making a quick reappearance following his third in a classified event here the previous day and racing off a career-high mark, did well to win given that the track bias all day had been towards those racing prominently, but it is probably significant that all the leaders dropped away in the closing stages, suggesting that they went too quick.
**Hidden Dragon(USA)** tracked the leaders on the inside but had to wait for a gap to appear before finishing strongly. He may have won had he been able to get a run earlier, but at least he proved once and for all that he stays seven furlongs well.
**Moayed**, who was held up and forced to challenge wide, ran a great race in defeat. A versatile sort with regards to distance, he is very much suited by a strongly-run race.
**Fiveoclock Express(IRE)** ran a pleasing race on his first start for his new stable, although he looks likely to struggle off his current mark for the time being.

**Lygeton Lad**, successful in this race last year, has struggled a little since being raised in the weights following his two wins before the turn of the year.
**Quito(IRE)**, another running off a career-high mark, ran on from the rear but never threatened the principals. He looks a better horse on Fibresand.
**Fast Gate(USA)** was popular in the market following Dettori's earlier successes on the card. He had every chance but was outpaced in the straight, in common with the pacesetters.
**Digital** got stuck behind a wall of horses inside the final furlong, and by the time the gap came the race was all but over. He ran a bit better than the bare form suggests.
**Arctic Desert**, a winner on the surface on his previous visit, was well supported beforehand but ran a disappointing race on his seasonal reappearance. He might have needed this more than was expected.
**Royal Dignitary(USA)** *Official explanation: jockey said gelding lost its action.*

## 1066 RICHARD GIBBS MEMORIAL H'CAP — 1m (P)
4:50 (4:51) (D) (0-85,82) 3-Y-0+ — £5,174 (£1,592; £796; £398) Stalls High

Form — RPR

30-1 **1** **Harrison Point (USA)**[28] 847 4-9-7 **76**................................ RHughes 4 85+
(PWChapple-Hyam) *lw: hld up: smooth hdwy 2f out: hrd rdn over 1f out: r.o to ld nr fin* **7/4**[1]

-305 **2** *hd* **Labrett**[45] 677 7-9-12 **81**..............................(tp) MFenton 11 90
(MissGayKelleway) *b. b.hind: prom: led 4f out: hrd rdn fnl f: kpt on: hdd nr fin* **14/1**

-340 **3** *nk* **Paragon Of Virtue**[25] 872 7-9-8 **77**.............................. JFanning 3 85
(PMitchell) *b.hind: lw: prom: jnd ldr 2f out: str chal fnl f: kpt on* **10/1**

-005 **4** *1/2* **Summer Recluse (USA)**[16] 961 5-9-8 **77**......................(p) DaneO'Neill 7 84
(BRJohnson) *b.hind: s.i.s: t.k.h towards rr: hdwy 2f out: styd on u.p fnl f* **9/1**[3]

6540 **5** *shd* **Dower House**[21] 915 9-9-10 **79**.............................. LDettori 6 86
(AndrewTurnell) *lw: hld up towards rr: hdwy on outside over 1f out: hrd rdn: r.o fnl f* **6/1**[2]

6101 **6** *2 1/2* **African Sahara (USA)**[16] 961 5-9-11 **80**......................(t) GCarter 10 81
(MissDMountain) *hld up in tch: trckd ldrs 3f out: hrd rdn over 1f out: no ex* **6/1**[2]

6601 **7** *3/4* **Kentucky King (USA)**[16] 961 4-9-12 **81**.............................. KDarley 2 80
(PWHiatt) *in tch: rdn 3f out: no hdwy fnl 2f* **9/1**[3]

500- **8** *1 1/2* **Onlytime Will Tell**[182] 5060 6-9-10 **79**.............................. JPMurtagh 9 75
(DNicholls) *b: dwlt: hld up in rr: rdn and sme hdwy over 1f out: nvr nr to chal* **14/1**

5212 **9** *5* **Caroubier (IRE)**[26] 862 4-9-7 **76**..............................(v) IMongan 12 61
(JGallagher) *dwlt: pushed along in rr 1/2-way: nvr nr ldrs* **20/1**

0-00 **10** *1 3/4* **Atahuelpa**[22] 911 4-9-13 **82**.............................. TQuinn 5 62
(MFHarris) *chsd ldrs tl wknd over 2f out* **66/1**

450- **11** *nk* **Racing Night (USA)**[197] 4707 4-9-10 **79**.............................. EAhern 1 59
(JRBest) *led 1f: wknd 3f out* **40/1**

201- **12** *13* **Super Song**[213] 4289 4-9-8 **77**.............................. SWKelly 8 27
(PDEvans) *led after 1f tl 4f out: wknd over 2f out* **33/1**

1m 38.18s (-1.33) **Going Correction** -0.05s/f (Stan) — **12** Ran SP% **119.0**
Speed ratings: **104,103,103,103,102 100,99,98,93,91 91,78**CSF £28.52 CT £203.36 TOTE £2.40: £1.30, £4.30, £3.10; EX 41.20 Place 6 £63.17, Place 5 £47.67.
**Owner** R E Sangster, M O'Donovan, F Cook **Bred** Creston Farm **Trained** Newmarket, Suffolk

**FOCUS**
A decent handicap, and the winner looks the sort to stay a step ahead of the Handicapper.

**NOTEBOOK**
**Harrison Point(USA)** ◆, who scored on his debut for his new stable last time out, won a shade more cosily than the official margin suggests as he had to make up a fair bit of ground on the leaders in the straight, something which had proved difficult all day. Each of his three career victories to date have come by just a head, making it difficult for the Handicapper to get a hold of him.
**Labrett**, up there all the way, ran an honest race, but he has never won off a mark in the 80s and the chances are he will continue to run into one or two rivals who are better handicapped.
**Paragon Of Virtue**, whose winning form is over 10 and 12 furlongs, had not raced over a trip as short as this for almost four years. He raced prominently throughout, though, and kept on well under pressure, posting a solid effort.
**Summer Recluse(USA)** ran a solid race, this time after being held up. On this occasion he might have been better off racing prominently.
**Dower House** was given a lot to do, having been held up way off the pace, especially as he is ideally suited by farther.
**African Sahara(USA)** came out on top in his battle with Kentucky King, with whom he dead-heated on identical terms last time.
**Super Song** *Official explanation: jockey said gelding ran too free to post and ran too keenly in the early stages.*
T/Plt: £98.70 to a £1 stake. Pool: £53,258.85. 393.80 winning tickets. T/Qpdt: £24.80 to a £1 stake. Pool: £3,646.20. 108.45 winning tickets. LM

# CURRAGH (R-H)
Sunday, March 21

**OFFICIAL GOING: Heavy**

## 1070a IRISH STALLION FARMS EUROPEAN BREEDERS FUND PARK EXPRESS STKS (LISTED RACE) (FILLIES) — 1m
3:45 (3:50) 3-Y-0+ — £34,383 (£10,088; £4,806; £1,637)

RPR

**1** **Alexander Goldrun (IRE)**[148] 5762 3-8-12 101.............................. KJManning 2 102
(JSBolger, Ire) *trckd ldrs on stands side: hdwy 3f out: led and qcknd clr under 2f out: kpt on u.p fnl f* **6/1**

**2** *1* **Blue Reema (IRE)**[134] 5960 4-9-12 92..............................(tp) TPO'Shea 10 97
(MHalford, Ire) *hld up: 7th and effrt 2f out: r.o strly fnl f: nrest at fin* **20/1**

**3** *1 1/2* **Royal Tigress (USA)**[213] 4328 3-8-9.............................. JPSpencer 6 94
(APO'Brien, Ire) *cl up: 3rd 1/2-way: led 2f out: sn hdd: kpt on u.p fnl f* **5/1**[3]

**4** *9* **Noahs Ark (IRE)**[148] 5762 3-8-9 96.............................. PJSmullen 5 76
(DKWeld, Ire) *trckd ldrs: 5th 3f out: kpt on fr 2f out* **11/2**

**5** *2 1/2* **Dossier**[189] 4915 4-10-1 103..............................(t) JPMurtagh 9 74
(JohnMOxx, Ire) *prom: led over 3f out: hdd 2f out: sn no ex* **7/4**[1]

**6** *3* **Twiggy's Sister (IRE)**[161] 5523 6-9-12 102.............................. JFEgan 4 65
(DermotMurphy, Ire) *hld up: kpt on one pce fr 2f out* **13/2**

**7** *10* **Genny Lim (IRE)**[134] 5956 4-9-12 94.............................. FMBerry 7 45
(JohnMOxx, Ire) *chsd ldrs: 5th 1/2-way: no imp fr over 2f out* **14/1**

**8** *9* **Takrice**[146] 5802 3-8-9 98.............................. DPMcDonogh 8 27
(KevinPrendergast, Ire) *hld up in tch: prog into 4th 3f out: rdn and wknd fr 2f out* **4/1**[2]

**9** *7* **Czaritza (IRE)**[497] 5681 5-9-12.............................. CatherineGannon 3 13
(JohnMOxx, Ire) *chsd ldrs: 4th 1/2-way: wknd fr 3f out* **20/1**

**10** *11* **Dixie Evans**[134] 5956 4-9-12 98..............................(b) DMGrant 1 —
(HRogers, Ire) *led: hdd over 3f out: wknd qckly* **12/1**

1m 51.2s **Going Correction** +1.25s/f (Soft)
**WFA** 3 from 4yo+ 17lb — **10** Ran SP% **139.9**
Speed ratings: **107,106,104,95,93 90,80,71,64,53**CSF £140.13 TOTE £7.60: £2.10, £7.70, £1.90; DF 166.20.
**Owner** Mrs N O'Callaghan **Bred** Dermot Cantillon **Trained** Coolcullen, Co Carlow

**NOTEBOOK**
**Alexander Goldrun(IRE)** had a busy time as a juvenile culminating an eight-race first season with a Listed success here in October. She has trained on well and went clear over the last quarter mile. She was never going to be caught although under pressure to keep going in the bad ground. She will stay further and could again pay to follow.
**Blue Reema(IRE)** showed improved form on her reappearance, staying on much the best of the opposition to be nearest at the end. She should be able to capitalise on this.
**Royal Tigress(USA)** got her head in front briefly before the winner went on. She will have benefited from this and could show marked improvement on better ground. It was not stamina that beat her.
**Noahs Ark(IRE)** needed this and did not appear to relish the ground.
**Dossier** had it to do with her penalty in this ground.
**Twiggy's Sister(IRE)** needed this.
**Takrice** weakened over the last two furlongs and was described as lame afterwards. *Official explanation: trainer said filly finished lame*

1071 - 1074a (Foreign Racing) - See Raceform Interactive

# 1035 WOLVERHAMPTON (A.W) (L-H)
Monday, March 22

**OFFICIAL GOING: Standard to slow**
Wind: mod across Weather: fine

## 1075 NEW SITE @ BETDIRECT.CO.UK BANDED STKS — 5f (F)
2:15 (2:18) (H) 3-Y-0+ — £1,445 (£413; £206) Stalls Low

Form — RPR

5300 **1** **Torrent**[6] 1033 9-9-7 45..............................(b) ACulhane 5 55
(DWChapman) *hld up: rdn and hdwy whn bmpd over 1f out: led ins fnl f: rdn out* **11/2**[3]

0040 **2** *1* **Soaked**[21] 941 11-9-7 45..............................(b) SSanders 10 52
(DWChapman) *a.p: rdn over 2f out: led 1f out tl ins fnl f: nt qckn* **9/1**

2654 **3** *3 1/2* **Hagley Park**[25] 893 5-9-7 45..............................(v) DHolland 6 39
(MQuinn) *led early: chsd ldrs: rdn over 2f out: edgd rt over 1f out: one pce fnl f* **11/4**[1]

5400 **4** *3* **So Sober (IRE)**[22] 938 6-9-7 45.............................. RWinston 4 29
(DShaw) *mid-div: rdn over 3f out: kpt on ins fnl f* **3/1**[2]

6040 **5** *1* **The Leather Wedge (IRE)**[22] 938 5-9-2 45.............................. PBradley(5) 11 25
(ABerry) *sn led: hdd after 1f: chsd ldr: rdn to ld again 2f out: hdd 1f out: wknd ins fnl f* **16/1**

0/0- **6** *1 3/4* **Abbiejo (IRE)**[301] 1864 7-9-7 40..............................(p) VSlattery 8 19
(GFierro) *s.i.s: outpcd: hdwy fnl f: nrst fin* **50/1**

0-00 **7** *nk* **Valazar (USA)**[22] 938 5-9-7 45..............................(b[1]) GDuffield 9 18
(DWChapman) *led after 1f: rdn and hdd 2f out: wknd fnl f* **10/1**

-306 **8** *1* **Mangus (IRE)**[24] 905 10-9-7 35..............................(be) NCallan 2 15
(KOCunningham-Brown) *in tch: rdn over 2f out: wknd over 1f out* **16/1**

4241 **9** *hd* **White O' Morn**[21] 944 5-9-7 40..............................(tp) GGibbons 12 14
(BAMcmahon) *sn outpcd* **7/1**

00-0 **10** *1 1/4* **La Vigna (IRE)**[13] 998 3-8-9 30..............................(p) CCatlin 7 10
(MrsLucindaFeatherstone) *sn bhd* **50/1**

6-50 **11** *1 1/2* **Rellim**[42] 721 5-9-7 45.............................. DeanMcKeown 1 4
(PABlockley) *chsd ldrs: rdn 2f out: wknd over 1f out* **11/2**[3]

00-0 **12** *shd* **Bond Domingo**[22] 936 5-9-7 40..............................(b) FLynch 3 4
(BSmart) *outpcd* **14/1**

63.51 secs (0.91) **Going Correction** +0.40s/f (Slow)
**WFA** 3 from 5yo+ 12lb — **12** Ran SP% **136.4**
Speed ratings: **108,106,100,96,94 91,91,89,89,87 84,84**CSF £63.35 TOTE £7.40: £1.80, £3.20, £2.00; EX 35.30.
**Owner** David W Chapman **Bred** Mrs Mary Taylor **Trained** Stillington, N Yorks

**FOCUS**
A decent winning time for the grade, the front pair are useful at this level and the form is a shade better than the usual standard.

**NOTEBOOK**
**Torrent** stayed on strongly in the final furlong to win this going away, posting a decent time in the process. He has enjoyed the slip into banded racing of late and can win again at this level if not handicapped out of the grade.
**Soaked** could not match his stablemate in the final furlong, but still acquitted himself with credit and was clear of the rest.
**Hagley Park** ran her race, but seems to have lost her way of late, as her best form would have seen her go much closer.
**So Sober(IRE)** showed more for this drop in grade. However, he has not built on his course-and-distance win in January and is hard to catch right.

## 1076 BETDIRECT.CO.UK CLAIMING STKS — 7f (F)
2:50 (2:52) (H) 3-Y-0+ — £1,459 (£417; £208) Stalls High

Form — RPR

-004 **1** **Travel Tardia (IRE)**[14] 993 6-9-9 35..............................(t) THamilton(3) 8 57
(IAWood) *w ldr: led over 5f out: rdn 3f out: all out* **10/1**

1364 **2** *hd* **Legalis (USA)**[8] 1025 6-9-12 55..............................(b) NCallan 6 56
(KARyan) *s.i.s: hdwy over 5f out: rdn over 2f out: c wd st: kpt on ins fnl f* **9/4**[1]

0030 **3** *5* **Headland (USA)**[35] 799 6-9-12 53..............................(b) ACulhane 10 44
(DWChapman) *a.p: wnt 2nd over 4f out: rdn over 2f out: wknd ins fnl f* **11/4**[2]

0000 **4** *nk* **Waterline Dancer (IRE)**[21] 940 4-9-5 35..............................(t) RWinston 9 36
(PDEvans) *towards rr: rdn over 4f out: hdwy on outside over 2f out: styd on ins fnl f* **14/1**

0400 **5** *1 3/4* **Welsh Whisper**[14] 994 5-9-0 35.............................. LPKeniry(3) 1 30
(SABrookshaw) *hld up in tch: rdn and hdwy over 2f out: wknd over 1f out* **25/1**

5400 **6** *1/2* **Dancing King (IRE)**[5] 1039 8-9-3 49.............................. PMakin(7) 2 35
(PWHiatt) *led over 1f: prom: rdn over 3f out: wknd over 1f out* **7/1**

-406 **7** *6* **Lively Felix**[8] 1021 7-9-1 40..............................(v) BSwarbrick(7) 4 18
(DGBridgwater) *prom: rdn over 4f out: wknd 3f out* **20/1**

066- **8** *3 1/2* **Lady Xanthia**[294] 2058 3-8-4 40.............................. GDuffield 7 7
(IAWood) *sn rdn along: bhd fnl 5f* **20/1**

00- **9** *6* **Toddeano**[198] 4734 8-9-8..............................(p) VSlattery 3 —
(GFierro) *s.i.s: rdn over 5f out: a bhd* **50/1**



The Form Book, Raceform Ltd, Compton, RG20 6NL

4150 **10** *1* **Muqtadi (IRE)**[14] 988 6-9-12 50 DHolland 5 —
(MQuinn) *outpcd: sn wl bhd* **7/2**[3]

1m 34.88s (4.68) **Going Correction** +0.40s/f (Slow)
**WFA** 3 from 4yo+ 15lb **10** Ran SP% **123.2**
Speed ratings: **89,88,83,82,80 80,73,69,62,61**CSF £33.43 TOTE £7.90: £3.30, £1.10, £1.30; EX 66.70.The winner was claimed for £5,000 by J T Billson
**Owner** Neardown Stables **Bred** Tally-Ho Stud **Trained** Upper Lambourn, Berks

**FOCUS**
A poor claimer which saw the front pair finish clear. The winner is back to some sort of form but the Handicapper is likely to react.

**NOTEBOOK**
**Travel Tardia(IRE)** enjoyed being allowed to lead after two furlongs and showed a resolute attitude to repel the runner-up late on. This was by far his best effort for some time and he can remain competitive at this level, but is a moody character and not one to trust for a follow-up bid. *Official explanation: trainer's representative said, regarding the improved form shown, horse benefited from being fitted with a tongue strap for the first time*
**Legalis(USA)**, officially the highest rated in the field, blew his chance with a sluggish start. He is worth another chance in this grade.
**Headland(USA)** ran his race with no excuses on this occasion.
**Waterline Dancer(IRE)** ran probably his best race to date on this surface, but has regressed badly in the past couple of months and is one to avoid at present.
**Muqtadi(IRE)** was later reported by his jockey to have hated the kickback. *Official explanation: jockey said gelding would not face the kickback.*

## 1077 SPECIAL OFFERS @ BETDIRECT.CO.UK BANDED STKS 1m 4f (F)
3:25 (3:27) (H) 4-Y-0+ £1,445 (£413; £206) Stalls Low

Form RPR
602- **1** **Isa'Af (IRE)**[188] 4968 5-8-7 45 PMakin(7) 11 64+
(PWHiatt) *hld up: smooth hdwy 6f out: led on bit over 3f out: clr over 2f out: v easily* **11/2**[3]
2212 **2** *7* **Buz Kiri (USA)**[14] 992 6-9-0 45 PDoe 3 47
(AWCarroll) *bhd: pushed along 8f out: rdn and hdwy on outside over 4f out: wnt 2nd over 1f out: no ch w wnr* **5/4**[1]
00-0 **3** *7* **Ersaal (USA)**[23] 914 4-8-12 45 (b) NCallan 1 37
(JJay) *led: rdn and hdd over 3f out: sn btn* **8/1**
000- **4** *1 1/4* **Bid Spotter (IRE)**[19] 6168 5-9-0 45 (p) GDuffield 12 35
(MrsLucindaFeatherstone) *hld up in tch: rdn over 6f out: wknd over 2f out* **25/1**
00-5 **5** *1/2* **Vitelucy**[34] 812 5-8-9 45 AQuinn(5) 10 34
(MissSJWilton) *hld up and bhd: rdn 7f out: hdwy over 1f out: n.d* **14/1**
0/11 **6** *4* **Dafa**[20] 947 8-9-0 45 SWKelly 7 28
(BJCurley) *hld up: rdn 6f out: bhd fnl 4f* **4/1**[2]
0035 **7** *2 1/2* **Top Of The Class (IRE)**[4] 1042 7-9-0 45 (v) JoannaBadger 2 24
(PDEvans) *prom: rdn over 5f out: wknd over 2f out* **11/1**
40-3 **8** *nk* **Nassau Street**[34] 814 4-8-12 40 (v) CCatlin 5 24
(DJSFrenchDavis) *prom: rdn over 4f out: wknd over 2f out* **20/1**
-532 **9** *18* **Dora Corbino**[14] 991 4-8-12 40 ACulhane 4 —
(RHollinshead) *hld up in tch: rdn 8f out: bhd fnl 6f: t.o* **20/1**
50/0 **10** *5* **Paarl Rock**[17] 973 9-9-0 45 (v) GGibbons 9 —
(STLewis) *chsd ldr tl rdn over 5f out: wknd over 4f out: t.o* **20/1**
055- **11** *2* **Singularity**[157] 5611 4-8-12 45 MTebbutt 6 —
(KFClutterbuck) *hld up towards rr: hdwy over 4f out: rdn and edgd lft over 3f out: sn wknd: t.o* **33/1**
000- **12** *dist* **Sandy Bay (IRE)**[247] 3079 5-9-0 45 RWinston 8 —
(RAllan) *a bhd: t.o fnl 4f out: virtually p.u fnl f* **25/1**

2m 46.53s (5.03) **Going Correction** +0.40s/f (Slow)
**WFA** 4 from 5yo+ 2lb **12** Ran SP% **130.9**
Speed ratings: **99,94,89,88,88 85,84,83,71,68 67,—**CSF £12.86 TOTE £7.10: £2.30, £1.10, £2.50; EX 35.30.
**Owner** Miss Maria McKinney **Bred** T Monaghan **Trained** Hook Norton, Oxon
■ Stewards Enquiry : M Tebbutt one-day ban: careless riding (Apr 2)

**FOCUS**
A fair time for the grade in a contest that saw the field finish well strung out behind the easy winner, who looks back to somewhere near his best.

**NOTEBOOK**
**Isa'Af(IRE)**, off for 188 days previously, ran away with this banded event and is clearly over the problems that saw him sidelined prior to this. He will now have to step up in grade, but remains one to keep on the right side of.
**Buz Kiri(USA)** kept on late from well off the pace, but the winner had flown. His best form is at this track, he was clear of the rest and will not always bump into such a rival as the winner in this grade.
**Ersaal(USA)** had the run of the race and improved slightly for the re-application of blinkers.
**Dafa** was never on terms in this slightly better race over this longer trip.

## 1078 BET IN RUNNING @ BETDIRECT.CO.UK MEDIAN AUCTION MAIDEN STKS 7f (F)
4:00 (4:02) (H) 3-5-Y-0 £1,431 (£409; £204) Stalls High

Form RPR
000- **1** **Riley Boys (IRE)**[140] 5906 3-8-9 64 MFenton 4 53
(JGGiven) *mde all: rdn over 2f out: drvn out* **3/1**[2]
5-42 **2** *3/4* **Bundaberg**[36] 779 4-9-10 45 ACulhane 7 51
(PWHiatt) *a.p: chsd wnr over 4f out: rdn and ev ch fnl 2f: nt qckn ins fnl f* **11/2**
0233 **3** *4* **Angelo's Pride**[8] 1022 3-8-9 59 SWKelly 2 41
(JAOsborne) *chsd ldrs: rdn 4f out: one pce fnl 3f* **5/4**[1]
56-0 **4** *16* **Fayr Firenze (IRE)**[8] 1020 3-8-9 49 (b) SRighton 5 1
(MFHarris) *hld up: hdwy over 4f out: rdn over 3f out: wknd over 2f out* **12/1**
**5** *9* **Sybill** 4-9-5 JQuinn 6 —
(JWUnett) *s.i.s: outpcd* **16/1**
6- **6** *1 3/4* **Vaudevire**[340] 1103 3-8-6 THamilton(3) 3 —
(RPElliott) *rdn over 5f out: sn bhd* **20/1**
00- **7** *17* **Spartan Odyssey**[227] 3950 3-8-9 NCallan 8 —
(ASenior) *w wnr tl rdn over 4f out: sn wknd: t.o* **100/1**
5-54 **8** *8* **Jacob (IRE)**[8] 1022 3-8-9 60 DeanMcKeown 1 —
(PABlockley) *chsd ldrs tl rdn and wknd over 3f out: t.o* **9/2**[3]

1m 33.65s (3.45) **Going Correction** +0.40s/f (Slow)
**WFA** 3 from 4yo 15lb **8** Ran SP% **122.3**
Speed ratings: **96,95,90,72,62 60,40,31**CSF £21.60 TOTE £4.50: £1.40, £1.60, £1.10; EX 44.50.
**Owner** Paul Riley **Bred** P J Makin **Trained** Willoughton, Lincs

**FOCUS**
A dire maiden contest featuring largely out-of-form runners.

**NOTEBOOK**
**Riley Boys(IRE)** led from pillar to post over what looks his optimum trip. Although he will come on again for this outing, according to official figures he should have beaten the runner-up more comfortably and does look flattered by his current mark.
**Bundaberg** ran another fair race, but again was unable to quicken late on. He may go up in the weights for this effort and that will make life tough in handicap company.
**Angelo's Pride** shaped as though he needs to step back up in trip, as he was badly outpaced turning for home.
**Jacob(IRE)** again showed he is flattered by his current official rating and was very disappointing. *Official explanation: trainer said gelding had bled from the nose.*

## 1079 BET DIRECT ON 0800 32 93 93 BANDED STKS 1m 1f 79y(F)
4:35 (4:36) (H) 3-Y-0+ £1,452 (£415; £207) Stalls Low

Form RPR
0-01 **1** **Jake Black (IRE)**[16] 940 4-9-7 45 (v1) DHolland 6 52
(JJQuinn) *hld up: rdn over 5f out: gd hdwy on outside over 2f out: led ins fnl f: r.o* **9/4**[2]
-610 **2** *nk* **Wilson Bluebottle (IRE)**[22] 939 5-9-7 45 (b) DaleGibson 5 51
(MWEasterby) *led after 1f: rdn wl over 1f out: hdd ins fnl f: r.o* **9/1**
-113 **3** *6* **Mrs Cube**[8] 1024 5-9-7 45 RWinston 1 39
(PHowling) *led 1f: prom: rdn over 5f out: wknd fnl f* **5/4**[1]
260- **4** *1 1/2* **Got To Be Cash**[154] 5672 5-9-0 45 BSwarbrick(7) 3 36
(WMBrisbourne) *hld up: rdn over 4f out: hdwy 3f out: n.m.r over 2f out: sn wknd* **4/1**[3]
0-04 **5** *1 1/2* **Morning Hawk (USA)**[39] 752 3-8-2 45 DKinsella 7 33
(JSMoore) *hld up in rr: rdn over 5f out: hdwy on ins wl over 1f out: wknd fnl f* **16/1**
65-2 **6** *nk* **Red Moor (IRE)**[27] 878 4-9-7 45 ACulhane 2 32
(RHollinshead) *hld up: rdn over 4f out: hdwy 3f out: wknd over 1f out* **10/1**
5-55 **7** *6* **Midnight Mambo (USA)**[13] 996 4-9-7 45 (b1) SSanders 4 20
(RGuest) *prom: rdn over 3f out: wknd over 2f out* **16/1**

2m 7.37s (4.47) **Going Correction** +0.40s/f (Slow)
**WFA** 3 from 4yo+ 19lb **7** Ran SP% **126.1**
Speed ratings: **96,95,90,89,87 87,82**CSF £25.65 TOTE £2.80: £1.10, £6.60; EX 25.20.
**Owner** G A Lucas **Bred** Yeomanstown Stud **Trained** Settrington, N Yorks

**FOCUS**
A weak event that produced a cracking finish between the front pair, who were clear of the rest. The form is average for the grade.

**NOTEBOOK**
**Jake Black(IRE)** did not looks to be responding positively to the first-time visor at halfway, but stayed on stoutly in the straight to record back-to-back wins at the track.
**Wilson Bluebottle(IRE)** improved on recent form for this switch to this track, but did look weak inside the final furlong and is a fragile sort. That said, he was clear of the third and can find a weak race.
**Mrs Cube** now looks exposed, as she had the run of the race, and has not built on her two wins earlier this month.
**Got To Be Cash**, off four 154 days previously, ran a fair race and will come on for this outing.

## 1080 BET DIRECT ON SKY ACTIVE BANDED STKS 1m 100y(F)
5:10 (5:11) (H) 3-Y-0+ £1,470 (£420; £210) Stalls Low

Form RPR
4160 **1** **Fraamtastic**[8] 1020 7-9-4 40 (p) BReilly(3) 13 47
(BAPearce) *chsd ldrs: rdn to ld over 2f out: sn clr: eased cl home* **8/1**
060- **2** *1 1/4* **Six Pack (IRE)**[86] 4247 6-9-7 40 CCatlin 12 44
(AndrewTurnell) *mid-div: rdn 5f out: hdwy over 2f out: edgd lft and r.o ins fnl f: nt trble wnr* **8/1**
0463 **3** *6* **Zahunda (IRE)**[5] 1036 5-9-2 40 MSavage(5) 1 31
(WMBrisbourne) *led: rdn and hdd over 3f out: wknd ins fnl f* **7/2**[2]
0532 **4** *3/4* **Neutral Night (IRE)**[8] 1021 4-9-7 40 (v) DHolland 8 30
(RBrotherton) *a.p: led over 4f out: rdn and hdd over 2f out: wknd ins fnl f* **4/1**[3]
-005 **5** *nk* **Youngs Forth**[20] 946 4-9-7 40 JQuinn 4 29
(AWCarroll) *hld up: rdn over 4f out: hdwy over 3f out: wknd ins fnl f* **10/1**
40-3 **6** *nk* **Rahjel Sultan**[42] 729 6-9-7 40 (tp) GGibbons 2 29
(BAMcmahon) *chsd ldrs: rdn over 3f out: wknd 1f out* **10/1**
-052 **7** *7* **Regency Malaya**[13] 999 3-8-4 40 (bt) SRighton 11 14
(MFHarris) *bhd: rdn over 6f out: hdwy on ins over 3f out: wknd over 1f out* **10/1**
5-40 **8** *1/2* **Cumbrian Princess**[45] 700 7-9-7 30 DSweeney 9 13
(MBlanshard) *hld up: hdwy 6f out: rdn 4f out: wknd over 1f out* **14/1**
000- **9** *shd* **Sarn**[105] 6143 5-9-7 40 SWKelly 6 13
(MMullineaux) *bhd: rdn over 6f out: hdwy 4f out: wknd over 2f out* **12/1**
0-06 **10** *3/4* **Un Autre Espere**[14] 994 5-9-7 30 SSanders 10 11
(TWall) *rdn over 6f out: sn bhd* **50/1**
-000 **11** *1* **Illustrious Duke**[24] 903 6-9-4 40 LisaJones(3) 5 9
(MMullineaux) *w ldr: led over 6f out tl over 4f out: wknd over 3f out* **3/1**[1]
-005 **12** *8* **Garnock Belle (IRE)**[14] 994 3-8-4 30 DaleGibson 3 —
(ABerry) *a bhd* **50/1**
0-00 **13** *16* **Altares**[35] 787 3-8-4 40 SWhitworth 7 —
(PHowling) *a bhd: t.o* **33/1**

1m 54.74s (3.74) **Going Correction** +0.40s/f (Slow)
**WFA** 3 from 4yo+ 17lb **13** Ran SP% **137.9**
Speed ratings: **97,95,89,89,88 88,81,80,80,80 79,71,55**CSF £81.45 TOTE £10.60: £3.20, £4.00, £2.80; EX 85.10 Place 6 £39.83, Place 5 £18.21.
**Owner** Richard J Gray **Bred** Bloodhorse International Limited **Trained** Newchapel, Surrey

**FOCUS**
Little strength in depth to this poor event and the field were well strung out behind the ready winner.

**NOTEBOOK**
**Fraamtastic** ◆ improved for this switch back to Fibresand and won cosily. She showed a good turn of foot off the home turn and could well follow-up on this.
**Six Pack(IRE)**, a winner over fences in December, stayed on well in the straight without looking a danger to the winner. He may be of interest over farther in this grade.
**Zahunda(IRE)** had every chance if good enough, but had nothing left when challenged three out and finished tired.
**Neutral Night(IRE)**, who had been placed over seven furlongs the last twice, ran out of steam over this extra furlong.
**Illustrious Duke**, dropping into this grade for the first time, showed very little and has lost the plot of late.

T/Plt: £19.50 to a £1 stake. Pool: £44,274.30. 1,651.40 winning tickets. T/Qpdt: £7.60 to a £1 stake. Pool: £2,639.70. 253.80 winning tickets. KH

## [1059]LINGFIELD (L-H)

Tuesday, March 23

**OFFICIAL GOING: Standard**

Wind: mod hlf against Weather: fair

### 1081 BET DIRECT CHAMPS LEAGUE CASHBACKS AMATEUR RIDERS' H'CAP 1m 5f (P)

**2:00** (2:01) (F) (0-55,55) 4-Y-O+ **£2,961** (£846; £423) **Stalls** Low

Form RPR

32-0 **1** **Great View (IRE)**[19] 966 5-10-5 **46** oh1...(v) MrSWalker 14 56
(MrsALMKing) *lw: hdwy 4f out: led over 1f out: drvn out* **11/1**

6000 **2** *1 1/4* **Golden Dual**[23] 931 4-10-2 **53**...(v[1]) MrDHutchison(7) 4 61
(SDow) *gd hdwy 3f out: pressing ldrs whn hmpd and swtchd rt over 1f out: styd on to take 2nd ins fnl f* **20/1**

3123 **3** *3* **Sungio**[6] 1041 6-10-4 **52**...(b) MrsRPowell(7) 11 56
(BGPowell) *prom: jnd ldr after 4f: led 3f out tl over 1f out: one pce* **16/1**

053/ **4** *2* **Ffiffiffer (IRE)**[192] 6-11-0 **55**... MrNickyTinkler 6 56
(CTinkler) *led tl 3f out: rdn and ev ch over 1f out: no ex* **9/2[2]**

0145 **5** *1/2* **Free Style (GER)**[14] 995 4-9-13 **46** oh1... MrSDobson(3) 1 47
(KRBurke) *b: in tch: n.m.r and lost pl over 4f out: swtchd wd and sme hdwy 3f out: styd on fnl f* **14/1**

2205 **6** *nk* **Our Glenard**[28] 878 5-10-0 **46** oh1... MissALTurner(5) 9 46
(SLKeightley) *wd: hld up in tch: outpcd 3f out: kpt on fnl f* **16/1**

155- **7** *hd* **Classic Millennium**[132] 5982 6-9-12 **46**... MissJPledge(7) 3 46
(WJMusson) *s.s: hld up in rr: gd late hdwy: nvr in chalng position* **10/1**

0035 **8** *5* **Makarim (IRE)**[18] 973 8-11-0 **55**...(p) MrsSBosley 5 48
(MRBosley) *in rr and wd: sme hdwy 7f out: rdn and btn 3f out* **9/1[3]**

203- **9** *2 1/2* **Jenavive**[60] 5375 4-10-0 **49**... MrLNewnes(5) 7 38
(NJHawke) *stdd s: hld up in midfield: hdwy 5f out: wknd 3f out* **14/1**

2441 **10** *2* **Chocolate Boy (IRE)**[9] 1016 5-10-6 **50** 5ex...(be) MrEDehdashti(3) 8 37
(GLMoore) *lw: in tch: pushed along and struggling to hold pl whn squeezed 5f out: sn drvn along and bhd* **13/8[1]**

600/ **11** *1 1/2* **Estuary (USA)**[557] 156 9-10-9 **53**... MsAEmbiricos(3) 12 37
(MsAEEmbiricos) *chsd ldrs tl wknd 3f out* **66/1**

204- **12** *nk* **Fletcher**[224] 4061 10-9-12 **46** oh1... MissGDGracey-Davison(7) 13 30
(HMorrison) *bit bkwd: prom 7f* **20/1**

-440 **13** *4* **Essay Baby (FR)**[14] 995 4-9-8 **46** oh1... MissCNosworthy(7) 10 24
(PDCundell) *lw: plld hrd: w ldrs 3f: stdd bk in tch: wknd 5f out* **33/1**

2m 48.06s (-0.02) **Going Correction** -0.025s/f (Stan)
**WFA** 4 from 5yo+ 3lb **13** Ran SP% **122.8**
Speed ratings: **99,98,96,95,94 94,94,91,89,88 87,87,85**CSF £221.18 CT £3502.37 TOTE £12.30: £2.40, £8.00, £4.80; EX 480.00.
**Owner** All The Kings Horses **Bred** Terry McGrath **Trained** Wilmcote, Warwicks

**FOCUS**
No more than a moderate handicap and, as is often the case in these amateur events, it proved worth following one of the best riders in the race. The form looks reliable for the grade and the winner should remain well treated.

**NOTEBOOK**
**Great View(IRE)**, racing from 1lb out of the handicap and effectively 2lb lower than when winning at Newbury last season, had the visor re-fitted, was partnered by one of the best amateurs in the race and the combination made no mistake. He is lightly raced at this sort of trip, but gets it well and should be competitive off higher marks, including back on turf.
**Golden Dual** made his debut in handicap company off a mark of 74, but has tumbled in the weights since and gained his best placing to date off a career-low mark in a first-time visor. He can be considered slightly unlucky for he had to be switched out to get a run, but hopefully he can build on this.
**Sungio** has gained his last two wins in selling company and did not look to have any excuses.
**Ffiffiffer(IRE)**, three times a winner in Spain, was given a positive ride on his return to this country and shaped well. This was his first run in 192 days, and although he looked fit, he should improve.
**Free Style(GER)** was short of room about half a mile out and was well held.
**Classic Millennium** never once threatened after starting slowly, but ran better than his finishing position suggests.
**Chocolate Boy(IRE)** was reported to have been struck into. *Official explanation: vet said gelding had been struck into.*

### 1082 CASHBACKS @ BET DIRECT ON SKY ACTIVE H'CAP (DIV I) 6f (P)

**2:30** (2:31) (E) (0-70,70) 3-Y-O+ **£3,415** (£1,051; £525; £262) **Stalls** Low

Form RPR

1233 **1** **Mayzin (IRE)**[4] 1057 4-9-6 **62**...(p) DSweeney 7 73
(RMFlower) *pressed ldr: led over 2f out: hrd rdn 1f out: hld on wl* **5/1[1]**

2534 **2** *1/2* **Spindor (USA)**[32] 834 5-9-2 **58**...(b) DHolland 11 67
(JAOsborne) *lw: outpcd towards rr: fin strly to take 2nd nr fin* **12/1**

-400 **3** *shd* **Polar Force**[4] 1051 4-9-0 **59**... DCorby(3) 2 68
(MRChannon) *lw: prom: rdn 1/2-way: drvn to press wnr fnl f: kpt on* **13/2[3]**

2410 **4** *1/2* **Hard To Catch (IRE)**[4] 1057 6-9-7 **70**...(b) LTreadwell(7) 6 77
(DKIvory) *lw: towards rr: rdn and hdwy 2f out: pressed ldrs over 1f out: kpt on* **6/1[2]**

-525 **5** *1/2* **Amelia (IRE)**[54] 626 6-8-0 **49**... BSwarbrick(7) 4 55
(WMBrisbourne) *prom: sltly outpcd over 2f out: kpt on u.p fnl f* **16/1**

5201 **6** *nk* **A Teen**[26] 896 6-8-11 **53**... RWinston 13 58
(PHowling) *b. b.hind: lw: dwlt: swtchd to ins: sn in midfield: drvn along 1/2-way: styd on fr over 1f out* **14/1**

5063 **7** *1/2* **Ladies Knight**[7] 1027 4-8-13 **55**... DarrenWilliams 3 58
(DShaw) *dwlt: sn in tch: outpcd 1/2-way: styd on fr over 1f out* **10/1**

0126 **8** *1* **Sounds Lucky**[4] 1051 8-9-1 **57**...(b) SSanders 12 57
(AndrewReid) *b: b.hind: awkward leaving stalls and s.s: sn in midfield: effrt over 1f out: nvr able to chal* **16/1**

0006 **9** *shd* **Law Maker**[21] 951 4-7-9 **40** oh5...(b) LisaJones(3) 9 40
(MABuckley) *prom tl hrd rdn and btn over 1f out* **66/1**

030- **10** *shd* **Davids Mark**[142] 5892 4-9-1 **57**... WRyan 5 57
(JRJenkins) *bit bkwd: in tch: effrt over 2f out: wd st: no ex ent fnl f* **9/1**

-112 **11** *nk* **Mynd**[25] 904 4-9-10 **66**... DeanMcKeown 1 65
(RMWhitaker) *led tl over 2f out: hrd rdn and wknd over 1f out* **8/1**

-405 **12** *1* **Legal Set (IRE)**[15] 987 8-9-0 **56**... RHughes 10 52
(WJMusson) *wd: hld up in tch: lost pl 1/2-way: shkn up and no hdwy fnl 2f* **10/1**

630- **13** *2 1/2* **Jagged (IRE)**[115] 6094 4-9-4 **60**... GBaker 14 48
(KRBurke) *b.hind: wd: a rr gp: no ch fr 1/2-way* **33/1**

00-0 **14** *3* **Roy McAvoy (IRE)**[18] 967 6-8-13 **55**... JoannaBadger 8 34
(MrsGHarvey) *dwlt: a bhd: no ch fr 1/2-way* **50/1**

1m 12.11s (-0.81) **Going Correction** -0.025s/f (Stan) **14** Ran SP% **116.1**
Speed ratings: **104,103,103,102,101 101,100,99,99,99 98,97,94,90**CSF £61.99 CT £405.70 TOTE £5.50: £2.50, £5.00, £1.70; EX 99.80.
**Owner** Ms Zoe Watkins **Bred** John McEnery **Trained** Jevington, E Sussex

**FOCUS**
Only a moderate handicap, but competitive nonetheless.

**NOTEBOOK**
**Mayzin(IRE)** had gained his only previous win in a maiden over seven furlongs round here, but he is equally effective over this shorter trip and ran out a determined winner. Rated just 52 on turf, he looks well worth another try on that surface.
**Spindor(USA)** did not run to his best on his only previous try on this surface, but he handled the Polytrack well on this occasion and was just held. He is on a winning mark.
**Polar Force**, at one point rated 109, ran respectably but is quite simply a very disappointing sort.
**Hard To Catch(IRE)**, with the blinkers back on, ran his race but has never won off a mark this high.
**Amelia(IRE)** did not run a bad race, but is not quite at the top of her game just now.
**Mynd** has gained both his previous wins over five furlongs, but was below form even allowing for the extra furlong.

### 1083 CASHBACKS @ BETDIRECT.CO.UK MAIDEN STKS 6f (P)

**3:00** (3:02) (D) 3-Y-O **£3,731** (£1,148; £574; £287) **Stalls** Low

Form RPR

033- **1** **Presto Shinko (IRE)**[162] 5548 3-9-0 **78**... RHughes 3 70+
(RHannon) *lw: trckd ldrs: led over 2f out: qcknd clr fnl f: easily* **11/8[1]**

**2** *3* **King Of Diamonds** 3-9-0 ... NPollard 6 61+
(JRBest) *unf: lw: sn bhd: gd late hdwy: tk 2nd nr fin* **20/1**

60- **3** *3/4* **Torquemada (IRE)**[182] 5142 3-9-0 ... PDoe 8 59
(WJarvis) *lw: t.k.h: rapid hdwy to join ldrs over 3f out: nt pce of wnr fnl f* **13/2**

020- **4** *2 1/2* **Bold Wolf**[150] 5746 3-9-0 **54**... ADaly 2 51
(JLSpearing) *led 2f: one pce fnl 2f* **25/1**

6 **5** *1/2* **Simpsons Mount (IRE)**[38] 764 3-9-0 ... RLMoore 11 50
(RMFlower) *dwlt: bhd: rdn and styd on fnl 2f: nt rch ldrs* **20/1**

0-00 **6** *nk* **Sussex Style (IRE)**[38] 766 3-9-0 ... DSweeney 7 49
(RMFlower) *hld up in midfield: effrt over 1f out: no imp* **50/1**

46-4 **7** *nk* **Imperium**[23] 927 3-9-0 **75**...(t) SDrowne 1 48
(MrsStefLiddiard) *chsd ldrs: rdn over 2f out: no ex over 1f out* **3/1[2]**

435- **8** *1* **Sworn To Secrecy**[222] 4112 3-8-9 **69**... DHolland 9 40
(SKirk) *bit bkwd: chsd ldrs: drvn along whn nt clr run over 2f out: no ex over 1f out* **6/1[3]**

0-00 **9** *1/2* **Top Place**[36] 791 3-8-9 ...(p) CCogan 4 38
(CADwyer) *in tch: n.m.r 4f out: no hdwy fnl 2f* **50/1**

**10** *1 1/2* **Mr Hullabalou (IRE)** 3-9-0 ... SSanders 5 39
(RIngram) *w'like: bit bkwd: s.s: outpcd: a in rr* **33/1**

0000 **11** *2* **Fora Smile**[25] 907 3-9-0 **45**... WRyan 10 33
(MDIUsher) *prom: led 4f out tl over 2f out: sn wknd* **50/1**

1m 13.07s (0.15) **Going Correction** -0.025s/f (Stan) **11** Ran SP% **116.9**
Speed ratings: **98,94,93,89,89 88,88,86,86,84 81**CSF £36.20 TOTE £2.30: £1.10, £4.10, £2.20; EX 39.30.
**Owner** Major A M Everett **Bred** Mrs S O'Riordan **Trained** East Everleigh, Wilts

**FOCUS**
Not that strong a maiden in depth, contested mainly by handicap types, but the winner could be quite useful and the second can do better.

**NOTEBOOK**
**Presto Shinko(IRE)** confirmed the promise he showed as a two-year-old to get off the mark with a comfortable victory. He was value for a lot more than the winning margin and there should be more to come.
**King Of Diamonds** showed real signs of greenness, but also shaped with some promise. Bred to be suited by much further, he never once threatened the winner but picked up well in the straight to grab second close home. He is bound to improve on this.
**Torquemada(IRE)** showed promise on both his starts at two, but did not really progress on this reappearance. However, he is now qualified for a handicap mark and could improve.
**Bold Wolf** hinted at ability as a two-year-old and, with the tongue-tie left off for this reappearance, again offered encouragement.
**Simpsons Mount(IRE)** made his debut in an eye-shield but the headgear was left off on this occasion. He shaped with promise but is unlikely to come into his own until handicapped.
**Imperium** only had 3lb to find with the winner at the weights, but did not perform and is becoming disappointing.
**Fora Smile** *Official explanation: jockey said colt lost its action*

### 1084 CASHBACKS @ BET DIRECT INTERACTIVE CLAIMING STKS 1m 2f (P)

**3:30** (3:31) (F) 3-Y-O **£2,884** (£824; £412) **Stalls** Low

Form RPR

0-20 **1** **Regulated (IRE)**[32] 835 3-9-1 **65**... DHolland 7 63
(JAOsborne) *t.k.h: in tch: led over 1f out: drvn out* **4/1[2]**

0-20 **2** *1* **Platinum Pirate**[55] 622 3-8-9 **55**...(b) GFaulkner 2 56
(KRBurke) *stdd s: plld hrd: sn prom: led 3f out tl over 1f out: rdn and hung rt: nt qckn* **8/1**

06-2 **3** *shd* **Caspian Dusk**[9] 1022 3-8-6 **53**... CHaddon(7) 8 59
(WGMTurner) *lw: hdwy 3f out: hrd rdn over 1f out: styd on fnl f* **11/2[3]**

6-04 **4** *hd* **Foot Fault (IRE)**[9] 1017 3-8-8 **57**... WRyan 11 54
(NACallaghan) *stdd s: hld up in rr: stdy hdwy 3f out: drvn to press ldrs over 1f out: kpt on* **5/2[1]**

5-00 **5** *5* **Frambo (IRE)**[35] 804 3-8-4 **49**...(p) RLMoore 1 41
(JGPortman) *led and set mod pce: hdd 3f out: no ex fnl 2f* **10/1**

-004 **6** *3/4* **Doctored**[9] 1015 3-8-10 **50**...(b) BReilly(3) 5 48
(BAPearce) *b: chsd ldrs: outpcd fnl 3f* **7/1**

5200 **7** *nk* **Quarry Island (IRE)**[5] 1046 3-7-5 **45**...(b[1]) BSwarbrick(7) 10 33
(PDEvans) *prom: rdn 3f out: btn 2f out* **20/1**

000- **8** *7* **Bunino Ven**[169] 5422 3-8-9 ... PaulEddery 4 30
(SCWilliams) *bit bkwd: hdwy 5f out: rdn 3f out: sn wknd* **8/1**

0005 **9** *2 1/2* **Mystic Promise (IRE)**[28] 877 3-8-4 **30**...(vt) HayleyTurner(5) 3 25
(MrsNMacauley) *hld up in midfield: n.m.r and dropped to rr 5f out: bhd fnl 3f* **50/1**

2m 12.07s (4.68) **Going Correction** -0.025s/f (Stan) **9** Ran SP% **114.5**
Speed ratings: **80,79,79,78,74 74,74,68,66**CSF £35.57 TOTE £5.70: £1.80, £2.40, £2.20; EX 68.20.
**Owner** Richard Leslie **Bred** Churchtown House Stud **Trained** Upper Lambourn, Berks

**FOCUS**
Not a very good claimer and the early pace was very steady.

**NOTEBOOK**
**Regulated(IRE)** was the best in at the weights and, despite wandering round a little in the closing stages, he made the most of this opportunity to get off the mark. This was his first run in a claimer and things are likely to be harder outside of this grade.
**Platinum Pirate**, 4lb wrong at the weights with the winner, appreciated the drop back into claiming company and ran a reasonable race. He did not help his chance, however, by hanging right in the closing stages and was also keen early on.
**Caspian Dusk**, who had 10lb to find with the winner at the weights, was making his Polytrack debut and stepping up to ten furlongs for the first time. This was a promising effort and, still lightly raced, there could be further improvement to come.
**Foot Fault(IRE)**, well held in fourth when stepped up to this trip for the first time in a handicap on her previous run, travelled stylishly and simply found a few too strong.

**Frambo(IRE)** did not look to improve for the switch to Polytrack.

## 1085 CASHBACKS @ ATTHERACES TEXT PAGE 410 H'CAP (DIV I) 1m 2f (P)
**4:00** (4:01) (E) (0-75,75) 3-Y-0+ **£3,376** (£1,039; £519; £259) **Stalls** Low

Form RPR

-042 **1** **Say What You See (IRE)**$^{19}$ 964 4-9-11 72 MHills 1 81
(JWHills) *lw: mde all: hrd rdn and edgd rt fnl f: hld on wl* **11/4**$^{1}$

250- **2** *nk* **Siena Star (IRE)**$^{122}$ 6052 6-10-0 75 RHughes 6 83
(PFICole) *lw: hld up: hdwy 2f out: drvn to press wnr ins fnl f: jst hld* **10/3**$^{2}$

46-0 **3** *nk* **Katiypour (IRE)**$^{19}$ 964 7-9-8 69 SSanders 3 77
(MissBSanders) *chsd ldrs: n.m.r on rail ent st: hrd rdn over 1f out: styd on fnl f* **13/2**

3-60 **4** *1* **Silvaline**$^{19}$ 964 5-9-4 65 GCarter 2 71
(TKeddy) *prom: rdn over 2f out: one pce appr fnl f* **9/2**$^{3}$

1-40 **5** *½* **Lyrical Way**$^{52}$ 650 5-9-1 62 (v) SDrowne 9 67
(PRChamings) *dwlt: bhd: hrd rdn over 2f out: hdwy over 1f out: nt rch ldrs* **12/1**

244- **6** *1 ½* **Compton Aviator**$^{153}$ 5452 8-8-9 56 (t) DHolland 5 59
(AWCarroll) *hld up towards rr: effrt 2f out: no imp* **8/1**

00/6 **7** *3 ½* **Hallings Overture (USA)**$^{27}$ 882 5-9-2 63 PaulEddery 7 59
(CAHorgan) *wd: t.k.h: in tch: pressed ldr over 3f out tl 2f out: wknd over 1f out* **14/1**

0561 **8** *7* **Haithem (IRE)**$^{21}$ 949 7-7-9 45 (t) LisaJones(3) 4 29
(DShaw) *t.k.h: prom 7f* **20/1**

2m 5.39s (-2.00) **Going Correction** -0.025s/f (Stan) **8** Ran SP% **111.5**
Speed ratings: **107,106,106,105,105 104,101,95**CSF £11.32 CT £50.65 TOTE £3.80: £1.50, £2.10, £1.50; EX 12.80.
**Owner** Richard Tufft & Ken Wilkinson **Bred** Killeen Castle Stud **Trained** Upper Lambourn, Berks

**FOCUS**
A tight little handicap and the form should stand up.

**NOTEBOOK**
**Say What You See(IRE)** is at his best when able to dominate and gained his first win in a handicap having been able to do just that. There was nothing to spare at the finish, but his yard appear in good form and he should remain competitive off higher marks.
**Siena Star(IRE)**, 3lb higher than when last successful over this course and distance, but on the same mark as when successful at Leicester last year, ran a fine race, especially considering he was struck on the nose in the closing stages - an action that Hughes thought might have made a difference.
**Katiypour(IRE)** has never won on this surface, but he did little wrong on this occasion and things would have been even closer had he not been short of room at the top of the straight.
**Silvaline** is well handicapped on this surface and this was not a bad effort.
**Lyrical Way**, 5lb higher than when winning over course and distance in December, was not beaten that far but never really looked like getting to the front.

## 1086 CASHBACKS @ SKY TEXT PAGE 372 FILLIES' H'CAP 7f (P)
**4:30** (4:32) (E) (0-70,69) 3-Y-0 **£3,464** (£1,066; £533; £266) **Stalls** Low

Form RPR

342 **1** **Alexander Ambition (IRE)**$^{19}$ 959 3-9-2 64 RHughes 3 69+
(SKirk) *chsd ldr: led over 1f out: drvn out* **7/1**

2253 **2** *nk* **Park Ave Princess (IRE)**$^{15}$ 983 3-8-11 59 DHolland 1 63
(NPLittmoden) *led tl over 1f out: hrd rdn and ev ch fnl f: kpt on* **9/2**$^{2}$

41 **3** *1 ½* **Kryssa**$^{19}$ 963 3-8-12 60 RLMoore 9 65+
(GLMoore) *hld up in midfield: effrt and nt clr run over 1f out: swtchd wd: nrst fin* **4/1**$^{1}$

0036 **4** *shd* **Docklands Blue (IRE)**$^{15}$ 983 3-8-6 54 CCatlin 5 54
(NPLittmoden) *hld up in rr: rdn and r.o fnl 2f: nvr nrr* **10/1**

1200 **5** *1* **Jaolins**$^{5}$ 1047 3-8-8 56 SDrowne 2 53
(PGMurphy) *dwlt: hld up in midfield: drvn to chse ldrs over 1f out: styd on same pce* **25/1**

00-0 **6** *hd* **Man Crazy (IRE)**$^{24}$ 917 3-8-12 60 JMackay 10 57
(RMBeckett) *bit bkwd: towards rr and wd: hdwy 3f out: styd on same pce fnl 2f* **20/1**

656- **7** *shd* **The Stick**$^{150}$ 5744 3-8-12 63 SHitchcott(3) 4 59
(MRChannon) *chsd ldrs: rdn 3f out: one pce appr fnl f* **16/1**

06-6 **8** *¾* **La Petite Chinoise**$^{34}$ 816 3-9-7 69 (b$^{1}$) SSanders 12 63
(RGuest) *chsd ldrs: hrd rdn over 1f out: no ex* **16/1**

-006 **9** *nk* **Trompe L'Oeil (IRE)**$^{9}$ 1017 3-8-12 60 (p) SCarson 8 54
(AndrewReid) *b: b.hind: dwlt: bhd: rdn and hdwy over 1f out: r.o* **33/1**

3222 **10** *hd* **Sonderborg**$^{9}$ 1020 3-8-0 51 (be) LisaJones(3) 7 44
(GLMoore) *chsd ldrs: outpcd over 2f out: sn btn* **11/2**$^{3}$

4406 **11** *1 ¼* **Lady Predominant**$^{23}$ 927 3-7-5 46 oh1 BSwarbrick(7) 11 36
(AndrewReid) *b: b.hind: hld up towards rr: shkn up over 1f out: nvr nr to chal* **25/1**

000- **12** *2* **Danifah (IRE)**$^{163}$ 5496 3-8-12 60 SWKelly 15 44
(PDEvans) *dwlt: in rr: rdn 3f out: wd st: n.d* **50/1**

600- **13** *2 ½* **Spring Dancer**$^{165}$ 5471 3-9-5 67 JQuinn 6 45
(APJarvis) *bit bkwd: chsd ldrs 5f* **12/1**

5203 **14** *1 ¾* **Zonnebeke**$^{21}$ 946 3-7-12 46 oh1 DaleGibson 13 19
(KRBurke) *in tch 4f* **20/1**

660- **15** *1* **Yamato Pink**$^{120}$ 6058 3-7-12 46 JoannaBadger 14 16
(KRBurke) *prom 5f* **50/1**

1m 26.04s (0.04) **Going Correction** -0.025s/f (Stan) **15** Ran SP% **118.7**
Speed ratings: **98,97,95,95,94 94,94,93,93,92 91,89,86,84,83**CSF £34.32 CT £148.06 TOTE £7.20: £2.80, £2.70, £1.90; EX 28.60.
**Owner** Mrs N O'Callaghan **Bred** Mountarmstrong Stud **Trained** Upper Lambourn, Berks

**FOCUS**
A run-of-the-mill fillies' handicap, although the winner can hold her own off higher marks. The third was unlucky and can be rated higher.

**NOTEBOOK**
**Alexander Ambition(IRE)**, runner-up in a mile handicap round here on her previous run, confirmed that promise to gain her first success to date. This will have boosted her paddock value.
**Park Ave Princess(IRE)** continues to run well but keeps finding one too good. A drop back into claiming company may be what is required.
**Kryssa**, who confirmed her debut promise to get off the mark over five furlongs here on her latest run, has to be considered unlucky on this handicap debut. She got no luck in running and would have finished a lot closer with a clearer passage.
**Docklands Blue(IRE)**, still a maiden, ran well enough and suggested she may get a mile.
**Jaolins** showed a bit more than she did on her last two starts.
**Sonderborg** was a long way below his recent form.
**Spring Dancer** *Official explanation: jockey said filly had hung left*

## 1087 CASHBACKS @ BET DIRECT ON SKY ACTIVE H'CAP (DIV II) 6f (P)
**5:00** (5:01) (E) (0-70,66) 3-Y-0+ **£3,415** (£1,051; £525; £262) **Stalls** Low

Form RPR

0242 **1** **Double M**$^{4}$ 1057 7-9-0 56 (v) RHughes 1 68
(MrsLRichards) *lw: trckd ldrs: rdn to ld ins fnl f: readily* **11/4**$^{1}$

1260 **2** *1 ¾* **Tayif**$^{31}$ 847 8-9-9 65 (t) SCarson 9 72
(AndrewReid) *b: b.hind: s.i.s: gd hdwy over 1f out: r.o to take 2nd ins fnl f* **6/1**$^{2}$

4050 **3** *½* **New Options**$^{27}$ 884 7-8-12 57 (p) LisaJones(3) 2 63
(WJMusson) *hld up in tch: effrt over 1f out: styd on to take 3rd ins fnl f* **12/1**

60-0 **4** *hd* **Woodbury**$^{24}$ 917 5-8-11 53 GBaker 7 58
(KRBurke) *pressed ldr: hrd rdn and ev ch over 1f out: one pce* **12/1**

0600 **5** *¾* **Teyaar**$^{26}$ 897 8-8-8 55 HayleyTurner(5) 3 58
(MrsNMacauley) *b: b.hind: led: hrd rdn and hdd ins fnl f: one pce* **16/1**

2114 **6** *1 ½* **Long Weekend (IRE)**$^{9}$ 1018 6-8-6 48 (v) DarrenWilliams 8 46
(DShaw) *hld up in midfield: effrt 2f out: styd on same pce* **8/1**

0350 **7** *1* **Illusive (IRE)**$^{4}$ 1057 7-9-4 60 (b) GCarter 12 55
(MWigham) *towards rr: wd and effrt ent st: no imp* **14/1**

3400 **8** *¾* **Pheckless**$^{4}$ 1055 5-9-10 66 DHolland 6 59
(JMBradley) *plld hrd: sn prom: hrd rdn over 1f out: no ex* **12/1**

232- **9** *4* **Salon Prive**$^{131}$ 5988 4-9-9 65 SSanders 11 46
(CACyzer) *in tch: rdn 1/2-way: wknd wl over 1f out* **15/2**

-044 **10** *shd* **Carlton (IRE)**$^{32}$ 833 10-8-10 57 RThomas(5) 13 38
(CRDore) *bhd: rdn over 2f out: nvr nr ldrs* **20/1**

10/0 **11** *shd* **Happy Camper (IRE)**$^{69}$ 519 4-9-4 60 DSweeney 5 40
(MRHoad) *prom to 1/2-way* **50/1**

0-00 **12** *3 ½* **Firework**$^{15}$ 987 6-9-2 58 JQuinn 10 28
(JAkehurst) *chsd ldrs to 1/2-way* **20/1**

-036 **13** *½* **Our Chelsea Blue (USA)**$^{36}$ 794 6-8-6 51 (t) RMiles(3) 4 19
(IAWood) *s.s and awkward leaving stalls: swtchd wd 1/2-way: a bhd* **13/2**$^{3}$

1m 12.14s (-0.78) **Going Correction** -0.025s/f (Stan) **13** Ran SP% **124.3**
Speed ratings: **104,101,101,100,99 97,96,95,90,89 89,85,84**CSF £18.50 CT £184.97 TOTE £3.50: £1.80, £4.50, £3.90; EX 17.40.
**Owner** Bryan Mathieson **Bred** M G Tebbitt **Trained** Funtington, W Sussex

**FOCUS**
Maybe just the weaker of the two divisions, but the best effort for some time by the winner.

**NOTEBOOK**
**Double M** gained deserved compensation for an unlucky effort when runner-up here on his last start. This is the highest mark he has ever won off and he is clearly at the top of his game.
**Tayif** returned to form after a couple of moderate efforts, but was readily brushed aside by the winner.
**New Options**, beaten in selling company on his last two runs, ran well in first-time cheekpieces. However, he has yet to win in this country.
**Woodbury** did not appear to have any excuses.
**Teyaar** is back on a winning mark and did not go too badly.

## 1088 CASHBACKS @ ATTHERACES TEXT PAGE 410 H'CAP 1m 2f (P)
**5:30** (5:32) (E) (0-75,75) 3-Y-0+ **£3,376** (£1,039; £519; £259) **Stalls** Low

Form RPR

2131 **1** **Steely Dan**$^{19}$ 966 5-9-3 64 NPollard 2 73+
(JRBest) *hld up in rr: smooth hdwy to ld ins fnl f: easily* **9/4**$^{1}$

-634 **2** *¾* **Burgundy**$^{23}$ 932 7-8-10 57 (b$^{1}$) RLMoore 9 65
(PMitchell) *s.s: hld up in rr: hdwy and ev ch 1f out: nt pce of wnr* **10/1**

0130 **3** *nk* **True Companion**$^{28}$ 870 5-9-5 66 DHolland 6 73
(NPLittmoden) *hld up in rr: nt clr run on rail ent st: swtchd rt: gng on wl at fin* **11/2**$^{3}$

0223 **4** *½* **Absolute Utopia (USA)**$^{19}$ 964 11-9-2 63 ADaly 4 70
(JLSpearing) *hld up in tch: effrt over 1f out: one pce* **12/1**

00-0 **5** *nk* **Rebate**$^{28}$ 872 4-9-9 70 PDobbs 8 76
(RHannon) *plld hrd: hld up in midfield: effrt and swtchd lft over 1f out: no imp* **14/1**

0000 **6** *½* **Adalar (IRE)**$^{27}$ 887 4-9-7 68 SWKelly 7 73
(PDEvans) *lw: chsd ldrs: rdn over 2f out: ev ch over 1f out: sltly hmpd ent fnl f: one pce* **16/1**

43-6 **7** *1* **Captain Darling (IRE)**$^{32}$ 834 4-9-1 62 RHughes 5 65
(RMHCowell) *led 3f: led over 1f out tl ins fnl f: no ex* **9/1**

0101 **8** *shd* **Scotty's Future (IRE)**$^{26}$ 894 6-10-0 75 JPMurtagh 3 78
(DRLoder) *b: dwlt: hld up in rr: effrt on outside ent st: sn btn* **4/1**$^{2}$

-240 **9** *1 ¼* **My Maite (IRE)**$^{27}$ 882 5-8-9 56 (vt) SSanders 1 57
(RIngram) *chsd ldr: led after 3f tl wknd over 1f out* **9/1**

2m 6.60s (-0.79) **Going Correction** -0.025s/f (Stan) **9** Ran SP% **115.5**
Speed ratings: **102,101,101,100,100 100,99,99,98**CSF £26.08 CT £111.59 TOTE £3.20: £1.10, £4.90, £3.50; EX 36.00 Place 6 £177.75, Place 5 £13.47.
**Owner** E A Condon **Bred** Mrs S E Barclay And L B Snowden **Trained** Hucking, Kent

**FOCUS**
A modest handicap won by the bang in-form Steely Dan, who is still well handicapped on his old form.

**NOTEBOOK**
**Steely Dan** continues in fine form and gained his third win since the turn of the year with a cheeky success. He remains worth keeping on the right side of.
**Burgundy** had blinkers on for the first time and ran a good race. He is, however, without a win in a handicap since July 2002.
**True Companion** would have been much closer with better luck in running, but would probably not have beaten the winner.
**Absolute Utopia(USA)** goes well over course and distance and ran well, but this race was a little too competitive for him.
**Rebate** ran better than he did last time and could be coming to hand.
**Scotty's Future(IRE)** continues to regress.
T/Plt: £79.20 to a £1 stake. Pool: £44,627.65. 410.95 winning tickets. T/Qpdt: £4.00 to a £1 stake. Pool: £4,955.10. 894.50 winning tickets. LM

# 1042 SOUTHWELL (L-H)
Tuesday, March 23

**OFFICIAL GOING: Standard**
Wind: mod hlf bhd Weather: overcast

## 1089 NEW SITE @ BETDIRECT.CO.UK BANDED STKS 5f (F)
**2:10** (2:11) (H) 3-Y-0+ **£1,452** (£415; £207) **Stalls** High

Form RPR

0000 **1** **Caronte (IRE)**$^{14}$ 998 4-9-7 30 (b) JBramhill 10 41
(SRBowring) *outpcd: hdwy over 1f out: r.o to ld nr fin* **33/1**

0000 **2** *¾* **Tuscan Dream**$^{22}$ 944 9-9-2 30 PBradley(5) 6 38
(ABerry) *led: hdd over 3f out: rdn to ld over 1f out: edgd lft and hdd nr fin* **20/1**

0400 **3** *shd* **Flying Faisal (USA)**$^{22}$ 941 6-9-7 35 PFitzsimons 5 38
(JMBradley) *chsd ldrs: rdn over 1f out: r.o* **5/1**$^{3}$

0-06 **4** *1 ½* **Mind The Time**$^{38}$ 774 3-8-9 35 MTebbutt 11 32
(JHetherton) *dwlt: outpcd: r.o ins fnl f: nrst fin* **20/1**

0004 **5** *nk* **Levelled**[14] 1000 10-9-7 35........(b) ACulhane 9 31
(DWChapman) *chsd ldrs: rdn and ev ch over 1f out: no ex ins fnl f* **4/1**[2]
0643 **6** *½* **Lone Piper**[22] 944 9-9-7 35........ SWhitworth 4 30
(JMBradley) *chsd ldrs: rdn and ev ch over 1f out: no ex ins fnl f* **9/4**[1]
00-0 **7** *hd* **Mr Uppity**[28] 876 5-9-0 35........(e[1]) MHalford(7) 8 29
(JulianPoulton) *sn outpcd: r.o ins fnl f: nvr nrr* **10/1**
/500 **8** *hd* **Magic Eagle**[35] 813 7-9-7 35........(v[1]) RFitzpatrick 2 28
(PTMidgley) *dwlt: rcvrd to ld over 3f out: rdn and hdd over 1f out: no ex ins fnl f* **11/1**
0-00 **9** *hd* **Burkees Graw (IRE)**[39] 762 3-8-9 35........ GDuffield 12 28
(MrsSLamyman) *mid-div: rdn and edgd lft 1/2-way: nvr trbld ldrs* **20/1**
000- **10** *¾* **The Lady Would (IRE)**[176] 5280 5-9-0 35........ DerekNolan(7) 3 25
(DGBridgwater) *outpcd fr 1/2-way* **10/1**
0-06 **11** *7* **Diamond Racket**[22] 944 4-9-7 30........(b) KDalgleish 7 —
(DWChapman) *dwlt: outpcd* **16/1**
0-00 **12** *nk* **Gruff**[37] 780 5-9-7 30........ GParkin 1 —
(PTMidgley) *s.i.s: outpcd* **40/1**

61.50 secs (1.20) **Going Correction** +0.175s/f (Slow)
**WFA** 3 from 4yo+ 12lb **12** Ran SP% **119.5**
Speed ratings: **97,95,95,93,92 91,91,91,91,89 78,78**CSF £554.62 TOTE £43.20: £8.80, £4.50, £2.10; EX 291.50.
**Owner** D H Bowring **Bred** John Grogan **Trained** Edwinstowe, Notts
■ Stewards Enquiry : J Bramhill two-day ban: used whip with excessive frequency (Apr 3,5)

**FOCUS**
A poor race full of disappointing sorts and a moderate pace.

**NOTEBOOK**
**Caronte(IRE)** finally broke his duck at the 36th attempt. Down in trip, and equipped with a hood to accompany the blinkers, he was nearly last at halfway but stayed on against the near rail to get up.
**Tuscan Dream** did nothing at all wrong and, having seen off several challengers, was a little unfortunate to be nailed near the line.
**Flying Faisal(USA)** was without the headgear tis time. He normally operates over farther and found this too sharp, although he was running on at the end.
**Mind The Time** stayed on quite well late in the day and the drop back to five furlongs was not the answer. He needs to break better than he has been doing, but this was only his fourth run and there might be a little race for him.
**Levelled** has been sharpened up by the blinkers on his last two runs and he ran his race with no excuses.
**Lone Piper** was always in the front rank but could never quite get his head in front.

## 1090 BETDIRECT.CO.UK AMATEUR RIDERS' CLAIMING STKS 1m (F)
**2:40** (2:41) (H) 4-Y-O+ **£1,459** (£417; £208) **Stalls** Low

Form RPR
3240 **1** **Our Destiny**[36] 800 6-10-3 50........(v) MissETucker(7) 6 48
(DBurchell) *a.p: chsd ldr over 4f out: led over 2f out: styd on wl* **13/2**
5450 **2** *3½* **Sea Ya Maite**[9] 1026 10-10-12 35........(t) MrsMMorris 7 43
(SRBowring) *chsd ldrs: rdn over 2f out: styd on* **11/1**
6-00 **3** *2½* **Prince Minata (IRE)**[19] 966 9-10-3 40........ MissAHockley(7) 9 36
(PWHiatt) *chsd ldrs: outpcd over 2f out: styd on ins fnl f* **12/1**
6160 **4** *shd* **Iamback**[18] 972 4-10-0 48........(p) GBartley(7) 5 33
(MissGayKelleway) *prom: rdn over 3f out: kpt on* **10/1**
4525 **5** *½* **Red Delirium**[9] 1024 8-10-7 50........(b) MrShaunJohnson(7) 3 39
(PABlockley) *hld up: effrt over 2f out: nt rch ldrs* **5/1**[3]
3-35 **6** *nk* **Levantine (IRE)**[22] 941 7-10-12 40........(p) MissCHannaford 13 36
(AGNewcombe) *mde most over 5f: wknd ins fnl f* **4/1**[2]
0355 **7** *¾* **Noble Pursuit**[5] 1043 7-10-9 53........ StaceyRenwick(5) 10 37
(PABlockley) *chsd ldrs: rdn over 2f out: sn btn* **3/1**[1]
00-0 **8** *3½* **Rathmullan**[76] 465 5-10-7 35........ MrCWitheford(7) 12 30
(EAWheeler) *w ldr to 1/2-way: wknd over 2f out* **50/1**
0-00 **9** *8* **Crown City (USA)**[26] 894 4-10-4 35........(t) MissKellyHarrison(3) 1 7
(BPJBaugh) *hld up: n.d* **28/1**
0/05 **10** *2* **Mr Perry (IRE)**[13] 940 8-10-1 30........ MrKFord(7) 4 4
(MrsPFord) *bhd fr 1/2-way* **22/1**
0-00 **11** *27* **Tern Intern (IRE)**[14] 998 5-10-1 30........ MissFionaBrown(7) 2 —
(MissJFeilden) *s.s: a bhd* **33/1**
3/ **12** *14* **Betterthedeviluno**[8] 2702 5-10-5........ MrDFWilliams(7) 8 —
(DMccain) *dwlt: hdwy 6f out: wknd 1/2-way* **40/1**

1m 48.41s (3.81) **Going Correction** +0.30s/f (Slow) **12** Ran SP% **115.3**
Speed ratings: **92,88,86,85,85 85,84,80,72,70 43,29**CSF £69.00 TOTE £3.60: £1.90, £2.40, £5.80; EX 27.00.The winner was claimed by Dennis Deacon for £3,000.
**Owner** Three Acres Racing **Bred** D A And Mrs Hicks **Trained** Briery Hill, Blaenau Gwent

**FOCUS**
A dire race with the favourite running below form.

**NOTEBOOK**
**Our Destiny** was unable to adopt his usual front-running tactics over this shorter trip, but got to the lead early in the straight and was pushed out to land this abysmal contest. Subsequently claimed, he is likely to join Tony Carroll.
**Sea Ya Maite** kept plugging on, but this extended his losing sequence to 41 races.
**Prince Minata(IRE)** ran a better race with a couple of outings under his belt, staying on after being outpaced. His rider, it has to be said, looked no more than a passenger.
**Iamback**, back in cheekpieces having worn an eyeshield on her last couple of runs, stayed on under pressure against the far rail.
**Red Delirium**, an inconsistent performer, was slow to find his stride and could never land a blow.
**Levantine(IRE)**, back in cheekpieces, was collared by the eventual winner with over a furlong to run and was run out of the placings inside the last.
**Noble Pursuit** had a chance at the weights, but he is not running well at present.
**Tern Intern(IRE)** *Official explanation: jockey said gelding was unsuited by the going*

## 1091 SPECIAL OFFERS @ BETDIRECT.CO.UK BANDED STKS 1m 3f (F)
**3:10** (3:12) (H) 4-Y-O+ **£1,449** (£414; £207) **Stalls** Low

Form RPR
0-50 **1** **Cumwhitton**[9] 1026 5-9-1 30........(p) PHanagan 4 51
(RAFahey) *dwlt: sn chsng ldrs: led and hung lft wl over 1f out: rdn clr* **8/1**
000- **2** *7* **That's Racing**[185] 5069 4-9-0 35........ GDuffield 8 40
(JHetherton) *chsd ldr 9f out: led over 3f out: hdd wl over 1f out: sn outpcd* **7/1**
00B2 **3** *8* **Spiders Web**[15] 994 4-9-0 35........(b) NCallan 5 27
(TKeddy) *chsd ldrs: rdn and hung lft 2f out: sn wknd* **6/1**[3]
-533 **4** *2½* **Samar Qand**[9] 1026 5-9-1 35........(t) MTebbutt 2 23
(JulianPoulton) *chsd ldrs: rdn and nt clr run over 3f out: wknd 2f out* **3/1**[1]
-040 **5** *2* **Trojan Wolf**[9] 1026 9-9-1 35........ ACulhane 3 20
(PHowling) *led over 7f: wknd over 2f out* **7/1**
5404 **6** *1* **Mathmagician**[9] 1026 5-8-12 35........(b) LFletcher(3) 9 18
(RFMarvin) *sn drvn along in rr: nvr nrr* **9/2**[2]
4030 **7** *1½* **Think Quick (IRE)**[9] 1026 4-8-7 35........ RKennemore(7) 7 16
(RHollinshead) *s.i.s: hld up: wknd over 3f out* **16/1**
000- **8** *4* **Wethaab (USA)**[298] 1968 7-9-1 35........(tp) AnnStokell 6 9
(MissAStokell) *hld up: wknd over 3f out* **12/1**
0-00 **9** *13* **Samba Beat**[20] 952 5-9-1 35........(b) PMcCabe 1 —
(RFMarvin) *s.s: hld up: plld hrd: wknd 4f out* **20/1**

2m 32.26s (3.36) **Going Correction** +0.30s/f (Slow)
**WFA** 4 from 5yo+ 1lb **9** Ran SP% **111.9**
Speed ratings: **99,93,88,86,84 84,83,80,70**CSF £60.09 TOTE £6.00: £2.40, £3.80, £1.70; EX 46.20.
**Owner** J Roundtree **Bred** Peter Storey **Trained** Musley Bank, N Yorks

**FOCUS**
This was run at a moderate pace, but the winner looks above average for the level of race.

**NOTEBOOK**
**Cumwhitton** was always going best and she came clear once striking the front despite edging over to the far rail. The cheekpieces would appear to have had a galvanising effect and she might win again in lowly company. *Official explanation: trainer's representative had no explanation for the improved form shown*
**That's Racing**, having his first run since September, was left trailing by the mare but himself finished clear of the others. This run at least proved that he acts on Fibresand.
**Spiders Web**, upped in trip, had his chance but was unable to quicken up. He is not straightforward, but is a half-brother to Rigmarole and his future could lie over hurdles.
**Samar Qand**, who had today's winner behind her last time out, gave trouble in the preliminaries. In the race her lack of pace was again all too evident.
**Samba Beat** *Official explanation: jockey said mare was hanging left*

## 1092 BET IN RUNNING @ BETDIRECT.CO.UK BANDED STKS 6f (F)
**3:40** (3:41) (H) 3-Y-O+ **£1,438** (£411; £205) **Stalls** Low

Form RPR
2030 **1** **Above Board**[23] 936 9-9-4 45........(t) LFletcher(3) 9 53
(RFMarvin) *chsd ldrs: rdn to ld wl ins fnl f* **16/1**
-033 **2** *1¾* **Largs**[7] 1032 4-9-7 45........ JEdmunds 6 48+
(JBalding) *sn outpcd: hdwy over 1f out: r.o* **2/1**[1]
0001 **3** *hd* **On The Trail**[15] 990 7-9-7 45........ ACulhane 4 47
(DWChapman) *chsd ldrs: rdn to ld over 1f out: hdd wl ins fnl f* **5/1**[2]
3350 **4** *2* **Bells Boy's**[23] 936 5-9-7 40........(p) NCallan 8 41
(KARyan) *led over 4f: no ex ins fnl f* **12/1**
6503 **5** *2* **Heathyardsblessing (IRE)**[23] 938 7-9-0 45 StephanieHollinshead(7) 7 35
(RHollinshead) *hld up: rdn 1/2-way: nvr trbld ldrs* **17/2**[3]
3010 **6** *nk* **Evangelist (IRE)**[15] 990 4-9-7 45........(tp) MFenton 5 34
(MrsStefLiddiard) *sn outpcd: styd on ins fnl f: nvr nrr* **10/1**
0-53 **7** *1* **Dusty Wugg (IRE)**[9] 1025 5-9-4 45........(p) ABeech(3) 10 31
(ADickman) *s.i.s: hdwy over 3f out: styd on same pce fnl 2f* **12/1**
-004 **8** *shd* **Malaah (IRE)**[21] 946 8-9-0 40........(b) MHalford(7) 1 31
(JulianPoulton) *chsd ldrs 4f* **11/1**
0653 **9** *3* **Attorney**[9] 1018 6-9-7 45........(v) GDuffield 3 22
(DShaw) *mid-div: drvn along over 3f out: sn wknd* **5/1**[2]
00-6 **10** *7* **Wub Cub**[23] 936 4-9-7 40........ PHanagan 2 1
(ADickman) *sn outpcd* **33/1**

1m 18.57s (1.77) **Going Correction** +0.30s/f (Slow) **10** Ran SP% **118.8**
Speed ratings: **100,97,97,94,92 91,90,90,86,76**CSF £49.20 TOTE £19.30: £8.00, £1.10, £1.30; EX 86.00.
**Owner** W I Bloomfield **Bred** Milton Park Stud **Trained** Southwell, Notts

**FOCUS**
Average form for the grade, and the pace was fair.

**NOTEBOOK**
**Above Board**, an in-and-out performer, ran on under pressure to secure only his second win in a career which began back in 1997. He would be no good thing to follow up.
**Largs** was left with too much to do, but she came home in decent style and snatched second place on the line. The drop back to six furlongs did not help and she remains in good heart.
**On The Trail** got to the front with over a furlong to run, but it was hard work and he was unable to hold on. He should continue to run with credit now he is in form.
**Bells Boy's**, tried in cheekpieces rather than blinkers, was three lengths to the good turning in before fading. He again shaped as if five furlongs would prove best.

## 1093 BET DIRECT ON 0800 32 93 93 BANDED STKS 1m (F)
**4:10** (4:11) (H) 3-Y-O+ **£1,449** (£414; £207) **Stalls** Low

Form RPR
4432 **1** **Printsmith (IRE)**[9] 1024 7-9-8 45........ JBramhill 6 51
(JRNorton) *hld up: rdn 1/2-way: hdwy over 2f out: rdn and hung lft fr over 1f out: styd on to ld wl ins fnl f* **8/1**
1111 **2** *1* **Smart Scot**[9] 1021 5-9-9 45........(p) MSavage(5) 5 55
(BPJBaugh) *w ldr: led over 3f out: rdn and hung lft fr over 1f out: hdd wl ins fnl f* **11/10**[1]
0144 **3** *5* **Mr Whizz**[23] 939 7-9-1 45........(be) DerekNolan(7) 7 39
(APJones) *w ldr: led 6f out: hdd over 3f out: hung lft and wknd over 1f out* **16/1**
3451 **4** *3½* **Kenny The Truth (IRE)**[9] 1024 5-10-0 40........(t) NCallan 1 38
(MrsJCandlish) *chsd ldrs: rdn over 2f out: wknd over 1f out* **3/1**[2]
-011 **5** *18* **Jake Black (IRE)**[1] 1079 4-9-11 45........(v[1]) LFletcher(3) 2 —
(JJQuinn) *led 2f: rdn 1/2-way: sn wknd* **7/2**[3]

1m 47.26s (2.66) **Going Correction** +0.30s/f (Slow) **5** Ran SP% **111.8**
Speed ratings: **98,97,92,88,70**CSF £17.85 TOTE £7.00: £2.60, £1.10; EX 20.50.
**Owner** Mrs Hazel Tattersall **Bred** Joseph O'Callaghan **Trained** High Hoyland, S Yorks

**FOCUS**
Average form for the grade. The winner was returning to form after a couple of below-par efforts.

**NOTEBOOK**
**Printsmith(IRE)** was being bustled along from halfway, but she stayed on under pressure to outpoint the favourite after a good duel. She is an honest sort.
**Smart Scot** was bidding for a course five-timer in banded events. Forced to battle once coming off the bridle, he hung left, although not as markedly as he had in previous runs, and had to concede defeat towards the finish. He is probably better over seven furlongs.
**Mr Whizz** found that the first two had his measure in the last quarter-mile.
**Kenny The Truth(IRE)** had Printsmith back in second when breaking his duck last time out, but was unable to repeat the dose on 6lb worse terms.
**Jake Black(IRE)** was unable to obtain an uncontested lead in the early stages and was beaten a long way out, probably feeling the effects of the previous day's exertions. *Official explanation: trainer was unable to offer any explanation for the poor form shown*

## 1094 BET DIRECT ON SKY ACTIVE BANDED STKS 7f (F)
**4:40** (4:41) (H) 3-Y-O+ **£1,452** (£415; £207) **Stalls** Low

Form RPR
004- **1** **Tee Jay Kassidy**[243] 3540 4-9-0 35........ MHalford(7) 13 41
(JulianPoulton) *chsd ldrs: rdn over 2f out: hung lft over 1f out: r.o to ld nr fin* **16/1**
000- **2** *shd* **Baytown Flyer**[130] 5995 4-9-0 35........ PMakin(7) 12 41
(PSMcentee) *w ldrs: bmpd wl over 1f out: sn led: rdn and hdd nr fin* **8/1**
3000 **3** *nk* **Mimas Girl**[14] 998 5-9-7 35........(tp) JBramhill 9 40
(SRBowring) *w ldr: rdn and ev ch whn edgd rt wl over 1f out: r.o* **7/1**[3]
0-00 **4** *1¾* **Monkey Or Me (IRE)**[28] 875 3-8-6 30........ RFitzpatrick 11 36
(PTMidgley) *s.i.s: bhd: hdwy and hung lft over 2f out: styd on* **33/1**

0600 **5** *1* **Caterham Common**[15] [994] 5-9-4 30..............................(b) LFletcher[(3)] 2 33
(DWChapman) *mde most over 5f: no ex wl ins fnl f* **16/1**
0-00 **6** *½* **Sennen Cove**[69] [527] 5-9-7 35........................................ KDalgleish 4 32
(RBastiman) *chsd ldrs: rdn over 1f out: no ex ins fnl f* **7/1**[3]
00-5 **7** *1* **Only For Gold**[22] [944] 9-9-7 30........................................ SWhitworth 8 29
(DrPPritchard) *chsd ldrs: outpcd 1/2-way: styd on ins fnl f* **5/1**[2]
0-06 **8** *2½* **Miss Millietant**[14] [998] 3-8-6 30........................................ GDuffield 1 23
(LMontagueHall) *chsd ldrs: rdn 1/2-way: wknd over 1f out* **11/1**
00/6 **9** *5* **Galaxy Fallon**[7] [1031] 6-9-4 30........................................ LEnstone[(3)] 5 11
(MDods) *outpcd* **20/1**
06-5 **10** *1½* **Sawah**[80] [422] 4-9-7 30........................................ NCallan 6 7
(DShaw) *sn outpcd* **9/2**[1]
440- **11** *½* **Miss Ocean Monarch**[174] [5304] 4-9-7 30........................................ ACulhane 3 6
(DWChapman) *hld up: nvr nr to chal* **7/1**[3]
0020 **12** *8* **Pooka's Daughter (IRE)**[14] [998] 4-9-7 30..................(p) PFitzsimons 10 —
(JMBradley) *chsd ldrs over 4f* **9/1**

1m 34.16s (3.36) **Going Correction** +0.30s/f (Slow)
**WFA** 3 from 4yo+ 15lb **12** Ran SP% **121.3**
Speed ratings: **92,91,91,89,88 87,86,83,78,76 75,66**CSF £141.68 TOTE £38.70: £16.00, £3.80, £2.80; EX 389.00 Place 6 £903.02, Place 5 £184.03.
**Owner** Meddler Bloodstock **Bred** Miss Jeanne M Brooks **Trained** Kentford, Suffolk

**FOCUS**
A dreadful race run at a slow pace.

**NOTEBOOK**
**Tee Jay Kassidy**, without any headgear for this first run since July, came between horses to lead near the line. He was under pressure some way out and might appreciate a step up in trip.
**Baytown Flyer** has returned to her first trainer after a spell with John Balding. Breaking better, she was always prominent but, having got to the front, was just touched off. This run proved her effectiveness on Fibresand.
**Mimas Girl** had every chance, but it will be a bad race that she wins.
**Monkey Or Me(IRE)** still looked green and hung when coming to deliver his challenge. This was a better run, however.
**Caterham Common** held a narrow lead until headed going to the final furlong.
**Sawah** was the subject of quite a gamble, but one that never looked like paying off. He got away from the stalls a bit better than he had in previous races but was soon struggling to go the pace. As he must have shown something at home it might be prudent to keep an eye out for him. *Official explanation: jockey said gelding did not act on the surface*
CR

## [1081]LINGFIELD (L-H)
### Wednesday, March 24

**OFFICIAL GOING: Standard**
Wind: mod hlf against first six race: almost nil last two Weather: sunny & heavy showers

## 1095 LENHAM WINNERS CUP H'CAP (DIV I) 1m (P)
**1:25** (1:26) (F ) (0-55,55) 3-Y-0+ **£2,940** (£840; £420) **Stalls** High

Form RPR
4123 **1** **Lucid Dreams (IRE)**[16] [988] 5-9-10 **55**..............................(p) JFanning 9 61+
(MWigham) *trckd ldrs: nt clr run over 2f out to wl over 1f out: rdn and r.o to ld last 100y: kpt on* **3/1**[2]
-001 **2** *nk* **Beltane**[30] [860] 6-9-1 **46** oh1........................................ SRighton 4 51
(WDeBest-Turner) *hld up in last pair: pushed along over 3f out: prog on outer 2f out: drvn to ld ins fnl f: sn hdd: kpt on* **14/1**
0232 **3** *1¾* **Lucayan Monarch**[24] [932] 6-9-10 **55**..............................(p) JPMurtagh 10 56
(PSMcentee) *pressed ldrs: rdn and effrt to ld wl over 1f out: hdd and nt qckn ins fnl f* **9/4**[1]
3055 **4** *1¾* **Pas De Surprise**[24] [926] 6-9-8 **53**........................................ SWKelly 5 50
(PDEvans) *trckd ldrs: rdn over 2f out: cl up jst over 1f out: wknd ins fnl f* **7/1**[3]
0-56 **5** *1¾* **Wodhill Be**[16] [982] 4-9-7 **52**........................................ DHolland 6 45
(DMorris) *hld up in last: rdn over 2f out: c wd in st: kpt on one pce over 1f out: no ch* **8/1**
0-34 **6** *3* **First Of May**[39] [766] 3-8-5 **53**........................................ MHenry 2 39
(MAJarvis) *led to wl over 1f out: sn wknd* **3/1**[2]
-003 **7** *1* **Lady Liesel**[30] [860] 4-8-10 **46** oh6........................................ JFMcDonald[(5)] 3 30
(JJBridger) *pressed ldr to 2f out: n.m.r sn after: wknd* **33/1**

1m 39.67s (0.16) **Going Correction** -0.075s/f (Stan)
**WFA** 3 from 4yo+ 17lb **7** Ran SP% **114.0**
Speed ratings: **96,95,93,92,90 87,86**CSF £41.73 CT £109.91 TOTE £4.20: £2.10, £3.40; EX 49.80.
**Owner** Reds Bar Four Partnership II **Bred** Dr Dean Harron **Trained** Newmarket, Suffolk
■ Stewards Enquiry : J P Murtagh caution: careless riding

**FOCUS**
A moderate handicap, but it did at least produce a close finish, although it is doubtful the winner needed to improve to score.

**NOTEBOOK**
**Lucid Dreams(IRE)**, 3lb higher than when winning over course and distance last month, has performed creditably since and squeezed through with a strong run to edge ahead in the final half a furlong. He held on well and should not be punished by the Handicapper too much for this.
**Beltane** improved on his win in a banded event for amateurs and went down fighting.
**Lucayan Monarch** ran another fair race without being good enough.
**Pas De Surprise** had every chance and ran respectably.
**Wodhill Be** was having only her fourth-ever start and shaped as though there will be better to come. She was forced to run wide in the straight.
**First Of May** dropped out disappointingly having led early.

## 1096 E.E.S. LIGHTNING MEDIAN AUCTION MAIDEN STKS 7f (P)
**1:55** (1:56) (F ) 3-4-Y-0 **£2,975** (£850; £425) **Stalls** Low

Form RPR
- **1** **Ifteradh** 3-8-9 ow1........................................ DHolland 10 77
(BHanbury) *w'like: bit bkwd: cmpt: t.k.h: pressed ldr after 1f: chal fr 2f out: pushed into ld ins fnl f: comf* **14/1**
042- **2** *¾* **Instructor**[161] [5572] 3-8-8 78........................................ RHughes 9 74
(RHannon) *lw: led: shkn up wl over 1f out: hdd ins fnl f: readily hld by wnr after* **4/6**[1]
3- **3** *3* **Warden Complex**[205] [4627] 3-8-8 ........................................ DaneO'Neill 4 66
(JRFanshawe) *bit bkwd: t.k.h early: restrained in midfield: effrt whn nt clr run wl over 1f out: pushed along and r.o to take 3rd last 5* **7/2**[2]
4 **4** *1* **Cheeky Chi (IRE)**[5] [1052] 3-8-0 ........................................ LisaJones[(3)] 8 58
(PSMcentee) *rrd s: sn chsd ldrs: shkn up and outpcd fr 2f out: one pce after* **20/1**
620- **5** *½* **Deign To Dance (IRE)**[172] [5362] 3-8-3 75........................................ RLMoore 5 57
(JGPortman) *restrained in midfield: effrt over 2f out: sn outpcd: shkn up and kpt on same pce after* **10/1**[3]
55 **6** *5* **Joans Jewel**[20] [963] 3-8-3 ........................................ AMcCarthy 3 43
(GGMargarson) *t.k.h: cl up: nt clr run wl over 1f out: sn outpcd: nudged along and lost further grnd fnl f* **25/1**
006 **7** *1¼* **Shalati Princess**[22] [948] 3-8-3 45........................................ RSmith 1 40
(JCFox) *s.v.s: racd in last: no ch fnl 2f: modest late prog* **100/1**
400- **8** *¾* **Bahama Reef (IRE)**[184] [5121] 3-8-8 67........................................ CCatlin 7 43
(BGubby) *t.k.h: restrained bhd ldrs: shkn up over 2f out: sn wknd* **33/1**
0- **9** *nk* **Bunyah (IRE)**[138] [5938] 3-8-3 ........................................ WSupple 2 37
(EALDunlop) *t.k.h: hld up in rr: pushed along and outpcd over 2f out: wknd over 1f out* **16/1**
00- **10** *2½* **Habitual (IRE)**[168] [5449] 3-8-8 ........................................ SSanders 6 35
(SirMarkPrescott) *bit bkwd: racd wd: a towards rr: rdn 3f out: wknd over 1f out* **50/1**

1m 25.75s (-0.25) **Going Correction** -0.075s/f (Stan) **10** Ran SP% **118.4**
Speed ratings: **98,97,93,92,92 86,84,84,83,80**CSF £23.57 TOTE £18.00: £2.90, £1.10, £1.40; EX 31.40.
**Owner** Hamdan Al Maktoum **Bred** Shadwell Estate Company Limited **Trained** Newmarket, Suffolk
■ Stewards Enquiry : Lisa Jones caution: careless riding

**FOCUS**
A fair maiden won by newcomer Ifteradh, who was kept off course with a fracture last season. However, some ordinary animals were not beaten that far, which suggests some caution is appropriate.

**NOTEBOOK**
**Ifteradh**, kept off the track as a two-year-old by a fracture, was with the hot favourite Instructor throughout and quickened up the better of the pair to win with something to spare. How the Handicapper will react to this cosy beating of a 78-rated performer will probably leave him struggling in handicaps, but he is undoubtedly a nice prospect.
**Instructor** boasted some very useful form as a juvenile, namely his second to UAE 2000 Guineas runner up Jack Sullivan over course and distance, and was fully expected by many to deliver. He did nothing wrong, but simply ran into a superior rival. He has a maiden in him, although handicaps are ultimately where his future will lay.
**Warden Complex** did not receive the clearest passage through and did nothing wrong in third. He shaped with promise on his sole outing as a juvenile as well and it will be disappointing if he can not get his head in front in the near future.
**Cheeky Chi(IRE)** was a cheap buy, but again shaped with promise as she had finished fourth on his debut at the course five days earlier.
**Bunyah(IRE)** is the type to do better once handicapped.
**Habitual(IRE)** will be best served by middle-distances once sent handicapping.

## 1097 L & M BODY REPAIRS ENGLISH ROSE CLASSIFIED STKS 1m 2f (P)
**2:25** (2:26) (F ) 4-Y-0+ **£2,933** (£838; £419) **Stalls** Low

Form RPR
4025 **1** **Blazing The Trail (IRE)**[28] [882] 4-9-0 59........................................ MHills 7 68
(JWHills) *lw: hld up towards rr: prog over 2f out: rdn and styd on wl to ld last 100y* **11/2**[3]
0213 **2** *½* **Fortune Point (IRE)**[24] [931] 6-9-0 60........................................ DHolland 12 67
(AWCarroll) *led: set fast pce tl stdd after 3f: kicked on again over 2f out: drvn over 1f out: hdd last 100y: kpt on* **4/1**[1]
0614 **3** *¾* **Raheel (IRE)**[20] [966] 4-9-0 57..............................(t) RLMoore 3 66
(PMitchell) *dwlt and rdn in last early: gd prog on wd outside 3f out: pressed ldr over 2f out: nt qckn and lost 2nd ins fnl f* **11/2**[3]
0310 **4** *hd* **Welsh Wind (IRE)**[20] [962] 8-9-0 60..............................(tp) JFanning 11 65
(MWigham) *t.k.h early: cl up: n.m.r on inner 2f out: shkn up and nt qckn over 1f out: styd on fnl f* **12/1**
0-02 **5** *hd* **Lara Falana**[5] [1053] 6-8-8 60........................................ LisaJones[(3)] 8 62
(MissBSanders) *s.i.s: hld up in rr: prog over 2f out: rdn to chse ldrs on outer fnl f: kpt on* **9/2**[2]
3566 **6** *nk* **Figura**[5] [1053] 6-8-11 58........................................ JQuinn 13 61
(RIngram) *hld up wl in rr: gd prog over 3f out to chse ldrs over 2f out: sn rdn: styd on same pce fr over 1f out* **10/1**
0221 **7** *2* **Meelup (IRE)**[16] [988] 4-9-0 59..............................(p) VSlattery 6 61
(JaneSouthcombe) *b: pressed ldr to 7f out: styd cl up: drvn over 2f out: wknd fnl f* **16/1**
310- **8** *1¼* **Decelerate**[99] [6200] 4-9-0 55........................................ RHughes 1 59
(ACharlton) *bit bkwd: hld up in midfield: lost pl on inner 2f out: pushed along and one pce after* **33/1**
5400 **9** *1¼* **Fen Gypsy**[5] [1055] 6-9-0 59..............................(b) RWinston 10 56
(PDEvans) *wl in rr whn rdn bnd after 1f: prog 6f out: chsd ldr 3f out to over 2f out: wknd over 1f out* **20/1**
0-45 **10** *½* **Must Be Magic**[35] [820] 7-9-0 60..............................(v) WSupple 14 55
(HJCollingridge) *b: b.hind: hld up in midfield: drvn and nt qckn 2f out: n.d fr over 1f out* **8/1**
024- **11** *1¼* **Half Inch**[174] [5328] 4-8-11 59........................................ SDrowne 4 50
(BICase) *settled in rr: rdn and no prog over 2f out: no ch fr over 1f out* **50/1**
000- **12** *6* **Arjay**[130] [5712] 6-9-0 59........................................ CCatlin 5 42
(AndrewTurnell) *hld up in midfield: rdn over 3f out: wknd over 2f out* **50/1**
00-0 **13** *17* **Linby Lad (IRE)**[20] [964] 4-9-0 60..............................(b[1]) DeanMcKeown 2 12
(JAGlover) *t.k.h: chsd ldr 7f out to 3f out: wknd rapidly: t.o* **33/1**

2m 5.82s (-1.57) **Going Correction** -0.075s/f (Stan) **13** Ran SP% **117.3**
Speed ratings: **103,102,102,101,101 101,99,98,97,97 96,91,78**CSF £25.81 TOTE £7.30: £2.90, £1.70, £2.00; EX 34.80.
**Owner** Sir John Robb **Bred** Irish National Stud **Trained** Upper Lambourn, Berks

**FOCUS**
They went a good gallop for this Classified event and it was the John Hills trained Blazing The Trail who came home the best. The field finished well bunched despite the fast pace.

**NOTEBOOK**
**Blazing The Trail(IRE)** was evidently suited by the good gallop set and stayed on well from the rear to edge ahead in the final half furlong. On this evidence he should be capable of getting an extra couple of furlongs.
**Fortune Point(IRE)** did well to finish where he did as he had set a strong pace. He deserves credit for his effort.
**Raheel(IRE)**, a disappointment last time when running too freely in the early part of the race, always looked to be struggling to go the pace, but came with a challenge on the turn into the straight and was not disgraced.
**Welsh Wind(IRE)** found himself a bit short of room turning in and lacked the pace to win.
**Lara Falana** stayed on without ever looking likely to win. *Official explanation: jockey said mare had stumbled on leaving the stalls.*
**Figura** ran a similar race to Lara Falana, staying on all too late.

## 1098 CHURCHILL INSURANCE H'CAP 7f (P)
**3:00** (3:01) (F ) (0-55,61) 3-Y-0+ **£3,010** (£860; £430) **Stalls** Low

Form RPR
-401 **1** **Stoic Leader (IRE)**[7] [1035] 4-9-12 **61** 6ex........................................ LFletcher[(3)] 8 74
(RFFisher) *chsd ldrs: pushed along 3f out: prog over 1f out: rdn to ld 150y out: hung lft and bmpd runner-up: sn clr* **12/1**

0-42 **2** 2 ½ **Ranny**[20] [960] 4-9-4 **50** ... JQuinn 2 56
(DrJDScargill) *prom: effrt 2f out: rdn to ld jst over 1f out: hdd and bmpd 150y out: no chancd w wnr after* **6/1**[2]

5003 **3** ½ **Frankskips**[24] [926] 5-9-9 **55** ... TQuinn 7 60
(MissBSanders) *hld up in rr: gng wl but stl in last trio wl over 1f out: weaved through fnl f: fin wl* **8/1**[3]

-002 **4** 1 **Lily Of The Guild (IRE)**[25] [918] 5-9-8 **54** ... NCallan 13 56
(WSKittow) *settled in rr: prog fr over 2f out: rdn and styd on fr over 1f out: nvr able to chal* **6/1**[2]

0450 **5** 1 **Balerno**[10] [1020] 5-9-4 **50** ... GCarter 6 49
(RIngram) *trckd ldrs on inner: n.m.r 2f out: swtchd rt and effrt over 1f out: styd on same pce fnl f* **12/1**

0104 **6** 1 **Gun Salute**[5] [1051] 4-9-7 **53** ... (p) RLMoore 12 50
(GLMoore) *lw: hld up towards rr: prog to trck ldrs 2f out: nt clr run and swtchd rt over 1f out: one pce after* **4/1**[1]

0640 **7** 1 ¾ **Zinging**[24] [933] 5-9-2 **48** ... SDrowne 3 40
(JJBridger) *prom: cl up 2f out: rdn over 1f out: wknd ins fnl f* **10/1**

0520 **8** shd **Master Rattle**[22] [946] 5-9-1 **47** ... (b[1]) VSlattery 4 39
(JaneSouthcombe) *pressed ldr: led over 2f out to jst over 1f out: wknd* **14/1**

-001 **9** ½ **Loch Laird**[10] [1020] 9-9-7 **53** 6ex ... GBaker 15 43
(MMadgwick) *settled in last pair: effrt over 2f out: no imp ldrs over 1f out* **20/1**

030- **10** ½ **Jakeal (IRE)**[17] [5202] 5-9-8 **54** ... DeanMcKeown 1 43
(RMWhitaker) *led to over 2f out: wknd over 1f out* **16/1**

00-5 **11** 1 **Dark Shah (IRE)**[29] [873] 4-9-9 **55** ... (p) MartinDwyer 10 41
(DMSimcock) *settled wl in rr: in last trio and rdn over 2f out: no prog* **33/1**

4100 **12** 1 ¾ **Badou**[22] [946] 4-9-1 **47** ... DHolland 14 28
(LMontagueHall) *w ldrs to 2f out: sn wknd* **14/1**

0002 **13** shd **Mutarafaa (USA)**[6] [1043] 5-9-5 **51** ... (v) WSupple 16 32
(DShaw) *racd wd early in midfield: shuffled along and lost pl 2f out: sn bhd* **20/1**

5415 **14** 4 **Foolish Thought (IRE)**[16] [993] 4-9-1 **52** ... (p) TEaves(5) 11 22
(IAWood) *chsd ldrs: rdn fr over 4f out: struggling over 2f out: sn wknd* **20/1**

000- **15** 14 **Brilliant Waters**[127] [6019] 4-9-6 **52** ... DaneO'Neill 9 —
(DWPArbuthnot) *settled in last pair: effrt over 2f out: sn wknd: t.o* **33/1**

1m 24.56s (-1.44) **Going Correction** -0.075s/f (Stan) **15** Ran SP% **123.5**
Speed ratings: **105,102,101,100,99 98,96,96,95,94 93,91,91,87,71**CSF £77.85 CT £625.31 TOTE £10.40: £3.60, £2.50, £2.80; EX 64.50.
**Owner** Great Head House Estates Limited **Bred** P J Higgins **Trained** Ulverston, Cumbria

**FOCUS**
Impressive winner Stoic Leader took advantage of his lower All-Weather mark.

**NOTEBOOK**
**Stoic Leader(IRE)**, who came right back to form at Wolverhampton last week, ran away with it in the final furlong despite hanging and bumping the runner up. This was a good effort under top-weight and he is clearly in great form at present.
**Ranny**, although done no favours by getting bumped, had every chance and was just unlucky to run into an in-form horse.
**Frankskips** should have finished second and only really got a clean run at things when the race was all over, finishing strongly.
**Lily Of The Guild(IRE)** kept on from the rear without ever looking likely to win.
**Balerno** may have been unlucky not to finish closer.
**Gun Salute** deserves another chance as he could not pick up again having been switched out wide.
**Brilliant Waters** *Official explanation: trainer said gelding had bled from the nose.*

## 1099 SCOTS CHALLENGE H'CAP 5f (P)

**3:35** (3:36) (D ) (0-85,85) 3-Y-O **£5,053** (£1,555; £777; £388) **Stalls** High

Form RPR

01-1 **1** **Peruvian Style (IRE)**[16] [986] 3-9-0 **78** ... DHolland 8 88
(NPLittmoden) *prom: chsd ldr 1/2-way: sustained chal fnl f: led last stride* **3/1**[2]

51-4 **2** shd **Green Manalishi**[16] [986] 3-8-12 **76** ... TQuinn 9 85
(DWPArbuthnot) *lw: led: rdn 2f out: kpt on wl fnl f: hdd last stride* **7/2**[3]

504- **3** ¾ **Only If I Laugh**[126] [6029] 3-8-1 **70** ... JFMcDonald(5) 5 76
(BJMeehan) *chsd ldrs: rdn and effrt over 2f out: styd on fnl f: jst unable to chal* **16/1**

00-2 **4** nk **Trick Cyclist**[16] [986] 3-8-10 **81** ... TBlock(7) 3 86
(AMBalding) *trckd ldrs: shkn up over 1f out: styd on fnl f: nvr able to mount a serious chal* **11/2**

1- **5** 2 ½ **Treasure Cay**[105] [6159] 3-8-13 **77** ... PaulEddery 4 72
(PWD'Arcy) *racd towards rr: rdn 1/2-way: no imp ldrs over 1f out* **5/2**[1]

320- **6** ¾ **La Vie Est Belle**[160] [5590] 3-8-12 **76** ... SDrowne 1 68
(BRMillman) *chsd ldr to 1/2-way: fdd over 1f out* **25/1**

326- **7** 3 ½ **Trotters Bottom**[105] [6159] 3-9-1 **82** ... J-PGuillambert(3) 6 60
(AndrewReid) *b: b.hind: s.i.s: a towards rr: drvn and effrt on outer 2f out: wknd over 1f out* **20/1**

010- **8** 1 ¾ **Dellagio (IRE)**[281] [2442] 3-9-4 **85** ... TPQueally(3) 2 56
(CADwyer) *s.i.s: a in rr: rdn 1/2-way: sn struggling* **33/1**

-116 **9** 3 ½ **Cut And Dried**[16] [986] 3-8-4 **68** ... MartinDwyer 10 25
(DMSimcock) *lft 12l s: nvr able to rcvr and allowed to complete in own time* **10/1**

58.83 secs (-0.95) **Going Correction** -0.075s/f (Stan) **9** Ran SP% **117.7**
Speed ratings: **104,103,102,102,98 96,91,88,82**CSF £13.93 CT £144.24 TOTE £2.90: £1.50, £1.40, £4.70; EX 13.70.
**Owner** M C S D Racing Ltd **Bred** Forenaghts Stud **Trained** Newmarket, Suffolk

**FOCUS**
An interesting sprint handicap, with the first two, who both had outside draws to overcome, both progressive.

**NOTEBOOK**
**Peruvian Style(IRE)** tracked Green Manalishi for most of the way before being locked in battle with him in a duel to the line that he got the better of in the dying strides. He is progressing nicely and will be seen to even better effect over six furlongs.
**Green Manalishi** is very fast and just about lasts out this trip. He lost nothing in defeat and connections are eyeing a handicap at Chester in May. That track will suit his style of running, but they will be hoping for a kinder draw.
**Only If I Laugh** was having his first outing of the season and ran a promising race.
**Trick Cyclist** shapes as though the step up to six furlongs will see him in a better light.
**Treasure Cay** was disappointing, failing to pick up when asked to go in pursuit of the principals. He is worth another chance as he had looked useful when winning on his debut and it may well be that things happened too quickly for him over this trip. *Official explanation: trainer said colt was later found to be coughing.*
**La Vie Est Belle** is entitled to improve on this first outing for a while.
**Cut And Dried** *Official explanation: jockey said gelding planted in the stalls.*

## 1100 PERFECT PANES (A BETTER BET FOR A WARMER HOME) H'CAP 1m 4f (P)

**4:10** (4:11) (D ) (0-85,79) 3-Y-O **£3,968** (£1,221; £610; £305) **Stalls** Low

Form RPR

0-1 **1** **Golden Quest**[19] [969] 3-9-7 **79** ... JFanning 2 82+
(MJohnston) *lw: chsd ldng pair: rdn and rn in snatches fr 5f out: wnt 2nd 2f out: drvn to ld last 150y: styd on strly* **9/4**[2]

040 **2** 1 ¼ **Champagne Shadow (IRE)**[25] [916] 3-8-7 **65** ... (b) RLMoore 5 66
(GLMoore) *racd wd: led ldng pair: rdn... *

0-00 **3** nk **Darn Good**[29] [871] 3-7-7 **56** oh4 ... (v[1]) JFMcDonald(5) 4 57
(RHannon) *hld up in 5th: rdn over 4f out: no prog u.p tl styd on fnl f: tk 3rd nr fin* **33/1**

11 **4** nk **Barathea Dreams (IRE)**[10] [1017] 3-8-5 **63** 6ex ... MartinDwyer 1 63
(JSMoore) *lw: led: gng best over 2f out: rdn over 1f out: wknd and hdd last 150y: lost 2 more pls nr fin* **5/4**[1]

-414 **5** 3 ½ **Another Con (IRE)**[16] [985] 3-8-8 **66** ... RHavlin 3 60
(MrsPNDutfield) *chsd ldr: rdn over 3f out: lost 2nd 2f out: wknd fnl f* **9/2**[3]

5-1 **6** nk **Rye (IRE)**[22] [948] 3-8-12 **70** ... CCatlin 6 64
(JAOsborne) *lw: chsd ldrs: rdn and dropped to last 5f out: lost tch over 3f out: one pce after* **12/1**

2m 33.53s (-0.45) **Going Correction** -0.075s/f (Stan) **6** Ran SP% **111.7**
Speed ratings: **98,97,96,96,94 94**CSF £26.91 TOTE £3.00: £1.40, £6.20; EX 31.40.
**Owner** Syndicate 2002 **Bred** Fittocks Stud **Trained** Middleham Moor, N Yorks

**FOCUS**
A good performance by the progressive winner and he will improve even more the further he goes back on turf.

**NOTEBOOK**
**Golden Quest** looks a typical progressive Mark Johnston trained three-year-old and defied a mark of 79 in impressive fashion. He is the type to do well back on turf and there should be more to come.
**Champagne Shadow(IRE)** seemed well served by this step up in trip.
**Darn Good** seemed to improve for the visor and has a race in him if the headgear has the same effect in future.
**Barathea Dreams(IRE)** had been impressive in two previous wins, but had stamina to prove at the trip and appeared to not get home.

## 1101 BET DIRECT CHAMPS LEAGUE CASHBACKS (S) STKS 1m 4f (P)

**4:45** (4:46) (G ) 4-Y-O+ **£2,541** (£726; £181; £181) **Stalls** Low

Form RPR

-642 **1** **Blue Savanna**[9] [997] 4-9-2 47 ... (p) RLMoore 10 40
(JGPortman) *led at sedate pce: hdd and outpcd 4f out: styd chsng clr ldr : clsd over 1f out: drvn ahd last 75y* **10/1**

3220 **2** 1 ¼ **Private Seal**[15] [995] 9-9-4 40 ... (t) DHolland 2 38
(JulianPoulton) *settled in last pair: outpcd 4f out: effrt 2f out: drvn and styd on fnl f to take 2nd nr fin* **5/1**[3]

-006 **3** nk **Birth Of The Blues**[33] [838] 8-8-11 30 ... DonnaBashton(7) 8 38
(ACharlton) *chsd ldng trio: outpcd 4f out: effrt 2f out: styd on steadily fnl f* **40/1**

-006 **3** dht **Top Tenor (IRE)**[16] [984] 4-9-2 65 ... (b) SWhitworth 7 38
(BRJohnson) *lw: tk ken hold: hld up in midfield: prog to ld 4f out and qcknd 5l clr: drvn over 1f out: wknd and hdd last 75y* **3/1**[2]

306/ **5** 2 **Malarkey**[483] [5804] 7-9-4 ... (p) DaneO'Neill 3 35
(ACrook) *dwlt: settled in rr: outpcd 4f out: no prog u.p 2f out: one pce after* **8/1**

05/0 **6** 2 ½ **Salford Flyer**[5] [1054] 8-9-4 70 ... (b[1]) VSlattery 4 31
(JaneSouthcombe) *b: t.k.h: hld up towards rr: outpcd 4f out: no prog u.p over 2f out: one pce after* **7/1**

00-0 **7** nk **Mikasa (IRE)**[57] [613] 4-8-13 45 ... LFletcher(3) 5 31
(RFFisher) *trckd ldng pair: outpcd 4f out: no prog over 2f out: wknd fnl f* **50/1**

000 **8** 1 ¼ **Alimiste (IRE)**[29] [871] 4-8-11 ... NCallan 9 24
(IAWood) *trckd ldr to jst over 4f out: sn outpcd: wknd over 1f out* **25/1**

0/50 **9** 1 ½ **Neptune**[30] [857] 8-9-4 35 ... PDobbs 6 27
(JCFox) *hld up in last pair: outpcd 4f out: struggling and no prog over 2f out* **25/1**

23/3 **10** 21 **Captain Crusoe**[8] [1031] 6-9-4 ... RWinston 1 —
(PHowling) *lw: b: hld up in midfield: outpcd 4f out: effrt over 2f out: lost action bdly over 1f out and virtually p.u* **11/4**[1]

2m 39.67s (5.69) **Going Correction** -0.075s/f (Stan)
**WFA** 4 from 6yo+ 2lb **10** Ran SP% **113.1**
Speed ratings: **78,77,76,76,75 73,73,72,71,57** CT £7.80 TOTE £1.60: £1.60, £; EX55.51 Trifecta £Place 3: Top Tenor 0.70, Birth of the Blues 4.60 1.There was no bid for the winner. Malarkey was claimed by Ms Cheryl Legg for £6,000. Top Tenor was claimed by Mr A Norman for £6,000.
**Owner** A S B Portman **Bred** Peter Nelson **Trained** Compton, Berks
■ Stewards Enquiry : R L Moore caution: used whip with excessive frequency

**FOCUS**
A poor race, run at a slow pace. The form is unlikely to work out.

**NOTEBOOK**
**Blue Savanna** made a lot of the early running until getting outpaced by Top Tenor, who kicked clear, but he is a trier and he kept plugging away. His effort was rewarded as he came back through to take it late on and win going away.
**Private Seal** stayed on all too late.
**Top Tenor(IRE)** went for home a long way out, but the effort told and he tied up late on.
**Birth Of The Blues** ran well at a big price given he would have been far better off in a handicap. He was probably flattered to get so close as a result of the slow gallop though.
**Captain Crusoe** *Official explanation: vet said gelding was lame on the left fore.*

## 1102 LENHAM WINNERS CUP H'CAP (DIV II) 1m (P)

**5:20** (5:21) (F ) (0-55,55) 3-Y-O+ **£2,933** (£838; £419) **Stalls** High

Form RPR

-212 **1** **Wanna Shout**[30] [855] 6-9-2 50 ... LisaJones(3) 4 66+
(RDickin) *prom: trckd ldr 5f out: effrt to chal 2f out: led last 150y : pushed out* **11/2**[3]

03/0 **2** 1 **Prime Offer**[8] [1032] 8-9-10 55 ... NCallan 9 69
(JJay) *led: rdn and pressed 2f out: hdd and unable qck last 150y* **20/1**

0-01 **3** 4 **Marnie**[10] [1019] 7-9-8 53 6ex ... JQuinn 1 58
(JAkehurst) *lw: hld up towards rr: effrt over 2f out: rdn and nt qckn wl over 1f out: kpt on to take 3rd ins fnl f: n.d* **13/2**

4040 **4** nk **Coppington Flyer (IRE)**[10] [1019] 4-9-2 47 ... RLMoore 5 51
(BWDuke) *hld up towards rr: effrt over 2f out: sn rdn and nt qckn: one pce fr wl over 1f out* **8/1**

3500 **5** 2 **Larad (IRE)**[10] [1019] 3-8-2 50 ... (b) DKinsella 3 49
(JSMoore) *chsd ldr to 5f out: rdn over 2f out: fdd over 1f out* **33/1**

1203 **6** ¾ **Indian Blaze**[10] [1019] 10-9-4 52 ... TPQueally(3) 7 50
(AndrewReid) *b: b.hind: trckd ldrs: drvn and cl up over 2f out: fdd over 1f out* **10/3**[2]

5610 **7** 1/2 **Haithem (IRE)**[1] 1085 7-9-1 46 oh1 ....................(t) DHolland 6 43
(DShaw) *hanging rt: hld up in rr: wnt wd 3f out and dropped to last: n.d after: modest late prog* **10/1**

0-12 **8** 1 3/4 **Thunderclap**[19] 967 5-9-10 55 .................... RWinston 8 48
(JJQuinn) *lw: cl up: chsd ldng pair over 3f out: drvn over 2f out: wknd over 1f out* **2/1**[1]

050- **9** 1/2 **Artzola (IRE)**[149] 5799 4-9-7 52 .................... PaulEddery 2 43
(CAHorgan) *b: b.hind: s.i.s: a in rr: rdn and brief effrt on outer over 1f out: no prog* **50/1**

**10** 2 1/2 **Newcorr (IRE)**[263] 2769 5-8-10 46 oh6 .................... JFMcDonald(5) 10 32
(JJBridger) *bit bkwd: a towards rr: no prog over 2f out: wknd over 1f out* **50/1**

1m 37.99s (-1.52) **Going Correction** -0.075s/f (Stan)
**WFA** 3 from 4yo+ 17lb **10** Ran SP% **117.0**
Speed ratings: **104,103,99,98,96 95,95,93,93,90**CSF £109.39 CT £744.91 TOTE £5.70: £1.90, £4.30, £1.80; EX 221.10 Place 6 £90.33, Place 5 £29.76.
**Owner** E R C Beech & B Wilkinson **Bred** C C Bromley And Son **Trained** Atherstone on Stour, Warwicks

**FOCUS**
A much better contest than the first division. The first two are well treated on old form.

**NOTEBOOK**
**Wanna Shout** has been running well in Banded events and handled this slight rise in grade well. She is in good form and can win again if finding a suitable opportunity.
**Prime Offer** ran well on this second start back after an absence and is weighted to soon be back to winning ways. He is due to be dropped 3lb.
**Marnie** stayed on from the rear to claim a moderate third.
**Coppington Flyer(IRE)** was well supported, but never looked like justifying it.
**Haithem(IRE)** *Official explanation: jockey said gelding had hung badly right down the back straight.*
**Thunderclap** had every chance and was disappointing.
T/Plt: £105.50 to a £1 stake. Pool: £40,662.30. 281.30 winning tickets. T/Qpdt: £15.00 to a £1 stake. Pool: £3,075.80. 151.20 winning tickets. JN

# DONCASTER (L-H)
## Thursday, March 25

**OFFICIAL GOING: Good**

## 1103 RACING SCHOOLS APPRENTICE H'CAP 1m 4f
1:50 (1:52) (E) (0-80,80) 4-Y-O+ **£3,571** (£1,099; £549; £274) **Stalls Low**

Form RPR

055- **1** **Middlethorpe**[61] 5920 7-8-7 62 ....................(b) PMulrennan(3) 6 73
(MWEasterby) *midfield: hdwy 4f out: led gng wl over 2 out: styd on u.p fnl f: all out* **4/1**[1]

-131 **2** hd **Robbie Can Can**[13] 867 5-8-10 62 .................... LisaJones 14 73
(AWCarroll) *dwlt: in tch whn hmpd and lost pl after 1f: hdwy over 3 out: styd on wl u.p fnl f: nt rch wnr* **12/1**

200- **3** 1 **Indian Solitaire (IRE)**[44] 4713 5-9-2 71 ....................(v[1]) THamilton(3) 7 80
(RAFahey) *midfield: effrt whn nt clr run over 3f out: chsd wnr over 1 out: styd on u.p: no ex ins last* **14/1**

002- **4** 1 **Blackthorn**[159] 5631 5-8-7 59 .................... ABeech 17 67
(MrsJRRamsden) *midfield: hdwy over 3f out: chsd ldrs fr over 1 out: kpt on ins last: nvr able to chal* **25/1**

2U-0 **5** 6 **Crown Agent (IRE)**[36] 818 4-9-7 75 .................... LPKeniry 21 74
(AMBalding) *hld up: hdwy 4f out: ch over 2 out: no further prog* **20/1**

000/ **6** 3 1/2 **Benbyas**[7] 1214 7-8-6 65 .................... DTudhope(7) 5 58
(DCarroll) *cl up: led after 3f tl hdd wl over 2 out: fdd* **5/1**[2]

0000 **7** 1/2 **Queen Excalibur**[23] 949 5-7-9 50 oh5 .................... JFMcDonald(3) 4 43
(CRoberts) *dwlt: rr div: styd on fnl 3f: n.d* **100/1**

000- **8** 1 3/4 **Rajam**[8] 5035 6-9-3 74 .................... LTreadwell(5) 8 64
(DNicholls) *chsd ldrs: rdn 4f out: fdd fnl 3f* **25/1**

0-00 **9** hd **Danakil**[29] 887 9-9-3 76 .................... JCoffill-Brown(7) 3 66
(SDow) *in tch: hdwy 4f out: rdn to ld wl over 2 out: sn hdd: wknd over 1 out* **40/1**

000- **10** 7 **Archie Babe (IRE)**[54] 5910 8-8-10 62 .................... SHitchcott 18 41
(JJQuinn) *sn rr divison: rdn over 4f out: no real hdwy* **9/1**

500- **11** 2 1/2 **Invitation**[19] 3699 6-9-10 76 .................... BReilly 12 52
(ACharlton) *dwlt: rr div: sme late hdwy: n.d* **25/1**

50/0 **12** 2 **Perestroika (IRE)**[28] 899 6-8-10 65 .................... TEaves(3) 10 38
(BEllison) *nvr bttr than mid-div* **66/1**

5221 **13** 3/4 **Glory Quest (USA)**[7] 1045 7-8-12 69 5ex ....................(v) PGallagher(5) 22 40
(MissGayKelleway) *sn disputing ld: rdn 4f out: sn wknd* **12/1**

000- **14** 14 **Iloveturtle (IRE)**[18] 6247 4-7-12 57 .................... RoryMoore(5) 1 7
(MCChapman) *chsd ldrs tl wknd over 3f out* **33/1**

050- **15** 1 **Champion Lion (IRE)**[138] 5952 5-9-4 77 .................... TO'Brien(7) 11 26
(MRChannon) *midfield whn hmpd and lost pl after 1f: n.d* **20/1**

564- **16** 2 **Kid'Z'Play (IRE)**[245] 3528 8-8-10 65 .................... NMackay(3) 23 11
(JSGoldie) *led or disp ld to 1/2-way: wknd over 4f out* **20/1**

4151 **17** 4 **Bella Pavlina**[9] 1030 6-9-0 71 5ex .................... BSwarbrick(5) 13 11
(WMBrisbourne) *midfield: rdn 4f out: sn wknd* **14/1**

15/ **18** 3 **Talk To Mojo**[567] 4417 7-10-0 80 .................... RMiles 20 15
(JHMGosden) *sn bhd* **13/2**[3]

-625 **19** 29 **My Bayard**[20] 967 5-8-2 58 ow3 .................... JDO'Reilly(7) 16 —
(JO'Reilly) *bhd most of way: t.o* **50/1**

5654 **20** 9 **King Priam (IRE)**[9] 1028 9-7-7 50 oh15 ....................(b) HayleyTurner(5) 9 —
(MJPolglase) *sn bhd: t.o* **100/1**

520- **21** 4 **Every Note Counts**[168] 5458 4-9-7 75 .................... LEnstone 15 —
(JJQuinn) *midfield to 1/2-way: sn bhd: t.o* **40/1**

0-60 **U** **Archirondel**[30] 874 6-7-9 52 .................... DFentiman(5) 2 —
(MDHammond) *towards rr whn hmpd and uns rdr after 1f* **40/1**

2m 35.17s (-0.71) **Going Correction** +0.15s/f (Good)
**WFA** 4 from 5yo+ 2lb **22** Ran SP% **130.2**
Speed ratings: **108,107,107,106,102 100,99,98,98,93 92,90,90,81,80 79,76,74,55,49 46,—**CSF £45.19 CT £645.56 TOTE £5.60: £1.50, £2.60, £3.90, £4.10; EX 54.10.
**Owner** J H Quickfall & A G Black **Bred** Alan Black And Co And M W Easterby **Trained** Sheriff Hutton, N Yorks
■ Stewards Enquiry : N Mackay seven-day ban: causing interference (Apr 5-8,10-12)
P Gallagher seven-day ban: causing interference (Apr 5-8,10-12)

**FOCUS**
A very competitive handicap run in a good time and the break-neck pace ensured this mile and a half took plenty of getting. There is no reason why this race should not work in similar events in the coming weeks.

**NOTEBOOK**
**Middlethorpe** had not won on the Flat since taking this race off a 3lb higher mark in 2002, but has been in good form over hurdles, including when winning at Wetherby in December of last year. He found himself in front too soon and is probably value for a little more than the winning margin. That said, he has never followed up a success on the level.
**Robbie Can Can**, back on the level after a slightly disappointing run over hurdles at Sandown, was 16lb higher than when winning a maiden handicap on his last start on the turf, having won twice on the Fibresand over the winter. He got hampered early and took a while to get going in the straight, but eventually picked up and was closing on the winner (who was getting lonely out in front) at the line.
**Indian Solitaire(IRE)** has not won since October 2001, but ran well in a first-time visor (he had been tried in blinkers). He had been in reasonable form over hurdles and looks like continuing in a similar vein on the Flat.
**Blackthorn**, having his first run since leaving Richard Fahey's yard, kept on well in the straight and pulled a long way clear of the remainder. He has never won in handicap company, but this run would suggest his new connections will find an opportunity for him.
**Crown Agent(IRE)** had a pipe opener at Lingfield last month and improved on what he showed there.
**Benbyas**, a tough handicapper over hurdles, has never been as good on the Flat but was worth trying back on the level given the way he has improved over obstacles. He needs to dominate and probably went off too fast in his bid to do so, but this was not a bad run and he could be worth another chance.
**Rajam** was hampered on the first bend but it did not look to affect his chance.
**Glory Quest(USA)** made a real dash for the lead going to the first bend and caused some interference. His rider got seven days.
**Iloveturtle(IRE)** got squeezed up rounding the first bend and lost his good early position.
**Kid'Z'Play(IRE)** was another who caused trouble trying to get a position on the first bend. His rider got seven days.
**Talk To Mojo**, having only his third-ever start at the age of seven, has been kept in training for a reason but showed little on this occasion. He is one to keep an eye on.
**Archirondel** suffered worse than any horse in the scramble for a good early position on the first bend.

## 1104 BADSWORTH MAIDEN STKS 1m (S)
2:20 (2:21) (D) 3-Y-O **£5,590** (£1,720; £860; £430) **Stalls High**

Form RPR

3- **1** **Gatwick (IRE)**[220] 4243 3-9-0 .................... TQuinn 6 87
(MRChannon) *sn towards rr and pushed along: hdwy 1/2-way: rdn over 2f out: styd on wl appr last: led last 100 yds* **4/1**[2]

**2** hd **Master Marvel (IRE)** 3-9-0 .................... RFfrench 15 87
(MJohnston) *trckd ldrs: hdwy 1/2-way: led over 1f out: sn rdn: hdd and no ex last 100 yds* **20/1**

05- **3** 3 **Appalachian Trail (IRE)**[258] 3190 3-9-0 .................... RWinston 3 80
(ISemple) *trckd ldrs: hdwy 3f out: rdn and ch over 1f out: one pce ins last* **33/1**

5- **4** 1 1/4 **Man Of Letters (UAE)**[141] 5925 3-9-0 .................... KDalgleish 11 77
(MJohnston) *led: rdn along 3f out: hdd over 1f out: wknd ent last* **33/1**

0- **5** shd **Panshir (FR)**[148] 5825 3-9-0 .................... GBaker 16 77
(CFWall) *hld up in tch: hdwy over 2f out: swtchd lft and effrt over 1f out: kpt on same pce* **66/1**

0- **6** 2 **Galvanise (USA)**[261] 3076 3-9-0 .................... RHughes 14 73
(BWHills) *hld up: hdwy 3f out: rdn 2f out and kpt on same pce* **7/2**[1]

06 **7** nk **Air Of Supremacy (IRE)**[28] 890 3-9-0 .................... SWKelly 12 72
(JNoseda) *hld up: hdwy on inner 2f out: rdn over 1f out: sn no imp* **50/1**

4- **8** 4 **Tudor Bell (IRE)**[141] 5923 3-9-0 .................... DSweeney 13 63
(JGMO'Shea) *hld up towards rr: hdwy 3f out: rdn along and no imp fnl 2f* **100/1**

4- **9** 1 1/2 **Doctorate**[299] 2001 3-9-0 .................... KDarley 5 60
(EALDunlop) *in tch: hdwy to chse ldrs 3f out: sn rdn and wknd 2f out* **4/1**[2]

2335 **10** nk **Amwell Brave**[26] 916 3-9-0 68 .................... MartinDwyer 9 59
(JRJenkins) *nvr nr ldrs* **33/1**

00- **11** 12 **Blaeberry**[139] 5940 3-8-9 .................... JFEgan 10 28
(PLGilligan) *rdn along and bhd fr 1/2-way* **100/1**

5- **12** 3/4 **Mudawin (IRE)**[139] 5938 3-9-0 .................... WSupple 8 31
(MPTregoning) *midfield: hdwy on outer over 3f out: sn rdn and wknd over 2f out* **4/1**[2]

04- **13** 1 3/4 **Ticero**[156] 5694 3-9-0 .................... DHolland 2 27
(CEBrittain) *cl up: rdn along 3f out: sn wknd* **12/1**[3]

**14** 4 **Byrd Island** 3-8-9 .................... PFitzsimons 4 14
(DMorris) *chsd ldrs: rdn along 1/2-way: sn wknd* **100/1**

0 **15** 7 **Mitzi Caspar**[11] 1022 3-8-9 .................... AMackay 7 —
(PLGilligan) *a bhd* **150/1**

**16** 1/2 **Hoops And Blades** 3-9-0 .................... JPMurtagh 1 —
(NPLittmoden) *prom on outer: rdn along 1/2-way: sn wknd* **40/1**

336- **17** 12 **Kalush**[187] 5067 3-9-0 66 .................... DeanMcKeown 17 —
(RonaldThompson) *cl up: rdn along over 3f out: sn wknd* **66/1**

1m 40.43s (-1.21) **Going Correction** -0.025s/f (Good) **17** Ran SP% **114.5**
Speed ratings: **105,104,101,100,100 98,98,94,92,92 80,79,77,73,66 66,54**CSF £84.67 TOTE £4.00: £1.60, £6.00, £7.50; EX 152.70.
**Owner** W H Ponsonby **Bred** M J Dargan **Trained** West Ilsley, Berks

**FOCUS**
Traditionally a decent maiden, and this latest running looks right up to scratch. Gatwick looks quite smart, and the race should produce plenty of future winners.

**NOTEBOOK**
**Gatwick(IRE)** ◆ has always been held in some regard and improved on his debut effort to get off the mark. Always stuck towards the outside, he had to be niggled along from an early stage, but will have been learning plenty in the process and picked up nicely when shown the whip. This effort should not be underestimated and he will come on a bundle for the experience. The French Guineas has been mentioned as a possible target.
**Master Marvel(IRE)** ◆, a half-brother a useful two-year-old in the US, out of a decent ten-furlong winner in France, was easy to back for this racecourse debut. He got stuck in behind his stablemate for much of the way, but lengthened well when in the clear and was just denied. He is bound to improve and should find a similar race.
**Appalachian Trail(IRE)** showed promise as a two-year-old for John Gosden and made a very pleasing debut for his new connections. Given normal improvement he should be placed to effect.
**Man Of Letters(UAE)** improved on the form he showed on his sole start last season and is the sort that should continue to progress.
**Panshir(FR)** stepped up on the form he showed on his only start last year and would have been closer with better luck in running.
**Galvanise(USA)** lacked a decisive change of pace and should improve when stepped up in trip.
**Air Of Supremacy(IRE)** ran a pleasing race without ever looking a threat to the principals. Things should be easier now he is qualified for a handicap mark.
**Doctorate** showed up well on his debut behind some useful sorts, but this was most disappointing and represents a step back.
**Mudawin(IRE)** raced wider than anything and failed to build on the form he showed on his only previous run.
**Ticero** *Official explanation: jockey said colt was unsuited by the yielding going*

## 1105 MIND GAMES BEARSTONE STUD BROCKLESBY CONDITIONS STKS 5f

2:55 (2:59) (C) 2-Y-O £7,398 (£2,806; £1,403; £637) Stalls High

Form RPR

1 **Next Time Around (IRE)** 2-8-11 ........ RWinston 5 84
(MrsLStubbs) *prom: rdn over 1f out: led ins last: all out* **9/1**

2 *nk* **Dance Night (IRE)** 2-8-11 ........ GGibbons 12 83
(BAMcmahon) *sn in tch: hdwy over 2f out: chal ent fnl f: disp ld and rdn ins last: no ex cl home* **6/1[2]**

3 *1 ¼* **Westbrook Blue** 2-8-11 ........ ADaly 4 78
(WGMTurner) *sn led: rdn over 1f out: hdd ins last: no ex* **8/1**

4 *1 ¾* **Mitchelland** 2-8-6 ........ JFanning 13 66
(JamesMoffatt) *midfield: keen: nt clr run after 2f: hdwy 2 out: r.o fnl f: nvr able to chal* **25/1**

3 5 *nk* **Windy Prospect**[5] 1060 2-8-11 ........ DeanMcKeown 11 70
(PABlockley) *chsd ldrs: rdn and ev ch over 1f out: fdd ins last* **9/2[1]**

6 *nk* **Gogetter Girl** 2-8-6 ........ NCallan 9 63+
(JGallagher) *sn towards rr and pushed along: hdwy over 1f out: r.o wl ins last: nrst fin* **50/1**

7 *shd* **Justaquestion** 2-8-6 ........ GDuffield 1 63
(IAWood) *sn towards rr and pushed along: hdwy 2f out: r.o wl ins fnl f: nrst fin* **7/1[3]**

8 *2 ½* **Yorkshire Lad (IRE)** 2-8-11 ........ RFitzpatrick 10 58
(DCarroll) *midfield: rdn 2f out: no hdwy* **11/1**

9 *hd* **Kathys Job** 2-8-1 ........ DFox[(5)] 16 52
(ADSmith) *prom to 1/2-way: fdd* **17/2**

10 *2* **Flossytoo** 2-8-6 ........ DRMcCabe 15 44
(JO'Reilly) *slowly away: wl bhd whn rn green and hung bdly lft after 1f: kpt on fnl 2f: n.d* **33/1**

11 *2* **Misty Princess** 2-8-6 ........ MartinDwyer 7 36
(MJPolglase) *sn bhd* **14/1**

12 *2* **Pennestamp (IRE)** 2-8-11 ........ RHavlin 14 33
(MrsPNDutfield) *chsd ldrs to 1/2-way: wknd over 1f out* **12/1**

13 *7* **Hiats** 2-8-4 ........ JDO'Reilly[(7)] 3 5
(JO'Reilly) *slowly away: bhd most of way* **40/1**

14 *shd* **Sahara Mist (IRE)** 2-8-6 ........ PHanagan 6 —
(DShaw) *s.i.s: a bhd* **40/1**

15 *3* **Berham Maldu (IRE)** 2-8-6 ........ KDarley 2 —
(MJWallace) *in tch: rdn 1/2-way: wknd 2f out* **11/1**

61.57 secs (0.31) **Going Correction** -0.025s/f (Good) **15** Ran SP% **121.3**
Speed ratings: **96,95,93,90,90 89,89,85,85,82 78,78,67,64,59**CSF £59.62 TOTE £14.80: £4.00, £2.50, £2.60; EX 94.20.
**Owner** T Osborne **Bred** Peter McCutcheon **Trained** Malton, N. Yorks
■ Stewards Enquiry : A Daly one-day ban: failed to keep straight from stalls (Apr 5); one-day ban: used whip without giving colt time to respond (Apr 6)

**FOCUS**
Last year's first six all subsequently won at least once and there is no reason why this should not produce a similar share of winners. The first seven pulled clear.

**NOTEBOOK**
**Next Time Around(IRE)** twice failed to attract a buyer at the sales and was bought privately for 6,000gns as a yearling. Out of a half-sister to a smart ten to 12-furlong performer in France, he showed bags of pace and kept on right the way to the line to make a winning debut. There should be some improvement left and he should be able to add to this.
**Dance Night(IRE)** ◆, a 16,500gns purchase, out of a half-sister to a two-year-old winner, was quite strong in the market and hailed from a stable that does well in this race. He ran a cracking race and should not be a maiden for too much longer.
**Westbrook Blue**, a 4,000gns purchase, half-brother to five multiple winners, including three as two-year-olds, had a near-fore plate removed at the start. He appeared to know his job and ran a fine race, suggesting he will soon be winning in maiden company. *Official explanation: jockey said colt had a shoe removed at the start and hung right throughout*
**Mitchelland**, a half-sister to a five furlong two-year-old winner, did the best of the fillies and can be considered unlucky not to have gone closer. She got stuck in behind horses and did not get a clear run, but finished well. It will be disappointing if she does not build on this.
**Windy Prospect** had the advantage of being the only runner with experience, but was simply not good enough on the day. There has to be a suspicion the Lingfield race he made his debut in was not that good, but then again this may have come too soon for him.
**Gogetter Girl**, whose dam won on the All-Weather at the age of five, cost just 800gns but made a very pleasing debut. She could not really go the early pace, but kept on right the way to the line and finished the last furlong very well. She should find a maiden.
**Justaquestion**, a 6,800gns yearling, sister to multiple seven to eight-furlong winner Temper Tantrum out of a useful two-year-old winner, was slowly away, stuck out wide from the lowest stall of all and ran green. However, she kept on nicely inside the final furlong and looks capable of improving on this.
**Yorkshire Lad(IRE)**, a 10,000euros two-year-old, out of a half-sister to two winners at up to a mile, was supported in the market but was well held.
**Kathys Job**, a half-brother to a five-furlong juvenile winner, was backed at long odds and showed some dash but did not get home.

## 1106 LESLEY GARRETT "SO DEEP IS THE NIGHT" H'CAP 6f

3:25 (3:27) (C) (0-90,90) 3-Y-0+ £9,946 (£3,060; £1,530; £765) Stalls High

Form RPR

200- 1 **Steel Blue**[120] 6078 4-9-6 **82** ........ MHills 3 89
(RMWhitaker) *racd far side: mde all: rdn over 1f out: styd on wl* **16/1**

1-55 2 *shd* **Law Breaker (IRE)**[47] 703 6-9-6 **85** ........ BReilly[(3)] 7 92
(JAGilbert) *in tch far side: hdwy over 1f out: rdn and styd on wl fnl f: jst failed* **9/1[3]**

004- 3 *½* **Endless Summer**[142] 5919 7-9-2 **78** ........ PFessey 2 83
(KARyan) *hld up far side: hdwy over 2f out: swtchd rt over 1f out: rdn and styd on wl fnl f* **33/1**

600- 4 *¾* **Consensus (IRE)**[110] 6132 5-9-4 **80** ........ TWilliams 5 83
(MBrittain) *chsd ldrs far side: hdwy over 2f out: rdn and nt qckn ins last* **25/1**

110- 5 *hd* **Cd Flyer (IRE)**[188] 5030 7-9-2 **83** ........ TEaves[(5)] 16 85
(BEllison) *towards rr stands side: gd hdwy 2f out: rdn and styng on wl whn hung lft ent last: nrst fin* **14/1**

000- 6 *1 ¼* **Plateau**[188] 5030 5-9-9 **85** ........ AlexGreaves 4 84
(DNicholls) *chsd wnr far side: rdn over 1f out: wknd ins last* **33/1**

5-00 7 *1 ¾* **Nashaab (USA)**[54] 647 7-9-12 **88** ........ RHavlin 14 81
(PDEvans) *s.i.s and behind stands side: gd hdwy 2f out: styd on strly ins last: nrst fin* **25/1**

0-00 8 *hd* **Chappel Cresent (IRE)**[41] 761 4-9-7 **90** ........ LTreadwell[(7)] 17 83
(DNicholls) *cl up stands side: led that gp briefly 2f out: sn rdn and hdd: kpt on same pce ins last* **66/1**

30-1 9 *¾* **Miss George**[6] 1056 6-9-13 **89** 6ex ........ DaneO'Neill 1 80
(DKIvory) *hld and bhd far side: hdwy 2f out: sn rdn and kpt on same pce* **14/1**

06-0 10 *¾* **Abbajabba**[12] 1007 8-9-9 **85** ........ JBramhill 6 73
(CWFairhurst) *towards rr far side: hdwy 2f out: sn rdn and no imp fnl f* **16/1**

04-5 11 *shd* **Branston Tiger**[12] 1013 5-9-3 **79** ........ MFenton 12 67
(JGGiven) *led stands side gp: rdn along over 2f out: sn hdd & wknd appr last* **7/1[1]**

0-00 12 *¾* **Winthorpe (IRE)**[59] 607 4-9-4 **80** ........ KDalgleish 9 66
(JJQuinn) *cl up far side: rdn along o ver 2f out: grad wknd* **50/1**

630- 13 *½* **Artie**[139] 5941 5-9-3 **79** ........ KDarley 11 63
(TDEasterby) *chsd ldrs stands side: rdn along 2f out: grad wknd* **8/1[2]**

023- 14 *hd* **Blackheath (IRE)**[180] 5216 8-9-9 **85** ........ JFanning 22 69
(DNicholls) *trckd ldrs stands side: effrt and cl up 2f out: sn rdn and wknd appr last* **12/1**

460- 15 *nk* **Young Mr Grace (IRE)**[161] 5597 4-8-13 **78** ........ DAllan[(3)] 8 61
(TDEasterby) *in tch far side: rdn along over 2f out: sn wknd* **50/1**

631- 16 *1* **Ridgeback**[320] 1522 4-9-4 **80** ........ RWinston 19 60
(ISemple) *chsd ldrs stands side: rdn along 2f out: grad wknd* **14/1**

000- 17 *1 ½* **Loyal Tycoon (IRE)**[180] 5210 6-9-10 **86** ........ ANicholls 21 61
(DNicholls) *chsd ldrs stands side: rdn 2f out: grad wknd* **16/1**

0100 18 *nk* **Type One (IRE)**[33] 841 6-9-2 **78** ........ DHolland 10 52
(JJQuinn) *chsd ldrs far side: rdn along over 2f out: sn wknd* **14/1**

460- 19 *shd* **Armagnac**[257] 3220 6-9-5 **81** ........ RFfrench 13 55
(MABuckley) *towards rr stands side: sme hdwy 2f out: sn rdn and wknd* **25/1**

210- 20 *2* **Namroud (USA)**[278] 2557 5-10-0 **90** ........ PHanagan 20 58
(RAFahey) *midfield stands side: pushed along over 2f out: sn wknd* **16/1**

340- 21 *2 ½* **Musical Fair**[190] 4990 4-9-2 **78** ........ RHughes 15 39
(JAGlover) *in tch stands side: effrt over 2f out: sn rdn and wknd* **20/1**

200- 22 *1 ¼* **Prince Cyrano**[236] 3784 5-10-0 **90** ........ WSupple 18 47
(WJMusson) *s.i.s and bhd stands side: hdwy over 2f out: sn rdn and wknd* **16/1**

1m 13.74s (-0.54) **Going Correction** -0.025s/f (Good) **22** Ran SP% **125.0**
Speed ratings: **102,101,101,100,99 98,95,95,94,93 93,92,91,91,91 89,87,87,87,84 81,79**CSF £136.27 CT £4688.35 TOTE £15.60: £3.90, £2.30, £9.70, £5.80; EX 119.40 TRIFECTA Not won..
**Owner** Country Lane Partnership **Bred** R T And Mrs Watson **Trained** Scarcroft, W Yorks

**FOCUS**
Those drawn low who raced on far side were at an advantage in this competitive sprint, though the winning time was modest for the grade.

**NOTEBOOK**
**Steel Blue** had the cheekpieces on for his final three starts last term but they were left off today and he looked as sweet as ever in making every yard. He will not go up much for this and remains worth having on your side.
**Law Breaker(IRE)**, 5lb higher than when winning this last year, ran another cracking race and only just failed to peg back the long-time leader and winner. *Official explanation: jockey said gelding hung right-handed*
**Endless Summer** looked to be regressing last year, including when beaten in a couple of claimers, but he has slipped to a reasonable mark as a result and ran a cracker. Connections will no doubt be hoping he can build on this.
**Consensus(IRE)** is on a winning mark and ran her race.
**Cd Flyer(IRE)** came clear of his group on the stands'-side rail and was closing down the winner at the finish. A fine effort on his first run since leaving Mick Channon.
**Nashaab(USA)** kept on after missing the kick.
**Branston Tiger** raced on the wrong side and the ground may also have been faster than he would have liked.

## 1107 FREEPHONE STANLEYBET DONCASTER MILE (LISTED RACE) 1m (R)

4:00 (4:01) (A) 4-Y-0+ £19,500 (£6,000; £3,000; £1,500) Stalls High

Form RPR

144- 1 **Sublimity (FR)**[145] 5872 4-8-12 102 ........ (t) JPMurtagh 4 115+
(SirMichaelStoute) *hld up in tch: hdwy over 2f out: led appr fnl f: styd on u.p ins last* **7/2[2]**

-260 2 *1 ¼* **Gateman**[19] 978 7-9-3 ........ KDalgleish 7 117
(MJohnston) *trckd ldr: led over 2f out: rdn and hdd appr fnl f: styd on* **10/3[1]**

00-3 3 *3 ½* **Rockets 'n Rollers (IRE)**[12] 1011 4-8-12 104 ........ DaneO'Neill 6 104
(RHannon) *sn trcking ldrs: ev ch appr fnl f: no ex u.p ins last* **25/1**

415- 4 *2 ½* **Suggestive**[173] 5385 6-8-12 109 ........ (v) ACulhane 10 99
(WJHaggas) *hld up in rr: hdwy over 3f out: chsd ldrs 2 out: no further prog* **7/1**

001- 5 *1 ¼* **Makhlab (USA)**[164] 5536 4-8-12 108 ........ WSupple 9 96
(BWHills) *hld up in tch: effrt 3f out: sn rdn: no hdwy* **9/2[3]**

121- 6 *1 ¼* **Lago D'Orta (IRE)**[158] 5663 4-9-1 109 ........ PRobinson 1 96
(CGCox) *sn trcking ldrs: rdn over 2f out: fdd* **6/1**

506- 7 *3* **Middlemarch (IRE)**[138] 5951 4-8-12 109 ........ TQuinn 3 87
(JSGoldie) *in tch: drvn along over 4f out: sn in rr* **25/1**

00-4 8 *2 ½* **Lundy's Lane (IRE)**[76] 485 4-8-12 107 ........ (b) DHolland 2 81
(CEBrittain) *led tl hdd over 2f out: wknd over 1 out* **25/1**

301- 9 *2 ½* **Excelsius (IRE)**[125] 6044 4-9-1 106 ........ KDarley 5 79
(JLDunlop) *hld up in rr: drvn along 4f out: sn btn* **12/1**

226- 10 *15* **Audience**[173] 5370 4-8-12 101 ........ JQuinn 8 43
(JAkehurst) *bhd and drvn along 1/2-way: t.o* **50/1**

1m 39.13s (-1.39) **Going Correction** +0.15s/f (Good) **10** Ran SP% **111.5**
Speed ratings: **112,110,107,104,103 102,99,96,94,79**CSF £14.09 TOTE £3.90: £1.70, £1.20, £4.20; EX 14.40.
**Owner** Saeed Suhail **Bred** Stratford Place And Watership Down Stud **Trained** Newmarket, Suffolk

**FOCUS**
A decent-looking conditions event run at a fair pace, and won by a progressive sort who looks capable of winning at a higher level.

**NOTEBOOK**
**Sublimity(FR)** ◆, lightly raced last season, looks typical of the sort his trainer does so well with. Beaten at this level last term, he looks to have found some improvement over the winter as this defeat of a good yardstick testifies. This trip looks his optimum for the present, and Group races such as the betfred.com Mile look on the agenda.
**Gateman**, fit from a campaign in Dubai, was unable to dominate early on this occasion, but got to the front halfway up the straight. However, despite running his race, the progressive winner was too good for him.
**Rockets 'n Rollers(IRE)**, fit from a run on the All-Weather, put up another creditable performance, if not quite getting home, and may be capable of finding a race at this level. A race like the Leicestershire Stakes back over seven may suit him.
**Suggestive** is not the easiest to win with, but this was a fair reappearance and he will appreciate a return to faster ground.
**Makhlab(USA)**, a Group Three winner as a juvenile but lightly raced last season, was travelling well early in the straight before finding little off the bridle. He may be better for the run and seems to appreciate cut in the ground.
**Lago D'Orta(IRE)** kept on steadily on this first outing for five months and should be better for the run.

**Excelsius(IRE)** *Official explanation: jockey said colt ran too free*

## 1108 BALBY H'CAP — 1m 2f 60y
4:30 (4:33) (D) (0-85,84) 3-Y-O — £5,652 (£1,739; £869; £434) Stalls Low

Form — RPR

331- **1** **Mutafanen**[163] 5557 3-9-7 **84** ...... WSupple 1 99+
*(EALDunlop) mde all: qcknd over 3f out: clr fnl 2f: v easily* **9/2[1]**

5-15 **2** 4 **Always Flying (USA)**[47] 704 3-8-6 **69** ...... JFanning 5 70
*(MJohnston) keen early: prom: chsd wnr fr over 3f out: kpt on: no imp* **9/1**

4323 **3** ¾ **Siegfrieds Night (IRE)**[22] 957 3-7-7 **61** oh6 ...... DFox(5) 2 61
*(MCChapman) trckd ldrs: rdn and outpcd over 2f out: styd on wl fnl f* **25/1**

640- **4** shd **Lochbuie (IRE)**[153] 5723 3-8-9 **72** ...... DHolland 10 71+
*(GWragg) hld up in rr: pushed along 1/2-way: styd on wl u.p fnl 2f: nvr able to chal* **8/1[3]**

010- **5** 1 ¼ **Mrs Pankhurst**[145] 5871 3-8-10 **73** ...... MHills 11 70
*(BWHills) dwlt: hld up in rr: gd hdwy 3f out: rdn over 1f out: no further prog* **7/1[2]**

041- **6** 2 ½ **Mr Midasman (IRE)**[142] 5915 3-8-9 **72** ...... NCallan 3 65
*(RHollinshead) midfield: hdwy to chse ldrs 3f out: sn rdn: no further prog* **16/1**

310- **7** 1 ½ **Coventina (IRE)**[164] 5551 3-9-5 **82** ...... KDarley 8 72
*(JLDunlop) trckd ldrs: effrt 4f out: rdn 3 out: fdd* **7/1[2]**

562- **8** 9 **In Deep**[176] 5309 3-9-0 **77** ...... RHavlin 9 51
*(MrsPNDutfield) prom: rdn over 3f out: sn wknd* **12/1**

212 **9** 3 ½ **Play Master (IRE)**[38] 798 3-8-11 **74** ...... PaulEddery 6 42
*(DHaydnJones) hld up: effrt over 3f out: sn btn* **8/1[3]**

0-60 **10** 1 ¼ **Infidelity (IRE)**[36] 822 3-8-7 **70** ...... GDuffield 7 35
*(ABailey) midfield: drvn along 4f out: sn btn* **25/1**

400- **11** ¾ **Indian Call**[153] 5725 3-8-3 **66** ...... GGibbons 4 30
*(BAMcmahon) bhd fr 1/2-way* **20/1**

000- **12** ¾ **Ace Coming**[168] 5459 3-7-12 **61** oh4 ...... (b) DaleGibson 12 24
*(DEddy) hld up: hdwy into midfield 3f out: sn rdn and wknd* **50/1**

-224 **13** 4 **Baawrah**[47] 704 3-8-7 **70** ...... CCatlin 14 25
*(MRChannon) midfield: effrt over 3f out: sn rdn and btn* **11/1**

251- **14** 5 **Bethanys Boy (IRE)**[103] 6175 3-8-13 **76** ...... RWinston 13 22
*(BEllison) midfield: rdn over 3f out: sn wknd* **16/1**

2m 13.4s (1.57) **Going Correction** +0.15s/f (Good) **14** Ran SP% **117.6**
Speed ratings: **99,95,95,95,94 92,90,83,80,79 79,78,75,71**CSF £40.98 CT £915.64 TOTE £4.90: £2.00, £3.20, £6.70; EX 49.50.
**Owner** Hamdan Al Maktoum **Bred** Shadwell Estate Company Limited **Trained** Newmarket, Suffolk

**FOCUS**
A fair handicap run at a steady pace early and totally dominated by the winner.

**NOTEBOOK**
**Mutafanen** ♦, who progressed with racing last season, was well supported despite shouldering top weight. Allowed to dictate the pace, as soon as he was asked for his effort the race was over. He is likely to go up a fair amount for this, but looks capable of winning again.
**Always Flying(USA)**, a winner on the All-Weather in January, was always in the right place, but could only chase the winner unavailingly for the final quarter mile. This was a fair effort and a good guide to the level of the form.
**Siegfrieds Night(IRE)**, also fit from the All-Weather, tracked the leaders but could only keep on at the one pace. He seems an improved performer since being stepped up in trip.
**Lochbuie(IRE)** was the eyecatcher of the race, keeping on well in the closing stages having run green. He was not given a hard race and should come on a fair amount for the outing.
**Mrs Pankhurst** reared slightly and missed the break, but after making good headway she then ran out of steam in the closing stages. She looks likely to stay even further in time.
**Mr Midasman(IRE)**, taking a fair step up in trip, ran well enough without ever looking like winning. He too should come on a for the outing.
**Coventina(IRE)** was easy in the market and, after showing up early, was struggling halfway up the straight.

## 1109 DAVID SCOTT & CO (PATTERN MAKERS) LADY RIDERS' H'CAP — 1m 2f 60y
5:00 (5:01) (E) (0-75,75) 4-Y-0+ — £3,659 (£1,126; £563; £281) Stalls Low

Form — RPR

1156 **1** **Brave Dane (IRE)**[21] 964 6-10-7 **68** ...... MrsSBosley 10 79+
*(AWCarroll) hld up and bhd: stdy hdwy on inner over 3f out: rdn to ld ins last: styd on wl* **7/1[2]**

0-00 **2** 2 **Oldenway**[21] 964 5-10-4 **70** ...... MissVTunnicliffe(5) 17 77
*(RAFahey) towards rr: n.m.r bnd at 1/2-way: hdwy 3f out: styd on and ch ent last: sn one pce* **12/1**

310- **3** 1 ½ **Eton (GER)**[204] 4660 8-10-6 **70** ...... MissKellyHarrison(3) 9 74
*(DNicholls) prom: smooth hdwy 3f out: led 2f out: rdn and edgd lft ent last: sn hdd and one pce* **25/1**

1024 **4** ½ **Sting Like A Bee (IRE)**[20] 967 5-8-12 **50** ...... MissDawnRankin(5) 18 53
*(JSGoldie) hld up and bhd: effrt and pushed along 3f out: rdn and hdwy 2f out: styd on ins last: nrst fin* **8/1[3]**

-025 **5** ½ **Noul (USA)**[35] 829 5-9-13 **60** ...... (b) MissSBrotherton 20 63
*(KARyan) in tch: hdwy to chse ldrs 3f out: rdn 2f and kpt on same pce appr last* **16/1**

050- **6** 1 ¾ **Dickie Deadeye**[96] 6220 7-9-4 **58** ...... MissJHannaford(7) 12 57
*(GBBalding) prom: effrt over 2f out: sn rdn and one pce* **14/1**

0/5- **7** 1 ¼ **Lunar Lord**[15] 639 8-9-4 **58** ...... MissETucker(7) 16 55
*(DBurchell) midfield: hdwy to chse ldrs over 3f out: rdn over 2f out and sn one pce* **25/1**

-330 **8** nk **Dance Party (IRE)**[29] 882 4-9-10 **64** ...... MissFCumani(7) 19 61
*(AMBalding) hld up towards rr: gd hdwy 3f out: swtchd rt and nt clr run 2f out: sn rdn and no imp* **25/1**

140- **9** 1 ¾ **Libre**[15] 5136 4-10-4 **70** ...... (tp) MissCMetcalfe(5) 5 63
*(RCGuest) hld up towards rr: n.m.r bnd at 1/2-way: hdwy to chse ldrs over 3f out: rdn and no imp fnl 2f* **14/1**

-150 **10** ¾ **Mi Odds**[5] 1062 8-10-9 **70** ...... MrsMMorris 8 62
*(MrsNMacauley) hld up towards rr: hdwy opn outer 3f out: sn rdn and nvr nr ldrs* **10/1**

3050 **11** ½ **Yenaled**[27] 903 7-9-10 **60** ...... MrsSOwen(3) 6 51
*(KARyan) s.i.s and bhd tl sme late hdwy* **33/1**

02-3 **12** 1 ¾ **Redspin (IRE)**[82] 413 4-10-11 **75** ...... MrsSMoore(3) 2 63
*(JSMoore) in tch: hdwy to chse ldrs over 3f out: sn rdn and wknd over 2f out* **33/1**

300- **13** 2 ½ **Crunchy (IRE)**[30] 6068 6-9-4 **54** ...... (tp) MissLEllison(3) 7 38
*(BEllison) bhd fr 1/2-way* **20/1**

106- **14** 4 **Forest Tune (IRE)**[39] 5379 6-10-1 **62** ...... (b) MsCWilliams 3 38
*(BHanbury) trckd ldrs: hdwy 4f out: rdn to ld wl over 2f out: drvn and hdd 2f out: wknd* **11/2[1]**

605- **15** 13 **Cryfield**[156] 5688 7-9-11 **65** ...... MissARothery(7) 1 18
*(NTinkler) led: rdn along over 3f out: sn hdd & wknd* **33/1**

0-30 **16** 1 ¾ **Intensity**[28] 902 8-9-13 **60** ...... MissCO'Neill 13 10
*(PABlockley) in tch on outer: pushed along 1/2-way: sn wknd* **20/1**

4025 **17** 3 ½ **Digger (IRE)**[28] 899 5-10-3 **64** ...... MissEJJones 11 7
*(MissGayKelleway) in tch: rdn along 4f out: sn wknd* **17/2**

3004 **18** 7 **Crusoe (IRE)**[7] 1043 7-9-10 **57** ...... (b) MrsCFord 4 —
*(ASadik) chsd ldrs: rdn along over 4f out and sn wknd* **40/1**

202/ **19** 9 **Esher Common (IRE)**[328] 2908 6-9-11 **65** (t) MissRachelReynolds(7) 14 —
*(AEPrice) plld hrd: cl up to 1/2-way: sn lost pl and bhd* **50/1**

2m 14.16s (2.33) **Going Correction** +0.15s/f (Good) **19** Ran SP% **119.8**
Speed ratings: **96,94,93,92,92 91,90,89,88,87 87,85,83,80,70 68,66,60,53**CSF £73.43 CT £1994.46 TOTE £8.90: £3.70, £3.80, £5.60, £2.10; EX 80.20 Place 6 £958.10, Place 5 £321.67.
**Owner** Gordon W Day **Bred** Gainsborough Stud Management Ltd **Trained** Wixford, Warwicks

**FOCUS**
A modest lady riders' handicap run at just an ordinary pace and dominated mostly by horses fit from the All-Weather.

**NOTEBOOK**
**Brave Dane(IRE)**, who had struggled on the All-Weather since being raised 10lb for his second successive victory in February, was given a fine ride and got a gap up the rail at the right time to score cosily. He had things go his way here and significant improvement seems unlikely.
**Oldenway**, who seems best in the spring, was another fit from the All-Weather and he stayed on well in the closing stages. He is on a fair mark at present and may find a small handicap before long.
**Eton(GER)**, who had shown form for an inexperienced rider before, travelled well for a long way until tiring in the closing stages. He looks a few pounds too high in the handicap at present.
**Sting Like A Bee(IRE)** seems to have discovered some form since switching to the All-Weather this winter, and he ran well back on turf off a 5lb lower mark.
**Noul(USA)**, a Fibresand specialist, has been tried over various trips but seems best at around a mile, and seemed not to last home after having every chance.
**Dickie Deadeye** showed up well on his first outing since December. He is not badly weighted now, and is one to bear in mind for a handicap when the conditions are testing.
**Forest Tune(IRE)**, who was fit from a spell over hurdles and fitted with blinkers for the first time since 2001, tracked the leaders going well, but dropped out tamely after leading briefly.
T/Jkpt: Not won. T/Plt: £995.20 to a £1 stake. Pool: £90,459.35. 66.35 winning tickets. T/Qpdt: £98.70 to a £1 stake. Pool: £5,783.80. 43.35 winning tickets. JF

# LONGCHAMP (R-H)
Thursday, March 25

**OFFICIAL GOING: Holding**

## 1110a PRIX LORD SEYMOUR (LISTED) — 1m 4f
2:50 (2:53) 4-Y-0+ — £15,845 (£6,338; £4,754; £3,169)

RPR

**1** **Foreign Affairs**[143] 5912 6-9-1 ...... J-BEyquem 2 104
*(SirMarkPrescott) made all, ridden out*

**2** ½ **Jazz D'Allier (FR)**[123] 7-8-11 ...... IMendizabal 6 99
*(EVagne, France)*

**3** nse **Kindjhal (FR)**[20] 4-8-11 ...... DBoeuf 4 101
*(ELellouche, France)*

**4** 1 **Billy The Kid (IRE)**[123] 6-8-11 ...... TThulliez 9 98
*(TClout, France)*

**5** nse **Clear Thinking**[20] 4-9-4 ...... CSoumillon 7 107
*(AFabre, France)*

**6** 2 **Paging The King (FR)**[142] 4-8-11 ...... OPeslier 3 97
*(MRolland, France)*

**7** hd **Idaho Quest**[164] 7-9-1 ...... GToupel 1 99
*(H-APantall, France)*

**8** ¾ **Craig's Falcon (FR)**[151] 5782 5-9-4 ...... (b) SPasquier 5 101
*(JDeRoualle, France)*

**9** 6 **Tiyango (GER)**[160] 5629 4-8-11 ...... FSpanu 8 87
*(EPilet, France)*

2m 40.6s **Going Correction** +0.65s/f (Yiel)
**WFA** 4 from 5yo+ 2lb **9** Ran
Speed ratings: **105,104,104,103,103 102,102,101,97.**
**Owner** Charles C Walker - Osborne House **Bred** Miss K Rausing **Trained** Newmarket, Suffolk

**NOTEBOOK**
**Foreign Affairs**, given a positive ride, won his second Listed race in France. This sort of ground is probably softer than ideal and he could well pick up another event of this type before returning to these shores.

# 1103 DONCASTER (L-H)
Friday, March 26

**OFFICIAL GOING: Good**
Wind: mod hlf against Weather: overcast

## 1111 MEXBOROUGH MAIDEN STKS — 7f
1:15 (1:16) (D) 3-Y-O — £5,621 (£1,729; £864; £432) Stalls High

Form — RPR

2- **1** **Zonus**[154] 5735 3-9-0 ...... MartinDwyer 10 83
*(BWHills) trckd ldrs: led over 1f out: readily* **10/11[1]**

**2** 2 ½ **South Face** 3-9-0 ...... DarrenWilliams 7 77
*(RMBeckett) leggy: unf: s.i.s: hdwy over 2f out: styd on to take 2nd ins last: no ch w wnr* **33/1**

5- **3** 1 ¾ **Tableau (USA)**[140] 5939 3-9-0 ...... RHughes 12 73
*(BWHills) w ldrs: led and qcknd 3f out: hdd over 1f out: nt qckn* **11/2[3]**

024- **4** 5 **Mission Man**[146] 5870 3-9-0 84 ...... KDarley 1 60
*(RHannon) swtchd lft after 1f and racd alone far side: w ldrs: wknd appr fnl f* **4/1[2]**

00-U **5** 3 **Dalida**[57] 628 3-8-9 ...... GFaulkner 3 48
*(PCHaslam) hld up: hdwy over 3f out: sn chsng ldrs: fdd over 1f out* **66/1**

000- **6** 2 ½ **Habitual Dancer**[217] 4355 3-8-7 ...... LeanneKershaw(7) 6 46
*(JeddO'Keeffe) sn outpcd and bhd: sme hdwy over 2f out: nvr on terms* **100/1**

50- **7** ½ **Stephano**[234] 3864 3-8-7 ...... KMay(7) 2 45
*(BWHills) sn outpcd and bhd: sme hdwy 2f out: nvr a factor* **20/1**

0- **8** 2 ½ **Compton Micky**[139] 5948 3-9-0 ...... JEdmunds 9 39
*(JBalding) mid-div: lost pl over 2f out* **100/1**

004- **9** hd **Simply Red**[217] 4335 3-9-0 30 ...... ADaly 11 38
*(RBrotherton) mid-div: nvr on terms* **100/1**

42-0 **10** ¾ **She's Our Lass (IRE)**[18] 983 3-8-9 56 ...... RFitzpatrick 4 31
*(DCarroll) mid-div: lost pl 3f out* **66/1**

**11** 5 **Inchloss (IRE)** 3-9-0 ...... TQuinn 8 24
*(BAMcmahon) cmpt: bit bkwd: w ldrs: lost pl over 2f out* **20/1**

-440 **12** *4* **Fayrz Please (IRE)**[23] 956 3-9-0 58 JBramhill 13 14
(MCChapman) *w ldrs: lost pl 3f out* **40/1**
2- **13** *3½* **Pink Supreme**[312] 1719 3-8-9 GDuffield 5 —
(IAWood) *set mod pce: hdd 3f out: sn lost pl* **14/1**

1m 28.59s (0.78) **Going Correction** +0.125s/f (Good) **13** Ran SP% **115.3**
Speed ratings: **100,97,95,89,86 83,82,79,79,78 72,68,64**CSF £48.73 TOTE £1.90: £1.10, £8.80, £1.80; EX 44.60.
**Owner** Concord Racing,Bonnycastle,Grant,Morton **Bred** T H Bletsoe And Son **Trained** Lambourn, Berks
■ Barry Hills saddled the winner for the fourth year running and for the fifth time in the last seven years.

**FOCUS**
Not a very competitive maiden with some poor animals not beaten far. The winner looked far superior to the rest and should prove better than the bare form.

**NOTEBOOK**
**Zonus**, runner-up at Newbury in October on his only previous outing, looked very fit and was on his toes beforehand. He travelled well within himself and took this with the minimum of fuss.
**South Face**, on the leg and narrow, picked up in good style to take second spot late on. A mile will suit him better.
**Tableau(USA)**, who had just one backend outing at two, is on the leg. He went on and quickened the pace but it was soon clear his stablemate was going to be too quick for him. He will improve when stepped up in trip.
**Mission Man**, a rangy type, is a moderate mover. He went to race by himself on the far side, but after matching strides with those on the stands' side he tired appreciably.
**Dalida**, a poor walker, showed limited ability and her future lies in handicap company.
**Habitual Dancer**, who is not very big, picked up late in the day. He needs further and will have better prospects in handicaps.
**Pink Supreme** *Official explanation: trainer said filly ran too free early on and failed to get the trip.*

## 1112 LAKESIDE H'CAP 2m 2f
**1:50** (1:52) (C ) (0-90,85) 4-Y-0+ **£9,755** (£3,001; £1,500; £750) **Stalls** Low

Form RPR
034- **1** **Rahwaan (IRE)**[16] 5490 5-9-12 83 JPMurtagh 10 92
(CWFairhurst) *mde all: qcknd 3f out: rdn wl over 1f out: kpt on wl fnl f* **9/2**[1]
626- **2** *¾* **Vicars Destiny**[20] 5017 6-8-8 65 GDuffield 1 73
(MrsSLamyman) *hld up and bhd: hdwy 5f out: n.m.r and swtchd rt over 2f out: sn rdn: styd on wl fnl f: nt rch wnr* **9/1**
/0-3 **3** *shd* **Ocean Tide**[29] 899 7-9-2 73 (v) KDarley 6 81
(RFord) *trckd ldrs: hdwy over 3f out: rdn to chse wnr and hung lft ent last: sn drvn and kpt on* **20/1**
4210 **4** *3* **Phantom Stock**[13] 1010 4-8-4 67 JQuinn 9 72
(WJarvis) *hld up and bhd: hdwy on outer over 3f out: rdn 2f out: kpt on: nrst fin* **14/1**
330- **5** *5* **Sahem (IRE)**[272] 2794 7-9-9 80 DaleGibson 8 80
(DEddy) *hld up and bhd: hdwy on inner over 3f out: sn rdn along: kpt on ins last: nt rch ldrs* **33/1**
040- **6** *1* **Bobsleigh**[33] 5639 5-9-8 79 SDrowne 12 78
(MrsAJPerrett) *trckd wnr: effrt and cl up 4f out: rdn along 3f out: grad wknd fnl 2f* **10/1**
2364 **7** *3* **George Stubbs (USA)**[10] 1030 6-8-8 65 TQuinn 7 61
(MJPolglase) *trckd ldng pair: hdwy to chse wnr 3f out: sn rdn: grad wknd fr wl over 1f out* **14/1**
3214 **8** *2½* **Altitude Dancer (IRE)**[29] 899 4-8-0 63 JBramhill 5 57
(PABlockley) *in tch: hdwy over 6f out: rdn along over 3f out: sn drvn and btn* **10/1**
060- **9** *11* **Riyadh**[240] 3685 6-10-0 85 (v) JFanning 2 68
(MJohnston) *hld up towards rr: smooth hdwy 5f out: rdn over 2f out: sn btn* **10/1**
4-23 **10** *10* **Northern Nymph**[13] 1010 5-9-6 77 WSupple 14 50
(RHollinshead) *midfield: effrt on outer 6f out: sn rdn along and nvr a factor* **20/1**
030- **11** *19* **Allez Mousson**[32] 5817 6-8-1 58 (p) PHanagan 3 12
(ABailey) *bhd fr 1/2-way* **16/1**
0- **12** *1* **Ridapour (IRE)**[33] 4807 5-8-3 60 JoannaBadger 4 13
(DJWintle) *a bhd* **100/1**
-111 **13** *4* **Sun Hill**[13] 1010 4-9-2 79 DSweeney 11 28
(MBlanshard) *in tch: rdn along 4f out: wknd 3f out* **13/2**[3]
011- **14** *2½* **Snow's Ride**[114] 6123 4-9-5 82 MartinDwyer 13 28
(WRMuir) *chsd ldrs: rdn along 5f out: sn wknd* **11/2**[2]

4m 1.78s (3.85) **Going Correction** +0.275s/f (Good)
**WFA** 4 from 5yo+ 6lb **14** Ran SP% **116.8**
Speed ratings: **102,101,101,100,98 97,96,95,90,85 77,76,75,74**CSF £41.14 CT £737.75 TOTE £5.40: £2.40, £3.90, £5.60; EX 73.20 Trifecta £598.70 Pool £843.30, 0.20 winning units - part won..
**Owner** Six Iron Partnership **Bred** Shadwell Estate Company Limited **Trained** Middleham Moor, N Yorks

**FOCUS**
A modest winning time for the grade. The form looks fairly solid but, as last year, the winner may struggle off higher marks.

**NOTEBOOK**
**Rahwaan(IRE)**, fresh from a recent win on his hurdling bow, dictated things from the front and was always doing just enough. A repeat bid in the Chester Cup beckons.
**Vicars Destiny**, progressive over hurdles, met traffic problems but was never going to quite get to grips with the winner. She stays all day.
**Ocean Tide**, a lot fitter for Southwell, raced handily but gave problems hanging.
**Phantom Stock**, who has a pronounced knee action, stuck on all the way to the line and stamina did not seem a problem.
**Sahem(IRE)**, having his first outing for nine months, stayed on from off the pace and will be sharper next time.
**Bobsleigh**, fit from hurdling, is still 10lb higher than his last win.
**Allez Mousson** *Official explanation: jockey said gelding was never travelling.*
**Sun Hill**, going into this after a hat-trick on the All-Weather, is a moderate mover and was in trouble some way out. *Official explanation: jockey said gelding failed to stay*
**Snow's Ride**, a scratchy mover, is clearly suited by the artificial surfaces. *Official explanation: trainer was unable to offer any explanation for the poor form shown.*

## 1113 VALUE PACKED YORKSHIRE SEASON TICKET H'CAP 5f
**2:20** (2:23) (B ) (0-105,100) 3-Y-0+ **£14,170** (£4,360; £2,180; £1,090) **Stalls** High

Form RPR
00-1 **1** **Maktavish**[38] 801 5-8-2 76 (p) PHanagan 18 90
(ISemple) *mde all stands' side: kpt on wl* **16/1**
000U **2** *¾* **Trinculo (IRE)**[34] 841 7-8-9 86 (p) J-PGuillambert(3) 21 97
(NPLittmoden) *racd stands' side: hld up: hdwy 2f out: styd on wl ins last* **25/1**
00-0 **3** *¾* **Piccled**[13] 1007 6-8-0 77 ow1 DAllan(3) 17 85
(EJAlston) *s.i.s: racd stands' side: sn chsng ldrs: nt qckn fnl f* **13/2**[1]
3543 **4** *nk* **Zarzu**[34] 841 5-8-0 74 JBramhill 12 81
(CRDore) *racd stands' side: sn outpcd and bhd: hdwy 2f out: hrd rdn and edgd rt 1f out: kpt on wl* **10/1**
000- **5** *2* **River Falcon**[189] 5030 4-8-6 80 WSupple 16 80
(JSGoldie) *racd stands' side: in tch: effrt over 2f out: kpt on fnl f* **20/1**
640- **6** *1¼* **Pax**[189] 5030 7-8-8 82 PMQuinn 20 78
(DNicholls) *racd stands' side: in rr: hdwy 2f out: styd on ins last* **66/1**
4004 **7** *1* **Bond Boy**[13] 1007 7-9-5 93 FLynch 11 85
(BSmart) *swtchd lft and racd far side: rr-div: kpt on fnl 2f: nt rch ldrs* **16/1**
012- **8** *½* **Caribbean Coral**[162] 5593 5-9-2 90 DarrenWilliams 15 80
(JJQuinn) *slowly in to stride: racd stands' side: hdwy 2f out: styd on wl ins last* **16/1**
220- **9** *½* **Cape Royal**[219] 4304 4-8-9 83 TQuinn 1 71
(MrsJRRamsden) *s.i.s: hld up far side: hdwy to ld that side 2f out: wknd ins last* **10/1**
001- **10** *½* **Ptarmigan Ridge**[181] 5216 8-8-6 85 NMackay(5) 19 72
(MissLAPerratt) *racd stands side: chsd ldrs: kpt on same pce fnl 2f* **40/1**
6211 **11** *shd* **No Time (IRE)**[6] 1061 4-9-7 98 6ex LFletcher(3) 14 84
(MJPolglase) *racd stands' side: chsd ldrs: outpcd fnl 2f* **8/1**[2]
500- **12** *hd* **Awake**[144] 5909 7-8-2 76 MartinDwyer 9 61
(DNicholls) *racd far side: chsd ldrs: one pce fnl 2f* **40/1**
101- **13** *1* **Willhewiz**[206] 4646 4-8-11 88 (v) TPQueally(3) 2 70
(CADwyer) *led far side tl 2f out: fdd* **20/1**
604- **14** *1* **Sierra Vista**[158] 5673 4-8-4 81 ow2 LEnstone(3) 4 59
(DWBarker) *racd far side: chsd ldrs over 3f: fdd* **16/1**
011- **15** *1½* **Smart Hostess**[153] 5743 5-9-5 93 RWinston 22 66
(JJQuinn) *racd stands side: bhd: hdwy over 2f out: hmpd and wknd 1f out* **9/1**[3]
5-05 **16** *2* **Chico Guapo (IRE)**[27] 912 4-8-3 77 (p) JQuinn 8 43
(JAGlover) *racd far side: in tch: fdd over 1f out* **12/1**
-135 **17** *¾* **Dancing Mystery**[34] 841 10-8-11 85 (b) SCarson 6 48
(EAWheeler) *racd far side: chsd ldrs: lost pl over 1f out* **9/1**[3]
600- **18** *5* **Kangarilla Road**[317] 1590 5-8-1 75 PFitzsimons 10 20
(MrsJRRamsden) *swtchd lft s: racd far side: hld up and bhd: nvr a factor* **33/1**
052- **19** *3½* **Pomfret Lad**[185] 5140 6-9-12 100 AlexGreaves 7 32
(DNicholls) *racd stands' side: chsd ldrs: lost pl 2f out* **50/1**
630- **20** *1¾* **Rectangle (IRE)**[283] 2447 4-8-9 83 ANicholls 3 9
(DNicholls) *racd far side: w ldr: wknd 2f out: eased* **20/1**

60.75 secs (-0.51) **Going Correction** +0.125s/f (Good) **20** Ran SP% **123.3**
Speed ratings: **109,107,106,106,102 100,99,98,97,96 96,96,94,93,90 87,86,78,72,70**CSF £380.12 CT £1743.76 TOTE £14.80: £3.60, £6.90, £1.80, £2.80; EX 431.20 Trifecta £752.60 Pool £1,060.10, 0.10 winning units - part won..
**Owner** D G Savala **Bred** V Robin Lawson **Trained** Carluke, S Lanarks

**FOCUS**
They split into two even groups, but the first six home raced on the stands' side. The form looks solid and the fourth has translated recent improvement to turf.

**NOTEBOOK**
**Maktavish**, a winner on the All-Weather 38 days previously, tends to hang right so was helped by the stands' side rail.
**Trinculo(IRE)**, taken to post early, was another fit from the All-Weather. He stayed on really well to hunt up the winner and would have preferred more give underfoot.
**Piccled** took this a year ago from a 3lb higher mark. After missing a beat at the start he stuck on well and is clearly weighted to regain winning brackets.
**Zarzu**, very keen to post, stayed on from off a strong pace and these days might be better suited by six.
**River Falcon** ran well on his return but he still looks weighted to the hilt.
**Pax** picked up in good style late on and should again pay his way this year, possibly in a lesser grade and on tracks with an uphill finish.
**Bond Boy**, the 2002 Stewards Cup winner, stayed on to finish first home on the far side. He seems better suited by six.
**Caribbean Coral**, having his first outing for his new stable, took the eye picking up nicely late on. He is one to bear in mind.
**Cape Royal**, who has clearly had problems at the start, sat down in the stalls. After showing ahead on the far side he tired late on. He loves fast ground and is worth bearing in mind, as he looks sure to uphold his family's tradition. *Official explanation: jockey said gelding sat down in the stalls and missed the break.*
**Smart Hostess** *Official explanation: trainer said mare had bled from the nose.*

## 1114 FREEPHONE STANLEYBET SPRING MILE (H'CAP) 1m (S)
**2:50** (2:54) (B ) 4-Y-0+ **£17,420** (£5,360; £2,680; £1,340) **Stalls** High

Form RPR
140- **1** **Autumn Glory (IRE)**[153] 5747 4-9-2 82 SDrowne 19 103+
(GWragg) *cl up stands side: hdwy and overall ldr over 2f out: pushed clr over 1f out: sn rdn and kpt on wl* **20/1**
315- **2** *1½* **St Petersburg**[148] 5838 4-9-2 82 GDuffield 20 96
(MHTompkins) *swtg: trckd ldrs stands side: hdwy to chse wnr 2f out: sn rdn and kpt* **33/1**
-102 **3** *2½* **Swift Tango (IRE)**[27] 922 4-9-8 88 WSupple 21 96
(EALDunlop) *lw: in tch stands side: hdwy over 2f out: swtchd lft wl over 1f out: sn rdn and nt qckn fnl f* **16/1**
1-02 **4** *1¾* **Linning Wine (IRE)**[51] 677 8-9-3 83 JPMurtagh 15 87
(BGPowell) *swtg: hld up stands side: hdwy 3f out: rdn 2f out: styd on wl fnl f: nrst fin* **16/1**
20-4 **5** *nk* **Danelor (IRE)**[13] 1009 6-9-7 87 PHanagan 24 91
(RAFahey) *cl up stands side: led that gp 1/2-way tl rdn and hdd over 2f out: drvn and kpt on same pce* **14/1**
110- **6** *2* **Strong Hand**[86] 6268 4-8-11 82 (t) PMulrennan(5) 22 81
(MWEasterby) *dwlt: sn in tch stands side: effrt and hdwy 3f out: sn rdn: kpt on fnl f* **50/1**
000- **7** *nk* **Everest (IRE)**[174] 5365 7-9-5 85 RWinston 11 83+
(BEllison) *hld up in rr far side: hdwy 3f out: rdn 2f out: kpt on ins last: nrst fin* **15/2**[3]
1016 **8** *¾* **African Sahara (USA)**[6] 1066 5-9-6 86 5ex (t) GCarter 7 83+
(MissDMountain) *in tch far side: hdwy to chse ldrs 3f out: rdn and kpt on same pce fnl 2f* **16/1**
15-4 **9** *nk* **Arry Dash**[27] 915 4-9-3 86 DCorby(3) 3 82+
(MRChannon) *hld up towards rr far side: hdwy over 3f out: rdn 2f out and kpt on same pce* **7/1**[2]
011- **10** *nk* **Thihn (IRE)**[146] 5873 9-9-10 90 ADaly 10 85+
(JLSpearing) *dwlt: hld up in rr far side: hdwy 3f out: rdn 2f out and sn no imp* **11/1**
11-2 **11** *shd* **Cardinal Venture (IRE)**[13] 1011 6-9-7 87 NCallan 2 82+
(KARyan) *overall ldr far side: rdn clr 3f out: hdd over 2f out: sn drvn and wknd wl over 1f out* **6/1**[1]

00-0 **12** 1 ½ **Compton Dragon (USA)**$^{7}$ [1056] 5-9-0 **80**.......................... ANicholls 23 71
(DNicholls) *hld up stands side: hdwy and pushed along whn n.m.r 3f out: sn rdn and no imp after* **40/1**

40-0 **13** 1 ½ **Krugerrand (USA)**$^{31}$ [872] 5-9-2 **82**.............................. MartinDwyer 18 70
(WJMusson) *chsd ldrs stands side: rdn along over 2f out: grad wknd* **33/1**

362- **14** 1 ¾ **Ace Of Hearts**$^{149}$ [5827] 5-9-4 **84**................................ JQuinn 8 68+
(CFWall) *in tch far side: hdwy over 3f out: rdn and wknd over 2f out* **14/1**

053- **15** 1 **Dunaskin (IRE)**$^{181}$ [5225] 4-9-7 **87**.......................... DaleGibson 17 69
(DEddy) *led stands side gp to 1/2-way: sn rdn along and wknd* **66/1**

0002 **16** nk **Internationalguest (IRE)**$^{31}$ [872] 5-9-1 **81**..................(b) KDarley 4 62+
(GGMargarson) *swtg: chsd ldrs far side: rdn wl over 2f out and sn wknd* **14/1**

534- **17** ½ **Marshman (IRE)**$^{125}$ [6050] 5-9-9 **89**....................... PRobinson 16 69
(MHTompkins) *in tch stands side: hdwy on outer to chse ldrs 3f out: sn rdn and wknd* **33/1**

105- **18** nk **Atlantic Ace**$^{150}$ [5814] 7-9-2 **82**.................................. FLynch 5 61+
(BSmart) *a rr far side* **16/1**

-004 **19** 2 ½ **Aventura (IRE)**$^{22}$ [961] 4-9-2 **85**........................ LFletcher$^{(3)}$ 6 58+
(MJPolglase) *chsd ldr far side: rdn along over 3f out: sn wknd* **20/1**

005- **20** 2 **Go Tech**$^{286}$ [2377] 4-9-2 **85**....................................... DAllan$^{(3)}$ 12 54+
(TDEasterby) *chsd ldrs far side: rdn along 3f out: sn wknd* **33/1**

420- **21** 6 **Jabaar (USA)**$^{195}$ [4879] 6-9-9 **89**......................... AlexGreaves 9 44+
(DNicholls) *a rr far side* **40/1**

00-0 **22** 5 **Sahaat**$^{13}$ [1009] 6-9-4 **84**.......................................... SWKelly 14 28
(JAOsborne) *a rr stands side* **33/1**

150- **23** nk **Unicorn Reward (IRE)**$^{13}$ [5252] 4-9-4 **84**...................... RHughes 1 27+
(MDHammond) *chsd ldrs far side: rdn along 1/2-way and sn wknd* **25/1**

030- **24** 20 **Sawwaah (IRE)**$^{237}$ [3785] 7-9-2 **82**........................ JoannaBadger 13 —+
(DNicholls) *a rr far side* **33/1**

1m 40.34s (-1.30) **Going Correction** +0.125s/f (Good) **24** Ran SP% **129.8**
Speed ratings: **111,109,107,105,104 102,102,101,101,101 101,99,98,96,95 95,94,94,91,89 83,78,78,58**CSF £557.59 CT £5251.75 TOTE £35.50: £8.50, £9.00, £3.60, £3.10; EX 899.40 Trifecta £3005.80 Pool £4,233.56, 0.50 winning units - part won..
**Owner** Mollers Racing **Bred** Margaret Conlon **Trained** Newmarket, Suffolk

**FOCUS**
They split into two groups but the first six home all raced on the stands' side. The form looks strong with the unexposed winner looking particularly interesting.

**NOTEBOOK**
**Autumn Glory(IRE)**, who had problems with a hind joint at three, is still relatively unexposed. He took a commanding lead and had only to be kept up to his work. There ought to be even better to come.
**St Petersburg**, 10lb higher than when successful at Redcar in October, is a keen type and he was very warm beforehand. He went after the winner and never gave up, albeit in hopeless pursuit.
**Swift Tango(IRE)**, who looked outstandingly well after his trip to Dubai, finds a mile his bare minimum.
**Linning Wine(IRE)**, very warm at the start, put in some sterling late work and is crying out for a return to further.
**Danelor(IRE)** keeps running well in this type of race but has only won once, and that was over two years ago now.
**Strong Hand**, last seen out on New Year's Eve, prefers more give underfoot.
**Everest(IRE)**, last of all on the far side at halfway, finished well to head home that group.
**Cardinal Venture(IRE)**, in fine form on the All-Weather, possibly went off too fast, leading on the far side. He fell in a heap with over a furlong left to run.

## 1115 BAWTRY MAIDEN (S) STKS 5f
**3:25** (3:28) (F) 2-Y-0 **£2,909** (£831; £415) **Stalls** High

Form RPR

**1** **Lisa Mona Lisa (IRE)** 2-8-9 ................................... JQuinn 6 50
(VSmith) *neat: chsd ldrs: styd on to ld last 100yds* **7/1**$^{2}$

**2** ½ **General Nuisance (IRE)** 2-9-0 ........................ MartinDwyer 1 53
(JSMoore) *cmpt unf: w ldrs: nt qckn ins last* **7/1**$^{2}$

**3** 1 ¼ **Little Wizzy** 2-8-9 ......................................... SWKelly 3 43
(PDEvans) *small: unf: s.i.s: sn chsng ldrs: hung bdly lft over 2f out: wnt to far side: nt qckn last 150yds* **11/1**

**4** nk **Grezie** 2-8-4 ................................................... DFox$^{(5)}$ 8 42
(ADSmith) *leggy: unf: s.i.s: sn bhd: stl last 1f out: fin wl* **10/1**$^{3}$

**5** nk **Emma's Venture** 2-8-4 ................................ PMulrennan$^{(5)}$ 2 41
(MWEasterby) *cmpt: s.i.s: sn chsng ldrs: led over 1f out: hdd 100yds out: wknd* **16/1**

**6** 1 ½ **Docklands Dude (IRE)** 2-9-0 ............................. KDarley 10 40
(MJWallace) *tall: unf: scope: s.i.s: hdwy to ld over 3f out: hdd over 1f out: wknd and eased ins last* **11/4**$^{1}$

**7** 1 ¾ **Concert Time** 2-8-9 ..................................... RFitzpatrick 5 28
(PTMidgley) *unf: sn outpcd and bhd: kpt on fnl 2f* **16/1**

**8** nk **Goldhill Prince** 2-9-0 ........................................ ADaly 9 31
(WGMTurner) *cmpt: led tl over 3f out: hung lft: wknd over 1f out* **11/4**$^{1}$

**9** ½ **Diatonic** 2-8-11 ............................................ LisaJones$^{(3)}$ 4 29
(WJMusson) *neat: trckd ldrs: lost pl 2f out* **12/1**

64.35 secs (3.09) **Going Correction** +0.125s/f (Good) **9** Ran SP% **115.2**
Speed ratings: **80,79,77,76,76 73,71,70,69** CT £8.40 TOTE £2.40: £2.40, £3.80, £; EX56.00
1.The winner was bought in for 6,000gns. Docklands Dude was claimed for £6,000 by M Meade, General Nuissance was claimed by Lynda Perratt for £6,000,
**Owner** Stephen Dartnell **Bred** A Geraghty **Trained** Exning, Suffolk
■ A first training success for former jockey Vince Smith.
■ Stewards Enquiry : P MulrennanM one-day ban: used whip down filly's shoulder in the forehand position (Apr 6)

**FOCUS**
A modest winning time, even for a juvenile seller and the form looks poor.

**NOTEBOOK**
**Lisa Mona Lisa(IRE)**, a February foal, is a smallish, close-coupled type. She knew her job and in the end did just enough to take what looked a fair race by selling standards.
**General Nuisance(IRE)**, a February foal, is very narrow. He was claimed after coming off just second best and heads for Scotland.
**Little Wizzy**, a March foal, is well named. She hung violently left and ended up racing hard against the far side rail. *Official explanation: jockey said filly hung left.*
**Grezie**, an April foal, was one of the biggest in the line-up. Green and clueless, she was hopelessly detached at halfway before finishing with a real flourish. She was claimed and joins John Best.
**Emma's Venture**, a March foal, did well to show ahead but was very leg weary inside the last.
**Docklands Dude(IRE)**, a March foal, is up in the air. He showed ability but tired badly and was eased late on. He was claimed.
**Goldhill Prince**showed plenty of toe but basically wanted to do nothing but hang left-handed.

## 1116 MALTBY MAIDEN STKS 1m 2f 60y
**4:00** (4:01) (D ) 3-Y-0 **£5,538** (£1,704; £852; £426) **Stalls** Low

Form RPR

42- **1** **King Of Dreams (IRE)**$^{167}$ [5489] 3-9-0 .......................... KDalgleish 6 88
(MJohnston) *trckd ldr: led 3f out: shkn up and edgd lft wl over 1f out: rdn and styd on wl fnl f* **11/8**$^{1}$

0-42 **2** 1 ½ **Keelung (USA)**$^{6}$ [1059] 3-9-0 ................................ PRobinson 5 85
(MAJarvis) *trckd ldrs: hdwy on inner over 3f out: n.m.r and swtchd lft over 1f out: rdn and kpt on fnl f* **9/2**$^{3}$

2- **3** 1 ½ **Flamboyant Lad**$^{149}$ [5825] 3-9-0 ................................ MHills 11 82
(BWHills) *lw: trckd ldrs gng wl: smooth hdwy over 3f out: chal 2f out: sn rdn and one pce* **15/8**$^{2}$

0- **4** 12 **Dancing Bear**$^{146}$ [5871] 3-9-0 ....................................... NCallan 2 61
(JulianPoulton) *hld up in midfield: hdwy 4f out: rdn along 3f out: nvr a factor* **66/1**

433- **5** 9 **Negwa (IRE)**$^{165}$ [5544] 3-8-6 74 ............................. DCorby$^{(3)}$ 4 40
(MRChannon) *led: rdn along and hdd 3f out: sn wknd* **10/1**

0- **6** 1 **Saameq (IRE)**$^{150}$ [5813] 3-9-0 ............................... DMcGaffin 10 43
(ISemple) *hld up and bhd: sme hdwy 4f out: nvr a factor* **66/1**

3443 **7** 5 **Katie's Role**$^{9}$ [1040] 3-8-9 57 ........................... DeanMcKeown 3 29
(IanEmmerson) *chsd ldng pair: rdn along over 4f out and sn wknd* **100/1**

050- **8** 2 **Danefonique (IRE)**$^{158}$ [5671] 3-8-9 53 ..................... RFitzpatrick 9 25
(DCarroll) *a rr* **100/1**

0- **9** 5 **Sir Bond (IRE)**$^{181}$ [5222] 3-9-0 ..................................... FLynch 8 21
(BSmart) *a rr* **40/1**

0-60 **10** 7 **Atlantic Tern**$^{27}$ [916] 3-9-0 53 ........................................ ADaly 1 9
(NMBabbage) *a rr* **100/1**

030- **11** 9 **Inchconnel**$^{141}$ [5934] 3-9-0 67 ..................................(b$^{1}$) JQuinn 7 —
(VSmith) *dwlt: sn in tch: rdn along 1/2-way and sn wknd* **50/1**

2m 13.55s (1.72) **Going Correction** +0.275s/f (Good) **11** Ran SP% **114.5**
Speed ratings: **104,102,101,92,84 84,80,78,74,68 61**CSF £7.79 TOTE £2.30: £1.10, £1.50, £1.50; EX 8.80 Place 6 £232.73, Place 5 £163.44.
**Owner** Saeed Buhaleeba **Bred** David Jamison Bloodstock And G Roddick **Trained** Middleham Moor, N Yorks

**FOCUS**
A useful maiden with the first three well clear.

**NOTEBOOK**
**King Of Dreams(IRE)**, who showed plenty of ability in two starts last year, lacks substance and looked very fit. He moved well to post and in the end ran out a decisive winner. He looks to have more stamina than speed.
**Keelung(USA)**, who carries condition, stayed on to follow home the winner. He was in no way unlucky but deserves to find a race.
**Flamboyant Lad**, runner-up in a backend maiden at Yarmouth, has plenty of scope. He seemed to travel better than the winner but began to tread water inside the last. He will improve a good deal for the outing and should have no trouble finding a race.
**Dancing Bear**, thrown in at the deep end on his sole outing at two, looks as if he needs more time yet.
**Negwa(IRE)**, placed in two of her three outings last year, is a tall, narrow filly. After setting the pace she dropped right away.
**Atlantic Tern** *Official explanation: jockey said colt hung right throughout.*
T/Jkpt: Not won. T/Plt: 755.60 to a £1 stake. Pool £80,478.40, 77.75 winning tickets T/Qpdt: 194.20 to a £1 stake. Pool 5,355.00, 20.40 winning tickets JR

# 1095 LINGFIELD (L-H)
Friday, March 26

**OFFICIAL GOING: Standard**
In contests up to a mile prominent racers appeared at an advantage - horses that either made all or raced close to the speed won the first four races.
Wind: lt hlf against Weather: fine & sunny

## 1117 BET DIRECT ON SKY ACTIVE MAIDEN AUCTION STKS 5f (P)
**2:00** (2:02) (E ) 2-Y-0 **£3,386** (£1,042; £521; £260) **Stalls** High

Form RPR

**1** **King After** 2-8-9 .............................................. NPollard 7 68
(JRBest) *leggy: trckd ldrs: effrt and swtchd to outer over 1f out: shkn up and styd on wl fnl f to ld last strides* **14/1**

**2** hd **Evanesce** 2-8-2 ow1.................................... SHitchcott$^{(3)}$ 9 63
(MRChannon) *leggy: hld up in tch: prog 1/2-way to join ldrs 2f out: rdn to ld jst over 1f out: kpt on: hdd last strides* **11/4**$^{1}$

**3** nk **Transaction (IRE)** 2-9-0 ........................................ JTate 2 71
(JMPEustace) *w'like: hanging rt thrght: disp ld: drvn and hdd jst over 1f out : ev ch nr fin: nt qckn* **7/2**$^{2}$

**4** 2 **Aunty Euro (IRE)** 2-8-9 ..................................... MFenton 1 58
(EJO'Neill) *w'like: unf: disp ld: hanging rt and hdd jst over 1f out: fdd ins fnl f* **10/1**

**5** ½ **Iceni Warrior** 2-8-10 ow1.................................. DHolland 3 57
(TGMills) *neat: bit bkwd: hld up: n.m.r and snatched up over 3f out: prog 2f out to chse ldrs over 1f out: pushed along and one pce f* **12/1**

5 **6** hd **Joe Ninety (IRE)**$^{6}$ [1060] 2-8-11 ............................. JDSmith 4 57
(JSMoore) *racd in midfield: pushed along 1/2-way: effrt wl over 1f out: one pce* **7/1**

**7** 3 ½ **Wizzskilad** 2-8-7 ................................................ RHavlin 8 39
(MrsPNDutfield) *unf: bit bkwd: racd towards rr: effrt 2f out: wknd over 1f out* **50/1**

**8** ½ **Turtle Magic (IRE)** 2-7-9 .................................. CHaddon$^{(7)}$ 5 32
(WGMTurner) *w'like: bit bkwd: chsd ldrs: pushed along 1/2-way: wknd over 1f out* **20/1**

**9** 7 **Droopys Joel** 2-8-4 ....................................... THamilton$^{(3)}$ 6 —
(RPElliott) *w'like: bit bkwd: s.i.s: a in rr: wknd wl over 1f out* **4/1**$^{3}$

61.06 secs (1.28) **Going Correction** -0.15s/f (Stan) **9** Ran SP% **111.6**
Speed ratings: **83,82,82,79,78 77,72,71,60**CSF £50.13 TOTE £18.50: £4.90, £1.60, £2.40; EX 84.00.
**Owner** D S Nevison **Bred** Mrs J McCreery **Trained** Hucking, Kent
■ Stewards Enquiry : J Tate one-day ban: used whip with excessive frequency (Apr 6)

**FOCUS**
Probably just an ordinary maiden and a moderate winning time.

**NOTEBOOK**
**King After**, a half-brother to five furlong two-year-old winner Animal Cracker, was easy to back. He was travelling better than anything turning for home, but had to be switched out for a run in the straight and did not look like getting there until lunging just yards from the line. This was a most pleasing debut and, with improvement likely, he should be competitive in a slightly higher grade.

**Evanesce**, a 10,000 euros purchase, out of a mare who was placed over eight and ten furlongs at three and was a half-sister to a Grade One winner in the US, was sent off favourite to make a winning debut. After travelling well and keeping on right the way to the finish, she was just denied. Although her stable will have plenty of better two-year-olds this season, she should find a maiden in the coming weeks.

**Transaction(IRE)**, a 19,000gns purchase, half-brother to a triple six furlong two-year-old winner Cheverak Forest, did not help his chance by hanging right, but still shaped with promise and should be able to go on from this. He was clear of the remainder.

**Aunty Euro(IRE)**, a 25,000 euros yearling, half-sister to a seven furlong two-year-old selling winner Great Blakeset, showed plenty of pace but proved no match for the front three in the closing stages.

**Iceni Warrior ◆**, out of a half-sister to a winner in Italy, had an eye-catching jockey booking but proved easy to back. He was outpaced in the final furlong, got behind and met trouble. However, he made up some of the lost ground turning into the straight before his run not surprisingly flattened out. He will know more next time and should improve on this.

**Joe Ninety(IRE)**, fifth in the first two-year-old race of the season over course and distance just six days previously, was a big drifter in the market and proved unable to build on that run. He was the only one with previous racecourse experience and this has to be considered disappointing.

**Droopys Joel**, a 4,500gns yearling, half-brother to three maidens with modest form, was supported in the market but missed the kick and never got competitive.

## 1118 PRESS INTERACTIVE TO BET DIRECT H'CAP — 1m (P)

2:30 (2:31) (E) (0-75,74) 4-Y-0+ — £3,513 (£1,081; £405; £405) Stalls High

Form — RPR

6-03 **1** **Katiypour (IRE)**[3] 1085 7-9-5 **69** ........ RMiles(3) 2 — 82
(MissBSanders) *lw: sn trckd ldr: led over 2f out: rdn 3l clr over 1f out: styd on wl* **11/2**[3]

0-00 **2** 1 1/2 **Concer Eto**[34] 847 5-9-7 **68** ........ (p) NPollard 3 — 78
(SCWilliams) *b.hind: stdd s: hld up wl in rr: gng easily 2f out: prog to chse wnr and edgd lft fnl f: kpt on: too much to do* **4/1**[2]

2-24 **3** 1 **Deeper In Debt**[31] 870 6-9-12 **73** ........ JMackay 9 — 80
(JAkehurst) *chsd ldng pair: rdn over 2f out: chsd wnr briefly over 1f out: one pce fnl f* **3/1**[1]

2032 **3** dht **Sir Laughalot**[31] 870 4-9-6 **70** ........ LPKeniry(3) 4 — 77
(MissECLavelle) *chsd ldrs: rdn over 2f out: effrt u.p over 1f out: one pce fnl f* **11/2**[3]

-144 **5** nk **Musical Gift**[32] 862 4-9-5 **69** ........ (p) BReilly(3) 11 — 76
(CNAllen) *b: b.hind: restrained after 1f and dropped to rr: effrt gng wl 2f out: no room wl over 1f out tl swtchd rt 1f out: kpt on:* **11/1**

415- **6** 3/4 **Night Wolf (IRE)**[300] 1997 4-9-5 **69** ........ SHitchcott(3) 5 — 74+
(MRChannon) *trckd ldrs: pushed along over 2f out: nt clr run wl over 1f out: swtchd rt fnl f: nt pce to chal after* **14/1**

136- **7** 4 **Trousers**[115] 6114 5-9-11 **72** ........ DHolland 10 — 68
(AndrewReid) *b: b.hind: chsd ldrs: rdn wl over 2f out: no imp over 1f out: wknd fnl f* **10/1**

100- **8** 1/2 **Indian Welcome**[134] 5991 5-9-13 **74** ........ (b) MFenton 12 — 68
(HMorrison) *sn led: hdd over 2f out: shuffled along and lost pl over 1f out* **12/1**

300- **9** 4 **Lifted Way**[188] 5082 5-9-13 **74** ........ WRyan 7 — 59
(PRChamings) *hld up in rr: rdn over 2f out: sn no prog: wknd over 1f out* **33/1**

00-0 **10** nk **Zeis (IRE)**[22] 961 4-9-12 **73** ........ ACulhane 6 — 58
(HMorrison) *dwlt: sn in last and detached bef 1/2-way: no ch after: kpt on fnl f* **50/1**

00-0 **11** 1/2 **Jools**[31] 870 6-9-9 **70** ........ DaneO'Neill 8 — 53
(DKIvory) *b: hld up in rr: rdn over 2f out: no prog: wknd over 1f out* **20/1**

2401 **12** 1 **Bressbee (USA)**[9] 1037 6-9-11 **72** 6ex ........ (b) VSlattery 1 — 53
(NPLittmoden) *dwlt: sn rdn in rr: a struggling* **20/1**

1m 37.1s (-2.41) **Going Correction** -0.15s/f (Stan) — **12** Ran SP% **122.0**

Speed ratings: **106,104,103,103,103 102,98,97,93,93 93,92**CSF £27.41 TOTE £8.20: £2.40, £1.30; EX 36.80 TRIFECTA Pl: DInD 1.00; Sir L 0.90; T/C - K-CE-DInD - 40.68; K-CE-SirL 59.81.

**Owner** Peter Crate **Bred** His Highness The Aga Khan's Studs S C **Trained** Epsom, Surrey

**FOCUS**

A modest but competitive handicap that appeared to favour those who raced near to the pace. The winning time was good and the form looks solid, with the runner-up well handicapped at present.

**NOTEBOOK**

**Katiypour(IRE)** had never previously won on this surface but he handles it as well as he does any other and won nicely and under a good ride from Miles, who kept things simple. This was compensation for a slightly unlucky run round here three days previously and he should continue to go well - a return to this course and distance is his next possible target.

**Concer Eto**, dropped 5lb off the back of a couple of poor efforts round here recently, was backed as though about to return to form and did so. He travelled as well as anything for most of the way, but was probably waited with for too long and the winner got first run. He should be able to confirm this promise next time given similar conditions, but there will be no flashy prices around.

**Deeper In Debt**, 6lb higher than when last winning on this surface, looked to have every chance and can have no excuses, but he was by no means knocked about when his chance of winning was gone.

**Sir Laughalot** continues in good form but also continues to struggle to get his head in front. Still a maiden, there are races to be won with despite the fact he is becoming frustrating.

**Musical Gift**, in cheekpieces for the first time, travelled nicely, well off the pace, but had to be switched for a run in the straight after making headway and never really looked like getting to the winner.

## 1119 BET DIRECT INTERACTIVE H'CAP — 7f (P)

3:00 (3:00) (E) (0-75,75) 3-Y-0 — £3,493 (£1,075; £537; £268) Stalls Low

Form — RPR

0-41 **1** **Eccentric**[26] 927 3-9-3 **71** ........ DHolland 1 — 75
(AndrewReid) *b: b.hind: mde virtually all: gng best 2f out: shkn up and clr over 1f out: comf* **7/4**[1]

14-6 **2** 1 1/2 **The Job**[79] 462 3-8-5 **59** ........ WRyan 6 — 59
(ADSmith) *t.k.h: hld up bhd ldrs: rdn and effrt over 2f out: chsd wnr 1f out: no imp* **7/1**

0364 **3** shd **Docklands Blue (IRE)**[3] 1086 3-8-0 **54** ........ CCatlin 4 — 54
(NPLittmoden) *hld up in last pair: prog over 2f out: drvn and styd on same pce fr over 1f out: nvr able to chal* **9/2**[3]

606- **4** 1/2 **Black Oval**[143] 5916 3-8-5 **62** ........ SHitchcott(3) 7 — 60
(MRChannon) *w wnr: rdn over 2f out: unable qck wl over 1f out: one pce after* **10/1**

04-1 **5** 3 **Generous Gesture (IRE)**[23] 956 3-9-7 **75** ........ JMackay 8 — 65
(MLWBell) *plld hrd early: w ldrs: rdn over 2f out: fdd jst over 1f out* **5/2**[2]

40-0 **6** 7 **Sachin**[29] 891 3-8-8 **65** ........ RMiles(3) 2 — 36
(JRBoyle) *s.i.s: racd in last pair and reminders early: struggling fr over 2f out* **16/1**

152- **7** 1 **Disco Diva**[151] 5789 3-9-1 **69** ........ DaneO'Neill 3 — 38
(MBlanshard) *t.k.h: trckd ldrs tl wknd over 2f out* **12/1**

30-0 **8** 3 1/2 **Wendy's Girl (IRE)**[13] 1008 3-8-10 **64** ........ TWoodley 5 — 23
(RPElliott) *racd v wd: chsd ldrs tl wknd wl over 2f out* **33/1**

1m 25.59s (-0.41) **Going Correction** -0.15s/f (Stan) — **8** Ran SP% **121.2**

Speed ratings: **96,94,94,93,90 82,81,77**CSF £16.16 CT £50.77 TOTE £2.60: £1.20, £3.10, £1.10; EX 12.10.

**Owner** A S Reid **Bred** A S Reid **Trained** Mill Hill, London NW7

**FOCUS**

This featured some disappointing sorts, but take nothing away from Eccentric, who won nicely and is progressing.

**NOTEBOOK**

**Eccentric**, off the mark under an enterprising ride in a course and distance maiden on his previous run, was not ridden with anywhere near as much force this time and won with a little bit to spare. He has beaten very little of note, but is progressing and remains one to have on your side.

**The Job** gained his only win to date in a seller but continues to acquit himself with credit outside of that grade.

**Docklands Blue(IRE)** appeared to run her race but is proving hard to win with.

**Black Oval** has not won since scoring on her debut last season. She tried to go with the winner but proved no match for that one and may well have needed this first run in 143 days.

**Generous Gesture(IRE)**, off the mark in a weak maiden over six furlongs at Southwell on her latest start, was far too keen on this step up to seven furlongs.

## 1120 LITTLEWOODS BET DIRECT CLASSIFIED STKS — 1m (P)

3:35 (3:35) (E) 3-Y-0 — £3,464 (£1,066; £533; £266) Stalls High

Form — RPR

-41 **1** **Certifiable**[29] 890 3-9-0 68 ........ DHolland 8 — 77
(AndrewReid) *b: b.hind: mde virtually all: rdn 2f out: hrd pressed fnl f: battled on wl last 100y* **6/1**

31-1 **2** 1/2 **Whitgift Rock**[79] 466 3-9-2 72 ........ PDoe 4 — 78
(SDow) *hld up in tch: prog 2f out: effrt on inner over 1f out: pressed wnr fnl f: nt qckn last 75y* **5/2**[1]

0-1 **3** 1 1/2 **Tiger Tiger (FR)**[34] 846 3-9-2 72 ........ PDobbs 1 — 75
(JamiePoulton) *hld up in last: prog 3f out: rdn and styd on fr over 1f out: tk 3rd last stride* **7/1**

0221 **4** nk **Alfridini**[18] 985 3-9-0 70 ........ DaneO'Neill 7 — 72
(DRCElsworth) *lw: t.k.h: pressed ldrs: rdn and effrt 2f out: chsd wnr briefly over 1f out: one pce fnl f* **3/1**[2]

63-2 **5** nk **Catalini**[12] 1015 3-9-5 75 ........ ACulhane 2 — 76
(MRChannon) *racd in last pair: pushed along over 4f out: drvn and effrt over 2f out : styd on fr over 1f out* **4/1**[3]

045- **6** 3 1/2 **Anduril**[145] 5886 3-9-1 71 ........ JTate 6 — 64
(JMPEustace) *t.k.h: chsd wnr 5f out to over 1f out: wknd* **25/1**

-521 **7** 3/4 **Hawkit (USA)**[13] 1012 3-9-1 71 ........ VSlattery 3 — 62
(JAOsborne) *chsd ldrs: rdn 3f out: fdd fnl 2f* **14/1**

036- **8** 11 **Stylish Sunrise (IRE)**[141] 5932 3-9-0 70 ........ MFenton 5 — 36
(MLWBell) *chsd wnr to 5f out: wknd 3f out: t.o* **25/1**

1m 38.47s (-1.04) **Going Correction** -0.15s/f (Stan) — **8** Ran SP% **114.7**

Speed ratings: **99,98,97,96,96 92,92,81**CSF £21.50 TOTE £6.10: £1.60, £1.40, £2.10; EX 22.70.

**Owner** A S Reid **Bred** A S Reid **Trained** Mill Hill, London NW7

**FOCUS**

An incredibly tight classified event with just 3lb separating the whole field on adjusted official figures. Five of the eight runners won last time and the form looks solid.

**NOTEBOOK**

**Certifiable**, something of a tricky customer in the past, has really taken to this Polytrack surface and followed up his course and distance maiden win with a fine effort from the front. He should keep improving.

**Whitgift Rock**, who claimed the scalp of the progressive Skidmark when last seen winning over this course and distance 79 days ago, had every chance to get to the winner in the straight but simply found that one too strong. He is entitled to be sharper next time.

**Tiger Tiger(FR)** got off the mark over this course and distance in maiden company on his previous outing and ran very creditably in this more competitive heat. He is lightly raced and open to further improvement.

**Alfridini**, 5lb higher than when winning over ten furlongs here on his latest outing, was a little keen on this drop back in trip and stuck out wide for much of the way. Despite that, he still had every chance in the straight but proved unable to quicken. He can be given another chance back up in trip.

**Catalini** probably failed to achieve a great deal when runner-up in a course and distance maiden on his debut on this surface and was always going to find this tougher. However, this was not a bad effort off top weight.

## 1121 BET RUGBY LEAGUE @ BETDIRECT.CO.UK CLAIMING STKS — 7f (P)

4:10 (4:11) (F) 3-Y-0+ — £3,017 (£862; £431) Stalls Low

Form — RPR

0-01 **1** **Supreme Salutation**[8] 1043 8-9-7 60 ........ ACulhane 5 — 67
(DWChapman) *dwlt: sn in midfield: rdn and effrt over 2f out: chsd ldng pair 1f out: styd on wl to ld last strides* **5/1**[2]

3500 **2** 3/4 **Illusive (IRE)**[3] 1087 7-9-9 60 ........ (b) MTebbutt 6 — 67
(MWigham) *t.k.h: prom: chsd ldr over 2f out: drvn to ld ins fnl f: hdd last strides* **14/1**

46-0 **3** nk **Foley Prince**[22] 965 3-8-7 67 ........ JMackay 4 — 65
(DFlood) *b: chsd ldr: led wl over 2f out and kicked on: hdd ins fnl f: kpt on* **5/1**[2]

-215 **4** 2 1/2 **Kinsman (IRE)**[37] 815 7-9-2 58 ........ (b) RMiles(3) 13 — 55
(TDMccarthy) *hld up in last pair: prog over 2f out: hanging but styd on fr over 1f out: nrst fin* **8/1**[3]

0-04 **5** 1 **Majhool**[30] 886 5-9-6 67 ........ DHolland 2 — 54
(GLMoore) *t.k.h: hld up: hit rail 5f out: effrt over 3f out: styd on fr over 1f out: nvr able to chal* **7/2**[1]

2323 **6** 1 3/4 **Lucayan Monarch**[2] 1095 6-9-4 55 ........ (p) BReilly(3) 12 — 50
(PSMcentee) *racd in midfield: drvn and effrt to chse ldrs 2f out: no imp fnl f* **8/1**[3]

2531 **7** nk **Lady Piste (IRE)**[22] 965 3-7-7 54 ........ (vt) BSwarbrick(7) 1 — 43
(PDEvans) *prom: rdn over 2f out: fdd over 1f out* **8/1**[3]

0030 **8** 1 **The Gay Fox**[12] 1020 10-9-1 45 ........ (bt) LPKeniry(3) 9 — 43
(BGPowell) *racd in midfield: n.m.r over 3f out: drvn over 2f out: one pce and n.d* **25/1**

0305 **9** 1 3/4 **Effective**[10] 1032 4-9-9 60 ........ (v[1]) DaneO'Neill 11 — 44
(APJarvis) *tk kene hold: pressed ldrs: rdn over 2f out: wknd over 1f out* **25/1**

000- **10** 1 1/2 **Eva Peron (IRE)**[154] 5729 4-8-9 59 ........ CHaddon(7) 3 — 33
(WGMTurner) *racd in midfield: rdn 1/2-way: no prog and btn 2f out* **33/1**

46-0 **11** 1 **Pagan Storm (USA)**[34] 847 4-9-2 67 ........ (b) KristinStubbs(7) 7 — 37
(MrsLStubbs) *a in rr: shuffled along and no prog over 1f out* **20/1**

0620 **12** 1 1/2 **Social Contract**[12] 1020 7-9-5 45 ........ (v) JFEgan 14 — 29
(SDow) *a in rr: rdn and no prog over 2f out* **33/1**

5456 **13** 3 1/2 **Back At De Front (IRE)**[8] 1047 3-8-3 59 ........ CCatlin 10 — 18
(NEBerry) *a wl in rr: struggling fr 3f out* **25/1**

0/0- **14** *5* **Orion's Belt**[166] 5509 4-8-13 55 .......... RThomas(5) 8 5
(GBBalding) *bit bkwd: t.k.h: prom tl wknd rapidly over 2f out* **50/1**

00-0 **15** *5* **Beenaboutabit**[52] 665 6-8-13 30 .......... (p) VSlattery 15 —
(MrsLCJewell) *led at fast pce to wl over 2f out: wknd rapidly* **66/1**

1m 24.3s (-1.70) **Going Correction** -0.15s/f (Stan)
**WFA** 3 from 4yo+ 15lb **15** Ran SP% **121.2**
Speed ratings: **103,102,101,98,97 95,95,94,92,90 89,87,83,78,72**CSF £65.35 TOTE £5.00: £2.40, £3.80, £2.30; EX 88.10.The winner was claimed by Dean Ivory for £8,000. Foley Prince was claimed by Steff Liddiard for £9,000
**Owner** David W Chapman **Bred** M I Marsh **Trained** Stillington, N Yorks

**FOCUS**
A very tricky claimer, with the favourite below form again, in which Supreme Salutation overcame a possible bias in favour of prominent racers over this sort of trip to follow up a recent Southwell success.

**NOTEBOOK**
**Supreme Salutation** had never previously won on this surface but had half a chance at the weights and made the most of it to follow up his recent success in this grade at Southwell. He was the only horse on this card in races up to a mile (there were five) to come from off the pace and emerges with real credit. He will now join Dean Ivory.
**Illusive(IRE)**, who had 6lb to find with the winner at weights, is incredibly hard to win but looked to have this in safe keeping half a furlong out. However, there was no answer when the winner pounced.
**Foley Prince**, second best in at the weights, was given a positive ride and looked to hold every chance.
**Kinsman(IRE)** never really threatened the principals and was also noted to be hanging. He does not win very often.
**Majhool**, the best in at the weights, was too keen and also ridden with more restraint than is often the case.

## 1122 NEW SITE @ BETDIRECT.CO.UK H'CAP 1m 4f (P)
**4:40** (4:40) (E) (0-75,73) 4-Y-0+ **£3,454** (£1,063; £531; £265) **Stalls** Low

Form RPR

4034 **1** **Classic Role**[30] 887 5-9-12 70 .......... (v1) ACulhane 1 84
(RIngram) *lw: hld up in tch and a gng wl: prog over 2f out: led wl over 1f out: rdn and styd on wl fnl f* **4/1**[3]

1311 **2** *1½* **Steely Dan**[3] 1088 5-9-12 70 6ex .......... NPollard 8 82
(JRBest) *lw: hld up in last pair: smooth prog over 2f out: shkn up to chse wnr jst over 1f out: kpt on but no imp* **5/2**[1]

2-10 **3** *3½* **So Vital**[36] 827 4-9-13 73 .......... RPrice 3 79
(JPearce) *lw: chsd ldrs: pushed along fr 1/2-way: effrt u.p 2f out: kpt on same pce* **25/1**

001- **4** *2½* **Grand Wizard**[87] 6259 4-9-12 72 .......... MTebbutt 2 74
(WJarvis) *hld up towards rr: nt clr run and lost pl 3f out: sn drvn: kpt on one pce fr over 1f out: no ch* **16/1**

0214 **5** *½* **Anyhow (IRE)**[7] 1053 7-9-6 64 .......... DHolland 7 65
(MissKMGeorge) *hld up in rr: pushed along and prog over 2f out: hemmed in against rail fr wl over 1f out to 1f out: nt rcvr* **3/1**[2]

-010 **6** *shd* **Private Benjamin**[30] 887 4-9-0 60 .......... DKinsella 4 61
(JamiePoulton) *prom: rdn to ld over 2f out: hdd & wknd wl over 1f out* **25/1**

0/12 **7** *3* **General**[10] 1030 7-9-7 65 .......... VSlattery 10 61
(NPLittmoden) *pressed ldr: rdn to ld over 3f out: hdd over 2f out: wknd wl over 1f out* **12/1**

03 **8** *3½* **Rainbow World (IRE)**[18] 984 4-9-10 70 .......... MFenton 9 61
(AndrewReid) *b: b.hind: racd in midfield: drvn to press ldrs over 2f out: wknd rapidly over 1f out* **25/1**

4-41 **9** *3* **Crossways**[27] 919 6-9-10 68 .......... DaneO'Neill 5 54
(PDEvans) *b: pressed ldng pair to 4f out: wknd 3f out* **11/2**

-234 **10** *2½* **Ellen Mooney**[45] 737 5-9-9 70 .......... THamilton(3) 6 52
(RPElliott) *led to over 3f out: sn wknd* **16/1**

2m 31.3s (-2.68) **Going Correction** -0.15s/f (Stan)
**WFA** 4 from 5yo+ 2lb **10** Ran SP% **120.0**
Speed ratings: **102,101,98,97,96 96,94,92,90,88**CSF £14.53 CT £212.01 TOTE £5.30: £1.40, £1.30, £5.00; EX 19.20 Place 6 £17.72, Place 5 £10.36.
**Owner** Pillar To Post Racing **Bred** P T Tellwright **Trained** Epsom, Surrey

**FOCUS**
Just a fair handicap with one or two looking a bit high in the weights off the back of maiden successes.

**NOTEBOOK**
**Classic Role** has generally been running well without winning this All-Weather season but, off his lowest every mark on this surface with a visor on for the first time, he ran out a clear-cut winner. This will have boosted his confidence.
**Steely Dan** has been in absolutely fantastic form this year, winning three races from seven furlongs to a mile two. This was his first run at the trip - his dam won over it - and he probably stayed, but he is a horse who does not find a lot off the bridle and was no match for the winner under his 6lb penalty for a success just three days previously.
**So Vital** left behind a shocking effort at Southwell to bounce back to form, but he does look a little high in the handicap.
**Grand Wizard**, did not have things go his way as he was short of room inside the final half mile but, on this evidence, he looks harshly treated for his maiden win.
**Anyhow(IRE)** was given a poor ride by Holland. He went for an ambitious run up the rail on turning for home, but was blocked and had to stop riding to avoid collision with the horse in front. When Anyhow finally got in the clear she was far from knocked about and can be rated much better than the bare form would suggest. *Official explanation: jockey said mare was unlucky in running.*
**Private Benjamin** *Official explanation: jockey said gelding hung left from the bend.*
**General**, a pound lower than when second in a Class C at Southwell on his latest run, failed to reproduce that sort of from on this faster surface.
**Rainbow World(IRE)** *Official explanation: jockey said colt had lost its action in the last 2 furlongs.*
T/Plt: £53.00 to a £1 stake. Pool £39,299.10, 540.95 winning tickets T/Qpdt: £23.30 to a £1 stake. Pool £3,214.00, 102.00 winning tickets JN

# 1111 DONCASTER (L-H)
Saturday, March 27

**OFFICIAL GOING: Good**
Wind: almost nil Weather: overcast

## 1123 MITSUBISHI DIAMOND VISION CONDITIONS STKS 1m (S)
**1:40** (1:40) (C) 3-Y-0 **£8,412** (£3,190; £1,595; £725) **Stalls** High

Form RPR

021- **1** **Divine Gift**[141] 5938 3-8-13 87 .......... PRobinson 5 102
(MAJarvis) *mde most: rdn and qcknd clr ent last: comf* **9/2**[3]

110- **2** *3½* **Gold History (USA)**[177] 5333 3-9-3 97 .......... JFanning 1 98
(MJohnston) *cl up: ev ch 2f out: sn rdn and one pce ent last* **7/2**[2]

43-0 **3** *¾* **Makfool (FR)**[7] 1063 3-8-13 96 .......... ACulhane 7 92
(MRChannon) *tacked ldrs on inner: effrt 2f out: sn rdn and one pce ent last* **11/2**

121- **4** *½* **New Mexican**[159] 5674 3-9-5 103 .......... (p) JPSpencer 2 97
(MrsJRRamsden) *trckd ldrs: effrt on outer over 2f out: sn rdn: drvn and one pce appr last* **3/1**[1]

334- **5** *1¼* **Kelucia (IRE)**[147] 5874 3-8-8 104 .......... RFfrench 6 84
(JSGoldie) *t.k.h: trckd ldrs: effrt 3f out: rdn and wknd over 1f out* **7/2**[2]

-203 **6** *9* **Fools Entire**[52] 675 3-8-8 69 .......... BReilly(3) 3 67
(JAGilbert) *plld hrd: chsd ldrs: rdn along 3f out and sn outpcd* **66/1**

00 **7** *5* **Well Knit**[7] 1063 3-8-6 .......... PaulEddery 8 51
(PWD'Arcy) *dwlt: a rr: pushed along and bhd fr 1/2-way* **100/1**

1m 41.44s (-0.20) **Going Correction** +0.075s/f (Good) **7** Ran SP% **105.5**
Speed ratings: **104,100,99,99,98 89,84**CSF £17.32 TOTE £6.00: £2.10, £2.30; EX 24.50.
**Owner** B E Nielsen **Bred** Bloomsbury Stud **Trained** Newmarket, Suffolk

**FOCUS**
A tactical affair with the first two one-two throughout. This is usually a decent event and the winner looked an improved performer.

**NOTEBOOK**
**Divine Gift**, a progressive juvenile who won here in November on his fourth and final start, is a robust-type who has a choppy action. He stepped up the gallop from the front and came clear entering the last. He will now take his chance in the Italian 2000 Guineas.
**Gold History(USA)**, who lost his unbeaten record in a Group Three at Newmarket in October, took on the winner but in the end proved no match. The outing will not be lost on him.
**Makfool(FR)**, having his second outing in a week, looked backward in his coat and was very warm at the start.
**New Mexican**, a tall type, wore cheekpieces for the first time. He was meeting Makfool on 6lb worse terms having defeated him just half a length in a Listed race at Pontefract in October.
**Kelucia(IRE)**, who had at least 12lb in hand all round on official ratings, has not grown at all and had two handlers in the paddock. She has something to prove now.

## 1124 KONICA EAST DONCASTER SHIELD (CONDITIONS STKS) 1m 4f
**2:10** (2:10) (B) 4-Y-0+ **£12,540** (£4,807; £2,403; £1,149) **Stalls** Low

Form RPR

06-0 **1** **Royal Cavalier**[84] 418 7-8-12 97 .......... WSupple 2 107
(RHollinshead) *trckd ldrs: hdwy on ins to ld over 2f out: kpt on wl* **33/1**

305- **2** *1* **Dunhill Star (IRE)**[252] 3400 4-8-10 108 .......... MHills 1 106
(BWHills) *hld up: n.m.r on inner over 4f out: edgd rt 2f out: styd on fnl f: no real imp* **3/1**[3]

255- **3** *1½* **Systematic**[189] 5073 5-8-12 111 .......... KDarley 7 103
(MJohnston) *chsd ldr: chal over 2f out: styd on same pce* **15/8**[1]

11/- **4** *2* **Forest Magic (IRE)**[511] 5594 4-8-10 .......... DHolland 5 100
(PWD'Arcy) *trckd ldrs: sltly hmpd 2f out: one pce* **11/1**

120- **5** *1¼* **Heisse**[307] 1857 4-8-10 .......... JPMurtagh 3 98
(DRLoder) *lw: hld up: effrt over 3f out: sn rdn: kpt on fnl f: nvr a threat* **5/2**[2]

310- **6** *3½* **King's Thought**[210] 4571 5-8-12 98 .......... RHughes 6 93
(SGollings) *led tl over 2f out: lost pl over 1f out* **33/1**

012- **7** *3* **Perfect Storm**[140] 5952 5-9-2 92 .......... NCallan 4 93
(MBlanshard) *hld up: smooth hdwy over 3f out: nvr rchd ldrs* **14/1**

100- **8** *2* **Ravenglass (USA)**[143] 5926 5-8-12 83 .......... RHavlin 8 86
(JGMO'Shea) *s.i.s: sn chsng ldrs: pushed along 6f out: outpcd fnl 3f* **125/1**

2m 33.87s (-2.01) **Going Correction** +0.075s/f (Good)
**WFA** 4 from 5yo+ 2lb **8** Ran SP% **110.0**
Speed ratings: **109,108,107,106,105 102,100,99**CSF £120.83 TOTE £21.80: £3.30, £1.40, £1.40; EX 90.60.
**Owner** The Three R'S **Bred** Longdon Stud Ltd **Trained** Upper Longdon, Staffs
■ Stewards Enquiry : M Hills four-day ban: careless riding (Apr 7,8,10,11)

**FOCUS**
A sound pace, but an unpredictable result with the highest-rated horses below par, and not form to take too literally.

**NOTEBOOK**
**Royal Cavalier**, the oldest horse in the line-up, has a good record round here. He crept through on the inner and, once in front, never really looked like being overhauled.
**Dunhill Star(IRE)**, below par on his final two starts at three, is a moderate walker. Left short of room on the inner turning in, he interfered with Forest Magic when making his way to the outside. He kept on in pursuit of the winner but was never going to get in a real blow. He at least showed he stays this trip.
**Systematic** looked fit and was much cooler than on some occasions in the past, although he planted himself and had to be dismounted and led the last 100 yards or so to the start. He had the leader covered, but under strong pressure, never looked like picking up sufficiently. How much of the ability he showed at three remains to be seen.
**Forest Magic(IRE)**, who won his final two starts at two, missed the whole of last year. Fitted with a cross noseband, he was going nowhere when nudged to one side by the runner-up two furlongs out. Last year he was not risked on fast ground.
**Heisse**, absent since finishing seventh in last year's Italian Derby, looked a picture of wellbeing but after being anchored at the back he ran very flat, only staying on when it was all over. He is surely capable of better than he showed here.
**King's Thought**, taken to post early, made this a true test, but he had plenty to find and has yet to show he stays this far.

## 1125 FREEPHONE STANLEYBET LINCOLN (HERITAGE H'CAP) 1m (S)
**2:45** (2:47) (B) 4-Y-0+ **£65,000** (£20,000; £10,000; £5,000) **Stalls** High

Form RPR

210- **1** **Babodana**[126] 6051 4-9-10 107 .......... PRobinson 23 116
(MHTompkins) *trckd ldrs stands side: swtchd lft and hdwy over 2f out: led 11/2f out: rdn ent last and styd on wl* **20/1**

-106 **2** *¾* **Quito (IRE)**[7] 1065 7-9-4 101 5ex .......... (b) ACulhane 16 108
(DWChapman) *bhd stands side: hdwy 2f out: str run ins last: nt rch wnr* **50/1**

400- **3** *hd* **Dark Charm (FR)**[155] 5732 5-8-7 90 .......... PHanagan 12 97
(RAFahey) *swtchd rt & rcd stands' side: hdwy 2f out: str run ent last: kpt on u.p* **20/1**

233- **4** *nk* **Wing Commander**[168] 5484 5-8-6 92 .......... THamilton(3) 24 98
(RAFahey) *towards rr stands side: hdwy over 2f out: rdn to chse ldrs over 1f out: kpt on fnl f* **33/1**

121- **5** *1½* **Alkaadhem**[240] 3720 4-9-3 100 .......... WSupple 5 110+
(MPTregoning) *trckd ldrs far side: hdwy over 2f out: led that gp 11/2f out and ev ch tl rdn and nt qckn ins last* **8/1**[2]

600- **6** *nk* **Jay Gee's Choice**[142] 5936 4-8-7 93 .......... DCorby(3) 14 95
(MRChannon) *bit bkwd: overall ldr stands side: rdn over 2f out: hdd 11/2f out and kpt on same pce* **40/1**

004- **7** *¾* **Blue Spinnaker (IRE)**[169] 5469 5-8-7 90 .......... DaleGibson 13 90+
(MWEasterby) *bit bkwd: swtchd rt and hmpd s: in tch stands side: hdwy over 2f out: sn rdn and kpt on: nrst fin* **66/1**

000- **8** *shd* **Unshakable (IRE)**[147] [5873] 5-8-9 **92** ........ JFEgan 19 92
(BobJones) *lw: hld up towards rr stands side: hdwy 2f out: sn rdn and kpt on ins last: nrst fin* **12/1**

110- **9** *shd* **Desert Opal**[147] [5873] 4-8-12 **95** ........ RHughes 2 102+
(JHMGosden) *dwlt: sn in tch far side: hdwy to trck ldrs 1/2-way: effrt and ev ch 2f out: sn rdn and one pce* **11/1**[3]

240- **10** *hd* **Pentecost**[175] [5365] 5-9-0 **100** ........ LPKeniry(3) 18 100
(AMBalding) *hld up stands side: hdwy over 2f out: rdn and kpt on fnl f: nrst fin* **40/1**

00-0 **11** *nk* **Serieux**[52] [677] 5-8-10 **93** ow1 ........ JPMurtagh 7 99+
(MrsAJPerrett) *cl up far side: effrt to ld that gp over 2f out: sn rdn: hdd over 1f out and grad wknd* **33/1**

110- **12** *shd* **Fremen (USA)**[182] [5210] 4-8-10 **93** ........ DHolland 10 99+
(SirMichaelStoute) *led far side: pushed along and hdd over 2f out: sn rdn and wknd over 1f out* **8/1**[2]

-156 **13** *1 1/4* **Blue Sky Thinking (IRE)**[7] [1062] 5-9-0 **97** 5ex ........ DarrenWilliams 4 100+
(KRBurke) *hld up far side: hdwy 3f out: rdn 2f out: kpt on same pce* **20/1**

03-0 **14** *nk* **Dumaran (IRE)**[28] [915] 6-8-9 **92** ........ MFenton 3 94+
(WJMusson) *bhd far side: hdwy over 2f out: styd on fnl f: nvr a factor* **66/1**

322- **15** *3/4* **Flighty Fellow (IRE)**[169] [5469] 4-8-9 **92** ........(b) SSanders 8 93+
(TDEasterby) *bhd far side tl styd on fnl 2f: nvr a factor* **25/1**

50- **16** *nk* **Craiova (IRE)**[147] [5873] 5-8-7 **90** ........ SDrowne 20 83
(BWHills) *in tch stands side: rdn along over 2f out: grad wknd* **25/1**

304- **17** *1 1/2* **El Coto**[175] [5366] 4-8-13 **96** ........ TQuinn 11 93+
(BAMcmahon) *hld up far side: hdwy to chse ldrs 3f out: rdn 2f out and sn btn* **20/1**

4/1- **18** *3/4* **Chivalry**[21] [5365] 5-8-12 **95** ........ GDuffield 1 90+
(JHowardJohnson) *cl up far side: rdn along 3f out: grad wknd fnl 2f* **16/1**

455- **19** *3 1/2* **Pablo**[147] [5872] 5-9-8 **105** ........ MHills 21 85
(BWHills) *midfield stands' side: hdwy to chse ldrs 3f out: rdn 2f out: hung lft; wknd appr fnl f* **7/1**[1]

00-0 **20** *7* **Onlytime Will Tell**[7] [1066] 6-8-12 **95** ........ JFanning 9 67+
(DNicholls) *swtg: a rr far side* **80/1**

000- **21** *3* **Norton (IRE)**[196] [4878] 7-9-1 **98** ........ KDarley 17 56
(TGMills) *swtg: prom stands side: rdn along 3f out: sn wknd* **11/1**[3]

330- **22** *3* **Tough Love**[245] [3589] 5-8-10 **93** ........ KDalgleish 22 45
(TDEasterby) *cl up stands side: rdn along and hung lft over 2f out: sn wknd* **14/1**

126- **23** *hd* **Convent Girl (IRE)**[175] [5365] 4-8-13 **96** ........ RHavlin 6 54+
(MrsPNDutfield) *chsd ldrs far side: rdn along 3f out and sn wknd* **25/1**

00-4 **24** *1* **Our Teddy (IRE)**[52] [677] 4-8-10 **93** ........(v[1]) MartinDwyer 15 49+
(AMBalding) *swtchd to far side s: sn cl up: rdn along 3f out and sn wknd* **14/1**

1m 40.15s (-1.49) **Going Correction** +0.075s/f (Good) **24** Ran SP% **125.8**
Speed ratings: **110,109,109,108,107 106,106,106,106,105 105,105,104,103,103 102,101,100,97,90 87,84,83,82**CSF £770.73 CT £18522.59 TOTE £32.80: £6.70, £8.60, £7.00, £7.30; EX 684.70 Trifecta £10864.20 Part won. Pool: £15,301.69 - 0.20 winning tickets..

**Owner** M P Bowring **Bred** Loan And Development Corporation **Trained** Newmarket, Suffolk

■ Babodana equalled Cataldi's weight-carrying record of 1985. The Lincoln is the first BHB-designated 'heritage handicap'.

■ Stewards Enquiry : R Hughes caution: used whip with excessive frequency

**FOCUS**

The usual solid handicap form; the field split into two groups and the first four home raced on the stands' side.

**NOTEBOOK**

**Babodana**, who was highly progressive at three, gave weight away all round from stall 23 of 24. He is now likely to try his hand in a Group Three in Germany.

**Quito(IRE)**, 9lb higher than when he won last year's Ayr Gold Cup, has proved himself better than ever on the All-Weather this winter. He burst through inside the last and clearly stays the mile.

**Dark Charm(FR)**, a keen sort, was having his first outing for his new yard. Loaded with the help of a rug, he came across to the stands' side group. He finished with quite a flourish and was clearly suited by the step up to a mile.

**Wing Commander**, out of luck since his two-year-old days, was having his first run for his new trainer and was drawn hard against the stands' side rail. He ran right up to his best but looks weighted to the limit.

**Alkaadhem** ◆, prepared in Italy, looked an absolute picture. He came out best of those on the far side and this lightly-raced individual deserves rich compensation.

**Jay Gee's Choice**, who looked in need of the outing, showed a very scratchy action. Gelded since last year, he showed bags of toe to take them along on the stands' side and seven furlongs might suit him better.

**Blue Spinnaker(IRE)**, who looked in need of the outing, was knocked out of his stride early on. Staying on in good style at the end, he should add to his record at five.

**Unshakable(IRE)**, now a gelding, took the eye beforehand. He stayed on in his own time and there is a nice prize to be won with him this year.

**Desert Opal**, a keen type, came out second best of the far side group. He still has plenty of potential.

**Fremen(USA)**, the ante-post favourite, was a negative on the day. He probably did too much in front on the far side and did not get home. He will bounce back.

**Craiova(IRE)** *Official explanation: jockey said horse hung left.*

**Pablo**, who took this a year ago from an 8lb lower mark, was sent off favourite to complete the double but he wanted to do nothing but hang left and ended up in the centre of the track. *Official explanation: jockey said horse hung left.*

## 1126 CAMMIDGE TROPHY (LISTED RACE) 6f

**3:15** (3:18) (A) 3-Y-0+ **£19,500** (£6,000; £3,000; £1,500) **Stalls** High

Form RPR

620- **1** **Goldeva**[140] [5953] 5-8-11 91 ........ ACulhane 16 101
(RHollinshead) *mid-div: effrt 2f out: r.o to ld 100yds out: hld on nr fin* **40/1**

006- **2** *nk* **Orientor**[155] [5732] 6-9-7 104 ........ JPMurtagh 17 110
(JSGoldie) *hld up towards rr: smooth hdwy 2f out: sn nt clr run: squeezed through ins last: jst hld* **6/1**[3]

365- **3** *nk* **The Kiddykid (IRE)**[231] [3979] 4-9-2 106 ........ JPSpencer 12 104
(PDEvans) *w ldrs: led 2f out tl last 100yds: no ex* **16/1**

010- **4** *3/4* **Chookie Heiton (IRE)**[224] [4176] 6-9-2 106 ........ RWinston 3 102
(ISemple) *rr div: hdwy on outer over 2f out: nt qckn fnl f* **10/1**

125- **5** *hd* **Monsieur Bond (IRE)**[148] [5866] 4-9-5 110 ........ FLynch 4 104
(BSmart) *sn in rr: nt clr run over 2f out tl r.o wl ins last* **11/1**

400- **6** *nk* **Smokin Beau**[177] [5331] 7-9-2 98 ........ MHenry 11 100
(NPLittmoden) *w ldrs: nt qckn fnl f* **25/1**

23-0 **7** *hd* **Fire Up The Band**[7] [1061] 5-9-2 106 ........ ANicholls 2 100
(DNicholls) *stmbld s: sn chsng ldrs: kpt on same pce fnl f* **7/2**[1]

063- **8** *nk* **Crimson Silk**[140] [5953] 4-9-2 102 ........ PaulEddery 7 99
(DHaydnJones) *s.i.s: bhd and pushed along: hdwy on wd outside 2f out: styd on same pce appr fnl f* **20/1**

-552 **9** *3/4* **Law Breaker (IRE)**[2] [1106] 6-9-2 85 ........ BReilly 5 97
(JAGilbert) *mid-div: hdwy over 2f out: sn chsng ldrs: one pce appr fnl f* **25/1**

044- **10** *hd* **Halmahera (IRE)**[129] [6034] 9-9-2 102 ........ NCallan 10 96
(KARyan) *in tch: outpcd fnl 2f* **25/1**

305- **11** *1 3/4* **Golden Nun**[140] [5953] 4-8-11 99 ........(p) KDarley 8 86
(TDEasterby) *sn bhd: styd on appr fnl f* **20/1**

261- **12** *shd* **Will He Wish**[152] [5791] 8-9-2 92 ........(b) RHughes 15 91
(SGollings) *hld up towards rr: nt clr run 2f out: styd on steadily ins last* **33/1**

00-0 **13** *1* **Striking Ambition**[7] [1061] 4-9-2 113 ........ DHolland 14 88
(GCBravery) *led tl 2f out: lost pl over 1f out* **5/1**[2]

350- **14** *1 1/2* **Coconut Penang (IRE)**[183] [5186] 4-9-2 98 ........ SDrowne 9 83
(BRMillman) *chsd ldrs: lost pl over 1f out* **33/1**

005- **15** *2* **Flashing Blade**[148] [5854] 4-8-11 85 ........ WSupple 13 72
(BAMcmahon) *chsd ldrs 3f: sn lost pl* **100/1**

3315 **16** *1* **Time N Time Again**[14] [1007] 6-9-2 74 ........(p) GDuffield 6 74
(EJAlston) *chsd ldrs: reminders 3f out: lost pl 2f out* **80/1**

140- **17** *1 3/4* **Capricho (IRE)**[167] [5527] 7-9-7 110 ........ TQuinn 1 74
(JAkehurst) *hld up and bhd: sme hdwy on outside 2f out: sn lost pl* **11/1**

1m 13.89s (-0.39) **Going Correction** +0.075s/f (Good) **17** Ran SP% **116.4**
Speed ratings: **105,104,104,103,102 102,102,101,100,100 98,98,96,94,92 90,88**CSF £232.35 TOTE £49.10: £8.80, £2.40, £4.90; EX 101.10 Trifecta £737.90 Pool: £1.455.20 - 1.40 winning tickets..

**Owner** M Pyle & Mrs T Pyle **Bred** Longdon Stud Ltd **Trained** Upper Longdon, Staffs

■ A very long-priced double for veteran trainer Reg Hollinshead, Goldeva supplementing the earlier win by Royal Cavalier.

■ Stewards Enquiry : A Culhane caution: careless riding

**FOCUS**

Up to scratch on paper, but a very rough and unsatisfactory contest won in a very modest time for the class.

**NOTEBOOK**

**Goldeva**, a half-sister to Royal Cavalier, had a dream run towards the stands' side and did just enough under a vintage ride. There were any amount of hard luck stories and this was her day.

**Orientor**, in the frame in the last two runnings of this event, as usual travelled strongly. Short of room at a crucial stage, he would have made it with a little further to go. However, a winner just four times now from 38 starts, that is the story of his life.

**The Kiddykid(IRE)**, who made great strides at three, was having his first run since August.

**Chookie Heiton(IRE)**, who finished lame on his final start last year, proved himself every bit as good as ever.

**Monsieur Bond(IRE)** ◆ was possibly the worst sufferer in a rough race. He is better suited by seven and his trainer has a race in Ireland coming up soon earmarked for him. He deserves a good prize.

**Smokin Beau**, third in this a year ago, has gone well when fresh in the past and connections will be hoping he stays sound.

**Fire Up The Band**, whose trainer has an awful record here, stumbled at the start and found himself racing towards the outside. This is best overlooked but he has a poor win-to-run ratio.

**Crimson Silk** showed his excellent effort here on his final start last year was no fluke, but he has not won since his two-year-old days.

**Law Breaker(IRE)**, who had a lot to find, seemed to run above himself.

**Will He Wish**, who had a lot to find, seemed to be ridden with another day in view. Seven suits him a lot better.

**Striking Ambition**, fit after an outing on the All-Weather, showed bags of toe before dropping right away. This must go down as a disappointing effort.

## 1127 POLYPIPE MAIDEN STKS 6f

**3:50** (3:50) (D) 3-Y-0 **£5,449** (£1,676; £838; £419) **Stalls** High

Form RPR

224- **1** **Local Poet**[154] [5740] 3-9-0 98 ........ GGibbons 2 71
(BAMcmahon) *trckd ldrs: hdwy 1/2-way: rdn to ld and edgd rt over 1f out: clr ins last* **4/9**[1]

0- **2** *2* **Volaticus (IRE)**[191] [5010] 3-9-0 ........ ANicholls 1 65
(DNicholls) *sn led: rdn along 2f out: hdd and swtchd lft over 1f out: sn drvn and kpt on same pce* **25/1**

4-05 **3** *1/2* **Blade's Edge**[38] [819] 3-9-0 59 ........ JFanning 5 64
(ABailey) *in tch: hdwy to chse ldrs 1/2-way: rdn along 2f out: kpt on same pce u.p ent last* **20/1**

0- **4** *nk* **Velocitas**[164] [5571] 3-8-11 ........ TPQueally(3) 3 63
(HJCollingridge) *chsd ldrs: rdn along 3f out: kpt on same pce u.p appr last* **33/1**

**5** *2 1/2* **Bollin Archie** 3-9-0 ........ KDarley 7 55
(TDEasterby) *rn green and sn pushed along towards rr: hdwy 1/2-way: styd on fnl 2f: nrst fin: bttr for r* **4/1**[2]

**6** *7* **Onyx** 3-9-0 ........ SRighton 4 34
(WDeBest-Turner) *s.i.s: t.k.h: in tch to 1/2-way: sn outpcd and bhd* **33/1**

2- **7** *2 1/2* **Diamond Shannon (IRE)**[206] [4655] 3-8-9 ........ RFitzpatrick 8 22
(DCarroll) *s.i.s: a bhd* **14/1**[3]

00 **8** *3 1/2* **Fly So High**[27] [927] 3-8-9 ........(v[1]) NCallan 6 11
(DShaw) *sn outpcd and bhd fr 1/2-way* **33/1**

1m 15.39s (1.11) **Going Correction** +0.075s/f (Good) **8** Ran SP% **113.4**
Speed ratings: **95,92,91,91,87 78,75,70**CSF £19.88 TOTE £1.70: £1.10, £3.00, £2.50; EX 17.10.

**Owner** J C Fretwell **Bred** Richard Brunger **Trained** Hopwas, Staffs

**FOCUS**

A poor maiden on paper offering an easy opportunity for the winner but he had to work harder than expected. The winning time was moderate.

**NOTEBOOK**

**Local Poet**, rated 98, scored in decisive fashion in the end but it was by no means straightforward. The third is rated just 59 which puts the overall form into context.

**Volaticus(IRE)**, quite an expensive purchase, had finished well beaten on his sole start at two. He split horses rated 98 and 59, so what the form is actually worth is anyone's guess.

**Blade's Edge**, who ran five times at two, has just a plater's mark.

**Velocitas**, bred for speed, had been well beaten on his sole start at two.

**Bollin Archie**, who has size and scope, will improve a good deal for the outing but he may need at least two more outings before he is ready to show his true worth.

## 1128 ORDERIT-ONLINE.COM MAIDEN AUCTION STKS 5f

**4:25** (4:26) (E) 2-Y-0 **£3,530** (£1,086; £543; £271) **Stalls** High

Form RPR

**1** **Dario Gee Gee (IRE)** 2-8-8 ........ NCallan 6 80
(KARyan) *w'like: cmpt: dwlt: sn trcking ldrs: led jst ins fnl f: sn clr* **14/1**

**2** *2 1/2* **Persian Rock (IRE)** 2-8-11 ........ DHolland 11 74
(JAOsborne) *w'like: lengthy: scope: chsd ldrs: outpcd over 2f out: styd on to go 2nd ins last: no ch w wnr* **7/2**[2]

**3** *hd* **Tiviski (IRE)** 2-8-3 ........ WSupple 2 65
(EJAlston) *leggy: unf: w ldrs: led 2f out: sn hdd: nt qckn ins last* **25/1**

**4** *2* **Next Time (IRE)** 2-8-4 ........ MartinDwyer 9 59
(MJPolglase) *neat: s.i.s: hdwy over 2f out: sn chsng ldrs: edgd lft: wknd fnl f* **16/1**



The Form Book, Raceform Ltd, Compton, RG20 6NL

5 *1* **Theatre Of Dreams** 2-8-7 ANicholls 5 58
(DNicholls) *cmpt: unf: dwlt: hdwy over 2f out: sn chsng ldrs: led over 1f out: hdd jst ins fnl f: wknd* **8/1**

6 *hd* **Von Wessex** 2-8-0 CHaddon(7) 3 58
(WGMTurner) *w'like: cmpt: led tl 2f out: wknd appr fnl f* **18/1**

7 *3/4* **Apologies** 2-8-7 GGibbons 1 55+
(BAMcmahon) *w'like: leggy: dwlt: hung lft and rn green: reminders after 1f: kpt on fnl 2f* **6/1[3]**

8 *hd* **Lord John** 2-8-7 DaleGibson 14 54
(MWEasterby) *chsd ldrs: hung lft 2f out: fdd* **33/1**

9 *3/4* **Bedtime Blues** 2-8-3 GDuffield 10 48
(JAGlover) *cmpt: dwlt: sn chsng ldrs: wknd 2f out* **25/1**

10 *3* **Brut** 2-8-5 LEnstone(3) 13 42
(DWBarker) *leggy: unf: scope: s.i.s: a in rr* **10/1**

11 *1 1/2* **Mindful** 2-8-7 JPSpencer 12 35
(MJPolglase) *leggy: unf: s.i.s: a bhd* **20/1**

12 *1 1/4* **Campeon (IRE)** 2-8-9 KDarley 8 33
(MJWallace) *w'like: leggy: lw: chsd ldrs: rdn 2f out: sn lost pl* **5/2[1]**

13 *1 1/2* **Champagne Brandy (IRE)** 2-8-2 JoannaBadger 4 21
(PDEvans) *small: unf: swvd lft s: a bhd* **33/1**

62.22 secs (0.96) **Going Correction** +0.075s/f (Good) **13** Ran SP% **121.4**
Speed ratings: **95,91,90,87,85 85,84,84,82,78 75,73,71**CSF £59.75 TOTE £23.90: £6.00, £2.60, £8.00; EX 81.20.
**Owner** Crewe And Nantwich Racing Club **Bred** John Malone **Trained** Hambleton, N Yorks

**FOCUS**
Probably a fair two-year-old event and the time was reasonable.

**NOTEBOOK**
**Dario Gee Gee(IRE)**, a March foal, is a short-backed, robust type. He knew his job and shot clear to take this above-average event in good style.
**Persian Rock(IRE)** ◆, a March foal, has size and scope. Fitted with a cross noseband, he was very green to post. He stayed on really well to snatch second spot and will be a lot sharper next time.
**Tiviski(IRE)**, a February foal, is on the leg and narrow. In time she will be suited by six.
**Next Time(IRE)**, a sister to No Time, who has done the stable so proud, is a smallish, close-coupled April foal. She will know more on her next outing.
**Theatre Of Dreams**, a March foal, was a springer in the market. After showing ahead he tired badly late on. He had presumably been showing plenty at home.
**Von Wessex**, an April foal, is already a gelding. He showed bags of toe but hung badly and may not be straightforward. *Official explanation: jockey said gelding hung right throughout.*
**Apologies**, a February foal, was drawn on the wide outside and looked very inexperienced both going to post and in the race itself.
**Campeon(IRE)**, a positive on the exchanges, is a leggy February foal who looked really fit and well. He was in trouble soon after halfway before dropping right away. He is surely better than he showed here.

## 1129 MARCH H'CAP 7f
5:00 (5:01) (D) (0-85,85) 3-Y-O **£5,746** (£1,768; £884; £442) **Stalls** High

Form RPR

120- **1** **Free Trip**[155] [5734] 3-9-0 **78** RHughes 22 87
(JHMGosden) *racd stands' side: chsd ldrs: led 3f out: hung lft: hld on nr fin* **3/1[1]**

5-1 **2** *nk* **Mount Vettore**[61] [606] 3-8-12 **76** JPSpencer 16 85+
(MrsJRRamsden) *racd stands' side: hld up towards rr: hdwy over 2f out: hrd rdn and r.o wl fnl f: jst hld* **7/2[2]**

401- **3** *2 1/2* **Granston (IRE)**[161] [5632] 3-8-8 **72** PRobinson 8 74
(JDBethell) *racd far side: chsd ldr: styd on to take charge that side last 75yds* **20/1**

423- **4** *3/4* **Imperialistic (IRE)**[144] [5916] 3-9-7 **85** DarrenWilliams 15 85
(KRBurke) *racd stands' side: mid-div: hdwy 2f out: edgd lft and kpt on ins last* **50/1**

223- **5** *3/4* **Distant Times**[201] [4770] 3-8-10 **74** KDarley 1 72
(TDEasterby) *led far side: hdd last 75 yds: eased towards fin* **16/1**

210- **6** *1/2* **Alpine Special (IRE)**[159] [5671] 3-8-8 **72** GFaulkner 20 69
(PCHaslam) *racd stands' side: s.i.s: hdwy 3f out: hung lft: nvr rchd ldrs* **33/1**

026- **7** *hd* **Cotosol**[140] [5950] 3-8-12 **76** WSupple 4 72
(BAMcmahon) *racd far side: chsd ldrs: one pce fnl 2f* **40/1**

033- **8** *1* **Another Bottle (IRE)**[182] [5221] 3-8-8 **72** DaleGibson 5 66
(TPTate) *racd far side: bhd: kpt on wl fnl 2f* **50/1**

043- **9** *1/2* **Red Birr (IRE)**[184] [5174] 3-8-13 **77** MartinDwyer 3 70
(AMBalding) *racd far side: chsd ldrs: one pce fnl 2f* **25/1**

160- **10** *1/2* **Cartronageeraghlad (IRE)**[105] [6172] 3-9-4 **82** (b) DHolland 11 73
(JAOsborne) *racd towards stands' side: w ldrs: wknd appr fnl f* **25/1**

212- **11** *1* **Kingsmaite**[91] [6242] 3-8-13 **77** JBramhill 14 66
(SRBowring) *racd stands' side: in tch: outpcd fnl 2f* **20/1**

003- **12** *3* **Gabana (IRE)**[141] [5940] 3-8-7 **71** SSanders 10 52
(CFWall) *swtchd rt and racd stands' side: bhd: sme hdwy 2f out: nvr on terms* **20/1**

21-3 **13** *shd* **Titus Salt (USA)**[24] [955] 3-8-11 **75** (b) DMernagh 18 56
(TDBarron) *racd stands' side: nvr on terms* **12/1**

516- **14** *nk* **Go Solo**[170] [5459] 3-9-0 **78** MHills 6 58
(BWHills) *racd far side: chsd ldrs: outpcd fnl 2f* **10/1**

502- **15** *nk* **Lets Get It On (IRE)**[144] [5916] 3-9-0 **78** KDalgleish 2 57
(JJQuinn) *racd far side: hld up in rr: sme hdwy 2f out: nvr a factor* **66/1**

336- **16** *3* **Morse (IRE)**[186] [5143] 3-9-3 **81** JPMurtagh 17 52
(JAOsborne) *racd stands' side: chsd ldrs: fdd fnl 2f* **14/1**

555- **17** *2 1/2* **Under My Spell**[213] [4500] 3-8-11 **75** SDrowne 19 40
(PDEvans) *racd stands' side: nvr nr ldrs* **20/1**

2-43 **18** *5* **West Country (UAE)**[44] [753] 3-9-1 **79** JFanning 21 31
(MJohnston) *racd stands' side: chsd ldrs: lost pl 3f out* **17/2[3]**

000- **19** *3/4* **Arfinnit (IRE)**[199] [4814] 3-8-11 **75** ACulhane 9 25
(MRChannon) *racd far side: a in rr* **40/1**

100- **20** *hd* **Redwood Rocks (IRE)**[154] [5741] 3-9-2 **80** FLynch 13 29
(BSmart) *racd stands' side: led tl 3f out: sn lost pl* **40/1**

620- **21** *hd* **Poppys Footprint (IRE)**[163] [5592] 3-9-7 **85** NCallan 12 34
(KARyan) *s.i.s: racd stands' side: a in rr* **40/1**

110- **22** *16* **Rules For Jokers (IRE)**[169] [5471] 3-9-4 **82** RWinston 7 —
(JAOsborne) *racd far side: chsd ldrs: sn pushed along: lost pl 3f out: sn bhd and eased: t.o* **28/1**

1m 28.37s (0.56) **Going Correction** +0.075s/f (Good) **22** Ran SP% **135.4**
Speed ratings: **99,98,95,94,94 93,93,92,91,91 89,86,86,85,85 82,79,73,72,72 72,54**CSF £11.04 CT £203.14 TOTE £5.20: £2.20, £2.00, £6.30, £8.30; EX 25.80 Place 6 £748.22, Place 5 £284.38..
**Owner** K Abdulla **Bred** Juddmonte Farms **Trained** Manton, Wilts

**FOCUS**
A solid and competitive 0-85 three-year-old handicap dominated by progressive horses that should throw up plenty of future winners.

**NOTEBOOK**
**Free Trip**, below his best on his final start at two, looked to have done plenty of work. Fitted with a cross noseband, he hung left, ending up in the centre and very nearly throwing it away.
**Mount Vettore**, happy to sit off the pace, went in pursuit of the winner. Sticking to the stands' side rail, he lacked company but in the end just failed to nail the errant winner. Both will have more to do in future, however.
**Granston(IRE)**, successful on his ninth and final outing at two, was first home on the far side.
**Imperialistic(IRE)** ran well under top-weight, but is likely to continue to struggle in handicap company from this sort of mark.
**Distant Times**, who was tried in blinkers at two, led them a merry dance on the far side and would have held on to fourth spot but for being eased near the line.
**Alpine Special(IRE)** stayed on despite a tendency to hang and will be suited by a return to a mile.
**Another Bottle(IRE)** ◆, a big type, stayed on steadily and should make his mark in handicap company, especially when stepped up in trip.
T/Plt: £1,868.50 to a £1 stake. Pool: £100,337.15. 39.20 winning tickets. T/Qpdt: £298.80 to a £1 stake. Pool: £6,501.00. 16.10 winning tickets. WG

# KEMPTON (R-H)
Saturday, March 27

**OFFICIAL GOING: Soft (good to soft in places)**
There was a strong bias towards horses racing against the far-side rail and up with the pace on the straight course.
Wind: nil Weather: overcast

## 1130 EBF FREEPHONE STANLEYBET 0808 100 1221 MAIDEN STKS 5f
2:05 (2:06) (D) 2-Y-O **£5,232** (£1,610; £805; £402) **Stalls** High

Form RPR

**1** **Lady Filly** 2-8-9 ADaly 1 73
(WGMTurner) *made virtually all: shkn up 2f out: kpt on wl fnl f* **20/1**

**2** *1* **Bibury Flyer** 2-8-9 CCatlin 2 69
(MRChannon) *chsng ldrs whn checked and snatched up after 1f: off the pce after: rdn and effrt 2f out: styd on to take 2nd last strides* **3/1[2]**

0 **3** *hd* **Grand Option**[7] [1060] 2-9-0 PDobbs 7 74
(BWDuke) *w wnr: shkn up and nt qckn 1f out: hld fnl f: lost 2nd last strides* **10/1**

**4** *2 1/2* **Tremar** 2-9-0 WRyan 6 65
(TGMills) *s.v.s: wl bhd and nt gng wl: pushed along and r.o fr over 1f out: nrst fin* **4/1[3]**

**5** *hd* **Polly Alexander (IRE)** 2-8-9 JMackay 4 59
(MJWallace) *w ldrs running green: edgd lft fr over 2f out: wknd fnl f* **16/1**

**6** *4* **Canton (IRE)** 2-9-0 DaneO'Neill 3 50
(RHannon) *s.s: rcvrd to chse ldrs over 3f out: hanging lft fr 2f out: wknd over 1f out* **9/4[1]**

**7** *3 1/2* **Bridge Place** 2-9-0 SWKelly 5 37
(BJMeehan) *s.i.s: a struggling: bhd fr 1/2-way* **11/2**

64.80 secs (3.44) **Going Correction** +0.55s/f (Yiel) **7** Ran SP% **110.9**
Speed ratings: **94,92,92,88,87 81,75**CSF £74.50 TOTE £15.30: £4.10, £2.10; EX 44.90.
**Owner** Mrs M S Teversham **Bred** Mrs M S Teversham **Trained** Sigwells, Somerset

**FOCUS**
Probably just an average maiden, but it should produce a couple of winners.

**NOTEBOOK**
**Lady Filly**, a half-sister to the very fast Justalord, out of a five-furlong juvenile winner, is bred purely for speed and showed plenty of that to make a winning debut. There are likely to be others in this race with more progression in them, but she looks up to holding her own in a better grade.
*Official explanation: jockey said filly had hung right*
**Bibury Flyer**, a 35,000gns yearling, sister to middle-distance winner Mojalid and half-sister to five sprint winners, out of a smart juvenile sprint scorer, was slowly away and, when trying to recover, got checked and snatched up after a furlong. She kept on for pressure and, although unable to get to the winner, she showed enough to suggest she will soon find a maiden.
**Grand Option**, well backed but disappointing in the first two-year-old race of the season just seven days previously, showed what he is capable of with the benefit of that experience. He had the rail to run against and showed plenty of dash, but this is probably as good as he is.
**Tremar**, a 26,000gns half-brother to a five-furlong two-year-old selling winner, out of a six-furlong juvenile winner, was well supported but lost any chance with a very slow start. However, he finished better than anything without being knocked about and this experience will not be lost on him.
**Polly Alexander(IRE)**, a 9,000gns yearling, half-sister to a seven-furlong two-year-old winner, was easy to back and well held on her debut. She showed pace, but also signs of inexperience, and should have learnt from this.
**Canton(IRE)**, a 30,000gns purchase, half-brother a two-year-old winner in Italy, has a Super Sprint entry and was sent off favourite to make a winning debut. However, he was slowly away, raced rather wide and was noted to be hanging. The market would suggest he is better than this, but he has it to prove.
**Bridge Place**, a 27,000gns purchase, half-brother to three juvenile sprint winners, was another to attract attention in the betting, but was a big disappointment. He missed the kick and never looked like getting competitive. He could, however, improve a bundle on this.

## 1131 STANLEYBET.COM H'CAP 5f
2:35 (2:37) (D) (0-80,81) 3-Y-O+ **£5,590** (£1,720; £860; £430) **Stalls** High

Form RPR

200- **1** **Further Outlook (USA)**[294] [2192] 10-9-9 **75** DaneO'Neill 9 92
(DKIvory) *mde all and sn racd against far side rail: clr fr 1/2-way: rdn over 1f out: unchal* **25/1**

000- **2** *5* **Seven No Trumps**[182] [5216] 7-9-8 **81** ow1 CJDavies(7) 10 83
(JMBradley) *prom far side: chsd wnr fr 1/2-way: rdn and no imp fnl 2f* **20/1**

1201 **3** *2* **Italian Mist (FR)**[11] [1027] 5-7-5 **50** oh5 (e) MHalford(7) 6 46
(JulianPoulton) *racd far side: towards rr: prog 1/2-way: carried hd high u.p but styd on fr over 1f out* **12/1**

6121 **4** *1 3/4* **Playtime Blue**[29] [905] 4-8-11 **63** GBaker 1 54
(KRBurke) *led nr side trio thrght: rdn over 1f out: kpt on: no ch w far side ldrs* **8/1**

-422 **5** *1/2* **Polish Emperor (USA)**[28] [912] 4-9-7 **73** PDobbs 7 62
(PWHarris) *racd on outer of far side gp: chsd wnr to 1/2-way: one pce fnl 2f* **5/1[1]**

44-0 **6** *shd* **Byo (IRE)**[81] [454] 6-9-0 **69** SHitchcott(3) 2 58
(MQuinn) *racd nr side: w ldr: rdn 1/2-way: kpt on same pce fnl 2f* **33/1**

5630 **7** *nk* **The Fisio**[8] [1051] 4-9-4 **75** NChalmers(5) 15 63
(AMBalding) *racd in midfield far side: rdn and no imp ldrs 2f out* **7/1[3]**

1010 **8** *hd* **Arogant Prince**[22] [968] 7-8-2 **54** (b) JQuinn 3 41
(AWCarroll) *racd nr side: w ldng pair: rdn wl over 1f out: kpt on same pce* **12/1**

6060 **9** *1* **Prime Recreation**[29] [905] 7-9-2 **68** SCarson 5 52
(PSFelgate) *racd on outer of far side gp: wl in rr: rdn and sme prog 1f out: no ch* **16/1**

5606 **10** 1 ½ **Bond Playboy**[14] 1007 4-9-11 **77** CCatlin 13 57
(BSmart) *racd far side: wl in rr and sn pushed along: nvr on terms* **12/1**

-050 **11** ½ **Ellens Lad (IRE)**[36] 836 10-8-13 **72** ARutter(7) 17 50
(WJMusson) *racd far side: n.m.r and snatched up after 1f: nvr on terms after* **20/1**

500- **12** 1 **Whistler**[193] 4972 7-10-0 **80** (p) PFitzsimons 8 55
(JMBradley) *prom far side for 3f: wknd* **20/1**

2123 **13** 2 **Justalord**[7] 1061 6-9-3 **69** (p) JEdmunds 4 38
(JBalding) *v restless in stalls: racd on outer of far side gp: nvr beyond midfield: n.d fnl 2f* **6/1**[2]

2-00 **14** 2 ½ **Roman Quintet (IRE)**[8] 1051 4-8-10 **62** SWKelly 16 24
(DWPArbuthnot) *prom far side: rdn bef 1/2-way: wknd wl over 1f out* **12/1**

5500 **15** 2 **Easily Averted (IRE)**[30] 891 3-8-7 **71** ADaly 14 27
(PButler) *s.i.s: racd far side: snatched up after 1f: wl in rr after* **40/1**

-500 **16** 2 **Abraxas**[30] 898 6-7-12 **50** oh10 (p) JMackay 12 —
(JAkehurst) *nvr beyond midfield far side: wknd 2f out* **100/1**

5-00 **17** 2 **Regal Song (IRE)**[30] 896 8-9-4 **70** (b) GCarter 11 14
(TJEtherington) *racd on outer of far side gp: sn rdn and struggling in rr* **12/1**

63.24 secs (1.88) **Going Correction** +0.55s/f (Yiel)
**WFA** 3 from 4yo+ 12lb **17** Ran SP% **123.4**
Speed ratings: **106,98,94,92,91 91,90,90,88,86 85,83,80,76,73 70,67**CSF £436.09 CT £6185.21 TOTE £35.30: £6.00, £4.20, £2.90, £2.90; EX 308.20.
**Owner** K T Ivory **Bred** Gainsborough Farm Inc **Trained** Radlett, Herts

**FOCUS**
This looked open, but when Further Outlook was fast away and bagged the favoured far-side rail nothing else could get into it. The trio who elected to race near side finished fourth, sixth and eighth. The distances were probably exaggerated by the ground.

**NOTEBOOK**
**Further Outlook(USA)**, not seen since June of 2003, absolutely pinged the gates, grabbed the far rail and never looked back. He is clearly on tremendous terms with himself and would be of interest if turned out under a penalty.
**Seven No Trumps** was a really frustrating sort when with Barry Hills, but this was a good effort on his debut for new connections.
**Italian Mist(FR)** has never won on turf but has been in fine form on Fibresand recently and ran well off a mark much lower than that of his All-Weather rating, even after taking into account he was out of the handicap. He should find a race on the grass.
**Playtime Blue** did just the best of the three horses that raced on the near side, but was never on terms with the runaway winner.
**Polish Emperor(USA)** tried to give chase to the winner, but never looked like getting to that one and was well held.
**Byo(IRE)** came out second best of the three to race on the near side.
**Arogant Prince** was last of the three on the near side, but only narrowly beaten in that group.
**Prime Recreation** has not won since taking this last year off a 2lb higher mark.
**Ellens Lad(IRE)** was unable to capitalise on a good draw against the favoured far-side rail after losing his place with four to run.
**Justalord** got a bit fractious in the stalls and proved unable to dominate from his low draw.

## 1132 FREEPHONE STANLEYBET 0808 100 1221 H'CAP 7f (J)

3:10 (3:11) (C) (0-95,94) 3-Y-O+ **£9,805** (£3,017; £1,508; £754) **Stalls** High

Form RPR

003- **1** **Zilch**[108] 6164 6-8-9 **76** ow1 DaneO'Neill 13 90
(MLWBell) *prom gng wl: led wl over 2f out: shkn up and in command over 1f out: styd on wl* **10/1**

132- **2** 2 ½ **Camberley (IRE)**[178] 5299 7-9-9 **90** JQuinn 8 98
(PFICole) *t.k.h: hld up in midfield: effrt gng easily 3f out: chsd wnr 2f out: sn rdn and nt qckn: no imp after* **9/2**[1]

02-0 **3** 4 **Digital**[7] 1065 7-9-12 **93** CCatlin 10 91
(MRChannon) *hld up in last: prog 3f out: rdn and kpt on one pce fnl 2f: nt pce to chal* **11/2**[2]

01-0 **4** ½ **Taranaki**[84] 417 6-8-9 **79** LisaJones(3) 12 76
(PDCundell) *dwlt: racd alone on inner: on terms w ldrs: ev ch over 2f out: one pce after* **16/1**

-033 **5** ½ **Sangiovese**[36] 837 5-8-1 **68** JMackay 3 64
(HMorrison) *pressed ldr to 3f out: rdn and grad fdd* **11/2**[2]

600- **6** 3 ½ **Marker**[182] 5210 4-9-11 **92** SCarson 9 79
(GBBalding) *trckd ldrs: rdn and cl up over 2f out: wknd wl over 1f out* **20/1**

163- **7** ¾ **Irony (IRE)**[211] 4555 5-9-3 **89** NChalmers(5) 7 74
(AMBalding) *mde most to wl over 2f out: grad wknd* **12/1**

50-0 **8** ½ **Ammenayr (IRE)**[77] 494 4-8-10 **77** WRyan 11 61
(TGMills) *trckd ldrs: rdn and cl up over 2f out: sn wknd* **25/1**

-005 **9** 3 **Hand Chime**[42] 770 7-8-11 **78** SWKelly 1 54
(WJHaggas) *plld hrd early: hld up in tch: rdn 3f out: sn wknd* **13/2**[3]

01-0 **10** 8 **Wood Fern (UAE)**[59] 624 4-8-10 **77** RLappin 5 33
(MRChannon) *hld up in rr: rdn and wknd 3f out* **50/1**

333- **11** 1 **Penny Cross**[182] 5213 4-9-2 **88** NMackay(5) 4 42
(JGGiven) *t.k.h early: pressed ldrs: rdn 1/2-way: wknd 3f out: eased fnl 2f* **10/1**

160- **12** ½ **Master Robbie**[154] 5747 5-9-10 **94** SHitchcott(3) 6 46
(MRChannon) *settled in tch: shkn up and btn 3f out: wknd* **14/1**

6-04 **13** 7 **Terraquin (IRE)**[56] 647 4-8-12 **79** NPollard 2 14
(JJBridger) *t.k.h early: hld up in tch: rdn and wknd 1/2-way* **16/1**

1m 32.55s (5.30) **Going Correction** +0.95s/f (Soft) **13** Ran SP% **117.2**
Speed ratings: **107,104,99,99,98 94,93,93,89,80 79,78,70**CSF £52.32 CT £278.01 TOTE £16.00: £3.10, £2.70, £2.50; EX 94.00.
**Owner** Mary Mayall, Linda Redmond, Julie Martin **Bred** Mrs Linda Corbett And Mrs Mary Mayall **Trained** Newmarket, Suffolk

**FOCUS**
A fair little handicap in which all bar fourth-placed Taranaki raced towards the stands' side in the straight. The winner was well treated on his old form.

**NOTEBOOK**
**Zilch** had not won since scoring on his seasonal reappearance as a three-year-old for Richard Hannon but, rated 21lb lower than when making his handicap debut back in June 2002 and back on his favoured soft ground, he ran out a most decisive winner. He only had four starts last season, but could win again if finding similar conditions.
**Camberley(IRE)**, 3lb higher than when last successful, ran a solid race on his first start in 178 days. He was no match for the winner but was well clear of the remainder and could be of interest in something like the Jubilee Stakes back here in May over a furlong further - his owner has won the last two renewals.
**Digital**, slightly unlucky at Lingfield on his reappearance, ran a respectable race back on turf and looks to be coming to hand. Interestingly, however, he has never won before May.
**Taranaki** raced away from the main group from the start and stayed towards the far rail in the straight. This was a good effort in the circumstances, but it could be worth keeping in mind he has never won off a mark this high.
**Sangiovese**, 8lb lower on turf than All-Weather, was disappointing.
**Hand Chime** was unable to get cover from his outside draw and pulled too hard.

## 1133 STANLEYBET.COM MAIDEN STKS 6f

3:45 (3:46) (D) 3-Y-O+ **£5,434** (£1,672; £836; £418) **Stalls** High

Form RPR

02- **1** **Bygone Days**[176] 5338 3-8-12 SWKelly 2 84+
(WJHaggas) *led after 1f: clr w one rival bef 1/2-way: shkn up and wl in command 2f out: rdn out* **3/1**[2]

3- **2** 5 **Rangoon (USA)**[148] 5850 3-8-12 DaneO'Neill 1 69+
(MrsAJPerrett) *dwlt: hld up and sn wl off the pce: prog on outer 3f out: rdn to chse clr ldng pair over 2f out: kpt on to take 2nd nr fin* **1/1**[1]

33 **3** 1 **Emsam Ballou (IRE)**[7] 1059 3-8-7 RSmith 10 61
(RHannon) *led for 1f: chsd wnr after and sn clr of rest: rdn and no imp 2f out: lost 2nd nr fin* **9/2**[3]

5- **4** 8 **Pompey Chimes**[167] 5508 4-9-11 SCarson 6 42
(GBBalding) *dwlt: outpcd bef 1/2-way: nvr on terms after* **20/1**

**5** ¾ **Silver Reign** 3-8-7 RThomas(5) 3 40
(GBBalding) *dwlt: outpcd and wl bhd: modest late prog* **50/1**

**6** nk **Scrunch** 3-8-7 PFitzsimons 8 34
(BJMeehan) *dwlt: t.k.h early: outpcd bef 1/2-way: no ch after* **12/1**

00 **7** 10 **Mandahar (IRE)**[19] 982 5-9-11 JQuinn 9 9
(AWCarroll) *sn outpcd: a wl bhd* **100/1**

**8** 3 **Triage (IRE)** 3-8-7 CCatlin 4 —
(MRChannon) *chsd ldrs over 2f: wknd wl over 2f out: sn wl bhd* **14/1**

00/ **9** 16 **Our Sion**[589] 3940 4-9-11 ADaly 7 —
(RBrotherton) *chsd ldrs 2f: wknd 1/2-way: t.o* **100/1**

1m 17.47s (4.30) **Going Correction** +0.55s/f (Yiel)
**WFA** 3 from 4yo+ 13lb **9** Ran SP% **116.2**
Speed ratings: **93,86,85,74,73 72,59,55,34**CSF £6.30 TOTE £5.50: £1.70, £1.10, £2.30; EX 11.60.
**Owner** J Hanson **Bred** J A E Hobby **Trained** Newmarket, Suffolk

**FOCUS**
On form this only concerned the first three, who finished well clear of the rest. The result should not be taken at face value however.

**NOTEBOOK**
**Bygone Days** showed promise on both his starts at two and confirmed that with a clear-cut success. Despite being drawn out wide, he was able to tack across and soon led against the favoured far-side rail. He is probably flattered by the winning margin, but is clearly going the right way.
**Rangoon(USA)**, third on his only start at two, was dropped out by O'Neill and could make no impression on the winner when asked. He is better than this and a stiffer track may suit.
**Emsam Ballou(IRE)** shaped encouragingly over seven furlongs and a mile on Polytrack, but was a little disappointing on this drop in trip. She gave up the far rail very easily to the eventual winner and could only find the one pace when asked.
**Pompey Chimes** shaped well on his debut in a weak maiden at Goodwood last year, but was unable to build on that. He should find things easier when handicapped.
**Silver Reign**, a 15,000gns purchase out of an unraced half-sister to eight winners, showed little on his debut.

## 1134 FREEPHONE STANLEYBET 0808 100 1221 CLASSIFIED STKS 1m 1f (R)

4:20 (4:22) (D) 3-Y-O **£5,408** (£1,664; £832; £416) **Stalls** High

Form RPR

31 **1** **African Dream**[35] 845 3-8-12 **81** JQuinn 8 99
(PWChapple-Hyam) *trckd ldng pair: led wl over 2f out: wl clr over 1f out: rdn out* **11/4**[1]

6112 **2** 9 **Red Lancer**[24] 957 3-8-4 **80** BSwarbrick(7) 10 80
(RJPrice) *t.k.h: hld up in midfield: effrt 3f out: sn rdn and nt qckn: kpt on to take 2nd nr fin* **6/1**[3]

41- **3** ¾ **Cimyla (IRE)**[164] 5578 3-9-0 **83** GBaker 4 81
(CFWall) *hld up in midfield: prog to chal 3f out: sn outpcd by wnr: lost 2nd nr fin* **5/1**[2]

162- **4** 6 **Le Tiss (IRE)**[158] 5698 3-8-10 **82** SHitchcott(3) 6 68
(MRChannon) *racd in rr: rdn over 3f out: sn outpcd: plugged on fnl 2f: no ch* **10/1**

554- **5** 1 ½ **Slavonic (USA)**[150] 5830 3-8-11 **79** PDobbs 9 63
(JHMGosden) *s.i.s: hld up in rr: effrt 3f out: rdn and wknd over 2f out* **9/1**

132- **6** 1 ¼ **Anuvasteel**[98] 6219 3-8-13 **82** WRyan 7 63
(NACallaghan) *trckd ldrs: rdn to chal 3f out: wknd over 2f out* **7/1**

412 **7** 3 **Heversham (IRE)**[35] 843 3-8-13 **82** SWKelly 5 57
(WJHaggas) *led to wl over 2f out: sn wknd* **7/1**

165- **8** 3 **Winners Delight**[246] 3560 3-9-0 **83** EStack 3 52
(APJarvis) *racd in last: rdn and lost tch over 3f out: wl bhd after* **33/1**

042- **9** 1 ¾ **Song Of Vala**[142] 5934 3-8-12 **81** DSweeney 2 46
(RCharlton) *chsd ldr to 3f out: wknd rapidly* **10/1**

2m 2.51s (7.71) **Going Correction** +0.95s/f (Soft) **9** Ran SP% **113.7**
Speed ratings: **103,95,94,89,87 86,83,81,79**CSF £18.90 TOTE £3.10: £1.30, £2.20, £2.60; EX 30.10.
**Owner** Franconson Partners **Bred** E Landi **Trained** Newmarket, Suffolk

**FOCUS**
There was nothing to separate these on ratings, but African Dream showed himself well ahead of the handicapper by winning impressively in a good time.

**NOTEBOOK**
**African Dream** ◆ followed up his recent win in a decent claimer with a mightily impressive success. His next target could be another classified event at Windsor and, as he will qualify off his current mark, he will be hard to beat.
**Red Lancer** has been in good form on the Fibresand since joining his current connections and did not run a bad race on this switch back to turf. He may, however, be better over further.
**Cimyla(IRE)**, off the mark in a modest maiden at Lingfield when last seen 164 days previously, ran respectably on this return to turf and was well clear of the remainder.
**Le Tiss(IRE)** had never previously raced on soft ground and he did not run to his best. He is entitled to improve on this, however.
**Slavonic(USA)** did not confirm the promise he showed in maidens on this reappearance. This ground may have been softer than ideal.

## 1135 FREEPHONE STANLEYBET H'CAP 1m 6f 92y

4:55 (4:55) (E) (0-75,73) 4-Y-O+ **£3,406** (£1,048; £524; £262) **Stalls** High

Form RPR

000- **1** **Linens Flame**[323] 797 5-8-9 **54** DSweeney 1 73
(BGPowell) *trckd ldr: led 8f out: rdn and jnd wl over 3f out: hung lft but asserted 2f out: forged clr over 1f out* **33/1**

22/2 **2** 5 **Belle Rouge**[27] 931 6-8-7 **52** JQuinn 13 65
(CAHorgan) *cl up: jnd wnr wl over 3f out and gng easily: rdn over 2f out: nt qckn and btn fnl 2f* **4/1**[1]

0-50 **3** 3 ½ **Turtle Valley (IRE)**[19] 981 8-9-11 **70** PDoe 2 78
(SDow) *settled in rr: prog to trck ldrs 4f out: rdn and outpcd wl over 2f out: one pce after* **7/1**[3]



The Form Book, Raceform Ltd, Compton, RG20 6NL

6436 **4** *2 ½* **Typhoon Tilly**[35] 844 7-9-11 **73** SHitchcott(3) 10 78
(CREgerton) *hld up in midfield: effrt to press ldrs 4f out: rdn and outpcd wl ovr 2f out: one pce after* **8/1**

4-55 **5** *1 ¼* **Lanos (POL)**[32] 867 6-8-9 **59** (t) NChalmers(5) 12 62
(MissSheenaWest) *trckd ldrs: rdn to chse ldng pair over 3f out: no imp: fdd fnl 2f* **14/1**

060- **6** *3* **San Hernando**[155] 5730 4-9-5 **73** RThomas(5) 3 72
(DRCElsworth) *s.s: hld up in last: gng wl enough but outpcd 4f out: shkn up and styd on fnl 2f: nvr nr ldrs* **8/1**

-331 **7** *9* **Boumahou (IRE)**[45] 743 4-9-6 **69** WRyan 6 57
(APJarvis) *racd in midfield: rdn over 3f out: wknd over 2f out* **11/2**[2]

2125 **8** *¾* **Unleaded**[40] 789 4-7-12 **47** oh7 JMackay 9 34
(JAkehurst) *prom: lost pl 8f out: renewed effrt 5f out: wknd wl over 2f out* **20/1**

3040 **9** *1 ½* **Munfarid (IRE)**[9] 1042 4-9-6 **69** (t) DKinsella 7 54
(PGMurphy) *racd in midfield: drvn wl over 3f out: sn wknd* **25/1**

06-0 **10** *2* **Our Imperial Bay (USA)**[19] 981 5-8-12 **64** (b) DerekNolan(7) 5 46
(RMStronge) *settled in rr: pushed along 5f out: wknd u.p 3f out* **16/1**

13-6 **11** *nk* **Aoninch**[23] 962 4-8-13 **62** SWhitworth 4 44
(MrsPNDutfield) *hld up in rr: effrt 4f out: sn rdn and wknd* **7/1**[3]

4110 **12** *6* **Mandoob**[22] 971 7-9-11 **73** J-PGuillambert(3) 11 47
(BRJohnson) *hld up in rr: effrt and sme prog 4f out: sn rdn and wknd* **16/1**

00-0 **13** *dist* **Go Classic**[19] 981 4-9-1 **64** SCarson 14 —
(AMHales) *prom: trckd wnr 8f out to 4f out: wknd rapidly: t.o* **20/1**

000- **P** **Polanski Mill**[184] 5171 5-9-3 **62** PDobbs 8 —
(CAHorgan) *led to 8f out: wknd rapidly and sn t.o: p.u 3f out* **20/1**

3m 30.87s (20.21) **Going Correction** +0.95s/f (Soft)
**WFA** 4 from 5yo+ 4lb **14** Ran SP% **122.1**
Speed ratings: **80,77,75,73,73 71,66,65,64,63 63,60,—,—**CSF £153.97 CT £1072.88 TOTE £65.50: £11.70, £2.00, £2.40; EX 746.20 Place 6 £97.46, Place 5 £22.31..
**Owner** D & J Newell **Bred** Mrs D B Mulley **Trained** Morestead, Hants

**FOCUS**
Just an ordinary staying handicap, and no great pace.

**NOTEBOOK**
**Linens Flame**, well held on all of his previous runs on the Flat, was returning to the level after a reasonable run on his hurdling debut at Wincanton 323-days previously and stepping up in trip. He is unexposed and promises to get even further, so might go in again. *Official explanation: trainer had no explanation for the improved form shown other than that gelding may have benefited from the step up in trip*
**Belle Rouge** had shaped well on her return from a long break at Lingfield last month and confirmed that promise with another solid effort.
**Turtle Valley(IRE)** had conditions to suit and was fit from a couple of recent spins on the All-Weather so there were no real excuses.
**Typhoon Tilly** did not run a bad race considering the ground was much softer than he would have liked.
**Lanos(POL)** has won on this ground in Poland so conditions were not a problem, but he was well held.
**Aoninch** *Official explanation: jockey said filly had ran too keen*
**Go Classic** *Official explanation: jockey said filly was unsuited by the ground*
T/Plt: £163.20 to a £1 stake. Pool: £45,350.60. 202.80 winning tickets. T/Qpdt: £7.50 to a £1 stake. Pool: £2,967.60. 292.55 winning tickets. JN

## 1075 WOLVERHAMPTON (A.W) (L-H)
### Saturday, March 27

**OFFICIAL GOING: Standard to slow**
Wind: nil Weather: fine

## 1136 BET DIRECT ON SKY ACTIVE H'CAP — 1m 4f (F)
**7:00** (7:00) (F) (0-55,62) 4-Y-O+ **£2,954** (£844; £422) **Stalls** Low

Form RPR

53/4 **1** **Ffiffiffer (IRE)**[4] 1081 6-9-7 **55** ACulhane 5 67
(CTinkler) *hld up in tch: rdn to ld over 2f out: rdn out* **7/2**[1]

321 **2** *2 ½* **Aveiro (IRE)**[10] 1041 8-10-0 **62** MFenton 11 70
(MissGayKelleway) *a.p: rdn over 5f out: led over 4f out tl over 2f out: one pce fnl f* **13/2**

-306 **3** *hd* **Kentucky Bullet (USA)**[9] 1042 8-8-10 **47** LPKeniry(3) 4 54
(AGNewcombe) *hld up in tch: rdn over 2f out: one pce fnl f* **7/1**

2134 **4** *nk* **Disabuse**[9] 1042 4-9-0 **55** PMulrennan(5) 3 62
(MWEasterby) *hld up and bhd: hdwy over 3f out: rdn over 2f out: styd on wl ins fnl f* **5/1**[3]

2200 **5** *2 ½* **Fight The Feeling**[23] 962 6-9-7 **55** (v) ADaly 2 58
(JWUnett) *t.k.h: prom: rdn 2f out: wknd ins fnl f* **11/1**

2122 **6** *7* **Buz Kiri (USA)**[5] 1077 6-8-7 **46** oh1 HayleyTurner(5) 1 39
(AWCarroll) *bhd: reminders 9f out: hdwy on ins 7f out: rdn over 5f out: wknd over 4f out* **9/2**[2]

5050 **7** *6* **Coolfore Jade (IRE)**[9] 1042 4-9-2 **52** CCatlin 6 36
(NEBerry) *set mod pce: hdd over 4f out: rdn over 3f out: wknd over 2f out* **16/1**

235- **8** *6* **Monsal Dale (IRE)**[74] 4782 5-8-12 **46** oh1 VSlattery 8 21
(NEBerry) *a bhd* **10/1**

0122 **9** *1 ½* **Prince Prospect**[36] 838 8-8-9 **50** KristinStubbs(7) 7 23
(MrsLStubbs) *a bhd* **14/1**

0054 **10** *4* **Santa Catalina (IRE)**[13] 1024 5-8-9 **46** oh6 BReilly(3) 10 13
(CADwyer) *a bhd* **50/1**

3-06 **11** *23* **Victory Vee**[22] 967 4-9-5 **55** RHavlin 9 —
(MBlanshard) *t.k.h in tch: rdn over 5f out: wknd over 4f out: t.o* **40/1**

2m 42.74s (1.24) **Going Correction** +0.175s/f (Slow)
**WFA** 4 from 5yo+ 2lb **11** Ran SP% **117.3**
Speed ratings: **102,100,100,100,98 93,89,85,84,82 66**CSF £26.19 CT £152.41 TOTE £4.00: £2.20, £2.70, £2.60; EX 17.90.
**Owner** George Ward **Bred** Miss B Galway-Greer **Trained** Compton, Berks

**FOCUS**
A fair handicap and the form should prove reliable.

**NOTEBOOK**
**Ffiffiffer(IRE)**, three times a winner on a similar surface at Mijas, was considered to be more at home here than on the Polytrack earlier in the week. Further improvement can be expected.
**Aveiro(IRE)** was again without the headgear for this return to a shorter trip. A 10lb rise in the weights proved too much and time may show he had plenty on his plate in trying to concede half a stone to the winner.
**Kentucky Bullet(USA)** showed signs of a return to form on what appears to be his favourite track.
**Disabuse** finished with a flourish and would probably have preferred a stronger-run race.
**Fight The Feeling**, reverting to Fibresand with the visor back on, proved difficult to settle because of the modest pace.
**Buz Kiri(USA)** may have had an off day but this was a step up in class.

## 1137 SPECIAL OFFERS @ BETDIRECT.CO.UK (S) STKS — 5f (F)
**7:30** (7:30) (G) 2-Y-O **£2,506** (£716; £358) **Stalls** Low

Form RPR

**1** **Little Biscuit (IRE)** 2-8-6 GFaulkner 1 49
(KRBurke) *s.i.s: sn rcvrd: wnt 2nd 3f out: rdn to ld 1f out: r.o wl* **9/4**[2]

**2** *1 ¼* **Nutty Times** 2-8-6 ADaly 6 45
(WGMTurner) *led: rdn over 2f out: hdd 1f out: nt qckn* **2/1**[1]

**3** *3 ½* **Petite Elle** 2-8-6 JQuinn 4 32
(PJMcbride) *bhd: pushed along over 3f out: rdn and sme hdwy on ins 2f out: wknd over 1f out* **3/1**[3]

**4** *11* **Marne (IRE)** 2-8-11 JTate 5 —
(JMPEustace) *chsd ldr tl rdn 3f out: wknd 2f out* **4/1**

65.50 secs (2.90) **Going Correction** +0.175s/f (Slow) **4** Ran SP% **109.1**
Speed ratings: **83,81,75,57**CSF £7.10 TOTE £2.20; EX 3.80.There was no bid for the winner.
**Owner** Mrs Elaine M Burke **Bred** Michael Mullins **Trained** Middleham Moor, N Yorks

**FOCUS**
The two horses who ran in the seller at Doncaster the previous day were scratched leaving four newcomers. The winning time was modest even for a contest like this.

**NOTEBOOK**
**Little Biscuit(IRE)**, the first foal of a five-furlong winner, is not very big. Her rider pulled his stick through in a flash when she was inclined to edge into the second as she took it up.
**Nutty Times** is a sister to Algunas Veces, a winner on Fibresand over five furlongs as a juvenile and a mile at three.
**Petite Elle** is a half-sister to a multiple winner in Denmark.

## 1138 PRESS INTERACTIVE TO BET DIRECT MAIDEN STKS — 1m 1f 79y(F)
**8:00** (8:00) (D) 3-Y-O+ **£3,396** (£1,045; £522; £261) **Stalls** Low

Form RPR

53- **1** **Slalom (IRE)**[183] 5195 4-9-12 (e1) MFenton 7 74
(MissGayKelleway) *s.i.s: sn rdn along: hdwy on ins over 2f out: led wl over 1f out: edgd rt ins fnl f: drvn out* **5/1**[2]

32- **2** *1 ½* **Golden Empire (USA)**[207] 4647 3-8-7 WSupple 4 71
(EALDunlop) *led after 1f: rdn over 4f out: hdd over 2f out: kpt on ins fnl f* **4/7**[1]

030/ **3** *1 ¾* **Pure Mischief (IRE)**[268] 5747 5-9-5 45 BSwarbrick(7) 6 67
(WMBrisbourne) *chsd ldrs: rdn to ld over 2f out: edgd lft and hdd wl over 1f out: no ex ins fnl f* **25/1**

66 **4** *3 ½* **Albee (IRE)**[50] 697 4-9-9 (p) LisaJones(3) 12 60
(MissGayKelleway) *mid-div: hdwy over 1f out: nvr nr to chal* **33/1**

44-5 **5** *shd* **Jarraaf**[37] 824 4-9-12 56 SWKelly 10 60
(JWUnett) *chsd ldrs: reminders over 7f out: rdn over 4f out: one pce fnl 3f* **6/1**[3]

553- **6** *6* **Menai Straights**[151] 5810 3-8-7 66 JFanning 8 48
(RFFisher) *prom: led over 3f out: rdn and hdd over 2f out: wknd over 1f out* **16/1**

5/ **7** *6* **Alpha Echo (USA)**[163] 5603 5-9-12 SRighton 11 36
(MFHarris) *prom: rdn and ev ch 3f out: wknd 2f out* **33/1**

0- **8** *5* **Spartan Principle**[299] 2066 4-9-7 CLowther 1 21
(RGuest) *a bhd* **80/1**

-060 **9** *5* **Un Autre Espere**[5] 1080 5-9-12 30 (b) LVickers 2 16
(TWall) *led 1f: wknd over 4f out* **100/1**

50 **10** *25* **Sunset Blues (FR)**[7] 1059 4-9-12 (be) RHavlin 3 —
(KOCunningham-Brown) *a bhd: t.o* **100/1**

**11** *dist* **Learn The Lingo**[17] 8-9-12 (tp) JFEgan 9 —
(MrsHDalton) *a bhd: t.o* **66/1**

000- **12** *dist* **Regal Ali (IRE)**[215] 5-9-12 30 VSlattery 5 —
(GAHam) *prom tl wknd qckly 5f out: t.o* **100/1**

2m 5.21s (2.31) **Going Correction** +0.175s/f (Slow)
**WFA** 3 from 4yo+ 19lb **12** Ran SP% **115.9**
Speed ratings: **96,94,93,90,89 84,79,74,70,48 —,—**CSF £7.76 TOTE £5.90: £1.50, £1.20, £3.40; EX 8.50.
**Owner** Hilton Guinle **Bred** Mrs D Hutch **Trained** Newmarket, Suffolk

**FOCUS**
The first two were below form, particularly the runner-up, in this ordinary maiden. The time was moderate.

**NOTEBOOK**
**Slalom(IRE)** was fitted with an eyeshield for this sand debut. The further he went the better he looked and Fenton certainly earned his winning percentage.
**Golden Empire(USA)** is a half-brother to Lear Spear, a Group Three and Listed winner at up to a mile and a half. He certainly shaped as if he needed a longer trip on this All-Weather debut.
**Pure Mischief(IRE)** had not been seen since unseating his rider over hurdles last July when trained by Martin Todhunter. This was a sound effort and he would not be the first to be rejuvenated by his present yard.
**Albee(IRE)** showed significant improvement, having lost ground at the start in his two previous outings over course and distance.
**Jarraaf** seems to reserve his best efforts for Dunstall Park.

## 1139 BETDIRECT.CO.UK H'CAP — 7f (F)
**8:30** (8:30) (D) (0-85,82) 3-Y-O+ **£4,030** (£1,240; £620; £310) **Stalls** High

Form RPR

2000 **1** **Flint River**[7] 1065 6-9-7 **78** ACulhane 9 92
(HMorrison) *hld up: hdwy on outside over 3f out: rdn to ld over 1f out: r.o wl* **11/4**[2]

-301 **2** *1 ¼* **Just A Glimmer**[14] 1013 4-9-11 **82** DHolland 3 93
(LGCottrell) *a.p: rdn over 2f out: ev ch over 1f out: nt qckn ins fnl f* **5/2**[1]

3052 **3** *1 ½* **Labrett**[7] 1066 7-9-11 **82** (tp) MFenton 8 89
(MissGayKelleway) *sn prom: rdn over 2f out: one pce fnl f* **4/1**[3]

0-50 **4** *½* **Romany Nights (IRE)**[22] 968 4-9-1 **72** (v) SWKelly 6 78
(JWUnett) *a.p: rdn to ld over 2f out: hdd over 1f out: wknd ins fnl f* **14/1**

0-20 **5** *1* **Pharoah's Gold (IRE)**[68] 564 6-8-5 **62** (e) WSupple 7 65
(DShaw) *hld up: hdwy over 2f out: c wd st: one pce fnl f* **16/1**

0515 **6** *8* **Ripple Effect**[8] 1057 4-9-5 **79** (t) TPQueally(3) 2 62
(CADwyer) *hld up: rdn over 2f out: wknd over 1f out* **16/1**

6-03 **7** *1* **Foley Prince**[1] 1121 3-7-12 **70** oh3 JMackay 4 51
(DFlood) *led: rdn and hdd over 2f out: wknd wl over 1f out* **14/1**

400- **8** *6* **Oases**[130] 6019 5-7-12 **58** (e1) LisaJones(3) 5 24
(DShaw) *s.i.s: hld up in rr: rdn 3f out: sn struggling* **25/1**

4610 **9** *nk* **Warden Warren**[14] 1013 6-9-0 **74** (p) BReilly(3) 1 39
(MrsCADunnett) *prom tl wknd over 3f out* **12/1**

1m 29.89s (-0.31) **Going Correction** +0.175s/f (Slow)
**WFA** 3 from 4yo+ 15lb **9** Ran SP% **111.9**
Speed ratings: **108,106,104,104,103 94,92,86,85**CSF £9.57 CT £25.30 TOTE £4.60: £1.40, £1.60, £1.90; EX 16.80.
**Owner** The Firm **Bred** P D Savill **Trained** East Ilsley, Berks

**FOCUS**
A finish fought out by a couple of course and distance specialists. The winning time was good.

**NOTEBOOK**
**Flint River** goes well for Culhane and bounced back to form on his favourite surface over the right sort of trip.
**Just A Glimmer**, raised 6lb, lost no caste in defeat against another useful performer over this course and distance.
**Labrett** seems to be a better horse on Polytrack and ran a sound race against a couple of Dunstall Park specialists.
**Romany Nights(IRE)** did not appear to quite get home on this demanding surface.
**Pharoah's Gold(IRE)** did not find a drop back to seven the answer.

## 1140 FREE #10 BET @ BET DIRECT INTERACTIVE CLAIMING STKS 6f (F)
**9:00** (9:00) (F) 4-Y-0+ **£2,919** (£834; £417) **Stalls** Low

Form RPR
0335 **1** **Gilded Cove**[22] 968 4-8-11 64 ACulhane 7 65
(RHollinshead) *hld up: hdwy over 3f out: rdn to ld wl over 1f out: drvn out* **5/4**[1]
6-30 **2** ½ **Rafters Music (IRE)**[22] 968 9-8-13 69 MFenton 3 65
(JulianPoulton) *hld up: rdn and hdwy over 1f out: ev ch ins fnl f: nt qckn* **6/1**[3]
4363 **3** ¾ **Aintnecessarilyso**[8] 1051 6-8-11 51 CCatlin 2 61
(NEBerry) *hld up: rdn over 3f out: hdwy over 2f out: kpt on u.str.p ins fnl f* **10/1**
6150 **4** 2 **Polar Haze**[40] 799 7-8-13 56 (v) JQuinn 5 57
(JPearce) *prom: rdn 2f out: wknd ins fnl f* **12/1**
1230 **5** shd **Blakeset**[14] 1013 9-8-10 72 DHolland 1 54
(TDBarron) *chsd ldr tl rdn over 2f out: wknd ins fnl f* **2/1**[2]
2-30 **6** 9 **Second Minister**[9] 1044 5-8-13 60 (bt) PFitzsimons 8 30
(DFlood) *led: rdn and hdd wl over 1f out: sn wknd* **20/1**

1m 15.82s (0.12) **Going Correction** +0.175s/f (Slow) **6** Ran SP% **113.6**
Speed ratings: **106,105,104,101,101 89**CSF £9.67 TOTE £2.10: £1.40, £2.10; EX 10.70.
**Owner** M Johnson **Bred** R Hollinshead And M Johnson **Trained** Upper Longdon, Staffs

**FOCUS**
A reasonable claimer and the winning time was decent.

**NOTEBOOK**
**Gilded Cove**, who is blind in his right eye, likes to race wide so he can see the other runners.
**Rafters Music(IRE)** came with a well-timed challenge but could not take advantage of a return to this grade.
**Aintnecessarilyso** had plenty to find at these weights. He stuck to his task but will certainly have known he had been in a race.
**Polar Haze** is another who would have been better off in a handicap.
**Blakeset**, well in on official figures, was without a visor for the first time in eight starts.

## 1141 CASHBACKS @ BETDIRECT.CO.UK H'CAP 1m 100y(F)
**9:30** (9:30) (E) (0-75,75) 3-Y-0+ **£3,283** (£938; £469) **Stalls** Low

Form RPR
-450 **1** **Del Mar Sunset**[23] 961 5-10-0 75 (p) DHolland 3 85
(WJHaggas) *mde all: rdn 2f out: edgd rt 1f out: drvn out* **15/8**[1]
33-2 **2** 1 **Active Account (USA)**[22] 970 7-9-5 66 JFEgan 4 74
(MrsHDalton) *hld up in tch: rdn 4f out: ev ch 1f out: nt qckn towards fin* **4/1**[3]
2041 **3** 5 **Danielle's Lad**[22] 967 8-9-11 72 (b) ACulhane 6 70
(BPalling) *prom: w wnr over 3f out: sn rdn: wknd over 1f out* **5/1**
0062 **4** 2 **Spark Up**[10] 1036 4-8-10 57 (v[1]) SWKelly 1 50
(JWUnett) *hld up in rr: rdn and hdwy on outside over 4f out: wknd 2f out* **8/1**
5110 **5** hd **Scottish River (USA)**[22] 970 5-9-12 73 ADaly 2 66
(MDIUsher) *dwlt: hld up: hdwy 3f out: rdn and hung lft over 1f out: wknd fnl f* **12/1**
-113 **6** 16 **Rare Coincidence**[11] 1029 3-8-6 70 (p) JFanning 5 29
(RFFisher) *s.i.s: hld up: rdn over 4f out: bhd fnl 3f: t.o* **7/2**[2]
404- **7** ½ **Clann A Cougar**[208] 4626 4-9-2 66 (p) THamilton(3) 7 24
(IAWood) *prom: rdn and wknd over 3f out: t.o* **33/1**

1m 51.72s (0.72) **Going Correction** +0.175s/f (Slow)
**WFA** 3 from 4yo+ 17lb **7** Ran SP% **115.4**
Speed ratings: **103,102,97,95,94 78,78**CSF £9.87 TOTE £3.30: £1.90, £2.40; EX 9.50 Place 6 £18.21, Place 5 £8.63..
**Owner** R A Dawson **Bred** Woodsway Stud And Chao Racing And Bloodstock Ltd **Trained** Newmarket, Suffolk

**FOCUS**
An ordinary handicap in which the winner had been given every chance.

**NOTEBOOK**
**Del Mar Sunset** took advantage of being given a chance by the Handicapper on this drop in class.
**Active Account(USA)** came up against a rival racing off a mark 10lb lower than when he scored over course and distance more than a year ago.
**Danielle's Lad** could not defy a 6lb rise in the ratings.
**Spark Up** had the headgear back on, but it was a visor instead of the blinkers.
**Scottish River(USA)** hung into the far rail in the home straight and gave the impression something may have been amiss.
T/Plt: £69.50 to a £1 stake. Pool £41,521.00. 435.80 winning tickets. T/Qpdt: £3.50 to a £1 stake. Pool £1,908.10. 403.30 winning tickets. KH

# 1001 NAD AL SHEBA (L-H)
### Saturday, March 27
**OFFICIAL GOING: Dirt course - fast; turf course - good to firm**

## 1142a GODOLPHIN MILE (GROUP 2) (DIRT) 1m
**1:40** (1:40) 3-Y-0+ **£335,195** (£111,731; £55,865; £27,932) **Stalls** Low

RPR
**1** **Firebreak**[104] 6187 5-9-0 (t) LDettori 8 120
(SaeedBinSuroor) *in tch in mid-div: stdy hdwy 4f out: rdn to ld 2f out: sn clr: pushed out* **3/1**[2]
**2** 4½ **Tropical Star (IRE)**[21] 974 4-9-0 (vt) RMullen 4 111
(AAlRaihe, UAE) *mid-div: nt clr run ent st: r.o fnl 1 1/2f: no ch w wnr* **14/1**
**3** 2¾ **Excessivepleasure (USA)**[63] 4-9-0 (bt) JKCourt 3 106
(DougO'Neill, U.S.A) *s.i.s: sn trckd ldrs ins: nt clr run and swtchd rt st: styd on nr fin* **12/1**
**4** 2¼ **Estimraar (USA)**[21] 974 7-9-0 (vt) GHind 5 101
(MAlKurdi, UAE) *disp ld: rdn to ld st: hdd 2f out: wknd fnl f* **20/1**
**5** 1½ **Inamorato (USA)**[44] 756 4-9-0 (vt) KMcEvoy 6 98
(SaeedBinSuroor) *towards rr: 8th and racd wd st: styd on fnl 2f: nvr trbld ldrs* **7/1**
**6** ¾ **During (USA)**[49] 4-9-0 (vt) JDBailey 1 97
(BBaffert, U.S.A) *disp ld tl hdd st: sn wknd* **2/1**[1]
**7** nk **Conflict (FR)**[8] 8-9-0 (vt) BDoyle 2 96
(MAlKurdi, UAE) *trckd ldrs: nt clr run ent st: effrt 2f out: wknd fnl f* **16/1**
**8** 2¾ **Cherry Pickings (USA)**[21] 974 7-9-0 (t) TEDurcan 7 90
(MAlKurdi, UAE) *towards rr: 7th and racd wd st: effrt 2f out: wknd nr fin* **5/1**[3]
**9** 11 **D'Anjou**[16] 1006 7-9-0 MJKinane 9 68
(JohnMOxx, Ire) *sn bhd and rdn along: last st: n.d* **16/1**

1m 35.82s **9** Ran SP% **118.4**
Speed ratings: .
**Owner** Godolphin **Bred** R P Williams **Trained** Newmarket, Suffolk

**NOTEBOOK**
**Firebreak**, winner of this race last season, had a tongue-tie on today and took his field apart in most impressive fashion. He has a good record on dirt and, given connections' excellent record at improving their older horses, there should be some more big races in him this year.
**Tropical Star(IRE)** reversed course form from earlier in the month with Cherry Pickings, but was no match for the winner. He would have been closer had he received a clean run through.
**Excessivepleasure(USA)** had a lot of ground to make up with favourite During on their running at Santa Anita earlier in the year, but he reversed form comprehensively and was slightly unlucky not get closer.
**Inamorato(USA)** ran on up the straight without ever posing a threat and is better further.
**During(USA)** was very disappointing, weakening having been up with the early pace. He is evidently better than this.
**Cherry Pickings(USA)** could not handle this rise in class having won at Listed level latest.

## 1143a UAE DERBY (GROUP 2) (DIRT) 1m 1f
**2:20** (2:20) 3-Y-0 **£670,391** (£223,463; £111,731; £55,865) **Stalls** Low

RPR
**1** **Lundy's Liability (BRZ)**[21] 975 3-9-4 WCMarwing 3 112
(MFDeKock, South Africa) *trckd ldrs: 3rd st: stdy hdwy 2f out: r.o wl to ld fnl 165yds: drvn out* **9/2**[3]
**2** ¾ **Petit Paris (CHI)**[21] 975 3-9-4 (t) JDBailey 7 111
(JBarton,) *led tl hdd st: rallied and ev ch 1f out: no ex nr fin* **4/1**[2]
**3** ¾ **Little Jim (ARG)**[21] 975 3-9-4 TEDurcan 9 109
(SSeemar, UAE) *trckd ldr: led st tl hdd fnl 165yds: wknd nr fin* **7/2**[1]
**4** 3¾ **Jack Sullivan (USA)**[51] 691 3-8-9 MJKinane 4 102
(GAButler) *mid-div outside: 6th st: styd on fnl 2f: nt rch ldrs* **13/2**
**5** ¾ **Ascertain (IRE)**[28] 913 3-8-9 EAhern 2 100
(NPLittmoden) *mid-div: rdn fr 1/2-way: styd on fnl 2f: nvr trbld ldrs* **12/1**
**6** 1¼ **Tamarillo**[16] 1005 3-8-5 GHind 8 94
(MAlKurdi, UAE) *trckd ldrs outside: 4th st: wknd fnl 2f* **8/1**
**7** 2¼ **Menhoubah (USA)**[16] 1005 3-8-5 ASolis 6 89
(CEBrittain) *mid-div: rdn fr 1/2-way: wknd st* **20/1**
**8** 7¾ **Great Exhibition (USA)**[193] 4965 3-8-9 (t) LDettori 1 78
(SaeedBinSuroor) *s.i.s: towards rr: 8th st: sn wknd* **6/1**
**9** 3 **Festive Style (SAF)**[16] 1005 3-9-0 RLMoore 5 68
(SSeemar, UAE) *a towards rr: last st: n.d* **12/1**

1m 50.83s **9** Ran SP% **119.3**
Speed ratings: .
**Owner** Stud TNT & Mrs M Slack **Bred** Stud Tnt **Trained** South Africa

**NOTEBOOK**
**Lundy's Liability(BRZ)** reversed recent course form with Petit Paris despite being 2lb worse off. He showed a great attitude in winning and has scope to get further.
**Petit Paris(CHI)** attempted to make all the running and very nearly managed to pull it off. He was momentarily passed by Little Jim, but battled back to give the winner most to think about.
**Little Jim(ARG)** only cried enough inside the final 100 yards and had run a very creditable race up to that point.
**Jack Sullivan(USA)** ran on without ever looking likely to trouble the front three.
**Ascertain(IRE)** was taking a big step up on the races he had been running in back in Britain, and was not altogether disgraced. Further looks sure to suit this gelding.
**Great Exhibition(USA)** was disappointing on this first start on the surface.

## 1144a DUBAI SHEEMA CLASSIC (GROUP 1) (TURF) 1m 4f
**3:10** (3:12) 4-Y-0+ **£670,391** (£223,463; £111,731; £55,865) **Stalls** Low

RPR
**1** **Polish Summer**[21] 980 7-8-11 GaryStevens 6 118
(AFabre, France) *mid-div: 7th st: smooth hdwy 1 1/2f out: rdn 1f out: r.o strly to ld wl ins fnl f* **10/3**[1]
**2** ½ **Hard Buck (BRZ)**[34] 5-8-11 JRVelazquez 10 117
(KMcpeek, U.S.A) *trckd ldr: 2nd st: styd on wl to ld 1f out: hdd wl ins fnl f* **9/1**
**3** ¾ **Scott's View**[16] 1003 5-8-11 SChin 7 116
(MJohnston) *towards rr: prog on ins 3 1/2f out: nt clr run and swtchd rt 1 1/2f out: r.o wl fnl f* **20/1**
**4** ¾ **Razkalla (USA)**[21] 976 6-8-11 TEDurcan 2 115
(DRLoder) *trckd ldrs: 3rd st: rdn and hdwy 2f out: styd on same pce* **16/1**
**5** ½ **Warrsan (IRE)**[104] 6185 6-8-11 MJKinane 9 114
(CEBrittain) *led: rdn st: hdd 1f out: wknd nr fin* **5/1**[2]
**6** 2¾ **Fair Mix (IRE)**[21] 976 6-8-11 OPeslier 12 110
(MRolland, France) *trckd ldrs outside: 4th st: rdn and effrt 2f out: sn wknd* **10/3**[1]
**7** hd **Grand Ekinoks (TUR)**[153] 6-8-11 (b) ASolis 8 110
(AyhanKasar, Turkey) *in rr: last and racd wd st: styd on fnl 2f: nt rch ldrs* **18/1**
**8** ½ **Rawyaan**[21] 976 5-8-11 (b) RHills 1 109
(JHMGosden) *mid-div: 6th st: grad wknd fnl 2f* **20/1**
**9** 1¼ **Delsarte (USA)**[221] 4270 4-8-11 KMcEvoy 3 109
(SaeedBinSuroor) *mid-div: lost pl over 4f out: 12th st: wknd fnl 2f* **16/1**
**10** nk **Compton Bolter (IRE)**[16] 1003 7-8-11 (b) EAhern 5 107
(GABulter) *a towards rr: 10th st: n.d* **28/1**
**11** 1 **Lunar Sovereign (USA)**[21] 976 5-8-11 (t) LDettori 4 105
(SaeedBinSuroor) *trckd ldrs: 5th st and rdn st: kpt on tl wknd fnl f* **8/1**[3]
**12** nk **Martaline**[181] 5249 5-8-11 JDBailey 11 105
(AFabre, France) *a towards rr: 11th st: n.d* **14/1**
**13** dist **Gorylla (BRZ)**[105] 6-8-11 AMota 13 —
(AAlvani, Brazil) *mid-div outside: rdn and wknd st* **40/1**

2m 31.09s
**WFA** 4 from 5yo+ 2lb **13** Ran SP% **123.0**
Speed ratings: .
**Owner** K Abdulla **Bred** Juddmonte Farms **Trained** France

**FOCUS**
Not the strongest Group One, but the winner appears to be improving at the age of seven.

**NOTEBOOK**
**Polish Summer**, a winner at Saint-Cloud earlier in the month, sat travelling strongly throughout and was only unleashed at the furlong pole. The response was what his rider would have been hoping for and he picked up in great style to cut down the runner-up late on.


The Form Book, Raceform Ltd, Compton, RG20 6NL

**Hard Buck(BRZ)** ran a brave race in defeat and ran right to the line.
**Scott's View ◆** was very unlucky and should have finished second at worse. He had nowhere to go on the inside for the majority of the straight, but once getting into the clear finished strongly. His progression continues.
**Razkalla(USA)** continues to improve with racing and produced another good performance.
**Warrsan(IRE)** had to make a lot of his own running and left himself a sitting duck as a consequence. There will be better to come from him this year.

## 1145a DUBAI GOLDEN SHAHEEN (GROUP 1) (DIRT) 6f

**3:50** (3:53) 3-Y-0+ **£670,391** (£223,463; £111,731; £55,865) **Stalls** High

RPR

1 **Our New Recruit (USA)**[55] 5-9-0 ........................(t) ASolis 10 121
(JWSadler, U.S.A) *a.p: rdn to ld 2f out: drew clr nr fin* **20/1**

2 2 **Alke (USA)**[49] 4-9-0 ........................ JRVelazquez 12 115
(TPletcher, U.S.A) *a.p: chsd wnr fr 2f out: kpt on: no ex nr fin* **9/2**[2]

3 1 1/2 **Conroy (USA)**[21] [977] 6-9-0 ........................ GaryStevens 9 111
(ASelvaratnam, UAE) *trckd ldrs: rdn and hdwy 1 1/2f out: nt rch ldrs* **20/1**

4 1/2 **Cajun Beat (USA)**[49] 4-9-0 ........................(vt) JDBailey 3 109
(SMargolis, U.S.A) *prom: ev ch 2f out: wknd fnl f* **13/8**[1]

5 3/4 **Meiner Select (JPN)**[76] 5-9-0 ........................(t) YTake 11 107
(HNakamura, Japan) *trckd ldrs: rdn 2 1/2f out: kpt on: nt rch ldrs* **8/1**

6 hd **Tsigane (FR)**[41] 5-9-0 ........................(t) DFlores 4 106
(JCanani, U.S.A) *trckd ldrs far side: rdn and ev ch 2f out: wknd fnl f* **16/1**

7 6 1/2 **State City (USA)**[154] 5-9-0 ........................(t) LDettori 7 87
(SaeedBinSuroor) *sn outpcd and rdn along: kpt on fnl f: nt rch ldrs* **9/1**

8 1 **Tour Of The Cat (USA)**[42] 6-9-0 ........................(t) JKCourt 5 84
(MMora, U.S.A) *chsd ldrs far side: wknd over 1f out* **33/1**

9 2 **Conceal**[8] 6-9-0 ........................ RHills 6 78
(RBouresly, Kuwait) *sn outpcd and rdn along: effrt over 2f out: wknd fnl f* **40/1**

10 6 1/4 **Feet So Fast**[16] [1004] 5-9-0 ........................ TEDurcan 8 59
(SSeemar, UAE) *un tch tl rdn and wknd 2 1/2f out* **10/1**

11 3/4 **Multidandy (AUS)**[14] 5-9-0 ........................(t) FCoetzee 1 57
(ASCruz, Hong Kong) *prom: rdn fr 1/2-way: wknd fnl 2f* **6/1**[3]

12 6 1/4 **Dantana (AUS)**[21] [977] 5-9-0 ........................(b) KMcEvoy 2 38
(PLeyshan, Macau) *prom: rdn and ev ch 2 1/2f out: wknd over 1f out* **40/1**

1m 10.3s **12** Ran SP% **124.0**
Speed ratings: .
**Owner** C R K Stable **Bred** Thomas A Groul **Trained** North America

**FOCUS**
A one-two for the Americans.

**NOTEBOOK**
**Our New Recruit(USA)**, who scored in claiming company in the USA back in October of last year, took this Group One contest with an impressive performance.
**Alke(USA)** has been in cracking form this year, and was able to confirm recent placings with Cajun Beat on 11lb worse terms than when beating him two and a half lengths over an extended six furlongs last month.
**Conroy(USA)** was staying on at the end, but never really threatened the winner.
**Cajun Beat(USA)**, last season's Breeders' Cup Sprint winner, was two and a half lengths behind Alke over an extended six furlongs at Gulfstream Park on his latest start but should have been able to reverse that form on 11lb better terms over this shorter distance. However, he did not run to his best and may not have been ideally suited by this straight track.
**State City(USA)** won this last year for another stable, but was never really going this time around.

## 1146a DUBAI DUTY FREE STKS (GROUP 1) (TURF) 1m 195y(T)

**4:30** (4:31) 3-Y-0+ **£446,927** (£446,927; £111,731; £55,865) **Stalls** Low

RPR

1 dht **Right Approach**[35] [853] 5-9-0 ........................(t) WCMarwing 7 120
(MFDeKock, South Africa) *towards rr: last st: rdn over 1 1/2f out: r.o strly fnl f: disp ld nr fin* **12/1**

1 **Paolini (GER)**[224] [4200] 7-9-0 ........................ EPedroza 4 120
(AWohler, Germany) *in tch towards rr: 9th on ins st: rdn and r.o strly fnl f: disp ld nr fin* **10/1**

3 nk **Nayyir**[161] [5638] 6-9-0 ........................ MJKinane 6 119
(GAButler) *mid-div: 5th st: rdn and hdwy over 1f out: led 110yds out tl hdd nr fin* **16/1**

4 1/2 **Crimson Palace (SAF)**[58] [636] 5-8-9 ........................ LDettori 2 113
(SaeedBinSuroor) *trckd ldrs: 3rd st: rdn 2f out: kpt on wl nr fin* **10/3**[2]

5 shd **Martillo (GER)**[223] [4232] 4-9-0 ........................ WMongil 9 118
(RSuerland, Germany) *trckd ldr: 2nd st: led 1f out tl hdd fnl 110yds: no ex nr fin* **20/1**

6 nk **Checkit (IRE)**[16] [1001] 4-9-0 ........................ TEDurcan 10 117
(MRChannon) *towards rr: 8th st: hdwy over 2f out: nt clr run 2f out: styd on nr fin* **14/1**

7 1 1/4 **Bright Sky (IRE)**[21] [980] 5-8-9 ........................ DBoeuf 11 110
(ELellouche, France) *towards rr outside: r.o fnl 1 1/2f: nt rch ldrs* **11/4**[1]

8 2 1/4 **Refuse To Bend (IRE)**[154] [5769] 4-9-0 ........................ KMcEvoy 3 110
(SaeedBinSuroor) *led tl hdd 1f out: sn wknd* **11/1**

9 3/4 **Evolving Tactics (IRE)**[28] [925] 4-9-0 ........................ PJSmullen 1 109
(DKWeld, Ire) *in tch on ins: 6th st: grad wknd fnl 1 1/2f* **10/1**

10 1 1/2 **Sarafan (USA)**[21] 7-9-0 ........................(t) GaryStevens 8 106
(NDrysdale, U.S.A) *trckd ldrs outside: 4th st: wknd over 2f out* **10/1**

11 2 1/4 **Surveyor (SAF)**[21] [978] 4-9-0 ........................(b) KShea 5 101
(MFDeKock, South Africa) *mid-div outside: rdn 2f out: sn wknd* **7/1**[3]

1m 49.36s **11** Ran SP% **122.9**
Speed ratings: .
**Owner** Frau C Ostermann-Richter **Bred** Mrs C Ostermann-Richter **Trained** Germany

**FOCUS**
This may not have been that strong a Group One but it provided a thrilling, blanket finish.

**NOTEBOOK**
**Paolini(GER)** is a regular in these big international contests and deserved to end a losing run stretching back to June 2001. *Official explanation: is a regular in these big international contests and deserved to end a losing run stretching back to June 2001.*
**Right Approach** never really fulfilled his potential when with Sir Michael Stoute, but won a Listed race on his debut in Dubai and followed up in this tougher contest with a fine effort.
**Nayyir** has always looked something of a seven-furlong specialist, but is bred to get this sort of trip and came so very close to winning his first Group One. He looks set for a big season. *Official explanation: has always looked something of a seven-furlong specialist, but is bred to get this sort of trip and came so very close to winning his first Group One. He looks set for a big season.*
**Crimson Palace(SAF)**, a winner on her debut in Dubai when with Mike De Kock, ran well on her first start for Godolphin in this better heat.
**Checkit(IRE)**, with the visor left off, ran well in the face of a stiff task.
**Bright Sky(IRE)** did not run to form and this ground may have been fast enough.
**Refuse To Bend(IRE)** had the run of the race.
**Evolving Tactics(IRE)** was not at his best, with no obvious excuse.

## 1147a DUBAI WORLD CUP (GROUP 1) (DIRT) 1m 2f

**5:20** (5:21) 3-Y-0+ **£2,011,173** (£670,391; £335,195; £167,597) **Stalls** Low

RPR

1 **Pleasantly Perfect (USA)**[56] 6-9-0 ........................(bt) ASolis 7 128
(RichardEMandella, U.S.A) *trckd ldrs: 3rd st: hdwy over 2f out: led over 1f out: styd on wl u.p* **5/2**[2]

2 3/4 **Medaglia D'Oro (USA)**[49] 5-9-0 ........................(t) JDBailey 11 127
(RJFrankel, U.S.A) *trckd ldr: led st: rdn over 2f out: hdd over 1f out: kpt on: nt pce of wnr* **2/1**[1]

3 5 **Victory Moon (SAF)**[21] [979] 5-9-0 ........................ WCMarwing 9 118
(MFDeKock, South Africa) *mid-div: 6th st: hdwy over 2f out: styd on fnl f: nt rch ldrs* **4/1**[3]

4 7 3/4 **Grand Hombre (USA)**[175] 4-9-0 ........................(t) LDettori 8 104
(SaeedBinSuroor) *trckd ldrs: 4th st: styd on same pce fnl 2f* **12/1**

5 4 **King's Boy (GER)**[78] 7-9-0 ........................(b) MJKinane 2 97
(JBarton,) *v.s.a: towards rr: prog on ins st: styd on fnl 2f: nt rch ldrs* **66/1**

6 4 **Domestic Dispute (USA)**[49] 4-9-0 ........................(t) GaryStevens 1 89
(PGallagher, U.S.A) *mid-div: 5th st: styd on same pce* **22/1**

7 nk **Fleetstreet Dancer (USA)**[56] 6-9-0 ........................(bt) JKCourt 10 89
(DougO'Neill, U.S.A) *led tl hdd st: wknd fnl 2f* **16/1**

8 2 1/4 **Admire Don (JPN)**[34] 5-9-0 ........................ KAndo 3 85
(HMatsuda, Japan) *mid-div: 7th st: wknd fnl 2f* **11/1**

9 1 3/4 **Regent Bluff (JPN)**[52] 8-9-0 ........................ YYoshida 5 82
(YOkubo, Japan) *a towards rr: last st: kpt on fnl 2f: nvr nr to chal* **40/1**

10 7 3/4 **Dinyeper**[21] [979] 5-9-0 ........................ HKaratas 4 68
(AyhanKasar, Turkey) *sn rdn along: trckd ldrs: wknd qckly fnl 4f* **40/1**

11 3 1/4 **State Shinto (USA)**[21] [979] 8-9-0 ........................(b) TEDurcan 12 62
(MAlKurdi, UAE) *mid-div tl wknd fr 1/2-way* **66/1**

12 13 **Silent Deal (JPN)**[34] 4-9-0 ........................ YTake 6 38
(YIkee, Japan) *v.s.a: a towards rr: n.d* **25/1**

2m 0.24s **12** Ran SP% **119.9**
Speed ratings: .
**Owner** Diamond A Racing Corporation **Bred** Clovelly Farm **Trained** USA

**FOCUS**
Not the strength in depth one would expect for the money, but the principals are two of the best dirt performers around and had the race to themselves in the straight.

**NOTEBOOK**
**Pleasantly Perfect(USA)** confirmed Breeders' Cup Classic placings with the runner-up and, not afraid to turn up and show what he is capable of, he once again proved himself a truly top-class dirt performer.
**Medaglia D'Oro(USA)** had slight question marks hanging over him with regard to this trip, especially given the particularly long straight, but he battled right the way to the line, pulling clear of some other classy performers in the process.
**Victory Moon(SAF)** has a good record on this track and had the advantage of a few prep runs, but he was simply not as good as the front two.
**Grand Hombre(USA)** did not run a bad race on his first start Saeed Bin Suroor, but does not look up to this class.

1148 - 1155a (Foreign Racing) - See Raceform Interactive

# LEOPARDSTOWN (L-H)

Sunday, March 28

**OFFICIAL GOING: Yielding**

## 1156a ALLEGED STKS (LISTED RACE) 1m 2f

**5:00** (5:01) 4-Y-0+ **£22,922** (£6,725; £3,204; £1,091)

RPR

1 **Brian Boru**[161] [5670] 4-9-7 117........................(t) JPSpencer 7 114
(APO'Brien, Ire) *settled 4th: 3rd st: led 2f out: veered lft under 1 1/2f out: kpt on wl fnl f* **1/2**[1]

2 3/4 **Napper Tandy (IRE)**[153] [5806] 4-9-3 109........................(b) KJManning 1 109
(JSBolger, Ire) *trckd ldrs in 3rd: chal st: sltly hmpd and swtchd over 1f out: kpt on wl* **7/1**[3]

3 3 **Dawn Invasion (IRE)**[14] [5588] 5-9-0 105........................ DPMcDonogh 6 101
(AnthonyMullins, Ire) *trckd ldrs in 5th: 6th st: kpt on wl fr over 1f out* **9/1**

4 2 1/2 **Jade Quest (IRE)**[141] [5960] 4-9-0 98........................ FMBerry 5 96
(CharlesO'Brien, Ire) *hld up: 7th st: kpt on fr 2f out* **20/1**

5 1 1/2 **Mkuzi**[22] [976] 5-9-3 110........................ MJKinane 3 96
(JohnMOxx, Ire) *sn led: hdd 2f out: wkng whn hmpd over 1f out* **6/1**[2]

6 nk **Tipperary All Star (FR)**[153] [5806] 4-9-3 106........................ TPO'Shea 4 96
(MHalford, Ire) *settled 2nd: chal st: no ex over 1f out* **14/1**

7 1 1/2 **Akshar (IRE)**[176] [5365] 5-9-0 109........................ PJSmullen 8 90
(DKWeld, Ire) *hld up: 6th and pushed along 4f out: wknd st* **10/1**

8 20 **Humilis (IRE)**[169] [5494] 4-9-0 96........................ PShanahan 2 54
(DKWeld, Ire) *a bhd: trailing st* **25/1**

2m 10.8s **Going Correction** +0.40s/f (Good) **8** Ran SP% **127.8**
Speed ratings: **114,113,111,109,107 107,106,90**CSF £6.05 TOTE £1.50: £1.10, £1.60, £3.50; DF 4.10.
**Owner** Mrs John Magnier **Bred** Juddmonte Farms **Trained** Ballydoyle, Co Tipperary
■ Stewards Enquiry : J P Spencer two-day ban: careless riding (Apr 10,11)

**NOTEBOOK**
**Brian Boru** coped adequately with this drop back in distance from the St Leger trip. He went with the pace throughout and got to the front, on the outer, two furlongs down. But with Spencer's stick in his right hand, he veered left across the three horses on his inner with under a furlong and a half left to race, causing plenty of inconvenience. He ran on well without quickening and the logical steps now are the Mooresbridge Stakes and then the Tattersalls Gold Cup, both at the Curragh. He is not short of pace over this trip.
**Napper Tandy(IRE)** was certainly impeded in his run by the winner's deviation but whether he would have won is doubtful.
**Dawn Invasion(IRE)**, successful over hurdles at Cork on his previous outing, ran well enough for a 105 handicapper.
**Jade Quest(IRE)** ran above himself, staying on from the rear without ever threatening.
**Mkuzi** appeared to be weakening when hampered but might have finished a place closer.
**Tipperary All Star(FR)** was still challenging when the winner went across, but he was not really affected.
**Akshar(IRE)** never really counted on ground that might not have suited.

1157 - 1162a (Foreign Racing) - See Raceform Interactive

# [1048] SAINT-CLOUD (L-H)

Sunday, March 28

**OFFICIAL GOING: Soft**

## 1163a PRIX EDMOND BLANC (GROUP 3) — 1m

**2:50** (3:31) 4-Y-0+ — **£25,704** (£10,282; £7,711; £5,141)

RPR

1 — **My Risk (FR)**[148] 5884 5-9-0 .......... CSoumillon 3 — 113
(J-MBeguigne, France) *held up, 9th straight, headway between horses over 2f out, ridden 1 1/2f out, hard driven to lead 100y out, just held on, a* — 3

2 *hd* **Art Moderne (USA)**[15] 1014 4-8-12 .......... (b) DBoeuf 8 — 111
(ELellouche, France) *held up, 7th straight, headway to lead 2f out, ridden 1 1/2f out, headed 100y out, rallied gamely under strong driving clos*

3 *snk* **Sarre (FR)**[15] 1014 4-8-8 .......... C-PLemaire 7 — 106
(PCostes, France) *last early, 8th straight on outside, headway down outside to go 2nd 1 1/2f out, stayed on*

4 *2* **Almond Mousse (FR)**[85] 5-8-8 .......... ELegrix 6 — 102
(RobertCollet, France) *held up in rear, last straight, taken to outside over 2f out, went 4th inside final f, kept on at one pace*

5 *nk* **Streamix (FR)**[194] 4-8-12 .......... TGillet 12 — 106
(JEHammond, France) *midfield on outside, 4th straight, hampered and lost paced 2f out, stayed on again final f*

6 *hd* **Puppeteer**[189] 4-8-12 .......... TJarnet 10 — 105
(ADeRoyer-Dupre, France) *raced in 4th, 5th straight, disputing 2nd over 1 1/2f out, one pace*

7 *2* **Special Kaldoun (IRE)**[105] 6187 5-9-2 .......... SPasquier 5 — 105
(DSmaga, France) *held up, 10th straight, effort when not much room over 1 1/2f out, kept on steadily final f* — 1

8 *1 1/2* **King's Drama (IRE)**[225] 4201 4-9-0 .......... DBonilla 4 — 100
(RobertCollet, France) *held up in rear, 11th straight, slightly hampered over 2f out, ridden and one pace from over 1f out*

9 *2* **Maxwell (FR)**[15] 1014 4-8-12 .......... OPeslier 2 — 94
(MmeCHead-Maarek, France) *tracked leader, 3rd straight, not much room when taken right and lost place over 2f out, no danger after* — 2

10 *1* **Nelson Creek (FR)**[15] 1014 4-8-12 .......... TThulliez 11 — 92
(HVanDePoele, France) *prominent, 2nd straight, still disputing 2nd over 1 1/2f out, weakened*

11 **Marshall (FR)**[30] 911 4-9-0 .......... MBlancpain 1 — 94
(CLaffon-Parias, France) *midfield against inside rail, 6th straight, no room and dropped back to last under 2f out, not recover* — 2

12 **Last Empress (FR)**[50] 4-8-8 .......... OPlacais 9 — 88
(JJNapoli, France) *set strong pace til headed 2f out, weakened quickly*

1m 43.0s **Going Correction** -0.40s/f (Firm) — **12** Ran SP% **146.7**
Speed ratings: **114,113,113,111,111 111,109,107,105,104 104,104.**
**Owner** R Monnier **Bred** R Monnier, D Forsans & D Bougarelle **Trained** France

### NOTEBOOK

**My Risk(FR)**, towards the tail of the field early, still had plenty to do in the straight and weaved through the field to challenge a furlong out. Under very strong pressure, he took the advantage in the last few strides and this was a very game effort, though his jockey was fined for excessive use of the whip. He now goes for the Prix du Muguet.
**Art Moderne(USA)**, blinkered for the first time, sat in mid-division early but made rapid progress in the straight to lead at the furlong marker. He battled on really well, but was just touched off the end. He will also go for the Muguet.
**Sarre(FR)**, held up for a late run, still had plenty to do entering the straight, but came with a storming late run a furlong out and finished best of all. She may also take her chance in the Muguet.
**Almond Mousse(FR)**, another to be held up in the early stages, was still well back turning into the straight and then made rapid progress up the centre of the track. This was a promising effort from this consistent mare.

# [1117] LINGFIELD (L-H)

Monday, March 29

**OFFICIAL GOING: Standard**
Wind: lt, hlf against Weather: fine & sunny

## 1164 BET DIRECT NO Q 08000 93 66 93 BANDED STKS — 1m 4f (P)

**2:00** (2:00) (H) 4-Y-0+ — **£1,477** (£422; £211) **Stalls** Low

Form — RPR

060/ **1** **Lissahanelodge**[563] 4593 5-9-2 40 .......... SWhitworth 8 — 46
(PRHedger) *s.s: hld up in last: gd prog on outer over 3f out: led wl over 1f out: rdn clr fnl f* — **20/1**

3140 **2** *2 1/2* **Little Richard (IRE)**[20] 995 5-9-2 40 .......... (p) VSlattery 3 — 42
(MWellings) *trckd ldrs: rdn and prog on inner to chal 2f out: chsd wnr over 1f out: no imp* — **9/2**[1]

05-0 **3** *2* **Anniversary Guest (IRE)**[42] 789 5-8-9 35 .......... DerekNolan(7) 11 — 39
(MrsLucindaFeatherstone) *dwlt: t.k.h: hld up towards rr: prog to join ldrs wl over 2f out: rdn and fnd nil wl over 1f out: one pce after* — **20/1**

0-00 **4** *shd* **Royale Pearl**[35] 855 4-9-0 40 .......... SDrowne 9 — 39
(RIngram) *hld up in rr: stdy prog 3f out: nvr rchd ldrs: drvn and styd on fr over 1f out* — **33/1**

3001 **5** *1 1/4* **Antony Ebeneezer**[11] 1042 5-8-11 40 .......... (t) RThomas(5) 14 — 37
(CRDore) *hld up in last trio: n.m.r 4f out: rdn and effrt to chse ldrs over 2f out: one pce and nvr able to chal* — **5/1**[2]

-030 **6** *1 1/4* **Giko**[20] 995 10-9-2 35 .......... (b) MartinDwyer 6 — 35
(JaneSouthcombe) *pressed ldrs: effrt to ld over 3f out: rdn and hdd wl over 1f out: wknd fnl f* — **14/1**

3244 **7** *2* **The Last Mohican**[18] 950 5-9-2 40 .......... (p) LDettori 1 — 32
(PHowling) *racd in midfield: rdn 3f out: one pce and nvr on terms w ldrs* — **9/2**[1]

00-0 **8** *7* **Fitz The Bill (IRE)**[10] 535 4-9-0 35 .......... JMackay 2 — 20
(NBKing) *racd in last trio: pushed along 1/2-way: struggling over 3f out: n.d* — **50/1**

0300 **9** *1 1/4* **Polka Princess**[20] 995 4-9-0 35 .......... (p) JQuinn 12 — 18
(MWellings) *nvr beyond midfield: rdn and no prog over 3f out: sn btn* — **20/1**

0-00 **10** *1/2* **Time Flyer**[37] 846 4-9-0 40 .......... SRighton 5 — 18
(WDeBest-Turner) *dwlt: plld hrd and prog on outer to trck ldrs after 5f: wknd wl over 2f out* — **50/1**

060- **11** *5* **Amethyst Rock**[216] 4486 6-9-2 40 .......... NPollard 10 — 10
(PLGilligan) *sn pressed ldr: led 1/2-way to 4f out: wknd 3f out* — **20/1**

2202 **12** *3/4* **Private Seal**[5] 1101 9-8-9 40 .......... (t) MHalford(7) 15 — 8
(JulianPoulton) *pressed ldrs: rdn and wknd rapidly 3f out* — **9/2**[1]

430- **13** *11* **Jezadil (IRE)**[228] 4105 6-8-9 40 .......... KristinStubbs(7) 13 — —
(MrsLStubbs) *s.s: t.k.h and plld way up to join ldrs after 3f: led 4f out to over 3f out: wknd rapidly over 2f out* — **7/1**[3]

0 **14** *28* **Newcorr (IRE)**[5] 1102 5-9-2 40 .......... GBaker 7 — —
(JJBridger) *led to 1/2-way: wknd rapidly 4f out: t.o* — **25/1**

2m 34.12s (0.14) **Going Correction** 0.0s/f (Stan)
**WFA** 4 from 5yo+ 2lb — **14** Ran SP% **120.1**
Speed ratings: **99,97,96,95,95 94,92,88,87,87 83,83,75,57**CSF £99.16 TOTE £25.20: £6.10, £1.90, £10.50; EX 135.50.
**Owner** J J Whelan **Bred** J J Whelan **Trained** Eastergate, W Sussex

### FOCUS

They went a decent pace here and set it up for those coming from behind. Probably just average form.

### NOTEBOOK

**Lissahanelodge**, having his first start since September 2002, had shown little in four maiden starts previously. Suited by the drop in grade and the way the race was run, he came through from the back of the field to run out a clear winner. His trainer reported that the reason the gelding had been off the track for so long was that he had needed time to develop physically, as opposed to injury, so he could well go on from here. *Official explanation: trainer had no explanation for the improved form shown*
**Little Richard(IRE)** got the good pace he needs at this trip but found the winner too strong. He is probably more effective over farther.
**Anniversary Guest(IRE)** needs to learn to settle if she is to get off the mark.
**Royale Pearl**, whose stamina was doubtful for this trip beforehand, appeared to improve for the step up in distance.
**Antony Ebeneezer** has never run as well on Polytrack as he has on Fibresand.
**Jezadil(IRE)** *Official explanation: jockey said mare hung right throughout*

## 1165 BET DIRECT NO Q BANDED STKS — 7f (P)

**2:30** (2:33) (H) 3-Y-0+ — **£1,484** (£424; £212) **Stalls** Low

Form — RPR

-320 **1** **Packin Em In**[43] 780 6-9-4 35 .......... DCorby(3) 7 — 49
(JRBoyle) *trckd ldr: led 1/2-way: kicked 2l clr wl over 1f out: rdn fnl f: hld on* — **25/1**

-013 **2** *hd* **Dial Square**[15] 1020 3-8-6 45 .......... (b) MHills 10 — 48
(PHowling) *trckd ldng pair: chsd wnr over 2f out: rdn and unable qck wl over 1f out: styd on fnl f: jst hld* — **5/1**[3]

0502 **3** *1 1/2* **Shirley Oaks (IRE)**[27] 951 6-9-2 40 .......... NChalmers(5) 11 — 44
(MissZCDavison) *racd towards rr: drvn and prog on wd outside 2f out: styd on fnl f: tk 3rd last strides* — **16/1**

6500 **4** *hd* **Vizulize**[29] 933 5-9-7 45 .......... JQuinn 3 — 43
(AWCarroll) *trckd ldng trio: rdn and effrt 2f out: nt qckn over 1f out: one pce after* — **20/1**

0254 **5** *1/2* **Single Track Mind**[15] 1020 6-9-7 45 .......... LDettori 9 — 42
(JRBoyle) *racd towards rr: rdn and sme prog over 2f out: kpt on one pce u.p* — **11/4**[2]

0300 **6** *3/4* **The Gay Fox**[3] 1121 10-9-7 40 .......... (tp) VSlattery 8 — 40
(BGPowell) *racd in midfield: rdn to chse ldrs over 2f out: one pce and no imp over 1f out* — **16/1**

0030 **7** *1/2* **Geespot**[15] 1020 5-9-7 40 .......... MartinDwyer 12 — 39
(DJSFfrenchDavis) *settled in last trio: sme prog 2f out: rdn and kpt on fnl f: n.d* — **16/1**

5306 **8** *1 1/2* **Estrella Levante**[29] 933 4-9-7 45 .......... (be) RLMoore 13 — 35
(GLMoore) *hld up wl in rr: rdn and kpt on same pce fr over 1f out: n.d* — **16/1**

0631 **9** *nk* **Gentle Response**[20] 998 4-9-7 45 .......... (b) SWhitworth 4 — 34
(BRJohnson) *wl in tch: trckd ldng quartet 3f out: gng wl enough whn nt clr run 2f out: shuffled along and lost pl fnl f* — **5/2**[1]

0040 **10** *4* **Malaah (IRE)**[6] 1092 8-9-0 40 .......... (b) MHalford(7) 6 — 23
(JulianPoulton) *led to 1/2-way: wknd wl over 1f out* — **20/1**

0030 **11** *nk* **Lady Liesel**[5] 1095 4-9-7 40 .......... GBaker 1 — 22
(JJBridger) *dwlt: racd in last: wl bhd over 2f out: no ch* — **33/1**

-000 **12** *5* **Brooklands Time (IRE)**[11] 1044 3-8-3 45 ow4 .......... GEdwards(7) 15 — 13
(IWMcinnes) *dwlt: rushed up on wd outside to press ldrs over 4f out: wknd over 2f out* — **50/1**

0-46 **13** *1 1/2* **Shamwari Fire (IRE)**[74] 536 4-9-0 45 .......... NataliaGemelova(7) 5 — 5
(IWMcinnes) *chsd ldrs: rdn 3f out: sn lost pl: wknd 2f out* — **12/1**

0106 **14** *7* **Evangelist (IRE)**[6] 1092 4-9-7 45 .......... (bt) SDrowne 16 — —
(MrsStefLiddiard) *a in rr: reminders over 4f out: struggling fr 1/2-way* — **20/1**

-404 **15** *12* **Janes Valentine**[35] 858 4-9-7 40 .......... NPollard 2 — —
(JJBridger) *in rr whn hmpd and hit rail jst over 4f out: nt rcvr* — **33/1**

1m 26.4s (0.40) **Going Correction** 0.0s/f (Stan)
**WFA** 3 from 4yo+ 15lb — **15** Ran SP% **129.1**
Speed ratings: **97,96,95,94,94 93,92,91,90,86 85,80,78,70,56**CSF £145.24 TOTE £38.30: £8.10, £2.20, £4.20; EX 267.20.
**Owner** City Industrial Supplies Ltd **Bred** Mrs M Upsdell **Trained** Epsom, Surrey

### FOCUS

A poor contest and a surprise result, with the lowest-rated horse showing much improved form to prevail narrowly.

### NOTEBOOK

**Packin Em In** appreciated the return to seven furlongs and the switch back to Polytrack. He was breaking his duck at the 17th attempt though, and does not appeal as the type to follow up.
**Dial Square** ran a better race back in the right grade. He is not one to discount in his present form in these banded contests as this was a good effort against his elders.
**Shirley Oaks(IRE)** ran another solid race and should continue to perform with credit in this grade.
**Vizulize** had the headgear left off this time and ran a better race than of late on this first outing in banded grade.
**Single Track Mind**, whose only win came almost three and a half years ago, is difficult to catch right as he needs to be held up way off the pace and produced late.
**Gentle Response** was fancied to follow up her recent course and distance success but, having travelled well down the hill, did not seem to handle the bend that well and her rider was not at all hard on her in the straight. She is better than this run suggests.
**Evangelist(IRE)** *Official explanation: jockey said filly had lost her action*

## 1166 LITTLEWOODS BET DIRECT BANDED STKS — 1m 2f (P)

**3:00** (3:01) (H) 3-Y-0+ — **£1,466** (£419; £209) **Stalls** Low

Form — RPR

-004 **1** **Oktis Morilious (IRE)**[20] 999 3-8-1 45 .......... JQuinn 7 — 53
(AWCarroll) *hld up in midfield: trckd ldrs 3f out: rdn to ld wl over 1f out: edgd rt fnl f: kpt on* — **10/1**

0-00 **2** *1* **Ryan's Bliss (IRE)**[27] 948 4-9-4 40 .......... J-PGuillambert(3) 11 — 51
(TDMccarthy) *hld up in rr: stdy prog 3f out: rdn and effrt wl over 1f out: chsd wnr fnl f: kpt on: a hld* — **50/1**

2036 **3** 2 **Theatre Lady (IRE)**[25] [966] 6-9-7 45.................. LDettori 5 47
(PDEvans) *settled towards rr: pushed along over 4f out: drvn and kpt on one pce fnl 2f* **9/4**[1]

00-0 **4** ½ **Eurolink Artemis**[86] [425] 7-9-0 40..................(p) MHalford(7) 12 47
(JulianPoulton) *hld up in rr: stdy prog 3f out: rdn and nt qckn wl over 1f out: one pce after* **33/1**

0050 **5** ¾ **Galey River (USA)**[12] [996] 5-9-4 40.................. DCorby(3) 2 45
(JJSheehan) *disp ld after 2f: rdn 4f out: defd advantage over 2f out: hdd and one pce wl over 1f out* **14/1**

6000 **6** 3½ **Mythical Charm**[35] [855] 5-9-7 45.................. NPollard 10 39
(JJBridger) *dwlt: hld up in rr: pushed along over 4f out: modest late prog: n.d* **12/1**

0-60 **7** 2½ **Steppenwolf**[34] [871] 3-8-1 45..................(p) SRighton 4 34
(WDeBest-Turner) *hld up in tch: trckd ldrs gng easily 3f out: rdn and fnd nil wl over 1f out: wknd* **11/1**

6506 **8** 3 **Pyrrhic**[20] [996] 5-9-7 45..................(b) RLMoore 8 29
(RMFlower) *dwlt: sn trckd ldrs: pushed along and lost pl 3f out: sn struggling* **9/2**[2]

5450 **9** nk **Wilom (GER)**[35] [855] 6-9-7 40.................. VSlattery 1 28
(MRHoad) *led: jnd after 2f: disp ld to over 2f out: steadily wknd* **14/1**

000/ **10** 1¾ **Barakana (IRE)**[127] 6-9-7 45..................(b) JMackay 3 25
(CTinkler) *trckd ldrs: rdn over 3f out: wknd over 2f out* **8/1**[3]

0-03 **11** 6 **Ersaal (USA)**[7] [1077] 4-9-7 45..................(b) SDrowne 9 14
(JJay) *pressed ldrs: rdn and reluctant 6f out: lost pl and last over 3f out: sn bhd* **9/1**

2m 8.28s (0.89) **Going Correction** 0.0s/f (Stan)
**WFA** 3 from 4yo+ 20lb **11** Ran SP% **113.4**
Speed ratings: **96,95,93,93,92 89,87,85,85,83 78**CSF £390.98 TOTE £13.00: £2.40, £8.50, £1.50; EX 331.50.
**Owner** Dennis Deacon **Bred** Lord Vestey **Trained** Wixford, Warwicks

**FOCUS**
An ordinary race with the three-year-old beating older rivals, and once again those who were held up off the pace fought out the finish.

**NOTEBOOK**
**Oktis Morilious(IRE)** had looked as though he would be suited by a step up in trip when fourth in a seller over a mile last time, and he confirmed that impression. This was a good effort against his elders and he is progressing.
**Ryan's Bliss(IRE)** found this drop in grade bringing about an improved display. She got the extra two furlongs well but the winner was always holding her challenge.
**Theatre Lady(IRE)**, who did not find a great deal under pressure, kept on well enough. However, this was a slightly disappointing effort given that this race appeared a fairly undemanding task in contrast to the handicap she contested last time.
**Eurolink Artemis**, having her first start for almost three months, travelled well into the straight, albeit wide of the rest, and kept on well enough. This run should bring him on and he could be up to winning a race of this nature.
**Galey River(USA)** did best of those who raced up with the pace but his overall record does not inspire.
**Pyrrhic** *Official explanation: trainer said gelding was found to be coughing after the race.*

## 1167 BETDIRECT.CO.UK BANDED STKS — 1m (P)
3:30 (3:32) (H) 3-Y-O+ — £1,456 (£416; £208) Stalls High

Form RPR

-400 **1** **Cumbrian Princess**[7] [1080] 7-9-3 30.................. RThomas(5) 5 44
(MBlanshard) *chsd ldrs: effrt over 2f out: drvn and styd on to ld last 100y: sn clr* **14/1**

00-2 **2** 1½ **Baytown Flyer**[6] [1094] 4-9-8 35.................. LDettori 10 41
(PSMcentee) *led: jnd over 2f out: shkn up and def advantage over 1f out: hdd and nt qckn last 100y* **9/2**[2]

/442 **3** 1¼ **Tiny Tim (IRE)**[20] [998] 6-9-1 35.................. RJKilloran(7) 4 38
(AMBalding) *trckd ldrs: gng easily over 2f out: effrt to press ldng pair 1f out: nt qckn and sn btn* **10/3**[1]

-003 **4** 1¼ **Tojoneski**[20] [998] 5-9-1 35..................(p) NataliaGemelova(7) 6 35
(IWMcinnes) *in tch: effrt to chse ldrs 3f out: rdn and kpt on same pce fnl 2f* **11/2**[3]

0000 **5** 1 **Hellbent**[27] [951] 5-9-2 35 ow1.................. SCrawford(7) 12 34
(JAOsborne) *s.s: t.k.h and hld up in last pair: sme prog 2f out: pushed along over 1f out: nvr rchd ldrs* **11/2**[3]

406/ **6** 1¼ **Mahlstick (IRE)**[518] [5495] 6-9-8 35.................. RLMoore 3 30
(DWPArbuthnot) *trckd ldr: chal and upsides over 2f out: rdn and nt qckn over 1f out: fdd* **12/1**

0003 **7** 1 **Platinum Boy (IRE)**[27] [947] 4-9-8 35..................(p) VSlattery 8 28
(MWellings) *chsd ldng pair: drvn over 3f out: steadily wknd u.p fnl 2f* **16/1**

0-00 **8** 1¾ **Out Of My Way**[40] [817] 3-8-5 30.................. RBrisland 2 24
(TMJones) *mostly in midfield: outpcd over 2f out: no ch after* **66/1**

055- **9** 3½ **Superclean**[290] [2319] 4-9-8 30.................. JQuinn 1 16
(AWCarroll) *dwlt: a towards rr: bhd fr over 2f out* **20/1**

0U0- **10** nk **Daphne's Doll (IRE)**[28] [5171] 9-9-1 30.................. LucyRussell(7) 9 15
(DrJRJNaylor) *chsd ldrs: lost pl over 3f out: bhd fnl 2f* **33/1**

0B23 **11** 1 **Spiders Web**[6] [1091] 4-9-8 35..................(b) GCarter 7 13
(TKeddy) *dwlt: a towards rr: bhd fr over 2f out* **11/2**[3]

4240 **12** ½ **All On My Own (USA)**[28] [940] 9-9-1 35..................(p) PPMathers(7) 11 12
(IWMcinnes) *dwlt: a in rr: bhd fr over 2f out* **10/1**

1m 40.36s (0.85) **Going Correction** 0.0s/f (Stan)
**WFA** 3 from 4yo+ 17lb **12** Ran SP% **125.9**
Speed ratings: **95,93,92,91,90 88,87,86,82,82 81,80**CSF £79.66 TOTE £16.30: £6.40, £1.80, £1.40; EX 306.20.
**Owner** David Sykes **Bred** Bishop's Down Farm **Trained** Upper Lambourn, Berks

**FOCUS**
The lowest grade and no great pace on, with those that raced prominently dominating.

**NOTEBOOK**
**Cumbrian Princess** was impossible to fancy on her recent form on Fibresand, but the switch to Polytrack sparked an improvement. This was her first victory since December 2001.
**Baytown Flyer**, second at Southwell on her reappearance, was soon in the lead and had every chance providing she got this longer trip. Although she held on for second, the suspicion is that she is better over shorter.
**Tiny Tim(IRE)** is still a maiden but he is running to a consistent level at present and deserves to pick up a race of this nature.
**Tojoneski** chased home Tiny Tim at a similar distance as he had over seven furlongs here last time out.
**Hellbent** did best of those who came from off the pace in a race run at a steady pace and which suited those who raced prominently. He is probably capable of better.

## 1168 BET DIRECT ON SKY ACTIVE CLAIMING STKS — 1m 2f (P)
4:00 (4:00) (H) 3-Y-O+ — £1,459 (£417; £208) Stalls Low

Form RPR

2234 **1** **Absolute Utopia (USA)**[6] [1088] 11-9-11 63.................. LDettori 4 61
(JLSpearing) *racd in 3rd: clsd over 3f out: led wl over 2f out: drvn clr over 1f out: styd on wl* **4/6**[1]

0050 **2** 5 **Itsonlyagame**[15] [1016] 4-9-12 45.................. SDrowne 5 53
(RIngram) *hld up in 5th: clsd over 3f out: hrd rdn over 2f out: kpt on one pce to take 2nd ins fnl f* **12/1**

0122 **3** 1¾ **Monduru**[20] [996] 7-9-12 47..................(be) RLMoore 6 50
(GLMoore) *hld up in 4th: clsd over 3f out: pushed along and nt qckn over 2f out: wnt 3rd nr fin* **3/1**[2]

-044 **4** ¾ **Foot Fault (IRE)**[6] [1084] 3-7-10 57.................. DFox(5) 2 44
(NACallaghan) *plld hrd: hld up in 2nd: clsd to ld over 3f out: hdd wl over 2f out: btn over 1f out: fdd ins fnl f* **5/1**[3]

**5** dist **Ivy House Lad (IRE)**[51] 4-9-2.................. PPMathers(7) 3 —
(IWMcinnes) *s.s: hld up in last: wknd 4f out: t.o* **50/1**

**6** 1½ **Sudden** 9-9-12.................. NPollard 1 —
(JJBridger) *plld hrd: led and sn clr: wknd rapidly and hdd over 3f out: sn t.o* **50/1**

2m 11.02s (3.63) **Going Correction** 0.0s/f (Stan)
**WFA** 3 from 4yo+ 20lb **6** Ran SP% **113.3**
Speed ratings: **85,81,79,79,—, —**CSF £10.77 TOTE £1.70: £1.10, £3.10; EX 8.20.The winner was claimed by Suzy Smith for £4,000. Foot Fault was claimed by Mark Gichero for £5,000
**Owner** M T Lawrance **Bred** Gainsborough Farm Inc **Trained** Kinnersley, Worcs

**FOCUS**
A slow time, 2.74 seconds slower than the earlier banded event over the trip. A poor race, and the winner did not need to be at his best.

**NOTEBOOK**
**Absolute Utopia(USA)** deserved to be a short-priced favourite in this grade against this opposition, and he won easily for his sixth course and distance success. Despite his advancing years he remains a useful tool in this company.
**Itsonlyagame** had the visor left off this time after it failed to do the job on his previous start. He had no business winning this on official ratings and ran as well as could be expected.
**Monduru** is a consistent type who once again ran his race. He would have been getting 17lb from the winner had this been a handicap, though.
**Foot Fault(IRE)** used up too much energy early, taking a keen hold, and that cost her in the closing stages.

## 1169 BET DIRECT NO Q DEMO 08000 837 888 MEDIAN AUCTION MAIDEN STKS — 6f (P)
4:30 (4:33) (H) 3-5-Y-O — £1,466 (£419; £209) Stalls Low

Form RPR

60- **1** **Kamanda Laugh**[215] [4495] 3-8-8.................. MHills 6 76
(BWHills) *cl up: trckd ldr wl over 2f out: rdn to chal over 1f out: r.o to ld last strides* **3/1**[1]

424- **2** hd **Buy On The Red**[142] [5948] 3-8-8 72.................. JQuinn 5 75
(WRMuir) *led: rdn wl over 1f out: r.o fnl f: hdd last strides* **3/1**[1]

2400 **3** 13 **Onefortheboys (IRE)**[21] [987] 5-9-7 40.................. SWhitworth 2 36
(DFlood) *outpcd in rr: wl adrift 1/2-way: plugged on u.p fnl f to take remote 3rd nr fin* **25/1**

**4** ½ **Cedric Coverwell** 4-9-7.................. SDrowne 3 35
(DKIvory) *dwlt: outpcd in rr: wl adrift 1/2-way: kpt on one pce fr over 1f out* **25/1**

006- **5** 1½ **Miss Judgement (IRE)**[128] [6045] 3-8-3 58.................. JMackay 10 25
(WRMuir) *wnt rt s: pressed ldrs: rdn over 2f out: sn outpcd: wknd ins fnl f* **6/1**[3]

0- **6** 1¼ **Lady Oriande**[305] [1948] 3-8-4 ow1.................. RLMoore 9 22
(AMBalding) *racd in midfield: drvn and outpcd 1/2-way: no ch after* **11/2**[2]

0-00 **7** 1¼ **La Vigna (IRE)**[7] [1075] 3-8-3 30 ow2..................(p) DerekNolan(7) 8 25
(MrsLucindaFeatherstone) *s.i.s: racd in midfield: drvn and outpcd 1/2-way: no ch whn nt clr run 1f out* **100/1**

00- **8** 2½ **Quintillion**[147] [5911] 3-8-8.................. GCarter 4 15
(TJEtherington) *sn outpcd: a bhd* **50/1**

05-6 **9** 1¼ **Bahamian Belle**[10] [1057] 4-9-2 48.................. LDettori 7 6
(PSMcentee) *chsd ldr to wl over 2f out: sn btn: eased ins fnl f* **11/2**[2]

**10** 3½ **Half A Handful** 3-8-5.................. DCorby(3) 1 1
(MJWallace) *s.v.s: a bhd* **12/1**

1m 12.06s (-0.86) **Going Correction** 0.0s/f (Stan)
**WFA** 3 from 4yo+ 13lb **10** Ran SP% **113.4**
Speed ratings: **105,104,87,86,84 83,81,78,76,71**CSF £10.80 TOTE £4.10: £1.60, £1.10, £4.50; EX 13.60 Place 6 £128.17, Place 5 £37.11.
**Owner** John Sillett **Bred** Miss K Rausing **Trained** Lambourn, Berks

**FOCUS**
A very smart time for the grade of contest and the first two came well clear.

**NOTEBOOK**
**Kamanda Laugh**, who has switched stables, battled on well under pressure to get his head in front in the last strides. Both he and the runner-up finished well clear of the rest, and he could be one for an early-season turf handicap.
**Buy On The Red**, who set the standard, ran a brave race in second, finishing a long way clear of the rest in the process. It goes without saying that he is eminently capable of winning a similar race.
**Onefortheboys(IRE)** had no chance on official ratings, and did as much as could have been expected by staying on past beaten horses for third.
**Cedric Coverwell**, whose dam is a half-sister to fair sprinter Prime Recreation, got going late in the day and is entitled to come on for the run.
**Miss Judgement(IRE)** needs dropping in grade.

T/Plt: £129.00 to a £1 stake. Pool £34,131.65, 193.10 winning tickets T/Qpdt: £3.00 to a £1 stake. Pool £3,117.20, 751.35 winning tickets JN

# NEWCASTLE (L-H)

Monday, March 29

**OFFICIAL GOING: Straight course - good to soft (soft in places); round course - soft**

The ground appeared to be much slower on the stands' side in the straight than on the far side.

Wind: light, half across Weather: cloudy, overcast

## 1170 EUROPEAN BREEDERS FUND MAIDEN STKS 5f

2:10 (2:10) (D) 2-Y-O £4,361 (£1,342; £671; £335) Stalls High

Form RPR

1 **Tara Tara (IRE)** 2-8-9 RWinston 4 81+
(JJQuinn) *hld up: effrt whn no room fr over 1f out tl wl ins last: swtchd lft and qcknd to ld cl home: comf* **10/1**

2 nk **Stanbury (USA)** 2-9-0 TEDurcan 7 78
(MRChannon) *cl up: rdn over 2f out: led ent last to wl ins last: r.o* **6/5**[1]

3 3/4 **Word Perfect** 2-8-9 DaleGibson 6 70
(MWEasterby) *prom: rdn 2f out: kpt on fnl f* **33/1**

4 3/4 **Bold Marc (IRE)** 2-9-0 DarrenWilliams 9 73
(KRBurke) *led to ent fnl f: kpt on same pce* **7/1**[3]

5 nk **Indibraun (IRE)** 2-9-0 GFaulkner 8 72
(PCHaslam) *trckd ldrs: rdn and edgd lft ins fnl f: one pce* **5/1**[2]

6 8 **Kilkenny Kitten (IRE)** 2-8-9 (t) KimTinkler 3 39
(NTinkler) *cl up tl rdn and wknd fr 2f out* **50/1**

7 3 **Kristikhab (IRE)** 2-9-0 KDarley 5 33
(ABerry) *s.i.s and outpcd: nvr on terms* **11/1**

8 6 **Verstone (IRE)** 2-8-9 JFanning 2 7
(RFFisher) *bhd and sn pushed along: no ch fr 1/2-way* **25/1**

9 6 **No Commission (IRE)** 2-8-11 LFletcher(3) 1 —
(RFFisher) *wnt bdly lft s: rn green and sn struggling* **16/1**

66.00 secs (4.47) **Going Correction** +0.35s/f (Good) 9 Ran SP% **106.7**

Speed ratings: **78,77,76,75,74 61,57,47,37**CSF £19.45 TOTE £8.00: £1.80, £1.10, £7.30; EX 30.40.

**Owner** Tara Leisure **Bred** Miss Roseanne Millett And Paul McEnery **Trained** Settrington, N Yorks

**FOCUS**

A very slow winning time. The first five finished in a heap, well clear of the rest, and the form looks nothing special.

**NOTEBOOK**

**Tara Tara(IRE)** is out of a mare who has produced numerous winners, including evergreen sprinter Don Fayruz and decent middle-distance performer Bolino Star. With nowhere to go at a crucial stage, she would have been an unlucky loser, but the gap appeared late on and she readily quickened up to score.

**Stanbury(USA)**, a 135,000 gns yearling, is a January foal with size and scope. He did little wrong, and faster ground and possibly an extra furlong, should see him off the mark.

**Word Perfect**, a filly from the first crop of Diktat, stayed on under pressure in the last quarter of a mile. She will know more next time.

**Bold Marc(IRE)** led against the rail and stuck on willingly when headed. A half-brother to three winners at 12 furlongs plus, out of a dam who won over two miles, he ought to get another furlong at least.

**Indibraun(IRE)** travelled well until coming off the bridle and should step up on this next time.

## 1171 SALTWELL SIGNS CLAIMING STKS 6f

2:40 (2:40) (F) 3-Y-0+ £3,059 (£874; £437) Stalls High

Form RPR

140- 1 **American Cousin**[180] [5301] 9-9-7 60 ANicholls 7 64
(DNicholls) *hld up: effrt over 2f out: led ins fnl f: kpt on wl* **10/1**

/-00 2 3/4 **Speedy James (IRE)**[60] [626] 8-8-11 40 LTreadwell(7) 6 59?
(DNicholls) *cl up stands rail: led 1/2-way: edgd lft over 1f out: hdd ins fnl f: kpt on* **25/1**

0000 3 2 **Only One Legend (IRE)**[21] [987] 6-9-9 60 (p) NCallan 1 58
(KARyan) *hld up: hdwy over 1f out: kpt on: nt rch ldrs* **5/2**[2]

2562 4 hd **Speedfit Free (IRE)**[15] [1025] 7-9-4 58 (b) PHanagan 8 52
(ISemple) *keen: cl up: rdn 2f out: kpt on same pce fnl f* **9/4**[1]

202- 5 1 **Pawan (IRE)**[164] [5627] 4-9-9 62 KimTinkler 3 54
(NTinkler) *cl up tl rdn and one pce fr over 1f out* **10/1**

-041 6 11 **Miss Wizz**[43] [780] 4-8-6 40 (p) RoryMoore(7) 2 11
(WStorey) *cl up tl wknd fr 2f out* **12/1**

03-0 7 1 **Flying Tackle**[83] [453] 6-9-4 51 (p) LEnstone(3) 5 16
(MDods) *keen: prom: hung lft and wknd fr 2f out* **7/2**[3]

00-0 8 8 **Wilheheckaslike**[15] [1024] 3-8-5 45 (v) DRMcCabe 4 —
(WStorey) *led to 1/2-way: sn lost pl* **50/1**

1m 21.37s (6.24) **Going Correction** +0.35s/f (Good)

**WFA** 3 from 4yo+ 13lb 8 Ran SP% **113.2**

Speed ratings: **72,71,68,68,66 52,50,40**CSF £209.13 TOTE £8.70: £3.20, £4.60, £1.10; EX 99.80.

**Owner** Middleham Park Racing Xiv **Bred** J W Parker And K Wills **Trained** Sessay, N Yorks

**FOCUS**

A painfully slow winning time, 4.93 seconds slower than the concluding handicap, and form to be sceptical about for the time being.

**NOTEBOOK**

**American Cousin** usually takes a few runs to strike form, but he was good enough to win this weak race on his seasonal bow, staying on better than his stable companion.

**Speedy James(IRE)**, a stablemate of the winner, is better over the minimum trip and he was only able to go up and down on the spot when headed. Despite finishing second he still looks a light of former days.

**Only One Legend(IRE)**, beaten in a Polytrack seller last time, wore cheekpieces instead of blinkers. He made late progress without reaching the Nicholls pair.

**Speedfit Free(IRE)**, who has been busy on the sand tracks, did not help his cause by racing keenly.

**Pawan(IRE)**, a maiden who has only previously run on fast ground, probably needs seven furlongs.

## 1172 GARY ROBSON MEMORIAL STKS (H'CAP) 1m 2f 32y

3:10 (3:11) (D) (0-80,80) 3-Y-0+ £5,811 (£1,788; £894; £447) Stalls High

Form RPR

64-3 1 **Ofaraby**[34] [872] 4-9-13 79 PRobinson 10 92+
(MAJarvis) *trckd ldrs: led over 1f out: edgd lft ins last: pushed out* **9/2**[1]

330- 2 2 **Shares (IRE)**[23] [3316] 4-8-4 56 RFfrench 5 66
(PMonteith) *chsd ldrs: led briefly wl over 1f out: kpt on same pce ins last* **9/1**

510- 3 3/4 **Captain Clipper**[200] [4848] 4-9-6 72 ANicholls 11 81
(DNicholls) *midfield: effrt over 2f out: kpt on same pce fnl f* **20/1**

56-5 4 6 **Melodian**[55] [671] 9-8-2 60 ow1 (b) MLawson(7) 6 60
(MBrittain) *keen: mde most to wl over 1f out: sn outpcd* **13/2**[2]

40-0 5 5 **Libre**[4] [1109] 4-9-4 70 (tp) DeanMcKeown 2 60
(RCGuest) *missed break: bhd tl hdwy over 2f out: no imp fnl f* **12/1**

060- 6 3/4 **Tony Tie**[168] [5537] 8-9-6 72 WSupple 9 61
(JSGoldie) *hld up: stdy hdwy over 2f out: outpcd fr over 1f out: bttr for r* **20/1**

0-60 7 6 **Fiddlers Creek (IRE)**[29] [679] 5-8-8 60 (p) PHanagan 14 39
(RAllan) *hld up: hdwy over 2f out: edgd lft and sn no imp* **14/1**

8 1 3/4 **Meteorite Sun (USA)**[858] 6-9-9 75 JFEgan 13 51
(MrsJRRamsden) *missed break: pushed along in rr whn hmpd over 2f out: n.d* **25/1**

104- 9 3 1/2 **Rotuma (IRE)**[144] [5935] 5-8-11 66 (b) LEnstone(3) 1 36
(MDods) *trckd ldrs: rdn over 2f out: sn no ex* **7/1**[3]

0/0- 10 3/4 **Lucky Largo (IRE)**[10] [5188] 4-9-2 68 (b) KDarley 12 36
(SGollings) *hld up and a bhd* **33/1**

000- 11 1/2 **Graft**[147] [5910] 5-8-8 65 PMulrennan(5) 7 33
(MWEasterby) *midfield: pushed along and lost pl over 3f out: n.d after* **14/1**

/11- 12 2 **Silvertown**[72] [2702] 9-9-2 68 DMcGaffin 8 32
(LLungo) *trckd ldrs tl wknd over 3f out* **9/1**

422- 13 25 **Love In Seattle (IRE)**[349] [1073] 4-10-0 80 JFanning 4 —
(MJohnston) *disp ld to 1/2-way: wknd over 2f out* **7/1**[3]

2120 14 23 **Desert Heat**[24] [970] 6-9-6 72 (v) RWinston 3 —
(ISemple) *in tch tl wknd wl over 2f out* **25/1**

2m 16.14s (4.34) **Going Correction** +0.55s/f (Yiel) 14 Ran SP% **117.7**

Speed ratings: **104,102,101,97,93 92,87,86,83,82 82,80,60,42**CSF £39.57 CT £740.41 TOTE £5.10: £2.00, £2.20, £5.60; EX 68.40 Trifecta £949.00 Pool £1,336.70, 0.20 winning units - part won..

**Owner** T G Warner **Bred** Red House Stud **Trained** Newmarket, Suffolk

**FOCUS**

A fair handicap run at a decent pace.

**NOTEBOOK**

**Ofaraby** had not run on turf since his racecourse debut last May, but he is a proven All-Weather performer. He ran on strongly for a decisive victory and can win again given cut in the ground.

**Shares(IRE)**, who was with Gerard Butler last Flat season, won over hurdles earlier this month. He ran a solid race on his return to the level and is well at home in soft ground.

**Captain Clipper** made a promising return to action, unable to quicken up in the final furlong but finishing clear of the fourth horse. He handles fast ground too and will pay his way this season.

**Melodian**, fit from a run on the sand, made much of the running but was never allowed any peace up front and the game was up once he was headed.

**Libre** won twice for Frank Jordan last season, but has not shown much either on the Flat or over hurdles since joining this yard. He came from the rear as usual, this time after missing the kick, but could not get in a blow at the principals.

**Tony Tie** is nicely handicapped again and there should be improvement in him with this run under his belt.

**Meteorite Sun(USA)**, a winner in heavy ground in the French provinces when last in action in November 2001, lost any chance he had when caught in scrimmaging over a quarter of a mile out.

## 1173 PUTTER AND FLUTTER H'CAP 2m 19y

3:40 (3:40) (E) (0-70,70) 4-Y-0+ £3,614 (£1,112; £556; £278) Stalls High

Form RPR

040- 1 **Acceleration (IRE)**[16] [5675] 4-8-13 60 (v) PHanagan 9 69
(RAllan) *prom: rdn 3f out: rallied to ld ins fnl f: styd on wl* **25/1**

110/ 2 2 **Magic Combination (IRE)**[30] [4759] 11-9-9 70 PMulrennan(5) 7 77
(LLungo) *hld up: smooth hdwy to ld over 2f out: edgd lft over 1f out: hdd ins fnl f: one pce* **12/1**

3 1 **Zoltano (GER)**[9] 6-9-9 65 RWinston 11 71
(MTodhunter) *prom: rdn over 3f out: r.o fnl f* **12/1**

0-35 4 hd **Toni Alcala**[12] [1041] 5-9-4 63 LFletcher(3) 4 69
(RFFisher) *hld up: hdwy over 1f out: kpt on: no imp last 50yds* **8/1**

1434 5 nk **Paddy Mul**[15] [1023] 7-7-12 40 (t) JBramhill 1 45
(WStorey) *bhd: hdwy over 1f out: squeezed through ins fnl f: r.o* **12/1**

/421 6 1 **Doctor John**[38] [839] 7-8-3 45 CCatlin 5 49
(AndrewTurnell) *trckd ldrs: n.m.r over 2f out: sn outpcd: rallied over 1f out: nt qckn fnl f* **7/1**[3]

460- 7 1 **Flame Of Zara**[177] [5375] 5-8-7 54 TEaves(5) 12 57
(MrsMReveley) *prom: smooth hdwy to dispute ld over 2f out: no ex fr over 1f out* **5/1**[2]

0060 8 2 1/2 **Moyne Pleasure (IRE)**[15] [1026] 6-7-5 40 (p) DFentiman(7) 2 40
(PaulJohnson) *hld up: hdwy and ev ch over 2f out: wknd over 1f out* **20/1**

005/ 9 1 1/4 **Almnadia (IRE)**[19] [5365] 5-8-9 51 KDarley 3 49
(SGollings) *in tch tl lost pl 3f out: n.d after* **5/1**[2]

53-5 10 1 1/4 **Danny Leahy (FR)**[18] [583] 4-9-1 65 LEnstone(3) 10 62
(MDHammond) *hld up: effrt and edgd lft over 2f out: sn n.d* **33/1**

2140 11 3 **Altitude Dancer (IRE)**[3] [1112] 4-9-2 63 NCallan 8 56
(PABlockley) *keen: cl up tl wknd over 2f out* **4/1**[1]

0-60 12 2 **Homeric Trojan**[32] [902] 4-7-13 46 DMernagh 6 37
(MBrittain) *mde most to over 2f out: sn btn* **50/1**

3m 59.57s (24.80) **Going Correction** +0.55s/f (Yiel)

**WFA** 4 from 5yo+ 5lb 12 Ran SP% **113.5**

Speed ratings: **60,59,58,58,58 57,57,56,55,54 53,52**CSF £277.82 CT £3746.33 TOTE £23.40: £4.80, £3.50, £4.90; EX 788.00.

**Owner** Kim Marshall, Sue Rigby, Susan Warren **Bred** Cliveden Stud Ltd **Trained** Cornhill-on-Tweed, Northumberland

■ Stewards Enquiry : J Bramhill one-day ban: careless riding (Apr 10)

**FOCUS**

A very slow time indeed. The race turned into something of a sprint and the form is suspect.

**NOTEBOOK**

**Acceleration(IRE)**, fit from hurdling, took a little time to find full stride before running on well to collar the leader inside the last. His trainer believes he is not an out-and-out stayer, so the steady gallop suited him.

**Magic Combination(IRE)** showed the best turn of foot to go a couple of lengths to the good but was cut down. He was successful off this mark when last running on the Flat in 2002 but had not shown much over hurdles through the winter.

**Zoltano(GER)** won over ten furlongs in Germany but this was his first run on the Flat in this country. Fit from hurdling, he appeared to stay given the way he finished, but this was a falsely-run race.

**Toni Alcala** was a pound lower than when finishing runner-up in this event a year ago. He was last turning into the straight which left him with too much to do given the way the race turned into a sprint.

**Paddy Mul**, fit from an All-Weather campaign, was doing his best work in the closing stages, in common with a number of others.

**Altitude Dancer(IRE)** failed to settle, which proved costly in what was a falsely-run race.

## 1174 SHARP MINDS BETFAIR MAIDEN STKS 7f
4:10 (4:13) (D) 3-Y-0+ £3,584 (£1,103; £551; £275) Stalls High

Form RPR
4- **1** **Etmaam**[186] [5174] 3-8-11 RHills 4 77+
(MJohnston) *mde all far side: rdn and styd on wl fnl f* **10/11**[1]
0- **2** *2* **Henndey (IRE)**[157] [5733] 3-8-11 PRobinson 5 72+
(MAJarvis) *cl up far side: chal over 1f out: kpt on: hld towards fin* **7/2**[2]
36-0 **3** *1 ¾* **High Cane (USA)**[34] [871] 4-9-7 65 DarrenWilliams 16 63
(MDHammond) *led stands side: rdn and r.o fnl 2f: nt rch far side ldrs* **25/1**
-0 **4** *5* **Imperial Dragon (USA)**[9] [1059] 4-9-12 KDarley 6 56
(WAO'Gorman) *prom far side: rdn over 2f out: one pce over 1f out* **20/1**
**5** *shd* **Lucky Piscean** 3-8-11 JFanning 2 55
(CWFairhurst) *hld up far side: effrt over 2f out: no imp fnl f* **50/1**
**6** *2 ½* **Indi Ano Star (IRE)** 3-8-4 DTudhope(7) 11 49
(DCarroll) *s.i.s: effrt centre over 1f out: n.d* **66/1**
**7** *shd* **Nounou** 3-8-11 CCatlin 3 49
(DJDaly) *sn outpcd far side: n.d* **25/1**
- **8** *½* **Baba (IRE)** 3-8-11 DaleGibson 1 48
(TPTate) *cl up far side tl wknd over 1f out* **20/1**
305- **9** *shd* **Senor Eduardo**[23] [5444] 7-9-12 54 PHanagan 14 47
(SGollings) *prom stands side tl wknd fr 2f out* **16/1**
000- **10** *shd* **Nafferton Heights (IRE)**[203] [4770] 3-8-6 PMulrennan(5) 7 47
(MWEasterby) *hld up far side: shkn up over 2f out: no imp over 1f out* **100/1**
05- **11** *14* **Glencairn Star**[168] [5533] 3-8-11 WSupple 13 12
(JSGoldie) *in tch stands side: shkn up over 2f out: sn outpcd* **11/1**[3]
4/0 **12** *1* **Miss Fleurie**[11] [1044] 4-9-2 TEaves(5) 9 5
(RCraggs) *sn outpcd stands side: nvr on terms* **100/1**
**13** *6* **Fast Lane (IRE)**[415] 5-9-12 LVickers 12 —
(JSWainwright) *cl up stands side: hung lft and wknd fr over 2f out* **100/1**
00- **14** *½* **Anicaflash**[167] [5556] 3-8-6 ow3 LEnstone(3) 10 —
(MDods) *in tch stands side to over 2f out: sn btn* **100/1**
**15** *½* **Ice Planet** 3-8-11 RWinston 8 —
(DNicholls) *missed break: a bhd far side* **25/1**
**16** *5* **Young Warrior (IRE)** 3-8-11 ANicholls 15 —
(DNicholls) *unruly bef s: prom stands side to 1/2-way: sn btn* **25/1**

1m 31.36s (3.32) **Going Correction** +0.35s/f (Good)
**WFA** 3 from 4yo+ 15lb **16 Ran SP% 121.1**
Speed ratings: **95,92,90,85,84 82,81,81,81,81 65,63,57,56,55 50**CSF £3.04 TOTE £1.80: £1.10, £2.00, £5.80; EX 5.70.
**Owner** Hamdan Al Maktoum **Bred** Hawkers Stud **Trained** Middleham Moor, N Yorks

**FOCUS**
A modest winning time for the grade of contest. They split into two groups and the market leaders on the far side came out on top.

**NOTEBOOK**
**Etmaam**, who displayed plenty of promise on his sole run at two, was always showing ahead up the far rail but it was only in the last half-furlong that he pulled away from the runner-up. He will stay a mile plus and ought to improve.
**Henndey(IRE)**, out of a smart racemare, has been gelded since finishing last on his debut at the backend. He travelled well for much of the way and was not knocked about when the favourite took his measure in the last 100 yards.
**High Cane(USA)** is officially rated 65 and she holds down the form. That said, she ran well to finish nicely clear of the remainder to race up the stands' rail.
**Imperial Dragon(USA)** showed more than on his recent debut on Polytrack and looks to be going the right way.
**Lucky Piscean** is a half-brother to Prix Star and Ringside Jack, both good servants to the Fairhurst yard. He stayed on steadily and should pay his way granted more experience.
**Indi Ano Star(IRE)** was running on down the centre of the track in the closing stages, and this was a decent effort considering that he had been slow to find his stride.

## 1175 RAMSIDE EVENT CATERING H'CAP 6f
4:40 (4:43) (E) (0-75,75) 3-Y-0+ £4,173 (£1,284; £642; £321) Stalls High

Form RPR
2131 **1** **Up Tempo (IRE)**[32] [897] 6-9-4 65 (b) NCallan 5 77
(KARyan) *midfield far side: sn pushed along: hdwy over 1f out: kpt on to ld towards fin* **9/2**[1]
05-0 **2** *nk* **If By Chance**[81] [480] 6-9-3 64 (b) JFanning 4 75
(RCraggs) *led far side: clr over 1f out: kpt on: hdd cl home* **10/1**
133- **3** *2* **Highland Warrior**[145] [5924] 5-9-1 62 WSupple 2 67
(JSGoldie) *hld up midfield far side: gd hdwy over 1f out: kpt on: no ex wl ins fnl f* **6/1**[2]
4011 **4** *4* **Stoic Leader (IRE)**[5] [1098] 4-9-7 71 6ex LFletcher(3) 17 64
(RFFisher) *led stands side: rdn and edgd lft over 1f out: no imp fnl f* **8/1**[3]
0-00 **5** *hd* **Raymond's Pride**[41] [801] 4-9-10 71 (b) PFessey 8 63
(KARyan) *prom far side: rdn over 2f out: one pce fnl f* **33/1**
4325 **6** *2 ½* **Soba Jones**[45] [761] 7-9-11 72 JEdmunds 12 57
(JBalding) *trckd far side ldrs tl outpcd over 1f out* **12/1**
600- **7** *1 ½* **Fair Shake (IRE)**[146] [5918] 4-9-6 67 DaleGibson 6 47
(DEddy) *outpcd far side: hdwy 2f out: nvr rchd ldrs* **8/1**[3]
600- **8** *1* **Quicks The Word**[171] [5473] 4-9-4 70 TEaves(5) 1 47
(CWThornton) *cl up far side tl wknd fr 2f out* **14/1**
1-10 **9** *1 ½* **Wainwright (IRE)**[75] [526] 4-9-2 63 DeanMcKeown 11 36
(PABlockley) *bhd and pushed along far side: nvr rchd ldrs* **12/1**
300- **10** *4* **Certa Cito**[126] [6056] 4-9-0 64 DAllan(3) 20 25
(TDEasterby) *cl up stands side tl rdn and outpcd fr 2f out* **25/1**
000- **11** *2* **Border Artist**[204] [4753] 5-9-3 64 ANicholls 9 19
(DNicholls) *prom far side tl wknd over 2f out* **22/1**
320- **12** *nk* **Tre Colline**[242] [3730] 5-10-0 75 KimTinkler 7 29
(NTinkler) *a bhd far side* **50/1**
0/0- **13** *8* **Stormville (IRE)**[343] [1144] 7-7-8 62 MLawson(7) 13 —
(MBrittain) *in tch far side tl wknd fr 3f out* **40/1**
104- **14** *½* **The Wizard Mul**[153] [5821] 4-9-3 64 DRMcCabe 19 —
(WStorey) *bhd and outpcd stands side: nvr on terms* **50/1**
022 **15** *10* **African Spur (IRE)**[29] [938] 4-9-5 73 (t) DTudhope(7) 3 —
(DCarroll) *missed break: a bhd far side* **20/1**
0/0- **16** *1* **Get Stuck In (IRE)**[193] [5007] 8-9-12 73 KDarley 16 —
(MissLAPerratt) *cl up stands side tl wknd over 1f out* **50/1**
400- **17** *½* **Nemo Fugat (IRE)**[147] [5909] 5-9-9 70 AlexGreaves 15 —
(DNicholls) *cl up stands side tl lost pl over 2f out* **25/1**
000- **18** *5* **Extinguisher**[200] [4846] 5-9-2 70 LTreadwell(7) 14 —
(DNicholls) *prom stands side to over 2f out: wknd* **66/1**
-400 **U** **Ronnie From Donny (IRE)**[35] [862] 4-9-9 70 RWinston 10 —
(BEllison) *uns rdr leaving stalls* **10/1**

1m 16.44s (1.31) **Going Correction** +0.35s/f (Good) **19 Ran SP% 124.5**
Speed ratings: **105,104,101,96,96 93,91,89,87,82 79,79,68,67,54 53,52,45,—**CSF £43.56 CT £226.94 TOTE £5.80: £1.70, £2.80, £1.80, £3.50; EX 94.90 Place 6 £248.72, Place 5 £162.06.
**Owner** Yorkshire Racing Club & Derek Blackhurst **Bred** T Burns **Trained** Hambleton, N Yorks

**FOCUS**
A competitive handicap and solid form, although only a fair winning time for the grade. They split into two groups, and the six on the stands' side had little chance.

**NOTEBOOK**
**Up Tempo(IRE)** was being pushed along from an early stage, but Callan's hard work eventually paid off. The return to seven furlongs would not inconvenience him.
**If By Chance**, who won over course and distance in the autumn off a 5lb higher mark, looked to have it in the bag but was just caught.
**Highland Warrior** found his form when dropped to sprint distances at the backend and this was an encouraging reappearance on ground that is ideal for him.
**Stoic Leader(IRE)**, on a hat-trick after two seven-furlong wins on sand, ran a cracker to finish clear of the rest to race on the wrong side. He is at the top of his game.
**Raymond's Pride** was fit from an All-Weather campaign.
**Fair Shake(IRE)** never promised to supplement his win on this card last year.
T/Jkpt: Not won. T/Plt: £203.70 to a £1 stake. Pool £47,483.80, 170.10 winning tickets T/Qpdt: £54.50 to a £1 stake. Pool £3,536.90, 48 winning tickets RY

# 1136 WOLVERHAMPTON (A.W) (L-H)
### Monday, March 29

**OFFICIAL GOING: Standard to slow**
There was no apparent track bias at this meeting.
Wind: almost nil Weather: overcast

## 1176 NEW & IMPROVED BETDIRECT.CO.UK H'CAP 7f (F)
2:20 (2:20) (F) (0-55,53) 3-Y-0+ £2,933 (£838; £419) Stalls High

Form RPR
0306 **1** **Bulawayo**[11] [1043] 7-9-1 46 (b[1]) GGibbons 3 57
(AndrewReid) *sn pushed along: rdn and hdwy over 3f out: led over 1f out: drvn out* **8/1**
1406 **2** *nk* **Aguila Loco (IRE)**[29] [930] 5-9-8 53 (p) MFenton 6 63
(MrsStefLiddiard) *led early: w ldr: led over 3f out: rdn over 2f out: hdd over 1f out: rallied and edgd lft towards fin* **4/1**[2]
-000 **3** *1* **Rocinante (IRE)**[11] [1043] 4-9-4 49 EAhern 2 57
(JJQuinn) *rdn and hdwy over 3f out: kpt on ins fnl f* **16/1**
2251 **4** *1* **Silver Mascot**[21] [993] 5-9-8 53 DHolland 11 58
(RHollinshead) *sn led: hdd over 3f out: rdn over 2f out: no ex fnl f* **11/4**[1]
/0-6 **5** *5* **Abbiejo (IRE)**[7] [1075] 7-8-10 44 oh4 (p) RMiles(3) 12 37
(GFierro) *racd wd: sn wl bhd: hdwy on stands' side over 1f out: nvr nrr* **33/1**
0000 **6** *2 ½* **Illustrious Duke**[7] [1080] 6-8-6 44 oh4 (b[1]) PVarley(7) 4 30
(MMullineaux) *w ldrs: sn rdn along: wknd over 3f out* **33/1**
6200 **7** *½* **Social Contract**[3] [1121] 7-9-0 45 (v) DSweeney 7 30
(SDow) *chsd clr ldrs: short-lived effrt over 2f out* **9/1**
463- **8** *nk* **Chantry Falls (IRE)**[168] [5545] 4-9-4 49 GDuffield 8 33
(JGGiven) *rdn and hdwy over 3f out: wknd 2f out* **14/1**
003- **9** *9* **Parisian Playboy**[152] [5832] 4-9-6 51 DaneO'Neill 9 13
(JeddO'Keeffe) *bhd fnl 4f* **7/1**
400/ **10** *2 ½* **Pharaoh Hatshepsut (IRE)**[483] [5476] 6-8-13 44 oh4 KDalgleish 1 —
(JamesMoffatt) *sn wl bhd* **25/1**
000- **11** *hd* **Frenchmans Lodge**[200] [4835] 4-9-7 52 ACulhane 10 7
(JMBradley) *sn wl bhd* **12/1**
2605 **12** *27* **Robin Sharp**[15] [1020] 6-9-0 45 (v) MTebbutt 5 —
(JAkehurst) *sn wl bhd: t.o* **13/2**[3]

1m 31.83s (1.63) **Going Correction** +0.225s/f (Slow) **12 Ran SP% 123.6**
Speed ratings: **99,98,97,96,90 87,87,86,76,73 73,42**CSF £41.09 CT £514.32 TOTE £8.50: £1.90, £2.10, £4.50; EX 56.10.
**Owner** A S Reid **Bred** D J Allen **Trained** Mill Hill, London NW7

**FOCUS**
A furious pace early with the leading trio going off like scalded cats, although they suffered in the latter stages and the overall time was moderate.

**NOTEBOOK**
**Bulawayo** was blinkered for the first time, having worn a visor on three of his five previous starts, and took advantage of a slipping mark. A fast-run seven furlongs seems to suit him well.
**Aguila Loco(IRE)** has been running reasonably well at Lingfield since scoring over this course and distance last month. This is probably his optimum surface.
**Rocinante(IRE)** showed definite signs of a return to form but needs to go back up to a mile.
**Silver Mascot** had got things his own way when landing a seller over course and distance last time.

## 1177 BETDIRECT.CO.UK APPRENTICE CLAIMING STKS 1m 100y(F)
2:50 (2:50) (F) 4-Y-0+ £2,870 (£820; £410) Stalls Low

Form RPR
2401 **1** **Our Destiny**[6] [1090] 6-8-7 50 SHitchcott 5 61
(AWCarroll) *w ldr: led over 6f out: hdd over 4f out: rdn over 3f out: led again over 1f out: r.o wl* **11/8**[1]
4006 **2** *2* **Dancing King (IRE)**[7] [1076] 8-8-0 47 BSwarbrick(5) 3 55
(PWHiatt) *led: hdd over 6f out: w ldr: rdn over 3f out: ev ch over 1f out: nt qckn ins fnl f* **5/1**
1604 **3** *1 ½* **Iamback**[6] [1090] 4-7-8 48 ow1 (p) DeanWilliams(7) 1 48
(MissGayKelleway) *w ldrs tl n.m.r on ins bnd 7f out: rdn over 3f out: sltly outpcd over 2f out: hdwy on ins over 1f out: one pce* **7/2**[2]
5000 **4** *¾* **Port St Charles (IRE)**[24] [968] 7-8-10 72 JFMcDonald(3) 6 58
(PRChamings) *stdd s: hdwy over 6f out: led over 4f out: rdn 3f out: hdd over 1f out: wknd fnl f* **4/1**[3]
005- **5** *hd* **Peregian (IRE)**[150] [5846] 6-8-3 49 ow1 MCoumbe(7) 2 55
(JAkehurst) *hld up: rdn over 3f out: kpt on same pce fnl f* **11/1**
0340 **6** *13* **Dundonald**[12] [1037] 5-8-5 35 (bt) RMiles 7 22
(MAppleby) *prom: rdn over 4f out: wknd over 3f out: eased fnl f* **20/1**

1m 52.99s (1.99) **Going Correction** +0.225s/f (Slow) **6 Ran SP% 114.1**
Speed ratings: **99,97,95,94,94 81**CSF £9.02 TOTE £1.60: £1.10, £2.30; EX 7.80.The winner was the subject of a friendly claim
**Owner** Dennis Deacon **Bred** D A And Mrs Hicks **Trained** Wixford, Warwicks

**FOCUS**
An ordinary claimer with a pace to match.

**NOTEBOOK**
**Our Destiny** fought back well after losing the lead at the end of the back straight and was nicely on top in the end.
**Dancing King(IRE)**, despite being unable to dominate, appeared to appreciate being back up to a mile.
**Iamback** was 4lb better off than when over six lengths behind the winner in an amateurs' event at Southwell last week.
**Port St Charles(IRE)** stood out on BHB ratings, but his stamina limitations were exposed.
**Peregian(IRE)** likes fast ground and never posed a real threat on this surface.

## 1178 NEW SITE @ BETDIRECT.CO.UK FILLIES' H'CAP 5f (F)

**3:20** (3:20) (E) (0-75,75) 3-Y-0+ **£3,701** (£1,139; £569; £284) **Stalls** Low

Form RPR

4445 **1** **Blakeshall Quest**[38] 834 4-8-11 58 (v) DHolland 8 74
(RBrotherton) *a.p: rdn to ld 1f out: r.o wl* **8/1**

2065 **2** 2½ **River Days (IRE)**[15] 1018 6-7-9 45 (vt) LisaJones(3) 4 52
(MissGayKelleway) *w ldrs: rdn and cl 3rd whn nt clr run 1f out: r.o ins fnl f: nt trble wnr* **4/1**[1]

2403 **3** 1½ **Cloudless (USA)**[12] 1039 4-8-8 55 DaneO'Neill 7 57
(JWUnett) *hld up: rdn and hdwy on outside over 1f out: r.o* **6/1**[3]

-000 **4** *nk* **Frascati**[41] 801 4-10-0 75 FLynch 1 76
(ABerry) *led: rdn whn edgd rt and hdd 1f out: no ex* **16/1**

5255 **5** ½ **Amelia (IRE)**[6] 1082 6-7-9 49 BSwarbrick(7) 10 48
(WMBrisbourne) *racd wd: sn rdn and bhd: nt clr run jst over 1f out: swtchd rt and hdwy ins fnl f: nrst fin* **5/1**[2]

0122 **6** 1¼ **Emaradia**[16] 1008 3-8-1 60 (b) GDuffield 11 55
(AWCarroll) *prom: rdn 3f out: one pce fnl 2f* **7/1**

3560 **7** ½ **Lady Pekan**[30] 912 5-8-10 60 (b) BReilly(3) 3 53
(PSMcentee) *hdwy on ins over 2f out: wknd ins fnl f* **7/1**

-440 **8** *shd* **Inching**[15] 1018 4-8-2 49 MHenry 5 41
(RMHCowell) *sn chsng ldrs: rdn over 2f out: wknd over 1f out* **16/1**

2620 **9** *nk* **Tigress (IRE)**[26] 954 5-8-13 60 (b) SWKelly 6 51
(JWUnett) *prom: rdn 3f out: wknd wl over 1f out* **13/2**

0650 **10** 3½ **Marabar**[15] 1018 6-8-2 49 (p) SCarson 2 28
(DWChapman) *sn outpcd* **14/1**

000/ **11** 5 **Miss Dangerous**[1302] 4211 9-7-12 45 DKinsella 9 7
(MQuinn) *a bhd* **40/1**

62.23 secs (-0.37) **Going Correction** +0.225s/f (Slow)
**WFA** 3 from 4yo+ 12lb **11** Ran SP% **121.3**
Speed ratings: **111,107,104,104,103 101,100,100,99,94 86**CSF £41.34 CT £212.56 TOTE £11.20: £2.90, £1.60, £2.00; EX 46.00.
**Owner** Droitwich Jokers **Bred** M P Bishop **Trained** Elmley Castle, Worcs

**FOCUS**
This did not look the strongest of handicaps but the clear-cut winner recorded a very fast time for the grade.

**NOTEBOOK**
**Blakeshall Quest** had not run over the minimum trip since her two-year-old days. Even her trainer was surprised that she possessed the speed to win in this manner. She will switch back to turf as soon as a suitable opening can be found on soft ground.
**River Days(IRE)** was done no favours by Frascati but would probably not have beaten the winner in any case. She is well handicapped at the moment.
**Cloudless(USA)** may have broken her duck over course and distance in December, but showed why she has been running over longer trips.
**Frascati** already had the winner bearing down on her when she came off a true line.
**Amelia(IRE)** met with traffic problems in the home straight and is one to bear in mind when returning to six.
**Emaradia** was unable to get to the front against these older rivals.

## 1179 SPECIAL OFFERS @ BETDIRECT.CO.UK MAIDEN STKS 1m 4f (F)

**3:50** (3:51) (D) 3-Y-0 **£3,487** (£1,073; £536; £268) **Stalls** Low

Form RPR

005 **1** **Our Little Rosie**[47] 739 3-8-9 58 DSweeney 3 62
(MBlanshard) *hld up in tch: wnt 2nd over 4f out: sn rdn: led ins fnl f: r.o* **8/1**

-223 **2** 1¼ **Bond Moonlight**[16] 1012 3-9-0 63 FLynch 2 65
(BSmart) *w ldr: led 8f out: rdn wl over 1f out: hdd ins fnl f: nt qckn towards fin* **5/4**[1]

056- **3** 15 **Semelle De Vent (USA)**[121] 6087 3-8-9 63 DaneO'Neill 7 38
(JHMGosden) *hld up in tch: rdn over 4f out: wknd over 3f out* **10/3**[2]

040- **4** 5 **Valiant Air (IRE)**[184] 5222 3-9-0 57 DHolland 5 35
(JRWeymes) *hld up: wnt 2nd over 5f out: sn rdn: wknd over 3f out* **20/1**

**5** 5 **Knight Of Hearts (IRE)** 3-9-0 GDuffield 4 28
(REPeacock) *s.i.s: sn prom: wknd over 5f out* **100/1**

0 **6** 23 **Stage Two (IRE)**[10] 1050 3-9-0 KDalgleish 1 —
(MJohnston) *led 4f: 2nd tl rdn and wknd over 5f out: t.o* **11/2**[3]

550- **P** **Argent**[234] 3971 3-9-0 62 RFitzpatrick 6 —
(DCarroll) *hld up: bhd whn lost action and p.u 4f out* **10/1**

2m 45.28s (3.78) **Going Correction** +0.225s/f (Slow) **7** Ran SP% **108.9**
Speed ratings: **96,95,85,81,78 63,**—CSF £16.74 TOTE £10.80: £5.90, £1.40; EX 16.20.
**Owner** Mrs R G Wellman **Bred** Biddestone Stud And Partner **Trained** Upper Lambourn, Berks

**FOCUS**
A weak maiden with only a modest winning time. The runner-up looks the guide to the form.

**NOTEBOOK**
**Our Little Rosie** found the combination of a switch to Fibresand and a step up in distance doing the trick.
**Bond Moonlight**, back up in distance, was going better than the winner on the home turn but seemed to get outstayed.
**Semelle De Vent(USA)** was in trouble a long way out, and the problem may have been the surface rather than the distance.
**Argent** *Official explanation: jockey said colt had lost his action*

## 1180 CASHBACKS @ BETDIRECT.CO.UK (S) STKS 5f (F)

**4:20** (4:20) (G) 3-Y-0+ **£2,555** (£730; £365) **Stalls** Low

Form RPR

2210 **1** **Blueberry Rhyme**[13] 1033 5-9-12 65 (v) DSweeney 7 61
(PJMakin) *a.p: rdn 1f out: rn to ld cl home* **7/2**[1]

0405 **2** ½ **The Leather Wedge (IRE)**[7] 1075 5-9-2 45 PBradley(5) 8 54
(ABerry) *led: rdn wl over 1f out: hdd cl home* **25/1**

0402 **3** 1 **Soaked**[7] 1075 11-9-7 45 (b) ACulhane 3 51
(DWChapman) *chsd ldr: rdn over 2f out: nt qckn ins fnl f* **9/2**[2]

0020 **4** 2½ **King's Ballet (USA)**[13] 1033 6-9-7 47 (p) DaneO'Neill 5 42
(PRChamings) *s.i.s: rdn and hdwy over 1f out: nt rch ldrs* **7/1**[3]

5035 **5** ¾ **Heathyardsblessing (IRE)**[6] 1092 7-9-0 45 StephanieHollinshead(7) 9 39
(RHollinshead) *mid-div: hdwy wl over 1f out: kpt on same pce fnl f* **40/1**

6436 **6** 1 **Lone Piper**[6] 1089 9-9-0 35 BSwarbrick(7) 2 36
(JMBradley) *mid-div: rdn and hdwy wl over 1f out: wknd ins fnl f* **25/1**

0100 **7** *nk* **Arogant Prince**[2] 1131 7-9-12 59 (b) DHolland 10 40
(AWCarroll) *prom tl wknd 2f out* **7/2**[1]

06-0 **8** 1 **Arabian Knight (IRE)**[21] 987 4-9-7 60 EAhern 6 31
(RJHodges) *sn bhd: sme hdwy 1f out: nvr nr to chal* **20/1**

3001 **9** ½ **Torrent**[7] 1075 9-9-12 45 (b) GDuffield 1 34
(DWChapman) *chsd ldrs tl wknd over 2f out* **8/1**

4003 **10** *shd* **Flying Faisal (USA)**[6] 1089 6-9-7 35 PFitzsimons 12 29
(JMBradley) *a bhd* **40/1**

6543 **11** 4 **Hagley Park**[7] 1075 5-9-2 45 (v) SWKelly 11 10
(MQuinn) *prom tl rdn and wknd 2f out* **9/1**

6505 **12** 2 **Jalouhar**[15] 1025 4-9-12 49 (v) MTebbutt 4 13
(BPJBaugh) *s.i.s: outpcd* **25/1**

62.89 secs (0.29) **Going Correction** +0.225s/f (Slow) **12** Ran SP% **117.4**
Speed ratings: **106,105,103,99,98 96,96,94,93,93 87,84**CSF £100.58 TOTE £5.20: £1.80, £3.60, £2.20; EX 82.90.There was no bid for the winner. Arogant Prince was claimed by Jeff Pearce for £6,000
**Owner** Mrs P J Makin **Bred** Red House Stud **Trained** Ogbourne Maisey, Wilts

**FOCUS**
A very decent winning time for a seller. The winner is a class apart when in the mood, and the placed horses are the guide to the form.

**NOTEBOOK**
**Blueberry Rhyme** was favoured by the weights and took advantage of being dropped into a seller for the first time.
**The Leather Wedge(IRE)** likes to front-run and would have been receiving another 15lb from the winner in a handicap.
**Soaked**, like the runner-up, would have been getting another 15lb from the winner in a handicap.
**King's Ballet(USA)** could not overcome an indifferent start on this drop into a seller.
**Heathyardsblessing(IRE)** could never make his presence felt over this trip.
**Hagley Park** *Official explanation: jockey said mare had lost her action in the closing stages.*

## 1181 BET DIRECT ON SKY ACTIVE H'CAP 1m 1f 79y(F)

**4:50** (4:51) (F) (0-55,52) 3-Y-0+ **£2,919** (£834; £417) **Stalls** Low

Form RPR

150 **1** **Sorbiesharry (IRE)**[26] 953 5-9-8 **48** (p) PMcCabe 7 55
(MrsNMacauley) *t.k.h: wnt 2nd over 3f out: rdn to ld wl over 1f out: drvn out* **10/1**

-410 **2** ½ **Jade Star (USA)**[30] 914 4-9-12 **52** MFenton 5 58
(MissGayKelleway) *prom: lost pl bnd 7f out: rdn and hdwy over 3f out: kpt on towards fin* **5/1**[3]

-033 **3** ½ **Call Of The Wild**[11] 1043 4-9-8 **51** (v[1]) THamilton(3) 6 56
(RAFahey) *hld up in rr: reminders over 6f out: rdn and hdwy over 3f out: ev ch ins fnl f: nt qckn* **4/1**[2]

3024 **4** 1 **Danger Bird (IRE)**[31] 909 4-9-11 **51** (p) ACulhane 1 54
(RHollinshead) *led 7f out: rdn and hdd wl over 1f out: nt qckn fnl f* **6/1**

4511 **5** 11 **Landescent (IRE)**[20] 996 4-9-10 **50** DHolland 2 31
(MissKMGeorge) *led over 1f: prom: rdn 5f out: wknd wl over 1f out* **4/1**[2]

6150 **6** 6 **Red Storm**[8] 874 5-9-7 **50** (bt) RMiles(3) 4 19
(JRBoyle) *prom: rdn over 4f out: wknd over 2f out* **7/1**

-051 **7** 9 **Sinjaree**[21] 989 6-9-6 **46** GDuffield 3 —
(MrsSLamyman) *chsd ldrs tl wknd over 3f out: eased whn no ch over 1f out* **7/2**[1]

2m 5.55s (2.65) **Going Correction** +0.225s/f (Slow) **7** Ran SP% **114.8**
Speed ratings: **97,96,96,95,85 80,72**CSF £58.83 TOTE £10.10: £3.20, £3.30; EX 89.00 Place 6 £128.17, Place 5 £37.11.
**Owner** Mrs Liz Nelson **Bred** Mrs R I Nelson **Trained** Sproxton, Leics

**FOCUS**
A weak handicap with a modest winning time.

**NOTEBOOK**
**Sorbiesharry(IRE)** was off the same mark as when landing a similar event over the stretch mile here last month. He just managed to last home after racing very keenly.
**Jade Star(USA)**, 4lb higher than when successful over course and distance last month, could not quite peg back the winner.
**Call Of The Wild**, fitted with a visor instead of cheekpieces, ran his race despite having to be woken up quite early on.
**Danger Bird(IRE)** was meeting Jade Star on a pound better terms than when beaten a neck here last month.
**Sinjaree** *Official explanation: jockey said gelding was never travelling; trainer later reported gelding had pulled a muscle in its shoulder.*
T/Plt: £266.10 to a £1 stake. Pool £37,064.40, 101.65 winning tickets T/Qpdt: £38.10 to a £1 stake. Pool £3,292.20, 63.90 winning tickets KH

# 1058 MAISONS-LAFFITTE (R-H)

Monday, March 29

**OFFICIAL GOING: Soft**

## 1182a PRIX RIGHT ROYAL (LISTED) 1m 7f 110y

**2:50** (2:49) 4-Y-0+ **£15,845** (£6,338; £4,754; £3,169)

RPR

**1** **Le Carre (USA)**[18] 6-9-2 CSoumillon 7 106
(ADeRoyer-Dupre, France)

**2** *snk* **Risk Seeker**[155] 5782 4-9-2 DBoeuf 6 111
(ELellouche, France) 1

**3** 2½ **Foreign Affairs**[4] 1110 6-9-2 SSanders 1 104
(SirMarkPrescott) 2

**4** *nk* **Grey Glitters (FR)**[18] 4-8-13 OPeslier 3 105
(PDemercastel, France)

**5** 1½ **Bailamos (GER)**[128] 6053 4-8-13 WMongil 2 104
(PSchiergen, Germany)

**6** ¾ **Terrazzo (USA)**[18] 9-8-13 SLadjadj 4 98
(JVanHandenhove, France)

**7** ½ **Salutare (IRE)**[132] 4-8-6 C-PLemaire 5 95
(JEPease, France)

3m 25.2s
**WFA** 4 from 6yo+ 4lb **7** Ran SP% **47.6**
Speed ratings: .
**Owner** J-R De Aragao Bozano **Bred** Haras Santa Maria De Araras **Trained** France

**NOTEBOOK**
**Foreign Affairs** was tackling a longer trip and has been more successful over trips around a mile and a half.



The Form Book, Raceform Ltd, Compton, RG20 6NL

# FOLKESTONE (R-H)

Tuesday, March 30

**OFFICIAL GOING: Good to soft (soft in places)**

As usual on the straight course the runners switched to the far rail. On the round course, those racing prominently seemed to have an advantage.

Wind: fresh against Weather: fine & sunny

## 1183 NEW TURF SEASON MEDIAN AUCTION MAIDEN STKS 5f

**2:20** (2:20) (F) 2-Y-O **£2,898** (£828; £414) **Stalls** Low

Form RPR

1 **Bright Moll** 2-8-9 ........ IMongan 4 73+
(MLWBell) *chsd ldrs: pushed along 1/2-way: effrt 2f out: led jst over 1f out: rdn clr* **9/4**[2]

2 4 **Colonel Bilko (IRE)** 2-9-0 ........ SDrowne 2 62
(BRMillman) *s.i.s: sn chsd ldr but hanging rt thrght: ev ch over 1f out: one pce fnl f* **2/1**[1]

3 *shd* **Smokincanon** 2-8-11 ........ RMiles(3) 1 62
(WGMTurner) *racd against nr side rail: led: rdn and hdd jst over 1f out: one pce and sn btn* **10/1**

4 11 **Veneer (IRE)** 2-9-0 ........ RHughes 3 18
(RHannon) *outpcd in last pair over 3f out: nvr a factor* **7/2**[3]

5 *nk* **Kissing A Fool** 2-8-7 ........ CHaddon(7) 5 16
(WGMTurner) *dwlt: outpcd in last pair over 3f out: nvr a factor* **12/1**

6 7 **Justenjoy Yourself** 2-8-9 ........ SSanders 6 —
(CADwyer) *chsd ldrs for 2f: wknd 1/2-way* **12/1**

64.07 secs (3.37) **Going Correction** +0.60s/f (Yiel) **6** Ran **SP%** **110.8**
Speed ratings: **97,90,90,72,72 61**CSF £6.96 TOTE £3.20: £1.50, £1.70; EX 6.40.
**Owner** A Buxton **Bred** Lostford Manor Stud **Trained** Newmarket, Suffolk

**FOCUS**
A decent time for a juvenile event at this stage of the season and probably above average form

**NOTEBOOK**
**Bright Moll**, whose dam also won at two over five furlongs, was the most expensive of these at auction. She won in good style and could go in again before the better two-year-olds appear on the scene.
**Colonel Bilko(IRE)** ◆, whose dam won at two and is a half-sister to very useful two-year-old winner Scarteen Fox, stood out in the paddock and was well supported in the market but ran green in the race itself. The experience should bring him on.
**Smokincanon**, a half-brother to middle-distance winner Molly's Secret, set a decent pace for a long way and will be interesting on a sharper track.
**Veneer(IRE)**, whose dam won over ten and 11 furlongs in France, found everything happening too quickly on his debut. He should do better with the run behind him.

## 1184 VISIT PORT LYMPNE & HOWLETTS H'CAP 6f

**2:50** (2:52) (E) (0-70,70) 3-Y-O **£3,445** (£1,060; £530; £265) **Stalls** Low

Form RPR

0350 1 **Ask The Clerk (IRE)**[47] [747] 3-9-3 **66** ........ MTebbutt 11 74
(VSmith) *trckd ldrs: effrt to chse ldr wl over 1f out: drvn to ld last 150y: hld on nr fin* **9/1**

430 2 *nk* **Siera Spirit (IRE)**[11] [1052] 3-7-13 **55** ........ NicolPolli(7) 9 62+
(MGQuinlan) *trckd ldrs: prog on inner to trck ldng pair whn nt clr run 1f out: swtchd lft and r.o last 150y: gaining fin: too much to d* **5/1**[2]

0-50 3 1 1/4 **Instinct**[22] [982] 3-8-13 **62** ........ RHughes 4 65
(RHannon) *reluctant to enter stalls: dwlt: sn rcvrd to press ldrs: led wl over 2f out: kicked on wl over 1f out: hdd and one pce last* **5/1**[2]

000- 4 4 **Goblin**[158] [5734] 3-9-1 **64** ........ SSanders 7 55
(DECantillon) *settled in last trio: pushed along and prog over 2f out: kpt on steadily fr over 1f out: nvr nr ldrs* **10/1**

-530 5 3/4 **Phluke**[41] [816] 3-9-7 **70** ........ SCarson 13 59
(RFJohnsonHoughton) *w ldrs 2f: sn lost pl: rdn over 2f out: one pce after* **6/1**[3]

0601 6 1 1/2 **Joy And Pain**[22] [983] 3-8-10 **59** ow1 ........ DaneO'Neill 6 44
(GLMoore) *restless in stalls: racd on outer: trckd ldrs: rdn and outpcd 2f out: n.d after* **10/1**

-265 7 1 1/4 **Mister Completely (IRE)**[22] [983] 3-8-2 **51** ........ MartinDwyer 8 32
(JRBest) *racd in last trio: rdn and struggling 3f out: modest late prog* **4/1**[1]

-360 8 1/2 **Jasmine Pearl (IRE)**[22] [983] 3-8-4 **53** ........ CCatlin 10 32
(TMJones) *chsd ldrs: rdn over 2f out: wknd over 1f out* **25/1**

2-26 9 2 1/2 **Velvet Touch**[55] [673] 3-8-11 **60** ........ LDettori 5 32
(JRJenkins) *led after 1f to wl over 2f out: wknd wl over 1f out* **9/1**

66-0 10 1 **Sparkling Clear**[12] [1047] 3-7-8 **48** oh2 ow1 ........(v) JFMcDonald(5) 3 17
(RMHCowell) *a wl in rr: last and drvn 1/2-way: no ch after* **50/1**

4-05 11 1 3/4 **Averami**[26] [965] 3-8-10 **59** ........(v) SDrowne 12 23
(AMBalding) *led for 1f: lost pl bef 1/2-way: wknd 2f out* **16/1**

0604 12 2 **Livia (IRE)**[22] [983] 3-8-4 **53** ........ RLMoore 1 11
(JGPortman) *racd on outer: in tch to 1/2-way: sn wknd* **20/1**

1m 17.38s (3.78) **Going Correction** +0.60s/f (Yiel) **12** Ran **SP%** **122.3**
Speed ratings: **98,97,95,90,89 87,85,85,81,80 78,75**CSF £54.25 CT £262.20 TOTE £10.50: £3.30, £2.90, £3.10; EX 58.20.
**Owner** R J Baines **Bred** M A Begley And Mrs T Stack **Trained** Exning, Suffolk

**FOCUS**
A moderate time for the grade. The whole field tacked over to race next to the far-side rail.

**NOTEBOOK**
**Ask The Clerk(IRE)** had a good pitch throughout and got a good lead from the eventual third. This is his trip as his record over the distance now reads 454331, whereas over all other distances he is 526037050.
**Siera Spirit(IRE)** may have been an unlucky loser as she had to wait for a run, and by the time she got going the winner was just beyond reach. She has shown promise on each of her starts to date, and there is a minor contest to be won with her off her current mark.
**Instinct** kicked for home too soon and did not get home. He has the ability to win a race off his current mark but perhaps it will be on a sharper track.
**Goblin**, who kept on well in the closing stages, has been given a chance by the Handicapper, who has dropped him 9lb since last season.
**Phluke** looked to have plenty in his favour, but he has proved a frustrating horse to follow and once again let his supporters down.
**Joy And Pain**, whose rider put up 1lb overweight, was not helped by having to race on the outside of the field.
**Mister Completely(IRE)** was expected to appreciate the drop back to six furlongs on his return to turf, but that did not look the case in the race itself.

## 1185 FOLKESTONE-RACECOURSE.CO.UK H'CAP 6f

**3:20** (3:21) (D) (0-80,80) 3-Y-O+ **£5,573** (£1,715; £857; £428) **Stalls** Low

Form RPR

460- 1 **Maddie's A Jem**[119] [6119] 4-9-0 **66** ........ SWKelly 12 75
(JRJenkins) *trckd ldrs: effrt to ld over 1f out: clr ins fnl f: rdn out* **20/1**

00-0 2 1 1/2 **Oases**[3] [1139] 5-8-6 **58** ........ SWhitworth 8 63
(DShaw) *dwlt: racd in rr: rdn and prog over 2f out: chsd wnr jst ins fnl f: styd on but nvr able to chal* **16/1**

4000 3 *nk* **Pheckless**[7] [1087] 5-8-5 **57** ........ SCarson 16 61
(JMBradley) *dwlt: hld up in last pair: eased to outside and smooth prog 2f out: gng easily over 1f out: rdn and kpt on fnl f: hopeless* **11/1**

000- 4 1 1/4 **Kingscross**[150] [5875] 6-9-7 **73** ........ DSweeney 10 73
(MBlanshard) *racd in midfield: effrt 2f out: rdn to dispute 2nd pl 1f out: one pce fnl f* **5/1**[1]

5005 5 3/4 **Scarrottoo**[31] [918] 6-8-2 **54** ........ MartinDwyer 9 52
(SCWilliams) *chsd ldrs: pushed along fr 1/2-way: nt pce to rch ldrs over 1f out: kpt on* **14/1**

-500 6 1 1/4 **Cashel Mead**[45] [770] 4-9-11 **77** ........ LDettori 11 71
(JLSpearing) *racd against far rail in midfield: prog 2f out: drvn and one pce over 1f out* **5/1**[1]

000- 7 *hd* **Kew The Music**[176] [5427] 4-9-1 **67** ........ TEDurcan 4 61
(MRChannon) *trckd ldrs: rdn and cl up over 1f out: wknd fnl f* **33/1**

100- 8 1 1/4 **Fort McHenry (IRE)**[176] [5427] 4-9-8 **74** ........ WRyan 2 64
(NACallaghan) *w ldr: led after 2f: rdn and hdd over 1f out: wknd rapidly ins fnl f* **25/1**

0/0- 9 *nk* **Antonio Canova**[150] [5875] 8-10-0 **80** ........ OUrbina 15 69
(BobJones) *racd in rr: rdn and effrt over 2f out: keeping on one pce and no ch whn nt clr run ins fnl f* **8/1**[3]

404- 10 1 3/4 **Waterside (IRE)**[101] [6225] 5-9-5 **71** ........ MHills 3 55
(JWHills) *pressed ldrs: rdn and cl up over 1f out: wknd rapidly fnl f* **6/1**[2]

300- 11 1 1/2 **Pedro Jack (IRE)**[274] [2855] 7-9-4 **75** ........ JFMcDonald(5) 14 54
(BJMeehan) *a in rr: rdn and no prog over 2f out* **10/1**

000- 12 1 1/2 **Ben Lomand**[150] [5875] 4-9-10 **76** ........ RLMoore 6 51
(BWDuke) *racd on outer: a in rr: rdn and struggling over 2f out: wknd* **50/1**

02-0 13 3 1/2 **Jonny Ebeneezer**[13] [1035] 5-9-11 **77** ........(p) EAhern 13 41
(RMHCowell) *led for 2f: styd prom against far rail: wkng whn hmpd over 1f out: eased* **8/1**[3]

0044 14 2 **Juwwi**[27] [954] 10-8-13 **65** ........(p) CCatlin 5 23
(JMBradley) *a wl in rr: struggling fr 1/2-way* **25/1**

000- 15 1/2 **Tappit (IRE)**[213] [4574] 5-9-3 **69** ........ PFitzsimons 1 26
(JMBradley) *racd alone on nr side: nt on terms fnl 2f* **40/1**

1m 16.95s (3.35) **Going Correction** +0.60s/f (Yiel) **15** Ran **SP%** **119.6**
Speed ratings: **101,99,98,96,95 94,94,92,91,89 87,85,80,78,77**CSF £288.41 CT £3760.06 TOTE £26.30: £6.70, £7.00, £4.10; EX 1017.30 Trifecta £2552.90 Pool £3,595.71, 0.60 w/u - part won..
**Owner** Mrs Wendy Jenkins **Bred** The Peel Stud **Trained** Royston, Herts

**FOCUS**
Quite a modest time for the grade of contest. All but one headed over to the far side.

**NOTEBOOK**
**Maddie's A Jem** was well drawn and appreciated the drop back to six furlongs on her reappearance. But she was racing off a career-low mark and would be difficult to fancy when reassessed.
**Oases** did not show much on the sand over the winter but this was much more encouraging. He runs his best races with a bit of cut in the ground.
**Pheckless**, given his ideal draw, was not given the best of rides to capitalise on his good fortune. In the end he challenged wide, which was not the place to be, and was not at all disgraced in finishing third.
**Kingscross** had his ground and came to have his chance, albeit on the outside of the field, but he flattened out pretty quickly and perhaps the run was needed. He is well treated these days.
**Scarrottoo**, twice a course winner and potentially well treated, is happier on a faster surface.
**Cashel Mead** was well fancied with the ground in her favour, but she found disappointingly little under pressure.
**Fort McHenry(IRE)** crossed over to bag the rail and lead, and probably took too much out of himself in the process.

## 1186 SELLINGE MAIDEN FILLIES' STKS (DIV I) 1m 1f 149y

**3:50** (3:50) (D) 3-Y-O **£3,701** (£1,139; £569; £284) **Stalls** Low

Form RPR

6- 1 **Gretna**[277] [2747] 3-8-11 ........ TQuinn 8 77
(JLDunlop) *mde virtually all: shkn up and jnd whn lft clr wl over 1f out: styd on strly* **12/1**

2 5 **On Cloud Nine** 3-8-6 ........ HayleyTurner(5) 1 68+
(MLWBell) *s.s and rn green in last trio: gd prog on outer over 3f out: jnd wnr whn veered sharply lft wl over 1f out: nt rcvr* **33/1**

045- 3 3 1/2 **Chara**[102] [6216] 3-8-11 64 ........ MartinDwyer 5 61
(JRJenkins) *settled in midfield: effrt whn nt clr run over 2f out: shkn up and styd on one pce fr over 1f out* **14/1**

333- 4 11 **Concert Hall (USA)**[145] [5934] 3-8-11 75 ........ RHughes 2 40
(MrsAJPerrett) *trckd wnr after 2f tl over 2f out: wknd rapidly over 1f out* **5/2**[1]

00 5 *nk* **Avertaine**[11] [1052] 3-8-11 ........ RLMoore 9 40
(GLMoore) *racd in last trio: sme prog over 3f out: sn outpcd and btn* **33/1**

0- 6 5 **Saucy**[253] [3469] 3-8-11 ........ LDettori 4 30
(BJMeehan) *chsd wnr for 2f: styd prom tl wknd rapidly jst over 2f out* **8/1**[3]

0- 7 19 **North Sea (IRE)**[157] [5750] 3-8-11 ........ TEDurcan 3 —
(MRChannon) *racd in midfield: effrt to chse ldrs 3f out: sn rdn and wknd rapidly: t.o* **4/1**[2]

8 5 **Observation** 3-8-11 ........ PRobinson 7 —
(MAJarvis) *w ldrs tl wknd rapidly over 2f out: t.o* **5/2**[1]

9 1 **Boot 'n Toot** 3-8-11 ........ SSanders 6 —
(CACyzer) *ssn rdn in last trio: nvr on terms: wknd 3f out: t.o* **20/1**

10 10 **Love Of Life** 3-8-11 ........ DRMcCabe 10 —
(MGQuinlan) *s.s: rcvrd into midfield after 2f: wknd 4f out: t.o* **20/1**

2m 12.43s (7.43) **Going Correction** +0.85s/f (Soft) **10** Ran **SP%** **118.0**
Speed ratings: **104,100,97,88,88 84,68,64,64,56**CSF £352.92 TOTE £8.90: £2.00, £7.50, £4.30; EX 148.00.
**Owner** Capt J Macdonald-Buchanan **Bred** The Lavington Stud **Trained** Arundel, W Sussex

**FOCUS**
A decent winning time, a quarter of a second faster then the second division. The formis best assessed through the third.

**NOTEBOOK**
**Gretna**, always in the right place, had her task made easier when the eventual runner-up threw away her chance by running green, but this was still a pleasing display. She is a half-sister to mile-six winner Dilsaa, Jay Gee's Choice and Kootenay, and is likely to get farther than this in time.

**On Cloud Nine** may have given the winner a race had she not veered violently over to the left and towards the stands'-side rail turning for home. Greenness may have beaten her this time, but she clearly has the ability to win a maiden on this evidence.
**Chara** had it to do in this company on what she had done to date, and was not disgraced in the circumstances. She will be better employed in handicaps, though.
**Concert Hall(USA)**, whose stamina was far from guaranteed over this longer trip, looked a blatant non-stayer.
**Avertaine** should not receive too harsh a rating judged on her three runs to date, and can now run in handicaps.
**Observation** is fairly well bred and was supported in the market, but she was weakening out of contention on the turn into the straight on this debut.

## 1187 WEALDEN ADVERTISER GETS RESULTS CLASSIFIED STKS 1m 1f 149y
4:20 (4:21) (E) 4-Y-0+ £3,367 (£1,036; £518; £259) Stalls Low

Form RPR
056- **1** **Miss Pebbles (IRE)**[92] [6255] 4-9-2 70 NPollard 7 74
(BRJohnson) *trckd ldr: rdn 2f out: led over 1f out: styd on wl fnl f* **5/1[3]**
001- **2** 1 ½ **Dash For Cover (IRE)**[229] [4124] 4-9-4 69 RHughes 5 73
(RHannon) *led: set mod pce: kicked on over 2f out: hdd over 1f out: pressed wnr tl no ex fnl 100y* **8/1**
1034 **3** 1 ¼ **Eastborough (IRE)**[25] [970] 5-9-0 62 SWhitworth 4 67
(BGPowell) *trckd ldng trio: rdn and unable qck 2f out: styd on ins fnl f: unable to chal* **9/2[2]**
3012 **4** 1 ¾ **Galloway Mac**[14] [1032] 4-9-0 60 JPMurtagh 8 63
(WAO'Gorman) *trckd ldng pair: rdn and nt qckn over 2f out: one pce after* **5/2[1]**
50-0 **5** *nk* **Cuddles (FR)**[11] [1053] 5-8-11 65 (p) TEDurcan 3 60
(CEBrittain) *racd in 6th: rdn and outpcd over 2f out: one pce after* **6/1**
0-00 **6** *hd* **Pure Speculation**[26] [964] 4-8-11 65 IMongan 6 60
(MLWBell) *t.k.h: hld up in last trio: effrt on outer 3f out: one pce and btn wl over 1f out* **9/1**
550- **7** *nk* **Voice Mail**[196] [4960] 5-9-2 70 LPKeniry(3) 1 67
(AMBalding) *hld up in last: rdn and effrt 2f out: one pce and nvr rchd ldrs* **10/1**
0000 **8** ¾ **Easter Ogil (IRE)**[25] [967] 9-9-0 56 VSlattery 2 61
(JaneSouthcombe) *settled in 8th pl: rdn over 2f out: one pce after: no ch whn n.m.r over 1f out* **16/1**
/0-5 **9** 10 **El Hamra (IRE)**[13] [1035] 6-9-0 40 SDrowne 9 42
(MJHaynes) *racd in 5th pl: rdn and wknd over 2f out* **50/1**

2m 13.62s (8.62) **Going Correction** +0.85s/f (Soft) **9** Ran SP% **115.8**
Speed ratings: **99,97,96,95,95 95,94,94,86**CSF £44.59 TOTE £8.20: £3.10, £2.00, £1.80; EX 91.20.
**Owner** A A Lyons **Bred** A Lyons Bloodstock **Trained** Epsom, Surrey

**FOCUS**
A fairly modest time, about a second slower than both divisions of the three-year-old fillies' maiden, and those who raced up with the pace remained there throughout.

**NOTEBOOK**
**Miss Pebbles(IRE)** did not look particularly well handicapped on the All-Weather, but the switch to turf brought about an improved display and she won a shade cosily. The way the race was run suited her, but the Handicapper cannot be too harsh on her for this.
**Dash For Cover(IRE)** got his own way in front and set a steady pace. His stamina was a doubt for this trip coming into the race and he still has it to prove judged on this performance.
**Eastborough(IRE)**, who would have been suited by a better pace, stayed on in his own time.
**Galloway Mac**, making his turf debut, was expected to appreciate this longer trip. He travelled well enough for a long way, but found disappointingly little under pressure. The chances are he is better suited by a stronger pace.
**Cuddles(FR)** is an inconsistent type who is difficult to catch right.

## 1188 STOWTING APPRENTICE H'CAP 1m 4f
4:50 (4:50) (F) (0-70,70) 3-Y-0+ £2,898 (£828; £414) Stalls Low

Form RPR
0-00 **1** **Madhahir (IRE)**[22] [981] 4-9-0 **58** TPQueally 9 67
(CADwyer) *led or disp ld: drvn and def advantage over 2f out: jnd 2f out and again 1f out: battled on gamely u.p* **12/1**
300- **2** *hd* **Man The Gate**[101] [6226] 5-8-10 **55** NChalmers(3) 3 64
(PDCundell) *hld up in rr: prog over 2f out: drvn to join wnr 1f out: ev ch after: jst hld* **3/1[1]**
6310 **3** 2 ½ **Miss Koen (IRE)**[11] [1053] 5-8-13 **55** (t) DCorby 1 60
(DLWilliams) *s.i.s: hld up in last trio: smooth prog over 3f out: jnd wnr 2f out: nt qckn and btn ent fnl f* **11/1**
-615 **4** 3 ½ **Gemi Bed (FR)**[15] [981] 9-8-7 **49** (b) RMiles 2 49
(GLMoore) *hld up in midfield: effrt over 2f out: sn rdn and nt qckn: one pce after* **9/2[2]**
300- **5** ¾ **Galandora**[162] [5682] 4-7-12 **52** ow7 (t) LucyRussell(10) 4 51
(DrJRJNaylor) *t.k.h in midfield: pushed along and outpcd over 2f out: no imp on ldrs after* **20/1**
014- **6** *shd* **Val De Fleurie (GER)**[13] [5079] 9-8-11 **58** LTreadwell(5) 5 56
(JGMO'Shea) *disp ld to over 2f out: fdd over 1f out* **5/1[3]**
0-00 **7** 6 **Environment Audit**[16] [671] 5-9-4 **70** JJeffrey(10) 7 59
(JRJenkins) *hld up in last: detached fr remainder 6f out: sn bhd* **16/1**
400/ **8** ¾ **Tragic Dancer**[15] [2207] 8-8-5 **47** SHitchcott 8 35
(DJWintle) *chsd ldrs: rdn and btn over 2f out: heavily eased ins fnl f* **9/1**
0002 **9** *dist* **Golden Dual**[7] [1081] 4-8-6 **60** (v) JCoffill-Brown(10) 6 —
(SDow) *t.k.h: trckd ldng pair tl wknd 5f out: t.o* **11/2**

2m 52.41s (12.11) **Going Correction** +0.85s/f (Soft)
**WFA** 4 from 5yo+ 2lb **9** Ran SP% **111.9**
Speed ratings: **93,92,91,88,88 88,84,83**,—CSF £46.10 CT £409.67 TOTE £14.30: £3.70, £1.70, £2.00; EX 111.30.
**Owner** M M Foulger, I Dodd, G Darrall **Bred** Shadwell Estate Company Limited **Trained** Newmarket, Suffolk
■ Stewards Enquiry : J Jeffrey one-day ban: used whip when out of contention (Apr 10)
T P Queally two-day ban: used whip with excessive frequency (Apr 10,11)

**FOCUS**
A moderate event and extremely slow final winning time.

**NOTEBOOK**
**Madhahir(IRE)** showed good battling qualities to fight off two challenges and keep his nose in front at the line. He stays farther than this and his stamina saw him through.
**Man The Gate**, running off a career-low mark, came through to challenge the winner and had every chance, but he lost out in the battle. He should be able to win a race off this sort of mark.
**Miss Koen(IRE)**, whose run needs to be delivered as late as possible, got to a challenging position too soon on this occasion.
**Gemi Bed(FR)**, who won this race last year, came here in good form having won on the All-Weather and over fences over the last five weeks, but he was racing off a 10lb higher mark this time around.
**Galandora**, who remains a maiden after 18 starts, was not helped by her rider putting up 7lb overweight.
**Val De Fleurie(GER)** got the worst of the argument with the winner for the lead and dropped out of contention on the turn into the straight.
**Environment Audit** *Official explanation: trainer said gelding had lost both front shoes.*

## 1189 SELLINGE MAIDEN FILLIES' STKS (DIV II) 1m 1f 149y
5:20 (5:20) (D) 3-Y-0 £3,692 (£1,136; £568; £284) Stalls Low

Form RPR
0- **1** **Bowstring (IRE)**[185] [5218] 3-8-11 DaneO'Neill 2 84+
(JHMGosden) *trckd ldr: led 4f out: drew wl clr fr 2f out: pushed out* **9/1[3]**
**2** 10 **High School** 3-8-11 JPMurtagh 7 65+
(DRLoder) *s.s: sn trckd ldng pair: effrt 3f out: rdn and outpcd 2f out: kpt on to take 2nd last 100y* **8/11[1]**
2- **3** 1 ½ **Kali**[125] [6072] 3-8-11 DSweeney 4 63+
(RCharlton) *trckd ldrs: effrt to join wnr over 2f out: sn rdn and brushed aside: lost 2nd last 100y* **3/1[2]**
00- **4** 1 **Illeana (GER)**[218] [4434] 3-8-11 MartinDwyer 1 61
(WRMuir) *t.k.h: hld up in midfield: rdn and effrt to chse ldrs 3f out: sn outpcd and btn* **20/1**
**5** ½ **Olympias (IRE)** 3-8-11 SDrowne 3 60
(HMorrison) *s.s: racd in midfield: outpcd and dropped to rr over 3f out: plugged on again fr over 1f out* **10/1**
0-00 **6** 3 ½ **Mystic Moon**[52] [702] 3-8-11 SWhitworth 5 53?
(JRJenkins) *hld up in last: outpcd over 3f out: rdn and no prog after* **66/1**
**7** 4 **Pella** 3-8-11 SSanders 6 45
(MBlanshard) *dwlt: hld up in last pair: effrt over 3f out: wknd 2f out* **25/1**
00 **8** 8 **Diverted**[11] [1052] 3-8-11 PMcCabe 8 30
(MGQuinlan) *racd in midfield: in tch 3f out: sn shkn up and wknd* **100/1**
00 **9** *dist* **Alianna (FR)**[10] [1059] 3-8-11 CCatlin 9 —
(SDow) *led to 4f out: wknd rapidly: t.o* **100/1**

2m 12.68s (7.68) **Going Correction** +0.85s/f (Soft) **9** Ran SP% **114.1**
Speed ratings: **103,95,93,93,92 89,86,80**,—CSF £15.63 TOTE £10.30: £2.20, £1.10, £1.10; EX 24.90 Place 6 £1,841.79, Place 5 £1,465.79.
**Owner** R E Sangster & Mrs J Magnier **Bred** Juddmonte Farms **Trained** Manton, Wilts

**FOCUS**
A quarter of a second slower than the first division, but still a decent time for the grade. The winner was impressive, but there were some moderate performers close behind the market leaders, who may not have run to form.

**NOTEBOOK**
**Bowstring(IRE)** ◆, who is closely related to smart French 12-furlong performer Tailfeather and two other winners, all of whom stayed two miles plus, including high-class hurdler/chaser Upgrade, won easily on her reappearance. She has an Oaks entry and, while that is perhaps flying a bit high, she is clearly talented and looks up to winning a conditions event, providing there is some cut in the ground.
**High School** is particularly well bred, being a sister to four Group winners, including In The Wings, but her appearance at this track for her debut rather than one of the more prestigious venues should have set alarm bells ringing. She is clearly nowhere near as good as her pedigree suggests, but she can surely be found a little race somewhere.
**Kali** set a fair standard on her second in a Polytrack maiden in November, but she was easily seen off by the winner. Run out of second close home, she might be worth dropping back in trip slightly.
**Illeana(GER)** did not show a lot in two outings as a juvenile but this was more promising. She is now eligible for handicaps.
**Olympias(IRE)**, who is a half-sister to five winners in France and Germany, came in for some support in the market. She looks a stayer through and through.
T/Plt: £3,728.00 to a £1 stake. Pool: £34,471.50. 6.75 winning tickets. T/Qpdt: £294.80 to a £1 stake. Pool: £2,430.70. 6.10 winning tickets. JN

# 1089 SOUTHWELL (L-H)
### Tuesday, March 30

**OFFICIAL GOING: Standard**

## 1190 NEW & IMPROVED BETDIRECT.CO.UK BANDED STKS 5f (F)
2:10 (2:10) (H) 3-Y-0+ £1,435 (£410; £205) Stalls High

Form RPR
-500 **1** **Pleasure Time**[30] [930] 11-9-7 40 (v) RFitzpatrick 6 47
(CSmith) *mde all: rdn clr ent last: kpt on wl* **6/1**
0002 **2** 2 ½ **Tuscan Dream**[7] [1089] 9-9-2 30 PBradley(5) 8 38
(ABerry) *chsd ldrs: rdn along 2f out: styd on to chse wnr ins last: no imp* **9/2[3]**
0-00 **3** ¾ **Bond Domingo**[8] [1075] 5-9-0 40 (v) MStainton(7) 9 35
(BSmart) *hld up in tch stands side: hdwy wl over 1f out: sn rdn and kpt on ins last: nrst fin* **9/1**
6100 **4** 1 **Danakim**[35] [876] 7-9-0 40 (be) DFentiman(7) 2 32
(JRWeymes) *cl up: rdn 2f out: drvn and wknd appr last* **11/2**
0045 **5** 1 ¼ **Levelled**[7] [1089] 10-9-7 35 (b) ACulhane 1 28
(DWChapman) *cl up: disp ld 1/2-way: rdn along wl over 1f out: sn wknd* **4/1[2]**
3250 **6** *hd* **Spy Master**[16] [1025] 6-9-0 35 (tp) MLawson(7) 5 27
(JParkes) *chsd ldrs: rdn along 2f out: kpt on same pce appr last* **3/1[1]**
000- **7** 2 **Dress Pearl**[105] [6201] 3-8-9 40 MFenton 4 20
(RPElliott) *dwlt and squeezed out s: a rr* **12/1**
0000 **8** 1 ¼ **Meticulous**[20] [823] 6-9-7 30 LVickers 3 15
(MCChapman) *sn outpcd and bhd* **40/1**
-060 **9** 8 **Diamond Racket**[7] [1089] 4-9-7 30 (b) JQuinn 7 —
(DWChapman) *chsd ldrs: rdn along 1/2-way: sn wknd and eased fnl f* **25/1**

63.77 secs (3.47) **Going Correction** +0.625s/f (Slow)
**WFA** 3 from 4yo+ 12lb **9** Ran SP% **116.8**
Speed ratings: **97,93,91,90,88 87,84,82,69**CSF £33.57 TOTE £6.50: £2.00, £1.10, £2.90; EX 52.00.
**Owner** C Smith **Bred** John David Abell **Trained** Temple Bruer, Lincs

**FOCUS**
A poor race even in the context of this lowly level.

**NOTEBOOK**
**Pleasure Time** had not won since November 2001 and had been out of form so far this year but, dropped back into banded company, he ran out a decisive winner. One could not, however, back him with much confidence to follow up.
**Tuscan Dream** bounced back to form when runner-up over course and distance on his previous outing, but he proved unable to build on that effort this time around.
**Bond Domingo** has not won since his two-year-old days and has been out of form lately, but this was a bit better.
**Danakim** has won a similar race over this course and distance, but he has been below his best on his last three starts now.
**Levelled** has not won in this country since 1999 and dropped out after showing pace.

**Spy Master** was unable to justify market support. He had the cheekpieces on instead of blinkers, but was well held.
**Diamond Racket** *Official explanation: jockey said saddle had slipped.*

## 1191 BETDIRECT.CO.UK BANDED STKS 6f (F)
2:40 (2:43) (H) 3-Y-O+ £1,456 (£416; £208) Stalls Low

Form RPR
00-6 1 **Indian Music**[42] [810] 7-9-7 40 FLynch 8 47
(ABerry) *bhd: wd st: gd hdwy 2f out: str run ent last: rdn and styd on to ld post* **12/1**
0-00 2 shd **Mr Uppity**[7] [1089] 5-9-4 35 (e) LisaJones(3) 11 47
(JulianPoulton) *in tch: gd hdwy over 2f out: rdn to ld over 1f out: drvn ins last: hdd on post* **18/1**
5324 3 shd **Neutral Night (IRE)**[8] [1080] 4-9-7 40 (v) DHolland 12 46
(RBrotherton) *dwlt and racd wd: gd hdwy over 2f out: rdn to chal over 1f out and ev ch tl drvn and nt qckn nr line* **11/2**[3]
0646 4 6 **Emarati's Image**[21] [1000] 6-9-7 40 KDarley 10 28
(RMStronge) *cl up: led over 2f out: rdn and hdd over 1f out: sn drvn and wknd* **5/1**[2]
0-50 5 ½ **Aboustar**[30] [934] 4-9-0 35 MLawson(7) 5 27
(MBrittain) *chsd ldrs: bmpd after 2f and sn rdn along: drvn 2f out: kpt on same pce u.p appr last* **25/1**
06U3 6 1½ **Brilliantrio**[16] [1021] 6-9-7 40 LVickers 7 22
(MCChapman) *dwlt and squeezed out s: towards rr and rdn along 1/2-way: nvr a factor* **12/1**
-150 7 3½ **Mount Superior (USA)**[36] [860] 8-9-7 40 (b) PaulEddery 4 12
(PWD'Arcy) *bhd tl sme late hdwy* **5/1**[2]
0-00 8 ¾ **Valuable Gift**[56] [670] 7-9-7 40 (bt) JFEgan 3 10
(RCGuest) *cl up: ev ch 2f out: sn rdn and wknd* **14/1**
0003 9 nk **Dances In Time**[29] [942] 4-9-0 40 (b) MHalford(7) 2 9
(CNKellett) *s.i.s: a rr* **33/1**
0-22 10 2 **Baytown Flyer**[1] [1167] 4-9-0 35 PMakin(7) 9 3
(PSMcentee) *alway towards rr* **8/1**
0-00 11 9 **Compton Bay**[30] [936] 4-9-2 40 (b[1]) TEaves(5) 6 —
(MBrittain) *chsd ldrs: rdn along over 2f out: sn wknd* **33/1**
3504 12 8 **Bells Boy's**[7] [1092] 5-9-7 40 (p) NCallan 1 —
(KARyan) *led: rdn along 1/2-way: sn hdd & wknd* **7/2**[1]

1m 19.35s (2.55) **Going Correction** +0.35s/f (Slow) 12 Ran SP% **119.1**
Speed ratings: **97,96,96,88,88 86,81,80,80,77 65,54**CSF £205.84 TOTE £12.90: £3.50, £5.60, £1.70; EX 131.50.
**Owner** Alan Berry **Bred** Miss K Rausing **Trained** Cockerham, Lancs
■ Stewards Enquiry : F Lynch caution: used whip down the shoulder with whip in forehand position

**FOCUS**
The leaders appeared to go off too fast in this very ordinary contest. The overall time was moderate.

**NOTEBOOK**
**Indian Music** has been campaigned at around a mile in recent starts but, with the cheekpieces left off and dropped in trip, he gained his first win since August 2002. He should be just as effective over seven furlongs
**Mr Uppity**, still a maiden, was narrowly denied the spoils. He did nothing wrong and should win at this level in his turn.
**Neutral Night(IRE)** was given every chancy by Holland but remains without a win in 28 starts. *Official explanation: jockey said filly hung right.*
**Emarati's Image** did best of those who raced up with the pace.
**Aboustar** seemed to appreciate this drop back to sprinting, but his chance was not helped when he was hampered after a couple of furlongs.
**Bells Boy's** was well supported, but he went off very fast and dropped out tamely. *Official explanation: trainer's representative said gelding was never travelling.*

## 1192 NEW SITE @ BETDIRECT.CO.UK MEDIAN AUCTION MAIDEN STKS 1m (F)
3:10 (3:12) (H) 3-5-Y-O £1,445 (£413; £206) Stalls Low

Form RPR
6-23 1 **Caspian Dusk**[7] [1084] 3-8-7 58 ACulhane 8 70
(WGMTurner) *cl up: led 1/2-way: pushed clr 2f out: easily* **5/2**[2]
634- 2 14 **Gold Card**[146] [5925] 3-8-7 71 KDarley 6 42
(JRWeymes) *chsd ldrs: hdwy over 2f out: sn rdn to chse wnr and no imp* **9/4**[1]
03- 3 1 **Be Wise Girl**[175] [5439] 3-8-2 GDuffield 2 35
(JGGiven) *cl up on inner: rdn along over 3f out: drvn: flashed tail and kpt on same pce fnl 2f* **5/1**[3]
400- 4 7 **Bonjour Bond (IRE)**[145] [5932] 3-8-7 67 FLynch 4 26
(BSmart) *led: rdn along and hdd 1/2-way: sn wknd* **5/1**[3]
5 11 **Plattocrat** 4-9-10 DHolland 7 4
(RPElliott) *s.i.s: sn in tch: rdn along over 3f out and sn btn* **8/1**
0- 6 ½ **Airedale Lad (IRE)**[294] [2247] 3-8-8 ow1 VHalliday 9 4
(JRNorton) *a rr* **40/1**
0-0 7 6 **Maria Maria (IRE)**[71] [563] 3-8-2 JoannaBadger 1 —
(MrsNMacauley) *sn outpcd and bhd* **33/1**
8 dist **Hello Tiger** 3-8-7 GFaulkner 3 —
(JASupple) *s.i.s: a bhd* **18/1**
6-6 9 1¼ **Vaudevire**[8] [1078] 3-8-4 THamilton(3) 5 —
(RPElliott) *cl up: rdn along 1/2-way: sn wknd* **40/1**

1m 46.15s (0.55) **Going Correction** +0.35s/f (Slow)
**WFA** 3 from 4yo 17lb 9 Ran SP% **116.9**
Speed ratings: **106,92,91,84,73 72,66,—,—**CSF £8.57 TOTE £3.30: £1.10, £1.20, £2.40; EX 7.90.
**Owner** P Nabavi **Bred** P Nabavi And Mrs M Nabavi **Trained** Sigwells, Somerset

**FOCUS**
A very fast time for the grade, but a very weak race and the runaway winner is likely to be punished by the Handicapper.

**NOTEBOOK**
**Caspian Dusk**, third in a weak claimer over ten furlongs at Lingfield on his previous run, ran away with this maiden on this drop back in trip and return to Fibresand. He beat little, but recorded a good time and could be competitive in a slightly higher grade.
**Gold Card** showed promise in maiden company on turf last year, but this was disappointing. He looks badly flattered by his rating of 71.
**Be Wise Girl**, well beaten into third over this course and distance when last seen 146 days previously, was again well held. Handicapping is likely to be her game.
**Bonjour Bond(IRE)** did not shape too badly on turf last year, but he does not look to be progressing now and did nothing to justify his rating of 67.

## 1193 SPECIAL OFFERS @ BETDIRECT.CO.UK BANDED STKS 2m (F)
3:40 (3:41) (H) 4-Y-O+ £1,442 (£412; £206) Stalls Low

Form RPR
5331 1 **Stravmour**[16] [1023] 8-9-3 45 DaleGibson 1 44
(RHollinshead) *hld up in rr: gd hdwy 6f out: trckd ldrs over 3f out: rdn 2f out: drvn to ld ent last: styd on* **2/1**[1]
-406 2 1½ **Berkeley Heights**[16] [1023] 4-8-12 35 NCallan 9 42
(MrsJCandlish) *in tch: hdwy over 4f out: led wl over 1f out: rdn and hdd ent last: sn drvn and one pce* **16/1**
0-55 3 1¼ **Vitelucy**[8] [1077] 5-8-12 45 AQuinn(5) 6 41
(MissSJWilton) *in tch: pushed along and outpcd 5f out: gd hdwy to chse ldrs over 2f out: rdn over 1f out and kpt on same pce* **8/1**
0/0- 4 6 **Golfagent**[15] [5682] 6-9-3 40 (t) DHolland 10 34
(MissKMarks) *prom: led 5f out: rdn and hdd wl over 1f out: grad wknd* **4/1**[3]
0500 5 11 **Western Command (GER)**[12] [1042] 8-9-3 30 RFitzpatrick 3 20
(MrsNMacauley) *chsd ldrs: rdn along over 4f out: sn wknd* **33/1**
4046 6 hd **Mathmagician**[7] [1091] 5-9-3 35 (p) DeanMcKeown 4 20
(RFMarvin) *hld up: hdwy 1/2-way: rdn along to chse ldrs 5f out: wknd 3f out* **16/1**
35-0 7 14 **Monsal Dale (IRE)**[3] [1136] 5-8-12 45 MSavage(5) 8 3
(NEBerry) *cl up: rdn along 5f out: sn wknd* **3/1**[2]
005- 8 6 **Rhetoric (IRE)**[306] [447] 5-8-10 40 BSwarbrick(7) 7 —
(DGBridgwater) *led: rdn along and hdd 5f out: drvn and wknd over 2f out* **18/1**
000- 9 dist **Errol**[64] [3865] 5-9-3 30 ACulhane 5 —
(JFCoupland) *prom: rdn along 1/2-way: sn wknd* **33/1**
050- 10 nk **Quinn**[253] [3461] 4-8-9 45 LisaJones(3) 2 —
(CWFairhurst) *a rr: bhd fr 1/2-way* **25/1**

3m 50.94s (-1.56) **Going Correction** +0.35s/f (Slow)
**WFA** 4 from 5yo+ 5lb 10 Ran SP% **116.2**
Speed ratings: **97,96,95,92,87 87,80,77,—,—**CSF £36.29 TOTE £3.00: £1.10, £4.80, £2.10; EX 52.80.
**Owner** E Bennion **Bred** E Bennion **Trained** Upper Longdon, Staffs

**FOCUS**
An ordinary race, run in a moderate time, in which the front three were clear.

**NOTEBOOK**
**Stravmour** hails from a stable in fantastic form and followed up his recent success in a similar race over a mile six. He had to work pretty hard to get on top and did not have that much to spare, but his confidence will be high and it would be no surprise to be see him go well outside of banded company.
**Berkeley Heights**, still a maiden, got closer to the winner than she did on her previous run on this first attempt at two miles and did not look to fail through lack of stamina. There could be a similar contest in her.
**Vitelucy**, stepping back up in trip from a mile and a half, travelled strongly into the straight but proved one paced when asked.
**Golfagent** has been in good form over hurdles recently, winning his last two starts over obstacles but, switched back to the level, he was well held.
**Western Command(GER)** kept on past beaten horses.
**Monsal Dale(IRE)** should have been suited by this step up from a mile and a half, but he disappointed.

## 1194 CASHBACKS @ BETDIRECT.CO.UK (S) STKS 1m 3f (F)
4:10 (4:11) (H) 4-Y-O+ £1,445 (£413; £206) Stalls Low

Form RPR
6-00 1 **Our Imperial Bay (USA)**[3] [1135] 5-9-1 58 (p) GDuffield 8 53
(RMStronge) *chsd ldrs: rdn along 4f out: hdwy u.p 2f out: drvn over 1f out: styd on to ld last 50 yds* **7/1**[2]
5255 2 hd **Red Delirium**[7] [1090] 8-9-1 50 (b) NCallan 3 53
(PABlockley) *hld up in rr: gd hdwy on outer over 4f out: chal 2f out: sn rdn and ev ch: drvn and styd on ins last* **8/1**[3]
-000 3 ½ **Forty Forte**[36] [861] 8-8-10 48 AQuinn(5) 5 52
(MissSJWilton) *mde most: rdn along and jnd 2f out: drvn and hung rt over 1f out: hdd and no ex last 50 yds* **20/1**
-262 4 3 **Elegant Gracie (IRE)**[14] [1031] 4-8-9 65 DHolland 2 42
(RGuest) *cl up on inner: effrt to chal and ev ch 2f out: sn rdn drvn and wknd ent last* **4/6**[1]
5000 5 17 **Ipledgeallegiance (USA)**[12] [1042] 8-9-1 35 ACulhane 4 20
(DWChapman) *chsd ldrs: pushed along 1/2-way: sn wknd* **18/1**
0300 6 3½ **Think Quick (IRE)**[7] [1091] 4-8-2 30 HFellows(7) 1 10
(RHollinshead) *a rr* **50/1**
0041 7 10 **Travel Tardia (IRE)**[8] [1076] 6-9-6 35 (t) DeanMcKeown 6 4
(PABlockley) *trckd ldrs: hdwy gng wl 4f out: rdn along over 2f out and wknd qckly* **20/1**
00-0 8 5 **Wethaab (USA)**[7] [1091] 7-9-1 35 (tp) AnnStokell 7 —
(MissAStokell) *in tch: rdn along 6f out: sn wknd* **50/1**

2m 33.83s (4.93) **Going Correction** +0.35s/f (Slow)
**WFA** 4 from 5yo+ 1lb 8 Ran SP% **102.3**
Speed ratings: **96,95,95,93,80 78,71,67**CSF £43.60 TOTE £7.30: £4.70, £5.00, £6.40; EX 46.50.The winner was bought in for 3,000gns
**Owner** Mrs Bernice Stronge **Bred** G Watts Humphrey Jnr & Louise I Humphrey **Trained** Beedon, Berks

**FOCUS**
A poor seller run at a moderate pace, in which few had much chance on official ratings.

**NOTEBOOK**
**Our Imperial Bay(USA)** had not achieved a great deal since being claimed out of Amanda Perrett's yard in October 2002 but, dropped into selling company, he ran out a narrow winner. He is not as good as he was, but is two from two on Fibresand and will be of interest back here in similar company.
**Red Delirium** has never won beyond a mile but gets this sort of trip well and was just held. He raced right against the stands'-side rail in the straight, whereas the winner raced down the centre of the track.
**Forty Forte** has not been in very good form lately but, stepped up in trip and dropped back into selling company, this was a better effort than of late.
**Elegant Gracie(IRE)**, third in a similar race over course and distance on his previous outing, was clear on the ratings but failed to build on that and has to be considered disappointing.
**Travel Tardia(IRE)**, claimed out of Ian Wood's yard after winning over seven furlongs at Wolverhampton on his previous run, did not stay this mile three.

## 1195 PRESS INTERACTIVE TO BET DIRECT TRI-BANDED STKS 1m (F)
4:40 (4:41) (H) 3-Y-O £1,424 (£407; £203) Stalls Low

Form RPR
4060 1 **Lady Predominant**[7] [1086] 3-8-7 45 BSwarbrick(7) 2 45
(AndrewReid) *cl up on inner: shkn up 2f out: sn rdn and styd on to ld ent last: r.o* **11/4**[2]

4054 **2** 2 **Secret Bloom**[13] [1040] 3-9-0 45 ....(v) DarrenWilliams 3 41
(JRNorton) *trckd ldrs: wd st: effrt to chal 2f out: sn rdn and hung lft: drvn ins last: nt qckn* **2/1**[1]

600- **3** 1 ½ **Roman The Park (IRE)**[147] [5915] 3-8-6 40 .... DAllan(3) 5 33
(TDEasterby) *led: qcknd 3f out: rdn 2f out: drvn and hdd ent last: one pce* **7/2**[3]

-004 **4** 6 **Heathyards Joy**[29] [942] 3-8-4 30 .... DeanMcKeown 4 16
(RHollinshead) *hld up: hdwy and wd st: rdn and ch 2f out: sn wknd* **8/1**

0500 **5** 21 **Dandy Jim**[27] [958] 3-8-4 30 .... JQuinn 1 —
(DWChapman) *trckd ldrs: pushed along 1/2-way: sn outpcd and b ehind* **9/2**

1m 49.31s (4.71) **Going Correction** +0.35s/f (Slow) **5** Ran SP% **111.5**
Speed ratings: **90,88,86,80,59**CSF £8.80 TOTE £4.80: £4.00, £1.10; EX 6.00 Place 6 £159.98, Place 5 £51.22.
**Owner** A S Reid **Bred** B Walters **Trained** Mill Hill, London NW7

**FOCUS**
An awful race run in a slow time.

**NOTEBOOK**
**Lady Predominant** appreciated the drop back into banded company and ran out a decisive winner of a very bad race. Things will almost certainly be tougher next time.
**Secret Bloom**, beaten in selling company on his latest run, did not look keen when put under pressure and was readily held.
**Roman The Park(IRE)** had the run of the race and can have no excuses.
**Heathyards Joy** can have no real excuses.
**Dandy Jim** was slowly away and never landed a blow.
T/Plt: £224.80 to a £1 stake. Pool £26,629.95. 86.45 winning tickets T/Qpdt: £19.50 to a £1 stake. Pool £2,469.00. 93.60 winning tickets JR

# CATTERICK (L-H)
## Wednesday, March 31

**OFFICIAL GOING: Good**
Wind: slt, hlf against Weather: fine & sunny

## 1196 TOTE BIG SCREEN IS HERE CLASSIFIED STKS 5f
2:20 (2:20) (F) 3-Y-O **£2,942** (£840; £420) **Stalls** Low

Form RPR

030- **1** **Linda Green**[187] [5197] 3-8-8 58 .... DeanMcKeown 8 60
(PABlockley) *midfield: hdwy appr fnl f: r.o wl ins last to ld clsng stages* **10/1**

500- **2** ¾ **Mr Wolf**[170] [5535] 3-8-10 62 .... LEnstone(3) 9 62
(DWBarker) *chsd ldrs: hdwy u.p over 1f out: edgd lft fnl f: led wl ins last: hdd clsng stages* **16/1**

503- **3** hd **Willjojo**[171] [5512] 3-8-5 54 .... THamilton(3) 5 56
(RAFahey) *prom: led jst ins fnl f: hdd wl ins last: no ex* **15/2**

06-4 **4** 1 **Black Oval**[5] [1119] 3-8-7 62 .... SHitchcott(3) 11 55+
(MRChannon) *midfield: hdwy over 1f out: styng on whn nt clr run jst ins fnl f and wl ins last: nvr able to chal* **7/2**[1]

50-4 **5** nk **Laconia (IRE)**[27] [963] 3-8-13 65 .... JDSmith 7 57+
(JSMoore) *chsd ldrs: styng on whn hmpd wl ins fnl f: nvr able to chal* **8/1**

0-00 **6** shd **Lord Baskerville**[63] [620] 3-8-11 60 .... DRMcCabe 6 54+
(WStorey) *towards rr: hdwy over 1f out: nt clr run and swtchd rt ins last: nvr able to chal* **33/1**

00-6 **7** ¾ **Killerby Nicko**[28] [956] 3-8-8 59 .... DAllan(3) 3 52
(TDEasterby) *prom: led 2f out: hdd jst ins fnl f: no ex* **11/1**

560- **8** ¾ **Reversionary**[298] [2184] 3-8-11 56 .... DaleGibson 10 49
(MWEasterby) *s.i.s: bhd: styd on fnl f: n.d* **33/1**

-053 **9** 2 **Blade's Edge**[4] [1127] 3-8-11 59 .... GDuffield 1 42
(ABailey) *prom: ev ch and rdn 2f out: sn btn* **11/2**[2]

200- **10** ½ **Lady Sunset (IRE)**[256] [3402] 3-8-13 65 ....(b1) NCallan 4 42
(KARyan) *trckd ldrs: effrt 2f out: sn ev ch: wknd fnl f* **6/1**[3]

-053 **11** ½ **Lavish Times**[37] [865] 3-8-11 51 ....(b) RWinston 2 38
(ABerry) *led tl hdd 2f out: nt clr run appr fnl f: eased whn no ch ins last* **12/1**

00-0 **12** 18 **Katie's Bath Time**[50] [731] 3-8-8 40 .... JBramhill 13 —
(IanEmmerson) *s.i.s: a bhd: t.o* **100/1**

61.64 secs (0.94) **Going Correction** +0.10s/f (Good) **12** Ran SP% **112.6**
Speed ratings: **96,94,94,92,92 92,91,89,86,85 85,56**CSF £149.33 TOTE £11.10: £3.00, £6.20, £2.20; EX 232.90.
**Owner** Stephen Roots **Bred** Colin Tinkler **Trained** Southwell, Notts

**FOCUS**
A moderate classified sprint that saw plenty of hard luck stories in the final furlong.

**NOTEBOOK**
**Linda Green**, making her debut for current connections, kept to her task gamely inside the final furlong to register a career-first success. She is all speed and this track suited, but she does not look an obvious type to follow up.
**Mr Wolf** did himself no favours by edging left inside the final furlong and that cost him. However, he still put in his best display to date, over a trip that looks his optimum, and he can be placed to advantage before long.
**Willjojo** ran another solid race, but can have no excuses and he does find it hard to win.
**Black Oval**, who looked backward in her coat, was slightly unlucky in that she had nowhere to go when seemingly full of running. She shaped as though a more galloping track would be to her advantage and is not one to write off just yet.
**Laconia(IRE)** was unlucky. She was hampered badly when mounting a serious challenge inside the last furlong, and would have gone close but for that. She looks the one to take out of the race.
**Blade's Edge**
**Lavish Times** *Official explanation: jockey said colt hung left handed from half way*

## 1197 FORCETT (S) STKS 7f
2:50 (2:51) (G) 3-Y-0+ **£2,646** (£756; £378) **Stalls** Low

Form RPR

000- **1** **Zhitomir**[116] [6128] 6-9-6 49 .... SWKelly 14 56
(MDods) *midfield: hdwy 2f out: led ins fnl f: styd on* **10/1**

00-0 **2** nk **Luke After Me (IRE)**[52] [717] 4-9-6 53 .... RWinston 2 55
(GASwinbank) *towards rr: gd hdwy over 1f out: ch ins fnl f: no ex clsng stages* **20/1**

550- **3** 1 **City General (IRE)**[114] [6147] 3-8-5 57 ....(p) DeanMcKeown 10 52
(JSMoore) *sn midfield: hdwy u.p over 1f out: r.o ins last: nvr able to chal* **16/1**

3030 **4** 1 ¼ **Tinian**[31] [939] 6-9-12 56 .... GFaulkner 5 55
(KRBurke) *dwlt: sn midfield: hdwy 2f out: styd on u.p fnl f: nvr able to chal* **14/1**

-530 **5** hd **Dusty Wugg (IRE)**[8] [1092] 5-8-12 45 ....(p) ABeech(3) 8 44
(ADickman) *in tch: hdwy over 2f out: ch appr fnl f: no ex ins last* **20/1**

53-0 **6** ½ **Mister Mal (IRE)**[37] [866] 8-9-3 55 ....(be) THamilton(3) 9 47
(BEllison) *led after 2f tl rdn and hdd ins fnl f: no ex* **9/1**

1236 **7** hd **Xaloc Bay (IRE)**[15] [1032] 6-9-6 56 .... DarrenWilliams 4 47
(BPJBaugh) *trckd ldrs: ev ch and rdn appr fnl f: no ex ins last* **7/1**[1]

206- **8** 1 ¼ **Royal Windmill (IRE)**[195] [5015] 5-9-3 50 ....(p) LEnstone(3) 18 44
(MDHammond) *in tch: hdwy over 2f out: rdn and ch over 1 out: no ex ins last* **14/1**

5624 **9** ¾ **Speedfit Free (IRE)**[2] [1171] 7-9-12 58 ....(b) GDuffield 13 48
(ISemple) *in tch: rdn 2f out: fdd fnl f* **8/1**[3]

0-01 **10** 1 ¼ **King Nicholas (USA)**[17] [1025] 5-9-5 50 ....(tp) MLawson(7) 6 44
(JParkes) *towards rr: kpt on fnl 2f: n.d* **15/2**[2]

0-60 **11** shd **Open Handed (IRE)**[37] [861] 4-9-7 35 ....(t) TEaves(5) 1 44
(BEllison) *nvr bttr than mid-div* **33/1**

5000 **12** 2 ½ **Magic Eagle**[8] [1089] 7-9-6 35 .... RFitzpatrick 17 32
(PTMidgley) *nvr bttr than mid-div* **66/1**

060- **13** 2 **Tancred Arms**[245] [3683] 8-9-7 45 .... TWilliams 16 27
(DWBarker) *rr div most of way* **14/1**

-450 **14** shd **Blunham**[21] [612] 4-9-12 53 .... LVickers 7 32
(MCChapman) *led 2f: remained cl up tl wknd wl over 1f out* **14/1**

0410 **15** 3 **Travel Tardia (IRE)**[1] [1194] 6-9-7 30 ....(t) DNolan(5) 11 24
(PABlockley) *prom: rdn over 2f out: sn wknd* **12/1**

0000 **16** 1 ½ **Brooklands Time (IRE)**[2] [1165] 3-7-7 45 .... NataliaGemelova(7) 3 9
(IWMcinnes) *s.i.s: a rr div* **33/1**

560- **17** nk **Miss Lyvennet**[327] [1478] 3-8-0 60 .... RFfrench 15 9
(MTodhunter) *rr div most of way* **50/1**

0560 **P** **Lion's Domane**[23] [993] 7-9-12 57 .... NCallan 12 —
(ABerry) *prom whn p.u over 5f out: sddle slipped* **14/1**

1m 27.95s (0.35) **Going Correction** -0.025s/f (Good)
**WFA** 3 from 4yo+ 15lb **18** Ran SP% **120.2**
Speed ratings: **97,96,95,94,93 93,93,91,90,89 89,86,84,83,80 78,78,—**CSF £205.88 TOTE £14.70: £4.80, £4.50, £8.00; EX 335.90.There was no bid for the winner.
**Owner** M J K Dods **Bred** Serpentine Bloodstock Et Al **Trained** Piercebridge, Co Durham

**FOCUS**
An ordinary pace, and with lowly rated horses close up the form is not great.

**NOTEBOOK**
**Zhitomir** appreciated this drop in trip and into selling company, to score all out from his unfavourable wide draw. He has started the current turf season on a fair-looking mark, but this looks to be about his level nowadays.
**Luke After Me(IRE)** was helped by the generous early gallop and ran his best race for sometime. However, he had the draw on this occasion and remains a maiden after 15 starts.
**City General(IRE)** ran a fair race against his elders and, on this evidence, can find a similar race at this level.
**Tinian** ◆ was not helped by a sluggish start and was finishing best of all. This was his best display since switching from Germany and he should be placed to advantage at this level soon.
**Dusty Wugg(IRE)** ran well enough at the weights, but is a fiendishly hard horse to win with.
**Mister Mal(IRE)** showed plenty of zip on this drop into selling company and can go in over six furlongs.
**Xaloc Bay(IRE)** was not allowed to dominate as he prefers and does look a better proposition on the All-Weather.
**Lion's Domane** *Official explanation: jockey said saddle slipped.*

## 1198 CATTERICKBRIDGE.CO.UK H'CAP 1m 5f 175y
3:20 (3:20) (D) (0-80,80) 4-Y-0+ **£5,508** (£1,695; £847; £423) **Stalls** Low

Form RPR

434- **1** **Court Of Appeal**[95] [6247] 7-9-3 **70** ....(t) TEaves(5) 1 82
(BEllison) *in tch: pushed along 5f out: hdwy 4 out: led appr fnl f: pushed out* **13/2**[3]

025- **2** 2 ½ **Tiyoun (IRE)**[185] [5258] 6-9-11 **73** .... GDuffield 4 81
(JeddO'Keeffe) *in tch: effrt over 3f out: styd on u.p to go 2nd ins fnl f: no imp on wnr* **20/1**

230/ **3** 2 **Calatagan (IRE)**[16] [5641] 5-8-10 **58** .... RWinston 11 63
(JMJefferson) *sn led: rdn and hdd appr fnl f: no ex* **7/1**

5552 **4** 2 ½ **Theatre Tinka (IRE)**[41] [825] 5-8-12 **60** ....(p) DaleGibson 13 62
(RHollinshead) *trckd ldrs: wnt 2nd 4f out: no imp on ldr: kpt on same pce* **12/1**

55-1 **5** 1 ¼ **Middlethorpe**[6] [1103] 7-8-9 **62** ....(b) PMulrennan(5) 8 62
(MWEasterby) *slowly away: towards rr: styd on fnl 3f: nvr able to chal* **5/1**[2]

00-0 **6** nk **Rajam**[6] [1103] 6-9-12 **74** .... AlexGreaves 14 74
(DNicholls) *prom: rdn over 3f out: fdd* **25/1**

00-0 **7** 2 ½ **Duc's Dream**[23] [984] 6-8-8 **56** .... DMcGaffin 5 52
(DMorris) *bhd: styd on fnl 3f: n.d* **20/1**

240- **8** ¾ **Spitting Image (IRE)**[142] [5972] 4-8-10 **62** .... ACulhane 9 57
(MrsMReveley) *hld up: effrt whn nt clr run and stmbld sltly 2f out: n.d* **16/1**

00-0 **9** 3 **Banningham Blaze**[14] [671] 4-8-2 **54** ....(b1) JBramhill 6 45
(CRDore) *rr div: hdwy into midfield 5f out: no further prog* **25/1**

054- **10** 2 ½ **Best Port (IRE)**[166] [5624] 8-8-1 **56** ow2 .... MLawson(7) 7 43
(JParkes) *hld up: sme hdwy 5f out: wknd over 2 out* **20/1**

040- **11** ½ **Bolshoi Ballet**[95] [5682] 6-8-8 **56** ....(b1) NCallan 10 43
(JMackie) *prom tl wknd 3f out* **8/1**

060- **12** 2 **Edmo Yewkay (IRE)**[13] [5910] 4-8-11 **66** .... DAllan(3) 12 50
(TDEasterby) *rr div most of way* **11/1**

210- **13** 13 **The Persuader (IRE)**[169] [5558] 4-10-0 **80** .... RFfrench 3 46
(MJohnston) *prom to 1/2-way: sn wknd: t.o* **10/3**[1]

3m 2.03s (-2.87) **Going Correction** -0.025s/f (Good)
**WFA** 4 from 5yo+ 4lb **13** Ran SP% **120.6**
Speed ratings: **107,105,104,103,102 102,100,100,98,97 96,95,88**CSF £136.27 CT £939.25 TOTE £8.60: £2.30, £6.20, £2.50; EX 163.10.
**Owner** Spring Cottage Syndicate No 2 **Bred** John And Susan Davis **Trained** Norton, N Yorks

**FOCUS**
A competitive staying handicap run at a generous gallop. The form looks sound.

**NOTEBOOK**
**Court Of Appeal**, who looked backward in his coat, landed the gamble in style and was value for more than the official winning margin. He has slipped to a winning mark of late and does go well at this track.
**Tiyoun(IRE)** ◆ made a pleasing comeback, having been off for 185 days previously, but had no chance with the winner. He is a likeable sort who looks capable of scoring off this lenient mark in the near future.
**Calatagan(IRE)**, who has been in good heart over hurdles during the winter, set the decent gallop and deserves credit for not folding late on. A drop in trip will suit and he looks on a reasonable mark at present.
**Theatre Tinka(IRE)** found his stamina stretched by the decent gallop and will be better over shorter.
**Middlethorpe** was not helped by a sluggish start, but recovered to have every chance if good enough and never looked like following up his latest success.


The Form Book, Raceform Ltd, Compton, RG20 6NL

**Spitting Image(IRE)** *Official explanation: jockey said, regarding the running, his orders were to settle filly in and do his best, adding that filly was not suited by the sharp track and that on entering the straight he was twice short of room - but it had no affected his placing; trainer's representative confirmed orders, adding that filly used to be keen in her races and had been taught to settle, which in handsight had not helped her on this sharp track*

**The Persuader(IRE)**, a progressive handicapper last season, ran too badly to be true. He shaped as though something may have been amiss. *Official explanation: trainer had no explanation for the poor form shown*

## 1199 GODS SOLUTION H'CAP — 7f

**3:50** (3:50) (D ) (0-85,84) 3-Y-O+ — **£5,687** (£1,750; £875; £437) **Stalls** Low

| Form | | | | Jockey | RPR |
|---|---|---|---|---|---|
| 000- | **1** | | **Nathan Brittles (USA)**[182] 5301 4-8-9 **72** (TDBarron) *in tch: hdwy over 1f out: rdn to ld ins fnl f: styd on* **50/1** | PMakin(7) 16 | 83 |
| 42-4 | **2** | *½* | **Sarraaf (IRE)**[18] 1013 8-8-12 **68** (ISemple) *midfield: hdwy over 1f out: styd on u.p to go 2nd wl ins last* **6/1**[1] | RWinston 10 | 78 |
| 040- | **3** | *1 ½* | **Watching**[144] 5946 7-9-6 **83** (DNicholls) *in tch: hdwy to chse ldrs over 1f out: styd on fnl f* **16/1** | LTreadwell(7) 5 | 89 |
| 0-00 | **4** | *¾* | **Lincoln Dancer (IRE)**[48] 749 7-9-7 **77** (DNicholls) *chsd ldrs: rdn to ld appr fnl f: hdd ins last: no ex* **12/1** | AlexGreaves 1 | 81 |
| 400U | **5** | *nk* | **Ronnie From Donny (IRE)**[2] 1175 4-8-9 **70** (BEllison) *towards rr: hdwy 2f out: styd on u.p fnl f* **12/1** | TEaves(5) 12 | 73 |
| 014- | **6** | *hd* | **Distant Country (USA)**[155] 5820 5-9-5 **75** (MrsJRRamsden) *hld up towards rr: styd on wl fnl 2f: nrst fin* **14/1** | PFitzsimons 9 | 78 |
| -050 | **7** | *1* | **No Grouse**[18] 1013 4-9-2 **75** (RAFahey) *hld up: hdwy over 2f out: rdn over 1 out: no further prog* **8/1**[3] | THamilton(3) 18 | 75 |
| 0006 | **8** | *¾* | **Flying Treaty (USA)**[44] 795 7-8-10 **66** (MissAStokell) *chsd ldrs: rdn 2f out: fdd* **33/1** | AnnStokell 2 | 64 |
| 530- | **9** | *1 ¾* | **Sir Don (IRE)**[230] 4119 5-8-11 **67** (DNicholls) *led tl rdn and hdd appr fnl f: wknd ins last* **16/1** | (v) ANicholls 6 | 60 |
| 000- | **10** | *1 ¼* | **Bailieborough (IRE)**[185] 5260 5-9-0 **70** (DNicholls) *slowly away: bhd: sme late hdwy: n.d* **33/1** | PMQuinn 15 | 60 |
| 223- | **11** | *nk* | **Raphael (IRE)**[148] 5918 5-9-3 **76** (TDEasterby) *midfield: rdn 2f out: no hdwy* **13/2**[2] | DAllan(3) 11 | 65 |
| 150- | **12** | *hd* | **Acomb**[166] 5626 4-8-9 **65** (MWEasterby) *prom: rdn 2f out: sn wknd* **16/1** | DaleGibson 13 | 54 |
| -300 | **13** | *1 ½* | **Royal Grand**[34] 900 4-8-10 **66** (TDBarron) *nvr bttr than mid-div* **10/1** | DMernagh 3 | 51 |
| 410- | **14** | *hd* | **Atlantic Quest (USA)**[158] 5749 5-9-8 **83** (GAHarker) *rr div most of way* **14/1** | PMulrennan(5) 14 | 67 |
| 340- | **15** | *¾* | **Rifleman (IRE)**[186] 5225 4-9-10 **80** (MrsADuffield) *midfield tl wknd 2f out* **14/1** | GDuffield 7 | 63 |
| 205- | **16** | *1* | **Sea Storm (IRE)**[182] 5299 6-10-0 **84** (DRMacleod) *sn bhd: nt clr run over 1f out: n.d* **16/1** | ACulhane 8 | 64 |
| 3000 | **17** | *1 ½* | **Grandma Lily (IRE)**[43] 803 6-8-6 **67** (MCChapman) *midfield tl wknd 2f out* **25/1** | DFox(5) 17 | 43 |
| 103- | **18** | *18* | **H Harrison (IRE)**[158] 5747 4-9-5 **82** (IWMcinnes) *prom tl wknd qckly 2f out: t.o* **10/1** | NataliaGemelova(7) 4 | 11 |

1m 26.75s (-0.85) **Going Correction** -0.025s/f (Good) **18** Ran SP% **127.5**

Speed ratings: **103,102,100,99,99 99,98,97,95,93 93,93,91,91,90 89,87,67**CSF £335.34 CT £5220.73 TOTE £37.40: £8.70, £2.00, £6.00, £3.70; EX 347.50 TRIFECTA Not won..

**Owner** Steve Vickers **Bred** Marvin Little Jr, And James H Iselin **Trained** Maunby, N Yorks

**FOCUS**

A fair-looking field and a solid pace to this competitive handicap should ensure the form is sound.

**NOTEBOOK**

**Nathan Brittles(USA)**, off for 182 days prior to this, showed a great atttitude to score doggedly on this comeback. The fact that he had never previously run beyond five furlongs suggests he has improved over the winter, and he could progress farther, especially when dropped back a furlong.

**Sarraaf(IRE)** stayed on to have every chance and ran another sound race. He is tricky customer, but he will come on for this and, on this evidence, there are still races to be won with him.

**Watching** threatened briefly approaching the final furlong, but lacked the change of gear to trouble the leaders. He is another who will improve for the outing, and although on a long losing run, could pop up one day.

**Lincoln Dancer(IRE)** has started the season on a decent mark, and shaped as though he can capitalise on that when getting his favoured cut in the ground.

**Ronnie From Donny(IRE)** did best of those to be held up and was finishing nicely. However, he is the sort who needs everything to fall just right.

**Distant Country(USA)** caught the eye finishing strongly and would have been closer with a more prominent ride. He looks one to keep on the right side of in the coming weeks and will do better with the cheekpieces re-applied. *Official explanation: jockey said, regarding the running and riding, he held gelding up as ordered but when a gap appeared at about the furlong marker the gelding hung away from the whip causing him to take a pull to avoid interference*

**Raphael(IRE)** looked backward in her coat.

## 1200 TOYTOP MAIDEN STKS — 5f 212y

**4:20** (4:21) (D ) 3-Y-O+ — **£3,376** (£1,039; £519; £259) **Stalls** Low

| Form | | | | Jockey | RPR |
|---|---|---|---|---|---|
| 2- | **1** | | **Place Cowboy (IRE)**[280] 2687 3-8-11 (JAOsborne) *cmpt: lengthy: lw: dwlt: sn trcking ldrs: led over 1f out: rdn and styd on fnl f* **5/2**[1] | SWKelly 1 | 64 |
| | **2** | *¾* | **Extremely Rare (IRE)** 3-7-13 (TDEasterby) *lengthy: unf: dwlt: sn midfield: hdwy 2f out: wnt 2nd ins fnl f: clsng on wnr towards fin* **20/1** | AMullen(7) 10 | 57 |
| 6466 | **3** | *1 ½* | **Amanda's Lad (IRE)**[17] 1025 4-9-10 45 (MCChapman) *prom: ev ch and rdn 2f out: kpt on same pce* **50/1** | LVickers 11 | 57? |
| 54- | **4** | *shd* | **Top Line Dancer (IRE)**[222] 4353 3-8-11 (MJohnston) *in tch: rdn 2f out: styd on fnl f* **5/2**[1] | RFfrench 5 | 57 |
| -30 | **5** | *1 ½* | **Uhuru Peak**[13] 1044 3-8-6 (MWEasterby) *midfield: kpt on fnl f: n.d* **25/1** | PMulrennan(5) 7 | 52 |
| 000- | **6** | *hd* | **Orion Express**[257] 3382 3-8-11 (MWEasterby) *bhd: styd on fnl 2f: n.d* **33/1** | DaleGibson 6 | 52 |
| 230- | **7** | *2* | **Fox Covert (IRE)**[170] 5535 3-8-8 71 (DWBarker) *led tl hdd over 4f out: led again 2 out: sn hdd: wkng whn stmbld ins fnl f* **4/1**[2] | LEnstone(3) 8 | 46 |
| 00-0 | **8** | *3* | **Strangely Brown (IRE)**[40] 835 3-8-11 (SCWilliams) *dwlt: a rr div* **20/1** | JBramhill 9 | 37 |
| 400- | **9** | *nk* | **Leopard Creek**[155] 5818 3-8-6 (MrsJRRamsden) *dwlt: plld hrd in rr early: pushed along 1/2-way: no hdwy* **10/1**[3] | ACulhane 3 | 31 |
| 44- | **10** | *1 ¾* | **Song Koi**[333] 1347 3-8-6 (JGGiven) *cl up: led after 2f: jinked over 2 out: sn hdd & wknd* **10/1**[3] | GDuffield 2 | 25 |
| | **11** | *29* | **Stoneacre** 4-9-5 (DNicholls) *rangy: unf: dwlt: a bhd: t.o* **14/1** | ANicholls 4 | — |

1m 14.72s (0.62) **Going Correction** -0.025s/f (Good)

**WFA** 3 from 4yo 13lb **11** Ran SP% **120.3**

Speed ratings: **94,93,91,90,88 88,85,81,81,79 40**CSF £62.05 TOTE £3.90: £1.10, £3.50, £10.10; EX 112.70.

**Owner** Mountgrange Stud **Bred** John Bourke And Rodger O Callaghan **Trained** Upper Lambourn, Berks

**FOCUS**

A modest time for the grade of contest, and a lowly-rated runner close up in third, but the first two can improve on this form.

**NOTEBOOK**

**Place Cowboy(IRE)**, who had shown ability on his only start as a juvenile last year, recovered from a slow start to win with a bit in hand. He is no superstar, but can progress on this in handicap company and may be better suited by a slightly stiffer test.

**Extremely Rare(IRE)**, was another to miss the break, but shaped nicely on this debut and will come on plenty for the experience.

**Amanda's Lad(IRE)** ran his best race for some time, but he is well exposed and does give the form a dodgy look.

**Top Line Dancer(IRE)** looked to be struggling for pace, but kept on well enough and will be of interest over farther now he qualifies for handicaps.

**Fox Covert(IRE)** was beating a retreat when he stumbled late on. He had some fair juvenile form, despite looking exposed, but still has to prove he has trained on.

**Leopard Creek** *Official explanation: jockey said filly hung right handed badly throughout.*

## 1201 YARM H'CAP — 1m 3f 214y

**4:50** (4:50) (E ) (0-75,75) 3-Y-O — **£3,445** (£1,060; £530; £265) **Stalls** Low

| Form | | | | Jockey | RPR |
|---|---|---|---|---|---|
| 006- | **1** | | **Liquidate**[173] 5467 3-8-5 **62** (HMorrison) *trckd ldrs: drvn along over 3f out: styd on wl u.p fnl f: led cl home* **13/2** | LFletcher(3) 10 | 71 |
| 2121 | **2** | *½* | **Yankeedoodledandy (IRE)**[28] 957 3-9-4 **72** (PCHaslam) *lw: trckd ldrs: rdn over 2f out: led ins fnl f: styd on u.p: hdd cl home* **4/1**[1] | GFaulkner 7 | 80 |
| 3233 | **3** | *1* | **Siegfrieds Night (IRE)**[6] 1108 3-7-10 **55** (MCChapman) *led 1f: remained cl up: drvn along over 3 out: ev ch ins fnl f: 3rd and hld whn hmpd cl home* **6/1**[3] | DFox(5) 2 | 61 |
| 400- | **4** | *2* | **Woody Valentine (USA)**[159] 5726 3-9-7 **75** (MJohnston) *led after 1f: rdn 2 out: hdd ins fnl f: no ex* **5/1**[2] | RFfrench 6 | 78 |
| -606 | **5** | *4* | **Bill Bennett (FR)**[41] 829 3-9-0 **68** (JJay) *hld up: hdwy over 4f out: rdn 2 out: no further prog* **12/1** | NCallan 1 | 65 |
| -125 | **6** | *2 ½* | **Come What July (IRE)**[23] 985 3-9-5 **73** (RGuest) *midfield: hdwy 5f out: chsd ldrs and rdn 2 out: wknd fnl f* **8/1** | (b) RWinston 3 | 66 |
| 350- | **7** | *7* | **Classic Event (IRE)**[149] 5906 3-8-8 **65** (TDEasterby) *bhd: styd on fnl 2f: n.d* **12/1** | DAllan(3) 4 | 47 |
| 50-P | **8** | *11* | **Argent**[2] 1179 3-8-8 **62** (DCarroll) *trckd ldrs: rdn 4f out: sn wknd* **33/1** | RFitzpatrick 11 | 26 |
| | **9** | *1 ¼* | **Friends Hope**[187] 5205 3-8-2 **56** (PABlockley) *sn midfield: rdn 4f out: sn wknd* **25/1** | GDuffield 12 | 18 |
| 56-0 | **10** | *1 ¼* | **The Stick**[8] 1086 3-8-6 **63** (MRChannon) *hld up: hdwy 5f out: wknd 3 out* **5/1**[2] | SHitchcott(3) 5 | 23 |
| 0-33 | **11** | *10* | **Vesta Flame**[51] 730 3-7-8 **55** oh17 ow3 (PABlockley) *prom tl wknd 5f out: sn bhd* **40/1** | SYourston(7) 8 | — |
| 600- | **12** | *4* | **Northern Summit (IRE)**[171] 5510 3-7-13 **53** oh12 ow1 (JRNorton) *bhd most of way* **66/1** | JBramhill 9 | — |

2m 37.77s (-1.93) **Going Correction** -0.025s/f (Good) **12** Ran SP% **118.2**

Speed ratings: **105,104,104,102,100 98,93,86,85,84 78,75**CSF £31.68 CT £167.09 TOTE £7.50: £2.10, £1.80, £2.40; EX 67.70 Place 6 £2,574.22, Place 5 £416.80.

**Owner** The Phantom Partnership **Bred** T D Holland-Martin **Trained** East Ilsley, Berks

■ Stewards Enquiry : L Fletcher caution: careless riding

**FOCUS**

A fair three-year-old handicap and a decent time for the grade.

**NOTEBOOK**

**Liquidate**, making his handicap debut, improved markedly on his previous three outings and relished this step up in trip. He can improve again, but will no doubt take a rise in the weights for this effort. *Official explanation: trainer's representative said, regarding the improved form shown, this was gelding's first run for the yard*

**Yankeedoodledandy(IRE)** narrowly failed to defy a 7lb rise for winning on the All-Weather last time. He again ran his race and has become a consistent performer.

**Siegfrieds Night(IRE)** did not look straightforward and failed to reverse terms with the runner-up on these better terms. However, he would have been a bit closer but for meeting trouble in the closing stages.

**Woody Valentine(USA)** held every chance if good enough, but could not quicken when it mattered under top weight.

**The Stick** is not a good mover.

JF

# [1164] LINGFIELD (L-H)

### Wednesday, March 31

**OFFICIAL GOING: Standard**

Wind: It across Weather: fine & sunny

## 1202 BET DIRECT ON SKY ACTIVE MAIDEN STKS — 7f (P)

**2:00** (2:02) (D ) 3-Y-O — **£3,750** (£1,154; £577; £288) **Stalls** Low

| Form | | | | Jockey | RPR |
|---|---|---|---|---|---|
| 3 | **1** | | **Instant Recall (IRE)**[12] 1052 3-9-0 (BJMeehan) *t.k.h: trckd ldr: rdn to ld over 1f out: narrowly hdd ins fnl f: rallied to ld again nr fin* **5/4**[1] | DHolland 3 | 77 |
| 023- | **2** | *hd* | **Emtilaak**[167] 5587 3-9-0 79 (BHanbury) *t.k.h: hld up in cl tch: chsd ldng pair over 2f out: rdn to ld ins fnl f: kpt on: hdd nr fin* **5/1**[3] | RHills 5 | 76 |
| 20-2 | **3** | *2* | **Finders Keepers**[12] 1052 3-9-0 84 (EALDunlop) *dwlt: t.k.h and hld up in midfield: prog over 2f out: rdn to chse ldng pair fnl f: no imp* **3/1**[2] | EAhern 7 | 71 |
| | **4** | *¾* | **Sylva Royal (IRE)** 3-8-6 (CEBrittain) *s.i.s: sn trckd ldrs: shkn up and outpcd 2f out: kpt on fnl f* **33/1** | LisaJones(3) 2 | 64 |
| 00 | **5** | *2 ½* | **Saintly Scholar (USA)**[12] 1052 3-8-9 (EALDunlop) *s.s: wl in rr tl prog into midfield over 2f out: effrt to chse ldrs over 1f out: wknd fnl f* **40/1** | RLMoore 6 | 58 |
| 2 | **6** | *1 ¾* | **King Of Diamonds**[8] 1083 3-9-0 (JRBest) *rluctant to go to post: t.k.h: led: rdn and hdd over 1f out: wknd rapidly* **7/1** | NPollard 10 | 58 |
| 5 | **7** | *2* | **Farnborough (USA)**[17] 1015 3-9-0 (DRCElsworth) *dwlt: hld up in rr: sme prog into midfield over 2f out: wknd over 1f out* **20/1** | DaneO'Neill 11 | 53 |

000- **8** 1 ½ **Airgusta (IRE)**[175] 5448 3-9-0 PRobinson 9 49
(CREgerton) *settled towards rr: no prog over 2f out: no ch after* **33/1**
666- **9** ¾ **Indian Edge**[153] 5836 3-9-0 62 DKinsella 12 47
(BPalling) *t.k.h: pressed ldrs: drvn over 2f out: sn wknd* **40/1**
**10** ½ **Pins 'n Needles (IRE)** 3-8-9 SWhitworth 1 41
(CACyzer) *s.s: a in rr: bhd fnl 2f* **33/1**
505- **11** 4 **Dr Fox (IRE)**[177] 5415 3-9-0 61 MTebbutt 8 35
(KAMorgan) *a in last trio: wl bhd 2f out* **50/1**

1m 26.24s (0.24) **Going Correction** +0.025s/f (Slow) **11** Ran SP% **119.0**
Speed ratings: **99,98,96,95,92 90,88,86,85,85 80**CSF £7.39 TOTE £2.20: £1.40, £2.10, £1.10; EX 7.50.
**Owner** Mrs Susan Roy **Bred** Frank Dunne **Trained** Upper Lambourn, Berks

**FOCUS**
Fair form from the principals, and probably a reasonable maiden, although one or two behind may have been flattered.

**NOTEBOOK**
**Instant Recall(IRE)** confirmed the promise of his debut on this track and impressed in the way he fought back after being headed. He should develop into a nice handicapper at around a mile.
**Emtilaak**, gelded since last seen in October and making his sand debut, came with a perfectly-timed effort to win his race but he did have questions over his stamina and did not quite get home. He is becoming frustrating.
**Finders Keepers** travelled really well behind the leaders, but once pulled out for his effort and given a crack with the whip the tail went and he found absolutely nothing.
**Sylva Royal(IRE)** ◆, resold for 37,000gns as a yearling, is related to decent performers such as Startino and Barathea Guest. She showed plenty of ability herself on this debut and should be suited by further.
**Saintly Scholar(USA)** again failed to get home over the trip, but at least can now be handicapped.
**King Of Diamonds**, stepping up a furlong from his promising debut, was not on good terms with himself before the start. After doing too much too soon he paid for it late on.

## 1203 PRESS INTERACTIVE TO BET DIRECT CLASSIFIED STKS 1m 4f (P)
**2:30** (2:31) (E ) 4-Y-0+ **£3,376** (£1,039; £519; £259) **Stalls** Low

Form RPR
3112 **1** **Steely Dan**[5] 1122 5-9-6 64 NPollard 2 80+
(JRBest) *hld up in last pair: gng easily over 2f out: effrt over 1f out: coaxed along and squeezed through fnl f to ld last 50y* **5/2**[1]
3-10 **2** nk **Rasid (USA)**[63] 618 6-9-0 67 DHolland 1 74
(CADwyer) *trckd ldng pair: effrt over 2f out: drvn to ld ins fnl f: hdd last 50y* **8/1**[3]
1510 **3** ¾ **Bella Pavlina**[6] 1103 6-8-8 74 BSwarbrick(7) 4 74
(WMBrisbourne) *trckd ldr: rdn to chal over 2f out: ev ch 1f out: nt qckn* **7/1**[2]
3-12 **4** hd **Moon Shot**[13] 1045 8-9-1 71 VSlattery 5 73
(AGJuckes) *hld up bhd ldrs: effrt over 2f out: rdn and cl up over 1f out : nt qckn and hld after* **10/1**
3-20 **5** ½ **Doris Souter (IRE)**[12] 1053 4-8-11 72 DaneO'Neill 3 71
(RHannon) *led at mod pce: rdn over 2f out: hdd ins fnl f: one pce* **7/1**[2]
11- **6** 1 ¼ **Kingkohler (IRE)**[84] 1627 5-9-2 75 RMiles(3) 7 75
(KAMorgan) *trckd ldrs: rdn and effrt on outer over 2f out: hanging and nt qckn over 1f out: btn after* **5/2**[1]
256- **7** 15 **Distant Cousin**[159] 5727 7-9-4 74 (v) SSanders 6 50
(MABuckley) *hld up in last pair: rdn over 3f out: wknd over 2f out: t.o* **12/1**

2m 36.23s (2.25) **Going Correction** +0.025s/f (Slow)
**WFA** 4 from 5yo+ 2lb **7** Ran SP% **110.0**
Speed ratings: **93,92,92,92,91 91,81**CSF £21.65 TOTE £3.30: £1.90, £3.80; EX 34.00.
**Owner** E A Condon **Bred** Mrs S E Barclay And L B Snowden **Trained** Hucking, Kent

**FOCUS**
A pedestrian winning time for the grade.

**NOTEBOOK**
**Steely Dan**, switched right off out the back, was suited by the moderate pace as it enabled him to use his ten-furlong speed at the business end. He had to wait for a gap to appear, but fortunately a nice one appeared between the eventual second and third and he quickly seized the opportunity.
**Rasid(USA)**, like the winner, has shown his best form over ten furlongs so he was also suited by the modest pace and was only just denied. There should be another race for him on this surface.
**Bella Pavlina**, in such fine form on Fibresand this year, is a thorough stayer so the moderate pace on this faster surface would not have been ideal. Under the circumstances this was not a bad effort.
**Moon Shot**, a winner on the old Equitrack here five years ago, could not quicken when the pace lifted and would prefer an end-to-end gallop on a slower surface these days.
**Doris Souter(IRE)**, trying her longest trip to date, had her own way out in front and did her best to hold on but was ultimately swamped.
**Kingkohler(IRE)**, back on the Flat after a couple of decent efforts over hurdles, had every chance in the straight but lacked the required turn of foot. Like so many others in this contest, he would have preferred a proper test.

## 1204 ALAN MORGAN REMEMBERED BY HIS FRIENDS H'CAP 7f (P)
**3:00** (3:01) (E ) (0-70,70) 3-Y-0+ **£3,532** (£1,087; £543; £271) **Stalls** Low

Form RPR
5342 **1** **Spindor (USA)**[8] 1082 5-9-2 58 (b) DHolland 10 68+
(JAOsborne) *hld up towards rr: nt clr run on inner 3f out: plld out and gd prog over 1f out: sustained run to ld last strides* **6/1**[2]
5002 **2** nk **Illusive (IRE)**[5] 1121 7-9-2 58 (b) MTebbutt 2 67
(MWigham) *settled in midfield: effrt 2f out: clsd on ldrs and nt clr run 1f out: swtchd rt and r.o last 100y: jst outpcd by wnr* **10/1**
0630 **3** ½ **Quantum Leap**[49] 745 7-9-6 62 (v) RLMoore 8 70
(SDow) *sn prom: led 1/2-way: drvn 2l clr wl over 1f out: hdd last strides* **25/1**
21-0 **4** shd **Cold Climate**[39] 847 9-9-9 65 OUrbina 6 73
(BobJones) *trckd ldrs: effrt to chse ldr 2f out: ev ch ins fnl f: outpcd nr fin* **10/1**
4104 **5** shd **Hard To Catch (IRE)**[8] 1082 6-9-7 70 MHoward(7) 13 77
(DKIvory) *racd in midfield: prog on outer fr 3f out: rdn to chal 1f out: ev ch ins fnl f: no ex nr fin* **16/1**
1414 **6** 1 ¼ **Zafarshah (IRE)**[39] 847 5-9-6 62 SSanders 9 66+
(PDEvans) *hld up in midfield: stmbld over 2f out: sme prog over 1f out: rdn and styd on ins fnl f: nt rch ldrs* **8/1**
00-6 **7** nk **Fearby Cross (IRE)**[39] 847 8-9-7 66 LisaJones(3) 12 69
(WJMusson) *sn wl in rr and pushed along: prog 2f out: styd on fr over 1f out: nrst fin* **14/1**
1021 **8** ¾ **Nearly A Fool**[15] 1032 6-9-6 62 (v) NPollard 11 63
(GGMargarson) *racd in midfield: pushed along and no prog wl over 3f out: one pce and nvr on terms after* **11/2**[1]
2545 **9** 1 ¼ **Single Track Mind**[2] 1165 6-7-10 45 KarenPeippo(7) 1 43
(JRBoyle) *s.s: racd in last pair and bhd: nudged along and kpt on fnl 2f: no ch* **25/1**
-000 **10** 2 **Sir Francis (IRE)**[39] 847 6-9-11 67 EAhern 4 60
(JNoseda) *led: rdn and hdd 1/2-way: wknd 2f out* **7/1**[3]
-436 **11** 1 ¼ **Parker**[14] 1039 7-9-7 63 (b) DKinsella 5 53
(BPalling) *w ldrs: rdn wl over 2f out: wknd wl over 1f out: eased* **14/1**
6215 **12** 1 **Feast Of Romance**[37] 861 7-9-2 58 (p) PRobinson 14 45
(CNAllen) *sn pressed ldrs on outer: rdn 3f out: wknd 2f out* **10/1**
4-55 **13** 1 ¼ **Star Fern**[31] 927 3-8-3 60 ow1 SWhitworth 3 44
(JAkehurst) *s.v.s: a wl bhd* **20/1**
2-42 **14** 19 **Super Canyon**[14] 1035 6-9-10 66 (vt) RHills 7 —
(JPearce) *sn struggling and wl in rr: t.o* **9/1**

1m 25.64s (-0.36) **Going Correction** +0.025s/f (Slow)
**WFA** 3 from 5yo+ 15lb **14** Ran SP% **122.2**
Speed ratings: **103,102,102,101,101 100,100,99,97,95 94,92,91,69**CSF £64.23 CT £1438.69 TOTE £6.30: £2.20, £4.80, £5.40; EX 50.80.
**Owner** Paul J Dixon **Bred** Juddmonte Farms Inc **Trained** Upper Lambourn, Berks

**FOCUS**
A decent pace, but a blanket finish with less than a length covering the front five.

**NOTEBOOK**
**Spindor(USA)** confirmed the promise of his effort here eight days earlier, but did not appear to be in a promising position at all turning in. Switched widest of all, he made up a tremendous amount of ground to get up in the dying strides and is value for more than the winning margin.
**Illusive(IRE)** tends to find one to beat him, but on this occasion it was not entirely his fault as he had to be switched at a vital stage, whereas the winner had a clear path down the outside.
**Quantum Leap**, better known as a ten-furlong performer these days, travelled really well up with the pace and had the lead turning for home, but despite trying his best was just run out of it. This was a good effort over an inadequate trip.
**Cold Climate**, 7lb higher than for his last win here, did nothing wrong and only just lost out.
**Hard To Catch(IRE)**, with the blinkers removed this time, came to win his race at just the right time but lacked a killer punch where it mattered.
**Zafarshah(IRE)**ran better than his final placing suggests as he was travelling well on the inside just behind the pace when taking a bad step two and a half furlongs from home. He did not see much daylight after that and, by the time he did, it was too late.
**Fearby Cross(IRE)** ◆ was noted staying on down the straight and is one to watch in the market from now on.
**Nearly A Fool** was a little short of room over the last couple of furlongs, but it would be pushing things to say his chances of winning were affected.
**Sir Francis(IRE)** is brilliantly handicapped on his form here a couple of years ago, but is not getting home so well these days.
**Star Fern** lost all chance at the start.

## 1205 CASHBACKS @ BETDIRECT.CO.UK RATED STKS (H'CAP) 5f (P)
**3:30** (3:30) (D ) (0-85,83) 3-Y-0+ **£4,805** (£1,822; £911; £414) **Stalls** High

Form RPR
6112 **1** **Forever Phoenix**[12] 1051 4-9-13 83 EAhern 4 99
(RMHCowell) *trckd ldr: led 2f out: pushed along 1f out: hrd pressed last 100y: rdn and flashed tail: jst hld on* **11/4**[1]
0-01 **2** shd **Magic Glade**[43] 806 5-9-2 77 RThomas(5) 3 93
(CRDore) *trckd ldng pair: effor 2f out: drvn to chse wnr 1f out: styd on wl nr finisg: jst failed* **4/1**[2]
1-61 **3** 3 ½ **Turibius**[32] 912 5-9-11 81 JFEgan 6 83
(TEPowell) *racd in last trio: rdn and effrt over 2f out: kpt on one pce fr over 1f out: no ch w ldng pair* **11/4**[1]
2000 **4** 1 **Prince Of Blues (IRE)**[33] 905 6-8-3 66 oh5 (p) PVarley(7) 2 64
(MMullineaux) *led to 2f out: wknd u.p 1f out* **20/1**
040- **5** 1 ¼ **Zargus**[201] 4867 5-8-13 69 DaneO'Neill 7 62
(WRMuir) *hld up in last: rdn and effrt over 2f out: no prog and btn over 1f out* **8/1**[3]
5132 **6** ½ **Sea The World (IRE)**[15] 1033 4-8-7 66 oh3 (v) LisaJones(3) 5 57
(DShaw) *dwlt: a in last trio: struggling 2f out* **10/1**
004- **7** 1 **Multiple Choice (IRE)**[176] 5441 3-9-1 83 DHolland 8 70
(NPLittmoden) *chsd ldrs: rdn 1/2-way: wknd wl over 1f out* **8/1**[3]

58.95 secs (-0.83) **Going Correction** +0.025s/f (Slow)
**WFA** 3 from 4yo+ 12lb **7** Ran SP% **109.4**
Speed ratings: **107,106,101,99,97 96,95**CSF £12.61 CT £28.42 TOTE £3.80: £1.60, £2.60; EX 16.00.
**Owner** J M Greetham **Bred** J M Greetham **Trained** Six Mile Bottom, Cambs

**FOCUS**
A decent pace and not many got into it. The winner improved again, and the second is back to something like his best.

**NOTEBOOK**
**Forever Phoenix**, dropping to the minimum trip for the first time and racing off a 13lb higher mark than for her last win, looked set to score by a decent margin when sent for home in the straight but, with the runner-up finishing to some purpose, she showed her dislike of being hit with the whip by flashing her tail and only managed to hold on by a nostril. She is much improved this year and it will be fascinating to see how she performs back on grass.
**Magic Glade** ◆, 4lb higher than for his Southwell win, stalked the front pair and his strong finish only just failed. He still does not look badly handicapped and should soon be winning again.
**Turibius**, up 4lb for his course-and-distance victory last time, was given more to do on this occasion and could never quite make up the ground.
**Prince Of Blues(IRE)** blazed a trail but basically set the race up for others. He is without a win for two years and even tumbling down the handicap is not bringing about much improvement in his fortunes.
**Zargus**, making his sand debut, is very well handicapped on the best of his turf form but he seemed to find everything happening too quickly for him on this occasion.
**Sea The World(IRE)** did his chances little good with a tardy start and was always fighting an uphill battle thereafter.

## 1206 BETDIRECT.CO.UK (S) STKS 6f (P)
**4:00** (4:00) (G ) 3-Y-0+ **£2,590** (£740; £370) **Stalls** Low

Form RPR
0156 **1** **Bells Beach (IRE)**[23] 987 6-9-8 54 RHills 2 56
(PHowling) *trckd ldrs: effrt to chse ldr over 1f out: drvn to ld last 150y: sn in command* **7/2**[2]
0041 **2** 1 ¼ **Kilmeena Star**[17] 1018 6-9-13 48 (b) RLMoore 1 57
(JCFox) *mde most: kicked on 2f out: rdn and hdd last 150y: one pce* **10/1**
/0-0 **3** nk **Orion's Belt**[5] 1121 4-9-8 55 RHavlin 5 51
(GBBalding) *dwlt: hld up in last: smooth prog 2f out: chsd ldrs 1f out: rdn and one pce fnl f: too much to do* **33/1**
1260 **4** 2 ½ **Sounds Lucky**[8] 1082 8-9-13 57 (b) DHolland 6 49
(AndrewReid) *hld up in last trio: smooth prog over 2f out: drvn and nt qckn over 1f out* **15/8**[1]
0005 **5** ½ **Hinchley Wood (IRE)**[22] 998 5-9-8 35 NPollard 4 42
(JRBest) *chsd ldrs: pushed along and lost pl 1/2-way: nt clr run and last over 2f out: kpt on again fnl f* **16/1**
4204 **6** ¾ **Lizhar (IRE)**[13] 1047 3-8-9 57 EAhern 8 40
(MJPolglase) *sn w ldrs: drvn over 2f out: wknd over 1f out* **7/2**[2]
6530 **7** 2 ½ **Attorney**[8] 1092 6-9-10 46 (v) LisaJones(3) 9 38
(DShaw) *hld up: prog to press ldrs over 2f out: drvn and fnd nil wl over 1f out: hung lft and wknd* **14/1**


The Form Book, Raceform Ltd, Compton, RG20 6NL

0P- **8** *6* **My Wild Rover**[296] 2225 4-9-5 ............(tp) RMiles[(3)] 3 15
(KAMorgan) *pressed ldr to over 2f out: sn wknd* **100/1**

0-00 **9** *nk* **Miss Trinity**[15] 1027 4-9-3 57............(p) PRobinson 7 9
(CNAllen) *pressed ldrs tl wknd over 2f out* **8/1**[3]

1m 13.48s (0.56) **Going Correction** +0.025s/f (Slow)
**WFA** 3 from 4yo+ 13lb **9** Ran SP% **115.9**
Speed ratings: **97,95,94,91,90 89,86,78,78**CSF £38.41 TOTE £5.70: £2.50, £3.10, £6.80; EX 53.20.There was no bid for the winner.
**Owner** Richard Berenson **Bred** Philip Mahon **Trained** Newmarket, Suffolk

**FOCUS**
A modest seller, contested mainly by exposed sorts. Several of the form horses were below their best.

**NOTEBOOK**
**Bells Beach(IRE)**, back down in class, was always in the ideal position to pounce and in the end won with a degree of comfort. This was her third course-and-distance victory of the year.
**Kilmeena Star**, badly in at the weights, nonetheless made a bold bid to make all from pole position, but the winner's turn of foot proved far too much down the home straight.
**Orion's Belt**, making his first appearance in a seller, made the frame for the first time at the ninth attempt and is at least less exposed on the surface than his rivals.
**Sounds Lucky**, a standing dish here over the years, travelled supremely well just off the pace and looked sure to take a hand in the finish, but did not find anything like as much off the bridle as looked likely.
**Hinchley Wood(IRE)**, racing over his shortest trip to date, stayed on late but not much should be read into this.
**Lizhar(IRE)**, racing for the 25th time, was always struggling to stay with the pace from her wide draw.

## 1207 NEW SITE @ BETDIRECT.CO.UK H'CAP 1m (P)
**4:30** (4:31) (F) (0-55,61) 3-Y-0+ **£2,933** (£838; £419) **Stalls** High

Form RPR

000- **1** **Samuel Charles**[183] 5291 6-9-10 55............ NPollard 1 66
(WMBrisbourne) *dwlt but sn rcvrd to press ldng pair: effrt 2f out: rdn to ld 1f out: carried hd high but kpt on wl* **14/1**

-415 **2** *1 1/4* **Titian Lass**[34] 895 5-9-1 46............(b) RHills 12 54
(CEBrittain) *racd wd: hld up in rr: smooth prog over 2f out: rdn 1f out: chsd wnr last 100y: no imp: too much to do* **16/1**

0000 **3** *1/2* **Londoner (USA)**[27] 962 6-9-8 53............ RLMoore 5 60
(SDow) *prom: disp ld 5f out to 1f out: one pce after* **16/1**

3/02 **4** *1* **Prime Offer**[7] 1102 8-9-0 52............ BSwarbrick[(7)] 2 57
(JJay) *led: jnd 5f out: disp ld after to 1f out: one pce* **7/2**[2]

1231 **5** *1 1/2* **Lucid Dreams (IRE)**[7] 1095 5-10-2 61 6ex............(p) GCarter 7 62
(MWigham) *t.k.h: hld up in tch: prog to press ldrs over 2f out: cl up over 1f out: fdd fnl f* **5/1**[3]

4500 **6** *1/2* **Amnesty**[27] 966 5-9-1 49............(be) LisaJones[(3)] 10 49
(GLMoore) *settled in rr: outpcd 2f out: shkn up and kpt on fr over 1f out: no ch* **16/1**

2036 **7** *1 1/2* **Indian Blaze**[7] 1102 10-9-7 52............ SSanders 3 49
(AndrewReid) *pressed ldrs: rdn over 2f out: wknd fnl f* **10/1**

0033 **8** *shd* **Frankskips**[7] 1098 5-9-10 55............ DHolland 9 51+
(MissBSanders) *t.k.h: hld up in rr: effrt whn nt clr run and snatched up over 2f out: nt rcvr* **5/2**[1]

412- **9** *1* **Lucefer (IRE)**[218] 4487 6-8-12 50............(t) DeanWilliams[(7)] 11 44
(GCHChung) *t.k.h: hld up in last: shuffled along 2f out: kpt on same pce: no ch* **14/1**

0-00 **10** *2* **Roy McAvoy (IRE)**[8] 1082 6-9-10 55............(p) EAhern 8 44
(MrsGHarvey) *dwlt: t.k.h and sn in midfield: wknd 2f out* **20/1**

00-0 **11** *5* **Hektikos**[16] 818 4-8-12 50............ JCoffill-Brown[(7)] 4 28
(SDow) *chsd ldrs for 3f: sn lost pl: bmpd along and wknd over 2f out* **66/1**

000- **12** *4* **Sunset King (USA)**[10] 6094 4-9-7 52............ DaneO'Neill 6 21
(JCFox) *pressed ldrs tl wknd 3f out* **16/1**

1m 39.12s (-0.39) **Going Correction** +0.025s/f (Slow) **12** Ran SP% **119.7**
Speed ratings: **102,100,100,99,97 97,95,95,94,92 87,83**CSF £221.48 CT £3641.91 TOTE £20.30: £3.30, £6.80, £4.30; EX 275.80 Place 6 £578.49, Place 5 £513.92.
**Owner** J F Thomas **Bred** Sheikh Mohammed Obaid Al Maktoum **Trained** Great Ness, Shropshire

**FOCUS**
A competitive if low-grade handicap, run at a fair pace.

**NOTEBOOK**
**Samuel Charles**, the only one of these never to have raced on sand before, had not been seen since September but was making his debut for a yard in fine form and he looked a different horse. The trip looked ideal and on this showing he can win again.
**Titian Lass**, back over probably her best trip, came from well off the pace and finished well down the outside, but the unexposed winner had already gone beyond recall.
**Londoner(USA)** has plummeted in the handicap and is now 37lb lower than for his last win on turf 18 months ago. This was his best effort for a long time, but has never been the most reliable of sorts.
**Prime Offer** again was given a positive ride, but may not have been helped by being taken on for the lead from a long way out and had little left for the final furlong.
**Lucid Dreams(IRE)**, carrying a 6lb penalty for his course-and-distance victory seven days earlier, had every chance but was safely held in the last furlong.
**Amnesty** is dropping down the weights and was doing all his best work late over this shorter trip. He is still a maiden after 19 attempts, but there could be a small race in him.
**Frankskips** was just starting to make his move from the rear when running into the back of the weakening Sunset King on the home bend and there was no way back from that. *Official explanation: jockey said filly had run too free; trainer later said gelding was found to have bled from the nose after race*
**Sunset King(USA)** *Official explanation: jockey said colt had hung left.*
JN

# NOTTINGHAM (L-H)
Wednesday, March 31

**OFFICIAL GOING: Good (good to firm in places in back straight)**
There was quite a strong following wind.

## 1208 EBF MAIDEN STKS 5f 13y
**2:10** (2:10) (D) 2-Y-0 **£4,176** (£1,285; £642; £321) **Stalls** High

Form RPR

**1** **Alvarinho Lady** 2-8-9............ PaulEddery 3 68
(DHaydnJones) *w ldr: led over 1f out: r.o wl* **11/2**[3]

**2** *1 1/2* **Dante's Diamond (IRE)** 2-9-0............ JPMurtagh 4 68+
(FJordan) *s.s: outpcd: swtchd lft and r.o ins fnl f: nrst fin* **10/1**

**3** *shd* **Edge Fund** 2-9-0............ SDrowne 2 67
(BRMillman) *chsd ldrs: rdn and hung lft fr 1/2-way: ev ch over 1f out: no ex ins fnl f* **4/5**[1]

**4** *3/4* **Weet Yer Tern (IRE)** 2-9-0............ KDarley 5 65
(PABlockley) *led: hung lft: rdn and hdd over 1f out: no ex ins fnl f* **7/2**[2]

**5** *3 1/2* **Town House** 2-8-9............ JFanning 1 47
(BPJBaugh) *chsd ldrs: rdn over 1f out: wknd ins fnl f* **40/1**

60.99 secs (-0.91) **Going Correction** -0.45s/f (Firm) **5** Ran SP% **104.7**
Speed ratings: **89,86,86,85,79**CSF £45.01 TOTE £6.80: £4.60, £1.90; EX 36.30.
**Owner** Mick White **Bred** Whitsbury Manor Stud **Trained** Efail Isaf, Rhondda C Taff

**FOCUS**
Not a great bunch in the paddock and the winning time was modest.

**NOTEBOOK**
**Alvarinho Lady**, a sister to juvenile winner All Nines as well as useful stayer Lago, travelled well and saw this trip out in a manner that suggested she will have no trouble staying further.
**Dante's Diamond(IRE)**, a half-brother to several winners, looked the most likely to benefit from the outing.
**Edge Fund**, a half-brother to winning stayer Forever Loved, did not impress to post and ran green during the race itself.
**Weet Yer Tern(IRE)**, from the same family as smart sprinters Weet-A-Minute and Now Look Here, showed plenty of pace, but also a tendency to run with his head on one side. He should certainly benefit from the experience and can find a small race in due course.
**Town House** looked in need of both the outing and experience, but did show some speed.

## 1209 BOTTESFORD H'CAP 5f 13y
**2:40** (2:40) (E) (0-75,75) 3-Y-0 **£3,520** (£1,083; £541; £270) **Stalls** High

Form RPR

215- **1** **Johnny Parkes**[181] 5334 3-9-7 75............ JPMurtagh 2 88+
(MrsJRRamsden) *dwlt and hmpd s: plld hrd: hdwy over 3f out: led ins fnl f: r.o wl* **6/4**[1]

-060 **2** *3* **Demolition Molly**[36] 868 3-8-13 70............(tp) TPQueally[(3)] 7 70
(RFMarvin) *s.i.s: outpcd: hdwy over 1f out: no ch w wnr* **17/2**

0-04 **3** *shd* **Kuringai**[42] 819 3-9-4 72............ TQuinn 9 72
(BWDuke) *led: hdd over 3f out: swtchd lft ins fnl f: kpt on* **7/1**[2]

1-64 **4** *1 1/4* **Scottish Exile (IRE)**[64] 610 3-9-0 68............(v) KDalgleish 4 64
(KRBurke) *wnt lft s: chsd ldrs: led over 3f out: rdn over 1f out: hdd & wknd ins fnl f* **12/1**

50-0 **5** *1* **Smart Danny**[28] 956 3-7-12 52............ PHanagan 1 44
(JJQuinn) *chsd ldrs: hmpd 4f out: sn lost pl and outpcd: styd on ins fnl f* **7/1**[2]

333- **6** *1/2* **Flash Ram**[319] 1655 3-9-3 71............ KDarley 6 61
(TDEasterby) *unruly stalls: chsd ldrs to 1/2-way* **8/1**[3]

-130 **7** *hd* **Desert Light (IRE)**[13] 1047 3-7-8 53............(v) JFMcDonald[(5)] 8 42
(DShaw) *chsd ldrs: rdn 1/2-way: wknd over 1f out* **8/1**[3]

000- **8** *5* **Short Chorus**[187] 5185 3-7-13 53............ CCatlin 3 24
(JBalding) *hmpd s: outpcd* **14/1**

59.53 secs (-2.37) **Going Correction** -0.45s/f (Firm) **8** Ran SP% **112.1**
Speed ratings: **100,95,95,93,91 90,90,82**CSF £14.30 CT £67.50 TOTE £2.20: £1.10, £1.90, £2.30; EX 17.70.
**Owner** Joseph Heler **Bred** Joseph Heler **Trained** Sandhutton, N Yorks

**FOCUS**
An ordinary sprint full of disappointing types, and a modest time, but a decent performance from the winner.

**NOTEBOOK**
**Johnny Parkes**, who took a while to lose his maiden tag, travelled strongly through the race and won with plenty in hand. He may do better still when upped in class, where he will get a lead for longer.
**Demolition Molly** turned in a sound enough effort, but she does not look one to rely on.
**Kuringai** is basically a disappointing sort.
**Scottish Exile(IRE)** has yet to convince she is as good on turf as on the All-Weather.
**Smart Danny**, done no favours as the winner made his ground, stayed on in pleasing fashion. He is not without ability, and comes from a family that get better with age.
**Flash Ram** got upset in the stalls and can be forgiven this effort.

## 1210 COLSTON BASSETT STKS (H'CAP) 2m 9y
**3:10** (3:10) (D) (0-80,80) 3-Y-0+ **£5,606** (£1,725; £862; £431) **Stalls** Low

Form RPR

06/5 **1** **Malarkey**[7] 1101 7-8-13 65............ SDrowne 9 72
(MrsStefLiddiard) *hld up: hdwy over 3f out: led over 1f out: rdn out* **16/1**

36-0 **2** *nk* **King Flyer (IRE)**[23] 981 8-9-7 78............ NMackay[(5)] 8 85
(MissJFeilden) *a.p: rdn and ev ch over 1f out: styd on* **13/2**

26-0 **3** *1/2* **Nawow**[16] 523 4-9-5 76............ KDalgleish 2 82
(PDCundell) *hld up: hdwy over 2f out: styd on* **13/2**

2223 **4** *nk* **Jadeeron**[32] 919 5-8-12 64............(p) FLynch 7 70
(MissDAMchale) *hld up: hdwy and edgd rt over 1f out: edgd lft ins fnl f: styd on* **8/1**

225- **5** *3* **Sonoma (IRE)**[183] 5287 4-9-1 72............ JMackay 6 74
(MLWBell) *led 2f: remained handy: led over 3f out: rdn and hdd over 1f out: no ex ins fnl f* **11/2**[3]

030- **6** *2* **Simon's Seat (USA)**[32] 5730 5-9-1 67............ DSweeney 5 67
(CDrew) *hld up: hdwy 2f out: no imp fnl f* **20/1**

431- **7** *1 1/2* **The Ring (IRE)**[182] 5298 4-8-13 70............ KDarley 1 68
(MrsMReveley) *hld up in tch: rdn and ev ch 2f out: wknd fnl f* **4/1**[1]

221- **8** *hd* **Greenwich Meantime**[161] 5703 4-9-9 80............ JPMurtagh 3 78
(MrsJRRamsden) *hld up: hdwy over 2f out: hmpd over 1f out: sn btn* **9/2**[2]

00-0 **9** *17* **Litzinsky**[18] 743 6-8-3 55............ JMcAuley 11 33
(CBBBooth) *chsd ldrs: rdn over 3f out: wknd 2f out* **16/1**

460- **10** *10* **Termonfeckin**[236] 3973 6-8-6 58............ JoannaBadger 4 24
(PWHiatt) *dwlt: plld hrd and sn w ldrs: led 5f out: hdd over 3f out: wknd over 2f out* **33/1**

0005 **11** *10* **Muraqeb**[17] 1023 4-7-13 56 oh5 ow1............(b) CCatlin 10 10
(MrsBarbaraWaring) *plld hrd: led after 2f: hdd 5f out: wknd over 3f out* **40/1**

3m 30.65s (-2.85) **Going Correction** -0.025s/f (Good)
**WFA** 4 from 5yo+ 5lb **11** Ran SP% **113.3**
Speed ratings: **106,105,105,105,103 102,102,102,93,88 83**CSF £109.99 CT £750.48 TOTE £13.50: £3.50, £2.00, £3.20; EX 136.40.
**Owner** A Liddiard **Bred** M E Wates **Trained** Great Shefford, Berks
■ Stewards Enquiry : N Mackay two-day ban: used whip from above shoulder height (Apr 13,14)

**FOCUS**
Quite a competitive staying contest, and the overall time was fair for the grade.

**NOTEBOOK**
**Malarkey** is clearly a tricky customer, but there is no doubt he has his fair share of ability when he cares to use it. This was his first start for his new connections and it remains to be seen whether he will put it all in next time.
**King Flyer(IRE)**, 3lb higher than when runner-up in this last year, never really gets going much before June, so with that in mind this looked a fair effort.
**Nawow**, fit from hurdling, proved he stayed this trip.
**Jadeeron** appeared to put up a new personal best on the figures, but he does not always find as much as he should, and that looked the case again.

**Sonoma(IRE)** looked as though the race would do her good.
**The Ring(IRE)** may have needed this, as he folded quite badly in the latter stages.
**Greenwich Meantime**, making his debut for new connections, did not have the best of runs and remains one to keep an eye on.

## 1211 APRIL CONDITIONS STKS — 5f 13y
3:40 (3:41) (D) 3-Y-0+ — £5,378 (£1,655; £827; £413) Stalls High

| Form | | | | RPR |
|---|---|---|---|---|
| 606- | 1 | | **Bahamian Pirate (USA)**[178] 5402 9-9-1 114 JPMurtagh 2 | 101 |
| | | | (DNicholls) *trckd ldrs: rdn to ld ins fnl f: r.o* 5/2[1] | |
| 000- | 2 | 1 1/4 | **Fromsong (IRE)**[113] 6154 6-9-10 90 SDrowne 3 | 105 |
| | | | (BRMillman) *chsd ldr: led over 1f out: hdd and unable qck ins fnl f* 16/1 | |
| 513- | 3 | 1 | **Henry Hall (IRE)**[158] 5743 8-9-1 93 KimTinkler 4 | 92 |
| | | | (NTinkler) *chsd ldrs: swtchd lft over 1f out: styd on* 8/1 | |
| 500- | 4 | 1/2 | **Indian Spark**[144] 5953 10-9-1 98 TQuinn 6 | 91 |
| | | | (JSGoldie) *sn outpcd: hdwy over 1f out: nt rch ldrs* 9/2[3] | |
| 00U2 | 5 | 1 3/4 | **Trinculo (IRE)**[5] 1113 7-8-12 86 (p) J-PGuillambert(3) 5 | 84 |
| | | | (NPLittmoden) *chsd ldrs: rdn 1/2-way: outpcd over 1f out* 6/1 | |
| 054- | 6 | 3/4 | **Withorwithoutyou (IRE)**[152] 5851 3-7-12 90 JMackay 7 | 77 |
| | | | (BAMcmahon) *led over 3f: wknd ins fnl f* 10/1 | |
| 360- | 7 | 3/4 | **Proud Boast**[167] 5591 6-8-10 95 KDarley 8 | 74 |
| | | | (DNicholls) *s.i.s: sn chsng ldrs: wkng whn n.m.r ins fnl f* 7/2[2] | |

57.98 secs (-3.92) **Going Correction** -0.45s/f (Firm) course record
**WFA** 3 from 5yo+ 12lb — 7 Ran SP% **109.3**
Speed ratings: **113,111,109,108,105 104,103** CSF £38.42 TOTE £2.10: £1.90, £5.90; EX 32.20.
**Owner** Lucayan Stud **Bred** Trackside Farm & Liberation Farm & G A Seelbinder **Trained** Sessay, N Yorks

**FOCUS**
A decent conditions event that was run at a sound pace throughout and produced a fast time.

**NOTEBOOK**
**Bahamian Pirate(USA)**, tackling easier company than he is used to, made no mistake. This was nothing like his best form, but it will have done his confidence good and there could be more prizes to be won with him
**Fromsong(IRE)** had a hopeless task at the weights and emerged with plenty of credit. However, he is likely to pay for this with the Handicapper.
**Henry Hall(IRE)**, although badly in with the winner, really ought to have beaten the runner-up on these terms. However, this will put an edge on him and he should pay his way again.
**Indian Spark**, on ground which was lively enough for him, especially over this trip, was doing his best work in the closing stages. Easier ground and an extra furlong will see him in a better light.
**Trinculo(IRE)** had plenty to find with the field on these terms and will certainly find easier openings.
**Withorwithoutyou(IRE)** had the benefit of the rail to help and showed plenty of pace before getting tired. However, off her current rating she will not be easy to place this year.
**Proud Boast** looked below her best. However, her new trainer Dandy Nicholls is a master at training sprinters and it will be no surprise to see her step up on this in due course.

## 1212 HBLB "FURTHER FLIGHT" STKS (LISTED RACE) — 1m 6f 15y
4:10 (4:10) (A) 4-Y-0+ — £17,400 (£6,600; £3,300; £1,500) Stalls Low

| Form | | | | RPR |
|---|---|---|---|---|
| 024- | 1 | | **Alcazar (IRE)**[144] 5951 9-9-0 118 MFenton 2 | 106+ |
| | | | (HMorrison) *trckd ldrs: led over 1f out: r.o wl* 11/8[1] | |
| 325- | 2 | 3 1/2 | **Dusky Warbler**[145] 5942 5-9-0 107 TQuinn 6 | 99+ |
| | | | (MLWBell) *led: rdn and hung rt wl over 1f out: sn hdd: styd on same pce* 11/4[3] | |
| 310- | 3 | 1/2 | **Hilbre Island**[158] 5752 4-8-13 111 MHills 4 | 101+ |
| | | | (BJMeehan) *hld up: hdwy over 3f out: edgd lft over 2f out: rdn to ld wl over 1f out: sn hdd and outpcd* 7/4[2] | |
| 005 | 4 | 1 3/4 | **Qudrah (IRE)**[12] 1053 4-8-5 81 JCarroll 1 | 91 |
| | | | (EJO'Neill) *hld up: outpcd over 3f out: styd on appr fnl f: nvr trbld ldrs* 50/1 | |
| 505- | 5 | 5 | **Taffrail**[7] 5023 6-9-0 86 (p) RPrice 3 | 90 |
| | | | (DBurchell) *chsd ldr: rdn whn hmpd over 2f out: sn wknd* 40/1 | |
| | 6 | 14 | **Celtic Vision (IRE)**[22] 8-9-0 (t) SRighton 5 | 71 |
| | | | (MAppleby) *dwlt: sn prom: wknd over 3f out* 150/1 | |

3m 3.08s (-4.12) **Going Correction** -0.025s/f (Good)
**WFA** 4 from 5yo+ 4lb — 6 Ran SP% **110.2**
Speed ratings: **110,108,107,106,103 95** CSF £5.33 TOTE £2.00: £1.10, £1.70; EX 5.50.
**Owner** J Repard,F Melrose,O Pawle,M Stokes,R Black **Bred** J Repard **Trained** East Ilsley, Berks

**FOCUS**
This run at a steady pace early, but the overall time was fair. The first three are all useful, but the fourth and fifth were a bit close for comfort.

**NOTEBOOK**
**Alcazar(IRE)** had little difficulty following up last year's success, despite the drying ground. Providing he can get his toe in, there are more prizes to be won with him.
**Dusky Warbler** had a soft lead, but was easily brushed aside when the winner picked up. Without a win the whole of last year, he certainly deserves to find a race, but the lack of a change of gear will always be against him.
**Hilbre Island** was a shade disappointing, having come to win his race. He may have just needed the outing.
**Qudrah(IRE)** had plenty to find on these terms, but was far from disgraced. This trip looked well within his compass.

## 1213 ROSELAND GROUP CLASSIFIED STKS — 1m 1f 213y
4:40 (4:40) (E) 4-Y-0+ — £3,551 (£1,092; £546; £273) Stalls Low

| Form | | | | RPR |
|---|---|---|---|---|
| 2-40 | 1 | | **Lawood (IRE)**[18] 1013 4-9-0 72 TQuinn 1 | 77 |
| | | | (KARyan) *hld up: swtchd rt and hdwy over 1f out: led ins fnl f: r.o* 7/1[2] | |
| -002 | 2 | 1/2 | **Oldenway**[6] 1109 5-8-12 70 PHanagan 12 | 74+ |
| | | | (RAFahey) *hld up: nt clr run over 3f out: hdwy over 1f out: r.o* 11/10[1] | |
| 033- | 3 | 1 | **Sir Haydn**[274] 2870 4-8-13 71 WRyan 10 | 73 |
| | | | (JRJenkins) *hld up: hdwy over 2f out: rdn and ev ch ins fnl f: unable qck* 16/1 | |
| 2-56 | 4 | nk | **Skibereen (IRE)**[60] 651 4-8-7 72 PPMathers(7) 14 | 74 |
| | | | (IWMcinnes) *dwlt: sn chsng ldr: led over 2f out: hdd and edgd lft ins fnl f: no ex* 33/1 | |
| /120 | 5 | 2 | **General**[5] 1122 7-8-12 73 TPQueally(3) 4 | 71 |
| | | | (NPLittmoden) *hld up: hdwy over 3f out: rdn over 1f out: styd on same pce* 12/1 | |
| 000- | 6 | 1 3/4 | **Mount Benger**[163] 5683 4-8-12 65 KDarley 11 | 64 |
| | | | (RMBeckett) *led over 7f: styng on same pce whn hmpd ins fnl f* 12/1 | |
| 34-0 | 7 | 1/2 | **Traveller's Tale**[74] 559 5-8-13 71 SDrowne 3 | 65 |
| | | | (PGMurphy) *hld up: plld hrd: rdn over 2f out: nt trble ldrs* 10/1[3] | |
| 000- | 8 | 1 1/4 | **Prince Of Gold**[167] 5597 4-9-0 72 WSupple 6 | 63 |
| | | | (RHollinshead) *hld up: hdwy 6f out: rdn over 1f out: sn wknd* 14/1 | |
| 0-00 | 9 | 1/2 | **Mamore Gap (IRE)**[42] 820 6-8-8 73 PGallagher(7) 5 | 63 |
| | | | (RHannon) *prom: plld hrd: lost pl 6f out: n.d after* 12/1 | |
| 000- | 10 | nk | **Lunar Leader (IRE)**[70] 6100 4-8-6 70 (p) BReilly(3) 7 | 57 |
| | | | (MJGingell) *prom over 7f* 33/1 | |
| 560- | 11 | nk | **Maritime Blues**[183] 5291 4-8-12 68 MFenton 2 | 59 |
| | | | (JGGiven) *chsd ldrs 8f* 12/1 | |
| 060- | 12 | 3/4 | **Eastern Hope (IRE)**[151] 5875 5-8-12 69 DSweeney 9 | 58 |
| | | | (MrsLStubbs) *s.i.s: hld up: a in rr* 33/1 | |
| 640- | 13 | nk | **Rocky Reppin**[155] 5815 4-8-12 60 (b[1]) JEdmunds 13 | 57? |
| | | | (JBalding) *prom: plld hrd: wknd wl over 1f out* 66/1 | |
| 000- | 14 | 11 | **Eastern Magenta (IRE)**[144] 5946 4-8-5 70 KristinStubbs(7) 8 | 36 |
| | | | (MrsLStubbs) *s.i.s: a in rr* 40/1 | |

2m 10.32s (0.72) **Going Correction** -0.025s/f (Good) — 14 Ran SP% **125.3**
Speed ratings: **96,95,94,94,92 91,91,90,89,89 89,88,88,79** CSF £15.06 TOTE £20.90: £3.70, £1.10, £4.80; EX 29.40.
**Owner** Mrs Norah Kennedy **Bred** Miss Alison Jones **Trained** Hambleton, N Yorks

**FOCUS**
A field in which many had question marks over them, and a very modest time for the grade. The first five were covered by just 3lb on official ratings.

**NOTEBOOK**
**Lawood(IRE)** looked to have improved for this step up in trip and was always doing enough to hold on. There could well be more to come from him.
**Oldenway** did not have the best of runs and should find compensation before long.
**Sir Haydn**, not seen since last summer made a pleasing return to action. Providing he remains sound there are sure to be openings for him.
**Skibereen(IRE)** has not always looked straightforward, but this was not a bad effort if he can build on this.
**General** has taken on a new lease of life since switching to the Flat. However, he looks as though he is getting used to it now.
**Mount Benger** *Official explanation: jockey said gelding hung in the latter stages.*

## 1214 NOTTINGHAM RACECOURSE CONFERENCE CENTRE H'CAP — 1m 54y
5:10 (5:11) (E) (0-70,70) 3-Y-0 — £3,606 (£1,109; £554; £277) Stalls Low

| Form | | | | RPR |
|---|---|---|---|---|
| 3014 | 1 | | **Dispol Veleta**[37] 864 3-8-10 64 NMackay(5) 3 | 71 |
| | | | (TDBarron) *hld up: hdwy over 1f out: r.o to ld nr fin* 9/1[3] | |
| 1613 | 2 | shd | **Jakarmi**[33] 909 3-8-13 62 PHanagan 4 | 69 |
| | | | (BPalling) *chsd ldrs: led ins fnl f: hdd nr fin* 15/2[2] | |
| 000- | 3 | 1/2 | **Another Choice (IRE)**[144] 5950 3-8-13 65 (t) TPQueally(3) 7 | 71 |
| | | | (NPLittmoden) *hld up: hdwy over 2f out: rdn and ev ch ins fnl f: styd on* 14/1 | |
| 1 | 4 | 1 1/4 | **Quickstyx**[60] 644 3-9-6 69 TEDurcan 6 | 72 |
| | | | (MRChannon) *s.i.s: sn chsng ldr: rdn to ld 1f out: sn edgd lft: hdd and unable qck* 7/2[1] | |
| 4-62 | 5 | 1 3/4 | **The Job**[5] 1119 3-8-10 59 WRyan 5 | 58 |
| | | | (ADSmith) *a.p: rdn over 2f out: styd on same pce ins fnl f* 12/1 | |
| 000- | 6 | shd | **Balearic Star (IRE)**[170] 5551 3-9-7 70 GBaker 9 | 68 |
| | | | (BRMillman) *s.i.s: hld up and bhd: hdwy over 2f out: styd on* 16/1 | |
| -260 | 7 | nk | **Kings Rock**[23] 985 3-9-0 63 PFessey 1 | 61 |
| | | | (KARyan) *mid-div: outpcd over 2f out: styd on u.p fnl f* 12/1 | |
| 40-6 | 8 | 1 1/4 | **Penel (IRE)**[36] 869 3-8-11 60 (b[1]) DSweeney 12 | 55 |
| | | | (BRMillman) *chsd ldrs: led 2f out: rdn and hdd 1f out: sn wknd* 33/1 | |
| 005- | 9 | 1 3/4 | **Satsu (IRE)**[253] 3479 3-8-11 60 MFenton 2 | 51 |
| | | | (JGGiven) *s.i.s: sn pushed along in rr: hdwy over 2f out: sn rdn and hung lft: wknd fnl f* 33/1 | |
| 600- | 10 | 2 1/2 | **Suchwot (IRE)**[193] 5078 3-8-10 59 JFanning 16 | 44 |
| | | | (FJordan) *hld up: effrt over 3f out: n.d* 50/1 | |
| 030- | 11 | 1 1/4 | **Mr Belvedere**[144] 5950 3-9-7 70 PDobbs 10 | 52 |
| | | | (RHannon) *w ldrs: rdn over 2f out: sn wknd* 16/1 | |
| 303- | 12 | nk | **Thadea (IRE)**[177] 5421 3-9-0 63 JPMurtagh 14 | 45 |
| | | | (JGGiven) *mde most 6f: wknd fnl f* 10/1 | |
| 2036 | 13 | 2 1/2 | **Fools Entire**[4] 1123 3-9-3 69 BReilly(3) 18 | 45 |
| | | | (JAGilbert) *hld up: plld hrd: n.d* 20/1 | |
| 002- | 14 | 1 1/2 | **Military Two Step (IRE)**[148] 5913 3-9-4 67 KDalgleish 15 | 39 |
| | | | (KRBurke) *hld up: bhd fr 1/2-way* 25/1 | |
| 500- | 15 | 1 | **Faraway Echo**[212] 4623 3-8-12 61 TQuinn 8 | 31 |
| | | | (MLWBell) *sn pushed along: a in rr* 10/1 | |
| 006- | 16 | 2 | **Insubordinate**[155] 5824 3-8-10 59 WSupple 17 | 24 |
| | | | (JSGoldie) *hld up: a in rr* 20/1 | |
| 300- | 17 | nk | **Perfect Balance (IRE)**[186] 5219 3-8-11 60 KimTinkler 13 | 25 |
| | | | (NTinkler) *bhd fr 1/2-way* 50/1 | |
| -314 | 18 | 4 | **Book Matched**[15] 1029 3-9-7 70 FLynch 11 | 26 |
| | | | (BSmart) *w ldr tl wknd over 2f out* 14/1 | |

1m 44.63s (-1.87) **Going Correction** -0.025s/f (Good) — 18 Ran SP% **125.8**
Speed ratings: **108,107,107,106,104 104,104,102,101,98 97,96,94,92,91 89,89,85** CSF £70.53 CT £961.68 TOTE £15.70: £4.30, £1.90, £3.40, £1.50; EX 132.80 Place 6 £237.13, Place 5 £24.14.
**Owner** W B Imison **Bred** B N And Mrs Toye **Trained** Maunby, N Yorks

**FOCUS**
With a couple of them taking each other on up front, this was run at a good gallop and the form looks solid enough. The first seven home had single figure draws.

**NOTEBOOK**
**Dispol Veleta**, ridden with plenty of confidence, had a dream run up the far rail to get her head in front almost on the line. As this was only her second run on turf, there should be plenty of improvement to come.
**Jakarmi**, has done most of his racing on the All-Weather surfaces. There was plenty of promise in this effort and he should have no trouble scoring off his current mark.
**Another Choice(IRE)**, 6lb lower than when last seen, showed enough to suggest he has a small race in him.
**Quickstyx** travelled well, but still looked a little green when she came off the bridle. On this showing her Oaks entry looks highly optimistic.
**The Job** looks as though he will have to return to selling company if he is to add to his solitary success.
**Balearic Star(IRE)** had plenty to do, but stuck on in willing fashion and may be one to keep an eye on as he steps up in trip.
**Thadea(IRE)** *Official explanation: jockey said filly ran keenly*
**Military Two Step(IRE)** *Official explanation: jockey said gelding hung right.*
**Book Matched** *Official explanation: jockey said gelding changed his legs in the home straight.*
T/Plt: £82.80 to a £1 stake. Pool: £30,393.30. 267.85 winning tickets. T/Qpdt: £7.60 to a £1 stake. Pool: £2,852.00. 276.40 winning tickets. CR

1215 - 1217a (Foreign Racing) - See Raceform Interactive

## 1162 SAINT-CLOUD (L-H)

Wednesday, March 31

**OFFICIAL GOING: Good**

### 1218a PRIX OMNIUM II (LISTED) (C&G) 1m
2:35 (2:36) 3-Y-O £15,845 (£6,338; £4,754; £3,169)

| | | | | RPR |
|---|---|---|---|---|
| 1 | | **American Post**[158] 5739 3-9-2 | RHughes 5 | 106+ |
| | | (MmeCHead-Maarek, France) *rcd in 2nd, led after 3f, pushed along & hdd over 1 1/2f out, qckned readily to ld again 150 yards out, sn clr, pushed out* | | |
| 2 | 4 | **Joursanvault (FR)**[12] 1058 3-9-2 | CSoumillon 3 | 98 |
| | | (ADeRoyer-Dupre, France) | | |
| 3 | 1/2 | **Blackdoun (FR)**[138] 3-9-2 | J-BEyquem 4 | 97 |
| | | (J-LPelletan, France) | | |
| 4 | 1/2 | **Richon (IRE)**[123] 3-9-2 | TGillet 1 | 96 |
| | | (RodCollet, France) | | |
| 5 | shd | **Svedov (FR)**[138] 3-9-2 | DBoeuf 2 | 96 |
| | | (ELellouche, France) | | |

1m 43.0s **Going Correction** -0.60s/f (Hard) **5** Ran
Speed ratings: **106,102,101,101,100.**
**Owner** K Abdulla **Bred** Juddmonte Farms **Trained** France

**NOTEBOOK**
**American Post** made a successful reappearance with the minimum of fuss and is on target for the Poule d'Essai des Poulains. The trainer is also keen to return to Britain for the Vodafone Derby.

## LEICESTER (R-H)

Thursday, April 1

**OFFICIAL GOING: Good to soft (good in places)**

### 1219 LEVY BOARD KNIGHTON MEDIAN AUCTION MAIDEN STKS 5f 2y
2:10 (2:16) (F) 2-Y-O £3,297 (£942; £471) Stalls Low

| Form | | | | | RPR |
|---|---|---|---|---|---|
| | 1 | | **Berkhamsted (IRE)** 2-9-0 | DHolland 1 | 79 |
| | | | (JAOsborne) *racd in 3rd pl and rn green: rdn over 1f out and qcknd to ld wl ins fnl f: hld on nr fin* **13/8**[2] | | |
| | 2 | shd | **Laconicos (IRE)** 2-9-0 | JPMurtagh 3 | 79 |
| | | | (DRLoder) *led tl rdn and hdd wl ins fnl f: rallied nr fin* **6/4**[1] | | |
| | 3 | 3 1/2 | **Georgie Belle (USA)** 2-8-9 | EAhern 4 | 61 |
| | | | (CTinkler) *trckd ldr: rdn 2f out: weakedned fnl f* **16/1** | | |
| | 4 | 5 | **Langston Boy** 2-9-0 | LDettori 2 | 48 |
| | | | (MLWBell) *swvd rt s: wl bhd fnl 2f* **10/3**[3] | | |
| | 5 | 5 | **Emerald Penang (IRE)** 2-9-0 | SDrowne 5 | 30 |
| | | | (BRMillman) *outpcd and lost tch 2f out* **33/1** | | |

63.75 secs (2.65) **Going Correction** +0.275s/f (Good) **5** Ran SP% **110.0**
Speed ratings: **89,88,83,75,67**CSF £4.43 TOTE £3.00: £1.50, £1.10; EX 3.50.
**Owner** Richard Leslie **Bred** E Lonergan **Trained** Upper Lambourn, Berks

**FOCUS**
Probably not a bad maiden for the time of year, although the pace was slow, and the front two pulled nicely clear.

**NOTEBOOK**
**Berkhamsted(IRE)**, a 50,000euros first foal, whose dam is out of a half-sister to the dam of Arazi and Noverre, justified some strong market support to make a winning debut. He showed signs of inexperience, most notably when drifting right under pressure, and should find plenty of improvement.
**Laconicos(IRE)**, a 28,000euros foal whose dam was placed over seven furlongs at two, and is a sister to the very useful ten-furlong performer Carry The Flag, had the rail to run against and appeared to know his job. This was a pleasing introduction and he should soon be winning.
**Georgie Belle(USA)**, an 11,000gns purchase, out of an unraced close relative to the useful two-year-old seven to eight-furlong performer Shuhrah, showed up well to halfway but proved unable to go with the front two. This was a satisfactory introduction and she should win an ordinary maiden.
**Langston Boy**, a 50,000gns yearling, out of a sister to a quite useful five-furlong two-year-old, struggled to go the early pace and never threatened the principals. This experience should bring him on.
**Emerald Penang(IRE)**, a 38,000gns first foal, out of a half-sister to a Listed winner, was easy to back and showed little.

### 1220 BURTON OVERY (S) STKS 5f 218y
2:45 (2:45) (G) 3-Y-O £2,618 (£748; £374) Stalls Low

| Form | | | | | RPR |
|---|---|---|---|---|---|
| 2060 | 1 | | **Stamford Blue**[28] 965 3-8-12 56 | (b) BSwarbrick(7) 6 | 60 |
| | | | (JSMoore) *w.w: hdwy 2f out: carried rt ins fnl f: led fnl 50yds* **11/1** | | |
| 5343 | 2 | 1/2 | **Soul Provider (IRE)**[18] 1015 3-8-9 56 | DeanMcKeown 5 | 49 |
| | | | (PABlockley) *led after 1f: hung rt u.p. fnl f: hdd fnl 50yds* **10/3**[1] | | |
| 0-00 | 3 | shd | **Barbilyrifle (IRE)**[14] 1047 3-9-2 63 | (p) LFletcher(3) 7 | 58 |
| | | | (HMorrison) *alwways chsng ldrs: ev ch appr fnl f: rallied ins fnl 50yds* **5/1**[3] | | |
| 300- | 4 | 3 1/2 | **United Union (IRE)**[188] 5191 3-9-0 65 | PaulEddery 1 | 43+ |
| | | | (DHaydnJones) *led for 1f: styd prom tl wknd fnl f* **9/2**[2] | | |
| 03-6 | 5 | 6 | **He's A Rocket (IRE)**[86] 452 3-9-0 40 | (v) GFaulkner 9 | 25 |
| | | | (MrsCADunnett) *s.i.s: sn prom: wknd appr fnl f* **25/1** | | |
| 0053 | 6 | 2 | **Son Of Rembrandt (IRE)**[14] 1046 3-8-7 64 | MHoward(7) 2 | 19 |
| | | | (DKIvory) *in tch: rdn 1/2-way: wknd over 1f out* **7/1** | | |
| 02-0 | 7 | 1/2 | **Queen Of Bulgaria (IRE)**[34] 905 3-9-0 61 | RPrice 3 | 17 |
| | | | (JPearce) *sn outpcd: rdn 1/2-way: a bhd* **11/2** | | |
| 000 | 8 | 8 | **Divina**[13] 1050 3-8-9 | PRobinson 4 | — |
| | | | (SLKeightley) *outpcd thrght* **16/1** | | |
| 60-0 | 9 | 5 | **Your Just Lovely (IRE)**[24] 983 3-8-9 60 | MartinDwyer 8 | — |
| | | | (AMBalding) *a struggling in rr* **8/1** | | |

1m 15.83s (2.43) **Going Correction** +0.275s/f (Good) **9** Ran SP% **115.0**
Speed ratings: **94,93,93,88,80 77,77,66,59**CSF £47.46 TOTE £24.50: £5.90, £1.90, £2.00; EX 78.90.There was no bid for the winner. Soul Provider was the subject of a friendly claim by Paul Blockley for £6,000.
**Owner** Miss Karen Theobald **Bred** Mrs Wendy Miller **Trained** East Garston, Berks

**FOCUS**
Just a weak seller, but the pace was good and the form should work out at a similar level.

**NOTEBOOK**
**Stamford Blue**, back on turf after an unsuccessful winter on the All-Weather, doubled his career tally with a narrow success. He has never won outside of this grade and would be one to take on in better company.
**Soul Provider(IRE)**, third in a Polytrack maiden over a mile on her latest start, showed plenty of speed on this drop back in trip and was only caught in the final strides. There should be a similar race in her. *Official explanation: jockey said filly lost a shoe*
**Barbilyrifle(IRE)**, who raced away from the front two against the near-side rail, had to be ridden from some way out but had every chance. He is becoming disappointing.
**United Union(IRE)** ran respectably on his first start in a seller and should improve for the outing, his first in 188 days.
**He's A Rocket(IRE)** may need dropping into regional company.
**Queen Of Bulgaria(IRE)** has won in this grade, but was below his best.

### 1221 RETHINK SEVERE MENTAL ILLNESS MAIDEN STKS 1m 3f 183y
3:20 (3:21) (D) 3-4-Y-O £4,764 (£1,466; £733; £366) Stalls High

| Form | | | | | RPR |
|---|---|---|---|---|---|
| 222- | 1 | | **Arresting**[187] 5227 4-9-12 85 | JPMurtagh 4 | 76 |
| | | | (JRFanshawe) *w.w: stdy hdwy fr 1/2-way: wnt 2nd 3f out: edgd lft and kpt up to work to ld wl ins fnl f* **4/9**[1] | | |
| | 2 | 3/4 | **Gran Dana (IRE)** 4-9-12 | JFanning 7 | 75 |
| | | | (MJohnston) *trckd ldr: led over 3f out: rdn and kpt on: hdd wl ins fnl f* **12/1** | | |
| 00 | 3 | 13 | **Lakaam**[13] 1050 3-8-1 | RBrisland 1 | 49 |
| | | | (GPEnright) *racxed keenly: sn bhd: styd on past btn horse to go poor 3rd ins fnl f* **100/1** | | |
| 00-0 | 4 | 2 1/2 | **Queen's Fantasy**[73] 563 3-8-2 ow1 | PaulEddery 6 | 46 |
| | | | (DHaydnJones) *mid-div: one pce fnl 3f* **66/1** | | |
| 2 | 5 | shd | **Muzio Scevola (IRE)**[13] 1050 3-8-6 | TEDurcan 8 | 50 |
| | | | (MRChannon) *chsd ldrs: rdn and wknd wl over 2f out* **6/1**[2] | | |
| 53- | 6 | 6 | **Hashid (IRE)**[251] 3558 4-9-12 | DaneO'Neill 5 | 40 |
| | | | (PCRitchens) *v.s.a: effrt on outside over 4f out: sn btn* **11/1**[3] | | |
| 00-0 | 7 | 5 | **Ameyrah (IRE)**[33] 916 3-8-1 | CCatlin 9 | 27 |
| | | | (MRChannon) *led: hdd over 3f out: sn wknd* **16/1** | | |
| 0 | 8 | 19 | **Baroque**[18] 1022 3-8-6 | RFitzpatrick 3 | 2 |
| | | | (CSmith) *a in rr* **100/1** | | |
| | 9 | 20 | **Court Emperor**[25] 4-9-12 | VSlattery 2 | — |
| | | | (RJPrice) *slowly away: plld hrd and sn prom: wknd 1/2-way* **40/1** | | |

2m 39.84s (4.64) **Going Correction** +0.475s/f (Yiel)
**WFA** 3 from 4yo 21lb **9** Ran SP% **111.4**
Speed ratings: **103,102,93,92,92 88,84,72,58**CSF £6.42 TOTE £1.20: £1.02, £2.90, £8.10; EX 7.30.
**Owner** Mrs Andrew Wates & Tim Vestey **Bred** T R G Vestey **Trained** Newmarket, Suffolk

**FOCUS**
Second favourite Muzio Scevola did not perform and, the front two apart, this was a very weak race.

**NOTEBOOK**
**Arresting** shaped well in maiden company last year, most notably when runner-up to Phoenix Reach at Newbury, but he did not really impress in getting off the mark. He pulled upsides the runner-up, but appeared to think twice about going through with his effort and flashed his tail when hit with the whip. However, he should get further and probably beat a fair sort in the runner-up, so he may hold his own in a higher grade.
**Gran Dana(IRE)** ◆, an IR60,000gns yearling, brother to a couple of ten-furlong winners, made a pleasing, albeit belated, racecourse debut. He made the winner work quite hard despite appearing inexperienced when put under pressure, and pulled a mile clear of the remainder. He should find a similar race.
**Lakaam** should find things easier now she is qualified for a handicap mark.
**Queen's Fantasy** did not really improve for this step up in trip.
**Muzio Scevola(IRE)** shaped well on his debut on the Polytrack and had the edge over some of these on fitness. However, he was disappointingly below form.

### 1222 "VISIT JELSONS' SHOWHOME AT THE FURLONGS" H'CAP 1m 1f 218y
3:55 (3:56) (E) (0-75,75) 3-Y-O £3,610 (£1,111; £555; £277) Stalls High

| Form | | | | | RPR |
|---|---|---|---|---|---|
| 014- | 1 | | **Swagger Stick (USA)**[184] 5290 3-9-3 71 | KDarley 13 | 84+ |
| | | | (JLDunlop) *a.p: led over 3f out: rdn and r.o wl fnl f* **11/2**[2] | | |
| 031- | 2 | 1 1/4 | **Hazyview**[153] 5845 3-8-13 67 | JPMurtagh 10 | 77+ |
| | | | (NACallaghan) *hld up: hmpd 7f out: rdn and hdwy to chse wnr fnl f* **5/2**[1] | | |
| 346- | 3 | 4 | **Bumptious**[146] 5940 3-9-7 75 | GDuffield 16 | 78 |
| | | | (MHTompkins) *a in tch: styd on fnl f: no ch w first 2* **11/1** | | |
| 006- | 4 | nk | **Late Opposition**[171] 5532 3-8-9 63 ow1 | LDettori 5 | 66 |
| | | | (EALDunlop) *trckd ldrs: ev ch 2 f out: rdn and nt qckn after* **10/1** | | |
| 531- | 5 | 3/4 | **Keep On Movin' (IRE)**[124] 6087 3-9-2 73 | RMiles(3) 11 | 74 |
| | | | (TGMills) *towards rr: hdwy on outside 3f out: styd on ins fnl 2f: nvr nrr* **25/1** | | |
| 650- | 6 | shd | **Mister Trickster (IRE)**[203] 4843 3-8-9 63 | SRighton 12 | 64 |
| | | | (RDickin) *slowly away: styd on ins fnl 2f: nvr nr to chal* **33/1** | | |
| 30-3 | 7 | 4 | **Charlie Tango (IRE)**[24] 985 3-9-3 71 | TEDurcan 9 | 65 |
| | | | (MRChannon) *mid-div: hdwy over 2f out: wknd ins fnl f* **11/1** | | |
| 016- | 8 | 4 | **Ermine Grey**[125] 6083 3-9-7 75 | (b) PaulEddery 8 | 62 |
| | | | (DHaydnJones) *in tch: wnt 2n briefly 2f out: rdn and sn btn* **33/1** | | |
| 0-25 | 9 | 3 | **Hsi Wang Mu (IRE)**[19] 1012 3-7-12 52 oh2 | DaleGibson 1 | 33 |
| | | | (RBrotherton) *a in rr* **33/1** | | |
| -126 | 10 | 3 1/2 | **Desert Image (IRE)**[38] 864 3-9-7 75 | EAhern 2 | 50 |
| | | | (CTinkler) *a towards rr* **20/1** | | |
| 00-1 | 11 | 1/2 | **Glendale**[45] 790 3-8-11 68 | LisaJones(3) 18 | 42 |
| | | | (CADwyer) *mid-div: nvr nr to chal* **33/1** | | |
| 500- | 12 | 15 | **Killoch Place (IRE)**[201] 4882 3-8-2 56 ow1 | MartinDwyer 15 | 3 |
| | | | (JAGlover) *a bhd* **28/1** | | |
| -434 | 13 | 3 1/2 | **Ashstanza**[29] 957 3-8-9 63 | (p) PRobinson 17 | 4 |
| | | | (MAJarvis) *prominenet tl wknd 3f out* **10/1** | | |
| 030- | 14 | 1 | **Nick The Silver**[159] 5754 3-9-2 70 | SDrowne 6 | 9 |
| | | | (GBBalding) *slowly away: a bhd* **25/1** | | |
| 221- | 15 | 12 | **Habanero**[178] 5421 3-9-4 72 | DHolland 4 | — |
| | | | (RHannon) *a bhd* **6/1**[3] | | |
| 10 | 16 | 6 | **Grouville**[33] 913 3-9-4 72 | (b[1]) TQuinn 7 | — |
| | | | (BJMeehan) *led tl hdd over 3f out: sn wknd and eased whn btn* **25/1** | | |
| 035- | 17 | nk | **Troubleinparadise (IRE)**[245] 3726 3-8-7 61 | MFenton 14 | — |
| | | | (JGGiven) *prom early: sn bhd* **50/1** | | |
| 00-0 | 18 | 3 1/2 | **Indian Call**[7] 1108 3-8-12 66 | SSanders 3 | — |
| | | | (BAMcmahon) *a bhd* **50/1** | | |

2m 12.18s (3.48) **Going Correction** +0.475s/f (Yiel) **18** Ran SP% **128.5**
Speed ratings: **105,104,100,100,99 99,96,93,91,88 87,75,73,72,62 57,57,54**CSF £17.63 CT £156.44 TOTE £8.90: £2.70, £1.50, £1.90, £3.30; EX 24.70.
**Owner** Robin F Scully **Bred** Clovelly Farms **Trained** Arundel, W Sussex

**FOCUS**
Quite a competitive handicap, run at a decent pace. The time was fair for the type of contest and the race should work out in the short term.
**NOTEBOOK**
**Swagger Stick(USA)** is a half-brother to the Breeders' Cup Classic and Dubai World Cup winner Pleasantly Perfect, so you could be forgiven for thinking he would be better off running on the dirt. He defied a handicap mark 4lb higher than when winning at Yarmouth last year and is going the right way.
**Hazyview**, 5lb higher than when winning on his final start at two at Brighton 153 days ago, made a pleasing return and was nicely clear of the remainder.
**Bumptious** showed promise in maiden company last season but had no easy task off 75 on this handicap debut. This was a good effort and, lightly raced, he is the sort that should progress.
**Late Opposition**, racing for the first time in 171 days, made a satisfactory handicap debut and is another that should be capable of improvement.
**Keep On Movin'(IRE)** has never raced on ground this soft before, but this was a reasonable effort and she should stay farther.
**Charlie Tango(IRE)** shaped well at Lingfield on his latest start but, after travelling strongly, he found little. *Official explanation: jockey said gelding hung right in the closing stages*
**Ermine Grey** had never previously run beyond a mile. He came there strongly but did not get home.
**Habanero**, a winner on his last start at two off a 4lb lower mark, was disappointing on this first start in 178 days.
**Grouville** *Official explanation: jockey said gelding ran too free in the early stages*

## 1223 LODDINGTON CONDITIONS STKS — 5f 218y
4:30 (4:32) (D) 3-Y-O — £7,059 (£2,172; £1,086; £543) Stalls Low

Form — RPR
132- **1** **Sevillano**[222] 4386 3-8-12 99 ... SSanders 1 — 109+
(PDCundell) *mde all: clr ent fnl f: unchal* **5/2**[2]
040- **2** 10 **Harry Up**[173] 5480 3-9-2 93 ... MFenton 2 — 81
(JGGiven) *outpcd in rr: styd on to chse easy wnr fnl f* **8/1**
-221 **3** 1 1/2 **Hatch**[24] 982 3-9-0 79 ... DHolland 3 — 75
(RMHCowell) *outpcd in rr: rdn and passed btn horses fnl f* **11/2**
020- **4** 3/4 **Vienna's Boy (IRE)**[180] 5371 3-9-0 92 ... DaneO'Neill 6 — 72
(RHannon) *sn prom: chsd wnr fr over 3f out to over 2f out: wknd over 1f out* **2/1**[1]
232- **5** 2 **Mac Love**[159] 5740 3-9-0 106 ... TQuinn 4 — 66
(JAkehurst) *prom: chsd wnr over 2f out: tl rdn and wknd fnl f* **7/2**[3]
-530 **6** 11 **Beau Jazz**[24] 986 3-8-10 62 ... SRighton 5 — 29
(WDeBest-Turner) *trakced wnr for over 2f: rdn and sn bhd* **66/1**

1m 13.68s (0.28) **Going Correction** +0.275s/f (Good) **6 Ran SP% 112.1**
Speed ratings: **109,95,93,92,90 75**CSF £21.78 TOTE £3.30: £1.60, £3.30; EX 31.00.
**Owner** Pedro Rosas **Bred** Miss C Green **Trained** Compton, Berks
**FOCUS**
A clear-cut winner and a smart time for the grade, although the winner will be weighted out of most handicaps after this.
**NOTEBOOK**
**Sevillano**, who showed some very useful form as a juvenile last season, failing to finish out of the first three in four attempts, was able to lead at a steady gallop and came right away from the field when asked for his effort. He had the run of the race and may have been flattered by the winning margin, but there is no doubting this represented an improvement on juvenile form and he could hold his own in better company.
**Harry Up** looked a little rusty on this seasonal debut and will be better off back on a faster surface.
**Hatch** had fitness on his side, but was not good enough over the trip.
**Vienna's Boy(IRE)** was disappointing, but is worth another chance as it was his first start of the year.
**Mac Love** was officially rated 7lb clear of his closest rival, but ran disappointingly on this first start since leaving Mick Channon. His stable are out of form at present so much better can be expected.

## 1224 SIMON DE MONTFORT MAIDEN STKS — 1m 1f 218y
5:05 (5:06) (D) 3-Y-O+ — £4,862 (£1,496; £748; £374) Stalls High

Form — RPR
4/2 **1** **Jorobaden (FR)**[37] 871 4-9-12 ... GBaker 2 — 79+
(CFWall) *hld up: hdwy 2f out: hmpd ins fnl f: led fnl 75yds: drvn out* **16/1**
63- **2** 1 **Ganymede**[170] 5563 3-8-7 ... DHolland 11 — 77+
(MLWBell) *mid-div: stdy hdwy over 3f out: carried lft and bmpd but led ent fnl f: rdn and hdd fnl 75yds* **9/4**[1]
0- **3** 1 **Bayhirr**[152] 5867 3-8-7 ... PRobinson 14 — 75+
(MAJarvis) *hld up: hdwy over 4f out: bdly hmpd over 1f out: styd on wl fnl f* **12/1**
22- **4** 4 **Just A Fluke (IRE)**[243] 3775 3-8-7 ... KDalgleish 16 — 68+
(MJohnston) *sn led: clr 3f out: swvd bdly lft after reminder over 1f out and hdd ent fnl f: wnt lft again jst ins and no ex* **5/1**[2]
30- **5** 3 **Absolutely Soaked (IRE)**[211] 4664 3-7-13 ... LisaJones(3) 15 — 58
(DrJDScargill) *trckd ldrs: wnt 2nd over 2f out: swtchd rt over 1f out: wknd fnl f* **50/1**
**6** 3 **Panzer (GER)** 3-8-7 ... SDrowne 6 — 57+
(RCharlton) *hld up in rr: hdwy and swtchd rt over 3f outg and lft over 2f out: nvr on terms* **50/1**
0- **7** 2 **Frankies Wings (IRE)**[110] 6175 3-8-4 ... RMiles(3) 10 — 54
(TGMills) *mid-div: nvr nr to chal* **22/1**
62- **8** 2 1/2 **Rarefied (IRE)**[147] 5932 3-8-7 ... RHughes 12 — 49
(RCharlton) *trckd ldr tl wknd over 2f out* **8/1**
**9** 3/4 **Amankila (IRE)** 3-8-2 ... JMackay 1 — 43
(MLWBell) *v.s.a: a bhd* **50/1**
4/5- **10** shd **Ipsa Loquitur**[428] 408 4-9-7 ... MartinDwyer 4 — 43
(SCWilliams) *a towards rr* **50/1**
00- **11** 7 **Calomeria**[152] 5868 3-8-2 ... GDuffield 5 — 30
(RMBeckett) *bhd thrght* **66/1**
6/5- **12** 1 1/4 **Dancing Pearl**[27] 605 6-9-7 ... VSlattery 17 — 28
(CJPrice) *s.i.s: a in rr* **33/1**
40/ **13** 5 **Enchanted Ocean (USA)**[888] 5484 5-9-7 ... RHavlin 9 — 19
(GBBalding) *slowly away: a bhd* **10/1**
000- **14** 2 **Littlestar (FR)**[191] 5137 3-8-7 ... SSanders 8 — 20
(JLDunlop) *mid-div: rdn over 3f out: sn btn* **25/1**
0- **15** 10 **Crystal Choir**[150] 5907 4-9-7 ... JPMurtagh 7 — —
(NJHenderson) *hld up: a bhd* **15/2**[3]
60- **16** 5 **Saint Lazare (IRE)**[155] 5830 3-8-7 ... MFenton 13 — —
(JGGiven) *trckd ldrs tl wknd over 3f out* **66/1**
**17** dist **Moonshaft (USA)** 3-8-7 ... EAhern 3 — —
(EALDunlop) *a bhd: t.o* **12/1**

2m 12.03s (3.33) **Going Correction** +0.475s/f (Yiel)
**WFA** 3 from 4yo+ 19lb **17 Ran SP% 122.6**
Speed ratings: **105,104,103,100,97 95,93,91,91,91 85,84,80,78,70 66,—**CSF £48.62 TOTE £23.50: £5.00, £2.10, £3.10; EX 100.70.
**Owner** The Storm Again Syndicate **Bred** R Le Poder **Trained** Newmarket, Suffolk

**FOCUS**
This is usually a decent maiden. A fair pace was set by Just A Fluke before he caused considerable interference down the straight and the result was somewhat messy, despite the field being strung out.
**NOTEBOOK**
**Jorobaden(FR)**, second at Lingfield on his first start since a juvenile, won despite conceding plenty of weight-for-age and being hampered when pacesetter Just A Fluke hung left. He clearly has plenty of ability and should make his mark in handicaps.
**Ganymede** was also caught up in the trouble and did nothing wrong in defeat. He will be more at home in handicaps.
**Bayhirr** ran well on this three-year-old debut and will get further.
**Just A Fluke(IRE)**, too big and backward to do himself justice as a two-year-old, looked to be travelling strongly with three to run, but swerved violently left after receiving a reminder, and after repeating the action again inside the final furlong, unsurprisingly blew his chance. He showed a similar tendency at two, but if it can be ironed out he will make his mark in handicaps.

## 1225 SAFFIE JOSEPH & SONS H'CAP — 7f 9y
5:40 (5:40) (D) (0-85,81) 3-Y-O+ — £5,525 (£1,700; £850; £425) Stalls Low

Form — RPR
1-04 **1** **Taranaki**[5] 1132 6-9-11 79 ... SSanders 10 — 87
(PDCundell) *a.p: led appr fnl f: rdn out* **13/2**[3]
-200 **2** 3/4 **Mistral Sky**[27] 968 5-8-12 66 ... (v) MFenton 1 — 72
(MrsStefLiddiard) *prom on ins tl outpcd over 2f out: swtchd rt overe 1f out and r.o to go 2nd ins fnl f* **10/1**
0-00 **3** shd **Ammenayr (IRE)**[5] 1132 4-9-9 77 ... KDarley 13 — 83
(TGMills) *chsd ldrs: led wl over 1f out tl hdd appr fnl f: kpt on* **10/1**
020- **4** 3/4 **Oh So Rosie (IRE)**[121] 6119 4-7-13 60 ... BSwarbrick(7) 9 — 64
(JSMoore) *hld up: hdwy on outside over 2f out: ev ch ent fnl f: kpt on one pce* **25/1**
000- **5** 1 3/4 **Oakley Rambo**[270] 3031 5-9-12 80 ... RHughes 2 — 79
(RHannon) *led to 1/2-way: shkn up over 1f out: eased whn hld wl ins fnl f* **20/1**
31-0 **6** nk **Dumnoni**[12] 1063 3-8-13 81 ... NCallan 15 — 80
(JulianPoulton) *chsd ldrs: nt qckn entereing fnl f* **25/1**
-205 **7** 1/2 **Pharoah's Gold (IRE)**[5] 1139 6-7-9 52 ... (v) LisaJones(3) 5 — 49
(DShaw) *hld up: effrt over 1f out: nvr nr to chal* **20/1**
560- **8** nk **Snow Bunting**[171] 5540 6-7-7 54 ... LeanneKershaw(7) 16 — 50
(JeddO'Keeffe) *plld hrd: hld up and nvr nr to chal* **25/1**
000- **9** 1/2 **Grey Cossack**[145] 5946 7-9-9 77 ... GParkin 11 — 72
(PTMidgley) *trckd ldr: led 1/2-way: hdd wl over 1f out: wknd fnl f* **33/1**
-053 **10** 1/2 **Barzak (IRE)**[56] 681 4-8-8 62 ... (bt) JBramhill 4 — 56
(SRBowring) *a bhd* **10/1**
024- **11** 2 1/2 **Jacaranda (IRE)**[168] 5597 4-9-4 72 ... SDrowne 12 — 59
(MrsALMKing) *wnt lft s: a struggling in rr* **25/1**
-032 **12** 1 **Middleton Grey**[19] 1013 6-8-10 64 ... (b) MartinDwyer 3 — 49
(AGNewcombe) *a bhd* **7/1**
130- **13** 1/2 **Kelseas Kolby (IRE)**[162] 5704 4-8-3 57 ... GGibbons 8 — 40
(JAGlover) *s.i.s: a bhd* **33/1**
00-6 **14** 2 **Kareeb (FR)**[28] 961 7-9-10 78 ... JPMurtagh 6 — 56
(WJMusson) *prom tl rdn over 1f out: wknd qckly* **9/2**[1]
000- **15** hd **Red Galaxy (IRE)**[271] 3016 4-9-12 80 ... (t) LDettori 14 — 58
(DWPArbuthnot) *a bhd* **20/1**
020- **16** 1 1/2 **Fleetwood Bay**[283] 2644 4-9-9 77 ... GBaker 7 — 51
(BRMillman) *chsd ldrs tl wknd over 2f out* **40/1**
1- **17** 10 **Soliniki**[218] 4495 3-8-12 80 ... DHolland 17 — 28
(JAOsborne) *chsd ldrs tl rdn 1/2-way: sn dropped rr* **5/1**[2]

1m 29.77s (3.67) **Going Correction** +0.275s/f (Good)
**WFA** 3 from 4yo+ 14lb **17 Ran SP% 125.9**
Speed ratings: **90,89,89,88,86 85,85,84,84,83 80,79,79,76,76 74,63**CSF £61.42 CT £684.36 TOTE £8.80: £2.30, £3.30, £3.90, £3.60; EX 103.90 Place 6 £18.30, Place 5 £14.56.
**Owner** Eric Evers **Bred** E D Evers **Trained** Compton, Berks
■ Stewards Enquiry : B Swarbrick two-day ban: used whip with excessive frequency (Apr 12, May 18))
**FOCUS**
A very moderate time indeed for the grade of contest. The form is nothing special and the winner simply ran up to his mark, but there were one or two eyecatching performances and it should produce a winner or two.
**NOTEBOOK**
**Taranaki** was always bang there and ran on well once taking it up to record the ninth win of his career and a double on the day for his trainer.
**Mistral Sky** stayed on again to get up for second having been tapped for toe.
**Ammenayr(IRE)** just got caught for second on the line. This was a decent effort.
**Oh So Rosie(IRE)** was there if good enough, but could only stay om.
**Oakley Rambo ◆** ran very well under top-weight on this first start since July and is one to note for the future, as he is now 3lb lower than when last winning.
**Kareeb(FR)** failed to confirm the promise of his comeback run at Lingfield and will be better with more reserved tactics. *Official explanation: jockey said gelding was unsuited by the soft ground*
**Solinik**i, a winner at Ascot on his sole start to date, fell right away and something was clearly amiss. *Official explanation: jockey said gelding lost its action*
T/Plt: £43.80 to a £1 stake. Pool: £28,077.80. 467.10 winning tickets. T/Qpdt: £29.20 to a £1 stake. Pool: £1,893.50. 47.90 winning tickets. JS

# 1202 LINGFIELD (L-H)
Friday, April 2

**OFFICIAL GOING: Standard**

## 1226 BETDIRECT.CO.UK MEDIAN AUCTION MAIDEN STKS (DIV I) — 1m (P)
1:40 (1:41) (F) 3-4-Y-O — £2,905 (£830; £415) Stalls High

Form — RPR
326- **1** **Fancy Foxtrot**[152] 5886 3-8-8 82 ow1 ... LDettori 1 — 83
(BJMeehan) *mde all: drew clr fr wl over 1f out: impressive* **2/1**[1]
5- **2** 7 **Extra Cover (IRE)**[147] 5940 3-8-7 ... SDrowne 5 — 66
(RCharlton) *sn chsd wnr: rdn over 2f out: outpcd and wl btn over 1f out* **5/2**[2]
05- **3** 1 1/4 **Beach Party (IRE)**[168] 5623 3-8-2 ... JFanning 10 — 58
(MLWBell) *hld up in tch: prog to chse ldng pair over 3f out: rdn over 2f out: kpt on same pce* **20/1**
**4** 1/2 **Trifti** 3-8-7 ... SWhitworth 3 — 62
(CACyzer) *hld up in midfield: prog 3f out: chsd ldng trio over 2f out: kpt on steadily fr over 1f out* **50/1**
-462 **5** 5 **Sewmore Character**[41] 846 4-9-8 70 ... DSweeney 6 — 50
(MBlanshard) *racd in midfield: rdn and outpcd 3f out: no ch after* **7/2**[3]
0- **6** 1 1/4 **Donastrela (IRE)**[141] 5984 3-8-2 ... MartinDwyer 2 — 42
(AMBalding) *prom tl rdn and grad wknd fr 3f out* **33/1**

0 **7** shd **Apollonious**[19] [1015] 3-8-7 ........ DaneO'Neill 8 47
(DRCElsworth) *dwlt: a in rr: struggling over 3f out* **9/1**
**8** 2 1/2 **Antigiotto (IRE)** 3-8-2 ........ NMackay(5) 9 41
(LMCumani) *s.s: rn green and a in last trio* **14/1**
**9** 8 **Laurens Girl (IRE)** 3-8-3 ow1 ........ DRMcCabe 7 19
(MGQuinlan) *s.i.s: a wl in rr: t.o* **66/1**
00-0 **10** 3 **Habitual (IRE)**[9] [1096] 3-8-7 ........ SSanders 4 16
(SirMarkPrescott) *chsd ldrs to 1/2-way: sn wknd: t.o* **50/1**

1m 37.02s (-2.49) **Going Correction** -0.075s/f (Stan)
**WFA** 3 from 4yo 15lb **10** Ran SP% **113.9**
Speed ratings: **109,102,100,100,95 94,93,91,83,80**CSF £6.58 TOTE £2.30: £1.20, £1.30, £4.70; EX 8.40.
**Owner** Joe L Allbritton **Bred** J G Fitzgerald **Trained** Upper Lambourn, Berks

**FOCUS**
The first division of this mile maiden was won impressively in a fast time. It should throw up its share of winners, without being the strongest of contests.

**NOTEBOOK**
**Fancy Foxtrot** ◆ pinged out of the gates and was never headed at any stage en-route to a ready success, posting a decent time. This was a promising comeback and he has clearly trained on well from last season, so he could be in for a fair year over this trip. He may head to the Listed Easter Stakes at Kempton later this month.
**Extra Cover(IRE)**, who had shown promise on his only previous outing last year, shaped well just behind the leaders for a long way before showing signs of greenness in the straight. He can lose his maiden tag in a similar contest.
**Beach Party(IRE)** ◆, unplaced in two fast-ground six-furlong maidens last year, shaped much better for this step up in trip and could be one to look out for now that she qualifies for handicaps.
**Trifti** was another to shape with promise on this debut, but never looked a danger at any stage. He will improve and was staying on at the end.
**Sewmore Character**, the sole four-year-old in the field, was disappointing as he was never going the pace and found little under pressure. He had the best Polytrack form going into this event and, with an All-Weather rating of 70, he has a lot to prove now.

## 1227 BETDIRECT.CO.UK MEDIAN AUCTION MAIDEN STKS (DIV II) 1m (P)
**2:10** (2:11) (F) 3-4-Y-O **£2,898** (£828; £414) **Stalls** High

Form RPR
42-2 **1** **Instructor**[9] [1096] 3-8-8 78 ow1 ........ RHughes 4 78
(RHannon) *mde virtually all: shkn up over 1f out: drew clr fnl f: comf* **4/5**[1]
624- **2** 2 1/2 **Sunisa (IRE)**[206] [4801] 3-7-11 82 ........ AMedeiros(5) 2 66
(BWHills) *chsd wnr for 1f: racd in 3rd after: shkn up and unable qckn over 2f out: styd on to take 2nd last 100y: no ch w wnr* **11/2**[3]
05 **3** 3/4 **Ballinger Express**[13] [1059] 4-9-3 ........ MartinDwyer 3 64
(AMBalding) *t.k.h: trckd wnr after 1f: rdn over 3f out: no imp 1f out: lost 2nd last 100y* **5/1**[2]
**4** 2 **Solor** 3-8-9 ow2 ........ DHolland 1 67
(DJCoakley) *s.s: wl in rr tl prog 3f out: drvn and c wd bnd 2f out: styd on fnl f: nrst fin* **12/1**
000- **5** hd **Stop The Nonsense (IRE)**[184] [5297] 3-8-7 ........ JFanning 8 64?
(EJO'Neill) *sn chsd ldng trio: rdn and no imp 3f out: one pce after* **50/1**
46- **6** 4 **Raheed (IRE)**[204] [4834] 3-8-7 ........ EAhern 5 55
(EALDunlop) *settled in last trio: wl bhd 1/2-way: shkn up over 1f out: styd on steadily fnl f: do bttr* **12/1**
00 **7** 8 **Fresh Connection**[65] [620] 3-8-2 ........ AMcCarthy 6 32
(GGMargarson) *nvr on terms w ldrs: drvn and struggling over 3f out: wknd* **66/1**
**8** 8 **Witches Broom** 3-8-3 ow1 ........ SWhitworth 9 14
(CACyzer) *towards rr: effrt to chse ldrs 5f out: sn rdn: wknd 3f out: wl bhd over 1f out* **25/1**
0- **9** 3 **Fiddles Music**[212] [4655] 3-8-2 ........ CCatlin 7 6
(MRChannon) *nvr on terms: rdn bef 1/2-way: sn wknd and wl bhd* **33/1**

1m 37.96s (-1.55) **Going Correction** -0.075s/f (Stan)
**WFA** 3 from 4yo 15lb **9** Ran SP% **113.2**
Speed ratings: **104,101,100,98,98 94,86,78,75**CSF £5.13 TOTE £1.30: £1.02, £2.10, £1.50; EX 6.40.
**Owner** Highclere Thoroughbred Racing IX **Bred** Cheveley Park Stud Ltd **Trained** East Everleigh, Wilts

**FOCUS**
This second division of the maiden did not look as strong as the first on paper, and that impression was backed up by the significantly slower time. The runner-up looks badly handicapped.

**NOTEBOOK**
**Instructor** had run into a hot-pot at this track nine days previously, and that form entitled him to score as he did over this extra furlong. He looks the type to improve with racing, but he will need to as he looks on a fairly stiff mark for handicaps and may go up again for this display.
**Sunisa(IRE)**, the highest of these on official ratings, made a satisfactory debut on this step up to a mile and stayed on well enough having been a touch keen early.
**Ballinger Express**, the only four-year-old in the line-up, ran her best race to date and now qualifies for handicaps.
**Solor** ◆, making his debut, was the eye-catcher of the race. He was slowly away and being hard ridden from an early stage, but he made up quite a bit of ground before the turn for home and finished nicely. He was not given a hard time in the straight when his winning chance had diminished and will be a lot sharper next time.
**Raheed(IRE)** was another to miss the break but was doing all of his best work late in that day and now qualifies for a handicap mark.

## 1228 NEW SITE @ BETDIRECT.CO.UK MAIDEN STKS 5f (P)
**2:45** (2:46) (D) 3-Y-0+ **£3,692** (£1,136; £568; £284) **Stalls** High

Form RPR
22-2 **1** **Shrink**[37] [881] 3-8-8 68 ow1 ........ DHolland 4 69
(MLWBell) *hld up in cl tch: effrt wl over 1f out: drvn and kpt on fnl f to ld last strides* **4/1**[2]
6-40 **2** shd **Imperium**[10] [1083] 3-8-12 75 ........ TQuinn 5 73
(MrsStefLiddiard) *trckd ldr: led 2f out: drvn over 1f out: hdd last strides* **8/1**
65 **3** 3/4 **Simpsons Mount (IRE)**[10] [1083] 3-8-12 ........ RLMoore 9 70
(RMFlower) *s.i.s: racd in last trio: prog 2f out: rdn and styd on fr over 1f out: nrst fin* **33/1**
-242 **4** 1 **Multahab**[29] [963] 5-9-9 60 ........ RHughes 6 66
(MissGayKelleway) *hld up in cl tch: effrt 2f out: hanging rt over 1f out: nt qckn and hld after* **3/1**[1]
**5** 1 1/4 **Four Kings** 3-8-12 ........ JTate 8 61
(JMPEustace) *settled in rr: effrt 2f out: rdn and kpt on same pce fr over 1f out: nvr able to chal* **9/2**[3]
5-6 **6** 2 1/2 **Horizontal (USA)**[72] [574] 4-9-9 ........ SSanders 7 51
(VSmith) *racd on outer: sn pressed ldrs: hanging rt and c wd bnd 2f out: wknd over 1f out* **9/2**[3]
330- **7** hd **Point Calimere (IRE)**[265] [3200] 3-8-12 85 ........ SDrowne 10 50
(CREgerton) *pressed ldrs tl wknd wl over 1f out* **8/1**
405- **8** 1 **Ryan's Quest (IRE)**[225] [4310] 5-9-1 48 ........ J-PGuillambert(3) 1 41
(TDMccarthy) *led to 2f out: wknd u.p over 1f out* **25/1**
0360 **9** nk **Confuzed**[25] [987] 4-9-9 45 ........ (e) PFitzsimons 2 45
(DFlood) *stdd s: hld up in last: shkn up briefly ent fnl f: nvr nr ldrs* **20/1**

59.15 secs (-0.63) **Going Correction** -0.075s/f (Stan)
**WFA** 3 from 4yo+ 11lb **9** Ran SP% **115.1**
Speed ratings: **102,101,100,99,97 93,92,91,90**CSF £34.59 TOTE £2.40: £1.10, £4.10, £8.40; EX 22.40.
**Owner** Billy Maguire **Bred** T K & Mrs P A Knox **Trained** Newmarket, Suffolk

**FOCUS**
This was an ordinary sprint maiden, but it was run at a solid pace. The winner showed improved form, and there were no excuses for any of the runners.

**NOTEBOOK**
**Shrink**, runner-up on her previous three outings, stuck to her task gamely to get on top in the final strides. She had lost all chance with a slow start over course-and-distance in February, but was much smarter from the gates and settled a lot better.
**Imperium** made most of the running on this drop to the minimum trip and was only just caught. This was by far his best effort for current connections, with the tongue tie left off, and he is worth another chance in a similar contest.
**Simpsons Mount(IRE)** stepped up on the form of his previous two outings and could be placed to advantage now he qualifies for handicaps.
**Multahab** held every chance if good enough but, not for the first time, did not look the strongest of finishers. He is a frustrating character.
**Point Calimere(IRE)**, top rated on official figures, showed plenty of early pace but dropped away tamely on this comeback from an absence of 265 days. His rider later reported that he was unsuited by the track. *Official explanation: jockey said gelding was unsuited by the track*

## 1229 BET IN RUNNING @ BETDIRECT.CO.UK FILLIES' H'CAP 7f (P)
**3:20** (3:20) (E) (0-75,75) 3-Y-O+ **£3,445** (£1,060; £530; £265) **Stalls** Low

Form RPR
540- **1** **Artistry**[154] [5856] 4-8-10 57 ........ DHolland 12 69
(BJMeehan) *trckd ldrs: effrt 2f out: rdn to ld 1f out: sn in command: comf* **16/1**
55-0 **2** 1 1/2 **Michelle Ma Belle (IRE)**[29] [960] 4-10-0 75 ........ RHughes 10 83
(SKirk) *hld up: prog on outer 1/2-way: chsd ldng pair over 2f out: drvn and styd on to take 2nd last 100y: no imp on wnr* **9/1**
2555 **3** 1/2 **Amelia (IRE)**[4] [1178] 6-7-9 49 ........ BSwarbrick(7) 5 56
(WMBrisbourne) *racd in midfield: t.k.h after 3f: effrt on outer wl over 1f out: styd on to take 3rd nr fin* **11/2**[2]
0624 **4** shd **And Toto Too**[29] [960] 4-9-1 69 ........ (b) SJDonohoe(7) 9 76
(PDEvans) *sn pushed along in rr: effrt u.p 2f out: styd on wl fnl f: nrst fin* **6/1**[3]
030- **5** 3/4 **Dixie Dancing**[155] [5838] 5-8-13 60 ........ SSanders 11 65
(CACyzer) *trckd ldr: led wl over 2f out: hrd rdn and hdd 1f out: wknd last 100y* **25/1**
640- **6** hd **A Woman In Love**[118] [6127] 5-8-7 54 ow1 ........ SDrowne 1 58
(MissBSanders) *s.i.s: t.k.h and hld up wl in rr: nt clr run over 2f out and over 1f out: styd on fnl f: no ch* **8/1**
500- **7** 1/2 **Just One Look**[161] [5734] 3-8-12 73 ........ DSweeney 4 76
(MBlanshard) *racd towards rr: rdn and no prog wl over 2f out: kpt on one pce over 1f out* **20/1**
6-05 **8** 3/4 **I Wish**[29] [960] 6-9-0 61 ........ GBaker 6 62
(MMadgwick) *hld up in rr: prog on wd outside over 2f out: no hdwy over 1f out* **7/1**
440- **9** 1 3/4 **Poppyline**[164] [5688] 4-8-11 58 ........ MartinDwyer 8 54
(WRMuir) *trckd ldrs: rdn 3f out: struggling and btn 2f out* **25/1**
340- **10** 2 **Sahara Storm (IRE)**[158] [5789] 3-8-13 74 ........ LDettori 3 65
(LMCumani) *prom: rdn 3f out: lost pl and btn 2f out* **3/1**[1]
21-0 **11** nk **Miss Poppets**[34] [917] 4-9-6 67 ........ TQuinn 7 57
(DRCElsworth) *led to wl over 2f out: hanging rt and nt run on sn after* **14/1**
3635 **12** 1 **Estimation**[16] [1036] 4-9-6 67 ........ EAhern 2 55
(RMHCowell) *hld up bhd ldrs: lost pl on inner over 4f out: no prog 2f out* **14/1**

1m 25.62s (-0.38) **Going Correction** -0.075s/f (Stan)
**WFA** 3 from 4yo+ 14lb **12** Ran SP% **120.0**
Speed ratings: **99,97,96,96,95 95,94,94,92,89 89,88**CSF £150.75 CT £913.93 TOTE £22.00: £8.40, £2.30, £1.90; EX 131.20.
**Owner** Wyck Hall Stud **Bred** Wyck Hall Stud Ltd **Trained** Upper Lambourn, Berks

**FOCUS**
This was a fair handicap, run at a solid pace, and the winner improved on her debut for a new yard.

**NOTEBOOK**
**Artistry** ◆, off for 154 days prior to this, showed a good turn of foot in the straight to win readily on this debut for current connections. She had shown promise on turf last season over farther, but this drop in trip proved ideal and she looks the type who could improve and win again.
**Michelle Ma Belle(IRE)** ran much better than on her comeback over course and distance in March and can capitalise off this mark, but is a tricky ride over this trip and looks worth a try back at six furlongs.
**Amelia(IRE)** just held third place and ran her race despite being a touch keen for the first half of the contest. She is another who looks better over six furlongs.
**And Toto Too** was held up and came too late on the scene. She looks in need of a drop in the weights.
**Dixie Dancing** made a satisfactory comeback effort and was only beaten for fitness inside the last furlong.
**A Woman In Love** ◆ was very keen on this reappearance and was last turning for home, but she picked up well late on and was full of running passing the line. With this run under her belt she will go closer next time.

## 1230 LITTLEWOODS BET DIRECT H'CAP 6f (P)
**3:55** (3:56) (E) (0-75,74) 3-Y-O+ **£3,464** (£1,066; £533; £266) **Stalls** Low

Form RPR
3050 **1** **Effective**[7] [1121] 4-8-12 **58** ........ (v) DHolland 1 69
(APJarvis) *led for 1f: styd prom: rdn 2f out: kpt on u.p fnl f to ld last strides* **10/1**
000- **2** 1/2 **Goodenough Mover**[141] [5987] 8-9-5 **65** ........ RHavlin 3 75
(JSKing) *prom: rdn 2f out: kpt on u.p to ld last 150y: hdd fnl strides* **25/1**
00-1 **3** 1 **Further Outlook (USA)**[6] [1131] 10-9-13 **73** 7ex ........ DaneO'Neill 6 80
(DKIvory) *led after 1f: hanging rt fr 2f out: hdd and nt qckn last 150y* **7/1**[3]
2331 **4** nk **Mayzin (IRE)**[10] [1082] 4-9-9 **69** 7ex ........ (p) DSweeney 4 75
(RMFlower) *prom: chsd ldr 1/2-way: drvn to chal and ev ch ent fnl f: nt qckn last 150y* **10/1**
2004 **5** shd **Madrasee**[14] [1057] 6-9-5 **65** ........ RLMoore 2 70
(LMontagueHall) *trckd ldrs: rdn and effrt 2f out: cl up ent fnl f: nt qckn* **9/1**
0022 **6** 2 1/2 **Illusive (IRE)**[2] [1204] 7-8-12 **58** ........ (b) JFanning 7 56
(MWigham) *dwlt: rchd midfield over 3f out: drvn and hanging rt fr wl over 1f out: nvr able to chal* **7/1**[3]

210- **7** *2 ½* **Don't Tell Rosey**[268] 3097 4-10-0 **74**........................ NCallan 5 64
(MBlanshard) *racd in midfield: drvn over 2f out: no prog wl over 1f out* **40/1**

5005 **8** *hd* **Cormorant Wharf (IRE)**[14] 1051 4-9-12 **72**........................ JFEgan 9 62
(TEPowell) *sn rdn in rr: no prog over 2f out: kpt on fnl f* **12/1**

0-41 **9** *shd* **Another Glimpse**[14] 1057 6-9-13 **73**........................(t) TQuinn 10 62
(MissBSanders) *racd in rr: effrt on wd outside over 2f out: no prog wl over 1f out* **9/2**[1]

60-3 **10** *shd* **Dunn Deal (IRE)**[17] 1033 4-8-13 **59**........................ SWKelly 11 48
(WMBrisbourne) *t.k.h: hld up wl in rr: rdn 2f out: no prog* **25/1**

2421 **11** *½* **Double M**[10] 1087 7-9-4 **64** 7ex........................(v) RHughes 12 52
(MrsLRichards) *bmpd s: swtchd to inner and hld up towards rr: outpcd 2f out: pushed along and no prog over 1f out* **11/2**[2]

0550 **12** *2 ½* **Sharp Hat**[17] 1027 10-8-9 **62**........................(b) PMakin(7) 13 42
(DWChapman) *bmpd s: a towards rr: rdn and struggling over 2f out* **25/1**

216- **13** *hd* **B A Highflyer**[150] 5918 4-9-2 **62**........................ CCatlin 8 42
(MRChannon) *sn rdn in rr: a struggling* **20/1**

2602 **14** *½* **Tayif**[10] 1087 8-9-5 **65**........................(t) SCarson 14 43
(AndrewReid) *hld up: prog to chse ldrs 1/2-way: wknd over 2f out* **10/1**

1m 11.41s (-1.51) **Going Correction** -0.075s/f (Stan) **14** Ran SP% **122.3**
Speed ratings: **107,106,105,104,104 101,97,97,97,97 96,93,93,92**CSF £248.98 CT £1876.59 TOTE £15.30: £5.10, £8.70, £3.30; EX 316.20.
**Owner** Eurostrait Ltd **Bred** Peter Balding **Trained** Twyford, Bucks

**FOCUS**
A typical sprint handicap for the track, run at a solid gallop and producing a decent time. The winner was back to his best in a visor, and the first five were clear at the finish.

**NOTEBOOK**
**Effective**, handy throughout from his inside draw, gamely stuck to his task inside the final furlong to score all-out. He has dropped a total of 17lb since the start of his All-Weather campaign last October and the visor seemed to help his concentration on this drop in trip.
**Goodenough Mover**, who was unable to dominate over this trip, had to come wide off the home turn in order to mount his challenge and that cost him victory. He has plummeted in the weights and could be one to side with when he steps up another furlong with this race under his belt.
**Further Outlook(USA)** made a bold bid from the front under his penalty and only gave in close home under his penalty for winning on turf last time. He is in good heart at present.
**Mayzin(IRE)** ran another sound race, but found things tougher under the penalty for his win in a weaker race over course and distance ten days previously.
**Madrasee** could not quite go the pace on this occasion and is a better horse on turf.

## 1231 BET DIRECT ON SKY ACTIVE (S) STKS — 1m 2f (P)
**4:30** (4:30) (G) 3-Y-0+ — **£2,520** (£720; £360) **Stalls** Low

Form — RPR

U **1** **Dissident (GER)**[54] 784 6-9-9 73........................(v[1]) PFitzsimons 8 57
(DFlood) *hld up in tch: smooth prog to trck ldr over 2f out: led over 1f out: sn rdn clr* **11/2**[3]

6050 **2** *3 ½* **Paradise Valley**[16] 1041 4-9-13 52........................(t) SDrowne 9 55
(MrsStefLiddiard) *hld up in last: prog to chse ldng pair 2f out: styd on to take 2nd nr fin: no ch w wnr* **7/2**[2]

0-34 **3** *nk* **Senor Toran (USA)**[18] 894 4-9-6 47........................ LPKeniry(3) 4 50
(PBurgoyne) *dwlt: rcvrd to ld after 2f: rdn over 2f out: hdd over 1f out: one pce and lost 2nd nr fin* **8/1**

1500 **4** *3 ½* **Muqtadi (IRE)**[11] 1076 6-9-13 50........................ SSanders 1 48
(MQuinn) *in tch: lost pl 1/2-way: last and nt qckn 3f out: kpt on fr over 1f out: n.d* **8/1**

0005 **5** *nk* **Ipledgeallegiance (USA)**[3] 1194 8-9-2 35........................ PMakin(7) 2 44
(DWChapman) *chsd ldrs: drvn 3f out: sn outpcd and btn* **16/1**

5060 **6** *5* **Pyrrhic**[4] 1166 5-9-9 45........................(b) EAhern 7 35
(RMFlower) *in tch: outpcd wl over 2f out: shuffled along and wknd over 1f out* **10/1**

00-0 **7** *18* **Prince Ivor**[18] 663 4-9-9 35........................(b[1]) PDobbs 5 2
(JCFox) *led for 2f: pressed ldr to 3f out: wkng rapidly whn n.m.r on inner over 2f out: t.o* **66/1**

10-0 **8** *21* **Decelerate**[9] 1097 4-9-13 55........................ RHughes 6 —
(ACharlton) *trckd ldrs: losing pl whn n.m.r 2f out: eased over 1f out: t.o: lame* **7/4**[1]

2m 7.67s (0.28) **Going Correction** -0.075s/f (Stan) **8** Ran SP% **112.7**
Speed ratings: **95,92,91,89,88 84,70,53**CSF £24.29 TOTE £3.60: £2.60, £1.10, £2.10; EX 42.50.The winner was bought in for 7,200gns
**Owner** Mrs Ruth M Serrell **Bred** Gestut Rottgen **Trained** Upper Lambourn, Berks

**FOCUS**
A weak event run at a moderate early pace, and the time was modest. It turned into a sprint about three furlongs from home, and with the form horse below his best the winner had little to beat.

**NOTEBOOK**
**Dissident(GER)**, a dual winner over shorter on sand in Germany in 2001, was restrained early and was perfectly placed to mount his challenge when the tempo increased. This was a pleasing British debut and he responded well to the first-time visor, but this took little winning and still has to prove he is worthy of his official rating of 73. He was bought back in by connections for £7,200.
**Paradise Valley** was held up last for a big part of the race and may have been better served by racing more prominently on this drop in class, as he is proven over farther. That said, he is rated 21lb lower than the winner according to official figures and ran as well as could have been expected at the weights.
**Senor Toran(USA)** set a modest pace until headed approaching the final furlong and had the run of the race, so he may be a touch flattered.
**Prince Ivor** *Official explanation: vet said gelding was found to be coughing*
**Decelerate** was bang there until the pace increased, but dropped out alarmingly in the straight as though something was amiss. *Official explanation: vet said colt finished lame*

## 1232 BET DIRECT INTERACTIVE APPRENTICE H'CAP — 1m 2f (P)
**5:05** (5:13) (E) (0-80,80) 3-Y-0+ — **£4,719** (£1,452; £726; £363) **Stalls** Low

Form — RPR

0010 **1** **Tight Squeeze**[14] 1054 7-10-0 **80**........................ PMakin 1 89
(PWHiatt) *mde all: set slow pce but sn 10l clr: stdd after 4f: pushed clr again over 2f out: unchal* **13/2**

1222 **2** *3 ½* **Bank On Him**[37] 882 9-8-3 **62**........................ JemmaMarshall(7) 2 65
(GLMoore) *t.k.h: hld up bhd clr ldr: in tch 6f out: nt qckn wl over 2f out: one pce after* **9/2**[3]

600- **3** *1 ¼* **Giunchiglio**[191] 5157 5-8-10 **62**........................ BSwarbrick 5 62
(WMBrisbourne) *hld up in 3rd: nvr on terms w wnr: outpcd 3f out: one pce and n.d after* **6/1**

1524 **4** *1* **Barry Island**[38] 872 5-9-12 **78**........................ MLawson 3 77
(DRCElsworth) *t.k.h: hld up in last and wl off the pce: rdn 3f out: no ch* **5/2**[1]

0640 **5** *1 ½* **Brilliant Red**[14] 1054 11-9-8 **79**........................(t) MHalford(5) 6 75
(JamiePoulton) *s.s: hld up in 4th: nvr on terms: rdn over 2f out: no prog* **8/1**

3403 **6** *¾* **Paragon Of Virtue**[13] 1066 7-9-11 **77**........................ SJDonohoe 7 72
(PMitchell) *hld up in 5th and nvr on terms w wnr: rdn 3f out: no prog* **11/4**[2]

2m 8.76s (1.37) **Going Correction** -0.075s/f (Stan)
**WFA** 3 from 5yo+ 19lb **6** Ran SP% **112.2**
Speed ratings: **91,88,87,86,85 84**CSF £34.83 TOTE £7.60: £2.70, £1.90; EX 26.20 Place 6 £190.90, Place 5 £126.41.
**Owner** Anthony Harrison **Bred** Anthony Harrison **Trained** Hook Norton, Oxon

**FOCUS**
This apprentice handicap was run at a shambolic early gallop and the form is highly suspect.

**NOTEBOOK**
**Tight Squeeze** led under sufferance in the first furlong and, as her other rivals were being restrained, she gained about a ten-length lead and was never headed from that point. This form is obviously extremely suspect, but she was winning the race for the second successive year off a 21lb higher mark and both she and rider deserve maximum credit.
**Bank On Him** tried to close the gap as the pace quickened about five out, but was totally unsuited by the way the race was run and had no chance with the winner.
**Giunchiglio** was another who tried to bridge the gap all too late and this run will bring him on plenty as he had been off for 191 days.
**Barry Island** was held up last off the farcical gallop and this run is best ignored.
T/Plt: £229.80 to a £1 stake. Pool: £30,513.45. 96.90 winning tickets. T/Qpdt: £417.70 to a £1 stake. Pool: £2,257.90. 4.00 winning tickets. JN

# 1190 SOUTHWELL (L-H)
Friday, April 2

**OFFICIAL GOING: Standard**
The centre of the track was the place to be on the straight course.

## 1233 BLOOR HOMES FISKERTON AMATEUR RIDERS' H'CAP — 1m (F)
**2:20** (2:21) (F) (0-55,56) 3-Y-0+ — **£2,954** (£844; £422) **Stalls** Low

Form — RPR

00-1 **1** **Rust En Vrede**[33] 939 5-10-5 53........................ MissDAllman(7) 16 67
(DCarroll) *a in tch: wnt 2nd over 2f out: led over 1f out: sn clr: v easily* **10/1**

6102 **2** *3 ½* **Wilson Bluebottle (IRE)**[11] 1079 5-10-5 46 oh1.(b) MissSBrotherton 10 53
(MWEasterby) *a.p: led over 4f out: hdd over 1f out: nt pce of wnr* **11/2**[3]

0 **3** *3 ½* **Secam (POL)**[12] 867 5-10-1 47........................ MrsCThompson(5) 14 47
(MrsPTownsley) *a.p: rdn over 2f out: one pce after* **33/1**

501 **4** *nk* **Sorbiesharry (IRE)**[4] 1181 5-10-13 54 6ex........................(p) MrsMMorris 3 53
(MrsNMacauley) *hld up in rr: styd on fnl 2f: nvr nrr* **7/1**

006- **5** *½* **Nimbus Twothousand**[129] 6067 4-10-2 46 oh1.....(b) MrEDehdashti(3) 4 44
(PRWood) *in rr: hdwy on outside over 3f out: no ex ins fnl 2f* **25/1**

4011 **6** *2 ½* **Our Destiny**[4] 1177 6-11-1 56 6ex........................(v) MrsSBosley 15 49
(AWCarroll) *in tch: rdn over 2f out: one pce after* **9/2**[2]

0026 **7** *¾* **Kumakawa**[19] 1019 6-10-1 49........................(b) MrCWitheford(7) 11 41
(EAWheeler) *hld up: one pce and little ch fnl 3f* **16/1**

0040 **8** *2 ½* **Crusoe (IRE)**[8] 1109 7-10-9 55........................(b) MrLNewnes(5) 12 42
(ASadik) *in tch tl bhd fnl 3f* **9/1**

0020 **9** *nk* **Mutarafaa (USA)**[9] 1098 5-10-12 53........................(e) MsCWilliams 13 39
(DShaw) *slowly away: hdwy over over 4f out: wknd 3f out* **4/1**[1]

-003 **10** *2 ½* **Prince Minata (IRE)**[10] 1090 9-9-12 46 oh6........................ MissAHockley(7) 9 27
(PWHiatt) *a towards rr* **14/1**

0006 **11** *¾* **Illustrious Duke**[4] 1176 6-9-12 46 oh6........................(b) MissMMullineaux(7) 7 26
(MMullineaux) *led tl hdd over 4f out: wknd qckly over 2f out* **20/1**

0-00 **12** *5* **Hoh's Back**[56] 700 5-10-9 55........................(p) MrPEvans(5) 5 25
(PaulJohnson) *prom tl wknd wl over 2f out* **16/1**

0616 **13** *nk* **Ace-Ma-Vahra**[38] 878 6-10-4 48........................(p) MissKellyHarrison(3) 2 17
(SRBowring) *a in rr* **14/1**

0/0- **14** *2* **Sunridge Fairy (IRE)**[381] 215 5-10-5 51........................ MissJFoster(5) 8 16
(AJLockwood) *a bhd* **25/1**

-000 **15** *14* **Tern Intern (IRE)**[10] 1090 5-9-12 46 oh16........................(b) MissFionaBrown(7) 6 —
(MissJFeilden) *v.s.a: a bhd: t.o* **50/1**

1m 46.87s (2.27) **Going Correction** +0.275s/f (Slow) **15** Ran SP% **127.6**
Speed ratings: **99,95,92,91,91 88,87,85,85,82 81,76,76,74,60**CSF £63.83 CT £1842.50 TOTE £15.50: £7.30, £2.30, £8.20; EX 100.50.
**Owner** Alan Mann **Bred** T J Cooper **Trained** Warthill, N Yorks
■ A first winner for Diane Allman.
■ Stewards Enquiry : Mrs S Bosley one-day ban: careless riding (Apr 19)

**FOCUS**
A moderate amateurs' event run at just a fair gallop. The winner looks capable of completing the hat-trick.

**NOTEBOOK**
**Rust En Vrede** has really taken to this surface and repeated his recent success in a banded event with an emphatic victory. He will no doubt be going up a fair few pounds for this, but looks capable of winning again back here.
**Wilson Bluebottle(IRE)**, who has been showing form in banded events, ran his race but is now handicapped out of those races and will not find things easy in better races. That said, he seems to appreciate Wolverhampton's nine furlongs better.
**Secam(POL)**, a former turf winner in Poland, ran much his best race in Britain on his first encounter with this surface. This is his trip and, if dropped a couple of pounds, he will be interesting in a banded event.
**Sorbiesharry(IRE)**, fresh from a win at Wolverhampton on Monday, was out with the washing and under strong pressure turning in. He kept on to good effect and was closest at the finish, but seems more effective on the West Midlands track these days.
**Nimbus Twothousand**, having her first run for over four months, did not perform too badly and may find an opportunity in banded company.
**Our Destiny**, trying to complete a hat-trick under a 6lb penalty, never got to the front on this occasion.
**Mutarafaa(USA)**, with the eyeshield reapplied, never got competitive after being slow to hit his stride.

## 1234 ESP EXPERIENCE CHALLENGE MAIDEN AUCTION FILLIES' STKS — 5f (F)
**2:55** (2:55) (F) 2-Y-O — **£2,863** (£818; £409) **Stalls** High

Form — RPR

**1** **Nova Tor (IRE)** 2-7-9........................ RoryMoore(7) 7 52
(PCHaslam) *hung lft thrght: chsd ldrs: edgd lft but r.o to ld ins fnl f* **4/1**[3]

**2** *¾* **Lady Erica** 2-8-4........................ GFaulkner 6 52
(KRBurke) *mde most tl hung bdly lft and hdd ins fnl f* **7/2**[2]

2 **3** *1 ¼* **Nutty Times**[6] 1137 2-8-2........................ ADaly 2 45
(WGMTurner) *w ldrs for 2f: outpcd: rallied and r.o wl fnl f* **10/3**[1]

**4** *1 ¼* **Glasson Lodge** 2-8-2........................ PHanagan 4 41
(PDEvans) *outpcd and wl bhd tl r.o wl fnl f* **10/1**

5 ½ **Voice Of An Angel (IRE)** 2-8-2 .......... GDuffield 3 39
(ABerry) *squeezed out s: swtchd lft and sn w ldrs: hung lft and wknd appr fnl f* **11/2**

0 6 1 ¾ **Sahara Mist (IRE)**[8] 1105 2-8-1 .......... LisaJones(3) 5 34
(DShaw) *plld hrd: w ldrs tl rdn and btn sn after 1/2-way* **16/1**

6 7 shd **Kilkenny Kitten (IRE)**[4] 1170 2-8-4 .......... (t) KimTinkler 1 34
(NTinkler) *disp ld tl rdn and wknd over 1f out* **4/1**[3]

63.09 secs (2.79) **Going Correction** +0.175s/f (Slow) **7 Ran SP% 115.7**
Speed ratings: **84,82,80,78,78 75,75**CSF £18.82 TOTE £6.20: £2.70, £2.20; EX 37.40.
**Owner** Blue Lion Racing III **Bred** Newlands House Stud **Trained** Middleham Moor, N Yorks

**FOCUS**
A very moderate-looking fillies' contest run 2.43sec slower than the later three-year-old handicap. The form looks poor with the third having previously been beaten in a seller.

**NOTEBOOK**
**Nova Tor(IRE)**, a cheaply bought half-sister to three juvenile winners, upheld the family tradition by making a winning debut. She was quite green in the race and may have some improvement in her, but this was a very ordinary race and she may need to find improvement to follow up.
**Lady Erica**, who has speed in her pedigree and is by a proven All-Weather sire, showed plenty of pace but drifted under pressure and could not hold off the late surge of the winner. She may be able to pick up a similar contest on this surface.
**Nutty Times**, beaten in a seller on her debut, was outpaced in the middle of the race before staying on. She is the guide to the level of the form.
**Glasson Lodge** was taken off her feet in the first half of the race but then finished best of all. She will have learnt a lot and may be the one to take out of the race.
**Voice Of An Angel(IRE)** showed plenty of pace after missing a beat at the start and should benefit from the experience.

## 1235 BETDIRECT.CO.UK MAIDEN STKS — 1m 4f (F)
**3:30** (3:30) (D) 3-Y-0+ — **£3,701** (£1,139; £569; £284) **Stalls Low**

Form — RPR

1 **Dance World**[246] 4-9-8 .......... BReilly(3) 6 69
(MissJFeilden) *a in tch: wnt 2nd over 2f out: led over 1f out: sn clr* **4/1**[3]

30-0 2 2 ½ **Masjoor**[29] 962 4-9-11 59 .......... JPMurtagh 2 65
(NAGraham) *trckd ldr tl over 2f out: hrd rdn to chse wnr over 1f out* **9/4**[2]

6-66 3 3 ½ **Pepe (IRE)**[50] 746 3-8-0 48 .......... DaleGibson 7 54
(RHollinshead) *led tl hdd over 2f out: wknd fnl f* **50/1**

000- 4 7 **Prairie Sun (GER)**[161] 5722 3-8-2 ow2 .......... GDuffield 4 45
(MrsADuffield) *in tch on outside: rdn 4f out: no hdwy u.p fnl 2f* **20/1**

0-52 5 13 **It Must Be Speech**[15] 1042 3-8-5 65 .......... ANicholls 1 27
(SLKeightley) *a in rr: lost tch over 3f out* **4/1**[3]

00 6 21 **Marino Mou (IRE)**[56] 697 4-9-11 .......... (b[1]) GCarter 5 —
(MissDMountain) *slowly away: sn wl bhd: t.o* **66/1**

3 7 13 **Border Saint**[14] 1050 3-8-5 .......... JMackay 3 —
(MLWBell) *trckd ldrs: wknd 3f out: eased over 1f out: t.o* **15/8**[1]

2m 44.07s (1.97) **Going Correction** +0.275s/f (Slow)
**WFA** 3 from 4yo 21lb **7 Ran SP% 113.8**
Speed ratings: **104,102,100,95,86 72,64**CSF £13.28 TOTE £5.70: £2.10, £2.00; EX 24.30.
**Owner** Stowstowquickquickstow Partnership **Bred** Juddmonte Farms **Trained** Exning, Suffolk

**FOCUS**
Just a fair pace for this maiden, and little strength in depth, but the winner scored with something in hand.

**NOTEBOOK**
**Dance World ◆**, a formerly French-trained cast-off from the Khalid Abdulla string, was always travelling well and won with the minimum of fuss. Apparently he has been working well with All-Weather horse of the year Najaaba, so if he proves anywhere near as good as his stable companion, could prove a useful acquisition for the yard. He would be interesting in handicaps off a mark in the mid-60s
**Masjoor** ran another fair race on his first encounter with this surface. He had no chance with the winner, but looks a real galloper who may appreciate another couple of furlongs.
**Pepe(IRE)** ran a decent race against his elders and seemed to appreciate the positive tactics. He will be better off in handicaps or, if the Handicapper relents a little, banded events.
**It Must Be Speech**, runner-up in an apprentice handicap here last month, had a clear chance on official ratings but was beaten turning in.
**Border Saint**, third in a maiden on Polytrack on his debut, appeared not to handle this surface. That said, the form of that race is not working out so far. *Official explanation: vet found gelding was 'tying up behind'*

## 1236 LITTLEWOODS BET DIRECT H'CAP — 5f (F)
**4:05** (4:05) (E) (0-70,70) 3-Y-0 — **£3,721** (£1,145; £572; £286) **Stalls High**

Form — RPR

0602 1 **Demolition Molly**[2] 1209 3-8-10 **62** .......... (tp) LFletcher(3) 2 71
(RFMarvin) *mde all: drvn clr fnl f* **5/2**[2]

1300 2 3 **Desert Light (IRE)**[2] 1209 3-8-1 **53** .......... (v) LisaJones(3) 3 51
(DShaw) *chsd wnr thrght: no imp fnl f* **13/2**[3]

3-00 3 1 ¼ **Blue Power (IRE)**[58] 678 3-8-13 **62** .......... DarrenWilliams 6 56
(KRBurke) *chsd ldrs: rdn 1/2-way: chsd ldng pair fnl 2f* **13/2**[3]

04-3 4 1 **Only If I Laugh**[9] 1099 3-9-2 **70** .......... JFMcDonald(5) 7 60
(BJMeehan) *chsd ldrs: edgd lft over 1f out: nt qckn* **7/4**[1]

206- 5 nk **Loveisdangerous**[173] 5512 3-8-6 **55** .......... KimTinkler 1 44
(DonEnricoIncisa) *chsd ldrs: fdd 2f out* **16/1**

0530 6 ¾ **Lavish Times**[2] 1196 3-8-2 **51** .......... (b) GDuffield 4 37
(ABerry) *spd for 3f* **10/1**

0640 7 2 ½ **Indrani**[15] 1047 3-7-5 **47** oh2 .......... DFentiman(7) 5 24
(JohnAHarris) *outpcd fr 1/2-way* **25/1**

-004 8 9 **Lakeside Guy (IRE)**[37] 881 3-8-8 **57** .......... (t) OUrbina 8 2
(PSMcentee) *outpcd after 2f* **14/1**

60.66 secs (0.36) **Going Correction** +0.175s/f (Slow) **8 Ran SP% 117.1**
Speed ratings: **104,99,97,95,95 93,89,75**CSF £19.80 CT £95.86 TOTE £2.70: £1.80, £3.30, £2.20; EX 31.80.
**Owner** D Blott **Bred** Mrs E M Charlton **Trained** Southwell, Notts

**FOCUS**
A modest sprint run at a fair pace, where the advantage was with those racing towards the centre of the track.

**NOTEBOOK**
**Demolition Molly**, who showed a return to form on turf last time, was able to run off an 8lb lower mark on Fibresand and took full advantage. She will unfortunately not get another chance to race on the All-Weather before she is re-assessed.
**Desert Light(IRE)**, who has been punished for a couple of good efforts in claimers and banded company, put up another good performance but would have preferred an extra furlong.
**Blue Power(IRE)**, a nursery winner here in December, appeared to run his race without being good enough.
**Only If I Laugh** was not helped by having to race towards the stands' side when the track advantage and the pace appeared to be up the centre. He can be given a chance to atone.
**Loveisdangerous**, having her first try on this surface, did not fare badly and may be of interest back on fast turf off what looks a reasonable mark.

## 1237 £10 FREE BET @ BETDIRECT.CO.UK (S) STKS — 6f (F)
**4:40** (4:41) (G) 3-Y-0+ — **£2,541** (£726; £363) **Stalls Low**

Form — RPR

0013 1 **On The Trail**[10] 1092 7-9-13 45 .......... ACulhane 5 56
(DWChapman) *a.p: led over 1f out: drvn out* **7/2**[2]

02-5 2 1 ¼ **Pawan (IRE)**[4] 1171 4-9-9 62 .......... KimTinkler 2 48
(NTinkler) *outpcd: rdn and hdwy to chse wnr over 1f out* **5/1**

0-00 3 2 **Rathmullan**[10] 1090 5-9-2 35 .......... (b) LiamJones(7) 7 42
(EAWheeler) *racd wd: chsd ldrs but n.d fnl 2f* **33/1**

0-30 4 10 **Festive Affair**[64] 625 6-9-9 47 .......... FLynch 3 12
(BSmart) *trckd ldr: led wl over 2f out: hdd over 1f out: wknd rapidly and eased* **9/2**

1504 5 1 **Polar Haze**[6] 1140 7-9-13 56 .......... (b) RPrice 1 13
(JPearce) *outpcd thrght* **5/2**[1]

4060 6 1 ¼ **Keltic Flute**[24] 998 5-9-4 30 .......... (v) DNolan(5) 6 6
(MrsLucindaFeatherstone) *stmbld s: sn prom: hrd rdn 1/2-way: wknd 2f out* **20/1**

0-06 7 7 **Czar Wars**[59] 670 9-9-6 63 .......... (b) LFletcher(3) 4 —
(JBalding) *led: hdd wl over 2f out: sn btn* **4/1**[3]

1m 18.91s (2.11) **Going Correction** +0.275s/f (Slow) **7 Ran SP% 113.3**
Speed ratings: **96,94,91,78,77 75,66**CSF £20.81 TOTE £5.10: £2.30, £2.50; EX 34.00.There was no bid for the winner. Pawan was claimed by Ann Stokell for £6,000
**Owner** J M Chapman **Bred** Ian Bellamy **Trained** Stillington, N Yorks

**FOCUS**
A poor seller run at an ordinary gallop but a good effort by the winner judged on official ratings.

**NOTEBOOK**
**On The Trail**, who has rediscovered his form in banded races of late, had a difficult task on official ratings but proved too strong for his more highly-rated rival in the closing stages. He should continue to give a good account.
**Pawan(IRE)** had a fine chance on offical ratings on this drop into selling company, but was making his All-Weather debut. He ran quite well and appeared to handle the surface, but is clearly not as good as his rating suggests.
**Rathmullan** ran his best race so far on this drop into a seller with the blinkers reapplied, despite racing wide throughout. Off his current mark, banded stakes look to offer his best opportunity.
**Festive Affair** stopped quickly in the closing stages, as he did last time, and may have a problem. *Official explanation: jockey said gelding had a breathing problem*
**Polar Haze** normally goes well on this track, but was very disappointing and made no show. *Official explanation: jockey said gelding lost a shoe and was never travelling.*
**Czar Wars**, another with a big chance on official ratings, seemed to pay the penalty for taking on Festive Affair in the early stages. *Official explanation: vet found gelding to be distressed.*

## 1238 SPONSORS DAY H'CAP — 1m 6f (F)
**5:15** (5:16) (F) (0-55,61) 4-Y-0+ — **£2,996** (£856; £428) **Stalls Low**

Form — RPR

2010 1 **Jungle Lion**[15] 1042 6-8-8 46 oh1 .......... (t) DeanMcKeown 9 57
(JohnAHarris) *trckd ldrs: led over 1f out: drvn clr* **18/1**

02-1 2 3 ½ **Isa'Af (IRE)**[11] 1077 5-8-13 51 6ex .......... ACulhane 12 57
(PWHiatt) *trckd ldr: led over 3f out: hdd over 1f out: nt qckn fnl f* **9/4**[1]

2212 3 ½ **The Beduth Navi**[19] 1026 4-8-6 47 oh2 .......... DaleGibson 4 52
(DGBridgwater) *led: hdd over 4f out: rdn and rallied 2f out: styd on fnl f* **11/1**

1112 4 nk **Broughton Knows**[33] 937 7-8-13 54 .......... (b) LisaJones(3) 6 59
(WJMusson) *stdd s and in rr tl hdwy over 2f out: styd on: nvr nr to chal* **17/2**

5005 5 shd **Western Command (GER)**[3] 1193 8-8-8 46 oh16..(p) JoannaBadger 14 51?
(MrsNMacauley) *hld up: hung rt thrght: hdwy 6f out: outpcd 3f out: styd on ins fnl 2f* **50/1**

/03- 6 9 **Light Brigade**[212] 4654 5-8-11 49 .......... JMackay 10 42
(JMPEustace) *trckd ldrs: ev ch 2f out: sn wknd* **16/1**

3125 7 10 **Lampos (USA)**[57] 684 4-9-0 55 .......... RWinston 16 35
(MissJACamacho) *dwlt: sn in tch: rdn 1m out: n.d fnl 3f* **4/1**[3]

50/0 8 5 **Broughtons Flush**[36] 889 6-8-8 46 oh1 .......... FLynch 5 20
(WJMusson) *a bhd* **25/1**

00/4 9 hd **Swing West (USA)**[16] 1041 10-8-8 46 oh16 .......... (p) SRighton 11 19
(AEJones) *slowly away: alway in rr* **80/1**

3/41 10 3 **Ffiffiffer (IRE)**[6] 1136 6-9-6 61 6ex .......... SHitchcott(3) 7 30
(CTinkler) *prom: rdn over 4f out: sn btn* **7/2**[2]

3010 11 2 **East Cape**[19] 1023 7-8-8 46 oh1 .......... KimTinkler 15 13
(DonEnricoIncisa) *a bhd* **22/1**

-034 12 3 ½ **Fortunes Favourite**[33] 937 4-8-5 46 oh9 .......... NPollard 8 8
(GMMoore) *prom: led over 4f out: hdd over 3f out: rdn and wknd qckly 2f out* **40/1**

00-4 13 5 **Bid Spotter (IRE)**[11] 1077 5-8-8 46 oh1 .......... (p) GDuffield 3 2
(MrsLucindaFeatherstone) *chsd ldrs: rdn over 1m out: sn wknd* **50/1**

04-4 14 dist **Morvern (IRE)**[18] 449 4-8-10 51 .......... (v) MFenton 13 —
(JGGiven) *chsd ldrs: tl wknd 5f out: t.o* **20/1**

0-50 15 dist **Star Seventeen**[25] 984 6-8-9 50 .......... DCorby(3) 1 —
(MrsNSSharpe) *a bhd: t.o* **50/1**

-026 P **Sean's Memory (USA)**[36] 889 4-8-9 50 .......... (p) GFaulkner 2 —
(MrsCADunnett) *chsd ldrs tl wknd 6f out: p.u: broke knee: dead* **33/1**

3m 11.75s (2.15) **Going Correction** +0.275s/f (Slow)
**WFA** 4 from 5yo+ 3lb **16 Ran SP% 128.4**
Speed ratings: **104,102,101,101,101 96,90,87,87,85 84,82,79,—,— —**CSF £57.06 CT £510.19 TOTE £30.50: £3.80, £1.90, £3.80, £2.60; EX 155.10 Place 6 £183.17, Place 5 £48.37.
**Owner** Mick Rowley **Bred** Buckram Thoroughbred Enterprises Inc **Trained** Eastwell, Leics

**FOCUS**
More than half of the field were out of the proper handicap, although some of them only narrowly, and the winner had a good chance on the weights. The gallop was decent and the time fair, but the proximity of a horse 16lb 'wrong' in fifth is a worry.

**NOTEBOOK**
**Jungle Lion**, a runaway course winner in banded company in February, was only a pound higher and, always travelling well, had no trouble staying the longer trip. He will be interesting back on turf, particularly if the ground is testing.
**Isa'Af(IRE)**, an easy winner of a banded event after a long break last time, was racing on this track for the first time and seemed unable to pick up after having every chance. He stays this trip on turf, but possibly finds 12 furlongs his limit on sand.
**The Beduth Navi**, who is progressing with racing, put up another courageous performance from the front, and did not give up when headed. He stays really well and should find further opportunities in what is a weak staying division.
**Broughton Knows**, beaten seven lengths by the winner in a banded stakes in February, was having his first run since and was worse off in the weights as a result of his earlier exploits. In the circumstances, he did well to finish so close.
**Western Command(GER)** is on a losing run that stretches back two years. He ran surprisingly well, especially considering he was racing from 16lb out of the handicap.
**Lampos(USA)**, a course and distance winner in January, was having his first race for eight weeks but looks too high in the weights now.

**Broughtons Flush** *Official explanation: jockey said, regarding the running and riding, orders were not to rush gelding early on, ease to the outside to avoid kickback and get into race as it developed but he could not get to the outside until back straight where despite constant pushing the gelding failed to progress; he added that gelding took a big blow turning into home straight and he felt it prudent not to perservere too strongly in view of gelding's tiredness*
**Ffiffiffer(IRE)**, a sand winner in Spain and successful on his Fibresand debut at Wolverhampton last week, put up a below-par effort and may have found this third race in ten days too much.
T/Plt: £804.70 to a £1 stake. Pool: £30,483.10. 27.65 winning tickets. T/Qpdt: £31.70 to a £1 stake. Pool: £2,470.20. 57.50 winning tickets. JS

# 1226 LINGFIELD (L-H)

Saturday, April 3

**OFFICIAL GOING: Standard**

## 1239 SHADWELL STUD INTERNATIONAL TRIAL STKS (LISTED RACE) 1m (P)

**1:55** (1:55) (A) 3-Y-O **£26,000** (£8,000; £4,000; £2,000) **Stalls** High

Form — RPR

16- **1** **Leitrim House**[204] 4863 3-8-11 SDrowne 5 106
(BJMeehan) *trckd ldrs: rdn to chse ldr over 2f out: drvn to ld jst ins fnl f: styd on wl* **20/1**

511- **2** 1 1/4 **Milk It Mick**[168] 5640 3-9-0 118 DHolland 7 106+
(JAOsborne) *hld up in last trio: prog on outer over 2f out: rdn and nt qckn over 1f out: kpt on to take 2nd last 100y: no imp on wnr* **7/4**[1]

-211 **3** shd **Skidmark**[38] 883 3-8-11 92 JPMurtagh 9 103+
(DRCElsworth) *hld up and last to 3f out: gng easily 2f out: plld out and effrt over 1f out: r.o wl fnl f: too much to do* **8/1**[3]

311 **4** 1 **Rosencrans (USA)**[14] 1063 3-8-11 (vt) LDettori 2 101
(SaeedBinSuroor) *led: shkn up over 1f out: hdd jst ins fnl f: fdd* **2/1**[2]

116- **5** 1 1/2 **Kings Point (IRE)**[248] 3686 3-8-11 107 RHughes 6 97
(RHannon) *lw: unf: hld up in last pair: pushed along over 2f out: effrt over 1f out: one pce and no imp on ldrs* **10/1**

05-0 **6** 1/2 **Crocodile Dundee (IRE)**[14] 1063 3-8-11 90 JFEgan 1 96
(JamiePoulton) *lw: trckd ldrs: rdn 3f out: fdd over 1f out* **33/1**

11-6 **7** 1/2 **Bravo Maestro (USA)**[14] 1063 3-8-11 95 TQuinn 3 95
(DWPArbuthnot) *t.k.h: hld up in tch: squeezed through to chse ldr 3f out to over 2f out: wknd over 1f out* **9/1**

165- **8** 1 1/2 **Parkview Love (USA)**[248] 3686 3-8-11 104 SChin 4 91
(MJohnston) *trckd ldrs: rdn over 2f out: wknd over 1f out* **16/1**

4241 **9** 23 **Ile Facile (IRE)**[40] 856 3-8-11 67 SWKelly 8 39
(NPLittmoden) *t.k.h: sn trckd ldr: wknd 3f out: t.o* **200/1**

1m 37.16s (-2.35) **Going Correction** -0.10s/f (Stan) **9** Ran SP% **114.0**
Speed ratings: **107,105,105,104,103 102,102,100,77**CSF £54.18 TOTE £19.80: £5.20, £1.10, £2.30; EX 77.10.
**Owner** Gallagher Equine Ltd **Bred** Whitsbury Manor Stud **Trained** Upper Lambourn, Berks

**FOCUS**
An interesting Listed race, but a steady early pace contributed to a surprise result. The Spring Cup representatives ran roughly to form, indicating this was a better race.

**NOTEBOOK**
**Leitrim House**, who made a winning debut at Newmarket last summer, had not been seen since finishing last in the Champagne Stakes at Doncaster, four lengths behind Milk It Mick. He was always close to the pace, but never appeared to be travelling that well. However, when asked for an effort, he found plenty and was always holding the favourite in the straight. A mile looks his optimum trip and connections are favouring a crack at one of the continental mile classics rather than Newmarket.
**Milk It Mick**, the surprise winner of last season's Dewhurst, seemed to travel well enough on this debut on this surface but was making no impression on the winner up the straight. Connections believe he settles better the more he races, and so he will have another outing in one of the Guineas trials before going to Newmarket at the beginning of next month.
**Skidmark** ◆, who has done all his racing on this surface, was held up as usual and was probably unsuited by the way the race was run. He is progressive and has already won over ten furlongs, and this Dante and Derby entry will no doubt soon be making his debut on turf.
**Rosencrans(USA)**, winner of the Ladbrokes.com Spring Cup at the Winter Derby meeting here, once again tried to dictate from the front, but found these arguably better rivals too strong. He is dirt bred and is now likely to make his way back to race in his native USA.
**Kings Point(IRE)**, who won a Group Three last season, has not looked quite up to that level in two subsequent runs now.

## 1240 BETDIRECT.CO.UK MAIDEN AUCTION STKS 5f (P)

**2:30** (2:30) (E ) 2-Y-O **£3,376** (£1,039; £519; £259) **Stalls** High

Form — RPR

6 **1** **Canton (IRE)**[7] 1130 2-9-0 DaneO'Neill 5 84
(RHannon) *lw: s.s: sn in tch: trckd ldr 1/2-way: rdn to ld over 1f out: sn in command: r.o wl* **3/1**[2]

2 **2** 1 1/2 **Evanesce**[8] 1117 2-8-2 CCatlin 2 66
(MRChannon) *trckd ldr: led 1/2-way: rdn and hdd over 1f out: no ch w wnr fnl f* **1/1**[1]

**3** 6 **Majestical (IRE)** 2-9-0 MartinDwyer 1 54
(WRMuir) *leggy: s.s: rn green early and hld up in last: effrt 1/2-way: sn outpcd: one pce fr over 1f out* **12/1**

4 **4** 1 1/2 **Cubic Confessions (IRE)**[14] 1060 2-8-6 SWKelly 3 40
(JAOsborne) *chsd ldrs: rdn 1/2-way: wl btn over 1f out: wknd* **9/2**[3]

6 **5** 5 **Von Wessex**[7] 1128 2-8-0 CHaddon(7) 4 21
(WGMTurner) *hanging rt thrght: led to 1/2-way: virtually rn off the crse bnd 2f out: bhd after* **6/1**

59.25 secs (-0.53) **Going Correction** -0.10s/f (Stan) **5** Ran SP% **115.2**
Speed ratings: **100,97,88,85,77**CSF £6.82 TOTE £4.10: £2.90, £1.10; EX 10.80.
**Owner** Louis Stalder **Bred** Yeomanstown Stud **Trained** East Everleigh, Wilts

**FOCUS**
An ordinary juvenile contest, but run at a decent pace and a good final time. Stable won this with a useful sort in 2003, and this one could be a similar type.

**NOTEBOOK**
**Canton(IRE)**, well beaten when favourite on his debut at Kempton, again missed the break but had clearly learnt from her first outing and picked up really well off the home turn to win going away. He looks capable of adding to this victory.
**Evanesce**, narrowly beaten in a similar race here on her debut, again started favourite and had every chance. However, she was brushed aside by the winner and connections will be keen to get a win under her belt sooner rather than later.
**Majestical(IRE)**, a half-brother to the sprinters Double Quick and Speedy James, was totally clueless in the early stages but kept on well in the straight and should come on a lot for the experience.
**Cubic Confessions(IRE)** again showed pace but dropped away rather tamely at the end.
**Von Wessex** gave his rider a torrid time by hanging away from the inside, as he had done on his debut. *Official explanation: jockey said gelding hung violently right throughout*

## 1241 NEW SITE @ BETDIRECT.CO.UK CLASSIFIED STKS 1m (P)

**3:05** (3:06) (E) 3-Y-O+ **£3,474** (£1,069; £534; £267) **Stalls** High

Form — RPR

1121 **1** **Steely Dan**[3] 1203 5-10-0 75 LDettori 10 89
(JRBest) *lw: hld up in last trio: plenty to do over 2f out: gd prog wl over 1f out: urged along and r.o wl to ld last stride* **10/3**[1]

-031 **2** shd **Katiypour (IRE)**[8] 1118 7-9-5 75 RMiles(3) 3 83
(MissBSanders) *trckd ldr: led 3f out: jnd 2f out: rdn 2l clr 1f out: r.o fnl f: hdd last stride* **10/3**[1]

-243 **3** 3 **Deeper In Debt**[8] 1118 6-9-6 73 GCarter 8 74
(JAkehurst) *cl up: effrt 3f out: rdn to join ldr 2f out: unable qck over 1f out: one pce after: jst hld on for 3rd* **5/1**[2]

03-3 **4** 1/2 **College Delinquent (IRE)**[63] 647 5-9-3 66 (t) DaneO'Neill 7 70
(KBell) *racd in midfield: pushed along 3f out: no imp ldrs 2f out: kpt on same pce fr over 1f out* **12/1**

-32L **5** shd **Spinning Dove**[42] 846 4-9-0 67 JPMurtagh 5 67
(NAGraham) *reluctant to s and lost 6l: hld up in last: effrt over 2f out: taken to wd outside over 1f out: kpt on fnl f* **14/1**

0300 **6** shd **Greenwood**[15] 1055 6-9-6 73 DKinsella 2 73
(PGMurphy) *cl up: rdn to chse ldng pair over 2f out: no imp over 1f out: one pce after* **20/1**

054- **7** shd **Redi (ITY)**[169] 5607 3-7-11 69 NMackay(5) 4 69
(LMCumani) *dwlt: sn rcvrd to chse ldrs: rdn over 2f out: one pce and nvr rchd ldrs* **14/1**

22-4 **8** 1 **The Best Yet**[63] 648 6-9-8 75 SWhitworth 9 72
(AGNewcombe) *dwlt: hld up in rr: prog over 2f out: chsd ldrs over 1f out: no imp after* **6/1**[3]

-060 **9** 4 **Agilis (IRE)**[49] 770 4-9-3 70 SDrowne 12 58
(JamiePoulton) *hld up in rr: rdn wl over 2f out: no prog: wknd over 1f out* **25/1**

600- **10** 7 **Omaha City (IRE)**[194] 5122 10-9-8 75 RHughes 11 47
(BGubby) *trckd ldrs: wknd 3f out: eased* **20/1**

300- **11** 1 1/4 **Desert Dance (IRE)**[161] 5749 4-9-3 65 DHolland 1 39
(GWragg) *lw: tk fierce hold early: trckd ldrs tl wknd wl over 2f out* **20/1**

2210 **12** 2 **Meelup (IRE)**[10] 1097 4-9-3 59 (p) VSlattery 6 34
(JaneSouthcombe) *led to 3f out: sn wknd* **28/1**

1m 37.6s (-1.91) **Going Correction** -0.10s/f (Stan)
**WFA** 3 from 4yo+ 15lb **12** Ran SP% **119.7**
Speed ratings: **105,104,101,101,101 101,101,100,96,89 87,85**CSF £12.52 TOTE £3.10: £1.30, £1.90, £1.70; EX 19.70.
**Owner** E A Condon **Bred** Mrs S E Barclay And L B Snowden **Trained** Hucking, Kent

**FOCUS**
A competitive classified event run 0.44sec slower than the earlier Listed race over the same trip. The form should prove reliable.

**NOTEBOOK**
**Steely Dan** has been in sparkling form on this surface this year and recorded his fifth win off his highest mark for two years. He just about handled the drop in trip from a mile and a half and is clearly still at the top of his game.
**Katiypour(IRE)** ◆, another in good form, did everything right and was only caught on the line. He looks capable of gaining compensation for this narrow defeat.
**Deeper In Debt** ◆ finished further behind the runner-up on this occasion, despite being on better terms, than he did here last month. Nevertheless, he is running consistently well, and a return to turf may see him get his head in front.
**College Delinquent(IRE)** ◆, having his first run for nine weeks, ran as if the outing will bring him on. He is one to keep an eye on back on turf, as he is rated 10lb lower.
**Spinning Dove** refused to race last time and nearly did the same again. However, when she did consent to co-operate she put up a decent performance. That said, she is not one to rely on.
**Greenwood** has been trying longer trips since switching to sand. His handicap mark is slipping, and it will be interesting to see if connections return him to sprinting back on turf.
**Redi(ITY)**, the only three-year-old in the line-up, showed promise but his current handicap mark looks a little high for what he has achieved.
**The Best Yet**, trying his longest trip for some while, seemed to not get home.
**Desert Dance(IRE)** *Official explanation: jockey said gelding hung left throughout*

## 1242 LITTLEWOODS BET DIRECT CONDITIONS STKS 7f (P)

**3:35** (3:36) (C) 4-Y-O+ **£9,604** (£3,643; £1,821; £828) **Stalls** Low

Form — RPR

5565 **1** **Lygeton Lad**[14] 1065 6-8-12 102 (t) MFenton 6 106
(MissGayKelleway) *b.nr fore: b.hind: t.k.h early: disp ld: def advantage wl over 1f out: drvn 2l clr fnl f: hld on wl* **4/1**[2]

00-2 **2** 1 **Hidden Dragon (USA)**[14] 1065 5-9-3 100 DeanMcKeown 1 108
(PABlockley) *b.hind: trckd ldng pair: effrt over 2f out: hanging lft and nt clr run over 1f out: chsd wnr ins fnl f: a hld* **7/1**

040- **3** nk **Vanderlin**[169] 5615 5-9-7 107 MartinDwyer 4 112
(AMBalding) *dwlt: sn pressed ldrs: pushed along 3f out: effrt to dispute 2nd ent fnl f: one pce* **8/1**

1136 **4** 1 1/4 **Grey Pearl**[15] 1056 5-8-7 81 SDrowne 2 94
(MissGayKelleway) *b.off fore: dwlt: sn trckd ldrs: pushed along 3f out: effrt u.p over 1f out: no imp fnl f* **25/1**

1062 **5** 3/4 **Quito (IRE)**[7] 1125 7-8-12 105 (b) ACulhane 3 97
(DWChapman) *hld up in last pair: gng wl enough over 2f out: effrt wl over 1f out: one pce and no ch* **5/1**[3]

-111 **6** shd **Aleutian**[21] 1011 4-9-3 104 JPMurtagh 5 102
(DRLoder) *disp ld to wl over 1f out: fdd fnl f* **7/4**[1]

0-10 **7** 3/4 **Miss George**[9] 1106 6-8-8 85 ow1 DaneO'Neill 8 91
(DKIvory) *b.hind: dwlt: hld up in last: gng wl enough over 2f out: effrt on wd outside over 1f out: one pce and no ch* **16/1**

61-0 **8** 5 **Will He Wish**[7] 1126 8-9-3 92 (b) DHolland 7 87
(SGollings) *chsd ldrs: rdn wl over 2f out: wknd wl over 1f out* **16/1**

1m 24.53s (-1.47) **Going Correction** -0.10s/f (Stan) **8** Ran SP% **112.3**
Speed ratings: **104,102,102,101,100 100,99,93**CSF £30.64 TOTE £5.50: £1.80, £2.60, £2.20; EX 33.70.
**Owner** J McGonagle & B J McGonagle **Bred** Khalifa Abdulla Dasmal **Trained** Newmarket, Suffolk

**FOCUS**
A decent conditions event, but run at only an ordinary gallop and the principals all raced close to the pace, which makes the form potentially unreliable.

**NOTEBOOK**
**Lygeton Lad** appreciated the switch from his usual hold-up tactics and seemed to enjoy himself at the head of affairs. He picked up well when asked and was always in command in the straight.
**Hidden Dragon(USA)** ◆, touched off on his return to action here last month, was in the right place but did not get a clear opening early in the straight. He appeared to be making no impression in the closing stages, but this was another useful performance and, fit and in-form, he will be interesting returned to turf.
**Vanderlin**, who had the highest official rating in the race, ran well on his first outing since October and should pay his way in similar events and Listed races in due course.

**Grey Pearl** had no chance on official ratings and did well to finish where she did. She is exposed as just a useful handicapper, and it is to be hoped the assessor does not overreact to this performance.
**Quito(IRE)** , held up in rear, was probably in the wrong place in a race run steadily early.
**Aleutian** has won at this level but the opposition was tougher on this occasion and his limitations were exposed. He will not find life easy off his current handicap mark.

## 1243 BET DIRECT ON SKY ACTIVE MAIDEN STKS 6f (P)
**4:20** (4:21) (D ) 3-Y-O **£3,760** (£1,157; £578; £289) **Stalls** Low

Form RPR
002- **1** **Bohola Flyer (IRE)**[147] 5947 3-8-9 74 ... RHughes 7 67
(RHannon) *mde virtually all: kicked 2l clr over 1f out: jst hld on* **7/1**[3]
26 **2** *shd* **King Of Diamonds**[3] 1202 3-9-0 ... JPMurtagh 1 72+
(JRBest) *w'like: plld hrd early: hld up in rr: nt clr run on inner 2f out: swtchd rt over 1f out: r.o fnl f: jst failed* **11/2**[2]
44 **3** *2 ½* **Cheeky Chi (IRE)**[10] 1096 3-8-9 ... LDettori 4 60
(PSMcentee) *b.nr fore: pressed wnr to over 1f out: one pce fnl f* **8/1**
- **4** *1 ½* **Andaluza (IRE)** 3-8-9 ... MartinDwyer 9 55
(PDCundell) *settled towards rr: effrt over 2f out: rdn and styd on fr over 1f out: nvr able to chal* **16/1**
4- **5** *1* **Alderney Race (USA)**[162] 5733 3-9-0 ... SDrowne 6 57
(RCharlton) *lw: trckd ldrs: rdn 2f out: sn nt qckn and btn: one pce after* **4/6**[1]
00-0 **6** *1* **Samara Sound**[53] 732 3-9-0 40 ... SWhitworth 2 54?
(AGNewcombe) *t.k.h: trckd ldrs: effrt 2f out: sn outpcd* **20/1**
-006 **7** *¾* **Sussex Style (IRE)**[11] 1083 3-9-0 53 ... DSweeney 5 52
(RMFlower) *trckd ldng gp: n.m.r 2f out: sn outpcd* **50/1**
**8** *½* **Radlett Lady** 3-8-3 ow1 ... MHoward(7) 10 46
(DKIvory) *b.nr fore: hld up in rr: prog on outer over 2f out: c wd bnd sn after: no hdwy over 1f out* **33/1**
000- **9** *4* **Hatch A Plan (IRE)**[162] 5735 3-9-0 ... MTebbutt 3 38
(RMBeckett) *b.hind: s.s: detached last tl 2f out: nvr a factor* **20/1**
050- **10** *1 ¾* **Nebraska City**[220] 4495 3-9-0 69 ... CCatlin 8 33
(BGubby) *sn w ldrs: wknd wl over 2f out* **20/1**
0 **11** *nk* **Adorata (GER)**[31] 956 3-8-2 ... BSwarbrick(7) 11 27
(JJay) *a in rr: struggling fr 1/2-way* **100/1**
**12** *7* **Sapphire Sky** 3-8-6 ... RMiles(3) 12 —
(DKIvory) *w'like: b.off fore: wnt rt s: sn rcvrd to press ldrs: wknd rapidly over 2f out* **50/1**

1m 13.16s (0.24) **Going Correction** -0.10s/f (Stan) **12** Ran SP% **127.0**
Speed ratings: **94,93,90,88,87 85,84,84,78,76 76,66**CSF £45.37 TOTE £7.60: £2.70, £2.60, £1.80; EX 37.50.
**Owner** William Durkan **Bred** Swordlestown Stud **Trained** East Everleigh, Wilts

**FOCUS**
A ordinary-looking maiden run at a slow pace and a modest final time. The proximity of the lowly-rated sixth casts doubts over the form.

**NOTEBOOK**
**Bohola Flyer(IRE)**, runner-up in a maiden at the end of last turf season that has produced three subsequent winners, dictated the pace and then found a little extra to hold off the late surge of the runner-up. She looks to be progressing with racing.
**King Of Diamonds**, who finished behind a stable companion of the winner on his debut, ran much better held up on this occasion than he had when making the running here earlier in the week. He should be able to gain compensation for this narrow defeat before long.
**Cheeky Chi(IRE)**, dropped a furlong, again ran well and now qualifies for a handicap mark.
**Andaluza(IRE)**, making her debut and from a yard in good form, ran as if the experience will bring her on.
**Alderney Race(USA)**, who showed plenty of promise in a Newbury maiden that has produced three subsequent winners, seemed to have every chance but failed to pick up off the home turn. This was a disappointing effort, but it is possible the track did not suit him.
**Hatch A Plan(IRE)** *Official explanation: jockey said he was struck in face by gelding's head when stalls opened causing gelding to be slowly away*

## 1244 BILL REVELL 80TH BIRTHDAY FILLIES' H'CAP 1m (P)
**4:55** (4:55) (F ) (0-55,57) 3-Y-O+ **£2,947** (£842; £421) **Stalls** High

Form RPR
4064 **1** **My Lilli (IRE)**[20] 1019 4-9-2 **49** ... DHolland 2 61
(PMitchell) *pushed up to ld: mde all: kicked 3l clr 3f out: drvn over 1f out: kpt on wl* **4/1**[2]
2121 **2** *2* **Wanna Shout**[10] 1102 6-9-7 **57** ... LisaJones(3) 4 64
(RDickin) *trckd ldrs: effrt to chse wnr over 2f out: shkn up over 1f out: kpt on but nvr able to chal* **7/2**[1]
600- **3** *hd* **Seejay**[137] 6022 4-9-1 **48** ... CCatlin 3 55
(MAAllen) *hld up in rr: prog over 2f out: rdn and styd on fr over 1f out: nrst fin* **40/1**
0135 **4** *1* **Miss Peaches**[20] 1019 6-9-0 **47** ... AMcCarthy 9 52
(GGMargarson) *hld up towards rr: prog on outer 2f out: styd on fr over 1f out: nrst fin* **12/1**
4152 **5** *½* **Titian Lass**[3] 1207 5-8-13 **46** ...(b) RHills 11 49
(CEBrittain) *b.hind: hld up in tch: prog 3f out: chsd ldrs 2f out: one pce after* **4/1**[2]
003- **6** *2 ½* **Kindness**[169] 5611 4-9-5 **52** ... DSweeney 12 50
(ADWPinder) *hld up in rr: effrt 2f out: one pce and n.d* **33/1**
610- **7** *¾* **Summerise**[179] 5440 3-8-4 **52** ow2 ... DeanMcKeown 5 48
(HJCollingridge) *dwlt: sn in midfield: rdn over 2f out: no imp ldrs after* **33/1**
0363 **8** *1 ¾* **Theatre Lady (IRE)**[5] 1166 6-8-13 **46** oh1 ... RHavlin 1 38
(PDEvans) *chsd ldrs: rdn 3f out: wknd over 1f out* **14/1**
-013 **9** *nk* **Marnie**[10] 1102 7-9-4 **51** ... TQuinn 8 42
(JAkehurst) *chsd wnr: rdn fr 5f out: lost 2nd and wknd over 2f out* **8/1**
5004 **10** *nk* **Vizulize**[5] 1165 5-8-13 **46** oh1 ... ACulhane 6 37
(AWCarroll) *trckd ldrs: lost pl over 5f out: in rr 3f out: n.d after* **14/1**
5440 **11** *1 ½* **Taiyo**[36] 910 4-9-0 **47** ... JPMurtagh 10 34
(JWPayne) *chsd ldrs: drvn 3f out: wknd 2f out* **11/1**
006- **12** *12* **Lark In The Park (IRE)**[193] 5136 4-8-9 **49** ... BSwarbrick(7) 7 9
(WMBrisbourne) *lost pl on outer over 5f out: drvn and struggling over 3f out: t.o* **7/1**[3]

1m 38.55s (-0.96) **Going Correction** -0.10s/f (Stan)
**WFA** 3 from 4yo+ 15lb **12** Ran SP% **123.5**
Speed ratings: **100,98,97,96,96 93,93,91,91,90 89,77**CSF £19.01 CT £434.60 TOTE £5.60: £2.40, £1.40, £11.80; EX 23.10 Place 6 £43.61, Place 5 £22.13.
**Owner** M Vickers **Bred** Dr Dean Harron **Trained** Epsom, Surrey

**FOCUS**
A moderate fillies' handicap run nearly 1.4sec slower than the open Listed race over the same trip. Not a race that is likely to have much bearing on the future.

**NOTEBOOK**
**My Lilli(IRE)** reversed recent course running with Marnie despite being no better off at the weights. However, on this occasion she was allowed an uncontested lead and Holland stole a lead running down towards the home turn which she never looked like surrendering. She is fairly exposed and may struggle to follow up off higher marks.
**Wanna Shout** has taken well to this surface and she again performed with credit off a 7lb higher mark. However, whether she can improve enough to win from this rating remains to be seen.
**Seejay** had shown little in three outings at the end of last season, but put up an improved effort dropped in trip on this handicap debut. She may have enough improvement in her to find a little handicap.
**Miss Peaches** ran close to recent course form with the winner, and would not have been helped by the steady early pace.
**Titian Lass** has been running well on this track of late, and did so again before tiring in the closing stages. She only needs to drop a pound to qualify for banded stakes once again.
T/Plt: £54.20 to a £1 stake. Pool: £34,040.20. 457.70 winning tickets. T/Qpdt: £16.00 to a £1 stake. Pool: £1,955.90. 90.20 winning tickets. JN

# 1170 NEWCASTLE (L-H)
### Saturday, April 3

**OFFICIAL GOING: Heavy (soft in places)**
Wind: fairly strong, half across Weather: cloudy

## 1245 CANTORSPORT.CO.UK H'CAP 1m 4f 93y
**1:40** (1:40) (E ) (0-75,75) 3-Y-O+ **£5,128** (£1,578; £789; £394**Stalls** Far side

Form RPR
00-0 **1** **Archie Babe (IRE)**[9] 1103 8-9-1 **61** ... KDarley 9 75
(JJQuinn) *cl up gng wl: led 3f out: pushed out over 1f out* **5/1**[3]
5310 **2** *6* **Bramantino (IRE)**[30] 962 4-8-12 **59** ...(b) PHanagan 14 65
(RAFahey) *in tch: hdwy over 4f out: chsd wnr over 1f out: kpt on: no imp* **12/1**
1225 **3** *5* **Nakwa (IRE)**[54] 724 6-8-7 **56** ... DAllan(3) 10 55
(EJAlston) *keen: cl up: led over 4f to 3f out: outpcd over 1f out* **4/1**[2]
354/ **4** *8* **Lucky Judge**[737] 688 7-9-0 **60** ... RWinston 11 47
(GASwinbank) *hld up: effrt over 4f out: no imp fr 2f out* **20/1**
0255 **5** *13* **Noul (USA)**[9] 1109 5-8-13 **59** ...(p) NCallan 3 28
(KARyan) *hld up: effrt u.p over 3f out: nvr rchd ldrs* **10/1**
320- **6** *1 ½* **Scurra**[131] 6057 5-8-7 **53** ... RFfrench 1 20
(ACWhillans) *cl up tl lost pl 1/2-way: n.d after* **33/1**
-354 **7** *2* **Toni Alcala**[5] 1173 5-9-0 **63** ... LFletcher(3) 4 27
(RFFisher) *hld up: rdn over 4f out: nvr on terms* **10/1**
600- **8** *nk* **Regal Vintage (USA)**[21] 5227 4-9-5 **69** ...(v) THamilton(3) 7 33
(CGrant) *bhd and early reminders: nvr on terms* **66/1**
15-4 **9** *7* **Easibet Dot Net**[36] 908 4-9-0 **61** ...(p) DMcGaffin 2 15
(ISemple) *in tch: rdn 1/2-way: wknd over 3f out* **14/1**
00-0 **10** *7* **La Muette (IRE)**[24] 666 4-9-7 **75** ... DFentiman(7) 8 19
(MAppleby) *bhd and pushed along: sme hdwy 1/2-way: wknd over 4f out* **33/1**
550- **11** *3* **Weaver Of Dreams (IRE)**[266] 3210 4-8-1 **48** ... DaleGibson 12 —
(GASwinbank) *hld up wd: hdwy 1/2-way: wknd over 4f out* **25/1**
353- **12** *7* **Staff Nurse (IRE)**[165] 5696 4-7-12 **45** ... KimTinkler 6 —
(DonEnricoIncisa) *hld up: rdn and wknd over 4f out* **20/1**
00-0 **13** *4* **Dark Cut (IRE)**[49] 765 4-8-3 **50** ... RLappin 13 —
(HAlexander) *hld up: hdwy 1/2-way: wknd over 4f out* **40/1**
-60U **14** *6* **Archirondel**[9] 1103 6-8-6 **52** ... JFanning 15 —
(MDHammond) *keen: cl up: led 1/2-way to over 4f out: sn struggling* **33/1**
231- **P** **Alnaja (USA)**[189] 5220 5-9-10 **70** ... MHills 5 —
(WJHaggas) *led to 1/2-way: sn struggling: t.o whn p.u and dismntd ins fnl f* **3/1**[1]

2m 58.6s (15.40) **Going Correction** +1.375s/f (Soft)
**WFA** 4 from 5yo+ 1lb **15** Ran SP% **120.3**
Speed ratings: **103,99,95,90,81 80,79,79,74,69 67,63,60,56,**—CSF £56.41 CT £267.70 TOTE £6.10: £1.90, £8.10, £2.10; EX 64.60.
**Owner** Bowett Lamb & Kelly **Bred** Golden Vale Stud **Trained** Settrington, N Yorks

**FOCUS**
An ordinary handicap run in gruelling conditions and not surprisingly the pace was on the steady side. With the favourite disappointing this took less winning than had previously looked likely.

**NOTEBOOK**
**Archie Babe(IRE)**, not seen to best effect on from a wide draw on ground quicker than ideal at Doncaster last time, relished these conditions and ran right up to his best. He is not the most consistent, though and would be no certainty to follow up from a higher mark on less testing ground next time.
**Bramantino(IRE)** likes a good test and ran his race (with the blinkers back on) back on turf, proving that he handles very testing conditions. He looks capable of winning a run of the mill handicap on grass.
**Nakwa(IRE)** goes well at this course and, although proved he could handle the conditions with just a fair effort, left the impression that he would be more at home on less-testing ground.
**Lucky Judge**, a Flat and hurdles winner on a sound surface, showed he retains ability on this first start for just over two years, but would almost certainly prefer less testing conditions. He is in good hands and is likely to be placed to best advantage.
**Noul(USA)**, with cheekpieces replacing blinkers, could not reproduce his fair Doncaster effort over this trip in this very testing ground, and his stamina over this far remains an issue.
**Scurra** has form in testing ground but is an inconsistent maiden who was a long way below his very best for this reappearance run.
**Toni Alcala**, who had shaped well in a slowly-run race over two miles at this course earlier in the week, failed by a long chalk to reproduce that effort over this shorter trip on this heavy ground. He is not one to place much faith in.
**Alnaja(USA)**, progressive on soft ground last year, looked to have plenty in his favour for this reappearance run but dropped out as though something was amiss and it subsequently emerged he had swallowed his tongue. He will presumbably be tried in a tongue-tie next time and is worth another chance. *Official explanation: jockey said gelding swallowed its tongue*

## 1246 BETFRED SPRINT SERIES H'CAP (QUALIFIER) 7f
**2:10** (2:11) (C ) (0-95,94) 3-Y-O+ **£13,728** (£4,224; £2,112; £1,056) **Stalls** High

Form RPR
60-0 **1** **Tidy (IRE)**[43] 836 4-8-8 **74** ... DarrenWilliams 3 85
(MDHammond) *prom: led over 2f out: r.o strly: eased cl home* **66/1**
03-1 **2** *1* **Zilch**[7] 1132 6-9-3 **83** ... SSanders 5 92
(MLWBell) *a cl up: led 1/2-way to over 2f out: styd upsides: kpt on: hld last 75yds* **9/4**[1]
1263 **3** *2 ½* **Moayed**[14] 1065 5-9-0 **80** ...(bt) EAhern 10 83
(NPLittmoden) *hld up: smooth hdwy to chse ldrs over 2f out: one pce over 1f out* **8/1**
2-03 **4** *2 ½* **Digital**[7] 1132 7-9-9 **92** ... SHitchcott(3) 14 89
(MRChannon) *prom: hdwy to chal 1/2-way: hung lft fr 2f out: sn one pce* **13/2**[3]

-000 **5** 1/2 **Chappel Cresent (IRE)**[9] 1106 4-9-0 **87** LTreadwell(7) 13 82
(DNicholls) *trckd ldrs tl rdn and outpcd fr 2f out* **20/1**

10-0 **6** *nk* **Namroud (USA)**[9] 1106 5-9-8 **88** PHanagan 8 83
(RAFahey) *hld up: hdwy and swtchd over 1f out: nvr able to chal* **33/1**

30-0 **7** 3/4 **Tough Love**[7] 1125 5-9-11 **91** KDalgleish 6 84
(TDEasterby) *hld up: hdwy over 1f out: no imp* **16/1**

161- **8** 1 1/4 **Flowerdrum (USA)**[170] 5597 4-8-11 **77** MHills 11 67
(WJHaggas) *hld up: effrt 1/2-way: no imp fr 2f out* **11/4**[2]

05-0 **9** 1/2 **Go Tech**[8] 1114 4-9-0 **83** DAllan(3) 9 72
(TDEasterby) *keen early in rr: rdn 1/2-way: n.d* **25/1**

00-0 **10** 5 **Fair Shake (IRE)**[5] 1175 4-8-1 **67** DaleGibson 7 44
(DEddy) *chsd ldrs tl wknd 2f out* **16/1**

056- **11** 7 **Colemanstown**[161] 5747 4-8-3 **74** TEaves(5) 15 34
(BEllison) *hld up: rdn over 2f out: sn btn* **20/1**

041- **12** 24 **Fantasy Believer**[185] 5299 6-10-0 **94** KDarley 12 —
(JJQuinn) *keen: cl up tl wknd over 2f out* **12/1**

/0-5 **13** 15 **Silver Seeker (USA)**[21] 1011 4-9-9 **89** (p) RWinston 1 —
(ISemple) *led to 1/2-way: sn lost pl* **33/1**

1m 34.48s (6.44) **Going Correction** +1.10s/f (Soft) **13** Ran SP% **122.1**
Speed ratings: **107,105,103,100,99 99,98,96,96,90 82,55,38**CSF £205.00 CT £1456.17 TOTE £74.70: £13.90, £1.20, £3.80; EX 179.90.
**Owner** P Davies and L Crowther **Bred** Mick McGinn And James Waldron **Trained** Middleham, N Yorks

**FOCUS**
A bunch of mainly exposed handicappers for this valuable prize and the whole field tacked centre to far side. The gallop was on the steady side and once again it paid to race up with the pace. With not many able to show their form in the conditions the form looks dubious.

**NOTEBOOK**
**Tidy(IRE)**, back on turf and back on testing ground, turned in a career-best effort to win with a bit more in hand than the official mark suggests. Although he handles a sound surface, he seems to relish testing conditions and he came to hand early last year. He should continue to go well at up to this trip.
**Zilch** fully confirmed the form of his Kempton win from this 7lb higher mark and goes well on a soft surface. He will be up in the weights again but, given the way he travelled for much of the way, may be capable of winning again.
**Moayed** was anything but disgraced, especially as he fared the best of those coming from off the pace but once again did not look the most enthusiastic off the bridle and would not be one to be lumping on at short odds.
**Digital**, a consistent sort, could not reverse recent placings with Zilch, despite having a fair pull in the weights. Although not disgraced he did not look entirely happy in this ground and is probably more effective on a sound surface.
**Chappel Cresent(IRE)** again shaped as though retaining ability and, although he has not won for some time, will be one to keep an eye on at up to this trip when his stable are in better form.
**Namroud(USA)** fared a little better on this second start for Richard Fahey and back over this more suitable trip. Although he seemed to handle the ground he may well be more effective back on a sound surface and he is not one to write off yet.
**Tough Love** showed more this time than at Doncaster on his reappearance and proved himself in the ground but, although he will be suited by the return to a mile, he may well have to come down the weights a bit more before regaining the winning thread.
**Flowerdrum(USA)**, a lightly raced sort who is open to further improvement, goes well fresh but was almost certainly found out by these very testing conditions on this first start since last October. She is not one to write off yet, though.

## 1247 CANTORODDS.CO.UK H'CAP — 1m 3y(S)
2:40 (2:42) (D) (0-80,80) 3-Y-O+ — **£8,303** (£2,555; £1,277; £638) **Stalls** High

Form — RPR

36-0 **1** **Trousers**[8] 1118 5-8-3 **55** GDuffield 4 64
(AndrewReid) *mde all far side: rdn and r.o strly fnl f* **15/2**[2]

000- **2** 3 **Top Dirham**[158] 5821 6-9-4 **70** DaleGibson 17 73
(MWEasterby) *trckd stands side ldr: led that gp over 1f out: kpt on: nt rch far side* **20/1**

12-0 **3** *nk* **Reap**[56] 705 6-9-1 **67** PRobinson 16 69
(JPearce) *led stands side to over 1f out: rallied: kpt on fnl f* **7/1**[1]

-563 **4** 1 1/2 **Goodbye Mr Bond**[36] 910 4-7-13 **51** JMackay 5 50
(EJAlston) *cl up far side: ev ch over 2f out: one pce fnl f* **8/1**[3]

200- **5** 1/2 **Commitment Lecture**[173] 5534 4-7-13 **51** (t) RFfrench 13 49
(MDods) *hld up far side: hdwy over 1f out: nvr rchd ldrs* **33/1**

542- **6** 6 **Megan's Magic**[155] 5856 4-8-8 **60** DRMcCabe 11 46
(WStorey) *bhd far side tl hdwy over 1f out: n.d* **16/1**

305- **7** 1 1/4 **Torrid Kentavr (USA)**[155] 4678 7-8-4 **61** ow1 TEaves(5) 6 45
(BEllison) *hld up: rdn over 2f out: n.d* **10/1**

0-00 **8** *hd* **Hov**[53] 735 4-9-9 **75** EAhern 12 59
(JJQuinn) *prom far side tl rdn and outpcd fr 2f out* **16/1**

366- **9** 11 **Hula Ballew**[185] 5300 4-8-9 **61** PHanagan 8 23
(MDods) *hld up far side: rdn 3f out: nvr on terms* **16/1**

024- **10** 1 1/4 **Apache Point (IRE)**[149] 5937 7-8-8 **60** KimTinkler 1 19
(NTinkler) *in tch far side to over 2f out: sn btn* **9/1**

003 **11** 7 **Harry Potter (GER)**[15] 1055 5-9-4 **70** (v) DarrenWilliams 2 15
(KRBurke) *chsd far side ldrs tl hung lft and wknd 2f out* **16/1**

00-3 **12** 4 **Creskeld (IRE)**[21] 1009 5-9-6 **72** FLynch 19 9
(BSmart) *chsd stands side ldrs: outpcd over 3f out: sn btn* **7/1**[1]

6-50 **13** 8 **Shifty**[39] 874 5-8-1 **53** ow1 (b) ANicholls 7 —
(DNicholls) *a bhd far side* **25/1**

000- **14** 1 1/4 **Celtic Romance**[278] 2851 5-8-11 **63** JCarroll 14 —
(MrsMReveley) *a bhd far side* **33/1**

15-6 **15** *dist* **Night Wolf (IRE)**[8] 1118 4-9-0 **69** SHitchcott(3) 10 —
(MRChannon) *cl up far side tl lost pl qckly over 3f out: t.o* **8/1**[3]

006- **U** **Tagula Blue (IRE)**[158] 5814 4-10-0 **80** (t) SSanders 9 —
(JAGlover) *dwlt: swvd bdly lft and uns rdr s* **14/1**

1m 50.18s (8.28) **Going Correction** +1.10s/f (Soft) **16** Ran SP% **122.8**
Speed ratings: **102,99,98,97,96 90,89,89,78,77 70,66,58,56,—** —CSF £157.00 CT £1147.01 TOTE £9.40: £2.00, £8.90, £1.30, £2.60; EX 400.90.
**Owner** A S Reid **Bred** A S Reid **Trained** Mill Hill, London NW7

**FOCUS**
Another run-of-the-mill handicap in which the three that raced on the stands side seemed at no disadvantage compared with the main group on the far side. The gallop was sensible again and it paid to race up with the pace. The winner looks to have transferred his All-Weather form to turf.

**NOTEBOOK**
**Trousers** had the run of the race on the far side, but turned in a much-improved effort on this first run on very testing ground and will be still after reassessment in similar company on soft ground.
**Top Dirham**, whose form tailed off at the end of last year, shaped really well on this reappearance run in these testing conditions to emerge best of the trio that raced on the stands' side and will be of interest in near-to-hand engagements. He seems to act on any ground.
**Reap** had the run of the race on the stands side group and returned to form, thus proving his effectiveness in ground as testing as this. He is capable of winning again when allowed his own way in front in ordinary company.
**Goodbye Mr Bond**'s form on sand has a patchy look to it but, although he had the run of the race on this occasion, ran creditably back on grass and he does seem more effective with cut in the ground.
**Commitment Lecture**, a course and distance winner on easy ground in May last year, was tongue-tied for the first time and fared the best of those that attempted to come from off the pace. He is one to keep an eye on in similar company.
**Megan's Magic**, a fairly consistent sort, ran a typical race and was not disgraced on this reappearance. She is almost certainly better on a sound surface but, given her style of racing, does need things to fall just right.
**Apache Point(IRE)** had conditions to suit for this reappearance and has a history of going well fresh, but was a long way below his best on this first starts since last November.
**Creskeld(IRE)** *Official explanation: jockey said gelding was unsuited by the heavy ground*

## 1248 E.B.F./CANTORINDEX.CO.UK NOVICE STKS — 5f
3:15 (3:16) (D) 2-Y-O — **£5,021** (£1,545; £772; £386) **Stalls** High

Form — RPR

4 **1** **Mitchelland**[9] 1105 2-8-7 JFanning 3 74
(JamesMoffatt) *keen: trckd ldr: led over 1f out: pushed clr: readily* **9/4**[2]

2 **2** 5 **Bibury Flyer**[7] 1130 2-8-4 SHitchcott(3) 4 59
(MRChannon) *led to over 1f out: one pce* **4/6**[1]

**3** 3 1/2 **Procrastinate (IRE)** 2-8-9 LFletcher(3) 5 54
(RFFisher) *trckd ldrs: rdn 1/2-way: outpcd over 1f out* **14/1**

**4** 3 1/2 **Mount Ephram (IRE)** 2-8-12 SRighton 1 43
(RFFisher) *wnt lft s: sn prom: rdn and wknd 1/2-way* **12/1**[3]

67.52 secs (5.99) **Going Correction** +1.10s/f (Soft) **4** Ran SP% **105.1**
Speed ratings: **96,88,82,76**CSF £3.95 TOTE £3.70; EX 5.90.
**Owner** R R Whitton **Bred** P G Airey And R R Whitton **Trained** Cartmel, Cumbria

**FOCUS**
An uncompetitive event, with Mitchelland fully confirming debut promise by easily beating her only serious rival. She should stay further and may be able to win again before the better juveniles start to appear.

**NOTEBOOK**
**Mitchelland** fully confirmed debut promise in this much softer ground and, although this was a most uncompetitive race, she may be able to win again before the better juveniles start to appear. She remains likely to stay five furlongs.
**Bibury Flyer** had the run of the race but failed to build on her debut effort and was readily left behind as the winner asserted. However, she is in good hands and may well be capable of better on less testing ground. *Official explanation: trainer said filly was unsuited by the heavy ground*
**Procrastinate(IRE)** has several winners in his pedigree and, although showing a modicum of ability on this racecourse debut, will have to improve a fair bit on this effort if he is to win in similar company.
**Mount Ephram(IRE)**, a half-brother to dual sprint winner Happy Camper, ran green and floundered in the conditions on this racecourse debut.

## 1249 CANTORSPORT.CO.UK MAIDEN STKS — 1m 4f 93y
4:05 (4:13) (D) 3-Y-O+ — **£3,740** (£1,151; £575; £287) **Stalls** Far side

Form — RPR

3/2- **1** **October Mist (IRE)**[28] 5914 10-9-13 SSanders 5 74
(MrsMReveley) *cl up: led 4f out: styd on strly* **11/1**

4- **2** 2 1/2 **Templet (USA)**[161] 5755 4-9-12 RWinston 6 70
(ISemple) *in tch: drvn over 4f out: rallied to chse wnr 2f out: kpt on: no ex wl ins last* **8/1**

20- **3** 9 **Nofa's Magic (IRE)**[323] 1629 4-9-7 KDarley 3 52
(JLDunlop) *chsd ldrs: effrt 3f out: outpcd fr 2f out* **5/4**[1]

**4** 4 **Southern Star (GER)**[24] 4-9-12 NCallan 8 52
(RCGuest) *hld up: hdwy over 5f out: outpcd fr 3f out* **20/1**

030- **5** 2 1/2 **Transit**[18] 3039 5-9-8 65 (p) TEaves(5) 1 48
(BEllison) *hld up: rdn over 3f out: nvr on terms* **16/1**

6 **6** 8 **Celtic Vision (IRE)**[3] 1212 8-9-13 (t) SRighton 7 37
(MAppleby) *led to 4f out: wknd 3f out* **33/1**

1264 **7** *dist* **Fiddlers Ford (IRE)**[15] 1050 3-8-6 72 EAhern 2 —
(JNoseda) *hld up in tch: rdn along 4f out: sn btn* **11/2**[3]

022- **8** 3/4 **Hathlen (IRE)**[150] 5925 3-8-3 77 SHitchcott(3) 4 —
(MRChannon) *chsd ldrs: struggling 1/2-way: sn btn* **4/1**[2]

3m 5.00s (21.80) **Going Correction** +1.75s/f (Heav)
**WFA** 3 from 4yo 21lb 4 from 5yo+ 1lb **8** Ran SP% **112.9**
Speed ratings: **97,95,89,86,85 79,—,—**CSF £91.86 TOTE £10.90: £1.50, £1.80, £1.10; EX 73.60.
**Owner** Mrs E A Murray **Bred** Michael Maye **Trained** Lingdale, N Yorks

**FOCUS**
With the three market leaders all disappointing this race took less winning than seemed likely beforehand. However as a result October Mist should not be too harshly treated for handicaps.

**NOTEBOOK**
**October Mist(IRE)** back on the Flat, had the run of the race but revelled in the conditions and turned in an improved effort in this sphere. He is a relentless galloper when on song and will be interesting granted similar conditions in run-of-the-mill handicaps over further in the near future.
**Templet(USA)**, who shaped with promise on his sole start last year for John Gosden, ran creditably on this first outing for his new and capable trainer and is sure to pick up an ordinary race over middle distances in due course.
**Nofa's Magic(IRE)** shaped as though retaining a fair bit of ability on this first start since May of last year but found a combination of this trip in this ground too much this time. It will be an ordinary race she wins, though.
**Southern Star(GER)**, having his first run on the Flat for his current stable, again hinted at ability and will be of more interest in modest handicap company on less testing ground.
**Transit** is a keen sort who will continue to look vulnerable in this grade.
**Celtic Vision(IRE)** had the run of the race but continues out of sorts.
**Fiddlers Ford(IRE)**, having his first start on heavy ground, floundered in the conditions and, although he may not be straightforward, is best not judged too harshly on this poor effort. *Official explanation: trainer said gelding was unsuited by the heavy ground*
**Hathlen(IRE)**, a most consistent sort last time, was the first beaten on this first run on heavy ground and, although conditions were almost certainly to blame, he may not be easy to place from his current mark of 77. *Official explanation: trainer said colt was unsuited by the heavy ground*

## 1250 CANTORODDS.CO.UK MAIDEN FILLIES' STKS — 1m 3y(S)
4:40 (4:40) (D) 3-Y-O+ — **£3,838** (£1,181; £590; £295) **Stalls** High

Form — RPR

**1** **Glen Innes (IRE)** 3-8-8 NPollard 8 91
(DRLoder) *keen early: in tch: smooth hdwy to ld over 1f out: sn clr* **9/4**[2]

**2** 11 **Lyford Lass** 3-8-8 PHanagan 3 69
(ISemple) *keen: cl up: outpcd over 2f out: kpt on fnl f: no ch w wnr* **10/1**

430- **3** 1 1/4 **Shardda**[187] 5275 4-9-9 65 JFanning 9 66
(FWatson) *prom: outpcd over 2f out: no imp fnl f* **20/1**

43-4 **4** *hd* **Miss Adelaide (IRE)**[14] 1059 3-8-8 80 MHills 7 66
(BWHills) *led to over 1f out: edgd lft and sn outpcd* **11/8**[1]

00- **5** 6 **Charmatic (IRE)**[152] 5905 3-8-8 SSanders 1 54
(JAGlover) *hld up wd: effrt over 2f out: sn btn* **14/1**

00- **6** *8* **Saratoga Splendour (USA)**[152] 5911 3-8-1 ......... LeanneKershaw(7) 5 38
(JeddO'Keeffe) *keen: in tch to 3f out: sn btn* **50/1**
00- **7** *5* **Barton Flower**[199] 4989 3-8-3 ......... PMulrennan(5) 2 28
(MWEasterby) *prom to 3f out: sn wknd* **25/1**
04- **8** *2* **Baboushka (IRE)**[152] 5911 3-8-8 ......... RWinston 6 24
(MissJACamacho) *cl up tl wknd over 2f out* **13/2**[3]

1m 55.98s (14.08) **Going Correction** +1.625s/f (Heav)
**WFA** 3 from 4yo 15lb **8** Ran SP% **112.5**
Speed ratings: **94,83,81,81,75 67,62,60**CSF £23.44 TOTE £3.40: £1.30, £3.10, £4.80; EX 27.50 Place 6 £163.15, Place 5 £73.48.
**Owner** Sheikh Mohammed **Bred** Darley **Trained** Newmarket, Suffolk

**FOCUS**
With Miss Adelaide again performing below expectations this took less winning than seemed likely but nevertheless a highly pleasing debut effort from the well-bred Glen Innes.

**NOTEBOOK**
**Glen Innes(IRE)**, a well-related sort, is an unfurnished type but showed plenty of ability to spreadeagle a modest field on this racecourse debut. Although this was not much of a race she is in very good hands and is sure to be placed to advantage.
**Lyford Lass**, a half-sister to mile and mile and a quarter winner Lennel, attracted support and shaped creditably on this racecourse debut. She is in good hands and may well be capable of better.
**Shardda** was not disgraced on this reappearance run, but is likely to continue to look vulnerable in anything but the worst maiden races and should be seen to better effect in modest handicaps in due course.
**Miss Adelaide(IRE)** had the run of the race but was a big disappointment and, although the very testing conditions may well be to blame, she will not be easy to place successfully given her current rating of 80.
**Charmatic(IRE)** from a stable that has struggled to find its feet this year, was well beaten on this reappearance run and modest handicaps will be more her level.
**Baboushka(IRE)** travelled strongly for a long way until tiring badly in the conditions. She is now qualified for a handicap mark and may do better in due course.
T/Plt: £414.40 to a £1 stake. Pool: £35,231.75. 62.05 winning tickets T/Qpdt: £246.10 to a £1 stake. Pool: £1,696.40. 5.10 winning tickets RY

1251 - 1253a (Foreign Racing) - See Raceform Interactive

## 1067 CURRAGH (R-H)
Sunday, April 4

**OFFICIAL GOING: Straight course - soft; round course - yielding to soft**

### 1254a CASTLEMARTIN/LA LOUVIERE STUDS GLADNESS STKS (GROUP 3) 7f
**3:45** (3:50) 4-Y-0+ **£32,091** (£9,366; £4,436; £1,478)

RPR
**1** **Monsieur Bond (IRE)**[8] 1126 4-9-0 ......... FLynch 10 119
(BSmart) *a cl up: 2nd travelling wl 1/2-way: led 2f out: sn rdn clr: easily* **3/1**[1]
**2** *7* **Steenberg (IRE)**[148] 5953 5-9-0 ......... PRobinson 8 103
(MHTompkins) *hld up in tch: nt clr run 2f out: kpt on fr over 1f out* **8/1**
**3** *3/4* **Rockets 'n Rollers (IRE)**[10] 1107 4-9-0 ......... DaneO'Neill 6 101
(RHannon) *chsd ldrs: 3rd 2f out: kpt on u.p* **12/1**
**4** *shd* **Orientor**[8] 1126 6-9-3 ......... JPMurtagh 3 104
(JSGoldie) *hld up: prog 2f out: 2nd over 1f out: kpt on same pce* **5/1**[3]
**5** *3/4* **Latino Magic (IRE)**[160] 5806 4-9-0 105 ......... RMBurke 2 99
(RJOsborne, Ire) *s.i.s and towards rr: rdn 3f out: kpt on wl* **10/1**
**6** *5* **Twentytwoandchange (IRE)**[14] 1071 5-9-0 97 ......... JPSpencer 9 88
(APO'Brien, Ire) *in tch to 2 1/2f out: sn wknd* **12/1**
**7** *shd* **Abunawwas (IRE)**[238] 4027 4-9-3 109 ......... DPMcDonogh 5 90
(KevinPrendergast, Ire) *nvr a factor: kpt on one pce fr 2f out* **9/2**[2]
**8** *2 1/2* **Dossier**[14] 1070 4-8-11 103 ......... (t) CatherineGannon 4 79
(JohnMOxx, Ire) *led: rdn over 3f out: hdd & wknd 2f out* **14/1**
**9** *nk* **Sea Dart (USA)**[183] 5385 4-9-6 107 ......... MJKinane 1 87
(JohnMOxx, Ire) *cl up on stands side: rdn and wknd over 2f out* **10/1**
**10** *3* **One More Round (USA)**[29] 977 6-9-0 109 ......... (b) PJSmullen 11 74
(DKWeld, Ire) *hld up: effrt over 2f out: sn wknd* **8/1**
**11** *1 1/2* **Avorado (IRE)**[148] 5958 6-9-3 110 ......... KJManning 7 74
(JSBolger, Ire) *a bhd* **9/1**
**12** *shd* **Tender Cove (IRE)**[14] 1071 6-9-0 87 ......... TPO'Shea 13 70
(JohnRafferty, Ire) *chsd ldrs on outer: rdn bef 1/2-way: sn wknd* **10/1**
**13** *9* **Desert Fantasy (IRE)**[225] 4397 5-9-0 107 ......... (bt) FMBerry 12 50
(CRoche, Ire) *bhd and trailing fr 3f out* **13/2**

1m 28.5s **Going Correction** +0.45s/f (Yiel) **13** Ran SP% **147.6**
Speed ratings: **116,108,107,107,106 100,100,97,97,93 92,91,81**CSF £35.56 TOTE £4.50: £2.80, £3.50, £3.70; DF 55.80.
**Owner** R C Bond **Bred** T Burns **Trained** Hambleton, N Yorks

**NOTEBOOK**
**Monsieur Bond(IRE)** ripped this field apart over the last furlong. He travelled so well over a quarter mile down that his jockey had no option but to go on. The ground and trip represented no problem and he won with any amount in hand.
**Steenberg(IRE)** encountered traffic problems two furlongs out but ran on with some purpose although never in a position to challenge the winner. This wouldn't have been his ideal ground.
**Rockets 'n Rollers(IRE)** stepped up on his Doncaster effort but was struggling in third place once the winner went on.
**Orientor** improved to chase the winner over a furlong out but could never get in any sort of a blow.
**Latino Magic(IRE)** was a much improved handicapper last season and looked as though he might come on from this, especially over a longer trip.
**Dossier** made the running. She will be interesting over further when she comes to hand.

### 1256a OAK LODGE & HAMFORD SIRES LOUGHBROWN STKS (LISTED RACE) 7f
**4:45** (4:46) 3-Y-0 **£22,922** (£6,725; £3,204; £1,091)

RPR
**1** **Newton (IRE)**[160] 5802 3-9-0 103 ......... JPSpencer 7 101
(APO'Brien, Ire) *settled 5th: impr into 3rd and rdn 2f out* **5/2**[2]
**2** *1/2* **Dabiroun (IRE)**[14] 1074 3-9-0 ......... MJKinane 5 100
(JohnMOxx, Ire) *led: rdn and kpt on wl fr 2f out: hdd cl home* **7/2**[3]
**3** *3/4* **Amarula Ridge (IRE)**[162] 5758 3-9-0 ......... DPMcDonogh 2 98
(KevinPrendergast, Ire) *prom: 2nd 1/2-way: chal 2f out: no imp fnl f: kpt on* **7/1**
**4** *4* **Wathab (IRE)**[203] 4914 3-9-0 115 ......... PJSmullen 4 88
(DKWeld, Ire) *hld up: 6th 3f out: rdn and no imp fr 2f out* **7/4**[1]
**5** *2 1/2* **Miss Childrey (IRE)**[206] 4840 3-8-11 100 ......... JAHeffernan 1 79
(FrancisEnnis, Ire) *chsd ldrs in 5th: prog 3f out: no ex fr 2f out* **10/1**
**6** *4 1/2* **Jemmy's Brother (IRE)**[14] 1073 3-9-0 96 ......... PCosgrave 3 —
(GMLyons, Ire) *prom: 3rd 1/2-way: wknd 2f out* **14/1**
**7** *3* **Have A Heart (IRE)**[14] 1069 3-8-11 ......... KJManning 6 —
(JSBolger, Ire) *a bhd: trailing fr over 2f out* **20/1**

1m 31.0s **Going Correction** +0.45s/f (Yiel) **7** Ran SP% **120.2**
Speed ratings: **102,101,100,96,93 88,84**CSF £12.66 TOTE £4.30: £2.10, £2.40; DF 19.50.
**Owner** Mrs John Magnier **Bred** Pacelco S A & Samac **Trained** Ballydoyle, Co Tipperary

**NOTEBOOK**
**Newton(IRE)** appeared amenable to hold-up tactics and certainly found plenty under pressure when asked to quicken inside the last. He was always going to get up and should improve a deal on this.
**Dabiroun(IRE)**, impressive when taking his maiden here two weeks previous, tried to make all. He didn't flinch under pressure but didn't have as hard a race as the winner.
**Amarula Ridge(IRE)** won a backend maiden here last season and has obviously trained on There is plenty of scope for further improvement.
**Wathab(IRE)** was disturbingly easy in the market Held up, he made absolutely no impression over the last furlong and a half. The ground mightn't have suited but this was a disappointing run from one which had got to within a length of One Cool Cat in a Group 1 last September when trained by Kevin Prendergast.

1255 - 1258a (Foreign Racing) - See Raceform Interactive

## BREMEN
Sunday, April 4

**OFFICIAL GOING: Good**

### 1259a GROSSER PREIS DER BREMER WIRTSCHAFT (GROUP 3) 1m 2f 110y
**3:35** (3:52) 4-Y-0+ **£22,535** (£9,155; £4,577; £2,465)

RPR
**1** **Olaso (GER)**[154] 5903 5-9-0 ......... OUrbina 16 111
(PVovcenko, Germany) *held up in rear, 12th straight, headway between horses from over 2 1/2f out, went 3rd inside final f, ran on strongly to le*
**2** *1/2* **Flambo (GER)**[184] 5352 4-9-0 ......... MO'Reilly 15 110
(PSchiergen, Germany) *always prominent, 3rd straight, went 2nd 3f out, led 1 1/2f out, headed and no extra last 20 yards*
**3** *1 1/2* **Winning Dash (GER)**[154] 5901 4-8-12 ......... AHelfenbein 9 105
(WKujath, Germany) *mid division early, headway to go 4th well over 3f out, stayed on at one pace under pressure from over 2f out* **3**
**4** *hd* **Soldier Hollow**[322] 1700 4-9-0 ......... FilipMinarik 6 107
(PSchiergen, Germany) *midfield, 8th straightm taken to wide outside over 2f out, stayed on* **2**
**5** *1 1/2* **Fleurie Domaine**[145] 5974 5-8-7 ......... J-PCarvalho 13 97
(MarioHofer, Germany) *9th early, 5th straight, kept on at one pace final 2 1/2f*
**6** *1 1/2* **King Of Boxmeer (GER)**[189] 5263 5-8-9 ......... IFerguson 12 97
(WBaltromei, Germany) *held up in rear, 14th straight, kept on steadily from over 2f out*
**7** *nk* **Russian Samba (IRE)**[586] 5-8-5 ......... DSmith 1 92
(LordJFitzgerald, Germany) *prominent early, 7th straight, one pace final 3f*
**8** *nk* **Levirat (GER)**[252] 3631 5-8-12 ......... VPanov 8 99
(MarioHofer, Germany) *set strong pace and soon 3 lengths clear, headed 1 1/2f out, one pace*
**9** *nk* **Liquido (GER)**[134] 6053 5-8-9 ......... SChin 2 95
(HSteinmetz, Germany) *raced in 8th, 11th straight, never a factor*
**10** *5* **Near Honor (GER)**[219] 4566 6-8-9 ......... ABest 14 86
(TimGibson, Germany) *raced in 2nd, ridden and beaten 3f out*
**11** *1/2* **Well Made (GER)**[168] 5666 7-8-12 ......... WMongil 3 89
(HBlume, Germany) *held up in rear, last straight, some headway on inside over 2f out, one pace final f* **1**
**12** *1 3/4* **Orfisio**[336] 1389 5-8-9 ......... SWKelly 4 83
(AndreasLowe, Germany) *held up, 13th straight, never a factor*
**13** *3/4* **Syracruz (GER)**[140] 4-8-9 ......... SJadwiszczak 11 81
(MTrinker, Germany) *towards rear, 10th straight, never a factor*
**14** *13* **Rajpute (GER)**[154] 5901 4-8-12 ......... ASuborics 7 61
(ASchutz, Germany) *raced in 5th, 6th straight, soon weakened*
**15** *17* **Palmridge (GER)**[154] 5901 4-8-12 ......... LHammer-Hansen 10 32
(DKRichardson, Germany) *raced in 10th, 9th straight, soon weakened, tailed off final f*

2m 17.86s **15** Ran SP% **130.4**
Speed ratings: .
**Owner** Stall Silbersee **Bred** M Beining **Trained** Germany

1260 - (Foreign Racing) - See Raceform Interactive

## 1110 LONGCHAMP (R-H)
Sunday, April 4

**OFFICIAL GOING: Good to soft**

### 1261a PRIX D'HARCOURT (GROUP 2) 1m 2f
**2:45** (2:47) 4-Y-0+ **£42,148** (£16,268; £7,764; £5,176)

RPR
**1** **Vangelis (USA)**[140] 6008 5-8-12 ......... CSoumillon 9 118
(ADeRoyer-Dupre, France) *held up, 6th straight, moved outside 2f out, steady progress to lead 150yds out, ran on well*
**2** *3/4* **Execute (FR)**[140] 6008 7-8-12 ......... TJarnet 1 117
(JEHammond, France) *settled 3rd, not clear run on rail 1 1/2f out, switched left, hard ridden & led briefly over 150yds out, ran on same pace*
**3** *1 1/2* **Short Pause**[183] 5383 5-8-12 ......... GaryStevens 5 114
(AFabre, France) *held up in rear early, moved up to dispute 3rd after 3f, 4th straight, kept on to take 3rd close home* **1**
**4** *1/2* **Nysaean (IRE)**[29] 980 5-8-12 ......... RHughes 7 113
(RHannon) *tracked leader, 2nd straight, led well over 1f out, hard ridden & headed over 150yds out, lost 3rd close home*
**5** *2 1/2* **Policy Maker (IRE)**[182] 5406 4-9-1 ......... DBoeuf 2 112
(ELellouche, France) *pulled early, raced in 5th to straight, kept on but never able to challenge* **2**
**6** *1/2* **Samando (FR)**[29] 980 4-8-8 ......... C-PLemaire 3 104
(FDoumen, France) *held up, 7th straight, never a factor*
**7** *shd* **Coroner (IRE)**[30] 4-9-1 ......... ELegrix 6 111
(J-CRouget, France) *held up, last straight, always in rear* **3**

8 ¾ **Weightless**[112] [6188] 4-9-1 ........ TThulliez 4 110
(PBary, France) *soon led, headed well over 1f out, eased when beaten final f* **1**

2m 2.60s **Going Correction** -0.175s/f (Firm) **8** Ran SP% **170.5**
Speed ratings: **115,114,113,112,110 110,110,109.**
**Owner** H Guy **Bred** Gainesway Thoroughbreds Ltd, M & J Hernon Et Al **Trained** France

**NOTEBOOK**
**Vangelis(USA)** would have appreciated this ground and confirmed he goes well fresh with a narrow victory. He could now go for the Prix Ganay and has the Arlington Million as a long-term target.
**Execute(FR)** posted a fine performance considering he would have preferred testing ground. The Ganay will no doubt be the next target.
**Short Pause** missed the kick and was held up early on, but he finished to good effect to grab a place late on. He has been entered in the Audemars Piguet QE II Cup at Sha Tin on April 25.
**Nysaean(IRE)** was given every chance by Hughes and ran pleasingly. Softer ground would have been an advantage.

## 1233 SOUTHWELL (L-H)
### Monday, April 5

**OFFICIAL GOING: Good to soft(good in places)**
Wind: fresh bhd Weather: heavy shower before race 6

## 1262 FESTIVAL OF GOOD LUCK H'CAP 5f (F)
**2:30** (2:34) (F) (0-55,53) 3-Y-0+ **£2,961** (£846; £423) **Stalls** High

Form RPR
6452 **1** **Never Without Me**[20] [1027] 4-8-8 **48** ........ KJackson(7) 13 61
(PJMcbride) *a.p: led over 1f out: rdn and edgd lft ins fnl f: r.o wl* **11/2**[1]
2130 **2** 1¾ **Henry Tun**[20] [1027] 6-8-13 **51** ........(p) MSavage(5) 2 58
(NEBerry) *a.p: rdn over 2f out: ev ch over 1f out: r.o one pce* **9/1**[3]
3300 **3** *hd* **Playful Spirit**[48] [803] 5-8-9 **45** ........(v) DAllan(3) 12 51
(JBalding) *dwlt: hdwy 3f out: sn rdn: swtchd rt over 1f out: r.o ins fnl f* **20/1**
4023 **4** ½ **Soaked**[7] [1180] 11-8-7 **47** ........(b) PMakin(7) 7 51
(DWChapman) *led: rdn over 2f out: hdd over 1f out: nt qckn* **8/1**[2]
0630 **5** *nk* **Ladies Knight**[13] [1082] 4-9-6 **53** ........ NCallan 8 56
(DShaw) *a.p: rdn over 2f out: kpt on same pce fnl f* **8/1**[2]
-644 **6** *1* **River Lark (USA)**[20] [1033] 5-9-1 **48** ........ RFrench 6 48
(MABuckley) *chsd ldrs: rdn 3f out: one pce fnl 2f* **8/1**[2]
5203 **7** ½ **Nanna (IRE)**[38] [906] 3-8-6 **50** ........ GDuffield 11 48
(RHollinshead) *prom: rdn over 2f out: wknd over 1f out* **25/1**
-234 **8** *nk* **Off Hire**[20] [1027] 8-9-1 **48** ........(v) RFitzpatrick 14 45
(CSmith) *sn outpcd: hdwy fnl f: r.o* **11/1**
0360 **9** *2* **Our Chelsea Blue (USA)**[13] [1087] 6-9-1 **48** ........(t) SRighton 5 37
(IAWood) *dwlt: nvr nrr* **11/1**
0602 **10** 2½ **Ejay**[41] [876] 5-8-6 **46** ........ MHalford(7) 10 26
(JulianPoulton) *nvr trbld ldrs* **10/1**
000- **11** *nk* **Tancred Times**[210] [4773] 9-9-2 **52** ........ LEnstone(3) 3 31
(DWBarker) *chsd ldrs: rdn over 3f out: hung lft over 2f out: sn wknd* **20/1**
0-56 **12** 1½ **Maggie Maquette**[32] [963] 4-9-5 **52** ........ EAhern 9 26
(WSKittow) *slowly into stridde: a bhd* **14/1**
1200 **13** *hd* **Cark**[36] [938] 6-9-2 **49** ........(p) JEdmunds 15 22
(JBalding) *chsd ldrs: wkng whn hung lft over 1f out* **16/1**
0301 **14** *1* **Above Board**[13] [1092] 9-9-3 **50** ........(t) DeanMcKeown 4 20
(RFMarvin) *sn bhd* **16/1**
/00- **15** 1¾ **Mandy's Collection**[409] [591] 5-8-12 **45** ........ SWhitworth 16 8
(AGNewcombe) *dwlt: a bhd* **16/1**
300- **16** *3* **Grasslandik**[152] [5924] 8-8-12 **45** ........(v) AnnStokell 1 —
(MissAStokell) *outpcd* **25/1**

58.67 secs (-1.63) **Going Correction** -0.325s/f (Stan)
**WFA** 3 from 4yo+ 11lb **16** Ran SP% **126.0**
Speed ratings: **100,97,96,96,95 94,93,92,89,85 85,82,82,80,77 73**CSF £51.70 CT £978.48 TOTE £8.00: £1.40, £4.50, £8.30, £2.40; EX 97.20.
**Owner** P J McBride **Bred** Miss Nathalie Lismonde **Trained** Newmarket, Suffolk

**FOCUS**
A run-of-the-mill low-grade sprint handicap in which it paid to race down the centre of the track. The form looks fairly solid for the level.

**NOTEBOOK**
**Never Without Me**, always up with the pace, made it tenth time lucky and was well handled by his apprentice. These are his ideal conditions.
**Henry Tun**, with only cheekpieces on this time as opposed to a visor or blinkers, is a regular in this type of contest and ran right up to his best, especially as a very low draw in a big field over the straight five here is not an advantage.
**Playful Spirit**, who usually races over further these days, finished well down the stands' rail and would probably be happier back over six, but her strike rate in recent seasons does not inspire confidence.
**Soaked** , who had the run of the race, showed his usual pace from his good draw and took the field along for almost half a mile, but could not last home and victories for him these days are getting fewer and further between.
**Ladies Knight** broke on terms this time and was never that far away, but he still could not make it pay and this trip is looking on the sharp side for him now.
**River Lark(USA)** ran well enough from her good draw, but does not strike as a winner waiting to happen.

## 1263 ST JULIANA OF LIEGE'S AMATEUR RIDERS' CLAIMING STKS 1m 4f
**3:00** (3:02) (G) 4-Y-0+ **£2,954** (£844; £422) **Stalls** Low

Form RPR
65/6 **1** **Maniatis**[9] [1030] 7-10-10 90 ........(v) MrDWeekes(7) 10 75
(MrsJCandlish) *led tl rn wd bnd over 8f out: chsd ldr: led again over 4f out: hrd rdn over 3f out: hung rt over 2f out: r.o wl* **3/1**[1]
0/4- **2** 2½ **Sir Ninja (IRE)**[97] [6262] 7-10-6 75 ........ MissMGunstone(5) 7 65
(SKirk) *hld up mid-div: hdwy over 4f out: kpt on ins fnl f* **11/2**[2]
1254 **3** 1½ **Grand Lass (IRE)**[9] [1037] 5-10-6 53 ........(p) MissEJJones 9 58
(ASadik) *hld up: hdwy over 5f out: wnt 2nd 3f out: rdn over 1f out: no ex ins fnl f* **6/1**[3]
0030 **4** *13* **Prince Minata (IRE)**[3] [1233] 9-10-0 40 ........ MissAHockley(7) 12 40
(PWHiatt) *prom: led over 8f out tl over 4f out: rdn over 3f out: wknd over 1f out* **66/1**
3406 **5** 2½ **Dundonald**[7] [1177] 5-10-0 35 ........(bt) MissFTurner(7) 3 36
(MAppleby) *bhd: hdwy on ins over 2f out: nvr nr ldrs* **40/1**
046/ **6** 1¼ **Kildare Chiller (IRE)**[28] [1074] 10-10-0 ........ MissEKemp(7) 11 34
(PRHedger) *s.i.s: hdwy on outside 3f out: no further prog fnl 2f* **12/1**
504/ **7** *3* **Lord Conyers (IRE)**[555] [4322] 5-9-9 ........ MrCLidster(7) 1 24
(BEllison) *hld up mid-div: sme hdwy on ins 3f out: n.d* **16/1**
0-00 **8** *nk* **Mikasa (IRE)**[12] [1101] 4-10-3 45 ........ KJMercer(3) 14 29
(RFFisher) *wnt bdly rt s: a bhd* **40/1**
**9** *5* **Mister Graham**[45] 9-10-5 ow5 ........(p) MrNHyde(7) 6 26
(KFClutterbuck) *dwlt: a bhd* **40/1**
055/ **10** *hd* **Roman King (IRE)**[387] [2683] 9-10-4 70 ........ DRCook(7) 13 25
(BDLeavy) *a bhd* **16/1**
**11** 1¼ **Mystery Solved (USA)**[264] [3319] 4-10-10 50 ........ StaceyRenwick(5) 5 28
(PABlockley) *hld up: hdwy 4f out: wknd wl over 1f out* **14/1**
6421 **12** *6* **Blue Savanna**[12] [1101] 4-10-5 47 ........(p) MrLNewnes(5) 8 14
(JGPortman) *prom tl wknd over 4f out* **8/1**
5334 **13** *7* **Samar Qand**[13] [1091] 5-10-2 35 ........(t) MrMatthewSmith(5) 4 —
(JulianPoulton) *prom: rdn 5f out: wknd 3f out* **12/1**
00/0 **14** *9* **Estuary (USA)**[13] [1081] 9-11-4 45 ........ MsAEmbiricos(3) 2 —
(MsAEEmbiricos) *prom: reminders over 5f out: wknd over 4f out* **20/1**

2m 49.33s (9.03) **Going Correction** +0.60s/f (Yiel)
**WFA** 4 from 5yo+ 1lb **14** Ran SP% **117.6**
Speed ratings: **93,91,90,81,80 79,77,76,73,73 72,68,64,58**CSF £16.83 TOTE £3.80: £1.50, £2.00, £1.70; EX 24.50.
**Owner** Racing For You Limited **Bred** A Christodoulou **Trained** Basford, Staffs
■ Stewards Enquiry : Mr N Hyde two-day ban: used whip when out of contention (Apr 19,24)
Miss M Gunstone two-day ban: careless riding (Apr 19,24)

**FOCUS**
A poor contest featuring many well past thier prime, in which the front three finished a very long way clear of the rest.

**NOTEBOOK**
**Maniatis**, miles ahead of the others on official ratings, loves this ground and won in good style despite hanging right for much of the contest. He needed the stands' rail in order to keep him straight in the final couple of furlongs and is value for more than the winning margin, but given his physical problems he is never going to be given to lump on.
**Sir Ninja(IRE)**, given time since his reappearance from a long layoff in December, ran with credit but probably not as well as his proximity to a 90-rated rival would suggest, especially given that horse's problems, and it is probably better to assess the performance through the third. He is without a win since October 1999.
**Grand Lass(IRE)** ◆, suited by the trip and the ground, ran well at the weights and pulled right away from the fourth. There may be a small race in her under similar conditions.
**Prince Minata(IRE)**, given a positive ride, had nothing more to offer after the winner went past him half a mile from home and his rider earned few marks for style. His best recent form has been on Fibresand and his best form on turf has been on fast ground, so he may have found this trip in the conditions stretching his stamina.
**Dundonald**, who boasts a record of one win from 35 starts under either code, achieved very little here.
**Kildare Chiller(IRE)**, racing on the Flat for the first time in nearly three years, made a little late headway in the second half of the contest and this should have helped bring him on again for when he returns to hurdles.
**Blue Savanna** showed up for a while, but dropped away very tamely.

## 1264 NATIONAL RAISIN AND SPICE BAR DAY MAIDEN AUCTION STKS 5f (F)
**3:30** (3:32) (F) 2-Y-0 **£2,919** (£834; £417) **Stalls** High

Form RPR
3 **1** **Westbrook Blue**[11] [1105] 2-8-0 ........ CHaddon(7) 5 71
(WGMTurner) *mde all: rdn over 1f out: drvn out* **4/7**[1]
**2** 1½ **Unlimited** 2-8-10 ........ GDuffield 6 69
(MrsADuffield) *chsd wnr: rdn 2f out: nt qckn ins fnl f* **33/1**
**3** *nk* **Why Harry** 2-8-7 ........ RWinston 1 65
(JJQuinn) *a.p: rdn 2f out: r.o one pce fnl f* **11/2**[2]
**4** *6* **Dane's Rock (IRE)** 2-8-10 ........ GFaulkner 3 46
(PCHaslam) *prom: rdn over 2f out: wknd over 1f out* **8/1**[3]
**5** 2½ **Ronnies Lad** 2-8-7 ........ VHalliday 4 34
(JRNorton) *sn outpcd: nvr trbld ldrs* **33/1**
0 **6** *1* **Mindful**[9] [1128] 2-8-10 ........ EAhern 8 33
(MJPolglase) *chsd ldrs: rdn over 2f out: wknd wl over 1f out* **20/1**
**7** *5* **Marcela Zabala** 2-8-5 ........ NPollard 2 10
(JGGiven) *dwlt: outpcd* **14/1**
0 **8** *3* **Verstone (IRE)**[7] [1170] 2-8-8 ........ SRighton 7 3
(RFFisher) *dwlt: outpcd* **66/1**

59.88 secs (-0.42) **Going Correction** -0.325s/f (Stan) **8** Ran SP% **109.0**
Speed ratings: **91,88,88,78,74 72,64,60**CSF £28.52 TOTE £1.30: £1.02, £4.70, £1.30; EX 18.40.
**Owner** Bob Chandler **Bred** B Minty **Trained** Sigwells, Somerset

**FOCUS**
A modest maiden, but fair form for the track, in which previous experience counted for plenty and the front three finished well clear.

**NOTEBOOK**
**Westbrook Blue**, third in the Brocklesby, made his experience count by pinging the stalls and he never saw another rival, though it was far from easy. He may well now go to Chester.
**Unlimited**, a 7,000gns yearling and first foal of the eight-time winner Cabcharge Blue, showed plenty of ability on this debut and should not be hard to place.
**Why Harry**, a 5,000gns half-brother to Fibresand winner Bold Blade out of a three-time winner in Italy, showed enough to suggest he has an aptitude for this surface as well.
**Dane's Rock(IRE)**, an 11,000euros half-brother to six-furlong winner Cut Ridge, should do better over further in time.
**Ronnies Lad**, whose half-brother Deceives The Eye won on this surface, cost only 800gns as a yearling and offered little immediate promise.
**Mindful** showed up for a while, but did not really progress from his debut.

## 1265 BATTLE OF NAFELS H'CAP 7f
**4:00** (4:00) (E) (0-75,75) 3-Y-0+ **£4,202** (£1,293; £646; £323) **Stalls** Low

Form RPR
0210 **1** **Nearly A Fool**[5] [1204] 6-9-6 **65** ........(v) NPollard 14 76
(GGMargarson) *hld up and bhd: rdn and gd hdwy on outside over 1f out: str run to ld cl home* **12/1**
3-60 **2** ¾ **Captain Darling (IRE)**[13] [1088] 4-9-2 **61** ........(p) EAhern 7 70
(RMHCowell) *a.p: rdn to ld 2f out: edgd lft over 1f out: edgd rt and hdd cl home* **10/1**
000/ **3** *2* **Sea Mark**[628] [2700] 8-9-1 **60** ........ RWinston 12 64+
(BEllison) *hld up and bhd: hdwy whn nt clr run jst over 1f out: r.o wl ins fnl f* **50/1**
-152 **4** ¾ **Mufreh (USA)**[23] [1007] 6-9-1 **60** ........ SWhitworth 5 62
(AGNewcombe) *hld up and bhd: rdn and hdwy 2f out: r.o ins fnl f* **4/1**[1]
21 **5** *2* **Marinaite**[62] [668] 3-9-2 **75** ........ KDalgleish 4 72
(SRBowring) *led over 1f: remained prom: rdn and ev ch 2f out: wknd ins fnl f* **7/1**[3]
334- **6** *shd* **Lucayan Dancer**[163] [5742] 4-9-6 **65** ........ AlexGreaves 1 61
(DNicholls) *a.p: rdn and ev ch 2f out: wknd ins fnl f* **20/1**
0413 **7** 1¾ **Danielle's Lad**[9] [1141] 8-9-7 **73** ........(b) SJDonohoe(7) 9 65
(BPalling) *led over 5f out: rdn and hdd 2f out: wknd ins fnl f* **12/1**

620- **8** *hd* **Sabalara (IRE)**[191] 5224 4-9-4 **63** NCallan 6 54
(PWHarris) *hld up mid-div: no hdwy fnl 2f* **9/1**

2002 **9** *1* **St Ivian**[19] 1039 4-9-5 **64** (v) PMcCabe 11 53
(MrsNMacauley) *hld up mid-div: rdn 3f out: no hdwy fnl 2f* **20/1**

502- **10** *1* **Lord Of The East**[163] 5742 5-9-6 **65** ANicholls 10 51
(DNicholls) *prom: rdn 4f out: edgd lft over 1f out: wknd fnl f* **33/1**

5/ **11** *½* **Brigadier Monty (IRE)**[257] 3637 6-9-2 **61** GDuffield 3 46
(MrsSLamyman) *t.k.h: in tch: rdn and ev ch 2f out: wknd fnl f* **33/1**

201- **12** *6* **Merdiff**[142] 6005 5-9-3 **62** SWKelly 13 31
(WMBrisbourne) *hld up in tch: rdn and wknd 2f out* **8/1**

0114 **13** *4* **Stoic Leader (IRE)**[7] 1175 4-9-6 **68** LFletcher(3) 16 27
(RFFisher) *prom: rdn over 3f out: hung lft over 2f out: wknd over 1f out* **5/1**[2]

660- **14** *3* **One Last Time**[173] 5573 4-9-13 **72** HBastiman 8 23
(RBastiman) *s.i.s: a bhd* **40/1**

300- **15** *2* **Jimmy Byrne (IRE)**[182] 5416 4-9-6 **70** TEaves(5) 15 16
(BEllison) *hld up: rdn 4f out: bhd fnl 3f* **20/1**

-302 **16** *1 ¼* **Rafters Music (IRE)**[9] 1140 9-9-7 **66** GFaulkner 2 9
(JulianPoulton) *hld up: rdn over 3f out: sme hdwy over 2f out: wknd over 1f out* **14/1**

1m 32.77s (3.57) **Going Correction** +0.60s/f (Yiel)
**WFA** 3 from 4yo+ 14lb **16** Ran SP% **126.0**
Speed ratings: **103,102,99,99,96 96,94,94,93,92 91,84,80,76,74 72**CSF £120.76 CT £5957.30 TOTE £13.50: £2.70, £3.30, £10.20, £2.20; EX 141.30.
**Owner** J Burns **Bred** Mrs S Shaw **Trained** Newmarket, Suffolk

**FOCUS**
A competitive handicap run at a solid gallop and the best effort from the winner since his three-year-old days.

**NOTEBOOK**
**Nearly A Fool** had not won on turf since June 2000, but he has been in brilliant from on sand this year and transferred the improvement back on to the grass. He had to be restrained off the pace from his high draw, but his strong late run down the outside of the track carried the day.
**Captain Darling(IRE)** would probably have preferred faster ground, but still looked to have stolen it when kicked clear on the inside two furlongs from home. However he started to hang right in the closing stages and the winner mugged him.
**Sea Mark ◆**, rated as high as 85 three years ago, was running for the first time in 21 months and making his debut for the yard. He ran a blinder too, emerging from behind a wall of horses to snatch third place. He is sure to come on from this and it would be no great surprise to see him winning again before too long. Faster ground would help him as well.
**Mufreh(USA)**, yet to win on turf from just four attempts before this, stayed on in the closing stages but much too late to bother the front pair.
**Marinaite**, making her turf debut after two runs on sand here, showed for a long way but was done for foot in the latter stages. She looks more of a galloper which is probably why the Fibresand appears to suit her better.
**Stoic Leader(IRE)** stays this trip on sand, but seems to struggle over it on turf and did not look happy from some way out.

## 1266 BOOKER T WASHINGTON CLASSIFIED STKS 6f
**4:30** (4:31) (E) 3-Y-O **£3,367** (£1,036; £518; £259) **Stalls** Low

Form RPR

1212 **1** **Piccolo Prince**[18] 1047 3-8-12 65 WSupple 6 71
(EJAlston) *a.p: sustained chal fnl 2f: hrd rdn to ld nr fin* **85/40**[2]

3421 **2** *nk* **Monte Major (IRE)**[17] 1052 3-9-3 70 NCallan 2 75
(MAJarvis) *led: rdn over 1f out: hdd nr fin* **2/1**[1]

05-0 **3** *1 ¾* **Munaawesh (USA)**[22] 1015 3-8-10 70 PMakin(7) 7 70
(DWChapman) *s.i.s: hld up: rdn and hdwy over 1f out: styd on fnl f* **12/1**

404- **4** *shd* **Impulsive Bid (IRE)**[149] 5947 3-8-10 66 PHanagan 1 63
(JeddO'Keeffe) *prom: rdn over 3f out: kpt on fnl f* **6/1**

0-00 **5** *2 ½* **Wendy's Girl (IRE)**[10] 1119 3-8-6 60 THamilton(3) 4 54
(RPElliott) *s.i.s: hld up: rdn and hdwy over 1f out: wknd ins fnl f* **22/1**

13-3 **6** *6* **Chickado (IRE)**[80] 547 3-8-9 65 PaulEddery 3 36
(DHaydnJones) *t.k.h: prom: rdn 3f out: wknd 2f out* **5/1**[3]

46-0 **7** *1* **Blue Emperor (IRE)**[33] 956 3-8-10 66 ow2 DNolan(5) 5 39
(PABlockley) *prom: rdn and hung lft 2f out: sn wknd* **22/1**

1m 19.99s (3.89) **Going Correction** +0.60s/f (Yiel) **7** Ran SP% **112.7**
Speed ratings: **98,97,95,95,91 83,82**CSF £6.57 TOTE £3.50: £1.90, £1.50; EX 7.50.
**Owner** The Burlington Partnership **Bred** Theobalds Stud **Trained** Longton, Lancs

**FOCUS**
A tight race on the figures but only two really mattered from a long way out.

**NOTEBOOK**
**Piccolo Prince** was beaten in a selling nursery on his last start on turf, but he has progressed since changing stables and really found his form on sand over the winter, winning twice, and this performance on his return to the turf confirmed that improvement.
**Monte Major(IRE)** made the running as usual on this turf debut. He only lost out narrowly and perhaps he can make amends when reverting to his winning distance of seven furlongs.
**Munaawesh(USA)**, whose breeding suggests that he should be suited by a trip of around a mile, was putting in his best work at the finish over this shorter distance.
**Impulsive Bid(IRE)**, who ran a decent race on her last start at two, kept on well under pressure. This was a good effort against match-fit rivals.
**Wendy's Girl(IRE)**, an exposed performer, is vulnerable to more progressive types.
**Chickado(IRE)** has yet to run as well on turf as she has on Fibresand.

## 1267 ST VINCENT FERRER'S DAY H'CAP 1m 2f
**5:00** (5:01) (F) (0-55,55) 3-Y-O **£2,947** (£842; £421) **Stalls** Low

Form RPR

00-6 **1** **Habitual Dancer**[10] 1111 3-9-1 **52** PHanagan 8 61+
(JeddO'Keeffe) *hld up: hdwy over 5f out: hrd rdn 3f out: led over 1f out: edgd rt ins fnl f: drvn out* **7/1**[3]

540- **2** *1* **Daggers Canyon**[96] 6266 3-9-4 **55** NCallan 7 62
(JulianPoulton) *hld up: hdwy over 4f out: hrd rdn and edgd rt over 1f out: r.o* **10/1**

50-0 **3** *4* **Danefonique (IRE)**[10] 1116 3-9-2 **53** RFitzpatrick 5 53
(DCarroll) *hld up: hdwy 5f out: rdn over 3f out: swtchd lft ins fnl f: eased whn btn towards fin* **16/1**

-400 **4** *5* **Heartbeat**[49] 798 3-8-8 **52** KJackson(7) 4 43
(PJMcbride) *prom: wnt 2nd over 6f out: led over 2f out tl over 1f out: wknd fnl f* **20/1**

3440 **5** *3* **Myannabanana (IRE)**[20] 1029 3-9-4 **55** (p) RWinston 6 41
(JRWeymes) *hld up: lost pl and hmpd over 5f out: hdwy over 3f out: n.d* **8/1**

0-00 **6** *hd* **Poacher's Paradise**[33] 958 3-8-4 **46** oh1 PMulrennan(5) 13 31
(MWEasterby) *led: rdn and hdd over 2f out: wknd over 1f out* **11/2**[1]

-000 **7** *8* **Atlantic Breeze**[33] 955 3-9-1 **52** JoannaBadger 14 23
(MrsNMacauley) *a bhd* **22/1**

0001 **8** *5* **Stonor Lady (USA)**[19] 1040 3-8-11 **48** EAhern 3 10
(PWD'Arcy) *hld up: hdwy over 4f out: wknd over 2f out* **13/2**[2]

06-0 **9** *¾* **Timbuktu**[91] 445 3-8-4 **46** oh6 TEaves(5) 12 6
(CWThornton) *a bhd* **33/1**

-005 **10** *¾* **Frambo (IRE)**[13] 1084 3-8-6 **46** oh1 (b[1]) BReilly(3) 9 —
(JGPortman) *a bhd* **9/1**

000- **11** *8* **Lenwade**[188] 5290 3-9-2 **53** AMcCarthy 11 —
(GGMargarson) *hld up and bhd: hdwy 6f out: wknd over 2f out* **9/1**

000- **12** *5* **Royal Upstart**[160] 5816 3-8-9 **46** SWKelly 2 —
(WMBrisbourne) *chsd ldrs tl lost pl over 6f out* **14/1**

4430 **13** *11* **Katie's Role**[10] 1116 3-9-4 **55** DeanMcKeown 1 —
(IanEmmerson) *chsd ldr over 3f: wknd over 5f out* **10/1**

0-04 **14** *23* **Hymns And Arias**[20] 1031 3-8-10 **47** ANicholls 10 —
(RonaldThompson) *hld up in tch: wknd over 5f out: t.o* **16/1**

2m 20.8s (5.80) **Going Correction** +0.60s/f (Yiel) **14** Ran SP% **121.0**
Speed ratings: **96,95,92,88,85 85,79,75,74,73 67,63,54,36**CSF £73.81 CT £1096.42 TOTE £6.70: £2.10, £4.20, £4.00; EX 59.30.
**Owner** The Country Stayers **Bred** Mrs A Yearley **Trained** Middleham Moor, N Yorks

**FOCUS**
A low-grade contest, but the first two, who were unexposed at the trip, came clear and could be fairly treated.

**NOTEBOOK**
**Habitual Dancer**, whose dam won over ten furlongs and whose sire was a middle-distance performer, had given every indication in his starts over six and seven furlongs at two that a step up to this sort of trip would bring about big improvement. He lived up to the expectation and there could be scope for further improvement as he was racing off a pretty lowly mark here. *Official explanation: trainer said, regarding the improved form shown, gelding had benefited from the step up in trip*
**Daggers Canyon** was not certain to improve for this step up in trip but he certainly appreciated it. He did look as though he would appreciate a faster surface, though.
**Danefonique(IRE)** ran her best race to date and now appears to have found her level.
**Heartbeat**, who went without the visor this time, failed the stamina test.
**Myannabanana(IRE)**, beaten in sellers when last seen on turf, has improved on the sand over the winter. His form to date has suggested that a mile is his best trip, though.
**Poacher's Paradise**, having never raced beyond six furlongs before, was taking a half-mile step up in trip and, despite the stamina doubts, was supported into favouritism. In the event he failed to get home, but on this evidence he could well go in off this sort of mark back over a mile.
**Hymns And Arias** *Official explanation: jockey said filly hung right-handed under pressure*

## 1268 HAPPY BIRTHDAY LITTLE JIMMY OSMOND H'CAP 6f
**5:30** (5:33) (F) (0-55,55) 3-Y-O+ **£2,961** (£846; £423) **Stalls** Low

Form RPR

000- **1** **Balakiref**[181] 5438 5-9-3 **53** FLynch 9 73+
(MDods) *hld up: hdwy over 2f out: rdn to ld over 1f out: sn edgd lft: r.o wl* **11/2**[2]

0440 **2** *3* **Carlton (IRE)**[13] 1087 10-8-13 **54** RThomas(5) 4 63+
(CRDore) *chsd ldrs: rdn 2f out: wnt 2nd and edgd lft ins fnl f: no imp* **11/2**[2]

1040 **3** *2* **Kennington**[20] 1032 4-9-0 **55** (v) HayleyTurner(3) 3 58
(MrsCADunnett) *chsd ldrs: rdn over 3f out: ev ch 2f out: one pce* **12/1**

2453 **4** *hd* **Boavista (IRE)**[18] 1044 4-8-12 **55** SJDonohoe(7) 5 57
(PDEvans) *prom: led over 4f out: rdn over 2f out: hdd and edgd rt over 1f out: one pce* **8/1**[3]

300- **5** *2* **Summer Special**[174] 5561 4-9-2 **55** LEnstone(3) 14 51
(DWBarker) *dwlt: hld up: hdwy whn swtchd rt 2f out: put hd in air: rdn and no real prog* **14/1**

1100 **6** *nk* **Mount Royale (IRE)**[19] 1039 6-9-3 **53** (vt) KimTinkler 13 49
(NTinkler) *racd wd: chsd ldrs: rdn over 2f out: wknd over 1f out* **8/1**[3]

200- **7** *1 ¼* **The Old Soldier**[166] 5706 6-9-2 **55** ABeech(3) 8 47
(ADickman) *hmpd s: sn chsng ldrs: wknd wl over 1f out* **12/1**

500- **8** *1 ¾* **Jazzy Millennium**[188] 5286 7-9-5 **55** (b) GBaker 2 42
(BRMillman) *hld up and bhd: hdwy on ins over 2f out: wknd over 1f out* **16/1**

3-00 **9** *3 ½* **Percy Douglas**[49] 794 4-9-3 **53** (p) AnnStokell 10 29
(MissAStokell) *prom tl wknd wl over 1f out* **33/1**

4062 **10** *¾* **Aguila Loco (IRE)**[7] 1176 5-9-3 **53** (p) EAhern 11 27
(MrsStefLiddiard) *prom: rdn over 2f out: wknd wl over 1f out* **3/1**[1]

5645 **11** *3* **Cleveland Way**[20] 1033 4-8-11 **52** (v) DNolan(5) 6 17
(DCarroll) *led over 1f: prom: rdn over 2f out: wknd wl over 1f out* **10/1**

6005 **12** *4* **Teyaar**[13] 1087 8-9-3 **53** PMcCabe 12 6
(MrsNMacauley) *chsd ldrs tl rdn and wknd over 3f out* **20/1**

-000 **13** *½* **Tanaffus**[20] 1032 4-8-9 **52** PMakin(7) 7 3
(DWChapman) *fly-jmpd and hmpd s: rdn over 2f out: a bhd* **33/1**

1m 19.62s (3.52) **Going Correction** +0.60s/f (Yiel) **13** Ran SP% **125.7**
Speed ratings: **100,96,93,93,90 90,88,86,81,80 76,71,70**CSF £37.10 CT £370.00 TOTE £7.20: £2.70, £2.60, £5.70; EX 50.70 Place 6 £53.20, Place 5 £19.02.
**Owner** Septimus Racing Group **Bred** S R Hope And D Erwin **Trained** Piercebridge, Co Durham

**FOCUS**
A modest but competitive contest, but the winner was well-handicapped on his best form and could be open to further improvement and the second is also well treated.

**NOTEBOOK**
**Balakiref**, who was beginning this season off a 23lb lower mark than he started last year's campaign on, enjoyed the easy ground and ran out a clear winner. There are more races to be won with him when he can get his toe in, and he should remain fairly handicapped even after being reassessed.
**Carlton(IRE)** has not won outside of claiming company since 1999, but he has not run off a lower mark than this since 1998, and this performance suggests that, despite his advancing years, he can still be placed to win in the right company.
**Kennington**, who ran his best races on the sand from the front, ran a fair race on his turf debut. It will be interesting to see how he gets on when connections choose to ride him more positively.
**Boavista(IRE)**, who has had plenty of chances, is not a win-only proposition.
**Summer Special** is a long-standing maiden who has his own ideas about the game.
**Mount Royale(IRE)** has done all his winning over seven furlongs.
**Aguila Loco(IRE)**, an improved performer on the All-Weather over the winter, was returning to the turf on a 13lb higher mark than when last racing on the surface in September. *Official explanation: jockey said gelding ran too free early on*

T/Plt: £59.30 to a £1 stake. Pool: £32,268.35. 396.60 winning tickets. T/Qpdt: £17.50 to a £1 stake. Pool: £2,209.60. 93.40 winning tickets. KH

# WINDSOR (R-H)

Monday, April 5

**OFFICIAL GOING: Good to soft (soft in places)**

The ground was riding quite testing and five of the seven winners were fit from a recent All-Weather campaign. Distances were also exaggerated.

## 1269 FRENCH BROTHERS MEDIAN AUCTION MAIDEN STKS — 5f 10y

**2:10** (2:12) (E) 2-Y-O — **£3,454** (£1,063; £531; £265) **Stalls** High

Form — RPR

**1** **Cornus** 2-9-0 ........ RHughes 4 — 84
(RHannon) *trckd ldr: shkn up to ld over 1f out: clr fnl f: readily* **8/1**[3]

**2** 2 1/2 **Goodricke** 2-9-0 ........ JPMurtagh 5 — 74+
(DRLoder) *s.s: in tch in rr: effrt 2f out: r.o to chse wnr ins fnl f: no imp* **2/1**[1]

4 **3** 1/2 **Tremar**[9] 1130 2-8-11 ........ RMiles(3) 8 — 72
(TGMills) *reluctant to enter stalls: s.s: pushed along in rr: effrt wl over 1f out: r.o fnl f: nrst fin* **7/2**[2]

0 **4** 3 **Wizzskilad**[10] 1117 2-9-0 ........ RHavlin 7 — 60
(MrsPNDutfield) *led to over 1f out: fdd fnl f* **66/1**

**5** 2 1/2 **Cummiskey (IRE)** 2-9-0 ........ DHolland 6 — 50
(JAOsborne) *trckd ldrs: pushed along 2f out: no imp and btn 1f out* **2/1**[1]

**6** 1 1/4 **High Dawn (IRE)** 2-9-0 ........ SSanders 3 — 45
(RMBeckett) *dwlt: pushed along to stay in tch: rdn and btn on outer whn hmpd over 1f out* **20/1**

**7** 5 **Leonalto (IRE)** 2-8-9 ........ JFMcDonald(5) 2 — 25
(BJMeehan) *pressed ldrs: losing pl u.p whn hung lft over 1f out* **33/1**

**8** 24 **Big Bambo (IRE)** 2-9-0 ........ SDrowne 1 — —
(MrsPNDutfield) *dwlt: sn outpcd and bhd: t.o* **40/1**

64.53 secs (3.33) **Going Correction** +0.525s/f (Yiel) **8 Ran SP% 111.6**
Speed ratings: **94,90,89,84,80 78,70,32**CSF £23.24 TOTE £6.50: £2.40, £2.00, £1.50; EX 45.40.
**Owner** David Mort **Bred** G Russell **Trained** East Everleigh, Wilts

**FOCUS**
On paper this looked like quite a hot maiden, with both the Jamie Osborne and David Loder juveniles fancied in the betting to make a winning debut, but it was the relatively unsupported Cornus who came home in front. It is difficult to know what to make of the form, but some of those in behind are surely capable of better.

**NOTEBOOK**
**Cornus**, a 16,000gns purchase, out of an unraced half-sister to a dual six-furlong three-year-old winner, went off relatively unsupported but knew his job, had the run of the race and ran out a clear-cut winner. He should be competitive in novice company, but there may just be one or two in this race capable of more improvement.
**Goodricke ◆**, a 110,000gns yearling, brother to 2003 smart triple six-furlong two-year-old winner Pastoral Pursuits, out of a five-furlong two-year-old winner, was very slowly away and could never quite get to the eventual winner. This was a pleasing enough introduction and he should be winning soon.
**Tremar** really caught the eye on his debut at Kempton, finishing to good effect after missing the kick, but he was unable to build on that and would appear to dislike the stalls. He was very reluctant to both enter and leave the gates and when he finally got going he needed plenty of stoking and never looked like picking up. He clearly has the ability to win a maiden but will need to learn to break on terms.
**Wizzskilad**, well beaten in a weaker race than this on his racecourse debut, represented last year's winning trainer who took this with Rosina May. He is flattered to finish fourth, for he broke well and soon had the rail to run against, but he is at least going the right way.
**Cummiskey(IRE)**, a 180,000euros purchase, half-brother to a fair winning miler in France, was very strong in the market but proved disappointing. He broke on terms and looked to have every chance when it mattered, but found little for pressure and appeared to drift to his left. He is probably capable of better, but has something to prove.
**High Dawn(IRE)**, a 15,500gns purchase, half-brother to six-furlong two-year-old winners Pink Sapphire and Niagara, was slowly away and never really threatened. He will have learnt plenty and promises to stay further.
**Leonalto(IRE)**, a 14,000gns yearling, whose dam was placed over six furlongs at two, has a Super Sprint entry but was very easy to back. He travelled well enough but found next to nothing under pressure.

## 1270 WELCOME TO ROYAL WINDSOR 2004 H'CAP — 6f

**2:40** (2:40) (E) (0-75,75) 3-Y-O — **£3,513** (£1,081; £540; £270) **Stalls** High

Form — RPR

2203 **1** **Muy Bien**[23] 1008 3-9-1 **69** ........ (b) LDettori 4 — 79
(JRJenkins) *mde all far side and sn wl clr of gp: overall ldr 2f out: wknd ins fnl f: hld on* **7/1**[3]

0601 **2** 1 **Stamford Blue**[4] 1220 3-8-1 **62** 6ex ........ (b) BSwarbrick(7) 3 — 69
(JSMoore) *racd far side: chsd ldrs: chsd wnr 1/2-way: clsd u.p fr over 1f out: gaining fin* **12/1**

00-0 **3** 6 **Arfinnit (IRE)**[9] 1129 3-9-4 **72** ........ TEDurcan 2 — 61
(MRChannon) *racd far side: last of gp and wl outpcd: styd on fnl 2f: no ch w ldng pair* **25/1**

0-31 **4** 3/4 **Royal Pavillion (IRE)**[51] 774 3-9-2 **70** ........ MFenton 15 — 57
(WJMusson) *racd nr side: rr of gp and pushed along after 2f: effrt 2f out: drvn to ld gp ins fnl f: no ch w far side ldrs* **7/2**[1]

-400 **5** nk **Head Boy**[54] 741 3-8-4 **58** ........ RLMoore 8 — 44
(SDow) *last of nr side gp and sn rdn: effrt over 2f out: prog and nt clr run 1f out: r.o fnl f: no ch w far side* **40/1**

040- **6** 2 1/2 **Night Worker**[172] 5590 3-8-11 **65** ........ PDobbs 12 — 43
(RHannon) *w nr side ldr to over 1f out: wknd ins fnl f* **12/1**

005- **7** hd **Perfect Hindsight (IRE)**[276] 2967 3-8-8 **62** ........ RSmith 11 — 40
(CGCox) *chsd nr side ldrs: rdn 1/2-way: no prog whn bmpd 1f out* **20/1**

00-0 **8** 2 1/2 **Spring Dancer**[13] 1086 3-8-9 **63** ........ EStack 1 — 33
(APJarvis) *chsd wnr far side to 1/2-way: wknd 2f out* **20/1**

-503 **9** 1 3/4 **Instinct**[6] 1184 3-8-8 **62** ........ RHughes 6 — 27
(RHannon) *led nr side gp: overall ldr to 2f out: lost gp ld 1f out: wknd and eased* **6/1**[2]

0103 **10** 2 **Head Of State**[18] 1047 3-8-6 **60** ........ (v) JMackay 5 — 19
(RMBeckett) *racd far side: chsd ldrs: wknd 2f out* **16/1**

60-3 **11** shd **Torquemada (IRE)**[13] 1083 3-9-0 **68** ........ PDoe 9 — 27
(WJarvis) *bmpd s: racd nr side: effrt fr rr to chse ldrs 2f out: sn wknd* **12/1**

253- **12** shd **Party Princess (IRE)**[181] 5432 3-8-9 **63** ........ DHolland 13 — 21
(JAGlover) *chsd nr side ldrs: hanging lft u.p fr over 1f out: sn wknd* **7/1**[3]

0-63 **13** shd **Off Beat (USA)**[40] 885 3-9-7 **75** ........ (b) SCarson 7 — 33
(RFJohnsonHoughton) *racd in midfield of nr side gp: effrt to chse ldrs over 2f out: sn wknd* **20/1**

553- **14** 7 **My Michelle**[149] 5948 3-9-6 **74** ........ KDarley 14 — 11
(BPalling) *a in rr of nr side gp: rdn and struggling after 2f* **8/1**

140- **15** 1 1/4 **Melody King**[220] 4550 3-9-1 **69** ........ (b) RHavlin 10 — —
(PDEvans) *racd nr side: nvr beyond midfield: wknd over 2f out* **40/1**

1m 17.53s (3.83) **Going Correction** +0.525s/f (Yiel) **15 Ran SP% 124.6**
Speed ratings: **96,94,86,85,85 81,81,78,76,73 73,73,72,63,61**CSF £82.01 CT £1284.68 TOTE £9.30: £2.60, £4.00, £9.80; EX 120.00.
**Owner** Kevin Reddington **Bred** K J Reddington **Trained** Royston, Herts

**FOCUS**
This appeared to be quite a competitive sprint handicap, but the field split into two groups and the form wants treating with caution. Those drawn in the bottom five stalls opted to raced towards the far side of the track and were at a distinct advantage.

**NOTEBOOK**
**Muy Bien** had gained both his previous wins on Fibresand but has become quite frustrating on that surface in recent months. Switched to the turf and favourably drawn to race on the favoured far side of the track, he was given a very positive ride and was always going to hold off the runner-up's late effort. He has a tendency to hang left, so the rail was ideally positioned.
**Stamford Blue** is another who appears sweetened up by a recent switch to the turf and, under a 6lb penalty for his recent selling success, he ran respectably. He was closing at the finish, but the winner had built up too much of a lead.
**Arfinnit(IRE)** was drawn on what turned out to be the right side, but he struggled to go the pace and is flattered to have finished third. He could be worth another try over farther.
**Royal Pavillion(IRE)**, off the mark over this trip on Fibresand on his previous outing, came out best of those who raced on the near side.
**Head Boy**, out of form on Polytrack on his last two runs, posted a respectable effort on this switch back to turf.
**Party Princess(IRE)** *Official explanation: jockey said filly lost her action*

## 1271 SWEET & MAXWELL ARCHBOLD MAIDEN STKS — 1m 2f 7y

**3:10** (3:11) (D) 3-Y-O — **£4,173** (£1,284; £642; £321) **Stalls** Low

Form — RPR

**1** **Bull Run (IRE)** 3-9-0 ........ JPMurtagh 3 — 100
(DRLoder) *trckd ldr: led wl over 3f out: pushed clr over 2f out: in n.d fr over 1f out: eased fnl f* **9/4**[1]

4- **2** 9 **Larkwing (IRE)**[159] 5825 3-9-0 ........ DHolland 11 — 84
(GWragg) *settled towards rr: prog wl over 3f out: shkn up to chse wnr over 2f out: styd on but no imp* **9/4**[1]

**3** 7 **Springtime Romance (USA)** 3-8-9 ........ LDettori 6 — 67
(EALDunlop) *trckd ldrs: effrt over 3f out: chsd ldng pair over 2f out: sn outpcd: kpt on* **10/1**[3]

0- **4** 5 **Obay**[185] 5345 3-9-0 ........ SDrowne 5 — 63
(EALDunlop) *racd in midfield: shkn up and outpcd 3f out: no imp after: kpt on fnl f* **11/2**[2]

5- **5** nk **Magic Sting**[159] 5831 3-9-0 ........ IMongan 7 — 62
(MLWBell) *racd in midfield: rdn over 3f out: chsd clr ldng trio 2f out: no imp* **25/1**

-343 **6** 1 1/4 **Ground Patrol**[47] 822 3-9-0 70 ........ MartinDwyer 9 — 60
(AMBalding) *racd in midfield: rdn and outpcd 3f out: no ch after: kpt on fnl f* **20/1**

00- **7** 1 **Patrixtoo (FR)**[159] 5830 3-9-0 ........ PRobinson 1 — 58
(MHTompkins) *led to wl over 3f out: wknd fr 2f out* **16/1**

00- **8** 7 **Grist Mist (IRE)**[151] 5934 3-8-9 ........ RHavlin 4 — 40
(MrsPNDutfield) *settled in last gp: outpcd 4f out: shuffled along and no ch after* **66/1**

-245 **9** 3/4 **Looks The Business (IRE)**[16] 1064 3-9-0 69 ........ (t) ACulhane 8 — 44
(WGMTurner) *prom: rdn wl over 3f out: sn wknd* **16/1**

0-6 **10** 1 1/2 **Scriptorium**[16] 1064 3-9-0 ........ TEDurcan 14 — 41
(LMCumani) *settled in rr: outpcd 4f out: hanging and sn bhd* **33/1**

0 **11** 1/2 **Cool Clear Water (USA)**[17] 1052 3-8-9 ........ MHills 10 — 35
(BJMeehan) *racd in midfield: rdn wl over 3f out: sn wknd* **25/1**

0- **12** 1 **Persian Dagger (IRE)**[163] 5754 3-9-0 ........ TQuinn 12 — 39
(JLDunlop) *settled in rr: rdn and lost tch 4f out: bhd after* **33/1**

00- **13** 22 **No Dilemma (USA)**[151] 5934 3-9-0 ........ KDarley 2 — —
(EALDunlop) *wl in rr: last and pushed along 1/2-way: sn struggling: t.o* **50/1**

0 **14** dist **Red Silk**[86] 492 3-8-9 ........ SSanders 13 — —
(MrsAJPerrett) *racd towards rr: rdn and wknd over 4f out: t.o* **66/1**

2m 15.78s (7.58) **Going Correction** +0.80s/f (Soft) **14 Ran SP% 121.1**
Speed ratings: **102,94,89,85,84 83,83,77,76,75 75,74,56,—**CSF £5.84 TOTE £3.30: £1.30, £1.90, £2.20; EX 11.10.
**Owner** Sheikh Mohammed **Bred** Hesmonds Stud Ltd **Trained** Newmarket, Suffolk

**FOCUS**
Probably not too bad a maiden, in which the field raced towards the far side in the straight. There is no doubt the soft ground exaggerated the distances, but even so it was hard not to be impressed by Bull Run.

**NOTEBOOK**
**Bull Run(IRE) ◆**, a 180,000gns purchase, half-brother to a ten-furlong All-Weather winner, and high-class eight to ten-furlong scorer Claxon, was considered too backward to race at two. Never too far off the pace, he found plenty when asked and, relishing the soft ground, he pulled right away for an impressive success. Connections plan to step him up in class next time and he could make up into something like an Italian Derby horse.
**Larkwing(IRE)**, an encouraging fourth in a fair Yarmouth maiden on his sole start last season, did not appear to do anything wrong on this reappearance but was simply left behind by the winner. He was clear of the remainder and should find a maiden.
**Springtime Romance(USA)**, a half-sister a very useful miler, a smart six-furlong two-year-old and a French ten-furlong scorer, made a satisfactory debut. She was beaten a long way but should progress.
**Obay** shaped well on his debut in a reasonable-looking Newmarket maiden last season, but made a somewhat disappointing return. He did not run badly, but did not show much progression from that initial outing.
**Magic Sting**, who made his debut in a division of the maiden Larkwing ran in last season, travelled quite nicely but did not find a great deal under pressure. He can be expected to improve on this first run in 159 days.

## 1272 HBLB CHARLTON ATHLETIC FC H'CAP — 1m 3f 135y

**3:40** (3:40) (D) (0-85,84) 3-Y-O+ — **£5,622** (£1,730; £865; £432) **Stalls** Low

Form — RPR

3030 **1** **Cruise Director**[20] 1030 4-9-9 **80** ........ MFenton 4 — 93
(WJMusson) *hld up in rr: stdy prog over 3f out: chsd clr ldr 2f out: rdn and styd on wl to ld last 75y* **12/1**

0341 **2** 1 **Classic Role**[10] 1122 5-9-5 **75** ........ (v) ACulhane 12 — 86+
(RIngram) *trckd ldrs: led 3f out: sn kicked 5l clr: drvn over 1f out: hdd fnl 75y* **5/1**[1]

25-0 **3** 5 **Bucks**[68] 618 7-8-8 **71** ........ MHoward(7) 3 — 74
(DKIvory) *settled towards rr: prog 3f out: shkn up and kpt on fr 2f out: tk 3rd nr fin* **33/1**

446- **4** 1 1/4 **Lady McNair**[176] 5505 4-9-7 **78** ........ SSanders 20 — 79
(PDCundell) *trckd ldrs: prog gng easily over 3f out: chsd ldr briefly over 2f out: sn nt qckn and btn* **14/1**

/20- **5** *6* **Skelligs Rock (IRE)**[277] [2928] 4-9-7 **78** RLMoore 9 70
(BWDuke) *racd in midfield: prog 3f out: rdn to dispute 2nd pl briefly over 2f out: sn btn* **40/1**

00-0 **6** *nk* **Invitation**[11] [1103] 6-9-4 **74** RHughes 5 65
(ACharlton) *racd in midfield: effrt and sme prog 3f out: no imp ldrs over 1f out* **20/1**

-000 **7** *2* **Midshipman**[20] [1030] 6-9-5 **75** (v[1]) IMongan 19 63
(AWCarroll) *pushed up to go prom: rdn to chal over 3f out: wknd 2f out* **66/1**

U-05 **8** *1 1/4* **Crown Agent (IRE)**[11] [1103] 4-8-13 **73** LPKeniry(3) 13 59
(AMBalding) *trckd ldrs: effrt gng easily over 3f out: wknd 2f out* **10/1**

4- **9** *3* **Kirov King (IRE)**[179] [5465] 4-9-7 **78** JPMurtagh 11 59
(BGPowell) *settled in rr: gng wl enough over 3f out: sn outpcd: nvr nr ldrs after* **25/1**

0020 **10** *2* **Internationalguest (IRE)**[10] [1114] 5-9-8 **78** (b) PRobinson 10 56
(GGMargarson) *racd in midfield: effrt 3f out: rdn and no prog over 2f out: wknd* **11/2**[2]

04-3 **11** *2* **Kylkenny**[20] [1030] 9-9-6 **76** SDrowne 18 51
(HMorrison) *pressed ldr: led 1/2-way: hdd 3f out: wknd 2f out* **13/2**[3]

050- **12** *2 1/2* **Persian King (IRE)**[205] [4186] 7-10-0 **84** DaneO'Neill 7 55
(JABOld) *hld up wl in rr: rdn wl over 3f out: nvr on terms* **33/1**

600- **13** *9* **Ribbons And Bows (IRE)**[155] [5889] 4-9-7 **80** MartinDwyer 15 37
(CACyzer) *prom tl wknd over 3f out* **50/1**

0-00 **14** *3* **Sahaat**[10] [1114] 6-9-1 **78** SCrawford(7) 17 30
(JAOsborne) *dwlt: hld up: last to 1/2-way: nvr a factor* **40/1**

350- **15** *7* **Makulu (IRE)**[249] [3721] 4-9-6 **77** LDettori 14 18
(BJMeehan) *dwlt: sn chsd ldrs: n.m.r bnd 5f out: sn rdn and struggling* **7/1**

210- **16** *1* **Claradotnet**[192] [5193] 4-9-11 **82** TEDurcan 16 21
(MRChannon) *a towards rr: rdn and wknd over 3f out* **25/1**

-050 **17** *4* **Bowing**[32] [964] 4-9-1 **72** DKinsella 1 5
(PGMurphy) *dwlt: a in rr: wknd 3f out* **40/1**

030 **18** *12* **Rainbow World (IRE)**[10] [1122] 4-9-1 **75** TPQueally(3) 6 —
(AndrewReid) *chsd ldrs: rdn and wknd over 4f out: sn bhd* **50/1**

2132 **19** *dist* **Fortune Point (IRE)**[12] [1097] 6-8-8 **64** ow2 DHolland 2 —
(AWCarroll) *le to 1/2-way: weakene 4f out: t.o* **9/1**

020- **20** *dist* **Royal Trigger**[243] [3897] 4-9-3 **74** CCatlin 8 —
(IanWilliams) *a in rr: rdn after 4f: dropped to last 1/2-way: sn t.o: virtually p.u* **33/1**

2m 40.75s (10.75) **Going Correction** +0.80s/f (Soft)
**WFA** 4 from 5yo+ 1lb **20 Ran SP% 125.3**
Speed ratings: **96,95,92,91,87 86,85,84,82,81 80,78,72,70,65 65,62,54,—,—**CSF £62.54 CT £1985.97 TOTE £18.10: £4.60, £1.80, £7.60, £4.40; EX 187.60 TRIFECTA Not won..
**Owner** K A Cosby **Bred** Biddestone Stud **Trained** Newmarket, Suffolk

**FOCUS**
Quite a competitive race, but once again the field raced towards the far-side rail and finished well strung out. Decent efforts from the first two, although the winning time was very modest for the grade of contest.

**NOTEBOOK**
**Cruise Director**, 6lb higher than when winning over this course and distance when last seen on turf nearly a year ago, was fit from the All-Weather and picked up well to collar the favourite inside the last furlong. He is two from four on turf and must be respected next time.
**Classic Role** took well to a first-time visor when winning at Lingfield on his previous start and, bidding to follow up off a 5lb higher mark on this very different surface, he looked all over the winner when kicked to the front three out, but probably got there too soon as he did little in front and was caught close home.
**Bucks**, back on turf, ran respectably and could be of interest if stepped back up to two miles.
**Lady McNair** was too high in the weights last term off the back of a successful juvenile campaign, but she hails from a yard in good form and made a satisfactory return.
**Skelligs Rock(IRE)**, considered a Derby horse by his trainer this time last season, is still a maiden and was well held on ground that really should have suited.
**Fortune Point(IRE)** *Official explanation: jockey said gelding was unsuited by today's good to soft ground*
**Royal Trigger** *Official explanation: jockey said gelding made a noise*

## 1273 COLLIERS CRE LICENCE & LEISURE CLASSIFIED STKS 1m 67y
4:10 (4:10) (D) 3-Y-O+ **£5,541** (£1,705; £852; £426) **Stalls** High

Form RPR

0-00 **1** **Jools**[10] [1118] 6-9-4 78 TQuinn 5 87
(DKIvory) *settled in midfield: prog over 2f out: hrd rdn to chse ldr fnl f: styd on to ld last strides* **33/1**

000- **2** *nk* **Soyuz (IRE)**[185] [5341] 4-9-6 82 PRobinson 12 88
(MAJarvis) *t.k.h: trckd ldr for 2f: styd prom: rdn to ld over 1f out: hrd drvn fnl f: hdd last strides* **11/4**[1]

6010 **3** *1* **Kentucky King (USA)**[16] [1066] 4-9-9 85 ACulhane 3 89+
(PWHiatt) *dwlt: t.k.h: hld up in last trio: effrt and nt clr run over 2f out: r.o fr over 1f out: gaining at fin* **16/1**

30-5 **4** *3* **Climate (IRE)**[17] [1055] 5-9-4 77 (v[1]) DSweeney 8 78
(JRBoyle) *hld up in tch: effrt to trck ldrs over 2f out: rdn and nt qckn wl over 1f out: one pce after* **25/1**

62-0 **5** *nk* **Ace Of Hearts**[10] [1114] 5-9-7 83 SSanders 10 80
(CFWall) *trckd ldr after 2f: rdn to chal over 2f out: ev ch over 1f out: no ex* **11/2**[3]

0160 **6** *1 1/4* **African Sahara (USA)**[10] [1114] 5-9-9 85 (t) GCarter 11 80+
(MissDMountain) *hld up in rr: n.m.r over 4f out: effrt and nt clr run over 2f out: swtchd rt: styd on wl fnl f* **9/1**

0022 **7** *1/2* **Te Quiero**[23] [1009] 6-9-6 82 (tp) SDrowne 2 76
(MissGayKelleway) *mde most to over 1f out: wknd ins fnl f* **11/2**[3]

034- **8** *2* **Welcome Stranger**[182] [5416] 4-9-4 78 JTate 9 69
(JMPEustace) *pressed ldrs: rdn wl over 2f out: fdd over 1f out* **25/1**

310- **9** *1* **Aimee's Delight**[261] [3410] 4-9-1 80 MFenton 13 64
(JGGiven) *chsd ldrs: rdn over 3f out: no prog and btn 2f out* **33/1**

0-00 **10** *nk* **Krugerrand (USA)**[10] [1114] 5-9-1 80 LisaJones(3) 4 67
(WJMusson) *hld up in rr: effrt 3f out: rdn and no prog over 2f out* **25/1**

101- **11** *1/2* **Anglo Saxon (USA)**[244] [3860] 4-9-8 84 JPMurtagh 14 70
(DRLoder) *racd in midfield: shkn up and no prog over 2f out: fdd* **9/2**[2]

1- **12** *4* **Red Spell (IRE)**[144] [5986] 3-8-3 79 RLMoore 7 57
(RHannon) *chsd ldrs: rdn over 3f out: wknd 2f out* **25/1**

-431 **13** *9* **Topton (IRE)**[41] [870] 10-9-4 80 (b) KDarley 6 38
(PHowling) *hld up in rr: rdn over 3f out: no prog over 2f out: sn wknd* **16/1**

1m 51.27s (5.77) **Going Correction** +0.80s/f (Soft)
**WFA** 3 from 4yo+ 15lb **13 Ran SP% 120.7**
Speed ratings: **103,102,101,98,98 97,96,94,93,93 92,88,79**CSF £118.47 TOTE £22.10: £6.50, £1.40, £5.70; EX 215.80.
**Owner** Anthony W Parsons **Bred** Tsarina Stud **Trained** Radlett, Herts

**FOCUS**
A fair handicap run at a good, solid pace throughout, but this looks typical early-season result and the Form may be turned around in a few weeks.

**NOTEBOOK**
**Jools**, below his best in a couple of runs on the All-Weather at Lingfield recently, bounced right back to form with a narrow victory. Travelling well, he had to be switched out for a run but found plenty for pressure and gradually wore down the eventual runner-up.
**Soyuz(IRE)**, below form in first-time blinkers when last seen 185 days earlier, was seen to much better effect with the headgear left off this time. He was a little keen early on, but had every chance when it mattered.
**Kentucky King(USA)**, racing on turf for only the third time in his career, ran a pleasing enough race. He finished to good effect and promises to get a little farther.
**Climate(IRE)** had been tried in blinkers in the past but this was his first run in a visor. Fit from a recent spin on the All-Weather, this was a respectable effort.
**Ace Of Hearts** has not won since 2002 or on this sort of ground.
**African Sahara(USA)** had to be switched out for a run and was unlucky not to have finished a little closer.
**Te Quiero** had every chance from the front.
**Anglo Saxon(USA)** found little for pressure and has suffered with a breathing problem in the past.
**Topton(IRE)** *Official explanation: trainer said gelding was unsuited by today's good to soft ground*

## 1274 COME RACING AT ROYAL WINDSOR (S) STKS 1m 67y
4:40 (4:41) (G) 3-Y-O+ **£2,996** (£856; £428) **Stalls** High

Form RPR

5006 **1** **Amnesty**[5] [1207] 5-9-6 56 (be) RLMoore 3 62
(GLMoore) *dwlt and nt gng wl in last early: prog over 3f out: chsd ldr 2f out: drvn and styd on to ld last 100y* **4/1**[2]

4000 **2** *1* **Fen Gypsy**[12] [1097] 6-9-12 60 RHavlin 6 66
(PDEvans) *pressed ldrs: led 3f out: rdn over 1f out: hdd and one pce last 100y* **5/1**[3]

0116 **3** *7* **Our Destiny**[3] [1233] 6-9-9 40 SHitchcott(3) 11 52
(AWCarroll) *t.k.h: mde most to 3f out: rdn and one pce fr over 2f out* **12/1**

0651 **4** *3* **Over To You Bert**[27] [999] 5-9-12 45 VSlattery 12 46
(RJHodges) *chsd ldrs: rdn and effrt 3f out: one pce fr over 2f out* **20/1**

5004 **5** *2 1/2* **Muqtadi (IRE)**[3] [1231] 6-9-12 50 SSanders 8 41
(MQuinn) *wl in rr: prog to chse ldrs 3f out: sn one pce and btn* **12/1**

0545 **6** *3/4* **Ballyrush (IRE)**[20] [1031] 4-8-13 57 RKeogh(7) 1 34
(KRBurke) *trckd ldrs: carried wd bnd 5f out: one pce fr 3f out* **14/1**

2-00 **7** *nk* **Espada (IRE)**[75] [575] 8-9-12 77 DHolland 7 39
(JAOsborne) *w ldrs: wnt sharply to far rail 5f out: ev ch over 2f out: sn wknd* **11/4**[1]

/05- **8** *27* **Prince Albert**[398] [669] 6-9-6 (t) JFEgan 5 —
(JRJenkins) *a in rr: wknd 3f out: t.o* **20/1**

0260 **9** *1/2* **Kumakawa**[3] [1233] 6-8-13 40 (b) LiamJones(7) 10 —
(EAWheeler) *a in rr: hanging and t.o 3f out* **20/1**

**10** *1 1/2* **Jem's Law**[15] 5-8-8 (v[1]) JJeffrey(7) 9 —
(JRJenkins) *a in rr: wknd 3f out: t.o* **66/1**

3023 **11** *1 3/4* **Just Wiz**[19] [1037] 8-9-12 40 (b) TGMcLaughlin 2 —
(NPLittmoden) *racd in midfield: rdn over 3f out: sn wknd and eased: t.o* **9/1**

000- **12** *2* **Whiplash (IRE)**[182] [5421] 3-8-5 60 RSmith 4 —
(RHannon) *a towards rr: wknd over 3f out: t.o* **12/1**

0040 **13** *11* **Miss Celerity**[34] [949] 4-9-1 35 SDrowne 13 —
(MJHaynes) *w ldrs to over 3f out: wknd and heavily eased: t.o* **40/1**

1m 51.29s (5.79) **Going Correction** +0.80s/f (Soft)
**WFA** 3 from 4yo+ 15lb **13 Ran SP% 121.3**
Speed ratings: **103,102,95,92,89 88,88,61,60,59 57,55,44**CSF £22.99 TOTE £5.20: £1.80, £3.00, £2.70; EX 24.80.The winner was bought in for 3,600gns.
**Owner** G A Jackman, J F Jackman **Bred** Lord Halifax **Trained** Woodingdean, E Sussex

**FOCUS**
A very moderate race with the market leaders all struggling for form, but the winning time was decent for a seller. Again, they all raced towards the far side in the straight.

**NOTEBOOK**
**Amnesty**, dropped into selling company for the first time, was not exactly the most willing of partners for Moore - he appeared reluctant to race when the stalls opened and needed plenty of stoking to get past Fen Gypsy - but did what was required to get off the mark at the 20th attempt.
**Fen Gypsy**, with the blinkers off on this switch back to the turf, had conditions to suit and ran well. He was well clear of the remainder.
**Our Destiny** has been in good form on Fibresand recently and this was by no means a bad effort switched back to the turf. He is rated just 40 on turf and would be of interest in a regional race.
**Over To You Bert**, successful in a poor seller at Lingfield on his latest start, had a bit to do at the weights but acquitted himself with credit.
**Muqtadi(IRE)** is very hard to win with.
**Espada(IRE)**, the best in at the weights, travelled well enough but found very little when asked. This was disappointing.

## 1275 CANONS HEALTH CLUB STOKE POGES H'CAP 1m 67y
5:10 (5:20) (E) (0-75,75) 3-Y-O+ **£4,355** (£1,340; £670; £335) **Stalls** High

Form RPR

2120 **1** **Caroubier (IRE)**[16] [1066] 4-9-7 **68** TEDurcan 11 82
(JGallagher) *wl off the pce in last pair: rdn and gd prog fr over 2f out: styd on to ld ins fnl f: sn clr* **16/1**

466- **2** *5* **Soller Bay**[192] [5194] 7-10-0 **75** DarrenWilliams 14 79+
(KRBurke) *pushed up to press ldr: led 4f out and styd in centre: drvn and hdd wl over 1f out: upsides ins fnl f: no ch wnr* **13/2**[3]

20-4 **3** *nk* **Oh So Rosie (IRE)**[4] [1225] 4-8-6 **60** BSwarbrick(7) 13 63
(JSMoore) *dwlt: prog fr rr on inner 5f out: styd centre st: hdwy to ld wl over 1f out: hdd and no ex ins fnl f* **7/1**

500- **4** *6* **Tiber Tiger (IRE)**[182] [5416] 4-9-7 **75** (v) StevenHarrison(7) 17 65
(NPLittmoden) *trckd ldrs: effrt and wl in tch over 2f out: sn bmpd along and btn* **25/1**

4410 **5** *8* **Realism (FR)**[38] [909] 4-9-4 **65** ACulhane 6 38
(PWHiatt) *hld up towards rr: rdn 4f out: kpt on one pce u.p fnl 3f: no ch* **25/1**

100- **6** *1 1/4* **Phred**[52] [5577] 4-9-5 **66** SCarson 10 37
(RFJohnsonHoughton) *trckd ldrs: effrt 3f out: rdn and fnd nil 2f out: no ch after* **16/1**

1445 **7** *1 3/4* **Musical Gift**[10] [1118] 4-9-8 **69** (p) PRobinson 18 36
(CNAllen) *trckd ldrs: wl in tch 3f out: sn rdn and btn* **5/1**[1]

3-00 **8** *1 1/2* **Karathaena (IRE)**[17] [1055] 4-9-7 **68** TQuinn 3 32
(JWHills) *racd in last pair: sme prog against far rail whn n.m.r 2f out: n.d* **33/1**

01-0 **9** *2* **Super Song**[16] [1066] 4-9-12 **73** (t) RHavlin 2 33
(PDEvans) *led at fast pce to 4f out: wknd 3f out* **25/1**

00-6 **10** *1 1/2* **Liberty Royal**[65] [647] 5-9-8 **69** SSanders 1 26
(PJMakin) *nvr beyond midfield: rdn and struggling in rr 4f out* **14/1**

003- **11** *9* **Gracia**[150] 5945 5-9-6 **67** ........ MartinDwyer 8 5
(SCWilliams) *pressed ldng pair: rdn and wknd over 3f out* **10/1**

1-00 **12** *5* **Wood Fern (UAE)**[9] 1132 4-9-6 **70** ........ DCorby(3) 16 —
(MRChannon) *chsd ldrs: rdn and no imp over 3f out: sn wknd* **28/1**

060/ **13** *5* **Bakiri (IRE)**[21] 3789 6-10-0 **75** ........ LDettori 4 —
(AndrewReid) *a wl in rr: rdn and struggling over 3f out* **12/1**

00-0 **14** *12* **Turn Around**[88] 476 4-9-2 **63** ........ KDarley 9 —
(BWHills) *sn pushed along in midfield: struggling 4f out: sn bhd* **16/1**

01- **15** *2 1/2* **Enchanted Princess**[252] 3648 4-9-11 **72** ........ MHills 7 —
(WJHaggas) *chsd ldrs: rdn 5f out: wknd over 3f out: sn bhd* **6/1**[2]

0/00 **16** *7* **Trusted Instinct (IRE)**[41] 870 4-9-8 **72** ........(t) TPQueally(3) 12 —
(CADwyer) *a in rr: rdn and struggling 4f out: sn bhd* **40/1**

040- **17** *22* **Oh Boy (IRE)**[277] 2929 4-9-7 **68** ........ RHughes 5 —
(RHannon) *nvr gng wl: rdn 5f out: t.o* **20/1**

240- **18** *30* **Bishopstone Man**[166] 5712 7-9-5 **73** ........ CCavanagh(7) 15 —
(HCandy) *racd in midfield tl wknd 4f out: t.o* **12/1**

1m 51.63s (6.13) **Going Correction** +0.80s/f (Soft) **18** Ran SP% **130.7**
Speed ratings: **101,96,95,89,81 80,78,77,75,73 64,59,54,42,40 33,11,**—CSF £113.81 CT £827.48 TOTE £19.60: £3.80, £1.80, £2.20, £8.00; EX 148.80 Place 6 £184.17, Place 5 £117.66.

**Owner** C R Marks (banbury) **Bred** J K Grimes **Trained** Chastleton, Oxon

**FOCUS**
The field raced towards the centre-to-far side of the track in the straight in this modest contest. The early pace was strong, but the extended distances suggest this should not be taken literally.

**NOTEBOOK**
**Caroubier(IRE)**, on the same mark as when last successful on turf, benefited from being held up off the strong pace and won going well clear. The winning margin probably flatters him, but he would be of interest if turned out under a penalty.
**Soller Bay** loves racing prominently on this sort of ground and did just that. However, he may have been forced to go a little quicker than he would have liked and had no answer to the winner's late burst.
**Oh So Rosie(IRE)** raced more towards the centre of the track than some of the others, but still had every chance.
**Tiber Tiger(IRE)** made a pleasing enough return to action and should be better for this first run in 182 days.
**Realism(FR)**, racing on turf for only the second time, was well beaten.
**Musical Gift** failed to perform on his turf debut.
**Oh Boy(IRE)** *Official explanation: jockey said colt was never travelling*
T/Jkpt: Not won. T/Plt: £854.70 to a £1 stake. Pool: £48,241.05. 41.20 winning tickets. T/Qpdt: £27.80 to a £1 stake. Pool: £3,289.60. 87.50 winning tickets. JN

# 1239 LINGFIELD (L-H)
## Tuesday, April 6

**OFFICIAL GOING: Standard**

## 1276 BETDIRECT.CO.UK MAIDEN AUCTION STKS 5f (P)
**2:30** (2:30) (H) 2-Y-O **£1,284** (£367; £183) **Stalls** High

Form RPR

3 **1** **Smokincanon**[7] 1183 2-8-11 ........ RMiles(3) 8 62
(WGMTurner) *mde all: drew 3l clr wl over 1f out: pushed out fnl f: unchal* **4/1**[2]

**2** *1 1/2* **Lateral Thinker (IRE)** 2-8-9 ........ SWKelly 6 51
(JAOsborne) *chsd ldrs: prog 1/2-way: rn green and wd bnd 2f out: chsd wnr over 1f out: kpt on but nvr able to chal* **11/1**

**3** *1 3/4* **Gaudalpin (IRE)** 2-8-9 ........ TEDurcan 5 44
(MJWallace) *chsd ldrs: pushed along 1/2-way: kpt on same pce fr over 1f out* **7/2**[1]

4 **4** *1/2* **Grezie**[11] 1115 2-8-9 ........ NPollard 10 42
(JRBest) *chsd wnr: rdn over 3f out: one pce and lost 2nd over 1f out* **4/1**[2]

**5** *1/2* **Speed Dial Harry (IRE)** 2-9-0 ........ DarrenWilliams 4 45
(KRBurke) *chsd ldrs: shkn up and no imp over 2f out: kpt on fnl f* **10/1**[3]

**6** *1 3/4* **Zachy Boy** 2-9-0 ........ MartinDwyer 9 38
(JSMoore) *dwlt: in rr tl prog on outer 2f out: no hdwy over 1f out* **12/1**

**7** *3/4* **Comintrue (IRE)** 2-8-6 ........ TPQueally(3) 3 30
(EJO'Neill) *chsd ldng pair to 2f out: wknd fnl f* **16/1**

**8** *4* **Il Pranzo** 2-9-0 ........ RHughes 2 19
(SKirk) *racd in midfield: nudged along and outpcd 2f out: no ch after* **4/1**[2]

**9** *2 1/2* **Faithfull Girl (IRE)** 2-8-4 ........ NChalmers(5) 7 4
(MissZCDavison) *s.i.s: outpcd and a bhd* **25/1**

**10** *1 1/4* **She's My Dream (IRE)** 2-8-9 ........ JDSmith 1 —
(JSMoore) *s.i.s: outpcd and a bhd* **50/1**

60.67 secs (0.89) **Going Correction** 0.0s/f (Stan) **10** Ran SP% **119.0**
Speed ratings: **92,89,86,86,85 82,81,74,70,68**CSF £48.62 TOTE £5.10: £2.40, £3.90, £2.50; EX 31.60.

**Owner** D A Drake **Bred** D A Drake **Trained** Sigwells, Somerset

**FOCUS**
A fair time for the grade with the winner running to his debut form. As is often the case in races like this at this stage of the season, previous experience was the key.

**NOTEBOOK**
**Smokincanon**, with experience on his side, confirmed the promise of his Folkestone effort and made every yard. He was inclined to hang slightly to his right on the home bend, but besides that this effort could not be faulted.
**Lateral Thinker(IRE)**, a half-sister to Polytrack winner Best Before out of a half-sister to Shambo, showed ability despite not handling the turn into the straight very well. A less turning track and eventually a longer trip should suit her.
**Gaudalpin(IRE)**, whose dam won three times including once on sand, was never far away but could never get on terms with the winner. How much she will come on from this is difficult to say as she was backed as though fitness was not a problem.
**Grezie**, fourth in a Doncaster seller on her debut for a different yard, was bustled along to take a handy position from her outside draw but could not maintain the gallop. Despite this only being a Regional maiden auction event, it may still have been a better race.
**Speed Dial Harry(IRE)**, out of a winning sister to Magic Of Love, did not set the world alight but may do better over further in time.

## 1277 NEW SITE @ BETDIRECT.CO.UK BANDED STKS 1m 2f (P)
**3:00** (3:01) (H) 4-Y-0+ **£1,452** (£415; £207) **Stalls** Low

Form RPR

0505 **1** **Galey River (USA)**[8] 1166 5-8-11 40 ........ DCorby(3) 6 45
(JJSheehan) *racd in midfield: rdn and outpcd 3f out: gd prog u.p over 1f out: styd on wl to ld last 75y* **5/1**[1]

306- **2** *3/4* **Candy Anchor (FR)**[284] 2741 5-9-0 35 ........(b) IMongan 4 44
(REPeacock) *t.k.h: hld up in midfield: prog to chse ldng pair over 2f out: rdn to chal 1f out: styd on same pce* **33/1**

/100 **3** *hd* **Ndola**[28] 996 5-9-0 40 ........ SWKelly 2 44
(BJCurley) *pressed ldr over 8f out: poised to chal gng easily over 2f out: rdn and fnd nil over 1f out: upsides fnl f: nt qckn* **5/1**[1]

-010 **4** *1/2* **Kingsdon (IRE)**[35] 947 7-9-0 40 ........(vt) MartinDwyer 13 43
(TJFitzgerald) *led after 1f and set gd pce: rdn over 2f out: kpt on wl tl hdd & wknd last 75y* **6/1**[2]

-002 **5** *1 3/4* **Ryan's Bliss (IRE)**[8] 1166 4-8-11 40 ........ J-PGuillambert(3) 8 40
(TDMcCarthy) *chsd ldrs: prog over 2f out: drvn and cl up on inner over 1f out: fdd fnl f* **13/2**[3]

0005 **6** *1* **Hellbent**[8] 1167 5-8-11 35 ........ LFletcher(3) 12 38
(JAOsborne) *s.s: wl in rr tl prog to chse ldrs 3f out: sn rdn: c wd bnd 2f out: nt qckn over 1f out* **10/1**

0030 **7** *3/4* **Platinum Boy (IRE)**[8] 1167 4-9-0 35 ........(p) VSlattery 14 36
(MWellings) *racd in last trio: drvn and struggling over 4f out: kpt on fnl 2f: no ch* **25/1**

0-66 **8** *3/4* **Prince Du Soleil (FR)**[35] 949 8-9-0 35 ........[1] RHughes 5 35
(JRJenkins) *trckd ldrs: gng wl enough over 2f out: rdn and nt qckn over 1f out: fdd* **7/1**

00-0 **9** *4* **Sweet Reflection (IRE)**[28] 996 4-8-11 40 ........(t) LisaJones(3) 3 28
(WJMusson) *dwlt: wl in rr: rdn and no prog 3f out* **20/1**

0-04 **10** *3/4* **Eurolink Artemis**[8] 1166 7-8-7 40 ........(p) MHalford(7) 10 27
(JulianPoulton) *trckd ldrs tl wknd over 2f out* **10/1**

400- **11** *1 1/2* **Dances With Angels (IRE)**[230] 4297 4-9-0 35 ........ PMQuinn 1 24
(MrsALMKing) *sn pushed along towards rr: struggling u.p 4f out* **12/1**

-000 **12** *shd* **Time Flyer**[8] 1164 4-9-0 40 ........ SRighton 11 24
(WDeBest-Turner) *dwlt: t.k.h and hld up in rr: no prog over 2f out* **33/1**

0540 **13** *5* **Santa Catalina (IRE)**[10] 1136 5-8-11 40 ........(p) TPQueally(3) 9 15
(CADwyer) *led for 1f: chsd ldng pair to over 2f out: wknd rapidly* **12/1**

00-0 **14** *5* **Shaamit's All Over**[91] 449 5-8-11 40 ........ BReilly(3) 7 6
(BAPearce) *s.i.s: a in rr: wknd rapidly over 2f out* **20/1**

2m 8.62s (0.77) **Going Correction** 0.0s/f (Stan) **14** Ran SP% **126.3**
Speed ratings: **96,95,95,94,93 92,92,91,88,87 86,86,82,78**CSF £189.82 TOTE £7.70: £2.20, £8.80, £2.00; EX 243.50.

**Owner** D J Dowling **Bred** Gainesway Thoroughbreds Ltd **Trained** Ashington, W Sussex

**FOCUS**
A very modest contest, but at least one run at a true pace.

**NOTEBOOK**
**Galey River(USA)**, ridden with much more restraint this time, still had plenty to do once in line for home but then produced a rare turn of foot to snatch the race. He was getting off the mark at the 18th attempt, but could pick up a similar contest in his current mood.
**Candy Anchor(FR)** ◆, a long-standing maiden, had every chance and this was not a bad effort considering she was returning from a ten-month break. She looks up to winning a race like this.
**Ndola**, dropped slightly in grade, despite his Wolverhampton victory put up arguably his best ever performance here, but that is not saying very much.
**Kingsdon(IRE)** had to do quite a lot early on in order to bag the early lead from his wide stall and, given the margins between the principals at the end, emerges with a little credit.
**Ryan's Bliss(IRE)** was unable to confirm the form with the winner from their last meeting here and is going to find it hard to win a race.
**Hellbent** was trying his longest trip to date and looked to be hanging right at various stages.
**Shaamit's All Over** *Official explanation: jockey said mare resented the kickback in the back straight*

## 1278 BET IN RUNNING @ BETDIRECT.CO.UK BANDED STKS 1m (P)
**3:30** (3:31) (H) 3-Y-0+ **£1,645** (£470; £235) **Stalls** High

Form RPR

0346 **1** **Ballare (IRE)**[23] 1020 5-9-7 45 ........(v) OUrbina 2 56
(BobJones) *t.k.h: trckd ldng pair: effrt to ld over 1f out: drvn clr* **3/1**[1]

5450 **2** *3 1/2* **Single Track Mind**[6] 1204 6-9-7 45 ........ MartinDwyer 9 48
(JRBoyle) *s.i.s: hld up last of main gp: nt clr run over 2f out: hanging rt but prog wl over 1f out: r.o to take 2nd nr fin* **11/2**[3]

0132 **3** *1* **Dial Square**[8] 1165 3-8-6 45 ........(b) CCatlin 8 46
(PHowling) *reluctant to enter stalls: t.k.h: pressed ldng pair: effrt to chal over 2f out: hung rt bnd wl over 1f out: nt qckn* **4/1**[2]

2-04 **4** *3/4* **Cooden Beach (IRE)**[28] 996 4-9-2 45 ........ HayleyTurner(5) 11 44
(MLWBell) *chsd ldrs: cl up over 2f out: rdn and one pce wl over 1f out* **9/1**

5005 **5** *3/4* **Larad (IRE)**[13] 1102 3-8-6 45 ........(b) DKinsella 3 42
(JSMoore) *racd in midfield: nt clr run on inner and lost pl over 2f out: drvn and kpt on fnl f* **12/1**

-020 **6** *3/4* **Harbour House**[40] 895 5-9-7 45 ........ NPollard 10 41
(JJBridger) *t.k.h: led for 1f: led again 3f out to over 1f out: fdd* **13/2**

0520 **7** *1 1/4* **Regency Malaya**[15] 1080 3-8-6 40 ........(bt) SRighton 12 38
(MFHarris) *sn rdn to stay in tch in rr: effrt u.p over 2f out: no prog over 1f out* **16/1**

504- **8** *1/2* **Brandywine Bay (IRE)**[148] 5973 4-9-7 45 ........(p) GHannon 6 37
(APJones) *hld up in rr: prog into midfield gng easily over 2f out: bmpd along and nt qckn over 1f out: no ch* **16/1**

50-0 **9** *3 1/2* **Stagecoach Ruby**[48] 822 3-8-6 45 ........(e) RLMoore 1 28
(GLMoore) *hld up in rr: rdn and no prog over 2f out* **16/1**

0-03 **10** *1* **Westmead Etoile**[56] 737 4-9-7 40 ........(v) RHughes 4 26
(JRJenkins) *racd in midfield: lost pl u.p over 2f out* **12/1**

LL-0 **11** *25* **Silver Louie (IRE)**[38] 914 4-9-7 45 ........ SCarson 5 —
(GBBalding) *rel to r and lft 20l a t.o* **33/1**

4500 **12** *2* **Wilom (GER)**[8] 1166 6-9-7 40 ........(b[1]) DaneO'Neill 7 —
(MRHoad) *pushed up to ld after 1f: hdd & wknd rapidly 3f out: t.o* **16/1**

1m 39.7s (0.15) **Going Correction** 0.0s/f (Stan)
**WFA** 3 from 4yo+ 15lb **12** Ran SP% **125.6**
Speed ratings: **99,95,94,93,93 92,91,90,87,86 61,59**CSF £20.61 TOTE £4.50: £1.60, £2.20, £1.70; EX 30.50.

**Owner** The Ballare Partnership **Bred** Oyster Farm **Trained** Wickhambrook, Suffolk

**FOCUS**
A fair race of its type and the pace was solid. The winner reproduced his best turf form.

**NOTEBOOK**
**Ballare(IRE)** ◆, back over probably his best trip, was well backed and could be called the winner some way out. The only question was whether a gap would appear when he needed it, but fortunately it did and once he went through it the race was over. This may have been his 17th attempt at getting off the mark, but such was the ease of his victory that he may well follow up.
**Single Track Mind** came from a long way back to snatch second and could be said to have run an encouraging race, but he has done this before and not built on it.
**Dial Square** is performing consistently well in this type of contest and ran right up to his best.
**Cooden Beach(IRE)**, back in trip, had every chance but did not find much off the bridle.
**Larad(IRE)**, ridden differently this time, did not enjoy the clearest of passages. He finished well but does look very moderate.
**Harbour House**, given a positive ride, went for home off the final bend but again did not appear to see out the trip.
**Brandywine Bay(IRE)** *Official explanation: jockey said filly had a breathing problem*

## 1279 LITTLEWOODS BET DIRECT (S) STKS 7f (P)
4:00 (4:02) (H) 3-Y-O+ £1,288 (£368; £184) Stalls Low

Form RPR

-600 **1** **Somerset West (IRE)**[29] 987 4-9-7 50 DaneO'Neill 12 51
(MrsLStubbs) *sn prom on outer: led 3f out: rdn 2f out: hdd ent fnl f: rallied to ld again nr fin* **16/1**

4050 **2** *hd* **Legal Set (IRE)**[14] 1082 8-9-7 53 RHughes 10 50
(WJMusson) *led 1f: w ldrs after: trckd ldr gng easily 3f out: led ent fnl f: shkn up and hdd nr fin* **3/1**[2]

05-5 **3** *nk* **Peregian (IRE)**[8] 1177 6-9-0 49 MCoumbe(7) 1 50
(JAkehurst) *dwlt: t.k.h: hld up in rr: prog on inner 2f out: shuffled along and styd on wl fnl f: gaining fin: too much to do* **7/1**

0055 **4** *1 ¾* **Hinchley Wood (IRE)**[6] 1206 5-9-7 35 (b¹) NPollard 8 45
(JRBest) *dwlt: settled in rr: prog over 2f out: drvn and kpt on fr over 1f out: nvr able to chal* **14/1**

3236 **5** *nk* **Lucayan Monarch**[11] 1121 6-9-12 54 (p) SWKelly 11 49
(PSMcentee) *pushed along in rr early: prog to chse ldrs over 2f out: no imp over 1f out* **11/4**[1]

0/00 **6** *nk* **Happy Camper (IRE)**[14] 1087 4-9-7 55 IMongan 4 44
(MRHoad) *t.k.h: trckd ldrs: nt clr run and lost pl over 2f out: styd on again u.p fnl f* **14/1**

4003 **7** *2* **Onefortheboys (IRE)**[8] 1169 5-9-7 40 SWhitworth 9 38
(DFlood) *dwlt: settled in rr: prog over 2f out: no imp ldrs over 1f out* **12/1**

0000 **8** *1 ¾* **Definitely Special (IRE)**[28] 1000 6-8-11 35 (p) MSavage(5) 5 29
(NEBerry) *chsd ldrs: fdd u.p fr over 2f out* **33/1**

500- **9** *3 ½* **Out Of Tune**[232] 4241 4-9-4 45 DCorby(3) 3 25
(CWeedon) *t.k.h: hld up in cl tch: wknd 2f out* **66/1**

4060 **10** *8* **Lively Felix**[15] 1076 7-9-2 35 (b¹) DNolan(5) 6 4
(DGBridgwater) *pushed up to ld after 1f: hdd 3f out: sn wknd* **50/1**

4150 **11** *6* **Foolish Thought (IRE)**[13] 1098 4-9-7 49 (tp) TEaves(5) 7 —
(IAWood) *chsd ldrs tl wknd 3f out: sn bhd* **12/1**

-340 **12** *1* **Abuelos**[50] 791 5-9-2 45 DFox(5) 2 —
(TPMcgovern) *rel to r and lft 20l a wl bhd* **6/1**[3]

1m 26.83s (0.89) **Going Correction** 0.0s/f (Stan) **12 Ran SP% 119.4**
Speed ratings: **94,93,93,91,91 90,88,86,82,73 66,65** CT £23.60 TOTE £4.40: £1.90, £1.90, £; EX114.20 1.The winner was sold for 4,000gns to John Best. Legal Set was claimed for £4,000 by Ann Stokell. Peregian was claimed by Andrew Reid for £4,000
**Owner** Mrs L Stubbs **Bred** Broguestown Stud **Trained** Malton, N. Yorks

**FOCUS**
A poor seller and a modest winning time with the form horses below their best.\n\x\x .

**NOTEBOOK**
**Somerset West(IRE)**, appreciating both the step up in trip and return to positive tactics, bravely fought back to snatch the contest near the line and now joins John Best.
**Legal Set(IRE)**, who has become devilishly difficult to win with, was at the head of affairs from the off but did not go off at a rate of knots and his rider seemed determined to settle him amongst the leaders. Appearing to be going better than the eventual winner, he fought his way back to the front in plenty of time only to have the race snatched away from him close to the line. He was claimed by Ann Stokell, but went down with colic in the stables afterwards. *Official explanation: jockey said his orders were to jump well, as he was drawn high, get across to the rail, kid along gelding and let it think it is going well, adding that he did break well and was given a lead, going well on the bridle, by Lively Felix but did want to be in front at that stage; when he did eventually pick up, and head, Somerset West in last 100yds he was unable to maintain his momentum and was beaten on the line*
**Peregian(IRE)** came from a long way back from the home turn and was finishing in good style, but could never quite get to the leaders in time and would probably have preferred an extra furlong. He now joins Andrew Reid.
**Hinchley Wood(IRE)**, who is still to finish in the front three, ran with a degree of credit in the first-time blinkers.
**Lucayan Monarch**, having his 14th start of the year, had every chance but could not deliver a telling blow.
**Happy Camper(IRE)**showed his first glimpse of ability since arriving from Spain and ran as though he would prefer further.

## 1280 BET DIRECT ON SKY ACTIVE BANDED STKS 6f (P)
4:30 (4:33) (H) 3-Y-O+ £1,631 (£466; £233) Stalls Low

Form RPR

5023 **1** **Shirley Oaks (IRE)**[8] 1165 6-9-2 40 NChalmers(5) 1 51
(MissZCDavison) *sn rdn in last: prog fr 1/2-way: sustained run on outer fr over 1f out to ld last 75y* **5/1**[2]

-600 **2** *¾* **Night Cap (IRE)**[37] 930 5-9-4 45 J-PGuillambert(3) 2 49
(TDMccarthy) *dwlt: prog fr rr to chse ldrs 1/2-way: sn rdn: effrt to ld jst ins fnl f: kpt on: hdd last 75y* **11/2**[3]

63-0 **3** *2* **Ballygriffin Kid**[35] 946 4-9-2 45 DFox(5) 5 43
(TPMcgovern) *hld up in midfield: nt clr run on inner over 2f out: styd on wl fnl f: nrst fin* **6/1**

0060 **4** *½* **Law Maker**[14] 1082 4-9-7 40 (v¹) MartinDwyer 9 41
(MABuckley) *plld hrd: sn w ldrs: led wl over 1f out: hdd & wknd jst ins fnl f* **14/1**

-000 **5** *1* **Top Place**[14] 1083 3-8-2 45 (p) HelenSmith(7) 4 38
(CADwyer) *trckd ldr: shuffled along and nt qckn over 1f out: kpt on* **33/1**

6-04 **6** *shd* **Fayr Firenze (IRE)**[15] 1078 3-8-9 45 (v¹) SRighton 3 38
(MFHarris) *hld up in rr: effrt over 2f out: one pce and nvr rchd ldrs* **20/1**

-660 **7** *2 ½* **Westmead Tango**[43] 859 4-9-7 40 RHughes 8 30
(JRJenkins) *mde most to wl over 1f out: fdd* **10/1**

00-0 **8** *hd* **The Lady Would (IRE)**[14] 1089 5-9-2 35 DNolan(5) 6 30
(DGBridgwater) *chsd ldrs: drvn over 2f out: wknd over 1f out* **50/1**

660- **9** *1* **Travellers Joy**[230] 4288 4-9-7 45 VSlattery 7 27
(RJHodges) *chsd ldrs tl wknd u.p over 1f out* **33/1**

0200 **10** *1 ½* **Tripti (IRE)**[18] 1051 4-9-7 45 NPollard 10 22
(JJBridger) *w ldrs: ev ch 2f out: sn wknd* **10/1**

3600 **11** *5* **Confuzed**[4] 1228 4-9-7 45 (e) OUrbina 11 7
(DFlood) *hld up in rr: shkn up and no rspnse 2f out: sn bhd* **7/1**

3201 **12** *6* **Packin Em In**[8] 1165 6-9-10 35 DCorby(3) 12 —
(JRBoyle) *hld up in rr: wknd and eased 2f out* **4/1**[1]

1m 13.37s (0.45) **Going Correction** 0.0s/f (Stan)
**WFA** 3 from 4yo+ 12lb **12 Ran SP% 116.3**
Speed ratings: **97,96,93,92,91 91,87,87,86,84 77,69**CSF £30.73 TOTE £5.00: £2.20, £4.30, £1.10; EX 29.40.
**Owner** The Secret Circle **Bred** Miss Honora Corridan **Trained** Ashurstwood, W Sussex

**FOCUS**
A routine banded event run at a fair pace and the form for the grade looks reliable.

**NOTEBOOK**
**Shirley Oaks(IRE)** has shown her best form over seven furlongs before now, but the solid pace enabled her to be played late and her wide run in the final furlong gained her the day. She should continue to do well in this sphere.
**Night Cap(IRE)**, with the blinkers left off and making his debut at this level, made progress racing down the false straight and looked to have made a race-winning move passing the furlong pole, but the winner's late challenge proved irresistible. This looks to be his grade now.
**Ballygriffin Kid** ◆ ran a good deal better on this second start back and was noted making good late progress against the inside rail. He is worth noting for a similar contest over seven.
**Law Maker**, who had finished no closer than sixth in 15 previous attempts, looked to be going well before hitting the front over a furlong out but did not get home. He is obviously very moderate, but may be worth another try over the minimum trip in a similar contest.
**Top Place** is less exposed that her rivals, but is still to show any worthwhile ability.
**Westmead Tango** made the early running, but faded tamely in the home straight and has lost her form badly this winter.
**Confuzed** has not built on a promising effort here in February.

## 1281 BET DIRECT INTERACTIVE APPRENTICE BANDED STKS 1m 5f (P)
5:00 (5:00) (H) 4-Y-O+ £1,477 (£422; £211) Stalls Low

Form RPR

0063 **1** **Birth Of The Blues**[13] 1101 8-8-11 40 DonnaBashton(5) 12 45
(ACharlton) *hld up in rr: last 5f out: rapid prog on outer over 3f out: pushed into ld jst over 1f out: in command after* **25/1**

60/1 **2** *1 ¼* **Lissahanelodge**[8] 1164 5-9-8 40 NChalmers 6 49
(PRHedger) *dwlt: hld up in rr: rapid prog on outer 4f out: rdn to join ldr 2f out: hanging and nt qckn jst over 1f out* **15/8**[1]

1402 **3** *nk* **Little Richard (IRE)**[8] 1164 5-9-2 40 (p) MSavage 1 43
(MWellings) *w ldrs: drvn to ld over 3f out: jnd 2f out: hanging and hdd jst over 1f out: nt qckn* **9/2**[2]

334- **4** *1 ¼* **Mercurious (IRE)**[106] 6233 4-9-0 40 DNolan 2 41
(JMackie) *prom in chsng gp: rdn 3f out: one pce and nvr able to chal* **8/1**

0/0- **5** *nk* **Ressource (FR)**[47] 5576 5-9-2 40 (be) AQuinn 11 41
(GLMoore) *hld up in rr: rdn and outpcd 3f out: styd on fr over 1f out: nrst fin* **25/1**

10-0 **6** *1 ¼* **Sariba**[46] 839 5-8-13 35 HayleyTurner(3) 3 39
(ACharlton) *led to over 5f out: styd chsng ldrs: one pce u.p fr 3f out* **33/1**

0/0- **7** *1 ¾* **Mantilla**[150] 635 7-8-13 30 (v) SCrawford(3) 10 36
(IanWilliams) *hld up in tch: rdn 5f out: outpcd 3f out: no imp ldrs after* **9/1**

2440 **8** *5* **The Last Mohican**[8] 1164 5-8-13 40 (p) SJDonohoe(3) 5 29
(PHowling) *pressed ldr: led over 5f out to over 3f out: wknd wl over 1f out* **12/1**

000- **9** *hd* **Dash For Glory**[256] 3567 5-9-2 40 JFMcDonald 13 29
(MBlanshard) *prom tl lost pl 1/2-way: last and struggling over 4f out* **20/1**

0000 **10** *2 ½* **Alimiste (IRE)**[13] 1101 4-9-0 40 TEaves 8 26
(IAWood) *racd in midfield: outpcd u.str.p over 3f out: wknd 2f out* **50/1**

0015 **11** *2* **Antony Ebeneezer**[8] 1164 5-9-2 40 (t) RThomas 4 23
(CRDore) *hld up in tch: rdn and wknd 3f out* **7/1**[3]

/0-0 **12** *5* **Elle Royal (IRE)**[28] 996 5-9-2 40 DFox 7 16
(TPMcgovern) *dwlt: sn pushed along in rr: wknd over 3f out* **66/1**

30-0 **13** *¾* **Jezadil (IRE)**[8] 1164 6-8-13 40 (p) KristinStubbs(3) 9 15
(MrsLStubbs) *dwlt: in tch: bmpd along 4f out: wknd 3f out* **20/1**

2m 49.22s (1.14) **Going Correction** 0.0s/f (Stan)
**WFA** 4 from 5yo+ 2lb **13 Ran SP% 117.9**
Speed ratings: **96,95,95,94,94 93,92,89,89,87 86,83,82**CSF £67.24 TOTE £15.20: £2.70, £1.30, £2.10; EX 98.40 Place 6 £52.32, Place 5 £25.54.
**Owner** J M Sancaster **Bred** G Middlebrook **Trained** Collingbourne Ducis, Wilts
■ Donna Bashton's first winner since becoming an apprentice.
■ Stewards Enquiry : T Eaves two-day ban: used whip with excessive force (Apr 17,18)

**FOCUS**
A poor contest run at an even gallop.

**NOTEBOOK**
**Birth Of The Blues**, held up out the back early, shadowed the favourite as he made his move from a similar position and, under a cool ride from his pilot, who has been victorious on him before, found plenty when asked. He may have been aided to a certain extent by the second and third barging into each other in the final furlong, but was nonetheless a worthy winner and this trip proved ideal.
**Lissahanelodge** tried the same tactics that proved successful here eight days earlier, making a sudden move from the back half a mile from home, but the eventual winner was sat right on his tail and found more than him when asked in the home straight. He did not help his chances by constantly hanging into the third in the final furlong, but it did not make the difference between victory and defeat. He did not appear to bounce.
**Little Richard(IRE)** stays further than this and tried to make his stamina tell, but was done for quick in the straight and getting involved in a barging match with the favourite may have cost him second.
**Mercurious(IRE)**, returning from a four-month break, stayed on to finish fourth and there appeared no stamina problems on this occasion.
**Ressource(FR)**, returning to the Flat after a spell over hurdles, may have found this an insufficient test of stamina.
T/Plt: £138.70 to a £1 stake. Pool £32,461.90, 170.80 winning tickets T/Qpdt: £6.20 to a £1 stake. Pool £2,663.50, 317.50 winning tickets JN

# PONTEFRACT (L-H)
Tuesday, April 6

**OFFICIAL GOING: Good to soft changing to soft after race 2 (2.50)**

## 1282 BETFAIR.COM APPRENTICE SERIES (ROUND ONE) H'CAP 1m 4f 8y
2:20 (2:20) (E) (0-70,70) 3-Y-O+ £4,221 (£1,299; £649; £324) Stalls Low

Form RPR

00/6 **1** **Benbyas**[12] 1103 7-9-4 **65** DTudhope(5) 3 78
(DCarroll) *mde all: clr 4f out: hld on wl u.p fnl f* **5/1**[3]

005- **2** *3 ½* **Tom Bell (IRE)**[171] 5635 4-7-13 **45** CHaddon(3) 11 53
(JGMO'Shea) *midfield: hdwy and in tch over 3f out: styd on to go 2nd clsng stages* **50/1**

1111 **3** *nk* **Sendintank**[74] 592 4-9-0 **60** DeanWilliams(3) 8 67
(SCWilliams) *in tch: chsd first 2 fr 4f out: chsd wnr ins fnl f: no ex* **7/2**[2]

1411 **4** *4* **Jair Ohmsford (IRE)**[47] 829 5-9-5 **66** ARutter(5) 15 67
(WJMusson) *towards rr: hdwy 2f out: styd on wl fnl f: nrst fin* **6/1**

0-01 **5** *¾* **Archie Babe (IRE)**[3] 1245 8-9-11 **67** 6ex DFentiman 5 67
(JJQuinn) *in tch: hdwy to chse wnr over 4f out: sn rdn: no imp: wknd ins fnl f* **10/3**[1]

00-2 **6** *4* **That's Racing**[14] 1091 4-7-11 **45** oh6 ow4 AReilly(5) 1 39
(JHetherton) *hld up: hdwy over 3f out: no further prog fnl 2f* **16/1**

040- **7** *1 ½* **Protocol (IRE)**[9] 5013 10-7-7 **40** oh10 (t) SYourston(5) 14 32
(MrsSLamyman) *rr div: hdwy into midfield 3f out: no further prog* **33/1**

5342 **8** *15* **Bevier**[29] 989 10-7-13 **46** ow6 KGhunowa(5) 2 15
(TWall) *in tch: outpcd over 3f out: n.d* **25/1**

060- **9** *6* **Annakita**[106] 6234 4-8-0 **48** LauraPike(5) 10 8
(WJMusson) *n.d* **50/1**

10-3 **10** ½ **Eton (GER)**[12] [1109] 8-9-11 **70** MHoward(3) 6 30
(DNicholls) *in tch tl fdd fnl 3f* **12/1**

/60- **11** *11* **Fatehalkhair (IRE)**[346] [802] 12-9-1 **62** DSwift(5) 13 5
(BEllison) *n.d* **25/1**

/06- **12** *3½* **Niagara (IRE)**[181] [1716] 7-9-8 **69** SaleemGolam(5) 16 7
(MHTompkins) *n.d* **18/1**

65-0 **13** ¾ **Piste Bleu (FR)**[19] [1042] 4-8-7 **55** LiamJones(5) 4 —
(RFord) *dwlt: rr div: hdwy into midfield 4f out: no further prog* **33/1**

30-4 **14** *3* **Commander Flip (IRE)**[32] [969] 4-8-8 **58** HFellows(7) 17 —
(RHollinshead) *sn bhd* **33/1**

0/0- **15** *1½* **Washington Pink (IRE)**[161] [5819] 5-8-4 **51** ow1 RKeogh(5) 9 —
(CGrant) *sn bhd* **66/1**

5046 **16** *7* **Turftanzer (GER)**[23] [1024] 5-7-10 **45** oh5 ow5......(t) JaniceWebster(7) 12 —
(DonEnricoIncisa) *chsd wnr tl wknd qckly over 4f out* **66/1**

-105 **17** *4* **Call Me Sunshine**[19] [1045] 4-9-1 **65** DWakenshaw(7) 7 —
(PCHaslam) *chsd ldrs tl wknd 5f out* **20/1**

2m 51.73s (11.68) **Going Correction** +1.05s/f (Soft)
**WFA** 4 from 5yo+ 1lb **17** Ran SP% **123.3**
Speed ratings: **103,100,100,97,97 94,93,83,79,79 71,69,69,67,66 61,58**CSF £249.29 CT £1002.66 TOTE £5.80: £1.10, £14.80, £1.90, £1.50; EX 171.00.
**Owner** C H Stephenson & Partners **Bred** C Stephenson **Trained** Warthill, N Yorks
■ Stewards Enquiry : Dean Williams one-day ban: used whip down the shoulder in the forehand position (Apr 17)

**FOCUS**
A moderate apprentice handicap run at a solid pace and the field were well strung out behind the winner. The form looks fairly reliable.

**NOTEBOOK**
**Benbyas** pinged out of the gates and made every post a winning one in dogged style. He is a tough, versatile performer who was suited by today's conditions and he could well follow up on this, granted his favoured soft ground, as he escapes a penalty for this success.
**Tom Bell(IRE)** stayed on late and made a pleasing return, posting a career-best effort, having been off for 171 days prior to this. He is entitled to improve on this and appreciated the underfoot conditions on this occasion.
**Sendintank**, progressive on the All-Weather during the winter, ran a fair race on this return to turf and should come on a bit for the run.
**Jair Ohmsford(IRE)** was given a fair bit to do on this occasion and was finishing well at the end. He is another who has improved on the sand during the winter (he is 10lb higher on the All-Weather) and can strike over this trip off his current turf mark.
**Archie Babe(IRE)**, a convincing winner three days previously, looked to find this coming too soon, and finished tired. He has frequently tried in the past to quickly follow up on his wins, before the Handicapper can react, but he has failed on most occasions.
**That's Racing** *Official explanation: jockey said saddle slipped*

## 1283 JASON & RACHEL JOINT 30TH BIRTHDAY (S) STKS 6f
**2:50** (2:52) (E) 3-Y-O+ **£3,857** (£1,187; £593; £296) **Stalls** Low

Form RPR

6500 **1** **Marabar**[8] [1178] 6-9-2 70 (b) ACulhane 17 56
(DWChapman) *towards rr: gd hdwy 2f out: led fnl 100yds: r.o strly* **7/1**[1]

0-00 **2** *3* **Alastair Smellie**[23] [1021] 8-9-7 45 (v) PMcCabe 11 52
(SLKeightley) *dwlt: hld up: gd hdwy over 2f out: led over 1 out: edgd rt and hdd fnl 100yds: no ex* **33/1**

000- **3** *1½* **Compton Princess**[189] [5289] 4-9-2 45 GDuffield 10 43
(MrsADuffield) *midfield: drvn along and hdwy 2f out: r.o fnl f: nvr able to chal* **33/1**

0-60 **4** *1¾* **Grand View**[58] [713] 8-9-7 35 (p) DHolland 1 42
(JRWeymes) *prom: rdn and ev ch over 1f out: no ex ins last* **40/1**

0-61 **5** *1* **Indian Music**[7] [1191] 7-9-12 40 FLynch 5 44
(ABerry) *in tch: drvn along over 2f out: chsd ldrs appr fnl f: no ex ins last* **16/1**

-403 **6** *1¾* **Tickle**[50] [791] 6-9-2 57 (vt) SSanders 4 29
(PJMakin) *mde most tl hdd over 1f out: wknd ins last* **15/2**[2]

5305 **7** *8* **Dusty Wugg (IRE)**[6] [1197] 5-8-13 40 (p) ABeech(3) 6 5
(ADickman) *dwlt: sn midfield: rdn 2f out: no hdwy* **25/1**

000- **8** *1¼* **Rileys Dream**[152] [5937] 5-9-2 52 SDrowne 7 1
(BJLlewellyn) *in tch: rdn 2f out: wknd fnl f* **14/1**

0503 **9** *2½* **New Options**[14] [1087] 7-9-7 57 (p) MFenton 16 —
(WJMusson) *cl up: rdn and ev ch 2f out: wknd fnl f* **7/1**[1]

6240 **10** ½ **Speedfit Free (IRE)**[6] [1197] 7-9-7 58 (b) PHanagan 9 —
(ISemple) *nvr bttr than mid-div* **9/1**[3]

5250 **11** *1¼* **Mizhar (USA)**[50] [799] 8-9-7 55 RWinston 8 —
(JJQuinn) *nvr bttr than mid-div* **10/1**

-000 **12** ¾ **Gruff**[14] [1089] 5-9-7 30 RFitzpatrick 14 —
(PTMidgley) *sn towards rr* **100/1**

-000 **13** *4* **Valuable Gift**[7] [1191] 7-9-7 40 (tp) JFEgan 13 —
(RCGuest) *towards rr most of way* **33/1**

0-00 **14** *4* **Sugar Cube Treat**[37] [936] 8-9-2 30 KDalgleish 18 —
(MMullineaux) *slowly away: a rr div* **50/1**

00-0 **15** *4* **Dancing Ridge (IRE)**[29] [990] 7-9-7 35 TWilliams 12 —
(ASenior) *towards rr most of way* **100/1**

-002 **16** *3½* **Speedy James (IRE)**[8] [1171] 8-9-0 40 LTreadwell(7) 3 —
(DNicholls) *midfield tl wknd 2f out* **14/1**

40-1 **17** *15* **American Cousin**[8] [1171] 9-9-12 60 ANicholls 15 —
(DNicholls) *chsd ldrs tl wknd over 2f out: virtually p.u ins fnl f* **7/1**[1]

1m 26.13s (8.83) **Going Correction** +1.30s/f (Soft) **17** Ran SP% **106.6**
Speed ratings: **93,89,87,84,83 81,70,68,65,64 63,62,56,51,46 41,21**CSF £193.31 TOTE £7.60: £2.40, £7.80, £8.10; EX 188.10.There was no bid for the winner.
**Owner** Miss N F Thesiger **Bred** Mrs M T Dawson **Trained** Stillington, N Yorks

**FOCUS**
A modest winning time to this selling sprint, which saw the field well strung out at the finish. Despite this the winner is nowhere near as good as her current official mark.

**NOTEBOOK**
**Marabar**, who has been regressive on the sand during the winter, stayed on strongly inside the final furlong to score her first victory since winning a maiden in 1999. Best in at the weights, she has run at this level on the All-Weather, but this was her first run in selling class on turf and she was aided by her high draw on this occasion.
**Alastair Smellie**, beaten in banded stakes the last twice, gave an improved display with the visor back on. He has not been victorious for just over two years now, but was suited by the soft ground and shaped as though he could end his losing run at this level.
**Compton Princess**, rated 25lb inferior to the winner, ran a solid race at the weights and proved she can go on soft ground. She will come on plenty for this outing.
**Grand View ◆**, winless since 2001, held every chance and only dropped out late on. He is the one to take out of the race, as he had the lowest draw, all of his best form is on much faster ground and he looked to have a stiff task at these weights.
**Indian Music**, winner of a banded stakes last time, never looked like following up form his low draw. However, he was not disgraced and the recent drop in trip has brought about improvement.
**Tickle** ran better than the bare form would suggest, as she quickly crossed to the far side form her low draw and lost ground in the process. She has not won since 2000, but can do better in this grade.
**Gruff** *Official explanation: jockey said gelding had a breathing problem*
**American Cousin** looked to have a solid chance on recent form and at the weights, but dropped out alarmingly having been up with the pace for the first few furlongs. It is possible that the conditions were too testing, but this was still a most disappointing effort. *Official explanation: trainer had no explanation for poor form shown*

## 1284 PONTEFRACT PARK STKS (H'CAP) 1m 4y
**3:20** (3:21) (C ) (0-95,94) 3-Y-O+ **£9,442** (£3,581; £1,790; £814) **Stalls** Low

Form RPR

15-2 **1** **St Petersburg**[11] [1114] 4-9-6 **86** PRobinson 12 100
(MHTompkins) *cl up gng wl: led over 1f out: styd on wl to draw clr ins last* **7/2**[1]

0-45 **2** *4* **The Bonus King**[18] [1056] 4-9-4 **84** JFanning 9 90
(MJohnston) *led 2f: remained cl up: led again 1/2-way: hdd over 1 out: chsd wnr after: no imp* **11/1**

10-6 **3** *5* **Strong Hand**[11] [1114] 4-9-0 **80** KDarley 6 76
(MWEasterby) *trckd ldrs: rdn and ev ch over 1f out: wknd ins last* **6/1**

50-0 **4** *5* **Unicorn Reward (IRE)**[11] [1114] 4-9-0 **80** ACulhane 4 66
(MDHammond) *hmpd sn after s: hld up in rr: pushed along and hdwy 2f out: styd on fnl f: nvr able to chal* **20/1**

300- **5** *3* **Shot To Fame (USA)**[157] [5872] 5-10-0 **94** SDrowne 10 74
(PWHarris) *hld up in rr: drvn along over 2f out: kpt on fnl f: n.d* **9/1**

22-0 **6** *2* **Flighty Fellow (IRE)**[10] [1125] 4-9-12 **92** SSanders 8 68
(TDEasterby) *midfield: rdn over 2f out: no hdwy* **5/1**[3]

000- **7** *1½* **Broadway Score (USA)**[178] [5484] 6-9-10 **90** DaleGibson 1 63
(MWEasterby) *led after 2f: hdd 1/2-way: wknd over 1 out* **20/1**

406- **8** *2½* **Mezuzah**[167] [5709] 4-9-6 **86** DHolland 2 54
(GWragg) *hld up rr div: drvn along over 2f out: no hdwy* **4/1**[2]

004- **9** *2½* **Cherished Number**[148] [5967] 5-9-1 **81** RWinston 7 44
(ISemple) *midfield: keen early: hdwy and ch 2f out: sn rdn and wknd* **14/1**

210- **10** *13* **Les Arcs (USA)**[209] [4819] 4-9-5 **85** JFEgan 5 22
(RCGuest) *hld up towards rr: drvn along over 2f out: sn btn* **25/1**

**11** ¾ **Jahia (NZ)**[180] 5-8-9 **75** NCallan 11 11
(RCGuest) *rr div: drvn along over 2f out: sn btn* **80/1**

**12** *1¾* **Huxley (IRE)**[47] [5763] 5-9-5 **85** PMcCabe 3 17
(MGQuinlan) *keen early: trckd ldrs tl wknd over 2f out* **25/1**

1m 54.21s (8.61) **Going Correction** +1.30s/f (Soft) **12** Ran SP% **116.6**
Speed ratings: **108,104,99,94,91 89,87,85,82,69 68,67**CSF £38.62 CT £228.84 TOTE £4.40: £1.60, £2.70, £2.70; EX 44.50 Trifecta £243.60 Pool £3,082.09, 8.40 w/u.
**Owner** P Heath **Bred** Kirtlington Stud Ltd **Trained** Newmarket, Suffolk

**FOCUS**
A downpour prior to this event saw the ground changed to 'soft'. This was a decent handicap run at a solid pace and the field finished strung out behind the comfortable winner, who has improved with every race over the past year.

**NOTEBOOK**
**St Petersburg**, 4lb higher for finishing runner-up in the Spring Mile at Doncaster last time, confirmed the promise of that run with a smooth success on this softer ground. He is progressing well and the plan is to carry a penalty in the Spring Cup at Newbury later this month, where he should have every chance, as long as the ground is not fast.
**The Bonus King** made a bold bid from the front, but had no answer to the winner when challenged approaching the final furlong. This was an improved effort on recent All-Weather outings, he seemd to get this trip well in these conditions and he was nicely clear of the rest.
**Strong Hand** failed to reverse recent form with the winner on 6lb better terms. He held every chance in the straight, but could only muster the one pace and was not given a hard time late on.
**Unicorn Reward(IRE)** was done no favours at the start and can be considered slightly better than the bare form would suggest. All of his best form is on fast going, but he seemed to go through the ground well on this occasion. *Official explanation: jockey said gelding suffered interference at the start*
**Shot To Fame(USA)** was restrained at the back of the pack for most of the race and although he stayed on late in the day, was never a threat. He should improve for this outing.
**Flighty Fellow(IRE)**, drawn on the wrong side in the Lincoln last time, had the blinkers left off on this occasion and ran a poor race.
**Mezuzah** was the disappointment of the race. He had the form to go well in this type of event and has been gelded since last year, but he never looked happy at any stage and has it all to prove now.
**Huxley(IRE)** *Official explanation: jockey said gelding had a breathing problem*

## 1285 YORKSHIRE RACING CLUB MEDIAN AUCTION MAIDEN STKS 1m 2f 6y
**3:50** (3:50) (E) 3-Y-0 **£4,075** (£1,254; £627; £313) **Stalls** Low

Form RPR

**1** **Winged D'Argent (IRE)** 3-9-0 JFanning 8 71
(MJohnston) *led or disp ld tl drvn ahd over 1f out: styd on u.p: all out* **11/2**[2]

4-0 **2** *hd* **Tudor Bell (IRE)**[12] [1104] 3-9-0 DSweeney 2 71
(JGMO'Shea) *trckd ldrs: drvn along over 2f out: chsd wnr over 1 out: styd on wl towards fin: jst hld* **25/1**

**3** *1¼* **At Your Request** 3-9-0 WSupple 1 69
(EALDunlop) *hld up: hdwy 3f out: rdn 2 out: disp 2nd fnl f: styd on: no ex clsng stages* **14/1**

00- **4** *11* **Crociera (IRE)**[157] [5870] 3-9-0 PRobinson 3 50
(MHTompkins) *keen early: led or disp ld tl rdn and wknd over 1f out* **8/1**[3]

000- **5** *5* **Hernando's Boy**[154] [5915] 3-9-0 ACulhane 6 42
(MrsMReveley) *keen early: trckd ldrs: effrt 3f out: outpcd by ldng quartet fnl 2f* **14/1**

0-00 **6** *dist* **Polish Rhapsody (IRE)**[29] [982] 3-8-9 48 GFaulkner 5 —
(JASupple) *hld up in rr: drvn along 3f out: lost tch 2 out: t.o* **66/1**

0-6 **7** *18* **Saameq (IRE)**[11] [1116] 3-9-0 DMcGaffin 7 —
(ISemple) *cl up: keen early: effrt 3f out: sn rdn and wknd: t.o* **33/1**

**8** *dist* **Serengeti Sky (USA)** 3-9-0 LDettori 4 —
(DRLoder) *drvn along early: sn trcking ldrs: drvn along again 3f out: sn btn: bhd whn eased fnl 2f: t.o* **4/7**[1]

2m 29.25s (15.34) **Going Correction** +1.30s/f (Soft) **8** Ran SP% **111.8**
Speed ratings: **90,89,88,80,76** —,—,—CSF £115.86 TOTE £6.90: £1.10, £3.90, £1.90; EX 123.10.
**Owner** Daniel A Couper **Bred** Daniel A Couper And George Hosie **Trained** Middleham Moor, N Yorks

**FOCUS**
A moderate winning time, 4.64 seconds slower than the following classified stakes, but the first three were well clear. However, this was probably a below-par renewal of what is usually a decent maiden.



The Form Book, Raceform Ltd, Compton, RG20 6NL

**NOTEBOOK**
**Winged D'Argent(IRE)** overcame greenness to make a winning debut. A half-brother to the useful stayer Mana D'Argent, he shaped on this occasion as though he will get farther and had no problems with this testing ground. It is hard to know what to make of the form, but he is entitled to improve.
**Tudor Bell(IRE)** made a pleasing comeback, stepping up on his juvenile form over this longer trip and on this soft ground.
**At Your Request** ran distinctly green in the early stages on this debut, but the penny gradually dropped and he shaped nicely in the end. This experience will bring him on leaps and bounds and he can lose his maiden tag granted similar conditions soon.
**Crociera(IRE)** paid for running too keen in the early part of the race on this step up in trip. He now qualifies for handicaps and will likely fare better in that sphere.
**Serengeti Sky(USA)**, the heavily backed favourite, was never travelling in this ground and was very disappointing. However, he was heavily eased at the top of the straight when his winning chance had gone, and it would be no surprise were this half-brother to the high-class stayer Mamool to leave this form behind in due course on better ground. *Official explanation: jockey said colt was unsuited by the soft ground*

## 1286 HIGH-RISE CLASSIFIED STKS — 1m 2f 6y
4:20 (4:20) (C) 3-Y-O+ — £9,210 (£3,493; £1,746; £794) Stalls Low

Form | | | | | RPR
---|---|---|---|---|---
| 1 | | **Akash (IRE)**[205] 4916 4-9-8 90 | JFanning 2 | 101
| | | (MJohnston) *mde virtually all: hrd pressed fnl 2f: styd on u.p: all out* | **9/1** |
350- | 2 | shd | **Bourgeois**[27] 5274 7-9-13 95 | KDarley 5 | 106
| | | (TDEasterby) *in tch: hdwy to trck wnr 4f out: chal over 2 out: disp ld: rdn and ev ch fnl f: jst hld* | **12/1** |
33-4 | 3 | 15 | **Wing Commander**[10] 1125 5-9-11 93 | PHanagan 8 | 79
| | | (RAFahey) *hld up: drvn along and hdwy 3f out: chsd first 2 fr over 1 out: no imp* | **4/1**[1] |
1023 | 4 | 11 | **Swift Tango (IRE)**[11] 1114 4-9-8 90 | (v) WSupple 9 | 57
| | | (EALDunlop) *hld up: hdwy 3f out: rdn 2 out: sn btn* | **9/2**[2] |
122- | 5 | 3 1/2 | **Prince Holing**[59] 4408 4-9-8 89 | ACulhane 7 | 51
| | | (MissVenetiaWilliams) *hld up: hdwy to chse first 2 3f out: sn rdn: wknd over 1 out* | **12/1** |
31- | 6 | 1 3/4 | **Argonaut**[297] 2373 4-9-8 88 | FLynch 10 | 48
| | | (SirMichaelStoute) *hld up in rr: drvn along over 4f out: no real hdwy* | **4/1**[1] |
/40- | 7 | 29 | **Wahchi (IRE)**[249] 3748 5-9-8 90 | DaleGibson 3 | —
| | | (GPKelly) *s.i.s: hld up towards rr: sme hdwy over 3f out: wknd over 2 out: t.o* | **80/1** |
13/ | 8 | 9 | **Love You Always (USA)**[555] 4948 4-9-13 95 | LDettori 6 | —
| | | (DRLoder) *prom: drvn along 4f out: wknd 3 out: t.o* | **11/2**[3] |
214- | 9 | dist | **Amandus (USA)**[226] 4409 4-9-13 95 | DHolland 1 | —
| | | (DRLoder) *prom tl wknd over 3f out: sn bhd: lost tch and eased fnl 2f: t.o* | **7/1** |

2m 24.61s (10.70) **Going Correction** +1.30s/f (Soft) **9** Ran SP% **112.7**
Speed ratings: **109,108,96,88,85 83,60,53,**—CSF £107.13 TOTE £11.00: £2.70, £2.80, £1.60; EX 64.50.
**Owner** Markus Graff **Bred** His Highness The Aga Khan's Studs S C **Trained** Middleham Moor, N Yorks

**FOCUS**
A useful looking line-up to this classified event which produced a great finish between the first two, who were well clear of the rest. The form is suspect as several behind failed to give their running.

**NOTEBOOK**
**Akash(IRE)** showed he is tough by gamely making all of the running on this debut for his new connections. He had some fair form in handicaps over 12 furlongs last year, but had not won since his juvenile days prior to this success. He handles testing ground well and can build on this success over farther.
**Bourgeois**, fit from a hurdling campaign over the winter, was only just denied. The testing ground helped bring out his stamina over this trip and this was a very solid effort, as he was miles clear of the rest.
**Wing Commander**, fourth in the Lincoln last time, disappointed and failed to run up to form on this soft ground. He can do better on quicker ground, but is not easy to win with.
**Swift Tango(IRE)**, who has been running well in Dubai over the winter, was another who failed to run to his best in this testing ground.
**Prince Holing** moved well for a long way, but found nil off the bridle with two furlongs to run. He is worthy of another chance on better ground.
**Argonaut** was disappointing, but his rider later reported that his mount was unsuited by the soft ground. He is another who could leave this form behind, but is clearly no star. *Official explanation: jockey said gelding was unsuited by the soft going*
**Love You Always(USA)** fell in a hole approaching three out and clearly has his limitations. *Official explanation: jockey said gelding was unsuited by the soft going*
**Amandus(USA)** *Official explanation: jockey said gelding was unsuited by the soft going*

## 1287 JAMAICAN FLIGHT H'CAP — 2m 1f 216y
4:50 (4:50) (E) (0-75,74) 4-Y-O+ — £4,143 (£1,275; £637; £318) Stalls Low

Form | | | | | RPR
---|---|---|---|---|---
400- | 1 | | **Green 'N' Gold**[7] 2672 4-7-12 50 oh1 | PHanagan 1 | 60
| | | (MDHammond) *hld up in rr: smooth hdwy 4f out: led 2 out: styd on u.p* | **25/1** |
26-2 | 2 | 3 1/2 | **Vicars Destiny**[11] 1112 6-9-6 67 | GDuffield 9 | 73
| | | (MrsSLamyman) *in tch: hdwy 5f out: led wl over 2 out: rdn and hdd 2 out: chsd wnr after: styd on: no imp fnl f* | **11/4**[2] |
344- | 3 | 5 | **Ringside Jack**[17] 5926 8-8-5 52 | JFanning 4 | 53
| | | (CWFairhurst) *trckd ldrs: ev ch 2 out: sn rdn: no ex* | **12/1** |
-344 | 4 | 12 | **Jamaican Flight (USA)**[19] 1045 11-8-5 52 | JFEgan 8 | 41
| | | (MrsSLamyman) *led tl rdn and hdd wl over 2f out: sn btn* | **14/1** |
010- | 5 | 1/2 | **Accepting**[20] 5675 7-8-6 53 | (b[1]) RWinston 2 | 42
| | | (JMackie) *midfield: drvn along over 5f out: kpt on fnl 3f: nvr able to chal* | **16/1** |
0/0- | 6 | 28 | **Charming Admiral (IRE)**[17] 1920 11-8-3 50 | JMackay 15 | 11
| | | (MrsADuffield) *towards rr: drvn along 1/2-way: n.d* | **33/1** |
0-06 | 7 | 17 | **Rajam**[6] 1198 6-9-11 72 | AlexGreaves 12 | 16
| | | (DNicholls) *cl up tl rdn and wknd 3f out* | **20/1** |
-401 | 8 | 19 | **Bustling Rio (IRE)**[26] 666 8-8-11 65 | RoryMoore(7) 6 | —
| | | (PCHaslam) *hld up: drvn along 4f out: sn btn* | **12/1** |
3-50 | 9 | 8 | **Danny Leahy (FR)**[8] 1173 4-8-13 65 | KDalgleish 3 | —
| | | (MDHammond) *in tch tl rdn and wknd over 3f out* | **50/1** |
/62- | 10 | dist | **My Line**[24] 5189 7-9-0 61 | (b) DHolland 10 | —
| | | (MrsMReveley) *bhd and drvn along 1/2-way: sn lost tch: t.o* | **9/4**[1] |
601- | 11 | 3/4 | **Killing Joke**[122] 6139 4-9-8 74 | MFenton 14 | —
| | | (JGGiven) *prom tl wknd qckly over 4f out: t.o* | **14/1** |
| 12 | 22 | **Ontos (GER)**[81] 8-9-9 70 | LDettori 13 | —
| | | (MissVScott) *in tch tl wknd 4f out: t.o* | **14/1** |
30-0 | 13 | 28 | **Allez Mousson**[11] 1112 6-8-9 56 | SSanders 7 | —
| | | (ABailey) *bhd and drvn along 1/2-way: sn lost tch: t.o* | **11/1**[3] |

4m 22.11s (19.11) **Going Correction** +1.30s/f (Soft)
**WFA** 4 from 5yo+ 5lb **13** Ran SP% **120.5**
Speed ratings: **109,107,105,99,99 87,79,71,67,**— —,—,—CSF £91.16 CT £913.02 TOTE £30.20: £4.50, £1.80, £2.90; EX 272.10.
**Owner** E Whalley **Bred** Micky Hammond Racing Ltd And S Branklin **Trained** Middleham, N Yorks

**FOCUS**
This was a real test of stamina and most of the field finished legless, but it produced decent winning time for the grade. Its relevance formwise is dubious.

**NOTEBOOK**
**Green 'N' Gold**, 1lb out of the handicap, travelled sweetly and could have been called the winner a long way from home. She came into this with fitness on her side, having finished third over hurdles seven days previously, and although this was a first ever win on the level, the manner of her victory would suggest she can go in again.
**Vicars Destiny** ran another solid race and finished nicely clear of the rest. This dour stayer has started the turf campaign in great heart and deserves to get her head in front soon.
**Ringside Jack** only tired late on and can capitalise on this mark when dropping slightly in trip.
**Jamaican Flight(USA)** made this a true test, but was soon beating a retreat in the straight and was unsuited by the soft ground.
**My Line** never looked a threat at any stage and was disappointing. *Official explanation: jockey said gelding was never travelling*

## 1288 PONTEFRACT-RACES.CO.UK MAIDEN FILLIES' STKS — 6f
5:20 (5:21) (D) 3-Y-O — £5,473 (£1,684; £842; £421) Stalls Low

Form | | | | | RPR
---|---|---|---|---|---
025- | 1 | | **Capetown Girl**[168] 5691 3-8-11 67 | GFaulkner 1 | 79?
| | | (KRBurke) *racd alone ins: led 1/2-way: clr 2 out: edgd rt over 1 out: r.o u.p* | **9/2**[2] |
| 2 | 8 | **Crathes** 3-8-11 | MFenton 6 | 55
| | | (JGGiven) *dwlt: towards rr: hdwy 1/2-way: rdn 2f out: wnt 2nd wl ins fnl f: no ch w wnr* | **10/1** |
0- | 3 | nk | **Cefira (USA)**[271] 3142 3-8-11 | PRobinson 8 | 54
| | | (MHTompkins) *trckd ldrs: led main gp 2f out: chsd wnr and rdn after: no imp: lost 2nd wl ins fnl f* | **10/3**[1] |
30 | 4 | 18 | **Pickle**[62] 673 3-8-11 | KDarley 5 | —
| | | (SCWilliams) *led to 1/2-way: continued to ld main gp tl hdd 2f out: sn wknd* | **7/1**[3] |
03-4 | 5 | 2 | **Graceful Air (IRE)**[20] 1038 3-8-11 64 | RWinston 7 | —
| | | (JRWeymes) *chsd ldrs main gp: drvn along 1/2-way: sn wknd* | **9/2**[2] |
000- | 6 | 19 | **Blade's Daughter**[202] 4985 3-8-11 | NCallan 10 | —
| | | (KARyan) *prom main gp: rdn 1/2-way: sn wknd* | **25/1** |
60- | 7 | 4 | **Estihlal**[152] 5929 3-8-11 | RHills 3 | —
| | | (EALDunlop) *in tch main gp: rdn over 2f out: sn wknd* | **9/2**[2] |
000- | 8 | 15 | **Savannah River (IRE)**[278] 2919 3-8-11 | (t) DMernagh 2 | —
| | | (CWThornton) *s.i.s: sn wl bhd: t.o* | **50/1** |
0-0 | 9 | 23 | **Pick A Berry**[18] 1052 3-8-11 | DHolland 4 | —
| | | (GWragg) *sn bhd: lost tch fnl 2f: t.o* | **14/1** |
660- | 10 | 26 | **Designer City (IRE)**[144] 5997 3-8-11 57 | JCarroll 11 | —
| | | (ABerry) *slowly away: sn t.o* | **20/1** |

1m 24.53s (7.23) **Going Correction** +1.30s/f (Soft) **10** Ran SP% **116.5**
Speed ratings: **103,92,91,67,65 39,34,14,**—,—CSF £47.46 TOTE £6.70: £2.10, £3.70, £1.70; EX 65.10 Place £838.41, Place 5 £462.46.
**Owner** Danum Racing **Bred** Genesis Green Stud Ltd **Trained** Middleham Moor, N Yorks

**FOCUS**
A poor maiden which saw the winner race alone on the inside to post an easy success. This form is most likely a nonsense.

**NOTEBOOK**
**Capetown Girl** was the only one to race on the inside and that proved most decisive as she scooted clear of the far-side group to win easily. She likes this ground and has obviously trained on from last year, but this form is seriously suspect and her next outing will tell us more.
**Crathes** won the battle on the far side and made a satisfactory debut. She will come on a fair bit for this experience.
**Cefira(USA)** showed good early pace and only tired late on in the testing conditions. She can be expected to improve on better ground.
**Pickle** set the pace for a long way, but tamely faded two out and finished well beaten. She now qualifies for handicaps.
**Estihlal** was disappointing and still has to prove she has trained on, but may be worth another chance on less testing ground.
T/Jkpt: Not won. T/Plt: £2,470.80 to a £1 stake. Pool: £51,616.70. 15.25 winning tickets. T/Qpdt: £34.60 to a £1 stake. Pool: £3,226.80. 68.85 winning tickets. JF

# 1182 MAISONS-LAFFITTE (R-H)
Tuesday, April 6

**OFFICIAL GOING: Holding**

## 1289a PRIX DJEBEL (LISTED) (C&G) (STRAIGHT) — 7f (S)
1:20 (1:23) 3-Y-O — £15,845 (£6,338; £4,754; £3,169)

| | | | | RPR
---|---|---|---|---
1 | | **Whipper (USA)**[158] 5865 3-9-2 | CSoumillon 3 | 115
| | (RobertCollet, France) | **1** |
2 | 8 | **Red Mo (USA)**[167] 5713 3-9-2 | OPeslier 6 | 95
| | (MmeCHead-Maarek, France) | |
3 | 4 | **Always King (FR)**[18] 1058 3-9-2 | IMendizabal 1 | 85
| | (J-CRouget, France) | |
4 | snk | **Doric (USA)**[146] 5983 3-9-2 | C-PLemaire 5 | 85
| | (MmeCHead-Maarek, France) | |
5 | 5 | **Le Boss (FR)**[8] 3-9-2 | ELegrix 2 | 72
| | (RobertCollet, France) | |
6 | 4 | **Chopoulou (FR)**[18] 3-9-2 | RMarchelli 4 | 62
| | (ABonin, France) | |

1m 28.7s **6** Ran SP% **76.9**
Speed ratings: .
**Owner** R C Strauss **Bred** Flaxman Holdings Ltd **Trained** France

**NOTEBOOK**
**Whipper(USA)**, last season's Prix Morny winner and fifth in the Middle Park, made an impressive start to his three-year-old season with an easy success. He is on course for the 2000 Guineas at Newmarket, and looks to have a decent chance, especially if the ground is softer than good.

## 1290a PRIX IMPRUDENCE (LISTED) (FILLIES) (STRAIGHT) 7f (S)
1:50 (1:50) 3-Y-O £15,845 (£6,338; £4,754; £3,169)

| | | | | RPR |
|---|---|---|---|---|
| 1 | | **Onda Nova (USA)**[176] 3-9-0 (DSepulchre, France) | SPasquier 6 | 114 |
| 2 | 2 | **Dolma (FR)**[21] [1034] 3-9-0 (NClement, France) | C-PLemaire 8 | 109 |
| 3 | 2 1/2 | **Petit Calva (FR)**[172] 3-9-0 (RGibson, France) | TJarnet 5 1 | 103 |
| 4 | 4 | **Southern Queen**[167] [5713] 3-9-0 (MmeCHead-Maarek, France) | OPeslier 7 | 93 |
| 5 | shd | **Double Coeur (FR)**[24] 3-9-0 (YDeNicolay, France) | FSpanu 3 | 93 |
| 6 | 1/2 | **Ouimonamour (FR)**[154] 3-9-0 (FHead, France) | (b) DBonilla 2 | 91 |
| 7 | snk | **Leila (FR)**[18] 3-9-0 (PBary, France) | TThulliez 4 | 91 |

1m 32.2s **7** Ran SP% **14.3**
Speed ratings: .
**Owner** Niarchos Family **Bred** Flaxman Holdings Ltd **Trained** France

**NOTEBOOK**
**Onda Nova(USA)**, out of the high-class Northern Trick, took this trial in good fashion and connections are looking at the Poule d'Essai des Pouliches, although the owners already have Denebola in that contest. Although she is by a sprinter, there is plenty of stamina on her dam's side.

# 1183 FOLKESTONE (R-H)
Wednesday, April 7

**OFFICIAL GOING: Good to soft (soft in places)**

## 1292 EUROPEAN BREEDERS FUND TENTERDEN MAIDEN STKS 5f
2:10 (2:10) (D) 2-Y-O £4,069 (£1,252; £626; £313) Stalls Low

| Form | | | | | RPR |
|---|---|---|---|---|---|
| | 1 | | **Observer (IRE)** 2-9-0 (DRLoder) *uns rdr in saddling boxes: mde all: rdn and pressed 1f out: kpt on wl* 4/7[1] | LDettori 2 | 81 |
| | 2 | 1/2 | **Norcroft** 2-9-0 (NACallaghan) *chsd wnr after 2f: shkn up to chal 1f out: kpt on wl but a hld* 2/1[2] | EAhern 3 | 79 |
| | 3 | 12 | **Dustini (IRE)** 2-9-0 (WGMTurner) *chsd wnr for 2f: sn outpcd and hanging rt: no ch fnl 2f* 12/1[3] | ADaly 1 | 36 |
| | 4 | 6 | **Gryskirk** 2-9-0 (PWD'Arcy) *green in preliminaries: dwlt and wnt rt s: rcvrd and in tch 1/2-way: wknd wl over 1f out: eased* 33/1 | PaulEddery 4 | 14 |

64.03 secs (3.33) **Going Correction** +0.575s/f (Yiel) **4** Ran SP% **107.6**
Speed ratings: **96,95,76,66**CSF £1.92 TOTE £1.30; EX 1.60.
**Owner** Sheikh Mohammed **Bred** Viejo Pueblo **Trained** Newmarket, Suffolk

**FOCUS**
Softish ground made this a test for these juveniles. The form is possibly a shade above average.

**NOTEBOOK**
**Observer(IRE)**, a February foal, may have played up in the preliminaries, but in the race itself he did a professional job, making every yard. Both he and the runner-up came clear and he should progress from here.
**Norcroft**, whose dam was a very useful and progressive handicapper who stayed middle distances, made a pleasing start to his career but was always playing second fiddle to the winner. Judged on this effort, he can find a little race.
**Dustini(IRE)**, a half-brother to a mile winner in Italy, ran green and looked in need of the experience.
**Gryskirk**, a February foal, was too green to do himself justice and is bred to do much better over farther in time.

## 1293 BARHAM MEDIAN AUCTION MAIDEN STKS 6f
2:40 (2:41) (F) 3-Y-O £2,968 (£848; £424) Stalls Low

| Form | | | | | RPR |
|---|---|---|---|---|---|
| | 1 | | **Petite Rose (IRE)** 3-8-9 (JHMGosden) *racd far side: mde all: shkn up over 1f out: clr fnl f: comf* 11/4[2] | LDettori 13 | 88+ |
| 3-3 | 2 | 4 | **Warden Complex**[14] [1096] 3-9-0 (JRFanshawe) *cl up far side: chsd wnr 1/2-way: shkn up and kpt on fnl 2f but no imp* 5/2[1] | DaneO'Neill 12 | 81 |
| | 3 | 8 | **Wunderbra (IRE)** 3-8-9 (MLWBell) *dwlt: wl in rr far side: rdn whn nt clr run and swtchd lft over 2f out: kpt on to chse clr ldng pair over 1f out: no ch* 16/1 | IMongan 8 | 52 |
| 03- | 4 | 3 | **Nafferton Girl (IRE)**[250] [3764] 3-8-9 (JAOsborne) *racd on outer of far side gp and rn green: outpcd fr 1/2-way: no ch fnl 2f* 33/1 | SWKelly 7 | 43+ |
| | 5 | shd | **Indian Lily** 3-8-9 (CFWall) *s.i.s: wl in rr far side: sme prog over 2f out: no ch w ldrs* 25/1 | GBaker 10 | 43 |
| 5 | 6 | 6 | **Silver Reign**[11] [1133] 3-8-9 (GBBalding) *racd far side: in tch: chsd clr ldng pair over 2f out tl wknd over 1f out* 33/1 | RThomas(5) 11 | 30 |
| 0- | 7 | 1 1/4 | **Delightfully**[264] [3368] 3-8-9 (BWHills) *chsd nr side ldrs: led gp ins fnl f: no ch* 9/1 | EAhern 6 | 21 |
| 0-6 | 8 | 1/2 | **Lady Oriande**[9] [1169] 3-8-9 (AMBalding) *s.s and restrained: racd far side: a bhd* 16/1 | MartinDwyer 15 | 19 |
| 0-35 | 9 | 3/4 | **Power To Burn**[57] [732] 3-9-0 52 (KBell) *racd far side: chsd ldrs to 1/2-way: wknd* 33/1 | (v) DRMcCabe 9 | 22 |
| 60- | 10 | shd | **Turtle Patriarch (IRE)**[273] [3101] 3-9-0 (MrsAJPerrett) *dwlt: prom nr side thrght: no ch* 10/1 | SSanders 2 | 22 |
| 000- | 11 | 1/2 | **Eight Ellington (IRE)**[166] [5734] 3-9-0 59 (MissGayKelleway) *s.i.s: led nr side gp to ins fnl f: nvr on terms w far side* 33/1 | PRobinson 1 | 20 |
| 0 | 12 | 3/4 | **Half A Handful**[9] [1169] 3-8-11 (MJWallace) *chsd wnr on far side to 1/2-way: wknd rapidly* 33/1 | DCorby(3) 14 | 18 |
| 00- | 13 | 3/4 | **Pat's Nemisis (IRE)**[100] [6250] 3-8-4 (BRJohnson) *racd nr side: prom 2f: sn lost pl: no ch* 100/1 | NChalmers(5) 4 | 11 |
| 204- | 14 | 1/2 | **Seguidilla (IRE)**[275] [3051] 3-8-9 84 (GCBravery) *t.k.h: prom nr side tl wknd fnl f: no ch* 8/1[3] | TQuinn 3 | 9 |
| 0 | 15 | 3 | **Mr Hullabalou (IRE)**[15] [1083] 3-9-0 (RIngram) *uns rdr bef ent stalls: s.v.s: racd nr side and a wl bhd* 66/1 | GCarter 5 | 5 |

1m 15.25s (1.65) **Going Correction** +0.575s/f (Yiel) **15** Ran SP% **118.2**
Speed ratings: **112,106,96,92,91 83,82,81,80,80 79,78,77,77,73**CSF £8.88 TOTE £4.50: £1.40, £1.30, £7.10; EX 8.10.
**Owner** Salem Suhail **Bred** Quay Bloodstock, Peter Magnier And Dr M Wallace **Trained** Manton, Wilts

**FOCUS**
A truly outstanding time for a race of this class and probably above-average efforts from first two. The far side dominated.

**NOTEBOOK**
**Petite Rose(IRE)**, a sister to July Cup runner-up Lincoln Dancer, who always enjoyed soft ground, was well drawn and made every yard for a successful debut. This did not look a great race beforehand, but she won easily and in a quick time, and it will be a surprise if she cannot hold her own in better company.
**Warden Complex** set the standard on his pair of thirds in maiden company over seven furlongs, but this drop back in trip was a slight worry. In the circumstances the step back in distance was not the cause of his defeat, he just met a smart one in the winner. He has the ability to win a similar contest, but handicaps are now an option, too.
**Wunderbra(IRE)**, whose sire was a miler, is a half-sister to five-furlong winners Grand Lad, Galloway Boy and La Stellina, out of a mare who won four times over the minimum trip. She was well beaten in third but still showed enough to suggest that an average minor maiden could come her way.
**Nafferton Girl(IRE)** looked unlikely to appreciate the drop back in trip based on her staying-on effort over seven furlongs on her final start last season, and her performance in the race itself appeared to support that view. However, she is now eligible for a handicap mark.
**Indian Lily**, a half-sister to four winners over various distances, kept on well having been slowly away. She should come on for her debut.
**Delightfully** came home first of the stands'-side group, who were never really in contention. She would probably have fared better had she been drawn higher.
**Seguidilla(IRE)** *Official explanation: jockey said saddle slipped.*

## 1294 VISIT PORT LYMPNE WILD ANIMAL PARK CLASSIFIED STKS 7f (S)
3:10 (3:10) (E) 3-Y-O+ £3,415 (£1,051; £525; £262) Stalls Low

| Form | | | | | RPR |
|---|---|---|---|---|---|
| 3014 | 1 | | **Chateau Nicol**[19] [1056] 5-9-3 68 (BGPowell) *t.k.h: hld up in last: prog on inner 2f out: effrt to ld fnl 100y: rdn out* 7/1 | (v) SSanders 1 | 81+ |
| 5-02 | 2 | 1 1/2 | **Michelle Ma Belle (IRE)**[5] [1229] 4-9-5 75 (SKirk) *led: set stdy pce tl hdd 4f out: styd prom: rdn to ld again over 1f out: edgd lft and hdd last 100y: nt qckn* 5/1[3] | RHughes 2 | 79 |
| 1- | 3 | 1 3/4 | **Perfect Portrait**[177] [5545] 4-9-7 74 (DRLoder) *pressed ldr: led 4f out to 3f out: shkn up to ld again over 2f out: rn green and hdd over 1f out: nt qckn* 11/8[1] | LDettori 3 | 77 |
| 0-26 | 4 | 3/4 | **Baker Of Oz**[25] [1012] 3-8-5 72 (RHannon) *t.k.h: cl up: rdn over 2f out: nt qckn and lost pl wl over 1f out: one pce after* 16/1 | RLMoore 6 | 73 |
| -003 | 5 | nk | **Ammenayr (IRE)**[6] [1225] 4-9-8 75 (TGMills) *chsd ldrs: hrd rdn fr wl over 2f out: no imp over 1f out* 5/2[2] | IMongan 5 | 75 |
| 036- | 6 | 13 | **Among Friends (IRE)**[251] [3714] 4-9-5 72 (BPalling) *t.k.h: cl up: led 3f out to over 2f out: sn wknd: heavily eased fnl f* 33/1 | TQuinn 4 | 40 |

1m 31.16s (3.36) **Going Correction** +0.575s/f (Yiel)
**WFA** 3 from 4yo+ 14lb **6** Ran SP% **108.7**
Speed ratings: **103,101,99,98,98 83**CSF £37.98 TOTE £9.90: £5.60, £1.80; EX 18.90.
**Owner** Basingstoke Commercials **Bred** Aston House Stud **Trained** Morestead, Hants

**FOCUS**
A steadily-run race and on paper a tight affair, the winner confirming recent improvement.

**NOTEBOOK**
**Chateau Nicol** had to wait for a gap to appear next to the rail, but as soon as the leader rolled off a straight line he soon settled the issue. He enjoyed a very successful winter on the All-Weather and is rated much lower on turf now, so there could well be more to come before the Handicapper catches up.
**Michelle Ma Belle(IRE)** enjoyed the run of the race and did well to battle back after being headed. She is consistent but difficult to win with.
**Perfect Portrait**, who did not have the benefit of a previous run like his main rivals, took a keen hold off the steady pace. He showed signs of inexperience under pressure and faster ground may see him in a better light.
**Baker Of Oz** had it to do against his elders on ground softer than he had run on before.
**Among Friends(IRE)** was always wanting to do too much off this steady pace and did not get home. He will be happier back over sprint distances.

## 1295 FOLKESTONE-RACECOURSE.CO.UK MAIDEN STKS 7f (S)
3:40 (3:43) (D) 3-Y-O+ £3,848 (£1,184; £592; £296) Stalls Low

| Form | | | | | RPR |
|---|---|---|---|---|---|
| | 1 | | **Wistman (UAE)** 3-8-7 (DRLoder) *dwlt: settled wl in rr: swtchd to outer and prog fr 2f out: shkn up and styd on fnl f: led last stride* 10/1 | LDettori 1 | 76 |
| 3-2 | 2 | hd | **Rangoon (USA)**[11] [1133] 3-8-7 (MrsAJPerrett) *taken down early: racd in midfield: pushed along wl over 2f out: styd on fr over 1f out: rdn to ld last strides: hdd on pos* 9/4[1] | RHughes 7 | 75 |
| 40 | 3 | nk | **The King's Bishop**[30] [982] 3-8-7 (SCWilliams) *chsd ldrs: pushed along wl over 2f out: r.o fr over 1f out: led ent fnl f: hung lft after: hdd last strides* 33/1 | GCarter 11 | 74 |
| 34- | 4 | 1 | **Royal Prince**[203] [4997] 3-8-7 (JRFanshawe) *dwlt: racd in midfield: pushed along wl over 2f out: prog wl over 1f out: ch ins fnl f: no ex nr fin* 11/4[2] | MartinDwyer 2 | 72 |
| 5/4- | 5 | 1 1/2 | **Isaz**[177] [5545] 4-9-7 75 (HCandy) *pressed ldrs: rdn and ev ch 1f out: hld whn sltly hmpd last 100y* 8/1 | DaneO'Neill 10 | 68 |
| 62- | 6 | 1 | **Photofit**[254] [3648] 4-9-7 (JLDunlop) *led to 4f out: shkn up to ld again over 2f out: hdd & wknd ent fnl f* 11/2[3] | TQuinn 13 | 66 |
| 6-0 | 7 | 3/4 | **Mutassem (FR)**[18] [1059] 3-8-7 (EALDunlop) *pressed ldr: led 4f out to over 2f out: stl there w ch 1f out: wknd fnl 100y* 20/1 | RHills 12 | 64 |
| | 8 | 1 | **Generous Spirit (IRE)** 3-8-7 (JAOsborne) *cl up: rdn over 2f out: cl up over 1f out: wknd fnl f* 50/1 | SWKelly 9 | 61 |
| | 9 | 3 | **Beauchamp Star** 3-8-2 (GAButler) *wl in rr: pushed along and no prog over 2f out: one pce after* 66/1 | RLMoore 4 | 49 |
| 05- | 10 | 1 3/4 | **Russian Symphony (USA)**[231] [4280] 3-8-7 (CREgerton) *rn green in rr: rdn and bhd over 2f out: n.d after* 16/1 | PRobinson 5 | 49 |
| 0- | 11 | 1 1/4 | **Compton Eagle**[300] [2306] 4-9-7 (GAButler) *chsd ldrs: rdn and wknd 2f out* 50/1 | TEDurcan 6 | 46 |

054- **12** ¾ **Grumpyintmorning**[167] 5719 5-9-7 53 PDobbs 8 44
(MrsPTownsley) *taken down early: racd in midfield: rdn over 2f out: sn wknd* **66/1**

5-4 **13** 6 **Pompey Chimes**[11] 1133 4-9-7 SCarson 3 29
(GBBalding) *a bhd: last and struggling 3f out* **40/1**

0 **14** 17 **Love Of Life**[8] 1186 3-8-3 ow1 DRMcCabe 14 —
(MGQuinlan) *dwlt: chsd ldrs to 1/2-way: wknd u.p: t.o* **100/1**

1m 31.92s (4.12) **Going Correction** +0.575s/f (Yiel)
**WFA** 3 from 4yo+ 14lb **14** Ran SP% **116.9**
Speed ratings: **99,98,98,97,95 94,93,92,89,87 85,84,77,58**CSF £30.31 TOTE £10.00: £4.60, £1.10, £8.40; EX 26.50.
**Owner** Sheikh Mohammed **Bred** Darley Dubai **Trained** Newmarket, Suffolk
■ Stewards Enquiry : T E Durcan caution: allowed gelding to coast home with no assistance from the saddle

**FOCUS**
The whole field tacked over to the far side and the leaders appeared to go too fast for their own good. This was still fair form with several likely to leave this form behind.

**NOTEBOOK**
**Wistman(UAE)** was poorly drawn but, with the whole field tacking over to the far side and the leaders going too fast, the race was run to suit those held up. His dam is a half-sister to smart middle-distance performer Husyan, and there is every chance that he will get farther than this in time.
**Rangoon(USA)** appreciated the step up to seven furlongs having found six too short last time. He is now eligible for handicaps.
**The King's Bishop**, a son of Bishop Of Cashel, improved for the switch to turf and easy ground. He is now eligible for a mark.
**Royal Prince** has run well on each of his starts, but he took his time to get going and looks likely to be suited by a further step up in distance.
**Isaz**, who has clearly had his training problems, ran a fair race, but handicaps look more his game.
**Photofit** paid for helping to set a pace which proved too hot. He is better than his finishing position suggests.
**Mutassem(FR)** also fell away after being up with the strong gallop for a long way. He is another who should be rated better than his final placing.

## 1296 COME RACING IN KENT (S) H'CAP 7f (S)
4:10 (4:10) (F) (0-60,60) 3-Y-O **£2,513** (£718; £359) **Stalls** Low

Form RPR
0046 **1** **Doctored**[15] 1084 3-9-4 57 (p) LDettori 5 61
(BAPearce) *urged into ld: mde all: hrd rdn 2f out: kpt on and in command fnl f* **11/2**[3]

303 **2** 2 **Brother Cadfael**[50] 802 3-7-10 40 JFMcDonald(5) 4 39
(JohnAHarris) *trckd ldrs: rdn and effrt over 2f out: nt qckn wl over 1f out: no imp wnr fnl f* **13/2**

50-3 **3** nk **City General (IRE)**[7] 1197 3-9-4 57 (p) MartinDwyer 6 55
(JSMoore) *mostly chsd wnr: rdn and nt qckn over 2f out: no imp after* **2/1**[1]

00-0 **4** hd **Whiplash (IRE)**[2] 1274 3-9-7 60 DaneO'Neill 7 58
(RHannon) *hld up: prog 3f out: sn rdn: hanging lft and fnd nil 2f out: one pce after* **12/1**

0000 **5** 2½ **Fora Smile**[15] 1083 3-8-6 45 ADaly 3 37
(MDIUsher) *chsd ldrs: rdn and nt qckn over 2f out: fdd fnl f* **14/1**

0032 **6** 28 **Fox Hollow (IRE)**[21] 1040 3-7-13 41 ow1 RMiles(3) 1 —
(MJHaynes) *chsd ldrs: wknd u.p 1/2-way: t.o* **3/1**[2]

6400 **7** 2½ **Dulce De Leche**[35] 958 3-8-8 50 (be) BReilly(3) 2 —
(SCWilliams) *t.k.h: in tch tl wknd wl over 2f out: eased over 1f out : t.o* **10/1**

1m 32.86s (5.06) **Going Correction** +0.575s/f (Yiel) **7** Ran SP% **110.5**
Speed ratings: **94,91,91,91,88 56,53**CSF £37.44 TOTE £4.60: £3.00, £3.30; EX 46.20.The winner was bought in for 3,600gns.
**Owner** T M J Keep **Bred** Wickfield Farm Partnership **Trained** Newchapel, Surrey
■ Stewards Enquiry : B Reilly caution: allowed gelding to coast home with no assistance from saddle

**FOCUS**
A poor field who, collectively, could boast only one win from their previous 65 starts. The winner improved on recent All-Weather efforts.

**NOTEBOOK**
**Doctored**, who had the cheekpieces back on and was dropping down in trip, was soon taken to the front and made all. The slower ground may have helped, but his record suggests he is not one to back to follow up.
**Brother Cadfael**, regularly exposed in selling company on sand, ran his best race to date on turf, but this was a poor heat.
**City General(IRE)** was the only previous winner in the field but his best form is on a firmer surface.
**Whiplash(IRE)**, making a quick reappearance having been stuffed in a Windsor seller two days earlier, looked another unsuited by the easy conditions.

## 1297 HBLB LUNCH IN THE LOOKOUT RESTAURANT FILLIES' H'CAP 1m 4f
4:40 (4:40) (E) (0-70,70) 3-Y-O+ **£3,415** (£1,051; £525; £262) **Stalls** Low

Form RPR
2/22 **1** **Belle Rouge**[11] 1135 6-8-13 54 LDettori 5 63
(CAHorgan) *mde all: set decent pce tl stdd 1/2-way: kicked on again 3f out: rdn fnl f: jst hld on* **5/4**[1]

006- **2** hd **Starry Mary**[100] 6254 6-8-12 53 SSanders 1 62
(RMBeckett) *trckd ldrs but rn in snatches: rdn 3f out: no prog tl r.o wl fr over 1f out: jst failed* **8/1**[2]

3-20 **3** 1¼ **Resonance**[39] 916 3-8-2 64 JoannaBadger 2 71
(NATwiston-Davies) *dwlt: t.k.h: hld up in midfield: prog 4f out: effrt to chal 2f out: hanging lft and nt qckn over 1f out* **12/1**

3300 **4** ½ **Dance Party (IRE)**[13] 1109 4-9-8 64 PRobinson 9 70
(AMBalding) *trckd wnr for 2f: styd prom: chsd wnr again 3f out: rdn over 1f out: nt qckn and hld fnl f* **8/1**[2]

3-60 **5** 5 **Aoninch**[11] 1135 4-9-5 61 RHavlin 7 60
(MrsPNDutfield) *t.k.h: hld up in rr: prog over 3f out: shkn up 2f out: one pce and nvr rchd ldrs* **11/1**

00-5 **6** 2½ **Galandora**[8] 1188 4-7-10 45 (t) LucyRussell(7) 8 40
(DrJRJNaylor) *t.k.h: trckd wnr after 2f to 3f out: fdd 2f out* **25/1**

5-16 **7** 1¾ **Rye (IRE)**[14] 1100 3-8-8 70 SWKelly 4 63
(JAOsborne) *nvr gng wl: in last pair and rdn 7f out: struggling fr over 2f out* **14/1**

3103 **8** 4 **Miss Koen (IRE)**[8] 1188 5-8-11 55 (t) DCorby(3) 3 42
(DLWilliams) *dwlt: racd in midfield: rdn and wknd over 2f out* **9/1**[3]

0-05 **9** 2 **Cuddles (FR)**[8] 1187 5-9-10 65 (p) TEDurcan 6 49
(CEBrittain) *trckd ldrs: rdn and wknd 3f out* **10/1**

6001 **10** 28 **Angelica Garnett**[29] 995 4-8-5 47 JFEgan 10 —
(TEPowell) *dwlt: racd in last pair: rdn 7f out: wknd over 3f out: t.o* **12/1**

2m 52.43s (12.03) **Going Correction** +1.05s/f (Soft)
**WFA** 3 from 4yo 21lb 4 from 5yo+ 1lb **10** Ran SP% **120.0**
Speed ratings: **101,100,100,99,96 94,93,90,89,70**CSF £12.24 CT £88.98 TOTE £1.90: £1.10, £3.20, £1.70; EX 16.30.
**Owner** Mrs B Woodford **Bred** Whitsbury Manor Stud **Trained** Ogbourne Maisey, Wilts
■ Stewards Enquiry : S Sanders caution: used whip with excessive frequency

**FOCUS**
Dettori completed a 947/1 five-timer in this modest handicap, who got his front-running tactics on the favourite just right. The form looks fairly solid.

**NOTEBOOK**
**Belle Rouge**, whose Kempton form had been given a boost by the third going in at Warwick just over half an hour earlier, was soon sent to the front by Dettori, who dictated the gallop throughout. He kicked the mare on turning into the straight and got a gap, but the advantage was diminishing fast as the line approached. She probably did not like being in front for so long and is probably better than the margin of victory suggests.
**Starry Mary**, who has changed stables, is at her best on an easy surface. She finished well and would have got up in another few strides.
**Resonance** came there to have every chance, but she hung under pressure and does not look one who can be wholly trusted to go through with her effort.
**Dance Party(IRE)**, who is a consistent type but still a maiden, had every chance, but she was one-paced when it mattered.
**Aoninch** needs fast ground to show her best form.
**Angelica Garnett** *Official explanation: jockey said filly hung left.*

## 1298 CLICK ON HOWLETTS.NET H'CAP 1m 1f 149y
5:10 (5:10) (E) (0-70,70) 4-Y-O+ **£3,523** (£1,084; £542; £271) **Stalls** Low

Form RPR
0/0- **1** **Royal Racer (FR)**[182] 5452 6-8-5 47 NPollard 9 56
(JRBest) *led for 1f: trckd ldr tl led again over 3f out and kicked on: drvn over 1f out: edgd lft last 75y: jst hld on* **33/1**

0000 **2** nk **Easter Ogil (IRE)**[8] 1187 9-9-0 56 RHughes 11 65
(JaneSouthcombe) *settled wl in rr: outpcd and plenty to do 3f out: prog fr 2f out: r.o fnl f: jst failed* **25/1**

0251 **3** hd **Blazing The Trail (IRE)**[14] 1097 4-9-9 65 RHills 5 73
(JWHills) *s.i.s: wl in rr tl prog over 4f out: rdn and outpcd over 2f out: styd on fr over 1f out: jst hld* **8/1**[3]

24-0 **4** nk **Half Inch**[14] 1097 4-9-0 59 (p) DCorby(3) 1 67
(BICase) *trckd ldrs: rdn and outpcd over 2f out: kpt on fr over 1f out: nvr quite able to chal* **25/1**

50-6 **5** 2 **Dickie Deadeye**[13] 1109 7-8-10 57 RThomas(5) 7 61
(GBBalding) *settled wl in rr: outpcd and bhd 3f out: styd on wl fr over 1f out: too much to do* **7/1**[2]

0124 **6** nk **Galloway Mac**[8] 1187 4-9-4 60 TEDurcan 3 63
(WAO'Gorman) *prom: jnd wnr gng easily over 3f out: rdn and nt qckn 2f out: wknd ins fnl f* **10/1**

5-10 **7** 1¾ **Jack Of Trumps (IRE)**[77] 577 4-9-11 67 SSanders 6 67
(GWragg) *racd in midfield: outpcd 3f out: drvn and effrt 2f out: no imp ldrs fnl f* **14/1**

-006 **8** 3 **Icannshift (IRE)**[74] 602 4-8-12 54 RLMoore 4 49
(SDow) *wl in rr: sme prog to midfield 4f out: outpcd 3f out: one pce and no hdwy after* **25/1**

4-20 **9** 9 **To Wit To Woo**[51] 800 4-9-2 58 (p) EAhern 10 37
(BWHills) *trckd ldrs: rdn and outpcd 3f out: sn wknd* **7/1**[2]

06-0 **10** 3 **Forest Tune (IRE)**[13] 1109 6-9-5 61 PRobinson 15 34
(BHanbury) *trckd ldrs: rdn and wknd 3f out* **5/1**[1]

004- **11** 1 **Madame Marie (IRE)**[285] 2745 4-8-12 54 PaulEddery 13 26
(SDow) *s.s: racd in detached last: outpcd over 3f out: bhd after* **50/1**

0-05 **12** 6 **Rebate**[15] 1088 4-10-0 70 PDobbs 14 31
(RHannon) *prom tl wknd over 3f out* **12/1**

-330 **13** dist **Zalkani (IRE)**[56] 745 4-9-0 56 LDettori 2 —
(BGPowell) *pushed up to ld after 1f: hdd and weakend rapidly over 3f out: t.o* **5/1**[1]

4010 **P** **Bressbee (USA)**[12] 1118 6-8-11 53 (v) SWKelly 8 —
(NPLittmoden) *lost pl after 2f: p.u 6f out: dismntd* **7/1**[2]

2m 14.6s (9.44) **Going Correction** +1.05s/f (Soft) **14** Ran SP% **121.8**
Speed ratings: **104,103,103,103,101 101,100,97,90,88 87,82,—,—**CSF £681.40 CT £7062.33 TOTE £46.10: £8.30, £5.20, £3.20; EX 468.60 Place 6 £183.69, Place 5 £113.30.
**Owner** Mr & Mrs R Dawbarn **Bred** Mme Renee Geffroy **Trained** Hucking, Kent

**FOCUS**
A decent pace for this modest handicap.

**NOTEBOOK**
**Royal Racer(FR)** can take plenty of credit for this performance as he helped force a decent pace and was able to hang on from a pack of closers in the final stages. He was also conceding race fitness to his rivals and hopefully he can build on this.
**Easter Ogil(IRE)**, who has not won on turf in this country for almost four years, had the race run to suit and finished strongly. He is the type who needs everything to fall just right.
**Blazing The Trail(IRE)**, another suited by the way the race was run, was returning to the turf on a 7lb lower mark than when last running on the surface.
**Half Inch** appreciated the return to the turf and looks on a feasible mark at present.
**Dickie Deadeye** had the ground to suit but was given too much to do. He looks capable of winning a race off his current mark when everything drops right.
**Galloway Mac** looked to have the race run to suit and came there to have his chance. He is proving disappointing.
**Bressbee(USA)** *Official explanation: jockey said gelding was lame*
T/Plt: £72.60 to a £1 stake. Pool: £31,342.50. 314.85 winning tickets. T/Qpdt: £37.50 to a £1 stake. Pool: £1,711.50. 33.70 winning tickets. JN

# WARWICK (L-H)
Wednesday, April 7

**OFFICIAL GOING: Soft (good to soft in places)**
Wind: mod against. Weather: shower race 6.

## 1299 EUROPEAN BREEDERS FUND MAIDEN FILLIES' STKS 5f
2:30 (2:30) (D) 2-Y-O **£4,361** (£1,342; £671; £335) **Stalls** Low

Form RPR
5 **1** **Polly Alexander (IRE)**[11] 1130 2-8-11 KDarley 3 67
(MJWallace) *w ldr: rdn over 2f out: swtchd lft over 1f out: led ins fnl f: drvn out* **10/3**[3]

6 **2** ½ **Gogetter Girl**[13] 1105 2-8-11 NCallan 1 65
(JGallagher) *led: edgd rt fr over 2f out: rdn and wandered over 1f out: r.o* **5/2**[1]

4 **3** 2 1/2 **Aunty Euro (IRE)**[12] 1117 2-8-11 MFenton 6 58
(EJO'Neill) *chsd ldrs: rdn over 3f out: hung lft fr over 1f out: kpt on ins fnl f* **12/1**

**4** 3/4 **Seasons Estates** 2-8-11 SDrowne 8 55
(BRMillman) *wnt rt s: racd wd: hdwy over 2f out: sn rdn: r.o one pce fnl f* **12/1**

**5** 2 1/2 **Iam Foreverblowing** 2-8-11 ANicholls 5 48
(SCBurrough) *chsd ldrs: rdn over 3f out: wknd ins fnl f* **33/1**

**6** 1 1/4 **Ribbons Of Gold** 2-8-11 DHolland 4 44
(JAOsborne) *prom: rdn over 2f out: wknd ins fnl f* **11/4**[2]

**7** 2 **Artadi** 2-8-8 TPQueally(3) 2 38
(PMPhelan) *dwlt: outpcd* **20/1**

**8** 13 **Kindlelight Dream (IRE)** 2-8-11 DSweeney 7 —
(DKIvory) *dwlt: rn green: a bhd* **25/1**

**9** 5 **Elvina Hills (IRE)** 2-8-11 ACulhane 9 —
(WGMTurner) *carried rt s: bhd fnl 3f* **10/1**

66.73 secs (6.53) **Going Correction** +1.175s/f (Soft) **9** Ran SP% **114.3**
Speed ratings: **94,93,89,88,84 82,78,58,50**CSF £11.64 TOTE £4.90: £1.10, £1.30, £3.60; EX 11.00.
**Owner** Mrs T A Foreman **Bred** Mrs T A Foreman **Trained** Newmarket, Suffolk

**FOCUS**
Only a fair fillies' maiden, but one that is sure to produce winners. The first three places were filled by the trio with previous experience, with the runner-up running close to Brocklesby form.

**NOTEBOOK**
**Polly Alexander(IRE)**, who showed distinct signs of inexperience on her debut at Kempton, was soon into her stride on the shoulder of the favourite and, despite getting outpaced on the turn into the straight, came home strongly. The step up to six furlongs is sure to suit this daughter of Foxhound and there should be more to come.
**Gogetter Girl** had finished sixth in the Brocklesby on her debut and came into this as the one to beat. She was soon at the head of affairs and looked to have it in the bag straightening for home, but she showed signs of inexperience in wandering under pressure and ended up being run out of it. She should have little difficulty picking up a similar race.
**Aunty Euro(IRE)**, the third and final member of the line-up with previous experience under her belt, did not look in love with the ground and hung in the straight. Six furlongs will see her in a better light.
**Seasons Estates** showed more than enough to suggest she can win races on this racecourse debut and will appreciate better ground.
**Iam Foreverblowing**, related to several sprint winners, showed up well for most of the way and is entitled to improve for the outing.
**Ribbons Of Gold**, a speedily-bred filly, was clearly expected to fare better than she did, but given it was her debut, can be given another chance.
**Kindlelight Dream(IRE)** *Official explanation: jockey said bit slipped though filly's mouth*

## 1300 WARDINGTON H'CAP — 7f 26y
**3:00** (3:01) (F) (0-55,55) 3-Y-O — **£3,206** (£916; £458) **Stalls** Low

Form RPR

2-00 **1** **She's Our Lass (IRE)**[12] 1111 3-9-3 **54** RFitzpatrick 2 63
(DCarroll) *a.p: swtchd lft and rdn to ld jst over 1f out: r.o wl* **15/2**[3]

60-4 **2** 1 1/2 **Knickyknackienoo**[20] 1046 3-9-0 **51** SWhitworth 11 56
(AGNewcombe) *s.i.s: hld up: sn swtchd lft: nt clr run over 2f out: swtchd rt and hdwy over 1f out: hrd rdn and r.o wl ins* **10/1**

4302 **3** 1 1/4 **Siera Spirit (IRE)**[8] 1184 3-9-4 **55** SDrowne 6 57
(MGQuinlan) *a.p: rdn and ev ch 1f out: nt qckn* **15/8**[1]

20-4 **4** 2 1/2 **Bold Wolf**[15] 1083 3-9-3 **54** KDarley 4 50
(JLSpearing) *led: rdn and hdd jst over 1f out: wknd ins fnl f* **16/1**

-000 **5** shd **Backlash**[57] 731 3-8-9 **46** oh1 SRighton 1 42
(AWCarroll) *hld up mid-div: hdwy on ins over 2f out: nvr able to chal* **11/1**

6040 **6** 3/4 **Livia (IRE)**[8] 1184 3-9-3 **54** ACulhane 9 48
(JGPortman) *chsd ldr: rdn over 2f out: ev ch jst over 1f out: wknd ins fnl f* **20/1**

500- **7** 1 3/4 **Upthedale (IRE)**[155] 5915 3-8-11 **48** PHanagan 13 37
(JRWeymes) *hld up mid-div: rdn 3f out: no hdwy fnl 2f* **33/1**

3643 **8** nk **Docklands Blue (IRE)**[12] 1119 3-9-3 **54** DHolland 7 43
(NPLittmoden) *hld up and bhd: c wd and hdwy over 2f out: one pce fnl f* **9/2**[2]

2005 **9** 1 1/2 **Jaolins**[15] 1086 3-9-3 **54** DKinsella 3 39
(PGMurphy) *s.s: plld hrd: short-lived effrt on ins over 2f out* **20/1**

0040 **10** 1 1/2 **Parallel Lines (IRE)**[29] 1000 3-8-12 **49** (v) RWinston 8 30
(PDEvans) *s.i.s: plld hrd: hmpd over 5f out: a bhd* **12/1**

00-6 **11** 1/2 **I Wish I Knew**[37] 942 3-9-4 **55** WSupple 12 35
(DJCoakley) *plld hrd: prom: rdn and edgd lft wl over 1f out: sn wknd* **28/1**

4000 **12** shd **Taranai (IRE)**[38] 926 3-8-11 **48** (b[1]) MFenton 5 28
(BWDuke) *s.i.s: sn mid-div: rdn 3f out: sn bhd* **33/1**

000- **13** 6 **Scenic Flight**[211] 4802 3-9-4 **55** CCatlin 10 20
(MrsAJBowlby) *plld hrd: prom: rdn and wknd wl over 1f out* **33/1**

000- **14** 5 **Jesse Samuel**[174] 5595 3-8-6 **50** JJeffrey(7) 14 —
(JRJenkins) *a bhd* **40/1**

1m 29.28s (4.38) **Going Correction** +0.425s/f (Yiel) **14** Ran SP% **120.0**
Speed ratings: **91,89,87,85,84 84,82,81,79,78 77,77,70,65**CSF £73.04 CT £206.66 TOTE £9.50: £1.80, £3.80, £1.30; EX 143.80.
**Owner** We-Know Partnership **Bred** Illuminatus Investments **Trained** Warthill, N Yorks

**FOCUS**
A poor handicap and not strong form, but a good performance from winning filly She's Our Lass, who found a change of pace around a furlong out that sealed the race.

**NOTEBOOK**
**She's Our Lass(IRE)** saved ground by racing towards the inside throughout and produced a good burst of speed to quicken into the lead around a furlong out. This represented a step up on previous form and there is every chance she can follow up. *Official explanation: trainer said, regarding the improved form shown, filly ran last time over the Doncaster straight but today appeared better suited by the drop in class and by being covered up on a tight track*
**Knickyknackienoo** was unlucky not to finish closer, having been slow to find his stride and denied a clear run on more than one occasion once finding it. He finished well, but is pretty exposed and does not do much for the form.
**Siera Spirit(IRE)** continues to run well without winning and may appreciate a return to six furlongs.
**Bold Wolf** showed up well for a long way before getting a little tired late on.
**Backlash** improved on recent All-Weather form and is evidently going to be better suited by turf.
**Livia(IRE)** was bang there with every chance in the straight, but failed to see out her race.
**Docklands Blue(IRE)** was always trailing and never got involved.

## 1301 WARWICK COURIER MAIDEN STKS (DIV I) — 1m 22y
**3:30** (3:32) (D) 3-Y-O — **£3,672** (£1,130; £565; £282) **Stalls** Low

Form RPR

00- **1** **Hasayis**[166] 5733 3-8-9 WSupple 6 69+
(JLDunlop) *hld up: hdwy 4f out: swtchd lft over 2f out: led wl over 1f out: jinked lft 1f out: all out* **9/4**[1]

**2** 3/4 **Cesare** 3-9-0 KDarley 4 72+
(JRFanshawe) *hld up and bhd: rdn and hdwy over 2f out: r.o ins fnl f* **11/4**[2]

0-00 **3** 5 **Prince Valentine**[64] 660 3-9-0 57 MTebbutt 3 62
(DBFeek) *chsd ldr 2f: rdn over 2f out: one pce* **12/1**

0 **4** 1 1/4 **Master Mahogany**[56] 744 3-9-0 VSlattery 7 60
(RJHodges) *hld up: rdn over 2f out: hdwy over 1f out: no imp fnl f* **33/1**

5-06 **5** 2 **Dante's Devine (IRE)**[40] 906 3-9-0 56 JBramhill 5 56
(ABailey) *led: wl clr after 2f: hdd wl over 1f out: wknd fnl f* **20/1**

**6** nk **Premier Dream (USA)** 3-9-0 JFanning 2 55
(MJohnston) *hld up: rdn over 3f out: short-lived effrt on ins wl over 1f out* **3/1**[3]

**7** 7 **Purple Rain (IRE)** 3-8-9 JMackay 1 36
(MLWBell) *chsd clr ldr after 2f: hung rt and c v wd st: sn wknd* **8/1**

0- **8** 28 **Hilly Be**[161] 5830 3-8-9 SWhitworth 9 —
(JRJenkins) *a bhd: t.o fnl 2f* **20/1**

1m 46.79s (7.49) **Going Correction** +0.95s/f (Soft) **8** Ran SP% **113.7**
Speed ratings: **100,99,94,93,91 90,83,55**CSF £8.31 TOTE £2.90: £1.30, £1.30, £3.70; EX 20.60.
**Owner** Hamdan Al Maktoum **Bred** Shadwell Estate Company Limited **Trained** Arundel, W Sussex

**FOCUS**
With the morning favourite Andean being a non-runner, the strength of the race was lessened. Hasayis showed a determined attitude in winning and is likely now to go handicapping off what should be a modest mark.

**NOTEBOOK**
**Hasayis**, who showed promise in better races as a juvenile, was helped by the absence of favourite Andean and held on well having taken it up under a quarter of a mile out. She still showed signs of inexperience a furlong out, jinking to her left, and is likely to take the handicap route.
**Cesare**, a half-brother to Exit To Nowhere, came from a fair way back to thrown down a challenge to the winner and it briefly looked as though he may get there before the winner pulled out more. This was an encouraging debut and he is sure to pick up a similar race.
**Prince Valentine** finishing third does not enhance the form, but he improved on his All-Weather form and will be better served in handicaps.
**Dante's Devine(IRE)** *Official explanation: jockey said gelding hung badly in the early stages*
**Premier Dream(USA)**, a well-related colt, is bred to appreciate better ground and should be given another chance.
**Purple Rain(IRE)** forfeited many lengths turning into the straight, hanging to her right and coming very wide. She is worth another chance to show her true form.

## 1302 SCOTTISH EQUITABLE / JOCKEYS ASSOCIATION H'CAP — 1m 6f 213y
**4:00** (4:00) (D) (0-80,80) 3-Y-O+ — **£5,824** (£1,792; £896; £448) **Stalls** Low

Form RPR

-503 **1** **Turtle Valley (IRE)**[11] 1135 8-9-3 **69** PDoe 4 80
(SDow) *hld up mid-div: hdwy over 3f out: rdn over 2f out: edgd lft and led 1f out: sn hung lft: r.o* **9/2**[2]

6/51 **2** shd **Malarkey**[7] 1210 7-9-0 **66** 6ex SDrowne 1 77+
(MrsStefLiddiard) *hld up: hdwy and nt clr run 3f out: rdn 2f out: ev ch ins fnl f: r.o* **11/2**[3]

3640 **3** 4 **George Stubbs (USA)**[12] 1112 6-8-7 **62** LFletcher(3) 9 68
(MJPolglase) *prom: led over 8f out: rdn over 2f out: hdd 1f out: wknd ins fnl f* **7/1**

105- **4** 5 **Moonshine Beach**[234] 4216 6-8-11 **63** ACulhane 12 62
(PWHiatt) *hld up and bhd: hdwy over 3f out: rdn over 2f out: wknd fnl f* **14/1**

006- **5** 1 **Heir To Be**[252] 3685 5-9-8 **74** KDarley 13 72
(JLDunlop) *hld up in tch: wnt 2nd over 3f out: rdn over 2f out: ev ch over 1f out: sn sltly hmpd: wknd fnl f* **9/2**[2]

500- **6** 3 **Whist Drive**[18] 2326 4-8-11 **66** CCatlin 3 60
(MrsNSmith) *hld up: rdn over 7f out: nvr nr ldrs* **16/1**

000- **7** 3/4 **Don Fernando**[20] 5639 5-10-0 **80** DHolland 8 73
(MCPipe) *prom: rdn over 4f out: wknd over 3f out* **4/1**[1]

000- **8** 3/4 **Muskatsturm (GER)**[24] 5949 5-9-11 **80** TPQueally(3) 11 72
(BJCurley) *a bhd* **25/1**

116- **9** dist **Vin Du Pays**[76] 6061 4-8-6 **61** ow2 NCallan 10 —
(MBlanshard) *hld up in tch: rdn over 4f out: wknd over 3f out: t.o* **25/1**

1110 **10** 2 1/2 **Sun Hill**[12] 1112 4-9-11 **80** DSweeney 5 —
(MBlanshard) *chsd ldr: rdn over 4f out: lost 2nd over 3f out: wknd 2f out: t.o* **9/1**

0400 **11** 2 **Munfarid (IRE)**[11] 1135 4-8-11 **66** (t) DKinsella 2 —
(PGMurphy) *led: hdd over 8f out: rdn over 5f out: wknd over 2f out: t.o* **50/1**

3m 31.26s (16.06) **Going Correction** +0.95s/f (Soft)
**WFA** 4 from 5yo+ 3lb **11** Ran SP% **116.5**
Speed ratings: **95,94,92,90,89 88,87,87,—,— —**CSF £28.61 CT £171.67 TOTE £5.30: £1.90, £1.60, £2.70; EX 26.10 Trifecta £159.30 Pool of £1,144.60 - 5.10 winning units..
**Owner** Cazanove Clear Height Racing **Bred** Kilfrush Stud Ltd **Trained** Epsom, Surrey
■ Stewards Enquiry : P Doe caution: careless riding

**FOCUS**
A fair handicap producing an exciting finish that resulted in a stewards' enquiry due the the front pair coming close inside the final furlong.

**NOTEBOOK**
**Turtle Valley(IRE)** revels in this ground and was recording the sixth Flat win of his career. He had to survive a stewards' enquiry though as he hung into the runner-up close home, but it was deemed not to have affected the result.
**Malarkey** was an unlucky loser, not getting a break when he wanted one and being slightly impeded close home. He was running off only a pound higher mark than when winning at Nottingham last week and should not go up much for this.
**George Stubbs(USA)** ran his race, leading to just over a furlong out, but was no match for the front pair.
**Moonshine Beach** ran well on this first start since August, looking a possible danger turning in before the lack of a recent run told up the straight. He is sure to come on for the outing.
**Heir To Be**, another having his first start of the season, made a most pleasing reappearance and should reverse form with most of these were they to meet again.
**Whist Drive**, who has been running well over hurdles of late, was struggling from a long way out and could only plug on through beaten horses.
**Don Fernando** was a disappointing favourite, failing to see out the trip.

## 1303 DUNCHURCH CLASSIFIED STKS — 6f 21y
**4:30** (4:33) (E) 3-Y-O — **£3,656** (£1,125; £562; £281) **Stalls** Low

Form RPR

23-5 **1** **Distant Times**[11] 1129 3-9-0 73 KDarley 1 81
(TDEasterby) *w ldr: led over 3f out: rdn and r.o wl fnl f* **5/4**[1]

2031 **2** 2 1/2 **Muy Bien**[2] 1270 3-9-3 69 (b) DHolland 3 77
(JRJenkins) *a.p: rdn over 2f out: chsd wnr jst over 1f out: no imp* **9/4**[2]

00-6 **3** 2 **Senor Bond (USA)**[22] 1029 3-8-13 72 FLynch 5 67
(BSmart) *hld up: rdn and nt clr run jst over 1f out: swtchd rt: kpt on ins fnl f* **18/1**

351- **4** *1 ¾* **La Landonne**[123] 6129 3-8-5 70 .......... TPQueally(3) 4 56
(PMPhelan) *led over 2f: ev ch over 2f out: wknd 1f out* **11/1**

240- **5** *2 ½* **Tyzack (IRE)**[155] 5913 3-8-12 71 .......... MFenton 2 53
(JGGiven) *hld up: rdn over 2f out: no rspnse* **7/1**[3]

20-4 **6** *1 ½* **Crewes Miss Isle**[75] 591 3-8-10 72 .......... SWhitworth 6 46
(AGNewcombe) *prom: rdn over 2f out: wknd fnl f* **11/1**

1m 14.5s (2.20) **Going Correction** +0.425s/f (Yiel) **6** Ran SP% **109.6**
Speed ratings: **102,98,96,93,90 88**CSF £3.98 TOTE £2.10: £1.10, £1.50; EX 2.80.
**Owner** Times Of Wigan **Bred** Times Of Wigan Ltd **Trained** Great Habton, N Yorks

**FOCUS**
A fair event in which Distant Times delivered as expected and warrants being stepped back up in grade.

**NOTEBOOK**
**Distant Times** was the clear form pick on his fifth at Doncaster last week and always looked set to win. He did not beat much, but should be capable of running well back up in grade.
**Muy Bien** proved his effectiveness on this ground when winning at Windsor two days earlier and did nothing wrong in second.
**Senor Bond(USA)** ◆ looked to be struggling early, but came good in the straight and was unlucky not to finish closer. He was denied a clear run just as he was getting going and, if going on from this, should be capable of winning back in handicap company.
**La Landonne** appeared to need this first outing of the year.

## 1304 WARWICK COURIER MAIDEN STKS (DIV II) 1m 22y
**5:00** (5:01) (D) 3-Y-O **£3,656** (£1,125; £562; £281) **Stalls** Low

Form RPR

6- **1** **City Palace**[166] 5735 3-9-0 .......... ACulhane 2 76
(BWHills) *a.p: rdn 2f out: led ins fnl f: drvn out* **6/4**[2]

30- **2** *1* **Oh Golly Gosh**[157] 5886 3-9-0 .......... KDarley 8 74
(NPLittmoden) *s.i.s: hld up: hdwy over 4f out: rdn over 2f out: led jst over 1f out tl ins fnl f: nt qckn* **14/1**[3]

5-4 **3** *1 ¼* **Man Of Letters (UAE)**[13] 1104 3-9-0 .......... KDalgleish 6 72+
(MJohnston) *a.p: wnt 2nd over 4f out: rdn to ld 2f out: hdd jst over 1f out: no ex ins fnl f* **11/10**[1]

00- **4** *10* **Land Of Nod (IRE)**[146] 5984 3-8-6 .......... TPQueally(3) 3 47
(GAButler) *hld up: bhd fnl 4f* **14/1**[3]

000- **5** *9* **Rebel Rouser**[160] 5836 3-9-0 .......... SDrowne 7 34
(WRMuir) *a bhd* **66/1**

0-6 **6** *½* **Saucy**[8] 1186 3-8-6 .......... LPKeniry(3) 1 28
(BJMeehan) *led: rdn and hdd 2f out: wknd qckly over 1f out* **20/1**

**7** *6* **Alexei** 3-9-0 .......... JDSmith 9 21
(JRFanshawe) *s.s: a bhd* **20/1**

04-0 **8** *24* **Simply Red**[12] 1111 3-9-0 40 .......... (v1) GDuffield 4 —
(RBrotherton) *chsd ldr over 3f: wknd over 3f out: t.o* **66/1**

**9** *dist* **Summer Joy** 3-8-3 ow1 .......... MHoward(7) 5 —
(DKIvory) *unruly and sat down in stalls: a wl t.o* **66/1**

1m 46.78s (7.48) **Going Correction** +0.95s/f (Soft) **9** Ran SP% **115.0**
Speed ratings: **100,99,97,87,78 78,72,48,—**CSF £20.24 TOTE £2.50: £1.20, £2.90, £1.02; EX 30.20.
**Owner** K Abdulla **Bred** Juddmonte Farms **Trained** Lambourn, Berks
■ Stewards Enquiry : A Culhane two-day ban: used whip with excessive frequency (Apr 19,20)

**FOCUS**
The front three pulled 14 lengths clear of the third in what was nothing more than a fair maiden.

**NOTEBOOK**
**City Palace**, who showed plenty of promise when sixth on his sole start as a two-year-old, has clearly gone the right way from two to three and stayed on well to edge clear in the final half-furlong. It is highly unlikely he is up to pattern level and handicaps are likely to present the best opportunities for him.
**Oh Golly Gosh** showed promise in two starts on the All-Weather without setting the world alight, but this represented an improved effort. He is evidently better on turf, and looks the type to do well in handicaps.
**Man Of Letters(UAE)**, who made a pleasing comeback run at Doncaster, was done no favours by an early bump and had done too much running by the time he got into contention. He understandably could offer no more in the straight, and is another likely to be seen to better effect in handicaps.
**Land Of Nod(IRE)** is now qualified for a mark.
**Saucy** was in the process of running a good race, but stopped very sharply a furlong out as though something were amiss.

## 1305 DRAYCOTE H'CAP 1m 2f 188y
**5:30** (5:31) (F) (0-45,55) 3-Y-0+ **£3,500** (£1,000; £500) **Stalls** Low

Form RPR

111/ **1** **Cristoforo (IRE)**[140] 5971 7-9-3 48 .......... TPQueally(3) 7 69+
(BJCurley) *hld up: stdy hdwy over 3f out: c wd st: led 1f out: pushed out* **11/4**[1]

2-01 **2** *2* **Great View (IRE)**[15] 1081 5-9-11 53 .......... (v) GDuffield 8 63
(MrsALMKing) *hld up in tch: led 2f out: sn rdn: edgd lft and hdd 1f out: nt qckn* **9/1**

520- **3** *1 ¼* **Moonshine Bill**[184] 5419 5-9-10 52 .......... ACulhane 16 60
(PWHiatt) *hld up: hdwy over 3f out: rdn and ev ch over 1f out: one pce* **16/1**

3630 **4** *2 ½* **Theatre Lady (IRE)**[4] 1244 6-9-8 50 .......... KDarley 18 54
(PDEvans) *hld up and bhd: rdn and hdwy over 1f out: nt rch ldrs* **20/1**

000- **5** *4* **Rutland Chantry (USA)**[103] 5823 10-9-5 47 .......... KDalgleish 20 44
(SGollings) *hld up and bhd: rdn over 3f out: hdwy over 1f out: styd on fnl f* **40/1**

0333 **6** *1 ½* **Call Of The Wild**[9] 1181 4-9-12 54 .......... (v) PHanagan 11 48
(RAFahey) *prom: rdn over 4f out: wknd over 1f out* **14/1**

000- **7** *1* **Imtihan (IRE)**[17] 5502 5-9-9 51 .......... ANicholls 3 44
(SCBurrough) *bhd: sn pushed along: hdwy over 1f out: nvr trbld ldrs* **11/2**[2]

00-0 **8** *7* **Bojangles (IRE)**[47] 838 5-9-5 50 .......... LFletcher(3) 15 31
(RBrotherton) *prom: led over 5f out: rdn and hdd over 2f out: wknd over 1f out* **33/1**

0003 **9** *1 ½* **Forty Forte**[8] 1194 8-9-1 48 .......... AQuinn(5) 19 26
(MissSJWilton) *prom tl rdn and wknd wl over 1f out* **50/1**

200- **10** *2 ½* **The Loose Screw (IRE)**[140] 6026 6-9-6 48 .......... MFenton 4 22
(GMMoore) *led 2f: wknd over 3f out* **28/1**

0003 **11** *1 ¾* **Rocinante (IRE)**[9] 1176 4-9-7 49 .......... RWinston 1 20
(JJQuinn) *hld up: rdn and hdwy over 2f out: wknd over 1f out* **28/1**

0-05 **12** *¾* **Paula Lane**[64] 666 4-9-10 55 .......... SHitchcott(3) 14 25
(RCurtis) *led after 2f tl over 5f out: ev ch 3f out: sn rdn: wknd wl over 1f out* **33/1**

2543 **13** *2 ½* **Grand Lass (IRE)**[2] 1263 5-9-11 53 .......... (p) DHolland 9 18
(ASadik) *a bhd* **15/2**[3]

0502 **14** *nk* **Paradise Valley**[5] 1231 4-9-10 52 .......... (t) SDrowne 5 17
(MrsStefLiddiard) *a bhd* **11/1**

0504 **15** *nk* **Spy Gun (USA)**[21] 1039 4-9-10 52 .......... RFfrench 2 16
(TWall) *chsd ldrs: rdn over 2f out: sn wknd* **50/1**

/00- **16** *9* **Dream Falcon**[45] 5270 4-9-8 50 .......... VSlattery 17 —
(RJHodges) *rdn over 7f out: a bhd* **16/1**

0232 **17** *2 ½* **Orinocovsky (IRE)**[22] 1028 5-9-13 55 .......... NCallan 6 —
(NPLittmoden) *prom: rdn 4f out: wknd 2f out* **15/2**[3]

0-36 **18** *7* **On Guard**[29] 995 6-9-13 55 .......... (v) DKinsella 13 —
(PGMurphy) *a bhd* **14/1**

4-1 **19** *dist* **Heathyards Pride**[95] 424 4-9-11 53 .......... WSupple 12 —
(RHollinshead) *a bhd: t.o fnl 3f* **20/1**

2m 29.41s (10.01) **Going Correction** +0.95s/f (Soft) **19** Ran SP% **137.7**
Speed ratings: **101,99,98,96,93 92,92,87,85,84 82,82,80,80,80 73,71,66,—**CSF £27.49 CT £373.19 TOTE £4.50: £2.40, £2.10, £4.10, £3.40; EX 62.20 Place 6 £6.96, Place 5 £4.23.
**Owner** P Byrne **Bred** Bill Dwan And Tom Lynch **Trained** Newmarket, Suffolk

**FOCUS**
This looked a fairly competitive race to end, but Cristoforo brushed aside the opposition to win in decisive fashion.

**NOTEBOOK**
**Cristoforo(IRE)**, whose support in the ring was significant given his connections, was always travelling strongly and came with a well-timed challenge to take it up around a furlong out, only having to be ridden out to score. He is likely to be punished for this, but how severely only the Handicapper knows.
**Great View(IRE)** faced a stiff task giving 8lb to the winner and ran as well as could have been expected.
**Moonshine Bill** was far from disgraced on this first outing since October and can only come on for the run.
**Theatre Lady(IRE)** has been kept busy of late and ran respectably.
**Rutland Chantry(USA)** shapes as though he would ideally prefer a stiffer test these days.
**Imtihan(IRE)**, who has been in hot form over hurdles of late, was never really going and appeared to find this trip on the sharp side. He is worth giving another chance to.
T/Jkpt: £9,452.20 to a £1 stake. Pool: £19,969.50. 1.50 winning tickets. T/Plt: £8.40 to a £1 stake. Pool: £42,789.30. 3,683.95 winning tickets. T/Qpdt: £3.30 to a £1 stake. Pool: £2,423.90. 533.00 winning tickets. KH

# SAN SIRO (R-H)
Wednesday, April 7

**OFFICIAL GOING: Good**

## 1306a PREMIO ANGELO GARDENGHI (UNRACED) 1m 1f
**4:30** (4:40) 3-Y-O **£8,803** (£3,873; £2,113; £1,056)

RPR

**1** **Electrocutionist (USA)** 3-9-2 .......... EBotti 9 —
(VValiani, Italy)

**2** *6* **Herakles (GER)** 3-9-2 .......... GBietolini 1 —
(RRohne, Germany)

**3** *4* **Petrovski (GER)** 3-9-2 .......... LHammer-Hansen 12 —
(DKRichardson, Germany)

**4** *1 ¾* **Ca Turtle (GER)** 3-9-2 .......... ACarboni 10 —
(PCaravati, Italy)

**5** *6* **Boltraffio (FR)** 3-9-2 .......... LSorrentino 8 —
(OPessi, Italy)

**6** *1 ½* **Strong Cat (IRE)** 3-9-2 .......... APitzalis 11 —
(MCiciarelli, Italy)

**7** *nk* **Milan All Stars (IRE)** 3-9-2 .......... SMulas 2 —
(BGrizzetti, Italy)

**8** *4* **Darvish (FR)** 3-9-2 .......... IRossi 5 —
(LBatzella, Italy)

**9** *7* **Waluck (ITY)** 3-9-2 .......... MSanna 7 —
(GColleo, Italy)

**10** *1 ¼* **Cazenove** 3-9-2 .......... APolli 15 —
(MGQuinlan) *missed break and towards rear, progress approaching straight, 5th and pressed leaders straight, soon weakened*

**11** *1 ¼* **Sesamoid (IRE)** 3-9-2 .......... DPorcu 6 —
(MGuarnieri, Italy)

**12** *1 ¾* **Azuni (IRE)** 3-9-2 .......... MEsposito 14 —
(VCaruso, Italy)

**13** *3 ½* **Lord Of Flowers** 3-9-2 .......... MTellini 4 —
(PPaciello, Italy)

**14** *12* **River Dominie (IRE)** 3-8-13 .......... CColombi 3 —
(LD'Auria, Italy)

**15** *4* **Mamone (IRE)** 3-9-2 .......... MMonteriso 13 —
(GRomano, Italy)

1m 51.4s **15** Ran
Speed ratings: .
**Owner** Earle I Mack **Bred** Compagnia Generale Srl **Trained** Italy

**NOTEBOOK**
**Cazenove**, making his debut in this newcomers' event, showed some ability after being slowly away, but tired in the closing stages.

# BATH (L-H)
Thursday, April 8

**OFFICIAL GOING: Good**

## 1307 SEVERN VALLEY CATERING CLAIMING STKS 5f 11y
**2:20** (2:21) (F) 2-Y-O **£3,066** (£876; £438) **Stalls** Low

Form RPR

**1** **Treat Me Wild (IRE)** 2-8-6 .......... RLMoore 9 59
(RHannon) *outpcd: bhd: hdwy over 2f out: drvn and str run to ld jst ins fnl f: r.o wl* **5/2**[1]

0 **2** *nk* **Im Spartacus**[19] 1060 2-8-9 .......... GDuffield 8 61
(IAWood) *outpcd and bhd: rdn 3f out: gd hdwy ins fnl 2f: fin strly: nt quite get up* **20/1**

23 **3** *1 ½* **Nutty Times**[6] 1234 2-7-7 .......... CHaddon(7) 6 47
(WGMTurner) *w ldr tl hung bdly rt bnd over 3f out: sn rcvrd: led 2f out: shkn up and hdd jst ins last: one pce* **8/1**

0 **4** *1* **Goldhill Prince**[13] 1115 2-8-4 .......... (p) ADaly 3 47
(WGMTurner) *made most tl hdd 2f out: outpcd ins fnl f* **16/1**

**5** *3* **Zimbali** 2-8-1 .......... JBramhill 5 34
(JMBradley) *disp ld 3f: wknd fnl f* **40/1**

2 **6** ¾ **General Nuisance (IRE)**[13] 1115 2-8-9 DKinsella 7 39
(PGMurphy) *s.i.s: sn rcvrd to chse ldrs: wknd over 1f out* **5/1**[2]

3 **7** 2 **Little Wizzy**[13] 1115 2-8-4 SWKelly 10 27
(PDEvans) *w ldrs whn carried rt bnd over 3f out: swtchd lft sn after: chsd ldrs and rdn 2f out: wknd over 1f out* **7/1**[3]

6 **8** 6 **Docklands Dude (IRE)**[13] 1115 2-8-7 VSlattery 2 8
(MMeade) *s.i.s: sn rcvrd to chse ldrs: wknd 2f out* **5/1**[2]

**9** 9 **Petite Noire** 2-8-6 EAhern 1 —
(JGPortman) *s.i.s: sn in tch: effrt 1/2-way: sn wknd* **11/1**

0 **10** 2½ **Berham Maldu (IRE)**[14] 1105 2-8-9 TQuinn 4 —
(MJWallace) *early spd: sn bhd* **16/1**

66.26 secs (3.76) **Going Correction** +0.55s/f (Yiel) **10** Ran SP% **112.8**
Speed ratings: **91,90,88,86,81 80,77,67,53,49**CSF £56.57 TOTE £2.90: £1.40, £4.90, £2.40; EX 72.40.General Nuisance was claimed by Mr J. S. Moore for £10,000. The winner was claimed by David John Brown (Friendly) £12,000
**Owner** The Old Downton Partnership **Bred** David John Brown **Trained** East Everleigh, Wilts

**FOCUS**
Those who had already run had shown just moderate form and the newcomer Treat Me Wild proved good enough. The leaders appeared to go off too fast and the third is the guide to the level of the form.

**NOTEBOOK**
**Treat Me Wild(IRE)**, a 2,000gns half-sister the quirky five-furlong juvenile selling winner Rehia, struggled to go the early pace, but the leaders appeared to go off a little too fast and she picked up well to make a successful debut. This would appear to be her grade, an opinion backed up by her connections.
**Im Spartacus**, well held in the first two-year-old race of the season at Lingfield, showed the benefit of that experience and ran well. He was another who proved unable to go the early gallop but finished to good effect, will be suited by a stiffer track and should stay farther in time.
**Nutty Times**, beaten in a seller on her debut, was racing on turf for the first time. She hung to her right throughout and did not handle the bend at all well, but still fared best of those to race up with the gallop and emerges with credit. She is only moderate but should find a small contest, possibly on a straight track or back on the All-Weather.
**Goldhill Prince**, stablemate of the third, showed more than when second last in a Doncaster seller on his debut, reversing form with a couple of these in the process. However, he was ultimately comfortably held.
**Zimbali**, a 1,000gns yearling, out of a half-sister to a five-furlong two-year-old winner, is bred for speed and showed plenty of it.
**General Nuisance(IRE)** failed to build on the promise he showed on his debut in selling company on this first start for Pat Murphy and was claimed afterwards by his original trainer, Stan Moore.
**Little Wizzy** is another who has not progressed, and being carried wide on the turn cannot be used as an excuse.
**Docklands Dude(IRE)** did not improve on what he showed on his first start on this debut for new connections.

## 1308 TOTETRIFECTA H'CAP — 1m 2f 46y
**2:50** (2:51) (E) (0-75,75) 3-Y-O+ **£4,192** (£1,290; £645; £322) **Stalls** Low

Form RPR

-201 **1** **War Owl (USA)**[43] 882 7-8-10 **60** LisaJones(3) 12 78
(IanWilliams) *s.i.s: hld up in rr: stdy hdwy on outside over 2f out: led over 1f out: clr ins last: easily* **4/1**[1]

620- **2** 7 **Castaway Queen (IRE)**[191] 5291 5-9-0 **61** LDettori 11 66
(WRMuir) *hld up in rr: haedway on outside over 2f out: styd on to chse wnr jst ins fnl f but no ch* **10/1**

300- **3** ¾ **Bluegrass Boy**[101] 6255 4-9-2 **63** SCarson 18 67
(GBBalding) *bhd: hdwy on outside fr 3f out: styd on wl fr over 1f out: nt qckn ins last* **25/1**

0343 **4** 3 **Eastborough (IRE)**[9] 1187 5-9-1 **62** SWhitworth 14 61
(BGPowell) *bhd: hdwy over 3f out: kpt on fr over 1f out but nt pce to trble ldrs* **8/1**[3]

0421 **5** nk **Say What You See (IRE)**[16] 1085 4-9-12 **73** RHills 8 71
(JWHills) *sn led: hdd 1m out: styd chsng ldr tl drvn to ld ins fnl 3f: hdd over 1f out: sn btn* **5/1**[2]

4-00 **6** 1¾ **Traveller's Tale**[8] 1213 5-9-10 **71** SDrowne 10 66
(PGMurphy) *bhd: t.k.h: hdwy 4f out: rdn and styd on same pce fnl 2f* **14/1**

5/06 **7** 2½ **Salford Flyer**[15] 1101 8-8-13 **60** (b) SSanders 2 50
(JaneSouthcombe) *led after 2f: hdd ins fnl 3f: wknd 2f out* **50/1**

043- **8** 7 **Kernel Dowery (IRE)**[160] 5848 4-8-13 **60** (p) TQuinn 9 38
(PWHarris) *chsd ldsrs: rdn over 3f out: wknd over 2f out* **10/1**

000- **9** 1¾ **Dexileos (IRE)**[251] 3753 5-9-4 **65** DSweeney 4 40
(ADWPinder) *t.k.h: in tch: rdn 3f out: wknd over 2f out* **50/1**

200- **10** 3 **Sninfia (IRE)**[179] 5500 4-9-4 **65** GDuffield 17 34
(GAHam) *t.k.h: hld up mid-div: hdwy 4f out: rdn ins fnl 3f: sn btn* **33/1**

01-2 **11** nk **Dash For Cover (IRE)**[9] 1187 4-9-8 **69** RHughes 6 38
(RHannon) *chsd ldrs: rdn over 3f out: sn wknd* **10/1**

-000 **12** 1¼ **Tally (IRE)**[56] 748 4-8-8 **58** LFletcher(3) 16 24
(MJPolglase) *chsd ldrs over 6f* **66/1**

-045 **13** 2½ **Springalong (USA)**[35] 964 4-9-6 **67** RHavlin 13 29
(PDEvans) *chsd ldrs over 6f* **16/1**

/55- **14** ½ **In Tune**[20] 313 4-8-8 **55** ANicholls 5 16
(SCBurrough) *sn bhd* **50/1**

-001 **15** 5 **Karaoke (IRE)**[35] 964 4-9-13 **74** DaneO'Neill 3 26
(SKirk) *chsd ldrs 6f* **16/1**

030- **16** 2½ **Desert Island Disc**[158] 5890 7-10-0 **75** JTate 15 23
(JJBridger) *chsd ldrs 6f* **18/1**

100- **17** 5 **Jack Durrance (IRE)**[20] 5276 4-9-13 **74** JQuinn 1 13
(GAHam) *s.i.s: a bhd* **40/1**

60/ **18** dist **Among Equals**[13] 5008 7-10-0 **75** VSlattery 7 —
(MMeade) *virtually ref to r: t.o* **12/1**

2m 13.62s (2.62) **Going Correction** +0.45s/f (Yiel) **18** Ran SP% **123.0**
Speed ratings: **107,101,100,98,98 96,94,89,87,85 85,84,82,81,77 75,71,**—CSF £41.22 CT £910.65 TOTE £5.30: £1.60, £2.40, £5.50, £2.30; EX 71.60 Trifecta £785.80 Pool of £1,106.80 - 0.30 winning tickets..
**Owner** Mrs Glennie Braune **Bred** Wertheimer Et Frere **Trained** Portway, Warwicks
■ Stewards Enquiry : R Havlin caution: allowed gelding to coast home with no assistance from saddle

**FOCUS**
A fair handicap in which the leaders went off very fast and the first four home all came from well off the pace. A smart time for the grade of contest.

**NOTEBOOK**
**War Owl(USA)**, a winner in France, he gained his first win in this country when scoring over ten furlongs on the Polytrack on his previous outing. Switched to turf, he got a strong pace that helped him settle and ran out a most decisive winner. He would be hard to beat if turned out under a penalty.
**Castaway Queen(IRE)**, racing for the first time in 191 days, had every chance and made a pleasing reappearance. However, she was simply no match for the winner and remains a maiden after 29 starts.
**Bluegrass Boy**, also still a maiden, travelled well enough and came there with every chance, but he was readily outpaced by the eventual winner and this first run in 101 days is sure to sharpen him up.
**Eastborough(IRE)** ♦, successful in a claimer at Wolverhampton during the winter, is 4lb lower than when last successful on turf and was unlucky not to have finished closer. He had to be snatched up about four and a half furlongs out before having to wait for a gap in the straight and, when finally in the clear, the principals were already in full stride.
**Say What You See(IRE)** is at his best when able to dominate and, unable to do so, he had to go faster than he would have liked to race prominently. To his credit, he did best of those to race up with the pace early.

## 1309 BATHWICK TYRES FILLIES' H'CAP — 1m 5y
**3:20** (3:21) (E) (0-75,73) 3-Y-O **£3,623** (£1,115; £418; £418) **Stalls** Low

Form RPR

0-24 **1** **Time To Relax (IRE)**[21] 1044 3-8-12 **64** TQuinn 7 69
(JJQuinn) *trckd ldrs: rdn and swtchd rt appr fnl f: r.o strly ins last to ld last strides* **7/1**[3]

150- **2** hd **Rabitatit (IRE)**[173] 5632 3-8-7 **62** RMiles(3) 9 67
(JGMO'Shea) *chsd ldr after 3f: rdn to chal fr over 2f out tl led wl ins last: ct last strides* **16/1**

062- **3** nk **Keshya**[160] 5845 3-8-11 **63** WSupple 2 67
(DJCoakley) *in tch: chsd ldrs 3f out: rdn and outpcd ins fnl 2f: rallied and r.o wl fnl f: fin wl: nt quite get up* **9/1**

230- **3** dht **Mystical Girl (USA)**[167] 5722 3-9-7 **73** SChin 15 77
(MJohnston) *chsd ldrs: rdn and str chal ins fnl f: nt qckn last strides* **11/2**[1]

030- **5** 1¼ **Carte Noire**[157] 5906 3-8-10 **62** EAhern 1 63
(JGPortman) *sn led: rdn to keep narrow advantage tl hdd wl ins fnl f: wknd cl home* **25/1**

03-0 **6** ¾ **Gabana (IRE)**[12] 1129 3-9-3 **69** SSanders 13 68
(CFWall) *bhd: hdwy fr 4f out: styd on u.p to chse ldrs over 1f out: outpcd ins last* **6/1**[2]

-005 **7** 2½ **Even Easier**[47] 845 3-8-8 **60** (p) RLMoore 5 54
(GLMoore) *s.i.s: bhd: hdwy over 2f out: kpt on fr over 1f out but nt rch ldrs* **14/1**

0060 **8** 1 **Trompe L'Oeil (IRE)**[16] 1086 3-7-9 **52** (p) JFMcDonald(5) 8 43
(AndrewReid) *s.i.s: bhd: hdwy on rails and n.m.r over 2f out: swtchd rt over 1f out: kpt on but nvr trbld ldrs* **12/1**

260- **9** ¾ **Desert Daisy (IRE)**[163] 5824 3-8-13 **65** SWKelly 10 54
(IAWood) *chsd ldrs: rdn 3f out: wknd ins fnl 2f* **33/1**

06-0 **10** 2 **Kilcullen Lass (IRE)**[42] 890 3-7-12 **50** oh3 JoannaBadger 3 35
(PDEvans) *s.i.s: bhd: sme hdwy on outside over 2f out: nvr nr ldrs* **66/1**

-223 **11** ¾ **Archerfield (IRE)**[42] 890 3-9-3 **69** DaneO'Neill 12 52
(JWHills) *chsd ldrs: rdn and effrt over 2f out: sn wknd* **7/1**[3]

440- **12** 3 **Barabella (IRE)**[196] 5167 3-9-0 **66** JPMurtagh 11 42
(RJHodges) *in tch: rdn 3f out: wknd over 2f out* **8/1**

024- **13** 1¼ **Miskina**[160] 5844 3-8-0 **59** BSwarbrick(7) 4 32
(WMBrisbourne) *mid-div: wknd ins fnl 3f* **10/1**

30-0 **14** hd **Hana Dee**[20] 1052 3-9-4 **70** TEDurcan 14 43
(MRChannon) *s.i.s: a bhd* **20/1**

22-0 **15** nk **Russalka**[89] 492 3-8-11 **63** NCallan 6 35
(JulianPoulton) *in tch: rdn 1/2-way: sn wknd* **20/1**

1m 45.55s (4.55) **Going Correction** +0.45s/f (Yiel) **15** Ran SP% **122.9**
Speed ratings: **95,94,94,94,93 92,90,89,88,86 85,82,81,81,80**CSF £107.94 TOTE £9.40: £2.90, £3.70; EX 144.40 Place 3: Mystical Girl 1.40, Kehsya 1.90; Tricast: Time to Relax/Rabitatit/Mystical Girl 343.15, Time to Relax/Rabitat/Keshya 526.92.
**Owner** Grahame Liles **Bred** Shay Ryan **Trained** Settrington, N Yorks

**FOCUS**
An ordinary but competitive fillies' handicap. The early pace was not that good and, given that the first four home finished in a bit of a heap, the form is not strong and wants treating with a little caution.

**NOTEBOOK**
**Time To Relax(IRE)** suggested this sort of trip would suit when showing promise in a couple of starts over six furlongs on Fibresand last month, and confirmed that with a narrow success. She had to be switched out for a run in the straight and picked up well to get there literally on the line. There should be more to come and she may well improve in a more strongly-run race.
**Rabitatit(IRE)**, a particularly tough sort in her juvenile campaign, including when scoring over course and distance off a 3lb lower mark, made a pleasing return to action, showing she has trained on in the process.
**Mystical Girl(USA)**, who showed promise in maiden company last term, again offered encouragement despite having no easy task off top weight on this first run since last October.
**Keshya**, runner-up in a Brighton nursery on her final start at two, ran well on this first start in 160 days. She took a while to pick up, but was flying at the finish and is another who should benefit from a stronger pace.
**Carte Noire** did nothing wrong from the front and should improve for the outing.
**Gabana(IRE)** kept on well enough for pressure, but was grabbing at the ground a little and could never quite get on terms. A more galloping track may suit her better.
**Archerfield(IRE)** looked to have every chance but was disappointing.

## 1310 LETHEBY & CHRISTOPHER MAIDEN STKS (DIV I) — 1m 5y
**3:50** (3:54) (D) 3-Y-O+ **£3,555** (£1,094; £547; £273) **Stalls** Low

Form RPR

0-36 **1** **Rahjel Sultan**[17] 1080 6-9-11 40 (t) GGibbons 7 57
(BAMcmahon) *chsd ldrs tl rdn: outpcd and lost position over 2f out: rallied and str run fr over 1f out to ld wl ins fnl f* **100/1**

0- **2** 1 **Captain Marryat**[153] 5940 3-8-10 EAhern 3 55
(PWHarris) *bhd:pushed along after 2f:hdwy on outside fr 3f out:slt ld appr fnl f: kpt on u.p: hdd cl home* **33/1**

**3** hd **Credit (IRE)** 3-8-10 DaneO'Neill 8 54
(RHannon) *s.i.s: bhd: rdn and hdwy 3f out: drvn to chal ins fnl f: no ex cl home* **8/1**

04- **4** 2 **Alyousufeya (IRE)**[159] 5868 3-8-5 RHills 11 45
(JLDunlop) *sn prom: led over 2f out: sn rdn: hdd appr fnl f wknd ins last* **7/2**[2]

00- **5** shd **Zonic Boom (FR)**[259] 3534 4-9-11 JPMurtagh 1 49
(JRFanshawe) *hld up in rr: nt clr run 2f out and over 1f out: swtchd rt and r.o wl fnl f: gng on cl home* **9/2**[3]

-233 **6** 3½ **Pacific Ocean (ARG)**[52] 797 5-9-11 60 (t) SDrowne 5 41
(MrsStefLiddiard) *in tch: chsd ldrs over 3f out: one pce fnl 2f* **10/1**

0-5 **7** ¾ **Panshir (FR)**[14] 1104 3-8-10 GBaker 9 40
(CFWall) *plld hrd: chsd ldrs: rdn over 2f out: wknd over 1f out* **10/3**[1]

**8** ¾ **Miss Librate**[46] 6-9-6 RLMoore 10 33
(JMBradley) *chsd ldr to 1/2-way: styd prom tl wknd ins fnl 2f* **100/1**

050 **9** nk **Bennanabaa**[44] 869 5-9-11 57 (t) ANicholls 2 37
(SCBurrough) *in tch tl wknd over 2f out* **100/1**

0- **10** *6* **Mix It Up**[176] [5578] 3-8-5 ........ GDuffield 6 18
(RMBeckett) *led tl hdd over 2f out: sn wknd* **66/1**

1m 46.01s (5.01) **Going Correction** +0.45s/f (Yiel)
**WFA** 3 from 4yo+ 15lb **10** Ran SP% **91.1**
Speed ratings: **92,91,90,88,88 85,84,83,83,77**CSF £1231.88 TOTE £50.40: £8.20, £3.80, £2.40; EX 44.30.
**Owner** Mrs J McMahon **Bred** B A McMahon **Trained** Hopwas, Staffs

**FOCUS**
A difficult race to work out, the time was very slow for the grade of contest and the form wants treating with caution. At first glance this would not look like a race to pay much attention to in terms of future contests with the 40-rated Rahjel Sultan getting off the mark at the 17th attempt. However, a couple of those in behind could be capable of better than they showed on this occasion.

**NOTEBOOK**
**Rahjel Sultan**, beaten over eight lengths in a banded stakes at Wolverhampton on his previous run, clearly improved for the removal of cheekpieces and return to turf. Sure to take a significant rise in the weights for this, he would be interesting if turned out under a penalty in a handicap or regional race, but is far from guaranteed to confirm this improvement in future.
**Captain Marryat**, well beaten on his debut last November, still looked quite inexperienced when put under pressure and should improve.
**Credit(IRE)**, a 100,000gns yearling, and half-brother to a fairly useful seven-furlong two-year-old winner out of a middle-distance scorer, was very easy to back. He was given every chance, but showed his inexperience when hitting the front and is going to come on a lot for the outing.
**Alyousufeya(IRE)** failed to build on the promise she showed at two and did not impress at the start when playing up and throwing Richard Hills off.
**Zonic Boom(FR)**, comfortably held in a couple of maidens last year, did not shape too badly on this reappearance. He did not get the clearest of runs but finished well enough and, now qualified for a mark, looks the type to do better in handicaps.
**Panshir(FR)** was far too keen and proved unable to build on the promise he showed at Doncaster on his previous start. *Official explanation: jockey said gelding ran too free early on*

## 1311 LETHEBY & CHRISTOPHER MAIDEN STKS (DIV II) 1m 5y
**4:20** (4:23) (D) 3-Y-0+ **£3,555** (£1,094; £547; £273) **Stalls** Low

Form RPR
02-4 **1** **Just Tim (IRE)**[19] [1064] 3-8-10 78 ........ DaneO'Neill 11 70
(RHannon) *sn led: narrowly hdd over 3f out: styd pressing ldr tl led again over 1f out: rdn and hld on wl fnl f* **11/2**[3]
6- **2** *nk* **Sailmaker (IRE)**[154] [5934] 3-8-10 ........ SDrowne 10 70
(RCharlton) *w wnr tl slt ld over 3f out: rdn and hdd over 1f out: kpt on wl but no ex cl home* **16/1**
2- **3** *nk* **Brindisi**[213] [4777] 3-8-5 ........ RHills 6 64
(BWHills) *hld up in rr: hdwy 3f out: rdn to chse ldrs and edgd lft over 1f out: hung lft ins last: kpt on again cl home* **2/1**[2]
54-5 **4** *3* **Slavonic (USA)**[12] [1134] 3-8-10 79 ........ (b[1]) RHughes 2 62
(JHMGosden) *chsd ldrs: shkn up and one pce fnl 2f* **6/1**
43-4 **5** *½* **Rood Boy (IRE)**[36] [955] 3-8-10 57 ........ IMongan 3 61?
(JSKing) *chsd ldrs: rdn 3f out: styd on one pce fnl 2f* **33/1**
**6** *3* **Fire Finch** 3-8-5 ........ TEDurcan 5 49
(MRChannon) *bhd: hdwy fr 2f out but n.d* **25/1**
**7** *3½* **Logger Rhythm (USA)** 4-9-11 ........ GDuffield 1 46
(RDickin) *bhd: sme hdwy fnl 2f: nt a danger* **66/1**
5- **8** *nk* **Chambray (IRE)**[227] [4434] 3-8-5 ........ MartinDwyer 7 40
(AMBalding) *rdn over 3f out: a in rr* **20/1**
3- **9** *2* **Stakhanovite (IRE)**[365] [982] 4-9-11 ........ JPMurtagh 8 41
(DRLoder) *plld hrd: chsd ldrs tl wknd qckly fr 2f out* **7/4**[1]
00- **10** *10* **Bold Ridge (IRE)**[100] [6259] 4-9-11 ........ PDobbs 4 18
(SKirk) *a bhd* **66/1**
\- **11** *3* **Zambezi River**[208] 5-9-11 ........ RLMoore 9 11
(JMBradley) *a in rr* **100/1**

1m 45.47s (4.47) **Going Correction** +0.45s/f (Yiel)
**WFA** 3 from 4yo+ 15lb **11** Ran SP% **120.8**
Speed ratings: **95,94,94,91,90 87,84,84,82,72 69**CSF £80.91 TOTE £6.60: £2.20, £3.60, £1.50; EX 56.60.
**Owner** D J Walker **Bred** Mrs S Joint **Trained** East Everleigh, Wilts

**FOCUS**
A moderate winning time, but it was still 0.54 seconds faster than the first division and this was the better race. The fifth looks the best guide to the level of the form.

**NOTEBOOK**
**Just Tim(IRE)** had shown enough in similar company to entitle him to pick up a race of this standard and, back on turf and dropped back two furlongs in trip, he ran out a narrow winner. He will find things tougher in handicap company but this will have boosted his confidence.
**Sailmaker(IRE)** confirmed the promise he showed on his sole start at two and should be up to winning a similar contest.
**Brindisi**, entered in the Oaks, failed to build on the promise she had shown when runner-up to subsequent Listed winner Spotlight. She came there with every chance, but did not look the toughest of individuals and was hanging to her left under pressure.
**Slavonic(USA)**, fitted with blinkers for the first time, looked very one paced.
**Rood Boy(IRE)** has done most of his racing on the All-Weather, but there is no reason to think he did not run to form on this switch to turf.
**Stakhanovite(IRE)**, a full-brother to Mark Of Esteem, had shown reasonable form on his debut behind a couple of useful sorts despite returning with a cut to his off-hind. However, reappearing after a year off, he was far too keen and then lost his action. Things are not going his way. *Official explanation: jockey said colt lost its action*

## 1312 BBC RADIO BRISTOL H'CAP 5f 11y
**4:50** (4:50) (E) (0-70,65) 3-Y-0 **£3,516** (£1,082; £541; £270) **Stalls** Low

Form RPR
2013 **1** **Ivory Lace**[57] [744] 3-9-2 60 ........ DSweeney 1 68
(SWoodman) *in tch: rdn and hdwy over 1f out: qcknd chal wl ins fnl f: led cl home* **20/1**
0-45 **2** *nk* **Laconia (IRE)**[8] [1196] 3-9-7 65 ........ MartinDwyer 3 72
(JSMoore) *trckd ldr: rdn to ld over 1f out: hrd drvn ins last: ct cl home* **14/1**
413 **3** *2* **Kryssa**[16] [1086] 3-9-2 60 ........ RLMoore 9 60+
(GLMoore) *carried rt s: outpcd and bhd: rdn 1/2-way: hdwy over 1f out: kpt on fnl f but nt pce to rch ldrs* **5/4**[1]
1003 **4** *nk* **Princess Kai (IRE)**[64] [678] 3-8-12 56 ........ (b) TQuinn 4 55
(RIngram) *led: rdn 1/2-way: hdd over 1f out: outpcd ins last* **20/1**
6-44 **5** *1* **Black Oval**[8] [1196] 3-9-0 61 ........ SHitchcott(3) 5 56
(MRChannon) *bhd: pushed along 1/2-way: hdwy over 1f out: kpt on ins last but nt trble ldrs* **7/2**[2]
30-3 **6** *nk* **Comeraincomeshine (IRE)**[43] [881] 3-9-4 62 ........ LDettori 8 56
(TGMills) *carried rt s: sn rcvrd and in tch: chsd ldrs 1/2-way: wknd ins fnl f* **4/1**[3]
00-0 **7** *¾* **Danifah (IRE)**[16] [1086] 3-8-11 55 ........ SWKelly 2 46
(PDEvans) *chsd ldrs: rdn 1/2-way: wknd fnl f* **16/1**
2046 **8** *3½* **Lizhar (IRE)**[8] [1206] 3-8-10 54 ........ GDuffield 6 33
(MJPolglase) *wnt rt s: sn rcvrd to chse ldrs: wknd appr fnl f* **20/1**
00-4 **9** *7* **United Union (IRE)**[7] [1220] 3-9-7 65 ........ (b[1]) PaulEddery 7 18
(DHaydnJones) *carried rt s: t.k.h and stmbld after 1f: a bhd* **22/1**

65.47 secs (2.97) **Going Correction** +0.55s/f (Yiel) **9** Ran SP% **117.8**
Speed ratings: **98,97,94,93,92 91,90,84,73**CSF £253.83 CT £616.53 TOTE £18.70: £3.40, £4.80, £1.10; EX 273.80.
**Owner** Christopher J Halpin **Bred** D R Tucker **Trained** East Lavant, W Sussex

**FOCUS**
A modest sprint run at a good pace but the form does not look strong. Lizhar carried the three horses drawn on her outside wide when the stalls opened.

**NOTEBOOK**
**Ivory Lace**, successful in a Polytrack seller two starts back for Dean Ivory, looked as good as ever on this switch back to turf on her first run in two months. She appeared to win a shade cosily and should continue to go well in similar events.
**Laconia(IRE)** confirmed she was unlucky in a similar event at Catterick on her previous start with a solid effort, reversing form with Black Oval in the process. Her yard is in good form.
**Kryssa** had shown herself to be versatile with regard to trip on the Polytrack recently, winning over five furlongs and placing over seven on her previous outing but, back down in distance, she was carried right at the start and could never get back on terms. A tough, lightly-raced sort, she always seems to give her running and one could follow worse fillies this season.
**Princess Kai(IRE)** looked to have every chance against the rail and ran her race.
**Black Oval** could never muster the pace to get on terms and may be worth another try over a little farther.
**Comeraincomeshine(IRE)**, making her handicap debut, was one of those carried right at the start but was disappointing in any case.
**Lizhar(IRE)** *Official explanation: jockey said filly hung left throughout*
**United Union(IRE)** *Official explanation: jockey said gelding stumbled shortly after the start*

## 1313 SCREENCHINA CLASSIFIED STKS 5f 161y
**5:20** (5:21) (E) 3-Y-0+ **£3,623** (£1,115; £557; £278) **Stalls** Low

Form RPR
600- **1** **Devise (IRE)**[251] [3751] 5-9-7 72 ........ TGMcLaughlin 13 81
(MSSaunders) *s.i.s: bhd: rapid hdwy on outside fr 2f out to ld appr fnl f: hung lft u.p ins last: drvn out* **25/1**
6300 **2** *1½* **The Fisio**[12] [1131] 4-9-5 70 ........ (v) MartinDwyer 7 74
(AMBalding) *sn led: hdd appr fnl f: one pce whn carried lft and swtchd rt ins last: hld on wl for 2nd* **9/1**
5434 **3** *¾* **Zarzu**[13] [1113] 5-9-4 74 ........ RThomas(5) 14 76
(CRDore) *bhd: hdwy 2f out: chsd ldrs over 1f out: one pce whn carried lft ins fnl f* **3/1**[1]
0004 **4** *1¼* **Port St Charles (IRE)**[10] [1177] 7-9-5 70 ........ RHughes 8 67
(PRChamings) *bhd: hdwy on rails fr 2f out: n.m.r whn styng on jst ins last: sn one pce* **16/1**
1045 **5** *shd* **Hard To Catch (IRE)**[8] [1204] 6-8-12 70 ........ MHoward(7) 3 67
(DKIvory) *chsd ldrs: rdn 2f out: one pce fnl f* **10/1**
061- **6** *nk* **Full Spate**[178] [5553] 9-9-2 69 ........ SHitchcott(3) 9 66
(JMBradley) *bhd: hdwy over 1f out: kpt on ins last but nt trble ldrs* **14/1**
6-00 **7** *nk* **Arabian Knight (IRE)**[10] [1180] 4-9-5 57 ........ VSlattery 6 65
(RJHodges) *behund: haedway over 1f out: r.o ins last but nt a danger* **66/1**
40-0 **8** *2½* **Ridicule**[63] [681] 5-9-5 66 ........ (b) RHavlin 11 57
(JGPortman) *bhd: hdwy and nt clr run 2f out: styd on fnl f* **33/1**
4606 **9** *1½* **Sundried Tomato**[34] [968] 5-9-5 73 ........ LFletcher(3) 4 55
(PWHiatt) *chsd ldrs: outpcd 2f out: sn n.m.r: n.d after* **15/2**[3]
40-5 **10** *hd* **Zargus**[8] [1205] 5-9-5 69 ........ JQuinn 5 51
(WRMuir) *chsd ldrs tl wknd ins fnl 2f* **20/1**
-402 **11** *¾* **Imperium**[6] [1228] 3-8-9 72 ........ SDrowne 16 51
(MrsStefLiddiard) *bhd: effrt on outside 1/2-way: n.d* **16/1**
04-0 **12** *1* **Waterside (IRE)**[9] [1185] 5-9-6 71 ........ RHills 1 47
(JWHills) *s.i.s: sn rcvrd on rails to chse ldrs: wknd fr 2f out* **12/1**
5306 **13** *2½* **Beau Jazz**[7] [1223] 3-8-7 62 ........ SRighton 15 37
(WDeBest-Turner) *chsd ldrs to 1/2-way* **100/1**
000- **14** *2½* **Brantwood (IRE)**[173] [5634] 4-9-5 70 ........ (t) WSupple 10 29
(BAMcmahon) *chsd ldrs 3f* **8/1**
00-0 **15** *6* **Tappit (IRE)**[9] [1185] 5-9-5 69 ........ RLMoore 12 9
(JMBradley) *s.i.s: a bhd* **25/1**
4225 **16** *1¾* **Polish Emperor (USA)**[12] [1131] 4-9-7 72 ........ (b) TQuinn 2 5
(PWHarris) *pressed ldrs 3f* **9/2**[2]

1m 13.88s (2.74) **Going Correction** +0.55s/f (Yiel)
**WFA** 3 from 4yo+ 12lb **16** Ran SP% **129.2**
Speed ratings: **103,101,100,98,98 97,97,94,92,91 90,89,86,82,74 72**CSF £238.01 TOTE £33.40: £9.00, £2.50, £2.30; EX 449.70 Place 6 £368.43, Place 5 £160.84.
**Owner** D Naylor **Bred** Clody Norton And Mrs Con Collins **Trained** Haydon, Somerset
■ Stewards Enquiry : T G McLaughlin three-day ban: careless riding (Apr 19,21)

**FOCUS**
This had the look of a competitive sprint, but few got into it and Devise caused a little bit of trouble when hanging left inside the final furlong. The form looks just fair.

**NOTEBOOK**
**Devise(IRE)**, 4lb higher than when winning at Windsor last June, quickened up well on the outside of the field on this first run in 251 days to get back to winning form. He had to be switched out wide for a run and then hung left-handed close home, causing a bit of trouble in behind. He is not very consistent and cannot be guaranteed to repeat this next time.
**The Fisio**, who has not won on turf since June 2002, had a visor back on. He was done no favours when carried left by the winner close home, but it did not affect the result.
**Zarzu** appeared to get the strong pace he needs and ran respectably off a mark 12lb lower than his All-Weather rating. He may have been intimidated by the winner drifting to his left, but it made no difference.
**Port St Charles(IRE)**, another on quite a long losing run on turf, looked to travel well under a typically confident ride from Hughes, but was held when squeezed up against the rail close home.
**Hard To Catch(IRE)** wins in his turn and, although not beaten that far, never really looked like taking this.
**Full Spate** finished well but never really threatened. He often needs a run or two to put him spot on and did well in the circumstances.
**Zargus** *Official explanation: jockey said gelding was hampered at halfway*
**Polish Emperor(USA)** showed speed before dropping out. This was disappointing. *Official explanation: jockey said gelding stopped quickly*

T/Jkpt: Not won. T/Plt: £440.30 to a £1 stake. Pool: £47,982.10. 79.55 winning tickets. T/Qpdt: £73.10 to a £1 stake. Pool: £2,443.00. 24.70 winning tickets. ST

# MUSSELBURGH (R-H)

Thursday, April 8

**OFFICIAL GOING: Good to firm (good in places on straight course; firm in places on round course)**

## 1314 KATHLEEN AND KEVIN DEVINE PRE-BIRTHDAY MAIDEN AUCTION STKS 5f

2:40 (2:40) (F) 2-Y-O £3,347 (£1,030; £515; £257) Stalls Low

Form RPR

4 **1** **Bold Marc (IRE)**[10] [1170] 2-8-11 ............ DarrenWilliams 8 79
*(KRBurke) cl up: led on bit 1/2-way: clr ent last* **11/4**[2]

**2** *2* **Forfeiter (USA)** 2-8-11 ............ KDarley 3 72
*(TDBarron) wnt rt s: sn pushed along and outpcd: hdwy 2f out out: swtchd rt over 1f out and styd on wl fnl f* **11/2**[3]

**3** *5* **Rightprice Premier (IRE)** 2-8-4 ............ PFessey 6 47
*(KARyan) led: rdn along and hdd 1/2-way: sn one pce* **11/2**[3]

**4** *3 1/2* **Favouring (IRE)** 2-8-9 ............ PHanagan 2 39
*(RAFahey) dwlt: rn green and sn outpcd: bhd and pushed along 1/2-way: gd hdwy over 1f out: fin strly* **5/2**[1]

**5** *3/4* **Beverley Beau** 2-8-7 ............ RWinston 1 35
*(MrsLStubbs) cl up: rdn along over 2f out: sn wknd* **16/1**

0 **6** *1 1/4* **Brut**[12] [1128] 2-8-6 ............ LEnstone(3) 7 32
*(DWBarker) dwlt: sn chsng ldrs: rdn along over 2f out and sn wknd* **33/1**

**7** *11* **Eternally** 2-8-8 ow1 ............ DHolland 4 —
*(RMHCowell) wnt rt s: a outpcd and bhd* **16/1**

**8** *6* **Steal The Thunder** 2-8-10 ow3 ............ FLynch 5 —
*(ABerry) s.i.s: a bhd* **14/1**

62.29 secs (1.89) **Going Correction** +0.25s/f (Good) **8** Ran SP% **107.4**

Speed ratings: **94,90,82,77,76 74,56,46**CSF £15.90 TOTE £3.00: £1.20, £1.40, £2.10; EX 10.00.

**Owner** Market Avenue Racing Club 1 **Bred** Eamon D Delany **Trained** Middleham Moor, N Yorks

**FOCUS**

A fair time for the grade, and an impressive display from the winner.

**NOTEBOOK**

**Bold Marc(IRE)** ◆, one of two with previous experience in the field, raced up with the pace travelling strongly for the first half of the race before cruising clear on the bridle and quickening away in great style. This was a very good performance and he looks worth his place in a better grade of race.

**Forfeiter(USA)**, one of the more interesting newcomers, showed signs of inexperience early and was a bit tapped for toe. Once it fell into place though, he picked up well and was finishing in good style, suggesting he should find a similar race.

**Rightprice Premier(IRE)**, the only filly in the line-up, showed good early speed but was no match for the winner. She was passed for second in final half a furlong.

**Favouring(IRE)** ◆, whose sire gets plenty of speedy juveniles, looked short on experience and was running green for the early part of the race. He, like the runner up, came home strongly and looks another future winner waiting to happen.

**Beverley Beau**, officially still three weeks short of his second birthday, can only improve for the experience and is sure to do better in time.

**Brut** showed up well for a long way before weakening and improved on his debut effort.

## 1315 DM HALL H'CAP 1m

3:10 (3:10) (D) (0-80,72) 3-Y-O+ £5,395 (£1,660; £830; £415) Stalls Low

Form RPR

663- **1** **Brief Goodbye**[199] [5117] 4-9-10 **72** ............ MFenton 6 81
*(JohnBerry) trckd ldrs: hdwy 2f out: rdn to ld ent last: kpt on* **11/1**

/10- **2** *1 3/4* **Queen Charlotte (IRE)**[195] [5194] 5-9-6 **68** ............ JFanning 2 73
*(MrsKWalton) led: rdn along 2f out: hdd ent last: sn drvn and nt qckn* **7/2**[3]

2-42 **3** *1 3/4* **Sarraaf (IRE)**[8] [1199] 8-9-6 **68** ............ RWinston 5 69
*(ISemple) hld up: hdwy 3f out: effrt and n.m.r wl over 1f out: sn rdn and one pce* **5/2**[2]

040- **4** *hd* **Regent's Secret (USA)**[178] [5537] 4-9-5 **67** ............ RFfrench 4 68
*(JSGoldie) trckd ldrs: hdwy 3f out: swtchd lft and rdn wl over 1f out: kpt on same pce* **14/1**

336- **5** *shd* **Cool Temper**[99] [6268] 8-9-8 **70** ............ (t) KDarley 3 70
*(PFICole) trckd ldr: hdwy to chal and ever ch tl rdn wl over 1f out and sn wknd* **15/8**[1]

500- **6** *12* **Repulse Bay (IRE)**[187] [5373] 6-8-9 **57** ............ CCatlin 1 30
*(JSGoldie) a rr* **25/1**

1m 43.55s (0.85) **Going Correction** +0.35s/f (Good) **6** Ran SP% **104.4**

Speed ratings: **109,107,105,105,105 93**CSF £42.11 TOTE £11.90: £2.70, £2.90; EX 54.00.

**Owner** J McCarthy **Bred** Chippenham Lodge Stud Ltd **Trained** Newmarket, Suffolk

**FOCUS**

A decent winning time for the class, despite the modest early gallop, but the form may not be all that reliable.

**NOTEBOOK**

**Brief Goodbye** defied top weight in good fashion on this seasonal return, taking it up around a furlong out and staying on well. He should be capable of holding his own at a higher level.

**Queen Charlotte(IRE)**, a winner on her seasonal debut last year, had the run of the race from the front but was unable to capitalise on it.

**Sarraaf(IRE)** would have prefered a stronger gallop.

**Regent's Secret(USA)** remains a maiden after 18 starts and could only keep on.

**Cool Temper** shaped as though possibly in need of this seasonal return, fading having come there with every chance.

## 1316 MUSSELBURGH TOWN H'CAP 2m

3:40 (3:40) (D) (0-85,85) 4-Y-O+ £6,708 (£2,064; £1,032; £516) Stalls Low

Form RPR

3 **1** **Zoltano (GER)**[10] [1173] 6-8-8 **65** ............ RWinston 10 76
*(MTodhunter) mde all: qcknd clr over 3f out: rdn over 1f out: kpt on* **20/1**

110/ **2** *2* **Plutocrat**[83] [1266] 8-8-13 **70** ............ KDalgleish 1 79
*(LLungo) hld up in tch: hdwy over 4f out: chsd wnr 2f out: sn rdn and kpt on ins last: nt rch wnr* **8/1**

404/ **3** *shd* **Mirjan (IRE)**[12] [5031] 8-10-0 **85** ............ KRenwick 7 93
*(LLungo) hld up and bhd: hdwy on outer 3f out: rdn along wl over 1f out: styd on strly ins last: nrst fin* **66/1**

0-33 **4** *1* **Ocean Tide**[13] [1112] 7-9-1 **75** ............ (v) LEnstone(3) 4 82
*(RFord) trckd wnr: effrt 3f out: sn rdn along and one pce fnl 2f* **3/1**[2]

/02- **5** *5* **Overstrand (IRE)**[26] [5926] 5-9-7 **78** ............ KDarley 3 79
*(MrsMReveley) in tch: effrt 3f out: sn rdn along and no impression* **11/4**[1]

40-1 **6** *hd* **Acceleration (IRE)**[10] [1173] 4-8-5 **66** 6ex ............ (v) PHanagan 9 67
*(RAllan) in tch on inner: effrt over 3f out: sn rdn and no imp* **6/1**[3]

0445 **7** *2* **Macaroni Gold (IRE)**[26] [1010] 4-8-3 **64** ............ CCatlin 6 63
*(WJarvis) hld up and b ehind tl sme late hdwy* **12/1**

60-0 **8** *6* **Riyadh**[13] [1112] 6-9-12 **83** ............ (v) JFanning 5 74
*(MJohnston) trckd ldrs: effrt over 3f out: sn riddcen along and wknd 2f out* **6/1**[3]

000- **9** *11* **Sono**[17] [5558] 7-9-4 **75** ............ ACulhane 11 53
*(PDNiven) chsd ldrs on inner: n.m.r and rdn along bnd ov er 4f out: sn outpcd and bhd* **33/1**

00/0 **10** *9* **Pharaoh Hatshepsut (IRE)**[10] [1176] 6-7-5 **55** oh15 ............ DFentiman(7) 8 22
*(JamesMoffatt) a rr* **100/1**

3m 37.95s (4.25) **Going Correction** +0.35s/f (Good)

**WFA** 4 from 5yo+ 4lb **10** Ran SP% **109.2**

Speed ratings: **103,102,101,101,98 98,97,94,89,84**CSF £156.74 CT £9195.56 TOTE £16.30: £3.80, £3.40, £6.70; EX 143.50.

**Owner** Leeds Plywood And Doors Ltd **Bred** Gestut Hof Ittlingen **Trained** Orton, Cumbria

■ Stewards Enquiry : K Dalgleish two-day ban: careless riding (Apr 19,20)

**FOCUS**

Zoltano and Robert Winston took full advantage of the modest gallop and went on a long way from home. In view of that the form may not work out.

**NOTEBOOK**

**Zoltano(GER)** was given an canny ride by Winston, taking a clear lead some way from home off the medium gallop and sealing it when quickening under half a mile out. He held on well, giving his all, and proved his effectiveness on this fast surface for the first time.

**Plutocrat**, having his first start on the Flat since May 2000, has been running reasonably well over hurdles and stayed on for second without ever really threatening to get to the winner. He was caught out when the winner quickened.

**Mirjan(IRE)**, a stablemate of the second, ran well at a huge price and, looking at the way he finished, may well have won had there been a stronger gallop.

**Ocean Tide** could not muster the speed when he needed to.

**Overstrand(IRE)** was disappointing, but another who would have been unsuited by the gallop.

**Riyadh** seems to have had enough of racing.

## 1317 ROBIN COOK AND UIA CLASSIFIED STKS 7f 30y

4:10 (4:11) (D) 3-Y-O+ £5,343 (£1,644; £822; £411) Stalls Low

Form RPR

2213 **1** **Hatch**[7] [1223] 3-8-8 79 ............ DHolland 1 93
*(RMHCowell) mde all: rdn wl over 1f out: clr ins last: styd on wl* **3/1**[2]

0001 **2** *5* **Flint River**[12] [1139] 6-9-4 74 ............ ACulhane 7 76
*(HMorrison) trckd ldrs: hdwy to chse wnr over 1f out: sn rdn and kpt on same pce* **11/4**[1]

0500 **3** *nk* **No Grouse**[8] [1199] 4-9-1 75 ............ THamilton(3) 4 75
*(RAFahey) chsd ldrs: hdwy 3f out: rdn wl over 1f out and kpt on same pce* **7/1**

-431 **4** *5* **What-A-Dancer (IRE)**[19] [1065] 7-9-8 79 ............ RWinston 3 66
*(GASwinbank) hld up in tch: hdwy on outer 3f out: rdn wl over 1f out and sn btn* **3/1**[2]

455- **5** *4* **High Finance (IRE)**[204] [4993] 4-9-5 79 ............ KDarley 6 53
*(JWHills) hld up in rr: pushed along and hdwy 2f out: hmpd wl over 1f out and nt rcvr* **6/1**[3]

005- **6** *6* **Coustou (IRE)**[60] [4006] 4-9-4 75 ............ (p) PFessey 2 36
*(ARDicken) chsd wnr: rdn along 3f out: drvn and wkng whn hung rt wl over 1f out: sn b ehind* **66/1**

6-00 **7** *3* **Pagan Storm (USA)**[13] [1121] 4-8-11 70 ............ (b) KristinStubbs(7) 5 28
*(MrsLStubbs) keen: a rr* **66/1**

1m 30.72s (1.19) **Going Correction** +0.35s/f (Good)

**WFA** 3 from 4yo+ 14lb **7** Ran SP% **106.4**

Speed ratings: **107,101,100,95,90 83,80**CSF £9.97 TOTE £4.00: £2.00, £1.70; EX 11.40.

**Owner** Blue Metropolis **Bred** Meon Valley Stud **Trained** Six Mile Bottom, Cambs

■ Stewards Enquiry : P Fessey one-day ban: careless riding (Apr 19)

**FOCUS**

A tight little handicap run at a decent pace and a much-improved effort from the winner.

**NOTEBOOK**

**Hatch**, moved up to an official rating of 84 since being entered, would not have qualified for this off his new mark and was therefore very well in. Back over a more suitable trip on his favoured ground, he appears to have turned the corner mentally for his new stable and there were no signs of the quirks he has shown in the past. Making just about all, he fairly bolted up and these tactics seem to suit him perfectly.

**Flint River**, officially rated 9lb lower on turf than he is on sand, was a little awkward on the home bend but had every chance and just found the winner far too strong. He may be better going left-handed.

**No Grouse** ◆ had no chance with the winner, but with the fast ground in his favour still ran his best race for some time and it was around this time last year that he struck form.

**What-A-Dancer(IRE)** likes to come from off the pace in a strongly-run race where the leaders come back to him, but they were not doing that here.

**High Finance(IRE)** ◆, held up out the back, was staying on when getting into a spot of bother passing the two-furlong pole and was not persevered with after that. This was her first outing for seven months, meaning she did not have the fitness edge of those that finished in front of her, and should come on for this.

## 1318 JOHN RICHARD MEMORIAL MAIDEN STKS 1m 1f

4:40 (4:41) (D) 3-Y-O+ £4,735 (£1,457; £728; £364) Stalls Low

Form RPR

2 **1** **Master Marvel (IRE)**[14] [1104] 3-8-7 ............ RFfrench 6 79
*(MJohnston) cl up: led after 4f: pushed along and hdd 2f out: sn rdn and wandered: styd on to ld ent last: drvn and kpt on* **8/13**[1]

4/2- **2** *3* **Khanjar (USA)**[318] [1862] 4-9-10 82 ............ (v[1]) DHolland 9 73
*(DRLoder) led 4f: cl up tl led again 2f out: sn rdn: hdd ent last and one pce* **7/4**[2]

43- **3** *1 3/4* **Par Indiana (IRE)**[108] [6230] 3-8-2 ............ PHanagan 3 64
*(ISemple) in tch: rdn along over 2f out: styd on appr last: nrst fin* **25/1**

0/0- **4** *1* **King's Envoy (USA)**[129] [5012] 5-9-10 50 ............ DMcGaffin 1 67
*(MrsJCMcgregor) bhd: hdwy on inner 3f out: swtchd outside and styd on to chse ldrs ent last: nrst fin* **200/1**

-564 **5** *1* **Skibereen (IRE)**[8] [1213] 4-9-3 72 ............ PPMathers(7) 5 65
*(IWMcinnes) chsd ldrs: rdn along over 2f out: sn one pce* **18/1**[3]

**6** *12* **My Ace**[27] 6-9-5 ............ (bt) JFanning 11 36
*(JamesMoffatt) chsd ldrs: rdn along 3f out: sn wknd* **50/1**

000- **7** *nk* **Islands Farewell**[174] [5625] 4-9-10 ............ MFenton 2 40
*(MrsMReveley) a rr* **100/1**

00-0 **8** *6* **Sandy Bay (IRE)**[17] [1077] 5-9-7 40 ............ (p) LEnstone(3) 8 28
*(RAllan) a rr* **200/1**

00- **9** *1* **Lapdancing**[166] [5744] 3-8-2 ............ PFessey 7 21
*(MissLAPerratt) s.i.s: a rr* **100/1**

000- **10** *nk* **Optimum Night**[352] [1172] 5-9-10 ............ RWinston 4 26
*(PDNiven) in tch: rdn along 1/2-way: sn wknd* **150/1**



The Form Book, Raceform Ltd, Compton, RG20 6NL

P- **11** 1 1/2 **Queenslander (IRE)**[298] [2394] 3-8-2 ........ DMernagh 10 18
(GASwinbank) *chsd ldrs to 1/2-way: sn lost pl and bhd* **66/1**

1m 55.5s (2.30) **Going Correction** +0.35s/f (Good)
**WFA** 3 from 4yo+ 17lb **11** Ran SP% **114.5**
Speed ratings: **103,100,98,97,97 86,86,80,79,79 78**CSF £1.74 TOTE £2.00: £1.02, £1.10, £3.10; EX 2.60.
**Owner** Maktoum Al Maktoum **Bred** Gainsborough Stud Management Ltd **Trained** Middleham Moor, N Yorks

**FOCUS**
A race in which only the front pair could be given a chance according to the market and so it proved as they had the race to themselves from the start. Overall a modest maiden.

**NOTEBOOK**
**Master Marvel(IRE)** ◆ confirmed the promise of his Doncaster debut, but at various stages in the home straight it looked as though he was getting the worst of the argument with the runner-up and he was hanging all over the track, but his raw ability eventually got him home by a decent margin. There is every reason to believe there is still plenty more in the locker.
**Khanjar(USA)**, reappearing from a break of 11 months in the first-time visor, did his best under a positive ride but his progressive three-year-old rival proved far too good. He will be lucky to find many races less competitive than this and his stable's runners do not normally come to the track undercooked, so he is unlikely to come on much from this.
**Par Indiana(IRE)** stayed on nicely and will appreciate further. She now qualifies for handicaps, and connections will be hoping the Handicapper uses the official mark of the fourth rather than the runner-up as a guide.
**King's Envoy(USA)**, who has shown little on the Flat or over hurdles since a promising debut three years ago, was doing all his best work late and his rider seemed to accept his final position a little early. He seemed to run way above his official rating, but something often does in contests like this and a literal interpretation of the form could be dangerous. *Official explanation: jockey said he suffered from cramp in closing stages and so could not ride out to the line*
**Skibereen(IRE)** was entitled to finish third on the best of his form and it was disappointing that he could not even manage that. He looks one to well and truly swerve.
**Queenslander(IRE)** *Official explanation: jockey said filly had hung left throughout*

## 1319 HONEST TOUN FILLIES' H'CAP 5f
5:10 (5:10) (E) (0-75,67) 3-Y-O+ **£4,017** (£1,236; £618; £309) **Stalls** Low

Form RPR
0004 **1** **Frascati**[10] [1178] 4-9-10 **67** ........ FLynch 4 76
(ABerry) *cl up: led 2f out: rdn ins last and kpt on* **5/1**[3]
5600 **2** 1 1/4 **Lady Pekan**[10] [1178] 5-9-3 **60** ........ (p) DHolland 1 64
(PSMcentee) *led: rdn along 1/2-way: sn hdd: drvn and one pce fnl f* **3/1**[1]
060- **3** 3/4 **Tender (IRE)**[131] [6094] 4-9-1 **58** ........ CCatlin 6 59
(DJDaly) *in tch: hdwy 2f out: sn rdn and kpt on same pce* **7/2**[2]
006- **4** 3 1/2 **College Maid (IRE)**[155] [5924] 7-8-10 **53** ........ (b) RFfrench 3 40
(JSGoldie) *outpcd and pushed along 1/2-way: sme hdwy appr last: nvr a factor* **5/1**[3]
-000 **5** 10 **Tamarella (IRE)**[39] [930] 4-9-2 **59** ........ AMcCarthy 2 6
(GGMargarson) *cl up: rdn along over 2f out and sn wknd* **3/1**[1]

61.87 secs (1.47) **Going Correction** +0.25s/f (Good) **5** Ran SP% **105.6**
Speed ratings: **98,96,94,89,73**CSF £18.26 TOTE £3.80: £1.30, £1.90; EX 13.90 Place 6 £314.83, Place 5 £176.24.
**Owner** Lord Crawshaw **Bred** Exors Of The Late Lord Crawshaw **Trained** Cockerham, Lancs

**FOCUS**
A modest contest, the winner taking advantage of a lower turf mark, and the form is unlikely to add up to much.

**NOTEBOOK**
**Frascati**, whose four previous victories have all been on the Southwell Fibresand, was able to race off an 8lb lower mark on this return to grass and was not hard pressed to score her first victory on turf. This was a poor race though, and she will do very well to find another one like it.
**Lady Pekan**, with cheekpieces replacing the usual blinkers, showed speed against the stands' rail but was firmly put in her place by the winner. She has not been at her best on sand of late and this probably was not much of an improvement.
**Tender(IRE)**, off since November, stayed on to finish third but probably did not achieve much and remains out of form despite a plummeting handicap mark.
**College Maid(IRE)** is very well handicapped on her best form, but that is because she has been below her best for some time now and she did not show much on this occasion.
**Tamarella(IRE)**, off a mark 3lb lower than for her last win a year ago, has not been running that well on sand this winter and this was a poor effort on her return to turf. *Official explanation: trainer had no explanation for the filly's disappointing run*
JR

1218

# SAINT-CLOUD (L-H)
### Friday, April 9

**OFFICIAL GOING: Good**

## 1320a PRIX PENELOPE (GROUP 3) (FILLIES) 1m 2f 110y
1:50 (1:50) 3-Y-O **£25,704** (£10,282; £7,711; £5,141)

RPR
**1** **Ask For The Moon (FR)**[34] 3-9-0 ........ IMendizabal 4 95+
(J-CRouget, France) *held up in 3rd, 2nd straight, smooth headway to lead 1 1/2f out, shaken up to go clear 1f out, pushed out, easily* 1
**2** 2 **Super Lina (FR)**[22] [1048] 3-9-0 ........ CSoumillon 3 91
(YDeNicolay, France) *2nd early, 3rd straight, ridden over 1 1/2f out, stayed on gamely under pressure to go 2nd 100 yards out, no chance with wi* 1
**3** nk **Miss France (FR)**[22] [1048] 3-9-0 ........ DBoeuf 5 91
(ELellouche, France) *raced in 5th, 4th straight, effort on outside over 1 1/2f out, hard ridden to dispute 2nd briefly 100 yards out, no extra c* 3
**4** 1/2 **Trinity Joy**[22] [1048] 3-9-0 ........ TJarnet 6 90
(RGibson, France) *set good pace, headed 1 1/2f out, lost 2nd 100 yards out* 2
**5** 3 **Kalatuna (FR)**[27] 3-9-0 ........ TThulliez 1 85
(JVanHandenhove, France) *raced in 4th, 5th straight, ridden and no impression from 2f out*
**6** 6 **Kate Winslet (USA)**[153] [5962] 3-9-0 ........ LProietti 2 74
(CLigerot, France) *held up in last, outpaced from 2f out*

2m 17.1s **Going Correction** +0.05s/f (Good) **6** Ran SP% **191.4**
Speed ratings: **115,113,113,112,110 106**.
**Owner** J-P Dubois **Bred** Mme Gilles Forien & Jean Francois Gribomont **Trained** France

**NOTEBOOK**
**Ask For The Moon(FR)** took this in excellent style and looks a high-class filly in the making. After taking control half-way up the straight, she was never in danger and ran out an easy winner. She will now be given a brief rest with her main target being the Prix de Diane.
**Super Lina(FR)** was outpaced early in the straight but ran on under strong pressure without ever looking like catching the winner.
**Miss France(FR)** came with a progressive but one-paced effort in the straight and was run out of second place in the final stages.
**Trinity Joy** tried to make very yard but lacked a change of pace.

# HAYDOCK (L-H)
### Saturday, April 10

**OFFICIAL GOING: Soft (heavy in places)**
After a wet week the going was described as 'heavy but not tacky'.
Wind: Slt, hlf behind Weather: Overcast

## 1321 BET365 CALL 08000 322 365 CLASSIFIED STKS 1m 2f 120y
2:00 (2:00) (D) 3-Y-0+ **£5,606** (£1,725; £862; £431) **Stalls** High

Form RPR
304- **1** **Zero Tolerance (IRE)**[169] [5724] 4-10-1 85 ........ MFenton 3 94+
(TDBarron) *trckd ldr: led 4f out: wnt clr over 2f out: drvn rt out* **7/2**[1]
5-40 **2** 1 1/4 **Arry Dash**[15] [1114] 4-10-1 85 ........ TEDurcan 9 92?
(MRChannon) *hld up: hdwy over 2f out: wnt 2nd 1f out: styd on strly* **11/2**
63-5 **3** 5 **Weet A Head (IRE)**[47] [864] 3-8-8 84 ........ WSupple 7 82
(RHollinshead) *sn trcking ldrs: effrt over 3f out: styd on same pce* **25/1**
031- **4** 3/4 **Fernery**[285] [2850] 4-9-10 83 ........ TQuinn 5 77
(LMCumani) *lw: trckd ldrs: outpcd over 2f out: styd on ins last* **5/1**[3]
220- **5** 3/4 **Tawny Way**[253] [3745] 4-9-11 84 ........ ACulhane 6 76+
(WJarvis) *hld up: effrt on inner over 4f out: sn chsng ldrs: one pce fnl 2f* **9/1**
1124 **6** 5 **Intricate Web (IRE)**[36] [971] 8-9-7 78 ........ DAllan(3) 8 67
(EJAlston) *rr-div: drvn along over 4f out: nvr rchd ldrs* **16/1**
000- **7** hd **Cat's Whiskers**[210] [4879] 5-10-0 84 ........ DaleGibson 11 71
(MWEasterby) *bit bkwd: plld hrd: sn trcking ldrs: lost pl over 1f out* **12/1**
-452 **8** 5 **The Bonus King**[4] [1284] 4-10-0 84 ........ JFanning 1 62
(MJohnston) *led tl 4f out: lost pl over 2f out: eased* **4/1**[2]
403- **9** 3/4 **Leighton (IRE)**[169] [5724] 4-9-11 81 ........ BDoyle 10 58
(JDBethell) *t.k.h in rr: effrt over 3f out: wknd 2f out: eased* **14/1**
0040 **10** 8 **Aventura (IRE)**[15] [1114] 4-9-6 83 ........ KGhunowa(7) 2 46
(MJPolglase) *plld v hrd: sn trcking ldrs: lost pl over 3f out: eased* **33/1**

2m 23.05s (5.32) **Going Correction** +0.50s/f (Yiel)
**WFA** 3 from 4yo+ 20lb **10** Ran SP% **111.3**
Speed ratings: **100,99,95,94,94 90,90,86,86,80**CSF £21.52 TOTE £5.30: £1.70, £2.20, £4.80; EX 22.20.
**Owner** The Hornsey Warriors Racing Syndicate **Bred** Cliveden Stud Ltd **Trained** Maunby, N Yorks

**FOCUS**
A decent, competitive classified event on paper, but they finished strung out in the soft ground and the winning time was only modest.. An improved effort from the winner though and the form looks sound.

**NOTEBOOK**
**Zero Tolerance(IRE)** ◆, whose three-year-old career was curtailed after being struck into at Royal Ascot, looked very fit and was full of himself beforehand. He took a fierce grip but, after quickening clear, he had to be kept up to his work. He looks sure to enjoy further success.
**Arry Dash**, out of luck with the draw at Doncaster, still looked backward in his coat. He went second about five lengths down on Zero Tolerance a furlong out, and finished with a real flourish but much too late to trouble the idling winner.
**Weet A Head(IRE)** finished a creditable third but will continue to struggle in handicap company from this sort of mark.
**Fernery**, winner of her third and final start at three in a maiden at Pontefract in June, looked really well. Her lack of experience showed and she can do much better when stepped up to a mile and a half.
**Tawny Way**, a tall filly, did not reappear after disappointing at Goodwood in August.
**The Bonus King** dropped out in a matter of strides and this trip looks beyond him. *Official explanation: trainer's representative had no explanation for the poor form shown*

## 1322 BIGWIGS BLOODSTOCK RACING CLUB RATED STKS (H'CAP) 1m 30y
2:30 (2:31) (C) (0-90,87) 3-Y-0 **£10,010** (£3,080; £1,540; £770) **Stalls** Low

Form RPR
23-4 **1** **Imperialistic (IRE)**[14] [1129] 3-9-4 **84** ........ (p) DarrenWilliams 3 94
(KRBurke) *trckd ldrs: led far side 2f out: hung lft and wandered: led overall appr fnl f: styd on* **7/2**[2]
1122 **2** 1 1/4 **Red Lancer**[14] [1134] 3-8-7 **80** ........ BSwarbrick(7) 7 87
(RJPrice) *hld up: hdwy on ins 4f out: ev ch 2f out: n.m.r ins last: nt qckn* **8/1**
015- **3** 1 1/2 **Oddsmaker (IRE)**[166] [5789] 3-8-7 **73** oh1 ........ SWKelly 6 77
(PDEvans) *sn trcking ldrs: t.k.h and hung rt: led overall and c wd over 4f out: edgd lft and hdd appr fnl f* **25/1**
120- **4** 5 **Saffron Fox**[161] [5874] 3-9-7 **87** ........ ACulhane 9 81
(JGPortman) *mid-div: pushed along 4f out: styd on fnl f* **13/2**[3]
42-2 **5** nk **Gjovic**[21] [1064] 3-9-0 **80** ........ KDarley 4 73
(BJMeehan) *led tl over 4f out: one pce fnl 2f* **7/1**
124- **6** 1 1/4 **Royal Distant (USA)**[179] [5557] 3-8-13 **79** ........ DaleGibson 8 70
(MWEasterby) *sn outpcd and pushed along: kpt on fnl 3f: nvr nr ldrs* **20/1**
-240 **7** 1 **Western Roots**[33] [985] 3-8-13 **79** ........ TQuinn 5 68
(PFICole) *trckd ldrs: t.k.h: lost pl 2f out* **16/1**
5-12 **8** 1 3/4 **Mount Vettore**[14] [1129] 3-9-2 **82** ........ EAhern 1 67
(MrsJRRamsden) *trckd ldrs: drvn along over 4f out: no rspnse* **15/8**[1]
313- **9** 14 **The Violin Player (USA)**[179] [5562] 3-9-0 **80** ........ MTebbutt 2 37
(WJarvis) *t.k.h towards rr: rdn 3f out: carried hd high and no imp: eased fnl f* **20/1**

1m 48.5s (2.95) **Going Correction** +0.50s/f (Yiel) **9** Ran SP% **113.2**
Speed ratings: **105,103,102,97,96 95,94,92,78**CSF £29.62 CT £598.22 TOTE £5.20: £1.80, £2.30, £3.60; EX 40.40.
**Owner** Bigwigs Bloodstock II **Bred** B H Bloodstock **Trained** Middleham Moor, N Yorks

**FOCUS**
Just a fair gallop and a reasonable time for the grade, but not a great race for the class.

**NOTEBOOK**
**Imperialistic(IRE)**, still backward in her coat, had the cheekpieces back on. She ducked and dived, but in the end did more than enough for the sponsors to win back their prizemoney.
**Red Lancer**, very fit and on his toes, stuck to his guns. Left short of room by the winner, he was beaten entirely on merit. Another couple of furlongs would not come amiss.
**Oddsmaker(IRE)**, who looked rough in his coat, was on his toes beforehand. He had difficulty making the turn and, after being pulled wide to race alone, he edged back to the main body of the field before fading late on. *Official explanation: jockey said gelding hung right round the bend*
**Saffron Fox**, backward in her coat, stayed on late in the day and will be suited by middle distances.
**Gjovic**, who looked very fit, will be suited by further and much better ground.
**Royal Distant(USA)**, having her first outing for her new stable, looked some way short of peak fitness.

**Mount Vettore**, loaded first, had finished ahead of the winner at Doncaster but he ran no race at all. The ground was not solely to blame. *Official explanation: trainer had no explanation for the poor form shown*

## 1323 FIELD MARSHAL RATED STKS (H'CAP) (LISTED RACE) 5f
**3:00** (3:00) (A) (0-110,104) 3-Y-O **£17,850** (£6,600; £3,300; £1,500) **Stalls** Centre

Form RPR
205- **1** **If Paradise**205 5009 3-9-3 **100** RLMoore 1 105
(RHannon) *h.d.w: trckd ldr: qcknd to ld over 1f out: r.o wl* **7/1**
655- **2** 2½ **Crafty Fancy (IRE)**162 5851 3-8-7 **90** oh5 TQuinn 5 87
(DJSFfrenchDavis) *sn outpcd: hdwy over 1f out: kpt on to take 2nd nr line* **4/1**3
40-2 **3** *shd* **Harry Up**9 1223 3-8-9 **92** MFenton 2 89
(JGGiven) *led: edgd lft and hdd over 1f out: kpt on same pce* **3/1**2
212- **4** 1¼ **Nights Cross (IRE)**182 5480 3-9-7 **104** TEDurcan 4 97
(MRChannon) *trckd ldrs: effrt 2f out: sn rdn and nt qckn* **2/1**1
001- **5** 2½ **Lake Garda**207 4964 3-8-7 **90** oh5 GGibbons 3 75
(BAMcmahon) *h.d.w: w ldrs: swtchd rt after 1f and racd alone stands' side: rdn 2f out: edgd lft: wknd and eased ins last* **11/2**
63.32 secs (1.25) **Going Correction** +0.375s/f (Good) **5** Ran SP% **106.2**
Speed ratings: **105,101,100,98,94**CSF £31.11 TOTE £8.80: £3.30, £2.40; EX 51.30.
**Owner** Mrs J Wood **Bred** G E Amey **Trained** East Everleigh, Wilts

**FOCUS**
A poor turnout for a £30,000 prize with just three of the five runners running from their correct mark. The time was ordinary for the grade and the form looks nothing special.

**NOTEBOOK**
**If Paradise**, who has strengthened and grown during the winer, travelled supremely well and found the heavy ground no problem at all.
**Crafty Fancy(IRE)**, who has not grown much from two to three, was running from 5lb out of the handicap. She found the ground no problem and pinched second place prizemoney on the line.
**Harry Up**, regularly put in his place by Nights Cross at two, looked very fit but may not want the ground as soft as this.
**Nights Cross(IRE)**, a tough customer at two, looked fit but was under pressure and going nowhere soon after halfway.
**Lake Garda**, 5lb 'wrong', is now a good-looking sprinter. He was brought to race alone on the stands' side but seemed to resent the lack of company.

## 1324 HAYDOCK PARK ANNUAL BADGEHOLDERS MAIDEN AUCTION STKS 5f
**3:35** (3:36) (E) 2-Y-O **£3,770** (£1,160; £580; £290) **Stalls** Centre

Form RPR
0 **1** **Apologies**14 1128 2-8-7 GGibbons 3 77
(BAMcmahon) *w ldr: led and edgd lft 2f out: hrd rdn and edgd righht fnl f: kpt on wl* **13/2**
**2** *1* **Mystical Land (IRE)** 2-8-11 RHavlin 7 78+
(JHMGosden) *w'like: sn drvn along: hdwy 3f out: styd on wl appr fnl f: nt qckn last 100yds* **5/1**1
**3** ¾ **Cammies Future** 2-8-11 AMcCarthy 6 75+
(PWChapple-Hyam) *neat: unf: sn trcking ldrs: ev ch over 1f out: hit on hd several times by winning rdr's whip: no ex ins last* **11/2**2
**4** *2* **Chiselled (IRE)** 2-8-11 DarrenWilliams 1 68
(KRBurke) *w'like: comp: swvd lft s: sn trcking ldrs: effrt on inner whn hmpd 2f out: kpt on same pce appr fnl f* **6/1**3
**5** ¾ **Special Gold** 2-9-0 KDarley 9 68
(TDEasterby) *w'like: leggy: scope: dwlt sn trcking ldrs: styd on same pce fnl f: improve* **6/1**3
2 **6** 1¼ **I'm Aimee**21 1060 2-8-2 SCarson 10 52
(PDEvans) *led tl 2f out: wknd jst ins fnl f: eased nr fin* **5/1**1
**7** 2½ **Gifted Gamble** 2-8-7 NCallan 5 48
(KARyan) *lengthy: unf: scope: s.s: sn bhd and detached in last: styd on appr fnl f* **10/1**
4 **8** 1¾ **Veneer (IRE)**11 1183 2-8-9 RLMoore 2 44
(RHannon) *sn outpcd and in rr* **14/1**
**9** *1* **Fantasy Defender (IRE)** 2-8-7 RWinston 4 39
(JJQuinn) *w'like: leggy: sn outpcd and bhd* **25/1**
0 **10** *17* **Droopys Joel**15 1117 2-8-7 JFanning 8 —
(RPElliott) *chsd ldrs: edgd lft and wknd 2f out: sn bhd* **16/1**
64.74 secs (2.67) **Going Correction** +0.375s/f (Good) **10** Ran SP% **116.1**
Speed ratings: **93,91,90,87,85 83,79,77,75,48**CSF £38.84 TOTE £7.90: £2.20, £2.10, £2.30; EX 65.60.
**Owner** J C Fretwell **Bred** Wyck Hall Stud **Trained** Hopwas, Staffs
■ Stewards Enquiry : G Gibbons seven-day ban: careless riding (Apr 21-27)

**FOCUS**
Probably a fair juvenile event likely to throw up future winners, although the time was ordinary.

**NOTEBOOK**
**Apologies**, still very inexperienced going to post, ducked and dived but did not flinch under a hard ride.
**Mystical Land(IRE)** ◆, a February foal, is quite a well-made type. He took an age to pick up but put in some sterling work inside the last. He will surely be able to go one better.
**Cammies Future**, a March foal, lacks size and susbstance. He travelled strongly, but not surprisingly hung fire when hit over the head by the winning rider's whip inside the last. This was not the happiest of debut experiences.
**Chiselled(IRE)**, a February foal, is a close-coupled individual. He banged against the running rail soon after halfway, and deserves credit for the way he stuck to his task.
**Special Gold** ◆, a March foal, is very much on the leg. He ran a pleasing first race and will be a lot wiser next time.
**I'm Aimee** looked backward in her coat and did not improve on her initial effort.

## 1325 RUNCORN MAIDEN STKS 1m 30y
**4:10** (4:11) (D) 3-Y-O **£5,902** (£1,816; £908; £454) **Stalls** Low

Form RPR
026- **1** **Baffle**206 4986 3-8-9 77 TQuinn 12 73
(JLDunlop) *mde all: shkn up 1f out: styd on wl* **9/4**1
02- **2** *3* **Tytheknot**168 5744 3-9-0 TEDurcan 6 72
(JeddO'Keeffe) *trckd wnr: kpt on fnl f* **13/2**
**3** *2* **Foolish Groom** 3-9-0 ACulhane 1 68
(RHollinshead) *leggy: unf: s.i.s: hdwy 5f out: sn chsng ldrs: edgd lft and kpt on same pce fnl f* **20/1**
0 **4** 1¾ **Inchloss (IRE)**15 1111 3-9-0 WSupple 10 65
(BAMcmahon) *hld up and bhd: hdwy over 3f out: kpt on fnl 2f* **20/1**
50- **5** 2½ **Burning Moon**218 4706 3-9-0 EAhern 8 60
(JNoseda) *lw: sn bhd and pushed along: styd on fnl 3f: nvr rchd ldrs* **3/1**2
6 **6** *nk* **Indi Ano Star (IRE)**12 1174 3-9-0 RFitzpatrick 5 59
(DCarroll) *s.i.s: kpt on fnl 3f: nvr nr ldrs* **10/1**
5- **7** 1¼ **Top Achiever (IRE)**267 3363 3-9-0 RWinston 2 56
(MrsLStubbs) *chsd ldrs: wknd over 1f out* **20/1**
0 **8** *8* **Go Green**65 683 3-8-9 SWKelly 7 35
(PDEvans) *chsd ldrs: wknd over 2f out* **33/1**
00- **9** *5* **Zabadou**155 5940 3-8-9 TEaves(5) 11 30
(CBBBooth) *mid-div: edgd lft and lost pl over 3f out: sn bhd* **100/1**
000- **10** *5* **True To Yourself (USA)**172 5689 3-9-0 JMackay 4 20
(JGGiven) *s.s: a in rr* **50/1**
00-0 **11** *4* **Royal Nite Owl**28 1012 3-8-7 JDO'Reilly(7) 3 12
(JO'Reilly) *plld v hrd: trckd ldrs: lost pl over 3f out: sn bhd* **50/1**
000- **P** **Grande Terre (IRE)**197 5185 3-8-9 MFenton 9 —
(JGGiven) *sn chsng ldrs: p.u over 3f out: dismntd* **6/1**3
1m 49.12s (3.57) **Going Correction** +0.50s/f (Yiel) **12** Ran SP% **114.6**
Speed ratings: **102,99,97,95,92 92,91,83,78,73 69**,—CSF £15.10 TOTE £3.00: £1.90, £2.00, £3.30; EX 15.30.
**Owner** Plantation Stud **Bred** Plantation Stud **Trained** Arundel, W Sussex

**FOCUS**
A modest maiden run at just a steady gallop and doubtful the winner ran up to her official mark.

**NOTEBOOK**
**Baffle**, a lengthy-type, had the worst of the draw. Making her way to the running rail, she always looked in total command but it was not a strong event.
**Tytheknot**, runner-up at Musselburgh in October on his second and final start at two, is a tall type. He chased the winner throughout but was never going to get in a serious blow.
**Foolish Groom**, an immature newcomer, showed ability and can do a bit better in time.
**Inchloss(IRE)** still looked on the backward side. By no means knocked, about he needs another outing to qualify for a handicap mark.
**Burning Moon**, who had just two outings at two, took the eye in the paddock but he showed very little only staying on when it was all over. Connections will be hoping for better over possibly much further in handicaps.
**Indi Ano Star(IRE)**, nicely backed at long odds, never threatened to enter the argument.
**Go Green** *Official explanation: jockey said filly hung right-handed*
**Grande Terre(IRE)** *Official explanation: jockey said filly lost her action behind*

## 1326 RECTANGLE GROUP H'CAP 1m 6f
**4:45** (4:46) (D) (0-85,80) 4-Y-O+ **£5,752** (£1,770; £885; £442) **Stalls** Low

Form RPR
0/61 **1** **Benbyas**4 1282 7-8-4 **65** DTudhope(7) 1 86+
(DCarroll) *led: clr 8f out: qcknd over 4f out: styd on wl: unchal* **7/2**1
2253 **2** *7* **Nakwa (IRE)**7 1245 6-8-1 **58** ow3 DAllan(3) 7 67
(EJAlston) *a chsng wnr: kpt on fnl 2f: no imp* **9/1**
000- **3** 1½ **Thewhirlingdervish (IRE)**196 5214 6-9-3 **78** AMullen(7) 3 85
(TDEasterby) *rr-div: hdwy 6f out: one pce fnl 2f* **50/1**
661- **4** 2½ **Cara Fantasy (IRE)**280 3008 4-9-9 **80** TQuinn 11 84+
(JLDunlop) *sn chsng ldrs: pushed along 6f out: one pce fnl 2f* **9/1**
/5-0 **5** ¾ **Dancing Pearl**9 1224 6-7-5 **52** oh12 BSwarbrick(7) 6 55
(CJPrice) *sn bhd: hdwy on wd outside 2f out: kpt on ins last* **20/1**
5-15 **6** ¾ **Middlethorpe**10 1198 7-8-8 **67** (b) PMulrennan(5) 2 69
(MWEasterby) *hld up in mid-div: effrt over 3f out: kpt on fnl f: nvr on terms* **14/1**
44-3 **7** *1* **Ringside Jack**4 1287 8-7-12 **52** JMackay 12 53
(CWFairhurst) *in tch: effrt over 3f out: nvr rchd ldrs* **13/2**3
-230 **8** ½ **Northern Nymph**15 1112 5-9-7 **75** (t) ACulhane 13 75
(RHollinshead) *hld up and bhd: sme hdwy 3f out: nvr a factor* **20/1**
5031 **9** 1¾ **Turtle Valley (IRE)**3 1302 8-9-7 **75** 6ex PDoe 10 73
(SDow) *hld up and bhd: hdwy 7f out: sn chsng ldrs: edgd lft and lost pl over 1f out* **4/1**2
50-0 **10** *6* **Champion Lion (IRE)**16 1103 5-9-7 **75** TEDurcan 5 65
(MRChannon) *hld up in rr: stdy hdwy 3f out: shkn up and wknd 1f out: eased* **14/1**
60-0 **11** *4* **Edmo Yewkay (IRE)**10 1198 4-8-8 **65** (b) WSupple 9 50
(TDEasterby) *chsd ldrs: lost pl 3f out* **16/1**
000- **12** *6* **Lillebror (GER)**75 5146 6-8-11 **65** SWKelly 8 42
(BJCurley) *lw: sn trcking ldrs: lost pl 6f out: sn in rr* **40/1**
410- **13** *dist* **Nobratinetta (FR)**310 2135 5-9-9 **77** KDarley 4 —
(MrsMReveley) *trckd ldrs: lost pl 5f out: sn in rr and eased: t.o* **8/1**
3m 12.45s (6.30) **Going Correction** +0.50s/f (Yiel)
**WFA** 4 from 5yo+ 3lb **13** Ran SP% **119.8**
Speed ratings: **102,98,97,95,95 94,94,94,93,89 87,83**,—CSF £33.84 CT £1358.61 TOTE £5.40: £2.50, £3.30, £10.60; EX 64.90 Place 6 £459.66, Place 5 £181.87.
**Owner** C H Stephenson & Partners **Bred** C Stephenson **Trained** Warthill, N Yorks

**FOCUS**
A fair handicap and sound form with an improved effort from winner, who is in good heart.

**NOTEBOOK**
**Benbyas**, without a penalty, steered an erratic path in front but, keeping the gallop up all the way to the line, was never going to be seriously threatened.
**Nakwa(IRE)** chased the winner throughout and the trip was not a problem.
**Thewhirlingdervish(IRE)**, who looks as if he needs some sun on his back, ran really well considering the trip was on the short side and he prefers much better ground.
**Cara Fantasy(IRE)**, 5lb higher than when last seen out winning at Leicester in July, looked fit but she may not want the ground as testing as this.
**Dancing Pearl**, 12lb 'wrong' stayed on really well late on. A winner three times over hurdles, she will relish a stiff test of stamina.
**Middlethorpe**, 5lb higher than Doncaster, never got competitive.
**Turtle Valley(IRE)**, making a quick reappearance, ran very flat.
**Nobratinetta(FR)** *Official explanation: jockey said mare was never travelling*
T/Plt: £357.30 to a £1 stake. Pool: £57,023.95. 116.50 winning tickets. T/Qpdt: £51.40 to a £1 stake. Pool: £2,914.45. 41.95 winning tickets. WG

# 1130 KEMPTON (R-H)
### Saturday, April 10

**OFFICIAL GOING: Good to soft**
Wind: Cold Weather: Sunny becoming overcast

## 1327 TURFTOURS.COM MASAKA STKS (LISTED RACE) (FILLIES) 1m (J)
**1:35** (1:35) (A) 3-Y-O **£17,400** (£6,600; £3,300; £1,500) **Stalls** High

Form RPR
122- **1** **Hathrah (IRE)**168 5750 3-8-8 103 RHills 4 109+
(JLDunlop) *lw: sn trcking ldr: chal over 3f out: led wl over 2f out: pushed clr appr fnl f: easily* **10/11**1
441- **2** *9* **Coqueteria (USA)**169 5734 3-8-8 80 SDrowne 3 89
(GWragg) *in tch: hdwy to chse ldrs 3f out: swtchd rt and styd on to chse wnr over 1f out but no ch* **25/1**
311- **3** ½ **Halicardia**233 4327 3-8-8 97 DHolland 7 88
(PWHarris) *chsd ldrs: hrd drvn fr over 2f out: styd on same pce* **9/2**2
116- **4** 1½ **Doctrine**172 5699 3-8-8 99 LDettori 8 85
(JHMGosden) *s.i.s: plld hrd and n.m.r after 1f: sme hdwy u.p over 2f out: nvr nr ldrs* **8/1**3


The Form Book, Raceform Ltd, Compton, RG20 6NL

210- **5** *6* **Fadeela (IRE)**[122] 6160 3-8-8 69 ........ PaulEddery 1 72
(PWD'Arcy) *led: rdn 3f out: hdd over 2f out: sn outpcd: wknd over 1f out* **66/1**
01- **6** *5* **Spring Surprise**[155] 5939 3-8-8 ........ KFallon 9 62
(BWHills) *a bhd: pushed along 1/2-way: lost tch fr over 2f out* **12/1**
201- **7** *6* **Zerlina (USA)**[163] 5834 3-8-8 86 ........ DaneO'Neill 2 49
(RHannon) *s.i.s: a bhd: lost tch fr over 2f* **20/1**
102- **8** *2* **Why Dubai (USA)**[189] 5362 3-8-8 89 ........ RHughes 6 45
(RHannon) *chsd ldrs tl wknd qckly over 2f out* **9/1**
610- **9** *11* **Betty Stogs (IRE)**[168] 5750 3-8-8 84 ........ SSanders 5 22
(DRCElsworth) *a bhd: lost tch fr over 2f out* **20/1**

1m 42.47s (2.85) **Going Correction** +0.60s/f (Yiel) **9** Ran SP% **114.2**
Speed ratings: **109,100,99,98,92 87,81,79,68**CSF £33.87 TOTE £1.80: £1.10, £5.50, £1.20; EX 38.70.
**Owner** Hamdan Al Maktoum **Bred** Kildaragh Stud **Trained** Arundel, W Sussex
■ Stewards Enquiry : R Hughes caution: careless riding

**FOCUS**
An easy win for Hathrah, but doubtful she beat much and this event is unlikely to prove much of a 1000 Guineas pointer. The time was just fair for the grade and the runners tacked over to the stands' side in the home straight.

**NOTEBOOK**
**Hathrah(IRE)** secured the lead against the stands' rail early in the home straight and came right away from her rivals. The softish ground might well have exaggerated the winning margin, but this was still a useful performance from a filly who also acts on a sound surface. She will stay further and is entered in the Oaks as well as the 1000 Guineas.
**Coqueteria(USA)**, who looked like she would improve for the run, stayed on but was no match at all for the easy winner. This was a step up on her juvenile form.
**Halicardia** stayed on under pressure in the straight and looks in need of an extra furlong or two at this stage.
**Doctrine**, who looked fit enough, was rather free early on and became short of room. She kept on without getting to the placed horses and looks in need of slightly farther.
**Fadeela(IRE)**, a 69-rated filly whose win came in a Fibresand nursery, was without the eyeshield she has been wearing on the All-Weather. After making the running and bringing the field over to the stands' side in the straight, she was soon passed by the eventual winner and faded out of contention.
**Spring Surprise**, a comeback ride for Kieren Fallon, was in trouble soon after halfway.
**Zerlina(USA)**, who has not grown much over the winter, was reluctant to make her way down to the start.
**Why Dubai(USA)**, who looked fit enough, was reported by Hughes to have stumbled and knocked herself. *Official explanation: jockey said filly stumbled and knocked herself*

## 1328 CORAL ROSEBERY STKS (HERITAGE H'CAP) 1m 2f (J)
**2:10** (2:12) (B ) (0-105,105) 4-Y-0+ **£23,200** (£8,800; £4,400; £2,000) **Stalls** High

Form RPR
325- **1** **Silence Is Golden**[177] 5589 5-8-13 **95** ........ JFMcDonald(5) 19 105
(BJMeehan) *bhd: hdwy 3f out: drvn to chnace ldrs over 1f out: led ins last: hld on wl* **11/1**
3-00 **2** *3/4* **Dumaran (IRE)**[14] 1125 6-8-13 **90** ........ KFallon 5 99
(WJMusson) *bhd: hdwy 4f out: swtchd rt and styd on fr 2f out: str run ins last: nt rch wnr* **8/1**[2]
110- **3** *nk* **Counsel's Opinion (IRE)**[162] 5853 7-9-12 **103** ........ SSanders 20 111
(CFWall) *s.i.s: bhd: hdwy 4f out: drvn to press ldrs over 1f out: chsd wnr ins last: nt qckn nr fin* **14/1**
430- **4** *nk* **Blythe Knight (IRE)**[203] 5074 4-9-7 **98** ........ LDettori 7 106
(EALDunlop) *lw: chsd ldrs: led over 1f out: sn hrd drvn hdd and nt qckn ins last* **5/1**[1]
-640 **5** *1 1/4* **Bonecrusher**[28] 1009 5-10-0 **105** ........(v) JPMurtagh 3 111
(DRLoder) *in ttch: hdwy 4f out: drvn to chse ldrs over 1f out: one pce fnl f* **12/1**
200- **6** *1 1/4* **Putra Kuantan**[182] 5484 4-9-2 **93** ........ PRobinson 9 96
(MAJarvis) *bit bkwd: trckd ldrs: chal 3f out tl led over 2f out:edgd lft ins fnl 2f: hdd over 1f out: sn one pce* **10/1**
105- **7** *4* **Vengeance**[227] 4498 4-9-0 **91** ........ GDuffield 6 87
(MrsAJPerrett) *hmpd and dropped rr after 2f: hdwy on stands rails whn hmpd ins fnl 2f: nt rcvr and one pce fnl f* **25/1**
10-6 **8** *1 3/4* **King's Thought**[14] 1124 5-9-7 **98** ........ DHolland 2 91
(SGollings) *w ldr: led after 2f: hdd over 2f out: wknd over 1f out* **9/1**[3]
440- **9** *1 1/4* **Prince Nureyev (IRE)**[195] 5253 4-9-6 **97** ........ SDrowne 17 88
(BRMillman) *b: bhd: kpt on fnl 2f: nt trble ldrs* **14/1**
21-0 **10** *2 1/2* **Turbo (IRE)**[42] 915 5-9-3 **94** ........(p) MartinDwyer 14 80
(GBBalding) *bhd: kpt on fnl 2f: nt a danger* **12/1**
00-0 **11** *3* **Unshakable (IRE)**[14] 1125 5-8-13 **90** ........ JFEgan 18 71
(BobJones) *b: chsd ldrs: rdn 3f out: wknd over 2f out* **8/1**[2]
102- **12** *1/2* **Trust Rule**[177] 5588 4-9-7 **98** ........ RHills 8 78
(BWHills) *bit bkwd: bhd: rdn 3f out: nvr in contention* **10/1**
240- **13** *1/2* **Tizzy May (FR)**[140] 6051 4-9-5 **96** ........ DaneO'Neill 16 75
(RHannon) *chsd ldrs: rdn 4f out: wknd* **16/1**
0-00 **14** *9* **Serieux**[14] 1125 5-8-13 **90** ........ RHughes 10 53
(MrsAJPerrett) *chsd ldrs 6f* **16/1**
040- **15** *1 1/4* **Gallery God (FR)**[182] 5484 8-9-9 **100** ........ PaulEddery 13 61
(SDow) *a in rr* **40/1**
550- **16** *10* **Tycoon Hall (IRE)**[231] 4369 4-8-13 **90** ........ PDobbs 12 33
(RHannon) *led 2f: styd prom tl wknd fr 4f out* **33/1**
-000 **17** *11* **Arabie**[42] 922 6-9-1 **92** ........ KDalgleish 1 15
(MJohnston) *b.hind: chsd ldrs over 6f* **25/1**

2m 10.38s (4.24) **Going Correction** +0.60s/f (Yiel) **17** Ran SP% **129.0**
Speed ratings: **107,106,106,105,104 103,100,99,98,96 93,93,93,85,84 76,68**CSF £97.67 CT £1278.38 TOTE £14.30: £2.80, £1.90, £4.00, £1.70; EX 106.30 Trifecta £2481.10 Part won. Pool: £3,494.64. 0.90 winning tickets..
**Owner** Miss J Semple **Bred** Mrs M T Dawson **Trained** Upper Lambourn, Berks

**FOCUS**
A classy, competitive handicap, effectively a 90+, run at a sound pace and the form looks solid. They again crossed over to the near rail in the straight.

**NOTEBOOK**
**Silence Is Golden**, who has not been easy to place, recorded her first win for nearly two years, coming with a run down the outer to get on top inside the final furlong. A tough and consistent filly, who has been covered by Medicean, she will now go for a Listed race, having been runner-up in that grade last autumn.
**Dumaran(IRE)**, who raced on what turned out to be the wrong side in the Lincoln, stayed on under hard driving from Fallon once switched widest of all in the straight. This ground was ideal for him.
**Counsel's Opinion(IRE)** ran a cracking race from a career-high mark especially as he prefers faster ground. He stays farther than this, but his 100 plus rating will not make him easy to place.
**Blythe Knight(IRE)**, who was well backed, travelled as well as anything before taking it up but was soon headed and unable to produce any extra. There did not appear to be a great deal wrong with his application this time.
**Bonecrusher** had plenty on under top weight and this was a thoroughly respectable effort. He appreciated the return to turf after competing on various artificial surfaces
**Putra Kuantan**, whose wins have come on fast ground, made a promising seasonal return and should strip fitter next time.
**Vengeance**, who should improve for the run, did well to finish where he did after meeting trouble on two occasions. A genuine sort who stays farther, there should be a decent handicap in him especially if he is dropped a pound or two.
**King's Thought**, who went early to post, adopted his usual front-running tactics before fading once headed.
**Prince Nureyev(IRE)** found this trip insufficient but was staying on in the latter stages.
**Turbo(IRE)**, who is more effective at a mile and a half, kept on in the last couple of furlongs without getting in a blow.
**Trust Rule** should improve with this run under his belt and when stepped back up to a mile and a half.

## 1329 ALANBRAZILRACING.COM QUEEN'S PRIZE (H'CAP) 2m
**2:40** (2:42) (C ) (0-100,99) 4-Y-0+ **£9,873** (£3,038; £1,519; £759) **Stalls** High

Form RPR
222- **1** **Anak Pekan**[154] 5949 4-8-4 **80** ........ PRobinson 17 99+
(MAJarvis) *mde all: pushed along 2f out: c clr appr fnl f: unchal* **9/4**[1]
133- **2** *5* **Teresa**[162] 5855 4-8-0 **76** ........ JQuinn 4 85
(JLDunlop) *chsd ldrs: rdn to chse wnr appr fnl 2f: no imp and sn one pce* **16/1**
0002 **3** *1 1/2* **High Point (IRE)**[59] 743 6-8-8 **80** ow1 ........ DaneO'Neill 5 87
(GPEnright) *mid-div after 6f: hdwy to chse ldrs fr 5f out: rdn and kpt on same pce fnl 2f* **20/1**
1132 **4** *3/4* **Cold Turkey**[22] 1054 4-8-3 **79** ........ SWhitworth 16 85
(GLMoore) *t.k.h: hld up in rr: gd hdwy on outside over 4f out: chsd ldrs over 2f out: one pce u.p appr fnl f* **16/1**
414/ **5** *1/2* **Hawadeth**[23] 1514 9-8-8 **80** ........(p) RHughes 6 86
(VRADartnall) *chsd ldrs: rdn 3f out: kpt on same pce fnl 2f* **8/1**[3]
613- **6** *7* **Reveillez**[190] 5349 5-9-7 **93** ........ LDettori 13 90
(JRFanshawe) *b: chsd ldrs: rdn 3f out: wknd over 1f out* **12/1**
40-5 **7** *1* **Red Wine**[36] 971 5-9-8 **94** ........ DHolland 9 90
(JAOsborne) *in tch: outpcd and rdn 6f out: styd on again fnl 3f but nvr gng pce to rch ldrs* **14/1**
131- **8** *1* **Ponderon**[154] 5949 4-9-1 **91** ........ GDuffield 12 86
(RFJohnsonHoughton) *b: chsd wnr: rdn 3f out: wknd 2f out: n.m.r sn after* **15/2**[2]
0-06 **9** *6* **Moon Emperor**[36] 600 7-9-1 **87** ........(v[1]) SDrowne 18 75
(JRJenkins) *bhd: sme hdwy 6f out: n.d after* **33/1**
4364 **10** *4* **Typhoon Tilly**[14] 1135 7-7-13 **71** ........ CCatlin 10 54
(CREgerton) *mid-div: hdwy 1/2-way: wknd fr 3f out* **20/1**
015- **11** *1 1/2* **Establishment**[154] 5949 7-8-7 **79** ........ SSanders 7 60
(CACyzer) *bit bkwd: in tch: rdn 5f out: wknd 3f out* **33/1**
206- **12** *1* **Mostarsil (USA)**[181] 5502 6-7-11 **71** ow1 ........(p) LisaJones(3) 11 52
(GLMoore) *a in rr* **33/1**
40-6 **13** *3/4* **Bobsleigh**[15] 1112 5-8-4 **76** ........ PHanagan 14 55
(MrsAJPerrett) *lw: nvr bttr than mid-div* **25/1**
20-5 **14** *11* **Heisse**[14] 1124 4-9-7 **97** ........ JPMurtagh 8 63
(DRLoder) *lw: a in rr and n.d* **12/1**
621- **15** *1 1/4* **Bid For Fame (USA)**[123] 6156 7-9-0 **86** ........ WRyan 15 50
(NTinkler) *bhd most of way* **25/1**
11-0 **16** *3 1/2* **Snow's Ride**[15] 1112 4-8-5 **81** ........ MartinDwyer 2 41
(WRMuir) *chsd ldrs tl wknd 4f out* **33/1**
0000 **17** *3* **Midshipman**[5] 1272 6-8-3 **75** ........(v) PaulEddery 1 32
(AWCarroll) *t.k.h: bhd fr 1/2-way* **100/1**
606- **18** *1/2* **Gulf (IRE)**[155] 5942 5-9-13 **99** ........ KFallon 3 55
(DRCElsworth) *stdd s and taken to ins rail: bhd: rdn 1/2-way: no rspnse* **12/1**

3m 39.22s (8.86) **Going Correction** +0.75s/f (Yiel)
**WFA** 4 from 5yo+ 4lb **18** Ran SP% **125.1**
Speed ratings: **107,104,103,103,103 99,99,98,95,93 92,92,92,86,85 84,82,82**CSF £35.75 CT £617.05 TOTE £3.40: £1.50, £3.00, £5.30, £3.70; EX 52.20 Trifecta £1028.60 Pool: £2,752.70. 1.90 winning units..
**Owner** H R H Sultan Ahmad Shah **Bred** Mrs Rebecca Philipps **Trained** Newmarket, Suffolk

**FOCUS**
The winner dictated the pace and few got into this from behind. However, the form still looks solid.

**NOTEBOOK**
**Anak Pekan** did not look fully wound up for this return to action. Under a fine ride from Robinson, who dictated a steady pace, he quickened up in the home straight and nothing could ever get to him. Still progressing, he has shown he acts on a fast surface but cut in the ground is ideal.
**Teresa**, who looked fit enough, ran well to finish best of the rest. She has plenty of stamina and had no problem handling this different ground.
**High Point(IRE)**, targeted at this race following a Polytrack campaign, had no problem with this ground and stayed on quite well without threatening the winner.
**Cold Turkey** improved to the tune of 23lb on the All-Weather through the winter and was 7lb higher here than when last running on turf. He was one of the few to get into contention from off the pace, although having arrived on the scene he was eventually found wanting for stamina. There are races to be won on turf with him over a little shorter.
**Hawadeth** was his trainer's first-ever runner on the Flat and had himself not appeared on the level for three years, when trained in Ireland. With the cheekpieces he wore at Cheltenham retained, this was a decent effort.
**Reveillez**, racing from a career-high mark, raced up with the pace before weakening out of contention. His best form is on faster ground and he is worth another chance at this trip on a sound surface.
**Ponderon** beat Anak Pekan two and a half lengths at Doncaster in November and was 6lb worse off today. After chasing that rival, he faded out of the picture in the final furlong and a half.

## 1330 ALANBRAZILRACING.COM EASTER STKS (LISTED RACE) (C&G) 1m (J)
**3:10** (3:11) (A ) 3-Y-O **£17,400** (£6,600; £3,300; £1,500) **Stalls** High

Form RPR
155- **1** **Privy Seal (IRE)**[196] 5208 3-8-11 105 ........ LDettori 3 112
(JHMGosden) *hld up in rr: hdwy 3f out: chsd wnr over 1f out: stl 3l down whn str run ins last: led fnl 100yds: readily* **9/1**
212- **2** *1* **Mutahayya (IRE)**[211] 4870 3-8-8 104 ........ RHills 7 107
(JLDunlop) *trckd ldrs: led over 2f out: drvn 3l clr fnl f: hdd and outpcd fnl 100yds* **3/1**[1]
412- **3** *7* **Psychiatrist**[213] 4814 3-8-8 105 ........ RHughes 6 92
(RHannon) *bit bkwd: led tl hdd over 2f out: sn pushed along: outpcd and no ch appr fnl f* **4/1**[3]
21-1 **4** *1* **Divine Gift**[14] 1123 3-8-8 104 ........ PRobinson 1 90
(MAJarvis) *w ldrs 2f: styd front rnk: rdn over 2f out: sn outpcd and no ch appr fnl f* **10/3**[2]
143- **5** *1 1/4* **Barbajuan (IRE)**[174] 5665 3-8-13 110 ........ JPMurtagh 2 93
(NACallaghan) *in tch: rdn over 2f out: sn btn* **11/2**
11- **6** *2* **Nero's Return (IRE)**[168] 5740 3-8-11 ........ KDalgleish 5 86
(MJohnston) *w ldr 2f: styd prom tl wknd over 2f out* **12/1**

42- 7 1 3/4 **Gravardlax**[190] 5345 3-8-8 ................ KFallon 4 80
(BJMeehan) *bit bkwd: bmpd s and sn pushed along in rr: rdn again 4f out: nvr gng pce to rch ldrs: wknd over 2f out* **10/1**

1m 42.8s (3.18) **Going Correction** +0.60s/f (Yiel) **7** Ran SP% **110.2**
Speed ratings: **108,107,100,99,97 95,94**CSF £33.52 TOTE £11.80: £3.80, £2.40; EX 68.50.
**Owner** Sheikh Mohammed **Bred** A Butler **Trained** Manton, Wilts

**FOCUS**
Possibly a decent renewal of this event, with useful efforts from first two, although the time was slower than the earlier fillies' trial. Once more the action took place up the near side in the home straight.

**NOTEBOOK**
**Privy Seal(IRE)** was found wanting at this trip as a juvenile, but there were no problems in that department here. He went after the leader in the home straight and, although he still had a bit to do entering the final furlong, cut him down to win going away in the end. He looks to have improved from two to three and may go for the Sandown Classic Trial now, but would have to be supplemented if he was to run in the Derby.
**Mutahayya(IRE)** looked fit enough, but was on his toes in the preliminaries. Once going on he soon established what looked a race-winning advantage, only to be mown down in the last half-furlong. He should stay farther than this.
**Psychiatrist**, a winner over this trip at two, represented a yard with a good record in this event. Making the running but not helped by being taken on, he was soon left behind when the favourite collared him.
**Divine Gift** had race-fitness on his side following his Doncaster win, but he was found out in this better company.
**Barbajuan(IRE)** was the best of these at two but was conceding a Group Three penalty for his win in the Solario last August, where he beat Milk It Mick. The only one of this field to hold a Guineas entry, he was disappointing, especially as he is proven on a softish surface.
**Nero's Return(IRE)** raced close to the pace until finding himself quickly shuffled back through the field once into the home straight. The mile ought not have been a problem, but the ground could have been a different matter.
**Gravardlax** became involved in a bumping match leaving the stalls and was always toiling in rear. This was one of those days and he probably deserves another chance.

## 1331 TURFTOURS.COM EBF MAIDEN STKS 5f
3:45 (3:45) (D) 2-Y-O £5,245 (£1,614; £807; £403) **Stalls** High

Form RPR
1 **Prince Charming** 2-9-0 ................ LDettori 2 77+
(JHMGosden) *w'like: lw: s.i.s: sn rcvrd to trck ldrs: chal 1f out: qcknd under hand driving to assert fnl 100yds: readily* **4/6**[1]
03 2 3/4 **Grand Option**[14] 1130 2-9-0 ................ PDobbs 1 74
(BWDuke) *w ldr tl led appr fnl 2f: styd on wl whn rdn fr over 1f out: hdd and no ex fnl 100yds* **6/1**[3]
3 1 3/4 **Earl Of Links (IRE)** 2-9-0 ................ RHughes 3 68
(RHannon) *w'like: s.i.s: sn rcvrd and trckd ldrs: drvn and effrt appr fnl f: nt qckn ins last* **9/2**[2]
4 4 **Art Legend** 2-9-0 ................ SSanders 5 54
(DRCElsworth) *unf: t.k.h: hld up in rr: shkn up and green 2f out: hung lft over 1f out: nvr gng pce to rch ldrs* **7/1**
0 5 1 **Leonalto (IRE)**[5] 1269 2-9-0 ................ KFallon 4 50
(BJMeehan) *slt ld tl hdd appr fnl 2f: wknd appr fnl f* **14/1**

63.68 secs (2.47) **Going Correction** +0.30s/f (Good) **5** Ran SP% **111.6**
Speed ratings: **92,90,88,81,80**CSF £5.34 TOTE £1.70: £1.10, £2.20; EX 5.30.
**Owner** Sheikh Mohammed **Bred** Mrs R D Peacock **Trained** Manton, Wilts

**FOCUS**
A fair maiden for this time of year, with the runner-up the guide to the form. We have not heard the last of the winner.

**NOTEBOOK**
**Prince Charming** ◆, a half-brother to six individual winners, has plenty of speed in his pedigree, but only asserted well inside the final furlong. He should come on for this experience and already looks one of the better early-season juveniles. What used to be the Garter Stakes at Ascot is reportedly the next target.
**Grand Option** had the edge on experience with the winner and ran another solid race. He was only mastered close home and is clearly capable of winning.
**Earl Of Links(IRE)**, a half-brother to two middle-distance winners, showed enough pace to suggest he can win juvenile races before stepping up in trip.
**Art Legend** looked clueless in the early stages and will clearly benefit from the experience. His breeding suggests he will need further in time and he is certainly not one to give up on just yet.
**Leonalto(IRE)**, who made his debut five days previously, helped force the pace in the early stages, but dropped right away.

## 1332 SURREY HERALD SNOWDROP FILLIES' STKS (LISTED RACE) 1m (J)
4:20 (4:20) (A) 4-Y-O+ £17,400 (£6,600; £3,300; £1,500) **Stalls** High

Form RPR
340- 1 **Beneventa**[177] 5589 4-8-9 95 ................ SSanders 7 107
(JLDunlop) *led: drvn and hdd jst ins fnl f: rallied gamely to ld again last strides* **14/1**[3]
245- 2 hd **Soviet Song (IRE)**[196] 5212 4-8-9 114 ................ JPMurtagh 5 106
(JRFanshawe) *hld up in rr: stdy hdwy fr 2f out: led jst ins last: sn rdn: no ex and hdd last strides* **4/11**[1]
422- 3 2 **Monturani (IRE)**[151] 5974 5-8-9 104 ................ DHolland 3 102
(GWragg) *prom: rdn over 2f out: kpt on ins fnl f but nvr gng pce to trble ldrs* **6/1**[2]
3- 4 2 1/2 **Cote Quest (USA)**[148] 6000 4-8-9 ................ MartinDwyer 8 97
(SCWilliams) *trckd wnr: rdn over 2f out: wknd ins fnl f* **33/1**
1151 5 6 **Najaaba (USA)**[24] 1036 4-8-9 78 ................ BReilly 4 84
(MissJFeilden) *bhd: rdn 3f out: nvr gng pce to rch ldrs* **33/1**
300- 6 3 **Dame De Noche**[168] 5747 4-8-9 92 ................ LDettori 2 78
(JGGiven) *chsd ldrs: rdn and effrt over 2f out: sn btn* **14/1**[3]
/65- 7 5 **Almaviva (IRE)**[251] 3814 4-8-9 92 ................ RHughes 1 67
(JNoseda) *bhd: sme hdwy 3f out: n.d and sn rr* **33/1**
0-00 8 5 **La Muette (IRE)**[7] 1245 4-8-9 75 ................ SRighton 6 57
(MAppleby) *lw: rdn 4f out: a bhd* **150/1**

1m 43.11s (3.49) **Going Correction** +0.60s/f (Yiel) **8** Ran SP% **110.4**
Speed ratings: **106,105,103,101,95 92,87,82**CSF £18.67 TOTE £18.00: £3.20, £1.02, £1.30; EX 38.80.
**Owner** R N Khan **Bred** R N And Mrs Khan **Trained** Arundel, W Sussex

**FOCUS**
A good renewal of this fillies' Listed event, but the early pace was not strong, it was the slowest of the three races over the trip, and it paid to be up with the pace. The runner-up was well below her best.

**NOTEBOOK**
**Beneventa**, who looked hard fit, clearly had the run of the race having set a steady gallop and grabbing the stands' rail. However, she was headed inside the final furlong and showed a tremendous attitude to battle back. She stays further than this and should find plenty of opportunities given her versatility.
**Soviet Song(IRE)**, who held her own in the top grade without winning last season, had everything in her favour on her seasonal debut. She looked sure to score when hitting the front after travelling smoothly, but was just outbattled by a fitter rival. However, official figures suggested she had 19lb in hand of the winner and this still has to go down as disappointing.
**Monturani(IRE)**, proven in this grade and on the ground, is becoming quite hard to win with.
**Cote Quest(USA)**, making her debut for current connections having been bought from France, ran as well as could be expected. She can be expected to progress and will surely be one of the flagships for her talented trainer.
**Najaaba(USA)**, who had shown bags of improvement on the All-Weather during the winter, could not handle the step up in class back on turf.
**Dame De Noche**, who was taken quite wide in the early stages, had shown all her best form on faster ground.

## 1333 TURFTOURS.COM H'CAP 6f
4:55 (4:56) (D) (0-85,85) 3-Y-O £5,642 (£1,736; £868; £434) **Stalls** High

Form RPR
16-4 1 **Petardias Magic (IRE)**[42] 913 3-8-13 77 ................ KFallon 11 90
(EJO'Neill) *lw: racd far side: trckd ldrs: led 2f out and overall: drvn out ins last* **5/1**[2]
36-0 2 1 1/2 **Morse (IRE)**[14] 1129 3-9-1 79 ................ JPMurtagh 14 87
(JAOsborne) *racd far side: rdn to chse ldrs fr 1/2-way: chsd wnr fnl f but no imp* **11/1**
420- 3 1 3/4 **Stormy Nature (IRE)**[254] 3728 3-8-12 76 ................ PRobinson 15 79
(PWHarris) *racd far side: led after 2f: hdd 2f out: styd on same pce fnl f* **16/1**
02-1 4 3/4 **Bohola Flyer (IRE)**[7] 1243 3-8-9 73 ................ RHughes 10 74
(RHannon) *racd far side: chsd ldrs: hung lft to stands side fr 3f out: led that gp over 1f out: kpt on but no ch w far side* **12/1**
102- 5 1/2 **Four Amigos (USA)**[156] 5931 3-8-13 77 ................ LDettori 13 76
(JGGiven) *chsd ldrs far side: styd on same pce u.p fr over 1f out* **8/1**[3]
051- 6 1 1/2 **After The Show**[164] 5829 3-8-5 69 ................ MartinDwyer 16 64
(JRJenkins) *led far side 2f: hung lft to stands side fr 3f out: styd front rnk tl outpcd fnl f* **16/1**
410- 7 1/2 **Motu (IRE)**[168] 5751 3-8-13 77 ................ SSanders 12 70
(JLDunlop) *racd far side: chsd ldrs: outpcd fnl f* **9/1**
-043 8 1/2 **Kuringai**[10] 1209 3-8-8 72 ................ OUrbina 2 64
(BWDuke) *racd stands side and pressed ldrs that gp over 4f* **33/1**
530- 9 1 1/4 **Bathwick Bill (USA)**[213] 4814 3-9-7 85 ................ SDrowne 3 73
(BRMillman) *in tch stands side: effrt whn nt clr run on rails over 1f out: swtchd rt: nt rcvr* **40/1**
-314 10 1/2 **Royal Pavillion (IRE)**[5] 1270 3-8-6 70 ................ PaulEddery 4 56
(WJMusson) *chsd ldrs stands side over 4f* **10/1**
-411 11 hd **Eccentric**[15] 1119 3-8-12 76 ................ DHolland 5 62
(AndrewReid) *b: b.hind: chsd ldrs stands side: led that gp 2f out but nt pce of far side: hdd over 1f out and sn wknd* **10/1**
60-0 12 1/2 **Cartronageeraghlad (IRE)**[14] 1129 3-8-9 80 ................ RKeogh(7) 8 64
(JAOsborne) *lw: racd stands side: outpcd fr 1/2-way* **33/1**
210- 13 5 **Alchera**[189] 5371 3-8-11 75 ................ (b) JQuinn 1 44
(RFJohnsonHoughton) *sn led stands side: hdd 2f out: wknd over 1f out* **50/1**
00-5 14 5 **Haydn (USA)**[67] 669 3-9-2 80 ................ JFEgan 9 34
(PWChapple-Hyam) *racd far side: in tch tl wknd over 1f out* **4/1**[1]
510- 15 1 3/4 **Pink Sapphire (IRE)**[211] 4865 3-8-8 72 ................ DaneO'Neill 7 21
(DRCElsworth) *racd fars side: sn outpcd* **25/1**
3221 16 4 **Global Achiever**[43] 906 3-8-8 72 ................ RFfrench 6 9
(GCHChung) *spd stands side 4f* **20/1**

1m 14.46s (1.39) **Going Correction** +0.30s/f (Good) **16** Ran SP% **122.6**
Speed ratings: **102,100,97,96,96 94,93,92,91,90 90,89,82,76,73 68**CSF £54.94 CT £589.69 TOTE £7.50: £1.90, £2.70, £2.80, £2.90; EX 90.00 Place 6 £13.58, Place 5 £10.18.
**Owner** Miss Sarah Diane Warren **Bred** Mountarmstrong Stud **Trained** Newmarket, Suffolk

**FOCUS**
A fair handicap and a clean-sweep for the high-drawn horses, with the first seven home coming from the seven double-figure boxes. The form looks solid enough.

**NOTEBOOK**
**Petardias Magic(IRE)**, back over the right trip on his handicap debut, soon got over to the favoured far-side rail, was prominent throughout and won fairly easily. He had plenty in his favour this time as he was racing off a 7lb lower mark than his All-Weather rating and he looks capable of building on this.
**Morse(IRE)**, down 2lb and with the benefit of a previous run under his belt, had a good draw and ran a decent race. He is probably better suited by a stiffer track.
**Stormy Nature(IRE)**, also well drawn, was making her handicap debut and seasonal reappearance. This was a promising start to the campaign and a drop back to five could see her off the mark.
**Bohola Flyer(IRE)**, a winner of a Polytrack maiden on her seasonal reappearance, did herself no favours by hanging across to the stands' side. She can win a handicap off this mark if the steering can be sorted out. *Official explanation: jockey said filly had hung left-handed*
**Four Amigos(USA)** is at his best over the minimum trip.
**After The Show** was another who threw away any chance he had by hanging over to the stands' side. In the circumstances he did not do too badly. *Official explanation: jockey said colt hung left-handed*
**Bathwick Bill(USA)** is worth rating better than his finishing position as he failed to get a run inside the final two furlongs. *Official explanation: jockey said gelding suffered interference in running*
**Haydn(USA)**, 4lb lower, was disappointing, even allowing for his average draw. He should not be written off yet, though.

T/Plt: £18.30 to a £1 stake. Pool: £87,485.45. 3,472.45 winning tickets. T/Qpdt: £7.30 to a £1 stake. Pool: £3,422.60. 342.40 winning tickets. ST

1334 - 1339a (Foreign Racing) - See Raceform Interactive

# 1314 MUSSELBURGH (R-H)
Sunday, April 11

**OFFICIAL GOING: Good to firm (good in places on straight course; firm in places on round course)**

## 1340 SHARP MINDS BETFAIR MAIDEN STKS 5f
2:40 (2:40) (D) 2-Y-O £4,745 (£1,460; £730; £365) **Stalls** Low

Form RPR
1 **Joseph Henry** 2-9-0 ................ JFanning 7 80
(MJohnston) *trckd ldrs: hdwy hafway: led over 1f out: pushed out* **4/1**[3]
2 4 **Nee Lemon Left** 2-8-2 ................ PPMathers(7) 6 60
(ABerry) *chsd ldrs: hdwy 2f out: swtchd rt and rdn over 1f out: kpt on ins last* **50/1**
3 1/2 **Monsieur Mirasol** 2-9-0 ................ NCallan 4 63
(KARyan) *dwlt and towards rr: hdwy 1/2-way: swtchd rt and rdn over 1f out: kpt on wl fnl f: nrst fin* **10/1**
3 4 shd **Tiviski (IRE)**[15] 1128 2-8-9 ................ WSupple 5 58
(EJAlston) *cl up: ev ch 2f out: sn rdn and wknd appr last* **2/1**[1]

4 **5** *1* **Next Time (IRE)**[15] [1128] 2-8-9 .... DHolland 1 54
(MJPolglase) *led: rdn along 2f out: hdd over 1f out and wknd ins last* **10/3**[2]

**6** *nk* **City Torque (USA)** 2-8-2 .... PMakin(7) 3 53
(TDBarron) *prom: rdn along over 2f out: grad wknd* **16/1**

3 **7** *6* **Procrastinate (IRE)**[8] [1248] 2-9-0 .... LDettori 8 37
(RFFisher) *dwlt: sn outpcd and a rr* **6/1**

61.21 secs (1.81) **Going Correction** +0.125s/f (Good) **7** Ran SP% **107.6**
Speed ratings: **90,83,82,82,81 80,70**CSF £123.42 TOTE £4.50: £2.40, £3.70; EX 108.60.
**Owner** John Brown & Megan Dennis **Bred** John Brown & Megan Dennis **Trained** Middleham Moor, N Yorks

**FOCUS**
The proximity of those with previous experience indicated the form of the placed horses downwards was nothing special, but the winner looks above average and the type to improve again. The whole field raced towards the stands' side and the gallop was fair.

**NOTEBOOK**
**Joseph Henry ◆**, out of a five-furlong winner, is from a stable that has been among the winners and, despite getting fractious beforehand, he created a very favourable impression on this racecourse debut. He looks a typical sort from this stable in that he is open to bags of improvement and is one to keep on the right side. He should prove equally effective over six furlongs.
**Nee Lemon Left**, nearly the youngest in the field, has speed in her pedigree and shaped well without posing any threat to the ready winner. She is entitled to come on for this experience and is capable of picking up a small event.
**Monsieur Mirasol**, who has a mixture of speed and stamina in his pedigree, shaped creditably, despite his obvious experience, and is the sort to be placed to best advantage by his shrewd handler in due course.
**Tiviski(IRE)** was a bit disappointing in view of her encouraging Doncaster debut run and, although not disgraced, may prove better suited by six furlongs in due course.
**Next Time(IRE)** had the run of the race and got a bit closer to Tiviski than she had done on her debut at Doncaster last month. She was the youngest in this field and may be capable of a bit better in due course.
**City Torque(USA)**, the first foal of an unraced half-sister to smart middle-distance performer Santillana, was easy to back and only hinted at ability on this racecourse debut but is likely to leave this form behind over further in due course.
**Procrastinate(IRE)**, on much faster ground than on his debut, had the services of Frankie Dettori but showed precious little this time.

## 1341 SHARP MINDS WINNERS WELCOME H'CAP 1m 6f
**3:10** (3:10) (E) (0-70,70) 3-Y-0+ **£4,065** (£1,251; £625; £312) **Stalls** High

Form RPR
400- **1** **Tandava (IRE)**[155] [5949] 6-10-0 **70** .... GDuffield 4 78
(ISemple) *set stdy pce: qcknd 4f out: pushed along and qcknd over 2f out: rdn wl over 1f out: drvn and styd on wl fnl f* **10/1**

3540 **2** *½* **Toni Alcala**[8] [1245] 5-9-4 **63** .... LFletcher(3) 6 70
(RFFisher) *trckd ldrs: hdwy 3f out: rdn 2f out: drvn and kpt on fnl f* **7/1**

40-0 **3** *1* **Spitting Image (IRE)**[11] [1198] 4-9-3 **62** .... ACulhane 9 68
(MrsMReveley) *trckd wnr: pushed along 3f out: edgd lft and rdn 2f out: sn drvn and kpt on fnl f* **10/1**

2234 **4** *nk* **Jadeeron**[11] [1210] 5-9-9 **65** .... (p) DHolland 1 70
(MissDAMchale) *trckd ldrs on inner:lost pl bnd 5f out: hdwy 3f out: nt clr run 2f out: swtchd lft and rdn ent last: kpt on: nrst fin* **10/3**[1]

40-0 **5** *hd* **Gargoyle Girl**[30] [693] 7-8-10 **52** .... (p) WSupple 3 57
(JSGoldie) *trckd ldrs: hdwy to chse wnr over 4f out: chal over 2f out: sn rdn and ev ch tl drvn and wknd ent last* **11/2**[2]

506- **6** *1¾* **Tbm Can**[185] [5463] 5-9-2 **65** .... BSwarbrick(7) 7 67
(WMBrisbourne) *hld up in rr: hdwy 3f out: sn rdn: kpt on appr last: nrst fin* **6/1**[3]

-600 **7** *5* **Fiddlers Creek (IRE)**[13] [1172] 5-9-1 **57** .... (t) RWinston 5 52
(RAllan) *hld up towards rr: effrt and hdwy 3f out: rdn and one pce fnl 2f* **10/1**

00-0 **8** *6* **Bridewell (USA)**[28] [1026] 5-7-12 **40** .... RFfrench 8 27
(FWatson) *prom: rdn along over 4f out: sn wknd* **66/1**

-005 **9** *5* **Majlis (IRE)**[23] [1054] 7-9-12 **68** .... EAhern 2 48
(RMHCowell) *hld up: hdwy 4f out: rdn over 2f out: sn btn* **6/1**[3]

060- **10** *21* **Howards Dream (IRE)**[195] [5274] 6-7-12 **40** .... (t) PFessey 10 —
(DANolan) *a rr* **33/1**

3m 8.06s (2.46) **Going Correction** +0.30s/f (Good)
**WFA** 4 from 5yo+ 3lb **10** Ran SP% **111.2**
Speed ratings: **104,103,103,102,102 101,99,95,92,80**CSF £74.29 CT £699.89 TOTE £11.40: £2.70, £3.40, £3.10; EX 206.60.
**Owner** Woodspeen Sport & Leisure **Bred** Newberry Stud Company **Trained** Carluke, S Lanarks

**FOCUS**
A modest handicap on paper but a dubious-looking race as a form guide as Tandava was allowed to dictate his own pace and, given his record, he would be no certainty to confirm this effort from a higher mark next time. Those held up were at a disadvantage.

**NOTEBOOK**
**Tandava(IRE)**, with the visor left off for this reappearance run, was allowed the run of the race but showed the right attitude in the closing stages. This is a dubious form guide though and, given his record, he would be no certainty to confirm this from a higher mark next time.
**Toni Alcala**, who got bogged down in heavy ground last time, was wisely ridden close to the steady pace and elected to put his best foot forward. This is arguably his best trip but his inconsistency and the fact that this bare form may flatter him means he is not one to lump on next time.
**Spitting Image(IRE)** had the run of the race and was not disgraced in terms of form but left the impression that a much stiffer test of stamina over this trip would have been in her favour. She looks worth another try over two miles and may be capable of picking up a small race in the North.
**Jadeeron** has proved most consistent on sand and on turf and looks a bit better than this bare form as he was in a most unpromising position when the tempo increased and he is one to keep an eye on in similar company when a stronger gallop is likely.
**Gargoyle Girl** has a good record at this course and, although having the run of the race, returned to form, despite racing freely. She is another that will be suited by a stronger gallop and she is capable of winning another race from this mark.
**Tbm Can** confirmed he retains most of his ability on this first start since October and is better than the bare form as this race suited those that raced close to the pace. A strong pace suits him ideally and he is one to keep an eye on in races where that looks likely.
**Fiddlers Creek(IRE)**, tried in a first-time tongue-tie, did not have the race run to suit, but has become a bit disappointing and did not really show enough to suggest he will be of interest in the near future.

## 1342 SHARP MINDS BETFAIR: BET IN RUNNING MAIDEN STKS 7f 30y
**3:40** (3:42) (D) 3-Y-0+ **£4,862** (£1,496; £748; £374) **Stalls** Low

Form RPR
0-23 **1** **Finders Keepers**[11] [1202] 3-8-8 **80** .... LDettori 6 81+
(EALDunlop) *v free and sn led: mde virtually all: rdn wl over 1f out: styd on* **1/1**[1]

5- **2** *2* **Never Will**[184] [5470] 3-8-8 .... KDalgleish 12 72+
(MJohnston) *chsd ldng pair: wd st: hdwy to chal 2f out and ev ch tl rdn: wandered and one pce appr last* **7/1**[3]

0-02 **3** *6* **Luke After Me (IRE)**[11] [1197] 4-9-8 **51** .... RWinston 4 56
(GASwinbank) *s.i.s and bhd: hdwy over 2f out: kpt on fnl f: nrst fin* **10/1**

450- **4** *1* **One 'N' Only (IRE)**[176] [5632] 3-8-3 **57** .... PHanagan 10 48
(MissLAPerratt) *midfield: rdn along 1/2-way: kpt on u.p fnl 2f: nrst fin* **40/1**

005- **5** *¾* **East Riding**[234] [4315] 4-9-3 **50** .... AnnStokell 11 46
(MissAStokell) *in tch: rdn along 3f out: wknd fnl 2f* **33/1**

0-60 **6** *1½* **Frimley's Mattery**[47] [877] 4-9-3 **45** .... PMulrennan(5) 3 47
(REBarr) *chsd ldrs: rdn over 3f out: sn wknd* **100/1**

56- **7** *2½* **Colloseum**[158] [5923] 3-8-8 .... DHolland 9 40
(TJEtherington) *bhd tl styd on fnl 2f* **40/1**

3- **8** *1* **Pass Go**[123] [6159] 3-8-8 .... EAhern 5 38
(GAButler) *chsd wnr: rdn along 3f out: sn wknd* **3/1**[2]

000- **9** *shd* **Constable Burton**[172] [5700] 3-8-8 .... GDuffield 1 38
(MrsADuffield) *a rr* **66/1**

**10** *½* **Clouds Of Gold (IRE)** 3-8-3 .... DRMcCabe 13 31
(JSWainwright) *v.s.a: a rr* **100/1**

006- **11** *8* **Environmentalist**[202] [5130] 5-9-5 **58** .... (t) DAllan(3) 2 15
(DANolan) *chsd ldrs: rdn and wknd 3f out* **66/1**

**12** *20* **Casey's House** 4-8-12 .... TEaves(5) 7 —
(FWatson) *s.i.s: a bhd* **100/1**

50- **13** *nk* **Musiotal**[206] [5010] 3-8-8 .... WSupple 8 —
(JSGoldie) *a bhd* **100/1**

1m 30.66s (1.13) **Going Correction** +0.30s/f (Good)
**WFA** 3 from 4yo+ 14lb **13** Ran SP% **111.4**
Speed ratings: **105,102,95,94,93 92,89,88,88,87 78,55,55**CSF £7.59 TOTE £2.00: £1.02, £2.50, £2.10; EX 12.70.
**Owner** Maktoum Al Maktoum **Bred** Gainsborough Stud Management Ltd **Trained** Newmarket, Suffolk

**FOCUS**
An uncompetitive maiden and, with Pass Go disappointing on this turf debut, this race did not take as much winning as had seemed likely, and moderate horses in third to sixth places set the level of the form. Fair performances from the first two who were clear, although form choice Finders Keepers had the run of the race and may not be easy to place successfully from a mark of 80 in handicap company.

**NOTEBOOK**
**Finders Keepers** again raced keenly but had the run of the race and, with his main market rival disappointing on his turf debut, was faced with a straightforward task. However life will be tougher in handicaps from his current rating of 80 and he will have to settle better if he is to follow up in competitive company next time.
**Never Will** fared better on this reappearance run than on his debut at York last year over this longer trip and is the type to improve again for current connections. He can pick up a small race race on this evidence.
**Luke After Me(IRE)**, placed in a Catterick seller last time, looked up against it in this company but attracted support and ran creditably, faring the best of those that came from off the pace. However he is likely to be seen to best effect back in handicap company.
**One 'N' Only(IRE)** was not totally disgraced on this reappearance outing but is exposed as modest and is another that will continue to look vulnerable in this grade.
**East Riding** was not totally disgraced on this first start for nearly eight months but is another that is exposed as modest and it will be a poor race in this grade she wins.
**Frimley's Mattery** has proved most disappointing and will invariably be one to field against in this company.
**Pass Go**, up to what had looked on pedigree a more suitable trip for this turf debut, failed to settle and proved most disappointing. He has ability but looks one to avoid taking a short price about from now on. *Official explanation: trainer had no explanation for the poor form shown*
**Constable Burton** *Official explanation: jockey said gelding right-handed all the way up the home straight*

## 1343 SHARP MINDS BETFAIR H'CAP 5f
**4:10** (4:12) (C) (0-100,95) 3-Y-0+ **£13,754** (£4,232; £2,116; £1,058) **Stalls** Low

Form RPR
-012 **1** **Magic Glade**[11] [1205] 5-8-6 **78** .... RThomas(5) 2 94
(CRDore) *trckd ldrs stands side: smooth hdwy over 1f out: rdn ent last and qcknd wl to ld last 100 yds* **4/1**[1]

0-11 **2** *1½* **Maktavish**[16] [1113] 5-9-0 **81** .... (p) PHanagan 11 91
(ISemple) *overall ldr far side: rdn over 1f out: hdd and nt qckn last 100 yds* **7/1**[2]

04-0 **3** *1¼* **Sierra Vista**[16] [1113] 4-8-7 **77** .... (p) LEnstone(3) 4 82
(DWBarker) *cl up stands side: ev ch over 1f out: sn rdn and one pce ins last* **12/1**

600- **4** *nk* **Viewforth**[160] [5908] 6-8-11 **78** .... (b) RWinston 5 82
(ISemple) *chsd ldrs stands side: hdwy over 1f out: sn rdn and kpt on towards fin* **20/1**

062- **5** *nk* **Chairman Bobby**[184] [5472] 6-7-10 **70** .... RoryMoore(7) 7 73
(DWBarker) *cl up stands side: rdn wewll over 1f out: drvn and one pce ent last* **20/1**

20-0 **6** *nk* **Cape Royal**[16] [1113] 4-9-1 **82** .... DHolland 8 83
(MrsJRRamsden) *trckd ldrs stands side: effrt and swtchd rt over 1f out: sn rdn: hung rt and one pce* **4/1**[1]

00-5 **7** *nk* **River Falcon**[16] [1113] 4-8-12 **79** .... WSupple 12 79
(JSGoldie) *chsd ldrs far side: rdn over 1f out: kpt on same pce* **16/1**

01-0 **8** *2½* **Ptarmigan Ridge**[16] [1113] 8-9-3 **84** .... JCarroll 3 74
(MissLAPerratt) *in tch stands side: effrt whn carried rt over 1f out: sn rdn and wknd* **33/1**

000- **9** *1¾* **Obe One**[160] [5909] 4-8-3 **77** .... PPMathers(7) 16 60
(ABerry) *chsd ldrs far side: rdn along 2f out: grad wknd* **50/1**

2110 **10** *shd* **No Time (IRE)**[16] [1113] 4-10-0 **95** .... LDettori 9 78
(MJPolglase) *led stands side gp: rdn along 2f out: wknd appr last* **10/1**

054- **11** *1½* **Inter Vision (USA)**[169] [5743] 4-9-4 **88** .... ABeech(3) 1 65
(ADickman) *racd stands side: n.d* **20/1**

000- **12** *1* **Beyond The Clouds (IRE)**[169] [5743] 8-9-1 **82** .... DRMcCabe 6 55
(JSWainwright) *in tch centre: rdn along 1/2-way: sn btn* **33/1**

011- **13** *1¼* **Peters Choice**[142] [6037] 3-8-1 **79** .... PFessey 13 47
(ISemple) *chsd ldrs far side: rdn along 2f out: sn wknd* **25/1**

/0-0 **14** *1¼* **Get Stuck In (IRE)**[13] [1175] 8-8-2 **69** .... RFfrench 10 32
(MissLAPerratt) *chsd ldrs stands side: rdn along 1/2-way and sn wknd* **100/1**

160- **15** *hd* **Seafield Towers**[205] [5030] 4-8-11 **78** .... (p) KDalgleish 14 40
(MissLAPerratt) *racd far side: bhd fr 1/2-way* **50/1**

0-03 **16** 1 1/4 **Piccled**[16] 1113 6-8-11 **78** ........ EAhern 15 35
(EJAlston) *chsd ldr far side: rdn 2f out: wknd over 1f out* **8/1**[3]

59.56 secs (-0.84) **Going Correction** +0.125s/f (Good)
**WFA** 3 from 4yo+ 11lb **16** Ran SP% **115.2**
Speed ratings: **111,108,106,106,105 105,104,100,97,97 95,93,91,89,89 87**CSF £25.07 CT £321.00 TOTE £5.90: £2.00, £1.90, £2.10, £3.60; EX 46.80 Trifecta £346.90 Pool of £1,905.55 - 3.90 winning units..
**Owner** P O'Gorman **Bred** Juddmonte Farms **Trained** West Pinchbeck, Lincs
■ Stewards Enquiry : D Holland one-day ban: careless riding (Apr 22)

**FOCUS**
A decent, competitive handicap run at a strong pace in a fast time. The bulk of the runners, including the winner came up the stands' side but the proximity of runner-up Maktavish showed there was no disadvantage in racing on the far side. The form should work out and the winner can hold his own in better company on this evidence and is one to keep on the right side.

**NOTEBOOK**
**Magic Glade**, an improved performer on All-Weather surfaces this winter, turned in his best effort yet back in trip and again caught the eye with the way he went through the race. He showed a bright turn of foot to win going away and looks the sort to be able to hold his own in better handicap company. He is still relatively lightly raced and remains one to keep on the right side.
**Maktavish** showed blistering speed on the far side and fully confirmed his Doncaster run from this 5lb higher mark. He has not proved entirely reliable on the Flat and may be vulnerable to progressive sorts but is more than capable of winning again from this mark in the near future.
**Sierra Vista**, poorly drawn on her reappearance at Doncaster, was better berthed this time and got much closer to Maktavish. Although she has not won for some time, she may be capable of picking up a small event from this mark.
**Viewforth** proved easy to back for this reappearance outing but shaped as though retaining most of his ability and is entitled to come on for the run. He goes on any ground and looks the type to pick up a decent handicap this term, especially granted a stiffer test of stamina.
**Chairman Bobby**, a tough and progressive sort last year, shaped creditably on this reappearance run under suitable conditions but does look vulnerable to progressive or well handicapped sorts from this mark.
**Cape Royal**, from a family that do well with age, is capable of winning from this mark when things go his way, but once again looked a less than easy ride and he may not be one to be taking too short a price about in this sort of company.
**River Falcon** ◆ shaped really well considering five furlongs at a sharp course on quick ground is probably too much of a test of speed for him and, although he is high enough in the weights at present, appeals as the type to win a fair handicap this term with more cut in the ground over this trip or over six furlongs.
**Piccled** was a long way below his Doncaster run and, as he is proven on fast ground and his draw can not really be forwarded as an excuse for defeat, there were no obvious reasons for this below-par effort. *Official explanation: jockey said gelding lost its action*

## 1344 SHARP MINDS PHONE 0870 90 80 121 MAIDEN STKS — 1m 4f
4:40 (4:40) (D) 3-Y-O+ **£4,735** (£1,457; £728; £364) **Stalls** High

| Form | | | | RPR |
|---|---|---|---|---|
| 2 | **1** | | **Gran Dana (IRE)**[10] 1221 4-9-12 ........ JFanning 7 | 69+ |
| | | | (MJohnston) *led: hdd over 4f out and sn pushed along: rdn 3f out and sn led again: drvn over 1f out and kpt on wl* **8/11**[1] | |
| 32-2 | **2** | 3/4 | **Golden Empire (USA)**[15] 1138 3-8-6 78 ........ (v[1]) WSupple 4 | 68+ |
| | | | (EALDunlop) *cl up: led over 4f out: rdn and hdd wl over 2f out: ev ch tl drvn: put hd in air and nt run on fnl f* **9/4**[2] | |
| 6232 | **3** | 5 | **Next Flight (IRE)**[28] 1023 5-9-13 45 ........ DHolland 2 | 60 |
| | | | (REBarr) *chsd ldng pair: rdn along over 3f out: kpt on same pce* **16/1**[3] | |
| 06 | **4** | 5 | **Stage Two (IRE)**[13] 1179 3-8-6 ........ KDalgleish 1 | 52+ |
| | | | (MJohnston) *chsd ldrs: rdn along over 3f out: drvn and no imp fnl 2f* **16/1**[3] | |
| 40-4 | **5** | 3 | **Valiant Air (IRE)**[13] 1179 3-8-6 55 ........ (v[1]) PHanagan 5 | 47 |
| | | | (JRWeymes) *nvr a factor* **50/1** | |
| | **6** | 1/2 | **Illicium (IRE)**[14] 5-9-8 ........ ACulhane 9 | 41 |
| | | | (MrsMReveley) *s.i.s: a rr* **20/1** | |
| | **7** | 13 | **Stravonian** 4-9-12 ........ DMcGaffin 10 | 26 |
| | | | (DANolan) *s.i.s: a rr* **33/1** | |
| | **8** | 1 | **Archenko**[29] 4-9-5 ........ PPMathers[(7)] 3 | 24 |
| | | | (ABerry) *in tch: rdn along 1/2-way: sn outpcd* **66/1** | |
| 620- | **9** | 16 | **Eyes Dont Lie (IRE)**[223] 4622 6-9-13 35 ........ PFessey 6 | — |
| | | | (DANolan) *a rr: bhd fr 1/2-way* **66/1** | |

2m 40.16s (2.14) **Going Correction** +0.30s/f (Good)
**WFA** 3 from 4yo 21lb 4 from 5yo+ 1lb **9** Ran SP% **113.1**
Speed ratings: **104,103,100,96,94 94,85,85,74**CSF £2.21 TOTE £1.60: £1.10, £1.30, £2.10; EX 3.00.
**Owner** Mrs I Bird **Bred** Grangemore Stud **Trained** Middleham Moor, N Yorks
■ Stewards Enquiry : P P Mathers caution: allowed gelding to coast home with no assistance from the saddle

**FOCUS**
Only two serious players in this otherwise modest event and, although the pair occupied the first two placings, the proximity of 45-rated Next Flight holds the form down. The winner is in good hands and open to improvement and is likely to win more races. The overall gallop was only fair.

**NOTEBOOK**
**Gran Dana(IRE)** did not have to improve on his debut effort to win an ordinary event in workmanlike fashion. However he is in very good hands and is open to plenty of improvement so it would be no surprise to see him build on this in handicap company.
**Golden Empire(USA)**, up in trip for this return to turf, was not disgraced, despite again being below his best, but left the impression that he was not giving it his best shot and, while he looks capable of winning a modest race in this grade, does not look one to be lumping on at short odds.
**Next Flight(IRE)** faced a stiff task at these weights back on turf but again ran creditably. However his best chance of success surely lies in low-grade handicap company around this trip.
**Stage Two(IRE)** showed his first worthwhile form on this turf debut but he will continue to look vulnerable on that evidence in this company. Modest handicaps and a step up in trip may well be the answer.
**Valiant Air(IRE)**, tried in a visor, again showed little and will continue to look vulnerable in this grade.
**Illicium(IRE)**, who has only hinted at ability in bumpers, offered little on this Flat debut and low-grade handicaps in due course will offer her best chance of success.

## 1345 SHARP MINDS BETFAIR: BACK AND LAY H'CAP — 7f 30y
5:10 (5:11) (D) (0-85,83) 3-Y-O+ **£6,825** (£2,100; £1,050; £525) **Stalls** Low

| Form | | | | RPR |
|---|---|---|---|---|
| 005- | **1** | | **Kirkby's Treasure**[148] 6006 6-7-13 55 ........ PHanagan 3 | 64 |
| | | | (ABerry) *hld up and bhd: gd hdwy 3f out: effrt and edgd lft 2f out: rdn to ld over 1f out: hung lft ins last: drvn out* **33/1** | |
| -423 | **2** | 3/4 | **Sarraaf (IRE)**[3] 1315 8-9-1 71 ........ NCallan 5 | 78 |
| | | | (ISemple) *hld up in tch: hdwy 3f out: rdn over 1f out: styng on whn hmpd ins last: drvn and kpt on to take 2nd nr line* **5/1**[3] | |
| 33-3 | **3** | shd | **Highland Warrior**[13] 1175 5-8-7 63 ........ WSupple 10 | 70 |
| | | | (JSGoldie) *hld up in rr: hdwy 1/2-way: effrt 2f out: sn rdn and ev ch over 1f out: nt qckn ins last* **7/2**[1] | |
| -006 | **4** | 4 | **Beauteous (IRE)**[42] 934 5-8-9 65 ........ LDettori 8 | 61 |
| | | | (MJPolglase) *cl up: effrt and ev ch over 2f out: rdn and wknd appr last* **4/1**[2] | |
| 05-0 | **5** | 1 | **Sea Storm (IRE)**[11] 1199 6-9-13 83 ........ (p) DHolland 2 | 76 |
| | | | (DRMacleod) *hld up and bhd: hdwy 3f out: rdn and kpt on fnl 2f: nrst fin* **10/1** | |
| 03-0 | **6** | 1/2 | **H Harrison (IRE)**[11] 1199 4-9-5 82 ........ PPMathers[(7)] 13 | 74 |
| | | | (IWMcinnes) *chsd ldrs: hdwy on outer 3f out: rdn 2f out and ev ch tl drvn: edgd lft and wknd appr last* **14/1** | |
| 0060 | **7** | 1/2 | **Flying Treaty (USA)**[11] 1199 7-8-7 63 ........ AnnStokell 7 | 54 |
| | | | (MissAStokell) *chsd ldrs: rdn along 3f out: sn btn* **25/1** | |
| 4502 | **8** | shd | **Malahide Express (IRE)**[39] 954 4-8-1 60 ow3 ........ DAllan[(3)] 6 | 50 |
| | | | (EJAlston) *led: rdn along 3f out: hdd & wknd over 1f out* **20/1** | |
| 500- | **9** | 3 | **The Gambler**[139] 6057 4-7-6 55 ........ (p) DFentiman[(7)] 14 | 37 |
| | | | (PaulJohnson) *a rr* **50/1** | |
| 025- | **10** | 3 | **Anthemion (IRE)**[209] 4942 7-8-6 62 ........ DMcGaffin 9 | 36 |
| | | | (MrsJCMcgregor) *bhd fr 1/2-way* **40/1** | |
| 154- | **11** | 1 1/2 | **Ballyhurry (USA)**[169] 5747 7-8-11 74 ........ JCurrie[(7)] 12 | 44 |
| | | | (JSGoldie) *hld up in rr: effrt and sme hdwy 3f out: sn rdn and btn* **10/1** | |
| 600- | **12** | 1 3/4 | **Desert Arc (IRE)**[172] 5702 6-8-2 58 ow1 ........ GDuffield 11 | 23 |
| | | | (WMBrisbourne) *trckd ldrs: effrt 3f out and sn ev ch: rdn 2f out and sn wknd* **16/1** | |
| 215- | **13** | 5 | **True Night**[204] 5059 7-9-10 80 ........ ANicholls 4 | 32 |
| | | | (DNicholls) *a rr* **10/1** | |

1m 30.78s (1.25) **Going Correction** +0.30s/f (Good) **13** Ran SP% **114.7**
Speed ratings: **104,103,103,98,97 96,96,96,92,89 87,85,79**CSF £177.46 CT £763.75 TOTE £21.80: £4.70, £1.70, £2.20; EX 214.10 Place 6 £171.91, Place 5 £23.24.
**Owner** Kirkby Lonsdale Racing **Bred** Mrs J M Berry **Trained** Cockerham, Lancs

**FOCUS**
A run-of-the-mill handicap contested by mainly exposed horses and one in which the pace seemed sound. However consistency has never been the winner's strongest suit and it remains to be seen whether this will be reproduced next time.

**NOTEBOOK**
**Kirkby's Treasure**, whose previous wins had been with cut in the ground, had the race run to suit and elected to put his best foot forward, despite edging off a true line, to win an ordinary handicap. However he has not always proved consistent and may not be one to lump on at shortish odds next time.
**Sarraaf(IRE)** has his quirks but is a capable performer when things go his way and, after getting the decent pace he seems to need, elected to give it his best shot. He is capable of winning again from this mark but is another that would not be one to lump on next time, though.
**Highland Warrior** confirmed his reappearance promise and, although effective over this trip on a sound surface, gives the impression that a strongly-run race with cut in the ground over six may be his ideal requirements.
**Beauteous(IRE)**, having his first run for Mark Polglase, was not disgraced and may be a bit better than the bare form as he fared the best of those that raced up with the decent gallop. He can win again when getting his own way in front.
**Sea Storm(IRE)**, with the cheekpieces back on, was not disgraced from his wide draw, especially as he usually races close to the pace. He has slipped to a fair mark for his current stable.
**H Harrison(IRE)** fared a good deal better than on his reappearance but, although he may be a bit better than the bare form, may have to drop in the weights a few pounds before he returns to winning ways.
T/Jkpt: Not won. T/Plt: £170.50 to a £1 stake. Pool: £57,685.15. 246.95 winning tickets. T/Qpdt: £4.70 to a £1 stake. Pool: £3,623.70. 569.85 winning tickets. JR

1346 - 1349a (Foreign Racing) - See Raceform Interactive

# [1260]LONGCHAMP (R-H)
Sunday, April 11

**OFFICIAL GOING: Good to soft**

## 1350a PRIX NOAILLES (GROUP 2) (3YO COLTS & FILLIES) — 1m 3f
2:45 (2:46) 3-Y-O **£42,148** (£16,268; £7,764; £3,882)

| | | | RPR |
|---|---|---|---|
| **1** | | **Voix Du Nord (FR)**[155] 5962 3-9-2 ........ CSoumillon 2 | 112 |
| | | (DSmaga, France) *disputed 3rd, 3rd straight, pushed along to lead over 1 1/2f out, driven clear over 1f out, readily* 1 | |
| **2** | 3 | **Cherry Mix (FR)**[24] 1049 3-9-2 ........ GaryStevens 4 | 107 |
| | | (AFabre, France) *raced in 7th, disputing 6th straight, pushed along 1 1/2f out, stayed on under pressure from over 1f out to take 2nd close* | |
| **3** | snk | **Fast And Furious (FR)**[36] 3-9-2 ........ IMendizabal 9 | 107 |
| | | (J-CRouget, France) *held up in 8th, driven along entering straight, not much room over 1f out, stayed on down outside final f, nearest finish* 2 | |
| **4** | shd | **Marnhac (FR)**[24] 1049 3-9-2 ........ C-PLemaire 1 | 107 |
| | | (PKhozian, France) *raced in 5th, disputing 3rd on inside straight, pushed along 2f out, disputing 2nd 1f out, stayed on* | |
| **4** | dht | **Young Tiger (FR)** 3-9-2 ........ OPeslier 3 | 107 |
| | | (FRohaut, France) *raced in 6th, disputing 6th straight, pushed along over 1 1/2f out, ridden to take 2nd just inside final f, no extra final* | |
| **6** | 2 1/2 | **Malevitch (IRE)**[138] 3-9-2 ........ DBoeuf 6 | 103 |
| | | (ELellouche, France) *disputed 3rd, disputing 4th straight, pushed along over 1 1/2f out, one pace* 3 | |
| **7** | 3 | **Kensington (GER)**[24] 1049 3-9-2 ........ (b) ELegrix 8 | 98 |
| | | (AJunk, France) *led after 1f, went 4 lengths clear after 3f, joined straight, headed over 1 1/2f out, weakened* | |
| **8** | 6 | **Nite Trippa (FR)**[12] 3-9-2 ........ TJarnet 7 | 88 |
| | | (RobertCollet, France) *raced in last, never a factor* | |
| **9** | snk | **Alcinos (FR)**[131] 3-9-2 ........ (b) SPasquier 5 | 88 |
| | | (DSmaga, France) *led 1f, raced in 2nd, pushed along to dispute lead entering straight, soon driven and weakened* 1 | |

2m 17.47s **Going Correction** -0.10s/f (Good) **9** Ran SP% **167.8**
Speed ratings: **113,110,110,110,110 108,106,102,102.**
**Owner** Baron T Van Zuylen De Nyevelt **Bred** Baron Thierry Van Zuylen De Nyevelt **Trained** France

**NOTEBOOK**
**Voix Du Nord(FR)** put up a faultless performance and was certain of victory by the furlong marker. Tucked in behind the leaders early on, he came to the fore one and a half out before striding out well to the line. He has quite clearly trained on could well make his mark at the highest level. His next target is the Prix Lupin as a prelude to the Prix du Jockey-Club.
**Cherry Mix(FR)** was a bit free early on and never really threatened the winner when it mattered. This was, however, still a promising run.
**Fast And Furious(FR)**, slightly hampered at the furlong marker, finished fastest of all. The jockey reported that he still has plenty to learn and he could now go for the Prix Hocquart.
**Young Tiger(FR)** came with a promising run from one and a half out and held second place until well inside the final furlong.
**Marnhac(FR)** still had plenty to do at the two-furlong marker and only made late progress to share fourth place on the line.

1351 - (Foreign Racing) - See Raceform Interactive

## [1327]KEMPTON (R-H)

Monday, April 12

**OFFICIAL GOING: Good to soft (good in places)**

## 1352 STPP MAIDEN STKS 7f (J)

**2:10** (2:11) (D) 3-Y-0+ **£5,590** (£1,720; £860; £430) **Stalls** High

| Form | | | | RPR |
|---|---|---|---|---|
| 04- | 1 | | **Poule De Luxe (IRE)**[252] 3844 3-8-6 ........ TQuinn 14<br>*(JLDunlop) lw: chsd ldrs: pushed along 3f out: chal over 1f out: led ins last: drvn out* **6/1**[2] | 69 |
| 0/60 | 2 | *nk* | **Hallings Overture (USA)**[20] 1085 5-9-11 60 ........ RHills 4<br>*(CAHorgan) trckd ldrs: led over 2f out: sn drvn: hdd ins fnl f: kpt on wl: no ex cl home* **16/1** | 73 |
| | 3 | *1 1/4* | **Kauri Forest (USA)** 3-8-11 ........ LDettori 8<br>*(JRFanshawe) str: scope: lw: in tch: chsd ldrs fr 1/2-way: rdn 2f out: nt qckn fnl f* **10/3**[1] | 70 |
| 36- | 4 | *1/2* | **Evaluator (IRE)**[151] 5984 3-8-11 ........ KDarley 5<br>*(TGMills) swtg: t.k.h: chsd ldrs: rdn over 2f out: styd on one pce ins fnl f* **8/1** | 69 |
| 43- | 5 | *1 1/2* | **Day To Remember**[205] 5078 3-8-11 ........ PMcCabe 12<br>*(ACStewart) hld up in rr: gd hdwy fr 2f out: shkn up to trck ldrs over 1f out: nt qckn ins last and eased cl home* **13/2**[3] | 69+ |
| | 6 | *1 1/4* | **Keyaki (IRE)** 3-8-6 ........ RMullen 11<br>*(CFWall) leggy: s.i.s: bhd: hdwy fr 2f out: kpt on wl fnl f: nt rch ldrs* **40/1** | 57 |
| 403/ | 7 | *2 1/2* | **El Chaparral (IRE)**[523] 5639 4-9-4 ........ MHoward(7) 17<br>*(DKIvory) chsd ldrs: rdn over 2f out: wknd fnl f* **25/1** | 56 |
| 6- | 8 | *3/4* | **Dr Synn**[156] 5947 3-8-11 ........ PDoe 13<br>*(JAkehurst) bhd: rdn over 2f out: kpt on fr over 1f out: nt trble ldrs* **14/1** | 54 |
| 00- | 9 | *1/2* | **Planters Punch (IRE)**[170] 5757 3-8-11 ........ KFallon 9<br>*(RHannon) bhd: pushed along 3f out: kpt on fnl f but n.d* **8/1** | 52 |
| -04 | 10 | *2 1/2* | **Imperial Dragon (USA)**[14] 1174 4-9-11 ........ DHolland 16<br>*(WAO'Gorman) s.i.s: sn in tch: rdn over 2f out: wknd over 1f out* **20/1** | 46 |
| 60 | 11 | *2 1/2* | **Sunset Dreamer (USA)**[79] 597 3-8-6 ........ JFanning 6<br>*(PMitchell) nvr bttr than mid-div* **66/1** | 35 |
| 050- | 12 | *shd* | **Catch The Fox**[270] 3338 4-9-11 45 ........ JTate 7<br>*(JJBridger) chsd ldrs tl wknd 2f out* **100/1** | 40 |
| 5- | 13 | *3 1/2* | **Royal Flight**[163] 5867 3-8-11 ........ EAhern 2<br>*(PWHarris) h.d.w: bkwd: bhd most of way* **14/1** | 31 |
| 20- | 14 | *shd* | **Colour Code (IRE)**[139] 6069 3-8-11 ........ MartinDwyer 1<br>*(MPTregoning) bit bkwd: chsd ldrs tl wknd qckly 2f out* **14/1** | 31 |
| 440- | 15 | *1* | **Lady Franpalm (IRE)**[222] 4656 4-9-3 54 ........ RMiles(3) 3<br>*(MJHaynes) s.i.s: sn mid-div: wd into st fr 3f out and sn wknd* **50/1** | 23 |
| 000 | 16 | *10* | **Mandahar (IRE)**[16] 1133 5-9-11 ........ MTebbutt 10<br>*(AWCarroll) in tch over 4f* **66/1** | — |
| 4 | 17 | *2 1/2* | **Cedric Coverwell**[14] 1169 4-9-11 ........ WRyan 15<br>*(DKIvory) led tl hdd & wknd qckly over 2f out* **50/1** | — |

1m 28.57s (1.30) **Going Correction** +0.375s/f (Good)

**WFA** 3 from 4yo+ 14lb **17 Ran SP% 117.7**

Speed ratings: **107,106,105,104,102 101,98,97,97,94 91,91,87,87,86 74,71**CSF £88.01 TOTE £7.10: £3.00, £7.20, £2.20; EX 168.70.

**Owner** D K Thorpe (Susan Abbott Racing) **Bred** M L Page **Trained** Arundel, W Sussex

**FOCUS**

Not a strong maiden for the track as the runner-up is exposed as modest.

**NOTEBOOK**

**Poule De Luxe(IRE)**, bred to appreciate this longer trip, duly stepped up on her previous form, but this was not a great maiden and she looks nothing special.

**Hallings Overture(USA)** had not been getting home over ten furlongs on the sand and appreciated this drop back in trip and return to the turf. He would probably be better employed in handicaps off his current sort of mark.

**Kauri Forest(USA)**, whose dam is a half-sister to Tillerman, was coltish in the preliminaries but ran well enough in the race itself, staying on well for third. He looks one for handicaps in time.

**Evaluator(IRE)** raced keenly on his reappearance and turf debut. He should not get too high a mark now and will be of more interest in handicap company.

**Day To Remember** looks as though he will improve for a step up in trip when he goes handicapping, and on the basis of his three runs to date he should not be burdened with too high a rating.

**Keyaki(IRE)** showed her inexperience at the start but kept on well enough in the latter stages. She should come on for this racecourse debut.

**Planters Punch(IRE)** looks as though he will need farther in handicap company.

## 1353 QUAIL CONDITIONS STKS 6f

**2:45** (2:45) (C) 3-Y-0+ **£8,343** (£3,164; £1,582; £719) **Stalls** Low

| Form | | | | RPR |
|---|---|---|---|---|
| 000- | 1 | | **Baron's Pit**[177] 5638 4-9-2 114 ........ KFallon 1<br>*(RHannon) lw: in tch: pushed along 1/2-way: hdwy over 2f out: led over 1f out: drvn out* **15/8**[1] | 109 |
| 00-6 | 2 | *2* | **Smokin Beau**[16] 1126 7-9-2 98 ........ TGMcLaughlin 7<br>*(NPLittmoden) lw: racd alone far side and a up w pce: styd on wl for 2nd fnl f but nt pce of wnr* **6/1**[3] | 103 |
| 3-00 | 3 | *nk* | **Fire Up The Band**[16] 1126 5-9-2 105 ........ ANicholls 4<br>*(DNicholls) s.i.s: sn in tch: hdwy 2f out: swtchd rt and r.o fnl f: tk 3rd cl home but no imp on wnr* **9/4**[2] | 102 |
| -055 | 4 | *nk* | **Fruit Of Glory**[44] 921 5-8-11 ........ DHolland 2<br>*(JRJenkins) trckd ldr: drvn to chal 2f out: led sn after: hdd over 1f out: sn one pce: ct for 3rd cl home* **14/1** | 96 |
| 1-00 | 5 | *2* | **Will He Wish**[9] 1242 8-9-10 92 ........ IMongan 5<br>*(SGollings) outpcd: rdn and sme hdwy 2f out: nvr gng pce to rch ldrs: outpcd fnl f* **50/1** | 103? |
| 100- | 6 | *2* | **Mazepa (IRE)**[171] 5732 4-9-2 96 ........ LDettori 3<br>*(NACallaghan) lw: b: sn led: hdd ins fnl 2f: wknd fnl f* **8/1** | 89 |
| 00-4 | 7 | *3* | **Indian Spark**[12] 1211 10-9-2 96 ........ TQuinn 6<br>*(JSGoldie) bhd: rdn and effrt 1/2-way: nvr gng pce to rch ldrs and wknd appr fnl f* **10/1** | 80 |

1m 12.36s (-0.71) **Going Correction** +0.075s/f (Good) **7 Ran SP% 108.7**

Speed ratings: **107,104,103,103,100 98,94**CSF £12.17 TOTE £2.80: £1.70, £3.70; EX 11.60.

**Owner** J T & K M Thomas **Bred** J T And Mrs Thomas **Trained** East Everleigh, Wilts

**FOCUS**

Not a terribly competitive race, and the ratings choice ran out a decisive winner without having to be at his best.

**NOTEBOOK**

**Baron's Pit** had the weights in his favour but it was his ability to handle the easier ground which was the doubt. He coped with conditions well, though, and won in decisive fashion. The Duke Of York Stakes, followed by the Golden Jubilee are his immediate targets.

**Smokin Beau ◆**, whose rider's decision to take his mount to race alone next to the far-side rail initially looked a shrewd move, given the result of the sprint over the course and distance two days earlier, eventually found the winner too strong on the stands' side. Given the result of the following handicap, it could be that he was not racing on the quicker ground after all and, seeing as the weights were against him here, he looks one to keep in mind for a similar contest.

**Fire Up The Band**, second best in at the weights, came home second on the stands' side and appears to be slowly hitting form. Small-field conditions races do not really bring out the best in him, though.

**Fruit Of Glory**, who is at her best on fast ground, got run out of the places close home but performed as well as could be expected on these terms.

**Will He Wish**, up against it at these weights, is another who would have been suited by faster ground. He also ideally needs another furlong.

## 1354 SHARP MINDS BETFAIR STKS (H'CAP) 6f

**3:15** (3:17) (C) (0-95,95) 4-Y-0+ **£9,759** (£3,003; £1,501; £750) **Stalls** Low

| Form | | | | RPR |
|---|---|---|---|---|
| 620- | 1 | | **Persario**[163] 5875 5-8-11 78 ........ LDettori 5<br>*(JRFanshawe) racd stands side: s.i.s: bhd: hdwy 1/2-way: swtchd rt ins last: str run to ld nr fin* **10/1**[2] | 97+ |
| 3-12 | 2 | *1/2* | **Zilch**[9] 1246 6-9-6 87 ........ IMongan 3<br>*(MLWBell) lw: racd stands side: trckd ldrs: led ins fnl 2f: sn hrd drvn: hdd cl home* **10/1**[2] | 104+ |
| 144- | 3 | *4* | **High Reach**[184] 5487 4-9-8 89 ........ KDarley 13<br>*(TGMills) racd far side: trckd ldrs: hdwy to ld that grp 2f out: kpt on wl but nt pce of stands side* **7/1**[1] | 94 |
| -041 | 4 | *1/2* | **Taranaki**[11] 1225 6-9-2 83 ........ KFallon 15<br>*(PDCundell) racd far side: trckd ldrs: rdn and effrt fr 2f out: kpt on wl fnl f: nt pce of stands side* **7/1**[1] | 87 |
| 00-2 | 5 | *3/4* | **Seven No Trumps**[16] 1131 7-9-1 82 ........ DHolland 18<br>*(JMBradley) led far side 4f: styd prom tl outpcd ins fnl f* **7/1**[1] | 83 |
| 305- | 6 | *nk* | **Winning Venture**[205] 5063 7-9-5 86 ........ WRyan 1<br>*(AWCarroll) racd stands side: bhd: swtchd rt and gd hdwy 1f out:fin wl: nt rch ldrs* **40/1** | 86 |
| 60-0 | 7 | *3/4* | **Armagnac**[18] 1106 6-8-12 79 ........ JFanning 7<br>*(MABuckley) pressed ldrs stands side: ev ch over 1f out tl wknd ins last* **33/1** | 77 |
| 00-6 | 8 | *1* | **Marker**[16] 1132 4-9-4 90 ........ RThomas(5) 17<br>*(GBBalding) racd far side: s.i.s: bhd: hdwy 2f out: kpt on same pce ins last* **12/1**[3] | 85 |
| -000 | 9 | *nk* | **Nashaab (USA)**[18] 1106 7-9-6 87 ........ TGMcLaughlin 16<br>*(PDEvans) racd far side and outpcd: hdwy 2f out: kpt on fnl f but nt a danger* **16/1** | 81 |
| 0-13 | 10 | *shd* | **Further Outlook (USA)**[10] 1230 10-8-13 87 ........ MHoward(7) 8<br>*(DKIvory) b: b.hind: disp ld stands side over 4f* **20/1** | 81 |
| 6-00 | 11 | *1* | **Abbajabba**[18] 1106 8-9-2 83 ........ JBramhill 2<br>*(CWFairhurst) racd stands side: sn rdn and outpcd: kpt on fnl f but nt a danger* **25/1** | 74 |
| 3110 | 12 | *shd* | **Polar Kingdom**[59] 761 6-8-11 78 ........ EAhern 11<br>*(TDBarron) racd stand side: rdn and effrt 1/2-way: sn outpcd* **12/1**[3] | 69 |
| 100- | 13 | *1* | **Material Witness (IRE)**[240] 4177 7-9-7 88 ........ MartinDwyer 9<br>*(WRMuir) slt ld stands side tl hdd ins fnl 2f: sn wknd* **33/1** | 76 |
| 00- | 14 | *2* | **Free Wheelin (IRE)**[164] 5854 4-8-13 80 ........ MTebbutt 6<br>*(WJarvis) lw: racd stands side: outpcd* **33/1** | 62 |
| 00-0 | 15 | *shd* | **Prince Cyrano**[18] 1106 5-9-5 86 ........ RMullen 19<br>*(WJMusson) lw: racd far side: s.i.s: sn rcvrd: outpcd 1/2-way* **14/1** | 67 |
| 240- | 16 | *hd* | **Little Venice (IRE)**[205] 5077 4-8-4 78 ........ SO'Hara(7) 12<br>*(CFWall) racd far side: a outpcd* **33/1** | 59 |
| 00-1 | 17 | *1* | **Steel Blue**[18] 1106 4-9-5 86 ........ RHills 4<br>*(RMWhitaker) lw: chsd ldrs stands side over 3f* **12/1**[3] | 64 |
| 100- | 18 | *nk* | **Mitcham (IRE)**[296] 2557 8-9-11 95 ........ RMiles(3) 20<br>*(TGMills) racd far side: spd 3f* **12/1**[3] | 72 |
| -040 | 19 | *3 1/2* | **Terraquin (IRE)**[16] 1132 4-8-11 78 ........ ANicholls 10<br>*(JJBridger) b: racd stands side: s.i.s: sn rcvrd: wknd 2f out* **33/1** | 44 |
| 340- | 20 | *12* | **Landing Strip (IRE)**[125] 6154 4-8-10 77 ........ JTate 14<br>*(JMPEustace) racd far side: spd to 1/2-way* **33/1** | 7 |

1m 12.44s (-0.63) **Going Correction** +0.075s/f (Good) **20 Ran SP% 127.7**

Speed ratings: **107,106,101,100,99 98,97,96,96,96 94,94,93,90,90 90,88,88,83,67**CSF £97.06 CT £781.79 TOTE £11.30: £2.70, £2.20, £2.30, £2.10; EX 93.20 Trifecta £1612.90 Part won. Pool £2,271.80 - 0.20 winning units..

**Owner** Barford Bloodstock **Bred** Mrs C Handscombe **Trained** Newmarket, Suffolk

**FOCUS**

The draw advantage, which had favoured high boxes two days earlier, saw the low numbers coming out on top this time. This was useful handicap form with first two clear, and should prove reliable.

**NOTEBOOK**

**Persario**, who is only lightly raced for a five-year-old, is bred to appreciate a bit of give, and the drop back to six furlongs appeared to suit. She had been finding seven just beyond her last year and could be open to more improvement at this distance.

**Zilch**, up another 4lb, pulled clear of the rest of the field and once again confirmed his current good form. If anything, he would have been suited by even softer ground.

**High Reach**, a progressive handicapper last season, came home first on the far side. He has clearly returned in good heart and should be kept in mind for a similar race in the coming weeks.

**Taranaki**, ideally suited by seven furlongs, is also a capable performer over this shorter trip. He is a consistent type but has never won off a mark in the 80s.

**Seven No Trumps**, with the benefit of a recent outing, made the running on the far side. His strike rate is not great, but on each occasion he has won a race following a barren spell, he has also followed up next time.

**Winning Venture** ran well over a trip too short on his first start for his new stable, but he has flattered to deceive before.

**Armagnac** ran a more promising race and is slowly dropping back to a winning mark.

**Abbajabba** *Official explanation: jockey said gelding hung right-handed*

## 1355 MAGNOLIA STKS (LISTED RACE) 1m 2f (J)

**3:50** (3:50) (A) 4-Y-0+ **£17,400** (£6,600; £3,300; £1,500) **Stalls** High

| Form | | | | RPR |
|---|---|---|---|---|
| 1013 | 1 | | **Scott's View**[16] 1144 5-9-0 115 ........ SChin 6<br>*(MJohnston) hld up in rr: rapid hdwy on outside fr over 2f out: led over 1f out: clr ins last: readily* **5/1**[2] | 116 |
| 42-3 | 2 | *3* | **Bustan (IRE)**[23] 1062 5-8-11 107 ........ RHills 9<br>*(MPTregoning) lw: trckd ldrs: rdn over 2f out: kpt on to chse wnr ins fnl f but no ch: kpt on wl for 2nd* **7/2**[1] | 109 |
| 432- | 3 | *1 3/4* | **Island House (IRE)**[205] 5058 8-8-11 113 ........ DHolland 5<br>*(GWragg) hld up in rr: pushed along 4f out: swtchd lft and hdwy fr 2f out: rdn and hung rt fnl f: r.o cl home* **13/2** | 106 |
| 440- | 4 | *1* | **Landinium (ITY)**[157] 5943 5-8-6 104 ........ RMullen 4<br>*(CFWall) awkward after s and rdn: bhd: hdwy and hung lft bnd 3f out: hung rt over 1f out: r.o ins last: nt rch ldrs* **50/1** | 99 |

0-54 **5** ½ **Nysaean (IRE)**[8] [1261] 5-9-2 115 ........ KDarley 1 109
(RHannon) *lw: led 2f: styd trcking ldrs tl led again over 3f out: kpt on u.p tl hdd over 1f out: wknd ins last* **11/2[3]**

0002 **6** 2½ **Easter Ogil (IRE)**[5] [1298] 9-8-11 56 ........ ANicholls 7 100?
(JaneSouthcombe) *bhd: hdwy 2f out: kpt in fnl f but nvr gng pce to trble ldrs* **100/1**

3-30 **7** 1¾ **Corriolanus (GER)**[23] [1062] 4-8-11 104 ........ JFanning 2 97
(PMitchell) *lw: bhd: hdwy and rdn 3f out: nvr gng pce to rch ldrs: wknd fnl f* **50/1**

103- **8** 2 **Piano Star**[192] [5346] 4-8-11 103 ........ KFallon 11 94
(SirMichaelStoute) *mid-div: rdn 1/2-way: wknd over 2f out* **11/2[3]**

464- **9** 1¼ **Chancellor (IRE)**[191] [5383] 6-8-11 110 ........ LDettori 10 92
(JLDunlop) *w ldrs: rdn and ev ch over 2f out: wknd over 1f out* **7/2[1]**

1/06 **10** 1 **Lion Hunter (USA)**[48] [872] 5-8-11 84 ........ MartinDwyer 12 91
(MissECLavelle) *led after 2f: hdd over 3f out: styd pressing ldrs tl wknd ins fnl 2f* **100/1**

320- **11** 5 **Rocket Force (USA)**[297] [2515] 4-8-11 104 ........ EAhern 8 83
(EALDunlop) *mid-div: rdn 4f out: sn wknd* **33/1**

650- **12** 21 **Tuning Fork**[177] [5643] 4-8-11 100 ........ TQuinn 3 52
(JAkehurst) *chsd ldrs over 6f* **33/1**

2m 7.53s (1.39) **Going Correction** +0.375s/f (Good) **12** Ran SP% **117.0**
Speed ratings: **109,106,105,104,104 102,100,99,98,97 93,76**CSF £21.89 TOTE £6.00: £2.30, £1.80, £2.50; EX 28.30.

**Owner** Great Escape Partnership **Bred** Cliveden Stud Ltd **Trained** Middleham Moor, N Yorks

**FOCUS**
There was a decent pace on for this well-contested Listed race, which produced a classy effort from the winner and the race overall is well up to scratch for the grade.

**NOTEBOOK**
**Scott's View**, fit from racing in the desert, proved suited by the decent pace as he ideally wants a bit farther than this, and came through to score in good style. Apparently, he is now off to Hong Kong for the Queen Elizabeth II Cup, and indeed he looks just the sort of tough campaigner who will thrive on a busy, international campaign this season.
**Bustan(IRE)** still has some supporters out there, and was well backed again, but he is a disappointing sort for whom there is always some excuse or other.
**Island House(IRE)** ◆ is a solid perfomer in this grade, but he was at a fitness disadvantage with many of his rivals and that found him out. This should have put an edge on him, though, and he should be kept in mind for Chester and/or Goodwood next month.
**Landinium(ITY)** ran fair races in this grade against her own sex last season, and this was a decent performance on her reappearance. Her inability to handle the bend and tendency to hang were big negatives, though.
**Nysaean(IRE)** looked to have plenty in his favour but he may have done too much too soon as he tired in the closing stages and the winner came from off the pace. He reportedly returned home with a 'mucky throat'.
**Easter Ogil(IRE)** should have been completely out of his depth in this company and ran way above expectations to finish sixth.
**Chancellor(IRE)**, who has changed stables, can be excused his disappointing run as he returned lame on his right foreleg. *Official explanation: vet said horse finished lame on the right fore; trainer said colt had lost its off fore shoe during the race*

## 1356 STPP MEDIA MAIDEN STKS — 1m 3f 30y
**4:25** (4:26) (D) 3-Y-O — **£5,434** (£1,672; £836; £418) **Stalls** High

Form RPR

34- **1** **Bukit Fraser (IRE)**[220] [4706] 3-9-0 ........ KDarley 4 71
(PFICole) *t.k.h: sn trcking ldr:drvn to ld wl over 1f out and j. path: c clr ins last: readily* **5/4[1]**

60- **2** 3 **Sunny Lady (FR)**[121] [6175] 3-8-9 ........ EAhern 1 61
(EALDunlop) *hld up in rr: rdn and hdwy over 2f out: edgd rt and r.o ins last: tk 2nd cl home but no ch w wnr* **20/1**

033- **3** nk **Tannoor (USA)**[166] [5831] 3-9-0 80 ........ PRobinson 3 66
(MAJarvis) *lw: led: rdn over 2f out: hdd wl over 1f out: one pce ins last: ct for 2nd cl home* **2/1[2]**

560- **4** 1½ **Scarrabus (IRE)**[203] [5112] 3-9-0 67 ........ TQuinn 7 64
(BGPowell) *bhd: hdwy 4f out: rdn to chse ldrs 2f out: one pce whn hmpd ins last* **20/1**

0- **5** 6 **Cleaver**[166] [5825] 3-9-0 ........ MTebbutt 2 54
(WJarvis) *lw: chsd ldrs: rdn over 3f out: wknd 2f out* **14/1**

0-0 **6** 1½ **Frankies Wings (IRE)**[11] [1224] 3-8-11 ........ RMiles(3) 5 52
(TGMills) *lw: stdd rr after 2f: rdn and effrt 3f out: nvr gng pce to rch ldrs: wknd fr 2f out* **15/2[3]**

0035 **7** ½ **Almost Welcome**[29] [1017] 3-9-0 45 ........ PDoe 10 51
(SDow) *in tch: rdn over 3f out: sn one pce: wknd fr 2f out* **33/1**

0 **8** ½ **Pella**[13] [1189] 3-8-9 ........ KFallon 9 45
(MBlanshard) *chsd ldrs: rdn 3f out: wknd qckly over 1f out* **16/1**

06- **9** 1½ **Nina Fontenail (FR)**[203] [5113] 3-8-9 ........ JBramhill 6 43
(NJHawke) *rr stalls and slowly away: plld hrd and sn rcvrd: rapid hdwy to chse ldrs 5f out: wknd ins fnl 2f* **100/1**

0 **10** 18 **Harry Came Home**[24] [1050] 3-9-0 ........ PMcCabe 8 19
(JCFox) *swtg: a bhd: lost tch fnl 2f* **100/1**

2m 29.68s (6.63) **Going Correction** +0.475s/f (Yiel) **10** Ran SP% **116.5**
Speed ratings: **94,91,91,90,86 85,84,84,83,70**CSF £34.43 TOTE £2.40: £1.20, £2.80, £1.50; EX 36.40.

**Owner** H R H Sultan Ahmad Shah **Bred** H R H Sultan Ahmad Shah **Trained** Whatcombe, Oxon
■ Stewards Enquiry : E Ahern caution: used whip in an incorrect place

**FOCUS**
A modest maiden in which there was no great gallop and the final time was modest. The form is unlikely to prove reliable.

**NOTEBOOK**
**Bukit Fraser(IRE)** only got into his stride in the closing stages, and although this was not a true test at the trip, he looked as though he will be even more effective over a mile and a half.
**Sunny Lady(FR)** improved for the step up in trip and was staying on well in the closing stages. She looks the type who will be suited by the stronger pace she is more likely to get in handicap company.
**Tannoor(USA)** raced keenly in front and was in the right place to benefit from the slow early gallop, but in the end he did not see it out as well as the winner. He has now started at 9-4 or shorter on each of his four starts to date, and must be classed as disappointing.
**Scarrabus(IRE)** appeared to step up on his previous form, but there is a good chance he was flattered by the way the race was run.
**Cleaver** is bred to improve with age and a test of stamina. The best of him is unlikely to be seen, however, until he begins running in handicaps.
**Frankies Wings(IRE)**, a half-brother to high-class three-year-old Frenchman's Bay, is now eligible for a mark.

## 1357 SHARP MINDS BETFAIR H'CAP — 1m 1f (R)
**5:00** (5:01) (D) (0-85,82) 3-Y-O — **£5,681** (£1,748; £874; £437) **Stalls** High

Form RPR

552- **1** **Show No Fear**[167] [5810] 3-8-6 **67** ........ WRyan 11 74
(HRACecil) *lw: hld up in rr: stdy hdwy fr 2f out: qckn ins last: drvn to ld cl home* **10/1**

541- **2** ½ **Celtic Heroine (IRE)**[121] [6172] 3-9-3 **78** ........ KDarley 13 84
(MAJarvis) *trckd ldrs: pushed along 3f out: drvn to ld wl over 1f out: hdd cl home* **5/2[1]**

321- **3** 1¼ **Momtic (IRE)**[182] [5548] 3-9-5 **80** ........ MTebbutt 6 83
(WJarvis) *hld up in rr. stdy hdwy on outside fr 3f out: shkn up and r.o wl fnl f: kpt on cl home* **33/1**

0- **4** ½ **Malibu (IRE)**[169] [5776] 3-9-1 **76** ........ PDoe 10 78
(SDow) *bhd: rdn and hdwy fr 2f out: r.o fnl f: kpt on cl home* **33/1**

066- **5** ½ **Peruvian Breeze (IRE)**[207] [5020] 3-7-13 **60** ........ JBramhill 7 61
(NPLittmoden) *chsd ldrs: wnt 2nd 4f out: rdn and ev ch ins fnl 2f: outpcd fnl f* **66/1**

002- **6** 1¾ **Carriacou**[121] [6175] 3-9-0 **75** ........ PRobinson 2 73
(PWD'Arcy) *led: rdn over 2f out: hdd wl over 1f out: wknd fnl f* **9/1**

0421 **7** nk **Hazewind**[43] [928] 3-8-1 **62** ........ (t) JFanning 9 59
(PDEvans) *bhd: rdn 3f out: r.o fnl 2f: nt rch ldrs* **9/1**

6-1 **8** 2½ **Gretna**[13] [1186] 3-9-7 **82** ........ TQuinn 5 74
(JLDunlop) *lw: chsd ldr 5f: wknd ins fnl 2f* **13/2[3]**

65-0 **9** hd **Winners Delight**[16] [1134] 3-9-5 **80** ........ EStack 3 72
(APJarvis) *stdd rr s: bhd: kpt on fnl 2f: nt trble ldrs* **33/1**

31- **10** 1 **Miss Langkawi**[156] [5947] 3-8-13 **74** ........ DHolland 12 64
(GWragg) *bhd most of way* **9/2[2]**

-120 **11** 1¾ **Pick Of The Crop**[47] [885] 3-8-13 **74** ........ LDettori 8 60
(JRJenkins) *hld up in rr: pushed along over 2f out: nvr in contention* **20/1**

501- **12** 1 **Anousa (IRE)**[194] [5297] 3-9-4 **79** ........ KFallon 4 63
(PHowling) *h.d.w: bit bkwd: chsd ldrs: rdn 3f out: sn wknd* **8/1**

20-1 **13** 8 **Count Dracula**[29] [1015] 3-8-9 **70** ........ MartinDwyer 1 38
(AMBalding) *chsd ldrs: rdn 4f out: wknd 3f out* **14/1**

1m 57.27s (2.94) **Going Correction** +0.475s/f (Yiel) **13** Ran SP% **122.0**
Speed ratings: **105,104,103,103,102 101,100,98,98,97 95,95,87**CSF £34.33 CT £856.13 TOTE £12.70: £3.20, £1.70, £11.90; EX 67.00 Place 6 £28.18, Place 5 £12.34..

**Owner** Colin Davey **Bred** Cheveley Park Stud Ltd **Trained** Newmarket, Suffolk
■ Stewards Enquiry : E StackJ nine-day ban: failed to obtain best possible placing (Apr 23-May 1)

**FOCUS**
There was a good pace on here, for what looked a decent event which, although not quite as strong as usual, should produce its share of winners.

**NOTEBOOK**
**Show No Fear**, who has changed stables since last season, was racing on the softest ground he has encountered and produced an improved display to break his maiden tag. This looked a fair handicap of its type beforehand and the chances are there is more to come from him.
**Celtic Heroine(IRE)**, who was strong in the market, was another who stepped up on her previous form on this easier surface. There was no disgrace in her narrow defeat, but she will go up in the weights again for this effort.
**Momtic(IRE)**, for whom the longer trip was a doubt, got the extra distance well. He has clearly returned in good heart and faster ground should suit.
**Malibu(IRE)**, who was trained in Ireland at two, made a promising start for his new stable. He was without the blinkers he wore on each of his last three starts as a juvenile on this occasion.
**Peruvian Breeze(IRE)** had shown little in maiden company at two, but performed much better on this handicap debut. He could be open to more improvement.
**Carriacou** set a decent pace in front and it was not too much of a surprise to see her weaken out of it in the closing stages.
**Gretna** was very disappointing given that she had a fitness edge on many of her rivals and that conditions looked ideal for her.
**Winners Delight**, who was held up in rear for most of the race, finished well under a far from energetic ride. Stack's lack of effort caught the Stewards' eye and the result was that the gelding was banned from racing for 40 days under the non-triers' rule. The rider was also banned for nine days, and the trainer fined £1,200. *Official explanation: 40-day ban: (Apr 15-May 24)*
**Miss Langkawi** *Official explanation: jockey said filly was never travelling*
T/Jkpt: Not won. T/Plt: £33.20 to a £1 stake. Pool: £66,270.95. 1,455.60 winning tickets. T/Qpdt: £7.60 to a £1 stake. Pool: £2,981.50. 288.00 winning tickets. ST

# REDCAR (L-H)
Monday, April 12

**OFFICIAL GOING: Soft**

## 1358 BANK HOLIDAY CLASSIFIED STKS — 7f
**2:20** (2:21) (E) 3-Y-O+ — **£3,571** (£1,099; £549; £274) **Stalls** Centre

Form RPR

1311 **1** **Up Tempo (IRE)**[14] [1175] 6-9-9 71 ........ (b) NCallan 13 81
(KARyan) *trckd ldrs: hdwy over 2f out: rdn to chal over 1f out: kpt on u.p to ld ins last: drvn out* **11/4[1]**

-000 **2** ½ **Hov**[9] [1247] 4-9-10 72 ........ RWinston 6 81
(JJQuinn) *cl up: rdn along 2f out and ev ch tl drvna nd nt qckn wl ins last* **8/1**

60-0 **3** hd **Young Mr Grace (IRE)**[18] [1106] 4-9-10 75 ........ DAllan(3) 9 84
(TDEasterby) *led: rdn along over 2f out: jnd and drvn over 1f out: hdd ins last: kpt on* **20/1**

400- **4** 2 **Hills Of Gold**[167] [5821] 5-9-3 66 ........ PMulrennan(5) 5 74
(MWEasterby) *chsd ldrs: rdn along 2f out: one pce appr last* **20/1**

00U5 **5** 4 **Ronnie From Donny (IRE)**[12] [1199] 4-9-3 70 ........ TEaves(5) 3 64
(BEllison) *hld up: hdwy 3f out: rdn and kpt on fnl 2f: nrst fin* **10/1**

00-0 **6** 2 **Bailieborough (IRE)**[12] [1199] 5-9-8 69 ........ AlexGreaves 11 59
(DNicholls) *s.i.s and bhd: hdwy 1/2-way: shkn up to chse ldrs over 2f out: sn no imp* **20/1**

60-0 **7** 2½ **Eastern Hope (IRE)**[12] [1213] 5-9-1 67 ........ KristinStubbs(7) 7 52
(MrsLStubbs) *bhd tl styd on u.p fnl 2f: nvr a factor* **25/1**

00-0 **8** ½ **Celtic Romance**[9] [1247] 5-9-5 59 ........ JCarroll 8 48
(MrsMReveley) *s.i.s: a rr* **50/1**

0050 **9** shd **Hand Chime**[16] [1132] 7-9-13 75 ........ PHanagan 2 56
(WJHaggas) *dwlt: sn in tch: effrt 3f out: sn rdn and btn* **7/2[2]**

220 **10** 1¼ **African Spur (IRE)**[14] [1175] 4-9-1 70 ........ (t) DTudhope(7) 1 48
(DCarroll) *in tch on outer: rdn along 3f out: sn wknd* **33/1**

20-0 **11** 3½ **Tre Colline**[14] [1175] 5-9-10 72 ........ KimTinkler 4 41
(NTinkler) *a rr* **25/1**

54-4 **12** hd **Top Line Dancer (IRE)**[12] [1200] 3-8-8 70 ........ RFfrench 12 38
(MJohnston) *chsd ldrs: rdn along wl over 2f out and sn wknd* **7/1[3]**



The Form Book, Raceform Ltd, Compton, RG20 6NL

030- **13** *13* **Looking Down**[117] 6206 4-9-5 70 ........................ GFaulkner 10 3
(PCHaslam) *chsd ldrs: rdn along 3f out and sn wknd: eased* **12/1**

1m 30.68s (5.78) **Going Correction** +1.00s/f (Soft)
**WFA** 3 from 4yo+ 14lb **13** Ran SP% **116.2**
Speed ratings: **106,105,105,102,98 96,93,92,92,91 87,86,72**CSF £21.38 TOTE £3.40: £1.10, £3.90, £6.40; EX 44.20.
**Owner** Yorkshire Racing Club & Derek Blackhurst **Bred** T Burns **Trained** Hambleton, N Yorks
■ Stewards Enquiry : D Allan two-day ban: used whip with excessve frequency (Apr 23-24)

**FOCUS**
A tight little classified event, but the pace appeared just ordinary and it was best not to be too far off the speed.

**NOTEBOOK**
**Up Tempo(IRE)**, in fine form over six furlongs recently, showed himself just as effective over this extra furlong. He travelled better than anything through the early part of the contest but had to work pretty hard to get on top and would probably have been suited by a stronger pace.
**Hov** is back on a winning mark and returned to form with a solid effort. He has gained both his previous wins on Fibresand but is just as effective on turf and should find a race in the coming weeks.
**Young Mr Grace(IRE)** was well beaten on his reappearance, but he showed the benefit of that run to post an encouraging effort.
**Hills Of Gold** has only ever won on good to firm so this was not a bad performance on ground that may have been softer than ideal.
**Ronnie From Donny(IRE)** has never won on turf and was well held.
**Hand Chime** is well handicapped on some of his form but continues below his best.

## 1359 FREE EGG GIVE AWAY MAIDEN STKS 5f
2:55 (2:56) (D) 2-Y-O £3,503 (£1,078; £539; £269) **Stalls** Centre

Form RPR
**1** **Bigalos Bandit** 2-9-0 ........................ RWinston 3 67+
(JJQuinn) *trckd ldrs: hdwy 2f out: rdn to ld ins last: styd on* **2/1**[1]
5 **2** *1 ½* **Speed Dial Harry (IRE)**[6] 1276 2-9-0 ........................ DarrenWilliams 2 63
(KRBurke) *led: rdn along over 1f out: drvn: hdd and hung rt ins last: one pce* **2/1**[1]
**3** *nk* **Paris Bell** 2-8-7 ........................ AMullen[(7)] 4 62+
(TDEasterby) *dwlt: sn pulling hrd and chsd ldrs: n.m.r 2f out: styng on on inner whn hmpd ins last: swtchd lft and r.o* **12/1**
**4** *1 ¾* **Keepasharplookout (IRE)** 2-9-0 ........................ PHanagan 1 56
(MrsLStubbs) *cl up: pushed along 2f out: rdn over 1f out and sn one pce* **6/1**[3]
**5** *1 ½* **Misty Miller** 2-8-11 ........................ DAllan[(3)] 6 52
(TDEasterby) *hld up: effrt and hdwy 2f out: rdn and wknd ins last* **9/2**[2]
0 **6** *5* **Hiats**[18] 1105 2-8-7 ........................ JDO'Reilly[(7)] 5 37
(JO'Reilly) *keen: cl up tl wandered and wknd fnl 2f* **16/1**

64.61 secs (5.91) **Going Correction** +1.00s/f (Soft) **6** Ran SP% **112.7**
Speed ratings: **92,89,89,86,83 75**CSF £6.07 TOTE £2.60: £2.10, £1.10; EX 4.40.
**Owner** Ian Buckley **Bred** David John Boughton **Trained** Settrington, N Yorks
■ Stewards Enquiry : Darren Williams one-day ban: failed to keep straight from stalls (Apr 23)

**FOCUS**
Probably just an ordinary maiden, but the winner is a likeable type and most of these in behind should improve.

**NOTEBOOK**
**Bigalos Bandit**, a 13,500gns yearling, half-brother to two juvenile winners, was forced to race towards the outside throughout but he overcame that and made a very pleasing debut. A likeable sort, he could well be placed to follow up.
**Speed Dial Harry(IRE)**, fifth in a fair Polytrack maiden on his debut, appeared to improve on that effort. A minor race should come his way.
**Paris Bell**, a half-brother to several winners, out of a ten-furlong winner, should have finished closer. He recovered from a slow start to race keenly for most of the way, but he struggled for a run and only got in the clear well inside the final furlong. If he can break on terms and settle better in future, a maiden will come his way.
**Keepasharplookout(IRE)**, out of an unraced daughter of mile two-year-old winner and Chester Cup scorer Doyce, showed pace in the early stages and should progress.
**Misty Miller**, a 17,000gns purchase, brother to a dual five-furlong two-year-old winner, offered encouragement and should improve.

## 1360 EASTER H'CAP 1m 2f
3:25 (3:26) (E) (0-75,73) 3-Y-O £4,238 (£1,304; £652; £326) **Stalls** Low

Form RPR
-202 **1** **Platinum Pirate**[20] 1084 3-7-10 55 ........................ (v[1]) RoryMoore[(7)] 9 63
(KRBurke) *hld up in tch: smooth hdwy 4f out: rdn to ld 2f out: hung bdly rt over 1f out: sn clr: rdn out* **9/1**
00-4 **2** *5* **Woody Valentine (USA)**[12] 1201 3-9-7 73 ........................ RFfrench 7 72
(MJohnston) *bhd: gd hdwy 1/2-way: led 3f out: rdn and hdd 2f out: sn drvn and one pce* **5/2**[1]
050- **3** *¾* **Third Empire**[175] 5671 3-8-10 62 ........................ RWinston 6 60
(CGrant) *hld up towards rr: gd hdwy 4f out: effrt and ev ch 2f out: sn rdn and one pce* **20/1**
400- **4** *5* **Athollbrose (USA)**[219] 4727 3-8-4 56 ........................ GFaulkner 2 46+
(TDEasterby) *bhd: hdwy 3f out: swtchd rt 2f out and kpt on: nt rch ldrs* **25/1**
6-00 **5** *3 ½* **Sir Galahad**[25] 1044 3-8-1 56 ow1 ........................ DAllan[(3)] 1 40
(TDEasterby) *hld up towards rr: gd hdwy 1/2-way: chsd ldrs over 3f out: sn rdn and weakended over 2f out* **6/1**[3]
030- **6** *2 ½* **Spring Breeze**[195] 5290 3-8-4 56 ........................ PFessey 5 35
(MDods) *chsd ldrs: rdn along over 3f out and sn wknd* **16/1**
14- **7** *6* **Rock Lobster**[205] 5061 3-9-7 73 ........................ DMcGaffin 4 42
(JGGiven) *chsd ldrs: rdn along over 3f out: sn wknd* **10/1**
05-0 **8** *4* **Satsu (IRE)**[12] 1214 3-8-6 58 ........................ NCallan 10 20
(JGGiven) *prom: led 4f out: rdn and hdd 3f out: sn wknd* **20/1**
2232 **9** *18* **Bond Moonlight**[14] 1179 3-8-11 63 ........................ FLynch 11 —
(BSmart) *trckd ldrs: hdwy to chal 4f out: sn rdn and wknd* **5/1**[2]
403- **10** *12* **Bargain Hunt (IRE)**[170] 5745 3-8-2 54 ow1 ........................ (v) DRMcCabe 8 —
(WStorey) *led: rdn along and hdd 4f out: sn wknd* **20/1**
06-0 **11** *8* **Artisticimpression (IRE)**[29] 1015 3-9-2 68 ........................ PHanagan 3 —
(EALDunlop) *chsd ldrs: rdn along 4f out: sn wknd* **7/1**
200- **12** *16* **Beamsley Beacon**[182] 5535 3-8-5 57 ........................ DaleGibson 12 —
(GMMoore) *a rr: bhd fr 1/2-way* **40/1**

2m 16.85s (10.05) **Going Correction** +1.00s/f (Soft) **12** Ran SP% **117.6**
Speed ratings: **99,95,94,90,87 85,80,77,63,53 47,34**CSF £29.00 CT £451.10 TOTE £9.40: £2.30, £1.80, £7.90; EX 24.40.
**Owner** Platinum Racing Club Limited **Bred** Llety Stud **Trained** Middleham Moor, N Yorks
■ Stewards Enquiry : Rory Moore five-day ban: used whip down the shoulder in the forehand position (Apr 23-27)

**FOCUS**
Just a modest handicap, but an imprved effort from the winner and they finished well strung out.

**NOTEBOOK**
**Platinum Pirate** was beginning to look pretty exposed on the All-Weather recently and was held in just an ordinary claimer at Lingfield on his previous outing. However, switched back to the turf and partnered for the first time by the promising Rory Moore, he ran out a most decisive winner. He will do well to follow up once reassessed and would therefore be of interest under a penalty.
**Woody Valentine(USA)** had never before raced on soft ground, but he appeared to handle it and can have no excuses.
**Third Empire** offered some encouragement in maiden company last term and confirmed that with a reasonable effort. He is lightly raced and should improve.
**Athollbrose(USA)**, stepping up in trip and making his handicap debut, showed there is ability there but never threatened the principals.
**Sir Galahad** had a very similar profile to that of his stablemate Athollbrose (fourth) for he was stepping up in trip for his handicap debut. He offered some encouragement but was ultimately well beaten.
**Beamsley Beacon** *Official explanation: jockey said gelding hung right handed throughout.*

## 1361 EASTER BUNNY H'CAP 6f
4:00 (4:01) (D) (0-80,78) 3-Y-O+ £9,074 (£2,792; £1,396; £698) **Stalls** Centre

Form RPR
00-0 **1** **Grey Cossack**[11] 1225 7-9-10 75 ........................ GParkin 6 86
(PTMidgley) *bhd: hdwy centre 1/2-way: swtchd rt over 1f out: rdn and styd on to ld ins last: edgd lft: r.o* **10/1**
2-52 **2** *½* **Pawan (IRE)**[10] 1237 4-8-7 58 ........................ AnnStokell 8 68
(MissAStokell) *chsd ldrs centre: hdwy 2f out: led over 1f out: hdd and nt qckn ins last* **50/1**
-004 **3** *nk* **Lincoln Dancer (IRE)**[12] 1199 7-9-11 76 ........................ AlexGreaves 12 85
(DNicholls) *in tch centre: hdwy over 2f out: rdn to chal wl over 1f out: ev ch tl drvn and nt qckn ins last* **10/1**
5-02 **4** *3* **If By Chance**[14] 1175 6-8-12 68 ........................ (b) TEaves[(5)] 9 68
(RCraggs) *cl up centre: ev ch 2f out: sn rdn and one pce appr last* **12/1**
4041 **5** *nk* **Quiet Times (IRE)**[30] 1007 5-9-2 67 ........................ (b) NCallan 7 66
(KARyan) *chsd ldrs centre: rdn along and lost pl 1/2-way: styd on again u.p fnl f* **11/2**[2]
02- **6** *1 ½* **Quantica (IRE)**[173] 5706 5-9-1 66 ........................ KimTinkler 11 60
(NTinkler) *in tch centre: rdn along 2f out: kpt on same pce appr last* **7/1**[3]
30-0 **7** *3 ½* **Artie**[18] 1106 5-9-8 76 ........................ DAllan[(3)] 2 60
(TDEasterby) *overall ldr centre: rdn along 2f out: hdd & wknd over 1f out* **15/2**
1- **8** *¾* **Palace Theatre (IRE)**[298] 2498 3-8-7 77 ........................ PMakin[(7)] 13 58
(TDBarron) *dwlt: sn in tch stands side: pushed along over 2f out: edgd lft and no imp* **16/1**
00-1 **9** *½* **Balakiref**[7] 1268 5-8-5 59 6ex ........................ THamilton[(3)] 16 39
(MDods) *chsd ldrs stands side: rdn 2f out: kpt on same pce appr last* **5/1**[1]
-000 **10** *3 ½* **Winthorpe (IRE)**[18] 1106 4-9-13 78 ........................ DaleGibson 5 47
(JJQuinn) *in tch centre: rdn along and outpcd 1/2-way: kpt on appr last: nvr a factor* **66/1**
000- **11** *½* **Undeterred**[185] 5473 8-9-12 77 ........................ PFessey 15 45
(TDBarron) *towards rr stands side: hdwy 2f out: nvr nr ldrs* **33/1**
00-0 **12** *3* **Quicks The Word**[14] 1175 4-8-11 67 ........................ PMulrennan[(5)] 10 26
(CWThornton) *chsd ldrs centre: rdn along over 2f out: sn btn* **50/1**
00-0 **13** *nk* **Certa Cito**[14] 1175 4-8-3 61 ........................ AMullen[(7)] 1 19
(TDEasterby) *prom centre: rdn along over 2f out: sn wknd* **33/1**
4-50 **14** *½* **Branston Tiger**[18] 1106 5-9-12 77 ........................ PHanagan 20 34
(JGGiven) *chsd ldrs stands side: rdn along over 2f out: sn btn* **8/1**
-034 **15** *1* **Majik**[67] 686 5-8-9 60 ........................ RFfrench 4 14
(DJSFfrenchDavis) *a rr* **10/1**
6060 **16** *½* **Bond Playboy**[16] 1131 4-9-7 72 ........................ FLynch 3 24
(BSmart) *hmpd s: a rr* **25/1**
1000 **17** *1* **Type One (IRE)**[18] 1106 6-9-13 78 ........................ RWinston 18 27
(JJQuinn) *racd stands side: bhd fr 1/2-way* **50/1**
2-00 **18** *8* **Jonny Ebeneezer**[13] 1185 5-9-7 75 ........................ (p) LEnstone[(3)] 19 —
(RMHCowell) *led stands side gp: rdn along 1/2-way: sn wknd* **33/1**
000- **19** *13* **Dizzy In The Head**[173] 5702 5-8-11 69 ........................ JDO'Reilly[(7)] 17 —
(JO'Reilly) *s.i.s: sn prom stands side: rdn and hung rt 1/2-way: sn wknd* **14/1**

1m 16.0s (4.30) **Going Correction** +1.00s/f (Soft)
**WFA** 3 from 4yo+ 12lb **19** Ran SP% **135.0**
Speed ratings: **111,110,109,105,105 103,98,97,97,92 91,87,87,86,85 84,83,72,55**CSF £479.73 CT £5128.57 TOTE £10.50: £1.80, £10.40, £3.00, £3.10; EX 557.50.
**Owner** Robert E Cook **Bred** R E And Mrs G M Cook **Trained** Westow, N Yorks
■ A first training success for ex-jockey Paul Midgley.
■ Stewards Enquiry : J D O'Reilly one-day ban: careless riding (Apr 23)

**FOCUS**
A competitive sprint handicap and a very decent time in the conditions. The form looks solid.

**NOTEBOOK**
**Grey Cossack** did not shape too badly on his reappearance and built on that promise to get back to winning form. There was not a great deal in it at the line, but this is his time of year - he has now won three times in April and three times in May - and a follow up cannot be ruled out.
**Pawan(IRE)**, runner-up in a seller on Fibresand on his latest start, coped well in this better race and only just failed to get off the mark. He is lightly raced and open to more improvement.
**Lincoln Dancer(IRE)** has not won since May 2000, but he has started this turf season in good form and, although clearly not easy to predict, he should soon end that losing run if maintaining this level of form.
**If By Chance** did not look to have any excuses, but is high enough in the weights.
**Quiet Times(IRE)**, trying to exploit a mark 21lb lower than that of his All-Weather rating, ran respectably, especially considering he lost his place with about three to run, but he is quite simply not as good on turf.
**Balakiref**, under a 6lb penalty for a recent Southwell (turf) success, failed to run to form.

## 1362 GO RACING IN YORKSHIRE MEDIAN AUCTION MAIDEN STKS 5f
4:35 (4:38) (D) 3-Y-O £3,357 (£1,033; £516; £258) **Stalls** Centre

Form RPR
443 **1** **Cheeky Chi (IRE)**[9] 1243 3-8-9 66 ........................ RWinston 7 61
(PSMcentee) *trckd ldrs: effrt and nt clr run over 1f out: swtchd lft and rdn to ld ins last: kpt on* **5/1**[3]
00-2 **2** *nk* **Mr Wolf**[12] 1196 3-8-11 62 ........................ LEnstone[(3)] 5 65
(DWBarker) *cl up: led 11/2f out: sn rdn: hdd and nt qckn ins last* **4/1**[2]
5- **3** *3 ½* **Bond Shakira**[261] 3608 3-8-9 ........................ FLynch 2 48
(BSmart) *wnt lft s: chsd ldrs: hdwy 2f out: sn rdn and hung lft over 1f out: kpt on same pce* **7/1**
432- **4** *1 ¼* **Fishlake Flyer (IRE)**[229] 4508 3-8-9 71 ........................ (v[1]) PHanagan 6 44
(JGGiven) *cl up: ev ch 2f out tl rdn and wknd ent last* **5/2**[1]
60- **5** *2* **Scooby Dooby Do**[167] 5818 3-8-9 ........................ VHalliday 9 37
(RMWhitaker) *s.i.s and bhd: hdwy over 2f out: styd on aproaching last: nrst fin* **12/1**

000- **6** *3* **Tapleon**[160] 5913 3-8-4 ........ TEaves(5) 4 27
(CJTeague) *dwlt: a rr* **66/1**

00- **7** *3 1/2* **Aguilera**[183] 5510 3-8-9 ........ RFfrench 3 15
(MDods) *chsd ldrs to 1/2-way: sn wknd* **14/1**

00-0 **8** *1/2* **Lady Sunset (IRE)**[12] 1196 3-8-9 62 ........ NCallan 8 13
(KARyan) *led: rdn along 2f out: hdd & wknd over 1f out* **7/1**

200- **9** *hd* **Queens Square**[242] 4118 3-8-9 50 ........ KimTinkler 1 13
(NTinkler) *bmpd s: bhd fr 1/2-way* **9/1**

63.99 secs (5.29) **Going Correction** +1.00s/f (Soft) **9** Ran SP% **116.1**
Speed ratings: **97,96,90,88,85 80,75,74,74**CSF £25.48 TOTE £5.80: £1.90, £2.10, £3.10; EX 19.10.

**Owner** Mrs R L McEntee **Bred** Miss Catriona Browne **Trained** Newmarket, Suffolk

**FOCUS**
Just a modest maiden featuring a number of exposed performers. The runner-up was the only colt in the field.

**NOTEBOOK**
**Cheeky Chi(IRE)** showed promise in just ordinary maidens over six and seven furlongs on the Polytrack and, switched to the turf and dropped in trip, she proved good enough to get off the mark. She will find things harder in handicaps, but is going the right way and should be competitive.

**Mr Wolf** has started the season in good form and, for the second race running, was just denied. A small race will come his way.

**Bond Shakira** showed little on her only start at two, but this was a little better. She did not help her chance by hanging under pressure, but shaped as though in need of another furlong in any case.

**Fishlake Flyer(IRE)**, a slightly frustrating sort last term, did not run to her mark of 71 on this reappearance in a first-time visor.

**Scooby Dooby Do** was well held, but may improve over farther in handicaps.

## 1363 REDCARRACING.CO.UK H'CAP 1m

**5:10** (5:11) (F) (0-55,55) 3-Y-O **£3,474** (£1,069; £534; £267) **Stalls** Centre

Form RPR

00-0 **1** **Perfect Balance (IRE)**[12] 1214 3-9-5 55 ........ KimTinkler 5 63
(NTinkler) *midfield: pushed along 1/2-way: hdwy ov er 2f out: sn rdn and styd on wl appr last: hung lft and led last 100 yds* **33/1**

0-46 **2** *1 1/2* **Biscar Two (IRE)**[55] 804 3-8-10 46 oh1 ........ VHalliday 1 51
(RMWhitaker) *slowly away: sn bhd and drvn along: swtchd rt 1/2-way: hdwy over 2f out: styd on u.p to chal ent last: kpt on* **25/1**

00-0 **3** *1 1/4* **Ace Coming**[18] 1108 3-9-0 55 ........(b) PMulrennan(5) 14 57
(DEddy) *cl up: swed rt to stands rail and led 2f out: rdn over 1f out: drvn ins last: hdd & wknd last 100 yds* **12/1**

300- **4** *1/2* **Pay Attention**[200] 5175 3-8-13 52 ........ DAllan(3) 7 53
(TDEasterby) *hmpd s and bhd: stdy hdwy over 2f out: rdn and ch over 1f out: drvn and one pce ins last* **16/1**

0-U5 **5** *3* **Dalida**[17] 1111 3-9-2 52 ........ GFaulkner 3 47
(PCHaslam) *trckd ldrs centre gng wl: hdwy to chal 2f out and ev ch tl rdn: edgd rt and wknd ent last* **9/1**[3]

045- **6** *6* **Salut Saint Cloud**[126] 6147 3-9-0 50 ........(v) DarrenWilliams 6 33
(MissVHaigh) *prom: rdn along over 2f out: grad wknd* **40/1**

006- **7** *5* **Plausabelle**[216] 4788 3-8-8 51 ........ AMullen(7) 16 24
(TDEasterby) *in tch stands side: pushed along and outpcd 1/2-way: swtchd lft 2f out and kpt on ins last: n.d* **50/1**

003- **8** *1* **Tancred Imp**[207] 5006 3-8-5 46 oh1 ........ TEaves(5) 13 17
(DWBarker) *cl up: rdn along over 3f out: grad wknd* **33/1**

060- **9** *1 3/4* **Tiz Wiz**[173] 5701 3-8-10 46 ........ DRMcCabe 12 14
(WStorey) *led: rdn along 3f out: hdd 2f out and wknd appr last* **50/1**

-006 **10** *nk* **Poacher's Paradise**[7] 1267 3-8-10 46 oh1 ........ DaleGibson 9 13
(MWEasterby) *chsd ldrs centre: rdn along 1/2-way: wknd 3f out* **11/1**

004- **11** *2 1/2* **Holly Walk**[207] 5021 3-8-11 50 ........ LEnstone(3) 8 12
(MDods) *midfield: rdn along 1/2-way: sn wknd* **16/1**

4405 **12** *nk* **Myannabanana (IRE)**[7] 1267 3-9-5 55 ........(p) RWinston 4 16
(JRWeymes) *cahsed ldrs on outer: rdn along over 3f out: sn wknd* **11/1**

00-2 **13** *5* **Reedsman (IRE)**[75] 620 3-9-3 53 ........(p) NCallan 10 4
(RCGuest) *a rr* **9/1**[3]

60-1 **14** *2* **Poker**[55] 802 3-9-5 55 ........ PHanagan 2 2
(WJHaggas) *trckd ldrs: smooth hdwy 3f over 3f out and sn ev ch: rdn over 2f out: sn btn and eased* **6/4**[1]

606- **15** *13* **Saros (IRE)**[188] 5439 3-9-3 53 ........ FLynch 15 —
(BSmart) *midfield: rdn along 1/2-way: sn wknd* **8/1**[2]

600- **16** *7* **Delta Lady**[178] 5621 3-8-10 46 ........ RFfrench 11 —
(RBastiman) *midfield: rdn along 1/2-way: sn wknd* **33/1**

1m 48.67s (10.97) **Going Correction** +1.00s/f (Soft) **16** Ran SP% **126.3**
Speed ratings: **85,83,82,81,78 72,67,66,65,64 62,61,56,54,41 34**CSF £696.16 CT £10400.65 TOTE £58.70: £6.50, £6.80, £2.70, £2.10; EX 1386.90 Place 6 £1,252.40, Place 5 £555.54..

**Owner** Alec & Pat Findlay **Bred** Lodge Park Stud **Trained** Langton, N Yorks

**FOCUS**
A poor handicap run in a slow time that is unlikely to produce many future winners.

**NOTEBOOK**
**Perfect Balance(IRE)** shaped well on his debut but had failed to build on that subsequently. He was 5lb lower than when well beaten on his reappearance and ran out a clear-cut winner. His starting price would suggest this was not expected and it remains to be seen if he can build on this.

**Biscar Two(IRE)**, dropped back three furlongs in trip, ran his best race to date and is on a mark that qualifies him for regional racing.

**Ace Coming**, dropped 6lb for a poor effort at Doncaster on his latest outing, had his chance and ran well enough.

**Pay Attention** appeared to lose his way towards the end of last season, but this was a respectable return.

**Dalida** travelled well but found little.

**Poacher's Paradise** *Official explanation: jockey said gelding hung right from three furlongs out.*

**Poker**, who landed a gamble when making a winning handicap debut over a mile at Southwell 55 days previously, failed to build on that on this switch back to turf. He is, however, obviously capable of better. *Official explanation: jockey said gelding was unsuited by the soft ground*

**Saros(IRE)** *Official explanation: jockey said colt lost its action*

T/Plt: £238.70 to a £1 stake. Pool: £26,375.25. 80.65 winning tickets. T/Qpdt: £148.40 to a £1 stake. Pool: £1,665.20. 8.30 winning tickets. JR

# 1299 WARWICK (L-H)

Monday, April 12

**OFFICIAL GOING: Good to soft**

Wind: nil Weather: fine but becoming cloudy

## 1364 SUNRISE MEDIAN AUCTION MAIDEN FILLIES' STKS 5f

**2:15** (2:16) (E) 2-Y-O **£3,818** (£1,175; £587; £293) **Stalls** Low

Form RPR

0 **1** **Justaquestion**[18] 1105 2-8-11 ........ GDuffield 5 71
(IAWood) *chsd ldrs: rdn over 2f out: led jst over 1f out: drvn out* **6/4**[1]

**2** *1 1/4* **Chilly Cracker** 2-8-11 ........ DSweeney 11 66+
(RHollinshead) *s.i.s: sn swtchd lft: outpcd: hdwy 2f out: sn edgd lft: rn ins fnl f: nt trble wnr* **25/1**

**3** *1 1/2* **Withering Lady (IRE)** 2-8-11 ........ RHavlin 7 60
(MrsPNDutfield) *hld up in tch: rdn over 2f out: hdwy over 1f out: kpt on ins fnl f* **12/1**

5 **4** *1 1/2* **Zimbali**[4] 1307 2-8-11 ........ SCarson 4 54
(JMBradley) *w ldrs: rdn over 2f out: no ex fnl f* **22/1**

**5** *nk* **Lady Misha** 2-8-11 ........ KDalgleish 6 53
(JeddO'Keeffe) *hld up: rdn over 2f out: hdwy fnl f: r.o* **40/1**

**6** *1* **Straffan (IRE)** 2-8-11 ........ DaneO'Neill 9 49
(EJO'Neill) *hld up on outside: rdn and no hdwy fnl 2f* **16/1**

5 **7** *1/2* **Town House**[12] 1208 2-8-11 ........ ACulhane 2 47
(BPJBaugh) *led: rdn and hdd jst over 1f out: wknd ins fnl f* **20/1**

**8** *2 1/2* **Stan's Girl** 2-8-11 ........ TEDurcan 8 37
(MRChannon) *dwlt: outpcd: nvr nr ldrs* **9/2**[2]

**9** *4* **Fantastic Star** 2-8-11 ........ MFenton 3 21
(JGGiven) *w ldr 2f: sn rdn: wknd 2f out* **8/1**[3]

**10** *5* **Blade Runner (IRE)** 2-8-11 ........ PaulEddery 10 1
(DHaydnJones) *s.i.s: outpcd* **8/1**[3]

**11** *1 1/4* **Champagne In Paris** 2-8-11 ........ GGibbons 1 —
(JAGlover) *prom: rdn over 2f out: wknd over 1f out* **16/1**

63.37 secs (3.17) **Going Correction** +0.425s/f (Yiel) **11** Ran SP% **115.3**
Speed ratings: **91,89,86,84,83 82,81,77,70,62 60**CSF £51.54 TOTE £2.20: £1.10, £4.60, £5.40; EX 55.10.

**Owner** Christopher Shankland **Bred** A S Reid **Trained** Upper Lambourn, Berks

**FOCUS**
This looked an ordinary event but it is of course possible that time may prove otherwise.

**NOTEBOOK**
**Justaquestion**, all the better for the experience she gained in the Brocklesby, was kept up to her work to score with a bit in hand.

**Chilly Cracker ◆**, a half-sister to dual six-furlong winner Run On, showed definite signs of inexperience and should derive considerable benefit from the outing.

**Withering Lady(IRE)** is a half-sister to five-furlong juvenile winner Midnight Arrow. She shaped as though she will appreciate another furlong.

**Zimbali**, making a quick reappearance, appears to be struggling to get home at the moment.

**Lady Misha** is bred to need further and was doing her best work late on.

**Straffan(IRE)** is a half-sister to the mile All-Weather specialist Miss Champers.

**Fantastic Star** *Official explanation: jockey said filly became unbalanced 1 1/2f furlongs out.*

## 1365 SHREWLEY H'CAP 1m 2f 188y

**2:50** (2:56) (E) (0-70,70) 3-Y-O **£3,997** (£1,230; £615; £307) **Stalls** Low

Form RPR

6065 **1** **Bill Bennett (FR)**[12] 1201 3-9-2 65 ........ GBaker 6 71
(JJay) *hld up and bhd: hdwy over 2f out: rdn and swtchd rt over 1f out: r.o to ld cl home* **9/1**

066 **2** *1/2* **Zaffeu**[24] 1050 3-9-3 69 ........ J-PGuillambert(3) 3 74
(NPLittmoden) *hld up: hdwy on ins over 4f out: nt clr run briefly over 2f out: sn rdn: ev ch 1f out: kpt on towards fin* **25/1**

045- **3** *nk* **Glide**[181] 5565 3-9-7 70 ........ SDrowne 1 75
(RCharlton) *a.p: rdn to ld over 2f out: edgd lft over 1f out: hdd ins fnl f: r.o* **7/1**[2]

50-0 **4** *shd* **Mambina (USA)**[46] 890 3-9-2 65 ........ TEDurcan 5 69
(MRChannon) *hld up mid-div: hdwy on ins over 4f out: rdn over 2f out: led ins fnl f: hdd and nt qckn cl home* **14/1**

00-0 **5** *1* **The King Of Rock**[84] 561 3-8-8 57 ........ SWhitworth 16 61+
(AGNewcombe) *dwlt: bhd tl hdwy over 3f out: rdn 2f out: ev ch whn hmpd 1f out: nt rcvr* **50/1**

00-0 **6** *1 1/2* **Suchwot (IRE)**[12] 1214 3-8-7 56 ........ SWKelly 8 56
(FJordan) *dwlt: bhd tl hdwy on ins over 3f out: hrd rdn and ev ch 1f out: no ex towards fin* **20/1**

550- **7** *8* **Spectested (IRE)**[168] 5792 3-8-13 65 ........ LPKeniry(3) 7 52
(BJMeehan) *s.i.s: hdwy over 4f out: nt clr run 3f out: rdn and carrying hd high 2f out: hung lft over 1f out: nt run on* **14/1**

1260 **8** *nk* **Desert Image (IRE)**[11] 1222 3-9-4 70 ........ DCorby(3) 19 56
(CTinkler) *hld up towards rr: rdn and sme hdwy on outside over 2f out: no further prog* **40/1**

1105 **9** *2 1/2* **Smart Boy Prince (IRE)**[25] 1046 3-8-11 65 ........ DNolan(5) 2 47
(PABlockley) *led after 2f: rdn and hdd over 2f out: wknd over 1f out* **22/1**

500- **10** *3* **Charlie Bear**[182] 5547 3-9-6 69 ........ MHills 9 46
(EALDunlop) *nvr trbld ldrs* **7/2**[1]

4145 **11** *3/4* **Another Con (IRE)**[19] 1100 3-9-3 66 ........ RHavlin 12 41
(MrsPNDutfield) *a mid-div* **14/1**

-663 **12** *5* **Pepe (IRE)**[10] 1235 3-7-13 55 ow6 ........ StephanieHollinshead(7) 11 22
(RHollinshead) *prom tl wknd over 2f* **25/1**

50-6 **13** *4* **Mister Trickster (IRE)**[11] 1222 3-9-0 63 ........ SRighton 13 23
(RDickin) *prom: rdn over 3f out: wknd over 2f out* **8/1**[3]

-003 **14** *1* **Darn Good**[19] 1100 3-9-6 69 ........(v) DaneO'Neill 18 27
(RHannon) *a bhd* **12/1**

1350 **15** *3* **Keepers Knight (IRE)**[40] 957 3-9-3 66 ........ ACulhane 4 19
(PFICole) *prom: rdn over 3f out: wknd over 2f out* **14/1**

235- **16** *3/4* **Petite Colleen (IRE)**[136] 6082 3-9-5 68 ........ PaulEddery 14 20
(DHaydnJones) *prom tl wknd over 4f out* **40/1**

00-0 **17** *22* **Killoch Place (IRE)**[11] 1222 3-8-2 51 ........(b[1]) SCarson 10 —
(JAGlover) *led 2f: prom tl wknd qckly over 3f out: t.o* **40/1**

35-0 **18** *6* **Troubleinparadise (IRE)**[11] 1222 3-8-9 58 ........(b[1]) MFenton 17 —
(JGGiven) *mid-div: rdn over 7f out: sn bhd: t.o* **40/1**

0051 **19** *dist* **Our Little Rosie**[14] 1179 3-8-11 60 ........ DSweeney 15 —
(MBlanshard) *bhd fnl 6f: virtually p.u fnl 2f* **12/1**

2m 24.83s (5.43) **Going Correction** +0.425s/f (Yiel) **19** Ran SP% **126.4**
Speed ratings: **97,96,96,96,95 94,88,88,86,84 83,80,77,76,74 73,57,53,—**CSF £229.35 CT £1691.20 TOTE £10.80: £3.50, £4.60, £2.60, £3.30; EX 653.30.

**Owner** Mr & Mrs Jonathan Jay **Bred** J Jay **Trained** Newmarket, Suffolk

■ Stewards Enquiry : S Drowne one-day ban: careless riding (Apr 23)

**FOCUS**
A fair handicap in which most of these were well exposed. This slowly-run affair produced a somewhat messy result.

**NOTEBOOK**
**Bill Bennett(FR)** was a winner over the extended nine furlongs at Wolverhampton just before Christmas. He lived up to his trainer's belief that he prefers the turf to Fibresand.
**Zaffeu** had shown signs of ability in three maidens on the Polytrack and seems to be going the right way.
**Glide**, gelded since last year, was stepping up from a mile on his handicap debut. Not beaten for a lack of stamina, he may have preferred a stronger gallop.
**Mambina(USA)** had shown promise at Newmarket last November prior to disappointing on the Polytrack. She looked far more at home back on turf.
**The King Of Rock**, taking a big step up in distance, was the unlucky horse of the race. Apparently unfancied in the ring, he deserves another chance.
**Suchwot(IRE)**, nibbled at in the market, may have found this longer trip stretching him to the limit.
**Keepers Knight(IRE)** *Official explanation: jockey said colt lost its action in the closing stages.*
**Our Little Rosie** *Official explanation: jockey said filly was struck into and was lame behind.*

## 1366 GEOFF WOODWARD "LIFETIME IN RACING" MAIDEN STKS (DIV I) 7f 26y
**3:20** (3:26) (D) 3-Y-O **£3,705** (£1,140; £570; £285) **Stalls** Low

Form RPR
524- **1** **River Treat (FR)**[185] 5470 3-9-0 85 SDrowne 4 86+
(GWragg) *t.k.h: sn prom: led jst ins fnl f: rdn and r.o* **10/11**[1]
355- **2** *hd* **Cello**[165] 5836 3-9-0 78 PDobbs 3 86+
(RHannon) *w ldr: led 4f out: rdn over 1f out: hdd jst ins fnl f: r.o* **5/1**[3]
000- **3** *10* **Marksgold (IRE)**[128] 6129 3-9-0 MHills 7 57
(PFICole) *led 3f: w ldr tl rdn over 2f out: wknd over 1f out* **28/1**
3432 **4** *1 1/2* **Soul Provider (IRE)**[11] 1220 3-8-8 52 ow4 DNolan(5) 9 52
(PABlockley) *w ldrs tl rdn and wknd over 1f out* **9/1**
00 **5** *1/2* **Accendere**[24] 1052 3-9-0 DSweeney 2 52
(RMBeckett) *hld up and bhd: sme hdwy 3f out: nvr nr to chal* **100/1**
550- **6** *2* **Verkhotina**[195] 5285 3-8-9 75 DaneO'Neill 13 42
(RCharlton) *hld up: hdwy over 4f out: rdn over 2f out: wknd over 1f out* **9/2**[2]
000- **7** *shd* **Snow Joke (IRE)**[283] 2950 3-8-9 RHavlin 12 41
(MrsPNDutfield) *hld up mid-div: rdn over 2f out: wknd over 1f out* **25/1**
0- **8** *1* **Doringo**[156] 5948 3-9-0 ADaly 5 44
(JLSpearing) *bhd fnl 4f* **33/1**
000- **9** *1 1/2* **Don Argento**[203] 5112 3-8-11 DCorby(3) 6 40
(MrsAJBowlby) *s.s: hdwy over 3f out: wknd over 1f out* **100/1**
0 **10** *1 3/4* **Justice Jones**[30] 1012 3-8-11 LisaJones(3) 8 35
(JLSpearing) *a bhd* **50/1**
0-00 **11** *nk* **Indian Call**[11] 1222 3-9-0 60 GGibbons 11 34
(BAMcmahon) *chsd ldrs: sn rdn along: wknd over 3f out* **14/1**
0 **12** *13* **Golnessa**[29] 1022 3-8-9 PaulEddery 10 —
(MrsNMacauley) *a bhd* **150/1**

1m 26.57s (1.67) **Going Correction** +0.425s/f (Yiel) **12 Ran SP% 118.7**
Speed ratings: **107,106,95,93,93 90,90,89,87,85 85,70**CSF £5.39 TOTE £1.70: £1.10, £1.90, £3.40; EX 5.70.
**Owner** Peter R Pritchard **Bred** Tarworth Bloodstock Ltd **Trained** Newmarket, Suffolk

**FOCUS**
Despite the fact this was over a second quicker than the other division, this was an uncompetitive affair although the front two are probably decent.

**NOTEBOOK**
**River Treat(FR)** was disappointing when beaten at 2/5 on the last of three runs over six furlongs last year. He had to work a bit harder than anticipated after going smoothly to the front but the first two did pull well clear.
**Cello** made sure the favourite did not have things all his own way and ought to be capable of taking a similar event.
**Marksgold(IRE)**, who has been gelded since changing stables, could not live with the two principals in the short home straight.
**Soul Provider(IRE)** is fully exposed and was only second in a seller last time.
**Accendere** ◆ had shown nothing in a couple of outings over 7f on the Polytrack. Tenderly handled, he was the subject of a Stewards' enquiry into his running and riding and the long-winded explanations were noted. He seems likely to do better in handicaps. *Official explanation: jockey said, regarding the running and riding, gelding is big and backward and orders were to hold it up, let it find its feet, get it balanced and get it to finish in first six for its handicap mark, but not to hit it, adding that gelding broke well but could not go the initial pace and could not get a clear run up the rail, adding that trainer thought gelding would be unsuited by the ground and the sharp track*

## 1367 "WEST MIDLANDS" CONDITIONS STKS 7f 26y
**3:55** (3:56) (C) 4-Y-O+ **£10,115** (£3,836; £1,918; £872) **Stalls** Low

Form RPR
55-0 **1** **Pablo**[16] 1125 5-8-8 103 (p) MHills 1 70
(BWHills) *led over 5f out: rdn and hdd over 1f out: led wl ins fnl f: drvn out* **2/1**[1]
-333 **2** *nk* **Rockets 'n Rollers (IRE)**[8] 1254 4-8-8 104 DaneO'Neill 2 69
(RHannon) *a.p: rdn to ld 1f out: hdd wl ins fnl f: r.o* **5/2**[2]
20/- **3** *1* **Kool (IRE)**[562] 4937 5-8-8 SDrowne 3 67
(PFICole) *hld up: hdwy 2f out: rdn and r.o one pce fnl f* **16/1**
0240 **4** *2* **Queens Rhapsody**[23] 1065 4-8-8 85 TEDurcan 7 62
(ABailey) *hld up: hdwy over 1f out: one pce fnl f* **16/1**
0625 **5** *1 1/4* **Quito (IRE)**[9] 1242 7-9-6 103 (b) ACulhane 8 71
(DWChapman) *hld up in tch: hdwy over 3f out: wnt 2nd over 2f out: rdn over 1f out: wknd fnl f* **6/1**
0062 **6** *nk* **Dancing King (IRE)**[14] 1177 8-8-9 46 LisaJones(3) 6 62?
(PWHiatt) *led over 1f: w wnr tl over 2f out: rdn and wknd over 1f out* **100/1**
3012 **7** *3* **Just A Glimmer**[16] 1139 4-8-3 84 ADaly 10 46
(LGCottrell) *prom tl wknd over 2f out* **20/1**
130- **8** *2* **Hit's Only Money (IRE)**[205] 5060 4-8-8 100 ow5 DNolan(5) 5 51
(PABlockley) *prom: rdn over 2f out: sn wknd* **4/1**[3]
065- **9** *1 1/2* **Takes Tutu (USA)**[243] 4075 5-8-8 83 KDalgleish 9 42
(KRBurke) *a bhd* **40/1**
66 **10** *1/2* **Celtic Vision (IRE)**[9] 1249 8-8-8 SRighton 4 41
(MAppleby) *s.i.s: a bhd* **150/1**

1m 25.67s (0.77) **Going Correction** +0.425s/f (Yiel) **10 Ran SP% 116.8**
Speed ratings: **112,111,110,108,106 106,103,100,99,98**CSF £6.98 TOTE £3.20: £1.40, £1.10, £4.70; EX 9.30.
**Owner** Guy Reed **Bred** G Reed **Trained** Lambourn, Berks

**FOCUS**
A good quality event run in a fast time, although the proximity of the sixth casts doubt over the form.

**NOTEBOOK**
**Pablo**, who wore cheekpieces after hanging in the Lincoln, held off a strong challenge from the runner-up slightly more easily than the narrow margin would suggest. Cut in the ground is a must.
**Rockets 'n Rollers(IRE)** had a good chance at the weights and just missed out. He is running well so far this term without winning, and the competition is set to become increasingly tough.
**Kool(IRE)** had trip and ground to suit for this first run since September 2002. He had been gelded in the interim and this was a highly encouraging return to action.
**Queens Rhapsody** proved his effectiveness on turf and this was a good run considering he would have been 18lb better off with Pablo in a handicap.
**Quito(IRE)** was not disgraced conceding weight all round.
**Dancing King(IRE)** ran a decent race considering he had no chance at the weights.
**Hit's Only Money(IRE)**, stepping up in trip for this seasonal return, was not helped by having to carry 5lb overweight.
**Celtic Vision(IRE)** *Official explanation: jockey said gelding had a breathing problem.*

## 1368 PEARSE H'CAP 5f
**4:30** (4:33) (E) (0-70,70) 3-Y-O+ **£4,013** (£1,235; £617; £308) **Stalls** Low

Form RPR
0-30 **1** **Dunn Deal (IRE)**[10] 1230 4-9-3 59 TEDurcan 4 69+
(WMBrisbourne) *hld up: hdwy on ins 2f out: nt clr run briefly jst over 1f out: rdn to ld nr fin* **20/1**
1120 **2** *nk* **Mynd**[20] 1082 4-9-6 62 MHills 8 71
(RMWhitaker) *w ldrs: rdn to ld 1f out: hdd nr fin* **9/2**[1]
1214 **3** *1 1/4* **Playtime Blue**[16] 1131 4-9-7 63 GBaker 7 68
(KRBurke) *led over 2f: rdn and ev ch ins fnl f: r.o* **9/2**[1]
4534 **4** *shd* **Boavista (IRE)**[7] 1268 4-8-13 55 RHavlin 13 59
(PDEvans) *hld up: hdwy over 2f out: rdn over 1f out: kpt on towards fin* **20/1**
115- **5** *3/4* **Astrac (IRE)**[182] 5540 13-8-9 51 PMQuinn 6 53
(MrsALMKing) *hld up: hdwy over 2f out: rdn over 1f out: ev ch ins fnl f: no ex towards fin* **33/1**
4210 **6** *nk* **Double M**[10] 1230 7-8-7 49 (v) ADaly 12 50
(MrsLRichards) *hld up and bhd: hdwy fnl f: r.o* **10/1**[3]
0050 **7** *shd* **Taboor (IRE)**[45] 904 6-9-1 57 (b) KDalgleish 16 57
(JWPayne) *plld hrd towards rr: rdn and hdwy over 1f out: edgd lft ins fnl f: nt rch ldrs* **12/1**
6446 **8** *1/2* **River Lark (USA)**[7] 1262 5-8-3 48 LisaJones(3) 9 46
(MABuckley) *bhd tl hdwy over 2f out: r.o one pce fnl f* **25/1**
4451 **9** *hd* **Blakeshall Quest**[14] 1178 4-9-2 58 (v) ACulhane 5 56
(RBrotherton) *chsd ldrs: rdn 2f out: one pce fnl f* **11/2**[2]
0004 **10** *hd* **Prince Of Blues (IRE)**[12] 1205 6-9-2 58 (p) SWKelly 3 55
(MMullineaux) *w ldr: led over 2f out: edgd lft over 1f out: sn rdn and hdd: wknd towards fin* **16/1**
0204 **11** *2* **King's Ballet (USA)**[14] 1180 6-9-0 56 (p) SDrowne 10 46
(PRChamings) *hld up: rdn over 2f out: hdwy over 1f out: eased whn btn wl ins fnl f* **16/1**
102- **12** *2 1/2* **Stokesies Wish**[164] 5849 4-9-10 66 GCarter 14 47
(JLSpearing) *mid-div: wknd over 1f out* **25/1**
6-00 **13** *hd* **Shady Deal**[42] 944 8-8-10 52 SCarson 2 33
(JMBradley) *chsd ldrs: rdn over 1f out: wknd fnl f* **25/1**
256- **14** *1 1/4* **Pulse**[231] 4468 6-9-5 61 (p) MFenton 20 37
(JMBradley) *racd wd: chsd ldrs: c stands' side: wknd 1f out* **25/1**
0600 **15** *nk* **Prime Recreation**[16] 1131 7-9-9 65 DaneO'Neill 15 40
(PSFelgate) *prom: rdn 2f out: wknd 1f out* **33/1**
00-0 **16** *1 1/4* **Brantwood (IRE)**[4] 1313 4-10-0 70 GGibbons 19 41
(BAMcmahon) *racd wd: rdn 2f out: sn bhd* **16/1**
0240 **17** *1/2* **Bali-Star**[34] 1000 9-8-3 45 PaulEddery 11 14
(RJHodges) *chsd ldrs: rdn over 2f out: wknd wl over 1f out* **33/1**
005- **18** *3/4* **Boanerges (IRE)**[262] 3556 7-9-6 62 GDuffield 17 28
(JMBradley) *chsd ldrs: c stands' side: wknd over 1f out* **16/1**
0020 **19** *1 3/4* **St Ivian**[7] 1265 4-9-8 64 (v) JoannaBadger 18 24
(MrsNMacauley) *a bhd* **16/1**

62.65 secs (2.45) **Going Correction** +0.425s/f (Yiel) **19 Ran SP% 131.7**
Speed ratings: **97,96,94,94,93 92,92,91,91,91 87,83,83,81,81 79,78,77,74**CSF £102.96 CT £498.67 TOTE £19.60: £4.00, £1.90, £1.70, £4.20; EX 159.40.
**Owner** Raymond McNeill **Bred** John Cullinan **Trained** Great Ness, Shropshire

**FOCUS**
An ordinary sprint handicap but the time was unexceptional. The runner-up translated his ll-Weather form to turf.

**NOTEBOOK**
**Dunn Deal(IRE)** was back over his ideal trip as he failed to stay six furlongs on his most recent start. He was briefly denied a run on the fence going to the furlong pole but the gap appeared in time.
**Mynd**, like the winner happier over this trip, has been in good form on the Fibresand and returned to turf on a handy mark. He was always in the front rank but, having got his head in front, was just unable to hold on.
**Playtime Blue** ran well from an unfavourable draw at Kempton and remains in good form.
**Boavista(IRE)**, who was doing her best work at the finish, remains a maiden but is consistent enough.
**Astrac(IRE)** is ideally suited by farther these days. This is his twelfth season on the track, and in that time he has run at every British Flat course apart from Chepstow.
**Double M** is a stone lower on turf than he is on the All-Weather.
**Taboor(IRE)**, who was fourth in this event last year, became warm in the preliminaries.

## 1369 "ISLE OF INISFREE" H'CAP 1m 2f 188y
**5:05** (5:06) (E) (0-75,75) 4-Y-O+ **£4,338** (£1,335; £667; £333) **Stalls** Low

Form RPR
1303 **1** **True Companion**[20] 1088 5-9-1 65 J-PGuillambert(3) 2 73
(NPLittmoden) *hld up and bhd: stdy hdwy on ins over 3f out: rdn over 1f out: led wl ins fnl f: r.o* **10/1**
3412 **2** *1* **Classic Role**[7] 1272 5-10-0 75 (v) ACulhane 14 82+
(RIngram) *hld up: sn in tch: rdn to ld over 1f out: hdd wl ins fnl f: r.o* **7/2**[2]
2011 **3** *1/2* **War Owl (USA)**[4] 1308 7-9-2 66 6ex LisaJones(3) 19 72+
(IanWilliams) *hld up and bhd: hmpd over 3f out: hdwy on outside over 1f out: sn rdn: r.o ins fnl f* **2/1**[1]
0350 **4** *1/2* **Top Of The Class (IRE)**[21] 1077 7-8-11 58 (v) SDrowne 1 63
(PDEvans) *hld up mid-div: hdwy on ins over 3f out: rdn 2f out: r.o one pce fnl f* **33/1**
114- **5** *2 1/2* **Lennel**[241] 4157 6-9-7 68 TEDurcan 7 69
(ABailey) *s.i.s: bhd tl hdwy on ins over 1f out: nvr able to chal* **16/1**
0000 **6** *1 3/4* **Queen Excalibur**[18] 1103 5-7-7 45 DFox(5) 16 43
(CRoberts) *hld up mid-div: rdn over 3f out: hdwy 2f out: one pce fnl f* **50/1**
6342 **7** *shd* **Burgundy**[20] 1088 7-8-11 58 KDalgleish 20 56
(PMitchell) *hld up towards rr: rdn and hdwy 2f out: swtchd lft over 1f out: one pce fnl f* **12/1**
U1 **8** *shd* **Dissident (GER)**[10] 1231 6-9-9 70 (v) DaneO'Neill 9 67
(DFlood) *prom: rdn to ld 2f out: hdd over 1f out: wknd fnl f* **9/1**[3]
1461 **9** *nk* **Game Guru**[27] 1031 5-8-8 62 (b) SYourston(7) 10 59
(PABlockley) *prom: rdn over 2f out: wknd 1f out* **33/1**

-126 **10** *5* **Cool Bathwick (IRE)**[77] 609 5-8-12 **59** ........ GBaker 13 47
(BRMillman) *prom: lost pl over 3f out: n.d after* **12/1**

230- **11** *1 1/2* **Pay The Silver**[165] 5839 6-9-12 **73** ........(p) GDuffield 8 59
(IAWood) *hld up mid-div: hdwy 4f out: sn rdn: wknd 2f out* **40/1**

450- **12** *7* **Summer Bounty**[116] 5291 8-9-3 **64** ........ SWKelly 6 38
(FJordan) *s.s: stdy hdwy over 6f out: rdn over 3f out: wknd 2f out* **33/1**

33-6 **13** *2 1/2* **Rozanee**[58] 767 4-9-1 **62** ........ MHills 11 32
(JWPayne) *led 1f: w ldr: led again over 5f out: rdn and hdd 2f out: wknd over 1f out* **25/1**

0- **14** *3/4* **Nautical**[32] 3699 6-9-1 **62** ........ DSweeney 5 30
(AWCarroll) *hld up in tch: rdn over 2f out: sn wknd* **66/1**

000- **15** *1 1/2* **Leitrim Rock (IRE)**[196] 5281 4-8-8 **55** ........ SWhitworth 3 21
(AGNewcombe) *s.v.s: a bhd* **25/1**

-000 **16** *shd* **La Muette (IRE)**[2] 1332 4-9-9 **70** ........ SRighton 17 36
(MAppleby) *s.i.s: a bhd* **50/1**

22-5 **17** *2 1/2* **Ember Days**[36] 464 5-9-3 **64** ........(b[1]) GCarter 4 25
(JLSpearing) *plld hrd: hdwy 8f out: rdn over 2f out: wknd wl over 1f out* **33/1**

600- **18** *3/4* **King's Mountain (USA)**[268] 3393 4-8-13 **60** ........ PMQuinn 12 20
(MrsALMKing) *a bhd* **66/1**

020- **19** *dist* **Burley Firebrand**[199] 5200 4-8-13 **60** ........ MFenton 18 —
(JGGiven) *bhd fnl 5f: t.o* **33/1**

/00- **20** *12* **Ace In The Hole**[332] 1638 4-7-13 **46** ........(p) JoannaBadger 15 —
(FJordan) *led after 1f tl over 5f out: wknd qckly over 4f out: t.o* **66/1**

2m 23.86s (4.46) **Going Correction** +0.425s/f (Yiel) **20 Ran SP% 129.1**
Speed ratings: **100,99,98,98,96 95,95,95,95,91 90,85,83,82,81 81,79,79,—,—**CSF £41.81 CT £103.57 TOTE £10.00: £2.40, £2.00, £1.10, £5.10; EX 57.90.
**Owner** Novowel Racing **Bred** S J Simmons **Trained** Newmarket, Suffolk

**FOCUS**
A fair handicap but run at only a steady pace and the form cannot be taken literally.

**NOTEBOOK**
**True Companion**, who has been in good form on the Lingfield Polytrack through the winter, had plenty to do turning in but came with a good run against the far rail to strike the front in the final 50 yards. All his wins to date have been for this jockey.
**Classic Role** was racing from the same mark as when runner-up at Windsor, and suffered a similar fate in that he looked in command but was run out of it. He does not find much in front and it might be better to hold him up for longer.
**War Owl(USA)**, under his penalty, had a lot of ground to make up after being hampered. He ran on well once in line for home, but at the same time was wandering and he did not look a straightforward ride. He remains in good form and should be kept on the right side.
**Top Of The Class(IRE)** was returning to the turf after failing to hit the target during a 13-run sand campaign.
**Lennel**, minus the blinkers on this first run since the autumn, made decent late progress. He prefers faster ground to this.
**Ember Days** *Official explanation: jockey said mare ran too free in the early stages.*

## 1370 GEOFF WOODWARD "LIFETIME IN RACING" MAIDEN STKS (DIV II) 7f 26y
5:35 (5:40) (D) 3-Y-O £3,688 (£1,135; £567; £283) Stalls Low

Form RPR

52- **1** **Key Partners (IRE)**[185] 5470 3-8-9 ........ DNolan(5) 1 73
(PABlockley) *a.p: led 3f out: hrd rdn fnl f: all out* **9/2**[3]

50- **2** *nk* **River Of Babylon**[166] 5830 3-8-9 ........ ACulhane 3 67
(MLWBell) *a.p: rdn 2f out: ev ch 1f out: r.o* **5/2**[1]

0 **3** *2 1/2* **Beauchamp Star**[5] 1295 3-8-9 ........ SCarson 9 61
(GAButler) *hld up: swtchd lft sn after s: hdwy over 3f out: one pce fnl f* **25/1**

0- **4** *2* **Burley Flame**[158] 5932 3-9-0 ........ MFenton 5 61
(JGGiven) *prom tl wknd over 1f out* **14/1**

000- **5** *1* **Daydream Dancer**[195] 5285 3-8-9 ........ RSmith 7 53
(CGCox) *mid-div: sn pushed along: hdwy 2f out: no imp fnl f* **28/1**

0- **6** *1* **General Flumpa**[168] 5792 3-9-0 ........ GBaker 10 56
(CFWall) *swtchd lft sn after s: rdn over 2f out: sme hdwy over 1f out: kpt on ins fnl f* **12/1**

60- **7** *shd* **The Fun Merchant**[291] 2714 3-9-0 ........ GDuffield 12 56
(WJarvis) *hld up and bhd: pushed along and sme hdwy over 1f out: n.d* **10/1**

00-0 **8** *6* **Roving Vixen (IRE)**[39] 965 3-8-9 ........ ADaly 11 36
(JLSpearing) *a bhd* **50/1**

**9** *5* **Rocket (IRE)** 3-9-0 ........ PDobbs 8 28
(RHannon) *prom: rdn over 2f out: sn wknd* **7/1**

6- **10** *1* **The Butterfly Boy**[245] 4051 3-9-0 ........ MHills 4 26
(PFICole) *led: hdd 3f out: rdn and rn green over 1f out: sn wknd* **11/4**[2]

00- **11** *10* **Rosie Maloney (IRE)**[150] 5993 3-8-6 ........ J-PGuillambert(3) 2 —
(NPLittmoden) *a bhd* **50/1**

0-0 **12** *8* **Pertemps Red**[24] 1050 3-8-9 ........ DFox(5) 6 —
(ADSmith) *a bhd* **50/1**

1m 27.74s (2.84) **Going Correction** +0.425s/f (Yiel) **12 Ran SP% 122.5**
Speed ratings: **100,99,96,94,93 92,92,85,79,78 66,57**CSF £16.12 TOTE £6.30: £1.80, £2.40, £4.50; EX 28.90 Place 6 £28.09, Place 5 £14.40..
**Owner** John Wardle **Bred** Michael Munnelly **Trained** Southwell, Notts

**FOCUS**
A weak maiden, run in a time more than a second slower than the first division and the form looks modest.

**NOTEBOOK**
**Key Partners(IRE)** was reluctant to enter the stalls. Always in the leading quintet, he stuck to the inner in the straight, where he had the rail to help him, and held on under a hard ride.
**River Of Babylon** raced up the centre in the home straight and just missed out to a rival who was helped by having the rail to race against. Handicaps are an option now.
**Beauchamp Star**, having her third run, was dropped in at the start from her high draw. She did best of those to race in the second bunch, some way off the leading five, and shaped as if in need of a bit farther.
**Burley Flame**, a half-brother to five winners, has been gelded since making his debut in the last week of the turf season.
**Daydream Dancer**, who raced at the head of the second wave of runners, was not disgraced.
**The Butterfly Boy** again ran green, as he had on his previous run, although this trip might have taxed him too. *Official explanation: jockey said colt lost its action in the closing stages.*
**Pertemps Red** *Official explanation: jockey said colt was never travelling.*
T/Plt: £17.60 to a £1 stake. Pool: £25,612.60. 1,059.60 winning tickets. T/Qpdt: £3.80 to a £1 stake. Pool: £1,705.10. 325.70 winning tickets. KH

# YARMOUTH (L-H)
Monday, April 12

**OFFICIAL GOING: Good to firm**
Wind: mod against Weather: overcast

## 1371 SHARP MINDS BETFAIR MAIDEN STKS 1m 3y
2:05 (2:09) (D) 3-Y-0+ £3,451 (£1,062; £531; £265) Stalls High

Form RPR

6- **1** **Andean**[279] 3076 3-8-9 ........ JPMurtagh 12 101+
(DRLoder) *mde all: clr 2f out: easily* **11/4**[2]

2- **2** *7* **Maclean**[246] 4004 3-8-9 ........ BDoyle 3 73+
(SirMichaelStoute) *hld up: hdwy 1/2-way: outpcd fnl 2f* **9/4**[1]

**3** *1 1/2* **Leg Spinner (IRE)** 3-8-6 ........ SHitchcott(3) 4 70
(MRChannon) *s.i.s: outpcd: hdwy over 2f out: nt trble ldrs* **50/1**

000- **4** *nk* **King Of Knight (IRE)**[166] 5830 3-8-9 ........ OUrbina 16 69
(GProdromou) *hld up: hdwy over 2f out: rdn over 1f out: no imp* **100/1**

40- **5** *hd* **La Persiana**[182] 5539 3-8-4 ........ JQuinn 15 63
(WJarvis) *plld hrd and prom: hmpd over 5f out: sn lost pl: n.d after* **33/1**

**6** *6* **Coppice (IRE)** 3-8-9 ........ RLMoore 7 55
(LMCumani) *s.i.s: hld up: hdwy 1/2-way: wknd 2f out* **25/1**

**7** *1* **Spector (IRE)** 4-9-7 ........ LFletcher(3) 13 52?
(JJSheehan) *sn outpcd: styd on ins fnl f: nvr nrr* **100/1**

**8** *nk* **Iktitaf (IRE)** 3-8-9 ........ WSupple 11 52
(JHMGosden) *trckd ldrs tl wknd wl over 1f out* **8/1**

52- **9** *2 1/2* **Habshan (USA)**[199] 5196 4-9-7 ........ ABeech(3) 20 46
(NAGraham) *chsd ldrs: hmpd over 5f out: wknd wl over 1f out* **9/1**

**10** *1 1/4* **Cunning Pursuit** 3-8-9 ........ JMackay 8 43
(MLWBell) *sn outpcd* **50/1**

**11** *1/2* **Star Magnitude (USA)** 3-8-9 ........ RHughes 9 42
(JHMGosden) *prom over 5f* **5/1**[3]

**12** *1* **Celebre Citation (IRE)** 3-8-9 ........ JDSmith 19 40
(JRFanshawe) *dwlt: nvr trbld ldrs* **33/1**

6 **13** *nk* **Suvari**[24] 1052 3-8-4 ........ CCatlin 5 34
(GCBravery) *prom over 5f* **50/1**

0- **14** *2* **Native Turk (USA)**[202] 5139 3-8-9 ........ SSanders 18 34
(JARToller) *s.i.s: sn prom: wknd over 2f out* **16/1**

0- **15** *8* **Tsarbuck**[224] 4611 3-8-9 ........ MHenry 10 16
(RMHCowell) *chsd ldrs over 5f* **100/1**

0000 **16** *6* **Time Flyer**[6] 1277 4-9-10 **40** ........ JFEgan 6 2
(WDeBest-Turner) *chsd ldrs over 5f* **100/1**

0 **17** *nk* **Byrd Island**[18] 1104 3-8-1 ........ TPQueally(3) 17 —
(DMorris) *hld up: hdwy 1/2-way: wknd wl over 2f out* **100/1**

-0 **18** *18* **Heyward Place**[88] 541 4-9-2 ........(t) BReilly(3) 1 —
(TKeddy) *sn outpcd* **100/1**

0 **19** *shd* **Hello Tiger**[13] 1192 3-8-9 ........ NPollard 14 —
(JASupple) *chsd ldrs: hung rt over 5f out: wknd over 3f out* **100/1**

1m 40.14s (0.44) **Going Correction** +0.325s/f (Good)
**WFA** 3 from 4yo 15lb **19 Ran SP% 123.6**
Speed ratings: **110,103,101,101,101 95,94,93,91,89 89,88,88,86,78 72,71,53,53**CSF £8.70 TOTE £3.90: £1.90, £2.20, £5.30; EX 12.50.
**Owner** Sheikh Mohammed **Bred** Darley **Trained** Newmarket, Suffolk

**FOCUS**
Probably not much strength in depth and the early pace was only moderate, but the winner quickened away impressively and is likely to prove a useful performer. The time was 2.18 seconds faster than the following fillies' handicap and there appeared to be no draw bias.

**NOTEBOOK**
**Andean ◆**, who holds entries in both the Dante and Derby, made short work of these. Always travelling supremely well, he came clear in effortless style, and even though he may not have beaten much, he left quite an impression.
**Maclean**, gelded over the winter, has yet to come in his coat and and left the impression he would benefit from the outing.\n\x\x While he is nothing special, he should be able to find a little race somewhere.
**Leg Spinner(IRE)**, an unfurnished newcomer, ran a race full of promise and will certainly do better as he gets stronger.
**King Of Knight(IRE)** didn't shape too badly on this return to action, but while he may not be good enough to win a maiden, he should hold his own in handicaps off his current mark.
**La Persiana**, who had shown promise as a juvenile, was a bit too fresh for her own good. She will have more options open to her now she is eligible to go handicapping.
**Coppice(IRE)**, a half-brother to winning juvenile Sheriff Shift, was very green in the paddock. He didn't shape too badly and is sure to have learnt plenty from the experience.
**Spector(IRE)**, a half-brother to a couple of middle-distance winners, took a while to get the hang of things. He is sure to have learnt plenty from this and will benefit from a step up in trip.
**Iktitaf(IRE)**, a half-brother to middle-distance winner Mostabshir, as well as seven-furlong winner Shahm, has yet to come in his coat and should do better as the season goes on.
**Star Magnitude(USA)**, a brother to Group 1 Queen Elizabeth Stakes winner Observatory, carried plenty of condition and wasn't knocked around when his chance had gone.

## 1372 CUSTOM KITCHENS FILLIES' H'CAP 1m 3y
2:40 (2:41) (D) (0-85,84) 3-Y-0+ £5,512 (£1,696; £848; £424) Stalls High

Form RPR

61-0 **1** **Flowerdrum (USA)**[9] 1246 4-9-7 **76** ........ RHughes 2 91+
(WJHaggas) *trckd ldrs: led on bit over 1f out: comf* **15/8**[1]

1- **2** *1* **Solar Power (IRE)**[203] 5118 3-8-10 **80** ........ JDSmith 7 86+
(JRFanshawe) *trckd ldrs: plld hrd: nt clr run over 1f out: sn rdn and ev ch: styd on* **16/1**

340- **3** *1 1/4* **Odabella (IRE)**[226] 4579 4-9-0 **69** ........ OUrbina 10 72
(JohnBerry) *s.i.s: hld up: hdwy over 1f out: styd on same pce ins fnl f* **40/1**

000- **4** *3/4* **Richemaur (IRE)**[135] 6101 4-9-11 **80** ........ MHenry 6 81
(MHTompkins) *w ldr: led 1/2-way: rdn and hdd over 1f out: styd on same pce* **12/1**

40-1 **5** *3* **Artistry**[10] 1229 4-8-2 **62** ........ JFMcDonald(5) 1 56
(BJMeehan) *chsd ldrs: rdn and ev ch over 1f out: wknd ins fnl f* **8/1**[2]

1364 **6** *1* **Grey Pearl**[9] 1242 5-10-0 **83** ........(t) SSanders 3 75
(MissGayKelleway) *chsd ldrs: rdn and ev ch over 1f out: wknd ins fnl f* **14/1**

03-0 **7** *1/2* **Gracia**[7] 1275 5-8-9 **67** ........ BReilly(3) 4 58
(SCWilliams) *hld up in tch: rdn and hmpd over 1f out: wknd fnl f* **12/1**

6350 **8** *nk* **Estimation**[10] 1229 4-8-13 **68** ........ WSupple 11 58
(RMHCowell) *mid-div: rdn over 2f out: wknd over 1f out* **33/1**

10-0 **9** *2 1/2* **Aimee's Delight**[7] 1273 4-9-11 **80** ........ BDoyle 12 64
(JGGiven) *chsd ldrs: rdn over 2f out: wknd fnl f: eased* **33/1**

0-34 **10** *3/4* **Brazilian Terrace**[24] 1055 4-9-1 **75** ........ HayleyTurner(5) 8 58
(MLWBell) *chsd ldrs over 6f* **10/1**

135- **11** *1 1/4* **Cheese 'n Biscuits**[145] 6034 4-9-13 **82** .......... RLMoore 13 62
(GLMoore) *hld up: a in rr* **10/1**

626- **12** *4* **Vas Y Carla (USA)**[163] 5869 3-9-0 **84** .......... JPMurtagh 5 55
(DRLoder) *w ldrs: rdn and ev ch over 2f out: wknd over 1f out* **9/1**[3]

120- **13** *12* **Jubilee Treat (USA)**[182] 5550 4-9-9 **78** .......... JFEgan 9 21
(GWragg) *led to 1/2-way: wkng whn n.m.r over 2f out* **20/1**

060- **14** *1/2* **Sister Sophia (USA)**[268] 3397 4-8-13 **68** .......... CCatlin 14 10
(WJMusson) *hld up: wknd 3f out* **25/1**

1m 42.32s (2.62) **Going Correction** +0.325s/f (Good) **14** Ran SP% **118.9**
**WFA** 3 from 4yo+ 15lb
Speed ratings: **99,98,96,96,93 92,91,91,88,87 86,82,70,70**CSF £31.93 CT £952.27 TOTE £2.70: £1.30, £3.20, £8.20; EX 28.90.
**Owner** J Caplan **Bred** Derry Meeting Farm & Christophe Clement **Trained** Newmarket, Suffolk

**FOCUS**
This looked quite a competitive contest on paper and the form appears solid enough, although the pace was only steady.

**NOTEBOOK**
**Flowerdrum(USA)** looks an improved filly and won with more in hand than the official verdict suggests. This faster ground suited well and she looks one to keep on the right side of.
**Solar Power(IRE)** ◆ lacked the experience of her rivals, and did not have the best of luck in running. However, she looks a filly of some promise and should find other openings.
**Odabella(IRE)** had shown promise for John Gosden last year and shaped well enough on this first outing for current connections. She can be found an opening before too long.
**Richemaur(IRE)** found this more her level after facing some stiff tasks last term. She is clearly on good terms with herself at present and although her only victory came with plenty of give underfoot, this faster surface wasn't a problem.
**Artistry** came into this in good form and although somewhat disappointing in the end, may have been unsuited to the steady pace.
**Grey Pearl** had no excuses other than she is probably more effective over seven furlongs.

## 1373 SALTWELL SIGNS H'CAP 7f 3y
**3:10** (3:12) (F) (0-55,55) 3-Y-O+ **£3,374** (£964; £482) **Stalls** High

Form RPR

0055 **1** **Scarrottoo**[13] 1185 6-9-0 **51** .......... BReilly(3) 5 61
(SCWilliams) *hld up: hdwy over 2f out: rdn to ld ins fnl f: r.o* **8/1**[3]

4505 **2** *1/2* **Balerno**[19] 1098 5-8-13 **47** .......... RHughes 15 56
(RIngram) *trckd ldrs: rdn over 1f out: r.o* **9/1**

2150 **3** *2* **Feast Of Romance**[12] 1204 7-9-0 **48** .......... SSanders 10 51
(CNAllen) *led to 1/2-way: rdn to ld over 1f out: hdd and unable qck ins fnl f* **25/1**

4402 **4** *nk* **Carlton (IRE)**[7] 1268 10-9-1 **54** .......... JFMcDonald(5) 19 56+
(CRDore) *hld up: nt clr run 1/2-way: swtchd lft and hdwy over 1f out: r.o* **15/2**[2]

513- **5** *shd* **Sky Dome (IRE)**[140] 6055 11-9-5 **53** .......... (b) JPMurtagh 16 55
(MHTompkins) *hld up: nt clr run over 2f out: r.o ins fnl f: nt rch ldrs* **12/1**

1354 **6** *3/4* **Miss Peaches**[9] 1244 6-8-13 **47** .......... AMcCarthy 4 47
(GGMargarson) *mid-div: hdwy and n.m.r over 1f out: styd on same pce ins fnl f* **16/1**

0162 **7** *1 3/4* **Acorazado (IRE)**[24] 1055 5-9-7 **55** .......... (be) RLMoore 9 50
(GLMoore) *trckd ldrs: rdn and ev ch 2f out: no ex fnl f* **13/2**[1]

12-0 **8** *1 1/4* **Lucefer (IRE)**[12] 1207 6-8-6 **47** .......... DeanWilliams(7) 11 39
(GCHChung) *chsd ldrs over 5f* **10/1**

-565 **9** *hd* **Wodhill Be**[19] 1095 4-9-2 **50** .......... WSupple 7 42
(DMorris) *hld up: hmpd 1/2-way: hdwy over 1f out: wknd ins fnl f* **40/1**

3461 **10** *1/2* **Ballare (IRE)**[6] 1278 5-9-6 **54** 6ex .......... (v) OUrbina 1 44
(BobJones) *trckd ldrs: plld hrd: ev ch 2f out: wknd fnl f* **8/1**[3]

05-0 **11** *shd* **Senor Eduardo**[14] 1174 7-9-6 **54** .......... NPollard 13 44
(SGollings) *hld up: n.d* **33/1**

0012 **12** *nk* **Beltane**[19] 1095 6-9-0 **48** .......... JFEgan 8 37
(WDeBest-Turner) *mid-div: pushed along 1/2-way: wknd wl over 1f out* **25/1**

0000 **13** *1/2* **Jamestown**[48] 878 7-8-9 **50** .......... KGhunowa(7) 2 38
(MJPolglase) *prom over 5f* **50/1**

60-0 **14** *1 3/4* **Snow Bunting**[11] 1225 6-8-12 **53** .......... LeanneKershaw(7) 3 36
(JeddO'Keeffe) *hld up: plld hrd: effrt over 1f out: sn wknd* **17/2**

-422 **15** *1 1/4* **Ranny**[19] 1098 4-9-3 **51** .......... JQuinn 12 31
(DrJDScargill) *w ldr: led 1/2-way: hdd & wknd over 1f out* **15/2**[2]

000- **16** *shd* **Fantasy Crusader**[202] 5135 5-9-1 **49** .......... JMackay 18 28
(JAGilbert) *hld up: nt clr run 1/2-way: n.d* **33/1**

03-0 **17** *1/2* **Parisian Playboy**[14] 1176 4-9-2 **50** .......... CCatlin 6 28
(JeddO'Keeffe) *s.s: sn chsng ldrs: wknd over 1f out* **12/1**

0-00 **18** *nk* **Roan Raider (USA)**[55] 805 4-8-12 **49** .......... (v) LFletcher(3) 14 26
(MJPolglase) *prom over 4f* **50/1**

-000 **19** *3* **Miss Trinity**[12] 1206 4-9-1 **52** .......... TPQueally(3) 17 21
(CNAllen) *w ldrs tl wknd wl over 1f out* **66/1**

1m 28.18s (1.68) **Going Correction** +0.325s/f (Good) **19** Ran SP% **131.4**
Speed ratings: **103,102,100,99,99 98,96,95,95,94 94,94,93,91,90 90,89,89,85**CSF £77.53 CT £1819.94 TOTE £10.80: £2.60, £3.80, £5.90, £2.50; EX 174.20.
**Owner** Michael Peacock **Bred** Freedom Farm Stud **Trained** Newmarket, Suffolk
■.

**FOCUS**
A moderate contest run at a steady pace and no advantage to be gained by the draw.

**NOTEBOOK**
**Scarrottoo**, is much happier when he can hear his feet rattle, and as he hadn't won for nearly two years had become well handicapped as a result.
**Balerno** is being kept busy, and is holding his form quite well having been on the go for over a year. This was another sound effort over a trip which could be sharp enough for him.
**Feast Of Romance**, something of an All-Weather specialist, has yet to win on turf, but this was a sound enough effort.
**Carlton(IRE)** did not have much luck in running, but showed more than enough to be of interest in similar company in the near future.
**Sky Dome(IRE)** has become well treated on the best of his form, and despite his advancing years still looks capable, although it looks as though this trip is the bare minimum for him now.

## 1374 RACECOURSE VIDEO SERVICES MAIDEN AUCTION STKS 5f 43y
**3:45** (3:46) (F) 2-Y-O **£2,919** (£834; £417) **Stalls** High

Form RPR

65 **1** **Von Wessex**[9] 1240 2-8-0 .......... CHaddon(7) 5 58
(WGMTurner) *mde all: rdn over 1f out: edgd lft ins fnl f: r.o* **20/1**

**2** *hd* **Monashee Prince (IRE)** 2-8-11 .......... NPollard 3 61+
(JRBest) *chsd wnr: rdn and ev ch fr over 1f out: edgd lft: r.o* **10/1**

**3** *1 3/4* **Red Affleck (USA)** 2-8-11 .......... AMcCarthy 4 55+
(PWChapple-Hyam) *s.i.s: sn prom: rdn and ev ch over 1f out: styd on same pce ins fnl f* **10/11**[1]

22 **4** *nk* **Evanesce**[9] 1240 2-8-4 .......... CCatlin 6 47+
(MRChannon) *chsd ldrs: rdn over 1f out: styd on same pce* **5/2**[2]

**5** *3* **Silver Visage (IRE)** 2-8-7 .......... BReilly(3) 7 42+
(MissJFeilden) *in tch: effrt over 1f out: wknd ins fnl f* **50/1**

**6** *hd* **Miss Truant** 2-8-6 .......... JMackay 8 37+
(MLWBell) *s.s: hdwy and nt clr run over 1f out: hung lft and wknd ins fnl f* **11/2**[3]

6 **7** *2 1/2* **Zachy Boy**[6] 1276 2-8-4 .......... SHitchcott(3) 9 29+
(JSMoore) *chsd ldrs over 3f* **40/1**

0 **8** *1 1/4* **She's My Dream (IRE)**[6] 1276 2-7-11 .......... JFMcDonald(5) 2 20
(JSMoore) *sn outpcd: hdwy over 1f out: wknd fnl f* **100/1**

**9** *1 3/4* **Miss Good Time** 2-8-2 .......... JQuinn 1 14
(JGGiven) *prom: racd keenly: ev ch 2f out: wknd over 1f out* **66/1**

65.79 secs (3.09) **Going Correction** +0.325s/f (Good) **9** Ran SP% **117.1**
Speed ratings: **88,87,84,84,79 79,75,73,70**CSF £194.35 TOTE £20.40: £3.30, £1.80, £1.50; EX 140.00.
**Owner** Darren Coombes **Bred** Helshaw Grange Stud Ltd **Trained** Sigwells, Somerset

**FOCUS**
This looked an ordinary contest for the track and the time was slow.

**NOTEBOOK**
**Von Wessex**, who had hung badly right on both previous starts, soon got across to the stands' side rail to help keep him straight. He showed a willing enough attitude when tackled, but will need to find improvement if he is to add to this.
**Monashee Prince(IRE)**, who is out of an unraced mare, is an early foal and showed plenty of pace. He is sure to find improvement from this and can find a small race in due course.
**Red Affleck(USA)**, out of a mare that won in the USA, attracted plenty of support, but that proved wide of the mark. While this didn't look that strong a contest, he is from a yard that makes few mistakes and no doubt they will find an opening for him somewhere.
**Evanesce** doesn't appear to be progressing.
**Silver Visage(IRE)**, a half-brother to seven-furlong winner Indian Giver, is sure to improve for the experience and may do better when stepped up in trip.
**Miss Truant**, a half-sister to winning sprinter The Fugative, was as green as grass and can only improve.

## 1375 BENNETTS ELECTRICAL TOSHIBA (S) STKS 1m 2f 21y
**4:20** (4:20) (G) 3-Y-O **£2,520** (£720; £360) **Stalls** Low

Form RPR

0-0 **1** **Fiddles Music**[10] 1227 3-8-6 .......... SHitchcott(3) 5 49
(MRChannon) *chsd ldr: led over 1f out: rdn out* **9/1**[3]

6-40 **2** *1 1/2* **Scorch**[72] 644 3-9-0 **51** .......... JQuinn 4 51
(VSmith) *led: rdn and hdd over 1f out: styd on same pce towards fin* **9/4**[2]

2243 **3** *1/2* **Princess Ismene**[29] 1017 3-9-1 **55** .......... (b) JFEgan 2 51
(PABlockley) *plld hrd and prom: rdn over 2f out: styd on* **10/11**[1]

00-0 **4** *shd* **Bunino Ven**[20] 1084 3-8-11 .......... (v[1]) BReilly(3) 6 50?
(SCWilliams) *s.i.s: hld up: hdwy 4f out: rdn over 2f out: styd on same pce ins fnl f* **9/1**[3]

000 **5** *4* **Fresh Connection**[10] 1227 3-8-9 .......... (p) AMcCarthy 3 38
(GGMargarson) *prom: rdn over 3f out: wknd fnl f* **14/1**

00 **6** *23* **Captain Fearless**[58] 769 3-8-9 .......... HayleyTurner(5) 1 1
(MrsCADunnett) *plld hrd and prom: wknd 4f out* **25/1**

2m 13.21s (5.24) **Going Correction** +0.075s/f (Good) **6** Ran SP% **113.7**
Speed ratings: **82,80,80,80,77 58**CSF £30.18 TOTE £7.40: £2.70, £1.90; EX 45.10.The winner was bought in for 4,400gns.
**Owner** M Channon **Bred** F Rowland **Trained** West Ilsley, Berks

**FOCUS**
A poor seller run at a steady pace in a very slow time. The form needs treating with caution.

**NOTEBOOK**
**Fiddles Music** stayed this longer trip well enough, but the way the race was run hardly put the emphasis on stamina.
**Scorch** had a soft lead and had no excuses. It will have to be a poor contest if he is to get his head in front.

## 1376 SALTWELL SIGNS GREAT NORTH AIR AMBULANCE H'CAP 1m 3f 101y
**4:55** (4:55) (E) (0-70,70) 3-Y-O+ **£3,721** (£1,145; £572; £286) **Stalls** Low

Form RPR

500- **1** **Wellington Hall (GER)**[138] 6076 6-8-11 **53** .......... AMcCarthy 4 65+
(PWChapple-Hyam) *chsd ldrs: led over 2f out: rdn clr over 1f out* **4/1**[3]

000- **2** *5* **Transcendantale (FR)**[216] 4800 6-8-0 **42** ow2 .......... CCatlin 5 46
(MrsSLamyman) *hld up: hdwy over 4f out: rdn over 1f out: styd on same pce* **28/1**

-001 **3** *3/4* **Madhahir (IRE)**[13] 1188 4-9-4 **63** .......... TPQueally(3) 7 66
(CADwyer) *led after 1f: rdn over 2f out: hdd over 1f out: styd on same pce* **6/1**

53 **4** *1/2* **Kashimo (GER)**[16] 962 5-9-2 **58** .......... RLMoore 2 60
(GLMoore) *chsd ldrs: rdn over 4f out: outpcd over 2f out: styd on ins fnl f* **9/4**[1]

00-3 **5** *1 1/2* **Toledo Sun**[21] 735 4-8-3 **45** .......... JQuinn 1 45
(VSmith) *led 1f: w ldr: rdn over 2f out: wknd over 1f out* **11/2**

1211 **6** *hd* **Steely Dan**[9] 1241 5-10-0 **70** .......... NPollard 6 69
(JRBest) *hld up: effrt over 2f out: no imp* **10/3**[2]

00-0 **7** *2 1/2* **Court One**[25] 1042 6-7-8 **41** oh5 ow1 .......... JFMcDonald(5) 8 36
(RJPrice) *dwlt: sn prom: rdn over 2f out: sn edgd lft and wknd* **28/1**

4065 **8** *10* **Dundonald**[7] 1263 5-7-7 **40** oh5 .......... (bt) HayleyTurner(5) 3 19
(MAppleby) *hld up: rdn and wknd over 3f out* **50/1**

2m 27.24s (-0.16) **Going Correction** +0.075s/f (Good) **8** Ran SP% **112.4**
Speed ratings: **103,99,98,98,97 97,95,88**CSF £99.48 CT £658.63 TOTE £5.10: £1.80, £3.90, £1.90; EX 80.00 Place 6 £134.70, Place 5 £ 87.07..
**Owner** Allan Darke & Tom Matthews **Bred** Baron G Von Ullmann **Trained** Newmarket, Suffolk

**FOCUS**
This was not that competitive, but the time was a fair one for the grade and the winner scored easily.

**NOTEBOOK**
**Wellington Hall(GER)**, making his debut for a new stable, handled this faster surface well and won with plenty in hand. It would be no surprise to see him turn out under a penalty.
**Transcendantale(FR)** is well exposed and lacks consistency. However, she is now running off her lowest mark on turf for nearly two years and if building on this would be no forlorn hope in a small contest.
**Madhahir(IRE)** was not disgraced off this 5lb higher mark than when winning at Folkestone, on ground which could well have been quick enough for him.
**Kashimo(GER)**, shaped as though a step up in trip should be well within his compass.
**Toledo Sun** is of limited ability and did not show enough to be of interest in the near future, despite his fall in the weights.
**Steely Dan** looked wonderfully well, despite his busy time of late. However, this was a disappointing effort and he does not look as good on turf as he is on the All-Weather.
T/Plt: £364.60 to a £1 stake. Pool: £23,399.55. 46.85 winning tickets. T/Qpdt: £110.90 to a £1 stake. Pool: £1,244.00. 8.30 winning tickets. CR

# [1346]CORK (R-H)

Monday, April 12

**OFFICIAL GOING: Flat course - yielding; jumps courses - good**

## 1379a CORK STKS (LISTED RACE) 5f

2:55 (3:00) 3-Y-O+ **£22,922** (£6,725; £3,204; £1,091)

RPR

1 **Moon Unit (IRE)**[183] [5519] 3-8-7 95 DMGrant 6 107
(HRogers, Ire) *a.p: mainly cl 2nd: rdn and led 1 1/2f out: styd on wl u.p ins fnl f* **11/1**

2 1 1/2 **Dragon Flyer (IRE)**[23] [1061] 5-9-4 JAHeffernan 9 102
(MQuinn) *chsd ldrs: 5th 1/2-way: rdn to chal in 3rd 1 1/2f out: 2nd 1f out and kpt on wl ins fnl f* **11/2**[2]

3 nk **Peace Offering (IRE)**[22] [1068] 4-9-7 99 (p) PCosgrave 5 104
(DeclanGillespie, Ire) *chsd ldrs: 4th 1/2-way: rdn to chal fr 1 1/2f out: kpt on wl u.p* **14/1**

4 1/2 **Revenue (IRE)**[199] [5186] 4-9-7 (t) KJManning 3 102
(TimothyRPinfield, Ire) *trckd ldrs in 3rd: rdn to chal fr under 2f out: kpt on one pce u.p* **12/1**

5 shd **Tiger Royal (IRE)**[22] [1068] 8-9-7 106 (b) PJSmullen 2 102
(DKWeld, Ire) *chsd ldrs: 6th 1/2-way: 5th 2f out: kpt on same pce u.p ins fnl f* **11/2**[2]

6 2 **Colonel Cotton (IRE)**[156] [5953] 5-9-11 MJKinane 4 99
(NACallaghan) *towards rr: rdn and kpt on same pce fr 2f out* **11/4**[1]

7 1/2 **Blue Crush (IRE)**[190] [5394] 3-8-7 101 NGMcCullagh 7 90
(EdwardLynam, Ire) *led: rdn and hdd 1 1/2f out: sn no ex* **8/1**[3]

8 3 **Sun Slash (IRE)**[183] [5523] 4-9-4 99 (t) PShanahan 8 79
(MsJoannaMorgan, Ire) *towards rr: rdn and no imp fr 2f out* **14/1**

61.10 secs
**WFA** 3 from 4yo+ 11lb **8 Ran SP% 97.9**
Speed ratings: CSF £48.69 TOTE £34.30: £6.50, £2.10, £2.70.
**Owner** Mrs Paula Davison **Bred** Ivan W Allan **Trained** Ardee, Co. Louth

**NOTEBOOK**
**Moon Unit(IRE)** demonstrated a level of form that she hadn't hinted at before, going on a furlong and a half down to win well.
**Dragon Flyer(IRE)**, weak in the market, did not have the clearest of runs, but she got going again late and finished quite well. Apparently held up in her work, she has a Bath sprint confined to mares on her agenda.
**Peace Offering(IRE)** finished with a rattle on his second outing in this country.
**Revenue(IRE)**showed that there is still plenty of life in him but he'll be hard to place.
**Tiger Royal(IRE)** ran on but needs the extra furlong these days.
**Colonel Cotton(IRE)**, rather a surprise favourite, never appeared to go the pace and needs it faster.

1380 - 1381a (Foreign Racing) - See Raceform Interactive

# NEWMARKET (R-H)

Tuesday, April 13

**OFFICIAL GOING: Good to soft**

## 1382 GILES FOX AT NEWMARKET RACECOURSE MAIDEN STKS 1m 2f

1:45 (1:46) (D) 3-Y-O **£5,473** (£1,684; £842; £421) **Stalls High**

Form RPR

1 **Ecomium (IRE)** 3-9-0 EAhern 8 103+
(JNoseda) *cmpt: scope: trckd ldrs: led over 1f out: r.o wl* **7/1**[3]

24- 2 5 **Buckeye Wonder (USA)**[179] [5612] 3-9-0 PRobinson 5 90
(MAJarvis) *chsd ldr: led over 2f out: rdn and hdd over 1f out: edgd lft ins fnl f: styd on same pce* **7/1**[3]

3 1 1/2 **Parliament Square (IRE)** 3-9-0 JPMurtagh 10 87
(DRLoder) *gd sort: leggy: hld up: hdwy over 3f out: rdn over 1f out: styd on* **13/8**[1]

5- 4 3 **Gironde**[159] [5932] 3-9-0 KFallon 6 82
(SirMichaelStoute) *b.bkwd: s.i.s: hld up: shkn up over 2f out: nvr trbld ldrs* **10/1**

2- 5 1 1/4 **Coming Again (IRE)**[172] [5733] 3-9-0 MHills 2 80+
(BWHills) *hld up: hdwy over 3f out: rdn and hung lft fnl 2f: wknd ins fnl f* **3/1**[2]

30- 6 4 **Sharaab (USA)**[199] [5219] 3-9-0 RHills 11 72
(BHanbury) *lw: led over 7f: wknd over 1f out* **14/1**

0 7 3 1/2 **Moonshaft (USA)**[12] [1224] 3-9-0 SDrowne 7 66
(EALDunlop) *lw: hld up in tch: rdn over 3f out: wknd wl over 1f out* **100/1**

503- 8 1/2 **Distant Connection (IRE)**[172] [5734] 3-9-0 75 DHolland 3 65
(APJarvis) *hld up: a in rr* **33/1**

9 3 **Nietzsche (IRE)** 3-9-0 RHughes 4 60
(JNoseda) *w'like: scope: chsd ldrs: rdn over 3f out: wknd wl over 1f out* **33/1**

44- 10 3 1/2 **Young Patriarch**[221] [4703] 3-8-11 LPKeniry(3) 9 54
(BJMeehan) *b.bkwd: s.i.s: hld up: wknd over 2f out* **50/1**

4 11 20 **Trifti**[11] [1226] 3-9-0 SSanders 1 18
(CACyzer) *hld up: racd keenly: wknd 3f out* **66/1**

2m 7.70s (2.01) **Going Correction** +0.375s/f (Good) **11 Ran SP% 114.2**
Speed ratings: **106,102,100,98,97 94,91,91,88,85 69**CSF £51.83 TOTE £12.00: £3.10, £2.10, £1.10; EX 58.10.
**Owner** Fieldspring Racing **Bred** Tower Bloodstock **Trained** Newmarket, Suffolk

**FOCUS**
This was run at a fair pace in a good time. It looks a useful maiden and should throw up several winners..

**NOTEBOOK**
**Ecomium(IRE)** ◆ is related to several winners, including Group 1 winner Scenic. A nice colt, he was always travelling well and showed a smart turn of foot to settle this in a matter of strides. Plenty more will be heard of him.
**Buckeye Wonder(USA)** got quite warm in the pre-parade ring, but that didn't stop him turning in a solid effort. He looks a resolute galloper who is likely to benefit from a step up in trip.
**Parliament Square(IRE)**, a half-brother to Group 1 juvenile winner Beckett, is very much on the leg at present. He was green to post and in the race itself and can only improve as he gets stronger.
**Gironde** still looked a little on the green side and better can be expected of him as he steps up in trip.
**Coming Again(IRE)**, a good-looking colt, looked a big threat as he launched his challenge down the centre of the course, but as the afternoon unfolded, that wasn't the place to be. He got very tired in the end and finished up near the stands'-side rail. He will show his true colours back on a faster surface. *Official explanation: jockey said colt hung left handed*

**Sharaab(USA)**, keen to post, was allowed to bowl along and just got tired in the ground. He should have more opportunities now he is eligible for handicaps.

## 1383 FEDERATION OF BLOODSTOCK AGENTS CONDITIONS STKS 5f

2:20 (2:20) (C) 2-Y-O **£7,186** (£2,725; £1,362; £619) **Stalls High**

Form RPR

1 1 **Cornus**[8] [1269] 2-9-2 RHughes 8 89+
(RHannon) *chsd ldr: led over 1f out: pushed clr: eased nr fin* **11/10**[1]

1 2 hd **Dario Gee Gee (IRE)**[17] [1128] 2-9-2 NCallan 7 84
(KARyan) *lw: s.i.s: sn prom: rdn over 1f out: r.o: no ch w wnr* **7/2**[2]

1 3 1 3/4 **Next Time Around (IRE)**[19] [1105] 2-9-4 RWinston 5 80
(MrsLStubbs) *led over 3f: hung lft and no ex ins fnl f* **4/1**[3]

62 4 1/2 **Gogetter Girl**[6] [1299] 2-8-7 TEDurcan 3 67
(JGallagher) *chsd ldrs: rdn over 1f out: styd on same pce* **16/1**

0 5 1 1/4 **Campeon (IRE)**[17] [1128] 2-8-12 KFallon 2 67
(MJWallace) *lw: hld up: pushed along 1/2-way: styd on: nvr able to chal* **12/1**

1 6 2 **King After**[18] [1117] 2-9-2 NPollard 1 64
(JRBest) *prom: pushed along 1/2-way: sn outpcd* **16/1**

0 7 4 **Comintrue (IRE)**[7] [1276] 2-8-7 JQuinn 6 41
(EJO'Neill) *plld hrd and prom: wknd over 1f out* **66/1**

8 3 **Our Choice (IRE)** 2-8-9 DHolland 4 32
(NPLittmoden) *leggy: wl grwn: bhd fnl 3f* **25/1**

62.77 secs (2.36) **Going Correction** +0.375s/f (Good) **8 Ran SP% 114.6**
Speed ratings: **96,95,92,92,90 86,80,75**CSF £5.08 TOTE £2.00: £1.10, £1.70, £1.50; EX 6.20.
**Owner** David Mort **Bred** G Russell **Trained** East Everleigh, Wilts

**FOCUS**
With four winners in the field, this looked a competitive little heat. They didn't go that quick here and the winner had the benefit of the far rail to race against.

**NOTEBOOK**
**Cornus** confirmed the promise of his debut and won with far more in hand than the official verdict suggested, for his rider took things far too easy in the latter stages.
**Dario Gee Gee(IRE)**, although flattered by his proximity to the winner, turned in a solid effort and already looks to need a sixth furlong.
**Next Time Around(IRE)** , giving weight away all round, hung quite badly in the latter stages, but was far from disgraced. He may need better ground than he faced here.
**Gogetter Girl** is learning all the time and looks to have a little race in her.
**Campeon(IRE)** still looked quite green here, but he stuck well enough to his task on meeting the rising ground and looks sure to benefit from an extra furlong.
**King After** can be forgiven this effort as he didn't have the best of draws and looked all at sea on the softened ground.

## 1384 DAVID OLDREY CONDITIONS STKS 7f

2:55 (2:55) (C) 3-Y-O **£8,502** (£3,225; £1,612; £733) **Stalls High**

Form RPR

12- 1 **Iqte Saab (USA)**[220] [4723] 3-9-1 RHills 4 109+
(JLDunlop) *lw: hld up in tch: plld hrd: nt clr run fr over 2f out: led ins fnl f: r.o wl* **5/4**[1]

13-0 2 3 **Glaramara**[24] [1063] 3-9-1 94 KFallon 3 96
(ABailey) *lw: hld up: hdwy 2f out: rdn and ev ch 1f out: sn outpcd* **16/1**

120- 3 1 1/4 **Ithaca (USA)**[199] [5209] 3-8-10 102 RHughes 1 88
(HRACecil) *lw: hld up in tch: pushed along 2f out: styd on same pce fnl f* **7/2**[2]

3-03 4 1/2 **Makfool (FR)**[17] [1123] 3-9-1 95 TEDurcan 7 91
(MRChannon) *led over 4f: wknd ins fnl f* **14/1**

24-1 5 1 **Local Poet**[17] [1127] 3-9-1 98 GGibbons 6 89
(BAMcmahon) *plld hrd: w ldrs: led over 1f out: hdd & wknd ins fnl f* **10/1**[3]

1- 6 1 1/4 **Two Step Kid (USA)**[169] [5797] 3-9-1 EAhern 5 86
(JNoseda) *b.bkwd: w ldr: led over 2f out: rdn and hdd over 1f out: wknd ins fnl f* **7/2**[2]

000 7 16 **Well Knit**[17] [1123] 3-8-6 JFEgan 2 35
(PWD'Arcy) *chsd ldrs 4f* **150/1**

1m 28.58s (2.11) **Going Correction** +0.375s/f (Good) **7 Ran SP% 111.2**
Speed ratings: **102,98,97,96,95 94,75**CSF £22.92 TOTE £2.10: £1.30, £5.00; EX 23.60.
**Owner** Hamdan Al Maktoum **Bred** Shadwell Farm Llc **Trained** Arundel, W Sussex

**FOCUS**
An unsatisfactory race which was run at a steady pace.

**NOTEBOOK**
**Iqte Saab(USA)** turned in a smart performance and simply outclassed his rivals. A strong-travelling type, with a useful turn of foot, it is debatable how much further he will want to go.
**Glaramara** settled much better without the blinkers this time and came to have every chance, before the winner quickened up. While this ground may well have been soft enough for him, off his current mark he is likely to be hard to place this year.
**Ithaca(USA)** has not grown much, if at all, over the winter. In what was a steadily-run race, she looked to lack pace and she is certain to be suited by a stiffer test than she faced here.
**Makfool(FR)** looked more exposed than his rivals and couldn't take advantage of his edge in fitness. He is likely to be hard to place this term.
**Local Poet**, tackling this trip for the first time, didn't give himself much of a chance to last home having pulled so hard.
**Two Step Kid(USA)** was something of a disappointment, dropping away tamely. He is well regarded and deserves another chance on better ground.

## 1385 GRANTCHESTER RATED STKS (H'CAP) 7f

3:25 (3:26) (B) (0-105,102) 4-Y-O+ **£12,441** (£4,719; £2,359; £1,072) **Stalls High**

Form RPR

11-0 1 **Thihn (IRE)**[18] [1114] 9-8-9 90 ADaly 12 101
(JLSpearing) *racd far side: hld up: hdwy 2f out: led ins fnl f: r.o* **8/1**[2]

0005 2 1/2 **Chappel Cresent (IRE)**[10] [1246] 4-8-4 85 ANicholls 3 95
(DNicholls) *lw: led stands' side: rdn over 1f out: r.o* **25/1**

34-0 3 nk **Marshman (IRE)**[18] [1114] 5-8-8 89 PRobinson 4 98
(MHTompkins) *racd stands' side: chsd ldrs: chal over 1f out: r.o* **14/1**

105- 4 shd **Greenslades**[213] [4884] 5-8-8 89 SSanders 10 98
(PJMakin) *lw: racd far side: chsd ldrs: led over 2f out: hdd ins fnl f: styd on* **12/1**

32-2 5 1 **Camberley (IRE)**[17] [1132] 7-8-11 92 KFallon 13 98
(PFICole) *racd far side: hld up: hdwy over 2f out: rdn over 1f out: styd on same pce ins fnl f* **6/1**[1]

644- 6 1 1/4 **Flying Express**[157] [5946] 4-8-6 87 MHills 11 90
(BWHills) *lw: racd far side: mid-div: hdwy over 2f out: styd on same pce fnl f* **8/1**[2]

0-00 7 1/2 **Tough Love**[10] [1246] 5-8-8 89 WSupple 9 91
(TDEasterby) *racd far side: hld up: hdwy and nt clr run over 1f out: nt rch ldrs* **16/1**

220- 8 nk **Manaar (IRE)**[194] [5331] 4-8-5 86 EAhern 15 87
(JNoseda) *racd far side: prom: outpcd over 2f out: r.o ins fnl f* **20/1**

612- **9** ½ **Miss Ivanhoe (IRE)**[179] 5628 4-9-7 **102** ............ DHolland 6 102
(GWragg) *racd far side: hld up: hdwy over 1f out: nt trble ldrs* **8/1**[2]

314- **10** ¾ **Calcutta**[179] 5618 8-9-5 **100** ............ RHills 19 98
(BWHills) *lw: racd far side: chsd ldrs: rdn over 1f out: no ex* **25/1**

003- **11** ½ **Hurricane Floyd (IRE)**[179] 5618 6-8-9 **89** ow1 ............ JPMurtagh 20 86
(DRLoder) *racd far side: prom: rdn over 2f out: styd on same pce appr fnl f* **10/1**[3]

26-0 **12** *nk* **Audience**[19] 1107 4-9-4 **99** ............ TQuinn 16 94
(JAkehurst) *racd far side: chsd ldrs: rdn over 2f out: no ex over 1f out* **25/1**

-102 **13** *shd* **Dawn Piper (USA)**[25] 1056 4-8-4 **85** oh1 ............(v) DRMcCabe 18 80
(DRLoder) *racd far side: chsd ldr: led over 4f out: hdd over 2f out: wknd fnl f* **14/1**

456- **14** *nk* **St Pancras (IRE)**[201] 5168 4-9-0 **95** ............ WRyan 7 89
(NACallaghan) *racd stands' side: outpcd* **40/1**

126- **15** *nk* **Royal Storm (IRE)**[166] 5838 5-9-0 **95** ............ RHughes 17 89
(MrsAJPerrett) *led far side: hdd over 4f out: wknd fnl f* **12/1**

604- **16** *shd* **Tedstale (USA)**[227] 4578 6-8-4 **85** ............ JQuinn 8 78
(TDEasterby) *racd far side: hld up: n.d* **33/1**

41-0 **17** 1¼ **Fantasy Believer**[10] 1246 6-8-13 **94** ............ KDarley 5 84
(JJQuinn) *lw: racd stands' side: chsd ldrs over 5f* **25/1**

52-0 **18** *nk* **Arctic Desert**[24] 1065 4-8-9 **90** ............ MartinDwyer 2 79
(AMBalding) *b. racd stands'side: chsd ldrs over 5f* **20/1**

60-0 **19** *nk* **Master Robbie**[17] 1132 5-8-10 **91** ............ SHitchcott(3) 1 83
(MRChannon) *racd stands' side: chsd ldrs: rdn 3f out: wknd over 1f out* **25/1**

030- **20** 1½ **Secret Formula**[171] 5756 4-8-1 **85** oh3 ............ LisaJones(3) 14 70
(SKirk) *racd far side: chsd ldrs over 5f* **50/1**

1m 27.87s (1.40) **Going Correction** +0.375s/f (Good) **20** Ran SP% **127.4**
Speed ratings: **107,106,106,105,104 103,102,102,101,101 100,100,100,99,99 99,97,97,97,95**CSF £201.48 CT £2841.27 TOTE £9.50: £2.00, £8.40, £3.40, £3.80; EX 826.50 Trifecta £3313.60 Part won. Pool £4,667.15 - 0.10 winning units..
**Owner** The Square Milers **Bred** Shadwell Estate Company Limited **Trained** Kinnersley, Worcs

**FOCUS**
A competitive handicap in which the field split into two, with no apparent advantage to either side. This race should throw up its fair share of winners in the coming months.

**NOTEBOOK**
**Thihn(IRE)** was winning off a career-high mark, and at the age on nine is clearly as good as ever. He seems to go particularly well for Alan Daly, who has partnered him to his last three victories.
**Chappel Cresent(IRE)**, who hasn't won since making a winning debut as a juvenile, again gave signs that he retains his abilty and may have been a shade unlucky, as he was one of only six to race on the stands' side.
**Marshman(IRE)** off a career-high mark now, confirmed he is a progressive performer. Equally at home on a fast surface, there should be plenty of opportunities in the coming months.
**Greenslades** has done all of his winning over six furlongs, but confirmed here that he does stay this far. Lightly raced, there should still be more to come from him.
**Camberley(IRE)**, who looked magnificent beforehand, ran a fine race and had no excuses. He looks to be in the grip of the Handicapper for the time being.
**Flying Express** was probably done no favours by having to race more towards the centre of the track. Twice a winner as a juvenile, he suffered at the hands of the Handicapper last year. He starts this season on what looks a favourable mark and it will be a surprise if connections can't find a decent prize for him.
**Tough Love**, who is arguably better over an extra furlong, and on a faster surface, was doing his best work in the closing stages and looks set for another successful season.
**Manaar(IRE)**

## 1386 ALEX SCOTT MAIDEN STKS (C&G) 7f
**4:00** (4:01) (D) 3-Y-O **£5,473** (£1,684; £842; £421) **Stalls** High

Form RPR

**1** **Davorin (JPN)** 3-8-11 ............ JPMurtagh 6 79
(DRLoder) *gd sort: leggy: scope: chsd ldrs: rdn 1/2-way: styd on to ld wl ins fnl f* **4/1**[2]

24-4 **2** *hd* **Mission Man**[18] 1111 3-8-11 82 ............ DaneO'Neill 2 78
(RHannon) *h.d.w: trckd ldrs: rdn to ld over 1f out: edgd rt and hdd wl ins fnl f* **9/2**[3]

0- **3** *nk* **Moors Myth**[158] 5938 3-8-11 ............ RHughes 4 77
(BWHills) *chsd ldrs: rdn and ev ch ins fnl f: r.o* **20/1**

02- **4** *nk* **Star Pupil**[164] 5867 3-8-11 ............ MartinDwyer 11 76
(AMBalding) *h.d.w: chsd ldrs: rdn to ld 2f out: hdd over 1f out: r.o* **8/1**

**5** 2 **Marsh Orchid** 3-8-11 ............ MTebbutt 3 71+
(WJarvis) *neat: hld up: outpcd over 2f out: r.o ins fnl f: eased towards fin* **66/1**

0- **6** 2½ **Gold Mask (USA)**[269] 3411 3-8-11 ............ DHolland 7 65
(JHMGosden) *lw: led 5f: edgd lft and wknd ins fnl f* **4/1**[2]

**7** ¾ **Imtalkinggibberish** 3-8-11 ............ SWKelly 5 63
(JRJenkins) *wl grwn: s.i.s: sn prom: wknd over 1f out* **66/1**

**8** 3 **Submissive** 3-8-11 ............ RHills 10 55
(BWHills) *w'like: scope: hld up: outpcd fr 1/2-way* **33/1**

**9** *shd* **Blake Hall Lad (IRE)** 3-8-8 ............ BReilly(3) 12 55
(MissJFeilden) *hld up: bhd fr 1/2-way* **66/1**

65- **10** *shd* **Scientist**[306] 2302 3-8-11 ............ KFallon 9 54
(JHMGosden) *h.d.w: chsd ldrs over 5f* **11/4**[1]

**11** *nk* **Gustavo** 3-8-11 ............ MHills 8 54
(BWHills) *gd sort: free to post: dwlt: outpcd* **33/1**

00-0 **12** 2 **Unprecedented (IRE)**[56] 802 3-8-11 50 ............ SDrowne 1 48
(TTClement) *hld up: bhd fnl 4f* **100/1**

1m 29.37s (2.90) **Going Correction** +0.375s/f (Good) **12** Ran SP% **112.1**
Speed ratings: **98,97,97,97,94 91,91,87,87,87 87,84**CSF £19.91 TOTE £3.50: £1.90, £1.50, £4.00; EX 21.60.
**Owner** Sheikh Mohammed **Bred** Shoei Co Ltd **Trained** Newmarket, Suffolk

**FOCUS**
Some taking individuals, but with less than a length covering the first four home the form does not look that strong by Newmarket maiden standards.

**NOTEBOOK**
**Davorin(JPN)**, a brother to the high-class Diktat, was as green as grass, but he has a willing attitude and should find plenty of improvement from this.
**Mission Man** had the edge in experience and didn't do anything wrong, but he is finding it hard to get his head in front.
**Moors Myth**, a half-brother to juvenile winner Salcombe, shaped well enough and should have little difficulty winning his maiden.
**Star Pupil** is quite speedily bred, but he had no trouble with this trip and will have plenty of options open to him now in handicaps.
**Marsh Orchid**, out of a mare that won over five furlongs, shaped quite well, despite running green.
**Gold Mask(USA)** looked to flounder in the ground and is one to keep an eye on when he goes handicapping and tackles a faster surface.
**Imtalkinggibberish**, a half-brother to winning sprinter Maddie's A Gem, travelled well for a long way and should benefit from the experience.
**Scientist** ran as though he needed the outing after a long break. However, connections will have more options open to them now in handicaps.

## 1387 WARREN HILL MAIDEN STKS 1m 4f
**4:35** (4:37) (D) 3-Y-O **£5,317** (£1,636; £818; £409) **Stalls** High

Form RPR

32- **1** **Percussionist (IRE)**[167] 5830 3-9-0 ............ KDarley 8 93+
(JHMGosden) *chsd ldrs: rdn over 4f out: styd on u.p to ld ins fnl f* **4/6**[1]

0- **2** 1½ **Chaplin**[203] 5139 3-9-0 ............ RHughes 3 90+
(BWHills) *lw: hld up: hdwy over 7f out: led over 1f out: hdd and unable qck ins fnl f* **12/1**

0-22 **3** 4 **Vantage (IRE)**[24] 1064 3-9-0 80 ............ DHolland 6 79
(NPLittmoden) *led: rdn and hdd over 1f out: no ex* **5/1**[2]

30 **4** *hd* **Border Saint**[11] 1235 3-9-0 ............ IMongan 2 79
(MLWBell) *hld up: swtchd lft and hdwy over 1f out: styd on same pce ins fnl f* **33/1**

**5** ½ **Dallool** 3-9-0 ............ PRobinson 5 78+
(MAJarvis) *w'like: b. prom: effrt over 2f out: styd on same pce appr fnl f* **14/1**

3 **6** 4 **Springtime Romance (USA)**[8] 1271 3-8-9 ............ JPMurtagh 7 67
(EALDunlop) *lw: chsd ldrs tl hung lft and wknd over 1f out* **13/2**[3]

53- **7** 11 **Turn 'n Burn**[169] 5792 3-9-0 ............ KFallon 4 55
(CACyzer) *plld hrd: trckd ldr: chal 4f out: rdn over 2f out: edgd lft and wknd over 1f out* **14/1**

30-0 **8** 24 **Inchconnel**[18] 1116 3-9-0 60 ............(b) MTebbutt 1 19
(VSmith) *hld up: pushed along 7f out: bhd fnl 5f* **50/1**

2m 40.11s (6.65) **Going Correction** +0.375s/f (Good) **8** Ran SP% **115.9**
Speed ratings: **92,91,88,88,87 85,77,61**CSF £10.73 TOTE £1.60: £1.10, £2.30, £1.60; EX 9.30.
**Owner** Exors of the late R E Sangster **Bred** Swettenham Stud **Trained** Manton, Wilts

**FOCUS**
The first two are likely to prove better than this, but there was not much strength in depth. The pace was only steady and the final time was slow.

**NOTEBOOK**
**Percussionist(IRE)** took quite a bit of winding up, but he has a willing attitude and should go on from here. However, he doesn't do anything quickly and may appreciate more use being made of him.
**Chaplin**, out of a mare that stayed 11 furlongs, found this trip well within his compass. He should have no trouble winning his maiden.
**Vantage(IRE)** is consistent enough, but he is beginning to look somewhat exposed.
**Border Saint**, having his first outing on turf, wasn't disgraced and looks to have a little race in him.
**Dallool**, a half-brother to 10-furlong winner Satyr and 11-furlong winner Muwassi, is sure to be all the wiser for the experience.
**Springtime Romance(USA)** dropped away tamely and may have found this coming too soon. Her future lies in handicaps.

## 1388 EXNING STKS (H'CAP) 6f
**5:10** (5:11) (C) (0-100,100) 3-Y-O **£9,665** (£2,974; £1,487; £743) **Stalls** High

Form RPR

010- **1** **Saristar**[178] 5630 3-8-1 **80** ............ JQuinn 15 89
(PFICole) *trckd ldrs: rdn over 1f out: r.o to ld post* **25/1**

115- **2** *hd* **Danzig River (IRE)**[186] 5471 3-8-7 **93** ............ KMay(7) 18 102
(BWHills) *lw: chsd ldrs: led over 1f out: ct post* **20/1**

6-41 **3** ¾ **Petardias Magic (IRE)**[3] 1333 3-8-5 **84** 7ex ............ EAhern 11 91
(EJO'Neill) *hld up: plld hrd: hdwy over 2f out: r.o* **4/1**[2]

163- **4** 2 **Moss Vale (IRE)**[208] 5009 3-9-7 **100** ............ MHills 2 101+
(BWHills) *edgd rt s: hld up: hdwy over 1f out: nt rch ldrs* **11/1**

150- **5** ½ **Molcon (IRE)**[203] 5143 3-7-8 **78** ............ DFox(5) 19 77
(NACallaghan) *w ldr tl led over 2f out: rdn and hdd over 1f out: no ex ins fnl f* **12/1**

432- **6** 3½ **Bentley's Ball (USA)**[179] 5613 3-8-13 **92** ............ RHughes 10 81
(RHannon) *s.s: hld up: hdwy and swtchd rt over 1f out: nt rch ldrs* **8/1**[3]

43-0 **7** 1 **Shielaligh**[36] 986 3-8-5 **84** ow1 ............(t) MFenton 9 70
(MissGayKelleway) *lw: chsd ldrs: rdn over 1f out: sn btn* **33/1**

033- **8** 1 **Compton's Eleven**[175] 5697 3-8-11 **90** ............ TEDurcan 13 73
(MRChannon) *lw: chsd ldrs over 4f* **25/1**

104- **9** 1¾ **Convince (USA)**[175] 5697 3-9-1 **94** ............ SDrowne 7 71
(MABuckley) *lw: hld up: nt clr run over 1f out: n.d* **25/1**

1-11 **10** *nk* **Peruvian Style (IRE)**[20] 1099 3-8-2 **81** ............ MartinDwyer 17 57
(NPLittmoden) *mde most over 3f: wknd over 1f out* **10/1**

221- **11** *shd* **Granato (GER)**[201] 5174 3-8-8 **87** ............ KFallon 3 63
(ACStewart) *lw: hmpd s: sn chsng ldrs: wknd over 1f out* **11/4**[1]

046- **12** *nk* **Wyatt Earp (IRE)**[165] 5850 3-7-9 **77** ............ LisaJones(3) 5 52
(JARToller) *mid-div: rdn over 2f out: wknd over 1f out* **25/1**

3501 **13** 1¼ **Ask The Clerk (IRE)**[14] 1184 3-7-5 **77** oh6 ............ BSwarbrick(7) 1 48
(VSmith) *mid-div: sn pushed along: wknd over 1f out* **25/1**

-113 **14** *hd* **Tag Team (IRE)**[36] 986 3-7-12 **77** ............ CCatlin 16 48
(AMBalding) *chsd ldrs over 4f* **20/1**

132- **15** 1½ **Dolce Piccata**[229] 4522 3-8-13 **92** ............ TQuinn 8 58
(BJMeehan) *keen to post: chsd ldrs 3f* **16/1**

04-0 **16** ½ **Multiple Choice (IRE)**[13] 1205 3-8-0 **79** ............ JBramhill 12 44
(NPLittmoden) *prom 4f* **33/1**

420- **17** ½ **Mac The Knife (IRE)**[269] 3402 3-8-7 **86** ............ PDobbs 4 49
(RHannon) *lw: s.i.s: hld up: a in rr* **33/1**

436- **18** 1 **Who's Winning (IRE)**[211] 4936 3-7-12 **77** oh2 ............ JMackay 14 37
(CADwyer) *mid-div: wkng whn hmpd wl over 1f out* **50/1**

10-0 **19** ½ **Dellagio (IRE)**[20] 1099 3-8-1 **83** ow1 ............ TPQueally(3) 6 42
(CADwyer) *b.bkwd: hld up: plld hrd: a in rr* **50/1**

1m 14.38s (1.29) **Going Correction** +0.375s/f (Good) **19** Ran SP% **130.3**
Speed ratings: **106,105,104,102,101 96,95,94,91,91 91,90,89,88,86 86,85,84,83**CSF £447.44 CT £2495.45 TOTE £55.40: £8.70, £6.20, £2.30, £3.10; EX 833.30 Place 6 £37.39, Place 5 £24.81.
**Owner** R A Instone **Bred** R A Instone **Trained** Whatcombe, Oxon

**FOCUS**
Another competitive handicap with the field eventually electing to race over on the far side. There looked to be plenty of pace on and it seemed to favour those drawn high. Strong form, and a likely source of plenty of winners.

**NOTEBOOK**
**Saristar**, tackling her softest surface too date, found this trip well within her compass. She showed a nice attitude to reel in the runner-up and she looks to be on the upgrade.
**Danzig River(IRE)** looked to have things under control when striking the front, only to be worried out of it in the shadow of the post. Already proven on a faster surface, there should be plenty of opportunities for him.
**Petardias Magic(IRE)** turned in a solid effort off this 7lb higher mark and is clearly on the upgrade.
**Moss Vale(IRE)**, who was found out at Listed level last year, ran a cracker from his poor draw, but as he is rated 100 he will have limited opportunities in handicaps and he may well have to step back up to Listed company in the future.

**Molcon(IRE)** showed plenty of speed against the far rail even though the ground may have been softer than ideal. Granted a fast surface, he shouldn't be difficult to place.
**Bentley's Ball(USA)** came home in good style, but the damage was done at the start. Although he handles some cut in the ground, he looks better suited to a faster surface.
T/Jkpt: £6,288.70 to a £1 stake. Pool: £48,715.50. 5.50 winning tickets. T/Plt: £97.90 to a £1 stake. Pool: £62,144.60. 463.10 winning tickets. T/Qpdt: £66.10 to a £1 stake. Pool: £2,677.30. 29.95 winning tickets. CR

# BEVERLEY (R-H)

Wednesday, April 14

**OFFICIAL GOING: Good to soft (good in places)**

The going was reckoned to be just on the slow side of good, the times were relatively slow due to quite a stiff breeze.

Weather: fine & sunny

## 1389 START OF THE SEASON (S) STKS — 1m 100y

**2:10** (2:11) (G ) 3-Y-0+ — **£2,625** (£750; £375) **Stalls** High

| Form | | | | RPR |
|---|---|---|---|---|
| -600 | **1** | | **Open Handed (IRE)**[14] 1197 4-9-7 35 ....(t) TEaves(5) 13<br>(BEllison) *mid-div: hdwy over 2f out: swtchd lft 1f out: r.o wl to ld towards fin* **20/1** | 64 |
| 0-20 | **2** | ½ | **Nod's Nephew**[27] 1043 7-9-12 58 .... JFEgan 12<br>(DECantillon) *trckd ldrs: qcknd to ld appr fnl f: hdd nr fin* **11/2**[2] | 63 |
| -164 | **3** | *nk* | **Weet Watchers**[48] 900 4-9-12 67 .... NCallan 17<br>(PABlockley) *trckd ldrs: styd on fnl f: kpt on towards fin* **4/1**[1] | 62 |
| 4004 | **4** | *shd* | **Heartbeat**[9] 1267 3-8-0 52 .... DaleGibson 10<br>(PJMcbride) *bhd and pushed along: hdwy 2f out: styd on wl ins last* **16/1** | 51 |
| /0-0 | **5** | ½ | **Lucky Largo (IRE)**[16] 1172 4-9-6 65 ....(b) IMongan 6<br>(SGollings) *mid-div: hdwy to chse ldrs 2f out: kpt on wl ins last* **9/1** | 55 |
| 5066 | **6** | 2 | **Vermilion Creek**[57] 814 5-8-8 50 .... StephanieHollinshead(7) 7<br>(RHollinshead) *bhd: styd on wl fnl 2f: nt rch ldrs* **25/1** | 46 |
| 640- | **7** | ¾ | **Fine Frenzy (IRE)**[117] 5564 4-8-10 47 .... AQuinn(5) 2<br>(MissSJWilton) *led tl appr fnl f: fdd* **40/1** | 44 |
| 00-0 | **8** | *shd* | **Eva Peron (IRE)**[19] 1121 4-9-1 55 .... ADaly 3<br>(WGMTurner) *chsd ldr: wknd appr fnl f* **14/1** | 44 |
| 0304 | **9** | *nk* | **Tinian**[14] 1197 6-9-12 54 .... DarrenWilliams 11<br>(KRBurke) *chsd ldrs: one pce fnl 2f* **15/2**[3] | 54 |
| 2336 | **10** | 1 | **Frank's Quest (IRE)**[37] 988 4-9-9 50 .... LPKeniry(3) 4<br>(PBurgoyne) *swtg: in tch: effrt over 2f out: nvr rchd ldrs* **20/1** | 52 |
| 036- | **11** | 2½ | **Lord Of Methley**[147] 6026 5-9-12 50 ....(v) VHalliday 15<br>(RMWhitaker) *mid-div: effrt over 2f out: nvr a threat* **9/1** | 47 |
| 0-40 | **12** | *shd* | **Shotley Dancer**[45] 934 5-8-8 40 .... SuzanneFrance(7) 1<br>(NBycroft) *s.i.s: nvr on terms* **40/1** | 36 |
| 06-0 | **13** | 2 | **Royal Windmill (IRE)**[14] 1197 5-9-5 48 ....(p) DFentiman(7) 9<br>(MDHammond) *bhd: effrt over 2f out: nvr a factor* **14/1** | 43 |
| 0-03 | **14** | *hd* | **Gwazi**[60] 776 4-9-3 40 ....(t) SHitchcott(3) 16<br>(MissDAMchale) *chsd ldrs: wknd over 1f out* **25/1** | 36 |
| 244- | **15** | *hd* | **Good Loser (IRE)**[307] 2313 4-9-6 60 ....(t) JBramhill 14<br>(CRDore) *promint: effrt over 2f out: wknd over 1f out* **8/1** | 36 |
| 00-0 | **16** | 30 | **Finningley Connor**[29] 1032 4-9-6 50 .... MFenton 5<br>(RonaldThompson) *mid-div: lost pl over 2f out: eased* **33/1** | — |
| 0 | **17** | 29 | **Fast Lane (IRE)**[16] 1174 5-9-6 40 ....(p) ACulhane 8<br>(JSWainwright) *mid-div: hmpd over 5f out: hungIft and bhd over 3f out: eased* **40/1** | — |

1m 51.26s (3.96) **Going Correction** +0.425s/f (Yiel)
**WFA** 3 from 4yo+ 15lb — **17** Ran SP% **125.0**
Speed ratings: **97,96,96,96,95 93,92,92,91 88,88,86,86,86 56,27** CT £23.40 TOTE £3.90: £2.00, £2.80, £; EX372.70 1.There was no bid for the winner. Lucky Largo (IRE) was claimed by Miss Linda Perratt for £6000. Weet Watcher
**Owner** Mrs Andrea M Mallinson **Bred** Citadel Stud **Trained** Norton, N Yorks

**FOCUS**
A moderate seller with a pace to match, the winner had dropped a lot in the official ratings since last turf season.

**NOTEBOOK**
**Open Handed(IRE)**, who had the least chance of all on official figures, was given a fine ride to get up near the line.
**Nod's Nephew**, as usual taken to post early, looked to have it in the bag when going a length up but he was found out by the winner's late burst.
**Weet Watchers**, who has broken blood vessels in the past, was unable to dominate and deserves credit for his fightback all the way to the line. David Nicholls was certainly impressed.
**Heartbeat**, backward in her coat, stayed on from an impossible position and will be suited by a return to a mile two.
**Lucky Largo(IRE)**, top on official ratings, only really found his stride inside the last. He was claimed and will now campaign under the Scottish flag.
**Vermilion Creek**, who looked in good nick beforehand, stayed on from a hopeless position turning in.
**Fast Lane(IRE)** *Official explanation: jockey said gelding hung left handed throughout the race*

## 1390 BEVERLEY-RACECOURSE.CO.UK MAIDEN AUCTION STKS — 5f

**2:45** (2:46) (E ) 2-Y-0 — **£3,653** (£1,124; £562; £281) **Stalls** High

| Form | | | | RPR |
|---|---|---|---|---|
| 2 | **1** | | **Dance Night (IRE)**[20] 1105 2-8-11 .... GGibbons 9<br>(BAMcmahon) *chsd ldr: led over 1f out: styd on wl: readily* **1/1**[1] | 86 |
| 0 | **2** | 3 | **Turtle Magic (IRE)**[19] 1117 2-7-9 .... CHaddon(7) 15<br>(WGMTurner) *sn chsng ldrs: wnt 2nd 1f out: kpt on: no ch w wnr* **20/1** | 67 |
| 3 | **3** | 5 | **Georgie Belle (USA)**[13] 1219 2-8-4 .... GDuffield 12<br>(CTinkler) *chsd ldrs: kpt on same pce fnl 2f* **6/1**[3] | 51 |
| 0 | **4** | 1¾ | **Lord John**[18] 1128 2-8-7 .... DaleGibson 11<br>(MWEasterby) *swvd lft s: bhd tl styd on fnl 2f* **16/1** | 48 |
| | **5** | *shd* | **Tiffin Deano (IRE)** 2-8-9 .... GFaulkner 16<br>(PCHaslam) *led tl over 1f out: sn weakend* **8/1** | 50 |
| | **6** | *nk* | **Mirage Prince (IRE)** 2-8-9 .... DarrenWilliams 14<br>(WMBrisbourne) *leggy: unf: sn in tch: kpt on same pce fnl 2f* **33/1** | 49 |
| | **7** | 1¼ | **Welcome Dream** 2-8-2 .... JQuinn 13<br>(MrsADuffield) *s.i.s: kpt on fnl 2f: nvr nr ldrs* **40/1** | 37 |
| 0 | **8** | 7 | **Bedtime Blues**[18] 1128 2-8-3 .... THamilton(3) 5<br>(JAGlover) *sn outpcd and bhd: nvr nrr* **50/1** | 17 |
| | **9** | 6 | **Victimised (IRE)** 2-8-6 .... LPKeniry(3) 7<br>(PBurgoyne) *s.i.s: m green and wnt lft over 2f out: nvr a factor* **66/1** | — |
| | **10** | ¾ | **Dramatic Review (IRE)** 2-8-2 .... RoryMoore(7) 10<br>(PCHaslam) *bmpd s: a in rr* **33/1** | — |
| | **11** | 3½ | **Silver Phantom (IRE)** 2-9-0 .... NPollard 8<br>(DRLoder) *chsd ldrs: lost pl over 2f out* **9/2**[2] | — |
| | **12** | ¾ | **Frisby Ridge (IRE)** 2-8-1 ow2 .... DAllan(3) 2<br>(TDEasterby) *cmpt: s.s and carried lft s: a bhd* **66/1** | — |
| | **13** | 5 | **Tartatartufata** 2-8-4 .... PHanagan 6<br>(DShaw) *mid-div: hung lft and lost pl over 2f out: sn bhd: eased* **66/1** | — |
| | **14** | 9 | **Brace Of Doves** 2-8-2 .... PMakin(7) 4<br>(TDBarron) *unruly in stalls: sn chsng ldrs: hung lft and lost pl over 2f out: sn bhd and eased* **33/1** | — |
| | **15** | *nk* | **Ruby Rebel** 2-8-4 ow2 .... RFitzpatrick 3<br>(PTMidgley) *lengthy: swvd bdly lft s: a bhd: eased* **100/1** | — |

67.13 secs (3.13) **Going Correction** +0.50s/f (Yiel) — **15** Ran SP% **122.9**
Speed ratings: **94,89,81,78,78 77,75,64,54,53 48,46,38,24,24**CSF £29.72 TOTE £1.80: £1.30, £4.60, £1.80; EX 30.70.
**Owner** J C Fretwell **Bred** Peter McClutcheon **Trained** Hopwas, Staffs

**FOCUS**
Probably just a modest event but a clear-cut and decisive winner.

**NOTEBOOK**
**Dance Night(IRE)**, chased home by two subsequent winners on the Town Moor, made this look very straightforward.
**Turtle Magic(IRE)**, an April foal, is quite a keen type. Drawn one off the rail, she improved a good deal on her debut effort on the All-Weather.
**Georgie Belle(USA)**, awkward to load, had a high draw so she had no real excuse.
**Lord John**, not born until May 1st, put in some solid late work and looks the type to appreciate a sixth furlong already.
**Tiffin Deano(IRE)** had the plum draw and this March foal showed bags of toe to lead them before becoming leg-weary in the final furlong. He should last longer next time.
**Mirage Prince(IRE)**, an April foal, is immature and will appreciate six furlongs plus in due course.
**Silver Phantom(IRE)**, a February foal, is not that big. He dropped right out at halfway and showed no immediate promise.
**Tartatartufata** *Official explanation: jockey said filly hung left throughout.*
**Brace Of Doves** *Official explanation: jockey said colt hung left from half way.*

## 1391 FLYING FIVE CLASSIFIED STKS — 5f

**3:20** (3:20) (C ) 3-Y-0+ — **£9,431** (£2,902; £1,451; £725) **Stalls** High

| Form | | | | RPR |
|---|---|---|---|---|
| 60-0 | **1** | | **Proud Boast**[14] 1211 6-9-2 92 .... ACulhane 10<br>(DNicholls) *chsd ldrs: n.m.r 1f out: r.o wl to ld last 75yds* **7/1** | 98 |
| 12-0 | **2** | ¾ | **Caribbean Coral**[19] 1113 5-9-3 90 .... DarrenWilliams 13<br>(JJQuinn) *dwlt: sn trcking ldrs: smooth hdwy to ld 1f out: rdn and edgd lft: hdd and no ex last 75yds* **9/2**[2] | 97 |
| 00-0 | **3** | ¾ | **Ikan (IRE)**[25] 1061 4-9-1 89 ow1 .... TGMcLaughlin 5<br>(NPLittmoden) *hld up and bhd: hdwy 2f out: n.m.r 1f out: styd on wl towards fin* **50/1** | 92 |
| 0010 | **4** | *nk* | **Johnston's Diamond (IRE)**[32] 1007 6-9-3 85 .... JQuinn 2<br>(EJAlston) *bhd: hdwy on outer over 1f out: kpt on wl ins last* **33/1** | 93+ |
| 300- | **5** | 1¼ | **Simianna**[186] 5482 5-9-0 89 .... GDuffield 7<br>(ABerry) *sn bhd: hdwy on outer over 2f out: nvr rchd ldrs* **14/1** | 86 |
| 0040 | **6** | 1¼ | **Bond Boy**[19] 1113 7-9-5 92 .... FLynch 8<br>(BSmart) *hld up: hdwy whn nt clr run over 1f out: styd on ins last* **4/1**[1] | 86 |
| 50-0 | **7** | *nk* | **Coconut Penang (IRE)**[18] 1126 4-9-8 95 .... NPollard 12<br>(BRMillman) *led 1f: chsd ldr: wkng whn n.m.r 1f out* **11/2**[3] | 88 |
| 000- | **8** | 1¼ | **Vita Spericolata (IRE)**[186] 5479 7-9-0 86 .... RWinston 4<br>(JSWainwright) *led after 1f: hdd 1f out: wknd and eased ins last* **28/1** | 76 |
| 00- | **9** | *hd* | **Matty Tun**[158] 5953 5-9-3 87 .... JBramhill 6<br>(JBalding) *hld up: hdwy on inner over 2f out: nt clr run 1f out: nvr rchd ldrs* **20/1** | 78 |
| 13-3 | **10** | 1¾ | **Henry Hall (IRE)**[14] 1211 8-9-6 93 .... KimTinkler 3<br>(NTinkler) *quite keen: trckd ldrs: fdd appr fnl f* **14/1** | 75 |
| 0U25 | **11** | 3 | **Trinculo (IRE)**[14] 1211 7-9-0 89 ....(p) J-PGuillambert(3) 11<br>(NPLittmoden) *chsd ldrs: wknd and eased 1f out* **8/1** | 61 |
| /10- | **12** | 2½ | **Arctic Burst (USA)**[291] 2779 4-9-3 90 ....(t) PHanagan 1<br>(DShaw) *s.i.s: swtchd rt after s: a bhd* **100/1** | 53 |
| 4-U3 | **13** | *nk* | **Ok Pal**[32] 1007 4-9-3 90 .... IMongan 9<br>(TGMills) *chsd ldrs: lost pl and n.m.r 2f out* **6/1** | 52 |

65.86 secs (1.86) **Going Correction** +0.50s/f (Yiel) — **13** Ran SP% **118.9**
Speed ratings: **105,103,102,102,100 98,97,95,95,92 87,83,83**CSF £36.60 TOTE £9.20: £2.40, £2.40, £14.20; EX 31.50.
**Owner** P D Savill **Bred** J Gittins And Capt J H Wilson **Trained** Sessay, N Yorks

**FOCUS**
A tight-knit affair with 11 of the runners rated within 4lb of each other on official figures and the draw again crucial.

**NOTEBOOK**
**Proud Boast**, marginally top on official ratings, was having her second outing for her new connections. She proved as brave as ever, capitalising on a favourable draw to record her sixth career win.
**Caribbean Coral**, still backward in his coat, had the plum draw but he missed a beat at the start. He took it up looking all over a winner but came off a straight line and was edged out. There will be other days.
**Ikan(IRE)** found her form with a vengeance and deserves full marks from an unfavourable draw.
**Johnston's Diamond(IRE)**, one of only two who had something to find on official ratings, looked backward in his coat and was walked to post. Drawn one off the outside, he did really well especially considering he was pushed even wider by the runner-up late on.
**Simianna** looked fairly straight on her first outing since October. She did well considering she had to make her effort on the outside.
**Bond Boy** had no luck at all but it is worth bearing in mind that his seventh and last career victory was in October 2002.
**Coconut Penang(IRE)**, who had a favourable draw, showed all his old speed but the fact remains he has not tasted success since his juvenile days.
**Vita Spericolata(IRE)** showed all her old speed to lead overall from her stall just three from the outside.

## 1392 NEW MINSTER ENCLOSURE STKS (H'CAP) — 7f 100y

**3:55** (3:55) (E ) (0-75,75) 3-Y-0 — **£3,718** (£1,144; £572; £286) **Stalls** High

| Form | | | | RPR |
|---|---|---|---|---|
| 5305 | **1** | | **Phluke**[15] 1184 3-8-13 **67** .... SCarson 16<br>(RFJohnsonHoughton) *led: sltly hdd over 2f out: styd on to ld post* **12/1** | 71 |
| 00-1 | **2** | *shd* | **Riley Boys (IRE)**[23] 1078 3-8-10 **64** .... MFenton 11<br>(JGGiven) *w ldr: slt ld over 2f out: hdd last stride* **14/1** | 68 |
| -156 | **3** | ½ | **Wings Of Morning (IRE)**[48] 900 3-8-12 **66** .... NCallan 8<br>(PABlockley) *trckd ldrs: styd on wl ins last* **20/1** | 69 |
| 354- | **4** | *nk* | **Charnock Bates One (IRE)**[214] 4893 3-8-10 **64** .... JQuinn 13<br>(TDEasterby) *in tch on ins: effrt over 2f out: kpt on wl ins last* **9/1**[3] | 66 |
| 14 | **5** | 1 | **Quickstyx**[14] 1214 3-9-1 **69** .... ACulhane 7<br>(MRChannon) *s.i.s: hdwy over 2f out: styd on fnl f* **11/4**[1] | 68 |
| 00-6 | **6** | *shd* | **Orion Express**[14] 1200 3-8-12 **66** .... DaleGibson 15<br>(MWEasterby) *hld up in mid-div: effrt over 2f out: styd in same pce whn n.m.r ins last* **14/1** | 65 |
| 45-6 | **7** | ½ | **Anduril**[19] 1120 3-9-2 **70** .... JTate 14<br>(JMPEustace) *s.i.s: t.k.h: sn trcking ldrs: hung rt 2f out: kpt on same pce* **16/1** | 68 |

050- **8** 1 ½ **Auroville**[210] 4997 3-9-0 **68** ........ IMongan 2 62
(MLWBell) *sn bhd: styd on fnl 2f: nvr nr ldrs* **22/1**
41-6 **9** ½ **Mr Midasman (IRE)**[20] 1108 3-9-3 **71** ........ DSweeney 3 64
(RHollinshead) *lw: s.i.s: hdwy over 2f out: kpt on wl ins last* **16/1**
150- **10** 1 ¾ **Cheverak Forest (IRE)**[158] 5950 3-8-12 **66** ........ KimTinkler 10 54
(DonEnricoIncisa) *sn bhd: hdwy over 2f out: one pce fnl f* **25/1**
346- **11** 2 ½ **Rigonza**[247] 4046 3-9-3 **74** ........ DAllan(3) 5 56
(TDEasterby) *s.i.s: bhd tl sme hdwy fnl 2f* **33/1**
0-63 **12** 1 ½ **Senor Bond (USA)**[7] 1303 3-9-4 **72** ........ FLynch 4 50
(BSmart) *hld up in rr: hdwy on wd outside over 4f out: lost pl 2f out* **16/1**
1-12 **13** 3 ½ **Whitgift Rock**[19] 1120 3-9-7 **75** ........ (v[1]) PDoe 12 45
(SDow) *chsd ldrs: hung lft bnd over 5f out: lost pl over 2f out* **9/2**[2]
2450 **14** 2 ½ **Looks The Business (IRE)**[9] 1271 3-8-8 **69** ........ (t) CHaddon(7) 1 32
(WGMTurner) *hdwy 6f out: sn chsng ldrs: hung lft and lost pl over 2f out* **50/1**
53-6 **15** ½ **Menai Straights**[18] 1138 3-8-11 **65** ........ GDuffield 9 27
(RFFisher) *sn trcking ldrs: lost pl over 2f out* **12/1**
3-25 **16** 12 **Bold Blade**[82] 595 3-8-9 **70** ........ (b) MStainton(7) 6 2
(BSmart) *swtg: a in rr: eased fnl f* **25/1**

1m 36.8s (2.50) **Going Correction** +0.425s/f (Yiel) **16** Ran SP% **122.9**
Speed ratings: **102,101,101,100,99 99,99,97,96,94 92,90,86,83,82 69**CSF £156.43 CT £3471.14 TOTE £15.40: £2.50, £2.00, £4.20, £1.90; EX 149.70.
**Owner** Mrs R F Johnson Houghton **Bred** Mrs R F Johnson Houghton **Trained** Blewbury, Oxon
■ Stewards Enquiry : J Quinn two-day ban: careless riding (Apr 25-26)

**FOCUS**
A modest handicap but run at a fair pace, and the first two, both drawn in double figures, were one-two throughout.

**NOTEBOOK**
**Phluke**, placed in five of his previous ten starts, is not that big. Helped by the best draw, he dictated the pace and came off just best in a very tight finish. His action suggests a bit of give underfoot suits him best.
**Riley Boys(IRE)**, another favourably drawn, took on the winner from start to finish and in the end only just missed out.
**Wings Of Morning(IRE)**, a keen type, was never far away. He stuck on well and was closing the first two down at the line. A full mile will suit him even better.
**Charnock Bates One(IRE)**, well drawn, found herself stuck on the inner with little room to work. She would not need to improve much to find a race.
**Quickstyx**, not that well drawn, made this even tougher with a tardy break. She was staying on when it was all over, and a step up in distance will suit this inexperienced filly.
**Orion Express**, with plenty to do at the weights, stayed on in his own time before running out of racing room well inside the last. He is still learning the ropes.
**Anduril**, a keen type, seemed to make his own trouble.
**Whitgift Rock**, in a first-time visor, hung out badly starting the turn for home and may be much better served going the other way round. *Official explanation: jockey said colt was hanging.*

## 1393 NEW COURSE ENCLOSURE STKS (H'CAP) 1m 1f 207y
4:30 (4:32) (E) (0-75,71) 3-Y-O+ **£3,896** (£1,199; £599; £299) **Stalls** High

Form RPR
30/3 **1** **Calatagan (IRE)**[14] 1198 5-8-12 **58** ........ PHanagan 13 69
(JMJefferson) *sn chsng ldrs: led 1f out: hld on towards fin* **6/1**[2]
60-6 **2** ½ **Tony Tie**[16] 1172 8-9-11 **71** ........ NCallan 12 81
(JSGoldie) *in tch: hdwy over 2f out: n.m.r 1f out: kpt on towards fin* **8/1**
23-3 **3** 2 **Trouble Mountain (USA)**[92] 516 7-9-5 **70** ........ PMulrennan(5) 16 76
(MWEasterby) *hmpd and lost pl after 2f: hdwy over 2f out: styd on wl fnl f* **3/1**[1]
430- **4** ½ **Grey Clouds**[200] 5215 4-9-4 **67** ........ DAllan(3) 17 73
(TDEasterby) *hmpd and lost pl after 2f: hdwy over 2f out: kpt on same pce fnl f* **10/1**
6-54 **5** 1 ¾ **Melodian**[16] 1172 9-8-13 **59** ........ (b) TWilliams 9 61
(MBrittain) *trckd ldrs: led over 2f out: hdd 1f out: wknd towards fin* **7/1**[3]
00-0 **6** ¾ **Graft**[16] 1172 5-9-0 **60** ........ DaleGibson 11 61
(MWEasterby) *bhd: styd on nicely fnl 2f: nt rch ldrs* **20/1**
60-0 **7** 1 **Maritime Blues**[14] 1213 4-9-5 **65** ........ MFenton 6 64
(JGGiven) *in rr: hdwy on outer over 2f out: kpt on: nvr rchd ldrs* **25/1**
60U0 **8** 5 **Archirondel**[11] 1245 6-8-1 **50** ........ RMiles(3) 1 40
(MDHammond) *bhd: sme hdwy on inner and n.m.r 2f out: nvr a factor* **25/1**
006- **9** 5 **Gifted Flame**[211] 4966 5-9-6 **66** ........ JQuinn 15 47
(TDBarron) *s.i.s: hdwy on inner whn nt clr run 2f out: nvr on terms* **9/1**
530- **10** ½ **Rockerfella Lad (IRE)**[89] 5225 4-9-8 **68** ........ GDuffield 4 48
(MTodhunter) *chsd ldrs. reminder 6f out: wknd 2f out* **40/1**
500- **11** 3 **Encounter**[175] 5712 8-8-3 **49** ........ DRMcCabe 2 24
(JHetherton) *mid-div: effrt on outer over 2f out: sn wknd* **16/1**
0540 **12** ¾ **Daimajin (IRE)**[48] 902 5-8-11 **62** ........ DNolan(5) 14 36
(MrsLucindaFeatherstone) *mid-div: effrt on outer over 2f out: sn wknd* **40/1**
/0-0 **13** ½ **Washington Pink (IRE)**[8] 1282 5-8-3 **52** ow2 ........ THamilton(3) 3 25
(CGrant) *bhd: sme hdwy 2f out: nvr a factor* **100/1**
050- **14** 1 ¼ **Face The Limelight (IRE)**[90] 5672 5-9-6 **66** ........ IMongan 8 36
(JeddO'Keeffe) *a bhd* **25/1**
20-0 **15** 2 **Every Note Counts**[20] 1103 4-9-10 **70** ........ RWinston 7 37
(JJQuinn) *hmpd and lost pl after 2f: nvr on terms after* **28/1**
-343 **16** nk **Senor Toran (USA)**[12] 1231 4-8-7 **56** ........ LPKeniry(3) 19 22
(PBurgoyne) *hmpd and lost pl after 2f: n.d after* **25/1**
000- **17** ½ **Mount Pekan (IRE)**[229] 4543 4-8-3 **49** ........ RFfrench 10 14
(JSGoldie) *led tl over 6f out: lost pl over 2f out* **33/1**
050- **18** 1 ½ **Ben Hur**[159] 5945 5-8-12 **58** ........ NPollard 5 21
(WMBrisbourne) *w ldrs: wknd over 2f out* **16/1**
500- **19** 7 **Mexican (USA)**[34] 3769 5-7-10 **49** ........ (p) DFentiman(7) 18 —
(MDHammond) *trckd ldrs: led over 6f out tl over 2f out: sn lost pl* **12/1**

2m 10.13s (2.93) **Going Correction** +0.425s/f (Yiel) **19** Ran SP% **133.8**
Speed ratings: **105,104,103,102,101 100,99,95,91,91 89,88,88,87,85 85,84,83,77**CSF £51.63 CT £182.25 TOTE £8.50: £2.40, £2.00, £1.30, £2.50; EX 69.00.
**Owner** Mr & Mrs J M Davenport **Bred** Mrs S Camacho **Trained** Norton, N Yorks

**FOCUS**
A modest handicap and not a strong pace early, although the overall time was decent. A concertina effect early on involving at least four horses with Grey Clouds possibly the worst sufferer.

**NOTEBOOK**
**Calatagan(IRE)**, happy to get a lead, in the end did just enough. The drop back in trip if anything seemed to be in his favour.
**Tony Tie**, who still looked wintry, had to squeeze through to mount his challenge. In the end he was just held at bay and, though he is not as good as when in his prime, his heart remains in the right place.
**Trouble Mountain(USA)** ◆, having his first outing for three months, was attempting to repeat last year's win in this from a 1lb lower mark this time. He had a favourable draw again but was on the back foot after being involved in a melee early on. In an impossible position turning in, he must be rated somewhat unlucky.
**Grey Clouds** did well after being put out of the contest in early scrimmaging. Much improved at three and suited by this particular track, she should enjoy further success this year.
**Melodian**, an old warhorse, was having his 61st career start. He raced handily but, after striking for home, the old legs were weary late on. He runs some of his best races here.
**Graft**, who has not won for over two years and was the stable's second string, caught the eye staying on nicely. Connections will know just where and when to put their money down.
**Maritime Blues**, poorly drawn, had to make his effort towards the outside. He kept on in willing fashion and all his best efforts have come on much quicker ground.
**Face The Limelight(IRE)** *Official explanation: jockey said gelding lost its action.*

## 1394 RACING HERE AGAIN NEXT THURSDAY STKS (FILLIES' H'CAP) 1m 4f 16y
5:05 (5:05) (E) (0-75,73) 3-Y-O **£3,575** (£1,100; £550; £275) **Stalls** High

Form RPR
45-3 **1** **Chara**[15] 1186 3-8-12 **64** ........ IMongan 7 65
(JRJenkins) *hld up: pushed along 6f out: hdwy over 2f out: edgd rt fnl f: led nr fin* **9/2**[2]
0-10 **2** nk **Varuni (IRE)**[37] 985 3-8-12 **64** ........ ACulhane 2 64
(JGPortman) *hld up: hdwy 6f out: edgd rt over 1f out: led last 75yds: hdd nr fin* **14/1**
56-3 **3** nk **Semelle De Vent (USA)**[16] 1179 3-8-6 **58** ........ RHavlin 10 58
(JHMGosden) *w ldr: led over 5f out: qcknd over 3f out: hdd and no ex last 75yds* **6/1**[3]
00-4 **4** hd **Prairie Sun (GER)**[12] 1235 3-8-4 **56** ........ GDuffield 1 56
(MrsADuffield) *chsd ldrs: rn in snatches: outpcd over 2f out: styd on wl ins last* **16/1**
445- **5** 1 ¼ **Dolly Wotnot (IRE)**[151] 6003 3-9-1 **67** ........ TGMcLaughlin 8 65
(NPLittmoden) *sn chsng ldrs: n.m.r over 1f out: kpt on same pce* **25/1**
640- **6** 1 **Signora Panettiera (FR)**[218] 4794 3-8-3 **58** ........ SHitchcott(3) 5 54
(MRChannon) *chsd ldrs: effrt over 2f out: bmpd over 1f out: kpt on* **9/1**
602- **7** 10 **Macchiato**[197] 5290 3-8-4 **56** ........ SCarson 9 37
(RFJohnsonHoughton) *led tl over 5f out: hung lft bnd 4f out: lost pl over 1f out* **8/1**
31-5 **8** nk **Keep On Movin' (IRE)**[13] 1222 3-9-4 **73** ........ RMiles(3) 4 54
(TGMills) *sn trcking ldrs: effrt over 4f out: hung rt and lost pl over 2f out* **15/8**[1]
00-6 **9** 2 **Moments I Treasure (USA)**[31] 1015 3-9-1 **67** ........ PHanagan 3 45
(EALDunlop) *sn trcking ldrs: lost pl 2f out* **10/1**
0-04 **10** nk **Ciacole**[64] 736 3-8-5 **64** ........ JDO'Reilly(7) 6 41
(RonaldThompson) *rrd s: hld up in rr: effrt on outside over 2f out: sn wknd* **33/1**

2m 48.89s (9.59) **Going Correction** +0.425s/f (Yiel) **10** Ran SP% **116.8**
Speed ratings: **85,84,84,84,83 82,76,76,74,74**CSF £65.63 CT £383.28 TOTE £5.80: £1.70, £3.30, £2.30; EX 75.70 Place 6 £191.91, Place 5 £70.04.
**Owner** M Ng **Bred** Michael Ng **Trained** Royston, Herts

**FOCUS**
A very modest 0-73 fillies' handicap run at just a steady pace to past halfway. The final time was pedestrian and the form looks weak.

**NOTEBOOK**
**Chara** looks still to have a bit to learn. She made things tough for her jockey but in the end did just enough. The stiffer test was definitely in her favour.
**Varuni(IRE)**, winner of an All-Weather claimer at Lingfield in February on only her second career start, worked hard to get her head in front but at the line was narrowly denied.
**Semelle De Vent(USA)**, quite a big filly, went on and soon stepped up the gallop but in the end was simply not good enough. Her rider deserves full marks though.
**Prairie Sun(GER)**, unplaced in four previous starts, was on and off the bridle but she finished best of all at the line. A stronger pace would have suited her.
**Dolly Wotnot(IRE)**, a leggy, narrow type, looked weighted to the limit on her handicap bow. Stamina did not seem an issue.
**Signora Panettiera(FR)**, who showed strictly limited ability in three starts at two, looked on a feasible handicap mark, but after lying handy in a moderately-run event she was going nowhere when bumped coming to the final furlong.
**Macchiato** *Official explanation: jockey said filly had lost her action.*
**Keep On Movin'(IRE)**, a tall filly, found herself carried towards the centre coming off the final bend and she looked all at sea. This track just did not suit her at all.
T/Plt: £61.80 to a £1 stake. Pool: £33,102.05. 390.75 winning tickets. T/Qpdt: £17.60 to a £1 stake. Pool: £2,400.00. 100.90 winning tickets. WG

# [1382] NEWMARKET (R-H)
### Wednesday, April 14

**OFFICIAL GOING: Good**
Weather: fine

## 1395 TURFTOURS.COM WOOD DITTON STKS 1m
1:10 (1:12) (D) 3-Y-O **£6,955** (£2,140; £1,070; £535) **Stalls** High

Form RPR
**1** **United Nations** 3-9-0 ........ JPMurtagh 3 92
(DRLoder) *w'like: scope: racd centre: chsd ldr: led 2f out: rdn out* **11/2**[3]
**2** 2 ½ **Denounce** 3-9-0 ........ RHughes 4 86
(HRACecil) *wl grwn: b.bkwd: sn led centre: hdd 2f out: unable qck ins fnl f* **4/1**[2]
**3** 1 ¾ **Marbush (IRE)** 3-9-0 ........ PRobinson 15 82
(MAJarvis) *w'like: led duo far side: rdn over 1f out: styd on same pce* **10/3**[1]
**4** 1 ½ **Diamond Lodge** 3-8-9 ........ SWKelly 5 74
(JNoseda) *w'like: lw: chsd ldrs centre: rdn and edgd rt over 1f out: styd on same pce* **50/1**
**5** 1 ½ **Maharaat (USA)** 3-9-0 ........ (t) WSupple 17 75
(SirMichaelStoute) *w'like: b.bkwd: chsd ldr far side: rdn over 2f out: sn outpcd* **20/1**
**6** 1 **Grand But One (IRE)** 3-9-0 ........ MHills 8 73
(BWHills) *w'like: scope: racd centre: sn pushed along in rr: hdwy over 1f out: nvr nrr* **16/1**
**7** ½ **Kaska (IRE)** 3-8-9 ........ DHolland 7 67
(BWHills) *w'like: leggy: chsd ldrs centre: wknd 2f out* **33/1**
**8** 2 **Balimaya (IRE)** 3-8-9 ........ EAhern 13 62
(JNoseda) *lt-f: leggy: hld up: effrt over 2f out: n.d* **33/1**
**9** 1 ½ **Rawdon (IRE)** 3-9-0 ........ LDettori 6 64
(JHMGosden) *gd sort: lw: s.i.s: racd centre: hdwy over 6f out: wknd over 2f out* **15/2**
**10** ½ **High Frequency (IRE)** 3-9-0 ........ RMullen 14 63
(WRMuir) *w'like: bkwd: racd centre: chsd ldrs over 5f* **66/1**
**11** 4 **Mustakhlas (USA)** 3-9-0 ........ RHills 12 53
(JLDunlop) *leggy: scope: lw: racd centre: sn outpcd* **10/1**
**12** hd **Key In** 3-8-9 ........ KDarley 10 48
(BWHills) *w'like: scope: racd centre: chsd ldrs 5f* **40/1**

**13** *½* **Tumbaga (USA)** 3-9-0 ........ SDrowne 9 52
(RCharlton) *gd sort: b.bkwd: raecd centre: hld up: hdwy over 3f out: wknd over 2f out* **10/1**

**14** *3* **Hinode (IRE)** 3-9-0 ........ SSanders 1 45
(JARToller) *gd sort: s.s: racd centre: a in rr* **50/1**

**15** *2* **Hilltop Rhapsody** 3-8-9 ........ CCatlin 16 35
(DJDaly) *leggy: scope: hld up: plld hrd: swtchd to r centre: wknd 3f out* **100/1**

**16** *4* **Dorset (USA)** 3-8-9 ........ MartinDwyer 2 26
(AMBalding) *w'like: unf: chsd ldrs centre: lost pl 5f out: sn bhd* **50/1**

**17** *15* **Protecting Heights (IRE)** 3-9-0 ........ TQuinn 11 —
(JLDunlop) *cmpt: scope: racd centre: outpcd* **50/1**

1m 40.06s (0.66) **Going Correction** +0.25s/f (Good) **17** Ran SP% **117.7**
Speed ratings: **106,103,101,100,98 97,97,95,93,93 89,89,88,85,83 79,64**CSF £24.42 TOTE £6.10: £2.10, £2.20, £1.60; EX 23.60.

**Owner** Sheikh Mohammed **Bred** Cyril Humphris **Trained** Newmarket, Suffolk

**FOCUS**

A race for previously unraced three-year-olds. The winning time was decent for a race of its type, which suggests this was an above-average renewal, full of future winners.

**NOTEBOOK**

**United Nations**, who cost 140,000gns as a foal, raced up with the pace throughout, showed a good attitude when he hit the front two out and ran on readily. On breeding this looks his optimum trip, but he shaped on this occasion as though he may get a bit farther and it would be a suprise were he not to build on this display.

**Denounce** ◆, a towering individual, travelled well on the pace throughout, before he ran green off the bridle and was always held by the winner. Still immature, he will have learnt plenty from this experience and could prove to be useful.

**Marbush(IRE)** ◆, a half-brother to the smart Sublimity, raced on the far side and would have been closer had he had more company inside the last two furlongs. He was doing a bit too much in front early on and that dented his turn of foot, but he is a nice prospect who will stay further and it would come as no suprise were to reverse this form in the future.

**Diamond Lodge** did the best of the fillies and was staying on well late on after a slow start. This will bring her on plenty and she is another who will benefit from farther in time.

**Maharaat(USA)** ◆ was travelling sweetly until he met the rising ground and he looked all at sea from then on. He will benefit from this run, has a decent middle-distance pedigree and looks a surefire future winner.

**Grand But One(IRE)** ◆ ran green at the back of the pack through the first couple of furlongs, but once the penny dropped, really found his stride and was finishing nicely. This colt looks well suited by the mile and looks a certainty for a maiden over that trip.

**Kaska(IRE)** was done for speed approaching the final two furlongs and will be seen to better effect when tackling further.

**Balimaya(IRE)**

**Rawdon(IRE)**, whose dam won the Group One Coronation Stakes, was sluggish at the start and made up ground too quickly to get to the leaders. He ran green late on and shaped as though he will come into his own over another couple of furlongs.

## 1396 VICTOR CHANDLER EUROPEAN FREE H'CAP (LISTED RACE) 7f

**1:45** (1:47) (A ) 3-Y-O **£17,400** (£6,600; £3,300; £1,500) **Stalls** High

Form RPR

215- **1** **Brunel (IRE)**[195] [5333] 3-8-13 **105** ........ DHolland 4 115
(WJHaggas) *h.d.w: racd far side: mde virtually all: clr over 1f out: rdn out* **9/1**

113- **2** *5* **Moonlight Man**[172] [5740] 3-8-13 **105** ........ RLMoore 6 102
(RHannon) *h.d.w: racd far side: prom: chsd wnr 2f out: sn rdn and no imp* **14/1**

65-0 **3** *nk* **Parkview Love (USA)**[11] [1239] 3-8-12 **104** ........ JFanning 11 100
(MJohnston) *racd far side: chsd wnr 5f: styd on same pce* **14/1**

344- **4** *nk* **Tahreeb (FR)**[172] [5739] 3-9-2 **108** ........ MartinDwyer 3 103
(MPTregoning) *lw: led centre: rdn over 1f out: no ex* **8/1**

144- **5** *½* **Azarole (IRE)**[195] [5333] 3-9-2 **108** ........ JPMurtagh 9 102
(JRFanshawe) *b.bkwd: racd far side: s.i.s: hdwy and swtchd lft over 1f out: nt trble ldrs* **6/1**[2]

165- **6** *6* **Mokabra (IRE)**[166] [5865] 3-9-1 **107** ........ TEDurcan 10 86
(MRChannon) *lw: racd far side: hld up: n.d* **20/1**

115- **7** *½* **Carrizo Creek (IRE)**[227] [4605] 3-9-4 **110** ........ KFallon 5 87
(BJMeehan) *h.d.w: racd centre: prom: rdn to chse ldr of that gp over 2f out: wknd fnl f* **4/1**[1]

60-0 **8** *nk* **Spanish Ace**[25] [1063] 3-9-0 **106** ........ MHills 2 82
(AMBalding) *b. racd centre: chsd ldrs 4f* **40/1**

503- **9** *5* **Blue Tomato**[186] [5485] 3-8-12 **104** ........ LDettori 7 67
(PFICole) *s.i.s: swtchd to r centre over 5f out: rdn 3f out: a in rr* **6/1**[2]

211- **10** *10* **Russian Valour (IRE)**[300] [2479] 3-9-7 **113** ........ KDarley 1 50
(MJohnston) *racd centre: chsd ldr of that gp tl wknd over 2f out* **7/1**[3]

40-5 **11** *11* **Venables (USA)**[25] [1063] 3-9-0 **106** ........(t) RHughes 8 15
(RHannon) *lw: racd far side: chsd ldrs 5f* **9/1**

1m 26.45s (-0.02) **Going Correction** +0.25s/f (Good) **11** Ran SP% **112.7**
Speed ratings: **110,104,103,103,103 96,95,95,89,78 65**CSF £122.51 CT £1769.15 TOTE £11.70: £3.40, £5.60, £5.20; EX 288.10 TRIFECTA Not won..

**Owner** Highclere Thoroughbred Racing X **Bred** Philip Brady **Trained** Newmarket, Suffolk

**FOCUS**

A decent time recorded by Brunel, who ran out a convincing winner.

**NOTEBOOK**

**Brunel(IRE)** may have enjoyed the run of the race, but the way he won suggests he was different class to the rest of these. He comprehensively turned the tables on Azarole, who had finished in front of him in the Somerville Tattersall Stakes last autumn, on 3lb better terms, and has clearly made giant strides over the winter. He is not entered in our Guineas, and his trainer plans to go down the German and Italian Guineas route instead, a path he successfully followed with Dupont in 2002.

**Moonlight Man** proved suited by the step back up to seven furlongs and battled on well to hold second. The winner was in a different league, though.

**Parkview Love(USA)** had the benefit of race fitness over the majority of his rivals, having had a run on the All-Weather lately. His form has a pretty exposed look to it and he may prove difficult to place this season.

**Tahreeb(FR)** finished clear of the group which he led down the centre of the track. It could be that he needs give in the ground to be seen at his best.

**Azarole(IRE)** was 3lb worse off with Brunel, whom he beat in the Somerville Tattersall Stakes last autumn, but that form was comprehensively overturned this time. He finished clear of the rest, but is another who may prove difficult to place this season.

**Carrizo Creek(IRE)** ran a long way below expectations and it could be that he needed this outing more than was thought.

**Russian Valour(IRE)** was very disappointing, even allowing for the question marks regarding his stamina coming into the race. His trainer was inclined to blame the change of training regime, which has been geared around trying to get him to stay farther than sprint trips, but it might just as likely be that he has yet to fully recover from the effects of the injury he sustained last year.

**Venables(USA)**reportedly returned home with mucus in his throat. *Official explanation: jockey said colt would not face the tongue strap*

## 1397 WEATHERBYS EARL OF SEFTON STKS (GROUP 3) 1m 1f

**2:20** (2:20) (A ) 4-Y-O+ **£29,000** (£11,000; £5,500; £2,500) **Stalls** High

Form RPR

2602 **1** **Gateman**[20] [1107] 7-8-13 112 ........ KDalgleish 3 117
(MJohnston) *b. hind: led over 7f: rallied to ld ins fnl f: r.o* **3/1**[2]

202- **2** *1* **Kalaman (IRE)**[194] [5347] 4-8-10 119 ........ KFallon 6 112
(SirMichaelStoute) *h.d.w: b.bkwd: trckd ldrs: led over 1f out: hdd and unable qck ins fnl f* **4/5**[1]

205- **3** *3* **Hurricane Alan (IRE)**[235] [4368] 4-8-10 110 ........ RHughes 2 106
(RHannon) *lw: trckd ldrs: racd keenly: rdn and ev ch over 1f out: wknd nr fin* **7/1**[3]

21-6 **4** *2½* **Lago D'Orta (IRE)**[20] [1107] 4-8-10 109 ........ PRobinson 5 101
(CGCox) *s.i.s: hld up: effrt over 2f out: wknd over 1f out* **16/1**

4120 **5** *1½* **Eastern Breeze (IRE)**[25] [1062] 6-8-10 102 ........ PaulEddery 1 98
(PWD'Arcy) *trckd wnr 7f: wknd over 1f out* **25/1**

2/1 **6** *21* **Wake (USA)**[25] [1059] 4-8-10 90 ........ LDettori 7 56
(BJMeehan) *hld up: wknd over 2f out* **16/1**

1m 52.77s (0.86) **Going Correction** +0.25s/f (Good) **6** Ran SP% **108.7**
Speed ratings: **106,105,102,100,98 80**CSF £5.37 TOTE £4.40: £1.90, £1.20; EX 7.90.

**Owner** Kennet Valley Thoroughbreds V **Bred** Miss K Rausing **Trained** Middleham Moor, N Yorks

**FOCUS**

A modest final time for a Group Three. The race is best viewed through Gateman, who ran right up to his best.

**NOTEBOOK**

**Gateman** got his own way in front, dictated a gallop to suit himself and, when the challenge from the favourite came, saw him off in game style. This was a good performance under his penalty and he looks just the type who could serve his stable well this season, plundering Group contests abroad.

**Kalaman(IRE)** had begun last season in good style and was unlucky in the St James's Palace Stakes. He disappointed, however, in the International Stakes though, and his defeat at HQ in the autumn left a question mark hanging over him. Although he lacked the winner's race fitness, this looked an ideal opportunity to get back on the winning trail and his defeat suggests that he may have been overrated.

**Hurricane Alan(IRE)** won the Craven Stakes here on his debut last season and ran a decent race in defeat on this occasion. He had a chance a furlong out, but could not pick up and was allowed to coast home once the front two had asserted. A drop back to a mile will probably suit him.

**Lago D'Orta(IRE)** improved slightly for his reappearance outing and put in some fair late work.

**Eastern Breeze(IRE)** was out of his depth in this grade.

## 1398 SHADWELL STUD NELL GWYN STKS (GROUP 3) (FILLIES) 7f

**2:55** (2:56) (A ) 3-Y-O **£29,000** (£11,000; £5,500; £2,500) **Stalls** High

Form RPR

000- **1** **Silca's Gift**[193] [5371] 3-8-9 103 ........ TEDurcan 2 106
(MRChannon) *racd centre: hld up: hdwy over 3f out: led that gp 2f out: overall ldr over 1f out: rdn out* **25/1**

61- **2** *3* **Incheni (IRE)**[167] [5833] 3-8-9 75 ........ SDrowne 13 99
(GWragg) *racd far side: hld up: hdwy over 1f out: led that gp ins fnl f: r.o* **50/1**

606- **3** *1* **Roseanna (FR)**[162] [5922] 3-8-9 ........ KDarley 11 96
(MmeCHead-Maarek, France) *w'like: racd far side: hld up: hdwy over 1f out: r.o* **14/1**

41- **4** *1¼* **Malvern Light**[160] [5930] 3-8-9 ........ DHolland 9 93
(WJHaggas) *h.d.w: racd far side: chsd ldr: rdn over 1f out: no ex ins fnl f* **5/1**[2]

103- **5** *hd* **Lucky Pipit**[216] [4840] 3-8-9 103 ........ MHills 10 92
(BWHills) *overall ldr far side tl hdd over 1f out: wknd ins fnl f* **10/1**

100- **6** *1* **Bay Tree (IRE)**[179] [5642] 3-8-9 105 ........ JPMurtagh 12 90
(DRLoder) *lw: racd far side: chsd ldrs: rdn over 2f out: styd on same pce appr fnl f* **13/2**[3]

31-0 **7** *½* **Valjarv (IRE)**[25] [1063] 3-8-9 95 ........ TPQueally 8 88
(NPLittmoden) *racd far side: chsd ldrs: rdn over 1f out: wknd ins fnl f* **50/1**

11- **8** *3½* **Top Romance (IRE)**[193] [5363] 3-8-9 ........ KFallon 1 79
(SirMichaelStoute) *racd centre: hld up: hdwy and hung lft over 2f out: sn rdn and edgd rt: wknd over 1f out* **5/1**[2]

210- **9** *1* **Totally Yours (IRE)**[195] [5332] 3-8-9 93 ........ MartinDwyer 3 77
(WRMuir) *racd centre: chsd ldrs 5f* **50/1**

120- **10** *1½* **Qasirah (IRE)**[216] [4840] 3-8-9 102 ........ PRobinson 5 73
(MAJarvis) *lw: racd centre: chsd ldrs over 4f* **14/1**

112- **11** *nk* **Snow Goose**[179] [5642] 3-8-9 105 ........ TQuinn 7 72
(JLDunlop) *lw: racd centre: hld up: hdwy over 2f out: wknd wl over 1f out* **4/1**[1]

210- **12** *2½* **Danclare (USA)**[192] [5404] 3-8-9 84 ........ LDettori 4 65
(JHMGosden) *led centre 5f: sn wknd* **20/1**

2- **13** *1¾* **St Francis Wood (USA)**[165] [5874] 3-8-9 ........ EAhern 6 61
(JNoseda) *racd centre: hld up: hmpd 5f out: effrt over 2f out: sn wknd* **13/2**[3]

1m 26.81s (0.34) **Going Correction** +0.25s/f (Good) **13** Ran SP% **116.9**
Speed ratings: **108,104,103,102,101 100,100,96,94,93 92,90,88**CSF £893.80 TOTE £30.10: £7.10, £9.60, £4.00; EX 958.90 Trifecta £9358.10 Part won. Pool £13,180.46 - 0.90 winning units..

**Owner** Aldridge Racing Limited **Bred** Limestone Stud **Trained** West Ilsley, Berks

**FOCUS**

A fair time for a race of its type, but a contest which will probably provide more clues towards the winners of the minor continental Guineas than the English version.

**NOTEBOOK**

**Silca's Gift** ran out a clear winner, but the impression given was that the race was not a particularly strong heat. She got the trip well, though, and her trainer does not rule out supplementing her for the 1,000 Guineas, although the German equivalent was originally the target.

**Incheni(IRE)**, a workmanlike Polytrack maiden winner on her final start last year, stepped up considerably on that form and looks likely to improve even further over a longer trip, for her dam won over a mile and her sire over a mile and a half.

**Roseanna(FR)**, whose trainer rarely brings no-hopers over, was running on well at the end of the race. She had looked nothing special in France as a juvenile and her performance probably underlines the fairly modest nature of the race. The Italian Guineas is her target.

**Malvern Light**, winner of a backend maiden, was the subject of good support throughout the day and her price shortened even further following the success of her galloping companion Brunel in the Free Handicap. She looked well beforehand and ran largely up to expectaions. There should be better to come. *Official explanation: jockey said filly ran too free*

**Lucky Pipit**, who made the running, may prove difficult to place this season.

**Bay Tree(IRE)**, who has changed stables since last season, just stayed on past beaten rivals.

**Valjarv(IRE)** is a pretty exposed performer who looks below this class. She is going to be hard to place this season.

**Top Romance(IRE)** may have been flattered by her Listed-grade success last backend, but this was still a disappointing effort.

**Snow Goose**, who set the standard on her second place in the Rockfel, was disappointing. The vet reported that she returned lame, but John Dunlop made no such excuse for her and said she was fine. *Official explanation: vet said filly was lame*
**St Francis Wood(USA)** *Official explanation: jockey said filly had hung left handed*

## 1399 INTERIOR PLC MAIDEN FILLIES' STKS — 5f
3:30 (3:33) (D) 2-Y-O — **£4,706** (£1,448; £724; £362) **Stalls** High

Form — RPR

1 **Siena Gold** 2-8-11 ........ LDettori 7 — 88
(BJMeehan) *neat: mde all: shkn up over 1f out: r.o wl* **10/3**[1]

2 *5* **Dance Away** 2-8-11 ........ JMackay 2 — 68
(MLWBell) *small: cmpt: b.hind: outpcd: hdwy 1/2-way: chsd wnr over 1f out: sn outpcd* **4/1**[3]

3 *1 1/2* **Miss Cassia** 2-8-11 ........ PDobbs 3 — 62
(RHannon) *leggy: unf: s.i.s: sn chsng ldrs: rdn over 1f out: no ex* **11/2**

3 — 4 *2* **Gaudalpin (IRE)**[8] 1276 2-8-11 ........ KFallon 8 — 54
(MJWallace) *chsd ldrs: rdn 2f out: wknd ins fnl f* **7/2**[2]

0 — 5 *1 1/2* **Misty Princess**[20] 1105 2-8-8 ........ LFletcher(3) 1 — 48
(MJPolglase) *hld up in tch: rdn and wknd over 1f out: edgd rt ins fnl f* **25/1**

6 *3* **Waterline Lover** 2-8-11 ........ SDrowne 9 — 36
(PDEvans) *cmpt: bkwd: s.i.s: sn chsng ldrs: outpcd fr 1/2-way* **25/1**

7 *3/4* **Beautiful Maria (IRE)** 2-8-11 ........ TQuinn 4 — 33
(PFICole) *w'like: chsd ldrs: sn rdn: wknd over 1f out* **6/1**

8 *2 1/2* **Cilla's Smile** 2-8-11 ........ KDarley 5 — 23
(MABuckley) *w'like: leggy: s.i.s: sn chsng ldrs: hung lft fnl 3f: wknd over 1f out* **20/1**

62.60 secs (2.19) **Going Correction** +0.25s/f (Good) — **8** Ran SP% **107.4**
Speed ratings: **92,84,81,78,76 71,70,66**CSF £14.58 TOTE £4.30: £1.70, £1.40, £2.00; EX 14.90.
**Owner** N Attenborough & Mrs L Mann **Bred** Limestone Stud **Trained** Upper Lambourn, Berks

**FOCUS**
The field raced more towards the centre of the track despite the stalls being on the far side. Winner apart, these are probably an average bunch.

**NOTEBOOK**
**Siena Gold**, a half-sister to several winners at between six and nine furlongs, clearly knew her job and showed a nice turn of foot to stretch clear. She is clearly a filly of some promise and connections intend taking the Hilary Needler/Queen Mary route with her.
**Dance Away**, who is out of a mare that won twice over this trip as a juvenile, has a quick action that may be better suited to a faster surface.
**Miss Cassia** is a half-sister to five winners, including ten-furlong German winner Metaxas, as well as seven- to eight-furlong performer Top Dirham. She is likely to stay further than this in time, so the fact that she showed some early pace augurs well for the future.
**Gaudalpin(IRE)** had the benefit of a run, but was easily shaken off as the winner quickened up. She is clearly of limited ability.
**Misty Princess**, a sister to winning sprinter Singsong, had clearly learnt from her debut and showed up well for much of the trip. Similar improvement should see her win a little race.
**Waterline Lover**, a half-sister to sprinters Branston Berry and Price Of Passion as well as mile winner Tough Love, has only just passed her second birthday this week. She can only improve for the experience.
**Beautiful Maria(IRE)** is out of a mare that stayed two-and-a-half miles, so this trip was hardly likely to bring out the best in her.

## 1400 GEOFFREY BARLING MAIDEN FILLIES' STKS — 7f
4:05 (4:06) (D) 3-Y-O — **£5,486** (£1,688; £844; £422) **Stalls** High

Form — RPR

2- 1 **Relaxed (USA)**[184] 5541 3-8-11 ........ KFallon 7 — 80
(SirMichaelStoute) *lw: racd stands' side: trckd ldrs: rdn to ld that gp over 1f out: r.o to be overall ldr nr fin* **7/1**[2]

3- 2 *1/2* **Red Top (IRE)**[337] 1576 3-8-11 ........ DaneO'Neill 14 — 79
(RHannon) *racd far side: hld up in tch: rdn over 1f out: r.o* **20/1**

34- 3 *shd* **Kind (IRE)**[193] 5367 3-8-11 ........ RHughes 16 — 78
(RCharlton) *led far side: rdn over 1f out: hdd nr fin* **12/1**

4- 4 *hd* **Attune**[230] 4531 3-8-11 ........ SDrowne 2 — 78
(BJMeehan) *racd stands' side: chsd ldrs: rdn and ev ch fr over 1f out: r.o* **50/1**

3- 5 *1* **Halabaloo (IRE)**[148] 6018 3-8-11 ........ DHolland 4 — 75
(GWragg) *lw: racd stands' side: hld up: hdwy over 1f out: r.o* **14/1**

6 *nk* **Capestar (IRE)** 3-8-11 ........ TQuinn 1 — 75
(BGPowell) *w'like: racd stands' side: s.s: hdwy 4f out: rdn and ev ch over 1f out: no ex ins fnl f* **50/1**

4- 7 *nk* **Cara Bella**[337] 1576 3-8-11 ........ JPMurtagh 3 — 74
(DRLoder) *lw: led stands' side 6f out: rdn and hdd over 1f out: styd on same pce ins fnl f* **8/1**[3]

8 *1/2* **Aricia (IRE)** 3-8-11 ........ LDettori 10 — 72
(JHMGosden) *w'like: racd far side: chsd ldrs: rdn over 2f out: no ex ins fnl f* **10/1**

9 *nk* **Sharp Needle** 3-8-11 ........ EAhern 13 — 72
(JNoseda) *gd sort: neat: racd far side: chsd ldrs: outpcd over 1f out: styd on ins fnl f* **66/1**

4- 10 *shd* **Zaqrah (USA)**[281] 3076 3-8-11 ........ RHills 11 — 71
(JLDunlop) *raecd far side: chsd ldr: chal 3f out: rdn over 1f out: no ex wl ins fnl f: lame* **4/5**[1]

11 *nk* **Antigua Bay (IRE)** 3-8-8 ........ LisaJones(3) 15 — 71
(JARToller) *w'like: scope: racd far side: prom: outpcd 2f out: r.o ins fnl f* **100/1**

20- 12 *1 3/4* **Speedbird (USA)**[165] 5868 3-8-11 ........ TEDurcan 17 — 66
(GWragg) *h.d.w: racd far side: chsd ldrs: rdn 2f out: wknd ins fnl f* **66/1**

13 *1* **Stocking Island** 3-8-11 ........ PRobinson 8 — 63
(BHanbury) *leggy: scope: racd stands' side: led 1f: wknd wl over 1f out* **66/1**

14 *7* **Sea Of Gold** 3-8-11 ........ MartinDwyer 5 — 45
(HJCyzer) *neat: racd stands' side: s.i.s: a in rr* **66/1**

15 *1 1/2* **Khafayif (USA)** 3-8-11 ........ WSupple 6 — 41
(BHanbury) *cmpt: racd stands' side: hld up: hdwy over 2f out: sn wknd* **25/1**

16 *1* **Miss Inkha** 3-8-11 ........ SSanders 9 — 39
(RGuest) *w'like: dwlt: racd stands' side: a in rr* **100/1**

050- 17 *1 3/4* **Shebaan**[193] 5362 3-8-11 58 ........ SWKelly 12 — 34
(PSMcentee) *raecd far side: hld up in tch: wknd wl over 1f out* **100/1**

1m 28.89s (2.42) **Going Correction** +0.25s/f (Good) — **17** Ran SP% **124.1**
Speed ratings: **96,95,95,95,93 93,93,92,92,92 91,89,88,80,79 77,75**CSF £145.15 TOTE £7.60: £2.00, £4.30, £3.00; EX 100.20.
**Owner** K Abdulla **Bred** Juddmonte Farms Inc **Trained** Newmarket, Suffolk

**FOCUS**
The field split into two here with no advantage to either side. This was the slowest of the three races to be run over this trip though the other two were the Free Handicap and Nell Gwyn. Just three and a half lengths covered the first 11 home.

**NOTEBOOK**
**Relaxed(USA)** confirmed the promise shown as a juvenile, and probably won with a little more up her sleeve than the verdict suggested. With improvement to come as she steps up in trip, she looks to have a bright future.
**Red Top(IRE)** took a while to hit top stride, but was finishing better than most. She looked a little unlucky, for she won her race on the far side. Compenstaion awaits.
**Kind(IRE)** showed plenty of pace and, although touched off, stayed this trip well. She deserves to find a race.
**Attune** showed enough to suggest she can win her maiden, possibly over a little further.
**Halabaloo(IRE)** ◆ is learning all the time, and with improvement to come over an extra furlong she looks to have a bright future.
**Capestar(IRE)**, out of a mare who won a Group 3, is a half-sister to several winners. She was very green and flashed her tail repeatedly, but she does have her fair share of ability and, providing she goes the right way, should win a little race.
**Cara Bella** looked as though another furlong wouldn't come amiss.
**Aricia(IRE)** ◆, a half-sister to Group 2 winner Cassandra Go, as well as Group 3 winner Verglas, was off the bridle some way out, but stuck well enough to her task in a manner which suggested she should stay further. She should find any amount of improvement from this.
**Zaqrah(USA)**, who came out of a hot maiden last year on her only start (six winners have come out of the race), was all the rage here but performed well below expectations, fading after holding every chance. The vet subsequently reported that she was lame, but according to John Dunlop it was nothing more serious than a bruised foot. *Official explanation: vet said filly was lame*
**Antigua Bay(IRE)** ◆, a half-sister to 12-furlong winner Largesse, shaped with plenty of promise and showed enough to suggest she can find a race when stepping up in trip.
**Shebaan** *Official explanation: jockey said filly lost her action*

## 1401 BABRAHAM H'CAP — 1m 4f
4:40 (4:43) (C) (0-95,95) 4-Y-O+ — **£9,665** (£2,974; £1,487; £743) **Stalls** High

Form — RPR

231- 1 **Sentry (IRE)**[154] 5978 4-9-1 **82** ........ LDettori 10 — 89
(JHMGosden) *lw: hld up: hdwy over 2f out: hung lft over 1f out: r.o to ld cl home* **10/1**

610- 2 *hd* **Prins Willem (IRE)**[166] 5855 5-9-6 **86** ........ KFallon 16 — 93
(JRFanshawe) *hld up in tch: rdn over 1f out: ev ch wl ins fnl f: r.o* **10/1**

010- 3 *hd* **Prairie Falcon (IRE)**[173] 5730 10-8-11 **82** ........ AMedeiros(5) 5 — 89
(BWHills) *lw: led: hdd over 1f out: rallied to ld ins fnl f: hdd cl home* **33/1**

015- 4 *3/4* **Bagan (FR)**[214] 4881 5-9-5 **85** ........ WRyan 7 — 90
(HRACecil) *hld up in tch: led over 1f out: hdd and unable qck ins fnl f* **9/1**[3]

10-4 5 *1/2* **Flotta**[26] 1054 5-9-6 **86** ........ TEDurcan 17 — 91
(MRChannon) *hld up: hdwy and edgd rt over 1f out: styd on* **12/1**

4/21 6 *1 1/2* **Jorobaden (FR)**[13] 1224 4-9-2 **83** ........ GBaker 6 — 85
(CFWall) *hld up: hdwy and n.m.r over 1f out: styd on* **16/1**

413- 7 *1 1/4* **Gold Ring**[158] 5952 4-9-4 **85** ........ SDrowne 12 — 85
(GBBalding) *lw: chsd ldrs: rdn over 2f out: styd on same pce appraoching fnl f* **12/1**

1011 8 *3 1/2* **Millville**[26] 1054 4-9-6 **87** ........ PRobinson 15 — 82
(MAJarvis) *hld up: hdwy 2f out: no imp fnl f* **3/1**[1]

014- 9 *nk* **Wunderwood (USA)**[158] 5952 5-9-10 **90** ........ SSanders 20 — 84
(LadyHerries) *hld up in tch: rdn over 3f out: wknd over 1f out* **6/1**[2]

216- 10 *1* **Mephisto (IRE)**[198] 5274 5-9-8 **88** ........ DHolland 13 — 81
(LMCumani) *lw: hld up: nt clr run over 2f out: effrt and hmpd over 1f out: nvr trbld ldrs* **25/1**

100- 11 *nk* **Annambo**[237] 4325 4-9-4 **85** ........ (v) JPMurtagh 11 — 77
(DRLoder) *chsd ldrs tl wknd over 1f out* **14/1**

1 12 *1 3/4* **Dance World**[12] 1235 4-8-10 **80** ........ BReilly(3) 14 — 69
(MissJFeilden) *prom: rdn over 2f out: edgd lft and wknd over 1f out* **14/1**

0301 13 *1/2* **Cruise Director**[9] 1272 4-9-0 **84** 4ex ........ LisaJones(3) 3 — 73
(WJMusson) *lw: hld up: hdwy over 3f out: wknd over 1f out* **12/1**

010- 14 *3 1/2* **Ring Of Destiny**[207] 5071 5-10-0 **94** ........ TQuinn 4 — 77
(PWHarris) *chsd ldrs over 9f* **33/1**

106- 15 *3/4* **High Action (USA)**[91] 4921 4-10-0 **95** ........ CCatlin 19 — 77
(IanWilliams) *b.bkwd: hld up: rdn 5f out: a in rr* **66/1**

426- 16 *1 1/4* **Wait For The Will (USA)**[193] 5253 8-9-10 **90** ........ (b) RLMoore 2 — 70
(GLMoore) *lw: s.s: hld up: a in rr* **33/1**

016- 17 *1/2* **Dovedon Hero**[172] 5738 4-8-13 **80** ........ MHills 18 — 59
(PJMcbride) *dwlt: hld up: plld hrd: a in rr* **25/1**

2-16 18 *1/2* **Harelda**[27] 1045 4-8-11 **81** ........ LFletcher(3) 8 — 59
(HMorrison) *lw: chsd ldrs over 9f* **25/1**

10-0 19 *11* **The Persuader (IRE)**[14] 1198 4-8-11 **78** ........ JFanning 1 — 39
(MJohnston) *lw: mid-div: hdwy 1/2-way: wknd over 2f out* **20/1**

350- 20 *25* **Island Light (USA)**[217] 4823 4-9-9 **90** ........ KDarley 9 — 11
(MrsMReveley) *hld up: plld hrd: a in rr: eased fnl 2f* **40/1**

2m 33.98s (0.52) **Going Correction** +0.25s/f (Good)
**WFA** 4 from 5yo+ 1lb — **20** Ran SP% **138.8**
Speed ratings: **108,107,107,107,106 105,105,102,102,101 101,100,100,97,97 96,96,95,88,71**CSF £106.97 CT £3276.60 TOTE £9.40: £2.50, £3.50, £14.70, £3.00; EX 155.40 Place 6 £2,353.13, Place 5 £1,769.69.
**Owner** Highclere Thoroughbred Racing IV **Bred** Mrs G Doyle **Trained** Manton, Wilts

**FOCUS**
This was a competitive contest run at a sound pace and it should throw up its fair share of winners.

**NOTEBOOK**
**Sentry(IRE)** ◆, gelded over the winter, needed his mind making up for him, but he did what was required in the end and won a shade more cosily than the verdict suggested. There looks to be plenty more to come from him.
**Prins Willem(IRE)** has needed an outing for the past couple of years to put him right, but there was plenty to like about this effort here. Although he is on a career-high mark, he still looks more than capable of holding his own.
**Prairie Falcon(IRE)** had plenty of use made of him over this inadequate trip, and only gave best in the shadow of the post. Now into the veteran stage, he still retains his enthusiasm and looks sure to pay his way for another season.
**Bagan(FR)** looked the likely winner when going on, but found little on the final climb. It could be that he just needed this outing to put an edge on him.
**Flotta** was probably done no favours by having to make up his ground down the centre of the track. Proven over further, he looks set for a decent summer.
**Jorobaden(FR)** lacked the experience of many of his rivals, but there was much to like about this effort, over a trip which proved well within his compass. With more to come, he looks set to pay his way in handicaps, although he probably wouldn't want the ground too quick.
**Gold Ring** hasn't got a great win-to-run ratio, but he turned in a sound enough effort in this and can be expected to strip sharper next time.
**Millville**, having his first outing on turf, didn't shape too badly and can be expected to show improvement from this, probably over a little further.

**Dance World** *Official explanation: jockey said gelding was unsuited by the good ground*
T/Jkpt: Not won. T/Plt: £1,670.10 to a £1 stake. Pool: £65,662.70. 28.70 winning tickets. T/Qpdt: £103.80 to a £1 stake. Pool: £4,735.60. 33.75 winning tickets. CR

## 1276 LINGFIELD (L-H)
### Thursday, April 15

**OFFICIAL GOING: Standard**
Wind: lt bhnd races 1-3, nil remaining races. Weather: fine & sunny

### 1402 BETDIRECT.CO.UK BANDED STKS — 1m 4f (P)
5:05 (5:05) (H) 4-Y-0+ — £1,473 (£421; £210) Stalls Low

Form — RPR

0-60 **1** **Leophin Dancer (USA)**$^{90}$ [446] 6-9-1 35 ........ BDoyle 4 — 44
(PWHiatt) *w ldrs tl restrained after 4f: effrt again 3f out: rdn to ld wl over 1f out: jnd fnl f: edgd rt but hld on* **7/1**

/500 **2** *shd* **Neptune**$^{22}$ [1101] 8-9-1 35 ........ RSmith 3 — 44
(JCFox) *s.s: hld up in rr: smooth prog over 3f out: rdn to join wnr ins fnl f: nt qckn nr fin* **10/1**

0056 **3** *1 ½* **Hellbent**$^{9}$ [1277] 5-9-1 35 ........ DSweeney 12 — 43
(JAOsborne) *dwlt: hld up in last pair: smooth prog 3f out: rdn to chal 1f out: fnd nil and btn fnl f* **4/1**$^{1}$

0/0- **4** *3* **Full Egalite**$^{19}$ [679] 8-9-1 30 ........(b) NPollard 2 — 42
(BRJohnson) *trckd ldrs: pushed along over 4f out: effrt to chse ldng pair over 2f out: nt qckn and btn 1f out* **7/1**

000- **5** *nk* **Smarter Charter**$^{306}$ [2372] 11-8-8 35 ........ KristinStubbs(7) 11 — 42
(MrsLStubbs) *dwlt: t.k.h: prog 1/2-way: led over 3f out: bmpd along and hdd wl over 1f out: wknd fnl f* **14/1**

660- **6** *5* **Sharp Spice**$^{74}$ [5500] 8-9-1 35 ........(v) SWhitworth 5 — 39
(DLWilliams) *v s.i.s: hld up in rr: effrt but outpcd 3f out: n.d after* **5/1**$^{3}$

0306 **7** *nk* **Giko**$^{17}$ [1164] 10-8-12 35 ........(b) DCorby(3) 6 — 39
(JaneSouthcombe) *w ldrs: led over 5f out: rdn and hdd over 3f out: wknd 2f out* **9/2**$^{2}$

065- **8** *2* **Oriental Moon (IRE)**$^{3}$ [6229] 5-8-12 35 ........(v$^{1}$) SHitchcott(3) 9 — 38
(MJGingell) *trckd ldrs: cl up 3f out: wknd over 2f out* **12/1**

00-6 **9** *½* **Leyaaly**$^{11}$ [722] 5-8-12 30 ........ BReilly(3) 1 — 38
(BAPearce) *a towards rr: rdn over 4f out: btn over 3f out* **33/1**

55-0 **10** *nk* **Superclean**$^{17}$ [1167] 4-8-7 30 ........ MLawson(7) 7 — 38
(AWCarroll) *a in rr: rdn and no prog 4f out* **16/1**

00-0 **11** *7* **Dances With Angels (IRE)**$^{9}$ [1277] 4-9-0 35 ........(p) PMQuinn 10 — 34
(MrsALMKing) *forced to r wd but led: hdd over 5f out: sn struggling* **12/1**

3000 **12** *12* **Polka Princess**$^{17}$ [1164] 4-9-0 35 ........(b$^{1}$) VSlattery 8 — 28
(MWellings) *t.k.h: w ldrs to over 5f out: sn wknd* **20/1**

2m 35.33s (1.09) **Going Correction** 0.0s/f (Stan)
**WFA** 4 from 5yo+ 1lb — **12** Ran SP% **124.6**
Speed ratings: **96,95,94,92,92 89,89,87,87,87 82,74**CSF £79.29 TOTE £6.70: £3.60, £4.00, £3.10; EX 70.10.
**Owner** Clive Roberts **Bred** Clovelly Farms **Trained** Hook Norton, Oxon

**FOCUS**
A truly awful affair, even in the context of this poor grade.

**NOTEBOOK**
**Leophin Dancer(USA)** had never previously won on the Flat and only had a selling hurdle success to his name in 49 career starts going into this. Returning to the level for this first start in 90 days, he ran out a very game winner to finally get off the mark on the level.
**Neptune**, well beaten in a course and distance seller on his previous start, returned to form in what was a worse race and was just denied.
**Hellbent** is not exactly progressing but this would have been one of the easiest tasks he has ever faced. However, having travelled well, he only had a small gap to go through between the eventual first and second in the straight and seemed unwilling to take it.
**Full Egalite** has not won on the level since taking a seller back in June of 2000 and had recently been refusing in point-to-points. He was gambled on and ran respectably, but his proximity is further proof of what a bad race this was.
**Smarter Charter**, racing for the first time in 306 days, ran a bit too free.
**Sharp Spice**, pulled up on her last two starts over hurdles, ran poorly on this switch back to the Flat.
**Giko** was below form.

### 1403 NEW SITE @ BETDIRECT.CO.UK BANDED STKS — 7f (P)
5:35 (5:35) (H) 3-Y-0+ — £1,267 (£362; £181) Stalls Low

Form — RPR

-220 **1** **Baytown Flyer**$^{16}$ [1191] 4-8-11 35 ........ BReilly(3) 10 — 43
(PSMcentee) *t.k.h: trckd ldr: led wl over 2f out: drvn 2l clr wl over 1f out: kpt on* **7/1**

0 **2** *1 ½* **Top Style (IRE)**$^{60}$ [783] 6-8-11 30 ........ DCorby(3) 2 — 39
(MJWallace) *s.i.s: racd in last pair: pushed along 4f out: plenty to do 2f out: styd on wl fr over 1f out: tk 2nd nr fin* **5/2**$^{2}$

06/6 **3** *nk* **Mahlstick (IRE)**$^{17}$ [1167] 6-8-11 35 ........ SHitchcott(3) 6 — 38
(DWPArbuthnot) *t.k.h: hld up: prog 1/2-way: rdn to chse wnr 2f out: no imp fnl f: lost 2nd nr fin* **11/1**

0064 **4** *1* **Beauteous (IRE)**$^{4}$ [1345] 5-9-0 35 ........ CLowther 7 — 36
(MJPolglase) *pushed up to go prom and sn plld hrd: rdn over 2f out: nt qckn over 1f out* **6/4**$^{1}$

4423 **5** *¾* **Tiny Tim (IRE)**$^{17}$ [1167] 6-8-7 35 ........ RJKilloran(7) 8 — 34
(AMBalding) *t.k.h: hld up in rr: stdy prog over 2f out: nt qckn over 1f out: one pce after* **7/2**$^{3}$

0000 **6** *2 ½* **Definitely Special (IRE)**$^{9}$ [1279] 6-8-9 35 ........(p) MSavage(5) 3 — 27
(NEBerry) *chsd ldrs: hrd rdn over 2f out: hanging and fnd nil wl over 1f out: eased last 100y* **25/1**

00-0 **7** *1 ¾* **Kafil (USA)**$^{72}$ [665] 10-8-9 35 ........(b) NChalmers(5) 4 — 23
(JJBridger) *t.k.h: n.m.r and dropped to rr after 1f: rdn 3f out: one pce after* **50/1**

0600 **8** *3* **Un Autre Espere**$^{19}$ [1138] 5-8-7 30 ........(b) BSwarbrick(7) 5 — 15
(TWall) *drvn in last pair and sn struggling: nvr a factor: kpt on fnl f* **50/1**

005- **9** *1 ½* **Superpridetwo**$^{208}$ [5068] 4-9-0 35 ........(v) SWhitworth 1 — 11
(PDNiven) *led to wl over 2f out: wknd rapidly wl over 1f out* **33/1**

0400 **10** *5* **Miss Celerity**$^{10}$ [1274] 4-8-11 35 ........ RMiles(3) 9 — —
(MJHaynes) *pressed ldrs to 1/2-way: nt run on: wl bhd over 1f out* **33/1**

1m 26.86s (0.92) **Going Correction** 0.0s/f (Stan) — **10** Ran SP% **125.3**
Speed ratings: **94,92,91,90,89 87,85,81,79,74**CSF £26.02 TOTE £10.90: £1.70, £1.40, £2.90; EX 92.00.
**Owner** J Doxey **Bred** B Minty **Trained** Newmarket, Suffolk

**FOCUS**
Probably just ordinary form.

**NOTEBOOK**
**Baytown Flyer** is at her best when able to race prominently but was unable to do so over six furlongs on Fibresand on her latest start. Stepped up in trip and switched to Polytrack, she benefited from a positive ride from Reilly and ran out a clear-cut winner.
**Top Style(IRE)**, a beaten favourite on his debut in this country over a mile three on Fibresand, could never get into it on this drop in trip and change in surface. A mile may suit better.
**Mahlstick(IRE)** was a little keen early and could only find the one pace in the straight.
**Beauteous(IRE)** was pushed along early in order to get a handy position but ended up running into the back of horses and needed to be snatched up quite drastically. This was not too bad an effort considering.
**Tiny Tim(IRE)**, down a furlong in trip, travelled well enough but found little.

### 1404 ANNE GURNEY BIRTHDAY BANDED STKS — 1m 2f (P)
6:05 (6:06) (H) 4-Y-0+ — £1,617 (£462; £231) Stalls Low

Form — RPR

00-5 **1** **Husky (POL)**$^{101}$ [446] 6-8-11 45 ........(p) BDoyle 2 — 50
(RMHCowell) *chsd ldr: clsd to ld wl over 3f out: rdn and pressed 2f out: edgd rt thrght fnl f: hld on* **7/2**$^{3}$

0/0- **2** *shd* **Kings Topic (USA)**$^{347}$ [1374] 4-8-4 45 ........ RJKilloran(7) 5 — 50
(PBurgoyne) *t.k.h: racd wd: in tch: effrt to chse wnr 3f out: shkn up to chal 2f out: edgd rt fnl f: nt qckn nr fin* **14/1**

0006 **3** *3* **Mythical Charm**$^{17}$ [1166] 5-8-6 40 ........ NChalmers(5) 6 — 44
(JJBridger) *dwlt: hld up: effrt to chse ldng pair wl over 2f out: sn rdn and nt qckn* **10/3**$^{2}$

5-43 **4** *5* **El Pedro**$^{67}$ [715] 5-8-9 45 ow3 ........ MSavage(5) 1 — 38
(NEBerry) *in tch: rdn 3f out: sn outpcd and btn* **9/4**$^{1}$

/00- **5** *¾* **Sylvan Twister**$^{396}$ [679] 5-8-11 35 ........ NPollard 7 — 34
(PMitchell) *restless in stalls and s.s: hld up in last: rdn over 3f out: one pce and no ch* **16/1**

0606 **6** *11* **Pyrrhic**$^{13}$ [1231] 5-8-11 40 ........(b) DSweeney 4 — 14
(RMFlower) *trckd ldrs: wl there 3f out: sn rdn and wknd* **6/1**

000/ **7** *2* **Courtledge**$^{3}$ [5894] 9-8-8 35 ........(v) SHitchcott(3) 3 — 11
(MJGingell) *led and sn clr: drvn and hdd wl over 3f out: wknd* **25/1**

2m 8.46s (0.61) **Going Correction** 0.0s/f (Stan) — **7** Ran SP% **106.8**
Speed ratings: **97,96,94,90,89 81,79**CSF £42.01 TOTE £6.10: £3.00, £7.80; EX 66.80.
**Owner** Mrs J M Penney **Bred** R Polec **Trained** Six Mile Bottom, Cambs

**FOCUS**
They went a good pace in what was a pretty uncompetitive race.

**NOTEBOOK**
**Husky(POL)**, a winner in Poland at up to seven furlongs, gained his first win in this country with a narrow success. Never too far off the pace, he travelled well and found plenty when asked. This will have boosted his confidence and he should continue to go well, especially if allowed to be kept to this level. *Official explanation: trainer said gelding had hung right*
**Kings Topic(USA)** had shown little in maiden company for Geoff Wragg, but this was a pleasing debut for new connections. He should improve on this given that it was his first run in 347 days and a similar race may come his way.
**Mythical Charm** travelled as well as anything but found disappointingly little when asked.
**El Pedro**, down in trip and switched from Fibresand to Polytrack, never threatened.
**Sylvan Twister** was never a danger after starting slowly.
**Pyrrhic** dropped out tamely.

### 1405 LITTLEWOODS BET DIRECT BANDED STKS — 1m 2f (P)
6:35 (6:35) (H) 3-Y-0 — £1,603 (£458; £229) Stalls Low

Form — RPR

0055 **1** **Larad (IRE)**$^{9}$ [1278] 3-8-4 45 ........(b) BSwarbrick(7) 1 — 50
(JSMoore) *prom: effrt to chse ldr over 2f out: hanging rt but led ins fnl f: drvn out* **7/2**$^{2}$

0041 **2** *½* **Oktis Morilious (IRE)**$^{17}$ [1166] 3-8-11 45 ........ JQuinn 3 — 49
(AWCarroll) *settled towards rr: prog 3f out: drvn and effrt over 1f out: kpt on u.p: a hld* **5/4**$^{1}$

5200 **3** *½* **Regency Malaya**$^{9}$ [1278] 3-8-11 40 ........(bt) SRighton 6 — 48
(MFHarris) *t.k.h: sn w ldr: led wl over 3f out: 2l clr and gng wl over 2f out: drvn over 1f out: hdd ins fnl f: one pce* **12/1**

0060 **4** *¾* **Shalati Princess**$^{22}$ [1096] 3-8-11 45 ........ RSmith 8 — 47
(JCFox) *settled in last: rdn 3f out: gd prog to chse ldrs 2f out: one pce u.p fnl f: nvr nr enough to chal* **8/1**

0-00 **5** *3 ½* **Stagecoach Ruby**$^{9}$ [1278] 3-8-11 45 ........(e) RBrisland 7 — 41
(GLMoore) *trckd ldrs: rdn and effrt wl over 2f out: nt qckn and btn over 1f out* **8/1**

-045 **6** *1* **Morning Hawk (USA)**$^{24}$ [1079] 3-8-11 45 ........ SWhitworth 5 — 39
(JSMoore) *settled towards rr: effrt and sme prog over 2f out: wknd over 1f out* **6/1**$^{3}$

0005 **7** *9* **Fora Smile**$^{8}$ [1296] 3-8-11 45 ........(v$^{1}$) DSweeney 4 — 23
(MDIUsher) *sn led: rdn and hdd wl over 3f out: wknd over 2f out* **14/1**

000- **8** *22* **Webbington Lass (IRE)**$^{192}$ [5424] 3-8-11 45 ........ SCarson 2 — —
(DrJRJNaylor) *chsd ldrs: rdn over 4f out: wknd over 3f out: t.o* **25/1**

2m 8.95s (1.10) **Going Correction** 0.0s/f (Stan) — **8** Ran SP% **121.4**
Speed ratings: **95,94,94,93,90 90,82,65**CSF £8.86 TOTE £4.80: £1.50, £1.10, £3.90; EX 11.30.
**Owner** A P Crook **Bred** Mrs E Thompson **Trained** East Garston, Berks

**FOCUS**
The pace was just ordinary and the first four finished very close together.

**NOTEBOOK**
**Larad(IRE)**, still a maiden going into this, was having only his second start over a trip this far, but it suited well. He had little in hand at the finish and is no sure thing to follow up.
**Oktis Morilious(IRE)**, successful in a similar race over course and distance on his previous run, looked to have every chance to follow up.
**Regency Malaya**, still a maiden, was a little keen early on but was allowed to do her own thing. She was clear three out and things would have been interesting had Righton kicked for home there and then.
**Shalati Princess**, trying this trip for the first time, travelled well but was given plenty to do and could never get on terms.
**Stagecoach Ruby** looked to have every chance.

### 1406 BET DIRECT ON SKY ACTIVE BANDED STKS — 6f (P)
7:05 (7:05) (H) 3-Y-0+ — £1,260 (£360; £180) Stalls Low

Form — RPR

00-4 **1** **Crafty Politician (USA)**$^{60}$ [782] 7-9-0 40 ........(b) RLMoore 4 — 51
(GLMoore) *trckd ldr: effrt to ld 2f out: rdn clr fnl f* **4/1**$^{3}$

0554 **2** *2 ½* **Hinchley Wood (IRE)**$^{9}$ [1279] 5-9-0 35 ........(b) NPollard 3 — 44
(JRBest) *trckd ldng pair: effrt 2f out: drvn over 1f out: nt qckn and no imp fnl f* **4/1**$^{3}$

3053 **3** *nk* **Sotonian (HOL)**$^{37}$ [1000] 11-8-11 40 ........ SHitchcott(3) 1 — 43
(PSFelgate) *led at mod pce: rdn and hdd 2f out: one pce after* **3/1**$^{2}$

0-52 **4** *4* **Maron**$^{45}$ [944] 7-9-0 40 ........(b) DaneO'Neill 2 — 31
(FJordan) *dwlt: prog to chse ldrs 1/2-way: drvn and nt qckn 2f out: sn btn* **11/4**$^{1}$

050- **5** 4 **Technician (IRE)**185 5540 9-9-0 40 (b) CLowther 5 19
(MissKMGeorge) *dwlt: racd in last: outpcd and drvn over 3f out: no ch after* **11/2**

000/ **6** 1/2 **Chakra**84 4629 10-8-11 30 RMiles(3) 6 17
(CJGray) *chsd ldrs: outpcd and drvn over 3f out: sn bhd* **20/1**

1m 12.81s (-0.11) **Going Correction** 0.0s/f (Stan) **6** Ran SP% **111.8**
Speed ratings: **100,96,96,90,85 84**CSF £19.89 TOTE £7.40: £1.80, £2.80; EX 18.80.
**Owner** Raymond Gross, Ms Adrienne Gross **Bred** M Prentiss **Trained** Woodingdean, E Sussex

**FOCUS**
The early pace was just steady in what was a weak sprint, but the final winning time was fair.

**NOTEBOOK**
**Crafty Politician(USA)**, with the blinkers refitted on this drop in trip and return to Polytrack, had the race run to suit and ran out a decisive winner of a weak event. This is his level.
**Hinchley Wood(IRE)**, beaten in sellers on his last two starts, ran respectably but never looked like getting to the winner.
**Sotonian(HOL)** was given every opportunity by Hitchcott but was simply not good enough.
**Maron** travelled strongly but found nothing when asked.
**Technician(IRE)** showed nothing on this first venture into regional racing over a trip that may have been shorter than ideal.

## 1407 BET DIRECT INTERACTIVE BANDED STKS 1m (P)
**7:35** (7:35) (H) 3-Y-O+ **£1,449** (£414; £207) **Stalls** High

| Form | | | | RPR |
|---|---|---|---|---|
| 4001 | **1** | | **Cumbrian Princess**17 1167 7-9-7 40 DSweeney 6<br>(MBlanshard) *chsd ldrs: effrt to chse clr ldr over 2f out: styd on u.p to ld last 75y* **9/4**2 | 45 |
| 426- | **2** | 1 1/2 | **Benjamin (IRE)**192 4340 6-9-7 40 (bt1) VSlattery 1<br>(JaneSouthcombe) *pressed ldr: led 1/2-way: kicked 4l clr over 2f out: wknd and hdd last 75y* **10/1** | 42 |
| 500 | **3** | hd | **Sunset Blues (FR)**19 1138 4-9-7 40 (be) DaneO'Neill 9<br>(KOCunningham-Brown) *v restless in stalls: racd in last pair and wl off the pce: prog 2f out: kpt on wl u.p fnl f: nrst fin* **20/1** | 41 |
| -000 | **4** | nk | **Lucretius**44 946 5-9-0 40 MHoward(7) 2<br>(DKIvory) *hld up in last trio: plenty to do over 3f out: prog to chse ldng pair 2f out: shkn up over 1f out: nt qckn fnl f* **25/1** | 40 |
| 0-52 | **5** | 2 1/2 | **Due To Me**44 949 4-9-7 40 (e) RLMoore 8<br>(GLMoore) *settled in rr: outpcd and rdn over 3f out: kpt on one pce fnl 2f : no ch* **7/4**1 | 35 |
| 00 | **6** | 4 | **Newcorr (IRE)**17 1164 5-9-2 35 NChalmers(5) 4<br>(JJBridger) *racd in midfield: drvn and no imp ldrs 3f out: wknd over 1f out* **33/1** | 25 |
| 0-52 | **7** | 6 | **A Bit Of Fun**45 945 3-8-6 35 PMQuinn 5<br>(JJQuinn) *chsd ldrs: pushed along 4f out: wknd over 2f out* **7/1** | 12 |
| 0/0- | **8** | 5 | **Tong Ice**366 1063 5-9-7 40 (p) RBrisland 3<br>(BAPearce) *led to 1/2-way: wknd rapidly over 2f out* **25/1** | — |
| 0055 | **P** | | **Youngs Forth**24 1080 4-9-7 40 (v1) JQuinn 7<br>(AWCarroll) *chsd ldrs: hrd rdn over 4f out: wknd p.u over 2f out: dismntd* **5/1**3 | — |

1m 40.58s (1.03) **Going Correction** 0.0s/f (Stan)
**WFA** 3 from 4yo+ 15lb **9** Ran SP% **120.8**
Speed ratings: **94,92,92,92,89 85,79,74,**—CSF £24.57 TOTE £2.50: £1.40, £2.70, £3.70; EX 25.50 Place 6 £247.15, Place 5 £99.84.
**Owner** David Sykes **Bred** Bishop's Down Farm **Trained** Upper Lambourn, Berks

**FOCUS**
A poor race but a decent effort from Cumbrian Princess, who continues in good heart.

**NOTEBOOK**
**Cumbrian Princess**, a winner in similar company over course and distance on her previous outing, had to work quite hard to follow up. The eventual runner-up had got away from her, but she kept on well in the straight to get on top under a strong ride. She could complete the hat-trick at this level.
**Benjamin(IRE)**, back on the level after a couple of unsuccessful spins over hurdles, and with blinkers on for the first time, nearly stole this under a positive ride from Slattery. He could pick up a similar race in his turn.
**Sunset Blues(FR)** did not show a great deal in maidens, but this was a respectable effort. He was doing his best work at the finish and promises to get farther.
**Lucretius**, with the cheekpieces left off this time, was given a lot to do but did appear to travel quite well. However, he found little for pressure in the straight.
**Due To Me**, with the blinkers left off this time, failed to build on the encouragement she showed on his previous run.
**Youngs Forth** *Official explanation: vet said filly had bled*
T/Plt: £563.70 to a £1 stake. Pool: £23,745.85. 30.75 winning tickets. T/Qpdt: £112.80 to a £1 stake. Pool: £2,561.30. 16.80 winning tickets. JN

# 1395 NEWMARKET (R-H)
Thursday, April 15

**OFFICIAL GOING: Good**
Wind: fresh hlf bhnd Weather: fine

## 1408 BET365 CALL 08000 322365 H'CAP 7f
**1:10** (1:12) (C) (0-95,95) 3-Y-O **£9,704** (£2,986; £1,493; £746) **Stalls** Low

| Form | | | | RPR |
|---|---|---|---|---|
| 1- | **1** | | **Oasis Star (IRE)**171 5785 3-8-1 75 MartinDwyer 2<br>(PWHarris) *a.p: rdn to ld wl ins fnl f: r.o* **20/1** | 88 |
| -1 | **2** | nk | **Ifteradh**22 1096 3-8-9 83 RHills 17<br>(BHanbury) *lw: chsd ldrs: rdn and edgd lft over 1f out: led ins fnl f : sn hdd: styd on* **10/1**3 | 96 |
| 231- | **3** | 1 1/4 | **Taruskin (IRE)**252 3917 3-8-8 82 RLMoore 8<br>(NACallaghan) *lw: chsd ldrs: outpcd over 2f out: rallied and swtchd rt ins fnl f: r.o* **33/1** | 91 |
| 31- | **4** | 1/2 | **Iffraaj**208 5078 3-8-12 86 PRobinson 1<br>(MAJarvis) *b.bkwd: sn led: rdn over 1f out: hdd and unable to quciken ins fnl f* **7/1**2 | 94 |
| 634- | **5** | 4 | **Lyca Ballerina**174 5734 3-7-13 73 JMackay 5<br>(BWHills) *hld up: r.o ins fnl f: nt rch ldrs* **20/1** | 71 |
| 20-1 | **6** | hd | **Free Trip**19 1129 3-8-11 85 RHughes 13<br>(JHMGosden) *chsd ldrs: rdn over 1f out: styd on same pce: edgd lft nr fin* **7/2**1 | 82 |
| 622- | **7** | 1 1/4 | **Mister Saif (USA)**138 6090 3-8-13 87 PDobbs 3<br>(RHannon) *prom: rdn over 2f out: styd on same pce appr fnl f* **33/1** | 81 |
| 10-5 | **8** | shd | **Fadeela (IRE)**5 1327 3-7-7 72 oh3 DFox(5) 18<br>(PWD'Arcy) *sn w ldr: rdn and ev ch 2f out: wkng whn hmpd over 1f out: and nr fin* **25/1** | 66 |
| -113 | **9** | hd | **Secret Place**54 843 3-8-10 84 EAhern 10<br>(EALDunlop) *hld up: plld hrd: nt clr run over 2f out: swtchd rt and hdwy over 1f out: nt trble ldrs* **25/1** | 77 |
| 31 | **10** | 2 | **Instant Recall (IRE)**15 1202 3-8-6 80 DHolland 9<br>(BJMeehan) *hld up in tch: wknd over 1f out* **14/1** | 68 |
| 20-0 | **11** | nk | **Poppys Footprint (IRE)**19 1129 3-8-9 83 NCallan 11<br>(KARyan) *s.i.s: sn pushed along in rr: nvr nrr* **66/1** | 70 |
| 01- | **12** | 3/4 | **Hezaam (USA)**166 5867 3-8-4 78 IMongan 6<br>(JLDunlop) *slowly into stride: hld up: nvr nrr* **14/1** | 63 |
| 626- | **13** | nk | **Go Yellow**177 5694 3-8-1 75 JFanning 4<br>(PDEvans) *chsd ldrs: rdn over 2f out: sn wknd* **50/1** | 59 |
| 221- | **14** | 1 1/2 | **Outer Hebrides**244 4160 3-8-9 83 (v) JPMurtagh 16<br>(DRLoder) *b.bkwd: hld up in tch: rdn over 2f out: wknd over 1f out* **12/1** | 63 |
| 261- | **15** | 1 1/4 | **Benny The Ball (USA)**142 6069 3-8-8 85 J-PGuillambert(3) 15<br>(NPLittmoden) *b.hind: chsd ldrs over 5f* **33/1** | 62 |
| 104- | **16** | 2 | **Sweet Reply**201 5223 3-8-8 82 ow2 KFallon 7<br>(IAWood) *chsd ldrs 5f* **33/1** | 54 |
| 211- | **17** | 2 1/2 | **Mahmoom**181 5614 3-9-4 92 TEDurcan 14<br>(MRChannon) *hld up: plld hrd: wknd over 2f out* **7/2**1 | 57 |
| 310- | **18** | 3 | **Tranquil Sky**257 3786 3-9-0 88 WRyan 19<br>(NACallaghan) *lw: hld up: n.d* **66/1** | 46 |
| 2110 | **19** | 1 1/4 | **Toronto Heights (USA)**50 885 3-8-5 79 JQuinn 12<br>(PWChapple-Hyam) *lw: mid-div: plld hrd: lost pl 4f out: n.d after* **20/1** | 33 |
| 1-14 | **20** | 1 | **Bettalatethannever (IRE)**26 1063 3-9-7 95 DaneO'Neill 20<br>(SDow) *sn prom: rdn and wknd wl over 1f out* **16/1** | 47 |

1m 26.66s (0.19) **Going Correction** +0.05s/f (Good) **20** Ran SP% **131.6**
Speed ratings: **100,99,98,97,93 92,91,91,91,88 88,87,87,85,84 81,78,75,74,72**CSF £195.72 CT £6644.76 TOTE £28.70: £4.60, £2.70, £8.00, £2.10; EX 252.40 TRIFECTA Not won..
**Owner** R J Creese **Bred** James Gleeson **Trained** Ringshall, Bucks

**FOCUS**
A well contested handicap sure to throw up plenty of winners. The field soon converged to race up the stands' side and not many got into it.

**NOTEBOOK**
**Oasis Star(IRE)**, winner of her only start at two, quickened up well to go through a gap and got on top in the last half-furlong. She is an honest filly who is probably open to more improvement.
**Ifteradh ◆**, who like the winner had been successful on his only previous start, was keen to post. Having tacked across from his wide draw, he briefly showed in front and stuck on willingly when headed. This was a highly promising turf debut.
**Taruskin(IRE)** ran a promising race, keeping on nicely once switched round the leading trio. He shapes as if another furlong would suit him.
**Iffraaj** made the running against the rail and kept on once headed in a manner which suggests he will stay farther. Faster ground should prove to his benefit.
**Lyca Ballerina**, one of just two maidens in the field, finished strongly from the back of the field without getting close to the leading quartet. *Official explanation: jockey said filly suffered interference early on in the race*
**Free Trip**, who went up 7lb for winning at Doncaster, was found wanting from his higher mark but ran respectably. He hung to his left when held, but not to the same extent as he had on Town Moor. *Official explanation: jockey said colt hung left-handed*
**Fadeela(IRE)**, who was theoretically 11lb well in, might be worth dropping back to six furlongs.
**Secret Place ◆** caught the eye making late progress after encountering trouble in running. He looks capable of bettering this in the near future.
**Instant Recall(IRE)** *Official explanation: jockey said colt ran too free early on*
**Sweet Reply** *Official explanation: jockey said filly hung right*
**Mahmoom** failed to settle and was in trouble a good way out.

## 1409 NGK SPARK PLUGS ABERNANT STKS (LISTED RACE) 6f
**1:45** (1:46) (A) 3-Y-O+ **£17,400** (£6,600; £3,300; £1,500) **Stalls** Low

| Form | | | | RPR |
|---|---|---|---|---|
| 263- | **1** | | **Arakan (USA)**180 5638 4-9-4 111 KFallon 5<br>(SirMichaelStoute) *lw: trckd ldrs: led and edgd lft over 1f out: r.o* **5/2**1 | 115+ |
| 611- | **2** | 1/2 | **Frizzante**182 5591 5-9-3 99 LDettori 1<br>(JRFanshawe) *lw: hld up: swtchd rt and hdwy over 1f out: edgd lft and chsd wnr ins fnl f: r.o* **3/1**2 | 113+ |
| 410- | **3** | 1 1/2 | **Ashdown Express (IRE)**159 5953 5-9-10 111 SSanders 4<br>(CFWall) *swtg: hld up in tch: nt clr run over 1f out: n.m.r ins fnl f: r.o* **11/1** | 115+ |
| 06-1 | **4** | 4 | **Bahamian Pirate (USA)**15 1211 9-9-4 112 JPMurtagh 2<br>(DNicholls) *lw: chsd ldrs: rdn over 1f out: hmpd ins fnl f: sn wknd* **6/1**3 | 97 |
| 15-4 | **5** | 1 1/4 | **Suggestive**21 1107 6-9-4 107 (b) DHolland 8<br>(WJHaggas) *sn pushed along in rr: effrt over 1f out: n.d* **8/1** | 93 |
| 515- | **6** | 3/4 | **Bonus (IRE)**228 4603 4-9-10 108 RHughes 6<br>(RHannon) *w ldrs: rdn and ev ch over 1f out: sn n.m.r: wknd ins fnl f* **9/1** | 97 |
| 65-3 | **7** | 3 | **The Kiddykid (IRE)**19 1126 4-9-4 104 NCallan 7<br>(PDEvans) *disp ld over 3f out: wkng whn hmpd 1f out* **15/2** | 82 |
| 63-0 | **8** | 8 | **Crimson Silk**19 1126 4-9-4 102 PaulEddery 3<br>(DHaydnJones) *lw: mde most over 4f: wkng whn hmpd ins fnl f* **20/1** | 58 |

1m 12.37s (-0.72) **Going Correction** +0.05s/f (Good) **8** Ran SP% **113.8**
Speed ratings: **106,105,103,98,96 95,91,80**CSF £9.98 TOTE £3.30: £1.20, £1.50, £3.70; EX 8.80.
**Owner** Niarchos Family **Bred** Flaxman Holdings Ltd **Trained** Newmarket, Suffolk
■ Stewards Enquiry : L Dettori caution: careless riding
K Fallon two-day ban: careless riding (Apr 26,27)

**FOCUS**
Though the final time was ordinary, this was run at a strong pace early, which played into the hands of the hold-up horses.

**NOTEBOOK**
**Arakan(USA)** was tackling this trip for the first time since his juvenile season. Well suited by the way the race panned out, he took first run and, edging left in front, was always going to hold the runner-up. A first Group win is overdue.
**Frizzante**, progressive last season, ran a sound race on this return to action, but the winner had taken first run on her by the time she went after him. She may return here for the Palace House but the drop to the minimum trip is not certain to suit.
**Ashdown Express(IRE)**, conceding a Group Three penalty, sweated up in the preliminaries and was taken early to post. Held up as usual, he had to wait for a run and by the time a clear passage had opened up ahead of him the first and second had flown. He finished well to match his third in this event last year and should enjoy a good season.
**Bahamian Pirate(USA)** tracked the leaders on the rail but lacked the necessary pace to go with them on ground which was faster than ideal for him.
**Suggestive** found things happening a shade quickly for him and will be happier back at seven furlongs.
**Bonus(IRE)**, penalised for his Group Three win in Ireland last season, made a satisfactory reappearance before lack of peak fitness took its toll. However, he reportedly scoped badly on his return home.
**The Kiddykid(IRE)** *Official explanation: jockey said gelding was unsuited by the good ground*

## 1410 BET365 CRAVEN STKS (GROUP 3) (C&G) 1m
**2:20** (2:21) (A) 3-Y-O **£29,750** (£11,000; £5,500; £2,500) **Stalls** Low

| Form | | | | RPR |
|---|---|---|---|---|
| 133- | **1** | | **Haafhd**180 5640 3-8-9 115 RHills 2<br>(BWHills) *h.d.w: mde all: qckned 2f out: sn clr: r.o wl* **10/3**2 | 121 |

312- 2 5 **Three Valleys (USA)**[180] 5640 3-8-9 118 ........ RHughes 1 110
(RCharlton) *h.d.w: plld hrd and prom: rdn to chse wnr over 1f out: sn outpcd* **2/1**[1]
111- 3 1 1/4 **Peak To Creek**[174] 5731 3-8-9 111 ........ EAhern 4 107
(JNoseda) *hld up: swtchd rt over 2f out: rdn over 1f out: no imp* **6/1**[3]
116- 4 2 1/2 **Imperial Stride**[180] 5640 3-8-9 113 ........ KFallon 5 101
(SirMichaelStoute) *h.d.w: trckd ldrs: plld hrd: rdn 2f out: sn btn* **7/1**
112- 5 4 **Fantastic View (USA)**[173] 5739 3-8-9 113 ........ PDobbs 3 92
(RHannon) *lw: chsd wnr over 6f: wknd qckly* **10/3**[2]
1m 38.33s (-1.07) **Going Correction** +0.05s/f (Good) **5** Ran SP% **106.3**
Speed ratings: **107,102,100,98,94**CSF £9.65 TOTE £4.60: £1.80, £1.60; EX 10.70.
**Owner** Hamdan Al Maktoum **Bred** Shadwell Estate Company Limited **Trained** Lambourn, Berks

**FOCUS**
The winner Haafhd was able to set his own pace, but there was no denying that he was an impressive winner despite the final time only being average.

**NOTEBOOK**
**Haafhd** finished behind Three Valleys in the Dewhurst but turned the tables in emphatic style here. Allowed to set his own pace, he wound it up from halfway before quickening into the Dip. He soon had all his opponents in trouble and stretched clear to score in impressive fashion. While the muddling pace means that this was an unsatisfactory race in some ways, it was still a taking trial for the 2000 Guineas, for which he now appears the leading home-based candidate, although Craven winners have a poor recent record in the first Classic.
**Three Valleys(USA)**, who lost his Middle Park victory after testing positive for Clenbuterol, was rather keen on this return to action. He moved into second pace approaching the final furlong, but by then the winner had taken control and he was unable to close the gap. He is entitled to stay a mile on pedigree but the way he races suggests he could be a sprinter.
**Peak To Creek**, who had a busy and highly successful first season, kept on once switched to the outside but could not get to the first two. A small individual, this was his first attempt at a mile and it did not tell us whether or not he stayed.
**Imperial Stride**, who lost his unbeaten record in the Dewhurst, was unable to find cover in the small field. Likely to derive improvement from the outing, he will appreciate a step up in trip.
**Fantastic View(USA)** was immediately on the retreat once the pace quickened. He is well regarded and it might be prudent to forgive him this, as he scoped badly on returning home.

## 1411 BET365 FEILDEN STKS (LISTED RACE) 1m 1f
**2:55** (2:56) (A) 3-Y-O **£17,400** (£6,600; £3,300; £1,500) **Stalls** Low

Form RPR
10-2 1 **Gold History (USA)**[19] 1123 3-8-11 100 ........ JFanning 3 102
(MJohnston) *mde all: rdn over 2f out: styd on gamely* **10/3**[3]
12-3 2 3/4 **Psychiatrist**[5] 1330 3-8-11 105 ........ RHughes 4 100
(RHannon) *trckead ldrs: racd keenly: rdn and ev ch fr over 1f out: edgd lft: unable qck towards fin* **3/1**[2]
513- 3 1/2 **Temple Place (IRE)**[187] 5478 3-8-11 91 ........ IMongan 7 99
(MLWBell) *hld up: racd keenly: hdwy over 3f out: nt clr run over 1f out: r.o* **8/1**
14- 4 1 1/4 **Isidore Bonheur (IRE)**[246] 4081 3-8-11 ........ (b[1]) MHills 6 97
(BWHills) *lw: trckd wnr: racd keenly: rdn and ev ch over 1f out: no ex ins fnl f* **14/1**
21-4 5 nk **New Mexican**[19] 1123 3-9-0 102 ........ LDettori 5 99
(MrsJRRamsden) *hld up: hdwy over 2f out: nvr able to chal* **7/1**
01- 6 1 **Roehampton**[169] 5830 3-8-11 ........ KFallon 1 94
(SirMichaelStoute) *h.d.w: s.i.s: sn prom: rdn over 2f out: styd on same pce fnl f* **11/4**[1]
353- 7 10 **Naaddey**[177] 5694 3-8-11 92 ........ TEDurcan 2 74
(MRChannon) *h.d.w: hld up in tch: wknd 2f out* **16/1**
1m 53.89s (1.98) **Going Correction** +0.05s/f (Good) **7** Ran SP% **110.9**
Speed ratings: **93,92,91,90,90 89,80**CSF £12.88 TOTE £4.60: £2.00, £2.30; EX 9.80.
**Owner** Abdulla Buhaleeba **Bred** W S Farish And E J Hudson Jr Irrevocable Trust **Trained** Middleham Moor, N Yorks

**FOCUS**
Not a strong renewal of this event and Classic clues were thin on the ground. The winning time was dire for a race of its class.

**NOTEBOOK**
**Gold History(USA)**, whose two wins as a juvenile came when he allowed his own way up front, was able to establish an uncontested lead once seeing off Isidore Bonheur. He stuck on in honest fashion to see it out and will stay farther than this, but this looked a long way removed from Classic form.
**Psychiatrist**, making a quick return to action, adopted different tactics from Kempton where he had made the running. He had his chance but was unable to find a change of gear inside the last.
**Temple Place(IRE)** did not enjoy the best of runs and had to be switched before staying on. Likely to get farther, he gave the impression that he might have been keeping a little back for himself, and may now go for the Chester Vase which will tell us more.
**Isidore Bonheur(IRE)** was fitted with blinkers for this return to action, having found nothing off the bridle on his last start at two, but was perhaps a little keen as a result.
**New Mexican**, burdened with a penalty for his win at this level last year, was without the cheekpieces that he wore on his reappearance. He appeared to race lazily and it could be that the headgear needs to be deployed again.
**Roehampton** was not given a hard time once his measure had been taken, but he is entitled to improve with this run under his belt. A half-brother to, amongst others, Bin Rosie and Generous Libra, he still looked inexperienced.
**Naaddey** dropped right away and it is difficult to see where connections will take it from here.

## 1412 CREATURE COMFORTS EBF MAIDEN STKS (C&G) 5f
**3:30** (3:30) (D) 2-Y-O **£4,771** (£1,468; £734; £367) **Stalls** Low

Form RPR
1 **Blue Dakota (IRE)** 2-8-11 ........ EAhern 9 98+
(JNoseda) *gd sort: leggy: trckd ldrs: shkn up to ld over 1f out: qcknd clr* **10/11**[1]
2 5 **Turnkey** 2-8-11 ........ TEDurcan 2 78
(MRChannon) *w'like: s.i.s: sn chsng ldrs: swtchd rt over 1f out: kpt on: no ch w wnr* **9/2**[2]
3 1/2 **Alpaga Le Jomage (IRE)** 2-8-11 ........ LDettori 5 76
(BJMeehan) *gd sort: lw: chsd ldr: rdn and ev ch over 1f out: sn outpcd* **14/1**
4 3/4 **Cavorting** 2-8-11 ........ JPMurtagh 3 73
(DRLoder) *cmpt: b.bkwd: led over 3f: no ex ins fnl f* **9/2**[2]
5 3 **The Crooked Ring** 2-8-11 ........ KFallon 6 61
(PDEvans) *neat: unf: chsd ldrs: pushed along 1/2-way: wknd over 1f out* **25/1**
4 6 2 **Gryskirk**[8] 1292 2-8-11 ........ PaulEddery 7 53
(PWD'Arcy) *s.s: hld up: n.d* **50/1**
7 2 **Destinate (IRE)** 2-8-11 ........ RHughes 8 45
(RHannon) *neat: s.i.s: sn chsng ldrs: wknd over 1f out* **10/1**[3]
8 1 1/4 **Countrywide Sun** 2-8-11 ........ DHolland 4 40
(NPLittmoden) *cmpt: unf: chsd ldrs: rdn 1/2-way: sn wknd* **33/1**
60.64 secs (0.23) **Going Correction** +0.05s/f (Good) **8** Ran SP% **113.3**
Speed ratings: **100,92,91,90,85 82,78,76**CSF £5.06 TOTE £1.90: £1.10, £1.40, £2.40; EX 5.90.
**Owner** A F Nolan, Mrs J M Ryan, Mrs P Duffin **Bred** Michael O'Donnell **Trained** Newmarket, Suffolk

**FOCUS**
Hard to know what to make of this as the winner was different class to the others. In terms of the winning time, this was the best performance against the clock by a juvenile so far this season.

**NOTEBOOK**
**Blue Dakota(IRE)** ◆, a half-brother to Group 3 winner Tarwiya, was all the rage beforehand and did not let his supporters down. Travelling well throughout, he quickened up like a serious horse when asked and soon left his rivals for dead. More will be heard of him.
**Turnkey**, a half-brother to winning stayer Forzair, stayed on nicely without ever threatening to take a hand. Already looking in need of a sixth furlong, there will be plenty of opportunities for him.
**Alpaga Le Jomage(IRE)**, out of a winning sprinter, was the oldest in the field having been foaled on February 12th. He looked to know what he was doing, but should still benefit from the experience.
**Cavorting**, a half-brother to winning sprinter Firework, was a bit edgy in the paddock, but went to post nicely enough. He showed plenty of pace on the rails before getting tired and will certainly benefit from the outing.
**The Crooked Ring**, a half-brother to winning juvenile My Lovely, found this company a bit hot for him and will need to lower his sights.

## 1413 BET365 CALL 08000 322365 MAIDEN STKS 6f
**4:05** (4:05) (D) 3-Y-O **£5,382** (£1,656; £828; £414) **Stalls** Low

Form RPR
22- 1 **Fun To Ride**[167] 5850 3-8-9 ........ MHills 2 98
(BWHills) *lw: mde all: clr 1f out: jst hld on* **8/1**
2 hd **Soldier's Tale (USA)** 3-9-0 ........ EAhern 9 102
(JNoseda) *gd sort: wl grwn: hld up: hdwy over 2f out: chsd wnr over 1f out: r.o* **11/4**[1]
0- 3 7 **Majorca**[174] 5735 3-9-0 ........ LDettori 4 81
(JHMGosden) *lw: s.i.s: hld up: pushed along 1/2-way: swtchd rt over 2f out: styd on fnl f: nvr trbld ldrs* **5/1**[3]
200- 4 3/4 **Farewell Gift**[265] 3564 3-9-0 92 ........ DaneO'Neill 8 79
(RHannon) *h.d.w: chsd ldrs: rdn over 2f out: wknd fnl f* **10/1**
0- 5 2 **Pizazz**[209] 5036 3-9-0 ........ DHolland 10 73
(BJMeehan) *sn pushed along and prom: wknd over 1f out* **11/1**
536- 6 1 1/4 **Midnight Ballard (USA)**[166] 5870 3-9-0 84 ........ SCarson 1 69
(RFJohnsonHoughton) *chsd wnr over 4f: sn wknd* **14/1**
20- 7 3/4 **Three Secrets (IRE)**[238] 4322 3-8-9 ........ JPMurtagh 7 62
(PWChapple-Hyam) *b.hind: prom: plld hrd: wknd over 1f out* **10/3**[2]
0-3 8 hd **Cefira (USA)**[9] 1288 3-8-9 ........ PRobinson 3 61
(MHTompkins) *chsd ldrs over 4f* **33/1**
52- 9 1/2 **Swinbrook (USA)**[177] 5697 3-8-11 ........ LisaJones[(3)] 5 65
(JARToller) *mid-div: hdwy over 2f out: n.m.r and wknd wl over 1f out* **14/1**
10 nk **Evoque** 3-8-9 ........ JQuinn 6 59
(HJCollingridge) *w'like: s.i.s: hld up: a in rr* **100/1**
1m 12.15s (-0.94) **Going Correction** +0.05s/f (Good) **10** Ran SP% **112.2**
Speed ratings: **108,107,98,97,94 93,92,91,91,90**CSF £29.04 TOTE £6.90: £2.30, £1.80, £2.00; EX 44.30.
**Owner** Abdulla Buhaleeba **Bred** Gainsborough Stud Management Ltd **Trained** Lambourn, Berks
■ Stewards Enquiry : E Ahern one-day ban: used whip in an incorrect place (Apr 26)

**FOCUS**
Not much strength in depth, but the time was very good indeed and the front pair pulled nicely clear.

**NOTEBOOK**
**Fun To Ride** had the benefit of the rail to help and made her experience count. There is no reason why she can't go on from here.
**Soldier's Tale(USA)** ◆, out of a winning miler, had a poor draw and had plenty to do going into the dip, but he never stopped trying only to find the post arrive a shade too soon. He can make amends before too long.
**Majorca** ◆ was doing his best work in the closing stages and looks a ready-made winner when stepping up in trip.
**Farewell Gift** showed plenty of pace before getting tired. He looks to have something to prove now, but he is from a family that get better with age, so all may not be lost just yet.
**Pizazz**, not helped by his wide draw, was always being taken along faster than ideal and may benefit from a step up in trip.

## 1414 BET365 CALL 08000 322365 H'CAP 1m 2f
**4:40** (4:41) (C) (0-95,90) 3-Y-O **£9,646** (£2,968; £1,484; £742) **Stalls** Low

Form RPR
31-2 1 **Hazyview**[14] 1222 3-7-13 73 ........ DFox[(5)] 11 87
(NACallaghan) *lw: chsd ldr: led over 5f out: rdn clr over 1f out: r.o wl* **9/2**[2]
331- 2 5 **Hello It's Me**[160] 5940 3-9-0 83 ........ JQuinn 3 88
(HJCollingridge) *plld hrd and prom: chsd wnr over 2f out: styd on same pce appr fnl f* **25/1**
51- 3 2 **Daytime Girl (IRE)**[201] 5218 3-8-7 76 ........ MHills 4 77
(BWHills) *chsd ldrs: pushed along over 3f out: styd on same pce fnl f* **10/1**
152- 4 shd **Mocca (IRE)**[185] 5544 3-8-7 76 ........ DHolland 2 77+
(DJCoakley) *hld up: nt clr run over 1f out: r.o ins fnl f: nrst fin* **25/1**
021- 5 1 1/2 **Prime Powered (IRE)**[194] 5355 3-9-6 89 ........ RLMoore 10 87
(GLMoore) *s.i.s: hld up: hdwy over 2f out: no ex fnl f* **20/1**
261- 6 6 **Mr Tambourine Man (IRE)**[173] 5744 3-9-0 83 ........ LDettori 12 70
(PFICole) *hld up: hdwy over 2f out: wknd over 1f out* **7/2**[1]
613- 7 5 **Spin King (IRE)**[258] 3755 3-8-13 82 ........ IMongan 7 60
(MLWBell) *hld up: hdwy 1/2-way: wknd over 1f out* **14/1**
031- 8 nk **Muhaymin (USA)**[184] 5565 3-9-2 85 ........ RHills 9 63
(JLDunlop) *lw: chsd ldrs: rdn over 2f out: wkng whn edgd lft and rdr dropped whip over 1f out* **10/1**
631- 9 3 **Golden Grace**[166] 5870 3-9-7 90 ........ JPMurtagh 5 62
(EALDunlop) *b.bkwd: hld up: a in rr* **16/1**
044- 10 hd **Screenplay**[174] 5723 3-8-8 77 ow2 ........ KFallon 6 49
(SirMichaelStoute) *hld up in tch: wknd over 2f out* **11/1**
42-1 11 nk **King Of Dreams (IRE)**[20] 1116 3-9-6 89 ........ KDalgleish 1 60
(MJohnston) *lw: led over 4f: wknd over 2f out* **5/1**[3]
41-3 12 hd **Cimyla (IRE)**[19] 1134 3-9-0 83 ........ RHughes 13 54
(CFWall) *hld up: hdwy 1/2-way: wkng whn n.m.r over 1f out* **12/1**
0-10 13 2 1/2 **Glendale**[14] 1222 3-7-9 67 oh2 ........ LisaJones[(3)] 8 34
(CADwyer) *lw: prom: lost pl 4f out: sn bhd* **33/1**
011- 14 1/2 **Breathing Sun (IRE)**[217] 4843 3-8-9 78 ........ EAhern 14 44
(WJMusson) *hw: hld up: hdwy 1/2-way: wknd and eased over 1f out* **16/1**
2m 5.67s (-0.02) **Going Correction** +0.05s/f (Good) **14** Ran SP% **125.1**
Speed ratings: **102,98,96,96,95 90,86,86,83,83 83,83,81,80**CSF £123.48 CT £1101.94 TOTE £6.70: £2.20, £4.00, £4.20; EX 196.80 Place 6 £37.03, Place 5 £6.18.
**Owner** T Mohan **Bred** N E Poole **Trained** Newmarket, Suffolk

**FOCUS**
A competitive handicap on paper with several unexposed types, but it was won in runaway style by the most experienced runner in the field.



The Form Book, Raceform Ltd, Compton, RG20 6NL

**NOTEBOOK**
**Hazyview**, with six runs under his belt, was the most experienced runner in the field. He was given a cracking ride from his young pilot, who soon managed to get across from his wide draw. While he is sure to face the wrath of the Handicapper for this effort, it would come as no surprise if he was capable of further improvement, especially as he looks as though he will stay further still.
**Hello It's Me** did well to finish as close as he did for he was far too free early on. Now he has had a run and got the buzz out of him, he can be placed to advantage.
**Daytime Girl(IRE)**, tackling handicappers for the first time, was off the bridle some way out and is sure to have learnt plenty from the experience.
**Mocca(IRE)** ◆ had no luck in running and would almost certainly have filled the runner-up spot had she anything like a clear run. She stayed ten furlongs as a juvenile, so there must be a fair chance she will get a bit further now she has another year on her back. *Official explanation: jockey said filly suffered interference in running*
**Prime Powered(IRE)** missed a beat at the start and was probably done no favours by having to lauch his challenge out wide. With this outing under his belt, he can be placed to advantage.
**Mr Tambourine Man(IRE)** looked a picture on his way to post, but ran as though he was in need of the outing. A winner on fast ground as a juvenile, there will be plenty of opportunities for him in the summer.
**Cimyla(IRE)** *Official explanation: jockey said colt lost its action*
T/Jkpt: Not won. T/Plt: £61.80 to a £1 stake. Pool: £66,579.80. 786.20 winning tickets. T/Qpdt: £10.10 to a £1 stake. Pool: £4,142.60. 301.50 winning tickets. CR

# RIPON (R-H)
## Thursday, April 15

**OFFICIAL GOING: Good (good to soft in places)**
Weather: fine

## 1415 EBF SHAROW MAIDEN STKS — 5f
**2:10** (2:10) (D) 2-Y-O — **£5,395** (£1,660; £830; £415) **Stalls** Low

Form — RPR
3 **1** **Word Perfect**[17] 1170 2-8-9 ..... DaleGibson 6 — 77
(MWEasterby) *drvn along to disp ld after 1f: rdn over 1 out: led ent fnl f: r.o* **4/1**[1]
2 **2** *1½* **Dante's Diamond (IRE)**[15] 1208 2-9-0 ..... SWKelly 5 — 76
(FJordan) *dwlt: sn w ldrs: slt ld 2f out: rdn and hdd appr fnl f: no ex* **4/1**[1]
**3** *2* **Smiddy Hill** 2-8-9 ..... RFfrench 8 — 63
(RBastiman) *leggy: scope: chsd ldrs: rdn and ch appr fnl f: no ex ins last* **33/1**
**4** *3* **Prince Namid** 2-9-0 ..... GDuffield 2 — 56
(MrsADuffield) *cmpt: unf: midfield: drvn along over 1f out: styd on fnl f: nvr able to chal* **9/1**[3]
**5** *1* **Lincolneurocruiser** 2-9-0 ..... DRMcCabe 9 — 52
(JO'Reilly) *leggy: unf: s.i.s: bhd: hdwy 1/2-way: drvn along over 1f out: styd on fnl f: nvr able to chal* **33/1**
**6** *1½* **King's Gait** 2-8-11 ..... DAllan(3) 7 — 46
(TDEasterby) *w'like: cmpt: s.i.s: towards rr: styd on fr over 1f out: n.d* **33/1**
3 **7** *½* **Why Harry**[10] 1264 2-9-0 ..... RWinston 11 — 44
(JJQuinn) *chsd ldrs: rdn over 1f out: wknd fnl f* **9/2**[2]
**8** *5* **Wonderful Mind** 2-9-0 ..... KDarley 1 — 24
(TDEasterby) *neat: unf: led or dispputed ld tl wknd 2f out* **4/1**[1]
**9** *1½* **Ice Ruby** 2-8-9 ..... PHanagan 4 — 13
(DShaw) *lt-fr: unf: s.i.s: a towards rr* **33/1**
**10** *1¾* **Morning World** 2-9-0 ..... SDrowne 12 — 11
(JRWeymes) *small: neat: midfield tl wknd over 1f out* **14/1**
**11** *8* **Serene Pearl (IRE)** 2-8-9 ..... NicolaTopper 3 — —
(GMMoore) *cmpt: unf: s.i.s: a rr* **40/1**
**12** *3½* **Urabande** 2-8-9 ..... MFenton 10 — —
(JulianPoulton) *leggy: unf: bhd fr 1/2-way* **16/1**

60.61 secs (0.41) **Going Correction** +0.025s/f (Good) **12** Ran SP% **114.9**
Speed ratings: **97,94,91,86,85 82,81,73,71,68 55,50**CSF £18.15 TOTE £4.70: £1.90, £1.20, £6.20; EX 11.30.
**Owner** Mrs Jean Turpin **Bred** Mrs Jean Turpin **Trained** Sheriff Hutton, N Yorks

**FOCUS**
The going was described as 'on the easy side of good' and there was a brisk tailwind in the home straight.
**NOTEBOOK**
**Word Perfect**, on her toes beforehand, was quite keen to post. She still has something to learn but was firmly in command at the line.
**Dante's Diamond(IRE)**, who had to be dragged round the paddock, took a narrow advantage but, tending to hang right, in the end was very much second best.
**Smiddy Hill**, an April foal, is bred exclusively for speed. On the leg, she ran a pleasing first race, finishing a good third behind two with previous experience.
**Prince Namid**, a March foal, is a close-coupled individual. From a stable at last finding form, he stayed on nicely from an unpromising position.
**Lincolneurocruiser**, a February foal, is on the leg and narrow. After a sluggish break, he was picking up in his own time in the closing stages and should improve given more time and a stiffer test.
**King's Gait**, an April foal, is a sharp, active type. Backward in his coat, after losing ground at the start he put in some sterling late work. There should be much better to come.
**Wonderful Mind**, a February foal, is not very big. After showing bags of toe he dropped right away with fully two furlongs left to run.

## 1416 MARK COCKER MEMORIAL H'CAP — 1m 4f 60y
**2:45** (2:46) (D) (0-85,85) 3-Y-O — **£5,397** (£1,660; £830; £415) **Stalls** High

Form — RPR
40-4 **1** **Lochbuie (IRE)**[21] 1108 3-8-8 **72** ..... JFEgan 3 — 83
(GWragg) *hld up: drvn along 6f out: hdwy 4 out: rdn to chal and edgd rt appr fnl f: sn led: styd on: all out* **9/2**[2]
04-1 **2** *½* **Absolutelythebest (IRE)**[96] 492 3-8-9 **73** ..... WSupple 9 — 83
(EALDunlop) *hld up in rr: gd hdwy to ld over 6f out: hrd pressed and rdn 2 out: hdd ent fnl f: styd on* **12/1**
46-3 **3** *3½* **Bumptious**[14] 1222 3-8-11 **75** ..... GDuffield 5 — 79
(MHTompkins) *a cl up: ev ch and rdn 2f out: no ex whn sltly hmpd appr fnl f* **7/1**
2-1 **4** *½* **Settlement Craic (IRE)**[27] 1050 3-9-7 **85** ..... KDarley 11 — 89
(TGMills) *hld up: nt clr run and swtchd to outside 4f out: ch and rdn 2 out: no ex fnl f* **7/1**
1-45 **5** *2* **Nessen Dorma (IRE)**[78] 622 3-8-11 **75** ..... MFenton 8 — 75
(JGGiven) *led 1f: remained prom: drvn along over 5f out: kpt on same pce fnl 3f* **33/1**
22-0 **6** *nk* **Hathlen (IRE)**[12] 1249 3-8-13 **77** ..... ACulhane 6 — 77
(MRChannon) *hld up: sme hdwy whn nt clr run over 3f out: styd on fnl 2f: nvr able to chal* **25/1**
0-11 **7** *6* **Golden Quest**[22] 1100 3-9-4 **82** ..... SChin 10 — 72
(MJohnston) *sn pushed along towards rr: outpcd and drvn 1/2-way: kpt on fnl 3f: n.d* **4/1**[1]
10-0 **8** *3½* **Coventina (IRE)**[21] 1108 3-9-3 **81** ..... TQuinn 7 — 66
(JLDunlop) *hld up midfield: effrt whn sltly hmpd 4f out: sn rdn and btn* **7/1**
31- **9** *10* **Messe De Minuit (IRE)**[141] 6074 3-8-13 **77** ..... SDrowne 4 — 46
(RCharlton) *midfield: drvn along over 5f out: sn bhd* **18/1**
06-1 **10** *12* **Liquidate**[15] 1201 3-8-3 **67** ..... CCatlin 1 — 17
(HMorrison) *sn prom: drvn along 6f out: wknd 4 out* **6/1**[3]
440- **11** *9* **Wing Collar**[189] 5459 3-8-1 **68** ow2 ..... DAllan(3) 2 — 3
(TDEasterby) *keen early: led after 1f tl hdd over 6 out: wknd qckly 4 out* **40/1**

2m 40.23s (0.33) **Going Correction** +0.125s/f (Good) **11** Ran SP% **112.1**
Speed ratings: **103,102,100,100,98 98,94,92,85,77 71**CSF £53.30 CT £368.19 TOTE £3.80: £1.60, £3.40, £2.30; EX 56.20.
**Owner** Mollers Racing **Bred** M Fahy **Trained** Newmarket, Suffolk

**FOCUS**
The gallop was just steady to halfway.
**NOTEBOOK**
**Lochbuie(IRE)**, a moderate mover, did well coming from off the pace in a race not run at a true gallop to halfway. He looked somewhat unhappy on the undulating track but showed a fighting spirit and should improve again.
**Absolutelythebest(IRE)**, who looked very fit, stepped up the gallop once in line for home and in the end made the winner dig deep. The experience will not be lost on him.
**Bumptious**, running from the same mark, ran with credit but was held when nudged sideways coming to the final furlong. He will continue to struggle from this sort of rating.
**Settlement Craic(IRE)**, a rangy, rather lightly-made individual, looked to have plenty on his plate on his handicap bow. Left short of room and forced to check once in line for home, he came wide to make his effort. He stuck on without ever looking likely to pick up but gave the impression he still has something to learn.
**Nessen Dorma(IRE)**, who looked backward in his coat, was having only his second outing on turf on his first run for 11 weeks.
**Hathlen(IRE)**, still carrying condition, proved much better suited by this much better ground. He didn't have the run of the race but is finding it difficult to lose the maiden tag.
**Golden Quest**, a very narrow individual, did not impress at all going to post. Soon behind and driven along, he stayed on when it was all over. After this there are questions to answer. *Official explanation: trainer had no explanation for the poor form shown*
**Coventina(IRE)**, who looks as if she needs more time to come to herself, slipped on the turn for home. *Official explanation: jockey said filly slipped on the bend*

## 1417 RIPON SILVER BOWL FILLIES' STKS (LISTED RACE) — 6f
**3:20** (3:20) (A) 3-Y-O — **£17,850** (£6,600; £3,300; £1,500) **Stalls** Low

Form — RPR
232- **1** **Bonne De Fleur**[176] 5707 3-8-11 78 ..... FLynch 3 — 98
(BSmart) *lw: mde virtually all: rdn 2f out: hld on wl fnl f: all out* **22/1**
1 **2** *½* **Petite Rose (IRE)**[8] 1293 3-8-11 ..... RHavlin 1 — 96
(JHMGosden) *w ldr: rdn 2f out: ev ch ins fnl f: no ex* **6/4**[1]
113- **3** *2* **Birthday Suit (IRE)**[282] 3074 3-8-11 102 ..... KDarley 4 — 90
(TDEasterby) *chsd ldrs: rdn and ch over 1f out: kpt on same pce* **7/2**[3]
125- **4** *2* **Needles And Pins (IRE)**[187] 5480 3-9-1 105 ..... MFenton 2 — 88
(MLWBell) *dwlt: rr but in tch: drvn along 2f out: no hdwy fnl f* **15/8**[2]
54-6 **5** *2* **Withorwithoutyou (IRE)**[15] 1211 3-8-11 87 ..... WSupple 5 — 78
(BAMcmahon) *rr but in tch: drvn along and sme hdwy over 2f out: wknd fnl f* **11/1**

1m 12.61s (-0.29) **Going Correction** +0.025s/f (Good) **5** Ran SP% **109.7**
Speed ratings: **102,101,98,96,93**CSF £55.42 TOTE £23.40: £5.80, £1.10; EX 52.50.
**Owner** Miss N Jefford **Bred** Miss N A Jefford **Trained** Hambleton, N Yorks

**FOCUS**
A weak turnout for the second running of this Listed race confined to three-year-old fillies. The winning time was modest.
**NOTEBOOK**
**Bonne De Fleur**, who had a stone and a half to find on RPR, looked really fit and well. She made virtually every yard and showed a real battling spirit. This could turn out to be her one day of fame though.
**Petite Rose(IRE)**, a moderate mover, had the rail to help but in the end had to settle for second best.
**Birthday Suit(IRE)**, who fractured a cannon bone when third in the Cherry Hinton, is quite a robust type but she doesn't look to have grown much over the winter. Soon driven along, she tended to hang to her right and was never going to get in a telling blow at the first two.
**Needles And Pins(IRE)**, who hasn't yet come in her coat, had to give 4lb away all round. After missing a beat at the start and getting messed slightly, she never posed a threat.
**Withorwithoutyou(IRE)**, a narrow type, was again well below the level of form she showed at two.

## 1418 RIPON "COCK O' THE NORTH" H'CAP — 1m
**3:55** (3:55) (C) (0-90,79) 3-Y-O — **£8,542** (£3,240; £1,620; £736) **Stalls** High

Form — RPR
01-3 **1** **Granston (IRE)**[19] 1129 3-9-1 **73** ..... TQuinn 10 — 81
(JDBethell) *cl up: plld hrd early: rdn to ld over 1f out: styd on* **9/2**[2]
251- **2** *1¼* **Lets Roll**[197] 5295 3-8-11 **69** ..... TWilliams 2 — 74
(CWThornton) *hld up in rr: hdwy over 3f out: styd on u.p fr over 1 out: no imp on wnr ins last* **25/1**
0141 **3** *½* **Dispol Veleta**[15] 1214 3-8-6 **67** ..... NMackay(3) 6 — 71
(TDBarron) *hld up in midfield: effrt whn nt clr run 2f out: hdwy over 1 out: styd on fnl f* **7/1**
1- **4** *3* **Catherine Howard**[327] 1827 3-9-2 **74** ..... ACulhane 8 — 71
(MRChannon) *trckd ldrs: bmpd over 4f out: led 2 out: sn rdn and hdd: no ex* **8/1**
4-1 **5** *5* **Etmaam**[17] 1174 3-9-5 **77** ..... WSupple 7 — 63
(MJohnston) *towards rr: drvn along 1/2-way: styd on fnl 2f: n.d* **9/4**[1]
021- **6** *¾* **Attacca**[178] 5676 3-9-6 **78** ..... (p) SDrowne 1 — 62
(JRWeymes) *led tl rdn and hdd 2f out: fdd* **50/1**
04-1 **7** *¾* **Alfonso**[62] 760 3-9-7 **79** ..... KDarley 11 — 61
(BWHills) *in tch: drvn along over 3f out: chsng ldrs and rdn 2 out: fdd* **5/1**[3]
230- **8** *nk* **Dark Day Blues (IRE)**[174] 5734 3-8-13 **71** ..... DarrenWilliams 3 — 52
(MDHammond) *s.i.s: rr: kpt on u.p fnl 2f: n.d* **33/1**
330- **9** *2½* **Toparudi**[159] 5950 3-8-13 **71** ..... GDuffield 9 — 47
(MHTompkins) *hld up: plld hrd early: rdn over 2f out: no ch whn hmpd appr fnl f* **11/1**
51-0 **10** *3½* **Bethanys Boy (IRE)**[21] 1108 3-9-3 **75** ..... RWinston 5 — 43
(BEllison) *cl up tl rdn and wknd 2f out* **16/1**
130- **11** *8* **Magical Mimi**[173] 5750 3-9-7 **79** ..... MFenton 4 — 28
(JeddO'Keeffe) *bhd fr 1/2-way* **25/1**

1m 40.47s (-0.63) **Going Correction** +0.125s/f (Good) **11** Ran SP% **116.0**
Speed ratings: **108,106,106,103,98 97,96,96,93,90 82**CSF £115.37 CT £795.95 TOTE £5.80: £2.00, £5.70, £2.10; EX 110.90.
**Owner** The Four Players Partnership **Bred** Yeomanstown Stud **Trained** Middleham Moor, N Yorks

**FOCUS**
Just a steady pace in the early stages and overall a rather unsatisfactory contest. However, in the end a decisive winner in a pretty decent winning time that was much faster than the two divisions of the maiden.

**NOTEBOOK**
**Granston(IRE)**, very keen early on, in the end took this in decisive fashion. Chester is the next step.
**Lets Roll**, who looked very backward in his coast, was last turning in. He stayed on well to snatch second spot inside the last and will be suited by a step up in trip in due course.
**Dispol Veleta**, who looked very fit, is a keen-going type. She was constantly denied a clear run otherwise she would have given the winner more to do. She deserves to find another race.
**Catherine Howard**, injured after winning her only previous start, a maiden at Lingfield in May, looked backward in her coat. After working her way to the front she could not hang on but there is surely better to come from this highly-rated filly.
**Etmaam**, who lacks any scope, was soon being driven along in the rear. He only stayed on when it was all over.
**Alfonso**, a decent type, was noisy in the paddock. He tended to hang right and, like his brother Pablo, is the type to appreciate genuine soft ground.

## 1419 SKELTON MAIDEN STKS (DIV I) — 1m
4:30 (4:31) (D) 3-Y-O — **£4,040** (£1,243; £621; £310) **Stalls** High

Form — RPR

4- **1** **Ashwaaq (USA)**$^{166}$ [5869] 3-8-9 ........ WSupple 3 — 70
(JLDunlop) *dwlt: sn trcking ldrs: nt clr run over 2f out: swtchd lft over 1 out: styd on wl u.p to ld wl ins fnl f* **4/6**$^{1}$

0- **2** ½ **Thara'A (IRE)**$^{124}$ [6175] 3-8-9 ........ SDrowne 7 — 69
(EALDunlop) *rangy: unf: dwlt: sn trcking ldrs: qckned to ld 2f out: rdn and hdd wl ins fnl f* **100/1**

000- **3** 1 ¾ **Hoh Nelson**$^{176}$ [5708] 3-8-11 ........ LFletcher(3) 4 — 70
(HMorrison) *cl up: led 3f out: hdd 2 out: rdn and ev ch ent fnl f: no ex ins last* **22/1**

0- **4** nk **Little Bob**$^{160}$ [5939] 3-9-0 ........ TQuinn 9 — 69
(JDBethell) *slowly away: hld up in rr: rdn over 1f out: styd on wl ins last: nvr able to chal* **33/1**

0- **5** ½ **Mouftari (USA)**$^{237}$ [4348] 3-9-0 ........ KDarley 2 — 68
(BWHills) *lw: prom: rdn and ch 2f out: kpt on same pce* **5/2**$^{2}$

6 **6** ½ **Premier Dream (USA)**$^{8}$ [1301] 3-9-0 ........ SChin 6 — 67
(MJohnston) *led tl hdd 3f out: ch and rdn appr fnl f: no ex ins last* **20/1**$^{3}$

**7** 2 ½ **Wedowannagiveuthat (IRE)** 3-8-9 ........ GFaulkner 11 — 56
(TDEasterby) *midfield: drvn along 3f out: no hdwy* **50/1**

00- **8** 1 ¾ **Theatre Belle**$^{201}$ [5218] 3-8-9 ........ JFEgan 5 — 52
(TDEasterby) *midfield: drvn along over 3f out: no hdwy* **50/1**

**9** ¾ **Trysting Grove (IRE)** 3-8-9 ........ GParkin 8 — 51
(KARyan) *leggy: unf: dwlt: towards rr: effrt 3f out: no hdwy* **50/1**

0 **10** 2 ½ **Purple Rain (IRE)**$^{8}$ [1301] 3-8-9 ........ FLynch 10 — 45
(MLWBell) *lengthy: unf: hld up in rr: hung rt fnl 4f: n.d* **25/1**

**11** 7 **Ghantoot** 3-8-11 ........ NMackay(3) 1 — 34
(LMCumani) *w'like: lengthy: scope: s.i.s: hld up: effrt over 3f out: wknd over 2 out* **20/1**$^{3}$

1m 43.58s (2.48) **Going Correction** +0.125s/f (Good) — **11** Ran SP% **116.1**
Speed ratings: **92,91,89,89,88 88,85,84,83,80 73**CSF £135.28 TOTE £1.50: £1.02, £20.90, £5.50; EX 80.80.
**Owner** Hamdan Al Maktoum **Bred** Shadwell Farm Llc **Trained** Arundel, W Sussex

**FOCUS**
A moderate winning time for the grade and the slower of the two divisions, but almost certainly the stronger in depth.

**NOTEBOOK**
**Ashwaaq(USA)**, a tall half-sister to the top miler Bahri, looked a bit of a handful in the paddock. She had to switch for a run but showed a nice turn of foot to take the spoils. This should have taught her plenty.
**Thara'A(IRE)**, a narrow type, is a poor walker. Unsighted on her only previous outing on the All-Weather in December, she went ahead travelling strongly but in the end found the winner too good.
**Hoh Nelson**, who had three outings at two, is officially rated just 64. He has presumably improved a few pounds over the winter.
**Little Bob**, whose dam won the Lincoln for the stable, was still plumb last three furlongs out. He finished to some effect and should improve a fair bit given more time.
**Mouftari(USA)**, who showed ability in one start at two, looked in good trim and, though he had no excuse on the day, he is the type to do better in due course.
**Premier Dream(USA)**, fitted with a cross noseband, has a short stride. He improved on his debut effort but had the run of the race.
**Purple Rain(IRE)** *Official explanation: jockey said filly hung right-handed throughout*

## 1420 SKELTON MAIDEN STKS (DIV II) — 1m
5:00 (5:01) (D) 3-Y-O — **£4,032** (£1,240; £620; £310) **Stalls** High

Form — RPR

05-3 **1** **Appalachian Trail (IRE)**$^{21}$ [1104] 3-9-0 76........ RWinston 5 — 79
(ISemple) *cl up: led 2f out: styd on wl* **7/4**$^{1}$

05- **2** 2 ½ **Fossgate**$^{164}$ [5905] 3-9-0 ........ CCatlin 3 — 73
(JDBethell) *led tl rdn and hdd 2f out: chsd wnr after: styd on: no imp fnl f* **8/1**

23-2 **3** 1 ¼ **Emtilaak**$^{15}$ [1202] 3-9-0 79........ WSupple 7 — 70
(BHanbury) *hld up: plld hrd early: gd hdwy 3f out: ev ch and rdn over 1 out: no ex fnl f* **5/2**$^{2}$

**4** 1 ½ **Queen Lucia (IRE)** 3-8-9 ........ TQuinn 6 — 62
(JGGiven) *cmpt: hld up towards rr: drvn along and hdwy to chse ldrs 2f out: kpt on fnl f: nvr able to chal* **20/1**

000- **5** 3 **Princess Kiotto**$^{191}$ [5439] 3-8-2 ........ AMullen(7) 2 — 55
(TDEasterby) *trckd ldrs: rdn wl over 1f out: sn btn* **50/1**

00- **6** 10 **Fourswainby (IRE)**$^{335}$ [1622] 3-8-9 ........ TEaves(5) 9 — 37
(BEllison) *dwlt: rr: outpcd over 3f out: n.d* **50/1**

5- **7** 1 ½ **Sweet Repose (USA)**$^{169}$ [5825] 3-8-9 ........ SDrowne 8 — 29
(EALDunlop) *trckd ldrs: plld hrd early: hmpd after 2f: drvn along 3 out: sn btn* **8/1**

00-0 **8** 4 **Anicaflash**$^{17}$ [1174] 3-8-6 ........ LEnstone(3) 10 — 19
(MDods) *hld up: keen early: hmpd after 2f: outpcd over 3 out: rr and rdn whn short of room 2 out* **100/1**

**U** **Vibe** 3-9-0 ........ RFfrench 1 — —
(MJohnston) *rangy: unf: jinked lft and uns rdr leaving stalls* **11/2**$^{3}$

1m 42.55s (1.45) **Going Correction** +0.125s/f (Good) — **9** Ran SP% **112.2**
Speed ratings: **97,94,93,91,88 78,77,73,—**CSF £15.64 TOTE £3.50: £1.30, £2.30, £1.20; EX 20.20.
**Owner** G L S Partnership **Bred** Swettenham Stud **Trained** Carluke, S Lanarks
■ Stewards Enquiry : A Mullen two-day ban: careless riding (Apr 26,27)

**FOCUS**
The quicker division, but still a modest time for the grade and a very ordinary maiden lacking any strength in depth.

**NOTEBOOK**
**Appalachian Trail(IRE)**, rated 76 after Doncaster, took this with the minimum of fuss. He should build on this.
**Fossgate**, who showed some ability on his second start at two, looked backward in his coat. He had his own way in front but in the end the winner proved different gear. At least he is now qualified for handicaps.
**Emtilaak**, a big type, wouldn't settle. After moving up looking a real threat he seemed to hang fire, hanging right and finding little. He has the ability but does he have the right approach?
**Queen Lucia(IRE)**, who lacks size and scope, stayed on in her own time and will appreciate further.
**Princess Kiotto**, who showed little in three outings at two, looked in need of the outing and was fitted with a cross noseband. Her future lies in low-grade handicaps.
**Sweet Repose(USA)** *Official explanation: jockey said filly was hampered by a loose horse several times*
**Vibe**, a narrow newcomer, stands over plenty of ground. A lazy walker and a moderate mover, he dumped his rider leaving the stalls.

## 1421 NEWBY APPRENTICE H'CAP — 5f
5:30 (5:30) (E) (0-70,70) 4-Y-O+ — **£4,180** (£1,286; £643; £321) **Stalls** Low

Form — RPR

1202 **1** **Mynd**$^{3}$ [1368] 4-9-3 62........ DTudhope(3) 5 — 72
(RMWhitaker) *prom: led 2f out: r.o wl* **7/2**$^{1}$

050- **2** 1 ¼ **Joyce's Choice**$^{178}$ [5673] 5-8-5 52........ KGhunowa(5) 19 — 58
(JSWainwright) *racd towards far side: prom: r.o wl to ld gp wl ins fnl f: no imp on wnr* **25/1**

050- **3** nk **Catch The Cat (IRE)**$^{125}$ [6170] 5-9-4 68........(b) AReilly(8) 2 — 72
(JSWainwright) *w ldrs: ev ch appr fnl f: no ex ins last* **20/1**

5-60 **4** ½ **Bahamian Belle**$^{17}$ [1169] 4-8-11 56........(t) DeanWilliams(3) 20 — 59
(PSMcentee) *racd towards far side: a.p: led gp appr fnl f: no ex clsng stages* **33/1**

000- **5** nk **Valiant Romeo**$^{188}$ [5472] 4-8-7 54........ SaleemGolam(5) 6 — 56
(RBastiman) *mde most tl hdd 2f out: kpt on fnl f* **33/1**

-030 **6** nk **Vijay (IRE)**$^{41}$ [968] 5-9-4 60........ WHogg 18 — 60
(ISemple) *racd towards far side: led gp tl appr fnl f: no ex* **14/1**

000- **7** shd **Fairgame Man**$^{224}$ [4677] 6-8-3 50........ StevenHarrison(5) 8 — 50
(JSWainwright) *chsd ldrs: drvn along 2f out: no ex fnl f* **40/1**

4521 **8** 1 ¼ **Never Without Me**$^{10}$ [1262] 4-8-5 55 7ex........ KJackson(8) 14 — 51
(PJMcbride) *midfield: drvn along 1/2-way: no hdwy* **14/1**

0010 **9** hd **Torrent**$^{17}$ [1180] 9-8-7 49........(b) CHaddon 4 — 44
(DWChapman) *midfield: effrt 2f out: no hdwy* **20/1**

6320 **10** nk **Park Star**$^{47}$ [917] 4-8-12 60........ DawnWatson(6) 1 — 54
(DShaw) *midfield: drvn along 2f out: no hdwy* **11/1**

220- **11** ½ **Yomalo (IRE)**$^{176}$ [5702] 4-9-1 67........ RMills(10) 11 — 59
(RGuest) *s.i.s: bhd: styd on fr over 1f out: n.d* **25/1**

230- **12** ½ **Aahgowangowan (IRE)**$^{176}$ [5706] 5-9-1 60........(t) AMullen(3) 10 — 50
(MDods) *chsd ldrs tl wknd appr fnl f* **20/1**

06-4 **13** nk **College Maid (IRE)**$^{7}$ [1319] 7-8-3 53........(b) JCurrie(8) 7 — 42
(JSGoldie) *nvr bttr than mid-div* **11/1**

3002 **14** ¾ **The Fisio**$^{7}$ [1313] 4-9-6 70........(v) TBlock(8) 9 — 56
(AMBalding) *chsd ldrs: drvn along 1/2-way: wknd over 1 out* **6/1**$^{2}$

6020 **15** nk **Ejay**$^{10}$ [1262] 5-7-10 46........ MHalford(8) 17 — 31
(JulianPoulton) *racd towards far side most of way: in tch tl wknd over 1f out* **40/1**

4003 **16** 1 ½ **Polar Force**$^{23}$ [1082] 4-8-8 60........ TDean(10) 3 — 40
(MRChannon) *slowly away: a bhd* **13/2**$^{3}$

0000 **17** nk **Grandma Lily (IRE)**$^{15}$ [1199] 6-8-13 63........ AndrewWebb(8) 13 — 42
(MCChapman) *midfield: drvn along 1/2-way: sn btn* **16/1**

0135 **18** 3 ½ **Cash**$^{30}$ [1027] 6-9-0 56........(v$^{1}$) DFentiman 15 — 22
(PaulJohnson) *sn bhd* **20/1**

640- **19** ½ **Petongski**$^{203}$ [5178] 6-8-3 50........(be) RKeogh(5) 16 — 14
(BEllison) *sn bhd* **33/1**

000- **20** 2 ½ **Shirley Not**$^{194}$ [5374] 8-7-13 46........ BO'Neill(5) 12 — —
(DNicholls) *in tch tl wknd 2f out* **33/1**

59.89 secs (-0.31) **Going Correction** +0.025s/f (Good) — **20** Ran SP% **129.1**
Speed ratings: **103,101,100,99,99 98,98,96,96,95 95,94,93,92,92 89,89,83,82,78**CSF £102.87 CT £1626.46 TOTE £4.30: £1.20, £5.40, £4.90, £12.60; EX 170.00 Place 6 £65.39, Place 5 £36.85.
**Owner** Derek And Jean Clee **Bred** John Rose **Trained** Scarcroft, W Yorks

**FOCUS**
Four raced middle to far side and they finished second, fourth and sixth.

**NOTEBOOK**
**Mynd**, an improved performer on the All-Weather this winter, went one better than Warwick. He is suited by a bit of give underfoot and should continue to give a good account of himself at this level.
**Joyce's Choice**, whose only previous success was asa two-year-old, was first home on the far side on his first outing for his new yard.
**Catch The Cat(IRE)**, who usually needs an outing or two to reach peak fitness, was 4lb higher than his last success.
**Bahamian Belle**, in a first-time tongue tie, appreciated the return to turf but the fact remains she is still a maiden after 23 attempts now.
**Valiant Romeo**, a winner three times at two, has slipped down to a very lenient mark and here he showed that at least some of the old speed remains. All his wins were on fast ground.
**Vijay(IRE)**, who led the other three on the far side, is still on a learning curve for his new yard.
T/Plt: £74.80 to a £1 stake. Pool: £26,543.30. 258.75 winning tickets. T/Qpdt: £18.40 to a £1 stake. Pool: £1,865.60. 75.00 winning tickets. JF

# 1262 SOUTHWELL (L-H)
Thursday, April 15

**OFFICIAL GOING: Standard**

## 1422 NEW SITE @ BETDIRECT.CO.UK CLASSIFIED STKS — 1m (F)
5:20 (5:21) (F) 3-Y-O — **£2,947** (£842; £421) **Stalls** Low

Form — RPR

00-4 **1** **Goblin**$^{16}$ [1184] 3-9-2 62........ SSanders 11 — 73
(DECantillon) *chsd ldrs: rdn along 1/2-way: hdwy and hung lft 2f out: drvn and styd on ins last to ld nr fin* **3/1**$^{1}$

6132 **2** hd **Jakarmi**$^{15}$ [1214] 3-9-4 64........ PHanagan 7 — 75
(BPalling) *chsd ldrs: hdwy to ld 3f out: clr 2f out: sn rdn: drvn and edgd lft ins last: hdd nr fin* **7/2**$^{2}$

1050 **3** 7 **Smart Boy Prince (IRE)**$^{3}$ [1365] 3-9-0 65........ DNolan(5) 10 — 62
(PABlockley) *cl up: led after 2f tl rdn along and hdd 3f out: drvn and kpt on same pce fnl 2f* **12/1**

2433 **4** 4 **Princess Ismene**$^{3}$ [1375] 3-8-11 55........(b) NCallan 2 — 46
(PABlockley) *midfield: hdwy on outer over 3f out: rdn 2f out and sn no imp* **14/1**



The Form Book, Raceform Ltd, Compton, RG20 6NL

-201 **5** *1* **Regulated (IRE)**[23] 1084 3-9-5 65 SWKelly 6 52
(JAOsborne) *s.i.s and bhd: hdwy on outer over 3f out: rdn and kpt on fnl 2f: nrst fin* **10/1**

606- **6** *shd* **Dance To My Tune**[188] 5470 3-8-6 57 PMulrennan(5) 9 44
(MWEasterby) *chsd ldrs: rdn long 3f out: sn btn* **25/1**

360- **7** *5* **I'm Dancing**[203] 5175 3-8-8 60 (e1) DAllan(3) 4 34
(TDEasterby) *led 2f: cl up tl rdn along and wknd over 2f out* **20/1**

045- **8** *3 1/2* **Considine (USA)**[177] 5687 3-9-0 60 JTate 5 30
(JMPEustace) *s.i.s: a bhd* **7/1**3

5-03 **9** *1/2* **Munaawesh (USA)**[10] 1266 3-8-12 65 PMakin(7) 13 34
(DWChapman) *a bhd* **12/1**

0-00 **10** *1 1/2* **Jango Malfoy (IRE)**[64] 741 3-9-0 57 OUrbina 8 26
(BWDuke) *a bhd* **66/1**

440- **11** *1 3/4* **Rajayoga**[227] 4612 3-9-2 62 MHenry 12 24
(MHTompkins) *a outpcd and bhd* **33/1**

532 **12** *nk* **Zuloago (USA)**[33] 1012 3-8-11 60 ANicholls 14 19
(SLKeightley) *a bhd* **9/1**

030- **13** *4* **Apollo Gee (IRE)**[185] 5547 3-8-13 64 JFMcDonald(5) 3 18
(BJMeehan) *chsd ldrs to 1/2-way: sn wknd* **10/1**

1m 43.95s (-0.65) **Going Correction** -0.025s/f (Stan) **13** Ran SP% **123.0**
Speed ratings: **102,101,94,90,89 89,84,81,80,79 77,77,73**CSF £13.02 TOTE £4.60: £1.80, £1.50, £2.80; EX 16.50.
**Owner** Mrs E M Clarke **Bred** G W Turner And Miss S J Turner **Trained** Carlton, Cambs
■ Stewards Enquiry : S Sanders two-day ban: used whip with excessive frequency (Apr 26,27)

**FOCUS**
A good finish to this Classified event, with only a head separating the front two. There was a seven-length gap back to the third.

**NOTEBOOK**
**Goblin**, who had a slight question mark hanging over him as to whether this trip is what he wanted, having looked a non-stayer over it last season, managed to get up late on despite hanging and seeming to dislike the surface. He will reportedly avoid this surface from now on and should win again in a similar grade.
**Jakarmi** looked all over the winner when going clear, but was nabbed by the winner late on. He remains in good form and pulled seven lengths clear of the third.
**Smart Boy Prince(IRE)** proved no match for the front pair, but was not disgraced and came four lengths clear of the fourth.
**Princess Ismene** was a well beaten fourth.
**Regulated(IRE)** made some late headway from the rear and was edging closer with every stride.
**Rajayoga** *Official explanation: jockey said colt was never travelling*

## 1423 BET DIRECT NO Q ON 08000 93 66 93 CLAIMING STKS 6f (F)
**5:50** (5:51) (F) 3-Y-O+ **£2,891** (£826; £413) **Stalls** Low

Form RPR

3120 **1** **Sergeant Slipper**[33] 1011 7-9-7 51 (v) RFitzpatrick 9 58
(CSmith) *bhd: hdwy on outer 1/2-way: rdn 2f out: styd on wl ent fnl f: led nr fin* **10/1**

2514 **2** *nk* **Silver Mascot**[17] 1176 5-9-5 52 DaleGibson 4 55
(RHollinshead) *led: clr over 2f out: rdn ins last: hdd and no ex nr fin* **7/1**3

2305 **3** *5* **Blakeset**[19] 1140 9-9-3 68 (v) SSanders 3 38
(TDBarron) *chsd ldrs: rdn along 2f out: sn drvn and one pce* **6/5**1

15-0 **4** *3* **Queen Of Night**[101] 436 4-8-11 74 ACulhane 8 23
(DWChapman) *in tch: effrt 3f out: sn rdn along and no imp fnl 2f* **4/1**2

400- **5** *2 1/2* **Give Him Credit (USA)**[253] 3892 4-9-9 68 GDuffield 7 28
(MrsADuffield) *in tch: rdn along hafway: wknd 2f out* **16/1**

3010 **6** *hd* **Above Board**[10] 1262 9-9-2 50 (t) TGMcLaughlin 1 20
(RFMarvin) *a rr* **20/1**

0016 **7** *3* **Scary Night (IRE)**[30] 1027 4-9-9 63 (p) JEdmunds 6 18
(JBalding) *promient: rdn along 1/2-way: wknd 2f out* **7/1**3

5246 **8** *3/4* **Zak Facta (IRE)**[28] 1044 4-9-4 50 (v) VHalliday 2 11
(MissDAMchale) *chsd ldr: rdn along over 2f out: sn wknd* **14/1**

00-0 **9** *20* **Limited Magician**[86] 569 3-8-4 JBramhill 5 —
(CSmith) *s.i.s: a bhd* **100/1**

1m 16.89s (-0.01) **Going Correction** -0.025s/f (Stan)
**WFA** 3 from 4yo+ 12lb **9** Ran SP% **117.8**
Speed ratings: **99,98,91,87,84 84,80,79,52**CSF £79.44 TOTE £18.90: £2.40, £2.50, £1.10; EX 48.80.
**Owner** C Smith **Bred** P And Mrs Russell **Trained** Temple Bruer, Lincs

**FOCUS**
Another close finish with the leader once again being caught close home.

**NOTEBOOK**
**Sergeant Slipper**, who had recorded all his previous wins at five furlongs, was produced with a well timed run to take it up late on, seeming well suited by the test.
**Silver Mascot** atempted to make full use of his proven stamina and kicked on just under halfway, only to be worn down close home.
**Blakeset** was disappointing and should have done better given he had plenty in hand on the front two on the ratings.
**Queen Of Night** had the highest official rating and, although likely to improve for this, was a little disappointing.

## 1424 BETDIRECT.CO.UK H'CAP 7f (F)
**6:20** (6:21) (D ) (0-80,74) 3-Y-O+ **£5,343** (£1,644; £822; £411) **Stalls** Low

Form RPR

6100 **1** **Warden Warren**[19] 1139 6-9-6 **73** (p) HayleyTurner(5) 5 83
(MrsCADunnett) *a.p: effrt 2f out: rdn to ld over 1f out: hung lft ins last: kpt on* **7/1**

1006 **2** *3/4* **Mount Royale (IRE)**[10] 1268 6-8-13 **61** (vt) KimTinkler 8 69
(NTinkler) *led: rdn along over 2f out: hdd over 1f out: swtchd rt ins last: drvn and kpt on* **11/4**1

1510 **3** *6* **Eager Angel (IRE)**[48] 909 6-8-9 **57** (p) RFitzpatrick 4 50
(RFMarvin) *in tch: hdwy over 2f out: sn rdn: edgd lft and one pce ins last* **11/2**3

4000 **4** *3/4* **Air Mail**[33] 1013 7-9-10 **72** (v) PMcCabe 3 63
(MrsNMacauley) *in tch on inner: swtchd rt and hdwy 2f out: sn rdn and kpt on same pce appr last* **10/1**

4024 **5** *2 1/2* **Carlton (IRE)**[3] 1373 10-8-1 **54** RThomas(5) 6 39
(CRDore) *hld up: hdwy 1/2-way: rdn along over 2f out: sn no imp* **7/2**2

50-4 **6** *3/4* **Teehee (IRE)**[61] 772 6-9-4 **66** (b) MFenton 1 49
(BPalling) *keen: trckd ldrs on inner: effrt over 2f out: sn rdn: drvn and wknd wl over1f out* **13/2**

04-0 **7** *1* **Clann A Cougar**[19] 1141 4-8-12 **60** GDuffield 7 41
(IAWood) *chsd ldrs to 1/2-way: sn wknd* **11/1**

245- **8** *3 1/2* **Banners Flying (IRE)**[292] 2781 4-9-12 **74** ACulhane 2 46
(DWChapman) *chsd ldrs: pushed along 1/2-way: sn wknd* **12/1**

1m 30.76s (-0.04) **Going Correction** -0.025s/f (Stan) **8** Ran SP% **115.2**
Speed ratings: **99,98,91,90,87 86,85,81**CSF £26.84 CT £115.52 TOTE £6.60: £2.10, £1.90, £3.30; EX 29.40.
**Owner** Annwell Inn Syndicate **Bred** R G Percival **Trained** Hingham, Norfolk

**FOCUS**
Modest stuff and a slow winning time for the grade.

**NOTEBOOK**
**Warden Warren** bounced back to form after a couple of disappointing efforts, winning off his highest ever mark in the process.
**Mount Royale(IRE)** ran well in defeat, having led for most of the way before sticking on well and pulling six lengths clear of the third.
**Eager Angel(IRE)** left a disappointing effort at Wolverhampton behind and stuck on for third.
**Air Mail** failed to achieve much in finishing fourth.
**Carlton(IRE)** is without a win in nearly a year and did nothing to suggest that run is going to end.
**Teehee(IRE)** raced too keenly early on and did not see out his race as a result.
**Banners Flying(IRE)** *Official explanation: trainer said colt was found to be lame on returning home*

## 1425 LITTLEWOODS BET DIRECT MEDIAN AUCTION MAIDEN STKS 7f (F)
**6:50** (6:54) (F ) 3-4-Y-O **£2,891** (£826; £413) **Stalls** Low

Form RPR

00-0 **1** **Constable Burton**[4] 1342 3-8-12 GDuffield 7 66
(MrsADuffield) *mde all: rdn clr 2f out: styd on* **14/1**3

0-3 **2** *2 1/2* **My Paris**[94] 506 3-8-12 NCallan 1 60
(KARyan) *trckd ldrs: hdwy to chse wnr over 2f out: sn rdn and no imp fnl f* **6/5**1

-422 **3** *5* **Bundaberg**[24] 1078 4-9-12 55 ACulhane 3 47
(PWHiatt) *hld up: hdwy 3f out: rdn to chse ldrs 2f out: wknd over 1f out* **2/1**2

0-6 **4** *12* **Airedale Lad (IRE)**[16] 1192 3-8-12 VHalliday 10 17
(JRNorton) *chsd ldrs on outer: rdn along 1/2-way: edgd lft and sn wknd* **50/1**

6-00 **5** *1 3/4* **Blue Emperor (IRE)**[10] 1266 3-8-9 60 ow2 DNolan(5) 6 15
(PABlockley) *plld hrd: chsd wnr: rdn along over 2f out and sn wknd* **14/1**3

000- **6** *3/4* **Mr Moon**[166] 5876 3-8-12 PHanagan 4 11
(MDHammond) *in tch: rdn along 3f out and sn wknd* **50/1**

5 **7** *13* **Sybill**[24] 1078 4-9-7 SWKelly 2 —
(JWUnett) *a outpcd and wl bhd fr 1/2-way* **40/1**

1m 30.55s (-0.25) **Going Correction** -0.025s/f (Stan)
**WFA** 3 from 4yo 14lb **7** Ran SP% **98.5**
Speed ratings: **100,97,91,77,75 74,60**CSF £22.99 TOTE £10.10: £2.80, £1.30; EX 17.80.
**Owner** Turf 2000 Limited **Bred** D R Botterill **Trained** Constable Burton, N Yorks

**FOCUS**
A uncompetitive and poor maiden.

**NOTEBOOK**
**Constable Burton** appreciated this easier task than when ninth in a maiden at Musselburgh at the weekend and made every yard for a comfy success. On this evidence he should have little trouble picking up a small handicap.
**My Paris** was the one to beat on the back of his third at Wolverhampton in January, but may have just been caught out by fitness on this first outing since.
**Bundaberg** was always going to be vulnerable to something with any improvement in it and was attempting to give a stone away.
**Blue Emperor(IRE)** *Official explanation: jockey said gelding ran too freely in the early stages*

## 1426 £10 FREE BET @ BETDIRECT.CO.UK H'CAP 1m 4f (F)
**7:20** (7:20) (F ) (46-55,55) 4-Y-O+ **£2,954** (£844; £422) **Stalls** Low

Form RPR

5-26 **1** **Red Moor (IRE)**[24] 1079 4-8-9 46 oh1 ACulhane 7 53
(RHollinshead) *trac ked ldrs: hdwy to ld over 3f out: rdn wl over 1f out: drvn ins last and styd on gamely* **10/1**

55-0 **2** *1* **Classic Millennium**[23] 1081 6-8-7 46 LisaJones(3) 3 52
(WJMusson) *hld up in rr: hdwy 3f out: rdn wl over 1f out: styd on wl fnl f* **2/1**1

560- **3** *hd* **Red Forest (IRE)**[152] 5680 5-8-11 47 (t) DaleGibson 5 52
(JMackie) *hld up pulling hrd: effrt: outpcd and n.m.r over 3f out: hdwy 2f out: sn rdn and styd on wl fnl f* **16/1**

500- **4** *3/4* **Sea Cove**[65] 5179 4-8-9 46 oh11 PHanagan 11 50
(JMJefferson) *s.i.s and bhd: stdy hdwy 1/2-way: chsd ldrs over 2f out: rdn and ch over 1f out: drvn and one pce ins last* **28/1**

2552 **5** *1/2* **Red Delirium**[16] 1194 8-8-13 49 (b) NCallan 8 52
(PABlockley) *hld up towards rr: hdwy on outer over 4f out: wd st: chsd ldrs 2f out: sn rdn and edgd rt 1f out: kpt on same pce* **8/1**

0101 **6** *hd* **Jungle Lion**[13] 1238 6-9-3 53 (t) SSanders 6 56
(JohnAHarris) *trckd ldrs: hdwy 3f out: rdn and ev ch over 1f out: drvn and one pce ins last* **7/2**2

03-6 **7** *2* **Light Brigade**[13] 1238 5-8-10 46 JTate 10 46
(JMPEustace) *trac ked ldrs: hdwy 4f out: chsd ldrs over 2f out: sn rdn and wknd ent last* **7/1**3

-001 **8** *12* **Our Imperial Bay (USA)**[16] 1194 5-9-5 55 (v) GDuffield 9 37
(RMStronge) *prom: rdn along 4f out and sn wknd* **8/1**

53-0 **9** *3* **Staff Nurse (IRE)**[12] 1245 4-8-9 46 oh6 KimTinkler 1 24
(DonEnricoIncisa) *prom on inner: rdn along 5f out: sn wknd* **20/1**

600- **10** *5* **Welsh And Wylde (IRE)**[7] 5542 4-9-1 52 MFenton 4 22
(BPalling) *led: rdn along 5f out: hdd over 3f out and sn wknd* **20/1**

330 **11** *9* **Spanish Star**[28] 1042 7-8-13 49 (v) PMcCabe 2 6
(MrsNMacauley) *midfield: pushed along and lost pl 1/2-way: sn bhd* **14/1**

2m 42.01s (-0.09) **Going Correction** -0.025s/f (Stan)
**WFA** 4 from 5yo+ 1lb **11** Ran SP% **124.9**
Speed ratings: **99,98,98,97,97 97,95,87,85,82 76**CSF £31.45 CT £343.02 TOTE £11.60: £3.70, £1.30, £5.70; EX 39.80.
**Owner** The C H F Partnership **Bred** Camogue Stud Ltd **Trained** Upper Longdon, Staffs

**FOCUS**
Red Moor should have more to offer now he has finally got his head in front.

**NOTEBOOK**
**Red Moor(IRE)** was suited by the return to this trip and plugged on bravely for his first ever success. He is only four and can pick up another weak race.
**Classic Millennium** looks to be back to form and it should not be long before she is getting her head in front again.
**Red Forest(IRE)** shaped as though this first run since pulling up over hurdles at Uttoxeter in November was needed and better can be expected next time.
**Sea Cove ◆** ran well given she was a bit slow away and she should be open to improvement, this being only her fifth ever start.
**Red Delirium** has not won a handicap for nearly three and a half years.
**Jungle Lion** was a long way off defying a 7lb penalty for winning at the course last time.

## 1427 BET IN RUNNING @ BETDIRECT.CO.UK H'CAP 1m (F)
**7:50** (7:50) (E ) (0-70,70) 3-Y-O+ **£3,474** (£1,069; £534; £267) **Stalls** Low

Form RPR

-015 **1** **Mission Affirmed (USA)**[30] 1029 3-8-8 63 DaleGibson 14 76
(TPTate) *trckd ldrs: hdwy 3f out: led over 1f out: rdn ent last and styd on wl* **12/1**

3463 **2** *1* **Quiet Reading (USA)**[41] 967 7-9-6 65....................(v) HayleyTurner(5) 9 76
(MRBosley) *in tch: hdwy to chse ldrs over 2f out: rdn to chal ent last: drvn and nt qckn towards fin* **8/1**[3]

2050 **3** *6* **Pharoah's Gold (IRE)**[14] 1225 6-9-6 60....................(e) DarrenWilliams 4 59
(DShaw) *bhd: hdwy on outer 2f out: sn rdn and styd on appr last: nrst fin* **10/1**

0500 **4** *½* **Yenaled**[21] 1109 7-9-1 55.................................................. NCallan 5 53
(KARyan) *bhd: hdwy over 2f out: styd on u.p appr last: nt rch ldrs* **12/1**

00-0 **5** *1 ¼* **Prince Of Gold**[15] 1213 4-9-11 65.......................................... ACulhane 3 61
(RHollinshead) *trckd ldrs: effrt 2f out and sn rdn: drvn and one pce appr last* **10/1**

5-61 **6** *nk* **Hold The Line**[32] 1022 3-8-10 65.........................................(p) ADaly 10 60
(WGMTurner) *bhd: hdwy 2f out: kpt on fnl f: nrst fin* **16/1**

4105 **7** *½* **Realism (FR)**[10] 1275 4-9-4 65............................................ PMakin(7) 12 59
(PWHiatt) *cl up: led over 2f out: sn rdn: hdd over 1f out and sn wknd* **14/1**

1136 **8** *½* **Rare Coincidence**[19] 1141 3-8-12 70..........................(p) LFletcher(3) 13 63
(RFFisher) *cl up: rdn over 2f out: sn wknd* **14/1**

1246 **9** *5* **Galloway Mac**[8] 1298 4-9-6 60............................................ SSanders 7 43
(WAO'Gorman) *hld up towards rr: effrt and pushed along whn n.m.r 1/2-way: sn btn* **7/2**[1]

6110 **10** *6* **Qobtaan (USA)**[84] 582 5-9-2 56............................................ GBaker 11 27
(MRBosley) *dwlt: a rr* **16/1**

2114 **11** *1 ½* **Simply The Guest (IRE)**[30] 1032 5-9-6 60......................(t) KimTinkler 6 28
(DonEnricoIncisa) *a bhd* **12/1**

4321 **12** *5* **Printsmith (IRE)**[23] 1093 7-8-10 50....................................... JBramhill 8 8
(JRNorton) *chsd ldrs to 1/2-way: sn wknd* **16/1**

23-4 **13** *3* **Brandy Cove**[93] 512 7-9-10 64............................................ FLynch 2 16
(BSmart) *led: rdn along and hdd over 2f out: sn wknd* **7/1**[2]

1112 **14** *15* **Smart Scot**[23] 1093 5-9-0 54............................................(p) MTebbutt 1 —
(BPJBaugh) *a rr: pushed along and bhd fr 1/2-way* **10/1**

1m 43.12s (-1.48) **Going Correction** -0.025s/f (Stan)
**WFA** 3 from 4yo+ 15lb **14** Ran SP% **127.2**
Speed ratings: **106,105,99,98,97 96,96,95,90,84 83,78,75,60**CSF £110.78 CT £1052.45 TOTE £15.30: £5.50, £2.80, £3.90; EX 296.40 Place 6 £46.10, Place 5 £26.17.
**Owner** T P Tate **Bred** Whisper Hill Farm **Trained** Tadcaster, N Yorks

**FOCUS**
The only really unexposed runner in the line-up, and only three-year-old, Mission Affirmed won with something in hand and should continue to pay his way.

**NOTEBOOK**
**Mission Affirmed(USA)** ◆, the only three-year-old in the line-up, may have done too much early when attempting to lead throughout last time and appreciated a slightly more restrained ride. He won with something in hand and will win again off his lowly rating despite a rise.
**Quiet Reading(USA)** usually runs his race without quite being good enough and it was once again the same scenario. He leaves the race with some credit though as he came clear of the third.
**Pharoah's Gold(IRE)** was six lengths adrift in third, but gaining with every stride towards the finish. He may be worth chancing over nine or ten furlongs.
**Yenaled** has not won for a while, but is weighted to do so.
**Galloway Mac** was not going to win, but may have reached third, when finding himself short of space. This ended any chance he had. *Official explanation: jockey said colt hung right-handed*
T/Plt: £117.30 to a £1 stake. Pool: £32,990.50. 205.25 winning tickets. T/Qpdt: £32.30 to a £1 stake. Pool: £2,460.70. 56.30 winning tickets. JR

1428 - 1434a (Foreign Racing) - See Raceform Interactive

# [1349]LONGCHAMP (R-H)
Thursday, April 15

**OFFICIAL GOING: Good**

## 1435a PRIX DE LA PORTE DE MADRID (LISTED) — 1m 4f
**2:50** (2:52) 4-Y-0+ **£15,845** (£6,338; £4,754; £3,169)

RPR

**1** **Kindjhal (FR)**[21] 1110 4-8-12 .................................... DBoeuf 9 111
(ELellouche, France)

**2** *snk* **Touch Of Land (FR)**[179] 5662 4-8-12 ........................... OPeslier 11 111
(H-APantall, France)

**3** *2* **Clear Thinking**[21] 1110 4-8-12 ................................ GaryStevens 1 108
(AFabre, France)

**4** *¾* **Foreign Affairs**[17] 1182 6-9-2 .................................. J-BEyquem 4 110
(SirMarkPrescott) *tracked leader, led entering straight, headed 1f out, one pace*

**5** *¾* **Snow Cap (FR)**[41] 5-8-12 .......................................... ELegrix 8 105
(DSmaga, France)

**6** *shd* **Jazz D'Allier (FR)**[21] 1110 7-8-12 ............................ IMendizabal 3 105
(EVagne, France)

**7** *¾* **Millenium Mambo (FR)**[182] 5605 4-8-12 ........................ SPasquier 12 104
(JDeRoualle, France)

**8** *¾* **Gatewick (IRE)**[181] 5629 4-8-12 ................................ MBlancpain 6 103
(CLaffon-Parias, France)

**9** *4* **Le Vernan (FR)**[21] 4-8-12 .......................................... TGillet 10 97
(JBertranDeBalanda, France)

**10** *1 ½* **Desert Plus (IRE)**[35] 5-8-12 ...................................... ABadel 7 94
(MmeMBollack-Badel, France)

**11** **Billy The Kid (IRE)**[21] 1110 6-8-12 ............................ TThulliez 5 94
(TClout, France)

2m 30.4s
**WFA** 4 from 5yo+ 1lb **11** Ran
Speed ratings: .
**Owner** F Bianco **Bred** Frederic Bianco **Trained** France

**NOTEBOOK**
**Foreign Affairs**, who looked extremely well in the paddock, could not get to the lead early on and settled in third place for much of the race. Quickening up, he took the lead early in straight and stayed on bravely on the far rail, but he was outpaced in the latter stages. He may now have a break after three recent outings in France.

# NEWBURY (L-H)
Friday, April 16

**OFFICIAL GOING: Good (good to soft in places in back straight)**
Weather: fine and warm

## 1436 PERTEMPS EUROPEAN BREEDERS FUND MAIDEN STKS — 5f 34y
**2:10** (2:11) (D) 2-Y-0 **£5,694** (£1,752; £876; £438) **Stalls** High

Form RPR

**1** **Tournedos (IRE)** 2-9-0 .............................................. TEDurcan 5 93
(MRChannon) *tall: unf: scope: trckd ldrs: rdn over 2f out: styd on wl fnl f: led cl home* **10/1**[3]

**2** *¾* **Moscow Music** 2-9-0 .................................................. RLMoore 4 90
(MGQuinlan) *leggy: scope: bit bkwd: trckd ldrs: chal fr 1/2-way: led wl over 1f out: kpt on fnl f: ct cl home* **25/1**

**3** *1* **Planet Tomato (IRE)** 2-9-0 .......................................... KFallon 3 86
(PFICole) *tall: str: scope: bit bkwd: s.i.s: rcvrd 1/2-way: hdwy on outside over 1f out: kpt on fnl f: nt qckn nr fin* **11/4**[1]

**4** *3* **Simplify** 2-9-0 ....................................................... JPMurtagh 1 74
(DRLoder) *neat: lw: led: c over to stands side after 1f: rdn and hdd wl over 1f out: wknd ins last* **3/1**[2]

**5** *¾* **Marching Song** 2-9-0 ................................................ RHughes 6 71
(RHannon) *str: bit bkwd: slowly into tride: sn rcvrd and in tch: shkn up and effrt 2f out: sn one pce* **10/1**[3]

**6** *½* **Detonate** 2-9-0 ....................................................... DHolland 8 69
(IAWood) *leggy: unf: s.i.s: bhd: pushed along after 2f: kpt on fnl f: nt a danger* **12/1**

**7** *2 ½* **Peninsular (FR)** 2-9-0 ............................................... LDettori 2 59
(JHMGosden) *neat: pressed ldrs: ev ch 2f out: wknd fnl f* **3/1**[2]

**8** *9* **Cree** 2-9-0 .............................................................. MartinDwyer 7 23
(WRMuir) *leggy: scope: bhd: lost tch 1/2-way* **25/1**

63.20 secs (0.55) **Going Correction** -0.025s/f (Good) **8** Ran SP% **110.2**
Speed ratings: **94,92,91,86,85 84,80,66**CSF £199.19 TOTE £11.10: £2.40, £4.20, £1.10; EX 139.00.
**Owner** Ridgeway Downs Racing **Bred** Pat Grogan **Trained** West Ilsley, Berks

**FOCUS**
Probably one of the best maidens so far, and a race that should produce some winners.

**NOTEBOOK**
**Tournedos(IRE)**, a 30,000euros purchase, whose dam won seven sprints at ages four and five, was allowed to go off at quite a big price but proved good enough to make a winning debut. He is well worth a try in a higher grade and his trainer thinks five furlongs will prove to be his best trip.
**Moscow Music** ◆, a 23,000gns yearling, half-brother to four winners, but none as two-year-olds, shaped well. He showed plenty of pace and kept on right the way to the line. A maiden is his for the taking.
**Planet Tomato(IRE)** ◆, a half-brother to a seven-furlong two-year-old winner, looked magnificent in the paddock and made a pleasing start to his career. After missing a beat at the start he just had to be niggled along early, but he responded well and stuck on without being knocked about. He will know a lot more next time and should soon be winning.
**Simplify**, a 280,000gns purchase, first foal of a quite useful 12-furlong winner who was unraced at two, showed plenty of pace in the early stages but proved no match for the front three. His trainer should find an opportunity for him.
**Marching Song**, a half-brother to Green Line and Snow Bunting, both seven-furlong winners, out of a useful five-furlong two-year-old winner, made an encouraging debut and looks well up to finding a similar race.
**Detonate**, out of a maiden half-sister to a seven-furlong Group Three two-year-old winner, and a very useful sprinter, made a pleasing introduction. He could never quite get on terms with the leaders after missing half a stride at the start but kept on under a hands and heels ride and should know more next time.
**Peninsular(FR)**, a half-brother to eight winners, including juvenile Group One winners Blue Duster (Cheveley Park) and Zeiten (Middle Park), is not very big at all and, after taking a walk in the betting, was not given too hard a ride and finished well beaten.

## 1437 DUBAI DUTY FREE FINEST SURPRISE RATED STKS (H'CAP) — 1m (S)
**2:45** (2:45) (C) (0-95,94) 3-Y-0 **£10,343** (£3,923; £1,961; £891) **Stalls** High

Form RPR

311 **1** **African Dream**[20] 1134 3-9-7 **94**.......................................... JQuinn 14 114
(PWChapple-Hyam) *hld up in tch: hdwy 3f out: chal 2f out: led sn after: pushed out fnl f* **6/1**

1222 **2** *2* **Red Lancer**[6] 1322 3-8-4 **80**............................................ RMiles(3) 15 95
(RJPrice) *trckd ldr: led over 4f out: rdn 2f out: sn hdd: kpt on fnl f: no imp on wnr* **16/1**

3-1 **3** *1 ¾* **Gatwick (IRE)**[22] 1104 3-8-10 **83**........................................ TQuinn 1 94
(MRChannon) *lw: s.i.s: sn rcvrd to trck ldrs: pushed along fr 3f out: styd on fnl 2f but nvr gng pce of ldrs* **4/1**[1]

2-1 **4** *½* **Zonus**[21] 1111 3-8-10 **83**................................................ MHills 12 93
(BWHills) *lw: bhd: hdwy over 2f out: styd on fnl f: kpt on cl home* **11/2**[3]

1-0 **5** *5* **Red Spell (IRE)**[11] 1273 3-8-6 **79**...................................... RLMoore 8 77
(RHannon) *mid-div: rdn 1/2-way: kpt on fnl 2f: nt pce of ldrs* **40/1**

400- **6** *1 ¾* **Frank Sonata**[167] 5871 3-9-3 **90**........................................ LDettori 6 84
(MGQuinlan) *bit bkwd: in tch: pushed along whn bmpd ins fnl 3f: kpt on fnl f: nt a danger* **20/1**

420- **7** *1* **Freak Occurence (IRE)**[111] 6242 3-8-12 **85**......................... SDrowne 13 77
(MissECLavelle) *sn mid-div: rdn over 2f out: n.d* **40/1**

61-0 **8** *¾* **Border Music**[28] 1056 3-8-2 **80**....................................... NChalmers(5) 11 70
(AMBalding) *bhd: rdn 3f out: styd on fnl 2f but nvr nr ldrs* **25/1**

111- **9** *¾* **Jedburgh**[185] 5562 3-9-6 **93**.......................................... MJKinane 10 82
(JLDunlop) *lw: in tch: edgd lft ins fnl 3f: rdn and hung lft again whn chsng ldrs 2f out: sn wknd* **5/1**[2]

21- **10** *5* **Seneschal**[368] 1054 3-9-7 **94**.......................................... TEDurcan 9 71
(MRChannon) *bhd: hdwy whn nt clr run ins fnl 3f: n.d after* **14/1**

446- **11** *1 ½* **Horner (USA)**[209] 5075 3-8-10 **83**..................................... KFallon 3 57
(PFICole) *bit bkwd: s.i.s: nt clr run over 4f out and swtchd to stands rail: nvr in contention* **16/1**

10-0 **12** *11* **Treasure House (IRE)**[27] 1063 3-9-7 **94**.............................. DHolland 2 42
(BJMeehan) *racd alone and led centre crse: hdd over 4f out: wknd fr 3f out* **20/1**

01- **13** *6* **Watamu (IRE)**[218] 4847 3-8-8 **81**....................................... SSanders 7 16
(PJMakin) *lw: slowly itno stride: sn rcvrd to trck ldrs: hmpd ins fnl 3f: wkng whn hmpd again 2f out* **16/1**

300- **14** *2* **Flip Flop And Fly (IRE)**[219] 4814 3-9-3 **90**........................... RHughes 4 20
(SKirk) *chsd ldrs over 5f* **20/1**



The Form Book, Raceform Ltd, Compton, RG20 6NL

15- **15** *1 ¼* **Lommel (UAE)**[232] 4525 3-9-6 **93**........................ JPMurtagh 5 20
(DRLoder) *t.k.h: chsd ldrs over 5f* **12/1**

1m 39.53s (-1.30) **Going Correction** -0.025s/f (Good) **15** Ran SP% **121.4**
Speed ratings: **105,103,101,100,95 94,93,92,91,86 85,74,68,66,64**CSF £88.02 CT £442.67 TOTE £7.30: £2.60, £3.80, £2.30; EX 58.40.
**Owner** Franconson Partners **Bred** E Landi **Trained** Newmarket, Suffolk

**FOCUS**
This had the look of a really competitive three-year-old handicap, and it was, but the progressive African Dream made it look easy. He looks Listed class at least.

**NOTEBOOK**
**African Dream ◆** defied a 13lb rise in the weights for his recent success in a classified event at Kempton with another impressive victory. He has improved with every start to date and, providing he continues to do so, could prove to be better than a handicapper. In the meantime, however, races like the Silver Bowl at Haydock and the Britannia at Royal Ascot look obvious targets.
**Red Lancer** is a real credit to his current trainer for all he has done is progress since being claimed out of a Wolverhampton seller back in October. He was unsurprisingly unable to reverse recent Kempton placings with the winner, but is holding his form really well and should continue to earn good money for his connections in similar events.
**Gatwick(IRE)**, off the mark in pleasing style on his reappearance at Doncaster in a maiden that is working out well enough, had been spoken of as a French Guineas possible but, unable to win off 83, that now looks unlikely. This was still a decent effort, however, as he fared best of those drawn low, and he promises to get further as he was a little one-paced in the closing stages. *Official explanation: jockey said colt hung right*
**Zonus**, a winner in taking style at Doncaster on his reappearance, got plenty of cover behind the leaders (maybe a little too much) but he took a while to hit top gear when given some more space and was doing his best work close home. He was nicely clear of the fifth and looks to have a decent prize in him.
**Red Spell(IRE)**, unfancied and second last on his reappearance at Windsor, shaped with a lot more encouragement this time but may just need dropping in grade.
**Frank Sonata** did best of those having their first run of the year.
**Jedburgh** ended his two-year-old season in fine form, winning his last three starts, but this was a little disappointing. He drifted to his left under pressure and never really looked like picking up.
**Treasure House(IRE)** *Official explanation: jockey said colt ran too free*

## 1438 DUBAI DUTY FREE FULL OF SURPRISES RATED STKS (H'CAP) 5f 34y
**3:15** (3:16) (B) (0-110,108) 4-Y-0+ **£12,095** (£4,587; £2,293; £1,042) **Stalls** High

Form RPR

153- **1** **Bishops Court**[218] 4845 10-9-7 **108**........................ LDettori 4 116
(MrsJRRamsden) *hld up in tch: hdwy over 1f out: drvn to ld wl ins last: hld on wl* **14/1**

6000 **2** *shd* **Peruvian Chief (IRE)**[27] 1061 7-8-8 **95**..................(v) DHolland 6 103
(NPLittmoden) *s.i.s: bhd: gd hdwy over 1f out: str run on outside fnl f: fin fast: jst failed* **13/2**[3]

-316 **3** *1* **Pic Up Sticks**[36] 1004 5-8-9 **96**........................ TEDurcan 11 100+
(MRChannon) *rrd s: bhd: hdwy over 1f out: nt clr run jst ins fnl f and swtchd lft: fin wl* **15/2**

00-2 **4** *hd* **Fromsong (IRE)**[16] 1211 6-8-8 **95**........................ SDrowne 2 99
(BRMillman) *chsd ldrs: chal over 1f out: led ins last: hdd and outpcd wl ins last* **7/1**

056- **5** *shd* **Whitbarrow (IRE)**[220] 4798 5-8-6 **93**........................ RLMoore 5 96
(JMBradley) *chsd ldr: rdn to ld 1f out: hdd ins last: outpcd cl home* **33/1**

243- **6** *hd* **Ringmoor Down**[175] 5732 5-8-7 **94** ow1........................ DaneO'Neill 9 97+
(DWPArbuthnot) *lw: s.i.s: bhd: stdy hdwy over 1f out: nt clr run and swtchd lft jst ins fnl f: kpt on but nt rcvr* **7/1**

143- **7** *nk* **Fanny's Fancy**[183] 5591 4-8-4 **91**........................ JQuinn 10 93+
(CFWall) *h.d.w: lw: hld up in tch: hot clr run fr over 1f out and ins last: squeezed through nr fin but nt rcvr* **7/2**[1]

25-5 **8** *shd* **Little Edward**[27] 1061 6-8-7 **97**........................ LPKeniry(3) 3 98
(BGPowell) *chsd ldrs: ev ch fr over 1f out tl outpcd wl ins last* **10/1**

010- **9** *1 ¼* **Repertory**[194] 5402 11-9-7 **108**........................ TGMcLaughlin 1 105
(MSSaunders) *pressed ldrs tl wknd ins fnl f: eased cl home* **16/1**

216- **10** *1 ¾* **Dubaian Gift**[209] 5072 5-9-5 **106**........................ MartinDwyer 8 96
(AMBalding) *b: led tl hdd 1f out: wknd ins last* **6/1**[2]

U250 **11** *5* **Trinculo (IRE)**[2] 1391 7-8-4 **91** oh2........................(b) NPollard 7 63
(NPLittmoden) *chsd ldrs over 3f* **20/1**

62.01 secs (-0.64) **Going Correction** -0.025s/f (Good) **11** Ran SP% **115.9**
Speed ratings: **104,103,102,101,101 101,100,100,98,96 88**CSF £100.84 CT £754.70 TOTE £10.60: £2.90, £2.60, £2.70; EX 65.80 Trifecta £1437.60 Pool of £14,781.88 - 7.30 winning tickets.
**Owner** D R Brotherton **Bred** D R Brotherton **Trained** Sandhutton, N Yorks

**FOCUS**
A really tight race and plenty of hard-luck stories. As the cliché goes, 'if you were to run this again you probably get a different result'. The winning time was moderate for the grade.

**NOTEBOOK**
**Bishops Court** had not won in handicap company since June 2001 but he showed himself to still be at the top of his game with a fine effort under top weight. You need a lot of luck in a race like this and he got plenty of it with the gaps appearing at just the right time. However, he has not followed up a success since 1998 and could be one to take on next time.
**Peruvian Chief(IRE)** showed little in Dubai over the winter and did not look at his best on his return to this country at Lingfield on his previous run. However, back on the same mark as when taking this race last year, and reunited with Holland, who has won on him four times from what is now nine rides, he was one of a few unlucky losers. Slowly away, he had to be switched out wide round the entire field and flew at the finish, just losing out on the nod.
**Pic Up Sticks**, unlike the runner-up, took well to racing in Dubai and landed a handicap out there off a mark of 91. Settled well off the pace early after rearing in the stalls, he got no luck in running and the gaps appeared all too late. This is a run, however, to treat with caution, as he is the type to often look unlucky and needs everything to fall just right for him.
**Fromsong(IRE)** has never won a handicap but confirmed just how well he is with another fine effort.
**Whitbarrow(IRE)** has been underachieving for the past two seasons but if anyone is going to get the best out of him it is his new trainer, Milton Bradley. This was a pleasing effort and he looks one to keep in mind for similar events.
**Ringmoor Down**, racing over a trip a little shorter than ideal, would have finished closer with better luck. One to keep an eye on when she steps up to six furlongs.
**Fanny's Fancy** has only ever won on Polytrack, but she is just as effective on turf and would have finished much closer with a better run.
**Dubaian Gift** was very disappointing but should improve given that it was his first start in 209 days.

## 1439 ARABIAN INTERNATIONAL RACEDAY CONDITIONS STKS 1m 2f 6y
**3:45** (3:45) (C) 3-Y-0 **£8,687** (£3,212; £1,606; £730) **Stalls** Low

Form RPR

12- **1** **Let The Lion Roar**[210] 5039 3-8-11........................ MJKinane 4 113
(JLDunlop) *lw: trckd ldrs in 3rd: gd hdwy to ld ins fnl 3f: idled and rdn over 1f out: kpt on u.p whn chal fnl f* **6/4**[1]

624- **2** *½* **Top Seed (IRE)**[160] 5962 3-8-11 108........................ TEDurcan 1 112
(MRChannon) *trckd ldr: chal 4f out: sn led: hdd ins fnl 3f: rallied to chal fnl f: no ex cl home* **10/3**[2]

1- **3** *17* **Mac Regal (IRE)**[177] 5714 3-8-11........................ LDettori 2 80
(MGQuinlan) *lengthy: bit bkwd: bhd: rdn and hung lft over 2f out: styd on for mod 3rd* **9/1**

214- **4** *3 ½* **White Hawk**[245] 4162 3-8-11 100........................ JPMurtagh 3 73
(DRLoder) *led tl hdd ins fnl 4f: wknd fr 3f out* **6/1**

1- **5** *1* **Manyana (IRE)**[268] 3505 3-8-11........................ MartinDwyer 5 71
(MPTregoning) *bkwd: bhd: rdn and effrt 4f out: nvr nr ldrs and sn wknd* **7/2**[3]

2m 8.27s (-0.44) **Going Correction** +0.20s/f (Good) **5** Ran SP% **109.6**
Speed ratings: **109,108,95,92,91**CSF £6.65 TOTE £1.80: £1.50, £1.60; EX 5.70.
**Owner** L Neil Jones **Bred** Abergwaun Farm **Trained** Arundel, W Sussex

**FOCUS**
Despite the small field they appeared to go a good gallop and the winning time was very smart. Although those in behind are surely capable of better, it is unlikely they would have got anywhere near the front two had they been right.

**NOTEBOOK**
**Let The Lion Roar**, a Dante and Derby entry, confirmed the promise he showed as a juvenile with a fine effort. He looked all set to pull well clear when hitting the front in the straight, but Top Seed would not go away and he had to show a good attitude to get the better of that one. The front two were 17 lengths clear of the remainder and he fully deserves to step up in grade for either the Chester Vase or the Lingfield Derby Trial.
**Top Seed(IRE)** only managed one win in 11 starts last term despite showing smart form such as when runner-up to Bago in a Group One. This was, however, a most pleasing reappearance. Never too far off the pace, he stuck with the winner when challenged and only gave way just yards from the line. He was a mile clear of the remainder and could surely add to that sole success before too much longer.
**Mac Regal(IRE)**, a winner on his only start to date in an Italian contest for unraced colts and geldings over nine furlongs, did not appear to want to let himself down and was hanging badly when asked for his effort. Given softer ground he could well improve significantly.
**White Hawk**, a winner of a Wolverhampton nursery off a mark of 90 last term, showed little on this reappearance. *Official explanation: jockey said colt ran too free early on*
**Manyana(IRE)**, a winner of a Sandown maiden on his only start at two, was well supported but failed to run to form. He probably needed this and should be capable of better, but even so, this was a poor effort. *Official explanation: jockey said colt had a breathing problem*

## 1440 STAN JAMES TELEBETTING MAIDEN FILLIES' STKS 1m 2f 6y
**4:20** (4:20) (D) 3-Y-0 **£5,616** (£1,728; £864; £432) **Stalls** Low

Form RPR

**1** **Winds Of March (IRE)** 3-8-11........................ LDettori 5 89
(JHMGosden) *lengthy: str :lw: s.i.s: sn rcvrd: hld up in rr: hdwy 4f out: chal fr 2f out: led appr fnl f: hld on wl* **9/4**[1]

0- **2** *shd* **Crystal (IRE)**[167] 5874 3-8-11........................ MHills 4 89
(BJMeehan) *bit bkwd: led: rdn over 2f out:styd on wl whn strly chal sn after: hdd appr 1f out: rallied gamely u.p: nt quite get up* **5/1**[2]

03- **3** *7* **Karamea (SWI)**[182] 5612 3-8-11........................ MJKinane 7 76
(JLDunlop) *hld up in rr: hdwy on outside over 3f out: rdn to chse ldrs 3f out: outpcd fnl 2f* **5/1**[2]

**4** *1 ½* **Modesta (IRE)** 3-8-11........................ RHughes 1 73
(HRACecil) *rangy: hld up mid-div: rdn 3f out: outpcd fnl 2f* **8/1**

32- **5** *4* **Cherubim (JPN)**[288] 2930 3-8-11........................ JPMurtagh 6 65
(DRLoder) *chsd ldr tl over 3f out: rdn over 2f out and sn wknd* **5/1**[2]

62- **6** *1* **Serramanna**[235] 4434 3-8-11........................ WRyan 3 63
(HRACecil) *in tch: chsd ldrs 3f out: sn wknd* **13/2**[3]

000- **7** *1 ¼* **Wee Dinns (IRE)**[174] 5754 3-8-11........................ TQuinn 10 61
(SKirk) *s.i.s: a in rr* **40/1**

00-0 **8** *1 ¼* **Calomeria**[15] 1224 3-8-11........................ SSanders 2 59
(RMBeckett) *chsd ldrs: rdn 3f out: hung bdly lft u.p and wknd qckly wl over 2f out* **66/1**

**9** *nk* **Apron (IRE)** 3-8-11........................ SDrowne 8 58
(RCharlton) *leggy: unf: bhd: rdn 4f out: nvr in contention and sn bhd* **20/1**

006- **10** *5* **Cloudingswell**[176] 5721 3-8-11 63........................ SWhitworth 9 49
(DLWilliams) *a bhd* **66/1**

2m 10.47s (1.76) **Going Correction** +0.20s/f (Good) **10** Ran SP% **115.4**
Speed ratings: **100,99,94,93,89 89,88,87,86,82**CSF £13.01 TOTE £3.50: £1.80, £1.50, £1.70; EX 17.70.
**Owner** Greenbay Stables Ltd **Bred** C H Wacker Iii **Trained** Manton, Wilts

**FOCUS**
A decent fillies' maiden and the first two home look particularly nice.

**NOTEBOOK**
**Winds Of March(IRE) ◆**, not sold at 760,000gns, is a sister to ten-furlong winner Curtain Time, and a half-sister to Group One winners Ali-Royal, Sleepytime and Taipan. She was easy to back on course but was still sent off favourite. Having travelled very nicely throughout for Dettori, she picked up in good style to get the better of the long-time leader Crystal. The pair were clear and she looks a very nice prospect. The Ribblesdale and Irish Oaks are her targets if all goes well, but in the meantime she will return to Newbury for a Listed race.
**Crystal(IRE) ◆** showed ability on her only start as a juvenile when eighth in a Listed race at Newmarket. Dropped into a more realistic grade for this first run in 167 days, she ran a fine race. She was sent to the front from the off and, after setting a reasonable enough gallop, kept on all the way to the line, pulling seven lengths clear of the third in the process. A ready-made maiden winner before stepping back up in class.
**Karamea(SWI)** well supported to confirm the promise she showed at two, travelled nicely well off the pace and looked likely to pose a big threat at one stage. However, she could never quite muster the pace to go with the front two. An Oaks entry, she does not look up to that class but should find a maiden at least before too much longer.
**Modesta(IRE)**, an impeccably bred half-sister to Reams Of Verse and Elmaamul, out of an unraced half-sister to Zafonic, was nibbled at in the ring and offered some encouragement. She never looked like taking this particular contest but, given normal improvement, it would be most disappointing if she did not find a race.
**Cherubim(JPN)** was runner-up behind Punctilious on her second start at two, but failed to progress from that on this first start in 288 days and is probably flattered by the bare result of that Yarmouth contest. That said, this run should bring her on.
**Serramanna** failed to build on the encouragement she showed at two.
**Wee Dinns(IRE)** should find things easier in handicaps.

## 1441 BRIDGET MAIDEN FILLIES' STKS 7f (S)
**4:50** (4:53) (D) 3-Y-0 **£5,850** (£1,800; £900; £450) **Stalls** High

Form RPR

**1** **Illustrious Miss (USA)** 3-8-11........................ JPMurtagh 9 88
(DRLoder) *gd sort: str: rangy: lw: trckd ldrs: led over 1f out: pushed clr ins last: comf* **7/2**[1]

**2** *3 ½* **Lucky Spin** 3-8-11........................ PDobbs 8 79
(RHannon) *w'like: scope: chsd ldrs: rdn over 2f out: styd on to chse wnr ins fnl f but no ch* **20/1**

3 1 **Dashiki (USA)** 3-8-11 ........ RHughes 12 76
(BWHills) *unf: scope: b.hind: chsd ldr tl led over 4f out: rdn 2f out: hdd over 1f out: outpcd and lost 2nd ins last* **7/1**[3]

4 1 **Pinching (IRE)** 3-8-11 ........ WRyan 14 74
(HRACecil) *w'like: in tch: hmpd over 2f out: hdwy over 1f out: hung lft and kpt on ins last* **10/1**

5 3 **Tree Tops** 3-8-11 ........ LDettori 4 66
(JHMGosden) *str: scope: bit bkwd: bhd: pushed along 1/2-way: hdwy fr 2f out: kpt on fnl f but nt trble ldrs* **4/1**[2]

6 2 **Shazana** 3-8-11 ........ MHills 11 61
(BWHills) *neat: led tl hdd over 4f out: styd chalng tl over 2f out: wknd ins fnl quarter m* **7/1**[3]

7 1 ½ **Vamp** 3-8-11 ........ SSanders 7 57
(RMBeckett) *leggy: unf: s.i.s: bhd: styd on fnl 2f but nvr in contention* **25/1**

8 ¾ **Woman In White (FR)** 3-8-11 ........ KFallon 13 55
(JHMGosden) *lengthy: unf: slowly away: bhd: swtchd lft to outside over 3f out: kpt on fnl 2f but n.d* **8/1**

9 1 **Set Alight** 3-8-11 ........ SCarson 1 52
(MissKBBoutflower) *w'like: bit bkwd: pushed along and bhd 1/2-way: kpt on fr over 1f out: nt a danger* **33/1**

10 1 ½ **Private Jessica** 3-8-11 ........ DaneO'Neill 5 48
(JRFanshawe) *lengthy: bkwd: chsd ldrs 5f* **12/1**

11 1 ¾ **Miss Shangri La** 3-8-11 ........ DHolland 3 44
(GWragg) *leggy: angular: slowly away: a in rr* **8/1**

12 ¾ **Cotton Easter** 3-8-11 ........ CCatlin 2 42
(MrsAJBowlby) *rangy: bkwd: in tch: rdn and effrt into mid-div 1/2-way: sn wknd* **33/1**

13 3 ½ **Dulcimer** 3-8-11 ........ SDrowne 6 33
(GBBalding) *neat: in tch: rdn 3f out: sn wknd* **25/1**

1m 26.96s (-0.26) **Going Correction** -0.025s/f (Good) **13 Ran SP% 124.6**
Speed ratings: **100,96,94,93,90 88,86,85,84,82 80,79,75**CSF £82.74 TOTE £3.90: £1.80, £8.50, £2.40; EX 118.10.

**Owner** Sheikh Mohammed **Bred** W S Farish And E J Hudson Jr Irrevocable Trust **Trained** Newmarket, Suffolk

■ Stewards Enquiry : P Dobbs two-day ban: careless riding (Apr 27,28)

**FOCUS**
A race for previously unraced fillies. With no form to go on it is guesswork as to how this maiden will work out, but it will be most disappointing if it does not produce its share of future winners.

**NOTEBOOK**
**Illustrious Miss(USA)**, a $600,000 purchase, half-sister to a Graded winner, made an impressive start to her racing career. She quickened up in good style and should be able to hold her own in a higher grade.

**Lucky Spin**, 16,500gns yearling, half-sister to four winners, raced up with the pace throughout but just lacked the change of pace the winner showed. It will be disappointing if she does not find a maiden.

**Dashiki(USA)**, a full-sister to Dewhurst winner Distant Music, was given every chance under a positive ride from Hughes and was simply not good enough. She should progress and can pick up a maiden.

**Pinching(IRE)** ◆, a 55,000gns purchase, is closely related to a high-class Italian juvenile winner and made a good introduction. She had to be switched out to her left for a run and showed signs of inexperience, but she was not given a hard time and should improve enough to win at least a maiden.

**Tree Tops**, out of a six-furlong two-year-old winner who later proved effective at up to a mile six, had to be niggled at a long way from home and never really threatened. She could, however, be capable of significant improvement.

## 1442 PETER SMITH MEMORIAL MAIDEN STKS — 1m 3f 5y
5:20 (5:21) (D) 3-Y-O — £5,486 (£1,688; £844; £422) Stalls Low

Form — RPR

05- 1 **Graham Island**[212] 4997 3-9-0 ........ DHolland 4 84
(GWragg) *lw: trckd ldr 5f:chal and nt clr run over 3f out:swtchd rt and str run fr 2f out: led appr fnl f: pushed clr* **5/4**[1]

2 2 **Strike** 3-9-0 ........ LDettori 3 81
(JHMGosden) *unf: slowly away: sn rcvrd: wnt 2nd 6f out: chal 4f out: led over 3f out: hdd over 1f out: styd on wl for 2nd: no ch w wnr* **9/2**[3]

3 nk **Yaahomm** 3-9-0 ........ JPMurtagh 5 80
(DRLoder) *unf: scope: trckd ldrs: rdn to chal 3f out: stl ev ch over 1f out: outpcd fnl f* **9/4**[2]

4- 4 4 **Turnstile**[162] 5932 3-9-0 ........ RHughes 2 74
(RHannon) *led tl hdd over 3f out: wknd ins fnl 2f* **7/1**

25 5 10 **Muzio Scevola (IRE)**[15] 1221 3-9-0 ........ TEDurcan 1 58
(MRChannon) *a bhd: lost tch fnl 3f* **16/1**

2m 27.96s (5.15) **Going Correction** +0.20s/f (Good) **5 Ran SP% 111.8**
Speed ratings: **89,87,87,84,77**CSF £7.45 TOTE £2.30: £1.20, £2.70; EX 7.00 Place 6 £64.75, Place 5 £26.49.

**Owner** Mollers Racing **Bred** Plantation Stud **Trained** Newmarket, Suffolk

**FOCUS**
This is often a useful maiden, but the time was very slow.

**NOTEBOOK**
**Graham Island** offered encouragement over seven furlongs as a juvenile and, stepped up to a more suitable trip, he was able to confirm that by scoring decisively, despite having to be switched for a run. His immediate future is probably in the hands of the assessor.

**Strike**, out of a seven-furlong two-year-old winner who progressed to become smart over middle-distances, was not too inconvenienced by a slow start for the early pace was just ordinary and he had every chance when it mattered. Given normal improvement he should win a maiden.

**Yaahomm**, a full-brother to the top-class ten-furlong filly Zahrat Dubai, out of a Group-winning miler in Germany, ran well on this racecourse debut. He looked to be coming to win his race two out, but proved unable to sustain his effort and was one paced in the closing stages. Like the second, he should win his maiden.

**Turnstile** fared best of those who raced off the pace on his debut at Nottingham last year, but this did not appear to represent progression. He had every chance from the front but could only post a lacklustre effort when it mattered.

**Muzio Scevola(IRE)** showed ability on his debut but has done nothing since.

T/Jkpt: Not won. T/Plt: £112.30 to a £1 stake. Pool £53,788.35, 349.5 winning tickets T/Qpdt: £13.00 to a £1 stake. Pool £3,206.90, 181.70 winning tickets ST

# 1422 SOUTHWELL (L-H)
Friday, April 16

**OFFICIAL GOING: Standard**
Having recently been watered, the track was not riding as deep as usual and there was a big bias against those that raced closest to the inside rail.
Wind: fresh bhd Weather: showery

## 1443 NEW SITE @ BETDIRECT.CO.UK BANDED STKS — 5f (F)
5:05 (5:05) (H) 3-Y-O+ — £1,445 (£413; £206) Stalls High

Form — RPR

5300 1 **Attorney**[16] 1206 6-9-6 45 ........ (v) GDuffield 2 55
(DShaw) *chsd ldrs: rdn to ld 1f out: edgd rt: r.o* **9/2**[3]

-000 2 2 **Valazar (USA)**[25] 1075 5-9-6 40 ........ ACulhane 9 48
(DWChapman) *chsd ldrs: led 1/2-way: rdn and hdd 1f out: edgd lft and no ex* **11/2**

5430 3 3 **Hagley Park**[18] 1180 5-9-6 45 ........ DSweeney 5 38
(MQuinn) *w ldrs: rdn adn ev ch over 1f out: wknd wl ins fnl f* **13/2**

3-03 4 shd **Ballygriffin Kid**[10] 1280 4-9-1 45 ........ JFMcDonald(5) 1 37
(TPMcgovern) *w ldrs: rdn 1/2-way: styd on same pce appr fnl f* **7/2**[1]

0022 5 shd **Tuscan Dream**[17] 1190 9-9-1 35 ........ PBradley(5) 6 37
(ABerry) *w ldrs: rdn and ev ch over 1f out: wknd ins fnl f* **8/1**

5001 6 ½ **Pleasure Time**[17] 1190 11-9-6 45 ........ (v) RFitzpatrick 4 35
(CSmith) *mde most to 1/2-way: rdn and ev ch over 1f out: wknd ins fnl f* **4/1**[2]

0455 7 shd **Levelled**[17] 1190 10-8-13 35 ........ CHaddon(7) 8 35
(DWChapman) *s.i.s: hld up: rdn over 1f out: no imp* **12/1**

1004 8 1 **Danakim**[17] 1190 7-8-13 40 ........ (be) DFentiman(7) 3 31
(JRWeymes) *w ldrs: rdn 1/2-way: wknd over 1f out* **14/1**

59.79 secs (-0.61) **Going Correction** -0.175s/f (Stan) **8 Ran SP% 114.6**
Speed ratings: **97,93,89,88,88 87,87,86**CSF £29.42 TOTE £5.50: £1.70, £3.20, £2.00; EX 22.00.

**Owner** K Nicholls **Bred** J R And Mrs P Good **Trained** Averham, Notts

**FOCUS**
A moderate contest in which those behind the front pair finished in a heap. There may have been an advantage in racing down the centre of the track.

**NOTEBOOK**
**Attorney** has a truly awful strike rate, but found a race he could win. The key to this victory may have been racing down the centre of the track, usually an advantage here, so much of the credit must go down to his wily rider.

**Valazar(USA)** ran his best race for a while and can be given a little extra credit, as having to race against the stands' rail is not usually favoured over the straight five here these days. He probably retains enough ability to nick a race like this.

**Hagley Park** showed her usual speed, but was up against it as soon as she was unable to get the early lead on her own.

**Ballygriffin Kid** was not helped at all by the drop to the minimum trip.

**Tuscan Dream** is another that needs to be able to dominate to show his best.

**Pleasure Time**, who had a couple of these behind when winning over course and distance last month, attempted the same tactics but the old legs could not carry him home this time.

## 1444 £10 FREE BET @ BETDIRECT.CO.UK BANDED STKS — 1m (F)
5:40 (5:40) (H) 3-Y-O+ — £1,449 (£414; £207) Stalls Low

Form — RPR

1601 1 **Fraamtastic**[25] 1080 7-9-4 45 ........ (p) BReilly(3) 6 53
(BAPearce) *broke wl: sn stdd: hdwy u.p over 2f out: chsd ldr over 1f out: styd on to ld wl ins fnl f* **9/4**[1]

5560 2 1 ¼ **Air Of Esteem**[47] 939 8-9-0 40 ........ DFentiman(7) 8 51
(IanEmmerson) *chsd ldrs: rdn to ld 2f out: hdd wl ins fnl f* **9/2**[3]

-606 3 6 **Desires Destiny**[67] 730 6-9-0 35 ........ MLawson(7) 3 39
(MBrittain) *w ldr: rdn 1/2-way: led over 2f out: sn hdd: wknd over 1f out* **8/1**

4502 4 1 ¼ **Sea Ya Maite**[24] 1090 10-9-7 40 ........ (t) JBramhill 4 36
(SRBowring) *s.i.s: hdwy 6f out: rdn over 2f out: wknd over 1f out* **4/1**[2]

040- 5 ½ **Cezzaro (IRE)**[214] 4948 6-9-0 35 ........ MNem(7) 5 35
(SRBowring) *led 6f out: hdd over 2f out: wknd over 1f out* **20/1**

0-65 6 6 **Abbiejo (IRE)**[18] 1176 7-9-7 40 ........ (p) VSlattery 7 23
(GFierro) *prom over 4f* **9/1**

4/00 7 shd **Miss Fleurie**[18] 1174 4-9-7 45 ........ GDuffield 1 23
(RCraggs) *sn led: hdd 6f out: wknd over 2f out* **12/1**

006- 8 dist **Delaware Trail**[221] 4771 5-9-7 45 ........ ACulhane 2 —
(JSWainwright) *prom to 1/2-way* **9/1**

1m 44.56s (-0.04) **Going Correction** -0.025s/f (Stan) **8 Ran SP% 112.5**
Speed ratings: **99,97,91,90,90 84,83,—**CSF £11.95 TOTE £3.00: £1.10, £2.60, £2.30; EX 10.40.

**Owner** Richard J Gray **Bred** Bloodhorse International Limited **Trained** Newchapel, Surrey

**FOCUS**
A routine banded stakes where once again it paid to race down the centre of the track.

**NOTEBOOK**
**Fraamtastic** has taken a real liking to this sort of racing, especially on Fibresand, and was winning her third such contest of the year from five outings having previously won only one of her first 35 contests under both codes. Despite breaking well, her rider was keen to drop her out and settle her, enabling him to produced her with a late wide swoop in the home straight.

**Air Of Esteem** looked to have a great chance of winning when sent into the lead soon after turning for home but, after a brief tussle, could not withstand the mare's late challenge. He has become very hard to win with and is nothing like the horse he was.

**Desires Destiny**, up there from the start, managed to hang on for third despite racing in the deep ground on the inside and then hanging right as she got tired inside the last furlong. This was her first placing at the eighth attempt, but that is not saying much.

**Sea Ya Maite** stretched his long losing run, but probably ran his race and is the benchmark to the value of the form.

**Cezzaro(IRE)**, making his debut at this level, dropped away after making much of the running but can be forgiven to a certain extent as this was his first run since September.

**Delaware Trail** *Official explanation: jockey said gelding lost its action*

## 1445 BETDIRECT.CO.UK BANDED STKS — 6f (F)
6:10 (6:11) (H) 3-Y-O+ — £1,435 (£410; £205) Stalls Low

Form — RPR

0644 1 **Beauteous (IRE)**[1] 1403 5-8-7 35 ........ KGhunowa(7) 8 69
(MJPolglase) *w ldr: led over 3f out: rdn clr over 1f out* **11/2**[3]

6450 2 7 **Cleveland Way**[11] 1268 4-8-7 45 ........ (v) DTudhope(7) 3 48
(DCarroll) *s.i.s: sn chsng ldrs: rdn over 2f out: styd on same pce* **5/2**[2]

2000 3 ¾ **Eternal Bloom**[47] 936 6-8-7 45 ........ MLawson(7) 6 46
(MBrittain) *s.i.s: sn chsng ldrs: rdn 1/2-way: wknd over 1f out* **10/1**

-615 **4** 1 1/4 **Indian Music**[10] 1283 7-9-0 45 FLynch 7 42
(ABerry) *s.s: hld up: rdn over 2f out: nrst fin* **9/4**[1]
0040 **5** 3/4 **Indian Warrior**[39] 990 8-9-0 45 (b) GDuffield 2 40
(JJay) *hld up: nvr nrr* **15/2**
-003 **6** 1 1/4 **Bond Domingo**[17] 1190 5-8-7 35 (b) MStainton(7) 5 36
(BSmart) *bmpd s: chsd ldrs: rdn and wknd over 2f out* **14/1**
00-0 **7** 10 **Firecat**[93] 529 5-9-0 45 DSweeney 4 6
(APJones) *led: hdd over 3f out: wknd 2f out* **14/1**
0001 **8** 5 **Caronte (IRE)**[24] 1089 4-9-0 40 (b) JBramhill 1 —
(SRBowring) *s.i.s: a in rr: wknd over 3f out* **10/1**

1m 16.41s (-0.49) **Going Correction** -0.025s/f (Stan) **8 Ran SP% 118.0**
Speed ratings: **102,92,91,90,89 87,74,67**CSF £20.38 TOTE £7.30: £1.60, £2.00, £2.60; EX 28.80.
**Owner** Paul J Dixon **Bred** Mrs Jill M Harley **Trained** Southwell, Notts

**FOCUS**
A decent winning time for a race of its type, but an uncompetitive affair and the winner is rated 30lb higher on turf.

**NOTEBOOK**
**Beauteous(IRE)** ◆, possibly a little unlucky when a beaten favourite on the Polytrack 24 hours earlier, broke well this time and helped force the pace. As soon as he made his break for home racing off the final bend, it was obvious he had his rivals well and truly cooked. In this mood he can win again at this level.
**Cleveland Way**, never far away, was ultimately firmly put in his place by the winner but the margin between the pair may have been exacerbated by racing tight against the inside rail and the way the track was riding that was going to be an almighty handicap.
**Eternal Bloom** has developed a habit of giving away ground at the start and even at this level she can ill afford to do that.
**Indian Music** missed the break and was then struggling to go the pace. He managed to stay on past a few, but was never in the same parish as the winner and over this trip he probably needs the track to be riding much deeper than it was here. *Official explanation: jockey said gelding was slowly away from the start*
**Indian Warrior** was another that seemed to find everything happening too quickly for him over this trip.

## 1446 BLOOR HOMES FISKERTON BANDED STKS 7f (F)
**6:40** (6:41) (H) 3-Y-0+ **£1,480** (£423; £211) **Stalls** Low

Form RPR
/40- **1** **Red Flyer (IRE)**[167] 582 5-9-7 40 GFaulkner 5 49
(PCHaslam) *s.s: outpcd: hdwy u.p over 2f out: styd on to ld wl ins fnl f: eased nr fin* **7/2**[2]
0060 **2** 1 3/4 **Illustrious Duke**[14] 1233 6-9-0 40 (b) PVarley(7) 1 45
(MMullineaux) *chsd ldrs: led over 4f out: hdd over 1f out: sn bmpd: led ins fnl f: sn hdd and no ex* **6/1**
3243 **3** hd **Neutral Night (IRE)**[17] 1191 4-9-7 40 (b1) ACulhane 3 44
(RBrotherton) *chsd ldrs: hrd rdn over 2f out: ev ch fr over 1f out: no ex ins fnl f* **2/1**[1]
536 **4** 5 **Countrywide Girl (IRE)**[52] 875 5-9-7 30 FLynch 2 32
(ABerry) *led: hdd over 4f out: rdn to ld and hung lft over 1f out: hdd & wknd ins fnl f* **13/2**
-000 **5** 3 **Compton Bay**[17] 1191 4-9-0 35 MLawson(7) 7 24
(MBrittain) *hld up: plld hrd: hdwy u.p over 2f out: wknd over 1f out* **25/1**
0003 **6** 3 1/2 **Mimas Girl**[24] 1094 5-9-7 35 (tp) JBramhill 6 15
(SRBowring) *chsd ldrs: hung lft and wknd over 2f out* **5/1**[3]
0606 **7** 5 **Keltic Flute**[14] 1237 5-9-2 30 (v) DNolan(5) 4 3
(MrsLucindaFeatherstone) *chsd ldrs over 4f* **12/1**

1m 32.19s (1.39) **Going Correction** -0.025s/f (Stan) **7 Ran SP% 111.4**
Speed ratings: **91,89,88,83,79 75,69**CSF £23.13 TOTE £4.60: £2.70, £3.00; EX 91.50.
**Owner** Mrs C Barclay **Bred** Scuderia Cesare Turri **Trained** Middleham Moor, N Yorks

**FOCUS**
A moderate winning time, even for a banded stakes.

**NOTEBOOK**
**Red Flyer(IRE)**, who has been performing at up to two and a half miles over hurdles since his last run on the Flat more than a year ago, was racing for the first time in five months. This was an amazing performance under such different conditions, especially as he completely fluffed the start, but being kept wide and challenging widest of all almost certainly proved crucial in what was a truly dismal contest.
**Illustrious Duke** probably did well to hold on for second considering he could not establish an uncontested lead from the off and was racing on the slowest part of the track, but this was such a bad race that the form means little.
**Neutral Night(IRE)**, a long-standing maiden, was disappointing and can have no excuses as she had the run of the race and was given every opportunity to make use of the track bias.
**Countrywide Girl(IRE)**, who is a very poor mare these days, was given a positive ride but hung all over the place as she got tired in the last couple of furlongs.
**Mimas Girl** is another long-standing maiden, but did not even run up to the form of her last outing.

## 1447 BET DIRECT NO Q ON 08000 93 66 93 TRI-BANDED STKS 1m (F)
**7:10** (7:10) (H) 3-Y-0 **£1,435** (£410; £205) **Stalls** Low

Form RPR
00-3 **1** **Roman The Park (IRE)**[17] 1195 3-8-9 40 GDuffield 4 39
(TDEasterby) *trckd ldrs: led over 2f out: drvn out* **9/4**[1]
-004 **2** 1 1/4 **Monkey Or Me (IRE)**[24] 1094 3-8-4 30 RFitzpatrick 5 31
(PTMidgley) *hld up: hdwy over 2f out: sn rdn: styd on* **5/1**[3]
0050 **3** hd **Mystic Promise (IRE)**[24] 1084 3-7-13 30 (t) HayleyTurner(5) 3 31
(MrsNMacauley) *w ldr: led over 4f out: rdn and hdd over 2f out: styd on u.p* **25/1**
0542 **4** 1/2 **Secret Bloom**[17] 1195 3-9-0 45 (b1) DarrenWilliams 1 40
(JRNorton) *trckd ldrs: rdn over 2f out: styd on u.p* **7/2**[2]
0-06 **5** 5 **Niteowl Express (IRE)**[30] 1038 3-8-9 40 DRMcCabe 2 25
(JO'Reilly) *led: hdd over 4f out: rdn over 2f out: wknd ins fnl f* **9/4**[1]
066 **6** 9 **Harbour Princess**[50] 898 3-8-9 40 SRighton 6 7
(MFHarris) *prom: rdn 1/2-way: wknd over 2f out* **11/1**

1m 46.31s (1.71) **Going Correction** -0.025s/f (Stan) **6 Ran SP% 112.6**
Speed ratings: **90,88,88,88,83 74**CSF £14.06 TOTE £3.20: £2.10, £2.20; EX 17.20.
**Owner** Middleham Park Racing Ii **Bred** Dermot Brennan **Trained** Great Habton, N Yorks

**FOCUS**
One of the worst races ever run on the Flat in Britain. Some of these are barely three-years old, yet they are sadly already rated below 45 and as deep into the basement as you can get.

**NOTEBOOK**
**Roman The Park(IRE)** battled on well to win a truly awful contest decisively and had at least run his best previous race under identical conditions. The fact that he reversed the form of that race with Secret Bloom suggests he may be improving, though that should be kept within context.
**Monkey Or Me(IRE)**came from off the pace to snatch second and probably ran to the level of his last start here, but he was racing on the fastest part of the track and the form means little.
**Mystic Promise(IRE)**, unplaced in all 11 of his previous starts, was not beaten far and that accurately illustrates the true nature of the form.
**Secret Bloom**, wearing blinkers rather than the usual visor, had the winner behind him when runner-up in an identical contest here last time, but he is not progressive in any way and his attitude is also questionable.
**Niteowl Express(IRE)**, making his debut at this level after finishing down the field in three Class D six-furlong maidens, raced tight against the unfavoured inside rail and failed to get home. He might be given one more chance to show that he is not as bad as this.

## 1448 LITTLEWOODS BET DIRECT BANDED STKS 1m 4f (F)
**7:40** (7:40) (H) 4-Y-0+ **£1,445** (£413; £206) **Stalls** Low

Form RPR
3311 **1** **Stravmour**[17] 1193 8-8-13 45 DaleGibson 9 57+
(RHollinshead) *s.i.s: hld up in tch: racd keenly: led over 2f out: sn pushed clr: eased nr fin* **5/2**[2]
1033 **2** 7 **Seraph**[19] 1042 4-8-5 45 (p) RoryMoore(7) 3 46
(JohnAHarris) *w ldrs: led over 3f out: hdd over 2f out: sn outpcd* **11/2**[3]
0055 **3** 1 **Western Command (GER)**[14] 1238 8-8-13 45 (p) JoannaBadger 1 45
(MrsNMacauley) *chsd ldrs: led over 6f out: rdn and hdd over 3f out: styd on same pce fnl 2f* **16/1**
2122 **4** 5 **Galley Law**[46] 943 4-8-12 45 JQuinn 6 37
(RCraggs) *hld up in tch: rdn over 3f out: wknd over 1f out* **11/8**[1]
500/ **5** 9 **Zelea (IRE)**[486] 5925 5-8-6 40 (t) MLawson(7) 8 24
(JParkes) *s.i.s: sn pushed along in rr: wknd over 3f out* **33/1**
-600 **6** 6 **Homeric Trojan**[18] 1173 4-8-5 45 DTudhope(7) 7 15
(MBrittain) *w ldrs: led over 8f out: hdd over 6f out: wknd over 2f out* **16/1**
6540 **7** 1 3/4 **King Priam (IRE)**[22] 1103 9-8-13 35 (b) ACulhane 5 12
(MJPolglase) *sn outpcd and bhd* **12/1**
00-0 **8** nk **Dash For Glory**[10] 1281 5-8-13 40 DSweeney 4 11
(MBlanshard) *chsd ldrs: rdn over 5f out: wknd over 3f out* **16/1**
00-0 **9** 8 **Mister Rushby**[87] 572 4-8-12 35 DarrenWilliams 2 —
(MissVHaigh) *led over 3f: rdn and wknd over 5f out* **28/1**

2m 42.55s (0.45) **Going Correction** -0.025s/f (Stan)
**WFA** 4 from 5yo+ 1lb **9 Ran SP% 117.8**
Speed ratings: **97,92,91,88,82 78,77,76,71**CSF £17.25 TOTE £3.60: £1.10, £2.10, £2.40; EX 11.90.
**Owner** E Bennion **Bred** E Bennion **Trained** Upper Longdon, Staffs

**FOCUS**
A messy race with the lead changing hands several times, but in the end a very easy winner.

**NOTEBOOK**
**Stravmour**, had no problem with the drop back in trip in his hat-trick bid and was cruising all over his rivals from some way out. His days in banded stakes' are probably now numbered.
**Seraph** seemed to be travelling well in front on the turn for home, but the winner was stalking him and when set alight it proved no contest. He did at least turn previous Wolverhampton form around with Galley Law in no uncertain terms and is probably happier here.
**Western Command(GER)** was having his 118th race on sand alone and seems to run just about every week these days. He has now run two fair races back-to-back at this track and halved the deficit with Stravmour compared with their meeting here two outings ago, but is hardly a winner waiting to happen.
**Galley Law** was off the bridle and going nowhere a fair way from home. This was his first genuinely poor effort at this level and perhaps conditions were not testing enough for him.
**Zelea(IRE)** almost certainly needed this after 16 months off, but did not offer any promise at all.
T/Plt: £118.80 to a £1 stake. Pool: £20,800.25. 127.75 winning tickets. T/Qpdt: £93.50 to a £1 stake. Pool: £2,097.50. 16.60 winning tickets. CR

# THIRSK (L-H)
### Friday, April 16

**OFFICIAL GOING: Good to soft (good in places)**
After persistent rain the ground was reckoned to be soft and a bit loose.
Wind: almost nil Weather: persistent rain turning to lt drizzle

## 1449 EBF ALEC BORROWS 90TH BIRTHDAY NOVICE FILLIES' STKS 5f
**2:30** (2:35) (D) 2-Y-0 **£5,486** (£1,688; £844; £422) **Stalls** High

Form RPR
1 **1** **Lady Filly**[20] 1130 2-8-10 AQuinn(5) 5 87
(WGMTurner) *mde virtually all: pushed clr appr last: styd on wl* **4/5**[1]
**2** 3 1/2 **World At My Feet** 2-8-1 SuzanneFrance(7) 6 66
(NBycroft) *cmpt: unf: hld up: swtchd to wd outside and hdwy over 1f out: kpt on ins last: no ch w wnr* **50/1**
26 **3** hd **I'm Aimee**[6] 1324 2-8-8 RHavlin 8 65
(PDEvans) *trckd ldrs: swtchd lft and hdwy over 1f out: sn rdn and kpt on ins last* **11/2**[2]
1 **4** 1 3/4 **Lisa Mona Lisa (IRE)**[21] 1115 2-8-10 GDuffield 3 60
(VSmith) *cl up: rdn along 2f out: sn wknd* **11/1**
2 **5** 1 **Lady Erica**[14] 1234 2-8-8 DarrenWilliams 2 54
(KRBurke) *chsd ldrs: effrt over 2f out: sn rdn and btn over 1f out* **12/1**
**6** 3/4 **Mimi Mouse** 2-8-5 DAllan(3) 7 51
(TDEasterby) *neat: s.i.s: hung lft through: hdwy to chse ldrs 1/2-way: sn rdn along and wknd* **16/1**
**7** 5 **Gypsy Fair** 2-8-8 KDarley 1 31
(TDBarron) *cmpt: cl up: rdn along 1/2-way: wknd wl over 1f out* **15/2**[3]
**8** 1/2 **Lucy Parkes** 2-8-8 WSupple 4 29
(EJAlston) *cmpt: unf: in tch: pushed along 1/2-way: sn outpcd* **16/1**

64.31 secs (4.41) **Going Correction** +0.75s/f (Yiel) **8 Ran SP% 112.5**
Speed ratings: **94,88,88,85,83 82,74,73**CSF £48.55 TOTE £1.60: £1.02, £9.50, £1.90; EX 59.30.
**Owner** Mrs M S Teversham **Bred** Mrs M S Teversham **Trained** Sigwells, Somerset

**FOCUS**
A modest juvenile event but an easy winner in a race which her trainer has farmed in recent years

**NOTEBOOK**
**Lady Filly**, easily the paddock pick, made this look pretty straightfoward - her trainer's third win in succession in this event. Six furlongs will not be a problem.
**World At My Feet**, a March foal, is a close-coupled, narrow type. Soon towards the rear, she switced widest of all before staying on to snatch second spot on the line.
**I'm Aimee**, who did not impress at all beforehand, may be best suited by the Polytrack.
**Lisa Mona Lisa(IRE)**, who gave her rider problems going to the start, had her limitations fully exposed.
**Lady Erica**, taken quietly to post, found this better company much too tough. A seller or claimer looks more her mark.
**Mimi Mouse**, a March foal, is a smallish, close-coupled filly. She showed very little on this debut run.

## 1450 HYGICARE MAIDEN STKS 1m 4f
**3:05** (3:06) (D) 3-Y-0 **£5,408** (£1,664; £832; £416) **Stalls** Low

Form RPR
0-4 **1** **Obay**[11] 1271 3-9-0 WSupple 4 75
(EALDunlop) *mde all: rdn clr over 3f out: styd on wl: unchal* **2/1**[2]

0- **2** *11* **Bollin Annabel**[202] [5218] 3-8-6 .......... DAllan(3) 5 53
(TDEasterby) *hld up: hdwy over 3f out: rdn and edgd lft 2f out: styd on fnl f: no ch w wnr* **16/1**[3]

63-2 **3** *8* **Ganymede**[15] [1224] 3-9-0 80 .......... IMongan 6 46
(MLWBell) *trckd ldrs: hdwy to chse wnr 5f out: rdn long over 3f out sn btn* **4/7**[1]

0-0 **4** *9* **Sir Bond (IRE)**[21] [1116] 3-9-0 .......... FLynch 1 33
(BSmart) *lengthy: unf: wnt lft s: a rr* **50/1**

00- **5** *16* **Over The Years (USA)**[144] [6059] 3-9-0 .......... DaleGibson 2 9
(TPTate) *rangy: unf: chsd wnr: rdn along over 4f out and sn wknd* **66/1**

55 **6** *11* **Harry Lad**[42] [969] 3-9-0 .......... RHavlin 3 —
(PDEvans) *chsd ldrs: pushed along 1/2-way: wknd over 4f out* **40/1**

2m 48.7s (13.50) **Going Correction** +0.95s/f (Soft) **6** Ran SP% **108.8**
Speed ratings: **93,85,80,74,63 56**CSF £25.60 TOTE £3.00: £1.40, £4.00; EX 35.30.
**Owner** Abdulla Buhaleeba **Bred** W S Farish And E J Hudson Jr Irrevocable Trust **Trained** Newmarket, Suffolk

**FOCUS**
A pedestrian winning time for the grade, the favourite was below form and the winner probably beat little.

**NOTEBOOK**
**Obay** has a round action and seemed suited by the rain-soaked ground. He had it won before the home turn and would have scored by double the official margin but for being eased right up.
**Bollin Annabel**, who had just one backend outing at two, was on her toes beforehand. She stayed on to finish clear second best and looks a real stayer.
**Ganymede**, a narrow type, is a poor walker. Sent in pursuit of the winner going into the final turn, he was soon flat out and floundering. His rider reported that he was unsuited by the soft ground. *Official explanation: jockey said colt was unsuited by the ground*
**Sir Bond(IRE)** has now been well beaten on all his three starts.
**Over The Years(USA)**, a big type, looks green and slow.
**Harry Lad** had finished well beaten in two starts on the All-Weather.

## 1451 CARPENTERS ARMS FELIXKIRK STKS (H'CAP) 1m
**3:35** (3:36) (E) (0-75,75) 3-Y-0+ **£3,692** (£1,136; £568; £284) **Stalls** Low

Form RPR

0030 **1** **Harry Potter (GER)**[13] [1247] 5-9-6 67 .......... (v) DarrenWilliams 5 76
(KRBurke) *trckd ldr: hdwy 2f out: rdn over 1f out: drvn and edgd lft ins last: styd on to ld nr line* **33/1**

-000 **2** *nk* **Hoh's Back**[14] [1233] 5-8-10 60 .......... (p) LisaJones(3) 7 68
(PaulJohnson) *cl up: led wl over 2f out: rdn and edgd rt over 1f out: sn drvn: hdd and no ex nr line* **33/1**

00-2 **3** *1 ½* **Top Dirham**[13] [1247] 6-9-10 71 .......... DaleGibson 2 76
(MWEasterby) *tra cked ldrs: hdwy over 2f out: rdn to chal over 1f out and ev ch tld riven and one pce ins last* **10/3**[1]

30-0 **4** *3* **Jakeal (IRE)**[23] [1098] 5-8-10 57 .......... MTebbutt 13 56
(RMWhitaker) *swtg: chsd ldrs: rdn over 2f out: drvn and one pce appr last* **40/1**

4232 **5** *nk* **Sarraaf (IRE)**[5] [1345] 8-9-10 71 .......... NCallan 18 69
(ISemple) *stdd and swtchd lft s: hdwy on inner over 3f out: swtchd rt and rdn wl over 1f out: kpt on ins last* **8/1**

14-6 **6** *1 ¼* **Distant Country (USA)**[16] [1199] 5-10-0 75 .......... JFEgan 8 70
(MrsJRRamsden) *in tch: hdwy over 2f out: rdn to chse ldrs wl over 1f out: wknd ent last* **11/2**[3]

0-06 **7** *¾* **Bailieborough (IRE)**[4] [1358] 5-9-1 69 .......... LTreadwell(7) 3 63
(DNicholls) *in tch: effrt over 2f out: sn rdn and no imp* **16/1**

05-0 **8** *1* **Cryfield**[22] [1109] 7-9-1 62 .......... KimTinkler 10 54
(NTinkler) *towards rr: hdwy over 2f out: kpt on ins last: nrst fin* **20/1**

-602 **9** *3 ½* **Captain Darling (IRE)**[11] [1265] 4-9-0 61 .......... (p) EAhern 14 45
(RMHCowell) *midfield: gd hdwy on outer 3f out: rdn and ev ch over 1f out: sn wknd* **15/2**

1-00 **10** *2 ½* **Super Song**[11] [1275] 4-9-12 73 .......... (t) RHavlin 12 52
(PDEvans) *in tch: pushed along and sltly outpcd over 2f out: sn rdn and no imp* **50/1**

00-0 **11** *3* **Border Artist**[18] [1175] 5-9-0 61 .......... ANicholls 15 34
(DNicholls) *bit bkwd: n.d* **25/1**

0-40 **12** *½* **Semper Paratus (USA)**[67] [719] 5-8-9 56 .......... (b) MFenton 11 28
(VSmith) *bhd: hdwy on wd outside over 2f out: sn rdn and wknd wl over 1f out* **33/1**

40-0 **13** *hd* **Rocky Reppin**[16] [1213] 4-8-10 57 .......... (b) JEdmunds 4 28
(JBalding) *chsd ldrs: rdn along over 2f out: grad wknd* **50/1**

0-30 **14** *5* **Creskeld (IRE)**[13] [1247] 5-9-11 72 .......... FLynch 9 33
(BSmart) *towards rr: rdn along 1/2-way: nvr a factor* **12/1**

126- **15** *3* **Newcorp Lad**[259] [3760] 4-9-12 73 .......... WSupple 6 27
(MrsGSRees) *bit bkwd: mde most tl rdn along and hdd wl over 2f out: grad wknd* **33/1**

1022 **16** *½* **Penwell Hill (USA)**[62] [775] 5-8-10 57 .......... KDarley 1 10
(TDBarron) *cl up: disp ld over 4f out: rdn along over 3f out and sn wknd* **9/2**[2]

6-03 **17** *5* **High Cane (USA)**[18] [1174] 4-9-2 63 .......... KDalgleish 17 6
(MDHammond) *stdd s: a rr* **20/1**

1m 46.52s (6.82) **Going Correction** +0.95s/f (Soft) **17** Ran SP% **124.6**
Speed ratings: **103,102,101,98,97 96,95,94,91,88 85,85,85,80,77 76,71**CSF £847.01 CT £4555.35 TOTE £38.10: £6.00, £6.70, £1.50, £6.90; EX 626.80.
**Owner** F Jeffers **Bred** Wilh Jackson **Trained** Middleham Moor, N Yorks
■ Stewards Enquiry : Darren Williams one-day ban: careless riding (Apr 25)

**FOCUS**
A modest handicap but run in a fair time for the grade and the form looks sound.

**NOTEBOOK**
**Harry Potter(GER)**, who did not shine on the All-Weather, came off a straight line but in the end did just enough.
**Hoh's Back**, out of sorts on the All-Weather, only just missed out.
**Top Dirham** looked a real danger at one stage but in this ground could not raise his game. Other opportunities will come his way on better ground.
**Jakeal(IRE)**, very warm beforehand, finds this trip streching his stamina to the very limit.
**Sarraaf(IRE)** was having his third race in just nine days and had the worst of the draw here.
**Distant Country(USA)**, whose Catterick performance has come under scrutiny, had the cheekpieces left off and the ground had turned against him.
**Creskeld(IRE)** hit his head on the stalls and on this ground never figured. *Official explanation: jockey said gelding hit its head on the stalls*

## 1452 SINDERBY STKS (H'CAP) 7f
**4:10** (4:10) (E) (0-75,77) 3-Y-0+ **£3,750** (£1,154; £577; £288) **Stalls** Low

Form RPR

26-0 **1** **Cotosol**[20] [1129] 3-9-1 75 .......... WSupple 12 82
(BAMcmahon) *lw: chsd ldrs: hdwy 2f out: rdn wl over 1f out: styd on u.p ins last to ld nr fin* **11/2**[2]

046- **2** *¾* **Efidium**[212] [5002] 6-8-11 65 .......... SuzanneFrance(7) 3 70
(NBycroft) *keen: hld up and bhd on inner: swtchd wd and gd hdwy over 2f out: styd on wl fnl f* **14/1**

02-0 **3** *shd* **Lord Of The East**[11] [1265] 5-8-11 65 .......... LTreadwell(7) 16 70
(DNicholls) *set str pce: rdn along over 2f out: drvn ins last: wknd last 100 yds: hdd nr fin* **20/1**

3111 **4** *shd* **Up Tempo (IRE)**[4] [1358] 6-10-2 77 6ex .......... (b) NCallan 14 82
(KARyan) *bhd: hdwy 2f out: sn rdn and styd on wl fnl f* **5/1**[1]

24-0 **5** *1* **Jacaranda (IRE)**[15] [1225] 4-9-9 70 .......... EAhern 8 72
(MrsALMKing) *chsd ldrs: rdn 2f out: kpt on appr last* **11/1**

50-0 **6** *2 ½* **Acomb**[16] [1199] 4-8-12 64 .......... PMulrennan(5) 4 60
(MWEasterby) *chsd ldr: rdn along 3f out: wkndfnl 2f* **11/2**[2]

56-0 **7** *2 ½* **Colemanstown**[13] [1246] 4-9-6 72 .......... TEaves(5) 6 62
(BEllison) *in tch: effrt 3f out: rdn and no imp fnl 2f* **9/1**

450- **8** *3* **Bundy**[177] [5702] 8-9-5 66 .......... PHanagan 9 48
(MDods) *a rr* **10/1**

0-06 **9** *1 ½* **Pride Of Kinloch**[80] [613] 4-9-1 65 .......... THamilton(3) 1 43
(JHetherton) *chsd ldrs: rdn along over 2f out: sn wknd* **25/1**

30-0 **10** *¾* **Sir Don (IRE)**[16] [1199] 5-9-5 66 .......... (v) ANicholls 11 42
(DNicholls) *chsd ldng pair: rdn over 2f out: sn wknd* **13/2**[3]

00-0 **11** *2 ½* **Pays D'Amour (IRE)**[31] [1027] 7-9-4 65 .......... AlexGreaves 13 35
(DNicholls) *bit bkwd: a rr* **12/1**

000- **12** *22* **Wahoo Sam (USA)**[265] [3611] 4-9-2 70 .......... (b[1]) PMakin(7) 15 —
(TDBarron) *s.i.s: a bhd* **16/1**

1m 32.51s (5.41) **Going Correction** +0.95s/f (Soft)
**WFA** 3 from 4yo+ 13lb **12** Ran SP% **117.0**
Speed ratings: **107,106,106,105,104 101,99,95,93,93 90,65**CSF £79.11 CT £1455.43 TOTE £7.10: £2.30, £3.80, £5.00; EX 106.20.
**Owner** J P Hames, G Pickering, RJH Limited **Bred** R And Mrs S J Turner **Trained** Hopwas, Staffs

**FOCUS**
A fair handicap and a decent winning time. The winner is improving and the form looks sound.

**NOTEBOOK**
**Cotosol**, a three-year-old taking on his elders, looked really well and was skilfully handled to put his head in front where it matters most.
**Efidium**, who has struck up a good understanding with his girl rider, pulled like a train. Making his way to the outside, he finished with quite a flourish. The partnership needs everything to fall just right.
**Lord Of The East**, taken to post early, had a stable attendant with him at the start. Worst drawn, he flew out of the stalls but, after looking likely to hold on, was reeled in near the line. The sharper the track the better with him.
**Up Tempo(IRE)**, winner of four of his last five starts, tried to come from off what was strong pace. He stayed on under his big weight but was never quite going to pull it off.
**Jacaranda(IRE)**, having his second outing for his new yard, likes to dominate and prefers much better ground.
**Acomb**, a keen type, ran as if still needing the outing. A mile suits him better.
**Colemanstown**, still backward in his coat, ran a lot better than on his return at Newcastle.

## 1453 FEVERSHAM ARMS MEDIAN AUCTION MAIDEN STKS 6f
**4:40** (4:40) (E) 3-4-Y-0 **£3,682** (£1,133; £566; £283) **Stalls** High

Form RPR

340- **1** **Commando Scott (IRE)**[195] [5371] 3-8-13 80 .......... FLynch 12 72
(ABerry) *lw: led to 1/2-way: cl up: swtchd lft over 1f out: qckng to ld ent last: rdn and hung rt: drvn and edgd lft: kpt on* **7/1**[3]

**2** *nk* **Catherine Wheel** 3-8-8 .......... EAhern 13 66
(JRFanshawe) *w'like: rangy: scope: dwlt: sn trcking ldrs gng wl: hdwy whn nt clr run and squeezed through over 1f out: rdn and hung lft* **10/3**[2]

**3** *3* **Mister Regent** 3-8-13 .......... NCallan 4 62
(KARyan) *leggy: unf: in tch: pushed along and nt clr run over 1f out: swtchd rt ins last: sn rdn and styd on wl nr fin* **50/1**

000- **4** *½* **Trojan Flight**[260] [3728] 3-8-13 .......... JFEgan 7 61
(MrsJRRamsden) *chsd ldrs: swtchd lft: nt clr run and hmpd over 1f out: rdn and kpt on ins last* **25/1**

4663 **5** *1 ¼* **Amanda's Lad (IRE)**[16] [1200] 4-9-10 49 .......... LVickers 14 57
(MCChapman) *cl up: rdn and hung lft 2f out and over 1f out: sn drvn and wknd ins last* **33/1**

0-0 **6** *shd* **Compton Micky**[21] [1111] 3-8-13 .......... JEdmunds 3 57
(JBalding) *chsd ldrs on out: rdn along whn hmpd over 1f out: one pce after* **100/1**

05-0 **7** *shd* **Flashing Blade**[20] [1126] 4-9-5 85 .......... WSupple 11 51
(BAMcmahon) *prom: hdwy to dispute ld 2f out: ev ch whn rdn and bmpd over 1f out: sn wknd* **5/2**[1]

000- **8** *4* **Raysoot (IRE)**[175] [5735] 3-8-13 .......... PMcCabe 10 44
(ACStewart) *bit bkwd: outpcd and bhd tl styd on fnl 2f* **11/1**

006- **9** *1 ½* **Stavros (IRE)**[182] [5625] 4-9-10 46 .......... DRMcCabe 1 40
(JSWainwright) *cl up: led 1/2-way: rdn: hmpd and wandered over 1f out: sn wknd* **20/1**

**10** *1 ¼* **Ragazzi (IRE)** 3-8-13 .......... KDarley 6 36
(TDBarron) *rangy: unf: scope: chsd ldrs on outer: rdn along 2f out: grad wknd* **16/1**

5 **11** *3* **Bollin Archie**[20] [1127] 3-8-13 .......... KDalgleish 8 27
(TDEasterby) *outpcd and bhd fr 1/2-way* **16/1**

2- **12** *5* **Gasparini (IRE)**[334] [1692] 3-8-10 .......... DAllan(3) 5 12
(TDEasterby) *midfield: oushed along 1/2-way: n.d* **18/1**

000- **13** *6* **Dame Nova (IRE)**[187] [5510] 3-8-1 .......... DWakenshaw(7) 9 —
(PCHaslam) *sn outpcd and bhd* **66/1**

0-2 **14** *3* **Volaticus (IRE)**[20] [1127] 3-8-13 .......... ANicholls 2 —
(DNicholls) *chsd ldrs: hdwy on outer and ch 2f out: sn rdn: hung lft and wknd* **9/1**

1m 18.78s (6.28) **Going Correction** +0.75s/f (Yiel)
**WFA** 3 from 4yo 11lb **14** Ran SP% **115.5**
Speed ratings: **88,87,83,82,81 81,81,75,73,72 68,61,53,49**CSF £27.48 TOTE £8.10: £2.50, £1.60, £14.70; EX 26.50.
**Owner** Mrs Ann Morris **Bred** Noel Finegan **Trained** Cockerham, Lancs

**FOCUS**
A very poor winning time for a race of its class and the form horses on paper ran below their best.

**NOTEBOOK**
**Commando Scott(IRE)**, who showed a fair level of ability at two, looked in really good trim. After getting into a bumping match he did just enough, and the pair finished clear.
**Catherine Wheel ◆**, bred exclusively for speed, is a nice type with size and scope. After missing a beat at the start she squeezed through to take it up hard on the steel, but when shaken up she edged left and just missed out. This will have taught her plenty and she will have no trouble going one better.
**Mister Regent**, on the leg and narrow, was keen to post. After an unhappy passage he stayed on bang on the inside to snatch third spot near the line. A seventh furlong will be in his favour.
**Trojan Flight**, who had three outings at two, is a robust type who was fitted with a cross noseband. He met plenty of trouble, and the way he was keeping on at the line suggests a mile will suit in handicap company.

**Amanda's Lad(IRE)** was trying to break his duck at the 42nd attempt.
**Compton Micky**, having his third outing, is now qualified to ply his trade in low-grade handicaps.
**Flashing Blade**, not disgraced in much stronger company at Doncaster, was already feeling the strain when collecting a bump. She will struggle in handicap company if her rating remains in the mid-80s.
**Raysoot(IRE)**, who had three outings at two, is a grand type but he looks to like his food. Still green to post, he stayed on in his own time and ought to be capable of a fair bit better in handicap company over further.

## 1454 HAMBLETON CLASSIFIED STKS 5f
**5:10** (5:10) (D) 3-Y-0+ **£5,460** (£1,680; £840; £420) **Stalls** High

Form RPR
-112 **1** **Maktavish**[5] [1343] 5-9-4 81 ... (p) PHanagan 1 93
(ISemple) *qckly away and swtchd rt to stands rail: mde all: rdn over 1f out and kpt on wl* **3/1**[1]
630- **2** *1* **Hiccups**[202] [5216] 4-9-3 80 ... (p) JFEgan 6 89
(MrsJRRamsden) *in tch: hdwy 2f out: sn rdn: kpt on fnl f* **14/1**
1121 **3** *hd* **Forever Phoenix**[16] [1205] 4-9-3 83 ... EAhern 9 88
(RMHCowell) *hld up: swtchd wd and hdwy 2f out: sn rdn and kpt on* **7/2**[2]
23-0 **4** *2 1/2* **Blackheath (IRE)**[22] [1106] 8-9-7 84 ... AlexGreaves 11 83
(DNicholls) *bit bkwd: chsd ldrs: rdn along 2f out: kpt on same pce* **11/2**
01-0 **5** *3/4* **Willhewiz**[21] [1113] 4-9-5 85 ... (v) TPQueally(3) 12 81
(CADwyer) *chsd wnr: rdn along 2f out: grad wknd* **5/1**[3]
40-6 **6** *shd* **Pax**[21] [1113] 7-8-11 81 ... LTreadwell(7) 7 77
(DNicholls) *blindfold removed late whn stalls opened and wnt lft s: bhd tl styd on fnl 2f: nrst fin* **8/1**
000- **7** *12* **John O'Groats (IRE)**[308] [2341] 6-9-4 81 ... SWKelly 10 35
(MDods) *in tch: rdn along 1/2-way: sn outpcd and eased* **16/1**
30-0 **8** *9* **Rectangle (IRE)**[21] [1113] 4-9-3 80 ... ANicholls 2 3
(DNicholls) *chsd ldrs on outer: rdn along 1/2-way: sn wknd* **16/1**
630- **9** *3/4* **Tommy Smith**[217] [4867] 6-9-3 77 ... (b) RWinston 5 —
(JSWainwright) *bit bkwd: cl up: rdn 1/2-way: sn wknd* **16/1**

62.70 secs (2.80) **Going Correction** +0.75s/f (Yiel) **9 Ran SP% 114.7**
Speed ratings: **107,105,105,101,99 99,80,66,64**CSF £45.63 TOTE £3.60: £1.60, £2.80, £1.80; EX 76.40 Place 6 £177.38, Place 5 £131.02.
**Owner** D G Savala **Bred** V Robin Lawson **Trained** Carluke, S Lanarks
■ Stewards Enquiry : P Hanagan 15-day ban (takes into account previous offences; three days deferred): failed to keep straight from stalls (May 14-25)

**FOCUS**
A decent classified sprint run at a good pace and the form looks solid.

**NOTEBOOK**
**Maktavish**, who hangs right, had the worst possible draw. He was across to the rails in no time at all and never really looked like being overhauled. His rider's enterprise will not go down with the magistrates.
**Hiccups**, backward in his coat, had a stable attendant with him at the stalls. He kept on really well and is better suited by either a stiffer track or six furlongs.
**Forever Phoenix**, who has won at up to a mile on the All-Weather, travelled hard on the steel and stuck on in willing fashion. Her four wins have been on the artificial surfaces but she can surely find an opening on turf.
**Blackheath(IRE)** still looked to be carrying condition, but he is 8lb higher than his last success in handicap company.
**Willhewiz** had the plum draw but he could not dominate and prefers better ground in any case.
**Pax** still had the hood on when the stalls opened and ran well in the circumstances.
**John O'Groats(IRE)** *Official explanation: jockey said gelding was unsuited by the ground*
T/Plt: £522.60 to a £1 stake. Pool: £32,722.20. 45.70 winning tickets. T/Qpdt: £104.00 to a £1 stake. Pool: £3,220.10. 22.90 winning tickets. JR

# 1436 NEWBURY (L-H)
Saturday, April 17

**OFFICIAL GOING: Good (good to soft in places)**
Wind: Mod, hlf against Weather: Fine

## 1455 DUBAI IRISH VILLAGE STKS (REGISTERED AS THE JOHN PORTER STAKES) (GROUP 3) 1m 4f 5y
**1:40** (1:40) (A) 4-Y-0+ **£29,000** (£11,000; £5,500; £2,500) **Stalls** Low

Form RPR
513- **1** **Dubai Success**[175] [5752] 4-8-11 110 ... MHills 3 117
(BWHills) *h.d.w: lw: hld up in tch: stdy hdwy to trck ldr 2f out: rdn to chal ins fnl f: led fnl 125yds: hld on all out* **10/1**[3]
123- **2** *shd* **Gamut (IRE)**[161] [5951] 5-8-12 117 ... (t) KFallon 15 117
(SirMichaelStoute) *lw: trckd ldrs: led ins fnl 3f: rdn and styd on fr over 1f out: hdd fnl 125yds: rallied gamely: jst failed* **7/2**[1]
110- **3** *3* **Imperial Dancer**[125] [6185] 6-9-5 117 ... TEDurcan 4 119
(MRChannon) *hld up in rr: nt clr run 3f out: hdwy and hmpd appr fnl 2f: rdn and r.o to chse ldrs fnl f: no imp* **11/1**
21- **4** *1/2* **Sayadaw (FR)**[320] [2051] 4-8-11 ... (t) WRyan 6 111
(HRACecil) *h.d.w: bit bkwd: hld up in rr: hdwy on outside fr 3f out: hung lft to far rail over 1f out: styd on but nt pce of ldrs* **20/1**
60-5 **5** *2 1/2* **Pugin (IRE)**[28] [1062] 6-8-12 105 ... JPMurtagh 13 107
(DRLoder) *lw: bhd: rdn hung lft and carried hd high ins fnl 3f: styd on u.p fr over 1f out: nt rch ldrs* **10/1**[3]
243- **6** *2* **Salsalino**[241] [4300] 4-8-11 107 ... ACulhane 10 104
(AKing) *bhd: rdn along 4f out: styd on fnl 2f: nt rch ldrs* **10/1**[3]
452- **7** *3/4* **The Whistling Teal**[161] [5951] 8-8-12 107 ... DHolland 5 103
(GWragg) *hld up in rr: hdwy on oustide fr over 2f out: nt rch ldrs* **11/1**
540- **8** *1* **Let Me Try Again (IRE)**[217] [4880] 4-8-11 107 ... KDarley 7 101
(TGMills) *mid-div: rdn and hdwy over 2f out: styd on same pce fnl f* **25/1**
1/-4 **9** *2* **Forest Magic (IRE)**[21] [1124] 4-8-11 100 ... PRobinson 11 98
(PWD'Arcy) *in tch: rdn fr 4f out: wknd ins fnl 2f* **40/1**
-020 **10** *3* **Dutch Gold (USA)**[42] [976] 4-8-11 ... LDettori 9 93
(CEBrittain) *in tch: rdn over 3f out: wknd 2f out* **16/1**
442- **11** *2* **Bandari (IRE)**[284] [3075] 5-8-12 114 ... RHills 17 90
(MJohnston) *sn led: hdd ins fnl 3f: wknd 2f out* **11/2**[2]
114- **12** *2 1/2* **Barolo**[280] [3223] 5-8-12 98 ... MartinDwyer 12 86
(PWHarris) *chsd ldrs: wnt 2nd 7f out to 5f out: wknd over 2f out* **33/1**
0342 **13** *1 1/4* **Anani (USA)**[28] [1062] 4-8-11 106 ... EAhern 16 84
(EALDunlop) *in tch: rdn to chse ldrs and hung lft over 2f out: sn wknd* **20/1**
015- **14** *nk* **Distinction (IRE)**[202] [5253] 5-8-12 107 ... SDrowne 2 84
(SirMichaelStoute) *chsd ldrs: rdn 3f out: wknd over 2f out* **25/1**
541/ **15** *3 1/2* **Jelani (IRE)**[643] [2994] 5-8-12 ... FLynch 14 78
(AndrewTurnell) *bit bkwd: chsd ldrs: rdn to chal 3f out: wknd qckly over 2f out* **25/1**
10-3 **16** *nk* **Hilbre Island**[17] [1212] 4-8-11 111 ... RHughes 8 78
(BJMeehan) *sn in tch: chsd ldrs: rdn and edgd lft over 2f out: wknd qckly* **20/1**
12-0 **17** *13* **Perfect Storm**[21] [1124] 5-8-12 92 ... SSanders 1 57
(MBlanshard) *a bhd* **66/1**

2m 35.54s (-0.75) **Going Correction** +0.30s/f (Good)
**WFA** 4 from 5yo+ 1lb **17 Ran SP% 120.1**
Speed ratings: **114,113,111,111,109 108,108,107,106,104 102,101,100,100,97 97,88**CSF £37.70 TOTE £11.50: £3.40, £2.00, £3.70; EX 39.40.
**Owner** Maktoum Al Maktoum **Bred** Watership Down Stud **Trained** Lambourn, Berks
■ Stewards Enquiry : R Hills three-day ban: careless riding (Apr 28-30)

**FOCUS**
A well contested renewal run at a sound pace. Improved form from the winner and strong form overall.

**NOTEBOOK**
**Dubai Success**, who did not run in his juvenile season, has done well physically from three to four. Travelling nicely, he edged ahead of the favourite in the last half-furlong after a fine tussle but would have been pegged back with a little further to go.
**Gamut(IRE)** made a winning return on this course on each of the last two seasons and just failed to repeat the trick. Rallying in brave style after being headed inside the last half-furlong, he was back in front a stride after the line. This trip looks a minimum for him now and he will appreciate a faster surface.
**Imperial Dancer** carried a Group One penalty for his success in the Premio Roma in the autumn, and it just seemed to anchor him in the closing stages. Having said that, he would have finished closer to the leading pair had the breaks come for him at the right time, and this was a highly encouraging return to action. *Official explanation: jockey said horse suffered interference in running*
**Sayadaw(FR)** ran a cracker on only his third start, having been off the track since landing a Leicester maiden last June. He hung to his right that day, and went left on this occasion after having made up a lot of ground from the rear to reach third place with a furlong to run.
**Pugin(IRE)**, returning to the turf, stayed on down the outer in the last furlong and a half, but his head carriage hinted that he was not putting in maximum effort. He is able but may remain hard to win with.
**Salsalino** , who missed the St Leger with a shoulder injury, has been gelded since his last run when finishing third in the Ebor. After finding himself outpaced, he stayed on without getting to the leaders.
**The Whistling Teal**, whose 2003 campaign did not begin until September, made a promising return to action but lack of race fitness told in the final furlong.
**Bandari(IRE)**, who has reportedly had a chip removed from a fetlock, was warm in the preliminaries. After setting a strong pace, he weakened disappointingly and has yet to recapture his three-year-old form.
**Jelani(IRE)** should improve with this run under his belt, having been out of action since winning a Haydock listed race in the summer of 2002.

## 1456 STANJAMESUK.COM SPRING CUP H'CAP 1m (S)
**2:15** (2:16) (B) (0-105,105) 4-Y-0+ **£23,200** (£8,800; £4,400; £2,000) **Stalls** Centre

Form RPR
04-0 **1** **El Coto**[21] [1125] 4-9-3 **94** ... SSanders 26 110
(BAMcmahon) *lw: mid-div on rail: rdn and hdwy 2f out: led 1f out: hung lft: rdn clr* **20/1**
-000 **2** *1 3/4* **Serieux**[7] [1328] 5-8-11 **88** ... KDarley 25 100
(MrsAJPerrett) *lw: chsd ldrs: nt clr run over 2f out: led briefly over 1f out: nt pce of wnr fnl f* **25/1**
512- **3** *1 1/4* **King's County (IRE)**[168] [5873] 6-9-4 **95** ... DHolland 8 104+
(LMCumani) *in tch: effrt and ev ch 2f out: one pce appr fnl f* **14/1**
21-5 **4** *nk* **Alkaadhem**[21] [1125] 4-9-9 **100** ... RHills 24 108+
(MPTregoning) *lw: hld up in midfield: effrt and nt clr run over 1f out: r.o fnl f* **7/4**[1]
00-0 **5** *2* **Norton (IRE)**[21] [1125] 7-9-2 **96** ... RMiles(3) 19 100
(TGMills) *w ldrs: led 4f out tl over 1f out: no ex* **33/1**
400- **6** *nk* **Star Sensation (IRE)**[190] [5469] 4-8-9 **86** ... RLMoore 18 89
(PWHarris) *hld up in rr: rdn and hdwy over 1f out: nt rch ldrs* **33/1**
30-1 **7** *3/4* **Uhoomagoo**[51] [900] 6-8-5 **82** ... (b) PHanagan 1 83
(KARyan) *bhd: hdwy and nt clr run over 1f out: nrst fin* **33/1**
10-0 **8** *shd* **Desert Opal**[21] [1125] 4-9-4 **95** ... RHughes 10 96
(JHMGosden) *towards rr: hdwy 3f out: hrd rdn over 1f out: one pce* **10/1**[2]
335- **9** *3/4* **Fisio Therapy**[279] [3242] 4-8-6 **83** ... JFanning 23 82
(MJohnston) *w ldrs tl wknd over 1f out* **25/1**
022- **10** *hd* **Impeller (IRE)**[172] [5814] 5-8-10 **87** ... MartinDwyer 22 86
(WRMuir) *towards rr: hdwy in midfield whn bdly hmpd over 1f out: nt rcvr* **33/1**
1-01 **11** *1/2* **Thihn (IRE)**[4] [1385] 9-9-4 **95** 5ex ... ADaly 2 93
(JLSpearing) *hld up in rr: gd hdwy 2f out: no ex over 1f out* **14/1**
0-56 **12** *3/4* **Golden Chalice (IRE)**[91] [556] 5-8-13 **90** ... KFallon 4 86
(AMBalding) *hld up in midfield: rdn and no hdwy fnl 2f* **20/1**
204- **13** *nk* **Finished Article (IRE)**[168] [5873] 7-8-13 **90** ... DaneO'Neill 6 85
(DRCElsworth) *hld up and bhd: shkn up 2f out: nvr in chalng position: bttr for r* **33/1**
141- **14** *shd* **Spanish Don**[175] [5756] 6-8-6 **86** ... LPKeniry(3) 9 81
(DRCElsworth) *mid-div: effrt over 2f out: no imp* **16/1**
0-00 **15** *shd* **Mystic Man (FR)**[35] [1009] 6-8-10 **87** ... PFessey 11 82
(KARyan) *towards rr: rdn over 2f out: n.d* **33/1**
-034 **16** *shd* **Digital**[14] [1246] 7-9-0 **91** ... TEDurcan 21 86
(MRChannon) *hld up in rr: rdn and styd on fnl 2f: nt trble ldrs* **25/1**
1110 **17** *1 3/4* **Vortex**[28] [1062] 5-9-6 **97** ... (t) MFenton 17 88
(MissGayKelleway) *b.hind: hld up towards rr: effrt 2f out: styng on in midfield whn hmpd 1f out: nt rcvr* **33/1**
00-5 **18** *3/4* **Shot To Fame (USA)**[11] [1284] 5-9-1 **92** ... SDrowne 3 81
(PWHarris) *mid-div: rdn and no imp fnl 2f* **33/1**
110- **19** *1 3/4* **Chinkara**[282] [3138] 4-9-1 **92** ... LDettori 14 77
(BJMeehan) *chsd ldrs: effrt over 2f out: wknd over 1f out* **14/1**
0 **20** *1 3/4* **Huxley (IRE)**[11] [1284] 5-8-6 **83** ... DRMcCabe 16 64
(MGQuinlan) *s.s: bhd: hmpd wl over 1f out: nvr nr ldrs* **100/1**
5-21 **21** *1 3/4* **St Petersburg**[11] [1284] 4-9-2 **93** ... PRobinson 12 70
(MHTompkins) *swtg: prom over 6f* **12/1**[3]
50-0 **22** *hd* **Craiova (IRE)**[21] [1125] 5-8-13 **90** ... (p) MHills 7 66
(BWHills) *lw: a towards rr* **25/1**
00-6 **23** *1/2* **Jay Gee's Choice**[21] [1125] 4-8-11 **91** ... DCorby(3) 27 66
(MRChannon) *lw: led 4f: wknd 2f out: wl btn whn hmpd over 1f out* **16/1**
600/ **24** *1* **Prizeman (USA)**[1011] [2943] 6-9-4 **95** ... RHavlin 15 68
(GBBalding) *bkwd: mid-div: outpcd over 2f out: steadily lost pl* **100/1**
505- **25** *8* **Iberus (GER)**[29] [2775] 6-8-8 **85** ... IMongan 13 40
(SGollings) *lw: towards rr: plld outside and mod effrt over 2f out: sn wknd* **100/1**
23-0 **26** *4* **Yakimov (USA)**[28] [1065] 5-9-1 **92** ... ACulhane 20 37
(DJWintle) *in tch 5f* **66/1**

0-40 **27** 1 1/4 **Lundy's Lane (IRE)**[23] [1107] 4-10-0 **105**.................................. WSupple 5 48
(CEBrittain) *racd alone in centre early: chsd ldrs 5f* **66/1**

1m 40.99s (0.16) **Going Correction** +0.225s/f (Good) **27** Ran SP% **139.3**
Speed ratings: **108,106,105,104,102 102,101,101,100,100 100,99,99,98,98 98,97,96,94,92 91,90,90,89,81 77,76**CSF £454.69 CT £7136.41 TOTE £25.90: £5.00, £6.30, £3.10, £1.50; EX 288.90 TRIFECTA Not won..
**Owner** R J H Ltd & J P Hames **Bred** J H Widdows **Trained** Hopwas, Staffs

**FOCUS**
The field all raced down the stands' side and this was a rough race with numerous hard-luck stories. A high draw was greatly favoured.

**NOTEBOOK**
**El Coto**, whose owners won this twelve months ago with Mystic Man, was down the field on the wrong side in the Lincoln. Drawn one off the rail, he quickened well to strike the front and, after hanging left, was soon straightened up and scored decisively. Things went his way here.
**Serieux**, favourably drawn and 5lb lower than when reappearing in the Lincoln, briefly showed ahead before the winner pounced. He could be worth another chance over ten furlongs.
**King's County(IRE)** ran an excellent race from the wrong half of the draw and there is surely a good handicap in him.
**Alkaadhem**, the moral winner of the Lincoln, again had the fates conspire against him. Sent off the shortest priced favourite in Spring Cup history, he had a favourably high draw but was unable to take advantage and found himself locked away in midfield. Coming off the rail two furlongs out but finding his path blocked, he was then angled in again to get a run, by which time it was too late, although he did run on nicely. An unlucky loser, he will step up to ten furlongs in Listed grade now.
**Norton(IRE)**, who has been edging down the weights, was always in the front rank from a decent draw and had no excuses.
**Star Sensation(IRE)**, a pound above her last winning mark, had ground conditions to suit and ran a good race, especially given that her hold-up tactics were not ideal the way this race was run.
**Uhoomagoo** won off a mark 15lb lower on Fibresand in February but is not getting any help from the handicapper on turf. He was involved in the scrimmaging before running on takingly inside the last.
**Desert Opal** was unfavourably drawn, as he had been in the Lincoln, and this was a satisfactory effort in the circumstances.
**Impeller(IRE)** was one of the worst affected by the stacking up in the last quarter-mile and was badly hampered by the favourite. This run can be written off. *Official explanation: jockey said gelding lost its action*
**Finished Article(IRE)** ◆ made a highly pleasing reappearance without ever reaching a challenging position. *Official explanation: jockey said, regarding the running and riding, his orders were to drop in, get cover and come late but he had nowhere to go at the 1f marker and the gaps came too late; trainer confirmed gelding is always ridden in this manner*
**Vortex** was 23lb higher than when last in action on grass, following a fine winter on the sand. The eyeshield dispensed with, he was just beginning his effort when the door closed on him and that was that.
**St Petersburg** *Official explanation: jockey said gelding suffered interference in running*

## 1457 CANTORSPORT.CO.UK H'CAP — 2m
**2:45** (2:47) (C) (0-90,90) 4-Y-O+ **£9,958** (£3,064; £1,532; £766) **Stalls** Low

Form RPR
/512 **1** **Malarkey**[10] [1302] 7-8-8 **70**........................................ SDrowne 4 80
(MrsStefLiddiard) *lw: hld up mid-div: stdy hdwy over 2f out: swtchd rt appr fnl f: led jst ins last: pushed out* **9/1**[3]
143- **2** 2 1/2 **Tomina**[268] [3533] 4-8-9 **75**........................................ DHolland 8 82
(NAGraham) *bhd: nt clr run ins fnl 3f: swtchd rt to outside and hdwy 2f out: hung lft fnl f:tk 2nd cl home:no ch w wnr* **9/1**[3]
6-02 **3** *hd* **King Flyer (IRE)**[17] [1210] 8-9-4 **80**.................................. SWhitworth 16 87
(MissJFeilden) *bhd: rdn and hdwy fr 3f out: styd on wl u.p fr 2f out: chsd wnr inswd last: no imp:ct for 2nd cl home* **14/1**
60-6 **4** 3/4 **San Hernando**[21] [1135] 4-8-7 **73**.................................. DaneO'Neill 2 79
(DRCElsworth) *hld up in rr: hdwy on outside 5f out: drvn to take narrow ld wl over 2f out: hdd jst ins last: one pce* **16/1**
6-03 **5** 3 **Nawow**[17] [1210] 4-8-11 **77**........................................ SSanders 14 80
(PDCundell) *lw: hld up mid-div: 5f out: qcknd to chal wl over 2f out: stl ev ch u.p over 1f out: wknd fnl f* **13/2**[2]
00-0 **6** 1 3/4 **Ravenglass (USA)**[21] [1124] 5-9-7 **83**.................................. RHavlin 11 83
(JGMO'Shea) *chsd ldrs: rdn to chal fr 3f out: stl ev ch ins fnl 2f: wknd ins fnl f* **25/1**
250- **7** 3/4 **Random Quest**[182] [5639] 6-10-0 **90**.................................. RHughes 7 90
(BJLlewellyn) *chsd ldrs: rdn to chal ins fnl 3f tl wl over 1f out: wknd fnl f* **16/1**
25-5 **8** 5 **Sonoma (IRE)**[17] [1210] 4-8-6 **72**.................................. MFenton 10 66
(MLWBell) *trckd ldr tl led over 4f out: hdd wl over 2f out: wknd appr fnl f* **16/1**
0-00 **9** 5 **Riyadh**[9] [1316] 6-9-2 **78**........................................(v) KDalgleish 9 66
(MJohnston) *s.i.s: sn rcvrd and in tch: rdn over 3f out: wknd 2f out* **16/1**
404- **10** *shd* **Promoter**[176] [5730] 4-9-8 **88**........................................ EAhern 18 75
(JNoseda) *bhd: stl plenty to do 3f out: sn pushed along and mod hdwy fnl 2f: nvr a danger* **9/2**[1]
050- **11** 5 **Sparkling Water (USA)**[195] [3810] 5-8-13 **75**.................. JPMurtagh 1 56
(DLWilliams) *mid-div: dropped rr 6f out: n.d after* **50/1**
0222 **12** 2 **Madiba**[43] [973] 5-7-7 **60**........................................ JFMcDonald(5) 13 39
(PHowling) *chsd ldrs: rdn to chal 3f out: wknd qckly 2f out* **16/1**
21-0 **13** 4 **Bid For Fame (USA)**[7] [1329] 7-9-9 **85**.................................. WRyan 17 59
(NTinkler) *lw: bhd: rdn and effrt on outside over 3f out: nvr in contention and sn bhd* **25/1**
06-5 **14** *nk* **Heir To Be**[10] [1302] 5-8-12 **74**........................................ KDarley 3 48
(JLDunlop) *in tch: rdn along 5f out: wknd over 3f out* **9/1**[3]
2-30 **15** 10 **Redspin (IRE)**[23] [1109] 4-8-7 **73**..............................(p) MartinDwyer 6 35
(JSMoore) *lw: reminders 1/2-way: a in rr* **50/1**
-416 **16** 6 **Stolen Song**[20] [734] 4-7-9 **64** oh2.................................. LisaJones(3) 5 19
(MJRyan) *chsd ldrs: rdn 5f out: wknd 3f out* **14/1**
210- **17** 3/4 **Mersey Sound (IRE)**[176] [5730] 6-8-1 **70**.................................. JDWalsh(7) 12 24
(SKirk) *bit bkwd: s.i.s: bhd: rdn and lost tch 5f out* **25/1**
50-0 **18** 17 **Makulu (IRE)**[12] [1272] 4-8-10 **76**..............................(b) LDettori 15 9
(BJMeehan) *led tl hdd over 4f out: wknd 3f out* **20/1**

3m 37.17s (1.74) **Going Correction** +0.30s/f (Good)
**WFA** 4 from 5yo+ 4lb **18** Ran SP% **124.5**
Speed ratings: **107,105,105,105,103 102,102,100,97,97 94,93,91,91,86 83,83,74**CSF £81.32 CT £1146.37 TOTE £6.10: £1.50, £2.80, £2.60, £4.80; EX 75.90.
**Owner** A Liddiard **Bred** M E Wates **Trained** Great Shefford, Berks

**FOCUS**
Quite a competitive handicap and the pace was decent.

**NOTEBOOK**
**Malarkey** ◆ is a fine example of his trainer's skills at rejuvenating other stables cast-offs. Claimed out of a Lingfield seller for £6,000, he has gone from strength to strength since joining Stef Liddiard and this may well have been the hat-trick up had he got a better run when short-head second at Warwick on his previous outing. This was an impressive success and, in form of his life, he will be hard to beat if turned out under a penalty.
**Tomina** offered plenty of promise in a light season last year and confirmed that on this step up to two miles and first run in 268 days. He had to be switched to the outside for a run and did not held Holland by lugging to his left under pressure. Softer ground will surely suit and he looks well up to winning a similar race granted those conditions.
**King Flyer(IRE)** is 5lb higher than when last successful and has never won off a mark this high. He proved unable to reverse recent Nottingham placings with the winner, but this was still a decent enough effort - he will just always be vulnerable to improvers.
**San Hernando** only has a maiden win to his name but this was a promising effort and it will be disappointing if he does not pay his way this season.
**Nawow**, held by the winner and the third at Nottingham recently, proved unable to reverse the form with either of them. He travelled very strongly, but found little when asked.
**Promoter**, racing for the first time in 176 days, was given plenty to do and never threatened the principals. He is better than he showed on this occasion.
**Makulu(IRE)** *Official explanation: jockey said gelding ran too free early on*

## 1458 DUBAI DUTY FREE STKS (REGISTERED AS THE FRED DARLING STAKES) (GROUP 3) — 7f (S)
**3:15** (3:17) (A) 3-Y-O **£29,000** (£11,000; £5,500; £2,500) **Stalls** Centre

Form RPR
312- **1** **Majestic Desert**[198] [5332] 3-9-0 111.................................. KFallon 6 110
(MRChannon) *lw: prom: qcknd to ld 1f out: pushed out* **6/4**[1]
110- **2** 1 **Nyramba**[198] [5332] 3-9-0 109........................................ LDettori 5 107
(JHMGosden) *t.k.h in rr: effrt over 1f out: r.o to take 2nd fnl 50 yds* **6/1**[3]
13- **3** 1 **Nataliya**[252] [3988] 3-9-0 ........................................ SSanders 9 104
(JLDunlop) *bit bkwd: plld hrd early: hld up in rr: hdwy 2f out: pressed wnr ins fnl f: nt qckn* **12/1**
121- **4** 1 1/4 **Spotlight**[168] [5874] 3-9-0 101.................................. JPMurtagh 7 101
(JLDunlop) *led and set stdy pce: qcknd over 2f out: rdn and hdd 1f out: one pce* **10/3**[2]
314- **5** 1 **Ruby Rocket (IRE)**[198] [5332] 3-9-0 105.................................. DHolland 1 99
(HMorrison) *lw: chsd ldrs: effrt over 2f out: no ex 1f out* **12/1**
01- **6** 1/2 **Phantom Wind (USA)**[184] [5587] 3-9-0 .................................. RHughes 8 97
(JHMGosden) *lw: stdd s: sn trcking ldr: rdn and ev ch 1f out: wknd fnl f* **13/2**
126- **7** 3/4 **Unshooda**[196] [5363] 3-9-0 95........................................ RHills 3 95
(BWHills) *t.k.h in rr: swtchd outside and effrt 2f out: no ex over 1f out* **20/1**
105- **8** 11 **Fragrant Star**[259] [3790] 3-9-0 81.................................. TEDurcan 4 67
(CEBrittain) *stdd s: bhd fnl 2f* **66/1**

1m 29.51s (2.29) **Going Correction** +0.225s/f (Good) **8** Ran SP% **112.3**
Speed ratings: **95,93,92,91,90 89,88,76**CSF £10.58 TOTE £2.10: £1.10, £2.30, £2.80; EX 10.60.
**Owner** Jaber Abdullah **Bred** Bloodhorse International Limited **Trained** West Ilsley, Berks

**FOCUS**
A pedestrian winning time for the grade of contest, 2.54 seconds slower than the Greenham. The stalls were in the centre but the runners tacked over to the stands' rail.

**NOTEBOOK**
**Majestic Desert** is more highly regarded by Channon than his Nell Gwyn winner Silca's Gift. Quickening up smartly to go through a gap at the furlong pole, she did it nicely. She has an exemplary attitude and the extra furlong at Newmarket should not pose her any problems.
**Nyramba** found cover in rear before running on strongly, but the winner had flown by the time she got going. This longer trip was not a problem and she will step up to a mile in the French Guineas now, not holding an entry at Newmarket.
**Nataliya** was not fully fit for this seasonal return. Keen early on, she stayed on pleasingly in the latter stages and will benefit from the step up to a mile.
**Spotlight** dictated the pace against the rail but had no answers when the winner went by her at the furlong pole. She won at a mile last season and will appreciate the return to that trip.
**Ruby Rocket(IRE)** was held in the final furlong. She has the build of a sprinter and a pedigree to match.
**Phantom Wind(USA)** was bang there at the furlong pole but soon faded out of the picture. Her trainer reported her to be only 70% fit and she will take her chance at Newmarket.
**Unshooda** again failed to settle satisfactorily but was not disgraced.

## 1459 LANE'S END GREENHAM STKS (GROUP 3) (C&G) — 7f (S)
**3:45** (3:46) (A) 3-Y-O **£29,000** (£11,000; £5,500; £2,500) **Stalls** Centre

Form RPR
1- **1** **Salford City (IRE)**[175] [5757] 3-9-0 .................................. JPMurtagh 11 118+
(DRCElsworth) *gd sort: h.d.w: bit bkwd: hld up in rr: hdwy 2f out: drvn and qcknd to ld wl ins fnl f: readily* **10/3**[2]
20-2 **2** 1 3/4 **Fokine (USA)**[28] [1063] 3-9-0 114.................................. MHills 5 110
(BWHills) *lw: trckd ldrs: led ins fnl 2f: rdn and hdd wl ins last: styd on: nt pce of wnr* **11/2**
41- **3** *shd* **So Will I**[176] [5733] 3-9-0 ........................................ WSupple 9 110
(MPTregoning) *hld up in rr: hdwy over 2f out: drvn to chal and hung lft ins fnl f: kpt on: nt pce of wnr* **14/1**
1- **4** 1/2 **Fort Dignity (USA)**[255] [3904] 3-9-0 .................................. KFallon 10 108
(SirMichaelStoute) *bit bkwd: hld up rr but in tch: rdn and hdwy 2f out: chsd ldrs over 1f out: styd on same pce ins last* **7/1**
11-2 **5** 1 3/4 **Milk It Mick**[14] [1239] 3-9-0 118.................................. DHolland 1 104
(JAOsborne) *t.k.h: hld up rr but in tch: hdwy to chse ldrs ins fnl 2f: rdn appr fnl f: wknd wl ins last* **3/1**[1]
2123 **6** 1 **Bahiano (IRE)**[28] [1063] 3-9-0 95.................................. EAhern 8 101
(CEBrittain) *chsd ldrs: rdn over 2f out: wknd ins fnl f* **25/1**
13- **7** *nk* **Mukafeh (USA)**[220] [4817] 3-9-0 .................................. RHills 2 101
(JLDunlop) *lw: led tl hdd ins fnl 2f: wknd fnl f* **9/2**[3]
11-6 **8** 1 1/2 **Nero's Return (IRE)**[7] [1330] 3-9-0 .................................. KDalgleish 7 97
(MJohnston) *disp 2nd 4f: styd chsng ldrs tl wknd appr fnl f* **33/1**
102- **9** 8 **Jazz Scene (IRE)**[190] [5471] 3-9-0 88.................................. TEDurcan 3 76
(MRChannon) *chsd ldrs tl wknd fr 2f out* **50/1**
16-5 **10** 1 1/4 **Kings Point (IRE)**[14] [1239] 3-9-0 107.................................. DaneO'Neill 4 73
(RHannon) *chsd ldrs tl wknd wl over 2f out* **16/1**

1m 26.97s (-0.25) **Going Correction** +0.225s/f (Good) **10** Ran SP% **115.4**
Speed ratings: **110,108,107,107,105 104,103,102,92,91**CSF £21.46 TOTE £3.80: £1.70, £2.30, £3.30; EX 23.60.
**Owner** M Tabor **Bred** Dr D Davis **Trained** Whitsbury, Hants

**FOCUS**
A good time for the grade, 2.54 seconds faster than the Fred Darling. The action took place down the centre of the track.

**NOTEBOOK**
**Salford City(IRE)** ◆ was sold to Michael Tabor after impressing in his maiden win here last backend. Dropping a furlong in trip, he was a little slow to find his stride and was still only fifth passing the furlong pole, but he picked up in fine style when asked and won going away. He still looked green and the undulations of Newmarket may find him out, a comment which also applies to Epsom, although the Derby trip should not be a problem for this high-class prospect.
**Fokine(USA)** posted his second good effort of the campaign, getting to the front before being put in his place by the winner. Faster ground will help his cause.

**So Will I**, sold for 160,000gns after winning his maiden here in the autumn, carried the Hamdan second colours on this occasion. This was a promising effort and the seventh furlong was not a problem, but he did hang markedly to his left when attempting to challenge.
**Fort Dignity(USA)** should improve for the run, like a number of his stablemates to have appeared so far this season, and a longer trip will be to his advantage.
**Milk It Mick** again failed to settle despite the stronger pace than at Lingfield. He seemed to have no real excuses although fast ground could be what he needs.
**Bahiano(IRE)** rather holds the form down, although he has improved considerably on the sand through the winter and could still be progressing.
**Mukafeh(USA)** faded after making the running and may have found the ground on the easy side.
**Nero's Return(IRE)**, down a furlong, ran a little better than he had at Kempton but was still one of the first beaten.

## 1460 DUBAI DUTY FREE H'CAP — 1m 2f 6y

**4:20** (4:20) (D) (0-85,85) 4-Y-0+ — **£6,110** (£1,880; £940; £470) **Stalls** Low

Form — RPR

530- **1** **Ionian Spring (IRE)**[175] 5753 9-10-0 **85** ........ PRobinson 10 — 98
(CGCox) *stdd s: plld hrd towards rr: hdwy over 2f out: led over 1f out: rdn clr: drvn out fnl 75 yds* **12/1**

6-25 **2** *1 ¼* **Street Life (IRE)**[85] 589 6-9-0 **71** ........ WSupple 12 — 82
(WJMusson) *hld up towards rr: rdn and hdwy fnl 2f: r.o to take 2nd fnl 75 yds* **20/1**

5244 **3** *1 ¾* **Barry Island**[15] 1232 5-9-7 **78** ........ DaneO'Neill 17 — 85
(DRCElsworth) *s.s: hld up in rr: rdn and r.o fnl 2f: nrst fin* **16/1**

044- **4** *nk* **Dream Magic**[163] 5936 6-9-7 **78** ........ EAhern 19 — 85
(MJRyan) *prom: led briefly wl over 1f out: one pce* **14/1**

-604 **5** *nk* **Silvaline**[25] 1085 5-9-4 **75** ........ TEDurcan 16 — 81
(TKeddy) *led 2f: mainly chsd ldr: rdn and ev ch 2f out: one pce* **20/1**

1/1- **6** *nk* **Balkan Knight**[213] 4995 4-9-9 **80** ........(v) JPMurtagh 9 — 86
(DRLoder) *h.d.w: bit bkwd: in tch: drvn along and sltly outpcd 4f out: styd on same pce fnl 2f* **4/1**[1]

260- **7** *¾* **Freeloader (IRE)**[176] 5724 4-9-3 **74** ........ RHills 18 — 78
(JWHills) *lw: hld up in midfield: hdwy to press ldrs 2f out: no ex over 1f out* **25/1**

500- **8** *3 ½* **Guilded Flyer**[196] 5379 5-9-7 **81** ........ LPKeniry[(3)] 6 — 79
(WSKittow) *led after 2f: wnt 6l clr 1/2-way: hdd wl over 1f out: sn wknd* **50/1**

**9** *1 ½* **Shamdian (IRE)**[91] 4-10-0 **85** ........ KFallon 3 — 80
(NJHenderson) *prom tl wknd over 1f out: eased whn btn* **8/1**[3]

4-00 **10** *shd* **Briareus**[94] 523 4-9-9 **80** ........ MartinDwyer 13 — 74
(AMBalding) *in tch: drvn along 4f out: no imp* **20/1**

0010 **11** *½* **Karaoke (IRE)**[9] 1308 4-9-1 **72** ........ JDSmith 4 — 66
(SKirk) *in tch: outpcd 3f out: n.d after* **50/1**

0103 **12** *3 ½* **Kentucky King (USA)**[12] 1273 4-10-0 **85** ........ RHughes 14 — 72
(PWHiatt) *prom: hrd rdn over 2f out: sn wknd* **16/1**

4-30 **13** *hd* **Kylkenny**[12] 1272 9-9-4 **75** ........(t) JFanning 1 — 61
(HMorrison) *lw: chsd ldrs over 6f* **14/1**

426- **14** *1* **Alrafid (IRE)**[129] 6162 5-9-13 **84** ........ RLMoore 8 — 69
(GLMoore) *mid-div: effrt 3f out: n.d fnl 2f* **12/1**

1606 **15** *¾* **African Sahara (USA)**[12] 1273 5-10-0 **85** ........(t) GCarter 20 — 68
(MissDMountain) *towards rr: sme hdwy on outside 3f out: wknd 2f out* **16/1**

5405 **16** *1* **Dower House**[28] 1066 9-9-8 **79** ........(t) LDettori 2 — 60
(AndrewTurnell) *stdd s: t.k.h towards rr: hrd rdn over 2f out: nvr a factor* **12/1**

451- **17** *¾* **Best Be Going (IRE)**[188] 5506 4-9-6 **77** ........ DHolland 5 — 57
(PWHarris) *chsd ldrs tl wknd over 2f out* **7/1**[2]

000- **18** *6* **Silver Prophet (IRE)**[11] 6121 5-9-8 **79** ........(t) GBaker 15 — 47
(MRBosley) *s.s: hrd rdn 4f out: a bhd* **50/1**

53-1 **19** *4* **Slalom (IRE)**[21] 1138 4-9-5 **76** ........ MFenton 7 — 37
(MissGayKelleway) *s.s: towards rr: rdn 4f out: no ch fnl 3f* **12/1**

210- **20** *13* **Count Walewski**[188] 5498 4-9-1 **72** ........ WRyan 11 — 8
(SDow) *plld hrd: rdn 4f out: a bhd* **66/1**

2m 11.55s (2.84) **Going Correction** +0.30s/f (Good) **20 Ran SP% 130.9**
Speed ratings: **100,99,97,97,97 96,96,93,92,92 91,89,88,88,87 86,86,81,78,67**CSF £247.48 CT £3866.51 TOTE £13.70: £2.70, £6.00, £4.00, £4.20; EX 205.40.
**Owner** Elite Racing Club **Bred** Ballymacoll Stud Farm Ltd **Trained** Lambourn, Berks

**FOCUS**
A competitive handicap but the pace was just ordinary until about half way. The winning time was only modest for the class of contest. The first five home were drawn in double figure stalls.

**NOTEBOOK**
**Ionian Spring(IRE)** had not won since taking this race off a 6lb lower mark last season and was a beaten favourite over this very course and distance on his final outing in 2003. However, fresh from a winter's break, he returned to action as good as ever. Having looked likely to pull clear when hitting the front, he only really did just enough and was being closed down at the finish. Things will be much harder when he is reassessed.
**Street Life(IRE)** has not won since June 2002 but this was a good effort on ground that would have been faster than ideal. He appeared to hang slightly in the closing stages and softer ground will suit much better.
**Barry Island** has been in fair form on Polytrack recently and this not a bad effort switched back to turf. He would have been suited by a stronger end-to-end gallop, but has yet to win on turf in any case.
**Dream Magic** is 2lb lower than when last successful and did not make a bad reappearance. He does not, however, win very often.
**Silvaline**, fit from the All-Weather, had every chance.
**Balkan Knight** has surely had his problems for this was just the fourth start of his career. He never really looked like picking up and a stronger pace would probably have suited.
**Kylkenny** *Official explanation: jockey said gelding lost its action*

## 1461 DUBAI INTERNATIONAL AIRPORT MAIDEN STKS — 1m (S)

**4:55** (4:57) (D) 3-Y-0 — **£6,240** (£1,920; £960; £480) **Stalls** Centre

Form — RPR

5-0 **1** **Mudawin (IRE)**[23] 1104 3-9-0 ........ WSupple 10 — 89
(MPTregoning) *trckd ldrs: led 1/2-way: pushed along and styd on wl fr over 1f out: readily* **20/1**

**2** *2 ½* **Rehearsal** 3-9-0 ........ PRobinson 9 — 83
(CGCox) *lengthy: str: scope: trckd ldrs: chsd wnr over 1f out: kpt on wl for 2nd but no imp ins* **33/1**

2- **3** *¾* **Akimbo (USA)**[245] 4175 3-9-0 ........ RHughes 15 — 82
(HRACecil) *hld up in tch: trckd ldrs 3f out: rdn and effrt over 1f out: kpt on same pce ins last* **8/11**[1]

5- **4** *2 ½* **Dr Thong**[207] 5139 3-9-0 ........ LDettori 3 — 76
(PFICole) *t.k.h: trckd ldrs 2f out: wknd ins fnl f* **9/1**[3]

0- **5** *½* **Whitsbury Cross**[168] 5870 3-9-0 ........ JPMurtagh 12 — 75
(DRCElsworth) *h.d.w: bit bkwd: s.i.s: bhd: pushed along over 2f out: styd on wl fnl f but nt rch ldrs* **16/1**

0- **6** *½* **Laabbij (USA)**[175] 5757 3-9-0 ........ JFanning 18 — 74
(MPTregoning) *bhd: hdwy fr 3f out: styd on fr over 1f out: nt rch ldrs* **50/1**

**7** *nk* **He Jaa (IRE)** 3-8-9 ........ TEDurcan 13 — 68
(CEBrittain) *lengthy: str: scope: bit bkwd: s.i.s: bhd: pushed along: 3f out and green: hdwy fr 2f out: kpt on wl fnl f but nt trble ldr* **66/1**

**8** *shd* **Fuel Cell (IRE)** 3-9-0 ........ DaneO'Neill 8 — 73
(RHannon) *cmpt: bhd: hdwy on far side fr 2f out: kpt on ins last: nt a danger* **50/1**

64- **9** *1 ¾* **Admiral (IRE)**[163] 5934 3-9-0 ........ KFallon 2 — 69
(SirMichaelStoute) *chsd ldrs: shkn up 2f out: fdd fnl f* **14/1**

03- **10** *½* **Albinus**[129] 6158 3-9-0 ........ MartinDwyer 7 — 68
(AMBalding) *led to 1/2-way: wknd over 1f out* **66/1**

- **11** *½* **Dandygrey Russett (IRE)** 3-8-9 ........ RLMoore 19 — 61
(GLMoore) *unf: scope: in tch: pushed along over 2f out: styd on same pl* **66/1**

4- **12** *1 ½* **Saharan Song (IRE)**[192] 5448 3-8-9 ........ MHills 1 — 58
(BWHills) *pushed lft s: sn in tch: pushed along and one pce fnl 2f* **66/1**

**13** *¾* **Principal Witness (IRE)** 3-9-0 ........ MFenton 4 — 61
(WRMuir) *wl grwn: bit bkwd: chsd ldrs tl wknd over 1f out* **100/1**

**14** *shd* **Ogilvy (USA)** 3-9-0 ........ WRyan 16 — 61
(JHMGosden) *str: bit bkwd: scope: s.i.s: bhd: kpt on fnl 2f* **33/1**

**15** *nk* **News Sky (USA)** 3-9-0 ........ EAhern 6 — 60
(BWHills) *leggy: unf: s.i.s: sn in tch: trckd ldrs over 3f out: wknd 2f out* **25/1**

4- **16** *3 ½* **Latif (USA)**[280] 3199 3-9-0 ........ RHills 17 — 52
(JHMGosden) *bit bkwd: chsd ldrs over 5f* **9/2**[2]

**17** *5* **Lucky Again (IRE)** 3-9-0 ........ GCarter 5 — 41
(JLDunlop) *small: slowly away: a in rr and n.d* **66/1**

**18** *½* **Anna Pallida** 3-8-9 ........ DHolland 11 — 35
(PWHarris) *tall: str: bit bkwd: sn pushed along: a in rr* **16/1**

2 **19** *7* **Mystic Lad**[63] 766 3-9-0 ........ KDalgleish 14 — 24
(JamiePoulton) *prom early: bhd fr 1/2-way* **33/1**

1m 42.56s (1.73) **Going Correction** +0.225s/f (Good) **19 Ran SP% 134.3**
Speed ratings: **100,97,96,94,93 93,92,92,91,90 90,88,87,87,87 83,78,78,71**CSF £572.10 TOTE £62.40: £9.10, £5.00, £1.40; EX 1098.70 Place 6 £271.16, Place 5 £114.07..
**Owner** Hamdan Al Maktoum **Bred** Shadwell Estate Company Limited **Trained** Lambourn, Berks

**FOCUS**
Hard to know what to make of this maiden that featured some Guineas, Dante, Oaks and Derby entrants. The form taken at face value may not be worth a great deal, particularly with the well-regarded Akimbo failing to progress from two to three, but it would not surprise if there were one or two in behind capable of improvement.

**NOTEBOOK**
**Mudawin(IRE)** ran poorly on his reappearance at Doncaster but showed the benefit of that run to get off the mark in decisive fashion. He had everything go his way and was always ideally placed for the way the race was run so things will be much harder next time, especially given the Handicapper is going to have his say. *Official explanation: trainer said, regarding the improved form shown, gelding was better suited by being ridden more prominently*
**Rehearsal**, a 47,000gns purchase, half-brother to three 12 furlong winners, made a very pleasing debut over a trip that would have been plenty short enough. He clearly has the ability to win a similar race.
**Akimbo(USA)**, a Guineas entry, has always been held in high regard but, for the second time in two career starts, failed to deliver. Sent off the same price he was today for his only start at two, he offered plenty of encouragement then, but proved unable to progress from that and now has it all to prove.
**Dr Thong** shaped nicely on his debut at Newmarket last term and again ran well. He is nothing special, but it will be disappointing if he does pick up at least a maiden.
**Whitsbury Cross** ◆ showed little on his only start at two but he has subsequently been given a Guineas entry and duly showed improved form. He could never muster the pace to get on terms but was keeping on nicely at the finish and should know a lot more next time. Possibly one to take out of the race.
**News Sky(USA)**, a Derby entry, half-brother to 1000 Guineas winner Sayyedati, is bred to be better than he showed on this occasion.
**Latif(USA)**, a Dante entry, was returning from 280 days off and showed little. He should, however, improve with this run under his belt.
**Anna Pallida** showed little on this racecourse debut but, a 300,000gns purchase and Oaks entry, this half-sister to Prix Marcel Boussac winner Sulk, could well be capable of better.
T/Plt: £377.10 to a £1 stake. Pool: £96,743.00. 187.25 winning tickets. T/Qpdt: £129.40 to a £1 stake. Pool: £3,429.50. 19.60 winning tickets. ST

# 1208 NOTTINGHAM (L-H)

Saturday, April 17

**OFFICIAL GOING: Good**
The going was described as 'just on the fast side of good' but the times were affected by a brisk almost head-on wind.
Wind: fresh hlf against Weather: fine

## 1462 NOTTINGHAM RACECOURSE CONFERENCE CENTRE MAIDEN STKS — 5f 13y

**5:15** (5:16) (D) 2-Y-0 — **£3,682** (£1,133; £566; £283) **Stalls** High

Form — RPR

2 **1** **Norcroft**[10] 1292 2-8-9 ........ DFox[(5)] 9 — 79
(NACallaghan) *chsd ldrs: styd on to ld jst ins fnl f: r.o wl* **11/10**[1]

**2** *2* **On The Waterline (IRE)** 2-8-9 ........ GDuffield 5 — 67
(PDEvans) *small unf: chsd ldrs: kpt on wl fnl f: no imp* **25/1**

032 **3** *1* **Grand Option**[7] 1331 2-9-0 ........ PDobbs 10 — 68
(BWDuke) *chsd ldrs: nt qckn appr fnl f* **16/1**

**4** *hd* **Sharp N Frosty** 2-9-0 ........ SWKelly 1 — 67
(WMBrisbourne) *cmpt: sn outpcd and bhd: hdwy 2f out: styd on wl ins last* **100/1**

**5** *1* **Fiefdom (IRE)** 2-9-0 ........ RFfrench 6 — 64
(MJohnston) *neat: mid-div: outpcd over 2f out: kpt on wl fnl f* **5/2**[2]

**6** *½* **Joe Jo Star** 2-9-0 ........ PHanagan 3 — 62
(PABlockley) *leggy: unf: mid-div: kpt on appr fnl f* **80/1**

**7** *hd* **Sea Hunter** 2-9-0 ........ CCatlin 11 — 61
(MRChannon) *neat: unf: s.s: bhd tl styd on fnl 2f: nvr nr ldrs* **14/1**

**8** *3* **Coleorton Dancer** 2-9-0 ........ GParkin 8 — 51
(KARyan) *leggy: led: hung bdly lft over 2f out: hdd jst ins fnl f: wknd* **40/1**

**9** *1* **Rasa Sayang (USA)** 2-9-0 ........ KDarley 4 — 47
(TDBarron) *w'like: cmpt: chsd ldrs: wknd over 1f out* **8/1**[3]

2 **10** *hd* **Colonel Bilko (IRE)**[18] 1183 2-9-0 ........ SDrowne 2 — 46
(BRMillman) *w ldr: hung bdly lft over 2f out: wknd fnl f* **10/1**

11 2½ **Hiamovi (IRE)** 2-9-0 .......... BDoyle 7 37
(RMHCowell) *rangy: s.s: a last* **100/1**

63.52 secs (1.72) **Going Correction** +0.20s/f (Good) **11** Ran SP% **118.4**
Speed ratings: **94,90,89,88,87 86,86,81,79,79 75**CSF £39.90 TOTE £2.10: £1.02, £6.60, £5.90; EX 56.30.
**Owner** Norcroft Park Stud **Bred** Norcroft Park Stud **Trained** Newmarket, Suffolk

**FOCUS**
Just an ordinary maiden, although the winner scored nicely.

**NOTEBOOK**
**Norcroft** ◆, the pick of the paddock, did it in good style in the end. His dam won at up to a mile six and he will relish a sixth furlong.
**On The Waterline(IRE)**, an April foal, is only small and was very backward in her coat. She kept on well to follow the winner home putting a question mark over the overall value of the form.
**Grand Option** was having his fourth start and is already looking fully exposed.
**Sharp N Frosty**, a March foal, is a close-coupled newcomer whose dam ran in bumpers and points. He will need a much stiffer test.
**Fiefdom(IRE)**, a January foal, is not very big and was inclined to be noisy beforehand. He stuck on in his own time and, a son of Singspiel, he will appreciate at least six furlongs.
**Colonel Bilko(IRE)** *Official explanation: jockey said colt hung badly left throughout*

## 1463 RICHARD BENSON FINAL FLING H'CAP 1m 6f 15y
**5:45** (5:46) (F) (0-55,55) 4-Y-0+ **£3,178** (£908; £454) **Stalls** Low

Form RPR
54-0 **1** **Best Port (IRE)**[17] 1198 8-8-9 **53** .......... MLawson(7) 12 63
(JParkes) *hld up: stdy hdwy over 3f out: hung lft and swtchd rt 1f out: kpt on to ld nr fin* **8/1**
-300 **2** ½ **Intensity**[23] 1109 8-9-4 **55** .......... SWKelly 6 64
(PABlockley) *trckd ldrs: smooth hdwy to ld 1f out: sn rdn: hdd nr fin* **20/1**
1-00 **3** ½ **Only For Sue**[82] 609 5-9-0 **51** .......... (b¹) IMongan 5 59
(WSKittow) *led tl 1f out: kpt on wl* **28/1**
60-0 **4** 1½ **Flame Of Zara**[19] 1173 5-9-2 **53** .......... KDarley 1 59
(MrsMReveley) *bhd: hdwy on outer 3f out: styd on wl fnl f* **8/1**
4-04 **5** shd **Astromancer (USA)**[51] 889 4-8-4 **50** .......... SaleemGolam(7) 11 56
(MHTompkins) *chsd ldrs: wnt 2nd over 3f out: kpt on same pce fnl 2f* **12/1**
616- **6** 6 **Field Spark**[182] 5635 4-9-2 **55** .......... (p) GDuffield 13 53
(JAGlover) *bhd: hdwy on outer 6f out: edgd lft and one pce fnl 2f* **14/1**
560- **7** 1¼ **Romil Star (GER)**[18] 5220 7-9-3 **54** .......... PHanagan 4 51
(KRBurke) *sn chsng ldrs: drvn along 6f out: sn outpcd and n.d* **11/1**
1016 **8** shd **Jungle Lion**[2] 1426 6-8-13 **50** .......... (t) SDrowne 9 47
(JohnAHarris) *chsd ldrs: wknd over 2f out* **7/1**[3]
05-2 **9** shd **Tom Bell (IRE)**[11] 1282 4-8-8 **47** .......... DSweeney 16 44
(JGMO'Shea) *mid-div: hdwy 7f out: sn chsng ldrs: wknd 3f out* **13/2**[2]
00-5 **10** shd **Rutland Chantry (USA)**[10] 1305 10-8-7 **47** .......... BReilly(3) 10 43
(SGollings) *in tch: drvn along 4f out: sn outpcd* **14/1**
1030 **11** 4 **Miss Koen (IRE)**[10] 1297 5-8-13 **53** .......... (t) DCorby(3) 8 44
(DLWilliams) *bhd: hdwy 6f out: nvr nr ldrs* **20/1**
6-26 **12** 3 **Retail Therapy (IRE)**[43] 549 4-8-9 **48** .......... RFfrench 7 35
(MABuckley) *mid-div: drvn along 5f out: nvr on terms* **33/1**
346- **13** 4 **Sunnyside Royale (IRE)**[42] 2575 5-8-10 **47** oh1 ow1 .......... (t) SSanders 17 29
(RBastiman) *a in rr* **6/1**[1]
5-00 **14** 1¼ **Monsal Dale (IRE)**[18] 1193 5-8-9 **51** ow1 .......... (p) MSavage(5) 15 32
(NEBerry) *sn w ldr: lost pl over 4f out: sn bhd* **28/1**
60-0 **15** 6 **Termonfeckin**[17] 1210 6-9-4 **55** .......... JoannaBadger 3 28
(PWHiatt) *s.s: hld up and a bhd* **40/1**
0020 **16** 4 **Golden Dual**[18] 1188 4-9-2 **55** .......... (v) PaulEddery 14 23
(SDow) *s.i.s: a bhd* **20/1**
0-00 **17** dist **Dark Cut (IRE)**[14] 1245 4-8-9 **48** .......... JCarroll 18 —
(HAlexander) *bhd: t.o 5f out* **66/1**

3m 5.73s (-1.47) **Going Correction** -0.025s/f (Good)
**WFA** 4 from 5yo+ 2lb **17** Ran SP% **119.8**
Speed ratings: **103,102,102,101,101 98,97,97,97,97 94,93,90,90,86 84,—**CSF £162.63 CT £4221.94 TOTE £10.50: £2.20, £2.70, £2.20, £1.90; EX 243.80.
**Owner** M Wormald **Bred** Lord Harrington **Trained** Upper Helmsley, N Yorks

**FOCUS**
A selling handicap in all but name but the pace was decent.

**NOTEBOOK**
**Best Port(IRE)**, whose last success a year and a half ago was from a 4lb higher mark, was given a fine ride and his head was put in front where is really matters. He has a useful turn of finishing speed for one rated so lowly.
**Intensity**, twice a winner on fast ground over hurdles in the winter, travelled supremely well and looked all over a winner when sent to the front, but he had no answer to the winner's late burst.
**Only For Sue**, in first-time blinkers, was quite keen in front and made this a true test. He kept on surprisingly well.
**Flame Of Zara** stayed on late up the wide outside and is well worth another try over two miles.
**Astromancer(USA)** ran with credit, but the fact remains she is still a maiden after 13 starts now.
**Rutland Chantry(USA)** *Official explanation: trainer said gelding was unsuited by the drying ground*
**Sunnyside Royale(IRE)**, a recent winner over hurdles, tended to hang right in the home straight and never figured. *Official explanation: jockey said gelding hung left in the home straight*
**Dark Cut(IRE)** *Official explanation: jockey said gelding lost its action*

## 1464 SKY BET PRESS RED TO BET FILLIES' H'CAP 6f 15y
**6:15** (6:18) (E) (0-75,75) 3-Y-0 **£3,629** (£1,116; £558; £279) **Stalls** High

Form RPR
31- **1** **Beejay**[382] 886 3-9-3 **71** .......... JQuinn 2 77
(PFICole) *racd far side: bhd: hdwy over 2f out: r.o wl to ld last 75yds* **14/1**
215 **2** 1¼ **Marinaite**[12] 1265 3-9-5 **73** .......... JBramhill 10 75
(SRBowring) *swtchd lft and led overall on far side: hdd and no ex wl ins last* **9/1**[3]
542- **3** shd **Whistful (IRE)**[180] 5676 3-8-13 **67** .......... SSanders 9 69
(CFWall) *racd far side: hld up: hdwy over 2f out: styd on ins last* **16/1**
060- **4** nk **Gojo (IRE)**[163] 5930 3-8-13 **67** .......... KDarley 11 68
(BPalling) *swtchd rt and led stands' side: kpt on wl fnl f* **20/1**
1- **5** nk **Missus Links (USA)**[137] 6118 3-9-2 **70** .......... RSmith 8 70
(RHannon) *racd far side: chsd ldrs: edgd lft 1f out: unable qckn* **9/2**[1]
4-15 **6** ¾ **Generous Gesture (IRE)**[22] 1119 3-9-6 **74** .......... IMongan 7 72
(MLWBell) *racd far side: w ldrs: edgd lft 1f out: nt qckn* **10/1**
044- **7** shd **Urban Rose**[178] 5707 3-8-13 **67** .......... SWKelly 17 64
(JWUnett) *racd stands' side: hdwy over 2f out: kpt on wl fnl f* **22/1**
00-0 **8** hd **Just One Look**[15] 1229 3-9-3 **71** .......... DSweeney 20 68
(MBlanshard) *racd stands' side: chsd ldrs: nt qckn fnl f* **7/1**[2]
35-0 **9** nk **Sworn To Secrecy**[25] 1083 3-8-13 **67** .......... PDobbs 5 63
(SKirk) *racd far side: chsd ldrs: nt qckn fnl f* **28/1**
55-0 **10** shd **Under My Spell**[21] 1129 3-9-1 **72** .......... BReilly(3) 6 68
(PDEvans) *racd far side: chsd ldrs: no ex whn n.m.r 1f out* **20/1**
-445 **11** hd **Black Oval**[9] 1312 3-8-5 **59** .......... CCatlin 1 54
(MRChannon) *racd far side: outpcd and bhd tl kpt on fnl 2f* **14/1**
04-4 **12** 2 **Impulsive Bid (IRE)**[12] 1266 3-8-10 **64** .......... PHanagan 13 53
(JeddO'Keeffe) *racd stands' side: w ldr: fdd over 1f out* **22/1**
0-00 **13** nk **Chiqitita (IRE)**[51] 891 3-8-5 **59** ow1 .......... (b¹) RPrice 3 47
(TTClement) *s.s: racd far side: nvr nrr* **66/1**
01- **14** 1¼ **Chorus Beauty**[110] 6250 3-8-12 **66** .......... SDrowne 4 50
(GWragg) *racd far side: in rr: effrt 2f out: nvr a factor* **10/1**
510- **15** 1½ **Alice Blackthorn**[165] 5916 3-9-1 **69** .......... RFfrench 18 49
(BSmart) *racd stands' side: chsd ldrs: wknd over 1f out* **20/1**
0-61 **16** 2 **Showtime Annie**[31] 1038 3-8-10 **64** .......... AMackay 15 38
(ABailey) *swvd lft s: nvr a factor* **25/1**
0-06 **17** 1½ **Man Crazy (IRE)**[25] 1086 3-9-0 **68** .......... GDuffield 16 37
(RMBeckett) *racd stands' side: in tch: wknd over 1f out* **20/1**
4560 **18** nk **Back At De Front (IRE)**[22] 1121 3-8-11 **70** .......... MSavage(5) 19 38
(NEBerry) *racd stands' side: a in rr* **20/1**
20-5 **19** ¾ **Deign To Dance (IRE)**[24] 1096 3-9-5 **73** .......... JCarroll 12 39
(JGPortman) *racd stands' side: chsd ldrs: lost pl over 1f out* **28/1**
030- **20** ½ **Annie Harvey**[161] 5950 3-9-0 **75** .......... MStainton(7) 14 40
(BSmart) *bmpd s: sn chsng ldrs: edgd lft and lost pl 2f out* **33/1**

1m 16.35s (1.55) **Going Correction** +0.20s/f (Good) **20** Ran SP% **125.8**
Speed ratings: **97,95,95,94,94 93,93,93,92,92 92,89,89,87,85 82,80,80,79,78**CSF £108.49 CT £2114.13 TOTE £13.00: £2.50, £3.20, £2.40, £5.00; EX 134.70.
**Owner** A H Robinson **Bred** A H And C E Robinson Partnership **Trained** Whatcombe, Oxon

**FOCUS**
The field split into two even groups but the first three were on the far side. A large blanket would have covered the first 11 at the line.

**NOTEBOOK**
**Beejay**, who did not reappear after winning her maiden on the Polytrack at Lingfield a year ago, stayed on from off the pace to win going away in the end. Seven furlongs will not come amiss, and this rather delicate filly is still something of an unknown quantity.
**Marinaite**, who elected to race on the far side, led overall but had no answer to the winner's late burst. Her sole win was over seven on the All-Weather and she may benefit from a slightly more patient ride.
**Whistful(IRE)**, progressive at two, picked up in good style inside the last.
**Gojo(IRE)**, who had just the three outings at two, elected to come down the stands' side and led that group throughout. She deserves credit for this.
**Missus Links(USA)**, who won her only previous start a maiden on the Polytrack at Lingfield in December, ran well and the experience will not be lost on her.
**Generous Gesture(IRE)**, who looked very fit, edged left under pressure and could find no more.
**Urban Rose** put in some solid late work finishing second best on the stands' side.

## 1465 COLWICK PARK H'CAP 1m 1f 213y
**6:45** (6:47) (F) (0-55,61) 3-Y-0 **£3,129** (£894; £447) **Stalls** Low

Form RPR
03-3 **1** **Be Wise Girl**[18] 1192 3-8-4 **47** .......... GDuffield 6 56
(JGGiven) *mde all: styd on wl* **7/1**[3]
0-03 **2** 3 **Danefonique (IRE)**[12] 1267 3-8-9 **52** .......... RFitzpatrick 1 55
(DCarroll) *chsd ldrs: edgd rt over 1f out: styd on to go 2nd ins last* **7/1**[3]
00-0 **3** 1¼ **Savannah River (IRE)**[11] 1288 3-8-3 **46** oh1 .......... (t) PHanagan 14 47
(CWThornton) *in tch: kpt on wl fnl 2f* **33/1**
006- **4** ½ **Cherokee Nation**[179] 5687 3-8-11 **54** .......... PaulEddery 11 54
(PWD'Arcy) *trckd ldrs: t.k.h: wnt 2nd over 3f out: rdn and hung lft 2f out: fnd little* **9/2**[1]
056- **5** 2 **Incisor**[198] 5325 3-8-8 **51** .......... PDobbs 12 47
(SKirk) *mid-div: styd on fnl 2f* **14/1**
0-01 **6** 1½ **Perfect Balance (IRE)**[5] 1363 3-9-4 **61** 6ex .......... KimTinkler 3 54
(NTinkler) *sn rr div: sme hdwy over 4f out: styd on fnl 2f: nvr rchd ldrs* **6/1**[2]
6-00 **7** 2½ **Timbuktu**[12] 1267 3-8-3 **46** oh6 .......... JQuinn 9 35
(CWThornton) *bhd: styd on fnl 2f: nvr nrr* **50/1**
4050 **8** 3 **Myannabanana (IRE)**[5] 1363 3-8-2 **52** .......... (p) DFentiman(7) 2 35
(JRWeymes) *s.s: bhd tl kpt on fnl 3f* **14/1**
550- **9** 1 **Northern Spirit**[200] 5290 3-8-12 **55** .......... GParkin 4 36
(KARyan) *bhd: sme hdwy 3f out: nvr a factor* **20/1**
00-0 **10** hd **Lenwade**[12] 1267 3-8-8 **51** .......... AMcCarthy 7 32
(GGMargarson) *s.i.s: nvr on terms* **22/1**
006- **11** shd **Calara Hills**[168] 5877 3-8-9 **52** .......... SWKelly 10 33
(WMBrisbourne) *mid-div: outpcd 5f out: nvr a factor after* **28/1**
-550 **12** 5 **Numpty (IRE)**[53] 871 3-8-3 **46** oh6 .......... (t) JoannaBadger 8 17
(NTinkler) *chsd ldrs: lost pl over 2f out* **33/1**
4334 **13** ¾ **Princess Ismene**[2] 1422 3-8-12 **55** .......... (b) JBramhill 16 25
(PABlockley) *chsd ldrs: lost pl over 3f out* **7/1**[3]
030- **14** 3 **Miss Hoofbeats**[245] 4185 3-8-5 **51** .......... BReilly(3) 5 15
(MissJFeilden) *in tch: effrt over 4f out: lost pl 3f out* **14/1**
00-5 **15** 30 **Rumour Mill (IRE)**[100] 482 3-8-12 **55** .......... CCatlin 15 —
(NEBerry) *sn bhd: t.o* **33/1**
0-04 **16** dist **Queen's Fantasy**[16] 1221 3-8-12 **55** .......... (b¹) SSanders 13 —
(DHaydnJones) *s.i.s: j. path and lost pl 6f out: sn t.o: virtually p.u* **14/1**

2m 8.97s (-0.53) **Going Correction** -0.025s/f (Good) **16** Ran SP% **120.0**
Speed ratings: **101,98,97,97,95 94,92,90,89,89 88,84,84,81,57** —CSF £49.85 CT £1532.23 TOTE £6.70: £1.70, £2.30, £6.00, £1.70; EX 65.50.
**Owner** Be Wise Racing **Bred** B Freiha **Trained** Willoughton, Lincs

**FOCUS**
In effect a 0-61 handicap run at just a fair pace and the winner dominated.

**NOTEBOOK**
**Be Wise Girl**, on her handicap bow, made every yard and in the end won going away. She should improve again.
**Danefonique(IRE)** showed her improved Southwell turf effort was no fluke.
**Savannah River(IRE)**, tailed off on her return, showed a lot more staying from from an unpromising position.
**Cherokee Nation**, who had the mandatory three outings at two, did not lack market support. After taking a keen grip, he moved up looking the likely winner but when asked a question the response was strictly limited.
**Incisor**, on his handicap debut, was putting in his best work late on and will appreciate further.
**Perfect Balance(IRE)**, dropping back in trip, could never enter the argument.
**Princess Ismene** dropped right away early in the straight, and three runs in the space of a week was a case of going to the well once too often. *Official explanation: jockey said filly ran flat having had three runs in the previous seven days*
**Queen's Fantasy** *Official explanation: jockey said filly stumbled twice in the back straight and lost its action*

## 1466 WORLD WATCH DEPARTS MEDIAN AUCTION MAIDEN STKS 1m 1f 213y
**7:15** (7:19) (F) 3-Y-0 **£3,178** (£908; £454) **Stalls** Low

Form RPR
0- **1** **Woodcracker**[183] 5612 3-9-0 .......... IMongan 10 79
(MLWBell) *in tch: gd hdwy 3f out: led over 1f out: styd on strly: readily* **9/1**

2- **2** 2 ½ **Mountain Meadow**$^{175}$ 5757 3-9-0 ........ KDarley 14 74
(MrsAJPerrett) *sn chsng ldrs: effrt 3f out: ev ch over 1f out: nt pce of wnr* **4/5**$^{1}$
4-02 **3** 2 ½ **Tudor Bell (IRE)**$^{11}$ 1285 3-9-0 75........ DSweeney 4 69
(JGMO'Shea) *w ldrs: led 4f out tl over 1f out: one pce* **15/2**$^{3}$
**4** ½ **Our Jaffa (IRE)** 3-8-10 ow1........ JPMurtagh 12 65
(DJDaly) *tall: unf: scope: s.i.s: hdwy to trck ldrs 6f out: kpt on same pce fnl 2f* **13/2**$^{2}$
00- **5** ½ **Peak Of Perfection (IRE)**$^{167}$ 5887 3-9-0 ........ PRobinson 8 68
(MAJarvis) *t.k.h: led 1f: trckd ldrs: kpt on fnl 2f: improve* **16/1**
003- **6** *nk* **Mustang Ali (IRE)**$^{151}$ 6021 3-9-0 66........ PDobbs 13 67
(SKirk) *in tch: effrt over 3f out: kpt on same pce* **33/1**
00-0 **7** 8 **Blaeberry**$^{23}$ 1104 3-8-9 ........ JFEgan 5 47
(PLGilligan) *sn bhd: hdwy over 3f out: nvr nr ldrs* **80/1**
000- **8** 4 **Winslow Boy (USA)**$^{152}$ 6012 3-9-0 ........ JQuinn 7 44
(CFWall) *mid-div: nvr a threat* **100/1**
0-4 **9** 3 **Dancing Bear**$^{22}$ 1116 3-9-0 ........ SSanders 11 39
(JulianPoulton) *sn trcking ldrs: fdd fnl 2f* **25/1**
000- **10** 2 ½ **Pearl Of York (DEN)**$^{185}$ 5571 3-8-9 ........ GDuffield 6 29
(RGuest) *a in rr* **80/1**
**11** 6 **Muslin** 3-8-9 ........ JDSmith 3 17
(JRFanshawe) *unf: scope: uns rdr and rn loose gng to s: s.i.s: a bhd* **11/1**
**12** 1 ½ **Miss St Albans** 3-8-9 ........ RPrice 1 15
(TTClement) *unf: s.i.s: a bhd* **100/1**
00 **13** 20 **Baroque**$^{16}$ 1221 3-9-0 ........ RFitzpatrick 2 —
(CSmith) *led after 1f: hdd 4f out: wknd qckly: sn bhd: t.o* **200/1**
00-5 **14** 19 **Stop The Nonsense (IRE)**$^{15}$ 1227 3-9-0 65........ JCarroll 9 —
(EJO'Neill) *chsd ldrs: lost pl over 3f out: bhd whn heavily eased 2f out: t.o* **50/1**

2m 8.88s (-0.62) **Going Correction** -0.025s/f (Good) **14** Ran SP% **118.6**
Speed ratings: **101,99,97,96,96 95,89,86,83,81 77,75,59,44**CSF £15.96 TOTE £12.10: £2.50, £1.10, £2.30; EX 23.70.
**Owner** Sir Thomas Pilkington **Bred** Sir Thomas Pilkington **Trained** Newmarket, Suffolk

**FOCUS**
The first two have some potential and the sixth is the key to the value of the form.

**NOTEBOOK**
**Woodcracker ◆**, who showed ability in one backend outing at two, stands over a fair amount of ground. He travelled nicely, quickened up well and will go on from here.
**Mountain Meadow**, who followed Salford City home at Newbury in October on his only start at two, is a lengthy, robust type. Green beforehand, he had to be stoked up to get into top gear but in the end the winner proved much too good. His action suggests give underfoot will suit and he should find an opening.
**Tudor Bell(IRE)** kicked on once in line for home but in the end simply met a couple too good.
**Our Jaffa(IRE)**, a tall, narrow newcomer, shaped nicely and was by no means knocked about. She should improve given a little more time.
**Peak Of Perfection(IRE) ◆**, who showed little in a couple of outings last year, is now a gelding. A thick-set type, he was on the backward side and stuck on under hands and heels. He is worth bearing in mind in a handicap over further.
**Mustang Ali(IRE)** had finished third in a claimer on his final outing at two.
**Dancing Bear** *Official explanation: trainer's representative said gelding lost its action*
**Stop The Nonsense(IRE)** *Official explanation: trainer said colt had a breathing problem*

## 1467 SKY VEGAS LIVE ON CHANNEL 295 H'CAP — 1m 54y
7:45 (7:48) (F) (0-55,60) 3-Y-O — £3,143 (£898; £449) Stalls Low

Form — RPR
000- **1** **Dagola (IRE)**$^{197}$ 5339 3-9-2 **55**........ PRobinson 9 65
(CGCox) *trckd ldrs: qcknd to ld 1f out: sn clr: readily* **14/1**
050- **2** 3 **Ask The Driver**$^{204}$ 5192 3-9-1 **54**........ KDarley 5 57
(DJSFfrenchDavis) *s.i.s: hdwy whn nt clr run over 3f out: styd on wl fnl f: tk 2nd nr fin* **7/2**$^{1}$
-001 **3** *nk* **She's Our Lass (IRE)**$^{10}$ 1300 3-9-7 **60**........ RFitzpatrick 3 63
(DCarroll) *trckd ldrs: nt clr run on inner 2f out: styd on ins last* **9/2**$^{2}$
300- **4** ¾ **Breezit (USA)**$^{194}$ 5415 3-9-1 **54**........ JBramhill 12 55
(SRBowring) *hld up in rr: rapid hdwy to ld over 2f out: hdd 1f out: nt qckn* **16/1**
0-00 **5** ½ **Three Welshmen**$^{31}$ 1040 3-9-1 **54**........(b$^{1}$) SDrowne 2 54
(BRMillman) *hld up towards rr: hdwy over 3f out: styd on same pce fnl f* **25/1**
032 **6** 3 ½ **Brother Cadfael**$^{10}$ 1296 3-8-2 **46** oh6........ RThomas$^{(5)}$ 10 38
(JohnAHarris) *set modest pce: hdd 3f out: fdd appr fnl f* **12/1**
603- **7** 1 ¼ **Welsh Empress**$^{172}$ 5816 3-8-13 **52**........ JFEgan 7 41
(PLGilligan) *hld up and bhd: sme hdwy over 2f out: nvr on terms* **7/1**$^{3}$
-006 **8** ½ **Mystic Moon**$^{18}$ 1189 3-9-2 **55**........ SWKelly 14 43
(JRJenkins) *s.i.s: bhd tl sme hdwy over 2f out: hung lft: nvr a factor* **25/1**
40-2 **9** ¾ **Daggers Canyon**$^{12}$ 1267 3-9-5 **58**........ SSanders 11 44
(JulianPoulton) *hld up and bhd: hdwy 4f out: nvr on terms* **7/1**$^{3}$
60-0 **10** 3 **Reversionary**$^{17}$ 1196 3-9-2 **55**........ DaleGibson 1 34
(MWEasterby) *trckd ldrs: sn drvn along: lost pl over 2f out* **14/1**
05-0 **11** *nk* **Dr Fox (IRE)**$^{17}$ 1202 3-8-9 **55**........ PMakin$^{(7)}$ 13 33
(KAMorgan) *t.k.h: sn trcking ldrs: led 3f out: sn hdd and btn* **25/1**
0601 **12** 1 ¼ **Lady Predominant**$^{18}$ 1195 3-8-11 **50**........ GDuffield 8 26
(AndrewReid) *trckd ldrs: nt clr run 3f out: hung lft and lost pl over 1f out* **8/1**
020- **13** 6 **Delcienne**$^{145}$ 6058 3-8-13 **52**........(t) AMcCarthy 6 14
(GGMargarson) *chsd ldrs: lost pl over 2f out* **12/1**

1m 46.63s (0.23) **Going Correction** -0.025s/f (Good) **13** Ran SP% **122.7**
Speed ratings: **97,94,93,92,92 88,87,87,86,83 83,81,75**CSF £62.81 CT £261.61 TOTE £18.00: £5.10, £1.70, £2.50; EX 108.80 Place 6 £150.88, Place 5 £75.93..
**Owner** The Originals **Bred** Patrick Hughes **Trained** Lambourn, Berks

**FOCUS**
In effect a 0-60 handicap not run at a strong pace in the early stages. Apart from the winner the form looks modest.

**NOTEBOOK**
**Dagola(IRE) ◆**, who showed little in four starts at two, looks to have done himself proud over the winter. Confidently ridden, he quickened up in good style and in the end scored with a fair bit in hand. He seemed to appreciate the quickish ground and will stay further in due course. He is worth keeping on the right side. *Official explanation: trainer said, regarding the improved form shown, gelding had strengthened up over the winter and had benefited from the step up in trip*
**Ask The Driver**, unplaced in three outings at two, stayed on well late on and will be suited by a much stiffer test.
**She's Our Lass(IRE)**, 6lb higher and racing on totally different ground, ran with credit especially as she was a shade out of luck.
**Breezit(USA)**, whose one success at two was on firm ground, was rushed to the front so it was no surprise that she had no more to give when headed. Seven furlongs and a more patient ride might suit her.
**Three Welshmen**, back on turf, had the headgear on for the first time but he does not look straightforward.
**Brother Cadfael**, 6lb out of the handicap, was handed a soft lead but still did not truly see out the mile.
T/Plt: £186.80 to a £1 stake. Pool: £21,345.85. 83.40 winning tickets. T/Qpdt: £19.70 to a £1 stake. Pool: £2,510.00. 94.00 winning tickets. WG

# 1449 THIRSK (L-H)
Saturday, April 17

**OFFICIAL GOING: Soft**

## 1468 CHRIS BAILEY AND GEOFF FLAVELL 60TH BIRTHDAY CLAIMING STKS — 5f
2:30 (2:31) (E) 2-Y-O — £3,575 (£1,100; £550; £275) Stalls High

Form — RPR
1 **1** **Little Biscuit (IRE)**$^{21}$ 1137 2-8-10 ........ DarrenWilliams 2 52
(KRBurke) *cl up: led 2f out: pushed clr appr last: styd on wl* **3/1**$^{1}$
5 **2** 2 ½ **Emma's Venture**$^{22}$ 1115 2-8-5 ........ PMulrennan$^{(5)}$ 3 43
(MWEasterby) *trckd ldrs: hdwy to chse wnr wl over 1f out: sn rdn and kpt on same pce* **8/1**
**3** 3 **Maureen's Lough (IRE)** 2-9-0 ........ NCallan 1 37
(TDBarron) *chsd ldrs: hdwy 2f out: sn rdn and one pce appr last* **10/1**
**4** 1 ½ **Alice King (IRE)** 2-7-11 ........ CHaddon$^{(7)}$ 6 22
(WGMTurner) *dwlt: sn trcking ldrs: effrt and swtchd lft wl over 1f out: rdn and hung lft appr last: no imp* **9/2**$^{3}$
**5** 8 **Bowland Bride (IRE)** 2-8-6 ........ JCarroll 8 —
(ABerry) *prom: pushed along 1/2-way: sn wknd* **12/1**
**6** 2 **Our Louis** 2-8-10 ........ RWinston 9 —
(JSWainwright) *led: rdn along 1/2-way: hdd 2f out and grad wknd* **14/1**
**7** 4 **Fold Walk** 2-8-2 ........ DaleGibson 5 —
(MWEasterby) *s.i.s: a rr* **25/1**
**8** 1 ¾ **Joshar** 2-8-7 ........ DAllan$^{(3)}$ 7 —
(MWEasterby) *sn outpcd and bhd* **25/1**
**9** *shd* **Karita** 2-8-5 ........ JMackay 10 —
(MLWBell) *slowly away: a bhd* **7/2**$^{2}$
**10** 15 **Boracay Beauty** 2-8-10 ........ JQuinn 4 —
(JRWeymes) *chsd ldrs: rdn along and wknd 1/2-way: eased* **33/1**

65.14 secs (5.24) **Going Correction** +0.775s/f (Yiel) **10** Ran SP% **110.6**
Speed ratings: **89,85,80,77,65 61,55,52,52,28**CSF £25.13 TOTE £2.70: £1.10, £2.80, £2.50; EX 13.10.The winner was the subject of a friendly claim
**Owner** Mrs Elaine M Burke **Bred** Michael Mullins **Trained** Middleham Moor, N Yorks

**FOCUS**
A poor claimer unlikely to produce many future winners and the pair with previous experience filled the first two places. Unusually those drawn low dominated, with the front trio coming from the three lowest stalls.

**NOTEBOOK**
**Little Biscuit(IRE)**, winner of a four-runner Fibresand seller on her debut, showed the benefit of that experience to win in decent style after racing prominently the whole way. The soft ground was almost certainly in her favour, but she will be a very difficult filly to place from now on.
**Emma's Venture** did not do much wrong though it is debatable whether she improved much on her Doncaster debut. She is nothing special, but may be worth another chance on better ground.
**Maureen's Lough(IRE)**, a half-sister to Fruitana and Warlingham, was well held by the front pair but did best of the eight newcomers and there is a small amount of encouragement in that.
**Alice King(IRE)**, from a stable that does particularly well with its juveniles here, ran a little green though she was entitled to in these conditions. She is out of a dual sprint winner, but is also a half-sister to a winner over 12 furlongs, suggesting she will get further in time.
**Bowland Bride(IRE)**, a half-sister to a couple of winners abroad, showed up until tiring from halfway.
**Karita**, whose dam won three times over sprint trips as a juvenile, was unable to make use of her plum draw after missing the break. She is likely to show herself to be better than this when encountering a sounder surface.

## 1469 HARLEQUIN CLEAR AIR CONDITIONS STKS — 1m
3:00 (3:00) (C) 4-Y-O+ — £8,502 (£3,225; £1,612; £733) Stalls Low

Form — RPR
000- **1** **Heretic**$^{163}$ 5936 6-9-1 105........ OUrbina 7 113
(JRFanshawe) *in tch: gd hdwy over 3f out: led wl over 1f out: pushed clr: comf* **15/8**$^{2}$
406- **2** ½ **Mine (IRE)**$^{168}$ 5872 6-8-9 99........ RWinston 4 106
(JDBethell) *hld up: hdwy over 2f out: swtchd ins and nt clr run wl over 1f out: swtchd rt and styd on fnl f: nt rch wnr* **10/3**$^{3}$
1/3- **3** 5 **Mysterinch**$^{413}$ 646 4-8-9 ........ JFEgan 3 96
(JeddO'Keeffe) *chsd ldr: hdwy to ld 3f out: rdn and hdd wl over 1f out: kpt on same pce* **16/1**
230- **4** 3 **Selective**$^{304}$ 2460 5-8-9 104........ TQuinn 6 90
(ACStewart) *hld up: hdwy 3f out: chsd ldrs 2f out: sn rdn and btn* **7/4**$^{1}$
1/4- **5** 8 **Lady Mytton**$^{366}$ 1101 4-8-4 87........ JMackay 2 69
(ABailey) *led: rdn along over 3f out: sn hdd & wknd* **25/1**
**6** 3 **Caribe (FR)**$^{217}$ 5-8-7 ........ PBradley$^{(5)}$ 8 71
(ABerry) *n.d* **50/1**
100- **7** 23 **Gala Sunday (USA)**$^{238}$ 4363 4-9-1 95........ DaleGibson 1 28
(MWEasterby) *in tch: rdn along over 3f out and sn wknd* **20/1**

1m 45.99s (6.29) **Going Correction** +0.975s/f (Soft) **7** Ran SP% **110.7**
Speed ratings: **107,106,101,98,90 87,64**CSF £7.88 TOTE £2.70: £2.10, £1.90; EX 9.40.
**Owner** Barford Bloodstock **Bred** Mrs C Handscombe **Trained** Newmarket, Suffolk

**FOCUS**
Only three had a chance at the weights, but still a contest run at a sound pace and the front pair should make their presence felt in some decent handicaps this season.

**NOTEBOOK**
**Heretic** ended last season disappointingly, but with the ground in his favour started this campaign on a winning note. The narrow winning margin was mainly due to him idling after going clear, and he should enjoy further success this season when he has conditions to suit.
**Mine(IRE)**, meeting the winner on the same terms as he would have in a handicap, did not enjoy a clear passage on the inside when trying to make headway in the home straight. Once switched, he finished in good style and was bearing down on the idling winner at the line. He is likely to come on from this and should win a decent handicap this term.
**Mysterinch**, making his debut for the yard and racing for the first time in 13 months, was given a positive ride and ran a blinder under the circumstances. This would have been the softest ground he has encountered and his next outing should tell us a lot more.
**Selective**, best in at the weights, tried to get into the contest down the home straight but never got competitive. This was his first outing for ten months, but he has a good record fresh so he may not necessarily improve much from this. His rider also reported that he was not suited by the ground. *Official explanation: jockey said gelding hung left and was unsuited by the ground*
**Lady Mytton**, racing for the first time in a year, set a decent pace before not surprisingly blowing up.

## 1470 GILLAMOOR CLASSIFIED STKS — 1m 4f
3:30 (3:30) (E) 3-Y-0+ £3,555 (£1,094; £547; £273) Stalls Low

Form RPR

10-3 **1** **Captain Clipper**[19] 1172 4-9-11 75 ANicholls 4 82
(DNicholls) *hld up: hdwy on outer 3f out: rdn to ld over 1f out: edgd lft ent last and styd on wl* **7/2**[2]

-401 **2** 2 **Lawood (IRE)**[17] 1213 4-9-11 75 NCallan 5 79
(KARyan) *trckd ldrs: hdwy 3f out: effrt to chal 2f out: sn rdn and ev ch tl one pce ent last* **3/1**[1]

-102 **3** shd **Rasid (USA)**[17] 1203 6-9-9 75 TPQueally(3) 7 79
(CADwyer) *prom: pushed along 3f out: rdn and sltly outpcd 2f out: swtchd rt and drvn over 1f out: kpt on wl towards fin* **6/1**[3]

000- **4** 4 **Vicious Prince (IRE)**[186] 5558 5-9-12 75 MTebbutt 1 73
(RMWhitaker) *set stdy pce: qcknd over 4f out: rdn along 3f out: drvn 2f out: sn hdd and grad wknd* **3/1**[1]

126- **5** 5 **Rutters Rebel (IRE)**[186] 5557 3-8-6 74 ow1 RWinston 2 66
(GASwinbank) *in tch on inner: effrt 3f out: rdn along and styng on whn nt clr run over 1f out: n.d* **6/1**[3]

06/- **6** 1 ½ **Saspys Lad**[98] 2505 7-9-7 70 TGMcLaughlin 6 59
(WMBrisbourne) *hld up: rapid hdwy on outer to chse ldr over 4f out: rdn along 3f out: wknd fnl 2f* **16/1**

**7** 17 **Zan Lo (IRE)**[81] 4-9-3 65 JFEgan 3 33
(BSRothwell) *prom: rdn along over 4f out: wknd 3f out* **25/1**

2m 53.67s (18.47) **Going Correction** +0.975s/f (Soft)
**WFA** 3 from 4yo 20lb 4 from 5yo+ 1lb **7** Ran SP% **110.5**
Speed ratings: **77,75,75,72,69 68,57**CSF £13.40 TOTE £3.30: £1.90, £2.20; EX 10.00.
**Owner** Clipper Group Holdings **Bred** Dunchurch Lodge Stud Co **Trained** Sessay, N Yorks

**FOCUS**
A tight classified event on paper, but a desperately slow time for the class of contest.

**NOTEBOOK**
**Captain Clipper**, all the better for his Newcastle reappearance, has already shown he can handle this sort of ground. Given a patient ride before delivering his effort wide in the home straight, he saw the trip out much better than when he tried it in similar conditions at Ripon a year ago. The modest pace may have helped him, but he would probably get it just as well in a stronger-run race on better ground anyway.
**Lawood(IRE)**, up 3lb for his Nottingham win, was stepping up in trip again and ran well enough, but the moderate pace means that his true ability to see it out remains somewhat unproven.
**Rasid(USA)**, fighting fit from the sand, is already proven on soft ground, but ran here as though he would very much have preferred a proper end-to-end gallop.
**Vicious Prince(IRE)** tried to steal this from the front, setting a moderate gallop before making a break for home rounding the final bend. However, lack of a recent run counted against him in the conditions and he was eventually swallowed up. He has dropped to a very favourable mark after several disappointments and this was a bit better, but the way the race was run does not make it a reliable predictor for his future prospects.
**Rutters Rebel(IRE)**, stepping up half a mile for this seasonal reappearance, did not enjoy the clearest of runs against his elders and looks worth persevering with over this sort of trip back against his own age group.

## 1471 MICHAEL FOSTER MEMORIAL CONDITIONS STKS — 6f
4:05 (4:06) (C) 3-Y-0+ £8,363 (£3,172; £1,586; £721) Stalls High

Form RPR

426- **1** **Welsh Emperor (IRE)**[150] 6034 5-9-1 109 (b) DaleGibson 4 110
(TPTate) *mde all: rdn ent last: r.o wl* **11/2**

44-0 **2** 1 **Halmahera (IRE)**[21] 1126 9-9-1 101 (b) NCallan 7 107
(KARyan) *trckd ldrs: effrt 2f out: rdn over 1f out: kpt on ins last* **5/1**[3]

316- **3** 4 **Circuit Dancer (IRE)**[189] 5488 4-9-1 89 FLynch 5 95
(ABerry) *in tch: hdwy 2f out: sn rdn and kpt on ins last* **16/1**

-003 **4** hd **Fire Up The Band**[5] 1353 5-9-1 105 (v[1]) ANicholls 2 94
(DNicholls) *cl up: pushed along 2f out: rdn over 1f out and grad wknd* **3/1**[2]

6-24 **5** 3 **Orientor**[13] 1254 6-9-8 109 TQuinn 1 92
(JSGoldie) *chsd ldng pair: chsd along 1/2-way: rdn and wknd wl over 1f out* **7/4**[1]

206- **6** 9 **Dazzling Bay**[201] 5272 4-9-1 105 JFEgan 8 58
(TDEasterby) *trckd ldng pair: effrt 2f out: sn rdn and wknd* **7/1**

012- **7** 4 **Smirfys Systems**[242] 4273 5-9-1 80 TGMcLaughlin 9 46
(WMBrisbourne) *sn outpcd and bhd fr 1/2-way* **33/1**

1m 16.01s (3.51) **Going Correction** +0.775s/f (Yiel) **7** Ran SP% **114.7**
Speed ratings: **107,105,100,100,96 84,78**CSF £32.94 TOTE £7.90: £3.40, £3.40; EX 41.20.
**Owner** Mrs Sylvia Clegg **Bred** Times Of Wigan Ltd **Trained** Tadcaster, N Yorks

**FOCUS**
A decent conditions event run at a good pace in the conditions, but ability to handle soft ground was paramount.

**NOTEBOOK**
**Welsh Emperor(IRE)**, who relishes these conditions and who was best in at the weights, made full use of his rails draw by bouncing out of the gates and making every yard. Already a winner in Listed company and Group placed on the continent, he will undoubtedly be back there this season when conditions are in his favour.
**Halmahera(IRE)** came on from his Doncaster reappearance and ran much better with the blinkers back on. He has won on this sort of ground in the distant past, but does look better suited by a sound surface these days and is likely to make his presence felt in at least one of the top sprint handicaps later in the season.
**Circuit Dancer(IRE)** ran a cracker considering he was very badly in at the weights and has never shown much in his limited encounters with soft ground. He was consistent over this trip last season and will be suited by a return to faster ground, but form shown in this type of races is notoriously misleading and it will be interesting to see what the Handicapper does with him now.
**Fire Up The Band**, visored for the first time, showed up until fading in the latter stages and would have preferred faster ground. He is also probably at his best in big-field handicaps.
**Orientor**, a talented sprinter though never the easiest to predict, had every chance but seems to have gone backwards since his promising seasonal reappearance. He can have no excuses with regards to the ground either.

## 1472 KEN DURNIN MEMORIAL MAIDEN STKS — 5f
4:35 (4:35) (D) 3-Y-0 £5,395 (£1,660; £830; £415) Stalls High

Form RPR

0- **1** **Tizzy's Law**[207] 5142 3-8-9 JBramhill 2 68
(MABuckley) *trckd ldrs: hdwy over 2f out: rdn to ld and edgd rt ins last: styd on* **14/1**

24-2 **2** ¾ **Buy On The Red**[19] 1169 3-9-0 72 JQuinn 7 71
(WRMuir) *sn led: rdn along wl over 1f out: hdd ins last: drvn and kpt on* **10/11**[1]

0 **3** 1 **Ice Planet**[19] 1174 3-9-0 RWinston 9 68
(DNicholls) *s.i.s and bhd: gd hdwy 2f out: swtchd lft over 1f out: sn rdn and edgd lft ins last: kpt on* **28/1**

4 ½ **Urban Calm** 3-8-9 MHenry 8 62
(RMHCowell) *trckd ldrs: effrt 2f out: sn rdn and n.m.r over 1f out: kpt on u.p ins last* **14/1**

306- **5** ¾ **True Magic**[172] 5818 3-8-6 65 DAllan(3) 4 59
(JDBethell) *cl up: rdn and ev ch 2f out: drvn and wknd appr last* **7/1**[3]

-452 **6** 1 **Laconia (IRE)**[9] 1312 3-8-6 69 NMackay(3) 5 56
(JSMoore) *chsd ldrs: rdn along 2f out: sn one pce* **11/4**[2]

2-0 **7** 5 **Diamond Shannon (IRE)**[21] 1127 3-8-2 DTudhope(7) 6 41
(DCarroll) *s.i.s: a rr* **25/1**

00- **8** 1 ¼ **Reno's Magic**[197] 5342 3-8-2 CHaddon(7) 3 38
(WGMTurner) *swtchd lft s: a rr* **25/1**

63.67 secs (3.77) **Going Correction** +0.775s/f (Yiel) **8** Ran SP% **116.0**
Speed ratings: **100,98,97,96,95 93,85,83**CSF £27.41 TOTE £18.80: £3.00, £1.40, £5.50; EX 40.20.
**Owner** North Cheshire Trading & Storage Ltd **Bred** North Cheshire Trading And Storage Ltd **Trained** Castle Bytham, Lincs

**FOCUS**
A routine maiden though a couple of these may turn into fair handicappers.

**NOTEBOOK**
**Tizzy's Law**, a half-sister to several winners including Blue Iris and Abbajabba, showed nothing in her sole start at two but has improved over the winter and was a different proposition here. Relishing the soft ground, she won as though another furlong will not be a problem and she should do well in sprint handicap company when conditions are in her favour.
**Buy On The Red**, with the benefit of a previous outing this term, again showed plenty of speed from the gate but he has never raced on ground this soft before and it may have just found him out. He is always going to be vulnerable to an improver in races like this and may be worth a try in handicap company.
**Ice Planet ◆**, as on his debut, missed the break but at least he managed to get into the race this time despite the two-furlong drop in trip. He is gradually getting the hang of things and will be of interest back over further, especially when handicapped.
**Urban Calm ◆**, out of a winning half-sister to the Goodwood Cup winner Tioman Island, showed plenty of promise on this belated debut and will be much better suited by further.
**True Magic**, encountering soft ground for the first time, probably needs further than this but should have derived benefit from this first outing in six months.
**Laconia(IRE)**, who had far more racecourse experience than any of her rivals, had never raced on this sort of ground before and it did not appear to suit. She is beginning to look exposed.

## 1473 THOMAS LORD STKS (H'CAP) — 5f
5:10 (5:11) (C) (0-90,85) 3-Y-0 £9,665 (£2,974; £1,487; £743) Stalls High

Form RPR

02-5 **1** **Four Amigos (USA)**[7] 1333 3-8-13 77 TQuinn 2 86
(JGGiven) *towards rr: pushed along 1/2-way: gd hdwy wl over 1f out: rdn to ld ins last: edgd rt and styd on wl* **10/3**[1]

042- **2** 3 ½ **Baron Rhodes**[175] 5746 3-8-4 68 PMQuinn 3 67
(JSWainwright) *in tch on outer: hdwy 2f out: rdn to ld over 1f out: hdd and nt qckn ins last* **14/1**

123- **3** 1 ½ **A Little Bit Yarie**[304] 2470 3-9-6 84 DarrenWilliams 11 78
(KRBurke) *in tch: rdn along and wandered wl over 1f out: styd on u.p ins last: nrst fin* **6/1**[3]

020- **4** nk **Elliot's Choice (IRE)**[288] 2967 3-8-1 72 ow1 DTudhope(7) 12 65
(DCarroll) *towards rr: hdwy 2f out: swtchd lft and kpt on ins last: nrst fin* **25/1**

31- **5** shd **Fiddle Me Blue**[187] 5547 3-8-10 77 LFletcher(3) 15 70
(HMorrison) *cl up: led 1/2-way: rdn and hung bdly lft over 1f out: sn hdd & wknd* **7/2**[2]

003- **6** 1 ¼ **Baylaw Star**[171] 5829 3-8-12 76 JEdmunds 13 65
(JBalding) *chsd ldrs: rdn along 2f out: kpt on same pce appr last* **14/1**

216- **7** 2 **Tyne**[280] 3225 3-9-4 85 NMackay(3) 5 68
(TDBarron) *towards rr: hdwy 2f out: edgd lft ins last: nt rch ldrs* **10/1**

02-0 **8** nk **Lets Get It On (IRE)**[21] 1129 3-8-13 77 RWinston 6 59
(JJQuinn) *s.i.s and bhd tl styd on appr last* **14/1**

501- **9** 2 ½ **Jadan (IRE)**[193] 5432 3-8-10 74 ANicholls 8 49
(EJAlston) *cl up: ev ch 2f out: sn rdn and wknd appr last* **25/1**

100- **10** nk **Eastern Pearl**[189] 5480 3-8-9 76 TPQueally(3) 10 50
(MrsLStubbs) *cl up: rdn along 1/2-way: sn wknd* **20/1**

000- **11** 3 **Louisiade (IRE)**[172] 5824 3-8-5 72 DAllan(3) 7 37
(TDEasterby) *a rr* **12/1**

11-0 **12** ¾ **Peters Choice**[6] 1343 3-9-1 79 NCallan 9 42
(ISemple) *cl up: rdn along 1/2-way: sn wknd* **9/1**

025- **13** 14 **Mrs Spence**[256] 3864 3-8-4 68 DaleGibson 16 —
(MWEasterby) *led to 1/2-way: sn wknd and eased fnl f* **12/1**

63.40 secs (3.50) **Going Correction** +0.775s/f (Yiel) **13** Ran SP% **126.5**
Speed ratings: **103,97,95,94,94 92,89,88,84,84 79,78,55**CSF £52.91 CT £287.09 TOTE £4.40: £2.40, £3.80, £2.20; EX 30.10 Place 6 £101.40, Place 5 £46.03..
**Owner** Bailey Booth Boorer Nelson **Bred** Heatherwold Stud **Trained** Willoughton, Lincs
■ Stewards Enquiry : D Tudhope 7-day ban (reduced from 28 days on appeal): failed to take all reasonable and permissible measures throughout race to obtain best possible placing (Jul 15-Jul 22)

**FOCUS**
A fairly competitive three-year-old handicap run at a good pace in the conditions.

**NOTEBOOK**
**Four Amigos(USA)** was back over his winning trip, but it still took some getting in the conditions and after coming from well off the pace, hit the front inside the final furlong and pulled right away in the closing stages. He would probably have a better chance of seeing out the sixth furlong if ridden this way.
**Baron Rhodes**, whose only previous victory came over course and distance when there was cut in the ground, obviously likes it here and ran very well on this seasonal reappearance. She can win a race like this under similar conditions.
**A Little Bit Yarie**, apart from becoming rather wayward over a furlong from home, did very little wrong on this first start in ten months. His only previous victory was with cut in the ground and he is one to watch out for with this run under his belt, whilst an extra furlong under similar conditions should see him in an even better light.
**Elliot's Choice(IRE)**, reappearing after a nine-month break and making his debut on soft ground, was one of only two maidens in the field, but he stayed on really well in the latter stages and should come on for the run.
**Fiddle Me Blue**, the least experienced in the line-up, had shown ability in soft ground on her debut but, after showing good early speed, she got tired in the conditions on this first start in six months. She also still showed signs of greenness, so is probably capable of better and looks worth persevering with over this trip.
**Mrs Spence** *Official explanation: jockey said filly lost its action*

T/Plt: £185.90 to a £1 stake. Pool: £34,995.35. 137.40 winning tickets. T/Qpdt: £45.80 to a £1 stake. Pool: £2,415.50. 39.00 winning tickets. JR

# $^{1176}$WOLVERHAMPTON (A.W) (L-H)

Saturday, April 17

**OFFICIAL GOING: Standard**

Most of the races tended to unfold towards the centre of the track, which incidentally looked to be riding a little faster than normal.

Wind: almost nil Weather: fine

## 1474 BET DIRECT NO Q ON 08000 93 66 93 CLAIMING STKS 5f (F)

6:00 (6:00) (F) 3-Y-O+ £2,877 (£822; £411) Stalls Low

Form RPR

3351 **1** **Gilded Cove**$^{21}$ [1140] 4-9-6 64 ACulhane 7 65
(RHollinshead) *chsd ldrs: rdn to ld and edgd rt wl ins fnl f: r.o: fin lame* **10/11**$^{1}$

0050 **2** *nk* **Teyaar**$^{12}$ [1268] 8-8-11 53 HayleyTurner(5) 5 60
(MrsNMacauley) *w ldrs: rdn to ld ins fnl f: sn hdd: r.o* **16/1**

1044 **3** *1 ½* **Best Lead**$^{61}$ [796] 5-9-3 57 (b) RoryMoore(7) 6 63
(IanEmmerson) *led over 3f out: hdd and hung rt ins fnl f: no ex* **5/1**$^{3}$

0652 **4** *½* **River Days (IRE)**$^{19}$ [1178] 6-8-12 46 (vt) LisaJones(3) 1 52
(MissGayKelleway) *chsd ldrs: rdn over 1f out: styd on* **4/1**$^{2}$

0014 **5** *nk* **Star Lad (IRE)**$^{40}$ [990] 4-9-6 46 (b) ADaly 3 56
(RBrotherton) *led: hdd over 3f out: rdn over 1f out: styd on* **20/1**

0440 **6** *1 ½* **Juwwi**$^{18}$ [1185] 10-9-6 60 SCarson 2 51
(JMBradley) *sn outpcd: hdwy over 1f out: no imp fnl f* **12/1**

0-00 **7** *4* **Telepathic (IRE)**$^{50}$ [905] 4-9-3 56 PPMathers(7) 8 41
(ABerry) *chsd ldrs over 3f* **25/1**

240- **8** *5* **Moscow Mary**$^{113}$ [6237] 3-8-5 55 SWhitworth 4 14
(AGNewcombe) *s.i.s: outpcd* **20/1**

62.78 secs (-0.02) **Going Correction** 0.0s/f (Stan)
**WFA** 3 from 4yo+ 10lb 8 Ran SP% **116.0**
Speed ratings: **100,99,97,96,95 93,87,79**CSF £17.88 TOTE £2.00: £1.10, £4.50, £2.60; EX 26.80.
**Owner** M Johnson **Bred** R Hollinshead And M Johnson **Trained** Upper Longdon, Staffs

**FOCUS**
Quite a competitive claimer, run in a fair time for the grade.

**NOTEBOOK**
**Gilded Cove**, who is equally at home over an extra furlong, was made to work hard to repel the persistent Teyaar. However, he returned to the winner's enclosure lame.
**Teyaar** appreciated the drop in class and, while this was a sound effort, he has done all of his winning over an extra furlong.
**Best Lead**, freshened up by a break, showed plenty of pace and is entitled to strip sharper next time.
**River Days(IRE)** ◆ reserves her winning for here and was far from disgraced in this, for she had plenty to find on these terms. She is clearly in good heart at present and is worth bearing in mind for a similar contest in the near future.
**Star Lad(IRE)**, who has yet to win over this trip, had a stiff task at the weights. He is a pacy sort who should win again in his right grade.
**Juwwi** is very much on the downgrade nowadays.

## 1475 LITTLEWOODS BET DIRECT APPRENTICE H'CAP 1m 100y(F)

6:30 (6:31) (E) (0-85,84) 3-Y-O+ £3,539 (£1,089; £544; £272) Stalls Low

Form RPR

1-00 **1** **Nimello (USA)**$^{35}$ [1009] 8-10-0 **84** NChalmers 4 95
(AGNewcombe) *hld up: hdwy over 2f out: led and edgd lft 1f out: rdn out* **4/1**$^{2}$

00-1 **2** *1* **Samuel Charles**$^{17}$ [1207] 6-8-1 **60** BSwarbrick(3) 1 69
(WMBrisbourne) *unruly stalls: w ldrs: led over 2f out: sn edgd lft: rdn and hdd 1f out: sn n.m.r: kpt on* **6/1**$^{3}$

214- **3** *1 ½* **Lauro**$^{203}$ [5225] 4-9-1 71 PMulrennan 5 77
(MissJACamacho) *chsd ldrs: rdn over 3f out: styd on* **6/1**$^{3}$

0624 **4** *1 ¾* **Spark Up**$^{21}$ [1141] 4-7-13 **55** (b) JFMcDonald 6 57
(JWUnett) *hld up: hmpd 6f out: styd on appr fnl f: nvr nrr* **14/1**

2222 **5** *1 ¼* **Bank On Him**$^{15}$ [1232] 9-8-6 **62** AQuinn 8 62
(GLMoore) *chsd ldr: led 4f out: hdd over 2f out: wknd fnl f* **7/2**$^{1}$

0004 **6** *1 ¼* **Air Mail**$^{2}$ [1424] 7-8-13 **72** (v) RoryMoore(3) 3 69
(MrsNMacauley) *chsd ldrs: rdn over 2f out: wknd over 1f out* **10/1**

0523 **7** *1 ¾* **Labrett**$^{21}$ [1139] 7-9-12 **82** (tp) DNolan 7 75
(MissGayKelleway) *sn led: hdd 4f out: wknd wl over 1f out* **7/2**$^{1}$

5645 **8** *7* **Skibereen (IRE)**$^{9}$ [1318] 4-8-6 **65** (p) NataliaGemelova(3) 2 44
(IWMcinnes) *s.s: hdwy 6f out: wknd over 2f out* **20/1**

1m 50.52s (-0.57) **Going Correction** 0.0s/f (Stan) 8 Ran SP% **113.5**
Speed ratings: **102,101,99,97,96 95,93,86**CSF £27.68 CT £142.06 TOTE £5.70: £2.30, £1.60, £2.50; EX 34.40.
**Owner** Ms Gerardine P O'Reilly **Bred** Glencrest Farm **Trained** Yarnscombe, Devon
■ Stewards Enquiry : Natalia Gemelova caution: careless riding

**FOCUS**
A decent contest for an apprentice handicap and, although they did not appear to go that quick, the time was respectable.

**NOTEBOOK**
**Nimello(USA)** found this much more his level having been outclassed the last twice. He is clearly at the top of his game at present, but can expect no favours from the Handicapper.
**Samuel Charles**, who gave trouble in the stalls, did not appear to do much wrong during the race itself, and may have done better still had he not raced tight to the far rails once in line for home.
**Lauro**, who has yet to finish out of the frame here in four outings, is entitled to strip sharper for this effort, her first for nearly seven months.
**Spark Up**, done no favours when Skibereen tightened her up at around the six-furlong point, stuck to her task well and clearly found this trip no problem. She is probably not one to rely on too heavily, but there is no doubt that she does have ability.
**Bank On Him**, who does most of his racing on the Polytrack, always looked to be doing just a bit too much and as a consequence just did not get home.
**Air Mail**, having gone over two-years without winning has become well handicapped, but there was still little encouragement for connections.
**Labrett** ran a lacklustre race and is better when he can have a lead.

## 1476 BETDIRECT.CO.UK MAIDEN STKS 1m 100y(F)

7:00 (7:00) (D) 3-Y-O+ £3,419 (£1,052; £526; £263) Stalls Low

Form RPR

24-2 **1** **Sunisa (IRE)**$^{15}$ [1227] 3-8-6 72 DHolland 2 73
(BWHills) *chsd ldr: led over 3f out: rdn and hung rt wl over 1f out: drvn clr fnl f* **4/5**$^{1}$

00- **2** *7* **Landucci**$^{197}$ [5345] 3-8-11 SWhitworth 8 63
(JWHills) *hld up: hdwy over 4f out: rdn and ev ch wl over 1f out: wknd fnl f* **9/4**$^{2}$

**3** *2 ½* **Bansha Bru (IRE)**$^{36}$ 4-9-11 ACulhane 7 58
(MissECLavelle) *s.i.s: outpcd: hdwy 4f out: rdn over 2f out: hung lft and wknd wl over 1f out* **25/1**

0- **4** *4* **Puri**$^{348}$ [1394] 5-9-11 MFenton 1 50
(JGGiven) *son led: hdd over 3f out: wknd wl over 1f out* **12/1**

5-5 **5** *3* **Magic Sting**$^{12}$ [1271] 3-8-11 JMackay 4 43
(MLWBell) *chsd ldrs over 6f* **13/2**$^{3}$

0 **6** *6* **Princess Bankes**$^{34}$ [1015] 3-8-3 60 LisaJones(3) 6 26
(MissGayKelleway) *prom over 5f* **25/1**

-0 **7** *4* **Zambezi River**$^{9}$ [1311] 5-9-8 ow4 CJDavies(7) 5 26
(JMBradley) *chsd ldrs 6f* **100/1**

0 **8** *dist* **Miss Librate**$^{9}$ [1310] 6-9-6 SCarson 3 —
(JMBradley) *sn pushed along in rr: wknd 5f out* **33/1**

1m 51.19s (0.10) **Going Correction** 0.0s/f (Stan)
**WFA** 3 from 4yo+ 14lb 8 Ran SP% **119.0**
Speed ratings: **100,99,89,85,82 76,72,—**CSF £2.83 TOTE £1.70: £1.10, £1.20, £4.50; EX 3.70.
**Owner** Ray Richards **Bred** H De Bromhead **Trained** Lambourn, Berks

**FOCUS**
This lacked strength in depth, and the front pair apart the others will find it difficult to win a race of any description. The winner is no more than fairly treated on current mark.

**NOTEBOOK**
**Sunisa(IRE)** found a really soft race to get off the mark and, while clearly nothing special, her trainer should be able to exploit her current mark of 72.
**Landucci** is sure to strip fitter for the outing and will certainly have more options open to him now in handicaps. This effort should ensure he starts off on a fair mark.
**Bansha Bru(IRE)** cut little ice in a couple of bumpers and, while she picked up some prizemoney, achieved little in doing so.
**Puri** must have shown connections something for them to have kept him in training as a five-year-old but, while he is open to improvement, he will need to.
**Magic Sting**, bandaged in front will have more option open to him now in handicaps, but he will need to leave this effort behind if he is to trouble the judge.
**Miss Librate** *Official explanation: jockey said mare finished distressed*

## 1477 NEW SITE @ BETDIRECT.CO.UK H'CAP 6f (F)

7:30 (7:30) (E) (0-70,68) 3-Y-O+ £3,656 (£1,125; £562; £281) Stalls Low

Form RPR

2013 **1** **Italian Mist (FR)**$^{21}$ [1131] 5-9-9 63 (e) GFaulkner 12 70
(JulianPoulton) *chsd ldrs: rdn to ld ins fnl f: r.o* **6/1**$^{2}$

3-20 **2** *½* **Zagala**$^{60}$ [803] 4-9-9 63 (t) ACulhane 5 69
(SLKeightley) *hld up: hdwy 1/2-way: rdn over 1f out: r.o* **13/2**$^{3}$

0620 **3** *nk* **Aguila Loco (IRE)**$^{12}$ [1268] 5-9-1 55 (p) MFenton 8 60
(MrsStefLiddiard) *w ldrs: edgd lft over 3f out: rdn and ev ch fr over 1f out: r.o* **12/1**

0403 **4** *shd* **Kennington**$^{12}$ [1268] 4-8-9 54 (v) HayleyTurner(5) 11 58
(MrsCADunnett) *mde most tl hdd ins fnl f: r.o* **16/1**

0501 **5** *2* **Effective**$^{15}$ [1230] 4-9-8 62 (v) EStack 4 60
(APJarvis) *prom: edgd lft: hmpd over 3f out: sn lost pl: hdwy u.p over 1f out: no ex ins fnl f* **8/1**

0130 **6** *nk* **Sabana (IRE)**$^{34}$ [1018] 6-8-8 48 (b) SCarson 10 45
(JMBradley) *hld up in tch: rdn over 1f out: styd on same pce* **16/1**

3421 **7** *¾* **Spindor (USA)**$^{17}$ [1204] 5-9-7 61 (b) DHolland 9 56
(JAOsborne) *swtchd rt sn after s: hdwy over 4f out: outpcd and hung lft 2f out: styd on u.p ins fnl f* **4/1**$^{1}$

-522 **8** *1 ¾* **Pawan (IRE)**$^{5}$ [1361] 4-9-1 55 AnnStokell 2 45
(MissAStokell) *s.i.s: in rr whn bdly hmpd over 3f out: n.d* **9/1**

56-0 **9** *shd* **Pulse**$^{5}$ [1368] 6-9-2 56 (p) RLMoore 1 46
(JMBradley) *hld up: n.m.r over 3f out: n.d* **20/1**

5553 **10** *2 ½* **Amelia (IRE)**$^{15}$ [1229] 6-8-1 48 BSwarbrick(7) 13 30
(WMBrisbourne) *w ldrs over 3f: wknd over 1f out* **15/2**

03-0 **11** *hd* **Laurel Dawn**$^{93}$ [540] 6-9-0 61 PPMathers(7) 6 43
(IWMcinnes) *s.s: outpcd* **33/1**

-000 **12** *8* **Noble Locks (IRE)**$^{54}$ [866] 6-9-11 68 LisaJones(3) 7 26
(JWUnett) *sn outpcd* **16/1**

30-1 **13** *5* **Caustic Wit (IRE)**$^{96}$ [509] 6-8-13 56 RMiles(3) 3 —
(MSSaunders) *prom: bmpd over 3f out: wknd wl over 1f out: eased* **7/1**

1m 15.79s (-0.01) **Going Correction** 0.0s/f (Stan) 13 Ran SP% **126.0**
Speed ratings: **100,99,98,98,96 95,94,92,92,88 88,78,71**CSF £47.49 CT £484.06 TOTE £8.10: £3.00, £2.20, £3.80; EX 19.80.
**Owner** S P Shore **Bred** Mrs Hilary Trigg & Mr John Veil **Trained** Kentford, Suffolk
■ Stewards Enquiry : M Fenton three-day ban: careless riding (Apr 28-30)

**FOCUS**
A competitive low-grade contest and a triumph for the Handicapper, with less than a length covering the first four home and the winner putting up a career-best effort.

**NOTEBOOK**
**Italian Mist(FR)** does not always impress with his high head carriage, but he knuckled down well enough to win off a career-high mark. He is in fine form at present and may be capable of exploiting a much lower mark on turf.
**Zagala** was doing her best work in the closing stages and was probably unlucky to come up against a horse at the top of his game at present. She can find compensation before long.
**Aguila Loco(IRE)**, who ran too free last time, was never able to dominate, but he battled on well and no doubt his astute handler will find another opening for him somewhere.
**Kennington** turned in a solid effort considering he was harried for the lead all the way.
**Effective**, 4lb higher than when winning at Lingfield, was done no favours as Aguila Loco came across him leaving the back straight.
**Sabana(IRE)** travelled really well off this sound pace, but this was a little more competitive than he normally cares for. While he is not one to rely on, he would be of interest if dropping back into selling company.
**Spindor(USA)**, even allowing for the fact that this trip may be sharp enough for him, does not look one to place too much faith in.
**Pawan(IRE)** got mugged leaving the back straight and did well to remain upright. Although he is still a maiden he is not without ability, but he looks to need further than this.
**Caustic Wit(IRE)** *Official explanation: jockey said gelding lost its action leaving the stalls*

## 1478 £10 FREE BET @ BETDIRECT.CO.UK (S) STKS 7f (F)

8:00 (8:00) (G) 3-Y-O £2,527 (£722; £361) Stalls High

Form RPR

5110 **1** **Lady Mo**$^{44}$ [965] 3-8-12 60 NCallan 8 75
(KARyan) *chsd ldrs: led over 2f out: rdn clr: eased ins fnl f* **11/8**$^{1}$

-005 **2** *12* **Wendy's Girl (IRE)**$^{12}$ [1266] 3-8-4 57 THamilton(3) 3 40
(RPElliott) *w ldr: led 1/2-way: hdd & wknd over 2f out* **12/1**

0536 **3** *3* **Son Of Rembrandt (IRE)**$^{16}$ [1220] 3-8-5 53 MHoward(7) 5 38
(DKIvory) *outpcd: nvr nrr* **12/1**

00-5 **4** *nk* **Flying Spud**$^{31}$ [1038] 3-8-12 47 ADaly 7 37
(JLSpearing) *dwlt: outpcd: nvr nrr* **9/1**$^{3}$

305- **5** *5* **Venetian Romance (IRE)**$^{183}$ [5620] 3-8-5 56 ow1 SHitchcott(3) 2 20
(APJones) *s.i.s: outpcd* **16/1**

10-0 **6** *5* **Rules For Jokers (IRE)**[21] 1129 3-9-3 80 DHolland 4 17
(JAOsborne) *chsd ldrs: rdn 1/2-way: wknd over 2f out* **2/1**[2]
-005 **7** *9* **Blue Emperor (IRE)**[2] 1425 3-8-7 60 (b[1]) DNolan(5) 6 —
(PABlockley) *s.i.s: outpcd* **16/1**
30-0 **8** *2* **Apollo Gee (IRE)**[2] 1422 3-8-7 64 (b[1]) JFMcDonald(5) 1 —
(BJMeehan) *sn led: hdd 1/2-way: wknd wl over 2f out* **11/1**
1m 30.41s (0.09) **Going Correction** 0.0s/f (Stan) **8** Ran SP% **120.9**
Speed ratings: **99,85,81,81,75 70,59,57**CSF £21.34 TOTE £2.20: £1.20, £2.80, £2.50; EX 28.30.There was no bid for the winner.
**Owner** Wooster Partnership **Bred** Mrs M S Teversham **Trained** Hambleton, N Yorks

**FOCUS**
A decent winning time for the class of contest, and although this looks an improved effort, the form may need treating with caution.

**NOTEBOOK**
**Lady Mo** is a tough filly who has plenty of form at this level. She stays further than this so was well suited to the strong pace and, as her rivals dropped away, she was left to win as she liked.
**Wendy's Girl(IRE)** had no chance of keeping up the strong pace she had helped set.
**Son Of Rembrandt(IRE)** managed to get into the frame, but achieved little in doing so.
**Flying Spud**, who is out of a winning hurdler, will be suited by a stiffer test than he faced here.
**Rules For Jokers(IRE)** looks to have lost his way for the time being. Out of a mare that is a sister to smart middle-distance performer The Miller, it may be that he will need a stiffer test in time.
*Official explanation: jockey said gelding was never travelling*

## 1479 BET IN RUNNING @ BETDIRECT.CO.UK H'CAP 1m 1f 79y(F)
**8:30** (8:30) (F) (0-55,55) 4-Y-O+ **£2,933** (£838; £419) **Stalls** Low

Form RPR
0244 **1** **Danger Bird (IRE)**[19] 1181 4-9-0 50 ACulhane 6 60
(RHollinshead) *chsd ldrs: led over 2f out: drvn out* **13/2**[3]
1223 **2** *2* **Monduru**[19] 1168 7-8-11 47 (be) RLMoore 9 53
(GLMoore) *hld up: hdwy over 3f out: chsd wnr and hung lft over 1f out: nt run on* **9/1**
062- **3** *2* **Champain Sands (IRE)**[179] 5696 5-8-5 48 BSwarbrick(7) 7 50
(WMBrisbourne) *a.p: rdn over 2f out: one pce fnl f* **4/1**[1]
0400 **4** *2* **Crusoe (IRE)**[15] 1233 7-8-10 51 (b) JFMcDonald(5) 4 49
(ASadik) *chsd ldrs: outpcd over 2f out: styd on ins fnl f* **14/1**
/006 **5** *shd* **Bought Direct**[45] 952 5-8-13 52 RMiles(3) 13 50
(RJSmith) *prom: rdn whn hmpd 2f out: styd on same pce* **12/1**
4102 **6** *nk* **Jade Star (USA)**[19] 1181 4-9-3 53 (p) MFenton 5 50
(MissGayKelleway) *chsd ldrs: led over 3f out: hdd over 2f out: wknd fnl f* **13/2**[3]
10-0 **7** *3/4* **Mezereon**[16] 602 4-8-12 55 DTudhope(7) 10 51
(DCarroll) *s.i.s: hld up: rdn 4f out: nvr trbld ldrs* **10/1**
1220 **8** *nk* **Prince Prospect**[21] 1136 8-8-6 49 KristinStubbs(7) 12 44
(MrsLStubbs) *outpcd: styd on appr fnl f: nvr nrr* **20/1**
040- **9** *shd* **Down To The Woods (USA)**[202] 5258 6-9-0 50 RFfrench 3 45
(RDEWoodhouse) *prom: lost pl over 5f out: n.d after* **7/1**
1022 **10** *3/4* **Wilson Bluebottle (IRE)**[15] 1233 5-8-8 49 (b) PMulrennan(5) 2 42
(MWEasterby) *sn led: hdd over 3f out: wknd over 1f out* **13/2**[3]
5014 **11** *nk* **Sorbiesharry (IRE)**[15] 1233 5-9-0 50 (p) PMcCabe 8 43
(MrsNMacauley) *hld up: effrt over 2f out: sn wknd* **6/1**[2]
000- **12** *9* **Maravedi (IRE)**[290] 2898 4-8-8 47 LisaJones(3) 1 22
(SLKeightley) *chsd ldrs: lost pl over 5f out: sn bhd* **28/1**
-506 **13** *3/4* **Better Off**[31] 1035 6-9-2 52 (p) JoannaBadger 11 25
(MrsNMacauley) *s.s: hld up: hdwy 3f out: sn wknd* **33/1**
2m 1.90s (-1.10) **Going Correction** 0.0s/f (Stan) **13** Ran SP% **131.4**
Speed ratings: **104,102,100,98,98 98,97,97,97,96 96,88,87**CSF £69.33 CT £276.77 TOTE £9.60: £3.30, £5.30, £2.20; EX 84.30 Place 6 £46.59, Place 5 £33.47..
**Owner** The C H F Partnership **Bred** Christian Healy **Trained** Upper Longdon, Staffs

**FOCUS**
This was no better than a seller, but it was run at a good pace.

**NOTEBOOK**
**Danger Bird(IRE)**, a long-standing maiden, finally got her act together and, despite some fairly vigorous tail-swishing, never looked likely to be reeled in.
**Monduru** has been running well enough of late, but he left the impression he is saving a bit for himself.
**Champain Sands(IRE)**, having his first outing for current connections, did not shape too badly on this return to action and, off his present mark, they are sure to find an opening for him.
**Crusoe(IRE)** is well treated on the best of his form, and there was a little more promise here than of late.
**Bought Direct**, a dual-winning miler in Ireland, has cut little ice in his three previous outings here. However, he is slipping in the weights and would have finished a deal closer had he not been squeezed out once in line for home.
**Jade Star(USA)** was entitled to finish close to the winner on their running here back in February (3lb worse off for a neck).
T/Plt: £105.60 to a £1 stake. Pool: £30,929.00. 213.70 winning tickets. T/Qpdt: £18.50 to a £1 stake. Pool: £1,979.40. 79.10 winning tickets. CR

1480 - 1484a (Foreign Racing) - See Raceform Interactive

# 1151 LEOPARDSTOWN (L-H)
Sunday, April 18

**OFFICIAL GOING: Soft**

## 1485a LEOPARDSTOWN 1,000 GUINEAS TRIAL STKS (LISTED RACE) (FILLIES) 7f
**3:00** (3:00) 3-Y-O **£22,922** (£6,725; £3,204; £1,091)

RPR
**1** **Royal Tigress (USA)**[28] 1070 3-8-11 JPSpencer 4 101
(APO'Brien, Ire) *chsd ldrs: 3rd and rdn ent st: 2nd 1f out: kpt on wl u.p to ld on line* **5/2**[1]
**2** *shd* **Takrice**[28] 1070 3-8-11 98 DPMcDonogh 1 101
(KevinPrendergast, Ire) *3rd to 1/2-way: lost pl ent st: hdwy on inner 1 1/2f out: led over 1f out: kpt on wl: hdd on line* **11/1**
**3** *2* **Misty Heights**[210] 5103 3-8-11 105 PJSmullen 5 96
(DKWeld, Ire) *hld up in 5th: 4th and hdwy on outer early st: chal over 1f out: kpt on same pce* **3/1**[2]
**4** *1 1/2* **Treasure The Lady (IRE)**[176] 5762 3-8-11 MJKinane 3 92
(JohnMOxx, Ire) *disp ld: hdd 1/2-way: regained ld early st: wandered abt u.p: hdd and no ex over 1f out* **5/2**[1]
**5** *1 1/2* **Danelissima (IRE)**[174] 5801 3-8-11 (b[1]) KJManning 7 88
(JSBolger, Ire) *hld up: 6th into st: kpt on ins fnl f* **10/1**[3]
**6** *1/2* **Alexander Duchess (IRE)**[162] 5955 3-8-11 98 JPMurtagh 6 87
(JGBurns, Ire) *disp ld: led 1/2-way: hdd early st: no ex over 1f out* **10/1**[3]
**7** *14* **Brazilian Sun (IRE)**[174] 5801 3-8-11 NGMcCullagh 2 52
(EdwardLynam, Ire) *s.i.s and a in rr* **16/1**
1m 39.2s **Going Correction** +1.25s/f (Soft) **7** Ran SP% **114.5**
Speed ratings: **110,109,107,105,104 103,87**CSF £30.46 TOTE £3.70: £1.80, £3.90; DF 45.30.
**Owner** Mrs John Magnier **Bred** Pacelco Sa & Chelston Ireland **Trained** Ballydoyle, Co Tipperary
■ Stewards Enquiry : J P Spencer one-day ban: used whip with excessive frequency (May 2)

**NOTEBOOK**
**Royal Tigress(USA)** showed progress from her Curragh reappearance and her fitness saw her assert close home. She got through this bad ground but her trainer is hoping for a better surface for her Curragh 1,000 bid.
**Takrice** finished tailed off and lame in the same race that the winner contested at the Curragh last month but showed no ill effects of that disappointing run here. She came a second time on the inner to lead over a furlong out and was only headed on the line.
**Misty Heights** beat the winner some five lengths in a maiden last season and on looks certainly has the scope to turn it around with the first pair in the future.
**Treasure The Lady(IRE)** was made plenty of use off and got tired inside the last. She might improve.
**Danelissima(IRE)** was not asked much of a question in this ground.
**Alexander Duchess(IRE)** was in the first pair to the straight before tiring. She did not like the ground either.

## 1487a LEOPARDSTOWN 2,000 GUINEAS TRIAL STKS (LISTED RACE) (C&G) 1m
**4:00** (4:00) 3-Y-O **£22,922** (£6,725; £3,204; £1,091)

RPR
**1** **Grey Swallow (IRE)**[174] 5802 3-9-2 PJSmullen 5 110
(DKWeld, Ire) *cl up in 4th: 3rd and chal early st: led ins fnl f: kpt on wl whn pressed cl home* **4/9**[1]
**2** *hd* **Meath (IRE)**[183] 5649 3-8-11 JPSpencer 6 105
(APO'Brien, Ire) *set slow pce: hdd 2f out: rallied u.p fnl f: jst failed* **3/1**[2]
**3** *3 1/2* **Amarula Ridge (IRE)**[14] 1256 3-8-11 DPMcDonogh 1 98
(KevinPrendergast, Ire) *cl 2nd: led 2f out: hdd ins fnl f: sn no ex* **8/1**[3]
**4** *1* **Medicinal (IRE)**[192] 5464 3-8-11 PShanahan 2 96
(DKWeld, Ire) *settled 3rd: rdn and no imp early st: kpt on hands and heals fnl f* **12/1**
**5** *11* **Loch Garman (IRE)** 3-8-11 KJManning 3 74
(JSBolger, Ire) *dwlt and slowly away: sn in tch: wknd st* **25/1**
1m 51.6s **Going Correction** +1.25s/f (Soft) **5** Ran SP% **116.9**
Speed ratings: **114,113,110,109,98**CSF £2.38 TOTE £1.40: £1.10, £1.90; DF 2.60.
**Owner** Mrs Rochelle Quinn **Bred** Mrs C L Weld **Trained** The Curragh, Co Kildare

**NOTEBOOK**
**Grey Swallow(IRE)** is a difficult horse to judge on looks. He would not have impressed all in the paddock but there is something to work on although he was fit enough. Challenging on the outer from two furlongs down, he got a flick off Amarula Ridge's rider's whip across his nose early inside the last but that barely affected his concentration and he kept on strongly enough. At face value this was nowhere good enough to win a 2,000 Guineas anywhere but on better ground he will almost certainly show the benefit of this careful run. Time is against him, more than anything else.
**Meath(IRE)** could be judged an improver and he was certainly sharper looking than the winner. He flattered inside the last but Grey Swallow's narrow advantage was maintained to the line.
**Amarula Ridge(IRE)**, in front over a furlong and a half out, was between horses early inside the last but was soon outpaced.
**Medicinal(IRE)** could be the major improver out of this race, especially over further.

## 1489a P.W.MCGRATH MEMORIAL BALLYSAX STKS (GROUP 3) 1m 2f
**5:00** (5:02) 3-Y-O **£34,063** (£9,415; £4,485)

RPR
**1** **Yeats (IRE)**[210] 5101 3-9-0 JPSpencer 4 117+
(APO'Brien, Ire) *mde all: qcknd clr 1 1/2f out: eased fnl f: impressive* **1/3**[1]
**2** *10* **Dabiroun (IRE)**[14] 1256 3-9-0 MJKinane 3 96
(JohnMOxx, Ire) *racd in 2nd: effrt ent st: no imp fr 1 1/2f out: one pce* **5/2**[2]
**3** *14* **Lord Admiral (USA)**[239] 4396 3-9-0 96 FMBerry 2 72
(CharlesO'Brien, Ire) *hld up in 3rd: tk clsr order 3f out: rdn ent st: sn wknd* **20/1**[3]
2m 23.4s **Going Correction** +1.675s/f (Heavy) **3** Ran SP% **108.4**
Speed ratings: **115,107,95**CSF £1.50 TOTE £1.30; DF 1.20.
**Owner** Mrs John Magnier **Bred** Barronstown Stud & Orpendale **Trained** Ballydoyle, Co Tipperary

**NOTEBOOK**
**Yeats(IRE)** really is not a great deal to look at, there is not a lot of him. He handled the ground well enough, came wide into the straight and wasn't in any danger at all from a furlong and a half down. Eased heavily inside the last, he won unchallenged. Epsom in June will be an entirely matte, but there is no doubt as to the esteem in which he is held within Ballydoyle and it is difficult to imagine a queue eager to take him on when he reappears next in the Derrinstown Stud Derby Trial here on May 9th.
**Dabiroun(IRE)** might have had a fitness advantage after two previous outings but that counted for nothing here and he was readily outpaced after coming under pressure before the straight.
**Lord Admiral(USA)** was not a contender in the straight.

1490 - 1491a (Foreign Racing) - See Raceform Interactive

# 1402 LINGFIELD (L-H)
Monday, April 19

**OFFICIAL GOING: Standard**
Wind: almost nil Weather: overcast, thundery, becoming bright

## 1492 BET DIRECT ON 0800 32 93 93 BANDED STKS 1m 4f (P)
**2:20** (2:25) (H) 4-Y-O+ **£1,617** (£462; £231) **Stalls** Low

Form RPR
-163 **1** **Montosari**[41] 995 5-8-13 45 DHolland 3 54
(PMitchell) *prom: trckd ldr 7f out: led wl over 3f out: pushed wl clr: easily* **6/4**[1]
103- **2** *10* **Quest On Air**[270] 3541 5-8-13 45 LDettori 1 38
(JRJenkins) *trckd ldr to 7f out: rdn to chse wnr over 3f out: no imp over 2f out* **4/1**[2]
325- **3** *1 3/4* **Bosphorus**[180] 5089 5-8-8 45 (v) DNolan(5) 7 35
(DGBridgwater) *t.k.h: hld up: prog to dispute 2nd pl over 3f out: sn rdn and one pce: no ch after* **9/2**[3]
0631 **4** *1 1/4* **Birth Of The Blues**[13] 1281 8-8-13 45 RHughes 4 33
(ACharlton) *stdd s: hld up in last: outpcd over 3f out: shuffled along and one pce fr over 2f out* **5/1**
0-46 **5** *11* **Cadwallader (USA)**[36] 1016 4-8-5 45 (p) RJKilloran(7) 6 16
(PBurgoyne) *in tch tl outpcd 4f out: sn bhd* **33/1**
/0-4 **6** *1* **Full Egalite**[4] 1402 8-8-13 30 (b) KFallon 2 14
(BRJohnson) *chsd ldrs: rdn 4f out: wknd 3f out* **10/1**


The Form Book, Raceform Ltd, Compton, RG20 6NL

000- 7 1 1/2 **Little Sky**[161] 5972 7-8-8 45 HayleyTurner(5) 5 12
(DMullarkey) *led to wl over 3f out: wknd and sn bhd* **12/1**
2m 32.85s (-1.39) **Going Correction** -0.025s/f (Stan)
**WFA** 4 from 5yo+ 1lb **7** Ran SP% **114.6**
Speed ratings: **103,96,95,94,87 86,85**CSF £7.74 TOTE £2.10: £1.70, £2.10; EX 9.60.
**Owner** Caterham Racing (jdrp) **Bred** S Gollogly **Trained** Epsom, Surrey
■ Stewards Enquiry : R J Killoran caution: used whip when out of contention

**FOCUS**
Not a very competitive race, but a good performance from the winner in a decent time for the grade.

**NOTEBOOK**
**Montosari** had been a beaten favourite on his two previous starts in similar company, but he could hardly fail to win this. Always well placed, he came right away and won unchallenged. He may now be given another try over hurdles, which is probably not a bad idea considering connections will be doing well to find a race as weak as this for his next start on the Flat, as they are likely to be forced back into handicaps.
**Quest On Air**, successful in a turf handicap off a mark of 42 last year, was disappointing on this first attempt in regional racing. The booking of Dettori suggested he must have been fit enough for this first run in 270 days, but he never once threatened the winner.
**Bosphorus**, returned to the level after a couple of unsuccessful starts over hurdles, travelled well but found very little when asked. He is likely to improve for the outing and is probably better over.
**Birth Of The Blues** failed to run to the form he showed when winning an apprentice banded stakes on his previous outing and, not that consistent, is not one to place much faith in.
**Cadwallader(USA)** did not improve for the fitting of cheekpieces.

## 1493 £10 FREE BET @ BET DIRECT SKY ACTIVE BANDED STKS 1m 2f (P)
2:50 (2:55) (H ) 3-Y-0+ **£1,260** (£360; £180) **Stalls** Low

Form RPR
-600 1 **Lady At Leisure (IRE)**[56] 855 4-9-8 35 SWhitworth 2 40
(MJRyan) *trckd ldrs: prog to ld wl over 3f out: 3l clr ent fnl f: hrd rdn: jst hld on* **9/1**[2]
02 2 hd **Top Style (IRE)**[4] 1403 6-9-8 30 KFallon 3 40
(MJWallace) *chsd ldrs: pushed along over 6f out: dropped to last 5f out: effrt on outer over 2f out: chsd wnr fnl f: kpt on: jst failed* **4/9**[1]
-006 3 5 **Sennen Cove**[27] 1094 5-9-8 30 (t) SSanders 4 31
(RBastiman) *settled in rr: stdy prog to chse wnr 3f out: shkn up and no imp over 1f out: eased ins fnl f* **14/1**
66-0 4 3 1/2 **Lady Xanthia**[28] 1076 3-8-5 35 EAhern 1 24
(IAWood) *led to wl over 3f out: sn hrd rdn and wknd* **16/1**
00-5 5 1 1/4 **Sylvan Twister**[4] 1404 5-9-8 35 NPollard 7 22
(PMitchell) *trckd ldrs: pushed along 4f out: struggling and btn wl over 2f out* **11/1**[3]
0/06 6 3/4 **Te Anau**[60] 823 7-9-1 30 LauraPike(7) 6 21
(WJMusson) *trckd ldr to over 4f out: lost pl: shuffled along and btn 3f out* **33/1**
B230 7 1/2 **Spiders Web**[21] 1167 4-9-8 35 (b) GCarter 5 20
(TKeddy) *dwlt: hld up in rr: rdn over 3f out: sn wknd* **9/1**[2]
2m 8.49s (0.64) **Going Correction** -0.025s/f (Stan)
**WFA** 3 from 4yo+ 17lb **7** Ran SP% **113.1**
Speed ratings: **96,95,91,89,88 87,87**CSF £13.20 TOTE £10.00: £3.80, £1.10; EX 18.60.
**Owner** The Aldora Partnership **Bred** Bo Helander **Trained** Newmarket, Suffolk

**FOCUS**
Just moderate stuff, but at least the pace was fair and the form should work out at this sort of level.

**NOTEBOOK**
**Lady At Leisure(IRE)**, making her debut for Mick Ryan, showed improved form to gain her first-ever win. Under a good ride, she made the most of the favourite Top Style struggling to hold his position when kicking for home over three out and had a decisive lead turning into the straight, just enough to hold him off at the line. This will have provided her with a nice confidence boost.
**Top Style(IRE)** was very disappointing on his British debut over a mile and a half at Southwell, but offered encouragement switched to Polytrack over seven furlongs on his previous outing. Stepped up to what should have been a more suitable trip, he lost his position down the back straight and by the time he hit full stride, the eventual winner was already clear. There is certainly a race in him, but he is proving expensive to follow.
**Sennen Cove**, with the tongue-tie re-fitted on this step up in trip and return to Polytrack, ran his race but was no match for the front two and has had plenty of chances.
**Lady Xanthia**, trying a trip this far for the first time and switched back to Polytrack, ran better than she did on her reappearance.
**Sylvan Twister** continues to struggle.

## 1494 BET DIRECT INTERACTIVE BANDED STKS 1m (P)
3:20 (3:25) (H ) 3-Y-0+ **£1,267** (£362; £181) **Stalls** High

Form RPR
-525 1 **Due To Me**[4] 1407 4-9-0 40 (p) SWhitworth 1 47
(GLMoore) *settled in 4th: prog to trck ldr over 2f out: led jst over 1f out: idled in front but rdn clr* **9/4**[2]
26-2 2 3 **Benjamin (IRE)**[4] 1407 6-9-0 40 (bt) VSlattery 5 40
(JaneSouthcombe) *t.k.h: w ldr: led 5f out: rdn and hdd jst over 1f out : nt qckn* **11/4**[3]
0011 3 shd **Cumbrian Princess**[4] 1407 7-9-6 40 DSweeney 2 46
(MBlanshard) *hld up in 3rd: chsd ldr over 3f out to over 2f out: rdn and nt qckn over 1f out* **5/4**[1]
0300 4 2 1/2 **Lady Liesel**[21] 1165 4-9-0 40 JTate 4 34
(JJBridger) *hld up in last: effrt 3f out: sn shkn up and no imp ldrs* **12/1**
0-00 5 19 **Hektikos**[19] 1207 4-9-0 40 RLMoore 3 —
(SDow) *pushed up to ld: hdd 5f out: hrd rdn and wknd over 3f out: t.o* **25/1**
1m 40.59s (1.04) **Going Correction** -0.025s/f (Stan) **5** Ran SP% **113.4**
Speed ratings: **93,90,89,87,68**CSF £9.12 TOTE £3.60: £1.70, £1.90; EX 7.30.
**Owner** Mrs Sheila Clarke **Bred** Exors Of The Late R M West **Trained** Woodingdean, E Sussex

**FOCUS**
Just an average race for the grade and a modest winning time.

**NOTEBOOK**
**Due To Me** was run off her feet when disappointing in a similar event over course and distance on her previous run (behind today's second and third placed horses) but, with cheekpieces replacing the eye-shield, she was able to confirm the promise she had shown round here two starts back and gained her first win. She may not be that consistent, but could well follow up in a similar race.
**Benjamin(IRE)** reversed recent course form with the third Cumbrian Princess on 6lb better terms, but effectively lost his chance when taken on for the lead. There is a race to be won with him, and a forceful ride when granted an uncontested lead could be the answer.
**Cumbrian Princess**, successful on her two previous outings in similar events, failed to confirm recent form with the runner-up and winner. She took a while to pick up and was below form.
**Lady Liesel** never threatened.

## 1495 BET DIRECT ON SKY ACTIVE TRI-BANDED STKS 1m (P)
3:50 (3:55) (H ) 3-Y-O **£1,603** (£458; £229) **Stalls** High

Form RPR
1323 1 **Dial Square**[13] 1278 3-9-0 45 KFallon 1 54
(PHowling) *settled in last trio: nt clr run over 3f out: prog over 2f out: rdn to ld jst over 1f out: edgd rt but drvn clr* **6/4**[1]
2003 2 2 **Regency Malaya**[4] 1405 3-8-9 40 (bt) LDettori 6 44
(MFHarris) *racd wd 1st 3f: led: gng easily over 2f out: shkn up over 1f out: sn hdd and fnd nil* **5/2**[2]
0551 3 2 **Larad (IRE)**[4] 1405 3-9-3 45 (b) LPKeniry(3) 4 51
(JSMoore) *trckd ldr to over 2f out: n.m.r sn after and drvn: nt qckn over 1f out: fdd fnl f* **8/1**
-005 4 3/4 **Stagecoach Ruby**[4] 1405 3-8-9 40 RLMoore 3 38
(GLMoore) *cl up: effrt to chse ldr over 2f out to over 1f out: wknd ins fnl f* **12/1**
0005 5 1 **Backlash**[12] 1300 3-9-0 45 DHolland 2 41
(AWCarroll) *hld up in tch: rdn over 3f out: effrt and in tch over 2f out: wknd fnl f* **4/1**[3]
5-00 6 27 **Oboe**[82] 620 3-8-6 40 J-PGuillambert(3) 5 —
(TKeddy) *in tch tl wknd 3f out: t.o* **14/1**
1m 39.9s (0.35) **Going Correction** -0.025s/f (Stan) **6** Ran SP% **114.0**
Speed ratings: **97,95,93,92,91 64**CSF £5.63 TOTE £2.20: £1.20, £1.40; EX 4.40.
**Owner** Rory Murphy **Bred** J And Mrs Bowtell **Trained** Newmarket, Suffolk

**FOCUS**
They appeared to go a good pace and the winner may be better than this level.

**NOTEBOOK**
**Dial Square**, with the blinkers left off and ridden with more restraint than is often the case, ran out an emphatic winner. This was a good effort, but it will be harder for him if forced back into handicaps now
**Regency Malaya** raced away from the main group through the early part of the race and was wide on the first bend. Dropped back from ten furlongs, she was given a chance but proved unable to go with the winner, and is probably worth another try over further.
**Larad(IRE)** appreciated the step up to ten furlongs when winning round here on his previous outing and the return to a mile did not appear to suit. He travelled well but lacked the pace of the winner.
**Stagecoach Ruby**, down two furlongs in trip and with the eye-shield left off, was given every chance.
**Backlash** did not improve for this switch back to Polytrack and step up to a mile.

## 1496 NEW SITE @ BETDIRECT.CO.UK CLAIMING STKS 7f (P)
4:20 (4:25) (H ) 3-Y-0+ **£1,277** (£365; £182) **Stalls** Low

Form RPR
5033 1 **Free Option (IRE)**[53] 894 9-9-1 65 LauraPike(7) 6 63
(WJMusson) *racd in last trio: prog on outer over 2f out: cajoled along and r.o to ld last 100y: edgd lft but sn clr* **5/1**[3]
2365 2 1 3/4 **Lucayan Monarch**[13] 1279 6-9-8 52 (p) LDettori 7 58
(PSMcentee) *mde most: drvn over 1f out: hdd and nt qckn last 100y* **2/1**[2]
5030 3 1 1/4 **New Options**[13] 1283 7-9-8 56 (p) KFallon 3 55
(WJMusson) *plld hrd: hld up bhd ldrs: prog to chal over 1f out: urged along and sn fnd nil* **7/4**[1]
0 4 3 **Rocket (IRE)**[7] 1370 3-8-9 PDobbs 8 47
(RHannon) *trckd ldrs: effrt 2f out: one pce over 1f out: fdd fnl f* **14/1**
/006 5 1 1/4 **Happy Camper (IRE)**[13] 1279 4-9-8 50 DSweeney 2 44
(MRHoad) *pressed ldr tl wl over 1f out: sn wknd* **20/1**
50/ 6 2 1/2 **Last Rebel (IRE)**[8] 2399 5-9-6 79 EAhern 5 35
(RTPhillips) *trckd ldrs tl wknd 2f out* **10/1**
0-03 7 1 **Orion's Belt**[19] 1206 4-9-6 49 RHavlin 1 33
(GBBalding) *v s.i.s: t.k.h and hld up: in tch tl wknd over 2f out* **10/1**
00-0 8 2 1/2 **Scenic Flight**[12] 1300 3-7-13 50 ow1 (t) CCatlin 4 18
(MrsAJBowlby) *t.k.h: hld up in last trio: wknd over 2f out* **33/1**
1m 26.51s (0.57) **Going Correction** -0.025s/f (Stan)
**WFA** 3 from 4yo+ 13lb **8** Ran SP% **118.9**
Speed ratings: **95,93,91,88,86 83,82,79** CT £7.50 TOTE £2.10: £1.90, £1.10, £; EX20.80 1.The winner was the subject of a friendly claim. Lucayan Monarch was claimed by Mrs S M Johnson for £5,000. Rocket was the subject of a fri
**Owner** W J Musson **Bred** Grange Stud (uk) **Trained** Newmarket, Suffolk

**FOCUS**
A moderate claimer with a pace to match.

**NOTEBOOK**
**Free Option(IRE)**, a beaten favourite in selling company on his last two starts, was the second best in at the weights for this claimer and had an apprentice taking over from Fallon (who was on the stablemate and favourite). He responded kindly to his inexperienced rider but is no sure thing to follow up.
**Lucayan Monarch** had 13lb to find with the winner at the weights, but gave a good account of himself. He has been kept very busy of late, however, and is on a bit of a losing run.
**New Options**, stablemate of the winner, was very well backed but proved disappointing. He was keen early but had every chance when it mattered and is quite simply very hard to win with.
**Rocket(IRE)**, dropped in grade, showed more than he did on his debut and is open to further improvement.
**Happy Camper(IRE)** had plenty to find at the weights and was well held. *Official explanation: jockey said gelding hung right throughout*

## 1497 BETDIRECT.CO.UK BANDED STKS 6f (P)
4:50 (4:55) (H ) 3-Y-0+ **£1,610** (£460; £230) **Stalls** Low

Form RPR
3001 1 **Attorney**[3] 1443 6-9-13 45 (v) KFallon 2 61
(DShaw) *settled towards rr: effrt on inner over 1f out: r.o to ld last 150y: sn clr* **4/1**[2]
1000 2 1 1/2 **Badou**[26] 1098 4-9-7 45 (v) DHolland 4 51
(LMontagueHall) *mde most: sltly hmpd by loose horse over 1f out: hdd and no ex last 150y* **9/2**[3]
0206 3 1/2 **Harbour House**[13] 1278 5-9-7 45 JTate 1 49
(JJBridger) *t.k.h: trckd ldrs: effrt to chal over 1f out: nt qckn fnl f* **14/1**
-055 4 nk **Lydia's Look (IRE)**[51] 917 7-9-7 45 JFanning 9 48
(TJEtherington) *trckd ldrs: lost pl over 2f out: effrt over 1f out: styd on same pce* **10/1**
6310 5 nk **Gentle Response**[21] 1165 4-9-7 45 (b) SWhitworth 7 47
(BRJohnson) *dwlt: t.k.h and hld up in rr: prog on wd outside over 2f out: chal over 1f out: one pce fnl f* **3/1**[1]
5542 6 3/4 **Hinchley Wood (IRE)**[4] 1406 5-9-7 45 (b) NPollard 6 45
(JRBest) *dwlt: in rr: drvn 1/2-way: no prog tl kpt on fnl f* **12/1**
6002 7 2 **Night Cap (IRE)**[13] 1280 5-9-4 45 J-PGuillambert(3) 8 39
(TDMccarthy) *t.k.h: w ldr to wl over 1f out: wknd u.p* **5/1**
3600 8 1 **Our Chelsea Blue (USA)**[14] 1262 6-9-0 45 (t) MHoward(7) 5 36
(IAWood) *dwlt and hmpd s: last tl rapid prog to chse ldng pair 1/2-way: wknd over 1f out* **5/1**

00-0 **U** **Mandy's Collection**[14] 1262 5-9-7 45 CCatlin 3 —
(AGNewcombe) *swvd and uns rdr s* **33/1**

1m 13.46s (0.54) **Going Correction** -0.025s/f (Stan) **9** Ran SP% **122.9**
Speed ratings: **95,93,92,91,91 90,87,86,**—CSF £24.07 TOTE £3.70: £3.20, £2.50, £8.00; EX 22.10 Place 6 £9.47, Place 5 £6.55.
**Owner** K Nicholls **Bred** J R And Mrs P Good **Trained** Averham, Notts

**FOCUS**
Quite a competitive sprint, with the winner returning to his 2003 form and capable of form in a higher grade.

**NOTEBOOK**
**Attorney** is not a very easy ride and had never previously followed up a success, but Fallon made it look easy and the pair scored convincingly. The winner coped well with the penalty for his recent Southwell success and would obviously be of interest if turned out again in this grade, but things will obviously be a lot tougher when he is forced back into handicaps.
**Badou** returned to form under a positive ride with the visor re-fitted, simply finding the winner too strong.
**Harbour House** has not won since taking a maiden back in 2001, but this was a respectable effort.
**Lydia's Look(IRE)**, a beaten favourite on her last start in this grade, ran respectably but again found a few too good.
**Gentle Response**, like a lot of horses at this level, is not that consistent and did not run to form.
**Our Chelsea Blue(USA)** was far too keen.
**Mandy's Collection** jinked left leaving the stalls and got rid of Catlin.
T/Plt: £12.90 to a £1 stake. Pool: £31,370.50. 1,772.65 winning tickets. T/Qpdt: £6.70 to a £1 stake. Pool: £1,957.85. 214.80 winning tickets. JN

# 1282 PONTEFRACT (L-H)
## Monday, April 19

**OFFICIAL GOING: Soft (heavy in places)**
After a wet weekend the ground was very soft.

## 1498 TOTESPORT BIG SCREEN MEDIAN AUCTION MAIDEN FILLIES' STKS 5f
**2:40** (2:46) (E) 2-Y-O **£5,447** (£1,676; £838; £419) **Stalls** Low

Form RPR
1 **Society Music (IRE)** 2-8-8 LEnstone(3) 8 79
(MDods) *trckd ldrs: pushed along and outpcd over 2f out: hdwy over 1f out styd on wl to ld last 75 yds* **14/1**
2 1 1/4 **Sapphire Dream** 2-8-11 RWinston 1 75
(ABailey) *trckd ldrs: smooth hdwy 2f out: rdn tgo ld ins last: hdd and nt qckn last 75 yds* **16/1**
3 1 1/2 **Mary Read** 2-8-11 FLynch 9 69
(BSmart) *cl up: led 2f out: sn rdn: hdd ins last and kpt on same pce* **8/1**[3]
4 1 1/4 **Alta Petens** 2-8-11 IMongan 10 65
(MLWBell) *trckd ldrs: hdwy 1/2-way: ev ch whn pushed along: rn green and sltly outpcd wl over 1f out: kpt on ins last* **3/1**[1]
5 4 **Rockburst** 2-8-11 DarrenWilliams 5 51
(KRBurke) *bhd tl styd on fnl 2f: nrst fin* **8/1**[3]
6 3 **Megell (IRE)** 2-8-11 DRMcCabe 11 41
(MGQuinlan) *chsd ldrs on outer: rdn along 1/2-way: sn outpcd* **9/2**[2]
7 7 **Danehill Fairy (IRE)** 2-8-11 GDuffield 4 16
(MrsADuffield) *sn outpcd and bhd fr 1/2-way* **25/1**
00 8 3 1/2 **Verstone (IRE)**[14] 1264 2-8-8 LFletcher(3) 2 4
(RFFisher) *led: rdn along 1/2-way: sn hdd & wknd* **50/1**

69.84 secs (6.04) **Going Correction** +1.025s/f (Soft) **8** Ran SP% **83.8**
Speed ratings: **92,90,87,85,79 74,63,57**CSF £108.60 TOTE £10.80: £3.00, £2.30, £2.30; EX 64.50.
**Owner** M J K Dods **Bred** John Weld **Trained** Piercebridge, Co Durham
■ Stewards Enquiry : F Lynch caution: careless riding

**FOCUS**
An ordinary juvenile event run at a modest pace in the conditions.

**NOTEBOOK**
**Society Music(IRE)**, a February foal, is still on the leg. Tapped for toe turning in, she made ground on the outer and poker her head in front in the closing stages. Six furlongs will suit her even better.
**Sapphire Dream**, a March foal, travelled strongly and looked nailed on when taking charge, but in the end the winner saw it out just the better in the conditions.
**Mary Read**, a March foal, knew her job but after showing ahead did not see it out nearly as well as the first two.
**Alta Petens**, an April foal, stuck on after running green and being tapped for toe once in line for home. The experience will not be lost on her, but basically she needs six already.
**Rockburst**, a March foal, stayed on when it was all over. She will know more in future.
**Megell(IRE)**, an April foal, had the worst of the draw.

## 1499 FRIENDLY SERVICE (S) STKS 1m 4f 8y
**3:10** (3:11) (E) 3-Y-O **£3,692** (£1,136; £568; £284) **Stalls** Low

Form RPR
-210 1 **Ceasar (IRE)**[47] 957 3-9-4 55 (p) GFaulkner 1 56
(PCHaslam) *hld up: gd hdwy 1/2-way: chal 2f out: shkn up over 1f out: led ins last: cleverly* **5/1**[2]
0-45 2 3/4 **Valiant Air (IRE)**[8] 1344 3-8-12 55 RWinston 6 49
(JRWeymes) *cl up: led over 4f out: rdn 2f out: drvn and hdd ins last: kpt on wl* **8/1**[3]
-040 3 8 **Ciacole**[5] 1394 3-8-7 64 DeanMcKeown 7 33
(RonaldThompson) *hld up: hdwy 1/2-way: chsd ldrs 3f out: rdn 2f out and kpt on same pce* **12/1**
-266 4 25 **Bretton**[33] 1040 3-8-12 45 (b) DaleGibson 5 3
(RHollinshead) *hld up: hdwy 1/2-way: rdn along to chse ldrs over 3f out: wknd over out* **11/1**
-450 5 6 **Given A Chance**[71] 713 3-8-7 40 RThomas(5) 8 —
(MrsSLamyman) *chsd ldrs: rdn along over 3f out: sn wknd* **25/1**
0050 6 1 **Frambo (IRE)**[14] 1267 3-8-7 45 (p) PHanagan 2 —
(JGPortman) *hld up: hdwy to chse ldrs over 4f out: rdn and btn 3f out* **8/1**[3]
0-04 7 dist **Bunino Ven**[7] 1375 3-8-12 (v) KDarley 9 —
(SCWilliams) *led: rdn along and hdd over 4f out: sn wknd* **5/1**[2]
40-6 8 11 **Signora Panettiera (FR)**[5] 1394 3-8-5 58 ow1 SHitchcott(3) 4 —
(MRChannon) *hld up in tch: effrt 1/2-way: rdn along and weakeneed qckly over 4f out: sn t.o* **13/8**[1]

2m 53.0s (12.95) **Going Correction** +1.025s/f (Soft) **8** Ran SP% **113.5**
Speed ratings: **97,96,91,74,70 69,—,—**CSF £43.40 TOTE £7.20: £1.70, £3.10, £2.50; EX 71.40.The winner was sold to Nigel Shields for 9,000gns
**Owner** Wilson Imports **Bred** Mrs R D Peacock **Trained** Middleham Moor, N Yorks

**FOCUS**
A poor seller but a clear winner.

**NOTEBOOK**
**Ceasar(IRE)**, who had plenty to find on official figures, moved up on the bridle and simply toyed with the runner-up. He attracted plenty of interest at the auction and his new owner is sure to place him shrewdly.
**Valiant Air(IRE)**, with the visor left off on his first outing in a seller, seemed to appreciate the soft ground but the winner simply toyed with him.
**Ciacole** had 20lb in hand of the winner and a stone better chance than the runner-up on official figures, but it did not work out that way.
**Bretton** has yet to show he stays beyond nine furlongs and he looks to have gone off the boil.
**Bunino Ven** *Official explanation: trainer had no explanation for the poor form shown*
**Signora Panettiera(FR)** ran badly and this may have come too soon for her after Beverley. *Official explanation: jockey said gelding was unsuited by the heavy going*

## 1500 TOTEPOOL H'CAP 6f
**3:40** (3:41) (C) (0-90,90) 3-Y-O+ **£9,349** (£3,546; £1,773; £806) **Stalls** Low

Form RPR
-122 1 **Zilch**[7] 1354 6-9-11 87 IMongan 4 103
(MLWBell) *towards rr: gd hdwy 1/2-way: rdn to ld ins last: styd on* **9/4**[1]
10-5 2 1 1/4 **Cd Flyer (IRE)**[25] 1106 7-9-7 83 RWinston 7 95
(BEllison) *hld up in rr: hdwy over 2f out: swtchd rt over 1f out: sn rdn and edgd lft ins last: styd on* **9/1**
0141 3 1/2 **Chateau Nicol**[12] 1294 5-9-0 76 (v) GDuffield 18 87
(BGPowell) *hld up in rr: hdwy on outer 2f out: styd on appr last: nrst fin* **7/1**[3]
0043 4 1/2 **Lincoln Dancer (IRE)**[7] 1361 7-9-0 76 AlexGreaves 1 85
(DNicholls) *cl up on inner: led over 2f out: sn rdn: hdd ins last: kpt on same pce* **9/1**
0-01 5 2 1/2 **Tidy (IRE)**[16] 1246 4-9-4 80 DarrenWilliams 14 82
(MDHammond) *chsd ldrs tl rdn along and outpcd over 2f out: styd on under pessure ins last: nrst fin* **5/1**[2]
00-0 6 nk **Awake**[24] 1113 7-8-10 72 KDarley 12 73
(DNicholls) *trckd ldrs gng wl: smooth hdwy to chal wl over 1f out: ev ch tl rdn and wknd ent last* **16/1**
00-0 7 3/4 **Loyal Tycoon (IRE)**[25] 1106 6-9-0 83 LTreadwell(7) 2 81
(DNicholls) *in tch: poushed along over 2f out: n.m.r over 1f out: sn rdn and kpt on ins last* **40/1**
0600 8 3 **Bond Playboy**[7] 1361 4-8-10 72 FLynch 11 61
(BSmart) *s.i.s and bhd tl styd on fnl 2f* **40/1**
000- 9 1/2 **Gdansk (IRE)**[213] 5030 7-8-11 73 JCarroll 13 61
(ABerry) *chsd ldrs: rdn along 2f out: edgd lft and wknd over 1f out* **16/1**
/0-0 10 1 1/2 **Antonio Canova**[20] 1185 8-8-13 75 FNorton 9 58
(BobJones) *in tch: rdn along 1/2-way: sn wknd* **25/1**
500- 11 4 **Bollin Janet**[168] 5909 4-8-11 76 DAllan(3) 5 47
(TDEasterby) *cl up: rdn along over 2f out: grad wknd* **40/1**
000- 12 15 **Online Investor**[182] 5673 5-8-8 70 ANicholls 10 —
(DNicholls) *s.i.s and bhd: gd hdwy on inner over 2f out: rdn and wknd wl over 1f out* **20/1**
-000 13 3/4 **Abbajabba**[7] 1354 8-9-7 83 JBramhill 16 7
(CWFairhurst) *prom on outer: rdn along over 2f out: sn wknd* **9/1**
54-0 14 6 **Inter Vision (USA)**[8] 1343 4-9-9 88 ABeech(3) 15 —
(ADickman) *racd wd: led: rdn along and hdd over 2f out: sn wknd* **50/1**
10-0 15 27 **Arctic Burst (USA)**[5] 1391 4-10-0 90 (t) MFenton 17 —
(DShaw) *a bhd: t.o fr 1/2-way* **50/1**

1m 22.21s (4.91) **Going Correction** +1.025s/f (Soft) **15** Ran SP% **121.5**
Speed ratings: **108,106,105,105,101 101,100,96,95,93 88,68,67,59,23**CSF £21.36 CT £129.46 TOTE £3.60: £1.70, £2.90, £3.00; EX 37.00 Trifecta £118.00 Pool £1,728.86, 10.40 w/u.
**Owner** Mary Mayall, Linda Redmond, Julie Martin **Bred** Mrs Linda Corbett And Mrs Mary Mayall **Trained** Newmarket, Suffolk

**FOCUS**
A decent handicap run at a good pace. This was strong form for the track, and should prove solid.

**NOTEBOOK**
**Zilch** loves soft ground and a stiff six furlongs suits him just as well as seven.
**Cd Flyer(IRE)**, who gave his new trainer plenty of encouragement first time, was unlucky not to give the winner more to do. As things developed it turned out to be expensive.
**Chateau Nicol** continues in fine form and a return to seven will be in his favour.
**Lincoln Dancer(IRE)**, suited by the ground, is running better but is now a pale shadow of his best, when he was runner-up in the 2000 July Cup.
**Tidy(IRE)**, suited by the soft, seemed to find this too sharp and really needs seven
**Loyal Tycoon(IRE)**shaped well on ground totally against him. His time will come.
**Abbajabba** *Official explanation: jockey said gelding hung right-handed*
**Arctic Burst(USA)** *Official explanation: trainer said gelding was unsuited by the heavy ground*

## 1501 TOTEPLACEPOT MARATHON H'CAP 2m 5f 122y
**4:10** (4:13) (E) (0-70,65) 4-Y-O+ **£6,873** (£2,115; £1,057; £528) **Stalls** Low

Form RPR
203- 1 **Great As Gold (IRE)**[58] 6033 5-9-6 55 (p) RWinston 14 65+
(BEllison) *hld up towards rr: stdy hdwy over 6f out: effrt over 2f out: rdn to ld over 1f out: edgd lft ins last and kpt on wl* **9/2**[2]
/0-6 2 2 1/2 **Charming Admiral (IRE)**[13] 1287 11-8-13 48 (b) GDuffield 6 56
(MrsADuffield) *in tch: hdwy over 6f out: led 3f out: rdn and hde over 1f out: drvn and kpt on fnl f* **10/1**
5402 3 17 **Toni Alcala**[8] 1341 5-9-11 63 LFletcher(3) 1 54
(RFFisher) *a.p: rdn along 3f out: drvn and plugged on same pce fnl 2f* **20/1**
3444 4 9 **Jamaican Flight (USA)**[13] 1287 11-9-2 51 JQuinn 3 33
(MrsSLamyman) *led: clr 1/2-way: rdn along 4f out: hdd 3f out: wd st and sn outpcd* **12/1**
00-0 5 7 **Regal Vintage (USA)**[16] 1245 4-9-7 65 (v) THamilton(3) 2 40
(CGrant) *hld up and bhd: hdwy and rdn along 6f out: drvn and no imp over 3f out* **50/1**
260/ 6 1/2 **Mccracken (IRE)**[11] 356 8-9-9 58 (t) LVickers 4 32
(RFord) *in tch: rdn along and rn in snatches: hdwy to chse ldrs 4f out sn drvn and wknd* **20/1**
05-4 7 5 **Moonshine Beach**[12] 1302 6-9-7 63 PMakin(7) 11 32
(PWHiatt) *chsd ldrs: hdwy 6f out: rdn along 4f out and sn wknd* **10/1**
3212 8 6 **Aveiro (IRE)**[23] 1136 8-9-3 52 MFenton 5 15
(MissGayKelleway) *chsd ldrs: hdwy 6f out: rdn along over 3f out: wknd over 2f out* **10/1**
40-0 9 dist **Protocol (IRE)**[13] 1282 10-7-10 36 oh3 ow3 (t) RThomas(5) 12 —
(MrsSLamyman) *prom: rdn along 6f out: wknd over 4f out* **14/1**
00-1 10 3 1/2 **Green 'N' Gold**[13] 1287 4-9-2 57 PHanagan 13 —
(MDHammond) *hld up and bhd: stdy hdwy over 6f out: chsd ldrs 4f out: sn rdn and wknd* **7/2**[1]
000- 11 24 **Ulshaw**[47] 6017 7-9-5 57 SHitchcott(3) 10 —
(BJLlewellyn) *hld up and bhd: hdwy 1/2-way: chsd ldrs over 5f out: sn rdn and wknd: virtually p.u fnl 2f* **25/1**

0-26 **12** *dist* **That's Racing**[13] [1282] 4-7-5 **39** oh4................................ DFentiman(7) 8 —
(JHetherton) *chsd clr ldr: rdn along over 7f out: sn wknd: virtually p.u over 2f out* **7/1**[3]

10-5 **13** *dist* **Accepting**[13] [1287] 7-9-2 **51**.................................................(b) KDarley 7 —
(JMackie) *in tch: chsd ldrs 1/2-way: sn rdn along and wknd over 6f out: virtually p.u over 2f out* **11/1**

5m 18.81s (21.21) **Going Correction** +1.025s/f (Soft)
**WFA** 4 from 5yo+ 6lb **13** Ran SP% **118.2**
Speed ratings: **102,101,94,91,89 88,87,84,—,— —,—,—**CSF £45.97 CT £824.08 TOTE £6.90: £2.00, £3.40, £4.90; EX 61.10.
**Owner** Keith Middleton **Bred** Rathasker Stud **Trained** Norton, N Yorks

**FOCUS**
An extreme test of stamina, even though it was run at just a fair gallop. The winner was back to his best under ideal conditions.

**NOTEBOOK**
**Great As Gold(IRE)**, runner-up in this a year ago, has since won three times over hurdles. He has stamina in abundance and the first two finished a long way clear.
**Charming Admiral(IRE)**, better known as a jumper these days, won this event three years ago.
**Toni Alcala** handles soft ground but all his best efforts have come on a fast surface.
**Jamaican Flight(USA)** took this a year ago, defeating the winner from a 6lb higher mark, but the ground had turned against him this time.
**Green 'N' Gold**, 6lb higher, was not in the same sort of form this time. *Official explanation: jockey said filly was unsuited by the heavy going*
**Accepting** *Official explanation: jockey said gelding finished distressed*

## 1502 LADIES IN RED CLASSIFIED STKS — 1m 4y
**4:40** (4:45) (F) 3-Y-O+ **£4,338** (£1,335; £667; £333) **Stalls** Low

Form RPR

05-0 **1** **Torrid Kentavr (USA)**[16] [1247] 7-9-5 59.............................. RWinston 7 73
(BEllison) *hld up in rr: hdwy 1/2-way: swtchd lft over 1f out: rdn to ld eneringlast: styd on wl* **6/1**[1]

00-5 **2** *1* **Charmatic (IRE)**[16] [1250] 3-8-2 60.......................................... GDuffield 4 68
(JAGlover) *towards rr and pushed along on inner 1/2-way: swtchd outside and rdn 2f out: str run to chal ent last: edgd lft and nt qckn* **20/1**

2034 **3** *1* **He Who Dares (IRE)**[50] [926] 6-9-5 60.................................. JQuinn 2 69
(AWCarroll) *hld up and bhd: hdwy 1/2-way: rdn to chse ldrs over 1f out: styng on whn n.m.r ins last* **13/2**[2]

-006 **4** *8* **Pure Speculation**[20] [1187] 4-9-4 62..................................... IMongan 1 52
(MLWBell) *trckd ldrs: hdwy to ld over 1f out: sn rdn: hdd wknd ent last* **7/1**[3]

34-6 **5** *2 ½* **Lucayan Dancer**[14] [1265] 4-9-8 63.............................. AlexGreaves 12 51
(DNicholls) *chsd ldrs: rdn along 2f out: sn btn* **15/2**

-361 **6** *4* **Rahjel Sultan**[11] [1310] 6-9-7 62........................................(t) GGibbons 11 42
(BAMcmahon) *in tch: hdwy to chse ldrs 3f out: rdn 2f out: sn edgd lft and wknd* **12/1**

500- **7** *1 ½* **Parnassian**[165] [5937] 4-9-0 58.......................................... RThomas(5) 13 37
(GBBalding) *trckd ldrs: hdwy to ld briefly 2f out: sn rdn and wknd* **11/1**

24-0 **8** *½* **Apache Point (IRE)**[16] [1247] 7-9-5 60............................. KimTinkler 14 36
(NTinkler) *dwlt: bhd tl styd on fnl 2f* **8/1**

-500 **9** *¾* **Shifty**[16] [1247] 5-9-5 51.......................................................(v[1]) ANicholls 8 35
(DNicholls) *keen: midfield: hdwy to chse ldrs 3f out: sn rdn and wknd over 2f out* **25/1**

0-02 **10** *22* **Locombe Hill (IRE)**[95] [542] 8-9-2 64.......................... LTreadwell(7) 9 —
(DNicholls) *led: rdn along and hdd 2f out: sn wknd* **11/1**

2420 **11** *19* **Surdoue**[52] [903] 4-9-5 56..................................................... KDarley 5 —
(PHowling) *cl up: rdn along over 3f out: sn wknd* **11/1**

450- **12** *11* **Esteban**[238] [4458] 4-9-5 57................................................... MFenton 17 —
(JJQuinn) *in tch on outer: pushed along 1/2-way: sn wknd* **22/1**

655- **13** *2 ½* **General Smith**[210] [5129] 5-9-0 59.............................. PMulrennan(5) 16 —
(GAHarker) *in tch on outer: rdn along 1/2-way: sn wknd* **20/1**

060- **14** *dist* **Eastern Dagger**[220] [4872] 4-9-5 60.......................... DeanMcKeown 6 —
(PABlockley) *chsd ldrs: rdn along and wkng whn hmpd over 3f out and sn bhd* **18/1**

1m 52.63s (7.03) **Going Correction** +1.025s/f (Soft)
**WFA** 3 from 4yo+ 14lb **14** Ran SP% **118.7**
Speed ratings: **105,104,103,95,92 88,87,86,85,63 44,33,31,—**CSF £127.80 TOTE £6.90: £2.30, £8.00, £2.30; EX 213.70.
**Owner** Graeme Redpath **Bred** Ford Farm Bloodstock **Trained** Norton, N Yorks
■ Stewards Enquiry : R Winston two-day ban: careless riding (Apr 30, May 3)

**FOCUS**
A fair winning time for the grade, given the conditions. The winner is well treated on last year's form; an improved effort from the second against her elders.

**NOTEBOOK**
**Torrid Kentavr(USA)**, a winner over both hurdles and fences, handles the soft and is battle-hardened. He now goes for the Swinton Hurdle at Haydock.
**Charmatic(IRE)**, a three-year-old taking on her elders, and having only her fourth career start, deserves plenty of credit.
**He Who Dares(IRE)**, in good form on the All-Weather, handles the soft and was a shade unfortunate not to finish closer.
**Pure Speculation**, who goes well on soft ground, was dropping back in trip but failed to see it out. She does not find much off the bridle.
**Lucayan Dancer**, having his second run for his present trainer, has not won since his juvenile days and he has been tried over a variety of trips.

## 1503 PUNTERS CHOICE H'CAP — 1m 2f 6y
**5:10** (5:11) (E) (0-75,74) 4-Y-O+ **£4,192** (£1,290; £645; £322) **Stalls** Low

Form RPR

-545 **1** **Melodian**[5] [1393] 9-8-13 **59**................................................(b) TWilliams 2 68
(MBrittain) *led: rdn over 2f out: hdd wl over 1f out: drvn and rallied ins last to ld last 100 yds* **5/1**[3]

0-65 **2** *2* **Dickie Deadeye**[12] [1298] 7-8-5 **56**.................................... RThomas(5) 6 62
(GBBalding) *a.p: rdn along 2f out: styd on u.p fnl f* **7/2**[2]

0 **3** *1 ½* **Meteorite Sun (USA)**[21] [1172] 6-9-10 **70**............................. JFEgan 5 73
(MrsJRRamsden) *hld up in tch: gd hdwy on inner over 2f out: led wl over 1f out and sn rdn: drvn ins last: hdd & wknd last 100 yds* **8/1**

00-0 **4** *1* **Jimmy Byrne (IRE)**[14] [1265] 4-9-8 **68**............................. RWinston 12 69
(BEllison) *hld up and bhd: hdwy 3f out: rdn 2f out: kpt on ins last: nrst fin* **20/1**

04-0 **5** *nk* **Rotuma (IRE)**[21] [1172] 5-9-2 **65**.........................................(b) LEnstone(3) 10 66
(MDods) *chsd ldrs: rdn over 2f out: sn drvn and one pce* **8/1**

0510 **6** *2 ½* **Sinjaree**[21] [1181] 6-7-13 **45**................................................ JQuinn 11 42
(MrsSLamyman) *towards rr: hdwy 3f out: sn rdn and no imp* **8/1**

20-3 **7** *2* **Moonshine Bill**[12] [1305] 5-8-3 **52**.................................... DAllan(3) 9 45
(PWHiatt) *trckd ldrs: pushed along 3f out: rdn 2f out and sn btn* **11/4**[1]

000- **8** *14* **Liberty Seeker (FR)**[61] [5194] 5-9-4 **64**.............................. GParkin 4 33
(PDNiven) *chsd ldrs: rdn 3f out: sn wknd* **16/1**

5400 **9** *dist* **Daimajin (IRE)**[5] [1393] 5-9-2 **62**........................................... ANicholls 8 —
(MrsLucindaFeatherstone) *hld up in rr: hdwy on outer over 3f out: rdn to chal over 2f out: sn wknd and eased* **33/1**

2m 26.76s (12.85) **Going Correction** +1.025s/f (Soft) **9** Ran SP% **112.5**
Speed ratings: **89,87,86,85,85 83,81,70,—**CSF £22.10 CT £135.37 TOTE £5.30: £1.90, £1.10, £2.60; EX 19.30 Place 6 £325.46, Place 5 £84.25.
**Owner** Mel Brittain **Bred** Northgate Lodge Stud Ltd **Trained** Warthill, N Yorks

**FOCUS**
A moderate handicap and a slow winning time. The winner was suited by the conditions and returned to his best.

**NOTEBOOK**
**Melodian**loves this type of ground and he responds well to his jockey's vigorous style.
**Dickie Deadeye**, whose one win was on similar going, missed two seasons but is finding his feet now. He is crying out for further, but time is running out ground-wise.
**Meteorite Sun(USA)**, dropped 5lb, did not quite see it out. A winner in testing ground in France, he would not need to improve much on this to regain the winning thread.
**Jimmy Byrne(IRE)** had his stamina and ability to handle this type of ground to prove, but on both charges the answer looks in the positive.
**Rotuma(IRE)** loves this type of ground but is still 5lb higher than her last success.
**Moonshine Bill**, 1llb higher than when winning here in the soft last summer, was disappointing, dropping out on the home turn.
**Daimajin(IRE)** *Official explanation: jockey said gelding ran too free*
T/Jkpt: Not won. T/Plt: £1,736.00 to a £1 stake. Pool: £64,329.55. 27.05 winning tickets. T/Qpdt: £28.40 to a £1 stake. Pool: £6,647.30. 173.00 winning tickets. JR

# 1269 WINDSOR (R-H)
### Monday, April 19
**OFFICIAL GOING: Good to soft (soft in places)**

## 1504 WELCOME TO MONDAY EVENINGS AT WINDSOR APPRENTICE H'CAP — 6f
**5:20** (5:20) (E) (0-85,82) 3-Y-O+ **£4,329** (£1,332; £666; £333) **Stalls** High

Form RPR

263- **1** **Mine Behind**[201] [5307] 4-9-1 **72**.......................................... MSavage 20 84
(JRBest) *mde most on sands side: rdn over 1f out: hung lft cl home and jst hld on* **20/1**

2130 **2** *½* **Whippasnapper**[68] [742] 4-7-13 **61**.............................. DeanWilliams(5) 4 71
(JRBest) *s.i.s: sn in tch: hdwy over 2f out: led centre gp appr fnl f: kpt on but nt pce of wnr stands side* **8/1**[2]

-324 **3** *2* **Savile's Delight (IRE)**[80] [637] 5-8-2 **64**........................ BO'Neill(5) 12 68
(RBrotherton) *chsd ldrs in centre crse: led that grnd 2f out tl appr fnl f: one pce ins last* **22/1**

0340 **4** *hd* **Majik**[7] [1361] 5-7-12 **60**...............................................(p) LiamJones(5) 19 63
(DJSFfrenchDavis) *racd stands side and chsd ldrs: rdn and edgd to centre fr 2f out: nt qckn ins last* **20/1**

6020 **5** *3 ½* **Tayif**[17] [1230] 8-8-2 **62**....................................................(t) BSwarbrick(3) 14 55
(AndrewReid) *in tch centre crse: hrd rdn 2f out: r.o fnl f: no imp on ldrs* **12/1**[3]

2016 **6** *hd* **A Teen**[27] [1082] 6-8-6 **63**................................................ HayleyTurner 15 55
(PHowling) *racd centre crse: bhd: rdn over 2f out: r.o fnl f: nt rch ldrs* **22/1**

0-24 **7** *2* **Trick Cyclist**[26] [1099] 3-8-8 **81**......................................... TBlock(5) 18 67
(AMBalding) *racd stands side and chsd wnr fr 1/2-way: outpcd fnl f* **16/1**

000- **8** *¾* **Idle Power (IRE)**[172] [5838] 6-9-3 **74**..................................... AQuinn 3 58
(JRBoyle) *in tch centre crse: rdn over 2f out: one pce over 1f out* **7/1**[1]

-000 **9** *½* **Arabian Knight (IRE)**[11] [1313] 4-7-12 **60**......................... CHaddon(5) 5 43
(RJHodges) *racd alone far side: chsd gd spd tl wknd appr fnl f* **25/1**

010- **10** *1 ½* **Prince Hector**[204] [5252] 5-9-1 **79**........................ DanielleDeverson(7) 8 57
(WJHaggas) *outpcd in rr: styd on fr over 1f out: nt a danger* **16/1**

02-0 **11** *1 ½* **Stokesies Wish**[7] [1368] 4-8-7 **66** ow1.......................... PGallagher(5) 16 41
(JLSpearing) *broke wl and wnt to ld gp in centre crse tl hdd 2f out: wknd over 1f out* **33/1**

0-25 **12** *1* **Seven No Trumps**[7] [1354] 7-9-6 **82**.................................. CJDavies(5) 13 53
(JMBradley) *chsd ldrs: rdn and wknd fnl 2f* **8/1**[2]

336- **13** *nk* **Nivernais**[252] [4054] 5-9-5 **81**........................................... CCavanagh(5) 11 51
(HCandy) *nvr gng pce to rch ldrs* **7/1**[1]

20-0 **14** *hd* **Fleetwood Bay**[18] [1225] 4-9-1 **75**..................................... MLawson(3) 1 44
(BRMillman) *pressed ldrs over 3f* **20/1**

0044 **15** *5* **Port St Charles (IRE)**[11] [1313] 7-8-11 **68**....................... JFMcDonald 7 22
(PRChamings) *chsd ldrs over 3f* **8/1**[2]

00-0 **16** *nk* **Rise**[82] [619] 3-8-2 **70**...........................................................(b) NMackay 10 23
(AndrewReid) *chsd ldrs over 3f* **33/1**

0-6 **17** *nk* **Margalita (IRE)**[51] [917] 4-9-4 **75**..................................(t) NChalmers 2 27
(PMitchell) *chsd ldrs: rdn 1/2-way: sn wknd* **20/1**

1005 **18** *shd* **Mr Spliffy (IRE)**[50] [938] 5-8-2 **59**......................................... DFox 17 11
(MCChapman) *sn outpcd* **33/1**

0-60 **19** *2* **Kareeb (FR)**[18] [1225] 7-9-2 **78**........................................... ARutter(5) 6 24
(WJMusson) *bhd fr 1/2-way* **14/1**

40-0 **20** *28* **Landing Strip (IRE)**[7] [1354] 4-9-1 **77**........................ SaleemGolam(5) 9 —
(JMPEustace) *chsd ldrs over 3f* **33/1**

1m 18.89s (5.02) **Going Correction** +0.85s/f (Soft)
**WFA** 3 from 4yo+ 11lb **20** Ran SP% **127.8**
Speed ratings: **100,99,96,96,91 91,88,87,87,85 83,81,81,81,74 74,73,73,70,33**CSF £152.53 CT £3623.55 TOTE £20.20: £5.50, £3.10, £8.60, £3.70; EX 142.70.
**Owner** D Gorton, M Folan, R Crampton **Bred** Hesmonds Stud Ltd **Trained** Hucking, Kent

**FOCUS**
A big difference of opinion as to where the best ground was. The larger group stayed mid-track, though there was a lot of switching of positions during the course of the contest. Despite the runner-up coming from a low draw, six of the first seven home came from the nine highest stalls. The form does not look that strong.

**NOTEBOOK**
**Mine Behind**, reappearing after a six-month break and dropping back from a mile, stuck to the stands' rail from his draw and made just about all the running to hold on from his stable companion despite hanging left near the line. As meritorious as this performance was, the way the race panned out makes the value of the form hard to evaluate.
**Whippasnapper**, racing off an 8lb lower mark than on sand, was patiently ridden in the group that raced down the centre of the track. Making his effort entering the last quarter-mile, he came through to lead that group and pulled right away from those on his side, but his stable companion had already gone beyond recall and he could not quite get there.
**Savile's Delight(IRE)**, 3lb higher than for his last start on turf and 5lb higher than on sand, was returning from a three-month break. He ran his usual consistent race, but keeps on finding one or two to beat him.
**Majik**, rated 8lb lower on turf than on sand, started off tracking the winner on the stands' side, gradually drifted out into the centre of the track. He could never really land a blow.

**Tayif**, fit from the Polytrack, ran his race but this is as good as he is.
**Idle Power(IRE)** goes in the ground, but could never get competitive from his low stall.
**Seven No Trumps** *Official explanation: trainer said gelding was unable to be covered up behind horses*
**Nivernais** was returning from an eight-month break, but has won after a similar layoff in the past so can have no excuses on that score. More likely is that he is 8lb higher than for his last win, and overall his best form has been on faster ground.
**Margalita(IRE)** *Official explanation: vet said filly finished lame*

## 1505 WINDSOR-RACECOURSE.CO.UK MAIDEN STKS 5f 10y
5:50 (5:52) (D) 2-Y-O £3,425 (£1,054; £527; £263) Stalls High

Form RPR
1 **Beaver Patrol (IRE)** 2-9-0 SCarson 8 82
(RFJohnsonHoughton) *wnt rt s: bhd: gd hdwy 3f out: led 1f out: drvn out ins last* 9/2[3]
2 1/2 **Chalison (IRE)** 2-9-0 RHughes 2 80
(RHannon) *led: rdn and hdd 1f out: styd pressing wnr tl no ex cl home* 3/1[2]
3 3 2 1/2 **Edge Fund**[19] [1208] 2-9-0 SDrowne 5 71
(BRMillman) *w ldrs: rdn 2f out: outpcd fnl f* 5/2[1]
4 nk **Catwalk Cleric (IRE)** 2-9-0 SSanders 9 70
(MJWallace) *bhd: headway and hung lft over 1f out: r.o ins last: nt pce to trble ldrs* 12/1
4 5 shd **Glasson Lodge**[17] [1234] 2-8-9 RHavlin 6 65
(PDEvans) *w ldrs: rdn over 2f out: outpcd appr fnl f* 16/1
6 1 3/4 **Chateau Istana** 2-9-0 EAhern 7 63
(NPLittmoden) *n.m.r s: sn outpcd: nvr gng pce to rch ldrs* 6/1
7 7 **Fair Along (GER)** 2-9-0 TQuinn 1 39
(WJarvis) *s.i.s: sn rcvrd to chse ldrs: wknd ins fnl 2f* 14/1
8 3/4 **Whistling Along** 2-9-0 RLMoore 4 36
(JMBradley) *slowly into into stride: sn drvn: outpcd fr 1/2-way* 33/1
9 1/2 **Caly Dancer (IRE)** 2-9-0 DaneO'Neill 3 35
(DRCElsworth) *slowly away: hdwy to chse ldrs 1/2-way: wknd ins fnl 2f* 14/1

65.77 secs (4.57) **Going Correction** +0.85s/f (Soft) 9 Ran SP% **115.9**
Speed ratings: **97,96,92,91,91 88,77,76,75** CSF £18.48 TOTE £4.70: £2.00, £1.80, £1.10; EX 19.60.
**Owner** G C Stevens **Bred** Kevin B Lynch **Trained** Blewbury, Oxon

**FOCUS**
Probably a fair maiden of its type, and the winner was very well fancied in the market. The whole field went to the far side.

**NOTEBOOK**
**Beaver Patrol(IRE)**, an 18,000euros yearling, is out of a winner over 13 furlongs, but nonetheless showed plenty of speed on this debut. Backed in from 16/1, he was done no favours by Catwalk Cleric at the start, but still travelled well on the outside of the field and came with his effort just after halfway. Despite the runner-up sticking to him, he showed the right attitude to prevail and now reportedly heads to Chester.
**Chalison(IRE)** ◆, a 42,000gns half-brother to Low Cloud, is out of a dual 12-furlong winner in France. He showed the sort of speed more associated with his sire Anabaa on this debut though, and fought back really well when the winner came to challenge. He should not be long in winning.
**Edge Fund**, with the benefit of previous experience, was more organised than on his debut but found a couple of newcomers too good for him. There should be a small race in him and he may get a bit further, though maidens of this grade will not get any easier in the future.
**Catwalk Cleric(IRE)**, a 26,000gns yearling, is out of a three-time winner at around a mile in Ireland who later went on to win over hurdles. Wayward leaving the stalls, he ran green in the race but still showed enough to suggest he can win his maiden. He should also get further in time.
**Glasson Lodge**, the only filly in the line-up, probably improved on the form of her Fibresand debut, but her previous experience would have counted for plenty in this field.
**Chateau Istana**, an 85,000euros yearling, is a half-brother to Mandobi out of a winner in the US. He ran as though needing this debut and should come into his own over a bit further.

## 1506 BUGLER DEVELOPMENTS H'CAP 1m 67y
6:20 (6:21) (D) (0-85,79) 3-Y-O £5,687 (£1,750; £875; £437) Stalls High

Form RPR
2120 1 **Play Master (IRE)**[25] [1108] 3-8-13 **71** PaulEddery 1 76
(DHaydnJones) *bhd: rdn 3f out: str run on outside fr 2f out: styd on wl to ld nr fin* 8/1
064- 2 3/4 **Rondelet (IRE)**[208] [5144] 3-9-4 **76** SSanders 3 79
(RMBeckett) *in tch: hdwy 3f out: styd on u.p fnl 2f to ld wl ins last: ct cl home* 7/1
1-06 3 nk **Dumnoni**[18] [1225] 3-9-7 **79** DHolland 4 81
(JulianPoulton) *chsd ldr: rdn over 2f out: n.m.r 1f out and ins last: swtchd rt wl ins last: gng on cl home* 13/2[3]
02-1 4 1 **Honest Injun**[98] [506] 3-9-7 **79** EAhern 6 79
(BWHills) *led: grad wnt to far side fr 3f out: rdn over 1f out: hdd wl ins last: wknd cl home* 11/4[1]
3-45 5 3 **Rood Boy (IRE)**[11] [1311] 3-7-8 **57** JFMcDonald[(5)] 9 51
(JSKing) *chsd ldrs tl nt act rnd bnd 6f out and lost postion: rdn and hdwy 3f out: one pce fnl 2f* 13/2[3]
31- 6 dist **The Way We Were**[175] [5798] 3-9-2 **77** RMiles[(3)] 5 —
(TGMills) *chsd ldrs: hung lft bnd 6f out: styd prom tl wknd qckly ins fnl 3f: t.o* 4/1[2]
040- 7 4 **Desert Diplomat (IRE)**[173] [5831] 3-8-10 **68** KFallon 2 —
(SirMichaelStoute) *chsng ldrs whn pushed wd bnd 6f out: wknd rapidly ins fnl 3f: t.o* 8/1
6-06 8 3 1/2 **Wares Home (IRE)**[81] [631] 3-8-12 **70** RHughes 7 —
(KRBurke) *chsd ldrs tl wknd qckly ins fnl 3f: t.o* 14/1

1m 52.71s (7.11) **Going Correction** +0.875s/f (Soft) 8 Ran SP% **114.7**
Speed ratings: **99,98,97,96,93** —,—,— CSF £62.39 CT £386.74 TOTE £10.30: £2.30, £2.80, £2.30; EX 64.60.
**Owner** Jason Weston **Bred** R N Auld **Trained** Efail Isaf, Rhondda C Taff

**FOCUS**
A fair handicap, run at just an average pace. The whole field made for the far side turning for home, though not all at the same time.

**NOTEBOOK**
**Play Master(IRE)** has been running very well on Fibresand so this softer ground was probably in his favour. Content to sit out the back, he needed every yard of this trip to forge his way to the front and should be suited by further given the right conditions. *Official explanation: trainer's representative said, regarding the improved form shown, gelding settled better over today's shorter trip*
**Rondelet(IRE)**, returning from a seven-month break and making his handicap debut, was like the winner given a patient ride and came through to hit the front inside the last furlong. He did little wrong and saw out the extra furlong, but Play Master's late surge proved just too much.
**Dumnoni**, fit from the sand, was never far away and was staying on in the closing stages after having to be switched inside the last furlong. She was probably unlucky not to finish second and stayed the longer trip well enough. *Official explanation: jockey said filly hung left-handed*
**Honest Injun**, up in trip, made the running but did not cross over to the far side as quickly as the others on turning in, preferring to follow a straight line from the home bend over to the far rail. Whether that made any difference is hard to say, as he was still in front when joining the others, and it was only inside the last furlong that he was overhauled. He did not quite appear to see out the extra furlong in the conditions.
**Rood Boy(IRE)**, still a maiden, did not take the home bend as well the others when in a good position and lost ground as a result. From that point, and not for the first time, he was then made to look very one-paced.
**The Way We Were**, off since October, ran poorly on this first encounter with soft ground. *Official explanation: trainer's representative said colt was unsuited by the soft ground*
**Wares Home(IRE)** *Official explanation: jockey said colt lost its action*

## 1507 DINE IN THE CASTLE RESTAURANT MAIDEN FILLIES' STKS 1m 67y
6:50 (6:52) (D) 3-Y-O £4,290 (£1,320; £660; £330) Stalls High

Form RPR
3- 1 **Classical Dancer**[260] [3811] 3-8-11 DaneO'Neill 17 77
(HCandy) *in tch: hdwy on outside to ld ins fnl 2f: drvn out* 5/4[1]
00- 2 1 1/2 **Hidden Hope**[187] [5572] 3-8-11 DHolland 4 74
(GWragg) *trcking ldrs whn lost pl bnd 6f out: hdwy fr 3f out: styd on to chse wnr ins last but no imp* 16/1
43- 3 1 **Nukhbah (USA)**[217] [4950] 3-8-11 SSanders 13 72
(LadyHerries) *s.i.s: sn rcvrd: racd alone stands side and styd up w pce: no ex ins fnl f* 14/1
4 3/4 **Empress Eugenie (FR)** 3-8-11 JTate 7 70
(JMPEustace) *s.i.s: hdwy 4f out: chsd ldrs 2f out: kpt on same pce ins last* 50/1
3- 5 shd **Principessa**[165] [5932] 3-8-11 SDrowne 2 70
(BPalling) *in tch: rdn: swtchd rt and hdwy over 2f out: kpt on ins last: nt rch ldrs* 16/1
034- 6 5 **Lorien Hill (IRE)**[194] [5449] 3-8-11 71 EAhern 5 59
(BWHills) *chsd ldrs: rdn over 2f out: sn one pce: wknd fnl f* 14/1
43- 7 nk **True (IRE)**[254] [3994] 3-8-11 MartinDwyer 15 59
(MPTregoning) *lef 7f out: rdn 3f out: hdd ins fnl 2f: hung lft and wknd fnl f* 9/2[2]
000- 8 4 **Cashema (IRE)**[229] [4664] 3-8-11 RHavlin 9 50
(MrsPNDutfield) *bhd: styd on fr over 2f out: nt trble ldrs* 100/1
00- 9 1/2 **St Tropez (IRE)**[202] [5284] 3-8-11 SWhitworth 10 49
(BGPowell) *s.i.s: bhd: hdwy over 3f out: sn in tch: wknd fr 2f out* 66/1
00- 10 nk **Ellina**[164] [5940] 3-8-11 RPrice 11 49
(JPearce) *s.i.s: bhd: sme prog fnl 2f* 100/1
0-6 11 14 **Donastrela (IRE)**[17] [1226] 3-8-6 NChalmers[(5)] 6 19
(AMBalding) *bhd: styd on fnl 2f but nvr a danger* 66/1
0 12 3/4 **Observation**[20] [1186] 3-8-11 PRobinson 18 18
(MAJarvis) *chsd ldrs tl wknd over 2f out* 20/1
0- 13 6 **Portmanteau**[189] [5539] 3-8-11 KFallon 16 5
(SirMichaelStoute) *chsd ldrs tl wknd qckly ins fnl 3f* 6/1[3]
46- 14 2 **Reign Of Fire (IRE)**[172] [5833] 3-8-8 LPKeniry[(3)] 8 1
(BJMeehan) *in tch over 5f* 33/1
00 15 1 1/4 **Mitzi Caspar**[25] [1104] 3-8-8 RMiles[(3)] 1 —
(PLGilligan) *led tl 7f out: wknd rapidly ins fnl 3f* 100/1
00-0 16 1 **Genuinely (IRE)**[61] [816] 3-8-11 RMullen 3 —
(WJMusson) *n.d* 100/1
000- 17 15 **St George's Girl**[195] [5440] 3-8-4 JJeffrey[(7)] 12 —
(JRJenkins) *nvr bttr than mid-div: bhd fnl 3f* 100/1
18 dist **Collada (IRE)** 3-8-11 RHughes 14 —
(JHMGosden) *chsd ldrs tl wknd qckly over 3f out: virtually p.u: lame* 12/1

1m 52.28s (6.68) **Going Correction** +0.875s/f (Soft) 18 Ran SP% **127.3**
Speed ratings: **101,99,98,97,97 92,92,88,87,87 73,72,66,64,63 62,47,—** CSF £25.45 TOTE £2.50: £1.30, £4.00, £4.70; EX 30.20.
**Owner** Jim Strange **Bred** Launceston Stud **Trained** Wantage, Oxon

**FOCUS**
Probably a fair fillies' maiden and several are likely to improve. All but one of the field went far side in the home straight.

**NOTEBOOK**
**Classical Dancer** ◆ confirmed the promise of her sole start last season and had no problem with either the longer trip or softer ground. She won with more in hand than the official margin would suggest and can go on to better things.
**Hidden Hope** ◆ ran a lot better than in her two starts as a juvenile and appreciated the longer trip. If anything she looks as though she will appreciate even further and now qualifies for a handicap mark.
**Nukhbah(USA)** ◆, who was placed over nine furlongs as a juvenile, appreciated the easier ground and ran a fine race on this reappearance, especially as she was the only one to stay stands' side in the straight and was not beaten very far. How she would have fared had she gone with the others is anybody's guess, but this was still promising and she could be very interesting in handicap company.
**Empress Eugenie(FR)**, whose three siblings have all won, ran a cracker on this belated debut. Her half-sister won at up to 14 furlongs, so there is every reason to believe she will be suited by further, and she is sure to improve.
**Principessa** saw the trip out better than in her sole juvenile start, despite having a speedy pedigree. She may be capable of further improvement given better ground.
**Lorien Hill(IRE)**, who showed ability in three starts as a juvenile, did not seem to see out the trip in the ground. She may be better off in handicap company.
**True(IRE)**, off since August, had shown enough in two starts as a juvenile to have done better than this and might have needed it.
**Collada(IRE)** *Official explanation: jockey said filly finished lame*

## 1508 SPONSORS EVENING MAIDEN STKS 1m 2f 7y
7:20 (7:23) (D) 3-Y-O £4,173 (£1,284; £642; £321) Stalls Low

Form RPR
5- 1 **Vinando**[170] [5870] 3-9-0 SDrowne 5 81
(CREgerton) *in tch: rdn over 4f out: styd on fr 3f out: chsd clr ldr over 2f out: r.o wl to ld last half f: readily* 11/2[3]
5-2 2 3 1/2 **Extra Cover (IRE)**[17] [1226] 3-9-0 RHughes 12 75
(RCharlton) *led: drvn clr 4f out: 8l ahd 3f out: wknd over 1f out: hdd and no ex last half f* 9/2[2]
0- 3 2 1/2 **Midshipman Easy (USA)**[174] [5813] 3-9-0 DHolland 3 70
(PWHarris) *in tch: rdn and lost position 5f out: styd on again fr 3f out: kpt on ins last: nt rch ldrs* 20/1
0- 4 1 1/4 **Irish Blade (IRE)**[145] [6072] 3-9-0 DaneO'Neill 6 68
(HCandy) *s.i.s: bhd: pushed along over 5f out: styd on wl fnl 2f: nt rch ldrs* 20/1
22- 5 shd **Notable Guest (USA)**[188] [5565] 3-9-0 KFallon 2 68
(SirMichaelStoute) *chsd ldrs: wnt 2nd over 5f out: rdn to chse clr ldr over 3f out and no imp: wknd fr 2f out* 5/6[1]
40- 6 2 1/2 **Fitting Guest (IRE)**[165] [5932] 3-9-0 PRobinson 9 63
(GGMargarson) *in tch 6f out: sn lost position: hdwy over 3f out: kpt on fnl 2f* 33/1

0-0 **7** *hd* **Persian Dagger (IRE)**[14] [1271] 3-9-0 .................................. GCarter 11 63
(JLDunlop) *hld up in rr: hdwy fr 3f out: kpt on fnl 2f but nt a danger* **40/1**

000 **8** *3 ½* **La Concha (IRE)**[68] [739] 3-8-9 .................................. JFMcDonald(5) 10 57?
(MrsLCJewell) *plld hrd: chsd ldrs: rdn 3f out: sn one pce* **100/1**

34- **9** *1 ½* **Majestic Vision**[156] [6003] 3-9-0 .................................. TQuinn 4 54
(PWHarris) *chsd ldrs: rdn 3f out: sn btn* **14/1**

00- **10** *2* **Regal Performer (IRE)**[177] [5757] 3-9-0 .................................. PDobbs 1 50
(SKirk) *mid-div: hdwy over 3f out: wknd 2f out* **50/1**

**11** *2 ½* **Singitta** 3-8-9 .................................. EAhern 7 41
(BPalling) *s.i.s: n.d* **33/1**

00- **12** *2* **Good Article (IRE)**[177] [5754] 3-9-0 ..................................(e[1]) DSweeney 13 42
(APJones) *bhd: sme hdwy 3f out: wknd 2f out* **100/1**

643- **13** *23* **Kitley**[214] [5021] 3-9-0 65 .................................. SWhitworth 8 —
(BGPowell) *rrd stalls: bhd most of way* **33/1**

**14** *10* **Jelly Baby** 3-8-9 .................................. JFanning 15 —
(WJHaggas) *slowly away: t.k.h and sn chsng ldrs: wknd 4f out* **25/1**

2m 21.15s (12.85) **Going Correction** +1.20s/f (Soft) **14** Ran SP% **123.4**
Speed ratings: **96,93,91,90,90 88,87,85,83,82 80,78,60,52**CSF £28.36 TOTE £6.90: £1.50, £1.80, £4.40; EX 50.10.
**Owner** Mrs Evelyn Hankinson **Bred** Miss K Rausing **Trained** Chaddleworth, Berks

**FOCUS**
A modest time, even allowing for the ground, but while some caution should be exercised regarding the form, several look likely improvers. Once again the whole field went far side in the straight.

**NOTEBOOK**
**Vinando ◆**, stepping up three furlongs from his sole juvenile start, needed every yard of it as it looked for a long time as though he would not pick up the clear leader. However, the further he went the better he was going, and he eventually got there in plenty of time. This may not have been a great race, but he can only improve.
**Extra Cover(IRE)**, fit from the sand, was given a most enterprising ride, making the running and then quickening into what looked an unassailable lead starting up the home straight. However, the distress signals were being sent out passing the quarter-mile pole and he was very tired when the winner went past him inside the final furlong. This trip in the conditions looked beyond him, but he should be able to find a small race and now qualifies for handicaps.
**Midshipman Easy(USA)** ran a good deal better than on his only juvenile start and saw the longer trip out well. He should come into his own once handicapped.
**Irish Blade(IRE)** was doing all of his best work late on and looks a likely type for middle-distance handicaps.
**Notable Guest(USA)**, beaten at long odds-on on his second and final start at two, had every chance but disappointed again and the longer trip and easier ground appeared to find him out.

## 1509 BOOK YOUR DISCOUNTED TICKETS ON LINE H'CAP 1m 3f 135y
**7:50** (7:50) (E) (0-75,73) 3-Y-0 **£3,523** (£1,084; £542; £271) **Stalls** Low

Form RPR

0-30 **1** **It's Blue Chip**[68] [739] 3-8-6 **58** ..................................(e) PaulEddery 2 68
(PWD'Arcy) *hld up in rr: pushe along and hdwy over 2f out: drvn and str run fnl f: led fnl 75yds* **33/1**

06-4 **2** *nk* **Late Opposition**[18] [1222] 3-8-11 **63** .................................. LDettori 14 73
(EALDunlop) *hld up in tch: hdwy to ld appr fnl 2f: pushed out ins last: hdd and no ex fnl 75yds* **3/1**[1]

300- **3** *7* **Pangloss (IRE)**[169] [5887] 3-9-6 **72** .................................. RLMoore 4 72
(GLMoore) *hld up in rr: gd hdwy 4f out: chal fr 2f out: rdn: carried hd high and wknd fnl f* **16/1**

560- **4** *5* **Cadeaux Rouge (IRE)**[224] [4764] 3-8-13 **65** .................................. RHavlin 11 57
(MrsPNDutfield) *in tch: rdn over 3f out: styd on same pce* **25/1**

0620 **5** *3* **Jackie Kiely**[36] [1017] 3-8-3 **58** .................................. RMiles(3) 1 46
(TGMills) *wl bhd: stl plenty to do over 2f out: styd on but nvr a danger* **16/1**

2333 **6** *¾* **Siegfrieds Night (IRE)**[19] [1201] 3-8-0 **57** .................................. DFox(5) 9 43
(MCChapman) *chsd ldrs: led over 3f out: hdd appr fnl 2f: wknd over 1f out* **11/2**[3]

630- **7** *shd* **Wilfred (IRE)**[196] [5421] 3-9-6 **72** .................................. EAhern 7 58
(JonjoO'Neill) *led tl hdd over 6f out: styd chsng ldr: ev ch ins fnl 3f: wknd fr 2f out* **16/1**

005- **8** *1* **Bakhtyar**[168] [5911] 3-8-11 **63** .................................. SDrowne 5 48
(RCharlton) *bhd: hdwy 3f out: nvr rchd ldrs: wknd fr 2f out* **8/1**

605- **9** *hd* **Bosco (IRE)**[185] [5607] 3-9-1 **67** .................................. PDobbs 12 51
(RHannon) *chsd ldrs tl wknd 3f out* **33/1**

00-0 **10** *dist* **Littlestar (FR)**[18] [1224] 3-8-8 **60** .................................. SSanders 10 —
(JLDunlop) *chsd ldr: pushed along to ld over 6f out: hdd over 3f out: sn btn: t.o* **16/1**

052- **11** *21* **Blue Hills**[203] [5271] 3-9-7 **73** .................................. JFanning 3 —
(MJohnston) *chsd ldr: rdn 6f out: wknd over 4f out: t.o* **7/2**[2]

2214 **12** *hd* **Alfridini**[24] [1120] 3-9-4 **70** .................................. DaneO'Neill 6 —
(DRCElsworth) *in tch 1m: t.o* **6/1**

2m 44.19s (14.09) **Going Correction** +1.20s/f (Soft) **12** Ran SP% **121.3**
Speed ratings: **101,100,96,92,90 90,90,89,89,— —,—**CSF £131.52 CT £1709.69 TOTE £47.50: £12.30, £1.50, £3.90; EX 572.60 Place 6 £266.07, Place 5 £56.27.
**Owner** Blue Chip Feed Ltd **Bred** G C Neate **Trained** Newmarket, Suffolk

**FOCUS**
A messy handicap in which several failed to handle the conditions. The field edged over to the far rail in the straight, though much more gradually than in previous races. The front pair finished well clear and may suffer in the ratings as a result.

**NOTEBOOK**
**It's Blue Chip** caused a real shock, despite not appearing likely to figure for a long time, relishing the trip in the conditions and gradually wearing down the favourite. His best previous effort had come on Fibresand, so the testing ground was probably in his favour, and he looks as though he will get further.
**Late Opposition** travelled really well and looked the likely winner when cruising to the front. His rival saw the trip out just the better, but it would be hard to criticise this effort as he pulled right away from the others. He should make amends.
**Pangloss(IRE)**, trying beyond a mile for the first time, ran better than in his final two starts of last season, but he did not look to be fancying it in the last furlong or so and may need better ground.
**Cadeaux Rouge(IRE)**, unplaced in four starts at two, emerged with some credit but, with several not handling the conditions, she may not have achieved a lot.
**Jackie Kiely**, fit from the sand, merely ran on past beaten horses.
**Siegfrieds Night(IRE)**, having his 21st start already and his eighth of the year, raced prominently for a long way but the way he faded suggests he did not enjoy the ground.
**Bakhtyar**, making his handicap debut, ran as though not seeing out this longer trip in the ground.
**Blue Hills**, who has already shown his ability to handle cut in the ground, was beaten so far out that he must have had a problem.
**Alfridini**, making his turf debut on his seventh outing, ran appallingly and either hated the ground or something was amiss.
T/Plt: £832.30 to a £1 stake. Pool: £45,038.90. 39.50 winning tickets. T/Qpdt: £117.20 to a £1 stake. Pool: £4,421.30. 27.90 winning tickets. ST

# [1474] WOLVERHAMPTON (A.W) (L-H)
Monday, April 19

**OFFICIAL GOING: Standard**
Wind: fine Weather: nil

## 1510 NEW SITE @ BETDIRECT.CO.UK AMATEUR RIDERS' BANDED STKS 6f (F)
**5:35** (5:36) (H) 4-Y-0+ **£1,438** (£411; £205) **Stalls** Low

Form RPR

2201 **1** **Baytown Flyer**[4] [1403] 4-10-13 35 .................................. MissJCDuncan(7) 9 50
(PSMcentee) *led 1f: chsd ldr: led 2f out: r.o wl* **7/1**[3]

-002 **2** *1 ½* **Alastair Smellie**[13] [1283] 8-10-9 35 ..................................(v) MissALTurner(5) 2 39
(SLKeightley) *s.i.s: t.k.h: hdwy over 4f out: chsd wnr fnl f: r.o one pce* **7/2**[2]

364 **3** *2 ½* **Countrywide Girl (IRE)**[3] [1446] 5-10-12 30 ow5.......... MrGGibson(7) 10 37
(ABerry) *chsd ldrs: kpt on same pce fnl f* **12/1**

0030 **4** *1 ½* **Flying Faisal (USA)**[21] [1180] 6-11-0 35 ..................................(b) MrSWalker 4 27
(JMBradley) *s.i.s: hdwy on outside over 2f out: one pce fnl f* **11/4**[1]

2506 **5** *hd* **Spy Master**[20] [1190] 6-10-11 35 ..................................(bt) MissKellyHarrison(3) 3 26
(JParkes) *hld up: hdwy 2f out: one pce fnl f* **7/2**[2]

4005 **6** *2* **Welsh Whisper**[28] [1076] 5-11-0 35 .................................. TJMalone 6 20
(SABrookshaw) *hld up: rdn wl over 1f out: nvr trbld ldrs* **9/1**

0-00 **7** *shd* **The Lady Would (IRE)**[13] [1280] 5-10-9 35..............(b[1]) MrLNewnes(5) 11 20
(DGBridgwater) *led after 1f: rdn and hdd 2f out: wknd fnl f* **12/1**

050- **8** *6* **Point Man (IRE)**[189] [5542] 4-10-7 30..............(b[1]) MissJWilmot-Smith(7) 5 —
(JWPayne) *s.i.s: a bhd* **20/1**

500/ **9** *1 ¼* **Real Ting**[1386] [2485] 8-10-7 30 .................................. DrHMcCarthy(7) 7 —
(MsDeborahJEvans) *bhd fnl 4f* **33/1**

000/ **10** *1 ¾* **Expectedtofli (IRE)**[630] [3439] 6-10-7 35 ..................................(t) MrMHowells(7) 8 —
(TWall) *sn prom: wknd qckly 2f out* **50/1**

00/- **11** *8* **Tea For Texas**[504] [5829] 7-11-0 30 .................................. MissEJJones 1 —
(IWMcinnes) *chsd ldrs: rdn 3f out: sn wknd* **40/1**

1m 18.03s (2.23) **Going Correction** -0.10s/f (Stan) **11** Ran SP% **121.1**
Speed ratings: **81,79,75,73,73 70,70,62,60,58 47**CSF £31.74 TOTE £5.00: £1.40, £2.00, £4.10; EX 22.30.
**Owner** J Doxey **Bred** B Minty **Trained** Newmarket, Suffolk
■ A first winner for Jane Duncan.

**FOCUS**
A dire contest the produced a slow winning time, even for a race of its type.

**NOTEBOOK**
**Baytown Flyer ◆** won decisively under a positive ride and followed up her win on the Polytrack four days previously. She was defying a 6lb penalty on this occasion, proving she has the speed to win over the trip at this level. While it was a dire event, she will be hard to beat next time, especially if reverting to seven furlongs.
**Alastair Smellie** lost all chance with a slow start and by racing too keenly in the early stages. However, although he is on a long losing run and is in decline, this was his best effort on the surface and he is in good heart at present.
**Countrywide Girl(IRE)**, not for the first time, was made to look very one paced. She ran her race and did little wrong, but is a very difficult horse to win with.
**Flying Faisal(USA)**, with the blinkers back on, was another who missed the break but recovered to have every chance if good enough.
**Spy Master**, with the blinkers replacing the cheekpieces on this occasion, never looked like getting to the leaders and was again disappointing.
**Tea For Texas** *Official explanation: jockey said mare finished lame*

## 1511 BET DIRECT NO Q ON 08000 93 66 93 BANDED STKS 1m 1f 79y(F)
**6:05** (6:05) (H) 3-Y-0+ **£1,435** (£410; £205) **Stalls** Low

Form RPR

-040 **1** **Eurolink Artemis**[13] [1277] 7-9-0 40 ..................................(p) NCallan 2 49
(JulianPoulton) *hld up: hdwy over 3f out: led over 2f out: rdn wl over 1f out: r.o wl* **3/1**[2]

0034 **2** *1 ¾* **Tojoneski**[21] [1167] 5-9-0 35 ..................................(p) RFfrench 5 46
(IWMcinnes) *a.p: rdn over 2f out: kpt on ins fnl f: nt trble wnr* **5/2**[1]

60-0 **3** *1 ½* **Amethyst Rock**[21] [1164] 6-9-0 35 .................................. FLynch 6 43
(PLGilligan) *sn led: hdd 6f out: led over 4f out: rdn and hdd over 2f out: no ex fnl f* **10/1**

0000 **4** *3 ½* **Jamestown**[7] [1373] 7-8-7 40 .................................. KGhunowa(7) 3 36
(MJPolglase) *plld hrd: led early: hld up: sddle sn slipped: hdwy over 5f out: rdn over 2f out: wknd fnl f* **7/2**[3]

0-00 **5** *17* **Wethaab (USA)**[20] [1194] 7-9-0 30 ..................................(vt) AnnStokell 4 —
(MissAStokell) *w ldr: led 6f out: rdn and hdd over 4f out: wknd 3f out* **33/1**

000- **6** *¾* **Ali Pasha**[179] [5717] 5-9-0 35 .................................. SWKelly 1 —
(WMBrisbourne) *hld up: hdwy over 4f out: rdn 3f out: wknd over 2f out* **3/1**[2]

2m 3.30s (0.30) **Going Correction** -0.10s/f (Stan) **6** Ran SP% **112.8**
Speed ratings: **94,92,91,88,72 72**CSF £11.05 TOTE £5.40: £2.50, £1.40; EX 10.60.
**Owner** Roberto Favarulo **Bred** Mrs Carolyn Antoniades **Trained** Kentford, Suffolk

**FOCUS**
A very weak heat featuring out of form and regressive performers.

**NOTEBOOK**
**Eurolink Artemis**, restrained early at the back of the field, put her best foot forward in the straight and stayed on well to record a first victory since December 2002. Although she is an in-and-out performer, she is likely to reappear in this grade at Chepstow later in the week and could go close as long as the ground is not too testing.
**Tojoneski** was clear of the rest in second, but had no answer to the winner over this longer trip. He seemed to stay the distance well enough, but may need to revert to shorter in order to score at this level.
**Amethyst Rock**, dropping in trip, could only muster the one pace in the straight having been handy throughout. He looks very slow and on this evidence it is hard to know what his ideal distance may be.
**Jamestown** pulled his way to the front and had little chance when his saddle slipped before halfway. He is running out of excuses and looks one to avoid at all costs. *Official explanation: jockey said saddle slipped*

## 1512 BETDIRECT.CO.UK BANDED STKS 2m 46y(F)
**6:35** (6:35) (H) 4-Y-0+ **£1,438** (£411; £205) **Stalls** Low

Form RPR

34-4 **1** **Mercurious (IRE)**[13] [1281] 4-8-10 40 .................................. DaleGibson 3 51
(JMackie) *hld up: hdwy over 6f out: rdn and wnt 2nd over 2f out: led wl ins fnl f: styd on wl* **9/2**[2]

4216 **2** *2* **Doctor John**[21] [1173] 7-8-11 45 ..................................(p) DCorby(3) 2 49
(AndrewTurnell) *hld up: hdwy 10f out: led over 5f out: rdn over 2f out: hdd and no ex wl ins fnl f* **10/11**[1]

4062 **3** *12* **Berkeley Heights**[20] [1193] 4-8-10 45........................................(v[1]) NCallan 5 35
(MrsJCandlish) *hld up: hdwy 10f out: rdn over 4f out: wknd over 1f out* **8/1**[3]

1250 **4** *15* **Unleaded**[23] [1135] 4-8-10 40.................................................... JMackay 1 17
(JAkehurst) *chsd ldrs: led 8f out: rdn over 6f out: hdd over 5f out: wknd over 3f out* **8/1**[3]

-341 **5** *2 ½* **Mysterium**[42] [992] 10-8-11 45........................................(v) TPQueally[(3)] 7 14
(NPLittmoden) *hld up and bhd: rdn over 5f out: sn struggling* **9/2**[2]

6006 **6** *dist* **Homeric Trojan**[3] [1448] 4-8-5 45 ow2................................ DTudhope[(7)] 4 —
(MBrittain) *sn chsng ldr: rdn and wknd over 6f out: sn t.o* **33/1**

0/00 **7** *dist* **Paarl Rock**[18] [1077] 9-9-0 40...............................................(v) FLynch 6 —
(STLewis) *led: hdd 8f out: sn lost pl: t.o fnl 6f* **50/1**

3m 39.62s (-2.68) **Going Correction** -0.10s/f (Stan)
**WFA** 4 from 7yo+ 4lb **7** Ran SP% **115.9**
Speed ratings: **102,101,95,87,86** —,—CSF £9.26 TOTE £7.60: £2.30, £1.30; EX 14.70.
**Owner** Gwen K Dot.com **Bred** Miss Jill Finegan **Trained** Church Broughton, Derbys

**FOCUS**
A decent winning time for the grade and the front pair pulled well clear of the rest in the straight. The winner is likely to be handicapped out of this grade in future.

**NOTEBOOK**
**Mercurious(IRE)** ◆ showed the benefit of her recent comeback run and registered a first career win in gritty style. She was attempting this trip for this first time and that brought about the improvement, and although she beat little on this occasion, she can build on this display at this lowly level.
**Doctor John**, with the cheekpieces back on, tired badly inside the final furlong and had nothing left when challenged. This was slightly disappointing, but he was well clear of the rest and can win a similar race in due course.
**Berkeley Heights** failed to run up to the form of her latest effort over this trip at Southwell in the first-time visor. The jury is still out as to whether she truly stays this trip.
**Paarl Rock** *Official explanation: jockey said gelding changed its legs down the back straight*

## 1513 LITTLEWOODS BET DIRECT BANDED STKS 1m 100y(F)
7:05 (7:06) (H) 3-Y-0+ £1,438 (£411; £205) Stalls Low

Form RPR

6441 **1** **Beauteous (IRE)**[3] [1445] 5-9-6 35.................................... KGhunowa[(7)] 5 69
(MJPolglase) *mde all: rdn clr over 2f out: unchal* **1/2**[1]

04-1 **2** *13* **Tee Jay Kassidy**[27] [1094] 4-9-0 40.................................... MHalford[(7)] 3 36
(JulianPoulton) *hld up: rdn over 2f out: c wd st: wnt 2nd 1f out: no ch w wnr* **11/4**[2]

0650 **3** *2* **Dundonald**[7] [1376] 5-9-7 35................................................(bt) SRighton 1 32
(MAppleby) *sn chsng wnr: rdn over 5f out: wknd over 2f out* **12/1**[3]

055/ **4** *11* **Power And Demand**[329] [333] 7-9-7 35.............................. RFfrench 2 9
(KGWingrove) *chsd ldr early: prom: rdn 4f out: sn wknd* **66/1**

2400 **5** *5* **All On My Own (USA)**[21] [1167] 9-9-0 35............(b) NataliaGemelova[(7)] 6 —
(IWMcinnes) *s.s: hdwy on ins over 3f out: wknd over 2f out* **12/1**[3]

1m 49.69s (-1.40) **Going Correction** -0.10s/f (Stan) **5** Ran SP% **110.2**
Speed ratings: **103,90,88,77,72**CSF £2.13 TOTE £1.60: £1.02, £1.60; EX 2.70.
**Owner** Paul J Dixon **Bred** Mrs Jill M Harley **Trained** Southwell, Notts

**FOCUS**
A decent winning time for a banded stakes and the field were well strung out behind the easy winner, whose performance was well above average for the grade.

**NOTEBOOK**
**Beauteous(IRE)** ◆ came home in splendid isolation on this step up to a mile to follow-up his success only three days previously. On recent evidence he looks more suited to the Fibresand, but he has won his last two outings by a combined 20 lengths and will be hard to beat when attempting the hat-trick, wherever he turns up.
**Tee Jay Kassidy** was held up to get the trip but, by the time he had got into his full stride, the winner had gone beyond all recall. He came very wide on the home turn and did well to run on as he did, so can be considered slightly better than the bare form suggests.
**Dundonald** did not improve for the drop back into banded company and is one to avoid. *Official explanation: jockey said gelding had lost interest in the race*

## 1514 £10 FREE BET @ BETDIRECT.CO.UK BANDED STKS 1m 4f (F)
7:35 (7:36) (H) 4-Y-0+ £1,435 (£410; £205) Stalls Low

Form RPR

-030 **1** **Ersaal (USA)**[21] [1166] 4-8-10 40........................................(t) NCallan 4 43
(JJay) *sn led: hdd over 8f out: prom: rdn to ld over 1f out: edgd rt ins fnl f: r.o* **11/4**[2]

-265 **2** *¾* **Fairmorning (IRE)**[55] [880] 5-8-8 40................................ LisaJones[(3)] 8 42
(JWUnett) *hld up: rdn over 4f out: hdwy on ins wl over 1f out: nt qckn towards fin* **11/8**[1]

030- **3** *hd* **Lady Lakshmi**[195] [5435] 4-8-10 40.................................... JMackay 5 42
(RGuest) *hld up: rdn and hdwy over 3f out: nt qckn ins fnl f* **11/2**[3]

05-0 **4** *1* **Rhetoric (IRE)**[20] [1193] 5-8-8 35 ow2.............................. DNolan[(5)] 3 42
(DGBridgwater) *prom: led over 8f out: rdn over 2f out: hdd over 1f out: one pce fnl f* **12/1**

0/0- **5** *7* **Kimoe Warrior**[35] [372] 6-8-11 35........................................(b) SWKelly 7 30
(MMullineaux) *prom: wnt 2nd 5f out: rdn and ev ch 2f out: wknd 1f out* **10/1**

5320 **6** *7* **Dora Corbino**[28] [1077] 4-8-3 40......................... StephanieHollinshead[(7)] 2 19
(RHollinshead) *led early: chsd ldrs: rdn over 4f out: wknd over 3f out* **9/1**

0-03 **7** *dist* **Final Lap**[42] [994] 8-8-11 30............................................ GGibbons 6 —
(STLewis) *prom tl wknd qckly 5f out: t.o* **16/1**

005/ **8** *12* **Manny**[562] [5104] 4-8-10 35.............................................. AnnStokell 1 —
(MissAStokell) *hld up and bhd: hung rt and lost tch over 7f out: sn t.o* **40/1**

2m 41.12s (-0.68) **Going Correction** -0.10s/f (Stan)
**WFA** 4 from 5yo+ 1lb **8** Ran SP% **119.3**
Speed ratings: **98,97,97,96,92 87**,—,—CSF £7.27 TOTE £3.10: £1.10, £1.50, £1.80; EX 9.90.
**Owner** G Knight **Bred** Shadwell Farm Inc **Trained** Newmarket, Suffolk

**FOCUS**
A desperate affair full of exposed runners and the first four were clear.

**NOTEBOOK**
**Ersaal(USA)**, despite hanging inside the final furlong, stuck his head out where it matted to score his first ever success with the tongue tie replacing the blinkers on this occasion. He has shown plenty of temperament in the past and this was a very weak event, so he hardly appeals as the type to follow-up.
**Fairmorning(IRE)** had every chance, but once again lacked the resolution to go through with her effort late on. She remains a maiden after 16 attempts.
**Lady Lakshmi** ◆, off for 195-days prior to this, could only keep on at the one pace late on. This was not a bad effort in the circumstances, she will improve plenty for this, and looks the one to take out of the race.
**Rhetoric(IRE)** ran an improved race on this drop in trip. However, he is still a maiden and totally exposed, so his proximity at the finish sums up the form.
**Manny** *Official explanation: jockey said gelding hung right-handed throughout*

## 1515 BET IN RUNNING @ BETDIRECT.CO.UK BANDED STKS 7f (F)
8:05 (8:05) (H) 3-Y-0+ £1,445 (£413; £206) Stalls High

Form RPR

0-40 **1** **Gilly's General (IRE)**[48] [946] 4-9-7 40.............................. GGibbons 9 49
(JWUnett) *prom: led 4f out: hrd rdn fnl f: jst hld on* **25/1**

-640 **2** *shd* **Dasar**[70] [725] 4-9-0 45........................................(v[1]) DTudhope[(7)] 10 49
(MBrittain) *hdwy over 5f out: w wnr and rdn over 2f out: ev ch fnl f: r.o* **9/1**

0003 **3** *5* **Eternal Bloom**[3] [1445] 6-9-0 45........................................ MLawson[(7)] 4 36
(MBrittain) *chsd ldrs: rdn and one pce fnl 3f* **10/1**

-002 **4** *hd* **Mr Uppity**[20] [1191] 5-9-4 40........................................(e) LisaJones[(3)] 8 35
(JulianPoulton) *hld up: hung rt over 3f out: hdwy over 1f out: one pce fnl f* **10/3**[2]

053- **5** *5* **Lieuday**[223] [4792] 5-9-7 45................................................(p) SWKelly 6 22
(WMBrisbourne) *hdwy 5f out: hmpd over 3f out: sn rdn: wknd over 1f out* **7/4**[1]

-656 **6** *nk* **Abbiejo (IRE)**[3] [1444] 7-9-4 40.......................................... DCorby[(3)] 5 21
(GFierro) *s.i.s: outpcd and bhd: sme hdwy over 1f out: n.d* **25/1**

6050 **7** *8* **Robin Sharp**[21] [1176] 6-9-7 45.............................................(v) PDoe 2 1
(JAkehurst) *prom early: sn rdn along and bhd* **6/1**[3]

560P **8** *4* **Lion's Domane**[19] [1197] 7-9-7 40........................................ FLynch 1 —
(ABerry) *led over 2f: n.m.r on ins over 3f out: wknd over 2f out* **10/1**

5200 **9** *13* **Master Rattle**[26] [1098] 5-9-7 45.........................................(b) VSlattery 7 —
(JaneSouthcombe) *sn w ldr: led briefly over 4f out: wknd 3f out* **8/1**

1m 30.55s (0.23) **Going Correction** -0.10s/f (Stan) **9** Ran SP% **120.7**
Speed ratings: **94,93,88,87,82 81,72,68,53**CSF £241.00 TOTE £29.70: £15.70, £5.80, £5.60; EX 163.90 Place 6 £59.28, Place 5 £16.37.
**Owner** Gillian Rosano & Partners **Bred** Terry Farrell **Trained** Wolverhampton, W Midlands

**FOCUS**
A poor contest run at just a fair pace and the first two were clear at the finish.

**NOTEBOOK**
**Gilly's General(IRE)**, who had run poorly in first-time blinkers previously, bravely registered his first win at the 15th attempt. This is his level and he may be able to build on this, but is not one to trust for the follow-up bid.
**Dasar** only just failed and was a little unlucky, as she came right away from the others. The first-time visor helped bring about some improvement.
**Eternal Bloom**, broke well on this occasion, but held every chance if good enough and was made to look very one paced in the straight. She has regressed since winning on her comeback in January, looks better at Southwell and this trip tends to stretch her stamina.
**Mr Uppity** looked a tricky ride on this occasion and failed to build on his latest effort at Southwell, which gave him every chance in this event.
T/Plt: £185.00 to a £1 stake. Pool £33,936.80 T/Qpdt: Not won KH

# 1292 FOLKESTONE (R-H)
### Tuesday, April 20

**OFFICIAL GOING: Soft (good to soft in places)**
Wind: lt across Weather: fine & sunny

## 1516 LEVY BOARD APPRENTICE H'CAP 6f
2:10 (2:10) (G) (0-55,55) 3-Y-0+ £3,059 (£874; £437) Stalls Low

Form RPR

1000 **1** **Arogant Prince**[22] [1180] 7-9-11 **52**................................ SaleemGolam 2 67
(JPearce) *racd against nr side rail: mde all: rdn clr fnl f* **16/1**

060- **2** *3 ½* **Halcyon Magic**[148] [6055] 6-9-8 **49**................................(b) LauraPike 5 54
(MissJFeilden) *racd nr side: towards rr of gp: urged along and styd on fr over 1f out: tk 2nd last strides* **33/1**

30-0 **3** *1* **Davids Mark**[28] [1082] 4-9-6 **55**........................................ JJeffrey[(8)] 1 57
(JRJenkins) *cl up nr side: chsd wnr over 2f out: rdn to chal over 1f out: outpcd fnl f* **25/1**

0045 **4** *½* **Muqtadi (IRE)**[15] [1274] 6-9-6 **47**........................................ KMay 3 47
(MQuinn) *dwlt: last of nr side gp: no prog tl r.o fnl f: nrst fin* **33/1**

000- **5** *½* **Tatweer (IRE)**[120] [6232] 4-9-8 **49**................................(v) LiamJones 15 48
(DShaw) *led far side gp: c towards centre fr 1/2-way: hanging lft and nt qckn over 1f out* **14/1**

0332 **6** *5* **Largs**[28] [1092] 4-8-13 **48**............................................ KPierrepont[(8)] 8 32
(JBalding) *cl up far side: drvn and effrt 2f out: c towards centre and wknd fnl f* **12/1**

0131 **7** *4* **Italian Mist (FR)**[3] [1477] 5-9-9 **53** 7ex................................(e) MHalford[(3)] 6 25
(JulianPoulton) *chsd wnr nr side to over 2f out: bmpd along and wknd over 1f out* **7/2**[1]

-000 **8** *½* **Shady Deal**[8] [1368] 8-9-11 **52**........................................ KGhunowa 13 22
(JMBradley) *prom far side: c towards centre frm 1/2-way: wknd wl over 1f out* **20/1**

1561 **9** *½* **Bells Beach (IRE)**[20] [1206] 6-9-7 **48**................................ KJackson 16 17
(PHowling) *prom far side: c towards centre fr 1/2-way: wknd wl over 1f out* **8/1**

100- **10** *shd* **Holly Rose**[183] [5672] 5-10-0 **55**........................................(p) MHoward 10 23
(DECantillon) *dwlt: racd far side: trckd ldrs after 2f: pushed along and wknd wl over 1f out* **33/1**

1146 **11** *3 ½* **Long Weekend (IRE)**[28] [1087] 6-9-4 **48**....................(v) DawnWatson[(3)] 14 6
(DShaw) *dwlt: racd far side: a wl in rr* **7/1**[3]

1503 **12** *2* **Feast Of Romance**[8] [1373] 7-9-2 **48**................................ SArcher[(5)] 7 —
(CNAllen) *racd on outer of nr side gp: a in last pair and struggling* **12/1**

1306 **13** *shd* **Sabana (IRE)**[3] [1477] 6-9-7 **51** ow4................................(b) CJDavies[(3)] 11 2
(JMBradley) *chsd far side ldrs: in centre of crse fr 1/2-way: wknd 2f out* **12/1**

1046 **14** *½* **Gun Salute**[27] [1098] 4-9-1 **50**........................................(p) JemmaMarshall[(8)] 12 —
(GLMoore) *dwlt: sn trckd ldrs far side: wknd 2f out* **9/2**[2]

0000 **15** *9* **Gone'N'Dunnett (IRE)**[53] [904] 5-9-13 **54**........................(v) DeanWilliams 9 —
(MrsCADunnett) *racd far side: a in rr of gp: wknd over 2f out* **16/1**

1m 16.62s (3.02) **Going Correction** +0.50s/f (Yiel) **15** Ran SP% **123.0**
Speed ratings: **99,94,93,92,91 85,79,79,78,78 73,70,70,70,58**CSF £483.89 CT £6502.92 TOTE £14.80: £4.50, £10.60, £4.20; EX 452.80.
**Owner** Chris Marsh **Bred** Miss Julie Self **Trained** Newmarket, Suffolk
■ Stewards Enquiry : Dean Williams one-day ban: failed to keep straight from stalls (May 3)
K Pierrepont one-day ban: failed to keep straight from stalls (May 3)

**FOCUS**
A moderate heat in which, surprisingly perhaps, a low draw proved a big advantage.

**NOTEBOOK**
**Arogant Prince**, well drawn as it turned out, had the blinkers left off for a change, stuck to the near-side rail throughout and made every yard. He likes a bit of cut in the ground and saw this longer trip out well.
**Halcyon Magic** goes with cut in the ground but is probably happier on a faster surface. Well drawn. he stayed on well, and a step back up to seven with this run under his belt should suit.

**Davids Mark**, well drawn, had never run on ground softer than good before. However, he coped well with these conditions and clearly likes it here, as his only previous success on turf came over the course and distance.

**Muqtadi(IRE)**, who is often slowly away, came with his usual late run, but he is a difficult horse to win with. His best form recently has been in selling grade, in which the form of his most recent outings reads 21441545

**Tatweer(IRE)** had faced stiff tasks on his two previous starts on turf, the last of which was in Listed grade. He did best of those drawn high and who raced towards the far side to halfway, finished clear of the rest, and is one to bear in mind for a similarly poor heat now that he has a run under his belt. *Official explanation: jockey said gelding had hung left*

**Italian Mist(FR)** looked to have plenty in his favour, including the draw, and was disappointing.

## 1517 KM EGG CUP CLAIMING STKS — 5f

2:40 (2:40) (F) 3-Y-O — £2,905 (£830; £415) Stalls Low

Form — RPR

3-65 **1** **He's A Rocket (IRE)**[19] [1220] 3-8-8 40 ........................(b[1]) LisaJones[(3)] 5 — 55
(MrsCADunnett) *mde virtually all: jnd and hrd rdn fnl f: jst hld on* **50/1**

0-00 **2** *hd* **A Bid In Time (IRE)**[68] [747] 3-8-7 48 ow1 ........................ NCallan 6 — 50
(DShaw) *started awkwardly: hld up in last pair: effrt 2f out: drvn to join wnr ins fnl f: edgd lft: nt qckn last strides* **16/1**

4450 **3** *1 ½* **Black Oval**[3] [1464] 3-8-3 59 ........................ SHitchcott[(3)] 4 — 44
(MRChannon) *cl up: rdn to join wnr 1f out: ev ch whn squeezed out last 75y: nt rcvr* **5/2**[1]

00-0 **4** *hd* **Short Chorus**[20] [1209] 3-8-4 50 ........................(p) SWKelly 3 — 41
(JBalding) *hld up in last pair: hrd drvn and swtchd rt over 1f out: clsng on ldrs whn rn out of room on inner last 75y* **13/2**

-003 **5** *3* **Blue Power (IRE)**[18] [1236] 3-9-5 60 ........................ GFaulkner 1 — 46
(KRBurke) *racd against nr side rail: cl up: effrt to chal whn hmpd over 1f out: nt rcvr* **6/1**

61-6 **6** *2* **Tictactoe**[98] [514] 3-8-2 57 ........................ CCatlin 2 — 22
(DJDaly) *chsd ldrs: rdn and no prog whn bmpd over 1f out: wknd* **11/2**[3]

3440 **7** *hd* **Pardon Moi**[69] [744] 3-7-11 45 ........................ HayleyTurner[(5)] 8 — 21
(MrsCADunnett) *racd on wd outside: chsd ldrs tl fdd over 1f out* **16/1**

4-34 **8** *13* **Only If I Laugh**[18] [1236] 3-9-0 75 ........................(b) JFMcDonald[(5)] 7 — —
(BJMeehan) *bmpd s: sn pressed ldr: wknd rapidly 2f out* **3/1**[2]

64.19 secs (3.49) **Going Correction** +0.50s/f (Yiel) **8** Ran SP% **110.3**

Speed ratings: **92,91,89,88,84 80,80,59**CSF £626.42 TOTE £23.00: £3.70, £2.40, £1.10; EX 404.50.He's A Rocket (no.3) was claimed by Karl Burke for £8,000. Black Oval (no.5) was claimed by Simon Dow for £8,000.

**Owner** Mrs Christine Dunnett **Bred** Lemongrove Stud **Trained** Hingham, Norfolk

■ Stewards Enquiry : Lisa Jones one-day ban: careless riding (May 3)

### FOCUS

Poor form, but the winner showed admirable battling qualities. The form may not be that reliable.

### NOTEBOOK

**He's A Rocket(IRE)** had little to recommend him on form, but the first-time blinkers appeared to spark improvement, and the soft ground was always likely to suit this son of Indian Ridge. *Official explanation: trainer said, regarding the improved form shown, colt was blinkered for the first time today*

**A Bid In Time(IRE)**, who scored her only success with cut in the ground, appreciated the easy surface. In theory her rider's 1lb overweight cost her, but in reality she had every chance to go past the battling winner.

**Black Oval** would have finished closer but for being squeezed up inside the last, but she had every chance to win. She has been a beaten favourite four times since winning her maiden and is proving expensive to follow.

**Short Chorus** ran a better race in the first-time cheekpieces and handled the softer conditions well enough.

**Blue Power(IRE)** went for a non-existent gap next to the near-side rail and had to be snatched up. He deserves rating better than his finishing position, but whether he would have threatened for the victory is doubtful.

## 1518 FOLKESTONE-RACECOURSE.CO.UK CLASSIFIED STKS — 5f

3:10 (3:10) (E) 3-Y-O+ — £3,396 (£1,045; £522; £261) Stalls Low

Form — RPR

60-1 **1** **Maddie's A Jem**[21] [1185] 4-9-2 72 ........................ SWKelly 3 — 81
(JRJenkins) *hld up bhd ldrs: smooth prog to chse ldr over 1f out: drvn and edgd lft ent fnl f: led last 150y: sn clr* **5/2**[2]

4-06 **2** *2 ½* **Byo (IRE)**[24] [1131] 6-9-3 67 ........................ SDrowne 2 — 73
(MQuinn) *disp ld to 3f out: styd chsng ldr: drvn and unable qck over 1f out: kpt on to take 2nd nr fin* **6/1**

020- **3** *½* **Roxanne Mill**[157] [6001] 6-9-5 75 ........................ RLMoore 5 — 73
(JMBradley) *disp ld tl def advantage 3f out: rdn over 1f out: hdd & wknd last 150y* **11/2**[3]

0020 **4** *1 ½* **The Fisio**[5] [1421] 4-9-5 72 ........................(v) MartinDwyer 1 — 68
(AMBalding) *pushed along to press ldrs: rdn and outpcd fr 2f out: no imp after* **2/1**[1]

130- **5** *5* **Tapau (IRE)**[202] [5310] 6-9-3 73 ........................ SCarson 8 — 49
(JMBradley) *dwlt: chsd ldrs: rdn 1/2-way: sn struggling and btn: wknd fnl f* **8/1**

4036 **6** *nk* **Tickle**[14] [1283] 6-9-0 54 ........................(bt[1]) DSweeney 6 — 44
(PJMakin) *chsd ldrs: outpcd 1/2-way: sn bhd: kpt on same pce fnl f* **25/1**

5000 **7** *¾* **Abraxas**[24] [1131] 6-9-3 40 ........................(p) JQuinn 4 — 45
(JAkehurst) *s.i.s: outpcd in last and hanging: nvr a factor: kpt on fnl f* **66/1**

/6P- **8** *13* **Foley Millennium (IRE)**[428] [560] 6-9-3 50 ........................ NPollard 7 — —
(MQuinn) *w ldrs to 1/2-way: wknd rapidly 2f out* **50/1**

62.61 secs (1.91) **Going Correction** +0.50s/f (Yiel) **8** Ran SP% **110.0**

Speed ratings: **104,100,99,96,88 88,87,66**CSF £16.23 TOTE £3.60: £1.02, £2.30, £3.70; EX 16.20.

**Owner** Mrs Wendy Jenkins **Bred** The Peel Stud **Trained** Royston, Herts

### FOCUS

A fai race and they went a decent pace. The winner seems improved this year.

### NOTEBOOK

**Maddie's A Jem**, who won at the track three weeks earlier, scored comfortably despite the drop back in trip. She was joint best in at the weights so was entiteld to run a big race, but she is also clearly in great heart at present.

**Byo(IRE)** had a bit to find with one or two on these terms, and he ran a solid race in defeat. He takes his racing well but his strike-rate is not great.

**Roxanne Mill** goes well with give in the ground and was racing over her ideal trip. Her stable's runners usually need a few runs before they hit top form though, and in the circumstances this was a fair effort.

**The Fisio**, for whom the visor appears to have lost its effect, is becoming disappointing.

**Tapau(IRE)** needs farther than this.

## 1519 KENTISH EXPRESS MAIDEN STKS — 7f (S)

3:40 (3:40) (D) 3-Y-O+ — £3,857 (£1,187; £593; £296) Stalls Low

Form — RPR

4-0 **1** **Doctorate**[26] [1104] 3-8-10 ........................ EAhern 12 — 78
(EALDunlop) *racd far side: cl up: trckd ldr gng easily 3f out: shkn up 2f out: styd on to ld last 100y* **9/2**[3]

0-2 **2** *1* **Henndey (IRE)**[22] [1174] 3-8-10 ........................ NCallan 9 — 75
(MAJarvis) *trckd far side ldr: led 1/2-way: drvn over 1f out: hdd and one pce last 100y* **7/2**[2]

040- **3** *½* **Flying Adored**[190] [5541] 3-8-5 74 ........................ TQuinn 7 — 69
(JLDunlop) *racd on outer of far side grop: prom: rdn 2f out: wandered over 1f out: kpt on to take 3rd nr fin* **7/1**

**4** *¾* **Nistaki (USA)** 3-8-10 ........................ JFEgan 5 — 72
(MissVHaigh) *towards rr far side: prog 3f out: hrd rdn to chal over 1f out: one pce fnl f* **10/1**

3-22 **5** *6* **Rangoon (USA)**[13] [1295] 3-8-10 78 ........................ RHughes 2 — 57
(MrsAJPerrett) *led nr side trio thrght: clr of rivals after 3f: no ch w far side ldrs fnl 2f* **2/1**[1]

30- **6** *3 ½* **Kensington (IRE)**[270] [3585] 3-8-10 77 ........................ MartinDwyer 13 — 48
(RGuest) *t.k.h: trckd far side ldrs tl wknd wl over 1f out* **14/1**

40-0 **7** *1 ½* **Lady Franpalm (IRE)**[8] [1352] 4-9-4 54 ........................ RLMoore 8 — 39
(MJHaynes) *dwlt: racd far side: in rr: outpcd 3f out: no ch after* **50/1**

0- **8** *3* **Rawalpindi**[171] [5870] 3-8-7 ........................ LisaJones[(3)] 3 — 37
(JARToller) *dwlt and swvd lft s: racd nr side: nvr on terms w ldr* **33/1**

5 **9** *nk* **Indian Lily**[13] [1293] 3-8-5 ........................ JQuinn 10 — 31
(CFWall) *racd far side: towards rr: outpcd 3f out: shuffled along and one pce after* **25/1**

000 **10** *8* **Diverted**[21] [1189] 3-8-5 ........................ SWKelly 6 — 11
(MGQuinlan) *racd far side: a in rr: bhd fnl 3f* **66/1**

00- **11** *5* **Buckenham Stone**[132] [6163] 5-9-4 ........................ RPrice 1 — —
(JPearce) *racd nr side: nvr on terms: struggling after 3f* **100/1**

00-0 **12** *4* **Pat's Nemisis (IRE)**[13] [1293] 3-8-5 ........................ NPollard 4 — —
(BRJohnson) *swtchd to r far side after 1f: a wl bhd* **66/1**

00-0 **13** *1 ½* **Frenchmans Lodge**[22] [1176] 4-9-9 45 ........................ PDoe 11 — —
(JMBradley) *leed far side gp to 1/2-way: wknd and eased sn after* **66/1**

1m 30.51s (2.71) **Going Correction** +0.50s/f (Yiel)

**WFA** 3 from 4yo+ 13lb **13** Ran SP% **116.2**

Speed ratings: **104,102,102,101,94 90,88,85,85,75 70,65,63**CSF £19.30 TOTE £6.10: £3.20, £2.40, £3.70; EX 35.60.

**Owner** P G Goulandris **Bred** Chippenham Lodge Stud Ltd **Trained** Newmarket, Suffolk

### FOCUS

A fair maiden despite the favourite disappointing.

### NOTEBOOK

**Doctorate** put behind him a fairly disappointing reappearance on this drop back to seven furlongs. This looked just a fair maiden though, and handicaps look the likely path for him.

**Henndey(IRE)** had plenty in his favour and appeared to run up to the form of his previous outing. He should get a mark in the mid-to-high 70s and could be interesting in handicap company.

**Flying Adored**, racing on soft ground for the first time, stayed on late in the day and should be capable of improving on this showing with a run behind her.

**Nistaki(USA)**, who changed hands for 30,000gns as a two-year-old, was the subject of support in the market at big prices and was bang there until weakening inside the last. He was clearly ready for this debut.

**Rangoon(USA)** had no chance with the far-side group as it turned out and was well held in fifth. He is becoming expensive to follow but faster ground may help.

**Kensington(IRE)** did not get home over this longer trip.

**Frenchmans Lodge** *Official explanation: jockey said gelding was unsuited by the going (soft, good to soft in places)*

## 1520 WESTENHANGER H'CAP — 1m 7f 92y

4:10 (4:11) (E) (0-70,70) 4-Y-O+ — £3,513 (£1,081; £540; £270) Stalls High

Form — RPR

00-1 **1** **Linens Flame**[24] [1135] 5-9-8 64 ........................ DSweeney 6 — 72+
(BGPowell) *mde all: drew clr over 2f out: in n.d after: pushed out* **5/2**[1]

/60- **2** *3 ½* **Mister Putt (USA)**[64] [1332] 6-9-4 60 ........................(b) CCatlin 9 — 64
(MrsNSmith) *settled towards rr: pushed along 7f out: nt clr run 4f out: prog 3f out: chsd wnr over 1f out: kpt on: nvr able to chal* **13/2**

006 **3** *1* **Marino Mou (IRE)**[18] [1235] 4-7-7 43 oh13 ........................ DFox[(5)] 8 — 46
(MissDMountain) *rn in snatches in last pair: prog over 3f out: rdn to dispute 2nd over 1f out: kpt on one pce fnl f* **66/1**

60/0 **4** *9* **Bakiri (IRE)**[15] [1275] 6-10-0 70 ........................ SCarson 3 — 62
(AndrewReid) *cl up: chsd wnr over 3f out: sn rdn and no imp: wknd over 1f out* **16/1**

443- **5** *2* **Henry Island (IRE)**[183] [5675] 11-9-13 69 ........................ EAhern 7 — 59
(MrsAJBowlby) *hld up in last pair: effrt over 3f out: no imp and btn 2f out* **7/1**

-050 **6** *18* **Paula Lane**[13] [1305] 4-8-4 52 ........................ SHitchcott[(3)] 2 — 20
(RCurtis) *chsd wnr: rdn over 5f out: wknd over 3f out* **20/1**

6/ **7** *21* **Windsor Beauty (IRE)**[110] [3320] 6-8-10 52 ........................ PDoe 5 — —
(RRowe) *in tch: reminder 8f out: drvn over 6f out: sn wknd: t.o 3f out* **22/1**

/410 **8** *dist* **Ffiffiffer (IRE)**[18] [1238] 6-9-3 59 ........................ RHughes 10 — —
(CTinkler) *chsd ldrs: rdn 4f out: wknd over 2f out: 7th and wl btn whn virtually p.u over 1f out: t.o* **9/2**[3]

31-P **9** *dist* **Alnaja (USA)**[17] [1245] 5-10-0 70 ........................(vt[1]) RHills 1 — —
(WJHaggas) *reminder sn after s: prom: drvn over 5f out: sn wknd: t.o whn virtually p.u 2f out* **7/2**[2]

3m 40.42s (13.22) **Going Correction** +0.90s/f (Soft)

**WFA** 4 from 5yo+ 3lb **9** Ran SP% **111.3**

Speed ratings: **100,98,97,92,91 82,70,—,—**CSF £17.92 CT £797.52 TOTE £2.80: £1.20, £2.10, £8.80; EX 22.60.

**Owner** D & J Newell **Bred** Mrs D B Mulley **Trained** Morestead, Hants

### FOCUS

A modest handicap that was a pretty uncompetitive race as it turned out.

### NOTEBOOK

**Linens Flame** defied a 10lb higher mark with ease. Making every yard, he would have won by even farther had his rider not allowed him to coast home. He is a progressive type and could well defy a penalty.

**Mister Putt(USA)**, twice successful over hurdles in heavy ground, ran his last three races over fences. He was never a threat to the winner but stayed on well, and clearly he is suited by a good test of stamina.

**Marino Mou(IRE)** ran far better than he should have given that he was 13lb out of the handicap. The step up in trip clearly suited, but connections will no doubt be hoping that the Handicapper does not take this form literally.

**Bakiri(IRE)** was taking a significant step up in trip and did not get home, despite the fact that he won over two and a half miles over hurdles last month.

**Henry Island(IRE)** probably needed this reappearance outing, and his best form is on faster ground anyway.

**Alnaja(USA)**, tongue tied and visored for the first time, once again disappointed, and he seems to have a problem.

## 1521 ROMNEY MARSH MAIDEN FILLIES' STKS 1m 4f

**4:40** (4:41) (D) 3-Y-O+ **£3,740** (£1,151; £575; £287) **Stalls** High

Form RPR

0- **1** **Marine City (JPN)**$^{171}$ [5869] 3-8-4 MHenry 5 75
(MAJarvis) *dwlt: hld up: chsd ldrs 4f out: brought to wd outside in st: effrt 2f out: rdn to ld last 100y: styd on* **20/1**

**2** *1* **Light Of Morn** 3-8-4 MartinDwyer 6 73
(RGuest) *trckd ldrs: effrt 3f out: c wd st and effrt to chal 2f out: ev ch hanging lft after: nt qckn fnl 100y* **3/1**$^{2}$

540- **3** *hd* **Portrait Of A Lady (IRE)**$^{179}$ [5722] 3-8-4 69 WRyan 7 73
(HRACecil) *hld up in midfield: prog 3f out: effrt and forced to come wd wl over 1f out: styd on same pce fnl f* **12/1**

03- **4** *hd* **Al Beedaa (USA)**$^{203}$ [5284] 3-8-4 RHills 8 73
(JLDunlop) *dwlt: sn trckd ldrs: rdn and nt qckn 2f out: flashed tail and swtchd to inner over 1f out: kpt on one pce* **6/1**$^{3}$

000- **5** *nk* **Sea Plume**$^{133}$ [6156] 5-9-10 75 RHughes 1 72
(LadyHerries) *led: kicked on over 3f out: flashed tail under presssure fnl 2f: hdd & wknd last 100y* **6/1**$^{3}$

2 **6** *2 ½* **High School**$^{21}$ [1189] 3-8-4 NPollard 4 69
(DRLoder) *pressed ldr: rdn to chal over 2f out: ev ch after: fnd nil u.p over 1f out: wknd ins fnl f* **2/1**$^{1}$

000- **7** *23* **Rovella**$^{232}$ [4623] 3-8-4 JFEgan 2 37?
(MrsHDalton) *settled in last: outpcd 4f out: nudged along and no prog after* **66/1**

5 **8** *16* **Olympias (IRE)**$^{21}$ [1189] 3-8-4 JQuinn 3 14
(HMorrison) *dwlt: rn green: in tch tl wknd u.p 4f out: t.o* **10/1**

2m 49.57s (9.17) **Going Correction** +0.90s/f (Soft)
**WFA** 3 from 5yo 20lb **8 Ran SP% 109.9**
Speed ratings: **105,104,104,104,103 102,86,76**CSF £73.56 TOTE £45.30: £7.30, £2.10, £3.30; EX 77.60.
**Owner** Saif Ali **Bred** Darley Stud Management, L L C **Trained** Newmarket, Suffolk

**FOCUS**
Not a great maiden despite the presence of some well-bred types. The third provides a guide to the level of the form.

**NOTEBOOK**
**Marine City(JPN)**, a half-sister to top-class and consistent stayer Marienbard, had shown little on her only previous start at two, but she came with a late rattle to land the spoils on her three-year-old debut despite running green. She is well bred and this win can be considered job done.
**Light Of Morn**, a half-sister to smart staying filly Moments Of Joy, is out of a mare who won the Prix Vermeille and Yorkshire Oaks. This was a pleasing debut, but her Oaks entry looks highly optimistic on the back of this effort.
**Portrait Of A Lady(IRE)** had more experience than most of these and was bred to be suited by the step up to a mile and a half. She ran a solid race but only confirmed the impression that she is nothing special.
**Al Beedaa(USA)**, who may have not been suited by the softer conditions, flashed her tail under pressure but kept on well enough.
**Sea Plume** is an exposed maiden who stays two miles. The fact that she came in for support in the market and ran well suggests the race was not that strong.
**High School**, sent off favourite, once again let her supporters down. She had every chance and is running far below the level that should be expected of her given her breeding.

## 1522 SAFFIE JOSEPH & SONS H'CAP 1m 1f 149y

**5:10** (5:10) (E) (0-70,70) 4-Y-O+ **£3,581** (£1,102; £551; £275) **Stalls** High

Form RPR

0061 **1** **Amnesty**$^{15}$ [1274] 5-9-0 56 (be) RLMoore 11 68
(GLMoore) *settled in midfield: prog 3f out: rdn to ld over 1f out: drvn clr* **5/1**$^{2}$

0060 **2** *3* **Icannshift (IRE)**$^{13}$ [1298] 4-8-8 50 WRyan 5 56
(SDow) *sn led and set str pce: rdn and hdd over 1f out: kpt on again ins fnl f* **9/1**

/0-1 **3** *hd* **Royal Racer (FR)**$^{13}$ [1298] 6-8-8 50 NPollard 7 56
(JRBest) *wl in tch: prog to chse ldr 3f out: rdn to chal and ev ch over 1f out: sn no ch w wnr: one pce after* **6/1**

56-1 **4** *1 ¾* **Miss Pebbles (IRE)**$^{21}$ [1187] 4-10-0 70 RHughes 10 73
(BRJohnson) *hld up in rr: prog 3f out: chsd ldrs 2f out: shkn up and no imp over 1f out: one pce after* **9/2**$^{1}$

0026 **5** *¾* **Easter Ogil (IRE)**$^{8}$ [1355] 9-9-1 57 VSlattery 1 59
(JaneSouthcombe) *lost pl and in rr after 1f: pushed along 6f out: prog on wd outside 3f out: drvn and one pce fnl 2f* **6/1**

10-0 **6** *7* **Mcqueen (IRE)**$^{83}$ [618] 4-9-4 60 JFEgan 4 49
(MrsHDalton) *racd in midfield: rdn 4f out: effrt to chse ldrs 2f out: sn btn: eased ins fnl f* **9/1**

000- **7** *5* **Havantadoubt (IRE)**$^{90}$ [5507] 4-9-9 65 GBaker 2 45
(MRBosley) *hld up in rr: effrt 3f out: sn outpcd and btn: wknd over 1f out* **33/1**

2336 **8** *5* **Pacific Ocean (ARG)**$^{12}$ [1310] 5-8-13 55 (t) SDrowne 6 26
(MrsStefLiddiard) *a in rr: pushed along 4f out: wknd 2f out* **14/1**

4100 **9** *4* **Coronado Forest (USA)**$^{62}$ [820] 5-8-9 51 JQuinn 12 15
(MRHoad) *chsd ldrs: rdn over 3f out: wknd over 2f out* **12/1**

00-0 **10** *hd* **Dexileos (IRE)**$^{12}$ [1308] 5-9-4 60 DSweeney 9 23
(ADWPinder) *pressed ldng pair tl wknd wl over 2f out* **33/1**

05-0 **11** *½* **Prince Albert**$^{15}$ [1274] 6-7-5 40 (t) JJeffrey$^{(7)}$ 8 2
(JRJenkins) *rrd bdly s and lost 15l: reecovered and jst in tch 5f out: outpcd and btn over 3f out* **33/1**

4501 **12** *18* **Del Mar Sunset**$^{24}$ [1141] 5-9-12 68 (p) RHills 3 —
(WJHaggas) *w ldr to jst over 3f out: wknd rapidly: t.o* **11/2**$^{3}$

2m 11.74s (6.58) **Going Correction** +0.90s/f (Soft) **12 Ran SP% 122.0**
Speed ratings: **109,106,106,105,104 98,94,90,87,87 87,72**CSF £50.37 CT £276.80 TOTE £8.10: £2.80, £3.10, £2.10; EX 53.80 Place 6 £1,942.22, Place 5 £62.76..
**Owner** G A Jackman, J F Jackman **Bred** Lord Halifax **Trained** Woodingdean, E Sussex

**FOCUS**
They went a good pace and the final time was quick for the grade. Although it was a modest heat, the form should work out well and the winner is well treated on last season's form.

**NOTEBOOK**
**Amnesty**, who followed up his success in selling grade in good style, looks to have improved since switching stables and returning to the turf. He took an age to get off the mark but could well notch up a hat-trick while in this mood.
**Icannshift(IRE)** ◆, who often races keenly, is usually held up in his races and the change to front-running tactics brought about an improved display. Given that he set a decent pace, he did well to keep on for second. He is well handicapped at present and could soon go one better.
**Royal Racer(FR)**, a shock winner on his reappearance, ran a solid race off a 3lb higher mark. He is clearly well suited by ease in the ground.
**Miss Pebbles(IRE)**, who had the race run to suit when successful over course and distance last time out, had her rating left unchanged after that. This was not a bad performance for a filly under top weight and she should continue to run well while in this form.
**Easter Ogil(IRE)**, flattered by his performance in Listed grade last time out, ran to his true level on this occasion.
**Mcqueen(IRE)** failed to translate his improved sand form to the turf.
**Dexileos(IRE)** *Official explanation: jockey said gelding hung left in the final 2f*
T/Plt: £1,677.40 to a £1 stake. Pool: £34,468.35. 15.00 winning tickets. T/Qpdt: £40.40 to a £1 stake. Pool: £3,127.10. 57.20 winning tickets. JN

# 1245 NEWCASTLE (L-H)

Tuesday, April 20

**OFFICIAL GOING: Heavy (soft in places)**

## 1523 BENFIELD ALFA ROMEO MAIDEN STKS 5f

**2:20** (2:21) (D) 2-Y-O **£4,351** (£1,339; £669; £334) **Stalls** High

Form RPR

**1** **Elsie Hart (IRE)** 2-8-9 WSupple 2 72
(TDEasterby) *trckd ldrs: drvn to ld appr fnl f: hung lft: drew clr ins last* **7/2**$^{2}$

**2** *3* **Spirit Of France (IRE)** 2-9-0 RFfrench 6 67
(MJohnston) *led: rdn and hung lft over 1f out: hdd appr fnl f: no ex* **2/1**$^{1}$

**3** *½* **Almaty Express** 2-9-0 RWinston 4 65
(MTodhunter) *slowly away: rr: pushed along 1/2-way: styd on fr over 1f out: nvr able to chal* **8/1**

**4** *3 ½* **Vision Victory (GER)** 2-9-0 DaleGibson 1 53
(TPTate) *chsd ldrs: drvn along 1/2-way: fdd fnl 2f* **4/1**$^{3}$

**5** *1 ¾* **Uredale (IRE)** 2-9-0 GDuffield 3 46
(MrsADuffield) *w ldr: drvn along 1/2-way: wknd over 1f out* **13/2**

**6** *6* **Lane Marshal** 2-8-9 TEaves$^{(5)}$ 5 25
(MESowersby) *dwlt: rr: drvn along 1/2-way: sn lost tch* **12/1**

66.15 secs (4.62) **Going Correction** +0.65s/f (Yiel) **6 Ran SP% 107.7**
Speed ratings: **73,68,67,61,59 49**CSF £10.00 TOTE £3.70: £1.60, £1.60; EX 9.60.
**Owner** C H Stevens **Bred** Cas **Trained** Great Habton, N Yorks

**FOCUS**
The ground was testing for this field of newcomers and the time was very slow, probably due to the whole field staying stands' side on what was almost certainly softer ground. It is hard to know the strength of the form, but the front three were clear.

**NOTEBOOK**
**Elsie Hart(IRE)** made a pleasing debut to win going away. She ran green in the early stages, but once the penny dropped she found her stride, went through a gap and quickly settled the issue inside the final furlong. She is a sister to heavy-ground juvenile winner Magic Myth, so it is no surprise that these conditions suited, and this speedy type can progress.
**Spirit Of France(IRE)** ◆, a scopey juvenile, was easy to back in the betting ring and ran as though this experience was very much needed. He is bred to appreciate further in time, so this was not a bad effort in the circumstances, and his stable's juveniles often improve for their debut outing.
**Almaty Express** lost all chance with at the start, but ran on well in the closing stages and will have learnt plenty from this experience. He is bred to make his mark as a two-year-old and may prefer better ground.
**Vision Victory(GER)**, despite veering left at the start, showed early speed but tired quickly approaching two out. He should improve with more experience, but looks modest.
**Uredale(IRE)** broke smartly, but was readily outpaced at the halfway stage and already looks in need of farther.

## 1524 JAMES FLETCHER MARQUEES AND PAVILION HIRE MAIDEN STKS 1m 2f 32y

**2:50** (2:50) (D) 3-Y-O **£3,477** (£1,070; £535; £267) **Stalls** High

Form RPR

-422 **1** **Keelung (USA)**$^{25}$ [1116] 3-9-0 85 PRobinson 5 83+
(MAJarvis) *keen early: mde virtually all: wl clr whn pushed along over 1f out: eased ins fnl f* **1/4**$^{1}$

**2** *16* **Twofan (USA)** 3-9-0 JFanning 3 55
(MJohnston) *prom: pushed along 1/2-way: outpcd over 3f out: kpt on u.p to go 2nd 2 out: no ch w wnr* **11/2**$^{2}$

0- **3** *9* **Silver Rhythm**$^{199}$ [5369] 3-8-9 VHalliday 6 35
(KRBurke) *trckd ldrs: drvn along and outpcd 4f out: n.d after* **20/1**$^{3}$

0- **4** *8* **Beaver Diva**$^{353}$ [1336] 3-8-2 BSwarbrick$^{(7)}$ 4 21
(WMBrisbourne) *cl up: keen early: drvn along 4f out: outpcd by wnr 3 out: wknd 2 out* **40/1**

**5** *dist* **Blue Nun** 3-8-9 GDuffield 1 —
(MrsADuffield) *s.s: a bhd: lost tch fnl 4f: t.o* **20/1**$^{3}$

2m 23.45s (11.85) **Going Correction** +0.775s/f (Yiel) **5 Ran SP% 107.3**
Speed ratings: **83,70,63,56,—**CSF £1.68 TOTE £1.30: £1.02, £2.30; EX 2.30.
**Owner** Norman Cheng **Bred** N Cheng And Tony Feng **Trained** Newmarket, Suffolk

**FOCUS**
Very little strength in depth to this weak maiden. The field were well strung out behind the easy winner and though the time was very slow, that is purely down to the favourite being heavily eased.

**NOTEBOOK**
**Keelung(USA)**, who has shown fair form in maidens on turf and the Polytrack prior to this, lost his maiden tag at the fifth attempt. He came right away from his moderate-looking rivals to win at a canter, and was value for much more than the official winning margin. Little new has been learnt by this, apart from that he handles this ground, but his confidence will be high and he may be capable of progressing in handicaps.
**Twofan(USA)**, a backward type who was unraced at two, was clear of the rest but had no chance with the winner. He got the hang of things late on, will appreciate better ground and come on plenty for this, but looks only modest.
**Silver Rhythm** was in-turn clear of the remainder, but shaped as though he may need farther and looks slow.

## 1525 WEATHERBYS INSURANCE H'CAP 5f

**3:20** (3:21) (D) (0-80,78) 3-Y-O+ **£5,902** (£1,816; £908; £454) **Stalls** High

Form RPR

-005 **1** **Raymond's Pride**$^{22}$ [1175] 4-9-3 69 (b) PFessey 2 84
(KARyan) *trckd ldrs far side: rdn over 1f out: led jst ins fnl f: r.o* **14/1**

3-33 **2** *1 ¾* **Highland Warrior**$^{9}$ [1345] 5-8-11 63 WSupple 3 73
(JSGoldie) *dwlt: hld up far side: hdwy 2f out: slt ld appr fnl f: rdn and hdd jst ins last: no ex* **4/1**$^{2}$

5220 **3** *1 ¼* **Pawan (IRE)**$^{3}$ [1477] 4-8-6 58 AnnStokell 4 64
(MissAStokell) *midfield far side: rdn 2f out: r.o fnl f* **7/1**$^{3}$

00-4 **4** *1 ¼* **Viewforth**$^{9}$ [1343] 6-9-12 78 (b) RWinston 5 80
(ISemple) *trckd ldrs far side: drvn along and outpcd 2f out: r.o ins fnl f* **10/3**$^{1}$

5020 **5** *hd* **Malahide Express (IRE)**[9] 1345 4-8-5 **57**............................ GDuffield 6 59
(EJAlston) *racd far side: led 1f: remained cl up: rdn and ev ch appr fnl f: no ex ins last* **14/1**

440- **6** *nk* **Karminskey Park**[183] 5673 5-8-10 **62**.................................. JFanning 13 63
(TJEtherington) *led stands side: clr of gp whn hung bdly lft to join far side appr fnl f: no further prog ins last* **11/1**

30-0 **7** *1 ¼* **Aahgowangowan (IRE)**[5] 1421 5-8-8 **60**...........................(t) RFfrench 8 57
(MDods) *racd far side: led after 1f: rdn and hdd appr fnl f: fdd ins last* **12/1**

40-0 **8** *2 ½* **Petongski**[5] 1421 6-7-12 **50**.............................................(be) PHanagan 1 40
(BEllison) *s.i.s: racd far side: bhd and rdn after 2f: n.d* **15/2**

140- **9** *2* **Proud Western (USA)**[181] 5706 6-7-5 **50**....................... DFentiman(7) 7 34
(BEllison) *dwlt: racd far side: n.d* **25/1**

000- **10** *2* **Rosie's Result**[211] 5129 4-7-11 **54**.................................... RThomas(5) 9 32
(MTodhunter) *in tch stands side: kpt on u.p fnl 2f: n.d* **50/1**

1350 **11** *6* **Cash**[5] 1421 6-8-6 **61** ow5...............................................(p) LFletcher(3) 12 21
(PaulJohnson) *prom stands side: rdn 2f out: sn btn* **20/1**

0-00 **12** *10* **Get Stuck In (IRE)**[9] 1343 8-8-12 **69**............................... TEaves(5) 10 —
(MissLAPerratt) *prom stands side to 1/2-way: sn btn* **33/1**

000- **13** *8* **I T Consultant**[158] 5998 6-7-9 **50** oh1.............................. NMackay(3) 11 —
(MissLAPerratt) *dwlt: racd stands side: a bhd* **50/1**

62.38 secs (0.85) **Going Correction** +0.65s/f (Yiel) **13** Ran SP% **112.2**
Speed ratings: **103,100,98,96,95 95,93,89,86,83 73,57,44**CSF £61.59 CT £343.41 TOTE £14.00: £3.70, £1.70, £2.90; EX 49.00 Trifecta £186.00 Pool £1,310.10 - 5 winning units..
**Owner** R E Robinson **Bred** Mrs Wendy Robinson **Trained** Hambleton, N Yorks
■ Stewards Enquiry : P Fessey two-day ban: careless riding (May 3,4)

**FOCUS**
A modest sprint which saw all bar one of the first ten home drawn low. The form may be suspect, but the relaible runner-up provides the best guide.

**NOTEBOOK**
**Raymond's Pride** relised the return to this trip and testing ground to score. He reversed recent form with the runner-up on 3lb better terms and, although he was aided by his low draw, this was a game effort.
**Highland Warrior** ◆ failed to confirm recent course form with the winner on this drop in trip. He may have prospered from racing more handily, but did himself no favours with a sluggish start, and this was another sound effort. He needs everything to fall right, but is getting ever closer to scoring and could be one to be with when reverting to another furlong.
**Pawan(IRE)**, who had excuses for his run on the All-Weather latest, posted another creditable effort on this drop to the minimum trip. He was aided by his low draw on this occasion and will take a rise in the weights for this, but is in good heart at present.
**Viewforth** tended to run in snatches and was staying on again all too late in the day.
**Malahide Express(IRE)**, who failed to get home over seven furlongs last time, improved for this drop in trip. He has fallen in the weights of late, but has only an All-Weather maiden win to his name from 29 outings, and is very hard to predict.
**Karminskey Park** ◆, who did best of the high numbers, ran a fine race on ground that was plenty soft enough. She showed plenty of early speed on the stands' side, and was clear of that group before she lost all chance by hanging across to the far side. She was still not beaten far and this has to rate as an encouraging return to action. *Official explanation: jockey said mare hung left throughout*

## 1526 SHARP MINDS BETFAIR H'CAP 6f
**3:50** (3:51) (E) (0-70,70) 3-Y-O+ **£3,974** (£1,223; £611; £305) **Stalls** High

Form RPR

3-06 **1** **Mister Mal (IRE)**[20] 1197 8-8-8 **50**...............................(be) PHanagan 14 61
(BEllison) *dwlt: sn led: clr and rdn 1f out: all out* **14/1**

0245 **2** *nk* **Carlton (IRE)**[5] 1424 10-8-9 **56**........................................ RThomas(5) 13 66
(CRDore) *in tch: hdwy u.p over 1f out: chsd wnr fnl f: jst hld* **11/1**

0-00 **3** *1 ¾* **Formeric**[103] 474 8-7-12 **40** oh5.........................................(v) PFessey 10 45
(MissLCSiddall) *towards rr: hdwy 2f out: r.o wl u.p fnl f: nrst fin* **100/1**

-010 **4** *1 ½* **King Nicholas (USA)**[20] 1197 5-8-4 **53** ow3...................(tp) MLawson(7) 5 53
(JParkes) *towards rr: swtchd rt and hdwy over 1f out: r.o fnl f: nrst fin* **7/1**[3]

0415 **5** *nk* **Quiet Times (IRE)**[8] 1361 5-9-11 **67**...................................(b) RWinston 9 66
(KARyan) *towards rr: hdwy 2f out: r.o fnl f: nrst fin* **5/1**[1]

626- **6** *nk* **Old Bailey (USA)**[186] 5626 4-8-4 **49**.................................(b) NMackay(3) 6 48
(TDBarron) *chsd ldrs: rdn 2f out: no ex fnl f* **8/1**

4600 **7** *shd* **Pilgrim Princess (IRE)**[34] 1039 6-8-3 **45**........................... GDuffield 15 43
(EJAlston) *prom: rdn 2f out: fdd fnl f* **20/1**

000- **8** *1 ¼* **Downland (IRE)**[174] 5832 8-8-10 **52**.................................. KimTinkler 11 47
(NTinkler) *sn towards rr: kpt on fnl 2f: n.d* **12/1**

1410 **9** *8* **Redoubtable (USA)**[37] 1020 13-8-3 **45**............................... JFanning 17 16
(DWChapman) *prom: chsd wnr fr 2f out tl wknd fnl f* **25/1**

020- **10** *nk* **William's Well**[181] 5702 10-9-8 **64**..................................(b) DaleGibson 8 34
(MWEasterby) *midfield: effrt 2f out: no hdwy* **9/1**

0U55 **11** *nk* **Ronnie From Donny (IRE)**[8] 1358 4-9-9 **70**.................... TEaves(5) 12 39
(BEllison) *nvr bttr than mid-div* **12/1**

-006 **12** *1* **Lord Baskerville**[20] 1196 3-8-7 **60**................................... DRMcCabe 16 26
(WStorey) *nvr bttr than mid-div* **33/1**

00-0 **13** *1 ¼* **The Old Soldier**[15] 1268 6-8-8 **53**........................................ ABeech(3) 4 15
(ADickman) *dwlt: nvr bttr than mid-div* **16/1**

200 **14** *¾* **African Spur (IRE)**[8] 1358 4-9-7 **70**...............................(t) DTudhope(7) 7 30
(DCarroll) *sn towards rr* **33/1**

200- **15** *shd* **Friar Tuck**[181] 5706 9-8-10 **52**.......................................... RFfrench 2 11
(MissLAPerratt) *midfield tl wknd 2f out* **14/1**

142- **16** *20* **Just One Smile (IRE)**[159] 5987 4-9-7 **63**.............................. KDarley 3 —
(TDEasterby) *prom tl wknd qckly 2f out: eased and lost tch fnl f* **6/1**[2]

1m 17.62s (2.58) **Going Correction** +0.65s/f (Yiel)
**WFA** 3 from 4yo+ 11lb **16** Ran SP% **123.0**
Speed ratings: **92,91,89,87,86 86,86,84,74,73 73,71,70,69,69 42**CSF £153.41 CT £13969.04 TOTE £15.30: £2.50, £3.10, £27.10, £2.90; EX 181.30.
**Owner** Mrs Andrea M Mallinson **Bred** Denis Cleary **Trained** Norton, N Yorks
■ Stewards Enquiry : J Fanning caution: careless riding

**FOCUS**
The first three home were drawn high which reversed the bias of the five-furlong sprint earlier on the card. The form looks modest and time was slow due to the whole field migrating over to the far side. The form is not particularly strong.

**NOTEBOOK**
**Mister Mal(IRE)** recovered well from a sluggish start, displayed plenty of early toe to get across to the favoured far side and showed guts to hold off the runner-up close home. He had gone too fast over seven last time and this does look like his optimum trip, but it was his first win since May 2001, and he cannot be recommended as a likely sort to follow up.
**Carlton(IRE)** was another to run well from an unfavoured high draw and went down all guns blazing. He is in good heart at present and goes best with cut in the ground, so could be placed to advantage soon.
**Formeric**, 5lb out of the handicap, ran his best race since winning his maiden in 2002. However, his proximity at the finish raises a big doubt as to the form of this contest, and he will face a rise in the weights for this.
**King Nicholas(USA)** improved on his latest effort over an extra furlong and appreciated the return to this softer ground. However, he does not look an easy ride and may need to drop in grade to score.
**Quiet Times(IRE)** did not look entirely happy on this ground, but has now failed to capitalise on his significantly lower turf mark (23lb higher on the sand) in two outings and has a bit to prove now.
**Old Bailey(USA)** travelled well just off the pace before he blew up two out on this return from a 186-day break. He will come on plenty for this outing and can be placed to strike before long.
**Pilgrim Princess(IRE)**
**Downland(IRE)** *Official explanation: trainer said gelding struck into itself*
**Lord Baskerville** *Official explanation: trainer said colt was unsuited by the going*
**Just One Smile(IRE)** *Official explanation: jockey said filly was unsuited by the heavy going*

## 1527 SALTWELL SIGNS H'CAP 1m 2f 32y
**4:20** (4:22) (F) (0-55,55) 3-Y-O+ **£3,416** (£976; £488) **Stalls** High

Form RPR

30/3 **1** **Pure Mischief (IRE)**[24] 1138 5-9-2 **54**.......................... BSwarbrick(7) 14 68
(WMBrisbourne) *hld up in tch: smooth hdwy to ld 2f out: hrd pressed and rdn fnl f: hld on wl* **6/1**[2]

2314 **2** *nk* **Double Ransom**[43] 988 5-9-10 **55**.................................(b) PHanagan 1 68
(MrsLStubbs) *hld up in tch: hdwy 2f out: rdn to chal ins fnl f: no ex clsng stages* **11/2**[1]

0115 **3** *1 ¼* **Jake Black (IRE)**[28] 1093 4-9-5 **50**...................................... RWinston 6 61
(JJQuinn) *in tch: chsng ldrs and rdn 2f out: styd on wl fnl f* **9/1**

0104 **4** *5* **Kingsdon (IRE)**[14] 1277 7-9-1 **46** oh6.............................(vt) GDuffield 16 49
(TJFitzgerald) *a.p: ev ch and rdn 2f out: wknd fnl f* **10/1**

00-5 **5** *3* **Summer Special**[15] 1268 4-9-3 **51**...................................... LEnstone(3) 3 49
(DWBarker) *hld up in rr: hdwy over 3f out: rdn over 2 out: no further prog fr over 1 out* **16/1**

360/ **6** *1 ¾* **Spree Vision**[15] 4352 8-9-7 **52**.............................................. RFfrench 12 47
(PMonteith) *chsd ldrs: rdn 2f out: no ex* **8/1**

050- **7** *1 ¾* **Stellite**[189] 5560 4-9-1 **46** oh1................................................ WSupple 15 38
(JSGoldie) *hld up in rr: hdwy into midfield over 4f out: in tch and rdn 2 out: no further prog* **33/1**

0 **8** *4* **Berrywhite (IRE)**[33] 1042 6-8-12 **46** oh6........................... THamilton(3) 7 31
(CGrant) *midfield: drvn along 1/2-way: no hdwy* **20/1**

00-0 **9** *1 ¼* **The Loose Screw (IRE)**[13] 1305 6-9-1 **46** oh1..................... JFanning 13 29
(GMMoore) *led 1f: remained cl up: led 4 out: rdn and hdd 2 out: sn wknd* **20/1**

00-0 **10** *3* **Business Matters (IRE)**[66] 767 4-9-5 **50**............................ RLappin 10 28
(HAlexander) *towards rr: drvn into midfield over 4f out: no further prog* **33/1**

0100 **11** *3 ½* **East Cape**[18] 1238 7-9-1 **46** oh1.......................................... KimTinkler 9 18
(DonEnricoIncisa) *towards rr most of way* **10/1**

04/0 **12** *1 ¼* **Lord Conyers (IRE)**[15] 1263 5-9-1 **46** oh6........................... VHalliday 17 16
(BEllison) *midfield: rdn 4f out: wknd over 2 out* **25/1**

20-6 **13** *2 ½* **Scurra**[17] 1245 5-9-1 **51**............................................................ TEaves(5) 2 16
(ACWhillans) *hld up: drvn along in midfield over 4f out: wknd 3 out* **16/1**

00-0 **14** *11* **The Gambler**[9] 1345 4-9-7 **55**.........................................(p) LFletcher(3) 11 —
(PaulJohnson) *led after 1f tl hdd over 5 out: wknd 4 out* **33/1**

0006 **15** *12* **Balalaika Tune (IRE)**[37] 1026 5-9-1 **46** oh6........................ DRMcCabe 8 —
(WStorey) *prom: led over 5f out tl hdd 4 out: sn wknd* **33/1**

010- **16** *5* **Border Terrier (IRE)**[167] 5928 6-9-10 **55**.............................. KDarley 5 —
(MDHammond) *rr div most of way* **7/1**[3]

2m 20.1s (8.50) **Going Correction** +0.775s/f (Yiel) **16** Ran SP% **118.4**
Speed ratings: **97,96,95,91,89 87,86,83,82,79 77,76,74,65,55 51**CSF £33.99 CT £291.50 TOTE £6.50: £2.50, £1.40, £2.60, £2.10; EX 26.50.
**Owner** The Cartmel Syndicate **Bred** T F Lacy **Trained** Great Ness, Shropshire

**FOCUS**
A modest handicap with all bar nine of the 17 runners racing from out of the handicap. The first three were clear, but no significance should be given to the time being more than three seconds faster than the earlier maiden. The runner-up is the best guide to the form.

**NOTEBOOK**
**Pure Mischief(IRE)** showed the benefit of his recent comeback outing on the Fibresand to score a first-ever win on the level. He travelled well throughout and showed a resolute attitude to hold off the challenge of the runner-up close home. He clearly needs soft ground, but his stable do very well with this type and he may have more to offer.
**Double Ransom** travelled every bit as well as the winner, but could not get past that rival when push came to shove late on. This was another fine effort however, over a trip that just stretches him, and he can gain compensation granted similar conditions over slightly shorter.
**Jake Black(IRE)**, who has been in fair form on the All-Weather of late, made a satisfactory return to turf. He got going all too late on this occasion, but finished convincingly and was clear of the rest.
**Kingsdon(IRE)**, who has been running in banded stakes recently, held every chance and ran a fair race at the these weights.
**Summer Special**, who has mainly been campaigned at around six furlongs, did not stay this trip. However, he ran well in the circumstances and will be capable of better when dropped to around a mile.
**Balalaika Tune(IRE)** *Official explanation: jockey said mare was unsuited by the going*

## 1528 SALTWELL SIGNS MEDIAN AUCTION MAIDEN STKS 1m 3y(S)
**4:50** (4:53) (F) 3-4-Y-O **£3,087** (£882; £441) **Stalls** High

Form RPR

2 **1** **Lyford Lass**[17] 1250 3-8-7 ...................................................... PHanagan 5 66
(ISemple) *led tl rdn and hdd ins fnl f: styd on wl to ld again cl home* **9/2**[3]

30-2 **2** *nk* **Oh Golly Gosh**[13] 1304 3-8-12 76........................................... KDarley 6 70
(NPLittmoden) *dwlt: sn trcking ldrs: effrt 2f out: rdn to ld ins fnl f: hdd cl home* **7/4**[1]

**3** *2* **Into The Shadows**[8] 4-9-2 ..................................................... TEaves(5) 3 61
(MrsMReveley) *dwlt: sn in tch: rdn 2f out: sn chsng first 2: no imp fnl f* **6/1**

**4** *nk* **Alcaidesa** 3-8-12 ........................................................................ JFanning 8 66
(MissJACamacho) *dwlt: hld up: hdwy over 2f out: styd on fnl f: nvr able to chal* **33/1**

**5** *8* **Nod's Star** 3-8-7 .......................................................................... RWinston 4 45
(MissJACamacho) *dwlt: towards rr: hdwy into midfield 1/2-way: drvn along and outpcd 3f out: n.d* **20/1**

66 **6** *2* **Indi Ano Star (IRE)**[10] 1325 3-8-5 ...................................... DTudhope(7) 7 46
(DCarroll) *dwlt: sn in tch: effrt 2f out: sn btn* **9/1**

U **7** *1 ¾* **Vibe**[5] 1420 3-8-12 ...................................................................... RFfrench 2 42
(MJohnston) *cl up: rdn over 2f out: sn wknd* **4/1**[2]

00-0 **8** *12* **Barton Flower**[17] 1250 3-8-7 ............................................. DaleGibson 10 13
(MWEasterby) *towards rr: effrt over 3f out: lost tch over 2 out* **33/1**

0- **9** *9* **Yorkshire Spirit**[226] 4755 3-8-12 ........................................ KimTinkler 11 —
(NTinkler) *towardts rr: effrt over 3f out: lost tch over 2 out* **33/1**

00/4 **10** *17* **Bettys Valentine**[51] 935 4-9-4 30.......................................... LEnstone(3) 1 —
(DWBarker) *in tch tl wknd 3f out: t.o* **66/1**

11 *9* **Paula**[23] 4-9-4 ........ THamilton(3) 9 —
(MDods) *sn bhd: lost tch 1/2-way: t.o* **20/1**

1m 48.8s (7.60) **Going Correction** +0.65s/f (Yiel)
**WFA** 3 from 4yo 14lb **11** Ran SP% **118.7**
Speed ratings: **72,71,69,69,61 59,57,45,36,19 10**CSF £11.93 TOTE £5.90: £2.00, £1.10, £2.80; EX 12.80 Place 6 £37.39, Place 5 £25.62..
**Owner** Evelyn Duchess Of Sutherland **Bred** Exors Of The Late Duke Of Sutherland **Trained** Carluke, S Lanarks

**FOCUS**
An ordinary maiden run at a fair gallop, but the time was slow mainly because the whole field drifted over to the far side. The conditions were testing and the field were well strung out at the finish. The form does not look particularly strong.

**NOTEBOOK**
**Lyford Lass**, a remote second behind an easy winner on her debut over course-and-distance last time, showed the benefit of that experience to score all out. She showed a tough attitude to rally when challenged inside the final furlong and should be capable of further progress, but must have these underfoot conditions to be seen at her best.
**Oh Golly Gosh** came there with every chance approaching the final furlong and looked like scoring when edging to the front, but had no more to give when the eventual winner rallied. He has the ability to win a maiden over this trip, but is still immature and looks a tricky ride.
**Into The Shadows** found things happening all too quickly from the gates, but responded to pressure and was staying on well in the final furlong. She should be a lot sharper next time, but may be one to watch until she qualifies for handicaps.
**Alcaidesa** ◆ caught the eye travelling nicely off the pace, before being unable to quicken with the principals when his lack of experience told. This was a decent debut performance, he should get farther in time and he looks one to take out of the race
**Vibe** dropped out tamely having helped set the pace for most of the way. This was a disappointing effort but he looked green as grass.
T/Plt: £18.80 to a £1 stake. Pool: £33,951.40. 1,317.20 winning tickets. T/Qpdt: £11.30 to a £1 stake. Pool: £2,486.40. 161.70 winning tickets. JF

# 1443 SOUTHWELL (L-H)
Tuesday, April 20

**OFFICIAL GOING: Good to soft (soft in places)**

## 1529 LA DOLCE VITA H'CAP — 1m 2f
2:00 (2:00) (F) (0-55,61) 3-Y-0 — £2,961 (£846; £423) Stalls Low

| Form | | | | RPR |
|---|---|---|---|---|
| 0 | 1 | | **Friends Hope**[20] 1201 3-8-10 **52** ........ DNolan(5) 12 | 55 |
| | | | (PABlockley) *s.s: hld up: hdwy over 1f out: r.o to ld wl ins fnl f* **14/1** | |
| 005 | 2 | ½ | **Avertaine**[21] 1186 3-8-13 **50** ........ IMongan 10 | 53 |
| | | | (GLMoore) *hld up in tch: led over 1f out: rdn and hdd wl ins fnl f* **16/1** | |
| 2021 | 3 | nk | **Platinum Pirate**[8] 1360 3-9-3 **61** 6ex ........ (v) RoryMoore(7) 5 | 63 |
| | | | (KRBurke) *trckd ldrs: racd keenly: swtchd lft over 1f out: sn rdn: styd on u.p* **7/4**[1] | |
| 0060 | 4 | 1½ | **Mystic Moon**[3] 1467 3-9-4 **55** ........ JPMurtagh 7 | 54 |
| | | | (JRJenkins) *hld up: hdwy over 3f out: rdn over 1f out: no ex wl ins fnl f* **9/1** | |
| -250 | 5 | 1¼ | **Hsi Wang Mu (IRE)**[19] 1222 3-8-12 **49** ........ ADaly 2 | 46 |
| | | | (RBrotherton) *led over 4f: rdn and ev ch over 1f out: no ex ins fnl f* **7/1**[3] | |
| 10-0 | 6 | 1 | **Summerise**[17] 1244 3-9-4 **55** ........ DeanMcKeown 8 | 50 |
| | | | (HJCollingridge) *chsd ldrs: rdn over 2f out: styd on same pce appr fnl f* **12/1** | |
| 0000 | 7 | shd | **Atlantic Breeze**[15] 1267 3-8-10 **47** ........ DarrenWilliams 11 | 42 |
| | | | (MrsNMacauley) *dwlt: hld up: hdwy u.p over 1f out: nvr trbld ldrs* **33/1** | |
| 00-4 | 8 | 1¾ | **Pay Attention**[8] 1363 3-8-12 **52** ........ DAllan(3) 1 | 44 |
| | | | (TDEasterby) *trckd ldrs: rdn over 2f out: looked hld whn hmpd wl over 1f out* **5/1**[2] | |
| 2-35 | 9 | 1¾ | **Comic Genius**[34] 1040 3-8-9 **46** oh6 ........ PaulEddery 9 | 35 |
| | | | (DHaydnJones) *hld up: effrt over 2f out: n.d* **50/1** | |
| -040 | 10 | 2½ | **Hymns And Arias**[15] 1267 3-8-9 **46** oh1 ........ MFenton 6 | 30 |
| | | | (RonaldThompson) *chsd ldrs: led over 5f out: rdn and hdd over 1f out: sn wknd* **50/1** | |
| 0-00 | 11 | 5 | **Ameyrah (IRE)**[19] 1221 3-9-4 **55** ........ TEDurcan 3 | 30 |
| | | | (MRChannon) *hld up: wknd over 2f out* **15/2** | |

2m 20.0s (6.10) **Going Correction** +0.325s/f (Good) **11** Ran SP% **114.4**
Speed ratings: **88,87,87,86,85 84,84,82,81,79 75**CSF £208.81 CT £584.96 TOTE £17.10: £6.00, £4.30, £1.10; EX 166.40.
**Owner** M J Wiley **Bred** Huish Bloodstock **Trained** Southwell, Notts
■ Stewards Enquiry : Rory Moore four-day ban: careless riding (May 1-4)

**FOCUS**
A moderate handicap and the early pace was steady resulting in a slow winning time. The form is not strong.

**NOTEBOOK**
**Friends Hope** ◆, a winner of a seven-furlong claimer in Ireland last year, was well beaten on her British debut at Catterick but improved on that to score a shade cosily. Having travelled strongly under a confident ride from Nolan, she found plenty when asked and won with something to spare. She is lightly raced and there should be more to come.
**Avertaine** found this easier than the maidens she has been contesting recently, but is flattered to get to within half a length of the winner. She showed enough to suggest she can win a similar race.
**Platinum Pirate** won nicely at Redcar on his previous outing and was 3lb lower than in future under his 6lb penalty for that success. However, he was unable to take advantage and could struggle off his new mark.
**Mystic Moon** ran respectably and would appear to be going the right way.
**Hsi Wang Mu(IRE)**, still a maiden, is not exactly progressing but this was a reasonable effort considering she was quite keen early.

## 1530 FESTIVAL OF FABULOUS WILDWOMEN MAIDEN STKS — 6f
2:30 (2:36) (D) 3-Y-0 — £3,523 (£1,084; £542; £271) Stalls Low

| Form | | | | RPR |
|---|---|---|---|---|
| 435- | 1 | | **Primo Way**[221] 4865 3-9-0 80 ........ MHills 4 | 75 |
| | | | (BWHills) *chsd ldrs: led 2f out: clr 1f out: rdn out* **10/11**[1] | |
| 50-0 | 2 | 1 | **Get To The Point**[98] 514 3-9-0 63 ........ JPMurtagh 14 | 72 |
| | | | (PWD'Arcy) *hld up: hdwy over 1f out: r.o wl* **25/1** | |
| 543- | 3 | 2½ | **Ela Paparouna**[176] 5785 3-8-9 76 ........ DaneO'Neill 12 | 60 |
| | | | (HCandy) *dwlt: hld up: nt clr run 2f out: r.o ins fnl f: nrst fin* **9/2**[2] | |
| 30-0 | 4 | 1 | **Point Calimere (IRE)**[18] 1228 3-9-0 82 ........ DHolland 9 | 62 |
| | | | (CREgerton) *led: hdd over 3f out: styd on same pce appr fnl f* **8/1**[3] | |
| | 5 | 1 | **Artie's Lad (IRE)** 3-9-0 ........ ANicholls 5 | 59 |
| | | | (DNicholls) *s.i.s: sn prom: wknd ins fnl f* **33/1** | |
| 360- | 6 | ½ | **Scarlett Rose**[143] 6090 3-8-9 71 ........ CLowther 1 | 52 |
| | | | (DrJDScargill) *hld up: styd on appr fnl f: nvr nrr* **20/1** | |
| 2 | 7 | 1¾ | **Extremely Rare (IRE)**[20] 1200 3-8-6 ........ DAllan(3) 8 | 47 |
| | | | (TDEasterby) *chsd ldrs: rdn over 2f out: wknd fnl f* **16/1** | |
| 5 | 8 | 1¼ | **Four Kings**[18] 1228 3-9-0 ........ JTate 2 | 48 |
| | | | (JMPEustace) *chsd ldrs over 4f* **16/1** | |
| 0- | 9 | ½ | **Dawn Duel (IRE)**[264] 3728 3-8-9 ........ TEDurcan 11 | 42 |
| | | | (BSmart) *s.i.s: outpcd: nvr nrr* **50/1** | |
| 0-4 | 10 | ¾ | **Velocitas**[24] 1127 3-8-11 ........ TPQueally(3) 3 | 44 |
| | | | (HJCollingridge) *chsd ldr: led over 3f out: hdd 2f out: sn rdn and wknd* **25/1** | |
| 00 | 11 | 1 | **Half A Handful**[13] 1293 3-9-0 ........ RHavlin 6 | 41 |
| | | | (MJWallace) *s.i.s: hld up: effrt over 2f out: n.d* **100/1** | |
| -622 | 12 | 2 | **Brown Dragon**[34] 1038 3-9-0 63 ........ PaulEddery 10 | 35 |
| | | | (DHaydnJones) *mid-div: pushed along 1/2-way: sn wknd* **16/1** | |
| 000- | 13 | ½ | **Pererin**[231] 4638 3-9-0 ........ JBramhill 7 | 34 |
| | | | (IAWood) *mid-div: sn pushed along: wknd over 2f out* **100/1** | |
| 5-3 | 14 | shd | **Bond Shakira**[8] 1362 3-8-9 ........ FLynch 13 | 28 |
| | | | (BSmart) *mid-div: rdn 1/2-way: sn wknd* **25/1** | |

1m 17.1s (1.00) **Going Correction** +0.325s/f (Good) **14** Ran SP% **122.5**
Speed ratings: **106,104,101,100,98 98,95,94,93,92 91,88,87,87**CSF £37.40 TOTE £1.90: £1.40, £6.80, £1.80; EX 56.20.
**Owner** D M James **Bred** Mrs P A Reditt And M J Reditt **Trained** Lambourn, Berks

**FOCUS**
Probably just an ordinary maiden and a race to treat with a little caution given the proximity of the 63-rated Get To The Point, despite the fact there appeared little fluke about that one's running.

**NOTEBOOK**
**Primo Way** showed promise in maidens and in a valuable sales race at Doncaster last term, and was able to confirm that promise faced with his easiest task to date. He was being closed down at the finish and will probably have to show improved form to win off a mark of 80, given that he had just a length to spare over a 63-rated rival.
**Get To The Point**, last in a Fibresand claimer on his previous outing 98 days ago, had the visor left off this time and was switched back to turf. Rated 63, he had no right to finish where he did, but there did not appear to be any fluke about it and, given the Handicapper is sure to put him up for this, he would have to be of interest if turned out before he is reassessed.
**Ela Paparouna**, beaten at odds-on in a Leicester maiden that is working out quite well on her third and final start at two, made an eye-catching reappearance. Held right up towards the rear after missing the break, she appeared to travel as well as anything and was still on the bridle two and half out. However, she got going too late and never once threatened the winner. There is a similar race in her.
**Point Calimere(IRE)** was most disappointing on the Polytrack on his latest start, but was reported to have been unsuited by the track that day and showed that running to be all wrong with a better effort.
**Artie's Lad(IRE)**, a 26,000euros yearling, half-brother to a ten-furlong winner, made a pleasing debut. He is the type to improve with time.

## 1531 NATIONAL SECRETARY DAY H'CAP — 7f
3:00 (3:03) (E) (0-75,75) 3-Y-0+ — £4,394 (£1,352; £676; £338) Stalls Low

| Form | | | | RPR |
|---|---|---|---|---|
| 0410 | 1 | | **Hurricane Coast**[38] 1007 5-9-5 **66** ........ (b) DaneO'Neill 12 | 81+ |
| | | | (DFlood) *trckd ldrs: led over 1f out: r.o wl* **12/1** | |
| 0-10 | 2 | 2 | **Balakiref**[8] 1361 5-9-1 **62** ........ FLynch 2 | 69 |
| | | | (MDods) *hld up: nt clr run over 1f out: r.o wl ins fnl f: nt rch wnr* **5/1**[3] | |
| 0-30 | 3 | nk | **Bannister**[46] 968 6-8-13 **60** ........ MFenton 6 | 66 |
| | | | (MrsStefLiddiard) *hld up: hdwy and hung lft over 1f out: r.o* **33/1** | |
| 4610 | 4 | 1¼ | **Ballare (IRE)**[8] 1373 5-8-1 **48** ........ TWilliams 10 | 51 |
| | | | (BobJones) *mid-div: hdwy over 2f out: rdn and ev ch over 1f out: styd on same pce* **12/1** | |
| 16-0 | 5 | ¾ | **B A Highflyer**[18] 1230 4-9-5 **66** ........ TEDurcan 9 | 67 |
| | | | (MRChannon) *chsd ldrs: rdn 4f out: styd on u.p* **16/1** | |
| 5040 | 6 | ½ | **Spy Gun (USA)**[13] 1305 4-8-1 **53** ow3 ........ NChalmers(5) 15 | 53 |
| | | | (TWall) *chsd ldrs: led 2f out: sn hdd: no ex fnl f* **40/1** | |
| 1-3 | 7 | hd | **Perfect Portrait**[13] 1294 4-9-13 **74** ........ JPMurtagh 1 | 74+ |
| | | | (DRLoder) *trckd ldrs: nt clr run over 1f out: swtchd rt ins fnl f: styd on same pce* **9/2**[2] | |
| 5-66 | 8 | ¾ | **Horizontal (USA)**[18] 1228 4-8-13 **60** ........ MTebbutt 13 | 58 |
| | | | (VSmith) *s.i.s: sn chsng ldrs: rdn over 2f out: btn whn n.m.r ins fnl f* **11/1** | |
| 5103 | 9 | nk | **Eager Angel (IRE)**[5] 1424 6-8-10 **57** ........ (p) DeanMcKeown 3 | 54 |
| | | | (RFMarvin) *hld up: rdn over 2f out: n.d* **33/1** | |
| 0-15 | 10 | 1 | **Artistry**[8] 1372 4-9-1 **62** ........ DHolland 8 | 56 |
| | | | (BJMeehan) *plld hrd and prom: lost pl over 4f out: hdwy 2f out: btn whn hmpd ins fnl f* **12/1** | |
| 000- | 11 | ¾ | **Zamyatina (IRE)**[222] 4838 5-8-3 **53** ........ DAllan(3) 7 | 46 |
| | | | (PLClinton) *s.i.s: hld up: n.d* **66/1** | |
| 1524 | 12 | shd | **Mufreh (USA)**[15] 1265 6-8-13 **60** ........ SWhitworth 5 | 52 |
| | | | (AGNewcombe) *s.i.s: sn pushed along in rr: nt clr run 3f out: nvr trbld ldrs* **7/2**[1] | |
| 610- | 13 | 1¾ | **Xpres Digital**[164] 5950 3-9-1 **75** ........ (t) JBramhill 4 | 63 |
| | | | (SRBowring) *chsd ldrs: rdn over 2f out: wkng whn hmpd 1f out* **50/1** | |
| -030 | 14 | 1¼ | **Munaawesh (USA)**[5] 1422 3-8-9 **69** ........ SSanders 14 | 54 |
| | | | (DWChapman) *hld up: effrt over 2f out: sn wknd* **50/1** | |
| 120- | 15 | 2½ | **Hollow Jo**[226] 4752 4-9-11 **72** ........ IMongan 11 | 51 |
| | | | (JRJenkins) *led 5f: wknd ins fnl f* **6/1** | |

1m 31.26s (2.06) **Going Correction** +0.325s/f (Good)
**WFA** 3 from 4yo+ 13lb **15** Ran SP% **122.4**
Speed ratings: **101,98,98,96,96 95,95,94,94,92 92,91,89,88,85**CSF £69.12 CT £2007.41 TOTE £15.40: £4.70, £3.50, £6.50; EX 106.90.
**Owner** Mrs Ruth M Serrell **Bred** Ian H Wills **Trained** Upper Lambourn, Berks

**FOCUS**
Just a modest handicap but with some well treated runners.

**NOTEBOOK**
**Hurricane Coast**, returning to turf off the back of a busy and quite successful campaign on the All-Weather this winter, is 16lb lower on this surface and ran out a ready winner. He had more luck in running than some of these and the winning margin probably flatters him, but even so there are more races to be won with him on turf and he now heads for a Leicester handicap before taking in a conditions race at Newmarket.
**Balakiref**, up a furlong in trip, returned to form and would have been much closer with better luck in running.
**Bannister** improved on his recent efforts on only his second start for Stef Liddiard, but could have been closer. He travelled well, but did not appear keen to let himself down and could not go with the winner. *Official explanation: jockey said gelding hung left*
**Ballare(IRE)** was 6lb lower than when well beaten at Yarmouth on his previous outing and ran respectably.
**B A Highflyer** did not run a bad race on this switch back to turf and could be coming to hand.
**Perfect Portrait**, making his handicap debut, was disappointingly one paced in the straight and faster ground may suit him better.
**Artistry** *Official explanation: jockey said filly did not get a clear run in the final furlong*
**Mufreh(USA)** had plenty to do after missing the break and, under an ambitious ride, did not get that clear a run in the straight. *Official explanation: jockey said gelding lost its action in the closing stages*
**Hollow Jo** *Official explanation: jockey said gelding lost a hind shoe going into the stalls*

## 1532 BOSTON MARATHON MEDIAN AUCTION MAIDEN STKS 1m 2f
3:30 (3:31) (F) 3-Y-O £2,940 (£840; £420) Stalls Low

Form RPR

1 **Fling** 3-8-9 DaneO'Neill 8 76+
(JRFanshawe) *s.s: hld up: hdwy over 5f out: led over 1f out: r.o wl* **13/2**

230- 2 7 **Jarvo**[179] [5725] 3-9-0 66 DHolland 9 63
(NPLittmoden) *chsd ldr: led 8f out: rdn and hdd over 1f out: no ex* **9/2**[3]

0 3 *nk* **Amankila (IRE)**[19] [1224] 3-8-9 IMongan 3 57
(MLWBell) *a.p: chsd ldr over 4f out: rdn over 2f out: ev ch over 1f out: edgd lft and no ex fnl f* **5/1**

03- 4 5 **Maria Bonita (IRE)**[210] [5138] 3-8-9 SSanders 6 48
(RMBeckett) *hld up: hdwy over 6f out: wknd 2f out* **7/2**[2]

3350 5 1 1/4 **Amwell Brave**[26] [1104] 3-9-0 65 (v) JPMurtagh 4 51
(JRJenkins) *chsd ldrs: rdn over 2f out: wknd over 1f out* **3/1**[1]

33-4 6 2 1/2 **Keltic Rainbow (IRE)**[103] [482] 3-8-9 57 PaulEddery 7 42
(DHaydnJones) *hld up: rdn 1/2-way: wknd over 3f out* **12/1**

00-4 7 22 **Bonjour Bond (IRE)**[21] [1192] 3-9-0 64 FLynch 2 7
(BSmart) *led 2f: wknd over 5f out* **16/1**

000- 8 1/2 **Lawgiver (IRE)**[169] [5905] 3-9-0 MFenton 1 6
(TJFitzgerald) *hld up: plld hrd: wknd 6f out* **66/1**

36-0 9 2 **Kalush**[26] [1104] 3-9-0 64 DeanMcKeown 5 3
(RonaldThompson) *prom 6f* **20/1**

2m 14.9s (1.00) **Going Correction** +0.325s/f (Good) **9 Ran SP% 115.2**
Speed ratings: **109,103,103,99,98 96,78,78,76**CSF £35.75 TOTE £4.00: £2.80, £1.80, £1.70; EX 27.00.
**Owner** Cheveley Park Stud **Bred** Cheveley Park Stud Ltd **Trained** Newmarket, Suffolk

**FOCUS**
Not a very competitive maiden with a 66-rated performer in second, but the final time was very good. The winner looks a decent prospect and finished nicely clear.

**NOTEBOOK**
**Fling**, a full-sister to an eight-furlong two-year-old winner out of a ten-furlong three-year-old scorer, was very easy to back and things did not look good when she missed the break. However, she was given plenty of time to find her stride and, well placed when it mattered, she picked up nicely and came right away in the closing stages. This was not a very good race, but there should be plenty of improvement in her and she should be competitive in a higher grade.
**Jarvo** showed promise last term between six furlongs and a mile but, stepped up in trip for this first start in 179 days, he was disappointing. This trip should not have been a problem and this run may just have been needed.
**Amankila(IRE)** showed the benefit of her debut run but was made to look one paced by the winner. If she continues to go the right way there could be a similar race in her, but she will always be vulnerable in this grade to something half decent.
**Maria Bonita(IRE)**, stepped up from a mile, failed to confirm the promise she showed on her final start at two in a Newmarket maiden. She looked unlikely to win a long way from home and has plenty to prove now.
**Amwell Brave** did not improve for the re-fitting of a visor and has had plenty of chances.

## 1533 ST. PETER MARTYR'S DAY (S) STKS 7f
4:00 (4:01) (G) 3-Y-O+ £2,667 (£762; £381) Stalls Low

Form RPR

0002 1 **Fen Gypsy**[15] [1274] 6-9-0 60 SJDonohoe(7) 6 64
(PDEvans) *a.p: chsd ldr 4f out: rdn to ld over 1f out: r.o: eased nr fin* **7/4**[1]

-000 2 2 **Jonny Ebeneezer**[8] [1361] 5-9-7 75 BDoyle 8 59
(RMHCowell) *s.i.s: hld up: hdwy 2f out: r.o ins fnl f: nt rch wnr* **6/1**

5142 3 1 1/4 **Silver Mascot**[5] [1423] 5-9-12 48 FLynch 2 61
(RHollinshead) *led: clr 4f out: rdn and hdd over 1f out: styd on same pce* **5/1**[3]

4 2 1/2 **Enna (POL)**[181] 5-8-11 51 NChalmers(5) 10 45
(AGJuckes) *s.i.s: hld up: hdwy and hung lft over 1f out: nvr trbld ldrs* **25/1**

00-0 5 *nk* **Rileys Dream**[14] [1283] 5-9-2 49 RHavlin 7 44
(BJLlewellyn) *hld up: rdn over 2f out: n.d* **25/1**

6 3/4 **My Country Club**[188] 7-9-7 53 DaneO'Neill 11 47
(AGJuckes) *hld up: styd on appr fnl f: nvr nr to chal* **14/1**

5001 7 2 **Marabar**[14] [1283] 6-9-7 65 (b) SSanders 4 42
(DWChapman) *sn pushed along in rr: nvr nrr* **9/2**[2]

0000 8 10 **Meticulous**[21] [1190] 6-9-7 30 LVickers 13 17
(MCChapman) *chsd ldrs to 1/2-way* **100/1**

0-50 9 1 **Mabel Riley (IRE)**[102] [487] 4-9-2 45 JBramhill 1 10
(MABuckley) *mid-div: hdwy 1/2-way: wknd 2f out* **20/1**

600/ 10 1/2 **Home By Socks (IRE)**[817] [275] 5-8-9 AndrewWebb(7) 5 8
(MCChapman) *s.i.s: outpcd* **50/1**

0-00 11 *hd* **Finningley Connor**[6] [1389] 4-9-7 50 DeanMcKeown 9 13
(RonaldThompson) *chsd ldrs over 4f* **80/1**

00-0 12 1 3/4 **Shirley Not**[5] [1421] 8-9-7 46 ANicholls 3 8
(DNicholls) *sn pushed along in rr: wknd over 2f out* **20/1**

1m 30.8s (1.60) **Going Correction** +0.325s/f (Good) **12 Ran SP% 113.6**
Speed ratings: **103,100,99,96,96 95,92,81,80,79 79,77**CSF £10.59 TOTE £2.60: £1.10, £1.90, £1.90; EX 15.90.The winner was bought in for 4,000gns. Silver Mascot subject to a friendly claim of £6,000.
**Owner** P D Evans **Bred** Juddmonte Farms **Trained** Pandy, Gwent

**FOCUS**
A modest seller and a race to treat with caution as the only one to keep tabs on long-time leader was Fen Gypsy, the winner. The winning time was fair for the grade.

**NOTEBOOK**
**Fen Gypsy**, runner-up to a subsequent winner in this grade at Windsor on his previous outing, was dropping a furlong in trip and it did not inconvenience him. The only one to keep tabs on the long-time leader right the way into the straight, he may be slightly flattered but would remain worthy of respect if kept to this level.
**Jonny Ebeneezer** was ridden with more restraint than is often case (possibly not by design as he reared in the stalls and missed the break) and it suited well. However, he was unlucky that those up with the pace were allowed to get away from the chasing pack. He is not as good as he was, but there is a similar race in him on this sort of ground.
**Silver Mascot** goes well in this grade when granted an uncontested lead had everything in his favour. He was simply not good enough.
**Enna(POL)**, a winner on similar ground in her native Poland, made a respectable British debut. This would appear to be her level.
**Rileys Dream** travelled well but could never get to the leaders - they were given too much rope in front.
**Marabar** was a long way below his best.
**Shirley Not** *Official explanation: jockey said gelding lost its action*

## 1534 HAROLD LLOYD'S BIRTHDAY H'CAP 2m
4:30 (4:32) (F) (0-55,55) 4-Y-O+ £3,010 (£860; £430) Stalls Low

Form RPR

0-56 1 **Galandora**[13] [1297] 4-7-13 46 oh1 LucyRussell(7) 7 55
(DrJRJNaylor) *hld up: plld hrd: hdwy 4f out: led over 1f out: styd on* **33/1**

06-2 2 1/2 **Starry Mary**[13] [1297] 6-9-5 55 SSanders 4 63
(RMBeckett) *chsd ldrs: outpcd 3f out: rallied to chse wnr over 1f out: r.o* **6/1**[3]

/42- 3 2 **Totally Scottish**[23] [2296] 8-8-10 45 DHolland 6 52
(MrsMReveley) *hld up: pushed along 1/2-way: hdwy u.p over 1f out: nt rch ldrs* **3/1**[1]

2123 4 2 1/2 **The Beduth Navi**[18] [1238] 4-8-7 47 ADaly 2 50
(DGBridgwater) *a.p: led over 3f out: rdn and hdd over 1f out: no ex ins fnl f* **11/2**[2]

043/ 5 2 1/2 **Castanet**[12] [5849] 5-8-7 45 RMiles(3) 5 46
(AEPrice) *hld up: hmpd over 5f out: hdwy over 2f out: sn rdn and no imp* **20/1**

010- 6 3/4 **Little Tobias (IRE)**[157] [5817] 5-8-12 51 DCorby(3) 12 50
(AndrewTurnell) *chsd ldrs: rdn over 2f out: wknd fnl f* **12/1**

1250 7 1/2 **Lampos (USA)**[18] [1238] 4-9-0 54 (v) FLynch 13 53
(MissJACamacho) *hld up: hdwy over 5f out: wknd 2f out* **8/1**

60-0 8 3 1/2 **Romil Star (GER)**[3] [1463] 7-9-4 54 (v[1]) DarrenWilliams 3 48
(KRBurke) *trckd ldrs tl lost pl and hmpd over 3f out* **6/1**[3]

/60- 9 16 **I Got Rhythm**[73] [3391] 6-8-10 45 TEDurcan 1 21
(MrsMReveley) *s.i.s: hld up: rdn over 4f out: wknd over 3f out* **11/1**

4-52 10 8 **Sashay**[43] [981] 6-8-3 45 StephanieHollinshead(7) 8 12
(RHollinshead) *led 11f: wknd over 2f out* **15/2**

0050 11 *nk* **Muraqeb**[20] [1210] 4-8-10 50 IMongan 9 15
(MrsBarbaraWaring) *hld up: plld hrd: rdn over 5f out: wknd over 3f out* **50/1**

640/ 12 3/4 **Eviyrn (IRE)**[40] [5531] 8-8-10 42 oh7 (v) MFenton 11 10
(JRJenkins) *chsd ldr: led 5f out: hdd over 3f out: sn wknd* **33/1**

3m 44.99s (7.79) **Going Correction** +0.325s/f (Good) **12 Ran SP% 120.5**
**WFA** 4 from 5yo+ 4lb
Speed ratings: **93,92,91,90,89 88,88,86,78,74 74,74**CSF £218.90 CT £793.47 TOTE £37.00: £13.80, £2.30, £1.90; EX 486.50.
**Owner** Michael Olpin **Bred** Trevor Calver **Trained** Shrewton, Wilts
■ A first winner for New Zealander Lucy Russell.

**FOCUS**
A very moderate handicap and a slow time. The runner-up is reliable at this level and provides a reasonable guide to the form.

**NOTEBOOK**
**Galandora** pulled for most of the way and was given a good ride in the circumstances. This was her first win, but she is weighted to go in again, although her tendency to race keenly is always going to make things tougher than they have to be.
**Starry Mary**, back up in trip, took a while to hit top stride and it cost her. She has not won for a long time but it will be disappointing if she does not find a similar race.
**Totally Scottish**, three times a winner over hurdles, has never won on the Flat but this was a reasonable effort. He needed plenty of driving and a stiffer track may suit better.
**The Beduth Navi**, in decent form on the All-Weather recently, did not appear to have any excuses.
**Castanet**, back on the Flat for the first time since December 2001, was easily held.
**Eviyrn(IRE)** *Official explanation: jockey said gelding was not striding out in the closing stages*

## 1535 TELETEXT RACING "HANDS AND HEELS" APPRENTICE H'CAP 1m 3f
5:00 (5:01) (G) (0-70,70) 4-Y-O+ £2,940 (£840; £420) Stalls Low

Form RPR

2-12 1 **Isa'Af (IRE)**[18] [1238] 5-8-10 55 PMakin(3) 3 64
(PWHiatt) *a.p: led over 1f out: r.o* **7/2**[2]

U10 2 1 **Dissident (GER)**[8] [1369] 6-9-11 70 (v) LTreadwell(3) 8 78
(DFlood) *trckd ldrs: plld hrd: ev ch over 1f out: styd on* **12/1**

3-33 3 2 1/2 **Trouble Mountain (USA)**[6] [1393] 7-10-0 70 PMulrennan 4 74
(MWEasterby) *hld up: hdwy over 1f out: nt rch ldrs* **5/2**[1]

/4-2 4 2 1/2 **Sir Ninja (IRE)**[15] [1263] 7-9-2 65 JDaly(7) 7 65
(SKirk) *hld up: rn wd over 3f out: hdwy over 2f out: one pce fnl f* **14/1**

4610 5 1 **Game Guru**[8] [1369] 5-9-6 62 (b) DNolan 9 61
(PABlockley) *led: hdd over 8f out: remained handy: led over 2f out: hdd over 1f out: wknd ins fnl f* **16/1**

500- 6 4 **Most-Saucy**[125] [6208] 8-9-6 65 SCrawford(3) 5 58
(IAWood) *hld up and bhd: styd on appr fnl f: nvr trbld ldrs* **10/1**[3]

3504 7 1 1/2 **Top Of The Class (IRE)**[8] [1369] 7-9-0 59 ow1 (v) SJDonohoe(3) 12 49
(PDEvans) *plld hrd: led over 8f out: hdd over 2f out: wknd over 1f out* **12/1**

5430 8 1/2 **Grand Lass (IRE)**[13] [1305] 5-8-11 53 (b) NChalmers 1 43
(ASadik) *hld up in tch: pushed along over 2f out: wknd over 1f out* **25/1**

050- 9 2 1/2 **Paradise Garden (USA)**[228] [4704] 7-7-8 43 oh5 ow3. RKennemore(7) 6 29
(PLClinton) *s.i.s: hld up: hdwy over 7f out: ev ch 2f out: wknd fnl f* **40/1**

0466 10 1/2 **Mathmagician**[21] [1193] 5-7-12 47 oh10 ow7 (b) HFellows(7) 11 32
(RFMarvin) *hld up: hdwy 7f out: wknd over 2f out* **66/1**

5524 11 6 **Theatre Tinka (IRE)**[20] [1198] 5-8-12 57 (p) StephanieHollinshead(3) 2 33
(RHollinshead) *chsd ldrs to 1/2-way* **7/2**[2]

00-0 12 12 **Lunar Leader (IRE)**[20] [1213] 4-9-9 65 (p) AQuinn 10 23
(MJGingell) *prom: chsd ldrs 8f out: wknd 3f out* **33/1**

2m 30.42s **12 Ran SP% 120.8**
Speed ratings: CSF £44.78 CT £125.64 TOTE £3.90: £2.00, £5.40, £1.10; EX 74.20 Place 6 £69.49, Place 5 £36.49..
**Owner** Miss Maria McKinney **Bred** T Monaghan **Trained** Hook Norton, Oxon
■ Stewards Enquiry : P Makin one-day ban: careless riding (May 3)

**FOCUS**
Just a modest handicap and the pace was steady.

**NOTEBOOK**
**Isa'Af(IRE)** has been in fine form on the All-Weather recently and continued that good run back on turf. He had never previously won off a mark this high, so things will be tougher next time, but he is one to have on your side whilst in this form.
**Dissident(GER)**, successful in a seller on Polytrack two starts back, was keen early but still posted a decent effort under his big weight.
**Trouble Mountain(USA)** has now been a beaten favourite on his last five starts and has not won for a year. This was a fair effort but he is clearly not one to place much faith in.
**Sir Ninja(IRE)** ran well under his inexperienced pilot but is on a very long losing run.
**Game Guru** did not appear to have any excuses.
**Most-Saucy** made a satisfactory return to action on ground a little softer than ideal, shaping as though she will stay a little further in the process.
T/Jkpt: Not won. T/Plt: £64.00 to a £1 stake. Pool: £39,189.20. 446.55 winning tickets. T/Qpdt: £34.50 to a £1 stake. Pool: £2,095.60. 44.90 winning tickets. CR

1536 - (Foreign Racing) - See Raceform Interactive

# EPSOM (L-H)

Wednesday, April 21

**OFFICIAL GOING: Soft**

## 1537 BLUE SQUARE 0800 587 0200 H'CAP — 5f

1:50 (1:52) (C ) (0-95,90) 3-Y-O+ — £9,117 (£3,458; £1,729; £786) Stalls High

Form — RPR

0-06 **1** **Cape Royal**[10] 1343 4-9-4 **82** .......... LDettori 9 — 93
(MrsJRRamsden) *trckd ldrs: pushed along 2f out: qcknd to ld 1f out: drive and r.o wl fnl f* **5/1**[1]

6002 **2** *2* **Lady Pekan**[13] 1319 5-7-9 **62** oh2 .......... (b) LisaJones(3) 11 — 67
(PSMcentee) *sn led: rdn 2f out: edgd lft fr ins fnl 2f: hdd 1f out: kpt on but nt pce of wnr ins last* **12/1**

0554 **3** *½* **Fruit Of Glory**[9] 1353 5-9-12 **90** .......... DHolland 12 — 94+
(JRJenkins) *s.i.s: bhd: n.m.r ins fnl 2f: nt clr over 1f out: qckند ins last and r.o cl home: no rch ldrs* **5/1**[1]

0040 **4** *shd* **Prince Of Blues (IRE)**[9] 1368 6-7-6 **63** oh4 ow1 .......... (p) PVarley(7) 6 — 66
(MMullineaux) *in tch: chsd ldrs 1/2-way: rdn and styd on fr over 1f out: nt qckn ins last* **25/1**

0-06 **5** *½* **Awake**[2] 1500 7-8-8 **72** .......... KFallon 2 — 74
(DNicholls) *bhd: hdwy over 1f out: r.o ins last: nt rch ldrs* **5/1**[1]

-240 **6** *2* **Blue Knight (IRE)**[33] 1057 5-8-9 **73** .......... RHughes 5 — 69
(APJarvis) *hld up in rr: hdwy and nt clr run over 1f out: kpt on ins last but nt a danger* **10/1**

0045 **7** *½* **Madrasee**[19] 1230 6-9-0 **78** .......... RLMoore 4 — 72
(LMontagueHall) *in tch early: sn outpcd: styd on again fnl f: nt a danger* **9/1**[3]

-050 **8** *½* **Chico Guapo (IRE)**[26] 1113 4-8-11 **75** .......... (p) DeanMcKeown 13 — 68
(JAGlover) *chsd ldrs tl wknd fnl f* **13/2**[2]

-410 **9** *½* **Another Glimpse**[19] 1230 6-8-5 **69** .......... (t) JQuinn 8 — 60
(MissBSanders) *lw: s.i.s: a outpcd* **16/1**

-006 **10** *hd* **Palawan**[60] 841 8-9-4 **85** .......... LPKeniry(3) 7 — 76
(AMBalding) *b: in tch: n.m.r ins fnl 2f: effrt 1f out: nt rch ldrs and wknd ins last* **25/1**

2040 **11** *2½* **King's Ballet (USA)**[9] 1368 6-7-12 **62** oh6 .......... (p) JMackay 10 — 45
(PRChamings) *s.i.s: a bhd* **16/1**

1350 **12** *5* **Dancing Mystery**[26] 1113 10-9-6 **84** .......... (b) SCarson 1 — 52
(EAWheeler) *s.i.s: a bhd* **14/1**

015- **13** *3½* **Izmail (IRE)**[247] 4239 5-8-10 **74** .......... JPMurtagh 3 — 32
(DNicholls) *w ldr 2f: styd prom tl wknd ins fnl 2f* **50/1**

58.96 secs (3.28) **Going Correction** +0.85s/f (Soft) — **13** Ran SP% **118.2**

Speed ratings: **107,103,103,102,102 98,98,97,96,96 92,84,78**CSF £64.11 CT £260.71 TOTE £5.90: £2.00, £2.90, £2.20; EX 57.20.

**Owner** D R Brotherton **Bred** D R Brotherton **Trained** Sandhutton, N Yorks

■ Stewards Enquiry : Lisa Jones caution: used whip with excessive frequency

**FOCUS**

The top weight was rated just 90 in this 0-95 and the form is probably nothing special, although the lightly-raced winner is interesting.

**NOTEBOOK**

**Cape Royal** had never previously raced on ground worse than good, but he handled it well. He may not have beaten a great deal but should be in for a good season in similar races.

**Lady Pekan** is well handicapped on some of her best turf form and, with the blinkers replacing cheekpieces, she ran well from 2lb out of the handicap. She may need dropping slightly in grade, but should find a race.

**Fruit Of Glory** lost her chance with a slow start and did not get the clearest of runs. However, she finished to good effect and is in good heart. This going did not inconvenience, but her overall record suggests she is better on fast ground. *Official explanation: jockey said mare suffered interference in running*

**Prince Of Blues(IRE)** has not won for a long time and would appear to be regressing, but this was a fair effort from 4lb out of the handicap.

**Awake** had conditions to suit and did not run badly. However, he has not won since July 2002. *Official explanation: jockey said gelding hung left and was unsuited by the downhill track*

## 1538 WEATHERBYS BLUE RIBAND TRIAL STKS (CONDITIONS RACE) — 1m 2f 18y

2:20 (2:20) (B ) 3-Y-O — £12,679 (£4,499; £2,249; £1,022) Stalls Low

Form — RPR

1 **1** **Bull Run (IRE)**[16] 1271 3-8-13 .......... JPMurtagh 3 — 115+
(DRLoder) *lw: hld up in tch and disp cl 3rd: hdwy to ld wl over 2f out: pushed clr over 1f out: impressive* **13/8**[1]

0-1 **2** *15* **Bowstring (IRE)**[22] 1189 3-8-8 **95** .......... LDettori 4 — 84
(JHMGosden) *led after 2f:hdd 7f out: styd w ldr tl rdn:rn green and lost pl 2f out: swtchd lft and kpt on to take poor 2nd ins last* **7/1**

31-1 **3** *1* **Mutafanen**[27] 1108 3-8-11 **100** .......... RHills 1 — 85
(EALDunlop) *lw: led 2f: led again 7f out: rdn and hdd wl over 2f out: sn no ch w wnr: lost mod 2nd ins last* **15/8**[2]

2113 **4** *5* **Skidmark**[18] 1239 3-9-1 **102** .......... KFallon 2 — 81
(DRCElsworth) *disp cl 3rd: rdn and effrt 3f out: wknd wl over 2f out* **7/2**[3]

2m 20.44s (11.74) **Going Correction** +1.375s/f (Soft) — **4** Ran SP% **107.6**

Speed ratings: **108,96,95,91**CSF £11.54 TOTE £2.50; EX 5.60.

**Owner** Sheikh Mohammed **Bred** Hesmonds Stud Ltd **Trained** Newmarket, Suffolk

**FOCUS**

A very impressive performance from Bull Run despite those in behind not running true to form and the soft ground exaggerating the distances. Not a bad time given the conditions, more than a second quicker than the City And Suburban, and the winner is above average for the race.

**NOTEBOOK**

**Bull Run(IRE)** ◆ again showed himself a very smart prospect. Always travelling very strongly for Murtagh, he pulled right away in the straight for a most impressive success, recording a good time in the process. Switched to Godolphin afterwards, he is a colt with a future and could run in the Predominate (his dam and half-sister both won the Lupe). If the ground looks like being on the soft side for the Derby he would be well worth supplementing, but the Italian Derby looks an obvious alternative.

**Bowstring(IRE)** was most impressive in what is turning out to be just an ordinary Folkestone maiden on her reappearance on good to soft but, on much easier ground, she failed to build on that. She did not show the most fluent action in the closing stages and looked quite tired, suggesting the conditions were a bit much for her.

**Mutafanen**, raised 16lb for hacking up in what appeared to be quite a competitive handicap at Doncaster on his reappearance, was fully entitled to take this step up in grade (not least because there would be few handicap options open for him), but he did not run to form. Time may show the Handicapper overreacted, but even so he should have run better than this and possibly failed to handle conditions. He can be given another chance.

**Skidmark**, a Dante and Derby entry, had been in great form on the Polytrack this winter, including when third over an inadequate mile in Listed company on his previous outing. However, making his debut on turf, he never really travelled that well and was not knocked about when it became obvious he was not going to pick up. This ground may well have been against him and he should be given another chance.

## 1539 BET@BLUESQ.COM GREAT METROPOLITAN STKS (H'CAP) — 1m 4f 10y

2:55 (2:58) (C ) (0-95,95) 3-Y-O+ — £15,892 (£6,028; £3,014; £1,370) Stalls Centre

Form — RPR

1324 **1** **Cold Turkey**[11] 1329 4-8-12 **79** .......... SWhitworth 14 — 89
(GLMoore) *hld up in rr: hdwy on rails whn nt clr run and swtchd lft appr fnl 2f: led wl over 1f out: drvn out* **11/2**[1]

1205 **2** *3* **General**[21] 1213 7-8-2 **71** ow2 .......... TPQueally(3) 18 — 77
(NPLittmoden) *chsd ldrs: wnt 2nd over 4f out: led appr fnl 2f: hdd wl over 1f out: styd on same pce* **20/1**

05-0 **3** *1½* **Vengeance**[11] 1328 4-9-9 **90** .......... DaneO'Neill 13 — 94
(MrsAJPerrett) *lw: in tch: hdwy 5f out: chsd ldrs over 2f out: kep on same pce fnl f* **7/1**[3]

40-3 **4** *½* **Pagan Dance (IRE)**[60] 844 5-9-10 **90** .......... (p) LDettori 11 — 93+
(MrsAJPerrett) *hld up in rr: hdwy whn bdly bmpd over 2f out and hung lft: continued to hang but kpt on fnl f* **9/1**

0-00 **5** *2* **Champion Lion (IRE)**[11] 1326 5-8-1 **70** .......... SHitchcott(3) 6 — 70+
(MRChannon) *bhd: hdwy 5f out: chsd ldrs 2f out: kpt on same pce* **14/1**

4-31 **6** *½* **Ofaraby**[23] 1172 4-9-5 **86** .......... PRobinson 2 — 86+
(MAJarvis) *chsd ldrs: rdn 3f out: wknd ins fnl 2f* **13/2**[2]

14-5 **7** *1½* **Lennel**[9] 1369 6-8-2 **68** .......... (b) FNorton 19 — 66
(ABailey) *bhd: hdwy 4f out: n.m.r appr fnl 2f: kpt on same pce fnl f* **14/1**

513- **8** *5* **Individual Talents (USA)**[173] 5852 4-8-2 **69** .......... MartinDwyer 8 — 60
(SCWilliams) *bhd: hdwy on rails over 2f out: kpt on but nt rch ldrs* **10/1**

-000 **9** *1* **Danakil**[27] 1103 9-8-7 **73** .......... RLMoore 3 — 62
(SDow) *bhd: hdwy 4f out: nvr gng pce to rch ldrs* **20/1**

00-0 **10** *4* **Muskatsturm (GER)**[14] 1302 5-8-9 **75** .......... SWKelly 7 — 59
(BJCurley) *bhd: rdn and effrt over 3f out: n.d* **25/1**

5-03 **11** *1* **Bucks**[16] 1272 7-8-5 **71** .......... CCatlin 16 — 53
(DKIvory) *chsd ldrs: rdn 4f out: wknd fr 3f out* **20/1**

2430 **12** *4* **Ezz Elkheil**[33] 1054 5-8-8 **74** .......... DHolland 9 — 51
(JRJenkins) *chsd ldr: led 5f out: hdd over 2f out and sn wknd* **16/1**

200- **13** *7* **Football Crazy (IRE)**[8] 5827 5-9-3 **83** .......... (b) KFallon 5 — 50
(PBowen) *bit bkwd: in tch: n.m.r and lost pl after 2f: sn rcvrd and in tch: wknd 3f out* **14/1**

50-0 **14** *10* **Persian King (IRE)**[16] 1272 7-9-1 **81** .......... SDrowne 15 — 34
(JABOld) *a in rr* **50/1**

103- **15** *10* **Mexican Pete**[172] 5066 4-8-6 **76** .......... RMiles(3) 12 — 15
(PWHiatt) *b: bhd: sme hdwy 4f out: wknd ins fnl 3f* **33/1**

253- **16** *3* **Jeepstar**[179] 5738 4-8-10 **77** .......... JMackay 17 — 12
(TDEasterby) *led 7f: wknd 3f out* **20/1**

0-50 **17** *2* **Heisse**[11] 1329 4-10-0 **95** .......... (v[1]) JPMurtagh 10 — 27
(DRLoder) *sn prom: rdn 5f out: wknd 4f out* **12/1**

434- **18** *8* **Stolen Hours (USA)**[62] 5703 4-8-8 **75** .......... TQuinn 4 — —
(JAkehurst) *bit bkwd: a in rr* **33/1**

0-00 **19** *3½* **Lunar Leader (IRE)**[1] 1535 4-7-9 **65** .......... (p) LisaJones(3) 20 — —
(MJGingell) *sn bhd* **50/1**

020- **20** *dist* **Sergeant Cecil**[228] 4713 5-9-8 **88** .......... RHughes 1 — —
(BRMillman) *chsd ldrs 6f: wknd rapidly 6f out: t.o* **20/1**

2m 53.93s (15.21) **Going Correction** +1.375s/f (Soft)

**WFA** 4 from 5yo+ 1lb — **20** Ran SP% **131.3**

Speed ratings: **104,102,101,100,99 99,98,94,94,91 90,88,83,76,70 68,66,61,59,—**CSF £120.58 CT £809.15 TOTE £6.20: £1.70, £5.50, £2.60, £2.90; EX 152.40 Trifecta £709.50 Pool £1,599.04 - 1.60 winning units..

**Owner** A Grinter **Bred** Worksop Manor Stud **Trained** Woodingdean, E Sussex

■ Stewards Enquiry : S Whitworth four-day-ban: careless riding (May 2-5)

**FOCUS**

Quite a competitive handicap, but several of these would not have been at home on the soft ground. The winner was translating his improved All-Weather form to turf.

**NOTEBOOK**

**Cold Turkey** may not have stayed two miles on his previous outing, but he got the stronger pace that suits him well on this drop in trip and weaved his way through to score most decisively. He should still be reasonably treated compared to his All-Weather mark when reassessed and may now go for a race over a mile six at Goodwood.

**General** loves this sort of ground and ran a fine race against a well-treated winner, sticking on gamely when headed and emerging with plenty of credit. He is worthy of plenty of respect on this ground.

**Vengeance** had never raced on ground this soft and has done all of his winning good to firm. However, conditions did not appear to be a problem and he ran well.

**Pagan Dance(IRE)** has won on good to soft but, like his stablemate (third), had never raced on ground this bad. He did not help his chance by hanging.

**Champion Lion(IRE)** travelled quite strongly but proved one paced in the straight.

**Football Crazy(IRE)** *Official explanation: jockey said gelding suffered interference in running*

**Jeepstar** *Official explanation: jockey said gelding was unsuited by the soft ground*

**Heisse** *Official explanation: jockey said colt had a breathing problem*

**Stolen Hours(USA)** *Official explanation: jockey said colt had suffered interference in running*

## 1540 BLUE SQUARE CITY AND SUBURBAN STKS (H'CAP) — 1m 2f 18y

3:30 (3:35) (B ) (0-105,104) 4-Y-O+ — £17,400 (£6,600; £3,300; £1,500) Stalls Low

Form — RPR

30-4 **1** **Blythe Knight (IRE)**[11] 1328 4-9-9 **99** .......... LDettori 6 — 109
(EALDunlop) *lw: hld up in rr: hdwy on outside over 4f out: trckd ldrs over 2f out: qcknd to ld appr fnl f: hld on all out* **9/2**[1]

6405 **2** *shd* **Bonecrusher**[11] 1328 5-10-0 **104** .......... JPMurtagh 9 — 114
(DRLoder) *lw: hld up in rr: hdwy on outside fr 4f out: n.m.r and swtchd lft over 2f out: str chal ins last:no ex cl home* **10/1**

410- **3** *5* **Shahzan House (IRE)**[179] 5753 5-9-4 **94** .......... PRobinson 5 — 96
(MAJarvis) *prom: rdn to press ldrs 2f out: outpcd fnl f* **9/1**

0-60 **4** *nk* **King's Thought**[11] 1328 5-9-6 **96** .......... DHolland 3 — 97
(SGollings) *sn led: rdn 3f out: hdd appr fnl f: sn outpcd* **8/1**[3]

6045 **5** *6* **Silvaline**[4] 1460 5-7-13 **75** .......... DaleGibson 1 — 66
(TKeddy) *chsd ldr after 4f: rdn 3f out: wknd 2f out* **14/1**

1105 **6** *1* **Scottish River (USA)**[25] 1141 5-7-7 **74** oh1 .......... HayleyTurner(5) 15 — 63
(MDIUsher) *bhd: hdwy on outside 4-4f out: styd on fr 2f out but nvr nr ldrs* **50/1**

0-05 **7** *2* **Norton (IRE)**[4] 1456 7-9-3 **96** .......... RMiles(3) 10 — 82
(TGMills) *in tch: rdn and effrt over 2f out: nvr rch ldrs and sn wknd* **12/1**

305- **8** *3* **Crow Wood**[193] 5484 5-9-2 **92** .......... MFenton 12 — 73
(JGGiven) *chsd ldrs: rdn 3f out: sn wknd* **20/1**

450- **9** *11* **Recount (FR)**[328] 1945 4-8-2 **78** ow1 .......... NPollard 16 — 40
(JRBest) *disp ld 1f: styd in tch tl dropped to mid-div 1/2-way: sn rdn and n.d after* **14/1**

4122 **10** *1 1/2* **Classic Role**[9] 1369 5-8-3 **79**....(v) JQuinn 4 38
(RIngram) *lw: bhd: sme hdwy over 3f out: nvr bttr than mid-div and sn bhd* **8/1**[3]

5104 **11** *11* **Mad Carew (USA)**[44] 984 5-8-3 **79**....(be) RLMoore 14 20
(GLMoore) *sn bhd* **25/1**

310- **12** *5* **Harcourt (USA)**[165] 5952 4-8-12 **88**.... KFallon 2 20
(PFICole) *chsd ldrs 7f* **10/1**

-402 **13** *2* **Arry Dash**[11] 1321 4-8-11 **87**.... TEDurcan 13 16
(MRChannon) *bhd whn n.m.r bnd 4f out: nvr in contention* **6/1**[2]

2203 **14** *28* **Northside Lodge (IRE)**[53] 915 6-8-7 **83**.... MartinDwyer 11 —
(PWHarris) *lw: chsd ldrs: rdn 5f out: sn wknd* **12/1**

320- **15** *1 1/2* **Prairie Wolf**[175] 5827 8-8-10 **86**.... IMongan 8 —
(MLWBell) *a in rr* **33/1**

-300 **16** *14* **Corriolanus (GER)**[9] 1355 4-10-0 **104**....(b) JFanning 7 —
(PMitchell) *sn chsng ldr: wknd 6f out* **25/1**

2m 21.6s (12.90) **Going Correction** +1.375s/f (Soft) **16** Ran SP% **128.9**
Speed ratings: **103,102,98,98,93 93,91,89,80,79 70,66,64,42,41 29**CSF £49.08 CT £409.01 TOTE £5.50: £1.60, £2.80, £3.20, £3.20; EX 39.20 Trifecta £912.10 Pool £1,798.60 - 1.40 winning units..
**Owner** Maktoum Al Maktoum **Bred** Gainsborough Stud Management Ltd **Trained** Newmarket, Suffolk

**FOCUS**
A competitive handicap run at a fair pace. The first four had it between them some way out. The distances probably should not be taken too literally, but race should work out well.

**NOTEBOOK**
**Blythe Knight(IRE)** was always travelling really well under Dettori, who pulled a master-stroke when coming wide round the bend to grab the stands' rail. The front two came right away in the last furlong and, considering he does not do much in front, there should be more to come. He seems to have improved this season for the switch to softer ground, although he did win twice on a faster surface last year.
**Bonecrusher**, closely matched with the winner on their previous running in Kempton's Rosebery Stakes, had to switch from the favoured stands' rail to deliver his challenge and was touched off in a bob of heads. Racing without his usual visor, he is still on a feasible mark and will continue to be competitive in this sort of event.
**Shahzan House(IRE)**, a course and distance winner, posted a most promising reappearance, travelling smoothly before lack of fitness told. He has done most of his racing on fast ground but clearly appreciates some ease. There is more improvement in him and he can win a big handicap. Something like the John Smith's Cup would be an ideal long-term target.
**King's Thought**, who stays further than this, soon grabbed his customary place at the head of affairs and set a good gallop. Although he was never going to hold the front two, he boxed on really well and should win more races, especially on similar ground.
**Silvaline**, fifth in a similar event at Newbury five days previously, again ran well without ever threatening to trouble the front two.
**Scottish River(USA)**, who has been busy on the All-Weather, appeared to be helped by racing against the stands' rail down the straight and may be a little flattered by this effort.
**Norton(IRE)**, fifth in the Spring Cup at Newbury four days previously, goes well on this sort of ground, but failed to see out the trip in the conditions. He is worth another try at the trip on better ground and, having edged down the weights, is one to bear in mind for all the big handicaps.
**Crow Wood**, who probably prefers faster ground, ran with a degree of promise and will certainly strip fitter next time.
**Corriolanus(GER)** *Official explanation: jockey said colt lost its action*

## 1541 DRIVERS JONAS MAIDEN STKS 1m 114y
**4:00** (4:04) (D) 3-Y-O+ **£5,369** (£1,652; £826; £413) **Stalls** Low

Form RPR
55-2 **1** **Cello**[9] 1366 3-8-9 78.... PDobbs 10 88
(RHannon) *trckd ldr: led 4f out: rdn and hung lft ins fnl 2f: continued to edge lft and r.o wl fnl f* **7/4**[1]

25- **2** *2* **Desert Cristal (IRE)**[230] 4691 3-8-4.... MartinDwyer 5 79
(JRBoyle) *sn trcking ldrs: wnt 2nd over 2f out: rdn and effrt whn hung lft fr over 1f out: nt qckn ins last but kpt on for clr 2nd* **11/4**[2]

3355 **3** *13* **Resplendent King (USA)**[57] 869 3-8-6 67.... RMiles[(3)] 7 57
(TGMills) *led tl hdd 4f out: wknd qckly 2f out* **7/1**

00- **4** *1/2* **Embassy Sweets (USA)**[133] 6158 3-8-4.... RLMoore 2 50
(PFICole) *bhd: stl in rr whn n.m.r on rails and swtchd lft over 2f out: r.o fnl f to take modest 4th cl home* **20/1**

000- **5** *shd* **Second Warning**[189] 5571 3-8-9.... CCatlin 1 55
(DJDaly) *bit bkwd: in tch: chsd ldrs 1/2-way: wknd qckly over 2f out* **33/1**

0- **6** *2 1/2* **Moscow Blue**[257] 3965 3-8-9.... RHughes 3 50
(JHMGosden) *chsd ldrs: rdn over 2f out: sn btn* **3/1**[3]

0-0 **7** *19* **Tsarbuck**[9] 1371 3-8-9.... DaleGibson 6 10
(RMHCowell) *a wl bhd* **50/1**

0/0- **8** *21* **Boozy Douz**[133] 252 4-9-5.... SDrowne 4 —
(HSHowe) *a wl behind* **50/1**

1m 56.63s (10.89) **Going Correction** +1.375s/f (Soft)
**WFA** 3 from 4yo 15lb **8** Ran SP% **112.2**
Speed ratings: **106,104,92,92,92 89,73,54**CSF £6.36 TOTE £2.40: £1.10, £1.40, £1.90; EX 5.10.
**Owner** Louis Stalder **Bred** Normandy Developments Ltd **Trained** East Everleigh, Wilts

**FOCUS**
An uncompetitive maiden full of dead wood and several failed to act on the ground. However, the front two did pull well clear and the winner franked previous Warwick form.

**NOTEBOOK**
**Cello**, who pushed an 85-rated rival all the way at Warwick, was always up with the pace and led them over to the stands' side. He always looked in control and may have had a bit up his sleeve.
**Desert Cristal(IRE)**, who looked fit on her seasonal debut, did not appear to be totally suited by the ground and certainly has a small race in her on this evidence.
**Resplendent King(USA)**, with the blinkers left off, was the only runner to stay tight to the rail coming down the hill. Although he tracked over to the stands' side, he was soon left behind.
**Embassy Sweets(USA)** came flying through from the rear, but what she actually achieved is open to debate.
**Second Warning** found the ground against him and should also come on for the run.
**Moscow Blue**, who was coltish in the paddock, had run in a hot Newmarket maiden on his only start at two, but dropped away very tamely. This ground may not have suited, but this was still disappointing.

## 1542 PHILIP HALL MEMORIAL CLASSIFIED STKS 1m 114y
**4:30** (4:31) (E) 3-Y-O+ **£4,745** (£1,460; £730; £365) **Stalls** Low

Form RPR
0-13 **1** **Tiger Tiger (FR)**[26] 1120 3-8-4 72.... JFEgan 2 87
(JamiePoulton) *hld up rr: hdwy over 4f out: led far side ins fnl 3f: overall advantage 2f out: drvn clr fnl f* **7/1**

2501 **2** *12* **The Gaikwar (IRE)**[33] 1055 5-8-12 68....(b) MSavage[(5)] 10 61
(NEBerry) *in tch: c stands side and hdwy over 2f out: no ch w wnr far side fnl f but kpt on wl for 2nd* **14/1**

36-5 **3** *3/4* **Cool Temper**[13] 1315 8-9-3 69.... KFallon 8 60
(PFICole) *lw: chsd ldrs: styd far side and ev ch ins fnl 3f: chsd wnr over 2f out: no ch fr over 1f out: lost 2nd ins last* **3/1**[1]

3-00 **4** *3 1/2* **Gracia**[9] 1372 5-9-0 66.... MartinDwyer 4 50
(SCWilliams) *chsd ldrs: styd far side: wknd over 2f out* **5/1**[3]

2433 **5** *1/2* **Deeper In Debt**[18] 1241 6-9-3 70.... GCarter 9 52
(JAkehurst) *chsd ldrs: c stands side: wknd over 2f out* **12/1**

0-60 **6** *3* **Liberty Royal**[16] 1275 5-9-3 66.... SSanders 7 46
(PJMakin) *sn drvn to ld: hdd over 3f out and c stands side: wknd over 2f out: hung lft fr over 1f out* **20/1**

5651 **7** *7* **Lygeton Lad**[18] 1242 6-9-7 74....(t) MFenton 5 36
(MissGayKelleway) *b: b.hind: a bhd* **5/1**[3]

0312 **8** *6* **Katiypour (IRE)**[18] 1241 7-9-2 72.... RMiles[(3)] 6 22
(MissBSanders) *lw: trckd ldrs: slt ld over 3f out: c stands side and lost overall ld 2f out: wknd qckly* **4/1**[2]

50-0 **9** *15* **Voice Mail**[22] 1187 5-9-0 68.... LPKeniry[(3)] 1 —
(AMBalding) *rr: styd far side and lost tch fnl 3f* **12/1**

1m 57.06s (11.32) **Going Correction** +1.375s/f (Soft)
**WFA** 3 from 5yo+ 15lb **9** Ran SP% **117.6**
Speed ratings: **104,93,92,89,89 86,80,74,61**CSF £100.32 TOTE £4.90: £2.00, £5.40, £1.60; EX 127.50 Place 6 £53.82, Place 5 £24.98..
**Owner** R W Huggins **Bred** Pierre Talvard And Jean-Claude Seroul **Trained** Telscombe, E Sussex

**FOCUS**
A messy event where the field split into two groups in the straight for the first time on the day. The far side seemed to have a definite advantage and the form looks unreliable.

**NOTEBOOK**
**Tiger Tiger(FR)**, making his turf debut, was given a canny ride by Egan, who made his mind up to stay far side and drew right away. This colt was the only three-year-old in the field, so this effort has to be given some credit, but it is not hard to pick holes in it.
**The Gaikwar(IRE)**, fit from the All-Weather, comes out with plenty of credit. He was first home on the stands' side by some way and, considering he is better on faster ground, he should be up to winning soon.
**Cool Temper**, another to stick to the far side, did not appear to be suited to the ground and the writing was on the wall from some way out. He will be better on faster ground, but it would be unwise to give him much credit for this.
**Gracia**, another better suited to faster ground, owed her finishing position to the decision to stay on the far side.
**Lygeton Lad** did not handle the descent well.
T/Jkpt: £6,684.20 to a £1 stake. Pool: £108,266.00. 11.50 winning tickets. T/Plt: £28.00 to a £1 stake. Pool: £81,267.35. 2,116.10 winning tickets. T/Qpdt: £8.50 to a £1 stake. Pool: £5,352.90. 461.10 winning tickets. ST

# 1492 LINGFIELD (L-H)
### Wednesday, April 21

**OFFICIAL GOING: Standard**
Wind: lt bhd Weather: overcast, heavy downpour after race 1, becoming sunny

## 1543 NEW SITE @ BETDIRECT.CO.UK BANDED STKS 1m 4f (P)
**5:15** (5:15) (H) 3-Y-O+ **£1,260** (£360; £180) **Stalls** Low

Form RPR
0/50 **1** **Buying A Dream (IRE)**[38] 1026 7-9-9 35.... CCatlin 4 40
(AndrewTurnell) *chsd ldrs: rdn 4f out: no prog tl r.o u.p over 1f out: led last 75y: sn clr* **16/1**

-601 **2** *1 1/2* **Leophin Dancer (USA)**[6] 1402 6-10-1 35.... BDoyle 3 44
(PWHiatt) *cl up: trckd ldr over 2f out: rdn and no imp over 1f out: kpt on same pce* **5/2**[2]

4400 **3** *shd* **The Last Mohican**[15] 1281 5-9-9 30....(p) JFanning 1 38
(PHowling) *led for 2f: led again over 5f out: drvn 3l clr over 1f out: nt run on fnl f: hdd last 75y* **6/1**

5002 **4** *1 1/2* **Neptune**[6] 1402 8-9-9 35.... RSmith 6 36
(JCFox) *hld up in 6th: rdn and no rspnse 3f out: kpt on fnl f: no ch* **9/4**[1]

05-0 **5** *nk* **Royal Axminster**[106] 455 9-9-2 35.... AmyBaker[(7)] 2 35
(MrsPNDutfield) *led after 2f to over 5f out: chsd ldr to over 2f out: one pce* **5/1**[3]

5660 **6** *3* **Broughtons Mill**[9] 994 9-9-9 30....(p) WSupple 5 31
(JASupple) *cl up: rdn over 3f out: wknd over 1f out* **12/1**

00-5 **7** *nk* **Smarter Charter**[6] 1402 11-9-2 35.... KristinStubbs[(7)] 7 30
(MrsLStubbs) *s.s: hld up in last: shuffled along 3f out: no prog* **11/2**

2m 37.62s (3.38) **Going Correction** 0.0s/f (Stan) **7** Ran SP% **119.3**
Speed ratings: **88,87,86,85,85 83,83**CSF £59.20 TOTE £19.80: £9.30, £1.90; EX 89.90.
**Owner** Robinson Webster (holdings) Ltd **Bred** James Kavanagh **Trained** Malton, N Yorks

**FOCUS**
A poor race run at a sedate pace and a slow winning time.

**NOTEBOOK**
**Buying A Dream(IRE)**, who would have eaten these on his two-year-old form, seemed to appreciate the switch to this surface after a couple of modest efforts on Fibresand. He took an age to respond to pressure, but in the end he was well on top. The slow time is some cause for concern, but it may be that he has now found his niche.
**Leophin Dancer(USA)** confirmed recent form here with a couple of these, but ran into a rival with latent ability.
**The Last Mohican** did the right thing in trying to make use of his undoubted stamina, but in the end his woeful lack of pace was again his undoing. He is still to win after 40 attempts. *Official explanation: vet said gelding lost a shoe.*
**Neptune**, 6lb better off with Leophin Dancer for a short-head defeat over course and distance, was beaten further this time and is not that reliable.
**Royal Axminster** showed up for a while, but is not on top of his game at present.

## 1544 £10 FREE BET @ BETDIRECT.CO.UK BANDED STKS 7f (P)
**5:45** (5:45) (H) 3-Y-O+ **£1,435** (£410; £205) **Stalls** Low

Form RPR
2011 **1** **Baytown Flyer**[2] 1510 4-9-6 35.... LDettori 5 53
(PSMcentee) *mde all: pushed clr fr 2f out: unchal* **2/1**[2]

0-41 **2** *2 1/2* **Crafty Politician (USA)**[6] 1406 7-9-6 40....(b) RLMoore 2 46
(GLMoore) *chsd wnr for 2f: rdn to go 2nd again over 2f out: no imp wl over 1f out* **11/8**[1]

0666 **3** *3* **Harbour Princess**[5] 1447 3-8-1 40.... SRighton 3 32
(MFHarris) *sn in last: rdn over 4f out: kpt on u.p fnl 2f: no ch* **33/1**

6/63 **4** *1 1/4* **Mahlstick (IRE)**[6] 1403 6-8-11 35....(t) SHitchcott[(3)] 1 29
(DWPArbuthnot) *cl up: effrt to chse wnr briefly wl over 2f out: sn fnd nil and btn* **5/1**[3]

-050 **5** *7* **Bar Of Silver (IRE)**[51] 941 4-9-0 40....(v) DHolland 4 11
(RBrotherton) *s.i.s: rcvrd to chse wnr after 2f to wl over 2f out: wknd* **11/2**

1m 25.93s (-0.01) **Going Correction** 0.0s/f (Stan)
**WFA** 3 from 4yo+ 13lb **5** Ran SP% **110.4**
Speed ratings: **100,97,93,92,84**CSF £5.17 TOTE £1.80: £1.10, £2.00; EX 3.30.

**Owner** J Doxey **Bred** B Minty **Trained** Newmarket, Suffolk

**FOCUS**

A modest little banded event, but the pace was good and the time was fair for the grade. The winner is in cracking form.

**NOTEBOOK**

**Baytown Flyer**, weak in the market, bounced out of the stalls in front and was never in any danger. This completed a six-day hat-trick for the filly, and it shows how effective she can be when able to establish an uncontested lead.

**Crafty Politician(USA)**, back up in trip and well backed, moved up approaching the home bend, but the winner quickened again and quickly left him standing.

**Harbour Princess** came from off the pace to make the frame for the first time, but may not have achieved much.

**Mahlstick(IRE)** is still to get off the mark and this is as good as he is.

**Bar Of Silver(IRE)**, another maiden, is exposed and looks slow.

## 1545 BETDIRECT.CO.UK BANDED STKS 1m 2f (P)

6:15 (6:16) (H) 3-Y-0+ £1,638 (£468; £234) Stalls Low

Form RPR

/0-2 **1** **Kings Topic (USA)**[6] 1404 4-9-5 45 LPKeniry(3) 9 50
(PBurgoyne) *trckd ldrs: prog to ld over 2f out: kicked clr wl over 1f out: rdn out* **8/1**

60-2 **2** 1 1/4 **Six Pack (IRE)**[30] 1080 6-9-8 45 CCatlin 7 48
(AndrewTurnell) *prom: rdn and unable qck over 2f out: chsd wnr over 1f out: kpt on* **4/1**[2]

0025 **3** *nk* **Ryan's Bliss (IRE)**[15] 1277 4-9-5 45 J-PGuillambert(3) 5 47
(TDMccarthy) *racd in midfield: prog 3f out: nt clr run over 2f out: drvn over 1f out: edgd rt and nt qckn fnl f* **16/1**

2056 **4** 3/4 **Our Glenard**[29] 1081 5-9-8 45 DHolland 1 46
(SLKeightley) *racd in midfield: outpcd and rdn in last trio over 4f out: effrt u.p over 2f out: kpt on same pce* **7/2**[1]

2020 **5** 1 1/2 **Private Seal**[23] 1164 9-9-8 45 (t) NCallan 8 43
(JulianPoulton) *hld up in last: rdn and outpcd over 4f out: effrt u.p over 2f out: one pce wl over 1f out* **10/1**

5051 **6** 4 **Galey River (USA)**[15] 1277 5-9-5 45 DCorby(3) 4 36
(JJSheehan) *prom: rdn and lost pl over 4f out: struggling fr over 2f out* **9/2**[3]

06-2 **7** 4 **Candy Anchor (FR)**[15] 1277 5-9-8 45 (b) LDettori 3 29
(REPeacock) *t.k.h: hld up bhd ldrs tl prog to ld and qcknd 5f out: hdd & wknd over 2f out* **7/2**[1]

/116 **8** 2 1/2 **Dafa**[30] 1077 8-9-8 40 (b[1]) SWKelly 6 24
(BJCurley) *led to 5f out: rdn and wknd over 3f out: eased* **8/1**

-006 **9** 6 **Polish Rhapsody (IRE)**[15] 1285 3-8-5 45 WSupple 2 13
(JASupple) *a in last trio: rdn and outpcd over 4f out: bhd fnl 3f* **25/1**

2m 8.37s (0.52) **Going Correction** 0.0s/f (Stan)

**WFA** 3 from 4yo+ 17lb 9 Ran SP% **123.7**

Speed ratings: **97,96,95,95,93 90,87,85,80**CSF £43.03 TOTE £7.30: £3.90, £1.80, £4.00; EX 42.60.

**Owner** Topics Tarts **Bred** Marvin Delfiner And Fred Seitz **Trained** Collingbourne Ducis, Wilts

**FOCUS**

A fair race of its type, run at a solid pace.

**NOTEBOOK**

**Kings Topic(USA)** ◆ was a candidate for the 'bounce' factor after his good effort here last week following a long layoff, but there was no sign of it and the race was over once he was kicked into the lead on the home bend. He still has a little scope and can win again in this grade.

**Six Pack(IRE)**, tried over a variety of trips in his career, including over hurdles and fences, had every chance but lacked toe where it mattered. He probably needs a stiffer test.

**Ryan's Bliss(IRE)**, still looking for her first win, was stuck behind a wall of horses turning for home and would probably have finished second otherwise.

**Our Glenard** lacked foot and probably needs a greater stamina test these days.

**Galey River(USA)**, who finished in front of a couple of these when winning over course and distance earlier this month, again hit a flat spot mid-race but on this occasion he could never get back on terms.

**Candy Anchor(FR)** seemed to be travelling well in front racing down the false straight, but the winner then ranged alongside and she was soon on the retreat. This was a better banded stakes than she has been running in. *Official explanation: jockey said mare ran too freely.*

## 1546 BET DIRECT INTERACTIVE BANDED STKS 5f (P)

6:45 (6:48) (H) 3-Y-0+ £1,610 (£460; £230) Stalls High

Form RPR

-003 **1** **Maromito (IRE)**[35] 1035 7-9-7 40 SSanders 5 56
(RBastiman) *mde all: drew clr fr 2f out: rdn out* **4/5**[1]

0604 **2** 3 **Law Maker**[15] 1280 4-9-7 40 (v) DHolland 7 45
(MABuckley) *cl up: chsd wnr 3f out: rdn over 2f out: sn outpcd* **4/1**[2]

-002 **3** 2 1/2 **Avit (IRE)**[43] 1000 4-9-7 40 JFEgan 1 36
(PLGilligan) *trckd ldrs: effrt but outpcd over 2f out: kpt on same pce fr over 1f out* **5/1**[3]

2400 **4** 1 **Bali-Star**[9] 1368 9-9-7 40 SDrowne 2 33
(RJHodges) *cl up: rdn 3f out: outpcd and btn over 2f out* **10/1**

/0-5 **5** 3 **Second Generation (IRE)**[73] 718 7-9-7 30 RLMoore 6 22
(RJHodges) *s.i.s: outpcd and bhd: effrt u.p 1/2-way: sn no prog* **33/1**

0030 **6** 1 1/2 **Onefortheboys (IRE)**[15] 1279 5-9-7 40 SWhitworth 3 16
(DFlood) *s.i.s: outpcd and wl bhd 3f out: plugged on fnl f* **11/2**

3060 **7** 2 1/2 **Mangus (IRE)**[30] 1075 10-9-7 35 (be) CCatlin 4 —
(KOCunningham-Brown) *pressed wnr to 3f out: wknd over 2f out* **25/1**

3000 **8** 11 **Philly Dee**[38] 1025 3-8-8 40 ow2 (b) MSavage(5) 8 —
(NEBerry) *v s.i.s: drvn to try to rcvr over 3f out: wknd 2f out* **25/1**

59.00 secs (-0.78) **Going Correction** 0.0s/f (Stan)

**WFA** 3 from 4yo+ 10lb 8 Ran SP% **127.3**

Speed ratings: **106,101,97,95,90 88,84,66**CSF £5.10 TOTE £1.60: £1.10, £1.40, £1.70; EX 5.20.

**Owner** Mrs P Bastiman **Bred** Joseph Finnegan **Trained** Cowthorpe, N Yorks

**FOCUS**

A gamble landed, and a very smart winning time for a banded stakes.

**NOTEBOOK**

**Maromito(IRE)** ◆, very well backed, was once a fair sprint handicapper but has been in freefall down the handicap within the past year. He very much appreciated the drop back from seven furlongs here though and, breaking smartly from the gate, travelled very well in front and found plenty when shaken up in the home straight. He looks much better than banded class and will probably not get many more chances at this level.

**Law Maker** appeared to be travelling well on the shoulder of the favourite for much of the way, but not for the first time did not find as much as had looked likely. To be fair to him, the winner is a better sort than you normally get in races like this.

**Avit(IRE)** did her best and probably ran to form. This was her tenth race and the first time she had started at less than 20/1.

**Bali-Star** was always being taken along faster than he cares for and probably needs a slower surface than this.

**Onefortheboys(IRE)** was always struggling and remains a maiden after 21 attempts.

## 1547 BET DIRECT ON SKY ACTIVE (S) STKS 2m (P)

7:15 (7:17) (H) 4-Y-0+ £1,456 (£416; £208) Stalls Low

Form RPR

0-06 **1** **Sariba**[15] 1281 5-8-11 35 PDobbs 6 41
(ACharlton) *led to 1/2-way: led again over 3f out: drvn 3f clr wl over 1f out: kpt on* **8/1**[3]

**2** 1 3/4 **Indian Chase**[44] 7-8-9 (v[1]) LucyRussell(7) 2 44
(DrJRJNaylor) *hld up in last pair: rdn and struggling 5f out: wl bhd 3f out: r.o over 1f out: tk 2nd nr fin* **33/1**

0010 **3** 1/2 **Our Imperial Bay (USA)**[6] 1426 5-9-7 55 (v) ADaly 5 48
(RMStronge) *hld up towards rr: rdn 5f out: sn struggling: kpt on fnl 2f to take 3rd nr fin* **4/1**[2]

0 **4** 1/2 **Mister Graham**[16] 1263 9-8-13 BReilly(3) 4 43
(KFClutterbuck) *s.s: sn chsd clr ldrs: clsd 4f out: w wnr 3f out: sn nt qckn: btn over 1f out* **33/1**

1233 **5** *nk* **Sungio**[29] 1081 6-9-7 52 (b) KFallon 7 47
(BGPowell) *settled bhd clr ldrs: clsd over 3f out: sn rdn: chsd wnr wl over 1f out: no imp: wknd ins fnl f* **4/9**[1]

-000 **6** 9 **Monsal Dale (IRE)**[4] 1463 5-8-11 40 (p) MSavage(5) 1 32
(NEBerry) *pressed ldr: led 1/2-way: clr 5f out: hdd over 3f out: wknd 2f out* **8/1**[3]

200- **7** 10 **Regal Repose**[250] 4161 4-8-0 50 CHaddon(7) 3 15
(AJChamberlain) *plld hrd: hld up in last pair: wknd 4f out: t.o* **16/1**

3m 29.04s (0.46) **Going Correction** 0.0s/f (Stan)

**WFA** 4 from 5yo+ 4lb 7 Ran SP% **123.2**

Speed ratings: **98,97,96,96,96 91,86**CSF £208.51 TOTE £10.20: £3.50, £5.60; EX 151.30.The winner was bought in for 2,600gns.

**Owner** Woodhaven Racing Syndicate **Bred** The Woodhaven Stud **Trained** Collingbourne Ducis, Wilts

**FOCUS**

A poor seller run at an even pace.

**NOTEBOOK**

**Sariba** stays all day and, given her usual positive ride, was very brave when the challengers arrived. She is only modest and with the favourite running so poorly this probably took little winning, but being able to lead on a fast surface does bring out the best in her.

**Indian Chase**, placed in bumpers, has had a disastrous time of it over hurdles and fences but found stamina coming to his rescue on this Flat debut in the first-time visor. He may be worth a try over this trip on Fibresand.

**Our Imperial Bay(USA)** is very inconsistent these days and has never shone over this sort of trip. He might have had a problem though, as he was dismounted immediately after the line. *Official explanation: trainer said gelding finished distressed.*

**Mister Graham** is still to get off the mark and did not achieve much.

**Sungio** is a dual winner on this surface but no world-beater, and he started plenty short enough. He needed plenty of driving to get into a challenging position, and had nothing more to offer down the home straight. *Official explanation: trainer said gelding was found to be lame the following morning*

**Regal Repose** *Official explanation: trainer later said filly had come heavily into season*

## 1548 £10 FREE BET @ BET DIRECT SKY ACTIVE BANDED STKS 1m (P)

7:45 (7:46) (H) 3-Y-0+ £1,256 (£359; £179) Stalls High

Form RPR

4411 **1** **Beauteous (IRE)**[2] 1513 5-9-13 35 LDettori 5 56+
(MJPolglase) *fly-jmpd s: racd wd 1st 2f: led over 5f out: drew clr fr 3f out: canter* **1/4**[1]

4235 **2** 5 **Tiny Tim (IRE)**[6] 1403 6-9-0 35 RJKilloran(7) 6 38
(AMBalding) *cl up: chsd wnr over 3f out: no ch fnl 2f* **5/1**[2]

006 **3** *nk* **Newcorr (IRE)**[6] 1407 5-9-2 35 NChalmers(5) 3 37
(JJBridger) *in tch: rdn 1/2-way: chsd ldng pair over 2f out: one pce* **33/1**

0000 **4** 8 **Divina**[20] 1220 3-8-7 30 (v[1]) DHolland 1 19
(SLKeightley) *led for 1f: cl up tl wknd wl over 2f out* **25/1**

006/ **5** 7 **Moose Malloy**[9] 3497 7-9-7 30 (p) SWhitworth 4 3
(MJRyan) *led after 1f to over 5f out: lost pl rapidly and sn t.o in last* **33/1**

0063 **6** 6 **Sennen Cove**[2] 1493 5-9-7 30 (bt) SSanders 2 —
(RBastiman) *cl up tl wknd rapidly fr 3f out: eased: t.o* **10/1**[3]

1m 41.26s (1.71) **Going Correction** 0.0s/f (Stan)

**WFA** 3 from 5yo+ 14lb 6 Ran SP% **115.5**

Speed ratings: **91,86,85,77,70 64**CSF £2.07 TOTE £1.20: £1.10, £1.80; EX 2.20 Place 6 £207.08, Place 5 £64.35..

**Owner** Paul J Dixon **Bred** Mrs Jill M Harley **Trained** Southwell, Notts

**FOCUS**

An uncompetitive event and a slow time. The winner was different class.

**NOTEBOOK**

**Beauteous(IRE)**, bidding for a six-day hat-trick, jumped up in the air as the stalls opened and gave his five rivals a start, but was still able to circle them to lead before halfway and ultimately thrash them without turning a hair. He is finding these types of races all too easy at present.

**Tiny Tim(IRE)**has had his chances and is still looking for his first win after 28 races, but he was unlucky to run into a rival at the top of his form.

**Newcorr(IRE)**, whose sole win so far came on heavy ground in Ireland, has only ever raced on this surface since arriving in this country, but does look very moderate nonetheless.

T/Plt: £343.10 to a £1 stake. Pool: £26,086.65. 55.50 winning tickets. T/Qpdt: £26.50 to a £1 stake. Pool: £2,792.10. 77.70 winning tickets. JN

# 1358 REDCAR (L-H)

Wednesday, April 21

**1549 Meeting Abandoned** - Waterlogged

# 1389 BEVERLEY (R-H)

Thursday, April 22

**OFFICIAL GOING: Good to soft (soft in places)**

The going was more testing than the official description indicated.

## 1556 WE APPRECIATE OUR WIVES CLAIMING STKS 5f

2:20 (2:20) (F) 2-Y-0 £3,045 (£870; £435) Stalls High

Form RPR

30 **1** **Why Harry**[7] 1415 2-8-13 RWinston 5 58
(JJQuinn) *trckd ldrs: effrt and nt clr run over 1f out:squeezed through to ld ins last: sn rdn and kpt on* **15/8**[1]

| | | | | | |
|---|---|---|---|---|---|
| | **2** | *nk* | **Story Of One (IRE)** 2-9-1 .......... DeanMcKeown 3<br>(RonaldThompson) *green: outpcd and sn pushed along: hdwy on outer 2f out: rdn to chal and hung rt ins last: styd on wl towards fin* **25/1** | 59+ |
| 6 | **3** | *3½* | **Straffan (IRE)**$^{10}$ 1364 2-8-10 .......... JCarroll 7<br>(EJO'Neill) *cl up: bmpd 2f out: sn rdn and slt ld over 1f out tl hdd & wknd ins last* **7/2$^{3}$** | 40 |
| 0 | **4** | *2* | **Fold Walk**$^{5}$ 1468 2-8-3 ow2 .......... PMulrennan$^{(5)}$ 1<br>(MWEasterby) *s.i.s and bhd: rdn along 1/2-way: hdwy over 1f out: kpt on ins last: nrst fin* **50/1** | 30 |
| 0 | **5** | *2½* | **Frisby Ridge (IRE)**$^{8}$ 1390 2-8-7 .......... DAllan$^{(3)}$ 4<br>(TDEasterby) *hmpd s: sn chsng ldrs: hdwy on inner over 1f out: nt clr run appr last and nt rcvr* **10/1** | 22 |
| 651 | **6** | *2* | **Von Wessex**$^{10}$ 1374 2-8-10 .......... AQuinn$^{(5)}$ 2<br>(WGMTurner) *cl up: effrt 2f out: rdn and edgd rt over 1f out: sn wknd* **11/4$^{2}$** | 19 |
| | **7** | *nk* | **Hunipot** 2-8-9 .......... TEaves$^{(5)}$ 8<br>(MESowersby) *sn outpcd and bhd tl sme late hdwy* **14/1** | 17 |
| 6 | **8** | *1* | **Our Louis**$^{5}$ 1468 2-8-7 .......... LEnstone$^{(3)}$ 6<br>(JSWainwright) *led: rdn along and edgd lft 2f out: drvn and hdd appr last: sn wknd* **20/1** | 9 |

1m 11.4s (7.40) **Going Correction** +1.25s/f (Soft) **8** Ran SP% **110.0**
Speed ratings: **90,89,83,80,76 73,73,71**CSF £50.45 TOTE £2.90: £1.10, £8.10, £1.40; EX 47.00.Story of One (IRE) was claimed by Nick Littmoden for £10,000.
**Owner** Derrick Bloy **Bred** J W Ford **Trained** Settrington, N Yorks

**FOCUS**
This proved quite a test of stamina in the prevailing ground.

**NOTEBOOK**
**Why Harry**, whose two previous outings were in better company, had to find room to make his final effort. After looking in charge, he had nothing to spare at the line.
**Story Of One(IRE)**, not yet two, was fairly clueless early on. Warming to his task, in the end he made the winner pull out all the stops. He was claimed.
**Straffan(IRE)**, who made her debut in better company, did not see it out on this bad ground on this uphill track.
**Fold Walk**, making a quick return to the track, was again slowly away. She showed a fair bit more this time and should improve again.
**Frisby Ridge(IRE)**, a close-coupled filly who is not that big, had no luck at all.
**Von Wessex**, who did not have the rail to help him this time, again came off a straight line. The heavy ground was probably against him too. *Official explanation: jockey said gelding was unsuited by the soft ground*

## 1557 CONSTANT SECURITY MAIDEN STKS — 1m 100y
**2:50** (2:50) (D) 3-Y-O+ — **£4,186** (£1,288; £644; £322) **Stalls** High

| Form | | | | RPR |
|---|---|---|---|---|
| 2 | **1** | | **Cesare**$^{15}$ 1301 3-8-11 .......... JPMurtagh 8<br>(JRFanshawe) *trckd ldrs: smooth hdwy 3f out: led ins last: comf* **1/2$^{1}$** | 73+ |
| | **2** | *1¾* | **Chanteloup** 3-8-6 .......... KDarley 10<br>(JRFanshawe) *towards rr: hdwy on outer 3f out and sn pushed along: rdn over 1f out: kpt on wl* **6/1$^{2}$** | 64+ |
| 66 | **3** | *1* | **Premier Dream (USA)**$^{7}$ 1419 3-8-11 .......... JFanning 7<br>(MJohnston) *led: rdn along 2f out: drvn and hdd ins last* **14/1** | 67 |
| | **4** | *shd* | **Estepona** 3-8-11 .......... JQuinn 9<br>(MissJACamacho) *s.i.s and bhd: gd hdwy 2f out: rdn and kpt on ins last: nrst fin* **50/1** | 67 |
| 0- | **5** | *1¼* | **Snowed Under**$^{167}$ 5940 3-8-11 .......... CCatlin 5<br>(JDBethell) *towards rr tl styd on fnl 2f: nrst fin* **66/1** | 64 |
| 000- | **6** | *½* | **Kalishka (IRE)**$^{234}$ 4627 3-8-11 .......... WSupple 2<br>(AndrewTurnell) *in tch: hdwy 3f out: rdn and one pce fnl 2f* **33/1** | 63 |
| 5-0 | **7** | *½* | **Top Achiever (IRE)**$^{12}$ 1325 3-8-11 .......... RWinston 3<br>(MrsLStubbs) *in tch: hdwy 3f out: swtchd ins 2f out: sn rdn and btn* **25/1** | 62 |
| 5 | **8** | *7* | **Lucky Piscean**$^{24}$ 1174 3-8-11 .......... KDalgleish 12<br>(CWFairhurst) *in tch: rdn along 3f out: sn wknd* **20/1** | 47 |
| 6 | **9** | *11* | **Illicium (IRE)**$^{11}$ 1344 5-9-6 .......... JCarroll 1<br>(MrsMReveley) *s.i.s: a rr* **50/1** | 19 |
| 4- | **10** | *1* | **Adees Dancer**$^{183}$ 5701 3-8-6 .......... RFfrench 4<br>(BSmart) *chsd ldrs: rdn along 3f out: sn wknd* **8/1$^{3}$** | 17 |
| 400- | **11** | *7* | **Let's Party (IRE)**$^{168}$ 5933 4-9-3 52 .......... (t) DAllan$^{(3)}$ 6<br>(PLClinton) *chsd ldr: rdn along 3f out: sn wknd* **66/1** | 2 |

1m 53.59s (6.29) **Going Correction** +0.75s/f (Yiel)
**WFA** 3 from 4yo+ 14lb **11** Ran SP% **117.2**
Speed ratings: **98,96,95,95,93 93,92,85,74,73 66**CSF £3.37 TOTE £1.50: £1.10, £1.60, £2.20; EX 5.70.
**Owner** Cheveley Park Stud **Bred** Cheveley Park Stud Ltd **Trained** Newmarket, Suffolk

**FOCUS**
A modest maiden but the first two should progress.

**NOTEBOOK**
**Cesare** is not very big but is well put together. He made this look simple and connections will be hoping for a realistic handicap mark. His action suggests he will be even better on much less testing ground.
**Chanteloup** made a pleasing bow and this late foal will improve, especially over further. She should find a race or two.
**Premier Dream(USA)**, who finished some way behind the winner at Warwick two outings ago, had the run of the race but was still nowhere near good enough.
**Estepona**, a late foal, showed ability on his debut and will be suited by further in due course.
**Snowed Under**, who showed next to nothing in one backend outing at two, stayed on in his own time and this will have taught him something.
**Kalishka(IRE)** showed a fait bit more than he had done in three starts at two.
**Top Achiever(IRE)** ran his best race to date on this third start and is now qualified for handicaps.
**Lucky Piscean** *Official explanation: jockey said gelding hung right-handed in the straight*

## 1558 JAGUAR CENTRE STKS (H'CAP) — 7f 100y
**3:20** (3:20) (C) (0-90,90) 3-Y-O — **£9,486** (£2,919; £1,459; £729) **Stalls** High

| Form | | | | RPR |
|---|---|---|---|---|
| 3-41 | **1** | | **Imperialistic (IRE)**$^{12}$ 1322 3-9-7 **90** .......... (p) KDalgleish 3<br>(KRBurke) *dwlt: hld up in tch: hdwy on inner over 2f out rdn to chal ent last: drvn and kpt on to ld nr fin* **9/4$^{1}$** | 97 |
| 5-43 | **2** | *shd* | **Man Of Letters (UAE)**$^{15}$ 1304 3-8-4 **73** .......... RFfrench 5<br>(MJohnston) *chsd ldr: led 2f out: sn rdn: drvn and edgd rt ins last: hdd nr fin* **7/2$^{2}$** | 80 |
| 1 | **3** | *1¾* | **Wistman (UAE)**$^{15}$ 1295 3-8-11 **80** .......... JPMurtagh 6<br>(DRLoder) *trckd ldrs: hdwy 3f out: swtchd lft and effrt over 1f out: sn rdn and one pce ins last* **9/4$^{1}$** | 82 |
| 12-0 | **4** | *8* | **Kingsmaite**$^{26}$ 1129 3-8-5 **74** .......... JBramhill 1<br>(SRBowring) *chsd ldrs: pushed along over 2f out: rdn over 1f out and sn btn* **8/1$^{3}$** | 56 |
| 4-30 | **5** | *1¼* | **Wavertree Girl (IRE)**$^{39}$ 1015 3-8-11 **80** .......... KDarley 2<br>(NPLittmoden) *a rr* **20/1** | 59 |
| 413- | **6** | *1¼* | **Vademecum**$^{183}$ 5708 3-8-13 **82** .......... FLynch 7<br>(BSmart) *led: rdn along and hdd 2f out: sn wknd* **16/1** | 58 |
| 24-6 | **7** | *hd* | **Royal Distant (USA)**$^{12}$ 1322 3-8-10 **79** .......... DaleGibson 4<br>(MWEasterby) *a rr* **16/1** | 55 |

1m 37.69s (3.39) **Going Correction** +0.75s/f (Yiel) **7** Ran SP% **111.4**
Speed ratings: **110,109,107,98,97 95,95**CSF £9.79 TOTE £3.50: £2.00, £1.80; EX 12.40 Trifecta £1045.20 Part won. Pool of £1,472.16 - 0.30 winning tickets..
**Owner** Bigwigs Bloodstock II **Bred** B H Bloodstock **Trained** Middleham Moor, N Yorks

**FOCUS**
A smart time for the grade, and useful looking form. The first three were well clear.

**NOTEBOOK**
**Imperialistic(IRE)**, 6lb higher, followed up by the skin of her teeth. She deserves a short break now.
**Man Of Letters(UAE)**, on his handicap bow, took it up but came off a straight line giving the winner a second bite at the cherry. Hopefully this will have made a man of him.
**Wistman(UAE)** if anything proved suited by this slightly stiffer test. This will have taught him plenty.
**Kingsmaite** seems much better suited by the All-Weather.
**Wavertree Girl(IRE)** seems to have started life in handicap company from a stiff mark.
**Vademecum** looks harshly treated with an official rating of 82.
**Royal Distant(USA)** looks to need still more time.

## 1559 BIRTHDAY CELEBRATION H'CAP — 1m 1f 207y
**3:50** (3:50) (E) (0-75,75) 3-Y-O — **£4,550** (£1,400; £700; £350) **Stalls** High

| Form | | | | RPR |
|---|---|---|---|---|
| 00-3 | **1** | | **Another Choice (IRE)**$^{22}$ 1214 3-8-12 **66** .......... (t) KDarley 1<br>(NPLittmoden) *trckd ldrs: hdwy 3f out: ridden to ld appr last: sn clr* **6/1$^{2}$** | 83+ |
| 00-4 | **2** | *7* | **Athollbrose (USA)**$^{10}$ 1360 3-8-2 **56** .......... JQuinn 10<br>(TDEasterby) *chsd ldr: led 2f out: sn rdn: drvn and hdd appr last: nt match pce of wnr* **12/1** | 55 |
| 500- | **3** | *1½* | **Dunlea Dancer**$^{185}$ 5671 3-8-2 **56** .......... RFfrench 12<br>(MJohnston) *chsd ldrs on inner: hdwy 3f out: rdn and kpt on same pce appr last* **10/1$^{3}$** | 52 |
| 0-05 | **4** | *1¼* | **The King Of Rock**$^{10}$ 1365 3-8-3 **57** .......... SWhitworth 7<br>(AGNewcombe) *hld up in rr: hdwy 4f out: effrt to chse ldrs on outer 2f out: sn rdn and one pce* **9/2$^{1}$** | 51 |
| 00-0 | **5** | *1½* | **Nafferton Heights (IRE)**$^{24}$ 1174 3-7-12 **52** .......... DaleGibson 2<br>(MWEasterby) *led: rdn along 3f out: hdd 2f out and grad wknd* **20/1** | 43 |
| 0213 | **6** | *3* | **Platinum Pirate**$^{2}$ 1529 3-8-7 **61** 6ex .......... (v) FLynch 8<br>(KRBurke) *plld hrd: hld up towards rr: hdwy 3f out: rdn 2f out and sn one pce* **9/2$^{1}$** | 47 |
| 640- | **7** | *¾* | **Our Kid**$^{260}$ 3888 3-8-7 **64** .......... DAllan$^{(3)}$ 3<br>(TDEasterby) *s.i.s and bhd tl sme late hdwy* **40/1** | 49 |
| -241 | **8** | *2* | **Time To Relax (IRE)**$^{14}$ 1309 3-8-12 **66** .......... KDalgleish 9<br>(JJQuinn) *towards rr: hdwy 3f out:sn rdn and no imp fnl 2f* **9/2$^{1}$** | 47 |
| 00-5 | **9** | *6* | **Hernando's Boy**$^{16}$ 1285 3-8-8 **62** .......... JCarroll 5<br>(MrsMReveley) *bhd: gd hdwy on outer over 2f out: rdn and wknd over 1f out* **12/1** | 32 |
| 46-6 | **10** | *5* | **Raheed (IRE)**$^{20}$ 1227 3-8-12 **66** .......... WSupple 6<br>(EALDunlop) *midfield: hdwy to chse ldrs 3f out: rdn 2f out and grad wknd* **11/1** | 27 |
| 224- | **11** | *5* | **Named At Dinner**$^{183}$ 5708 3-9-7 **75** .......... GDuffield 4<br>(MrsADuffield) *prom: rdn along 3f out and sn wknd* **25/1** | 27 |
| 04-0 | **12** | *18* | **Baboushka (IRE)**$^{19}$ 1250 3-8-5 **59** .......... RWinston 11<br>(MissJACamacho) *midfield: rdn along over 3f out: sn wknd* **14/1** | — |

2m 12.26s (5.06) **Going Correction** +0.75s/f (Yiel) **12** Ran SP% **119.4**
Speed ratings: **109,103,102,101,100 97,97,95,90,86 82,68**CSF £74.66 CT £716.65 TOTE £7.20: £2.70, £3.60, £3.70; EX 77.00.
**Owner** A A Goodman **Bred** Lloyd Farm Stud **Trained** Newmarket, Suffolk

**FOCUS**
A very decent time for the grade.

**NOTEBOOK**
**Another Choice(IRE)**, worst drawn, seemed to be well suited by the step up in trip. He came right away and connections will be keen to turn him out under a penalty for he is re-assesed.
**Athollbrose(USA)** ran easily his best race so far, though in the end was left for dead.
**Dunlea Dancer**, dropped 8lb compared to his nursery debut, ran five times in all at two. He shaped a lot better and should improve for the outing.
**The King Of Rock**, out of luck last time, did best of the hold-up horses but remains a maiden after 11 starts.
**Nafferton Heights(IRE)**, having only his fifth outing and on his handicap bow, made the running but did not get home in the conditions. He has at least started at the right end of the handicap.
**Platinum Pirate**, having his second outing in three days, would not settle and never really entered the argument. He will struggle once his new mark kicks in.
**Time To Relax(IRE)**, 2lb higher, was stepping up in trip and never got competitive.
**Hernando's Boy** *Official explanation: jockey said gelding lost its action*

## 1560 RACING AGAIN ON SATURDAY 8TH MAY FILLIES' H'CAP — 1m 1f 207y
**4:20** (4:21) (E) (0-70,65) 4-Y-O+ — **£3,679** (£1,132; £566; £283) **Stalls** High

| Form | | | | RPR |
|---|---|---|---|---|
| 42-6 | **1** | | **Megan's Magic**$^{19}$ 1247 4-9-5 **60** .......... JBramhill 8<br>(WStorey) *slowly away and bhd: hdwy over 3f out: swtchd rt 2f out: nt clr run 11/2f out: sn rdn and styd on strly to ld iside last* **9/1** | 73 |
| 60-4 | **2** | *3* | **Got To Be Cash**$^{31}$ 1079 5-7-6 **40** .......... BSwarbrick$^{(7)}$ 6<br>(WMBrisbourne) *midfield: in tch 1/2-way: hdwy to chal 2f out: sn rdn: drvn to ld briefly ins last: sn hdd and one pce* **13/2$^{1}$** | 48 |
| 00-2 | **3** | *1* | **Transcendantale (FR)**$^{10}$ 1376 6-8-0 **41** ow1 .......... CCatlin 7<br>(MrsSLamyman) *in tch: rdn along 2f out: kpt on u.p ins last* **7/1$^{2}$** | 47 |
| 1026 | **4** | *1¾* | **Jade Star (USA)**$^{5}$ 1479 4-8-12 **53** .......... FLynch 9<br>(MissGayKelleway) *led: rdn along 3f out: drvn 2f out: hdd & wknd ins last* **12/1** | 56 |
| /00- | **5** | *¾* | **Untidy Daughter**$^{10}$ 5705 5-8-9 **55** .......... (b$^{1}$) TEaves$^{(5)}$ 13<br>(BEllison) *in tch: hdwy to chse ldrs on inner 3f out: rdn 2f out: kpt on same pce appr last* **7/1$^{2}$** | 57 |
| 010- | **6** | *nk* | **Life Is Beautiful (IRE)**$^{199}$ 5419 5-8-5 **46** .......... DaleGibson 1<br>(WHTinning) *prom: rdn along 3f out: grad wknd fnl 2f* **10/1** | 47 |
| 452- | **7** | *1¾* | **Olivia Rose (IRE)**$^{168}$ 5937 5-9-5 **60** .......... JQuinn 4<br>(JPearce) *hld up towards rr: hdwy 4f out: rdn over 2f out and sn no imp* **9/1** | 58 |
| | **8** | *shd* | **Acola (FR)**$^{108}$ 4-9-5 **60** .......... JPMurtagh 15<br>(RMHCowell) *in tch on inner: rdn along 3f out: sn drvn and one pce* **20/1** | 58 |
| 6063 | **9** | *nk* | **Desires Destiny**$^{6}$ 1444 6-8-4 **45** .......... TWilliams 3<br>(MBrittain) *keen: hld up: hdwy over 4f out: rdn along 3f out and n.d* **33/1** | 42 |
| 350- | **10** | *¾* | **Uno Mente**$^{211}$ 5151 5-9-7 **62** .......... KimTinkler 2<br>(DonEnricoIncisa) *a rr* **40/1** | 58 |
| 6251 | **11** | *2½* | **Dash Of Magic**$^{39}$ 1026 6-8-4 **45** .......... GDuffield 5<br>(JHetherton) *midfield: hdwy on outer to chse ldrs 4f out: rdn along 2f out and sn wknd* **15/2$^{3}$** | 36 |

4-04 **12** 1/2 **Half Inch**[15] [1298] 4-9-5 **60**.................................................(p) WSupple 14 51
(BICase) *midfield: hdwy to chse ldrs 3f out: sn rdn and wknd fnl 2f* **15/2**[3]
340- **13** 5 **Dormy Two (IRE)**[10] [5426] 4-9-0 **55**....................................(p) GParkin 10 37
(JSWainwright) *a rr: bhd fr 1/2-way* **33/1**
-000 **14** 1 **Karathaena (IRE)**[17] [1275] 4-9-3 **65**............................. HGemberlu(7) 11 45
(JWHills) *bhd fr 1/2-way* **16/1**
556- **15** hd **Green Ocean**[236] [4579] 4-9-3 **58**.......................................... RWinston 12 37
(JWUnett) *in tch: rdn along and n.m.r over 4f out: sn wknd* **50/1**

2m 14.32s (7.12) **Going Correction** +0.75s/f (Yiel) **15** Ran SP% **119.6**
Speed ratings: **101,98,97,96,95 95,94,94,93,93 91,90,86,86,85**CSF £62.23 CT £441.71 TOTE £8.60: £3.10, £2.30, £3.30; EX 83.50.
**Owner** Steve Howard And Tony Peters **Bred** Mrs N A Ward And W J Musson **Trained** Muggleswick, Co Durham

**FOCUS**
Just a steady gallop in what was in effect a 0-65 handicap.

**NOTEBOOK**
**Megan's Magic**, after a sluggish start, had to seek room. In the end she won going away.
**Got To Be Cash**, a long-standing maiden, did absolutely nothing wrong.
**Transcendantale(FR)**, runner-up a year ago from a 4lb higher mark, stuck to her task in willing fashion but has a poor win-to-run ratio.
**Jade Star(USA)**, in good heart on the All-Weather, seems to find this trip stretching her to the very limit, especially on a track with such a stiff uphill finish as this.
**Untidy Daughter**, improved over hurdles, wore blinkers instead of the usual cheekpieces. She is worth a try over a bit further.
**Life Is Beautiful(IRE)**, who likes it round here, had the worst of the draw. There will be other days.

## 1561 GO RACING IN YORKSHIRE SEASON TICKET MEDIAN AUCTION MAIDEN STKS 1m 4f 16y
**4:50** (4:50) (E) 3-Y-O **£3,523** (£1,084; £542; £271) **Stalls** High

Form RPR
-223 **1** **Vantage (IRE)**[9] [1387] 3-9-0 **80**................................................. KDarley 1 72+
(NPLittmoden) *trckd ldng pair: hdwy to ld 3f out: sn clr: styd on* **10/11**[1]
04-0 **2** 7 **Holly Walk**[10] [1363] 3-8-6 **50**...........................................(b[1]) LEnstone(3) 2 56?
(MDods) *trckd ldrs: hdwy on outer 3f out: rdn and styd on fnl 2f: no ch w wnr* **40/1**
3 **3** 14 **At Your Request**[16] [1285] 3-9-0 ............................................. WSupple 3 40
(EALDunlop) *cl up: led after 4f: rdn along and hdd 3f out: sn drvn and wknd* **7/4**[2]
0 **4** 18 **Serengeti Sky (USA)**[16] [1285] 3-9-0 ................................. JPMurtagh 4 13
(DRLoder) *green: led 4f: cl up and rdn along 1/2-way: drvn over 3f out and sn wknd* **5/1**[3]

2m 51.63s (12.33) **Going Correction** +0.75s/f (Yiel) **4** Ran SP% **107.9**
Speed ratings: **88,83,74,62**CSF £20.67 TOTE £2.10; EX 11.80 Place 6 £40.30, Place 5 £24.42.
**Owner** Mark Harniman **Bred** Michael Dalton **Trained** Newmarket, Suffolk

**FOCUS**
A very slow winning time and basically a one-horse race.

**NOTEBOOK**
**Vantage(IRE)** had easily the best credentials and made this look very simple. He was not winning out of turn.
**Holly Walk**, rated just 50 after five starts at two, wore blinkers for the first time and was taking a step up in trip. She had 19lb to find with the winner on RPR.
**At Your Request** finished a long way behind the runner-up, who is rated just 50, and his Pontefract form has taken a few knocks.
**Serengeti Sky(USA)** again ran badly. Connections must be clinging to the hope that testing ground has been responsible for his two dire efforts. *Official explanation: trainer said colt finished distressed*

T/Plt: £65.90 to a £1 stake. Pool: £34,879.40. 385.90 winning tickets. T/Qpdt: £33.70 to a £1 stake. Pool: £1,945.00. 42.60 winning tickets. JR

# SALISBURY (R-H)
Thursday, April 22
**1562 Meeting Abandoned** - Waterlogged

# 1510 WOLVERHAMPTON (A.W) (L-H)
Thursday, April 22

**OFFICIAL GOING: Standard**
Wind: almost nil Weather: fine

## 1568 £10 FREE BET @ BETDIRECT.CO.UK BANDED STKS 5f (F)
**5:45** (5:45) (H) 3-Y-O+ **£1,424** (£407; £203) **Stalls** Low

Form RPR
0225 **1** **Tuscan Dream**[6] [1443] 9-9-2 **35**......................................... PBradley(5) 2 41
(ABerry) *led: hdd over 3f out: led over 1f out: rdn out* **5/2**[1]
4550 **2** 1 1/4 **Levelled**[6] [1443] 10-9-7 **35**................................................ ACulhane 6 37
(DWChapman) *led over 3f out: hdd over 1f out: r.o* **5/2**[1]
6-60 **3** 5 **Vaudevire**[23] [1192] 3-8-8 **30**.............................................(b[1]) THamilton(3) 7 19
(RPElliott) *chsd ldrs: rdn 1/2-way: sn outpcd* **16/1**
0036 **4** 1/2 **Bond Domingo**[6] [1445] 5-9-0 **35**......................................(v) MStainton(7) 4 17
(BSmart) *chsd ldrs: rdn 1/2-way: sn outpcd* **3/1**[2]
0-00 **5** 1 1/4 **Dancing Ridge (IRE)**[16] [1283] 7-9-7 **30**......................... PHanagan 1 12
(ASenior) *prom: outpcd 1/2-way: n.d after* **14/1**
0000 **6** 5 **Mesmerised**[87] [608] 4-9-7 **30**...........................................(p) AnnStokell 5 —
(MissAStokell) *sn pushed along and prom: wknd 1/2-way* **12/1**
40-0 **7** 7 **Littleton Liberty**[53] [927] 3-8-8 **35**.....................................(p) TPQueally(3) 3 —
(AndrewReid) *bhd fr 1/2-way* **7/1**[3]

63.62 secs (0.82) **Going Correction** +0.025s/f (Slow)
**WFA** 3 from 4yo+ 10lb **7** Ran SP% **114.9**
Speed ratings: **94,92,84,83,81 73,62**CSF £9.06 TOTE £2.70: £1.30, £2.00; EX 5.30.
**Owner** Galaxy Moss Side Racing Clubs Limited **Bred** F Hines **Trained** Cockerham, Lancs

**FOCUS**
A routine banded stakes and the order did not change very much during the contest.

**NOTEBOOK**
**Tuscan Dream** broke well, but looked up against it when the runner-up took over in front before the end of the back straight. He does not normally show his best when taken on for the early lead, but dug deep and saw the race out the stronger, which shows how weak this race was.
**Levelled** was in front after a furlong and looked to be travelling very well in front, but he is a weak finisher these days and the winner had the legs of him in the home straight.
**Vaudevire**, unplaced in three maidens at up to a mile, managed to plod on for third but his best trip remains a mystery.
**Bond Domingo**, with the visor back on, had every chance but continues on the decline.

## 1569 £10 FREE BET @ BETDIRECT.CO.UK CLAIMING STKS 6f (F)
**6:15** (6:15) (H) 3-Y-O+ **£1,438** (£411; £205) **Stalls** Low

Form RPR
00-0 **1** **Pedro Jack (IRE)**[23] [1185] 7-9-3 **83**.................................. JFMcDonald(5) 6 64
(BJMeehan) *a.p: chsd ldr over 2f out: rdn to ld last strides* **5/6**[1]
0131 **2** nk **On The Trail**[20] [1237] 7-9-8 **50**........................................... ACulhane 2 63
(DWChapman) *led: edgd rt wl over 1f out: hdd last strides* **7/2**[2]
2400 **3** nk **Speedfit Free (IRE)**[16] [1283] 7-9-4 **52**...............................(b) PHanagan 3 58
(ISemple) *chsd ldrs: outpcd over 3f out: rallied over 1f out: ev ch ins fnl f: r.o* **7/1**[3]
0502 **4** 1 1/4 **Teyaar**[5] [1474] 8-9-3 **53**....................................................... HayleyTurner(5) 4 58
(MrsNMacauley) *a.p: chsd ldr over 3f out to over 2f out: styd on same pce appr fnl f* **7/1**[3]
30 **5** 3 1/2 **Pips Song (IRE)**[39] [1018] 9-8-13 **50**....................................... RMiles(3) 1 42
(PWHiatt) *chsd ldrs over 4f* **14/1**

1m 16.32s (0.52) **Going Correction** +0.025s/f (Slow)
**WFA** 3 from 7yo+ 11lb **5** Ran SP% **108.4**
Speed ratings: **97,96,96,94,89** CT £1.70 TOTE £1.10: £1.60, £; EX4.90 1.Pedro Jack was claimed by M A Buckley for £5,000. Teeyaar was claimed Mark Wallings for £3,000. Speedfit Free was claimed by Ann Stokell for £3,000.
**Owner** Michael F B Peart **Bred** Miss Laura G F Ferguson **Trained** Upper Lambourn, Berks

**FOCUS**
Only a modest claimer, despite being contested by better horses than you normally find at a Regional meeting.

**NOTEBOOK**
**Pedro Jack(IRE)** had a ton in hand of his four rivals at the weights, but it took him an age to get on top and he ran a long way below his 83 rating. That did not stop Mark Buckley from claiming him for £5,000, but he will not be easy to place and probably needs to stick to races like this.
**On The Trail** had a lot to do against the favourite at the weights but, given his usual positive ride, was mugged only in the last couple of strides. Finishing so close to a much higher-rated rival would normally be a disaster for his handicap mark, but his performance is likely to be measured through those that finished behind him.
**Speedfit Free(IRE)** usually goes well here and this performance was as good as anything he has shown over the past year or so, especially as he stuck to the inside down the home straight while the other pair raced wide. He now joins Ann Stokell.
**Teyaar**, who manages one win a year these days and was having his 88th race, did not run badly and seems to stand up to his very busy schedule well enough. He was subsequently claimed.
**Pips Song(IRE)** *Official explanation: jockey said gelding was never travelling*

## 1570 BETDIRECT.CO.UK TRI-BANDED STKS 1m 1f 79y(F)
**6:45** (6:45) (H) 3-Y-O **£1,421** (£406; £203) **Stalls** Low

Form RPR
5424 **1** **Secret Bloom**[6] [1447] 3-9-0 **45**...............................................(v) JFEgan 6 48
(JRNorton) *a.p: chsd ldr over 6f out: rdn to ld over 3f out: sn clr* **11/10**[1]
00-0 **2** 3 **True To Yourself (USA)**[12] [1325] 3-9-0 **45**......................... ACulhane 5 42
(JGGiven) *a.p: rdn to chse wnr over 2f out: no imp* **7/2**[2]
00-0 **3** 2 1/2 **Royal Upstart**[17] [1267] 3-9-0 **45**..........................................(b[1]) SWKelly 3 37
(WMBrisbourne) *sn led: hdd over 3f out: sn outpcd* **7/1**
00-0 **4** 3 **Upthedale (IRE)**[15] [1300] 3-9-0 **45**...................................... PHanagan 2 31
(JRWeymes) *chsd ldrs: outpcd 5f out: no ch whn rdr dropped whip over 1f out* **7/1**
6650 **5** shd **Platinum Chief**[53] [939] 3-8-7 **45**....................................... PPMathers(7) 4 31
(ABerry) *broke wl: sn outpcd and bhd* **6/1**[3]

2m 5.42s (2.42) **Going Correction** +0.025s/f (Slow) **5** Ran SP% **109.1**
Speed ratings: **90,87,85,82,82**CSF £5.05 TOTE £1.60: £1.10, £2.70; EX 7.90.
**Owner** Reddal Racing **Bred** J And Mrs Bowtell **Trained** High Hoyland, S Yorks

**FOCUS**
A poor contest and a moderate winning time, even for a race like this.

**NOTEBOOK**
**Secret Bloom** has not looked that enthusiastic in the past, but on this occasion his rider was not prepared to accept any messing about. Off the bridle racing down the back straight, his jockey kept riding him along vigorously even after the combination had taken the lead and set sail for home with three furlongs still to run. This was such a poor race that none of his rivals were able to get close enough to take advantage.
**True To Yourself(USA)**, beaten a total of 121 lengths in four previous outings, was down in class and up in trip and stayed on to finish second at a respectful distance without achieving very much.
**Royal Upstart**, who has been very disappointing since making the frame in a Haydock seller last spring, tried to be positive in the first-time blinkers, but once the winner was booted past him he looked very slow.
**Upthedale(IRE)** looks a very poor performer indeed.
**Platinum Chief** was quickly restrained over the longest trip he has attempted to date, but never got competitive after that.

## 1571 NEW SITE @ BETDIRECT.CO.UK TRI-BANDED STKS 6f (F)
**7:15** (7:15) (H) 3-Y-O **£1,431** (£409; £204) **Stalls** Low

Form RPR
0000 **1** **Little Flute**[54] [918] 3-9-0 **45**............................................ PDoe 3 51
(TKeddy) *chsd ldrs: rdn to ld over 1f out: edgd lft ins fnl f: r.o* **3/1**[1]
-046 **2** 2 **Fayr Firenze (IRE)**[16] [1280] 3-9-0 **45**................................(v) SRighton 7 45
(MFHarris) *w ldr: led 4f out: sn hdd: led over 2f out: rdn and hdd over 1f out: no ex ins fnl f* **3/1**[1]
00-0 **3** 5 **Dress Pearl**[23] [1190] 3-8-2 **35** ow1....................................(p) THamilton(3) 1 21
(RPElliott) *w ldrs: sn pushed along: led over 3f out: rdn and hdd over 2f out: wknd fnl f* **10/1**
6400 **4** 2 1/2 **Indrani**[20] [1236] 3-8-7 **45**.................................................. DFentiman(7) 2 23
(JohnAHarris) *chsd ldrs: rdn over 2f out: wknd over 1f out* **5/1**[3]
006- **5** 6 **Weaver Spell**[294] [2919] 3-8-9 **40**........................................ VHalliday 6 —
(JRNorton) *chsd ldrs over 3f* **20/1**
6-00 **6** 3 **Sparkling Clear**[23] [1184] 3-9-0 **45**....................................... MHenry 4 —
(RMHCowell) *led 2f: rdn and ev ch whn n.m.r 2f out: sn wknd* **7/1**
4-00 **7** 12 **Simply Red**[15] [1304] 3-8-10 **40** ow1....................................(v) ACulhane 5 —
(RBrotherton) *s.i.s: sn prom: wknd 1/2-way* **7/2**[2]

1m 16.93s (1.13) **Going Correction** +0.025s/f (Slow) **7** Ran SP% **115.2**
Speed ratings: **93,90,83,80,72 68,52**CSF £12.43 TOTE £5.90: £2.10, £2.40; EX 12.90.
**Owner** Mrs H Keddy **Bred** H Parkes And G Rock **Trained** Newmarket, Suffolk

**FOCUS**
A moderate contest, though the pace was fair.

**NOTEBOOK**
**Little Flute**, well backed, was making his debut at this level and had been gelded since his last run. He found the drop in grade doing the trick, but will probably need to stay at this level if he is to win again, and that is up to the Handicapper.
**Fayr Firenze(IRE)** ran his best race to date, but he has already looked exposed at this level and this effort demonstrates the weakness of the contest.
**Dress Pearl** was well beaten and has never really shown much aptitude for sand. Her best form to date has been on very soft ground on turf.
**Indrani**, making her debut at this level, never got competitive.



The Form Book, Raceform Ltd, Compton, RG20 6NL

**Simply Red**, stepping back from a mile and making his sand debut, did not go unbacked on this drop in class but was a beaten horse at halfway.

## 1572 BET DIRECT ON SKY ACTIVE BANDED STKS 1m 4f (F)
7:45 (7:45) (H) 3-Y-O+ £1,435 (£410; £205) Stalls Low

Form RPR
25-3 1 **Bosphorus**[3] 1492 5-9-0 45 (v) DNolan(5) 4 51
(DGBridgwater) *a.p: trckd ldr 6f out: led over 4f out: clr over 2f out : eased nr fin* 11/4[2]
-261 2 2 1/2 **Red Moor (IRE)**[7] 1426 4-9-10 45 AColhane 2 53
(RHollinshead) *a.p: rdn to chse wnr over 3f out: no imp fnl 2f* 5/2[1]
0553 3 9 **Western Command (GER)**[6] 1448 8-9-5 45 (p) JoannaBadger 6 34
(MrsNMacauley) *w ldr: plld hrd: led over 8f out: hdd over 4f out: wknd 3f out* 11/1
3420 4 9 **Bevier**[16] 1282 10-9-0 45 NChalmers(5) 1 20
(TWall) *hld up in tch: wknd over 4f out* 5/2[1]
-553 5 5 **Vitelucy**[23] 1193 5-9-0 40 (p) AQuinn(5) 5 13
(MissSJWilton) *led over 3f: wknd over 4f out* 5/1[3]
-005 6 20 **Wethaab (USA)**[3] 1511 7-9-5 30 (tp) AnnStokell 3 —
(MissAStokell) *hld up: wknd over 4f out* 50/1

2m 40.95s (-0.85) **Going Correction** +0.025s/f (Slow)
**WFA** 4 from 5yo+ 1lb 6 Ran SP% **110.8**
Speed ratings: **103,101,95,89,86 72**CSF £9.76 TOTE £2.90: £1.60, £1.50; EX 23.70.
**Owner** Led Astray Again Partnership **Bred** Juddmonte Farms **Trained** Winchcombe, Gloucs

**FOCUS**
A decent time for a banded stakes and the strong pace suited the proven stayers.

**NOTEBOOK**
**Bosphorus**, a maiden after 14 attempts going into this, goes well here and stays further. In a race run at a decent pace, that was all that was required.
**Red Moor(IRE)** pulled right away from the rest of the field along with the winner, but under his penalty could never quite get on terms with him and he may be better suited by the longer straight at Southwell.
**Western Command(GER)** pulled hard in front and did far too much too soon, but at least he made sure this was run at a true pace.
**Bevier** should have had no problem with the trip nor the track so this was a poor effort. There seemed no valid excuse, unless age is finally catching up with him.
**Vitelucy** ideally needs further, but this was still a moderate performance.

## 1573 BET IN RUNNING @ BETDIRECT.CO.UK BANDED STKS 7f (F)
8:15 (8:15) (H) 3-Y-O+ £1,435 (£410; £205) Stalls High

Form RPR
4111 1 **Beauteous (IRE)**[1] 1548 5-9-6 35 KGhunowa(7) 2 58+
(MJPolglase) *chsd ldrs: led over 4f out: clr over 1f out* 4/9[1]
0111 2 5 **Baytown Flyer**[1] 1544 4-9-10 35 BReilly(3) 7 45+
(PSMcentee) *led 1f: w ldr: rdn over 2f out: outpcd over 1f out* 7/2[2]
643 3 1 1/4 **Countrywide Girl (IRE)**[3] 1510 5-9-2 30 PBradley(5) 8 36
(ABerry) *led 6f out: hdd over 4f out: styng on same pce whn hung lft fnl f* 16/1[3]
0503 4 3 1/2 **Mystic Promise (IRE)**[6] 1447 3-8-3 30 (t) HayleyTurner(5) 3 27
(MrsNMacauley) *outpcd: styd on appr fnl f: nvr nrr* 50/1
6000 5 1/2 **Un Autre Espere**[7] 1403 5-9-7 30 (b) LVickers 6 26
(TWall) *chsd ldrs: outpcd over 5f out: n.d after* 100/1
0056 6 shd **Welsh Whisper**[3] 1510 5-9-2 35 NChalmers(5) 4 26
(SABrookshaw) *s.i.s: outpcd: hdwy 1/2-way: rdn over 2f out: wknd over 1f out* 66/1
-000 7 4 **Peartree House (IRE)**[73] 730 10-9-7 30 ACulhane 5 16
(DWChapman) *outpcd* 20/1
55/4 8 10 **Power And Demand**[3] 1513 7-9-7 35 (t) RFfrench 1 —
(KGWingrove) *outpcd* 80/1

1m 30.73s (0.41) **Going Correction** +0.025s/f (Slow)
**WFA** 3 from 4yo+ 13lb 8 Ran SP% **107.8**
Speed ratings: **98,92,90,86,86 86,81,70**CSF £1.73 TOTE £1.20: £1.02, £1.10, £2.30; EX 1.70 Place 6 £2.09, Place 5 £2.03.
**Owner** Paul J Dixon **Bred** Mrs Jill M Harley **Trained** Southwell, Notts

**FOCUS**
An above-average contest of its type with two horses coming into it looking for four-timers.

**NOTEBOOK**
**Beauteous(IRE)** continues to make hay at this level. He has already shown that he does not have to lead early, so it was not a problem to him here and once he took over at halfway, he was then always in total control. He is due to go up to 57 from Saturday, so it was a shrewd move to keep running him in these races and connections were fortunate there were so many regional meetings on sand during the past fortnight.
**Baytown Flyer**, like the winner bidding for a quick four-timer, did not seem to be helped by being taken on for the early lead and, although she was right there alongside the other two leaders for much of the way, it was obvious from some way out that the winner was running all over her. It has still been a successful eight days for her though.
**Countrywide Girl(IRE)**, without a win in three and a half years, was given a positive ride but found the winner far too good for her from halfway. This was a slightly more competitive event of its type than usual, but that does not mean she is a winner waiting to happen.
**Mystic Promise(IRE)** is very poor, though the drop back in trip would not have been in his favour.
T/Plt: £5.30 to a £1 stake. Pool: £32,481.40. 4,444.85 winning tickets. T/Qpdt: £3.10 to a £1 stake. Pool: £2,362.60. 552.20 winning tickets. CR

# 1435 LONGCHAMP (R-H)
Thursday, April 22

**OFFICIAL GOING: Good to soft**

## 1578a PRIX DE BARBEVILLE (GROUP 3) 1m 7f 110y
1:20 (1:19) 4-Y-O+ £25,704 (£10,282; £7,711; £5,141)

RPR
1 **Westerner**[179] 5782 5-9-6 DBoeuf 6 120+
(ELellouche, France) *held up in last, headway on outside over 1 1/2f out, edged right, led inside final f, pushed out, ran on strongly* 1
2 2 **Forestier (FR)**[42] 4-8-9 C-PLemaire 4 111
(EDanel, France) *raced in 4th, 3rd straight, ridden & slightly hampered 1f out, stayed on under pressure to take 2nd final strides* 3
3 shd **Idaho Quest**[28] 1110 7-8-11 OPeslier 5 109
(H-APantall, France) *raced keenly in 5th, effort over 1f out, still 5th 50yds out, stayed on down outside to take 3rd close home*
4 nse **Le Carre (USA)**[24] 1182 6-8-11 CSoumillon 1 109
(ADeRoyer-Dupre, France) *set slow pace, joined 3f out, hard ridden 1f out, soon headed but kept on gamely, lost 2nd final strides* 2
5 shd **Swing Wing**[172] 5903 5-8-13 IMendizabal 2 111
(PFICole) *pressed leader til joining him 3f out, ridden & every chance 1f out, kept on, lost 2nd close home*
6 10 **Victory Taita (FR)**[326] 2044 4-8-9 ELegrix 3 99
(XThomas-Demeaulte, France) *pulled hard in 3rd while tracking leader, 4th straight, weakened over 1 1/2f out*

3m 35.5s (10.00) **Going Correction** +0.55s/f (Yiel)
**WFA** 4 from 5yo+ 3lb 6 Ran SP% **115.0**
Speed ratings: **97,96,95,95,95 90.**
**Owner** Ecurie Wildenstein **Bred** Dayton Investments Ltd **Trained** France

**NOTEBOOK**
**Westerner** looked in splendid condition and totally outclassed the opposition. Settled in last place for much of the race, he came with a sweeping late run in the straight. He showed terrific finishing speed on this occasion and proved he could go on all ground. The main target now is the Ascot Gold Cup and he will have a run before in the Prix Vicomtesse Vigier.
**Forestier(FR)** settled behind the leaders for much of the race before starting his run from a furlong and half out. He stayed on well and this useful performer should win a similar race.
**Idaho Quest** looked very well in the paddock and showed he could stay this longer distance. Last but one early on, he was putting in his best work at the finish.
**Le Carre(USA)** was given a canny ride by his jockey, who set a slow early pace and rallied again when passed halfway up the straight. He battled on well to the line and would have been happier had the ground been softer.
**Swing Wing** was unsuited by the slow early pace and would have been seen to better effect had the gallop been stronger.

# CHEPSTOW (L-H)
Friday, April 23

**OFFICIAL GOING: Good to soft (soft in places)**
The first 'regional racing' meeting to be run on turf, and quite possibly Chepstow's worst ever card.
Weather: fine and warm, clouding over later

## 1579 SALTWELL SIGNS CLAIMING STKS 1m 4f 23y
5:40 (5:40) (H) 3-Y-O £1,477 (£422; £211) Stalls Low

Form RPR
006- 1 **Fleetfoot Mac**[184] 5710 3-9-3 59 NCallan 6 69
(PDEvans) *trckd ldrs: wnt 2nd 6f out: led over 3f out: drvn and styd on wl fnl 2f* 7/1[3]
2000 2 13 **Quarry Island (IRE)**[31] 1084 3-8-8 40 JoannaBadger 1 41
(PDEvans) *led: rdn and hdd over 3f out: no ch w wnr fnl 2f but hld on for poor 2nd* 14/1
0412 3 1 1/4 **Oktis Morilious (IRE)**[8] 1405 3-9-3 45 MFenton 3 48
(AWCarroll) *in tch: hdwy 6f out: rdn to chse ldrs 3f out: sn no ch w wnr and styd one pce for mod 3rd* 7/2[2]
-160 4 dist **Rye (IRE)**[16] 1297 3-8-12 65 DHolland 2 —
(JAOsborne) *chsd ldr: rdn 7f out: lost 2nd 6f out: lost tch 4f out: t.o* 1/1[1]
0- 5 dist **Grace Darling**[216] 5088 3-8-0 JFEgan 5 —
(MissECLavelle) *s.i.s: t.o fr 1/2-way* 33/1
-350 6 dist **Comic Genius**[3] 1529 3-8-1 40 NChalmers(5) 4 —
(DHaydnJones) *s.i.s: sn pushed along in rr: t.o fr 1/2-way* 7/1[3]

2m 51.62s (13.12) **Going Correction** +1.225s/f (Soft) 6 Ran SP% **106.8**
Speed ratings: **105,96,95,—,— —**CSF £79.13 TOTE £7.00: £2.10, £5.80; EX 46.80.
**Owner** M W Lawrence **Bred** Lloyd Farm Stud **Trained** Pandy, Gwent

**FOCUS**
The best race on the card and a decent winning time for the grade, but desperate stuff all the same.

**NOTEBOOK**
**Fleetfoot Mac**, tackling cut in the ground for the first time, went on with over three to run and, maintaining the gallop, slammed some weak opposition. With the favourite not running her race this took little winning.
**Quarry Island(IRE)**, without the headgear for this return to the turf, did the donkey work and plugged on for second once headed.
**Oktis Morilious(IRE)** was having his first run on grass. He was unable to get past the runner-up when second place looked his for the taking, and he probably failed to stay.
**Rye(IRE)** held a clear chance on official ratings, but she was in trouble a good way out and she trailed in well beaten. Holland reported that she was reluctant to race. *Official explanation: jockey said filly was reluctant to race*

## 1580 PREMIER RESTAURANT OPENING NIGHT APPRENTICE BANDED STKS 1m 2f 36y
6:10 (6:11) (H) 3-Y-O+ £1,470 (£420; £210) Stalls Low

Form RPR
0401 1 **Eurolink Artemis**[4] 1511 7-9-8 40 (p) MHalford(5) 3 57
(JulianPoulton) *hld up in rr: stdy hdwy on outside over 3f out: trckd leaader appr fnl 2f: led appr fnl f: sn clr: easily* 4/1[3]
1443 2 7 **Mr Whizz**[11] 1093 7-9-7 40 (p) LTreadwell 5 38
(APJones) *sn chsng ldrs: led 4f out: rdn 2f out: hdd appr fnl f: no ch w wnr ins last* 9/4[1]
0-00 3 17 **Jezadil (IRE)**[17] 1281 6-9-7 35 KristinStubbs 2 8
(MrsLStubbs) *led after 2f: hdd 4f out: sn rdn: wknd 2f out* 9/1
0563 4 9 **Hellbent**[8] 1402 5-9-7 40 SCrawford 6 —
(JAOsborne) *s.i.s: plld hrd and sn rcvrd: wknd qckly over 2f out* 7/2[2]
000- 5 5 **Jim Lad**[12] 4437 4-9-0 40 (v) LucyRussell(7) 7 —
(DrJRJNaylor) *in tch tl wknd qckly ins fnl 3f* 11/1
000- 6 4 **Fortuna Mea**[192] 5559 4-9-7 40 BSwarbrick 4 —
(WMBrisbourne) *sn led: hdd after 2f: rdn and wknd qckly ins fnl 3f* 15/2
554- 7 dist **Middlemiss (IRE)**[261] 3878 4-9-7 40 MLawson 1 —
(JWMullins) *prom early sn bhd: t.o fnl 4f* 25/1

2m 23.54s (13.94) **Going Correction** +1.225s/f (Soft) 7 Ran SP% **106.9**
Speed ratings: **93,87,73,66,62 59,—**CSF £11.63 TOTE £4.30: £2.80, £1.50; EX 10.30.
**Owner** Roberto Favarulo **Bred** Mrs Carolyn Antoniades **Trained** Kentford, Suffolk

**FOCUS**
A weak race and they went no pace, but the winner appears back in good heart.

**NOTEBOOK**
**Eurolink Artemis**, returning to turf after a busy winter on the sand, was easy to back but proved much too good for the opposition under a confident ride.
**Mr Whizz** won a selling hurdle earlier in the month in first-time cheekpieces. He edged ahead with half a mile to run, but took a couple of furlongs to shake off the attentions of Jezadil and was quickly put in his place by the winner going to the last.
**Jezadil(IRE)**, who became warm beforehand, was just headed half a mile from home but did not finally drop away for another couple of furlongs.
**Hellbent**, a keen sort who was equipped with a net muzzle, failed to stay.

## 1581 LETHEBY & CHRISTOPHER BANDED STKS — 1m 2f 36y
6:40 (6:40) (H) 3-Y-O+ — £1,477 (£422; £211) Stalls Low

Form — RPR

0400 **1** **Margarets Wish**[15] [994] 4-9-1 35 ... DHolland 5 43
(TWall) *hld up in tch: hdwy to ld 3f out: pushed clr over 1f out: readily* **5/1**[2]

1226 **2** 4 **Buz Kiri (USA)**[27] [1136] 6-9-1 35 ... PDoe 7 36
(AWCarroll) *hld up in rr: pushed along and hdwy 4f out: pressed ldrs 3f out: chsd wnr fnl 2f: no ch fr over 1f out: kpt on for clr 2nd* **4/5**[1]

646/ **3** 5 **Dancing Dolphin (IRE)**[545] [4246] 5-8-12 35 ... LisaJones(3) 3 27
(JulianPoulton) *chsd ldrs tl lost position 5f out: styd on again fnl 2f: nt trble ldrs* **12/1**

0/0- **4** 1 3/4 **Pharly Reef**[19] [1214] 12-9-1 30 ... RPrice 8 24
(DBurchell) *keen ho:d trckd ldr after 2f: led 4f out: hdd 3f out and sn rdn: wknd qckly 2f out* **11/1**[3]

00/0 **5** 1 1/2 **Tyrrellspass (IRE)**[44] [809] 7-9-1 30 ... (t) VSlattery 4 21
(JDFrost) *s.i.s: rr but in tch: styd on fnl 2f but nvr a danger* **11/1**[3]

5-00 **6** 3/4 **Superclean**[8] [1402] 4-8-10 30 ... (v[1]) MLawson(5) 1 20
(AWCarroll) *led 1f: styd in tch: rdn to press ldrs 3f out: sn wknd* **33/1**

0-60 **7** *dist* **Leyaaly**[8] [1402] 5-8-12 30 ... (tp) BReilly(3) 2 —
(BAPearce) *a bhd: t.o fnl 5f* **25/1**

0000 **8** 1 1/4 **Alimiste (IRE)**[17] [1281] 4-9-1 35 ... NCallan 6 —
(IAWood) *led after 1f: hdd 4f out: wknd qckly 3f out: t.o* **14/1**

2m 22.37s (12.77) **Going Correction** +1.225s/f (Soft) **8** Ran SP% **110.0**
Speed ratings: **97,93,89,88,87 86,—,—**CSF £8.61 TOTE £4.10: £1.50, £1.10, £1.50; EX 7.80.
**Owner** A H Bennett **Bred** A H Bennett **Trained** Harton, Shropshire

**FOCUS**
A very poor race run at an ordinary gallop.

**NOTEBOOK**
**Margarets Wish**, who failed to stay over hurdles last time, was a comfortable winner of this poor race. She seemed to like this ground and she may be able to win again in suitably lowly company.
**Buz Kiri(USA)** maintained his record of having been placed on each of his starts in banded grade, but he was no match for the winner on ground that may not have suited him.
**Dancing Dolphin(IRE)**, who had not run since the autumn of 2002, did keep on again having lost her pitch.
**Pharly Reef**, better known as a hurdler, showed ahead only briefly before the game was up.
**Tyrrellspass(IRE)**, runner-up in a selling hurdle here on his latest start, had not run on the Flat since August 2002, when he was trained in Ireland. After missing the break he was always struggling over this inadequate trip, although he did find his stride in the final quarter mile and was closing at the line.
**Superclean** showed no improvement in first-time headgear.
**Leyaaly** *Official explanation: jockey said mare had a breathing problem*
**Alimiste(IRE)** is a very small filly.

## 1582 BETFAIR SHARP MINDS BANDED STKS — 1m 14y
7:10 (7:11) (H) 3-Y-O+ — £1,512 (£432; £216) Stalls High

Form — RPR

0-00 **1** **Bojangles (IRE)**[16] [1305] 5-9-7 45 ... DHolland 8 52
(RBrotherton) *mde virtually all: drvn along 2f out: kpt on wl fnl f* **9/2**[2]

50-0 **2** 1 1/2 **Catch The Fox**[11] [1352] 4-9-7 45 ... JTate 5 49
(JJBridger) *bhd: hdwy over 2f out: chsd ldrs over 1f out: styd on to take 2nd cl home but no imp on wnr* **25/1**

4514 **3** 1/2 **Kenny The Truth (IRE)**[31] [1093] 5-9-7 45 ... (t) NCallan 6 48
(MrsJCandlish) *t.k.h: w wnr over 5f: rdn 2f out: outpcd fnl f: lost 2nd cl home* **3/1**[1]

0326 **4** 6 **Unsuited**[46] [989] 5-9-0 45 ... NataliaGemelova(7) 4 35
(JELong) *chsd ldrs: rdn over 2f out: sn btn* **14/1**

-050 **5** 5 **Kanz Wood (USA)**[46] [988] 8-9-7 45 ... PDoe 9 25
(AWCarroll) *trckd ldrs: swtchd lft and hdwy over 3f out: sn rdn to chse ldrs but no imp: wknd fr 2f out* **9/2**[2]

600- **6** *nk* **Grady**[176] [5426] 5-9-0 40 ... BSwarbrick(7) 1 24
(WMBrisbourne) *in tch: rdn and lost position 1/2-way: mod prog again fnl f* **11/1**

6514 **7** 5 **Over To You Bert**[18] [1274] 5-9-7 45 ... VSlattery 3 14
(RJHodges) *chsd ldrs tl wknd over 2f out* **11/2**[3]

6043 **8** 7 **Iamback**[25] [1177] 4-9-7 45 ... (p) MFenton 10 —
(MissGayKelleway) *hmpd sn after s: chsd ldrs tl wknd qckly fr 3f out* **15/2**

450- **9** 3 **Mantles Pride**[8] [5559] 9-9-7 45 ... DSweeney 7 —
(DrPPritchard) *v.s.a: a in rr* **25/1**

004- **10** 25 **Lady Dulcet**[305] [2628] 4-9-7 40 ... RPrice 2 —
(DBurchell) *chsd ldrs over 4f* **50/1**

1m 41.76s (5.86) **Going Correction** +0.80s/f (Soft) **10** Ran SP% **113.2**
Speed ratings: **102,100,100,94,89 88,83,76,73,48**CSF £109.22 TOTE £5.20: £1.70, £5.70, £1.70; EX 121.00.
**Owner** Roy Brotherton **Bred** C H Wacker Iii **Trained** Elmley Castle, Worcs
■ Stewards Enquiry : D Holland one-day ban: careless riding (May 4)

**FOCUS**
Another poor race, though the winning time was good for a banded stakes, and the first three finished clear.

**NOTEBOOK**
**Bojangles(IRE)** soon secured the lead against the stands' rail and was ridden out firmly to make sure. He has plummeted in the ratings and this was his first run at a mile.
**Catch The Fox** stayed on late to record the first placing of his career. He obviously handles softish ground.
**Kenny The Truth(IRE)**, who has shown very little in a limited numner of starts on turf, had his chance and there were no real excuses.
**Unsuited** ran her race but looks a very modest performer indeed.
**Kanz Wood(USA)** was disappointing, especially in that he was favourably drawn and ought to have handled the ground.
**Iamback** had the best of the draw, but she was hampered by the eventual winner inside the first 100 yards and never seemed happy thereafter.

## 1583 SALTWELL SIGNS BANDED STKS — 7f 16y
7:40 (7:40) (H) 3-Y-O+ — £1,477 (£422; £211) Stalls High

Form — RPR

0005 **1** **Un Autre Espere**[1] [1573] 5-9-0 30 ... (b) BSwarbrick(7) 5 41
(TWall) *mde all: rdn over 2f out: drvn out fnl f* **25/1**

6011 **2** 1 1/4 **Fraamtastic**[7] [1444] 7-9-10 40 ... (p) BReilly(3) 3 44
(BAPearce) *in tch:lost position 1/2-way and bhd:hdwy and rdn 2f out:chsd wnr appr fnl f: kpt on but no imp nr fin* **9/4**[1]

6503 **3** 3 **Dundonald**[4] [1513] 5-9-7 35 ... (t) SRighton 2 30
(MAppleby) *s.i.s: bhd: swtchd lft and hdwy over 3f out: sn chsng ldrs but no imp: one pce fnl f* **11/1**

0006 **4** 7 **Definitely Special (IRE)**[8] [1403] 6-9-2 35 ... (p) MSavage(5) 7 13
(NEBerry) *t.k.h: chsd ldrs: rdn 3f out: wknd 2f out* **9/1**[3]

4-12 **5** *shd* **Tee Jay Kassidy**[4] [1513] 4-9-7 40 ... JFEgan 1 13
(JulianPoulton) *bhd: hung lft and hdwy over 2f out: chsd wnr over 1f out but no imp: wknd qckly fnl f* **7/2**[2]

6400 **6** *hd* **Zinging**[30] [1098] 5-9-7 40 ... JTate 6 12
(JJBridger) *chsd ldrs tl rdn and wknd qckly 2f out* **9/4**[1]

466- **7** 2 1/2 **Miss Faye**[228] [4767] 4-9-7 40 ... (p) MFenton 4 6
(JMBradley) *s.i.s: rdn and hdwy to dispute 2nd 1/2-way: wknd over 2f out* **25/1**

1m 30.03s (6.83) **Going Correction** +0.80s/f (Soft) **7** Ran SP% **109.8**
Speed ratings: **92,90,87,79,79 78,75**CSF £74.93 TOTE £33.70: £7.80, £2.20; EX 115.90.
**Owner** Snax Catering Services Limited **Bred** Backfield Ltd **Trained** Harton, Shropshire

**FOCUS**
The winner set a moderate pace and the final time was modest. With a couple of fancied horses failing to run their race this looks pretty dubious form.

**NOTEBOOK**
**Un Autre Espere**, well beaten at 100/1 on Fibresand the previous evening, dictated an average pace and was driven out to hold on. The form means little with a couple of fancied horses below par.
**Fraamtastic**, who became warm in the preliminaries, lost her place at halfway and that cost her the race. She rallied to bustle up the winner but could not make up the lost ground.
**Dundonald**, who was missing his customary headgear, stayed on past beaten rivals in the closing stages.
**Definitely Special(IRE)**, a long-standing maiden, failed to prove that she handles a softish surface.
**Tee Jay Kassidy** is a better horse on Fibresand.
**Zinging** found nothing when asked to pick up.

## 1584 LETHEBY & CHRISTOPHER BANDED STKS — 5f 16y
8:10 (8:11) (H) 3-Y-O+ — £1,547 (£442; £221) Stalls High

Form — RPR

4004 **1** **Bali-Star**[2] [1546] 9-9-7 45 ... JFEgan 11 56
(RJHodges) *broke wl: rdn and outpcd 1/2-way: rdn and rapid hdwy fnl f: led cl home* **14/1**

0011 **2** 1/2 **Attorney**[4] [1497] 6-9-13 45 ... (v) KFallon 2 60
(DShaw) *bhd: hdwy 2f out: drvn to chal fr 1f out tl wl ins last: no ex cl home* **5/2**[1]

3633 **3** *shd* **Aintnecessarilyso**[27] [1140] 6-9-7 45 ... PDoe 3 54
(NEBerry) *in tch: hdwy fr 2f out: slt ld appr fnl f: hdd an no ex cl home* **9/2**[2]

4003 **4** 2 1/2 **Threat**[80] [665] 8-9-6 51 ow6 ... CJDavies(7) 9 51
(JMBradley) *bhd: hdwy 2f out: pressed ldrs over 1f out: outpcd ins fnl f* **16/1**

360- **5** 1 **Diamond Ring**[242] [4468] 5-9-2 45 ... NChalmers(5) 10 41
(MrsJCandlish) *bhd: hdwy 2f out: chsd ldrs over 1f out: wknd ins last* **14/1**

0304 **6** 1 1/4 **Flying Faisal (USA)**[4] [1510] 6-9-7 45 ... (b) DHolland 6 37
(JMBradley) *led after 1f: rdn 2f out: hdd appr fnl f: sn btn* **7/1**[3]

1302 **7** *hd* **Henry Tun**[18] [1262] 6-9-2 40 ... (p) MSavage(5) 5 36
(NEBerry) *sn pressing ldrs: ev chnace over 1f out: wknd ins last* **9/2**[2]

60-0 **8** 2 **Travellers Joy**[17] [1280] 4-9-7 40 ... MFenton 1 29
(RJHodges) *pressed ldrs over 3f* **40/1**

0200 **9** 1 1/2 **Ejay**[8] [1421] 5-9-4 45 ... LisaJones(3) 12 24
(JulianPoulton) *bhd fr 1/2-way* **12/1**

0-00 **10** 1 1/2 **Firecat**[7] [1445] 5-9-7 45 ... (p) DSweeney 8 19
(APJones) *led 1f: styd w ldr tl wknd ins fnl 2f* **33/1**

4366 **11** 9 **Lone Piper**[25] [1180] 9-9-0 45 ... (p) HazelBoyd(7) 4 —
(JMBradley) *spd to 1/2-way* **33/1**

000/ **12** 27 **Bright Mist**[674] [2277] 5-9-7 45 ... NCallan 7 —
(BPalling) *early spd* **33/1**

63.76 secs (4.26) **Going Correction** +0.80s/f (Soft) **12** Ran SP% **115.6**
Speed ratings: **97,96,96,92,90 88,88,84,82,80 65,22**CSF £46.53 TOTE £17.30: £4.30, £1.50, £2.00; EX 49.70 Place 6 £105.21, Place 5 £7.34.
**Owner** E W Carnell **Bred** E W Carnell **Trained** Charlton Adam, Somerset

**FOCUS**
Decent form for the grade. A high draw is usually an advantage on the straight course here, so the placed horses deserve credit.

**NOTEBOOK**
**Bali-Star**, well drawn on the stands' rail, came fast and late to snatch the race near the line. This was only his second win in 42 career starts, although he was short-headed on his last visit here.
**Attorney**, on a hat-trick after a couple of sand successes, was poorly drawn and conceding upwards of 6lb all round. Fallon's only ride of the night, he had his chance but, as he attempted to get past the leader on his outside, the winner mugged the pair of them close home.
**Aintnecessarilyso** , who has been largely consistent on turf through the winter, got his head in front approaching the final furlong but was relegated two places near the finish. His low draw was no help.
**Threat**, who was taken early to post, did best of his trainer's trio but is without a win for nearly two years.
**Diamond Ring** did not run badly on her first start since August, albeit in this poor race.
T/Plt: £142.60 to a £1 stake. Pool: £27,163.60. 139.05 winning tickets. T/Qpdt: £5.50 to a £1 stake. Pool: £2,704.15. 362.10 winning tickets. ST

# SANDOWN (R-H)
Friday, April 23

**OFFICIAL GOING: Good to soft**
Other races under Rules of National Hunt Racing.
Wind: almost nil Weather: sunny, warm

## 1585 JETAIR ESHER CUP (H'CAP) — 1m 14y
2:20 (2:21) (C) (0-100,96) 3-Y-O — £15,674 (£5,945; £2,972; £1,351) Stalls High

Form — RPR

114 **1** **Barathea Dreams (IRE)**[30] [1100] 3-7-12 **73** oh1 ... JQuinn 4 89
(JSMoore) *t.k.h: trckd ldr: led over 2f out: rdn and hdd over 1f out: rallied gamely to ld again nr fin* **14/1**

5-31 **2** *nk* **Appalachian Trail (IRE)**[8] [1420] 3-8-6 **81** 5ex ... RWinston 8 96
(ISemple) *cl up: effrt over 2f out: led over 1f out: drvn and r.o fnl f: hdd nr fin* **10/3**[2]

21-3 **3** 4 **Momtic (IRE)**[11] [1357] 3-8-5 **80** ... KDarley 6 87
(WJarvis) *t.k.h: hld up in tch: effrt over 2f out: rdn and nt qckn wl over 1f out: kpt on to take 3rd ins fnl f* **3/1**[1]

2-41 **4** 2 **Just Tim (IRE)**[15] [1311] 3-8-3 **78** ... RLMoore 2 81
(RHannon) *t.k.h: hld up bhd ldrs: effrt to chal over 2f out: uunable qck over 1f out: one pce after* **10/1**

-411 **5** 1 3/4 **Certifiable**[28] [1120] 3-8-0 **75** ow1 ... MartinDwyer 1 74?
(AndrewReid) *b: b.hind: lw: pressed ldrs: shkn up on outer 3f out: outpcd fr 2f out* **8/1**

122- **6** *8* **Colour Wheel**[205] 5313 3-9-1 **90** RHughes 3 72
(RCharlton) *hld up in last pair: rn wd bnd over 4f out: shkn up 3f out: wknd 2f out* **11/2**[3]

415- **7** *nk* **Overdrawn (IRE)**[168] 5944 3-9-7 **96** SWKelly 5 78
(JAOsborne) *bit bkwd: hld up in last pair: shkn up and effrt 3f out: wknd 2f out* **16/1**

140- **8** *6* **Baileys Dancer**[174] 5874 3-8-12 **87** JFanning 7 56
(MJohnston) *mde most to over 2f out: wknd rapidly* **7/1**

1m 46.04s (2.12) **Going Correction** +0.425s/f (Yiel) **8** Ran SP% **108.7**
Speed ratings: **106,105,101,99,97 89,89,83**CSF £54.55 CT £162.91 TOTE £14.70: £3.60, £1.40, £1.40; EX 60.40 Trifecta £272.50 Pool of £2,801.78 - 7.30 winning units.
**Owner** Mrs Fitri Hay **Bred** Shadwell Estate Company Limited **Trained** East Garston, Berks

**FOCUS**
A good finish to this tight little handicap, with the stronger stamina of Barathea Dreams winning him the day. The winning time was decent for the grade.

**NOTEBOOK**
**Barathea Dreams(IRE)**, a non-stayer over a mile and a half on his most recent outing, had previously been successful in both his other Polytrack starts but seemed to improve for this switch to turf. He showed a great attitude, grinding hard to get back up, and looks progressive.
**Appalachian Trail(IRE)** stepped up on his maiden success in second, just finding the winner too strong late on. He was four lengths clear of the third.
**Momtic(IRE)** has run well on both starts this season and is sure to have his turn.
**Just Tim(IRE)** was not entitled to win this on form and ran as well as one could have hoped. As a relation of the stable's formerly smart performer Umistim, he may improve as the season goes on.
**Certifiable** made all for both Polytrack wins and was unable to lead on this turf debut.
**Colour Wheel** was expected to need the outing and should be capable of much better next time.
**Overdrawn(IRE)** ran a little better than his finishing position suggested on this seasonal return, but may need to drop a few pound sbefore he is winning again.
**Baileys Dancer** was entitled to do better on last season's evidence but comes from a stable not yet firing and this can only bring her on.

## 1586 BETFRED CLASSIC TRIAL (GROUP 3) 1m 2f 7y
2:55 (2:56) (A) 3-Y-O **£29,750** (£11,000; £5,500; £2,500) **Stalls** High

Form RPR

3111 **1** **African Dream**[7] 1437 3-8-10 94 JQuinn 5 115
(PWChapple-Hyam) *cl up: trckd ldr over 2f out: led over 1f out and sn pushed clr: reminder and jinked lft ins fnl f: r.o wl* **7/2**[2]

55-1 **2** *3 ½* **Privy Seal (IRE)**[13] 1330 3-8-10 110 LDettori 3 109
(JHMGosden) *lw: w.w in last: shkn up and prog over 2f out: chsd wnr ent fnl f: r.o but no imp* **8/11**[1]

0-21 **3** *5* **Gold History (USA)**[8] 1411 3-8-10 98 JFanning 2 100
(MJohnston) *lw: led: rdn and hdd over 1f out: sn outpcd* **7/1**[3]

01- **4** *2 ½* **Mutawassel (USA)**[226] 4818 3-8-10 90 RHills 1 96
(BWHills) *cl up: shkn up 3f out: wandering and green after: flashed tail and outpcd fr 2f out: one pce after* **7/1**[3]

-104 **5** *21* **Forthright**[62] 848 3-8-10 92 RHughes 4 58
(CEBrittain) *chsd ldr to over 2f out: wknd rapidly: t.o* **33/1**

2m 12.93s (2.75) **Going Correction** +0.425s/f (Yiel) **5** Ran SP% **108.1**
Speed ratings: **106,103,99,97,80**CSF £6.26 TOTE £3.80: £1.80, £1.10; EX 6.90.
**Owner** Franconson Partners **Bred** E Landi **Trained** Newmarket, Suffolk

**FOCUS**
Far from the strongest Group Three and an ordinary renewal of this Classic Trial.

**NOTEBOOK**
**African Dream** has come a long way since being claimed at Lingfield in February. An impressive winner at Kempton next time on his turf debut, he again did it in style in handicap company at Newbury and made a smooth transition here into Group company. All credit to him, but he beat only Listed performers, and while capable of winning again in this company abroad, where soft ground is more likely to be found, he may struggle to win another back in this country.
**Privy Seal(IRE)** did it well in the Easter Stakes on his seasonal debut, but that was not a strong race and he looks a little flattered by his rating. He ran well enough, without suggesting he will win at this level in this country.
**Gold History(USA)** was always going to be vulnerable to something progressive and could not follow up his win in the Fielden, where he had run of the race and the rail to run against. He is an honest sort though and is bound to be placed successfully in pattern-company when his stable are in better form, possibly abroad.
**Mutawassel(USA)** was having his first run of the year and was always going to struggle against race-fit rivals. He should improve for the outing.
**Forthright** was outclassed and will be hard to place.

## 1587 SUNDERLANDS CONDITIONS STKS (C&G) 1m 14y
4:05 (4:06) (C) 3-Y-O **£8,928** (£3,168; £1,584; £720) **Stalls** High

Form RPR

1- **1** **Thajja (IRE)**[271] 3625 3-9-0 RHills 3 101
(JLDunlop) *hld up in last: prog to ld over 1f out: rdn and in command fnl f* **6/1**[3]

21- **2** *2* **Putra Sas (IRE)**[196] 5467 3-8-10 90 KFallon 4 93
(PFICole) *h.d.w: bit bkwd: mde most: rdn and hdd over 1f out: one pce after* **7/1**

1 **3** *4* **United Nations**[9] 1395 3-9-0 JPMurtagh 2 89
(DRLoder) *lw: restless in stalls: sn pressed ldr: shkn up over 2f out: nt qckn wl over 1f out: wknd ins fnl f* **10/11**[1]

1- **4** *5* **Warrad (USA)**[182] 5735 3-9-0 LDettori 1 78
(GAButler) *trckd ldng pair: shkn up over 2f out: wknd over 1f out* **11/4**[2]

1m 47.84s (3.92) **Going Correction** +0.425s/f (Yiel) **4** Ran SP% **105.8**
Speed ratings: **97,95,91,86**CSF £35.24 TOTE £6.30; EX 22.10.
**Owner** Hamdan Al Maktoum **Bred** Shadwell Estate Company Limited **Trained** Arundel, W Sussex

**FOCUS**
Four unexposed horses and probably useful form, although the winning time was ordinary and it's hard to be sure.

**NOTEBOOK**
**Thajja(IRE)**, a doubtful stayer on pedigree, quickened up best of all and was suited by the way the race was run. Both his wins have come in small fields and he has still to prove his stamina for a truly run mile.
**Putra Sas(IRE)** ◆ was receiving 4lb off his three rivals, but shaped with much promise in second and will be suited by a stiffer test. He would reverse form with the winner were they to meet again in a more strongly-run race.
**United Nations**, impressive winner of the Wood Ditton at Newmarket, a race that often looks better than it is, was not on the best of terms with himself and disappointed. He may be hard to place.
**Warrad(USA)**, who looked fit beforehand, is well thought of by connections, but ran way below expectations. He may be capable of better when the yard are in better order.

## 1588 BETFRED "DOUBLE RESULT ON SINGLES AND MULTIS" H'CAP 1m 2f 7y
4:35 (4:36) (C) (0-90,87) 3-Y-O **£8,700** (£3,300; £1,650; £750) **Stalls** High

Form RPR

1-21 **1** **Hazyview**[8] 1414 3-8-8 **79** 6ex DFox[(5)] 4 96
(NACallaghan) *lw: pressed ldr: led wl over 2f out: shkn up and hdd over 1f out: kpt on wl fnl f: led again last strides* **1/1**[1]

2222 **2** *shd* **Red Lancer**[7] 1437 3-9-1 **84** RMiles[(3)] 10 101
(RJPrice) *hld up in midfield: smooth prog over 2f out: rdn to ld over 1f out: kpt on fnl f: hdd last strides* **7/2**[2]

402- **3** *4* **Cutting Crew (USA)**[191] 5578 3-9-1 **81** MartinDwyer 8 91
(PWHarris) *trckd ldrs: rdn and unable qck over 2f out: styd on same pce fr over 1f out* **14/1**

321- **4** *¾* **Camrose**[226] 4821 3-9-3 **83** TQuinn 1 91
(JLDunlop) *bit bkwd: hld up in rr: rdn 3f out: prog 2f out: styd on same pce fr over 1f out* **14/1**

1 **5** *3 ½* **Winged D'Argent (IRE)**[17] 1285 3-9-0 **80** JFanning 2 82
(MJohnston) *lw: cl up: rdn 4f out: lost pl and struggling 3f out: one pce after* **10/1**

51-2 **6** *1* **Lets Roll**[8] 1418 3-8-3 **69** TWilliams 9 69
(CWThornton) *racd in last pair: pushed along over 3f out: no imp ldrs over 2f out* **8/1**[3]

20-4 **7** *4* **Saffron Fox**[13] 1322 3-9-7 **87** TJMurphy 6 80
(JGPortman) *settled in midfield: brief effrt over 2f out: sn wknd* **20/1**

1- **8** *7* **Laawaris (USA)**[311] 2449 3-9-5 **85** JPMurtagh 7 66
(JAOsborne) *bit bkwd: s.s and lost 6l: a bhd: rdn and no prog 3f out* **20/1**

21-0 **9** *23* **Habanero**[22] 1222 3-8-5 **71** RLMoore 5 10
(RHannon) *led to wl over 2f out: wknd rapidly wl over 1f out: t.o* **20/1**

2m 13.6s (3.42) **Going Correction** +0.425s/f (Yiel) **9** Ran SP% **120.0**
Speed ratings: **103,102,99,99,96 95,92,86,68**CSF £4.53 CT £26.54 TOTE £2.10: £1.40, £1.70, £3.10; EX 6.90 Place 6 £235.31, Place 5 £44.90.
**Owner** T Mohan **Bred** N E Poole **Trained** Newmarket, Suffolk

**FOCUS**
A decent handicap, dominated by two well-treated horses. Hazyview remains progressive, and just edged it.

**NOTEBOOK**
**Hazyview**, who slaughtered the opposition at Newmarket last week, had to pull out all the stops to follow up, just doing enough when the line came. However, he has scope to progress again and will be suited by another step up in distance.
**Red Lancer** deserves to get his head in front, having finished second the last five times against some progressive types. He continues to climb the weights as a result though.
**Cutting Crew(USA)**, who looked fit for this reappearance, ran well on this handicap debut and shaped very much as though in need of further.
**Camrose** will stay further and should come on for this.
**Winged D'Argent(IRE)** ran respectably on this handicap debut, having won a maiden on his only previous outing earlier in the month. His breeding suggests further is required.
T/Jkpt: £7,477.70 to a £1 stake. Pool: £10,532.00. 0.50 winning tickets. T/Plt: £179.40 to a £1 stake. Pool: £69,038.05. 280.90 winning tickets. T/Qpdt: £18.20 to a £1 stake. Pool: £4,668.80. 189.10 winning tickets. JN

# 1364 WARWICK (L-H)
### Friday, April 23

**OFFICIAL GOING: Good (good to soft in places)**
Wind: almost nil Weather: fine

## 1589 CUBBINGTON MAIDEN AUCTION STKS 5f
5:25 (5:27) (H) 2-Y-O **£1,666** (£476; £238) **Stalls** Low

Form RPR

54 **1** **Zimbali**[11] 1364 2-8-2 SCarson 15 64
(JMBradley) *mde all: rdn over 1f out: r.o* **14/1**

2 **2** *2* **Lateral Thinker (IRE)**[17] 1276 2-8-6 SWKelly 16 61
(JAOsborne) *chsd wnr: rdn and ev ch over 1f out: unable qck ins fnl f* **11/4**[1]

02 **3** *2* **Turtle Magic (IRE)**[9] 1390 2-7-11 CHaddon[(7)] 11 52
(WGMTurner) *chsd ldrs: rdn over 1f out: styd on same pce* **11/4**[1]

**4** *nk* **Ninah's Intuition** 2-8-9 ANicholls 9 56
(JMBradley) *chsd ldrs: rdn and ev ch whn j. path and lost action over 1f out: nt rcvr* **50/1**

60 **5** *nk* **Zachy Boy**[11] 1374 2-8-9 EAhern 1 55
(JSMoore) *chsd ldrs: rdn 1/2-way: one pce fnl f* **20/1**

04 **6** *nk* **Wizzskilad**[18] 1269 2-8-7 RHavlin 14 52
(MrsPNDutfield) *trckd ldrs: racd keenly: rdn over 1f out: styd on same pce* **7/1**[2]

**7** *1 ½* **Princely Vale (IRE)** 2-8-9 ADaly 10 48
(WGMTurner) *dwlt: outpcd: styd on ins fnl f: nvr nrr* **11/1**[3]

**8** *¾* **Lady Chef** 2-8-4 AMcCarthy 2 40
(BRMillman) *dwlt: outpcd: styd on ins fnl f: nrst fin* **33/1**

0 **9** *2* **Ice Ruby**[8] 1415 2-8-3 PHanagan 3 32
(DShaw) *chsd ldrs: outpcd 3f out: n.d after* **40/1**

**10** *2 ½* **Higgys Prince** 2-8-7 TPQueally[(3)] 7 30
(DFlood) *sn outpcd* **16/1**

**11** *2 ½* **Muestra (IRE)** 2-8-5 FNorton 5 16
(MrsPNDutfield) *s.s: outpcd* **40/1**

**12** *hd* **Lord Chalfont (IRE)** 2-8-11 (b[1]) SWhitworth 13 22
(DFlood) *s.s: outpcd* **12/1**

**13** *1 ¼* **Faithisflying** 2-8-11 SSanders 12 17
(CADwyer) *dwlt: outpcd* **20/1**

**14** *nk* **Ryans Lil Ol Gal** 2-8-3 JMackay 6 8
(ABCoogan) *s.i.s: outpcd* **40/1**

**15** *1 ¼* **Mrs Willy Nilly** 2-8-2 CCatlin 8 2
(JMBradley) *s.s: outpcd* **50/1**

62.16 secs (1.96) **Going Correction** +0.05s/f (Good) **15** Ran SP% **118.1**
Speed ratings: **86,82,79,79,78 78,75,74,71,67 63,63,61,60,58**CSF £47.04 TOTE £17.90: £7.40, £1.40, £1.60; EX 120.40.
**Owner** J M Bradley **Bred** Matthew Sharkey **Trained** Sedbury, Gloucs
■ Stewards Enquiry : S W KellyM three-day ban: used whip with excessive force (May 4-6)

**FOCUS**
An ordinary contest run at a slow pace, in which most of the runners were too green or backward to do themselves justice. Although the front two had the race to themselves for much of the trip, it would be wrong to assume that a high draw was an advantage.

**NOTEBOOK**
**Zimbali** had the benefit of a couple of runs and quickly got across from her outside draw. While she is nothing much to look at she does have plenty of speed, and her heart is in the right place.
**Lateral Thinker(IRE)**, only just turned two, still looked as though the race would not be lost on her.
**Turtle Magic(IRE)**, like the winner, had the edge in experience, but lacked the pace over this sharp five to take advantage.
**Ninah's Intuition**, a cheap foal, was the first of the colts home. He showed plenty of dash, despite his inexperience, and was still in with a shout when jumping the path going to the furlong pole causing him to lose his action. While he is probably no great shakes, he did show enough to suggest he can win a little race.
**Zachy Boy** will need to find improvement if he is to get his head in front, but a step up in trip may help.

**Wizzskilad**, dropped in this time, was always doing a bit too much on the heels of the leaders.
**Princely Vale(IRE)** did not run too badly considering how colty he had been in the paddock.

## 1590 MITIE SWEEP (S) STKS — 1m 2f 188y

5:55 (5:57) (H) 3-Y-O+ — £1,582 (£452; £226) Stalls Low

| Form | | | | RPR |
|---|---|---|---|---|
| 100- | 1 | | **Barton Sands (IRE)**[45] [5150] 7-9-7 61 ........(vt) NMackay(3) 4 (MCPipe) *hld up and bhd: hdwy over 2f out: shkn up to ld 1f out: hung lft: rdn clr* **15/8**[1] | 58 |
| -202 | 2 | 2 ½ | **Nod's Nephew**[9] [1389] 7-9-10 58 ........ TGMcLaughlin 7 (DECantillon) *hld up: hdwy 4f out: led 2f out: rdn and hdd 1f out: styd on same pce* **15/8**[1] | 54 |
| 0006 | 3 | ¾ | **Queen Excalibur**[11] [1369] 5-9-5 45 ........ EAhern 3 (CRoberts) *chsd ldrs: rdn and ev ch over 1f out: styd on same pce* **5/1**[2] | 48 |
| 0162 | 4 | 1 ½ | **Heathers Girl**[37] [1037] 5-9-10 45 ........ PaulEddery 5 (DHaydnJones) *sn chsng ldr: rdn and ev ch over 1f out: no ex fnl f* **8/1**[3] | 50 |
| 0/0- | 5 | nk | **Prayerful**[12] [894] 5-9-2 40 ........(p) SHitchcott(3) 2 (BNDoran) *sn led: rdn and hdd 2f out: no ex fnl f* **33/1** | 45 |
| 500/ | 6 | 7 | **Yallambie**[563] [5167] 5-9-5 57 ........(t) PHanagan 1 (KAMorgan) *traked ldrs: plld hrd: rdn and wknd over 1f out* **25/1** | 33 |
| 0-00 | 7 | 7 | **Termonfeckin**[6] [1463] 6-9-10 55 ........ BDoyle 6 (PWHiatt) *s.v.s and rel to r: hdwy 4f out: wknd 3f out* **10/1** | 26 |

2m 26.61s (7.21) **Going Correction** +0.35s/f (Good) **7** Ran SP% **113.2**
Speed ratings: **87,85,84,83,83 78,73** CT £3.00 TOTE £2.00: £2.20, £; EX6.80 1.The winner was bought by I.Chim for 2,000gns. Prayerful was bought by R.Flint for £4,000. Queen Excalibur was bought by Nigel Brown for £4,000. Nod's Nephew
**Owner** Stuart M Mercer **Bred** Patrick Cassidy **Trained** Nicholashayne, Devon

**FOCUS**
A poor contest, run at a steady pace, and a slow time.

**NOTEBOOK**
**Barton Sands(IRE)** was best in on official figures, and showed a nice turn of foot to settle the issue. There is no reason why he should not score again at this level.
**Nod's Nephew** flattered briefly when going to the front, but the winner had him covered and showed much the better turn of foot. He has a good win-to-run ratio, for one of his abilty and it would be a surprise if he cannot improve on that in this company.
**Queen Excalibur**, a long-standing maiden, had plenty to find on these terms, but was far from disgraced.
**Heathers Girl**, tackling grass for only the second time, did not run at all badly at the weights, but left the impression this trip may be far enough for her.
**Prayerful** had a soft lead, but was easily shaken off when the pace quickened.

## 1591 HARBURY BANDED STKS — 6f 21y

6:25 (6:27) (H) 3-Y-O+ — £1,540 (£440; £220) Stalls Low

| Form | | | | RPR |
|---|---|---|---|---|
| 1112 | 1 | | **Baytown Flyer**[1] [1573] 4-9-12 35 ........ TGMcLaughlin 2 (PSMcentee) *mde virtually all: rdn out* **9/4**[2] | 57 |
| -604 | 2 | 1 ¾ | **Grand View**[17] [1283] 8-9-6 40 ........(p) PHanagan 9 (JRWeymes) *a.p: rdn over 2f out: chsd wnr fnl f: no imp* **2/1**[1] | 46 |
| 3060 | 3 | 1 ¾ | **Xsynna**[40] [1021] 8-9-6 40 ........(v) CLowther 10 (TTClement) *chsd ldrs: rdn over 2f out: styd on same pce fnl f* **10/1** | 41 |
| 0004 | 4 | ¾ | **Lucretius**[8] [1407] 5-8-13 40 ........ MHoward(7) 1 (DKIvory) *outpcd: hdwy and hung rt over 1f out: r.o* **8/1** | 39 |
| 0005 | 5 | hd | **Top Place**[17] [1280] 3-8-9 40 ........(p) EAhern 8 (CADwyer) *chsd wnr 5f: no ex* **7/1**[3] | 38 |
| 0000 | 6 | ¾ | **Time Flyer**[11] [1371] 4-9-6 35 ........(b[1]) ADaly 7 (WDeBest-Turner) *s.i.s: outpcd: r.o ins fnl f: nrst fin* **40/1** | 36 |
| 6566 | 7 | 2 ½ | **Abbiejo (IRE)**[4] [1515] 7-9-1 40 ........ AQuinn(5) 6 (GFierro) *sn outpcd: effrt and hung rt over 1f out: n.d* **16/1** | 28 |
| 0-00 | 8 | 1 ¼ | **Moonglade (USA)**[52] [951] 4-9-6 30 ........(t) JMcAuley 5 (MissJFeilden) *chsd ldrs: rdn over 2f out: wknd over 1f out* **66/1** | 24 |
| 650- | 9 | 2 | **Sweet Talking Girl**[165] [5969] 4-9-6 40 ........ SCarson 3 (JMBradley) *outpcd* **28/1** | 18 |
| 504/ | 10 | 13 | **Bound To Please**[522] [5733] 9-9-6 40 ........(v) AnnStokell 4 (MissAStokell) *sn outpcd* **25/1** | — |

1m 13.42s (1.12) **Going Correction** +0.35s/f (Good)
**WFA** 3 from 4yo+ 11lb **10** Ran SP% **113.9**
Speed ratings: **106,103,101,100,100 99,95,94,91,74**CSF £6.68 TOTE £2.80: £1.60, £1.10, £2.70; EX 7.30.
**Owner** J Doxey **Bred** B Minty **Trained** Newmarket, Suffolk

**FOCUS**
Not a strong contest, but the winner is on the upgrade and was winning for the 4th time in just over a week. The winning time was very good for a banded stakes and the form looks reliable.

**NOTEBOOK**
**Baytown Flyer**, none the worse for her busy schedule, continues in fine form. She has plenty of pace and proved just as suited by this trip, as the seven she has been racing over the last twice.
**Grand View** is running well enough at present and was probably a little unlucky to bump into a filly at the top of her game.
**Xsynna** lacks consistency and could not be relied upon to turn in a similar effort.
**Lucretius** had plenty to do turning for home and clearly found this trip, around a track as sharp as this, an insufficient test.
**Top Place** was soon toiling when the race began in earnest.

## 1592 CLAVERDON BANDED STKS — 1m 22y

6:55 (6:56) (H) 3-Y-O+ — £1,540 (£440; £220) Stalls Low

| Form | | | | RPR |
|---|---|---|---|---|
| -035 | 1 | | **Extemporise (IRE)**[37] [1039] 4-9-7 40 ........ TGMcLaughlin 6 (TTClement) *a.p: rdn to chse ldr fnl f: r.o to ld post* **5/1**[2] | 46 |
| 0342 | 2 | shd | **Tojoneski**[4] [1511] 5-9-7 35 ........(p) RFfrench 7 (IWMcinnes) *led: rdn clr over 1f out: hdd post* **6/1**[3] | 46 |
| 4005 | 3 | 2 | **All On My Own (USA)**[4] [1513] 9-9-7 35 ........(b) LVickers 4 (IWMcinnes) *hld up: hdwy over 2f out: rdn over 1f out: styd on u.p* **33/1** | 41 |
| 460- | 4 | 1 ½ | **Sea Jade (IRE)**[216] [5070] 5-9-7 40 ........ EAhern 11 (JWPayne) *chsd ldr: rdn over 1f out: no ex* **9/1** | 38 |
| 0006 | 5 | 3 | **Chickasaw Trail**[37] [1037] 6-9-7 40 ........ DaleGibson 5 (RHollinshead) *hld up: effrt over 2f out: no imp over 1f out* **20/1** | 31 |
| 4633 | 6 | 3 | **Zahunda (IRE)**[32] [1080] 5-9-7 40 ........ SWKelly 2 (WMBrisbourne) *hld up: nt clr run 3f out: nvr trbld ldrs* **11/4**[1] | 24 |
| 3334 | 7 | ½ | **Newclose**[81] [653] 4-9-7 40 ........(t) KimTinkler 8 (NTinkler) *hld up: outpcd 1/2-way: n.d* **5/1**[2] | 23 |
| 500- | 8 | 1 ½ | **Dunmidoe**[220] [4973] 4-9-7 40 ........ GCarter 9 (CDrew) *chsd ldrs tl wknd over 1f out* **50/1** | 20 |
| 5-24 | 9 | 1 ½ | **Sadlers Swing (USA)**[46] [989] 8-9-2 40 ........ AQuinn(5) 10 (JJSheehan) *hld up: wknd over 2f out* **7/1** | 16 |
| -000 | 10 | 5 | **Crown City (USA)**[31] [1090] 4-9-7 40 ........(t) MTebbutt 3 (BPJBaugh) *chsd ldrs over 5f* **25/1** | 5 |

1m 43.52s (4.22) **Going Correction** +0.35s/f (Good) **10** Ran SP% **110.3**
Speed ratings: **92,91,89,88,85 82,81,80,78,73**CSF £31.32 TOTE £7.90: £3.10, £1.90, £4.90; EX 50.40.
**Owner** Ms K Sadler **Bred** Paradime Ltd **Trained** Newmarket, Suffolk

**FOCUS**
With five wins from 206 runs between them, this is about as bad as it gets and the time was modest.

**NOTEBOOK**
**Extemporise(IRE)**, without the tongue strap this time, took a while to find top stride, but he stuck to his task well to nail the runner-up in the shadow of the post. While he is clearly of limited ability, he is lightly-raced and should be open to some improvement.
**Tojoneski** had more use made of him and it clearly suited. While he is no great shakes, he should be capable of adding to his tally at this level.
**All On My Own(USA)**, a long-standing maiden, turned in one of his better efforts.
**Sea Jade(IRE)** did not look that keen when push came to shove, and she is clearly one to have reservations about.
**Chickasaw Trail**, another long-standing maiden, is now 47 not out.
**Zahunda(IRE)** did not have the best of runs turning for home and is capable of better than she showed here.

## 1593 BARFORD BANDED STKS — 1m 6f 213y

7:25 (7:25) (H) 4-Y-O+ — £1,582 (£452; £226) Stalls Low

| Form | | | | RPR |
|---|---|---|---|---|
| 0-00 | 1 | | **Court One**[11] [1376] 6-8-9 35 ........ JFMcDonald(5) 9 (RJPrice) *s.s: hld up: hdwy over 3f out: rdn to ld ins fnl f: r.o* **9/2**[2] | 44 |
| 0406 | 2 | 1 | **Amanpuri (GER)**[53] [945] 6-9-0 35 ........ DeanMcKeown 3 (PABlockley) *chsd ldrs: led 2f out: rdn and hdd ins fnl f: edgd lft and kpt on* **7/1**[3] | 43 |
| 3206 | 3 | 6 | **Dora Corbino**[4] [1514] 4-8-11 40 ........ PHanagan 5 (RHollinshead) *led: rdn and hdd 2f out: styd on same pce* **25/1** | 35 |
| 5-03 | 4 | shd | **Anniversary Guest (IRE)**[25] [1164] 5-9-0 40 ........ CCatlin 8 (MrsLucindaFeatherstone) *hld up: plld hrd: hdwy 4f out: rdn over 2f: edgd lft and styd on same pce* **20/1** | 35 |
| 4-41 | 5 | 5 | **Mercurious (IRE)**[4] [1512] 4-9-3 40 ........ DaleGibson 1 (JMackie) *hld up in tch: rdn over 2f out: wknd over 1f out* **5/4**[1] | 34 |
| /0-4 | 6 | 5 | **Golfagent**[13] [1193] 6-8-11 40 ........(t) SHitchcott(3) 2 (MissKMarks) *hld up: hdwy over 3f out: wknd wl over 1f out* **8/1** | 22 |
| 360- | 7 | 30 | **River Of Fire**[191] [5576] 6-9-0 35 ........(v) JMackay 4 (CNKellett) *chsd ldrs over 11f* **16/1** | — |
| 000- | 8 | ¾ | **Rose Tea (IRE)**[8] [4639] 5-9-0 40 ........(b[1]) SSanders 7 (NAGraham) *chsd ldrs tl wknd over 2f out* **8/1** | — |
| 0056 | 9 | 12 | **Wethaab (USA)**[1] [1572] 7-9-0 30 ........(tp) AnnStokell 6 (MissAStokell) *prom over 8f* **66/1** | — |

3m 22.44s (7.24) **Going Correction** +0.35s/f (Good)
**WFA** 4 from 5yo+ 3lb **9** Ran SP% **113.3**
Speed ratings: **94,93,90,90,87 84,68,68,62**CSF £34.24 TOTE £6.00: £2.10, £2.30, £4.10; EX 46.10.
**Owner** Derek & Cheryl Holder **Bred** Mrs C R Holder **Trained** Ullingswick, H'fords

**FOCUS**
A moderate contest with the field finishing well strung out, although it was run at an ordinary pace.

**NOTEBOOK**
**Court One** looked to be in a right mood for he did not want to go out onto the course, and then he walked out of the stalls. However, you could not fault his attitude at the business end and he always looked like holding on.
**Amanpuri(GER)** looked much happier on this return to turf and certainly stayed this trip well enough.
**Dora Corbino** was given a positive ride, but she is only slow and will have a job to find a race.
**Anniversary Guest(IRE)**, a long-standing maiden, was far too free to give herself a chance.
**Mercurious(IRE)** seemed to run a little flat and may have found this coming too soon after her victory at Wolverhampton on Monday.

## 1594 HASELEY TRI-BANDED STKS — 7f 26y

7:55 (7:55) (H) 3-Y-O — £1,477 (£422; £211) Stalls Low

| Form | | | | RPR |
|---|---|---|---|---|
| 0365 | 1 | | **Courant D'Air (IRE)**[66] [808] 3-8-9 40 ........ GFaulkner 1 (PCHaslam) *mde virtually all: rdn and edgd lft over 1f out: styd on gamely* **5/2**[1] | 42 |
| 0044 | 2 | hd | **Heathyards Joy**[24] [1195] 3-8-4 30 ........ DaleGibson 2 (RHollinshead) *chsd ldrs: rdn and ev ch fr over 1f out: r.o* **25/1** | 36 |
| 0042 | 3 | ¾ | **Monkey Or Me (IRE)**[7] [1447] 3-8-5 31 ow1 ........ RFitzpatrick 3 (PTMidgley) *hld up: hdwy over 2f out: rdn and ev ch fr over 1f out: edgd lft ins fnl f: kpt on* **7/2**[2] | 36 |
| 00-0 | 4 | 1 ¼ | **Jesse Samuel**[16] [1300] 3-9-0 45 ........ SWKelly 6 (JRJenkins) *hld up: hdwy u.p over 1f out: unable qck wl ins fnl f* **10/1** | 41 |
| 0462 | 5 | 1 ¼ | **Fayr Firenze (IRE)**[1] [1571] 3-9-0 45 ........(v) DeanMcKeown 4 (MFHarris) *w ldr to 1/2-way: rdn and ev ch over 1f out: hmpd and no ex ins fnl f* **5/1**[3] | 38 |
| 326 | 6 | 4 | **Brother Cadfael**[6] [1467] 3-8-9 40 ........ SSanders 5 (JohnAHarris) *chsd ldrs over 5f* **5/2**[1] | 23 |

1m 27.48s (2.58) **Going Correction** +0.35s/f (Good) **6** Ran SP% **109.0**
Speed ratings: **99,98,97,96,95 90**CSF £52.54 TOTE £4.00: £1.80, £4.50; EX 92.00 Place 6 £53.89, Place 5 £37.40.
**Owner** M T Buckley **Bred** Tally-Ho Stud **Trained** Middleham Moor, N Yorks
■ Stewards Enquiry : G Faulkner four-day ban: used whip with excessive force (May 4-7)

**FOCUS**
A competitive low-grade contest, but not a bad time.

**NOTEBOOK**
**Courant D'Air(IRE)**, given a positive ride, just had enough in reserve to repel the persistent runner-up. However, he did have quite a hard race and will need to find more if he is to follow up.
**Heathyards Joy**, having only her second run on turf, stuck to her task well and was only just denied. If she can build on this she may well pick up a similar event.
**Monkey Or Me(IRE)** has now strung together a couple of promising efforts, albeit at a low level, and looks to have a small race in him.
**Jesse Samuel**, taking quite a drop in class, never looked likely to reel the leaders in
**Fayr Firenze(IRE)**, who showed a little promise last time, was already beaten when squeezed out in the latter stages. He is beginning to look exposed.
**Brother Cadfael** got rather warm beforehand and ran no sort of race.
T/Plt: £89.40 to a £1 stake. Pool: £24,817.85. 202.60 winning tickets. T/Qpdt: £44.60 to a £1 stake. Pool: £1,693.60. 28.10 winning tickets. CR

## 1568 WOLVERHAMPTON (A.W) (L-H)

Friday, April 23

**OFFICIAL GOING: Standard**

Wind: almost nil Weather: fine

### 1595 NEW SITE @ BETDIRECT.CO.UK CLASSIFIED STKS — 7f (F)

**2:05** (2:06) (F) 3-Y-0+ — **£2,947** (£842; £421) **Stalls** High

Form — RPR

6250 **1** **My Bayard**$^{29}$ [1103] 5-9-12 65 ........ WSupple 1 — 77
*(JO'Reilly) mde all: rdn wl over 1f out: drvn out* **8/1**

0062 **2** *1 ½* **Mount Royale (IRE)**$^{8}$ [1424] 6-9-8 61 ........(vt) KimTinkler 3 — 69
*(NTinkler) a.p: chsd wnr wl over 1f out: sn rdn: nt qckn fnl f* **5/1**$^{3}$

4210 **3** *1 ¼* **Spindor (USA)**$^{6}$ [1477] 5-9-8 61 ........(b) DHolland 5 — 66
*(JAOsborne) hld up mid-div: hdwy over 3f out: hrd rdn 2f out: one pce fnl f* **4/1**$^{2}$

1620 **4** *¾* **Acorazado (IRE)**$^{11}$ [1373] 5-9-11 64 ........(be) SWhitworth 8 — 67
*(GLMoore) hld up and bhd: hdwy over 3f out: rdn over 2f out: one pce fnl f* **7/2**$^{1}$

0520 **5** *1 ¾* **Dispol Peto**$^{63}$ [833] 4-9-7 59 ........(p) JBramhill 7 — 59
*(IanEmmerson) racd wd: hld up and bhd: hdwy on outside over 1f out: nt rch ldrs* **25/1**

4360 **6** *shd* **Parker**$^{23}$ [1204] 7-9-8 61 ........ IMongan 10 — 60
*(BPalling) hld up mid-div: rdn 3f out: hdwy over 1f out: nvr trbld ldrs* **7/1**

6203 **7** *hd* **Aguila Loco (IRE)**$^{6}$ [1477] 5-9-7 55 ........(p) MFenton 2 — 58
*(MrsStefLiddiard) w wnr: rdn over 2f out: lost 2nd wl over 1f out: wknd ins fnl f* **9/1**

025- **8** *5* **Siraj**$^{125}$ [6221] 5-9-11 64 ........ ACulhane 6 — 50
*(NAGraham) hld up mid-div: rdn 3f out: sn bhd* **11/2**

005- **9** *3* **Jubilee Street (IRE)**$^{221}$ [4952] 5-9-7 51 ........ GDuffield 4 — 38
*(MrsADuffield) prom tl wknd over 3f out* **33/1**

-060 **10** *4* **Victory Vee**$^{27}$ [1136] 4-9-7 52 ........ DSweeney 9 — 28
*(MBlanshard) prom: rdn over 3f out: sn wknd* **20/1**

1m 29.6s (-0.72) **Going Correction** -0.10s/f (Stan) — **10** Ran SP% **119.4**
Speed ratings: **100,98,96,96,94 93,93,87,84,79**CSF £47.83 TOTE £7.80: £2.90, £2.00, £1.50; EX 55.50.
**Owner** Burntwood Sports Ltd **Bred** G And Mrs Middlebrook **Trained** Brierley, S Yorks

**FOCUS**
A modest but competitive event, although the pace was unexceptional.

**NOTEBOOK**
**My Bayard**, back to the right sort of trip, found a drop in class enabling him to live up to the promise of his two good efforts here in February.
**Mount Royale(IRE)** did nothing wrong and simply met one too good.
**Spindor(USA)**, disappointing over six last time, seems best at this trip nowadays.
**Acorazado(IRE)** handles this surface but has been campaigned mainly on the Polytrack of late.
**Dispol Peto** had the cheekpieces fitted having sported blinkers last time.
**Parker** was without his usual blinkers for the third time in his last four outings.

### 1596 LITTLEWOODS BET DIRECT MAIDEN CLAIMING STKS — 5f (F)

**2:40** (2:40) (F) 3-Y-0+ — **£2,863** (£818; £409) **Stalls** Low

Form — RPR

4-30 **1** **Lucius Verrus (USA)**$^{72}$ [738] 4-9-13 48 ........ WSupple 1 — 55
*(DShaw) chsd ldrs: wnt 2nd wl over 1f out: hrd rdn to ld wl ins fnl f: r.o* **13/8**$^{1}$

2030 **2** *nk* **Nanna (IRE)**$^{18}$ [1262] 3-8-12 48 ........ GDuffield 2 — 49
*(RHollinshead) led: rdn and edgd lft jst over 1f out: hdd wl ins fnl f: r.o* **9/4**$^{2}$

6-0 **3** *4* **The Butterfly Boy**$^{11}$ [1370] 3-9-3 ........ SSanders 4 — 40
*(PFICole) w ldr: rdn and lost 2nd wl over 1f out: wknd ins fnl f* **7/2**$^{3}$

40-0 **4** *5* **Minirina**$^{57}$ [898] 4-8-10 45 ........ RFitzpatrick 5 — 5
*(CSmith) w ldrs: rdn over 2f out: wknd wl over 1f out* **16/1**

540- **5** *3* **Campbells Lad**$^{194}$ [5512] 3-8-11 45 ........ FLynch 6 — 5
*(ABerry) hld up: rdn 2f out: no rspnse* **16/1**

05-5 **6** *½* **East Riding**$^{12}$ [1342] 4-9-8 50 ........ AnnStokell 7 — 4
*(MissAStokell) hung rt sn after s: rdn over 3f out: sn bhd* **12/1**

0P-0 **7** *15* **My Wild Rover**$^{23}$ [1206] 4-8-13 ........(tp) PHanagan 3 — —
*(KAMorgan) hld up in tch: rdn and wknd over 2f out* **25/1**

62.60 secs (-0.20) **Going Correction** -0.10s/f (Stan) — **7** Ran SP% **114.4**
**WFA** 3 from 4yo+ 10lb
Speed ratings: **97,96,90,82,77 76,52**CSF £5.49 TOTE £1.90: £1.60, £1.30; EX 4.00.
**Owner** Swann Racing Ltd **Bred** Pacelco S A **Trained** Averham, Notts

**FOCUS**
A weak maiden claimer and an ordinary pace.

**NOTEBOOK**
**Lucius Verrus(USA)** has been beset with problems and is never going to live up to his illustrious pedigree. He justified sustained support in the market on this return to the minimum trip.
**Nanna(IRE)** made the winner work hard on this return to claiming company.
**The Butterfly Boy** was down in both grade and distance on this sand debut.

### 1597 BETDIRECT.CO.UK MEDIAN AUCTION MAIDEN STKS — 7f (F)

**3:15** (3:15) (F) 3-Y-0 — **£2,891** (£826; £413) **Stalls** High

Form — RPR

-4 **1** **Andaluza (IRE)**$^{20}$ [1243] 3-8-9 ........ SSanders 5 — 67
*(PDCundell) a.p: rdn over 2f out: led ins fnl f: drvn out* **5/2**$^{2}$

420- **2** *1* **Magic Amigo**$^{223}$ [4882] 3-9-0 75 ........ DHolland 6 — 69
*(JRJenkins) a.p: rdn over 2f out: kpt on ins fnl f* **2/1**$^{1}$

355- **3** *nk* **Carry On Doc**$^{216}$ [5080] 3-9-0 75 ........ SWhitworth 1 — 68
*(JWHills) hld up in tch: rdn over 2f out: chal ins fnl f: nt qckn cl home* **4/1**$^{3}$

354- **4** *2* **Aliba (IRE)**$^{268}$ [3679] 3-9-0 66 ........ FLynch 4 — 63
*(BSmart) led: rdn over 2f out: hdd and no ex ins fnl f* **14/1**

0 **5** *1 ½* **Nounou**$^{25}$ [1174] 3-9-0 ........ CCatlin 2 — 59
*(DJDaly) n.m.r after 1f: sn bhd: hrd rdn 3f out: n.d* **16/1**

00-3 **6** *nk* **Marksgold (IRE)**$^{11}$ [1366] 3-9-0 ........ ACulhane 3 — 58
*(PFICole) hld up: rdn over 3f out: wknd wl over 1f out* **4/1**$^{3}$

1m 30.35s (0.03) **Going Correction** -0.10s/f (Stan) — **6** Ran SP% **114.5**
Speed ratings: **95,93,93,91,89 89**CSF £8.19 TOTE £2.80: £1.80, £1.30; EX 4.10.
**Owner** Pedro Rosas **Bred** Dr Dean Harron **Trained** Compton, Berks

**FOCUS**
A fair maiden for Dunstall Park although there is some doubt as to whether those behind the winner can run to their current marks.

**NOTEBOOK**
**Andaluza(IRE)** was all the better for her Polytrack debut and appreciated the extra furlong.
**Magic Amigo**, who showed promise on turf last year, shaped as though he will get a mile on this switch to the sand.
**Carry On Doc** was another making his All-Weather debut who should do better over a longer trip.
**Aliba(IRE)** may need more patient tactics to be effective at this trip.

### 1598 NEW SITE @ BETDIRECT.CO.UK H'CAP — 1m 100y(F)

**3:50** (3:51) (E) (0-75,72) 3-Y-0+ — **£3,711** (£1,142; £571; £285) **Stalls** Low

Form — RPR

6244 **1** **Spark Up**$^{6}$ [1475] 4-8-11 55 ........(b) SSanders 7 — 66
*(JWUnett) sn led: rdn and edgd rt over 1f out: drvn out* **16/1**

4632 **2** *1 ¼* **Quiet Reading (USA)**$^{8}$ [1427] 7-9-2 65 ........(v) HayleyTurner$^{(5)}$ 9 — 73
*(MRBosley) hld up: hdwy over 5f out: rdn over 2f out: wnt 2nd over 1f out: nt qckn ins fnl f* **7/2**$^{2}$

4130 **3** *½* **Danielle's Lad**$^{18}$ [1265] 8-10-0 72 ........ ACulhane 10 — 79
*(BPalling) a.p: rdn over 2f out: nt qckn ins fnl f* **9/1**

3360 **4** *2* **Frank's Quest (IRE)**$^{9}$ [1389] 4-8-6 53 ........ LPKeniry$^{(3)}$ 8 — 56
*(PBurgoyne) a.p: rdn over 3f out: one pce fnl 2f* **25/1**

3-22 **5** *2 ½* **Active Account (USA)**$^{27}$ [1141] 7-9-11 69 ........ IMongan 6 — 67
*(MrsHDalton) bhd: rdn 7f out: hdwy over 1f out: n.d* **3/1**$^{1}$

620- **6** *1 ¼* **Summer Shades**$^{258}$ [3990] 6-8-13 64 ........ BSwarbrick$^{(7)}$ 1 — 59
*(WMBrisbourne) led early: prom tl wknd over 3f out* **16/1**

0503 **7** *½* **Pharoah's Gold (IRE)**$^{8}$ [1427] 6-9-2 60 ........(e) WSupple 4 — 54
*(DShaw) hld up and bhd: rdn 3f out: hdwy wl over 1f out: n.d* **10/1**

0046 **8** *9* **Air Mail**$^{6}$ [1475] 7-10-0 72 ........(v) PMcCabe 3 — 47
*(MrsNMacauley) prom: rdn 4f out: wknd over 3f out* **16/1**

0002 **9** *½* **Hoh's Back**$^{7}$ [1451] 5-8-4 51 ........(p) LisaJones$^{(3)}$ 2 — 25
*(PaulJohnson) stmbld s: bhd fnl 5f* **4/1**$^{3}$

-120 **10** *½* **Thunderclap**$^{30}$ [1102] 5-8-11 55 ........ PHanagan 5 — 28
*(JJQuinn) hld up: pushed along over 6f out: rdn over 4f out: bhd fnl 2f* **11/2**

1m 49.24s (-1.85) **Going Correction** -0.10s/f (Stan) — **10** Ran SP% **123.2**
Speed ratings: **105,103,103,101,98 97,97,88,87,87**CSF £75.56 CT £450.40 TOTE £11.70: £3.60, £1.40, £3.20; EX 115.80.
**Owner** Christopher Chell **Bred** Cheveley Park Stud Ltd **Trained** Wolverhampton, W Midlands

**FOCUS**
A modest handicap run in a good time for the grade, and the first two look fairly treated.

**NOTEBOOK**
**Spark Up** appreciated a change of tactics and dictated matters from the front.
**Quiet Reading(USA)** could not peg back the winner despite the fact he was set to go up 4lb in future handicaps.
**Danielle's Lad** was 6lb higher than when successful over course and distance last month on another rare run without the blinkers.
**Frank's Quest(IRE)** was not beaten as far as had seemed likely turning in and ideally wants a shade further.
**Active Account(USA)**, raised 3lb, was disappointing after a couple of good seconds over this course and distance.
**Hoh's Back** *Official explanation: trainer's representative said gelding stumbled leaving the stalls and then resented the kickback*

### 1599 BET DIRECT ON SKY ACTIVE APPRENTICE (S) STKS — 1m 4f (F)

**4:25** (4:26) (G) 4-Y-0+ — **£2,520** (£720; £360) **Stalls** Low

Form — RPR

2320 **1** **Orinocovsky (IRE)**$^{16}$ [1305] 5-8-11 55 ........ StevenHarrison$^{(8)}$ 1 — 65
*(NPLittmoden) mde all: clr 2f out: sn shkn up: easily* **8/15**$^{1}$

0230 **2** *9* **Just Wiz**$^{18}$ [1274] 8-8-8 58 ........(b) KJackson$^{(5)}$ 4 — 46
*(NPLittmoden) hld up: stdy hdwy over 5f out: wnt 2nd over 2f out: sn no ch w wnr* **7/4**$^{2}$

0/0- **3** *12* **Myrtus**$^{171}$ [5917] 5-8-10 ........ DFentiman$^{(3)}$ 3 — 28
*(JRWeymes) chsd wnr: rdn over 4f out: lost 2nd over 2f out: wknd wl over 1f out* **25/1**$^{3}$

00/ **4** *19* **Tolaga Bay**$^{503}$ [5855] 6-8-8 ........ DTudhope 2 — —
*(TJFitzgerald) hld up: rdn over 4f out: sn struggling* **40/1**

2m 39.52s (-2.28) **Going Correction** -0.10s/f (Stan) — **4** Ran SP% **107.9**
Speed ratings: **103,97,89,76**CSF £1.69 TOTE £1.20; EX 1.40.There was no bid for the winner.
**Owner** Nigel Shields **Bred** N Chatzigrigoriou **Trained** Newmarket, Suffolk

**FOCUS**
A dreadful seller with the anticipated match failing to materialise. The pace was fair for the grade.

**NOTEBOOK**
**Orinocovsky(IRE)** gets this trip well and was ridden accordingly.
**Just Wiz** had his stamina limitations exposed by the winner.

### 1600 BET IN RUNNING @ BETDIRECT.CO.UK H'CAP — 1m 1f 79y(F)

**5:00** (5:00) (F) (0-55,55) 3-Y-0 — **£2,870** (£820; £410) **Stalls** Low

Form — RPR

2333 **1** **Angelo's Pride**$^{32}$ [1078] 3-9-2 55 ........ GDuffield 7 — 59
*(JAOsborne) hld up: hdwy over 5f out: led over 2f out: sn rdn: r.o wl* **3/1**$^{2}$

0326 **2** *2* **Fox Hollow (IRE)**$^{16}$ [1296] 3-8-12 51 ........ ACulhane 6 — 51
*(MJHaynes) prom: rdn over 4f out: outpcd over 3f out: rallied fnl f: nt trble wnr* **8/1**

5513 **3** *2 ½* **Larad (IRE)**$^{4}$ [1495] 3-8-12 51 6ex ........(b) JDSmith 4 — 46
*(JSMoore) a.p: rdn over 3f out: ev ch over 2f out: one pce* **5/1**$^{3}$

06-4 **4** *2* **Cherokee Nation**$^{6}$ [1465] 3-8-12 54 ........(e$^{1}$) LPKeniry$^{(3)}$ 2 — 45
*(PWD'Arcy) t.k.h: led: rdn and hdd over 2f out: wknd ins fnl f* **7/4**$^{1}$

00-5 **5** *3 ½* **Rebel Rouser**$^{16}$ [1304] 3-8-8 47 ........ IMongan 1 — 31
*(WRMuir) prom: rdn over 4f out: sn wknd* **12/1**

006- **6** *1* **Scorchio (IRE)**$^{186}$ [5676] 3-8-7 46 ........ SRighton 3 — 28
*(MFHarris) prom: lost pl 7f out: rdn over 5f out: sn bhd* **50/1**

03-4 **7** *dist* **Nafferton Girl (IRE)**$^{16}$ [1293] 3-8-11 50 ........ DaneO'Neill 5 — —
*(JAOsborne) a bhd: rdn over 4f out: sn lost tch: t.o* **11/2**

2m 3.09s (0.09) **Going Correction** -0.10s/f (Stan) — **7** Ran SP% **114.2**
Speed ratings: **95,93,91,89,86 85,—**CSF £26.59 TOTE £4.40: £2.40, £2.30; EX 15.90 Place 6 £53.56, Place 5 £23.55.
**Owner** J A Osborne **Bred** Mrs Kathleen Panayiotou **Trained** Upper Lambourn, Berks

**FOCUS**
A weak handicap run at a moderate pace and not a race to place much faith in.

**NOTEBOOK**
**Angelo's Pride** appreciated being back up to this trip on his handicap debut.
**Fox Hollow(IRE)** was attempting this distance for the first time and may get even further.
**Larad(IRE)** was trying to overcome a penalty on this first try on Fibresand.
**Cherokee Nation** ran too freely in the first-time eyeshield.
**Nafferton Girl(IRE)** *Official explanation: trainer's representaive said filly had shown signs of coming into season*

T/Plt: £35.80 to a £1 stake. Pool: £23,532.05. 479.55 winning tickets. T/Qpdt: £9.50 to a £1 stake. Pool: £1,417.10. 110.20 winning tickets. KH

# [1321]HAYDOCK (L-H)

Saturday, April 24

**OFFICIAL GOING: Soft (good to soft in places)**

The going was reckoned to be 'dead and tacky'.

Wind: almost nil Weather: fine and sunny

## 1601 EUROPEAN BREEDERS FUND MAIDEN FILLIES' STKS 5f

5:45 (5:45) (D) 2-Y-O **£4,719** (£1,452; £726; £363) **Stalls** Centre

Form RPR

0 **1** **Flossytoo**[30] 1105 2-8-4 ........ JDO'Reilly(7) 5 69
(JO'Reilly) *trckd ldr: wnt rt and led 2f out: sn rdn and hung lft: kpt on* **4/1**[2]

3 **2** 1 1/2 **Rightprice Premier (IRE)**[16] 1314 2-8-11 ........ NCallan 3 64
(KARyan) *trckd ldrs: swtchd rt and hmpd 2f out: kpt on same pce fnl f* **10/3**[1]

0 **3** 2 1/2 **Stan's Girl**[12] 1364 2-8-8 ........ SHitchcott(3) 7 55
(MRChannon) *chsd ldrs: one pce fnl 2f* **4/1**[2]

**4** 3 1/2 **Make Us Flush** 2-8-4 ........ PPMathers(7) 1 43
(ABerry) *leggy: unf: s.i.s: bhd tl styd on fnl 2f* **10/1**

**5** 1 1/2 **Tantien** 2-8-11 ........ RWinston 6 38
(JohnAHarris) *tall: unf: s.i.s: sme hewaday 2f out: hung lft: nvr on terms* **12/1**

**6** 3 **Mytton's Dream** 2-8-8 ........ BReilly(3) 8 27
(ABailey) *leggy: unf: s.i.s: nvr wnt pce* **6/1**[3]

**7** 11 **Gloria Nimbus** 2-8-11 ........ SRighton 4 —
(MMullineaux) *rangy: scope: led tl 2f out: sn wknd* **25/1**

**8** 1 1/2 **Houdini Bay (IRE)** 2-8-8 ........ THamilton(3) 2 —
(RPElliott) *sn drvn along: lost pl 2f out: sn bhd* **12/1**

62.00 secs (-0.07) **Going Correction** -0.125s/f (Firm) 8 Ran SP% **105.7**
Speed ratings: **95,92,88,83,80 75,58,55**CSF £14.95 TOTE £5.20: £1.60, £1.10, £1.90; EX 12.20.
**Owner** J Saul **Bred** J Saul **Trained** Brierley, S Yorks

**FOCUS**
A modest event run at a fair pace in the conditions that compares well with the following three-year-old race.

**NOTEBOOK**
**Flossytoo**, up in the air and narrow, ducked and dived but in the end took this very modest event in convincing fashion.
**Rightprice Premier(IRE)**, quite a big, leggy type, was very much on her toes beforehand. Left short of room by the winner, she never seemed to really buckle down. She will benefit if given plenty more time to strengthen and fill her frame.
**Stan's Girl** improved on her debut effort but she looks to have strictly limited ability.
**Make Us Flush**, who continually swished her tail in the paddock, was backward in her coat and showed a round action. A February foal, she looks as though she needs more time yet.
**Tantien**, an April foal, is very much up in the air. The experience will not be lost on her.
**Mytton's Dream**, a March foal, looks very weak and showed next to nothing on her debut.

## 1602 DIANE ORGAN 40TH BIRTHDAY H'CAP 5f

6:15 (6:15) (D) (0-85,85) 3-Y-O **£5,541** (£1,705; £852; £426) **Stalls** Centre

Form RPR

102- **1** **Foursquare (IRE)**[178] 5829 3-9-6 **84** ........ NCallan 1 93
(JMackie) *mde all: shkn up 2f out: styd on wl* **7/1**[3]

2121 **2** 3 **Piccolo Prince**[19] 1266 3-8-4 **68** ........ WSupple 2 67
(EJAlston) *chsd wnr: styd on same pce appr fnl f: no real imp* **4/1**[1]

01-5 **3** nk **Lake Garda**[14] 1323 3-9-7 **85** ........ SWKelly 4 83
(BAMcmahon) *chsd ldrs: effrt 2f out: kpt on wl ins last* **6/1**[2]

20-4 **4** 3/4 **Elliot's Choice (IRE)**[7] 1473 3-8-1 **72** ow1 ........ DTudhope(7) 3 67
(DCarroll) *trckd ldrs: swtchd lft over 1f out: kpt on wl* **4/1**[1]

0-04 **5** 4 **Point Calimere (IRE)**[4] 1530 3-9-4 **82** ........ EAhern 6 64
(CREgerton) *chsd ldrs: fdd over 1f out* **9/1**

25-0 **6** 1 1/2 **Mrs Spence**[7] 1473 3-8-4 **68** ........ DaleGibson 5 45
(MWEasterby) *s.i.s: sn outpcd: kpt on fnl 2f: nvr on terms* **33/1**

23-3 **7** 5 **A Little Bit Yarie**[7] 1473 3-9-6 **84** ........ DarrenWilliams 7 44
(KRBurke) *sn trcking ldrs: drvn along over 2f out: sn lost pl* **4/1**[1]

00-0 **8** 1/2 **Eastern Pearl**[7] 1473 3-8-9 **73** ........ RWinston 8 31
(MrsLStubbs) *chsd ldrs: lost pl over 1f out* **25/1**

4-00 **9** 15 **Multiple Choice (IRE)**[11] 1388 3-8-8 **75** ........ J-PGuillambert(3) 9 —
(NPLittmoden) *sn outpcd: lost pl 2f out: eased* **9/1**

61.37 secs (-0.70) **Going Correction** -0.125s/f (Firm) 9 Ran SP% **113.6**
Speed ratings: **100,95,94,93,87 84,76,75,51**CSF £34.51 CT £177.77 TOTE £8.70: £2.90, £1.50, £2.40; EX 35.10.
**Owner** Tim Kelly **Bred** C Farrell **Trained** Church Broughton, Derbys

**FOCUS**
A competitive handicap although the time was ordinary. The winner is very speedy and will now step up in class.

**NOTEBOOK**
**Foursquare(IRE)**, taken to post early, was keen to get on with the job. He came right away and, very speedy, will now tackle something better.
**Piccolo Prince**, dropping back to the minimum trip, could never summon the pace to get in a real blow.
**Lake Garda** was putting in his best work at the finish and will be suited by a return to six furlongs.
**Elliot's Choice(IRE)**, a tall type, was quite keen. After being switched he kept on in his own time, and he will be suited by a step up to six furlongs.
**Point Calimere(IRE)**, making a quick return, did not improve for the drop back in trip.
**A Little Bit Yarie**, fitted with a cross noseband, had two handlers in the paddock. He dropped right away and connections felt this came too soon just a week after Thirsk. *Official explanation: trainer had no explanation for the poor form shown other than that race may have come too soon after previous outing seven days ago*

## 1603 REDNAL CLASSIFIED STKS 6f

6:45 (6:47) (D) 3-Y-O+ **£5,655** (£1,740; £870; £435) **Stalls** Centre

Form RPR

31/- **1** **Zoom Zoom**[543] 5528 4-9-3 70 ........ RWinston 5 80
(MrsLStubbs) *t.k.h: led over 2f: led over 1f out: hrd rdn and kpt on wl* **4/1**[2]

1114 **2** 1 **Up Tempo (IRE)**[8] 1452 6-9-5 77 ........ (b) NCallan 4 79
(KARyan) *stmbld after 1 1/2f: hdwy to chse wnr over 1f out: kpt on: no imp* **1/1**[1]

00-0 **3** 6 **Free Wheelin (IRE)**[12] 1354 4-9-3 75 ........ MTebbutt 6 59
(WJarvis) *t.k.h: sn trcking ldrs: effrt 2f out: kpt on same pce* **10/1**

304- **4** 1 1/2 **Sewmuch Character**[201] 5427 5-9-3 72 ........ DSweeney 2 55
(MBlanshard) *rrd s: w ldr: led over 3f out tl over 1f out: fdd* **11/2**[3]

-000 **5** 2 1/2 **Sugar Cube Treat**[18] 1283 8-9-0 30 ........ (p) SRighton 1 44?
(MMullineaux) *rrd s: trckd ldrs: lost pl 3f out: n.d after* **100/1**

1/00 **6** 1 3/4 **Full Pitch**[64] 836 8-9-3 60 ........ VSlattery 7 42
(WJenks) *chsd ldrs: outpcd over 2f out: sn lost pl* **50/1**

100- **7** 1 3/4 **Cross Ash (IRE)**[226] 4846 4-9-4 76 ........ DaleGibson 8 38
(RHollinshead) *chsd ldrs: lost pl over 2f out* **33/1**

00-0 **U** **Gdansk (IRE)**[5] 1500 7-8-10 73 ........ PPMathers(7) 3 —
(ABerry) *swvd bdly rt s and sn uns rdr* **7/1**

1m 16.14s (1.25) **Going Correction** -0.125s/f (Firm) 8 Ran SP% **112.9**
Speed ratings: **86,84,76,74,71 69,66,**—CSF £8.14 TOTE £3.90: £1.30, £1.20, £2.00; EX 8.00.
**Owner** Des Thurlby **Bred** Simon Curtis **Trained** Malton, N. Yorks

**FOCUS**
The winning time was very pedestrian for the grade, but the first two finished clear and they should continue to give a good account of themselves.

**NOTEBOOK**
**Zoom Zoom ◆**, a big type, has suffered two fractures since he won at two. Fitted with stick-on shoes, he was very keen, but after showing his inexperience in front he really buckled down under a powerful ride. There should be even better to come.
**Up Tempo(IRE)**, who is bang in form, was playing catch-up after stumbling early on. He stuck on really well but in the winner was meeting an unexposed and potentially useful sort.
**Free Wheelin(IRE)**, fitted with a cross noseband, was taken very quietly to post. He was very keen, but in the end was left trailing by the first two.
**Sewmuch Character**, who came out of the stalls on his back legs, showed plenty of toe but seemed to blow up on his first outing this time.
**Sugar Cube Treat**, most reluctant leaving the paddock, had to be led down to the start. She had three stone to find in order to figure.

## 1604 FORTON RATED STKS (H'CAP) 1m 2f 120y

7:15 (7:16) (C) (0-90,88) 4-Y-O+ **£9,938** (£3,058; £1,529; £764) **Stalls** High

Form RPR

140- **1** **Red Fort (IRE)**[204] 5349 4-9-7 **88** ........ PRobinson 6 101
(MAJarvis) *sn trcking ldrs: hung lft 2f out: led over 1f out: hld on towards fin* **11/2**[3]

610- **2** nk **La Sylphide**[168] 5952 7-8-10 **77** ........ SWKelly 5 89
(GMMoore) *led: qcknd 5f out: hdd over 1f out: kpt on wl* **20/1**

550- **3** 5 **Kentucky Blue (IRE)**[49] 5952 4-9-4 **85** ........ RWinston 3 89
(TDEasterby) *in tch: rdn and outpcd over 4f out: hdwy on ins over 2f out: sn swtchd rt: kpt on same pce* **6/1**

35-0 **4** 1/2 **Fisio Therapy**[7] 1456 4-9-1 **82** ........ JFanning 8 85
(MJohnston) *chsd ldrs: rdn over 3f out: one pce* **9/2**[2]

0113 **5** 1 1/4 **War Owl (USA)**[12] 1369 7-8-7 **74** ........ NCallan 9 75
(IanWilliams) *s.i.s: bhd tl hdwy on wd outside over 3f out: nvr nr ldrs* **4/1**[1]

530- **6** 9 **Telemachus**[168] 5952 4-9-7 **88** ........ MFenton 1 73
(JGGiven) *sn drvn along: sn w ldr: lost pl over 1f out* **9/1**

1246 **7** 7 **Intricate Web (IRE)**[14] 1321 8-8-9 **76** ........ WSupple 10 49
(EJAlston) *hld up: hdwy 6f out: sn chsng ldrs: rdn and hung lft over 3f out: sn wknd* **16/1**

44-4 **8** 16 **Dream Magic**[7] 1460 6-8-11 **78** ........ EAhern 7 24
(MJRyan) *stdd s: hld up: effrt over 4f out: lost pl over 2f out: eased* **11/2**[3]

00-0 **9** hd **Broadway Score (USA)**[18] 1284 6-9-7 **88** ........ DaleGibson 2 34
(MWEasterby) *sn drvn along: lost pl 6f out: sn bhd* **25/1**

**10** 29 **Arawan (IRE)**[224] 4901 4-9-0 **86** ........ PMulrennan(5) 4 —
(MWEasterby) *rr-div: lost pl over 6f out: sn bhd: t.o* **28/1**

2m 17.95s (0.22) **Going Correction** +0.25s/f (Good) 10 Ran SP% **111.2**
Speed ratings: **109,108,105,104,103 97,92,80,80,59**CSF £106.41 CT £657.63 TOTE £6.60: £2.20, £3.50, £2.80; EX 87.30.
**Owner** The Red Fort Partnership **Bred** Genesis Green Stud Ltd **Trained** Newmarket, Suffolk

**FOCUS**
A decent handicap run at just a steady gallop to halfway, but the overall time was up well up to scratch and the first two were clear.

**NOTEBOOK**
**Red Fort(IRE)**, a big type, was encountering easy ground for the first time. He travelled best but was always inclined to hang in, and his rider did an exceptionally good job of keeping him off the runner-up.
**La Sylphide**, a big mare, tried to pinch it from the front. She stuck on in brave fashion but at the line was just second best. She looks better than ever at seven.
**Kentucky Blue(IRE)**, fit from hurdling, could have done with a much stronger pace.
**Fisio Therapy**, who looked very fit, did not improve on his comeback effort. The softer the ground the better for him.
**War Owl(USA)**, 8lb higher and up in class, sat off the pace in what was not a strongly-run event. This is best overlooked.
**Telemachus**, well backed, is now a gelding. Suited by the ground, he took on the leader but tired badly late on as if needing this first outing of the campaign.
**Dream Magic** *Official explanation: jockey said gelding was unsuited by the soft ground*

## 1605 SLEAP MAIDEN STKS 1m 3f 200y

7:45 (7:45) (D) 3-Y-O **£5,395** (£1,660; £830; £415) **Stalls** High

Form RPR

5 **1** **Dallool**[11] 1387 3-9-0 ........ PRobinson 1 78+
(MAJarvis) *lw: set mod pce: hung bdly rt bnd over 4f out and hdd: led over 3f out: styd on wl fnl f* **5/6**[1]

**2** 2 1/2 **Woolly Back (IRE)** 3-9-0 ........ DaleGibson 4 74
(RHollinshead) *w'like: scope: trckd ldrs: pushed along 4f out: styd on to take 2nd nr line* **20/1**

**3** 1/2 **Cumbria** 3-8-9 ........ JFanning 3 69
(MJohnston) *tall: unf: scope: trckd ldr: lft in ld bnd over 4f out: hdd over 3f out: hung lft and fdd fnl f* **4/1**[3]

2-22 **4** 18 **Golden Empire (USA)**[13] 1344 3-9-0 77 ........ (v) WSupple 2 47
(EALDunlop) *stdd s: hld up: effrt and hung lft over 2f out: fnd nthing and sn lost pl: eased ins last* **11/4**[2]

2m 42.91s (7.75) **Going Correction** +0.25s/f (Good) 4 Ran SP% **106.0**
Speed ratings: **84,82,82,70**CSF £13.88 TOTE £2.00; EX 16.40.
**Owner** Sheikh Ahmed Al Maktoum **Bred** Plantation Stud **Trained** Newmarket, Suffolk

**FOCUS**
Just a steady gallop and a slow time which makes the form difficult to rate, but a most convincing winner who will improve again.

**NOTEBOOK**
**Dallool ◆**, a tall, rangy type, has an action ideally suited by give. Having only his second outing, he seemed to suffer a panic attack on the home turn. Given time to get his act back together, in the end he took this modest event going right away to give his trainer his fifth winner on the day. He will go on from here.
**Woolly Back(IRE)**, whose dam was a five-furlong performer, looked green going down. He stuck on after being tapped for toe to take second spot near the line. This was a pleasing bow.
**Cumbria**, a half-sister to the smart hurdler Copeland, is very much up in the air and weak-looking. Backward in her coat, she tired late on and will need more time yet.
**Golden Empire(USA)**, who looked very fit indeed, had the visor on again. He hung the minute he was asked for an effort and found nothing at all. He needs to completely change his attitude.



The Form Book, Raceform Ltd, Compton, RG20 6NL

## 1606 HIGH ERCALL FILLIES' H'CAP — 1m 30y
8:15 (8:15) (E) (0-75,75) 3-Y-O+ £3,809 (£1,172; £586; £293) Stalls Low

| Form | | | | | RPR |
|---|---|---|---|---|---|
| 00-5 | 1 | | **Commitment Lecture**[21] 1247 4-8-11 **51** (t) WSupple 11 | | 64 |
| | | | (MDods) *hld up: hdwy over 3f out: led over 1f out: hld on towards fin* | 4/1[1] | |
| 0666 | 2 | ½ | **Vermilion Creek**[10] 1389 5-8-1 **48** StephanieHollinshead(7) 6 | | 60 |
| | | | (RHollinshead) *hld up and bhd: hdwy and nt clr run 2f out: wnt 2nd ins last: styd on wl towards fin* | 16/1 | |
| 0-43 | 3 | 7 | **Oh So Rosie (IRE)**[19] 1275 4-9-1 **60** JFMcDonald(5) 10 | | 58 |
| | | | (JSMoore) *bhd: styd on fnl 2f: nvr nrr* | 13/2[3] | |
| 6336 | 4 | 1 | **Zahunda (IRE)**[1] 1592 5-7-9 **40** DFox(5) 4 | | 36 |
| | | | (WMBrisbourne) *led tl hdd & wknd over 1f out* | 10/1 | |
| 3210 | 5 | 1¾ | **Printsmith (IRE)**[9] 1427 7-8-5 **45** JBramhill 8 | | 38 |
| | | | (JRNorton) *in tch: effrt over 3f out: one pce* | 10/1 | |
| 4033 | 6 | 1½ | **Cloudless (USA)**[26] 1178 4-9-1 **55** SWKelly 7 | | 45 |
| | | | (JWUnett) *trckd ldrs: smooth hdwy to go 2nd 3f out: rdn over 1f out: fnd little* | 11/1 | |
| 20-0 | 7 | 3 | **Sabalara (IRE)**[19] 1265 4-9-7 **61** EAhern 1 | | 45 |
| | | | (PWHarris) *trckd ldrs: lost pl over 1f out* | 10/1 | |
| 0-00 | 8 | 5 | **Celtic Romance**[12] 1358 5-9-1 **55** JCarroll 14 | | 29 |
| | | | (MrsMReveley) *bhd: hdwy on wd outside 3f out: nvr nr ldrs* | 25/1 | |
| 2340 | 9 | 1½ | **Ellen Mooney**[29] 1122 5-9-7 **64** THamilton(3) 3 | | 35 |
| | | | (RPElliott) *mid-div: sn drvn along: nvr a factor* | 8/1 | |
| 200- | 10 | shd | **Sienna Sunset (IRE)**[40] 4625 5-9-6 **60** JFEgan 12 | | 30 |
| | | | (MrsHDalton) *mid-div: hung lft and lost pl over 2f out* | 25/1 | |
| 06-0 | 11 | 1¾ | **Lark In The Park (IRE)**[21] 1244 4-8-7 **47** PMQuinn 2 | | 14 |
| | | | (WMBrisbourne) *in tch: effrt over 3f out: lost pl 2f out* | 20/1 | |
| 25-1 | 12 | 6 | **Capetown Girl**[18] 1288 3-9-7 **75** DarrenWilliams 9 | | 30 |
| | | | (KRBurke) *trckd ldrs: hung lft over 3f out: lost pl over 2f out* | 9/2[2] | |
| 000- | 13 | 8 | **Milk And Sultana**[215] 5117 4-8-13 **58** PMulrennan(5) 13 | | — |
| | | | (WMBrisbourne) *chsd ldrs: lost pl over 2f out: eased* | 33/1 | |
| 0-00 | 14 | 8 | **Thumamah (IRE)**[47] 988 5-9-0 **54** (t) MTebbutt 5 | | — |
| | | | (BPJBaugh) *s.i.s: a in rr: virtually p.u ins last* | 50/1 | |

1m 46.84s (1.29) **Going Correction** +0.25s/f (Good)
**WFA** 3 from 4yo+ 14lb **14** Ran SP% **121.5**
Speed ratings: **103,102,95,94,92 91,88,83,81,81 79,73,65,57**CSF £65.22 CT £418.35 TOTE £5.50: £2.30, £6.30, £2.70; EX 161.90 Place 6 £31.54, Place 5 £24.18.
**Owner** Mrs B Riddell **Bred** Mrs Ian Pilkington **Trained** Piercebridge, Co Durham

**FOCUS**
In effect a 0-64 handicap, but fair for the grade, and the first two out on their own at the line.

**NOTEBOOK**
**Commitment Lecture**, whose Newcastle effort has been well advertised, took what looked a decisive lead but at the line there was next to nothing to spare.
**Vermilion Creek**, only sixth in a seller on her previous start, had to seek an opening and, after making up several lengths, was in the end just held at bay.
**Oh So Rosie(IRE)**, a winner three times at two, likes easy ground and stamina did not seem to be a problem.
**Zahunda(IRE)**, who ran the previous night, was ridden totally differently this time, but in the end she fell in a heap.
**Printsmith(IRE)**, a winner twice in banded races, found this beyond her on her return to turf.
**Cloudless(USA)**, on her toes beforehand, looked to have the leader covered but, after moving upsides, she found next to nothing when asked a question.
**Capetown Girl**, backward in her coat, seemed to find this extended trip well beyond her.
T/Plt: £94.30 to a £1 stake. Pool: £30,967.25. 239.70 winning tickets. T/Qpdt: £39.70 to a £1 stake. Pool: £2,045.70. 38.05 winning tickets. WG

# 1219 LEICESTER (R-H)
## Saturday, April 24

**OFFICIAL GOING: Good to soft**
Wind: almost nil Weather: fine & sunny

## 1607 "ORIGINAL" MEDIAN AUCTION MAIDEN STKS — 5f 2y
2:10 (2:11) (E) 2-Y-O £3,542 (£1,090; £545; £272) Stalls Low

| Form | | | | | RPR |
|---|---|---|---|---|---|
| 2 | 1 | | **Goodricke**[19] 1269 2-9-0 LDettori 3 | | 83+ |
| | | | (DRLoder) *s.s: rcvrd to ld 4f out: pushed clr fnl f: eased towards fin* | 1/5[1] | |
| 4 | 2 | 5 | **Langston Boy**[23] 1219 2-9-0 IMongan 2 | | 55 |
| | | | (MLWBell) *a.p: rdn 1/2-way: chsd wnr over 1f out: sn outpcd* | 7/1[2] | |
| 44 | 3 | 2 | **Grezie**[18] 1276 2-8-9 NPollard 4 | | 42 |
| | | | (JRBest) *led 1f: remained handy: rdn over 1f out: sn btn* | 20/1[3] | |
| | 4 | 5 | **Mauro (IRE)** 2-8-6 TPQueally(3) 5 | | 22 |
| | | | (PMPhelan) *chsd ldrs over 3f* | 33/1 | |
| | 5 | 6 | **Listen To Me** 2-9-0 PaulEddery 1 | | — |
| | | | (DHaydnJones) *sn outpcd* | 33/1 | |

63.00 secs (2.07) **Going Correction** +0.275s/f (Good) **5** Ran SP% **106.5**
Speed ratings: **94,86,82,74,65**CSF £1.64 TOTE £1.10: £1.02, £2.10; EX 1.40.
**Owner** Sheikh Mohammed **Bred** Red House Stud **Trained** Newmarket, Suffolk

**FOCUS**
A less than competitive heat and modest form behind the winner. The pace was only steady.

**NOTEBOOK**
**Goodricke**, as on his debut, gave away ground at the start. However, soon on an even keel, he simply outclassed his rivals. He will not get away with giving better opposition a start.
**Langston Boy**, a well-grown colt, is getting the hang of things and better can be expected as he steps up in trip.
**Grezie** has already had three outings even though she has not quite reached two yet. She was far from disgraced and will certainly find easier openings.
**Mauro(IRE)**, out of a mare that was placed as a juvenile, showed plenty of dash on the outside until getting tired.

## 1608 TIGER BEST BITTER H'CAP — 5f 218y
2:40 (2:41) (D) (0-80,80) 3-Y-O+ £5,772 (£1,776; £888; £444) Stalls Low

| Form | | | | | RPR |
|---|---|---|---|---|---|
| 1302 | 1 | | **Whippasnapper**[5] 1504 4-8-9 **61** NPollard 15 | | 73 |
| | | | (JRBest) *racd stands' side: hld up: hdwy over 1f out: qcknd to ld nr fin* | 5/1[1] | |
| 00-4 | 2 | ¾ | **Kingscross**[25] 1185 6-9-6 **72** DSweeney 11 | | 82 |
| | | | (MBlanshard) *racd stands' side: hld up: hdwy over 2f out: r.o to ld wl ins fnl f: hdd nr fin* | 13/2[3] | |
| -504 | 3 | nk | **Romany Nights (IRE)**[28] 1139 4-9-9 **75** (v) SWKelly 7 | | 84 |
| | | | (JWUnett) *racd stands' side: a.p: rdn over 1f out: r.o* | 20/1 | |
| 000- | 4 | nk | **Mr Malarkey (IRE)**[215] 5120 4-9-13 **79** (b) ANicholls 20 | | 87 |
| | | | (MrsCADunnett) *led far side duo: rdn and hung lft fr over 1f out: hdd nr fin* | 25/1 | |
| 53-6 | 5 | ½ | **Dorchester**[61] 866 7-9-5 **74** LisaJones(3) 16 | | 81 |
| | | | (WJMusson) *racd stands' side: chsd ldrs: rdn over 1f out: styd on* | 20/1 | |
| 4101 | 6 | nk | **Hurricane Coast**[4] 1531 5-9-7 **73** 7ex (b) DaneO'Neill 19 | | 79 |
| | | | (DFlood) *s.i.s: racd stands'side: hld up: hdwy over 2f out: rdn over 1f out: styd on same pce* | 11/2[2] | |
| 61-6 | 7 | ½ | **Full Spate**[16] 1313 9-9-2 **68** RLMoore 2 | | 72 |
| | | | (JMBradley) *s.s: racd stands' side: nt clr run and r.o ins fnl f: nrst fin* | 16/1 | |
| -500 | 8 | 2½ | **Branston Tiger**[12] 1361 5-9-10 **76** LDettori 8 | | 73 |
| | | | (JGGiven) *racd stands' side: mid-div: sn drvn along: swtchd rt ins fnl f: nt rch ldrs* | 8/1 | |
| 20-0 | 9 | 1¼ | **Hollow Jo**[4] 1531 4-9-6 **72** FLynch 3 | | 65 |
| | | | (JRJenkins) *disp ld stands' side tl led that gp over 2f out: hdd and no ex over 1f out* | 14/1 | |
| 00-0 | 10 | 1¼ | **Kew The Music**[25] 1185 4-8-13 **65** CCatlin 12 | | 54 |
| | | | (MRChannon) *racd stands' side: mid-div: effrt over 2f out: n.d* | 25/1 | |
| 110- | 11 | nk | **Bob's Buzz**[217] 5077 4-9-4 **70** RMullen 13 | | 58 |
| | | | (SCWilliams) *racd stands side: a in rr: bhd whn hmpd ins fnl* | 25/1 | |
| 0-00 | 12 | 1 | **Ridicule**[16] 1313 5-8-11 **63** (v) SDrowne 14 | | 48 |
| | | | (JGPortman) *racd stands' side: chsd ldrs over 4f* | 33/1 | |
| 000- | 13 | hd | **Elidore**[191] 5597 4-9-12 **78** SSanders 18 | | 63 |
| | | | (BPalling) *chsd ldr far side: rdn 1/2-way: sn outpcd* | 33/1 | |
| 15-0 | 14 | ¾ | **True Night**[13] 1345 7-9-6 **79** LTreadwell(7) 5 | | 62 |
| | | | (DNicholls) *racd stands' side: mid-div: sn drvn along: n.d* | 25/1 | |
| 5006 | 15 | ½ | **Cashel Mead**[25] 1185 4-9-7 **73** ADaly 10 | | 54 |
| | | | (JLSpearing) *s.s: racd stands' side: outpcd* | 16/1 | |
| 033- | 16 | 3½ | **Pinchbeck**[179] 5811 5-9-10 **76** MHenry 6 | | 47 |
| | | | (MAJarvis) *racd stands' side: chsd ldrs over 4f* | 14/1 | |
| 6-50 | 17 | 3½ | **Goodwood Prince**[101] 526 4-9-2 **68** WRyan 1 | | 28 |
| | | | (SDow) *led stands' side over 3f: sn wknd* | 33/1 | |
| 3200 | U | | **Park Star**[9] 1421 4-8-6 **58** WSupple 9 | | — |
| | | | (DShaw) *racd stands' side: mid-div: lost pl over 3f out: bhd whn hmpd and uns rdr ins fnl f* | 33/1 | |
| -015 | U | | **Tidy (IRE)**[5] 1500 4-10-0 **80** RHughes 17 | | — |
| | | | (MDHammond) *racd stands' side: prom: rdn over 1f out: styng on same pce but disputing 3rd whn sddle slipped and uns rdr ins fnl f* | 8/1 | |

1m 14.28s (0.88) **Going Correction** +0.275s/f (Good) **19** Ran SP% **129.4**
Speed ratings: **105,104,103,103,102 102,101,98,96,94 94,93,92,91,91 86,81,—,—**CSF £32.65 CT £623.35 TOTE £5.40: £1.90, £1.80, £5.50, £6.20; EX 56.60.
**Owner** Miss Vanessa Church **Bred** Acrum Lodge Stud **Trained** Hucking, Kent
■ Stewards Enquiry : D Sweeney two-day ban: used whip with excessive frequency and without allowing sufficient time to respond (May 5,6)

**FOCUS**
Quite a competitive sprint and plenty of drama, but the form looks sound. Although the field split, there were only two that elected to race on the far side.

**NOTEBOOK**
**Whippasnapper** showed a smart turn of foot and although a narrow winner, looked to have plenty in hand. Although he stays seven furlongs, this strongly-run six proved ideal, and he will still be well treated under a penalty, compared with his All-Weather rating.
**Kingscross** looked to have done everything just right until collared right on the line. He is well treated on his best form and is one to keep in mind for a similar contest.
**Romany Nights(IRE)** turned in a sound effort on this return to turf, and as he is just 1lb higher than when successful at Newbury, he looks one to keep an eye on as the ground dries up.
**Mr Malarkey(IRE)**, who elected to race on the far side, showed plenty of pace, but as he got tired on ground which could well have been soft enough for him, tended to drift towards the main bunch. He is sure to strip sharper next time.
**Dorchester** shaped quite well considering he has yet to win before July.
**Hurricane Coast** was a little disappointing, but having missed the kick raced more towards the centre of the course where he possibly saw too much daylight.
**Full Spate** made up no end of ground in the closing stages having missed the break. While he is getting no younger, he still retains plenty of ability.
**Tidy(IRE)**, who lost his jockey inside the final furlong, can be rated as though finishing around fifth or sixth place.

## 1609 EVERARDS POPULAR PUBS H'CAP — 1m 3f 183y
3:15 (3:15) (C) (0-90,85) 3-Y-O £9,568 (£2,944; £1,472; £736) Stalls High

| Form | | | | | RPR |
|---|---|---|---|---|---|
| 14-1 | 1 | | **Swagger Stick (USA)**[23] 1222 3-9-7 **80** SSanders 5 | | 94+ |
| | | | (JLDunlop) *trckd ldr tl led 2f out: styd on wl* | 8/11[1] | |
| -455 | 2 | 3 | **Nessen Dorma (IRE)**[9] 1416 3-9-1 **74** LDettori 3 | | 81 |
| | | | (JGGiven) *led: rdn and hdd 2f out: styd on same pce fnl f* | 15/2[3] | |
| 1- | 3 | 5 | **Yoshka**[222] 4950 3-9-5 **78** RFfrench 2 | | 78 |
| | | | (MJohnston) *slowly in to stride: hld up: hdwy 7f out: rdn over 4f out: outpcd over 2f out: styd on ins fnl f* | 5/1[2] | |
| 2231 | 4 | 1½ | **Vantage (IRE)**[2] 1561 3-9-9 **85** 5ex TPQueally(3) 1 | | 82 |
| | | | (NPLittmoden) *plld hrd and prom: rdn over 2f out: wknd over 1f out* | 5/1[2] | |
| 14-0 | 5 | 27 | **Rock Lobster**[12] 1360 3-8-12 **71** BDoyle 4 | | 28 |
| | | | (JGGiven) *chsd ldrs: lost pl 7f out: wknd over 2f out* | 25/1 | |

2m 36.29s (1.61) **Going Correction** +0.175s/f (Good) **5** Ran SP% **106.8**
Speed ratings: **101,99,95,94,76**CSF £6.24 TOTE £1.60: £1.10, £2.60; EX 6.90.
**Owner** Robin F Scully **Bred** Clovelly Farms **Trained** Arundel, W Sussex

**FOCUS**
This wasn't that competitive and was run at a steady pace, but the winner continues on the upgrade.

**NOTEBOOK**
**Swagger Stick(USA)** would not have been ideally suited by the steady pace, but still proved too strong for his rivals. With better to come when faced with a stiffer test, he looks one to keep on the right side of.
**Nessen Dorma(IRE)** had a soft lead and could well be flattered by this effort.
**Yoshka** was not suited by the steady pace and will need more use making of him over this sort of trip.
**Vantage(IRE)** looked to run a little flat and this third run in just over a week may have caught up with him.

## 1610 TOTESPORT LEICESTERSHIRE STKS (LISTED RACE) — 7f 9y
3:50 (3:51) (A) 4-Y-O+ £17,400 (£6,600; £3,300; £1,500) Stalls Low

| Form | | | | | RPR |
|---|---|---|---|---|---|
| 605- | 1 | | **Tout Seul (IRE)**[146] 6102 4-8-12 113 SCarson 8 | | 109 |
| | | | (RFJohnsonHoughton) *chsd ldrs: shkn up to ld ins fnl f: r.o* | 7/2[2] | |
| 100- | 2 | 1¾ | **Polar Ben**[175] 5872 5-9-3 112 OUrbina 1 | | 110 |
| | | | (JRFanshawe) *hld up: hdwy u.p over 1f out: r.o: nt rch wnr* | 3/1[1] | |
| 3332 | 3 | nk | **Rockets 'n Rollers (IRE)**[12] 1367 4-8-12 104 DaneO'Neill 5 | | 104 |
| | | | (RHannon) *chsd ldrs: rdn to ld over 1f out: hdd and unable qck ins fnl f* | 8/1 | |
| 6-14 | 4 | ¾ | **Bahamian Pirate (USA)**[9] 1409 9-8-12 112 LDettori 6 | | 102 |
| | | | (DNicholls) *trckd ldrs: rdn over 1f out: styd on same pce* | 8/1 | |
| 01-5 | 5 | shd | **Makhlab (USA)**[30] 1107 4-8-12 108 WSupple 3 | | 102 |
| | | | (BWHills) *chsd ldrs: rdn and ev ch over 1f out: no ex ins fnl f* | 9/2[3] | |

-005 **6** *1 1/4* **Will He Wish**$^{12}$ [1353] 8-8-12 92 .......... IMongan 9 99
(SGollings) *chsd ldr: rdn to ld wl over 1f out: sn hdd and no ex* **25/1**

0/-3 **7** *1* **Kool (IRE)**$^{12}$ [1367] 5-8-12 .......... SDrowne 4 96
(PFICole) *trckd ldrs: racd keenly: rdn over 2f out: styd on same pce appr fnl f* **12/1**

001- **8** *2 1/2* **Riva Royale**$^{178}$ [5832] 4-8-7 84 .......... TPQueally 11 85
(IAWood) *led: hdd wl over 1f out: sn btn* **100/1**

520- **9** *3 1/2* **Starbeck (IRE)**$^{190}$ [5616] 6-8-9 84 ow2 .......... PMcCabe 10 78
(PHowling) *hld up: rdn over 2f out: n.d* **66/1**

3-00 **10** *1/2* **Crimson Silk**$^{9}$ [1409] 4-8-12 102 .......... PaulEddery 7 80
(DHaydnJones) *hld up: rdn over 2f out: a in rr* **28/1**

1116 **11** *1 1/2* **Aleutian**$^{21}$ [1242] 4-8-12 104 .......... NPollard 2 76
(DRLoder) *s.i.s: hld up: rdn over 2f out: a in rr* **20/1**

1m 26.31s (0.21) **Going Correction** +0.275s/f (Good) **11 Ran SP% 109.9**
Speed ratings: **109,107,106,105,105 104,103,100,96,95 93**CSF £12.52 TOTE £4.50: £1.70, £2.30, £2.00; EX 13.20.
**Owner** Eden Racing **Bred** Johnston King **Trained** Blewbury, Oxon

**FOCUS**
Downgraded to just Listed level now, this still looked a decent contest. Just an ordinary pace for the class of animals on show.

**NOTEBOOK**
**Tout Seul(IRE)**, who faced some stiff tasks as a three-year-old, bounced back to form over what is probably his optimum trip. This can only have done his confidence good, but he will need placing with care.
**Polar Ben**, whose yard has won this three times in the last five years with Warningford, was far from disgraced under his Group Three penalty, and may have been a little unlucky not to add to that record, for he had those around him covered only to find the winner had flown on the outside of the field. There will be other days for him.
**Rockets 'n Rollers(IRE)** had a little to find with some of his rivals on these terms and comes out of this with plenty of credit. While he will need placing with care, there should be enough opportunities for him this term.
**Bahamian Pirate(USA)** was not disgraced over a trip which is beyond his best.
**Makhlab(USA)**, a poor mover in his slower paces, had no excuses and may have to go abroad during the summer to get his favoured soft surface.
**Will He Wish** had plenty to do with the principals on these terms and was far from disgraced. A progressive handicapper last term, he will be difficult to place this time around.

## 1611 PICK EVERARD H'CAP — 1m 1f 218y
**4:25** (4:25) (E) (0-75,75) 3-Y-0+ **£3,659** (£1,126; £563; £281) **Stalls** High

Form RPR

0602 **1** **Icannshift (IRE)**$^{4}$ [1522] 4-8-3 50 .......... RLMoore 3 62
(SDow) *mde virtually all: rdn over 1f out: r.o* **8/1**

U102 **2** *1 1/4* **Dissident (GER)**$^{4}$ [1535] 6-9-4 65 .......... (v) DaneO'Neill 7 75
(DFlood) *chsd wnr: rdn over 1f out: hung rt ins fnl f: nt run on* **9/2**$^{3}$

-252 **3** *1 1/2* **Street Life (IRE)**$^{7}$ [1460] 6-10-0 75 .......... RMullen 6 82
(WJMusson) *hld up: hdwy over 2f out: nt rch ldrs* **5/1**

/5-0 **4** *3/4* **Ipsa Loquitur**$^{23}$ [1224] 4-8-13 60 .......... SDrowne 10 66
(SCWilliams) *hld up: hdwy u.p over 3f out: nt rch ldrs* **20/1**

00-2 **5** *1/2* **Man The Gate**$^{25}$ [1188] 5-8-12 59 .......... SSanders 9 64
(PDCundell) *chsd ldrs: rdn over 2f out: hung lft over 1f out: styd on same pce* **7/2**$^{1}$

33-3 **6** *1 1/4* **Sir Haydn**$^{24}$ [1213] 4-9-10 71 .......... WRyan 8 74
(JRJenkins) *s.i.s: hld up: hdwy and nt clr run over 1f out: eased whn btn towards fin* **22/1**

0-00 **7** *1 1/2* **Maritime Blues**$^{10}$ [1393] 4-9-1 62 .......... BDoyle 11 62
(JGGiven) *chsd ldrs: rdn over 3f out: styd on same pce fnl 2f* **8/1**

43-0 **8** *3/4* **Kernel Dowery (IRE)**$^{16}$ [1308] 4-8-11 58 .......... (p) IMongan 5 57
(PWHarris) *chsd ldrs: rdn over 3f out: wknd over 1f out* **20/1**

300- **9** *1* **Lucky Leo**$^{201}$ [5425] 4-9-7 68 .......... CCatlin 4 65
(IanWilliams) *hld up in tch: lost pl over 6f out: n.d after* **25/1**

11/1 **10** *shd* **Cristoforo (IRE)**$^{17}$ [1305] 7-8-6 56 .......... TPQueally$^{(3)}$ 2 53
(BJCurley) *dwlt: hld up: effrt over 3f out: n.d* **4/1**$^{2}$

2220 **11** *6* **Sonderborg**$^{32}$ [1086] 3-7-7 62 oh3 .......... DFox$^{(5)}$ 1 48
(MissAMNewton-Smith) *hld up: a in rr* **50/1**

2m 9.23s (0.83) **Going Correction** +0.175s/f (Good)
**WFA** 3 from 4yo+ 17lb **11 Ran SP% 119.0**
Speed ratings: **103,102,100,100,99 98,97,97,96,96 91**CSF £41.13 CT £202.81 TOTE £10.30: £2.80, £1.60, £2.20; EX 54.30.
**Owner** R E Anderson **Bred** Piercetown Stud **Trained** Epsom, Surrey

**FOCUS**
An ordinary handicap in which it paid to be up with the pace. The winner is potentially well handicapped.

**NOTEBOOK**
**Icannshift(IRE)** had a soft lead and showed plenty of resolution when it mattered. This time last year, when in the care of Peter Harris, he was racing off a 44lb higher mark, so he may be capable of stepping up on this.
**Dissident(GER)**, the only one to keep tabs on the winner, did not look that keen to go by in the latter stages.
**Street Life(IRE)**, given enough to do in what was a steadily-run event, stuck to his task resolutely, but never had a hope of catching the front pair.
**Ipsa Loquitur**, tackling handicappers for the first time, does not look badly treated, but she may be suited by a stiffer test than she faced here.
**Man The Gate** goes particularly well here, but the steady early pace was no good to him.
**Cristoforo(IRE)** *Official explanation: jockey had no explanation for the poor form shown*

## 1612 BEACON BITTER MAIDEN STKS — 1m 1f 218y
**5:00** (5:01) (D) 3-Y-0+ **£5,746** (£1,768; £884; £442) **Stalls** High

Form RPR

0-3 **1** **Bayhirr**$^{23}$ [1224] 3-8-8 ow1 .......... LDettori 2 81
(MAJarvis) *trckd clr ldr: led over 3f out: clr 2f out: comf* **1/1**$^{1}$

0- **2** *2 1/2* **Sunset Mirage (USA)**$^{214}$ [5138] 3-8-2 .......... RLMoore 8 71
(EALDunlop) *hld up: hdwy over 3f out: wnt 2nd over 1f out: no ch w wnr* **20/1**

**3** *1 1/4* **Nunki (USA)** 3-8-7 .......... WRyan 3 74
(HRACecil) *chsd ldrs: rdn over 2f out: styd on same pce fnl f* **8/1**$^{3}$

**4** *3 1/2* **Race The Ace** 3-8-7 .......... SSanders 4 67
(JLDunlop) *s.s: hld up: hdwy over 3f out: nt rch ldrs* **16/1**

00-0 **5** *4* **Patrixtoo (FR)**$^{19}$ [1271] 3-8-0 .......... SaleemGolam$^{(7)}$ 1 60
(MHTompkins) *prom: jnd wnr 3f out: sn rdn: wknd wl over 1f out* **25/1**

**6** *7* **Talwandi (IRE)** 3-8-7 .......... BDoyle 12 47
(SirMichaelStoute) *chsd ldrs over 7f* **11/1**

000- **7** *1 1/2* **Kalanisha (IRE)**$^{210}$ [5227] 4-9-10 .......... PaulEddery 10 45
(NAGraham) *outpcd: nvr nrr* **100/1**

**8** *3/4* **I'Ll Fly**$^{38}$ 4-9-10 .......... OUrbina 11 43
(JRFanshawe) *hld up: hdwy over 3f out: wknd over 2f out* **12/1**

0 **9** *3/4* **Court Emperor**$^{23}$ [1221] 4-9-7 .......... TPQueally$^{(3)}$ 13 42
(RJPrice) *s.i.s: rdn over 3f out: a in rr* **150/1**

**10** *3/4* **Helm (IRE)** 3-8-4 .......... NMackay$^{(3)}$ 5 41
(LMCumani) *sn pushed along: a in rr* **25/1**

00/ **11** *hd* **Lake Of Dreams**$^{528}$ [5698] 5-9-3 .......... LucyRussell$^{(7)}$ 14 40
(DrJRJNaylor) *chsd ldrs over 7f* **150/1**

0 **12** *1/2* **Logger Rhythm (USA)**$^{16}$ [1311] 4-9-10 .......... DaneO'Neill 9 39
(RDickin) *a in rr* **66/1**

**13** *2 1/2* **Choir Leader** 3-8-7 .......... RMullen 6 35
(WJHaggas) *s.s: effrt over 3f out: sn wknd* **11/2**$^{2}$

**14** *dist* **Ba Clubman (IRE)** 4-9-10 .......... (b$^{1}$) SDrowne 7 —
(SCWilliams) *led and sn clr: hung lft over 5f out: wknd and hdd over 3f out* **40/1**

**15** *dist* **Atlantic Waltz** 4-9-7 .......... (t) DCorby$^{(3)}$ 15 —
(JJSheehan) *sn outpcd and bhd* **100/1**

2m 9.00s (0.60) **Going Correction** +0.175s/f (Good)
**WFA** 3 from 4yo+ 17lb **15 Ran SP% 118.1**
Speed ratings: **104,102,101,98,95 89,88,87,87,86 86,85,83,—,—**CSF £29.67 TOTE £1.80: £1.30, £4.70, £2.50; EX 16.50.
**Owner** Sheikh Ahmed Al Maktoum **Bred** Darley **Trained** Newmarket, Suffolk

**FOCUS**
This didn't look that strong a maiden, although the time was reasonable and the winner is almost certainly capable of better.

**NOTEBOOK**
**Bayhirr**, a half-brother to Cheveley Park winner Embassy as well as ten-furlong winner Tarfshi, gained compensation for what looked an unlucky outing over course and distance last time. While he may not have beaten much, he won with authority and is open to further improvement.
**Sunset Mirage(USA)**, a half-sister to several winners including Loving Pride, winner over a mile in France, plugged on her own time, and her future looks to lie in handicaps.
**Nunki(USA)**, from the same family as the high-class pair Machiavellian and Exit To Nowhere, did not shape too badly and should certainly improve for the experience, but he will need to.
**Race The Ace**, a half-brother to useful stayer Give Notice, turned in a sound first effort and will undoubtedly step up on this when tackling further in handicap company.
**Patrixtoo(FR)**, whose future appears to lie in handicaps, looks as though he will appreciate a step up in trip.
**Talwandi(IRE)**, a May foal, has some catching up to do and will no doubt do better as he gets stronger.

## 1613 PERFICK H'CAP — 1m 9y
**5:30** (5:30) (E) (0-75,74) 3-Y-0 **£3,844** (£1,183; £591; £295) **Stalls** High

Form RPR

30-0 **1** **Toparudi**$^{9}$ [1418] 3-8-9 69 .......... SaleemGolam$^{(7)}$ 14 72
(MHTompkins) *chsd ldrs: rdn over 1f out: r.o to ld post* **12/1**

3051 **2** *shd* **Phluke**$^{10}$ [1392] 3-9-3 70 .......... SCarson 16 73
(RFJohnsonHoughton) *led: rdn and edgd lft over 1f out: hdd post* **4/1**$^{1}$

300- **3** *2 1/2* **Lady Georgina**$^{168}$ [5950] 3-9-4 71 .......... DaneO'Neill 12 69
(JRFanshawe) *chsd ldrs: rdn and ev ch over 1f out: one pce ins fnl f* **8/1**$^{3}$

050- **4** *1* **Morag**$^{168}$ [5950] 3-9-0 70 .......... TPQueally$^{(3)}$ 13 66
(IAWood) *hld up in tch: hmpd over 2f out: rdn over 1f out: styd on same pce ins fnl f* **33/1**

00-4 **5** *1/2* **King Of Knight (IRE)**$^{12}$ [1371] 3-9-3 70 .......... OUrbina 5 65
(GProdromou) *hld up: hdwy over 2f out: styd on under presure* **12/1**

4005 **6** *2 1/2* **Head Boy**$^{19}$ [1270] 3-8-4 57 .......... PDoe 4 46
(SDow) *hld up: hdwy 3f out: rdn and edgd rt over 1f out: no ex* **9/1**

16-0 **7** *2* **Ermine Grey**$^{23}$ [1222] 3-9-6 73 .......... (b) PaulEddery 9 58
(DHaydnJones) *hld up: plld hrd: hmpd 3f out: rdn over 1f out: nvr trbld ldrs* **10/1**

400- **8** *1* **Ablaj (IRE)**$^{173}$ [5905] 3-8-7 60 .......... SDrowne 8 43
(EALDunlop) *chsd ldrs: lost pl over 4f out: hmpd 3f out: n.d after* **14/1**

634- **9** *shd* **Nantucket Sound (USA)**$^{136}$ [6158] 3-9-0 70 .......... NMackay$^{(3)}$ 15 53
(MCPipe) *dwlt: hld up: hmpd 3f out: n.d* **16/1**

140- **10** *1/2* **Susiedil (IRE)**$^{201}$ [5421] 3-8-12 65 .......... BDoyle 2 47
(PWHarris) *chsd ldrs over 5f* **33/1**

224- **11** *13* **Danish Monarch**$^{205}$ [5325] 3-9-4 74 .......... DCorby$^{(3)}$ 11 28
(ADWPinder) *chsd ldr: rdn and ev ch over 2f out: sn wknd* **20/1**

051- **12** *6* **Aesculus (USA)**$^{158}$ [6018] 3-9-5 72 .......... LDettori 10 14
(LMCumani) *mid-div: hdwy 3f out: sn wknd* **9/2**$^{2}$

406- **13** *4* **Erte**$^{195}$ [5503] 3-8-11 64 .......... CCatlin 1 —
(MRChannon) *bhd fr 1/2-way* **20/1**

-250 **14** *dist* **Bold Blade**$^{10}$ [1392] 3-8-12 65 .......... (b) FLynch 6 —
(BSmart) *bhd fr 1/2-way* **20/1**

000- **15** *20* **Growler**$^{168}$ [5950] 3-8-8 61 .......... SSanders 7 —
(JLDunlop) *hld up: rdn 1/2-way: sn wknd* **14/1**

00-0 **U** **Hatch A Plan (IRE)**$^{21}$ [1243] 3-8-13 66 .......... RMullen 3 —
(RMBeckett) *chsd ldrs: n.m.r: stmbld and uns rdr 3f out* **20/1**

1m 44.14s (1.54) **Going Correction** +0.175s/f (Good) **16 Ran SP% 127.9**
Speed ratings: **99,98,96,95,94 92,90,89,89,88 75,69,65,—,— —**CSF £56.21 CT £334.33 TOTE £16.90: £4.70, £1.30, £2.10, £15.40; EX 83.00 Place 6 £14.98, Place 5 £14.62.
**Owner** M P Bowring **Bred** M P Bowring **Trained** Newmarket, Suffolk

**FOCUS**
An ordinary contest run at a steady pace and the first four home all had double figure draws..

**NOTEBOOK**
**Toparudi**, dropped 2lb since his seasonal debut, took advantage of his high draw. If he is to go on from this, he will need to learn to settle better.
**Phluke** had the best of the draw and made a bold bid to follow up his Beverley success. However, despite having a soft time of it up front, he was just unable to repel the persistent winner.
**Lady Georgina**, who had shown her best form as a juvenile on a fast surface, may have just found this ground against her. However, she will be much sharper next time.
**Morag** turned in a sound enough effort, but was one of the many who would have been suited by a proper gallop.
**King Of Knight(IRE)**, tackling handicappers for the first time, was not disgraced from his low draw and may have done better had he not tried to come down the centre of the track once in line for home.
**Head Boy** has yet to convince at this trip.
**Aesculus(USA)** *Official explanation: jockey said filly had lost her action*
**Growler** *Official explanation: jockey said gelding was bumped approaching the turn out of the back straight and was never travelling thereafter*

T/Plt: £13.00 to a £1 stake. Pool: £27,847.30. 1,551.80 winning tickets. T/Qpdt: £5.30 to a £1 stake. Pool: £1,341.10. 185.40 winning tickets. CR

# [1415]RIPON (R-H)

## Saturday, April 24

**OFFICIAL GOING: Good to soft**

### 1614 RIPON FUTURE SPRINT STARS H'CAP 6f

2:00 (2:01) (C) (0-95,93) 3-Y-O £8,572 (£3,251; £1,625; £739) Stalls Low

| Form | | | | RPR |
|---|---|---|---|---|
| 020- | 1 | | **High Voltage**[219] 5009 3-9-5 91 (t) DarrenWilliams 10 (KRBurke) *mde all far side: drew clr fr 2f out* 40/1 | 103 |
| 016- | 2 | 3 | **Red Romeo**[218] 5033 3-8-2 74 DaleGibson 4 (GASwinbank) *led stands side gp: rdn and kpt on fr 2f out: nt rch far side wnr* 25/1 | 77 |
| 3-51 | 3 | ½ | **Distant Times**[17] 1303 3-8-7 79 KDarley 14 (TDEasterby) *trckd far side ldrs: effrt 2f out: kpt on fnl f: no imp* 7/4[1] | 81 |
| 10-0 | 4 | 1 | **Xpres Digital**[4] 1531 3-8-3 75 (t) JBramhill 2 (SRBowring) *chsd stands side ldrs: rdn over 2f out: kpt on fnl f* 33/1 | 74 |
| 2-00 | 5 | 1¼ | **Lets Get It On (IRE)**[7] 1473 3-8-5 77 RWinston 12 (JJQuinn) *bhd far side: rdn 1/2-way: kpt on fnl f: no imp* 20/1 | 72 |
| 154- | 6 | shd | **Iskander**[210] 5232 3-9-7 93 (b) NCallan 13 (KARyan) *s.i.s: bhd far side: rdn 1/2-way: nvr rchd ldrs* 25/1 | 87 |
| -413 | 7 | hd | **Petardias Magic (IRE)**[11] 1388 3-8-13 85 JCarroll 11 (EJO'Neill) *in tch far side tl rdn and outpcd fr 2f out* 5/2[2] | 79 |
| 100- | 8 | hd | **Bright Sun (IRE)**[190] 5613 3-9-0 86 KimTinkler 6 (NTinkler) *chsd stands side ldrs tl outpcd fr over 2f out* 28/1 | 79 |
| 2-51 | 9 | 1 | **Four Amigos (USA)**[7] 1473 3-9-1 87 JFanning 7 (JGGiven) *pressed wnr far side tl rdn and wknd ent fnl f* 6/1[3] | 77 |
| 0-00 | 10 | 1½ | **Poppys Footprint (IRE)**[9] 1408 3-8-8 80 GParkin 9 (KARyan) *hld up outside of far side gp: rdn over 2f out: btn ins fnl f* 33/1 | 66 |
| 032- | 11 | 1½ | **Mrs Moh (IRE)**[168] 5950 3-8-4 83 AMullen(7) 5 (TDEasterby) *cl up stands side tl wknd 2f out* 14/1 | 64 |
| 000- | 12 | 1¼ | **Reidies Choice**[178] 5829 3-8-5 77 MFenton 3 (JGGiven) *dwlt: n.d stands side* 33/1 | 55 |
| 000- | 13 | 2 | **George The Best (IRE)**[208] 5273 3-8-10 82 EAhern 1 (MDHammond) *a bhd stands side* 25/1 | 54 |
| 30-0 | 14 | 1 | **Fox Covert (IRE)**[24] 1200 3-7-12 70 oh1 (p) PHanagan 8 (DWBarker) *cl up far side to 1/2-way: sn wknd* 25/1 | 39 |

1m 14.15s (1.25) **Going Correction** +0.25s/f (Good) **14 Ran SP% 120.7**
Speed ratings: **101,97,96,95,93 93,92,92,91,89 87,85,83,81**CSF £776.96 CT £2758.99 TOTE £47.80: £10.80, £4.10, £1.10; EX 586.50.
**Owner** Mrs K Halsall **Bred** D P Martin **Trained** Middleham Moor, N Yorks

**FOCUS**
Few progressive performers in this fairly valuable handicap but a wide-margin winner. Although the winner raced on the far side there was no particular advantage in the draw (stalls 1 to 6 raced stands side and the remainder tacked over to the far side) and very few got into it from off the pace.

**NOTEBOOK**
**High Voltage**, under an enterprising ride, turned in a much-improved performance on his reappearance with the tongue tie on for only the second time. This was a smart effort, but he will find life much tougher in a more competitive race after reassessment.
**Red Romeo ◆**, back in trip and on this first start on easy ground, was easy to back, but fared the best of those that raced on the stands'-side group and will be of interest in similar company next time, especially if returned to seven furlongs.
**Distant Times**, who had the rub of a very uncompetitive race last time, was anything but disgraced after being upped 6lb, but is likely to continue to look vulnerable from his current mark in similar handicap company.
**Xpres Digital**, a proven performer on easy ground, bettered his reappearance effort returned to six furlongs but, on this evidence, looks worth another try over that longer trip.
**Lets Get It On(IRE)**fared the best of those that attempted to come from off the pace, so may be a bit better than the bare form, but she has not always looked straightforward and looks plenty high enough in the weights at present.
**Iskander** was not disgraced after losing ground at the start on this reappearance run, but he looks on a very stiff mark at present and will almost certainly need some leniency in handicaps if he is to regain the winning thread.
**Petardias Magic(IRE)** looked to have solid claims on his recent easy-ground form over this trip but was below that level on this more undulating track. He is certainly capable of better and is not one to write off yet.
**George The Best(IRE)** *Official explanation: jockey said gelding hung left throughout*

### 1615 C. B. HUTCHINSON MEMORIAL CHALLENGE CUP (HANDICAP STKS) 2m

2:35 (2:36) (C) (0-90,89) 4-Y-O+ £8,642 (£3,278; £1,639; £745) Stalls Low

| Form | | | | RPR |
|---|---|---|---|---|
| 6403 | 1 | | **George Stubbs (USA)**[17] 1302 6-7-10 62 JFMcDonald(5) 17 (MJPolglase) *keen: hld up ins: hdwy whn n.m.r over 2f out: led over 1f out: hld on wl* 14/1 | 71 |
| 31-0 | 2 | nk | **The Ring (IRE)**[24] 1210 4-8-5 70 ow1 KDarley 12 (MrsMReveley) *prom: effrt over 2f out: ev ch ins fnl f: kpt on: jst hld* 8/1[3] | 79 |
| 21-0 | 3 | 1¼ | **Greenwich Meantime**[24] 1210 4-9-0 79 ACulhane 7 (MrsJRRamsden) *hld up and bhd: hdwy ins over 2f out: swtchd and kpt on fnl f* 12/1 | 87 |
| 00-3 | 4 | shd | **Thewhirlingdervish (IRE)**[14] 1326 6-8-10 78 AMullen(7) 16 (TDEasterby) *hld up: hdwy over 2f out: effrt over 1f out: kpt on fnl f* 9/1 | 85 |
| 233- | 5 | 1 | **Kristensen**[171] 5926 5-9-8 83 (p) JQuinn 8 (DEddy) *hld up: hdwy 3f out: rdn and kpt on fnl f: nrst fin* 16/1 | 89 |
| 6-50 | 6 | 3½ | **Heir To Be**[7] 1457 5-8-11 72 PRobinson 3 (JLDunlop) *keen early: prom: effrt over 2f out: hung rt: wknd over 1f out* 8/1[3] | 74 |
| 2344 | 7 | ½ | **Jadeeron**[13] 1341 5-8-3 67 ow2 (p) SHitchcott(3) 9 (MissDAMchale) *keen early: prom tl rdn and outpcd fr over 2f out* 14/1 | 68 |
| 114- | 8 | ½ | **Dr Sharp (IRE)**[14] 2873 4-8-6 71 DaleGibson 13 (TPTate) *led to 3f out: outpcd over 1f out* 15/2[2] | 72 |
| 660- | 9 | nk | **Freedom Now (IRE)**[77] 5617 6-9-1 76 DarrenWilliams 11 (MDHammond) *hld up: effrt whn n.m.r 3f out: edgd rt and sn n.d* 33/1 | 76 |
| -000 | 10 | 3½ | **Riyadh**[7] 1457 6-8-4 72 (v) WHogg(7) 1 (MJohnston) *hld up: hdwy and in tch 3f out: hung rt and wknd wl over 1f out* 25/1 | 68 |
| 433- | 11 | hd | **Mana D'Argent (IRE)**[222] 4941 7-10-0 89 JFanning 15 (MJohnston) *cl up: led 3f out to over 1f out: sn btn* 16/1 | 85 |
| 406- | 12 | 3½ | **Mr Fortywinks (IRE)**[213] 5146 10-7-12 59 oh3 PHanagan 2 (BEllison) *midfield: rdn over 4f out: nvr rchd ldrs* 16/1 | 51 |
| 6-22 | 13 | ½ | **Vicars Destiny**[9] 1287 6-8-8 69 EAhern 5 (MrsSLamyman) *midfield: effrt over 3f out: sn no imp* 7/1[1] | 60 |
| 660 | 14 | 1 | **Celtic Vision (IRE)**[12] 1367 8-7-13 60 (t) SRighton 14 (MAppleby) *hld up: hdwy over 3f out: wknd over 2f out* 66/1 | 50 |
| 01-0 | 15 | ½ | **Killing Joke**[18] 1287 4-8-8 73 MFenton 10 (JGGiven) *prom tl wknd fr over 3f out* 33/1 | 62 |
| 0/ | 16 | 8 | **Always Rainbows (IRE)**[33] 5669 6-8-9 75 (v) TEaves(5) 4 (BSRothwell) *cl up tl wknd fr over 3f out* 50/1 | 55 |
| 31 | 17 | 8 | **Zoltano (GER)**[16] 1316 6-8-8 69 RWinston 6 (MTodhunter) *prom: rdn over 3f out: sn btn* 8/1[3] | 39 |

3m 34.9s (1.40) **Going Correction** +0.25s/f (Good)
**WFA** 4 from 5yo+ 4lb **17 Ran SP% 119.5**
Speed ratings: **106,105,105,105,104 102,102,102,102,100 100,98,98,97,97 93,89**CSF £113.88 CT £1401.15 TOTE £15.30: £3.70, £2.10, £3.00, £2.60; EX 171.70.
**Owner** Paul J Dixon **Bred** Woodlynn Farm Inc **Trained** Southwell, Notts

**FOCUS**
A fair handicap but, although the pace was only fair in the first half of the contest, those held up filled three of the first four placings. The chief protaganists either raced or made ground up close to the favoured far rail.

**NOTEBOOK**
**George Stubbs(USA)** is a tough sort who fully confirmed previous promise and showed the right attitude to win his first race over this trip and break a losing run. He should not be going up too much for this and should continue to give a good account.
**The Ring(IRE)**, who shaped as though his reappearance run was needed, had the run of the race and fared better this time. He has not always looked 100% straightforward, but is a consistent sort who is capable of winning again from a similar mark.
**Greenwich Meantime ◆** fared much better than on his reappearance and looks a bit better than the bare result, as he was set plenty to do in a race run at only a modest pace. On this evidence he looks sure to win more races.
**Thewhirlingdervish(IRE) ◆**, who has slipped to a fair mark, confirmed reappearance promise and, although he has not won for some time, looks capable of returning to winning ways at some point in the near future. He would have been suited by a stronger end-to-end gallop and is one to keep an eye on.
**Kristensen** is a consistent sort who again ran his race. He may be a bit better than the bare form as he was dropped out in a race run at a modest pace and fared the best of those that attempted to make ground in the centre of the course. However, he looks vulnerable from this mark and his losing run of over two years is a concern.
**Heir To Be** fared better in terms of form than at Newbury, but again did not look straightforward as he took a good hold and just wanted to hang under pressure. He is capable of winning from this mark but does not look one to rely on.
**Jadeeron**, who was not seen to best effect last time, was not totally disgraced but is almost certainly happier on much faster ground. He is a bit better than his last two runs suggest and is not one to write off yet.
**Mana D'Argent(IRE)** had the run of the race but showed enough to suggest he retains most of his ability. He is an Ascot specialist who usually comes into his own from summer onwards, and will be one to keep an eye on when returned to the Berkshire venue in due course.
**Vicars Destiny** was below her recent best, but she was not really suited by the way this race unfolded or by attempting to make ground in the centre of the course. This run is best overlooked. *Official explanation: jockey said mare was unsuited by the slow early pace and ran flat in the home straight*
**Zoltano(GER)** *Official explanation: vet said gelding finished lame*

### 1616 DISHFORTH NOVICE AUCTION FILLIES' STKS 5f

3:10 (3:10) (E) 2-Y-O £4,017 (£1,236; £618; £309) Stalls Low

| Form | | | | RPR |
|---|---|---|---|---|
| 51 | 1 | | **Polly Alexander (IRE)**[17] 1299 2-8-10 KDarley 3 (MJWallace) *mde all: drvn out fnl f* 8/11[1] | 78 |
| 224 | 2 | ½ | **Evanesce**[12] 1374 2-8-3 ow4 SHitchcott(3) 2 (MRChannon) *chsd ldrs: effrt and swtchd wl over 1f out: r.o fnl f* 3/1[2] | 72 |
| | 3 | 5 | **Angelofthenorth** 2-8-2 JFanning 4 (JDBethell) *chsd ldrs tl rdn and outpcd over 1f out* 12/1 | 48 |
| | 4 | 2 | **Chicago Nights (IRE)** 2-8-2 PHanagan 5 (PCHaslam) *prom to 1/2-way: sn rdn and outpcd* 15/2[3] | 40 |
| | 5 | ½ | **Balashova** 2-8-2 DaleGibson 1 (KRBurke) *sn outpcd: nvr on terms* 25/1 | 38 |

62.52 secs (2.32) **Going Correction** +0.25s/f (Good) **5 Ran SP% 106.2**
Speed ratings: **91,90,82,79,78**CSF £2.81 TOTE £1.70: £1.10, £1.60; EX 2.70.
**Owner** Mrs T A Foreman **Bred** Mrs T A Foreman **Trained** Newmarket, Suffolk

**FOCUS**
An uncompetitive event in which those with experience came to the fore and it is unlikely this race will be throwing up too many winners in the near future. The pace seemed fair and the winner had the run of the race against the stands rail.

**NOTEBOOK**
**Polly Alexander(IRE)** had the run of the race next to the stands' rail and probably did not have to improve to beat the only other in this modest field with experience. Although she did nothing wrong she is likely to look vulnerable in a more competitive event.
**Evanesce** is starting to look exposed, but ran another creditable race on this first start on easy ground with her rider putting up 4lb overweight. However, it will be a similarly modest and uncompetitive event she wins at this level.
**Angelofthenorth** is related to winners but, while she hinted at ability on this racecourse debut against a couple of more experienced rivals, did not really show enough to suggest she will be winning in the near future.
**Chicago Nights(IRE)**, the first foal of a mare who is a half-sister to juvenile seven-furlong winner Comfy, offered little immediate promise on this debut but is bred to do better over further in ordinary handicap company in due course.
**Balashova**, the first foal of a multiple six-furlong winner, was green and offered little immediate promise on this racecourse debut.

### 1617 BANDSTAND (S) STKS 1m 2f

3:45 (3:46) (F) 3-4-Y-O £3,241 (£926; £463) Stalls High

| Form | | | | RPR |
|---|---|---|---|---|
| 0340 | 1 | | **Fortunes Favourite**[22] 1238 4-9-5 40 EAhern 7 (GMMoore) *cl up: outpcd 3f out: rallied to ld over 1f out: pushed out* 7/2[1] | 50 |
| 000- | 2 | 2 | **Let It Be**[185] 5701 3-8-2 PHanagan 8 (MrsMReveley) *in tch: outpcd 4f out: rallied to ld chse wnr over 1f out: kpt on* 11/2 | 46 |
| 050- | 3 | 1¼ | **Senza Scrupoli**[12] 6177 4-9-10 70 (b) KDarley 6 (MDHammond) *hld up in tch: outpcd 1/2-way: rallied over 2f out: no imp fnl f* 9/2[3] | 49 |
| 60-0 | 4 | 3½ | **Littleton Valar (IRE)**[25] 445 4-9-3 30 DFentiman(7) 4 (JRWeymes) *led to 4f out: rallied: wknd over 1f out* 10/1 | 43 |
| 5456 | 5 | 7 | **Ballyrush (IRE)**[19] 1274 4-9-3 53 (p) RKeogh(7) 3 (KRBurke) *cl up: led 4f out to over 1f out: hung rt and sn btn* 4/1[2] | 30 |
| 00-0 | 6 | 23 | **Zabadou**[14] 1325 3-8-3 ow1 TEaves(5) 2 (CBBBooth) *in tch to 1/2-way: sn outpcd* 16/1 | — |
| | 7 | 4 | **Lucayan Belle** 3-7-11 (v[1]) HayleyTurner(5) 5 (MLWBell) *sn outpcd: nvr on terms* 5/1 | — |

000- **8** *6* **Lord Wishingwell (IRE)**[175] 5867 3-8-1 ow1....................(p) AReilly(7) 1 —
(JSWainwright) *cl up tl wknd over 4f out* **16/1**

2m 10.84s (2.84) **Going Correction** +0.25s/f (Good)
**WFA** 3 from 4yo 17lb **8** Ran SP% **113.3**
Speed ratings: **98,96,95,92,87 68,65,60**CSF £22.52 TOTE £4.90: £1.80, £1.20, £1.50; EX 26.20.There was no bid for the winner.
**Owner** Lucayan Stud **Bred** Lucayan Stud Ltd And Whatton Manor Stud **Trained** Middleham Moor, N Yorks

**FOCUS**
A weak race, even by selling standards, advertised by the fact that 40-rated Fortunes Favourite ran out a decisive winner after racing close to the far-side rail throughout. The pace was fair but it is a race unlikely to be throwing up many winners.

**NOTEBOOK**
**Fortunes Favourite** is only rated 40 but ran out a fairly convincing winner. The return to a mile and a half will suit and she is unexposed on turf, but this was a poor event and one that is unlikely to be throwing up too many winners.
**Let It Be**, upped in trip for this reappearance, probably ran her best race to date and should be suited by further. It will be a poor race she wins, but she is in good hands and is likely to be placed to best advantage.
**Senza Scrupoli**, a poor hurdler, confirmed himself as poor back on the Flat and, although his current rating of 70 is likely to take a considerable drop after reassessment, it will be a bad race he eventually wins.
**Littleton Valar(IRE)**, rated 30, was not disgraced back on the Flat but his proximity is further confirmation that this race is of the lowest standard.
**Ballyrush(IRE)**had a decent chance in this company on his best efforts but he looked less than straightforward under pressure and was again a long way below his best. He is one to tread carefully with.
**Zabadou** again showed nothing.
**Lucayan Belle** cost 25,000 guineas and is related to winners, but was sporting a first-time visor for this racecourse debut and showed absolutely nothing.

## 1618 RIPON-RACES.CO.UK CONDITIONS STKS 1m 4f 60y
4:20 (4:22) (C) 4-Y-0+ £10,332 (£3,666; £1,833; £833) Stalls High

Form RPR
035- **1** **Putra Sandhurst (IRE)**[168] 5951 6-8-9 104.......................... PRobinson 3 107
(MAJarvis) *mde all: rdn over 1f out: kpt on wl* **7/4**[1]
525/ **2** *1* **Grampian**[540] 5577 5-8-9 102............................................ MFenton 1 106
(JGGiven) *hld up in tch: hdwy to chse wnr over 1f out: r.o fnl f* **5/1**
/34- **3** *5* **Silver Gilt**[352] 1473 4-8-8 102.............................................. KDarley 2 98
(JHMGosden) *trckd ldrs: outpcd 3f out: n.d after* **3/1**[3]
131/ **4** *3/4* **Legal Approach**[581] 4792 5-8-9 ........................................... JFanning 4 97
(MJohnston) *trckd wnr: rdn over 3f out: wknd over 1f out* **5/2**[2]

2m 41.83s (1.93) **Going Correction** +0.25s/f (Good)
**WFA** 4 from 5yo+ 1lb **4** Ran SP% **106.6**
Speed ratings: **103,102,99,98**CSF £9.77 TOTE £2.90; EX 13.70.
**Owner** H R H Sultan Ahmad Shah **Bred** Neville O'Byrne **Trained** Newmarket, Suffolk

**FOCUS**
A fairly useful field but not a race to take at face value as the winner, who was one of only two to race last year, was allowed to dictate a moderate pace against the inside rail at a course that very much suits his style of racing.

**NOTEBOOK**
**Putra Sandhurst(IRE)** a smart performer, was bandaged heavily in front but looked in tremendous condition and was given a fine ride at a course that suits his style of racing. Although the bare result is potentially misleading, he is the type who will always be seen to best effect in single-figure fields when allowed to dominate.
**Grampian** had not been seen since 2002, but confirmed he retains a good deal of his ability and he is probably a bit better than the bare form. A stronger gallop over this trip would have suited and he should be better for the run, but he will have to improve to win a competitive handicap from his current mark.
**Silver Gilt** had shown he was capable of smart form but he was below his best on this first start for nearly a year. He may be better for this run and may be suited by the return to further but he might not be easy to place successfully.
**Legal Approach**, the winner of four of his five races, had not been seen since September 2002 but looked in magnificent shape for this reappearance. He showed he retains ability before lack of peak fitness told but, although he should come on for the run, is another that may not be the easiest to place successfully.

## 1619 ALDBOROUGH MAIDEN FILLIES' STKS 1m 2f
4:55 (4:57) (D) 3-Y-O £4,143 (£1,275; £637; £318) Stalls High

Form RPR
20- **1** **Maganda (IRE)**[175] 5874 3-8-11 ........................................... PRobinson 7 75+
(MAJarvis) *trckd ldrs: led 2f out: edgd rt: rdn out* **4/6**[1]
0 **2** *1 1/2* **Stocking Island**[10] 1400 3-8-11 ........................................ JCarroll 6 73
(BHanbury) *mde most to 2f out: kpt on ins fnl f* **16/1**
65- **3** *3* **Trullitti (IRE)**[203] 5369 3-8-11 .............................................. KDarley 1 67
(JLDunlop) *hld up in tch: hdwy to chal 2f out: one pce fnl f* **6/1**[3]
02- **4** *3 1/2* **Bubbling Fun**[190] 5619 3-8-11 ........................................... PHanagan 8 61
(EALDunlop) *keen: in tch: outpcd 3f out: no imp fr 2f out* **20/1**
3- **5** *1* **Exclusive Danielle**[185] 5701 3-8-11 .................................. ACulhane 5 59
(BWHills) *cl up: n.m.r and outpcd over 3f out: sn n.d* **9/2**[2]
0- **6** *1 1/4* **Citrine Spirit (IRE)**[175] 5868 3-8-11 ................................... RHavlin 2 57
(JHMGosden) *stdd s: keen: hld up: hdwy and ev ch 2f out: sn rdn and btn* **20/1**
**7** *5* **Jalousie Dream** 3-8-6 ......................................................... TEaves(5) 3 48
(GMMoore) *hld up in tch: rdn 4f out: wknd over 2f out* **100/1**
03- **8** *9* **Ctesiphon (USA)**[124] 6228 3-8-11 ......................................... MFenton 4 32
(JGGiven) *hung rt thrght: blkd after 3f: sn outpcd* **33/1**

2m 9.55s (1.55) **Going Correction** +0.25s/f (Good) **8** Ran SP% **111.8**
Speed ratings: **103,101,99,96,95 94,90,83**CSF £12.02 TOTE £1.70: £1.02, £4.40, £2.00; EX 14.50.
**Owner** N R A Springer **Bred** Barronstown Stud And Orpendale **Trained** Newmarket, Suffolk

**FOCUS**
Just a run-of-the-mill fillies' maiden in which the pace was on the steady side and one in which the winner did not have to improve to get off the mark.

**NOTEBOOK**
**Maganda(IRE)**, who is in very good hands, did not have to improve to get off the mark in workmanlike fashion. Although this was not much of a race, she is open to improvement and shaped as though the step up to a mile and a half would suit.
**Stocking Island** had the run of the race and bettered her debut form, but is likely to continue to look vulnerable against progressive sorts in this type of event.
**Trullitti(IRE)** again showed ability on this reappearance run and, although another that is likely to continue to look vulnerable against progressive types in this grade, may fare better in ordinary handicaps at up to a mile and a half.
**Bubbling Fun** was not totally disgraced on this reappearance run, despite failing to settle early on. She is likely to continue to look vulnerable in this grade, but may do better in ordinary handicaps in due course.
**Exclusive Danielle** failed to build on debut promise on this reappearance run but did meet trouble. She may do better in due course but it will be a similarly ordinary event in this grade she wins.
**Citrine Spirit(IRE)** is a bit better than the bare form as he was keen, raced wide and attempted to come from off the pace in a steadily-run event. She will have to settle to progress and will be seen to better effect in ordinary handicaps.

## 1620 BBC RADIO YORK SPORT H'CAP 1m
5:25 (5:27) (E) (0-70,69) 3-Y-0+ £3,935 (£1,211; £605; £302) Stalls High

Form RPR
00-4 **1** **Hills Of Gold**[12] 1358 5-9-10 66.......................................... KDarley 20 76
(MWEasterby) *prom: rdn to ld over 1f out: styd on wl* **5/1**[1]
2-61 **2** *3/4* **Megan's Magic**[2] 1560 4-9-9 65 5ex................................ DRMcCabe 14 73
(WStorey) *hld up: effrt and swtchd over 2f out: rdn over 1f out: r.o fnl f* **6/1**[2]
5634 **3** *1* **Goodbye Mr Bond**[21] 1247 4-8-9 51.................................... JFEgan 4 57+
(EJAlston) *hld up wd: effrt over 2f out: r.o fnl f* **9/1**
-060 **4** *2* **Pride Of Kinloch**[8] 1452 4-9-4 60................................ RFitzpatrick 19 62
(JHetherton) *in tch: rdn over 2f out: kpt on fnl f* **50/1**
66-0 **5** *shd* **Hula Ballew**[21] 1247 4-9-3 59............................................ JCarroll 17 60
(MDods) *led to over 2f out: rallied: one pce fnl f* **12/1**
5-00 **6** *1 1/4* **Cryfield**[8] 1451 7-9-4 60............................................... KimTinkler 10 59
(NTinkler) *keen in midfield: effrt over 2f out: kpt on: no imp ins fnl f* **16/1**
0-05 **7** *1 1/2* **Prince Of Gold**[9] 1427 4-9-13 69......................................... ACulhane 13 65
(RHollinshead) *cl up: led over 2f to over 1f out: outpcd ins last* **10/1**
0530 **8** *1 3/4* **Barzak (IRE)**[23] 1225 4-9-4 60.......................................(t) JBramhill 18 52
(SRBowring) *trckd ldrs tl rdn and outpcd fr wl over 1f out* **8/1**
46-2 **9** *5* **Efidium**[8] 1452 6-9-2 65.............................................. SuzanneFrance(7) 16 47
(NBycroft) *prom tl edgd rt and outpcd fr 2f out* **7/1**[3]
04-0 **10** *1 3/4* **The Wizard Mul**[26] 1175 4-8-13 62................................. DFentiman(7) 6 40
(WStorey) *cl up tl edgd rt and wknd over 1f out* **33/1**
0-04 **11** *1 3/4* **Jakeal (IRE)**[8] 1451 5-8-13 55.......................................... DeanMcKeown 9 29
(RMWhitaker) *in tch tl wknd over 2f out* **14/1**
506- **12** *1* **Basinet**[170] 5933 6-9-2 58.......................................................... PFessey 5 30
(JJQuinn) *swtchd sharply rt s: hld up: effrt over 2f out: nvr rchd ldrs* **25/1**
6001 **13** *1 3/4* **Open Handed (IRE)**[10] 1389 4-8-12 59...............................(t) TEaves(5) 8 27
(BEllison) *towards rr: rdn 3f out: n.d* **20/1**
60 **14** *1/2* **Soft Mist (IRE)**[92] 590 4-9-4 60.......................................... PHanagan 15 27
(JJQuinn) *midfield: outpcd 4f out: n.d after* **66/1**
00-0 **15** *3/4* **Arjay**[31] 1097 6-8-7 56.........................................................(b) AMullen(7) 1 22
(AndrewTurnell) *bhd: rdn 1/2-way: nvr on terms* **40/1**
6-20 **16** *3/4* **Futuristic**[57] 909 4-8-12 54.................................................. JQuinn 12 18
(JPearce) *in tch: lost pl 1/2-way: n.d after* **20/1**
6/5- **17** *nk* **Late Arrival**[466] 307 7-8-5 50.......................................... LEnstone(3) 3 14
(MDHammond) *a bhd* **100/1**
30-0 **18** *1* **Rockerfella Lad (IRE)**[10] 1393 4-9-4 65......................... RThomas(5) 7 26
(MTodhunter) *midfield: wknd fr 3f out* **40/1**
60-0 **19** *3* **One Last Time**[19] 1265 4-9-13 69........................................ HBastiman 11 24
(RBastiman) *a bhd* **50/1**
060- **20** *12* **Pepper Road**[169] 5945 5-8-10 52............................................. GParkin 2 —
(RBastiman) *racd wd in rr: nvr on terms* **40/1**

1m 41.86s (0.76) **Going Correction** +0.25s/f (Good) **20** Ran SP% **124.4**
Speed ratings: **106,105,104,102,102 100,99,97,92,90 89,88,86,85,85 84,84,83,80,68**CSF £29.31 CT £276.58 TOTE £4.50: £1.60, £2.00, £2.10, £11.30; EX 34.80 Place 6 £26.13, Place £11.50.
**Owner** G Hart, D Scott & G Sparkes **Bred** Gainsborough Stud Management Ltd **Trained** Sheriff Hutton, N Yorks

**FOCUS**
A field of mainly exposed handicappers and one in which the pace was soon sound. As is usually the case in big fields on the round course over this trip, those drawn high that can race up with the pace close to the inside rail have a big edge, so the runner-up and the third may be a bit better than the bare form.

**NOTEBOOK**
**Hills Of Gold** fully confirmed reappearance promise back on this less-testing ground and showed the right attitude, but it is worth remembering that he did have the run of the race on the inside rail from his favourable draw. However, he should not be going up too much for this and should continue to give a good account.
**Megan's Magic** ◆ back in trip and under a penalty, ran really well considering she had to switch to the unfavoured centre of the course to get a run. She will be suited by the return to a mile and a quarter and will remain of interest in her current form, even after reassessment.
**Goodbye Mr Bond** has not won for nearly a year but ran as well as he has done and can be rated a bit better than the bare form, as he was forced to race on the outside from his unfavourably low draw. Although his wins-to-runs ratio means he is not one to lump on, he will be of interest in similar company next time.
**Pride Of Kinloch** had the run of the race from her favourable draw and elected to give it her best shot, but she has yet to win a race and her inconsistency means she is far from sure to reproduce this next time.
**Hula Ballew** was another who had the run of the race from her high draw. However she should be spot on now after two outings this term and this mainly consistent sort will be of interest in modest company.
**Cryfield**, who has slipped back to a favourable mark, shaped as though coming to hand and is another to keep an eye out for in similar company.
T/Plt: £42.80 to a £1 stake. Pool: £40,207.40. 685.55 winning tickets. T/Qpdt: £3.40 to a £1 stake. Pool: £1,460.30. 316.80 winning tickets. RY

# 1585 SANDOWN (R-H)
Saturday, April 24

**OFFICIAL GOING: Good to soft (good in places)**
Other races under Rules of National Hunt Racing.
Wind: almost nil Weather: sunny, warm

## 1621 BETFRED.COM MILE (GROUP 2) 1m 14y
2:55 (2:56) (A) 4-Y-0+ £58,000 (£22,000; £11,000; £5,000) Stalls High

Form RPR
05-3 **1** **Hurricane Alan (IRE)**[10] 1397 4-9-0 110.................................. PDobbs 1 117
(RHannon) *t.k.h early in midfield: prog to trck ldng pair over 2f out: shkn up over 1f out: r.o to ld last 150y: styd on wl* **25/1**
6021 **2** *nk* **Gateman**[10] 1397 7-9-0 112........................................... KDalgleish 4 116
(MJohnston) *b.hind: led: rdn and hdd over 2f out: edgd lft fr over 1f out: rallied to ld jst over 1f out: hdd last 150y: battled on wl* **8/1**
45-2 **3** *1* **Soviet Song (IRE)**[14] 1332 4-8-11 114................................. JPMurtagh 2 111
(JRFanshawe) *hld up in last trio: effrt over 2f out: swtchd rt over 1f out: r.o fnl f: nrst fin* **5/2**[1]
360- **4** *hd* **Norse Dancer (IRE)**[210] 5212 4-9-0 117................................ TQuinn 10 113
(DRCElsworth) *t.k.h: hld up in midfield: prog on outer 2f out: rdn to chal ent fnl f: sn nt qckn and btn* **9/1**

100- **5** *2* **Indian Haven**[189] 5641 4-9-0 117 DHolland 8 109
(PWD'Arcy) *lw: trckd ldrs: rdn over 2f out: one pce and no imp over 1f out* **11/2[3]**

10-1 **6** *1 1/4* **Babodana**[28] 1125 4-9-0 111 GDuffield 9 107
(MHTompkins) *lw: trckd ldr: led gng easily over 2f out: rdn and hdd jst over 1f out: wknd fnl f* **7/1**

44-1 **7** *shd* **Sublimity (FR)**[30] 1107 4-9-0 110 (t) KFallon 3 106
(SirMichaelStoute) *swtg: s.i.s: sn t.k.h in midfield: rdn and effrt over 2f out: no prog over 1f out* **4/1[2]**

4336 **8** *nk* **Checkit (IRE)**[28] 1146 4-9-0 112 TEDurcan 5 106
(MRChannon) *settled in last pair: rdn 3f out: one pce and no imp ldrs fnl 2f* **12/1**

310- **9** *6* **Salselon**[160] 6007 5-9-0 MartinDwyer 6 93
(LMCumani) *w'like: leggy: bit bkwd: a wl in rr: last and rdn over 4f out: nvr on terms* **16/1**

5-01 **10** *2 1/2* **Pablo**[12] 1367 5-9-0 103 (p) MHills 7 88
(BWHills) *stmbld s: sn trckd ldng pair: rdn and wknd over 2f out* **25/1**

1m 43.67s (-0.25) **Going Correction** +0.35s/f (Good) **10 Ran SP% 118.8**
Speed ratings: **115,114,113,113,111 110,110,109,103,101**CSF £216.00 TOTE £27.50: £4.50, £2.20, £1.60; EX 134.50 Trifecta £387.90 Pool of £2,130.82 - 3.90 winning tickets.
**Owner** I A N Wight **Bred** Mrs Stephanie Hanly **Trained** East Everleigh, Wilts

**FOCUS**
Not a strong Group Two, but it was a competitive event with the first eight home covered by 7lb on official figures. The pace was even and up to standard for the grade.

**NOTEBOOK**
**Hurricane Alan(IRE)**, 3lb better off for a four-length beating by Gateman last time, had clearly benefited from that run and showed improved form. He had consistently been found out at this level last year, but was clearly going best two out and stayed on well to collar Gateman. He is clearly not going to be among the top milers this season, but it would be wrong to call this a fluke.
**Gateman** is as tough as can be and kept coming back for more after setting the pace. He has looked as good as ever this season since returning from Dubai and must have every chance of repeating his victory in the Diomed at Epsom on Derby day. He is one to keep on the right side of.
**Soviet Song(IRE)** was again well backed, despite her defeat in a Listed race at Kempton on her reappearance. She had a nice run up the fair rail, but lacked the toe to get to the leaders. A step up in trip is now on the cards, and although it might not be clutching at straws it is surely a move connections must have hoped would not be forced on them quite so soon.
**Norse Dancer(IRE)**, who only ran in Group One races last season, made a satisfactory reappearance. He was reportedly struck in the face with a flailing whip two out, but still had every opportunity to recover. His preparation had been interrupted, but he is becomng a 'nearly' horses and is without a win since his two-year-old season.
**Indian Haven**, who would have found the drying ground against him, was free enough in the early stages. He is entitled to come on for this first run of the year, but he may well have to be sent abroad to find his required soft ground.
**Babodana**, winner of the Lincoln off top weight on his previous start, was travelling as well as anything two out, but found less than expected up the hill. An easier track may be required in Group company.
**Sublimity(FR)** , who was badly off with Gateman on their Doncaster running, got worked up in the preliminaries. He is better than this.
**Salselon** did not show much on his first start for Luca Cumani.

## 1622 BETFRED GORDON RICHARDS STKS (GROUP 3) 1m 2f 7y
4:10 (4:12) (A) 4-Y-0+ **£29,000** (£11,000; £5,500; £2,500) **Stalls** High

Form RPR

64-0 **1** **Chancellor (IRE)**[12] 1355 6-8-10 110 KFallon 11 115
(JLDunlop) *cl up: rdn 2f out: effrt to chal over 1f out: drvn to ld last 50y* **13/2**

-545 **2** *nk* **Nysaean (IRE)**[12] 1355 5-8-13 112 PDobbs 2 117
(RHannon) *lw: hld up in midfield: smooth prog over 2f out: shkn up to ld jst over 1f out: hdd and hld last 75y* **16/1**

303- **3** *1 3/4* **Sunstrach (IRE)**[160] 6008 6-8-10 TQuinn 4 111
(LMCumani) *lengthy: leggy: t.k.h: pressed ldr after 3f: led over 2f out: rdn and hdd over 1f out: kpt on wl fnl f* **9/1**

110- **4** *shd* **Franklins Gardens**[322] 2190 4-8-10 108 GDuffield 6 111
(MHTompkins) *settled in last trio: rdn 3f out: prog and edgd rt over 1f out: r.o fnl f: nrst fin* **12/1**

6-04 **5** *2* **Bourgainville**[35] 1062 6-8-10 107 MartinDwyer 10 107
(AMBalding) *lw: racd in midfield: rdn over 3f out: prog 2f out: hanging rt over 1f out: styd on fnl f* **16/1**

1/1- **6** *2* **Persian Majesty (IRE)**[310] 2483 4-8-10 JPMurtagh 3 103
(PWHarris) *lw: settled in last pair: rdn 3f out: no prog tl styd on fnl f* **11/2[3]**

32-3 **7** *shd* **Island House (IRE)**[12] 1355 8-8-10 113 DHolland 7 103
(GWragg) *s.i.s: hld up in last pair: shkn up 3f out: effrt on inner wl over 1f out: one pce fnl f* **11/2[3]**

234- **8** *shd* **Muqbil (USA)**[189] 5643 4-8-10 113 TEDurcan 5 103
(JLDunlop) *mde most to over 2f out: wknd over 1f out* **5/1[2]**

2-32 **9** *1/2* **Bustan (IRE)**[12] 1355 5-8-10 107 (b[1]) RHills 9 102
(MPTregoning) *trckd ldrs: rdn over 2f out: wknd over 1f out* **9/2[1]**

632/ **10** *15* **Sir George Turner**[588] 4613 5-8-10 KDalgleish 1 75
(MJohnston) *chsd ldr for 3f: wknd over 2f out* **20/1**

110- **11** *5* **Yawmi**[249] 4270 4-8-10 110 MHills 8 66
(BWHills) *in tch tl wknd wl over 2f out: eased over 1f out* **16/1**

2m 11.19s (1.01) **Going Correction** +0.35s/f (Good) **11 Ran SP% 119.1**
Speed ratings: **109,108,107,107,105 104,104,103,103,91 87**CSF £106.55 TOTE £7.50: £3.00, £4.80, £3.50; EX 198.00.
**Owner** M J Al-Qatami **Bred** Norelands Bloodstock **Trained** Arundel, W Sussex

**FOCUS**
A competitive race on official ratings but the pace was ordinary.

**NOTEBOOK**
**Chancellor(IRE)** made it three from three at the track and won this event for the second time after his victory in 2002. The drying ground would not have been in his favour and he showed a good attitude to battle back and collar the runner-up. This is clearly his level, but he will probably have to venture abroad to ensure the soft ground he enjoys.
**Nysaean(IRE)**, another who would have preferred genuinely soft ground, probably hit the front too soon and was outbattled by the winner. This was his fourth start of the year and there is every chance several of those in behind will improve past him now. He is another who will struggle to get his ideal conditions in this country.
**Sunstrach(IRE)** ◆ is the one to take from the race. From a yard yet to find the winner's enclosure this season, he ran a fine race on his first start since arriving from Italy. He was fairly keen in the early stages and was perhaps in front a little too soon, but he is sure to improve and looks capable of winning a decent prize, especially on softer ground. There was a lot to like about this and it is interesting he represents the same connections as Falbrav.
**Franklins Gardens** not seen since getting jarred up in the Derby, ran a most encouraging race over a trip that would almost certainly be on the short side. He is one to keep on the right side of when back at a mile and a half.
**Bourgainville**, runner-up in the race last year, ran as well as could be expected. He has not won for nearly two years.
**Persian Majesty(IRE)**, a springer in the market, had not been seen since winning a Listed race at Royal Ascot on only his second start. He has obviously been hard to train, but is not one to give up on and should be suited by further in time.
**Island House(IRE)**, who won this race in 2001, has only won at Listed level since and is generally found wanting in Group races these days.
**Muqbil(USA)**, strangely for a horse with plenty of speed, tried to make all. He is not one to give up on just yet.
**Bustan(IRE)** is becoming terribly disappointing. He was keen in first-time blinkers and his jockey later reported that his mount was unsuited by the ground, but connections are running out of excuses. *Official explanation: jockey said horse was unsuited by the going - good to soft, good in places*

## 1623 BETFRED "TREBLE ODDS ON LUCKY'S" RATED STKS (H'CAP) 1m 14y
4:45 (4:48) (C ) (0-95,95) 4-Y-0+ **£12,586** (£4,774; £2,387; £1,085) **Stalls** High

Form RPR

0-00 **1** **Unshakable (IRE)**[14] 1328 5-9-0 88 FNorton 4 99+
(BobJones) *b.hind: hld up bhd ldrs: swtchd lft and rdn wl over 1f out: qcknd to ld jst over 1f out: sn clr: eased nr fin* **7/1[3]**

000- **2** *3/4* **Always Esteemed (IRE)**[203] 5366 4-9-7 95 MartinDwyer 9 104
(GWragg) *settled towards rr: shkn up and effrt over 2f out: prog wl over 1f out: r.o to chse wnr last 100y: gaining fin but no ch* **20/1**

00-2 **3** *1* **Soyuz (IRE)**[19] 1273 4-8-8 82 KFallon 11 89
(MAJarvis) *trckd ldrs: rdn over 2f out: effrt u.p over 1f out: styd on fnl f* **7/2[1]**

030- **4** *nk* **Dubrovsky**[251] 4211 4-8-11 85 RHills 13 91+
(JRFanshawe) *s.i.s: hld up in rr: last 3f out: shuffled to wd outside fr 2f out to over 1f out: r.o wl fnl f: hopeless task* **14/1**

-001 **5** *nk* **Jools**[19] 1273 6-8-4 81 RMiles(3) 1 87
(DKIvory) *b: racd wd: hld up in rr: rdn 3f out: prog on outer 2f out: styd on same pce fr over 1f out* **16/1**

006- **6** *nk* **Jazz Messenger (FR)**[170] 5936 4-9-7 95 TEDurcan 15 100
(GAButler) *hld up wl in rr: prog 2f out: clsng whn nt clr run 1f out: r.o last 100y: nt rcvr* **11/2[2]**

14-0 **7** *1/2* **Amandus (USA)**[18] 1286 4-9-7 95 JPMurtagh 14 99
(DRLoder) *cl up: rdn to ld wl over 1f out: hdd jst over 1f out: wknd last 100y* **20/1**

040- **8** *2* **Certain Justice (USA)**[154] 6050 6-8-3 82 NChalmers(5) 17 82
(PFICole) *hld up in rr: effrt on inner over 2f out: prog over 1f out: one pce fnl f* **16/1**

63-0 **9** *1/2* **Irony (IRE)**[28] 1132 5-8-12 89 LPKeniry(3) 12 88
(AMBalding) *mde most to wl over 1f out: wknd fnl f* **20/1**

040- **10** *1 1/4* **Impersonator**[175] 5875 4-8-6 80 TQuinn 2 76
(JLDunlop) *lw: settled in midfield: rdn over 2f out: no prog and btn over 1f out* **16/1**

055- **11** *hd* **Island Rapture**[185] 5709 4-8-5 79 AMcCarthy 3 75
(JARToller) *bit bkwd: wl in rr: effrt on outer and rdn 3f out: keeping on one pce whn nt clr run 1f out* **33/1**

44-6 **12** *2* **Flying Express**[11] 1385 4-8-12 86 MHills 8 77
(BWHills) *lw: pressed ldr tl wknd 2f out* **10/1**

600- **13** *hd* **Nuit Sombre (IRE)**[159] 6013 4-8-9 83 KDalgleish 10 74
(MJohnston) *bit bkwd: trckd ldrs: cruised up to chal 2f out: fnd nil over 1f out: wknd* **12/1**

00-5 **14** *3/4* **Oakley Rambo**[23] 1225 5-8-5 79 RSmith 7 68
(RHannon) *racd towards outer in rr: pushed along 3f out: hanging rt whn rdn 2f out: no prog* **16/1**

2-05 **15** *shd* **Ace Of Hearts**[19] 1273 5-8-7 81 JMackay 18 70
(CFWall) *hld up in midfield: effrt whn hmpd 2f out: nt rcvr: no ch whn nt clr run ent fnl f* **9/1**

00-4 **16** *3/4* **Richemaur (IRE)**[12] 1372 4-8-5 79 GDuffield 16 67
(MHTompkins) *trckd ldrs tl wknd u.p 2f out* **20/1**

6060 **17** *6* **African Sahara (USA)**[7] 1460 5-8-8 82 (t) GCarter 5 57
(MissDMountain) *hld up in rr: rdn over 2f out: wknd* **20/1**

1m 45.29s (1.37) **Going Correction** +0.35s/f (Good) **17 Ran SP% 133.8**
Speed ratings: **107,106,105,104,104 104,103,101,101,100 99,97,97,96,96 96,90**CSF £154.01 CT £595.32 TOTE £9.50: £2.60, £5.20, £1.50, £4.20; EX 261.10.
**Owner** Unshakable Partnership **Bred** Timothy Coughlan **Trained** Wickhambrook, Suffolk

**FOCUS**
A competitive handicap run at a decent gallop, but there was plenty of trouble and many horses were making their seasonal reappearance.

**NOTEBOOK**
**Unshakable(IRE)** is value for more than the winning margin as his jockey took his foot off the throttle inside the final furlong. He had a frustrating time last season, but has clearly benefited from being gelded. Although he did have race fitness on his side, it was hard not to be impressed and there could well be more to come.
**Always Esteemed(IRE)**, running in only his second handicap after spending much of the latter part of last season running in pattern company, rattled home, but was clearly flattered by his proximity to the winner. This was still a fair effort as he was conceding race fitness to the winner, but he will not find life easy off this sort of mark.
**Soyuz(IRE)** was not suited by the drying ground, but ran well enough. He is often placed, but is often caught out by his lack of toe. Soft ground seems vital for him.
**Dubrovsky** ◆ was the unluckiest horse of the race. Still at the back of the field going to two out, he was pulled right round the outside of the field, but although he rattled home when he finally saw daylight there was no hope of catching the winner. Only lightly raced, he looks to have improved and must be fancied to take a similar event.
**Jools**, who beat Soyuz on his previous start, ran a solid race from his outside draw, especially as he had to deliver his challenge wide.
**Jazz Messenger(FR)** usually races up with the pace but was dropped right out and got into all sorts of trouble. By the time he got out the race had gone, but there will be another day for him.
**Irony(IRE)** set the pace, but folded very tamely. He needs an easier mile than this.
**Ace Of Hearts** got into all sorts of trouble and this run is best ignored.
**African Sahara(USA)**was reported by his jockey to have never been travelling. *Official explanation: jockey said horse was never travelling*

## 1624 BETFRED "THE BONUS KING" FLAT V JUMP JOCKEYS H'CAP 1m 14y
5:20 (5:25) (E ) (0-75,75) 4-Y-0+ **£7,036** (£2,165; £1,082; £541) **Stalls** High

Form RPR

00-0 **1** **Lifted Way**[29] 1118 5-11-4 72 APMcCoy 5 87
(PRChamings) *trckd ldr: led 2f out: reminder ins fnl f: pushed out stylishly* **11/1**

0323 **2** *4* **Sir Laughalot**[29] 1118 4-11-2 70 MAFitzgerald 2 77
(MissECLavelle) *chsd ldrs: rdn 2f out: chsd wnr over 1f out: no imp* **9/1**

330- **3** *nk* **Mr Velocity (IRE)**[169] 5945 4-11-2 70 MartinDwyer 10 76
(ACStewart) *hld up in rr: rdn 3f out: prog on inner 2f out: drvn and kpt on fnl f* **7/1**

00-6 **4** *1 1/2* **Todlea (IRE)**[112] 419 4-11-7 75 BJGeraghty 12 78
(JAOsborne) *settled towards rr: rdn and effrt over 2f out: prog over 1f out: one pce fnl f* **14/1**

0100 **5** 3½ **Karaoke (IRE)**[7] [1460] 4-11-2 **70** JPMurtagh 11 65
(SKirk) *racd in midfield: rdn over 2f out: n.m.r over 1f out: btn after* **6/1**[3]

330- **6** 1 **Medallist**[266] [3798] 5-11-4 **72** CLlewellyn 3 65
(BEllison) *racd in midfield: rdn over 2f out: no prog and btn over 1f out* **12/1**

40-0 **7** ¾ **Bishopstone Man**[19] [1275] 7-11-3 **71** TEDurcan 4 63
(HCandy) *wl in rr: rdn 3f out: one pce and nvr rchd ldrs* **14/1**

000- **8** nk **Swift Alchemist**[166] [5970] 4-11-2 **70** TJMurphy 1 61
(MrsHSweeting) *led and sn clr: hdd & wknd 2f out* **20/1**

50-0 **9** 2½ **Racing Night (USA)**[35] [1066] 4-11-7 **75** RJohnson 8 61
(JRBest) *wl in rr: hrd rdn and effrt on outer 3f out: no prog 2f out* **14/1**

2116 **10** shd **Steely Dan**[12] [1376] 5-10-13 **67** MHills 7 53
(JRBest) *hld up last: shuffled along and effrt over 2f out: nvr a factor* **4/1**[1]

2330 **11** 2½ **Skylarker (USA)**[44] [915] 6-11-7 **75** GDuffield 9 55
(WSKittow) *chsd ldrs: rdn 3f out: wknd over 2f out* **9/1**

-050 **12** ¾ **Rebate**[17] [1298] 4-10-13 **67** KFallon 6 46
(RHannon) *t.k.h: chsd ldrs: rdn 3f out: wknd 2f out* **11/2**[2]

1m 46.07s (2.15) **Going Correction** +0.35s/f (Good) **12** Ran SP% **123.0**
Speed ratings: **103,99,98,97,93 92,91,91,89,89 86,85**CSF £110.40 CT £769.97 TOTE £15.90: £3.80, £2.30, £2.50; EX 167.00 Place 6 £602.56, Place 5 £337.99.
**Owner** Mrs Alexandra J Chandris **Bred** Mrs J Chandris **Trained** Baughurst, Hants

**FOCUS**
A modest event with many of the runners coming off the All-Weather. Riding arrangements were also unusual as it was a Flat v National Hunt jockeys challenge. The pace was good but the overall form is not strong.

**NOTEBOOK**
**Lifted Way** was always in the right position and drew clear when asked to do so by the champion jump jockey. This was a pleasing effort, but it is unlikely the form amounts to a great deal.
**Sir Laughalot**, who has been busy on the All-Weather, again ran his race. He always seems to find one or two too good, but he may be found a weak race somewhere.
**Mr Velocity(IRE)** got a nice run through to challenge, but never looked likely to get anywhere near the winner.
**Todlea(IRE)**, only lightly raced, had been highly tried when last seen on turf. He stays further than this and is certainly capable of winning a small race when faced with a stiffer test of stamina.
**Karaoke(IRE)** was a little short of room two furlongs out, but it didn't make much difference.
**Swift Alchemist** went off too fast for her own good.
**Steely Dan** has thrived on Polytrack during the winter, but is probably better on that surface than on turf and more effective over further. He is not a straightforward ride and was later reported by his jockey to have lost his action. *Official explanation: jockey said gelding lost its action*
T/Plt: £224.10 to a £1 stake. Pool: £137,406.70. 447.50 winning tickets. T/Qpdt: £76.90 to a £1 stake. Pool: £5,427.50. 52.20 winning tickets. JN

# [1595]WOLVERHAMPTON (A.W) (L-H)
Saturday, April 24

**OFFICIAL GOING: Standard**
Wind: nil Weather: sunny

## 1625 NEW SITE @ BETDIRECT.CO.UK AMATEUR RIDERS' H'CAP 6f (F)
**6:00** (6:00) (E ) (0-70,70) 4-Y-O+ **£3,435** (£1,057; £528; £264) **Stalls** Low

Form RPR

4510 **1** **Blakeshall Quest**[12] [1368] 4-10-6 65 (v) MrLNewnes(5) 9 77
(RBrotherton) *a.p: led over 3f out: c wd st: rdn out* **11/4**[1]

5344 **2** ½ **Boavista (IRE)**[12] [1368] 4-9-12 55 MissEFolkes(3) 3 66
(PDEvans) *a.p: rdn over 2f out: chsd wnr over 1f out: r.o* **13/2**[3]

240- **3** 3 **Val De Maal (IRE)**[206] [5310] 4-10-7 68 MrTThomas(7) 5 70
(GCHChung) *a.p: rdn 2f out: one pce fnl f* **10/1**

0000 **4** shd **Noble Locks (IRE)**[7] [1477] 6-10-7 66 MissJCWilliams(5) 8 67
(JWUnett) *racd wd: hld up: hdwy over 1f out: r.o ins fnl f* **9/1**

010- **5** hd **Bint Royal (IRE)**[186] [5685] 6-10-11 70 ow3 (p) MissVHaigh(5) 12 71
(MissVHaigh) *hld up and bhd: rdn and hdwy over 2f out: one pce fnl f* **12/1**

000- **6** shd **Boisdale (IRE)**[127] [6217] 6-9-2 47 MissALTurner(5) 10 47
(SLKeightley) *a.p: rdn over 1f out: one pce* **20/1**

0602 **7** nk **Illustrious Duke**[8] [1446] 6-8-7 40 (b) MissMMullineaux(7) 4 39
(MMullineaux) *led over 2f: prom tl wknd ins fnl f* **20/1**

6305 **8** ½ **Ladies Knight**[19] [1262] 4-9-13 53 MrsSBosley 6 51
(DShaw) *hld up: sn bhd: hdwy over 1f out: no imp fnl f* **6/1**[3]

15-5 **9** hd **Astrac (IRE)**[12] [1368] 13-9-10 50 MsCWilliams 2 47
(MrsALMKing) *hld up: hdwy over 1f out: no ex fnl f* **6/1**[2]

0160 **10** 5 **Scary Night (IRE)**[9] [1423] 4-10-1 58 (p) MrSDobson(3) 7 40
(JBalding) *prom: rdn over 2f out: wknd over 1f out* **12/1**

305 **11** 15 **Pips Song (IRE)**[2] [1569] 9-9-5 50 MrsMarieKing(5) 1 —
(PWHiatt) *s.i.s: hmpd on ins over 3f out: a bhd: t.o* **10/1**

1m 17.31s (1.51) **Going Correction** +0.05s/f (Slow) **11** Ran SP% **121.7**
Speed ratings: **91,90,86,86,85 85,85,84,84,77 57**CSF £21.04 CT £159.53 TOTE £4.00: £1.60, £1.80, £2.90; EX 33.90.
**Owner** Droitwich Jokers **Bred** M P Bishop **Trained** Elmley Castle, Worcs

**FOCUS**
The winner was not inconvenienced by being brought wide in the home straight.

**NOTEBOOK**
**Blakeshall Quest**, 7lb higher than when scoring here last month, did not mind a return back up to six.
**Boavista(IRE)** was 7lb better off than when just under two lengths in front of the winner at Warwick last time. She was another who was not inconvenienced by the extra furlong.
**Val De Maal(IRE)**, twice a winner over seven on this surface, ran a sound race on his seasonal debut.
**Noble Locks(IRE)** showed signs of a return to form off a mark only a pound higher than when winning over course and distance on Boxing Day.
**Bint Royal(IRE)** was having her first outing for six months and should be better for it.
**Boisdale(IRE)** was previously trained by Dandy Nicholls and was having his first run here for more than two and a half years.
**Ladies Knight** *Official explanation: jockey said gelding would not face the kickback*

## 1626 BETDIRECT.CO.UK CLASSIFIED STKS 5f (F)
**6:30** (6:30) (E ) 3-Y-O **£3,337** (£1,027; £513; £256) **Stalls** Low

Form RPR

0-46 **1** **Crewes Miss Isle**[17] [1303] 3-8-9 65 SWhitworth 3 71
(AGNewcombe) *chsd ldrs: hmpd on ins over 2f out: swtchd rt wl over 1f out: sn rdn: led ins fnl f: r.o* **11/2**[3]

341 **2** ½ **Sahara Silk (IRE)**[37] [1047] 3-8-12 68 (v) DHolland 2 72
(DShaw) *sn w ldr: rdn to ld jst over 1f out: hdd ins fnl f: nt qckn* **4/5**[1]

-644 **3** 3½ **Scottish Exile (IRE)**[24] [1209] 3-8-10 66 (v) IMongan 1 58
(KRBurke) *sn led: edgd lft over 2f out: sn rdn: hdd jst over 1f out: wknd ins fnl f* **9/4**[2]

000- **4** 1 **Obe Bold (IRE)**[179] [5824] 3-8-4 65 PBradley(5) 4 53
(ABerry) *led early: prom tl rdn and wknd over 1f out* **12/1**

63.29 secs (0.49) **Going Correction** +0.05s/f (Slow) **4** Ran SP% **109.4**
Speed ratings: **98,97,91,90**CSF £10.72 TOTE £6.70; EX 13.20.
**Owner** A McRoberts **Bred** Southill Stud **Trained** Yarnscombe, Devon
■ Stewards Enquiry : I Mongan two-day ban: careless riding (May 5,6)

**FOCUS**
The winner may have raced on faster ground after being forced to switch wide in the home straight.

**NOTEBOOK**
**Crewes Miss Isle** managed to overcome trouble in running despite the drop back to five.
**Sahara Silk(IRE)**, four times a winner at Southwell, was making her first visit to Dunstall Park.
**Scottish Exile(IRE)** carved up the winner on the apex of the bend at halfway and her rider was given a two-day ban for careless riding.
**Obe Bold(IRE)**, whose form deteriorated last autumn, was making her debut on the All-Weather.

## 1627 SWEENEY-STEVENSON FILLIES' H'CAP 1m 100y(F)
**7:00** (7:00) (E ) (0-75,70) 3-Y-O **£5,031** (£1,548; £774; £387) **Stalls** Low

Form RPR

3215 **1** **Daring Affair**[52] [955] 3-8-12 **61** GFaulkner 8 68
(KRBurke) *hld up in tch: rdn to ld over 2f out: edgd rt ins fnl f: drvn out* **5/1**

1101 **2** ¾ **Lady Mo**[7] [1478] 3-9-7 **70** FLynch 10 75
(KARyan) *hld up in tch: jnd wnr on bit over 2f out: rdn over 1f out: nt qckn ins fnl f* **9/2**[3]

24-0 **3** 2 **Miskina**[16] [1309] 3-8-1 **57** BSwarbrick(7) 11 58
(WMBrisbourne) *s.i.s: stdy hdwy over 5f out: rdn 3f out: kpt on same pce fnl f* **16/1**

02-6 **4** 1½ **Carriacou**[12] [1357] 3-9-6 **69** (e) DHolland 5 67
(PWD'Arcy) *a.p: rdn 3f out: one pce fnl 2f* **3/1**[1]

2-00 **5** 9 **Russalka**[16] [1309] 3-8-8 **60** LisaJones(3) 7 39
(JulianPoulton) *in rr: wl bhd 4f out: hdwy over 1f out: nvr nr ldrs* **20/1**

002- **6** 1¼ **Chase The Rainbow**[152] [6058] 3-8-7 **56** RFfrench 2 32
(ABerry) *led: rdn over 3f out: hdd over 2f out: wknd over 1f out* **10/1**

5-00 **7** 2 **Sworn To Secrecy**[7] [1464] 3-9-1 **64** SWhitworth 4 36
(SKirk) *chsd ldrs tl wknd 5f out* **16/1**

52-6 **8** 1 **Unintentional**[92] [593] 3-8-9 **58** ADaly 1 28
(RBrotherton) *a bhd* **20/1**

05-3 **9** 7 **Beach Party (IRE)**[22] [1226] 3-9-0 **63** IMongan 6 18
(MLWBell) *plld hrd: prom: rdn over 3f out: sn wknd* **4/1**[2]

450- **10** shd **Compassion (IRE)**[166] [5966] 3-8-2 **58** DeanWilliams(7) 9 13
(GCHChung) *prom: lost pl 6f out: wl bhd fnl 4f* **25/1**

5320 **11** 6 **Zuloago (USA)**[9] [1422] 3-8-8 **57** ANicholls 3 —
(SLKeightley) *bhd: rdn and short-lived effrt on ins 4f out* **16/1**

1m 52.1s (1.01) **Going Correction** +0.05s/f (Slow) **11** Ran SP% **120.0**
Speed ratings: **96,95,93,91,82 81,79,78,71,71 65**CSF £27.55 CT £281.58 TOTE £6.70: £2.00, £1.90, £6.70; EX 45.40.
**Owner** Nigel Shields **Bred** N R Shields And K R Burke **Trained** Middleham Moor, N Yorks

**FOCUS**
An ordinary handicap.

**NOTEBOOK**
**Daring Affair** put her disappointing run last time behind her on this first attempt at a mile.
**Lady Mo** found disappointingly little when the chips were down, but she was a stone higher than when last in a handicap.
**Miskina** gave the impression she will be suited by further on this All-Weather debut.
**Carriacou** was 6lb lower than when making a promising reappearance at Kempton.
**Sworn To Secrecy** *Official explanation: jockey said filly would not face the kickback*
**Zuloago(USA)** *Official explanation: jockey said filly was never travelling*

## 1628 SPECIAL OFFERS @ BETDIRECT.CO.UK MAIDEN STKS 1m 1f 79y(F)
**7:30** (7:30) (D ) 3-Y-O+ **£3,454** (£1,063; £531; £265) **Stalls** Low

Form RPR

**1** **First Dynasty (USA)**[136] [5764] 4-9-5 79 AQuinn(5) 5 80
(MissSJWilton) *t.k.h: chsd ldr: rdn to ld 2f out: edgd lft ins fnl f: drvn out* **9/2**[2]

00- **2** hd **Strider**[183] [5723] 3-8-9 BDoyle 3 80
(SirMichaelStoute) *led: rdn and hdd 2f out: swtchd rt ins fnl f: rallied cl home* **5/2**[1]

0-6 **3** 11 **General Flumpa**[12] [1370] 3-8-9 GBaker 4 58
(CFWall) *hld up: hdwy over 4f out: rdn over 3f out: sn wknd* **5/1**[3]

40-0 **4** 7 **State Of Balance**[84] [650] 6-9-5 62 IMongan 1 39
(KBell) *hld up: hdwy on ins 6f out: rdn over 3f out: sn wknd* **7/1**

5 **5** 2½ **Knight Of Hearts (IRE)**[26] [1179] 3-8-9 ANicholls 8 39
(REPeacock) *hld up: hdwy over 5f out: rdn over 3f out: sn wknd* **50/1**

000- **6** ½ **Adeeba (IRE)**[185] [5701] 3-8-4 SWhitworth 2 33
(EALDunlop) *prom: rdn over 3f out: sn wknd* **25/1**

**7** 15 **Dareneur (IRE)**[136] 4-9-5 TGMcLaughlin 9 —
(WMBrisbourne) *s.s: a bhd: t.o* **50/1**

0- **8** 1 **Salford Rocket**[185] [5711] 4-9-10 RFfrench 6 —
(GCHChung) *prom tl wknd 5f out: t.o* **50/1**

20-P **P** **Devil's Bite**[55] [927] 3-8-9 77 DHolland 7 —
(BWHills) *hld up in tch: wknd qckly 5f out: sn p.u: b.b.v* **5/2**[1]

2m 2.70s (-0.30) **Going Correction** +0.05s/f (Slow)
**WFA** 3 from 4yo+ 15lb **9** Ran SP% **114.2**
Speed ratings: **103,102,93,86,84 84,70,69,—**CSF £15.65 TOTE £7.30: £2.00, £1.30, £2.40; EX 30.70.
**Owner** John Pointon And Sons **Bred** And Mrs John C Mabee **Trained** Wetley Rocks, Staffs

**FOCUS**
This had already developed into a match by the time they left the back straight.

**NOTEBOOK**
**First Dynasty(USA)**, previously trained by Aidan O'Brien, had finished a well-beaten third for his new connections over hurdles at Newbury in December. He only just managed to hold the renewed effort of the runner-up.
**Strider** had to come off the rails after the winner went across him and only just failed to pull it out of the fire.
**Devil's Bite** *Official explanation: trainer's representative said colt had bled from the nose*

## 1629 BET DIRECT ON 0800 32 93 93 (S) STKS 1m 100y(F)
**8:00** (8:00) (G ) 3-Y-O+ **£2,555** (£730; £365) **Stalls** Low

Form RPR

1163 **1** **Our Destiny**[19] [1274] 6-9-10 52 SHitchcott(3) 2 67
(AWCarroll) *hld up in tch: rdn over 2f out: led wl over 1f out: r.o* **7/2**[2]

0-00 **2** 1½ **Turn Around**[19] [1275] 4-9-8 58 DHolland 5 59
(BWHills) *a.p: led over 2f out tl wl over 1f out: hrd rdn and carried high: nt qckn ins fnl f* **4/1**[3]

2360 **3** ¾ **Xaloc Bay (IRE)**[24] [1197] 6-9-10 56 LisaJones(3) 6 62
(BPJBaugh) *led: rdn and hdd over 2f out: no ex ins fnl f* **11/2**

1200 **4** 1 1/4 **Desert Heat**[26] 1172 6-9-13 64 (v) IMongan 4 60
(ISemple) *hld up: rdn over 3f out: hdwy over 1f out: one pce fnl f* **3/1**[1]
2302 **5** 2 1/2 **Just Wiz**[1] 1599 8-9-8 58 (b) TGMcLaughlin 7 49
(NPLittmoden) *s.i.s: hld up: hdwy over 3f out: rdn over 2f out: wknd over 1f out* **7/2**[2]
0030 **6** 11 **Forty Forte**[17] 1305 8-9-3 45 (tp) AQuinn(5) 3 26
(MissSJWilton) *prom tl wknd 3f out* **14/1**
000- **7** 8 **Mutabari (USA)**[274] 3581 10-9-1 45 AmyMyatt(7) 1 10
(JLSpearing) *sn wl bhd: t.o fnl 4f* **33/1**

1m 51.4s (0.31) **Going Correction** +0.05s/f (Slow) 7 Ran SP% **114.4**
Speed ratings: **100,98,97,96,94 83,75**CSF £17.89 TOTE £5.40: £2.00, £3.80; EX 37.70.There was no bid for the winner
**Owner** Dennis Deacon **Bred** D A And Mrs Hicks **Trained** Wixford, Warwicks

**FOCUS**
An ordinary seller.

**NOTEBOOK**
**Our Destiny** looked rather more willing than the runner-up.
**Turn Around**, dropped in class, gave the impression that he did not relish a battle.
**Xaloc Bay(IRE)** may have found the stretch mile just beyond his best.
**Desert Heat** never really seemed likely to take advantage of this return to selling company.
**Just Wiz** may not have recovered from his exertions over a distance beyond his best the previous day.

## 1630 BET DIRECT ON SKY ACTIVE H'CAP 1m 4f (F)
8:30 (8:30) (F) (0-55,53) 3-Y-0+ **£2,905** (£830; £415) **Stalls** Low

Form RPR
60-3 **1** **Red Forest (IRE)**[9] 1426 5-9-8 47 (t) ACulhane 8 62
(JMackie) *a.p: chsd ldr 6f out: led 3f out: sn clr: rdn and edgd rt fr over 1f out: drvn out* **5/2**[2]
5-02 **2** 6 **Classic Millennium**[9] 1426 6-9-4 46 LisaJones(3) 4 52
(WJMusson) *a.p: rdn and wnt 2nd 2f out: no ch w wnr* **9/4**[1]
640- **3** 15 **Shape Up (IRE)**[244] 4420 4-9-13 53 (b) PDoe 6 37
(TKeddy) *set slow pce tl qcknd clr 7f out: rdn and hdd 3f out: wknd 2f out* **20/1**
3306 **4** 1 3/4 **Ambersong**[75] 724 6-9-9 48 IMongan 3 29
(AWCarroll) *dwlt: hld up and bhd: rdn over 4f out: nvr nr ldrs* **4/1**[3]
5533 **5** 1/2 **Western Command (GER)**[2] 1572 8-9-4 43 oh3 (p) JoannaBadger 5 23
(MrsNMacauley) *chsd ldr tl rdn 6f out: wknd over 3f out* **20/1**
3063 **6** 1 3/4 **Kentucky Bullet (USA)**[28] 1136 8-9-8 47 SWhitworth 7 25
(AGNewcombe) *hld up: hdwy 4f out: wknd 3f out* **9/2**
5066 **7** 3 **E Minor (IRE)**[38] 1041 5-9-3 47 NChalmers(5) 2 20
(TWall) *sn prom: rdn over 4f out: wknd over 3f out* **16/1**
355- **8** 15 **French Risk (IRE)**[301] 2789 4-9-1 48 BSwarbrick(7) 1 —
(WMBrisbourne) *dwlt: a bhd: rdn over 6f out: t.o* **14/1**

2m 40.41s (-1.39) **Going Correction** +0.05s/f (Slow)
**WFA** 4 from 5yo+ 1lb 8 Ran SP% **119.6**
Speed ratings: **106,102,92,90,90 89,87,77**CSF £9.07 CT £86.70 TOTE £3.70: £2.10, £1.40, £6.40; EX 11.10 Place 6 £246.26, Place 5 £125.85.
**Owner** P Riley **Bred** Olympic B'Stock Ltd, Freynestown B'Stock And B Hi **Trained** Church Broughton, Derbys

**FOCUS**
A slowly-run race until the tempo increased significantly going out on the final circuit and the winning time was good for the grade.

**NOTEBOOK**
**Red Forest(IRE)** settled better this time and ran his field ragged, despite persistently drifting right in the home straight.
**Classic Millennium** had finished just in front of the winner on identical terms at Southwell last week but it was a very different story this time.
T/Plt: £278.80 to a £1 stake. Pool: £26,590.90. 69.60 winning tickets. T/Qpdt: £22.70 to a £1 stake. Pool: £2,075.80. 67.60 winning tickets. KH

1631 - 1633a (Foreign Racing) - See Raceform Interactive

# NAVAN (L-H)
Saturday, April 24

**OFFICIAL GOING: Yielding (yielding to soft in places)**

## 1634a IRISH STALLION FARMS EUROPEAN BREEDERS FUND SALSABIL STKS (LISTED) (F&M) 1m 2f
4:00 (4:01) 3-Y-0+ **£32,091** (£9,415; £4,485; £1,528)

RPR
**1** **All Too Beautiful (IRE)**[27] 1157 3-8-7 JPSpencer 5 105+
(APO'Brien, Ire) *trckd ldrs in 5th: smooth prog ent st: led 2f out: edgd lft 1 1/2f out: pushed out and qcknd clr 1f out: eased cl home* **4/7**[1]
**2** 2 1/2 **Queen Astrid (IRE)**[195] 5521 4-9-13 102 PJSmullen 7 103
(DKWeld, Ire) *led: rdn and hdd 2f out: kpt on wl u.p wout troubling wnr* **6/1**[2]
**3** 1 **Imoya (IRE)**[157] 6035 5-9-10 PCosgrave 2 98
(EndaKelly, Ire) *prom: 4th 1/2-way: 3rd and rdn early st: 5th 2f out: kpt on fnl f* **16/1**
**4** 3/4 **Miss Trish (IRE)**[34] 1071 4-9-10 93 DPMcDonogh 1 97
(KevinPrendergast, Ire) *hld up: 7th appr st: impr into 4th 2f out: rdn and one pced* **14/1**
**5** 5 **Sissy Slew (USA)**[196] 5494 4-9-10 NGMcCullagh 4 88
(MJGrassick, Ire) *s.i.s: hld up towards rr: 6th early st: no ex fr 2f out* **12/1**
**6** 7 **Blue Reema (IRE)**[13] 1347 4-9-10 96 (bt) TPO'Shea 3 75
(MHalford, Ire) *slowly away: hld up in rr: kpt on one pced st* **7/1**
**7** 11 **Classic Primrose (IRE)**[24] 1217 3-8-7 52 JEMoriarty 8 55
(PCluskey, Ire) *chsd ldrs: 3rd 1/2-way: rdn and wknd early st* **100/1**
**8** 10 **Dixie Evans**[34] 1070 4-9-10 98 (b) DMGrant 6 37
(HRogers, Ire) *hld up: 6th and rdn bef st: sn wknd* **12/1**
**S** **Sahara Sonnet (USA)**[24] 1215 3-8-7 (b[1]) MJKinane 9 —
(JohnMOxx, Ire) *cl up: 2nd into st: sn rdn: cl 3rd whn clipped heels and slipped up 1 1/2f out* **13/2**[3]

2m 16.5s
**WFA** 3 from 4yo+ 17lb 9 Ran SP% **132.7**
Speed ratings: CSF £6.07 TOTE £1.50: £1.10, £3.10, £7.90; DF 9.50.
**Owner** Michael Tabor **Bred** Sunderland Holdings/Abbey Bloo **Trained** Ballydoyle, Co Tipperary
■ Stewards Enquiry : J P Spencer four-day ban: careless riding (May 3,5-7)

**NOTEBOOK**
**All Too Beautiful(IRE)**, a sister to Galileo, showed the anticipated improvement from her Leopardstown maiden win. Edging left when still on the bridle a furlong and a half out, her rider got a 4 day ban for careless riding. She is a taking sort of filly but at this stage it isn't easy to translate the value of this form into anything vaguely resembling Classic standard. But she has a high home reputation, appears to be of an equitable temperament and is bred to appreciate further.
**Queen Astrid(IRE)** had to do her own donkey work before being outpaced by the winner. She needs further to be fully effective.
**Imoya(IRE)** stayed on well on her first Irish outing and will show more when the ground dries out.
**Miss Trish(IRE)** looked a bit out of her depth here but will improve for the run.
**Blue Reema(IRE)** never got involved.
**Sahara Sonnet(USA)** was hampered by the winner a furlong and a half down, clipped heels and slipped up.

1635 - 1637a (Foreign Racing) - See Raceform Interactive

# BRIGHTON (L-H)
Sunday, April 25

**OFFICIAL GOING: Good to firm (firm in places)**
Wind: lt hlf against Weather: hazy sun

## 1638 EUROPEAN BREEDERS FUND MAIDEN STKS 5f 59y
2:10 (2:11) (D) 2-Y-0 **£5,040** (£1,551; £775; £387) **Stalls** Low

Form RPR
02 **1** **Im Spartacus**[17] 1307 2-9-0 DHolland 1 68
(IAWood) *dwlt: sn outpcd in rr: hdwy over 1f out: led ins fnl f: idled: pushed out* **9/4**[1]
4 **2** 1 1/4 **Weet Yer Tern (IRE)**[25] 1208 2-9-0 DeanMcKeown 5 63
(PABlockley) *s.s and wnt rt: sn w ldrs: led over 2f out tl ins fnl f: nt qckn* **9/4**[1]
05 **3** 1 1/4 **Leonalto (IRE)**[15] 1331 2-9-0 (b[1]) KFallon 4 58
(BJMeehan) *t.k.h: w ldrs: rdn and ev ch 1f out: one pce* **7/1**
3 **4** 1 **Majestical (IRE)**[22] 1240 2-9-0 MartinDwyer 3 54
(WRMuir) *s.s: hdwy to ld 4f out: hdd over 2f out: hung rt: one pce* **4/1**[2]
3 **5** 5 **Dustini (IRE)**[18] 1292 2-9-0 ADaly 2 34
(WGMTurner) *led over 1f: wknd over 2f out* **11/2**[3]

63.68 secs (1.41) **Going Correction** +0.025s/f (Good) 5 Ran SP% **109.4**
Speed ratings: **89,87,85,83,75**CSF £7.36 TOTE £2.30: £1.40, £1.10; EX 5.70.
**Owner** John Purcell **Bred** John Purcell **Trained** Upper Lambourn, Berks

**FOCUS**
Once the slow starters had recovered and got themselves up with the pace after a furlong, they went a decent two-year-old gallop down the hill. A modest time for the grade and the form comes into the same catergory.

**NOTEBOOK**
**Im Spartacus** only came into his own on meeting the rising ground. He looks to need six furlongs already and is a little better than the bare form suggests.
**Weet Yer Tern(IRE)** is capable of winning a run-of-the-mill maiden.
**Leonalto(IRE)**, a bit free in the first-time visor, ran respectably.
**Majestical(IRE)** became a bit unbalanced, hanging up the camber in the home straight.
**Dustini(IRE)** was again easily left behind from halfway.

## 1639 BROADWATER MAILING (S) STKS 5f 213y
2:45 (2:45) (G) 3-Y-0+ **£2,583** (£738; £369) **Stalls** Low

Form RPR
3046 **1** **Flying Faisal (USA)**[2] 1584 6-9-6 45 (b) RLMoore 7 51
(JMBradley) *t.k.h: chsd ldrs: led over 2f out: rdn clr: drvn out fnl 100 yds* **13/2**[3]
5050 **2** 1 3/4 **Jalouhar**[27] 1180 4-9-12 46 (p) EAhern 3 52
(BPJBaugh) *led tl over 2f out: sn drvn along and outpcd by wnr: regained 2nd nr fin* **12/1**
0030 **3** nk **Polar Force**[10] 1421 4-8-13 60 BO'Neill(7) 1 45
(MRChannon) *dwlt: hld up in tch on rail: rdn to chse wnr over 1f out: nt qckn: lost 2nd nr fin* **11/10**[1]
-003 **4** 1 3/4 **Rathmullan**[23] 1237 5-8-13 40 (b) LiamJones(7) 4 40
(EAWheeler) *chsd ldr tl outpcd over 2f out: hung lft over 1f out: styd on same pce* **16/1**
-412 **5** 3/4 **Crafty Politician (USA)**[4] 1544 7-9-7 47 (b) AQuinn(5) 5 43
(GLMoore) *s.s: hdwy 3f out: one pce appr fnl f* **11/4**[2]
3660 **6** 1 1/4 **Lone Piper**[2] 1584 9-9-6 45 (p) CCatlin 2 34
(JMBradley) *plld hrd: stdd bk in tch: rdn 2f out: no ex over 1f out* **10/1**
**7** 20 **Dallington Brook**[35] 5-8-13 (b) LucyRussell(7) 6 —
(DrJRJNaylor) *dwlt: sn outpcd and bhd* **50/1**

1m 10.79s (0.69) **Going Correction** +0.025s/f (Good) 7 Ran SP% **112.2**
Speed ratings: **96,93,93,90,89 88,61**CSF £73.89 TOTE £7.90: £2.40, £4.40; EX 86.50.There was no bid for the winner. Polar Force was claimed by Miss Kirsty Boutflower for £6,000.
**Owner** Clifton Hunt **Bred** C S W Stables **Trained** Sedbury, Gloucs

**FOCUS**
A poor seller and a moderate early pace which increased at halfway.

**NOTEBOOK**
**Flying Faisal(USA)** won a weak race with a decisive move a quarter of a mile from home.
**Jalouhar** battled on well enough but his recent form tells the story of this race.
**Polar Force**, with a stone in hand of his rivals on official ratings, was a disappointment but not knocked about. Claimed for £6,000, he will be an interesting acquisition for his new stable if recapturing even a fraction of his old form.
**Rathmullan** plodded on dourly but has now finished in the first three only once in 16 outings.
**Crafty Politician(USA)** was not helped by the 6lb penalty for winning a poor banded All-Weather event ten days earlier.
**Lone Piper** is regressive, and blew any chance he might have had by racing too fiercely.

## 1640 BRIGHTON & HOVE ALBION CLASSIFIED STKS 1m 1f 209y
3:20 (3:24) (E) 3-Y-0 **£3,445** (£1,060; £530; £265) **Stalls** High

Form RPR
045- **1** **Meadaaf (IRE)**[244] 4440 3-9-3 71 KFallon 3 76
(ACStewart) *t.k.h: chsd ldrs: rdn 4f out: led ins fnl f: styd on* **7/1**[3]
1235 **2** 1/2 **Gavroche (IRE)**[53] 957 3-9-0 71 J-PGuillambert(3) 5 75
(CADwyer) *hmpd s: bhd: hdwy on outside and edgd lft 2f out: pressed wnr fnl 100 yds: r.o* **20/1**
031- **3** 1 1/2 **Kristal's Dream (IRE)**[188] 5671 3-9-4 75 TQuinn 4 73
(JLDunlop) *set mod pce 2f: chsd clr ldr: led over 1f out: hung lft and hdd ins fnl f: one pce* **6/5**[1]
4-54 **4** 3/4 **Slavonic (USA)**[17] 1311 3-9-4 72 (v[1]) DHolland 2 72
(JHMGosden) *chsd ldrs: rdn to press ldrs over 1f out: carried lft and no room jst ins fnl f: styd on same pce* **5/1**[2]
041- **5** 5 **Sound Blaster (IRE)**[223] 4934 3-9-7 75 MartinDwyer 7 65+
(AMBalding) *led after 2f: racd freely and sn 5l clr: hdd over 1f out: 4th and btn whn n.m.r on rail jst ins fnl f* **15/2**
406- **6** 1 3/4 **Canni Thinkaar (IRE)**[208] 5290 3-9-2 70 RLMoore 8 57
(PWHarris) *towards rr: rdn 1/2-way: nvr nr to chal* **20/1**
52-1 **7** 8 **Key Partners (IRE)**[13] 1370 3-8-11 70 DNolan(5) 6 42
(PABlockley) *wnt lft s: towards rr: mod effrt 3f out: wknd over 1f out* **15/2**

33-5 **8** *5* **Negwa (IRE)**[30] 1116 3-9-3 **74**........ TEDurcan 1 33
(MRChannon) *plld hrd early: mid-div: rdn over 3f out: no rspnse: eased whn no ch fnl f* **8/1**

2m 1.48s (-1.06) **Going Correction** +0.025s/f (Good) **8** Ran SP% **118.8**
Speed ratings: **105,104,103,102,98 97,91,87**CSF £133.10 TOTE £9.00: £2.50, £3.50, £1.10; EX 114.70.
**Owner** Sheikh Ahmed Al Maktoum **Bred** Gerrardstown House Stud **Trained** Newmarket, Suffolk

**FOCUS**
Kristal's Dream was a reluctant early leader, but Sound Blaster soon pulled himself into the lead and went a good gallop. However, the others let him go and do his own thing and eventually he capitulated. A fair time for the grade, but the form may not prove that reliable.

**NOTEBOOK**
**Meadaaf(IRE)** has the physical presence of a decent horse but his sights are having to be kept to a realistic level. However, this was a competent effort on a track which was probably not ideal, and there is a handicap or two in him.
**Gavroche(IRE)** sailed home down the centre of the track, avoiding all the trouble near the inside rail, but it was still a good performance to get so close to the unexposed winner.
**Kristal's Dream(IRE)** started to drift on the camber as she became tired. She will be sharper for this seasonal debut, and a mile and a half should not be a problem.
**Slavonic(USA)** was a shade unlucky in running, but he looks a tricky ride with a limited finishing effort.
**Sound Blaster(IRE)** has shown a tendency to pull too hard in all four races to date, and ended up running himself into the ground. More racing might reduce his impetuosity; if not, a return to a shorter trip would be an obvious option.
**Canni Thinkaar(IRE)** did not show a great deal and a step up in trip looks the best plan.
**Key Partners(IRE)** was ridden patiently to get the trip, but appeared not to last home up the hill.
**Negwa(IRE)**, the subject of a gamble, was the first beaten. She spread a plate before the start, which may be something of an excuse, but her seasonal debut was no more inspiring than this anyway. *Official explanation: jockey said filly spread a plate at the start*

## 1641 TOTESPORT.COM H'CAP — 7f 214y
**3:55** (3:56) (D) (0-85,84) 3-Y-O — **£5,499** (£1,692; £846; £423) **Stalls** Low

Form / RPR
31-3 **1** **Taruskin (IRE)**[10] 1408 3-9-7 **84**........ RLMoore 1 88
(NACallaghan) *trckd ldrs: nt clr run over 2f out: led over 1f out: rdn out* **4/11**[1]
554 **2** *½* **On The Waterfront**[48] 982 3-8-3 **66**........ EAhern 3 69
(JWHills) *hld up in rr: hdwy and nt clr run 2f out: squeezed through 1f out: ev ch fnl f: kpt on* **11/2**[2]
5-60 **3** *¾* **Anduril**[11] 1392 3-8-6 **69**........ JTate 5 70
(JMPEustace) *rrd s: hld up in tch: rdn to chse ldrs over 2f out: carried hd high: kpt on* **10/1**[3]
230- **4** *5* **Vamose (IRE)**[260] 3976 3-8-9 **72**........ MFenton 2 62
(MissGayKelleway) *led tl over 1f out: rdn and n.m.r on rail: sn btn* **16/1**
10- **5** *2½* **Lin In Gold (IRE)**[170] 5944 3-8-13 **81**........ DNolan(5) 4 65
(PABlockley) *s.s: hdwy to chse ldr over 5f out: wknd over 1f out* **16/1**

1m 34.71s (-0.29) **Going Correction** +0.025s/f (Good) **5** Ran SP% **109.6**
Speed ratings: **102,101,100,95,93**CSF £2.76 TOTE £1.30: £1.10, £2.10; EX 2.70.
**Owner** M Tabor **Bred** Myles Fitzpatrick **Trained** Newmarket, Suffolk
■ Stewards Enquiry : R L Moore caution:careless riding

**FOCUS**
A fair handicap run at a medium gallop, with the race finally developing two furlongs from home. The winner did not need to reproduce Newmarket form to win.

**NOTEBOOK**
**Taruskin(IRE)**, a progressive gelding, got the trip well and was holding the runner-up readily at the finish.
**On The Waterfront** made a promising turf debut following three fair efforts on the All-Weather. He travelled well and is certainly up to winning.
**Anduril** looks an awkward ride but ran well enough despite showing an unattractive head carriage.
**Vamose(IRE)** showed some promise last season and has reasonable prospects at this level. The interference, though not costing him a winning chance, finished him off more quickly than would have been the case.
**Lin In Gold(IRE)** won here last October but could do with dropping a few pounds.

## 1642 HARRY BLOOM MEMORIAL H'CAP — 5f 59y
**4:30** (4:30) (E) (0-75,70) 3-Y-O+ — **£3,474** (£1,069; £534; £267) **Stalls** Low

Form / RPR
0-05 **1** **Erracht**[58] 904 6-9-0 **60**........ GBaker 11 72
(MrsHSweeting) *led 1f: prom: led ins fnl f: rdn out* **25/1**
6-00 **2** *½* **Pulse**[8] 1477 6-9-0 **60**........(p) RLMoore 12 70
(JMBradley) *dwlt and unbalanced s: wd in midfield: hdwy over 1f out: chal ins fnl f: kpt on* **16/1**
2250 **3** *2* **Polish Emperor (USA)**[17] 1313 4-9-10 **70**........(b) DHolland 4 73
(PWHarris) *chsd ldrs: effrt and hung lft over 1f out: nt qckn ins fnl f* **11/2**[3]
0600 **4** *shd* **Panjandrum**[37] 1057 6-8-10 **56**........ PDoe 3 58
(NEBerry) *dwlt: outpcd and wl bhd: effrt whn hmpd and snatched up wl over 1f out: eased outside: fin wl* **25/1**
0500 **5** *½* **Taboor (IRE)**[13] 1368 6-8-11 **57**........(b) KFallon 8 58
(JWPayne) *mid-div: hdwy on outside 2f out: one pce fnl f* **5/1**[2]
020- **6** *1¾* **Ela Figura**[177] 5849 4-8-10 **56**........ SSanders 7 50
(AWCarroll) *hmpd s: towards rr: hdwy and hung lft over 1f out: styd on same pce* **25/1**
-100 **7** *shd* **Yorkie**[37] 1051 5-8-10 **56**........ DeanMcKeown 14 50
(PABlockley) *s.s: bhd: hdwy in midfield whn n.m.r and bmpd 1f out: nrst fin* **20/1**
3021 **8** *½* **Whippasnapper**[1] 1608 4-9-7 **67** 6ex........ NPollard 9 53
(JRBest) *dwlt: outpcd in midfield: nvr able to chal* **11/4**[1]
0022 **9** *shd* **Lady Pekan**[4] 1537 5-8-11 **60**........(b) LisaJones(3) 16 52
(PSMcentee) *led after 1f and wnt across to ins rail: hdd & wknd ins fnl f* **7/1**
0-50 **10** *1* **Zargus**[17] 1313 5-9-5 **65**........(b[1]) MartinDwyer 5 53
(WRMuir) *pressed ldr after 1f: rdn and hmpd over 1f out: sn wknd* **9/1**
0-00 **11** *½* **Tappit (IRE)**[17] 1313 5-9-4 **64**........(p) SCarson 10 50
(JMBradley) *chsd ldrs 3f* **25/1**
300/ **12** *2* **Louis Georgio**[182] 5-8-9 **55**........ JFEgan 6 34
(MRHoad) *outpcd: a towards rr* **20/1**
2000 **13** *½* **Tripti (IRE)**[19] 1280 4-8-8 **54**........ JTate 13 31
(JJBridger) *prom 3f* **50/1**
-566 **14** *hd* **Captain Cloudy**[59] 895 4-8-13 **62**........ LPKeniry(3) 1 39
(MMadgwick) *chsd ldrs: rdn and wkng whn bmpd 1f out* **20/1**
000- **15** *2* **Guns Blazing**[188] 5673 5-8-8 **61**........(v) MHoward(7) 2 31
(DKIvory) *in tch 2f: sn outpcd: btn in midfield whn hmpd over 1f out* **14/1**

61.18 secs (-1.09) **Going Correction** +0.025s/f (Good)
**WFA** 3 from 4yo+ 10lb **15** Ran SP% **125.4**
Speed ratings: **109,108,105,104,104 101,101,100,100,98 97,94,93,93,90**CSF £356.28 CT £2593.67 TOTE £23.70: £4.50, £3.30, £2.90; EX 252.70 Trifecta £4033.70 Pool of £24,429.52 - 4.30 winning units..
**Owner** P Sweeting **Bred** Downclose Stud **Trained** Marlborough, Wilts

**FOCUS**
A fair handicap in which Lady Pekan had to get across from the outside stall to make the running, and then set a good sprint pace. A decent time for the class of contest, but the first two will need to improve to win off revised marks.

**NOTEBOOK**
**Erracht**, making her debut for a new trainer, showed speed throughout and proved tenacious at the finish.
**Pulse**, whose rider nearly went out the side door leaving the stalls, gave the winner quite a start but ended up giving her a good race. He is back in form and close to his winning mark.
**Polish Emperor(USA)** looked unhappy on the camber, helping to cause much of the trouble near the rail as he drifted down the slope. He is not reliable, but could win again off his current mark on a good day. *Official explanation: jockey said gelding hung left*
**Panjandrum** flew home after a desperate run from the back. He looks on a handy mark on turf and is capable of landing a similar event.
**Taboor(IRE)** has become disappointing, but he is fairly handicapped at present and there were signs of a return to form. *Official explanation: jockey said gelding hung left*
**Ela Figura** is still a maiden after 24 attempts. She has shown a tendency to edge left at the business end, so this track was not ideal.
**Yorkie** had a rotten luck in running and became involved in a barging match with Captain Cloudy at the furlong pole. He can win off his present mark, particularly if returning to six furlongs.
**Whippasnapper** , a winner at Leicester the previous day, has been in good form but found five furlongs on fast ground too sharp. *Official explanation: jockey said race came too soon after gelding's run the previous day and that gelding found the distance too sharp*
**Lady Pekan** soon crossed from the outside stall to the inside rail to make the running. In the circumstances she made a bold , bid but that early effort was always likely to count against her.
**Zargus** *Official explanation: jockey said gelding hung left*

## 1643 WESTOWS PLAY & FOOTBALL IN HOVE H'CAP — 1m 1f 209y
**5:05** (5:08) (F) (0-55,58) 3-Y-O — **£2,898** (£828; £414) **Stalls** High

Form / RPR
56-5 **1** **Incisor**[8] 1465 3-8-13 **50**........ PDobbs 3 55
(SKirk) *hld up in tch: nt clr run 3f out: effrt 2f out: drvn to ld ins fnl f: hld on nr fin* **5/2**[2]
-040 **2** *hd* **Queen's Fantasy**[8] 1465 3-9-4 **55**........(v[1]) PaulEddery 2 60
(DHaydnJones) *dwlt: sn pressing ldr: drvn and outpcd over 1f out: rallied and r.o wl nr fin: jst hld* **14/1**
006- **3** *1¾* **Garston Star**[177] 5847 3-9-2 **53**........ MartinDwyer 4 54
(JSMoore) *led: hrd rdn over 1f out: hdd and no ex ins fnl f* **8/1**
005 **4** *nk* **Silver Cache (USA)**[64] 846 3-9-3 **54**........ EAhern 5 55
(JNoseda) *t.k.h: in tch: effrt over 2f out: one pce appr fnl f* **7/2**[3]
01 **5** *shd* **Friends Hope**[5] 1529 3-9-2 **58** 6ex........ DNolan(5) 6 59
(PABlockley) *hld up in rr: effrt on outside over 2f out: one pce appr fnl f* **5/4**[1]

2m 4.81s (2.27) **Going Correction** +0.025s/f (Good) **5** Ran SP% **113.0**
Speed ratings: **91,90,89,89,89**CSF £30.97 TOTE £3.90: £1.90, £2.70; EX 23.10.
**Owner** R Gander **Bred** J Godfrey **Trained** Upper Lambourn, Berks

**FOCUS**
A weak race and an unspectacular gallop, with the tempo increasing early in the straight. A modest winning time.

**NOTEBOOK**
**Incisor** travelled with confidence throughout and the bare result did not flatter him as he tired up the final climb. This was a weak contest, but he is lightly-raced and there is a bit of improvement in him. *Official explanation: trainer said, regarding the improved form shown, he thought gelding had run creditably on its previous start*
**Queen's Fantasy** appeared to have had enough a furlong from home, only to stage an unexpected rally. The visor achieved some success but she still looks a funny customer.
**Garston Star** was beaten in sellers last season but might do better now in that sphere if repeating this effort.
**Silver Cache(USA)** has shown signs of ability in her last two starts but will need to be kept at a sensible level.
**Friends Hope** was carrying a 6lb penalty for her win five days earlier. Given the close finish, that may have been the difference between victory and defeat.

## 1644 PLEASURE PALACE RACING LADY RIDERS' SERIES H'CAP — 1m 3f 196y
**5:35** (5:38) (F) (0-55,58) 3-Y-O+ — **£2,996** (£856; £428) **Stalls** High

Form / RPR
-012 **1** **Great View (IRE)**[18] 1305 5-11-0 **55**........(v) MsCWilliams 3 67
(MrsALMKing) *t.k.h: in tch: led over 3f out: pushed clr over 2f out: comf* **11/4**[1]
1455 **2** *2½* **Free Style (GER)**[33] 1081 4-10-3 **48**........ MissEFolkes(3) 4 56
(MrsHSweeting) *led 6f: rdn and lost pl 4f out: hung right over 2f out: rallied and styd on wl fnl f: wnt 2nd last 50 yds* **16/1**
1445 **3** *1½* **Delta Force**[75] 734 5-10-8 **49**........ MissCO'Neill 9 55
(PABlockley) *hld up in midfield: hdwy 5f out: chsd wnr over 2f out: one pce: lost 2nd last 50 yds* **9/1**
0-00 **4** *2* **Banningham Blaze**[13] 1198 4-10-8 **50**........(v) MissEJJones 12 53
(CRDore) *towards rr: hdwy 4f out: one pce fnl 2f* **8/1**[3]
04-0 **5** *1½* **Fletcher**[33] 1081 10-9-12 **45**........ MissGDGracey-Davison(7) 2 47
(HMorrison) *chsd ldr: led 6f out tl over 2f out: no ex* **16/1**
6314 **6** *1* **Birth Of The Blues**[6] 1492 8-10-0 **45**........ MissSarah-JaneDurman(5) 13 45
(AChariton) *hld up in rr: pushed along and styd on fnl 3f: nvr nrr* **11/1**
0/12 **7** *½* **Lissahanelodge**[19] 1281 5-9-12 **46**........ MissEKemp(7) 11 45
(PRHedger) *s.s: bhd tl rdn and styd on fnl 3f* **7/1**[2]
222- **8** *¾* **Short Change (IRE)**[147] 5720 5-10-13 **54**........ MrsSBosley 14 51
(AWCarroll) *prom: outpcd over 2f out: sn btn* **10/1**
-040 **9** *3* **Sammy's Shuffle**[52] 966 9-10-2 **48**........(b) MsDGoad(5) 6 41
(JamiePoulton) *mid div: rdn and btn 3f out* **12/1**
0666 **10** *3½* **Joely Green**[48] 981 7-10-2 **45**........ MrsEmmaLittmoden(3) 8 34
(NPLittmoden) *dwlt: bhd: hrd rdn over 2f out: n.d* **7/1**[2]
3002 **11** *2½* **Intensity**[8] 1463 8-10-12 **58**........ MissFayeBramley(5) 5 42
(PABlockley) *dwlt: sn chsng ldrs: outpcd 4f out: grad lost pl* **7/1**[2]
P060 **12** *8* **Geography (IRE)**[56] 931 4-9-11 **46** oh1........(p) MissSCassidy(7) 7 18
(PButler) *bhd fnl 5f* **50/1**
-600 **13** *nk* **Steppenwolf**[27] 1166 3-8-10 **48** ow3........(p) MrsIDeBest(5) 10 19
(WDeBest-Turner) *wd: bhd fnl 4f* **33/1**

2m 33.15s (1.05) **Going Correction** +0.025s/f (Good)
**WFA** 3 from 4yo 20lb 4 from 5yo+ 1lb **13** Ran SP% **127.1**
Speed ratings: **97,95,94,93,92 91,91,90,88,86 84,79,78**CSF £56.71 CT £374.08 TOTE £3.70: £2.10, £4.40, £4.70; EX 99.60 Place 6 £273.23, Place 5 £213.19.
**Owner** All The Kings Horses **Bred** Terry McGrath **Trained** Wilmcote, Warwicks

**FOCUS**
A surprisingly moderate gallop to halfway, with a notable injection of pace five furlongs from home.

**NOTEBOOK**
**Great View(IRE)**, given a polished ride, made a decisive move early in the straight, following which defeat was out of the question.


The Form Book, Raceform Ltd, Compton, RG20 6NL

**Free Style(GER)**, 5lb better off with the winner on recent Lingfield running, managed to get around five lengths closer. She runs as if an extra couple of furlongs would be in her favour.
**Delta Force** has won on sand at this trip and over two miles. He looked well handicapped for this reappearance on turf but was beaten on merit.
**Banningham Blaze** is on a winning mark but could not capitalise on that when push came to shove.
**Fletcher** tried to offset his lack of finishing speed over this trip by helping to make the running. However, he merely set things up nicely for the winner.
**Birth Of The Blues** was given quite a bit to do but the early pace was too pedestrian to bring his stamina into play.
T/Plt: £323.30 to a £1 stake. Pool: £31,689.50. 71.55 winning units. T/Qpdt: £36.00 to a £1 stake. Pool: £2,120.90. 43.50 winning units. LM

1645 - 1648a (Foreign Racing) - See Raceform Interactive

## 1251 CURRAGH (R-H)

Sunday, April 25

**OFFICIAL GOING: Soft**

### 1649a IRISH STALLION FARMS EUROPEAN BREEDERS FUND ATHASI STKS (GROUP 3) (FILLIES) 7f

**4:30** (4:32) 3-Y-0+ **£41,197** (£12,042; £5,704; £1,901)

RPR

1 **Lucky (IRE)**[10] 1434 3-8-8 ... JAHeffernan 2 104
(APO'Brien, Ire) *mde virtually all: rdn over 2f out: wandered abt fnl f: kpt on wl: comf* **11/8**[1]

2 1 ½ **Golden Nun**[29] 1126 4-9-7 ... (p) KDarley 1 100
(TDEasterby) *chsd ldrs in 4th: 5th and outpcd over 2f out: kpt on wl fnl f* **4/1**[2]

3 2 ½ **Megec Blis (IRE)**[28] 1152 3-8-8 ... PJSmullen 6 94
(DKWeld, Ire) *trckd ldrs in 3rd: rdn 2f out: kpt on same pce* **4/1**[2]

4 hd **Twiggy's Sister (IRE)**[35] 1070 6-9-7 102 ... JPMurtagh 3 93
(DermotMurphy, Ire) *hld up: effrt 2f out: 5th 1f out: kpt on u.p* **13/2**

5 ½ **Maroochydore (IRE)**[238] 4601 3-8-8 104 ... PCosgrave 5 92
(DavidWachman, Ire) *cl 2nd: chal over 2f out: no ex fnl f* **5/1**[3]

6 5 **Triton Dance (IRE)**[15] 1336 4-9-7 88 ... NGMcCullagh 4 80
(MJGrassick, Ire) *a in rr: no ex fr 2f out* **16/1**

1m 30.6s **Going Correction** +0.625s/f (Yiel)
**WFA** 3 from 4yo+ 13lb **6** Ran SP% **118.0**
Speed ratings: **109,107,104,104,103 97**CSF £7.79 TOTE £2.60: £1.50, £2.10; DF 8.60.
**Owner** Mrs John Magnier **Bred** Quay Bloodstock & J T Jones **Trained** Ballydoyle, Co Tipperary

**NOTEBOOK**
**Lucky(IRE)** was another Ballydoyle filly to make huge improvement following a maiden win ten days earlier She made virtually all and, despite running a bit green inside the last, was always in control.
**Golden Nun** looked to have had the waiting tactics overdone to an extent, as she ran on all too late.
**Megec Blis(IRE)** had Lucky just behind in third place when winning her Leopardstown maiden last month but there was no doubting which had made the most progress since.
**Twiggy's Sister(IRE)** got going late but possibly still needed this.
**Maroochydore(IRE)** will come on considerably for this outing.

1650 - 1651a (Foreign Racing) - See Raceform Interactive

## 1578 LONGCHAMP (R-H)

Sunday, April 25

**OFFICIAL GOING: Good to soft**

### 1652a PRIX DE LA GROTTE (GROUP 3) (FILLIES) 1m

**2:20** (2:19) 3-Y-0 **£25,704** (£10,282; £7,711; £5,141)

RPR

1 **Grey Lilas (IRE)**[21] 3-9-0 ... GaryStevens 5 106
(AFabre, France) *raced in close 2nd, disputing 2nd straight, smooth headway to lead 150y out, pushed out* 2

2 1 ½ **Petit Calva (FR)**[19] 1290 3-9-0 ... TJarnet 2 103
(RGibson, France) *led, pushed along 1 1/2f out, headed 150y out, kept on to just hold 2nd*

3 shd **Denebola (USA)**[203] 5404 3-9-0 ... C-PLemaire 4 103
(PBary, France) *sweating, disputing 5th on rail, close up disputing 4th straight, shaken up over 1f out, ran on final f, nearest at finish* 1

4 1 ½ **Via Milano (FR)**[28] 1162 3-9-0 ... TThulliez 1 100
(MmeJLaurent-JoyeRossi, France) *raced in 3rd, disputed 2nd straight, pushed along & slightly outpaced over 1f out, kept on under pressure final f*

5 1 **Grandes Illusions (FR)**[28] 1162 3-9-0 ... DBoeuf 3 98
(DSmaga, France) *raced in 4th, disputing 4th straight, ridden & effort 1 1/2f out, one pace final f*

6 2 ½ **Dalna (FR)**[173] 5922 3-9-0 ... OPeslier 8 92
(MmeCHead-Maarek, France) *held up in last, shaken up straight, never dangerous* 3

7 1 **Haskilclara (FR)**[238] 4605 3-9-0 ... CSoumillon 7 90
(YDeNicolay, France) *raced in 7th, pushed along 2f out, one pace final f*

8 4 **Firedance (GER)**[31] 3-9-0 ... ELegrix 6 82
(MDelzangles, France) *disputed 5th, 6th straight, pushed along over 1 1/2f out, no impression*

1m 38.4s **Going Correction** -0.10s/f (Good) **8** Ran SP% **120.4**
Speed ratings: **111,109,109,107,106 104,103,99.**
**Owner** Gestut Ammerland **Bred** Azienda Agricola Il Tiglio Di Amelia Prevedello **Trained** France

**NOTEBOOK**
**Grey Lilas(IRE)** ran quite free early on still managed to run out a clear-cut winner. A fast improving filly with a good turn of foot, she now goes for the Gainsborough Poule d'Essai des Pouliches.
**Petit Calva(FR)** tried to make all the running at just an ordinary pace but had nothing in reserve when the winner came sweeping past.
**Denebola(USA)** took a little time to balance in the straight, but made up some late ground and only lost second place by a narrow margin. This race will have brought her on a lot and she is still on target for the Pouliches.
**Via Milano(FR)** was outpaced early on the straight before running on throughout the final furlong and a half. Her pedigree suggests she may well be suited to a longer trip.

### 1653a PRIX DE FONTAINEBLEAU (GROUP 3) (COLTS) 1m

**2:50** (2:52) 3-Y-0 **£25,704** (£10,282; £7,711; £5,141)

RPR

1 **American Post**[25] 1218 3-9-2 ... CSoumillon 2 111+
(MmeCHead-Maarek, France) *made all, quickened over 1f out, ran on well* 1

2 2 **Blackdoun (FR)**[25] 1218 3-9-2 ... FSpanu 1 105
(J-LPelletan, France) *close up, 3rd on rail straight, pushed along over 1 1/2f out, one pace, finished 3rd, beaten 1l, 2l, placed 2nd*

3 ¾ **Diamond Green (FR)**[227] 4858 3-9-2 ... GaryStevens 3 103
(AFabre, France) *trckd wnr, pressed briefly over 1 1/2f out, one pace whn crossed & snatched up ins fnl f, fin 4th, btn 3 ¾l, placed 3rd* 2

4 1 **Antonius Pius (USA)**[190] 5640 3-9-2 ... JPSpencer 4 109
(APO'Brien, Ire) *racd in last, hdwy over 1f out, drvn to go 2nd fnl f, hung rt, ran on but no imp on wnr, fin 2nd, btn 1l, disq, pl last* 3

1m 38.5s **Going Correction** -0.10s/f (Good) **4** Ran SP% **123.3**
Speed ratings: **111,108,107,110.**
**Owner** K Abdulla **Bred** Juddmonte Farms **Trained** France
■ Stewards Enquiry : J P Spencer four-day ban: careless riding (May 4-7)

**NOTEBOOK**
**American Post** dominated this Classic trial from the moment he took the lead soon after the start and Soumillon never had to get too serious with him. He now heads for the Gainsborough Poule d'Essai des Poulains.
**Blackdoun(FR)** was promoted to the runners-up position after a Stewards enquiry. This provincially trained colt ran with great merit and he will probably be allowed to take his chance in the Poulains.
**Diamond Green(FR)** was a little free early on and proved unable to quicken. He had to be snatched up and nearly fell in the straight - he was promoted him to third. He will probably go for the Poulains.
**Antonius Pius(USA)** was always travelling easily and looked dangerous one and a half out. However, he hung right under pressure into Diamond Green and Blackdoun, and was also hampered in his run. He was disqualified as a result.

### 1654a PRIX GREFFUHLE (GROUP 2) (C&F) 1m 2f 110y

**3:20** (3:32) 3-Y-0 **£42,148** (£16,268; £7,764; £5,176)

RPR

1 **Millemix (FR)**[21] 1260 3-9-2 ... C-PLemaire 4 108+
(MmeCHead-Maarek, France) *disputed 3rd, close 3rd towards outside straight, led 1 1/2f out, ran on final f, driven out* 1

2 snk **Day Or Night**[24] 3-9-2 ... TGillet 3 104
(JEPease, France) *disputed 3rd early, pushed along 1 1/2f out, disputed 2nd from 1f out, finished 3rd, beaten 2l & snk, placed 2nd* 2

3 ¾ **Vassilievsky (IRE)**[26] 3-9-2 ... DBoeuf 5 103
(ELellouche, France) *held up in last, ran on from over 1f out to take 4th close home, beaten 2l, snk & ¾l, placed 3rd*

4 shd **Blue Canari (FR)**[21] 1260 3-9-2 ... TThulliez 1 103
(PBary, France) *raced in 7th, stayed on from over 1f out, crossed inside final f, nearest finish, finished 5th, 2l, snk, ¾l & shd, placed 4*

5 2 **Esperanto (IRE)**[21] 1252 3-9-2 ... JPSpencer 6 104
(APO'Brien, Ire) *raced in 5th, pushed along on outside straight, ridden over 1f out, wandered ins fnl f, fin 2nd 2l, disq, pl 5th*

6 nk **Hamriya** 3-9-2 ... CSoumillon 2 99
(J-CRouget, France) *raced in 6th, progress on inner from half-way, 4th straight, pushed along to close up over 1 1/2f out, no extra final 100y* 3

7 nk **Mythe (FR)**[20] 3-9-2 ... OPlacais 7 98
(MmeCHead-Maarek, France) *led, pushed along 2f out, headed 1 1/2f out, ridden 1f out, kept on one pace* 1

8 nk **Saville Row (USA)**[21] 1260 3-9-2 ... GaryStevens 8 98
(AFabre, France) *tracked leader, driven to disputed lead 1 1/2f out, ridden & ran on til no extra final 100y*

2m 12.9s **Going Correction** -0.10s/f (Good) **8** Ran SP% **144.1**
Speed ratings: **104,102,101,101,102 101,101,101.**
**Owner** Alec Head **Bred** A Head And Mme Alec Head **Trained** France
■ Stewards Enquiry : J P Spencer two-day ban: careless riding

**NOTEBOOK**
**Millemix(FR)** was always travelling well and, eased into the lead at the furlong marker, he won nicely - the result was never in doubt from that point. He should improve again and now looks like going for the Prix Lupin before the Prix du Jockey-Club.
**Day Or Night** was a little free due to the lack of pace. Hampered before just losing second place near the finish, the stewards moved him up to the runners-up position.
**Vassilievsky(IRE)** was keen in the early stages and still had plenty to do in the straight. He ran on well at the finish and was moved up to third place by the Stewards.
**Blue Canari(FR)** was slightly hampered by the initial runner-up and was eventually moved up to fourth place.
**Esperanto(IRE)** was responsible for stopping both Day or Night and Blue Canari from gaining the best possible place and was demoted from second to fifth position. He is not an easy ride.

## DIELSDORF (R-H)

Sunday, April 25

**OFFICIAL GOING: Good**

### 1655a SUPER GRAND PRIX BMW 1m 3f 110y

**2:00** (2:11) 4-Y-0+ **£10,859** (£4,344; £3,258; £2,172)

RPR

1 **Moonjaz**[581] 4858 7-8-11 ow2 ... EWehrel 8 —
(KKlein, Germany)

2 nk **Akash (IRE)**[19] 1286 4-9-6 ... JFanning 13 —
(MJohnston) *led, challenged by winner one furlong out, headed 100y out, ran on* 1

3 2 ½ **Syndaco (IRE)**[70] 786 5-8-9 ... RHavlin 2 —
(MWeiss, Switzerland)

4 1 ¼ **Glavalcour (FR)**[315] 2412 4-9-10 ... BJollivet 1 —
(KSchafflutzel, Switzerland) 2

5 1 ¼ **Standby Dancer (GER)**[334] 8-9-4 ... ASchikora 10 —
(DrABolte, Germany)

6 2 **Funward (FR)**[199] 5-9-8 ... MlleSeverineKalina 4 —
(KKlein, Germany)

7 **Kasai**[336] 1854 5-8-9 ... FlurinaWullschleger 5 —
(WFigge, Germany)

8 **Borsato (GER)**[427] 603 7-8-9 ... DMoffatt 9 —
(MissACasotti, Switzerland)

9 **Brother's Valcour (FR)**[70] 785 6-9-8 ............ BMarchand 11 —
(KSchafflutzel, Switzerland)
10 **Auenteufel (GER)**[70] 785 5-9-6 ............(b) DSweeney 7 —
(KarinSuter, Switzerland)
11 **Brigadier Du Pin (FR)**[70] 785 6-8-13 ............ NJeanpierre 6 —
(KSchafflutzel, Switzerland)
12 **Soul Of Magic (IRE)**[540] 5620 5-8-6 ............ BrigitteRenk 14 —
(KarinSuter, Switzerland)
D **Safin (GER)**[70] 785 4-8-9 ............ GBocskai 12 —
(CarmenBocksai, Germany) *Finished 7th, disqualified, placed last.* 3

2m 28.9s 13 Ran SP% **144.2**
Speed ratings: .
**Owner** Stall Brunau **Bred** Shadwell Estate Company Limited **Trained** Germany

**NOTEBOOK**
**Akash(IRE)**, a game winner on his British/seasonal debut at Pontefract, attempted to lead throughout and went down fighting in defeat. He did his best to get back at the eventual winner, but ran out of time. He will stay further and looks a horse connections are sure to have fun with in similar races.

## FRANKFURT (L-H)
Sunday, April 25

**OFFICIAL GOING: Good**

### 1656a FRUHJAHRSPREIS DES BANKHAUS METZLER - STADRAT ALBERT VON METZLER-RENNEN (GROUP 3) 1m 2f
**4:00** (4:20) 3-Y-O **£32,394** (£13,380; £7,042; £3,521)

RPR
1 **Apeiron (GER)**[168] 3-9-0 ............ J-PCarvalho 4 101
(MarioHofer, Germany) *pulled early in 4th, 5th straight, driven and headway 1f out, ran on well to lead last strides* 1
2 nk **Mensatiger (GER)**[168] 3-9-0 ............ AStarke 5 101
(THHansen, Germany) *tracked leader to straight, led 1 1/2f out, caught last strides*
3 1 3/4 **Siberion (GER)** 3-9-0 ............ IMongan 2 98
(MarioHofer, Germany) *raced in 3rd to straight, ran on one pace from over 1f out*
4 1 1/4 **Genios (GER)**[203] 3-9-0 ............ LHammer-Hansen 1 96
(DrABolte, Germany) *led to 1 1/2f out, kept on one pace*
5 nk **Egerton (GER)**[189] 5660 3-9-0 ............ AHelfenbein 3 95
(PRau, Germany) *held up, closed up over 3f out, 4th straight, stayed on but never able to challenge* 3
6 nk **Eleazar (GER)**[189] 5660 3-9-0 ............ WMongil 6 94
(HBlume, Germany) *held up in rear, last straight, never a factor*
7 3 1/2 **Armand (GER)**[35] 3-9-0 ............ THellier 7 88
(PSchiergen, Germany) *in touch on outside to over 3f out, 6th & weakening straight* 2

2m 8.74s 7 Ran SP% **131.1**
Speed ratings: .
**Owner** E Sauren **Bred** Gestut Karlshof **Trained** Germany

## SHA TIN (R-H)
Sunday, April 25

**OFFICIAL GOING: Good to firm**

### 1657a AUDEMARS PIGUET QE II CUP (GROUP 1) 1m 2f
**9:30** (9:42) 3-Y-0+ **£575,540** (£215,827; £107,914; £57,554)

RPR
1 **River Dancer (IRE)**[35] 5-9-0 ............ GSchofield 8 117
(JSize, Hong Kong) *raced in 6th, led 100 yards out, driven out* **57/1**
2 3/4 **Elegant Fashion (AUS)**[35] 6-8-10 ............ GMosse 2 112
(DHayes, Hong Kong) *raced in 5th, 3rd straight, disputed lead briefly 120 yards out, soon headed, stayed on at same pace* **39/10**[2]
3 shd **Scott's View**[13] 1355 5-9-0 ............ SChin 6 116
(MJohnston) *raced in 7th, taken gradually wide from 2f out, ridden and edged left approaching final furlong, stayed on well final furlo* **9/1**
4 3/4 **Bowman's Crossing (IRE)**[35] 5-9-0 ............ SDye 11 115
(DOughton, Hong Kong) *dropped out in last, ran on well down outside to take 4th 100 yards out, stayed on* **34/1**
5 3/4 **Right Approach**[29] 1146 5-9-0 ............ WCMarwing 3 113
(MFDeKock, South Africa) *raced in 8th, stayed on at same pace final 2f* **17/1**
6 3/4 **Lucky Owners (NZ)**[35] 4-9-0 ............ FCoetzee 9 112
(ACruz, Hong Kong) *raced in 4th, niggled along 4f out, 5th straight, effort and disputing 4th 1 1/2f out, soon lost place, stayed on again clo* **6/5**[1]
7 nse **Saturn (IRE)**[35] 4-9-0 ............ AMarcus 5 112
(IWAllan, Hong Kong) *led til headed 120 yards out, weakened* **15/1**
8 1 3/4 **Visorhill (FR)**[329] 6-9-0 ............ PPayne 7 109
(IWAllan, Hong Kong) *raced in 3rd, 2nd straight, ridden approaching final furlong, soon weakened* **42/1**
9 hd **Blue Stitch**[133] 6188 5-9-0 ............(v) RFradd 1 109
(ATMillard, Hong Kong) *raced in 9th, ridden and looked held when slightly hampered 1f out* **98/1**
10 nse **Bullish Luck (USA)**[35] 5-9-0 ............(b) ODoleuze 4 108
(ASCruz, Hong Kong) *raced in 10th, 11th straight, never a factor* **12/1**
11 2 3/4 **Ain't Here (AUS)**[35] 4-9-0 ............ BPrebble 12 104
(DHayes, Hong Kong) *raced in 12th, never a factor* **57/1**
12 nse **Sarafan (USA)**[29] 1146 7-9-0 ............ ASuborics 13 104
(NDrysdale, U.S.A) *raced in 11th, 10th on inside straight, never a factor* **26/1**
13 1/2 **Paolini (GER)**[29] 1146 7-9-0 ............ EPedroza 14 103
(AWohler, Germany) *raced in 13th, effort on inside 2f out, no impression* **29/1**
14 dist **Tiber (IRE)**[35] 4-9-0 ............ DWhyte 10 —
(JMoore, Hong Kong) *immediately pushed along to press leader on outside, 4th and weakening entering straight, eased approaching final furlong* **81/10**[3]

2m 1.40s 14 Ran SP% **123.0**
Speed ratings: .
**Owner** R J Arculli **Bred** Watership Down Stud **Trained** Hong Kong

**NOTEBOOK**
**River Dancer(IRE)** was known as Diaghilev when winning the 2002 Prix La Force for Aidan O'Brien. Finally got the fast pace that he needs and, always handy, ran on strongly in the straight to register a victory that was no fluke despite his odds of almost 58-1.
**Elegant Fashion(AUS)**is admirably game and consistent but, after hitting the front for a few strides inside the final furlong, simply found one too good.
**Scott's View**, an unlucky loser on his penultimate outing in the Sheema Classic, won in great style back in England last time and could again be called unlucky here. He was not given a good ride and ended up coming wide with his challenge. He would have won in another half a furlong and deserves to land a big prize.

## HAMILTON (R-H)
Monday, April 26

**OFFICIAL GOING: Good (good to soft in places)**

### 1658 DAILY RECORD PUNTER DAY MAIDEN AUCTION STKS (QUALIFIER FOR HAMILTON PARK 2YO SERIES FINAL) 5f 4y
**2:20** (2:21) (E) 2-Y-O **£3,461** (£1,065; £532; £266) **Stalls** High

Form RPR
2 1 **Monashee Prince (IRE)**[14] 1374 2-8-8 ............ NPollard 6 65+
(JRBest) *qckly away: mde all: rdn over 1f out: styd on wl* **7/4**[2]
2 1 **Exit Smiling** 2-8-9 ............ KDalgleish 4 62+
(MJohnston) *chsd wnr: rdn over 1f out: edgd rt and kpt on ins last* **13/8**[1]
0 3 1 1/4 **Gifted Gamble**[16] 1324 2-8-7 ............ NCallan 1 55
(KARyan) *chsd ldng pair: swtchd rt wl over 1f out: sn rdn and kpt on same pce* **8/1**[3]
0 4 2 **Our Choice (IRE)**[13] 1383 2-8-10 ............ TEDurcan 5 50
(NPLittmoden) *in tch: rdn along 2f out: kpt on same pce* **8/1**[3]
0 5 hd **Steal The Thunder**[18] 1314 2-8-8 ow1 ............ FLynch 3 47
(ABerry) *sn pushed along in rr: rdn 1/2-way: nvr a factor* **100/1**
6 7 **Lerida** 2-8-7 ............ KDarley 2 18
(TDBarron) *wnt rt s: in tch: rdn along 1/2-way: wknd wl over 1f out* **11/1**

61.62 secs (0.36) **Going Correction** -0.025s/f (Good) **6** Ran SP% **106.0**
Speed ratings: **96,94,92,89,88 77**CSF £4.33 TOTE £3.00: £1.10, £1.90; EX 5.60.
**Owner** Richmond Thoroughbreds **Bred** Mrs Dolores Gleeson **Trained** Hucking, Kent

**FOCUS**
An ordinary maiden run at a sound pace. The form looks no better than average for the grade.
**NOTEBOOK**
**Monashee Prince(IRE)**, with the benefit of previous experience and the far rail to help him, bounced out to make every yard and did this nicely. There should be more races in him, but he would be very unlikely to confirm the form with the runner-up were they to meet again.
**Exit Smiling ◆**, a 24,000gns Dr Fong colt out of a half-sister to Reason To Dance, was in vain pursuit of the winner the whole way but there is plenty of improvement in him and he is very likely to turn out the best of these.
**Gifted Gamble** improved from his debut on this better ground and should find a race in due course.
**Our Choice(IRE)**, last of eight in a hot Newmarket conditions event on his debut, was in more realistic company here but did not show very much despite the big drop in class.

### 1659 ROA SCOTLAND CONDITIONS STKS 5f 4y
**2:50** (2:50) (C) 3-Y-O **£8,963** (£3,400; £1,700; £772) **Stalls** High

Form RPR
32-1 1 **Sevillano**[25] 1223 3-8-12 106 ............ TEDurcan 6 94
(PDCundell) *mde all: shkn up wl over 1f out: rdn ent last: kpt on* **1/6**[1]
246- 2 1 3/4 **Celtic Thunder**[199] 5471 3-8-9 84 ............ RHavlin 4 85
(TJEtherington) *trckd wnr: rdn over 1f out: styd on ins last* **14/1**[2]
03-6 3 3 **Baylaw Star**[9] 1473 3-8-9 75 ............ JEdmunds 3 74
(JBalding) *cl up: rdn along 2f out:grad wknd* **25/1**[3]
3-30 4 5 **A Little Bit Yarie**[2] 1602 3-8-12 84 ............ DarrenWilliams 5 59
(KRBurke) *dwlt: sn chsng ldrs: rdn along 1/2-way: sn outpcd* **14/1**[2]
50-4 5 1 1/2 **One 'N' Only (IRE)**[15] 1342 3-8-4 55 ............ PHanagan 2 46
(MissLAPerratt) *sn outpcd and bhd* **100/1**
254- 6 7 **Balwearie (IRE)**[221] 5011 3-8-9 66 ............ JCarroll 1 26
(MissLAPerratt) *s.i.s: a rr* **66/1**

59.92 secs (-1.34) **Going Correction** -0.025s/f (Good) **6** Ran SP% **105.4**
Speed ratings: **109,106,101,93,91 79**CSF £2.50 TOTE £1.10: £1.02, £3.50; EX 2.80.
**Owner** H E Sheikh Rashid Bin Mohammed **Bred** Miss C Green **Trained** Compton, Berks

**FOCUS**
An uncompetitive event, but a decent pace and few got into it.
**NOTEBOOK**
**Sevillano** made very yard from his rails draw and, though nothing like as impressive as at Leicester, never looked like being beaten. The stiff track would have helped offset the drop to the minimum trip somewhat, as he is probably better over six, and it will be interesting to see how he would fare in Pattern company.
**Celtic Thunder ◆**, reappearing after a break of six months, ran a blinder at the weights and was snapping at the favourite's heels until the last half furlong. Unless the Handicapper takes this at face value he is one to keep in mind.
**Baylaw Star**, twice a winner over course and distance in a busy juvenile campaign, ran well considering he was badly in at the weights with those that finished around him, but he is relatively exposed and may be flattered by this.
**A Little Bit Yarie** should have done better at the weights, but was shaken off at halfway. Connections had suggested that the reason for his disappointing effort at Haydock 48 hours earlier may have been down to running him again too quickly following his reappearance from a long layoff, so his appearance here was rather strange.

### 1660 RACEGOERS CLUB RACECOURSE OF THE YEAR H'CAP 1m 1f 36y
**3:20** (3:20) (E) (0-75,67) 3-Y-O+ **£3,575** (£1,100; £550; £275) **Stalls** High

Form RPR
5030 1 **Pharoah's Gold (IRE)**[3] 1598 6-8-7 50 ............(v) TEDurcan 3 59
(DShaw) *stdd s and hld up in rr: gd hdwy on outer 3f out: str run appr last: styd on wl to ld nr fin* **14/1**
215/ 2 nk **Dispol Foxtrot**[426] 4758 6-9-8 65 ............ DMcGaffin 15 73
(MissVScott) *tracd ldrs: hdwy to ld wl over 1f out: rdn ent last: drvn and hdd nr fin* **16/1**
0-55 3 2 1/2 **Summer Special**[6] 1527 4-8-8 51 ............ PHanagan 11 54
(DWBarker) *dwlt and towards rr: hdwy 1/2-way: swtchd lft 3f out: sn rdn: styd on appr last: nrst fin* **10/1**[3]
4-50 4 1 **Lennel**[5] 1539 6-9-10 67 ............(b) FNorton 9 68
(ABailey) *hld up towards rr: hdwy 3f out: rdn and kpt on fnl 2f: nrst fin* **11/2**[2]
500- 5 1/2 **Jordans Elect**[181] 5821 4-9-9 66 ............ NPollard 12 66
(ISemple) *cl up: led 3f out: rdn and hdd wl over 1f out: grad wknd* **12/1**

0244 **6** ¾ **Sting Like A Bee (IRE)**[32] [1109] 5-8-7 **50** JFEgan 4 49
(JSGoldie) *towards rr: pushed along 1/2-way: hdwy u.p whn n.m.r 3f out: sn drvn: kpt on: nt rch ldrs* **5/1**[1]

00-0 **7** ½ **Encounter**[12] [1393] 8-8-3 **46** DaleGibson 13 44
(JHetherton) *chsd ldrs: rdn along over 2f out: swtchd rt and drvn ent last: one pce* **10/1**[3]

4-05 **8** 1¼ **Rotuma (IRE)**[7] [1503] 5-9-1 **65** (b) PMakin(7) 5 60
(MDods) *chsd ldrs: rdn along over 3f out: grad wknd* **10/1**[3]

300- **9** 5 **Forest Air (IRE)**[184] [5749] 4-8-6 **49** PFessey 8 34
(MissLAPerratt) *a rr* **50/1**

00-5 **10** 1½ **Inchinnan**[74] [650] 7-9-0 **57** ANicholls 1 39
(JamesMoffatt) *a towards rr* **20/1**

0/00 **11** ½ **Pharaoh Hatshepsut (IRE)**[18] [1316] 6-7-12 **41** oh6 PMQuinn 6 22
(JamesMoffatt) *led: rdn along 4f out: hdd 3f out and sn wknd* **100/1**

5525 **12** shd **Red Delirium**[11] [1426] 8-7-5 **41** oh1 (b) BSwarbrick(7) 14 22
(PABlockley) *in tchon inner: rdn along over 3f out: sn wknd* **12/1**

060- **13** nk **Millennium Hall**[213] [5189] 5-9-0 **57** RFfrench 7 37
(PMonteith) *prom: rdn along 4f out: wknd wl over 2f out* **11/1**

0-05 **14** ¾ **Lucky Largo (IRE)**[12] [1389] 4-9-1 **58** KDalgleish 10 37
(MissLAPerratt) *a rr* **25/1**

2555 **15** 3½ **Noul (USA)**[23] [1245] 5-9-1 **58** (p) NCallan 2 30
(KARyan) *a rr* **10/1**[3]

1m 58.99s (-0.61) **Going Correction** -0.025s/f (Good) **15** Ran SP% **116.2**
Speed ratings: **101,100,98,97,97 96,96,94,90,89 88,88,88,87,84**CSF £205.66 CT £2332.65 TOTE £16.90: £4.50, £2.40, £5.20; EX 327.90.
**Owner** The Whiteman Partnership **Bred** Rathbarry Stud **Trained** Averham, Notts
■ Stewards Enquiry : D McGaffin caution: used whip with excessive frequency

**FOCUS**
Quite a competitive if ordinary handicap run at an even pace.

**NOTEBOOK**
**Pharoah's Gold(IRE)**, well handicapped on his sand form, was stone last with half a mile to run but, once switched wide, ran past the entire field to nail the runner-up near the line. This year he seems to have found some stamina from somewhere.
**Dispol Foxtrot**, who has gained her last five wins at this track, was reappearing after a break of 14 months and looked to have done everything right, but despite pulling away from the others found the winner had the greater impetus at the end. It will be a surprise if she does not score again here this season.
**Summer Special**, a maiden after 24 attempts coming into this, dispelled any doubts over his ability to stay the trip and, on this better ground, was travelling as strongly at the line as he had at any stage. He looks worth persevering with over this sort of distance, though he will probably always need a sound surface.
**Lennel** was staying on well at the end, but has still not had his favoured fast ground yet this season.
**Jordans Elect** ◆ ran very well on this first start in six months and was in front racing up the straight before tiring as if just needing it. He has dropped to a reasonable mark and is one for the notebook.
**Sting Like A Bee(IRE)** did not see a great deal of daylight at various stages up the home straight, but lacked the speed to get him out of trouble and just stayed on at the one pace.

## 1661 TOTETRIFECTA STKS (H'CAP) 1m 4f 17y
**3:50** (3:51) (C ) (0-90,85) 4-Y-0+ **£10,387** (£3,196; £1,598; £799) **Stalls** High

Form RPR

604- **1** **King Revo (IRE)**[25] [6025] 4-9-3 **79** GFaulkner 8 88
(PCHaslam) *dwlt and in rr: hdwy over 4f out: swtchd lft over 2f out: rdn over 1f out: styd on strly ins last to ld last 100 yds* **8/1**[3]

13-0 **2** ¾ **Gold Ring**[12] [1401] 4-9-9 **85** RHavlin 7 93
(GBBalding) *in tch: hdwy over 2f out: rdn over 1f out: kpt on u.p ins last* **7/1**[2]

64-0 **3** ½ **Kid'Z'Play (IRE)**[32] [1103] 8-8-2 **63** JFEgan 10 70
(JSGoldie) *led: rdn over 2f out: drvn over 1f out: hdd and no ex last 100 yds* **25/1**

31-1 **4** hd **Sentry (IRE)**[12] [1401] 4-9-9 **85** KDarley 12 92
(JHMGosden) *in tch: effrt on outer 3f out: rdn to chal over 1f out and ev ch tld riven and no ex wl ins last* **7/4**[1]

0/31 **5** 2 **Calatagan (IRE)**[12] [1393] 5-8-2 **63** PHanagan 2 67
(JMJefferson) *chsd ldrs: rdn along over 2f out: styd on same pce appr last* **14/1**

343- **6** 1½ **Golden Boot**[211] [5258] 5-8-6 **67** (p) FNorton 9 69
(ABailey) *hld up in rr: hdwy on inner and nt clr run 4f out: styd on fnl 2f: nrst fin* **16/1**

30-5 **7** nk **Sahem (IRE)**[31] [1112] 7-8-10 **78** BSwarbrick(7) 6 79
(DEddy) *towards rr: hdwy over 3f out: rdn an d n.m.r 2f out: kpt on fnl f: nrst fin* **14/1**

60/6 **8** ½ **Spree Vision**[6] [1527] 8-7-12 **59** oh7 RFfrench 14 59
(PMonteith) *in tch on inner: gd hdwy 1/2-way: effrt to chal 3f out and ev ch tl rdn and wknd over 1f out* **100/1**

21 **9** ¾ **Gran Dana (IRE)**[15] [1344] 4-9-6 **82** KDalgleish 11 81
(MJohnston) *cl up: rdn along 4f out: wknd wl over 2f out* **14/1**

2052 **10** 3½ **General**[5] [1539] 7-8-8 **69** NCallan 4 63
(NPLittmoden) *in tch: effrt and rdn whn hmpd over 2f out: sn no imp* **7/1**[2]

3010 **11** 3½ **Cruise Director**[12] [1401] 4-9-9 **85** FLynch 1 74
(WJMusson) *a towards rr* **20/1**

54/4 **12** 2½ **Lucky Judge**[23] [1245] 7-7-12 **59** DaleGibson 3 44
(GASwinbank) *midfield: rdn along 4f out: sn wknd* **33/1**

0-16 **13** 1½ **Acceleration (IRE)**[18] [1316] 4-8-1 **63** (v) PMQuinn 5 46
(RAllan) *a rr* **50/1**

030- **14** 7 **Spectrometer**[10] [4862] 7-9-10 **85** TEDurcan 13 57
(RCGuest) *chsd ldrs: rdn along 4f out: wknd 3f out* **16/1**

2m 38.06s (-1.14) **Going Correction** -0.025s/f (Good)
**WFA** 4 from 5yo+ 1lb **14** Ran SP% **118.7**
Speed ratings: **102,101,101,101,99 98,98,98,97,95 93,91,90,85**CSF £59.19 CT £1351.03 TOTE £9.10: £2.40, £2.50, £7.00; EX 71.70 Trifecta £923.20 Part won. Pool of £1,300.00 - 0.70 winning units..
**Owner** Dick Renwick & Mrs C Barclay **Bred** Tom Radley **Trained** Middleham Moor, N Yorks
■ Stewards Enquiry : G Faulkner seven-day ban: used whip with excessive force and above shoulder height (4 days); careless riding (3 days) (May 8,10-11,12-15)

**FOCUS**
A decent-class and competitive handicap, but only an ordinary pace and a modest time for a race of this grade.

**NOTEBOOK**
**King Revo(IRE)**, in such good form over hurdles this winter, was given a patient ride before being produced with his effort widest of all up the straight. Despite hanging, his impetus was still enough to take him to the front and he won quite tidily in the end.
**Gold Ring** ◆ was tucked away behind the leader on the inside up the straight and had to wait to get a clear run. When he did get out, he stayed on really well but the winner enjoyed a clear passage down the outside and just had his measure. He deserves compensation.
**Kid'Z'Play(IRE)**, all the better for his reappearance effort, established his normal position out in front but set just a sensible gallop. That meant he was able to keep something in reserve and he hung in there for longer than would have been expected.
**Sentry(IRE)**, off a 3lb higher mark, had every chance but was always making hard work of it. It may be that this very different track to Newmarket was not suitable for him.
**Calatagan(IRE)**, 5lb higher for his Beverley win, had every chance but seemed to run out of puff at the end and, despite having won over hurdles, it may be that ten furlongs is his best trip on the Flat.
**Golden Boot** did not see a great deal on daylight on the inside, but was not stopped in his run to any great degree and just kept staying on. He is entitled to come on for this first race in seven months, but is still without a win since his third start as a juvenile.

## 1662 FAMOUS GROUSE MAIDEN STKS 1m 3f 16y
**4:20** (4:21) (D ) 3-4-Y-0 **£6,123** (£1,884; £942; £471) **Stalls** High

Form RPR

-224 **1** **Golden Empire (USA)**[2] [1605] 3-8-5 **77** TEDurcan 4 73
(EALDunlop) *led 4f: cl up tl led over 2f out: sn rdn and edgd rt: drvn ins last and kpt on* **3/1**[2]

30- **2** nk **Sadler's Pride (IRE)**[212] [5227] 4-9-10 JCarroll 8 73
(AndrewTurnell) *hld up towards rr: smooth hdwy 3f out: rdn to chal over 1f out and ev ch tld riven and nt qckn nr fin* **14/1**

4-2 **3** 2½ **Templet (USA)**[23] [1249] 4-9-10 PHanagan 7 69
(ISemple) *hld up: hdwy and pushed along over 4f out: hdwy on inner whn bdly hmpd 2f out: kpt on ins last* **10/11**[1]

5- **4** 2½ **Act Of The Pace (IRE)**[283] [3386] 4-9-5 KDalgleish 3 60
(MJohnston) *dwlt: sn pushed along and in tch: hdwy 4f out: rdn over 2f out and kpt on same pce* **9/1**[3]

**5** 9 **Jordans Spark** 3-8-7 ow2 NCallan 5 53
(ISemple) *keen: cl up tl led after 4f: rdn along 4f out: hdd: rdn and hung lft 2f out: sn drvn and wknd* **20/1**

66-5 **6** 1¾ **Peruvian Breeze (IRE)**[14] [1357] 3-8-5 59 NPollard 6 48
(NPLittmoden) *chsd ldrs: rdn along over 3f out: sn wknd* **10/1**

0 **7** 5 **Archenko**[15] [1344] 4-9-10 FLynch 1 40
(ABerry) *promonent: effrt and ev ch 3f out: sn rdn and wknd fnl 2f* **100/1**

**8** dist **Flying Red (IRE)** 3-7-7 BSwarbrick(7) 2 —
(PABlockley) *s.i.s: a rr: drvn along and bhd fnl 4f* **33/1**

2m 26.04s (-0.46) **Going Correction** -0.025s/f (Good)
**WFA** 3 from 4yo 19lb **8** Ran SP% **111.8**
Speed ratings: **100,99,97,96,89 88,84,**—CSF £39.96 TOTE £3.80: £1.10, £5.30, £1.10; EX 41.90.
**Owner** Ahmed Buhaleeba **Bred** D J Stable Llc **Trained** Newmarket, Suffolk

**FOCUS**
A moderate maiden and an ordinary time for the grade.

**NOTEBOOK**
**Golden Empire(USA)**, whose application has been very questionable this season, had the visor dispensed with and it seemed to do the trick. He had every chance to down tools when the runner-up ranged alongside two furlongs from home, but he dug deep and there was no problem with his resolution this time.
**Sadler's Pride(IRE)**, reappearing after a seven-month break, came to win his race but was outbattled by a horse that has looked irresolute in the past. He is given the benefit of the doubt in that he may have needed it, and he now qualifies for handicaps.
**Templet(USA)**, down in trip and on faster ground compared with his promising reappearance, tried for an audacious run between his stable companion and the inside rail passing the three-furlong pole, but the gap eventually closed and he was knocked backwards. He stayed on again towards the line, but the margin between himself and the front pair makes it impossible to say he would have won otherwise.
**Act Of The Pace(IRE)**, off since making her belated racecourse debut last summer, was not disgraced and must possess some ability given her trainer has chosen to persevere with her.
**Jordans Spark**, out of a winner in Italy, took a good hold in the first half of the race and probably did too much out in front for his own good. His biggest contribution was to squeeze his stable companion against the inside rail between the three and two-furlong markers as he started to tire, but he did show some ability in his own right and should be all the better for this.

## 1663 RECTANGLE GROUP H'CAP 6f 5y
**4:50** (4:50) (E ) (0-75,72) 3-Y-0+ **£3,867** (£1,190; £595; £297) **Stalls** High

Form RPR

600- **1** **Ulysees (IRE)**[142] [6135] 5-9-6 **64** PHanagan 1 79
(ISemple) *in tch: rdn along 1/2-way: hdwy over 1f out: sn rdn and str run ent last to ld last 100 yds* **33/1**

-102 **2** 2½ **Balakiref**[6] [1531] 5-9-4 **62** FLynch 8 69
(MDods) *in tch: rdn along 1/2-way: hdwy over 1f out: styng on strly whn hmpd wl ins last: kpt on nr fin* **9/4**[2]

000- **3** hd **Pirlie Hill**[173] [5924] 4-8-1 **45** RFfrench 5 51?
(MissLAPerratt) *chsd ldng pair: hdwy 2f out: rdn and ch ent last: sn drvn and one pce* **66/1**

00-0 **4** hd **Tancred Times**[21] [1262] 9-8-13 **57** NCallan 2 63
(DWBarker) *led to 1/2-way: cl up and rdn 2f out: drvn ins last and kpt on same pce* **22/1**

3545 **5** shd **Waltzing Wizard**[66] [833] 5-8-11 **55** TEDurcan 7 61
(ABerry) *outpcd and rdn along 1/2-way: hdwy over 1f out: styd on wl fnl f* **12/1**

63-1 **6** ½ **Mine Behind**[7] [1504] 4-10-0 **72** NPollard 10 76
(JRBest) *cl up: led 1/2-way: rdn over 1f out:d riven ins last: hdd & wknd last 100 yds* **7/4**[1]

00-0 **7** 5 **Friar Tuck**[6] [1526] 9-8-8 **52** KDalgleish 4 41
(MissLAPerratt) *a outpcd and bhd* **25/1**

0-02 **8** 2 **Oases**[27] [1185] 5-9-2 **60** FNorton 6 43
(DShaw) *dwlt and bhd: rdn along over 2f out: sn drvn and no imp* **11/2**[3]

50-2 **9** 3 **Joyce's Choice**[11] [1421] 5-8-3 **54** DTudhope(7) 9 28
(JSWainwright) *dwlt: plld hrd and hung bdly lft after 1f: a rr* **9/1**

05-6 **10** 2½ **Coustou (IRE)**[18] [1317] 4-9-11 **69** PFessey 3 36
(ARDicken) *sn outpcd and bhd* **50/1**

1m 12.21s (-0.89) **Going Correction** -0.025s/f (Good) **10** Ran SP% **114.8**
Speed ratings: **104,100,100,100,100 99,92,90,86,82**CSF £102.47 CT £5116.80 TOTE £33.10: £4.10, £1.40, £13.50; EX 225.50 Place 6 £104.14, Place 5 £89.51.
**Owner** John F Allan **Bred** Sweetmans Bloodstock **Trained** Carluke, S Lanarks

**FOCUS**
A competitive handicap run at a good pace and a most impressive winner.

**NOTEBOOK**
**Ulysees(IRE)** ◆, absent since putting in three modest efforts on sand towards the end of last year, showed his first sign of ability since arriving from Ireland on this drop back in trip. His winning margin was impressive considering he only hit the front half a furlong from home, which shows how strongly he was travelling at the line. He is one to watch closely.
**Balakiref**, came off the bridle some way out, but got stronger as the race progressed. His rider had to stop riding for a few strides when it looked as though he was going to meet trouble in the latter stages, but he got through to snatch second and that was the best position he was ever going to get. He looks worth another try over seven.

**Pirlie Hill**, still a maiden, raced up with the pace the whole way and ran a very creditable reappearance, but it is worth remembering that her form became gradually regressive after early promise last season.
**Tancred Times** helped force the pace for much of the way before done for foot in the closing stages, but this was still an improvement on her reappearance.
**Waltzing Wizard** found this trip too sharp and was under pressure soon after halfway. Tending to hang right when struck with the whip, it was not until his pilot put it down that he decided to run on and he would have been second in a few more strides. A return to further may see him end his losing run.
**Mine Behind**, off the same mark as at Windsor, again tried to utilise a rails draw under a positive ride. Despite doing his best, he could never establish a decisive enough advantage and he was run right out of it after leading past the half-furlong marker. The stiff track seemed to find him out.
**Friar Tuck** *Official explanation: jockey said gelding had a breathing problem*
T/Plt: £136.30 to a £1 stake. Pool: £31,167.75. 166.85 winning tickets. T/Qpdt: £456.60 to a £1 stake. Pool: £1,666.20. 2.70 winning tickets. JR

# 1523 NEWCASTLE (L-H)
Monday, April 26

**OFFICIAL GOING: Soft**
Wind: light, across Weather: persistent rain all races

## 1664 ST JAMES SECURITY MEDIAN AUCTION MAIDEN STKS 5f
**5:50** (5:51) (F) 3-Y-O **£3,234** (£924; £462) **Stalls High**

| Form | | | | RPR |
|---|---|---|---|---|
| 0-22 | **1** | | **Mr Wolf**[14] 1362 3-8-11 70 LEnstone(3) 5<br>(DWBarker) *mde all: styd on strly fnl f* **9/4**[1] | 77 |
| | **2** | 3 1/2 | **Frabrofen** 3-8-9 DeanMcKeown 6<br>(JamesMoffatt) *chsd ldrs: outpcd over 1f out: kpt on fnl f: no ch w wnr* **20/1** | 62 |
| 62- | **3** | 1/2 | **El Palmar**[266] 3833 3-9-0 KDarley 2<br>(TDBarron) *sn pressing wnr: shkn up over 1f out: no ex ins fnl f* **5/2**[2] | 65 |
| 400- | **4** | 8 | **Lady Of The Links (IRE)**[208] 5294 3-8-9 56 KimTinkler 3<br>(NTinkler) *sn pushed along bhd ldrs: struggling fr 1/2-way* **10/1**[3] | 36 |
| 000- | **5** | nk | **Sea Fern**[270] 3728 3-9-0 GDuffield 4<br>(DEddy) *keen: chsd ldrs to 1/2-way: sn wknd* **20/1** | 40 |
| 04-0 | **6** | 4 | **Seguidilla (IRE)**[19] 1293 3-8-9 82 ACulhane 1<br>(GCBravery) *in tch on outside: rdn 1/2-way: sn btn* **9/4**[1] | 23 |

62.84 secs (1.31) **Going Correction** +0.175s/f (Good) **6 Ran SP% 108.7**
Speed ratings: **96,90,89,76,76 69**CSF £39.06 TOTE £3.00: £1.10, £4.90; EX 65.70.
**Owner** P Asquith **Bred** P Asquith **Trained** Scorton, N Yorks

**FOCUS**
With Seguidilla failing to handle the rain-softened conditions and El Palmar looking to need this reappearance run it is unlikely that Mr Wolf had to improve to win this uncompetitive event. The pace was fair and all the runners raced close to the stands rail.

**NOTEBOOK**
**Mr Wolf**, a half-brother to Celtic Mill who has improved for being gelded over the winter, faced a straightforward task with his main market rivals either disappointing or looking to need the race. He showed bags of foot and, as he is unlikely to go up too much for this, he may be capable of better when returned to handicaps.
**Frabrofen** has some speedy sorts in her pedigree and, although easy to back, showed ability on this racecourse debut. She is open to improvement and may be capable of picking up a small race.
**El Palmar** confirmed he retains ability on this reappearance run and was not knocked about when tiring in the closing stages. He is in good hands and will be one to keep an eye on in ordinary handicaps.
**Lady Of The Links(IRE)**, having her first run since last October, is a modest performer and once again had her limitations exposed. She will have to drop in grade if she is to hold a realistic chance of winning a race.
**Sea Fern** again showed little on this reappearance run and it will be a very modest race he eventually wins.
**Seguidilla(IRE)** came into this race as the clear highest rated but turned in another most disappointing effort and, although these rain-softened conditions may not have suited, she looks one to tread very carefully with. *Official explanation: trainer had no explanation for the poor form shown*

## 1665 CANTORSPORT.CO.UK H'CAP 6f
**6:20** (6:22) (E) (0-75,75) 3-Y-O+ **£4,260** (£1,311; £655; £327) **Stalls High**

| Form | | | | RPR |
|---|---|---|---|---|
| 0051 | **1** | | **Raymond's Pride**[6] 1525 4-9-9 75 6ex (b) TEaves(5) 11<br>(KARyan) *in tch far side: smooth hdwy to ld appr fnl f: rdn and r.o strly* **9/1**[3] | 87 |
| 2452 | **2** | 1/2 | **Carlton (IRE)**[6] 1526 10-8-3 55 RThomas(5) 6<br>(CRDore) *midfield far side: pushed along 1/2-way: hdwy over 1f out: r.o fnl f* **8/1**[2] | 66 |
| 0-00 | **3** | 1 1/2 | **Fair Shake (IRE)**[23] 1246 4-9-4 65 (p) GDuffield 15<br>(DEddy) *led stands side gp: rdn and r.o wl fnl f: nt rch far side* **16/1** | 71 |
| -024 | **4** | hd | **If By Chance**[14] 1361 6-9-4 68 (b) DAllan(3) 9<br>(RCraggs) *cl up far side: effrt and ev ch over 1f out: no ex ins fnl f* **8/1**[2] | 73 |
| 2203 | **5** | shd | **Pawan (IRE)**[6] 1525 4-9-0 61 AnnStokell 8<br>(MissAStokell) *hld up outside of far side gp: rdn 1/2-way: gd hdwy over 1f out: kpt on fnl f* **10/1** | 66 |
| 0002 | **6** | 1 1/4 | **Hov**[14] 1358 4-9-6 72 (p) PMulrennan(5) 3<br>(JJQuinn) *towards rr far side: outpcd 1/2-way: gd heawday over 1f out: fin wl* **6/1**[1] | 73 |
| 50-3 | **7** | shd | **Catch The Cat (IRE)**[11] 1421 5-9-1 69 (b) AReilly(7) 4<br>(JSWainwright) *led far side to appr fnl f: no ex ins last* **14/1** | 70 |
| 040- | **8** | 1 1/4 | **Trinity (IRE)**[195] 5561 8-8-6 53 TWilliams 12<br>(MBrittain) *cl up far side tl rdn and no ex over 1f out* **20/1** | 50 |
| 26-6 | **9** | shd | **Old Bailey (USA)**[6] 1526 4-8-2 49 (b) DaleGibson 10<br>(TDBarron) *trckd far side ldrs: effrt over 2f out: outpcd whn n.m.r ins fnl f* **12/1** | 46 |
| 3404 | **10** | 1 | **Majik**[7] 1504 5-8-7 57 (v[1]) LEnstone(3) 17<br>(DJSFfrenchDavis) *cl up stands side: effrt that gp 2f out: no imp* **14/1** | 51 |
| 0-00 | **11** | 2 1/2 | **The Gambler**[6] 1527 4-7-12 52 (p) NataliaGemelova(7) 20<br>(PaulJohnson) *in tch stands side: outpcd 1/2-way: edgd lft over 1f out: nvr rchd ldrs* **50/1** | 39 |
| 0461 | **12** | 1 | **Far Note (USA)**[41] 1033 6-9-5 66 (b) JBramhill 16<br>(SRBowring) *pressed stands side ldr tl outpcd over 1f out* **20/1** | 50 |
| 50-0 | **13** | 1 | **Bundy**[10] 1452 8-9-4 65 KDarley 18<br>(MDods) *hld up in tch stands side: drvn 1/2-way: no imp* **12/1** | 46 |
| 3500 | **14** | 1/2 | **Cash**[6] 1525 6-8-1 55 (p) DFentiman(7) 2<br>(PaulJohnson) *bhd far side: drvn 1/2-way: sn btn* **20/1** | 34 |
| 100- | **15** | 3/4 | **Paddywack (IRE)**[122] 6235 7-9-5 73 (b) PMakin(7) 7<br>(DWChapman) *hld up midfield stands side: rdn and wknd fr 1/2-way* **22/1** | 50 |
| 0-00 | **16** | 1/2 | **Tre Colline**[14] 1358 5-9-8 69 KimTinkler 14<br>(NTinkler) *racd stands side: nvr on terms* **50/1** | 44 |
| 0303 | **17** | 1 | **New Options**[7] 1496 7-8-6 56 (p) LisaJones(3) 5<br>(WJMusson) *a bhd far side* **20/1** | 28 |
| -000 | **18** | 1/2 | **Drury Lane (IRE)**[41] 1032 4-9-4 65 (b) ACulhane 1<br>(DWChapman) *in tch far side to 1/2-way: sn btn* **25/1** | 36 |
| 2000 | **19** | 2 | **African Spur (IRE)**[6] 1526 4-9-4 65 (t) RFitzpatrick 13<br>(DCarroll) *missed break: a struggling far side* **50/1** | 30 |
| -030 | **20** | 25 | **High Cane (USA)**[10] 1451 4-8-13 60 DarrenWilliams 19<br>(MDHammond) *racd stands side: sn wl bhd* **20/1** | — |

1m 16.93s (1.89) **Going Correction** +0.275s/f (Good) **20 Ran SP% 128.1**
Speed ratings: **98,97,95,95,94 93,93,91,91,90 86,85,84,83,82 81,80,79,77,43**CSF £69.74 CT £1183.02 TOTE £11.60: £2.80, £2.30, £3.90, £2.70; EX 96.80.
**Owner** R E Robinson **Bred** Mrs Wendy Robinson **Trained** Hambleton, N Yorks

**FOCUS**
A run of the mill handicap in which the lowest 13 in the draw raced on the far side and the remainder came stands' side. The far-side group always had the edge.

**NOTEBOOK**
**Raymond's Pride**, with a penalty to carry and up in trip, appreciated the persistent rain that fell and turned in an improved effort. Given the way he travelled through this race he will be of interest, even after reassessment, on this sort of ground.
**Carlton(IRE)** has not won a handicap for a good number of years but came into the race in good form, was well drawn, had conditions to suit and gave it his best shot again. He should continue to go well when conditions are testing.
**Fair Shake(IRE)** ◆, from a stable that is coming back to form, had conditions to suit and ran an eyecatching race to finish clear of the group that raced on the stands side. He is one to keep a close eye on in similar company granted suitable conditions.
**If By Chance** is a reliable yardstick who goes well at Newcastle and gave it his best shot after having the run of the race. He does look vulnerable from his current mark to well handicapped or unexposed rivals, though.
**Pawan(IRE)**, who has been in good heart on soft ground this spring, shaped as though he is a bit better than the bare form and made up a considerable amount of ground from, an uncompromising position in the closing stages. He is capable of winning a similar event.
**Hov** had conditions to suit and a favourable draw but was taken off his feet in the first half of the contest dropped to this trip. The return to seven furlongs plus will be in his favour, and he is capable of winning again.
**Catch The Cat(IRE)** ran well from his favourable draw but left the strong impression that the return to five furlongs would be in his favour.
**Trinity(IRE)** shaped as though retaining ability on this first start since last October.
**New Options** *Official explanation: jockey said gelding was unsuited by the soft ground*

## 1666 CANTORSPORT.CO.UK CLAIMING STKS 5f
**6:50** (6:51) (F) 2-Y-O **£3,010** (£860; £430) **Stalls High**

| Form | | | | RPR |
|---|---|---|---|---|
| 5 | **1** | | **Kissing A Fool**[27] 1183 2-8-2 PMakin(7) 4<br>(WGMTurner) *mde all: rdn and hld on wl fnl f* **10/1** | 45 |
| 0 | **2** | 1 1/4 | **Danehill Fairy (IRE)**[7] 1498 2-8-4 (b[1]) GDuffield 5<br>(MrsADuffield) *cl up: effrt over 1f out: kpt on fnl f: hld towards fin* **20/1** | 36 |
| 0 | **3** | 1 1/4 | **Joshar**[9] 1468 2-8-4 DaleGibson 3<br>(MWEasterby) *sn rdn bhd ldng gp: no imp tl hdwy over 1f out: kpt on* **25/1** | 31 |
| 4 | **4** | 2 1/2 | **Alice King (IRE)**[9] 1468 2-7-7 CHaddon(7) 1<br>(WGMTurner) *racd wd in tch: hdwy 1/2-way: wknd ins fnl f* **5/1**[3] | 19 |
| | **5** | nk | **Belle Largesse** 2-8-6 KDarley 2<br>(CBBBooth) *prom: sn pushed along: effrt 1/2-way: btn ins fnl f* **9/1** | 23 |
| 52 | **6** | 3/4 | **Emma's Venture**[9] 1468 2-8-3 PMulrennan(5) 7<br>(MWEasterby) *trckd ldrs: rdn 1/2-way: wknd ins fnl f* **11/10**[1] | 23 |
| 5 | **U** | | **Balashova**[2] 1616 2-8-8 DarrenWilliams 6<br>(KRBurke) *s.i.s and already struggling whn lost action and uns rdr sn after s* **4/1**[2] | — |

67.51 secs (5.98) **Going Correction** +0.625s/f (Yiel) **7 Ran SP% 112.0**
Speed ratings: **77,75,73,69,68 67,—**CSF £163.17 TOTE £16.00: £4.60, £4.00; EX 46.40.
**Owner** Mascalls Stud **Bred** Mascalls Stud **Trained** Sigwells, Somerset

**FOCUS**
A weak race, even by selling standards, and the winning time was very slow even allowing for the conditions. The field raced stands' side and the gallop was fair, but it is unlikely this race will be throwing up many winners.

**NOTEBOOK**
**Kissing A Fool** bettered his debut effort and showed the right attitude in the closing stages but this was a very poor race and he would not be an obvious one to follow up in anything but the worst company.
**Danehill Fairy(IRE)**, with the blinkers fitted on only this second start, shaped better in this lower grade for a stable that has been going fairly well of late but it will be a similarly poor race she wins.
**Joshar** ran better than on her debut and will doubtlessly be placed to best advantage, but it is worth remembering that the form of this race amounts to very little.
**Alice King(IRE)** may be a little bit better than the bare form, as she raced the furthest away from the rail, but she did not really show enough to suggest she would be of any interest next time.
**Belle Largesse**, the first foal of a five-furlong juvenile winner, was not totally disgraced in a poor race on her debut and may be capable of better, but will have to show more before she is a betting proposition.
**Emma's Venture** looked the one to beat on Thirsk form, but she ran poorly in similar conditions and her below-par showing devalues further the worth of this form. It will be a very modest race she wins.
**Balashova**, surprisingly well backed after showing nothing on her debut only two days previously, was already starting to get left behind when losing both her action and her rider after about 100 yards.

## 1667 CANTOR SPORT SPREAD BETTING H'CAP 1m 3y(S)
**7:20** (7:22) (F) (0-55,55) 3-Y-O **£2,919** (£834; £417) **Stalls High**

| Form | | | | RPR |
|---|---|---|---|---|
| 0-03 | **1** | | **Ace Coming**[14] 1363 3-9-5 55 (b) GDuffield 1<br>(DEddy) *hld up: smooth hdwy 3f out: led over 1f out: drvn out* **11/2**[3] | 68 |
| -462 | **2** | 3 | **Biscar Two (IRE)**[14] 1363 3-8-12 48 VHalliday 10<br>(RMWhitaker) *bhd and sn outpcd: plenty to do fr 1/2-way: gd hdwy over 1f out: nt rch wnr* **9/2**[2] | 55 |
| -005 | **3** | 2 | **Sir Galahad**[14] 1360 3-9-0 53 DAllan(3) 9<br>(TDEasterby) *hld up in tch: drvn 1/2-way: rallied to ld over 2f out to over 1f out: no ex fnl f* **6/1** | 56 |
| 50-2 | **4** | 2 | **Ask The Driver**[9] 1467 3-9-4 54 KDarley 7<br>(DJSFfrenchDavis) *hld up: shkn up and hdwy over 2f out: ev ch over 1f out: outpcd ins fnl f* **4/1**[1] | 53 |
| 03-0 | **5** | 7 | **Tancred Imp**[14] 1363 3-8-7 46 oh1 LEnstone(3) 11<br>(DWBarker) *trckd ldrs tl wknd fr 2f out* **20/1** | 31 |
| 5-00 | **6** | 8 | **Satsu (IRE)**[14] 1360 3-9-5 55 ACulhane 8<br>(JGGiven) *prom: led briefly over 2f out: sn wknd* **7/1** | 24 |
| 0-00 | **7** | 6 | **Killoch Place (IRE)**[14] 1365 3-8-11 47 (v[1]) DeanMcKeown 3<br>(JAGlover) *cl up: ev ch tl wknd over 2f out* **16/1** | 4 |
| 000- | **8** | 5 | **Ego Trip**[189] 5671 3-8-13 54 PMulrennan(5) 12<br>(MWEasterby) *sn rdn in rr: no ch fr 1/2-way* **10/1** | 1 |

00-0 **9** *7* **Beamsley Beacon**[14] [1360] 3-8-12 **53**................................(b[1]) TEaves(5) 6 —
(GMMoore) *keen: led to over 2f out: wknd* **16/1**
5500 **10** *1 1/2* **Numpty (IRE)**[9] [1465] 3-8-10 **46** oh6..................................(t) KimTinkler 2 —
(NTinkler) *cl up tl wknd over 3f out* **25/1**
000- **11** *25* **Johnny Alljays (IRE)**[231] [4764] 3-8-7 **50**........................ DerekNolan(7) 4 —
(JSMoore) *prom to 1/2-way: sn wknd* **20/1**

1m 48.73s (7.53) **Going Correction** +0.625s/f (Yiel) **11** Ran SP% **114.6**
Speed ratings: **87,84,82,80,73 65,59,54,47,45 20**CSF £28.65 CT £156.08 TOTE £7.20: £1.90, £2.20, £2.60; EX 22.80.
**Owner** I R Clements **Bred** S J And Mrs Pembroke **Trained** Ingoe, Northumberland

**FOCUS**
A modest handicap in which the field raced in the centre of the course before all tacking over to the far side at halfway. The pace seemed fair in the ever-softening conditions, though the final time was slow.

**NOTEBOOK**
**Ace Coming** confirmed reappearance promise on ground he seems to like and, given that he travels strongly in his races, may be capable of a bit better when going up in grade.
**Biscar Two(IRE)** was not beaten far but did not look an easy ride. On this evidence the step up to a mile and a quarter should be in his favour, but he may not be one to place maximum faith in.
**Sir Galahad** was not disgraced in terms of form but turned in a laboured performance. He again did not see out his race, and it is not easy to assess accurately what his ideal trip is at present.
**Ask The Driver**'s run of steadily progressive efforts came to a halt but, although he did make up a fair amount of ground in a fairly short space of time in these conditions, it may be the case that he prefers a sounder surface.
**Tancred Imp** was again well beaten on soft ground and she may be happier back on a sound surface.
**Satsu(IRE)**, back in trip, travelled well for a long way but again failed to get home in the conditions, but would not be one to write off back on a sound surface.

## 1668 CANTOR SPORT GOOD LUCK PAUL HUNTER H'CAP 1m 6f 97y
**7:50** (7:55) (F) (0-55,55) 4-Y-0+ **£2,975** (£850; £425) **Stalls** High

Form RPR
2323 **1** **Next Flight (IRE)**[15] [1344] 5-8-12 **48**................................ RFitzpatrick 12 57
(REBarr) *keen: cl up: led 5f out: hld on gamely* **7/1**
030- **2** *1/2* **Cusp**[16] [5298] 4-8-8 **46** oh1.......................................... DeanMcKeown 11 54
(CWThornton) *prom: effrt 3f out: chsd wnr over 1f out: r.o* **16/1**
00 **3** *8* **Berrywhite (IRE)**[6] [1527] 6-8-10 **46** oh4.............................. GDuffield 9 44
(CGrant) *hld up: hdwy and prom over 3f out: rdn and outpcd over 1f out* **14/1**
0-00 **4** *1 1/4* **Washington Pink (IRE)**[12] [1393] 5-8-7 **46**...................... THamilton(3) 5 42
(CGrant) *hld up: hdwy and in tch over 2f out: outpcd over 1f out* **20/1**
200- **5** *1 3/4* **Exalted (IRE)**[231] [4775] 11-9-5 **55**..................................... DaleGibson 10 49
(TAKCuthbert) *prom tl outpcd fr wl over 1f out* **13/2**
1124 **6** *6* **Broughton Knows**[24] [1238] 7-9-1 **54**..............................(b) LisaJones(3) 6 40
(WJMusson) *hld up: effrt over 3f out: edgd lft over 2f out: nvr rchd ldrs* **6/1**[3]
/00- **7** *12* **Bulgaria Moon**[247] [3302] 4-8-8 **46** oh6.................................. JBramhill 8 16
(CGrant) *midfield: lost pl 1/2-way: n.d after* **40/1**
60-0 **8** *3* **I Got Rhythm**[6] [1534] 6-8-10 **46**.......................................... KDarley 2 12
(MrsMReveley) *hld up: effrt over 4f out: sn n.d* **11/2**[2]
-203 **9** *1 3/4* **Colonnade**[43] [1023] 5-9-0 **50**......................................... DarrenWilliams 1 14
(CGrant) *prom tl wknd over 3f out* **12/1**
2120 **10** *15* **Aveiro (IRE)**[7] [1501] 8-9-2 **52**.............................................. ACulhane 3 —
(MissGayKelleway) *mde most to 5f out: sn wknd* **5/1**[1]
2500 **11** *22* **Lampos (USA)**[6] [1534] 4-8-13 **54**.......................................(v) DAllan(3) 4 —
(MissJACamacho) *hld up: rdn 1/2-way: sn btn* **5/1**[1]
05/0 **12** *dist* **Manny**[7] [1514] 4-8-2 **47** oh11 ow1.................................(p) PPMathers(7) 7 —
(MissAStokell) *keen: prom to 6f out: sn lost tch* **40/1**

3m 27.47s (17.57) **Going Correction** +1.25s/f (Soft)
**WFA** 4 from 5yo+ 2lb **12** Ran SP% **118.7**
Speed ratings: **99,98,94,93,92 89,82,80,79,70 58,—**CSF £111.07 CT £1522.23 TOTE £8.20: £2.80, £6.30, £4.50; EX 231.10.
**Owner** Malcolm O'Hair **Bred** Michael Dalton **Trained** Seamer, N Yorks

**FOCUS**
A race that took little winning with the market leaders all under-performing but, although the gallop was only fair in the first half of the race, the field finished well strung out in the testing conditions.

**NOTEBOOK**
**Next Flight(IRE)**, a consistent sort, showed the right attitude to get off the mark at the 21st attempt. Although his main market rivals under-performed, he should continue to give a good account in ordinary handicaps around this trip.
**Cusp** turned in an improved effort back on the Flat and it looks as though the step up to this trip coupled with the soft conditions were the reason. She should stay two miles and can pick up a small race on this evidence.
**Berrywhite(IRE)**, a dual German Flat winner in 2002, ran his best race for his current stable but it will be a poor race he wins.
**Washington Pink(IRE)** ran his best race for some time but, given his record, would not be certain to reproduce this next time.
**Exalted(IRE)**, who had conditions to suit for this reappearance run, shaped as though in need of the race but also showed enough to suggest he retains all his ability, and he is capable of winning again on the Flat this term.
**Broughton Knows**, a moneyspinner on the sand this winter, had seen his turf rating go up in line with his All-Weather improvement but he never looked happy in the conditions and was soundly beaten. He may be happier on a sound surface.

## 1669 RAMSIDE EVENT CATERING CLASSIFIED STKS 1m 2f 32y
**8:20** (8:21) (E) 3-Y-0+ **£2,426** (£2,426; £571; £285) **Stalls** High

Form RPR
0-04 **1** *dht* **Jimmy Byrne (IRE)**[7] [1503] 4-9-4 68.................................... RWinston 1 78
(BEllison) *prom: rdn to chal over 2f out: kpt on: all out* **7/1**[3]
1023 **1** **Rasid (USA)**[9] [1470] 6-9-9 75.............................................. KDarley 5 83
(CADwyer) *prom: hdwy to ld over 3f out: jnd over 2f out: kpt on: all out* **13/2**[2]
0/6- **3** *15* **Konker**[80] [5910] 9-8-13 67.............................................. TEaves(5) 4 53
(MrsMReveley) *hld up: effrt over 2f out: chsd ldrs over 1f out: no imp* **10/1**
26-0 **4** *4* **Newcorp Lad**[10] [1451] 4-9-5 71............................................ ACulhane 6 47
(MrsGSRees) *hld up in tch: effrt over 3f out: hung lft over 2f out: sn outpcd* **16/1**
/611 **5** *2* **Benbyas**[9] [1326] 7-9-2 75...........................................(v) DTudhope(7) 2 47
(DCarroll) *led to over 3f out: sn btn* **4/7**[1]
1256 **6** *12* **Come What July (IRE)**[26] [1201] 3-8-1 70..........................(b) DaleGibson 3 22
(RGuest) *keen: cl up tl rdn and wknd fr over 3f out* **8/1**

2m 22.71s (11.11) **Going Correction** +1.25s/f (Soft)
**WFA** 3 from 4yo+ 17lb **6** Ran SP% **115.6**
Speed ratings: **105,105,93,89,88 78** Place 6 £13,257.90, Place 5 £5,168.28.
**Owner** Keith Middleton **Bred** Austin Well Stud **Trained** Norton, N Yorks

**FOCUS**
With Benbyas running a long way below his recent best, this did not take as much winning as seemed likely. The gallop was sound in the conditions.

**NOTEBOOK**
**Rasid(USA)**, who seems more consistent these days, appreciated the testing conditions and really stuck his head out in the closing stages. However he will have to improve to follow up on less testing ground back in handicap company.
**Jimmy Byrne(IRE)** turned in his best effort for his current stable and clearly goes well around this trip on soft ground, but he may have to improve to follow up back in handicap company after reassessment.
**Konker**, a proven mudlark, has only been lightly raced in the last couple of years, but did not show enough back on the Flat to suggest he would be of interest from his current mark back in handicaps in the near future.
**Newcorp Lad** was again well beaten but he may be better suited by a mile on a sounder surface. He won twice at Hamilton on a sound surface last year and may well be capable of better when he has conditions to suit.
**Benbyas** looked the one to beat on these terms, and in light of his recent efforts in testing ground on the Flat and over hurdles. However, he was a long way below his best and may have had enough for the time being. *Official explanation: trainer had no explanation for the poor form shown*
**Come What July(IRE)** pulled too hard and not surprisingly did not get home in the conditions. He is better than this but does not look particularly well treated in turf handicaps from a mark of 70.
T/Plt: £5,522.70 to a £1 stake. Pool: £34,800.60. 4.60 winning tickets. T/Qpdt: £352.30 to a £1 stake. Pool: £3,000.00. 6.30 winning tickets. RY

# 1504 WINDSOR (R-H)
Monday, April 26

**OFFICIAL GOING: Good (good to firm in places)**
Wind: almost nil Weather: sunny becoming cloudy

## 1670 WELCOME TO MONDAY EVENINGS AT WINDSOR MAIDEN AUCTION FILLIES' STKS 5f 10y
**5:35** (5:35) (F) 2-Y-0 **£3,513** (£1,081; £540; £270) **Stalls** High

Form RPR
**1** **High Chart** 2-8-4 ................................................................ AMcCarthy 9 71+
(GGMargarson) *trckd ldrs: effrt over 1f out: shkn up to ld nr fin: pushed out and jst hld on* **4/1**[1]
**2** *shd* **Agent Kensington** 2-8-2 ........................................................ RLMoore 7 68
(RHannon) *dwlt: wl in rr: last and rdn 2f out: prog and swtchd lft over 1f out: str run ins fnl f: jst failed* **7/1**[3]
22 **3** *shd* **Lateral Thinker (IRE)**[3] [1589] 2-7-13 ................................ JFMcDonald(3) 4 68
(JAOsborne) *w ldrs: shkn up over 1f out: styd on to ld wl ins fnl f: hdd nr fin* **9/2**[2]
**4** *nk* **Elisha (IRE)** 2-8-4 ................................................................ MartinDwyer 8 69
(DMSimcock) *w ldrs: led over 1f out: edgd lft after: hdd wl ins fnl f: one pce* **33/1**
**5** *1* **Baileys Applause** 2-8-6 ...................................................(p) JFanning 12 67
(CADwyer) *s.i.s: sn pressed ldrs: rdn and edgd lft fr over 1f out: kpt on same pce* **25/1**
6 **6** *3/4* **Miss Truant**[14] [1374] 2-8-6 ...................................................... JMackay 14 64
(MLWBell) *dwlt: rcvrd into midfield after 2f: no prog 2f out: styd on ins fnl f* **9/2**[2]
**7** *nk* **Celtic Spa (IRE)** 2-8-1 ............................................................ RMiles(3) 2 61
(MrsPNDutfield) *racd on outer: chsd ldrs: ch over 1f out: fdd ins fnl f* **20/1**
**8** *1 1/4* **Clinet (IRE)** 2-8-4 ...................................................................... SCarson 10 56
(PMPhelan) *dwlt: racd in last trio: swtchd sharply lft jst over 1f out: styd on: nvr nrr* **33/1**
**9** *1 1/4* **Aspen Ridge (IRE)** 2-8-6 .......................................................... SDrowne 13 53
(CTinkler) *pressed ldrs: lost pl sltly on inner and nt clr run wl over 1f out: no prog after* **12/1**
6 **10** *shd* **Waterline Lover**[12] [1399] 2-8-8 .............................................. MFenton 6 54
(PDEvans) *chsd ldrs: rn green and wknd over 1f out* **25/1**
**11** *2* **Ashes (IRE)** 2-8-4 ...................................................................... CCatlin 15 42
(KRBurke) *chsd ldrs: pushed along and outpcd over 1f out: n.d after* **9/1**
**12** *3/4* **Chutney Mary (IRE)** 2-8-8 ...................................................... DaneO'Neill 1 43
(JGPortman) *dwlt: a wl in rr* **50/1**
233 **13** *1/2* **Nutty Times**[18] [1307] 2-8-2 ........................................................ ADaly 11 35
(WGMTurner) *mde most to over 1f out: wknd* **10/1**
**14** *nk* **Heart Of Eternity (IRE)** 2-8-11 ................................................ JPMurtagh 5 43
(JRBoyle) *dwlt: a wl in rr* **14/1**
**15** *7* **Be Bop Aloha** 2-8-2 ................................................................ WSupple 3 6
(IAWood) *dwlt: rcvrd into midfield after 2f: wknd over 1f out* **16/1**

61.74 secs (0.54) **Going Correction** -0.025s/f (Good) **15** Ran SP% **128.5**
Speed ratings: **94,93,93,93,91 90,89,87,85,85 82,81,80,80,68**CSF £31.38 TOTE £5.80: £2.10, £3.40, £1.90; EX 85.60.
**Owner** Dennis Russell **Bred** Whitsbury Manor Stud **Trained** Newmarket, Suffolk
■ Stewards Enquiry : A Daly caution: careless riding

**FOCUS**
An average-looking contest of its type, although confidence in form governed by the fact first seven in a heap.

**NOTEBOOK**
**High Chart**, for whom there had been plenty of money throughout the day, came through to lead close home and make a successful debut. Well regarded by her trainer, he considers her a potential Listed-class filly, but she will have to progress a lot to prove that prediction correct. A step up to six furlongs is likely next time out.
**Agent Kensington**, bred to do best this year, kept on well in the latter stages having run green. She looks sure to come on a good deal for the run and a modest race should be within her ability.
**Lateral Thinker(IRE)** set a fair standard for the others to aim at, having finished runner-up in a couple of maidens already. She ran a solid race but will always be vulnerable to something with a bit more potential.
**Elisha(IRE)**, a half-sister to four winners, showed plenty of pace for one bred to appreciate farther in time.
**Baileys Applause**, for whom the application of cheekpieces on her debut was slightly worrying, is bred to be a speedy two-year-old.
**Miss Truant** was expected to come on for her debut outing, where she had been too green to do herself justice, but she was once again slowly away and the advantage of her high draw was lost.

## 1671 GIBBS AND DANDY CLASSIFIED STKS 1m 2f 7y
**6:05** (6:07) (D) 3-Y-0+ **£5,638** (£1,735; £867; £433) **Stalls** Low

Form RPR
20-5 **1** **Tawny Way**[16] [1321] 4-9-5 82.................................................. SDrowne 10 89
(WJarvis) *s.i.s: racd in midfield: rdn and prog wl over 1f out: led narrowly ins fnl f: drvn out* **7/1**[3]
123- **2** *shd* **Desert Royalty (IRE)**[197] [5505] 4-9-5 82.................................. LDettori 7 89
(EALDunlop) *trckd ldrs: rdn 2f out: effrt to chal fnl f: ev ch: jst pipped* **9/2**[2]

/060 **3** *shd* **Lion Hunter (USA)**[14] 1355 5-9-10 84 WSupple 8 94
(MissECLavelle) *trckd ldr: nt clr run over 2f out to over 1f out: sn led on inner: hdd ins fnl f: jst hld* **10/1**

30-0 **4** *2 1/2* **Desert Island Disc**[18] 1308 7-9-0 73 JFMcDonald(3) 1 82
(JJBridger) *settled towards rr: prog over 3f out: rdn to chal wl over 1f out: one pce fnl f* **50/1**

/41- **5** *shd* **Wiggy Smith**[283] 3373 5-9-6 80 DaneO'Neill 13 85
(HCandy) *sn chsd ldrs: lost pl 3f out: effrt again over 1f out: kpt on same pce: unable to chal* **7/2**[1]

350- **6** *3 1/2* **Barking Mad (USA)**[192] 5618 6-9-9 83 MFenton 12 81
(MLWBell) *led: kicked on over 3f out: hdd & wknd jst over 1f out* **10/1**

31-4 **7** *1 1/4* **Fernery**[16] 1321 4-9-5 82 TQuinn 2 75
(LMCumani) *trckd ldrs: effrt and cl up over 2f out: fdd over 1f out* **8/1**

20-3 **8** *shd* **Nofa's Magic (IRE)**[23] 1249 4-9-3 80 JPMurtagh 3 73
(JLDunlop) *hld up towards rr: effrt on outer over 2f out: no prog and btn over 1f out* **8/1**

1201 **9** *shd* **Caroubier (IRE)**[21] 1275 4-9-3 76 RMiles(3) 6 75
(JGallagher) *hld up in last trio: sme prog on wd outside over 2f out: no hdwy over 1f out* **16/1**

015/ **10** *5* **Ken's Dream**[389] 5023 5-9-6 80 PMcCabe 9 66
(MsAEEmbiricos) *t.k.h: hld up in midfield: rdn and effrt to press ldrs 2f out: wknd over 1f out* **50/1**

400/ **11** *shd* **Pardishar (IRE)**[19] 1172 6-9-11 85 RLMoore 11 71
(GLMoore) *racd in last: detached fr rest 1/2-way: drvn 3f out: nvr on terms* **12/1**

216- **12** *2* **Colophony (USA)**[260] 4019 4-9-6 79 (t) MartinDwyer 5 62
(KAMorgan) *hld up in last trio: effrt on outer 3f out: wknd over 2f out* **33/1**

4520 **13** *9* **The Bonus King**[16] 1321 4-9-10 84 JFanning 4 49
(MJohnston) *racd in ldng trio to 2f out: sn wknd and eased* **12/1**

2m 7.63s (-0.67) **Going Correction** +0.10s/f (Good) **13** Ran SP% **121.4**
Speed ratings: **106,105,105,103,103 100,99,99,99,95 95,94,86** CSF £38.79 TOTE £9.30: £2.90, £2.30, £4.60; EX 38.50.
**Owner** Rams Racing Club **Bred** K P Seow **Trained** Newmarket, Suffolk

**FOCUS**
A decent classified event producing a close finish, and run at in a time well up to stadard for the grade.

**NOTEBOOK**
**Tawny Way**, all the better for her reappearance outing at Haydock earlier this month, had more suitable ground this time and just edged the victory in a tight photo. Her trainer is hopeful that she will win a decent handicap this season.
**Desert Royalty(IRE)**, who seems to go on any ground, made a very pleasing reappearance. She stays farther than this and looks set for another good season.
**Lion Hunter(USA)** was out of his depth on his reapparance and found this grade far more suitable. He did well to get so close after suffering an interrupted passage over two furlongs out, and the more patient tactics appeared to work well.
**Desert Island Disc**, who has done her winning over a longer trip than this, had a bit to find with most of these at the weights and ran well in the circumstances. She will be suited by a step up to a mile and a half.
**Wiggy Smith**, not seen since July of last year, has clearly had a problem in the interim. This was a promising return though, and provided he can build on this he should soon be winning again.
**Barking Mad(USA)** ran a decent race for his reappearance outing, and should come on for the run.

## 1672 SHORTERM ENGINEERS H'CAP — 1m 3f 135y
**6:35** (6:35) (D) (0-85,81) 3-Y-O — **£5,508** (£1,695; £847; £423) **Stalls** Low

Form RPR

62-0 **1** **Rarefied (IRE)**[25] 1224 3-9-1 **75** SDrowne 4 83
(RCharlton) *cl up: pressed ldr 4f out: rdn to ld over 2f out: hung fire over 1f out: drvn out* **12/1**

6-42 **2** *1 1/2* **Late Opposition**[7] 1509 3-8-3 **63** WSupple 3 69
(EALDunlop) *hld up in tch: prog over 3f out: chsd wnr 2f out: hrd rdn and no imp fnl f* **5/2**[2]

1 **3** *1 1/2* **Jomacomi**[63] 863 3-9-6 **80** JFanning 6 84
(MJohnston) *trckd ldr: led after 4f: hanging lft over 3f out: hdd and outpcd over 2f out: kpt on fr over 1f out* **10/1**

01- **4** *1 1/4* **Zeitgeist (IRE)**[175] 5911 3-9-0 **77** NMackay(3) 8 79
(LMCumani) *towards rr: pushed along 4f out: kpt on same pce fr over 2f out: nvr able to chal* **12/1**

031- **5** *hd* **Dumfries**[203] 5414 3-9-7 **81** LDettori 10 82
(JHMGosden) *hld up in tch: trckd ldrs 4f out: rdn and nt qckn 2f out: btn whn stmbld 1f out* **2/1**[1]

5-55 **6** *1/2* **Magic Sting**[9] 1476 3-8-5 **65** JMackay 7 65
(MLWBell) *t.k.h: hld up in last: prog over 3f out: unable qck over 2f out: one pce after* **33/1**

5-31 **7** *3* **Chara**[12] 1394 3-8-6 **66** MartinDwyer 2 62
(JRJenkins) *led for 4f: chsd ldr to 4f out: lost pl and struggling wl over 2f out* **16/1**

0402 **8** *3/4* **Champagne Shadow (IRE)**[33] 1100 3-8-6 **66** (b) RLMoore 5 60
(GLMoore) *a in rr: last over 3f out: no imp ldrs after* **16/1**

31-0 **9** *3/4* **Miss Langkawi**[14] 1357 3-9-0 **74** DHolland 1 67
(GWragg) *trckd ldrs tl fdd fr over 2f out* **13/2**[3]

05-0 **10** *3* **Bosco (IRE)**[7] 1509 3-8-7 **67** PDobbs 9 55
(RHannon) *racd in midfield: pushed along and struggling 4f out: sn in rr* **33/1**

2m 31.79s (1.69) **Going Correction** +0.10s/f (Good) **10** Ran SP% **117.4**
Speed ratings: **98,97,96,95,95 94,92,92,91,89** CSF £42.47 CT £318.54 TOTE £10.90: £4.00, £1.40, £2.50; EX 55.60.
**Owner** K Abdulla **Bred** Juddmonte Farms **Trained** Beckhampton, Wilts

**FOCUS**
An interesting handicap but the time was nothing special.

**NOTEBOOK**
**Rarefied(IRE)**, whose dam was a Group Three winner over ten furlongs in France, stepped up on his maiden form on this handicap debut. His rider grabbed the rail and stole a march on his rivals, and the better ground appeared to suit him more than his main opponents.
**Late Opposition** looked to hold a strong chance on his last-time-out effort, but the ground was much quicker this time and his stamina was not as much use on this occasion. It looks like he needs soft ground to be seen at his best.
**Jomacomi**, making his turf debut, looks to have been lumbered with quite a high rating for what he achieved on the All-Weather. *Official explanation: jockey said colt was hanging left*
**Zeitgeist(IRE)**, a seven-furlong winner on his last start as a juvenile, appeared to find this trip on the short side. He may improve for a sterner test of stamina.
**Dumfries** won on officially firm ground last year, but the time of the race suggested the ground was not as fast as that. He certainly looked uncomfortable on this ground, and softer conditions may suit him better.

## 1673 REED & MACKAY CLASSIFIED STKS — 6f
**7:05** (7:07) (D) 3-Y-O+ — **£5,427** (£1,670; £835; £417) **Stalls** High

Form RPR

0434 **1** **Lincoln Dancer (IRE)**[7] 1500 7-9-3 78 PDobbs 7 87
(DNicholls) *chsd ldrs: lost pl 1/2-way: rdn over 2f out: prog over 1f out: led ent fnl f: drvn out* **9/1**

6-02 **2** *nk* **Morse (IRE)**[16] 1333 3-8-8 82 LDettori 10 88
(JAOsborne) *chsd ldr for 2f: lost pl and rdn 1/2-way: prog wl over 1f out: drvn to chal ent fnl f: styd on: jst hld* **9/4**[1]

-100 **3** *1* **Miss George**[23] 1242 6-9-3 83 DaneO'Neill 8 83+
(DKIvory) *s.i.s: hld up: nt clr run 2f out to 1f out: running on whn nt clr run and swtchd rt ins fnl f: nrst fin* **6/1**[3]

3-04 **4** *1 1/2* **Blackheath (IRE)**[10] 1454 8-9-5 82 AlexGreaves 3 81
(DNicholls) *t.k.h: cl up: bmpd along and ev ch 1f out: nt qckn* **10/1**

04-3 **5** *1 1/4* **Endless Summer**[32] 1106 7-9-3 80 DHolland 1 75
(KRBurke) *racd on outer: in tch: effrt 2f out: one pce over 1f out* **7/2**[2]

00-1 **6** *3/4* **Devise (IRE)**[18] 1313 5-9-3 78 TGMcLaughlin 6 73
(MSSaunders) *t.k.h: pressed ldr 4f out: ev ch 1f out: wknd* **12/1**

-U30 **7** *1 1/2* **Ok Pal**[12] 1391 4-9-5 85 RMiles(3) 9 73
(TGMills) *mde most tl hdd & wknd ent fnl f* **16/1**

100- **8** *3/4* **Mirasol Princess**[184] 5751 3-8-5 81 ow1 TQuinn 4 65
(DKIvory) *s.i.s: in tch: pushed along 2f out: n.m.r over 1f out: wknd* **16/1**

216- **9** *2 1/2* **Bahamian Breeze**[251] 4272 3-8-7 81 SWKelly 5 59
(JNoseda) *s.i.s: a in rr: rdn and no prog 2f out* **12/1**

000- **10** *2 1/2* **Golden Bounty**[208] 5310 5-8-10 80 PGallagher(7) 2 51
(RHannon) *racd on outer: in tch: cl enough wl over 1f out: sn wknd* **25/1**

1m 13.53s (-0.34) **Going Correction** -0.025s/f (Good)
**WFA** 3 from 4yo+ 11lb **10** Ran SP% **117.4**
Speed ratings: **101,100,99,97,95 94,92,91,88,84** CSF £29.75 TOTE £11.70: £3.60, £1.30, £2.40; EX 37.20.
**Owner** The Gardening Partnership **Bred** Joseph Keappock **Trained** Sessay, N Yorks

**FOCUS**
A decent classified stakes, but a fairly modest time for the grade.

**NOTEBOOK**
**Lincoln Dancer(IRE)** has been in good form this spring and finally got his head in front after a barren spell stretching back almost four years. His trainer is now eyeing the Victoria Cup, in which the gelding finished second in 2002.
**Morse(IRE)**, a previous course and distance winner, had every chance on his recent form and ran a solid race in defeat. He could gain compensation soon.
**Miss George** looked a little unlucky not to win, as she travelled well in behind but just could not get a gap when she needed it. She needs to be held up for a late run and the risk of a troubled passage is one her backers must accept. *Official explanation: jockey said mare lost a shoe at the start*
**Blackheath(IRE)** looks pretty high in the ratings at present, which will make things difficult when he returns to handicap company.
**Endless Summer** was slightly disappointing given his promising reappearance outing, although he was not helped by having to race widest of all in the straight.
**Devise(IRE)** will appreciate a drop back in trip as he did not appear to see out this six furlongs.

## 1674 WINDSOR-RACECOURSE.CO.UK MAIDEN STKS — 1m 2f 7y
**7:35** (7:37) (D) 3-Y-O — **£4,303** (£1,324; £662; £331) **Stalls** Low

Form RPR

0-2 **1** **Crystal (IRE)**[10] 1440 3-8-9 MHills 5 80+
(BJMeehan) *prom: trckd ldr 4f out: led over 2f out: in command over 1f out: pushed out* **1/1**[1]

0 **2** *1 3/4* **Nietzsche (IRE)**[13] 1382 3-9-0 SWKelly 16 82+
(JNoseda) *trckd ldrs gng wl: effrt 3f out: rdn and hung lft over 1f out : styd on to take 2nd ins fnl f: no imp wnr* **25/1**

5-4 **3** *1* **Gironde**[13] 1382 3-9-0 BDoyle 10 80+
(SirMichaelStoute) *s.i.s: sn trckd ldrs: prog 4f out: rdn to chse wnr wl over 1f out: rn green and no imp: lost 2nd last 100y* **9/2**[3]

2- **4** *5* **Sound Of Fleet (USA)**[290] 3190 3-9-0 SDrowne 12 70+
(PFICole) *dwlt: t.k.h and prog to ld after 3f: hdd over 2f out: fdd* **7/2**[2]

0- **5** *1 1/4* **Brough Supreme**[172] 5934 3-9-0 PDobbs 8 68
(HMorrison) *racd in midfield: pushed along and outpcd 3f out: kpt on steadily fnl 2f: no ch whn veered lft over 1f out* **66/1**

0 **6** *3/4* **Protecting Heights (IRE)**[12] 1395 3-9-0 GCarter 15 67
(JLDunlop) *settled towards rr: prog 1/2-way: chsd ldrs and rdn over 2f out: fdd over 1f out* **100/1**

**7** *3/4* **Silencio (IRE)** 3-9-0 VSlattery 7 65+
(AKing) *racd in midfield: outpcd over 3f out: pushed along and one pce fnl 2f* **66/1**

**8** *hd* **Masked (IRE)** 3-9-0 TQuinn 3 65+
(JWHills) *wl in rr: pushed along 4f out: no real prog tl styd on fr over 1f out: nvr nrr* **100/1**

0- **9** *nk* **Levitator**[192] 5612 3-9-0 DaneO'Neill 4 64
(SirMichaelStoute) *trckd ldrs: shkn up and outpcd over 2f out: grad fdd* **16/1**

**10** *6* **Idealistic (IRE)** 3-8-6 NMackay(3) 13 48
(LMCumani) *s.s: wl in rr: pushed along 3f out: nvr on terms* **50/1**

**11** *3/4* **Twelve Bar Blues** 3-8-9 LDettori 6 46
(JHMGosden) *a wl in rr: struggling over 4f out: no ch after* **10/1**

0-0 **12** *3/4* **Doringo**[14] 1366 3-9-0 ADaly 2 50
(JLSpearing) *racd in midfield: hrd rdn and btn 3f out* **100/1**

000- **13** *8* **Flying Patriarch**[149] 6091 3-9-0 RLMoore 9 35
(GLMoore) *led for 3f: wknd 4f out* **100/1**

**14** *1* **Oh So Hardy** 3-8-9 CCatlin 11 28
(MAAllen) *a wl in rr: wl bhd over 3f out* **100/1**

**15** *shd* **Maidstone Midas (IRE)** 3-9-0 MFenton 1 33
(WSKittow) *lost pl rapidly after 2f: wl in rr and struggling after* **100/1**

0- **16** *nk* **Seagold**[180] 5831 3-8-9 JMackay 14 27
(CFWall) *chsd ldrs tl wknd rapidly 4f out* **100/1**

2m 10.25s (1.95) **Going Correction** +0.10s/f (Good) **16** Ran SP% **121.1**
Speed ratings: **96,94,93,89,88 88,87,87,87,82 81,81,74,74,73 73** CSF £36.79 TOTE £1.90: £1.30, £6.50, £2.10; EX 59.30.
**Owner** F C T Wilson **Bred** Strawhill Farm **Trained** Upper Lambourn, Berks

**FOCUS**
This looked a fair maiden, although the time was ordinary, and the runner-up looks a sure-fire future winner.

**NOTEBOOK**
**Crystal(IRE)** held a big form chance on her Newbury second and did the business with the minimum of fuss. Whether she is up to the class her trainer believes her to be remains to be seen, but either way her Classic credentials are likely to be put on the line in the Lupe or Lingfield Oaks Trial.
**Nietzsche(IRE)** ◆ had finished over 12 lengths behind Gironde at Newmarket on his debut and showed big improvement to beat that rival on this occasion. Still green, there looks to be better still to come, and a maiden should be his for the taking.

**Gironde** appeared to run a solid race in defeat, although the eventual second's improvement to beat him this time suggests that he is not progressing as well as others. He is, however, now eligible for a handicap mark.
**Sound Of Fleet(USA)**, who was strong in the market considering this was his first outing since July, raced a touch keenly and had little left when challenged in the closing stages. He should come on a bit for the run.
**Brough Supreme**, who shapes as though he will be suited by farther than this in time, needs one more run for a mark.
**Masked(IRE)**, whose stable's runners are rarely at their best first time up, made steady headway down the outside in the straight and looks the type who could build on this in time.

## 1675 COME RACING AT ROYAL WINDSOR H'CAP 1m 67y
8:05 (8:06) (E) (0-70,70) 3-Y-O+ £3,649 (£1,123; £561; £280) Stalls High

Form RPR
323- **1** **Salinor**[234] [4702] 4-10-0 **70**............ LDettori 10 84
(ACStewart) *hld up in midfield: smooth prog over 2f out: rdn to chal over 1f out: led last 100y: styd on wl* **7/2**[2]
-001 **2** *hd* **Best Before (IRE)**[57] [932] 4-9-5 **61**............ SDrowne 17 75
(PDEvans) *chsd ldrs: pushed along 4f out: effrt and nt clr run over 2f out: drvn and prog to ld over 1f out: hdd last 100y: jst hld* **14/1**
00-5 **3** *2½* **Zonic Boom (FR)**[18] [1310] 4-9-6 **62**............ JPMurtagh 12 70
(JRFanshawe) *hld up bhd ldrs: effrt 3f out: nt clr run and taken towards centre 2f out: drvn and r.o fnl f: nrst fin* **2/1**[1]
01-0 **4** *½* **Duelling Banjos**[104] [512] 5-9-9 **65**............ TQuinn 8 72
(JAkehurst) *racd in midfield: pushed along 4f out: prog over 2f out: swtchd lft over 1f out: kpt on u.p* **25/1**
0611 **5** *½* **Amnesty**[6] [1522] 5-9-7 **63** 7ex............(be) RLMoore 3 68
(GLMoore) *s.i.s: settled wl in rr: effrt over 2f out: styd on fr over 1f out: unable to chal* **15/2**[3]
3434 **6** *nk* **Eastborough (IRE)**[18] [1308] 5-9-4 **60**............ DHolland 13 65
(BGPowell) *hld up wl in rr: stl in last pair wl over 2f out: rdn and styd on fr over 1f out: nvr nrr* **9/1**
1-20 **7** *nk* **Dash For Cover (IRE)**[18] [1308] 4-9-10 **66**............ PDobbs 6 70
(RHannon) *trckd ldrs: effrt over 2f out: cl up wl over 1f out: fdd fnl f* **33/1**
00-0 **8** *1½* **Parnassian**[7] [1502] 4-9-2 **58**............ MartinDwyer 5 59
(GBBalding) *s.s: wl in rr: prog on outer 3f out: no imp over 1f out: fdd ins fnl f* **20/1**
360- **9** *1¾* **Miss Grace**[217] [5122] 4-9-1 **60**............ DCorby(3) 2 57
(JJSheehan) *hld up wl in rr: rdn 3f out: one pce and nvr rchd ldrs* **50/1**
422- **10** *¾* **Spirit's Awakening**[185] [5729] 5-9-2 **58**............ CCatlin 11 53
(JAkehurst) *prom: rdn to chal 2f out: sn wknd* **16/1**
-011 **11** *¾* **Supreme Salutation**[31] [1121] 8-9-5 **68**............ MHoward(7) 1 61
(DKIvory) *s.v.s: prog on outer 1/2-way: chsd ldrs and ch 2f out: sn wknd* **25/1**
560- **12** *hd* **Bijou Dancer**[318] [2321] 4-9-3 **59**............ GBaker 16 52
(MRBosley) *s.i.s: racd towards rr: shkn up over 2f out: no prog over 1f out* **50/1**
2100 **13** *1* **Meelup (IRE)**[23] [1241] 4-9-4 **60**............(p) VSlattery 15 50
(JaneSouthcombe) *racd keenly: prom: led over 3f out to over 1f out: wknd tamely* **66/1**
-303 **14** *2* **Bannister**[6] [1531] 6-9-4 **60**............ MFenton 4 46
(MrsStefLiddiard) *settled in rr: rdn and effrt 3f out: no prog over 1f out: sn wknd* **25/1**
-000 **15** *6* **Espada (IRE)**[21] [1274] 8-9-9 **65**............ SWKelly 7 37
(JAOsborne) *chsd ldrs tl wknd wl over 2f out* **25/1**
020- **16** *9* **One Way Ticket**[179] [5837] 4-9-9 **65**............(p) SCarson 14 16
(JMBradley) *racd freely: led to over 3f out: wknd rapidly over 2f out* **50/1**
600- **17** *9* **Seal Of Office**[228] [4848] 5-9-11 **67**............ DaneO'Neill 9 —
(AMHales) *s.s: wl in rr: effrt on wd outside 3f out: sn wknd: eased over 1f out* **12/1**
4200 **18** *19* **Surdoue**[7] [1502] 4-9-0 **56**............ JFanning 18 —
(PHowling) *chsd ldrs to over 3f out: nt run on: sn bhd: eased and t.o* **25/1**

1m 44.76s (-0.84) **Going Correction** +0.10s/f (Good) **18** Ran SP% **131.9**
Speed ratings: **108,107,105,104,104 104,103,102,100,99 98,98,97,95,89 80,71,52**CSF £48.75 CT £135.61 TOTE £4.20: £1.30, £3.50, £1.70, £5.50; EX 186.10 Place 6 £330.37, Place 5 £16.96.
**Owner** M J C Hawkes & A Goddard **Bred** D P Martin **Trained** Newmarket, Suffolk

**FOCUS**
A modest handicap but a smart winning time for the class.

**NOTEBOOK**
**Salinor** looked a progressive type last season but was a beaten favourite on his final three starts. He looks to have done well over the winter and appears open to even further improvement.
**Best Before(IRE)**, a winner on the Polytrack last time, returned to the turf on what looked a very fair mark and, sticking to the rail in the straight, ran a fine race in defeat. He finished clear of the third and should be able to pick up a race off this sort of mark.
**Zonic Boom(FR)**, well supported throughout the day, ended up challenging towards the centre of the track after not enjoying the best of runs. It is unlikely he would have won with a clear passage, but he would have finished closer.
**Duelling Banjos**, for whom the ground cannot be too soft, found enough give in this surface to put up a solid performance off what had looked a high enough mark.
**Amnesty** is the type who needs everything to fall just right, and while he came with his usual late run, it was too late on this occasion. There was no disgrace in this effort, though.
**Eastborough(IRE)** was another who got going all too late, but in fairness this trip is on the short side for him. *Official explanation: jockey said gelding hung left*
**Surdoue** *Official explanation: jockey said gelding lost its action*
T/Jkpt: Not won. T/Plt: £14.60 to a £1 stake. Pool: £51,652.50. 2,579.70 winning tickets. T/Qpdt: £3.90 to a £1 stake. Pool: £3,178.10. 595.60 winning tickets. JN

# 1625 WOLVERHAMPTON (A.W) (L-H)
Monday, April 26

**OFFICIAL GOING: Standard**
There appeared to be a bias towards horses racing down the middle and towards the stands'-rail in the straight.
Wind: almost nil Weather: fine

## 1676 BET DIRECT NO Q DEMO 08000 837 888 H'CAP 6f (F)
2:30 (2:30) (F) (0-55,55) 3-Y-O £2,961 (£846; £423) Stalls Low

Form RPR
-206 **1** **Melaina**[76] [732] 3-8-9 **51**............(p) MSavage(5) 4 54
(MSSaunders) *w ldr: led over 4f out: rdn over 2f out: hdd wl over 1f out: r.o u.p to ld again cl home* **12/1**
00-5 **2** *½* **Savernake Brave (IRE)**[115] [408] 3-8-9 **46**............(b) GBaker 3 48
(MrsHSweeting) *a.p: rdn over 2f out: led wl over 1f out: edgd rt ent fnl f: hdd cl home* **16/1**
0-34 **3** *hd* **Wonky Donkey**[44] [1012] 3-9-2 **53**............ MFenton 8 54
(SCWilliams) *chsd ldrs: c wd st: rdn over 1f out: kpt on ins fnl f* **3/1**[1]
0-44 **4** *1* **Bold Wolf**[19] [1300] 3-9-3 **54**............ ADaly 7 52
(JLSpearing) *led over 1f: prom: rdn 3f out: one pce fnl f* **6/1**[3]
0-05 **5** *3* **Smart Danny**[26] [1209] 3-8-12 **49**............ RWinston 6 38
(JJQuinn) *a.p: rdn over 2f out: wknd fnl f* **9/2**[2]
2-30 **6** *nk* **Anisette**[105] [506] 3-9-4 **55**............ IMongan 5 43
(JulianPoulton) *sn pushed along and outpcd: rdn and hdd on ins over 2f out: no further prog* **10/1**
00-0 **7** *1¾* **Kedross (IRE)**[74] [751] 3-9-4 **55**............ MTebbutt 10 38
(JJay) *outpcd: sme hdwy fnl f: nvr trbld ldrs* **10/1**
4001 **8** *1¼* **Garnock Venture (IRE)**[39] [1046] 3-9-4 **55**............(b) DHolland 12 34
(ABerry) *bhd: short-lived effrt on outside 3f out* **8/1**
0-04 **9** *nk* **Short Chorus**[6] [1517] 3-8-13 **50**............(p) SWKelly 11 28
(JBalding) *mid-div: rdn and bhd fnl 3f* **8/1**
40-0 **10** *1¼* **Moscow Mary**[9] [1474] 3-8-13 **50**............ SWhitworth 1 24
(AGNewcombe) *outpcd* **20/1**
00-6 **11** *½* **Blade's Daughter**[20] [1288] 3-8-6 **46** oh1............(b[1]) SHitchcott(3) 9 19
(KARyan) *hmpd s: outpcd* **20/1**
0052 **P** **Wendy's Girl (IRE)**[9] [1478] 3-9-1 **55**............ THamilton(3) 2 —
(RPElliott) *broke wl: sddle sn slipped: p.u after 2f* **9/1**

1m 16.13s (0.33) **Going Correction** -0.05s/f (Stan) **12** Ran SP% **131.0**
Speed ratings: **95,94,94,92,88 88,86,84,83,82 81**,—CSF £208.62 CT £750.29 TOTE £16.30: £5.60, £23.20, £1.70; EX 428.20.
**Owner** Bali Royal Racing **Bred** Barry Minty **Trained** Haydon, Somerset

**FOCUS**
A very moderate sprint handicap with a time to match.

**NOTEBOOK**
**Melaina**, whose only previous success came in a course and distance seller as a juvenile, was returning from a 76-day break and ran out a game winner. After showing good pace from the off, she had to battle in the straight to get the better of the runner-up and there was little in it at the line. Things will be harder when she is reassessed.
**Savernake Brave(IRE)**, having his first start for a new trainer, improved on the form he showed on his previous run when well beaten in a seven furlong claimer 115 days ago. The stands'-side is often favoured at Wolverhampton and this one, unlike the winner, raced more towards the far side.
**Wonky Donkey**, dropped back from a mile for this handicap debut, ran respectably and should prove just as effective over another furlong.
**Bold Wolf** continues to find a few too good.
**Smart Danny** showed little on his only other start on Fibresand and was again disappointing.
**Garnock Venture(IRE)** *Official explanation: jockey said colt was very restless in the stalls*
**Wendy's Girl(IRE)** *Official explanation: jockey said saddle slipped*

## 1677 BET DIRECT NO Q ON 08000 93 66 93 CLAIMING STKS 1m 4f (F)
3:00 (3:01) (F) 4-Y-O+ £2,870 (£820; £410) Stalls Low

Form RPR
5/61 **1** **Maniatis**[8] [1263] 7-8-11 75............(v) NChalmers(5) 4 75
(MrsJCandlish) *hld up: wnt 2nd over 8f out: led 5f out: rdn over 3f out: c wd st: r.o wl* **7/4**[2]
1100 **2** *5* **Mandoob**[30] [1135] 7-8-7 71............(p) J-PGuillambert(3) 1 62
(BRJohnson) *dwlt: reminders after 2f: rdn and hdwy 4f out: tk 2nd ins fnl f: nt trble wnr* **13/8**[1]
3201 **3** *1¾* **Orinocovsky (IRE)**[3] [1599] 5-8-6 55............ StevenHarrison(7) 2 62
(NPLittmoden) *led: hdd 5f out: rdn over 3f out: ev ch over 1f out: wknd ins fnl f* **7/2**[3]
4300 **4** *11* **Grand Lass (IRE)**[6] [1535] 5-8-3 49 ow3............ TPQueally(3) 5 38
(ASadik) *chsd ldr over 3f: rdn 6f out: sn outpcd and struggling* **14/1**
5240 **5** *1¾* **Theatre Tinka (IRE)**[6] [1535] 5-9-2 59............(p) DSweeney 3 46
(RHollinshead) *prom: n.m.r on ins and plld out over 7f out: rdn 6f out: sn outpcd and struggling* **7/1**

2m 39.07s (-2.73) **Going Correction** -0.05s/f (Stan) **5** Ran SP% **115.8**
Speed ratings: **107,103,102,95,94**CSF £5.35 TOTE £2.70: £2.00, £1.70; EX 4.70.Maniatis was claimed by Andrew Reid for £10,000.
**Owner** Racing For You Limited **Bred** A Christodoulou **Trained** Basford, Staffs
■ Stewards Enquiry : J-P Guillambert caution: careless riding

**FOCUS**
Just an ordinary claimer, but a decent winning time for the grade.

**NOTEBOOK**
**Maniatis**, back on the Flat after an unsuccessful spin over hurdles, had a good chance at the weights and took it under a positive ride. He drifted over to the stands'-side rail in the straight and the width of the track separated him and the second and third placed horses, but he kept on right the way to the line. He will now join Andrew Reid and should continue to prove hard to beat, although it could be worth noting his former connections said he has bad knees.
**Mandoob**, with the cheekpieces re-fitted and switched from turf to Fibresand, was the best in at the weights (2lb better off with the winner) but proved disappointing. He was being ridden along some way from home and, when finally in top stride, stayed on the far side in the straight. *Official explanation: jockey said saddle slipped*
**Orinocovsky(IRE)**, who had 19lb to find with the winner at the weights, kept on well when headed by that one but was another to race towards the far side in the straight. This and selling company is his sort of level.
**Grand Lass(IRE)**, with no headgear on this time, was most disappointing. Her only previous win came over nine furlongs.
**Theatre Tinka(IRE)** is not that easy to win with, but was below his best in any case. *Official explanation: trainer's representative said gelding bled from the nose*

## 1678 AVOID THE QUEUES WITH BET DIRECT NO Q FILLIES' H'CAP 7f (F)
3:30 (3:30) (E) (0-70,62) 3-Y-O £3,435 (£1,057; £528; £264) Stalls High

Form RPR
644- **1** **Farriers Charm**[186] [5715] 3-9-1 **59**............ TPQueally(3) 1 63
(DJCoakley) *hld up in tch: rdn 3f out: led ins fnl f: r.o wl* **14/1**
-210 **2** *2½* **Could She Be Magic (IRE)**[54] [955] 3-9-6 **61**............(b[1]) SWKelly 4 59
(TDEasterby) *a.p: swtchd rt 4f out: sn chsng ldr: rdn 3f out: edgd lft over 1f out: ev ch ins fnl f: one pce* **9/4**[1]
060- **3** *1* **Miss Madame (IRE)**[213] [5185] 3-9-7 **62**............ PRobinson 5 58
(RGuest) *led: rdn over 1f out: hdd and no ex ins fnl f* **4/1**[3]
-610 **4** *2* **Showtime Annie**[9] [1464] 3-9-5 **60**............ GCarter 7 51
(ABailey) *outpcd and bhd: hdwy over 1f out: r.o* **4/1**[3]
004- **5** *3½* **Sharplaw Destiny (IRE)**[193] [5595] 3-9-0 **55**............ DHolland 2 37
(WJHaggas) *prom: rdn 3f out: wknd 2f out* **3/1**[2]
00-0 **6** *5* **Faraway Echo**[26] [1214] 3-9-2 **57**............ IMongan 3 26
(MLWBell) *chsd ldrs: rdn 5f out: wknd 3f out* **10/1**
000- **7** *11* **Tshukudu**[182] [5797] 3-8-6 **47** ow1............ DSweeney 6 —
(MBlanshard) *rdn 5f out: a bhd* **16/1**

1m 30.29s (-0.03) **Going Correction** -0.05s/f (Stan) **7** Ran SP% **117.4**
Speed ratings: **98,95,94,91,87 82,69**CSF £47.66 TOTE £20.40: £3.60, £1.20; EX 88.10.
**Owner** Alf Hall **Bred** Giles W Pritchard-Gordon (farming) Ltd **Trained** West Ilsley, Berks

**FOCUS**
A few unexposed sorts contested this fillies' handicap and one of those, Farriers Charm, won nicely. However, the form is probably just ordinary.

**NOTEBOOK**
**Farriers Charm** shaped well on her first two starts but was reportedly unsuited by the track at Brighton when disappointing on her third and final start at two. Making her handicap and Fibresand debut, she ran her best race to date, ending up a most decisive winner. This was her first run in 186 days and there should be more to come.
**Could She Be Magic(IRE)** did not look the most straightforward of rides in first-time blinkers. Hard ridden into the straight, she wandered around and proved no match for the winner.
**Miss Madame(IRE)** found this easier than some of the races she contested last season and shaped with promise. This was her first start in 213 days and it should bring her on.
**Showtime Annie** was disappointing back on turf on her previous outing and, although this was a little better, she was still well held. After starting slowly, she never got into it.
**Sharplaw Destiny(IRE)** caught the eye in a maiden on her third and final start last season, but she was a drifter on course and was well beaten.

## 1679 BET DIRECT NO Q MEDIAN AUCTION MAIDEN STKS — 1m 100y(F)
4:00 (4:00) (E ) 3-Y-O — £3,367 (£1,036; £518; £259) Stalls Low

Form — RPR
0 **1** **Submissive**[13] [1386] 3-8-7 ........ KMay(7) 2 — 70
(BWHills) *mde all: rdn over 2f out: hld on wl fnl f* **20/1**
0-0 **2** *nk* **Delightfully**[19] [1293] 3-8-9 ........ MHills 1 — 65
(BWHills) *w wnr thrght: rdn 3f out: nt qckn ins fnl f* **11/2**
00-5 **3** *3/4* **Peak Of Perfection (IRE)**[9] [1466] 3-9-0 73........ PRobinson 6 — 68
(MAJarvis) *a.p: rdn over 2f out: edgd lft over 1f out: nt qckn* **6/4**[1]
3- **4** *3 1/2* **Devious Ayers (IRE)**[119] [6250] 3-8-11 ........ TPQueally(3) 3 — 61
(GAButler) *hld up in tch: rdn over 2f out: wknd over 1f out* **3/1**[3]
30-2 **5** *11* **Jarvo**[6] [1532] 3-9-0 66........ DHolland 5 — 38
(NPLittmoden) *chsd ldrs: rdn over 3f out: sn wknd* **9/4**[2]
0 **6** *2 1/2* **Cunning Pursuit**[14] [1371] 3-9-0 ........ IMongan 4 — 32
(MLWBell) *in rr: rdn over 4f out: no ch fnl 3f* **11/1**

1m 50.15s (-0.94) **Going Correction** -0.05s/f (Stan) — 6 Ran SP% **124.2**
Speed ratings: **102,101,100,97,86 83**CSF £132.47 TOTE £10.80: £13.30, £3.20; EX 7.00.
**Owner** Guy Reed **Bred** G Reed **Trained** Lambourn, Berks

**FOCUS**
Not a great maiden, but competitive enough.

**NOTEBOOK**
**Submissive** found this easier than the Newmarket maiden he made his debut in, and got off the mark under a good ride from his apprentice jockey. The form is probably not worth a great deal and connections will be hoping the Handicapper does not overreact.
**Delightfully**, drawn on the wrong side at Folkestone on her previous run (she won her race on the stands'-side), did nothing wrong an looks capable of winning a similar race.
**Peak Of Perfection(IRE)** was not sure to be suited by this drop in trip but that was not the problem. He held every chance in the straight, but was inclined to hang to his left. He looks a bit harshly treated off his current rating of 73.
**Devious Ayers(IRE)** failed to build on his encouraging debut effort on this step up in trip and switch to Fibresand.
**Jarvo** was not suited by this switch to Fibresand and is basically disappointing. *Official explanation: jockey said gelding hung left-handed*

## 1680 BET IN RUNNING @ BETDIRECT.CO.UK (S) STKS — 7f (F)
4:30 (4:30) (G ) 3-Y-O+ — £2,520 (£720; £360) Stalls High

Form — RPR
2500 **1** **Mizhar (USA)**[20] [1283] 8-9-6 48........(p) RWinston 3 — 63
(JJQuinn) *hld up: rdn over 3f out: hdwy 2f out: led ins fnl f: r.o wl* **6/1**
2-50 **2** *2 1/2* **Bella Beguine**[86] [646] 5-9-1 67........(v) GCarter 1 — 52
(ABailey) *led: rdn over 2f out: hdd ins fnl f: one pce* **4/6**[1]
5360 **3** *1 1/4* **Chandelier**[57] [932] 4-9-1 51........ MSavage(5) 2 — 54
(MSSaunders) *s.i.s: jnd ldrs over 5f out: rdn and ev ch 2f out: edgd rt over 1f out: one pce* **3/1**[2]
40-0 **4** *6* **Fine Frenzy (IRE)**[12] [1389] 4-8-10 45........ AQuinn(5) 4 — 34
(MissSJWilton) *w ldr tl rdn over 2f out: sn wknd* **5/1**[3]

1m 30.66s (0.34) **Going Correction** -0.05s/f (Stan) — 4 Ran SP% **115.9**
Speed ratings: **96,93,91,84**CSF £11.56 TOTE £9.00; EX 11.60.There was no bid for the winner.
**Owner** Andrew Page **Bred** Shadwell Farm Inc **Trained** Settrington, N Yorks

**FOCUS**
A very moderate seller and the favourite Bella Beguine, who was well clear at the weights, failed to perform.

**NOTEBOOK**
**Mizhar(USA)**, beaten in this grade on his last five starts, had the cheekpieces back on returned to Fibresand and scored nicely. He had the race run to suit and, given that he has not followed up since 1998, he could be one to take on next time.
**Bella Beguine** had 24lb in hand over the winner at the weights, but was most disappointing. She is not one to follow.
**Chandelier**, with the blinkers left off on this drop in grade, can have no excuses.
**Fine Frenzy(IRE)** weakened tamely.

## 1681 BETDIRECT.CO.UK AMATEUR RIDERS' H'CAP — 1m 100y(F)
5:00 (5:00) (G ) (0-55,55) 4-Y-O+ — £2,982 (£852; £426) Stalls Low

Form — RPR
2245 **1** **Maggie's Pet**[57] [939] 7-10-0 46 oh1........(t) MissJoeyEllis(5) 11 — 56
(KBell) *w ldr: led over 4f out: clr 2f out: r.o wl* **9/1**
4004 **2** *1 1/2* **Crusoe (IRE)**[9] [1479] 7-10-9 50........(b) MissEJJones 9 — 57
(ASadik) *led: hdd over 4f out: rdn 3f out: kpt on same pce fnl f* **7/2**[1]
4224 **3** *1* **Donegal Shore (IRE)**[59] [910] 5-10-2 48........(vt) MrDWeekes(5) 10 — 53
(MrsJCandlish) *sn wl bhd: hrd rdn over 1f out: gd hdwy and edgd lft fnl f: nrst fin* **8/1**[3]
0065 **4** *1* **Bought Direct**[9] [1479] 5-10-5 51........ MrLNewnes(5) 13 — 54
(RJSmith) *a.p: rdn over 2f out: no ex ins fnl f* **9/2**[2]
540- **5** *1/2* **Saxe-Coburg (IRE)**[189] [5680] 7-10-6 54........ MrGDenvir(7) 1 — 56
(GAHam) *s.i.s: bhd tl hdwy over 1f out: one pce fnl f* **16/1**
400- **6** *4* **Rainstorm**[205] [5373] 9-10-2 46 oh1........ MrsSOwen(3) 7 — 39
(WMBrisbourne) *s.i.s: plld hrd: sn chsng ldrs: wknd fnl f* **12/1**
000- **7** *nk* **Encore Royale**[221] [5024] 4-10-2 50........ MrTThomas(7) 12 — 43
(JJay) *s.v.s: nvr nrr* **11/1**
000- **8** *nk* **Desert Fury**[180] [5832] 7-10-6 52........ MissRBastiman(5) 6 — 44
(RBastiman) *chsd ldrs: rdn over 3f out: wknd fnl f* **14/1**
1100 **9** *shd* **Qobtaan (USA)**[11] [1427] 5-11-0 55........ MrsSBosley 3 — 47
(MRBosley) *s.i.s: hdwy on ins 4f out: wknd fnl f* **10/1**
0554 **10** *1 1/4* **Pas De Surprise**[33] [1095] 6-10-8 52........ MissEFolkes(3) 2 — 41
(PDEvans) *hld up and bhd: hdwy over 3f out: wknd over 1f out* **9/2**[2]
0304 **11** *5* **Prince Minata (IRE)**[21] [1263] 9-9-12 46 oh6........ MissAHockley(7) 4 — 25
(PWHiatt) *chsd ldrs tl rdn and wknd over 4f out* **12/1**
420- **12** *1 1/2* **Smart Minister**[188] [5688] 4-10-10 51........ MrSWalker 5 — 27
(JJQuinn) *chsd ldrs: rdn 4f out: wknd 3f out* **8/1**[3]

1m 52.6s (1.51) **Going Correction** -0.05s/f (Stan) — 12 Ran SP% **136.2**
Speed ratings: **90,88,87,86,86 82,81,81,81,80 75,73**CSF £46.78 CT £286.08 TOTE £15.60: £7.60, £1.90, £2.50; EX 74.00 Place 6 £2388.45, Place 5 £752.20.
**Owner** Len Purdy **Bred** Mrs D J Hodges **Trained** Letcombe Regis, Oxon

**FOCUS**
A moderate handicap and the form is not strong.

**NOTEBOOK**
**Maggie's Pet**, who started her career in bumpers, finally got off the mark on the level. This will have boosted her confidence, but a rise in the weights will make things tougher.
**Crusoe(IRE)**, 11lb lower than when last successful, ran his race in second and is clearly handicapped to go in again.
**Donegal Shore(IRE)**, dropped 3lb since its last run, ran respectably and shaped as though he will stay a little further.
**Bought Direct** has never won in this country, but this was by no means a bad effort. He is now on a realistic mark.
**Saxe-Coburg(IRE)**, dropped back from a mile and a half, found this trip on the short side.
**Encore Royale** lost about 15 lengths at the start and did really well to finish where she did.
T/Plt: £736.40 to a £1 stake. Pool: £21,789.95. 21.60 winning tickets. T/Qpdt: £171.10 to a £1 stake. Pool: £1,433.70. 6.20 winning tickets. KH

1682 - (Foreign Racing) - See Raceform Interactive

# 1307 BATH (L-H)
Tuesday, April 27

**OFFICIAL GOING: Good (good to firm in places)**

## 1683 M J CHURCH MAIDEN STKS — 1m 2f 46y
2:00 (2:08) (D ) 3-Y-O — £3,620 (£1,114; £557; £278) Stalls Low

Form — RPR
4 **1** **Solor**[25] [1227] 3-9-0 ........ DHolland 19 — 81
(DJCoakley) *trckd ldrs: led over 2f out: sn rdn: hdd appr fnl f: rallied to ld ins last and styd on wl* **25/1**
3- **2** *1/2* **Magnetic Pole**[196] [5565] 3-9-0 ........ JPMurtagh 14 — 80
(SirMichaelStoute) *chsd ldrs: pressed ldrs 2f out: led over 1f out: rdn: hdd and no ex ins last* **7/4**[1]
0 **3** *2 1/2* **Iktitaf (IRE)**[15] [1371] 3-9-0 ........ RHills 11 — 76
(JHMGosden) *in tch: outpcd 6f out: hdwy over 2f out: str run fr over 1f out: fin wl: nt rch ldrs* **33/1**
42-0 **4** *3/4* **Gravardlax**[17] [1330] 3-9-0 89........ KDarley 4 — 74
(BJMeehan) *chsd ldrs: rdn fr over 3f out: styd on same pce fnl 2f* **6/1**[3]
04- **5** *1 1/4* **Moonlight Tango (USA)**[185] [5757] 3-8-9 ........ LDettori 13 — 67
(JHMGosden) *sn in tch: hdwy 3f out: one pce fnl 2f* **6/1**[3]
**6** *3* **Motorway (IRE)** 3-9-0 ........ DSweeney 1 — 67
(RCharlton) *bhd: hdwy fr 3f out: kpt on fnl 2f but nt trble ldrs* **25/1**
50- **7** *2* **Belisco (USA)**[181] [5830] 3-9-0 ........ DaneO'Neill 10 — 63
(MrsAJPerrett) *chsd ldrs: rdn over 3f out: wknd over 1f out* **50/1**
**8** *hd* **Uig** 3-8-9 ........ TEDurcan 3 — 58
(HSHowe) *mid-div: hdwy 3f out: kpt on same pce fnl 2f* **200/1**
04 **9** *1 3/4* **Master Mahogany**[20] [1301] 3-9-0 ........ VSlattery 18 — 59
(RJHodges) *bhd: kpt on fr over 2f out: nt a danger* **80/1**
0-5 **10** *1* **Opera Star (IRE)**[90] [621] 3-8-9 ........ MartinDwyer 8 — 53
(BWHills) *chsd ldrs: rdn 5f out: wknd over 2f out* **80/1**
3-5 **11** *1/2* **Principessa**[8] [1507] 3-8-9 ........ SDrowne 9 — 52
(BPalling) *chsd ldrs: rdn 4f out: wknd over 2f out* **12/1**
4- **12** *1/2* **Aqualung**[291] [3190] 3-9-0 ........ MHills 15 — 56
(BWHills) *led tl hdd over 2f out: wkng whn hmpd over 1f out* **4/1**[2]
00 **13** *shd* **Go Green**[17] [1325] 3-8-9 ........ RPrice 6 — 51
(PDEvans) *a in rr* **200/1**
00-0 **14** *2* **Grist Mist (IRE)**[22] [1271] 3-8-9 ........ RHavlin 5 — 47
(MrsPNDutfield) *t.k.h: chsd ldrs: wknd qckly over 2f out* **125/1**
000- **15** *1/2* **House Of Blues**[173] [5934] 3-9-0 ........ SWKelly 12 — 51
(JAOsborne) *nvr bttr than mid-div* **100/1**
00-0 **16** *shd* **Planters Punch (IRE)**[15] [1352] 3-9-0 ........ RLMoore 20 — 51
(RHannon) *bhd: sme hdwy into mid-div 3f out: n.d after* **50/1**
00 **17** *5* **Justice Jones**[15] [1366] 3-9-0 ........ ADaly 17 — 42
(JLSpearing) *sn bhd* **150/1**
**18** *5* **Ballyliffin (IRE)** 3-8-7 ........ JDWalsh(7) 7 — 33
(SKirk) *s.i.s: a in rr* **125/1**
00-0 **19** *1 1/2* **Regal Performer (IRE)**[8] [1508] 3-9-0 ........ TQuinn 16 — 30
(SKirk) *a in rr* **100/1**
**20** *19* **Forged (IRE)** 3-8-11 ........ NMackay(3) 2 — —
(LMCumani) *s.i.s: n.d* **40/1**

2m 11.54s (0.54) **Going Correction** +0.05s/f (Good) — 20 Ran SP% **117.3**
Speed ratings: **99,98,96,96,95 92,91,90,89,88 88,87,87,86,85 85,81,77,76,61**CSF £63.33 TOTE £24.70: £4.40, £1.40, £8.00; EX 230.40.
**Owner** Bolam Hurley Ross **Bred** Wretham Stud **Trained** West Ilsley, Berks

**FOCUS**
An ordinary maiden featuring mostly inexperienced horses, and the principals came right away in the closing stages. The time was moderate for the grade, being slowest of the three races over the trip on the day, and the form may not be all that reliable.

**NOTEBOOK**
**Solor** ◆ had run with plenty of promise on his debut on the Lingfield Polytrack, and showed the benefit of the experience. Always close to the pace, he took a narrow lead halfway up the straight but was quickly challenged by the favourite. However, he rallied well and got the upper hand in the last half-furlong. He looks capable of winning a decent race this season.
**Magnetic Pole** ◆ was well backed to build on the promise of his sole juvenile run and looked the winner when taking the advantage over a furlong out. However, the winner proved too resolute on this occasion, but he was well clear of the rest and, while his Derby entry is clearly optimistic, he should pick up a maiden before long.
**Iktitaf(IRE)** was noted running-on strongly for third after struggling early on. He can do better in time and looks likely to be suited by a more galloping track and possibly a longer trip.
**Gravardlax** appeared not to handle the turn into the straight, and just kept on steadily under pressure. He looks harshly handicapped judged on this performance.
**Moonlight Tango(USA)** caught the eye without ever troubling the leaders, and both should be better for the run.
**Motorway(IRE)**, a 270,000gns half-brother to Geminiani, was difficult to load but showed some promise despite running green.
**Aqualung** was somewhat disappointing, folding tamely after making the early running.
**Grist Mist(IRE)** *Official explanation: jockey said filly had a breathing problem and hung right*
**Regal Performer(IRE)** *Official explanation: jockey said gelding was never travelling*

## 1684 BET365 CALL 08000 322365 FILLIES' H'CAP — 1m 3f 144y

**2:30** (2:34) (D) (0-80,80) 4-Y-0+ — **£3,748** (£3,748; £882; £441) **Stalls** Low

Form — RPR

210- **1** *dht* **Etching (USA)**204 [5417] 4-8-6 **58** ........ EAhern 2 — 65
(JRFanshawe) *sn trcking ldr: rdn to ld ins fnl 2f: hdd wl ins last: rallied to force dead heat* **7/2**1

531- **1** **Wasted Talent (IRE)**5 [6214] 4-9-4 **70** ........ (p) RLMoore 9 — 77
(JGPortman) *led: qckd clr 6f out: rdn 3f out: hdd ins fnl 2f:rallied to ld again wl ins last: hld on wl for dead heat* **6/1**

556- **3** *nk* **Albavilla**307 [2678] 4-9-8 **74** ........ TQuinn 4 — 81
(PWHarris) *chsd ldrs: rdn over 3f out: hung lft fr over 1f out: styd on wl ins last: no ex cl home* **12/1**

2145 **4** *½* **Anyhow (IRE)**32 [1122] 7-8-9 **60** ........ DHolland 7 — 66+
(MissKMGeorge) *hld up in rr: hdwy on ins over 2f out: styng on wl whn n.m.r 1f out and thrght fnl f: kpt on: nt rcvr* **4/1**2

-000 **5** *5* **Nuzzle**90 [623] 4-7-12 **50** ........ FNorton 10 — 48
(MQuinn) *chsd ldrs: rdn over 2f out: wknd fnl f: eased whn no ch w ldrs ins last* **25/1**

00-6 **6** *3 ½* **Most-Saucy**7 [1535] 8-8-9 **65** ........ DNolan(5) 1 — 57
(IAWood) *in tch: hrd rdn and effrt on outside to chse ldrs over 3f out: wknd ins fnl 2f* **7/1**

00-0 **7** *3* **Sninfia (IRE)**19 [1308] 4-8-8 **60** ........ JQuinn 12 — 47
(GAHam) *s.i.s: bhd: rdn and hdwy over 2f out: nvr gng pce to rch ldrs: sn wknd* **20/1**

-103 **8** *7* **Maystock**39 [1053] 4-9-11 **77** ........ LDettori 11 — 53
(GAButler) *bhd: hdwy 3f out: nvr gng pce to rch ldrs:wknd over 2f out* **9/2**3

10-0 **9** *3* **Claradotnet**22 [1272] 4-10-0 **80** ........ TEDurcan 8 — 51
(MRChannon) *a in rr* **16/1**

035- **10** *8* **Fully Fledged**239 [4624] 4-7-7 **50** oh1 ........ RThomas(5) 3 — 9
(GBBalding) *chsd ldrs tl wknd over 4f out* **40/1**

2m 32.41s (2.11) **Going Correction** +0.05s/f (Good)
**WFA** 4 from 7yo+ 1lb — **10** Ran **SP% 111.8**
Speed ratings: **94,94,93,93,90 87,85,81,79,73** TRIFECTA Win: WT 3.00, E 2.60; Pl: WT 1.90, E 1.90, 3.10; Ex: WT/E 14.30, E/WT 14.20; CSF: WT/E 12.72, E/WT 11.43; Tri: W/E/A 119.57, E/WT/A.
**Owner** Wasted Talent Partnership **Bred** L And D Fox And Oak Lodge Stud **Trained** Compton, Berks

**FOCUS**
A fair fillies' handicap in which the early pace was steady and the time was moderate for the grade.

**NOTEBOOK**
**Wasted Talent(IRE)** had a fitness advantage having been busy over hurdles, but looked beaten when headed by the favourite. However, she refused to give in and battled back to share the spoils. Jumping seems to have improved her, and she will continue to alternate between hurdles and the Flat.
**Etching(USA)**tracked the leader from the start and took the advantage inside the two. However, she was having her first run for nearly seven months and in the end had to pull out all the stops to hold on. She stays two miles but this shorter trip proved no problem.
**Albavilla** has clearly had her problems, but she has ability and ran a fine race, despite looking in need of the outing on her first run since last June, to press the principals all the way to the line. If she remains sound, she can get off the mark before long.
**Anyhow(IRE)** adopted her usual waiting tactics and finished on the heels of the first three after not getting a clear run, and will be interesting on a more galloping track on turf. *Official explanation: jockey said mare ran out of room close home*
**Nuzzle** having her first outing for three months and now 12lb lower than when last seen on turf, has run well on this track before but probably found this trip stretching her stamina.
**Most-Saucy** was closer than usual turning in but failed to find an extra gear. She has dropped close to a winning mark, and is worth bearing in mind for a race at one of the switchback tracks, such as Epsom or Brighton.
**Maystock** never showed and the jockey reported the filly ran flat. *Official explanation: jockey said filly ran flat*

## 1685 EUROPEAN BREEDERS FUND LANSDOWN FILLIES' STKS (LISTED RACE) — 5f 11y

**3:00** (3:02) (A) 3-Y-0+ — **£17,400** (£6,600; £3,300; £1,500) **Stalls** Low

Form — RPR

43-6 **1** **Ringmoor Down**11 [1438] 5-9-0 93 ........ DaneO'Neill 13 — 106
(DWPArbuthnot) *bhd: swtchd to outside over 2f out: rapid hdwy over 1f out: led ins last: qcknd: readily* **11/2**1

11- **2** *¾* **La Cucaracha**347 [1631] 3-8-4 ........ MHills 14 — 103
(BWHills) *bhd: hdwy on outside whn bmpd over 2f out: qcknd to chal ins last: kpt on but nt pce of wnr* **6/1**2

10-2 **3** *2 ½* **Speed Cop**38 [1061] 4-9-0 100 ........ MartinDwyer 7 — 94
(AMBalding) *led tl hdd appr fnl f: rallied to ld again jst ins last: sn hdd and outpcd* **11/2**1

505- **4** *¾* **Curfew**290 [3196] 5-9-0 95 ........ JPMurtagh 6 — 92
(JRFanshawe) *s.i.s: hdwy 2f out: chsd ldrs and rdn over 1f out: one pce ins last* **12/1**

00-5 **5** *nk* **Simianna**13 [1391] 5-9-0 88 ........ FNorton 1 — 91
(ABerry) *in tch: hdwy 2f out: rdn to chse ldrs whn hmpd and hit rail 1f out: kpt on same pce* **33/1**

201- **6** *nk* **Incise**298 [2967] 3-8-4 93 ........ JFEgan 15 — 89
(BJMeehan) *in tch: swtchd rt and hdwy over 2f out: led appr fnl f: hdd & wknd jst ins last* **12/1**

0-42 **7** *¾* **Dragon Flyer (IRE)**15 [1379] 5-9-0 104 ........ SDrowne 4 — 87
(MQuinn) *chsd ldrs: ev ch whn hit over hd and hmpd appr fnl f: effrt and nt clr run wl ins last: nt rcvr* **11/2**1

0-01 **8** *1 ½* **Proud Boast**13 [1391] 6-9-0 94 ........ KDarley 5 — 81
(DNicholls) *chsd ldrs: n.m.r and wknd over 1f out* **8/1**3

0-03 **9** *¾* **Ikan (IRE)**13 [1391] 4-9-0 89 ........ TGMcLaughlin 11 — 79
(NPLittmoden) *outpcd and bhd: rdn 3f out: styd on fnl f: nt trble ldrs* **12/1**

116- **10** *1 ¾* **Vermilliann (IRE)**199 [5480] 3-8-4 98 ........ RLMoore 10 — 72
(RHannon) *bhd: effrt 1/2-way: nvr gng pce to rch ldrs: wknd over 1f out* **25/1**

103- **11** *¾* **Tentative (USA)**220 [5057] 3-8-4 92 ........ EAhern 16 — 70
(RCharlton) *t.k.h: hld up in rr: nvr gng pce to rch ldrs* **25/1**

2-16 **12** *½* **Dusty Dazzler (IRE)**38 [1061] 4-9-0 87 ........ LDettori 8 — 68
(WGMTurner) *chsd ldrs 3f* **14/1**

5-00 **13** *¾* **Flashing Blade**11 [1453] 4-9-0 78 ........ TQuinn 9 — 65
(BAMcmahon) *chsd ldrs 3f* **66/1**

4-65 **14** *5* **Withorwithoutyou (IRE)**12 [1417] 3-8-4 85 ........ WSupple 3 — 47
(BAMcmahon) *pressed ldr to 1/2-way* **40/1**

61.38 secs (-1.12) **Going Correction** +0.05s/f (Good)
**WFA** 3 from 4yo+ 10lb — **14** Ran **SP% 115.9**
Speed ratings: **110,108,104,103,103 102,101,99,97,95 93,93,91,83**CSF £34.23 TOTE £6.50: £2.50, £2.20, £2.00; EX 55.00 Trifecta £421.50 Pool of £1,1721.78 - 2.90 winning tickets.
**Owner** Prof C D Green **Bred** Pigeon House Stud **Trained** Upper Lambourn, Berks

■ Stewards Enquiry : J F Egan four-day ban: two cases of careless riding (May 8,10-12)

**FOCUS**
An interesting Listed fillies' sprint, run in a decent time, being 1.78sec faster than the later handicap. The first two are improving and overcame high draws and racing off the pace.

**NOTEBOOK**
**Ringmoor Down**, who had gained all her previous wins over six furlongs and needs to be held up, appreciated good early pace. She won nicely in the end, and this victory increases her paddock value. She will have plenty of options in similar events.
**La Cucaracha ◆** performed with plenty of credit on her first outing since last May, especially considering she was done no favours by Incise at halfway. She is clearly a speedy filly and looks capable of winning a similar race.
**Speed Cop** broke quickly from her middle draw, but despite beating off several rivals had no answer when the principals arrived on the scene.
**Curfew** was another returning from a long absence and did not want to go behind the stalls. However, she performed with credit, will appreciate longer trips, and the outing should not be lost on her.
**Simianna**, who had a fair amount to find on official ratings, ran another decent race without ever posing a serious threat.
**Incise** did well to throw down a challenge from her outside stall, but caused a fair bit of grief in doing so, hampering the runner-up when moving out to challenge then squeezing out Dragon Flyer when briefly hitting the front. Egan was given a four-day ban.
**Dragon Flyer(IRE)** still seemed likely to figure, although under pressure at the time, but the interference effectively ended her chance,

## 1686 EXXON MOBIL MAIDEN AUCTION STKS — 5f 11y

**3:30** (3:32) (F) 2-Y-0 — **£2,975** (£850; £425) **Stalls** Low

Form — RPR

**1** **Elgin Marbles** 2-8-9 ........ DaneO'Neill 11 — 77
(RHannon) *s.i.s: bhd: plenty to do 1/2-way: swtchd to outside and rapid hdwy over 1f out: str run ins last to ld last stride* **9/2**2

5 **2** *shd* **The Crooked Ring**12 [1412] 2-8-7 ........ KDarley 13 — 75
(PDEvans) *in tch: hdwy 2f out: ridden to ld ins fnl f: ct last stride* **11/2**3

**3** *1 ½* **Alsu (IRE)** 2-8-4 ........ MartinDwyer 7 — 66
(AMBalding) *chsd ldrs: rdn and kpt on wl fnl f: nt qckn nr fin* **14/1**

3 **4** *1* **Withering Lady (IRE)**15 [1364] 2-7-13 ........ JFMcDonald(3) 6 — 60
(MrsPNDutfield) *trckd ldr: led 1/2-way: styd on wl whn chal appr fnl f:hdd ins last and sn one pce* **13/2**

**5** *1 ¼* **Al Qudra (IRE)** 2-8-9 ........ LDettori 9 — 62
(BJMeehan) *in tch: hdwy 2f out: rdn and kpt on fr over 1f out: nt pce to rch ldrs* **3/1**1

023 **6** *nk* **Turtle Magic (IRE)**4 [1589] 2-7-9 ........ CHaddon(7) 4 — 54
(WGMTurner) *in tch: hdwy ins fnl 2f: rdn to chal 1f out: wknd ins last* **11/1**

**7** *1 ½* **Haroldini (IRE)** 2-8-7 ........ RHavlin 5 — 53
(MrsPNDutfield) *s.i.s: hdwy into mid-div 1/2-way: nvr gng pce to trble ldrs* **50/1**

**8** *2* **Granary Girl** 2-8-2 ........ JFEgan 2 — 40
(BPalling) *s.i.s: bhd: sme hdwy fr over 1f out: nt trble ldrs* **50/1**

04 **9** *2* **Goldhill Prince**19 [1307] 2-8-7 ........ (p) ADaly 1 — 37
(WGMTurner) *chsd ldrs to 1/2-way* **25/1**

4 **10** *1* **Seasons Estates**20 [1299] 2-8-6 ow2 ........ SDrowne 10 — 32
(BRMillman) *chsd ldrs 3f* **9/1**

**11** *½* **Mystery Maid (IRE)** 2-8-2 ........ JQuinn 8 — 26
(HSHowe) *a outpcd* **66/1**

**12** *shd* **Grand Welcome (IRE)** 2-8-7 ........ EAhern 14 — 30
(CTinkler) *s.i.s: outpcd* **16/1**

0 **13** *nk* **Cree**11 [1436] 2-8-7 ........ TQuinn 3 — 29
(WRMuir) *led to 1/2-way: sn wknd* **50/1**

**14** *2* **Ahaz** 2-8-7 ........ WSupple 12 — 21
(IAWood) *s.i.s: rdn and effrt 1/2-way: nvr bttr than mid-div: sn bhd* **50/1**

63.50 secs (1.00) **Going Correction** +0.05s/f (Good) — **14** Ran **SP% 116.0**
Speed ratings: **94,93,91,89,87 87,84,81,78,76 76,76,75,72**CSF £27.05 TOTE £5.50: £2.80, £3.10, £4.50; EX 35.90.
**Owner** Jumeirah Racing **Bred** Trickledown Stud **Trained** East Everleigh, Wilts

**FOCUS**
A fair juvenile maiden featuring few with experience, and the time was average, being 0.34sec slower than the concluding handicap.

**NOTEBOOK**
**Elgin Marbles**, a speedily-bred son of Lujain, did well to win having been behind early. He stayed on really strongly, will appreciate another furlong, and looks the type to come on a good deal for the experience.
**The Crooked Ring ◆**, who was well beaten on his debut in a decent race at Newmarket, did nothing wrong but was collared on the line. He should have no difficulty winning an ordinary maiden.
**Alsu(IRE)** was another debutante to make an encouraging start to her career. She is bred to make a two-year-old and should win races at an ordinary level.
**Withering Lady(IRE)** did best of those to race up with the early pace, she will not find things easy but may find her niche in nurseries later on.
**Al Qudra(IRE)** was doing his best work at the finish and will know more next time. He will appreciate a longer trip in time.
**Turtle Magic(IRE)**make their mark in nurseries later on.

## 1687 OVAL OF BATH, PEUGEOT, (S) STKS — 1m 2f 46y

**4:00** (4:00) (G) 3-Y-0+ — **£2,625** (£750; £375) **Stalls** Low

Form — RPR

2341 **1** **Absolute Utopia (USA)**29 [1168] 11-10-0 63 ........ JPMurtagh 5 — 63
(JLSpearing) *hld up in rr: stdy hdwy over 3f out: qcknd to chal fr 2f out: led jst ins last: shkn up: jst hld on* **11/4**1

1631 **2** *hd* **Our Destiny**3 [1629] 6-9-11 47 ........ SHitchcott(3) 8 — 63
(AWCarroll) *bhd: hdwy 4f out: slt ld 2f out: narrowly hdd jst ins last: rallied and kpt on: nt pce of wnr cl home* **8/1**

/060 **3** *7* **Salford Flyer**19 [1308] 8-9-10 54 ........ (b) EAhern 7 — 46
(JaneSouthcombe) *trckd ldrs: led ins fnl 3f: hdd 2f out: readily outpcd fnl f* **10/1**

030- **4** *3* **Mobo-Baco**198 [5498] 7-9-10 60 ........ SDrowne 1 — 41
(RJHodges) *t.k.h: trckd ldr 3f: styd front rnk: slt ld 3f out: sn hdd: wknd ins fnl 2f* **3/1**2

00/6 **5** *2 ½* **Chakra**12 [1406] 10-9-3 40 ........ CHaddon(7) 3 — 36
(CJGray) *t.k.h: chsd ldrs: wknd over 2f out* **66/1**

0-00 **6** *½* **Eva Peron (IRE)**13 [1389] 4-9-5 49 ........ ADaly 9 — 30
(WGMTurner) *s.i.s: bhd: mod hdwy fr over 1f out* **20/1**

500- **7** *1 ¾* **Breezer**30 [5945] 4-9-10 57 ........ RHavlin 6 — 32
(GBBalding) *a in rr* **11/1**

/5-0 **8** *9* **Lunar Lord**17 [1109] 8-9-10 57 ........ (p) RPrice 2 — 16
(DBurchell) *chsd ldrs: wnt 2nd after 3f to 4f out: wknd ins fnl 3f* **5/1**3

6/ **9** *3* **Devote**34 [4076] 6-9-10 ........ (b) SWhitworth 4 — 10
(JDFrost) *bhd fr 1/2-way* **25/1**

00-0 **10** *10* **Jack Durrance (IRE)**[19] 1308 4-9-10 65 (v[1]) JQuinn 10 —
(GAHam) *t.k.h: led: hdd 3f out: sn btn* **16/1**

2m 11.28s (0.28) **Going Correction** +0.05s/f (Good) **10** Ran SP% **112.9**
Speed ratings: **100,99,94,91,89 89,88,80,78,70**CSF £23.77 TOTE £3.00: £2.00, £3.00, £3.50; EX 9.90.There was no bid for the winner.
**Owner** M T Lawrance **Bred** Gainsborough Farm Inc **Trained** Kinnersley, Worcs

**FOCUS**
A very moderate seller dominated by two horses that have been making hay on the All-Weather. The winner did not have to be at his best to win.

**NOTEBOOK**
**Absolute Utopia(USA)** had 16lb in hand of Our Destiny on official ratings, but was made to work hard by his younger rival to gain his second successive win in this race. In the end his superior stamina may have made the difference and he clearly remains in good heart.
**Our Destiny**ran well considering the ground was faster than he may prefer and his optimum trip these days is a mile. He is likely to suffer in the ratings as a result, but he is likely to remain in sellers and claimers in any case.
**Salford Flyer** ran his best race for a while and was travelling as well as anything before being outpaced. He stays a good deal further and a long-distance seller would appear to offer his best chance of ending his losing run.
**Mobo-Baco** ran as if he would be better for this first outing in six months. He will also appreciate a drop back to a mile.
**Lunar Lord**, fitted with cheekpieces for the first time, seemed to run too free early and dropped right out.
**Jack Durrance(IRE)** ran too free in the first-time visor. *Official explanation: jockey said filly had run too freely*

## 1688 NATIONWIDE PROPERTY FINANCE H'CAP — 1m 2f 46y

4:30 (4:32) (E) (0-75,75) 3-Y-O — **£3,776** (£1,162; £581; £290) **Stalls** Low

Form RPR

0-31 **1** **Another Choice (IRE)**[5] 1559 3-9-4 **72** 6ex (t) KDarley 4 78
(NPLittmoden) *chsd ldrs: rdn and str run fr over 1f out: led cl home: rdn out* **15/8**[1]

1322 **2** *½* **Jakarmi**[12] 1422 3-8-10 **64** TQuinn 1 69
(BPalling) *chsd ldrs: nt clr run and lost pl over 2f out: swtchd rt and hdwy over 1f out: str run ins last: nt rch wnr* **9/1**

2600 **3** *hd* **Desert Image (IRE)**[15] 1365 3-8-11 **68** DCorby(3) 9 73
(CTinkler) *hld up in tch: hdwy on rails fr 3f out: chal 2f out tl led ins fnl f: hdd and no ex cl home* **50/1**

62-3 **4** *nk* **Keshya**[19] 1309 3-8-9 **63** DaneO'Neill 8 67
(DJCoakley) *chsd ldrs: led appr fnl 2f: hdd ins last: no ex cl home* **5/1**[2]

0-41 **5** *1 ¼* **Goblin**[12] 1422 3-8-8 **62** TEDurcan 14 64
(DECantillon) *bhd: hdwy and n.m.r 3f out: swtchd rt and r.o fnl 2f: nt rch ldrs* **15/2**

605- **6** *nk* **Alaloof (USA)**[210] 5288 3-8-13 **67** RHills 11 68
(JLDunlop) *slowly away: bhd: hdwy on outside 2f out: str run fr over 1f out: fin wl* **8/1**

00-4 **7** *3* **Illeana (GER)**[28] 1189 3-8-10 **64** MartinDwyer 12 59
(WRMuir) *mid-div: rdn to chse ldrs fr 4f out: stl chsng ldrs u.p 2f out: wknd fnl f* **22/1**

55-0 **8** *½* **Simonovski (USA)**[39] 1052 3-9-2 **70** SWKelly 13 64
(JAOsborne) *bhd: hdwy 3f out: sn rdn: wknd over 1f out* **33/1**

000- **9** *1 ½* **Rinneen (IRE)**[229] 4843 3-8-3 **57** RSmith 10 49
(RHannon) *broke wl: dropped rr after 3f: sme hdwy fnl 2f but nvr nr ldrs* **40/1**

1-33 **10** *2* **Dr Cerullo**[104] 522 3-9-7 **75** SDrowne 7 63
(CTinkler) *bhd most of way* **20/1**

020- **11** *1* **Smoothly Does It**[190] 5671 3-8-13 **67** EAhern 2 53
(MrsAJBowlby) *bhd: hdwy 3f out: sn rdn: wknd over 2f out* **66/1**

1450 **12** *1* **Another Con (IRE)**[15] 1365 3-8-8 **62** RHavlin 5 46
(MrsPNDutfield) *w ldr: led after 1f: styd w ldr tl wknd ins fnl 3f* **25/1**

064- **13** *16* **Neap Tide**[197] 5533 3-9-7 **75** JPMurtagh 3 29
(JHMGosden) *led 1f: styd w ldr tl led 4f out: hdd over 2f out and wknd qckly* **6/1**[3]

003- **14** *9* **Solo Sole (ITY)**[132] 6203 3-9-1 **72** NMackay(3) 6 9
(LMCumani) *in tch: rdn 4f out: wknd 3f out* **28/1**

2m 11.04s (0.04) **Going Correction** +0.05s/f (Good) **14** Ran SP% **123.8**
Speed ratings: **101,100,100,100,99 98,96,96,94,93 92,91,78,71**CSF £18.43 CT £671.43 TOTE £3.40: £1.10, £3.30, £15.20; EX 25.10.
**Owner** A A Goodman **Bred** Lloyd Farm Stud **Trained** Newmarket, Suffolk

**FOCUS**
An interesting three-year-old handicap on paper featuring a number of unexposed horses, and run fastest of the three races over the trip on the day, but ultimately dominated by those with plenty of experience.

**NOTEBOOK**
**Another Choice(IRE)** followed up his recent wide-margin Beverley success under a 6lb penalty. He finished strongly and has the look of a progressive individual, but will reportedly be given a short break now, and the Handicapper is sure to have his say.
**Jakarmi** has been busy of late and was touched off in his two previous starts. However, he holds his form well and, stepping up in trip, seemed to get it well enough.
**Desert Image(IRE)** appreciated this return to a sound surface and, back on a winning mark, got a good split up the rail and ran as well as could be expected.
**Keshya** ran well for a yard that has just hit form, and seemed to handle the faster surface and the longer trip.
**Goblin** beat today's runner-up on their last meeting, but after looking a danger halfway up the straight, could not pick up again and may have found this longer trip beyond him.
**Alaloof(USA)** was the gamble of the race, but lost her chance with a tardy start. She was keeping on nicely at the finish and looks capable of better than she has shown so far.
**Neap Tide** was keen in front early on and dropped away tamely as a result. *Official explanation: jockey said gelding had run too freely early on*

## 1689 SAFFIE JOSEPH & SONS H'CAP — 5f 11y

5:00 (5:00) (E) (0-70,69) 3-Y-O — **£3,750** (£1,154; £577; £288) **Stalls** Low

Form RPR

0131 **1** **Ivory Lace**[19] 1312 3-9-3 **65** DSweeney 15 69
(SWoodman) *in tch: hdwy 2f out: rdn to chal ins last: led cl home* **9/2**[2]

4526 **2** *hd* **Laconia (IRE)**[10] 1472 3-9-7 **69** MartinDwyer 10 72
(JSMoore) *chsd ldrs: led ins fnl 2f: styd on wl u.p: hdd cl home* **10/1**

5306 **3** *1 ½* **Lavish Times**[25] 1236 3-8-3 **51** (b) FNorton 8 49
(ABerry) *wnt lft sn after s: and w ldr: stl ev ch ins fnl 2f: nt qckn ins fnl f* **16/1**

500- **4** *½* **Best Force**[173] 5930 3-8-6 **57** TPQueally(3) 14 53
(GAButler) *in tch: hdwy to chse ldrs fr 2f out: one pce ins last* **14/1**

40-0 **5** *nk* **Barabella (IRE)**[19] 1309 3-8-12 **63** JFMcDonald(3) 9 58
(RJHodges) *rrd stalls and bhd: n.m.r over 2f out: swtchd rt to outside and hdwy over 1f out: fin wl* **25/1**

000- **6** *½* **Maxi's Princess (IRE)**[157] 6045 3-8-8 **56** DaneO'Neill 5 49
(PJMakin) *s.i.s: bhd: hdwy on outside over 1f out: fin wl: nt rch ldrs* **16/1**

366- **7** *1* **Gemini Girl (IRE)**[271] 3725 3-8-8 **56** TQuinn 7 46
(MDHammond) *sn chsng ldrs: rdn over 2f out: outpcd fnl f* **12/1**

006- **8** *hd* **Maluti**[185] 5746 3-8-5 **53** JMackay 1 42
(RGuest) *mid-div: styd on fnl 2f but nvr gng pce to trble ldrs* **14/1**

-002 **9** *hd* **A Bid In Time (IRE)**[7] 1517 3-8-2 **50** ow2 WSupple 4 38
(DShaw) *hld up in rr: hdwy and n.m.r over 2f out: nvr dagerous after* **9/1**

51-6 **10** *¾* **After The Show**[17] 1333 3-9-7 **69** JPMurtagh 6 54
(JRJenkins) *wnt lft after s and sn slt ld: hdd ins fnl 2f and sn wknd* **10/3**[1]

6544 **11** *shd* **Rehia**[64] 865 3-8-9 **57** RHills 3 42
(JWHills) *chsng ldrs whn nt clr run sn after s: styd in tch: outpcd fnl 2f* **16/1**

020 **12** *½* **Imperium**[19] 1313 3-9-6 **68** SDrowne 2 51
(MrsStefLiddiard) *hmpd sn after s and hit rail: outpcd fr 1/2-way* **15/2**[3]

0-06 **13** *1 ¼* **Samara Sound**[24] 1243 3-8-7 **55** SWhitworth 11 34
(AGNewcombe) *s.i.s: bhd: effrt 1/2-way: sn btn* **12/1**

3060 **14** *1 ¼* **Beau Jazz**[19] 1313 3-8-12 **60** SRighton 13 34
(WDeBest-Turner) *in to9uch: chsd ldrs 1/2-way: wknd ins fnl 2f* **40/1**

63.16 secs (0.66) **Going Correction** +0.05s/f (Good) **14** Ran SP% **124.8**
Speed ratings: **96,95,93,92,92 91,89,89,88,87 87,86,84,82**CSF £51.33 CT £702.05 TOTE £4.80: £2.10, £3.80, £4.90; EX 56.90 Place 6 £60.75, Place 5 £28.40.
**Owner** Christopher J Halpin **Bred** D R Tucker **Trained** East Lavant, W Sussex

**FOCUS**
A modest sprint run 1.78sec slower than the earlier Listed event. The first two repeated their recent course form virtually tro the pound.

**NOTEBOOK**
**Ivory Lace** repeated her course-and-distance victory earlier in the month, when she had beaten today's runner-up Laconia on 1lb better terms. She has done really well for connections since being claimed out of a seller at Lingfield, and should not go up too much for this.
**Laconia(IRE)**ran right up to her previous form and lost little in defeat. She looks well capable of winning a small sprint.
**Lavish Times**, who gained his sole win in a seller on similar going, was up with the pace throughout but his record suggests he is not guaranteed to repeat this effort next time.
**Best Force**, dropping in trip for her handicap debut, ran well enough if looking as though a return to six will be in her favour
**Barabella(IRE)**, who reared as the stalls opened, did well to finish on the heels of the placed horses. She is lightly raced and looks capable of stepping up on this.
**Maxi's Princess(IRE)**, with the tongue tie left off, also came from well back after being sluggish at the start and is another who can do better in time.
**After The Show** hung left leaving the stalls and hampered Imperium, but the interference was deemed accidental.
**Imperium** was done no favours when squeezed up early by the favourite. He can be given another chance.
T/Jkpt: Not won. T/Plt: £49.30 to a £1 stake. Pool: £50,933.40. 752.75 winning tickets. T/Qpdt: £12.60 to a £1 stake. Pool: £2,935.70. 171.35 winning tickets. ST

# 1543 LINGFIELD (L-H)

Tuesday, April 27

**OFFICIAL GOING: Standard**
Wind: almost nil Weather: sunny becoming hazy

## 1690 BET DIRECT NO Q DEMO 08000 837 888 BANDED STKS — 1m 4f (P)

5:25 (5:25) (H) 4-Y-O+ — **£1,274** (£364; £182) **Stalls** Low

Form RPR

0332 **1** **Seraph**[11] 1448 4-8-9 40 (p) DHolland 5 44
(JohnAHarris) *mde most at modest pce: pressed and rdn 3f out: hdd briefly over 2f out: narrow ld after: kpt on* **5/2**[1]

6012 **2** *shd* **Leophin Dancer (USA)**[6] 1543 6-8-10 40 BDoyle 3 44
(PWHiatt) *t.k.h: hld up bhd ldrs: effrt on inner to dispute ld 3f out: ev ch after: nt qckn nr fin* **11/4**[2]

0301 **3** *nk* **Ersaal (USA)**[8] 1514 4-9-1 40 (t) NCallan 2 49
(JJay) *hld up bhd ldrs: effrt over 3f out: led briefly over 2f out: rdn and ev ch after: nt qckn wl ins fnl f* **5/1**[3]

000- **4** *11* **Wayward Melody**[20] 2292 4-8-9 40 (be[1]) RLMoore 4 26
(GLMoore) *w wnr: rdn over 4f out: wknd over 3f out* **5/2**[1]

0-00 **5** *16* **Sweet Reflection (IRE)**[21] 1277 4-8-6 40 LisaJones(3) 1 —
(WJMusson) *dwlt: plld hrd: hld up bhd ldrs: jnd wnr over 5f out to 3f out: hanging and wknd rapidly after* **14/1**

2m 38.19s (3.95) **Going Correction** +0.05s/f (Slow)
**WFA** 4 from 6yo 1lb **5** Ran SP% **107.1**
Speed ratings: **88,87,87,80,69**CSF £9.08 TOTE £2.80: £1.90, £1.10; EX 8.70.
**Owner** M F Schofield **Bred** T R Lock **Trained** Eastwell, Leics
■ Stewards Enquiry : N Callan caution: used whip with whip arm raised above shoulder height

**FOCUS**
A very ordinary race, but still competitive. The time was pedestrian, even for a banded stakes.

**NOTEBOOK**
**Seraph** had been in fair form in this sort of company on the Fibresand recently, but this was his first start on Polytrack. Despite handling it well enough to win, he may just be better on the former surface as he could never quite muster the pace to get away from his rivals. He also shaped as though he will be suited by a step up in trip. He could, however, be out under a penalty back round here.
**Leophin Dancer(USA)**, off the mark on the Flat in an awful race over this course and distance two starts previously, continues to acquit himself well. However, despite his consistency, he is probably one to oppose in future as there is usually something better than him, even at this level.
**Ersaal(USA)**, off the mark in a similarly weak event over this trip at Wolverhampton on his previous outing, travelled as well as anything but proved unable to quicken. For that reason he may be slightly better suited by Fibresand.
**Wayward Melody**, twice a winner over hurdles since last seen on the Flat, including in a seller on her previous outing, was supported in the market but proved disappointing. The fitting of an eye-shield and blinkers may not have suited, but her overall record on the Flat suggests she is not one to have too much confidence in.
**Sweet Reflection(IRE)** had the tongue-tie left off this time. She was too keen and was also noted to be hanging. *Official explanation: jockey said filly hung badly right*

## 1691 BET DIRECT NO Q ON 08000 93 66 93 BANDED STKS — 1m 2f (P)

5:55 (5:55) (H) 3-Y-O+ — **£1,620** (£463; £231) **Stalls** Low

Form RPR

0-21 **1** **Kings Topic (USA)**[6] 1545 4-9-10 45 LPKeniry(3) 5 55
(PBurgoyne) *cl up: trckd ldr over 3f out: drvn over 1f out: kpt on to ld last 50y* **3/1**[2]

1631 **2** *nk* **Montosari**[8] 1492 5-9-13 45 DHolland 2 54
(PMitchell) *led at mod pce: kicked on over 3f out: drvn over 1f out: worn down last 50y* **4/5**[1]

0-51 **3** *2* **Husky (POL)**[12] 1404 6-9-7 45 (p) BDoyle 4 44
(RMHCowell) *t.k.h: trckd ldr to over 3f out: sn outpcd: kpt on and ch over 1f out: fnd nil* **4/1**[3]

-000 **4** *13* **Roy McAvoy (IRE)**[27] [1207] 6-9-7 45 ........ GBaker 1 21
(MrsGHarvey) *s.s and lost 6l: sn in tch: wknd 3f out* **11/1**

0300 **5** *5* **Platinum Boy (IRE)**[21] [1277] 4-9-7 35 ........ (p) VSlattery 3 12
(MWellings) *trckd ldrs tl wknd u.p over 3f out* **33/1**

2m 8.26s (0.41) **Going Correction** +0.05s/f (Slow) **5** Ran SP% **111.8**
Speed ratings: **100,99,98,87,83**CSF £5.96 TOTE £3.30: £3.00, £1.02; EX 8.20.
**Owner** Topics Tarts **Bred** Marvin Delfiner And Fred Seitz **Trained** Collingbourne Ducis, Wilts

**FOCUS**
Probably not that bad a race in the context of this lowly grade. The first two will both be out of banded class after this.

**NOTEBOOK**
**Kings Topic(USA)** has been in great form since returning from a lay-off and switching stables, and was able to follow up his recent and distance success. He had to work pretty hard, but this was a good performance to beat the in-from Montosari and, lightly raced, he should be capable of further improvement. Connections will wait to see how he is reassessed before deciding his next target.
**Montosari**, under a 6lb penalty for his recent ten-length success round here over a mile and a half, would not have been suited by this drop in trip and may have been better off setting a stronger pace. This was still not a bad effort and he will be of interest in this grade back over further.
**Husky(POL)** was 7lb better off with the winner than when beating that one a short-head on his previous outing, but he had a fitness edge that day and was unable to confirm placings.
**Roy McAvoy(IRE)** has well and truly lost his way.

## 1692 BET DIRECT NO Q BANDED STKS 7f (P)
6:25 (6:25) (H) 4-Y-0+ **£1,435** (£410; £205) **Stalls** Low

Form RPR

1121 **1** **Baytown Flyer**[4] [1591] 4-9-4 40 ........ TGMcLaughlin 2 58
(PSMcentee) *mde virtually all: drew 2l clr over 1f out: hung rt and drvn fnl f: jst hld on* **7/2**[2]

0420 **2** *hd* **Cargo**[62] [884] 5-8-9 45 ........ (tp) RMiles(3) 7 51
(BAPearce) *rrd sharply s: sn trckd ldrs: rdn over 2f out: chsd wnr fnl f: kpt on: jst failed* **4/1**[3]

4502 **3** *½* **Single Track Mind**[21] [1278] 6-8-12 45 ........ DHolland 1 50
(JRBoyle) *hld up towards rr: rdn over 2f out: styd on fnl f: nrst fin* **5/2**[1]

000- **4** *½* **A One (IRE)**[160] [6027] 5-8-12 45 ........ MFenton 6 49
(BPalling) *w wnr tl rn wd bnd wl over 1f out: sn rdn and nt qckn: one pce after* **10/1**

0405 **5** *1* **Indian Warrior**[11] [1445] 8-8-12 45 ........ NCallan 8 46
(JJay) *in tch: drvn on wd outside and effrt over 2f out: nt qckn wl over 1f out* **8/1**

3105 **6** *3* **Gentle Response**[8] [1497] 4-8-12 45 ........ (b) NPollard 4 38
(BRJohnson) *trckd ldrs: rdn and fnd nil 2f out: brief effrt over 1f out: sn wknd* **5/1**

000/ **7** *2 ½* **O'So Neet**[686] [2038] 6-8-9 30 ........ LPKeniry(3) 5 32
(PBurgoyne) *sn outpcd in last: drvn 4f out: no prog* **66/1**

4040 **8** *8* **Janes Valentine**[29] [1165] 4-8-12 40 ........ JTate 3 11
(JJBridger) *dwlt: sn in tch: wknd over 2f out* **25/1**

1m 26.96s (1.02) **Going Correction** +0.05s/f (Slow) **8** Ran SP% **113.0**
Speed ratings: **96,95,95,94,93 90,87,78**CSF £17.47 TOTE £3.00: £1.10, £2.20, £1.50; EX 14.10.
**Owner** J Doxey **Bred** B Minty **Trained** Newmarket, Suffolk

**FOCUS**
A pretty ordinary banded stakes, but another win for Baytown Flyer, who is likely to have to race at a higher level in future.

**NOTEBOOK**
**Baytown Flyer** made it five wins in the last 12 days with a narrow victory. The bare form may not be worth a great deal and she was not that impressive, but whilst in this sort of form will be hard to beat when making a quick reappearance back here over a furlong shorter.
**Cargo** was a disappointing favourite in a seller on his previous outing, but this was better with cheekpieces replacing blinkers and stepped up a furlong in trip. He reared at the start, but it did not affect the result.
**Single Track Mind**, dropped a furlong in trip, was again doing his best work at the finish. He has only ever won one race and that was back in November 2000.
**A One(IRE)**, well beaten on Fibresand in a seller on his previous run, shaped better this time but did not help his chance by running wide into the straight.
**Indian Warrior** was up in trip and had the blinkers left off, but he was well held.
**Janes Valentine** *Official explanation: jockey said filly had lost her action*

## 1693 AVOID THE QUEUES WITH BET DIRECT NO Q BANDED STKS 2m (P)
6:55 (6:55) (H) 4-Y-0+ **£1,463** (£418; £209) **Stalls** Low

Form RPR

4-05 **1** **Fletcher**[2] [1644] 10-9-2 45 ........ RLMoore 8 45+
(HMorrison) *trckd ldr: led over 2f out and kicked on: idled fnl f: jst hld on* **6/1**[3]

064- **2** *shd* **Prince Of The Wood (IRE)**[129] [5972] 4-8-12 45 ........ MFenton 5 45
(ABailey) *cl up: rdn over 3f out: chsd wnr over 2f out: kpt on wl fnl f: jst failed* **9/1**

-034 **3** *2 ½* **Anniversary Guest (IRE)**[4] [1593] 5-8-9 40 ........ (p) DerekNolan(7) 2 42
(MrsLucindaFeatherstone) *plld hrd: hld up: prog over 3f out: chsd ldng pair 2f out: cl up 1f out: nt qckn after* **12/1**

10-0 **4** *7* **Waverley Road**[20] [962] 7-9-2 45 ........ DHolland 9 34
(MMadgwick) *trckd ldrs: drvn over 4f out: outpcd wl over 2f out: no ch after* **6/4**[1]

4023 **5** *3 ½* **Little Richard (IRE)**[21] [1281] 5-9-2 40 ........ (p) VSlattery 1 29
(MWellings) *cl up: rdn over 3f out: sn outpcd and btn* **9/2**[2]

3415 **6** *1 ¾* **Mysterium**[8] [1512] 10-8-9 45 ........ (v) StevenHarrison(7) 6 27
(NPLittmoden) *settled towards rr: rdn over 3f out: fnd nil and btn after* **11/1**

60-0 **7** *nk* **Annakita**[21] [1282] 4-8-9 45 ........ LisaJones(3) 3 27
(WJMusson) *hld up in last: hmpd wl over 3f out: no ch after* **10/1**

0-00 **8** *2* **Dash For Glory**[11] [1448] 5-9-2 30 ........ NCallan 7 25
(MBlanshard) *led at sedate pce: kicked on over 4f out: hdd & wknd over 2f out* **33/1**

-465 **U** **Cadwallader (USA)**[8] [1492] 4-8-5 45 ........ RJKilloran(7) 4 —
(PBurgoyne) *hld up in last pair: in tch whn stmbld and uns rdr wl over 3f out* **33/1**

3m 31.62s (3.04) **Going Correction** +0.05s/f (Slow)
**WFA** 4 from 5yo+ 4lb **9** Ran SP% **113.5**
Speed ratings: **94,93,92,89,87 86,86,85,—**CSF £57.43 TOTE £5.90: £1.60, £2.60, £3.60; EX 71.60.
**Owner** Lady Margadale **Bred** Carroll Bloodstock Ltd **Trained** East Ilsley, Berks

**FOCUS**
A weak race with a couple not running to form and the pace was pretty ordinary.

**NOTEBOOK**
**Fletcher**, without a win since July 2002, or over this trip, was dropped into banded company for the first time. He had everything go his way and could struggle to follow up, but connections have put plans to retire him on hold.
**Prince Of The Wood(IRE)**, back on the Flat, appreciated the drop into banded company and did enough to suggest he can win a similar race.
**Anniversary Guest(IRE)** was very keen in the first-time cheekpieces but still held very chance in the straight. She will need to learn to settle better.
**Waverley Road**, a winner on his last start over this course and distance, was returned to the Flat after some unsuccessful spins over hurdles, but disappointed. *Official explanation: jockey said gelding hung left*
**Little Richard(IRE)** should have been suited by this step up in trip but did not run his race. A stronger pace may have suited.

## 1694 BET IN RUNNING @ BETDIRECT.CO.UK BANDED STKS 6f (P)
7:25 (7:25) (H) 3-Y-0+ **£1,253** (£358; £179) **Stalls** Low

Form RPR

6042 **1** **Grand View**[4] [1591] 8-9-0 30 ........ (p) DHolland 4 43
(JRWeymes) *outpcd and rdn wl over 3f out: clsd u.p 2f out: drvn over 1f out: led last 100y: kpt on* **1/1**[1]

2352 **2** *¾* **Tiny Tim (IRE)**[6] [1548] 6-8-7 35 ........ RJKilloran(7) 5 41
(AMBalding) *trckd ldng pair: smooth prog to ld wl over 1f out: shkn up ent fnl f: hdd and nt qckn last 100y* **11/4**[2]

0-55 **3** *1 ¾* **Second Generation (IRE)**[6] [1546] 7-9-0 30 ........ RLMoore 6 36
(RJHodges) *outpcd and pushed along wl over 3f out: clsd 2f out: drvn and effrt on outer over 1f out: nt qckn fnl f* **7/1**

/634 **4** *4* **Mahlstick (IRE)**[6] [1544] 6-9-0 35 ........ (t) BDoyle 1 24
(DWPArbuthnot) *led for 1f: chsd ldr: rdn and ev ch 2f out: sn wknd* **11/2**[3]

-040 **5** *shd* **Almara**[72] [780] 4-9-0 30 ........ (t) SCarson 3 23
(MissKBBoutflower) *outpcd in last 4f out: n.d fr over 2f out: kpt on fnl f* **20/1**

/0-0 **6** *8* **Tong Ice**[12] [1407] 5-9-0 30 ........ (b) RBrisland 2 —
(BAPearce) *drvn to ld after 1f and set str pce: hdd & wknd rapidly wl over 1f out* **25/1**

1m 13.58s (0.66) **Going Correction** +0.05s/f (Slow) **6** Ran SP% **113.2**
Speed ratings: **97,96,93,88,88 77**CSF £4.02 TOTE £2.20: £1.10, £1.80; EX 2.70.
**Owner** Sporting Occasions **Bred** The Wickfield Stud Ltd **Trained** Middleham Moor, N Yorks

**FOCUS**
Not a very strong race and the leaders set it up for those in behind by going too fast early on.

**NOTEBOOK**
**Grand View** proved unable to go the strong early pace (they went too fast) but he picked up and did what was required. One would not be in a rush to back him to follow up off the back of this performance, but there is every chance connections will find a race just as weak next time.
**Tiny Tim(IRE)**, down two furlongs in trip, had no problems going the pace but proved no match for the winner. He is without a win in 29 starts and one can afford to miss his maiden success.
**Second Generation(IRE)** needed this step up from five furlongs and may even get seven, as he again struggled to go the early gallop.
**Mahlstick(IRE)** appeared keen to get to the front but was unable to do so and found little when asked.
**Almara** had the cheekpieces left off and never threatened.
**Tong Ice** went five-furlong pace.

## 1695 BETDIRECT.CO.UK TRI-BANDED STKS 1m (P)
7:55 (7:55) (H) 3-Y-0 **£1,610** (£460; £230) **Stalls** High

Form RPR

3231 **1** **Dial Square**[8] [1495] 3-9-6 45 6ex ........ MHills 2 61+
(PHowling) *dwlt: hld up in last: prog on wd outside 2f out: pushed into ld last 150y: sn clr* **4/7**[1]

0-50 **2** *2 ½* **Joint Destiny (IRE)**[59] [918] 3-9-0 45 ........ DHolland 4 49
(EJO'Neill) *trckd ldng pair: effrt to chse ldr wl over 1f out: drvn to ld ent fnl f: sn hdd and outpcd* **7/2**[2]

0054 **3** *1 ½* **Stagecoach Ruby**[8] [1495] 3-8-9 40 ........ RLMoore 3 41
(GLMoore) *mde most: rdn 2f out: hdd & wknd ent fnl f* **8/1**[3]

0005 **4** *5* **Fresh Connection**[15] [1375] 3-8-4 35 ........ AMcCarthy 1 24
(GGMargarson) *chsd ldrs: rdn over 3f out: sn outpcd and btn* **16/1**

005- **5** *1* **David's Girl**[127] [6228] 3-8-4 35 ........ SCarson 5 22
(DMorris) *w ldr to 2f out: wknd rapidly* **14/1**

1m 39.83s (0.28) **Going Correction** +0.05s/f (Slow) **5** Ran SP% **109.5**
Speed ratings: **100,97,96,91,90**CSF £2.80 TOTE £1.20: £1.10, £2.30; EX 3.50 Place 6 £7.97, Place 5 £4.52..
**Owner** Rory Murphy **Bred** J And Mrs Bowtell **Trained** Newmarket, Suffolk

**FOCUS**
Not a very good contest but a decent time for a race of its type and a well above standard effort form winner.

**NOTEBOOK**
**Dial Square** followed up his recent course and distance victory with another straightforward success. Waiting tactics appear to suit, and he will be very hard to beat if bidding for a quick follow-up.
**Joint Destiny(IRE)** was suited by this step up in trip and had every chance.
**Stagecoach Ruby** is not doing anything wrong, she just keeps finding a couple too good.
**Fresh Connection** did not improve for the drop in trip, removal of cheekpieces or switch to Polytrack.
T/Plt: £24.10 to a £1 stake. Pool: £24,417.45. 739.45 winning tickets. T/Qpdt: £14.90 to a £1 stake. Pool: £2,045.40. 101.20 winning tickets. JN

# 1529 SOUTHWELL (L-H)
Tuesday, April 27

**OFFICIAL GOING: Standard to fast**

## 1696 LITTLEWOODS BET DIRECT APPRENTICE BANDED STKS 6f (F)
5:40 (5:41) (H) 3-Y-0+ **£1,435** (£410; £205) **Stalls** Low

Form RPR

2463 **1** **Larky's Lob**[57] [941] 5-9-2 45 ........ JDO'Reilly(5) 2 59
(JO'Reilly) *mde virtually all: rdn wl over 1f out: styd on wl fnl f* **3/1**[1]

4502 **2** *5* **Cleveland Way**[11] [1445] 4-9-4 45 ........ (v) DTudhope(3) 6 44
(DCarroll) *cl up: rdn 2f out and ev ch tl drvn and one pce ent fnl f* **7/2**[2]

0002 **3** *1 ¼* **Valazar (USA)**[11] [1443] 5-9-7 45 ........ PMakin 4 40
(DWChapman) *trckd ldng pair: smootyh hdwy to chal 2f out and ev ch tl rdn and wknd appr last* **7/2**[2]

6154 **4** *5* **Indian Music**[11] [1445] 7-7-9 45 ........ PPMathers 3 25
(ABerry) *sn outpcd and wl bhd: hdwy wl over 1f out: styd on ins last: nvr a factor* **6/1**[3]

0024 **5** *¾* **Mr Uppity**[8] [1515] 5-9-2 40 ........ (e) MHalford(5) 1 23
(JulianPoulton) *in tch: rdn along and outpcd 1/2-way: sn bhd* **8/1**

00-3 **6** *6* **Compton Princess**[21] [1283] 4-9-7 40 ........ SJDonohoe 5 5
(MrsADuffield) *in tch: rdn along 1/2-way: sn wknd* **6/1**[3]

1m 14.32s (-2.58) **Going Correction** -0.375s/f (Stan) **6** Ran SP% **109.1**
Speed ratings: **102,95,93,87,86 78**CSF £12.86 TOTE £2.80: £2.00, £1.50; EX 15.10.

**Owner** J O R Racing **Bred** P Balding **Trained** Brierley, S Yorks

**FOCUS**

A weak event that produced a good time for the grade, and the winner is approaching best for new yard.

**NOTEBOOK**

**Larky's Lob** won well under a positive ride on his debut for new connections. This was his first success since beating the runner-up in January at this venue and confirmed the form readily over this shorter trip. Banded stakes are about his level nowadays, but he is a fair yardstick and his confidence will be high after this effort.

**Cleveland Way** could not quicken with the winner late on, but ran up to form and has found some consistency of late over this course-and-distance. He may be worth a try back at Wolverhampton in this grade.

**Valazar(USA)** looked a threat entering the straight, but hung and found little under pressure approaching the final furlong. He is in good heart at present, and may be able to score when dropped back to the minimum trip.

**Indian Music**, well behind Cleveland Way over course-and-distance last time, again struggled to go the early pace and was staying on all to late in the day. He looks a tricky ride.

## 1697 BETDIRECT.CO.UK BANDED STKS — 1m (F)

**6:10** (6:10) (H) 3-Y-0+ — **£1,442** (£412; £206) **Stalls** Low

| Form | | | | RPR |
|---|---|---|---|---|
| 0-03 | 1 | | **Amethyst Rock**[8] 1511 6-9-4 35 ........ FLynch 7<br>(PLGilligan) *cl up: led after 3f: rdn out: drvn and edgd lft 1f out: hdd ins last: rallied gamely to ld on line* **4/1**[1] | 44 |
| 0664 | 2 | *shd* | **Dalriath**[51] 952 5-8-11 35 ........ AndrewWebb(7) 4<br>(MCChapman) *dwlt and hld up: smooth hdwy on inner over 3f out: chal over 1f out: rdn to ld ins last: drvn and hdd on line* **11/2**[2] | 44 |
| 4660 | 3 | 8 | **Mathmagician**[7] 1535 5-9-4 35 ........(b) DeanMcKeown 6<br>(RFMarvin) *towards rr and sn pushed along: hdwy 3f out: rdn 2f out and kpt on same pce* **13/2** | 28 |
| 00-0 | 4 | *nk* | **Sarn**[36] 1080 5-8-11 35 ........ PVarley(7) 8<br>(MMullineaux) *chsd ldrs: rdn along 3f out: drvn and kpt o n same pce fnl 2f* **11/1** | 27 |
| 0051 | 5 | 6 | **Un Autre Espere**[4] 1583 5-9-3 30 ........(b) BSwarbrick(7) 1<br>(TWall) *chsd ldrs: rdn along 3f out: sn drvn and one pce* **6/1**[3] | 21 |
| 40-5 | 6 | *shd* | **Cezzaro (IRE)**[11] 1444 6-9-4 35 ........ JBramhill 2<br>(SRBowring) *led 3f: cl up tl rdn along over 2f out and sn wknd* **6/1**[3] | 15 |
| 40-0 | 7 | 2 | **Miss Ocean Monarch**[35] 1094 4-9-4 30 ........ ACulhane 3<br>(DWChapman) *chsd ldrs: rdn along 1/2-way: wknd wl over 2f out* **12/1** | 11 |
| 0050 | 8 | ½ | **Morris Dancing (USA)**[10] 995 5-9-4 30 ........(p) JoannaBadger 10<br>(BPJBaugh) *in tch on outer: rdn aolong over 3f out and sn wknd* **14/1** | 10 |
| 0-00 | 9 | ½ | **Mister Rushby**[11] 1448 4-9-4 30 ........ RFitzpatrick 5<br>(MissVHaigh) *in tch: rdn along over 3f out and sn wknd* **33/1** | 9 |
| 2300 | 10 | 3½ | **Spiders Web**[8] 1493 4-9-4 35 ........(b) PDoe 9<br>(TKeddy) *in tch: rdn along and outpcd 1/2-way: wd st and sn bhd* **11/1** | 2 |

1m 42.92s (-1.68) **Going Correction** -0.375s/f (Stan) **10 Ran SP% 111.3**

Speed ratings: **93,92,84,84,78 78,76,76,75,72**CSF £24.05 TOTE £4.80: £2.30, £2.00, £2.10; EX 43.40.

**Owner** John Peters **Bred** J A Peters **Trained** Newmarket, Suffolk

**FOCUS**

A dire contest that saw a cracking finish and the first two pull well clear in the straight.

**NOTEBOOK**

**Amethyst Rock** rallied under pressure to get back up on the line and win his first-ever race. He has shown improvement since dropping in trip and may have more to offer in this grade.

**Dalriath** ◆ looked booked for success when hitting the front late on, but idled a touch and just failed. This was a fair effort and she was well clear of the rest, so should go close in this grade next time.

**Mathmagician** improved a touch for this drop in trip and return to the surface, but is well exposed and finds it hard to win at any trip.

**Sarn**

**Cezzaro(IRE)** dropped out alarmingly in the straight and has a lot to prove now.

**Miss Ocean Monarch** *Official explanation: jockey said filly was struck into behind*

## 1698 SPECIAL OFFERS @ BETDIRECT.CO.UK BANDED STKS — 1m 6f (F)

**6:40** (6:40) (H) 4-Y-0+ — **£1,442** (£412; £206) **Stalls** Low

| Form | | | | RPR |
|---|---|---|---|---|
| 46-0 | 1 | | **Sunnyside Royale (IRE)**[10] 1463 5-9-0 45 ........(t) RFfrench 4<br>(RBastiman) *cl up: led 1/2-way: rdn over 2f out: styd on strly* **7/1** | 52 |
| 2162 | 2 | 4 | **Doctor John**[8] 1512 7-9-0 45 ........ CCatlin 1<br>(AndrewTurnell) *in tch: pushed along after 5f: hdwy 5f out: rdn to chse wnr over 2f out: sn drvn and no imp* **1/1**[1] | 47 |
| 00-0 | 3 | 4 | **Iloveturtle (IRE)**[30] 1103 4-8-12 40 ........ GDuffield 2<br>(MCChapman) *in tch: smooth hdwy over 5f out: chsd wnr over 3f out: rdn and one pce fnl 2f* **14/1** | 42 |
| 0623 | 4 | 3 | **Berkeley Heights**[8] 1512 4-8-7 45 ........ NChalmers(5) 6<br>(MrsJCandlish) *chsd ldrs: rdn along and outpcd 5f out: drvn and plugged on fnl 2f* **9/2**[2] | 38 |
| 0/00 | 5 | 2½ | **Broughtons Flush**[25] 1238 6-9-0 45 ........ FLynch 3<br>(WJMusson) *hld up in rr: hdwy 4f out: rdn over 2f out and no futher prog* **13/2**[3] | 34 |
| 5400 | 6 | 18 | **King Priam (IRE)**[11] 1448 9-9-0 30 ........(b) RFitzpatrick 7<br>(MJPolglase) *led: rdn along and hdd 1/2-way: sn wknd* **20/1** | 11 |
| -434 | 7 | 5 | **El Pedro**[12] 1404 5-8-9 45 ........ MSavage(5) 5<br>(NEBerry) *keen: chsd ldrs: rdn along over 4f out: sn wknd* **9/1** | 5 |

3m 7.89s (-1.81) **Going Correction** -0.375s/f (Stan)

**WFA** 4 from 5yo+ 2lb **7 Ran SP% 115.4**

Speed ratings: **90,87,85,83,82 72,69**CSF £14.79 TOTE £8.00: £3.70, £1.10; EX 27.90.

**Owner** S Durkin, P Earnshaw & J Greenan **Bred** Tim Corby **Trained** Cowthorpe, N Yorks

**FOCUS**

A slow winning time to this poor staying event.

**NOTEBOOK**

**Sunnyside Royale(IRE)**, a winner over hurdles in February, stayed on stoutly having made his challenge in the straight to score a first win on the level. This was a big improvement on his recent form and, as it was his All-Weather debut, he may have more to offer still.

**Doctor John** was undone by the lack of early pace over this shorter than ideal distance. He kept on late in the day and can do better when upped in trip once again.

**Iloveturtle(IRE)** quickly found his stamina deserting him having made an effort four out. He will be seen to better effect when reverting to shorter.

**Berkeley Heights** was another to find the drop in trip against him.

## 1699 BET IN RUNNING @ BETDIRECT.CO.UK BANDED STKS — 5f (F)

**7:10** (7:10) (H) 3-Y-0+ — **£1,442** (£412; £206) **Stalls** High

| Form | | | | RPR |
|---|---|---|---|---|
| 0031 | 1 | | **Maromito (IRE)**[6] 1546 7-9-12 40 ........ HBastiman 1<br>(RBastiman) *led: hdd briefly 1/2-way: sn led again: rdn wl over 1f out: drvn wl ins last: jst hld on* **8/11**[1] | 54 |
| 0000 | 2 | *shd* | **Finger Of Fate**[44] 1018 4-9-6 40 ........(b) RFitzpatrick 2<br>(MJPolglase) *cl up: led briefly 1/2-way: rdn wl over 1f out: drvn and ev ch ins last: jst hld* **10/1** | 48 |
| 5502 | 3 | 3½ | **Levelled**[5] 1568 10-9-6 35 ........ ACulhane 10<br>(DWChapman) *dwlt: hdwy 1/2-way: rdn and styd on appr last: nrst fin* **11/1** | 36 |
| 0416 | 4 | 1½ | **Miss Wizz**[29] 1171 4-8-13 40 ........(p) DTudhope(7) 3<br>(WStorey) *in tch centre: hdwy 2f out: sn rdn and kpt on same pce* **9/1**[3] | 31 |
| 2251 | 5 | ½ | **Tuscan Dream**[5] 1568 9-9-7 40 ........ PBradley(5) 7<br>(ABerry) *chsd ldrs: rdn along 2f out: one pce appr last* **8/1**[2] | 35 |
| -005 | 6 | 1¾ | **Dancing Ridge (IRE)**[5] 1568 7-9-6 30 ........(v) GDuffield 9<br>(ASenior) *chsd ldrs: rdn along 2f out: grad wknd* **28/1** | 23 |
| 0040 | 7 | 1¼ | **Danakim**[11] 1443 7-8-13 40 ........ DFentiman(7) 8<br>(JRWeymes) *chsd ldrs: rdn along 2f out: sn wknd* **16/1** | 18 |
| 0010 | 8 | 2½ | **Caronte (IRE)**[11] 1445 4-9-6 40 ........(b) JBramhill 6<br>(SRBowring) *s.i.s: a rr* **16/1** | 10 |
| 0-00 | 9 | 1½ | **Wilheheckaslike**[29] 1171 3-8-7 40 ........(v) DAllan(3) 5<br>(WStorey) *cl up 2f: sn rdn along and wknd* **66/1** | 4 |
| 0-60 | 10 | *shd* | **Wub Cub**[35] 1092 4-9-3 35 ........ ABeech(3) 4<br>(ADickman) *dwlt: a rr* **66/1** | 4 |

59.29 secs (-1.11) **Going Correction** -0.275s/f (Stan)

**WFA** 3 from 4yo+ 10lb **10 Ran SP% 114.6**

Speed ratings: **97,96,91,88,88 85,83,79,76,76**CSF £8.58 TOTE £1.60: £1.10, £3.00, £2.80; EX 15.90.

**Owner** Mrs P Bastiman **Bred** Joseph Finnegan **Trained** Cowthorpe, N Yorks

■ Stewards Enquiry : R Fitzpatrick one-day ban: used whip with excessive frequency (May 8)

**FOCUS**

An weak sprint which produced a decent finish and was dominated from start to finish by the first two home. There should be better to come from the winner.

**NOTEBOOK**

**Maromito(IRE)** ◆ followed-up his win at Lingfield by the narrowest of margins. He was quickly away and looked to be booked for a comfortable success entering the final two furlongs, but idled when in the lead and had to work very hard to hold on at the death. His connections feel he is better suited by the Polytrack and he will be hard to beat in this grade if reverting to that surface over this trip when bidding for the hat-trick.

**Finger Of Fate** went with the winner for most of the contest and was only just denied. The drop into this grade helped bring about improvement on his recent efforts and, while connections have been struggling to find his best trip, he was clear of the rest and could go one better in a similar event.

**Levelled** lost his chance with a slow start, but kept on well enough late in the day and reversed recent Wolverhampton form with Tuscan Dream on this occasion.

**Miss Wizz** was unable to get serious at any stage on this drop to the minimum trip and will be much better suited by a return to six furlongs.

## 1700 BET DIRECT ON 0800 32 93 93 BANDED STKS — 1m 3f (F)

**7:40** (7:40) (H) 4-Y-0+ — **£1,456** (£416; £208) **Stalls** Low

| Form | | | | RPR |
|---|---|---|---|---|
| 5-04 | 1 | | **Rhetoric (IRE)**[8] 1514 5-8-8 35 ow1 ........ DNolan(5) 1<br>(DGBridgwater) *mde all: rdn along 3f out: drvn and styd on wl appr last* **4/1**[3] | 42 |
| 0600 | 2 | 2½ | **Moyne Pleasure (IRE)**[29] 1173 6-8-5 30 ........(p) DFentiman(7) 3<br>(PaulJohnson) *s.i.s: in rr tl hdwy over 3f out: rdn wl over 1f out: drvn and styd on ins last: nrst fin* **3/1**[1] | 37 |
| /501 | 3 | *hd* | **Buying A Dream (IRE)**[6] 1543 7-9-4 35 ........ CCatlin 2<br>(AndrewTurnell) *in tch: hdwy to chse wnr over 2f out: sn rdn and one pce appr last* **7/2**[2] | 43 |
| 00/5 | 4 | ¾ | **Zelea (IRE)**[11] 1448 5-8-5 35 ........(t) BSwarbrick(7) 5<br>(JParkes) *trckd ldrs: effrt 4f out: rdn along and outpcd over 2f out: drvn and plugged on appr last* **9/2** | 36 |
| 50-0 | 5 | 1¼ | **Paradise Garden (USA)**[7] 1535 7-8-12 35 ........ ACulhane 4<br>(PLClinton) *chsd ldrs: rdn along 3f out: wknd fnl 2f* **5/1** | 34 |
| 0-00 | 6 | 11 | **Elle Royal (IRE)**[21] 1281 5-8-12 35 ........(b[1]) GDuffield 6<br>(TPMcgovern) *chsd wnr: rdn along 4f out: edgd lft and wknd over 2f out* **16/1** | 17 |

2m 28.14s (-0.76) **Going Correction** -0.375s/f (Stan) **6 Ran SP% 108.0**

Speed ratings: **87,85,85,84,83 75**CSF £15.01 TOTE £4.60: £1.80, £1.70; EX 13.10.

**Owner** Alan A Wright **Bred** Marston Stud And Grange Nominees **Trained** Winchcombe, Gloucs

**FOCUS**

A pedestrian winning time, even for such a poor race.

**NOTEBOOK**

**Rhetoric(IRE)** made every yard a winning one to score his first-ever win on the level. He has struggled over farther recently and this trip suited, but he is no good thing to follow-up.

**Moyne Pleasure(IRE)** was given a fair bit to do on this occasion having missed the kick. He was staying on all too late in the day.

**Buying A Dream(IRE)** never looked like following-up his Lingfield win on this switch back to the Fibresand. He has run badly on all his attempts on this surface and looks a much better horse on the Polytrack.

**Zelea(IRE)** ran as though this outing would again bring her on, but it will be a dire contest this maiden wins.

## 1701 BET DIRECT ON SKY ACTIVE TRI-BANDED STKS — 7f (F)

**8:10** (8:10) (H) 3-Y-0 — **£1,435** (£410; £205) **Stalls** Low

| Form | | | | RPR |
|---|---|---|---|---|
| 06-0 | 1 | | **Saros (IRE)**[15] 1363 3-9-0 45 ........ FLynch 4<br>(BSmart) *cl up: led 3f out: rdn clr wl over 1f out: styd on strly* **9/2**[2] | 59 |
| 0-31 | 2 | 9 | **Roman The Park (IRE)**[11] 1447 3-9-0 45 ........ GDuffield 1<br>(TDEasterby) *trckd ldrs: hdwy to chse wnr 2f out: sn rdn and no imp* **5/4**[1] | 37 |
| 6505 | 3 | 5 | **Platinum Chief**[5] 1570 3-9-0 45 ........(b) ACulhane 2<br>(ABerry) *bmpd s and sn pushed along in rr: swtchd rt and hdwy over 2f out: sn rdn and plugged on same pce* **11/2**[3] | 24 |
| 0-00 | 4 | *nk* | **Royal Nite Owl**[17] 1325 3-8-7 45 ........ JDO'Reilly(7) 3<br>(JO'Reilly) *led: rdn along and hdd 3f out: sn wknd* **9/1** | 23 |
| 5034 | 5 | 1½ | **Mystic Promise (IRE)**[5] 1573 3-7-13 35 ........(t) HayleyTurner(5) 6<br>(MrsNMacauley) *in tch on outer: rdn along 3f out: sn wknd* **9/2**[2] | 10 |
| 06-5 | 6 | *shd* | **Weaver Spell**[5] 1571 3-8-9 40 ........ VHalliday 5<br>(JRNorton) *chsd ldrs: rdn along over 3f out: sn wknd* **25/1** | 14 |

1m 28.32s (-2.48) **Going Correction** -0.375s/f (Stan) **6 Ran SP% 110.0**

Speed ratings: **99,88,83,82,80 80**CSF £10.17 TOTE £5.40: £3.50, £1.60; EX 10.70 Place 6 £8.20, Place 5 £4.71..

**Owner** Pinnacle Desert Sun Partnership **Bred** Patrick K Stephens **Trained** Hambleton, N Yorks

**FOCUS**

A smart winning time for the grade, a decent effort from the winner, and the field were well strung out at the finish.

**NOTEBOOK**

**Saros(IRE)** relished the drop in trip and grade to win most readily. He had an excuse for his latest effort on turf, and on this evidence should go in again at this level, but the Handicapper will no doubt ensure a hefty rise in the weights for this. *Official explanation: trainer's representative said, regarding the improved form shown, colt had grown in confidence and the race was run to suit*

**Roman The Park(IRE)**, the winner of a dire contest last time, could not get near the winner over this shorter trip. However, he was well clear of the rest and can make amends over an extra furlong in this grade.

**Platinum Chief**, with the blinkers back on, was done few favours at the start, but was still disappointing nonetheless. He is one to avoid and seemed to resent the blinkers on this occasion.

T/Plt: £13.20 to a £1 stake. Pool: £26,102.65. 1,443.25 winning tickets. T/Qpdt: £5.10 to a £1 stake. Pool: £1,717.00. 248.00 winning tickets. JR

# ASCOT (R-H)

## Wednesday, April 28

**OFFICIAL GOING: Soft (good to soft in places)**

Plenty of rain overnight, 17mm in fact, turned the going testing.

## 1702 SODEXHO H'CAP 6f

2:10 (2:10) (D) (0-80,80) 3-Y-O **£6,041** (£1,859; £929; £464) **Stalls** Low

Form RPR

50-5 **1** **Molcon (IRE)**[15] 1388 3-9-4 **77** JPMurtagh 11 85
(NACallaghan) *bhd: hdwy 2f out: stl plenty to do over 1f out: str run ins last to ld fnl 50 yds* **15/2**[2]

5010 **2** ½ **Ask The Clerk (IRE)**[15] 1388 3-8-12 **71** MTebbutt 3 78
(VSmith) *chsd ldrs: wnt 2nd over 1f out: str chal u.p to ld ins fnl f: ct fnl 50yds* **20/1**

0312 **3** *nk* **Muy Bien**[21] 1303 3-9-3 **76** (b) DHolland 5 82
(JRJenkins) *sn led: rdn fr 2f out: hdd ins last: kpt on u.p but no ex nr fin* **10/1**

310- **4** 3 **Flipando (IRE)**[207] 5371 3-9-3 **76** KFallon 9 73
(TDBarron) *mid-div: hdwy over 2f out: no imp tl styd on ins fnl f: nt rch ldrs* **9/1**

042- **5** 6 **Out After Dark**[174] 5930 3-9-3 **76** RSmith 20 55
(CGCox) *lw: s.i.s: bhd: hdwy over 1f out: styd on fnl f but nvr gng pce to rch ldrs* **8/1**[3]

2-14 **6** *hd* **Bohola Flyer (IRE)**[18] 1333 3-9-0 **73** DaneO'Neill 6 51
(RHannon) *w ldrs: wnt 2nd over 2f out: sn rdn: wknd appr fnl f* **8/1**[3]

053- **7** 5 **Epaminondas (USA)**[179] 5867 3-9-2 **75** EAhern 12 38
(RHannon) *bit bkwd: bhd: styd on fr over 1f out but nvr a danger* **20/1**

-231 **8** 2 **Finders Keepers**[17] 1342 3-9-7 **80** LDettori 4 37
(EALDunlop) *lw: hld up in rr: stdy hdwy fr 1/2-way but nvr rchd ldrs: wknd ins fnl 2f* **5/1**[1]

20-3 **9** 1¾ **Stormy Nature (IRE)**[18] 1333 3-9-3 **76** TQuinn 8 28
(PWHarris) *chsd ldrs tl wknd 2f out* **8/1**[3]

40-6 **10** 1¼ **Night Worker**[23] 1270 3-8-4 **63** RLMoore 2 11
(RHannon) *bhd: mod prog fr over 1f out* **20/1**

10-0 **11** *hd* **Motu (IRE)**[18] 1333 3-9-2 **75** KDarley 19 23
(JLDunlop) *bhd: sn pushed along and nvr in contention* **20/1**

366- **12** 5 **Red Sovereign**[182] 5829 3-9-3 **76** WSupple 7 9
(IAWood) *chsd ldrs 4f* **33/1**

10-0 **13** ½ **Alchera**[18] 1333 3-9-0 **73** (b) SCarson 14 4
(RFJohnsonHoughton) *w ldrs: rdn and ev ch over 2f out: sn wknd* **25/1**

-405 **14** 1¼ **Smokin Joe**[62] 891 3-8-9 **68** IMongan 15 —
(JRBest) *lw: broke wl: sn rdn and outpcd: no ch fr 1/2-way* **25/1**

0-00 **15** 1¼ **Dellagio (IRE)**[15] 1388 3-8-9 **75** HelenSmith(7) 13 —
(CADwyer) *a outpcd* **66/1**

0-30 **16** 23 **Torquemada (IRE)**[23] 1270 3-8-6 **65** PDoe 16 —
(WJarvis) *s.i.s: sn rcvrd to press ldrs tl wknd ins fnl 3f* **40/1**

0-50 **17** 2 **Haydn (USA)**[18] 1333 3-9-4 **77** JFEgan 17 —
(PWChapple-Hyam) *sn bhd* **16/1**

1m 21.73s (5.74) **Going Correction** +1.10s/f (Soft) **17 Ran SP% 120.4**

Speed ratings: **105,104,103,99,91 91,85,82,80,78 78,71,70,69,67 36,34**CSF £152.95 CT £1567.92 TOTE £10.00: £2.90, £9.60, £1.70, £2.60; EX 578.20.

**Owner** Mark Venus **Bred** Noel O'Callaghan **Trained** Newmarket, Suffolk

■ Stewards Enquiry : D Holland three-day ban: used whip with excessive frequency and down the shoulder in the forehand position (May 10-12)

M Tebbutt one-day ban: excessive use of the whip (May 10)

**FOCUS**

A fair time for the grade, but the form is not great for the track and should be treated with caution on account of the ground.

**NOTEBOOK**

**Molcon(IRE)** ran well in a decent Newmarket handicap on his return and had been dropped 1lb subsequently. He finished with a rare rattle and clearly had no problem with the testing conditions, despite having done his previous winning on a good to firm surface.

**Ask The Clerk(IRE)** finished a long way behind the winner at Newmarket last time, but he had a good draw and the ground was in his favour, being a son of Turtle Island. This effort will not do his handicap mark any good, though.

**Muy Bien** likes soft ground and was another well drawn near the stands'-side rail. He made a bold bid to make every yard and is clearly in great heart at present. This performance will force his mark up again though, and he will have to find further improvement to defy the Handicapper.

**Flipando(IRE)**, making his handicap debut on his reappearance, ran a race full of promise and, as he has already proved his effectiveness on fast ground, he looks sure to progress into an useful handicapper this season.

**Out After Dark**, a brother to the very useful sprinter Move It, who made such huge progress as a three-year-old, shaped with promise from a poor draw. If his brother's preference is anything to go by, then he should do a lot better on faster ground.

**Bohola Flyer(IRE)** found this stiff six furlongs in this ground too much for her, but she should not be written off back on a sharper track.

**Epaminondas(USA)**, who looked in need of the run beforehand, will want farther than this six furlongs in time.

**Finders Keepers**, who raced keenly and made all for his maiden success, was surprisingly held up towards the rear on this occasion. He travelled well but could not pick up in this ground. He is probably capable of better than this back on faster ground.

**Torquemada(IRE)** *Official explanation: jockey said colt had been struck into*

## 1703 BOVIS HOMES SAGARO STKS (GROUP 3) 2m 45y

2:40 (2:40) (A) 4-Y-O+ **£29,000** (£11,000; £5,500; £2,500) **Stalls** High

Form RPR

20-2 **1** **Risk Seeker**[30] 1182 4-8-12 DBoeuf 13 121
(ELellouche, France) *lengthy: scope: lw: hld up in rr: hdwy on bit fr 4f out: trckd ldr 2f out: shkn up: sn led and clr: impressive* **11/2**[2]

25-2 **2** *18* **Dusky Warbler**[28] 1212 5-8-13 107 DHolland 9 100
(MLWBell) *sn led:hdd after 3f:styd w ldr:led again 4f out:pushed along and hdd ins fnl 2f:sn no ch w wnr: kpt on for clr2nd* **16/1**

042- **3** *11* **Millenary**[193] 5637 7-9-4 117 TQuinn 5 94
(JLDunlop) *lw: hdwy 10f out: trckd ldrs 6f out: wnt 2nd travelling wl appr fnl 2f: sn rdn and wknd* **3/1**[1]

40-0 **4** *11* **Let Me Try Again (IRE)**[11] 1455 4-8-9 105 RMiles 4 78
(TGMills) *in tch: rdn to chse ldrs 7f out: stl wl there over 3f out: wknd qckly sn after* **20/1**

001/ **5** *17* **Royal Rebel**[678] 2280 8-8-13 JPMurtagh 3 61
(MJohnston) *bhd: rdn 6f out: sme hdwy 4f out: nvr nr ldrs and wknd over 2f out* **20/1**

130- **6** *dist* **Darasim (IRE)**[185] 5782 6-9-4 114 (v) JFanning 8 —
(MJohnston) *lw: chsd ldrs tl wknd 7f out: t.o* **14/1**

355- **7** *dist* **Savannah Bay**[193] 5637 5-8-13 111 LDettori 6 —
(BJMeehan) *bhd: rdn and effrt 7f out: n.d: sn wknd: t.o* **12/1**

200- **8** *3* **Maktub (ITY)**[136] 6185 5-9-2 PRobinson 1 —
(MAJarvis) *str: lw: trckd ldrs tl wknd qckly 5f out: t.o* **13/2**[3]

611- **9** *dist* **Misternando**[175] 5927 4-8-9 101 SHitchcott 12 —
(MRChannon) *sn pushed along in rr: nvr travelling wl: t.o fnl 5f* **16/1**

021- **10** *dist* **Supremacy**[213] 5254 5-8-13 104 KFallon 14 —
(SirMichaelStoute) *chsd ldrs: rdn 6f out: wknd 5f out: t.o* **11/1**

0-30 **P** **Hilbre Island**[11] 1455 4-8-9 110 (b[1]) SDrowne 11 —
(BJMeehan) *t.k.h: chsd ldrs 7f: t.o fnl 7f: p.u fnl f* **33/1**

2U0- **P** **Morozov (USA)**[248] 4430 5-8-13 IMongan 10 —
(CNAllen) *neat: trckd ldrs tl wknd fr 3f out: t.o and p.u fnl f* **20/1**

101- **P** **Persian Punch (IRE)**[193] 5637 11-9-4 118 MartinDwyer 7 —
(DRCElsworth) *led after 3f: hdd 4f out: sn rdn: wknd over 2f out: collapsed and died fnl f* **11/1**

3m 49.97s (15.13) **Going Correction** +1.10s/f (Soft)

**WFA** 4 from 5yo+ 4lb **13 Ran SP% 113.7**

Speed ratings: **106,97,91,86,77 —,—,—,—,— —,—,—**CSF £79.85 TOTE £6.10: £2.10, £5.10, £2.00; EX 62.80 Trifecta £624.70 Pool of £1,372.73 - 1.56 winning tickets.

**Owner** Ecurie Wildenstein **Bred** Dayton Investments Ltd **Trained** France

■ Stewards Enquiry : D Boeuf £250 fine: removed colt's ear plugs during race

**FOCUS**

Beaten distances more familiar to the jumps scene as a result of the testing going, make this Group Three an unreliable form guide to the future and although mightily impressive in galloping his rivals into submission, Risk Seeker was the only runner who relished conditions and so it would be foolish to take the result at face-value.

**NOTEBOOK**

**Risk Seeker**, just touched off in Listed company on his seasonal return back home, was the only runner who appeared to relish these sapping conditions. He travelled strongly in rear for most of the way before looming up to go on early in the straight, and powered away in emphatic style. Whilst an impressive performance, several of his main rivals ran below form in the conditions, so it would be unwise to get carried away with the bare form, although he is undoubtedly a top staying prospect.

**Dusky Warbler** was nibbled at in the market beforehand and ran a brave race in defeat, despite proving no match for the winner. He beat the remainder well enough and will reportedly go in search of Group success abroad, where he should have little trouble winning.

**Millenary** has shown his best form on a sound surface, and whose rider reported he hung in this sloppy ground, and found this sort of test taxing his stamina. Better can be expected of him on a sounder surface. *Official explanation: jockey said horse was hanging in the ground*

**Let Me Try Again(IRE)** confirmed the good impression he gave on his seasonal return at Newbury with a decent effort in fourth. He was being niggled some way out and is not the most straightforward, but clearly has plenty of ability.

**Royal Rebel**, dual winner of the Ascot Gold Cup, was having his first start since winning the race back in 2002 and ran creditably. The run can only do him good, and it will be interesting to see how he fares next time.

**Darasim(IRE)** seemed to take few runs before he hit top form last year and this outing would have been needed.

**Savannah Bay**, who won this in the Stewards' room before losing it again at an appeal last season, wants good, fast ground. *Official explanation: trainer said gelding was unsuited by the soft (good to soft in places) going*

**Maktub(ITY)** was always going to struggle to last out the trip in this ground, but appeared to be beaten before stamina really became an issue. He was a very useful performer in Italy and should be capable of much better.

**Misternando**, a remarkable story last season, winning ten times, ran a lazy race, even for him, and may have found this ground too soft. He deserves another chance.

**Supremacy** has recorded all four of his wins on a decent surface and was another to dislike the ground.

**Persian Punch(IRE)**, one of the most popular horses of all time, was making his eagerly awaited seasonal debut, but sadly for those connected and the horse himself, he collapsed and died in front of the stands with a suspected heart attack. He had been a legend over the years, admired for his unique battling qualities and will be sorely missed by many a racing fan.

**Morozov(USA)**, a three-time Group winner when trained in France, ran well for a long way before getting tired and can be expected to improve for the run.

**Hilbre Island** failed to show any improvement in the first-time blinkers and was out of his league. *Official explanation: trainer said colt was unsuited by the soft (good to soft in places) going*

## 1704 CAREY GROUP SWINLEY STKS (LISTED RACE) (FILLIES) 1m (R)

3:15 (3:16) (A) 3-Y-O **£17,400** (£6,600; £3,300; £1,500) **Stalls** High

Form RPR

501- **1** **Shady Reflection (USA)**[212] 5271 3-8-11 75 LDettori 3 91
(JHMGosden) *h.d.w: lw: mde virtually all: rdn fr 2f out: styd on gamely u.p fnl f* **8/1**

1 **2** *shd* **Glen Innes (IRE)**[25] 1250 3-8-11 JPMurtagh 6 90+
(DRLoder) *hld up in rr:nt clr run ins fnl 2f tl swtchd lft to outer appr fnl f:edgd lft: finshed strly: jst failed* **2/1**[1]

3-2 **3** 1½ **Red Top (IRE)**[14] 1400 3-8-11 DaneO'Neill 7 87
(RHannon) *slowly away: sn rcvrd and in tch: hdwy over 2f out: styng on whn edgd rt over 1f out: kpt on wl: nt pce of ldrs ins last* **9/1**

1-2 **4** 1½ **Solar Power (IRE)**[16] 1372 3-8-11 83 EAhern 9 84
(JRFanshawe) *t.k.h: in tch: n.m.r ins fnl 2f and 1f out: swtchd rt and r.o ins last: nt rch ldrs* **7/1**[3]

310- **5** *hd* **Glebe Garden**[295] 3074 3-8-11 89 IMongan 11 84
(MLWBell) *chsd ldrs: rdn and hung rt fr over 1f out: one pce ins last* **25/1**

25-2 **6** 1 **Desert Cristal (IRE)**[7] 1541 3-8-11 MartinDwyer 5 82
(JRBoyle) *t.k.h: hld up in rr: c wd and hdwy into st: rdn and nt rch ldrs: wkng whn sltly hmpd wl ins last* **20/1**

212- **7** 1 **Nephetriti Way (IRE)**[194] 5614 3-8-11 87 SDrowne 1 80
(PRChamings) *chsd ldrs: rdn to chal over 2f out: wknd fnl f* **20/1**

31- **8** 3½ **Caveral**[180] 5850 3-8-11 RLMoore 4 73
(RHannon) *hld up in rr: hdwy over 2f out to chse ldrs over 1f out: wknd ins last* **11/1**

21- **9** ¾ **First Candlelight**[189] 5701 3-8-11 TQuinn 8 72
(JGGiven) *chsd ldrs: rdn over 2f out: wknd fnl f* **14/1**

4-4 **10** *19* **Attune**[14] [1400] 3-8-11 ........ KFallon 10 34
(BJMeehan) *lw: chsd ldrs tl wknd over 2f out* **14/1**

3-5 **11** *1* **Halabaloo (IRE)**[14] [1400] 3-8-11 ........ DHolland 2 32
(GWragg) *in tch: rdn over 3f out: wknd appr fnl 2f* **6/1**[2]

1m 51.07s (8.03) **Going Correction** +1.10s/f (Soft) **11** Ran SP% **116.3**
Speed ratings: **103,102,101,99,99 98,97,94,93,74 73**CSF £23.29 TOTE £7.50: £2.10, £1.50, £2.80; EX 19.80.
**Owner** Maktoum Al Maktoum **Bred** Gainsborough Farm Llc **Trained** Manton, Wilts

**FOCUS**
Not a strong Listed race, but nothing should be taken away from Shady Reflection's performance.

**NOTEBOOK**
**Shady Reflection(USA)**, who appeared to improve for softer conditions when getting off the mark at the third attempt as a juvenile, was not really entitled to win a Pattern event with her rating of 75, but it is more than likely this was a weak race by Listed standards. Under a positive ride from Dettori she made every yard and lengthened really well in the straight, running on strongly all the way to the line to hold on narrowly from the favourite. She will reportedly be stepped up to ten furlongs now and will avoid fast ground, but is likely to struggle to follow up.
**Glen Innes(IRE)**, a winner on her only start to date, a weak race in heavy ground at Newcastle early in the month, could be called an unlucky loser as she was short of room early in the straight and had to be switched out wide. She finished strongly is bound to improve for further.
**Red Top(IRE)**, one of four maidens in the line-up, was another running on well at the finish and was not helped by a slow start. She should have little trouble landing her maiden if asked to.
**Solar Power(IRE)** was unlucky not to finish closer, being caught a little short of room, and was closing with every stride at the line.
**Glebe Garden** ran well on this seasonal debut, despite running around a bit and appearing to hang. She was there with every chance over a furlong out and may have just got a little tired in the ground.
**Desert Cristal(IRE)**, who lacks the physical scope of some of these, ran well and should be winning her maiden before long.
**Nephetriti Way(IRE)** showed up well for a long way and should be placed to effect in handicaps.
**Caveral** made some good headway from the rear to look a likely danger two out, but got a little tired. She will come on for this.
**Halabaloo(IRE)** was very disappointing, soft ground being the only possible excuse.

## 1705 VELCOURT GROUP PARADISE STKS (LISTED RACE) 1m (R)
**3:50** (3:50) (A ) 4-Y-0+ **£18,600** (£6,600; £3,300; £1,500) **Stalls** High

Form RPR

010- **1** **Putra Pekan**[193] [5643] 6-9-0 106 ........ (b) KFallon 6 115
(MAJarvis) *lw: t.k.h: trckd ldr: drvn to ld over 1f out: c clr ins last: comf* **4/1**[3]

311- **2** *4* **New Seeker**[277] [3589] 4-9-0 103 ........ JPMurtagh 5 107
(CGCox) *lw: led: rdn 2f out: hdd over 1f out: sn no ch w wnr but kpt on to hold 2nd* **7/4**[1]

210- **3** *1 ¼* **Ikhtyar (IRE)**[207] [5383] 4-9-3 117 ........ WSupple 3 108
(JHMGosden) *bit bkwd: racd in 4th but wl in tch: rdn and hdwy to go 3rd over 3f out: sn no imp on ldrs and one pce* **3/1**[2]

00-1 **4** *21* **Heretic**[11] [1469] 6-9-0 105 ........ OUrbina 2 63
(JRFanshawe) *racd in 3rd tl wknd qckly appr fnl 2f* **3/1**[2]

1m 48.03s (4.99) **Going Correction** +1.10s/f (Soft) **4** Ran SP% **106.4**
Speed ratings: **119,115,113,92**CSF £10.96 TOTE £5.60; EX 12.90.
**Owner** H R H Sultan Ahmad Shah **Bred** Mrs Mary Taylor **Trained** Newmarket, Suffolk

**FOCUS**
Considering the conditions, a cracking time which was 3.04 seconds faster than the preceding three-year-old fillies' Listed event. Putra Pekan was winning first time up for the third successive season and winning for the first time in this company at the age of six.

**NOTEBOOK**
**Putra Pekan**, a winner first time out for the past two seasons and hailing from a bang in-form stable, tracked New Seeker throughout until taking it up and going clear with just over a furlong to run. He stayed on strongly for pressure to record his first win at this level, but it is unlikely to be repeated and both second and third should reverse the form were they to meet again with the run under their belts. Racing abroad may now represent the best opportunities for him.
**New Seeker**, a most progressive handicapper last term, was always going to be a sitting duck for anything with a change of pace in this ground and found the winner too strong on the day. Back on faster conditions under a more restrained ride, he will be capable of much better.
**Ikhtyar(IRE)**, who drifted right out in the betting, had to concede 3lb to his rivals and shaped as though in need of it. He showed plenty of useful form last season and, like the second, will be a better horse under less extreme conditions.
**Heretic**, who has a proven liking for this sort of ground, ran a shocker and something was evidently not right.

## 1706 BOVIS HOMES PAVILION STKS (LISTED RACE) 6f
**4:25** (4:25) (A ) 3-Y-0 **£17,400** (£6,600; £3,300; £1,500) **Stalls** Low

Form RPR

313- **1** **Millbag (IRE)**[187] [5731] 3-8-11 100 ........ TEDurcan 3 107
(MRChannon) *lw: trckd ldr: led ins fnl 3f: rdn and edgd rt 1f out: pushed out fnl f: readily* **3/1**[2]

13-2 **2** *3* **Moonlight Man**[14] [1396] 3-8-11 105 ........ DaneO'Neill 6 98
(RHannon) *chsd ldrs: rdn and ev ch 2f out: hung bdly lft fr 1f out: one pce and no ch w wnr* **2/1**[1]

55-2 **3** *¾* **Crafty Fancy (IRE)**[18] [1323] 3-8-6 88 ........ TQuinn 7 91
(DJSFfrenchDavis) *chsd ldrs: rdn over 2f out: kpt on fnl f but nt pce to rch ldrs* **4/1**[3]

32-5 **4** *2 ½* **Mac Love**[27] [1223] 3-8-11 105 ........ JQuinn 8 88
(JAkehurst) *t.k.h: stdd rr but in tch: hdwy to chse ldrs over 2f out: wknd fnl f* **10/1**

0-00 **5** *10* **Treasure House (IRE)**[12] [1437] 3-8-11 91 ........ DHolland 4 58
(BJMeehan) *t.k.h: hld up in tch: hdwy over 2f out: hung bdly rt and wknd over 1f out* **9/1**

11-0 **6** *23* **Russian Valour (IRE)**[14] [1396] 3-9-4 113 ........ KDalgleish 2 —
(MJohnston) *lw: led tl hdd ins fnl 3f: sn hung rt and wknd* **7/1**

1m 21.66s (5.67) **Going Correction** +1.10s/f (Soft) **6** Ran SP% **109.9**
Speed ratings: **106,102,101,97,84 53**CSF £9.01 TOTE £3.40: £2.00, £1.80; EX 11.20.
**Owner** Sheikh Ahmed Al Maktoum **Bred** Dermot Cantillon **Trained** West Ilsley, Berks

**FOCUS**
A highly promising performance from Millbag in the ground, action suggests he is very much a fast ground performer, and even more so given he was the sole runner making his seasonal debut. The form looks fair for the grade.

**NOTEBOOK**
**Millbag(IRE)**, who had some very useful form to his name as a juvenile, was the only runner in the field making his seasonal debut, but still proved good enough to win comfortably and looks a good sprinting prospect in the making. His assured stamina counted in the conditions, and it was impressive the way he quickened over a furlong out to seal the matter. A return to better ground will suit this son of Cape Cross, and we should be hearing much more about him in the future.
**Moonlight Man** had every right to be favourite on the back of his second to Brunel in the Free Handicap and, although no match for the winner, acquitted himself well. Further seems to suit ideally.
**Crafty Fancy(IRE)** had plenty to find with some of these on official ratings and was staying on at the death. She may be worth trying over seven furlongs.
**Mac Love** ran respectably for a stable who are struggling for form at present.
**Treasure House(IRE)** was reported to have run too freely early by his jockey. *Official explanation: jockey said colt ran too freely early on*
**Russian Valour(IRE)**, a top sprinting juvenile, suffered an injury over the winter and showed absolutely nothing on his seasonal reappearance in the Free Handicap. Sadly it was the same story here and one must now question whether he has trained on. As he is a big horse it is possible he is still a bit reluctant to let himself down after the injury, so he may not be one to give up on totally yet, although the signs do not look promising.

## 1707 BOVIS HOMES CONDITIONS STKS 5f
**5:00** (5:01) (C ) 2-Y-0 **£7,192** (£2,728; £1,364; £620) **Stalls** Low

Form RPR

1 **1** **Prince Charming**[18] [1331] 2-9-1 ........ LDettori 1 95+
(JHMGosden) *lw: hld up in tch: hdwy and hung rt fr over 1f out: continued to hang but qcknd to ld last half f: comf* **15/8**[2]

11 **2** *1 ¾* **Cornus**[15] [1383] 2-9-1 ........ RLMoore 3 89
(RHannon) *chsd ldrs: rdn to chal 1f out: slt ld jst ins last: hdd and nt pce of wnr last half f* **1/1**[1]

3 **3** *1 ¾* **Alpaga Le Jomage (IRE)**[13] [1412] 2-8-8 ........ JFMcDonald(3) 5 79
(BJMeehan) *lw: led: rdn 2f out: hdd jst ins last: kpt on one pce* **14/1**

6 **4** *1 ¾* **Detonate**[12] [1436] 2-8-11 ........ DHolland 4 73
(IAWood) *chsd ldrs: rdn and one pce fnl 2f* **40/1**

1 **5** *8* **Alvarinho Lady**[28] [1208] 2-8-10 ........ PaulEddery 8 44
(DHaydnJones) *wnt bdly rt s: sn in tch: rdn 1/2-way: nvr gng pce of ldrs and wknd qckly 2f out* **20/1**

21 **6** *7* **Norcroft**[11] [1462] 2-8-10 ........ DFox(5) 2 24
(NACallaghan) *chsd ldr tl wknd over 2f out* **5/1**[3]

67.53 secs (5.60) **Going Correction** +1.10s/f (Soft) **6** Ran SP% **115.3**
Speed ratings: **99,96,93,90,77 66**CSF £4.27 TOTE £2.50: £1.60, £1.60; EX 4.60.
**Owner** Sheikh Mohammed **Bred** Mrs R D Peacock **Trained** Manton, Wilts

**FOCUS**
This looked a decent heat beforehand; the ground made it a real test for these juveniles. It has been rated the joint best juvenile performance so far, along with Blue Dakota, although confidence in the form is tempered by the ground.

**NOTEBOOK**
**Prince Charming** did well to win as he still looked very green when asked to go and win his race, hanging all over the place. He won despite the ground and will be better suited by a faster surface. He is likely to have one more race before Royal Ascot, where the Coventry Stakes, in which his sire was successful in 1995, looks the obvious target.
**Cornus** had won his first two races on an easy surface with ease, but he was taking on tougher opposition here and, although he ran with credit, the far more testing ground appeared to find him out.
**Alpaga Le Jomage(IRE)** is out of a mare who won over six furlongs but who is a half-sister to Gold Cup winner Arcadian Heights, so there is some stamina in his pedigree. He made much of the running and, on the form he has shown to date behind the best early-season juveniles seen out so far, a maiden should be a formality.
**Detonate** was trying to bite off more than he could chew in this grade and in the circumstances did not disgrace himself.
**Alvarinho Lady**, whose trainer had stated the previous day that she would not turn out if there was any overnight rain, in fact ran in the race despite 17mm of the wet stuff falling on the course during the night.
**Norcroft** failed to handle these testing conditions.

## 1708 BOVIS HOMES STKS (H'CAP) 1m (S)
**5:30** (5:33) (D ) (0-80,80) 3-Y-0+ **£5,629** (£1,732; £866; £433) **Stalls** Low

Form RPR

212- **1** **Retirement**[167] [5991] 5-9-9 75 ........ JFanning 7 91
(MHTompkins) *lw: hld up: travelling wl 2f out: rdn: swtchd rt and qcknd to ld appr fnl f: drvn clr* **10/1**

350- **2** *5* **Lilli Marlane**[200] [5486] 4-9-6 72 ........ LDettori 3 78
(NACallaghan) *hld up towards rr: n.m.r over 2f out:swtchd rt and hdwy over 1f out: styd on to take 2nd wl ins last* **4/1**[1]

010- **3** *½* **Crail**[279] [3519] 4-9-6 72 ........ GBaker 6 77
(CFWall) *chsd ldrs: rdn 3f out: swtchd rt and hdwy over 1f out: kpt on to dispute 2nd ins last but no ch w wnr* **40/1**

1-20 **4** *1 ½* **J R Stevenson (USA)**[98] [577] 8-9-11 77 ........ SWKelly 9 79
(MWigham) *lw: hld up towards rr: hdwy on rails and nt clr run over 1f out: swtchd rt and kpt on ins last but nt pce to rch ldrs* **6/1**[2]

0400 **5** *2* **Terraquin (IRE)**[16] [1354] 4-9-10 76 ........ KDalgleish 10 74
(JJBridger) *b: mid-div: hdwy 2f out: rdn to chal over 1f out: wknd ins fnl f* **50/1**

0-50 **6** *2 ½* **Oakley Rambo**[4] [1623] 5-9-13 79 ........ DaneO'Neill 18 72
(RHannon) *wnt rt s: sn rcvrd to chse ldrs: led 5f out: hdd appr fnl f: wknd ins last* **16/1**

4-22 **7** *6* **Blue Trojan (IRE)**[102] [559] 4-9-5 78 ........ JDaly(7) 17 59
(SKirk) *racd wd but up w pce tl wknd appr fnl f* **25/1**

-001 **8** *¾* **Nimello (USA)**[11] [1475] 8-9-11 77 ........ SWhitworth 13 57
(AGNewcombe) *bhd: sme hdwy fnl 2f: n.d* **7/1**[3]

00 **9** *1 ½* **Huxley (IRE)**[11] [1456] 5-10-0 80 ........ (t) PMcCabe 19 57
(MGQuinlan) *hmpd s and bhd: nvr rchd ldrs* **50/1**

450- **10** *hd* **Craic Sa Ceili (IRE)**[191] [5681] 4-9-4 75 ........ MSavage(5) 15 51
(MSSaunders) *lw: sn in tch: wknd 2f out* **33/1**

0-54 **11** *2* **Climate (IRE)**[23] [1273] 5-9-11 77 ........ (v) RLMoore 20 49
(JRBoyle) *chsd ldrs: rdn 3f out: wknd qckly 2f out* **16/1**

360- **12** *5* **Band**[215] [5196] 4-9-8 74 ........ GGibbons 5 36
(BAMcmahon) *in tch: rdn and wknd over 2f out* **20/1**

-000 **13** *5* **Krugerrand (USA)**[23] [1273] 5-9-13 79 ........ PaulEddery 4 31
(WJMusson) *bhd: rdn and sme hdwy on outside over 2f out: n.d and sn wknd* **11/1**

62-6 **14** *10* **Photofit**[21] [1295] 4-9-6 72 ........ TQuinn 8 4
(JLDunlop) *lw: chsd ldrs over 5f* **14/1**

4310 **15** *dist* **Topton (IRE)**[23] [1273] 10-10-0 80 ........ (b) KFallon 1 —
(PHowling) *sn bhd: t.o* **14/1**

110- **16** *nk* **Out For A Stroll**[179] [5875] 5-9-11 77 ........ MartinDwyer 2 —
(SCWilliams) *led 3f: wknd 1/2-way: t.o* **16/1**

-222 **17** *dist* **Just Fly**[88] [648] 4-10-0 80 ........ JPMurtagh 12 —
(SKirk) *a bhd: t.o* **10/1**

00-0 **P** **Red Galaxy (IRE)**[27] [1225] 4-9-9 75 ........ (t) EAhern 11 —
(DWPArbuthnot) *prom early:t.o and dismntd ins fnl f* **50/1**

1m 51.07s (9.15) **Going Correction** +1.10s/f (Soft) **18** Ran SP% **124.2**
Speed ratings: **98,93,92,91,89 86,80,79,78,78 76,71,66,56,— —,—,—**CSF £46.78 CT £1569.13 TOTE £12.20: £2.50, £2.00, £12.80, £1.80; EX 67.00 Place 6 £69.37, Place 5 £17.72.
**Owner** Ben Allen **Bred** Woodsway Stud And Chao Racing And Bloodstock Ltd **Trained** Newmarket, Suffolk

**FOCUS**
A moderate time for the grade, even allowing for the conditions.

**NOTEBOOK**
**Retirement** has always gone well on soft ground, but it was something of a surprise to see him win this so easily. The Handicapper will almost certainly hammer him for this, and he will find things much tougher from now on, especially when the ground firms up.
**Lilli Marlane**, who was largely consistent last season but only won once, had been dropped 2lb for this reappearance. There was plenty of money for her during the day and she ran a solid race. Connections always have the option of stepping her back up to ten furlongs, as she looks equally effective over that trip.
**Crail**, lightly raced and not seen after disappointing in a Doncaster handicap last July, ran with a lot more promise on this occasion. He will need to improve on this to win off his current mark, though.
**J R Stevenson(USA)**, who likes this sort of ground, did not get the best of runs and would probably have finished second with a clear passage. He is not really one to make too many excuses for, though, as his strike-rate is poor.
**Terraquin(IRE)** ran well over a trip which stretches his stamina. His wins have come over seven furlongs and he will be happier back over that trip.
**Oakley Rambo** goes on this ground, but he was poorly drawn on this occasion and continues to look too high in the handicap.
**Blue Trojan(IRE)** did not do himself many favours by racing on his own towards the centre of the track. In the circumstances he was not disgraced.
**Photofit** *Official explanation: trainer said gelding was unsuited by the soft (good to soft in places) going*
T/Jkpt: Not won. T/Plt: £239.90 to a £1 stake. Pool: £78,898.90. 240.05 winning tickets. T/Qpdt: £76.50 to a £1 stake. Pool: £4,295.70. 41.50 winning tickets. ST

## [1498] PONTEFRACT (L-H)

### Wednesday, April 28

**OFFICIAL GOING: Heavy (soft in places)**
After 3" rain in April the going was soft and the riders had different views about where the best ground was. The 4.00 and 4.35 races used a flip-start.
Wind: fresh hlf against Weather: overcast & cool

### 1709 EUROPEAN BREEDERS FUND THORNE MAIDEN STKS — 5f
2:20 (2:20) (D ) 2-Y-O — £5,447 (£1,676; £838; £419) Stalls Low

Form — RPR
6 **1** — **King's Gait**[13] 1415 2-8-11 — DAllan(3) 6 — 73
(TDEasterby) *led or disp ld tl drvn ahd 2f out: c over to stands rail: styd on u.p: all out* — **5/1**[2]
5 **2** *nk* **Lincolneurocruiser**[13] 1415 2-8-7 — JDO'Reilly(7) 2 — 72
(JO'Reilly) *dwlt: sn in tch: rdn over 1f out: styd on u.p ins fnl f: clsng on wnr fin* — **7/1**
4 **3** *1/2* **Prince Namid**[13] 1415 2-9-0 — GDuffield 9 — 71
(MrsADuffield) *prom: rdn and ch over 1f out: styd on fnl f: no ex clsng stages* — **9/4**[1]
0 **4** *3* **Tartatartufata**[14] 1390 2-8-9 — PHanagan 1 — 55
(DShaw) *chsd ldrs: stuck to far rail in home st: rdn and ch over 1f out: no ex fnl f* — **20/1**
6 **5** *10* **Lane Marshal**[8] 1523 2-8-9 — TEaves(5) 5 — 25
(MESowersby) *leggy: scope: cl up: led over 3f out tl hdd 2 out: rdn and wknd over 1 out* — **25/1**
**6** *1/2* **Caitlin (IRE)** 2-8-9 — FLynch 8 — 18
(BSmart) *cmpt: dwlt: in rr and drvn along 1/2-way: n.d* — **6/1**[3]
**7** *1 1/4* **Robury** 2-8-11 — TPQueally(3) 3 — 19
(EJAlston) *angular: unf: dwlt: towards rr: rdn 2f out: no hdwy* — **16/1**
**8** *3 1/2* **Beacon Star (USA)** 2-9-0 — RFfrench 4 — 7
(MJohnston) *rangy: unf: scope: dwlt: sn in tch: drvn along 1/2-way: sn wknd* — **5/1**[2]
**9** *3/4* **Ellenare (IRE)** 2-8-2 — BSwarbrick(7) 7 — —
(MsDeborahJEvans) *unf: dwlt: a bhd* — **25/1**

68.09 secs (4.29) **Going Correction** +0.725s/f (Yiel) — **9** Ran SP% **109.2**
Speed ratings: **94,93,92,87,71 71,69,63,62**CSF £35.63 TOTE £7.20: £2.30, £2.80, £1.20; EX 38.40.
**Owner** Mrs E J Wills **Bred** Ian H Wills **Trained** Great Habton, N Yorks

**FOCUS**
An ordinary juvenile race run at a modest pace in the testing ground. The first three advertised the form of their Ripon race to some extent.

**NOTEBOOK**
**King's Gait** had clearly learnt plenty from his initial outing. He knew his job this time and, brought wide off the home turn, did just enough to take a very ordinary event.
**Lincolneurocruiser**, who finished ahead of the winner at Ripon, really found his stride inside the last and would have made it with a little further to go.
**Prince Namid**, who finished ahead of the first two at Ripon, will appreciate a sixth furlong.
**Tartatartufata**, a good-bodied filly, was drawn one and, after hanging left on her debut, she stuck to the far-side rail. She will improve again.
**Lane Marshal**, a February foal, is very much on the leg. He showed plenty of toe before tiring badly in the ground.
**Caitlin(IRE)**, a March foal, was very green to post and was fairly clueless on the way back.
**Beacon Star(USA)**, a February foal, stands over plenty of ground and is a lazy walker. After missing a beat at the start he was on the retreat at halfway. He is surely a lot better than he showed here, as the ground was probably against him.

### 1710 OSSETT (S) H'CAP — 1m 4y
2:50 (2:50) (F ) (0-55,52) 3-Y-0+ — £3,513 (£1,081; £540; £270) Stalls Low

Form — RPR
0030 **1** — **Rocinante (IRE)**[21] 1305 4-9-3 **46** — RWinston 6 — 56
(JJQuinn) *trckd ldrs: led over 2f out: clr over 1 out: drvn out* — **4/1**[1]
06-0 **2** *3/4* **Plausabelle**[16] 1363 3-8-3 **49** — (b[1]) DAllan(3) 4 — 57
(TDEasterby) *towards rr: drvn along and hdwy into midfield 2f out: styd on wl u.p fnl f: clsng on wnr fin* — **11/1**
302- **3** *2* **Rymer's Rascal**[223] 5015 12-9-6 **49** — GDuffield 1 — 53
(EJAlston) *midfield: keen early: effrt over 2f out: chsd wnr and rdn 1 out: no ex ins last* — **6/1**[3]
4/00 **4** *2 1/2* **Lord Conyers (IRE)**[8] 1527 5-8-9 **43** oh3 — TEaves(5) 5 — 42
(BEllison) *towards rr: drvn along and hdwy into midfield over 2f out: kpt on u.p fnl f: nvr able to chal* — **10/1**
066- **5** *1* **Astral Prince**[16] 5704 6-9-5 **48** — (b) RFfrench 2 — 45
(MrsKWalton) *midfield: drvn along and outpcd over 2f out: styd on fr over 1 out: n.d* — **12/1**
0000 **6** *2* **Peartree House (IRE)**[6] 1573 10-9-5 **48** — ACulhane 3 — 41
(DWChapman) *hld up: hdwy 3f out: rdn to chse wnr 2 out: wknd fnl f* **10/1**
3604 **7** *2* **Frank's Quest (IRE)**[5] 1598 4-9-4 **50** — LPKeniry(3) 9 — 39
(PBurgoyne) *hld up in rr: hdwy into midfield 2f out: sn rdn: no further prog* — **6/1**[3]
36-0 **8** *3/4* **Lord Of Methley**[14] 1389 5-9-7 **50** — (b) VHalliday 12 — 38
(RMWhitaker) *prom: slt ld 3f out: sn hdd: wknd 2 out* — **11/2**[2]
06-0 **9** *19* **Delaware Trail**[12] 1444 5-8-13 **45** — (p) LEnstone(3) 11 — —
(JSWainwright) *prom: slt ld over 3f out: sn hdd: wknd over 2 out: t.o* — **33/1**
5650 **10** *18* **Wodhill Be**[16] 1373 4-9-1 **47** — TPQueally(3) 7 — —
(DMorris) *midfield: hung bdly rt after 2f: wknd over 2 out: t.o* — **10/1**
00-0 **11** *7* **Let's Party (IRE)**[6] 1557 4-9-9 **52** — (bt[1]) DaleGibson 10 — —
(PLClinton) *led tl hdd over 3f out: sn wknd: t.o* — **20/1**

1m 52.92s (7.32) **Going Correction** +0.90s/f (Soft)
**WFA** 3 from 4yo+ 14lb — **11** Ran SP% **115.0**
Speed ratings: **99,98,96,93,92 90,88,88,69,51 44**CSF £47.71 CT £266.22 TOTE £7.00: £2.00, £3.70, £2.30; EX 73.50.There was no bid for winner.
**Owner** Mrs Marie Taylor **Bred** John Malone **Trained** Settrington, N Yorks

**FOCUS**
A rock bottom event.

**NOTEBOOK**
**Rocinante(IRE)**, back in trip and down in grade, grabbed the stands' side rail once in line for home. Four lengths clear a furlong out, he was tying up fast at the line.
**Plausabelle**, in first-time blinkers, took plenty of stoking up. She really found her stride inside the last and would have made it with a bit further to go.
**Rymer's Rascal**, keen as usual, showed that even in his 13th year he is no back number, at this level at least.
**Lord Conyers(IRE)**, who missed last year, did not go without support and ran easily her best race on her third start this term.
**Astral Prince**, whose sole win from 40 starts now was nearly three years ago, was last seen in action over fences.
**Peartree House(IRE)**, who is not in love with the All-Weather, was turned out in tip-top trim.

### 1711 FERRYBRIDGE FLYERS MAIDEN STKS — 6f
3:25 (3:27) (D ) 3-Y-0+ — £5,616 (£1,728; £864; £432) Stalls Low

Form — RPR
000- **1** — **Game Flora**[161] 6029 3-8-4 50 ow1 — TEaves(5) 2 — 55
(MESowersby) *cl up: led over 3f out: rdn over 1f out: r.o wl* — **25/1**
000- **2** *3* **Boris The Spider**[210] 5294 3-8-13 62 — ACulhane 1 — 50
(MDHammond) *swvd s: hld up: hdwy 3f out: chsd ldrs 2f out: sn rdn: wnt 2nd ins fnl f: no imp on wnr* — **9/1**[3]
0 **3** *3/4* **Clouds Of Gold (IRE)**[17] 1342 3-8-8 — JTate 5 — 43
(JSWainwright) *towards rr: hdwy over 2f out: styd on fnl f: nrst fin* — **50/1**
50 **4** *nk* **Bollin Archie**[12] 1453 3-8-13 — GDuffield 8 — 47
(TDEasterby) *mde most tl hdd over 3f out: rdn and ev ch 2 out: no ex fnl f* — **11/1**
066- **5** *hd* **Palvic Moon**[225] 4964 3-8-8 60 — RFitzpatrick 4 — 41
(CSmith) *w ldrs: rdn over 2f out: kpt on fnl f* — **14/1**
5- **6** *1 1/2* **The Warley Warrior**[346] 1692 3-8-8 — (b[1]) PMulrennan(5) 3 — 42
(MWEasterby) *s.i.s: sn chsng ldrs: drvn along 3f out: kpt on fnl f* — **8/1**[2]
000- **7** *nk* **Ligne D'Eau**[180] 5850 3-8-13 — RHavlin 10 — 41
(PDEvans) *towards rr: drvn along 3f out: kpt on fnl 2f: n.d* — **10/1**
23- **8** *3/4* **Artistic Style**[197] 5560 4-9-10 70 — RWinston 9 — 39
(BEllison) *prom: drvn along 3f out: wknd 2 out* — **1/1**[1]
0/00 **9** *2* **Lady Double U**[75] 760 4-9-2 — DAllan(3) 7 — 28
(TDEasterby) *chsd ldrs: rdn 3f out: sn btn* — **33/1**
00- **10** *16* **Someone's Angel (USA)**[187] 5722 3-8-8 — WRyan 6 — —
(EALDunlop) *keen early: a rr: lost tch fnl f: t.o* — **11/1**
06- **11** *16* **Bolshevik (IRE)**[266] 3896 3-8-13 — PHanagan 11 — —
(TDEasterby) *midfield: drvn along 3f out: sn wknd: lost tch appr fnl f: t.o* — **16/1**

1m 24.22s (6.92) **Going Correction** +0.90s/f (Soft)
**WFA** 3 from 4yo 11lb — **11** Ran SP% **118.2**
Speed ratings: **89,85,84,83,83 81,80,79,77,55 34**CSF £233.04 TOTE £45.50: £6.20, £2.70, £6.00; EX 322.00.
**Owner** The Southwold Set **Bred** R S Cockerill (farms) Ltd **Trained** Goodmanham, E Yorks

**FOCUS**
A moderate maiden and a very modest time, even in the conditions.

**NOTEBOOK**
**Game Flora**, who ran her best races at two on her first two outings, went to post early. She made the best of her way home and never looked like being overhauled. This was very likely her one day of glory.
**Boris The Spider**, who had four outings at two, is rated just 62. His action suggests he is ideally suited by soft ground.
**Clouds Of Gold(IRE)**, who showed nothing on his debut two weeks earlier, still looked short of peak condition. She stayed on steadily and should improve, but she needs one more outing to qualify for a handicap mark.
**Bollin Archie**, a lot sharper, showed a fair bit more and is now qualified to ply his trade in handicap company. He should get a realistic mark.
**Palvic Moon**, who is only small, seems suited by give underfoot.
**The Warley Warrior**, tried in blinkers this time, is a monkey at the stalls.
**Artistic Style** was one of the first to come under pressure and was a spent force turning in. Heavily supported and from a yard that knows the time of day, this was too bad to be true. *Official explanation: trainer said colt seems to want further than 6f*
**Bolshevik(IRE)** *Official explanation: jockey said gelding was unsuited by the going*

### 1712 PONTEFRACT BOROUGH H'CAP — 1m 2f 6y
4:00 (4:01) (D ) (0-85,82) 3-Y-0 — £9,349 (£3,546; £1,773; £806) Stalls Far side

Form — RPR
0-42 **1** — **Woody Valentine (USA)**[16] 1360 3-8-13 **74** — SChin 1 — 89
(MJohnston) *led: rdn and hdd appr fnl f: styd on wl to regain ld ins last* — **11/2**[2]
15-3 **2** *1 1/4* **Oddsmaker (IRE)**[18] 1322 3-8-12 **73** — DeanMcKeown 6 — 86
(PDEvans) *trckd ldrs: chal 2f out: led appr fnl f: rdn and hdd ins last: no ex* — **5/1**[1]
02-2 **3** *18* **Tytheknot**[18] 1325 3-9-0 **75** — PHanagan 4 — 57
(JeddO'Keeffe) *prom: ev ch and drvn along over 2f out: wknd over 1 out* — **8/1**
0-04 **4** *1* **Mambina (USA)**[16] 1365 3-8-5 **66** — CCatlin 10 — 47
(MRChannon) *rr: drvn along over 3f out: kpt on fnl 2f: n.d* — **9/1**
3-53 **5** *1* **Weet A Head (IRE)**[18] 1321 3-9-7 **82** — DSweeney 3 — 61
(RHollinshead) *midfield: drvn along and outpcd 3f out: n.d* — **8/1**
30-5 **6** *5* **Absolutely Soaked (IRE)**[27] 1224 3-8-0 **64** — LisaJones(3) 8 — 34
(DrJDScargill) *in tch tl drvn along and outpcd 3f out* — **14/1**
22-4 **7** *1 3/4* **Just A Fluke (IRE)**[27] 1224 3-9-2 **77** — (t) RFfrench 7 — 44
(MJohnston) *prom: drvn along over 3f out: wknd over 2 out* — **6/1**[3]
46-0 **8** *4* **Rigonza**[14] 1392 3-8-8 **72** — DAllan(3) 5 — 33
(TDEasterby) *towards rr: drvn along over 3f out: no hdwy* — **25/1**

10-5 **9** *dist* **Mrs Pankhurst**[34] [1108] 3-8-12 **73**.............................................. MHills 2 —
(BWHills) *midfield: drvn along over 3f out: sn wknd: t.o* **5/1**[1]

01- **10** *dist* **Red Skelton (IRE)**[190] [5689] 3-9-2 **77**.............................................. ACulhane 9 —
(WJHaggas) *rr: lost tch over 3f out: t.o whn virtually p.u 2 out* **9/1**

2m 20.1s (6.19) **Going Correction** +0.775s/f (Yiel) **10** Ran SP% **115.7**
Speed ratings: **106,105,90,89,89 85,83,80,—,—**CSF £32.90 CT £219.89 TOTE £6.70: £2.90, £2.40, £2.70; EX 53.70.
**Owner** Favourites Racing **Bred** J I Amos And Barbara F Amos **Trained** Middleham Moor, N Yorks

**FOCUS**
This 0-82 handicap was a flip-start due to the bad ground and was hand-timed. The resultant time was decent for the grade given the conditions.

**NOTEBOOK**
**Woody Valentine(USA)**, his fitness guaranteed, stuck towards the centre. His rider switched his whip with great alacrity inside the last, and in the end they won going away.
**Oddsmaker(IRE)**, still backward in his coat, travelled easily best but, after going a neck up, he hung left and in the end the winner saw out the extended trip much the better.
**Tytheknot**, on his handicap debut, failed to see out the extra two furlongs.
**Mambina(USA)**, who is not very big, looks likely to continue to struggle to make any impact from this sort of mark.
**Weet A Head(IRE)**, back against his contemporaries, ran a lifeless race, never threatening.
**Mrs Pankhurst**, warm on a cold day, dropped right away and finished hopelessly tailed off. Even if the ground was against her it was an abject display. *Official explanation: jockey said filly was unsuited by the going*

## 1713 BRIAN HUNTER - A LIFETIME IN RACING MAIDEN STKS — 1m 2f 6y
**4:35** (4:35) (D) 3-Y-O **£5,590** (£1,720; £860; £430) **Stalls** Far side

Form RPR

**1** **Master Wells (IRE)** 3-9-0 .............................................. CCatlin 6 84
(JDBethell) *w'like: cmpt: rr but in tch: effrt 3f out: wnt 2nd wl over 1 out: rdn to ld ins fnl f: styd on* **20/1**

**2** *1 ½* **Backgammon** 3-9-0 .............................................. NPollard 1 81
(DRLoder) *w'like: lengthy: trckd ldrs: led 2f out: rdn and hdd ins fnl f: no ex* **9/4**[2]

0- **3** *13* **Blaze Of Colour**[187] [5722] 3-8-9 .............................................. FLynch 5 54
(SirMichaelStoute) *trckd ldrs: ev ch over 2f out: sn rdn: outpcd by first 2 over 1 out* **2/1**[1]

00 **4** *3* **Moonshaft (USA)**[15] [1382] 3-9-0 .............................................. WRyan 7 54
(EALDunlop) *led tl rdn and hdd 2f out: sn wknd* **20/1**

0-2 **5** *5* **Bollin Annabel**[12] [1450] 3-8-6 .............................................. DAllan(3) 2 41
(TDEasterby) *w.r.s and lost 20l: rr but in tch after 2f: rdn and lost tch 3 out: no ch after* **8/1**

4 **6** *2 ½* **Empress Eugenie (FR)**[9] [1507] 3-8-9 .............................................. JTate 4 36
(JMPEustace) *cl up tl rdn and wknd over 2f out* **3/1**[3]

2m 28.6s (14.69) **Going Correction** +0.775s/f (Yiel) **6** Ran SP% **109.7**
Speed ratings: **72,70,60,58,54 52**CSF £62.11 TOTE £22.90: £4.70, £1.80; EX 43.20.
**Owner** Jordan Ellison Lund **Bred** Barronstown Stud And Orpendale **Trained** Middleham Moor, N Yorks

**FOCUS**
This very ordinary maiden was also a flip start and hand timed, but on this occasion the time was very pedestrian after no pace until the final half mile.

**NOTEBOOK**
**Master Wells(IRE)**, a son of Sadler's Wells, was cheaply bought and lacks size and substance. He went in pursuit of the leader and was firmly in command at the line.
**Backgammon**, another son of Sadler's Wells, is long in the back. He looked the likely winner when making his break for home, but in the end was worn down by the winner. The pair finished clear but the race lacked any strength in depth.
**Blaze Of Colour**, who had one backend outing at two, stands over plenty of ground. She looked in need of the outing and was going up and down in the same place with over a furlong left to run. She can do better in time, especially on much better ground.
**Moonshaft(USA)**, bred entirely for speed on his dam's side, set just a steady pace but stopped to nothing turning in. Now qualified for a handicap mark, it will be interesting to see if he now drops back in trip.
**Bollin Annabel** shied at the tape (the stalls could not be used because of the wet ground) and lost many lengths, but because of the pedestrian pace she soon caught up.
**Empress Eugenie(FR)**, who has not yet come in her coat, was stepping up in trip but stamina was not the real reason for this poor effort, just nine days after showing promise on her racecourse debut.

## 1714 SUSAN & BRIAN GREENWOOD 40TH ANNIVERSARY H'CAP — 1m 4f 8y
**5:05** (5:05) (D) (0-80,76) 3-Y-O **£5,330** (£1,640; £820; £410) **Stalls** Low

Form RPR

45-0 **1** **Considine (USA)**[13] [1422] 3-8-4 **59**.............................................. JTate 4 70
(JMPEustace) *led 4f: remained cl up: rdn to ld over 1 out: styd on u.p* **12/1**

0-61 **2** *5* **Habitual Dancer**[23] [1267] 3-8-4 **59**.............................................. PHanagan 3 63
(JeddO'Keeffe) *hld up in tch: keen early: drvn along 4f out: outpcd over 2 out: styd on fnl f to go 2nd clsng stages* **4/1**[2]

0-30 **3** *¾* **Crackleando**[70] [822] 3-8-2 **57**.............................................. JBramhill 2 60
(NPLittmoden) *cl up: led after 4f: rdn and hdd over 1 out: no ex* **25/1**

0662 **4** *shd* **Zaffeu**[16] [1365] 3-8-12 **70**.............................................. J-PGuillambert(3) 5 73
(NPLittmoden) *dwlt: sn trcking ldrs: effrt and ev ch 2f out: hung rt u.p appr fnl f: no ex* **11/2**[3]

51-3 **5** *dist* **Daytime Girl (IRE)**[13] [1414] 3-9-7 **76**.............................................. MHills 6 —
(BWHills) *trckd ldrs: drvn along 5f out: rdn and lost tch over 3 out: t.o* **1/1**[1]

2-06 **6** *2 ½* **Hathlen (IRE)**[13] [1416] 3-9-7 **76**.............................................. ACulhane 1 —
(MRChannon) *hld up in tch: tk clsr order 1/2-way: drvn along 4f out: lost tch over 2 out: t.o* **6/1**

2m 50.95s (10.90) **Going Correction** +0.775s/f (Yiel) **6** Ran SP% **111.2**
Speed ratings: **94,90,90,90,— —**CSF £57.11 TOTE £14.20: £4.20, £2.00; EX 70.30.
**Owner** Elias Haloute **Bred** D Considine **Trained** Newmarket, Suffolk

**FOCUS**
A 0-76 handicap run at a moderate pace resulting in a slow time even in the conditions.

**NOTEBOOK**
**Considine(USA)**, stepping up in trip on his handicap bow, did not go unbacked. On his toes beforehand and continually swishing his tail, he came right away in the closing stages.
**Habitual Dancer**, up 7lb and back on grass, was very keen and would have been suited by a much stronger pace.
**Crackleando**, having his first outing on grass on his sixth start, was having his first run for ten weeks and looked to be carrying a fair amount of condition.
**Zaffeu**, who looked very fit, did nothing to advertise the form of his Warwick race.
**Daytime Girl(IRE)**, backward in her coat, lacks substance. She opted to race wide and was in trouble at halfway. She soon dropped right out and, proven on soft at two, this was simply too bad to be true. *Official explanation: jockey said filly was unsuited by the gooing*
**Hathlen(IRE)**, weighted to the hilt, does not handle this type of ground and in the end completed in her own time.

## 1715 BETFAIR.COM APPRENTICE SERIES (ROUND 2) H'CAP — 1m 2f 6y
**5:35** (5:35) (E) (0-70,67) 3-Y-O+ **£4,085** (£1,257; £628; £314) **Stalls** Low

Form RPR

1153 **1** **Jake Black (IRE)**[8] [1527] 4-8-11 **50**.............................................. DTudhope 2 68
(JJQuinn) *cl up: led over 3f out: drvn clr over 1 out: in command after* **5/2**[1]

-652 **2** *11* **Dickie Deadeye**[9] [1503] 7-8-12 **56**.............................................. TBlock(5) 3 55
(GBBalding) *hld up: hdwy over 3f out: wnt 2nd over 2 out: styd on: no imp on wnr* **11/4**[2]

0000 **3** *10* **Midshipman**[18] [1329] 6-9-12 **65**..............................................(b[1]) CHaddon 8 47
(AWCarroll) *rr: effrt over 3f out: kpt on fnl 2f: n.d* **12/1**

0-05 **4** *1 ¼* **Libre**[30] [1172] 4-9-9 **67**..............................................(b) AReilly(5) 5 47
(RCGuest) *hld up: hdwy over 3f out: chsng first 2 and rdn 2 out: sn btn* **7/2**[3]

240- **5** *5* **Little Englander**[224] [4987] 4-9-4 **62**.............................................. CCavanagh(5) 4 33
(HCandy) *in tch: effrt over 3f out: wknd over 2 out* **14/1**

0600 **6** *11* **Marengo**[58] [945] 10-7-12 **40** oh7 ow3.............................................. KGhunowa(3) 7 —
(PaulJohnson) *slowly away: hld up: effrt over 3f out: sn btn* **16/1**

/00- **7** *24* **Furniture Factors (IRE)**[372] [1176] 4-9-4 **60**.............................................. JDO'Reilly(3) 1 —
(RonaldThompson) *trckd ldrs: ev ch 3f out: sn rdn and wknd: t.o* **50/1**

0460 **8** *11* **Turftanzer (GER)**[22] [1282] 5-7-12 **44** oh2 ow7......(t) JaniceWebster(7) 10 —
(DonEnricoIncisa) *prom tl wknd over 3f out: t.o* **25/1**

61-0 **9** *17* **Buscador (USA)**[107] [507] 5-9-2 **58**.............................................. SaleemGolam(3) 9 —
(WMBrisbourne) *led tl hdd over 3f out: wknd qckly: t.o* **13/2**

2m 19.4s (5.49) **Going Correction** +0.775s/f (Yiel) **9** Ran SP% **116.8**
Speed ratings: **109,100,92,91,87 78,59,50,36**CSF £9.70 CT £67.95 TOTE £3.50: £1.20, £1.40, £3.40; EX 8.70 Place 6 £483.71, Place 5 £315.88.
**Owner** G A Lucas **Bred** Yeomanstown Stud **Trained** Settrington, N Yorks

**FOCUS**
A moderate apprentice race but a runaway success and a smart winning time allowing for the testing conditions.

**NOTEBOOK**
**Jake Black(IRE)** handles this type of ground and came right away once in line for home. The plan is to turn out again without a penalty at Newcastle next Monday.
**Dickie Deadeye** went in pursuit of the winner but was left toiling once in line for home. He finished as far ahead of the rest as the margin the winner defeated him.
**Midshipman**, who ran over two miles last time, wore blinkers for the first time. His best days are some way behind him now.
**Libre**, wearing blinkers for just the second time, is now 1lb lower than his last success, but he is a quirky type who is hard to predict.
**Little Englander** does not appreciate conditions as testing as these.
T/Plt: £1,861.20 to a £1 stake. Pool: £26,389.65. 10.35 winning tickets. T/Qpdt: £587.90 to a £1 stake. Pool: £1,668.40. 2.10 winning tickets. JF

# AYR (L-H)
### Thursday, April 29

**OFFICIAL GOING: Good**

## 1717 KIDZPLAY MAIDEN AUCTION STKS — 5f
**5:50** (5:51) (H) 2-Y-O **£1,666** (£476; £238) **Stalls** Low

Form RPR

**1** **Handsome Lady** 2-8-3 .............................................. PHanagan 4 78
(ISemple) *in tch: smooth hdwy to ld over 1f out: drew clr fnl f* **5/1**[3]

3 **2** *5* **Smiddy Hill**[14] [1415] 2-8-3 .............................................. RFfrench 6 58
(RBastiman) *mde most to over 1f out: edgd lft and outpcd ins last* **5/2**[2]

52 **3** *1 ¼* **Speed Dial Harry (IRE)**[17] [1359] 2-8-8 .............................................. DarrenWilliams 3 58
(KRBurke) *cl up: sn pushed along: outpcd 1/2-way: kpt on fnl f* **7/4**[1]

**4** *1 ¼* **Bond Finesse (IRE)** 2-8-7 ow4.............................................. FLynch 1 52
(BSmart) *s.i.s: bhd tl styd on fnl f: nrst fin* **20/1**

5 **5** *7* **Beverley Beau**[21] [1314] 2-8-8 .............................................. RWinston 5 25
(MrsLStubbs) *cl up tl wknd wl over 1f out* **20/1**

3 **6** *2 ½* **Maureen's Lough (IRE)**[12] [1468] 2-8-3 .............................................. JFEgan 2 10
(TDBarron) *chsd ldrs: sn rdn along: struggling fr 1/2-way* **13/2**

61.14 secs (0.71) **Going Correction** -0.15s/f (Firm) **6** Ran SP% **104.5**
Speed ratings: **88,80,78,76,64 60**CSF £15.36 TOTE £7.90: £2.60, £1.10; EX 31.50.
**Owner** David Platt **Bred** David And Mrs Rachel Platt **Trained** Carluke, S Lanarks

**FOCUS**
A run of the mill maiden in which all the runners stayed on the far side from their draws but a most encouraging debut performance from Handsome Lady, who looks sure to win more races.

**NOTEBOOK**
**Handsome Lady** ◆, who has plenty of speed in her pedigree, created a most favourable impression on this racecourse debut. She is highly regarded by her very capable trainer, and is likely to be able to hold her own in slightly stronger company.
**Smiddy Hill**, who shaped well in a race that has thrown up winners on her debut, probably ran to a similar level and again showed plenty of foot. She should improve as she strengthens.
**Speed Dial Harry(IRE)**, who shaped well on soft ground last time, ran his race on this quicker surface but left the impression that a stiffer test of stamina would suit. It will be an uncompetitive race over this trip in this grade he wins.
**Bond Finesse(IRE)**, a half-sister to winning sprinter Landing Strip, hinted at ability after a tardy start on this racecourse debut and is entitled to come on for the experience.
**Beverley Beau**, who has plenty of speed in her pedigree, again showed little.
**Maureen's Lough(IRE)**, whose debut form on soft ground has taken a few knocks, was readily exposed in this better grade and on this quicker ground. However, she is in good hands and will be placed to best advantage in due course.

## 1718 HATS BY CHRISTINE (S) STKS — 1m
**6:20** (6:22) (H) 3-Y-O+ **£1,263** (£361; £180) **Stalls** Low

Form RPR

00-0 **1** **Forest Air (IRE)**[3] [1660] 4-8-12 49.............................................. PHanagan 6 52
(MissLAPerratt) *prom: rdn over 3f out: squeezed through over 1f out: kpt on to ld cl home* **5/1**[3]

2004 **2** *nk* **Desert Heat**[5] [1629] 6-9-8 66..............................................(b) RWinston 2 61
(ISemple) *s.i.s: hdwy 1/2-way: led and hung lft over 1f out: kpt on: hdd cl home* **3/1**[1]

0-60 **3** *1 ½* **Scurra**[9] [1527] 5-8-12 51.............................................. PMulrennan(5) 3 53
(ACWhillans) *hld up: effrt over 2f out: r.o fnl f* **8/1**

3040 **4** *2 ½* **Tinian**[15] [1389] 6-9-8 52..............................................(p) DarrenWilliams 8 52
(KRBurke) *keen: led 2f: disp ld tl no ex over 1f out* **4/1**[2]

6-00 **5** *1* **Royal Windmill (IRE)**[15] [1389] 5-9-3 47..............................................(p) GFaulkner 5 45
(MDHammond) *keen: led after 2f to over 1f out: no ex* **6/1**

0636 **6** *1 ¼* **Sennen Cove**[8] [1548] 5-9-3 40.............................................. RFfrench 7 42
(RBastiman) *in tch: rdn 3f out: one pce fr 2f out* **16/1**



The Form Book, Raceform Ltd, Compton, RG20 6NL

7 1 ½ **Smeorach** 3-8-1 ow3 ANicholls 1 36
(JamesMoffatt) *s.i.s: sme late hdwy: nvr on terms* **20/1**

0/40 **8** 1 ¼ **Bettys Valentine**[9] [1528] 4-8-9 30 (t) LEnstone(3) 10 30
(DWBarker) *prom tl rdn and wknd wl over 1f out* **66/1**

**9** 5 **Welcome Archie**[151] 4-8-12 TEaves(5) 4 24
(JSHaldane) *s.i.s: n.d* **66/1**

0-05 **10** 11 **Blue Bijou**[60] [935] 4-9-3 DeanMcKeown 9 —
(TTClement) *chsd ldrs tl hung lft and wknd fr 1/2-way* **20/1**

1m 44.6s (1.48) **Going Correction** -0.025s/f (Good)
**WFA** 3 from 4yo+ 14lb **10** Ran SP% **105.5**
Speed ratings: **91,90,89,86,85 84,82,81,76,65**CSF £16.90 TOTE £6.60: £1.80, £1.30, £2.50; EX 14.90.There was no bid for the winner. Desert Heat was claimed by John W. Payne for £4,000.
**Owner** Mrs K A Cullen **Bred** Auriga Partnership **Trained** Ayr, Strathclyde

**FOCUS**
An poor, uncompetitive seller in which the pace picked up after about three furlongs, but the final time was still slow and it is more likely the winner was below form than the others improved.

**NOTEBOOK**
**Forest Air(IRE)**, dropped in grade and in trip, turned in an improved effort to beat an unreliable rival in a very modest event, but would not look an obvious one to follow up in anything but the worst company.
**Desert Heat** looked to hold solid claims in a weak event but, although just touched off, was below his best form and did not look straightforward. He is not one to be lumping on at short odds, even in this grade.
**Scurra** bettered his two previous runs this season back on a sound surface and shaped as though the return to a mile and a quarter would suit. However, his inconsistency means he is not sure to put it all in next time.
**Tinian** looked to have a decent chance at these weights back on turf but, although he was not helped by being taken on for the lead, is one to tread carefully with, even in this grade.
**Royal Windmill(IRE)** got closer to Tinian than he had done on his two previous starts this term, but he did not do himself any favours by failing to settle and is not one to place much faith in.
**Sennen Cove** an inconsistent performer, was not totally disgraced in the face of a stiff task but a record of no wins from 28 starts confirms he is not one to be interested in.

## 1719 T LAWRIE AND PARTNERS BANDED STKS 6f
6:50 (6:51) (H) 3-Y-0+ £1,627 (£465; £232) Stalls Low

Form RPR

4100 **1** **Redoubtable (USA)**[9] [1526] 13-8-13 45 PMakin(7) 7 48
(DWChapman) *cl up: led over 2f out: r.o strly* **9/2**[3]

60-0 **2** 3 **Tiz Wiz**[17] [1363] 3-8-9 45 KDalgleish 2 39
(WStorey) *in tch: effrt over 2f out: r.o fnl f: no ch w wnr* **20/1**

0/0- **3** shd **Joshuas Boy (IRE)**[236] [4732] 4-9-6 45 (b1) RWinston 3 39
(KARyan) *prom: effrt over 2f out: kpt on fnl f* **5/2**[1]

00-3 **4** 1 **Pirlie Hill**[3] [1663] 4-9-6 45 RFfrench 8 36
(MissLAPerratt) *led to over 2f out: edgd rt and wknd ins fnl f* **6/1**

020- **5** 2 ½ **Petana**[236] [4732] 4-9-6 45 (b) FLynch 6 28
(MDods) *hld up: hdwy and shkn up 2f out: no imp* **14/1**

000- **6** 1 ¾ **Andreyev (IRE)**[214] [5257] 10-9-6 45 JFEgan 5 23
(JSGoldie) *chsd ldrs tl edgd lft and outpcd fr over 2f out* **10/1**

0421 **7** 7 **Grand View**[2] [1694] 8-9-12 40 (p) PHanagan 4 8
(JRWeymes) *prom tl rdn and wknd over 2f out* **3/1**[2]

000- **8** 5 **Square Dancer**[318] [2421] 8-9-6 40 (t) DMcGaffin 1 —
(DANolan) *disp ld 2f: sn lost pl* **66/1**

00-6 **9** 8 **Tapleon**[17] [1362] 3-8-4 40 TEaves(5) 9 —
(CJTeague) *chsd ldrs 2f: sn outpcd* **100/1**

1m 13.69s (-0.03) **Going Correction** -0.15s/f (Firm)
**WFA** 3 from 4yo+ 11lb **9** Ran SP% **109.0**
Speed ratings: **94,90,89,88,85 82,73,66,56**CSF £79.13 TOTE £5.50: £2.40, £2.90, £1.70; EX 136.00.
**Owner** David W Chapman **Bred** Wooden Horse Inv Inc And Post Syndicate **Trained** Stillington, N Yorks

**FOCUS**
A low-grade event in which the field again raced on the far side. The pace was sound.

**NOTEBOOK**
**Redoubtable(USA)** is at the veteran stage but had more in his favour than most in this field and won decisively in this lower grade. He will find life tougher back in handicaps, though.
**Tiz Wiz** looked to have a stiff task, but ran her best race to date and shaped as though the return to seven furlongs would be in her favour.
**Joshuas Boy(IRE)**, in the first-time blinkers, was well supported and showed his first worthwhile form. He is still relatively unexposed and looks capable of winning a modest race in this grade.
**Pirlie Hill**, very edgy in the preliminaries, failed by a long chalk to confirm reappearance promise three days earlier. She disappointed last year after an encouraging start and is one to tread carefully with.
**Petana**, an unreliable maiden, confirmed she retains ability on this reappearance and was not knocked about, but it will be a poor race she eventually wins.
**Andreyev(IRE)** is a shadow of his former self and this first run in banded company confirms he is not one to be interested in.
**Grand View**, who had been running creditably in weak events of late, showed exactly why he is an unreliable betting proposition.

## 1720 ALAN MACDONALD HAPPY BIRTHDAY BANDED STKS 7f 50y
7:20 (7:20) (H) 3-Y-0+ £1,624 (£464; £232) Stalls Low

Form RPR

50-0 **1** **Stellite**[9] [1527] 4-9-7 45 JFEgan 2 52
(JSGoldie) *hld up: hdwy 2f out: led appr fnl f: styd on wl* **7/1**[2]

250- **2** 1 **Hebenus**[248] [4454] 5-9-7 45 FLynch 1 49
(TAKCuthbert) *led to over 1f out: rallied: one pce wl ins last* **8/1**

060- **3** nk **Moonlight Song (IRE)**[225] [5002] 7-9-0 45 DFentiman(7) 4 48
(JohnAHarris) *prom: rdn over 2f out: edgd lft and hdwy over 1f out: r.o* **14/1**

60-0 **4** 5 **Tancred Arms**[29] [1197] 8-9-4 45 LEnstone(3) 6 35
(DWBarker) *hld up in tch: rdn and outpcd 3f out: rallied over 1f out: no imp* **15/2**[3]

003- **5** nk **Merlins Profit**[238] [4679] 4-9-7 45 RWinston 5 34
(MDods) *hld up in tch: outpcd over 3f out: r.o fnl f: no imp* **12/1**

000/ **6** 3 ½ **Goodbye Mrs Chips**[48] [5794] 5-9-2 45 (t) TEaves(5) 3 25
(MrsLBNormile) *chsd ldrs tl wknd fr 2f out* **16/1**

00-0 **7** 1 ¾ **Mexican (USA)**[7] [1393] 5-9-7 45 (p) PHanagan 8 21
(MDHammond) *prom to 2f out: sn rdn and wknd* **7/1**[2]

1306 **8** 1 ¾ **Rosti**[60] [939] 4-9-7 45 GFaulkner 7 16
(PCHaslam) *hld up: rdn over 2f out: nvr on terms* **11/8**[1]

1m 32.64s (0.17) **Going Correction** -0.025s/f (Good) **8** Ran SP% **110.2**
Speed ratings: **98,96,96,90,90 86,84,82**CSF £56.52 TOTE £10.40: £1.50, £2.50, £2.90; EX 36.70.
**Owner** J S Goldie **Bred** Cheveley Park Stud Ltd **Trained** Uplawmoor, E Renfrews

**FOCUS**
A modest race in which the market leader failed to translate his all-weather form to turf. The pace was on the steady side and favoured those racing prominently.

**NOTEBOOK**
**Stellite**, who hinted at ability on his reappearance, appreciated the drop in grade and the better ground and ran arguably his best race. He should prove equally effective at a mile and, as he is unexposed, may well be capable of better. *Official explanation: trainer said, regarding the improved form shown, gelding had matured over the winter*
**Hebenus**, having his first run for his current stable, had the run of the race on this reappearance outing but showed enough to suggest he can win a similar race in due course.
**Moonlight Song(IRE)** was not disgraced on this first start since September but, given her losing run and her career record, would not be certain to put her best foot forward next time.
**Tancred Arms** may be a little better than the bare form given the way this race unfolded, but he is not the most consistent and did not really show enough to suggest he would be of any interest next time.
**Merlins Profit** another inconsistent performer, did not really have the run of the race on this first start after a break and it will be a poor race he wins.
**Mexican(USA)**, dropped in grade and trip for this return to Flat duty, was well below his best and remains a frustrating individual. *Official explanation: jockey said horse had hung left-handed throughout*
**Rosti** looked to have fair claims if his Fibresand form could be translated to grass but, after attracting plenty of market support, ran poorly. He may do better returned to All-Weather surfaces. *Official explanation: jockey said gelding lost its action*

## 1721 CHRISTINE SADLER DESIGNER JEWELLERY BANDED STKS 1m 5f 13y
7:50 (7:50) (H) 3-Y-0+ £1,449 (£414; £207) Stalls Low

Form RPR

200- **1** **Righty Ho**[219] [5131] 10-9-10 40 RWinston 9 47
(WHTinning) *cl up: led over 2f out: hld on gamely fnl f* **9/1**

-000 **2** nk **Timbuktu**[12] [1465] 3-8-3 40 PHanagan 2 47
(CWThornton) *hld up in tch: hdwy and ev ch fr 2f out: kpt on: jst hld* **7/2**[1]

060- **3** 5 **Haystacks (IRE)**[131] [4216] 8-9-10 35 (p) ANicholls 4 40
(JamesMoffatt) *s.i.s: hld up: hdwy over 1f out: nt rch first two* **9/2**[2]

0060 **4** 1 **Balalaika Tune (IRE)**[9] [1527] 5-9-10 40 DarrenWilliams 8 38
(WStorey) *keen in tch: rdn and edgd lft over 2f out: no imp over 1f out* **16/1**

050/ **5** 1 ½ **Nautical Star**[96] [3251] 9-9-5 35 TEaves(5) 6 36
(ACWhillans) *led 3f: cl up tl wknd fr 2f out* **16/1**

65-0 **6** ½ **Copplestone (IRE)**[11] [471] 8-9-10 35 (p) KDalgleish 1 35
(WStorey) *keen: in tch: n.m.r 3f out: rdn and no imp fr 2f out* **10/1**

4062 **7** 1 **Amanpuri (GER)**[6] [1593] 6-9-10 35 DeanMcKeown 5 34
(PABlockley) *chsd ldrs: n.m.r over 2f out: sn rdn and lost pl: n.d after* **5/1**[3]

0055 **8** 7 **Ipledgeallegiance (USA)**[27] [1231] 8-9-3 35 PMakin(7) 3 24
(DWChapman) *hld up: rdn over 2f out: sn btn* **7/1**

-003 **9** 10 **Jezadil (IRE)**[6] [1580] 6-9-3 35 (p) KristinStubbs(7) 7 10
(MrsLStubbs) *s.i.s: hdwy to ld after 3f: hdd over 2f out: sn wknd* **14/1**

2m 56.61s (0.76) **Going Correction** -0.025s/f (Good)
**WFA** 3 from 5yo+ 21lb **9** Ran SP% **107.1**
Speed ratings: **96,95,92,92,91 90,90,85,79**CSF £35.52 TOTE £10.00: £2.80, £1.90, £2.00; EX 37.40.
**Owner** W H Tinning **Bred** B J Warren **Trained** Thornton-le-Clay, N Yorks
■ Stewards Enquiry : P Hanagan caution: used whip with excessive frequency

**FOCUS**
A low-grade contest in which the pace was only fair.

**NOTEBOOK**
**Righty Ho** looked to hold fair claims on his best form, has a good record fresh and, although he had the run of the race, showed the right attitude in the closing stages. He is likely to win again in this grade.
**Timbuktu**, upped in trip, was well supported and turned in an improved effort to pull clear of the remainder. On this evidence he is likely to win a small race when the emphasis is on stamina.
**Haystacks(IRE)**, a dual hurdles winner last term, was not disgraced after a break given the way this race suited those racing prominently, and he should be spot on now for the return to timber.
**Balalaika Tune(IRE)** was not totally disgraced but may well be a touch flattered given the way this race unfolded and, given her record, is not one to be interested in next time.
**Nautical Star** had the run of the race and should be better for this first run in over three months, but it will be a poor race he wins on the Flat.
**Copplestone(IRE)** is not really one to rely on, but would have preferred a much stronger end-to-end gallop over this trip.
**Amanpuri(GER)**, whose latest run looked to give him strong claims in this grade, was uneasy in the market and was a long way below that level. He is not one to rely on.

## 1722 RACING HERE ON SATURDAY 22ND MAY BANDED STKS 1m 2f
8:20 (8:20) (H) 3-Y-0+ £1,449 (£414; £207) Stalls Low

Form RPR

1044 **1** **Kingsdon (IRE)**[9] [1527] 7-9-7 40 (vt) JFEgan 4 52
(TJFitzgerald) *trckd ldrs: led over 2f out: drew clr over 1f out* **1/1**[1]

0-50 **2** 8 **Smarter Charter**[8] [1543] 11-9-0 35 KristinStubbs(7) 2 37
(MrsLStubbs) *s.i.s: keen: hld up: hdwy to chse wnr ins fnl f: no imp* **10/1**

00-0 **3** 5 **Optimum Night**[21] [1318] 5-9-7 40 RWinston 7 28
(PDNiven) *chsd ldrs: ev ch and rdn 3f out: one pce fr 2f out* **5/1**[2]

60-0 **4** 2 ½ **Howards Dream (IRE)**[18] [1341] 6-9-2 35 (t) TEaves(5) 6 23
(DANolan) *cl up: ev ch 3f out: one pce fr 2f out* **25/1**

0-04 **5** nk **Sir Bond (IRE)**[13] [1450] 3-8-7 43 ow3 FLynch 1 25
(BSmart) *led to over 2f out: sn outpcd* **6/1**[3]

0-00 **6** 7 **Bridewell (USA)**[18] [1341] 5-9-7 30 PHanagan 3 9
(FWatson) *hld up: drvn 1/2-way: btn over 2f out* **5/1**[2]

-060 **7** 1 ¾ **Anacapri**[74] [783] 4-9-4 35 LEnstone(3) 5 6
(WSCunningham) *prom tl rdn and wknd fr 3f out* **50/1**

2m 11.72s (-0.47) **Going Correction** -0.025s/f (Good)
**WFA** 3 from 4yo+ 17lb **7** Ran SP% **112.5**
Speed ratings: **100,93,89,87,87 81,80**CSF £11.99 TOTE £2.20: £1.80, £3.10; EX 6.90 Place 6 £61.19, Place 5 £21.62.
**Owner** Mike Browne **Bred** Barronstown Stud **Trained** Norton, N Yorks

**FOCUS**
A particularly weak event in which Kingsdon did not have to improve too much record a decisive success. The pace was fair at best.

**NOTEBOOK**
**Kingsdon(IRE)** looked to have plenty in his favour and ran out the very easy winner of this poor event. He is a fair sort for this grade.
**Smarter Charter** is not the most straightforward and probably ran to the level of his recent All-Weather form, but he is the type that needs things to fall right and is not one to rely on.
**Optimum Night** attracted support and ran a bit better on his first start in this grade but, on this evidence, it will be a very weak event he wins.
**Howards Dream(IRE)** was again below the pick of last year's form and did not show enough to suggest he would be of interest for the near future.
**Sir Bond(IRE)**, who had shown little in maidens, had the run of the race in this lower grade but this run confirms he is only of very limited ability.
**Bridewell(USA)** attracted a bit of support but again showed nothing and remains one to tread carefully with.
RY

# [1690]LINGFIELD (L-H)

Thursday, April 29

**OFFICIAL GOING: Standard**

## 1723 LITTLEWOODS BET DIRECT AMATEUR RIDERS' BANDED STKS 1m (P)

5:35 (5:35) (H ) 4-Y-O+ £1,449 (£414; £207) Stalls High

Form RPR

0200 1 **Littleton Zephir (USA)**[62] 903 5-10-9 45........... MrsCThompson(5) 11 53
(MrsPTownsley) *racd in midfield: prog over 3f out: led over 2f out: urged along and clr over 1f out: kpt on* **14/1**

0-00 2 1¾ **Gran Clicquot**[51] 996 9-10-7 40............................... MrJPemberton(7) 4 49
(GPEnright) *w.w towards rr: prog over 2f out: rdn over 1f out: chsd chsd wnr ins fnl f: kpt on* **16/1**

6304 3 1½ **Theatre Lady (IRE)**[22] 1305 6-10-11 40....................... MissEFolkes(3) 2 46
(PDEvans) *led to over 3f out: pushed along and nt qckn over 2f out: styd on again ins fnl f* **11/4**[1]

0500 4 shd **Robin Sharp**[10] 1515 6-10-7 45............................(p) MrSGascoyne(7) 12 45
(JAkehurst) *racd v wd: in tch: jnd wnr over 2f out: outpcd and unbalanced over 1f out* **12/1**

5023 5 2 **Single Track Mind**[2] 1692 6-10-9 45.......................(p) MrMPattinson(5) 5 41
(JRBoyle) *dwlt: settled in last of main gp and sn wl bhd: prog 2f out: one pce fnl f: hopeless task* **3/1**[2]

3040 6 ¾ **Prince Minata (IRE)**[3] 1681 9-10-7 40.................... MissAHockley(7) 10 39
(PWHiatt) *wl in rr: pushed along over 3f out: bmpd along and sme prog over 1f out: no ch* **7/1**[3]

3004 7 3½ **Lady Liesel**[10] 1494 4-10-8 40 ow1..................... MissDonnaHandley(7) 3 32
(JJBridger) *pressed ldr: led over 3f out to over 2f out: wknd over 1f out* **12/1**

00-0 8 1 **Maravedi (IRE)**[12] 1479 4-10-9 45.........................(v[1]) MissALTurner(5) 9 29
(SLKeightley) *dwlt: a towards rr: pushed along and one pce fr over 2f out* **33/1**

00-0 9 1¾ **Mutabari (USA)**[5] 1629 10-10-7 45............................. MrJohnEvans(7) 7 25
(JLSpearing) *racd wd: trckd ldrs: grad wknd fr wl over 1f out* **25/1**

54-0 10 nk **Middlemiss (IRE)**[6] 1580 4-10-9 40.......................................... MrJJBest(5) 8 24
(JWMullins) *racd in midfield: wknd 2f out* **25/1**

55-0 11 5 **Singularity**[25] 1077 4-10-11 40.......................................... MrLNewnes(3) 6 12
(KFClutterbuck) *s.i.s: sn prom: lost pl over 3f out: c v wd bnd 2f out: bhd after* **10/1**

000- 12 10 **Mr Loverman (IRE)**[216] 5203 4-10-10 45 ow1.............. MissVHaigh(5) 1 —
(MissVHaigh) *rel to r and lft 25l: a t.o* **16/1**

1m 41.14s (1.59) **Going Correction** +0.075s/f (Slow) 12 Ran SP% **117.7**
Speed ratings: **95,93,91,91,89 88,85,84,82,82 77,67**CSF £212.65 TOTE £17.70: £5.50, £2.80, £1.20; EX 259.40.

**Owner** Classic Security UK Ltd **Bred** Sierra Thoroughbreds **Trained** Dunsfold, Surrey

■ Stewards Enquiry : Miss V Haigh one-day ban: used whip when out of contention (May 19)

**FOCUS**

A very poor contest though at least the pace was solid. The form is average for the grade.

**NOTEBOOK**

**Littleton Zephir(USA)**, with the blinkers left off and in a banded stakes for the first time, had run well in her only previous try on this surface and won this modest event in good style. The trip would have been sharp enough.

**Gran Clicquot** is better over ten furlongs and stayed on to chase the winner home without ever looking a threat.

**Theatre Lady(IRE)**, never the easiest to predict, may be extra over an extra quarter mile these days and, after making the running, got caught for foot rounding the home bend before staying on again.

**Robin Sharp** is not the horse he was, but ran a creditable race until his rider appeared to be having problems staying aboard as things got tight amongst the placed horses down the home straight.

**Single Track Mind**, who again started a short-enough price considering his very long losing run, was given an awful lot to do. Though he did get into a challenging position turning for home, there was little more to come. His rider did look little more than a passenger.

**Prince Minata(IRE)** really needs a greater test of stamina than this and his final placing was as close as he got. His rider's style still requires plenty of work.

## 1724 BETDIRECT.CO.UK BANDED STKS 6f (P)

6:05 (6:06) (H ) 4-Y-O+ £1,438 (£411; £205) Stalls Low

Form RPR

0022 1 **Alastair Smellie**[10] 1510 8-8-12 35....................................(v) PMcCabe 2 46
(SLKeightley) *trckd ldng pair: led wl over 2f out: sn clr: easily* **8/1**[2]

1211 2 3½ **Baytown Flyer**[2] 1692 4-9-4 40...................................... LDettori 4 42
(PSMcentee) *led to wl over 2f out: sn outpcd and rdn: no imp wnr after* **4/11**[1]

0306 3 2 **Onefortheboys (IRE)**[8] 1546 5-8-12 40.......................... SWhitworth 5 30
(DFlood) *dwlt: outpcd in last and pushed along: kpt on to take 3rd over 1f out: n.d* **8/1**[2]

0533 4 2 **Sotonian (HOL)**[14] 1406 11-8-9 40.................................. SHitchcott(3) 3 24
(PSFelgate) *chsd ldr to 3f out: sn outpcd and btn* **12/1**[3]

0-06 5 ½ **Tong Ice**[2] 1694 5-8-12 30............................................. RBrisland 1 22
(BAPearce) *hld up in last pair: effrt 2f out: no prog over 1f out* **33/1**

1m 13.15s (0.23) **Going Correction** +0.075s/f (Slow) 5 Ran SP% **106.2**
Speed ratings: **101,96,93,91,90**CSF £10.86 TOTE £12.00: £3.30, £1.02; EX 10.20.

**Owner** Mrs C C Regalado-Gonzalez **Bred** Stetchworth Park Stud Ltd **Trained** Waltham-On-The-Wolds, Leics

**FOCUS**

A fair time for a banded takes and something of a turn-up, but there was no fluke about the result.

**NOTEBOOK**

**Alastair Smellie ◆**, rated 90 in his heyday, was beaten by Baytown Flyer at Wolverhampton last time, but circumstances conspired against him that day and this time around he was cantering all over the favourite from some way out. He can win again at this level.

**Baytown Flyer**, bidding for her sixth win in 15 days, soon established her usual position out in front with her rider keen to stay well away from the inside rail, but the winner cruised past her on the final bend and there was little she could do about it.

**Onefortheboys(IRE)** was never going the pace and his final placing was the best he could hope for.

**Sotonian(HOL)**, without a win in nearly three years, stumbled slightly on the turn for home as the favourite cut the corner in front of him and he lost his impetus for a couple of strides. The incident may have cost him third at best.

**Tong Ice** reverted to patient tactics, but the result was the same.

## 1725 BET IN RUNNING @ BETDIRECT.CO.UK TRI-BANDED STKS 6f (P)

6:35 (6:35) (H ) 3-Y-O £1,606 (£459; £229) Stalls Low

Form RPR

60-0 1 **Yamato Pink**[37] 1086 3-8-9 40............................................ GBaker 7 51
(MrsHSweeting) *s.s: hld up in last: gd prog over 2f out: drvn to ld over 1f out: sn clr* **11/2**

4625 2 2½ **Fayr Firenze (IRE)**[6] 1594 3-9-0 45.................................(v) SRighton 2 48
(MFHarris) *trckd ldng pair: lost pl and drvn over 2f out: kpt on u.p fr over 1f out: no ch w wnr* **4/1**[3]

0400 3 ¾ **Parallel Lines (IRE)**[22] 1300 3-9-0 45................................ KFallon 4 46
(PDEvans) *settled in rr: prog over 2f out: rdn to chse ldrs over 1f out: no imp wnr fnl f* **9/4**[1]

3600 4 ½ **Jasmine Pearl (IRE)**[30] 1184 3-9-0 45............................ SWhitworth 8 44
(TMJones) *trckd ldr: led 2f out: drvn and hdd over 1f out: one pce* **7/2**[2]

60-0 5 3 **Anatom**[66] 865 3-8-7 35 ow3............................................(t) LDettori 1 28
(PSMcentee) *hld up in rr: outpcd in last over 2f out: n.d after* **15/2**

5000 6 hd **Must Be So**[63] 891 3-8-9 45.......................................... NChalmers(5) 3 35
(JJBridger) *trckd ldng pair: rdn 2f out: wknd over 1f out* **14/1**

4004 7 3 **Indrani**[7] 1571 3-9-0 45..................................................(p) NPollard 5 26
(JohnAHarris) *led to 2f out: wkng whn n.m.r over 1f out* **14/1**

1m 13.12s (0.20) **Going Correction** +0.075s/f (Slow) 7 Ran SP% **113.5**
Speed ratings: **101,97,96,96,92 91,87**CSF £27.15 TOTE £7.20: £3.50, £2.80; EX 32.40.

**Owner** P Sweeting **Bred** Baldernock Bloodstock Ltd **Trained** Marlborough, Wilts

**FOCUS**

A weak race but a good pace and a decent time for a race of its type.

**NOTEBOOK**

**Yamato Pink ◆**, making her debut in banded company, was returning to sprinting. Content to sit right out he back early, she strode around the entire field on the home bend and had little difficulty in pulling clear. She looks better than a mere banded-class performer and will be hard to beat if given another chance in a similar contest.

**Fayr Firenze(IRE)** stayed on to finish second, but was up against an unexposed sort. He is not very good, but is consistent at this level and a fair guide to the form.

**Parallel Lines(IRE)** had every chance, but is exposed and has gone the wrong way since last summer.

**Jasmine Pearl(IRE)**, who has dropped 30lb since last autumn, was up there the whole way but looked woefully one paced in the latter stages.

**Anatom** was struggling the whole way and even the Dettori magic made little difference.

## 1726 SPECIAL OFFERS @ BETDIRECT.CO.UK TRI-BANDED STKS 1m 2f (P)

7:05 (7:05) (H ) 3-Y-O £1,431 (£409; £204) Stalls Low

Form RPR

2311 1 **Dial Square**[2] 1695 3-9-6 45 6ex.......................................... KFallon 3 54
(PHowling) *t.k.h: hld up in 3rd: effrt over 1f out: pushd into ld last 150y: idled and reminder nr fin* **1/4**[1]

06-6 2 ½ **Scorchio (IRE)**[6] 1600 3-9-0 45............................................ LDettori 1 47
(MFHarris) *led: stdd pce 1/2-way: kicked on over 2f out: drvn and hdd last 150y: kpt on* **7/1**[2]

0-00 3 2½ **Lenwade**[12] 1465 3-9-0 45................................................. JMackay 2 42
(GGMargarson) *trckd ldr: rdn and ev ch 2f out: hanging rt and nt qckn over 1f out* **7/1**[2]

-000 4 5 **Out Of My Way**[31] 1167 3-8-5 30 ow1.............................. SWhitworth 4 24
(TMJones) *settled in last: effrt 3f out: wknd wl over 1f out* **20/1**[3]

2m 12.15s (4.30) **Going Correction** +0.075s/f (Slow) 4 Ran SP% **109.8**
Speed ratings: **85,84,82,78**CSF £2.67 TOTE £1.10; EX 2.20.

**Owner** Rory Murphy **Bred** J And Mrs Bowtell **Trained** Newmarket, Suffolk

**FOCUS**

A weak race run at a crawl and a pedestrian winning time. It was noticeable how the whole field wanted to keep well away from the inside rail.

**NOTEBOOK**

**Dial Square** managed to complete the hat-trick and land the long odds-on, but it was not all plain sailing. Finding himself tucked away in a pocket for some time, he had to be quick to take advantage of a gap when it appeared, and even after getting to the front he decided to idle and received a crack with the whip to keep his mind on the job. His superiority was greater than the winning margin would suggest.

**Scorchio(IRE)**, unplaced in six previous outings but dropped in class, was allowed his own way out in front and did his best to run the finish out of the favourite rounding the home bend, but was nothing like good enough to do so. He is greatly flattered by his proximity at the line, especially as he had the run of the race.

**Lenwade**, another dropping in grade having never previously been placed, had every chance but hung right turning for home which opened the door for the favourite.

**Out Of My Way**, trying his longest trip to date, did not improve for it.

## 1727 BET DIRECT ON 0800 32 93 93 CLAIMING STKS 1m 2f (P)

7:35 (7:35) (H ) 3-Y-O+ £1,277 (£365; £182) Stalls Low

Form RPR

2232 1 **Monduru**[12] 1479 7-9-10 50..............................................(be) RLMoore 2 53
(GLMoore) *trckd ldng pair: effrt 2f out: squeezed through on inner to ld over 1f out: pushed clr* **4/5**[1]

3430 2 1¾ **Senor Toran (USA)**[15] 1393 4-9-7 47............................... LPKeniry(3) 7 50
(PBurgoyne) *trckd ldr: rdn over 2f out: unable qck over 1f out: kpt on* **2/1**[2]

0-00 3 3 **Fitz The Bill (IRE)**[31] 1164 4-9-2 30.................................(b[1]) JMackay 6 36
(NBKing) *led: kicked on 3f out: hanging rt wl over 1f out: sn hdd and btn* **16/1**

-000 4 1¼ **Island Star (IRE)**[45] 575 4-9-7 40........................................ RBrisland 4 39
(GPEnright) *t.k.h: trckd ldrs: outpcd over 2f out: n.d after* **16/1**

00 5 3½ **Sink Or Swim (IRE)**[41] 1055 6-9-0................................... NChalmers(5) 5 30
(JJBridger) *hld up in last: outpcd fr 3f out: no ch fnl 2f* **16/1**

04 6 13 **Mister Graham**[8] 1547 9-9-10 .......................................(p) OUrbina 3 10
(KFClutterbuck) *dwlt and early reminder: effrt to chse ldrs 1/2-way: rdn and nt run on over 3f out: sn t.o* **12/1**[3]

2m 9.33s (1.48) **Going Correction** +0.075s/f (Slow) 6 Ran SP% **114.2**
Speed ratings: **97,95,93,92,89 79**CSF £2.68 TOTE £1.50: £1.10, £1.80; EX 1.90.

**Owner** Pleasure Palace Racing **Bred** D J And Mrs Deer **Trained** Woodingdean, E Sussex

**FOCUS**

A poor claimer and a much faster time than the previous race, but still only an ordinary time for the grade. The market suggested it was a two-horse race and so it proved.

**NOTEBOOK**

**Monduru**, best in on adjusted official ratings, is a consistent performer in this grade. Always close to the pace, he was a little fortunate that the leader jinked right soon after turning for home, leaving him with a nice gap against the inside rail. He did not need a second invitation.

**Senor Toran(USA)**, always on the shoulder of the leader, had every chance but the favourite found much the better turn of foot. Getting a bump from Fitz The Bill a furlong and a half from home made no difference to the result.

**Fitz The Bill(IRE)**, well beaten on the Flat and over hurdles in her ten previous outings, was given a positive ride from the start in the first-time blinkers and tried to steal the race on the home turn, but could never establish a sufficient lead. She jinked to her right on reaching the home straight, cannoning into the runner-up and leaving a gap for the winner to come through.
**Island Star(IRE)**, who has shown precious little on the Flat and over hurdles over the past year or so, pulled far too hard early which would have compromised any chance he may have had.

## 1728 BET DIRECT ON SKY ACTIVE BANDED STKS 1m 5f (P)
8:05 (8:05) (H) 3-Y-O+ £1,477 (£422; £211) Stalls Low

| Form | | | | | RPR |
|---|---|---|---|---|---|
| -004 | 1 | | **Royale Pearl**[31] [1164] 4-9-9 40 ... DaneO'Neill 9 | | 47 |
| | | | (RIngram) *t.k.h: hld up in rr: outpcd 5f out: gd prog 3f out: led wl over 1f out: rdn out* | 14/1 | |
| 30-3 | 2 | 2 | **Lady Lakshmi**[10] [1514] 4-9-9 40 ... JMackay 8 | | 44 |
| | | | (RGuest) *hld up: outpcd 5f out: prog 3f out: drvn to chse wnr ins fnl f: kpt on* | 9/1 | |
| 0122 | 3 | 1 | **Leophin Dancer (USA)**[2] [1690] 6-9-10 40 ... BDoyle 4 | | 43 |
| | | | (PWHiatt) *trckd ldrs: outpcd 5f out: chsd clr ldng pair over 3f out: ev ch 2f out: chsd wnr wl over 1f out: one pce after* | 7/2[3] | |
| 0- | 4 | 2 ½ | **Eau Pure (FR)**[8] [937] 7-9-10 40 ... RLMoore 5 | | 39 |
| | | | (GLMoore) *racd in midfield: outpcd 5f out: drvn 3f out: kpt on one pce fr over 1f out: n.d* | 11/4[1] | |
| 0-55 | 5 | nk | **Sylvan Twister**[10] [1493] 5-9-10 35 ... NPollard 7 | | 39 |
| | | | (PMitchell) *hld up in last: outpcd 5f out: rdn over 3f out: kpt on same pce fnl 2f: no ch* | 50/1 | |
| 1160 | 6 | 1 ¼ | **Dafa**[8] [1545] 8-9-10 40 ...(b) SWKelly 2 | | 37 |
| | | | (BJCurley) *led at gd pce: jnd 6f out: clr w chalr fr 5f out: hdd wl over 1f out: hanging and wknd* | 14/1 | |
| 0343 | 7 | 1 ½ | **Anniversary Guest (IRE)**[2] [1693] 5-9-10 40 ... CCatlin 6 | | 35 |
| | | | (MrsLucindaFeatherstone) *t.k.h: hld up: plld way up to press ldng pair 7f out: outpcd 5f out: lost 3rd and fdd over 3f out* | 6/1 | |
| 6-04 | 8 | 3 ½ | **Lady Xanthia**[10] [1493] 3-8-3 35 ... PDoe 3 | | 30 |
| | | | (IAWood) *t.k.h: trckd ldr: chal 6f out: wknd rapidly 2f out* | 33/1 | |
| 3321 | 9 | dist | **Seraph**[2] [1690] 4-10-1 40 ...(p) KFallon 1 | | — |
| | | | (JohnAHarris) *chsd ldrs: rdn and wknd over 5f out: t.o* | 10/3[2] | |

2m 50.82s (2.74) **Going Correction** +0.075s/f (Slow) 9 Ran SP% **114.5**
**WFA** 3 from 4yo 21lb 4 from 5yo+ 1lb
Speed ratings: **94,92,92,90,90 89,88,86,—**CSF £131.48 TOTE £13.70: £2.60, £2.40, £2.10; EX 57.40 Place 6 £43.44, Place 5 £16.22.
**Owner** Glen Antill **Bred** G A And Mrs Antill **Trained** Epsom, Surrey

**FOCUS**
A modest pace for the first half of the race, but the tempo quickened considerably in the second. The form is no better than average for the grade.

**NOTEBOOK**
**Royale Pearl**, stepping up again in distance, had to prove her stamina conclusively due to the way the race was run and did so in style. She had quite a bit to do at halfway, but she got stronger as the race progressed and, as the front pair tired, she was the one that took full advantage. This was not a great race, but she is still relatively unexposed over this sort of trip.
**Lady Lakshmi**, in a race run to suit those coming from off the pace, utilised her stamina to come through and snatch second but found the winner much too good. She is not without hope for a similar contest when stamina is at a premium.
**Leophin Dancer(USA)**, a regular in this type of contest here lately, led the group chasing the two clear leaders and, although he managed to pick both of them up as they tired, found a couple seeing this slightly longer trip out just a little bit better.
**Eau Pure(FR)**, well beaten in her only Flat outing in this country at this venue a year ago, has enjoyed some success over hurdles since but seemed to find this an insufficient test of stamina despite the strong pace in the second half of the contest.
**Dafa**, trying his longest trip to date, made the running but was taken on before halfway and, in trying to shake his challenger off, only managed to run himself into the ground. *Official explanation: jockey said gelding hung right up the straight*
**Lady Xanthia**, stepping up another three furlongs in trip, took the leader on before halfway and went clear along with him, but that only resulted in bottoming the pair of them.
T/Plt: £15.70 to a £1 stake. Pool: £25,006.60. 1,161.35 winning tickets. T/Qpdt: £5.40 to a £1 stake. Pool: £1,630.80. 223.40 winning tickets. JN

# [1358] REDCAR (L-H)
Thursday, April 29
**1729 Meeting Abandoned** - Waterlogged

# [1696] SOUTHWELL (L-H)
Thursday, April 29
**OFFICIAL GOING: Standard to slow changing to standard after race 4 (4.00pm)**
Wind: fresh across Weather: overcast

## 1735 LITTLEWOODS BET DIRECT MAIDEN AUCTION STKS 5f (F)
2:30 (2:31) (F) 2-Y-O £2,954 (£844; £422) Stalls High

| Form | | | | | RPR |
|---|---|---|---|---|---|
| 2 | 1 | | **Unlimited**[24] [1264] 2-8-9 ... GDuffield 5 | | 65 |
| | | | (MrsADuffield) *chsd ldr: rdn to ld over 1f out: r.o* | 13/8[1] | |
| 0 | 2 | ½ | **Urabande**[14] [1415] 2-7-13 ... LisaJones(3) 3 | | 56 |
| | | | (JulianPoulton) *led: rdn: edgd rt and hdd over 1f out: r.o* | 50/1 | |
| 0 | 3 | 3 | **Eternally**[21] [1314] 2-8-9 ...(p) MHenry 6 | | 51 |
| | | | (RMHCowell) *chsd ldrs: rdn over 1f out: styd on same pce* | 20/1 | |
| | 4 | 2 ½ | **Zendaro** 2-8-2 ... BSwarbrick(7) 8 | | 41 |
| | | | (WMBrisbourne) *chsd ldrs: rdn over 1f out: wkng whn hung lft ins fnl f* | 10/3[2] | |
| | 5 | 3 | **Missed Turn** 2-8-9 ... PFessey 7 | | 29 |
| | | | (KARyan) *chsd ldrs over 3f* | 14/1 | |
| | 6 | 1 ½ | **Almost Perfect (IRE)** 2-8-3 ow1 ... EAhern 9 | | 17 |
| | | | (TDBarron) *sn outpcd* | 6/1[3] | |
| | 7 | 2 ½ | **Danehill Angel** 2-8-6 ... DHolland 11 | | 10 |
| | | | (MJPolglase) *dwlt: outpcd* | 14/1 | |
| 5 | 8 | nk | **Ronnies Lad**[24] [1264] 2-8-7 ... VHalliday 4 | | 10 |
| | | | (JRNorton) *sn outpcd* | 50/1 | |
| 0 | 9 | 5 | **Lord Chalfont (IRE)**[6] [1589] 2-8-9 ...(b) ACulhane 12 | | — |
| | | | (DFlood) *outpcd* | 14/1 | |
| | 10 | 1 | **Keresforth** 2-9-0 ... TEDurcan 10 | | — |
| | | | (TDEasterby) *s.s: outpcd* | 12/1 | |
| | 11 | 4 | **Metolica** 2-8-4 ow2 ... RFitzpatrick 2 | | — |
| | | | (CSmith) *s.s: outpcd* | 40/1 | |
| 0 | 12 | 6 | **Ryans Lil Ol Gal**[6] [1589] 2-8-2 ... DaleGibson 1 | | — |
| | | | (ABCoogan) *outpcd* | 80/1 | |

61.74 secs (1.34) **Going Correction** 0.0s/f (Stan) 12 Ran SP% **115.5**
Speed ratings: **89,88,83,79,74 72,68,67,59,58 51,42**CSF £117.90 TOTE £2.60: £1.10, £9.30, £6.00; EX 62.90.
**Owner** Mrs L J Tounsend **Bred** J Wise **Trained** Constable Burton, N Yorks

**FOCUS**
Not much strength in depth in what was predictably an ordinary maiden. The form is only fair, but there should be a couple in behind capable of picking up a similarly modest event.

**NOTEBOOK**
**Unlimited** is trained on the course and made his debut round here, so he knows the track well. He showed plenty of pace from the off and found enough under pressure to hold off the runner-up, confirming the promise of his initial outing in the process. Despite clearly acting on the surface, connections feel the deep ground does not help him and he could prove better on turf.
**Urabande**, a 2,600gns purchase, showed little on her debut but offered plenty of encouragement this time around. An ordinary maiden should come her way.
**Eternally** was well held on his debut at Musselburgh but had cheekpieces on this time and ran better. He was a little one paced in the closing stages, but should continue to progress.
**Zendaro**, a 6,500gns yearling, out of an unraced half-sister to the high-class mile to ten-furlong filly Donna Viola, was supported and ran well. He lacked the pace of the front two in the closing stages, but looks capable of improvement.
**Missed Turn**, a 14,000gns sister to a six-furlong two-year-old winner, never really posed a threat but did hint at ability. There should be plenty of improvement in her.

## 1736 BETDIRECT.CO.UK CLAIMING STKS 1m (F)
3:00 (3:00) (F) 3-Y-O £3,213 (£918; £459) Stalls Low

| Form | | | | | RPR |
|---|---|---|---|---|---|
| 0461 | 1 | | **Doctored**[22] [1296] 3-8-10 54 ...(p) BReilly(3) 5 | | 62 |
| | | | (BAPearce) *chsd ldrs: led over 2f out: rdn over 1f out: styd on* | 11/2[2] | |
| -231 | 2 | ¾ | **Caspian Dusk**[30] [1192] 3-9-1 70 ... ACulhane 2 | | 63 |
| | | | (WGMTurner) *chsd ldr 7f out: led 5f out: rdn and hdd over 2f out: unable qck ins fnl f* | 1/4[1] | |
| 0004 | 3 | 6 | **Divina**[8] [1548] 3-8-6 30 ...(v) FNorton 1 | | 42? |
| | | | (SLKeightley) *chsd ldrs: rdn over 2f out: sn outpcd* | 50/1 | |
| 2664 | 4 | 4 | **Bretton**[10] [1499] 3-8-7 45 ...(p) DaleGibson 4 | | 35 |
| | | | (RHollinshead) *sn outpcd and bhd* | 10/1[3] | |
| 000- | 5 | dist | **Shanghai Surprise**[192] [5679] 3-8-9 46 ... JEdmunds 3 | | — |
| | | | (JBalding) *led 3f: wknd over 2f out* | 25/1 | |

1m 47.09s (2.49) **Going Correction** +0.075s/f (Slow) 5 Ran SP% **110.3**
Speed ratings: **90,89,83,79,—**CSF £7.46 TOTE £5.20: £2.90, £1.02; EX 26.00.
**Owner** T M J Keep **Bred** Wickfield Farm Partnership **Trained** Newchapel, Surrey

**FOCUS**
A weak claimer that only concerned the first two home from the top of the straight. The winning time was slow for the grade.

**NOTEBOOK**
**Doctored**, off the mark in a seven-furlong seller at Folkestone on his previous outing, followed up with a hard-fought victory. He had 14lb to find with the winner at the weights, but proved too strong for that one and is clearly one to have on your side in these moderate events whilst in this sort of form.
**Caspian Dusk** bolted up in a course and distance maiden on his previous start and looked a good thing to follow up on the figures, for he had upwards of 14lb in hand of his rivals at the weights. He simply found one too good and his current rating of 70 looks to flatter him after this.
**Divina** had 17lb to find with the winner at the weights and was not surprisingly well beaten. Banded racing looks the way to go with this one.
**Bretton** was badly outpaced on this drop back in trip.
**Shanghai Surprise**, with the blinkers left off this time, was keen and found little in the straight.

## 1737 SPECIAL OFFERS @ BETDIRECT.CO.UK FILLIES' H'CAP 6f (F)
3:30 (3:30) (E) (0-75,75) 3-Y-O £3,740 (£1,151; £575; £287) Stalls Low

| Form | | | | | RPR |
|---|---|---|---|---|---|
| -156 | 1 | | **Generous Gesture (IRE)**[12] [1464] 3-9-6 74 ...(v[1]) IMongan 3 | | 84 |
| | | | (MLWBell) *sn pushed along in rr: hdwy over 3f out: hung lft and led over 1f out: rdn out* | 9/2 | |
| 2152 | 2 | 2 | **Marinaite**[12] [1464] 3-9-7 75 ... JBramhill 4 | | 79 |
| | | | (SRBowring) *trckd ldr: led on bit over 2f out: hdd over1f out: sn bmpd: unable qck ins fnl f* | 2/1[1] | |
| 00-4 | 3 | 7 | **Obe Bold (IRE)**[5] [1626] 3-8-11 65 ... FNorton 7 | | 48 |
| | | | (ABerry) *led over 3f: wknd over 1f out* | 25/1 | |
| 4431 | 4 | nk | **Cheeky Chi (IRE)**[17] [1362] 3-8-12 66 ... NCallan 5 | | 48 |
| | | | (PSMcentee) *chsd ldrs: rdn and ev ch over 2f out: wkng whn hung lft ins fnl f* | 4/1[3] | |
| 430- | 5 | ½ | **Turkish Delight**[141] [6160] 3-8-3 57 ... JEdmunds 6 | | 38 |
| | | | (JBalding) *chsd ldrs: outpcd over 4f out: n.d after* | 16/1 | |
| -260 | 6 | ½ | **Velvet Touch**[30] [1184] 3-8-1 55 ... JQuinn 1 | | 34 |
| | | | (JRJenkins) *hld up: hdwy u.p over 2f out: wknd over 1f out* | 14/1 | |
| 00-0 | 7 | 8 | **Queens Square**[17] [1362] 3-7-12 52 oh2 ... KimTinkler 8 | | 7 |
| | | | (NTinkler) *chsd ldrs over 3f* | 66/1 | |
| 412 | 8 | dist | **Sahara Silk (IRE)**[5] [1626] 3-9-0 68 ...(v) DHolland 2 | | — |
| | | | (DShaw) *in tch tl wknd wl over 3f out: eased over 1f out* | 7/2[2] | |

1m 17.27s (0.37) **Going Correction** +0.075s/f (Slow) 8 Ran SP% **111.6**
Speed ratings: **100,97,88,87,86 86,75,—**CSF £13.22 CT £193.89 TOTE £7.00: £3.20, £1.10, £7.00; EX 18.30.
**Owner** Mr & Mrs J & P Ransley **Bred** Bakewell Bloodstock **Trained** Newmarket, Suffolk

**FOCUS**
Just ordinary stuff, but probably quite a good performance from the front two - they were well clear of the remainder. The time was fair for the class of contest and sound-enough form.

**NOTEBOOK**
**Generous Gesture(IRE)** was ideally suited by the fitting of a visor and returned to winning form after a couple of ordinary efforts. The visor helped her concentrate, and she could well follow up if it has the same effect next time, especially if returned to this course and distance as she is two from two round here.
**Marinaite** did nothing wrong, she travelled well and came clear of all bar the winner in the straight.
**Obe Bold(IRE)** had every chance from the front but was not good enough to go with the front two in the closing stages. Her only win to date came over five furlongs and that trip may suit better.
**Cheeky Chi(IRE)**, off the mark over the minimum trip at Redcar on her latest start, proved disappointed over this extra furlong on her Fibresand debut. A drop back in trip may suit.
**Turkish Delight** has been given a chance by the Handicapper, but did not offer that much encouragement on her return from a 141-day break. She can, however, be expected to come on for the run.
**Sahara Silk(IRE)** weakened early on in the race and something may have been amiss. *Official explanation: jockey said filly was never travelling*

## 1738 BET IN RUNNING @ BETDIRECT.CO.UK H'CAP 5f (F)
4:00 (4:00) (E) (0-75,70) 3-Y-O+ **£3,760** (£1,157; £578; £289) **Stalls High**

Form RPR

4610 **1** **Far Note (USA)**[3] [1665] 6-10-0 70..........(b) JBramhill 1 82
(SRBowring) *s.i.s: sn chsng ldrs: rdn to ld and hung rt over 1f out: eased towards fin* **8/1**

-301 **2** *2* **Dunn Deal (IRE)**[17] [1368] 4-9-7 63.......... TEDurcan 4 69
(WMBrisbourne) *in rr: hdwy over 1f out: no ch w wnr* **7/1**[2]

-125 **3** *1 ½* **Empress Josephine**[62] [905] 4-9-1 60..........(v) DCorby(3) 7 62
(JRJenkins) *w ldr tl led 1/2-way: rdn and hdd over 1f out: no ex ins fnl f* **11/1**

1310 **4** *½* **Italian Mist (FR)**[9] [1516] 5-9-5 68..........(e) MHalford(7) 13 68
(JulianPoulton) *hld up: r.o ins fnl f: nt rch ldrs* **6/1**[1]

4052 **5** *hd* **The Leather Wedge (IRE)**[31] [1180] 5-8-5 47.......... FNorton 12 46
(ABerry) *chsd ldrs: rdn and ev ch over 1f out: no ex* **15/2**[3]

0002 **6** *hd* **Finger Of Fate**[2] [1699] 4-7-9 40..........(b) JFMcDonald(3) 5 39
(MJPolglase) *chsd ldrs: rdn and ev ch whn hmpd over 1f out: no ex* **7/1**[2]

4003 **7** *nk* **Speedfit Free (IRE)**[7] [1569] 7-8-10 52..........(v) AnnStokell 6 50
(MissAStokell) *sn outpcd: styd on ins fnl f: nvr nrr* **40/1**

0112 **8** *½* **Attorney**[6] [1584] 6-9-0 56 6ex..........(v) DHolland 3 52
(DShaw) *prom: rdn 3f out: hung lft fr 1/2-way: nt run on* **15/2**[3]

1326 **9** *½* **Sea The World (IRE)**[29] [1205] 4-9-7 63..........(v) NCallan 11 58
(DShaw) *dwlt: outpcd* **7/1**[2]

1030 **10** *¾* **Lady Protector**[73] [796] 5-8-6 48.......... JEdmunds 8 41
(JBalding) *led to 1/2-way: rdn and ev ch over 1f out: wknd ins fnl f* **16/1**

0001 **11** *7* **Arogant Prince**[9] [1516] 7-9-2 58..........(b) RPrice 9 30
(JPearce) *sn outpcd* **10/1**

2604 **12** *1* **Sounds Lucky**[29] [1206] 8-8-12 54..........(b) GGibbons 10 23
(AndrewReid) *dwlt: outpcd* **33/1**

59.83 secs (-0.57) **Going Correction** 0.0s/f (Stan) **12 Ran SP% 115.1**
Speed ratings: **104,100,98,97,97 96,96,95,94,93 82,80**CSF £61.15 CT £626.23 TOTE £9.20: £2.20, £3.10, £3.60; EX 68.20.
**Owner** Mrs A Potts **Bred** Juddmonte Farms **Trained** Edwinstowe, Notts
■ Stewards Enquiry : D Corby one-day ban: used whip down the shoulder in the forehand position (May 10)

**FOCUS**
Quite a competitive sprint handicap and the pace was fair.

**NOTEBOOK**
**Far Note(USA)** failed to handle soft ground at Newcastle on his previous start, but goes very well on Fibresand and returned to form off a mark 3lb higher than when winning over this course and distance two starts back. He may be switched back to the turf, but would clearly want to avoid ground too testing.
**Dunn Deal(IRE)**, 4lb higher than when winning at Warwick on his previous start, appeared to run his race on this switch back to Fibresand.
**Empress Josephine** is 7lb higher than when last successful and, although this was not a bad effort, she may just be in the Handicapper's grip.
**Italian Mist(FR)**, a winner on his last two starts on Fibresand, finished too good effect but it was all too late. Six furlongs may suit slightly better.
**The Leather Wedge(IRE)** continues on his long losing run.

## 1739 BET DIRECT ON 0800 32 93 93 (S) STKS 6f (F)
4:30 (4:31) (G) 3-Y-O+ **£2,534** (£724; £362) **Stalls Low**

Form RPR

1312 **1** **On The Trail**[7] [1569] 7-9-11 50.......... ACulhane 5 63
(DWChapman) *mde all: shkn up over 1f out: styd on* **11/4**[2]

3053 **2** *¾* **Blakeset**[14] [1423] 9-9-11 63.......... EAhern 3 61
(TDBarron) *trckd wnr: rdn over 1f out: r.o* **10/3**[3]

5210 **3** *shd* **Never Without Me**[14] [1421] 4-9-4 54.......... KJackson(7) 7 60
(PJMcbride) *chsd ldrs: hung lft over 1f out: r.o* **9/4**[1]

5610 **4** *2* **Bells Beach (IRE)**[9] [1516] 6-9-6 54.......... TEDurcan 2 49
(PHowling) *s.i.s: outpcd: hdwy u.p over 1f out: one pce fnl f* **6/1**

5045 **5** *3 ½* **Polar Haze**[27] [1237] 7-9-11 55..........(b) RPrice 6 44
(JPearce) *chsd ldrs over 3f* **9/1**

04/0 **6** *17* **Bound To Please**[6] [1591] 9-9-6 47..........(v) AnnStokell 1 —
(MissAStokell) *s.i.s: outpcd* **40/1**

1m 16.74s (-0.16) **Going Correction** +0.075s/f (Slow) **6 Ran SP% 107.2**
Speed ratings: **104,103,102,100,95 72**CSF £11.10 TOTE £4.10: £1.40, £2.00; EX 8.00.There was no bid for the winner.
**Owner** J M Chapman **Bred** Ian Bellamy **Trained** Stillington, N Yorks
■ Stewards Enquiry : E Ahern two-day ban: used whip with excessive frequency (May 10-11)

**FOCUS**
Only a few runners, but a competitive enough seller for the track. A fair winning time for the grade.

**NOTEBOOK**
**On The Trail** continued his tremendous run of form. He was there to be shot at, but kept on right the way to the line and remains one to have on your side at this level.
**Blakeset** is regressing and the drop into selling company did not prove the answer.
**Never Without Me**, well backed on this drop into selling company, threatened to pick up but could never quite get there.
**Bells Beach(IRE)** is at her best in this grade, but has been doing her winning on Polytrack recently and was below form switched to Fibresand.
**Polar Haze** continues to run below form.

## 1740 BET DIRECT ON SKY ACTIVE H'CAP 1m 4f (F)
5:00 (5:06) (F) (0-55,61) 3-Y-O **£2,877** (£822; £411) **Stalls Low**

Form RPR

6630 **1** **Pepe (IRE)**[17] [1365] 3-8-6 49.......... StephanieHollinshead(7) 2 57
(RHollinshead) *mde all: rdn clr over 2f out: hung rt over 1f out: styd on* **11/2**

00-5 **2** *4* **Princess Kiotto**[14] [1420] 3-9-3 53.......... TEDurcan 5 55
(TDEasterby) *trckd ldrs: rdn over 3f out: sn outpcd: styd on ins fnl f: nt trble wnr* **9/2**[3]

0000 **3** *3 ½* **Atlantic Breeze**[9] [1529] 3-8-11 47.......... RFitzpatrick 3 44
(MrsNMacauley) *chsd ldrs: outpcd over 3f out: styd on ins fnl f* **7/1**

-452 **4** *1 ½* **Valiant Air (IRE)**[10] [1499] 3-8-10 46 oh1.......... DHolland 8 41
(JRWeymes) *chsd wnr 9f out: rdn over 2 out: wknd fnl f* **11/4**[1]

3331 **5** *10* **Angelo's Pride**[6] [1600] 3-9-11 61 6ex.......... GDuffield 7 41
(JAOsborne) *hld up in tch: rdn over 2f out: sn wknd* **4/1**[2]

00-0 **6** *10* **Northern Summit (IRE)**[29] [1201] 3-8-10 46 oh6.......... FNorton 4 11
(JRNorton) *s.i.s: sn prom: pushed along 8f out: wknd 4f out* **50/1**

0-55 **7** *3* **Rebel Rouser**[6] [1600] 3-8-11 47.......... IMongan 6 7
(WRMuir) *hld up: hdwy over 4f out: wknd over 2f out* **10/1**

30-0 **8** *12* **Miss Hoofbeats**[12] [1465] 3-8-8 47.......... BReilly(3) 1 —
(MissJFeilden) *sn pushed along in rr: wknd over 5f out* **10/1**

2m 44.6s (2.50) **Going Correction** +0.075s/f (Slow) **8 Ran SP% 112.9**
Speed ratings: **94,91,89,88,81 74,72,64**CSF £29.56 CT £173.46 TOTE £5.70: £1.90, £2.70, £2.50; EX 35.10 Place 6 £76.65, Place 5 £36.87.
**Owner** J D Graham **Bred** Paul Starr **Trained** Upper Longdon, Staffs

**FOCUS**
A very weak handicap run at a moderate gallop.

**NOTEBOOK**
**Pepe(IRE)** shaped well when last seen on this surface and, returned to Fibresand in possibly a weaker race, her jockey made good use of her stamina and she was never going to be caught. She will stay even further and should be able to go on from this.
**Princess Kiotto** appeared suited by this step up from a mile, but got going too late to trouble the winner. There could be a similar race in her now connections appear to have found a trip that suits.
**Atlantic Breeze**, racing over a trip this far for the first time and returned to Fibresand, ran respectably but was beaten a long way.
**Valiant Air(IRE)** was being niggled along down the back straight and never really looked like picking up. This was disappointing, but he did not show his best on his previous try on this surface and maybe it does not suit.
**Angelo's Pride** was trying this trip for the first time and he did not appear to stay.
**Rebel Rouser** *Official explanation: jockey said gelding tired very rapidly in the closing stages*
**Miss Hoofbeats** *Official explanation: jockey said filly hung right*
T/Plt: £86.30 to a £1 stake. Pool: £35,787.65. 302.45 winning tickets. T/Qpdt: £64.20 to a £1 stake. Pool: £1,970.50. 22.70 winning tickets. CR

# 1652 LONGCHAMP (R-H)
Thursday, April 29

**OFFICIAL GOING: Soft**

## 1741a PRIX DE MONTRETOUT (LISTED) 7f
2:20 (2:27) 4-Y-O+ **£15,845** (£6,338; £4,754; £3,169)

RPR

**1** **Vasywait (FR)**[28] 5-9-2 .......... DBoeuf 8 111
(J-LGay, France)

**2** *nk* **Puppeteer**[32] [1163] 4-9-2 .......... CSoumillon 11 110
(ADeRoyer-Dupre, France)

**3** *1 ½* **Crystal Castle (USA)**[181] [5866] 6-9-2 .......... TGillet 13 107
(JEHammond, France) 1

**4** *shd* **Star Valley (FR)**[28] 4-9-2 .......... IMendizabal 10 107
(J-CRouget, France)

**5** *1 ½* **The Wise Lady (FR)**[48] 4-8-8 .......... SPasquier 5 96
(MNigge, France)

**6** *shd* **Charming Groom (FR)**[23] [1291] 5-8-12 .......... OPeslier 2 100
(FHead, France)

**7** *shd* **Dexterity (USA)**[291] [3256] 6-8-12 .......... C-PLemaire 6 100
(H-APantall, France)

**8** *¾* **La Tard (FR)**[35] 6-8-8 .......... TJarnet 1 94
(MlleBJoly, France)

**9** *shd* **Davyd Sho (FR)**[18] 7-8-12 .......... PSogorb 12 98
(HCarlus, France)

**10** *½* **Garlinote (FR)**[18] [1351] 4-8-13 ..........(b) FSpanu 7 98
(MmeCBarande-Barbe, France)

**11** *2 ½* **Cote Quest (USA)**[19] [1332] 4-8-8 .......... TThulliez 4 88
(SCWilliams) *raced in last place to over 1f out, no real progress*

**12** *¾* **L'Archonte (FR)**[209] 4-9-2 .......... MNobili 9 94
(M-FMathet, France)

**13** *1 ½* **Man O Desert (FR)**[199] 4-8-12 .......... GaryStevens 14 87
(AFabre, France)

**14** *5* **Fabuleux River (FR)**[28] 4-8-12 ..........(b) DBonilla 3 77
(NMadamet, France)

1m 20.9s **Going Correction** +0.05s/f (Good) **14 Ran SP% 5.6**
Speed ratings: **113,112,110,110,109 109,108,108,107,107 104,103,101,96**.
**Owner** Mme F Gay **Bred** Mlle Fanny Guedj **Trained** France

**NOTEBOOK**
**Cote Quest(USA)**, slowly into her stride, never really got a blow in. She still had plenty to do in the straight and did run on towards the finish, but the jockey felt she needed a longer trip, and she now heads for a handicap in England.

# 1340 MUSSELBURGH (R-H)
Friday, April 30

**OFFICIAL GOING: Straight course - good; round course - good (good to firm in places)**
The ground was reckoned to be almost good but very loose on top after light rain had fallen on watered ground.
Wind: fresh hlf bhd Weather: overcast, cold and light rain

## 1742 EAST LOTHIAN H'CAP 5f
2:20 (2:20) (E) (0-75,72) 3-Y-O **£4,104** (£1,263; £631; £315) **Stalls Low**

Form RPR

-651 **1** **He's A Rocket (IRE)**[10] [1517] 3-7-9 46 6ex oh3..........(b) LisaJones(3) 4 60
(KRBurke) *bmpd s: sn chsng ldrs: led over 1f out: wnt clr ins last* **7/1**

0034 **2** *3* **Princess Kai (IRE)**[22] [1312] 3-8-4 55..........(b) GDuffield 5 55
(RIngram) *bmpd s: sn w ldr: rdn and hung rt 2f out: kpt on ins last* **7/2**[1]

0010 **3** *shd* **Garnock Venture (IRE)**[4] [1676] 3-8-4 55..........(b) FNorton 8 55
(ABerry) *sn chsng ldrs: styd on same pce appr fnl f* **12/1**

30-1 **4** *2* **Linda Green**[30] [1196] 3-8-9 60.......... DeanMcKeown 1 52
(PABlockley) *sn chsng ldrs: hung rt and n.m.r over 1f out: styd on towards fin* **6/1**

1-00 **5** *½* **Peters Choice**[13] [1473] 3-9-7 72..........(p) NCallan 7 63
(ISemple) *led tl over 1f out: fdd ins last* **9/2**[2]

010- **6** *nk* **Feu Duty (IRE)**[188] [5746] 3-8-11 62.......... RHavlin 9 52
(TJEtherington) *sn chsng ldrs on outside: hung rt 1/2-way: wknd appr fnl f* **12/1**

0-60 **7** *4* **Blade's Daughter**[4] [1676] 3-7-13 50 oh4 ow1..........(p) PFessey 2 25
(KARyan) *sn outpcd and bhd: kpt on fnl 2f: nvr a factor* **14/1**

2210 **8** *5* **Global Achiever**[20] [1333] 3-9-5 70..........(b[1]) RFfrench 3 27
(GCHChung) *swvd rt s: a outpcd in rr* **5/1**[3]

600- **9** *8* **O'l Lucy Broon**[228] [4947] 3-8-5 56.......... JFEgan 6 —
(JSGoldie) *sn outpcd and bhd* **25/1**

61.25 secs (0.85) **Going Correction** +0.125s/f (Good) **9 Ran SP% 109.8**
Speed ratings: **98,93,93,89,89 88,82,74,61**CSF £29.17 CT £268.30 TOTE £8.00: £1.90, £1.60, £4.00; EX 22.70.
**Owner** Mrs Lorraine Charge **Bred** Lemongrove Stud **Trained** Middleham Moor, N Yorks

**FOCUS**
A modest race with a pace to match, but the winner is in top form and it looks sound enough.

**NOTEBOOK**

**He's A Rocket(IRE)** gave his new connections a quick return. Transformed by blinkers, he came right away inside the last but he will face much stiffer tasks in future.
**Princess Kai(IRE)**, who looked very fit indeed, took a bump at the start. She hung away from the running rail and in the end proved no match.
**Garnock Venture(IRE)** did nothing wrong in the stalls this time but he finds this his bare minimum.
**Linda Green**, best drawn, took a walk in the market. She did not have the run of the race but was found to be coughing afterwards. *Official explanation: vet said filly was coughing*
**Peters Choice**, who has slipped to a mark 2lb lower than his last success at two achieved on the All-Weather, wore first-time cheekpieces. They set him alight but in the end he did not really see it out.
**Feu Duty(IRE)**, on her toes beforehand, tended to hang right and looks on a stiff mark.
**O'l Lucy Broon** *Official explanation: jockey said filly hung right-handed throughout*

## 1743 ROYAL BANK OF SCOTLAND MEDIAN AUCTION MAIDEN STKS — 5f
2:50 (2:51) (E) 2-Y-O — £4,017 (£1,236; £618; £309) Stalls Low

Form — RPR

3 **1** **Mary Read**[11] [1498] 2-8-9 ........ FLynch 2 79
(BSmart) *mde virtually all: styd on wl ins last* **12/1**

4 **2** *1 ¼* **Chiselled (IRE)**[20] [1324] 2-9-0 ........ DarrenWilliams 3 79
(KRBurke) *dwlt: t.k.h: sn trcking ldrs: effrt 2f out: ev ch ins last: no ex* **3/1**[1]

3 **3** *2 ½* **Monsieur Mirasol**[19] [1340] 2-9-0 ........ NCallan 7 69
(KARyan) *rrd s: sn outpcd: hdwy over 2f out: wandered 1f out: kpt on same pce* **8/1**

**4** *3* **Secret Pact (IRE)** 2-9-0 ........ KDalgleish 8 57+
(MJohnston) *leggy:unf: scope: w ldrs: fdd over 1f out: will improve* **16/1**

**5** *hd* **Chilali (IRE)** 2-8-9 ........ FNorton 1 51
(ABerry) *neat: unf: w ldrs: hung rt 2f out: sn fdd* **33/1**

2 **6** *nk* **Forfeiter (USA)**[22] [1314] 2-9-0 ........ KDarley 5 55
(TDBarron) *outpcd and lost pl after 1f: hdwy and swtchd rt over 1f out: nvr nr ldrs* **7/2**[2]

**7** *shd* **Aza Wish (IRE)** 2-8-9 ........ SRighton 4 50
(MsDeborahJEvans) *cmpt: unf: s.s: bhd tl kpt on fnl 2f* **100/1**

5 **8** *½* **Tiffin Deano (IRE)**[16] [1390] 2-9-0 ........ GFaulkner 9 53
(PCHaslam) *w ldrs: lost pl over 1f out* **15/2**[3]

05 **9** *½* **Campeon (IRE)**[17] [1383] 2-9-0 ........ KFallon 6 51
(MJWallace) *chsd ldrs: edgd lft and lost pl over 1f out* **7/2**[2]

61.91 secs (1.51) **Going Correction** +0.125s/f (Good) **9 Ran SP% 109.8**
Speed ratings: **92,90,86,81,80 80,80,79,78**CSF £44.37 TOTE £12.00: £1.80, £2.10, £3.50; EX 53.60.
**Owner** S J F racing **Bred** A S Denniff **Trained** Hambleton, N Yorks

**FOCUS**
Probably an above average juvenile maiden for this track, although the pace was ordinary.

**NOTEBOOK**
**Mary Read**, much happier on this much less testing ground, led them a merry dance and in the end won going right away. She will improve again.
**Chiselled(IRE)** looked a lot fitter. He took a fierce grip early on but after working his way almost upsides, then found the winner much too good. He deserves to find a race.
**Monsieur Mirasol**was stood on his back legs when the stalls opened. He still has something to learn and the outing will have done him good.
**Secret Pact(IRE)**, a March foal, was very green to post. He showed bags of toe before tiring and will improve a fair bit.
**Chilali(IRE)**, an April foal, is bred purely for speed on her dam's side. She showed plenty of toe but lacks size and scope.
**Forfeiter(USA)**, a sharp type, was soon being run off his feet and this was disappointing after his good effort first time.
**Campeon(IRE)**, a sharp type, did not improve on his Newmarket effort and does not look a five-furlong horse.

## 1744 FAMOUS GROUSE H'CAP — 1m 6f
3:20 (3:20) (D) (0-85,85) 3-Y-O+ — £6,747 (£2,076; £1,038; £519) Stalls High

Form — RPR

4023 **1** **Toni Alcala**[11] [1501] 5-8-9 64 ........ KFallon 2 73+
(RFFisher) *trckd ldrs: led over 2f out: qcknd clr over 1f out: eased wl ins last* **5/2**[1]

060- **2** *3* **Highland Games (IRE)**[218] [5176] 4-10-0 85 ........ KDarley 1 90
(JGGiven) *sn w ldr: led over 3f out: edgd lft and hdd over 2f out: no ch w wnr* **6/1**[3]

34-3 **3** *7* **Compton Eclaire (IRE)**[105] [549] 4-8-0 57 ........(b) PHanagan 3 52
(GAButler) *hld up in rr: effrt over 4f out: kpt on: nvr nr ldrs* **10/3**[2]

000- **4** *10* **Autumn Fantasy (USA)**[307] [2784] 5-8-7 67 ........(t) TEaves(5) 4 48
(BEllison) *trckd ldrs: outpcd over 4f out: no ch after* **7/1**

311- **5** *3* **Kahyasi Princess (IRE)**[280] [3546] 4-9-13 84 ........ RFfrench 5 61
(MJohnston) *set mod pce: qcknd 6f out: hdd over 3f out: lost pl 2f out* **5/2**[1]

3m 13.02s (7.42) **Going Correction** +0.375s/f (Good)
**WFA** 4 from 5yo 2lb **5 Ran SP% 107.0**
Speed ratings: **93,91,87,81,79**CSF £16.06 TOTE £3.20: £1.60, £3.10; EX 21.80.
**Owner** Alan Willoughby **Bred** Mrs Agnes Steele Moore **Trained** Ulverston, Cumbria

**FOCUS**
Just an ordinary handicap, but no gallop until starting the home turn.

**NOTEBOOK**
**Toni Alcala** thrives on hard work and showed much the best turn of foot and, after shooting clear, was able to ease right up, value double the official margin.
**Highland Games(IRE)**, now a gelding, was having his first outing for his new stable. A lazy-type, he will come on for the outing and will be suited by quicker ground and a much stiffer test.
**Compton Eclaire(IRE)** made her move at the right time but she is only really plating-class and she could never get near the first two.
**Autumn Fantasy(USA)**, who won at three over two miles from a 9lb higher mark, has done little since and is best going left-handed.
**Kahyasi Princess(IRE)**, much improved at three, was 12lb higher than when running away with a two-mile handicap in the soft at Ascot in July. She looked backward in her coat and after setting just a steady pace she dropped right away. This was too bad to be true even though she made it an insufficient test. *Official explanation: trainer had no explanation for the poor form shown*

## 1745 ROYAL BANK OF SCOTLAND H'CAP — 7f 30y
3:50 (3:52) (C) (0-95,93) 3-Y-O — £11,505 (£3,540; £1,770; £885) Stalls Low

Form — RPR

00-0 **1** **Redwood Rocks (IRE)**[34] [1129] 3-8-6 78 ........ FLynch 1 85
(BSmart) *mde all: edgd lft fnl f: hld on towards fin* **12/1**

-432 **2** *½* **Man Of Letters (UAE)**[8] [1558] 3-8-1 73 ........ RFfrench 3 79
(MJohnston) *in tch: effrt over 3f out: sn outpcd: styd on wl appr fnl f: kpt on wl nr fin* **5/2**[1]

2131 **3** *nk* **Hatch**[22] [1317] 3-9-2 88 ........ PHanagan 4 93
(RMHCowell) *dwlt: hld up: hdwy 4f out: sn chsng ldrs: kpt on wl fnl f* **11/2**[3]

21-0 **4** *5* **Rydal (USA)**[41] [1063] 3-9-0 89 ........ TPQueally(3) 8 81
(GAButler) *hld up: effrt over 3f out: sn chsng ldrs: wknd fnl f* **12/1**

310- **5** *2* **Bessemer (JPN)**[259] [4144] 3-9-7 93 ........ KDalgleish 6 80
(MJohnston) *sn chsng wnr: effrt over 3f out: lost pl over 1f out* **16/1**

24-1 **6** *5* **River Treat (FR)**[18] [1366] 3-8-13 85 ........ KFallon 2 59
(GWragg) *t.k.h: hdwy on wd outside over 3f out: lost pl 2f out* **10/3**[2]

433- **7** *shd* **Imperial Echo (USA)**[209] [5371] 3-8-13 85 ........ KDarley 5 59
(TDBarron) *sn trcking ldrs: effrt over 3f out: n.m.r over 1f out: sn lost pl* **7/1**

15-0 **8** *23* **Lommel (UAE)**[14] [1437] 3-9-3 89 ........ DRMcCabe 7 3
(DRLoder) *s.v.s: hdwy on ins 3f out: sn lost pl and eased* **25/1**

1m 30.13s (0.60) **Going Correction** +0.375s/f (Good) **8 Ran SP% 104.6**
Speed ratings: **111,110,110,104,102 96,96,69**CSF £35.30 CT £145.99 TOTE £15.30: £4.80, £1.10, £1.70; EX 37.90 Trifecta £495.70 Pool £1,186.94, 1.70 w u.
**Owner** Dan Hall **Bred** 6c Stallions Ltd **Trained** Hambleton, N Yorks

**FOCUS**
A decent contest, but just a steady gallop with the narrow winner having things his own way out in front.

**NOTEBOOK**
**Redwood Rocks(IRE)**, now a gelding, was much more settled and took the eye beforehand. He was allowed to set his own pace and after drifting off the fence did just enough. His rider deserves full marks. *Official explanation: trainer said, regarding the improved form shown, gelding may have run too keen last time and possibly needed the run, its first for five months*
**Man Of Letters(UAE)**, due to race from a 3lb higher mark in future, took an age to get going and only really found his stride inside the last. A slightly stiffer test will be in his favour.
**Hatch**, who looked very fit indeed, was unable to dominate with totally different tactics adopted. He stuck to his task and was only found wanting inside the last. He is clearly going the right way.
**Rydal(USA)**, who has plenty of size and scope, was back in the right sort of grade but had the blinkers missing.
**Bessemer(JPN)**, who has been gelded, will need to settle better if he is to stay as far as his pedigree would suggest.
**River Treat(FR)** took a fierce grip and unable to get cover on the wide outside was very disappointing. *Official explanation: jockey said colt ran too freely in the early stages*
**Imperial Echo(USA)** looked fit and well but was disapointing and his chance had gone when messed about. He is surely capable of a fair bit better than he showed here.

## 1746 EDMONDS.CO.UK CLASSIFIED STKS — 1m
4:20 (4:21) (D) 3-Y-O+ — £5,382 (£1,656; £828; £414) Stalls Low

Form — RPR

22-0 **1** **Love In Seattle (IRE)**[32] [1172] 4-9-10 78 ........ KDalgleish 5 86
(MJohnston) *mde all: shkn up over 2f out: edgd lft fnl f: hld on nr fin* **14/1**

0-62 **2** *½* **Tony Tie**[16] [1393] 8-9-7 75 ........ JFEgan 3 82
(JSGoldie) *hld up: hdwy 5f out: swtchd lft over 1f out: styd on wl ins last* **11/2**[3]

-140 **3** *4* **Hail The Chief**[69] [842] 7-9-8 76 ........ KFallon 6 74
(DNicholls) *trckd wnr: effrt over 2f out: kpt on same pce* **4/1**[1]

/2-2 **4** *¾* **Khanjar (USA)**[22] [1318] 4-9-9 77 ........(v) DRMcCabe 4 73
(DRLoder) *s.i.s: t.k.h in rr: hdwy over 3f out: kpt on fnl 2f: nvr nr ldrs* **11/2**[3]

400- **5** *hd* **Astrocharm (IRE)**[160] [6052] 5-9-4 75 ........(b) MHenry 8 68
(MHTompkins) *sn trcking ldrs: effrt over 2f out: one pce* **6/1**

0-00 **6** *¾* **Aimee's Delight**[18] [1372] 4-9-7 78 ........ GDuffield 7 69
(JGGiven) *chsd ldrs: outpcd fnl 2f* **14/1**

2325 **7** *3* **Sarraaf (IRE)**[14] [1451] 8-9-7 72 ........ NCallan 1 62
(ISemple) *hld up and bhd: effrt over 3f out: wknd over 1f out* **9/2**[2]

30-0 **8** *2* **Sawwaah (IRE)**[35] [1114] 7-9-12 80 ........ ANicholls 2 62
(DNicholls) *chsd ldrs: edgd lft and wknd over 1f out* **14/1**

1m 43.34s (0.64) **Going Correction** +0.375s/f (Good) **8 Ran SP% 103.2**
Speed ratings: **111,110,106,105,105 104,101,99**CSF £72.16 TOTE £11.20: £3.00, £2.10, £1.80; EX 68.30.
**Owner** M Doyle **Bred** M P B Bloodstock Ltd **Trained** Middleham Moor, N Yorks

**FOCUS**
A fair contest and the pace was good for the grade. The winner is unexposed and can rate higher.

**NOTEBOOK**
**Love In Seattle(IRE)**, a bitter disappointment at three, had his own way in front and in the end did just enough. A more galloping track will suit him even better.
**Tony Tie**, a tough customer, had to come wide to find room to make his finishing effort. He closed the gap all the way to the line but in the end was just held. This trip is his bare minimum.
**Hail The Chief**, back on grass, was given every chance but this is as good as he is nowadays - on this surface at least.
**Khanjar(USA)**, who had the visor on again, took a keen hold but when asked for an effort the response was strictly limited.
**Astrocharm(IRE)**, who looked to have a good chance on the ratings, was back down in trip but she never looked a real threat.
**Sarraaf(IRE)** was nowhere near his best. *Official explanation: jockey said gelding did not handle the loose ground*

## 1747 ROYAL BANK OF SCOTLAND MAIDEN STKS — 1m 1f
4:50 (4:52) (D) 3-Y-O+ — £4,715 (£1,451; £725; £362) Stalls Low

Form — RPR

2-2 **1** **Maclean**[18] [1371] 3-8-9 ........ KFallon 1 71+
(SirMichaelStoute) *trckd ldrs: effrt 4f out: styd on to ld over 1f out: pushed out* **4/9**[1]

0 **2** *1* **Sharp Needle**[16] [1400] 3-8-5 ow1 ........ KDarley 5 65+
(JNoseda) *sn in rr and pushed along: hdwy to chse ldrs 6f out: styd on sam pce fnl f: no real imp* **11/2**[2]

/0-4 **3** *1* **King's Envoy (USA)**[22] [1318] 5-9-10 60 ........ DMcGaffin 7 67
(MrsJCMcgregor) *hld up: effrt over 3f out: nt clr and swtchd lft over 2f out: kpt on same pce fnl f* **33/1**

4 **4** *5* **Queen Lucia (IRE)**[15] [1420] 3-8-4 ........ GDuffield 4 52
(JGGiven) *t.k.h: led after 2f and qcknd pce: hdd over 1f out: fdd* **25/1**

53- **5** *5* **Salamba**[200] [5532] 3-8-9 ........ MHenry 8 47
(MHTompkins) *t.k.h: trckd ldrs: edgd lft over 2f out: wknd over 1f out* **20/1**

20- **6** *1 ¼* **Badr (USA)**[233] [4818] 3-8-9 ........ RFfrench 6 45
(MJohnston) *set mod pce: hdd after 2f: edgd rt over 2f out: sn lost pl* **8/1**[3]

**7** *12* **Columbian Emerald (IRE)** 3-8-9 ........ RHavlin 2 21
(TJEtherington) *rangy: bit bkwd: dwlt: a in rr: bhd fnl 3f* **150/1**

1m 57.4s (4.20) **Going Correction** +0.375s/f (Good)
**WFA** 3 from 4yo+ 15lb **7 Ran SP% 108.0**
Speed ratings: **96,95,94,89,85 84,73**CSF £2.54 TOTE £1.40: £1.10, £3.80; EX 3.10.
**Owner** The Queen **Bred** The Queen **Trained** Newmarket, Suffolk

**FOCUS**
An ordinary maiden but the pace was steady, and the third horse being rated just 60 puts a question mark over the value of the form.

**NOTEBOOK**
**Maclean**, inclined to swish his tail in the paddock, always looked to be doing enough and was hardly blowing afterwards. He now qualifies for handicaps and, with the third rated just 60, he might receive a realistic mark.

**Sharp Needle**, pushed along early, warmed to her task but in the end was very much second best. Another step up in trip will do her no harm.
**King's Envoy(USA)**, unplaced in eight previous starts, is rated just 60 so his proximity buts a cap on the overall value of the form.
**Queen Lucia(IRE)** would not settle so she was allowed to go on after the first quarter mile. She tired noticeably late on, suggesting she still needed the outing.
**Salamba**, who had just two outings at two, looked backward in his coat and needs more time yet.
**Badr(USA)**, a let down on his two starts as a juvenile, was keen to post. He came off a straight line and dropped away. He has an awful lot to prove now.

## 1748 SAFFIE JOSEPH & SONS H'CAP — 7f 30y

5:20 (5:20) (F) (0-55,55) 3-Y-0+ — £2,975 (£850; £425) Stalls Low

| Form | | | | RPR |
|---|---|---|---|---|
| 000- | 1 | | **Tap**[140] 6171 7-8-9 **50** ....(p) DFentiman(7) 11<br>(IanEmmerson) *chsd ldrs: led over 1f out: kpt on wl* 40/1 | 61 |
| 0622 | 2 | 3/4 | **Mount Royale (IRE)**[7] 1595 6-9-3 **51** ....(vt) KimTinkler 3<br>(NTinkler) *led tl over 1f out: kpt on same pce ins last* 7/1[3] | 60 |
| 5052 | 3 | 3/4 | **Balerno**[18] 1373 5-9-3 **51** .... KDarley 14<br>(RIngram) *in tch: effrt 3f out: styd on fnl f* 9/2[1] | 58 |
| 5000 | 4 | 3 | **Shifty**[11] 1502 5-9-3 **51** ....(v) AlexGreaves 7<br>(DNicholls) *chsd ldrs: one pce fnl 2f* 7/1[3] | 50 |
| 5455 | 5 | 1 1/4 | **Waltzing Wizard**[4] 1663 5-9-7 **55** .... FLynch 10<br>(ABerry) *hld and bhd: hdwy over 3f out: edgd rt 2f out: nvr nr ldrs* 6/1[2] | 51 |
| 5-56 | 6 | 1 1/2 | **East Riding**[7] 1596 4-9-1 **49** .... AnnStokell 8<br>(MissAStokell) *chsd ldrs: edgd lft over 2f out: one pce* 66/1 | 41 |
| 000- | 7 | 1 | **Yorkshire Blue**[197] 5596 5-9-2 **50** .... JFEgan 13<br>(JSGoldie) *mid-div: effrt 3f out: nvr nr ldrs* 10/1 | 40 |
| 0-00 | 8 | 2 1/2 | **Friar Tuck**[4] 1663 9-8-13 **52** .... TEaves(5) 5<br>(MissLAPerratt) *hld up towards rr: kpt on fnl 2f: nvr a factor* 20/1 | 35 |
| 2534 | 9 | 1 | **Magic Mamma's Too**[58] 953 4-9-1 **52** ....(v[1]) TPQueally(3) 12<br>(TDBarron) *bhd: hrd rdn 3f out: nvr a factor* 12/1 | 32 |
| -023 | 10 | 1 3/4 | **Luke After Me (IRE)**[19] 1342 4-9-3 **51** .... KFallon 1<br>(GASwinbank) *dwlt: swtchd rt after s: sme hewady on ins 3f out: nvr a factor* 8/1 | 27 |
| 5-53 | 11 | 1 1/4 | **Peregian (IRE)**[24] 1279 6-9-1 **49** .... GDuffield 2<br>(AndrewReid) *chsd ldrs: rdn over 3f out: lost pl over 2f out* 10/1 | 22 |
| 000- | 12 | 8 | **Due Diligence (IRE)**[192] 5688 5-9-2 **50** .... KDalgleish 6<br>(CWFairhurst) *chsd ldr: edgd lft and lost pl over 2f out* 33/1 | 2 |
| 000- | 13 | dist | **Xanadu**[191] 5706 8-9-2 **50** .... PHanagan 4<br>(MissLAPerratt) *hld up in rr: eased over 1f out: virtually p.u: t.o* 33/1 | — |

1m 31.32s (1.79) **Going Correction** +0.375s/f (Good) **13** Ran SP% **109.0**
Speed ratings: **104,103,102,98,97 95,94,91,90,88 87,78,—**CSF £268.17 CT £1440.68 TOTE £29.00: £7.40, £2.80, £1.20; EX 381.80 Place 6 £25.03, Place 5 £10.32.
**Owner** Trade Direct Bathrooms & Furniture **Bred** Fonthill Stud And Philip Wroughton **Trained** Holmside, Co Durham

**FOCUS**
A seller in all but name, although the pace was good and the form looks sound enough at an ordinary level.

**NOTEBOOK**
**Tap**, out of sorts on the All-Weather, had the cheekpieces on for the first time on his first outing since December. He lay close to the pace and in the end did just enough.
**Mount Royale(IRE)**, leniently treated compared to his All-Weather mark, did well to get in front from his outside draw. He fought back bravely and in the end was just held at bay.
**Balerno**, 4lb higher, again ran well but the fact remains he has now tasted success just once from 30 attempts.
**Shifty**, 7lb lower than his last success, ran better appreciating the quicker ground.
**Waltzing Wizard**, making a quick return to action, looked very fit indeed. Stepping up in trip he sat way off the pace, he did well to finish so close.
**East Riding**, who had run over five furlongs last time, has yet to hit the target in 14 attempts now.
**Luke After Me(IRE)** *Official explanation: jockey said gelding was unsuited by the loose ground*
**Xanadu** *Official explanation: jockey said gelding was unsuited by the loose going*
T/Jkpt: Not won. T/Plt: £62.60 to a £1 stake. Pool: £54,661.95. 636.75 winning tickets. T/Qpdt: £11.70 to a £1 stake. Pool: £3,128.80. 197.20 winning tickets. WG

# [1462]NOTTINGHAM (L-H)

Friday, April 30

**OFFICIAL GOING: Soft (heavy in places) changing to soft after race 5 (4.10)**
Wind: mod hlf bhd Weather: overcast

## 1749 BESTWOOD PARK MAIDEN STKS — 6f 15y

2:10 (2:13) (D) 3-Y-0 — £3,746 (£1,152; £576; £288) Stalls High

| Form | | | | RPR |
|---|---|---|---|---|
| 04 | 1 | | **Inchloss (IRE)**[20] 1325 3-9-0 .... WSupple 9<br>(BAMcmahon) *hld up: hdwy over 2f out: hung lft fr over 1f out: styd on u.p to ld wl ins fnl f* 11/2[2] | 74 |
| | 2 | 1 1/4 | **Snap** 3-9-0 .... JFanning 12<br>(MJohnston) *chsd ldrs: led over 3f out: rdn and hdd wl ins fnl f* 6/1[3] | 70 |
| 56- | 3 | nk | **Soviet Sceptre (IRE)**[156] 6072 3-9-0 .... KMcEvoy 7<br>(GAButler) *chsd ldrs: hmpd over 4f out: rdn over 2f out: r.o ins fnl f* 5/1[1] | 69 |
| | 4 | 1 | **Called Up** 3-9-0 .... DaneO'Neill 5<br>(HCandy) *s.i.s: sn chsng ldrs: outpcd 1/2-way: r.o ins fnl f* 9/1 | 66 |
| 66-0 | 5 | nk | **Indian Edge**[30] 1202 3-9-0 65 .... DSweeney 4<br>(BPalling) *hld up in tch: outpcd 1/2-way: hdwy and nt clr run 1f out: kpt on* 14/1 | 65 |
| 6-0 | 6 | nk | **Dr Synn**[18] 1352 3-9-0 .... PDoe 11<br>(JAkehurst) *prom: chsd ldr over 2f out: rdn and ev ch 1f out: no ex* 5/1[1] | 64 |
| 00 | 7 | 3/4 | **Adorata (GER)**[27] 1243 3-8-9 .... DBadel 1<br>(JJay) *chsd ldrs: rdn over 1f out: sn edgd lft and no ex* 66/1 | 57 |
| 0 | 8 | 1 1/4 | **Ghantoot**[15] 1419 3-8-11 .... NMackay(3) 8<br>(LMCumani) *sn outpcd: n.d* 25/1 | 58 |
| 0 | 9 | nk | **Private Jessica**[14] 1441 3-8-9 .... JPMurtagh 2<br>(JRFanshawe) *sn outpcd: hdwy over 1f out: wknd fnl f* 7/1 | 52 |
| | 10 | 10 | **Rene Barbier (IRE)** 3-9-0 .... PRobinson 6<br>(JAGlover) *dwlt: outpcd* 25/1 | 27 |
| 04- | 11 | 1/2 | **Spartan Spear**[175] 5938 3-9-0 .... JEdmunds 13<br>(JBalding) *hld up: rdn and wknd wl over 2f out* 16/1 | 26 |
| 0- | 12 | 12 | **Baychevelle (IRE)**[213] 5285 3-8-9 .... SSanders 10<br>(MrsHDalton) *spd to 1/2-way: wknd wl over 1f out* 16/1 | — |
| 600- | 13 | dist | **New Day Dawning**[212] 5296 3-8-9 48 .... RFitzpatrick 3<br>(CSmith) *led over 2f: wknd 2f out: eased* 50/1 | — |

1m 17.76s (2.96) **Going Correction** +0.375s/f (Good) **13** Ran SP% **115.1**
Speed ratings: **95,93,92,91,91 90,89,88,87,74 73,57,—**CSF £35.75 TOTE £5.00: £2.20, £4.20, £2.10; EX 38.40.
**Owner** R Thornhill **Bred** John McEnery **Trained** Hopwas, Staffs

**FOCUS**
Despite the stalls being on ths stands' side, the field elected to race over the far side. With the 65-rated Indian Edge a close up fifth this was probably an ordinary contest.

**NOTEBOOK**
**Inchloss(IRE)**, with a couple of runs under his belt already this term, had the edge in fitness over the majority of his rivals. This effort should ensure he does not start life off in handicaps on too stiff a mark.
**Snap**, a half-brother to useful middle-distance performer Shemozzle, shaped with plenty of promise over what will turn out to be an inadequate trip.
**Soviet Sceptre(IRE)** shaped as though this trip was on the sharp side for him, but will at least have more options open to him now in handicaps.
**Called Up**, who is out of a mare that won over middle distances, did not run too badly over what will have been an inadequate trip.
**Indian Edge** had only shown moderate form coming into this, and would certainly have finished closer had Adorata not hung across him at the furlong pole.
**Dr Synn**, a half-brother to middle-distance winner Gentleman Venture, just got tired in the ground having shown plenty of pace. He will have plenty of options open to him in handicap company.
**Baychevelle(IRE)** *Official explanation: jockey said filly was fractious, showing signs of being highly strung going to post*
**New Day Dawning** *Official explanation: jockey said filly hung right*

## 1750 NOTTINGHAMSHIRE CHAMBER OF COMMERCE AND INDUSTRY FILLIES' H'CAP — 6f 15y

2:40 (2:42) (E) (0-70,70) 3-Y-0+ — £3,707 (£1,140; £570; £285) Stalls High

| Form | | | | RPR |
|---|---|---|---|---|
| 5530 | 1 | | **Amelia (IRE)**[13] 1477 6-8-1 **50** .... BSwarbrick(7) 9<br>(WMBrisbourne) *mid-div: stmbld wl over 4f out: hdwy over 2f out: styd on to ld wl ins fnl f* 8/1 | 59 |
| 60-4 | 2 | 1 | **Gojo (IRE)**[13] 1464 3-9-0 **67** .... SSanders 8<br>(BPalling) *chsd ldrs: rdn to ld ins fnl f: sn hdd: kpt on* 6/1[2] | 73 |
| 0000 | 3 | 3/4 | **Grandma Lily (IRE)**[15] 1421 6-9-4 **60** .... LDettori 14<br>(MCChapman) *sn outpcd: hdwy over 1f out: edgd lft ins fnl f: r.o* 15/2[3] | 64 |
| 200U | 4 | 3 1/2 | **Park Star**[6] 1608 4-8-13 **58** .... JFMcDonald(3) 5<br>(DShaw) *sn outpcd: hdwy over 1f out: nt rch ldrs* 11/1 | 51 |
| 300- | 5 | shd | **Bowling Along**[178] 5916 3-8-3 **60** ow1 .... PMulrennan(5) 16<br>(MESowersby) *s.i.s: sn chsng ldrs: rdn over 1f out: sn wknd* 40/1 | 54 |
| 600- | 6 | 1 | **Glencoe Solas (IRE)**[207] 5427 4-9-12 **68** .... PDobbs 6<br>(SKirk) *led: wknd and hdd ins fnl f* 8/1 | 58 |
| 406- | 7 | 1 1/4 | **Tuscarora (IRE)**[220] 5133 5-9-1 **57** .... IMongan 10<br>(AWCarroll) *hld up: hdwy and nt clr run over 1f out: n.d* 16/1 | 43 |
| 0005 | 8 | 3/4 | **Sugar Cube Treat**[6] 1603 8-7-7 **40** oh10 ow2 ....(p) PVarley(7) 13<br>(MMullineaux) *dwlt: hdwy over 3f out: wknd wl over 1f out* 25/1 | 26 |
| 300- | 9 | 5 | **Medusa**[340] 1877 4-10-0 **70** .... JPMurtagh 12<br>(DMorris) *chsd ldrs 4f* 20/1 | 39 |
| 2-00 | 10 | 1/2 | **Queen Of Bulgaria (IRE)**[29] 1220 3-8-7 **60** .... RPrice 15<br>(JPearce) *chsd ldrs over 4f* 40/1 | 27 |
| 50-0 | 11 | 2 1/2 | **Silver Chime**[42] 1051 4-9-10 **69** .... NMackay(3) 2<br>(DMSimcock) *s.i.s: n.d* 9/1 | 29 |
| 00-0 | 12 | 2 1/2 | **Leopard Creek**[30] 1200 3-8-9 **62** .... ACulhane 1<br>(MrsJRRamsden) *hld up: rdn 4f out: n.d* 20/1 | 14 |
| /50- | 13 | 1 3/4 | **Lady Justice**[328] 2185 4-9-7 **70** .... DTudhope(7) 3<br>(WJarvis) *s.i.s: outpcd* 16/1 | 17 |
| 5101 | 14 | nk | **Blakeshall Quest**[6] 1625 4-9-7 **63** 6ex ....(v) DHolland 4<br>(RBrotherton) *chsd ldrs to 1/2-way* 11/2[1] | 9 |
| 305- | 15 | 2 1/2 | **Princess Erica**[340] 1877 4-9-2 **58** .... WSupple 11<br>(JBalding) *outpcd* 20/1 | — |
| 50-0 | 16 | 4 | **Sweet Talking Girl**[7] 1591 4-7-12 **40** .... JQuinn 7<br>(JMBradley) *dwlt: bhd fr 1/2-way* 25/1 | — |

1m 16.6s (1.80) **Going Correction** +0.375s/f (Good)
**WFA** 3 from 4yo+ 11lb **16** Ran SP% **120.6**
Speed ratings: **103,101,100,96,95 94,92,91,85,84 81,77,75,75,71 66**CSF £49.23 CT £380.30 TOTE £10.40: £3.10, £2.00, £2.00, £2.50; EX 82.70.
**Owner** Raymond McNeill **Bred** Ballyhane Stud **Trained** Great Ness, Shropshire

**FOCUS**
A modest handicap, and like the first race the field raced over the far side. This looked to to be run at a fair pace and not that many got into it and the form does not appeal as that strong.

**NOTEBOOK**
**Amelia(IRE)** is well exposed, but having been on the go through the winter had the edge in fitness over most of her rivals.
**Gojo(IRE)** looked to have done everything right, only to be worn down late on. Tackling older horse for the first time, she deserves plenty of credit for this effort having been up with the pace throughout.
**Grandma Lily(IRE)** is beginning to slip down the weights after some uninspiring efforts of late. Unable to go the early pace, she came home in good style and looks to be returning to some sort of form.
**Park Star** has done all of her winning over the minimum, but did enough to suggest that she does stay this far.
**Bowling Along** showed plenty of pace after missing the break until lack of a recent outing took its toll. While she probably isn't one to rely on, she showed enough from what would have been the worst of the draw, and is one to keep an eye on in a low-grade contest.
**Glencoe Solas(IRE)** soon tacked across to the far rails and showed plenty of speed without being asked to. Granted a less-testing surface, she should have no trouble getting back on the winning trail.
**Blakeshall Quest** was reported to have been unsuited by the ground. *Official explanation: jockey said filly was unsuited by the soft ground*

## 1751 DAMIAN WAKEFIELD STAG PARTY NOVICE MEDIAN AUCTION STKS — 5f 13y

3:10 (3:10) (F) 2-Y-0 — £3,115 (£890; £445) Stalls High

| Form | | | | RPR |
|---|---|---|---|---|
| 1 | 1 | | **Joseph Henry**[19] 1340 2-9-6 .... JFanning 7<br>(MJohnston) *chsd ldr: hung lft fnl 3f: led 2f out: sn clr* 4/11[1] | 90+ |
| 4 | 2 | 7 | **Mauro (IRE)**[6] 1607 2-8-7 .... JQuinn 4<br>(PMPhelan) *chsd ldrs: rdn 1/2-way: wknd and hung lft over 1f out* 25/1 | 52 |
| 541 | 3 | 3 | **Zimbali**[7] 1589 2-8-7 .... SCarson 6<br>(JMBradley) *swvd lft s: led: hung lft thrght: hdd 2f out: sn wknd* 4/1[2] | 42 |
| | 4 | 1/2 | **Our Fugitive (IRE)** 2-8-12 .... DHolland 2<br>(AWCarroll) *dwlt and edgd rt s: outpcd: hdwy 2f out: n.d* 14/1[3] | 45 |
| 06 | 5 | 7 | **Sahara Mist (IRE)**[28] 1234 2-8-7 .... WSupple 1<br>(DShaw) *sn outpcd* 25/1 | 15 |
| 0 | 6 | 10 | **Whistling Along**[11] 1505 2-8-12 .... JBramhill 3<br>(JMBradley) *hmpd s: outpcd* 25/1 | — |

62.57 secs (0.77) **Going Correction** +0.375s/f (Good) **6** Ran SP% **111.5**
Speed ratings: **108,96,92,91,80 64**CSF £14.58 TOTE £1.20: £1.10, £7.40; EX 8.90.
**Owner** John Brown & Megan Dennis **Bred** John Brown & Megan Dennis **Trained** Middleham Moor, N Yorks

**FOCUS**
Not a great race on paper, but the winner simply outclassed his rivals and, as the time was exceptional for the grade, he could be an Ascot juvenile.
**NOTEBOOK**
**Joseph Henry** showed plenty of pace, even on ground which he looked to be hating. He was clearly a cut above these and should be capable of holding his own in better company.
**Mauro(IRE)** making a quick return to action, was outclassed, but did manage to beat a previous winner.
**Zimbali** got in here unpenalised for having won at Warwick. She looked to be hating this surface, and this effort can be forgotten. *Official explanation: jockey said filly hung left throughout*
**Our Fugitive(IRE)** was as green as grass and should improve for the experience.

## 1752 DCM APEX FILLIES' H'CAP — 1m 1f 213y
3:40 (3:41) (D) (0-80,76) 3-Y-0+ £5,671 (£1,745; £872; £436) Stalls Low

Form | | | | RPR
52-0 **1** **Olivia Rose (IRE)**[8] [1560] 5-8-8 **60** JQuinn 7 70
(JPearce) *hld up: hdwy over 3f out: led ins fnl f: pushed out* **13/2**[2]
30-4 **2** *1* **Grey Clouds**[16] [1393] 4-9-1 **67** WSupple 4 75
(TDEasterby) *hld up: racd keenly: hdwy over 3f out: led over 1f out: hdd and unable qck ins fnl f* **5/2**[1]
321- **3** *1 1/4* **Polar Jem**[191] [5711] 4-9-8 **74** AMcCarthy 3 80
(GGMargarson) *hld up in tch: rdn over 1f out: styd on same pce ins fnl f* **9/1**[3]
241- **4** *1/2* **Maxilla (IRE)**[146] [6131] 4-9-6 **72** DHolland 6 77
(LMCumani) *chsd ldrs: led over 2f out: rdn and hdd over 1f out: no ex ins fnl f* **9/1**[3]
0-23 **5** *1 1/2* **Transcendantale (FR)**[8] [1560] 6-7-13 **51** oh5 ow1 CCatlin 8 54?
(MrsSLamyman) *hld up: effrt over 2f out: nvr trbld ldrs* **13/2**[2]
00-0 **6** *7* **Sienna Sunset (IRE)**[6] [1606] 5-8-8 **60** SCarson 10 51
(MrsHDalton) *sn chsng ldr: led over 3f out: hdd over 2f out: wknd fnl f* **11/1**
412- **7** *5* **Peruvia (IRE)**[41] [5537] 4-9-10 **76** SSanders 5 58
(RMBeckett) *chsd ldrs over 7f* **9/1**[3]
2441 **8** *2 1/2* **Spark Up**[7] [1598] 4-9-1 **67** 6ex SWKelly 9 45
(JWUnett) *led over 6f: wknd over 2f out* **11/1**
000- **9** *9* **Summer Wine**[184] [5828] 5-9-9 **75** GBaker 2 38
(CFWall) *s.s: hdwy 8f out: wknd over 2f out* **16/1**
2m 16.37s (6.87) **Going Correction** +0.525s/f (Yiel) **9** Ran SP% **107.8**
Speed ratings: **93,92,91,90,89 84,80,78,70**CSF £20.55 CT £124.15 TOTE £7.20: £2.30, £1.10, £2.80; EX 19.20.
**Owner** A Watford **Bred** Dermot Cantillon **Trained** Newmarket, Suffolk
**FOCUS**
A modest handicap and not a strong contest, but it should produce its fair share of winners in the right grade. It was run at a steady pace.
**NOTEBOOK**
**Olivia Rose(IRE)**, all the better for her run at Beverley, was ridden with plenty of confidence and it looked just a matter of when her jockey elected to go. This success will have done her good and if in the same mood should be capable of following up.
**Grey Clouds**, like the winner travelled well for much of the trip only to be worn down in the closing stages. She can find compensation before too long.
**Polar Jem**, tackling her softest surface to date, turned in a sound effort on this return to action.
**Maxilla(IRE)** did not shape too badly on this return to turf, although this ground may have been soft enough for her.
**Transcendantale(FR)** was not in the best place in a slowly-run contest, and never got in a blow.
**Sienna Sunset(IRE)**, due to be dropped 3lb in the future, was not suited to the steady early pace and is certainly capable of better than she showed here.
**Spark Up** *Official explanation: jockey said filly hung right*

## 1753 COLWICK MAIDEN FILLIES' STKS — 1m 54y
4:10 (4:10) (D) 3-Y-0 £3,738 (£1,150; £575; £287) Stalls Low

Form | | | | RPR
4- **1** **Pont Allaire (IRE)**[239] [4691] 3-8-11 DaneO'Neill 4 79
(HCandy) *chsd ldr: led over 1f out: rdn out* **13/8**[1]
5 **2** *3* **Tree Tops**[14] [1441] 3-8-11 LDettori 2 73+
(JHMGosden) *led: pushed along over 3f out: hdd over 1f out: eased whn btn towards fin* **5/2**[2]
4 **3** *2 1/2* **Pinching (IRE)**[14] [1441] 3-8-11 WRyan 6 68
(HRACecil) *trckd ldrs: rdn and hung lft over 2f out: styd on same pce appr fnl f* **4/1**[3]
**4** *3 1/2* **Lillianna (IRE)** 3-8-11 PaulEddery 7 61
(HRACecil) *hld up: hdwy over 2f out: wknd over 1f out* **25/1**
**5** *nk* **Soviet Spirit** 3-8-11 JPMurtagh 1 60
(JRFanshawe) *chsd ldrs: rdn over 2f out: wknd over 1f out* **11/1**
00 **6** *1 3/4* **Purple Rain (IRE)**[15] [1419] 3-8-11 IMongan 3 57
(MLWBell) *plld hrd and prom: rdn over 2f out: sn hung lft and wknd* **40/1**
0-2 **7** *2 1/2* **Thara'A (IRE)**[15] [1419] 3-8-11 SDrowne 5 52
(EALDunlop) *s.s: hld up: plld hrd: wknd over 2f out* **10/1**
1m 52.63s (6.23) **Going Correction** +0.525s/f (Yiel) **7** Ran SP% **110.4**
Speed ratings: **89,86,83,80,79 77,75**CSF £5.37 TOTE £2.60: £1.70, £1.40; EX 6.30.
**Owner** Britton House Stud Ltd **Bred** Britton House Stud Ltd **Trained** Wantage, Oxon
**FOCUS**
This did not look a strong maiden, despite representatives from some of the top yards. The pace was steady until past halfway.
**NOTEBOOK**
**Pont Allaire(IRE)** confirmed the promise shown on her only juvenile start. She was well suited by the step up in trip and, with further improvement to come, should be capable of scoring again.
**Tree Tops** had a soft time of things up front and was not knocked around when her chance had gone. However, while she is clearly nothing special, a step up in trip and a faster surface may bring about some improvement.
**Pinching(IRE)**, as she had on her debut, hung to the left and may not be entirely straightforward.
**Lillianna(IRE)**, a cheap yearling, will need to find plenty of improvement from this if she is to make her mark.
**Soviet Spirit**, from the same family as the top-class Pursuit Of Love, can only improve for the experience, but she will need to.
**Purple Rain(IRE)** was done no favours by the steady early pace, as she refused to settle. Still, she will have more options open to her now in handicaps.
**Thara'A(IRE)** did herself no favours by refusing to settle.

## 1754 NEWARK H'CAP — 1m 6f 15y
4:40 (4:40) (E) (0-70,70) 4-Y-0+ £3,809 (£1,172; £586; £293) Stalls Low

Form | | | | RPR
-121 **1** **Isa'Af (IRE)**[10] [1535] 5-8-6 **55** PMakin(7) 15 69
(PWHiatt) *a.p: chsd ldr over 3f out: led over 2f out: sn clr* **9/1**[3]
501- **2** *1 3/4* **Calamintha**[46] [5826] 4-8-13 **60** NMackay(3) 9 72
(MCPipe) *hld up in tch: rdn to chse wnr fnl f: styd on* **10/1**
4450 **3** *3 1/2* **Macaroni Gold (IRE)**[22] [1316] 4-9-2 **60** MTebbutt 12 67
(WJarvis) *mid-div: rn in snatches: hdwy 10f out: rdn to ld over 6f out: clr over 3f out: hdd over 2f out: no ex fnl f* **20/1**
033/ **4** *7* **Impish Jude**[12] [3862] 6-8-7 **49** DaleGibson 17 47
(JMackie) *hld up: hdwy 5f out: n.d* **16/1**
2300 **5** *1 1/4* **Northern Nymph**[20] [1326] 5-9-7 **70** StephanieHollinshead(7) 10 66
(RHollinshead) *hld up: hdwy 5f out: rdn over 2f out: n.d* **25/1**
3-62 **6** *hd* **Pipssalio (SPA)**[26] [812] 7-8-0 **45** (t) JFMcDonald(3) 13 41
(JamiePoulton) *hld up: bhd and rdn 10f out: styd on appr fnl f: nvr nrr* **5/1**[1]
0- **7** *1 3/4* **Lubinas (IRE)**[9] [1349] 5-8-5 **47** ow1 SWKelly 3 41
(FJordan) *hld up: rdn 6f out: nt clr run 2f out: nvr nrr* **20/1**
43-6 **8** *1 3/4* **Golden Boot**[4] [1661] 5-9-11 **67** (p) TEDurcan 5 59
(ABailey) *hld up: hdwy u.p over 2f out: n.d* **11/2**[2]
2/4- **9** *6* **Migration**[322] [2339] 8-9-4 **60** LVickers 6 44
(MPitman) *dwlt: hld up: hdwy over 3f out: rdn and wknd 2f out* **40/1**
0013 **10** *3* **Madhahir (IRE)**[18] [1376] 4-9-4 **62** DHolland 14 42
(CADwyer) *prom tl wknd 2f out* **14/1**
0-02 **11** *10* **Masjoor**[28] [1235] 4-9-1 **59** LDettori 18 26
(NAGraham) *hdwy to chse ldr after 2f: wknd 3f out* **12/1**
02-4 **12** *1/2* **Blackthorn**[36] [1103] 5-9-3 **59** JPMurtagh 2 25
(MrsJRRamsden) *prom 10f* **11/2**[2]
10-6 **13** *9* **Little Tobias (IRE)**[10] [1534] 5-8-9 **51** CCatlin 11 6
(AndrewTurnell) *chsd ldrs 8f* **16/1**
40-0 **14** *3 1/2* **Down To The Woods (USA)**[13] [1479] 6-8-3 **45** JQuinn 4 —
(RDEWoodhouse) *hld up: a bhd* **66/1**
200- **15** *3* **Saintly Thoughts (USA)**[185] [5817] 9-8-8 **50** (p) SDrowne 8 —
(RJHodges) *chsd ldrs to 1/2-way* **50/1**
6-22 **16** *4* **Starry Mary**[10] [1534] 6-8-13 **55** SSanders 1 —
(RMBeckett) *led over 7f: wknd over 3f out: eased* **9/1**[3]
105- **17** *5* **St Jerome**[254] [4279] 4-9-0 **58** TGMcLaughlin 7 —
(NPLittmoden) *hld up: effrt over 4f out: sn wknd: eased over 1f out* **33/1**
606- **18** *7* **Party Ploy**[168] [5999] 6-9-7 **63** IMongan 16 —
(KRBurke) *chsd ldrs over 10f: eased* **40/1**
3m 12.17s (4.97) **Going Correction** +0.525s/f (Yiel)
**WFA** 4 from 5yo+ 2lb **18** Ran SP% **127.3**
Speed ratings: **106,105,103,99,98 98,97,96,92,91 85,85,79,77,76 73,71,67**CSF £90.79 CT £1792.53 TOTE £14.50: £2.60, £3.10, £3.60, £3.20; EX 80.90.
**Owner** Miss Maria McKinney **Bred** T Monaghan **Trained** Hook Norton, Oxon
**FOCUS**
A m,odest handicap was not that competitive, but the time was decent and, with the runners strung out like three-mile chasers, the form looks sound.
**NOTEBOOK**
**Isa'Af(IRE)**, given a peach of a ride, had this sewn up some way out. He is at the top of his game at present and may be capable of more still.
**Calamintha**, none the worse for her fall at Stratford last time, won under similar conditions at Yarmouth last back-end. She looks reasonably treated at present, and no doubt connections will find another opening for her before too long.
**Macaroni Gold(IRE)**, again without the headgear, looked to run his race in snatches.
**Impish Jude**, off the bridle some way out, could probably have done better with a stronger pace.
**Northern Nymph** is none too reliable, and although flattering briefly down the centre of the track, he never really looked like taking a hand.
**Pipssalio(SPA)** had his conditions but, under pressure before halfway, never looked likely to land a blow.
**Madhahir(IRE)** *Official explanation: jockey said gelding raced in snatches*
**Party Ploy** *Official explanation: jockey said gelding finished exhausted*

## 1755 CARLTON HBLB H'CAP — 1m 54y
5:10 (5:10) (E) (0-70,70) 3-Y-0 £3,926 (£1,208; £604; £302) Stalls Low

Form | | | | RPR
0-12 **1** **Riley Boys (IRE)**[16] [1392] 3-9-3 **66** SSanders 4 71
(JGGiven) *w ldr: led 6f out: rdn and hdd wl ins fnl f: rallied to ld post* **13/2**[3]
0-52 **2** *shd* **Charmatic (IRE)**[11] [1502] 3-8-11 **60** JQuinn 12 65
(JAGlover) *plld hrd and a.p: rdn to ld wl ins fnl f: hdd post* **9/2**[1]
36-4 **3** *nk* **Evaluator (IRE)**[18] [1352] 3-9-7 **70** LDettori 6 74
(TGMills) *s.i.s: hld up: hdwy over 1f out: r.o* **6/1**[2]
50-0 **4** *1 1/2* **Auroville**[16] [1392] 3-9-3 **66** IMongan 17 67
(MLWBell) *hld up: hdwy over 2f out: rdn over 1f out: no ex nr fin* **14/1**
00-0 **5** *1 1/4* **Wee Dinns (IRE)**[14] [1440] 3-9-6 **69** PDobbs 7 68
(SKirk) *s.i.s: sn prom: rdn over 2f out: one pce fnl f* **11/1**
54-4 **6** *1/2* **Charnock Bates One (IRE)**[16] [1392] 3-9-2 **65** TEDurcan 3 63
(TDEasterby) *led 2f: rdn over 2f out: no ex ins fnl f* **15/2**
605- **7** *3/4* **Selebela**[178] [5915] 3-8-8 **60** NMackay(3) 10 56
(LMCumani) *mid-div: effrt over 2f out: styd on same pce appr fnl f* **20/1**
3505 **8** *1 1/4* **Amwell Brave**[10] [1532] 3-9-2 **65** DHolland 8 59
(JRJenkins) *hld up: nt clr run 2f out: r.o ins fnl f: nt rch ldrs* **10/1**
030- **9** *1 1/2* **Mr Independent (IRE)**[200] [5548] 3-9-2 **65** EAhern 14 56
(EALDunlop) *hld up: rdn over 3f out: nvr trbld ldrs* **20/1**
00-0 **10** *hd* **Airgusta (IRE)**[30] [1202] 3-9-1 **64** PRobinson 9 55
(CREgerton) *prom: rdn over 2f out: wknd over 1f out* **10/1**
1-60 **11** *4* **Mr Midasman (IRE)**[16] [1392] 3-9-6 **69** DaleGibson 18 52
(RHollinshead) *s.i.s: hld up: n.d* **20/1**
035- **12** *1 3/4* **Double Vodka (IRE)**[224] [5033] 3-9-4 **67** JPMurtagh 5 46
(MrsJRRamsden) *s.i.s: hld up: plld hrd: nt clr run 3f out: n.d* **20/1**
02-0 **13** *hd* **Military Two Step (IRE)**[30] [1214] 3-9-2 **65** ACulhane 11 44
(KRBurke) *plld hrd and prom: wknd wl over 1f out* **33/1**
506- **14** *3 1/2* **Beautiful Noise**[184] [5830] 3-9-0 **63** WSupple 1 35
(DMorris) *hld up: hdwy over 3f out: wknd over 1f out* **16/1**
000- **15** *6* **Desert Battle (IRE)**[212] [5313] 3-9-4 **67** DSweeney 15 27
(MBlanshard) *hld up: n.d* **50/1**
640- **16** *3* **Washbrook**[199] [5557] 3-9-1 **64** CCatlin 16 18
(AndrewTurnell) *chsd ldrs over 5f* **40/1**
450- **17** *3* **Joey Perhaps**[210] [5339] 3-9-1 **64** SWKelly 2 12
(JRBest) *prom: n.m.r and wknd 2f out* **25/1**
**18** *1* **Faith Healer (IRE)**[174] [5955] 3-9-2 **65** MTebbutt 13 11
(VSmith) *hld up: wknd 3f out* **18/1**
1m 51.17s (4.77) **Going Correction** +0.525s/f (Yiel) **18** Ran SP% **132.1**
Speed ratings: **97,96,96,95,93 93,92,91,89,89 85,83,83,80,74 71,68,67**CSF £34.03 CT £202.97 TOTE £8.40: £2.70, £1.20, £3.00, £4.10; EX 33.90 Place 6 £39.60, Place 5 £20.66.
**Owner** Paul Riley **Bred** P J Makin **Trained** Willoughton, Lincs
**FOCUS**
An ordinary contest, but competitive nonetheless. Ther field finished in a heap and the overall time was ordinary.
**NOTEBOOK**
**Riley Boys(IRE)** is a tough cookie and really had to dig deep to land this. He is progressing, but will need to find more again if he is to add to this.

**Charmatic(IRE)** had her ideal conditions and turned in a solid effort. She is clearly on good terms with herself at present and, granted some give underfoot, should have no trouble getting off the mark.
**Evaluator(IRE)** had plenty to do turning for home, but he stayed on in willing fashion and can be found an opening in the near future.
**Auroville**, done no favours by the draw, was 4lb better off with the winner compared with their running at Beverley, and managed to close the gap this time. He left the impression that this trip was just stretching him.
**Wee Dinns(IRE)** tackling handicappers for the first time, does not do anything quickly and may appreciate more of a test than she faced here.
**Charnock Bates One(IRE)** is consistent enough, but was just let down by a change of gear.
**Double Vodka(IRE)** *Official explanation: jockey said gelding was keen going to post and ran freely in the early stages*
T/Plt: £57.40 to a £1 stake. Pool: £39,091.55. 496.40 winning tickets. T/Qpdt: £16.20 to a £1 stake. Pool: £2,238.10. 102.20 winning tickets. CR

1756 - (Foreign Racing) - See Raceform Interactive

## 1601 HAYDOCK (L-H)

Saturday, May 1

**OFFICIAL GOING: Good**
Other races under Rules of Jump Racing.
Wind: almost nil Weather: fine

### 1757 FREEPHONE STANLEYBET FLAT V JUMP JOCKEYS H'CAP — 1m 30y
**2:10** (2:15) (E) (0-70,70) 4-Y-0+ — **£6,987** (£2,150; £1,075; £537) **Stalls** Low

Form — RPR
1140 **1** — **Stoic Leader (IRE)**[26] 1265 4-11-3 **66** — KDalgleish 2 — 85+
(RFFisher) *midfield: hdwy over 3f out: led 2f out: rdn clr and tail flashed over 1f out: eased down cl home* — **12/1**
0335 **2** *4* **Sangiovese**[35] 1132 5-11-3 **66** — TJMurphy 5 — 73
(HMorrison) *trckd ldrs: rdn over 2f out: swtchd rt over 1f out: wnt 2nd ins fnl f: no ch w wnr* — **5/1**[2]
1050 **3** *1* **Realism (FR)**[16] 1427 4-10-13 **62** — KMcEvoy 7 — 67
(PWHiatt) *prom: rdn 2f out: one pce over 1f out* — **25/1**
00-6 **4** *1* **Phred**[26] 1275 4-11-2 **65** — GLee 11 — 67
(RFJohnsonHoughton) *prom: rdn and ev ch 2f out: no ex fnl f* — **16/1**
404- **5** *1 3/4* **Oscar Pepper (USA)**[213] 5300 7-11-1 **64** — NFehily 9 — 62
(TDBarron) *hld up: rdn and hdwy over 2f out: one pce fnl f* — **12/1**
225 **6** *1 1/4* **Active Account (USA)**[8] 1598 7-11-3 **66** — BHarding 3 — 62
(MrsHDalton) *dwlt: bhd: rdn over 3f out: hdwy 2f out: nvr able to chal* — **12/1**
2200 **7** *1/2* **Yorker (USA)**[49] 1013 6-11-2 **65** — ACulhane 4 — 59
(MsDeborahJEvans) *midfield: rdn over 3f out: wknd over 2f out* — **16/1**
2-03 **8** *3/4* **Reap**[28] 1247 6-11-4 **67** — CLlewellyn 12 — 60
(JPearce) *led: rdn and hdd 2f out: wknd fnl f* — **11/2**[3]
0-06 **9** *1/2* **Acomb**[15] 1452 4-10-13 **62** — WSupple 1 — 53
(MWEasterby) *s.v.s: bhd: rdn and hdwy over 2f out: btn over 1f out* — **9/2**[1]
00-0 **10** *3* **Swift Alchemist**[7] 1624 4-11-4 **67** — GDuffield 8 — 52
(MrsHSweeting) *trckd ldrs: rdn over 2f out: sn wknd* — **12/1**
6-53 **11** *5* **Cool Temper**[10] 1542 8-11-6 **69** — (p) DaneO'Neill 10 — 42
(PFICole) *reminders after s: midfield: rdn over 2f out: sn wknd* — **7/1**
/31- **12** *19* **Buthaina (IRE)**[375] 1172 4-11-7 **70** — ADobbin 6 — —
(THCaldwell) *midfield: rdn and wknd over 2f out* — **20/1**

1m 43.61s (-1.94) **Going Correction** -0.225s/f (Firm) — **12** Ran SP% **113.9**
Speed ratings: **100,96,95,94,92 91,90,89,89,86 81,62**CSF £68.13 CT £1496.71 TOTE £14.50: £4.30, £2.50, £8.30; EX 104.80.
**Owner** Great Head House Estates Limited **Bred** P J Higgins **Trained** Ulverston, Cumbria
■ Stewards Enquiry : B Harding two-day ban: used whip with excessive force (May 12,13)

**FOCUS**
A moderate handicap for flat and jump jockeys, though run at a decent gallop. The form may not be the most solid.

**NOTEBOOK**
**Stoic Leader(IRE)**ran out the convincing winner on this step up in trip. This was his third win of the year, and he could be out again soon.
**Sangiovese**had nothing to offer the winner but nevertheless put in one of his better efforts on turf.
**Realism(FR)**put in a better effort compared to his most recent outings.
**Phred**is not one of the more consistent types but ran with a shade of encouragement.
**Oscar Pepper(USA)**ran well on his seasonal debut without really threatening. The six year-old, who has worn cheekpieces in the past but was without the aids in this race, is certainly up to scoring this term.
**Buthaina(IRE)** *Official explanation: jockey said filly lost its action*

### 1758 STANLEYBET.COM SPRING TROPHY STKS (LISTED RACE) — 7f 30y
**2:45** (2:46) (A) 3-Y-0+ — **£17,400** (£6,600; £3,300; £1,500) **Stalls** Low

Form — RPR
3323 **1** — **Rockets 'n Rollers (IRE)**[7] 1610 4-9-3 102 — DaneO'Neill 2 — 109
(RHannon) *mde all: rdn 2f out: all out* — **9/1**
00-2 **2** *shd* **Polar Ben**[7] 1610 5-9-10 112 — OUrbina 3 — 116+
(JRFanshawe) *hld up: hdwy over 3f out: r.o ins fnl f: jst failed* — **7/2**[1]
0-16 **3** *1 1/4* **Babodana**[7] 1621 4-9-7 111 — GDuffield 8 — 110
(MHTompkins) *in tch: sn trckd ldrs: rdn over 2f out: styd on u.p fnl f* — **7/2**[1]
1-55 **4** *shd* **Makhlab (USA)**[7] 1610 4-9-3 108 — WSupple 5 — 105
(BWHills) *prom: rdn 2f out: ev ch over 1f out: styd on u.p: hld whn n.m.r cl home* — **14/1**
4-01 **5** *3/4* **El Coto**[14] 1456 4-9-3 101 — GGibbons 4 — 104
(BAMcmahon) *trckd ldrs: rdn 3f out: styng on whn n.m.r and snatched up ins fnl f: nt rcvr* — **11/1**
6255 **6** *1/2* **Quito (IRE)**[19] 1367 7-9-3 103 — (b) ACulhane 9 — 102
(DWChapman) *bhd: rdn over 2f out: styd on fnl f: nt pce to chal* — **16/1**
0056 **7** *2 1/2* **Will He Wish**[7] 1610 8-9-3 95 — KDalgleish 1 — 96
(SGollings) *racd keenly: hld up: rdn over 2f out: nvr able to chal* — **50/1**
230- **8** *1/2* **Millennium Force**[280] 3589 6-9-3 111 — CCatlin 6 — 94
(MRChannon) *trckd ldrs: rdn over 2f out: sn wknd* — **11/2**[3]
241- **9** *2* **Meshaheer (USA)**[288] 3370 5-9-3 106 — (t) KMcEvoy 7 — 89
(SaeedBinSuroor) *racd keenly: hld up: hdwy over 3f out: rdn over 2f out: wknd over 1f out* — **4/1**[2]

1m 29.7s (-2.46) **Going Correction** -0.225s/f (Firm) — **9** Ran SP% **112.7**
Speed ratings: **105,104,103,103,102 101,99,98,96**CSF £39.45 TOTE £9.40: £2.10, £1.70, £1.80; EX 35.80.
**Owner** M Mulholland **Bred** S W D McIlveen **Trained** East Everleigh, Wilts
■ Stewards Enquiry : O Urbina one-day ban: used whip with excessive frequency (May 12)
G Duffield one-day ban: careless riding (May 12)

**FOCUS**
What appeared a decent race on paper was run at a steady pace, and the form is just fair for the grade.

**NOTEBOOK**
**Rockets 'n Rollers(IRE)** was the recipient of a positive ride from the front and just held on to reverse recent Leicester form with the runner-up. The ground proved no hindrance for the four year-old who has been busy of late.
**Polar Ben**just failed to nail the winner on 2 pound worse terms for their Leicester encounter. Compensation surely awaits this season over this trip with preferably some juice in the ground.
**Babodana**stuck on really well having been dropped in trip, but his last two wins were over a mile.
**Makhlab(USA)**held every chance, but probably found the ground lively enough.
**El Coto**was snatched up when trying to mount a challenge on the fence inside the final furlong, and would definitely finished closer. He lacked the pace to take advantage of a gap which existed momentarily between the winner and the rail, however without the trouble in running would have finished third. On this evidence a black type event awaits, probably over a mile.
**Meshaheer(USA)**, not for the first time, was too keen and in the end proved a bitter disappointment.

### 1759 FREEPHONE STANLEYBET CONDITIONS STKS — 6f
**3:20** (3:21) (C) 3-Y-0+ — **£8,729** (£3,311; £1,655; £752) **Stalls** Centre

Form — RPR
01-2 **1** — **Steenberg (IRE)**[27] 1254 5-9-11 110 — GDuffield 7 — 117
(MHTompkins) *hld up: hdwy over 2f out: led over 1f out: r.o wl* — **2/1**[2]
-144 **2** *3 1/2* **Bahamian Pirate (USA)**[7] 1610 9-9-7 110 — SWKelly 1 — 103
(DNicholls) *hld up: hdwy over 3f out: led over 2f out: rdn and hdd over 1f out: nt pce of wnr ins fnl f* — **11/2**[3]
/30- **3** *1 3/4* **Mister Links (IRE)**[364] 1343 4-8-13 109 — KMcEvoy 4 — 89
(SaeedBinSuroor) *cl up: rdn wl over 1f out: kpt on same pce fnl f* — **11/8**[1]
16-3 **4** *nk* **Circuit Dancer (IRE)**[14] 1471 4-8-13 92 — ACulhane 6 — 88
(ABerry) *trckd ldrs: rdn over 2f out: one pce fnl f* — **8/1**
0404 **5** *6* **Prince Of Blues (IRE)**[10] 1537 6-8-6 58 — (p) PVarley[(7)] 2 — 70?
(MMullineaux) *led: hdd over 3f out: rdn 2f out: wknd over 1f out* — **100/1**
2500 **6** *10* **Trinculo (IRE)**[15] 1438 7-8-10 86 — (p) J-PGuillambert[(3)] 3 — 40
(NPLittmoden) *prom: led over 3f out: rdn and hdd over 2f out: sn wknd* — **50/1**
010- **7** *23* **Tom Tun**[175] 5953 9-9-11 97 — (b) KDalgleish 5 — —
(JBalding) *dwlt: a bhd* — **20/1**

1m 13.04s (-1.85) **Going Correction** 0.0s/f (Good) — **7** Ran SP% **109.6**
Speed ratings: **112,107,105,104,96 83,52**CSF £12.02 TOTE £3.20: £2.20, £2.90; EX 8.10.
**Owner** Kenneth Macpherson **Bred** B Ryan **Trained** Newmarket, Suffolk

**FOCUS**
A decent conditions race run at a good pace, with the first two home both held up early.

**NOTEBOOK**
**Steenberg(IRE)** put in a useful performance in landing the spoils with authority over what appears his ideal trip. He is reportedly being aimed at the Duke Of York Stakes at York's Dante fixture.
**Bahamian Pirate(USA)** was back to a more suitable distance but lacked the pace of the winner.
**Mister Links(IRE)** performed with credit considering he ran up with the strong pace. He met with a setback last year and was having his first run for current connections. It would be folly to dismiss him after this his first run for a year and close inspection is definitely warranted again.
**Circuit Dancer(IRE)** ran well in what was a big ask at the weights and may prove difficult to place.

### 1760 FREEPHONE STANLEYBET H'CAP — 6f
**3:55** (3:55) (D) (0-85,82) 3-Y-0 — **£5,791** (£1,782; £891; £445) **Stalls** Centre

Form — RPR
120- **1** — **Benbaun (IRE)**[203] 5480 3-9-3 **81** — DCorby[(3)] 10 — 93
(MJWallace) *w ldrs: rdn to ld 2f out: sn edgd lft: r.o* — **10/1**
500- **2** *1 1/2* **Times Review (USA)**[238] 4712 3-9-4 **79** — WSupple 9 — 86
(TDEasterby) *sn chsd ldrs: rdn over 2f out: wnt 2nd ins fnl f: no imp on wnr* — **20/1**
-022 **3** *1/2* **Morse (IRE)**[5] 1673 3-9-7 **82** — SWKelly 1 — 88
(JAOsborne) *in rr: rdn and hdwy 2f out: styd on ins fnl f* — **3/1**[1]
105- **4** *1 1/2* **Lualua**[317] 2494 3-8-8 **76** — PMakin[(7)] 5 — 77
(TDBarron) *sweating: led: rdn and hdd 2f out: no ex ins fnl f* — **12/1**
-110 **5** *1/2* **Peruvian Style (IRE)**[18] 1388 3-9-3 **78** — KMcEvoy 3 — 78
(NPLittmoden) *broke wl: sn lost pl: swtchd rt and hdwy over 1f out: kpt on ins fnl f* — **4/1**[2]
00-0 **6** *1 1/2* **George The Best (IRE)**[7] 1614 3-9-3 **78** — ACulhane 4 — 73
(MDHammond) *chsd ldrs: rdn over 2f out: one pce* — **16/1**
0-00 **7** *3 1/2* **Just One Look**[14] 1464 3-8-8 **69** — DSweeney 2 — 54
(MBlanshard) *midfield: rdn 3f out: no imp* — **13/2**[3]
-430 **8** *3/4* **West Country (UAE)**[35] 1129 3-9-2 **77** — KDalgleish 7 — 59
(MJohnston) *midfield: outpcd over 3f out: swtchd lft 1f out: n.d* — **7/1**
060- **9** *hd* **Lupine Howl**[179] 5916 3-8-1 **62** — GGibbons 8 — 44
(BAMcmahon) *prom: rdn over 2f out: sn wknd* — **20/1**
21-6 **10** *6* **Attacca**[16] 1418 3-9-2 **77** — (p) GDuffield 6 — 41
(JRWeymes) *prom tl rdn and wknd over 2f out* — **10/1**

1m 15.37s (0.48) **Going Correction** 0.0s/f (Good) — **10** Ran SP% **112.1**
Speed ratings: **96,94,93,91,90 88,84,83,82,74**CSF £182.42 CT £758.17 TOTE £13.00: £3.00, £6.90, £1.30; EX 234.00.
**Owner** P Ransley **Bred** Dr T A Ryan **Trained** Newmarket, Suffolk

**FOCUS**
A difficult handicap on paper. The time was steady, although the form looks fair.

**NOTEBOOK**
**Benbaun(IRE)** proved he had speed to burn as a juvenile, winning twice at the minimum distance, and on this his three year-old debut, showed bags of pace and proficiency over an extra furlong. He seems to have a tendency to edge left in his races, a trait which was in evidence with this handsome victory. There may be more success to follow.
**Times Review(USA)** ran a solid enough race on his seasonal reappearance but could not match the toe of the winner.
**Morse(IRE)** stayed on from off the pace, looking as though he would not be inconvenienced by an easy seventh furlong.
**Lualua** got warm beforehand and set a good pace before giving way inside the final furlong. A return to five furlongs would see him in better light.
**Peruvian Style(IRE)** broke on terms and was then reined back by his jockey, in the end keeping on late. It is still possible he can perform over this trip on turf.
**Just One Look** *Official explanation: jockey said filly had spread a plate*
**Attacca** *Official explanation: vet said colt was found to be unsound*

### 1761 STANLEYBET.COM MAIDEN STKS — 1m 2f 120y
**4:30** (4:31) (D) 3-Y-0 — **£5,765** (£1,774; £887; £443) **Stalls** High

Form — RPR
22- **1** — **Destination Dubai (USA)**[219] 5177 3-9-0 — (v[1]) KMcEvoy 3 — 86+
(SaeedBinSuroor) *prom: led after 2f: hdd narrowly 4f out: regained ld over 2f out: rdn out* — **4/9**[1]
2 **2** *2* **Twofan (USA)**[11] 1524 3-9-0 — KDalgleish 5 — 82+
(MJohnston) *led for 2f: remained prom: led again narrowly 4f out: hdd over 2f out: rn green over 1f out: hung lft ins fnl f: nt qckn* — **6/1**[2]
0- **3** *6* **Mungo Jerry (GER)**[190] 5723 3-9-0 — WSupple 1 — 72+
(JGGiven) *hld up: hdwy over 3f out: rdn over 2f out: one pce over 1f out* — **12/1**[3]

4 1 ¼ **Corran Ard (IRE)**[202] 5517 3-9-0 .......... ACulhane 8 70
(MrsJohnHarrington, Ire) *in tch: rdn over 2f out: nvr able to chal* **33/1**

60- 5 2 ½ **Royal Approach**[235] 4794 3-8-9 .......... DSweeney 2 61
(MBlanshard) *trckd ldrs: rdn over 2f out: wknd over 1f out* **33/1**

6 6 **Acuzio** 3-9-0 .......... GDuffield 4 56
(WMBrisbourne) *dwlt: trckd ldrs: hung rt over 6f out: rdn 3f out: wknd 2f out* **40/1**

00-P 7 1 ¼ **Grande Terre (IRE)**[21] 1325 3-8-9 .......... OUrbina 6 48
(JGGiven) *in rr: rdn 3f out: no imp* **14/1**

8 14 **Now Look Away (IRE)** 3-9-0 .......... GGibbons 7 30
(BAMcmahon) *s.i.s: racd keenly: hld up: lft bhd 3f out* **16/1**

2m 15.78s (-1.95) **Going Correction** -0.225s/f (Firm) **8** Ran SP% **112.1**
Speed ratings: **98,96,92,91,89 85,84,74**CSF £3.21 TOTE £1.60: £1.10, £1.10, £1.90; EX 2.10 Place 6 £238.85, Place 5 £84.36..
**Owner** Godolphin **Bred** Calumet Farm **Trained** Newmarket, Suffolk
■ A first winner in britain for Australian Kerrin McEvoy.

**FOCUS**
An average maiden lacking any strength in depth.

**NOTEBOOK**
**Destination Dubai(USA)** looked a far from straightforward ride, racing lazily in the first time visor. He took his time mastering a green rival, although his jockey feels there is more improvement to come
**Twofan(USA)** ran with credit making the favourite fight despite showing signs of greenness. He looks the type to take a small event, though with his high knee action would appreciate a bit of cut.
**Mungo Jerry(GER)** was no match for the front two, but seemed suited by the step up in trip. He will be of interest when achieving a handicap mark.
T/Plt: £247.10 to a £1 stake. Pool: £55,412.45. 163.65 winning tickets. T/Qpdt: £27.10 to a £1 stake. Pool: £2,763.30. 75.30 winning tickets. DO

# 1408 NEWMARKET (R-H)
## Saturday, May 1

**OFFICIAL GOING: Good**
Wind: mod bhd Weather: overcast

## 1762 COUNTRYWIDE STEEL & TUBES RATED STKS (H'CAP) 1m 2f
**1:40** (1:43) (B) (0-100,103) 4-Y-0+ **£12,359** (£4,688; £2,344; £1,065) **Stalls** Low

Form RPR

132- 1 **Promotion**[273] 3800 4-8-7 **86** oh1 .......... MJKinane 2 101
(SirMichaelStoute) *dwlt: racd stands' side: hld up: hdwy over 2f out: led over 1f out: r.o wl* **12/1**

40-0 2 2 ½ **Tizzy May (FR)**[21] 1328 4-9-2 **95** .......... PDobbs 4 105
(RHannon) *racd stands' side: chsd ldrs: rdn and evc hance over 1f out: styd on* **20/1**

00-6 3 ½ **Putra Kuantan**[21] 1328 4-8-13 **92** .......... PRobinson 16 101+
(MAJarvis) *lw: led far side duo: rdn and ev ch over 1f out: no ex ins fnl f* **4/1**[1]

0-41 4 1 ½ **Blythe Knight (IRE)**[10] 1540 4-9-10 **103** .......... LDettori 10 109
(EALDunlop) *s.s: racd stands' side: hld up: hdwy over 2f out: rdn over 1f out: r.o: nt rch ldrs* **6/1**[2]

26-0 5 hd **Alrafid (IRE)**[14] 1460 5-8-7 **86** oh4 .......... RLMoore 3 92
(GLMoore) *lw: racd stands' side: hld up: hdwy and nt clr run over 1f out: r.o* **40/1**

-604 6 1 **King's Thought**[10] 1540 5-9-2 **95** .......... JPMurtagh 7 99
(SGollings) *led stands' side over 8f: wknd ins fnl f* **16/1**

/3-3 7 nk **Mysterinch**[14] 1469 4-9-1 **94** .......... JFEgan 8 97
(JeddO'Keeffe) *racd stands' side: chsd ldrs: rdn and ev ch over 1f out: wknd ins fnl f* **50/1**

56-0 8 1 ½ **St Pancras (IRE)**[18] 1385 4-8-11 **90** .......... WRyan 12 91
(NACallaghan) *racd stands' side: dwlt: hld up: hdwy over 1f out: nvr nrr* **12/1**

30-1 9 1 **Ionian Spring (IRE)**[14] 1460 9-8-11 **90** .......... RSmith 14 89
(CGCox) *racd stands' side: hld up: hdwy over 3f out: wknd over 1f out* **14/1**

2443 10 1 ½ **Barry Island**[14] 1460 5-8-2 **86** oh8 .......... RThomas[(5)] 6 82
(DRCElsworth) *racd stands' side: mid-div: rdn over 3f out: wknd over 1f out* **40/1**

030- 11 5 **Interceptor**[241] 4662 4-8-9 **88** .......... DHolland 19 74
(JWHills) *lw: chsd ldr far side: wknd over 1f out* **16/1**

12 12 1 **Akash (IRE)**[6] 1655 4-8-12 **91** .......... JFanning 1 75
(MJohnston) *racd stands' side: chsd ldr: rdn over 2f out: wknd over 1f out* **10/1**

00-0 13 ¾ **Everest (IRE)**[36] 1114 7-7-8 **86** oh1 .......... JPSpencer 15 69
(BEllison) *racd stands' side: hld up: hdwy over 2f out: wknd over 1f out* **13/2**[3]

161- 14 2 **Pagan Sky (IRE)**[189] 5753 5-8-4 **86** .......... LisaJones[(3)] 13 65
(JARToller) *racd stands' side: s.i.s: hld up: n.d* **12/1**

65-0 15 6 **Almaviva (IRE)**[21] 1332 4-8-11 **90** .......... EAhern 9 58
(JNoseda) *lw: racd stands' side: prom over 7f* **50/1**

16 ½ **Tresor Secret (FR)**[266] 4-8-2 **86** oh1 .......... DFox[(5)] 18 53
(NACallaghan) *swtchd to r stands' side: 9f out: hld up: n.d* **50/1**

020- 17 ½ **Famous Grouse**[19] 5365 4-9-7 **100** .......... SDrowne 17 66
(RCharlton) *swtchd to racd stands' side over 8f out: sn chsng ldrs: wknd wl over 2f out* **20/1**

/35- 18 ½ **Barrissimo (IRE)**[252] 4388 4-9-3 **96** .......... KFallon 5 61
(WJMusson) *swtg: racd stands' side: mid-div: wknd over 2f out* **33/1**

00-0 19 dist **Gala Sunday (USA)**[14] 1469 4-8-11 **90** .......... PJSmullen 11 —
(MWEasterby) *racd stands' side: mid-div: bhd fnl 4f* **66/1**

2m 4.35s (-1.34) **Going Correction** +0.075s/f (Good) **19** Ran SP% **122.9**
Speed ratings: **108,106,105,104,104 103,103,102,101,100 96,95,94,93,88 87,87,87,—**CSF £242.31 CT £1144.01 TOTE £12.60: £2.20, £3.40, £1.70, £1.30; EX 520.00 Trifecta £1248.60 Part won. Pool £1,758.60. 0.90 winning tickets..
**Owner** The Queen **Bred** The Queen **Trained** Newmarket, Suffolk

**FOCUS**
A competitive handicap in which the main body of the field raced up the stands' side. Just two runners, including the third home, raced up the far rail. The pace was fair and the form looks solid.

**NOTEBOOK**
**Promotion**, who has been gelded since a light campaign at three, overcame a tardy start to step up considerably on his three-year-old form and win decisively. Suited by the slightly easier ground on this occasion, he will have no problem with an extra quarter-mile and is obviously progressive.
**Tizzy May(FR)** became particularly warm in the preliminaries. Always prominent in the main bunch, this was a much better effort than his reappearance run but it is not going to bring him any relief from the Handicapper.
**Putra Kuantan** ◆ was one of only two to race up the far rail. He probably held the overall lead at one stage and this was a cracking effort in the circumstances.
**Blythe Knight(IRE)**, raised 4lb for his City And Suburban win, made progress from the rear without landing a blow at the leaders. He should continue to give a good account.
**Alrafid(IRE)**, racing from 4lb out of the handicap, picked up in good style late in the day after meeting with a spot of trouble. He is not easy to win with.
**King's Thought** bowled along in front as usual and only dropped away inside the last. He was 7lb above his highest winning mark here.
**St Pancras(IRE)**, who sweated up beforehand, was ridden to get the trip. He made late headway without conclusively proving that he stayed.
**Interceptor** was one of only two to race on the far side of the track.
**Everest(IRE)**, tackling this trip for the first time since 2001, did not appear to get home, but may be worth another chance over ten furlongs as he does tend to finish well over a mile.
**Gala Sunday(USA)** *Official explanation: jockey said gelding had a breathing problem*

## 1763 VICTOR CHANDLER PALACE HOUSE STKS (GROUP 3) 5f
**2:15** (2:17) (A) 3-Y-0+ **£29,000** (£11,000; £5,500; £2,500) **Stalls** Low

Form RPR

11-2 1 **Frizzante**[16] 1409 5-8-9 105 .......... JPMurtagh 1 116
(JRFanshawe) *outpcd: hdwy over 1f out: r.o u.p to ld post* **13/8**[1]

343- 2 shd **Avonbridge**[231] 4900 4-8-12 113 .......... SDrowne 5 119
(RCharlton) *h.d.w: chsd ldrs: nt clr run over 1f out: rdn to ld ins fnl f: hdd post* **7/1**[2]

341- 3 4 **Boogie Street**[226] 5009 3-8-3 107 .......... (t) RLMoore 9 104
(RHannon) *h.d.w: chsd ldrs: led over 1f out: hdd and no ex ins fnl f* **11/1**

0-24 4 hd **Fromsong (IRE)**[15] 1438 6-8-12 95 .......... LDettori 3 104
(BRMillman) *hld up: nt clr run 2f out: r.o ins fnl f: nt rch ldrs* **25/1**

00-0 5 ½ **Matty Tun**[17] 1391 5-8-12 87 .......... KFallon 13 102
(JBalding) *lw: s.i.s: outpcd: hdwy over 1f out: nt trble ldrs* **33/1**

100- 6 ½ **Baltic King**[197] 5615 4-8-12 105 .......... (t) DHolland 14 100
(HMorrison) *lw: hld up: hdwy 1/2-way: ev ch over 1f out: styd on same pce ins fnl f* **7/1**[2]

0-62 7 hd **Smokin Beau**[19] 1353 7-8-12 98 .......... TGMcLaughlin 7 99
(NPLittmoden) *chsd ldrs: rdn over 1f out: no ex* **16/1**

003- 8 hd **Fast Heart**[203] 5480 3-8-3 99 .......... (t) JFMcDonald 2 98
(BJMeehan) *lw: mid-div: sn pushed along: nt clr run over 1f out: kpt on* **50/1**

0002 9 1 ¼ **Peruvian Chief (IRE)**[15] 1438 7-8-12 97 .......... (v) EAhern 12 94
(NPLittmoden) *s.i.s: hdwy 3f out: styng on same pce whn n.m.r ins fnl f* **16/1**

30-6 10 nk **Colonel Cotton (IRE)**[19] 1379 5-8-12 109 .......... WRyan 8 93
(NACallaghan) *s.i.s: outpcd: nt clr run 1f out and ins fnl f : nvr trbld ldrs* **9/1**[3]

10-0 11 2 ½ **Repertory**[15] 1438 11-9-1 108 .......... JFanning 6 87
(MSSaunders) *w ldrs: rdn and ev ch over 1f out: wknd ins fnl f* **25/1**

16-0 12 ½ **Dubaian Gift**[15] 1438 5-8-12 105 .......... MartinDwyer 4 82
(AMBalding) *b: led: edgd rt and hdd over 1f out: wknd ins fnl f* **20/1**

012- 13 5 **Mornin Reserves**[224] 5072 5-8-12 108 .......... RWinston 10 64
(RAllan) *w ldrs: rdn and ev ch over 1f out: wkng whn hmpd ins fnl f* **14/1**

59.24 secs (-1.17) **Going Correction** +0.075s/f (Good)
**WFA** 3 from 4yo+ 9lb **13** Ran SP% **117.2**
Speed ratings: **112,111,105,105,104 103,103,102,100,100 96,95,87**CSF £11.17 TOTE £2.50: £1.70, £2.60, £2.70; EX 10.20 Trifecta £112.70 Pool £1,556.24 - 9.80 winning units..
**Owner** Mrs Jan Hopper & Mrs Elizabeth Grundy **Bred** Mrs J P Hopper And Mrs E M Grundy **Trained** Newmarket, Suffolk
■ Stewards Enquiry : J P Murtagh one-day ban: used whip without giving mare time to respond (May 12)

**FOCUS**
A strong renewal of this event, run at decent gallop. The first two finished clear and look capable of better still.

**NOTEBOOK**
**Frizzante** ◆, runner-up over six last time, was running over the minimum trip for the first time since 2002. Drawn against the rail, she almost inevitably met trouble in running, but she picked up really well when in the clear and got there on the line. She is progressing well.
**Avonbridge** ◆ ran a cracker on his first try at five furlongs, looking set to score when striking the front but just losing out to the mare. Likely to come on for the run, this half-brother to his stable companion Patavellian looks an improved performer and should be in for a good season.
**Boogie Street**, tackling his elders for the first time, got to the front but was cut down by the first two inside the last. He emerges with plenty of credit and has clearly trained on well.
**Fromsong(IRE)** was in last place when a little short of room at the quarter-mile pole but came home strongly. He is worth another try at six furlongs
**Matty Tun** struggled to go the pace after missing the break, but ran on well down the outside after momentarily finding himself short of room going into the Dip.
**Baltic King** improved down the outside at halfway but the effort flattened out inside the last. Although he should come on for the run, he may not be easy to place unless he finds improvement.
**Colonel Cotton(IRE)** was beginning to pick up when his path was blocked, otherwise he would have finished a few places closer. He is capable of winning a race of this nature but does require luck in running. *Official explanation: jockey said he was short of room in the closing stages*
**Dubaian Gift** showed bags of pace to lead for over three furlongs but weakened on this uphill finish.

## 1764 ULTIMATEBET.COM 2000 GUINEAS STKS (GROUP 1) (ENTIRE COLTS & FILLIES) 1m
**2:55** (2:59) (A) 3-Y-0 **£174,000** (£66,000; £33,000; £15,000) **Stalls** Centre

Form RPR

33-1 1 **Haafhd**[16] 1410 3-9-0 120 .......... RHills 4 126
(BWHills) *lw: trckd ldrs centre: led over 2f out: rdn and edgd rt over 1f out: r.o* **11/2**[2]

110- 2 1 ¾ **Snow Ridge (IRE)**[196] 5640 3-9-0 113 .......... LDettori 14 122
(SaeedBinSuroor) *hld up centre: hdwy over 2f out: rdn over 1f out: r.o* **8/1**[3]

1- 3 1 **Azamour (IRE)**[202] 5518 3-9-0 .......... MJKinane 11 119
(JohnMOxx, Ire) *gd sort: lw: hld up centre: hdwy over 1f out: r.o* **25/1**

1-1 4 1 **Grey Swallow (IRE)**[13] 1487 3-9-0 .......... PJSmullen 3 117
(DKWeld, Ire) *gd sort: lw: s.i.s: hld up centre: hdwy over 1f out: r.o* **10/1**

51-1 5 hd **Whipper (USA)**[25] 1289 3-9-0 .......... CSoumillon 8 117
(RobertCollet, France) *lw: trckd ldrs centre: ev ch 2f out: wknd ins fnl f* **9/1**

1-1 6 ½ **Salford City (IRE)**[14] 1459 3-9-0 115 .......... JPMurtagh 6 115
(DRCElsworth) *lw: outpcd: hdwy over 1f out: one pce ins fnl f* **11/2**[2]

334- 7 1 ½ **Bachelor Duke (USA)**[196] 5640 3-9-0 114 .......... SSanders 9 112
(JARToller) *h.d.w: chsd ldrs centre: rdn over 2f out: no ex fnl f* **20/1**

1-25 8 3 ½ **Milk It Mick**[14] 1459 3-9-0 114 .......... DHolland 1 104
(JAOsborne) *racd centre: s.i.s: hld up: plld hrd: rdn over 2f out: n.d* **12/1**

626- 9 8 **Tumblebrutus (USA)**[230] 4930 3-9-0 .......... PCosgrave 7 86
(APO'Brien, Ire) *gd sort: w ldr centre: evc hance over 2f out: wknd over 1f out* **200/1**

3-02 10 2 ½ **Glaramara**[18] 1384 3-9-0 96 .......... TEDurcan 12 80
(ABailey) *racd centre: outpcd* **200/1**

12-2 **11** ½ **Three Valleys (USA)**[16] [1410] 3-9-0 117 .................................. KFallon 2 79
(RCharlton) *lw: racd centre: mid-div: pushed along 1/2-way: effrt over 2f out: wknd over 1f out* **20/1**

43-5 **12** *shd* **Barbajuan (IRE)**[21] [1330] 3-9-0 110 .................................. PRobinson 10 78
(NACallaghan) *racd alone far side: chsd ldrs over 5f* **150/1**

111- **13** *dist* **One Cool Cat (USA)**[230] [4914] 3-9-0 .................................. JPSpencer 13 —
(APO'Brien, Ire) *gd sort: leggy: hld up centre: rdn 3f out: sn wknd and eased* **15/8**[1]

122- **14** *nk* **Golden Sahara (IRE)**[205] [5460] 3-9-0 96 ..................................(vt[1]) JCarroll 5 —
(SaeedBinSuroor) *lw: led centre over 5f: wknd qckly* **200/1**

1m 36.64s (-2.76) **Going Correction** +0.075s/f (Good) **14** Ran SP% **119.0**
Speed ratings: **116,114,113,112,112 111,110,106,98,96 95,95,—,—**CSF £46.44 CT £1046.41 TOTE £6.70: £2.50, £3.30, £4.50; EX 48.00 Trifecta £715.30 Pool £7,052.41 - 7.00 winning units..
**Owner** Hamdan Al Maktoum **Bred** Shadwell Estate Company Limited **Trained** Lambourn, Berks
■ Barry Hills's second win in the 2,000 Guineas, 25 years after his success with Tap On Wood.

**FOCUS**
A strong renewal of this Classic, but a strange race visually. The stalls were placed in the centre, but the runners were soon spread out across from the centre to the far side. The two pacemakers were quickly around ten lengths ahead of some of the fancied horses. The time was decent for a Guineas and Haafhd emerges second only to King's Best among recent winners on Racing Post Ratings.

**NOTEBOOK**
**Haafhd** ◆, who has always been held in the highest regard by Barry Hills, tracked the Godolphin pacemaker in the centre of the track before taking up the running. Quickening a couple of lengths to the good, he edged to his left but never looked likely to be caught. A high-class colt, he is not bred to get 12 furlongs so the Derby has been ruled out, and the St James's Palace Stakes is his immediate target.
**Snow Ridge(IRE)** ◆ , with Marcus Tregoning at two before joining Godolphin, impressed in a private trial in Dubai last month. Held up some way off the pace, he kept on well but the winner had taken first run and was not stopping. The Derby is his aim now and he ought to stay.
**Azamour(IRE)** ◆ was only eighth at the two-furlong pole but he ran on strongly. On pedigree he will struggle to stay a mile and half, but he should get ten furlongs, although his next race is likely to be in the Irish Guineas. Although he won the Beresford Stakes on yielding ground, his trainer considers him to be a much better colt on a fast surface.
**Grey Swallow(IRE)** had not pleased his trainer in the build-up to the race and should come on for the outing. Pushed along with three to run, he stayed on from off the pace and faster ground will be to advantage at the Curragh.
**Whipper(USA)** , who became rather warm in the preliminaries and was on his toes, showed knee action. Tracking the leaders in the centre before tacking over to the far side, he was still second passing the furlong pole before weakening as if failing to see out the stiff mile.
**Salford City(IRE)** was again slow to leave the stalls. Making his effort at the same time as Azamour, he was making no impression inside the last. This was a little disappointing, but he will appreciate a step up to ten furlongs which should offest his problem at the start.
**Bachelor Duke(USA)** ◆ ran a fine race for a maiden but was eventually found out by the final climb. He can win a nice race this season.
**Milk It Mick**, equipped with a net muzzle, was dropped in at the start. Always in rear until passing some beaten rivals, he did not appear to stay and will drop back in trip now.
**Three Valleys(USA)** was well enough placed, but he did not find much when asked for his effort and dropped away in disappointing fashion. He probably failed to stay.
**One Cool Cat(USA)** , a well-backed favourite, held up well off the pace, was immediately in trouble when asked to pick up three furlongs out and, showing no response, was eased down to finish tailed off. He clearly failed to run his race and, having been found to be suffering an irregular heartbeat, there will presumably be a period of recovery before he races again. *Official explanation: vet said colt had an irregular heartbeat*

## 1765 LADBROKES H'CAP 6f
**3:30** (3:32) (C) (0-95,92) 3-Y-O+ **£29,000** (£11,000; £5,500; £2,500) **Stalls** Low

Form RPR

2633 **1** **Moayed**[28] [1246] 5-8-13 80 ..................................(bt) EAhern 20 94
(NPLittmoden) *racd far side: chsd ldrs: rdn to ld ins fnl f: r.o* **25/1**

4634 **2** 1¾ **Ellens Academy (IRE)**[79] [749] 9-8-11 78 .................................. JFEgan 3 87
(EJAlston) *racd stands' side: chsd ldrs: rdn to ld that gp over 1f out: r.o* **33/1**

1100 **3** *hd* **Polar Kingdom**[19] [1354] 6-8-7 74 .................................. RHills 23 82
(TDBarron) *racd far side: hld up: hdwy over 1f out: r.o* **20/1**

05-4 **4** *shd* **Greenslades**[18] [1385] 5-9-9 90 .................................. SSanders 25 98
(PJMakin) *led far side: rdn over 1f out: hdd and unable qck ins fnl f* **10/1**[3]

110- **5** ½ **Tychy**[217] [5210] 5-9-6 90 .................................. BReilly[(3)] 19 96
(SCWilliams) *b: racd far side: chsd ldrs: rdn and ev ch over 1f out: styd on same pce ins fnl f* **33/1**

44-3 **6** *shd* **High Reach**[19] [1354] 4-9-8 89 .................................. LDettori 6 95
(TGMills) *racd stands' side: chsd ldrs: rdn over 2f out: r.o* **8/1**[2]

5543 **7** ¾ **Fruit Of Glory**[10] [1537] 5-9-9 90 .................................. DHolland 7 94
(JRJenkins) *racd stands' side: chsd ldrs: rdn over 1f out: no ex ins fnl f* **12/1**

0-00 **8** 1¼ **Beauvrai**[84] [703] 4-8-8 75 .................................. MTebbutt 29 75
(VSmith) *racd far side: chsd ldrs: rdn and ev ch over 1f out: no ex ins fnl f* **100/1**

0400 **9** *nk* **Aventura (IRE)**[21] [1321] 4-8-13 80 .................................. CSoumillon 28 79
(MJPolglase) *racd far side: chsd ldrs: outpcd over 2f out: r.o ins fnl f* **50/1**

00-4 **10** *nk* **Mr Malarkey (IRE)**[7] [1608] 4-8-13 80 ..................................(b) TGMcLaughlin 4 78
(MrsCADunnett) *racd stands' side: w ldrs: rdn and ev ch over 1f out: no ex* **25/1**

450- **11** *shd* **Najeebon (FR)**[175] [5946] 5-9-5 89 .................................. SHitchcott[(3)] 27 87
(MRChannon) *racd far side: chsd ldrs: rdn over 1f out: one pce* **25/1**

0-44 **12** *nk* **Viewforth**[11] [1525] 6-8-10 77 ..................................(b) SDrowne 1 74
(ISemple) *swtg: racd stands' side: chsd ldrs: rdn over 1f out: styd on same pce* **25/1**

0-60 **13** *nk* **Marker**[19] [1354] 4-9-7 88 .................................. RHavlin 21 84
(GBBalding) *lw: racd far side: chsd ldrs: rdn over 2f out: styd on same pce appr fnl f* **40/1**

0-00 **14** *shd* **Prince Cyrano**[19] [1354] 5-9-2 83 .................................. GCarter 30 79
(WJMusson) *racd far side: hld up: effrt over 1f out: nt trble ldrs* **50/1**

0-14 **15** ½ **Celtic Mill**[78] [761] 6-9-1 85 .................................. LEnstone[(3)] 14 79
(DWBarker) *led stands' side over 4f: wknd ins fnl f* **20/1**

00-0 **16** *nk* **Obe One**[20] [1343] 4-8-8 75 .................................. FNorton 5 68
(ABerry) *chsd ldrs stands' side: lost pl 1/2-way: n.d after* **66/1**

20-1 **17** ½ **Persario**[19] [1354] 5-9-5 86 .................................. JPMurtagh 8 78
(JRFanshawe) *racd stands' side: chsd ldrs over 4f* **4/1**[1]

203- **18** *nk* **Marsad (IRE)**[295] [3157] 10-9-9 90 .................................. PDoe 24 81
(JAkehurst) *racd far side: in tch: rdn over 1f out: sn btn* **14/1**

0-52 **19** *nk* **Cd Flyer (IRE)**[12] [1500] 7-9-4 85 .................................. RWinston 11 75
(BEllison) *racd stands' side: chsd ldrs to 1/2-way* **14/1**

35-0 **20** ¾ **Cheese 'n Biscuits**[19] [1372] 4-8-12 79 .................................. RLMoore 18 67
(GLMoore) *racd stands' side: a in rr* **50/1**

05-6 **21** *shd* **Winning Venture**[19] [1354] 7-9-5 86 .................................. WRyan 22 74
(AWCarroll) *racd far side: prom over 4f* **14/1**

40-3 **22** ¾ **Watching**[31] [1199] 7-9-2 83 .................................. PDobbs 12 68
(DNicholls) *lw: racd stands' side: chsd ldrs 4f* **20/1**

020- **23** *nk* **Bi Polar**[175] [5946] 4-8-11 78 .................................. MJKinane 9 62
(DRCElsworth) *lw: racd stands' side: chsd ldrs 4f* **33/1**

0-00 **24** *nk* **Master Robbie**[18] [1385] 5-9-11 92 .................................. TEDurcan 2 76
(MRChannon) *racd stands' side: hld up: n.d* **40/1**

0-10 **25** 1 **Steel Blue**[19] [1354] 4-9-5 86 ..................................(v[1]) MHills 10 67
(RMWhitaker) *racd stands' side: w ldr: rdn over 2f out: wknd over 1f out* **25/1**

2-25 **26** *nk* **Camberley (IRE)**[18] [1385] 7-9-11 92 .................................. KFallon 13 72
(PFICole) *racd stands' side: chsd ldrs to 1/2-way* **16/1**

0-16 **27** ½ **Devise (IRE)**[5] [1673] 5-8-11 78 .................................. MartinDwyer 16 56
(MSSaunders) *racd stands' side: a in rr* **40/1**

00-6 **28** 1 **Plateau**[37] [1106] 5-9-3 84 .................................. JCarroll 17 59
(DNicholls) *racd stands' side: prom 4f* **25/1**

1-00 **29** 1¼ **Fantasy Believer**[18] [1385] 6-9-11 92 .................................. JFanning 15 63
(JJQuinn) *lw: racd stands' side: chsd ldrs 4f* **40/1**

0-00 **30** 14 **Arctic Burst (USA)**[12] [1500] 4-9-4 85 ..................................(vt[1]) SWhitworth 26 14
(DShaw) *b.bhd: racd far side: bhd fnl 2f* **100/1**

1m 12.03s (-1.06) **Going Correction** +0.075s/f (Good) **30** Ran SP% **139.1**
Speed ratings: **110,107,107,107,106 106,105,103,103,103 102,102,102,101,101 100,100,99,99,98 98,97,96,96,95** 9CSF £693.01 CT £15566.49 TOTE £40.20: £7.50, £10.70, £11.00, £2.40; EX 2085.10 TRIFECTA Not won..
**Owner** Nigel Shields **Bred** Sentinal Bloodstock And Wong Chung Mat **Trained** Newmarket, Suffolk

**FOCUS**
A strong handicap in which the field split into two, 12 going over to the far rail, although they ended up spread across the track. There was no real advantage to either flank. The time was good for the grade and the form should work out.

**NOTEBOOK**
**Moayed**, who ran well back on turf last time, had never run over six furlongs before. Staying on strongly, he drifted away from the far rail to end up near the centre of the track and won decisively, showing career best form.
**Ellens Academy(IRE)** ◆ won the race on the stands' side, despite missing the break slightly. This was a very encouraging effort and faster ground will be to his benefit.
**Polar Kingdom**, suited by a stiff track at this trip, was keeping on well in the latter stages. He has not won on turf for three years but is nicely handicapped nowadays.
**Greenslades** ran a good race, making the running on the far side and sticking on well, but his consistency is going to continue to make life difficult for him with the Handicapper.
**Tychy** was 7lb above her highest winning mark and this was an excellent effort on her seasonal debut.
**High Reach** ◆ ran on strongly late in the day to finish second amongst the near-side group, and he remains in good form.
**Fruit Of Glory** had run well over five furlongs last time, but the way she finished suggested that a return to seven furlongs might not come amiss.
**Beauvrai**, formerly trained by John Quinn, shaped with promise and would have finished closer but for being eased when held. A drop back to five furlongs would not be a problem and he is on a decent mark now.
**Aventura(IRE)** signalled a return to form, staying on strongly when it was all over. She ran over an extended ten furlongs last time, and an intermediate trip of seven or a mile could prove best.
**Obe One** was staying on nicely once in the clear and the sixth furlong did not appear to be a problem.
**Persario**, from an 8lb higher mark, never looked likely to justify some strong market support.
**Camberley(IRE)** *Official explanation: jockey said gelding was never travelling*

## 1766 ROLLS-ROYCE MOTOR CARS LONDON NEWMARKET STKS (LISTED RACE) (COLTS) 1m 2f
**4:05** (4:05) (A ) 3-Y-O **£17,850** (£6,600; £3,300; £1,500) **Stalls** Low

Form RPR

-211 **1** **Hazyview**[8] [1588] 3-8-8 84 .................................. DHolland 6 111
(NACallaghan) *lw: mde all: shkn up over 1f out: r.o wl* **3/1**[2]

44-4 **2** 1½ **Tahreeb (FR)**[17] [1396] 3-8-8 108 .................................. MartinDwyer 4 108
(MPTregoning) *trckd ldrs: chal over 1f out: unable qck towards fin* **4/1**[3]

5-06 **3** 2½ **Crocodile Dundee (IRE)**[28] [1239] 3-8-8 93 .................................. JFEgan 3 103
(JamiePoulton) *hld up: plld hrd: hdwy over 3f out: rdn and ev ch over 1f out: no ex* **20/1**

14-4 **4** 2½ **Isidore Bonheur (IRE)**[16] [1411] 3-8-8 98 ..................................(b) MHills 5 98
(BWHills) *lw: trckd ldr: rdn and ev ch over 1f out: wknd ins fnl f* **9/1**

102- **5** 1 **Bayeux (USA)**[212] [5333] 3-8-8 112 ..................................(t) LDettori 1 96
(SaeedBinSuroor) *chsd ldrs: swtchd rt over 1f out: wknd fnl f* **11/10**[1]

2m 5.38s (-0.31) **Going Correction** +0.075s/f (Good) **5** Ran SP% **107.4**
Speed ratings: **104,102,100,98,98**CSF £14.11 TOTE £3.60: £1.50, £2.10; EX 19.20.
**Owner** T Mohan **Bred** N E Poole **Trained** Newmarket, Suffolk

**FOCUS**
This was run at a muddling pace and probably was not the strongest of Listed races, although the winner is improving and the form looks sound enough.

**NOTEBOOK**
**Hazyview** had plenty to find against these on official ratings, but was suited by having a soft time of things up front. However, it would be dangerous to underestimate him, for he is progressive and had looked in his two previous runs as if he would be suited by a stiffer test. Connections have suggested that they may be tempted to run him in the Chester Vase, where the likely small field and turning track may well make him difficult to peg back.
**Tahreeb(FR)**, tackling his furthest trip to date, had every chance, but was just outstayed towards the finish. This was only steadily run, so he did not really prove that he genuinely stays this far.
**Crocodile Dundee(IRE)** has faced some stiff tasks since winning his maiden, and he did himself no favours by taking a fierce grip. This was only his second outing on turf, but while he is open to improvement, he will not be easy to place off his current mark.
**Isidore Bonheur(IRE)** settled better in the blinkers this time, despite there not being much pace on. He had his chance going into the dip, but did not find anything off the bridle and looks to have something to prove now.
**Bayeux(USA)**, best in on official figures was most disappointing and was the first beaten. He was fitted with a tongue tie on his second start last year and failed to sparkle that day, so it could be that he does not get on with the aid.

## 1767 RUINART CHAMPAGNE CONDITIONS STKS 1m 2f
**4:40** (4:43) (B ) 4-Y-O+ **£12,267** (£4,653; £2,326; £1,057) **Stalls** Low

Form RPR

42-0 **1** **Bandari (IRE)**[14] [1455] 5-8-7 114 .................................. JFanning 8 111
(MJohnston) *mde all: rdn over 1f out: r.o gamely* **9/2**[2]

45-0 **2** 1 **Private Charter**[42] [1062] 4-8-7 110 .................................. MHills 10 109
(BWHills) *chsd ldrs: rdn and ev ch over 1f out: styd on* **10/1**

3/1- **3** ½ **Musanid (USA)**[349] [1695] 4-8-10 100 .................................. RHills 3 111
(SirMichaelStoute) *h.d.w: hld up: hdwy over 2f out: rdn over 1f out: styd on* **6/1**[3]

200- **4** 1 **Persian Lightning (IRE)**[183] [5853] 5-8-7 102 MJKinane 7 106
(JLDunlop) *h.d.w: trckd wnr: rdn and ev ch over 1f out: no ex towards fin* **13/2**

452- **5** 2 1/2 **Songlark**[232] [4861] 4-8-7 107 (vt[1]) LDettori 2 101
(SaeedBinSuroor) *h.d.w: hld up in tch: rdn over 1f out: nt run on* **4/1**[1]

/54- **6** 2 **Orange Touch (GER)**[352] [1616] 4-8-7 101 KFallon 6 98
(MrsAJPerrett) *lw: plld hrd and prom: outpcd wl over 1f out: styd on ins fnl f* **20/1**

324- **7** shd **Quiet Storm (IRE)**[227] [5000] 4-8-10 94 DHolland 9 100
(GWragg) *hld up: hdwy 2f out: no imp fnl f* **20/1**

3/0- **8** 1 1/4 **Beekeeper**[420] [691] 6-8-7 JPSpencer 1 95
(DRLoder) *lw: hld up: hdwy 2f out: wknd fnl f* **9/2**[2]

35-1 **9** 2 **Putra Sandhurst (IRE)**[7] [1618] 6-9-1 104 PRobinson 4 99
(MAJarvis) *b: lw: chsd ldrs tl wknd wl over 1f out* **9/1**

20-0 **10** 5 **Rocket Force (USA)**[19] [1355] 4-8-7 102 EAhern 5 82
(EALDunlop) *s.i.s: hld up: rdn over 2f out: sn wknd* **66/1**

2m 4.31s (-1.38) **Going Correction** +0.075s/f (Good) **10** Ran SP% **114.1**
Speed ratings: **108,107,106,106,104 102,102,101,99,95**CSF £46.29 TOTE £4.30: £2.20, £3.20, £2.10; EX 39.70.
**Owner** Hamdan Al Maktoum **Bred** Rathasker Stud **Trained** Middleham Moor, N Yorks

**FOCUS**
This was quite a hot conditions race, with Group Two and Three winners taking part, and the form looks up to minor Pattern-race level. All the same it was a steadily-run contest.

**NOTEBOOK**
**Bandari(IRE)** ◆, who found life difficult last year, albeit in the face of some stiff tasks, faced his easiest opening since his juvenile days. Able to dictate a steady pace, he gradually wound things up and showed plenty of resolution in the finish. This win will have done his confidence nothing but good.
**Private Charter** ◆ bounced back from a poor effort on his return to action, over a trip possibly short of his best. He has the ability to win a Listed event at the very least.
**Musanid(USA)** had no easy task giving weight away to some useful performers and comes out of this with plenty of credit. A lightly-raced colt, he clearly has plenty of ability and should not be too difficult to place this year, providing he remains sound.
**Persian Lightning(IRE)** could have done with a stronger pace over this trip, but nonetheless this was still a solid effort.
**Songlark**, fitted with a visor for the first time, did not impress when push came to shove and may be one to treat with caution.
**Orange Touch(GER)** again did himself no favours by taking a fair grip. However, he is not without ability and if consenting to settle should win his fair share.
**Quiet Storm(IRE)** had plenty to find with the majority of these and was far from disgraced, having been held up in a steadily-run contest.
**Beekeeper**, who stays further than this, would not have been suited by the steady early pace.

## 1768 THE CURRAGH "THE HOME OF THE IRISH CLASSICS" H'CAP 1m 4f
**5:15** (5:18) (C) (0-100,98) 4-Y-0+ **£8,572** (£3,251; £1,625; £739) **Stalls** Centre

Form RPR

1022 **1** **Dissident (GER)**[7] [1611] 6-8-0 **70** (v) JMackay 5 84
(DFlood) *a.p: chsd ldr over 3f out: led over 2f out: sn clr: rdn out* **20/1**

0-34 **2** 3 **Pagan Dance (IRE)**[10] [1539] 5-9-6 **90** (p) LDettori 16 99
(MrsAJPerrett) *hld up: hdwy and nt clr run over 2f out and over 1f out: r.o: nt rch wnr* **6/1**[3]

10-2 **3** hd **Prins Willem (IRE)**[17] [1401] 5-9-4 **88** JPMurtagh 1 97
(JRFanshawe) *hld up: hdwy over 2f out: r.o* **9/2**[2]

15-4 **4** 5 **Bagan (FR)**[17] [1401] 5-9-2 **86** WRyan 7 87
(HRACecil) *hld up in tch: plld hrd: rdn over 2f out: hung rt over 1f out: no ex* **4/1**[1]

2-00 **5** nk **Perfect Storm**[14] [1455] 5-9-8 **92** FNorton 19 93
(MBlanshard) *hld up: nt clr run over 2f out: swtchd lft over 1f out: r.o* **14/1**

02-0 **6** 1 1/4 **Trust Rule**[21] [1328] 4-10-0 **98** MHills 13 97
(BWHills) *lw: hld up in tch: plld hrd: effrt and hmpd over 1f out: nt trble ldrs* **11/1**

-005 **7** shd **Champion Lion (IRE)**[10] [1539] 5-8-1 **74** ow5 SHitchcott[(3)] 9 72
(MRChannon) *lw: s.i.s: hld up: hdwy over 2f out: no ex fnl f* **9/1**

15-0 **8** nk **Establishment**[21] [1329] 7-8-7 **77** SWhitworth 2 75
(CACyzer) *hld up: hdwy over 1f out: nvr nrr* **25/1**

323- **9** 3/4 **Montecristo**[231] [4895] 11-8-1 **74** LisaJones[(3)] 8 71
(RGuest) *hld up: styd on appr fnl f: nvr nrr* **40/1**

005- **10** 3 1/2 **Largo (IRE)**[195] [5659] 4-9-7 **91** MJKinane 12 82
(JLDunlop) *b.nr fore: hld up: nvr nr to chal* **33/1**

16-0 **11** nk **Dovedon Hero**[17] [1401] 4-8-9 **79** SSanders 3 70
(PJMcbride) *hld up: hdwy 2f out: wknd fnl f* **50/1**

-000 **12** hd **Environment Audit**[32] [1188] 5-7-6 **69** oh3 ow1 (v[1]) JJeffrey[(7)] 10 59
(JRJenkins) *led: clr 9f out: hdd over 2f out: wknd over 1f out* **100/1**

0231 **13** 1 **Rasid (USA)**[5] [1669] 6-8-9 **79** 4ex DHolland 6 68
(CADwyer) *b.nr hind: hld up: a in rr* **20/1**

-103 **14** 2 1/2 **So Vital**[36] [1122] 4-8-3 **73** (p) RPrice 11 58
(JPearce) *chsd ldrs 10f* **50/1**

6405 **15** 6 **Brilliant Red**[29] [1232] 11-8-8 **78** (t) EAhern 20 53
(JamiePoulton) *lw: dwlt: sn chsng ldrs: wknd over 3f out* **40/1**

26-0 **16** 3/4 **Wait For The Will (USA)**[17] [1401] 8-9-5 **89** (b) RLMoore 15 63
(GLMoore) *lw: hld up: wknd over 2f out* **25/1**

110- **17** 3 1/2 **Financial Future**[276] [3688] 4-10-0 **98** JFanning 14 66
(MJohnston) *chsd ldr to 1/2-way: wknd over 2f out* **14/1**

0212 **18** 11 **Hip Hop Harry**[66] [887] 4-9-2 **86** KFallon 18 37
(EALDunlop) *prom: rdn over 4f out: wknd over 2f out* **7/1**

40-0 **19** 1 1/2 **Wahchi (IRE)**[25] [1286] 5-9-1 **85** TLucas 17 33
(GPKelly) *hld up: hung rt and wknd 3f out* **100/1**

2m 32.81s (-0.65) **Going Correction** +0.075s/f (Good) **19** Ran SP% **127.6**
Speed ratings: **105,103,102,99,99 98,98,98,97,95 95,95,94,92,88 88,85,78,77**CSF £129.69 CT £659.05 TOTE £46.00: £9.10, £1.70, £1.50, £1.90; EX 516.70 Place 6 £430.59, Place 5 £185.33..
**Owner** Mrs Ruth M Serrell **Bred** Gestut Rottgen **Trained** Upper Lambourn, Berks

**FOCUS**
A difficult race to work out, but while very few got seriously involved it should produce its share of winners. The early pace was strong, but the overall time was unexceptional.

**NOTEBOOK**
**Dissident(GER)**, who had not looked that keen at Leicester, proved well suited by this strongly-run contest and found himself left in front some way out, as the runaway leader folded. Left with quite a lead, nothing ever looked likely to get to him.
**Pagan Dance(IRE)**, done no favours as Bagan hung across him, stuck well to his task, but the winner was beyond recall. There will be other days for him.
**Prins Willem(IRE)** ◆, like the runner-up, found the winner had flown before he had got going. A step back up in trip looks the key to him.
**Bagan(FR)** was a bit keen early on, but was one of the first to try to get after the winner before his run petered out. He does have ability, but he looks the sort who needs everything to fall just right for him.
**Perfect Storm** found this more his level and showed a bit more than of late. However, he looks as though he needs a bit of help from the Handicapper.
**Trust Rule** was done no favours as Bagan hung in the dip, causing Pagan Dance to give him a bump. However, there was plenty to like about this effort under his big weight.
**Largo(IRE)** did not have a hard time of things and can step up on this in due course.
**Hip Hop Harry** *Official explanation: jockey said colt was unsuited by the surface*
T/Plt: £512.70 to a £1 stake. Pool: £119,469.35. 170.10 winning tickets. T/Qpdt: £74.50 to a £1 stake. Pool: £4,593.15. 45.60 winning tickets. CR

# [1468]THIRSK (L-H)
Saturday, May 1

**OFFICIAL GOING: Good**
The ground appeared to be riding slower than the official going suggested.

## 1769 EUROPEAN BREEDERS FUND SUTTON NOVICE STKS 5f
**2:05** (2:06) (D ) 2-Y-0 **£5,473** (£1,684; £842; £421) **Stalls** High

Form RPR

2 **1** **World At My Feet**[15] [1449] 2-8-7 JQuinn 5 81
(NBycroft) *trckd ldrs: drvn along over 1f out: led ins fnl f: r.o wl* **12/1**

41 **2** 3 1/2 **Bold Marc (IRE)**[23] [1314] 2-9-0 DarrenWilliams 6 74
(KRBurke) *w ldr: led 2f out: drvn along and edgd lft appr fnl f: hdd ins last: no ex* **5/6**[1]

**3** 2 **Twice Nightly** 2-8-12 PHanagan 1 64
(JDBethell) *sn wl bhd: hdwy over 1f out: hung lft fnl f: r.o wl towards fin* **20/1**

5 **4** 2 **Special Gold**[21] [1324] 2-8-9 DAllan[(3)] 4 56
(TDEasterby) *slt ld tl hdd 2f out: sn rdn: wknd fnl f* **11/4**[2]

**5** 2 **Piddies Pride (IRE)** 2-8-4 TPQueally[(3)] 7 43
(IAWood) *s.i.s: sn wl bhd: kpt on fr over 1f out: nvr danger dangerous* **40/1**

31 **6** hd **Smokincanon**[25] [1276] 2-8-9 RMiles[(3)] 3 47
(WGMTurner) *dwlt: a bhd* **7/1**[3]

**6** dht **Melandre** 2-8-7 TWilliams 2 42
(MBrittain) *s.i.s: sn chsng ldrs: rdn and ch over 1f out: wknd ins last* **50/1**

62.68 secs (2.78) **Going Correction** +0.525s/f (Yiel) **7** Ran SP% **110.6**
Speed ratings: **98,92,89,86,82 82,82**CSF £21.33 TOTE £11.40: £3.50, £1.30; EX 17.00.
**Owner** Cavalier Racing **Bred** Mrs B Shirley **Trained** Brandsby, N Yorks

**FOCUS**
A fair race run in a decent time, although the favourite was probably unsuited by the ease in the ground.

**NOTEBOOK**
**World At My Feet**, a pleasing second on her debut, had come on for that run and appreciated the ease in the ground, eventually running out a clear winner. Sold for just 1,400gns as a foal, she looks like something of a bargain. The Hilary Needler at Beverley could now be on the cards.
**Bold Marc(IRE)**, withdrawn from his intended race at Ascot on Wednesday because of the soft ground, probably found this surface easier than he would ideally like. He should be given another chance back on fast ground. *Official explanation: jockey said colt hung left throughout*
**Twice Nightly**, bred to make a two-year-old, was conceding race experience to the first, second and fourth in what was a fair event. Running green, he took a while to get the hang of things, but when the penny finally dropped, he ran on well. He should come on quite a bit for the run and a modest maiden looks there for the taking.
**Special Gold** probably did too much in front and is capable of better than this bare form suggests.
**Smokincanon** might be better off going back on the All-Weather on this evidence.

## 1770 RYE MAIDEN STKS 1m 4f
**2:40** (2:41) (D ) 3-Y-0+ **£5,525** (£1,700; £850; £425) **Stalls** Low

Form RPR

03-3 **1** **Karamea (SWI)**[15] [1440] 3-8-0 82 JQuinn 1 69
(JLDunlop) *trckd ldrs: led 7f out: pushed clr fr over 2 out: comf* **1/2**[1]

5- **2** 2 1/2 **Calonnog (IRE)**[180] [5907] 4-9-5 PaulEddery 6 65
(HRACecil) *led 3f: remained cl up: rdn and ch 3 out: sn outpcd by wnr: styd on* **10/3**[2]

0- **3** 3 **Dawn Air (USA)**[182] [5869] 3-8-0 PFessey 4 60?
(KARyan) *towards rr: outpcd 4f out: kpt on u.p fr over 2 out: n.d* **25/1**

00 **4** 1 1/2 **Logger Rhythm (USA)**[7] [1612] 4-9-10 MFenton 2 63?
(RDickin) *hld up in rr: sme hdwy u.p 4f out: no further prog fr over 2 out* **50/1**

400- **5** 3 **Havetoavit (USA)**[190] [5726] 3-7-12 61 SShaw[(7)] 3 58
(JDBethell) *rrd bdly s and slowly away: plld hrd and sn in tch: rdn over 3f out: no hdwy* **14/1**[3]

0 **6** 12 **Paula**[11] [1528] 4-9-2 (p) THamilton[(3)] 7 34
(MDods) *prom tl rdn and wknd over 3f out* **100/1**

664 **7** 6 **Albee (IRE)**[35] [1138] 4-9-10 54 (p) IMongan 5 29
(MissGayKelleway) *cl up: led after 3f: hdd 7 out: wknd 3 out* **16/1**

0- **8** dist **Rocky Rambo**[192] [5710] 3-8-4 ow4 TEaves[(5)] 8 —
(RDEWoodhouse) *towards rr: outpcd 4f out: lost tch fr over 2 out: t.o* **100/1**

2m 47.21s (12.01) **Going Correction** +0.525s/f (Yiel)
**WFA** 3 from 4yo 19lb **8** Ran SP% **110.1**
Speed ratings: **80,78,76,75,73 65,61,—**CSF £2.05 TOTE £1.50: £1.02, £2.00, £6.70; EX 2.00.
**Owner** Mrs S Egloff **Bred** Gestut Sorenhof **Trained** Arundel, W Sussex

**FOCUS**
Uncompetitive stuff, and a poor time, but another boost for the Newbury maiden form of Winds Of March.

**NOTEBOOK**
**Karamea(SWI)** had run with credit behind two useful fillies on her reappearance at Newbury, and this task looked a lot simpler. In what was effectively a match, the trip proved no problem and she won with the minimum of fuss.
**Calonnog(IRE)**, who looked the only danger to the favourite on paper, could not match the pace of the winner but finished a clear second. There probably was not much quality behind her but, as a half-sister to Sunshine Street, she should stay farther still.
**Dawn Air(USA)**, a half-sister to several winners, notably Oaks third Midnight Line, never got into a competitive position but stayed on well. She looks the type who may do better once she has been given a mark.
**Logger Rhythm(USA)** ran her best race to date and now qualifies for a handicap mark.
**Havetoavit(USA)**, without the headgear he wore on his last three starts last year, did not do a lot right in the race and a stamina doubt remains.

## 1771 B F C BRAVA LTD MAIDEN STKS 7f
**3:15** (3:17) (D) 3-Y-0 **£5,785** (£1,780; £890; £445) **Stalls** Low

Form RPR

**1** **Night Air (IRE)** 3-8-11 TPQueally[(3)] 13 74
(DRLoder) *prom: rdn over 2f out: led ins fnl f: r.o: all out* **4/1**[2]

0-32 **2** *shd* **My Paris**[16] 1425 3-9-0 64 .......... NCallan 5 74
(KARyan) *prom: led 2f out: hdd ins fnl f: r.o u.p: jst hld* **12/1**

0-4 **3** *½* **Burley Flame**[19] 1370 3-9-0 .......... MFenton 9 73
(JGGiven) *prom: rdn and sltly outpcd over 2f out: rallied over 1f out r.o fnl f* **25/1**

320- **4** *5* **Sessay**[232] 4865 3-9-0 69 .......... ANicholls 7 60
(DNicholls) *chsd ldrs: drvn along over 2f out: kpt on: no hdwy* **33/1**

03 **5** *nk* **Ice Planet**[14] 1472 3-9-0 .......... AlexGreaves 6 59
(DNicholls) *in tch: drvn along over 2f out: kpt on: no hdwy* **16/1**

0-3 **6** *2* **Moors Myth**[18] 1386 3-9-0 .......... DeanMcKeown 2 54
(BWHills) *led tl rdn and hdd 2f out: hung lft: no ex* **1/1**[1]

0- **7** *5* **Adaikali (IRE)**[206] 5448 3-9-0 .......... BDoyle 1 41
(SirMichaelStoute) *sn midfield: drvn along over 2f out: no hdwy* **11/2**[3]

0 **8** *½* **Trysting Grove (IRE)**[16] 1419 3-8-9 .......... GParkin 3 34
(KARyan) *midfield: rn wd into home st over 3f out: sme hdwy over 2 out: no further prog fnl 2f* **100/1**

05- **9** *1 ¾* **Storm Clouds**[229] 4950 3-8-7 .......... AMullen(7) 8 35
(TDEasterby) *midfield: effrt 3f out: no hdwy* **100/1**

4 **10** *½* **Estepona**[9] 1557 3-9-0 .......... DRMcCabe 12 34
(MissJACamacho) *s.i.s: a towards rr* **20/1**

0 **11** *¾* **Antigiotto (IRE)**[29] 1226 3-8-11 .......... NMackay(3) 4 32
(LMCumani) *s.i.s: towards rr: drvn along 1/2-way: no hdwy* **33/1**

00- **12** *3* **Ravel (IRE)**[176] 5938 3-9-0 .......... IMongan 10 24
(MLWBell) *nvr bttr than mid-div* **33/1**

00-0 **13** *3 ½* **Theatre Belle**[16] 1419 3-8-6 .......... DAllan(3) 15 10
(TDEasterby) *s.i.s: a towards rr* **66/1**

0- **14** *16* **Mikes Mate**[140] 6175 3-8-9 .......... TEaves(5) 14 —
(CJTeague) *s.i.s: a rr div: t.o* **100/1**

**15** *dist* **Warbreck** 3-9-0 .......... PHanagan 11 —
(CREgerton) *a bhd: t.o* **14/1**

1m 29.87s (2.77) **Going Correction** +0.525s/f (Yiel) **15** Ran SP% **127.5**
Speed ratings: **105,104,104,98,98 95,90,89,87,87 86,82,78,60,—**CSF £50.07 TOTE £6.00: £1.90, £3.10, £4.30; EX 79.30.
**Owner** Sheikh Mohammed **Bred** Norelands Stud **Trained** Newmarket, Suffolk
■ Stewards Enquiry : M Fenton one-day ban: careless riding (May 12)

**FOCUS**
Only fair form on the face of it, but the time was decent for the grade.

**NOTEBOOK**
**Night Air(IRE)**, who cost 110,000gns, did well to defy his high draw on his debut, but in being all out to beat a 64-rated rival, the form probably does not amount to much.
**My Paris**, fit from the All-Weather, ran well in defeat on his turf debut and will be interesting in a handicap off this sort of mark.
**Burley Flame** ran another solid race, pulling nicely clear of the fourth, and he is now eligible for handicaps.
**Sessay** is bred for speed, so it was a little surprising to see him make his reappearance over seven furlongs.
**Ice Planet** looked likely to appreciate the return to seven furlongs on his reappearance and he is another who is now eligible for a mark.
**Moors Myth** was a disappointing favourite given the fact that he was well drawn, appeared to have trip and ground in his favour and was race-fit after a promising reappearance at Newmarket.
**Estepona** *Official explanation: jockey said gelding hung right throughout*

## 1772 TOTEPOOL H'CAP — 7f
**3:50** (3:50) (C ) (0-90,89) 3-Y-0+ **£9,782** (£3,010; £1,505; £752) **Stalls** Low

Form RPR

23-0 **1** **Raphael (IRE)**[31] 1199 5-9-0 75 .......... DaleGibson 7 85+
(TDEasterby) *hld up: hdwy whn nt clr run 2f out: styd on wl fnl f: led clsng stages* **12/1**

00-4 **2** *nk* **Fiveoclock Express (IRE)**[42] 1065 4-9-3 78 .......... (p) IMongan 11 87
(MissGayKelleway) *towards rr: hdwy 1/2-way: styd on wl to ld ins fnl f: hdd clsng stages* **8/1**[3]

026- **3** *¾* **Qualitair Wings**[171] 5981 5-8-11 72 .......... DMcGaffin 9 79
(JHetherton) *bhd: hdwy whn nt clr run 2f out: styd on wl fnl f: nrst fin* **20/1**

0-03 **4** *1 ½* **Young Mr Grace (IRE)**[19] 1358 4-8-11 75 .......... DAllan(3) 12 78
(TDEasterby) *a chsng ldrs: rdn over 2f out: kpt on wl fnl f* **12/1**

10-0 **5** *hd* **Atlantic Quest (USA)**[31] 1199 5-9-2 82 .......... PMulrennan(5) 10 85
(GAHarker) *midfield: effrt whn nt clr run over 1f out: r.o wl ins fnl f: nvr able to chal* **25/1**

5-00 **6** *hd* **Go Tech**[28] 1246 4-8-12 80 .......... AMullen(7) 6 82
(TDEasterby) *bhd and sn pushed along: hdwy appr fnl f: r.o wl ins last: nrst fin* **16/1**

1-20 **7** *hd* **Cardinal Venture (IRE)**[36] 1114 6-9-12 87 .......... NCallan 14 89
(KARyan) *sn prom: led over 3f out: rdn over 2 out: hdd ins fnl f: no ex* **9/2**[1]

0301 **8** *hd* **Harry Potter (GER)**[15] 1451 5-8-10 71 .......... (v) DarrenWilliams 5 72
(KRBurke) *midfield: rdn over 2f out: kpt on fnl f: nvr able to chal* **13/2**[2]

-560 **9** *1 ¼* **Golden Chalice (IRE)**[14] 1456 5-9-8 88 .......... NChalmers(5) 3 86
(AMBalding) *midfield: effrt over 2f out: no real hdwy* **13/2**[2]

5-00 **10** *¾* **True Night**[7] 1608 7-9-2 77 .......... AlexGreaves 13 73
(DNicholls) *nvr bttr than mid-div* **25/1**

331- **10** *dht* **King Harson**[179] 5918 5-9-7 82 .......... (v) PHanagan 4 78
(JDBethell) *cl up: led over 5f out: hdd over 3 out: wknd appr fnl f* **8/1**[3]

4-66 **12** *1 ¼* **Distant Country (USA)**[15] 1451 5-8-12 73 .......... (p) JQuinn 15 66
(MrsJRRamsden) *midfield: effrt over 2f out: no hdwy* **9/1**

00-0 **13** *7* **Online Investor**[12] 1500 5-8-6 67 .......... ANicholls 8 42
(DNicholls) *slowly away: bhd early: hdwy into midfield 1/2-way: styng on whn nt clr run and hmpd ins fnl f* **14/1**

00L- **14** *shd* **Time To Remember (IRE)**[196] 5636 6-8-8 69 .......... DRMcCabe 1 43
(DNicholls) *led tl hdd over 5f out: remained prom tl wknd over 1 out* **25/1**

010- **15** *3* **Wessex (USA)**[83] 2684 4-10-0 89 .......... DeanMcKeown 16 56
(JamesMoffatt) *in tch tl wknd 2f out* **33/1**

050- **16** *1 ¼* **Coranglais**[252] 4375 4-9-1 76 .......... SCarson 2 39
(JMBradley) *midfield tl wknd 2f out* **33/1**

1m 30.06s (2.96) **Going Correction** +0.525s/f (Yiel) **16** Ran SP% **127.2**
Speed ratings: **104,103,102,101,100 100,100,100,98,97 97,96,88,88,84 83**CSF £100.19 CT £1936.99 TOTE £11.10: £2.30, £1.80, £5.70, £3.10; EX 83.70.
**Owner** Mrs K Arton **Bred** Mrs B A Headon **Trained** Great Habton, N Yorks

**FOCUS**
They went a decent pace for this competitive affair, but the form is only ordinary for the grade.

**NOTEBOOK**
**Raphael(IRE)** did not have everything go smoothly during the race but overcame the difficulties to get up close home. She should not be dismissed lightly in the coming weeks now that she has hit form.
**Fiveoclock Express(IRE)** ◆ is not as good on the turf as he is on the All-Weather, but he had the race run to suit and performed well in defeat. The re-application of the visor may help, and it will be a surprise if his capable trainer does not get a win out of him while in this form.
**Qualitair Wings** ◆ ran a very promising race on his reappearance, finishing well having not enjoyed the best of runs. He is arguably better over a mile and should be ready to strike with this run under his belt.
**Young Mr Grace(IRE)** is better handicapped now than he was last year and ran a solid race in defeat.
**Atlantic Quest(USA)**, who did all his winning last year in some form of headgear or other, would have been happier over another furlong on faster ground. He ran well in the circumstances.
**Go Tech** suffered last year as a result of a successful juvenile campaign, but he looks better handicapped now and is beginning to show some form as a result.
**Cardinal Venture(IRE)** did too much too soon in front and only set it up for those finishing from off the pace.
**King Harson** shot his bolt in front.

## 1773 HYGICARE THIRSK HUNT CUP (H'CAP) — 1m
**4:25** (4:26) (C ) (0-95,90) 3-Y-0+ **£12,818** (£3,944; £1,972; £986) **Stalls** Low

Form RPR

04-0 **1** **Blue Spinnaker (IRE)**[35] 1125 5-9-5 90 .......... PMulrennan(5) 18 106
(MWEasterby) *hld up: gd hdwy 3f out: drvn to ld over 1 out: styd on wl* **11/1**

020- **2** *2 ½* **Vicious Warrior**[166] 6013 5-9-3 83 .......... DeanMcKeown 5 93
(RMWhitaker) *chsd ldrs: led 2f out: sn hdd: styd on: no imp on wnr fnl f* **20/1**

00-0 **3** *2* **Cat's Whiskers**[21] 1321 5-9-1 81 .......... DaleGibson 6 86
(MWEasterby) *trckd ldrs: chal 2f out: sn rdn: no ex fnl f* **5/1**[1]

04-0 **4** *1 ½* **Cherished Number**[25] 1284 5-8-13 79 .......... IMongan 1 81
(ISemple) *midfield: hdwy 3f out: ch and rdn over 1 out: no ex ins last* **14/1**

0052 **5** *½* **Chappel Cresent (IRE)**[18] 1385 4-9-7 87 .......... ANicholls 10 88
(DNicholls) *led tl hdd 2f out: no ex* **9/1**[3]

330- **6** *1* **Cripsey Brook**[204] 5468 6-9-6 86 .......... KimTinkler 16 85
(DonEnricoIncisa) *bhd: hdwy over 1f out: styd on wl ins last: nvr nr to chal* **20/1**

0-10 **7** *hd* **Uhoomagoo**[14] 1456 6-9-2 82 .......... (b) PFessey 7 80
(KARyan) *s.i.s: towards rr: hdwy 3f out: chsng ldrs and rdn over 1 out: no further prog* **10/1**

5-05 **8** *4* **Sea Storm (IRE)**[20] 1345 6-8-12 81 .......... (p) TPQueally(3) 12 70
(DRMacleod) *cl up: rdn 3f out: fdd fnl 2f* **33/1**

200- **9** *1 ¼* **Mister Arjay (USA)**[14] 6098 4-8-7 78 .......... TEaves(5) 17 64
(BEllison) *midfield: rdn and outpcd over 3f out: n.d* **25/1**

2404 **10** *¾* **Queens Rhapsody**[19] 1367 4-9-2 85 .......... NMackay(3) 8 69
(ABailey) *midfield: drvn along 3f out: no hdwy* **10/1**

05-0 **11** *nk* **Atlantic Ace**[36] 1114 7-9-0 80 .......... FLynch 11 64
(BSmart) *s.s: bhd: hdwy u.p into midfield 2f out: no further prog* **16/1**

04-0 **12** *hd* **Tedstale (USA)**[18] 1385 6-9-4 84 .......... JQuinn 2 67
(TDEasterby) *in tch: rdn 3f out: fdd fnl 2f* **10/1**

-000 **13** *1 ¾* **Mystic Man (FR)**[14] 1456 6-9-5 85 .......... NCallan 3 64
(KARyan) *midfield whn nt clr run 1/2-way: rdn 3f out: sn btn* **9/1**[3]

33-0 **14** *hd* **Penny Cross**[35] 1132 4-9-8 88 .......... MFenton 13 67
(JGGiven) *chsd ldrs tl wknd 2f out* **20/1**

65-0 **15** *1 ¾* **Takes Tutu (USA)**[19] 1367 5-9-0 80 .......... (v) DarrenWilliams 4 55
(KRBurke) *towards rr: rdn 3f out: sn btn* **11/1**

-000 **16** *hd* **Tough Love**[18] 1385 5-9-5 88 .......... DAllan(3) 15 62
(TDEasterby) *towards rr most of way* **8/1**[2]

640- **17** *3* **Gem Bien (USA)**[161] 6050 6-9-2 82 .......... PHanagan 9 49
(AndrewTurnell) *midfield tl wknd 2f out* **50/1**

1m 42.27s (2.57) **Going Correction** +0.525s/f (Yiel) **17** Ran SP% **127.3**
Speed ratings: **108,105,103,102,101 100,100,96,95,94 94,93,92,91,90 89,86**CSF £227.71 CT £1299.24 TOTE £17.40: £5.20, £7.80, £1.60, £4.20; EX 1801.10.
**Owner** G Sparkes G Hart S Curtis & T Dewhirst **Bred** M3 Elevage And Haras D'Etreham **Trained** Sheriff Hutton, N Yorks

**FOCUS**
Another soundly-run, competitive handicap. The pace was decent and the form looks strong.

**NOTEBOOK**
**Blue Spinnaker(IRE)** had looked high enough in the handicap beforehand, but on the back of a promising run in the Lincoln he won this in decisive style, defying top weight and the worst draw in the process. His connections now have a handicap at the York Dante meeting in mind for him.
**Vicious Warrior** has done his winning over ten furlongs but he is perfectly proficient over this shorter trip. He finished nicely clear of the favourite in third and can hopefully build on this.
**Cat's Whiskers**, racing off a mark just 1lb higher than when last successful, over this course and distance in fact, appreciated the drop back in trip and ran a solid race. He should continue to run well off this sort of rating.
**Cherished Number**, who was well drawn, ran his best race for a while. He could be just hitting form.
**Chappel Cresent(IRE)** continues to run to a consistent level but is struggling to get his head in front where it matters.
**Cripsey Brook**, a six-times winner over ten furlongs last season, ideally wants better ground than this. Over a trip too short and from a poor draw, he ran a very promising race.
**Uhoomagoo** takes a while to get into top gear and this sharp track is probably not ideal for him.
**Atlantic Ace** *Official explanation: jockey said gelding lost its action*

## 1774 DOUG MOSCROP RACING JOURNALIST OF THE YEAR H'CAP — 5f
**5:00** (5:01) (D ) (0-85,85) 3-Y-0+ **£5,707** (£1,756; £878; £439) **Stalls** High

Form RPR

0500 **1** **Chico Guapo (IRE)**[10] 1537 4-9-3 73 .......... IMongan 10 85
(JAGlover) *racd centre: mde virtually all: hld on wl fnl f* **33/1**

0-00 **2** *½* **Artie**[19] 1361 5-9-3 73 .......... DaleGibson 18 83
(TDEasterby) *prom stands side: rdn to ld gp 1f out: r.o: no ex clsng stages* **7/1**[2]

-332 **3** *½* **Highland Warrior**[11] 1525 5-8-6 65 .......... NMackay(3) 11 73
(JSGoldie) *in tch stands side: hdwy over 1f out: r.o u.p fnl f* **8/1**

0511 **4** *nk* **Raymond's Pride**[5] 1665 4-9-7 82 6ex .......... (b) TEaves(5) 14 89
(KARyan) *s.i.s: rr stands side: effrt whn nt clr run ent fnl f: r.o wl ins last: nvr nrr* **15/2**[3]

000- **5** *hd* **Palanzo (IRE)**[224] 5063 6-8-12 68 .......... PMQuinn 4 74
(DNicholls) *towards rr far side: hdwy 2f out: led gp ins fnl f: r.o* **50/1**

000- **6** *¾* **Brigadore**[213] 5301 5-8-9 68 .......... THamilton(3) 8 72
(JRWeymes) *racd centre: a.p: kpt on fnl f* **50/1**

62-5 **7** *¾* **Chairman Bobby**[20] 1343 6-8-11 70 .......... DAllan(3) 3 71
(DWBarker) *mde most far side gp tl hdd ins fnl f: no ex* **10/1**

0-66 **8** *nk* **Pax**[15] 1454 7-9-3 80 .......... LTreadwell(7) 7 80
(DNicholls) *chsd ldrs far side: drvn along 1/2-way: kpt on fnl f* **11/1**

2021 **9** *shd* **Mynd**[16] 1421 4-8-11 67 .......... DeanMcKeown 1 66
(RMWhitaker) *racd far side: dwlt: sn prom: fdd fnl f* **5/1**[1]

4-03 **10** *½* **Sierra Vista**[20] 1343 4-9-8 78 .......... (p) PHanagan 16 76
(DWBarker) *led stands side gp tl hdd ent fnl f: fdd* **8/1**

-250 **11** *hd* **Seven No Trumps**[12] 1504 7-9-10 80 .......... SCarson 12 77
(JMBradley) *chsd ldrs stands side: rdn over 1f out: no hdwy* **25/1**

00-0 **12** *nk* **Beyond The Clouds (IRE)**$^{20}$ [1343] 8-9-9 **79**.................. DRMcCabe 13 75
(JSWainwright) *racd stands side: hld up: keen early: nvr nr to chal* **33/1**

200- **13** *nk* **Zuhair**$^{252}$ [4367] 11-9-5 **75**.................................. AlexGreaves 5 70
(DNicholls) *sn towards rr far side: n.d* **40/1**

022- **14** *nk* **Dispol Katie**$^{190}$ [5725] 3-9-6 **85**........................................ NCallan 15 79
(TDBarron) *chsd stands side ldrs tl rdn and wknd appr fnl f* **10/1**

2-6 **15** *½* **Quantica (IRE)**$^{19}$ [1361] 5-8-10 **66**................................ KimTinkler 19 58
(NTinkler) *racd stands side: dwlt: a towards rr* **10/1**

00-0 **16** *nk* **John O'Groats (IRE)**$^{15}$ [1454] 6-9-6 **76**........................ FLynch 6 67
(MDods) *sn towards rr far side: n.d* **50/1**

00-0 **17** *nk* **Whistler**$^{35}$ [1131] 7-9-8 **78**........................................(p) MFenton 9 68
(JMBradley) *prom far side tl wknd over 1f out* **33/1**

000- **18** *nk* **Beyond Calculation (USA)**$^{201}$ [5553] 10-8-11 **67**................ JQuinn 20 56
(JMBradley) *rr stands side: nt clr run ent fnl f and ins last: n.d* **20/1**

15-0 **19** *2* **Izmail (IRE)**$^{10}$ [1537] 5-9-2 **72**........................................ ANicholls 17 53
(DNicholls) *prom stands side tl wknd appr fnl f* **25/1**

30-0 **20** *nk* **Tommy Smith**$^{15}$ [1454] 6-9-5 **75**........................................(b) GParkin 2 55
(JSWainwright) *prom far side tl wknd appr fnl f* **40/1**

61.75 secs (1.85) **Going Correction** +0.525s/f (Yiel)
**WFA** 3 from 4yo+ 9lb **20** Ran SP% **130.8**
Speed ratings: **106,105,104,103,103 102,101,100,100,99 99,98,98,98,97 96,96,95,92,92**CSF £242.22 CT £2115.87 TOTE £35.20: £5.30, £2.80, £1.90, £2.50; EX 427.50.

**Owner** 2nd Carlton Partnership **Bred** Hardys Of Kilkeel Ltd **Trained** Carburton, Notts

■ Stewards Enquiry : D R McCabeM 20-day ban: failed to take all reasonable and permissible measures to obtain best possible placing (May 12-31)

**FOCUS**
They split into three groups here and there appeared little bias. A decent handicap run at a good pace and the form looks solid.

**NOTEBOOK**
**Chico Guapo(IRE)**, whose last win came over this course and distance off a 5lb lower mark, made almost all the running down the centre of the track. He was without the usual cheekpieces on this occasion, but he has speed to burn and a sharp track suits him really well.

**Artie**, another 3lb lower, is really well handicapped at present and he will surely not be long in going one better. He came out on top of the stands'-side group on this occasion.

**Highland Warrior**, a versatile type who is effective at distances ranging from five to seven furlongs these days, but who has a victory over nine furlongs to his name in the dim and distant past, ran another sound race. He really is a most consistent animal.

**Raymond's Pride**, who could have done with the ground softer than this, was chasing the hat-trick off a 7lb higher mark. He ran well, especially as he did not get the best of runs, but things are not going to get any easier from now on, with the ground likely to get generally quicker soon.

**Palanzo(IRE)** ◆, who at his peak was racing off a mark of 108, is essentially an underachiever. He is currently racing off a mark a full 40lb lower though, and this performance, in which he came out on top of the far-side group. This gives plenty of hope that his trainer, an expert with sprint handicappers, has an animal to go to war with this season.

**Brigadore**, who kept the winner company up the centre of the track, looks fairly handicapped at present as he is 3lb lower than his last winning mark.

**Beyond The Clouds(IRE)** was not put into the race and the Stewards took a dim view. For breaking the non-triers rule, the trainer was fined £2,900, the jockey suspended for 20 days and the horse banned from running for 40 days. *Official explanation: 40-day ban (May 5-Jun 15)*

## 1775 LEVY BOARD CLASSIFIED STKS 6f
**5:35** (5:35) (E) 3-Y-O **£3,604** (£1,109; £554; £277) **Stalls** High

Form RPR

-221 **1** **Mr Wolf**$^{5}$ [1664] 3-9-4 70........................................ TEaves$^{(5)}$ 6 82
(DWBarker) *led tl hdd wl over 1f out: remained cl up: r.o wl u.p to regain ld clsng stages* **9/2**$^{2}$

501- **2** *1* **Mis Chicaf (IRE)**$^{227}$ [4985] 3-8-12 71.............................. DAllan$^{(3)}$ 4 71
(JSWainwright) *cl up: led wl over 1f out: sn hrd pressed and rdn: hdd clsng stages: no ex* **16/1**

1-5 **3** *hd* **Treasure Cay**$^{38}$ [1099] 3-9-8 75.................................. PaulEddery 2 77
(PWD'Arcy) *hld up: hdwy over 2f out: rdn to chal over 1 out: ev ch ins fnl f: no ex clsng stages* **9/2**$^{2}$

2-21 **4** *shd* **Shrink**$^{29}$ [1228] 3-9-0 70........................................ IMongan 1 69
(MLWBell) *trckd ldrs: chal over 1f out: ev ch and rdn ins fnl f: no ex clsng stages* **6/1**$^{3}$

040- **5** *¾* **Neon Blue**$^{186}$ [5824] 3-8-10 68.................................. DTudhope$^{(7)}$ 3 70
(RMWhitaker) *dwlt: hld up: hdwy over 2f out: chal over 1 out: ch ins fnl f: no ex clsng stages* **12/1**

0-1 **6** *1* **Tizzy's Law**$^{14}$ [1472] 3-9-0 70.................................. JBramhill 5 64
(MABuckley) *trckd ldrs: effrt 2f out: ch and rdn over 1 out: fdd fnl f* **13/2**

10-0 **7** *5* **Alice Blackthorn**$^{14}$ [1464] 3-9-0 67.............................. FLynch 8 49
(BSmart) *s.i.s: rr: effrt over 2f out: rdn over 1 out: sn btn* **16/1**

004- **8** *1 ¾* **Commander Bond**$^{213}$ [5294] 3-9-7 74.............................. DMcGaffin 7 51
(BSmart) *dwlt: rr: effrt over 2f out: no hdwy* **20/1**

4212 **9** *24* **Monte Major (IRE)**$^{26}$ [1266] 3-9-5 72.............................. NCallan 9 —
(MAJarvis) *prom: drvn along over 2f out: sn wknd: virtually p.u ins fnl f* **5/2**$^{1}$

1m 16.19s (3.69) **Going Correction** +0.525s/f (Yiel) **9** Ran SP% **116.8**
Speed ratings: **96,94,94,94,93 91,85,82,50**CSF £73.37 TOTE £6.80: £2.10, £4.90, £1.50; EX 68.00 Place 6 £198.10, Place 5 £125.13.

**Owner** P Asquith **Bred** P Asquith **Trained** Scorton, N Yorks

**FOCUS**
A competitive classified race and an improved effort from the winner.

**NOTEBOOK**
**Mr Wolf** followed up his recent win over a furlong shorter in battling style. He looks to be improving as he was worst in at the weights here.

**Mis Chicaf(IRE)**, who was joint best in at the weights, ran well on her reappearance and a drop back to five is likely to suit.

**Treasure Cay**, stepping up in trip on his turf debut, ran a fair race but, with handicaps in mind, may need to drop a few pounds before he is winning again.

**Shrink**, a winner over five on Polytrack last time, is another who may have found the combination of the step up to six furlongs and easier ground counting against her.

**Neon Blue**, who ran a number of respectable races last season, is still chasing that elusive first victory.

**Monte Major(IRE)** *Official explanation: jockey said gelding was unsuited by the track*

T/Plt: £437.20 to a £1 stake. Pool: £29,437.25. 49.15 winning tickets. T/Qpdt: £165.70 to a £1 stake. Pool: £1,970.90. 8.80 winning tickets. JF

# CAPANNELLE (R-H)
Saturday, May 1

**OFFICIAL GOING: Heavy**

## 1776a PREMIO CARLO CHIESA (GROUP 3) (F&M) 1m
**2:05** (2:07) 4-Y-O+ **£32,989** (£14,918; £8,255; £4,128)

RPR

**1** **Miss Nashwan (IRE)**$^{41}$ 4-8-11 .................................. MBelli 4 104
(MGrassi, Italy) *tracked leaders, 4th straight, headway on outside to lead 2f out, driven out*

**2** *1* **Sayuri (IRE)**$^{370}$ [1253] 4-8-11 .................................. MPasquale 5 103
(LBrogi, Italy) *held up in last, headway on outside 2f out, went 2nd over 1f out, stayed on* **2**

**3** *1* **Arlecchina (GER)**$^{27}$ 4-8-11 .................................. FMBerry 2 101
(UStoltefuss, Germany) *raced in 4th, every chance on inside 2f out, one pace* **3**

**4** *¾* **Marbye (IRE)**$^{41}$ 4-8-11 .................................. SMulas 7 100
(BGrizzetti, Italy) *raced in 6th, effort in centre 2f out, soon ridden & unable to quicken* **1**

**5** *½* **Sa Erola (ITY)**$^{349}$ [1705] 4-8-11 ..................................(b) PBorrelli 1 99
(GLigas, Italy) *led for 2 1/2f, 2nd straight, every chance 2f out, one pace*

**6** *3 ½* **She Breeze**$^{527}$ [5770] 4-8-11 .................................. MEsposito 6 94
(VCaruso, Italy) *led after 2 1/2f, headed 2f out & weakened*

**7** *9* **Ianina (IRE)**$^{27}$ 4-8-11 .................................. IRossi 3 80
(RRohne, Germany) *raced in 5th, never a factor*

1m 41.8s **7** Ran SP% **130.2**
Speed ratings: .
**Owner** Camma Di Schiavi Carlo Maria&c **Bred** Camma S A S Di Schiavi **Trained** Italy

## 1777a PREMIO PARIOLI ABN AMRO (GROUP 2) (COLTS) 1m
**3:05** (3:24) 3-Y-O **£112,113** (£56,796; £33,169; £16,585)

RPR

**1** **Spirit Of Desert (IRE)**$^{195}$ [5665] 3-9-2 .................................. MPasquale 3 110
(LBrogi, Italy) *always prominent, 4th straight, smooth headway to lead 2f out, soon 2l clear, ridden out, fin lame* **1**

**2** *2* **Bravo Tazio (IRE)**$^{139}$ [6189] 3-9-2 .................................. EBotti 10 106
(ABotti, Italy) *held up towards rear, 8th straight, headway down centre from over 2f out, stayed on well final f to take 2nd last 50yds* **2**

**3** *1* **Ceprin (IRE)** 3-9-2 .................................. IRossi 6 104
(SDioscuri, Italy) *led 2f, 2nd straight, led 3f out, headed & looked beaten 2f out, rallied inside final f to regain 3rd final strides*

**4** *½* **Pippo Di Lucilla (IRE)** 3-9-2 .................................. CFiocchi 8 103
(MariaRitaSalvioni, Italy) *always close up, 3rd straight, went 2nd just under 2f out, no extra & lost 2nd closing stages*

**5** *6* **Obed (IRE)**$^{217}$ [5244] 3-9-2 .................................. GBietolini 7 91
(BGrizzetti, Italy) *got loose before start, dwelt, in rear & came very wide entering straight, kept on at one pace from over 2f out but never n* **3**

**6** *½* **Whilly (IRE)**$^{195}$ [5665] 3-9-2 .................................. SMulas 5 90
(BGrizzetti, Italy) *held up in rear, headway over 2f out, soon one pace*

**7** *2 ½* **Kill Cat (IRE)**$^{209}$ [5398] 3-9-2 .................................. MEsposito 1 85
(APeraino, Italy) *close up, 5th 2f out, not pushed when beaten 1 1/2f out*

**8** *nse* **Golden Pivotal**$^{167}$ [6009] 3-9-2 .................................. DVargiu 11 85
(GFratini, Italy) *mid-division, 5th & came very wide entering straight, weakened over 2f out*

**9** *2* **Strezkov** 3-9-2 .................................. MMonteriso 2 81
(VValiani, Italy) *held up towards rear, effort 3f out, never a threat*

**10** *8* **Living Symbol (USA)** 3-9-2 .................................. PShanahan 4 65
(ARenzoni, Italy) *never a factor*

**11** *4* **Melon Rouge (IRE)**$^{139}$ [6189] 3-9-2 .................................. KDarley 9 57
(BGrizzetti, Italy) *led after 2f til headed 3f out, weakened quickly*

1m 41.2s **11** Ran SP% **147.1**
Speed ratings: .
**Owner** Allevamento La Nuova Sbarra **Bred** Scuderia Ascagnano Spa **Trained** Italy

## 1778a PREMIO REGINA ELENA (GROUP 2) (FILLIES) 1m
**4:05** (4:28) 3-Y-O **£116,901** (£60,387; £35,563; £17,782)

RPR

**1** **Rumba Loca (IRE)**$^{258}$ [4235] 3-8-11 .................................. DVargiu 19 103
(BGrizzetti, Italy) *dropped in from outside draw, midfield on inside, steady headway from over 3f out to lead approaching final f, quickened cl*

**2** *4 ½* **Super Bobbina (IRE)** 3-8-11 .................................. ACorniani 18 95
(IBugattella, Italy) *held up in rear, effort & not clear run 2f out, finished strongly to take 2nd 60y out*

**3** *1* **Dorr (ITY)** 3-8-11 .................................. ADiNapoli 1 94
(CMarinelli, Italy) *always close up, stayed on gamely under pressure final 3f*

**4** *1 ½* **Shoko**$^{202}$ [5531] 3-8-11 .................................. GBietolini 2 91
(BGrizzetti, Italy) *prominent, 2nd straight, one pace final 1 1/2f*

**5** *½* **Bond Deal (IRE)**$^{179}$ [5922] 3-8-11 .................................. PAragoni 6 90
(LRiccardi, Italy) *set strong pace, headed approaching final f, soon weakened*

**6** *1 ¼* **Rekindled Applause**$^{188}$ 3-8-11 .................................. J-LMartinez 17 88
(MGuarnieri, Italy) *covered up in rear, stayed on final 3f, never nearer*

**7** *1* **Kalifornia Blue (GER)**$^{202}$ [5529] 3-8-11 .................................. DPorcu 16 86
(PVovcenko, Germany) *midfield, wandered under pressure 3f out, kept on same pace*

**8** *3* **Looking Back (IRE)**$^{300}$ [3044] 3-8-11 .................................. GTemperini 10 81
(RBrogi, Italy) *midfield on inside, ridden & one pace from over 2f out*

**9** *hd* **Zona (ITY)** 3-8-11 .................................. MEsposito 4 81
(VCaruso, Italy) *close up, ridden over 2f out, soon weakened* **1**

**10** *1* **Roseanna (FR)**$^{17}$ [1398] 3-8-11 .................................. KDarley 14 79
(MmeCHead-Maarek, France) *held up, effort 3f out, unable to quicken* **2**

**11** *½* **Etroubles (FR)**$^{188}$ 3-8-11 .................................. MMonteriso 5 78
(MMonteriso, U.S.A) *mid-division, ridden & beaten over 2f out*

**12** *hd* **Stai Su**$^{300}$ [3044] 3-8-11 .................................. MPasquale 3 78
(LBrogi, Italy) *held up, ridden & beaten over 2f out*

**13** *6* **Jalys (ITY)**$^{217}$ [5242] 3-8-11 .................................. EBotti 8 67
(ABotti, Italy) *prominent, 5th straight, weakened over 2f out* **3**

**14** *2* **Vettori Loose (IRE)** 3-8-11 .................................. SMulas 13 64
(BGrizzetti, Italy) *close up in 2nd til weakened over 2f out*

15 4 **Halesia Carolina (USA)** 3-8-11 ........................................ FJovine 15 57
(GBietolini, Italy) *never a factor*
16 3 **Alopecurus (IRE)**[202] 5531 3-8-11 ........................................ AMonteriso 12 51
(APeraino, Italy) *never a factor*
17 5 **Enrika's Gift (IRE)** 3-8-11 ........................................ MBelli 11 43
(ARenzoni, Italy) *4th straight, weakened 3f out*
18 2 1/2 **Basic Woman** 3-8-11 ........................................ SDiana 7 38
(LCamici, Italy) *always in rear*
1m 42.6s **18** Ran SP% **145.2**
Speed ratings: .
**Owner** Scuderia Mack Ferrer **Bred** M Parola **Trained** Italy

# MULHEIM (R-H)
Saturday, May 1
**OFFICIAL GOING: Soft**

## 1779a MULHEIM STEHERCUP (LISTED) 1m 6f 165y
**4:25** (4:44) 4-Y-0+ **£8,451** (£3,099; £1,690; £845)

RPR
1 **Liquido (GER)**[27] 1259 5-9-4 ........................................ PHeugl 6 107
(HSteinmetz, Germany) 2
2 2 1/2 **Quebo (GER)**[216] 2882 6-8-11 ........................................ ADeVries 5 97
(UStoltefuss, Germany)
3 1/2 **Bailamos (GER)**[33] 1182 4-9-2 ........................................ FilipMinarik 3 103
(PSchiergen, Germany) 1
4 1 **Orfisio**[27] 1259 5-8-7 ........................................ PVanDeKeere 4 91
(AndreasLowe, Germany)
5 5 **Western Devil (IRE)**[209] 5400 4-9-0 ........................................ THellier 1 94
(ASchutz, Germany)
6 7 **Teresa**[21] 1329 4-8-9 ........................................ IFerguson 2 80
(JLDunlop) *led to over 2f out, weakened approaching final f* 3
3m 20.77s
**WFA** 4 from 5yo+ 2lb **6** Ran SP% **133.9**
Speed ratings: .
**Owner** G Engel **Bred** Gestut Evershorst **Trained** Germany

**NOTEBOOK**
**Teresa**, who gave an improved effort when running gallantly at Kempton most recently, was stepping up in grade but, on ground that should have suited, was disappointing. She is capable of better than this.

# [1716]SAINT-CLOUD (L-H)
Saturday, May 1
**OFFICIAL GOING: Very soft**

## 1780a PRIX DU MUGUET (GROUP 2) 1m
**3:10** (3:14) 4-Y-0+ **£42,148** (£16,268; £7,764; £5,176)

RPR
1 **Martillo (GER)**[35] 1146 4-9-1 ........................................ WMongil 2 118
(RSuerland, Germany) *pushed up on inside to go 3rd after 3f, close 5th straight, switched out well over 1f out, led 130 yards out, driven out* 2
2 hd **Sarre (FR)**[34] 1163 4-8-8 ........................................ IMendizabal 1 111
(PCostes, France) *held up, headway and 7th straight, not clear run over 2f out, ran on from over 1f out, finished well*
3 1 1/2 **Maxwell (FR)**[34] 1163 4-8-12 ........................................ C-PLemaire 8 112
(MmeCHead-Maarek, France) *led to over 2f out, led again 1f out to 130 yards out, ran on* 3
4 1/2 **Krataios (FR)**[30] 4-8-12 ........................................ OPeslier 3 111
(CLaffon-Parias, France) *always close up, 3rd straight, disputing 3rd when carried right and slightly impeded by winner 1 1/2f out, kept on same pac* 1
5 hd **My Risk (FR)**[34] 1163 5-8-12 ........................................ TJarnet 11 110
(J-MBeguigne, France) *8th straight, ridden and headway on outside from 2f out, no extra last 100 yards*
6 nse **Almond Mousse (FR)**[34] 1163 5-8-8 ........................................ SMaillot 10 106
(RobertCollet, France) *held up, 10th straight, kept on under strong pressure from distance, nearest at finish*
7 shd **King's Drama (IRE)**[34] 1163 4-8-12 ........................................ DBonilla 6 110
(RobertCollet, France) *disputed lead, 2nd straight, led over 2f out to 1f out, weakened and lost 4th close home*
8 3 **Marshall (FR)**[34] 1163 4-8-12 ........................................ MBlancpain 7 104
(CLaffon-Parias, France) *close up, 6th straight, one pace from well over 1f out* 3
9 1/2 **Mystic Melody (USA)**[214] 5292 4-8-8 ........................................ ACarre 14 99
(AFabre, France) *held up, last straight, never a factor*
10 2 1/2 **Special Kaldoun (IRE)**[34] 1163 5-9-1 ........................................ TThulliez 12 101
(DSmaga, France) *close up on outside, 4th straight, weakened well over 1f out*
11 **Saratan (IRE)**[182] 5884 7-8-12 ........................................ ELegrix 13 98
(MDelzangles, France) *prominent on outside to half-way, 8th straight, well behind final furlong*
1m 36.4s **Going Correction** -1.125s/f (Hard) **11** Ran SP% **111.4**
Speed ratings: **118,117,116,115,115 115,115,112,111,109 109**.
**Owner** Gestut Hony-Hof **Bred** Gestut Katharinenhof **Trained** Germany

**NOTEBOOK**
**Martillo(GER)** forced his way a little when extracted to challenge just over a furlong out. The colt then strode out and held off the late challenge of the runner-up. There was a long Stewards' enquiry but the result was left unchanged and he now heads to Royal Ascot for the Queen Anne Stakes.
**Sarre(FR)** found the gap at the furlong marker and finished like the proverbial train. She was cutting down the winner as the race came to an end and could have been first past the post with a better run.
**Maxwell(FR)** had the lead at the furlong marker and then stayed on gamely to the line.
**Krataios(FR)** looked exceptionally well in the paddock. He was towards the tail of the field early on and began to make progress rounding the final turn. He was slightly hampered when making his challenge at the furlong marker which could have cost him a place.

# CHURCHILL DOWNS (L-H)
Saturday, May 1
**OFFICIAL GOING: Dirt course - fast (8.57) changing to sloppy (11.04); turf course - yielding**

## 1781a KENTUCKY DERBY (GRADE 1) (DIRT) 1m 2f (D)
**11:04** (11:12) 3-Y-O **£511,061** (£94,972; £47,486; £25,140)

RPR
1 **Smarty Jones (USA)**[21] 3-9-0 ........................................ ShaneElliott 15 125
(JohnCServis, U.S.A) *Raced in 4th, went 2nd over 4f out, pressing leader over 2f out, led approaching final f out, ridden out* **41/10**[1]
2 2 3/4 **Lion Heart (USA)**[21] 3-9-0 ........................................ MESmith 3 120
(PLBiancone, U.S.A) *Set fast pace till headed approaching final f, kept on* **54/10**[2]
3 3 1/4 **Imperialism (USA)**[28] 3-9-0 ........................................(b) KDesormeaux 10 115
(KristinMulhall, U.S.A) *In rear, hampered 7f out, 13th 4f out, switched to outside over 2f out, stayed on well while drifting left final 1 1/2f* **109/10**
4 2 **Limehouse (USA)**[21] 3-9-0 ........................................ JSantos 1 111
(TPletcher, U.S.A) *Mid division, 6th 2f out, went 3rd 1 1/2f out, one pace* **42/1**
5 4 1/2 **The Cliff's Edge (USA)**[21] 3-9-0 ........................................ SSellers 11 103
(NZito, U.S.A) *In rear, 17th 2f out, late headway down outside* **82/10**
6 1 1/4 **Action This Day (USA)**[21] 3-9-0 ........................................ DFlores 4 101
(RichardEMandella, U.S.A) *Detached last to 4f out, 14th 2f out, stayed on* **44/1**
7 1 **Read The Footnotes (USA)**[49] 3-9-0 ........................................ RViolette 14 99
(RVioletteJr, U.S.A) *Raced in 5th or 6th, went 3rd over 2f out, soon outpaced* **23/1**
8 1/2 **Birdstone (USA)**[210] 5408 3-9-0 ........................................ EPrado 13 98
(NZito, U.S.A) *Midfield, 9th 2f out, soon ridden and unable to quicken* **21/1**
9 1/2 **Tapit (USA)**[21] 3-9-0 ........................................ RADominguez 18 97
(MDickinson, U.S.A) *Raced wide, in rear early, 10th straight, one pace* **64/10**[3]
10 1/2 **Borrego (USA)**[21] 3-9-0 ........................................(b) VEspinoza 12 97
(CBGreely, U.S.A) *Midfield, went 4th 2f out, soon weakened* **142/10**
11 1 1/4 **Song Of The Sword (USA)**[28] 3-9-0 ........................................(b) NArroyoJr 2 94
(JenniferLeigh-Pedersen, U.S.A) *Hampered first turn, never a factor* **56/1**
12 1 **Master David (USA)**[21] 3-9-0 ........................................ ASolis 8 93
(RJFrankel, U.S.A) *Midfield, hampered and lost place 4f out, no danger after* **106/10**
13 1 1/2 **Pro Prado (USA)**[21] 3-9-0 ........................................ JohnMcKee 19 90
(RHolthus, U.S.A) *Raced wide, headway to go 5th 2f out, soon weakened* **54/1**
14 5 1/2 **Castledale (IRE)**[28] 3-9-0 ........................................ JValdiviaJr 16 80
(JeffMullins, U.S.A) *Went right start, always towards rear* **22/1**
15 11 1/2 **Friends Lake (USA)**[49] 3-9-0 ........................................ RMigliore 6 60
(JKimmel, U.S.A) *Never a factor* **185/10**
16 1/2 **Minister Eric (USA)**[189] 5772 3-9-0 ........................................ PDay 7 59
(RichardEMandella, U.S.A) *Close up, 3rd 4f out, weakened 3f out* **23/1**
17 3 1/2 **Pollard's Vision (USA)**[28] 3-9-0 ........................................ JRVelazquez 17 53
(TPletcher, U.S.A) *Prominent early on outside, weakened 4f out* **24/1**
18 17 **Quintons Gold Rush (USA)**[28] 3-9-0 ........................................ CNakatani 20 24
(SAsmussen, U.S.A) *Prominent til hampered and weakened 4f out, eased* **51/1**
2m 4.06s **18** Ran SP% **119.6**
Speed ratings: .
**Owner** Someday Farm **Bred** Someday Farm **Trained** USA

**NOTEBOOK**
**Smarty Jones(USA)** braved the dreadful conditions and did exceptionally well from his wide draw. He was always just off the leaders and came through to challenge long-time leader Lion Heart two out. He stayed on the stronger of the pair and will presumably now head for the next leg of the Triple Crown.
**Lion Heart(USA)** led at a good clip throughout and simply could not find enough to repel Smarty Jones. He is sure to be back for another crack at the winner.
**Imperialism(USA)** did best of those who were held-up and stayed on well down the straight despite edging left.

# [1658]HAMILTON (R-H)
Sunday, May 2
**OFFICIAL GOING: Good (good to firm in places)**

## 1782 IAN STEVENSON EBF MAIDEN STKS (QUALIFIER FOR THE HAMILTON PARK 2-Y-O SERIES FINAL) 5f 4y
**1:45** (1:45) (D) 2-Y-O **£4,823** (£1,484; £742; £371) **Stalls** Low

Form RPR
0 1 **Sea Hunter**[15] 1462 2-9-0 ........................................ ACulhane 5 80
(MRChannon) *cl up: rdn to ld ins fnl f: hld on wl* **11/10**[1]
2 1/2 **Distinctly Game** 2-9-0 ........................................ GParkin 6 78
(KARyan) *sn outpcd: gd hdwy stands rail over 1f out: r.o wl: jst hld* **9/2**[3]
3 2 **Beckermet (IRE)** 2-8-9 ........................................ PBradley(5) 2 70
(RFFisher) *s.i.s: plld hrd and sn cl up: led over 1f out to ins fnl f: no ex* **33/1**
4 4 7 **Keepasharplookout (IRE)**[20] 1359 2-9-0 ........................................ PHanagan 4 42
(MrsLStubbs) *chsd ldrs to 1/2-way: sn rdn and btn* **7/1**
0 5 2 1/2 **No Commission (IRE)**[34] 1170 2-8-9 ........................................ DNolan(5) 1 32
(RFFisher) *led to over 1f out: wknd qckly* **25/1**
2 6 9 **Nee Lemon Left**[21] 1340 2-8-2 ........................................ PPMathers(7) 3 —
(ABerry) *keen: cl up to 1/2-way: sn rdn and wknd: eased whn btn fnl f* **10/3**[2]
60.78 secs (-0.48) **Going Correction** -0.125s/f (Firm) **6** Ran SP% **108.2**
Speed ratings: **98,97,94,82,78** **64**CSF £5.86 TOTE £1.90: £1.20, £2.40; EX 6.00.
**Owner** Sheikh Mohammed **Bred** Bearstone Stud **Trained** West Ilsley, Berks

**FOCUS**
An ordinary bunch on both looks and on the limited form available but the performance of the runner-up caught the eye. The gallop was sound and the whole field raced stands side.

**NOTEBOOK**
**Sea Hunter** is not very big but showed the right attitude and showed improved form to win an ordinary event. He is likely to prove effective over six furlongs but may look vulnerable in anything but modest company under a penalty.
**Distinctly Game** the first foal of a dam who won twice over five furlongs at three years, has physical scope and showed more than enough, despite his apparent greenness, to suggest he can win a similar race with this experience behind him.
**Beckermet(IRE)**, out of a seven furlong winner and a half-brother to a winner abroad, belied his starting price to run a fair race on this debut and pulled well clear of the remainder. He may do better over further when learning to settle.
**Keepasharplookout(IRE)** failed to confirm the bit of debut promise he showed under conditions that placed much more of an emphasis on speed. Given he is stoutly bred, he may do better over further in due course.
**No Commission(IRE)** fared a bit better than on his debut on this first start on a sound surface but it will be a poor race he wins in this grade.
**Nee Lemon Left**, an unfurnished type, failed by a long chalk to confirm the bit of debut promise shown at Musselburgh and, although she may do better on a more galloping track, she is likely to continue to look vulnerable in this grade.

## 1783 THE SUNDAY MAIL ANNUAL JUMP JOCKEYS H'CAP (TO BE RIDDEN BY NH JOCKEYS) (SERIES QUALIFIER) 1m 65y

**2:15** (2:17) (E) (0-70,63) 4-Y-0+ **£4,420** (£1,360; £680; £340) **Stalls** High

| Form | | | | | SP | RPR |
|---|---|---|---|---|---|---|
| 3142 | **1** | | **Double Ransom**[12] [1527] 5-11-3 **56** (MrsLStubbs) *hld up: hdwy over 2f out: led ent fnl f: r.o wl* | (b) GDuffield 7 | **4/1**[1] | 68 |
| 25-0 | **2** | *1* | **Anthemion (IRE)**[21] [1345] 7-11-4 **60** (MrsJCMcgregor) *midfield: effrt over 3f out: kpt on fnl f: nt rch wnr* | WDowling(3) 13 | **16/1** | 70 |
| 2103 | **3** | *shd* | **Spindor (USA)**[9] [1595] 5-11-8 **61** (JAOsborne) *hld up: rdn and swtchd 2f out: r.o fnl f: nrst fin* | (b) VSlattery 16 | **8/1**[3] | 70 |
| 1111 | **4** | *½* | **Beauteous (IRE)**[10] [1573] 5-11-7 **63** (MJPolglase) *led to ent fnl f: kpt on same pce* | LVickers(3) 3 | **6/1**[2] | 71 |
| 5004 | **5** | *1 ¼* | **Yenaled**[17] [1427] 7-11-3 **56** (KARyan) *s.i.s: bhd tl hdwy over 1f out: no imp fnl f* | JCrowley 11 | **8/1**[3] | 61 |
| 60-0 | **6** | *2* | **Millennium Hall**[6] [1660] 5-11-4 **57** (PMonteith) *bhd tl styd on fnl 2f: nvr rchd ldrs* | KRenwick 15 | **9/1** | 58 |
| 000- | **7** | *1 ¼* | **Francis Flute**[190] [5749] 6-10-11 **50** (BMactaggart) *cl up tl rdn and wknd over 1f out* | ADempsey 9 | **33/1** | 48 |
| -050 | **8** | *6* | **Lucky Largo (IRE)**[6] [1660] 4-11-2 **58** (MissLAPerratt) *trckd ldrs tl wknd fr over 2f out* | (b) BGibson(3) 6 | **25/1** | 42 |
| 0-00 | **9** | *3 ½* | **One Last Time**[8] [1620] 4-11-7 **63** (RBastiman) *s.i.s: struggling 1/2-way: nvr on terms* | HBastiman(3) 14 | **18/1** | 39 |
| 000- | **10** | *1 ½* | **Mehmaas**[155] [6099] 8-11-2 **55** (REBarr) *trckd ldrs: rdn 1/2-way: outpcd over 3f out: n.d after* | LEnstone 12 | **14/1** | 28 |
| 000- | **11** | *2 ½* | **Skiddaw Jones**[202] [5537] 4-10-12 **54** (MissLAPerratt) *chsd ldrs tl wknd over 2f out* | LMcGrath(3) 5 | **16/1** | 21 |
| -000 | **12** | *nk* | **Lunar Leader (IRE)**[11] [1539] 4-11-7 **60** (MJGingell) *towards rr: rdn 1/2-way: n.d* | (tp) ARoss 10 | **25/1** | 26 |
| 6-05 | **13** | *nk* | **Hula Ballew**[8] [1620] 4-11-5 **58** (MDods) *chsd ldrs tl rdn and wknd over 2f out* | RGarritty 1 | **12/1** | 24 |
| 0030 | **14** | *1 ½* | **Speedfit Free (IRE)**[3] [1738] 7-10-6 **52** (MissAStokell) *in tch tl wknd over 3f out* | AnnStokell(7) 8 | **14/1** | 14 |

1m 49.65s (0.35) **Going Correction** -0.025s/f (Good) **14** Ran SP% **115.2**
Speed ratings: **97,96,95,95,94 92,90,84,81,79 77,77,76,75**CSF £65.58 TOTE £3.70: £1.60, £5.90, £2.90; EX 153.90.
**Owner** Tyme Partnership **Bred** Limestone Stud **Trained** Malton, N. Yorks
■ Stewards Enquiry : Ann Stokell three-day ban: careless riding (May 13-15)
L Vickers two-day ban: used whip with excessive force (May 13,14)

**FOCUS**
A run of the mill handicap featuring mainly exposed types and one in which the pace was soon sound. The whole field raced centre to far side in the straight.

**NOTEBOOK**
**Double Ransom**, a consistent sort, did not have to improve on his recent form to win back over this shorter trip. He seems best with strong handling and should continue to give a good account in this company at up to a mile and a quarter.
**Anthemion(IRE)** is not the most consistent but put a poor reappearance run behind him over this longer trip. However he has not won for nearly four years, is vulnerable from his current mark and would be no certainty to put it all in next time.
**Spindor(USA)**, returned to turf, does not look the easiest of rides but turned in a creditable effort and proved his effectiveness over this trip. He looks the type that needs things to fall just right.
**Beauteous(IRE)**, in such good form in low-grade All-Weather races of late, had the run of the race and ran creditably from his low draw. He is capable of winning up to this trip on turf and seems best when allowed to dominate.
**Yenaled** is not a reliable betting proposition given his record and his style of running but confirms he retains ability back on turf. Strongly run races suit him ideally but he is not one to place too much faith in these days.
**Millennium Hall**, who has slipped back to a favourable mark, showed much more than on his reappearance and, although he is not the most consistent, is capable of winning a modest race this term.

## 1784 52ND LOWLAND REGIMENT CLAIMING STKS 1m 1f 36y

**2:50** (2:50) (E) 3-Y-0 **£3,737** (£1,150; £575; £287) **Stalls** High

| Form | | | | | SP | RPR |
|---|---|---|---|---|---|---|
| 5210 | **1** | | **Hawkit (USA)**[37] [1120] 3-9-3 74 (JAOsborne) *cl up: led on bit over 2f out: pushed out fnl f* | SWKelly 7 | **1/1**[1] | 64 |
| 03-0 | **2** | *1 ¾* | **Bargain Hunt (IRE)**[20] [1360] 3-8-3 50 (WStorey) *cl up: rdn over 2f out: chsd wnr over 1f out: r.o* | JBramhill 5 | **12/1** | 46 |
| 3-05 | **3** | *nk* | **Tancred Imp**[6] [1667] 3-7-12 45 (DWBarker) *in tch: effrt over 2f out: r.o fnl f: no imp* | RFfrench 8 | **7/1**[3] | 40 |
| 0-45 | **4** | *6* | **One 'N' Only (IRE)**[6] [1659] 3-8-12 55 (MissLAPerratt) *in tch: outpcd 3f out: n.d after* | PHanagan 2 | **10/1** | 42 |
| | **5** | *1 ¼* | **The Fox's Head (IRE)** 3-8-12 (BMactaggart) *in tch: drvn and outpcd over 3f out: sn btn* | JMcAuley 4 | **50/1** | 40 |
| 02-6 | **6** | *5* | **Chase The Rainbow**[8] [1627] 3-8-0 62 (ABerry) *chsd ldrs tl edgd rt and outpcd fr over 2f out* | PPMathers(7) 1 | **4/1**[2] | 25 |
| 0-4 | **7** | *1* | **Beaver Diva**[12] [1524] 3-7-5 (WMBrisbourne) *led to over 2f out: sn btn* | BSwarbrick(7) 6 | **16/1** | 14 |
| 00-0 | **8** | *14* | **Lapdancing**[24] [1318] 3-8-4 (MissLAPerratt) *hld up: rdn 1/2-way: sn btn* | PFessey 3 | **33/1** | — |

2m 0.87s (1.27) **Going Correction** -0.025s/f (Good) **8** Ran SP% **110.1**
Speed ratings: **93,91,91,85,84 80,79,66**CSF £13.48 TOTE £1.90: £1.10, £1.80, £1.80; EX 10.00.Hawkit (no.1) was claimed by P D Evans for £12,000.
**Owner** Paul J Dixon **Bred** Hargus Sexton And Sandra Sexton **Trained** Upper Lambourn, Berks

**FOCUS**
A weak race, even by claiming standards and one in which the winner did not have to improve to get off the mark on turf. It is unlikely this race will be throwing up many winners.

**NOTEBOOK**
**Hawkit(USA)** looked to have a clear-cut chance at these weights in this weak event returned to turf and he did not have to improve to win with the minimum of fuss. He will find life much tougher back in handicaps from his current mark, though.
**Bargain Hunt(IRE)** turned in a much better effort back on a sound surface but was flattered to get so close to the winner and is much better judged on his proximity to the 45-rated third. It will be a poor race he eventually wins.
**Tancred Imp**, down in grade and back on a sound surface, fared a little better but this bare form looks misleading and it will be a poor race she wins.
**One 'N' Only(IRE)**, back up in trip and down in grade, offered little encouragement and was beaten before her stamina over this trip became an issue. She will struggle to win a handicap from her 55 mark.
**The Fox's Head(IRE)**, related to some ordinary National Hunt performers, offered little immediate promise on this racecourse debut.
**Chase The Rainbow**, a seven furlong turf winner on a sound surface last year, was beaten before stamina became an issue. She did not look an easy ride and is another who may not be easy to place successfully.

## 1785 TOTEJACKPOT H'CAP 1m 5f 9y

**3:25** (3:25) (D) (0-85,84) 4-Y-0+ **£7,124** (£2,192; £1,096; £548) **Stalls** High

| Form | | | | | SP | RPR |
|---|---|---|---|---|---|---|
| 306/ | **1** | | **Colorado Falls (IRE)**[69] [4197] 6-8-13 **72** (PMonteith) *trckd ldrs: rdn 3f out: rallied to ld ins fnl f. r.o* | LEnstone(3) 11 | **12/1** | 84 |
| 2532 | **2** | *1 ½* | **Nakwa (IRE)**[22] [1326] 6-8-1 **60** (EJAlston) *led tl hung rt and hdd over 4f out: rallied and ev ch ins fnl f: r.o* | DAllan(3) 6 | **8/1** | 70 |
| 4031 | **3** | *3* | **George Stubbs (USA)**[8] [1615] 6-8-6 **65** (MJPolglase) *keen: hld up in tch: hdwy to ld over 3f out: hdd and no ex ins fnl f* | JFMcDonald(3) 3 | **11/2**[2] | 71 |
| 0-50 | **4** | *½* | **Sahem (IRE)**[6] [1661] 7-9-8 **78** (DEddy) *hld up: hdwy over 2f out: ev ch over 1f out: outpcd ins fnl f* | PHanagan 9 | **7/1** | 83 |
| 06-6 | **5** | *3* | **Tbm Can**[21] [1341] 5-8-2 **65** (WMBrisbourne) *hld up: hdwy and ev ch over 3f out: no ex over 1f out* | BSwarbrick(7) 2 | **5/1**[1] | 66 |
| 25-2 | **6** | *1* | **Tiyoun (IRE)**[32] [1198] 6-9-5 **75** (JeddO'Keeffe) *in tch tl rdn and no ex fr over 2f out* | KDalgleish 5 | **8/1** | 75 |
| 0-03 | **7** | *½* | **Spitting Image (IRE)**[21] [1341] 4-8-6 **62** (MrsMReveley) *cl up: led over 4f to over 3f out: lost pl and hung rt over 2f out* | SWKelly 4 | **16/1** | 61 |
| 00-6 | **8** | *3* | **Repulse Bay (IRE)**[24] [1315] 6-7-13 **55** (JSGoldie) *bhd: rdn 1/2-way: nvr on terms* | JoannaBadger 7 | **25/1** | 50 |
| 3-60 | **9** | *shd* | **Golden Boot**[2] [1754] 5-8-6 **67** (ABailey) *missed break: hld up: rdn 4f out: sn btn* | (p) TEaves(5) 10 | **7/1** | 61 |
| 00-1 | **10** | *1 ¾* | **Tandava (IRE)**[21] [1341] 6-9-3 **73** (ISemple) *trckd ldrs tl hung rt and wknd over 2f out* | GDuffield 1 | **6/1**[3] | 65 |

2m 50.44s (-2.96) **Going Correction** -0.025s/f (Good) **10** Ran SP% **111.0**
Speed ratings: **108,107,105,104,103 102,102,100,100,99**CSF £98.77 CT £570.69 TOTE £14.70: £3.40, £2.50, £1.90; EX 215.60.
**Owner** J W D Campbell **Bred** Airlie Stud **Trained** Rosewell, Midlothian

**FOCUS**
A field of exposed handicappers and one in which the pace, that was only fair at best, suited those racing prominently.

**NOTEBOOK**
**Colorado Falls(IRE)** confirmed recent Carlisle hurdles promise and showed himself none the worse for his Perth mishap with a gutsy success. He has not always proved consistent but looks worth a try over a bit further.
**Nakwa(IRE)**, back on a sound surface, did not look entirely at home on this track but showed the right attitude in the closing stages and looks capable of winning a similar race back on a more galloping course. He seems to go well at Newcastle.
**George Stubbs(USA)**, successful over 2m last time, was anything but disgraced back over this trip in a steadily run race. He is not one to write off yet when returned to a longer trip, especially when there looks like being a decent gallop.
**Sahem(IRE)** confirmed his return to form for a stable that has been going fairly well of late and may be a bit better than the bare form as he fared the best of those that came from off the pace. He may be vulnerable from this mark against progressive or well-handicapped types, though.
**Tbm Can** is another that may be a bit better than the bare form as he made his ground up off the steady pace in the centre of the course and would have been better suited by a stronger gallop. He is not one to write off yet.
**Tiyoun(IRE)**, from a stable among the winners, was not disgraced but did have the run of the race to a larger degree than some and will have to improve on recent efforts to win from his current mark in similar company.
**Tandava(IRE)**, who had the rub of things when successful last time, did not get to the front this time and did not look the most enthusiastic under pressure. He is not one to rely too heavily on.
*Official explanation: jockey said gelding was never travelling*

## 1786 JACQUI DALGLEISH 40TH BIRTHDAY MEDIAN AUCTION MAIDEN STKS 1m 4f 17y

**4:00** (4:00) (E) 3-5-Y-0 **£3,802** (£1,170; £585; £292) **Stalls** High

| Form | | | | | SP | RPR |
|---|---|---|---|---|---|---|
| 6-33 | **1** | | **Bumptious**[17] [1416] 3-8-7 75 (MHTompkins) *cl up: led and hrd pressed over 2f out: drvn out* | GDuffield 3 | **4/7**[1] | 72 |
| | **2** | *½* | **Recognise (IRE)** 3-8-7 (MJohnston) *trckd ldrs: rn green over 3f out: rallied over 1f out: r.o wl* | KDalgleish 8 | **7/1**[3] | 71 |
| 3 | **3** | *3* | **Into The Shadows**[12] [1528] 4-9-7 (MrsMReveley) *in tch: effrt and ev ch over 2f out: one pce ins fnl f* | ACulhane 9 | **11/2**[2] | 61 |
| | **4** | *4* | **Caymans Gift**[11] 4-9-12 (ACWhillans) *in tch: effrt over 3f out: outpcd fr over 2f out* | PHanagan 1 | **66/1** | 60 |
| 52-0 | **5** | *2 ½* | **Blue Hills**[13] [1509] 3-8-7 73 (MJohnston) *hld up: rdn 4f out: nvr rchd ldrs* | RFfrench 2 | **12/1** | 56 |
| 00 | **6** | *9* | **Archenko**[6] [1662] 4-9-7 (ABerry) *led after 2f: hdd & wknd over 2f out* | PBradley(5) 6 | **66/1** | 41 |
| 60 | **7** | *1 ¼* | **Illicium (IRE)**[10] [1557] 5-9-2 (MrsMReveley) *hld up: rdn 4f out: nvr on terms* | TEaves(5) 7 | **33/1** | 34 |
| | **8** | *23* | **Lange Bleu (FR)**[396] 5-9-12 (MrsSCBradburne) *towards rr: rdn 1/2-way: struggling fr 4f out* | (e[1]) VSlattery 5 | **33/1** | 2 |
| 0/0- | **9** | *30* | **Diligent Lad**[386] [1025] 4-9-9 57 (DWBarker) *led 2f: cl up tl wknd 4f out* | LEnstone(3) 10 | **50/1** | — |

2m 38.37s (-0.83) **Going Correction** -0.025s/f (Good)
**WFA** 3 from 4yo+ 19lb **9** Ran SP% **110.1**
Speed ratings: **101,100,98,96,94 88,87,72,52**CSF £4.31 TOTE £1.60: £1.02, £2.20, £1.60; EX 4.50.
**Owner** Mrs Beryl Lockey **Bred** P And Mrs Venner **Trained** Newmarket, Suffolk

**FOCUS**
An uncompetitive maiden run at just a fair pace and one in which Bumptious did not have to improve to get off the mark but would be no certainty to confirm placings with the runner-up should the pair meet again.
**NOTEBOOK**
**Bumptious**, a consistent performer at up to middle distances, had the run of the race and showed the right attitude to get off the mark but is likely to remain vulnerable from his current mark back in handicap company.
**Recognise(IRE)**, related to useful middle distance performers Romantic Affair and Gulf, showed more than enough on this racecourse debut, despite his inexperience, to suggest he can win a similar race at the very least. He is in good hands and is likely to stay further.
**Into The Shadows**, up in trip and back on a sound surface, again ran creditably and is likely to be seen to best effect in ordinary handicap company around middle distances in due course.
**Caymans Gift**'s proximity confirms this form is nothing special but, while he did have the run of the race, he shaped better than in bumpers and over hurdles and may do a bit better in low-grade handicaps in due course.
**Blue Hills**, who disappointed at Windsor on his handicap debut and reappearance, fared little better in this uncompetitive event and may not be the easiest to place successfully in the short term.
**Archenko**, who is now qualified for a handicap mark, again achieved little.

## 1787 DAVID COOPER H'CAP — 6f 5y
**4:35** (4:36) (E) (0-70,70) 3-Y-0+ — **£4,468** (£1,375; £687; £343) **Stalls** Low

Form — RPR
-000 **1** **Friar Tuck**[2] [1748] 9-8-9 **50** ........ RFfrench 15 — 63
(MissLAPerratt) *outpcd far side: gd hdwy centre over 1f out: styd on to ld wl ins fnl f* **12/1**
00-0 **2** ¾ **Xanadu**[2] [1748] 8-8-4 **50** ........ (p) PMulrennan(5) 14 — 61
(MissLAPerratt) *trckd far side ldrs: led over 1f out: r.o: hdd wl ins fnl f* **12/1**
000- **3** 1 **Golden Spectrum (IRE)**[202] [5550] 5-9-2 **57** ........ AlexGreaves 5 — 65
(DNicholls) *in tch stands side: effrt 2f out: hung rt: r.o wl fnl f* **25/1**
0-04 **4** 1 **Tancred Times**[6] [1663] 9-8-13 **57** ........ LEnstone(3) 8 — 62
(DWBarker) *swtchd to far side: w ldr: rdn 1/2-way: r.o fnl f* **7/1**[3]
-020 **5** nk **Flying Edge (IRE)**[78] [772] 4-9-6 **61** ........ ANicholls 2 — 65
(EJAlston) *cl up stands side: ev ch that gp over 1f out: r.o fnl f* **12/1**
-000 **6** nk **Telepathic (IRE)**[15] [1474] 4-9-6 **66** ........ PBradley(5) 13 — 69
(ABerry) *in tch far side: effrt over 2f out: no imp over 1f out* **40/1**
00-1 **7** ½ **Ulysees (IRE)**[6] [1663] 5-10-1 **70** 6ex ........ PHanagan 12 — 72
(ISemple) *bhd and outpcd: styd on over 1f out: n.d* **7/2**[1]
-000 **8** ½ **Pagan Storm (USA)**[24] [1317] 4-9-5 **67** ........ (b) KristinStubbs(7) 6 — 67
(MrsLStubbs) *outpcd stands side: sme hdwy over 1f out: n.d* **25/1**
0003 **9** 1½ **Only One Legend (IRE)**[34] [1171] 6-9-3 **58** ........ (p) ACulhane 9 — 54
(KARyan) *trckd far side ldrs tl edgd rt and no ex over 1f out* **9/1**
100- **10** ½ **Ballybunion (IRE)**[228] [4988] 5-9-6 **68** ........ LTreadwell(7) 16 — 62
(DNicholls) *mde most far side to over 1f out: sn outpcd* **18/1**
06-0 **11** 5 **Environmentalist**[21] [1342] 5-8-9 **50** ........ (t) DMcGaffin 10 — 29
(DANolan) *outpcd far side: nvr on terms* **66/1**
0502 **12** hd **Legal Set (IRE)**[26] [1279] 8-9-0 **55** ........ AnnStokell 4 — 34
(MissAStokell) *led stands side to over 1f out: wknd* **16/1**
044- **13** nk **Rosselli (USA)**[188] [5791] 8-8-1 **49** ow3 ........ PPMathers(7) 1 — 27
(ABerry) *prom stands side tl wknd fr 2f out* **50/1**
106- **14** 1¾ **Smirfys Party**[253] [4381] 6-9-1 **56** ........ JBramhill 3 — 28
(DNicholls) *cl up stands side tl wknd over 1f out* **33/1**
0306 **15** 3½ **Vijay (IRE)**[17] [1421] 5-9-4 **59** ........ (b) GDuffield 7 — 21
(ISemple) *in tch stands side tl wknd fr 2f out* **9/2**[2]

1m 12.3s (-0.80) **Going Correction** -0.125s/f (Firm) — **15** Ran SP% **113.7**
Speed ratings: **100,99,97,96,95 95,94,94,92,91 84,84,84,81,77**CSF £130.42 CT £3564.00 TOTE £16.20: £3.90, £3.30, £10.10; EX 36.10.
**Owner** Cree Lodge Racing Club **Bred** James Thom And Sons **Trained** Ayr, Strathclyde

**FOCUS**
A low-grade sprint in which the field split into two even groups (stands side and far side) but the winner made up his ground in the centre. There seemed little advantage in the draw.
**NOTEBOOK**
**Friar Tuck**, from a stable back among the winners, did well to come from an uncompromising position and came up the centre in the closing stages, so may be a bit better than the bare form, but his record suggests he is by no means certain to put it all in next time. *Official explanation: trainer said, regarding the improved form shown, gelding appreciated the firmer ground and was favoured by the draw*
**Xanadu**, who has a good record at this course and had conditions to suit, has slipped to a fair mark and ran his race. He had the rub of things more than the winner but, although inconsistent, is capable of adding to his tally this term.
**Golden Spectrum(IRE)**, inconsistent for Richard Hannon, starts life with new connections on a lenient mark and, in finishing ahead of those that raced on the stands side, showed more than enough on this reappearance run to suggest he can win races this term over this trip or over seven furlongs.
**Tancred Times**, who goes well at this course, is from a stable among the winners and was not disgraced after being switched to race with the far side group. She looks capable of winning again this term.
**Flying Edge(IRE)**, returned to turf after this short break, was not disgraced but does look vulnerable to well-handicapped or progressive types from his current mark.
**Telepathic(IRE)**, who has slipped a fair way in the weights since his sole success in 2002, was not totally disgraced but his inconsistency means he would not be one to get heavily involved with next time.
**Ulysees(IRE)**, a course-and-distance winner earlier in the week, was a fair way below that level under his penalty and, judging by his record to date, consistency does not look his strongest suit.
**Smirfys Party** *Official explanation: jockey said gelding hung right-handed*
**Vijay(IRE)** *Official explanation: trainer had no explanation for the poor form shown*

## 1788 DISCOVER SCOTTISH RACING H'CAP — 5f 4y
**5:10** (5:13) (E) (0-75,75) 3-Y-0 — **£3,851** (£1,185; £592; £296) **Stalls** Low

Form — RPR
6443 **1** **Scottish Exile (IRE)**[8] [1626] 3-8-11 **65** ........ (v) DarrenWilliams 1 — 71
(KRBurke) *trckd ldrs: led over 1f out: drvn out* **9/2**[3]
42-2 **2** nk **Baron Rhodes**[15] [1473] 3-8-11 **70** ........ TEaves(5) 8 — 75
(JSWainwright) *racd wd: prom: effrt 2f out: kpt on fnl f: jst hld* **4/1**[2]
0060 **3** ¾ **Lord Baskerville**[12] [1526] 3-8-3 **57** ........ JBramhill 4 — 59
(WStorey) *chsd ldng gp: hdwy on outside over 1f out: edgd lft ins last: r.o* **7/1**
040- **4** 1¼ **Open Mind**[223] [5127] 3-8-0 **54** ow2 ........ ANicholls 2 — 52
(EJAlston) *prominet: effrt and swtchd to stands rail over 1f out: r.o fnl f* **12/1**
50-0 **5** ½ **Musiotal**[21] [1342] 3-7-12 **52** oh4 ........ PFessey 5 — 48
(JSGoldie) *bhd tl swtchd and hdwy ins fnl f: r.o: nrst fin* **25/1**
3063 **6** hd **Lavish Times**[5] [1689] 3-7-12 **52** oh1 ........ (b) PHanagan 7 — 47
(ABerry) *cl up tl rdn and outpcd wl over 1f out* **7/2**[1]
000- **7** nk **Sir Ernest (IRE)**[230] [4943] 3-9-4 **75** ........ JFMcDonald(3) 6 — 69
(MJPolglase) *chsd ldrs tl rdn and wknd over 1f out* **5/1**
-533 **8** 9 **Shaymee's Girl**[46] [1038] 3-8-3 **57** ........ JoannaBadger 3 — 19
(MsDeborahJEvans) *led to over 1f out: sn btn* **10/1**

60.97 secs (-0.29) **Going Correction** -0.125s/f (Firm) — **8** Ran SP% **110.2**
Speed ratings: **97,96,95,93,92 92,91,77**CSF £21.10 CT £114.96 TOTE £4.50: £2.60, £1.40, £2.80; EX 8.70 Place 6 £104.30, Place 5 £69.90..
**Owner** Mrs Melba Bryce **Bred** D J And Mrs Deer **Trained** Middleham Moor, N Yorks
■ Stewards Enquiry : T Eaves caution: used whip with excessive frequency

**FOCUS**
A run of the mill handicap featuring mainly exposed performers and a race in which the field raced on the stands rail. The pace was sound and there was not much between the first seven home.
**NOTEBOOK**
**Scottish Exile(IRE)** had the run of the race next to the rail from her low draw back on turf and showed the right attitude to hold on in the closing stages. She has been consistent this year and should continue to give a good account.
**Baron Rhodes** confirmed reappearance promise back on a sound surface and may be a bit better than the bare form as she raced five deep from her wide draw for much of the contest. She is a reliable sort who looks capable of winning in similarly ordinary company.
**Lord Baskerville**, who got bogged down on heavy ground over six furlongs last time, showed more than enough dropped in trip and back on a sound surface to suggest he can win in modest company this term.
**Open Mind**, did not really have the rub of things for this reappearance run but shaped as though retaining all her ability and will be placed to best advantage by her capable trainer this term.
**Musiotal** showed his first worthwhile form from out of the handicap. He is only lightly raced and shaped as though he would improve granted a stiffer test of stamina.
**Lavish Times** looked to have fair claims on his latest Bath form but he is not the most consistent of performers and was below his best on this occasion. He does not look one to place too much faith in.
T/Plt: £306.30 to a £1 stake. Pool: £31,540.15. 75.15 winning tickets. T/Qpdt: £112.20 to a £1 stake. Pool: £1,728.70. 11.40 winning tickets. RY

# [1762] NEWMARKET (R-H)
Sunday, May 2

**OFFICIAL GOING: Good**

## 1789 CURTIS MEDICAL RATED STKS (H'CAP) — 6f
**1:30** (1:30) (B) (0-110,107) 4-Y-0+ — **£12,064** (£4,576; £2,288; £1,040) **Stalls** Low

Form — RPR
26-0 **1** **Royal Storm (IRE)**[19] [1385] 5-8-9 **95** ........ MJKinane 2 — 105
(MrsAJPerrett) *w ldr: rdn to ld 2f out: r.o* **9/1**
112- **2** hd **Seel Of Approval**[225] [5060] 5-9-3 **103** ........ DHolland 6 — 112
(RCharlton) *chsd ldrs: rdn and ev ch whn edgd rt ins fnl f: r.o* **9/2**[2]
00-6 **3** ¾ **Mazepa (IRE)**[20] [1353] 4-8-9 **95** ........ LDettori 7 — 102
(NACallaghan) *hld up in tch: rdn and ev ch over 1f out: unable qck nr fin* **8/1**
1221 **4** 2 **Zilch**[13] [1500] 6-8-7 **93** oh1 ........ IMongan 8 — 94
(MLWBell) *s.i.s: hld up: r.o ins fnl f: nt rch ldrs* **9/2**[2]
10-4 **5** 1½ **Chookie Heiton (IRE)**[36] [1126] 6-9-4 **104** ........ RWinston 3 — 101
(ISemple) *chsd ldrs: rdn and nt clr run over 1f out: styd on same pce* **4/1**[1]
100- **6** 3 **Border Subject**[302] [3002] 7-9-7 **107** ........ SDrowne 5 — 95
(RCharlton) *sn led: hdd 2f out: wknd ins fnl f* **8/1**
030- **7** ½ **Presto Vento**[176] [5953] 4-8-7 **93** oh3 ........ KDarley 9 — 79
(RHannon) *s.i.s: hld up: hdwy over 1f out: wknd ins fnl f* **16/1**
0406 **8** ½ **Bond Boy**[18] [1391] 7-8-7 **93** oh1 ........ FLynch 1 — 78
(BSmart) *hld up: effrt over 1f out: n.d* **7/1**[3]
054- **9** 9 **Crafty Calling (USA)**[248] [4523] 4-8-10 **96** ........ KFallon 4 — 54
(PFICole) *chsd ldrs over 4f* **16/1**

1m 12.0s (-1.09) **Going Correction** -0.025s/f (Good) — **9** Ran SP% **112.9**
Speed ratings: **106,105,104,102,100 96,95,94,82**CSF £48.01 CT £339.99 TOTE £13.60: £2.90, £2.00, £2.10; EX 102.30.
**Owner** The Cloran Family **Bred** E Campion **Trained** Pulborough, W Sussex

**FOCUS**
A competitive rated stakes run at a sound pace. Solid form.
**NOTEBOOK**
**Royal Storm(IRE)**, all the better for his pipe-opener at the Craven meeting, benefited from a positive ride and ran on to gain his first victory over the trip. This was a smart effort off a 7lb higher mark than he had ever previously won from, and as he thrived on his racing last season, we should be seeing plenty more of him.
**Seel Of Approval**, 11lb above his highest winning mark, ran a fine race on this first start for eight months, which is encouraging, as he has needed his first run after a break in the past. The problem is that his rating may make him difficult to place, especially as his consistency is unlikely to gain him much respite.
**Mazepa(IRE)**, ridden with more patience this time, could never quite land a telling blow but showed enough to suggest he will find a race before too long. Faster ground would have suited him better.
**Zilch**, 6lb higher for his Pontefract win, stayed on but could not get there in time and would have preferred easier ground. He will be freshened up now with the Wokingham in mind, going permitting.
**Chookie Heiton(IRE)** did not enjoy the clearest of runs though it is doubtful it made that much difference. He is not obviously well handicapped, but he has needed a couple of runs to put him right in the past so should not be written off.
**Border Subject**, reappearing after a ten-month break, tried to make all as usual but had nothing left in the closing stages and almost certainly needed it.

## 1790 LETHEBY & CHRISTOPHER DAHLIA STKS (GROUP 3) (F&M) — 1m 1f
**2:00** (2:00) (A) 4-Y-0+ — **£29,000** (£11,000; £5,500; £2,500) **Stalls** Low

Form — RPR
40-1 **1** **Beneventa**[22] [1332] 4-8-9 104 ........ SSanders 6 — 108
(JLDunlop) *chsd ldr: rdn to ld and edgd rt over 1f out: r.o wl* **7/2**[2]
25-1 **2** 2½ **Silence Is Golden**[22] [1328] 5-8-9 99 ........ KFallon 3 — 103
(BJMeehan) *s.i.s: pushed along 1/2-way: hdwy 2f out: r.o ins fnl f: nt rch wnr* **7/2**[2]
**3** nk **Special Delivery (IRE)**[21] [1351] 4-8-9 ........ DBonilla 2 — 102
(ELellouche, France) *hld up in tch: rdn and hung rt over 1f out: styd on* **7/1**[3]
011- **4** 1½ **Echoes In Eternity (IRE)**[211] [5364] 4-9-0 109 ........ (t) LDettori 5 — 104
(SaeedBinSuroor) *led: rdn and hdd over 1f out: wknd ins fnl f* **2/1**[1]
242- **5** 5 **Zietory**[182] [5889] 4-8-9 102 ........ SDrowne 7 — 89
(PFICole) *chsd ldrs tl wknd over 1f out* **16/1**
1515 **6** 2½ **Najaaba (USA)**[22] [1332] 4-8-9 82 ........ BReilly 1 — 84
(MissJFeilden) *hld up: rdn over 2f out: sn wknd* **66/1**
535- **7** 3½ **Felicity (IRE)**[159] [6071] 4-8-9 97 ........ MJKinane 4 — 77
(JHMGosden) *trckd ldrs: racd keenly: wknd over 1f out* **12/1**

413- **8** *7* **Chantress**[232] 4879 4-8-9 92 ........ JPMurtagh 8 63
(MrsJRRamsden) *hld up: wknd 3f out* **16/1**

1m 50.65s (-1.26) **Going Correction** -0.025s/f (Good) **8** Ran SP% **111.2**
Speed ratings: **104,101,101,100,95 93,90,84**CSF £15.24 TOTE £4.70: £1.80, £1.40, £1.70; EX 14.40.
**Owner** R N Khan **Bred** R N And Mrs Khan **Trained** Arundel, W Sussex

**FOCUS**
Not the strongest of Group Threes and the pace was only ordinary, resulting in a modest winning time.

**NOTEBOOK**
**Beneventa** continues in great form and, given a positive ride over this longer trip, accomplished this stiffer task in style. This was not the greatest of Group Threes, but she keeps on winning and a record of six wins from ten starts is creditable at any level. There should be plenty more opportunities for her either here or on the continent. *Official explanation: continues in great form and, given a positive ride over this longer trip, accomplished this stiffer task in style. This was not the greatest of Group Threes, but she keeps on winning and a record of six wins from ten starts is creditable at any level. There should be plenty more opportunities for her either here or on the continent.*
**Silence Is Golden**, placed at Listed level but better known as a handicapper, took her time in responding to pressure and her finishing position was as close as she got. Although a decent event on official figures, this was not quite her best form according to Racing Post Ratings. However, there could be improvement in her if she is tried again over a bit further. *Official explanation: , placed at Listed level but better known as a handicapper, took her time in responding to pressure and her finishing position was as close as she got. Although a decent event on official figures, this was not quite her best form according to Racing Post Ratings. However, there could be improvement in her if she is tried again over a bit further.*
**Special Delivery(IRE)**, a lightly raced French filly, ran as though finding this trip too sharp. *Official explanation: , a lightly raced French filly, ran as though finding this trip too sharp.*
**Echoes In Eternity(IRE)**, winner of a Group Two here last autumn, was allowed to set her own pace out in front but folded rather tamely once losing the lead. She ideally needs faster ground and, as she improved from her reappearance last season, it may be wise to give her the benefit of the doubt. *Official explanation: , winner of a Group Two here last autumn, was allowed to set her own pace out in front but folded rather tamely once losing the lead. She ideally needs faster ground and, as she improved from her reappearance last season, it may be wise to give her the benefit of the doubt.*
**Zietory**may have needed it, but this was also the longest trip she has attempted and she did not appear to stay. *Official explanation: may have needed it, but this was also the longest trip she has attempted and she did not appear to stay.*
**Felicity(IRE)** tended to take a keen hold early and probably compromised her chances by doing so. *Official explanation: tended to take a keen hold early and probably compromised her chances by doing so.*

## 1791 ULTIMATEBET.COM 1000 GUINEAS STKS (GROUP 1) (FILLIES) 1m
**2:40** (2:42) (A) 3-Y-O **£187,195** (£71,005; £35,502; £16,137) **Stalls** Centre

Form RPR

111- **1** **Attraction**[299] 3074 3-9-0 119 ........ KDarley 8 115
(MJohnston) *mde all towards far side: rdn and edgd rt over 1f out: styd on gamely* **11/2**[2]

12- **2** *1/2* **Sundrop (JPN)**[218] 5209 3-9-0 ........ KMcEvoy 1 114+
(SaeedBinSuroor) *racd centre: hld up: hdwy over 1f out: r.o wl* **16/1**

22-1 **3** *1/2* **Hathrah (IRE)**[22] 1327 3-9-0 111 ........ RHills 16 112
(JLDunlop) *racd towards far side: trckd ldrs: rdn over 1f out: styd on* **6/1**[3]

311- **4** *1 1/4* **Red Bloom**[218] 5209 3-9-0 113 ........ KFallon 7 110
(SirMichaelStoute) *racd towards far side: trckd ldrs: racd keenly: rdn over 1f out: styd on same pce ins fnl f* **4/1**[1]

11- **5** *1/2* **Secret Charm (IRE)**[190] 5750 3-9-0 ........ MHills 6 108+
(BWHills) *racd towards far side: hld up: nt clr run and dropped rr over 2f out: hdwy over 1f out: r.o ins fnl f: nvr able to chal* **14/1**

111- **6** *hd* **Carry On Katie (USA)**[213] 5332 3-9-0 ........ LDettori 10 108
(SaeedBinSuroor) *racd towards far side: chsd ldrs: hung rt and outpcd 2f out: styd on ins fnl f* **7/1**

13-3 **7** *1 1/4* **Nataliya**[15] 1458 3-9-0 104 ........ SSanders 14 105
(JLDunlop) *racd towards far side: hld up in tch: rdn over 2f out: no ex ins fnl f: hung rt nr fin* **20/1**

00-1 **8** *nk* **Silca's Gift**[18] 1398 3-9-0 ........ TEDurcan 15 104+
(MRChannon) *racd towards far side: chsd ldrs: rdn and ev ch over 1f out: no ex ins fnl f* **16/1**

12-1 **9** *hd* **Majestic Desert**[15] 1458 3-9-0 111 ........ DHolland 3 104
(MRChannon) *racd towards far side: prom: rdn over 2f out: wknd fnl f* **7/1**

11- **10** *2 1/2* **Cairns (UAE)**[197] 5642 3-9-0 ........ JCarroll 12 98
(SaeedBinSuroor) *racd towards far side: chsd ldrs: rdn over 2f out: wknd over 1f out* **25/1**

34-5 **11** *2* **Kelucia (IRE)**[36] 1123 3-9-0 100 ........ JFEgan 4 94
(JSGoldie) *racd towards far side: hld up: rdn over 2f out: n.d* **100/1**

110- **12** *3/4* **Necklace**[210] 5404 3-9-0 ........ JPMurtagh 13 92
(APO'Brien, Ire) *racd towards far side: chsd ldrs: rdn over 3f out: wknd wl over 1f out* **8/1**

1-00 **13** *2 1/2* **Valjarv (IRE)**[18] 1398 3-9-0 95 ........ TGMcLaughlin 5 86
(NPLittmoden) *racd towards far side: hld up: rdn over 2f out: sn wknd* **200/1**

61-2 **14** *3* **Incheni (IRE)**[18] 1398 3-9-0 103 ........ SDrowne 9 79
(GWragg) *racd towards far side: hld up: rdn over 3f out: n.d* **25/1**

1- **15** *1 1/2* **Jath**[191] 5722 3-9-0 ........ NCallan 11 76
(JulianPoulton) *s.i.s: hld up: effrt over 2f out: sn wknd* **100/1**

21-4 **16** *shd* **Spotlight**[15] 1458 3-9-0 101 ........ EAhern 2 76
(JLDunlop) *racd alone in centre: chsd ldrs: jnd main gp over 3f out: wknd over 2f out* **33/1**

1m 36.78s (-2.62) **Going Correction** -0.025s/f (Good) **16** Ran SP% **122.1**
Speed ratings: **112,111,111,109,109 109,107,107,107,104 102,102,99,96,95 94**CSF £85.58 CT £581.63 TOTE £7.10: £3.30, £4.50, £3.00; EX 166.80 Trifecta £2378.70 Pool £12,396.48 - 3.70 winning units..
**Owner** Duke Of Roxburghe **Bred** Floors Farming **Trained** Middleham Moor, N Yorks
■ A second English classic for both trainer Mark Johnston and jockey Kevin Darley, though a first 1000 Guineas for both.

**FOCUS**
A cracking 1000 Guineas run at a decent clip, and a creditable time for the grade. The field gratowards the far side, though at different intervals and unlike last year, there were not too many hard luck stories, so the form should be reliable. Attraction was a most worthy winner, although in the overall scheme of things she is probably no better than an average winner of the race.

**NOTEBOOK**
**Attraction** was the outstanding member of her sex at two but had questions to answer, having been sidelined by injury since winning the Cherry Hinton at last year's July Meeting. Returning in superb nick, she was ridden as if there were no reservations over her stamina and made every yard. Although her rivals kept on having a go at her, she always had the answers and the post arrived before the runner-up could get to her. Her ungainly action remains a talking point, but there is no debating her ability. Her immediate options include the French or Irish 1,000 Guineas, while at Royal Ascot connections can choose between the Golden Jubilee and the Coronation Stakes.
**Sundrop(JPN)** came home in great style and may well have won with a little further to go, especially as she hung to her left at a vital stage. She reversed last season's Fillies' Mile form with Red Bloom and will be popular for the Oaks after this, but although ten furlongs should be no problem, there is no guaranteeing she will stay further.
**Hathrah(IRE)** would have preferred softer ground than this and ran a cracking race under the circumstances. She was certainly not stopping at the end and, with ground conditions more likely to be in her favour, the Prix de Diane would look the obvious target.
**Red Bloom**, racing for the first time since winning the Fillies' Mile at Ascot last September, was always ideally placed but lacked the required pace where it mattered. She may well come on from this, but she does not look as good as her stable-companion Russian Rhythm was at the same stage last season. A step up in trip for the Prix de Diane is an obvious option.
**Secret Charm(IRE)** ◆, less experienced than most with this being only her third start, was possibly unlucky not to finish closer as she was stopped in her run before finishing in grand style. The Irish 1000, a race her stable has won before, is a possibility.
**Carry On Katie(USA)**, unbeaten in three starts at two and making her debut for Godolphin, was a similar type to the winner in that she was untried beyond six furlongs and making her seasonal reappearance, but unlike that rival she showed up for a while before getting outpaced and then ran on again. Given the speed she showed at two, this performance makes her absolute best trip somewhat perplexing.
**Nataliya** had every chance and was still fourth passing the furlong pole, but despite some hefty smacks there was little more to come, though she did reverse Fred Darling form with Majestic Desert. She should be able to make her mark in Pattern company.
**Silca's Gift**was a supplementary entry. Never far away against the far rail, she had every chance but stopped as though failing to last the extra furlong. A drop back in trip should see her winning again.
**Majestic Desert** had every chance, but did not find much when asked for maximum effort. She may have been flattered by her victory in a slowly run Fred Darling, and she may not have stayed, although connections wondered if the race came too soon after Newbury.
**Cairns(UAE)**, another unbeaten juvenile making her debut for Godolphin, either needed it or did not stay.
**Necklace** may need fast ground to show her best, but was still disappointing and completed a miserable couple of days for Ballydoyle.

## 1792 ULTIMATEBET.COM JOCKEY CLUB STKS (GROUP 2) 1m 4f
**3:15** (3:17) (A) 4-Y-O+ **£58,000** (£22,000; £11,000; £5,000) **Stalls** Centre

Form RPR

23-2 **1** **Gamut (IRE)**[15] 1455 5-8-9 117 ........ (t) KFallon 7 120
(SirMichaelStoute) *trckd ldrs: nt clr run over 2f out: shkn up to ld wl ins fnl f: r.o* **7/4**[1]

55-3 **2** *1 1/4* **Systematic**[36] 1124 5-8-9 109 ........ KDarley 3 118
(MJohnston) *trckd ldr: chal 3f out: rdn to ld over 1f out: hdd and unable qck wl ins fnl f* **11/1**

33-5 **3** *1 1/2* **Warrsan (IRE)**[36] 1144 6-9-0 117 ........ DHolland 6 121
(CEBrittain) *led: rdn 3f out: hdd over 1f out: no ex towards fin* **9/2**[3]

13-1 **4** *3/4* **Dubai Success**[15] 1455 4-8-9 110 ........ MHills 5 114
(BWHills) *hld up in tch: rdn over 2f out: styd on same pce fnl f* **10/3**[2]

24-0 **5** *1 1/2* **Martaline**[36] 1144 5-8-12 ........ LDettori 1 115
(AFabre, France) *hld up: hdwy over 2f out: rdn and hung rt over 1f out: styd on same pce* **8/1**

41/0 **6** *4* **Jelani (IRE)**[15] 1455 5-8-9 ........ MJKinane 2 106
(AndrewTurnell) *prom tl wknd over 1f out* **33/1**

115- **7** *6* **Moments Of Joy**[232] 4880 4-8-6 105 ........ SSanders 4 93
(RGuest) *hld up: wknd wl over 1f out* **8/1**

2m 29.77s (-3.69) **Going Correction** -0.025s/f (Good) **7** Ran SP% **111.1**
Speed ratings: **111,110,109,108,107 105,101**CSF £20.98 TOTE £2.60: £1.70, £3.30; EX 25.30.
**Owner** Mrs G Smith **Bred** Ballymacoll Stud Farm Ltd **Trained** Newmarket, Suffolk

**FOCUS**
A reasonable standard for a Group 2 and solid form from the principals, although the pace did not pick up until halfway.

**NOTEBOOK**
**Gamut(IRE)**, made up for his narrow defeat at Newbury by Dubai Success. Always travelling well, his only concern was that he was trapped behind the two leaders at a vital stage but he managed to ease his way out in plenty of time and came away under hands and heels riding. He looks set for a good season.
**Systematic** was out of sorts in an abbreviated 2003 campaign after such a successful season the year before, but this was much more like it. Never far away, he never stopped trying and if he is truly back then there should be more Group races to be won with him.
**Warrsan(IRE)**, winner of this last year, had a 5lb penalty this time and after making much of the running was worn down after a protracted battle with the runner-up. He is likely to attempt a repeat win in the Coronation Cup at Epsom.
**Dubai Success**, who beat Gamut narrowly in the John Porter at Newbury, did his best to try and keep that rival in a pocket when making his effort two furlongs from home, but could not do so and was soon found wanting for pace.
**Martaline**, held up early, tried to make an effort down the outside coming to the last quarter-mile but it came to nothing. He ideally needs softer ground.
**Jelani(IRE)** took a good hold early and then saw plenty of daylight. He is still below his best.
**Moments Of Joy** never moved out of last place and it remains to be seen whether she has trained on.

## 1793 R. L. DAVISON PRETTY POLLY STKS (LISTED RACE) (FILLIES) 1m 2f
**3:50** (3:53) (A) 3-Y-O **£17,400** (£6,600; £3,300; £1,500) **Stalls** Low

Form RPR

313- **1** **Ouija Board**[183] 5874 3-8-8 93 ........ KFallon 4 111+
(EALDunlop) *hld up: hdwy over 2f out: led over 1f out: rdn clr* **2/1**[1]

61- **2** *6* **Sahool**[178] 5934 3-8-8 86 ........ RHills 6 100
(MPTregoning) *prom: rdn to chse ldr over 2f out: styd on same pce fnl f* **13/2**

61- **3** *1/2* **Rave Reviews (IRE)**[190] 5754 3-8-8 81 ........ MJKinane 8 99
(JLDunlop) *hld up: hdwy 4f out: outpcd 2f out: styd on ins fnl f* **16/1**

2-3 **4** *1 1/4* **Brindisi**[24] 1311 3-8-8 ........ MHills 2 97
(BWHills) *led: clr over 2f out: hdd over 1f out: wknd ins fnl f* **12/1**

**5** *1/2* **Kisses For Me (IRE)**[200] 5582 3-8-9 ow1 ........ JPMurtagh 9 97
(APO'Brien, Ire) *chsd ldrs: rdn over 2f out: wknd over 1f out* **5/1**[3]

3- **6** *11* **Opera Comique (FR)**[224] 5103 3-8-8 ........ (t) LDettori 7 75
(SaeedBinSuroor) *trckd ldr over 6f: wknd over 2f out* **7/2**[2]

0- **7** *1 3/4* **Lady Peaches**[312] 2687 3-8-8 ........ JFanning 5 72
(DMullarkey) *s.i.s: hld up: wknd 3f out* **100/1**

1- **8** *5* **Rendezvous Point (USA)**[171] 5984 3-8-8 ........ KDarley 1 62
(JHMGosden) *s.i.s: sn chsng ldrs: wknd over 2f out* **16/1**

0 **P** **He Jaa (IRE)**[15] 1461 3-8-8 ........ DHolland 3 —
(CEBrittain) *hld up: p.u over 3f out* **20/1**

2m 2.92s (-2.77) **Going Correction** -0.025s/f (Good) **9** Ran SP% **110.8**
Speed ratings: **110,105,104,103,103 94,93,89,—**CSF £14.42 TOTE £3.00: £1.60, £1.80, £2.60; EX 19.10.
**Owner** Lord Derby **Bred** Stanley Estate And Stud Co **Trained** Newmarket, Suffolk

**FOCUS**
A steady early pace, but a decent overall time. Hard form to assess accurately, with so many unexposed fillies involved, but in all probability a smart effort from the winner.
**NOTEBOOK**
**Ouija Board** stepped up on her juvenile form to run out a facile winner, appreciating the step up in distance. She is clearly going the right way, and as she is from the same family of Teleprompter, she can be expected to improve as she gets older.
**Sahool**, looked the part on the way to post and turned in a sound enough effort even if the winner was in a different league.
**Rave Reviews(IRE)**, caught out as the tempo lifted, stayed on well when meeting the rising ground and looks sure to appreciate a step up in trip.
**Brindisi** had a soft time of things up front and tried to nick this going to the two-furlong pole, but that effort took its toll on her and she folded tamely in the latter stages. However, this was still a step in the right direction and she should have no trouble winning her race.
**Kisses For Me(IRE)**, even though probably stepping up on her maiden win, was still a little disappointing and was not the only runner from the O'Brien yard to be found wanting at this meeting.
**Opera Comique(FR)** stopped very quickly and clearly was not at her best.

## 1794 HASTINGS MAIDEN STKS — 1m
4:25 (4:28) (D) 3-Y-O — £7,046 (£2,168; £1,084; £542) Stalls Low

| Form | | | | RPR |
|---|---|---|---|---|
| 2 | 1 | | **Rehearsal**[15] 1461 3-9-0 ... PRobinson 18<br>(CGCox) *trckd ldrs: plld hrd: led 1f out: rdn out* **9/2**[2] | 89 |
| 5-2 | 2 | 2 ½ | **Never Will**[21] 1342 3-9-0 ... JFanning 24<br>(MJohnston) *led: rdn and hdd 1f out: no ex ins fnl f* **14/1** | 83 |
| 3 | 3 | shd | **Credit (IRE)**[24] 1310 3-9-0 ... KFallon 3<br>(RHannon) *chsd ldrs: rdn and ev ch over 2f out: hung rt and outpcd over 1f out: styd on ins fnl f* **10/1** | 83 |
| 2- | 4 | ½ | **Silent Hawk (IRE)**[183] 5870 3-9-0 ...(t) LDettori 20<br>(SaeedBinSuroor) *chsd ldrs: rdn and ev ch over 2f out: styd on same pce ins fnl f* **11/2**[3] | 82 |
| | 5 | 2 ½ | **Mikao (IRE)** 3-8-7 ... SaleemGolam(7) 16<br>(MHTompkins) *hld up: hdwy over 2f out: swtchd rt over 1f out: r.o* **100/1** | 76 |
| | 6 | 2 ½ | **Nassiria** 3-8-9 ... TEDurcan 19<br>(CEBrittain) *plld hrd and prom: outpcd over 2f out: r.o ins fnl f* **25/1** | 65 |
| 335- | 7 | hd | **Master Theo (USA)**[155] 6087 3-9-0 77 ... JQuinn 9<br>(HJCollingridge) *prom: outpcd over 2f out: r.o ins fnl f* **33/1** | 70 |
| 2 | 8 | ¾ | **Denounce**[18] 1395 3-9-0 ... WRyan 14<br>(HRACecil) *s.i.s: hld up: plld hrd: hdwy 1/2-way: ev ch over 2f out: sn rdn: wknd fnl f* **2/1**[1] | 68 |
| 0-22 | 9 | 1 ½ | **Oh Golly Gosh**[12] 1528 3-9-0 76 ...(p) KDarley 23<br>(NPLittmoden) *prom: rdn and ev ch over 2f out: wknd over 1f out* **14/1** | 65 |
| 6- | 10 | 1 ¼ | **Want (USA)**[191] 5733 3-9-0 ... MJKinane 22<br>(JHMGosden) *s.s: hld up: styd on appr fnl f: nvr nrr* **9/1** | 62 |
| | 11 | nk | **Hawaajes** 3-9-0 ... RHills 15<br>(BHanbury) *hld up: hdwy 1/2-way: rdn and ev ch over 2f out: wknd over 1f out* **20/1** | 61 |
| 0 | 12 | 1 | **Miss Inkha**[18] 1400 3-8-9 ... SDrowne 12<br>(RGuest) *hld up: nvr trbld ldrs* **100/1** | 54 |
| | 13 | 1 ½ | **Desert Hawk** 3-9-0 ... JPMurtagh 13<br>(RHannon) *sn pushed along in rr: n.d* **33/1** | 55 |
| 0 | 14 | nk | **Suspicious Minds**[43] 1059 3-8-9 ... DHolland 6<br>(GCBravery) *hld up: n.d* **50/1** | 50 |
| | 15 | 2 | **Miss Merenda** 3-8-9 ... JMackay 11<br>(DECantillon) *s.i.s: a in rr* **100/1** | 45 |
| | 16 | nk | **Killmorey** 3-9-0 ... OUrbina 8<br>(SCWilliams) *s.s: effrt 1/2-way: sn wknd* **66/1** | 49 |
| 0 | 17 | ¾ | **Hinode (IRE)**[18] 1395 3-9-0 ... SSanders 17<br>(JARToller) *prom over 5f* **100/1** | 48 |
| | 18 | nk | **Magic Verse** 3-8-9 ... CLowther 10<br>(RGuest) *s.i.s: a in rr* **100/1** | 42 |
| | 19 | 1 ¼ | **Unbridled's Dream (USA)** 3-9-0 ... GCarter 1<br>(HJCyzer) *s.i.s: a in rr* **66/1** | 44 |
| | 20 | 2 ½ | **Crocolat** 3-8-9 ... AMackay 4<br>(NACallaghan) *sn pushed along: a in rr* **50/1** | 33 |
| | 21 | 1 ½ | **Glencalvie (IRE)** 3-9-0 ... EAhern 5<br>(JNoseda) *s.i.s: hld up: pushed along 1/2-way: sn wknd* **33/1** | 35 |
| | 22 | 11 | **Eizawina Docklands** 3-9-0 ... TGMcLaughlin 2<br>(NPLittmoden) *dwlt: hdwy 6f out: wknd 3f out* **66/1** | 10 |
| | 23 | 1 ¼ | **Vicat Cole** 3-9-0 ... NCallan 21<br>(HJCyzer) *s.s: a in rr* **66/1** | 7 |
| 000 | 24 | 7 | **Mitzi Caspar**[13] 1507 3-8-9 ... JFEgan 7<br>(PLGilligan) *prom 5f* **100/1** | — |

1m 38.8s (-0.60) **Going Correction** -0.025s/f (Good) **24** Ran SP% **132.6**
Speed ratings: **102,99,99,98,96 93,93,92,91,90 89,88,87,87,85 84,84,83,82,80 78,67,66,59**CSF £62.91 TOTE £5.40: £2.10, £4.10, £3.00; EX 93.70.
**Owner** Elite Racing Club **Bred** Taker Bloodstock **Trained** Lambourn, Berks
**FOCUS**
Despite the stalls being placed on the stands' side the field elected to race up the centre. They didn't appear to go that quick in the early stages, but the overall time was decent. This is good maiden form, although possibly not quite up to the race's usual high standards.
**NOTEBOOK**
**Rehearsal**, keen both to post and during the race itself, clearly has his fair share of ability, but will need to settle if he is to cope with a step up in grade and fulfil his potential.
**Never Will** ◆ got this longer trip well and may have been a shade unlucky to bump into what could prove an above average rival. He should have no trouble getting off the mark.
**Credit(IRE)** ◆ had clearly learned from his debut. As he is out of a mare that stayed 12 furlongs, he is sure to benefit from a step up in trip.
**Silent Hawk(IRE)** had no excuses and looked as though this trip may be far enough for him.
**Mikao(IRE)**, out of a mare that won over 12 furlongs, shaped with plenty of promise and should not be too hard to place.
**Nassiria**, who is out of a mare that won over a mile as a juvenile, was a bit too keen for her own good early on, but did enough to suggest she can pay her way in due course.
**Master Theo(USA)** again hinted at having ability and can be found easier openings.
**Denounce** was far too keen for his own good and will need to learn to settle if he is to progress.
**Want(USA)** looks the sort to do better when he goes handicapping and when facing a stiffer test than he faced here.
**Hawaajes**
**Mitzi Caspar** *Official explanation: jockey said filly had got upset in the stalls*

## 1795 PORTLAND LODGE H'CAP — 1m
5:00 (5:03) (C) (0-100,94) 3-Y-O — £13,962 (£4,296; £2,148; £1,074) Stalls Low

| Form | | | | RPR |
|---|---|---|---|---|
| 21 | 1 | | **Master Marvel (IRE)**[24] 1318 3-8-9 82 ... JFanning 16<br>(MJohnston) *led: rdn and hdd over 1f out: rallied to ld wl ins fnl f* **6/1**[3] | 96 |
| 411- | 2 | ¾ | **Thyolo (IRE)**[191] 5726 3-9-3 90 ... PRobinson 19<br>(CGCox) *chsd ldrs: rdn and ev ch fr over 1f out: r.o* **5/1**[1] | 102 |
| 11-0 | 3 | nk | **Jedburgh**[16] 1437 3-9-6 93 ... MJKinane 15<br>(JLDunlop) *hld up: hdwy over 3f out: rdn to ld over 1f out: hdd wl ins fnl f* **25/1** | 105 |
| 13-0 | 4 | 3 ½ | **Spin King (IRE)**[17] 1414 3-8-7 80 ... JMackay 11<br>(MLWBell) *hld up: hdwy over 3f out: rdn over 1f out: styd on same pce* **20/1** | 84 |
| 314- | 5 | nk | **State Dilemma (IRE)**[199] 5592 3-9-2 89 ... MHills 8<br>(BWHills) *trckd ldr: rdn over 1f out: styd on same pce* **20/1** | 92 |
| 1-31 | 6 | ½ | **Granston (IRE)**[17] 1418 3-8-6 78 ow1 ... SDrowne 3<br>(JDBethell) *hld up: styd on u.p appr fnl f: nt rch ldrs* **12/1** | 81 |
| 241- | 7 | hd | **Secretary General (IRE)**[242] 4665 3-9-1 88 ... KFallon 17<br>(PFICole) *slowly in to stride: hld up: hdwy over 1f out: nt rch ldrs* **8/1** | 89 |
| 32-6 | 8 | nk | **Anuvasteel**[36] 1134 3-8-5 78 ... AMackay 21<br>(NACallaghan) *dwlt: hld up: hdwy over 1f out: nt trble ldrs* **25/1** | 79 |
| 15-0 | 9 | nk | **Overdrawn (IRE)**[9] 1585 3-9-7 94 ... DHolland 18<br>(JAOsborne) *s.s: hld up: hdwy u.p over 1f out: no ex ins fnl f* **33/1** | 94 |
| 26-1 | 10 | 2 ½ | **Fancy Foxtrot**[30] 1226 3-9-5 92 ... LDettori 4<br>(BJMeehan) *hld up: rdn over 1f out: n.d* **12/1** | 86 |
| -120 | 11 | nk | **Mount Vettore**[22] 1322 3-8-9 82 ... JPMurtagh 7<br>(MrsJRRamsden) *hld up: effrt and hung rt over 1f out: n.d* **12/1** | 75 |
| 4-10 | 12 | 1 | **Alfonso**[17] 1418 3-8-3 76 ... EAhern 6<br>(BWHills) *chsd ldrs: rdn 1/2-way: wknd wl over 1f out* **33/1** | 67 |
| 5-01 | 13 | shd | **Mudawin (IRE)**[15] 1461 3-9-3 90 ... RHills 1<br>(MPTregoning) *hld up: hdwy over 3f out: wknd over 1f out* **11/2**[2] | 81 |
| 11-0 | 14 | nk | **Mahmoom**[17] 1408 3-9-3 90 ... TEDurcan 12<br>(MRChannon) *hld up in tch: wknd and eased fnl f* **8/1** | 80 |
| 21-0 | 15 | 1 | **Outer Hebrides**[17] 1408 3-8-8 81 ...(v) DRMcCabe 2<br>(DRLoder) *hld up in tch: rdn over 2f out: wknd over 1f out* **50/1** | 69 |
| 10-0 | 16 | 4 | **Tranquil Sky**[17] 1408 3-8-13 86 ... WRyan 5<br>(NACallaghan) *hld up: nvr trbld ldrs* **66/1** | 65 |
| 30-0 | 17 | 12 | **Magical Mimi**[17] 1418 3-7-10 76 ... LeanneKershaw(7) 13<br>(JeddO'Keeffe) *s.i.s: hdwy 6f out: wknd over 2f out* **50/1** | 27 |
| 610- | 18 | 8 | **Tafaahum (USA)**[195] 5674 3-9-1 88 ... WSupple 20<br>(MJohnston) *mid-div: wknd 1/2-way* **50/1** | 21 |
| 613- | 19 | shd | **Mountcharge (IRE)**[152] 6115 3-8-7 80 ... JQuinn 9<br>(CNAllen) *chsd ldrs over 5f: eased* **33/1** | 12 |
| 22-0 | U | | **Mister Saif (USA)**[17] 1408 3-8-13 86 ... KDarley 14<br>(RHannon) *uns rdr leaving stalls* **33/1** | — |

1m 37.52s (-1.88) **Going Correction** -0.025s/f (Good) **20** Ran SP% **128.0**
Speed ratings: **108,107,106,103,103 102,102,102,101,99 99,98,97,97,96 92,80,72,72,**—CSF £31.63 CT £733.00 TOTE £6.80: £2.10, £1.60, £4.50, £6.50; EX 32.60 Place 6 £218.58, Place 5 £72.26..
**Owner** Maktoum Al Maktoum **Bred** Gainsborough Stud Management Ltd **Trained** Middleham Moor, N Yorks
**FOCUS**
As in the previous race, they elected to race up the centre, but on this occasion those drawn high appeared to have an advantage. The time was fair for the grade and it should throw up a fair few winners.
**NOTEBOOK**
**Master Marvel(IRE)** showed plenty of resolution to get his head back in front and looks a most progressive individual. He may be suited by a bit further in time.
**Thyolo(IRE)** turned in a sound effort on this return to action and was only just worried out of it. There will be other days for him.
**Jedburgh** stayed this trip well enough, but he has plenty of pace and would not be inconvenienced by a return to seven.
**Spin King(IRE)** showed a bit more here, but he has yet to convince he really stays this far.
**State Dilemma(IRE)** turned in a sound effort on this return to action and should strip sharper for the outing.
**Granston(IRE)** was far from disgraced in this better race and still looks to be on the upgrade.
**Secretary General(IRE)** was doing his best work late on and can be expected to leave this behind in due course.
**Anuvasteel** had plenty to do from a slow start and is capable of better.
**Overdrawn(IRE)** missed the break worst of all and did plenty of running going into the Dip, only to run out of steam up the hill. A return to seven furlongs could prove to be the answer to him.
**Tafaahum(USA)** *Official explanation: jockey said colt had made a noise*
**Mountcharge(IRE)** *Official explanation: jockey said gelding lost its action*
T/Jkpt: £18,805.40 to a £1 stake. Pool: £291,351.81. 11.00 winning tickets. T/Plt: £284.10 to a £1 stake. Pool: £107,842.45. 277.05 winning tickets. T/Qpdt: £49.00 to a £1 stake. Pool: £6,732.05. 101.60 winning tickets. CR

# SALISBURY (R-H)
Sunday, May 2

**OFFICIAL GOING: Soft**

## 1796 BUTLER & CO. EQUINE TAX PLANNING MAIDEN STKS — 6f
2:30 (2:34) (D) 3-Y-O+ — £5,843 (£1,798; £899; £449) Stalls Centre

| Form | | | | RPR |
|---|---|---|---|---|
| | 1 | | **Dafore** 3-8-12 ... RLMoore 17<br>(RHannon) *mid-div: swtchd rt and hdwy over 1f out: str run ins last to ld cl home* **12/1** | 83 |
| 4-5 | 2 | nk | **Alderney Race (USA)**[29] 1243 3-8-12 ... TQuinn 4<br>(RCharlton) *trckd ldrs: rdn over 2f out: led jst ins fnl f: kpt on: hdd and no ex cl home* **2/1**[1] | 82 |
| 00-4 | 3 | 1 ¼ | **Farewell Gift**[17] 1413 3-8-12 87 ... PDobbs 15<br>(RHannon) *prom: rdn and swtchd lft to rail over 1f out: n.m.r and swtchd rt jst ins last: r.o ins last: nt rch ldrs* **3/1**[2] | 78 |
| 00 | 4 | 1 | **Mr Hullabalou (IRE)**[25] 1293 3-8-12 ... MHenry 8<br>(RIngram) *sn trcking ldrs: rdn 2f out: styd on fnl f but nt pce of ldrs ins last* **66/1** | 75 |
| /4-5 | 5 | 2 ½ | **Isaz**[25] 1295 4-9-8 74 ... DaneO'Neill 11<br>(HCandy) *sn led: rdn 2f out: hdd jst ins last: wknd nr fin* **9/2**[3] | 68 |
| 03/0 | 6 | 2 ½ | **El Chaparral (IRE)**[20] 1352 4-9-8 74 ... MTebbutt 9<br>(DKIvory) *w ldrs: pushed along 2f out: wknd ins fnl f* **16/1** | 60 |
| 00- | 7 | ½ | **Pleasure Seeker**[199] 5590 3-8-7 ... ADaly 3<br>(MDIUsher) *s.i.s: bhd: hdwy over 1f out: r.o wl fnl f but nt rch ldrs* **50/1** | 54 |
| 054- | 8 | ½ | **Rockley Bay (IRE)**[166] 6018 3-8-12 ... DSweeney 19<br>(PJMakin) *chsd ldrs: ridden and swtchd lft over 1f out: wknd fnl f* **25/1** | 57 |
| 0 | 9 | 1 ¼ | **Generous Spirit (IRE)**[25] 1295 3-8-12 ... PaulEddery 14<br>(JAOsborne) *pressed ldrs: rdn over 1f out: sn wknd* **16/1** | 54 |
| 0 | 10 | 1 ¼ | **Dulcimer**[16] 1441 3-8-2 ... RThomas(5) 2<br>(GBBalding) *bhd: hdwy 1/2-way: styng on whn nt clr run appr fnl f: n.d after* **50/1** | 45 |

11 *2* **Batchworth Beau** 3-8-12 ........ SCarson 1 44
(EAWheeler) *s.i.s: bhd: pushed along 1/2-way: sme hdwy fnl f but nvr a danger* **50/1**

0-4 12 *1/2* **Bold Trump**[89] 660 3-8-9 ........ SHitchcott(3) 5 42
(Jean-ReneAuvray) *in tch: rdn 1/2-way: one pce whn n.m.r over 1f out and sn wknd* **20/1**

40 13 *3/4* **Cedric Coverwell**[20] 1352 4-9-8 ........ CCatlin 10 40
(DKIvory) *pressed ldrs: rdn 1/2-way: wknd fnl 2f* **66/1**

000- 14 *nk* **Miss Tilly**[240] 4705 3-8-7 ........ FNorton 12 34
(GBBalding) *nvr bttr than mid-div: rn green and wknd fnl 2f* **66/1**

15 *1* **Tipsy Lady** 3-8-7 ........ NPollard 16 31
(DRCElsworth) *v.s.a: mod hdwy 1/2-way: sn bhd* **10/1**

16 *10* **Strides Of Fire (IRE)** 3-8-12 ........ RHavlin 6 6
(JHMGosden) *s.i.s: a in rr* **9/1**

17 *2 1/2* **Fair Options** 3-8-12 ........ MFenton 13 —
(HJCyzer) *slowly away: wnt rt to stands rails sn after s: a bhd* **25/1**

1m 18.4s (3.46) **Going Correction** +0.575s/f (Yiel)
**WFA** 3 from 4yo 10lb **17** Ran SP% **137.9**
Speed ratings: **99,98,96,95,92 88,88,87,85,84 81,80,79,79,78 64,61**CSF £38.41 TOTE £20.90: £4.40, £1.50, £2.00; EX 41.10.
**Owner** Fieldspring Racing **Bred** C N Hart **Trained** East Everleigh, Wilts

**FOCUS**
Only an ordinary maiden.

**NOTEBOOK**
**Dafore**, a 260,000gns yearling, won what was only a modest maiden on this debut, but he is a well-bred individual who is sure to have more to offer. He may be difficult to place however, as it is unlikely he is up to Pattern company and may struggle in handicaps as he had a 87-rated performer back in third.
**Alderney Race(USA)** is now qualified to compete in handicaps, but is another who may not get the most generous of marks.
**Farewell Gift** did nothing wrong, but has become disappointing. He has had plenty of chances.
**Mr Hullabalou(IRE)** needed this for his handicap mark and was finishing with purpose.
**Isaz**, like the third placed horse, has had plenty of chances and did nothing for being ridden prominently.
**Strides Of Fire(IRE)** is evidently one of his stables lesser lights, but it would be surprising if he is not capable of a little better than this.

## 1797 SHARP MINDS BETFAIR RATED STKS (H'CAP) 6f
**3:00** (3:02) (B) (0-100,91) 3-Y-O **£12,238** (£4,642; £2,321; £1,055) **Stalls** Centre

Form RPR

021- 1 **Spliff**[197] 5630 3-8-13 **87** ........ DaneO'Neill 11 95
(HCandy) *hld up in rr: gd hdwy fr 2f out: str run to ld last half f: pushed out: readily* **4/1**[1]

02-4 2 *1 1/4* **Star Pupil**[19] 1386 3-8-6 **80** ........ MartinDwyer 7 84
(AMBalding) *in tch: pushed along 1/2-way: hdwy fr 2f out to ld jst ins last: hdd and outpcd last half f* **4/1**[1]

1-31 3 *3* **Taruskin (IRE)**[7] 1641 3-8-8 **87** 3ex ........ DFox(5) 10 82
(NACallaghan) *bhd: pushed along 1/2-way: hdwy over 2f out: str chal 1f out: one pce ins last* **4/1**[1]

100- 4 *hd* **Enford Princess**[219] 5185 3-9-2 **90** ........ RLMoore 9 84
(RHannon) *bhd and outpcd: rdn: swtchd rt and hdwy appr fnl f: fin wl but nt trble ldrs* **20/1**

601- 5 *2 1/2* **Enchantment**[191] 5725 3-8-7 **81** ........ CCatlin 8 68
(JMBradley) *w ldrs: rdn 2f out: stl ev ch 1f out: wknd ins last* **16/1**

30-0 6 *nk* **Bathwick Bill (USA)**[22] 1333 3-8-9 **83** ........ AMcCarthy 1 69
(BRMillman) *w ldrs: led over 3f out: hdd jst ins last and sn wknd* **16/1**

523- 7 *1* **King's Caprice**[214] 5311 3-9-0 **88** ........ SCarson 4 71
(GBBalding) *w ldrs: rdn over 2f out: wknd appr fnl f* **13/2**[2]

33-0 8 *nk* **Compton's Eleven**[19] 1388 3-8-12 **89** ........ SHitchcott(3) 2 71
(MRChannon) *mid-div: rdn to chse ldrs 3f out: edgd lft u.p 2f out: wknd over 1f out* **9/1**[3]

402- 9 *3/4* **Oro Verde**[144] 6159 3-9-3 **91** ........ PDobbs 6 71
(RHannon) *t.k.h: chsd ldrs 4f* **20/1**

20-0 10 *13* **Mac The Knife (IRE)**[19] 1388 3-8-9 **83** ........ RSmith 5 24
(RHannon) *a outpcd* **25/1**

00-0 11 *5* **Flip Flop And Fly (IRE)**[16] 1437 3-8-11 **85** ........ (b[1]) MFenton 3 11
(SKirk) *sn led:hdd over 3f out: wkng whn n.m.r on rails over 2f out* **16/1**

1m 17.78s (2.84) **Going Correction** +0.575s/f (Yiel) **11** Ran SP% **114.4**
Speed ratings: **104,102,98,98,94 94,93,92,91,74 67**CSF £17.70 CT £67.05 TOTE £4.60: £2.00, £1.70, £1.40; EX 15.80.
**Owner** H R Mould **Bred** R T And Mrs Watson **Trained** Wantage, Oxon
■ Stewards Enquiry : A McCarthy two-day ban: used whip with excessive frequency and without giving gelding time to respond (May 13,14)

**FOCUS**
A decent handicap dominated by two progressive sorts. A particularly good effort from Spliff, who looks sure to go on to bigger things.

**NOTEBOOK**
**Spliff ◆**, who showed plenty as a juvenile, winning on his final outing, took his time to get going on this seasonal debut, but once hitting top stride he came home strongly and ended up winning with a bit to spare. There should be plenty more to come from this colt.
**Star Pupil ◆**, whose stable are not quite in top-form at present, beat the remainder well enough, but just found the winner too pacey. He should have little trouble landing a race.
**Taruskin(IRE)** has been in good form and came into this on the back of a win last Sunday. He was in with every chance at the furlong pole, but could not muster the pace.
**Enford Princess** was making her three-year-old debut and shaped with plenty of promise. With the run entitled to bring her forward it will be interesting to see how she fares next time.
**Enchantment** showed herself to be all speed as a juvenile, and shaped well given the trip and going. Entitled to improve for this, she will be of interest when dropped back to the minimum.
**King's Caprice** is entitled to improve for this.

## 1798 CATISFIELD HINTON & STUD FILLIES' CONDITIONS STKS 5f
**3:35** (3:35) (C) 2-Y-O **£7,308** (£2,772; £1,386; £630) **Stalls** Centre

Form RPR

11 1 **Lady Filly**[16] 1449 2-8-10 ........ AQuinn(5) 2 87
(WGMTurner) *mde all: clr 2f out: unchal* **15/8**[1]

2 *4* **Azuree (IRE)** 2-8-6 ........ RLMoore 3 64
(RHannon) *bhd: swtchd rt 2f out: edgd rt and r.o to chse wnr ins fnl f: kpt on but no imp* **9/2**[3]

3 *5* **Speed Of Sound** 2-8-6 ........ MartinDwyer 7 47
(AMBalding) *s.i.s: sn in tch: pushed along 1/2-way: chsd wnr ins fnl 2f: no imp and lost 2nd ins last: wknd* **3/1**[2]

5 4 *5* **Iam Foreverblowing**[25] 1299 2-8-6 ........ LPKeniry(3) 6 32
(SCBurrough) *chsd wnr tl ins fnl 2f: wknd fnl f* **20/1**

5 *1 3/4* **Feminist (IRE)** 2-8-6 ........ CCatlin 4 23
(MRChannon) *sn chsng ldrs: rdn 1/2-way: sn wknd* **9/2**[3]

6 *13* **Spree (IRE)** 2-8-6 ........ DaneO'Neill 5 —
(RHannon) *slowly into strode: rcvrd to chse ldrs 1/2-way: sn wknd* **8/1**

63.60 secs (2.03) **Going Correction** +0.575s/f (Yiel) **6** Ran SP% **112.0**
Speed ratings: **106,99,91,83,80 60**CSF £10.63 TOTE £2.40: £2.10, £2.70; EX 13.10.
**Owner** Mrs M S Teversham **Bred** Mrs M S Teversham **Trained** Sigwells, Somerset

**FOCUS**
Probably a decent little juvenile event and an impressive display from the winner. The winning time was outstanding.

**NOTEBOOK**
**Lady Filly** completed her hat-trick in great fashion to complete the hat-trick. She clearly possesses bundles of speed and will reportedly be put away now for the Queen Mary at Royal Ascot.
**Azuree(IRE)**, who is bred to appreciate a little further, shaped as though she will improve for this, staying on well for a cosy second having been in rear and shoved along early. Six furlongs will see her in a better light.
**Speed Of Sound**, a half-sister to Speed Cop, comes from a stable who are not in great form at present and can be expected to leave this form behind in time.
**Iam Foreverblowing** will be better off once handicapped.
**Feminist(IRE)** was fancied to run much better than she did and better can be expected next time.
**Spree(IRE)** will require further to be seen to full effect.

## 1799 GODDARDS FIAT H'CAP 1m 1f 198y
**4:10** (4:10) (C) (0-100,93) 3-Y-O **£9,187** (£3,484; £1,742; £792) **Stalls** High

Form RPR

0-61 1 **Dancing Lyra**[64] 916 3-8-6 **78** ........ RLMoore 5 93
(JWHills) *in tch: styd far side and racd alone fr over 3f out: def overall advantage over 2f out: clr over 1f out: pushed out* **12/1**

-131 2 *8* **Tiger Tiger (FR)**[11] 1542 3-8-11 **83** ........ FNorton 1 84
(JamiePoulton) *hld up in rr:c stands side and hdwy over 2f out:styd on to ld that gp jst ins fnl f but no ch w wnr far side* **10/3**[2]

4221 3 *1 1/2* **Keelung (USA)**[12] 1524 3-8-13 **85** ........ MHenry 8 84
(MAJarvis) *led: c stand side and lost overall ld over 2f out but styd ahd stands side tl hdd jst ins last: one pce* **2/1**[1]

41- 4 *4* **Arkholme**[218] 5219 3-8-10 **82** ........ MFenton 4 74
(WJHaggas) *trckd ldr: c stands side and styd chsng that ldr tl over 1f out: wknd ins last* **7/1**[3]

316- 5 *2* **Torinmoor (USA)**[233] 4870 3-9-7 **93** ........ DaneO'Neill 3 82
(MrsAJPerrett) *hld up in rr: hdwy 4f out: c to stands side and wknd over 2f out* **9/1**

12 6 *shd* **Chasing The Dream (IRE)**[67] 883 3-8-2 **74** ........ MartinDwyer 10 62
(AMBalding) *bhd: hdwy to chse ldrs stands side 3f out: wknd qckly over 1f out* **7/1**[3]

61-6 7 *3 1/2* **Mr Tambourine Man (IRE)**[17] 1414 3-8-11 **83** ........ CCatlin 6 66
(PFICole) *t.k.h: c stands side and chsd ldrs tl wknd fnl 2f* **8/1**

21-0 8 *6* **Seneschal**[16] 1437 3-9-3 **92** ........ SHitchcott(3) 2 64
(MRChannon) *chsd ldrs: c stands side: wknd qckly over 2f out* **14/1**

2m 12.08s (3.76) **Going Correction** +0.575s/f (Yiel) **8** Ran SP% **116.9**
Speed ratings: **107,100,99,96,94 94,91,86**CSF £53.08 CT £116.28 TOTE £17.00: £4.30, £1.30, £1.70; EX 55.50.
**Owner** N N Browne **Bred** Shadwell Estate Company Limited **Trained** Upper Lambourn, Berks

**FOCUS**
An easy win for handicap debutant Dancing Lyra, who was the only one to stay far side. Although possibly flattered by the winning margin, he would have won regardless of where he raced.

**NOTEBOOK**
**Dancing Lyra**, who left a couple of disappointing efforts behind when getting off the mark on his most recent outing back in February, was the only runner who stayed far side and it paid dividends as he strolled home by eight lengths. Whilst flattered by the winning margin, it is hard to imagine he would not have won regardless of where he raced, and this progressive three-year-old has every chance of completing his hat-trick if the Handicapper does not overreact.
**Tiger Tiger(FR)** had been raised 11lb since bolting up in a conditions race at Epsom and is going the right way as he won the race on his side convincingly.
**Keelung(USA)** came home alone in an uncompetitive event last time and faced a stiffer task on this handicap debut. He was not disgraced and another couple of furlongs would not go amiss.
**Arkholme** ran a promising race on this seasonal debut and is entitled to come on for the outing.
**Torinmoor(USA)** faced no easy task under top weight on this first start since September and was done no favours by losing his position after being a bit tight for room.
**Chasing The Dream(IRE)** stopped quickly and may be one to leave alone until her trainer hits form.

## 1800 CITY CABS SALISBURY MAIDEN STKS 1m 4f
**4:45** (4:46) (D) 3-Y-O **£5,668** (£1,744; £872; £436) **Stalls** High

Form RPR

1 **Day Flight** 3-9-0 ........ PDobbs 8 81
(JHMGosden) *hld up in rr: hdwy fr 3f out: swtchd rt to rail and qcknd over 1f out to ld jst ins last: sn clr: easily* **7/1**

4- 2 *6* **River Gypsy**[182] 5887 3-8-11 ........ LPKeniry(3) 7 73
(DRCElsworth) *bhd: hdwy fr 3f out: rdn and styd on wl fr over 1f out: tk 2nd cl home but no ch w wnr* **8/1**

0-4 3 *nk* **Irish Blade (IRE)**[13] 1508 3-9-0 ........ DaneO'Neill 10 72
(HCandy) *led 1f: styd trcking ldr: rdn to chal and edgd lft ins 2f out and over 1f out: kpt on same pce* **9/2**[2]

4 *1/2* **Water Taxi** 3-9-0 ........ DSweeney 3 72
(RCharlton) *bhd: hdwy on outside fr 3f out: pressing ldrs whn bmpd ins fnl 2f and over 1f out: kpt on same pce* **14/1**

5 *1/2* **Light Wind** 3-8-9 ........ MartinDwyer 5 66
(MrsAJPerrett) *s.i.s: bhd: hdwy and pushed along 3f out: drvn and styd on fr over 1f out: kpt on cl home* **16/1**

2 6 *nk* **Strike**[16] 1442 3-9-0 ........ RHavlin 11 71
(JHMGosden) *led after 1f: reminder 6f out: rdn over 2f out: hdd jst ins last: kpt on same pce* **6/4**[1]

7 *1 1/4* **Massif Centrale** 3-9-0 ........ NPollard 1 69
(DRCElsworth) *slowly away: bhd: hdwy and rn green 3f out: rdn: swtchd rt and hdwy over 1f out: r.o ins last: nt rch ldrs* **6/1**[3]

3- 8 *2* **Victory Lap (GER)**[141] 6175 3-8-9 ........ CCatlin 13 61
(MRChannon) *chsd ldrs: rdn 3f out: wknd 2f out* **10/1**

0604 9 *10* **Shalati Princess**[17] 1405 3-8-9 **45** ........ RBrisland 12 47
(JCFox) *bhd: mod effrt 3f out: n.d and sn rr* **66/1**

10 *11* **Open Book** 3-8-9 ........ MFenton 6 32
(HMorrison) *t.k.h: bhd: sme hdwy on outside over 3f out: wknd over 2f out* **25/1**

0-00 11 *2 1/2* **Once Around (IRE)**[92] 644 3-8-11 ........ RMiles(3) 4 33
(TGMills) *chsd ldrs tl qwknd qckly 3f out* **40/1**

00 12 *nk* **Harry Came Home**[20] 1356 3-9-0 ........ RLMoore 2 33
(JCFox) *chsd ldrs 1m* **66/1**

2m 42.42s (6.07) **Going Correction** +0.575s/f (Yiel) **12** Ran SP% **127.0**
Speed ratings: **102,98,97,97,97 96,96,94,88,80 79,78**CSF £65.36 TOTE £10.50: £2.40, £3.00; EX 75.60.
**Owner** K Abdulla **Bred** Juddmonte Farms **Trained** Manton, Wilts

**FOCUS**
This looked a maiden packed with future middle-distance handicappers, the one possible exception being impressive winner Day Flight, who quickened nicely on this debut to win well.

**NOTEBOOK**
**Day Flight**, a stablemate of the favourite and making his debut, did it most impressively, quickening away a furlong out and coasting home. Evidently suited by the ground, being by Sadler's Wells, he looks worthy of a step up in grade.
**River Gypsy** ◆ stayed on well to get up for second and it will be disappointing if he can not win a similar race in the coming weeks. He should make up into a decent handicapper.
**Irish Blade(IRE)** ran a nice race when fourth at Windsor most recently and did nothing wrong in third. He is the type to improve for going handicapping.
**Water Taxi** made a promising debut, moving up promisingly down the outside of the field before appearing to get a little tired. He should come on for this and can pick up a maiden.
**Light Wind** fared best of the fillies in the line-up, staying on well for fifth having been slowly away. She can only improve.
**Strike** finished second in what was nothing more than an average maiden at Newbury on his most recent outing and did not look good enough on the day.
**Massif Centrale** looked in need of the experience on this racecourse debut and should fare better next time.

## 1801 102 SPIRE FM H'CAP — 1m 6f 15y
5:20 (5:21) (C) (0-90,85) 4-Y-0+ **£9,628** (£3,652; £1,826; £830) **Stalls** Far side

| Form | | | | | RPR |
|---|---|---|---|---|---|
| 226/ | 1 | | **The Last Cast**[43] 2763 5-9-0 **74** MFenton 14<br>(HMorrison) *mde all: rdn over 2f out: styd on gamely fnl f* **7/1**[3] | | 83 |
| -030 | 2 | 3/4 | **Bucks**[11] 1539 7-8-2 **69** MHoward(7) 17<br>(DKIvory) *bhd:hdwy fr 4f out:qcknd to chse ldrs over 1f out:n.m.r and travelling wl ins fnl f:nt rcvr: tk 2nd cl home* **33/1** | | 77+ |
| 1-14 | 3 | shd | **Sentry (IRE)**[6] 1661 4-9-10 **85** DaneO'Neill 15<br>(JHMGosden) *trckd ldrs: riddeen to chal ins finaal 2f: nt qckn ins fnl f: ct for 2nd cl home* **10/3**[1] | | 93 |
| 0-06 | 4 | 2 1/2 | **Invitation**[27] 1272 6-8-10 **70** RSmith 10<br>(ACharlton) *bhd: hdwy on ins whn nt clr run ins fnl 2f:swtchd lft and hdwy 1f out: nt pce to rch ldrs* **25/1** | | 75 |
| 1100 | 5 | 3/4 | **Sun Hill**[25] 1302 4-8-11 **72** DSweeney 16<br>(MBlanshard) *chsd ldrs: rdn 3f out: one pce fnl f* **25/1** | | 76 |
| 06-0 | 6 | nk | **Mostarsil (USA)**[22] 1329 6-8-10 **70** (p) RLMoore 2<br>(GLMoore) *bhd: hdwy fr 3f out: kpt on fnl f but nt rch ldrs* **25/1** | | 73 |
| 212- | 7 | 1 1/4 | **Laggan Bay (IRE)**[144] 3266 4-8-13 **77** LPKeniry(3) 9<br>(JCFox) *bhd: hdwy on rails over 2f out: kpt on but nvr gng pce to rch ldrs* **16/1** | | 79 |
| 356- | 8 | hd | **Stoop To Conquer**[176] 5949 4-8-9 **70** TQuinn 8<br>(JLDunlop) *plld hrd: chsd ldrs: rdn 3f out: wknd fnl f* **15/2** | | 71 |
| -050 | 9 | 3 | **Crown Agent (IRE)**[27] 1272 4-8-9 **70** MartinDwyer 19<br>(AMBalding) *mid-div: rdn and effrt fr 3f out: nvr gng pce to rch ldrs* **33/1** | | 67 |
| 0-64 | 10 | 1 3/4 | **San Hernando**[15] 1457 4-8-11 **72** NPollard 18<br>(DRCElsworth) *mid-div: rdn and effrt 3f out: wknd 2f out* **4/1**[2] | | 67 |
| 0-25 | 11 | 1 | **Man The Gate**[8] 1611 5-7-9 **58** LisaJones(3) 1<br>(PDCundell) *mid-div: rdn and sme hdwy 3f out: nvr rchd ldrs and wknd 2f out* **8/1** | | 52 |
| 0310 | 12 | 1 | **Turtle Valley (IRE)**[22] 1326 8-8-13 **73** PaulEddery 11<br>(SDow) *chsd wnr tl over 3f out: wknd over 2f out* **9/1** | | 66 |
| 10-0 | 13 | 1 1/2 | **Mersey Sound (IRE)**[15] 1457 6-8-7 **67** PDobbs 5<br>(SKirk) *n.d* **33/1** | | 58 |
| 140/ | 14 | nk | **Cloudy Sky (IRE)**[1675] 4674 8-9-6 **80** GBaker 3<br>(SimonEarle) *slowly away: a in rr* **66/1** | | 70 |
| 004- | 15 | 1 | **Theatre (USA)**[184] 5855 5-9-9 **83** FNorton 4<br>(JamiePoulton) *n.d* **20/1** | | 72 |
| 34-0 | 16 | 1/2 | **Stolen Hours (USA)**[11] 1539 4-8-9 **73** SHitchcott(3) 7<br>(JAkehurst) *in tch: rdn 4f out: sn wknd* **50/1** | | 61 |
| 01-4 | 17 | 3 | **Grand Wizard**[37] 1122 4-8-10 **71** MTebbutt 13<br>(WJarvis) *t.k.h: trckd ldrs tl wknd 3f out* **16/1** | | 55 |

3m 14.8s (8.80) **Going Correction** +0.575s/f (Yiel) **17 Ran SP% 128.8**
**WFA** 4 from 5yo+ 1lb
Speed ratings: **97,96,96,95,94 94,93,93,91,90 90,89,88,88,88 87,86**CSF £236.71 CT £932.73 TOTE £8.70: £2.40, £6.90, £1.60, £4.50; EX 377.00 Place 6 £23.39, Place 5 £15.16..
**Owner** D P Barrie **Bred** P A Mason **Trained** East Ilsley, Berks

**FOCUS**
A modest winning time for the grade.

**NOTEBOOK**
**The Last Cast**, a winner over hurdles back in March, was given positive ride by Michael Fenton, making all for a game success. He has the scope to stay further and he should continue to pay his way.
**Bucks** could be called an unlucky loser as he was travelling well with nowhere to go in the final furlong and could not reach the winner in time. A lesser race should be his for the taking.
**Sentry(IRE)** performed with credit under top weight, just being run out of it close home.
**Invitation** is not the quickest so having his run blocked when hitting top stride would have done him no favours.
**Sun Hill** ran respectably, but is undoubtedly better handicapped on the All-Weather.
**Mostarsil(USA)** ran on through beaten horses from the rear.
**San Hernando** never really made a show and failed to confirm the promise of his Newbury run.
**Man The Gate** looked a big danger at one point, but seemed to be found out by lack of stamina.
**Turtle Valley(IRE)** *Official explanation: jockey said gelding went lame*
T/Plt: £52.70 to a £1 stake. Pool: £36,543.95. 505.70 winning tickets. T/Qpdt: £38.60 to a £1 stake. Pool: £1,842.40. 35.30 winning tickets. ST

# COLOGNE (R-H)
Sunday, May 2

**OFFICIAL GOING: Soft**

## 1802a GERLING-PREIS (GROUP 2) — 1m 4f
4:10 (4:23) 4-Y-0+ **£28,169** (£10,563; £4,225; £2,817)

| | | | RPR |
|---|---|---|---|
| 1 | | **Olaso (GER)**[28] 1259 5-8-11 AStarke 10<br>(PVovcenko, Germany) *raced in 4th on inside, quickened to lead over 2f out, soon clear, ran on strongly* 1 | 115 |
| 2 | 3 1/2 | **Well Made (GER)**[28] 1259 7-8-11 WMongil 3<br>(HBlume, Germany) *raced in 5th, headway to go 2nd over 1 1/2f out, kept on but no chance with winner* 3 | 110 |
| 3 | 2 1/2 | **Senex (GER)**[217] 5263 4-8-11 ADeVries 5<br>(HBlume, Germany) *raced in 6th, headway over 2f out, went 3rd inside final f, kept on* | 107 |
| 4 | 1 3/4 | **Storm Trooper (GER)**[238] 4760 4-8-11 ASuborics 8<br>(ASchutz, Germany) *raced in 7th, headway on outside to take 3rd over 1f out, lost 3rd and one pace inside final f* 2 | 105 |
| 5 | 7 | **Foreign Affairs**[17] 1435 6-8-11 FJohansson 2<br>(SirMarkPrescott) *raced in 2nd, still 2nd over 1 1/2f out, weakened* | 96 |
| 6 | 5 | **Levirat (GER)**[28] 1259 5-8-11 AHelfenbein 1<br>(MarioHofer, Germany) *raced in 3rd on inside, weakened over 2f out* | 90 |
| 7 | 1 1/4 | **Palmridge (GER)**[28] 1259 4-8-11 LHammer-Hansen 7<br>(DKRichardson, Germany) *set strong pace til headed over 2f out, weakened quickly* | 88 |
| L | | **King Of Boxmeer (GER)**[28] 1259 5-8-11 IFerguson 6<br>(WBaltromei, Germany) *refused to race* | — |

2m 30.89s **8 Ran SP% 126.5**
Speed ratings: .
**Owner** Stall Silbersee **Bred** M Beining **Trained** Germany

**NOTEBOOK**
**Foreign Affairs** is not as good as he used to be and struggles in this sort of grade. Having again tried to make every post a winning one, the tactic was foiled a furlong and a half from home. Connections reported that he will be given a break now after a busy start to the season.

# 1741 LONGCHAMP (R-H)
Sunday, May 2

**OFFICIAL GOING: Very soft**

## 1803a PRIX VANTEAUX (GROUP 3) (FILLIES) — 1m 1f 55y
2:20 (2:21) 3-Y-0 **£25,704** (£10,282; £7,711; £5,141)

| | | | RPR |
|---|---|---|---|
| 1 | | **Latice (IRE)**[196] 5661 3-9-0 CSoumillon 1<br>(J-MBeguinge, France) *always close up, 3rd straight, led approaching final f, shaken up, ran on well* 1 | 111 |
| 2 | 1 | **Asti (IRE)**[27] 3-9-0 DBoeuf 3<br>(ELellouche, France) *held up in 5th to straight, headway to go close second 1f out, ran on but could make no impression on winner* 3 | 109 |
| 3 | 1 1/2 | **Green Swallow (FR)**[35] 1162 3-9-0 TGillet 2<br>(PDemercastel, France) *dwelt, last to straight, stayed on up outside final 1 1/2f, nearest at finish* | 106 |
| 4 | 1 1/2 | **Polyfirst (FR)**[35] 1162 3-9-0 OPeslier 5<br>(MmeCHead-Maarek, France) *tracked leader, led 3f out to approaching final f, one pace* 2 | 103 |
| 5 | 2 | **Bradamante**[35] 1162 3-9-0 C-PLemaire 4<br>(RGibson, France) *led over 1f, settled a close 3rd, 4th straight, never able to challenge* | 99 |
| 6 | 8 | **Trinity Joy**[23] 1320 3-9-0 TJarnet 6<br>(RGibson, France) *led 7f out to 3f out, 2nd straight, weakened over 1f out, eased inside final f* | 83 |

2m 1.30s **Going Correction** +0.825s/f (Soft) **6 Ran SP% 122.4**
Speed ratings: **108,107,105,104,102 95.**
**Owner** E Ciampi **Bred** Petra Bloodstock Agency Ltd **Trained** France

**NOTEBOOK**
**Latice(IRE)** confirmed that she is out of the top draw with this performance. In a falsely run race she was fourth early on and always relaxed and going easily. She took control of this Classic trial just before the furlong marker and was not extended when passing the post. Now unbeaten in three races, her main target is the Prix de Diane-Hermes. but she could take in the Prix Saint-Alary beforehand.
**Asti(IRE)** put up a fine effort. Fifth early on she made a forward move up the centre of the track from one and a half out but could never get to the winner. She looks sure to make further progress and a similar race looks in her grasp later in the year.
**Green Swallow(FR)** was slowly into her stride and last for the early part of this race. She was outpaced when things were quickened up early in the straight and was running on at the finish. This was a much better effort from this group winner.

## 1804a PRIX GANAY (GROUP 1) — 1m 2f 110y
3:05 (3:05) 4-Y-0+ **£80,479** (£32,197; £16,099; £8,042)

| | | | RPR |
|---|---|---|---|
| 1 | | **Execute (FR)**[28] 1261 7-9-2 TGillet 2<br>(JEHammond, France) *raced in 5th to straight, headway on rail over 1f out, led 150yds out, ran on well* **219/10** | 117 |
| 2 | 1 1/2 | **Vespone (IRE)**[57] 978 4-9-2 C-PLemaire 4<br>(SaeedBinSuroor) *led to 150 yards out, ran on same pace* **42/10**[2] | 114 |
| 3 | 1/2 | **Fair Mix (IRE)**[36] 1144 6-9-2 OPeslier 7<br>(MRolland, France) *raced in 4th to straight, headway 2f out, reached 3rd inside final f, kept on same pace* **46/10**[3] | 113 |
| 4 | 1/2 | **Vallee Enchantee (IRE)**[140] 6185 4-8-13 DBoeuf 5<br>(ELellouche, France) *held up, 7th straight, headway well over 1f out, looking for gap from distance to 100yds out, ran on* **56/10** | 109+ |
| 5 | 1/2 | **Polish Summer**[36] 1144 7-9-2 GaryStevens 8<br>(AFabre, France) *raced in 6th to straight, headway 2f out, kept on same pace from over 1f out* **11/10**[1] | 111 |
| 6 | nk | **Touch Of Land (FR)**[17] 1435 4-9-2 SPasquier 1<br>(H-APantall, France) *raced in 3rd to straight, went 2nd 1 1/2f out, weakened final f* **48/1** | 111 |
| 7 | 3 | **Vangelis (USA)**[28] 1261 5-9-2 CSoumillon 3<br>(ADeRoyer-Dupre, France) *held up in rear, last straight, ridden 1 1/2f out, no response* **66/10** | 106 |
| 8 | 3/4 | **Chancellor (IRE)**[8] 1622 6-9-2 TJarnet 6<br>(JLDunlop) *tracked leader, 2nd straight, soon ridden, weakened well over 1f out* **50/1** | 105 |

2m 14.6s **Going Correction** +0.375s/f (Good) **8 Ran SP% 121.4**
Speed ratings: **117,115,115,115,114 114,112,111.**
**Owner** Ecurie Chalhoub **Bred** Ecurie Kura **Trained** France

**NOTEBOOK**
**Execute(FR)** quickened impressively when a gap arrived halfway up the straight. The horse loved the cut in the ground and had the race won by the furlong marker. He is a game performer and is winning for the first time in over two years. There are no immediate plans, but no doubt his connections will be looking for soft ground.
**Vespone(IRE)** was asked to make all the running but couldn't quicken like the winner in the latter stages. He stayed on well and this effort augurs well for the future. The very soft ground certainly didn't suit him and he could have a crack at the Prix d'Isaphan.
**Fair Mix(IRE)** was given every possible chance. Fourth early on, he made a forward move one and a half out, but was rather one paced as the race came to a close. His trainer thought that racing him over 12 furlongs might have taken off an edge.

**Polish Summer** seemed to hold every chance and was disappointing.
**Chancellor(IRE)** was always well up behind the leader and going well until the straight. He found nothing under pressure and gradually dropped out of contention and this performance was certainly below par.

## 1306 SAN SIRO (R-H)
### Sunday, May 2

**OFFICIAL GOING: Soft**

**1805a** **PREMIO BAGGIO (LISTED) (FILLIES)** **1m 2f**
**4:20** (4:25) 3-Y-O **£24,648** (£10,845; £5,915; £2,958)

RPR
1 **Quilanga (GER)** 3-8-9 ... EBotti 6 102
(AWohler, Germany)
2 *4* **Entusiasmo (ITY)**[274] 3820 3-8-9 ... PConvertino 10 95
(JHeloury, Italy)
3 *3/4* **Oligarchica (GER)** 3-8-9 ... MEsposito 8 94
(RRohne, Germany)
4 *3* **Japigia (IRE)**[175] 5965 3-8-9 ... APolli 1 88
(MGQuinlan) *always in touch racing in 3rd or 4th, effort entering straight, kept on at one pace to line*
5 *3/4* **Martha Stewart (IRE)**[203] 5531 3-8-9 ... IRossi 9 87
(ABotti, Italy)
6 *3* **Salse Bravo** 3-8-9 ... DVargiu 4 82
(LBrogi, Italy)
7 *3 1/2* **Youthopia (IRE)** 3-8-9 ... DPorcu 2 76
(MGuarnieri, Italy)
8 *16* **Laona** 3-8-9 ... EPedroza 5 48
(AWohler, Germany)
9 *7* **Figuresti (IRE)** 3-8-9 ... MMonteriso 3 36
(EBorromeo, Italy)
10 *9* **Donna Francesca**[232] 4903 3-8-9 ... GBietolini 7 20
(LauraGrizzetti, Italy)

2m 8.60s **10** Ran
Speed ratings: .
**Owner** Stiftung Gestut Fahrhof **Bred** Stiftung Gestut Fahrhof **Trained** Germany

**NOTEBOOK**
**Japigia(IRE)** was unable to follow up her win last time but stayed on in a manner that suggests she may get farther. However, she will have to improve significantly to have any chance in the Oaks d'Italia..

## 1123 DONCASTER (L-H)
### Monday, May 3

**OFFICIAL GOING: Good to soft (soft in places)**

**1819** **NATIONAL FESTIVAL CIRCUS IS HERE TODAY NOVICE AUCTION STKS** **5f**
**2:00** (2:05) (E) 2-Y-O **£3,435** (£1,057; £528; £264) **Stalls** High

Form RPR
2 1 **Mystical Land (IRE)**[23] 1324 2-8-9 ... LDettori 6 90+
(JHMGosden) *trckd ldrs: effrt over 1f out: led ent fnl f: drvn out* **2/7**[1]
1 2 *3/4* **Bigalos Bandit**[21] 1359 2-9-3 ... KDarley 1 95
(JJQuinn) *led tl rdn and hdd ent fnl f: no ex* **9/1**[3]
3 *1 3/4* **Space Shuttle** 2-8-4 ... DAllan[(3)] 4 78+
(TDEasterby) *slowly away: sn rr of main gp: rdn 1/2-way: sme hdwy over 1f out: kpt on same pce ins last* **25/1**
01 4 *1 1/2* **Apologies**[23] 1324 2-8-12 ... GGibbons 2 77
(BAMcmahon) *cl up: rdn 2f out: no ex* **11/2**[2]
5 *dist* **Northern Revoque (IRE)** 2-8-2 ... DaleGibson 3 —
(ABerry) *slowly away: bhd: lost tch after 2f: t.o* **100/1**

61.47 secs (0.05) **Going Correction** +0.15s/f (Good) **5** Ran SP% **108.0**
Speed ratings: **105,103,101,98,**—CSF £3.43 TOTE £1.40: £1.10, £2.20; EX 2.90.
**Owner** Sheikh Mohammed **Bred** T A Scothern **Trained** Manton, Wilts

**FOCUS**
What looked a routine novice auction event beforehand, but a very impressive winning time for the grade and the front three especially look nice prospects.

**NOTEBOOK**
**Mystical Land(IRE)** ◆, all the better for his Haydock debut, appreciated the better ground and quickened up nicely when asked. He has very much a speed-oriented pedigree and there should be more to come.
**Bigalos Bandit** showed good early pace and never stopped trying when the favourite went past. There was no disgrace in this defeat given that he was trying to give 8lb to a potentially decent sort and he will not always meet such a rival.
**Space Shuttle** ◆, a half-brother to Polar Haze out of a half-sister to Lago Di Varano, was the real eyecatcher. After missing the break and giving away a good few lengths, he gradually got the hang of things and was staying on nicely in the closing stages. This was a smart debut against rivals that had already shown ability and he should not be difficult to place.
**Apologies**, who had beaten the winner at Haydock last time when he had the advantage of a previous outing, had every chance but could not confirm the form under his penalty and does not look as progressive as a couple of these.
**Northern Revoque(IRE)**, a half-sister to Katies Crown, was badly behaved beforehand and then missed the break. She was quickly tailed off and looked clueless. *Official explanation: jockey said saddle slipped*

**1820** **"UNICYCLIST" MAIDEN STKS** **7f**
**2:30** (2:33) (D) 3-Y-O+ **£6,256** (£1,925; £962; £481) **Stalls** High

Form RPR
5-4 1 **Dr Thong**[16] 1461 3-8-12 ... KDarley 14 80
(PFICole) *mde all: shkn up over 1f out: drvn out* **6/4**[1]
0 2 *1 1/4* **Star Magnitude (USA)**[21] 1371 3-8-12 ... LDettori 19 77
(JHMGosden) *sn trcking ldrs: effrt 2f out: nt qckn ins last* **7/1**[3]
0-50 3 *1 1/4* **Panshir (FR)**[25] 1310 3-8-12 73 ... RLMoore 20 74
(CFWall) *hld up in rr: hdwy over 2f out: styd on same pce fnl f* **11/2**[2]
4 *2 1/2* **Literatim** 4-9-7 ... NMackay[(3)] 5 68
(LMCumani) *mid-div: effrt over 2f out: kpt on same pce* **20/1**
6635 5 *5* **Amanda's Lad (IRE)**[17] 1453 4-9-10 65 ... LVickers 17 55
(MCChapman) *chsd ldrs: outpcd fnl 2f* **33/1**
6 *2 1/2* **Irusan (IRE)** 4-9-3 ... LeanneKershaw[(7)] 1 49
(JeddO'Keeffe) *in tch on outer: wknd over 1f out* **66/1**
0-4 7 *3/4* **Puri**[16] 1476 5-9-10 ... MFenton 6 47
(JGGiven) *trckd ldrs: wknd over 1f out* **40/1**
0 8 *1 1/2* **Gustavo**[20] 1386 3-8-12 ... RHills 16 43
(BWHills) *hld up and bhd: swtchd lft over 1f out: n.d* **10/1**
5 9 *shd* **Nod's Star**[13] 1528 3-8-7 ... DaleGibson 15 38
(MissJACamacho) *hld up and bhd: kpt on fnl 2f: n.d* **50/1**
2-0 10 *nk* **Gasparini (IRE)**[17] 1453 3-8-12 ... DSweeney 18 42
(TDEasterby) *trckd ldrs: fdd fnl 2f* **33/1**
4 11 *nk* **Alcaidesa**[13] 1528 3-8-12 ... DRMcCabe 9 41
(MissJACamacho) *s.s: hmpd over 5f out: swtchd lft over 1 out: n.d* **12/1**
P 12 *1* **Laura Lea**[76] 811 4-9-10 ... DeanMcKeown 11 39
(RonaldThompson) *chsd ldrs: lost pl over 2f out* **100/1**
U0 13 *2 1/2* **Vibe**[13] 1528 3-8-12 ... KDalgleish 12 33
(MJohnston) *w wnr: rdn and hung lft 1/2-way: lost pl over 1f out* **16/1**
0 14 *1/2* **Wedowannagiveuthat (IRE)**[18] 1419 3-8-4 ... THamilton[(3)] 13 26
(TDEasterby) *dwlt: a rr* **50/1**
15 *shd* **Pointed (IRE)** 3-8-4 ... DAllan[(3)] 7 26
(TDEasterby) *s.i.s: hmpd 1f out: n.d* **33/1**
0- 16 *1 1/2* **Mac's Elan**[259] 4250 4-9-10 ... JMcAuley 3 27
(ABCoogan) *in tch on outer: lost pl 1/2-way* **66/1**
0- 17 *3* **Mad Maurice**[259] 4248 3-8-12 ... SWKelly 8 20
(BJCurley) *a rr* **14/1**
50-0 18 *2 1/2* **Tata Naka**[65] 914 4-9-5 46 ... TGMcLaughlin 10 9
(MrsCADunnett) *w ldrs: wknd and eased 2f out* **50/1**
50 19 *8* **Lucky Piscean**[11] 1557 3-8-12 ... GGibbons 2 —
(CWFairhurst) *unruly s: mid-div: lost pl 1/2-way* **50/1**
050- 20 *7* **Ash Laddie (IRE)**[256] 4315 4-9-10 63 ... MHenry 4 —
(EJAlston) *chsd ldrs to 1/2-way: eased 2f out* **50/1**

1m 28.47s (0.66) **Going Correction** +0.15s/f (Good) **20** Ran SP% **127.0**
**WFA** 3 from 4yo+ 12lb
Speed ratings: **102,100,99,96,90 87,86,85,85,84 84,83,80,79,79 77,74,71,62,54**CSF £10.45 TOTE £2.60: £1.30, £2.30, £3.30; EX 12.20.
**Owner** Frank Stella **Bred** Mascalls Stud **Trained** Whatcombe, Oxon
■ Stewards Enquiry : R L Moore two-day ban (reduced from three on appeal): careless riding (May 14-15)

**FOCUS**
A fair maiden run at a sound pace and the whole field migrated over to the stands' side. Those drawn high enjoyed an advantage.

**NOTEBOOK**
**Dr Thong** probably only had to reproduce his Newbury effort to collect and the furlong shorter trip looked to be in his favour. Bagging pole position against the stands' rail early, he dominated from that point and found plenty to hold off his rivals when asked. He should continue to progress and handicaps are now an option for him.
**Star Magnitude(USA)** has come on a good deal from his Yarmouth debut and chased the winner all the way to the line. He needs one more run for a handicap mark and that is probably where his future lies.
**Panshir(FR)**, patiently ridden, settled much better than he did at Bath, but had to rather weave his way through to get a run and under the circumstances he did well so finish so close. He is going to be vulnerable to an improver in races like this and may be better off in handicap company.
**Literatim** ◆, a half-brother to Shamanic, ran a promising belated debut especially from his low draw and though comfortably held by the front three, still came right away from the others. Better is likely to be seen from him in time.
**Amanda's Lad(IRE)**, a long-standing maiden, did not achieve much in leading home the second group ahead of a bunch of backward and modest rivals.
**Irusan(IRE)** hinted at some ability on this belated racecourse debut, especially as he was probably starting from the worst draw.
**Mad Maurice** *Official explanation: jockey said gelding had suffered interference in running*
**Ash Laddie(IRE)** *Official explanation: jockey said gelding hung left and was never moving well*

**1821** **WILLIAM HILL 25 YEAR SERVICE H'CAP** **1m 2f 60y**
**3:05** (3:10) (C) (0-90,90) 3-Y-O+ **£10,270** (£3,160; £1,580; £790) **Stalls** Low

Form RPR
30-6 1 **Telemachus**[9] 1604 4-9-10 86 ... MFenton 6 96
(JGGiven) *in tch: effrt over 2f out: rdn to ld ent fnl f: styd on* **13/2**[2]
-000 2 *1* **Briareus**[16] 1460 4-9-2 78 ... KDarley 4 86
(AMBalding) *trckd ldrs: led over 2f out: rdn and hdd ent fnl f: styd on* **11/1**
20-0 3 *1* **Jabaar (USA)**[38] 1114 6-9-11 87 ... AlexGreaves 18 94
(DNicholls) *midfield: nt clr run briefly over 2f out: styd on u.p fnl 2f: nvr able to chal* **33/1**
63-1 4 *nk* **Brief Goodbye**[25] 1315 4-9-0 76 ... KDalgleish 11 82
(JohnBerry) *in tch: effrt 2f out: sn rdn: hung lft ins fnl f: styd on* **11/1**
0-00 5 *6* **Compton Dragon (USA)**[38] 1114 5-9-1 77 ... ANicholls 3 73
(DNicholls) *slowly away: rr div: hdwy over 3f out: styd on u.p fnl 2f: nvr nrr* **16/1**
150- 6 *hd* **Glimmer Of Light (IRE)**[240] 4719 4-9-2 78 ... RLMoore 5 74
(PWHarris) *midfield: effrt and swtchd rt over 3f out: kpt on same pce fnl 2f* **20/1**
0-05 7 *1/2* **Atlantic Quest (USA)**[2] 1772 5-9-1 82 ... PMulrennan[(5)] 2 77
(GAHarker) *hld up: hdwy and in tch over 2f out: no further prog* **7/1**[3]
53-0 8 *nk* **Dunaskin (IRE)**[38] 1114 4-9-9 85 ... FNorton 16 79
(DEddy) *w ldr: led wl over 3f out: hdd over 2 out: fdd* **16/1**
0-00 9 *4* **Broadway Score (USA)**[9] 1604 6-9-7 83 ... TGMcLaughlin 8 70
(MWEasterby) *towards rr: hdwy into midfield 2f out: no further prog* **25/1**
100- 10 *1/2* **Madamoiselle Jones**[201] 5577 4-8-4 66 ... DKinsella 17 53
(HSHowe) *prom: rdn over 2f out: wknd over 1 out* **33/1**
341- 11 *2* **Best Flight**[226] 5084 4-8-10 72 ... RHills 7 55
(BWHills) *trckd ldrs: rdn over 2f out: wknd over 1 out* **7/2**[1]
10-0 12 *6* **Les Arcs (USA)**[27] 1284 4-9-1 80 ... JFMcDonald[(3)] 12 53
(RCGuest) *sn towards rr: nt clr run over 3f out: n.d* **28/1**
310- 13 *nk* **Stallone**[191] 5463 7-8-8 73 ... THamilton[(3)] 10 45
(NWilson) *sn towards rr: n.d* **33/1**
20-0 14 *1 1/2* **Prairie Wolf**[12] 1540 8-9-9 85 ... NPollard 14 55
(MLWBell) *midfield: drvn along 3f out: no hdwy* **33/1**
06-0 15 *4* **High Action (USA)**[19] 1401 4-10-0 90 ... SWKelly 20 53
(IanWilliams) *midfield: rdn 3f out: sn btn* **40/1**
/03- 16 *1* **Derwent (USA)**[316] 2601 5-9-8 84 ... LDettori 15 45
(JDBethell) *sn towards rr: n.d* **14/1**
50-0 17 *1 1/4* **Island Light (USA)**[19] 1401 4-9-6 85 ... DAllan[(3)] 1 44
(MrsMReveley) *s.s: a bhd* **25/1**
05-0 18 *4* **Iberus (GER)**[16] 1456 6-9-4 80 ... (b[1]) GGibbons 13 32
(SGollings) *mde most tl hdd wl over 3f out: wknd qckly* **33/1**
41- 19 *8* **Bishopric**[343] 1862 4-9-12 88 ... DSweeney 19 27
(HCandy) *midfield tl wknd 3f out* **7/1**[3]

0 **20** *15* **Arawan (IRE)**[9] 1604 4-9-8 **84** DaleGibson 9 —
(MWEasterby) *midfield to 1/2-way: sn bhd* **50/1**

2m 12.58s (0.82) **Going Correction** +0.40s/f (Good) **20** Ran SP% **130.7**
Speed ratings: **112,111,110,110,105 105,104,104,101,100 99,94,94,93,89 89,88,84,78,66**CSF £69.69 CT £2264.58 TOTE £8.60: £1.80, £4.00, £7.80, £2.60; EX 115.90.
**Owner** The Travellers **Bred** Cheveley Park Stud Ltd **Trained** Willoughton, Lincs

**FOCUS**
A competitive handicap run at a decent pace and a good winning time for the grade.

**NOTEBOOK**
**Telemachus**, all the better for his reappearance effort at Haydock when getting tired in the deep ground, was always travelling well just behind the leaders and when a gap eventually appeared he quickened up nicely to score. This is his ideal trip and the gelding operation over the winter seems to have had the desired effect.
**Briareus** stays further than this so was rightly ridden prominently before making a break for home passing the two-furlong pole, but the winner was tailgating him and quickened up the better from the point. This was still a decent effort.
**Jabaar(USA)** ran much better back over a more suitable trip and is dropping to a reasonable mark. It will be a surprise if his yard do not find an opportunity for him before too long.
**Brief Goodbye**, up 4lb for his Musselburgh win, was caught in traffic for a while but was out in the clear in plenty of time and stayed on well despite running about a bit under pressure. He has not convinced over this trip in the past, but the way he pulled clear of the fifth horse suggests stamina was not a problem.
**Compton Dragon(USA)**, who was racing over as short as six furlongs last autumn, was trying this trip for the first time and ran as though he wanted every yard of it. He is miles below the form he was showing a couple of years ago, but his current mark reflects that and is in the ideal yard to help him rediscover any latent talent he may still have.
**Glimmer Of Light(IRE)** ◆, reappearing after an eight-month break, ran with credit under the circumstances and is still lightly raced so he may still have a bit of scope.
**Atlantic Quest(USA)**, back up in trip, was rather buried away in traffic but in reality did not find very much when seeing daylight. He may be best in a strongly run race over a mile.
**Best Flight**, not seen since winning a moderate maiden handicap on Fibresand last September, started short enough for a contest like this which may have been more down to potential and coming from a big yard rather than proven ability. After holding every chance, he faded tamely in the closing stages and this may be as good as he is.
**Bishopric** *Official explanation: jockey said gelding became upset in the stalls*

## 1822 DONCASTER RACECOURSE SPONSORSHIP CLUB CONDITIONS STKS 1m (R)
3:35 (3:35) (C) 3-Y-O **£9,151** (£3,247; £1,623; £738) **Stalls** High

Form RPR
310- **1** **Duke Of Venice (USA)**[198] 5640 3-9-1 106 (t) LDettori 1 110+
(SaeedBinSuroor) *trckd ldr: shkn up to ld over 1f out: rdn and styd on fnl f* **4/6**[1]
136- **2** *1 3/4* **Happy Crusader (IRE)**[177] 5962 3-8-12 104 KDalgleish 2 103
(PFICole) *led tl hdd over 1f out: styd on u.p* **3/1**[2]
13-3 **3** *19* **Birthday Suit (IRE)**[18] 1417 3-8-13 102 KDarley 3 64
(TDEasterby) *chsd first 2: rdn wl over 2f out: no imp: clr 3rd whn eased fnl f* **4/1**[3]
**4** *15* **Ses Seline** 3-8-4 PaulEddery 4 24
(JohnAHarris) *s.s: a wl bhd* **66/1**

1m 43.07s (2.52) **Going Correction** +0.40s/f (Good) **4** Ran SP% **106.5**
Speed ratings: **103,101,82,67**CSF £2.86 TOTE £1.50; EX 2.30.
**Owner** Godolphin **Bred** Forenaghts Stud **Trained** Newmarket, Suffolk

**FOCUS**
A truly run race despite there only being four runners.

**NOTEBOOK**
**Duke Of Venice(USA)**, a smart juvenile for Mark Johnston last season, was making his debut for Godolphin and sat in the slipstream of the leader for much of the way. He looked likely to win easily when moving alongside a furlong from home, but with that rival finding a bit more he had to be ridden right out to score. The likelihood is that he is capable of a good deal more than he showed here.
**Happy Crusader(IRE)**, making his seasonal reappearance, was allowed to set his own pace and battled back really well when the favourite came to challenge. This was a decent effort considering he is best on fast ground, but he may not be the easiest horse to place.
**Birthday Suit(IRE)**, stepping up two furlongs in trip, was easily left behind by the two market principals and probably did not stay.
**Ses Seline**, whose dam won over 14 furlongs and is a half-sister to the Group-race winning stayer Weld, found a tough race in which to make her belated debut and was left behind as soon as the stalls opened.

## 1823 JOE SIME MEMORIAL H'CAP 1m 6f 132y
4:10 (4:13) (D) (0-80,80) 3-Y-O **£5,395** (£1,660; £830; £415) **Stalls** Low

Form RPR
4552 **1** **Nessen Dorma (IRE)**[9] 1609 3-9-1 **74** MFenton 4 83+
(JGGiven) *led 3f: remained cl up: led again over 3 out: styd on u.p* **7/2**[2]
3336 **2** *2 1/2* **Siegfrieds Night (IRE)**[14] 1509 3-7-9 **57** oh2 NMackay(3) 1 63
(MCChapman) *hld up: effrt 3f out: disputing 2nd whn rdn over 1 out: kpt on fnl f: no imp on wnr* **5/1**
03-4 **3** *1 1/4* **Al Beedaa (USA)**[13] 1521 3-9-1 **74** RHills 7 78
(JLDunlop) *trckd ldrs: rdn over 2f out: kpt on same pce* **4/1**[3]
-301 **4** *11* **It's Blue Chip**[14] 1509 3-8-5 **64** (e) PaulEddery 2 54
(PWD'Arcy) *towards rr: effrt 4f out: sn rdn and btn* **10/3**[1]
0-44 **5** *2 1/2* **Prairie Sun (GER)**[19] 1394 3-7-12 **57** DaleGibson 6 44
(MrsADuffield) *led after 3f tl rdn and hdd over 3 out: sn wknd* **6/1**
255 **6** *dist* **Muzio Scevola (IRE)**[17] 1442 3-8-6 **68** SHitchcott(3) 5 —
(MRChannon) *slowly away: sn in tch: rdn 5f out: lost tch fr over 3 out: t.o* **10/1**
005- **7** *dist* **Opera Babe (IRE)**[248] 4557 3-8-13 **72** LDettori 8 —
(HSHowe) *slowly away: a bhd: lost tch fr 5f out: t.o* **12/1**

3m 15.22s (5.48) **Going Correction** +0.40s/f (Good) **7** Ran SP% **113.0**
Speed ratings: **101,99,99,93,91** —,—CSF £20.68 CT £71.13 TOTE £3.80: £2.20, £3.70; EX 32.70.
**Owner** Hokey Cokey Partnership **Bred** Robinski Bloodstock Limited **Trained** Willoughton, Lincs

**FOCUS**
A fair handicap run at an even pace.

**NOTEBOOK**
**Nessen Dorma(IRE)**, trying his longest trip to date, did not have an uncontested lead this time and had to show that he had the necessary stamina to win. This he did in good style and there should be more to come from him in staying handicaps.
**Siegfrieds Night(IRE)**, who was racing over five furlongs up until as recently as January, has been running with credit over much longer trips in recent months and certainly saw this trip out well enough, just not quite as well as the winner. He has the ability to win a similar contest.
**Al Beedaa(USA)**, making her handicap debut, did not fail through lack of stamina but does not look that enthusiastic under pressure. There is probably a small race in her, but she does not appeal as a betting proposition.
**It's Blue Chip** had looked as though he would appreciate this sort of trip, but he tended to race in snatches and it may be he needs softer ground than this.
**Prairie Sun(GER)** was given a positive ride over this longer trip, but did not get home.
**Opera Babe(IRE)** ran poorly and her rider reported that she gurgled. *Official explanation: jockey said filly had a breathing problem*

## 1824 CANNONS HEALTH CLUB CLAIMING STKS 6f
4:40 (4:48) (E) 4-Y-O+ **£3,620** (£1,114; £557; £278) **Stalls** High

Form RPR
0-00 **1** **Pays D'Amour (IRE)**[17] 1452 7-9-0 62 AlexGreaves 15 73
(DNicholls) *trckd ldrs: led gng wl over 1f out: clr fnl f: comf* **14/1**
0000 **2** *3 1/2* **Type One (IRE)**[21] 1361 6-9-10 75 (p) KDarley 14 72
(JJQuinn) *sn trcking ldrs: hdwy over 1f out: r.o u.p to chse wnr ins fnl f: no imp* **7/2**[1]
000- **3** *nk* **Red Leicester**[181] 5919 4-8-5 50 GGibbons 10 52
(JAGlover) *cl up: led 2f out: hdd over 1 out: no ex* **25/1**
05-0 **4** *shd* **Jubilee Street (IRE)**[10] 1595 5-8-7 49 ABeech(3) 3 57
(MrsADuffield) *rr div: hdwy over 1f out: r.o wl u.p fnl f: nrst fin* **33/1**
3020 **5** *1 1/2* **Rafters Music (IRE)**[28] 1265 9-8-10 63 MFenton 13 53
(JulianPoulton) *chsd ldrs: rdn over 1f out: kpt on same pce fnl f* **6/1**[2]
4460 **6** *1* **River Lark (USA)**[21] 1368 5-8-1 45 ow1 DAllan(3) 8 44
(MABuckley) *led tl hdd 2f out: no ex* **8/1**[3]
5156 **7** *nk* **Ripple Effect**[37] 1139 4-9-2 75 NMackay(3) 5 58
(CADwyer) *hld up in tch: effrt over 1f out: no hdwy u.p fnl f* **8/1**[3]
0-0U **8** *2 1/2* **Gdansk (IRE)**[9] 1603 7-9-4 70 FNorton 2 49
(ABerry) *dwlt: hld up: hdwy u.p to chse ldrs over 1f out: fdd fnl f* **6/1**[2]
0-01 **9** *3 1/2* **Pedro Jack (IRE)**[11] 1569 7-9-7 72 JFMcDonald(3) 16 45
(MABuckley) *rr div most of way* **10/1**
0-36 **10** *1 1/4* **Compton Princess**[6] 1696 4-7-13 45 DaleGibson 1 16
(MrsADuffield) *nvr bttr than mid-div* **20/1**
500- **11** *1 1/2* **Efimac**[425] 678 4-8-5 45 NPollard 9 17
(NBycroft) *dwlt: sn chsng ldrs: rdn over 2f out: wknd over 1 out* **50/1**
05-0 **12** *nk* **Princess Erica**[3] 1750 4-8-5 58 (p) JEdmunds 4 16
(JBalding) *s.s: sn midfield: wknd over 2f out* **16/1**
0000 **13** *1 1/4* **Meticulous**[13] 1533 6-8-4 30 RLMoore 6 12
(MCChapman) *sn bhd* **100/1**
306- **14** *1 1/4* **Zietzig (IRE)**[262] 4139 7-8-10 53 ANicholls 12 14
(DNicholls) *prom: rdn 2f out: wkng whn eased appr fnl f* **14/1**

1m 14.53s (0.25) **Going Correction** +0.15s/f (Good) **14** Ran SP% **115.8**
Speed ratings: **104,99,98,98,96 95,95,91,87,85 83,83,81,79**CSF £57.40 TOTE £16.10: £4.40, £2.30, £7.40; EX 85.60.
**Owner** The Inglenookers **Bred** James Wigan **Trained** Sessay, N Yorks

**FOCUS**
A fair claimer run at a decent pace and a clear-cut winner. Those drawn high had the advantage.

**NOTEBOOK**
**Pays D'Amour(IRE)**, who hit form at around this time last year, has been struggling in handicaps of late but bounced right back to form even though he was by no means best in at the weights. Pulling right away from his rivals, this was a decent performance considering he is best on fast ground and this looks to be his grade now.
**Type One(IRE)**, like the winner, has been struggling in handicaps this term but his two wins on sand during the winter were in claimers and a return to that grade, together with the application of cheekpieces, saw a much improved effort.
**Red Leicester**, unplaced in all five of her starts last season and returning from a six-month break, bagged the position next to the stands' rail and ran very well despite the inconvenience of a slipping noseband.
**Jubilee Street(IRE)**, one of the worst in on adjusted official ratings, came home best of all and would have been second in a few more strides. He did very much the best of those drawn low and if he can carry this form back into handicap company he would be a good bet, but on the other hand his previous record does not suggest he is one to lump on.
**Rafters Music(IRE)** ran his race, but has nothing in the way of improvement as his age.
**River Lark(USA)** made much of the running and put up a fair performance at the weights.
**Ripple Effect**, best in on adjusted official ratings, could never land a blow.
**Zietzig(IRE)** *Official explanation: jockey said gelding had lost its action*

## 1825 "CLOWNS" H'CAP 6f
5:15 (5:19) (D) (0-85,84) 3-Y-O+ **£5,931** (£1,825; £912; £456) **Stalls** High

Form RPR
0-42 **1** **Kingscross**[9] 1608 6-9-2 **73** DSweeney 9 83+
(MBlanshard) *hld up towards rr: nt clr run over 1f out: str run on ins to ld last 75yds: readily* **9/2**[2]
0-00 **2** *1 1/4* **Loyal Tycoon (IRE)**[14] 1500 6-9-6 **80** THamilton(3) 16 87
(DNicholls) *chsd ldrs: bmpd over 1f out: ev ch ins last: no ex* **16/1**
004- **3** *shd* **Look Here's Carol (IRE)**[214] 5336 4-9-12 **83** GGibbons 18 89
(BAMcmahon) *chsd ldrs: swtchd lft over 1f out: ev ch ins last: nt qckn* **8/1**[3]
33-0 **4** *shd* **Pinchbeck**[9] 1608 5-9-5 **76** MHenry 10 82
(MAJarvis) *chsd ldrs: led over 1f out: hdd 75yds out: no ex* **20/1**
0-00 **5** *2 1/2* **Online Investor**[2] 1772 5-8-10 **67** DRMcCabe 15 66
(DNicholls) *s.i.s: plld hrd in rr: nt clr run 2f out: styd on steadily ins last* **14/1**
5000 **6** *3/4* **Branston Tiger**[9] 1608 5-9-2 **73** MFenton 14 69
(JGGiven) *in tch: effrt over 2f out: kpt on same pce* **8/1**[3]
200- **7** *hd* **Ragamuffin**[333] 2138 6-9-3 **77** DAllan(3) 17 73
(TDEasterby) *sn bhd: styd on fnl 2f* **33/1**
0-00 **8** *nk* **Armagnac**[21] 1354 6-9-6 **77** KDalgleish 2 72
(MABuckley) *s.i.s: hdwy on outside over 2f out: nvr nr ldrs* **16/1**
402- **9** *1 1/2* **Magic Music (IRE)**[206] 5473 5-9-2 **73** NPollard 6 63
(MrsHDalton) *mde most: hdd over 1f out: fdd* **16/1**
400- **10** *shd* **Merlin's Dancer**[242] 4688 4-9-4 **75** AlexGreaves 13 65
(DNicholls) *trckd ldrs: kpt on same pce fnl 2f* **33/1**
430- **11** *2* **Million Percent**[171] 5992 5-9-12 **83** DarrenWilliams 19 67
(KRBurke) *hld up towards rr: sme hdwy on ins 2f out: nvr on terms* **33/1**
4341 **12** *2 1/2* **Lincoln Dancer (IRE)**[7] 1673 7-9-6 **84** 7ex LTreadwell(7) 1 60
(DNicholls) *s.i.s: hung lft over 1f out: nvr a factor* **10/1**
30-2 **13** *1* **Hiccups**[17] 1454 4-9-10 **81** (p) LDettori 8 54
(MrsJRRamsden) *unruly in stalls: rrd s: sme hdwy over 2f out: sn lost pl* **4/1**[1]
40-0 **14** *3/4* **Musical Fair**[39] 1106 4-9-6 **77** RLMoore 7 48
(JAGlover) *chsd ldrs towards outer: wknd over 1f out* **25/1**
440- **15** *8* **Vigorous (IRE)**[196] 5673 4-9-2 **73** CCogan 5 20
(DNicholls) *chsd ldrs: lost pl 2f out: eased* **33/1**
0000 **16** *2* **Winthorpe (IRE)**[21] 1361 4-9-4 **75** DaleGibson 4 16
(JJQuinn) *rr-div: sme hdwy on wd outside over 2f out: hung lft and sn lost pl: eased* **50/1**
0-00 **17** *1/2* **Sir Don (IRE)**[17] 1452 5-8-7 **64** (v) ANicholls 11 4
(DNicholls) *chsd ldr: lost pl over 2f out: sn wknd: eased* **33/1**

1m 14.45s (0.17) **Going Correction** +0.15s/f (Good) **17** Ran SP% **119.1**
Speed ratings: **104,102,102,102,98 97,97,97,95,94 92,88,87,86,75 73,72**CSF £61.72 CT £513.76 TOTE £5.00: £1.50, £4.90, £1.80, £3.70; EX 130.50 Place 6 £54.20, Place 5 £45.52.

**Owner** Mrs D Ellis **Bred** Mrs D Ellis **Trained** Upper Lambourn, Berks
■ Stewards Enquiry : G Gibbons one-day ban: careless riding (May 14)

**FOCUS**
A competitive handicap run in a similar time to the claimer. Once again the draw played its part with the first seven home coming from stall nine upwards.

**NOTEBOOK**
**Kingscross** has been threatening to win a race this season and managed to get it right, though he had to be switched in order to get a run. When he did reach the stands' rail, he fairly flew home and in the end scored with a bit to spare. *Official explanation: has been threatening to win a race this season and managed to get it right, though he had to be switched in order to get a run. When he did reach the stands' rail, he fairly flew home and in the end scored with a bit to spare.*
**Loyal Tycoon(IRE)** ran his best race for some time and deserves extra credit because, even though he was drawn high, he was racing furthest from the stands' rail of the front four. He has dropped to a very attractive mark and is worth watching out for with his stable in good form. *Official explanation: ran his best race for some time and deserves extra credit because, even though he was drawn high, he was racing furthest from the stands' rail of the front four. He has dropped to a very attractive mark and is worth watching out for with his stable in good form.*
**Look Here's Carol(IRE)**, returning from a seven-month break, appreciated the easier ground and ran well. She is another one to watch out for, but may be better over an extra furlong these days. *Official explanation: , returning from a seven-month break, appreciated the easier ground and ran well. She is another one to watch out for, but may be better over an extra furlong these days.*
**Pinchbeck** ran much better than on his seasonal reappearance and never stopped trying. He is not without hope despite still being 5lb above his highest winning mark. *Official explanation: ran much better than on his seasonal reappearance and never stopped trying. He is not without hope despite still being 5lb above his highest winning mark.*
**Online Investor ◆**, making a quick reappearance, again found all the trouble going before finishing strongly. His style of running, mainly as a result of constantly missing the break, does mean he needs luck, but he is so well handicapped at present that when things go his way he will surely end his losing run stretching back three years. *Official explanation: , making a quick reappearance, again found all the trouble going before finishing strongly. His style of running, mainly as a result of constantly missing the break, does mean he needs luck, but he is so well handicapped at present that when things go his way he will surely end his losing run stretching back three years.*
**Branston Tiger** has become well handicapped and ran his best race for a while. *Official explanation: has become well handicapped and ran his best race for a while.*
**Armagnac** deserves credit as he did best of those starting from the lowest stalls and also missed the break. *Official explanation: deserves credit as he did best of those starting from the lowest stalls and also missed the break.*
**Hiccups** *Official explanation: jockey said gelding got upset in the stalls*
**Sir Don(IRE)** *Official explanation: jockey said gelding was never travelling*
T/Plt: £77.10 to a £1 stake. Pool: £45,815.70. 433.50 winning tickets. T/Qpdt: £83.50 to a £1 stake. Pool: £2,297.30. 20.35 winning tickets. JF

## 1352 KEMPTON (R-H)

### Monday, May 3

**OFFICIAL GOING: Heavy**

### 1826 EBF SHARP MINDS BETFAIR MAIDEN STKS — 5f
**2:10** (2:13) (D) 2-Y-0 — **£5,388** (£1,658; £829; £414) **Stalls** High

| Form | Pos | Dist | Horse | Jockey | RPR |
|---|---|---|---|---|---|
| 2 | 1 | | **Turkney**[18] 1412 2-9-0 — (MRChannon) *trckd ldr: led ins fnl 2f: c clr fnl f: easily* **5/2**[2] | TEDurcan 4 | 94 |
| 3 | 2 | 11 | **Planet Tomato (IRE)**[17] 1436 2-9-0 — (PFICole) *sn led: rdn over 2f out: hdd ins fnl 2f: sn no ch w wnr but kpt on for 2nd* **6/4**[1] | KFallon 7 | 67 |
| | 3 | ½ | **Wilko (USA)** 2-9-0 — (JNoseda) *trckd ldrs: pushed along over 2f out: outpcd over 1f out* **3/1**[3] | EAhern 5 | 65 |
| | 4 | 3 | **Stedfast McStaunch (IRE)** 2-9-0 — (BJMeehan) *s.i.s: sn in tch: rdn 1/2-way: outpcd fnl 2f* **25/1** | SDrowne 1 | 58 |
| | 5 | 3½ | **Fortnum** 2-9-0 — (RHannon) *s.i.s: sn in tch: rdn 1/2-way: wknd over 1f out* **16/1** | DaneO'Neill 2 | 49 |
| | 6 | 1 | **Atsos (IRE)** 2-9-0 — (RHannon) *s.i.s: sn pushed along: wknd 1/2-way* **20/1** | PDobbs 6 | 47 |
| | 7 | 2 | **First Rule** 2-9-0 — (CFWall) *slowly in stride: sn rcvrd and in tch: outpcd 1/2-way: wknd qckly over 1f out* **33/1** | JQuinn 8 | 42 |
| | 8 | 6 | **Flying Pass** 2-9-0 — (DJSFfrenchDavis) *s.i.s: a outpcd: lost tch fr 1/2-way* **50/1** | TQuinn 3 | 27 |

66.30 secs (5.09) **Going Correction** +1.175s/f (Soft) **8** Ran SP% **113.0**
Speed ratings: **106,88,87,82,77 75,72,62**CSF £6.26 TOTE £3.90: £1.40, £1.10, £1.90; EX 6.50.
**Owner** Sheikh Mohammed **Bred** Mrs E M Charlton **Trained** West Ilsley, Berks

**FOCUS**
A good maiden that should produce plenty of future winners.

**NOTEBOOK**
**Turnkey**, five-length second to the very highly-regarded and Royal Ascot bound Blue Dakota on his debut at Newmarket, showed the benefit of that run and absolutely bolted up. He proved fully effective in the conditions and the winning margin does flatter him, but his trainer has a high opinion of him and could run him in something like the Norfolk or the Coventry at Ascot in June. He looks sure to stay six furlongs.
**Planet Tomato(IRE)** shaped well on his debut in a good maiden at Newbury and was much sharper this time. However, he was no match for the winner and has to be considered disappointing. The testing ground may not have suited and he can be given another chance back on a decent surface.
**Wilko(USA)** is a $35,000 foal out of a three-year-old winner. He played up before the start, dropping his rider and running loose for around 100 yards or so. In the race itself, he offered plenty of encouragement, but he lacked the winner's change of pace and, despite keeping on right the way to the line, was thought to have been unsuited by the soft ground. A good effort in the circumstances and he should find a similar contest.
**Stedfast McStaunch(IRE)**, a 32,000euros yearling and half-brother to Business Acumen who was placed over 12 furlongs and over hurdles, has a Weatherbys Super Sprint entry and clearly posses more speed than his brother. There should be plenty of improvement to come.
**Fortnum**, a 35,000gns purchase and half-brother to four winners including a couple of two-year-old winners, looked in need of this experience.
**Atsos(IRE)**, a 30,000euros purchase and half-brother to a five-furlong juvenile selling winner, ran a similar race to that of his stablemate and should be better for the outing.
**First Rule ◆**, a 37,000gns yearling and brother to a useful six-furlong juvenile winner and half-brother to four winners, ran much better than his finishing position suggests. He travelled quite strongly on the heels of the leaders for much of the way but could not get through the ground when asked to quicken. He will be interesting on a decent surface and could well find a maiden.

### 1827 STPP MEDIA MAIDEN STKS (DIV I) — 1m (J)
**2:40** (2:44) (D) 3-Y-0 — **£5,616** (£1,728; £864; £432) **Stalls** Low

| Form | Pos | Dist | Horse | Jockey | RPR |
|---|---|---|---|---|---|
| 6- | 1 | | **First Centurion**[208] 5448 3-9-0 — (JWHills) *in tch: rdn and hdwy fr 3f out: swtchd rt 2f out:str run to ld jst ins fnl f: sn clr: comf* **11/1** | EAhern 11 | 84 |
| 0-5 | 2 | 5 | **Pizazz**[18] 1413 3-9-0 — (BJMeehan) *sn w ldr: led 3f out: hdd and rn green over 2f out: hrd rdn to ld again over 1f out: hdd jst ins last: one pce* **4/1**[2] | DHolland 3 | 74 |
| 6-2 | 3 | 4 | **Sailmaker (IRE)**[25] 1311 3-9-0 — (RCharlton) *chsd ldrs: led over 2f out: sn rdn: hdd over 1f out: wknd ins fnl f* **7/2**[1] | SDrowne 4 | 66 |
| -0 | 4 | 3½ | **Dandygrey Russett (IRE)**[16] 1461 3-8-9 — (GLMoore) *slowly away: bhd: hdwy fr 3f out: kpt on wl fr over 1f out but nvr gng pce to rch ldrs* **33/1** | RBrisland 10 | 54 |
| | 5 | 1 | **Pass The Port** 3-9-0 — (JRFanshawe) *in tch: rdn to chse ldrs 3f out: wknd ins fnl 2f* **9/1**[3] | JPMurtagh 9 | 57 |
| | 6 | 5 | **Lucayan Legend (IRE)** 3-9-0 — (RHannon) *bhd: pushed along 1/2-way: kpt on fnl 2f but nvr a danger* **9/1**[3] | PDobbs 7 | 47 |
| | 7 | 10 | **High View (USA)** 3-9-0 — (FJordan) *slowly away and wnt lft s: mod prog fr over 1f out* **50/1** | JQuinn 1 | 27 |
| 0-00 | 8 | 1½ | **Tsarbuck**[12] 1541 3-9-0 — (RMHCowell) *mid-div: rdn 3f out: sn wknd* **100/1** | PDoe 12 | 24 |
| 32-0 | 9 | 2 | **Great Exhibition (USA)**[37] 1143 3-9-0 — (SaeedBinSuroor) *led tl hdd 3f out: wknd qckly over 2f out* **4/1**[2] | (t) KMcEvoy 5 | 20 |
| | 10 | 9 | **Heriot** 3-9-0 — (HCandy) *slowly away: sn drvn and a bhd* **14/1** | DaneO'Neill 6 | — |
| 0-2 | 11 | 13 | **Captain Marryat**[25] 1310 3-9-0 — (PWHarris) *chsd ldrs tl wknd fr 3f out* **14/1** | MartinDwyer 8 | — |
| 06- | 12 | 2½ | **Rubaiyat (IRE)**[187] 5831 3-9-0 — (GWragg) *chsd ldrs 5f* **33/1** | TEDurcan 2 | — |

1m 51.65s (12.03) **Going Correction** +1.55s/f (Heav) **12** Ran SP% **112.7**
Speed ratings: **101,96,92,88,87 82,72,71,69,60 47,44**CSF £50.99 TOTE £13.50: £2.60, £1.30, £1.70; EX 67.00.
**Owner** D M Kerr And N Brunskill **Bred** Abergwaun Farm **Trained** Upper Lambourn, Berks

**FOCUS**
Probably just an ordinary maiden and the heavy ground exaggerates the distances, but the winner looks a useful colt in the making.

**NOTEBOOK**
**First Centurion** caught the eye on his debut over seven furlongs on the Polytrack and confirmed that promise off the back of a 208-day break. The winning margin probably flatters him, but he is clearly a nice prospect and deserves to take his chance in a higher grade.
**Pizazz** was suited by this step up from a mile and showed enough to suggest there is a similar race in him. He has a slightly awkward head carriage, but looks to try hard enough.
**Sailmaker(IRE)**, made favourite off the back of a promising reappearance at Bath, did not see out his race and may not have been suited by this testing ground.
**Dandygrey Russett(IRE)** did not shape too badly on her debut at Newbury and again hinted at ability. She is going the right way, but may be best watched until she goes handicapping, that is unless she is found a particularly weak maiden.
**Pass The Port**, a 22,000gns purchase out of a sister to the very smart juvenile and Classic placed Relatively Special and half-sister to the top-class One So Wonderful, was easy to back but hinted at ability.
**Great Exhibition(USA)**, sent off just 6/1 for the UAE Derby on his latest start, was disappointing that day and again failed to perform. He did not pick up when asked and wandered around when shown the whip. He should be capable of better back on a decent surface, but does appeal as one to place too much faith in.

### 1828 JUBILEE STKS (H'CAP) — 1m (J)
**3:15** (3:15) (C) (0-100,98) 4-Y-0+ — **£9,390** (£3,561; £1,780; £809) **Stalls** Low

| Form | Pos | Dist | Horse | Jockey | RPR |
|---|---|---|---|---|---|
| 0-50 | 1 | | **Shot To Fame (USA)**[16] 1456 5-9-5 **89** — (PWHarris) *racd stands side rail: mde all: c clr ins fnl 2f: easily* **14/1** | EAhern 5 | 112 |
| -210 | 2 | 11 | **St Petersburg**[16] 1456 4-9-9 **93** — (MHTompkins) *racd stands side rail and chsd wnr thrght: rdn over 2f out: sn no ch but r.o strly for clr 2nd* **11/2**[2] | DHolland 1 | 94 |
| 0340 | 3 | 5 | **Digital**[16] 1456 7-9-6 **90** — (MRChannon) *racd stands side rail: bhd: hdwy over 2f out: r.o wl fr over 1f out but nvr gng pce to rch ldrs* **12/1** | TEDurcan 2 | 81 |
| -050 | 4 | 1 | **Norton (IRE)**[12] 1540 7-9-9 **93** — (TGMills) *chsd ldrs on stands side rail: rdn and outpcd 3f out: kpt on again fnl f but nvr a danger* **8/1** | WRyan 3 | 82 |
| 0-00 | 5 | 1 | **Desert Opal**[16] 1456 4-9-10 **94** — (JHMGosden) *racd stands side rail and chsd ldrs: rdn 3f out: wknd over 2f out* **7/2**[1] | SDrowne 6 | 81 |
| 1016 | 6 | 5 | **Hurricane Coast**[9] 1608 5-8-3 **73** — (DFlood) *racd stands side rail: t.k.h: rdn over 2f out: wknd wl over 1f* **14/1** | (b) JMackay 4 | 50 |
| 6-00 | 7 | 2½ | **Audience**[20] 1385 4-9-11 **95** — (JAkehurst) *racd far side rail: chsd ldrs tl wknd qckly fr 2f out* **25/1** | JQuinn 17 | 67 |
| 03-0 | 8 | 12 | **Hurricane Floyd (IRE)**[20] 1385 6-9-4 **88** — (DRLoder) *racd stands side rail: bhd most of way* **16/1** | JPMurtagh 7 | 36 |
| 10-0 | 9 | 6 | **Cornelius**[51] 1009 7-9-9 **98** — (PFICole) *racd far side rail: led that gp tl wknd ins fnl 3f* **14/1** | NChalmers[(5)] 16 | 34 |
| 030- | 10 | ½ | **Sri Diamond**[204] 5506 4-8-10 **80** — (SKirk) *racd far side rail: in tch: hdwy to chse ldrs 3f out: sn wknd* **33/1** | PDobbs 12 | 15 |
| 605- | 11 | 9 | **Devant (NZ)**[187] 5827 4-9-1 **85** — (MAJarvis) *racd far side rail: s.i.s: sn rcvrd and prom: wknd fr 3f out* **6/1**[3] | PRobinson 9 | — |
| 0-60 | 12 | 17 | **Jay Gee's Choice**[16] 1456 4-8-12 **89** — (MRChannon) *racd far side rail: w ldrs tl wknd fr 3f out* **20/1** | BO'Neill[(7)] 10 | — |
| 220- | 13 | 3 | **Night Kiss (FR)**[173] 5981 4-8-0 **70** oh4 ow2 — (RHannon) *racd stands side rail: a bhd* **33/1** | MartinDwyer 8 | — |
| 3-00 | 14 | 12 | **Yakimov (USA)**[16] 1456 5-9-5 **89** — (DJWintle) *racd far side rail: a bhd* **25/1** | DaneO'Neill 14 | — |

1m 50.07s (10.45) **Going Correction** +1.55s/f (Heav) **14** Ran SP% **114.9**
Speed ratings: **109,98,93,92,91 86,83,71,65,65 56,39,36,24**CSF £79.34 CT £670.84 TOTE £14.10: £4.30, £2.10, £3.20; EX 138.90 Trifecta £1371.80 Part won. Pool: £1,932.24. 0.50 winning tickets..
**Owner** The Conquistadors **Bred** Eric Puerari **Trained** Ringshall, Bucks

**FOCUS**
This looked a competitive handicap, but few horses handled the conditions and no horse handled the ground as well as the winner. For that reason he is obviously slightly flattered and the distances are exaggerated. The field split into two groups in the early part of the contest and the first six home raced towards the stands'-side rail.

**NOTEBOOK**
**Shot To Fame(USA)**, ridden much more positively than is often the case, had his ground for about only the fourth time since making a winning debut on a soft surface and ran out a very comfortable winner. He would obviously be of interest if turned out under a penalty as things will be very hard when he is reassessed, but give in the ground is obviously the key.
**St Petersburg**, 11lb higher than when runner-up in the Spring Mile and 7lb higher than when scoring at Pontefract two starts back, appeared to handle the conditions but was simply no match for the winner.
**Digital** is back on a winning mark and ran well. This is his time of year and he is one to keep an eye on for similar events.
**Norton(IRE)**, back two furlongs in trip, ran well considering this ground was softer than ideal. He is not badly handicapped on the pick of his form, but is not exactly progressing.
**Desert Opal** goes on soft ground, but this heavy surface may just have been against him. He has been a beaten favourite on two of his last four starts.
**Hurricane Coast** *Official explanation: trainer said gelding finished distressed*
**Hurricane Floyd(IRE)** *Official explanation: jockey said gelding had a breathing problem on the heavy ground*
**Devant(NZ)** has won on soft, but disappointed on that sort of ground in his previous run and again failed to perform under testing conditions.

## 1829 FULHAM F.C. FOOTBALL AND COMMUNITY SCHEME EBF FILLIES' CONDITIONS STKS 6f
3:45 (3:46) (C) 3-Y-O £8,383 (£3,180; £1,590; £722) Stalls High

| Form | | | | RPR |
|---|---|---|---|---|
| 151- | 1 | | **Autumn Pearl**[186] 5835 3-8-13 87 ... PRobinson 7 | 91 |
| | | | (MAJarvis) *mde all: clr over 1f out: drvn out ins last and hld on wl* **9/2**[3] | |
| 305- | 2 | 1 | **Cusco (IRE)**[184] 5874 3-8-13 87 ... PDobbs 1 | 88 |
| | | | (RHannon) *chsd ldrs: rdn to chse wnr 2f out: styd on wl fnl f: no imp cl home* **11/2** | |
| 004- | 3 | 1 ¼ | **Hilites (IRE)**[228] 5022 3-8-9 83 ... MartinDwyer 4 | 80 |
| | | | (JSMoore) *hld up rr but in tch: hdwy 2f out: styd on wl to chse ldrs ins last: no ex nr fin* **16/1** | |
| 11- | 4 | 9 | **La Coruna**[188] 5822 3-8-13 ... SDrowne 5 | 57 |
| | | | (RCharlton) *trckd wnr: rdn 1/2-way: wknd qckly 2f out* **2/1**[1] | |
| 32-0 | 5 | 2 | **Dolce Piccata**[20] 1388 3-8-9 89 ... TQuinn 6 | 47 |
| | | | (BJMeehan) *chsd ldrs: rdn over 2f out: wknd fnl quarter m* **11/1** | |
| 410- | 6 | 10 | **Our Gamble (IRE)**[331] 2187 3-8-13 90 ... DaneO'Neill 3 | 21 |
| | | | (RHannon) *s.i.s: bhd: brief effrt 1/2-way: sn wknd* **11/1** | |
| 221- | 7 | dist | **Bread Of Heaven**[199] 5623 3-8-13 81 ... DHolland 2 | — |
| | | | (MrsAJPerrett) *sn rdn and outpcd: lost tch fr 1/2-way and virtually p.u* **4/1**[2] | |

1m 21.39s (8.32) **Going Correction** +1.175s/f (Soft) **7 Ran SP% 109.4**
Speed ratings: **91,89,88,76,73 60,**—CSF £26.49 TOTE £4.80: £2.50, £2.70; EX 31.40.
**Owner** Mr & Mrs Kevan Watts **Bred** Bearstone Stud **Trained** Newmarket, Suffolk

**FOCUS**
Probably not too bad a race, but only a few handled the ground and several of these could prove hard to place. The winning time was modest.

**NOTEBOOK**
**Autumn Pearl** confirmed the promise she showed over five furlongs at two and had no problem staying this extra furlong. Ideally drawn to grab the favoured rail, she had everything go her way but is open to improvement and could add to her impressive wins-to-runs record whilst in this sort of form.
**Cusco(IRE)**, beaten in Listed company on her final two starts last term, was dropped back from a mile for this first start in 184 days and it suited well. She will not be easy to place off her current mark, however.
**Hilites(IRE)** handled the ground well and made a promising return. She is likely to be sharper for the outing, but is another who will not be easy to place.
**La Coruna**, racing on ground worse than good for the first time and dropped back from seven furlongs for this first start in 188 days, proved unable to quicken and may not have been suited by the surface. *Official explanation: jockey said filly was unsuited by the heavy ground*
**Dolce Piccata** gained her only win to date on good to firm ground.
**Bread Of Heaven** got off the mark on firm ground and clearly failed to act in these much worse conditions. *Official explanation: trainer's representative said filly was never travelling*

## 1830 STPP MEDIA MAIDEN STKS (DIV II) 1m (J)
4:20 (4:20) (D) 3-Y-O £5,616 (£1,728; £864; £432) Stalls Low

| Form | | | | RPR |
|---|---|---|---|---|
| 00- | 1 | | **Night Frolic**[177] 5947 3-8-9 ... EAhern 5 | 59 |
| | | | (JWHills) *in tch: lost position bnd 3f out: hdwy on rail 2f out:swtchd rt and qcknd over 1f out: drvn to ld wl ins last: styd on* **14/1** | |
| | 2 | nk | **Charleston** 3-9-0 ... JPMurtagh 3 | 64 |
| | | | (JHMGosden) *chsd ldr: reminder sn after s: chal over 2f out: def advantage ins fnl quarter m: hdd wl ins last: kpt on* **11/2**[3] | |
| | 3 | 1 ¾ | **Anatolian Queen (USA)** 3-8-9 ... JTate 2 | 55 |
| | | | (JMPEustace) *rr stalls: bhd: hdwy 2f out: nt clr run and swtchd rt wl over 1f out: str run to press ldrs ins last:nt qckn cl home* **12/1** | |
| 000- | 4 | shd | **Verasi**[170] 6003 3-9-0 ... DaneO'Neill 9 | 60 |
| | | | (RCharlton) *chsd ldrs: challened over 2f out: tl w ldrs ins last: no ex nr fin* **33/1** | |
| | 5 | 2 | **Motive (FR)** 3-9-0 ... KFallon 7 | 56 |
| | | | (SirMichaelStoute) *hld up in rr: shkn up over 2f out: stdy hdwy fr over 1f out: kpt on ins last: nt trble ldrs* **11/2**[3] | |
| 302- | 6 | ½ | **Bailaora (IRE)**[204] 5503 3-9-0 79 ... TQuinn 12 | 55 |
| | | | (BWDuke) *bhd: hdwy 2f out: sn n.m.r: rdn to chse ldrs over 1f out: kpt on same pce ins last* **9/2**[1] | |
| | 7 | 3 | **My Pension (IRE)** 3-9-0 ... TEDurcan 4 | 49 |
| | | | (PHowling) *bhd: nvr gng pce to rch ldrs* **20/1** | |
| 3-4 | 8 | 1 | **Devious Ayers (IRE)**[7] 1679 3-9-0 ... WRyan 6 | 47 |
| | | | (GAButler) *led tl hdd ins fnl 2f: wknd qckly fnl f* **14/1** | |
| | 9 | 6 | **Peter Paul Rubens (USA)** 3-9-0 ... DHolland 1 | 35 |
| | | | (PFICole) *mid-diviison: rdn over 2f out: sn wknd* **8/1** | |
| 00- | 10 | 8 | **My Hope (IRE)**[184] 5869 3-8-9 ... SDrowne 11 | 14 |
| | | | (RCharlton) *nvr bttr than mid-div* **5/1**[2] | |
| | 11 | dist | **Black Sabbeth** 3-9-0 ... JQuinn 10 | — |
| | | | (PJMakin) *wnt bdly rt s: sn rcvrd and in tch: wknd qckly fr 3f out* **20/1** | |

1m 54.06s (14.44) **Going Correction** +1.55s/f (Heavy) **11 Ran SP% 110.2**
Speed ratings: **89,88,86,86,84 84,81,80,74,66** —CSF £81.26 TOTE £21.50: £5.60, £3.10, £3.40; EX 197.60.
**Owner** The Wandering Stars **Bred** John Warren And Floors Farming **Trained** Upper Lambourn, Berks

**FOCUS**
Not much form to go on and this was probably just an ordinary maiden. A modest winning time for the class, 2.41 seconds slower than the first division.

**NOTEBOOK**
**Night Frolic** was reported to have a breathing problem on her first start last term and did not really improve for the fitting of a tongue-tie on her second and final outing of the year. Stepped up from six furlongs and racing on ground worse than good for the first time, she ran out a narrow winner. Her future lies in the hands of the Handicapper.
**Charleston**, a brother to a very useful two-year-old and half-brother to a smart middle distance filly, made an encouraging debut. It is hard to know what to make of the form, but it would be disappointing if he does not find a similar contest.
**Anatolian Queen(USA)**, a $75,000 purchase whose dam is a half-sister to Craven Stakes winner King Of Happiness, was stuck wider than most in the straight but still shaped with promise.
**Verasi** had shown little in his three previous starts but, returning from a 170-day break, he offered some promise. He got a little tired in the closing stages and should be sharper next time.
**Motive(FR)**, a 250,000gns yearling out of a high-class stayer, proved easy to back and was well held. He should, however, be capable of improvement and looks sure to stay further.
**Bailaora(IRE)**, with the blinkers left off on this first run in 204 days, did not run to form and was disappointing. *Official explanation: jockey said colt was unsuited by the heavy ground*

## 1831 SHARP MINDS BETFAIR H'CAP 1m 1f (R)
4:50 (4:52) (D) (0-85,82) 3-Y-O £5,824 (£1,792; £896; £448) Stalls High

| Form | | | | RPR |
|---|---|---|---|---|
| 01-0 | 1 | | **Anousa (IRE)**[21] 1357 3-9-2 77 ... (v[1]) KFallon 8 | 83 |
| | | | (PHowling) *bhd: rdn over 2f out:swtchd rt and str run appr fnl f: drvn to ld wl ins last* **14/1** | |
| 2352 | 2 | 1 ¼ | **Gavroche (IRE)**[8] 1640 3-8-7 71 ... J-PGuillambert(3) 3 | 75 |
| | | | (CADwyer) *hld up in rr: hdwy fr 3f out: rdn 2f out: str run to press ldrs ins fnl f: nt pce of wnr nr fin* **12/1** | |
| 20-0 | 3 | nk | **Freak Occurence (IRE)**[17] 1437 3-9-7 82 ... SDrowne 2 | 85 |
| | | | (MissECLavelle) *hld up rr: rdn and hdwy on stand rail ins fnl 2f: drvn and slt ld jst ins fnl f: hdd and outpcd wl ins last* **20/1** | |
| 2-14 | 4 | 2 | **Honest Injun**[14] 1506 3-9-3 78 ... MartinDwyer 6 | 77 |
| | | | (BWHills) *led 3f: styd trcking ldr tl led again wl over 1f out: hdd jst ins last: wknd cl home* **7/1**[3] | |
| 26-1 | 5 | 2 | **Baffle**[23] 1325 3-9-2 77 ... TQuinn 11 | 72 |
| | | | (JLDunlop) *led 7f out: rdn over 2f out: hdd wl over 1f out: wknd ins last* **6/1**[2] | |
| 13- | 6 | 1 ¾ | **Penzance**[212] 5355 3-9-3 78 ... EAhern 4 | 70+ |
| | | | (JRFanshawe) *chsd ldrs: rdn and styng on whn bdly hmpd ins fnl 2f: nt rcvr* **7/1**[3] | |
| 00-6 | 7 | 2 ½ | **Balearic Star (IRE)**[33] 1214 3-8-7 68 ... TEDurcan 12 | 55 |
| | | | (BRMillman) *bhd: rdn and hdwy fr 3f out: chsd ldrs 2f out: sn outpcd* **10/1** | |
| 52-1 | 8 | 1 ½ | **Show No Fear**[21] 1357 3-8-10 71 ... WRyan 13 | 55 |
| | | | (HRACecil) *chsd ldrs tl wknd appr fnl f* **3/1**[1] | |
| 01-0 | 9 | 5 | **Watamu (IRE)**[17] 1437 3-9-5 80 ... JQuinn 9 | 54 |
| | | | (PJMakin) *chsd ldrs tl wknd over 2f out* **20/1** | |
| 41- | 10 | 1 ¾ | **Salisbury Plain**[302] 3036 3-9-7 82 ... JPMurtagh 1 | 52 |
| | | | (DRLoder) *hld up in tch: hdwy on rails whn hung bdly rt ins fnl 2f: sn btn* **12/1** | |
| 045- | 11 | 6 | **Schapiro (USA)**[203] 5532 3-9-2 77 ... KMcEvoy 14 | 35 |
| | | | (JHMGosden) *a in rr* **20/1** | |
| 1-0 | 12 | hd | **Laawaris (USA)**[10] 1588 3-9-7 82 ... DaneO'Neill 5 | 40 |
| | | | (JAOsborne) *slowly away: a in rr* **33/1** | |
| 034- | 13 | 26 | **Thirteen Tricks (USA)**[183] 5886 3-9-0 75 ... DHolland 7 | — |
| | | | (MrsAJPerrett) *chsd ldrs tl wknd qckly over 2f out: virtually p.u fnl f* **20/1** | |

2m 7.10s (12.77) **Going Correction** +1.65s/f (Heavy) **13 Ran SP% 117.4**
Speed ratings: **109,107,107,105,104 102,100,98,94,92 87,87,64**CSF £153.59 CT £3438.96 TOTE £15.40: £3.00, £3.50, £8.60; EX 356.30.
**Owner** Arkland International (uk) Ltd **Bred** Michael Dalton **Trained** Newmarket, Suffolk

**FOCUS**
Quite a competitive handicap and a decent winning time in the conditions.

**NOTEBOOK**
**Anousa(IRE)** disappointed on his reappearance over this course and distance but returned to form in the first-time visor. He promises to stay further and should continue to run well if the headgear keeps working.
**Gavroche(IRE)**, having just his fourth start on turf, had never raced on ground this soft but handled it well. He has been in good form since switching stables.
**Freak Occurence(IRE)**, racing beyond a mile for the first time, ran better than he did on his reappearance and may have a race in him off his current mark.
**Honest Injun** gained his only win to date over seven furlongs and this nine furlong trip on heavy ground proved just a little too far.
**Baffle**, off the mark in a weak maiden at Haydock on her previous start, was racing over a furlong further this time and got a little tired in the closing stages.
**Show No Fear**, 4lb higher than when winning over course and distance on his previous start, ran disappointingly and may be best watched until his stable hits top form.

## 1832 KEITH WILLIAM ELMSLIE H'CAP 1m 6f 92y
5:25 (5:26) (D) (0-85,85) 3-Y-O+ £5,746 (£1,768; £884; £442) Stalls High

| Form | | | | RPR |
|---|---|---|---|---|
| /216 | 1 | | **Jorobaden (FR)**[19] 1401 4-9-12 83 ... JQuinn 1 | 98 |
| | | | (CFWall) *bhd: hdwy 4f out: rdn to chse ldrs and hung lft fr 2f out: swtchd rt and str run over 1f out: led ins last: rdn out* **7/2**[1] | |
| 0-11 | 2 | 3 ½ | **Linens Flame**[13] 1520 5-9-1 71 ... KFallon 8 | 82 |
| | | | (BGPowell) *chsd ldrs: led over 3f out: hrd drvn fr 2f out: hdd and no ex ins fnl f* **7/2**[1] | |
| 10 | 3 | 8 | **Dance World**[19] 1401 4-9-4 78 ... BReilly(3) 13 | 79 |
| | | | (MissJFeilden) *mid-div: hdwy 5f out: chsd ldrs 2f out: wknd fnl f* **20/1** | |
| 0221 | 4 | nk | **Dissident (GER)**[2] 1768 6-9-6 76 6ex ... (v) JMackay 4 | 77 |
| | | | (DFlood) *chsd ldrs: rdn 3f out: wknd fnl f* **6/1**[2] | |
| 050- | 5 | 8 | **Star Member (IRE)**[192] 5730 5-9-7 77 ... DHolland 9 | 68 |
| | | | (APJarvis) *chsd ldrs: rdn and effrt 3f out: wknd 2f out* **16/1** | |
| 5-50 | 6 | 6 | **Sonoma (IRE)**[16] 1457 4-8-8 70 ... HayleyTurner(5) 14 | 54 |
| | | | (MLWBell) *led tl hdd over 3f out: wknd over 2f out* **16/1** | |
| 4-0 | 7 | 5 | **Kirov King (IRE)**[28] 1272 4-9-1 75 ... LPKeniry(3) 5 | 53 |
| | | | (BGPowell) *bhd: nvr rch ldrs* **50/1** | |
| 20-5 | 8 | 6 | **Skelligs Rock (IRE)**[28] 1272 4-9-6 77 ... DaneO'Neill 11 | 48 |
| | | | (BWDuke) *bhd fr 1/2-way* **25/1** | |
| 422- | 9 | 22 | **Land 'n Stars**[204] 5504 4-9-4 75 ... TQuinn 7 | 19 |
| | | | (JamiePoulton) *a in rr* **20/1** | |
| 00-5 | 10 | hd | **Treasure Trail**[121] 413 5-9-3 73 ... PDobbs 10 | 17 |
| | | | (SKirk) *a in rr* **16/1** | |
| 22-1 | 11 | 6 | **Arresting**[32] 1221 4-10-0 85 ... JPMurtagh 12 | 22 |
| | | | (JRFanshawe) *mid-div: pushed along and hdwy over 4f out: wknd qckly 3f out: eased whn no ch* **6/1**[2] | |
| 30-3 | 12 | dist | **Rome (IRE)**[75] 818 5-8-13 69 ... MartinDwyer 2 | — |
| | | | (GPEnright) *chsd ldrs tl wknd qckly 4f out: t.o* **25/1** | |

-123 **13** *6* **Dolzago**[45] [1054] 4-8-12 **69**......(b) TEDurcan 3 —
(GLMoore) *bhd: hdwy 7f out: rdn 5f out: wknd qckly 3f out: eased whn no ch: t.o* **12/1**[3]

3m 34.78s (24.12) **Going Correction** +1.65s/f (Heav)
**WFA** 4 from 5yo+ 1lb **13** Ran SP% **117.5**
Speed ratings: **97,95,90,90,85 82,79,75,63,63 59,—,—**CSF £12.90 CT £214.29 TOTE £5.40: £2.10, £1.60, £4.20; EX 21.40 Place 6 £847.51, Place 5 £792.92.
**Owner** The Storm Again Syndicate **Bred** R Le Poder **Trained** Newmarket, Suffolk

**FOCUS**
A reasonable staying handicap, but they were well strung out and not many of them will have handled the ground. The winning time was slow.

**NOTEBOOK**
**Jorobaden(FR)**, up in trip and racing on heavy ground for the first time, travelled really strongly and found plenty for pressure. He could bid to follow up at the big York meeting if the ground does not dry out too much.
**Linens Flame** was 17lb higher than when winning over this course and distance two starts back and ran a cracker. He will go up again for this and the Handicapper looks to be catching up with him.
**Dance World** ran better than he did at Newmarket on his previous run on this step up in trip, but is on a stiff enough mark.
**Dissident(GER)** had the ground in his favour, but did not convince over this trip.
**Star Member(IRE)** has done most of his racing on fast ground and did not get home on this very different surface.
**Arresting** did not run to his best on this first run on heavy ground. *Official explanation: trainer's representative said gelding was unsuited by the heavy ground*
T/Jkpt: Not won. T/Plt: £3,962.80 to a £1 stake. Pool: £65,142.00. 12.00 winning tickets. T/Qpdt: £1,869.10 to a £1 stake. Pool: £2,525.90. 0.90 winning tickets. ST

## 1664 NEWCASTLE (L-H)
### Monday, May 3
**1833 Meeting Abandoned** - Waterlogged

## 1589 WARWICK (L-H)
### Monday, May 3

**OFFICIAL GOING: Soft**
Wind: slt across Weather: mainly sunny

### 1839 EUROPEAN BREEDERS FUND PRIMROSE MAIDEN FILLIES' STKS 5f
**2:15** (2:25) (D) 2-Y-O **£4,582** (£1,410; £705; £352) **Stalls** Far side

Form RPR
30 **1** **Little Wizzy**[25] [1307] 2-8-11 ...... JoannaBadger 7 58
(PDEvans) *w ldr: led over 2f out: sn rdn and hung lft: jst hld on* **33/1**
**2** *shd* **Alexander Capetown (IRE)** 2-8-11 ...... MHills 12 58
(BWHills) *s.i.s: hdwy over 2f out: c stands' side: r.o ins fnl f: jst failed* **7/2**[2]
**3** *nk* **Umniya (IRE)** 2-8-11 ...... CCatlin 5 57
(MRChannon) *s.i.s: gd hdwy fnl f: r.o* **8/1**
**4** *nk* **Ruby's Dream** 2-8-11 ...... SCarson 4 56
(JMBradley) *chsd ldrs: rdn over 2f out: edgd rt jst over 1f out: r.o one pce* **50/1**
**5** *2 1/2* **Ivana Illyich (IRE)** 2-8-11 ...... JDSmith 8 48
(SKirk) *towards rr: pushed along over 3f out: hdwy over 1f out: no ex fnl f* **12/1**
05 **6** *nk* **Misty Princess**[19] [1399] 2-8-11 ...... IMongan 1 48
(MJPolglase) *s.i.s: hdwy over 1f out: one pce fnl f* **12/1**
0 **7** *1* **Elvina Hills (IRE)**[26] [1299] 2-8-4 ...... CHaddon[(7)] 11 45
(WGMTurner) *mid-div: rdn and no hdwy fnl 2f* **33/1**
**8** *1/2* **Kashmar Flight** 2-8-11 ...... WSupple 3 43
(TDEasterby) *chsd ldrs: wnt 2nd and hung lft 2f out: wknd ins fnl f* **16/1**
**9** *nk* **Royal Accolade** 2-8-11 ...... SSanders 13 42
(BHanbury) *prom: rdn over 2f out: wknd fnl f* **6/1**[3]
624 **10** *2* **Gogetter Girl**[20] [1383] 2-8-11 ...... NCallan 6 36
(JGallagher) *led over 2f: wknd over 1f out* **11/4**[1]
60 **11** *2 1/2* **Waterline Lover**[7] [1670] 2-8-11 ...... RHavlin 9 29
(PDEvans) *s.i.s: sn rcvrd: wknd 2f out* **12/1**
0 **12** *3* **Mrs Willy Nilly**[10] [1589] 2-8-11 ...... JBramhill 2 20
(JMBradley) *hung lft over 3f out: sn bhd* **80/1**

65.90 secs (5.70) **Going Correction** +1.025s/f (Soft) **12** Ran SP% **112.3**
Speed ratings: **95,94,94,93,89 89,87,87,86,83 79,74**CSF £137.08 TOTE £20.80: £4.30, £2.10, £2.40; EX 85.70.
**Owner** E A R Morgans **Bred** E A R Morgans **Trained** Pandy, Gwent

**FOCUS**
A shambolic false start to this average fillies' maiden and a flag start means that this form is most unreliable, but the placed horses look capable of winning. The race was hand-timed.

**NOTEBOOK**
**Little Wizzy**, who was done no favours by the false start, showed the benefit of her previous experience by holding on grimly at the finish. Not for the first time, she hung under pressure and the form of this race looks highly suspect, but she has a fair bit of early pace and can build on this.
**Alexander Capetown(IRE)** ◆ would have probably won but for making a very sluggish start. As the penny dropped approaching two out she really found her stride, but the line came just too late for her. She is a half-sister to Power Elite, who won a Listed event over seven furlongs on his debut, and she will improve for further, but looks a ready made winner of a maiden over this trip.
**Umniya(IRE)** also lost ground at the start and was finishing with real effect late on. This half-sister to the smart sprinter Lady Links will come on plenty for this and should go close next time.
**Ruby's Dream** made a pleasing debut. She was not beaten at all far and the fact that her stable's juveniles usually need plenty of time bodes well for her chances of scoring in similar company.
**Gogetter Girl** unseated her rider at the start and when the tape went up, she ran too freely and had nothing left when push came to shove approaching the final furlong. This run can be excused, but she is starting to look exposed now.

### 1840 AXMINSTER CARPETS CLASSIFIED STKS 7f 26y
**2:45** (2:52) (D) 3-Y-O+ **£5,798** (£1,784; £892; £446) **Stalls** Low

Form RPR
0120 **1** **Just A Glimmer**[21] [1367] 4-9-2 80...... IMongan 11 88
(LGCottrell) *w ldr: rdn to ld 2f out: sn edgd lft: r.o* **8/1**
1020 **2** *2 1/2* **Dawn Piper (USA)**[20] [1385] 4-9-4 82......(v) TPQueally[(3)] 4 87
(DRLoder) *led: hdd 2f out: sn rdn: one pce fnl f* **8/1**
1413 **3** *nk* **Chateau Nicol**[14] [1500] 5-9-5 77......(v) SSanders 6 84
(BGPowell) *hld up and bhd: hdwy over 2f out: sn rdn: r.o ins fnl f* **7/2**[1]
3-06 **4** *3 1/2* **H Harrison (IRE)**[22] [1345] 4-8-12 80...... PPMathers[(7)] 12 75
(IWMcinnes) *prom: hung bdly lft over 1f out: nt run on* **25/1**
232- **5** *4* **Handsome Cross (IRE)**[198] [5630] 3-8-12 85...... OUrbina 8 70
(HMorrison) *hld up mid-div: rdn over 3f out: wknd 2f out* **6/1**[3]
40-0 **6** *1/2* **Certain Justice (USA)**[9] [1623] 6-9-5 80...... CCatlin 9 64
(PFICole) *prom: lost pl over 4f out: n.d after* **5/1**[2]
4000 **7** *1 3/4* **Aventura (IRE)**[2] [1765] 4-9-5 80...... JBramhill 2 60
(MJPolglase) *s.i.s: a bhd* **9/1**
000- **8** *5* **San Antonio**[188] [5820] 4-9-7 82...... MHills 10 49
(BWHills) *bhd fnl 3f* **8/1**
06-U **9** *1 1/4* **Tagula Blue (IRE)**[30] [1247] 4-9-5 80......(v[1]) WSupple 5 44
(JAGlover) *s.i.s: plld hrd: sn prom: rdn over 3f out: wknd over 2f out* **10/1**
013- **10** *8* **Liquid Form (IRE)**[206] [5468] 4-9-10 85...... AMcCarthy 3 29
(BHanbury) *a in rr* **25/1**

1m 28.91s (4.01) **Going Correction** +0.75s/f (Yiel)
**WFA** 3 from 4yo+ 12lb **10** Ran SP% **113.3**
Speed ratings: **107,104,103,99,95 94,92,86,85,76**CSF £68.32 TOTE £10.50: £2.60, £3.00, £1.70; EX 107.50.
**Owner** Manor Farm Packers Ltd **Bred** Mrs P A Reditt And M J Reditt **Trained** Dulford, Devon

**FOCUS**
A solid pace to this fair handicap saw the field strung out from an early stage.

**NOTEBOOK**
**Just A Glimmer**, who has done most of her racing on the All-Weather, appreciated the drop in grade to score her first turf success readily. She had been dropped 4lb since her last run and was given a positive ride on this occasion, relishing the ground, and looks capable of adding to this granted similar conditions.
**Dawn Piper(USA)** set the generous gallop and although he had no answer to the winner, he did well to stick to his task under pressure. This was the slowest ground he had encountered and he handled it well, so could be placed to advantage off his current mark.
**Chateau Nicol**, back up in trip, was given a fair bit to do from off the pace and got going all too late in the day. He is a consitent sort who seems at his best over this trip and his winning turn does not look far off.
**H Harrison(IRE)** travelled nicley on the bridle until he hung fire under pressure and his chance was lost from that point onwards. He has shown temperament in the past and is not one to trust, but he has talent and may do better on quicker ground.
**Handsome Cross(IRE)**, a tough and consistent juvenile last year, ran well over this trip on ground he did not look comfortable on. He will strip a lot fitter for this reappearance and looks one to be with over shorter on better ground.
**Liquid Form(IRE)** *Official explanation: jockey said gelding was unsuited by the soft ground*

### 1841 COVENTRY CUP H'CAP 7f 26y
**3:20** (3:23) (D) (0-80,78) 3-Y-O **£8,027** (£2,470; £1,235; £617) **Stalls** Low

Form RPR
030- **1** **Apex**[177] [5950] 3-9-2 **73**...... WSupple 2 82
(EALDunlop) *hld up and bhd: hdwy over 3 out: rdn 2 out: led wl ins fnl f: r.o* **9/1**
60-1 **2** *shd* **Kamanda Laugh**[35] [1169] 3-9-2 **73**...... MHills 6 82
(BWHills) *a.p: led over 2f out: rdn wl over 1f out: hdd wl ins fnl f: r.o* **5/1**[1]
100- **3** *1 1/4* **Mr Jack Daniells (IRE)**[213] [5339] 3-8-11 **71**...... RMiles[(3)] 4 77
(WRMuir) *hld up and bhd: gd hdwy over 1f out: r.o ins fnl f* **33/1**
130- **4** *2 1/2* **Leaping Brave (IRE)**[199] [5613] 3-9-6 **77**...... AMcCarthy 15 76
(BRMillman) *prom: lost pl over 4f out: hdwy over 1f out: kpt on ins fnl f* **66/1**
6-01 **5** *3/4* **Cotosol**[17] [1452] 3-9-6 **77**...... SSanders 12 75
(BAMcmahon) *chsd ldrs: rdn over 3f out: one pce fnl f* **11/2**[2]
423- **6** *1/2* **Dandouce**[153] [6118] 3-8-13 **70**...... BDoyle 14 66
(PWChapple-Hyam) *led over 1f: rdn 3f out: one pce fnl 2f* **8/1**[3]
0512 **7** *3/4* **Phluke**[9] [1613] 3-9-2 **73**...... SCarson 11 67
(RFJohnsonHoughton) *prom: rdn and ev ch over 1f out: wknd ins fnl f* **5/1**[1]
0-04 **8** *1 1/4* **Xpres Digital**[9] [1614] 3-9-3 **74**......(t) JBramhill 8 65
(SRBowring) *dwlt: rdn and hdwy over 2f out: no imp fnl f* **20/1**
0-00 **9** *3/4* **Cartronageeraghlad (IRE)**[23] [1333] 3-9-4 **78**......(b) TPQueally[(3)] 13 67
(JAOsborne) *led over 5f out: rdn and hdd over 2f out: wknd fnl f* **16/1**
03-0 **10** *3* **Distant Connection (IRE)**[20] [1382] 3-9-4 **75**...... EStack 16 57
(APJarvis) *prom: rdn and ev ch over 2f out: wknd over 1f out* **100/1**
6-56 **11** *2* **Diamond George (IRE)**[94] [640] 3-7-12 **60**...... DFox[(5)] 5 37
(JohnBerry) *a bhd* **33/1**
0-03 **12** *nk* **Arfinnit (IRE)**[28] [1270] 3-8-13 **70**...... CCatlin 10 46
(MRChannon) *bhd fnl 4f* **20/1**
03-0 **13** *3/4* **Thadea (IRE)**[33] [1214] 3-8-7 **64** ow1...... IMongan 9 38
(JGGiven) *mid-div: hmpd over 3f out: sn bhd* **33/1**
44-0 **14** *3* **Urban Rose**[16] [1464] 3-8-8 **65**...... OUrbina 7 32
(JWUnett) *hld up: hdwy over 3f out: wknd over 1f out: eased fnl f* **14/1**
53-0 **15** *3 1/2* **Among Dreams**[117] [462] 3-8-9 **66**...... NCallan 3 24
(AGNewcombe) *a bhd* **16/1**
240- **16** *3 1/2* **Ninah**[209] [5443] 3-8-7 **71**...... BSwarbrick[(7)] 1 20
(JMBradley) *a bhd* **40/1**
4210 **17** *7* **Hazewind**[21] [1357] 3-8-3 **60**...... JoannaBadger 17 —
(PDEvans) *a bhd* **9/1**

1m 30.2s (5.30) **Going Correction** +0.75s/f (Yiel) **17** Ran SP% **121.5**
Speed ratings: **99,98,97,94,93 93,92,90,90,86 84,83,83,79,75 71,63**CSF £48.64 CT £992.78 TOTE £13.60: £3.80, £2.10, £9.60, £10.50; EX 58.30.
**Owner** Patrick Milmo And Stuart Tilling **Bred** P D And Mrs C E Player And Jonathon Jay **Trained** Newmarket, Suffolk

**FOCUS**
A fair three-year-old handicap run at a fair pace.

**NOTEBOOK**
**Apex** gained a deserved first success in gritty fashion. He was given a well-judged and strong ride on this occasion and relished this ground, which looks the key to further success.
**Kamanda Laugh** gave his all in defeat and only just failed. He went through this ground well and should have no trouble going one better in a similar event over this trip.
**Mr Jack Daniells(IRE)** finished with real effect and had no problems on this testing ground. He should come on a lot physically for the run and progress again, but will go up in the weights for this.
**Leaping Brave(IRE)** did best of those to be drawn high and saw out this extra furlong well on the softest surface he had encountered to date.
**Cotosol** held every chance, and whilst this was disappointing, he was not disgraced off this 2lb higher mark for winning last time.
**Dandouce**, well-backed throughout the day, found very little off the bridle on this handicap debut. Connections will be praying that better ground brings about some improvement.
**Phluke** held every chance entering the straight, but a combination of this testing ground and his latest rise in the weights found him out.
**Thadea(IRE)** *Official explanation: jockey said filly suffered interference approaching the 4f marker*

### 1842 SPRING MEMBERSHIP MAIDEN FILLIES' STKS 1m 22y
**3:50** (3:54) (D) 3-Y-O+ **£4,127** (£1,270; £635; £317) **Stalls** Low

Form RPR
0- **1** **Dreaming Of You (IRE)**[203] [5539] 3-8-8 ...... BDoyle 7 75
(SirMichaelStoute) *a.p: rdn over 2f out: led wl ins fnl f: r.o* **14/1**

03 2 ½ **Beauchamp Star**[21] [1370] 3-8-8 SCarson 4 74
(GAButler) *t.k.h: mid-div: hdwy over 2f out: rdn over 1f out: ev ch fnl f* **7/1**
34-5 3 ½ **Lyca Ballerina**[18] [1408] 3-8-8 73 MHills 2 73
(BWHills) *hld up in tch: rdn over 2f out: led over 1f out: hdd and nt qckn wl ins fnl f* **9/4**[1]
43-3 4 2½ **Nukhbah (USA)**[14] [1507] 3-8-8 70 SSanders 15 68
(LadyHerries) *led: rdn over 2f out: hdd over 1f out: no ex ins fnl f* **9/2**[3]
4-0 5 3 **Cara Bella**[19] [1400] 3-8-5 TPQueally(3) 13 62
(DRLoder) *a.p: rdn over 2f out: wknd ins fnl f* **10/3**[2]
6 2 **Miss Monica (IRE)** 3-8-8 WSupple 10 58
(HRACecil) *prom: ev ch 2f out: sn rdn: wknd 1f out* **12/1**
7 2 **Trew Class** 3-8-8 NCallan 9 54
(MHTompkins) *hld up towards rr: sme hdwy over 1f out: n.d* **20/1**
0 8 1¼ **Dareneur (IRE)**[9] [1628] 4-9-2 MSavage(5) 1 52
(WMBrisbourne) *prom: wkng whn edgd rt over 1f out* **125/1**
9 1¾ **Danettie** 3-8-1 BSwarbrick(7) 8 48
(WMBrisbourne) *dwlt: nvr nr ldrs* **100/1**
0- 10 5 **Viola Da Braccio (IRE)**[199] [5612] 3-8-8 CCatlin 3 38
(DJDaly) *a bhd* **66/1**
5 11 ¾ **My Little Sophia**[63] [942] 4-9-0 PVarley(7) 6 37
(MMullineaux) *prom over 4f* **125/1**
12 ¾ **Tetchy** 4-9-7 IMongan 5 35
(JGGiven) *hld up and bhd: hdwy on ins 3f out: wknd over 1f out* **20/1**
- 13 8 **Kerristina** 3-8-8 JDSmith 14 19
(DJSFrenchDavis) *prom 5f* **66/1**
0- 14 3½ **Light The Dawn (IRE)**[208] [5454] 4-9-7 GBaker 11 12
(WMBrisbourne) *a bhd* **80/1**

1m 49.39s (10.09) **Going Correction** +1.10s/f (Soft)
**WFA** 3 from 4yo 13lb **14 Ran SP% 115.2**
Speed ratings: **93,92,92,89,86 84,82,81,79,74 73,73,65,61**CSF £99.84 TOTE £10.50: £3.30, £1.80, £1.50; EX 51.10.
**Owner** M Tabor & Mrs John Magnier **Bred** Ballymacoll Stud Farm Ltd **Trained** Newmarket, Suffolk

**FOCUS**
A modest winning time to this average fillies' maiden.

**NOTEBOOK**
**Dreaming Of You(IRE)** stayed on stoutly in the final furlong to get off the mark on her second outing. This half-sister to the smart hurdler/stayer on the Flat Landing Light had excuses on her sole juvenile start and looks the type to progress over middle-distances this year, without being one of her stable's leading lights.
**Beauchamp Star** improved on her previous two outings and was not beaten far, but was always looking held by the winner. She has plenty of stamina in her pedigree and can be placed to good effect now that she qualifies for handicaps.
**Lyca Ballerina**, who set the standard on previous form, came there with every chance approaching the final furlong, but could only muster the one pace under maximum pressure. She is now looking fully exposed.
**Nukhbah(USA)** ran her race with no obvious excuses. She did the best of those to be drawn high and may be worth a switch to handicap company now.
**Cara Bella** looked to be in with every chance entering the straight, but found less than expected under pressure and looked to be hating this ground late on. She is capable of better and now qualifies for handicaps.

## 1843 EDGECOTE H'CAP 1m 4f 134y
**4:25** (4:25) (E) (0-70,68) 3-Y-O **£4,582** (£1,410; £705; £352) **Stalls** Far side

Form RPR
0651 1 **Bill Bennett (FR)**[21] [1365] 3-9-6 **67** GBaker 8 83+
(JJay) *hld up: smooth hdwy on ins over 3f out: led on bit over 2f out: clr over 1f out: easily* **11/2**
0-03 2 7 **Savannah River (IRE)**[16] [1465] 3-7-13 **46** (t) CCatlin 9 47
(CWThornton) *a.p: rdn and ev ch over 2f out: one pce* **9/1**
06-0 3 ¾ **Calara Hills**[16] [1465] 3-7-10 **50** BSwarbrick(7) 4 50
(WMBrisbourne) *hld up: rdn and hdwy 3f out: kpt on same pce fnl 2f* **40/1**
0-42 4 5 **Athollbrose (USA)**[11] [1559] 3-8-9 **56** WSupple 2 49
(TDEasterby) *a.p: rdn over 2f out: wknd fnl f* **5/1**[3]
6205 5 nk **Jackie Kiely**[14] [1509] 3-8-6 **56** RMiles(3) 1 49
(TGMills) *hld up: hdwy over 4f out: rdn over 2f out: wknd fnl f* **10/1**
06-0 6 16 **Cloudingswell**[17] [1440] 3-8-13 **63** DCorby(3) 3 33
(DLWilliams) *hld up: hdwy over 7f out: ev ch over 2f out: wknd over 1f out* **20/1**
064 7 15 **Stage Two (IRE)**[22] [1344] 3-7-12 **45** RFfrench 10 —
(MJohnston) *hld up: rdn and dropped rr over 5f out: sn struggling* **4/1**[1]
-005 8 11 **Russalka**[9] [1627] 3-8-10 **57** NCallan 7 —
(JulianPoulton) *w ldr: led over 6f out: rdn and hdd over 2f out: wknd qckly* **33/1**
00-4 9 2½ **Crociera (IRE)**[27] [1285] 3-9-7 **68** SSanders 11 —
(MHTompkins) *hld up and bhd: rdn 4f out: short-lived effrt 3f out* **9/1**
006- 10 11 **Duke's View (IRE)**[178] [5938] 3-9-7 **68** IMongan 5 —
(MrsAJPerrett) *hld up in tch: wknd over 3f out: eased over 1f out* **9/2**[2]
0-40 11 21 **Bonjour Bond (IRE)**[13] [1532] 3-9-1 **62** FLynch 6 —
(BSmart) *led: rdn and hdd over 6f out: wknd over 4f out: eased whn no ch fnl 3f* **20/1**

2m 59.9s (16.60) **Going Correction** +1.10s/f (Soft) **11 Ran SP% 114.2**
Speed ratings: **92,87,87,84,83 74,64,58,56,49 36**CSF £49.62 CT £1779.81 TOTE £5.80: £2.30, £2.60, £14.50; EX 65.40.
**Owner** Mr & Mrs Jonathan Jay **Bred** J Jay **Trained** Newmarket, Suffolk

**FOCUS**
A weak handicap which produced modest winning time and the field were well strung out behind the easy winner.

**NOTEBOOK**
**Bill Bennett(FR)** followed-up on his previous win with ease racing off a 2lb higher mark. He has relished the switch to turf recently, is obviously in the form of his life at present, and although he will take a hike in the weights for this he is progressing quickly.
**Savannah River(IRE)** improved markedly again for this step up in trip, but had no chance with the winner.
**Calara Hills** showed her best form to date over this longer trip and enjoyed the underfoot conditions.
**Athollbrose(USA)** could not quicken on this ground and failed to improve on his latest effort which gave him an obvious chance in this.
**Stage Two(IRE)**, making his handicap debut, tailed himself off early and was never a threat at any stage. *Official explanation: trainer had no explanation for the poor form shown*
**Duke's View(IRE)** *Official explanation: trainer had no explanation for the poor form shown*
**Bonjour Bond(IRE)** *Official explanation: jockey said gelding had breathing problems*

## 1844 ROWANNA H'CAP 1m 22y
**4:55** (4:58) (F) (0-55,55) 3-Y-O **£3,318** (£948; £474) **Stalls** Low

Form RPR
-005 1 **Three Welshmen**[16] [1467] 3-9-1 **52** (b) IMongan 4 59
(BRMillman) *w ldr: led over 6f out: rdn over 1f out: r.o wl* **11/1**
-436 2 2½ **Turnberry (IRE)**[76] [802] 3-9-4 **55** (v[1]) MHills 12 57
(JWHills) *hld up: hdwy 2f out: chsd wnr over 1f out: chal ins fnl f: no ex* **5/1**[3]
0-06 3 2 **Summerise**[13] [1529] 3-9-2 **53** DeanMcKeown 8 51
(HJCollingridge) *a.p: rdn and one pce fnl 2f* **9/2**[2]
5133 4 1 **Larad (IRE)**[10] [1600] 3-8-3 **47** (b) DerekNolan(7) 7 43
(JSMoore) *led over 1f: prom: rdn over 3f out: once pce fnl 2f* **11/2**
0-54 5 ½ **Flying Spud**[16] [1478] 3-8-10 **47** NCallan 3 42
(JLSpearing) *prom: rdn over 4f out: wknd 1f out* **14/1**
0- 6 1 **Mr Strowger**[138] [6203] 3-8-13 **50** RSmith 1 43
(ACharlton) *bhd: styd on fnl f: n.d* **33/1**
005 7 3 **Accendere**[21] [1366] 3-9-1 **52** SSanders 5 39
(RMBeckett) *hld up: hdwy over 4f out: rdn 3f out: wknd fnl f* **10/3**[1]
3066 8 4 **Bookiesindexdotcom**[46] [1046] 3-8-13 **50** (v) WSupple 11 29
(JRJenkins) *hld up and bhd: hdwy on ins over 2f out: sn no imp* **16/1**
650- 9 ½ **Melinda's Girl**[213] [5339] 3-9-1 **52** EStack 15 30
(APJarvis) *prom: rdn over 3f out: sn wknd* **25/1**
05-5 10 5 **Venetian Romance (IRE)**[16] [1478] 3-9-4 **55** (be[1]) GHannon 13 23
(APJones) *a bhd* **33/1**
20-0 11 6 **Delcienne**[16] [1467] 3-8-10 **47** AMcCarthy 2 3
(GGMargarson) *a bhd* **20/1**
555- 12 4 **Elitista (FR)**[168] [6012] 3-8-12 **52** TPQueally(3) 14 —
(EJO'Neill) *t.k.h in tch: lost pl 4f out: sn bhd* **25/1**
0600 13 dist **Trompe L'Oeil (IRE)**[25] [1309] 3-8-13 **50** (p) SCarson 10 —
(AndrewReid) *bhd fnl 3f: t.o* **6/1**

1m 50.72s (11.42) **Going Correction** +1.10s/f (Soft) **13 Ran SP% 126.8**
Speed ratings: **86,83,81,80,80 79,76,72,71,66 60,56,—**CSF £65.21 CT £304.94 TOTE £16.50: £2.90, £2.80, £2.20; EX 72.00.
**Owner** Mouse Racing **Bred** Mouse Racing **Trained** Kentisbeare, Devon

**FOCUS**
A slow winning time to this low grade handicap.

**NOTEBOOK**
**Three Welshmen** appreciated the undefoot conditions and stayed on well under a postive ride to lose his maiden tag at the 11th attempt. He has improved for the application of blinkers the last twice and remains unexposed on this ground, but is inconsistent and not one to rely on for a follow-up bid.
**Turnberry(IRE)**, with the blinkers swapped for this visor on this occasion, looked the likely winner two out, but he quickly came under maximum pressure and could not quicken. He can make amends in this grade when dropped back to seven furlongs.
**Summerise** held every chance on this drop in trip, but lacked the change gears necessary to get to the leaders. She seemed to find ten furlongs beyond her last time, but shaped as though she may be worth another try.
**Larad(IRE)**
**Accendere** did not improve as expected on this handicap debut over this extra furlong. He may be worth another chance on better ground. *Official explanation: trainer said gelding was unsuited by the soft ground*
**Delcienne** *Official explanation: jockey said filly was unsuited by the ground*
**Trompe L'Oeil(IRE)** was reported by her rider to have been unsuited by the ground. *Official explanation: jockey said filly was unsuited by the ground*

## 1845 KNOWLE APPRENTICE H'CAP 1m 22y
**5:25** (5:28) (G) (0-85,84) 3-Y-O+ **£3,066** (£876; £438) **Stalls** Low

Form RPR
645- 1 **Heneseys Leg**[183] [5891] 4-7-13 **60** JDO'Reilly(5) 2 77
(JohnBerry) *hld up: hdwy over 2f out: hrd rdn and edgd rt wl over 1f out: sn led: edgd rt ins fnl f: r.o* **33/1**
0012 2 nk **Best Before (IRE)**[7] [1675] 4-8-0 **61** StevenHarrison(5) 7 77
(PDEvans) *plld hrd: prom: led over 4f out: rdn and hdd over 1f out: ev ch ins fnl f: r.o* **6/1**[3]
0-00 3 5 **Parnassian**[7] [1675] 4-8-0 **56** RThomas 12 62
(GBBalding) *hld up: hdwy over 2f out: rdn over 1f out: one pce* **10/1**
30-0 4 ¾ **Pay The Silver**[21] [1369] 6-8-12 **71** (p) BSwarbrick(3) 3 76
(IAWood) *hld up: hdwy over 2f out: one pce fnl f* **25/1**
00-0 5 4 **Nuit Sombre (IRE)**[9] [1623] 4-9-6 **81** WHogg(5) 10 78
(MJohnston) *hld up: hdwy 3f out: rdn over 1f out: wknd fnl f* **6/1**[3]
0-00 6 ½ **Fleetwood Bay**[14] [1504] 4-9-2 **72** DFox 11 68
(BRMillman) *led: hdd over 4f out: wknd over 1f out* **50/1**
1 7 1 **First Dynasty (USA)**[9] [1628] 4-9-9 **79** AQuinn 9 73
(MissSJWilton) *prom tl wknd over 1f out* **8/1**
0026 8 nk **Hov**[7] [1665] 4-9-2 **72** (p) NChalmers 4 65
(JJQuinn) *nvr nr ldrs* **7/2**[1]
3000 9 1½ **Ephesus**[59] [971] 4-9-6 **79** (v) SJDonohoe(3) 5 69
(MissGayKelleway) *prom tl wknd over 1f out* **16/1**
0-06 10 ¾ **Mr Dip**[50] [1022] 4-7-11 **58** CHaddon(5) 6 46
(AWCarroll) *plld hrd: broke wl: sn mid-div: bhd fnl 4f* **66/1**
5200 11 ½ **The Bonus King**[7] [1671] 4-9-7 **84** AElliott(7) 8 71
(MJohnston) *prom: rdn 3f out: sn wknd* **8/1**
1030 12 3 **Kentucky King (USA)**[16] [1460] 4-9-10 **83** PGallagher(3) 1 64
(PWHiatt) *s.i.s: a bhd* **11/2**[2]
005- 13 hd **Johannian**[220] [5187] 6-9-9 **84** CJDavies(5) 13 65
(JMBradley) *hld up mid-div: bhd fnl 3f* **33/1**
205- 14 13 **Anna Walhaan (IRE)**[174] [4960] 5-9-3 **76** ow1 SCrawford(3) 17 31
(IanWilliams) *sn prom: rdn over 3f out: wknd over 2f out* **33/1**
002- 15 5 **Adobe**[204] [5498] 9-8-13 **69** MSavage 16 14
(WMBrisbourne) *hld up: rdn over 2f out: sn bhd* **16/1**

1m 47.24s (7.94) **Going Correction** +1.10s/f (Soft) **15 Ran SP% 125.4**
Speed ratings: **104,103,98,97,93 92,91,91,89,88 88,85,85,72,67**CSF £220.86 CT £2229.63 TOTE £42.80: £8.80, £2.50, £3.20; EX 251.10 Place 6 £481.11, Place 5 £162.26.
**Owner** Peter J Skinner **Bred** J W Ford **Trained** Newmarket, Suffolk

**FOCUS**
Not a bad time under the circumstances, faster than the other two races over the same trip despite the deteriorating conditions.

**NOTEBOOK**
**Heneseys Leg**, off for 183-day previously, put her proven stamina to great effect late on to score all-out. Her best form last year was on fast ground over father, but these conditions played to her strength and she looks to have improved during the winter.
**Best Before(IRE)** paid for running too keen in the early stages, as he had no more to give when challenged late on. This was still another solid run however, on ground that was plenty soft enough, and he was clear of the rest.
**Parnassian** kept on at the one pace in the straight, but never looked like getting to the leaders. He remains a maiden after 20 outings and looks worth a drop into selling company.
**Pay The Silver** ran respectably over a trip short of his best and will come on again for the run.
**Nuit Sombre(IRE)** has lost her way of late and did nothing to suggest a return to form on this occasion.
**Hov** looked to have an obvious chance on his previous form, but was never going at any stage and proved most disappointing.

T/Plt: £641.30 to a £1 stake. Pool: £37,033.70. 42.15 winning tickets. T/Qpdt: £94.30 to a £1 stake. Pool: £2,384.40. 18.70 winning tickets. KH

1846 - (Foreign Racing) - See Raceform Interactive

## 1645 CURRAGH (R-H)

Monday, May 3

**OFFICIAL GOING: Straight course - good; round course - good to firm**

### 1847a ROCK OF GIBRALTAR EUROPEAN BREEDERS FUND TETRARCH STKS (GROUP 3) (C&F) 7f

**3:00** (3:00) 3-Y-O **£41,260** (£12,105; £5,767; £1,964)

RPR

1 **Leitrim House**[30] 1239 3-9-0 ........ MJKinane 2 116
(BJMeehan) *mde all: rdn and r.o wl fr 2f out: eased cl home: easily* **5/2**[1]

2 *3 ½* **Grand Reward (USA)**[213] 5348 3-9-0 111 ........ PJScallan 3 107
(APO'Brien, Ire) *cl up: 2nd fr 1/2-way: rdn and no imp fr 2f out: kpt on* **3/1**[2]

3 *2* **Mokabra (IRE)**[19] 1396 3-9-3 ........ ACulhane 4 105
(MRChannon) *cl up: 3rd rdn and outpcd over 2 1/2f out: kpt on fnl f* **9/2**[3]

4 *½* **Newton (IRE)**[29] 1256 3-9-0 105 ........ PCosgrave 5 101
(APO'Brien, Ire) *hld up in 4th: rdn and no imp fr over 2f out* **5/2**[1]

5 *4* **Noahs Ark (IRE)**[22] 1347 3-8-11 96 ........ PJSmullen 1 87
(DKWeld, Ire) *a bhd: trailing fr over 2f out* **12/1**

1m 22.3s **Going Correction** -0.45s/f (Firm) **5** Ran SP% **108.0**
Speed ratings: **114,110,107,107,102**CSF £9.80 TOTE £3.40: £1.80, £1.70; DF 6.50.
**Owner** Gallagher Equine Ltd **Bred** Whitsbury Manor Stud **Trained** Upper Lambourn, Berks

**NOTEBOOK**
**Leitrim House** made all under a positive ride to steal this. Recording a very fast time, helped by a strong tailwind, he possibly would not be without a chance in the Irish 2,000 Guineas.
**Grand Reward(USA)** was struggling in second place from three furlongs down.
**Mokabra(IRE)** could never get on terms over the last two and a half furlongs.
**Newton(IRE)** was never close enough to utilise his turn of foot.
**Noahs Ark(IRE)** *Official explanation: jockey said filly lost her action 2f out and was eased in the closing stages*

### 1849a GOLAN EUROPEAN BREEDERS FUND MOORESBRIDGE STKS (GROUP 3) 1m 2f

**4:00** (4:01) 4-Y-0+ **£41,197** (£12,042; £5,704; £1,901)

RPR

1 **Nysaean (IRE)**[9] 1622 5-9-4 ........ MJKinane 6 117
(RHannon) *trckd ldrs travelling wl: 3rd into st: qcknd into ld over 1f out: sn clr: easily* **6/4**[2]

2 *2 ½* **Latino Magic (IRE)**[8] 1647 4-9-0 104 ........ RMBurke 8 108
(RJOsborne, Ire) *hld up: 6th appr st: hdwy on outer 2f out: kpt on ins fnl f* **12/1**[3]

3 *1 ½* **Akshar (IRE)**[36] 1156 5-9-0 109 ........(b[1]) PJSmullen 4 105
(DKWeld, Ire) *chsd ldrs: 4th into st: sn rdn: kpt on fnl f* **14/1**

4 *2 ½* **Middlemarch (IRE)**[39] 1107 4-9-0 ........(p) JFEgan 5 101
(JSGoldie) *led: jnd bef 1/2-way: slt advantage st: hdd over 1f out: no ex* **25/1**

5 *shd* **Brian Boru**[36] 1156 4-9-7 117 ........(t) JAHeffernan 7 107
(APO'Brien, Ire) *cl up: disp ld bef 1/2-way: rdn and hdd ent st: rallied 2f out: no ex and wknd over 1f out* **5/4**[1]

6 *3* **Tacitus (IRE)**[8] 1647 4-9-0 100 ........ NGMcCullagh 2 95
(DTHughes, Ire) *chsd ldrs in 4th: 5th and rdn appr st: no ex over 1f out* **16/1**

7 *13* **Avorado (IRE)**[29] 1254 6-9-4 110 ........ KJManning 3 74
(JSBolger, Ire) *a bhd: trailing fr 2f out* **14/1**

2m 9.30s **Going Correction** +0.25s/f (Good) **7** Ran SP% **115.2**
Speed ratings: **110,108,106,104,104 102,91**CSF £20.15 TOTE £3.00: £1.30, £4.30; DF 40.80.
**Owner** Fieldspring Racing **Bred** Mme L Ades **Trained** East Everleigh, Wilts

**NOTEBOOK**
**Nysaean(IRE)** handled this drying ground without any problems and followed up his success in this race last year. Always travelling well, he went clear inside the last, and the Arc is now the main target this season
**Latino Magic(IRE)** continues his rate of improvement, although he was comfortably held by the winner.
**Akshar(IRE)** showed improved form in first-time blinkers.
**Middlemarch(IRE)** showed plenty of zest with the cheekpieces on. He ran in front until headed and outpaced by the winner.
**Brian Boru** was bluntly a disappointment after his first-time-out Leopardstown win over this trip when he was allowed to dominate. He took on the leader from halfway and never looked comfortable. He needs to be stepped up in trip.

1850 - 1852a (Foreign Racing) - See Raceform Interactive

## 1683 BATH (L-H)

Tuesday, May 4

**OFFICIAL GOING: Soft (good to soft in places)**

### 1853 EUROPEAN BREEDERS FUND MAIDEN STKS 5f 11y

**2:20** (2:23) (D) 2-Y-O **£4,585** (£1,411; £705; £352) **Stalls Low**

Form RPR

1 **Johnny Jumpup (IRE)** 2-9-0 ........ SSanders 2 85
(RMBeckett) *a.p: led over 2f out: rdn out* **12/1**

2 *2 ½* **Iceman** 2-9-0 ........ LDettori 8 76
(JHMGosden) *a.p: rdn to go 2nd 2f out: no imp fnl f* **11/8**[1]

35 3 *6* **Dustini (IRE)**[9] 1638 2-9-0 ........(b[1]) ADaly 10 55
(WGMTurner) *led tl hdd over 2f out: one pce after* **14/1**

4 *1 ¼* **Ms Polly Garter** 2-8-9 ........ RLMoore 4 46
(JMBradley) *trckd ldr to 2f out: one pce after* **20/1**

5 *¾* **Aberdeen Park** 2-8-9 ........ JoannaBadger 9 43
(MrsHSweeting) *towards rr: hdwy 1/2-way: wknd ins fnl f* **40/1**

6 *3* **Troublesome Gerri** 2-8-9 ........ VSlattery 12 33
(SCBurrough) *rdn 2f out: nvr bttre tham mid-div* **66/1**

7 *nk* **Make It Happen Now** 2-8-6 ........ DCorby[(3)] 3 31
(SCBurrough) *in tch tl rdn 2f out: sn btn* **50/1**

8 *2* **Alright My Son (IRE)** 2-9-0 ........ DaneO'Neill 7 29
(RHannon) *v.s.a: rdn over 3f out: no hdwy* **5/1**[2]

9 *2 ½* **Agilete** 2-9-0 ........ SDrowne 6 21
(LGCottrell) *prom tl wknd over 1f out* **13/2**[3]

0 10 *4* **Muestra (IRE)**[11] 1589 2-8-9 ........ FNorton 11 —
(MrsPNDutfield) *slowly away: a in rr* **50/1**

11 *2* **Pie Corner** 2-8-11 ........ LPKeniry[(3)] 15 —
(MMadgwick) *mid-div tl rdn and wknd over 2f out* **40/1**

5 12 *5* **Listen To Me**[10] 1607 2-9-0 ........ PaulEddery 5 —
(DHaydnJones) *sn mid-div: wknd 1/2-way* **40/1**

13 *1 ½* **Cleo Collins (IRE)** 2-8-9 ........ MartinDwyer 13 —
(SKirk) *slowly away: a in rr* **12/1**

14 *shd* **Amalgam (IRE)** 2-8-9 ........ RHavlin 1 —
(MrsPNDutfield) *slowly away: a wl in rr* **28/1**

66.79 secs (4.29) **Going Correction** +0.75s/f (Yiel) **14** Ran SP% **115.1**
Speed ratings: **95,91,81,79,78 73,72,69,65,59 56,48,45,45**CSF £25.77 TOTE £14.30: £3.40, £1.10, £2.50; EX 65.30.
**Owner** Mr & Mrs A Briars **Bred** Mill House Stud **Trained** Lambourn, Berks

**FOCUS**
Just an ordinary maiden, but the front two were nicely clear. There could be a couple in behind capable of improving the form they showed on this occasion.

**NOTEBOOK**
**Johnny Jumpup(IRE)**, an 11,00gns yearling and half-brother to six furlong/mile winner Ally Makbul, created a good impression on this racecourse debut - he seemed to know his job and always looked like holding off the favourite. There may be a few in behind who will have needed the experience more than him, but he should not be underestimated when he steps up in grade.
**Iceman**, a half-brother to a six furlong two-year-old winner, was backed to make a winning debut, but simply found one too good. He was clear of the third and should find a similar race.
**Dustini(IRE)** appeared to improve for the fitting of blinkers. He has a weak maiden in him, but looks one to oppose in the long run.
**Ms Polly Garter**, a 2,100gns yearling, first foal out of an unraced mare, hails from a stable that has not done too badly with it juveniles this season. She made a pleasing debut, faring the best of the fillies, and should be capable of improvement.
**Aberdeen Park**, out of a dual six-furlong All-Weather selling winner at two, hinted at ability but will need to improve to pick up a similar race.
**Alright My Son(IRE)**, a 28,000euros yearling and out of a mare placed in France at around a mile, was slowly away and never got competitive. He is likely to be capable of much better than this and will stay further.

### 1854 SALTWELL SIGNS CLAIMING STKS 5f 161y

**2:50** (2:52) (F) 3-Y-0 **£2,912** (£832; £416) **Stalls Low**

Form RPR

06-0 1 **Cornwallis**[90] 673 3-8-5 55 ........ RLMoore 10 67
(RGuest) *bhd: rdn 1/2-way: gd hdwy fr 2f out: drvn to ld ins fnl f: r.o wl* **12/1**

400- 2 *3 ½* **Borzoi Maestro**[193] 5725 3-9-1 77 ........ ADaly 4 67
(JLSpearing) *t.k.h early: trckd ldrs: led gng wl appr fnl f: sn rdn: hdd and outpcd ins last* **9/2**[2]

04 3 *1 ¾* **Rocket (IRE)**[15] 1496 3-8-11 ........ DaneO'Neill 5 57
(RHannon) *w ldrs: chal 3f out: sn rdn one pce fnl 2f* **11/1**

000- 4 *shd* **Jinksonthehouse**[189] 5816 3-8-4 60 ........ MartinDwyer 7 50
(MDIUsher) *chsd ldrs: rdn over 2f out: styd on same pce* **12/1**

0200 5 *5* **Imperium**[7] 1689 3-9-3 68 ........ TQuinn 9 48
(MrsStefLiddiard) *trckd ldrs: slt ld ins fnl 3f: hdd appr fnl f: wknd ins last* **9/2**[2]

0-36 6 *5* **Marksgold (IRE)**[11] 1597 3-9-1 60 ........ LDettori 6 31
(PFICole) *sn outpcd and pushed along in rr: a bhd* **11/2**[3]

0050 7 *½* **Jaolins**[27] 1300 3-8-6 52 ........ RHavlin 8 20
(PGMurphy) *in tch: rdn and wknd over 2f out* **11/1**

8 *1 ½* **Prince Renesis** 3-8-4 ........ DerekNolan[(7)] 3 21
(JSMoore) *slowly away: a bhd: lost tch fr 1/2-way* **33/1**

-003 9 *14* **Barbilyrifle (IRE)**[33] 1220 3-8-9 62 ........(p) SDrowne 1 —
(HMorrison) *racd alone far side: a wl bhd* **4/1**[1]

0000 10 *nk* **Ricky Martan**[57] 983 3-8-5 58 ........(v[1]) JBramhill 2 —
(GCBravery) *slt ld tl hdd jst ins fnl 3f: sn wknd* **12/1**

1m 15.99s (4.85) **Going Correction** +0.75s/f (Yiel) **10** Ran SP% **114.4**
Speed ratings: **97,92,90,89,83 76,75,73,55,54**CSF £64.10 TOTE £17.40: £5.50, £1.90, £2.40; EX 114.90.The winner was claimed by J S King for £5,000. Prince Renesis was claimed by I W McInnes for £8,000
**Owner** The Bricklayers Partnership **Bred** Mrs Susan Feddern **Trained** Newmarket, Suffolk

**FOCUS**
Not a very strong race, featuring some disappointing sorts. That said, the winner did the job nicely and is obviously the one to take from the race.

**NOTEBOOK**
**Cornwallis** did not show a great deal in maiden company on the All-Weather and had plenty to find with some of these at the weights, 12lb with the runner-up. Making his turf debut off the back off a 90-day break, he ran by far his best race to date, taking this weak event in good style. He would be of interest if turned out under a penalty as he is sure to take a significant rise in the weights.
**Borzoi Maestro** was no sure thing to have trained on. Although he showed himself still capable at the right level, this run suggested he is not as good as he was. He was ridden with more restraint than was often the case, but did not find that much when asked.
**Rocket(IRE)** did nothing wrong and, still gaining experience, there could be a similarly weak race in him.
**Jinksonthehouse** did not really progress at two, but this was a fair reappearance. She will need to step up on this, however, to find a similar race.
**Imperium** is a disappointing sort and the drop in grade was not the answer.
**Marksgold(IRE)** *Official explanation: jockey said gelding suffered interference soon after the start*
**Barbilyrifle(IRE)** continues to regress.

### 1855 OSWALD BAILEY FILLIES' H'CAP 5f 161y

**3:20** (3:21) (E) (0-70,70) 3-Y-0+ **£3,692** (£1,136; £568; £284) **Stalls Low**

Form RPR

330- 1 **Go Go Girl**[173] 5988 4-9-7 63 ........ FNorton 10 73
(LGCottrell) *a in tch: rdn over 1f out: r.o to ld nr fin* **16/1**

060- 2 *1* **Annijaz**[236] 4838 7-8-12 54 ........ RLMoore 16 61
(JMBradley) *hld up towards rr: rdn and rapid hdwy to ld jst ins finl f: kpt on: hdd nr fin* **25/1**

5301 3 *1 ¾* **Amelia (IRE)**[4] 1750 6-8-9 56 6ex ........ BSwarbrick[(5)] 2 58
(WMBrisbourne) *a.p: led wl over 1f out: rdn and hdd jst ins finl f: kpt on one pce* **5/1**[2]

-050 4 *1 ¼* **I Wish**[32] 1229 6-8-13 58 ........ LPKeniry[(3)] 13 56
(MMadgwick) *a.p: ev ch 2f out: sn rdn: one pce fnl f* **10/1**

005- 5 *3* **Calusa Lady (IRE)**[150] 6134 4-9-2 58 ........ RHavlin 7 47
(GBBalding) *mid-div: rdn and hdwy 2f out: r.o one pce after* **20/1**

0336 6 *½* **Cloudless (USA)**[10] 1606 4-8-11 53 ........ DaneO'Neill 8 41
(JWUnett) *towards rr: rdn and sme hdwy 2f out: nvr nr to chal* **9/1**

-604 7 *nk* **Bahamian Belle**[19] 1421 4-9-0 56 ........(t) LDettori 14 43
(PSMcentee) *t.k.h: racd mid-div: wknd approachng fnl f* **7/1**[3]

20-0 8 *1* **Yomalo (IRE)**[19] 1421 4-9-11 67 ........ SSanders 1 51
(RGuest) *slowly away: sn in tch: rdn 2f out: sn btn* **14/1**

0-42 9 *nk* **Gojo (IRE)**[4] 1750 3-9-1 67 ........ TQuinn 12 50
(BPalling) *led for 1f: rdn and ev ch 2f out: wknd appr fnl f* **7/2**[1]

0-05 **10** *nk* **Rileys Dream**[14] 1533 5-8-3 **45**.................................. DKinsella 11 27
(BJLlewellyn) *s.i.s: nvr bttr than mid-div* **20/1**

353- **11** *nk* **Charlottebutterfly**[245] 4641 4-9-5 **61**.................................. JMackay 4 42
(TTClement) *prom tl rdn and wknd over 1f out* **33/1**

20-6 **12** *shd* **Ela Figura**[9] 1642 4-8-11 **56**.................................. SHitchcott(3) 17 37
(AWCarroll) *a towards rr* **16/1**

-400 **13** *2 1/2* **Fiamma Royale (IRE)**[65] 930 6-8-5 **50**.................................. RMiles(3) 3 23
(MSSaunders) *s.i.s: sn prom: led over 2f out: hdd wl over 1f out: sn wknd* **25/1**

0-05 **14** *3* **Barabella (IRE)**[7] 1689 3-8-8 **63**.................................. JFMcDonald(3) 18 27
(RJHodges) *racd wd: sn outpcd in rr* **9/1**

-000 **15** *3/4* **Naughty Girl (IRE)**[84] 737 4-10-0 **70**.................................. KMcEvoy 9 32
(PDEvans) *prom tl wknd 2f out* **33/1**

0U3- **16** *20* **Royal Supremacy (IRE)**[225] 5114 3-8-4 **56**.................................. JBramhill 5 —
(JMBradley) *led after 1f: hdd over 2f out: wknd rapidly and eased fnl f* **40/1**

1m 16.27s (5.13) **Going Correction** +0.75s/f (Yiel)
**WFA** 3 from 4yo+ 10lb **16** Ran SP% **124.4**
Speed ratings: **95,93,91,89,85 85,84,83,82,82 82,81,78,74,73 46**CSF £377.32 CT £2386.64 TOTE £12.50: £2.90, £5.10, £2.10, £3.10; EX 363.70.
**Owner** H C Seymour **Bred** Mascalls Stud **Trained** Dulford, Devon

**FOCUS**
Just an ordinary handicap.

**NOTEBOOK**
**Go Go Girl**, still a maiden going into this, was dropped half a furlong in trip and returned to turf after an unsuccessful spin on Polytrack. She won going away and now she has got that first win under her belt, there could be more to come.
**Annijaz** has done all of her winning on fast ground or Fibresand, but she handled conditions well and ran a blinder on this first start in 236 days. She travelled really nicely and probably ended up going too soon. If she goes the right way from this, there will surely be a similar race in her before too much longer.
**Amelia(IRE)**, under a 6lb penalty for a recent Nottingham victory, did not look to have any excuses.
**I Wish** is not an easy horse to predict, but she ran a fair race and her turn may not be that far off.
**Calusa Lady(IRE)** is not running too badly, but is still looking for her first success. A maiden handicap would be ideal for her.
**Gojo(IRE)** started the season well with a couple of good efforts at Nottingham, but this represented a step backwards

## 1856 OVAL OF BATH, PEUGEOT H'CAP 1m 2f 46y
**3:50** (3:50) (F) (0-55,55) 3-Y-0+ **£3,580** (£1,023; £511) **Stalls** Low

Form RPR

40-5 **1** **Saxe-Coburg (IRE)**[8] 1681 7-9-4 **54**.................................. JFMcDonald(3) 10 66
(GAHam) *bhd: stdy hdwy 4f out: led ins fnl 2f: pushed clr ins last: readily* **28/1**

3242 **2** *3 1/2* **Diamond Orchid (IRE)**[9] 995 4-9-0 **47**.................................. SDrowne 6 53
(PDEvans) *chsd ldrs: rdn and outpcd over 2f out: styd on u.p fr over 1f out: chsd wnr ins last but no imp* **7/1**[3]

6021 **3** *2 1/2* **Icannshift (IRE)**[10] 1611 4-9-8 **55**.................................. RLMoore 19 57
(SDow) *chsd ldrs: wnt 2nd over 3f out: led over 2f out: hdd ins fnl quarter m: wknd and lost 2nd ins last* **9/2**[2]

6312 **4** *1 1/4* **Our Destiny**[7] 1687 6-8-13 **49**.................................. SHitchcott(3) 12 49
(AWCarroll) *chsd ldrs: hrd rdn and one pce fnl 2f* **7/1**[3]

1531 **5** *1/2* **Jake Black (IRE)**[6] 1715 4-9-3 **50**.................................. TQuinn 1 49
(JJQuinn) *in tch: snatched up 7f out: styd prom: rdn to press ldrs fr over 2f out: wknd qckly appr fnl f* **13/8**[1]

000- **6** *2* **Tidal**[195] 5705 5-9-1 **55**.................................. DerekNolan(7) 7 50
(AWCarroll) *slowly into strode: bhd: hdwy over 4f out: drvn to chse ldrs over 2f out: wknd appr fnl f* **25/1**

000- **7** *hd* **Deewaar (IRE)**[38] 4141 4-9-2 **49**.................................. RSmith 4 44
(JCFox) *bhd: pushed along and hdwy 3f out: nvr gng pce to rch ldrs* **66/1**

0002 **8** *nk* **Quarry Island (IRE)**[11] 1579 3-7-12 **46** oh11.................................. JoannaBadger 18 41
(PDEvans) *led after 2f: rdn over 3f out: hdd over 2f out: wknd qckly over 1f out* **40/1**

0-0 **9** *3/4* **Nautical**[22] 1369 6-9-8 **55**.................................. ADaly 11 48
(AWCarroll) *hld up in rr: styd on fnl 2f but nvr nr ldrs* **100/1**

-360 **10** *15* **On Guard**[27] 1305 6-9-5 **52**.................................. (v) DKinsella 5 20
(PGMurphy) *bhd: sme hdwy 4f out: n.d* **25/1**

600- **11** *5* **Danebank (IRE)**[50] 5787 4-9-5 **52**.................................. LDettori 16 11
(JMackie) *in tch: rdn and effrt over 3f out: nvr rchd ldrs and sn wknd* **16/1**

06-0 **12** *18* **Nina Fontenail (FR)**[22] 1356 3-8-3 **50** ow1.................................. EStack 2 —
(NJHawke) *s.i.s: bhd: hdwy 6f out: nvr rchd ldrs and sn wknd* **40/1**

00-0 **13** *3* **Esperance (IRE)**[90] 672 4-9-1 **48**.................................. SSanders 13 —
(JAkehurst) *chsd ldrs tl rdn and wknd rapidly over 3f out* **25/1**

5660 **14** *3/4* **Abbiejo (IRE)**[11] 1591 7-8-10 **46** oh16.................................. RMiles(3) 3 —
(GFierro) *prom early: sn bhd* **80/1**

600- **15** *7* **Multicolour**[358] 1557 4-9-8 **55**.................................. DaneO'Neill 15 —
(RHannon) *sn bhd* **66/1**

55-0 **16** *hd* **In Tune**[26] 1308 4-9-0 **50**.................................. (b[1]) LPKeniry(3) 8 —
(SCBurrough) *chsd ldrs tl wknd rapidly over 3f out* **100/1**

00-3 **17** *6* **Seejay**[31] 1244 4-9-2 **49**.................................. MartinDwyer 9 —
(MAAllen) *t.k.h: led 2f: styd chsng ldrs tl rdn and wknd 3f out* **33/1**

2m 18.67s (7.67) **Going Correction** +0.90s/f (Soft)
**WFA** 3 from 4yo+ 15lb **17** Ran SP% **116.2**
Speed ratings: **105,102,100,99,98 97,97,96,96,84 80,65,63,62,57 57,52**CSF £188.76 CT £1061.81 TOTE £25.30: £3.70, £1.10, £2.20, £2.00; EX 290.10.
**Owner** Sally & Tom Dalley **Bred** Sheikh Mohammed Bin Rashid Al Maktoum **Trained** Rooks Bridge, Somerset

**FOCUS**
A moderate handicap and as is often the case on this sort of ground, few will have really handled conditions.

**NOTEBOOK**
**Saxe-Coburg(IRE)**, 8lb higher than when winning a selling handicap at Windsor last year, was racing on soft ground for this first time and absolutely relished the conditions. He would be of interest if turned out under a penalty in a handicap given similar conditions.
**Diamond Orchid(IRE)**, with the visor left off and returned to the level off the back of a success in a claiming hurdle, was another who had no trouble in handling the ground and ran well.
**Icannshift(IRE)**, 5lb higher than when scoring nicely at Leicester on his previous start, was a little bit disappointing. He got quite tired in the closing stages and this ground was probably softer than ideal.
**Our Destiny** is running well enough, but he last won a handicap off a mark of 30.
**Jake Black(IRE)** was unpenalised for his recent heavy ground success in an apprentice handicap, but was a huge disappointment. Maybe this race came too soon for him. *Official explanation: jockey said gelding suffered interference in running*

## 1857 WEATHERBYS INSURANCE H'CAP 1m 5y
**4:20** (4:22) (E) (0-70,70) 3-Y-0+ **£4,455** (£1,371; £685; £342) **Stalls** Low

Form RPR

4-00 **1** **Lockstock (IRE)**[69] 882 6-9-6 **65**.................................. (p) RMiles(3) 16 77
(MSSaunders) *trckd ldr gng wl: led on bit over 2f out: kpt on strly* **20/1**

6115 **2** *3 1/2* **Amnesty**[8] 1675 5-9-6 **62**.................................. (be) RLMoore 4 67
(GLMoore) *t.k.h: hld up: hdwy and nt clr run over 2f out: swtchd rt over 1f out: r.o to chse wnr fnl f* **7/4**[1]

2-50 **3** *2* **Ember Days**[22] 1369 5-9-6 **62**.................................. (p) VSlattery 2 63
(JLSpearing) *racd keenly: hld up towards rr: hdwy over 2f out: swtchd lft over 1f out: r.o but no ch w first 2* **10/1**[3]

30-4 **4** *1 1/4* **Mobo-Baco**[7] 1687 7-9-4 **60**.................................. SDrowne 15 59
(RJHodges) *led tl hdd over 2f out: one pce after* **10/1**[3]

01-0 **5** *3/4* **Enchanted Princess**[29] 1275 4-10-0 **70**.................................. (v[1]) LDettori 13 67
(WJHaggas) *mid-div: rdn and hdwy over 2f out: wknd ins fnl f* **10/1**[3]

4-00 **6** *3/4* **Clann A Cougar**[19] 1424 4-9-2 **63**.................................. (b[1]) BSwarbrick(5) 5 59
(IAWood) *s.i.s: t.k.h: hdwy to chse ldrs 3f out: wknd wl over 1f out* **14/1**

0-00 **7** *2 1/4* **Sninfia (IRE)**[7] 1684 4-9-1 **60**.................................. JFMcDonald(3) 11 51
(GAHam) *slowly away: sn in tch: rdn 3f out: wknd 2f out* **16/1**

00-0 **8** *1 1/4* **Tuscan Treaty**[118] 469 4-9-4 **60**.................................. JMackay 14 49
(TTClement) *hld up in rr: rdn 4f out: nvr on terms* **66/1**

6-05 **9** *1/2* **B A Highflyer**[14] 1531 4-9-6 **65**.................................. SHitchcott(3) 1 53
(MRChannon) *prom: hrd rdn over 3f out: wknd appr fnl f* **7/1**[2]

0000 **10** *1/2* **Karathaena (IRE)**[12] 1560 4-9-4 **60**.................................. (v[1]) TQuinn 12 47
(JWHills) *trckd ldrs tl wknd appr fnl f* **14/1**

010- **11** *3/4* **Princess Magdalena**[18] 5507 4-9-1 **57**.................................. RHavlin 10 42
(LGCottrell) *trckd ldrs: rdn 3f out: wknd qckly 2f out* **25/1**

3606 **12** *11* **Parker**[11] 1595 7-9-6 **62**.................................. SSanders 6 25
(BPalling) *slowly away: sn in tch: rdn 3f out: sn wknd* **14/1**

5/0- **13** *7* **Night Driver (IRE)**[53] 3066 5-9-10 **66**.................................. DaneO'Neill 3 15
(GLMoore) *a struggling in rr* **14/1**

1m 49.04s (8.04) **Going Correction** +0.90s/f (Soft) **13** Ran SP% **118.8**
Speed ratings: **95,91,89,88,87 86,84,83,82,82 81,70,63**CSF £53.85 CT £409.54 TOTE £19.20: £5.30, £1.10, £2.90; EX 81.10 Trifecta £592.60 Pool £2,587.44, 3.10 winning units.
**Owner** Chris Scott **Bred** W H Joyce **Trained** Haydon, Somerset

**FOCUS**
Just a modest handicap and a slow time.

**NOTEBOOK**
**Lockstock(IRE)** handles this sort of ground well and, returning from a short break, he won nicely. However, he has never won off a mark higher than 67 and will have a tough task next time.
**Amnesty** did not run badly but gave the impression the Handicapper is catching up with him.
**Ember Days**, with the cheekpieces replacing blinkers, and down in trip, ran respectably on ground that would have suited.
**Mobo-Baco** has done all of his winning on firm or good to firm ground so this was by no means a bad performance.
**Enchanted Princess** ran better in the first-time visor, but does look on a high enough mark.
**Clann A Cougar** was too keen in the first-time blinkers.

## 1858 WWW.SALTWELLSIGNS.CO.UK H'CAP 1m 3f 144y
**4:50** (4:53) (F) (0-55,61) 4-Y-0+ **£3,066** (£876; £438) **Stalls** Low

Form RPR

-003 **1** **Only For Sue**[17] 1463 5-8-12 **53**.................................. (b) SDrowne 18 62
(WSKittow) *led 1f: styd trcking ldr tl led 3f out: rdn 2f out: styd on wl whn chal fr over 1f out* **11/1**

0121 **2** *1 1/2* **Great View (IRE)**[9] 1644 5-9-3 **61** 6ex.................................. (v) DCorby(3) 1 68
(MrsALMKing) *chsd ldrs: wnt 2nd over 3f out: rdn to chal 1f out: edgd lft u.p ins last and sn fnd no ex* **9/2**[2]

0603 **3** *8* **Salford Flyer**[7] 1687 8-8-8 **54**.................................. (b) AQuinn(5) 7 50
(JaneSouthcombe) *in tch: rdn over 3f out: styd on for 3rd but no ch w ldrs fnl 2f* **22/1**

22-0 **4** *1 1/4* **Short Change (IRE)**[9] 1644 5-8-10 **54**.................................. SHitchcott(3) 2 48
(AWCarroll) *in tch: rdn 5f out: nvr gng pce to rch ldrs* **10/1**

5020 **5** *nk* **Paradise Valley**[27] 1305 4-8-6 **47**.................................. (t) SSanders 15 41
(MrsStefLiddiard) *mid-div: hrd drvn and styd on fnl 3f: nvr nr ldrs* **25/1**

0-31 **6** *hd* **Red Forest (IRE)**[10] 1630 5-8-12 **53**.................................. (t) LDettori 10 46
(JMackie) *bhd: rdn and mod hdwy 5f out: nvr nr ldrs and styd on same pce fnl 3f* **3/1**[1]

1260 **7** *1 1/2* **Cool Bathwick (IRE)**[22] 1369 5-9-0 **55**.................................. (b[1]) MartinDwyer 12 46
(BRMillman) *led after 1f: hdd 3f out: wknd over 2f out* **14/1**

/00- **8** *6* **Western Ridge (FR)**[188] 821 7-8-12 **53**.................................. RHavlin 3 36
(BJLlewellyn) *a mid-div and n.d* **25/1**

004- **9** *5* **Purdey**[284] 3582 4-8-6 **50**.................................. JFMcDonald(3) 17 26
(HMorrison) *bhd: kpt on fnl 2f: nt a danger* **25/1**

000- **10** *1/2* **Java Dawn (IRE)**[323] 2417 4-8-7 **48**.................................. ADaly 14 23
(TEPowell) *hld up in rr: a bhd* **66/1**

44-6 **11** *3/4* **Compton Aviator**[42] 1085 8-9-0 **55**.................................. (t) RLMoore 9 29
(AWCarroll) *bhd most of way* **16/1**

4552 **12** *18* **Free Style (GER)**[9] 1644 4-8-7 **48**.................................. JoannaBadger 20 —
(MrsHSweeting) *t.k.h: chsd ldrs 6f* **12/1**

0502 **13** *2 1/2* **Itsonlyagame**[36] 1168 4-8-9 **50**.................................. (v) DaneO'Neill 4 —
(RIngram) *chsd ldrs 7f* **25/1**

0515 **14** *7* **Un Autre Espere**[7] 1697 5-8-5 **46** oh1.................................. (b) JMackay 11 —
(TWall) *chsd ldrs 6f* **50/1**

100- **15** *9* **Canatrice (IRE)**[20] 5848 4-8-11 **55**.................................. (p) J-PGuillambert(3) 5 —
(TDMccarthy) *s.i.s: a bhd* **33/1**

56-0 **16** *25* **Komati River**[103] 583 5-8-7 **48**.................................. TQuinn 16 —
(JAkehurst) *bhd: rdn and effrt 5f out: sn wknd* **8/1**[3]

0010 **17** *10* **Angelica Garnett**[27] 1297 4-8-6 **47**.................................. FNorton 6 —
(TEPowell) *chsd ldrs 6f* **33/1**

2m 40.8s (10.50) **Going Correction** +0.90s/f (Soft) **17** Ran SP% **121.0**
Speed ratings: **101,100,94,93,93 93,92,88,85,84 84,72,70,66,60 43,36**CSF £52.30 CT £1098.34 TOTE £10.80: £2.00, £2.10, £3.10, £2.40; EX 76.50 Place 6 £152.10, Place 5 £87.92.
**Owner** Ms Susan Arnesen **Bred** A W Schiff **Trained** Blackborough, Devon

**FOCUS**
This proved quite a stamina test and the field finished incredibly well strung out. Not a race to pay to much attention to with regards to future contests.

**NOTEBOOK**
**Only For Sue**, 8lb higher than when winning over a mile and a half at Wolverhampton late last year, proved very game under a positive ride. Very few got home and this is a race to treat with caution, so one would not want to take too short a price about him following up.
**Great View(IRE)** ran a fine race under his big weight, but the winner was just too strong. He is in cracking form.
**Salford Flyer**, beaten in a ten-furlong seller round here on his previous start, did not run badly, but was left behind by the front two.
**Short Change(IRE)** may have found this ground softer than ideal.
**Paradise Valley** is proving really frustrating.

**Red Forest(IRE)** was unable to reproduce his recent Fibresand form back on turf.
**Angelica Garnett** *Official explanation: jockey said filly hung badly left-handed*
T/Jkpt: Not won. T/Plt: £107.40 to a £1 stake. Pool: £39,051.90. 265.25 winning tickets. T/Qpdt: £25.10 to a £1 stake. Pool: £10,091.27. 297.15 winning tickets. ST

## 1638 BRIGHTON (L-H)
### Tuesday, May 4

**OFFICIAL GOING: Good**
Wind: fresh hlf against Weather: unsettled

### 1859 TOTEPLACEPOT BANDED STKS — 5f 59y
2:10 (2:19) (H) 3-Y-0+ — £1,638 (£468; £234) **Stalls** Low

Form — RPR
2063 **1** — **Harbour House**[15] 1497 5-9-7 45 — JTate 3 — 56
(JJBridger) *prom: led over 3f out: rdn to hold on fnl f* — **9/1**
6333 **2** ½ — **Aintnecessarilyso**[11] 1584 6-9-7 45 — PDoe 2 — 54
(NEBerry) *in tch: styd far side st: rdn to press wnr 2f out: ev ch ins fnl f: kpt on* — **2/1**[1]
4004 **3** 1¾ — **So Sober (IRE)**[43] 1075 6-9-7 45 — NCallan 8 — 48
(DShaw) *t.k.h towards rr: rdn and hdwy over 1f out: nrst fin* — **13/2**[3]
0034 **4** 1½ — **Threat**[11] 1584 8-9-4 45 — BReilly(3) 7 — 42
(JMBradley) *a.p: one pce appr fnl f* — **13/2**[3]
0600 **5** 1 — **Mangus (IRE)**[13] 1546 10-9-2 35 — (b) NChalmers(5) 4 — 39
(KOCunningham-Brown) *towards rr: rdn and hdwy over 1f out: nt pce to chal* — **33/1**
4125 **6** hd — **Crafty Politician (USA)**[9] 1639 7-9-7 45 — (b) WRyan 6 — 38
(GLMoore) *hld up in rr: effrt over 1f out: nt rch ldrs* — **10/3**[2]
0-00 **7** 2 — **Frenchmans Lodge**[14] 1519 4-9-0 45 — (b[1]) KGhunowa(7) 10 — 31
(JMBradley) *s.i.s: plld hrd: hdwy to press wnr over 3f out: rdn and btn wl over 1f out* — **25/1**
0461 **8** 3 — **Flying Faisal (USA)**[9] 1639 6-9-6 45 — (b) CJDavies(7) 5 — 26
(JMBradley) *hmpd s: rdn along in rr: sme hdwy on outside 3f out: hrd drvn and btn 2f out* — **11/1**
0023 **9** 6 — **Avit (IRE)**[13] 1546 4-9-7 40 — NPollard 9 — —
(PLGilligan) *chsd ldrs: rdn and edgd rt over 2f out: sn wknd* — **11/1**
0055 **10** ¾ — **Top Place**[11] 1591 3-8-12 40 — (p) JDSmith 1 — —
(CADwyer) *led over 1f: styd far side st: wknd 2f out: eased whn no ch fnl f* — **14/1**

65.49 secs (3.22) **Going Correction** +0.675s/f (Yiel)
**WFA** 3 from 4yo+ 9lb — **10** Ran SP% **123.2**
Speed ratings: **101,100,97,95,93 93,89,85,75,74**CSF £28.96 TOTE £9.60: £3.10, £1.10, £2.40; EX 36.10.
**Owner** Tommy Ware **Bred** Patrick Trant **Trained** Liphook, Hants

**FOCUS**
Not a bad time for a banded stakes. This was Harbour House's second career win.

**NOTEBOOK**
**Harbour House** was winning for the first-time since November 2001, this drop back in trip appearing to suit. He showed up well early, before finding extra to assert close home. Believed to appreciate the rain the course saw, he may be able to pick up a small handicap in the coming weeks.
**Aintnecessarilyso** continues to run well in defeat, but his turn will come again.
**So Sober(IRE)** remains without a win in 20 starts on turf.
**Threat** was comfortably held at the line.
**Mangus(IRE)**, the lowest rated in the field, ran respectably, but is not going to be getting any better at the age of ten.

### 1860 TOTEEXACTA BANDED STKS — 6f 209y
2:40 (2:40) (H) 4-Y-0+ — £1,288 (£368; £184) **Stalls** Low

Form — RPR
3522 **1** — **Tiny Tim (IRE)**[7] 1694 6-8-5 35 — TBlock(7) 3 — 43
(AMBalding) *trckd ldng pair: led over 2f out: rdn clr over 1f out: styd on* — **4/11**[1]
4-00 **2** 4 — **Middlemiss (IRE)**[5] 1723 4-8-12 35 — (p) SRighton 2 — 33
(JWMullins) *in tch: sltly outpcd 1/2-way: rallied to chse wnr 2f out: no imp over 1f out* — **10/1**[3]
66-0 **3** 12 — **Miss Faye**[11] 1583 4-8-9 35 — (p) BReilly(3) 4 — —
(JMBradley) *pressed ldr: led over 3f out tl over 2f out: wknd and hung rt wl over 1f out* — **4/1**[2]
500/ **4** 5 — **Mayfair Maundy**[578] 5061 4-8-5 35 — CHaddon(7) 1 — —
(WGMTurner) *led over 3f: wknd 2f out* — **14/1**

1m 27.5s (4.90) **Going Correction** +0.675s/f (Yiel) — **4** Ran SP% **109.1**
Speed ratings: **99,94,80,75**CSF £4.81 TOTE £1.40; EX 2.90.
**Owner** I A Balding **Bred** Denis Noonan **Trained** Kingsclere, Hants

**FOCUS**
Dreadful stuff.

**NOTEBOOK**
**Tiny Tim(IRE)** was winning at the 30th attempt. He had nothing to beat, but has been running consistently and should continue to earn his keep.
**Middlemiss(IRE)** was the only runner to have a crack at the winner, but never looked like it.
**Miss Faye** will struggle to ever win a race.
**Mayfair Maundy** folded tamely having raced keenly.

### 1861 TOTEQUADPOT BANDED STKS — 7f 214y
3:10 (3:10) (H) 3-Y-0+ — £1,295 (£370; £185) **Stalls** Low

Form — RPR
/354 **1** — **Adjiram (IRE)**[55] 945 8-9-4 30 — (v) WRyan 4 — 38
(AWCarroll) *led tl over 2f out: sn outpcd and hrd rdn: rallied over 1f out: styd on to ld fnl 100 yds* — **15/8**[1]
0063 **2** 1 — **Newcorr (IRE)**[13] 1548 5-8-13 35 — NChalmers(5) 2 — 36
(JJBridger) *chsd ldng pair: jnd ldr 3f out: led jst ins fnl f: hdd and one pce fnl 100 yds* — **7/2**[3]
50-0 **3** 2 — **Point Man (IRE)**[15] 1510 4-9-4 30 — NCallan 5 — 31
(JWPayne) *chsd ldr: led over 2f out tl jst ins fnl f: no ex* — **6/1**
6006 **4** 1½ — **Marengo**[6] 1715 10-8-11 30 — KGhunowa(7) 1 — 28
(PaulJohnson) *hld up in 4th: drvn to press ldrs over 1f out: no ex fnl f* — **6/1**
513- **5** 30 — **Haunt The Zoo**[245] 4643 9-9-4 35 — LVickers 3 — —
(JohnAHarris) *rrd bdly s: lost 15 l: a wl bhd* — **11/4**[2]

1m 43.04s (8.04) **Going Correction** +0.675s/f (Yiel) — **5** Ran SP% **112.2**
Speed ratings: **86,85,83,81,51**CSF £8.92 TOTE £2.70: £1.30, £2.10; EX 7.60.
**Owner** K Marshall **Bred** His Highness The Aga Khan's Studs S C **Trained** Wixford, Warwicks

**FOCUS**
They finished weary and a very slow winning time. It was early leader Adjiram who stayed on best of all to claim victory.

**NOTEBOOK**
**Adjiram(IRE)**, who was having his first run of the season on turf, looked beaten when passed around two furlongs, but his extra stamina saw him ok in a race where they finished tired. The visor which failed to spark any improvement last time seems to now be having the desired effect, and he can win again under suitable conditions.
**Newcorr(IRE)** was another who appreciated the morning rain. He seems to be going the right way now, having taken time to find his feet since arriving from Ireland and could sneak a race of this nature.
**Point Man(IRE)** has yet to find a trip that suits, but he has the ability to win a race when finding one.
**Marengo** ran his best race for a while.
**Haunt The Zoo** lost all chance when rearing leaving the stalls and badly missing the break.

### 1862 TOTEWIN BANDED STKS — 1m 3f 196y
3:40 (3:41) (H) 3-Y-0+ — £1,491 (£426; £213) **Stalls** High

Form — RPR
2262 **1** — **Buz Kiri (USA)**[11] 1581 6-9-10 35 — PDoe 6 — 50
(AWCarroll) *hdwy 5f out: led over 2f out: drvn clr* — **5/2**[1]
2063 **2** 4 — **Dora Corbino**[11] 1593 4-9-10 40 — TGMcLaughlin 8 — 44
(RHollinshead) *led tl over 2f out: kpt on same pce* — **16/1**
0-00 **3** hd — **Dances With Angels (IRE)**[19] 1402 4-9-10 40 — NCallan 4 — 44
(MrsALMKing) *in tch: chsd ldr over 4f out tl 3f out: sn outpcd by ldng pair: edgd lft 1f out: styd on nr fin* — **14/1**
1223 **4** 4 — **Leophin Dancer (USA)**[5] 1728 6-9-10 40 — LVickers 3 — 37
(PWHiatt) *chsd ldrs: hrd rdn 3f out: 4th and wl btn whn hung lft 1f out* — **3/1**[3]
-040 **5** 3 — **Bunino Ven**[15] 1499 3-8-2 40 — (be[1]) BReilly(3) 5 — 32
(SCWilliams) *plld hrd: outpcd and lost tch 5f out: mod 5th and sme hdwy whn hmpd on rail ins fnl f* — **10/1**
0004 **6** 11 — **Island Star (IRE)**[5] 1727 4-9-10 40 — RBrisland 1 — 15
(GPEnright) *bhd: mod effrt 4f out: 6th and no ch whn hung lft fnl 2f* — **20/1**
6002 **7** 2 — **Moyne Pleasure (IRE)**[7] 1700 6-9-3 40 — (p) KGhunowa(7) 7 — 12
(PaulJohnson) *chsd ldr tl outpcd 4f out: wknd over 2f out* — **5/1**
0002 **8** dist — **Timbuktu**[5] 1721 3-8-5 40 — NPollard 2 — —
(CWThornton) *prom 7f: sn bhd: no ch whn virtually p.u over 1f out* — **11/4**[2]

2m 40.4s (8.30) **Going Correction** +0.675s/f (Yiel)
**WFA** 3 from 4yo+ 19lb — **8** Ran SP% **123.3**
Speed ratings: **99,96,96,93,91 84,82,—**CSF £46.73 TOTE £3.10: £1.10, £2.40, £3.30; EX 61.40.
**Owner** Serafino Agodino **Bred** Jamm Ltd And W Lazy T Ltd **Trained** Wixford, Warwicks

**FOCUS**
Runners again finished tired.

**NOTEBOOK**
**Buz Kiri(USA)**, who has been out of the first three only once in 11 starts since the start of the year, appreciated stepping back up to a mile and a half having been beaten over shorter recently.
**Dora Corbino** was always likely to struggle for pace over this trip having appeared to find a mile seven too sharp last time. She plugged on for second.
**Dances With Angels(IRE)** was making the three for the first time and seemed to improve for the return to turf.
**Leophin Dancer(USA)** had every chance and hung under pressure.
**Bunino Ven**, sporting an eyeshield and blinkers for the first-time, pulled hard but saw he race out well, albeit back in fifth.
**Island Star(IRE)** *Official explanation: jockey said gelding hung left*
**Moyne Pleasure(IRE)** *Official explanation: trainer said gelding lost its action*
**Timbuktu** was never going and something presumably went amiss. *Official explanation: jockey said gelding did not handle the track*

### 1863 TOTEPLACE BANDED STKS — 7f 214y
4:10 (4:10) (H) 3-Y-0+ — £1,442 (£412; £206) **Stalls** Low

Form — RPR
0065 **1** — **Chickasaw Trail**[11] 1592 6-9-0 40 — StephanieHollinshead(7) 5 — 45
(RHollinshead) *bhd: hdwy 2f out: led ins fnl f: rdn out* — **11/1**
60-4 **2** ½ — **Sea Jade (IRE)**[11] 1592 5-9-7 40 — NCallan 6 — 44
(JWPayne) *plld hrd: in tch: led over 2f out tl ins fnl f: kpt on* — **7/4**[1]
0/65 **3** 6 — **Chakra**[7] 1687 10-9-0 40 — CHaddon(7) 8 — 30
(CJGray) *plld hrd: chsd ldrs: edgd lft fnl 2f: one pce* — **16/1**
6663 **4** 3½ — **Harbour Princess**[13] 1544 3-8-8 35 — SRighton 2 — 22
(MFHarris) *in tch: outpcd over 4f out: drvn and rallied 2f out: no imp* — **10/1**
4006 **5** 2 — **Zinging**[11] 1583 5-9-7 40 — JTate 7 — 17
(JJBridger) *led tl over 2f out: hrd rdn and wknd over 1f out* — **3/1**[2]
5000 **6** 11 — **Wilom (GER)**[28] 1278 6-9-7 40 — NPollard 1 — —
(MRHoad) *t.k.h: prom over 5f* — **7/1**
0064 **7** 2½ — **Definitely Special (IRE)**[11] 1583 6-9-7 35 — (p) PDoe 3 — —
(NEBerry) *prom 6f: eased whn btn* — **6/1**[3]
2600 **8** dist — **Kumakawa**[29] 1274 6-9-0 40 — (b) LiamJones(7) 4 — —
(EAWheeler) *sn bhd: no ch whn rdr dropped whip 3f out* — **8/1**

1m 42.5s (7.50) **Going Correction** +0.675s/f (Yiel)
**WFA** 3 from 5yo+ 13lb — **8** Ran SP% **122.6**
Speed ratings: **89,88,82,79,77 66,63,—**CSF £33.06 TOTE £14.80: £3.00, £1.02, £10.10; EX 48.50.
**Owner** Anthony White **Bred** Auldyn Stud Ltd **Trained** Upper Longdon, Staffs

**FOCUS**
Not a strong race in a slow time, advertised by the winner finally getting off the mark at the 48th attempt.

**NOTEBOOK**
**Chickasaw Trail**, still a maiden after 47 starts prior to this, made it 48th time lucky. She stayed on well to collar Sea Jade having made some good headway from the rear a quarter of a mile out.
**Sea Jade(IRE)** pulled six lengths clear of the third, but could not repel the winner.
**Chakra** looked a doubtful stayer, but plodded on for third despite pulling hard early.
**Harbour Princess** was not disgraced on this first start on turf.
**Zinging** was easily brushed aside.
**Kumakawa** was never going and something evidently went wrong. *Official explanation: jockey said gelding broke a blood vessel*

### 1864 TOTEPOOL TRI-BANDED STKS — 6f 209y
4:40 (4:40) (H) 3-Y-0 — £1,463 (£418; £209) **Stalls** Low

Form — RPR
00-0 **1** — **Pererin**[14] 1530 3-9-0 45 — NCallan 7 — 51
(IAWood) *hld up in 4th pl: hrd rdn and outpcd 3f out: styd on over 1f out: drvn to ld ins fnl f* — **2/1**[1]
6252 **2** 1¼ — **Fayr Firenze (IRE)**[5] 1725 3-9-0 45 — (v) SRighton 3 — 48
(MFHarris) *chsd ldrs: drvn to ld over 1f out: hdd ins fnl f: one pce* — **5/1**
0543 **3** ½ — **Stagecoach Ruby**[7] 1695 3-8-9 40 — WRyan 1 — 42
(GLMoore) *rdn to ld: sn 5 l clr: hdd over 1f out: one pce* — **11/4**[2]
0000 **4** 1¾ — **Taranai (IRE)**[27] 1300 3-8-9 45 — NChalmers(5) 2 — 42
(BWDuke) *chsd clr ldr: ev ch over 1f out: one pce* — **9/1**

0442 **5** *1 ½* **Heathyards Joy**[11] [1594] 3-8-4 35 ........ PDoe 4 28
(RHollinshead) *towards rr: rdn and hdwy 2f out: no ex over 1f out* **5/1**

3266 **6** *nk* **Brother Cadfael**[11] [1594] 3-8-9 40 ........ NPollard 6 32
(JohnAHarris) *in rr: hrd rdn and rdr dropped whip 3f out: nt pce to chal* **9/2**[3]

-006 **7** *dist* **Sparkling Clear**[12] [1571] 3-8-9 40 ........ (v) JDSmith 5 —
(RMHCowell) *sn t.o and moving bdly: virtually p.u* **20/1**

1m 27.76s (5.16) **Going Correction** +0.675s/f (Yiel) 7 Ran SP% **126.3**
Speed ratings: **97,95,95,93,91 90,**—CSF £14.49 TOTE £3.80: £3.60, £2.20; EX 33.90 Place 6 £30.68, Place 5 £17.45.
**Owner** Tyrnest Ltd **Bred** Barry Minty **Trained** Upper Lambourn, Berks

**FOCUS**
A field of exposed performers, the exception being Pererin.

**NOTEBOOK**
**Pererin**, who was well supported in the ring - 7/1 into 2/1- seemed beaten with two to run, but came home strongly and ended up winning with a bit to spare. He still has some learning to do, but can win again in similar company back on a more conventional track. *Official explanation: trainer's representative said colt had benefited from the drop in class*
**Fayr Firenze(IRE)** looks sure to be suited by a return to six furlongs.
**Stagecoach Ruby** had nothing left to offer from the furlong pole, having led at a decent pace.
**Taranai(IRE)** failed to quite see out the trip.
**Sparkling Clear** *Official explanation: jockey said filly lost its action*
T/Plt: £29.00 to a £1 stake. Pool: £24,347.60. 612.00 winning tickets. T/Qpdt: £20.50 to a £1 stake. Pool: £1,324.40. 47.80 winning tickets. LM

# 1742 MUSSELBURGH (R-H)

Tuesday, May 4

**OFFICIAL GOING: Good (good to soft in places on straight course)**

## 1865 BRUNTON HALL MAIDEN AUCTION STKS — 5f
**6:10** (6:11) (E) 2-Y-O — **£3,360** (£1,034; £517; £258) **Stalls** Low

Form — RPR

**1** **Dance Anthem** 2-8-8 ........ PMcCabe 5 71+
(MGQuinlan) *chsd ldrs: shkn up whn hmpd over 1f out: swtchd and qcknd to ld ins fnl f: comf* **7/2**[3]

35 **2** *1 ½* **Windy Prospect**[40] [1105] 2-8-8 ow3 ........ DNolan[(5)] 9 70
(PABlockley) *dwlt: sn prom on outside: hdwy and ev ch fr over 1f out: r.o fin* **11/4**[1]

**3** *nk* **Llamadas** 2-8-9 ........ FLynch 1 65
(MDods) *s.i.s and sn rdn: hdwy centre over 1f out: r.o fnl f* **3/1**[2]

0 **4** *½* **Coleorton Dancer**[17] [1462] 2-8-7 ........ GParkin 7 61
(KARyan) *led stands rail to ins fnl f: one pce* **11/2**

**5** *nk* **Lady Hopeful (IRE)** 2-8-3 ow3 ........ THamilton[(3)] 3 59
(RPElliott) *chsd ldrs: rdn 1/2-way: one pce fnl f* **10/1**

0 **6** *1* **Miss Good Time**[22] [1374] 2-8-2 ........ PHanagan 4 51
(JGGiven) *chsd ldrs tl rdn and no ex over 1f out* **50/1**

**7** *1 ¼* **Namking** 2-8-8 ........ DeanMcKeown 2 52
(CWThornton) *s.i.s: outpcd: shkn up whn hung rt over 1f out: kpt on: no imp* **50/1**

5 **8** *7* **Voice Of An Angel (IRE)**[32] [1234] 2-8-2 ........ DaleGibson 8 18
(ABerry) *cl up tl rdn and outpcd over 1f out* **12/1**

0 **9** *¾* **Gypsy Fair**[18] [1449] 2-8-5 ........ KDarley 6 18
(TDBarron) *sn wl bhd: nvr on terms* **14/1**

0 **10** *5* **Morning World**[19] [1415] 2-8-9 ........ KDalgleish 10 —
(JRWeymes) *w ldrs tl wknd over 1f out* **66/1**

61.57 secs (1.17) **Going Correction** +0.10s/f (Good) 10 Ran SP% **118.1**
Speed ratings: **94,91,91,90,89 88,86,75,73,65**CSF £13.71 TOTE £4.30: £1.50, £1.40, £2.30; EX 26.90.
**Owner** The Afternoon Syndicate **Bred** Newsells Park Stud Limited **Trained** Newmarket, Suffolk
■ Stewards Enquiry : P McCabe caution: used whip with excessive frequency

**FOCUS**
An average juvenile maiden run at a sound pace.

**NOTEBOOK**
**Dance Anthem** showed a fair turn of foot to score at the first time of asking. He was smartly away and can be considered better than the bare form, as he met interference approaching the final furlong, and did well to recover and win going away. He should score again.
**Windy Prospect**, carrying 3lb overweight, was not helped by a sluggish start from his wide draw, but still held every chance if good enough, and this must go down as a missed opportunity. He is in danger of becoming exposed, but certainly has a similar race within his compass.
**Llamadas** would have finished closer but for missing the kick and he had to come wide in order to deliver his challenge over a furlong out. This was a satisfactory debut effort and he will come on a lot for the experience and no doubt go close next time.
**Coleorton Dancer** tired inside the last after showing early speed, but improved on his debut form.
**Lady Hopeful(IRE)** showed a bit of early toe, but ran green late on and looks the type to improve with more experience.
**Namking** ran distinctly green and will be sharper next time out.

## 1866 LEN LOTHIAN LTD H'CAP — 2m
**6:40** (6:40) (F) (0-55,55) 4-Y-O+ — **£2,926** (£836; £418) **Stalls** Low

Form — RPR

0-05 **1** **Gargoyle Girl**[9] [1341] 7-8-13 **52** ........ KDarley 4 67
(JSGoldie) *hld up: hdwy over 3f out: led over 1f out: sn clr* **5/1**[2]

0-00 **2** *13* **Romil Star (GER)**[14] [1534] 7-8-11 **50** ........ (b[1]) DarrenWilliams 3 49
(KRBurke) *trckd ldrs gng wl: led 5f out: clr 3f out: hdd over 1f out: edgd lft and no ex* **6/1**

40-0 **3** *½* **Dormy Two (IRE)**[12] [1560] 4-8-8 **50** ........ (p) RWinston 9 49
(JSWainwright) *keen: hld up: hdwy over 3f out: no imp fr 2f out* **20/1**

6600 **4** *1 ½* **Celtic Vision (IRE)**[10] [1615] 8-8-11 **50** ........ (t) PHanagan 10 47
(MAppleby) *hld up: effrt 4f out: no imp over 2f out* **20/1**

06-0 **5** *½* **Mr Fortywinks (IRE)**[10] [1615] 10-8-11 **55** ........ TEaves[(5)] 8 51
(BEllison) *prom: rdn 1/2-way: one pce fr 4f out* **5/1**[2]

044/ **6** *20* **Western Bluebird (IRE)**[9] [2513] 6-8-7 **51** ........ PMulrennan[(5)] 6 23
(MissKateMilligan) *in tch: effrt over 4f out: wknd fr 3f out* **20/1**

0604 **7** *1 ¾* **Balalaika Tune (IRE)**[5] [1721] 5-8-0 **46** oh6 ........ DFentiman[(7)] 7 16
(WStorey) *keen: hld up: rdn over 4f out: sn btn* **20/1**

-045 **8** *10* **Astromancer (USA)**[17] [1463] 4-8-2 **51** ow1 ........ SaleemGolam[(7)] 1 9
(MHTompkins) *sn led: hdd 5f out: sn btn* **4/1**[1]

231- **9** *28* **Rouge Blanc (USA)**[49] [5675] 4-8-12 **54** ........ (p) DaleGibson 5 —
(GAHarker) *chsd ldrs 6f: sn lost pl: struggling over 4f out* **11/2**[3]

0063 **10** *13* **Marino Mou (IRE)**[14] [1520] 4-7-13 **48** oh1 ow2 ........ AReilly[(7)] 2 —
(MissDMountain) *racd wd: in tch: hdwy 1/2-way: rdn and wknd over 4f out* **12/1**

3m 37.15s (3.45) **Going Correction** +0.375s/f (Good)
**WFA** 4 from 5yo+ 3lb 10 Ran SP% **109.7**
Speed ratings: **106,99,99,98,98 88,87,82,68,61**CSF £30.17 CT £504.31 TOTE £6.10: £2.10, £2.60, £9.80; EX 39.50.
**Owner** Mrs C Brown **Bred** Aramstone Stud **Trained** Uplawmoor, E Renfrews

**FOCUS**
A moderate staying handicap which was run at a fast early gallop and suited those to be held up. The winning time was good for the grade, but the form may be suspect.

**NOTEBOOK**
**Gargoyle Girl**, who is best off a fast gallop, produced a nice turn of foot just over one out to win in decisive fashion. She has slipped to a winning mark , having lost her form of late, and was flattered by this as the early leaders went too quick. However, she would be of interest if turned out under a penalty, as her confidence will be sky high after this.
**Romil Star(GER)** kicked on and went clear with three furlongs to run, but tired approaching the final furlong and had nothing left when challenged by the winner. He may have prospered from a slightly more patient ride and is worth another chance over this trip.
**Dormy Two(IRE)** did not help her chances of staying by running freely early and could only muster the one pace from over two out.
**Astromancer(USA)** set the generous gallop and looked to go off too fast.
**Rouge Blanc(USA)** *Official explanation: jockey said filly had a breathing problem*

## 1867 HOLLIES CLAIMING STKS — 1m 4f
**7:10** (7:10) (F) 4-Y-O+ — **£2,884** (£824; £412) **Stalls** High

Form — RPR

2102 **1** **Platinum Charmer (IRE)**[48] [1041] 4-8-7 58 ........ (p) DarrenWilliams 1 52
(KRBurke) *trckd ldrs: smooth hdwy 3f out: drvn over 1f out: led ins fnl f: r.o wl* **9/4**[2]

000- **2** *3* **Arms Acrossthesea**[229] [5015] 5-8-9 40 ........ JCarroll 8 49
(ACWhillans) *hld up: hdwy 4f out: led over 1f out: hdd and no ex ins last* **16/1**

-000 **3** *6* **Mikasa (IRE)**[29] [1263] 4-8-6 40 ow3 ........ RWinston 6 37
(RFFisher) *led to over 2f out: wknd 1f out* **25/1**

310/ **4** *1 ½* **Minstrel Hall**[18] [4352] 5-9-1 ........ LEnstone[(3)] 5 46
(PMonteith) *hld up: rdn over 4f out: kpt on over 1f out: nvr rchd ldrs* **7/1**[3]

0-30 **5** *nk* **Eton (GER)**[28] [1282] 8-9-9 70 ........ AlexGreaves 2 51
(DNicholls) *cl up: led over 2f to over 1f out: sn wknd* **2/1**[1]

66-5 **6** *4* **Astral Prince**[6] [1710] 6-8-5 48 ........ (b) RFfrench 3 26
(MrsKWalton) *chsd ldrs tl wknd fr 1/2-way* **11/1**

500/ **7** *¾* **Iranoo (IRE)**[9] [4455] 7-8-3 ........ (t) PHanagan 7 23
(RAllan) *chsd ldrs: rdn over 4f out: sn btn* **20/1**

-004 **8** *4* **Washington Pink (IRE)**[8] [1668] 5-8-3 45 ow1 ........ THamilton[(3)] 4 20
(CGrant) *hld up: rdr over 4f out: sn btn* **12/1**

2m 41.87s (3.85) **Going Correction** +0.375s/f (Good) 8 Ran SP% **107.1**
Speed ratings: **102,100,96,95,94 92,91,88**CSF £32.18 TOTE £2.90: £1.40, £2.40, £7.40; EX 29.30.
**Owner** Platinum Racing Club Limited **Bred** F Hinojosa **Trained** Middleham Moor, N Yorks

**FOCUS**
A weak event lacking any strength in depth and the race suited those racing handy.

**NOTEBOOK**
**Platinum Charmer(IRE)** won comfortably under a confident ride to score his first win on the turf. He had the run of the race on this occasion and beat little, but should continue to pay his way at this sort of level.
**Arms Acrossthesea**, making his debut for new connections, had no answer to the winner when challenged. He is entitled to come on for this, as he was off for 229-days prior to this.
**Mikasa(IRE)** found little under pressure approaching the two furlong marker having set the pace until that point.
**Eton(GER)** can have no excuses and proved most disappointing.

## 1868 CONTINENTAL AIRLINES BIG APPLE H'CAP — 7f 30y
**7:40** (7:41) (E) (0-70,72) 3-Y-O+ — **£4,134** (£1,272; £636; £318) **Stalls** Low

Form — RPR

1401 **1** **Stoic Leader (IRE)**[3] [1757] 4-10-0 **72** 6ex ........ DNolan[(5)] 10 86+
(RFFisher) *trckd ldrs: led gng wl over 2f out: r.o strly: eased ins fnl f* **9/4**[1]

-000 **2** *1 ¾* **The Gambler**[8] [1665] 4-8-4 **50** ........ (p) DFentiman[(7)] 1 56
(PaulJohnson) *bhd: hdwy centre over 2f out: r.o fnl f: no ch w wnr* **33/1**

-060 **3** *hd* **Bailieborough (IRE)**[18] [1451] 5-10-0 **67** ........ AlexGreaves 12 72
(DNicholls) *sn in tch: effrt over 2f out: one pce ins fnl f* **10/1**

6-20 **4** *1* **Efidium**[10] [1620] 6-9-5 **65** ........ SuzanneFrance[(7)] 4 67
(NBycroft) *hld up: hdwy over 2f out: edgd rt over 1f out: no imp ins fnl f* **12/1**

6-60 **5** *1* **Old Bailey (USA)**[8] [1665] 4-8-3 **47** ........ (b) PMakin[(5)] 6 47
(TDBarron) *keen: prom: effrt over 2f out: one pce over 1f out* **9/1**[3]

0020 **6** *nk* **Hoh's Back**[11] [1598] 5-9-3 **63** ........ (p) NataliaGemelova[(7)] 13 62
(PaulJohnson) *chsd ldr tl rdn and no ex over 1f out* **12/1**

40-4 **7** *shd* **Regent's Secret (USA)**[26] [1315] 4-9-13 **66** ........ KDarley 2 65
(JSGoldie) *bhd tl sme late hdwy: nvr rchd ldrs* **12/1**

0004 **8** *1 ¾* **Shifty**[4] [1748] 5-8-12 **51** ........ PMQuinn 5 45
(DNicholls) *hld up: rdn 3f out: no imp fr 2f out* **10/1**

1-10 **9** *2* **Smith N Allan Oils**[97] [624] 5-9-7 **60** ........ (p) RWinston 8 49
(MDods) *midfield: drvn over 3f out: btn over 1f out* **8/1**[2]

55-0 **10** *2* **General Smith**[15] [1502] 5-9-5 **58** ........ KDalgleish 7 42
(GAHarker) *s.i.s: nvr rchd ldrs* **33/1**

60P0 **11** *5* **Lion's Domane**[15] [1515] 7-9-2 **55** ........ JCarroll 11 26
(ABerry) *set str pce tl hdd & wknd over 2f out* **14/1**

3-40 **12** *3* **Mon Secret (IRE)**[49] [1032] 6-9-4 **57** ........ FLynch 9 20
(BSmart) *prom tl wknd fr 2f out* **10/1**

0000 **13** *1 ¼* **African Spur (IRE)**[8] [1665] 4-9-5 **65** ........ (t) DTudhope[(7)] 3 25
(DCarroll) *bhd: rdn 1/2-way: nvr on terms* **50/1**

1m 32.16s (2.63) **Going Correction** +0.375s/f (Good) 13 Ran SP% **116.7**
Speed ratings: **99,97,96,95,94 94,94,92,89,87 81,78,76**CSF £94.64 CT £655.18 TOTE £3.10: £1.10, £11.00, £6.30; EX 104.60.
**Owner** Great Head House Estates Limited **Bred** P J Higgins **Trained** Ulverston, Cumbria

**FOCUS**
A modest handicap run at a solid pace.

**NOTEBOOK**
**Stoic Leader(IRE)** ◆ readily followed up his win three days previously under his 6lb penalty. This shorter trip proved no problem, he was value for more than the official winning margin and he will be hard to beat when going for the hat-trick.
**The Gambler** put up his best display for some time, having slipped to a fair mark of late, but will no doubt take a hike back up in the weights for this.
**Bailieborough(IRE)**, not for the first time, lost ground at the start. He recovered well however and improved on his recent form.
**Efidium** put a poor run last time behind her with a fair effort and could find a small race off his current mark.

**Old Bailey(USA)** gave himself little chance of staying this extra furlong by pulling too hard early. He is not one to write off just yet and may do better when reverting to six furlongs.
**Smith N Allan Oils** *Official explanation: trainer said gelding lost a front shoe*

## 1869 MILL LADE MAIDEN STKS 7f 30y
**8:10** (8:11) (D) 3-Y-O **£4,056** (£1,248; £624; £312) **Stalls** Low

Form RPR

4322 **1** **Man Of Letters (UAE)**[4] 1745 3-9-0 76 KDalgleish 4 69
(MJohnston) *prom: effrt and drvn 3f out: led 1f out: styd on* **2/5**[1]

3-45 **2** *2* **Graceful Air (IRE)**[28] 1288 3-8-9 62 RWinston 5 59
(JRWeymes) *bhd: outpcd 1/2-way: gd hdwy centre over 1f out: kpt on: no ch w wnr* **33/1**

55-2 **3** *3/4* **Joshua's Gold (IRE)**[57] 983 3-8-7 58 DTudhope(7) 2 62?
(DCarroll) *chsd ldrs: effrt and led briefly over 1f out: one pce ins last* **20/1**

2 **4** *3 1/2* **Crathes**[28] 1288 3-8-9 MFenton 6 48
(JGGiven) *chsd ldrs: rdn 3f out: no imp fr 2f out* **12/1**[3]

050- **5** *hd* **Canadian Storm**[187] 5836 3-8-7 70 SaleemGolam(7) 1 52
(MHTompkins) *led at decent gallop to over 1f out: sn btn* **16/1**

00- **6** *1/2* **Son Of Thunder (IRE)**[204] 5532 3-8-11 LEnstone(3) 8 51
(MDods) *hld up: rdn 3f out: no imp over 1f out* **100/1**

53-2 **7** *10* **Trench Coat (USA)**[57] 982 3-9-0 72 KDarley 7 25
(AMBalding) *w ldr to 3f out: wknd wl over 1f out* **5/1**[2]

0-0 **8** *dist* **Dawn Duel (IRE)**[14] 1530 3-8-9 FLynch 3 —
(BSmart) *s.i.s: outpcd: c wd st: t.o* **66/1**

1m 32.05s (2.52) **Going Correction** +0.375s/f (Good) **8** Ran SP% **111.9**
Speed ratings: **100,97,96,92,92 92,80,**—CSF £23.87 TOTE £1.40: £1.02, £7.00, £2.70; EX 18.90.
**Owner** Jumeirah Racing **Bred** Darley Dubai **Trained** Middleham Moor, N Yorks

**FOCUS**
A weak maiden and the form looks suspect.

**NOTEBOOK**
**Man Of Letters(UAE)** lost his maiden tag at the sixth attempt in workmanlike fashion. His rating of 76 set the standard, but he made heavy weather of this and may not have been totally suited by this sharp track.
**Graceful Air(IRE)** was not able to go with the early gallop, but stayed on nicely and proved she is best at this trip. She remains a maiden after 12 outings however, and is well exposed.
**Joshua's Gold(IRE)** held every chance over one out, but could not find the change of gears needed to stay with the eventual winner. He has resumed this season in fair form, but his proximity at the finish drags the form down.
**Trench Coat(USA)**, who was fairly well in at the weights, proved disappointing and is regressing. *Official explanation: jockey said colt hung both ways*
**Dawn Duel(IRE)** *Official explanation: jockey said filly hung violently left*

## 1870 GOOSE GREEN H'CAP 5f
**8:40** (8:41) (F) (0-55,55) 3-Y-O+ **£3,045** (£870; £435) **Stalls** Low

Form RPR

5000 **1** **Cash**[8] 1665 6-9-4 **55** (p) KDalgleish 13 65
(PaulJohnson) *cl up centre: led over 1f out: drvn out* **20/1**

00-5 **2** *1* **Valiant Romeo**[19] 1421 4-9-2 **53** RFfrench 2 59
(RBastiman) *cl up stands rail: ev ch and rdn over 1f out: kpt on fnl f* **5/1**[1]

-000 **3** *nk* **Roan Raider (USA)**[22] 1373 4-8-6 **46** oh1 (v) THamilton(3) 15 51
(MJPolglase) *racd centre: in tch: rdn 1/2-way: kpt on fnl f* **50/1**

0443 **4** *nk* **Best Lead**[17] 1474 5-8-8 **52** (b) DFentiman(7) 4 56
(IanEmmerson) *sn rdn in rr: hdwy and hung rt over 1f out: r.o: nrst fin* **10/1**

0205 **5** *nk* **Malahide Express (IRE)**[14] 1525 4-9-4 **55** DeanMcKeown 8 58
(EJAlston) *led to over 1f out: kpt on same pce* **6/1**[2]

6-40 **6** *1* **College Maid (IRE)**[19] 1421 7-8-13 **50** (b) KDarley 7 49
(JSGoldie) *chsd ldrs: ev ch over 1f out: one pce fnl f* **8/1**[3]

0300 **7** *1 1/4* **Lady Protector**[5] 1738 5-8-11 **48** JEdmunds 5 43
(JBalding) *midfield: rdn over 2f out: no imp over 1f out* **11/1**

00-0 **8** *nk* **Fairgame Man**[19] 1421 6-8-12 **49** RWinston 16 43
(JSWainwright) *chsd ldrs centre tl outpcd over 1f out* **16/1**

0100 **9** *1 1/2* **Torrent**[19] 1421 9-8-5 **47** (b) PMakin(5) 17 35
(DWChapman) *racd centre: in tch tl outpcd fr 2f out* **14/1**

3-00 **10** *1/2* **Laurel Dawn**[17] 1477 6-8-8 **52** PPMathers(7) 1 38
(IWMcinnes) *sn drvn along towards rr stands side: no imp fr 1/2-way* **12/1**

415- **11** *1 3/4* **Mystery Pips**[204] 5538 4-9-1 **52** (v) KimTinkler 6 32
(NTinkler) *chsd ldrs tl wknd over 1f out* **16/1**

40-0 **12** *shd* **Proud Western (USA)**[14] 1525 6-8-5 **47** TEaves(5) 12 27
(BEllison) *sn wl bhd centre: nvr on terms* **10/1**

06-0 **13** *3* **Stavros (IRE)**[18] 1453 4-8-9 **46** JCarroll 9 15
(JSWainwright) *hld up centre: rdn 1/2-way: nvr on terms* **50/1**

000- **14** *5* **Robwillcall**[182] 5919 4-9-1 **52** FLynch 3 3
(ABerry) *chsd ldrs tl lost pl qckly 1/2-way* **14/1**

0-20 **L** **Joyce's Choice**[8] 1663 5-8-10 **54** (p) AReilly(7) 11 —
(JSWainwright) *ref to r* **10/1**

60.89 secs (0.49) **Going Correction** +0.10s/f (Good) **15** Ran SP% **119.1**
Speed ratings: **100,98,97,97,96 95,93,92,90,89 86,86,81,73,**—CSF £113.86 CT £5026.70 TOTE £26.20: £7.00, £3.00, £17.10; EX 170.20 Place 6 £98.94, Place 5 £79.13.
**Owner** Insull, White, Pritchard & Johnson **Bred** F C T Wilson **Trained** White-le-Head, Co Durham
■ Stewards Enquiry : K Dalgleish one-day ban: used whip with excessive frequency (May 16)

**FOCUS**
A weak sprint run at a sound gallop and the field were tightly bunched at the finish.

**NOTEBOOK**
**Cash** appreciated this better ground and scored readily under a positive ride. This drop back to five proved ideal. *Official explanation: trainer's representative had no explanation for the improved form shown*
**Valiant Romeo** ran a sound race in defeat and showed enough to suggest his turn is not far off in this grade.
**Roan Raider(USA)**, dropping in trip, ran by far his best race for some time from 1lb out of the handicap.
**Best Lead** was unable to go the early pace and was doing all his best work too late in the day. He is fairly consistent in this grade and could win if dropped back to plating company.
**Malahide Express(IRE)** showed good early speed and only folded late on. He is a hard horse to catch right, but is on a fair mark and will pop up at a big price before long.
**College Maid(IRE)** showed enough on this occasion to suggest she could capitalise on her current lenient mark before long.
T/Plt: £43.10 to a £1 stake. Pool: £32,935.85. 556.95 winning tickets. T/Qpdt: £11.30 to a £1 stake. Pool: £2,218.20. 144.90 winning tickets. RY

# 1839 WARWICK (L-H)
### Tuesday, May 4

**OFFICIAL GOING: Heavy**
Meeting switched from Carlisle. Races 3-7 flip start and hand-timed.
Wind: fresh bhd Weather: heavy showers

## 1871 EUROPEAN BREEDERS FUND MAIDEN STKS 5f
**2:00** (2:00) (D) 2-Y-O **£5,027** (£1,547; £773; £386) **Stalls** Low

Form RPR

3 **1** **Earl Of Links (IRE)**[24] 1331 2-9-0 PDobbs 4 72
(RHannon) *mde virtually all: rdn over 1f out: hung rt ins fnl f: r.o* **9/4**[2]

**2** *hd* **Harvest Warrior** 2-8-11 DAllan(3) 5 71
(TDEasterby) *w wnr: rdn over 1f out: r.o* **12/1**[3]

**3** *3 1/2* **Dramaticus** 2-9-0 JPMurtagh 6 59
(DRLoder) *chsd ldrs: rdn over 1f out: styd on same pce* **8/13**[1]

4 **4** *3/4* **Ninah's Intuition**[11] 1589 2-9-0 ANicholls 3 56
(JMBradley) *chsd ldrs: rdn 1/2-way: no ex fnl f* **22/1**

**5** *6* **Limonia (GER)** 2-8-9 IMongan 2 30
(DKIvory) *s.s: sn prom: rdn over 1f out: sn wknd* **33/1**

**6** *10* **Clipper Hoy** 2-9-0 GBaker 1 —
(MrsHSweeting) *prom: rdn 1/2-way: hung lft and wknd 2f out* **33/1**

66.62 secs (6.42) **Going Correction** +1.025s/f (Soft) **6** Ran SP% **110.6**
Speed ratings: **89,88,83,81,72 56**CSF £24.09 TOTE £3.10: £1.10, £7.60; EX 14.40.
**Owner** Coriolan Links Partnership VIII **Bred** Michael Hanrahan **Trained** East Everleigh, Wilts

**FOCUS**
Desperate conditions for these two-year-olds - the race was run in a hailstorm.

**NOTEBOOK**
**Earl Of Links(IRE)**, who has plenty of stamina in his pedigree and had the benefit of race experience, made the most of those factors and led almost all the way. He will be suited by a longer trip in time and his trainer regards him as a nursery type.
**Harvest Warrior**, a half-brother to seven-furlong specialist Amber Fort and several juvenile sprint winners, hails from a stable whose runners usually need their first run, so this was a promising display.
**Dramaticus**, whose dam was a Listed winner and in soft ground, is by a soft-ground sire too, so there was every expectation that he would handle this ground. He was disappointing and is clearly thought better than this. Less testing conditions should see him in a better light.
**Ninah's Intuition** was taking on better opposition this time and was not disgraced in terrible conditions.

## 1872 WARWICK RACECOURSE CONFERENCE AND BANQUETING CENTRE CLASSIFIED STKS 5f
**2:30** (2:31) (F) 3-Y-O+ **£3,262** (£932; £466) **Stalls** Low

Form RPR

/006 **1** **Full Pitch**[10] 1603 8-9-3 55 MHills 19 77
(WJenks) *dwlt: outpcd: hdwy centre over 1f out: edgd lft and led wl ins fnl f: r.o* **50/1**

40-6 **2** *3* **Karminskey Park**[14] 1525 5-9-2 62 JFanning 10 67
(TJEtherington) *s.i.s: sn chsng ldrs: led 3f out: styd far side ent st: hdd and no ex wl ins fnl f* **9/2**[2]

-002 **3** *2 1/2* **Pulse**[9] 1642 6-9-3 60 (p) SCarson 13 61
(JMBradley) *chsd ldrs: c stands' side and led that gp ent st: no ex fnl f* **14/1**

0-00 **4** *1* **Quicks The Word**[22] 1361 4-9-6 63 (b) JPMurtagh 12 61
(CWThornton) *chsd ldrs: c stands' side ent st: sn rdn: styd on same pce appr fnl f* **11/1**

05-0 **5** *2* **Boanerges (IRE)**[22] 1368 7-9-3 59 CCatlin 3 52
(JMBradley) *chsd ldrs: c stands' side ent st: wknd ins fnl f* **28/1**

5/0 **6** *hd* **Brigadier Monty (IRE)**[29] 1265 6-9-3 59 EAhern 7 51
(MrsSLamyman) *chsd ldrs: c stands' side ent st: sn rdn: wknd ins fin al f* **25/1**

000- **7** *1/2* **Sholto**[195] 5706 6-8-12 62 (b) JDO'Reilly(7) 2 51
(JO'Reilly) *led 2f: styd far side ent st: nt clr run 2f out: sn hung lft and wknd* **10/1**[3]

00-0 **8** *1 1/4* **Guns Blazing**[9] 1642 5-8-11 61 MHoward(7) 16 47
(DKIvory) *hmpd s: outpcd: c stands' side ent st: nvr nrr* **33/1**

0-00 **9** *1/2* **Brantwood (IRE)**[22] 1368 4-9-6 63 (t) GGibbons 11 47
(BAMcmahon) *chsd ldrs: c stands' side ent st: wknd over 1f out* **20/1**

2143 **10** *hd* **Playtime Blue**[22] 1368 4-9-5 62 GBaker 9 46
(MrsHSweeting) *chsd ldrs: c stands' side ent st: wknd fnl f* **4/1**[1]

-000 **11** *1/2* **Percy Douglas**[29] 1268 4-9-3 50 (v) AnnStokell 8 42
(MissAStokell) *s.s: outpcd: c stands' side ent st: nvr trbld ldrs* **66/1**

5005 **12** *2* **Taboor (IRE)**[9] 1642 6-9-3 57 (b) KFallon 17 36
(JWPayne) *chsd ldrs: rdn and c stands' side ent st: wknd wl over 1f out* **10/1**[3]

0400 **13** *1/2* **King's Ballet (USA)**[13] 1537 6-9-3 54 (p) JQuinn 1 35
(PRChamings) *s.i.s: son chsng ldrs: rdn 3f out: sn wknd: styd far side ent st* **11/1**

2000 **14** *5* **Cark**[29] 1262 6-8-10 47 (p) KPierrepont(7) 5 20
(JBalding) *chsd ldrs: c stands' side ent st: wknd wl over 1f out* **50/1**

6004 **15** *3 1/2* **Panjandrum**[9] 1642 6-8-12 56 MSavage(5) 18 9
(NEBerry) *sn outpcd: c stands' side ent st* **20/1**

-301 **16** *nk* **Lucius Verrus (USA)**[11] 1596 4-9-3 54 WSupple 6 8
(DShaw) *outpcd whn c stands' side ent st* **16/1**

0010 **17** *7* **Marabar**[14] 1533 6-9-0 60 (b) ACulhane 14 —
(DWChapman) *edgd rt s: outpcd: c stands' side ent st* **14/1**

64.49 secs (4.29) **Going Correction** +1.025s/f (Soft) **17** Ran SP% **117.4**
Speed ratings: **106,101,97,95,92 92,91,89,88,88 87,84,83,75,69 69,58**CSF £237.29 TOTE £62.50: £17.30, £1.30, £4.40; EX 401.90.
**Owner** W Jenks **Bred** R Burton **Trained** Glazeley, Shropshire

**FOCUS**
Ability to handle the ground proved more important than the draw. The time was good for the grade.

**NOTEBOOK**
**Full Pitch** had not shown a lot since returning from a four-and-a-half year absence due to a broken pelvis, but he ran out a ready winner on this occasion on ground he clearly relishes. There was no fluke about this result.
**Karminskey Park** handles this sort of ground well and ran another fine race, having been beaten by the draw on her final start. She has a moderate strike-rate, but is primed to score.
**Pulse**, who has shown all his best form on a faster surface, has hit form and does not look too badly handicapped at present.
**Quicks The Word** rarely wins but this sort of ground suits him ideally and he ran a better race than of late with the blinkers back on.
**Boanerges(IRE)** dropped 13lb in the handicap last year and has lost another 3lb this season already. This ground would not have suited and in the circumstances it was a promising effort.

**Brigadier Monty(IRE)** found seven furlongs too far last time and this trip looked far more suitable for this ex-Irish gelding.
**Playtime Blue** was disappointing and it is likely that these very testing conditions proved too much for him.
**Cark** *Official explanation: jockey said gelding bled from the nose*

## 1873 KINGMAKER RESTAURANT H'CAP — 6f 21y
**3:00** (3:00) (E) (0-70,68) 3-Y-O+ — **£3,916** (£1,205; £602; £301) **Stalls** Far side

Form — RPR
3243 **1** **Savile's Delight (IRE)**[15] 1504 5-9-9 **64** ........ JPMurtagh 5 71
(RBrotherton) *w ldr tl led over 2f out: rdn over 1f out: r.o* **9/2**[1]
4522 **2** *1 3/4* **Carlton (IRE)**[8] 1665 10-8-13 **59** ........ RThomas(5) 3 61
(CRDore) *chsd ldrs: rdn over 2f out: styd on same pce ins fnl f* **7/1**
4-00 **3** *shd* **Waterside (IRE)**[26] 1313 5-9-13 **68** ........ MHills 4 69
(JWHills) *led over 3f: styd on same pce fnl f* **9/2**[1]
2103 **4** *3* **Never Without Me**[5] 1739 4-8-11 **52** ........ JQuinn 10 44
(PJMcbride) *chsd ldrs: rdn over 2f out: hung lft and wknd fnl f* **8/1**
1-60 **5** *6* **Full Spate**[10] 1608 9-9-13 **68** ........ JFEgan 9 42
(JMBradley) *sn pushed along in rr: sme hdwy over 1f out: wknd ins fnl f* **13/2**[3]
-020 **6** *6* **Oases**[8] 1663 5-9-5 **60** ........ WSupple 8 16
(DShaw) *chsd ldrs: rdn 1/2-way: hung lft and wknd wl over 1f out* **11/2**[2]
-000 **7** *hd* **Ridicule**[10] 1608 5-9-4 **59** ........(v) ACulhane 12 15
(JGPortman) *prom 4f* **10/1**
30-0 **8** *5* **Jagged (IRE)**[42] 1082 4-9-2 **57** ........ GBaker 13 —
(MrsHSweeting) *hld up: rdn and wknd over 2f out* **10/1**
360- **9** *6* **High Ridge**[204] 5553 5-9-3 **58** ........(p) SCarson 6 —
(JMBradley) *sn outpcd and bhd* **25/1**
100- **10** *23* **Compton Arrow (IRE)**[172] 5992 8-8-8 **63** ........ IMongan 1 —
(AWCarroll) *s.s: outpcd* **25/1**

1m 19.7s (7.40) **Going Correction** +1.35s/f (Soft)
**WFA** 3 from 4yo+ 10lb — **10 Ran SP% 114.6**
Speed ratings: **104,101,101,97,89 81,81,74,66,35** CSF £35.24 CT £132.37 TOTE £6.60: £1.60, £3.20, £1.60; EX 21.50.
**Owner** Roy Brotherton **Bred** Romany Investements Ltd **Trained** Elmley Castle, Worcs

**FOCUS**
There was a flip start to this race, and very few got into it.

**NOTEBOOK**
**Savile's Delight(IRE)** is a consistent type and, off the same mark as when third on his turf reappearance, battled on well to score for the third time in his career.
**Carlton(IRE)** has not won in handicap company since 1999 and always seems to find one or two too good, but he retains ability and while the ground is like this he should continue to run well.
**Waterside(IRE)** did not see the race out as well as the first two but this was his best performance of the season to date and he is entitled to step up on this form.
**Never Without Me** was only having his third outing on turf and showed his best form to date on the surface.
**Full Spate**, whose best form is on fast ground, is one to look out for when getting a favourable draw at his favourite track Windsor.
**Oases** had the ground to suit but ran a disappointing race.
**Compton Arrow(IRE)** *Official explanation: jockey said gelding was unsuited by the heavy ground*

## 1874 SPRING MEMBERSHIP H'CAP — 1m 22y
**3:30** (3:31) (E) (0-70,68) 3-Y-O — **£4,208** (£1,295; £647; £323) **Stalls** Far side

Form — RPR
663 **1** **Premier Dream (USA)**[12] 1557 3-9-6 **67** ........ JFanning 10 73
(MJohnston) *mde all: rdn over 1f out: r.o* **11/2**[3]
0-06 **2** *nk* **Suchwot (IRE)**[22] 1365 3-8-9 **56** ........ KFallon 4 62
(FJordan) *a.p: chsd wnr 3f out: sn rdn and ev ch: edgd lft ins fnl f: r.o* **10/3**[1]
4505 **3** *2 1/2* **Given A Chance**[15] 1499 3-7-7 **45** oh5........ RThomas(5) 8 46
(MrsSLamyman) *chsd ldrs: rdn over 1f out: styd on same pce* **33/1**
2151 **4** *3/4* **Daring Affair**[10] 1627 3-9-2 **66** ........ LisaJones(3) 11 65
(KRBurke) *hld up: rdn over 2f out: r.o ins fnl f: nt trble ldrs* **9/2**[2]
-003 **5** *3/4* **Prince Valentine**[27] 1301 3-8-13 **60** ........ MTebbutt 5 58
(DBFeek) *s.i.s: hld up: hdwy and nt clr run over 3f out: rdn over 1f out: styd on same pce* **14/1**
052- **6** *nk* **Miss Eloise**[182] 5915 3-8-8 **58** ........ DAllan(3) 2 55
(TDEasterby) *chsd ldrs: rdn over 2f out: wknd fnl f* **14/1**
4223 **7** *6* **Big Bad Burt**[61] 965 3-8-12 **66** ........ DeanWilliams(7) 15 51
(MissGayKelleway) *s.i.s: hld up: n.d* **11/1**
006- **8** *1 3/4* **Wake Up Henry**[162] 6059 3-8-13 **60** ........ DSweeney 6 41
(RCharlton) *hld up: n.d* **10/1**
0300 **9** *1/2* **Munaawesh (USA)**[14] 1531 3-9-5 **66** ........ ACulhane 1 46
(DWChapman) *hld up: effrt over 3f out: sn wknd* **12/1**
01-0 **10** *10* **Chorus Beauty**[17] 1464 3-9-3 **64** ........ JFEgan 9 24
(GWragg) *hld up: hdwy over 3f out: wknd over 1f out* **14/1**
6-00 **11** *22* **The Stick**[34] 1201 3-8-13 **60** ........ TEDurcan 17 —
(MRChannon) *chsd ldrs over 4f* **12/1**

1m 52.6s (13.30) **Going Correction** +1.35s/f (Soft) — **11 Ran SP% 118.0**
Speed ratings: **87,86,84,83,82 82,76,74,74,64 42** CSF £24.23 CT £568.14 TOTE £3.20: £1.50, £2.50, £11.00; EX 29.10.
**Owner** Lucayan Stud **Bred** T F Vanmeter Ii **Trained** Middleham Moor, N Yorks
■ Stewards Enquiry : K Fallon caution: used whip down the gelding's shoulder in the forehand position

**FOCUS**
Once again there were no stalls in use for this race. The time was slow even allowing for the conditions.

**NOTEBOOK**
**Premier Dream(USA)**, making his handicap debut after three starts in maiden company, made every yard. He looks nothing special but it would be unwise to assume that he needs ground this bad.
**Suchwot(IRE)** was racing off the same mark but, significantly, was down in trip having failed to stay ten furlongs on his previous start. This shorter distance is clearly important to him.
**Given A Chance** was another who looked happier over this shorter trip and this was a fair effort given that he was racing from 5lb out of the handicap.
**Daring Affair**, who came home strongly, has been in good form on the Fibresand of late and acquitted herself well off a 5lb higher mark and on a different surface.
**Prince Valentine**, who was making his handicap debut, gave away a few lengths at the start and did not shape too badly in the circumstances.
**Miss Eloise** ran a promising race on her seasonal reappearance, just weakening inside the last as lack of race fitness told in the conditions.
**Chorus Beauty** *Official explanation: jockey said filly was unsuited by the heavy ground*

## 1875 ZORN H'CAP (DIV I) — 1m 22y
**4:00** (4:03) (E) (0-70,68) 4-Y-O+ — **£3,737** (£1,150; £575; £287) **Stalls** Far side

Form — RPR
50-0 **1** **Summer Bounty**[22] 1369 8-9-6 **62** ........ JFanning 1 72
(FJordan) *hld up: hdwy over 3f out: led over 1f out: styd on wl* **25/1**
0626 **2** *2 1/2* **Dancing King (IRE)**[22] 1367 8-8-1 **46** ........ LisaJones(3) 6 51
(PWHiatt) *chsd ldr: led 6f out: rdn and hdd over 1f out: no ex ins fnl f* **8/1**[3]
-001 **3** *6* **Bojangles (IRE)**[11] 1582 5-8-6 **48** ........ EAhern 15 41
(RBrotherton) *led 2f: remained w ldr tl 2f out: rdn and wknd 1f out* **9/2**[1]
0-51 **4** *3* **Commitment Lecture**[10] 1606 4-9-1 **57** ........(t) WSupple 10 44
(MDods) *hld up: hdwy over 3f out: rdn and wknd over 1f out* **5/1**[2]
440- **5** *4* **Hilarious (IRE)**[216] 5308 4-8-9 **51** ........ AMcCarthy 5 30
(BRMillman) *prom: rdn over 2f out: wknd over 1f out* **33/1**
00-0 **6** *5* **Route Sixty Six (IRE)**[18] 412 8-7-10 **45** ........(p) LeanneKershaw(7) 3 14
(JeddO'Keeffe) *s.i.s: hld up: n.d* **16/1**
03-6 **7** *12* **Kindness**[31] 1244 4-8-10 **52** ........ DSweeney 14 —
(ADWPinder) *prom over 5f* **33/1**
6322 **8** *2* **Quiet Reading (USA)**[11] 1598 7-8-1 **48** ........(v) HayleyTurner(5) 7 —
(MRBosley) *sn pushed along in rr: hdwy 1/2-way: wknd 3f out* **8/1**[3]
0301 **9** *2 1/2* **Pharoah's Gold (IRE)**[8] 1660 6-8-13 **55** 6ex........(v) TEDurcan 2 —
(DShaw) *hld uyp: a in rr* **8/1**[3]
-200 **10** *6* **Dash For Cover (IRE)**[8] 1675 4-9-10 **66** ........ PDobbs 4 —
(RHannon) *mid-div: wknd 1/2-way* **11/1**
4000 **11** *1* **Daimajin (IRE)**[15] 1503 5-9-4 **60** ........ CCatlin 13 —
(MrsLucindaFeatherstone) *plld hrd and prom: wknd over 3f out* **50/1**
-660 **12** *1* **Horizontal (USA)**[14] 1531 4-9-1 **57** ........ MTebbutt 11 —
(VSmith) *chsd ldrs 5f* **14/1**
0604 **13** *16* **Pride Of Kinloch**[10] 1620 4-9-3 **59** ........ KFallon 8 —
(JHetherton) *chsd ldrs over 5f* **8/1**[3]
5012 **U** **The Gaikwar (IRE)**[13] 1542 5-9-7 **68** ........(b) MSavage(5) 12 —
(NEBerry) *s.s: in rr whn stmbld and uns rdr 6f out* **9/1**

1m 49.3s (10.00) **Going Correction** +1.35s/f (Soft) — **14 Ran SP% 121.9**
Speed ratings: **104,101,95,92,88 83,71,69,67,61 60,59,43,—** CSF £211.77 CT £1119.18 TOTE £12.80: £4.90, £3.00, £2.60; EX 191.90.
**Owner** Tim Powell **Bred** Berkshire Equestrian Services Ltd **Trained** Adstone, Northants

**FOCUS**
A ragged start to another race started without stalls.

**NOTEBOOK**
**Summer Bounty** may have done all his previous winning on fast ground, but he handles this sort of surface perfectly well, and he won this in good style having travelled strongly throughout.
**Dancing King(IRE)** had run well here in a conditions race last time and put in another good performance, finishing well clear of the rest having been up with the pace throughout. He takes his racing well.
**Bojangles(IRE)** found this tougher than the banded race he won at Chepstow last time and, having helped force the pace, did not see it out as well as some.
**Commitment Lecture** found the combination of a 6lb higher mark and taking on the boys too much to handle.
**Hilarious(IRE)**, who was making her seasonal reappearance, is still a maiden and is more effective on faster ground.
**Pharoah's Gold(IRE)** *Official explanation: jockey said gelding was unsuited by the heavy ground*
**Pride Of Kinloch** *Official explanation: trainer said filly was unsuited by the heavy ground*

## 1876 ZORN H'CAP (DIV II) — 1m 22y
**4:30** (4:32) (E) (0-70,68) 4-Y-O+ — **£3,721** (£1,145; £572; £286) **Stalls** Far side

Form — RPR
0110 **1** **Supreme Salutation**[8] 1675 8-9-12 68........ ACulhane 8 81
(DKIvory) *hld up: hdwy 1/2-way: led over 1f out: sn clr* **7/1**[3]
0021 **2** *10* **Fen Gypsy**[14] 1533 6-9-4 60........ KFallon 4 53
(PDEvans) *chsd ldrs: led 6f out: rdn and hdd over 1f out: sn btn* **6/4**[1]
-566 **3** *3 1/2* **East Riding**[4] 1748 4-8-3 45........ AnnStokell 13 31
(MissAStokell) *hld up: hdwy over 1f out: nvr trbld ldrs* **25/1**
000- **4** *5* **Explode**[38] 5933 7-8-10 52........ JQuinn 15 28
(MissLCSiddall) *prom tl wknd wl over 1f out* **20/1**
-200 **5** *4* **To Wit To Woo**[27] 1298 4-8-11 53........(p) MHills 3 21
(BWHills) *chsd ldrs over 5f* **4/1**[2]
0000 **6** *4* **Tally (IRE)**[26] 1308 4-9-0 56........ JPMurtagh 12 16
(MJPolglase) *chsd ldrs: rdn 1/2-way: wknd 3f out* **14/1**
3-00 **7** *nk* **Parisian Playboy**[22] 1373 4-8-6 48........ JFanning 5 7
(JeddO'Keeffe) *hld up: n.d* **20/1**
0064 **8** *4* **Pure Speculation**[15] 1502 4-9-3 59........ IMongan 1 10
(MLWBell) *chsd ldrs over 5f* **7/1**[3]
000- **9** *6* **Beneking**[161] 6063 4-9-3 59........ WSupple 6 —
(RHollinshead) *hld up: hdwy 1/2-way: wknd wl over 1f out* **16/1**
0-00 **10** *dist* **Dexileos (IRE)**[14] 1522 5-9-1 57........ DSweeney 11 —
(ADWPinder) *chsd ldrs over 5f* **20/1**
-000 **11** *dist* **Wood Fern (UAE)**[29] 1275 4-9-9 65........ TEDurcan 10 —
(MRChannon) *led 2f: pushed along 1/2-way: sn wknd* **20/1**

1m 48.8s (9.50) **Going Correction** +1.35s/f (Soft) — **11 Ran SP% 120.4**
Speed ratings: **106,96,92,87,83 79,79,75,69,—,—** CSF £16.74 CT £266.84 TOTE £8.80: £2.40, £1.10, £12.20; EX 24.20.
**Owner** Dean Ivory **Bred** M I Marsh **Trained** Radlett, Herts
■ Stewards Enquiry : M Hills caution: careless riding

**FOCUS**
No stalls for this race, and the runaway win of exposed performer Supreme Salutation suggests the form is questionable.

**NOTEBOOK**
**Supreme Salutation** relished the conditions and ran out a very easy winner on his second start for his new stable. Hopefully the Handicapper does not get carried away too much with this performance, but there is always the opportunity to go back into claiming company.
**Fen Gypsy** was well supported to follow up his recent win in selling grade, partly one assumes due to the replacement of his 7lb-claiming apprentice, who was down to ride him in the paper, with the Champion jockey. He did little wrong in second but just found the winner much too strong in the conditions.
**East Riding**, who remains a maiden, has shown in the past that she goes in this sort of ground.
**Explode**, who had an outing over hurdles in March, ran with a bit more promise than he did last season on the Flat.
**To Wit To Woo** seems to have lost his way since getting off the mark at Wolverhampton in November.
**Wood Fern(UAE)** *Official explanation: jockey said colt was unsuited by the heavy ground*

## 1877 HERR SOURCE CLASSIFIED STKS — 7f 26y
**5:00** (5:01) (E) 3-Y-O+ — **£3,932** (£1,210; £605; £302) **Stalls** Far side

Form — RPR
006- **1** **Azreme**[150] 6140 4-9-7 68........ IMongan 12 75
(DKIvory) *chsd ldrs: rdn to ld wl over 1f out: r.o: eased nr fin* **22/1**

1022 **2** *2* **Balakiref**[8] 1663 5-9-4 64 ... WSupple 4 67
(MDods) *hld up: hdwy over 2f out: rdn and ev ch whn hung lft over 1f out: no ex towards fin* **15/8**[1]

0-00 **3** *3* **Swift Alchemist**[3] 1757 4-9-3 67 ... GBaker 15 58
(MrsHSweeting) *hld up: rdn over 2f out: r.o ins fnl f: nt rch ldrs* **12/1**

100- **4** *2* **Cashneem (IRE)**[213] 5372 6-9-1 61 ... DAllan(3) 1 54
(WMBrisbourne) *chsd ldrs: rdn over 2f out: wknd over 1f out* **25/1**

0000 **5** *hd* **Sir Francis (IRE)**[34] 1204 6-9-4 65 ... EAhern 14 54
(JNoseda) *hld up: hdwy 1/2-way: wknd over 1f out* **5/1**[2]

021- **6** *6* **Didnt Tell My Wife**[174] 5976 5-9-1 64 ... LisaJones(3) 16 39
(CFWall) *hld up: nvr nrr* **5/1**[2]

622- **7** *9* **Nicholas Nickelby**[158] 6086 4-9-4 62 ... JPMurtagh 17 16
(MJPolglase) *led: hdd & wknd wl over 1f out* **14/1**

351- **8** *½* **In The Pink (IRE)**[196] 5693 4-9-3 67 ... TEDurcan 9 14
(MRChannon) *hld up: n.d* **14/1**

0002 **9** *8* **Jonny Ebeneezer**[14] 1533 5-9-7 68 ...(p) BDoyle 3 —
(RMHCowell) *w ldr: rdn and ev ch wl over 1f out: sn wknd* **10/1**[3]

0-00 **10** *½* **Bundy**[8] 1665 8-9-4 65 ... JQuinn 5 —
(MDods) *hld up: plld hrd: wknd over 2f out* **12/1**

-000 **11** *nk* **Tappit (IRE)**[9] 1642 5-9-4 64 ...(p) SCarson 7 —
(JMBradley) *chsd ldrs over 4f* **40/1**

20-0 **12** *1* **One Way Ticket**[8] 1675 4-9-4 65 ...(p) JFEgan 10 —
(JMBradley) *chsd ldrs: rdn and ev ch wl over 1f out: sn wknd* **14/1**

560- **13** *dist* **Logistical**[185] 5875 4-9-6 67 ... DSweeney 6 —
(ADWPinder) *hld up: a in rr: eased fnl f* **20/1**

1m 34.1s (9.20) **Going Correction** +1.35s/f (Soft)
**WFA** 3 from 4yo+ 12lb **13** Ran SP% **128.0**
Speed ratings: **101,98,95,93,92 85,75,75,65,65 65,63,**—CSF £65.30 TOTE £35.50: £5.20, £1.20, £6.20; EX 175.50 Place 6 £167.38, Place 5 £43.64.
**Owner** Halcyon Partnership **Bred** Miss Helen Mary Ann Omersa **Trained** Radlett, Herts

**FOCUS**
A tight classified heat on paper, with 7lb covering all the runners on adjusted ratings. The winner provided Dean Ivory with a 183-1 double on the card.

**NOTEBOOK**
**Azreme**, having his first outing for his new stable, stepped up on the form he was showing for his previous trainer towards the backend of last season, and hopefully he can now build on this.
**Balakiref** is taking his racing really well but he has gone up 11lb in the handicap during the last month and the Handicapper appears to be just in charge.
**Swift Alchemist** runs her best races from the front.
**Cashneem(IRE)** put up a creditable performance on his reappearance given that he is ideally served by fast ground.
**Sir Francis(IRE)** is currently on a career-low mark and shaped with a bit more promise than he had on the All-Weather earlier in the year.
**Didnt Tell My Wife** did not run too badly on his reappearance but he will have to step up considerably on this performance if he is to defy a mark as high as this back in handicap company.
**Nicholas Nickelby** *Official explanation: jockey said gelding was too keen in the early stages of the race*
**One Way Ticket** *Official explanation: jockey said colt was unsuited by the heavy ground*
**Logistical** *Official explanation: jockey said colt was unsuited by the heavy ground*
T/Plt: £23.60 to a £1 stake. Pool: £27,781.90. 857.95 winning tickets. T/Qpdt: £8.20 to a £1 stake. Pool: £2,352.80. 210.50 winning tickets. CR

# CHESTER (L-H)
## Wednesday, May 5

**OFFICIAL GOING: Good to soft changing to soft after race 3 (2.55)**
A change of format for Chester's May meeting, now held on Wednesday to Friday.
Wind: almost nil Weather: wet

## 1878 JOSEPH HELER CHESHIRE CHEESE LILY AGNES CONDITIONS STKS 5f 16y
**1:55** (1:56) (B) 2-Y-O **£12,325** (£4,675; £2,337; £1,062) **Stalls** Low

Form RPR

21 **1** **Dance Night (IRE)**[21] 1390 2-8-10 ... GGibbons 1 88+
(BAMcmahon) *trckd ldrs: rdn and swtchd rt over 1f out: sn led: r.o* **15/8**[1]

2 **2** *1 ½* **Sapphire Dream**[16] 1498 2-8-5 ... TEDurcan 2 77
(ABailey) *in tch: rdn whn nt clr run over 1f out: r.o ins fnl f* **8/1**

1 **3** *hd* **Beaver Patrol (IRE)**[16] 1505 2-8-13 ... SCarson 3 87+
(RFJohnsonHoughton) *lw: s.i.s: racd keenly: towards rr: nt clr run ins fnl f: r.o: nrst fin* **10/3**[2]

61 **4** *½* **Canton (IRE)**[32] 1240 2-8-10 ... DaneO'Neill 6 79
(RHannon) *lw: s.s: bhd: hdwy over 1f out: r.o wl fnl f: nrst fin* **7/1**[3]

21 **5** *nk* **Monashee Prince (IRE)**[9] 1658 2-8-10 ... NPollard 5 78
(JRBest) *led: rdn over 1f out: sn hdd: no ex ins fnl f* **14/1**

16 **6** *½* **King After**[22] 1383 2-8-10 ... LDettori 7 76
(JRBest) *w ldr: rdn whn bmpd over 1f out: wknd towards fin* **25/1**

263 **7** *1 ¼* **I'm Aimee**[19] 1449 2-8-7 ow2 ... SDrowne 8 68
(PDEvans) *prom: pushed along 2f out: wknd ins fnl f* **40/1**

1 **8** *hd* **Tara Tara (IRE)**[37] 1170 2-8-8 ... RWinston 9 68+
(JJQuinn) *s.i.s: towards rr: rdn over 1f out: no imp* **8/1**

41 **9** *1 ¼* **Mitchelland**[32] 1248 2-8-8 ... JFanning 4 63+
(JamesMoffatt) *trckd ldrs: rdn whn outpcd over 1f out: eased whn btn ins fnl f* **10/1**

62.72 secs (0.74) **Going Correction** +0.225s/f (Good) **9** Ran SP% **114.6**
Speed ratings: **103,100,100,99,99 98,96,95,93**CSF £17.63 TOTE £2.70: £1.30, £2.00, £1.60; EX 17.60.
**Owner** J C Fretwell **Bred** Peter McClutcheon **Trained** Hopwas, Staffs
■ Stewards Enquiry : G Gibbons one-day ban: careless riding (May 16)

**FOCUS**
A fair time given the conditions, and strong form. A one-two-three for the inside traps.

**NOTEBOOK**
**Dance Night(IRE)** had the perfect draw, got a good position tracking the pace and, when asked to go and win his race turning in, kicked nicely clear. He had things go his way on this occasion but can progress again.
**Sapphire Dream**, proven in the ground on her debut, kept on well to grab second close home. She should be able to find a maiden without too much trouble on this evidence.
**Beaver Patrol(IRE)**, constantly denied a run on the inside, was perhaps an unlucky loser. He should certainly have finished closer and there should be more to come from him back on a more conventional track.
**Canton(IRE)** was slowly away and trailed the field for most of the way, before making up ground on the outside in the straight. He too looks sure to improve on a more galloping track.
**Monashee Prince(IRE)** showed good pace early on but was done with early in the straight.
**Tara Tara(IRE)** could never get into it from her wide draw.

## 1879 LETHEBY & CHRISTOPHER CHESHIRE OAKS (LISTED RACE) (FILLIES) 1m 3f 79y
**2:25** (2:25) (A) 3-Y-O **£29,000** (£11,000; £5,500; £2,500) **Stalls** Low

Form RPR

00-2 **1** **Hidden Hope**[16] 1507 3-8-9 75 ... TEDurcan 1 106
(GWragg) *trckd ldr: rdn 3f out: led over 1f out: r.o* **14/1**

-230 **2** *2 ½* **Menhoubah (USA)**[39] 1143 3-8-9 ...(p) DHolland 2 102
(CEBrittain) *led: rdn over 2f out: hdd over 1f out: no ex ins fnl f* **7/1**

21- **3** *2* **Crystal Curling (IRE)**[189] 5825 3-8-9 ... MHills 4 99
(BWHills) *lw: in tch: hdwy over 3f out: rdn over 1f out whn chsng ldng pair: one pce ins fnl f* **7/2**[1]

1- **4** *6* **Si Si Amiga (IRE)**[186] 5868 3-8-9 ... MartinDwyer 8 89
(BWHills) *in rr: niggled along 6f out: styd on fr over 1f out: nvr nrr* **12/1**

20-0 **5** *5* **Qasirah (IRE)**[21] 1398 3-8-9 100 ...(b[1]) PRobinson 5 81
(MAJarvis) *racd keenly: hld up: effrt over 3f out: no imp* **12/1**

20-3 **6** *3* **Ithaca (USA)**[22] 1384 3-8-9 102 ... WRyan 6 76
(HRACecil) *midfield: rdn over 3f out: nvr trbld ldrs* **7/1**

6 **7** *11* **Alexander Duchess (IRE)**[17] 1485 3-8-9 ... JPMurtagh 7 59
(JGBurns, Ire) *a bhd* **11/1**

01- **8** *2* **Deraasaat**[218] 5284 3-8-9 95 ... RHills 9 56
(EALDunlop) *chsd ldrs tl rdn and wknd over 3f out* **11/2**[3]

1- **9** *dist* **Proud Tradition (USA)**[225] 5138 3-8-9 ... LDettori 3 —
(JHMGosden) *bit bkwd: prom: rdn 5f out: wknd fr 4f out: t.o* **5/1**[2]

2m 27.3s (1.81) **Going Correction** +0.225s/f (Good) **9** Ran SP% **109.7**
Speed ratings: **102,100,98,94,90 88,80,79,**—CSF £99.61 TOTE £12.80: £2.30, £3.20, £1.70; EX 147.40.
**Owner** Mrs Stephen Lussier **Bred** Hascombe And Valiant Studs **Trained** Newmarket, Suffolk

**FOCUS**
This looked a weak race for an Oaks trial, and the way the race was run adds further question marks to the worth of the form.

**NOTEBOOK**
**Hidden Hope** could have raced in a handicap off a mark of 75, but her trainer, who has a great record in this race, clearly knew he had a filly who was capable of better than that. The only one to go with the leader, she stayed on well to score and, although the way the race was run casts doubt on the value of the form, she clearly has plenty of ability, and the Ribblesdale now looks the likely target.
**Menhoubah(USA)** was given a canny ride by Holland, who set a steady pace to begin with before stretching the field in the back straight. He did everything right but the filly was not quite good enough. At least she proved she gets the trip, though.
**Crystal Curling(IRE)**, whose dam was runner-up in this race, looked to be given too much to do by her rider after the front two stole a decent lead in the back straight. She clearly stays this trip well and the Lancashire Oaks, in which her mother was successful, looks a suitable target.
**Si Si Amiga(IRE)**, whose trainer had been quoted saying that she had been slow to come to hand and would improve for the run, put in some nice late work, and better can be expected of her with this run under her belt.
**Qasirah(IRE)**, blinkered for the first time, took a keen hold in the early stages and may not have appreciated the ease in the ground. She is becoming disappointing.
**Ithaca(USA)** has been overrated ever since her maiden win and she looks as though she is going to be difficult to place this season.
**Alexander Duchess(IRE)** *Official explanation: vet said filly finished lame*
**Deraasaat** may have found the ground softer than ideal but this was still a disappointing effort as she was bred to appreciate this distance. *Official explanation: jockey said filly was unsuited by the ground*
**Proud Tradition(USA)** was another who did not run to her best on the softish ground. *Official explanation: jockey said filly was unsuited by the ground*

## 1880 TOTESPORT CHESTER CUP (HERITAGE H'CAP) 2m 2f 147y
**2:55** (2:55) (B) 4-Y-0+ **£69,600** (£26,400; £13,200; £6,000) **Stalls** High

Form RPR

22-1 **1** **Anak Pekan**[25] 1329 4-8-2 90 ... PRobinson 4 106+
(MAJarvis) *lw: racd keenly: a.p: led over 1f out: drew clr fnl f: r.o wl: eased cl home* **2/1**[1]

11-0 **2** *5* **Misternando**[7] 1703 4-8-10 101 ... SHitchcott(3) 18 107
(MRChannon) *hld up: hdwy 9f out: ridde along over 5f out: ev ch wl over 1f out: no ex fnl f* **33/1**

440- **3** *¾* **Big Moment**[49] 5639 6-8-12 96 ... DHolland 11 101+
(MrsAJPerrett) *swtg: hld up: rdn and hdwy 3f out: r.o fnl f: nrst fin* **7/1**[2]

303- **4** *½* **Distant Prospect (IRE)**[102] 5949 7-8-6 90 ... MartinDwyer 5 95
(AMBalding) *hld up: hdwy over 4f out: pushed along 3f out: styd on fnl f* **15/2**[3]

33-0 **5** *shd* **Mana D'Argent (IRE)**[11] 1615 7-8-5 89 ... JFanning 10 94
(MJohnston) *midfield: hdwy 6f out: nt clr run over 3f out: styd on fnl f* **28/1**

31-0 **6** *1 ½* **Ponderon**[25] 1329 4-8-1 89 ... SCarson 12 92
(RFJohnsonHoughton) *lw: in tch: prom after 5f out: led over 4f out: rdn over 2f out: hdd over 1f out: wknd fnl f* **12/1**

50-0 **7** *¾* **Random Quest**[18] 1457 6-8-4 88 ... FNorton 3 90
(BJLlewellyn) *lw: hld up: hdwy over 4f out: nt clr run over 3f out: rdn over 2f out: styd on fnl f* **12/1**

010- **8** *nk* **Numitas (GER)**[34] 5639 4-8-3 91 ... JMackay 2 93
(PJHobbs) *lw: midfield: lost pl over 7f out: styd on u.p fr 2f out: nt trble ldrs* **20/1**

33-5 **9** *2 ½* **Kristensen**[11] 1615 5-7-13 83 ...(p) JQuinn 15 83
(DEddy) *lw: in tch: nt clr run and lost pl 4f out: kpt on fr over 1f out* **16/1**

564- **10** *9* **Almizan (IRE)**[182] 5927 4-8-0 88 ... CCatlin 8 79
(MRChannon) *midfield: hdwy 6f out: rdn over 4f out: wknd over 2f out* **33/1**

303- **11** *¾* **Collier Hill**[60] 5927 6-8-12 96 ... EAhern 9 86
(GASwinbank) *hld up: pushed along and stdy hdwy 7f out: wknd wl over 1f out* **25/1**

02-0 **12** *11* **Gralmano (IRE)**[48] 844 9-8-1 85 ... PFessey 1 64
(KARyan) *b.nr hind: trckd ldrs tl rdn and wknd 5f out* **20/1**

400- **13** *9* **Archduke Ferdinand (FR)**[182] 5926 6-8-4 88 ... JFEgan 14 58
(PFICole) *midfield: nt clr run and lost pl 8f out: n.d* **33/1**

356- **14** *3* **Rayshan (IRE)**[38] 4898 4-9-2 104 ... RWinston 6 71
(JHowardJohnson) *in tch: rdn and wknd 6f out* **33/1**

00/0 **15** *3* **Gracilis (IRE)**[23] 899 7-7-9 82 oh2 ... LisaJones(3) 7 46
(GASwinbank) *a bhd* **25/1**

33-5 **16** *6* **Swing Wing**[13] 1578 5-9-10 108 ... KFallon 16 66
(PFICole) *prom tl rdn and wknd 3f out: eased 2f out* **16/1**

34-1 **17** *22* **Rahwaan (IRE)**[40] 1112 5-8-3 87 ... PHanagan 13 23
(CWFairhurst) *led: hdd over 4f out: wknd 3f out* **12/1**

4m 10.9s (5.52) **Going Correction** +0.225s/f (Good)
**WFA** 4 from 5yo+ 4lb **17** Ran SP% **124.9**
Speed ratings: **97,94,94,94,94 93,93,93,92,88 88,83,79,78,77 74,65**CSF £92.41 CT £399.27 TOTE £3.20: £1.50, £6.50, £2.10, £1.90; EX 100.40 Trifecta £617.60 £617.60 to a £1 stake. Pool of £4697.88 - 5.40 winning units..

**Owner** H R H Sultan Ahmad Shah **Bred** Mrs Rebecca Philipps **Trained** Newmarket, Suffolk

**FOCUS**

A competitive renewal, but not many got into it and the highly progressive favourite enjoyed a perfect trip throughout.

**NOTEBOOK**

**Anak Pekan**, who was the subject of a decent public gamble, had a good draw and used it to good effect, tracking the leader next to the rail for most of the way. Eased out turing for home, he drew clear in the straight for what was a comfortable win, and clearly he is a most progressive stayer. Another rise in the handicap will make things difficult, but he will surely still be a major player in the Northumberland Plate.

**Misternando** ran a blinder in second given that the ground looked to have gone against him, he was worst drawn of all and he was forced to race wide for much of the final circuit. Given a galloping track and fast ground, he could well win in Group company.

**Big Moment**, runner-up in last year's race off a 4lb lower mark, had to weave his way through the pack and ran well in the circumstances. He is a consistent type, but a horse of his ability should have won more races.

**Distant Prospect(IRE)**, who has not won a race on the Flat since the 2001 Cesarewitch, ran a creditable race given that this sharp track would not be ideal. A more galloping course will suit his style of running better.

**Mana D'Argent(IRE)** looked to be going well turning out of the back straight, but as the leaders kicked on he was left waiting for a gap to appear. It did not come until it was too late, but he stayed on well and looks like he is returning to form.

**Ponderon** gave the favourite 5lb and a two and a half length beating on his final start last year, and it is a measure of his rival's progress that he has reversed that form so comprehensively on his two starts this term.

**Random Quest**, a former course and distance winner, was well drawn and ran a fair race without suggesting that he is about to strike.

**Numitas(GER)** looks high enough in the weights at present.

**Archduke Ferdinand(FR)** *Official explanation: jockey said gelding ran too freely*

**Rahwaan(IRE)**, fourth in this last year off a 1lb lower mark, had to use up a fair degree of pace to get over from his wide draw to make the running. That early effort may have taken its toll, but the way he weakened quickly suggests there may have been something amiss. *Official explanation: jockey said gelding finished lame behind*

## 1881 TESS GRAHAM MEMORIAL H'CAP — 6f 18y

**3:30** (3:35) (C) (0-90,90) 3-Y-O — **£13,065** (£4,020; £2,010; £1,005) **Stalls** Low

| Form | Pos | Dist | Horse | Jockey | Odds | RPR |
|---|---|---|---|---|---|---|
| 1-53 | **1** | | **Lake Garda**[11] 1602 3-9-2 **85** (BAMcmahon) *w ldr: led over 3f out: drvn out* | GGibbons 1 | **8/1** | 96 |
| 22-1 | **2** | *1* | **Fun To Ride**[20] 1413 3-9-7 **90** (BWHills) *trckd ldrs: bmpd over 1f out: ev ch ins fnl f: nt qckn cl home* | MHills 5 | **3/1**[1] | 98 |
| 20-4 | **3** | *1* | **Sessay**[4] 1771 3-8-0 **69** (DNicholls) *hld up: hdwy over 3f out: swtchd rt to chal over 1f out: r.o same pce cl home* | ANicholls 6 | **25/1** | 74 |
| 310 | **4** | *1 ½* | **Instant Recall (IRE)**[20] 1408 3-8-9 **78** (BJMeehan) *hld up: hdwy over 1f out: r.o ins fnl f: nrst fin* | DHolland 2 | **5/1**[2] | 78 |
| 21- | **5** | *1* | **Ace Club**[220] 5255 3-8-6 **75** (WJHaggas) *hld up: hdwy whn nt clr run 2f out: styd on ins fnl f* | RHills 12 | **16/1** | 72 |
| 33-1 | **6** | *½* | **Presto Shinko (IRE)**[43] 1083 3-8-9 **78** (RHannon) *trckd ldrs: rdn and hung lft over 1f out: wknd ins fnl f* | KFallon 9 | **7/1**[3] | 74 |
| 301- | **7** | *3* | **Bo McGinty (IRE)**[275] 3833 3-8-10 **79** (RAFahey) *b.nr fore: uns rdr on way to post: midfield: pushed along 3f out: nvr able to chal* | PHanagan 15 | **25/1** | 66 |
| 20-1 | **8** | *3 ½* | **Benbaun (IRE)**[4] 1760 3-9-1 **87** 6ex (MJWallace) *led: hdd over 3f out: bmpd over 1f out: sn wknd* | DCorby(3) 3 | **5/1**[2] | 63 |
| 1212 | **9** | *shd* | **Piccolo Prince**[11] 1602 3-7-13 **68** (EJAlston) *midfield: hdwy 2f out: wknd fnl f* | JQuinn 10 | **12/1** | 44 |
| 20-6 | **10** | *1 ½* | **La Vie Est Belle**[42] 1099 3-8-7 **76** (BRMillman) *midfield: rdn 3f out: wknd over 1f out* | AMcCarthy 13 | **50/1** | 47 |
| 26-0 | **11** | *shd* | **Go Yellow**[20] 1408 3-8-4 **73** (PDEvans) *outpcd: swtchd lft and nt clr run ent fnl f: sn eased* | SCarson 4 | **16/1** | 44 |
| 40-1 | **12** | *shd* | **Commando Scott (IRE)**[19] 1453 3-8-9 **78** (ABerry) *chsd ldrs: lost pl after 1f: n.d after* | FLynch 11 | **33/1** | 49 |
| 140- | **13** | *8* | **Catch The Wind**[284] 3588 3-8-13 **82** (IAWood) *prom tl rdn and wknd over 2f out* | JPMurtagh 16 | **40/1** | 29 |
| 04-0 | **14** | *9* | **Ticero**[41] 1104 3-8-11 **80** (CEBrittain) *s.i.s: a outpcd* | TEDurcan 7 | **40/1** | — |

1m 15.9s (0.02) **Going Correction** +0.225s/f (Good) — **14** Ran SP% **118.9**

Speed ratings: **108,106,105,103,102 101,97,92,92,90 90,90,79,67**CSF £29.73 CT £589.38 TOTE £8.80: £2.20, £2.00, £5.90; EX 20.60.

**Owner** J C Fretwell **Bred** Capt J H Wilson **Trained** Hopwas, Staffs

■ Stewards Enquiry : A Nicholls one-day ban: careless riding (May 16)

**FOCUS**

On paper this was quite a competitive sprint, but once again the low draws had a huge advantage and the form may want treating with a little caution, especially away from Chester. At least the time was decent for the grade.

**NOTEBOOK**

**Lake Garda**, like his stablemate in the first, had the ideal draw and Gibbons once again made good use of it. He was suited by the step back up to six furlongs and gave the impression he could be in for a good season in these type of events. Despite that, he is not one to get carried away about, as everything went his way on this occasion.

**Fun To Ride**, off the mark in a fair Newmarket maiden on her previous start, got upsides the winner in the straight but that one was too strong. There should be more to come.

**Sessay ◆**, still a maiden, showed himself on a fair mark on this handicap debut with a good effort. He still looked a little inexperienced when battling for a position in the straight and should be capable of progressing.

**Instant Recall(IRE)** has done all of his racing over seven furlongs and, dropped back a furlong, he lost his chance with a slow start. He had to wait an age for a gap and was never going to make up the ground he lost when finally in the clear.

**Ace Club**, racing beyond five furlongs and on soft ground for the first time, did not get that clear a run and is probably capable of better than he showed on this occasion.

**Presto Shinko(IRE)** *Official explanation: jockey said saddle slipped*

**Piccolo Prince** *Official explanation: jockey said gelding lost its action*

**Go Yellow** *Official explanation: jockey said gelding was hanging right*

**Ticero** *Official explanation: jockey said colt lost a left hind shoe*

## 1882 WEATHERBYS BANK MAIDEN STKS (DIV I) — 5f 16y

**4:05** (4:06) (D) 2-Y-O — **£8,287** (£2,550; £1,275; £637) **Stalls** Low

| Form | Pos | Dist | Horse | Jockey | Odds | RPR |
|---|---|---|---|---|---|---|
| 4 | **1** | | **Catwalk Cleric (IRE)**[16] 1505 2-9-0 (MJWallace) *lw: trckd ldrs: burst through gap wl over 1f out: sn edgd rt: r.o to ld wl ins fnl f* | KFallon 3 | **1/1**[1] | 80 |
| 50 | **2** | *1* | **Town House**[23] 1364 2-8-9 (BPJBaugh) *led: rdn over 1f out: hdd and no ex wl ins fnl f* | JFanning 5 | **33/1** | 72 |
| 52 | **3** | *nk* | **The Crooked Ring**[8] 1686 2-9-0 (PDEvans) *prom: rdn 2f out: nt qckn fnl f* | KDarley 7 | **7/2**[2] | 75 |
| | **4** | *2* | **Victoria Peek (IRE)** 2-8-9 (DNicholls) *leggy: sn outpcd: hdwy over 1f out: styd on: nt pce of ldrs* | ANicholls 1 | **8/1** | 63 |
| 0 | **5** | *5* | **Aza Wish (IRE)**[5] 1743 2-8-9 (MsDeborahJEvans) *s.i.s: a outpcd* | SRighton 6 | **33/1** | 46 |
| 2 | **6** | *3 ½* | **Chilly Cracker**[23] 1364 2-8-9 (RHollinshead) *prom: rdn and ev ch whn bmpd wl over 1f out: sn wknd* | DaleGibson 4 | **5/1**[3] | 34 |
| | **7** | *15* | **The Terminator (IRE)** 2-9-0 (ABerry) *cmpt: bit bkwd: s.i.s: a outpcd* | FNorton 2 | **14/1** | — |

64.44 secs (2.46) **Going Correction** +0.375s/f (Good) — **7** Ran SP% **112.5**

Speed ratings: **95,93,92,89,81 76,52**CSF £37.94 TOTE £2.00: £1.70, £6.70; EX 71.70.

**Owner** Favourites Racing **Bred** Tony Mullins **Trained** Newmarket, Suffolk

**FOCUS**

A pretty ordinary maiden, although the winner will probably rate higher next time..

**NOTEBOOK**

**Catwalk Cleric(IRE)**, third to Beaver Patrol on his debut in a fair Windsor maiden, confirmed that promise with what was eventually a cosy enough victory. He needed plenty of stoking up, but was always going to get there when in full stride. He deserves to take his chance in a higher grade and will stay further, but things will be much tougher.

**Town House** managed to bag the favoured rail from her five stall and reversed recent Warwick form with Chilly Cracker, but she may have been flattered a little.

**The Crooked Ring** looks flattered by the bare form of Newmarket debut running, but should find a small race.

**Victoria Peek(IRE)**, a 20,000gns yearling, half-sister to a five-furlong two-year-old winner in Italy, out of a six furlong winner, was too inexperienced to make the most of stall one, but still shaped with promise.

**Aza Wish(IRE)** was again slowly away and well held.

**Chilly Cracker** was far too keen under Gibson and has not progressed from her debut.

## 1883 DAVID.M.ROBINSON DIAMOND DESIGN H'CAP — 5f 16y

**4:40** (4:41) (C) (0-100,100) 3-Y-O — **£13,682** (£4,210; £2,105; £1,052) **Stalls** Low

| Form | Pos | Dist | Horse | Jockey | Odds | RPR |
|---|---|---|---|---|---|---|
| 63-4 | **1** | | **Moss Vale (IRE)**[22] 1388 3-9-7 **100** (BWHills) *lw: midfield: hdwy 1f out: r.o to ld cl home* | MHills 7 | **5/1**[3] | 109 |
| 1-42 | **2** | *½* | **Green Manalishi**[42] 1099 3-7-13 **78** (DWPArbuthnot) *trckd ldrs: led over 1f out: hung lft ins fnl f: hdd cl home* | JQuinn 8 | **9/1** | 85 |
| 160- | **3** | *3* | **Wanchai Lad**[214] 5371 3-8-9 **88** (DNicholls) *outpcd: bhd: plenty to do 2f out: str run fnl f: nrst fin* | KDarley 14 | **50/1** | 86+ |
| 500- | **4** | *½* | **Embassy Lord**[177] 5966 3-7-13 **85** oh10 ow8 (b) (JO'Reilly) *towards rr: hdwy whn nt clr run 2f out: swtchd rt over 1f out: r.o ins fnl f* | JDO'Reilly(7) 5 | **50/1** | 82? |
| 02-1 | **5** | *nk* | **Foursquare (IRE)**[11] 1602 3-8-13 **92** (JMackie) *led: rdn and hdd over 1f out: wknd ins fnl f* | NCallan 6 | **4/1**[2] | 88 |
| 00-0 | **6** | *½* | **Sir Ernest (IRE)**[3] 1788 3-8-0 **79** oh2 ow2 (MJPolglase) *towards rr: pushed along 3f out: hdwy 2f out: styd on ins fnl f* | MartinDwyer 3 | **12/1** | 73 |
| 01-6 | **7** | *1 ½* | **Incise**[8] 1685 3-9-0 **93** (BJMeehan) *sn hmpd: bhd: hdwy wl over 1f out: one pce ins fnl f* | LDettori 11 | **14/1** | 83 |
| 4-15 | **8** | *½* | **Local Poet**[22] 1384 3-9-2 **95** (BAMcmahon) *outpcd: styd on fnl f: nt pce to trble ldrs* | GGibbons 15 | **33/1** | 83 |
| 0-23 | **9** | *2 ½* | **Harry Up**[25] 1323 3-8-11 **90** (JGGiven) *sn w ldr: rdn and ev ch over 1f out: wknd ins fnl f* | MFenton 1 | **10/3**[1] | 71 |
| 261- | **10** | *hd* | **Tribute (IRE)**[259] 4286 3-8-1 **83** ow3 (DRLoder) *hmpd and sn lost pl: towards rr: rdn over 2f out: hdwy whn hmpd over 1f out: no imp after* | TPQueally(3) 12 | **25/1** | 63 |
| 15-1 | **11** | *nk* | **Johnny Parkes**[35] 1209 3-8-4 **83** (MrsJRRamsden) *midfield: rdn over 1f out: sn btn* | PRobinson 9 | **13/2** | 62 |
| 161- | **12** | *1 ½* | **Divine Spirit**[233] 4943 3-8-4 **83** (MDods) *squeezed out sn after s: a bhd* | PHanagan 10 | **50/1** | 58 |
| 4314 | **13** | *3* | **Cheeky Chi (IRE)**[6] 1737 3-7-7 **77** oh11 (PSMcentee) *w ldrs: rdn 2f out: sn wknd* | DFox(5) 4 | **20/1** | 43 |
| 01-0 | **14** | *5* | **Jadan (IRE)**[18] 1473 3-7-12 **77** oh5 (EJAlston) *midfield: rdn and wknd 2f out* | JMackay 13 | **50/1** | 28 |
| 6021 | **15** | *¾* | **Demolition Molly**[33] 1236 3-7-9 **77** oh7 (tp) (RFMarvin) *w ldrs: rdn over 2f out: wknd over 1f out* | LisaJones(3) 2 | **12/1** | 25 |

63.21 secs (1.23) **Going Correction** +0.375s/f (Good) — **15** Ran SP% **124.5**

Speed ratings: **105,104,99,98,98 97,94,94,90,89 89,86,82,74,72**CSF £48.05 CT £2068.69 TOTE £7.30: £2.80, £4.70, £10.10; EX 144.10.

**Owner** John C Grant **Bred** Derek Veitch **Trained** Lambourn, Berks

**FOCUS**

A competitive sprint in which the very low stalls did not dominate like they had in some of the earlier sprints, but those in double figures once again had next to no chance. The form would want treating with a little caution for that reason alone, but the proximity of the fourth from out of the handicap is another worry, and there were the usual hard luck stories.

**NOTEBOOK**

**Moss Vale(IRE)**, who has an entry in the Group Two Duke Of York Stakes, has done most of his racing over six furlongs, but this drop in trip did not trouble him and he defied top weight with a narrow victory. It took him a while to catch the runner-up, and he may just be better served by another furlong when he steps back up in grade, which he will surely be forced to do off the back of this success. *Official explanation: , who has an entry in the Group Two Duke Of York Stakes, has done most of his racing over six furlongs, but this drop in trip did not trouble him and he defied top weight with a narrow victory. It took him a while to catch the runner-up, and he may just be better served by another furlong when he steps back up in grade, which he will surely be forced to do off the back of this success.*

**Green Manalishi**, a real speedy sort who only just gets five furlongs, he handled the soft ground well enough but would surely have been better served by a faster surface.

**Wanchai Lad ◆** shaped like being a pretty smart sprinter when winning on his first two starts last term, but lost his way after that. Having his first start since leaving Alan Jarvis, and encountering a soft surface for the first time, he ran a blinder. He came from a mile back to grab third close home and, if able to build on this, will be one to follow next time, and possibly after that.

**Embassy Lord** gained his only win so far over six furlongs and shaped as though a return to that trip will suit. This was a good effort from 10lb out of the handicap. *Official explanation: jockey said gelding had hung right*

**Foursquare(IRE)** gave the impression the Handicapper has been harsh putting him up 8lb for his latest success.

**Incise** was done no favours when hampered early on and ran a good race in the circumstances. *Official explanation: jockey said filly suffered from general bunching immediately after the start*

**Harry Up** missed the break and probably used up too much to get an early position. *Official explanation: jockey said colt lost a front shoe*

## 1884 WEATHERBYS BANK MAIDEN STKS (DIV II) — 5f 16y

**5:15** (5:16) (D) 2-Y-O — **£8,255** (£2,540; £1,270; £635) **Stalls** Low

| Form | Pos | Dist | Horse | Jockey | Odds | RPR |
|---|---|---|---|---|---|---|
| 34 | **1** | | **Tiviski (IRE)**[24] 1340 2-8-9 (EJAlston) *trckd ldrs: r.o to ld wl ins fnl f* | WSupple 5 | **12/1** | 74 |

33 2 1½ **Alpaga Le Jomage (IRE)**[7] [1707] 2-9-0 LDettori 6 74
(BJMeehan) *w ldr: rdn and hung lft over 1f out: ev ch ins fnl f: nt qckn* 4/6[1]

2 3 nk **On The Waterline (IRE)**[18] [1462] 2-8-9 SDrowne 9 68
(PDEvans) *in tch: rdn and outpcd 2f out: styd on ins fnl f* 6/1[2]

5 4 hd **Theatre Of Dreams**[39] [1128] 2-9-0 ANicholls 3 72
(DNicholls) *racd keenly: led: rdn over 1f out: hdd and no ex wl ins fnl f* 7/1[3]

5 2½ **Piper Lily** 2-8-9 FNorton 1 58+
(MBlanshard) *leggy: dwlt: pushed along and hdwy 3f out: one pce ins fnl f* 12/1

6 6 1¾ **Mytton's Dream**[11] [1601] 2-8-6 SHitchcott[(3)] 7 52
(ABailey) *sn outpcd: nvr trbld ldrs* 33/1

4 7 13 **Sharp N Frosty**[18] [1462] 2-9-0 TEDurcan 8 12
(WMBrisbourne) *a bhd* 20/1

64.86 secs (2.88) **Going Correction** +0.375s/f (Good) **7 Ran SP% 109.9**
Speed ratings: **91,88,88,87,83 81,60**CSF £19.04 TOTE £11.90: £3.20, £1.20; EX 18.10 Place 6 £56.00, Place 5 £40.56.
**Owner** The Selebians **Bred** Patrick J Fadden **Trained** Longton, Lancs

**FOCUS**
Like the first division, just ordinary form, although it looks reliable enough.

**NOTEBOOK**
**Tiviski(IRE)** was slightly disappointing at Musselburgh on her previous run having shaped so well on her debut, but this was more like it. She is flattered by the bare form of this (the favourite failed to handle the ground) but is entitled to step up in class.
**Alpaga Le Jomage(IRE)** had shaped well on both starts so far, most notably on his debut when third behind Blue Dakota and Turnkey, but he did not go through the soft ground and was unable to run to form. He is not one to give up on just yet as he will surely win his maiden on a better surface.
**On The Waterline(IRE)** did not really improve on the form she showed on her debut.
**Theatre Of Dreams**, given plenty of time from her first run, had every chance under a positive ride.
**Piper Lily**, out of a three times winner round Chester (good to soft twice, soft once), lost her chance with a slow start, but was noted keeping on quite nicely and will know a lot more next time.
T/Jkpt: Not won. T/Plt: £68.90 to a £1 stake. Pool: £104,706.85. 1,107.95 winning tickets.
T/Qpdt: £32.80 to a £1 stake. Pool: £4,252.20. 95.80 winning tickets. DO

## 1676 WOLVERHAMPTON (A.W) (L-H)

### Wednesday, May 5

**OFFICIAL GOING: Standard**
Wind: nil Weather: a few light showers

## 1885 WOLVERHAMPTON-RACECOURSE.CO.UK AMATEUR RIDERS' BANDED STKS 1m 1f 79y(F)
**6:00** (6:00) (H) 4-Y-0+ **£1,438** (£411; £205) **Stalls Low**

Form RPR

-600 1 **Leyaaly**[12] [1581] 5-10-7 30 MrGGallagher[(7)] 1 42
(BAPearce) *mde all: rdn 2f out: drvn out* 10/1

0020 2 1½ **Moyne Pleasure (IRE)**[1] [1862] 6-10-11 30 (p) MissKellyHarrison[(3)] 2 39
(PaulJohnson) *hld up in tch: swtchd rt 4f out: rdn 3f out: r.o ins fnl f: nt rch wnr* 5/2[1]

5033 3 nk **Dundonald**[12] [1583] 5-10-11 35 (bt) MrLNewnes[(3)] 3 38
(MAppleby) *chsd wnr: rdn 4f out: edgd lft 1f out: one pce* 4/1[3]

0/0- 4 5 **Classical Waltz (IRE)**[301] [3104] 6-10-7 35 MrJPemberton[(7)] 4 28
(JJSheehan) *hld up: rdn 6f out: hdwy on ins 3f out: no ex fnl f* 16/1

060- 5 2½ **Erupt**[190] [5819] 11-10-7 35 MissVBarr[(7)] 9 23
(REBarr) *hld up: hdwy 6f out: wknd fnl f* 7/1

5634 6 1¾ **Hellbent**[12] [1580] 5-11-0 35 MissSBeddoes 5 20
(JAOsborne) *dwlt: t.k.h in rr: hdwy on outside over 3f out: wknd over 1f out* 11/4[2]

0500 7 hd **Morris Dancing (USA)**[8] [1697] 5-10-11 30 MrEDehdashti[(3)] 8 20
(BPJBaugh) *prom tl rdn and lost pl over 5f out* 8/1

0-00 8 8 **Miss Ocean Monarch**[8] [1697] 4-10-7 30 MissRachelClark[(7)] 6 —
(DWChapman) *hld up in rr: no ch fnl 5f* 9/1

2m 7.17s (4.17) **Going Correction** -0.025s/f (Stan) **8 Ran SP% 123.8**
Speed ratings: **80,78,78,73,71 70,70,62**CSF £38.39 TOTE £16.70: £3.60, £1.60, £1.10; EX 127.30.
**Owner** Mervyn Merwood **Bred** N A Ovett **Trained** Newchapel, Surrey
■ This was Gordon Gallagher's first winner under Rules.
■ Stewards Enquiry : Mr G Gallagher five-day ban: used whip with excessive frequency (May 19,25, Jun 1,2,4)
Miss Rachel Clark one-day ban: used whip when out of contention (May 19)

**FOCUS**
The winner may have benefitted from a soft lead in this moderately run affair.

**NOTEBOOK**
**Leyaaly**, nibbled at in the ring, has suffered with all sorts of problems and was suited by a change to front-running tactics. Her rider picked up a five-day ban for excessive use of the whip. *Official explanation: trainer said mare had benefited from being ridden more prominently on this occasion*
**Moyne Pleasure(IRE)**, who was reported to have lost his action at Brighton the previous day, really wants further nowadays.
**Dundonald** had the blinkers refitted for this return to a longer trip.

## 1886 WEDDINGS AND RECEPTIONS AT DUNSTALL PARK BANDED STKS 5f (F)
**6:30** (6:30) (H) 3-Y-0+ **£1,431** (£409; £204) **Stalls Low**

Form RPR

4303 1 **Hagley Park**[19] [1443] 5-9-6 40 DHolland 5 52
(MQuinn) *mde all: rdn wl over 1f out: drew clr fnl f: r.o wl* 7/4[1]

2410 2 7 **White O' Morn**[44] [1075] 5-9-6 40 (p) RWinston 4 27
(JWUnett) *prom: rdn and wnt over 3f out: edgd lft over 1f out: wknd fnl f* 9/2[3]

0-00 3 shd **Travellers Joy**[12] [1584] 4-9-6 40 RLMoore 7 27
(RJHodges) *hld up: outpcd and bhd 3f out: gd hdwy fnl f: r.o* 11/1

0-04 4 ½ **Minirina**[12] [1596] 4-9-6 40 RFitzpatrick 2 25
(CSmith) *a.p: rdn over 2f out: rdr lost whip wl over 1f out: one pce* 14/1

2515 5 ¾ **Tuscan Dream**[8] [1699] 9-9-1 40 PBradley[(5)] 1 22
(ABerry) *hdwy on ins 3f out: sn rdn: one pce fnl 2f* 7/1

6464 6 1¼ **Emarati's Image**[36] [1191] 6-9-6 40 ACulhane 3 18
(BForsey) *hld up in tch: rdn over 2f out: sn wknd* 9/4[2]

0056 7 1 **Dancing Ridge (IRE)**[8] [1699] 7-8-13 30 (v) StephanieHollinshead[(7)] 6 14
(ASenior) *hld up: rdn over 3f out: sn bhd* 20/1

62.84 secs (0.04) **Going Correction** -0.025s/f (Stan) **7 Ran SP% 117.6**
Speed ratings: **98,86,86,85,84 82,81**CSF £10.68 TOTE £2.10: £1.10, £3.60; EX 13.10.
**Owner** Steven Astaire **Bred** Astaire & Partners (holdings) Ltd **Trained** Sparsholt, Oxon

**FOCUS**
This was the fastest time of the meeting compared with standard.

**NOTEBOOK**
**Hagley Park ♦** took full advantage of a drop to Band B. Holland has already made himself available to ride the mare when she returns here for a similar event on 17 May.
**White O' Morn** only just held on for second place after paying the penalty for trying to go with the winner.
**Travellers Joy** would have been second in another stride but the winner was home and dry.
**Minirina** could not take advantage of a drop in grade and the fact her rider lost his whip made little difference.
**Tuscan Dream** is at his best when able to dominate but that was always going to be difficult with Hagley Park in the field.

## 1887 COME EVENING RACING TO DUNSTALL PARK BANDED STKS 1m 6f 166y(F)
**7:00** (7:00) (H) 4-Y-0+ **£1,421** (£406; £203) **Stalls High**

Form RPR

0/5- 1 **My Legal Eagle (IRE)**[242] [4164] 10-8-9 40 BSwarbrick[(5)] 3 49
(RJPrice) *hld up: hdwy over 5f out: rdn over 3f out: led over 1f out: styd on wl* 2/1[1]

4003 2 5 **The Last Mohican**[14] [1543] 5-9-0 30 (p) RWinston 5 43
(PHowling) *led: rdn over 2f out: hdd over 1f out: no ex* 3/1[2]

60-0 3 5 **River Of Fire**[12] [1593] 6-9-0 30 DHolland 2 36
(CNKellett) *hld up: hdwy over 5f out: rdn over 3f out: wknd over 2f out* 13/2[3]

0235 4 10 **Little Richard (IRE)**[8] [1693] 5-9-0 40 (p) VSlattery 1 23
(MWellings) *hld up: hdwy over 5f out: sn rdn: wknd 4f out* 2/1[1]

0000 5 dist **Polka Princess**[20] [1402] 4-8-12 30 (p) ACulhane 4 —
(MWellings) *chsd ldr tl rdn and wknd over 4f out: t.o* 14/1

3m 21.4s (-0.10) **Going Correction** -0.025s/f (Stan)
**WFA** 4 from 5yo+ 2lb **5 Ran SP% 111.7**
Speed ratings: **99,96,93,88,**—CSF £8.45 TOTE £3.00: £1.40, £1.90; EX 8.40.
**Owner** E G Bevan **Bred** G J Freyne **Trained** Ullingswick, H'fords

**FOCUS**
A dreadful event even by "Regional Racing" standards.

**NOTEBOOK**
**My Legal Eagle(IRE)**, who has got over a little problem, was brought back on the Flat because he is considered too high in the handicap over hurdles.
**The Last Mohican** had no answer when the winner came to take his scalp.
**River Of Fire** had worn a visor when well beaten in a similar event at Warwick last month.

## 1888 JUNE SUMMER BALL AT DUNSTALL PARK BANDED STKS 1m 1f 79y(F)
**7:30** (7:30) (H) 3-Y-0+ **£1,445** (£413; £206) **Stalls Low**

Form RPR

0430 1 **Iamback**[12] [1582] 4-9-7 45 DHolland 5 51
(MissGayKelleway) *mde all: rdn over 1f out: r.o wl* 7/1

0516 2 2½ **Galey River (USA)**[14] [1545] 5-9-4 45 DCorby[(3)] 10 46
(JJSheehan) *w wnr thrght: rdn over 2f out: nt qckn fnl f* 16/1

4011 3 2½ **Eurolink Artemis**[12] [1580] 7-9-7 45 (p) NCallan 3 41
(JulianPoulton) *hld up: hdwy over 3f out: rdn over 2f out: kpt on same pce fnl f* 10/3[2]

0-22 4 2 **Six Pack (IRE)**[14] [1545] 6-9-7 45 CCatlin 6 37
(AndrewTurnell) *bhd: pushed along 7f out: hdwy 5f out: rdn and outpcd over 3f out: rallied over 1f out: styd on fnl f* 3/1[1]

030- 5 1¾ **Super Dominion**[280] [3697] 7-9-0 40 StephanieHollinshead[(7)] 4 34
(RHollinshead) *prom: rdn over 2f out: wknd wl over 1f out* 12/1

235- 6 1¾ **Time To Regret**[271] [3361] 4-9-7 45 RWinston 9 30
(JJQuinn) *sn prom: rdn over 3f out: wknd wl over 1f out* 4/1[3]

4204 7 2½ **Bevier**[13] [1572] 10-9-2 45 NChalmers[(5)] 8 25
(TWall) *hdwy 6f out: rdn over 4f out: sn wknd* 7/1

0-03 8 1¾ **Optimum Night**[6] [1722] 5-9-7 40 ACulhane 2 22
(PDNiven) *bhd: rdn over 4f out: short-lived effrt 3f out* 16/1

5335 9 5 **Western Command (GER)**[11] [1630] 8-9-7 40 (p) JoannaBadger 1 12
(MrsNMacauley) *prom tl rdn and lost pl over 5f out* 14/1

0-00 10 5 **Mutabari (USA)**[6] [1723] 10-9-0 40 AmyMyatt[(7)] 7 —
(JLSpearing) *hld up: hdwy on outside over 5f out: wknd over 3f out* 33/1

2m 3.10s (0.10) **Going Correction** -0.025s/f (Stan) **10 Ran SP% 122.1**
Speed ratings: **98,95,93,91,90 88,86,84,80,76**CSF £117.20 TOTE £10.00: £2.10, £4.00, £2.40; EX 89.50.
**Owner** Twilight Racing **Bred** Mrs J M F Dibben **Trained** Newmarket, Suffolk

**FOCUS**
The first two were at the head of affairs throughout.

**NOTEBOOK**
**Iamback**, with the headgear left off, appeared to enjoy herself out in front. She responded well to pressure and was nicely on top in the end.
**Galey River(USA)** reversed last month's Polytrack form with Six Pack but met one too good in the winner.
**Eurolink Artemis** was up to Band A on her bid to complete a hat-trick.
**Six Pack(IRE)**, who finished nearly seven lengths in front of Galey River at Lingfield last time, again gave the impression he wants further.
**Super Dominion** was without his usual tongue strap for this first outing since last July.

## 1889 CONFERENCES WITH RACING AT DUNSTALL PARK BANDED STKS 7f (F)
**8:00** (8:00) (H) 3-Y-0+ **£1,431** (£409; £204) **Stalls High**

Form RPR

2433 1 **Neutral Night (IRE)**[19] [1446] 4-9-7 40 (v) DHolland 2 47
(RBrotherton) *led 1f: prom: rdn to ld jst ins fnl f: r.o wl* 11/8[1]

00-0 2 3 **My Girl Pearl (IRE)**[69] [895] 4-9-7 40 VSlattery 8 39
(MSSaunders) *a.p: led over 3f out: sn rdn: hdd jst ins fnl f: one pce* 10/1

0034 3 1½ **Rathmullan**[10] [1639] 5-9-0 40 (b) LiamJones[(7)] 3 35
(EAWheeler) *prom: swtchd lft over 4f out: n.m.r on ins whn hit rails and stmbld over 3f out: sn rdn: one pce fnl f* 7/1

0-00 4 nk **Roving Vixen (IRE)**[23] [1370] 3-8-9 40 (p) ADaly 1 35
(JLSpearing) *prom: lost pl over 5f out: rdn over 4f out: hdwy over 2f out: one pce fnl f* 10/1

100- 5 2½ **Ben Kenobi**[212] [5419] 6-9-7 30 RFfrench 4 28
(MrsPFord) *hld up: hdwy over 3f out: rdn over 2f out: wknd over 1f out* 11/1

0006 6 1½ **Peartree House (IRE)**[7] [1710] 10-9-7 30 ACulhane 5 24
(DWChapman) *hld up: wl bhd 3f out: sme hdwy over 1f out: n.d* 6/1[3]

-030 7 8 **Westmead Etoile**[29] [1278] 4-9-4 40 (v) DCorby[(3)] 7 3
(JRJenkins) *led after 1f tl over 3f out: wknd over 2f out* 9/2[2]

00-0 **8** *10* **Dunmidoe**[12] 1592 4-9-7 35 GCarter 6 —
(CDrew) *a bhd: lost tch 3f out* **16/1**

1m 31.0s (0.68) **Going Correction** -0.025s/f (Stan)
**WFA** 3 from 4yo+ 12lb **8** Ran SP% **119.5**
Speed ratings: **95,91,89,89,86 84,75,64**CSF £17.75 TOTE £2.30: £1.40, £3.40, £2.70; EX 25.10.
**Owner** Raymond N R Auld **Bred** R N Auld **Trained** Elmley Castle, Worcs

**FOCUS**
Only two of the runners had ever previously scored.

**NOTEBOOK**
**Neutral Night(IRE)** finally broke her duck with the visor back on, having tried blinkers last time.
**My Girl Pearl(IRE)**, who had worn blinkers on her first two starts for her new trainer, ran much better, but this was a big drop in class.
**Rathmullan** ran out of room at the end of the back straight and his young rider must have wondered why he had switched to the inside.
**Roving Vixen(IRE)** was fitted with cheekpieces for this return to the sand.
**Ben Kenobi** was racing over a totally inadequate distance on this reappearance.

## 1890 STAY AT THE HOLIDAY INN DUNSTALL PARK BANDED STKS 6f (F)
8:30 (8:30) (H ) 3-Y-0+ £1,435 (£410; £205) **Stalls** Low

Form RPR
0566 **1** **Welsh Whisper**[13] 1573 5-9-1 30 NChalmers(5) 4 45
(SABrookshaw) *s.i.s: hdwy 3f out: rdn to ld wl over 1f out: drvn clr fnl f* **12/1**
433 **2** *6* **Countrywide Girl (IRE)**[13] 1573 5-9-1 35 PBradley(5) 2 27
(ABerry) *led: hdd wl over 1f out: sn edgd lft: one pce* **3/1**[3]
5023 **3** *3/4* **Levelled**[8] 1699 10-9-6 35 ACulhane 5 25
(DWChapman) *chsd ldrs: rdn and ev ch wl over 1f out: one pce* **5/2**[1]
-553 **4** *hd* **Second Generation (IRE)**[8] 1694 7-9-6 30 RLMoore 7 24
(RJHodges) *outpcd: hdwy fnl f: nrst fin* **4/1**
5221 **5** *nk* **Tiny Tim (IRE)**[1] 1860 6-8-13 35 (b[1]) RJKilloran(7) 1 23
(AMBalding) *w ldrs: ev ch 2f out: carried lft over 1f out: one pce* **11/4**[2]
000- **6** *5* **Madame Roux**[293] 3327 6-9-6 30 GCarter 6 8
(CDrew) *s.i.s: a bhd* **14/1**
-603 **7** *3* **Vaudevire**[13] 1568 3-8-7 30 (b) THamilton(3) 3 —
(RPElliott) *w ldrs: rdn and ev ch 2f out: wknd over 1f out* **14/1**

1m 16.19s (0.39) **Going Correction** -0.025s/f (Stan)
**WFA** 3 from 5yo+ 10lb **7** Ran SP% **121.3**
Speed ratings: **96,88,87,86,86 79,75**CSF £51.47 TOTE £19.00: £7.60, £2.00; EX 100.90 Place 6 £97.46, Place 5 £50.83.
**Owner** S A Brookshaw **Bred** Lloyd Bros **Trained** Uffington, Shropshire
■ Stewards Enquiry : P Bradley one-day ban: careless riding (May 16)

**FOCUS**
With three horses vying for the lead there was no hanging about.

**NOTEBOOK**
**Welsh Whisper** seemed to improve for the drop in trip and was able to come off a good pace after an indifferent start.
**Countrywide Girl(IRE)** could not live with the winner after leaning on Tiny Tim in the home straight.
**Levelled** could not raise his game after being obliged to race five wide on the home turn.
**Second Generation(IRE)** again ran as if he requires another furlong.
**Tiny Tim(IRE)**, who won an egg and spoon affair at Brighton over seven the previous day, should not be considered unlucky.
T/Plt: £90.60 to a £1 stake. Pool: £27,210.60. 219.10 winning tickets. T/Qpdt: £25.20 to a £1 stake. Pool: £2,015.40. 59.10 winning tickets. KH

1891 - 1892a (Foreign Racing) - See Raceform Interactive

# NAAS (L-H)
Wednesday, May 5

**OFFICIAL GOING: Yielding (good to yielding in places)**

## 1893a WWW.VICTORCHANDLER.IE WOODLANDS STKS (LISTED) 6f
6:30 (6:30) 3-Y-0+ £27,507 (£8,070; £3,845; £1,309)

RPR
**1** **Abunawwas (IRE)**[31] 1254 4-9-13 109 DPMcDonogh 14 112
(KevinPrendergast, Ire) *trckd ldrs on stand side: 6th 1/2-way: 3rd and chal fr over 1f out: kpt on wl u.p to ld on line* **7/1**[3]
**2** *shd* **Millybaa (USA)**[187] 5866 4-9-3 MJKinane 12 102
(RGuest) *trckd ldrs on stand side: prog into 2nd and rdn to chal 1 1/2f out: ev ch fnl f: led briefly nr fin: hdd on line* **5/2**[1]
**3** *hd* **Moon Unit (IRE)**[23] 1379 3-8-11 101 DMGrant 4 105
(HRogers, Ire) *cl up: led 1/2-way: rdn and strly pressed fr 1 1/2f out: hdd nr fin* **13/2**[2]
**4** *shd* **One Won One (USA)**[10] 1647 10-9-6 102 KJManning 13 104
(MsJoannaMorgan, Ire) *hld up: prog into 5th 1f out: r.o wl cl home* **12/1**
**5** *3* **Prince Monalulu (IRE)**[235] 4896 3-8-10 (t) CO'Donoghue 11 95
(EdwardLynam, Ire) *prom: 5th 1/2-way: 4th 1 1/2f out: no ex fnl f* **12/1**
**6** *shd* **Tiger Royal (IRE)**[23] 1379 8-9-6 104 (b) DJCasey 9 95
(DKWeld, Ire) *hld up: 7th 1f out: kpt on* **12/1**
**7** *nk* **Miss Serendipity (IRE)**[25] 1335 3-8-7 92 TPO'Shea 10 91
(MHalford, Ire) *s.i.s and towards rr: 9th 1f out: kpt on* **14/1**
**8** *1 1/2* **Anna Frid (GER)**[221] 5230 4-9-7 100 PJSmullen 8 90
(DKWeld, Ire) *prom to 2f out: 6th 1f out: no ex* **9/1**
**9** *3/4* **Danecare (IRE)**[11] 1631 4-9-6 95 JMO'Dwyer 1 87
(JGBurns, Ire) *s.i.s: nvr a factor* **20/1**
**10** *2 1/2* **Peace Offering (IRE)**[23] 1379 4-9-6 99 (p) PCosgrave 15 79
(DeclanGillespie, Ire) *plld hrd early: chsd ldrs on stand side: no ex fr 2f out* **12/1**
**11** *3* **Lady Portia (IRE)**[11] 1631 3-8-7 91 RMBurke 2 67
(JohnAQuinn, Ire) *led: rdn and hdd 1/2-way: sn wknd* **12/1**
**12** *1/2* **Sun Slash (IRE)**[23] 1379 4-9-3 99 PShanahan 3 66
(MsJoannaMorgan, Ire) *cl up to 1/2-way: wknd over 2f out* **20/1**
**13** *3* **Revenue (IRE)**[23] 1379 4-9-6 98 (t) JAHeffernan 7 60
(TimothyRPinfield, Ire) *nvr a factor* **14/1**

1m 12.2s **Going Correction** +0.125s/f (Good)
**WFA** 3 from 4yo+ 10lb **13** Ran SP% **125.7**
Speed ratings: **113,112,112,112,108 108,107,105,104,101 97,96,92**CSF £26.04 TOTE £6.20: £2.50, £1.50, £3.00; DF 29.90.
**Owner** Hamdan Al Maktoum **Bred** Airlie Stud **Trained** Friarstown, Co Kildare

**NOTEBOOK**
**Abunawwas(IRE)** got up on the outer in the last stride. The ground is the key but he still managed to erase that poor run behind Monsieur Bond in the Gladness Stakes.
**Millybaa(USA)** did everything right, as she got her nose in front close home but was just foiled by the winner's late surge. She could come back here for a five-furlong race in early June.
**Moon Unit(IRE)** fought off challengers from halfway before succumbing in the last strides.
**One Won One(USA)** is at the veteran stage now but showed a glimpse of his old zest with a strong late flurry.
**Prince Monalulu(IRE)** was outpaced inside the last.
**Tiger Royal(IRE)** is hard to place these days.

1894 - 1897a (Foreign Racing) - See Raceform Interactive

# 1780 SAINT-CLOUD (L-H)
Wednesday, May 5

**OFFICIAL GOING: Good to soft**

## 1898a PRIX LA FORCE (GROUP 3) 1m 2f
1:35 (1:35) 3-Y-0 £25,704 (£10,282; £7,711; £5,141)

RPR
**1** **Delfos (IRE)**[40] 3-9-2 OPeslier 1 111
(CLaffon-Parias, France) *raced in 2nd, pushed along 2 1/2f out, led just over 1 1/2f out, ran on well* 2
**2** *2 1/2* **Young Tiger (FR)**[24] 1350 3-9-2 J-BEyquem 4 107
(FRohaut, France) *held up in last, went 2nd just under 1 1/2f out, soon ridden, stayed on but no impression on winner*
**3** *2 1/2* **Kurm (IRE)**[48] 1049 3-9-2 IMendizabal 3 103
(J-CRouget, France) *led after 1f, set solid pace, ridden and headed just over 1 1/2f out, one pace* 1
**4** *2 1/2* **Joursanvault (FR)**[35] 1218 3-9-2 CSoumillon 2 98
(ADeRoyer-Dupre, France) *raced in 3rd, relegated to 4th 1 1/2f out, ridden adn unable to quicken inside final f, eased close home* 3

2m 8.40s **Going Correction** -0.35s/f (Firm) **4** Ran SP% **121.2**
Speed ratings: **113,111,109,107.**
**Owner** L Marinopoulos **Bred** Stilvi Compania Financiera S A **Trained** France

**NOTEBOOK**
**Delfos(IRE)**, settled in behind the leader in the early part of the race, made his challenge 300 metres from the post and strode out well in the final stages. He is definitely progressive, will stay further and could well be supplemented for the Prix du Jockey-Club next month.
**Young Tiger(FR)**, held up for the first part of the race, came with a progressive run in the straight but could never get to the winner. He held second place comfortably and may find a longer trip more to his liking.
**Kurm(IRE)**, smartly away, was soon at the head of affairs. He led into the straight, but had nothing in reserve when challenged by the winner and runner-up and was rather one-paced in the final stages.
**Joursanvault(FR)** was third until the straight, but was a spent force with two furlongs left to run. He definitely did not stay the trip and will soon revert to a mile.

# 1878 CHESTER (L-H)
Thursday, May 6

**OFFICIAL GOING: Good to soft**
Wind: almost nil Weather: overcast, shower race 3

## 1899 VICTOR CHANDLER H'CAP 1m 4f 66y
1:55 (1:55) (C ) (0-95,90) 3-Y-0 £10,432 (£3,210; £1,605; £802) **Stalls** Low

Form RPR
0-41 **1** **Lochbuie (IRE)**[21] 1416 3-8-9 **78** JFEgan 4 91
(GWragg) *lw: hld up: rdn and hdwy 3f out: led ent fnl f: r.o* **7/2**[1]
241- **2** *1/2* **Asiatic**[191] 5813 3-8-11 **80** KDalgleish 1 92
(MJohnston) *led after 2f: hdd after 3f: remained prom: rdn to regain ld 2f out: hdd ent fnl f: r.o* **5/1**[2]
31-5 **3** *7* **Dumfries**[10] 1672 3-8-12 **81** LDettori 5 82
(JHMGosden) *lw: prom: led after 3f: rdn and hdd 2f out: wknd ins fnl f* **5/1**[2]
1P0- **4** *3/4* **Akritas**[187] 5871 3-9-7 **90** TQuinn 10 90
(PFICole) *s.s: in rr: rdn and hdwy over 2f out: one pce fnl f* **12/1**
5-32 **5** *nk* **Oddsmaker (IRE)**[8] 1712 3-8-4 **73** DeanMcKeown 3 72
(PDEvans) *plld v hrd: handy: rdn 2f out: no ex fnl f* **6/1**
0-1 **6** *1 1/2* **Marine City (JPN)**[16] 1521 3-8-8 **77** PRobinson 2 74
(MAJarvis) *hld up: rdn and hdwy over 2f out: wknd fnl f* **11/2**[3]
2-01 **7** *22* **Rarefied (IRE)**[10] 1672 3-8-12 **81** 6ex SDrowne 8 43
(RCharlton) *lw: prom tl rdn and wknd over 2f out* **15/2**
-600 **8** *1/2* **Infidelity (IRE)**[42] 1108 3-7-9 **67** oh2 LisaJones(3) 7 28
(ABailey) *in tch: rdn and wknd 3f out* **50/1**
26-5 **9** *21* **Rutters Rebel (IRE)**[19] 1470 3-8-3 **72** EAhern 6 —
(GASwinbank) *led for 2f: remained prom tl rdn and wknd 3f out* **16/1**

2m 43.9s (3.38) **Going Correction** +0.40s/f (Good) **9** Ran SP% **112.5**
Speed ratings: **104,103,99,98,98 97,82,82,68**CSF £20.16 CT £85.06 TOTE £4.30: £2.00, £2.20, £1.70; EX 22.00.
**Owner** Mollers Racing **Bred** M Fahy **Trained** Newmarket, Suffolk

**FOCUS**
A good handicap where the front two pulled seven lengths clear of the third. The time was faster than for the Chester Vase later on the card.

**NOTEBOOK**
**Lochbuie(IRE)** ◆, off the mark at the fifth attempt in a 0-85 at Ripon last month, looked in trouble half a mile out, but he picked up strongly from the turn in and showed a good attitude in battling past Asiatic. He looks a progressive colt and should handle a further rise in grade.
**Asiatic** ◆, making his seasonal reappearance, had the best of the draw and went down fighting having raced prominently throughout. He pulled seven lengths clear of the third and with this run likely to bring him on a little, should be up to landing a similar race.
**Dumfries**, in need of the outing when only fifth at Windsor last month, raced prominently and had every chance. This was a slightly disappointing effort.
**Akritas** could never get into it having raced in rear for most of the journey. He was highly tried at two and seemed better suited by this drop down in grade.
**Oddsmaker(IRE)** lost all chance by pulling hard. He is better than this.
**Marine City(JPN)** won a poor maiden at Folkestone and although disappointing on this handicap debut, would not have been suited by the course. She is capable of better.
**Rarefied(IRE)** was very disappointing, failing to confirm Windsor form with Dumfries. *Official explanation: jockey said colt was unsuited by the ground*
**Rutters Rebel(IRE)** *Official explanation: jockey said gelding was unsuited by the ground*

## 1900 FREEPHONE STANLEYBET STKS (H'CAP) 7f 122y
2:25 (2:26) (C ) (0-100,100) 3-Y-0 £16,457 (£6,242; £3,121; £1,418) **Stalls** Low

Form RPR
1-1 **1** **Oasis Star (IRE)**[21] 1408 3-8-2 **81** MartinDwyer 2 91
(PWHarris) *midfield: hdwy over 2f out: rdn over 1f out: led ins fnl f: jst hld on* **5/1**[3]

2-14 **2** *hd* **Zonus**[20] 1437 3-8-4 **83** ........ RHills 9 92+
(BWHills) *towards rr: niggled along 6f out: hdwy over 1f out: edgd lft ins fnl f: r.o cl home: jst failed* **4/1**[1]

-020 **3** *¾* **Glaramara**[5] 1764 3-9-3 **96** ........ KFallon 4 103
(ABailey) *in tch: led over 2f out: sn rdn: hdd ins fnl f: styd on u.p: hld cl home* **8/1**

225- **4** *1¾* **Sew'N'So Character (IRE)**[199] 5674 3-9-3 **96** ........ FNorton 5 99+
(MBlanshard) *midfield: rdn and hdwy over 2f out: styng on wl whn n.m.r cl home* **20/1**

420- **5** *1½* **Desert Dreamer (IRE)**[239] 4817 3-8-9 **93** ........ AMedeiros(5) 16 92+
(BWHills) *hld up: hdwy over 1f out: styd on ins fnl f: nt rch ldrs* **50/1**

5-21 **6** *7* **Cello**[15] 1541 3-8-3 **82** ........ JFEgan 1 64
(RHannon) *trckd ldrs: rdn over 2f out: wknd 1f out* **9/2**[2]

2531 **7** *2* **St Savarin (FR)**[92] 675 3-7-12 **77** ........ DaleGibson 12 54
(JRBest) *trckd ldrs: rdn over 3f out: wknd over 2f out* **33/1**

3-00 **8** *¾* **Distant Connection (IRE)**[3] 1841 3-7-10 **80** oh2 ow3..... RThomas(5) 7 55
(APJarvis) *lw: prom: led over 3f out: hdd over 2f out: wknd over 1f out* **50/1**

-034 **9** *2½* **Makfool (FR)**[23] 1384 3-8-13 **92** ........ TEDurcan 6 61
(MRChannon) *in tch: rdn over 2f out: sn wknd* **14/1**

00-0 **10** *1* **Bright Sun (IRE)**[12] 1614 3-8-3 **82** ........ KimTinkler 10 48
(NTinkler) *midfield: rdn and wknd over 2f out* **66/1**

01- **11** *nk* **Ringsider (IRE)**[250] 4569 3-8-3 **82** ........ EAhern 8 47
(GAButler) *sqeezed out s: towards rr: pushed along over 2f out: nvr on terms* **16/1**

14-4 **12** *3½* **White Hawk**[20] 1439 3-9-7 **100** ........ JPMurtagh 18 57
(DRLoder) *lw: a bhd* **50/1**

0-16 **13** *4* **Free Trip**[21] 1408 3-8-7 **86** ow1........ LDettori 17 33
(JHMGosden) *towards rr: nt clr run over 2f out: nvr on terms* **12/1**

-312 **14** *7* **Appalachian Trail (IRE)**[13] 1585 3-8-7 **86** ........ RWinston 15 15
(ISemple) *in tch: hdwy over 4f out: wknd over 1f out* **9/1**

100- **15** *dist* **Skyharbor**[239] 4814 3-8-9 **88** ........ DHolland 3 —
(DNicholls) *led: hdd over 3f out: wknd qckly: hmpd over 2f out: t.o* **20/1**

1m 36.13s (1.38) **Going Correction** +0.40s/f (Good) **15** Ran SP% **116.0**
Speed ratings: **109,108,108,106,104 97,95,95,92,91 91,87,83,76,**—CSF £22.35 CT £161.37 TOTE £5.00: £2.00, £2.40, £1.90; EX 19.50 Trifecta £140.80 Pool of £2,718.36 - 13.70 winning tickets.
**Owner** R J Creese **Bred** James Gleeson **Trained** Ringshall, Bucks
■ Stewards Enquiry : Martin Dwyer caution: careless riding

**FOCUS**
A strong handicap producing a decent time for the grade, and another gritty display by the only filly in the line-up Oasis Star.

**NOTEBOOK**
**Oasis Star(IRE)**, who showed a determined attitude in winning on her reappearance at Newmarket, stepped up again off a 6lb higher mark, just holding off the strong late challenge of Zonus. She seems to only just do enough, which will play to her advantage, and nothing is to say she can not win again.
**Zonus** would have been the winner in another couple of strides, but just could not get going in time. He is a progressive colt with more to offer who can land a similar race before long.
**Glaramara**, down the field in the Guineas only five days previously, appreciated this first venture into handicap company and ran well in defeat.
**Sew'N'So Character(IRE)** faced a stiff task on this first start at three on his handicap debut off this mark, but he performed admirably and was not beaten far in fourth. He will be hard to place and needs to drop in the weights before he is winning.
**Desert Dreamer(IRE)** ran very well from a poor draw, staying on through tiring horses from the final bend. He can pick up a race if going the right way from this.
**Cello** was disappointing from the plum draw. He is better than he showed.
**Distant Connection(IRE)** was not totally disgraced at a big price and should be up to winning in a lesser grade.
**Ringsider(IRE)** lost his chance when being squeezed out at the start.
**Free Trip** never got involved from a poor draw.
**Appalachian Trail(IRE)** had little chance from his draw.
**Skyharbor** *Official explanation: jockey said gelding lost its action*

## 1901 MBNA EUROPE BANK CHESTER VASE (GROUP 3) (C&G) 1m 4f 66y
2:55 (2:55) (A) 3-Y-O £37,700 (£14,300; £7,150; £3,250) Stalls Low

Form RPR

2222 **1** **Red Lancer**[13] 1588 3-8-10 88 ........ RMiles 5 111+
(RJPrice) *hld up: hdwy 4f out: led 2f out: rdn clr 1f out: eased ins fnl f* **9/1**

5-12 **2** *5* **Privy Seal (IRE)**[13] 1586 3-8-10 110........ LDettori 4 100
(JHMGosden) *lw: in tch: rdn and ev ch over 2f out: no ex fnl f* **5/2**[1]

13-3 **3** *1¾* **Temple Place (IRE)**[21] 1411 3-8-10 100........ JPMurtagh 1 98
(MLWBell) *led for 1f: remained prom: regained ld wl over 4f out: rdn and hdd 2f out: wknd fnl f* **5/2**[1]

4-44 **4** *½* **Isidore Bonheur (IRE)**[5] 1766 3-8-10 98........(b) MHills 6 97
(BWHills) *led after 1f: hdd wl over 4f out: rdn whn n.m.r over 2f out: wknd over 1f out* **25/1**

01-6 **5** *14* **Roehampton**[21] 1411 3-8-10 97........(t) KFallon 7 76
(SirMichaelStoute) *sn niggled along: a bhd* **5/1**[3]

05-1 **6** *10* **Graham Island**[20] 1442 3-8-10 84........ DHolland 2 61
(GWragg) *unf: lw: trckd ldrs tl rdn and wknd over 3f out* **7/2**[2]

2m 44.33s (3.81) **Going Correction** +0.40s/f (Good) **6** Ran SP% **109.9**
Speed ratings: **103,99,98,98,88 82**CSF £30.36 TOTE £9.80: £2.80, £1.80; EX 23.40.
**Owner** Fox And Cub Partnership **Bred** Bishop Wilton Stud **Trained** Ullingswick, H'fords

**FOCUS**
Not a particularly good time for a Group Three and the form is to be taken with a pinch of salt.

**NOTEBOOK**
**Red Lancer**, ninth in a seller at Wolverhampton last October, has come a long way since and made the successful leap from handicap company in great style. Upped in trip, he won with any amount in hand, being eased down, but with many of the fancied horses running below expectations, one should not get carried away with the bare form. *Official explanation: trainer said, regarding the improved form shown, gelding appreciated the 1m4f trip and was very much suited by today's tight track*
**Privy Seal(IRE)** is nothing more than a Listed performer and will be suited by a return to better ground.
**Temple Place(IRE)** was disappointing even allowing for the fact this ground may have been against him. He holds a Derby entry, and is undoubtedly better than this, but has a bit to prove now.
**Isidore Bonheur(IRE)**, fourth in a Listed event at Newmarket five days earlier, attempted to make all, but was beaten with over half a mile to run. He was plugging on though when being squeezed up on the rail on turning in and was slightly unfortunate not to finish a little closer.
**Roehampton**, who reportedly looked a bit reluctant prior to the race, ran appallingly and was never travelling. There may well have been something amiss. *Official explanation: trainer had no explanation for the poor form shown*
**Graham Island** was another to run abysmally.

## 1902 BREITLING WATCHES & WALTONS OF CHESTER HUXLEY STKS (FOR THE TRADESMAN'S CUP) (LISTED RACE) 1m 2f 75y
3:30 (3:31) (A) 4-Y-O+ £20,300 (£7,700; £3,850; £1,750) Stalls High

Form RPR

2-01 **1** **Bandari (IRE)**[5] 1767 5-8-12 114........ RHills 7 117
(MJohnston) *swtg: chsd ldrs: lost pl after 2f: nt clr run over 4f out: rdn and hdwy over 3f out: r.o to ld wl ins fnl f* **10/3**[2]

262- **2** *1¾* **Parasol (IRE)**[292] 3400 5-8-12 114........(v) JPMurtagh 1 114
(DRLoder) *prom: led over 7f out: rdn over 1f out: hdd and no ex wl ins fnl f* **2/1**[1]

111- **3** *1¼* **Leporello (IRE)**[236] 4886 4-9-3 114........ TQuinn 9 116
(PWHarris) *lw: hld up: hdwy gng wl over 4f out: chsd ldr over 1f out: sn rdn: lost 2nd and ex ins fnl f* **5/1**[3]

6046 **4** *3½* **King's Thought**[5] 1762 5-8-12 95........ DHolland 11 105
(SGollings) *prom: hung rt on bnd after 2f: rdn over 2f out: no ex ins fnl f* **33/1**

-045 **5** *5* **Bourgainville**[12] 1622 6-8-12 107........ MartinDwyer 5 96
(AMBalding) *hld up: rdn over 3f out: hdwy over 1f out: one pce* **12/1**

312- **6** *2* **Hambleden**[221] 5253 7-8-12 101........ PRobinson 3 92
(MAJarvis) *bit bkwd: led: hdd over 7f out: remained prom: rdn over 2f out: wknd over 1f out* **12/1**

1-64 **7** *15* **Lago D'Orta (IRE)**[22] 1397 4-9-1 106........ DaneO'Neill 10 68
(CGCox) *s.s: in rr: sme hdwy over 2f out: sn wknd* **12/1**

52-5 **8** *5* **Margery Daw (IRE)**[113] 520 4-8-7 64........ LisaJones 8 51
(PSMcentee) *in tch: rdn 5f out: sn wknd* **150/1**

-210 **9** *1¼* **Grand Passion (IRE)**[47] 1062 4-8-12 103........ SDrowne 12 54
(GWragg) *trckd ldrs: lost pl 5f out: wknd over 3f out* **14/1**

03-0 **10** *2* **Piano Star**[24] 1355 4-8-12 100........(v[1]) KFallon 13 51
(SirMichaelStoute) *chsd ldrs: forced wd on bnd after 2f: rdn 6f out: wknd over 3f out* **14/1**

2m 14.4s (1.85) **Going Correction** +0.40s/f (Good) **10** Ran SP% **113.1**
Speed ratings: **108,106,105,102,98 97,85,81,80,78**CSF £9.99 TOTE £3.50: £1.50, £1.50, £2.00; EX 7.10.
**Owner** Hamdan Al Maktoum **Bred** Rathasker Stud **Trained** Middleham Moor, N Yorks

**FOCUS**
Another good renewal of this event, which is often superior to Listed grade. Bandari did remarkably well to win from the position he came from and continues his fight back to form.

**NOTEBOOK**
**Bandari(IRE)** ◆, a high-class three-year-old, looks to have come back to something like his best at the age of five, this being his second win in five days. Things did not appear to be going his way today, as he dropped back to nearer last than first early in the race, but he stuck to his task well and his extra stamina came into play. His confidence is back on a high and he deserves stepping back up to Group company.
**Parasol(IRE)** ran his usual consistent race and just got a little tired in the closing stages.
**Leporello(IRE)** should improve considerably for this first outing of the year on soft ground. A most progressive individual last season, he was cantering turning into the straight before appearing to get a little tired. There will be more to come from him this term.
**King's Thought** ran much better than his rating entitled him to, appreciating the ground.
**Bourgainville** usually runs respectably without proving good enough to win.
**Hambleden** would have found this ground on the slow side and ran well considering.
**Lago D'Orta(IRE)** lost all chance with a very slow start.
**Grand Passion(IRE)** *Official explanation: jockey said gelding was unsuited by the ground*
**Piano Star** *Official explanation: jockey said gelding was unsuited by the ground*

## 1903 WALKER SMITH WAY SOLICITORS RATED STKS (H'CAP) 1m 2f 75y
4:05 (4:05) (C) (0-95,95) 4-Y-O+ £11,932 (£4,526; £2,263; £1,028) Stalls High

Form RPR

00-0 **1** **Guilded Flyer**[19] 1460 5-8-6 **80**........ WSupple 5 91
(WSKittow) *mde all: rdn over 1f out: r.o wl* **14/1**

034- **2** *2½* **Petrula**[45] 4879 5-8-4 **78** oh1........(b) PFessey 2 85
(KARyan) *chsd wnr: rdn 3f out: no imp on wnr fnl f* **7/1**

05-0 **3** *1½* **Crow Wood**[15] 1540 5-9-4 **92**........ MFenton 4 96
(JGGiven) *midfield: hmpd after 2f: rdn and hdwy over 2f out: styd on ins fnl f: nt rch ldrs* **10/1**

-316 **4** *3* **Ofaraby**[15] 1539 4-8-12 **86**........ PRobinson 3 85
(MAJarvis) *racd keenly:in tch: rdn and hdwy over 2f out: one pce fnl f* **5/2**[1]

010- **5** *½* **Shayadi (IRE)**[33] 4478 7-8-5 **79**........(tp) FNorton 16 77
(BEllison) *hld up: rdn 3f out: styd on u.p fnl f: nvr trbld ldrs* **20/1**

650- **6** *nk* **Low Cloud**[232] 4998 4-8-4 **78** oh1........ ANicholls 14 75
(DNicholls) *hld up: hmpd after 2f: rdn and hdwy over 1f out: kpt on fnl f* **66/1**

310- **7** *5* **Stretton (IRE)**[194] 5756 6-8-4 **81**........ TPQueally(3) 13 69
(JDBethell) *hld up: effrt over 2f out: nvr on terms* **16/1**

-024 **8** *2½* **Linning Wine (IRE)**[41] 1114 8-8-9 **83**........ JPMurtagh 15 67
(BGPowell) *midfield: rdn over 2f out: wknd over 1f out* **14/1**

1111 **9** *1¼* **Consonant (IRE)**[68] 915 7-9-2 **90**........ KFallon 7 71
(DGBridgwater) *prom: rdn over 3f out: wknd over 1f out* **9/2**[2]

2030 **10** *14* **Northside Lodge (IRE)**[15] 1540 6-8-6 **80**........ EAhern 10 36
(PWHarris) *hld up: cl up tl rdn and wknd 3f out* **14/1**

00-0 **11** *4* **Blue Patrick**[103] 600 4-8-12 **86**........ JTate 8 35
(JMPEustace) *midfield: rdn and wknd 3f out* **66/1**

5-04 **P** **Fisio Therapy**[12] 1604 4-8-7 **81**........ JFanning 1 —
(MJohnston) *chsd ldrs for 2f: sn p.u: dead* **5/1**[3]

2m 14.73s (2.18) **Going Correction** +0.40s/f (Good) **12** Ran SP% **118.6**
Speed ratings: **107,105,103,101,101 100,96,94,93,82 79,**—CSF £107.62 CT £1036.41 TOTE £23.70: £5.50, £2.20, £3.50; EX 140.90.
**Owner** The Racing Guild **Bred** Catridge Farm Stud Ltd **Trained** Blackborough, Devon

**FOCUS**
Not as strong a race as it can sometimes be. Guilded Flyer had everything go his way and won with plenty in hand.

**NOTEBOOK**
**Guilded Flyer** was allowed a soft lead and, on ground he has shown a liking for in the past, was seen at his best. He had it under control from three furlongs out and stayed on well down the straight.
**Petrula**, a shock 66/1 winner of this race last year, ran well in defeat, sticking on all the way to the line after the winner had got a bit of a head start on him.
**Crow Wood** stayed on for third despite not getting the clearest of runs.
**Ofaraby** had every chance, but did race a little keenly in the early stages and that appeared to tell late on. *Official explanation: jockey said gelding was unsuited by the ground*
**Shayadi(IRE)** ideally appreciates further than this.
**Low Cloud** ran well at a big price, staying on having been hampered early.
**Consonant(IRE)** was found out by better horses back on turf.
**Fisio Therapy** tragically went wrong having slipped a stifle early in the race.

## 1904 STRATSTONE ASTON MARTIN MAIDEN FILLIES' STKS 7f 2y
4:40 (4:41) (D ) 3-Y-O £8,209 (£2,526; £1,263; £631) Stalls Low

| Form | | | | RPR |
|---|---|---|---|---|
| 2- | 1 | | **Sydney Star**[187] 5869 3-8-11 ... MHills 7 (BWHills) *b: b.hind: a.p: led 2f out: rdn and edgd lft over 1f out: r.o wl* **4/6**[1] | 86 |
| 0- | 2 | 1 3/4 | **Noora (IRE)**[180] 5947 3-8-11 ... RHills 2 (MPTregoning) *bit bkwd: trckd ldrs: rdn to take 2nd over 1f out: kpt on: nt trble wnr* **7/2**[2] | 82? |
| 063- | 3 | 6 | **Island Spell**[194] 5746 3-8-11 76 ... JPMurtagh 3 (CGrant) *bit bkwd: led: hdd 2f out: sn rdn: wknd fnl f* **9/1**[3] | 67 |
| 504- | 4 | shd | **Keeper's Lodge (IRE)**[223] 5190 3-8-11 72 ... GGibbons 4 (BAMcmahon) *bit bkwd: racd keenly: prom: rdn and ev ch 2f out: wknd fnl f* **10/1** | 67 |
| | 5 | 2 1/2 | **Prelude** 3-8-11 ... TEDurcan 8 (WMBrisbourne) *w'like: lengthy: hld up: rdn and wknd over 2f out* **33/1** | 61 |
| 5- | 6 | 6 | **Ballyboro (IRE)**[256] 4406 3-8-8 ... DCorby(3) 5 (MJWallace) *b: lw: dwlt: hld up: pushed along 3f out: sn lft bhd* **16/1** | 46 |

1m 30.95s (2.66) **Going Correction** +0.40s/f (Good) **6 Ran SP% 110.1**
Speed ratings: **100,98,91,91,88 81**CSF £3.06 TOTE £1.60: £1.30, £1.70; EX 2.60 Place 6 £28.78, Place 5 £19.58.
**Owner** Mohamed Obaida **Bred** Gainsborough Stud Management Ltd **Trained** Lambourn, Berks

**FOCUS**
Not much of a race and Sydney Star failed to achieve anything in winning.

**NOTEBOOK**
**Sydney Star** looked fit beforehand and won what was only a weak maiden well. It is highly unlikely however that she will be up to her Coronation Stakes entry, and she may be best off kept to a more realistic level.
**Noora(IRE)** has a similar race in her and should progress again.
**Island Spell** is well exposed and better off in handicaps.
**Keeper's Lodge(IRE)** is another going to be suited better by handicaps.
T/Jkpt: Not won. T/Plt: £60.60 to a £1 stake. Pool: £108,018.30. 1,300.15 winning tickets. T/Qpdt: £19.50 to a £1 stake. Pool: £4,231.90. 160.00 winning tickets. DO

1516
# FOLKESTONE (R-H)
Thursday, May 6

**OFFICIAL GOING: Soft (heavy in places)**
In all bar the first race, the far side of the track proved the place to be. On the straight course there appeared a bias towards prominent racers.

## 1905 CROSS CHANNEL MAIDEN AUCTION STKS 5f
2:05 (2:06) (E) 2-Y-O £3,454 (£1,063; £531; £265) Stalls Low

| Form | | | | RPR |
|---|---|---|---|---|
| | 1 | | **Striking Endeavour** 2-8-10 ... SSanders 1 (GCBravery) *mde virtually all: shkn up and hanging rt 2f out: jnd 1f out: rdn and styd on wl* **11/2**[2] | 79 |
| 2 | 2 | 2 1/2 | **Agent Kensington**[10] 1670 2-8-2 ... RLMoore 3 (RHannon) *cl up: trckd wnr 1/2-way: drvn to chal and upsides 1f out: unable qck* **1/2**[1] | 62 |
| 0 | 3 | 4 | **Artadi**[29] 1299 2-8-3 ... JQuinn 2 (PMPhelan) *hld up in tch: chsd ldng pair over 2f out: sn outpcd: drvn out to hold on to 3rd ins fnl f* **25/1** | 49 |
| | 4 | 3/4 | **Josear** 2-8-9 ... NCallan 5 (SCWilliams) *racd in last pair: outpcd bef 1/2-way: one pce and n.d fnl 2f* **25/1** | 52 |
| | 5 | 1/2 | **Dusty Dane (IRE)** 2-8-9 ... (t) ADaly 4 (WGMTurner) *w wnr for 2f: drvn 2f out: steadily wknd* **14/1** | 51 |
| | 6 | 5 | **Taipan Tommy (IRE)** 2-8-13 ... CCatlin 6 (SDow) *sn outpcd in last: nvr a factor* **33/1** | 37 |
| 56 | 7 | 3 | **Joe Ninety (IRE)**[41] 1117 2-8-2 ... DerekNolan(7) 7 (JSMoore) *racd on outer: spd 2f: sn wknd* **12/1**[3] | 23 |

64.79 secs (4.09) **Going Correction** +0.525s/f (Yiel) **7 Ran SP% 107.0**
Speed ratings: **88,84,77,76,75 67,62**CSF £7.55 TOTE £6.50: £2.90, £1.10; EX 12.40.
**Owner** Unicorn Free Spirit Partnership **Bred** A Walder **Trained** Newmarket, Suffolk

**FOCUS**
Probably just an ordinary maiden, but a good performance from the winner and there may well be minor races for some of the others. The time was modest for the grade. The whole field stayed towards the stands'-side rail.

**NOTEBOOK**
**Striking Endeavour**, a 16,000gns yearling, half-brother to four winners (none as two-year-olds), notably smart dirt performer Zanay, made a fine start to his racing career. He showed bags of pace and found plenty when challenged by the favourite. He looks up to holding his own in a higher grade.
**Agent Kensington**, narrowly denied in a pretty average Windsor maiden on her debut, did not appear to do a great deal wrong, but she just proved unable to go past the eventual winner. She was nicely clear of the remainder and should find a small race.
**Artadi** did not show that much on her debut at Warwick, but is bred to be a two-year-old and shaped better this time. She should continue to go the right way.
**Josear**, a 9,000gns yearling, half-brother to a couple of two-year-old winners, offered plenty of encouragement and should be capable of progression. The market may offer some clues when this one runs next time.
**Dusty Dane(IRE)**, a 9,400gns yearling, out of a half-sister to minor winners, several as two-year-olds, had a tongue-tie fitted for this racecourse debut. He showed plenty of pace before dropping out pretty tamely.

## 1906 TRANS-MANCHE MAIDEN STKS 5f
2:35 (2:36) (D ) 3-Y-O £3,740 (£1,151; £575; £287) Stalls Low

| Form | | | | RPR |
|---|---|---|---|---|
| | 1 | | **Eisteddfod** 3-9-0 ... SSanders 9 (PFICole) *racd far side: led gp: rdn and edgd lft over 1f out: overall ldr ins fnl f: styd on wl* **3/1**[1] | 77 |
| 4 | 2 | 3 | **Urban Calm**[19] 1472 3-8-9 ... MHenry 1 (RMHCowell) *overall ldr nr side: drvn over 1f out: lost overall ld ins fnl f: wkng nr fin* **5/1**[3] | 63 |
| 3- | 3 | nk | **General Feeling (IRE)**[241] 4779 3-9-0 ... PDobbs 2 (SKirk) *chsd nr side ldr: rdn 2f out: styd on fnl f* **7/2**[2] | 67 |
| 5- | 4 | 1 3/4 | **Ex Mill Lady**[152] 6129 3-8-9 ... NCallan 6 (JohnBerry) *pressed ldng pair nr side and clr of rest of gp after 2f: outpcd 1/2-way: kpt on again fnl f* **20/1** | 57 |
| 2606 | 5 | 1/2 | **Velvet Touch**[7] 1737 3-8-9 57 ... WRyan 12 (JRJenkins) *prom far side: chsd wnr fr 1/2-way: sn outpcd: wknd fnl f* **7/1** | 55 |
| 50 | 6 | 2 1/2 | **Indian Lily**[16] 1519 3-8-9 ... GBaker 11 (CFWall) *dwlt: last of far side gp and outpcd after 2f: shuffled along and kpt on fr over 1f out: nvr nrr* **33/1** | 48 |
| 00 | 7 | 1/2 | **Generous Spirit (IRE)**[4] 1796 3-9-0 ... PaulEddery 13 (JAOsborne) *chsd far side ldrs: drvn and outpcd 2f out: n.d after* **14/1** | 51 |
| 00- | 8 | 1 3/4 | **Cinnamon Ridge (IRE)**[281] 3698 3-8-11 ... LPKeniry(3) 10 (BJMeehan) *chsd wnr far side to 1/2-way: wknd rapidly fr over 1f out* **16/1** | 46 |
| 000- | 9 | 1 | **Willhego**[182] 5929 3-9-0 ... NPollard 8 (JRBest) *racd nr side: outpcd after 2f: nvr on terms w ldrs after* **16/1** | 43 |
| 0 | 10 | 3 | **Radlett Lady**[33] 1243 3-8-2 ... MHoward(7) 4 (DKIvory) *hld up nr side: outpcd after 2f: struggling fr 1/2-way* **25/1** | 29 |
| 50 | 11 | 3 | **Noble Mount**[101] 606 3-9-0 ... JMackay 5 (RGuest) *dwlt: racd on outer of nr side gp: nvr on terms: bhd fnl 2f* **25/1** | 25 |
| 0 | 12 | 16 | **Sapphire Sky**[33] 1243 3-8-9 ... BDoyle 3 (DKIvory) *s.s: racd nr side: a bhd: t.o* **50/1** | — |
| 3-0 | 13 | 2 | **Pass Go**[25] 1342 3-9-0 ... CCatlin 7 (GAButler) *chsd nr side ldrs: wknd bef 1/2-way: t.o* **20/1** | — |

63.21 secs (2.51) **Going Correction** +0.525s/f (Yiel) **13 Ran SP% 116.9**
Speed ratings: **100,95,94,91,91 87,86,83,81,77 72,46,43**CSF £15.54 TOTE £2.80: £2.10, £1.30, £1.60; EX 25.10.
**Owner** Elite Racing Club **Bred** Elite Racing Club **Trained** Whatcombe, Oxon

**FOCUS**
Probably just a modest maiden. The field split into two groups, the winner raced on the far side.

**NOTEBOOK**
**Eisteddfod**, a half-brother to the smart six- to eight-furlong performer Boston Lodge, out of a juvenile Listed winner, was sent off favourite to make a winning debut and did not disappoint. Always in the control of things on the far side, he picked up nicely to get the better of those on the near side who were in front at one stage. He has beaten little of note, but should be capable in handicaps if not too harshly treated.
**Urban Calm** shaped as though further would suit when fourth on her debut over this trip, but she showed plenty of pace and won her race on the near side. It is hard to know what she achieved, but she clearly posseses enough ability to win a minor race, probably when handicapped.
**General Feeling(IRE)**, only third when sent off 6/4 on his only start last term, was dropped a furlong in trip and racing on very different ground for this first start in 241 days. He offered some encouragement, but may be better served by a return to six furlongs.
**Ex Mill Lady** did not shape too badly on this first start in 152 days, but may be best watched until she goes handicapping.
**Velvet Touch**, rated 57, gives a guide to the strength of the form.

## 1907 EUROTUNNEL 10TH ANNIVERSARY FILLIES' H'CAP 6f
3:05 (3:07) (E) (0-75,73) 3-Y-O £3,591 (£1,105; £552; £276) Stalls Low

| Form | | | | RPR |
|---|---|---|---|---|
| 2061 | 1 | | **Melaina**[10] 1676 3-8-5 62 7ex ... (p) PMakin(5) 10 (MSSaunders) *mde all: pushed along fr 2f out: jst hld on* **10/1**[3] | 64 |
| 040- | 2 | hd | **Princess Galadriel**[192] 5789 3-7-12 50 ... DKinsella 9 (JRBest) *hld up rr: plenty to do whn effrt 2f out: rdn and rn green over 1f out: swtchd lft last 150y: hung lft but r.o wl: jst fail* **25/1** | 51 |
| 113- | 3 | 1 1/2 | **Intriguing Glimpse**[128] 6258 3-9-5 71 ... NCallan 3 (MissBSanders) *t.k.h: prom: rdn to chse wnr over 1f out: hld ins fnl f: lost 2nd nr fin* **11/1** | 68 |
| -146 | 4 | 1 1/4 | **Bohola Flyer (IRE)**[8] 1702 3-9-7 73 ... RSmith 8 (RHannon) *prom: rdn and disp 2nd pl fr 2f out to over 1f out: one pce* **3/1**[1] | 66 |
| -461 | 5 | 1 1/2 | **Crewes Miss Isle**[12] 1626 3-9-3 69 ... SWhitworth 2 (AGNewcombe) *s.i.s: hld up in last trio: plenty to do whn snatched up over 1f out: nudged along and kpt on steadily: nvr nr ldrs* **10/1**[3] | 57 |
| 0-00 | 6 | shd | **Rise**[17] 1504 3-8-7 64 ... (b) BSwarbrick(5) 5 (AndrewReid) *rn in snatches: drvn to chse ldrs 1/2-way: outpcd 2f out: kpt on fnl f* **16/1** | 52 |
| 00-4 | 7 | 1/2 | **Best Force**[9] 1689 3-8-5 57 ... CCatlin 4 (GABulter) *chsd wnr to over 1f out: wknd* **9/1**[2] | 43 |
| 00-4 | 8 | 7 | **Lady Of The Links (IRE)**[10] 1664 3-8-4 56 ... JQuinn 7 (NTinkler) *dwlt: a in rr: rdn 1/2-way: struggling after* **11/1** | 21 |
| 42-3 | 9 | 3 | **Whistful (IRE)**[19] 1464 3-9-2 68 ... SSanders 1 (CFWall) *pressed ldrs to 2f out: wknd and eased* **3/1**[1] | 24 |
| -000 | 10 | 6 | **Chiqitita (IRE)**[19] 1464 3-8-3 55 ... (b) RLMoore 6 (TTClement) *sed v awkwardly: drvn to rcvr after 2f: wknd 1/2-way: sn t.o* **14/1** | — |

1m 16.86s (3.26) **Going Correction** +0.525s/f (Yiel) **10 Ran SP% 111.2**
Speed ratings: **99,98,96,95,93 92,92,82,78,70**CSF £217.35 CT £2751.44 TOTE £15.10: £4.10, £5.70, £3.30; EX 115.30.
**Owner** Bali Royal Racing **Bred** Barry Minty **Trained** Haydon, Somerset
■ Stewards Enquiry : B Swarbrick one-day ban: careless riding (May 17)

**FOCUS**
Just a modest sprint handicap. The whole field raced towards the far side and those drawn high probably had a small egde.

**NOTEBOOK**
**Melaina**, 11lb higher than when winning over this trip at Wolverhampton on her previous start, was given an intelligent ride by Makin, who made the most of stall ten by switching to the far side and gaining an easy lead. She was all out to hang on and may be one to oppose next time.
**Princess Galadriel**, who hinted at ability at two, ran her best race to date on this first run in 192 days and would have won with a clearer run, or had he not hung left under pressure.
**Intriguing Glimpse**, racing for the first time in 128 days, posted a good effort from her low stall, especially considering she was keen on this first run on soft ground.
**Bohola Flyer(IRE)** was a little one-paced in the closing stages and may well be worth a try over the minimum trip.
**Crewes Miss Isle** kept on without being knocked about and is capable of better.
**Whistful(IRE)** was having her first start on soft ground and failed to run to form. *Official explanation: jockey said filly was unsuited by by the going (soft, heavy in places)*

## 1908 ENTENTE CORDIALE H'CAP 7f (S)
3:40 (3:40) (F) (0-55,59) 3-Y-O £2,968 (£848; £424) Stalls Low

| Form | | | | RPR |
|---|---|---|---|---|
| 304 | 1 | | **Pickle**[30] 1288 3-9-2 55 ... SSanders 1 (SCWilliams) *hld up in tch: prog to trck ldr wl over 2f out: shkn up to ld over 1f out: rdn and styd on wl fnl f* **13/2**[3] | 65 |
| 0-42 | 2 | 2 | **Knickyknackienoo**[29] 1300 3-9-0 53 ... SWhitworth 4 (AGNewcombe) *dwlt: hld up in rr: prog over 2f out: rdn to chse wnr jst over 1f out: fnd nil and btn fnl f* **4/1**[2] | 58 |
| 0051 | 3 | 6 | **Three Welshmen**[3] 1844 3-9-6 59 7ex ... (b) JQuinn 5 (BRMillman) *racd freely: led: rdn and hdd over 1f out: wknd fnl f* **7/2**[1] | 49 |
| 0-20 | 4 | 3 1/2 | **Vrisaki (IRE)**[97] 640 3-9-2 55 ... GCarter 8 (MissDMountain) *prom: rdn 3f out: sn outpcd and wl btn* **20/1** | 36 |
| 0056 | 5 | 1 3/4 | **Head Boy**[12] 1613 3-9-2 55 ... RLMoore 7 (SDow) *chsd ldrs: lost pl and struggling 4f out: bhd over 2f out: one pce after* **7/2**[1] | 32 |

1334 **6** *3 ½* **Larad (IRE)**[3] [1844] 3-8-2 **48** ow1 ....................(b) DerekNolan(7) 2 16
(JSMoore) *mostly chsd ldr to wl over 2f out: wknd* **7/1**

000- **7** *4* **Be My Alibi (IRE)**[150] [6147] 3-8-5 **49** .................... BSwarbrick(5) 6 7
(WMBrisbourne) *settled in rr: rdn 3f out: sn wknd* **33/1**

0-04 **8** *27* **Jesse Samuel**[13] [1594] 3-8-7 **46** oh1 .................... WRyan 3 —
(JRJenkins) *a in rr: wknd 3f out: t.o* **16/1**

0406 **9** *6* **Livia (IRE)**[29] [1300] 3-8-11 **50** ....................(b1) RHavlin 9 —
(JGPortman) *prom to 3f out: wknd rapidly: t.o* **11/1**

1m 31.85s (4.05) **Going Correction** +0.525s/f (Yiel) **9** Ran SP% **112.2**
Speed ratings: **97,94,87,83,81 77,73,42,35**CSF £31.46 CT £105.24 TOTE £5.60: £1.60, £1.10, £1.80; EX 21.40.
**Owner** S P Tindall **Bred** Simon Tindall **Trained** Newmarket, Suffolk

**FOCUS**
A low-grade handicap, but the first two finished clear.

**NOTEBOOK**
**Pickle** shaped well on her debut, but went the wrong way subsequently. Well supported on this handicap bow, she left behind her two latest efforts to get off the mark. Lightly raced, there could be more to come before she goes to the sales in July.
**Knickyknackienoo**, still a maiden, let the winner get first run and did not look that keen when put under pressure.
**Three Welshmen**, under a 7lb penalty for his success over a mile at Warwick just three days previously, did not appear too inconvenienced by this drop in trip, but was left behind by the front two. Maybe the race came too soon.
**Vrisaki(IRE)** looks to have dropped to a reasonable enough mark, but was beaten quite a way.
**Head Boy** gained his only win to date on fast ground and did not travel that well in these very different conditions.

## 1909 CHANNEL TUNNEL H'CAP 6f
**4:15** (4:15) (E) (0-70,68) 3-Y-O+ **£3,523** (£1,084; £542; £271) **Stalls** Low

Form RPR

0-10 **1** **Caustic Wit (IRE)**[19] [1477] 6-8-9 56 ....................(p) PMakin(5) 11 68
(MSSaunders) *mde all: qcknd 5l clr over 2f out: tired fnl f: jst hld on* **12/1**

4100 **2** *½* **Another Glimpse**[15] [1537] 6-9-11 67 ....................(t) NCallan 6 78
(MissBSanders) *hld up in midfield: outpcd over 2f out: rdn and prog wl over 1f out: chsd wnr last 75y: gaining at fin* **11/2**[2]

0205 **3** *1* **Tayif**[17] [1504] 8-9-3 59 ....................(t) SCarson 9 67
(AndrewReid) *cl up: outpcd over 2f out: rdn to chse wnr wl over 1f out: clsd fnl f: lost 2nd last 75y* **5/1**[1]

00-6 **4** *5* **Glencoe Solas (IRE)**[6] [1750] 4-9-12 68 .................... PDobbs 4 61
(SKirk) *settled in rear: outpcd over 2f out: shkn up & styd on fr over 1f out: no danger* **5/1**[1]

0010 **5** *3 ½* **Loch Laird**[43] [1098] 9-8-12 54 .................... GBaker 2 36
(MMadgwick) *dwlt: racd in last: rdn and struggling 1/2-way: styd on u.p fr over 1f out: n.d* **8/1**[3]

-000 **6** *3* **Firework**[44] [1087] 6-9-7 63 ....................(p) CCatlin 3 36
(JAkehurst) *mostly chsd wnr to wl over 1f out: wknd* **14/1**

0206 **7** *3 ½* **Oases**[2] [1873] 5-9-4 60 .................... SWhitworth 7 23
(DShaw) *dwlt: a in rr: pushed along and no prog 1/2-way: no ch after* **5/1**[1]

0000 **8** *1* **Arabian Knight (IRE)**[17] [1504] 4-9-2 58 .................... RLMoore 5 18
(RJHodges) *a in rr: struggling fr 1/2-way* **20/1**

-000 **9** *1* **Firecat**[13] [1584] 5-7-12 40 .................... DKinsella 8 —
(APJones) *prom tl wknd over 2f out* **22/1**

4611 **10** *1 ¾* **Doctored**[7] [1736] 3-8-9 61 ....................(p) BDoyle 1 12
(BAPearce) *drvn sn after s: struggling in rr after 2f: bhd after* **10/1**

3260 **11** *nk* **Sea The World (IRE)**[7] [1738] 4-8-11 53 ....................(v) JQuinn 10 3
(DShaw) *chsd ldrs: hanging lft and wknd wl over 2f out* **12/1**

1m 15.61s (2.01) **Going Correction** +0.525s/f (Yiel)
**WFA** 3 from 4yo+ 10lb **11** Ran SP% **116.7**
Speed ratings: **107,106,105,98,93 89,85,83,82,80 79**CSF £76.16 CT £386.47 TOTE £16.40: £6.60, £2.20, £2.40; EX 149.70.
**Owner** Mrs Sandra Jones **Bred** Gainsborough Stud Management Ltd **Trained** Haydon, Somerset

**FOCUS**
Just a modest handicap and again all the runners raced towards the far side.

**NOTEBOOK**
**Caustic Wit(IRE)** ran a shocker at Wolverhampton on his previous outing, but bounced right back to form under a really good, positive ride from his apprentice, who caught his rivals flat-footed when kicking for home inside the final three furlongs. He had to work hard to hang on and, not that consistent, would not be one to take too short a price about next time.
**Another Glimpse** appreciated the step up from five furlongs and was just denied. He is on a decent mark.
**Tayif** looked to run his race and can have no real excuses.
**Glencoe Solas(IRE)** has not won for nearly a year and was unable to muster the pace the pose a serious threat.
**Loch Laird** has not won over this trip since 1999.
**Oases** is 6lb higher than when last winning a year ago, but even allowing for that, was disappointing.
**Arabian Knight(IRE)** *Official explanation: jockey said gelding hung left*
**Sea The World(IRE)** *Official explanation: jockey said gelding hung left*

## 1910 SAMPHIRE HOE H'CAP 1m 1f 149y
**4:50** (4:51) (F) (0-55,53) 3-Y-O+ **£3,066** (£876; £438) **Stalls** Low

Form RPR

0-42 **1** **Got To Be Cash**[14] [1560] 5-8-9 **45** .................... BSwarbrick(5) 1 56
(WMBrisbourne) *hld up in last pair: smooth prog over 3f out: led over 1f out: hung lft but sn drew clr* **3/1**[2]

40-3 **2** *5* **Shape Up (IRE)**[12] [1630] 4-9-5 **50** ....................(b) PDoe 6 53
(TKeddy) *trckd ldr: chal and upsides 3f out: led briefly wl over 1f out : chsd wnr after: hung lft and no ch w wnr fnl f* **8/1**

2-00 **3** *1* **Lucefer (IRE)**[24] [1373] 6-8-8 **46** .................... DeanWilliams(7) 4 47
(GCHChung) *t.k.h: hld up in last: no prog tl pushed along over 2f out : styd on to take 3rd last 75y: no ch* **12/1**

0-50 **4** *2 ½* **Shaman**[52] [931] 7-9-0 **45** .................... RLMoore 5 42
(GLMoore) *trckd ldrs: rdn 3f out: nt qckn and btn over 2f out: one pce after* **9/2**[3]

00-0 **5** *2* **Encore Royale**[10] [1681] 4-9-5 **50** .................... NCallan 2 43
(JJay) *dwlt: t.k.h and sn chsd ldrs: rdn 3f out: fdd fnl 2f* **20/1**

0-13 **6** *2* **Royal Racer (FR)**[16] [1522] 6-9-5 **50** .................... NPollard 7 40
(JRBest) *led to wl over 1f out: wknd rapidly fnl f* **5/2**[1]

**7** *¾* **Dalon (POL)**[166] 5-9-8 **53** .................... MTebbutt 8 41
(DBFeek) *prom: lost pl after 3f: pushed along 1/2-way: wl in rr over 3f out: one pce u.p after* **9/1**

60-0 **8** *27* **Viva Atlas Espana**[124] [415] 4-9-0 **45** .................... SSanders 3 —
(MissBSanders) *hld up in rr: wknd over 3f out: eased: t.o* **25/1**

2m 12.92s (7.76) **Going Correction** +0.90s/f (Soft) **8** Ran SP% **109.2**
Speed ratings: **104,100,99,97,95 94,93,71**CSF £24.45 CT £223.42 TOTE £3.10: £1.10, £2.20, £3.60; EX 29.90.
**Owner** Mrs B Penton **Bred** Penton Haulage **Trained** Great Ness, Shropshire

**FOCUS**
An uncompetitive event, but an impressive performance from the winner.

**NOTEBOOK**
**Got To Be Cash** ◆ finally got her head in front at the 31st attempt. Although she only ran up to form, she did this easily and, with her confidence now sure to be on a high, she would be hard to beat under a penalty.
**Shape Up(IRE)** is still a maiden and had no chance when challenged by the winner.
**Lucefer(IRE)** has never won beyond a mile and he failed to prove his effectiveness over this sort of trip.
**Shaman**, last seen pulling up over hurdles in March, did not shape like a winner waiting to happen but is at least on a mark that qualifies him for regional racing.
**Encore Royale** is still a maiden.
**Royal Racer(FR)** had conditions to suit but ran poorly.

## 1911 COTE D'OPALE MEDIAN AUCTION MAIDEN STKS (DIV I) 1m 1f 149y
**5:25** (5:28) (F) 3-4-Y-O **£2,954** (£844; £422) **Stalls** Low

Form RPR

20-2 **1** **Magic Amigo**[13] [1597] 3-8-7 73 .................... WRyan 9 45
(JRJenkins) *wl in tch: trckd ldng pair 4f out: effrt to chal whn hmpd over 1f out: swtchd lft: rdn and r.o to ld last strides* **11/2**[2]

5-22 **2** *hd* **Extra Cover (IRE)**[17] [1508] 3-8-7 75 .................... PDobbs 2 44
(RCharlton) *led: hanging lft fr 4f out: rdn and veered sharply lft over 1f out: edgd lft again and hdd last strides* **2/5**[1]

**3** *1 ¾* **Play The Melody (IRE)** 3-8-7 .................... JQuinn 5 41
(CTinkler) *s.i.s: settled in rr: pushed along 3f out: plenty to do whn prog 2f out: styd on wl fr over 1f out: nrst fin* **14/1**[3]

/00- **4** *shd* **Maximinus**[56] [6022] 4-9-5 .................... LPKeniry(3) 7 41
(MMadgwick) *off the pce in midfield: effrt to chse ldng trio over 3f out: hrd rdn over 1f out: styd on same pce* **33/1**

00- **5** *6* **Vicario**[182] [5934] 3-8-7 .................... JMackay 3 30
(MLWBell) *chsd ldrs: drvn 4f out: one pce and no imp fnl 2f* **33/1**

**6** *1 ¼* **Kilindini** 3-8-8 ow1 .................... SSanders 10 29
(MissECLavelle) *restless stalls: prom: trckd ldr 1/2-way: rdn to chal 2f out: sltly hmpd over 1f out: wknd and eased* **16/1**

**7** *7* **Bayou Princess** 3-8-2 .................... CCatlin 4 10
(BDeHaan) *racd in midfield: rdn over 3f out: sn struggling* **40/1**

000- **8** *7* **Rainsborough Hill**[189] [5836] 3-8-7 .................... VSlattery 6 3
(AKing) *s.s: a in rr: rdn and no prog 4f out* **33/1**

0-0 **9** *9* **Salford Rocket**[12] [1628] 4-9-8 .................... TGMcLaughlin 1 —
(GCHChung) *a wl in rr: rdn and wknd 4f out* **50/1**

-00 **10** *dist* **Heyward Place**[24] [1371] 4-9-3 ....................(t) PDoe 8 —
(TKeddy) *chsd ldr to 1/2-way: wknd rapidly 4f out: t.o whn virtually p.u fnl f* **100/1**

2m 13.69s (8.53) **Going Correction** +0.90s/f (Soft)
**WFA** 3 from 4yo 15lb **10** Ran SP% **113.6**
Speed ratings: **101,100,99,99,94 93,87,82,75,—**CSF £7.61 TOTE £7.60: £1.70, £1.02, £4.20; EX 17.30.
**Owner** Kevin Reddington **Bred** Newgate Stud Co **Trained** Royston, Herts

**FOCUS**
A pretty weak maiden and not the first race to look at for future winners, particularly considering the proximity of the fourth. The pace was just ordinary.

**NOTEBOOK**
**Magic Amigo**, racing beyond seven furlongs for the first time, stayed the trip well but was a slightly fortunate winner as the runner-up threw the race away in the straight, hampering him in the process. He will struggle to follow up in a handicap off his current mark.
**Extra Cover(IRE)** was given every chance from the front, but he did not look that keen when asked to quicken, holding his head quite high and wandering around. He will win a race, but is not one to follow.
**Play The Melody(IRE)**, a half-brother to middle-distance/staying winners, out of a half-sister to 2000 Guineas winner Doyoun, fared best of the three newcomers and should win a minor race given normal improvement.
**Maximinus** did not run too badly over hurdles when last seen and, returned to the Flat, he ran above himself. His handicap mark may suffer though, despite him being flattered.
**Vicario** showed little but will find things easier now he is qualified for a handicap mark.

## 1912 COTE D'OPALE MEDIAN AUCTION MAIDEN STKS (DIV II) 1m 1f 149y
**6:00** (6:05) (F) 3-4-Y-O **£2,954** (£844; £422) **Stalls** Low

Form RPR

03 **1** **Amankila (IRE)**[16] [1532] 3-8-2 .................... JMackay 6 71
(MLWBell) *prom: trckd ldr 4f out: chalng and gng wl whn lft clr wl over 2f out: unchal after* **4/5**[1]

0 **2** *11* **Ballyliffin (IRE)**[9] [1683] 3-8-7 .................... PDobbs 9 57
(SKirk) *s.i.s and reminders sn after s: in rr: prog whn lft in 2nd pl wl over 2f out: no ch w wnr after* **33/1**

0 **3** *2 ½* **Muslin**[19] [1466] 3-8-5 ow3 .................... OUrbina 7 50
(JRFanshawe) *hld up in midfield: effrt to chse ldng pair whn hmpd wl over 2f out: no ch after: kpt on* **7/1**[3]

0 **4** *5* **Lucky Again (IRE)**[19] [1461] 3-8-7 .................... GCarter 2 43
(JLDunlop) *s.i.s: settled in last pair: effrt whn squeezed out over 3f out: hmpd wl over 2f out: kpt on one pce after* **10/1**

0 **5** *17* **Ba Clubman (IRE)**[12] [1612] 4-9-8 .................... RLMoore 1 12
(SCWilliams) *chsd ldr to 4f out: wkng whn hmpd wl over 2f out* **12/1**

04 **6** *18* **Serengeti Sky (USA)**[14] [1561] 3-8-4 .................... ABeech(3) 4 —
(DRLoder) *racd in midfield: shkn up 1/2-way: effrt whn bdly hmpd wl over 2f out: nt rcvr* **9/1**

0 **7** *4* **Miss St Albans**[19] [1466] 3-7-9 .................... NicolPolli(7) 5 —
(TTClement) *sddle slipped sn after s: chsd ldrs to 1/2-way: in rr and no ch whn forced wd bnd wl over 2f out* **50/1**

3 **S** **Bansha Bru (IRE)**[19] [1476] 4-9-8 .................... SSanders 3 —
(MissECLavelle) *led: rdn and hrd pressed whn collapsed wl over 2f out: dead* **11/2**[2]

00-0 **B** **Good Article (IRE)**[17] [1508] 3-8-7 ....................(e) SWhitworth 10 —
(APJones) *hmpd and lost pl after 1f: dropped to last pair: rdn and effrt in 5th whn b.d wl over 2f out* **20/1**

2m 13.75s (8.59) **Going Correction** +0.90s/f (Soft)
**WFA** 3 from 4yo 15lb **9** Ran SP% **119.9**
Speed ratings: **101,92,90,86,72 58,55,—,—**CSF £42.45 TOTE £1.80: £1.02, £14.60, £2.00; EX 77.30 Place 6 £108.56, Place 5 £100.47.
**Owner** Luke Lillingston **Bred** Mount Coote Stud **Trained** Newmarket, Suffolk
■ Frangipani (3/1) was withdrawn after breaking out of the stalls. Rule 4 applies, deduct 25p in the £. New market formed.

**FOCUS**
An incident-packed race. Leading fancy Frangipani had to be withdrawn after getting loose before the start and in the race itself, Bansha Blue collapsed on the final turn, causing trouble to all bar the first two home. All things taken into account, this was a very weak maiden, although the form looks better than division one.

**NOTEBOOK**
**Amankila(IRE)** avoided all the trouble and, although flattered by her winning margin, she would surely have won in any case. She is progressing with every race, but will face her toughest task to date when going handicapping.
**Ballyliffin(IRE)**, like the winner, avoided the trouble on the home bend, but was still well beaten. Handicapping is his game.
**Muslin** lost about four or five lengths and plenty of momentum when hampered on the bend.
**Lucky Again(IRE)** missed the break and looked held when badly hampered by the faller.
**Ba Clubman(IRE)** looked to be struggling when pushed wide on the final turn in a bid to avoid the trouble.
**Serengeti Sky(USA)** was almost taken out of the race by all of the trouble.
**Bansha Bru(IRE)** was under pressure when sadly taking a fatal fall.
T/Plt: £105.20 to a £1 stake. Pool: £22,517.45. 156.25 winning tickets. T/Qpdt: £49.80 to a £1 stake. Pool: £1,320.40. 19.60 winning tickets. JN

1735 **SOUTHWELL** (L-H)
Thursday, May 6

**OFFICIAL GOING: Standard**
Wind: mod across Weather: cloudy

## 1913 BATTLE OF WOUNDED KNEE BANDED STKS — 6f (F)
**2:15** (2:16) (H) 3-Y-0+ — **£1,449** (£414; £207) **Stalls** Low

Form — RPR
00-6 **1** **Boisdale (IRE)**[12] 1625 6-8-13 45 ........ LTreadwell(7) 3 — 63
(SLKeightley) *trckd ldrs: led over 2f out: rdn out* **7/1**[3]
4631 **2** 1 1/4 **Larky's Lob**[9] 1696 5-8-13 45 ........ JDO'Reilly(7) 2 — 59
(JO'Reilly) *s.i.s: hdwy over 3f out: rdn over 2f out: ev ch fr over 1f out: no ex towards fin* **4/7**[1]
4202 **3** 2 **Cargo**[9] 1692 5-9-3 45 ........(tp) BReilly(3) 7 — 53
(BAPearce) *unruly stalls: chsd ldrs: rdn over 2f out: styd on same pce fnl f* **9/2**[2]
4400 **4** 5 **Pardon Moi**[16] 1517 3-8-5 45 ........(p) HayleyTurner(5) 1 — 38
(MrsCADunnett) *sn pushed along and prom: wknd over 1f out* **25/1**
-500 **5** 1 **Lake Eyre (IRE)**[105] 584 5-9-6 45 ........ JEdmunds 4 — 35
(JBalding) *led over 3f: wknd over 1f out* **11/1**
630- **6** 1/2 **Glory Girl**[264] 4190 4-8-13 45 ........ DTudhope(7) 5 — 34
(MBrittain) *chsd ldrs over 4f* **33/1**
0-06 **7** 1 1/4 **Zabadou**[12] 1617 3-8-5 40 ........ TEaves(5) 8 — 30
(CBBBooth) *outpcd* **40/1**
0033 **8** 2 **Eternal Bloom**[17] 1515 6-9-6 45 ........ TWilliams 6 — 24
(MBrittain) *chsd ldrs over 4f* **16/1**

1m 16.02s (-0.88) **Going Correction** -0.20s/f (Stan)
**WFA** 3 from 4yo+ 10lb — **8** Ran SP% **117.8**
Speed ratings: **97,95,92,86,84 84,82,79**CSF £11.67 TOTE £9.20: £2.60, £1.02, £1.10; EX 22.30.
**Owner** Ms Sue Gray **Bred** G Ryan **Trained** Waltham-On-The-Wolds, Leics
■ Stewards Enquiry : J D O'Reilly two-day ban: used whip with excessive force (May 17,18)

**FOCUS**
This event was above average for the grade. It was run at a modest pace.

**NOTEBOOK**
**Boisdale(IRE)** greatly appreciated the drop into this grade and registered his first success since scoring over course-and-distance in June 2003. He was given a postive ride on this occasion and showed a good attitude to repel the runner-up late on.
**Larky's Lob** did himself no favours with a sluggish start, but still recovered to have every chance if good enough. He may not have been helped by sticking to the far-side rail, which is the slowest part of the straight, and was clear of the rest. He will be weighted out of banded races now due to his success last time.
**Cargo** played up in the stalls and raced wide for most of the contest. He is not one to rely on, but is probably capable of better.
**Pardon Moi**, down in grade, was made to look very one-paced in the straight, but was not totally disgraced against her elders.

## 1914 HOORAH FOR HATS & HORSES BANDED STKS — 1m 3f (F)
**2:45** (2:46) (H) 3-Y-0+ — **£1,459** (£417; £208) **Stalls** Low

Form — RPR
00/- **1** **Lago Di Como**[866] 5980 7-9-7 45 ........(t) ACulhane 1 — 63
(MrsPTownsley) *mde all: clr 9f out: drvn out: unchal* **10/1**
360- **2** 11 **Melograno (IRE)**[171] 6017 4-9-2 45 ........ DNolan(5) 6 — 47
(MarkCampion) *prom: chsd wnr over 6f out: rdn over 2f out: hung lft and wknd over 1f out* **15/2**
6-01 **3** 1 3/4 **Sunnyside Royale (IRE)**[9] 1698 5-9-13 45 ........(t) HBastiman 5 — 50
(RBastiman) *hld up: hdwy 1/2-way: rdn over 3f out: sn outpcd* **5/2**[2]
-351 **4** 10 **Misty Man (USA)**[104] 594 6-9-4 45 ........(b) BReilly(3) 7 — 29
(MissJFeilden) *hld up: rdn over 4f out: sn wknd* **4/1**[3]
400- **5** 2 1/2 **Tioga Gold (IRE)**[11] 5442 5-9-7 40 ........(p) VHalliday 4 — 25
(LRJames) *prom to 1/2-way* **16/1**
-501 **6** 4 **Cumwhitton**[44] 1091 5-9-4 45 ........(p) THamilton(3) 3 — 19
(RAFahey) *dwlt: hdwy 8f out: rdn and wknd over 3f out* **2/1**[1]
060- **7** dist **Noble Philosopher**[104] 3503 4-9-7 45 ........ JoannaBadger 2 — —
(KBell) *chsd wnr tl wknd over 6f out* **20/1**

2m 26.05s (-2.85) **Going Correction** -0.20s/f (Stan) — **7** Ran SP% **113.4**
Speed ratings: **102,94,92,85,83 80,**—CSF £78.70 TOTE £13.40: £4.10, £4.50; EX 43.20.
**Owner** M J Caldwell **Bred** F T Adams And E J Fenaroli **Trained** Dunsfold, Surrey

**FOCUS**
A fair time for a banded stakes and the field were strung out behind the winner at the finish.

**NOTEBOOK**
**Lago Di Como** ◆, off the track for a whopping 866 days previously, made a superb comeback by comfortably making all. He had dropped 6lb since his last run and therefore qualified for this grade, which he looks well capable of following up in.
**Melograno(IRE)** was the only one to try and go with the winner, but was soon shaken off. This was his first run for 171 days and he is entitled to improve on this.
**Sunnyside Royale(IRE)** never looked like following up his win nine days previously over this shorter trip.
**Misty Man(USA)** quickly lost his place on the turn for home and was disappointing. *Official explanation: jockey said gelding hung right throughout*
**Cumwhitton** *Official explanation: trainer's representative said mare had shown signs of coming into season*

## 1915 ST AVA'S DAY BANDED STKS — 7f (F)
**3:20** (3:20) (H) 3-Y-0+ — **£1,459** (£417; £208) **Stalls** Low

Form — RPR
1600 **1** **Sandorra**[67] 939 6-9-2 45 ........ TWilliams 6 — 50
(MBrittain) *mde all: drvn clr fnl f* **9/1**
-125 **2** 3 1/2 **Tee Jay Kassidy**[13] 1583 4-8-9 40 ........ MHalford(7) 3 — 41
(JulianPoulton) *hld up: nt much roon over 3f out: hdwy over 1f out: sn rdn and no imp* **8/1**
1544 **3** 1 1/4 **Indian Music**[9] 1696 7-9-2 45 ........ JCarroll 4 — 38
(ABerry) *hld up: hdwy over 1f out: styd on same pce ins fnl f* **8/1**
5602 **4** nk **Air Of Esteem**[20] 1444 8-8-9 45 ........ DFentiman(7) 7 — 37
(IanEmmerson) *chsd wnr: rdn over 2f out: styd on same pce fnl f* **2/1**[1]
2001 **5** 2 1/2 **Littleton Zephir (USA)**[7] 1723 5-9-8 45 ........ ACulhane 1 — 36
(MrsPTownsley) *chsd ldrs: rdn over 2f out: wknd fnl f* **4/1**[3]
5022 **6** 3 **Cleveland Way**[9] 1696 4-8-9 45 ........(v) DTudhope(7) 5 — 23
(DCarroll) *s.s: hdwy 5f out: rdn over 2f out: edgd lft and wknd over 1f out* **7/2**[2]
00- **7** 6 **North Landing (IRE)**[191] 5819 4-8-11 45 ........ TEaves(5) 2 — 7
(RCGuest) *chsd ldrs to 1/2-way* **14/1**

1m 30.13s (-0.67) **Going Correction** -0.20s/f (Stan) — **7** Ran SP% **114.4**
Speed ratings: **95,91,89,89,86 82,76**CSF £76.13 TOTE £10.60: £9.20, £4.30; EX 78.30.
**Owner** Mel Brittain **Bred** Theobalds Stud **Trained** Warthill, N Yorks

**FOCUS**
A weak heat which was run at a modest pace and did not suit those who were held up.

**NOTEBOOK**
**Sandorra** was yet another on the card to make all the running. The drop in trip worked the oracle and she was suited by this small field.
**Tee Jay Kassidy** stayed on all too late in the day. He did not get the best of runs around the bend, but the bird had already flown by that time and his hold-up tactics were against him on this occasion.
**Indian Music**, held up to get the trip, could not quicken late on and may need to revert to shorter.
**Air Of Esteem** never looked totally happy over this trip and may be capable of improvement when upped in distance.
**Cleveland Way** dwelt at the start and looked to use up too much energy when trying to join the leaders over two out. He can do better.

## 1916 SIGMUND FREUD BIRTHDAY TRI-BANDED STKS — 1m (F)
**3:55** (3:56) (H) 3-Y-0 — **£1,442** (£412; £206) **Stalls** Low

Form — RPR
6-01 **1** **Saros (IRE)**[9] 1701 3-8-13 45 6ex ........ MStainton(7) 3 — 62+
(BSmart) *chsd ldr tl led 5f out: rdn clr over 1f out* **5/6**[1]
0043 **2** 2 **Divina**[7] 1736 3-8-1 30 ........(v) BReilly(3) 7 — 42
(SLKeightley) *a.p: chsd wnr 1/2-way: rdn over 2f out: styd on* **12/1**
-312 **3** 5 **Roman The Park (IRE)**[9] 1701 3-8-11 45 ........ DAllan(3) 2 — 42
(TDEasterby) *s.i.s: sn chsng ldrs: rdn over 2f out: wknd over 1f out* **2/1**[2]
5053 **4** 10 **Platinum Chief**[9] 1701 3-8-9 40 ........(b) ACulhane 4 — 17
(ABerry) *chsd ldrs 6f* **9/1**[3]
0-64 **5** 7 **Airedale Lad (IRE)**[21] 1425 3-8-4 35 ........ JBramhill 6 — —
(JRNorton) *dwlt: hdwy over 3f out: sn wknd* **18/1**
00-0 **6** 2 **Delta Lady**[24] 1363 3-9-0 45 ........ RFfrench 5 — 4
(RBastiman) *outpcd* **20/1**
0400 **7** 12 **Hymns And Arias**[16] 1529 3-9-0 45 ........ SRighton 1 — —
(RonaldThompson) *led 3f: rdn and wknd over 3f out* **20/1**

1m 44.24s (-0.36) **Going Correction** -0.20s/f (Stan) — **7** Ran SP% **120.4**
Speed ratings: **93,91,86,76,69 67,55**CSF £14.35 TOTE £1.70: £1.40, £4.90; EX 16.60.
**Owner** Pinnacle Desert Sun Partnership **Bred** Patrick K Stephens **Trained** Hambleton, N Yorks

**FOCUS**
A very weak heat with no strength in depth, but it was run at a solid pace.

**NOTEBOOK**
**Saros(IRE)** got a decent early position and could have been called the winner from that point onwards. He was following up his facile win nine days previously and had no problems seeing out this extra furlong under his 6lb penalty. In great form at present, he has to step up in grade after this and life will be tougher in the future.
**Divina** kept on well late in the day without looking a danger to the winner. She can win a similar event.
**Roman The Park(IRE)**, beaten by today's winner last time, was never really travelling on this occasion and disappointed.
**Platinum Chief** ran much the same as when beaten by the winner last time out over shorter.
**Airedale Lad(IRE)** *Official explanation: jockey said gelding lost its action*

## 1917 SACK OF ROME BANDED STKS — 1m 4f (F)
**4:30** (4:31) (H) 3-Y-0+ — **£1,438** (£411; £205) **Stalls** Low

Form — RPR
0032 **1** **The Last Mohican**[1] 1887 5-9-5 30 ........(p) PMcCabe 5 — 42
(PHowling) *mde all: clr over 4f out: styd on wl* **9/4**[1]
/000 **2** 4 **Miss Fleurie**[20] 1444 4-9-2 35 ........ DAllan(3) 2 — 36
(RCraggs) *racd keenly: trckd ldr 5f: sn rdn: wnt 2nd over 2f out: kpt on* **14/1**
0202 **3** 5 **Moyne Pleasure (IRE)**[1] 1885 6-9-2 30 ........(p) LEnstone(3) 3 — 29
(PaulJohnson) *prom: chsd wnr 7f out: rdn over 2f out: styd on same pce* **3/1**[2]
0/54 **4** 7 **Zelea (IRE)**[9] 1700 5-9-5 35 ........ ACulhane 1 — 18
(JParkes) *hld up: rdn over 4f out: sn wknd* **6/1**[3]
0063 **5** 6 **Queen Excalibur**[13] 1590 5-9-0 35 ........ NChalmers(5) 6 — 9
(AGJuckes) *chsd ldrs: rdn over 4f out: wknd over 3f out* **3/1**[2]
46/3 **6** 3 1/2 **Dancing Dolphin (IRE)**[13] 1581 5-8-12 30 ........ MHalford(7) 4 — 4
(JulianPoulton) *s.i.s: hld up: lost tch 7f out* **8/1**

2m 41.75s (-0.35) **Going Correction** -0.20s/f (Stan) — **6** Ran SP% **112.8**
Speed ratings: **93,90,87,82,78 76**CSF £32.69 TOTE £4.10: £1.90, £5.50; EX 43.60.
**Owner** P Woodward **Bred** Miss S N Ralphs **Trained** Newmarket, Suffolk

**FOCUS**
A shocking event which saw yet another winner make all the running.

**NOTEBOOK**
**The Last Mohican** , who had finished second over further at Wolverhampton 24 hours prior to this, had the field strung out from an early stage and kept on well in the straight to register his first ever success. He beat very little on this occasion however, and would not be one to trust in a follow-up bid.
**Miss Fleurie** ran her best race to date over this longer trip. She has had training problems in the past and is only moderate, but is less exposed than most in this grade and was clear of the rest on this occasion.
**Moyne Pleasure(IRE)** never looked totally happy on this step up in trip. He has now run three times in as many days and found this coming too quick.
**Queen Excalibur** was all at sea on this Fibresand debut. She was made to look very one-paced when asked to quicken and is one to avoid.

## 1918 RUDOLPH VALENTINO BIRTHDAY BANDED STKS — 1m (F)
**5:05** (5:07) (H) 4-Y-0+ — **£1,438** (£411; £205) **Stalls** Low

Form — RPR
6642 **1** **Dalriath**[9] 1697 5-8-5 35 ........ AndrewWebb(7) 1 — 44
(MCChapman) *w ldrs: racd keenly: led 1/2-way: styd on wl* **5/2**[2]

0630 **2** *3* **Desires Destiny**[14] 1560 6-8-12 35 TWilliams 6 38
(MBrittain) *mde most to 1/2-way: rdn and ev ch over 2f out: styd on same pce fnl f* **4/1**[3]

0-00 **3** *3* **Shaamit's All Over**[30] 1277 5-8-9 35 (b[1]) BReilly(3) 5 32
(BAPearce) *hld up in tch: rdn and hung lft fr over 2f out: nt run on* **12/1**

0-05 **4** *3/4* **Paradise Garden (USA)**[9] 1700 7-8-9 35 (v) DAllan(3) 4 31
(PLClinton) *dwlt: outpcd: hdwy 1/2-way: styd on same pce fnl 2f* **14/1**

6603 **5** *3* **Mathmagician**[9] 1697 5-8-12 35 (b) DeanMcKeown 2 25
(RFMarvin) *w ldrs to 1/2-way: wknd 3f out* **8/1**

-031 **6** *1/2* **Amethyst Rock**[9] 1697 6-9-4 35 ACulhane 7 30
(PLGilligan) *chsd ldrs over 4f* **7/4**[1]

0064 **7** *1 1/4* **Marengo**[2] 1861 10-8-12 30 JoannaBadger 3 21
(PaulJohnson) *s.s: outpcd* **14/1**

1m 44.07s (-0.53) **Going Correction** -0.20s/f (Stan) **7** Ran SP% **117.1**
Speed ratings: **94,91,88,87,84 83,82**CSF £13.55 TOTE £3.30: £1.10, £4.20; EX 19.40 Place 6 £1,256.17, Place 5 £1,148.07.
**Owner** M B Gielty **Bred** Blakeshall Farm And Mike Channon Bloodstock Ltd **Trained** Market Rasen, Lincs

**FOCUS**
A race lacking any strength in depth and the pace was only moderate.

**NOTEBOOK**
**Dalriath** was always in a handy position and, despite racing keenly, found a fair turn of foot to settle the issue approaching the turn for home. This was her first win on the level and she is suited by this trip, but connections feel she may reach greater heights over hurdles, and that is where she is most likely to turn up next.
**Desires Destiny** enjoyed the switch back to the Fibresand, having run poorly on turf last time, but had no chance with the winner and is a most frustrating horse.
**Shaamit's All Over** looked to be all at sea in the first-time blinkers and may do better without them next time.
**Amethyst Rock**, who beat today's winner by a short head last time, was never going and dropped away as though something may have been amiss. *Official explanation: jockey said gelding was never travelling*
**Marengo** *Official explanation: vet said gelding was lame*
T/Plt: £1,652.20 to a £1 stake. Pool: £18,673.00. 8.25 winning tickets. T/Qpdt: £98.50 to a £1 stake. Pool: £1,398.30. 10.50 winning tickets. CR

1919 - 1921a (Foreign Racing) - See Raceform Interactive

## [1803]LONGCHAMP (R-H)
Thursday, May 6

**OFFICIAL GOING: Holding**

### 1922a PRIX D'HEDOUVILLE (GROUP 3) 1m 4f
**2:50** (2:50) 4-Y-O+ **£25,704** (£10,282; £7,711; £5,141)

RPR

**1** **Short Pause**[32] 1261 5-8-12 GaryStevens 6 115
(AFabre, France) *close up in 4th on outside, 3rd straight, ridden 2f out, hard driven to dispute lead 1f out, edged right, led 100y out, ran* 1

**2** *3/4* **Kindjhal (FR)**[21] 1435 4-8-9 DBoeuf 2 111
(ELellouche, France) *raced in 5th, short of room momentarily just over 2f out, hard ridden to dispute lead 1f out, headed 100y out, no extra* 3

**3** *1/2* **Maredsous (FR)**[25] 1351 4-8-6 IMendizabal 4 107
(DSepulchre, France) *held up in 7th, headway on outside to go 4th over 1 1/2f out, one pace final f*

**4** *1 1/2* **Whortleberry (FR)**[193] 5781 4-9-1 OPeslier 3 114
(FRohaut, France) *held up in last, stayed on steadily final 1 1/2f to take 4th close home*

**5** *snk* **Walkamia (FR)**[177] 5974 4-8-13 MSautjeau 7 112
(AFabre, France) *raced in 2nd til led just over 2f out, went 2 lengths clear, headed 1f out, weakened*

**6** *1* **Kalabar**[144] 6185 4-9-4 TThulliez 1 115
(PBary, France) *raced in 6th on inside, hampered and lost all chance 2f out, stayed on well closing stages* 1

**7** *5* **Craig's Falcon (FR)**[42] 1110 5-8-12 (b) SPasquier 5 102
(JDeRoualle, France) *led 1 1/2f, tracked leader on inside, 4th straight, hampered 2f out, weakened*

**8** *15* **Go Got (USA)**[450] 515 6-8-9 CSoumillon 8 76
(J-MBeguigne, France) *led after 1 1/2f, headed just over 2f out, soon weakened and eased* 2

2m 39.1s **Going Correction** +0.85s/f (Soft) **8** Ran SP% **162.3**
Speed ratings: **118,117,117,116,116 115,112,102.**
**Owner** K Abdulla **Bred** Juddmonte Farms **Trained** France

**NOTEBOOK**
**Short Pause**, who was always well placed, came with a progressive run from one and a half out and held on bravely at the line. There was contact with the runner-up but the Stewards left the result unchanged. He is a consistent horse who goes well on soft ground and the Grand Prix de Chantilly is now his target.
**Kindjhal(FR)** was short of room when challenging one out but then battled on very bravely to the line. He is brave and always has hard races so he will now be given a rest.
**Maredsous(FR)** was brought with a run on the outside and finished best of all. Judging by this outing, she has scope for improvement.
**Whortleberry(FR)** was dropped back in to last position where she stayed until the latter stages. Shaken up a furlong and a half out, she finished very well. She was carrying a Group Two penalty here and this outing augurs well for the future.

## [1899]CHESTER (L-H)
Friday, May 7

**OFFICIAL GOING: Good to soft**
Wind: mod against Weather: fine

### 1923 BANK OF SCOTLAND RATED STKS (H'CAP) 5f 16y
**1:55** (1:55) (B) (0-100,100) 4-Y-O+ **£15,381** (£5,834; £2,917; £1,326) **Stalls Low**

Form RPR

1-00 **1** **Ptarmigan Ridge**[26] 1343 8-8-1 **83** oh1 NMackay(3) 4 92
(MissLAPerratt) *in tch: hdwy whn nt clr run over 1f out: r.o to ld cl home* **14/1**

0-55 **2** *hd* **Simianna**[10] 1685 5-8-9 **88** (p) FNorton 2 96
(ABerry) *lw: pushed along and nt much sn after s: towards rr: hdwy over 2f out: ev ch wl ins fnl f: r.o* **8/1**[3]

1121 **3** *3/4* **Maktavish**[21] 1454 5-8-6 **85** (p) PHanagan 1 90
(ISemple) *led: rdn over 1f out: hdd cl home* **7/2**[1]

010- **4** *1/2* **Native Title**[223] 5210 6-8-4 **83** oh2 ANicholls 9 87
(DNicholls) *hld up in rr: hdwy over 1f out: r.o strly ins fnl f: nrst fin* **50/1**

000- **5** *hd* **Corridor Creeper (FR)**[195] 5743 7-8-11 **90** (p) DHolland 5 93
(JMBradley) *chsd ldr: rdn over 1f out: no ex cl home* **10/1**

0104 **6** *1* **Johnston's Diamond (IRE)**[23] 1391 6-8-10 **89** KFallon 3 88
(EJAlston) *chsd ldrs: rdn over 2f out: styd on same pce fnl f* **4/1**[2]

-061 **7** *1 3/4* **Cape Royal**[16] 1537 4-8-9 **88** LDettori 6 81
(MrsJRRamsden) *hld up: rdn 2f out: hdwy over 1f out: one pce ins fnl f* **7/2**[1]

000- **8** *3* **Talbot Avenue**[195] 5743 6-8-4 **83** oh1 WSupple 7 65
(MMullineaux) *b: b.hind: racd keenly: towards rr: hdwy over 1f out: nvr able to chal* **33/1**

00-0 **9** *1 1/2* **Vita Spericolata (IRE)**[23] 1391 7-8-7 **86** RWinston 12 63
(JSWainwright) *lw: chsd ldrs: sn rdn: wknd 1f out: eased whn btn ins fnl f* **25/1**

-620 **10** *shd* **Smokin Beau**[6] 1763 7-9-5 **98** TGMcLaughlin 11 74
(NPLittmoden) *midfield: hdwy over 3f out: rdn 2f out: wknd fnl f* **25/1**

-130 **11** *1* **Further Outlook (USA)**[25] 1354 10-8-7 **86** ACulhane 8 59
(DKIvory) *b: b.hind: midfield: rdn and wknd over 1f out* **25/1**

56-5 **12** *1 1/4* **Whitbarrow (IRE)**[21] 1438 5-8-13 **92** KDarley 10 60
(JMBradley) *lw: midfield: rdn 3f out: wknd over 1f out* **20/1**

0060 **13** *10* **Palawan**[16] 1537 8-8-5 **84** MHills 13 16
(AMBalding) *b: a towards rr* **66/1**

52-0 **14** *nk* **Pomfret Lad**[42] 1113 6-9-7 **100** AlexGreaves 14 31
(DNicholls) *a bhd* **66/1**

62.22 secs (0.24) **Going Correction** +0.425s/f (Yiel) **14** Ran SP% **115.5**
Speed ratings: **115,114,113,112,112 110,107,103,100,100 99,97,81,80**CSF £106.39 CT £387.47 TOTE £17.80: £3.80, £2.60, £1.60; EX 99.30.
**Owner** The Hon Miss Heather Galbraith **Bred** Miss Heather Galbraith **Trained** Ayr, Strathclyde

**FOCUS**
A cracking winning time for the grade, and a low draw once again proved a big advantage. This is solid handicap form.

**NOTEBOOK**
**Ptarmigan Ridge**, for whom a bit of cut has always been essential, had never before won off a mark in the 80s, but he had a good draw on this occasion and appreciated the strong gallop, getting up to score close home. A valuable handicap at Musselburgh towards the end of this month is the next target.
**Simianna**, a regular at this track, is another at her best with give in the ground, and she has now finished first, second and third on her three starts over five furlongs here. Her consistency makes life difficult for her with regard to the Handicapper, though.
**Maktavish** was never going to be ideally suited by this tight left-handed track as his tendency is to hang right. He showed terrific speed from the plum draw, but did hang right in the straight, letting the winner through on his inside. He will appreciate a return to a track where he can race against a right-handed rail. *Official explanation: jockey said gelding had hung right throughout*
**Native Title**, 2lb out of the handicap, did not have a great draw and needs farther than this, but the strong pace brought him into the argument late on. He should come on for this promising reappearance.
**Corridor Creeper(FR)** is a course and distance winner, but he needs some help from the Handicapper and his yard has yet to hit form this season.
**Johnston's Diamond(IRE)**, another course and distance winner, was 4lb higher for his promising reappearance. He was never happy on this occasion, though, as he struggled with the frenetic pace. Perhaps he needs six furlongs these days.
**Cape Royal**, racing off a 6lb higher mark, found the competition tougher here than at Epsom last time. *Official explanation: trainer said gelding missed the break and was unable to get into the race thereafter*

### 1924 JARDINE LLOYD THOMPSON DEE STKS (GROUP 3) (C&G) 1m 2f 75y
**2:25** (2:25) (A) 3-Y-O **£46,900** (£15,400; £7,700) **Stalls High**

Form RPR

1111 **1** **African Dream**[14] 1586 3-8-11 113 JQuinn 2 105+
(PWChapple-Hyam) *hld up in last pl: qcknd to ld 1f out: pushed out* **2/5**[1]

21-2 **2** *3/4* **Putra Sas (IRE)**[14] 1587 3-8-8 90 LDettori 5 101
(PFICole) *lw: trckd ldr: led wl over 2f out: sn rdn: hdd 1f out: styd on* **4/1**[2]

01-4 **3** *1 1/2* **Mutawassel (USA)**[14] 1586 3-8-8 95 RHills 4 98
(BWHills) *set stdy pce: hung rt: qcknd over 3f out: rdn and hdd wl over 2f out: styd on same pce fnl f* **6/1**[3]

2m 19.74s (7.19) **Going Correction** +0.425s/f (Yiel) **3** Ran SP% **105.7**
Speed ratings: **88,87,86**CSF £2.21 TOTE £1.40; EX 1.80.
**Owner** Franconson Partners **Bred** E Landi **Trained** Newmarket, Suffolk

**FOCUS**
A disappointing turnout for this Group Three event, with three withdrawals following the 48-hour declaration stage, and a pedestrian winning time for the grade. The winner had already shown form good enough to win an average running, but more likely he was brought down to their level than the others improved

**NOTEBOOK**
**African Dream** brought the best form to the table but a tactical affair was always a worry for connections. His superiority is not reflected in the winning margin and if he were to meet the other two on a more conventional track one would expect him to beat them with greater ease. As a gelding he is barred from running in the Derby, so the Eclipse Stakes is now to be his summer target, with ease in the ground a prerequisite.
**Putra Sas(IRE)** was expected to appreciate the step up in trip and he did so, running a decent race in defeat. The winner was too strong for him on this occasion but there are races to be won with him this season.
**Mutawassel(USA)**, whose rider is a master at the front-running game, set a pace to suit himself and attempted to steal the race from the front. The colt was not up to the task, though, and did not appear to handle the track very well.

### 1925 BETDAQ ORMONDE STKS (GROUP 3) 1m 5f 89y
**2:55** (2:56) (A) 4-Y-O+ **£43,500** (£16,500; £8,250; £3,750) **Stalls Low**

Form RPR

5-32 **1** **Systematic**[5] 1792 5-8-11 109 KDarley 7 118
(MJohnston) *lw: chsd ldr: led over 3f out: rdn over 2f out: styd on gamely* **5/2**[1]

52-0 **2** *1 3/4* **The Whistling Teal**[20] 1455 8-8-11 107 DHolland 5 116
(GWragg) *lw: midfield: hdwy over 5f out: ev ch fr 3f out: sn rdn: no ex towards fin* **7/2**[2]

4050 **3** *12* **Compton Bolter (IRE)**[41] 1144 7-8-11 108 LDettori 1 99
(GAButler) *hld up: hdwy over 4f out: rdn over 3f out: no imp on ldng pair* **15/2**

6-01 **4** *hd* **Royal Cavalier**[41] 1124 7-8-11 98 WSupple 6 98
(RHollinshead) *in tch: lost pl after 4f: n.m.r over 5f out: rdn over 3f out: kpt on one pce* **9/1**

/-40 **5** *1 3/4* **Forest Magic (IRE)**[20] 1455 4-8-11 100 EAhern 8 96
(PWD'Arcy) *in tch: rdn over 6f out: lost pl 4f out: n.d after* **25/1**

000/ **6** *5* **Limerick Boy (GER)**[20] 5078 6-8-11 TEDurcan 10 89
(MissVenetiaWilliams) *chsd ldrs: rdn over 5f out: wknd over 3f out* **33/1**

-160 **7** *3/4* **Rawyaan**[41] 1144 5-8-11 112 (b) RHills 2 88
(JHMGosden) *towards rr: hdwy 5f out: rdn over 3f out: wknd wl over 1f out* **14/1**

300- **8** *2* **Narrative (IRE)**[201] [5662] 6-8-11 108 ........ TPQueally 3 85
(DRLoder) *racd freely: led: sn clr: rdn and hdd over 3f out: wknd over 2f out* **12/1**

120- **9** *30* **First Charter**[215] [5406] 5-8-11 109 ........ KFallon 4 43
(SirMichaelStoute) *hld up: struggling 6f out: t.o* **5/1**[3]

2m 56.34s (0.95) **Going Correction** +0.425s/f (Yiel) **9** Ran SP% **110.4**
Speed ratings: **114,112,105,105,104 101,100,99,81**CSF £10.23 TOTE £3.10: £1.60, £1.70, £2.30; EX 9.20 Trifecta £30.50 Pool of £2646.46 - 61.46 winning units..

**Owner** Maktoum Al Maktoum **Bred** Gainsborough Stud Management Ltd **Trained** Middleham Moor, N Yorks

**FOCUS**
The ground made it quite a test in the conditions and very few got into it. This was a decent race for the grade and the form looks solid, with a big gap back to the third.

**NOTEBOOK**
**Systematic** had shaped as though back to his best at Newmarket last time, but he was pretty friendless in the market on this occasion. Stamina doubts were probably the reason for that but he confounded the doubters in no uncertain style. He and the runner-up enjoyed a good battle up the straight, but he was always holding his rival, and on this evidence he looks sure to play a major role in the Hardwicke Stakes at Royal Ascot.
**The Whistling Teal** loves to get his toe in and was representing the trainer responsible for sending out the last three winners of this race, so he had plenty in his favour. He threw down a determined challenge to the favourite on the final turn but eventually had to accept second best. Connections may now have to abroad in search of his ground.
**Compton Bolter(IRE)**, who failed to make much of an impression out in Dubai, was having his first outing of the year in this country. Second on fast ground in this race last season, he was never in contention for the win on this occasion but came out of the pack to grab the minor placing.
**Royal Cavalier**, a market mover, had looked flatterd by his win at Doncaster in March when he had Systematic back in third, and this result appears to confirm that impression. A galloping track suits his style of running better.
**Forest Magic(IRE)** had the ground in his favour but recent evidence suggests he is flattered by his current rating of 100.
**Limerick Boy(GER)**, better known as a smart two-mile hurdler, was having his first outing on the Flat in this country having originally been trained in Germany, where he won a ten-furlong Group Three race on heavy ground back in 2001.
**Rawyaan** may need better ground than this to show his best and never got competitive.
**Narrative(IRE)** came in for support in the market but his backers soon knew their fate as he failed to settle at all in front and shot his bolt well before the finish. A pacemaker for Godolphin last season, he needs to learn to settle if he is going to win anything this year.
**First Charter**, who looked to be quietly progressing last term on fast ground, can be forgiven this poor performance as he was found to be coughing after the race. *Official explanation: jockey said horse was hampered leaving the stalls and never got ino the race thereafter; vet found horse to be coughing*

## 1926 BOODLE & DUNTHORNE MAIDEN STKS — 1m 2f 75y
**3:30** (3:30) (D ) 3-Y-O **£8,287** (£2,550; £1,275; £637) **Stalls** High

Form RPR

03 **1** **Iktitaf (IRE)**[10] [1683] 3-9-0 ........ RHills 3 79
(JHMGosden) *trckd ldrs: nt clr run over 1f out: r.o to ld wl ins fnl f: drvn out* **3/1**[2]

**2** *½* **Line Drawing** 3-9-0 ........ KFallon 1 78?
(BWHills) *w'like: scope: bit bkwd: str: hld up: hdwy 5f out: led over 1f out: flashed tail: hung rt and hdd wl ins fnl f* **9/2**[3]

4-2 **3** *1 ¼* **Larkwing (IRE)**[32] [1271] 3-9-0 ........ DHolland 2 76
(GWragg) *hld up: hdwy over 1f out: hung lft ins fnl f: styng on whn sn nt clr run: swtchd lft cl home* **5/4**[1]

0-5 **4** *shd* **Mouftari (USA)**[22] [1419] 3-9-0 ........ MHills 8 76
(BWHills) *lw: sn led: rdn over 2f out: hdd over 1f out: styd on* **12/1**

0- **5** *1 ½* **Patrixprial**[191] [5831] 3-9-0 ........ NCallan 4 73
(MHTompkins) *racd keenly: hld up: rdn and hdwy over 1f out: kpt on* **33/1**

0 **6** *1 ½* **Balimaya (IRE)**[23] [1395] 3-8-9 ........ EAhern 5 65
(JNoseda) *lw: racd keenly: broke wl: lost pl after 2f: rdn and ev ch 2f out: btn 1f out* **8/1**

000 **7** *14* **Go Green**[10] [1683] 3-8-9 ........ JoannaBadger 7 40
(PDEvans) *s.i.s: hung rt thrght: sn prom: rdn 3f out: sn wknd* **66/1**

0- **8** *14* **Phoenix Eye**[183] [5932] 3-9-0 ........ WSupple 6 20
(MMullineaux) *bit bkwd: racd keenly: prom: losing pl whn hmpd over 5f out: bhd after* **100/1**

2m 17.2s (4.65) **Going Correction** +0.425s/f (Yiel) **8** Ran SP% **111.9**
Speed ratings: **98,97,96,96,95 94,82,71**CSF £16.03 TOTE £4.70: £1.50, £1.40, £1.10; EX 12.70.

**Owner** Hamdan Al Maktoum **Bred** Shadwell Estate Company Limited **Trained** Manton, Wilts

**FOCUS**
Not much pace on here for what looked a fair maiden.

**NOTEBOOK**
**Iktitaf(IRE)**, who had run with promise when stepped up to this trip at Bath last time, waited for a gap to appear next to the far rail and picked up well when the opportunity arrived. He shapes as though he will get farther than this.
**Line Drawing**, who is a half-brother to seven-furlong winner Fine Arts out of a mare who won her only start over 12 furlongs, was the favoured one of the Hills runners in the market. He ran well on his debut but hung right and flashed his tail under pressure. It was probably greenness as much as anything, and the experience should not be lost on him.
**Larkwing(IRE)** had shaped at Windsor as though finding this trip a bare minimum and this performance appeared to confirm that impression. He is now eligible for a handicap mark and will be open to improvement when he is tried over further.
**Mouftari(USA)**, the lesser-fancied of the Hills-trained pair, did not go a mad gallop in front and kept on fairly well. He too is now eligible for a mark.
**Patrixprial**, who is a half-brother to two middle-distance winners on the Flat who later won over obstacles, is entitled to come on for his reappearance, although he is likely to be seen at his best in handicap company.
**Balimaya(IRE)** still has a Ribblesdale entry but that looks highly optimistic on this evidence.

## 1927 WARWICK INTERNATIONAL RATED STKS (H'CAP) — 7f 122y
**4:05** (4:10) (C ) (0-90,90) 4-Y-O+ **£10,379** (£3,936; £1,968; £894) **Stalls** Low

Form RPR

0525 **1** **Chappel Cresent (IRE)**[6] [1773] 4-9-4 87 ........ ANicholls 1 102
(DNicholls) *mde all: rdn over 1f out: r.o wl* **15/2**[3]

0000 **2** *3* **Nashaab (USA)**[25] [1354] 7-9-4 87 ........ KFallon 4 95
(PDEvans) *n.m.r sn after s: towards rr: hdwy over 1f out: r.o ins fnl f: nt rch wnr* **5/1**[2]

12-1 **3** *½* **Retirement**[9] [1708] 5-8-9 78 3ex ........ DHolland 3 85
(MHTompkins) *in tch: rdn and hdwy over 1f out: styd on ins fnl f* **2/1**[1]

0012 **4** *1* **Flint River**[29] [1317] 6-8-7 76 ow2 ........ ACulhane 7 81
(HMorrison) *midfield: hdwy over 3f out: rdn over 1f out: styd on: one pce towards fin* **12/1**

-064 **5** *nk* **H Harrison (IRE)**[4] [1840] 4-8-11 80 ........ EAhern 2 84
(IWMcinnes) *trckd ldrs: rdn 3f out: n.m.r over 1f out: styd on: one pce towards fin* **14/1**

3403 **6** *1 ½* **Digital**[4] [1828] 7-9-4 90 ........ SHitchcott(3) 11 91
(MRChannon) *upset in stalls: towards rr: rdn and hdwy over 1f out: nt clr run ins f: styd on: nt rch ldrs* **12/1**

3150 **7** *2 ½* **Time N Time Again**[41] [1126] 6-8-5 74 ........ JQuinn 15 69
(EJAlston) *prom: rdn 3f out: wknd ins fnl f* **33/1**

000- **8** *hd* **Banjo Bay (IRE)**[239] [4846] 6-9-3 86 ........ AlexGreaves 9 80
(DNicholls) *racd keenly: trckd ldrs: rdn over 1f out: wknd ins fnl f* **50/1**

4040 **9** *¾* **Queens Rhapsody**[6] [1773] 4-9-2 85 ........ TEDurcan 6 78
(ABailey) *b: hld up: rdn over 1f out: kpt on fnl f: nvr on terms* **12/1**

00-0 **10** *nk* **Idle Power (IRE)**[18] [1504] 6-8-4 73 oh2 ........ (p) WSupple 8 65
(JRBoyle) *midfield: rdn whn hmpd over 1f out: no hdwy* **20/1**

3-01 **11** *1 ¼* **Raphael (IRE)**[6] [1772] 5-8-9 78 3ex ........ DaleGibson 12 67
(TDEasterby) *lw: midfield: rdn along 6f out: one pce fnl 2f* **16/1**

0-00 **12** *½* **Riska King**[71] [900] 4-8-3 75 ow1 ........ THamilton(3) 16 63
(RAFahey) *bhd: rdn over 2f out: kpt on one pce fnl f* **66/1**

00-6 **13** *1 ¾* **Dame De Noche**[27] [1332] 4-9-7 90 ........ MFenton 10 74
(JGGiven) *lw: trckd ldrs: rdn over 3f out: wknd 2f out* **33/1**

1403 **14** *3 ½* **Hail The Chief**[7] [1746] 7-8-7 76 ........ MHills 14 52
(DNicholls) *b: hld up: pushed along over 3f out: no imp* **28/1**

-200 **15** *nk* **Cardinal Venture (IRE)**[6] [1772] 6-9-4 87 ........ NCallan 18 62
(KARyan) *in tch: hdwy over 4f out: rdn over 2f out: n.m.r over 1f out: sn wknd* **25/1**

66-2 **16** *12* **Soller Bay**[32] [1275] 7-8-6 75 ........ DarrenWilliams 17 22
(KRBurke) *midfield: rdn over 3f out: wknd over 2f out* **25/1**

12-0 **17** *13* **Smirfys Systems**[20] [1471] 5-8-11 80 ........ RHills 5 —
(WMBrisbourne) *a bhd* **20/1**

1001 **18** *5* **Warden Warren**[22] [1424] 6-7-13 73 oh1 ........ (p) HayleyTurner(5) 13 —
(MrsCADunnett) *sn bhd* **33/1**

1m 36.03s (1.28) **Going Correction** +0.425s/f (Yiel) **18** Ran SP% **130.3**
Speed ratings: **110,107,106,105,105 103,101,101,100,99 98,98,96,92,92 80,67,62**CSF £42.10 CT £108.78 TOTE £8.40: £1.90, £1.90, £1.30, £2.80; EX 28.80.

**Owner** Mrs Ann D Coogan **Bred** Gerry Coogan **Trained** Sessay, N Yorks

**FOCUS**
A decent handicap, if not as competitive as the numbers suggested, and the draw once again played its part.

**NOTEBOOK**
**Chappel Cresent(IRE)** , who has been in good heart this spring but has struggled to last home, was back to the form he showed as a juvenile here. With the ground in his favour and drawn ideally for a front-runner, he set out to dictate from the gate and made every yard, eventually winning fairly easily. A drop back to seven furlongs will not inconvenience him.
**Nashaab(USA)** has not won for almost three years but his record at this track is a good one, his form now reading 1242. Despite being well drawn, he forfeited that advantage early on and got a luckless run, being stopped in his run a number of times on his way through from the rear. He is undoubtedly well handicapped, but is far from easy to catch right.
**Retirement**, who had just a 3lb penalty to carry for his Ascot romp, was well drawn but he struggled to keep hold of a good early position. He stayed on well for third but the impression given was that the trip was on the short side for him. He is due to go up another 6lb in future handicaps.
**Flint River** ran a sound race on ground plenty soft enough.
**H Harrison(IRE)**, who needs to drop a few pounds in the handicap, was another who would have ideally preferred better ground, but he was well drawn and ran a solid race
**Digital** ◆ did best of those drawn in double figures and once again gave the impression that he is ready to strike.
**Time N Time Again** does not stay this far.
**Soller Bay** *Official explanation: trainer had no explanation for the poor form shown*

## 1928 CHESHIRE REGIMENT H'CAP (SPONSORED BY THE ELIFAR FOUNDATION) — 1m 4f 66y
**4:40** (4:40) (D ) (0-80,78) 3-Y-O+ **£9,165** (£2,820; £1,410; £705) **Stalls** Low

Form RPR

34-1 **1** **Court Of Appeal**[37] [1198] 7-9-7 78 ........ (t) TEaves(5) 4 87
(BEllison) *in tch: hdwy over 4f out: rdn over 2f out: led over 1f out: r.o* **11/2**[2]

434- **2** *2 ½* **Aleron (IRE)**[181] [5949] 6-9-2 68 ........ EAhern 5 73
(JJQuinn) *in tch: hdwy 6f out: led over 2f out: hdd over 1f out: no ex towards fin* **9/2**[1]

03-0 **3** *¾* **Mexican Pete**[16] [1539] 4-9-8 74 ........ ACulhane 9 78
(PWHiatt) *hld up: hdwy over 3f out: rdn over 1f out: styd on ins fnl f* **25/1**

3031 **4** *½* **True Companion**[25] [1369] 5-9-2 71 ........ J-PGuillambert(3) 7 74
(NPLittmoden) *towards rr: hdwy 4f out: rdn over 1f out: styd on ins fnl f* **12/1**

-333 **5** *1* **Trouble Mountain (USA)**[17] [1535] 7-9-3 69 ........ (b) KFallon 6 71
(MWEasterby) *midfield: hdwy 4f out: n.m.r and outpcd 2f out: styd on ins fnl f* **9/2**[1]

0050 **6** *½* **Champion Lion (IRE)**[6] [1768] 5-9-0 69 ........ SHitchcott(3) 2 70
(MRChannon) *s.s: hld up: hdwy gng wl 4f out: rdn over 1f out: one pce ins fnl f* **9/2**[1]

450- **7** *13* **Movie King (IRE)**[242] [4772] 5-9-5 71 ........ DHolland 8 52
(SGollings) *trckd ldrs: led 7f out: hdd 6f out: regained ld over 4f out: rdn and hdd over 2f out: sn wknd* **16/1**

0/0 **8** *3 ½* **Always Rainbows (IRE)**[13] [1615] 6-9-4 70 ........ (p) MFenton 12 46
(BSRothwell) *bhd: rdn 4f out: nvr on terms* **50/1**

040- **9** *1 ¼* **Mr Lear (USA)**[46] [4800] 5-9-3 72 ........ THamilton(3) 3 46
(RAFahey) *prom: lft in ld wl over 7f out: sn hdd: rdn and wknd over 5f out* **12/1**

53-0 **10** *2 ½* **Jeepstar**[16] [1539] 4-9-11 77 ........ WSupple 14 47
(TDEasterby) *led: hung rt and hdd wl over 7f out: regained ld 6f out: hdd over 4f out: rdn and wknd over 2f out* **25/1**

0003 **11** *16* **Sudden Flight (IRE)**[50] [1045] 7-9-2 68 ........ MHills 10 14
(PDEvans) *in tch: rdn over 4f out: wknd 3f out* **10/1**[3]

0/04 **12** *1 ¾* **Bakiri (IRE)**[17] [1520] 6-9-1 67 ........ TEDurcan 1 11
(AndrewReid) *prom tl rdn and wknd over 4f out* **16/1**

2m 44.96s (4.44) **Going Correction** +0.425s/f (Yiel) **12** Ran SP% **115.8**
Speed ratings: **102,100,99,99,98 98,89,87,86,85 74,73**CSF £29.09 CT £571.16 TOTE £4.60: £1.90, £2.20, £6.20; EX 28.70 Place 6 £10.85, Place 5 £4.94.

**Owner** Spring Cottage Syndicate No 2 **Bred** John And Susan Davis **Trained** Norton, N Yorks

**FOCUS**
A competitive handicap and the form looks solid enough. The first two home were first and third in this race last year.

**NOTEBOOK**
**Court Of Appeal**, 8lb higher than when successful in this race last year, won in good style. He has returned better than ever this season and is clearly well suited by a sharp track, for his other wins on the Flat have come at Catterick and Kempton, and he has been successful over hurdles at Musselburgh.
**Aleron(IRE)**, third in this race last year, went one better this time around, although the winner's superiority over him on this occasion was greater. This was still a good performance on his seasonal reappearance, though, and he can surely be placed to win off his current mark.

**Mexican Pete** improved on his recent reappearance and, given that he has shown a distinct preference for faster ground in the past, he can surely build on this when the ground turns in his favour.
**True Companion** had his stamina to prove over this longer trip but he had shaped as though he would appreciate it when successful at Warwick off a 6lb lower mark last time. He appeared to stay the trip well enough.
**Trouble Mountain(USA)** has a poor strike-rate but rarely runs a bad race, which makes it difficult for the Handicapper to drop him much.
**Champion Lion(IRE)** not for the first time looked to have more in the tank than was actually the case when pressure was applied.
**Movie King(IRE)** looked a clear non-stayer. *Official explanation: jockey said gelding had hung left in the closing stages*
T/Jkpt: £14,090.10 to a £1 stake. Pool: £128,994.00. 6.50 winning tickets. T/Plt: £9.20 to a £1 stake. Pool: £112,723.70. 8,863.85 winning tickets. T/Qpdt: £4.10 to a £1 stake. Pool: £4,824.20. 851.60 winning tickets. DO

# 1782 HAMILTON (R-H)

## Friday, May 7

**OFFICIAL GOING: Good to soft**
Wind: It across Weather: cloudy but bright

## 1929 MITIE AMATEUR CLASSIFIED STKS (AMATEUR RIDERS) 6f 5y
6:10 (6:13) (F) 4-Y-O+ **£3,024** (£864; £432) **Stalls** High

Form RPR
4011 **1** **Stoic Leader (IRE)**$^{3}$ [1868] 4-11-11 66 KJMercer$^{(3)}$ 7 84
(RFFisher) *hld up: hdwy centre over 1f out: checked wl ins fnl f: sn led: r.o* **9/4**$^{1}$
2-03 **2** *nk* **Lord Of The East**$^{21}$ [1452] 5-11-2 65 MrJGee$^{(5)}$ 9 76
(DNicholls) *cl up far side: led over 1f out: swvd bdly lft and hdd wl ins fnl f: kpt on* **10/1**
0210 **3** *1 1/4* **Whippasnapper**$^{12}$ [1642] 4-11-4 65 MrEDehdashti$^{(3)}$ 10 72
(JRBest) *in tch: hdwy and edgd into centre over 1f out: kpt on fnl f* **5/2**$^{2}$
3323 **4** *1 3/4* **Highland Warrior**$^{6}$ [1774] 5-11-0 65 MrGGoldie$^{(7)}$ 2 67
(JSGoldie) *swtchd to far side s: hld up: nt clr run and swtchd centre 2f out: r.o fnl f: no imp* **8/1**
2101 **5** *2* **Blueberry Rhyme**$^{39}$ [1180] 5-11-2 62 (v) MissFayeBramley$^{(5)}$ 11 61
(PABlockley) *prom: rdn 1/2-way: no imp over 1f out* **20/1**
006- **6** *1* **Albashoosh**$^{208}$ [5515] 6-11-6 67 MissKellyHarrison$^{(3)}$ 1 60
(DNicholls) *led and sn tacked over to far side: hdd over 1f out: sn outpcd* **20/1**
0006 **7** *2* **Telepathic (IRE)**$^{5}$ [1787] 4-11-8 66 (b$^{1}$) MsCWilliams 3 53
(ABerry) *hld up centre: effrt 2f out: nt pce to chal* **50/1**
4155 **8** *3 1/2* **Quiet Times (IRE)**$^{17}$ [1526] 5-11-2 65 (b) MSeston$^{(5)}$ 5 42
(KARyan) *chsd centre ldrs: drvn 1/2-way: btn over 1f out* **13/2**$^{3}$
142- **9** *1 1/2* **Tuscan Flyer**$^{232}$ [5025] 6-11-2 64 MissRBastiman$^{(5)}$ 8 37
(RBastiman) *trckd ldrs to over 2f out: sn btn* **25/1**
000- **10** *nk* **Orangino**$^{208}$ [5516] 6-11-2 40 MissRDavidson$^{(5)}$ 6 36
(JSHaldane) *chsd ldrs tl wknd over 2f out* **100/1**
00-6 **11** *1/2* **Andreyev (IRE)**$^{8}$ [1719] 10-11-2 45 (p) MissDawnRankin$^{(5)}$ 12 35
(JSGoldie) *bhd far side: drvn 1/2-way: sn btn* **50/1**
00-0 **12** *9* **Square Dancer**$^{8}$ [1719] 8-11-0 40 (t) MrMMacdonald-Wagstaffe$^{(7)}$ 4 8
(DANolan) *hld up centre: rdn 1/2-way: sn btn* **150/1**

1m 14.5s (1.40) **Going Correction** +0.225s/f (Good) **12** Ran SP% **111.8**
Speed ratings: **99,98,96,94,91 90,87,83,81,80 80,68**CSF £22.01 TOTE £2.90: £1.30, £4.60, £1.40; EX 32.10.
**Owner** Great Head House Estates Limited **Bred** P J Higgins **Trained** Ulverston, Cumbria
■ Stewards Enquiry : Miss Kelly Harrison one-day ban: failed to keep straight from stalls (May 19)
Mr J Gee one-day ban: careless riding (May 19)

**FOCUS**
A run-of-the-mill handicap run at a decent clip in which the field raced centre to far side, but the main protagonists either hung into, or made ground in, the centre of the course in the last half of the contest. The form looks solid enough.

**NOTEBOOK**
**Stoic Leader(IRE)**, who had a good chance at the weights, is a versatile sort who put his best foot forward to notch his fifth win in his last seven starts. He looks a bit better than the bare form and, although up in the handicap from the following day, should continue to give a good account.
**Lord Of The East**, back in trip, confirmed his return to form and may well have prevailed had he not hung markedly in the closing stages. All his wins have been at Epsom and he may well be better in more experienced hands.
**Whippasnapper** looked to have plenty in his favour regarding recent form, ground, trip and draw and he confirmed his recent Brighton run to be all wrong. He is capable of winning again from his current mark in the mid 60s.
**Highland Warrior** ran creditably given he did not get the best of runs at a course that does not really suit his style of racing. He needs things to fall right but is capable of winning again in ordinary handicap company on easy ground.
**Blueberry Rhyme**, having his first run for his new yard, did not really improve for the return to six furlongs back on turf but, although the return to the minimum trip will suit, he is the type that needs things to fall right.
**Albashoosh**, who has slipped a fair way in the weights, showed more than enough from this draw and over this trip on his reappearance and first run for David Nicholls to suggest he can win races this term.

## 1930 MITIE MAIDEN AUCTION STKS (QUALIFIER FOR THE HAMILTON PARK 2-Y-O SERIES FINAL) 5f 4y
6:40 (6:41) (E) 2-Y-O **£4,160** (£1,280; £640; £320) **Stalls** High

Form RPR
**1** **Midnight Tycoon** 2-8-7 FLynch 2 68
(BSmart) *mde all: rdn and hld on wl fnl f* **2/1**$^{1}$
**2** *3/4* **Extra Mark** 2-8-7 NPollard 4 66
(JRBest) *w ldrs: rdn 1/2-way: rallied over 1f out: kpt on: hld cl home* **9/2**$^{3}$
**3** *9* **Mister Bell** 2-8-11 DSweeney 3 38
(JGMO'Shea) *dwlt: sn chsng ldrs: effrt 1/2-way: wknd over 1f out* **7/1**
**4** *2* **Mrs Kepple** 2-8-6 JFanning 6 26
(MJohnston) *w ldrs: outpcd 1/2-way: edgd lft and sn btn* **9/4**$^{2}$
0 **5** *3* **Kristikhab (IRE)**$^{39}$ [1170] 2-8-9 FNorton 1 19
(ABerry) *s.i.s: a outpcd* **9/1**

63.03 secs (1.77) **Going Correction** +0.225s/f (Good) **5** Ran SP% **104.8**
Speed ratings: **94,92,78,75,70**CSF £9.94 TOTE £3.30: £1.40, £1.80; EX 6.40.
**Owner** Pinnacle Marju Partnership **Bred** Executive Bloodlines **Trained** Hambleton, N Yorks

**FOCUS**
Hard to gauge the true merit of this form but the first two, who pulled clear of the remainder from halfway, look sure to win more races.

**NOTEBOOK**
**Midnight Tycoon**, the first foal of a sister to useful sprinter Midnight Escape, created a favourable impression on his racecourse debut. Always travelling strongly, he showed the right attitude when pressed and looks the type to win more races.
**Extra Mark** ◆, a half-brother to multiple winners New Options and Steely Dan, has plenty of scope for improvement and turned in a pleasing debut performance. Six furlongs will suit and he looks sure to win races.
**Mister Bell**, the first foal of a dam who has winners in her pedigree, was far from disgraced on this racecourse debut and, given the way he travelled for a long way, could pick up an ordinary race in due course.
**Mrs Kepple**, a half-sister to useful mile to ten-furlong performer Khibrah and fair dual five-furlong juvenile winner Red Power, was well beaten on this debut run but, given the market support, better was obviously expected and she is not one to write off yet.
**Kristikhab(IRE)** again offered no immediate encouragement.

## 1931 MITIE MILE FILLIES' STKS (H'CAP) 1m 65y
7:10 (7:13) (C) (0-90,85) 3-Y-O+ **£9,848** (£3,735; £1,867; £849) **Stalls** High

Form RPR
41-2 **1** **Celtic Heroine (IRE)**$^{25}$ [1357] 3-8-11 81 KDarley 15 98+
(MAJarvis) *trckd ldrs: smooth hdwy 3f out: led over 1f out: drvn out* **5/2**$^{1}$
14-3 **2** *1 1/4* **Lauro**$^{20}$ [1475] 4-9-2 73 RWinston 14 81
(MissJACamacho) *midfield: pushed along 1/2-way: effrt over 2f out: chsd wnr ins fnl fg: r.o* **14/1**
15/2 **3** *3* **Dispol Foxtrot**$^{11}$ [1660] 6-8-8 65 RFfrench 8 67
(MissVScott) *cl up: led 3f to over 1f out: one pce fnl f* **13/2**
1- **4** *3* **Salagama (IRE)**$^{392}$ [1008] 4-9-9 85 RThomas$^{(5)}$ 7 80
(PFICole) *keen: led after 1f to 3f out: no ex over 1f out* **11/2**$^{3}$
5156 **5** *nk* **Najaaba (USA)**$^{5}$ [1790] 4-9-8 82 BReilly$^{(3)}$ 1 77
(MissJFeilden) *hld up: hdwy over 2f out: no imp over 1f out* **25/1**
50-2 **6** *2 1/2* **Lilli Marlane**$^{9}$ [1708] 4-8-10 72 DFox$^{(5)}$ 2 62
(NACallaghan) *hld up: effrt over 2f out: nvr rchd ldrs* **5/1**$^{2}$
-612 **7** *shd* **Megan's Magic**$^{13}$ [1620] 4-8-12 69 JBramhill 5 58
(WStorey) *s.i.s: bhd tl styd on fr 2f out: no imp* **10/1**
21 **8** *1 3/4* **Lyford Lass**$^{17}$ [1528] 3-8-2 72 PHanagan 4 58
(ISemple) *hld up: rdn 3f out: n.d* **25/1**
40-3 **9** *1 3/4* **Odabella (IRE)**$^{25}$ [1372] 4-8-12 69 JFEgan 11 51
(JohnBerry) *hld up: rdn over 3f out: nt pce to chal* **20/1**
50-0 **10** *1 1/2* **Uno Mente**$^{15}$ [1560] 5-8-3 60 KimTinkler 13 39
(DonEnricoIncisa) *a bhd* **66/1**
410- **11** *shd* **Millagros (IRE)**$^{182}$ [5943] 4-9-9 80 DMcGaffin 9 59
(ISemple) *chsd ldrs tl wknd over 2f out* **25/1**
0-40 **12** *1/2* **Richemaur (IRE)**$^{13}$ [1623] 4-9-6 77 (b$^{1}$) KDalgleish 12 55
(MHTompkins) *keen in tch: rdn and hung rt over 2f out: sn wknd* **25/1**
3400 **13** *3/4* **Ellen Mooney**$^{13}$ [1606] 5-8-4 61 (b$^{1}$) SChin 10 37
(RPElliott) *led 1f: cl up tl wknd over 2f out* **33/1**
050- **14** *1/2* **Scotland The Brave**$^{233}$ [4993] 4-8-12 69 JFanning 6 44
(JDBethell) *in tch tl rdn and wknd over 2f out* **50/1**
30-3 **15** *17* **Shardda**$^{34}$ [1250] 4-8-3 65 BSwarbrick$^{(5)}$ 3 4
(FWatson) *dwlt: a bhd* **50/1**

1m 50.08s (0.78) **Going Correction** +0.225s/f (Good)
**WFA** 3 from 4yo+ 13lb **15** Ran SP% **118.2**
Speed ratings: **105,103,100,97,97 94,94,93,91,89 89,89,88,71,57**CSF £34.38 CT £213.77 TOTE £3.90: £1.60, £3.70, £2.60; EX 37.60.
**Owner** P D Savill **Bred** P D Savill **Trained** Newmarket, Suffolk

**FOCUS**
A fair fillies' handicap which was run at an ordinary pace and one in which those racing close to the pace were favoured. The form looks solid enough.

**NOTEBOOK**
**Celtic Heroine(IRE)**, with conditions to suit and the best of the draw, had the run of the race, but was always travelling smoothly and ran out a comfortable winner. She is in good hands and may well be capable of better.
**Lauro** fully confirmed reappearance promise and her effectiveness on an easy surface. A more galloping course could be more to her liking and she appeals as the type to win more races.
**Dispol Foxtrot**, up in the weights and in grade, fully confirmed reappearance promise at her favourite course and is likely to win more races away from progressive types in a lesser grade. She relishes cut in the ground.
**Salagama(IRE)**, not seen since winning on her sole start over a year ago, did not really settle and ran well for one so inexperienced on this handicap debut. She really took the eye in the paddock and, although high in the weights at present, looks sure to win races this term.
**Najaaba(USA)** was not disgraced given this race did not really play to the strengths of those coming from off the pace but, although she looks a bit better than the bare form, she does look high enough in the weights on turf.
**Lilli Marlane** failed to reproduce her improved Ascot effort in a race that favoured those racing prominently, and she will be worth another chance on a more conventional track.
**Megan's Magic** was another who was not really suited by the way things panned out and is also not one to write off yet.
**Millagros(IRE)** *Official explanation: jockey said filly lost its action in the final 3f*
**Scotland The Brave** *Official explanation: jockey said filly hung left-handed in the straight*

## 1932 MITIE SCOTTISH H'CAP 1m 1f 36y
7:40 (7:44) (E) (0-70,70) 3-Y-O **£4,338** (£1,335; £667; £333) **Stalls** High

Form RPR
-031 **1** **Ace Coming**$^{11}$ [1667] 3-8-12 61 6ex (b) PHanagan 3 71
(DEddy) *keen: sn in tch: hdwy to ld 2f out: edgd rt: drvn out* **7/2**$^{2}$
2410 **2** *5* **Time To Relax (IRE)**$^{15}$ [1559] 3-9-3 66 KDarley 10 66
(JJQuinn) *hld up: hdwy and ev ch over 1f out: no ex ins fnl f* **6/1**$^{3}$
0-04 **3** *7* **Upthedale (IRE)**$^{15}$ [1570] 3-7-5 47 oh7 DFentiman$^{(7)}$ 9 33
(JRWeymes) *hld up wd: effrt centre over 2f out: no imp over 1f out* **33/1**
1360 **4** *1 1/2* **Rare Coincidence**$^{22}$ [1427] 3-9-6 69 (p) JFEgan 2 52
(RFFisher) *led after 1f to 2f out: sn outpcd* **12/1**
-016 **5** *3* **Perfect Balance (IRE)**$^{20}$ [1465] 3-8-11 60 KimTinkler 4 37
(NTinkler) *prom: lost pl 1/2-way: n.d after* **12/1**
-152 **6** *1* **Always Flying (USA)**$^{43}$ [1108] 3-9-7 70 JFanning 5 45
(MJohnston) *cl up tl rdn and wknd over 2f out* **9/4**$^{1}$
4-03 **7** *1/2* **Miskina**$^{13}$ [1627] 3-8-3 57 BSwarbrick$^{(5)}$ 7 31
(WMBrisbourne) *trckd ldrs: lost pl 1/2-way: n.d after* **10/1**
030- **8** *7* **Musical Lyrics (USA)**$^{213}$ [5434] 3-9-4 67 RFfrench 6 27
(MJohnston) *hld up: hdwy 1f: cl up tl wknd over 3f out* **16/1**

2m 2.62s (3.02) **Going Correction** +0.225s/f (Good) **8** Ran SP% **100.6**
Speed ratings: **95,90,84,83,80 79,79,72**CSF £18.65 CT £377.96 TOTE £3.40: £1.20, £2.30, £7.20; EX 13.10.
**Owner** I R Clements **Bred** S J And Mrs Pembroke **Trained** Ingoe, Northumberland
■ Stewards Enquiry : R FfrenchE caution: careless riding

**FOCUS**
A run-of-the-mill handicap run at just an ordinary gallop but an improved performance from Ace Coming, who relishes cut in the ground.

**NOTEBOOK**

**Ace Coming**, with conditions to suit, turned in an improved performance under a penalty in this stronger grade. He is clearly in good heart but it remains to be seen whether he will be as effective when the ground dries out after reassessment.

**Time To Relax(IRE)** returned to form but left the impression that his optimum conditions would be a strongly-run race at around a mile on goodish ground.

**Upthedale(IRE)** was not totally disgraced from 7lb out of the handicap in a race that was not really run to suit and he will be of more interest at around this trip when dropped in grade.

**Rare Coincidence**, from a stable that has been among the winners, had the run of the race but left the impression that this trip on easy ground just stretched his stamina.

**Perfect Balance(IRE)** has not progressed since his Redcar soft-ground success in April and was again well beaten. He may not be one to place too much faith in.

**Always Flying(USA)**, although not especially well treated in handicaps, could have been expected to fare a good deal better than he did on ground he has handled in the past.

## 1933 MITIE MEDIAN AUCTION MAIDEN STKS — 1m 3f 16y

8:10 (8:10) (E) 3-Y-O — £3,396 (£1,045; £522; £261) Stalls High

| Form | | | | | RPR |
|---|---|---|---|---|---|
| -023 | 1 | | **Tudor Bell (IRE)**[20] [1466] 3-9-0 75 ... DSweeney 1 — (JGMO'Shea) *mde all: clr 2f out: pushed out* | 11/4[2] | 77 |
| 34-2 | 2 | 6 | **Gold Card**[38] [1192] 3-9-0 70 ... RWinston 5 — (JRWeymes) *trckd ldrs: rdn over 2f out: sn one pce* | 10/1 | 67 |
| 43-3 | 3 | 3/4 | **Par Indiana (IRE)**[29] [1318] 3-8-9 60 ... PHanagan 4 — (ISemple) *prom: effrt over 2f out: sn no imp* | 11/2[3] | 61 |
| 2 | 4 | 7 | **Recognise (IRE)**[5] [1786] 3-9-0 ... KDalgleish 2 — (MJohnston) *cl up: rdn over 3f out: sn outpcd* | 5/6[1] | 55 |
| 0-3 | 5 | 1 1/2 | **Silver Rhythm**[17] [1524] 3-8-9 ... DarrenWilliams 6 — (KRBurke) *hld up in tch: rdn over 3f out: sn btn* | 33/1 | 48 |
| 00- | 6 | 15 | **Roaming Vagabond (IRE)**[191] [5831] 3-8-9 ... DFox(5) 3 — (NACallaghan) *hld up: rdn over 3f out: sn btn* | 25/1 | 29 |

2m 29.18s (2.68) **Going Correction** +0.225s/f (Good) 6 Ran SP% **112.5**

Speed ratings: **99,94,94,89,87 77**CSF £28.46 TOTE £4.20: £1.40, £3.50; EX 40.40.

**Owner** K W Bell & Son Ltd **Bred** Michael Byrne **Trained** Elton, Gloucs

**FOCUS**

A fair maiden in which odds-on favourite Recognise failed by a long chalk to reproduce the promise of his recent debut run.

**NOTEBOOK**

**Tudor Bell(IRE)** , who had the run of the race, did not have to improve to get off the mark over this longer trip but may continue to look vulnerable against progressive sorts from a mark in the mid 70s back in handicap company.

**Gold Card**, returned to turf, was not disgraced but had to fight hard to finish just in front of a 60-rated rival and, on the evidence so far, is not going to be easy to place successfully in maidens or in handicaps from his current mark.

**Par Indiana(IRE)** looked sure to be suited by the step up to this trip but, while she was not disgraced in the face of a stiffish task, she will be seen to better effect in ordinary handicap company in due course. *Official explanation: jockey said filly hung left*

**Recognise(IRE)** looked the one to beat after his promising debut run at this course five days earlier but disappointed on this easier ground. However this run may have come too quickly and he is not one to write off just yet.

**Silver Rhythm** again offered little immediate encouragement but may fare a little better in low-grade handicaps from now on.

**Roaming Vagabond(IRE)** again showed nothing. *Official explanation: jockey said gelding hung left*

## 1934 MITIE H'CAP — 5f 4y

8:40 (8:40) (F) (0-55,62) 3-Y-O — £2,968 (£848; £424) Stalls High

| Form | | | | | RPR |
|---|---|---|---|---|---|
| -040 | 1 | | **Short Chorus**[11] [1676] 3-8-11 47 ... (p) KDarley 7 — (JBalding) *w ldrs: rdn 2f out: led ent fnl f: hld on wl* | 8/1[3] | 52 |
| 3002 | 2 | nk | **Desert Light (IRE)**[35] [1236] 3-9-3 53 ... (v) PHanagan 8 — (DShaw) *w ldrs: led 2f out to ent fnl f: kpt on* | 8/1[3] | 57 |
| 6511 | 3 | nk | **He's A Rocket (IRE)**[7] [1742] 3-9-7 62 7ex ... (b) BSwarbrick(5) 10 — (KRBurke) *trckd ldrs: nt clr run fr 1/2-way to ins fnl f: r.o strly* | 7/4[1] | 65+ |
| 052P | 4 | 2 1/2 | **Wendy's Girl (IRE)**[11] [1676] 3-9-5 55 ... SChin 1 — (RPElliott) *prom: effrt and ch appr fnl f: one pce* | 16/1 | 49 |
| 0-05 | 5 | shd | **Musiotal**[5] [1788] 3-8-12 48 ... JFEgan 4 — (JSGoldie) *bhd: pushed along 1/2-way: kpt on fnl f: nrst fin* | 6/1[2] | 42 |
| 0020 | 6 | nk | **A Bid In Time (IRE)**[10] [1689] 3-8-13 49 ... DarrenWilliams 2 — (DShaw) *s.i.s: effrt over 2f out: no imp fnl f* | 10/1 | 42 |
| 0103 | 7 | hd | **Garnock Venture (IRE)**[7] [1742] 3-9-5 55 ... (b) FLynch 3 — (ABerry) *racd wd: n.d* | 11/1 | 47 |
| 0636 | 8 | shd | **Lavish Times**[5] [1788] 3-9-1 51 ... (b) FNorton 9 — (ABerry) *led to 2f out: sn outpcd* | 9/1 | 42 |
| 346- | 9 | 1 1/4 | **Icenaslice (IRE)**[185] [5915] 3-9-5 55 ... RWinston 5 — (JJQuinn) *dwlt: keen and sn chsng ldrs: nt clr run 1/2-way: rdn and wknd over 1f out* | 12/1 | 42 |
| 06-5 | 10 | shd | **Loveisdangerous**[35] [1236] 3-9-3 53 ... KimTinkler 6 — (DonEnricolncisa) *chsd ldrs to 1/2-way: sn rdn and wknd* | 33/1 | 40 |

62.52 secs (1.26) **Going Correction** +0.225s/f (Good) 10 Ran SP% **116.8**

Speed ratings: **98,97,97,93,92 92,92,91,89,89**CSF £70.53 CT £161.06 TOTE £10.70: £2.20, £4.10, £1.50; EX 97.20 Place 6 £43.46, Place 5 £31.64.

**Owner** Watchman Racing **Bred** Catridge Farm Stud Ltd **Trained** Scrooby, Notts

**FOCUS**

A weak handicap in which the field raced centre to far side and one in which third-placed He's A Rocket looked a shade unfortunate not to win his third consecutive race.

**NOTEBOOK**

**Short Chorus**, back in trip, had the run of the race and showed the right attitude in the closing stages. She has not been the most consistent, though, and had little in hand, so may be one to field against after reassessment.

**Desert Light(IRE)**, a winner on Polytrack in January, showed more than enough on this second turf start to suggest he can win a similar race in this sphere.

**He's A Rocket(IRE)**, up 16lb in the weights, turned in a career-best effort and looked unlucky not to complete the three-timer as he got precious little room in the last half of the contest. He can make amends from this mark in similar company.

**Wendy's Girl(IRE)** was anything but disgraced from the worst draw, but she has yet to win in 18 starts and her record suggests she is far from certain to put it all in next time.

**Musiotal** ◆ fared the best of those that attempted to come from off the pace and once again left the strong impression that the step up to six furlongs would suit. He is better than his last two runs suggest and is one to keep an eye on.

**A Bid In Time(IRE)** was not disgraced, but this latest sluggish start meant he was always going to be up against it in a race that favoured those racing close to the pace.

T/Plt: £63.10 to a £1 stake. Pool: £42,923.20. 496.50 winning tickets. T/Qpdt: £27.40 to a £1 stake. Pool: £3,056.90. 82.50 winning tickets. RY

# [1723] LINGFIELD (L-H)

Friday, May 7

**OFFICIAL GOING: Turf course - soft (good to soft in places); all-weather - standard**

## 1935 SATURDAY NIGHT RACING AT LINGFIELD 29TH MAY H'CAP — 1m (P)

2:15 (2:19) (E) (0-75,75) 3-Y-O+ — £3,503 (£1,078; £539; £269) Stalls High

| Form | | | | | RPR |
|---|---|---|---|---|---|
| 0-01 | 1 | | **Lifted Way**[13] [1624] 5-9-13 74 ... SDrowne 7 — (PRChamings) *trckd ldr: effrt to ld over 1f out: drvn out ins fnl f: jst hld on* | 6/1[2] | 83 |
| 1561 | 2 | hd | **Brave Dane (IRE)**[43] [1109] 6-9-12 73 ... WRyan 8 — (AWCarroll) *hld up in last of main gp: gd prog over 2f out: str run on outer fnl f: jst failed* | 11/2[1] | 82 |
| -002 | 3 | nk | **Concer Eto**[42] [1118] 5-9-6 70 ... (p) BReilly(3) 6 — (SCWilliams) *cl up: trckd ldng pair 1/2-way: effrt over 1f out: pressed wnr ins fnl f: nt qckn and lost 2nd nr fin* | 6/1[2] | 78 |
| 1101 | 4 | nk | **Supreme Salutation**[3] [1876] 8-9-5 73 7ex ... MHoward(7) 4 — (DKIvory) *hld up in midfield: stdy prog over 2f out: trckd ldng trio wl over 1f out: hanging and shuffled along fnl f: nvr nrr* | 8/1 | 80 |
| 4036 | 5 | 2 1/2 | **Paragon Of Virtue**[35] [1232] 7-10-0 75 ... RLMoore 2 — (PMitchell) *lost pl after 2f and sn wl in rr: rdn 1/2-way: effrt 2f out: styd on fnl f: n.d* | 11/2[1] | 77 |
| 3-34 | 6 | 1/2 | **College Delinquent (IRE)**[34] [1241] 5-9-5 66 ... (t) MartinDwyer 5 — (KBell) *dwlt: t.k.h and hld up in midfield: rdn 3f out: nt qckn and no prog: one pce fr over 1f out* | 7/1[3] | 66 |
| 3500 | 7 | 1/2 | **Estimation**[25] [1372] 4-9-0 66 ... AQuinn(5) 9 — (RMHCowell) *t.k.h: hld up in midfield: prog to trck ldrs over 2f out: sn rdn: one pce over 1f out* | 25/1 | 65 |
| 500- | 8 | 2 | **Willheconquertoo**[193] [5796] 4-9-6 67 ... (t) SCarson 3 — (AndrewReid) *led at gd pce: hdd over 1f out: hanging and wknd* | 25/1 | 62 |
| 0600 | 9 | shd | **Agilis (IRE)**[34] [1241] 4-9-3 67 ... (v[1]) RMiles(3) 1 — (JamiePoulton) *settled in rr: pushed along 1/2-way: brief effrt 3f out: sn no imp and btn* | 16/1 | 61 |
| 5525 | 10 | 10 | **Superchief**[73] [870] 9-9-4 65 ... (bt) SSanders 11 — (MissBSanders) *racd wd: t.k.h and hld up in tch: rdn 3f out: sn struggling: wknd 2f out* | 11/1 | 36 |
| -250 | 11 | 15 | **Learned Lad (FR)**[61] [820] 6-9-5 66 ... CCatlin 10 — (JamiePoulton) *lost tch in last after 2f: sn t.o* | 20/1 | 3 |
| 10-0 | 12 | shd | **Count Walewski**[20] [1460] 4-9-9 70 ... TQuinn 12 — (SDow) *prom to 1/2-way: wknd rapidly wl over 2f out: t.o* | 40/1 | 7 |

1m 38.86s (-0.69) **Going Correction** 0.0s/f (Stan) 12 Ran SP% **112.1**

Speed ratings: **103,102,102,102,99 99,98,96,96,86 71,71**CSF £34.74 CT £204.18 TOTE £5.80: £2.50, £2.70, £2.30; EX 43.70.

**Owner** Mrs Alexandra J Chandris **Bred** Mrs J Chandris **Trained** Baughurst, Hants

**FOCUS**

An ordinary handicap run at an even pace.

**NOTEBOOK**

**Lifted Way**, raised 2lb for winning the Flat versus Jump jockeys challenge at Sandown on Betfred Gold Cup day under Tony McCoy, was always close to the pace and impressed with the way he held off several challenges in the home straight. This was a big improvement on his two previous tries on this surface, but is now likely to return to grass.

**Brave Dane(IRE)**, 5lb higher than for his Doncaster win, needs to be held up for a late run, but there was always the suspicion that he would not be helped by the drop back to a mile and his late effort down the outside just failed. He should be winning again when stepped back up in trip.

**Concer Eto** ran another good race over this course and distance and looked a big threat to all turning for home, but the winner would not be denied and he could not get to him despite trying his hardest.

**Supreme Salutation**, under a 7lb penalty for his Warwick victory in very soft ground three days earlier, was another doing all his best work late on. He did win a claimer over a furlong shorter here in March, but was entitled to do so at the weights and he probably needs a slower surface over this trip.

**Paragon Of Virtue** is another whose best form is over further and he did not get going until far too late.

**College Delinquent(IRE)**, whose only previous victory in 24 previous attempts came in a maiden over course and distance 16 months ago, did not help himself by pulling hard early but still looks held off his current mark.

**Superchief** *Official explanation: trainer said gelding had a muscular problem in its back.*

**Learned Lad(FR)** reportedly banged his head leaving the stalls and was never travelling thereafter. *Official explanation: jockey said gelding banged itself exiting the stalls and was never travelling*

## 1936 EUROPEAN BREEDERS FUND MAIDEN STKS — 5f

2:45 (2:46) (D) 2-Y-O — £4,212 (£1,296; £648; £324) Stalls High

| Form | | | | | RPR |
|---|---|---|---|---|---|
| 2 | 1 | | **Moscow Music**[21] [1436] 2-9-0 ... SDrowne 4 — (MGQuinlan) *mde all: shkn up over 1f out: in command fnl f* | 4/7[1] | 65+ |
| | 2 | 1 1/2 | **Bogaz (IRE)** 2-9-0 ... SSanders 1 — (RMBeckett) *chsd wnr: rdn 2f out: no imp and hld fnl f* | 8/1[3] | 60 |
| 5 | 3 | 3/4 | **Fortnum**[4] [1826] 2-9-0 ... RLMoore 3 — (RHannon) *sn pushed along in last pair: rdn 3f out: struggling fr 1/2-way: styd on ins fnl f* | 3/1[2] | 57 |
| 0 | 4 | 1 1/2 | **Heart Of Eternity (IRE)**[11] [1670] 2-8-9 ... MartinDwyer 2 — (JRBoyle) *sn pushed along in last pair and rn green: effrt 2f out: sn btn* | 11/1 | 47 |

62.32 secs (3.45) **Going Correction** +0.525s/f (Yiel) 4 Ran SP% **108.1**

Speed ratings: **93,90,89,87**CSF £5.59 TOTE £1.50; EX 4.40.

**Owner** O'Connor Racing **Bred** The Earl Cadogan **Trained** Newmarket, Suffolk

**FOCUS**

An uncompetitive maiden. The winning time confirmed that the going on the turf course was testing.

**NOTEBOOK**

**Moscow Music** boasted the best form going into this and made full use of his rails draw, bouncing out and making all the running to score with the minimum of fuss. He would not have been allowed to take his chance in the testing ground had it not been for so few rivals and he should carry on improving back on a sound surface.

**Bogaz(IRE)**, a 17,000gns yearling, ran a promising debut and chased the favourite all the way to the line. His dam is a half-sister to winners at up to 12 furlongs so he should get much further than this.

**Fortnum** did not appear to improve much from his Kempton debut just four days earlier, but he has only ever encountered testing conditions and faster ground may see him start to recoup some of his 35,000gns purchase price.

**Heart Of Eternity(IRE)**, as on her debut, dwelt in the stalls, but managed to stay in touch and held every chance. She was just not good enough.



The Form Book, Raceform Ltd, Compton, RG20 6NL

## 1937 TOTEPLACEPOT H'CAP 5f

3:20 (3:20) (D ) (0-85,85) 3-Y-0+ £7,046 (£2,168; £1,084; £542) Stalls High

Form RPR

1213 **1** **Forever Phoenix**[21] 1454 4-9-5 **81** AQuinn(5) 10 99
(RMHCowell) *trckd ldrs: led 2f out: pushed clr fnl f: comf* **9/2**[1]

20-3 **2** *3 ½* **Roxanne Mill**[17] 1518 6-9-3 **74** RLMoore 11 82
(JMBradley) *cl up: effrt to press wnr wl over 1f out: sn rdn: wl btn fnl f but hld on for 2nd* **13/2**[3]

1002 **3** *1 ¼* **Another Glimpse**[1] 1909 6-8-10 **67** (t) SSanders 6 71
(MissBSanders) *nt gng wl in rr early and reminder after 1f: prog u.p 2f out: chsd ldng pair 1f out: kpt on* **5/1**[2]

135- **4** *¾* **Cerulean Rose**[237] 4885 5-8-11 **68** WRyan 9 70
(AWCarroll) *settled towards rr: prog 2f out: nudged along and kpt on steadily fr over 1f out: nvr rchd ldrs* **7/1**

0450 **5** *2* **Madrasee**[16] 1537 6-9-6 **77** SDrowne 3 73
(LMontagueHall) *swtchd to inner after 1f and in rr: rdn and prog 2f out: chsd ldrs 1f out: no imp and eased* **12/1**

U300 **6** *4* **Ok Pal**[11] 1673 4-9-11 **85** RMiles(3) 8 69
(TGMills) *w ldr: led 3f out to 2f out: wknd over 1f out* **9/1**

100- **7** *¾* **Roses Of Spring**[234] 4972 6-10-0 **85** (p) BDoyle 7 67
(RMHCowell) *hld up in midfield: shkn up 2f out: sn wknd* **25/1**

3500 **8** *1 ½* **Dancing Mystery**[16] 1537 10-9-4 **82** (b) LiamJones(7) 12 59
(EAWheeler) *led to 3f out: wknd 2f out* **11/1**

0220 **9** *½* **Lady Pekan**[12] 1642 5-8-2 **62** (b) LisaJones(3) 5 38
(PSMcentee) *racd on outer: pressed ldrs to 1/2-way: sn struggling* **10/1**

-062 **10** *nk* **Byo (IRE)**[17] 1518 6-8-13 **70** MartinDwyer 1 45
(MQuinn) *racd on outer: a struggling: bhd fr 1/2-way* **14/1**

2500 **11** *2 ½* **Seven No Trumps**[6] 1774 7-9-9 **80** (p) SCarson 2 47
(JMBradley) *racd on outer: a struggling: bhd fr 1/2-way* **12/1**

-000 **12** *hd* **Blessed Place**[71] 896 4-8-0 **57** oh5 ow2 CCatlin 4 24
(DJSFrenchDavis) *racd on outer: nvr on terms w ldrs: wknd 1/2-way* **40/1**

59.75 secs (0.88) **Going Correction** +0.525s/f (Yiel) 12 Ran SP% 116.4
Speed ratings: **113,107,105,104,101 94,93,91,90,89 85,85**CSF £32.61 CT £154.37 TOTE £5.40: £1.80, £2.60, £3.30; EX 28.70.
**Owner** J M Greetham **Bred** J M Greetham **Trained** Six Mile Bottom, Cambs

**FOCUS**
A decent sprint handicap, but a high draw proved a big advantage with the first two coming from stalls 10 and 11 respectively. A cracking winning time for the class.

**NOTEBOOK**
**Forever Phoenix** has maintained her improved sard form back on to turf and still looks to be on the upgrade. Her rider was lobbing along on her from some way out and when he asked for her effort, she quickened away most impressively in the ground. She will be entered for both the valuable sprint handicap and the Group Two Temple Stakes at the Epsom Derby meeting.
**Roxanne Mill** confirmed the promise of her Folkestone reappearance and can be considered unlucky to have come up against such a progressive rival. She has not won for nearly two years, but is well handicapped at present and running well enough to take advantage.
**Another Glimpse** showed no ill effects from his narrow defeat at Folkestone the previous day, but he ideally needs another furlong and his final placing was as close as he got.
**Cerulean Rose** ran a blinder on her first start for eight months. Although she has won with cut, most of her five-timer last summer was achieved on fast ground, so she is very much one to watch out for with this effort under her belt.
**Madrasee** would have preferred faster ground, but was not entirely disgraced from her low draw.
**Ok Pal** showed up for a long way, but seemed to get tired in the ground despite his best previous form being achieved on it. He goes down 5lb in the handicap now which should be some help to him.

## 1938 R R RICHARDSON CLASSIFIED STKS 7f 140y

3:55 (3:55) (D ) 3-Y-0+ £5,638 (£1,735; £867; £433) Stalls Centre

Form RPR

0-23 **1** **Soyuz (IRE)**[13] 1623 4-9-9 82 PRobinson 3 92
(MAJarvis) *trckd ldr for 2f: effrt 3f out: rdn to ld 2f out: clr fnl f: styd on wl* **5/4**[1]

5-00 **2** *3 ½* **Cheese 'n Biscuits**[6] 1765 4-9-4 79 RLMoore 2 79
(GLMoore) *pushed along in last over 4f out: rdn 2f out: styd on fnl f to take 2nd nr fin: no ch w wnr* **7/2**[2]

0015 **3** *¾* **Jools**[13] 1623 6-9-5 81 RMiles(3) 4 81
(DKIvory) *sn led: hdd and rdn 2f out: sn no ch w wnr: lost 2nd nr fin* **7/2**[2]

40-0 **4** *2* **Impersonator**[13] 1623 4-9-7 78 (b[1]) TQuinn 1 76
(JLDunlop) *trckd ldr after 2f: rdn and ev ch over 2f out: fnd nil and sn btn* **5/1**[3]

1m 37.77s (6.31) **Going Correction** +0.525s/f (Yiel) 4 Ran SP% 105.6
Speed ratings: **89,85,84,82**CSF £5.48 TOTE £1.60; EX 5.20.
**Owner** N R A Springer **Bred** Mount Coote Stud **Trained** Newmarket, Suffolk

**FOCUS**
A tight race on adjusted official ratings, and only the winner looks to have shown his form. The four runners migrated over to the stands' rail after a quarter of a mile and the early pace was modest, resulting in a pedestrian winning time for the grade.

**NOTEBOOK**
**Soyuz(IRE)**, given a patient ride, eventually forged right away from his three rivals to score with ease. Being gelded appears to have done him a lot of good and he looks more than capable of adding to this, but cut in the ground does look a necessity.
**Cheese 'n Biscuits** stayed on to finish a respectable second after getting a bit outpaced at halfway. Both of her wins have been on Polytrack, but she has run well in very soft ground before and this effort confirms that she can handle it.
**Jools** was closely matched with Soyuz on the form of their two previous meetings this term, but it proved no contest this time despite getting the run of the race out in front.
**Impersonator** had already finished well behind Soyuz and Jools this season, but although the soft ground should have been in his favour, it is appearing more likely that he needs the ground to be virtually unraceable for him to show his best.

## 1939 WEATHERBYS INSURANCE MAIDEN STKS 7f

4:30 (4:31) (D ) 3-Y-0+ £4,199 (£1,292; £646; £323) Stalls High

Form RPR

2 **1** **Lucky Spin**[21] 1441 3-8-7 RLMoore 17 86
(RHannon) *cl up: led over 1f out: sn wl clr* **11/4**[2]

34- **2** *5* **Castleton**[282] 3686 3-8-12 MartinDwyer 8 78
(HJCyzer) *mde most to over 1f out: clr of remainder but no ch w wnr after* **5/2**[1]

00- **3** *7* **Wyoming**[205] 5571 3-8-7 WRyan 6 56
(JARToller) *racd in midfield: effrt 3f out: kpt on to take modest 3rd 1f out: no ch w ldng pair* **100/1**

0 **4** *¾* **My Pension (IRE)**[4] 1830 3-8-12 SDrowne 1 59
(PHowling) *s.i.s: hld up in last trio: stdy prog fr 1/2-way: styng on but no ch whn nt clr run 1f out: kpt on* **25/1**

0/3- **5** *3 ½* **Presumptive (IRE)**[309] 2922 4-9-10 TQuinn 16 50
(RCharlton) *sn trckd ldrs: rdn 3f out: outpcd 2f out: wknd over 1f out* **9/2**[3]

6 **6** *1 ¼* **Keyaki (IRE)**[25] 1352 3-8-8 ow1 SSanders 7 43
(CFWall) *s.s: rcvrd into midfield after 2f: rdn and effrt to chse ldrs over 2f out: wknd over 1f out* **7/1**

04-0 **7** *nk* **Madame Marie (IRE)**[30] 1298 4-9-2 50 LisaJones(3) 11 41
(SDow) *hld up wl in rr: wl bhd 1/2-way: nudged along and styd on wl fnl f: nvr nr ldrs* **66/1**

0- **8** *nk* **Grey Boy (GER)**[217] 5337 3-8-12 CCatlin 14 45
(GCBravery) *pressed ldr after 2f to 2f out: sn wknd* **20/1**

00 **9** *1 ½* **Forge Lane (IRE)**[71] 890 3-8-12 RBrisland 12 42
(GLMoore) *racd in midfield: outpcd and btn wl over 2f out: fdd* **66/1**

055 **10** *1 ¼* **Young Dynasty**[59] 997 4-9-3 45 (b[1]) LiamJones(7) 15 38
(EAWheeler) *wnt lft s: sn prom: rdn 3f out: wknd wl over 1f out* **66/1**

-550 **11** *3* **Star Fern**[37] 1204 3-8-7 57 NChalmers(5) 4 31
(JAkehurst) *a wl in rr: no ch fr over 2f out* **50/1**

0-0 **12** *1* **Mad Maurice**[4] 1820 3-8-12 (p) SWKelly 9 28
(BJCurley) *settled in rr: sme prog into midfield 3f out: nudged along and carried hd high over 2f out: wknd and eased over 1f out* **33/1**

0 **13** *2 ½* **Spector (IRE)**[25] 1371 4-9-7 DCorby(3) 3 22
(JJSheehan) *rn v green in last trio: sn struggling* **50/1**

0 **14** *1 ¾* **Blake Hall Lad (IRE)**[24] 1386 3-8-12 OUrbina 5 18
(MissJFeilden) *racd on outer: nvr on terms w ldrs: bhd fr over 2f out* **33/1**

3336 **15** *7* **Night Storm**[64] 959 3-8-7 70 PaulEddery 13 —
(SDow) *dwlt: a in rr: wl bhd fr over 2f out* **12/1**

**16** *20* **Wolf Cub** 3-8-12 CLowther 10 —
(MissGayKelleway) *pressed ldr for 2f: hanging rt and sn lost pl: wknd rapidly and eased 2f out: t.o* **33/1**

-00 **17** *hd* **Zambezi River**[20] 1476 5-9-10 SCarson 2 —
(JMBradley) *a towards rr: rdn and btn whn stmbld wl over 2f out: wknd after: t.o* **100/1**

1m 26.51s (2.30) **Going Correction** +0.525s/f (Yiel)
**WFA** 3 from 4yo+ 12lb 17 Ran SP% 121.4
Speed ratings: **107,101,93,92,88 87,86,86,84,83 79,78,75,73,65 42,42**CSF £8.81 TOTE £4.30: £1.60, £1.30, £47.10; EX 11.30.
**Owner** George C Scudder **Bred** Roland Hope **Trained** East Everleigh, Wilts

**FOCUS**
An uncompetitive maiden though a very impressive winner. Not many could be given a serious chance despite the size of the field.

**NOTEBOOK**
**Lucky Spin ◆** could hardly have been more impressive. She has obviously come on from her debut and it was the turn of foot she showed here on the rain-softened ground that made such an impression. Her trainer believes she is yet to come in her coat, so she is likely to have plenty of improvement still in her.
**Castleton** was made to look very one-paced by the winner after making much of the running, but still finished a long way clear of the others. He was entitled to need this first run since finishing fourth behind Lucky Story in a Group Two at Glorious Goodwood last July, but his St James's Palace entry still looks very optimistic.
**Wyoming ◆**, well beaten in two maidens won by fair sorts last season, has improved over the winter if this staying-on effort is anything to go by despite finishing well behind the front pair. There is stamina in her pedigree which suggests she will improve again over further and she also now qualifies for a handicap mark. She is one to keep a note of.
**My Pension(IRE) ◆**, turned out again quickly having only made his debut at Kempton four days earlier, was noted staying on nicely in the latter stages. He might have finished third had he not run into traffic over a furlong from home and is worth keeping an eye on. *Official explanation: jockey said gelding was unlucky in running*
**Presumptive(IRE)** has only managed one outing in each of his three seasons so far and offered only limited encouragement on this first start for his current yard. He must be thought capable of winning a race to be persevered with like this.
**Keyaki(IRE)** did not really improve from her debut and it may be that she needs better ground.
**Wolf Cub** *Official explanation: jockey said gelding was hanging right*

## 1940 COME TO THE DERBY TRIAL TOMORROW FILLIES' H'CAP 1m 2f (P)

5:05 (5:10) (E ) (0-70,70) 3-Y-0+ £3,474 (£1,069; £534; £267) Stalls Low

Form RPR

0-04 **1** **State Of Balance**[13] 1628 6-9-3 **59** CCatlin 9 67
(KBell) *dwlt: t.k.h: hld up in last trio: prog over 2f out: str run on outside fnl f to ld last strides* **12/1**

1454 **2** *nk* **Anyhow (IRE)**[10] 1684 7-9-3 **64** DNolan(5) 6 71
(MissKMGeorge) *racd in midfield: prog 2f out: drvn and r.o to chal wl ins fnl f: jst pipped* **6/1**[2]

0641 **3** *hd* **My Lilli (IRE)**[34] 1244 4-8-12 **54** RLMoore 5 61
(PMitchell) *prom: led gng easily 3f out: rdn 2l clr over 2f out: wknd ins fnl f: hdd last strides* **6/1**[2]

60-0 **4** *nk* **Miss Grace**[11] 1675 4-9-11 **70** DCorby(3) 7 76
(JJSheehan) *wl plcd: effrt over 2f out: rdn to chse ldr over 1f out: clsd and ev ch nr fin: one pce* **25/1**

5666 **5** *6* **Figura**[44] 1097 6-9-0 **56** SSanders 4 51
(RIngram) *trckd ldrs: effrt whn squeezed out over 2f out: nt rcvr: one pce over 1f out* **4/1**[1]

0355 **6** *1* **Alisa (IRE)**[64] 962 4-9-1 **57** (t) SWKelly 2 50
(BICase) *hld up bhd ldrs: rdn over 2f out: kpt on one pce fr over 1f out* **20/1**

1212 **7** *shd* **Wanna Shout**[34] 1244 6-8-13 **58** LisaJones(3) 8 51
(RDickin) *trckd ldrs: rdn to chse ldr over 2f out to over 1f out: wknd* **7/1**[3]

2-50 **8** *2* **Margery Daw (IRE)**[1] 1902 4-9-1 **64** DerekNolan(7) 1 53
(PSMcentee) *uns rdr and bolted on way to s: reluctant to enter stalls: in tch: nt qckn over 2f out: btn after* **16/1**

301- **9** *1 ¼* **Tetou (IRE)**[171] 6022 4-9-11 **70** JFMcDonald(3) 12 57
(BJMeehan) *trckd ldrs: lost pl over 4f out: rdn and no prog over 2f out* **12/1**

0 **10** *1* **Acola (FR)**[15] 1560 4-9-0 **56** BDoyle 14 41
(RMHCowell) *racd on outer: in tch: rdn 3f out: sn struggling* **14/1**

0005 **11** *2 ½* **Nuzzle**[10] 1684 4-8-8 **50** MartinDwyer 10 30
(MQuinn) *led after 2f to 3f out: wknd over 2f out* **14/1**

030- **12** *1* **Haribini**[199] 5696 4-8-1 **48** NChalmers(5) 13 26
(JJBridger) *s.v.s: a in rr: drvn and struggling over 4f out* **50/1**

20-2 **13** *1* **Castaway Queen (IRE)**[29] 1308 5-9-6 **62** SDrowne 11 38
(WRMuir) *settled in rr: rdn and struggling over 3f out: sn bhd* **11/1**

600- **14** *1 ½* **Dreaming Waters**[196] 5735 3-8-6 **63** SCarson 3 36
(RFJohnsonHoughton) *reluctant to enter stalls: led for 2f: steadily lost pl fr 1/2-way: wl bhd 2f out* **20/1**

2m 7.29s (-0.56) **Going Correction** 0.0s/f (Stan)
**WFA** 3 from 4yo+ 15lb 14 Ran SP% 119.3
Speed ratings: **102,101,101,101,96 95,95,94,93,92 90,89,88,87**CSF £77.86 CT £485.21 TOTE £25.70: £5.70, £2.70, £2.70; EX 191.80 Place 6 £24.22, Place 5 £13.15.
**Owner** North Farm Stud **Bred** Mrs S France **Trained** Letcombe Regis, Oxon

**FOCUS**
A modest fillies' handicap, but a thrilling conclusion with the front four all finishing in a heap.

**NOTEBOOK**
**State Of Balance** had never previously made the first three in six previous starts on the Flat, but did have some form over this course and distance. Given a patient ride, she fairly flew once switched to the outside in the home straight and got up near the line to gain what had looked an unlikely victory. This represented improved form, but she is likely to struggle back in mixed company.
**Anyhow(IRE)** did nothing wrong, but she may be better over 12 furlongs on this surface these days and the winner had the stronger finishing kick.
**My Lilli(IRE)** very nearly benefited from an enterprising ride. She was quickly kicked into a significant advantage turning for home and still looked like holding on for most of the home straight, but she got tired in the last half-furlong and had the race snatched from her. She does stay this trip.
**Miss Grace**, racing on Polytrack for the first time since winning a course-and-distance maiden for Barry Hills 14 months ago, ran by far her best race for her current yard.
**Figura** was still close to the leaders when getting seriously unbalanced on the home turn, but was being shoved along at the time so it is unlikely it made that much difference.
**Alisa(IRE)** was done no favours by the drop in trip.
**Wanna Shout** just about stays this trip, but all her wins have come over a mile.
T/Plt: £22.10 to a £1 stake. Pool: £25,247.95. 833.40 winning tickets. T/Qpdt: £7.80 to a £1 stake. Pool: £1,656.70. 156.60 winning tickets. JN

## 1749 NOTTINGHAM (L-H)
Friday, May 7

**OFFICIAL GOING: Soft changing to soft (heavy in places) after race 4 (3.40)**
Weather: sunshine, until rain broke through after race four.

### 1941 COME RACING AGAIN NEXT WEEKEND APPRENTICE H'CAP — 6f 15y
**2:05** (2:05) (F ) (0-55,57) 3-Y-O+ — **£3,248** (£928; £464) **Stalls High**

Form — RPR
0104 **1** **King Nicholas (USA)**[17] [1526] 5-8-12 **50**.....................(tp) RoryMoore(3) 1 57
(JParkes) *racd far side: chsd ldrs: rdn to ld that gp 1/2-way: styd on* **4/1**[1]
-400 **2** *½* **Semper Paratus (USA)**[21] [1451] 5-9-1 **53**...(b) StephanieHollinshead(3) 7 59
(VSmith) *racd far side: hld up: hdwy over 1f out: r.o* **10/1**[3]
0/0- **3** *hd* **Fenwicks Pride (IRE)**[206] [5561] 6-9-0 **54**.............................. DSwift(5) 9 59
(RAFahey) *racd far side: chsd ldrs: rdn: hung lft and ev ch fr over 1f out: styd on* **20/1**
00-1 **4** *2 ½* **Game Flora**[9] [1711] 3-8-12 **57** 7ex.......................................... PMulrennan 6 54
(MESowersby) *racd far side: a.p: chsd wnr over 2f out: rdn and ev ch over 1f out: wknd nr fin* **11/1**
2-00 **5** *nk* **Diamond Shannon (IRE)**[20] [1472] 3-8-0 **50**............. DawnWatson(5) 11 47
(DCarroll) *s.i.s: racd far side: sn pushed along in rr: hdwy over 1f out: r.o: nt rch ldrs* **20/1**
30-6 **6** *½* **Glory Girl**[1] [1913] 4-8-5 **45**................................................ DTudhope(5) 5 40
(MBrittain) *s.i.s: racd far side: outpcd: r.o ins fnl f: nvr nrr* **25/1**
1001 **7** *1* **Redoubtable (USA)**[8] [1719] 13-8-9 **47** 7ex....................(b) PMakin(3) 12 39
(DWChapman) *racd stands' side: chsd ldr: led that gp over 1f out: no ch w far side* **14/1**
606- **8** *½* **Speed On**[232] [5025] 11-8-7 **47** ow1................................. CCavanagh(5) 17 38
(HCandy) *led stands' side over 4f: no ex* **12/1**
60-2 **9** *nk* **Halcyon Magic**[17] [1516] 6-8-10 **50**...............................(b) LauraPike(5) 14 40
(MissJFeilden) *racd stands' side: in tch: rdn over 1f out: n.d* **8/1**[2]
0145 **10** *½* **Star Lad (IRE)**[20] [1474] 4-8-10 **48**..............................(b) PPMathers(3) 16 36
(RBrotherton) *racd stands' side: chsd ldrs over 4f* **16/1**
2460 **11** *½* **Zak Facta (IRE)**[22] [1423] 4-8-10 **50**................................ KGhunowa(5) 8 37
(MissDAMchale) *racd far side: hung lft and prom: rdn and wknd over 1f out* **33/1**
6160 **12** *1* **Ace-Ma-Vahra**[35] [1233] 6-8-12 **47**.......................................(b[1]) PBradley 13 31
(SRBowring) *swtchd lft to ld far side gp 5f out: hdd 1/2-way: wknd over 1f out* **40/1**
131- **13** *1 ¾* **Waterpark**[361] [1551] 6-8-8 **48**............................................ AMullen(5) 15 26
(RCraggs) *racd stands' side: chsd ldrs 4f* **8/1**[2]
0106 **14** *3* **Above Board**[22] [1423] 9-8-3 **45** oh10....................................... MNem(7) 4 14
(RFMarvin) *racd far side: outpcd* **33/1**
466- **15** *5* **Run On**[239] [4839] 6-9-5 **54**.................................................. DNolan 2 8
(DGBridgwater) *racd far side: prom: lost pl over 4f out: hdwy u.p over 2f out: wknd wl over 1f out* **12/1**
0041 **16** *nk* **Bali-Star**[14] [1584] 9-8-6 **46**............................................ CHaddon(5) 10 —
(RJHodges) *racd stands' side: chsd ldrs: hung lft and wknd 2f out* **14/1**
5-50 **17** *25* **Astrac (IRE)**[13] [1625] 13-8-10 **50**................................... DerekNolan(5) 3 —
(MrsALMKing) *racd far side: mid-div: wknd over 2f out* **10/1**[3]
1m 18.41s (3.61) **Going Correction** +0.55s/f (Yiel) **17** Ran SP% **125.0**
**WFA** 3 from 4yo+ 10lb
Speed ratings: **97,96,96,92,92 91,90,89,89,88 87,86,84,80,73 73,39**CSF £39.48 CT £764.30 TOTE £5.70: £2.50, £3.00, £3.10, £2.30; EX 89.80.
**Owner** M Wormald **Bred** Calumet Farm **Trained** Upper Helmsley, N Yorks
**FOCUS**
A poor contest, not much better than a seller, in which the field split into two, with the first six home all racing on the far side.
**NOTEBOOK**
**King Nicholas(USA)**, with the advantage of the far rail to help and one of the more experienced riders in the field on his back, made no mistake. This soft ground is ideal for him and granted similar conditions he could follow up in a similar contest.
**Semper Paratus(USA)** is hardly the most consistent horse in training, but he is handy enough at this level when things go his way.
**Fenwicks Pride(IRE)** had his ideal conditions and had no excuses. Well treated on the best of his form, he looks capable of scoring at this level.
**Game Flora**, who went up 7lb for winning at Pontefract, didn't quite get home.
**Diamond Shannon(IRE)**, tackling handicappers for the first time, did herself no favours by falling out of the stalls. However, she did come home well enough and should be able to win a little race, possibly over a little further.
**Glory Girl** shaped much better here than she did on the Fibresand the previous day, and the way she came home suggested she will be suited by further.
**Redoubtable(USA)** won the race on the stands' side and is clearly in good heart at present.
**Run On** *Official explanation: jockey said horse lost its action on the soft ground*
**Astrac(IRE)** *Official explanation: trainer said gelding was unsuited by the soft ground*

### 1942 BECOME AN ANNUAL MEMBER MEDIAN AUCTION MAIDEN STKS — 6f 15y
**2:35** (2:36) (E ) 3-Y-O — **£3,750** (£1,154; £577; £288) **Stalls High**

Form — RPR
4-42 **1** **Mission Man**[24] [1386] 3-9-0 82........................................... PDobbs 7 81
(RHannon) *w ldr: led 1/2-way: rdn clr over 1f out* **8/11**[1]
6-05 **2** *3 ½* **Indian Edge**[7] [1749] 3-9-0 65.......................................... DKinsella 11 71?
(BPalling) *s.i.s: hld up: hdwy u.p and hung lft fr over 1f out: nvr trbld wnr* **9/1**[3]
30-6 **3** *2 ½* **Kensington (IRE)**[17] [1519] 3-9-0 72...................................... JCarroll 10 63
(RGuest) *chsd ldrs: rdn over 1f out: wknd ins fnl f* **9/1**[3]
0 **4** *4* **Rene Barbier (IRE)**[7] [1749] 3-9-0 ........................................ GGibbons 2 51
(JAGlover) *prom: chsd wnr over 2f out: rdn over 1f out: sn wknd* **66/1**
06 **5** *3* **Cunning Pursuit**[11] [1679] 3-9-0 .......................................... IMongan 4 42
(MLWBell) *mid-div: sn pushed along: wknd 2f out* **33/1**
**6** *1 ¼* **Victoriana** 3-8-9 ........................................................ DeanMcKeown 9 33
(HJCollingridge) *chsd ldrs 4f* **20/1**
**7** *½* **Weir's Annie** 3-8-9 ........................................................... DaneO'Neill 8 32
(HCandy) *chsd ldrs: rdn over 2f out: wknd over 1f out* **5/1**[2]
6 **8** *1* **Onyx**[41] [1127] 3-9-0 ............................................................. SRighton 1 34
(WDeBest-Turner) *led to 1/2-way: wknd 2f out* **66/1**
000- **9** *nk* **Sam The Sorcerer**[204] [5595] 3-9-0 ......................................... VHalliday 12 33
(JRNorton) *hld up: rdn and hung lft wl over 1f out: sn wknd* **100/1**
0 **10** *5* **Strides Of Fire (IRE)**[5] [1796] 3-9-0 ...................................(b[1]) RHavlin 6 18
(JHMGosden) *s.s: outpcd* **25/1**
**11** *6* **Petrolina (IRE)** 3-8-9 ............................................................ JMackay 3 —
(HMorrison) *s.i.s: sn pushed along in rr: wknd 1/2-way* **14/1**
1m 18.12s (3.32) **Going Correction** +0.55s/f (Yiel) **11** Ran SP% **116.8**
Speed ratings: **99,94,91,85,81 80,79,78,77,70 62**CSF £7.36 TOTE £1.70: £1.10, £2.50, £2.40; EX 9.10.
**Owner** Lady Davis **Bred** Raffin Bloodstock **Trained** East Everleigh, Wilts
**FOCUS**
A fair maiden, although the winner and second apart these were probably a moderate bunch. Although the stalls were on the stands' side, the field elected to race over on the far side.
**NOTEBOOK**
**Mission Man**, facing his easiest task to date, won pretty much as he liked. While he wasn't winning out of turn, he won't be that easy to place off his current mark.
**Indian Edge** looked a difficult ride and may not be one to place too much faith in.
**Kensington(IRE)** at least picked up some prize money, but achieved little in doing so.
**Rene Barbier(IRE)** had clearly learnt from his debut, but looks the type do better wheh he goes handicapping.
**Cunning Pursuit** found things happening too quickly for him over this trip.
**Strides Of Fire(IRE)**, colty throughout, is clearly a couple of stones too heavy at present. However, a similar effort will ensure he doesn't start life off on too stiff a mark when going handicapping.
*Official explanation: jockey said mount behaved in a coltish manner*

### 1943 EUROPEAN BREEDERS FUND NOVICE MEDIAN AUCTION FILLIES' STKS — 5f 13y
**3:05** (3:06) (F ) 2-Y-O — **£3,474** (£1,069; £534; £267) **Stalls High**

Form — RPR
0 **1** **Celtic Spa (IRE)**[11] [1670] 2-8-8 ............................................... RHavlin 4 80
(MrsPNDutfield) *s.i.s and bmpd s: sn prom: chal over 1f out : r.o to ld post* **11/2**[3]
1 **2** *hd* **Bright Moll**[38] [1183] 2-8-12 .................................................. IMongan 3 83
(MLWBell) *trckd ldr: led 1/2-way: rdn and hdd post* **4/11**[1]
**3** *5* **Castelletto** 2-8-8 .................................................................. GGibbons 1 62
(BAMcmahon) *s.i.s: sn led: hdd 1/2-way: outpcd fnl f* **9/2**[2]
**4** *10* **Monashee Miss** 2-8-8 ........................................................ DeanMcKeown 5 27
(JAPickering) *edgd lft s: chsd ldrs: hung lft and outpcd fr 1/2-way* **33/1**
64.67 secs (2.87) **Going Correction** +0.55s/f (Yiel) **4** Ran SP% **109.8**
Speed ratings: **99,98,90,74**CSF £8.40 TOTE £10.70; EX 7.10.
**Owner** Steve Evans **Bred** Miss A R Byrne **Trained** Axmouth, Devon
**FOCUS**
A steady early pace which only lifted at halfway, but the winning time was excellent for the type of race and this is fairly decent early-season fillies' form.
**NOTEBOOK**
**Celtic Spa(IRE)** had clearly learnt from her debut and showed a nice turn of foot to wear down the leader. Out of a mare that stayed seven furlongs, she should be capable of improvement as she steps up in trip.
**Bright Moll** may have done better had she gone for home a little earlier.
**Castelletto**, a sister to six winners including Lake Garda and Baby Barry, was easily left behind when the tempo picked up. She should certainly benefit from the experience, and better ground.
**Monashee Miss**, an early foal, is quite a lengthy filly and can only go one way.

### 1944 ROBIN HOOD H'CAP — 1m 1f 213y
**3:40** (3:40) (D ) (0-80,75) 3-Y-O+ — **£6,077** (£1,870; £935; £467) **Stalls Low**

Form — RPR
0/31 **1** **Pure Mischief (IRE)**[17] [1527] 5-8-4 **58**.................................... DAllan(3) 1 68
(WMBrisbourne) *s.i.s: sn prom: chsd ldr over 2f out: rdn to ld over 1f out: r.o* **2/1**[1]
2513 **2** *1* **Blazing The Trail (IRE)**[30] [1298] 4-9-1 **66**............................... SWhitworth 5 74
(JWHills) *sn led: rdn and hdd over 1f out: styd on* **7/2**[3]
2-01 **3** *1* **Olivia Rose (IRE)**[7] [1752] 5-9-0 **65** 6ex......................................... JMackay 6 71
(JPearce) *hld up: hdwy over 2f out: styd on same pce ins fnl f* **11/4**[2]
050- **4** *5* **Smart John**[286] [3601] 4-8-9 **60**.............................................. DaneO'Neill 2 58
(WMBrisbourne) *prom: rdn over 1f out: wknd fnl f* **13/2**
1005 **5** *13* **Karaoke (IRE)**[13] [1624] 4-9-3 **68**............................................ JDSmith 3 44
(SKirk) *trckd ldr: racd keenly: rdn over 2f out: sn wknd* **6/1**
2m 19.4s (9.90) **Going Correction** +1.25s/f (Soft) **5** Ran SP% **109.8**
Speed ratings: **110,109,108,104,94**CSF £9.18 TOTE £2.70: £1.10, £2.80; EX 9.60.
**Owner** The Cartmel Syndicate **Bred** T F Lacy **Trained** Great Ness, Shropshire
**FOCUS**
Officially a 0-80, it was really a 0-68. A slowly-run race.
**NOTEBOOK**
**Pure Mischief(IRE)** had his ideal conditions and confirmed what a progressive individual he is, despite not having the race run to suit.
**Blazing The Trail(IRE)** is probably better coming from off the pace, but he did battle on well when headed and should be able to find another opening.
**Olivia Rose(IRE)** had similar conditions to last week and wasn't disgraced under her penalty.
**Smart John**, having his first outing for current connections, just got tired and can be expected to step up on this.
**Karaoke(IRE)** was too keen for his own good, on ground which would have been soft enough for him.

### 1945 HBLB MAIDEN FILLIES' STKS — 1m 54y
**4:15** (4:16) (D ) 3-Y-O — **£4,979** (£1,532; £766; £383) **Stalls Low**

Form — RPR
0-6 **1** **Citrine Spirit (IRE)**[13] [1619] 3-8-11 ........................................ RHavlin 4 77
(JHMGosden) *chsd ldr: led over 3f out: rdn clr over 1f out* **13/8**[1]
00- **2** *6* **Dark Raider (IRE)**[184] [5923] 3-8-11 ..................................... SWhitworth 7 65
(APJones) *a.p: chsd wnr over 2f out: wknd over 1f out* **5/2**[2]
50- **3** *1 ¼* **Inmom (IRE)**[241] [4794] 3-8-11 ............................................... GBaker 3 63?
(SRBowring) *hld up: hdwy u.p over 1f out: styd on same pce fnl f* **6/1**
0-00 **4** *8* **Maria Maria (IRE)**[38] [1192] 3-8-11 ........................................ PMcCabe 2 47?
(MrsNMacauley) *sn led: hung lft over 4f out: hdd over 3f out: wknd 2f out* **33/1**
4 **5** *5* **Ses Seline**[4] [1822] 3-8-11 .............................................. DeanMcKeown 5 37
(JohnAHarris) *chsd ldrs: pushed along 6f out: bhd fr 1/2-way* **10/1**

00 **6** *9* **Golnessa**[25] 1366 3-8-11 ........ RFitzpatrick 1 19
(MrsNMacauley) *prom over 4f* **25/1**
**7** *8* **Crimson Star (IRE)** 3-8-11 ........ DaneO'Neill 6 3
(CTinkler) *prom over 4f* **4/1**[3]

1m 57.34s (10.94) **Going Correction** +1.25s/f (Soft) **7** Ran SP% **116.8**
Speed ratings: **95,89,87,79,74 65,57**CSF £6.15 TOTE £1.80: £1.10, £3.10; EX 6.30.
**Owner** Salem Suhail **Bred** Edward Lynam **Trained** Manton, Wilts

**FOCUS**
The going had become quite testing for the remaining races due to heavy rain after previous race. This event lacked strength in depth and was slowly run.

**NOTEBOOK**
**Citrine Spirit(IRE)** handled the ground better than her rivals and had little difficulty in winning a dire contest. At least she will be worth more now to breed with.
**Dark Raider(IRE)** is entitled to strip sharper for the run, especially as the ground had become quite testing. She should find easier pickings when she goes handicapping.
**Inmom(IRE)**, tackling by far her softest surface to date, had plenty to do turning for home, and deserves some credit for finishing as close as she did. She does have a little ability and should do better when going handicapping.
**Maria Maria(IRE)** at least showed a bit more here than on her previous starts, but once headed dropped away tamely and may not have been suited to the testing ground.
**Crimson Star(IRE)**, a half-sister to nine-furlong winner Storm Shower, got very tired in the ground, but is open to improvement.

## 1946 NOTTINGHAM RACECOURSE CONFERENCE CENTRE H'CAP 1m 1f 213y
**4:50** (4:51) (F) (0-55,55) 3-Y-O **£3,234** (£924; £462) **Stalls** Low

Form RPR
006- **1** **Ilwadod**[174] 6003 3-8-5 **46** oh1 ........ RLappin 7 62
(MRChannon) *hld up in tch: rdn over 3f out: led ins fnl f: r.o* **14/1**
0-40 **2** *1 1/2* **Pay Attention**[17] 1529 3-8-7 **51** ........ DAllan(3) 11 64
(TDEasterby) *trckd ldrs: led over 2f out: rdn over 1f out: hdd and unable qck ins fnl f* **7/1**[3]
0-00 **3** *6* **Strangely Brown (IRE)**[37] 1200 3-9-0 **55** ........ GCarter 12 58
(SCWilliams) *hld up: plld hrd: hdwy over 4f out: styd on u.p fr over 1f out* **4/1**[1]
5053 **4** *6* **Given A Chance**[3] 1874 3-7-12 **46** oh6 ........ RoryMoore(7) 9 39
(MrsSLamyman) *led over 7f: wknd over 1f out* **11/2**[2]
00-2 **5** *1 3/4* **Let It Be**[13] 1617 3-8-5 **46** oh1 ........ JMackay 10 36
(MrsMReveley) *chsd ldrs: rdn and ev ch 3f out: wknd wl over 1f out* **15/2**
2-60 **6** *hd* **Unintentional**[13] 1627 3-9-0 **55** ........ ADaly 16 44
(RBrotherton) *hld up: bhd 1/2-way: styd on u.p fnl 2f* **16/1**
6000 **7** *1* **Steppenwolf**[12] 1644 3-8-5 **46** oh1 ........ SRighton 4 34
(WDeBest-Turner) *chsd ldrs: rdn over 3f out: wknd 2f out* **50/1**
-063 **8** *1 1/4* **Summerise**[4] 1844 3-8-12 **53** ........ DeanMcKeown 6 38
(HJCollingridge) *s.i.s: hld up: styd on appr fnl f* **15/2**
0003 **9** *shd* **Atlantic Breeze**[8] 1740 3-8-5 **46** oh1 ........ (p) RFitzpatrick 15 31
(MrsNMacauley) *chsd ldrs: rdn over 3f out: wknd wl over 1f out* **10/1**
03-0 **10** *1 1/2* **Ctesiphon (USA)**[13] 1619 3-8-11 **52** ........ IMongan 2 35
(JGGiven) *sn pushd along in rr: n.d* **16/1**
000- **11** *shd* **Romeo's Day**[197] 5716 3-8-6 **54** ........ LHarman(7) 14 37
(MRChannon) *hld up: a in rr* **33/1**
00-0 **12** *2* **Rovella**[17] 1521 3-8-5 **46** oh6 ........ DKinsella 8 25
(MrsHDalton) *hld up: rdn over 2f out: n.d* **40/1**
0000 **13** *9* **Well Knit**[24] 1384 3-8-11 **55** ........ LPKeniry(3) 13 19
(PWD'Arcy) *hld up: a in rr* **12/1**
0604 **14** *12* **Mystic Moon**[17] 1529 3-9-0 **55** ........ SWhitworth 5 —
(JRJenkins) *s.i.s: hld up: rdn over 3f out: sn wknd* **10/1**
0-00 **15** *17* **Inchconnel**[24] 1387 3-9-0 **55** ........ VSlattery 3 —
(VSmith) *prom over 5f* **20/1**
00-0 **16** *1* **Cashema (IRE)**[18] 1507 3-9-0 **55** ........ RHavlin 1 —
(MrsPNDutfield) *s.i.s: hld up: rdn and wknd over 4f out* **10/1**

2m 21.12s (11.62) **Going Correction** +1.25s/f (Soft) **16** Ran SP% **136.9**
Speed ratings: **103,101,97,92,90 90,89,88,88,87 87,85,78,69,55 54**CSF £118.88 CT £489.70 TOTE £18.60: £5.30, £3.30, £1.50, £1.40; EX 319.20.
**Owner** Sheikh Ahmed Al Maktoum **Bred** Darley **Trained** West Ilsley, Berks

**FOCUS**
A poor contest full of mainly exposed sorts, but the front two finished nicely clear.

**NOTEBOOK**
**Ilwadod**, tackling handicappers for the first time, was still very green when asked to go about his work and should be open to any amount of improvement. *Official explanation: trainer's representative said gelding could have benefited from a wind operation over the winter*
**Pay Attention** didn't have things fall right for her last time, when there was no gallop. She had a bit more use made of her here, which clearly suited, and she should be able to pick up a similar contest.
**Strangely Brown(IRE)**, tackling both handicap company and his furthest trip to date, shaped as though an even stiffer test would have suited better still.
**Given A Chance**, who had quite a hard race in similar conditions earlier in the week, failed to get home and may have found this coming too soon.
**Let It Be** found conditions too testing for her and ended up having quite a hard race.
**Unintentional** was doing her best work in the closing stages and shapes as though she will stay much further.
**Summerise** *Official explanation: jockey said filly was unsuited by the heavy ground*
**Cashema(IRE)** *Official explanation: jockey said filly was unsuited by the soft ground*

## 1947 SAFFIE JOSEPH & SONS H'CAP 1m 6f 15y
**5:20** (5:20) (E) (0-70,73) 3-Y-O **£3,653** (£1,124; £562; £281) **Stalls** Low

Form RPR
-303 **1** **Crackleando**[9] 1714 3-8-4 **57** ........ StevenHarrison(7) 9 63
(NPLittmoden) *chsd ldr: led 8f out: styd towards far side ent st: rdn over 3f out: wandered over 1f out: all out* **9/1**
6511 **2** *1/2* **Bill Bennett (FR)**[4] 1843 3-9-13 **73** 6ex ........ GBaker 5 78
(JJay) *hld up: hdwy over 5f out: c stands' side ent st: rdn and hung lft fr over 2f out: nt clr run ins fnl f: kpt on* **7/4**[1]
-334 **3** *1* **Nocatee (IRE)**[80] 804 3-7-10 **49** ........ RoryMoore(7) 10 53
(PCHaslam) *hld up: hdwy 9f out: chsd wnr 6f out: c stands' side ent st: rdn and hung lft fr over 2f out: no ex nr fin* **8/1**[3]
00-5 **4** *10* **Over The Years (USA)**[21] 1450 3-7-12 **44** oh4 ........ JMackay 7 35
(TPTate) *rn in snatches: prom: lost pl over 5f out: c stands' side ent st: styd on u.p fnl 3f* **28/1**
4-02 **5** *5* **Holly Walk**[15] 1561 3-8-2 **48** ........ (b) GGibbons 1 33
(MDods) *trckd ldrs: plld hrd: c stands' side ent st: wknd 3f out* **10/1**
50-0 **6** *shd* **Northern Spirit**[20] 1465 3-8-7 **53** ........ PFessey 2 37
(KARyan) *hld up: effrt and c stands' side ent st: sn wknd* **16/1**
60-4 **7** *13* **Cadeaux Rouge (IRE)**[18] 1509 3-9-3 **63** ........ RHavlin 8 30
(MrsPNDutfield) *hld up in tch: c stands' side ent st: sn wknd* **9/1**
0000 **8** *dist* **La Concha (IRE)**[18] 1508 3-8-9 **55** ........ DaneO'Neill 6 —
(MrsLCJewell) *s.i.s: sn pushed along in rr: rdn 5f out: c stands' side and wknd ent st* **16/1**
50-0 **9** *29* **Spectested (IRE)**[25] 1365 3-8-12 **61** ........ LPKeniry(3) 3 —
(BJMeehan) *hld up: rdn 8f out: c stands' side and wknd ent st* **11/1**
4524 **10** *dist* **Valiant Air (IRE)**[8] 1740 3-7-13 **45** ........ AMcCarthy 4 —
(JRWeymes) *led 6f: wknd 6f out: t.o and c stands' side ent st* **4/1**[2]

3m 27.39s (20.19) **Going Correction** +1.25s/f (Soft) **10** Ran SP% **120.1**
Speed ratings: **92,91,91,85,82 82,75,—,—,—**CSF £25.88 CT £139.25 TOTE £11.30: £3.20, £1.10, £2.20; EX 63.10 Place 6 £77.45, Place 5 £32.41.
**Owner** The Headquarters Partnership Ltd **Bred** Stowell Hill Ltd **Trained** Newmarket, Suffolk
■ Stewards Enquiry : L P Keniry one-day ban: used whip when out of contention (May 18)

**FOCUS**
Not a strong race, and the front three apart, the field were strung out like washing on a line. The winner stayed towards the far side entering the straight, while the remainder went over to the stands' side.

**NOTEBOOK**
**Crackleando** proved well suited to this stiffer test, and although running on empty for much of the final two furlongs, stayed on bravely. He has a big heart and should win again in the right company.
**Bill Bennett(FR)** came into this in the form of his life and was far from disgraced under his big weight, on what had become really testing ground. This trip wasn't a problem for him, but he looked as though he would appreciate a better surface.
**Nocatee(IRE)** stayed this longer trip well enough, but lack of a recent outing caught him out in the closing stages. There will be other days for him.
**Over The Years(USA)** is a hard ride and looks as though he will stay forever. Some form of headgear could prove beneficial.
**Holly Walk** was always doing too much on the heels of the leaders and didn't give herself a chance of lasting home.
**Valiant Air(IRE)** *Official explanation: jockey said gelding became distressed on the heavy ground*
T/Plt: £163.00 to a £1 stake. Pool: £22,448.35. 100.50 winning tickets. T/Qpdt: £45.50 to a £1 stake. Pool: £1,028.90. 16.70 winning tickets. CR

1948 - 1951a (Foreign Racing) - See Raceform Interactive

# [1756]CHANTILLY (R-H)
Friday, May 7

**OFFICIAL GOING: Soft**

## 1952a PRIX ALLEZ FRANCE (GROUP 3) (F&M) 1m 2f
**2:00** (2:05) 4-Y-O+ **£25,704** (£10,282; £7,711; £5,141)

RPR
**1** **Pride (FR)**[15] 4-8-7 ........ DBonilla 5 107
(ADeRoyer-Dupre, France) *close up in 4th, edged right and bumped with Aubonne 2f out, switched left, hard ridden to lead 1f out, driven out*
**2** *1 1/2* **Russian Hill**[26] 1351 4-8-7 ........ GaryStevens 9 104
(AFabre, France) *led til headed 1f out, kept on, just held on for 2nd* 3
**3** *shd* **Samando (FR)**[33] 1261 4-8-9 ........ C-PLemaire 6 106
(FDoumen, France) *raced in 5th, stayed on well on outside from over 1f, nearest finish*
**4** *1 1/2* **Aubonne (GER)**[22] 4-8-9 ........ CSoumillon 11 103
(ELibaud, France) *raced keenly in 2nd, tracking leader when switched left and bumped by winner 2f out, switched right, no extra inside final* 2
**5** *snk* **Visorama (IRE)**[193] 5809 4-9-0 ........ TFarina 3 108
(AFabre, France) *raced in 7th, 6th straight, stayed on at same pace final 2f*
**6** *3/4* **Actrice (IRE)**[26] 1351 4-8-9 ........ DBoeuf 10 102
(ELellouche, France) *held up in 10th, effort on outside from 2f out, kept on at one pace* 1
**6** *dht* **Amathia (IRE)**[178] 5974 5-8-9 ........ TJarnet 4 102
(RGibson, France) *tracked leader in 3rd, remained prominent on inside til no extra final f*
**8** *nk* **Seraphine (GER)**[180] 5963 4-8-7 ........ ELegrix 8 99
(WHimmel, Germany) *held up in rear, 9th straight, stayed on final 2f but never near leaders*
**9** *nk* **Salydora (FR)**[26] 1351 4-8-7 ........ OPeslier 7 99
(MmeCHead-Maarek, France) *pulled hard early, raced in 8th, 7th straight, one pace final 2f*
**10** *2* **Fleurie Domaine**[33] 1259 5-8-9 ........ J-PCarvalho 1 97
(MarioHofer, Germany) *held up in last, always in rear*
**11** **Sweet Stream (ITY)**[170] 6035 4-8-7 ........ (b) TGillet 2 95
(JEHammond, France) *raced in 5th, 8th and weakening straight, tailed off final 2f*

2m 6.90s **Going Correction** +0.40s/f (Good) **11** Ran SP% **121.6**
Speed ratings: **115,113,113,112,112 111,111,111,111,109 109.**
**Owner** Np Bloodstock Ltd **Bred** Np Bloodstock Ltd **Trained** France

**NOTEBOOK**
**Pride(FR)** ran out a really good winner of her first Group event. Dropped in behind the leaders early on, she challenged for the lead a furlong and a half out and dominated the final 50 yards. There looks to be more improvement in her and she now goes on to the Prix Corrida.
**Russian Hill** tried to go from pillar to post at a sensible pace. She was taken on by the winner a furlong and a half out but could not quicken as the race came to an end, but she held on bravely to second place.
**Samando(FR)**, settled in sixth place early on, made a forward move halfway up the straight. She was brought with a run up the centre of the track and was putting in her best work at the end.
**Aubonne(GER)** had to be snatched up when challenging before the furlong marker and then ran on one-paced. Her jockey objected to the winner but the Stewards left the result unchanged.

# JAGERSRO (R-H)
Thursday, May 6

**OFFICIAL GOING: Fast**

## 1953a SYDSVENSKAN SPRINT (LISTED) 6f
**7:15** (7:23) 3-Y-O+ **£18,634** (£6,211; £3,106; £1,941)

RPR
**1** **Glad To Be Fast (IRE)**[172] 6009 4-9-6 ........ ASuborics 3 —
(MarioHofer, Germany) 1
**2** *1* **Damachida (IRE)**[208] 5487 5-9-6 ........ KAndersen 7 —
(EvaSundbye, Sweden) 2
**3** *nse* **Hide And Seek (SWE)**[364] 1477 8-9-6 ........ P-AGraberg 1 —
(HLundell, Sweden)
**4** *3* **Waquaas**[235] 4928 8-9-6 ........ FJohansson 8 —
(RoyArneKvisla, Sweden)
**5** *shd* **Rex (IRE)**[364] 1477 7-9-6 ........ (b) PJarven 11 —
(FCastro, Sweden)

6 9 **Just Michael**[364] 1477 5-9-6 .................... NCordrey 2 —
(TPersson, Sweden)
7 hd **Grey Pearl**[24] 1372 5-9-2 .................... (b) FLynch 6 —
(MissGayKelleway) *broke well, led to 2f out, gradually weakened*
8 3 **Without Notice (USA)** 4-9-6 .................... (b) JJohansen 9 —
(LReuterskiold, Sweden)
9 hd **Ardbeg (IRE)** 5-9-6 .................... YvonneDurant 4 —
(FCastro, Sweden)
10 ½ **Steve's Champ (CHI)**[313] 4-9-6 .................... FDiaz 5 —
(RuneHaugen, Norway) 3

1m 12.5s **10** Ran SP% **125.6**
Speed ratings: .
**Owner** Stall Jenny **Bred** Gestut Romerhof **Trained** Germany

**NOTEBOOK**
**Grey Pearl** showed up well for most of the journey, but her early exertions took their toll late on. She is not up to this class.

## 1954a PRAMMS MEMORIAL (LISTED) 1m 120y
7:40 (7:55) 4-Y-0+ **£46,583** (£15,528; £7,764; £4,658)

RPR
1 **Vortex**[19] 1456 5-9-6 .................... NCordrey 7 —
(MissGayKelleway) *mid-division, moved up to third at half-way, led 1f out, just held on*
2 hd **Mandrake El Mago (CHI)**[235] 4926 5-9-6 .................... MSantos 3 —
(FCastro, Sweden) 1
3 8½ **Organizer (NOR)**[270] 4038 4-9-6 .................... FJohansson 10 —
(WidoNeuroth, Norway) 3
4 3½ **Rotulo (ARG)**[61] 974 6-9-6 .................... (b) GSolis 8 —
(DiegoLowther, Sweden)
5 1½ **Hanzano (IRE)**[228] 6-9-6 .................... KAndersen 11 —
(AreHyldmo, Norway)
6 hd **Honeysuckle Player (SWE)**[235] 4926 6-9-6 .......... (b) YvonneDurant 5 —
(FReuterskiold, Sweden)
7 1½ **Te Quiero**[31] 1273 6-9-6 .................... FLynch 1 —
(MissGayKelleway) *missed break, soon in mid-division, beaten 2f out*
8 ½ **Cabriac**[364] 1476 7-9-6 .................... MLarsen 4 —
(CarolineStromberg)
9 1 **Caluki**[47] 1062 7-9-6 .................... DVargiu 12 —
(LCamici, Italy) 2
10 1 **Buffalo Boy (IRE)** 6-9-6 .................... FDiaz 6 —
(BNeuman, Sweden)
11 4½ **Jubilation**[197] 5-9-6 .................... (b) LHammer-Hansen —
(NLindgren, Sweden)
12 7 **Capital Secret (USA)**[193] 5779 7-9-6 .................... ASuborics 2 —
(MarioHofer, Germany)

1m 49.0s **12** Ran SP% **127.1**
Speed ratings: .
**Owner** Coriolis Partnership **Bred** Juddmonte Farms **Trained** Newmarket, Suffolk

**NOTEBOOK**
**Vortex** was given a great ride by local pilot Cordrey. Always close up, he hit the front a furlong out and, much like in the Wolverhampton Lincoln Trial, looked set for a comfy win only for things to get very tight in the last few yards. An American campaign is now a possibility, with the Royal Hunt Cup as an alternative.
**Te Quiero** was scuppered as soon as he missed the break, as he never faced up to the kickback thereafter.

# 1556 BEVERLEY (R-H)
### Saturday, May 8

**OFFICIAL GOING: Heavy**
Weather: overcast

## 1955 COACHMAN CARAVANS CONDITIONS STKS 5f
1:50 (1:51) (C) 3-Y-0+ **£12,064** (£4,576; £2,288; £1,040) **Stalls** High

Form RPR
1442 1 **Bahamian Pirate (USA)**[7] 1759 9-9-2 108 .................... KDarley 5 110
(DNicholls) *trckd ldrs: effrt appr fnl f: r.o to ld last strides* **9/4**[1]
53-1 2 hd **Bishops Court**[22] 1438 10-9-9 111 .................... ACulhane 8 116
(MrsJRRamsden) *trckd ldrs: led 1f out: hrd rdn and edgd lft: jst ct* **10/3**[3]
0-00 3 5 **Vita Spericolata (IRE)**[1] 1923 7-8-7 86 .................... RWinston 3 85
(JSWainwright) *led tl hdd 1f out: fdd* **22/1**
4-02 4 1½ **Halmahera (IRE)**[21] 1471 9-8-12 102 .................... (b) NCallan 4 86
(KARyan) *trckd ldrs: effrt over 1f out: sn hung lft and wknd* **5/2**[2]
605- 5 6 **Tedburrow**[279] 3809 12-8-12 95 .................... WSupple 2 68
(EJAlston) *hld up: effrt over 2f out: rdn and wknd over 1f out* **20/1**
0-60 6 2½ **Colonel Cotton (IRE)**[7] 1763 5-9-9 109 .................... TEDurcan 6 71
(NACallaghan) *s.i.s: nvr on terms* **6/1**
44-0 7 5 **Rosselli (USA)**[6] 1787 8-8-7 46 .................... PBradley(5) 1 45
(ABerry) *chsd ldrs on outer: lost pl over 2f out* **200/1**
500- 8 dist **Absent Friends**[196] 5743 7-9-5 98 .................... JEdmunds 7 —
(JBalding) *chsd ldr: lost pl over 2f out: sn bhd: virtually p.u: t.o* **20/1**

67.21 secs (3.21) **Going Correction** +0.85s/f (Soft) **8** Ran SP% **111.1**
Speed ratings: **108,107,99,97,87 83,75,—**CSF £9.21 TOTE £3.00: £1.40, £1.10, £5.00; EX 11.50.
**Owner** Lucayan Stud **Bred** Trackside Farm & Liberation Farm & G A Seelbinder **Trained** Sessay, N Yorks

**FOCUS**
After overnight rain the ground was described as 'heavy and very testing'. This was a decent conditions sprint.

**NOTEBOOK**
**Bahamian Pirate(USA)**, a moderate mover, proved suited by the underfoot conditions. The opening came at just the right time and he nailed the runner-up near the line.
**Bishops Court**, third in this twice before, had the plum draw and travelled strongly. After being sent on he idled slightly and was just worried out of it. Ideally he needs hanging on to a bit longer.
**Vita Spericolata(IRE)**, who ran at Chester the previous day, showed all her old speed to lead from a draw just two from the outside. She doesn't want the ground anywhere near as soft as this and, dying in front, contributed to Bishops Court's demise.
**Halmahera(IRE)**, best in on official figures, had the blinkers back on. He got in the way of the winner before dropping away and these days probably prefers much better ground.
**Tedburrow**, now a veteran, has not been at his best for the last two seasons.
**Colonel Cotton(IRE)** missed the break slightly and never fired in this bad ground.

## 1956 LEISURE FURNISHINGS SPRINT (A RATED H'CAP) 5f
2:20 (2:21) (D) (0-80,82) 3-Y-0+ **£7,711** (£2,925; £1,462; £664) **Stalls** High

Form RPR
-002 1 **Artie**[7] 1774 5-9-5 75 .................... DaleGibson 18 89
(TDEasterby) *mde all far side: styd on strly fnl f* **7/2**[1]
0-30 2 3½ **Catch The Cat (IRE)**[12] 1665 5-8-12 68 .................... (b) RWinston 13 72
(JSWainwright) *racd far side: hdwy to chse wnr 2f out: nt qckn fnl f* **7/1**[3]
0100 3 1 **Marabar**[4] 1872 6-8-2 63 oh3 .................... (b) BSwarbrick(5) 16 64
(DWChapman) *racd far side: bhd: hdwy on ins 2f out: edgd lft and styd on strongly fnl f* **50/1**
00-0 4 2 **Paddywack (IRE)**[12] 1665 7-9-0 70 .................... (b) ACulhane 20 65
(DWChapman) *racd far side: mid-div: hdwy over 2f out: kpt on* **10/1**
5114 5 2½ **Raymond's Pride**[7] 1774 4-9-7 82 .................... (b) TEaves(5) 15 69
(KARyan) *racd far side: mid-div: kpt on same pce fnl 2f* **9/2**[2]
0-62 6 nk **Karminskey Park**[4] 1872 5-8-7 63 oh1 .................... OUrbina 9 49
(TJEtherington) *racd far side towards centre: chsd ldrs: outpcd fnl 2f* **12/1**
5500 7 1¼ **Sharp Hat**[36] 1230 10-8-8 64 .................... MFenton 10 46
(DWChapman) *racd far side: chsd ldrs: fdd over 1f out* **50/1**
351- 8 2 **Misaro (GER)**[184] 5929 3-8-11 79 .................... DNolan(3) 12 55
(PABlockley) *mid-div: effrt over 2f out: nvr nr ldrs* **50/1**
0210 9 nk **Mynd**[7] 1774 4-8-10 66 .................... DeanMcKeown 11 41
(RMWhitaker) *racd far side: in tch: effrt over 2f out: no hdwy* **12/1**
000- 10 ¾ **Prince Pyramus**[339] 2110 6-8-7 63 oh18 .................... TEDurcan 6 36
(CGrant) *racd far side: bhd tl kpt on fnl 2f* **100/1**
-065 11 1¼ **Awake**[17] 1537 7-9-1 71 .................... ANicholls 1 40
(DNicholls) *led other three on stands' side: rdn 2f out: eased whn no ch w far side ins last* **9/1**
0-01 12 1¼ **Grey Cossack**[26] 1361 7-9-10 80 .................... GParkin 14 46
(PTMidgley) *racd far side: sn outpcd and bhd: nvr on terms* **7/1**[3]
650- 13 hd **Candleriggs (IRE)**[322] 2574 8-9-2 72 .................... AlexGreaves 19 37
(DNicholls) *racd far side: sn outpcd and in rr* **16/1**
000- 14 5 **Sir Sandrovitch (IRE)**[185] 5924 8-8-4 63 oh3 .................... THamilton(3) 17 13
(RAFahey) *racd far side: hld up in rr* **28/1**
0234 15 ¾ **Soaked**[33] 1262 11-8-7 63 oh3 .................... (b) JBramhill 8 11
(DWChapman) *racd far side: chsd ldrs: lost pl over 2f out* **50/1**
00-4 16 5 **Consensus (IRE)**[44] 1106 5-9-10 80 .................... TWilliams 7 13
(MBrittain) *racd far side: chsd ldrs on outer: lost pl over 2f out: eased* **25/1**
0041 17 10 **Frascati**[30] 1319 4-9-1 71 .................... FLynch 3 —
(ABerry) *racd stands' side: chsd ldr: rdn over 2f out: sn btn* **33/1**
5-04 18 5 **Queen Of Night**[23] 1423 4-8-9 70 .................... PMakin(5) 2 —
(DWChapman) *unruly in stalls: rrd s: racd stands' side: sn chsng ldr: lost pl over 2f out* **40/1**
-030 19 3½ **Piccled**[27] 1343 6-9-5 78 .................... DAllan(3) 4 —
(EJAlston) *racd stands' side: sn outpcd and bhd: eased* **28/1**

67.80 secs (3.80) **Going Correction** +0.85s/f (Soft)
**WFA** 3 from 4yo+ 9lb **19** Ran SP% **130.7**
Speed ratings: **103,97,95,92,88 88,86,82,82,81 79,77,76,68,67 59,43,35,30**CSF £26.91 CT £1113.24 TOTE £5.40: £1.90, £2.00, £9.00, £2.10; EX 41.70.
**Owner** A Arton **Bred** Mrs D Ellis **Trained** Great Habton, N Yorks

**FOCUS**
As usual the draw played a pivotal part.

**NOTEBOOK**
**Artie**, 5lb lower than for his last success at York at three, likes the ground and had a plum draw. This will have done his confidence a power of good.
**Catch The Cat(IRE)**, who likes it here, was well supported in the betting ring and he ran a blinder to finish second best from stall 13. His very best form has been on much less testing ground.
**Marabar**, beaten out of sight on this ground just four days earlier, was in one of her going moods and made up many lengths on the first two late on. She too had a favourable draw.
**Paddywack(IRE)**, best drawn, ran a lot better and will no doubt pay his way again this year.
**Raymond's Pride** had a good draw but he is high enough in the ratings now.
**Karminskey Park**, making a quick return to action, deserves credit for this good effort from a single figure draw. She deserves a third career win.
**Awake**, drawn one, dominated throughout against the other three who chose the stands'-side route, but his cause was a lost one even before the final furlong.

## 1957 POWERPART H'CAP 1m 100y
2:55 (2:55) (E) (0-75,75) 3-Y-0 **£4,940** (£1,520; £760; £380) **Stalls** High

Form RPR
-522 1 **Charmatic (IRE)**[8] 1755 3-8-8 62 .................... DeanMcKeown 17 70
(JAGlover) *led tl over 2f out: led jst ins fnl f: kpt on wl* **5/1**[2]
-121 2 ½ **Riley Boys (IRE)**[8] 1755 3-9-1 69 .................... MFenton 14 76
(JGGiven) *trckd wnr: slt ld over 2f out: hdd jst ins last: no ex* **7/2**[1]
30-3 3 shd **Mystical Girl (USA)**[30] 1309 3-9-5 73 .................... KDalgleish 16 80
(MJohnston) *chsd ldrs: rdn over 2f out: styd on towards fin* **11/2**[3]
523- 4 3 **Silverhay**[186] 5915 3-8-9 68 .................... PMakin(5) 6 73+
(TDBarron) *mid-div: styd on strly appr fnl f: improve* **22/1**
00-4 5 1½ **Trojan Flight**[22] 1453 3-9-1 69 .................... ACulhane 9 67
(MrsJRRamsden) *sn trcking ldrs on ins: effrt over 2f out: kpt on same pce* **7/1**
106- 6 1½ **Futoo (IRE)**[193] 5822 3-8-9 63 .................... NPollard 15 58
(GMMoore) *chsd ldrs: rdn over 2f out: one pce* **33/1**
0-66 7 ¾ **Orion Express**[24] 1392 3-8-6 65 .................... PMulrennan(5) 10 58
(MWEasterby) *dwlt: swtchd rt s: hdwy over 4f out: sn chsng ldrs: fdd over 1f out* **12/1**
034- 8 3½ **Jerome**[248] 4664 3-9-4 75 .................... DAllan(3) 7 61
(TDEasterby) *in tch: effrt over 2f out: nvr rchd ldrs* **50/1**
-100 9 9 **Glendale**[23] 1414 3-8-8 62 .................... JDSmith 12 30
(CADwyer) *bhd: sme hdwy over 2f out: nvr a factor* **40/1**
0-30 10 1 **Charlie Tango (IRE)**[37] 1222 3-9-2 70 .................... TEDurcan 4 36
(MRChannon) *hld up in rr: sme hdwy on wd outside over 2f out: nvr a factor* **20/1**
6-43 11 ½ **Evaluator (IRE)**[8] 1755 3-9-4 72 .................... KDarley 1 37
(TGMills) *rr-div: effrt on outer over 2f out: nvr on terms* **8/1**
0151 12 5 **Mission Affirmed (USA)**[23] 1427 3-9-0 68 .................... DaleGibson 8 23
(TPTate) *rr-div: effrt over 4f out: nvr a factor* **10/1**
-600 13 2 **Mr Midasman (IRE)**[8] 1755 3-8-12 66 .................... WSupple 5 17
(RHollinshead) *bhd: sme hdwy over 4f out: nvr on terms* **33/1**
30-0 14 1 **Dark Day Blues (IRE)**[23] 1418 3-9-1 69 .................... PHanagan 13 18
(MDHammond) *sn in tch: effrt over 2f out: sn lost pl* **25/1**
000- 15 hd **Gallas (IRE)**[252] 4583 3-8-10 64 .................... (v[1]) RWinston 11 13
(JSWainwright) *dwlt: a bhd* **50/1**

 

05-2 **16** *14* **Fossgate**[23] 1420 3-9-6 **74** ........ CCatlin 3 —
(JDBethell) *a in rr: eased* **28/1**

1m 54.93s (7.63) **Going Correction** +1.15s/f (Soft) **16** Ran SP% **123.3**
Speed ratings: **107,106,106,103,101 100,99,96,87,86 85,80,78,77,77 63**CSF £20.34 CT £96.84 TOTE £6.50: £1.90, £1.10, £1.70, £4.90; EX 13.80.
**Owner** Advanced Brickwork Ltd **Bred** Patsy Byrne **Trained** Carburton, Notts

**FOCUS**
A decent time for the grade. The first two basically reproduced their Nottingham form. The first three were all well drawn and were the first three throughout.

**NOTEBOOK**
**Charmatic(IRE)**, marginally better off with Rileys Boys, had the best draw of all. She was given a canny ride, never leaving the rail, and in the end did just enough. She will stay further and might even prefer better ground than she encountered here.
**Riley Boys(IRE)**, on the outside of the winner throughout, went a neck up but in the end came off just second best.
**Mystical Girl(USA)**, the first of the first three to come under serious pressure, picked up best very late in the day and is worth a try over a bit further.
**Silverhay** ◆, progressive in three starts at two, had a single figure draw. He picked up in good style late on and is open to a fair amount of improvement. He is well worth keeping on the right side.
**Trojan Flight**, stepping up in trip on his handicap bow, overcame a single figure draw and was soon on the heels of the winner racing against the running rail. He did not truly see the trip out in these testing conditions.
**Futoo(IRE)**, whose sole win at two was on easy ground, had a good draw.
**Glendale** *Official explanation: trainer said gelding lost a shoe during the race.*

## 1958 C.G.I. STAYERS H'CAP 2m 35y
**3:25** (3:25) (E) (0-75,75) 4-Y-0+ **£4,654** (£1,432; £716; £358) **Stalls** High

Form RPR
14-0 **1** **Dr Sharp (IRE)**[14] 1615 4-9-6 **70** ........ DaleGibson 12 83
(TPTate) *trckd ldrs on ins: led 2f out: kpt on wl fnl f* **10/1**
03-1 **2** *3 ½* **Great As Gold (IRE)**[7] 1501 5-8-13 **60** ........(p) RWinston 14 69
(BEllison) *chsd ldrs: sn pushed along: chal 2f out: nt qckn fnl f* **9/4**[1]
1-02 **3** *7* **The Ring (IRE)**[14] 1615 4-9-8 **72** ........ KDarley 15 74
(MrsMReveley) *hld up in mid-div: hdwy 5f out: n.m.r over 2f out: kpt on same pce* **11/4**[2]
-334 **4** *6* **Ocean Tide**[30] 1316 7-10-0 **75** ........(v) KDalgleish 11 71
(RFord) *led tl 2f out: wknd over 1f out* **8/1**[3]
0/4- **5** *7* **Il Cavaliere**[49] 5258 9-9-2 **63** ........ JCarroll 3 52
(MrsMReveley) *hld up and bhd: sme hdwy 3f out: nvr a factor* **20/1**
3005 **6** *7* **Northern Nymph**[8] 1754 5-9-2 **68** ........ StephanieHollinshead(5) 1 50
(RHollinshead) *hld up and bhd: sme hdwy over 4f out: wknd over 2f out* **25/1**
650- **7** *21* **Kaparolo (USA)**[31] 3685 5-9-7 **68** ........ WSupple 2 29
(MrsAJPerrett) *chsd ldrs: wknd over 1f out: eased ins last* **10/1**
0130 **8** *1 ½* **Madhahir (IRE)**[8] 1754 4-8-12 **62** ........ MFenton 4 22
(CADwyer) *chsd ldrs: lost pl over 2f out* **20/1**
4-30 **9** *6* **Ringside Jack**[10] 1326 8-8-3 **50** ........ GGibbons 9 4
(CWFairhurst) *chsd ldrs: lost pl over 2f out: eased* **8/1**[3]
0-00 **10** *4* **The Persuader (IRE)**[24] 1401 4-9-10 **74** ........ RFfrench 10 24
(MJohnston) *chsd ldrs: outpcd over 4f out: wknd 2f out: eased* **10/1**
-561 **11** *9* **Galandora**[18] 1534 4-7-7 **50** ow1 ........ LucyRussell(7) 13 —
(DrJRJNaylor) *a towards rr: bhd fnl 3f* **16/1**

3m 56.23s (16.83) **Going Correction** +1.15s/f (Soft) **11** Ran SP% **126.2**
**WFA** 4 from 5yo+ 3lb
Speed ratings: **103,101,97,94,91 87,77,76,73,71 67**CSF £34.36 CT £85.08 TOTE £14.10: £4.00, £1.30, £1.60; EX 58.90.
**Owner** The Ivy Syndicate **Bred** Mrs Ann Fortune **Trained** Tadcaster, N Yorks

**FOCUS**
Not a strongly-run race, but a severe test of stamina in the conditions and they came in well strung out. The form looks sound.

**NOTEBOOK**
**Dr Sharp(IRE)**, who loves the mud, was given a canny ride. Tucked away on the heels of the leaders, the gap on the inside came at just the right moment and in the end he won going away.
**Great As Gold(IRE)**, 5lb higher than Pontefract, has since been seen out over hurdles. He was soon being pushed along, and though in the end he was clear second best he was never going to trouble the winner. Severe tests of stamina bring out the very best in him.
**The Ring(IRE)** had to check for a few strides when on the heels of the leaders with over two furlongs left to run. When called on for a serious effort he was soon going up and down in the same place. The heavy ground was not in his favour.
**Ocean Tide**, allowed to set just his own pace, was readily brushed aside and at the line he was a tired horse.
**Il Cavaliere**, who these days usually plies his trade under National Hunt rules, stayed on up the final hill but was never a factor.

## 1959 WANDERER (S) STKS 1m 1f 207y
**4:00** (4:00) (F) 3-Y-0 **£3,076** (£879; £439) **Stalls** High

Form RPR
0403 **1** **Ciacole**[19] 1499 3-8-7 50 ........ DeanMcKeown 6 48
(RonaldThompson) *led tl 5f out: led over 2f out: all out* **11/4**[2]
0-P0 **2** *1 ½* **Argent**[38] 1201 3-8-5 58 ........ DTudhope(7) 1 50
(DCarroll) *w ldr: led 5f out tl 3f out: no ex ins last* **4/1**[3]
-400 **3** *nk* **Bonjour Bond (IRE)**[5] 1843 3-8-12 62 ........(b[1]) DMcGaffin 2 50+
(BSmart) *trckd ldrs: drvn along over 4f out: styd on appr fnl f: nt clr run wl ins last* **7/1**
6644 **4** *5* **Bretton**[9] 1736 3-8-12 45 ........(b) DaleGibson 5 41
(RHollinshead) *plld hrd in rr: effrt over 3f out: sn hrd drvn: nvr rchd ldrs* **7/1**
000- **5** *4* **Warif (USA)**[161] 6087 3-8-12 ........ RFfrench 4 35
(EJO'Neill) *hld up: hdwy over 5f out: rdn over 3f out: hung rt: wknd over 1f out* **2/1**[1]
000 **6** *dist* **Baroque**[21] 1466 3-8-12 ........ RWinston 3 —
(CSmith) *chsd ldrs: pushed along 7f out: lost pl over 4f out: t.o 2f out* **25/1**

2m 22.31s (15.11) **Going Correction** +1.15s/f (Soft) **6** Ran SP% **108.8**
Speed ratings: **85,83,83,79,76** —CSF £13.12 TOTE £3.40: £1.10, £3.70; EX 13.30.There was no bid for the winner. Argent was claimed by Miss L.Perrett for £6,000.
**Owner** B Bruce **Bred** Hesmonds Stud Ltd **Trained** Stainforth, S Yorks

**FOCUS**
A pedestrian time for the grade, and they seemed to be in slow motion in the closing stages.

**NOTEBOOK**
**Ciacole** broke her duck at her ninth attempt for her third yard. She is at least willing but they don't come worse than this.
**Argent** went a neck up but after a dire war of attrition came off just second best. He took Linda Perratt's eye and now heads for Scotland.
**Bonjour Bond(IRE)**, bred for speed, wore blinkers for the first time and was having his second outing in five days after being reported to have a breathing problem. Trying for a run up the inner, he bounced off the rail and looked second best on merit.
**Bretton**, off the boil of late on the All-Weather, gave himself little chance, refusing point blank to settle.
**Warif(USA)**, who showed a glimmer of form in three starts in better company at two, was flat out at the foot of the hill and he seemed reluctant to go forward in a straight line.

## 1960 COACHMAN AMARA MEDIAN AUCTION MAIDEN STKS (DIV I) 5f
**4:30** (4:32) (E) 2-Y-0 **£4,472** (£1,376; £688; £344) **Stalls** High

Form RPR
**1** **Melalchrist** 2-9-0 ........ PHanagan 7 72
(JJQuinn) *cmpt: in tch: gd hdwy appr fnl f: str run to ld last 50yds* **14/1**
**2** *1 ¼* **Tagula Bay (IRE)** 2-8-6 ........ DAllan(3) 6 63
(TDEasterby) *leggy: scope:chsd ldrs: led over 1f out: hdd and no ex clsng stages* **14/1**
42 **3** *3* **Langston Boy**[14] 1607 2-9-0 ........ IMongan 12 57
(MLWBell) *led after 1f: hdd over 1f out: wknd ins last* **6/4**[1]
4 **4** *shd* **Bond Finesse (IRE)**[9] 1717 2-8-9 ........ FLynch 8 52
(BSmart) *in tch: hdwy 2f out: edgd lft 1f out: styd on same pce* **5/1**[3]
**5** *2* **Dixie Queen (IRE)** 2-8-6 ........ LEnstone(3) 10 45
(MDods) *cmpt: led 1f: w ldrs: wknd approching fnl f* **11/1**
**6** *shd* **Ming Vase** 2-8-7 ........ DTudhope(7) 11 49
(DCarroll) *leggy: scope: rn green and sn bhd: hdwy over 1f out: styd on ins last* **25/1**
**7** *3 ½* **Desert Buzz (IRE)** 2-9-0 ........ MTebbutt 4 37
(JHetherton) *leggy: unf: s.i.s: sme hdwy over 2f out: wknd over 1f out* **50/1**
**8** *1 ½* **Timmy** 2-8-9 ........ TEaves(5) 5 32
(MESowersby) *unf: chsd ldrs over 2f: sn lost pl* **33/1**
2 **9** *6* **Story Of One (IRE)**[16] 1556 2-9-0 ........ KDarley 9 11
(NPLittmoden) *w ldrs: lost pl over 2f out* **5/2**[2]
4 **10** *½* **Vision Victory (GER)**[18] 1523 2-9-0 ........ DaleGibson 2 9
(TPTate) *outpcd and lost pl after 2f* **16/1**
4 **11** *1* **Favouring (IRE)**[30] 1314 2-8-11 ........ THamilton(3) 1 —
(RAFahey) *dwlt: a in rr* **14/1**
**12** *5* **Miller Hill** 2-9-0 ........ TLucas 3 —
(MWEasterby) *unf: unruly and uns rdr in paddock: s.s: sme hdwy on outer over 2f out: sn lost pl and bhd* **33/1**

1m 11.82s (7.82) **Going Correction** +1.275s/f (Soft) **12** Ran SP% **131.1**
Speed ratings: **88,86,81,81,77 77,72,69,60,59 57,49**CSF £207.73 TOTE £16.60: £3.40, £4.00, £1.50; EX 363.50.
**Owner** T G S Wood **Bred** A C M Spalding **Trained** Settrington, N Yorks

**FOCUS**
A modest time for the class, 1.29 seconds slower than the second division.

**NOTEBOOK**
**Melalchrist**, a January foal, is a close-coupled type. He really picked up the bridle inside the last and in the end won going away. It was a modest event, much slower than the second division, but he will go on from here.
**Tagula Bay(IRE)**, a February foal, is on the leg. She took it up looking nailed on but in the end had no answer to the winner's finishing burst. She will appreciate less-testing ground and should improve and find a race.
**Langston Boy**, the clear paddock pick, had the plum draw but after showing ahead he completely failed to get home. He is well worth another chance on much better ground.
**Bond Finesse(IRE)** broke on terms this time, but in the ground came off a straight line.
**Dixie Queen(IRE)**, a February foal, is a sharp sort. She had a high draw and showed bags of toe until tiring. She is capable of better in less-testing conditions.
**Ming Vase**, noisy in the paddock, unseated his rider on the way down to the start. He was clueless but showed some promise, picking up nicely late in the day. This will have taught him a fair bit.
**Story Of One(IRE)**, having his first outing since being claimed, showed speed but dropped right out at the halfway mark. His new connections must have been hoping for a lot better effort.

## 1961 COACHMAN AMARA MEDIAN AUCTION MAIDEN STKS (DIV II) 5f
**5:05** (5:05) (E) 2-Y-0 **£4,472** (£1,376; £688; £344) **Stalls** High

Form RPR
**1** **Royal Island (IRE)** 2-9-0 ........ KDalgleish 10 87+
(MJohnston) *w'like: cmpt: led 1f: led over 2f out: rdn clr 1f out* **4/1**[3]
**2** *8* **Skippit John** 2-9-0 ........ DeanMcKeown 11 59
(RonaldThompson) *cmpt: sn outpcd: hdwy 2f out: styd on to go 2nd last 100yds* **14/1**
**3** *½* **Obe Gold** 2-9-0 ........ TEDurcan 5 57
(MRChannon) *leggy: unf: s.i.s: bhd: hdwy 2f out: kpt on ins last* **10/3**[2]
**4** *2* **Lady Dan (IRE)** 2-8-9 ........ TLucas 6 45
(MWEasterby) *neat: in tch: hdwy to chse wnr appr fnl f: fdd ins last* **25/1**
3 **5** *6* **Paris Bell**[26] 1359 2-8-11 ........ DAllan(3) 3 29
(TDEasterby) *led after 1f tl over 2f out: wknd appr fnl f* **3/1**[1]
6 **6** *1 ½* **Joe Jo Star**[21] 1462 2-8-11 ........ DNolan(3) 7 24
(PABlockley) *chsd ldrs: wknd over 1f out* **9/2**
**7** *5* **Niteowl Lad (IRE)** 2-8-7 ........ JDO'Reilly(7) 2 7
(JO'Reilly) *lengthy: unf: uns rdr gng to s: s.s: sme hdwy on outside over 2f out: hung rt and sn lost pl* **25/1**
0 **8** *3 ½* **Fantasy Defender (IRE)**[28] 1324 2-9-0 ........ PHanagan 4 —
(JJQuinn) *sn chsng ldrs: wknd fnl 2f* **14/1**
0 **9** *½* **Hunipot**[16] 1556 2-8-9 ........ GParkin 8 —
(MESowersby) *chsd ldrs: lost pl over 2f out* **50/1**
**10** *29* **La Bella Rosa (IRE)** 2-8-6 ........ LEnstone(3) 1 —
(JSWainwright) *leggy: s.i.s: a bhd: lost tch and eased* **25/1**

1m 10.53s (6.53) **Going Correction** +1.275s/f (Soft) **10** Ran SP% **113.1**
Speed ratings: **98,85,84,81,71 69,61,55,54,8**CSF £52.66 TOTE £4.30: £2.00, £2.50, £2.10; EX 36.50.
**Owner** Markus Graff **Bred** Mrs Bill O'Neill **Trained** Middleham Moor, N Yorks

**FOCUS**
A good time for the grade, 1.29 seconds faster than the first division, and a potentially very useful winner.

**NOTEBOOK**
**Royal Island(IRE)** ◆, a late-April foal, is a sturdy type. Noisy in the paddock, he certainly knew his job and, very professional, his rider kept him up to his work in the bad ground. Likely to be even better suited by six, he looks a bright prospect.
**Skippit John**, a bargain-basement buy, lacks size and scope. Making ground from the back, he never left the far rail.
**Obe Gold**, a March foal, lost ground at the start and was last of all after two furlongs. He grasped the nettle late on and this will have taught him plenty.
**Lady Dan(IRE)**, a February foal, is on the small side and looked backward in her coat. Her prominent showing underlines the lack of opposition facing the winner.
**Paris Bell**, well backed, showed bags of toe but, after taking charge, in this ground he rather fell in a heap. He had clearly been showing something better at home and is well worth another chance in less-testing conditions.

**Joe Jo Star** didn't show the same amount of ability this time on totally different ground.

## 1962 COACHMAN VIP LADY AMATEUR RIDERS' H'CAP — 1m 1f 207y

**5:35** (5:35) (E ) (0-70,69) 3-Y-0+ **£3,757** (£1,156; £578; £289) **Stalls** High

Form RPR

0045 **1** **Yenaled**[6] [1783] 7-9-12 **56** MissNCarberry(3) 11 71
(KARyan) *hld up: stdy hdwy over 2f out: led 1f out: pushed clr ins last* **7/1**[2]

5451 **2** 3 1/2 **Melodian**[19] [1503] 9-10-7 **62** (b) MsCWilliams 7 71
(MBrittain) *set str pce: hdd 5f out: nt qckn fnl f* **11/8**[1]

460- **3** 1 1/4 **Santiburi Lad (IRE)**[206] [4666] 7-9-8 **54** MrsNWilson(5) 8 61
(NWilson) *chsd ldrs: effrt over 2f out: styd on ins last* **16/1**

436- **4** 2 1/2 **The Fairy Flag (IRE)**[51] [5215] 6-10-1 **59** (p) MissKellyHarrison(3) 12 62
(ABailey) *w ldr: led 5f out tl 1f out: wknd* **7/1**[2]

000- **5** 1 1/4 **Pension Fund**[207] [5559] 10-9-6 **54** ow5 MissJCoward(7) 3 55
(MWEasterby) *sn chsng ldrs: edgd rt and kpt on fnl 2f* **9/1**

000- **6** 3/4 **Inchnadamph**[225] [5200] 4-9-9 **50** MissAElsey 4 49
(TJFitzgerald) *chsd ldrs: wknd over 1f out* **40/1**

160- **7** 1 3/4 **Wuxi Venture**[47] [5276] 9-10-6 **66** MissVTunnicliffe(5) 6 62
(RAFahey) *hld up and bhd: hdwy on outer over 2f out: edgd rt: nvr rchd ldrs* **15/2**[3]

600 **8** 10 **Soft Mist (IRE)**[14] [1620] 4-9-11 **57** MissDawnRankin(5) 5 36
(JJQuinn) *mid-div: effrt over 2f out: sn lost pl* **33/1**

00-0 **9** 1/2 **Blue Venture (IRE)**[66] [952] 4-9-9 **55** MissAArmitage(5) 1 33
(PCHaslam) *hld up: hdwy on outer over 2f out: wknd over 1f out* **12/1**

0564 **10** 15 **Our Glenard**[17] [1545] 5-8-13 **45** MissALTurner(5) 13 —
(SLKeightley) *s.s: hdwy 7f out: lost pl 2f out: sn bhd* **7/1**[2]

420- **11** 1 3/4 **Larking About (USA)**[186] [5920] 4-10-3 **65** MsAmyBoeder(7) 10 15
(WJMusson) *s.i.s: a last: t.o 4f out* **25/1**

2m 19.2s (12.00) **Going Correction** +1.275s/f (Soft) **11** Ran SP% **124.2**
Speed ratings: **103,100,99,97,96 95,94,86,85,73 72**CSF £17.70 CT £162.66 TOTE £9.30: £2.40, £1.10, £5.70; EX 24.80 Place 6 £21.10, Place 5 £11.95.
**Owner** The Fishermen **Bred** R S A Urquhart **Trained** Hambleton, N Yorks

**FOCUS**
A 0-66 handicap run at a furious pace and the winner was given an exceptional ride. The form looks sound.

**NOTEBOOK**
**Yenaled**, who in the past has won from a 10lb higher mark, was ridden with one eye on his unproven stamina. He was produced to show ahead a furlong out, and when his rider switched her whip hand inside the last he shot clear. It was a ride any professional would have been proud of.
**Melodian**, who likes it round here, is as tough as old boots. He went head to head with The Fairy Flag and deserves credit for sticking on so well.
**Santiburi Lad(IRE)**, having his first outing on the Flat since September, stayed on in willing fashion inside the last and stamina was clearly not a problem.
**The Fairy Flag(IRE)** went at it hammer and tongs with Melodian and she was out on her feet when the winner swept by.
**Pension Fund**, now in the veteran stage, gave his trainer's granddaughter a nice experience. Her day will come but the old boy's best days are behind him now.
T/Plt: £16.50 to a £1 stake. Pool: £65,982.00. 2,905.15 winning tickets. T/Qpdt: £6.10 to a £1 stake. Pool: £3,105.00. 376.60 winning tickets. WG

# 1935 LINGFIELD (L-H)

### Saturday, May 8

**OFFICIAL GOING: Soft (good to soft in places)**

## 1963 ANTONIA CRIDLAND OAKS TRIAL (LISTED RACE) (FILLIES) — 1m 3f 106y

**1:35** (1:35) (A ) 3-Y-O **£29,750** (£11,000; £5,500; £2,500) **Stalls** High

Form RPR

**1** **Baraka (IRE)**[238] [4902] 3-8-8 JPSpencer 5 107+
(APO'Brien, Ire) *gd sort: lw: s.i.s: sn rcvrd to trck ldr: chal on bit 2f out: led gng wl appr fnl f: v easily* **9/4**[2]

0-12 **2** 6 **Bowstring (IRE)**[17] [1538] 3-8-8 95 LDettori 2 86
(JHMGosden) *led: rdn over 3f: styd on wl whn strly chal fr 2f out: hdd appr fnl f: sn no ch w wnr* **10/11**[1]

035- **3** 10 **Rio De Jumeirah**[250] [4623] 3-8-8 78 DHolland 1 71
(CEBrittain) *chsd ldrs: rdn 4f out: no ch w ldrs fnl 3f* **16/1**

10- **4** 1 **Donna Vita**[216] [5404] 3-8-8 90 KFallon 4 70
(GAButler) *lw: rr but in tch: rdn 4f out: no ch fr over 3f out* **11/2**[3]

-310 **5** 7 **Chara**[12] [1672] 3-8-8 66 EAhern 3 59
(JRJenkins) *a bhd: no ch fnl 5f* **25/1**

2m 41.68s (12.16) **Going Correction** +1.10s/f (Soft) **5** Ran SP% **108.3**
Speed ratings: **99,94,87,86,81**CSF £4.50 TOTE £3.70: £1.80, £1.10; EX 5.00.
**Owner** Mrs David Nagle & Mrs John Magnier **Bred** Barronstown Stud And Orpendale **Trained** Ballydoyle, Co Tipperary

**FOCUS**
A modest winning time for the grade, 3.38 seconds slower than the Derby Trial, and no strength in depth. However, the winner looks useful.

**NOTEBOOK**
**Baraka(IRE)**, a very disappointing odds-on favourite in her only start last term, is a good bodied filly and was a completely different proposition this time. She was running all over the favourite down the home straight and when asked to quicken up the result was quickly settled. The slow winning time and the quality of the opposition, as well as the conditions, put several question marks over the value of the form and at this stage she remains all potential.
**Bowstring(IRE)** tried to dominate this from the start, but the winner was running all over her after the pair turned for home and, despite doing her best, was totally outclassed by her rival. Despite her Folkestone win coming on easy ground, this performance, together with her Epsom effort, suggests she does not want the ground as testing as this.
**Rio De Jumeirah**, reappearing after an eight-month break, was racing over trip more than half a mile further than she has ever tried before. Not being good enough on the day was probably a bigger problem than lack of stamina and her 260,000gns price tag is looking expensive.
**Donna Vita**, racing for the first time since finishing down the field in the Prix Marcel Boussac last October, still looked a bit weak and was beaten some way out. At this stage does not look as good as connections obviously think she is, but this was only her third start, and the stable has yet to strike form this year, so all is not completely lost.
**Chara**, beaten in a handicap last time, was totally outclassed but still picked up £1,250 for connections.

## 1964 TOTESPORT CHARTWELL FILLIES' STKS (GROUP 3) — 7f

**2:05** (2:07) (A ) 3-Y-0+ **£29,000** (£11,000; £5,500; £2,500) **Stalls** High

Form RPR

1 **1** **Illustrious Miss (USA)**[22] [1441] 3-8-5 TPQueally 11 111+
(DRLoder) *lw: hld up in rr: nt clr run ins fnl 2f: swtchd rt and rapid hdwy over 1f out: led ins fnl f: easily* **4/1**[2]

1-01 **2** 2 1/2 **Gonfilia (GER)**[58] [1002] 4-9-3 (t) LDettori 1 105
(SaeedBinSuroor) *lw: sn w ldr: led ins fnl 3f: rdn over 1f out: hdd ins last: kpt on but no ch w wnr* **3/1**[1]

5-02 **3** 4 **Golden Nun**[13] [1649] 4-9-3 96 (p) TQuinn 8 95
(TDEasterby) *lw: in tch: rdn and hdwy fr 2f out:chsng ldrs and one pce whn hung bdly lft ins fnl f* **7/1**

042- **4** 1 3/4 **Blaise Castle (USA)**[176] [6000] 4-9-3 90 SDrowne 9 91
(GAButler) *bit bkwd: in tch: rdn 3f out: styd on fr over 1f out but nvr gng pce to trble ldrs* **14/1**

461- **5** nk **Dowager**[190] [5851] 3-8-5 99 MartinDwyer 7 90
(RHannon) *chsd ldrs: rdn over 2f out: wnt 2nd ins fnl 2f but no imp: wknd fnl f* **12/1**

12-0 **6** shd **Miss Ivanhoe (IRE)**[25] [1385] 4-9-3 102 DHolland 2 90
(GWragg) *chsd ldrs: rdn fr 3f out: wknd fnl f* **9/2**[3]

20-0 **7** nk **Starbeck (IRE)**[14] [1610] 6-9-3 84 PMcCabe 12 89+
(PHowling) *b. s.i.s:bhd: rdn and sme hdwy whn nt clr run on rails ins fnl 2f: kpt on same pce ins last* **40/1**

41-4 **8** 2 1/2 **Malvern Light**[24] [1398] 3-8-5 99 RHills 10 83
(WJHaggas) *mid-div: hdwy over 2f out: nvr gng pce to rch ldrs: wknd ins fnl f* **7/1**

1003 **9** 2 1/2 **Miss George**[12] [1673] 6-9-3 83 DaneO'Neill 3 76
(DKIvory) *b.hind: s.i.s: bhd: sme hdwy over 2f out: nvr gng pce to rch ldrs: wknd over 1f out* **33/1**

01-0 **10** 2 1/2 **Riva Royale**[14] [1610] 4-9-3 84 JFanning 4 70
(IAWood) *mde most tl hdd ins fnl 3f: wknd fr 2f out* **50/1**

30-0 **11** 3 **Presto Vento**[6] [1789] 4-9-3 90 PDobbs 5 63
(RHannon) *s.i.s: bhd: hdwy 4f out: styng on one pce whn hmpd on rails ins fnl 2f: nt rcvr* **20/1**

1m 27.77s (3.56) **Going Correction** +0.875s/f (Soft)
**WFA** 3 from 4yo+ 12lb **11** Ran SP% **114.6**
Speed ratings: **114,111,106,104,104 104,103,100,98,95 91**CSF £15.33 TOTE £5.60: £2.00, £1.30, £2.30; EX 16.60 Trifecta £71.20 Pool of £1,585.22 - 15.80 winning units.
**Owner** Sheikh Mohammed **Bred** W S Farish And E J Hudson Jr Irrevocable Trust **Trained** Newmarket, Suffolk

**FOCUS**
A decent contest, run in a creditable time, and a fine performance from the winner, who achieved a Racing Post Rating on a par with the placed horses in the 1,000 Guineas.

**NOTEBOOK**
**Illustrious Miss(USA)** ◆, whose Newbury victory was given a big boost by the runner-up's impressive victory here the previous day, was equally impressive herself. She did not enjoy the clearest of runs and still had ground to make up when the favourite went for home, but the way she picked her up and then quickened away to eventually win comfortably had class written all over it. She still has bags of scope and could be very exciting indeed.
**Gonfilia(GER)**, a impressive winner in Dubai on her most recent start, looked to have won it when she was sent clear passing the quarter-mile pole but was swamped by the winner's turn of foot. Her draw would not have been ideal, but it probably made little difference to the result and she still pulled right away from the rest.
**Golden Nun** is yet to prove conclusively that she stays this trip, especially in these conditions. She has several placings in Listed and Group company to her name and again ran her race, if firmly put in her place by the front pair, but is without a win in 19 months.
**Blaise Castle(USA)**, proven in the conditions, did not run badly on this first start since November but may need further these days.
**Dowager** was encountering soft ground for the first time, which it was thought might suit her better, but lack of a run since October was probably a bigger problem. She should come on for this.
**Miss Ivanhoe(IRE)** relished similar conditions when winning a Listed contest in France last autumn so she should have had no excuses on that score. Perhaps she still needed this.
**Starbeck(IRE)** appeared to run very well at the weights, especially as she met traffic problems, but she was already proven in the ground and that would have counted for plenty.

## 1965 TOTESCOOP6 SPRINT (HERITAGE H'CAP) — 6f

**2:35** (2:36) (B ) (0-105,91) 3-Y-O **£34,800** (£13,200; £6,600; £3,000) **Stalls** High

Form RPR

0223 **1** **Morse (IRE)**[7] [1760] 3-8-13 **83** LDettori 4 90
(JAOsborne) *chsd ldrs: drvn over 3f out: qcknd to ld over 1f out: drvn out and hld on wl* **9/2**

4130 **2** hd **Petardias Magic (IRE)**[14] [1614] 3-9-1 **85** KFallon 3 91
(EJO'Neill) *lw: hld up in rr: hdwy over 2f out: str run u.p to chse wnr wl ins last: gng on cl home* **6/1**

3-16 **3** 3 **Presto Shinko (IRE)**[3] [1881] 3-8-8 **78** DHolland 1 75
(RHannon) *wnt lft and s.i.s s: sn trcking ldrs: rdn to chse wnr over 2f out: hung lft and wknd ins fnl f* **4/1**[3]

20-4 **4** 1 **Vienna's Boy (IRE)**[37] [1223] 3-9-5 **89** DaneO'Neill 5 83
(RHannon) *led: rdn fr 1/2-way: hdd over 1f out: wknd ins last* **12/1**

0-51 **5** 1/2 **Molcon (IRE)**[10] [1702] 3-8-6 **81** DFox(5) 6 74
(NACallaghan) *lw: chsd ldrs: rdn over 3f out: wknd fr 2f out* **3/1**[1]

02-0 **6** hd **Oro Verde**[6] [1797] 3-9-7 **91** PDobbs 2 83
(RHannon) *edgd lft s: bhd sme hedway over 2f out: nvr gng pce to rch ldrs* **50/1**

2-42 **7** 1 3/4 **Star Pupil**[6] [1797] 3-8-10 **80** (v1) MartinDwyer 7 67
(AMBalding) *nvr gng wl: a bhd* **10/3**[2]

1m 15.53s (3.88) **Going Correction** +0.875s/f (Soft) **7** Ran SP% **110.2**
Speed ratings: **109,108,104,103,102 102,100**CSF £28.78 TOTE £4.80: £1.80, £3.10; EX 27.20.
**Owner** Turf 2000 Limited **Bred** Auriga Partnership **Trained** Upper Lambourn, Berks

**FOCUS**
A fair winning time for the grade, but this was nothing like as competitive a race as it has been over the years, which was disappointing considering the money on offer.

**NOTEBOOK**
**Morse(IRE)**, proven in the ground, was being ridden along from some way out but he kept responding and after taking it up had the race won inside the last furlong, despite the narrowness of the margin. He may be better over a stiffer six and the soft ground probably compensated for the sharp track.
**Petardias Magic(IRE)**, held up early, had to be switched wide in order to get an run and then took time to organise himself. That proved crucial, as he was finishing strongly down the centre of the track but never looked like getting there.
**Presto Shinko(IRE)**, turned out again quickly, was awkward leaving the stalls but had every chance passing the furlong pole before tiring in the ground. A faster surface may suit him better.
*Official explanation: jockey said colt hung left*
**Vienna's Boy(IRE)**, who has paid the penalty for finishing in the frame in Listed company at two, took the field along for over half a mile before fading. He needs to come down in the weights a bit more yet.
**Molcon(IRE)**, encountering similar conditions to when winning at Ascot last time, was only 4lb higher but never really got into the race. Connections wondered if the race had come too soon for him.
**Oro Verde** is not receiving any help from the Handicapper.
**Star Pupil** failed to run up to his Salisbury form in the first-time visor and was the first beaten. He is likely to be returned to further now.



The Form Book, Raceform Ltd, Compton, RG20 6NL

## 1966 GALLAGHER GROUP LTD DERBY TRIAL STKS (GROUP 3) (C&G) 1m 3f 106y
**3:10** (3:10) (A) 3-Y-0 **£37,200** (£13,200; £6,600; £3,000) **Stalls** High

Form RPR

32-1 **1** **Percussionist (IRE)**[25] 1387 3-8-7 **88** ...................................... LDettori 1 116+
(JHMGosden) *trckd ldrs: wnt 2nd over 7f out: pressed ldr 5f out: led ins fnl 3f: rdn: hung bdly rt and c clr thrght fnl f* **11/4**[3]

2111 **2** *10* **Hazyview**[7] 1766 3-8-7 **84** ...................................... DHolland 5 104+
(NACallaghan) *lw: trckd ldr: led 1m out: rdn 4f out: hdd ins fnl 3f: styd w wnr to 2f out: no ch appr fnl f* **11/10**[1]

4- **3** *17* **Five Dynasties (USA)**[209] 5518 3-8-7 ...................................... JPSpencer 3 79+
(APO'Brien, Ire) *strong: hld up in tch: rdn 5f out: no ch w ldrs fnl 4f: eased whn no ch fnl 2f* **9/4**[2]

0 **4** *dist* **Maidstone Midas (IRE)**[12] 1674 3-8-7 ...................................... SDrowne 4 —
(WSKittow) *led tl hdd 1m out: sn lost tch and t.o* **100/1**

2m 38.3s (8.78) **Going Correction** +1.10s/f (Soft) **4 Ran SP% 106.0**
Speed ratings: **112,104,92,**—CSF £6.02 TOTE £3.00; EX 5.00.
**Owner** Exors of the late R E Sangster **Bred** Swettenham Stud **Trained** Manton, Wilts

**FOCUS**
A weakly contested Group Three, but a time 3.38 seconds faster than the Oaks Trial and a decent performance from the winner, who has been rated better than the winners of either of the week's Chester trials. North Light was an absentee due to the ground.

**NOTEBOOK**
**Percussionist(IRE)**, who was on his toes and got a little warm before, was travelling best from a long way out and when asked for maximum effort two furlongs from home, quickly put daylight between himself and the favourite. Despite some urgent smacks from his rider, he hung violently to his right in the closing stages, but that was probably a one-off, possibly caused by the proximity of the Channel 4 camera car on the adjacent AW track. The winning time compares favourably with the Oaks Trial, which suggests this was a true test, and he is likely to take his chance in the Derby, but he may well be more of a St Leger prospect.
**Hazyview** came into this in cracking form, but a combination of the longer trip, the softest ground he has ever raced on, and the step up in class all found him out and the winner was running all over him starting up the home straight. He has had a hard time of it in recent weeks and would probably benefit from a break.
**Five Dynasties(USA)**, off since October and not quite 100%, travelled well enough until suddenly coming off the bridle at the top of the hill and that was him finished. This was the second time he has disappointed on soft ground and his debut victory came under much faster conditions. *Official explanation: jockey said colt was unsuited by the ground*
**Maidstone Midas(IRE)** had his moment of glory early and managed to pick up £3,000 for his connections without harming his potential handicap mark.

## 1967 TESTERS OF EDENBRIDGE MAIDEN STKS 1m 2f
**3:40** (3:43) (D) 3-Y-0+ **£4,407** (£1,356; £678; £339) **Stalls** Low

Form RPR

2- **1** **Fine Palette**[187] 5907 4-9-12 ...................................... WRyan 7 83
(HRACecil) *lw: t.k.h: hld up in rr: hdwy over 2f out: rdn and kpt on wl to ld last half f* **7/2**[2]

2- **2** *1* **Seven Year Itch (IRE)**[172] 6022 4-9-12 ...................................... MartinDwyer 2 81
(MPTregoning) *t.k.h: led: hdd over 3f out:styd 2nd and sn rdn:rallied and led jst ins last:hdd: no ex and hung rt last half f* **13/2**

05- **3** *1 ½* **Pagan Magic (USA)**[192] 5830 3-8-8 ...................................... LisaJones(3) 6 78
(JARToller) *h.d.w: trckd ldr: led over 3f out: rdn over 2f out: hdd jst ins last: one pce whn carried rt last half f* **7/1**

3 **4** *2 ½* **Swainson (USA)**[70] 916 3-8-11 ...................................... DHolland 8 74
(PMitchell) *s.i.s: sn rcvrd to chse ldrs: rdn and outpcd over 2f out: styd on again ins last* **5/1**[3]

5 **5** *1 ¾* **Maharaat (USA)**[24] 1395 3-8-11 ......................................(t) RHills 3 71
(SirMichaelStoute) *chsd ldrs: rdn 4f out: wknd ins fnl 2f* **9/4**[1]

0-00 **6** *1 ¾* **Persian Dagger (IRE)**[19] 1508 3-8-11 ...................................... GCarter 4 68
(JLDunlop) *bhd: kpt on fnl 2f: n.d* **33/1**

0 **7** *1* **Masked (IRE)**[12] 1674 3-8-11 ...................................... TQuinn 5 67
(JWHills) *s.i.s: bhd: n.d* **14/1**

**8** *2* **Lucky Arthur (IRE)** 3-8-6 ...................................... DSweeney 1 58
(JGMO'Shea) *leggy: unf: sn bhd: n.d* **66/1**

0 **9** *26* **Starmix**[50] 1050 3-8-11 ...................................... KFallon 9 19
(PFICole) *chsd ldrs: rdn 5f out: sn btn* **20/1**

2m 21.72s (12.12) **Going Correction** +1.10s/f (Soft)
**WFA** 3 from 4yo 15lb **9 Ran SP% 111.4**
Speed ratings: **95,94,93,91,89 88,87,85,65**CSF £24.79 TOTE £4.50: £1.80, £1.80, £2.00; EX 23.40.
**Owner** Mrs Angela Scott **Bred** Addison Racing Ltd Inc **Trained** Newmarket, Suffolk

**FOCUS**
Not a particularly competitive maiden and a modest winning time. The first two were the only older horses in the line-up.

**NOTEBOOK**
**Fine Palette** had a bit to do turning for home, but he looks a stayer and the further they went, the better he was going. With the inside rail to help him, he made relentless progress down the home straight and he got up in the last half-furlong to score. He will appreciate further and could develop into a nice middle-distance handicapper.
**Seven Year Itch(IRE)**, runner-up on the Polytrack in his only previous outing last November, is a nice-type, but still a bit coltish. He was in and out of the lead the whole way, but after a protracted battle with the third he started to hang in the closing stages and the winner took full advantage. He does not look an easy ride, but is obviously not without ability either.
**Pagan Magic(USA)**, off since October, looked as though the run would bring him on. He was always up with the pace and got involved in a dour battle with the runner-up in the home straight, but could not quicken in the conditions. He was done few favours by that rival hanging into him in the closing stages, but it did not effect the result. He now qualifies for handicaps.
**Swainson(USA)**, making his turf debut, ran as though he will appreciate further and should improve for this.
**Maharaat(USA)**, joined a growing list of horses who have failed to uphold the Wood Dittton form, although in fairness he did not appear to see out this longer trip in the conditions.

## 1968 LINGFIELD-RACECOURSE.CO.UK H'CAP 7f
**4:15** (4:16) (B) (0-105,98) 4-Y-0+ **£12,319** (£4,672; £2,336; £1,062) **Stalls** High

Form RPR

5600 **1** **Golden Chalice (IRE)**[7] 1772 5-9-0 **86** ...................................... KFallon 14 99
(AMBalding) *lw: hld up in rr: n.m.r on rails and swtchd lft over 3f out: str run fr 2f out to ld 1f out: drvn clr ins last: readily* **8/1**[3]

-506 **2** *¾* **Oakley Rambo**[10] 1708 5-8-5 **77** ...................................... RLMoore 15 88
(RHannon) *lw: bhd on rails: swtchd lft to outside over 3f out: gd hdwy fr 2f out: str run to chse wnr ins last: no imp cl home* **12/1**

/11- **3** *½* **Polar Bear**[231] 5059 4-9-2 **88** ...................................... DHolland 10 101+
(WJHaggas) *h.d.w: hld up in tch: nt clr run fr over 2f out: swtchd lft and gd hdwy appr fnl f: kpt on wl but nt pce of ldrs* **5/2**[1]

-600 **4** *4* **Marker**[7] 1765 4-8-13 **85** ...................................... RHavlin 2 85
(GBBalding) *lw: chsd ldrs: rdn to chal over 1f out: outpcd ins last* **20/1**

/-30 **5** *½* **Kool (IRE)**[14] 1610 5-9-9 **95** ...................................... TQuinn 8 94
(PFICole) *b.bkwd: chsd ldrs: rdn over 2f out: outpacded appr fnl f* **12/1**

-000 **6** *1* **Prince Cyrano**[7] 1765 5-8-7 **79** ...................................... GCarter 13 75
(WJMusson) *rr stalls and bhd: kpt on fr over 1f out: nt trble ldrs* **33/1**

4-03 **7** *1* **Marshman (IRE)**[25] 1385 5-9-4 **90** ...................................... PRobinson 9 84
(MHTompkins) *lw: chsd ldrs: rdn over 2f out: wknd appr fnl f* **7/2**[2]

0414 **8** *shd* **Taranaki**[26] 1354 6-8-11 **83** ...................................... SSanders 11 76
(PDCundell) *trckd ldrs: led over 2f out: hdd 1f out and wknd qckly ins last* **8/1**[3]

034- **9** *2* **Camp Commander (IRE)**[131] 6252 5-9-10 **96** ......................(t) LDettori 1 84
(CEBrittain) *b.bkwd: s.i.s: bhd: sme hdwy fnl 2f but nvr a danger* **14/1**

10-0 **10** *nk* **Out For A Stroll**[10] 1708 5-8-5 **77** ...................................... JMackay 16 65
(SCWilliams) *a outpcd* **66/1**

00-0 **11** *1 ½* **Material Witness (IRE)**[26] 1354 7-9-0 **86** ...................................... MartinDwyer 6 70
(WRMuir) *sn w ldr: led over 4f out: hdd over 2f out: wknd wl over 1f out* **33/1**

-000 **12** *5* **Crimson Silk**[14] 1610 4-9-12 **98** ......................................(p) PaulEddery 12 69
(DHaydnJones) *prom 4f* **25/1**

0-42 **13** *8* **Fiveoclock Express (IRE)**[7] 1772 4-8-9 **81** ......................(v) SDrowne 7 32
(MissGayKelleway) *sn outpcd* **11/1**

40-3 **14** *5* **Val De Maal (IRE)**[14] 1625 4-8-1 **73** ...................................... AMcCarthy 5 12
(GCHChung) *lw: sn slt ld: hdd over 4f out: wknd qckly over 2f out* **66/1**

1m 28.77s (4.56) **Going Correction** +0.875s/f (Soft) **14 Ran SP% 120.9**
Speed ratings: **108,107,106,102,101 100,99,99,96,96 94,88,79,74**CSF £93.79 CT £312.54 TOTE £9.30: £3.00, £4.30, £1.90; EX 144.90.
**Owner** Holistic Racing Ltd **Bred** Killeen Castle Stud **Trained** Kingsclere, Hants

**FOCUS**
A competitive handicap in which things got predictably tight. Even though the front three came from double-figure draws, they all had to be switched wide in order to get a run.

**NOTEBOOK**
**Golden Chalice(IRE)**, who has not been setting the world alight so far this season, bounced back to his very best on this softer ground. He had to be switched in order to get a run, but when in clear daylight he quickened up nicely and definitely got first run on both the second and third. He now heads for the Victoria Cup.
**Oakley Rambo ◆**, who is starting to be given a chance by the Handicapper, had to be switched wide in order to see daylight, but the winner was already through and away by the time he did so and despite doing his best to bridge the gap, the margin was too great. This was his best effort for some time.
**Polar Bear ◆**, like the runner-up, had to be switched wide in order to see daylight enabling the winner to get first run on them both. He stayed on well towards the line and this was a decent effort considering he lacked a recent outing, unlike the front pair. He is one to bear in mind for a valuable handicap.
**Marker** is from a soft-ground family, though he has only shown limited ability on it himself. He has never won a handicap, but is being given a chance now and was far from disgraced. His low draw may not have been quite the disadvantage it may have looked given the way the race panned out.
**Kool(IRE)** ran with credit, but the way he was ridden meant that he got the run of the race.
**Prince Cyrano**, trying this trip for the first time since his second start as a juvenile, deserves some credit for reaching his final position after giving ground away at the start.
**Marshman(IRE)** has won on this ground, so was a little disappointing following his good effort at Newmarket.
**Taranaki**, up there from the start, did not get home in the ground.
**Crimson Silk** *Official explanation: trainer said gelding bled from the nose.*

## 1969 OCS GROUP LADIES STKS (H'CAP) (LADY AMATEUR RIDERS) 7f
**4:45** (4:49) (E) (0-75,74) 3-Y-0+ **£2,392** (£2,392; £563; £281) **Stalls** High

Form RPR

6001 **1** *dht* **Somerset West (IRE)**[32] 1279 4-9-10 **63** ...................... MissJFerguson(7) 7 72
(JRBest) *mde virtually all: hld on gamely fnl f for dead heat* **20/1**

0343 **1** **He Who Dares (IRE)**[19] 1502 6-10-0 **60** ...................... MrsSBosley 12 69
(AWCarroll) *s.i.s: bhd: hdwy over 2f out: str run appr fnl f: wnt 2nd ins last: styd on to force dead heat* **5/2**[1]

-003 **3** *¾* **Parnassian**[5] 1845 4-9-2 **55** ...................... MissJHannaford(7) 8 62
(GBBalding) *lw: bhd: hdwy fr 2f out: r.o fnl f: fin wl and gng on cl home* **11/2**[2]

0-60 **4** *1 ¾* **Fearby Cross (IRE)**[38] 1204 8-10-0 **67** ...................... MissJPledge(7) 3 70
(WJMusson) *in tch: hdwy and r.o fnl 2f: nt qckn ins last* **11/1**

2-64 **5** *1 ¼* **Carriacou**[14] 1627 3-9-10 **73** ...................... MissRD'Arcy(5) 13 73
(PWD'Arcy) *chsd ldrs: wnt 2nd over 2f out: no imp on ldr: wknd fnl f* **12/1**

0-64 **6** *hd* **Phred**[7] 1757 4-10-4 **64** ...................... MissEJohnsonHoughton 5 63
(RFJohnsonHoughton) *bhd: hdwy over 2f out: kpt on fnl f but nvr gng pce of ldrs* **14/1**

5222 **7** *1* **Carlton (IRE)**[4] 1873 10-9-10 **59** ...................... MrsEmmaLittmoden(3) 6 56
(CRDore) *lw: bhd: hdwy 3f out: kpt on fr over 1f out but nvr gng pce to rch ldrs* **13/2**

6510 **8** *3* **Lygeton Lad**[17] 1542 6-11-0 **74** ......................(t) MissEJJones 15 63
(MissGayKelleway) *chsd ldrs tl wknd fr 2f out* **13/2**

-433 **9** *2 ½* **Oh So Rosie (IRE)**[14] 1606 4-9-11 **60** ......................(p) MrsSMoore(3) 14 43
(JSMoore) *b. s.i.s: bhd: hdwy over 2f out: nvr rch ldrs and wknd over 1f out* **6/1**[3]

030- **10** *1* **Giverand**[176] 5998 5-8-6 **45** ...................... MissSophieDoyle(7) 2 25
(MissJacquelineSDoyle) *chsd ldrs over 4f* **50/1**

54-0 **11** *5* **Grumpyintmorning**[31] 1295 5-9-3 **54** ow1 ...................... MrsCThompson(5) 9 22
(MrsPTownsley) *sn outpcd* **33/1**

-400 **12** *8* **Yellow River (IRE)**[20] 834 4-9-0 **46** oh2 ow4 .........(p) MissSBeddoes 11 —
(RCurtis) *w ldr 4f: wknd qckly over 2f out* **66/1**

000/ **13** *14* **Frederick James**[1097] 1176 10-8-8 **45** oh2 ow3 ......... MissAWallace(5) 1 —
(HEHaynes) *bkwd: a in rr* **66/1**

6000 **P** **Karaoke King**[69] 928 6-9-9 **62** ...................... MissSCassidy(7) 4 —
(JELong) *sn bhd: t.o whn p.u and dismntd ins fnl f: dead* **33/1**

1m 31.15s (6.94) **Going Correction** +0.875s/f (Soft)
**WFA** 3 from 4yo+ 12lb **14 Ran SP% 123.2**
Speed ratings: **95,95,94,92,90 90,89,85,83,81 76,67,51,**— TRIFECTA W: SW 7.5,HW 1.90; Pl: SW 3.5,HW 1.30, 2.5; Ex: SW/HW 41.60,HW/SW 36.70; CSF: SW/HW 34.52,HW/SW 31.00;Tri: SW/HW/P 166.46 HW/SW/P 1.Place 6 £190.94, Place 5 £154.98
**Owner** Roger Clarke **Bred** John Osborne **Trained** Wixford, Warwicks
■ This was Jenny Ferguson's first winner.

**FOCUS**
A modest contest though the pace was fair in the conditions.

**NOTEBOOK**
**He Who Dares(IRE)** is not an easy ride, but had one of the most experience riders aboard. Needing to be delivered as late as possible, he was ridden to do so and, with the soft ground helping compensate for the inadequate trip, came from way back to share the spoils on the line.
**Somerset West(IRE)**, making his debut for the yard, was given a fine positive ride on ground in which he was unproven. He did nothing wrong and ran right to the line, but in the end had to be content with a dead heat after being joined on the line.

**Parnassian** handles this ground, but he was not helped by the furlong-shorter trip, especially on a sharp track like this, and his strong finishing effort was always going to be too late. A return to a mile will suit him, but he is still a maiden after 21 attempts.
**Fearby Cross(IRE)** is used to the feminine touch and had every chance, but did not appear to see out the trip in the conditions.
**Carriacou** stays further than this and also acts in the ground, yet did not get home on this occasion.
**Phred** ran with credit, but is better suited by a mile and faster ground.
**Lygeton Lad** is several leagues better on Polytrack, but even on turf this ground would not have been to his liking.
**Grumpyintmorning** *Official explanation: jockey said gelding was unsuitable by the ground*
T/Plt: £120.20 to a £1 stake. Pool: £69,890.40. 424.40 winning tickets. T/Qpdt: £60.10 to a £1 stake. Pool: £2,667.60. 32.80 winning tickets. ST

# 1769 THIRSK (L-H)
## Saturday, May 8

**OFFICIAL GOING: Good**

## 1970 CALVERTS CARPETS CLAIMING STKS — 5f
6:05 (6:08) (E) 2-Y-O — £3,623 (£1,115; £557; £278) Stalls High

Form — RPR
1 **1** **Nova Tor (IRE)**$^{36}$ [1234] 2-8-1 ........ RoryMoore(7) 6 — 66
(PCHaslam) *mde virtually all: edgd lft and rdn over 1f out: r.o wl fnl f* **9/2**$^{2}$
11 **2** *3* **Little Biscuit (IRE)**$^{21}$ [1468] 2-8-13 ........ DarrenWilliams 4 — 59
(KRBurke) *slowly away: sn trcking ldrs: effrt over 1f out: chsd wnr fnl f: mo imp* **2/1**$^{1}$
6516 **3** *1/2* **Von Wessex**$^{16}$ [1556] 2-8-1 ........ CHaddon(7) 3 — 52
(WGMTurner) *prom: rdn over 1f out: kpt on same pce fnl f* **8/1**$^{3}$
5 **4** *1 3/4* **Missed Turn**$^{9}$ [1735] 2-8-5 ........ PFessey 8 — 42
(KARyan) *slowly away: sn midfield: kpt on fnl 2f: n.d* **16/1**
**5** *1 1/4* **Snookered Again** 2-8-9 ........ PMulrennan(5) 11 — 46
(MWEasterby) *s.s: bhd tl r.o wl fr over 1f out: n.d* **20/1**
301 **6** *1 1/2* **Why Harry**$^{16}$ [1556] 2-8-8 ........ RWinston 1 — 34
(JJQuinn) *midfield: hdwy 2f out: ch and rdn appr fnl f: 4th and hld whn eased ins last* **9/2**$^{2}$
0 **7** *3/4* **Keresforth**$^{9}$ [1735] 2-8-13 ........ WSupple 7 — 36
(TDEasterby) *cl up: rdn over 1f out: fdd* **25/1**
03 **8** *nk* **Joshar**$^{12}$ [1666] 2-8-3 ........ RFfrench 5 — 25
(MWEasterby) *nvr bttr than mid-div* **33/1**
0 **9** *1* **Boracay Beauty**$^{21}$ [1468] 2-7-5 ........ DFentiman(7) 9 — 16
(JRWeymes) *mid-div tl wknd 2f out* **66/1**
5 **10** *2 1/2* **Bowland Bride (IRE)**$^{21}$ [1468] 2-8-2 ........ FNorton 2 — 10
(ABerry) *towards rr most of way* **66/1**
51 **11** *hd* **Kissing A Fool**$^{12}$ [1666] 2-8-3 ........ PMakin(5) 10 — 15
(WGMTurner) *cl up tl wknd 2f out* **9/1**

62.21 secs (2.31) **Going Correction** +0.30s/f (Good) — **11** Ran SP% **111.2**
Speed ratings: **93,88,87,84,82 80,79,78,76,72** CSF £12.33 TOTE £5.80: £2.10, £1.10, £2.10; EX 19.60
**Owner** Blue Lion Racing III **Bred** Newlands House Stud **Trained** Middleham Moor, N Yorks
■ Stewards Enquiry : C Haddon one-day ban: failed to keep straight from stalls
Rory Moore three-day ban: used whip when clearly winning (May 19-21)

**FOCUS**
Probably a fair claimer.

**NOTEBOOK**
**Nova Tor(IRE)**, successful on her debut in a maiden at Southwell, had little trouble following up on this drop into claiming company. She will stay further and may be up to winning a novice event.
**Little Biscuit(IRE)** has two wins and a second to her name in this sort of company and seemed to handle the fast ground well enough.
**Von Wessex** appreciated the return to this faster ground and kept on for third. He will be suited by six furlongs.
**Missed Turn** improved on her debut effort, syaing on for fourth. She should be up to winning in this company.
**Snookered Again**, the only newcomer in the line-up, made a most promising debut and should have little trouble winning in this sort of company.
**Why Harry** lost a couple of places in the final half-furlong as a result of being eased. *Official explanation: jockey said gelding hung left throughout*

## 1971 QUADNETICS H'CAP — 7f
6:35 (6:36) (F) (0-55,55) 3-Y-0+ — £3,101 (£886; £443) Stalls Low

Form — RPR
00-1 **1** **Tap**$^{8}$ [1748] 7-8-13 **54** ........ (p) DFentiman(7) 7 — 65
(IanEmmerson) *prom: led over 2f out: styd on wl u.p: all out* **8/1**$^{2}$
0230 **2** *1/2* **Luke After Me (IRE)**$^{8}$ [1748] 4-9-3 **51** ........ RWinston 9 — 61
(GASwinbank) *s.i.s: sn midfield: hdwy 2f out: ev ch and rdn ins fnl f: no ex clsng stages* **11/1**
6222 **3** *1 1/4* **Mount Royale (IRE)**$^{8}$ [1748] 6-9-5 **53** ........ (vt) KimTinkler 4 — 59
(NTinkler) *trckd ldrs: ev ch and rdn over 1f out: no ex fnl f* **11/2**$^{1}$
0551 **4** *1/2* **Scarrottoo**$^{26}$ [1373] 6-9-4 **55** ........ BReilly(3) 11 — 60
(SCWilliams) *bhd: hdwy 3f out: styd on wl u.p fr over 1 out: nvr able to chal* **11/2**$^{1}$
1004 **5** *1 1/2* **Classic Vision**$^{70}$ [917] 4-9-7 **55** ........ ACulhane 12 — 56
(WJHaggas) *towards rr: drvn along and hdwy 2f out: styd on fnl f: nvr able to chal* **9/1**$^{3}$
464- **6** *1/2* **Scramble (USA)**$^{134}$ [6241] 6-8-13 **52** ........ (t) TEaves(5) 3 — 52
(BEllison) *s.i.s: midfield: kpt on u.p fnl 2f: nvr able to chal* **9/1**$^{3}$
4555 **7** *1 1/4* **Waltzing Wizard**$^{8}$ [1748] 5-9-7 **55** ........ JCarroll 15 — 51
(ABerry) *midfield: hdwy u.p and in tch over 1f out: no further prog* **16/1**
06-0 **8** *nk* **Zietzig (IRE)**$^{5}$ [1824] 7-9-5 **53** ........ AlexGreaves 10 — 48
(DNicholls) *midfield: rdn 2f out: no hdwy* **25/1**
00-0 **9** *3* **Mr Bountiful (IRE)**$^{101}$ [624] 6-9-7 **55** ........ SWKelly 16 — 42
(MDods) *sn towards rr: n.d* **20/1**
40-0 **10** *1 3/4* **Trinity (IRE)**$^{12}$ [1665] 8-9-3 **51** ........ TWilliams 5 — 34
(MBrittain) *cl up tl rdn and wknd 2f out* **14/1**
4600 **11** *hd* **Zak Facta (IRE)**$^{1}$ [1941] 4-9-2 **50** ........ (v) DarrenWilliams 2 — 32
(MissDAMchale) *led tl hdd over 2f out: fdd* **16/1**
00-0 **12** *2 1/2* **Zamyatina (IRE)**$^{18}$ [1531] 5-8-13 **50** ........ DAllan(3) 6 — 25
(PLClinton) *midfield tl wknd over 2f out* **25/1**
30-0 **13** *1* **Kelseas Kolby (IRE)**$^{37}$ [1225] 4-9-7 **55** ........ (v) GGibbons 8 — 28
(JAGlover) *midfield whn n.m.r and dropped towards rr after 1f: n.d* **12/1**
60-0 **14** *3 1/2* **Pepper Road**$^{14}$ [1620] 5-9-2 **50** ........ RFfrench 1 — 13
(RBastiman) *prom tl wknd over 2f out* **12/1**
0-04 **15** *6* **Sarn**$^{11}$ [1697] 5-8-9 **50** ........ (p) PVarley(7) 13 — —
(MMullineaux) *sn wl bhd* **20/1**

1m 29.25s (2.15) **Going Correction** +0.475s/f (Yiel) — **15** Ran SP% **121.2**
Speed ratings: **106,105,104,103,101 101,99,99,95,93 93,90,89,85,78**CSF £87.91 CT £529.14 TOTE £8.50: £4.30, £3.50, £2.00; EX 176.60.
**Owner** Trade Direct Bathrooms & Furniture **Bred** Fonthill Stud And Philip Wroughton **Trained** Holmside, Co Durham
■ Stewards Enquiry : B Reilly two-day ban: used whip with excessive frequency and without giving gelding time to respond (May 19,20)

**FOCUS**
A fair winning time for the grade and the form looks sound.

**NOTEBOOK**
**Tap**, a shock 40/1 winner in cheekpieces at Musselburgh late last month, showed that to be no fluke with a gritty performance. The cheekpieces appear to have made a big difference.
**Luke After Me(IRE)** did himself no favours by being a bit slow at the start and only cried enough close home.
**Mount Royale(IRE)** continues to knock on the door, but could not reverse Musselburgh form with Tap, despite being slightly better off at the weights.
**Scarrottoo** won for the first time in a while at Yarmouth last month and was not disgraced in defeat. He has often shaped as though a mile will suit.
**Classic Vision** was having only her second start on turf and would have pleased connections with this effort. She seems versatile with regards to trip, but time may show her to be best at a mile.

## 1972 GLISTEN MAIDEN STKS — 1m
7:05 (7:08) (D) 3-Y-0+ — £5,798 (£1,784; £892; £446) Stalls Low

Form — RPR
**1** **Blue Oasis (IRE)** 3-8-6 ........ KDarley 2 — 71
(RGuest) *s.i.s: towards rr: hdwy 3f out: styd on wl u.p fnl f: led clsng stages* **10/1**$^{2}$
232- **2** *3/4* **Capped For Victory (USA)**$^{233}$ [5020] 3-8-11 **100** ........ KFallon 5 — 74
(SirMichaelStoute) *cl up: led 5f out: hrd pressed and rdn fnl 2f: hdd clsng stages* **1/3**$^{1}$
04- **3** *hd* **Arran Scout (IRE)**$^{183}$ [5940] 3-8-11 ........ RWinston 9 — 74
(MrsLStubbs) *trckd ldrs: chal and rdn 2f out: ev ch ins fnl f: no ex clsng stages* **33/1**
0-4 **4** *4* **Little Bob**$^{23}$ [1419] 3-8-11 ........ CCatlin 11 — 65
(JDBethell) *s.i.s: bhd: drvn along 1/2-way: styd on wl u.p fnl 2f: nvr able to chal* **14/1**$^{3}$
2- **5** *1/2* **Kelbrook**$^{300}$ [3244] 5-9-10 ........ WSupple 7 — 64
(ABailey) *dwlt: sn midfield: hdwy to chse ldrs 2f out: no further prog* **25/1**
23-0 **6** *1* **Artistic Style**$^{10}$ [1711] 4-9-5 **68** ........ TEaves(5) 14 — 61
(BEllison) *led 1f: remained prom: rdn over 2 out: fdd* **16/1**
60- **7** *2* **Commemoration Day (IRE)**$^{197}$ [5723] 3-8-11 ........ MFenton 13 — 57
(JGGiven) *s.i.s: bhd: drvn along 1/2-way: styd on u.p fnl 2f: n.d* **33/1**
000- **8** *1/2* **Koodoo**$^{210}$ [5489] 3-8-8 ........ LEnstone(3) 6 — 56?
(ACrook) *towards rr: kpt on u.p fnl 3f: n.d* **200/1**
2/0- **9** *3* **Blue Mariner**$^{151}$ [6153] 4-9-10 ........ BDoyle 8 — 49
(PWHarris) *trckd ldrs: rdn over 2f out: sn wknd* **14/1**$^{3}$
5- **10** *2* **Locator (IRE)**$^{172}$ [6020] 3-8-11 ........ JTate 12 — 44
(JMPEustace) *midfield: rdn over 2f out: sn btn* **33/1**
**11** *3* **Milly Golightly** 3-8-6 ........ SWKelly 4 — 32
(MDods) *s.s: a bhd* **100/1**
**12** *nk* **Grey Fortune** 5-9-5 ........ TWilliams 10 — 32
(MBrittain) *towards rr most of way* **100/1**
54- **13** *17* **Outward (USA)**$^{196}$ [5748] 4-9-13 ow3 ........ HBastiman 1 — —
(RBastiman) *led after 1f tl hdd 5 out: wknd 3 out: t.o* **66/1**
00- **14** *1* **Grey Orchid**$^{185}$ [5923] 3-8-6 ........ JFanning 3 — —
(TJEtherington) *midfield tl wknd 3f out: t.o* **200/1**

1m 43.34s (3.64) **Going Correction** +0.475s/f (Yiel)
**WFA** 3 from 4yo+ 13lb — **14** Ran SP% **120.5**
Speed ratings: **100,99,99,95,94 93,91,91,88,86 83,82,65,64**CSF £13.31 TOTE £12.30: £3.30, £1.02, £10.20; EX 22.80.
**Owner** E Duggan & D Churchman **Bred** Amdovra Way Partnership And Gaines-Centry Thorough **Trained** Newmarket, Suffolk
■ Stewards Enquiry : B Doyle caution: allowed colt to coast home with no assistance from the rider

**FOCUS**
An ordinary maiden producing probably fair form overall.

**NOTEBOOK**
**Blue Oasis(IRE)**, who has only just turned three, ran around a bit having been tardy at the start and showed signs of inexperience, as one would expect. She still proved good enough to overhaul the hot favourite and, given she is well bred, is likely to go in pursuit of some black type.
**Capped For Victory(USA)** has been turned over at 1/4 and 1/3 the last twice and is becoming disappointing. He does have a maiden in him, but is hardly one to follow and may be better in handicaps.
**Arran Scout(IRE)** showed some fair form on his second start at two and appears to have progressed. He will be of interest in handicap company.
**Little Bob** is now qualified for handicapping and should improve further for an extra quarter-mile.
**Kelbrook** is lightly raced for a five-year-old and has evidently not been easy to train.
**Commemoration Day(IRE)** is another not going to be seen at his best until handicapping.
**Blue Mariner** has been kept in training for a reason and is not one to give up on just yet.

## 1973 RIPLEY H'CAP — 2m
7:35 (7:37) (D) (0-85,80) 4-Y-0+ — £5,525 (£1,700; £850; £425) Stalls Low

Form — RPR
4/40 **1** **Lucky Judge**$^{12}$ [1661] 7-8-2 **55** ........ DaleGibson 9 — 60
(GASwinbank) *hld up: drvn along and gd hdwy to go prom 3f out: led over 1 out: styd on u.p* **28/1**
2220 **2** *1 3/4* **Madiba**$^{21}$ [1457] 5-8-2 **55** ........ JFanning 5 — 58
(PHowling) *cl up: led over 3f out: rdn and hdd over 1 out: styd on* **12/1**
0000 **3** *1 1/2* **Riyadh**$^{14}$ [1615] 6-9-3 **70** ........ (v) KDalgleish 6 — 71
(MJohnston) *s.s: hld up in rr: hdwy over 4f out: rdn 3 out: styd on wl fnl 2f: nvr able to chal* **7/1**
10-0 **4** *2* **Nobratinetta (FR)**$^{28}$ [1326] 5-9-9 **76** ........ KDarley 4 — 75
(MrsMReveley) *midfield: effrt over 3f out: styd on u.p fnl 2f: nvr able to chal* **25/1**
00-0 **5** *2* **Sono**$^{15}$ [1316] 7-9-6 **73** ........ (p) PHanagan 12 — 69
(PDNiven) *bhd and drvn along after 6f: styd on wl u.p fnl 3f: nrst fin* **50/1**
0231 **6** *nk* **Toni Alcala**$^{8}$ [1744] 5-9-1 **68** ........ KFallon 8 — 64
(RFFisher) *midfield: effrt over 3f out: sn rdn: kpt on same pce* **11/2**$^{3}$
515- **7** *1/2* **Skye's Folly (USA)**$^{209}$ [5502] 4-9-10 **80** ........ MFenton 1 — 75
(JGGiven) *led 1f: remained prom: chsng ldrs and rdn 2f out: fdd* **14/1**
-165 **8** *4* **Red Scorpion (USA)**$^{87}$ [743] 5-9-0 **72** ........ BSwarbrick(5) 2 — 63
(WMBrisbourne) *in tch: effrt over 3f out: sn rdn and btn* **11/1**
10-1 **9** *19* **Etching (USA)**$^{11}$ [1684] 4-8-4 **60** ........ EAhern 7 — 28
(JRFanshawe) *trckd ldrs: drvn along 4f out: rdn and wknd 3 out* **11/4**$^{1}$

0-34 **10** *nk* **Thewhirlingdervish (IRE)**$^{14}$ [1615] 6-9-5 **79** .................... AMullen$^{(7)}$ 11 46
(TDEasterby) *led after 1f tl hdd over 3f out: sn wknd* **3/1**$^{2}$

-106 **11** *½* **Vanbrugh (FR)**$^{79}$ [827] 4-8-8 **64** ..............................(t) DarrenWilliams 10 31
(MissDAMchale) *trckd ldrs: rdn over 3f out: sn wknd: bhd and eased fnl f* **33/1**

00-4 **12** *dist* **Autumn Fantasy (USA)**$^{8}$ [1744] 5-8-6 **64** ..........................(t) TEaves$^{(5)}$ 3 —
(BEllison) *towards rr: lost tch fr 6f out: t.o* **33/1**

3m 36.7s (5.50) **Going Correction** +0.475s/f (Yiel)
**WFA** 4 from 5yo+ 3lb **12** Ran SP% **117.4**
Speed ratings: **105,104,103,102,101 101,100,98,89,89 89,**—CSF £315.00 CT £2617.06 TOTE £37.00: £6.50, £2.50, £2.30; EX 363.10.
**Owner** Mrs I Gibson **Bred** K G Powter **Trained** Melsonby, N Yorks

**FOCUS**
A good performance from the seven-year-old Lucky Judge, who is back to form again having been off injured for a couple of years prior to this season. The form looks fair.

**NOTEBOOK**
**Lucky Judge**, who had been off for around two years prior to the start of this season, looks to be finding his feet again and, under a patient ride, came through to challenge before hitting the front and staying on strongly. He is well enough handicapped to win again off this sort of mark.
**Madiba** usually runs his race without being quite good enough to win. He did nothing wrong, but the winner was too strong on the day.
**Riyadh** has never had the best of attitudes towards racing, but he showed here he still has what it takes to win races and if kept sweet his turn will come.
**Nobratinetta(FR)** was having only her fifth start on the level and seemed to improve for the step up in trip on better ground.
**Sono**, who was being ridden some way from the finish, left some uninspiring efforts behind with a staying-on fifth. He remains without a win in this country - on the Flat and over hurdles - but on this evidence he is up to winning.
**Skye's Folly(USA)** ◆ is entitled to come on for this first start for his new stable and much better can be expected next time.
**Etching(USA)** was most disappointing, not putting up any sort of fight once in trouble half a mile out.
**Thewhirlingdervish(IRE)** was as disappointing as the favourite, folding tamely once beaten.

## 1974 DICK PEACOCK SPRINT H'CAP 6f
8:05 (8:07) (E) (0-75,75) 3-Y-0+ **£5,772** (£1,776; £888; £444) **Stalls** High

Form RPR

0244 **1** **If By Chance**$^{12}$ [1665] 6-9-2 **68** ..............................(b) TEaves$^{(5)}$ 8 76
(RCraggs) *racd far side: mde all: all out* **12/1**

460- **2** *nk* **Hartshead**$^{147}$ [6177] 5-9-2 **63** .................................... BDoyle 13 70
(GASwinbank) *dwlt: sn chsng stands side ldrs: rdn to ld gp over 1f out: edgd lft and r.o wl fnl f: nt rch wnr* **33/1**

1-0 **3** *1 ½* **Palace Theatre (IRE)**$^{26}$ [1361] 3-8-13 **75** ........................... PMakin$^{(5)}$ 9 78
(TDBarron) *racd alone centre: a.p: edgd lft fnl f: r.o* **14/1**

6101 **4** *1 ¼* **Far Note (USA)**$^{9}$ [1738] 6-9-5 **66** ....................................(b) JBramhill 6 65
(SRBowring) *in tch far side: chsng wnr and rdn appr fnl f: no ex ins last* **8/1**

0000 **5** *2 ½* **Pagan Storm (USA)**$^{6}$ [1787] 4-8-13 **67** ........................ KristinStubbs$^{(7)}$ 2 58
(MrsLStubbs) *in tch far side: hdwy 2f out: kpt on same pce fnl f* **50/1**

000- **6** *½* **Mister Sweets**$^{244}$ [4753] 5-9-5 **73** ............................ DTudhope$^{(7)}$ 16 63
(DCarroll) *midfield stands side: kpt on wl fnl f: nvr able to chal* **16/1**

00-5 **7** *shd* **Palanzo (IRE)**$^{7}$ [1774] 6-9-7 **68** ........................................ ANicholls 10 57
(DNicholls) *midfield stands side: drvn along 1/2-way: hdwy to chse ldrs over 1f out: kpt on same pce fnl f* **6/1**$^{1}$

5-60 **8** *nk* **Coustou (IRE)**$^{12}$ [1663] 4-9-3 **64** .............................................. PFessey 4 53
(ARDicken) *chsd wnr far side tl wknd over 1f out* **100/1**

0/0- **9** *½* **Hilltime (IRE)**$^{225}$ [5196] 4-9-4 **65** ...................................... RWinston 20 52
(JJQuinn) *racd stands side: dwlt: towards rr: kpt on fr over 1f out: n.d* **40/1**

00-0 **10** *½* **Zuhair**$^{7}$ [1774] 11-9-11 **72** .................................................... AlexGreaves 5 58
(DNicholls) *sn towards rr far side: n.d* **25/1**

000- **11** *½* **Roman Mistress (IRE)**$^{183}$ [5941] 4-9-4 **68** ........................ DAllan$^{(3)}$ 18 52
(TDEasterby) *prom stands side tl wknd over 1f out* **22/1**

20-0 **12** *½* **William's Well**$^{18}$ [1526] 10-9-2 **63** ...................................(b) DaleGibson 12 46
(MWEasterby) *cl up stands side tl wknd over 1f out* **25/1**

140- **13** *nk* **Mimic**$^{211}$ [5473] 4-9-4 **72** .......................................................... RMills$^{(7)}$ 15 54
(RGuest) *cl up stands side: led gp 1/2-way tl over 1f out: edgd lft and wknd fnl f* **16/1**

0L-0 **14** *½* **Time To Remember (IRE)**$^{7}$ [1772] 6-9-6 **67** ...................... ACulhane 14 47
(DNicholls) *chsd ldrs stands side tl wknd over 1f out* **25/1**

2-60 **15** *1 ½* **Quantica (IRE)**$^{7}$ [1774] 5-9-3 **64** ............................................. KimTinkler 7 40
(NTinkler) *dwlt: swtchd to stands side after 1f: a towards rr* **14/1**

0000 **16** *¾* **African Spur (IRE)**$^{4}$ [1868] 4-8-13 **63** ..............................(t) DNolan$^{(3)}$ 3 36
(DCarroll) *racd far side: sn bhd* **66/1**

260- **17** *shd* **Kings College Boy**$^{208}$ [5538] 4-9-2 **63** ............................... PHanagan 19 36
(RAFahey) *racd stands side: sn rr div* **20/1**

1550 **18** *1 ½* **Quiet Times (IRE)**$^{1}$ [1929] 5-9-4 **65** .....................................(b) NCallan 11 34
(KARyan) *racd stands side: sn rr div* **8/1**

2-50 **19** *¾* **Chairman Bobby**$^{7}$ [1774] 6-9-5 **69** ................................... LEnstone$^{(3)}$ 17 35
(DWBarker) *led stands side gp to 1/2-way: sn rdn and wknd* **7/1**$^{2}$

500- **20** *1 ¾* **Midnight Parkes**$^{209}$ [5515] 5-9-7 **68** ........................................ WSupple 1 29
(EJAlston) *prom far side tl wknd over 2f out* **15/2**$^{3}$

1m 13.8s (-2.03) **Going Correction** +0.30s/f (Good)
**WFA** 3 from 4yo+ 10lb **20** Ran SP% **124.0**
Speed ratings: **103,102,100,98,95 94,94,94,93,93 92,91,91,90,88 87,87,85,84,82**CSF £370.72 CT £5518.25 TOTE £11.30: £2.30, £6.00, £3.60, £2.70; EX 552.00.
**Owner** Ray Craggs **Bred** D R Tucker **Trained** Sedgefield, Co Durham

**FOCUS**
The field split, but the draw did not appear to make much difference. This was only a fair handicap and probably not great form.

**NOTEBOOK**
**If By Chance** stuck to the far side and found plenty for pressure under a positive ride from Eaves. This was the highest ever mark he has won off by 9lb, and he will not find things easy from now on, but he is consistent and should continue to pay his way.
**Hartshead** fared best of those racing stands side, just getting run out of it. His final run last season came over a mile and a half and this sort of trip seems to suit much better.
**Palace Theatre(IRE)**, the only three-year-old in the field, came down the centre alone and ran well considering he was having only his third start. There should be more to come from him.
**Far Note(USA)** is fully effective at this trip, although possibly better suited by five.
**Pagan Storm(USA)** ran well at a big price, and may be worth chancing over seven.
**Mister Sweets** ran well on this first start since September, and can only come on for the outing.
**Palanzo(IRE)** is in the right hands to recapture his best form and should not be long.
**Chairman Bobby** showed up well early, but was struggling from two out. *Official explanation: jockey said gelding became very unsettled in the stalls.*

## 1975 CATTERICK GARRISON MAIDEN STKS 6f
8:35 (8:38) (D) 3-Y-0+ **£5,200** (£1,600; £800; £400) **Stalls** High

Form RPR

2 **1** **Snap**$^{8}$ [1749] 3-8-11 ....................................................... JFanning 7 69
(MJohnston) *w ldr: led over 1f out: drvn out* **9/4**$^{1}$

503- **2** *½* **Flying Bantam (IRE)**$^{223}$ [5255] 3-8-8 71 ........................ THamilton$^{(3)}$ 8 68
(RAFahey) *slt ld tl hdd over 1f out: r.o u.p* **20/1**

0465 **3** *nk* **Dark Champion**$^{51}$ [1044] 4-9-7 60 ........................................ PHanagan 9 67
(REBarr) *chsd ldrs: rdn over 1f out: r.o* **33/1**

36-6 **4** *nk* **Midnight Ballard (USA)**$^{23}$ [1413] 3-8-11 82 ........................ SCarson 13 66
(RFJohnsonHoughton) *chsd ldrs: rdn over 1f out: r.o* **7/2**$^{2}$

530- **5** *2* **Oeuf A La Neige**$^{308}$ [3007] 4-9-7 70 ....................................... RFfrench 3 60
(GCHChung) *midfield: drvn along 1/2-way: kpt on fnl f: nvr able to chal* **28/1**

**6** *½* **Intavac Boy** 3-8-11 ............................................................. TWilliams 2 59
(CWThornton) *s.s: bhd: r.o u.p fnl 2f: nrst fin* **100/1**

026- **7** *2 ½* **Compton Plume**$^{208}$ [5538] 4-9-2 55 ................................... TEaves$^{(5)}$ 16 51
(WHTinning) *racd alone stands rail: chsd ldrs: drvn along over 2f out: no hdwy* **14/1**

3 **8** *¾* **Mister Regent**$^{22}$ [1453] 3-8-11 ........................................... NCallan 10 49
(KARyan) *s.s: sn drvn along in midfield: no hdwy* **9/1**$^{3}$

00-2 **9** *1 ¼* **Boris The Spider**$^{10}$ [1711] 3-8-11 61 .................................... ACulhane 5 45
(MDHammond) *nvr btr than mid-div* **25/1**

-0 **10** *hd* **Red Monarch (IRE)**$^{66}$ [956] 3-8-8 ................................... DNolan$^{(3)}$ 15 45
(PABlockley) *racd towards stands rail: prom tl hung lft and wknd over 1f out* **50/1**

5-6 **11** *8* **The Warley Warrior**$^{10}$ [1711] 3-8-6 ............................(b) PMulrennan$^{(5)}$ 11 21
(MWEasterby) *s.s: hdwy to chse ldrs 1/2-way: wknd 2f out* **50/1**

000- **12** *nk* **Sujosise**$^{224}$ [5221] 3-8-11 ................................................. RWinston 12 20
(JJQuinn) *sn bhd* **100/1**

65-0 **13** *nk* **Scientist**$^{25}$ [1386] 3-8-11 80 ............................................... KFallon 6 19
(JHMGosden) *s.i.s: mid-div: drvn along over 2f out: sn btn* **7/2**$^{2}$

P0- **14** *29* **From The North (IRE)**$^{220}$ [5294] 3-8-6 ............................... CCatlin 14 —
(ADickman) *sn bhd: lost tch fnl 2f: t.o* **100/1**

1m 15.21s (2.71) **Going Correction** +0.30s/f (Good)
**WFA** 3 from 4yo 10lb **14** Ran SP% **114.8**
Speed ratings: **93,92,91,91,88 88,84,83,82,81 71,70,70,31**CSF £52.94 TOTE £3.20: £1.70, £3.90, £9.10; EX 38.80 Place 6 £249.00, Place 5 £168.33.
**Owner** Lord Hartington **Bred** Side Hill Stud **Trained** Middleham Moor, N Yorks

**FOCUS**
A very modest winning time for the grade, 1.41 seconds slower than the preceding handicap. The third home holds down the form.

**NOTEBOOK**
**Snap**, who shaped with plenty of promise when second on his debut, went one better in good fashion, staying on well from the front to win with a little bit in hand. He will be suited by an extra furlong and should be up to winning in handicap company.
**Flying Bantam(IRE)** is without a win in six starts, just being run out of it in the final furlong. His turn will come.
**Dark Champion** has yet to win in 23 outings and does not do much for the form.
**Midnight Ballard(USA)** was not completely disgraced and will be better off back in handicaps.
**Oeuf A La Neige** is well exposed and it will be a weak race he wins.
**Intavac Boy** would have pleased connections on this racecourse debut, edging closer with every stride at the line.
**Scientist** was never going and may be in trouble off his current rating as he does not appear to be heading the right way.
T/Plt: £166.00 to a £1 stake. Pool: £35,806.15. 157.45 winning tickets. T/Qpdt: £115.60 to a £1 stake. Pool: £2,251.10. 14.40 winning tickets. JF

1976 - 1978a (Foreign Racing) - See Raceform Interactive

# 1484 LEOPARDSTOWN (L-H)
Sunday, May 9

**OFFICIAL GOING: Good to yielding**

## 1979a DERRINSTOWN STUD DERBY TRIAL STKS (GROUP 2) 1m 2f
4:00 (4:00) 3-Y-0 **£60,563** (£17,394; £8,239; £2,746)

RPR

**1** **Yeats (IRE)**$^{21}$ [1489] 3-9-0 ................................................ JPSpencer 5 111+
(APO'Brien, Ire) *mde all: edgd clr 3f out: rdn and kpt on wl st: comf* **1/5**$^{1}$

**2** *1 ½* **Relaxed Gesture (IRE)**$^{197}$ [5772] 3-9-0 107 ........................... PJSmullen 2 108
(DKWeld, Ire) *hld up in rr: hdwy on outer ent st: 2nd and kpt on wl fr over 1f out* **11/2**$^{2}$

**3** *1* **Medicinal (IRE)**$^{21}$ [1487] 3-9-0 ........................................... PShanahan 3 106
(DKWeld, Ire) *chsd ldrs in 3rd: rdn 3f out: outpcd early st: kpt on u.p fnl f* **20/1**

**4** *2 ½* **Barati (IRE)**$^{14}$ [1651] 3-9-0 ................................................ MJKinane 1 102
(JohnMOxx, Ire) *settled 2nd: rdn 3f out: one pce st* **8/1**$^{3}$

2m 10.3s **Going Correction** +0.125s/f (Good) **4** Ran SP% **114.6**
Speed ratings: **105,103,103,101**CSF £2.18 TOTE £1.20; DF 2.20.
**Owner** Mrs John Magnier **Bred** Barronstown Stud & Orpendale **Trained** Ballydoyle, Co Tipperary

**NOTEBOOK**
**Yeats(IRE)** put up another workmanlike performance. He was always doing enough, and won without being extended, and once again left little indication regarding his exact ability, which most of us believe is in excess of what he has shown to date. He goes to Epsom still very much a dark horse. He had a placid, relaxed demeanour and has not really come in his coat yet. He appears to have suffered a skin problem, but he was feisty enough after the race.
**Relaxed Gesture(IRE)**, having his first run since a disappointing Breeders' Cup effort, needed this. Waited with in last place, he looked a little too relaxed, came wide and, with second place assured from a furlong and a half down, the penny only dropped too late that this was a Group Two and a bit more effort resulted. He would not have beaten the winner, but he may have got to within a half length. He would need to be supplemented for Epsom and the Belmont Stakes appears to be the favoured option. There is plenty of improvement to come.
**Medicinal(IRE)**, second string to the runner-up and 10lb below him in the Classifications, ran well and built on his fourth behind Grey Swallow here last month.
**Barati(IRE)**won what was only an average Curragh maiden a fortnight previously and was supplemented for this. Under pressure before the straight, he was soon struggling but this still marked him as being on the upgrade..

## 1980a DERRINSTOWN STUD 1,000 GUINEAS TRIAL (GROUP 3) (FILLIES) 7f

4:30 (4:33) 3-Y-O £38,968 (£11,433; £5,447; £1,855)

RPR

1 **Alexander Goldrun (IRE)**[49] 1070 3-8-11 101 KJManning 1 99+
(JSBolger, Ire) *s.i.s: checked after 1 1/2 fs: 7th and rdn early st: 3rd 1f out: r.o wl between horses to ld nr fin* **4/1**[2]

2 *shd* **Misty Heights**[21] 1485 3-8-11 105 PJSmullen 5 99
(DKWeld, Ire) *trckd ldrs: 4th into st: rdn to ld 1f out: kpt on wl u.p: hdd nr fin* **5/1**[3]

3 *nk* **Miss Childrey (IRE)**[35] 1256 3-8-11 100 JAHeffernan 8 98
(FrancisEnnis, Ire) *attempted to make all: rdn early st: hdd 1f out: kpt on wl u.p* **14/1**

4 *3* **Lucky (IRE)**[14] 1649 3-8-11 104 JPSpencer 9 91
(APO'Brien, Ire) *prom: 3rd 1/2-way: rdn st: no imp whn hung rt 1 1/2f out: no ex fnl f* **9/4**[1]

5 *¾* **Summer Sunset (IRE)**[210] 5519 3-8-11 95 PShanahan 7 89
(DKWeld, Ire) *s.i.s and towards rr: kpt on fr 2f out* **16/1**

6 *shd* **Rihla (IRE)**[17] 1576 3-8-11 MJKinane 3 89
(JohnMOxx, Ire) *s.i.s and hld up: last and rdn ent st: kpt on one pced* **8/1**

7 *nk* **Sudden Silence (IRE)**[22] 1480 3-8-11 88 WSupple 2 88
(DeclanGillespie, Ire) *prom: 2nd into st: sn wknd* **16/1**

8 *2* **Maroochydore (IRE)**[14] 1649 3-8-11 104 (b[1]) JPMurtagh 4 83
(DavidWachman, Ire) *4th early: 5th 1/2-way: effrt and no imp early st: eased fnl f* **10/1**

9 *8* **Ulfah (USA)**[203] 5655 3-8-11 92 DPMcDonogh 6 63
(KevinPrendergast, Ire) *racd keenly: 6th 1/2-way: wknd ent st* **7/1**

1m 31.4s **Going Correction** +0.125s/f (Good) **9** Ran SP% **118.6**
Speed ratings: **109,108,108,105,104 104,103,101,92**CSF £25.11 TOTE £3.90: £1.40, £1.80, £7.20; DF 15.40.
**Owner** Mrs N O'Callaghan **Bred** Dermot Cantillon **Trained** Coolcullen, Co Carlow

**NOTEBOOK**
**Alexander Goldrun(IRE)** missed the break, was checked after a furlong and a half but was still able to come between horses to lead close home.
**Misty Heights** showed improvement on her last run here, got to the front a furlong out and will find more on better ground.
**Miss Childrey(IRE)** found front-running tactics showing her in a better light.
**Lucky(IRE)** found this a stiffer task than her Curragh Group Three win. She hung out with over a furlong to race and found nothing.
**Summer Sunset(IRE)** showed improved form on her three-year-old debut.

## 1982a AMETHYST STKS (LISTED RACE) 1m

5:30 (5:31) 3-Y-O+ £22,922 (£6,725; £3,204; £1,091)

RPR

1 **D'Anjou**[43] 1142 7-9-13 110 MJKinane 4 112
(JohnMOxx, Ire) *trckd ldr in 2nd: rdn to chal 2f out: led under 1 1/2f out: kpt on wl ins fnl f* **12/1**

2 *½* **Meath (IRE)**[21] 1487 3-8-9 106 JPSpencer 2 106
(APO'Brien, Ire) *led: strly pressed early st: hdd under 1 1/2f out: rallied u.p ins fnl f* **8/11**[1]

3 *shd* **Tolpuddle (IRE)**[14] 1647 4-9-11 105 WMLordan 3 109
(TStack, Ire) *trckd ldrs: 4th 1/2-way: 5th and rdn ent st: styd on wl ins fnl f* **11/2**[2]

4 *nk* **Eklim (IRE)**[14] 1647 4-9-8 105 DPMcDonogh 6 105
(KevinPrendergast, Ire) *settled 3rd: kpt on under rpessure fr 2f out* **13/2**[3]

5 *hd* **Twiggy's Sister (IRE)**[14] 1649 6-9-5 100 WSupple 8 102
(DermotMurphy, Ire) *chsd ldrs: 6th into st: kpt on wl fr over 1f out* **16/1**

6 *nk* **Multazem (USA)**[207] 5585 4-9-8 108 PJSmullen 7 104
(DKWeld, Ire) *towards rr: prog on outer early st: 4th 1f out: kpt on* **13/2**[3]

7 *1* **Livadiya (IRE)**[49] 1071 8-9-8 110 JPMurtagh 1 102
(HRogers, Ire) *hld up in rr: effrt and no imp st* **10/1**

8 *3* **One Won One (USA)**[4] 1893 10-9-8 102 KJManning 5 96
(MsJoannaMorgan, Ire) *hld up: no imp fr 2f out* **14/1**

9 *2* **Common World (USA)**[12] 2188 5-9-8 104 PShanahan 9 91
(NoelMeade, Ire) *hld up: prog into 4th 3f out: wknd st* **16/1**

1m 45.0s **Going Correction** +0.125s/f (Good)
**WFA** 3 from 4yo+ 13lb **9** Ran SP% **135.2**
Speed ratings: **102,101,101,101,100 100,99,96,94**CSF £24.95 TOTE £13.30: £2.30, £1.40, £1.80; DF 29.40.
**Owner** Barouche Stud Ireland Ltd **Bred** Barouche Stud Ltd **Trained** Currabeg, Co Kildare

**NOTEBOOK**
**D'Anjou** was fit from his desert sojourn but had a 5lb penalty for his Group Three success and really needs firm ground, but he led over a furlong out and held on gamely.
**Meath(IRE)** tried to make all and came back strongly inside the last after being headed by the winner. He would appreciate another couple of furlongs and will have his day.
**Tolpuddle(IRE)** finished well and would have liked it a lot softer.
**Eklim(IRE)** ran to his mark.
**Twiggy's Sister(IRE)** is ready to strike.
**Multazem(USA)** just might have needed this initial outing.
**Livadiya(IRE)** came with a wide run in the straight but it was never going to get her there.
T/Jkpt: @1,375.80 to a 50 cents stake. Pool of @16,510.50 - 9 winning units T/Plt: @13.00 to a 50 cents stake. Pool of @2,420.50 - 139 winning units II

1981 - 1982a (Foreign Racing) - See Raceform Interactive

# DUSSELDORF (R-H)

Sunday, May 9

**OFFICIAL GOING: Soft**

## 1983a HENKEL-RENNEN GERMAN 1000 GUINEAS (GROUP 2) (FILLIES) 1m

3:35 (3:38) 3-Y-O £80,989 (£30,986; £16,197; £8,451)

RPR

1 **Shapira (GER)**[29] 3-9-2 JPalik 13 104
(AndreasLowe, Germany) *held up in rear, 11th straight, strong run down outside from 2f out, led just over 1f out, edged right, ran on well*

2 *1¾* **La Ina (GER)**[27] 3-9-2 ADeVries 5 100
(ATrybuhl, Germany) *9th straight, went 5th 1 1/2f out, stayed on well down outside final f to take 2nd final 50 yards* 3

3 *¾* **Coqueteria (USA)**[29] 1327 3-9-2 SDrowne 1 99
(GWragg) *in touch on inside, 4th tracking leader entering straight, squeezed through to lead narrowly 1 1/2f out, headed just over 1*

4 *½* **Freedom (GER)** 3-9-2 THellier 15 98
(ASchutz, Germany) *held up, headway on outside to go 6th straight, pressing leader 2f out to 1f out, one pace*

5 *2* **La Hermana**[8] 3-9-2 FilipMinarik 10 94
(AWohler, Germany) *7th straight, effort on inside when hampered over 1 1/2f out, stayed on well against inside rail final f*

6 *½* **Chrisiida (GER)**[29] 3-9-2 LHammer-Hansen 14 93
(ASchutz, Germany) *in rear, last straight, ran on steadily under pressure final 1 1/2f*

7 *1¾* **Red Pearl (FR)** 3-9-2 JBojko 11 89
(HFanelsa, France) *close up, 3rd straight, every chance 2f out to 1 1/2f out, weakened final f*

8 *1¾* **Felicity (GER)** 3-9-2 ABoschert 2 86
(PRau, Germany) *close up, 5th straight, one pace final 2f*

9 *2* **Attilia (GER)**[273] 3-9-2 ASuborics 9 82
(PSchiergen, Germany) *held up, 10th straight, switched to inside and not much room 2f out, switched to outside, stayed on at one pace final f* 2

10 *1¼* **Night Lagoon (GER)**[27] 3-9-2 AStarke 6 79
(ASchutz, Germany) *raced in 2nd, led narrowly 2f out to 1 1/2f out, weakened* 1

11 *hd* **Apokalypse (GER)** 3-9-2 SChin 7 79
(ASchutz, Germany) *never a factor*

12 *1¼* **Acciacatura (USA)**[252] 4601 3-9-2 (b) JFEgan 8 76
(RGibson, France) *12th straight, soon ridden and no impression*

13 *4½* **Prunelle (GER)** 3-9-2 AHelfenbein 12 67
(PRau, Germany) *close up til weakened 2f out*

14 *1¼* **Letitzia (GER)**[247] 4711 3-9-2 (b) IFerguson 16 65
(WBaltromei, Germany) *always in rear*

15 *1¼* **Joyce (GER)**[200] 5713 3-9-2 (b) WMongil 4 62
(HSteinmetz, Germany) *set good pace to 2f out, weakened quickly*

1m 42.21s **15** Ran SP% **132.8**
Speed ratings: .
**Owner** Stall Granum **Bred** Gestut Schattauer Hof - Granum Zucht **Trained** Germany

**NOTEBOOK**
**Shapira(GER)** belied her odds, using a fine burst of speed to come from the rear to lead a furlong out. A mile could be the extent of her stamina.
**La Ina(GER)** was staying on strongly in the closing stages. She has been sold to continue her career in the US but her current trainer is hoping to keep her long enough to run in the German Oaks, where the extra three furlongs should be ideal.
**Coqueteria(USA)**, the only British raider, ran a good race in defeat and should have little trouble winning at Group level this season, her versatility with regards to ground being a bonus.

# 1826 KEMPTON (R-H)

Monday, May 10

**OFFICIAL GOING: Heavy**

## 1984 NATWEST MAIDEN AUCTION STKS 5f

2:10 (2:12) (H) 2-Y-O £1,522 (£435; £217) Stalls High

Form RPR

1 **Golden Anthem (USA)** 2-8-9 JQuinn 7 69
(JPearce) *s.s: rn green in rr: effrt whn nt clr run and swtchd lft over 2f out: prog over 1f out: led last 100y: rdn clr* **7/1**

4 2 *2½* **Ruby's Dream**[7] 1839 2-8-9 RLMoore 10 61
(JMBradley) *trckd ldrs: effrt to ld over 1f out: hdd and outpcd last 100y* **4/1**[1]

046 3 *5* **Wizzskilad**[17] 1589 2-9-0 RHavlin 8 51
(MrsPNDutfield) *racd against far rail: led to over 3f out: led again over 2f out to over 1f out: wknd ins fnl f* **6/1**

26 4 *½* **General Nuisance (IRE)**[32] 1307 2-8-7 DerekNolan[(7)] 4 50
(JSMoore) *racd on outer: in tch: rdn and outpcd 2f out: styd on again ins fnl f* **8/1**

5 *3½* **Tipsy Lillie** 2-8-6 LisaJones[(3)] 1 34
(JulianPoulton) *racd on outer: in rr: outpcd fr 1/2-way: kpt on one pce fnl f* **20/1**

6 *2½* **Queen's Glory (IRE)** 2-8-9 SDrowne 9 27
(WRMuir) *chsd ldrs: pushed along bef 1/2-way: wknd wl over 1f out* **16/1**

7 *1* **Russian Rocket (IRE)** 2-9-0 CCatlin 2 29
(MrsCADunnett) *dwlt: racd on outer: nvr on terms* **33/1**

00 8 *3* **Muestra (IRE)**[6] 1853 2-8-9 TEDurcan 5 15
(MrsPNDutfield) *s.s: a bhd* **66/1**

6 9 *1¾* **Bamboozled**[51] 1060 2-8-9 KFallon 6 9
(PDEvans) *chsd ldrs for 2f: sn wknd* **5/1**[2]

10 *5* **Sherbourne** 2-8-9 PaulEddery 11 —
(MGQuinlan) *s.s: rcvrd to chse ldrs after 2f: rdn and wkng whn hmpd over 1f out: eased* **11/2**[3]

605 11 *¾* **Zachy Boy**[17] 1589 2-9-0 MartinDwyer 3 —
(JSMoore) *pressed ldrs: led over 3f out to over 2f out: wknd and hung rt over 1f out* **12/1**

65.66 secs (4.45) **Going Correction** +0.775s/f (Yiel) **11** Ran SP% **112.7**
Speed ratings: **95,91,83,82,76 72,71,66,63,55 54**CSF £32.95 TOTE £10.50: £3.00, £1.80, £1.90; EX 51.10.
**Owner** S Birdseye **Bred** W A Hamilton **Trained** Newmarket, Suffolk

**FOCUS**
A low-grade maiden and a real test in the conditions for these juveniles, but front two appear slightly better than bottom grade.

**NOTEBOOK**
**Golden Anthem(USA)**, a half-sister to a juvenile mile winner in the US, overcame her early greenness to run out a tidy winner. She handled the testing conditions well and, although this was a weak maiden, is open to further improvement.
**Ruby's Dream** had run a fair race on her debut and set the standard. She ran well in defeat and a regional race looks within her capability.
**Wizzskilad** once again failed to get home and it is possible that faster ground will help him preserve his limited stamina.
**General Nuisance(IRE)**, beaten in a seller and claimer on his first two starts, kept going late on and should pay his way in the short term in banded grade.
**Tipsy Lillie** was not helped by her low draw in her debut.
**Queen's Glory(IRE)** hails from a stable whose juveniles usually improve for their debuts.

## 1985 CBFM TRI-BANDED STKS 6f
2:40 (2:40) (H) 3-Y-O £1,452 (£415; £207) Stalls High

Form RPR

4004 1 **Pardon Moi**[4] 1913 3-8-9 45........................................ HayleyTurner(5) 9 52
(MrsCADunnett) *racd against far rail: pressed ldr: led 2f out: edgd lft over 1f out: rdn and kpt on fnl f* 6/1[3]

0040 2 2 1/2 **Indrani**[11] 1725 3-9-0 45........................................ PaulEddery 2 46
(JohnAHarris) *trckd ldrs: effrt over 2f out: drvn to chse wnr 1f out: nt qckn and no imp last 100y* 10/1

00-0 3 2 1/2 **Lord Wishingwell (IRE)**[16] 1617 3-8-9 40....................(v[1]) SWhitworth 3 35
(JSWainwright) *pressed ldrs: rdn wl over 2f out: kpt on same pce fr over 1f out* 20/1

0-05 4 1 3/4 **Anatom**[11] 1725 3-8-5 36 ow1........................................(t) NPollard 5 26
(PSMcentee) *led to 2f out: wknd ins fnl f* 7/1

4425 5 nk **Heathyards Joy**[6] 1864 3-8-4 35........................................ JQuinn 1 24
(RHollinshead) *racd on outer: in rr: rdn 1/2-way: one pce and no imp ldrs* 9/2[2]

0004 6 1 **Taranai (IRE)**[6] 1864 3-8-9 45........................................ NChalmers(5) 4 32
(BWDuke) *a in rr: last and rdn over 3f out: struggling after* 7/2[1]

00-0 7 3/4 **St George's Girl**[21] 1507 3-7-11 30........................................ JJeffrey(7) 6 20
(JRJenkins) *rrd s: as in rr: bmpd along and no prog 2f out* 33/1

0006 8 1 3/4 **Must Be So**[11] 1725 3-8-9 40........................................ JTate 8 21
(JJBridger) *chsd ldrs: rdn 1/2-way: wknd over 1f out* 9/2[2]

0-00 9 1/2 **Scenic Flight**[21] 1496 3-9-0 45........................................(b[1]) CCatlin 7 24
(MrsAJBowlby) *chsd ldrs: rdn 1/2-way: wknd over 1f out* 9/1

1m 21.39s (8.32) **Going Correction** +0.775s/f (Yiel) **9** Ran SP% **112.2**

Speed ratings: **75,71,68,66,65 64,63,60,60**CSF £61.57 TOTE £9.20: £2.80, £4.50, £5.80; EX 76.30.

**Owner** Andy Middleton **Bred** Launceston Stud **Trained** Hingham, Norfolk

**FOCUS**

A painfully slow time, even allowing for the grade of contest and the testing conditions.

**NOTEBOOK**

**Pardon Moi**, one of only two previous winners in the race, made the most of her high draw and stuck to the far-side rail throughout. She scored well enough, but this race did not take much winning and she will find things tougher if her connections choose to take up an engagement in a Yarmouth handicap later in the week.

**Indrani** was without the cheekpieces which had little positive impact last time out. She ran a better race this time and soft ground clearly holds no fears.

**Lord Wishingwell(IRE)** did not get home over ten furlongs last time and a visor replaced the cheekpieces on this occasion. The drop in class and return to sprinting certainly brought about an improved display.

**Anatom** did not find the change of tactics bringing about any significant improvement. *Official explanation: jockey said filly hung badly left-handed*

**Heathyards Joy** failed to run up to his best on this softer ground.

**Taranai(IRE)** has now run poorly on both starts in testing conditions.

## 1986 COUTTS & CO BANDED STKS 7f (J)
3:15 (3:15) (H) 3-Y-O+ £1,550 (£443; £221) Stalls Low

Form RPR

0351 1 **Extemporise (IRE)**[17] 1592 4-9-5 45........................................ TGMcLaughlin 10 56
(TTClement) *racd on inner: pressed ldrs: led over 2f out: hung rt but in command over 1f out: drvn out* 10/1

3422 2 4 **Tojoneski**[17] 1592 5-9-5 40........................................(p) KFallon 12 46
(IWMcinnes) *w overall ldr on inner: led 3f out to over 2f out: chsd wnr after: no imp fnl f* 5/1[1]

0065 3 1 1/4 **Happy Camper (IRE)**[21] 1496 4-9-5 45........................................ DSweeney 16 43
(MRHoad) *racd on inner: in rr: outpcd 3f out: styd on fr over 1f out* 50/1

5251 4 nk **Due To Me**[21] 1494 4-9-5 45........................................(p) SWhitworth 17 42
(GLMoore) *trckd ldrs on inner: swtchd to outer 3f out and led gp: clr of rivals wl over 1f out: no ch* 14/1

0505 5 6 **Kanz Wood (USA)**[17] 1582 8-9-2 45........................................ SHitchcott(3) 14 27
(AWCarroll) *dwlt: racd in last pair on inner: drvn and effrt 3f out: no imp on ldrs 2f out: wknd fnl f* 10/1

0231 6 3/4 **Shirley Oaks (IRE)**[34] 1280 6-9-0 45........................................ NChalmers(5) 6 25
(MissZCDavison) *trckd ldrs on outer: c centre in st: effrt over 2f out: one pce and n.d* 9/1

0-02 7 8 **Catch The Fox**[17] 1582 4-9-5 45........................................ JTate 5 5
(JJBridger) *cl up on outer: chsd ldr 2f out: no imp: wknd over 1f out* 8/1[3]

0235 8 5 **Single Track Mind**[11] 1723 6-9-5 45........................................ MartinDwyer 7 —
(JRBoyle) *racd on outer: rr: rdn 3f out: nvr on terms* 14/1

0454 9 5 **Muqtadi (IRE)**[20] 1516 6-9-5 45........................................ LDettori 4 —
(MQuinn) *racd on outer: settled wl in rr: struggling fr over 2f out* 13/2[2]

0300 10 1/2 **Westmead Etoile**[5] 1889 4-9-5 45........................................(b[1]) CLowther 1 —
(JRJenkins) *pressed ldr on outer to over 2f out: wknd* 50/1

2010 11 4 **Packin Em In**[34] 1280 6-9-5 45........................................ MHenry 2 —
(JRBoyle) *led gp on outer to over 2f out: wknd rapidly over 1f out* 16/1

5004 12 2 1/2 **Robin Sharp**[11] 1723 6-9-5 35........................................(p) PDoe 13 —
(JAkehurst) *overall ldr on inner to 3f out: wknd rapidly wl over 1f out* 25/1

1252 13 3 **Tee Jay Kassidy**[4] 1915 4-9-2 40........................................ LisaJones(3) 11 —
(JulianPoulton) *racd in rr on gp on inner: swtchd to outer 3f out: nvr a factor* 20/1

0004 14 3 1/2 **Waterline Dancer (IRE)**[49] 1076 4-9-5 45........................................(vt) SDrowne 8 —
(PDEvans) *prom on outer to over 2f out: wknd rapidly* 33/1

4055 15 9 **Indian Warrior**[13] 1692 8-9-5 45........................................ KMcEvoy 15 —
(JJay) *dwlt: racd in last pair on gp on inner: swtchd to outer 3f out: shuffled along and sn wknd* 16/1

-003 16 1 1/2 **Formeric**[20] 1526 8-9-5 40........................................(v) JQuinn 3 —
(MissLCSiddall) *racd on outer: a in rr: wl bhd 3f out* 10/1

0400 17 15 **Janes Valentine**[13] 1692 4-9-5 35........................................ NPollard 9 —
(JJBridger) *rrd s: racd on outer: a bhd: t.o* 50/1

1m 36.75s (9.48) **Going Correction** +1.30s/f (Soft) **17** Ran SP% **120.9**

Speed ratings: **97,92,91,90,83 82,73,68,62,61 57,54,50,46,36 34,17**CSF £54.59 TOTE £19.60: £3.00, £2.00, £11.20; EX 95.70.

**Owner** Ms K Sadler **Bred** Paradime Ltd **Trained** Newmarket, Suffolk

**FOCUS**

The field split into two groups in the early stages and those drawn high who remained towards the inner dominated.

**NOTEBOOK**

**Extemporise(IRE)** stuck to the inside, which proved an advantage as it turned out, and followed up his recent success at Warwick in good style, running out a clear winner. He is clearly very much at home in the mud and so the drop back in trip was no problem.

**Tojoneski**, a narrow runner-up to Extemporise at Warwick, again had to settle for second behind that rival. He too benefited from racing on the favoured inside.

**Happy Camper(IRE)**, another to race on the favoured ground towards the inside, stayed on well enough without threatening to win.

**Due To Me** ran with credit given that her rider probably made the wrong decision in heading for the stands'-side rail turning in. She finished clear on her side.

**Kanz Wood(USA)** was beaten a fair way and her final position owes more to her racing on the favoured inner than anything.

**Shirley Oaks(IRE)** can take credit from the fact that she came out best of those who stuck to the outside throughout.

**Single Track Mind** *Official explanation: jockey said gelding was unsuited by the heavy ground*

**Muqtadi(IRE)** *Official explanation: jockey said gelding was unsuited by the heavy ground*

**Packin Em In** *Official explanation: jockey said horse was unsuited by the heavy ground*

## 1987 ONE ACCOUNT BANDED STKS 1m 2f (J)
3:50 (3:52) (H) 3-Y-O+ £1,505 (£430; £215) Stalls Low

Form RPR

3264 1 **Unsuited**[17] 1582 5-9-1 40........................................ NataliaGemelova(7) 9 61
(JELong) *hld up in rr: prog on inner 3f out: led over 1f out: sn wl clr : drvn out* 12/1

4432 2 17 **Mr Whizz**[14] 1580 7-9-1 40........................................(p) DerekNolan(7) 2 32
(APJones) *wl in tch: chsd ldr 3f out: rdn to chal 2f out: no ch w wnr fr over 1f out* 11/2[3]

5-00 3 3/4 **Prince Albert**[20] 1522 6-9-8 35........................................ WRyan 11 31
(JRJenkins) *racd in midfield: rdn and effrt 3f out: one pce fnl 2f* 16/1

0053 4 2 1/2 **All On My Own (USA)**[17] 1592 9-9-8 35........................................(b) LVickers 4 27
(IWMcinnes) *dwlt: racd in rr: rdn and prog 3f out: kpt on one pce u.p fnl 2f* 16/1

3514 5 nk **Misty Man (USA)**[4] 1914 6-9-5 40........................................(b) BReilly(3) 10 26
(MissJFeilden) *dwlt: t.k.h and sn prom: led 1/2-way: kicked clr over 3f out: hdd & wknd over 1f out* 6/1

6/36 6 2 **Dancing Dolphin (IRE)**[4] 1917 5-9-5 30........................................ LisaJones(3) 6 23
(JulianPoulton) *trckd ldrs: rdn over 2f out: sn fdd* 33/1

-502 7 5 **Smarter Charter**[11] 1722 11-9-1 35........................................ KristinStubbs(7) 1 14
(MrsLStubbs) *s.i.s: wl in rr: c centre st: bmpd along and no ch* 14/1

4001 8 hd **Margarets Wish**[17] 1581 4-9-8 40........................................ LDettori 8 14
(TWall) *hld up: prog to chse ldrs 3f out: wknd 2f out* 5/2[1]

00/0 9 22 **O'So Neet**[13] 1692 6-9-5 30........................................ LPKeniry(3) 12 —
(PBurgoyne) *a wl in rr: bhd fr 4f out: t.o* 66/1

6001 10 3/4 **Lady At Leisure (IRE)**[21] 1493 4-9-8 40........................................ SWhitworth 7 —
(MJRyan) *led to 1/2-way: wknd 3f out: t.o* 8/1

0651 11 1/2 **Chickasaw Trail**[6] 1863 6-9-9 40........................................ StephanieHollinshead(5) 13 —
(RHollinshead) *racd in midfield: wknd 3f out: t.o* 20/1

-041 12 5 **Rhetoric (IRE)**[13] 1700 5-9-5 40........................................ DNolan(3) 5 —
(DGBridgwater) *prom: rdn after 4f: sn lost pl: bhd 4f out: t.o* 5/1[2]

-004 13 3 **Roving Vixen (IRE)**[5] 1889 3-8-7 40........................................(p) ADaly 3 —
(JLSpearing) *s.i.s: a in rr: bhd fr 4f out: t.o* 25/1

2m 20.02s (13.88) **Going Correction** +1.30s/f (Soft)

**WFA** 3 from 4yo+ 15lb **13** Ran SP% **125.2**

Speed ratings: **96,82,81,79,79 77,73,73,56,55 55,51,48**CSF £77.81 TOTE £18.10: £7.30, £2.20, £3.50; EX 98.10.

**Owner** Amaroni Racing **Bred** Lawn Stud **Trained** Woldingham, Surrey

■ Stewards Enquiry : Natalia Gemelova caution: used whip when clearly winning

**FOCUS**

They went a decent pace here given the conditions and that played into the hands of the hold-up performers. The winner came right away and, if the Handicapper takes this effort seriously, banded races will be out of the question.

**NOTEBOOK**

**Unsuited** had shown nothing to suggest that she was capable of a performance such as this, but the combination of a fast pace, testing conditions and a step up in trip brought out the best in her. She may well be flattered by the bare result, but she is clearly worthy of consideration when getting similar ground in future.

**Mr Whizz** acts on this sort of surface having won his maiden on heavy ground. He probably went for home too soon as it happens, although it is difficult to imagine how he could have ever beaten the clear-cut winner.

**Prince Albert** has his quirks, but the strong pace and testing conditions saw him in his best light.

**All On My Own(USA)** often runs creditably without threatening to win, and it was the same story here.

**Misty Man(USA)** was given a far too aggressive ride in the conditions and, having kicked into a clear lead early in the straight, fell in a heap with over a furlong to run. He ran better than his final placing suggests.

**Margarets Wish** was disappointing as she seemed to have conditions in her favour. However, the gallop was stronger in this heat than at Chepstow last time.

## 1988 WEALTH MANAGEMENT BANDED STKS 5f
4:20 (4:22) (H) 3-Y-O+ £1,494 (£427; £213) Stalls High

Form RPR

6P-0 1 **Foley Millennium (IRE)**[20] 1518 6-9-3 45........................................ NPollard 10 54
(MQuinn) *mde all and racd in centre: drvn 3l clr over 1f out: all out* 25/1

2000 2 1 1/2 **Ejay**[17] 1584 5-9-0 40........................................ LisaJones(3) 4 49
(JulianPoulton) *in rr: rdn 1/2-way: prog wl over 1f out: chsd wnr ins fnl f: clsd nr fin but nvr able to chal* 16/1

0631 3 3 **Harbour House**[6] 1859 5-9-9 45........................................ JTate 3 46
(JJBridger) *prom: chsd wnr 1/2-way: rdn and no imp over 1f out: one pce after* 5/1[3]

0002 4 1 3/4 **Badou**[21] 1497 4-9-3 45........................................(v) KFallon 7 35
(LMontagueHall) *midfield: rdn 1/2-way: one pce and nvr rchd ldrs* 2/1[1]

4606 5 3/4 **River Lark (USA)**[7] 1824 5-9-3 45........................................ KMcEvoy 9 33
(MABuckley) *racd in midfield: effrt 2f out: no imp ldrs over 1f out* 7/2[2]

0344 6 1/2 **Threat**[6] 1859 8-9-3 45........................................ MartinDwyer 2 31
(JMBradley) *dwlt: racd in centre: outpcd and struggling 1/2-way: n.d after* 9/1

-000 7 6 **Frenchmans Lodge**[6] 1859 4-9-3 45........................................(b) PDoe 8 13
(JMBradley) *stdd s: hld up: prog 1/2-way: wknd over 1f out* 33/1

0412 8 1 **Kilmeena Star**[40] 1206 6-9-3 40........................................(b) RLMoore 5 10
(JCFox) *racd freely: chsd wnr to 1/2-way: wknd wl over 1f out* 7/1

0000 9 8 **Abraxas**[20] 1518 6-9-3 40........................................(p) CCatlin 1 —
(JAkehurst) *racd centre: outpcd and a bhd* 20/1

00/4 10 8 **Mayfair Maundy**[6] 1860 4-8-12 35........................................ AQuinn(5) 6 —
(WGMTurner) *prom 1f: sn lost pl: bhd fr 1/2-way: t.o* 33/1

65.38 secs (4.17) **Going Correction** +0.775s/f (Yiel) **10** Ran SP% **115.1**

Speed ratings: **97,94,89,87,85 85,75,73,61,48**CSF £350.75 TOTE £37.90: £7.40, £6.40, £2.20; EX 196.50.

**Owner** Mrs S G Davies **Bred** Elperefa Bloodstock **Trained** Sparsholt, Oxon

**FOCUS**

Strangely, Foley Millennium eschewed the far-side rail and brought the field down the centre of the track.

**NOTEBOOK**
**Foley Millennium(IRE)** was taking on much lesser opposition on this first outing in banded company and had clearly benefited from his recent reappearance at Folkestone. This ground may suit him better these days following the injury he sustained early last year. *Official explanation: trainer said, regarding the improved form shown, gelding tired badly in its previous race, that being its first for 14 months following an injury*
**Ejay** ran one of her best races to date and was cutting back the winner's advantage at the finish. She would not be one to go overboard about, though.
**Harbour House** is in form and ran a fair race, but he just met a couple who handled the ground better.
**Badou** found this drop back in trip providing an insufficient test of stamina, even in this ground.
**River Lark(USA)** looked to have less to do in this company, but her best form is on faster ground.

## 1989 ROYALTIES GOLD BANDED STKS — 1m 4f
**4:50** (4:50) (H) 3-Y-O+ — **£1,533** (£438; £219) **Stalls** Low

Form — RPR
2-36 **1** **Make My Hay**[10] [676] 5-9-8 40 ... TEDurcan 3 — 55
(JGallagher) *hld up in rr: prog 4f out: led over 2f out: sn pressed: drvn and kpt on wl fr over 1f out* **11/1**
-626 **2** *3* **Pipssalio (SPA)**[10] [1754] 7-9-8 45 ... (t) CCatlin 5 — 51
(JamiePoulton) *hld up: pushed along 7f out: rdn and prog 4f out: drvn to press wnr 2f out: no imp fnl f* **13/8**[1]
550/ **3** *13* **Sure Future**[9] [4269] 8-9-8 45 ... ADaly 8 — 33
(RMStronge) *hld up in rr: prog 5f out: rdn to chse ldrs over 3f out: one pce fnl 2f* **7/1**
0632 **4** *6* **Dora Corbino**[6] [1862] 4-9-8 40 ... TGMcLaughlin 11 — 24
(RHollinshead) *led at gd pce: hdd over 2f out: grad wknd* **16/1**
0024 **5** *nk* **Neptune**[19] [1543] 8-9-8 30 ... RLMoore 1 — 24
(JCFox) *hld up in rr: rdn and no prog 4f out: one pce and n.d after* **25/1**
00-0 **6** *3* **Kalanisha (IRE)**[16] [1612] 4-9-8 45 ... PaulEddery 9 — 20
(NAGraham) *trckd ldrs: pushed along 9f out: lost pl u.p over 4f out : n.d after* **11/2**[3]
000/ **7** *19* **Silver Mistress**[636] [3843] 5-9-8 45 ... VSlattery 7 — —
(BNDoran) *dwlt: t.k.h: hld up in midfield: prog to chse ldrs over 4f out: wknd wl over 2f out* **50/1**
005 **8** *dist* **Sink Or Swim (IRE)**[11] [1727] 6-9-8 30 ... JTate 4 — —
(JJBridger) *chsd ldrs tl wknd 4f out: t.o* **40/1**
0640 **9** *5* **Stage Two (IRE)**[7] [1843] 3-8-3 45 ... JFanning 10 — —
(MJohnston) *trckd ldr: chal 5f out: wknd over 3f out: t.o whn virtually p.u fnl f* **7/1**
3013 **10** *28* **Ersaal (USA)**[13] [1690] 4-9-8 45 ... (tp) KFallon 2 — —
(JJay) *trckd ldrs: reminders 6f out: sn btn: t.o* **5/1**[2]

2m 54.02s (19.02) **Going Correction** +1.525s/f (Heav)
**WFA** 3 from 4yo+ 19lb — **10** Ran SP% **117.6**
Speed ratings: **97,95,86,82,82 80,67,—,—,—**CSF £29.20 TOTE £11.90: £3.50, £1.10, £3.70; EX 31.80 Place 6 £1,649.38, Place 5 £781.92.
**Owner** Mrs Irene Clifford **Bred** The Valentines **Trained** Chastleton, Oxon

**FOCUS**
Once again the leaders went off too fast in the testing ground and the field was well strung out at the finish.

**NOTEBOOK**
**Make My Hay** had the race run to suit as the leaders came back to him. Given that he was getting off the mark at the 22nd attempt, one would not be confident about him following up, even in similar grade.
**Pipssalio(SPA)** had ground conditions as he likes them and the race run to suit, and so it was very disappointing to see him beaten by a long-standing maiden. He is clearly nowhere near the horse he used to be.
**Sure Future**, absent from the Flat for the best part of four years, did not really take to chasing earlier this year. He has always liked a bit of give and had the race run to suit, but he could only stay on one-paced.
**Dora Corbino** set too hot a pace in the conditions and paid the price in the straight. In the circumstances she was not disgraced in finishing fourth.
**Neptune** is of very limited ability and is not one to rely on.
**Kalanisha(IRE)** looked one of a few with potential improvement in him, but he soon beat a retreat once the race began in earnest.
T/Plt: £1,354.80 to a £1 stake. Pool: £34,613.30. 18.65 winning tickets. T/Qpdt: £96.90 to a £1 stake. Pool: £2,568.00. 19.60 winning tickets. JN

# 1358 REDCAR (L-H)
### Monday, May 10

**OFFICIAL GOING: Soft (heavy in places)**

## 1990 CROWS NEST RESTAURANT NOVICE MEDIAN AUCTION STKS — 5f
**2:20** (2:20) (F) 2-Y-O — **£2,934** (£838; £419) **Stalls** High

Form — RPR
43 **1** **Prince Namid**[12] [1709] 2-8-12 ... SCarson 2 — 64+
(MrsADuffield) *mde virtually all: pushed clr fnl f: comf* **1/4**[1]
**2** *5* **Mas O Menos (IRE)** 2-8-12 ... IMongan 4 — 47
(MsDeborahJEvans) *cl up: rdn to chse wnr over 1f out: no imp fnl f* **20/1**[3]
**3** *1 3/4* **Jane Jubilee (IRE)** 2-8-7 ... RFfrench 1 — 35
(MJohnston) *cl up: rdn 2f out: sn btn* **4/1**[2]

65.05 secs (6.35) **Going Correction** +1.125s/f (Soft) — **3** Ran SP% **104.8**
Speed ratings: **94,86,83**CSF £5.02 TOTE £1.30; EX 4.80.
**Owner** S Adamson **Bred** Mrs R D Peacock **Trained** Constable Burton, N Yorks

**FOCUS**
A depleted field as a result of the ground simplified Prince Namid's task.

**NOTEBOOK**
**Prince Namid**, who has experience under his belt and a proven ability to handle soft ground, never looked like doing anything else but winning and coasted home. He is a possible for a nursery.
**Mas O Menos(IRE)** ran respectably for the outsider of the three, sticking to his task well and has a small race in him.
**Jane Jubilee(IRE)** can only improve for this and will be seen to better effect next time.

## 1991 CLASSIC BOXES MAIDEN FILLIES' STKS — 6f
**2:50** (2:51) (D) 3-Y-O+ — **£3,623** (£1,115; £557; £278) **Stalls** High

Form — RPR
20 **1** **Extremely Rare (IRE)**[20] [1530] 3-8-8 ... DAllan(3) 7 — 60
(TDEasterby) *trckd ldrs: led over 1f out: styd on u.p fnl f: all out* **3/1**[2]
506- **2** *hd* **Green Ridge**[182] [5966] 3-8-11 70 ... KDarley 5 — 59
(PWD'Arcy) *cl up: led after 2f: hdd over 1f out styd on u.p: no ex clsng stages* **11/4**[1]
66-5 **3** *1* **Palvic Moon**[12] [1711] 3-8-11 56 ... RFitzpatrick 8 — 56
(CSmith) *chsd ldrs: rdn 2f out: styd on: no imp on first 2 fnl f* **6/1**[3]
0 **4** *3/4* **Akiramenai (USA)**[93] [708] 4-9-7 ... RWinston 2 — 54?
(MrsLStubbs) *drvn along in rr 1/2-way: styd on u.p fnl 2f: nvr able to chal* **9/1**
00- **5** *shd* **La Fonteyne**[179] [5990] 3-8-6 ... TEaves(5) 6 — 53
(CBBBooth) *chsd ldrs: rdn 1/2-way: kpt on u.p fnl f* **50/1**
000- **6** *17* **Pay Time**[267] [4220] 5-9-2 45 ... PMulrennan(5) 1 — 2
(REBarr) *in tch: rdn over 2f out: sn wknd: bhd and no ch whn eased ins fnl f* **33/1**
0- **7** *5* **Savannah Sue**[348] [1918] 3-8-11 ... VHalliday 3 — —
(JRNorton) *in tch: wkng whn hung bdly lft 2f out: wl bhd and no ch whn eased ins fnl f* **25/1**
622- **8** *1 1/2* **Champagne Cracker**[216] [5432] 3-8-11 65 ... PHanagan 4 — —
(MissLAPerratt) *led 2f: wknd 1/2-way: bhd and no ch whn eased ins fnl f* **3/1**[2]

1m 20.49s (8.79) **Going Correction** +1.125s/f (Soft)
**WFA** 3 from 4yo+ 10lb — **8** Ran SP% **109.7**
Speed ratings: **86,85,84,83,83 60,53,51**CSF £10.60 TOTE £4.70: £1.30, £1.70, £1.90; EX 16.80.
**Owner** Mrs M H Easterby **Bred** P Gilson **Trained** Great Habton, N Yorks

**FOCUS**
A good finish to what was a weak race and a slow winning time.

**NOTEBOOK**
**Extremely Rare(IRE)**, a disappointment last time having made a promising debut, got back on track with a narrow victory, staying on well to edge the favourite out of it.
**Green Ridge**, who was well thought of as a juvenile, failed to show his form on ground faster than ideal, but had her conditions today and it was disappointing she could not win. *Official explanation: trainer said filly was found to have a swelling of the left hind thigh muscle.*
**Palvic Moon** is well exposed and does nothing for the form.
**Akiramenai(USA)** ran as though further is required and needs one more run to qualify for a handicap mark.
**La Fonteyne** can now race in handicaps.
**Savannah Sue** *Official explanation: jockey said filly hung badly left-handed throughout*
**Champagne Cracker** was the disappointment of the race and, whilst better than this, is hardly one to follow. *Official explanation: jockey said filly was unsuited by the soft ground*

## 1992 TOTEEXACTA FILLIES' STKS (H'CAP) — 7f
**3:25** (3:25) (D) (0-80,73) 3-Y-O+ — **£7,007** (£2,156; £1,078; £539) **Stalls** High

Form — RPR
31-0 **1** **Waterpark**[3] [1941] 6-8-5 48 ... PFessey 8 — 62
(RCraggs) *mde most: rdn over 1f out: drew clr fnl f* **8/1**[3]
60-2 **2** *4* **Annijaz**[6] [1855] 7-8-11 54 ... SCarson 15 — 58
(JMBradley) *hld up in rr: hdwy 1/2-way: rdn to chse wnr over 1f out: no imp fnl f* **6/1**[1]
42-0 **3** *shd* **Just One Smile (IRE)**[20] [1526] 4-9-2 62 ... DAllan(3) 4 — 66
(TDEasterby) *in tch: hdwy 3f out: ev ch 2f out: sn rdn: kpt on same pce* **20/1**
00U4 **4** *nk* **Park Star**[10] [1750] 4-8-13 56 ... RWinston 11 — 59
(DShaw) *hld up: hdwy and in tch 3f out: kpt on u.p fnl f* **14/1**
-000 **5** *hd* **Celtic Romance**[16] [1606] 5-8-7 50 ... PHanagan 3 — 53
(MrsMReveley) *dwlt: hld up: hdwy 1/2-way: ch and rdn 2f out: no further prog* **9/1**
6001 **6** *1 3/4* **Sandorra**[4] [1915] 6-8-8 51 6ex ... TWilliams 2 — 49
(MBrittain) *w wnr tl rdn and outpcd 2f out: n.d after* **12/1**
2224 **7** *2 1/2* **Jessie**[57] [1021] 5-8-2 45 ... (t) KimTinkler 14 — 37
(DonEnricoIncisa) *dwlt: rdn in rr 4f out: styd on fnl 2f: n.d* **6/1**[1]
30-0 **8** *3/4* **Annie Harvey**[23] [1464] 3-9-4 73 ... FLynch 7 — 63
(BSmart) *dwlt: rr div: kpt on u.p fnl 2f: n.d* **14/1**
31-0 **9** *3* **Buthaina (IRE)**[9] [1757] 4-9-5 67 ... TEaves(5) 10 — 50
(THCaldwell) *midfield: rdn 3f out: sn btn* **33/1**
60-3 **10** *1 1/4* **Moonlight Song (IRE)**[11] [1720] 7-7-9 45 ... DFentiman(7) 9 — 24
(JohnAHarris) *chsd ldrs: rdn over 3f out: fdd* **11/1**
/000 **11** *3/4* **Pharaoh Hatshepsut (IRE)**[14] [1660] 6-7-12 41 oh6 ... (v[1]) PMQuinn 5 — 19
(JamesMoffatt) *chsd ldrs: rdn 3f out: sn btn* **50/1**
0300 **12** *2* **High Cane (USA)**[14] [1665] 4-8-13 56 ... KDalgleish 13 — 29
(MDHammond) *hld up towards rr: rdn 1/2-way: sn btn* **20/1**
1030 **13** *1/2* **Eager Angel (IRE)**[20] [1531] 6-8-11 54 ... (p) DeanMcKeown 6 — 25
(RFMarvin) *midfield: rdn 3f out: sn wknd* **14/1**
5-06 **14** *3 1/2* **Mrs Spence**[16] [1602] 3-8-8 63 ... DaleGibson 12 — 26
(MWEasterby) *towards rr most of way* **40/1**
0-00 **15** *dist* **Sabalara (IRE)**[16] [1606] 4-9-1 58 ... IMongan 1 — —
(PWHarris) *cl up to 1/2-way: sn wknd: lost tch and eased fnl f* **13/2**[2]

1m 32.31s (7.41) **Going Correction** +1.125s/f (Soft)
**WFA** 3 from 4yo+ 12lb — **15** Ran SP% **115.9**
Speed ratings: **102,97,97,96,96 94,91,87,86 85,83,82,78,—**CSF £49.43 CT £949.73 TOTE £9.80: £3.10, £2.20, £6.80; EX 48.70 Trifecta £517.60 Part won. Pool of £729.10 - 0.80 winning units..
**Owner** Ray Craggs **Bred** Cromlech Bloodstock **Trained** Sedgefield, Co Durham

**FOCUS**
A good performance and a decent time from Waterpark, who may not be the most consistent, but is a decent mare when in-form.

**NOTEBOOK**
**Waterpark** was winning her third race since the turn of the year and did it the simple way from the front. The way she scored suggests there are more races to be won with her in the short term.
**Annijaz** has found her form again and should be winning before long given her versatility with regards to trip.
**Just One Smile(IRE)** just got run out of second, but this was a good effort on ground she was reported to have been unsuited by on her previous outing.
**Park Star** ran on right the way to the line, but could not do it quickly enough.
**Celtic Romance** continues to creep back into form and may be nearing a win.
**Jessie** made some modest progress from the rear. *Official explanation: trainer said mare had lost a front shoe*
**Sabalara(IRE)** *Official explanation: vet said filly was found to be suffering from azatoria*

## 1993 CLASSIC SUITE H'CAP — 1m
**4:00** (4:00) (F) (0-55,55) 3-Y-O+ — **£3,220** (£920; £460) **Stalls** High

Form — RPR
0301 **1** **Rocinante (IRE)**[12] [1710] 4-9-3 51 ... RWinston 15 — 62
(JJQuinn) *in tch: smooth hdwy to ld over 1f out: hld on wl fnl f* **11/1**[3]
0U00 **2** *hd* **Archirondel**[26] [1393] 6-8-12 46 ... IMongan 9 — 57
(MDHammond) *hld up: swtchd lft and gd hdwy over 1f out: styd on wl u.p fnl f: jst hld* **25/1**
0-00 **3** *shd* **Encounter**[14] [1660] 8-8-9 46 oh1 ... DAllan(3) 3 — 56
(JHetherton) *hld up: hdwy 2f out: chsng ldrs and rdn appr fnl f: styd on wl ins last* **11/1**[3]
6343 **4** *1/2* **Goodbye Mr Bond**[16] [1620] 4-9-4 52 ... DeanMcKeown 12 — 61
(EJAlston) *trckd ldrs: nt clr run and lost pl over 3f out: hdwy 2f out: styd on wl u.p fnl f* **5/2**[1]



The Form Book, Raceform Ltd, Compton, RG20 6NL

0040 **5** ½ **Shifty**[6] 1868 5-9-1 **49** PMQuinn 10 57
(DNicholls) *midfield: hdwy to trck ldrs 2f out: ev ch and rdn appr fnl f: styd on wl ins last* **20/1**

00-1 **6** 3 **Zhitomir**[40] 1197 6-9-0 **51** LEnstone(3) 18 53
(MDods) *hld up towards rr: hdwy into midfield 3f out: styd on u.p fnl f: nvr able to chal* **14/1**

0-01 **7** ¾ **Stellite**[11] 1720 4-8-13 **47** KDarley 1 48
(JSGoldie) *held up: hdwy 1/2-way: chsng ldrs and rdn over 1f out: no ex fnl f* **9/1**[2]

0-01 **8** 2 **Forest Air (IRE)**[11] 1718 4-9-1 **49** RFfrench 14 46
(MissLAPerratt) *towards rr: drvn along 1/2-way: kpt on fnl 2f: n.d* **25/1**

00-4 **9** 1½ **Explode**[6] 1876 7-9-4 **52** KDalgleish 11 46
(MissLCSiddall) *vlose up: led 1/2-way: hdd over 1f out: sn wknd* **20/1**

000- **10** ¾ **Noble Penny**[201] 5705 5-9-2 **50** SChin 7 42
(MrsKWalton) *cl up: disp ld fr 1/2-way tl wknd over 1f out* **20/1**

2105 **11** 1 **Printsmith (IRE)**[16] 1606 7-8-12 **46** oh1 JBramhill 13 36
(JRNorton) *towards rr: hdwy into midfield over 2f out: edgd lft and no ex fr over 1f out* **16/1**

0-00 **12** 8 **Business Matters (IRE)**[20] 1527 4-8-12 **46** RLappin 17 20
(HAlexander) *in rr and drvn along after 3f: n.d* **33/1**

20-0 **13** 7 **Smart Minister**[14] 1681 4-9-3 **51** DaleGibson 16 11
(JJQuinn) *prom: drvn along 3f out: wknd 2f out* **20/1**

005- **14** nk **Dara Mac**[235] 5015 5-8-9 **50** (p) SuzanneFrance(7) 4 10
(NBycroft) *trckd ldrs: rdn 3f out: wknd 2f out* **33/1**

420- **15** 14 **Gemini Lady**[216] 5437 4-8-12 **46** oh1 ANicholls 19 —
(MrsGSRees) *midfield: tl rdn and wknd 3f out: t.o* **20/1**

1200 **16** 13 **Thunderclap**[17] 1598 5-9-2 **55** (p) PMulrennan(5) 8 —
(JJQuinn) *led tl hdd 1/2-way: sn wknd: t.o* **12/1**

00-0 **17** nk **Islands Farewell**[32] 1318 4-8-11 **50** TEaves(5) 2 —
(MrsMReveley) *midfield tl rdn and wknd over 3f out: t.o* **50/1**

00-0 **18** 1 **Mehmaas**[8] 1783 8-9-7 **55** (v) PHanagan 6 —
(REBarr) *towards rr and sn pushed along: hdwy into midfield over 3f out: wknd over 2f out: t.o* **12/1**

040- **19** nk **Hormuz (IRE)**[211] 5514 8-8-7 **48** DFentiman(7) 5 —
(PaulJohnson) *midfield to 1/2-way: wknd qckly: t.o* **25/1**

1m 46.31s (8.61) **Going Correction** +1.125s/f (Soft) **19** Ran SP% **126.4**
Speed ratings: **101,100,100,100,99 96,95,93,92,91 90,82,75,75,61 48,48,47,46**CSF £264.01 CT £3184.03 TOTE £11.10: £3.60, £3.20, £3.10, £1.10; EX 339.70.
**Owner** Mrs Marie Taylor **Bred** John Malone **Trained** Settrington, N Yorks

**FOCUS**
A moderate handicap but a fair gallop producing a tight finish, with the front three being separated by a head and a neck.

**NOTEBOOK**
**Rocinante(IRE)**, off a 5lb higher mark than when winning last month, appreciates this sort of ground and found plenty for pressure once hitting the front. He is unlikely to go up much for this.
**Archirondel** ran respectably and should not be long in winning.
**Encounter**, winner of this race last term, was never closer than at the line and returned to something near his best.
**Goodbye Mr Bond** was slightly unlucky, losing his place having been a bit short of room before running on well.
**Shifty** ran respectably and shaped as though he would appreciate a return to further.
**Stellite** travelled well enough, but had nothing left to offer when push came to shove.
**Thunderclap** *Official explanation: jockey said gelding bled from the nose*
**Mehmaas** *Official explanation: jockey said gelding missed the break*

## 1994 VOLTIGEUR RESTAURANT CLAIMING STKS — 6f
**4:30** (4:30) (F) 3-Y-O+ **£3,102** (£886; £443) **Stalls** High

Form RPR

00-0 **1** **Dizzy In The Head**[28] 1361 5-8-12 67 (e[1]) JDO'Reilly(7) 2 63
(JO'Reilly) *dwlt: sn cl up: led after 2f: rdn over 1 out: kpt on fnl f* **5/1**[3]

00-0 **2** ¾ **Downland (IRE)**[20] 1526 8-9-7 50 KimTinkler 10 63
(NTinkler) *hld up: hdwy 2f out: chsd first 2 ent fnl f: r.o strly ins fnl f to go 2nd clsng stages* **5/2**[1]

0000 **3** ½ **Shady Deal**[20] 1516 8-8-13 49 KDalgleish 3 54
(JMBradley) *trckd ldrs: hdwy to chse wnr over 2f out: ch and rdn over 1f out: no ex ins fnl f* **12/1**

406- **4** 5 **Mallia**[265] 4264 11-8-8 45 Laura-JayneCrawford(7) 1 41
(TDBarron) *prom: rdn over 2f out: no ex* **12/1**

1201 **5** hd **Sergeant Slipper**[25] 1423 7-9-9 46 (v) RFitzpatrick 11 48
(CSmith) *s.i.s: towards rr: effrt over 2f out: kpt on fnl f: n.d* **10/1**

-606 **6** 3½ **Frimley's Matterry**[29] 1342 4-8-8 45 PMulrennan(5) 7 27
(REBarr) *chsd ldrs tl outpcd 1/2-way: n.d after* **12/1**

0-00 **7** 1 **Petongski**[20] 1525 6-8-8 47 TEaves(5) 9 24
(BEllison) *in tch: drvn along 1/2-way: sn btn* **7/2**[2]

3060 **8** 2 **Sabana (IRE)**[20] 1516 6-9-5 45 SCarson 4 24
(JMBradley) *led 2f: remained prom tl wknd over 2f out* **16/1**

0 **9** ½ **Welcome Archie**[11] 1718 4-8-13 DaleGibson 5 17
(JSHaldane) *dwlt: a bhd* **100/1**

0-60 **10** 3 **Andreyev (IRE)**[3] 1929 10-8-13 40 (v) KDarley 6 8
(JSGoldie) *in tch tl wknd over 2f out* **14/1**

1060 **11** 4 **Above Board**[3] 1941 9-8-13 35 (t) DeanMcKeown 8 —
(RFMarvin) *a bhd* **25/1**

1m 16.99s (5.29) **Going Correction** +1.125s/f (Soft) **11** Ran SP% **117.0**
Speed ratings: **109,108,107,100,100 95,94,91,91,87 81**CSF £17.72 TOTE £8.70: £2.30, £1.70, £3.90; EX 26.00.
**Owner** Burntwood Sports Ltd **Bred** Bearstone Stud And T Herbert Jackson **Trained** Brierley, S Yorks

**FOCUS**
The front three finished five lengths clear of the fourth, and the winning time was decent given the conditions.

**NOTEBOOK**
**Dizzy In The Head**, sporting the first-time eyeshield, was up with the pace throughout and readily took it up two out. He found plenty under pressure and to win with a little bit in hand. If the eyeshield works again he may be able to defy a penalty.
**Downland(IRE)** finished with a real kick on ground he favours, but could not get there in time. He is not getting any better at the age of eight.
**Shady Deal** is without a win since 2002, but ran respectably.
**Mallia** was five lengths adrift back in fourth, being unable to give any more once headed.
**Sergeant Slipper** was tardy at the stalls and did well to finish where he did.
**Petongski** never really looked like getting involved and was disappointing.

## 1995 SAFFIE JOSEPH & SONS H'CAP — 1m 2f
**5:00** (5:01) (E) (0-70,70) 3-Y-O **£3,799** (£1,169; £584; £292) **Stalls** Low

Form RPR

-556 **1** **Magic Sting**[14] 1672 3-9-0 **63** IMongan 1 68
(MLWBell) *midfield: hdwy 2f out: styd on u.p to chal ent fnl f: led clsng stages* **4/1**[1]

60-0 **2** nk **I'm Dancing**[25] 1422 3-8-7 **59** DAllan(3) 5 64
(TDEasterby) *prom: led over 3f out: hrd pressed and rdn ent fnl f: hdd clsng strages* **16/1**

40-0 **3** 1¼ **Wing Collar**[25] 1416 3-9-2 **65** PHanagan 3 68
(TDEasterby) *hld up in rr: hdwy u.p 2f out: styd on wl ins fnl f: nrst fin* **33/1**

0165 **4** nk **Perfect Balance (IRE)**[3] 1932 3-8-11 **60** KimTinkler 4 62
(NTinkler) *in tch: hdwy 3f out: ev ch and rdn appr fnl f: no ex ins fnl last* **9/1**

2136 **5** 1¾ **Platinum Pirate**[18] 1559 3-8-10 **64** (v) PMulrennan(5) 8 63
(KRBurke) *midfield: hdwy over 3f out: ev ch and rdn 2f out: wknd appr fnl f* **5/1**[2]

4-05 **6** 3 **Rock Lobster**[16] 1609 3-9-2 **65** JBramhill 7 59
(JGGiven) *hld up in rr: hdwy and in tch over 2f out: hung rt and no further prog* **14/1**

0-50 **7** 2½ **Hernando's Boy**[18] 1559 3-8-8 **62** TEaves(5) 6 52
(MrsMReveley) *hld up: effrt over 3f out: sn btn* **8/1**[3]

2320 **8** 22 **Bond Moonlight**[28] 1360 3-8-11 **60** (p) FLynch 9 12
(BSmart) *trckd ldrs: ch and rdn 3f out: wknd qckly 2 out: t.o* **9/1**

50-3 **9** 10 **Third Empire**[28] 1360 3-8-13 **62** RWinston 10 —
(CGrant) *towards rr: drvn along 1/2-way: no hdwy: t.o* **5/1**[2]

420- **10** 3 **Pearl Pride (USA)**[228] 5175 3-9-7 **70** KDalgleish 11 —
(MJohnston) *led tl hdd over 3f out: sn wknd t.o* **10/1**

-043 **U** **Upthedale (IRE)**[3] 1932 3-7-5 **47** oh7 DFentiman(7) 2 —
(JRWeymes) *prom: wkng whn bdly hmpd and uns rdr 3f out* **14/1**

2m 16.01s (9.21) **Going Correction** +0.90s/f (Soft) **11** Ran SP% **115.7**
Speed ratings: **99,98,97,97,96 93,91,74,66,63** —CSF £68.78 CT £1840.79 TOTE £4.30: £1.80, £4.30, £10.40; EX 93.70 Place 6 £35.90, Place 5 £28.10.
**Owner** Mrs P T Fenwick **Bred** Michael Watt And Exors Of The Late Miss Jemima Joh **Trained** Newmarket, Suffolk
■ Stewards Enquiry : Kim Tinkler three-day ban: careless riding (May 21-23)

**FOCUS**
An ordinary contest and a modest time for the grade, but Magic Sting finished strongly to record his first victory.

**NOTEBOOK**
**Magic Sting**, sixth on his handicap debut latest, was dropping back in trip and finished well to collar I'm Dancing nearing the line. He will stay further and a follow up cannot be ruled out. *Official explanation: trainer's representative said, regarding the improved form shown, colt may have benefited from the drop in trip on this occasion*
**I'm Dancing** left some moderate efforts behind over this longer trip and has a small race in him.
**Wing Collar** shaped as though he is worth trying back over a mile and a half, as he finished strongly having been a little outpaced.
**Perfect Balance(IRE)** ran poorly only days ago, but showed that running to be all wrong with fourth place.
**Platinum Pirate** had his chance without proving good enough.
**Third Empire** never left the rear and is better than this.
**Pearl Pride(USA)** weakened tamely and is better than she showed, the ground being the only possible excuse.
T/Plt: £21.90 to a £1 stake. Pool: £28,277.70. 939.05 winning tickets. T/Qpdt: £15.50 to a £1 stake. Pool: £1,958.70. 93.10 winning tickets. JF

# 1670 WINDSOR (R-H)
Monday, May 10

**OFFICIAL GOING: Soft**

## 1996 SANDHURST MARQUEES NOVICE STKS — 5f 10y
**5:45** (5:45) (D) 2-Y-O **£4,108** (£1,264; £632; £316) **Stalls** High

Form RPR

1 **1** **Blue Dakota (IRE)**[25] 1412 2-9-5 LDettori 4 96+
(JNoseda) *mde all: c clr on bit ins fnl 2f: unchal* **1/8**[1]

0 **2** 6 **Alright My Son (IRE)**[6] 1853 2-8-12 DaneO'Neill 5 63
(RHannon) *chsd ldrs: outpcd after 2f: styd on and edgd lft over 1f out: tk 2nd wl ins last but no ch w wnr* **33/1**

301 **3** 2 **Little Wizzy**[7] 1839 2-9-0 JPMurtagh 2 58
(PDEvans) *wnt lft s: sn rcvrd to chse wnr: no ch ins fnl 2f: tired fnl f and sn lost 2nd* **25/1**

**4** 6 **Perianth (IRE)** 2-8-12 SDrowne 3 35
(BJMeehan) *in tch: rdn and btn 2f out* **20/1**[3]

**5** 6 **Come Good** 2-8-12 RHughes 1 14
(RHannon) *hampeded and carried lft s: rcvrd and in tch after 2f: wknd qckly 2f out* **12/1**[2]

65.12 secs (3.92) **Going Correction** +0.675s/f (Yiel) **5** Ran SP% **108.1**
Speed ratings: **95,85,82,72,63**CSF £7.79 TOTE £1.10: £1.02, £6.90; EX 6.60.
**Owner** A F Nolan, Mrs J M Ryan, Mrs P Duffin **Bred** Michael O'Donnell **Trained** Newmarket, Suffolk

**FOCUS**
The field finished well strung out behind the Royal Ascot-bound winner, whose time was up to standard for the grade.

**NOTEBOOK**
**Blue Dakota(IRE)** ◆ confirmed the impression of his debut success in grand style. He has plenty of early pace, and had this field strung out from an early stage on ground that looked plenty soft enough. This performance did little but confirm the impression that he is the best juvenile to have raced this season and he must go to the Norfolk Stakes at Royal Ascot with an obvious chance.
**Alright My Son(IRE)**, whose stable often introduce a fair juvenile in this event, ran green early on, but picked up nicely to grab second late in the day. This scopey colt will improve again for the experience, but will most likely come into his own over further.
**Little Wizzy** veered markedly left out of the gates, but quickly got back into her stride and showed good early speed to try and get to the eventual winner, which she paid for in the closing stages on this testing ground. She is a precocious filly who should win a minor race at the least when the ground is quicker.
**Perianth(IRE)** did not show too much on this debut, but can be expected to improve in time.
**Come Good** was done few favours at the start and was up against it from then on. It is wise to forgive this form, as he is probably capable of a lot better.

## 1997 FACTORTAME H'CAP — 1m 67y
**6:15** (6:15) (E) (0-70,69) 3-Y-O **£3,796** (£1,168; £584; £292) **Stalls** High

Form RPR

-030 **1** **Foley Prince**[44] 1139 3-9-3 **65** SDrowne 11 74
(MrsStefLiddiard) *mde all: hrd drvn fnl 2f: hld on gamely* **12/1**

20-0 **2** hd **Smoothly Does It**[13] 1688 3-9-2 **64** TEDurcan 4 73?
(MrsAJBowlby) *hung lft and lost pl after 2f: hdwy over 3f out: str run fr over 1f out: fin wl: nt quite get up* **25/1**

3222 **3** 1½ **Jakarmi**[13] 1688 3-9-3 **65** TQuinn 12 71
(BPalling) *sn chsng wnr: rdn and ev ch over 1f out: one pce ins last: outpcd cl home* **7/2**[1]

| Form | Pos | Dist | Horse | Jockey | RPR |
|---|---|---|---|---|---|
| 34-0 | **4** | ½ | **Nantucket Sound (USA)**[16] 1613 3-9-5 **67** (MCPipe) *s.i.s: bhd: hdwy over 2f out: swtchd lft 1f out and str run ins last: no ex nr fin* **8/1**[3] | DaneO'Neill 15 | 72 |
| 1-00 | **5** | 12 | **Habanero**[17] 1588 3-9-6 **68** (RHannon) *chsd ldrs: rdn 3f out: wknd ins fnl 2f* **14/1** | RLMoore 9 | 49 |
| -603 | **6** | 1 | **Anduril**[15] 1641 3-9-7 **69** (JMPEustace) *t.k.h: bhd: rdn 3f out: kpt on fr over 1f out: nt trble ldrs* **14/1** | JTate 2 | 48 |
| 00-2 | **7** | 1 | **Landucci**[23] 1476 3-9-6 **68** (JWHills) *chsd ldrs: rdn over 2f out: sn btn* **8/1**[3] | MHills 1 | 45 |
| 5050 | **8** | shd | **Amwell Brave**[10] 1755 3-9-0 **62** (JRJenkins) *in tch: rdn ande sme hdwy over 3f out: n.d and sn wknd* **9/1** | (v) LDettori 16 | 38 |
| 0-60 | **9** | 4 | **Night Worker**[12] 1702 3-8-12 **60** (RHannon) *chsd ldrs: rdn over 3f out: sn btn* **25/1** | PDobbs 18 | 28 |
| 40-0 | **10** | 5 | **Susiedil (IRE)**[16] 1613 3-9-1 **63** (PWHarris) *chsd ldrs 5f* **33/1** | BDoyle 7 | 21 |
| 550- | **11** | 4 | **Molinia**[290] 3552 3-9-3 **65** (RMBeckett) *s.i.s: sme hdwy 4f out: sn wknd* **33/1** | SSanders 17 | 15 |
| 466- | **12** | 1¼ | **Music Mix (IRE)**[143] 6216 3-9-1 **63** (EALDunlop) *bhd: rdn and sme hdwy into mid-div over 3f out: sn wknd* **7/1**[2] | JPMurtagh 8 | 11 |
| 03-0 | **13** | ½ | **Solo Sole (ITY)**[13] 1688 3-9-4 **69** (LMCumani) *a in rr* **33/1** | NMackay(3) 10 | 16 |
| 050- | **14** | ¾ | **Inchpast**[167] 6069 3-9-3 **65** (MHTompkins) *a in rr* **16/1** | PRobinson 14 | 10 |
| -625 | **15** | 6 | **The Job**[40] 1214 3-8-9 **57** (ADSmith) *sn bhd* **12/1** | JQuinn 3 | — |
| 43-0 | **16** | 5 | **Kitley**[21] 1508 3-9-3 **65** (BGPowell) *a in rr* **25/1** | SWhitworth 13 | — |
| 00-0 | **17** | 3½ | **Lord Greystoke (IRE)**[121] 490 3-8-12 **60** (CPMorlock) *nvr bttr than mid-div: bhd fr 1/2-way* **66/1** | RHavlin 6 | — |
| 0-04 | **18** | 3½ | **Whiplash (IRE)**[33] 1296 3-8-11 **59** (RHannon) *chsd ldrs over 4f* **33/1** | RSmith 5 | — |

1m 51.9s (6.30) **Going Correction** +0.975s/f (Soft) **18** Ran SP% **126.3**
Speed ratings: **107,106,105,104,92 91,90,90,86,81 77,76,75,75,69 64,60,57**CSF £296.53 CT £1327.63 TOTE £13.10: £2.90, £5.70, £1.30, £2.10; EX 565.10.
**Owner** Mrs Stef Liddiard **Bred** Foley Steelstock **Trained** Great Shefford, Berks

**FOCUS**
A modest handicap run at a strong pace and the winning time was decent in the conditions. The first four were clear.

**NOTEBOOK**
**Foley Prince**, making his debut for new connections, made all and showed a great attitude to hold off his challengers from two out. He has been beaten twice in claimers on the All-Weather this year, but looks to have improved for the recent change of scenery and may have more to offer, especially if dropped back to seven furlongs.
**Smoothly Does It** ◆ took time to hit top gear under pressure on this drop in trip, but was finishing fast and only just went down. He clearly likes this course and distance and excuses early on this time, so can find a similar race at this track in which to gain compensation and lose his maiden tag.
**Jakarmi** came there with every chance approaching the last furlong, but his stamina gave way and he could only keep on at the one pace. This was a stiff enough test and this consistent performer can make amends when faced with better ground.
**Nantucket Sound(USA)**, popular in the betting ring, gave himself too much to do after a slow start, but did finish well and looks well worth a try over farther. Not for the first time, he was slowly away and does look a tricky ride.
**Landucci**
**Kitley** *Official explanation: trainer said colt was unsuited by the soft ground*
**Lord Greystoke(IRE)** *Official explanation: jockey said colt was unsuited by the soft ground*

## 1998 KARINA LAWFORD MEMORIAL H'CAP — 1m 3f 135y
**6:45** (6:48) (E) (0-70,67) 3-Y-O — **£3,737** (£1,150; £575; £287) **Stalls** Low

| Form | Pos | Dist | Horse | Jockey | RPR |
|---|---|---|---|---|---|
| 06-1 | **1** | | **Fleetfoot Mac**[17] 1579 3-8-13 **59** (PDEvans) *mde all: hrd drvn fr over 2f out: edgd rt appr fnl f: styd on gamely to go clr ins last* **12/1** | NCallan 9 | 69 |
| -422 | **2** | 3 | **Late Opposition**[14] 1672 3-9-7 **67** (EALDunlop) *hld up up rr: stdy hdwy over 3f out: rdn to chse wnr fnl f: sn edgd lft and fnd no ex u.p* **4/1**[1] | LDettori 14 | 73 |
| 0-63 | **3** | ½ | **General Flumpa**[16] 1628 3-9-4 **64** (CFWall) *hld up in touhc: hdwy over 2f out: rdn to chse ldrs over 1f out: kpt on same pce ins last* **11/1**[3] | GBaker 4 | 69 |
| 500- | **4** | ½ | **Prenup (IRE)**[160] 6118 3-8-9 **58** (LMCumani) *chsd ldrs: wnt 2nd over 5f out: rdn over 2f out: no imp over 1f out and styd on same pce* **12/1** | NMackay(3) 1 | 62 |
| -044 | **5** | 3 | **Mambina (USA)**[12] 1712 3-9-6 **66** (MRChannon) *bhd: hdwy 3f out: styd on fnl 2f: nvr gng pce to rch ldrs* **20/1** | TEDurcan 17 | 66 |
| 3014 | **6** | 4 | **It's Blue Chip**[7] 1823 3-9-4 **64** (PWD'Arcy) *bhd: hdwy fr 3f out: styd on fnl 2f but nvr gng pce to rch ldrs* **6/1**[2] | (e) PaulEddery 2 | 59 |
| 0-00 | **7** | ½ | **Airgusta (IRE)**[10] 1755 3-9-1 **61** (CREgerton) *chsd ldrs: rdn fr 3f out: wknd fr 2f out* **14/1** | PRobinson 11 | 55 |
| 0-56 | **8** | 3 | **Absolutely Soaked (IRE)**[12] 1712 3-9-2 **62** (DrJDScargill) *bhd: hdwy fr 3f out: chsd ldrs 2f out: wknd appr fnl f* **33/1** | CLowther 18 | 52 |
| 00-0 | **9** | 1¾ | **Rinneen (IRE)**[13] 1688 3-8-8 **54** (RHannon) *bhd: hrd drvn fr 4f out: kpt on fnl 2f but nvr in contention* **16/1** | RLMoore 6 | 41 |
| 500- | **10** | shd | **Science Academy (USA)**[174] 6020 3-9-0 **60** (PFICole) *mid-div: hdwy and pushed along 3f out: nvr nr ldrs* **6/1**[2] | KFallon 20 | 47 |
| 0-60 | **11** | 6 | **Mister Trickster (IRE)**[28] 1365 3-9-1 **61** (RDickin) *bhd: kpt on fnl 3f: n.d* **33/1** | JQuinn 13 | 40 |
| 05-0 | **12** | 3 | **Bakhtyar**[21] 1509 3-9-1 **61** (RCharlton) *chsd ldrs tl wknd over 2f out* **12/1** | SDrowne 16 | 36 |
| 0-00 | **13** | 3 | **Littlestar (FR)**[21] 1509 3-8-10 **56** (JLDunlop) *chsd ldrs: rdn over 3f out: wknd qckly ins fnl 2f* **33/1** | (b1) SSanders 10 | 26 |
| 0-40 | **14** | 4 | **Illeana (GER)**[13] 1688 3-9-1 **61** (WRMuir) *chsd ldrs tl wknd 5f out* **33/1** | MartinDwyer 15 | 26 |
| 102 | **15** | ¾ | **Varuni (IRE)**[26] 1394 3-9-4 **64** (JGPortman) *hld up in tch: hdwy to trck ldrs over 5f out: wknd qckly over 2f out* **25/1** | PDobbs 3 | 28 |
| 45-5 | **16** | 5 | **Dolly Wotnot (IRE)**[26] 1394 3-9-7 **67** (NPLittmoden) *in tch: nt handle bnd and lost pl 7f out: hdwy 5f out: wknd 3f out* **40/1** | TGMcLaughlin 12 | 24 |
| 0-00 | **17** | 19 | **Grist Mist (IRE)**[13] 1683 3-8-13 **59** (MrsPNDutfield) *a in rr: wl bhd fnl 3f* **100/1** | (t) AMcCarthy 19 | — |
| 063- | **18** | 28 | **Polar Dancer**[163] 6091 3-9-5 **65** (MrsAJPerrett) *bhd fr 1/2-way* **20/1** | DaneO'Neill 8 | — |
| 00-0 | **19** | 2½ | **Desert Battle (IRE)**[10] 1755 3-9-4 **64** (MBlanshard) *mid-div 6f: wl bhd fnl 3f* **66/1** | DSweeney 5 | — |
| 6-33 | **20** | 4 | **Semelle De Vent (USA)**[26] 1394 3-8-12 **58** (JHMGosden) *chsd ldrs tl wknd qckly 4f out: wl bhd fnl 3f* **16/1** | RHavlin 7 | — |

2m 42.68s (12.58) **Going Correction** +0.975s/f (Soft) **20** Ran SP% **128.5**
Speed ratings: **97,95,94,94,92 89,89,87,86,86 82,80,78,75,74 71,58,40,38,35**CSF £55.11 CT £573.70 TOTE £13.80: £2.30, £1.40, £2.80, £5.50; EX 56.00.
**Owner** M W Lawrence **Bred** Lloyd Farm Stud **Trained** Pandy, Gwent

**FOCUS**
A solid gallop to this moderate handicap and few got into the argument.

**NOTEBOOK**
**Fleetfoot Mac** made all under a canny ride from Callan. He handles this ground well and this followed up his win in a claimer last time, so he is evidently on the up, but looks slightly flattered by the bare form.
**Late Opposition** again found one too good. He may have been left a bit to do, but did not help his rider under pressure and looked to down tools. He has now finished second over course and distance the last three times and does deserve to get his head in front, but is now well exposed and vunerable to improvers.
**General Flumpa**, making his handicap debut, found his stamina desert him over this trip, but shaped nicely until that point and could build on this if dropped in trip.
**Prenup(IRE)**, another making her handicap bow, ran her best race to date and is entitled to come on for this outing.
**Mambina(USA)** was held up to get the trip and having made good headway approaching two out, found this distance beyond her.
**Science Academy(USA)**, popular in the betting ring, was most reluctant to enter the stalls and once racing was forced wide for most of the way. She will come on a lot for this experience and can do better.

## 1999 TOTESPORT.COM ROYAL WINDSOR STKS (LISTED RACE) (C&G) — 1m 67y
**7:15** (7:15) (A) 3-Y-O+ — **£19,500** (£6,000; £3,000; £1,500) **Stalls** High

| Form | Pos | Dist | Horse | Jockey | RPR |
|---|---|---|---|---|---|
| 10-1 | **1** | | **Putra Pekan**[12] 1705 6-9-7 108 (MAJarvis) *plld hrd: rn wd and led bnd after 2f: rdn and styd on whn strly chal ins fnl 2f: in command ins last* **5/4**[1] | (b) PRobinson 4 | 114 |
| | **2** | 2½ | **Ancient World (USA)**[214] 4-9-2 (SaeedBinSuroor) *led tl rn wd and hdd after 2f: styd trcking wnr: chal ins fnl 2f: edgd rt u.p ins last:wknd cl home* **13/8**[2] | (t) LDettori 5 | 104 |
| 01-0 | **3** | 3½ | **Excelsius (IRE)**[46] 1107 4-9-7 106 (JLDunlop) *slowly away:sn in tch: hdwy 3f out: chsd ldrs 2f out: wknd fnl f but tk 3rd nr fin* **14/1** | TQuinn 6 | 102? |
| 3231 | **4** | hd | **Rockets 'n Rollers (IRE)**[9] 1758 4-9-7 106 (RHannon) *trckd ldrs: rdn and effrt over 2f out: no imp: wknd fnl f and lost 3rd cl home* **6/1**[3] | DaneO'Neill 3 | 102 |

1m 50.88s (5.28) **Going Correction** +0.975s/f (Soft) **4** Ran SP% **103.5**
Speed ratings: **112,109,106,105**CSF £3.21 TOTE £1.90; EX 3.10.
**Owner** H R H Sultan Ahmad Shah **Bred** Mrs Mary Taylor **Trained** Newmarket, Suffolk

**FOCUS**
A decent field for this Listed event that was run at a fair pace for the grade.

**NOTEBOOK**
**Putra Pekan** pulled his way to the front after two furlongs and never looked back from that point on. He followed up his Ascot Listed win on this occasion and will now most likely have to move back into Group company, which twice found him out last term, but he could not be in better form at present and relishes this testing ground.
**Ancient World(USA)** ran very much as though this race was needed, and would have strong claims of reversing the form with the winner with this outing under his belt. He evidently needs this ground, and while he is unlikely to prove one of his stable's leading lights, he looks a sure-fire winner of a similar contest.
**Excelsius(IRE)** lost all chance at the start, but shaped well late on and finished well. He is better than the bare form and should continue to pay his way at this level.
**Rockets 'n Rollers(IRE)** never looked like following up on his Listed success last time over this longer trip. He has found his form again this year and was not disgraced on this occasion, so may be worth another chance when dropped a furlong.

## 2000 BEECHCROFT ASSOCIATES CLASSIFIED STKS — 1m 2f 7y
**7:45** (7:45) (E) 4-Y-O+ — **£4,407** (£1,356; £678; £339) **Stalls** Low

| Form | Pos | Dist | Horse | Jockey | RPR |
|---|---|---|---|---|---|
| 1056 | **1** | | **Scottish River (USA)**[19] 1540 5-8-11 72 (MDIUsher) *hld up: hdwy over 3f out: drvn to ld and hung lft fr 1f out: kpt on wl* **40/1** | HayleyTurner(5) 15 | 81 |
| -064 | **2** | ¾ | **Invitation**[8] 1801 6-9-0 70 (ACharlton) *hld up in rr: headway over 2f out: r.o wl and hung lft ins fnl f: no imp on wnr cl home* **12/1** | RSmith 8 | 78 |
| 2523 | **3** | 1½ | **Street Life (IRE)**[16] 1611 6-9-4 74 (WJMusson) *bhd: hdwy 4f out: pushed along 3f out: hdwy 2f out: rdn to chal 1f out: no ex ins last* **9/4**[1] | KFallon 3 | 79 |
| 21-3 | **4** | 5 | **Polar Jem**[10] 1752 4-9-1 74 (GGMargarson) *chsd ldrs: rdn 4f out: slt ld appr fnl f: sn hdd: wknd ins last* **10/1** | AMcCarthy 14 | 68 |
| 00-0 | **5** | 1½ | **Silver Prophet (IRE)**[23] 1460 5-9-5 75 (MRBosley) *chsd ldrs: rdn 3f out: wknd over 1f out* **100/1** | GBaker 16 | 69 |
| 421- | **6** | shd | **Pequenita**[110] 5534 4-8-11 69 (GLMoore) *chsd ldrs: rn wd bnd 7f out: styd prom and chal 2f out: sn slt ld: hdd appr 1f out: wknd qckly* **14/1** | (b) RLMoore 10 | 61 |
| 6-14 | **7** | 2 | **Miss Pebbles (IRE)**[20] 1522 4-8-11 68 (BRJohnson) *led 1f: styd pressing ldr tl slt ld again over 2f out: hdd ins fnl 2f: sn wknd* **12/1** | NPollard 2 | 58 |
| 41-4 | **8** | shd | **Maxilla (IRE)**[10] 1752 4-8-13 72 (LMCumani) *led after 1f: hdd over 2f out: sn weakewned* **7/1**[2] | LDettori 12 | 59 |
| /54- | **9** | shd | **Shredded (USA)**[209] 5560 4-9-5 75 (JHMGosden) *chsd ldrs: wknd over 2f out* **14/1** | JPMurtagh 19 | 65 |
| 3-36 | **10** | ¾ | **Sir Haydn**[16] 1611 4-9-0 70 (JRJenkins) *bhd: kpt on u.p fnl 2f: nt rch ldrs* **20/1** | WRyan 9 | 59 |
| 0030 | **11** | nk | **Sudden Flight (IRE)**[3] 1928 7-9-0 68 (PDEvans) *chsd ldrs tl rdn and wknd 3f out* **25/1** | RHavlin 17 | 58 |
| 1135 | **12** | 5 | **War Owl (USA)**[16] 1604 7-8-13 72 (IanWilliams) *trckd ldrs: rdn 3f out: wknd over 2f out* **8/1**[3] | LisaJones(3) 13 | 52 |
| 216- | **13** | 9 | **My Galliano (IRE)**[64] 4446 8-8-11 68 (BGPowell) *nvr bttr than mid-div* **40/1** | LPKeniry(3) 7 | 35 |
| 3300 | **14** | 1¾ | **Skylarker (USA)**[16] 1624 6-9-2 72 (WSKittow) *bhd: rdn into mid-div: 1/2-way: wknd 4f out* **12/1** | NCallan 18 | 34 |
| -124 | **15** | 12 | **Moon Shot**[40] 1203 8-9-1 71 (AGJuckes) *sn bhd* **40/1** | VSlattery 5 | 12 |
| | **16** | 5 | **One Of Them**[27] 5-8-7 62 (JSMoore) *chsd ldrs over 6f* **100/1** | (b) DerekNolan(7) 11 | 3 |
| 350- | **17** | nk | **Chevronne**[174] 6025 4-9-0 70 (LGCottrell) *wnt rt s: sn rcvrd and in tch: wknd 3f out* **20/1** | (b1) SDrowne 20 | 2 |
| 0000 | **18** | 12 | **Dusty Carpet**[89] 743 6-9-0 65 (MJWeeden) *a bhd* **25/1** | MFenton 1 | — |


The Form Book, Raceform Ltd, Compton, RG20 6NL

056- **19** *16* **Den'S-Joy**[177] 6004 8-8-11 52 ............ SSanders 6 —
(VSmith) *bhd most of way* **33/1**

2m 17.33s (9.03) **Going Correction** +0.975s/f (Soft) **19** Ran SP% **129.3**
Speed ratings: **102,101,100,96,95 94,93,93,93,92 92,88,81,79,70 66,65,56,43**CSF £454.17 TOTE £36.70: £8.90, £4.40, £1.50; EX 549.70.

**Owner** M D I Usher **Bred** The Thoroughbred Corporation **Trained** Upper Lambourn, Berks

**FOCUS**
A fair handicap run at a strong early gallop and the first three were clear at the finish.

**NOTEBOOK**
**Scottish River(USA)**, despite hanging markedly left under pressure approaching the last furlong, saw off his rivals to score his first win on turf since 2001. He enjoyed a successful winter on the All-Weather, winning three times at Wolverhampton, and looks to have carried that forward onto the turf, so could still be well treated at present. *Official explanation: jockey said gelding hung left*
**Invitation** appreciated the drop in trip and improved on his most recent efforts, but looked reluctant to go through with his effort close home. There is no denying he is on a winning mark, but he is the type that needs everything to drop right.
**Street Life(IRE)**, who came into this having won three times from as many starts over course and distance, made good headway to get involved entering the straight to hold every chance if good enough, but could not quicken under pressure. He may have been better served by a more patient ride on this occasion and should not be written off.
**Polar Jem** ◆ ran right up to her mark over this slightly longer trip and was not disgraced. She is marginally better than the bare form suggests and is one to look out for off this mark when encountering faster ground.
**Maxilla(IRE)** raced alone in the straight up the stands' side rail and is better than the bare form would suggest, but this is her level.

## 2001 BDL GROUP MEDIAN AUCTION MAIDEN STKS 1m 2f 7y
**8:15** (8:17) (E) 3-Y-O **£3,669** (£1,129; £564; £282) **Stalls** Low

Form RPR
063- **1** **Incursion**[198] 5754 3-9-0 82 ............ RHughes 20 79
(AKing) *trckd ldrs: led over 3f out: drvn and r.o wl fnl f* **5/2**[1]
0-3 **2** *3* **Midshipman Easy (USA)**[21] 1508 3-9-0 ............ NCallan 14 74
(PWHarris) *sn trcking ldrs: chal 3f out: chsd wnr fr over 2f out: outpcd fnl f* **5/1**[3]
0-0 **3** *3 ½* **Lady Peaches**[8] 1793 3-8-9 ............ LDettori 7 63
(DMullarkey) *chsd ldrs: rdn and outpcd over 2f out: rallied: edgd lft and r.o fnl f: nt trble ldrs* **12/1**
00-0 **4** *hd* **Ellina**[21] 1507 3-8-9 ............ RPrice 1 63
(JPearce) *chsd ldrs: rdn to chal over 3f out: wknd appr fnl f* **25/1**
**5** *3* **Cultured** 3-8-9 ............ SDrowne 12 58
(MrsAJBowlby) *chsd ldrs: rdn and kpt on same pce fnl 2f* **33/1**
00 **6** *2 ½* **Pella**[28] 1356 3-8-9 ............ DSweeney 17 53
(MBlanshard) *chsd ldrs: pushed along 3f out: wknd ins fnl 2f* **100/1**
**7** *hd* **Honeymooning** 3-8-9 ............ WRyan 8 53
(HRACecil) *bhd: pushed along over 3f out: swtchd to outside and kpt on fnl 2f: nt a danger* **10/1**
00- **8** *1 ¼* **Young Love**[202] 5691 3-8-9 ............ MFenton 16 51
(MissECLavelle) *in tch: rdn and effrt 3f out: wknd 2f out* **66/1**
0 **9** *nk* **Crocolat**[8] 1794 3-8-9 ............ AMackay 11 50
(NACallaghan) *bhd tl r.o fnl 2f: nt a danger* **66/1**
0-6 **10** *½* **Laabbij (USA)**[23] 1461 3-9-0 ............ MartinDwyer 6 54
(MPTregoning) *bhd: hrd drvn 3f out: n.d* **7/2**[2]
00 **11** *hd* **Antigiotto (IRE)**[9] 1771 3-8-11 ............ NMackay[(3)] 13 54
(LMCumani) *bhd: kpt on fr over 2f out: nt a danger* **66/1**
6-0 **12** *1 ¼* **Wild Pitch**[107] 598 3-9-0 ............ RLMoore 18 52
(PMitchell) *mid-div: rdn and effrt 3f out: wknd fnl 2f* **33/1**
0 **13** *2 ½* **Silencio (IRE)**[14] 1674 3-9-0 ............ VSlattery 9 48
(AKing) *mid-div: pushed along over 4f out: n.d after* **25/1**
**14** *3* **Highlight Girl** 3-8-6 ............ SHitchcott[(3)] 4 38
(AWCarroll) *a in rr* **50/1**
00-0 **15** *3 ½* **St Tropez (IRE)**[21] 1507 3-8-9 ............ SWhitworth 10 32
(BGPowell) *t.k.h: hld up in rr: hdwy on rails fr 3f out: wknd over 1f out* **100/1**
000 **16** *¾* **Justice Jones**[13] 1683 3-9-0 ............ ADaly 3 35
(JLSpearing) *led 2f: styd chsng ldrs: chal over 3f out: sn wknd* **66/1**
0 **17** *2 ½* **Trew Class**[7] 1842 3-8-9 ............ PRobinson 2 26
(MHTompkins) *a in rr* **20/1**
**18** *14* **Pouilly Fume** 3-8-9 ............ AMcCarthy 15 2
(DJSFfrenchDavis) *sn bhd* **50/1**
5 **19** *½* **Soviet Spirit**[10] 1753 3-8-9 ............ JPMurtagh 19 2
(JRFanshawe) *led after 2f: t.k.h: hdd over 3f out: sn wknd* **7/1**
00 **20** *3 ½* **Second User**[89] 739 3-8-7 ............ JJeffrey[(7)] 5 1
(JRJenkins) *bhd fr 1/2-way* **100/1**

2m 21.04s (12.74) **Going Correction** +0.975s/f (Soft) **20** Ran SP% **127.9**
Speed ratings: **88,85,82,82,80 78,78,77,76,76 76,75,73,70,68 67,65,54,53,51**CSF £13.59 TOTE £3.50: £2.30, £2.30, £3.90; EX 20.30 Place 6 £29.09, Place 5 £26.13.

**Owner** Nigel Bunter **Bred** K J Mercer **Trained** Barbury Castle, Wilts

**FOCUS**
An ordinary maiden, lacking any strength in depth, and run in a slow time.

**NOTEBOOK**
**Incursion**, who showed promise on three outings as a juvenile last year, got off the mark with a comfortable success. He showed a liking for this ground and was given a well-judged ride on this occasion, suggesting he may get farther than this. He could make up into a useful handicapper over this sort of trip, but will need to keep improving, as he was already rated 82 prior to this and his entry for the King Edward VII stakes at Royal Ascot looks ambitious.
**Midshipman Easy(USA)** looked a threat in the straight, but could not quicken with the winner over this trip. He shaped as though he would appreciate further and although he is now qualified for handicaps, he may find himself starting on a fairly stiff mark, thanks to this effort.
**Lady Peaches**, outclassed in a Listed race last time, appreciated this drop in grade and ran her best race to date. She was another to suggest that farther will suit and, now that she qualifies for handicaps, she should be placed to advantage before long.
**Ellina** markedly improved on her previous form and looks to be gradually getting the hang of things, yet her proximity at the finish does drag the form down somewhat.
**Cultured** was not disgraced on her racecourse debut and will come on a fair bit for this experience, but looks only modest.
**Honeymooning**
**Laabbij(USA)** proved disappointing. He failed to improve on his previous two outings and was never at the races on this occasion, but may do better now he is eligible for handicaps.
T/Jkpt: Not won. T/Plt: £15.50 to a £1 stake. Pool: £54,856.25. 2,579.35 winning tickets. T/Qpdt: £9.40 to a £1 stake. Pool: £3,252.90. 255.20 winning tickets. ST

# 1885 WOLVERHAMPTON (A.W) (L-H)
Monday, May 10

**OFFICIAL GOING: Standard**
Wind: almost nil Weather: fine

## 2002 MIX BUSINESS WITH PLEASURE AT DUNSTALL PARK MAIDEN AUCTION FILLIES' STKS 5f (F)
**2:30** (2:33) (E) 2-Y-O **£3,445** (£1,060; £530; £265) **Stalls** Low

Form RPR
32 **1** **Rightprice Premier (IRE)**[16] 1601 2-8-6 ow1 ............ NCallan 7 74
(KARyan) *t.k.h: w ldr: led 3f out: qcknd clr wl over 1f out: pushed out* **9/4**[1]
**2** *½* **Wise Wager (IRE)** 2-8-3 ow3 ............ THamilton[(3)] 6 72
(RAFahey) *dwlt: hdwy 3f out: chsd wnr over 1f out: edgd lft ins fnl f: r.o* **7/1**[3]
5 **3** *7* **Baileys Applause**[14] 1670 2-8-7 ............ (p) SSanders 5 45
(CADwyer) *led 2f: sn rdn: wknd 1f out* **3/1**[2]
223 **4** *½* **Lateral Thinker (IRE)**[14] 1670 2-8-1 ............ JFMcDonald[(3)] 2 40
(JAOsborne) *chsd ldrs: rdn and outpcd over 2f out: sme hdwy over 1f out: n.d* **3/1**[2]
**5** *nk* **Docklands Grace (USA)** 2-8-3 ............ TPQueally[(3)] 4 41
(NPLittmoden) *s.i.s: sme hdwy fnl f: nvr nr ldrs* **12/1**
0236 **6** *4* **Turtle Magic (IRE)**[13] 1686 2-7-10 ............ CHaddon[(7)] 1 22
(WGMTurner) *sn outpcd* **12/1**
5 **7** *shd* **Chilali (IRE)**[10] 1743 2-8-4 ............ FNorton 3 22
(ABerry) *w ldrs: rdn over 2f out: wkng whn swtchd rt over 1f out* **20/1**

62.30 secs (-0.50) **Going Correction** -0.075s/f (Stan) **7** Ran SP% **113.4**
Speed ratings: **101,100,89,88,87 81,81**CSF £18.33 TOTE £2.40: £1.20, £1.90; EX 23.40.

**Owner** Rightprice Racing **Bred** Illuminatus Investments **Trained** Hambleton, N Yorks
■ Stewards Enquiry : N Callan £375 fine: weighed in 4lb heavier than weighing out

**FOCUS**
Just an ordinary maiden, but the time was very good for the grade and it should produce its share of future winners.

**NOTEBOOK**
**Rightprice Premier(IRE)** ◆ confirm the promise she showed on her two previous runs on turf on this Fibresand debut. She has bags of pace, is capable of progressing further and could well follow up in a higher grade.
**Wise Wager(IRE)**, a 3,500euros half-sister to a moderate maiden, missed the break, was soon pushed along and looked the first beaten. However, she responded well to pressure and, gradually getting the hang of things, was the only one that could go with Rightprice Premier in the straight. Her tendency to hang in behind the winner close home has to be a slight concern, but it will be disappointing if she cannot find a similar race.
**Baileys Applause** was reluctant to enter the stalls and proved disappointing in the race itself. Having shown pace in the early part of the contest, she was a little one-paced in the closing stages.
**Lateral Thinker(IRE)** never really got competitive and keeps finding a few too good. *Official explanation: jockey said filly was unsuited by the fibresand surface*
**Docklands Grace(USA)**, a 9,000gns half-sister to five winners in the US, looked in need of the experience and should improve, possibly over further.

## 2003 WINNING POST SPECIAL AT DUNSTALL PARK CLAIMING STKS 5f (F)
**3:00** (3:01) (F) 2-Y-O **£2,898** (£828; £414) **Stalls** Low

Form RPR
**1** **Key Secret** 2-8-3 ............ JMackay 4 53
(MDIUsher) *rn green and outpcd: gd hdwy on ins wl over 1f out: led ent fnl f: jst hld on* **12/1**
040 **2** *shd* **Goldhill Prince**[13] 1686 2-7-13 ............ (p) CHaddon[(7)] 2 56
(WGMTurner) *chsd ldrs: rdn over 2f out: edgd rt wl ins fnl f: r.o: jst failed* **9/2**[3]
63 **3** *1 ¼* **Straffan (IRE)**[18] 1556 2-8-5 ............ JCarroll 7 50
(EJO'Neill) *chsd ldrs: rdn over 2f out: r.o one pce fnl f* **7/2**[2]
25 **4** *½* **Lady Erica**[24] 1449 2-8-9 ............ DarrenWilliams 8 52
(KRBurke) *w ldr: rdn and ev ch over 1f out: nt qckn* **15/8**[1]
50 **5** *nk* **Voice Of An Angel (IRE)**[6] 1865 2-8-5 ............ FNorton 3 46
(ABerry) *led: edgd lft over 1f out: hdd ent fnl f: no ex* **12/1**
**6** *7* **Shish (IRE)** 2-8-0 ............ JFMcDonald[(3)] 1 16
(JAOsborne) *outpcd* **8/1**
00 **7** *2* **Ice Ruby**[17] 1589 2-7-11 ............ BSwarbrick[(5)] 5 7
(DShaw) *s.i.s: sn chsng ldrs: rdn and wknd 2f out* **20/1**
0 **8** *¾* **Houdini Bay (IRE)**[16] 1601 2-8-4 ............ THamilton[(3)] 6 9
(RPElliott) *w ldrs: rdn over 2f out: wknd wl over 1f out* **25/1**

63.05 secs (0.25) **Going Correction** -0.075s/f (Stan) **8** Ran SP% **110.3**
Speed ratings: **95,94,92,92,91 80,77,75**CSF £60.48 TOTE £14.90: £4.60, £1.90, £1.40; EX 75.50.Key Secret was the subject of a friendly claim of £8,000.

**Owner** I Sheward **Bred** Barry Minty **Trained** Upper Lambourn, Berks

**FOCUS**
Not a great race and, with about two lengths separating the first five home, the form looks modest and must be treated with caution.

**NOTEBOOK**
**Key Secret**, out a dual five-furlong selling juvenile winner, overcame her inexperience to make a winning debut. After missing the break, she ran very green towards the rear, but gradually got the hang of things and picked up well in the straight. She should remain competitive at this sort of level.
**Goldhill Prince**, dropped back into claiming company, did not do a great deal wrong but looks in need of another furlong.
**Straffan(IRE)** ran wider than anything in the straight but finished to good effect and is another who should get six furlongs.
**Lady Erica** did not get home and has not really progressed from her debut running.
**Voice Of An Angel(IRE)** wandered around when out under pressure, but looked to have every chance.

## 2004 SPONSOR A RACE AT DUNSTALL PARK H'CAP 1m 6f 166y(F)
**3:35** (3:38) (F) (0-55,51) 4-Y-O+ **£2,933** (£838; £419) **Stalls** High

Form RPR
0-35 **1** **Toledo Sun**[15] 1376 4-8-11 **51** ............ JoannaBadger 10 59
(VSmith) *prom: led after 3f: rdn 4f out: drvn out* **6/1**[3]
4-33 **2** *1* **Compton Eclaire (IRE)**[10] 1744 4-8-6 **49** ............ (v) TPQueally[(3)] 3 56
(GABulter) *s.i.s: hld up: stdy hdwy over 6f out: styd on and edgd lft ins fnl f: nt rch wnr* **13/2**
2612 **3** *1 ½* **Red Moor (IRE)**[18] 1572 4-8-8 **48** ............ ACulhane 6 53
(RHollinshead) *a.p: chsd ldr 8f out: rdn over 3f out: no ex ins fnl f* **5/1**[2]
/5-1 **4** *shd* **My Legal Eagle (IRE)**[5] 1887 10-8-3 **46** 6ex ............ BSwarbrick[(5)] 4 51
(RJPrice) *hld up and bhd: stdy hdwy over 7f out: rdn over 4f out: styd on same pce fnl 2f* **5/1**[2]

0-0 **5** *4* **Lubinas (IRE)**[10] 1754 5-8-8 **46**.................... SWKelly 1 45
(FJordan) *prom: rdn 7f out: no imp fnl 4f* **8/1**
6004 **6** *30* **Celtic Vision (IRE)**[6] 1866 8-8-12 **50**.................... (t) SRighton 8 10
(MAppleby) *rn in snatches: rdn and short-lived effrt over 6f out: lost tch 5f out: t.o* **22/1**
550- **7** *15* **Caliban (IRE)**[364] 1563 6-8-11 **49**.................... MFenton 5 —
(IanWilliams) *led 3f: rdn and wknd qckly 7f out: t.o fnl 5f* **12/1**
1234 **8** *19* **The Beduth Navi**[20] 1534 4-8-8 **48** ow1.................... SSanders 2 —
(DGBridgwater) *prom: rdn 7f out: wknd 4f out: sn eased: t.o* **7/2**[1]
00-6 **9** *dist* **Fortuna Mea**[17] 1580 4-8-2 **47** ow2.................... PMakin(5) 9 —
(WMBrisbourne) *hld up: rdn over 6f out: sn lost tch: t.o* **20/1**

3m 18.9s (-2.60) **Going Correction** -0.075s/f (Stan)
**WFA** 4 from 5yo+ 2lb **9** Ran **SP% 111.1**
Speed ratings: **103,102,101,101,99 83,75,65,**—CSF £42.06 CT £201.11 TOTE £9.90: £4.40, £1.30, £2.90; EX 49.20.
**Owner** Monkey A Month Racing **Bred** Natton House Thoroughbreds **Trained** Exning, Suffolk
■ Stewards Enquiry : Joanna Badger two-day ban: used whip in an incorrect place (close to gelding's rib-cage) (May 21-22)

**FOCUS**
A very moderate handicap, but a fair pace and only five got home.

**NOTEBOOK**
**Toledo Sun** proved very game in fending off all challengers to get his head in front for the first time. He had never previously run over a trip this far on the Flat, but promised to stay having run well over hurdles on his previous outing. His long-term future lies back over obstacles.
**Compton Eclaire(IRE)** travelled easily on the first circuit, but really needed stoking up second time round and did not look to be going anywhere until hitting top stride in the straight. She is probably worth another try over two miles, but does not look like one to follow.
**Red Moor(IRE)**, stepping out of regional racing, did not appear suited by this step up in trip.
**My Legal Eagle(IRE)** scored in banded company over this course and distance on his previous start but, up in grade, he was made to look pretty one paced.
**Lubinas(IRE)** did not offer much encouragement.
**The Beduth Navi** was never really going that well and returned lame. *Official explanation: vet said gelding finished lame on the left fore*

## 2005 COME RACING AGAIN TOMORROW AT DUNSTALL PARK FILLIES' H'CAP 1m 100y(F)
**4:10** (4:10) (E) (0-70,66) 3-Y-O **£3,396** (£1,045; £522; £261) **Stalls** Low

Form RPR
1514 **1** **Daring Affair**[6] 1874 3-9-7 **66**.................... DarrenWilliams 1 70
(KRBurke) *w ldr 2f: hld up in tch: rdn over 2f out: led wl over 1f out: sn hung persistently rt: jst hld on* **9/4**[2]
2-34 **2** *hd* **Keshya**[13] 1688 3-9-1 **63**.................... TPQueally(3) 3 67
(DJCoakley) *prom: rdn over 3f out: outpcd over 2f out: rallied over 1f out: r.o ins fnl f* **11/8**[1]
-100 **3** *1 ½* **Somewhere My Love**[67] 959 3-9-4 **66**.................... RMiles(3) 2 67
(TGMills) *chsd ldr after 2f: rdn over 2f out: nt qckn fnl f* **7/1**
040- **4** *1 ¼* **Stiletto Lady (IRE)**[189] 5905 3-9-4 **63**.................... MFenton 5 61
(JGGiven) *led: rdn over 2f out: hdd wl over 1f out: no ex ins fnl f* **13/2**[3]
6010 **5** *20* **Lady Predominant**[23] 1467 3-7-11 **47**.................... (t) BSwarbrick(5) 4 3
(AndrewReid) *prom: rdn over 3f out: wknd over 2f out* **10/1**

1m 51.43s (0.34) **Going Correction** -0.075s/f (Stan) **5** Ran **SP% 107.8**
Speed ratings: **95,94,93,92,72**CSF £5.48 TOTE £2.40: £1.10, £1.10; EX 4.70.
**Owner** Nigel Shields **Bred** N R Shields And K R Burke **Trained** Middleham Moor, N Yorks

**FOCUS**
A modest fillies' handicap in which the winner did nothing when sent to the front and is value for more than the winning margin.

**NOTEBOOK**
**Daring Affair**, 5lb higher than when winning on her previous start over this course and distance, travelled well for much of the race, but did nothing other than prick her ears and hang all over the track when sent to the front. She may do better ridden with more restraint and there are more races to be won with her, especially on sand.
**Keshya**, still a maiden and making her Fibresand debut, did not really do much wrong but is flattered to get so close to the winner as that one was idling in front.
**Somewhere My Love** returned to some sort of form after a couple of poor efforts. This was her first start on Fibresand but she seemed to handle the surface well.
**Stiletto Lady(IRE)**, racing for the first time in 189 days, making both her Fibresand and handicap debut, ran well for a long way and should improve.
**Lady Predominant**, whose only previous win came in banded company, was below form in a first-time tongue-tie.

## 2006 TATTERSALLS VALUE PACKAGE AT DUNSTALL PARK (S) STKS 7f (F)
**4:40** (4:41) (G) 3-Y-O+ **£2,639** (£754; £377) **Stalls** High

Form RPR
-002 **1** **Turn Around**[16] 1629 4-9-8 52.................... ACulhane 8 61
(BWHills) *a.p: led over 3f out: rdn over 2f out: drvn out* **7/2**[2]
3603 **2** *1 ¾* **Chandelier**[14] 1680 4-9-5 48.................... (p) RMiles(3) 7 56
(MSSaunders) *prom: rdn 4f out: outpcd 3f out: rallied ins fnl f* **6/1**
5001 **3** *nk* **Mizhar (USA)**[14] 1680 8-9-13 52.................... (p) DarrenWilliams 6 61
(JJQuinn) *sn bhd: rdn and hdwy over 2f out: kpt on one pce fnl f* **6/1**
-040 **4** *1* **Queen Of Night**[2] 1956 4-8-12 70.................... PMakin(5) 4 48
(DWChapman) *led over 3f: rdn over 2f out: no ex fnl f* **5/1**[3]
0404 **5** *8* **Tinian**[11] 1718 6-9-1 45.................... (b[1]) SBushby(7) 1 32
(KRBurke) *sn bhd* **14/1**
0-0 **6** *7* **Compton Eagle**[33] 1295 4-9-5.................... TPQueally(3) 5 14
(GAButler) *s.s: rdn 4f out: a bhd* **8/1**
000/ **7** *6* **Golden Legend (IRE)**[350] 4370 7-9-3 30.................... BSwarbrick(5) 2 —
(RJPrice) *stmbld s: a wl bhd* **66/1**
0002 **8** *dist* **Shadowfax**[53] 1044 4-9-8 58.................... (v[1]) MFenton 3 —
(MissGayKelleway) *w ldr: rdn over 3f out: sn wknd: virtually p.u wl over 1f out* **3/1**[1]

1m 30.51s (0.19) **Going Correction** -0.075s/f (Stan) **8** Ran **SP% 111.7**
Speed ratings: **95,93,92,91,82 74,67,**—CSF £23.52 TOTE £5.20: £1.10, £2.50, £2.80; EX 34.30.The winner was bought in for 7,200gns.
**Owner** Gryffindor (www.racingtours.co.uk) **Bred** Cheveley Park Stud Ltd **Trained** Lambourn, Berks

**FOCUS**
A weak seller which offers little for the future.

**NOTEBOOK**
**Turn Around** gained his first win since landing a Windsor maiden back in October 2002 with a decisive success. This will have boosted his confidence and he should continue to go well at this sort of level.
**Chandelier**, with the cheekpieces back on, could never really get on terms with the winner and may benefit from a step to a mile.
**Mizhar(USA)**, successful in a course and distance seller on his previous start, lacked a change of pace under his big weight and proved unable to follow up.
**Queen Of Night** did nothing wrong, but did not appear to stay the trip. She will be best served by a return to shorter distances.
**Tinian** had blinkers replacing the cheekpieces, but was never a threat.
**Shadowfax** *Official explanation: jockey said gelding lost its action*

## 2007 TELETEXT RACING "HANDS AND HEELS" APPRENTICE H'CAP 1m 1f 79y(F)
**5:10** (5:10) (F) (0-55,51) 3-Y-O+ **£2,947** (£842; £421) **Stalls** Low

Form RPR
635- **1** **Vandenberghe**[146] 6200 5-9-3 **48**.................... RKeogh(3) 7 58
(JAOsborne) *hld up: hdwy over 3f out: rdn over 2f out: r.o to ld wl ins fnl f* **4/1**[1]
6040 **2** *nk* **Frank's Quest (IRE)**[12] 1710 4-9-3 **50**.................... RJKilloran(5) 5 59
(PBurgoyne) *a.p: led 4f out: rdn over 1f out: hdd wl ins fnl f: nt qckn* **11/2**[3]
0-00 **3** *6* **Arjay**[16] 1620 6-9-9 **51**.................... MHoward 2 48
(AndrewTurnell) *led: hdd 4f out: rdn over 2f out: wknd over 1f out* **12/1**
3336 **4** *4* **Call Of The Wild**[33] 1305 4-9-6 **51**.................... (p) DSwift(3) 6 40
(RAFahey) *hld up: hdwy 6f out: rdn over 3f out: wknd over 2f out* **4/1**[1]
6262 **5** *hd* **Dancing King (IRE)**[6] 1875 8-9-4 **46**.................... MHalford 4 35
(PWHiatt) *prom tl rdn and wknd 2f out* **4/1**[1]
63-0 **6** *6* **Chantry Falls (IRE)**[42] 1176 4-9-6 **48**.................... LiamJones 8 25
(JGGiven) *hld up: hdwy 6f out: rdn and wknd over 2f out* **9/1**
0042 **7** *2 ½* **Crusoe (IRE)**[14] 1681 7-9-9 **51**.................... (b) KMay 1 23
(ASadik) *prom: lost pl 6f out: sn bhd* **5/1**[2]
0000 **8** *3* **Daimajin (IRE)**[6] 1875 5-9-3 **50**.................... TO'Brien(5) 3 16
(MrsLucindaFeatherstone) *s.i.s: hld up: rdn over 5f out: bhd fnl 4f* **20/1**

2m 3.07s (0.07) **Going Correction** -0.075s/f (Stan) **8** Ran **SP% 114.5**
Speed ratings: **96,95,90,86,86 81,79,76**CSF £26.19 CT £240.74 TOTE £4.00: £2.50, £1.30, £3.70; EX 36.20 Place 6 £69.51, Place 5 £31.84.
**Owner** D Marks **Bred** Douglas Marks **Trained** Upper Lambourn, Berks

**FOCUS**
A moderate handicap with pace to match, but the first two were clear.

**NOTEBOOK**
**Vandenberghe**, last seen 146 days previously running over two miles, was dropped back to the distance he gained his only previous win over and, off a 1lb lower mark than when gaining that success, ran out a narrow winner. He has a poor wins-to-runs record and may be one to take on next time.
**Frank's Quest(IRE)**, beaten in a seller on his previous run, travelled really strongly into the straight but proved unable to resist the winner's challenge. He was clear of the third and may have a small race in him.
**Arjay**, with the blinkers left off this time, ran respectably from the front, showing real signs of a return to form.
**Call Of The Wild**, with cheekpieces replacing a visor and returned to Fibresand, never really looked like picking up and has to be considered disappointing.
**Dancing King(IRE)** has done most of his racing over shorter and may not have been suited by this step up in trip.
T/Plt: £123.00 to a £1 stake. Pool: £23,685.70. 140.50 winning tickets. T/Qpdt: £20.70 to a £1 stake. Pool: £1,869.40. 66.70 winning tickets. KH

# 2002 WOLVERHAMPTON (A.W) (L-H)
Tuesday, May 11

**OFFICIAL GOING: Standard**
There was a bias against those that raced tight against the inside rail and it paid to race wide.

## 2012 EVENING RACING IS FUN AT DUNSTALL PARK BANDED STKS 6f (F)
**6:20** (6:20) (H) 3-Y-O+ **£1,445** (£413; £206) **Stalls** Low

Form RPR
0343 **1** **Rathmullan**[6] 1889 5-8-13 40.................... (b) LiamJones(7) 7 44
(EAWheeler) *racd wd: hdwy 2f out: edgd lft bef led 1f out: wnt lft again ins fnl f: hld on* **6/1**[3]
4331 **2** *nk* **Neutral Night (IRE)**[6] 1889 4-9-12 40.................... (v) IMongan 5 49
(RBrotherton) *chsd ldrs: chalng whn squeezed out over 1f out: carried lft ins fnl f but kpt on* **5/2**[1]
5443 **3** *1 ½* **Indian Music**[5] 1915 7-9-6 40.................... JCarroll 6 39
(ABerry) *bhd and racd wd: outpcd tl r.o fnl f: nvr nrr* **5/1**[2]
0026 **4** *1 ¼* **Finger Of Fate**[12] 1738 4-9-6 40.................... RFitzpatrick 1 35
(MJPolglase) *led after 1f: rdn and hdd 1f out: wknd after* **5/2**[1]
0-0U **5** *5* **Mandy's Collection**[22] 1497 5-9-6 40.................... SWhitworth 3 20
(AGNewcombe) *led for 1f: styd prom: rdn 2f out: wknd 1f out* **5/1**[2]
-600 **6** *½* **Blade's Daughter**[11] 1742 3-8-10 40.................... NCallan 4 18
(KARyan) *in tch: rdn and wknd over 2f out* **8/1**

1m 15.04s (-0.76) **Going Correction** -0.125s/f (Stan)
**WFA** 3 from 4yo+ 10lb **6** Ran **SP% 115.9**
Speed ratings: **100,99,97,95,89 88**CSF £22.22 TOTE £6.90: £1.90, £2.10; EX 34.50.
**Owner** E A Wheeler **Bred** Mrs M Chubb **Trained** Whitchurch-on-Thames, Oxon
■ Stewards Enquiry : Liam Jones two-day ban: careles riding (May 22,23); caution: separate instance of careless riding

**FOCUS**
A poor race, but a sound pace. The runner-up suffered at the hands of the winner who may have been fortunate to keep it.

**NOTEBOOK**
**Rathmullan**, 6lb better off with the runner-up for a beating of four-and-a-half lengths over an extra furlong here last time, was kept wide from his outside draw and managed to reverse the form, but he tended to edge left throughout the final furlong and certainly did his main rival no favours.
**Neutral Night(IRE)**, dropping back a furlong, was closely matched with the runner-up on their running here last time. She was short of room when coming with her effort between horses soon after turning for home and was then carried to her left by the winner all the way to the line. She may well have won otherwise, but the Stewards decided to leave the placings unaltered.
**Indian Music** was completely taken off his feet before running on past beaten horses to reach his final position. The track was riding fast for this meeting and he ideally needs it slower over this trip.
**Finger Of Fate**, who has tried more trips than Judith Chalmers, was given a positive ride but his best recent effort was over the minimum and he ran as though not staying. That seems amazing for a horse that has won over seven furlongs and been tried over two miles.
**Mandy's Collection** is another that has shown his very best form over five and he found the extra furlong too much after having been given a positive ride.

## 2013 STAY IN THE HOLIDAY INN DUNSTALL PARK (S) STKS 1m 100y(F)
**6:50** (6:51) (H) 3-Y-O+ **£1,463** (£418; £209) **Stalls** Low

Form RPR
0306 **1** **Forty Forte**[17] 1629 8-9-3 45.................... (tp) AQuinn(5) 5 56
(MissSJWilton) *a.p: led 6f out: hdd 2f out: led again u.p 1f out: drvn clr ins fnl f* **6/1**
0013 **2** *2 ½* **Mizhar (USA)**[1] 2006 8-9-13 52.................... (p) MFenton 2 56
(JJQuinn) *chsd ldrs: wnt 2nd over 3f out and ev ch 2f out: edgd lft u.p and no ex ins fnl f* **10/3**[2]


The Form Book, Raceform Ltd, Compton, RG20 6NL

5055 **3** 1 ½ **Kanz Wood (USA)**[1] [1986] 8-9-8 50 IMongan 6 48
(AWCarroll) *outpcd early: hdwy over 4f out: led 2f out: rdn and hdd 1f out: wknd after* **9/4**[1]
4045 **4** 5 **Tinian**[1] [2006] 6-9-8 45 (b[1]) NCallan 7 37
(KRBurke) *bhd tl hdwy over 3f out: wknd wl overe 1f out* **4/1**[3]
5060 **5** 8 **Better Off**[24] [1479] 6-9-8 48 JoannaBadger 4 20
(MrsNMacauley) *a towards rr: lost tch 1/2-way* **8/1**
00/6 **6** 13 **Yallambie**[18] [1590] 5-9-0 50 (t) DNolan(3) 3 —
(KAMorgan) *led tl hdd 6f out: sn rdn and wknd 1/2-way* **6/1**
4/06 **7** 15 **Bound To Please**[12] [1739] 9-9-8 40 (v) AnnStokell 1 —
(MissAStokell) *prom early: bhd fr 1/2-way* **25/1**

1m 51.15s (0.06) **Going Correction** -0.125s/f (Stan) **7** Ran SP% **117.4**
Speed ratings: **94,91,90,85,77 64,49**CSF £27.33 TOTE £7.20: £3.40, £2.00; EX 51.80.There was no bid for the winner.
**Owner** John Pointon And Sons **Bred** B Long **Trained** Wetley Rocks, Staffs

**FOCUS**
A bad race, but a brave winner.

**NOTEBOOK**
**Forty Forte**, whose last two wins came over this course and distance, established his usual position out in front after a couple of furlongs. His goose looked cooked when he was flanked by the placed horses soon after turning in, but they are hardly the most talented individuals in the world and he surprisingly found himself back in front before striding away for a clear-cut win.
**Mizhar(USA)**, making a quick reappearance having finished third over seven furlongs here the previous day, was trying this trip for the first time in his 65th start. He came to win his race at the ideal time, but then the petrol ran out and he patently failed to stay.
**Kanz Wood(USA)**, another making a quick reappearance having finished unplaced on turf the previous day, is not at the top of his game at present. Despite that, he still looked the one to beat when nosing ahead of the eventual winner turning for home, but then hit a brick wall.
**Tinian** has become very disappointing and the headgear failed to work again.
**Better Off** has dropped 27lb in the last 12 months and this effort shows why.

## 2014 ESP EXPERIENCE CHALLENGE TRI-BANDED STKS 1m 4f (F)
7:20 (7:20) (H) 3-Y-O £1,428 (£408; £204) Stalls Low

Form RPR
0-02 **1** **True To Yourself (USA)**[19] [1570] 3-8-9 40 MFenton 6 49
(JGGiven) *racd wd early: stdy hdwy u.p to ld 1f out: sn clr* **5/2**[1]
0-66 **2** 7 **Middleham Rose**[105] [611] 3-7-11 35 RoryMoore(7) 5 34
(PCHaslam) *hld up: hdwy 7f out: led over 4f out: rdn over 2f out: hdd 1f out: wknd after* **3/1**[2]
6444 **3** 5 **Bretton**[3] [1959] 3-9-0 45 NCallan 1 36
(RHollinshead) *led: hdd over 4f out: rdn and wknd over 2f out* **7/2**[3]
0405 **4** nk **Bunino Ven**[7] [1862] 3-8-9 40 RLMoore 4 31
(SCWilliams) *in tch: rdn over 5f out: n.d ins fnl 4f* **4/1**
6-62 **5** 3 **Scorchio (IRE)**[12] [1726] 3-9-0 45 SRighton 3 31
(MFHarris) *chsd ldrs: rdn 5f out: sn btn* **4/1**
0-06 **6** dist **Northern Summit (IRE)**[12] [1740] 3-8-4 35 FNorton 2 —
(JRNorton) *trckd ldr: rdn 6f out: sn wknd and struggling in rr: t.o* **20/1**

2m 42.56s (0.76) **Going Correction** -0.125s/f (Stan) **6** Ran SP% **120.6**
Speed ratings: **92,87,84,83,81** —CSF £11.35 TOTE £3.50: £1.70, £1.50; EX 8.90.
**Owner** Mike J Beadle **Bred** S D Plummer **Trained** Willoughton, Lincs

**FOCUS**
Only a modest early pace though things quickened up over the last half-mile.

**NOTEBOOK**
**True To Yourself(USA)** ♦, stepping up in trip again, did not look to be going as well as the eventual runner-up half a mile from home, but the further they went the better he was going. He ultimately he won going away and, the way the track was riding, hanging over to the stands' rail was probably in his favour. Stamina appears to be his forte and he can win a similar event if given the opportunity.
**Middleham Rose**, another stepping up in trip, looked to be travelling best when taking over in front half a mile from home, but she did not find much off the bridle and was comprehensively beaten by the winner. She might just have needed this after a three-month break and is worth another chance over this trip.
**Bretton** set the pace, but he is yet to really prove himself over this trip and when the front two collared him there was nothing more to come.
**Bunino Ven** had the headgear left off this time, but did not improve for it.
**Scorchio(IRE)**, flattered by his Lingfield effort, found the combination of a longer trip, a different surface, and not being able to lead ending his chances.

## 2015 CORPORATE HOSPITALITY IS A WINNER AT DUNSTALL PARK BANDED STKS 1m 1f 79y(F)
7:50 (7:50) (H) 3-Y-O+ £1,445 (£413; £206) Stalls Low

Form RPR
4301 **1** **Iamback**[6] [1888] 4-8-13 45 DeanWilliams(7) 5 54
(MissGayKelleway) *trckd ldr: led over 5f out: pushed out fnl f* **11/4**[2]
4565 **2** 2 **Ballyrush (IRE)**[17] [1617] 4-8-7 45 (b[1]) RKeogh(7) 2 44
(KRBurke) *trckd ldrs: wnt 2nd over 2f out: rdn and no imp fnl f* **3/1**[3]
5162 **3** 2 ½ **Galey River (USA)**[6] [1888] 5-8-11 45 DCorby(3) 1 39
(JJSheehan) *chsd ldrs: outpcd 3f out: kpt on but no imp fnl 2f* **2/1**[1]
3600 **4** ¾ **On Guard**[7] [1856] 6-9-0 40 DKinsella 3 38
(PGMurphy) *in rr: hdwy 6f out: wknd wl over 1f out* **11/4**[2]
5/00 **5** dist **Manny**[15] [1668] 4-8-7 35 (p) PPMathers(7) 4 —
(MissAStokell) *led tl hdd over 5f out: rdn and sn wknd: t.o* **33/1**

2m 1.64s (-1.36) **Going Correction** -0.125s/f (Stan) **5** Ran SP% **114.6**
Speed ratings: **101,99,97,96**,—CSF £11.80 TOTE £4.30: £1.30, £1.50; EX 9.90.
**Owner** Twilight Racing **Bred** Mrs J M F Dibben **Trained** Newmarket, Suffolk

**FOCUS**
A decent pace and a fair winning time for the grade.

**NOTEBOOK**
**Iamback**, who won nicely over course and distance six days ago, was given a similarly positive ride and saw her race out well, though being kept away from the inside rail probably swung things her way.
**Ballyrush(IRE)**, dropped into banded company for the first time, travelled really well and was still cruising turning for home, but found nothing off the bridle. He was racing tight against the inside rail and at this meeting that was a negative.
**Galey River(USA)** finished further behind Iamback than he did here last week, despite a 6lb pull in the weights.
**On Guard**, with the visor left off, had every chance but proved disappointing and looks very much on the downgrade.

## 2016 SPONSOR A RACE AT DUNSTALL PARK TRI-BANDED STKS 1m 1f 79y(F)
8:20 (8:22) (H) 3-Y-O £1,424 (£407; £203) Stalls Low

Form RPR
-520 **1** **A Bit Of Fun**[26] [1407] 3-8-4 35 PHanagan 3 47
(JJQuinn) *hld up in tch: hdwy to ld over 2f out: wnt clr fnl f* **2/1**[1]
0-03 **2** 5 **Royal Upstart**[19] [1570] 3-8-4 40 (b) BSwarbrick(5) 1 42
(WMBrisbourne) *chsd ldrs: outpcd 5f out: styd on and wnt 2nd ins fnl f* **4/1**[3]
4241 **3** ¾ **Secret Bloom**[19] [1570] 3-9-0 45 (v) DarrenWilliams 5 45
(JRNorton) *led over 4f out: hdd over 2f out: wknd over 1f out* **9/4**[2]
0534 **4** 1 ¾ **Platinum Chief**[5] [1916] 3-8-3 40 ow1 (p) PPMathers(7) 4 38
(ABerry) *sn outpcd: sme late prog* **14/1**
0032 **5** 5 **Regency Malaya**[22] [1495] 3-9-0 45 (bt) SRighton 2 32
(MFHarris) *led tl hdd over 4f out: wknd wl over 1f out* **11/2**
0345 **6** 2 ½ **Mystic Promise (IRE)**[14] [1701] 3-7-13 35 (t) HayleyTurner(5) 6 17
(MrsNMacauley) *a bhd: lost tch 1/2-way* **12/1**

2m 3.81s (0.81) **Going Correction** -0.125s/f (Stan) **6** Ran SP% **113.8**
Speed ratings: **91,86,85,84,79 77**CSF £10.66 TOTE £2.30: £2.60, £1.70; EX 20.90.
**Owner** The Fun Seekers **Bred** Lord Halifax **Trained** Settrington, N Yorks

**FOCUS**
Only a modest pace, but an authoritative winner and a gamble landed.

**NOTEBOOK**
**A Bit Of Fun**, whose best previous effort came when runner-up over this course and distance two starts back, was very well backed to go one better. Getting stronger as the race progressed, he had one anxious moment when Secret Bloom carried him wide on the home bend, but that meant he ended up on the fastest part of the track and he forged clear of his rivals. He races as though he would get further on this surface.
**Royal Upstart** got tapped for toe mid-race before getting his second wind in the home straight. He was never a threat though and probably achieved little.
**Secret Bloom**, whose course-and-distance win last month was boosted by the victory of the runner-up True To Yourself earlier on the card, may have been flattered by that effort. He seemed to be travelling best when taking over half a mile out, but he was awkward on the home bend and once the winner ranged alongside the race was over.
**Platinum Chief** was never nearer than at the line, but offered little encouragement.
**Regency Malaya**, who has been running well on Polytrack, has never shown the same aptitude for this surface and did not see out the trip.
**Mystic Promise(IRE)** *Official explanation: trainer said gelding had a breathing problem*

## 2017 TATTERSALLS VALUE PACKAGE AT DUNSTALL PARK BANDED STKS 7f (F)
8:50 (8:50) (H) 3-Y-O+ £1,456 (£416; £208) Stalls High

Form RPR
4332 **1** **Countrywide Girl (IRE)**[6] [1890] 5-9-7 35 FNorton 6 42
(ABerry) *mde all: hung lft appr fnl f: kpt on* **7/4**[1]
00-5 **2** 1 **Ben Kenobi**[6] [1889] 6-9-7 30 RFfrench 5 39
(MrsPFord) *outpcd early: hdwy outsiide 2f out: styd on strly to go 2nd ins fnl f* **17/2**
5661 **3** 1 ¼ **Welsh Whisper**[6] [1890] 5-9-8 30 NChalmers(5) 3 42
(SABrookshaw) *slow into stride: hdwy after 2f: wnt over 2f out: rdn and wknd fnl f* **5/2**[2]
0-03 **4** 6 **Point Man (IRE)**[7] [1861] 4-9-7 30 NCallan 8 21
(JWPayne) *in tch: rdn over 2f out: n.d after* **13/2**
-000 **5** 2 **Ellamyte**[85] [792] 4-9-4 35 DNolan(3) 4 15
(DGBridgwater) *trckd ldr tl rdn and wknd over 2f out* **11/2**[3]
/0-0 **6** 1 ¼ **Boozy Douz**[20] [1541] 4-9-7 30 (p) SWhitworth 2 12
(HSHowe) *in tch: sn outpcd and a bhd* **20/1**
0006 **7** 1 ¼ **Mesmerised**[19] [1568] 4-9-7 30 (p) AnnStokell 7 9
(MissAStokell) *trckd ldrs: outpacxed 1/2-way: sn bhd* **16/1**
/653 **8** 6 **Chakra**[7] [1863] 10-9-0 30 CHaddon(7) 1 —
(CJGray) *outpcd fr s a struggling wl in rr* **12/1**

1m 30.26s (-0.06) **Going Correction** -0.125s/f (Stan) **8** Ran SP% **122.5**
Speed ratings: **95,93,92,85,83 81,80,73**CSF £19.52 TOTE £2.90: £1.10, £2.80, £1.30; EX 17.00 Place 6 £63.92, Place 5 £26.70..
**Owner** Galaxy Moss Side Racing Clubs Limited **Bred** Ray Cullen **Trained** Cockerham, Lancs

**FOCUS**
Probably the most competitive event on the card, but only a fair pace.

**NOTEBOOK**
**Countrywide Girl(IRE)**, 6lb better off with Welsh Whisper for a six-length beating here last week, comprehensively reversed the form over this extra furlong. Making every yard, she stayed on bravely to the line despite tending to run about under pressure down the home straight.
**Ben Kenobi**, taken off his feet for much of the way, was finishing in good style down the stands' rail and again found the trip too sharp. He could be very interesting at this level in his current mood when stepped back up in distance.
**Welsh Whisper**, 6lb worse off with the winner having beaten her six lengths over six furlongs here last week, gave away ground at the start but she had ever chance starting up the home straight and did not seem to get home.
**Point Man(IRE)** ended up well beaten and again did little to help establish his best trip.
**Ellamyte** is nothing like the horse she was as a juvenile, despite having tried just about every piece of equipment in the meantime. She had no headgear or tongue tie on this occasion, but it did not improve matters.
T/Plt: £55.90 to a £1 stake. Pool: £29,645.55. 386.50 winning tickets. T/Qpdt: £12.80 to a £1 stake. Pool: £1,778.80. 102.20 winning tickets. JS

# YORK (L-H)
### Tuesday, May 11

**OFFICIAL GOING: Good to soft (good in places)**
Wind: slt hlf against Weather: overcast and cool

## 2018 NEWTON INVESTMENT MANAGEMENT RATED STKS (H'CAP) 1m 2f 88y
1:30 (1:31) (B) (0-100,90) 3-Y-O £12,841 (£4,870; £2,435; £1,107) Stalls Low

Form RPR
00-6 **1** **Frank Sonata**[25] [1437] 3-9-5 **88** RLMoore 5 101
(MGQuinlan) *trckd ldrs: nt clr run over 2f out: swtchd rt over 1f out: r.o to ld last 100yds* **33/1**
0-1 **2** 1 **Woodcracker**[24] [1466] 3-9-4 **87** IMongan 8 98
(MLWBell) *trckd ldrs: effrt over 3f out: led 1f out: hdd and nt qckn ins last* **16/1**
631- **3** 1 ¾ **Lord Mayor**[216] [5449] 3-9-5 **88** KFallon 6 96
(SirMichaelStoute) *trckd ldrs: effrt over 3f out: styd on same pce fnl f* **11/1**
31-0 **4** hd **Golden Grace**[26] [1414] 3-9-5 **88** LDettori 7 95
(EALDunlop) *lw: trckd ldr: ev ch tl nt qckn fnl f* **20/1**
0-31 **5** 2 **Bayhirr**[17] [1612] 3-9-4 **87** PRobinson 3 91
(MAJarvis) *lw: led tl 1f out: fdd* **10/3**[2]
515- **6** 3 ½ **Night Spot**[197] [5797] 3-8-13 **82** SDrowne 1 79
(RCharlton) *hld up: effrt over 3f out: kpt on fnl 2f: nvr nr to chal* **66/1**
-535 **6** dht **Weet A Head (IRE)**[13] [1712] 3-8-11 **80** WSupple 2 77
(RHollinshead) *chsd ldrs: effrt over 3f out: wknd 2f out* **33/1**
161- **8** ¾ **Top Spec (IRE)**[208] [5592] 3-9-4 **87** DaneO'Neill 10 83
(RHannon) *dwlt: bhd tl kpt on fnl 3f* **50/1**
6-1 **9** 6 **City Palace**[34] [1304] 3-8-9 **78** RHughes 9 63
(BWHills) *trckd ldrs: effrt over 3f out: wknd 2f out* **10/1**
11-2 **10** 1 ¾ **Thyolo (IRE)**[9] [1795] 3-9-7 **90** JPMurtagh 11 72
(CGCox) *trckd ldrs: effrt on outside over 2f out: sn rdn and wknd* **3/1**[1]

31-2 **11** *1 3/4* **Hello It's Me**[26] [1414] 3-9-2 **85** ........ JQuinn 13 64
(HJCollingridge) *hld up: effrt over 3f out: lost pl over 2f out* **8/1**[3]

211- **12** *shd* **Whispered Promises (USA)**[271] [4108] 3-8-13 **82** ........ KDalgleish 4 61
(MJohnston) *bit bkwd: in rr: sn drvn along: lost pl 4f out* **17/2**

210- **13** *dist* **Caracara (IRE)**[243] [4840] 3-9-2 **85** ........ JFanning 12 —
(MJohnston) *in rr: sn pushed along: lost pl over 4f out: sn wl bhd: t.o* **12/1**

2m 18.88s (9.44) **Going Correction** +1.075s/f (Soft) **13** Ran SP% **114.8**
Speed ratings: **105,104,102,102,101 98,98,97,92,91 90,89,—**CSF £456.48 CT £6054.48 TOTE £44.30: £8.50, £4.00, £3.50; EX 445.50 Trifecta £1371.90 Part won. Pool £1,932.30 - 0.60 winning tickets..

**Owner** Adams, Flynn, Arnold **Bred** Bishop Wilton Stud **Trained** Newmarket, Suffolk

**FOCUS**

A decent handicap, but the early gallop was not strong and those held up off the pace failed to get competitive.

**NOTEBOOK**

**Frank Sonata** ran with promise at Newbury on his reappearance and the form of that race has worked out very well. He showed a decent turn of foot when switched and looks the type who could go on from this.

**Woodcracker** ran well on just his third-ever start, although like the other main protagonists, he benefited from being ridden up with the pace. There is surely better still to come, however.

**Lord Mayor**, who has not grown much but looked fit for this reappearance, is bred to improve at this sort of trip but was weak in the market. He had a good pitch in behind the leader but could not quicken when the tap was turned.

**Golden Grace** has started off the season on a fairly stiff-looking mark and did not run badly. However, faster ground may suit him better.

**Bayhirr** had a good draw and was allowed to dictate at his own pace. Given that he had so much in his favour, it was disappointing to see him drop away with over a furlong to run.

**Night Spot** did best of those held up off the pace in a race run to suit those who raced prominently. He had never raced beyond six furlongs before, but kept on steadily and is worth another try over this distance.

**Thyolo(IRE)** was very disappointing and it now looks as if he needs a sound surface to show his best.

## 2019 WILLIAMHILLPOKER.COM STKS (H'CAP) 6f 217y

**2:00** (2:02) (B) (0-105,104) 3-Y-O **£19,500** (£6,000; £3,000; £1,500) **Stalls** Low

Form RPR

14-5 **1** **State Dilemma (IRE)**[9] [1795] 3-8-6 **89** ........ MHills 4 97
(BWHills) *hld up: hdwy over 3f out: styd on to ld last 100yds* **9/2**[2]

2-10 **2** *1 1/4* **Key Partners (IRE)**[16] [1640] 3-7-12 **81** oh11 ........ JBramhill 13 86
(PABlockley) *bhd: hdwy on wd outside over 2f out: nt qckn ins last* **66/1**

02-1 **3** *1/2* **Bygone Days**[45] [1133] 3-8-0 **83** ........ PHanagan 2 87+
(WJHaggas) *trckd ldrs: led over 2f out tl ins last: no ex* **5/2**[1]

146- **4** *1 1/4* **Fine Silver (IRE)**[211] [5551] 3-8-0 **83** ........ JQuinn 10 83
(PFICole) *sn trcking ldrs: ev ch over 1f out: kpt on same pce* **25/1**

2-0U **5** *1/2* **Mister Saif (USA)**[9] [1795] 3-8-3 **86** ........ RLMoore 11 85
(RHannon) *in rr whn hmpd and lost pl 3f out: hdwy over 1f out: kpt on wl* **40/1**

333- **6** *shd* **Danesmead (IRE)**[269] [4189] 3-8-13 **96** ........ KDarley 3 95
(TDEasterby) *sn chsng ldrs: nt qckn appr fnl f* **14/1**

1236 **7** *nk* **Bahiano (IRE)**[24] [1459] 3-9-3 **100** ........ KFallon 6 98
(CEBrittain) *chsd ldrs: n.m.r over 3f out: kpt on fnl 2f* **15/2**[3]

04-0 **8** *2 1/2* **Convince (USA)**[28] [1388] 3-8-7 **90** ........ SDrowne 8 82
(MABuckley) *hld up in rr: nt clr run over 2f out: kpt on fnl f* **25/1**

54-6 **9** *1 1/4* **Iskander**[17] [1614] 3-8-7 **90** ........(b) NCallan 12 78
(KARyan) *b: s.i.s: hld up and bhd: hdwy over 2f out: nvr nr to chal* **25/1**

0-00 **10** *1 1/4* **Bright Sun (IRE)**[5] [1900] 3-7-13 **82** ........ KimTinkler 5 67
(NTinkler) *led tl 2f out: weakend appr fnl f* **50/1**

263- **11** *1 3/4* **Varnay**[220] [5362] 3-8-3 **89** ........(v) TPQueally(3) 1 69
(DRLoder) *hld up: hdwy over 2f out: fdd over 1f out* **8/1**

5-03 **12** *11* **Parkview Love (USA)**[27] [1396] 3-9-7 **104** ........ JFanning 7 56
(MJohnston) *chsd ldrs: lost pl over 1f out: eased* **9/1**

0-01 **13** *1 1/2* **Redwood Rocks (IRE)**[11] [1745] 3-7-13 **82** ........ CCatlin 14 30
(BSmart) *trckd ldrs on outer: wknd over 2f out: eased* **12/1**

32-0 **14** *16* **Mrs Moh (IRE)**[17] [1614] 3-7-12 **81** ........ DaleGibson 9 —
(TDEasterby) *b.hind: unruly in stalls: mid-div: lost pl over 2f out: sn bhd and eased* **33/1**

1m 31.0s (7.69) **Going Correction** +1.30s/f (Soft) **14** Ran SP% **114.4**
Speed ratings: **108,106,106,104,104 103,103,100,99,97 95,83,81,63**CSF £282.73 CT £918.20 TOTE £4.80: £2.10, £13.00, £1.60; EX 372.10 Trifecta £1019.40 Pool £2,297.36 - 1.60 winning units..

**Owner** Maktoum Al Maktoum **Bred** Gainsborough Stud Management Ltd **Trained** Lambourn, Berks

**FOCUS**

A good, competitive handicap run at a decent gallop and the first two came from well off the pace. The form looks sound.

**NOTEBOOK**

**State Dilemma(IRE)** looked to have a fine chance on the form of his Newmarket run, where he was one of only two horses drawn in single figures to make the first nine, and the drop back in trip promised to help him. He appreciated the fast pace and won nicely, but better ground will surely suit him ideally.

**Key Partners(IRE)**, who won his maiden over this trip on good to soft ground, ran a blinder from 11lb out of the handicap. Clearly this trip suits him better than the ten furlongs over which he was beaten last time, although the Handicapper will surely take his revenge for this.

**Bygone Days**, a clear winner of his maiden on soft ground, did nothing wrong but just appeared to find the trip stretching his stamina. He will be interesting back over six furlongs as he travelled strongly for most of the race.

**Fine Silver(IRE)** ran a sound race on his seasonal debut despite starting the campaign on a high enough mark. Faster ground should suit.

**Mister Saif(USA)**, one of the more exposed runners in the field, kept on well from the back despite not getting much of a run.

**Danesmead(IRE)** did not see the trip out on this seasonal debut but is entitled to come on for the run, although he may need some leniency from the Handicapper.

**Bahiano(IRE)** hails from a stable struggling to hit form and ran well in the circumstances. He will be suited by another furlong.

**Convince(USA)** never got into the race but, on the plus side, his handicap mark should drop a pound or two for this.

## 2020 TATTERSALLS MUSIDORA STKS (GROUP 3) (FILLIES) 1m 2f 88y

**2:30** (2:31) (A) 3-Y-O **£31,900** (£12,100; £6,050; £2,750) **Stalls** Low

Form RPR

113- **1** **Punctilious**[227] [5209] 3-8-8 110 ........(t) LDettori 4 111+
(SaeedBinSuroor) *led: qcknd over 5f out: shkn up over 1f out: wnt lft: styd on* **8/11**[1]

12 **2** *6* **Glen Innes (IRE)**[13] [1704] 3-8-8 91 ........ KFallon 1 101
(DRLoder) *t.k.h: trckd wnr: effrt over 3f out: swtchd rt over 1f out: styd on: no imp* **9/4**[2]

00-6 **3** *1 3/4* **Bay Tree (IRE)**[27] [1398] 3-8-8 102 ........ TPQueally 2 98
(DRLoder) *trckd ldrs: rdn 3f out: kpt on same pce* **16/1**[3]

2 **4** *2* **Chanteloup**[19] [1557] 3-8-8 ........ JPMurtagh 3 95?
(JRFanshawe) *lw: hld up in tch: hdwy 4f out: one pce* **25/1**

155- **5** *7* **Asia Winds (IRE)**[220] [5362] 3-8-8 93 ........ MHills 5 83
(BWHills) *hld up: hdwy over 3f out: sn rdn weakend 2f out* **20/1**

6 **6** *dist* **Nassiria**[9] [1794] 3-8-8 ........ TEDurcan 6 —
(CEBrittain) *reluctant to load: chsd ldrs: rdn 4f out: sn lost pl and bhd: t.o* **33/1**

2m 22.33s (12.89) **Going Correction** +1.075s/f (Soft) **6** Ran SP% **106.1**
Speed ratings: **91,86,84,83,77** —CSF £2.09 TOTE £1.60: £1.20, £1.50; EX 2.50.

**Owner** Godolphin **Bred** Bjorn E Nielsen **Trained** Newmarket, Suffolk

**FOCUS**

A modest renewal of this Oaks trial. The winner had things her own way out in front and the opposition did not impress at all in the paddock. The winning time was pedestrian for the grade of contest, 3.45 seconds slower than the opening three-year-old handicap over the same trip.

**NOTEBOOK**

**Punctilious**, quite a big filly, looked very fit indeed. She was allowed to set just a steady pace and coming wide off the home turn stepped up the gallop. Given a flick with the whip one and a half furlongs out she swished her tail and went left. She had everything her own way here but will find it much tougher at Epsom and, in the 1000 Guineas runner-up Sundrop, Godolphin have another filly with equally strong claims.

**Glen Innes(IRE)**, who looks to have run up very light, was happy to let the winner give her a lead. Very keen due to the lack of pace, she never gave up in pursuit but in the end it was a very one-sided battle.

**Bay Tree(IRE)**, who is not very big, had her limitations ruthlessy exposed and it would be unwise to presume she stays this far on the evidence on show here. It was just a sprint up the home straight.

**Chanteloup**, runner-up in a Beverley maiden, gained some valuable black type. A much easier opportunity will surely be found to break her duck.

**Asia Winds(IRE)**, who is only small, dropped right away looking to run completely out of stamina.

**Nassiria**, awkward to load on just her second start, dropped right out as soon as the pace increased. This abject performance on the back of a good effort in maiden company on her racecourse debut just nine days earlier was put down to her coming into season. *Official explanation: trainer's representative said filly appeared to be in season after the race*

## 2021 DUKE OF YORK HEARTHSTEAD HOMES STKS (GROUP 2) 6f 3y

**3:00** (3:01) (A) 3-Y-O+ **£58,000** (£22,000; £11,000; £5,000) **Stalls** High

Form RPR

5-51 **1** **Monsieur Bond (IRE)**[37] [1254] 4-9-2 114 ........ FLynch 5 121
(BSmart) *sn chsng ldr: led over 1f out: edgd rt and lft: r.o wl* **4/1**[1]

1-21 **2** *1 1/2* **Steenberg (IRE)**[10] [1759] 5-9-2 110 ........ PRobinson 14 116+
(MHTompkins) *bmpd s: bhd: hdwy over 2f out: styd on wl to go 2nd ins last* **10/1**

63-1 **3** *1 3/4* **Arakan (USA)**[26] [1409] 4-9-2 111 ........ KFallon 9 111
(SirMichaelStoute) *sn chsng ldrs: sn drvn along: styd on fnl f* **11/2**[2]

26-1 **4** *hd* **Welsh Emperor (IRE)**[24] [1471] 5-9-2 109 ........(b) DaleGibson 10 110
(TPTate) *led tl over 1f out: edgd lft and kpt on same pce* **33/1**

20-1 **5** *1 3/4* **Goldeva**[45] [1126] 5-8-13 100 ........ ACulhane 11 102
(RHollinshead) *mid-div: swtchd lft over 1f out: kpt on wl* **66/1**

360- **6** *shd* **Airwave**[219] [5402] 4-8-13 117 ........ DaneO'Neill 8 102
(HCandy) *plld hrd towards rr: hdwy over 2f out: kpt on: nvr rchd ldrs* **6/1**[3]

210- **7** *1/2* **Somnus**[219] [5402] 4-9-9 117 ........ TEDurcan 6 110
(TDEasterby) *chsd ldrs: kpt on same pce fnl 2f* **12/1**

205- **8** *3 1/2* **Country Reel (USA)**[207] [5615] 4-9-2 110 ........(vt[1]) LDettori 7 93
(SaeedBinSuroor) *chsd ldrs: wknd over 1f out* **20/1**

-245 **9** *1 1/2* **Orientor**[24] [1471] 6-9-2 109 ........ KDarley 12 88
(JSGoldie) *hld up and bhd: kpt on fnl 2f: nvr on terms* **28/1**

4421 **10** *1* **Bahamian Pirate (USA)**[3] [1955] 9-9-2 110 ........ SWKelly 13 85
(DNicholls) *b.off hind: hld up in rr: effrt 2f out: nvr nr ldrs* **25/1**

15-6 **11** *5* **Bonus (IRE)**[26] [1409] 4-9-2 108 ........ MJKinane 15 70
(RHannon) *lw: wnt lft s: sn chsng ldrs: wknd over 1f out* **18/1**

10-3 **12** *2 1/2* **Ashdown Express (IRE)**[26] [1409] 5-9-2 111 ........ SSanders 2 63
(CFWall) *chsd ldrs on outer: lost pl over 1f out* **12/1**

10U- **13** *1 1/4* **Fayr Jag (IRE)**[207] [5615] 5-9-2 110 ........ WSupple 4 59
(TDEasterby) *chsd ldrs: fading whn hmpd over 1f out* **33/1**

615- **14** *2* **Trade Fair**[206] [5638] 4-9-2 120 ........ RHughes 1 53
(RCharlton) *chsd ldrs on outer: lost pl over 1f out* **12/1**

201- **15** *1/2* **Just James**[206] [5638] 5-9-6 113 ........ JPMurtagh 3 55
(JNoseda) *bhd: sme hdwy on outer over 2f out: sn lost pl* **11/1**

1m 16.39s (5.32) **Going Correction** +1.30s/f (Soft) **15** Ran SP% **114.9**
Speed ratings: **116,114,111,111,109 108,108,103,101,100 93,90,88,85,85**CSF £37.55 TOTE £5.10: £2.10, £3.80, £2.30; EX 44.20 Trifecta £187.40 Pool £4,119.19 - 15.60 winning units..

**Owner** R C Bond **Bred** T Burns **Trained** Hambleton, N Yorks

■ Stewards Enquiry : A Culhane two-day ban: careless riding (May 22,23)

**FOCUS**

A high-class renewal of this Group Two sprint, run in a time well up to standard. The conditions may have been a factor, as some would have preferred it faster, but the form looks solid.

**NOTEBOOK**

**Monsieur Bond(IRE)**, who really took the eye in the paddock, came into this with his confidence sky high after his Curragh success. He kept tabs on the leader but once in front saw it out well despite wandering both ways. He should continue to give a good account of himself in the top sprints.

**Steenberg(IRE)**, no match for the winner in Ireland, had it all to do after collecting a bump at the start. He stayed on really well to take clear second spot inside the last and deserves to find another good prize.

**Arakan(USA)**has a powerful action. He worked hard in pursuit of the leader and grabbed third spot on the line. A return to seven furlongs and quicker ground may bring out the very best in this most likeable individual.

**Welsh Emperor(IRE)**, who had the hood taken off in the nick of time, led them a merry dance and only missed out on third place near the line, recording a personal best. He loves the mud and is even better with a rail to run against. His trainer will have to scan the international pattern book to find him an opportunity.

**Goldeva** showed her much improved Doncaster win was no fluke and should have another Listed race in her.

**Airwave**, out of luck in her later starts at three, was much more settled than on some occasions in the past going to post. Anchored in the rear, she stayed on in her own time and will do much better with some sun on her back on quicker ground. If things fall into place she will be a serious candidate for top sprint honours again.

**Somnus**, lumbered with a 7lb penalty for his Group One Haydock success, lacked race sharpness but gave every indication that he is as good as ever. Connections will be hoping that it is not another dry summer.

**Country Reel(USA)**, in a first-time visor, has not tasted success since his Gimcrack win here in 2002.

**Trade Fair** looks every inch a sprinter, with full, rounded quarters, but he was drawn one and had the ground against him. The run will bring him on and connections will be expecting him to bounce back in a big way this summer.

## 2022 ARRIVA TRAINS STKS (H'CAP) 1m 3f 198y
3:35 (3:36) (C ) (0-95,94) 4-Y-0+ £10,738 (£3,304; £1,652; £826) Stalls Low

Form RPR
/1-6 1 **Balkan Knight**[24] 1460 4-8-11 **80**....(v) TPQueally(3) 4 91
(DRLoder) *lw: in tch: stdy hdwy to ld over 1f out: hld on towards fin* **5/1**[1]
0100 2 *nk* **Cruise Director**[15] 1661 4-9-3 **83**.... KFallon 8 93
(WJMusson) *swtg: mid-div: hdwy over 3f out: ev ch ins last: no ex towards fin* **12/1**
3-02 3 *1 ½* **Gold Ring**[15] 1661 4-9-7 **87**.... SDrowne 1 95
(GBBalding) *lw: chsd ldrs: ev ch over 1f out: nt qckn ins last* **5/1**[1]
030- 4 *nk* **Crathorne (IRE)**[199] 5738 4-9-0 **80**....(p) TQuinn 16 88
(JDBethell) *s.i.s: hdwy over 4f out: nt qckn appr fnl f* **16/1**
10-2 5 *2 ½* **La Sylphide**[17] 1604 7-9-2 **82**.... SWKelly 11 86
(GMMoore) *led tl over 1f out: wknd ins last* **16/1**
53-6 6 *nk* **Nowell House**[38] 513 8-8-11 **82**.... PMulrennan(5) 2 85
(MWEasterby) *racd keenly: trckd ldrs: ev chnace over 2f out: kpt on same pce* **14/1**
3-00 7 *12* **Dunaskin (IRE)**[8] 1821 4-9-5 **85**.... JPMurtagh 19 70
(DEddy) *s.i.s: bhd: hdwy 4f out: wknd fnl 2f* **33/1**
000- 8 *3* **Sporting Gesture**[185] 5952 7-8-9 **75**.... DaleGibson 3 56
(MWEasterby) *bit bkwd: in tch: effrt 4f out: wknd 2f out* **16/1**
00-3 9 *1* **Indian Solitaire (IRE)**[47] 1103 5-8-7 **73**....(v) PHanagan 7 52
(RAFahey) *bhd: hdwy over 3f out: wknd 2f out* **7/1**[3]
/611 10 *¾* **Maniatis**[15] 1677 7-8-10 **76**....(v) SSanders 13 54
(AndrewReid) *b: b.hind: trckd ldrs: rdn and wknd 2f out* **20/1**
10-0 11 *9* **Ring Of Destiny**[27] 1401 5-9-12 **92**.... MartinDwyer 10 57
(PWHarris) *bhd and drvn along 5f out: nvr a factor* **33/1**
50-3 12 *6* **Kentucky Blue (IRE)**[17] 1604 4-9-5 **85**.... TEDurcan 18 41
(TDEasterby) *sn chsng ldrs: wknd 2f out: eased* **25/1**
000- 13 *6* **Double Obsession**[199] 5738 4-10-0 **94**.... KDalgleish 9 41
(MJohnston) *bit bkwd: trckd ldrs: wknd 2f out: eased* **20/1**
115- 14 *3 ½* **Kuster**[221] 5349 8-9-8 **91**....(b) NMackay(3) 5 32
(LMCumani) *bit bkwd: hld up in rr: hdwy 4f out: lost pl over 2f out: eased* **25/1**
04-1 15 *25* **King Revo (IRE)**[15] 1661 4-9-5 **85**.... KDarley 12 —
(PCHaslam) *lw: sn bhd and pushed along: eased 3f out: t.o* **6/1**[2]
0-00 16 *10* **Wahchi (IRE)**[10] 1768 5-8-12 **78**.... TLucas 17 —
(GPKelly) *bhd whn hmpd over 6f out: t.o* **100/1**
0-31 17 *nk* **Captain Clipper**[24] 1470 4-8-13 **79**.... ANicholls 20 —
(DNicholls) *b: bhd: sme hdwy over 4f out: eased 3f out: t.o* **25/1**
110- 18 *¾* **Sovereign Dreamer (USA)**[251] 4660 4-9-2 **82**.... JBramhill 15 —
(PFICole) *chsd ldrs: lost pl 3f out: sn bhd: eased: t.o* **40/1**
P **Harambee (IRE)**[219] 4-9-0 **80**.... RWinston 14 —
(BSRothwell) *bit bkwd: bhd whn hmpd over 6f out: sn t.o and p.u* **66/1**

2m 38.72s (9.86) **Going Correction** +1.075s/f (Soft) 19 Ran SP% **124.0**
Speed ratings: **110,109,108,108,106 106,98,96,96,95 89,85,81,79,62 55,55,55,—**CSF £56.87 CT £325.07 TOTE £6.60: £1.60, £2.60, £2.00, £4.70; EX 83.40.
**Owner** Sheikh Mohammed **Bred** Sheikh Mohammed Bin Rashid Al Maktoum **Trained** Newmarket, Suffolk

**FOCUS**
A decent handicap, run at a good pace. The first six pulled well clear and the form should work out well.

**NOTEBOOK**
**Balkan Knight**, who had run with promise on his reappearance at Newbury, kept responding to pressure and ground out the victory. He certainly saw the trip out well and the ground clearly suited this son of Selkirk. Lightly raced, he can be expected to build on this, with the Duke of Edinburgh Handicap at Royal Ascot looking the next logical target.
**Cruise Director** is well suited by some decent cut in the ground and put a couple of poor performances on a quicker surface behind him. His form figures with the Champion on board now read 312.
**Gold Ring** continues to run well without winning. He had the ground to suit, and it looks as if the Handicapper may have his measure now.
**Crathorne(IRE)**, making his seasonal reappearance, is well suited by a strong gallop and came from the back to get into the places. He is a difficult horse to catch right, but these big-field handicaps bring out the best in him.
**La Sylphide** held off her rivals for a long way and confirmed herself to be in tip-top form at present. She will appreciate a drop back to ten furlongs.
**Nowell House**, twice successful over hurdles earlier this year, made a pleasing return to the Flat, finishing well clear of the rest.
**Dunaskin(IRE)** will surely be happier reverting to front-running tactics.
**King Revo(IRE)** was the disappointment of the race, failing to run up to the form of his Musselburgh win on this softer ground. *Official explanation: trainer had no explanation for the poor form shown*
**Captain Clipper** *Official explanation: jockey said gelding was unsuited by the dead ground*
**Sovereign Dreamer(USA)** *Official explanation: jockey said colt had a breathing problem*
**Harambee(IRE)** *Official explanation: trainer had no explanation for the poor form shown*

## 2023 GARBUTT & ELLIOTT COLIN FOSTER EBF NOVICE FILLIES' STKS 6f 3y
4:10 (4:12) (D ) 2-Y-0 £6,870 (£2,114; £1,057; £528) Stalls High

Form RPR
01 1 **Justaquestion**[29] 1364 2-8-9.... TPQueally(3) 2 81
(IAWood) *trckd ldrs: led over 1f out: jst hld on* **9/2**[3]
3 2 *shd* **Umniya (IRE)**[8] 1839 2-8-8.... TEDurcan 3 77
(MRChannon) *sn drvn along: sn chsng ldrs: ev ch fr over 1f out: kept on wl* **13/2**
1 3 *1 ½* **Elsie Hart (IRE)**[21] 1523 2-9-1.... WSupple 4 79
(TDEasterby) *hld up: hdwy and swtchd rt over 2f out: nt qckn ins fnl f* **10/3**[2]
1 4 *5* **High Chart**[15] 1670 2-8-10.... AMcCarthy 5 59
(GGMargarson) *trckd ldrs: t.k.h: effrt over 2f out: wknd fnl f* **9/2**[3]
0 5 *6* **Ashes (IRE)**[15] 1670 2-8-8.... DarrenWilliams 1 39
(KRBurke) *unruly gng to s: led tl over 1f out: hung lft and eased ins last* **28/1**
2 6 *dist* **Azuree (IRE)**[9] 1798 2-8-9 ow1.... RHughes 6 —
(RHannon) *sn trcking ldrs: rdn over 3f out: lost pl over 1f out: eased: t.o* **2/1**[1]

1m 19.64s (-11.07) **Going Correction** +1.30s/f (Soft) 6 Ran SP% **109.6**
Speed ratings: **94,93,91,85,77** —CSF £30.72 TOTE £7.20: £3.20, £2.50; EX 37.10.
**Owner** Christopher Shankland **Bred** A S Reid **Trained** Upper Lambourn, Berks

**FOCUS**
The first six-furlong two-year-old race of the season. Just a steady gallop, but the form should be reliable.

**NOTEBOOK**
**Justaquestion**, who stands over a fair amount of ground, is progressive and very game, but will find things tougher from now on.
**Umniya(IRE)**, a rangy-type, almost certainly stepped up a good deal on her debut effort a week earlier, proving well suited by the sixth furlong. She should improve again and is sure to find a race or two.
**Elsie Hart(IRE)**, giving weight away all round, had to be switched to make her effort. She gave her all but was simply not good enough.
**High Chart** would not settle as a result of the steady pace and failed to see out the extra furlong.
**Ashes(IRE)**, a real handful going to post, jumped out in front and soon dropped anchor. She hung when challenged and her rider called it a day inside the last. It is to be hoped her temperament does not get the better of her.
**Azuree(IRE)** was the first to come under pressure and, with her stride ever shortening, was in the end virtually pulled up. Something was clearly amiss after her promising debut effort. *Official explanation: trainer had no explanation for the poor form shown*

## 2024 THERIPLEYCOLLECTION.COM RACING JEWELLERY MAIDEN STKS (C&G) 5f 3y
4:45 (4:47) (D ) 2-Y-0 £4,855 (£1,494; £747; £373) Stalls High

Form RPR
1 **Brecon Beacon** 2-8-11.... KFallon 3 84
(PFICole) *w'like: w ldrs: led 2f out: styd on wl ins last* **10/3**[1]
2 *½* **Asian Tiger (IRE)** 2-8-11.... MJKinane 1 82
(RHannon) *unf: scope: bit bkwd: sn chsng ldrs: rdn to chal over 1f out: nt qckn ins last* **11/2**[3]
3 *2* **Adoration** 2-8-11.... JFanning 4 75+
(MJohnston) *w'like: sn chsng ldrs and drvn along: hung lft and outpcd over 2f out: kpt on wl fnl f* **7/1**
4 *1 ½* **Blue Kandora (IRE)** 2-8-11.... PRobinson 2 70
(MAJarvis) *w'like: b: dwlt: hld up: hdwy over 2f out: sn chsng ldrs: wknd fnl f* **11/2**[3]
5 *5* **Skywards** 2-8-11.... LDettori 7 53
(SaeedBinSuroor) *unf: scope: led tl over 3f out: chsd ldrs tl wknd over 1f out* **7/2**[2]
6 *1* **Komac** 2-8-11.... SSanders 8 49
(BAMcmahon) *cmpt: w ldrs: led over 3f out tl 2f out: wknd over 1f out* **16/1**
7 *1 ¼* **Mac Cois Na Tine** 2-8-11.... KDarley 6 45
(KARyan) *w'like: bit bkwd: s.i.s: sn drvn along: lost pl over 1f out* **20/1**
8 *5* **Prospect Court** 2-8-11.... TQuinn 5 27
(JDBethell) *w'like: sn drvn along: lost pl over 1f out: sn bhd* **9/1**

65.88 secs (7.14) **Going Correction** +1.30s/f (Soft) 8 Ran SP% **109.2**
Speed ratings: **94,93,90,87,79 78,76,68**CSF £19.82 TOTE £3.50: £1.20, £2.20, £2.40; EX 18.90 Place 6 £324.73, Place 5 £19.68..
**Owner** Elite Racing Club **Bred** Elite Racing Club **Trained** Whatcombe, Oxon

**FOCUS**
All newcomers, so a hard race to assess, but there were some nice types and the time looks all right for the grade, so it is probably a decent maiden.

**NOTEBOOK**
**Brecon Beacon**, a home-bred March foal, is a well-made, mature-type. He certainly knew his job and was always doing just enough. He will improve for the outing fitness wise and can take a novice event.
**Asian Tiger(IRE)**, an April foal, stands over plenty of ground. Noisy in the paddock, he went down fighting and is a ready-made winner of a maiden event.
**Adoration ◆**, born on April Fools day, is out of a mare that did the stable proud. Long in the back and lacking substance, he was upset in the paddock by the big television screen. After getting outpaced and showing his inexperience, he put in some solid late work. The experience will have taught him plenty and he is sure to find a race.
**Blue Kandora(IRE)**, an April foal, is a good walker. He moved up in good style after a missing a beat at the start, but became leg-weary in the final furlong. He looks capable of a fair bit better.
**Skywards**, a January foal and Godolphin's first juvenile to see a racecourse this year, is a quality colt who looked really well. He dropped away after making the running, but can be expected to do much better in due course especially over six or even seven furlongs.
**Komac**, a cheaply-bought March foal, is a good-bodied individual. He showed plenty of toe till fading and will do better in due course.
T/Jkpt: Not won. T/Plt: £699.50 to a £1 stake. Pool: £100,385.80. 104.75 winning tickets. T/Qpdt: £29.10 to a £1 stake. Pool: £8,356.00. 211.85 winning tickets. WG

2025 - 2027a (Foreign Racing) - See Raceform Interactive

# 1898 SAINT-CLOUD (L-H)
Tuesday, May 11

**OFFICIAL GOING: Soft**

## 2028a PRIX CLEOPATRE (GROUP 3) (FILLIES) 1m 2f 110y
1:50 (1:58) 3-Y-0 £25,704 (£10,282; £7,711; £5,141)

RPR
1 **Steel Princess (IRE)**[42] 3-8-9.... TJarnet 4 98
(RGibson, France) *tracked leaders, 5th straight, ridden & headway over 1 1/2f out, ran on under strong driving to lead close home*
2 *¾* **Love And Bubbles (USA)**[201] 3-8-9.... SMaillot 3 97
(RobertCollet, France) *prom, 3rd str, pushed along & hdwy over 1 1/2f out, rdn to ld appr fnl f, ran on til hdd cl hme*
3 *snk* **Barancella (FR)**[44] 3-8-9.... OPeslier 5 97
(FHead, France) *cl up, led appr str, pushed along over 2f out, rdn & ran on wl til hdd appr fnl f, kpt on u.p* 2
4 *1* **Popee (FR)** 3-8-9.... IMendizabal 8 95
(J-CRouget, France) *mid-division, 7th straight, stayed on from 1 1/2f out, took 4th final strides*
5 *shd* **Diamond Tango (FR)**[21] 3-8-9.... GaryStevens 7 95
(AFabre, France) *held up towards rear, 8th straight, stayed on from 1 1/2f out but never threatened leaders* 1
6 *½* **Pink Palace (IRE)**[40] 3-8-9.... SPasquier 1 94
(DSepulchre, France) *led 1f then settled tracking leaders, 4th straight, ridden 1 1/2f out, no extra final 150yds*
7 *1 ½* **Narcisse Du Rheu (FR)**[21] 3-8-9.... CSoumillon 10 91
(DProd'Homme, France) *towards rear, last straight, never dangerous*
8 *shd* **Miss France (FR)**[32] 1320 3-8-9.... DBoeuf 9 91
(ELellouche, France) *held up, 9th straight, pushed along 2f out, some late headway but never dangerous* 3
9 *1 ½* **Siberian Highness (FR)**[21] 3-8-9.... FSpanu 2 89
(J-VToux, France) *mid-division, 6th straight, effort 2f out, no impression*
10 *5* **Moonrise (GER)**[298] 3-8-9.... C-PLemaire 6 80
(H-APantall, France) *led after 1f, headed approaching straight, kept on under pressure til one pace from over 1f out*

2m 16.3s **Going Correction** -0.10s/f (Good) 10 Ran SP% **123.9**
Speed ratings: **112,111,111,110,110 110,109,109,107,104**.
**Owner** R F Barnes **Bred** Barronstown Stud & Orpendale **Trained** France

**NOTEBOOK**

**Steel Princess(IRE)** began a progressive run from one and a half out and took the lead at exactly the right moment inside the final furlong. This was a very game effort from the filly who is considered to need firm ground. She is now unbeaten in three races and goes on to the Prix de Diane.

**Love And Bubbles(USA)** made an effort two out to lead at the furlong marker. She was run out of fifth place at the final fifty metres and can only improve for this outing.

**Barancella(FR)** was always up in the leading group and took control of the race at the two furlong marker. She then battled courageously to the line and was finally beaten under a length. It is possible she may need a longer trip

**Diamond Tango(FR)** never once looked like following up her debut win and now has it all to prove.

## 1859 BRIGHTON (L-H)

Wednesday, May 12

**OFFICIAL GOING: Good to firm (firm in places)**

Wind: slt hlf against Weather: overcast

### 2029 HARDINGS BAR AND CATERING SERVICES MAIDEN STKS — 5f 213y

**2:10** (2:12) (D) 3-Y-0+ — **£3,464** (£1,066; £533; £266) **Stalls** Low

Form — RPR

4-22 **1** **Buy On The Red**[25] [1472] 3-8-9 72 ... RMiles(3) 5 — 79
(WRMuir) *prom: led 2f out: drvn clr 1f out: edgd rt fnl 100 yds* — **5/2**[2]

0-02 **2** 2 **Get To The Point**[22] [1530] 3-8-12 72 ... RLMoore 1 — 73
(PWD'Arcy) *chsd ldrs: pressed wnr 2f out: nt qckn fnl f* — **4/1**[3]

000- **3** 3 1/2 **All Quiet**[238] [4986] 3-8-7 ... PDobbs 8 — 58
(RHannon) *sn outpcd in midfield: styd on wl fr over 1f out: nrst fin* — **14/1**

04- **4** 1 1/2 **Fair Compton**[333] [2362] 3-8-8 ow1 ... DaneO'Neill 4 — 54
(RHannon) *chsd ldrs: hrd rdn over 1f out: one pce* — **8/1**

532- **5** 1 3/4 **Wychbury (USA)**[260] [4484] 3-8-9 79 ... DCorby(3) 2 — 53
(MJWallace) *prom: hmpd and stmbld over 4f out: wknd over 1f out* — **2/1**[1]

000 **6** 1 **Generous Spirit (IRE)**[6] [1906] 3-8-12 ... PaulEddery 6 — 50
(JAOsborne) *a abt same pl: rdn and no imp 2f out* — **20/1**

0 **7** 2 1/2 **Fair Options**[10] [1796] 3-8-12 ... GCarter 12 — 42
(HJCyzer) *wd: bhd tl styd on fnl 2f* — **66/1**

00-0 **8** 1/2 **Bold Ridge (IRE)**[34] [1311] 4-9-8 ... DSweeney 7 — 41
(SKirk) *outpcd towards rr: mod late hdwy* — **50/1**

00-0 **9** 2 1/2 **Cinnamon Ridge (IRE)**[6] [1906] 3-8-9 ... (b[1]) LPKeniry(3) 14 — 33
(BJMeehan) *hung lft: led tl 2f out: wknd over 1f out* — **25/1**

50-0 **10** 1/2 **Compassion (IRE)**[18] [1627] 3-8-7 62 ... (p) AMcCarthy 9 — 27
(GCHChung) *mid-div: drvn along and outpcd fr 1/2-way* — **33/1**

5363 **11** 1/2 **Son Of Rembrandt (IRE)**[25] [1478] 3-8-5 60 ... MHoward(7) 13 — 30
(DKIvory) *in tch to 1/2-way* — **33/1**

000- **12** hd **Quarrymount**[211] [5563] 3-8-5 ... SArcher(7) 10 — 30
(SirMarkPrescott) *stdd in rr s: a bhd* — **16/1**

**13** 1 **Flying With Eagles** 3-8-9 ... LisaJones(3) 15 — 27
(JJay) *s.s: a bhd* — **50/1**

00/0 **14** 1 3/4 **Our Sion**[46] [1133] 4-9-8 ... ADaly 3 — 21
(RBrotherton) *mid-div tl wknd 1/2-way* — **100/1**

68.33 secs (-1.77) **Going Correction** -0.075s/f (Good)
**WFA** 3 from 4yo 10lb — **14** Ran SP% **126.5**
Speed ratings: **108,105,100,98,96 95,91,91,87,87 86,86,84,82**CSF £12.85 TOTE £3.60: £1.20, £2.00, £4.70; EX 13.90.
**Owner** R Haim **Bred** J Gittins And Capt J H Wilson **Trained** Lambourn, Berks
■ Stewards Enquiry : L P Keniry two-day ban: careless riding (May 23,24)

**FOCUS**

A good tempo down the hill, with the field soon well strung out and half of the runners never threatening to get anywhere near the leaders. It produced a very smart winning time for the grade and the form looks sound.

**NOTEBOOK**

**Buy On The Red** acted well on the fast ground and used his speed to good effect. He drifted up the camber as he began to tire, but the race was in safe keeping by then.

**Get To The Point** has run some good races and is effective enough on turf to find a race at this level.

**All Quiet** made a satisfactory seasonal debut. Taken off her legs down the hill, she looks as if a stiffer test or longer trip would be in her favour.

**Fair Compton** made a fair first appearance of the season, her third in all. She was beaten on merit, and will have to be kept to low-grade events, but handicaps are now a possibility.

**Wychbury(USA)** was never comfortable after being squeezed for room on the home turn and deserves another chance.

**Generous Spirit(IRE)** has made little impact at a number of trips in maidens, so handicaps might be the next option.

**Fair Options** could be improving a little and his next run should be monitored to assess his prospects in future handicaps.

**Our Sion** *Official explanation: jockey said gelding lost its action*

### 2030 RACECOURSE VIDEO SERVICES H'CAP — 7f 214y

**2:40** (2:44) (E) (0-75,74) 3-Y-0+ — **£3,822** (£1,176; £588; £294) **Stalls** Low

Form — RPR

3120 **1** **Katiypour (IRE)**[21] [1542] 7-9-11 72 ... LisaJones(3) 6 — 83
(MissBSanders) *hld up in tch: effrt 2f out: edgd lft 1f out: drvn to ld ins fnl f: readily* — **8/1**[3]

506- **2** 1 **Analyze (FR)**[158] [6093] 6-10-0 72 ... RLMoore 5 — 80
(BGPowell) *hdwy over 2f out: chsd wnr ins fnl f: kpt on* — **16/1**

0-12 **3** shd **Samuel Charles**[25] [1475] 6-9-5 63 ... NPollard 11 — 71
(WMBrisbourne) *prom: chal and hung bdly lft fr 2f out: led briefly 1f out: nt qckn* — **8/1**[3]

0023 **4** 4 **Concer Eto**[5] [1935] 5-9-9 70 ... (p) BReilly(3) 2 — 69
(SCWilliams) *chsd ldrs: nt clr run and swtchd rt over 2f out: disputing 4th and hld whn n.m.r 1f out* — **7/2**[1]

2000 **5** 3/4 **Dash For Cover (IRE)**[8] [1875] 4-8-13 64 ... PGallagher(7) 9 — 61
(RHannon) *led: hrd rdn and hdd 1f out: no ex* — **20/1**

1033 **6** 1 **Spindor (USA)**[10] [1783] 5-9-3 61 ... (b) VSlattery 15 — 56
(JAOsborne) *mid-div: effrt and hung lft 2f out: no imp* — **11/1**

6020 **7** 1/2 **Captain Darling (IRE)**[26] [1451] 4-9-2 65 ... (p) AQuinn(5) 12 — 59
(RMHCowell) *in tch: outpcd over 2f out: sn btn* — **9/1**

5-60 **8** 1 1/4 **Night Wolf (IRE)**[39] [1247] 4-9-8 69 ... SHitchcott(3) 14 — 60
(MRChannon) *wd: chsd ldrs: rdn and btn 2f out* — **14/1**

00-2 **9** 3/4 **Treetops Hotel (IRE)**[102] [650] 5-8-11 60 ... NChalmers(5) 3 — 49
(BRJohnson) *stdd s: hld up in rr: rdn and sme hdwy over 2f out: nt rch ldrs* — **14/1**

4335 **10** 1 **Deeper In Debt**[21] [1542] 6-9-11 69 ... GCarter 10 — 56
(JAkehurst) *hld up in rr: rdn 3f out: nvr nr to chal* — **9/1**

0-04 **11** 2 **Pay The Silver**[9] [1845] 6-9-13 71 ... (p) IMongan 13 — 53
(IAWood) *sn rdn along towards rr: nvr a factor* — **10/1**

6000 **12** nk **Agilis (IRE)**[5] [1935] 4-9-1 62 ... (b) RMiles(3) 4 — 43
(JamiePoulton) *hld up in tch: rdn and wknd over 2f out* — **33/1**

230- **13** 2 1/2 **Chubbes**[162] [6115] 3-9-3 74 ... (v) DaneO'Neill 8 — 50
(MCPipe) *hld up in rr: rdn 3f out: nvr nr ldrs* — **13/2**[2]

054- **14** 3/4 **Ziet D'Alsace (FR)**[171] [5728] 4-8-11 55 ... SRighton 7 — 29
(AWCarroll) *stdd s: plld v hrd and fly-jmpd in rr: a bhd* — **33/1**

32-0 **15** 6 **Salon Prive**[50] [1087] 4-9-5 63 ... (b[1]) SWhitworth 1 — 23
(CACyzer) *plld hrd: pressed ldr tl wknd qckly over 2f out* — **25/1**

1m 33.85s (-1.15) **Going Correction** -0.075s/f (Good)
**WFA** 3 from 4yo+ 13lb — **15** Ran SP% **128.9**
Speed ratings: **102,101,100,96,96 95,94,93,92,91 89,89,86,86,80**CSF £132.38 CT £1101.70 TOTE £10.50: £3.10, £8.10, £3.40; EX 84.30.
**Owner** Peter Crate **Bred** His Highness The Aga Khan's Studs S C **Trained** Epsom, Surrey

**FOCUS**

An ordinary handicap and only a fair pace, with several hard pullers. The tempo increased turning down into the straight. The form looks sound.

**NOTEBOOK**

**Katiypour(IRE)** goes well on tracks like this and appreciated the fast ground. Given a tidy ride, he had to be stoked up to get there but was well in control near the finish.

**Analyze(FR)** proved disappointing over hurdles but is useful on the Flat, both on turf and sand. This was his first outing for five months and it showed he has retained his ability and enthusiasm.

**Samuel Charles** has an awkward head carriage and the camber accentuated his tendency to hang. In the circumstances he ran well enough, but he is likely to be most effective on a more conventional track.

**Concer Eto** had plenty in his favour, and the fact that he had to be switched cannot be used as an excuse, but he should continue to be there or thereabouts in similar events.

**Spindor(USA)** looked unhappy on the camber, which ultimately prevented him from mounting a serious challenge.

**Treetops Hotel(IRE)** tried to come from too far back off a moderate early pace. He took a good hold and will be better suited by a stronger tempo.

**Deeper In Debt**, though reported by his jockey to have never been travelling comfortably on this occasion, is most effective when ridden more prominently or bowling along in front. *Official explanation: jockey said gelding was never travelling*

**Ziet D'Alsace(FR)** was far too fresh in his first appearance for nearly six months. He needs a strong pace to stop him pulling like a maniac.

**Salon Prive** *Official explanation: jockey said gelding hung both ways*

### 2031 ALEXANDER CATERING (S) STKS — 1m 3f 196y

**3:10** (3:11) (G) 3-Y-0+ — **£2,548** (£728; £364) **Stalls** High

Form — RPR

-004 **1** **Banningham Blaze**[3] [1644] 4-8-12 50 ... (v) RThomas(5) 3 — 56
(CRDore) *hld up: hdwy over 2f out: drvn to ld ins fnl f* — **3/1**[2]

4410 **2** 1/2 **Chocolate Boy (IRE)**[50] [1081] 5-10-0 57 ... (b) RLMoore 5 — 66
(GLMoore) *hld up in tch: drvn to ld over 2f out: hdd ins fnl f: r.o* — **7/4**[1]

3124 **3** 8 **Our Destiny**[8] [1856] 6-9-11 62 ... SHitchcott(3) 1 — 53
(AWCarroll) *pressed ldr: led 1/2-way: hdd over 2f out: wknd over 1f out* — **7/2**[3]

0205 **4** 1 1/2 **Paradise Valley**[8] [1858] 4-9-11 47 ... (t) RMiles(3) 2 — 51
(MrsStefLiddiard) *hld up in rr: hdwy on outside 4f out: rdn and btn 2f out* — **8/1**

4302 **5** 6 **Senor Toran (USA)**[13] [1727] 4-9-5 53 ... (p) LPKeniry(3) 6 — 35
(PBurgoyne) *chsd ldng pair: wnt 2nd over 4f out tl 3f out: wknd 2f out* — **9/1**

3146 **6** 11 **Birth Of The Blues**[17] [1644] 8-9-1 45 ... PGallagher(7) 4 — 18
(ACharlton) *sn led: hdd 1/2-way: wknd over 2f out: remote 6th whn eased ins fnl f* — **10/1**

2m 32.25s (0.15) **Going Correction** -0.075s/f (Good) — **6** Ran SP% **113.8**
Speed ratings: **96,95,90,89,85 78**CSF £8.90 TOTE £4.50: £1.90, £1.60; EX 8.00.Banningham Blaze was sold to Mr. Dennis Deacon for 7,200gns.
**Owner** Crown Select **Bred** D J And Mrs Deer **Trained** West Pinchbeck, Lincs

**FOCUS**

A poor seller and a weak pace for the first half-mile, then a moderate one until the tempo quickened noticeably three furlongs from home.

**NOTEBOOK**

**Banningham Blaze**, who goes well on this ground, enjoyed the drop in class.

**Chocolate Boy(IRE)**, returning to selling class, tried to nick the race two furlongs from home. The tactics did not quite pay off but he made the winner go all the way, with the others well beaten off.

**Our Destiny** looks more effective over shorter trips, and the final hill found him out.

**Paradise Valley** had plenty to find on official figures, so ran as well as could have been expected at the weights.

**Senor Toran(USA)** looks better at ten furlongs.

**Birth Of The Blues** is essentially a banded-grade performer and had a tough task at the weights even in this selling grade.

### 2032 CELEBPOKER.COM H'CAP — 1m 3f 196y

**3:45** (3:46) (E) (0-70,70) 3-Y-0+ — **£3,802** (£1,170; £585; £292) **Stalls** High

Form — RPR

102- **1** **Flying Spirit (IRE)**[196] [3919] 5-9-2 58 ... RLMoore 15 — 71+
(GLMoore) *prom: led after 2f: drvn clr over 2f out: comf* — **4/1**[2]

0000 **2** 4 **Danakil**[21] [1539] 9-10-0 70 ... PDobbs 8 — 77
(SDow) *t.k.h towards rr: stdy hdwy over 3f out: hrd rdn 2f out: r.o to take 2nd on line* — **14/1**

0106 **3** shd **Private Benjamin**[47] [1122] 4-8-7 49 ... FNorton 6 — 55
(JamiePoulton) *t.k.h: hdwy 4f out: chsd wnr fnl 2f: no imp: lost 2nd on line* — **14/1**

433- **4** 3 1/2 **Merrymaker**[254] [4615] 4-9-3 59 ... NPollard 7 — 60
(WMBrisbourne) *chsd ldrs: hrd rdn and hung lft 2f out: no ex over 1f out* — **10/1**

0-66 **5** 1 1/4 **Most-Saucy**[15] [1684] 8-9-3 62 ... LPKeniry(3) 9 — 61
(IAWood) *hmpd s: bhd: rdn and styd on fnl 3f: nrst fin* — **14/1**

4346 **6** 3/4 **Eastborough (IRE)**[16] [1675] 5-9-4 60 ... DSweeney 1 — 58
(BGPowell) *dwlt: hdwy 4f out: rdn and hung lft 2f out: no imp* — **7/1**[3]

0-00 **7** 1 1/2 **Cantrip**[78] [867] 4-8-11 53 ... ADaly 17 — 48
(MissBSanders) *led 2f: prom tl wknd 3f out* — **20/1**

6-00 **8** 1 1/4 **Forest Tune (IRE)**[24] [1298] 6-9-3 59 ... DaneO'Neill 16 — 52
(BHanbury) *t.k.h towards rr: sme hdwy and hrd rdn 3f out: nt pce to chal* — **25/1**

00-1 **9** nk **Wellington Hall (GER)**[30] [1376] 6-9-7 63 ... AMcCarthy 4 — 56
(PWChapple-Hyam) *in tch: struggling to hold pl whn squeezed 5f out: n.d fnl 3f* — **7/4**[1]

0050 **10** nk **Majlis (IRE)**[31] [1341] 7-9-4 65 ... (b) AQuinn(5) 11 — 57
(RMHCowell) *bmpd s: hdwy to join ldrs after 4f: wknd 2f out: 6th and btn whn n.m.r ins fnl f* — **33/1**

-500 **11** 1 **Margery Daw (IRE)**[5] [1940] 4-9-5 64 ... LisaJones(3) 14 — 55
(PSMcentee) *rdn 4f out: a towards rr* — **66/1**

1002 **12** 2 1/2 **Mandoob**[16] [1677] 7-9-10 69 ... (p) J-PGuillambert(3) 3 — 56
(BRJohnson) *dwlt: rdn 4f out: a bhd* — **16/1**

666- **13** *6* **North Point (IRE)**[26] 4089 6-8-10 **55**..............(p) RMiles(3) 5 32
(RCurtis) *prom tl wknd 3f out* **25/1**
500- **14** *nk* **Gabor**[3] 6208 5-9-2 **58**.............. RBrisland 18 35
(GLMoore) *hld up in midfield: wknd over 4f out: sn bhd* **16/1**
503- **15** *12* **Summer Cherry (USA)**[442] 612 7-8-3 **45**..............(t) PDoe 12 —
(JamiePoulton) *s.s: sn in midfield: wknd over 3f out* **33/1**
44-0 **16** *20* **Young Patriarch**[29] 1382 3-8-2 **63**.............. DKinsella 13 —
(BJMeehan) *wnt lft s: plld hrd: chsd ldrs: drvn along over 4f out: sn wknd* **20/1**

2m 29.71s (-2.39) **Going Correction** -0.075s/f (Good)
**WFA** 3 from 4yo+ 19lb **16** Ran SP% **134.3**
Speed ratings: **104,101,101,98,98 97,96,95,95,95 94,93,89,88,80 67**CSF £60.65 CT £764.41 TOTE £6.30: £1.30, £3.90, £3.00, £2.40; EX 97.00.
**Owner** Richard Green (fine Paintings) **Bred** Sean Madigan **Trained** Woodingdean, E Sussex

**FOCUS**
An ordinary handicap run at a moderate early pace which quickened around the five-furlong pole.

**NOTEBOOK**
**Flying Spirit(IRE)** received an enterprising ride and was well up to the task. The Handicapper will take note but he gives the impression that he is still improving and should have a good season.
**Danakil** has become unreliable and this was his best effort for some time. Not ideally suited by the way the race was run, he should continue to run some good races when the ground is fast but will doubtless continue to be something of an enigma.
**Private Benjamin** goes well on switchback tracks like this and looks as if he will be one to consider in similar races this summer.
**Merrymaker** was with Sir Michael Stoute last season. Though handy throughout, he is not a strong finisher and the camber had him getting very unbalanced in the last quarter-mile. *Official explanation: jockey said gelding had hung left*
**Most-Saucy** is well handicapped on turf and ought to take advantage in the coming months. She was doing her best work at the end and a longer trip may be in her favour.
**Eastborough(IRE)** has a tendency to hang left, so circumstances were not ideal. A flat track and a slightly shorter trip would help.
**Forest Tune(IRE)**
**Wellington Hall(GER)** ran into traffic problems on thedescent to the straight, but it would be wrong to use that as an excuse. However, on the evidence of his Yarmouth win, he is capable of better. *Official explanation: trainer said gelding was unsuited to the Brighton track*
**Young Patriarch** had an immense task against older opponents over this trip at this stage of the season. He was reported to have lost his action and can do better if suffering no long-term effects. *Official explanation: jockey said colt lost its action*

## 2033 TOTEPLACEPOT H'CAP 5f 59y
**4:20** (4:20) (E ) (0-70,70) 3-Y-O **£3,666** (£1,128; £564; £282) **Stalls** Low

Form RPR
2005 **1** **Imperium**[8] 1854 3-9-2 **65**.............. FNorton 6 70
(MrsStefLiddiard) *chsd ldrs: effrt 2f out: r.o to ld fnl 50 yds* **11/1**
0342 **2** *3/4* **Princess Kai (IRE)**[12] 1742 3-8-4 **55** ow1..............(b) SHitchcott(3) 5 58
(RIngram) *w ldr: hrd rdn and ev ch fnl 2f: nt qckn last 50 yds* **6/1[2]**
5440 **3** *nk* **Rehia**[15] 1689 3-8-4 **53**.............. SWhitworth 1 54
(JWHills) *led: hrd rdn fnl f: hdd and one pce fnl 50 yds* **15/2[3]**
1311 **4** *nk* **Ivory Lace**[15] 1689 3-9-7 **70**.............. DSweeney 10 70
(SWoodman) *outpcd: hrd rdn and hdwy over 1f out: hung left: nrst fin* **6/1[2]**
1160 **5** *1/2* **Cut And Dried**[49] 1099 3-9-2 **68**.............. LPKeniry(3) 4 66
(DMSimcock) *pressed ldng pair: hrd rdn over 1f out: one pce* **11/2[1]**
1423 **6** *1* **Alizar (IRE)**[76] 891 3-8-10 **59**.............. DaneO'Neill 8 53
(SDow) *towards rr: styd on fnl f: nvr nrr* **11/2[1]**
3140 **7** *1/2* **Cheeky Chi (IRE)**[7] 1883 3-9-0 **66**.............. LisaJones(3) 2 58
(PSMcentee) *hmpd s: sn in midfield: effrt 2f out: no imp fnl f* **12/1**
0-52 **8** *1* **Savernake Brave (IRE)**[16] 1676 3-7-13 **48**..............(b) JoannaBadger 3 36
(MrsHSweeting) *wnt lft s: plld hrd in rr: unbalanced on trck: nvr rchd ldrs* **9/1**
00-6 **9** *1 1/4* **Maxi's Princess (IRE)**[15] 1689 3-8-5 **54**.............. RLMoore 9 37
(PJMakin) *dwlt: sn in midfield: rdn and btn over 1f out* **6/1[2]**
5000 **10** *2* **Easily Averted (IRE)**[46] 1131 3-9-2 **65**..............(p) IMongan 7 40
(PButler) *mid-div: drvn along 1/2-way: sn outpcd* **16/1**

61.67 secs (-0.60) **Going Correction** -0.075s/f (Good) **10** Ran SP% **117.3**
Speed ratings: **101,99,99,98,98 96,95,94,92,88**CSF £76.04 CT £545.96 TOTE £12.70: £3.80, £2.40, £3.30; EX 153.20.
**Owner** The Cross Keys Racing Club **Bred** Mrs H B Raw **Trained** Great Shefford, Berks

**FOCUS**
A fair handicap and a good, solid sprint pace from the word go. The form is not strong.

**NOTEBOOK**
**Imperium** was helped by the final hill and looks as if six furlongs should be no problem.
**Princess Kai(IRE)** ran her race and is capable of continuing to make an impact off her current mark.
**Rehia** has generally been a plater but proved a revelation with the front-running tactics. This was a game effort and a repeat performance would give her every chance.
**Ivory Lace** has been in good form and was raised 5lb for her last success - which may have made all the difference. In addition, the track did not suit her as well as Bath, so she did well in the circumstances.
**Cut And Dried** is handicapped up to his best, so this was a bright effort on his return to turf.
**Alizar(IRE)** has been running well on the sand, where two of her three wins were over six furlongs. She could have done with a bit farther, and gives the impression that a first turf success is within reach.
**Savernake Brave(IRE)** has run well on this tricky track before, but on this occasion he was far too headstrong under restraint, causing him to zig-zag all over the place on the downhill run into the straight. In the end, it was remarkable he got as close as he did.

## 2034 TELETEXT RACING "HANDS AND HEELS" APPRENTICE H'CAP 1m 1f 209y
**4:55** (4:56) (G ) (0-55,55) 3-Y-0+ **£2,674** (£764; £382) **Stalls** High

Form RPR
2225 **1** **Bank On Him**[25] 1475 9-8-10 **45**.............. JemmaMarshall(8) 7 58
(GLMoore) *t.k.h: trckd ldrs: pressed ldr over 2f out: qcknd to ld ins fnl f: pushed out* **7/1[3]**
00-0 **2** *2 1/2* **Holly Rose**[22] 1516 5-9-11 **52**..............(p) MHoward 5 61
(DECantillon) *led and restrained in front: rdn and hdd ins fnl f: nt pce of wnr* **15/2**
00-0 **3** *4* **Fantasy Crusader**[30] 1373 5-9-6 **47**.............. MHalford 2 48
(JAGilbert) *in tch: effrt over 2f out: one pce appr fnl f* **12/1**
-003 **4** *1* **Lucefer (IRE)**[6] 1910 6-9-2 **46**.............. DeanWilliams(3) 8 46
(GCHChung) *towards rr: sme hdwy on outside 3f out: styd on same pce fnl 2f* **11/2[2]**
35-1 **5** *shd* **Vandenberghe**[2] 2007 5-9-4 **48**.............. RKeogh(3) 10 47
(JAOsborne) *t.k.h in rr: rdn 3f out: styd on strly fnl f* **11/2[2]**
0-00 **6** *hd* **Fife And Drum (USA)**[105] 623 7-9-8 **49**..............(p) LauraPike 3 48
(MissJFeilden) *chsd ldr tl over 2f out: wknd 1f out* **20/1**
-211 **7** *3/4* **Kings Topic (USA)**[15] 1691 4-9-9 **55**.............. RJKilloran(5) 1 53
(PBurgoyne) *trckd ldrs: hmpd on rail and lost several pls over 4f out: rdn 3f out: wknd over 1f out* **11/1**
-006 **8** *1* **Eva Peron (IRE)**[6] 1687 4-9-4 **45**.............. BO'Neill 9 41
(WGMTurner) *chsd ldrs: rdn 3f out: wknd and hung lft 2f out* **33/1**
3420 **9** *3/4* **Burgundy**[30] 1369 7-10-0 **55**..............(v) StevenHarrison 6 49
(PMitchell) *dwlt: rn in snatches in rr: hdwy on rail 2f out: no imp fnl f* **9/2[1]**
-421 **10** *nk* **Got To Be Cash**[6] 1910 5-9-2 **51** 6ex.............. SamanthaDavies(8) 4 45
(WMBrisbourne) *mid-div: outpcd over 3f out: n.d after* **7/1[3]**
0400 **11** *9* **Sammy's Shuffle**[17] 1644 9-9-7 **48**..............(b) KJackson 11 26
(JamiePoulton) *t.k.h towards rr: rdn 3f out: sn bhd* **16/1**
-000 **12** *2* **Sholay (IRE)**[59] 1016 5-9-1 **50**.............. CrystalCaetano(8) 12 24
(PMitchell) *rdn 3f out: a bhd* **33/1**

2m 2.37s (-0.17) **Going Correction** -0.075s/f (Good) **12** Ran SP% **118.3**
Speed ratings: **97,95,91,91,90 90,90,89,88,88 81,79**CSF £57.29 CT £620.74 TOTE £12.50: £3.20, £2.90, £4.40; EX 92.20 Place 6 £359.44, Place 5 £195.15.
**Owner** Vetlab Supplies Ltd **Bred** Brook Stud Ltd **Trained** Woodingdean, E Sussex
■ This was Jemma Marshall's first winner.

**FOCUS**
A poor handicap run at a medium tempo until the race developed inside the last half mile.

**NOTEBOOK**
**Bank On Him**, given a admirable ride, finally won for the first time on turf at the age of nine - though to be fair it was only his 12th start compared with 48 on sand. However, it showed beyond doubt that he is perfectly effective on grass, and is he well-handicapped on it at present too.
**Holly Rose** usually misses the break, so it was amazing to see her bowling along from the word go. The change did her good too, and she put up one of her better performances under a well-judged ride.
**Fantasy Crusader** showed signs of a return to form and is fairly handicapped at present if he can find a bit more.
**Lucefer(IRE)** gets this trip well, but he was forced to come wide and always had a bit too much ground to make up.
**Vandenberghe**, unpenalised for his win in a similar contest on sand earlier in the week, switched off at the back, but was caught out when the pace quickened turning for home. Had he been just a few lengths closer at that point, he would have finished in the first three.
**Fife And Drum(USA)** is selling class nowadays but put up a bold show for a long way.
**Got To Be Cash** may have found the ground too lively. With a 6lb penalty also counting against her, she failed to reproduce her winning effort on soft ground six days earlier.
T/Plt: £978.10 to a £1 stake. Pool: £26,932.30. 20.10 winning tickets. T/Qpdt: £70.20 to a £1 stake. Pool: £1,603.80. 16.90 winning tickets. LM

# 1664 NEWCASTLE (L-H)
Wednesday, May 12

**OFFICIAL GOING: Heavy (soft in places)**
Wind: slt hlf bhd Weather: fine and sunny

## 2035 DALTON PARK TOP BRANDS MEDIAN AUCTION MAIDEN 6f
**6:15** (6:16) (E ) 2-Y-0 **£3,623** (£1,115; £557; £278) **Stalls** Centre

Form RPR
**1** **Selkirk Storm (IRE)** 2-8-9.............. PMulrennan(5) 3 73
(MWEasterby) *s.s: hdwy and swtchd to far side over 3f out: led over 1f out: sn rdn: styd on wl: eased nr fin* **33/1**
4 **2** *1 1/4* **Secret Pact (IRE)**[12] 1743 2-9-0.............. RFfrench 5 69
(MJohnston) *led in centre: hdd over 1f out: rallied ins last: r.o* **11/4[2]**
**3** *3 1/2* **Lorna Dune** 2-8-9.............. ACulhane 8 54
(MrsJRRamsden) *hld up: hdwy and swtchd to far side 3f out: sn w ldrs: fdd fnl f* **14/1**
5 **4** *3* **Tantien**[18] 1601 2-8-9.............. DeanMcKeown 7 45
(JohnAHarris) *chsd ldrs: outpcd and swtchd to far side over 2f out: kpt on fnl f* **8/1[3]**
4 **5** *1* **Mount Ephram (IRE)**[39] 1248 2-8-9.............. PBradley(5) 1 47
(RFFisher) *w ldrs: wknd over 1f out* **25/1**
30 **6** *hd* **Procrastinate (IRE)**[31] 1340 2-8-7.............. PPMathers(7) 2 46
(RFFisher) *w ldrs: wknd over 1f out* **10/1**
**7** *1* **Profit's Reality (IRE)** 2-8-11.............. DNolan(3) 4 43
(PABlockley) *in tch: outpcd over 2f out: kpt on fnl f* **8/1[3]**
3 **8** *1 1/4* **Almaty Express**[22] 1523 2-9-0.............. PHanagan 10 39
(MTodhunter) *hld up in centre: effrt over 2f out: sn rdn: nvr on terms* **5/2[1]**
**9** *15* **Ryedane (IRE)** 2-8-11.............. DAllan(3) 9 —
(TDEasterby) *sn chsng ldrs: outpcd 3f out: sn lost pl and bhd: eased* **14/1**
44 **10** *1/2* **Keepasharplookout (IRE)**[10] 1782 2-9-0.............. RWinston 6 —
(MrsLStubbs) *chsd ldrs on far side: lost pl 2f out: eased* **10/1**

1m 17.78s (2.74) **Going Correction** +0.35s/f (Good) **10** Ran SP% **115.8**
Speed ratings: **95,93,88,84,83 83,81,80,60,59**CSF £121.96 TOTE £42.90: £16.80, £1.02, £8.10; EX 65.70.
**Owner** Morecool Racing **Bred** Maurice Craig **Trained** Sheriff Hutton, N Yorks

**FOCUS**
The going on the straight course at least was reckoned to be not as testing as the official version. The far rail was the place to be all night and those who raced towards the middle were at a disadvantage.

**NOTEBOOK**
**Selkirk Storm(IRE)**, a February foal, is on the leg and narrow. He has a pronounced knee action and proved suited by the soft ground. After giving away ground at the start, he made his way to the far rail and in the end did enough. He will struggle under a penalty.
**Secret Pact(IRE)** made the running, but his rider made the mistake of sticking to the centre on the slower ground. He battled back well when headed and is virtually a winner without a penalty.
**Lorna Dune**, a February foal, is a close-coupled type. She looked short of peak condition and, after working her way on to the heels of the first two, tired noticeably in the closing stages.
**Tantien**, on her toes beforehand, looked to be struggling until reaching the favoured far side late on.
**Mount Ephram(IRE)**, last of four first time, at least showed a bit more but he had the best of the draw.
**Procrastinate(IRE)** was having his third race already.
**Almaty Express**, drawn ten of ten, was on the slower ground throughout and never fired.
**Keepasharplookout(IRE)** *Official explanation: jockey said colt was suffering from sore shins*

## 2036 ING REAL ESTATE DEVELOPMENT UK H'CAP 7f
**6:45** (6:46) (E ) (0-70,69) 3-Y-0 **£4,348** (£1,338; £669; £334) **Stalls** Centre

Form RPR
06-0 **1** **Insubordinate**[42] 1214 3-8-3 **56**.............. TEaves(5) 10 65
(JSGoldie) *hld up and bhd: hdwy and swtchd far side 2f out: led appr fnl f: kpt on wl* **12/1**
4-40 **2** *2* **Impulsive Bid (IRE)**[25] 1464 3-9-0 **62**.............. PHanagan 6 66
(JeddO'Keeffe) *trckd ldrs: ev ch 1f out: styd on same pce* **16/1**

1245 **3** 1 **Turf Princess**[96] [696] 3-8-2 **57** DFentiman[(7)] 4 59
(IanEmmerson) *w ldr: led over 3f out: hdd appr fnl f: no ex* **12/1**

0-45 **4** 4 **Trojan Flight**[4] [1957] 3-9-7 **69** KFallon 12 61
(MrsJRRamsden) *hld up: hdwy on ins over 3f out: rdn to chse ldrs over 2f out: wknd 1f out* **6/4**[1]

0-00 **5** 1 1/4 **Reversionary**[25] [1467] 3-8-5 **53** (b[1]) DaleGibson 9 41
(MWEasterby) *in tch: outpcd over 2f out: swtchd ins and kpt on appr fnl f* **20/1**

2600 **6** 2 1/2 **Kings Rock**[42] [1214] 3-8-13 **61** PFessey 1 43
(KARyan) *chsd ldrs on ins: hmpd over 2f out: no imp after* **9/2**[2]

53-0 **7** 3 **Party Princess (IRE)**[37] [1270] 3-8-12 **60** DeanMcKeown 8 35
(JAGlover) *hld up: hdwy over 2f out: sn chsng ldrs: rdn and wknd over 1f out* **14/1**

2102 **8** 2 **Could She Be Magic (IRE)**[16] [1678] 3-8-7 **58** DAllan[(3)] 7 28
(TDEasterby) *chsd ldrs: edgd lft and lost pl over 1f out* **9/1**[3]

2-00 **9** 20 **Military Two Step (IRE)**[12] [1755] 3-9-0 **62** (p) DarrenWilliams 13 —
(KRBurke) *racd wd: sn in rr and rdn along: bhd fnl 3f: eased* **10/1**

004- **10** 6 **Victorian Dancer (IRE)**[251] [4682] 3-8-11 **59** GParkin 11 —
(KARyan) *s.i.s: wl bhd fnl 2f* **40/1**

0-00 **11** 3 **Fox Covert (IRE)**[18] [1614] 3-8-13 **64** LEnstone[(3)] 3 —
(DWBarker) *led: hdd over 3f out: hrd rdn and edgd lft over 2f out: sn wknd and bhd: eased* **12/1**

1m 30.84s (2.82) **Going Correction** +0.35s/f (Good) 11 Ran SP% **120.1**
Speed ratings: **97,94,93,89,87 84,81,79,56,49 45**CSF £192.30 CT £2390.80 TOTE £14.00: £3.30, £5.00, £2.60; EX 322.10.
**Owner** J S Goldie **Bred** Charlock Farm Stud **Trained** Uplawmoor, E Renfrews

**FOCUS**
Again the far rail was the place to be.

**NOTEBOOK**
**Insubordinate**, an excitable sort, had two handlers in the paddock. He made his way to the far side rail and, in the end, ran out a convincing winner.
**Impulsive Bid(IRE)**, unplaced in five previous starts, raced towards the far side but paid the penalty for leaving the gap for the winner on her inside.
**Turf Princess**, absent since running on the All-Weather in February, showed bags of toe and stuck to her task.
**Trojan Flight**, drawn one off the outside, tried to make his way to the favoured far rail. He could never get there and when asked a serious question the response was limited to say the very least.
**Reversionary**, in first-time blinkers, struggled to keep up and only stayed on when he was switched to the far side rail coming to the final furlong. He looks as though he really needs every inch of a mile.

## 2037 DALTON-PARK.COM H'CAP — 1m 3y(S)
**7:15** (7:16) (F) (0-55,55) 3-Y-O — **£3,094** (£884; £442) **Stalls** Centre

Form RPR

06-6 **1** **Dance To My Tune**[27] [1422] 3-8-9 **54** PMulrennan[(5)] 4 63
(MWEasterby) *swvd lft s: hld up: smooth hdwy over 2f out: shkn up to ld if out: hld on wl* **8/1**[3]

06-1 **2** 3/4 **Ilwadod**[5] [1946] 3-8-11 **51** 6ex RLappin 6 58
(MRChannon) *trckd ldr: led over 2f out: hdd 1f out: nt qckn* **11/10**[1]

00-6 **3** 8 **Fourswainby (IRE)**[27] [1420] 3-8-3 **48** TEaves[(5)] 5 39
(BEllison) *s.i.s: hld up: hdwy over 2f out: sn chsng ldrs: wl outpcd fnl f* **14/1**

0053 **4** 9 **Sir Galahad**[16] [1667] 3-8-9 **52** DAllan[(3)] 2 25
(TDEasterby) *set modearte pce: qcknd 4f out: hdd over 2f out: wknd over 1f out* **7/4**[2]

0-40 **5** 1 1/2 **Lady Of The Links (IRE)**[6] [1907] 3-9-1 **55** (v[1]) KimTinkler 1 25
(NTinkler) *trckd ldrs: rdn over 2f out: sn lost pl* **16/1**

5005 **6** 2 1/2 **Dandy Jim**[43] [1195] 3-8-6 **46** oh16 ACulhane 3 11
(DWChapman) *sltly hmpd s: hld up: drvn along 3f out: sn lost pl* **25/1**

1m 46.43s (5.23) **Going Correction** +0.35s/f (Good) 6 Ran SP% **111.5**
Speed ratings: **87,86,78,69,67 65**CSF £17.20 TOTE £11.50: £2.50, £1.20; EX 37.70.
**Owner** R S Cockerill (Farms) Ltd **Bred** R S Cockerill (farms) Ltd **Trained** Sheriff Hutton, N Yorks

**FOCUS**
A 0-55 handicap run at just a steady pace to halfway.

**NOTEBOOK**
**Dance To My Tune**, placed twice in eight previous starts, was reluctant at first to go to the start. After going sideways leaving the stalls, she moved up on the bridle and had only to be kept up to her work.
**Ilwadod**, banged up 11lb after Nottingham, had just a 6lb penalty over this two-furlong-shorter trip. He went on and stepped up the gallop, but the filly always looked to have his every move covered.
**Fourswainby(IRE)**, unplaced in three previous starts, was making his handicap bow from what looked a stiff sort of mark.
**Sir Galahad**, on his toes beforehand, tried to steal a march from the front, but he was out on his feet with over a furlong left to run.
**Lady Of The Links(IRE)** was stepping up in trip in a first-time visor. She looks regressive.
**Dandy Jim**, unplaced in eight starts on the All-Weather, was making his turf debut.

## 2038 DALTON PARK 50% OFF BEST BRANDS H'CAP — 1m 4f 93y
**7:45** (7:45) (F) (0-55,58) 3-Y-O+ — **£3,409** (£974; £487) **Stalls** Far side

Form RPR

000- **1** **Royal Melbourne (IRE)**[317] [2861] 4-9-8 **51** RWinston 8 61
(MissJACamacho) *trckd ldr: t.k.h: shkn up to ld over 2f out: kpt on u.p: jst hld on* **25/1**

350- **2** shd **Cantemerle (IRE)**[158] [6139] 4-9-8 **51** (b) KFallon 10 61
(WMBrisbourne) *mid-div: effrt over 3f out: wnt 2nd 1f out: styd on wl: jst failed* **8/1**

0-06 **3** 3 **Millennium Hall**[10] [1783] 5-9-11 **54** KRenwick 1 60
(PMonteith) *hld up in last pl: hdwy 2f out: hung lft and styd on wl fnl f* **8/1**

3231 **4** 1 1/4 **Next Flight (IRE)**[16] [1668] 5-9-9 **52** RFitzpatrick 6 56
(REBarr) *led: qcknd 7f out: hdd over 2f out: one pce* **6/1**[3]

0-50 **5** shd **Inchinnan**[16] [1660] 7-9-6 **54** TEaves[(5)] 7 58
(JamesMoffatt) *mid-div: effrt over 2f out: styd on fnl f* **16/1**

1000 **6** 1 **East Cape**[22] [1527] 7-9-3 **46** oh6 KimTinkler 5 49
(DonEnricoIncisa) *chsd ldng pair: one pce fnl 2f* **16/1**

3401 **7** 1 1/2 **Fortunes Favourite**[18] [1617] 4-9-3 **46** oh1 EAhern 12 46
(GMMoore) *hld up in rr: sme hdwy over 2f out: nvr nr ldrs* **14/1**

350- **8** 3/4 **Mythical King (IRE)**[41] [2425] 7-9-5 **53** BSwarbrick[(5)] 9 52
(RLee) *chsd ldrs: stdy hdwy over 3f out: sn chsng ldrs: rdn over 2f out: hung lft and wknd over 1f out* **11/4**[1]

6-02 **9** 2 1/2 **Plausabelle**[14] [1710] 3-8-1 **52** (b) DAllan[(3)] 4 48
(TDEasterby) *bhd: drvn along 5f out: sme hdwy 3f out: lost pl 2f out* **10/1**

-051 **10** 1/2 **Gargoyle Girl**[8] [1866] 7-10-1 **58** 6ex KDarley 3 53
(JSGoldie) *t.k.h in rr: nvr a factor* **11/2**[2]

230- **11** 1 1/2 **Dubonai (IRE)**[232] [5135] 4-9-11 **54** CCatlin 2 47
(AndrewTurnell) *hld up towards rr: hdwy over 2f out: wknd and eased jst ins last* **25/1**

-553 **12** 2 **Summer Special**[16] [1660] 4-9-4 **50** LEnstone[(3)] 13 40
(DWBarker) *hld up in rr: effrt on outside over 2f out: no imp: eased ins last* **12/1**

2m 54.9s (2.60) **Going Correction** +0.675s/f (Yiel)
**WFA** 3 from 4yo+ 19lb 12 Ran SP% **121.5**
Speed ratings: **88,87,85,85,85 84,83,82,81,80 79,78**CSF £218.51 CT £1763.72 TOTE £35.30: £14.60, £3.70, £2.60; EX 363.90.
**Owner** Jamie Spence **Bred** Mrs S Camacho **Trained** Norton, N Yorks

**FOCUS**
Due to the ground the stalls could not be used and this race was hand timed. It was run at a very steady pace early on.

**NOTEBOOK**
**Royal Melbourne(IRE)**, well beaten in four previous outings, was having his first race for almost a year. He sat on the leader's heels pulling hard early because of the lack of pace. Sent for home at exactly the right time, he was three lengths clear a furlong out but, in the end, the post came just in time. His rider deserves full marks. *Official explanation: trainer said, regarding the improved form shown, gelding had matured over the winter*
**Cantemerle(IRE)**, who has slipped right down the ratings, was having her first outing since December. She went in pursuit of the winner a furlong out, but needed one more stride. She is just the type of moderate handicapper her trainer does so well with.
**Millennium Hall**, a winner just once from 20 previous starts, was stepping up in trip. He sat last of all in a race run at no pace early on, then made his effort on the wide outside towards the centre. He deserves full marks for this, unlike his rider.
**Next Flight(IRE)**, down in trip, dropped anchor in front but, in the sprint over the final three furlongs, was found sadly lacking.
**Inchinnan**, who last won in September 2001, was having just her second outing for her new yard. She stayed on when it was all over.
**East Cape** kept tabs on the first two, but proved simply too slow when the dash for home began in earnest. A true-run mile six may be needed now.
**Mythical King(IRE)**, who won over hurdles on heavy ground at Ascot in January, has won twice on the level, both on decent ground. He moved up smoothly once in line for home but, when called on for a final effort, seemed to flounder.

## 2039 DALTON PARK OUTLET SHOPPING CLASSIFIED STKS — 1m 2f 32y
**8:15** (8:18) (E) 3-Y-O+ — **£3,744** (£1,152; £576; £288) **Stalls** Low

Form RPR

34-2 **1** **Aleron (IRE)**[5] [1928] 6-9-11 68 (p) EAhern 1 78+
(JJQuinn) *led 1f: trckd ldrs gng wl: smooth hdwy to ld 150yds: shkn up and pushed out* **9/4**[1]

04/ **2** 1 1/2 **Turtle Dancer (IRE)**[614] [5716] 6-9-4 66 TEaves[(5)] 6 73
(BEllison) *trckd ldrs: led over 2f out: hdd jst ins fnl f: no ch w wnr* **20/1**

4512 **3** 1/2 **Melodian**[4] [1962] 9-9-8 62 (b) TWilliams 2 71
(MBrittain) *trckd ldrs: chal 2f out: styd on same pce fnl f* **9/2**

4-03 **4** 3/4 **Kid'Z'Play (IRE)**[16] [1661] 8-9-8 64 CCatlin 8 70
(JSGoldie) *led after 1f: set mod pce: hdd over 2f out: kpt on same pce* **10/1**

/311 **5** 7 **Pure Mischief (IRE)**[5] [1944] 5-9-9 58 BSwarbrick[(5)] 4 64
(WMBrisbourne) *hld up: hdwy 6f out: rdn over 2f out: wknd appr fnl f* **7/2**[2]

30-6 **6** 3/4 **Medallist**[18] [1624] 5-9-12 69 (be) RWinston 3 61
(BEllison) *awkward to load: dwlt: hdwy to chse ldrs after 3f: drvn along over 3f out: wknd appr fnl f* **14/1**

0-60 **7** 18 **Countykat (IRE)**[98] [679] 4-9-6 70 DonnaBashton[(7)] 5 31
(KRBurke) *hld up in rr: lost tch 3f out* **33/1**

0 **8** 1 1/4 **Zan Lo (IRE)**[25] [1470] 4-9-5 60 PHanagan 9 21
(BSRothwell) *rr-div: lost tch 3f out* **66/1**

006- **9** dist **Trilemma**[212] [5533] 3-8-5 63 ow1 (b[1]) SSanders 7 —
(SirMarkPrescott) *mid-div: reminders 6f out: no rspnse: lost tch over 3f out: virtually p.u: t.o* **4/1**[3]

2m 17.47s (5.87) **Going Correction** +0.675s/f (Yiel)
**WFA** 3 from 4yo+ 15lb 9 Ran SP% **116.1**
Speed ratings: **103,101,101,100,95 94,80,79,—**CSF £51.44 TOTE £2.90: £1.60, £4.40, £1.30; EX 86.00.
**Owner** Grahame Liles **Bred** Sheikh Mohammed Bin Rashid Al Maktoum **Trained** Settrington, N Yorks

**FOCUS**
No gallop but the winner travelled easily best throughout.

**NOTEBOOK**
**Aleron(IRE)**, in first-time cheekpieces, travelled supremely well and, produced as late as possible, had only to be nudged out. Now a gelding, connections are very hopeful he will come good over hurdles this time.
**Turtle Dancer(IRE)**, last seen over hurdles in September 2002, has shown he can handle testing conditions. He kicked for home, but it was soon obvious he was the mouse and the winner the cat.
**Melodian** made the mistake of not dominating. The pace was not strong and to compound his downfall, his rider elected to come up the middle in the home straight on the slower ground.
**Kid'Z'Play(IRE)** dawdled along in front and it was no surprise to see him totally tapped for toe when the dash for home started. A winner at up to a mile and a half, he should surely have gone off quicker.
**Pure Mischief(IRE)** had a bit to find and, after sitting off the pace, he could never take a hand and tired late on.
**Medallist**, very awkward to load, had both blinkers and eyeshields fitted, but he ran a sour sort of race. The promise he showed at three is history now.
**Trilemma**, in blinkers on her reappearance, did not want to know and looked to curl up completely when given some sharp reminders at halfway. It is not often one from this stable runs so badly.

## 2040 PANTHEON RETAIL ASSET MANAGERS DALTON PARK MEDIAN AUCTION MAIDEN — 5f
**8:45** (8:45) (F) 3-4-Y-O — **£3,248** (£928; £464) **Stalls** Centre

Form RPR

00-5 **1** **Tatweer (IRE)**[22] [1516] 4-9-9 47 (v) RWinston 6 57
(DShaw) *chsd ldrs: led and hung lft over 1f out: rdn out* **7/2**[2]

205- **2** 2 1/2 **Westborough (IRE)**[197] [5818] 3-9-0 56 KimTinkler 8 50
(NTinkler) *chsd ldrs: edgd lft and styd on fnl f: tk 2nd on line* **7/1**[3]

62-3 **3** shd **El Palmar**[16] [1664] 3-8-9 68 PMakin[(5)] 9 49
(TDBarron) *led over 1f: w ldrs: nt qckn appr fnl f* **6/4**[1]

6- **4** 3 1/2 **Take Good Time (IRE)**[213] [5509] 4-9-9 SChin 2 39
(JohnBerry) *hld up in mid-div: outpcd over 2f out: styd on ins fnl f* **8/1**

6-00 **5** nk **Stavros (IRE)**[8] [1870] 4-9-9 46 PHanagan 3 38
(JSWainwright) *w ldr: led over 3f out tl over 1f out: wkng whn sltly hmpd jst ins last* **16/1**

**6** 1 1/4 **Grey Gurkha** 3-9-0 GParkin 7 34
(PTMidgley) *s.i.s: bhd tl styd on appr fnl f* **12/1**

5-00 **7** 1 1/4 **Dr Fox (IRE)**[25] [1467] 3-9-0 51 EAhern 5 30
(KAMorgan) *mid-div: outpcd over 2f out: kpt on fnl f* **10/1**

0 **8** nk **Casey's House**[31] [1342] 4-8-13 TEaves[(5)] 4 24
(FWatson) *s.i.s: bhd tl kpt on fnl 2f: nvr a factor* **100/1**



The Form Book, Raceform Ltd, Compton, RG20 6NL

-340 **9** *5* **Knight To Remember (IRE)**[56] 1040 3-9-0 48......... DarrenWilliams 10 14
(KRBurke) *swtchd lft after s: hld up: effrt over 2f out: sn rdn and lost pl* **10/1**

P-00 **10** *24* **My Wild Rover**[19] 1596 4-9-4 .....................................(t) PMulrennan(5) 1 —
(KAMorgan) *mid-div: lost pl over 2f out: sn bhd and eased* **33/1**

63.01 secs (1.48) **Going Correction** +0.35s/f (Good)
**WFA** 3 from 4yo 9lb **10** Ran SP% **121.5**
Speed ratings: **102,98,97,92,91 89,87,87,79,40**CSF £29.79 TOTE £6.70: £2.30, £3.10, £1.10; EX 33.90 Place 6 £640.27, Place 5 £182.09.
**Owner** Swann Racing Ltd **Bred** Sean O'Keeffe **Trained** Averham, Notts

**FOCUS**
A low grade sprint maiden with the disapointing favourite never in quite the right place away from the far rail.

**NOTEBOOK**
**Tatweer(IRE)**, unplaced in ten previous starts and rated just 47, owes his trainer and jockey something. He hung left when hitting the front, putting himself on the best ground against the far side rail. His rider left nothing to chance.
**Westborough(IRE)**, having his first outing since October, stayed on against the far side rail to snatch second spot on the line.
**El Palmar**, who had 12lb in hand of the runner-up and 21lb in hand of the winner on official figures, is a keen type. He tended to race wide and could never get to the far side rail and, in the end, both the winner and the second went by him on his inside. Rated 68, he will struggle in handicaps from that sort of mark.
**Take Good Time(IRE)**, who started slowly in one backend start at two, is not that big but does look to possess some ability. He stayed on in his own time after getting outpaced and needs another run for handicaps.
**Stavros(IRE)**, a maiden after 24 starts, had the far side rail to help him, but his chance was slipping when left short of room by the runner-up just inside the last.
**Grey Gurkha**, a leggy newcomer, is a full-brother to the soft ground sprint-handicapper Grey Cossack. After a slow start, he showed some ability staying on late in the day. He looks to have a fair bit to learn.
T/Plt: £953.00 to a £1 stake. Pool: £37,665.90. 28.85 winning tickets. T/Qpdt: £25.30 to a £1 stake. Pool: £2,960.40. 86.50 winning tickets. WG

## [2018] YORK (L-H)
### Wednesday, May 12

**OFFICIAL GOING: Good to soft (good in places)**
The going was generally considered to be soft with a lush covering of grass.

## 2041 TOTESPORT.COM H'CAP — 5f 3y
1:30 (1:31) (B) (0-110,110) 3-Y-O+ **£14,820** (£4,560; £2,280; £1,140) **Stalls** High

Form RPR

0-50 **1** **River Falcon**[31] 1343 4-7-9 **80** oh2.................................... NMackay(3) 10 91
(JSGoldie) *chsd ldrs: effrt 2f out: rdn to ld over 1f out: hung lft ins last: kpt on* **16/1**

0-30 **2** *½* **Watching**[11] 1765 7-8-1 **83**.................................................... ANicholls 12 92
(DNicholls) *chsd ldrs: hdwy 2f out: rdn and ev ch ins last: kpt on* **16/1**

3-30 **3** *nk* **Henry Hall (IRE)**[28] 1391 8-8-11 **93**.................................. KimTinkler 11 101
(NTinkler) *midfield: gd hdwy 2f out: rdn to chal ent last and ev ch tl drvn: edgd lft and no ex last 100 yds* **25/1**

00-5 **4** *¾* **Corridor Creeper (FR)**[5] 1923 7-8-8 **90**..............................(p) CCatlin 19 95
(JMBradley) *pronent stands side: rdn over 1f out: ev ch ent last: sn drvn and nt qckn last 100 yds* **12/1**

0-05 **5** *½* **Matty Tun**[11] 1763 5-8-12 **94**.................................................. KFallon 2 97
(JBalding) *dwlt and sn outpcd far side: hdwy 2f out: styd on u.p ent last: nrst fin* **8/1**[3]

0610 **6** *½* **Cape Royal**[5] 1923 4-8-6 **88**...................................................... ACulhane 9 90
(MrsJRRamsden) *trckd ldrs centre: effrt wl over 1f out: sn rdn and kpt on same pce ins last* **10/1**

3-12 **7** *nk* **Bishops Court**[4] 1955 10-10-0 **110**........................................... LDettori 6 111
(MrsJRRamsden) *trckd ldrs centre: hdwy wl over 1f out: rdn and one pce ins last* **9/1**

-420 **8** *2 ½* **Dragon Flyer (IRE)**[15] 1685 5-9-5 **101**.............................. JPSpencer 8 93
(MQuinn) *cl up centre: rdn to ld briefly wl over 1f out: sn drvn : hdd & wknd* **12/1**

-030 **9** *1* **Sierra Vista**[11] 1774 4-7-12 **80** oh2.....................................(p) PHanagan 5 68
(DWBarker) *chsd ldrs centree: rdn wl over 1f out: grad wknd* **20/1**

43-0 **10** *1* **Fanny's Fancy**[26] 1438 4-8-9 **91**............................................ SSanders 20 75
(CFWall) *towards rr stands side: hdwy 2f out: rdn wl over 1f out and sn no imp* **11/2**[1]

100- **11** *1* **Night Prospector**[234] 5110 4-8-10 **92**.................................... NCallan 16 73
(JWPayne) *chsd ldrs stands side: rdn along 2f out: sn wknd* **50/1**

6-50 **12** *nk* **Whitbarrow (IRE)**[5] 1923 5-8-10 **92**...................................... SDrowne 4 72
(JMBradley) *chsd ldrs centre: rdn along over 2f out: sn wknd* **18/1**

4045 **13** *1* **Prince Of Blues (IRE)**[11] 1759 6-7-5 **80** oh18..................(p) PVarley(7) 1 56
(MMullineaux) *racd alone far rail: prom tl rdn along 1/2-way: sn wknd* **66/1**

03-0 **14** *hd* **Fast Heart**[11] 1763 3-8-8 **99**...............................................(t) MHills 3 74
(BJMeehan) *s.i.s: a rr* **25/1**

5006 **15** *¾* **Trinculo (IRE)**[11] 1759 7-8-3 **85**........................................(p) JBramhill 7 58
(NPLittmoden) *overall ldr centre: rdn along 1/2-way: hdd & wknd wl over 1f out* **33/1**

-030 **16** *¾* **Ikan (IRE)**[15] 1685 4-8-6 **88**.................................................... EAhern 18 58
(NPLittmoden) *in tch stands side: rdn along over 2f out: sn btn* **33/1**

5001 **17** *nk* **Chico Guapo (IRE)**[11] 1774 4-7-12 **80** oh3............................ JQuinn 15 49
(JAGlover) *led stands side: rdn along over 2f out: sn wknd* **18/1**

0021 **18** *2* **Artie**[4] 1956 5-7-13 **81** 6ex.................................................. DaleGibson 14 43
(TDEasterby) *upset in stalls: s.i.s: a bhd* **7/1**[2]

105- **19** *5* **Proud Native (IRE)**[238] 4991 10-8-5 **87**.............................. KDarley 13 31
(DNicholls) *in rr fr 1/2-way* **40/1**

205- **20** *5* **Salviati (USA)**[200] 5743 7-8-8 **90**........................................ SCarson 17 16
(JMBradley) *s.i.s: a b ehind* **50/1**

61.74 secs (3.00) **Going Correction** +0.825s/f (Soft)
**WFA** 3 from 4yo+ 9lb **20** Ran SP% **122.0**
Speed ratings: **109,108,107,106,105 104,104,100,98,97 95,95,93,93,92 90,90,87,79,71**CSF £223.09 CT £6247.02 TOTE £18.50: £4.60, £3.60, £6.00, £3.10; EX 402.50 Trifecta £1434.30 Pool: £2020.26. 0.10 winning tickets..
**Owner** S Bruce **Bred** Manor Farm Packers Ltd **Trained** Uplawmoor, E Renfrews
■ Stewards Enquiry : N Mackay one-day ban: used whip from above shoulder height (May 23)

**FOCUS**
The runners spread across the track but the first three home all raced down the centre.

**NOTEBOOK**
**River Falcon**, who caught the eye at Musselburgh, appreciated the cut in the ground and battled to the front close home. He may go for a valuable sprint back at at Musselburgh now, a race in which Matty Tun was successsful last year after winning here.
**Watching**, who had not run over the minimum trip for a year, likes this sort of ground and ran a sound race. He has not got his head in front nearly three years but obviously remains capable of rectifying that.
**Henry Hall(IRE)** had run respectably in this event for the past three seasons. This time it looked as if he would prevail as he took a slight lead inside the last, but he was relegated two places near the line.
**Corridor Creeper(FR)** did best of those drawn high. Although currently 5lb higher than when last getting his head in front, he looks capable of winning when his yard hits form.
**Matty Tun** went up 7lb for a good effort in the Group Three Palace House Stakes last time, putting him on a stone higher mark than when successful in this race twelve month ago. Again slow to go, he was running on well at the death and just missed the frame.
**Cape Royal** was never able to land a blow at Chester but this more conventional track produced a better run.
**Bishops Court**, who gave upwards of 9lb all round, performed with credit and finished a neck behind his half-brother.
**Dragon Flyer(IRE)** showed plenty of pace in the centre of the track before fading. She deserves to pick up a decent prize but may continue to prove hard to place.
**Fanny's Fancy**, done no favours by her stands' rail draw, also found the dead ground against her. *Official explanation: jockey said filly was unsuited by the dead ground*
**Artie**, under a 6lb penalty for his win at Beverley, became very upset in the stalls. The handler was a split second late in whipping off the blindfold as the gates opened and that was that.

## 2042 TOTEPOOL MIDDLETON STKS (GROUP 3) (F&M) — 1m 2f 88y
2:00 (2:00) (A) 4-Y-O+ **£29,000** (£11,000; £5,500; £2,500) **Stalls** Low

Form RPR

14 **1** **Crimson Palace (SAF)**[46] 1146 5-8-9 ..................................... LDettori 4 112
(SaeedBinSuroor) *hld up in tch: smooth hdwy 3f out: shkn up to ld over 1f out: sn rdn and kpt on* **6/4**[1]

0-11 **2** *¾* **Beneventa**[10] 1790 4-8-12 104.................................................. SSanders 3 114
(JLDunlop) *lw: trckd ldr: led over 3f out and sn qcknd: rdn and hdd over 1f out: rallied wl u.p ins last: kpt on* **10/3**[2]

302- **3** *11* **Summitville**[214] 5481 4-8-9 111............................................... KFallon 5 92
(JGGiven) *lw: trckd ldrs: rdn along and outpcd 4f out: kpt on u.p fnl 2f: no imp* **4/1**[3]

40-4 **4** *6* **Landinium (ITY)**[30] 1355 5-8-9 100........................................ RHughes 2 82
(CFWall) *chsd ldng pair: effrt and ev ch 3f out: sn rdn and outpcd fnl 2f* **25/1**

320- **5** *9* **Thingmebob**[245] 4816 4-8-9 104............................................ PRobinson 6 67
(MHTompkins) *hld up: pushed along and outpcd 1/2-way: sn bhd* **12/1**

146- **6** *2 ½* **Sun On The Sea (IRE)**[303] 3281 4-8-9 107........................... MJKinane 1 63
(BJMeehan) *bit bkwd: led: rdn along and hdd over 3f out: sn wknd* **9/1**

2m 15.68s (6.24) **Going Correction** +0.875s/f (Soft) **6** Ran SP% **104.6**
Speed ratings: **110,109,100,95,88 86**CSF £5.59 TOTE £2.20: £1.50, £2.40; EX 4.20.
**Owner** Godolphin **Bred** Adv A P Joubert **Trained** Newmarket, Suffolk
■ This event has been upgraded from listed status.

**FOCUS**
They went no great pace. The runners came up the centre once into the straight.

**NOTEBOOK**
**Crimson Palace(SAF)**, a top performer when trained in South Africa, is quite a tall, scopey mare and looked very fit for this domestic debut for Godolphin. She travelled really well and was always going to win once easing to the front, but she did not do it as easily as she had promised and the runner-up made her work a bit. Faster ground will suit her, and she will benefit from an enhanced programme of opportunites for older fillies this season.
**Beneventa** ran a fine race attempting to concede 3lb to a smart opponent, rallying in typically game style to make the favourite work for her victory. Her attitude to racing should ensure further success.
**Summitville** was rather disappointing, as she took a long time to pick up and then could only keep on at the same pace. Placed in the Epsom and Yorkshire Oaks last term, she was unsuited by the lack of a gallop over this shorter trip and will appreciate a return to a mile and a half.
**Landinium(ITY)**, who faced a difficult task at the weights, had no problem with the ground but was found wanting in this company.
**Thingmebob**, having her first run since September, was not helped by the lack of a true gallop over a trip on the short side for her.
**Sun On The Sea(IRE)**, trained last season by Brian Meehan, was having her first run since July. She had the run of the race in front, but capitulated rather tamely. The softish ground might have been against her, although her sire Bering's progeny usually handle give underfoot. *Official explanation: jockey said filly felt amiss and blew excessively*

## 2043 TOTESPORT DANTE STKS (GROUP 2) — 1m 2f 88y
2:30 (2:31) (A) 3-Y-O **£84,100** (£31,900; £15,950; £7,250) **Stalls** Low

Form RPR

21- **1** **North Light (IRE)**[231] 5153 3-8-11 ........................................... KFallon 1 120+
(SirMichaelStoute) *keen: hld up in tch: hdwy to ld over 4f out: qcknd 3f out: rdn 2f out: kpt on wl* **6/1**

113- **2** *½* **Rule Of Law (USA)**[228] 5208 3-8-11 110...............................(t) LDettori 3 118
(SaeedBinSuroor) *in tch: pushed along and outpcd 3f out: hdwy 2f out: swtchd lft over 1f out: sn rdn and kpt on wl* **8/1**

12-1 **3** *2 ½* **Let The Lion Roar**[26] 1439 3-8-11 108................................... MJKinane 9 114
(JLDunlop) *pushed along in rr 1f: niggled along 1/2-way: hdwy on outer 4f out: rdn to chse ldrs 2f out: sn drvn and kpt on same pce* **3/1**[1]

24-2 **4** *1* **Top Seed (IRE)**[26] 1439 3-8-11 108....................................... TEDurcan 6 112
(MRChannon) *trckd ldrs: hdwy 3f out: rdn 2f out and kpt on same pce* **8/1**

6-1 **5** *6* **Andean**[30] 1371 3-8-11 .......................................................... TPQueally 7 101
(DRLoder) *keen: in tch: hdwy 4f out: rdn to chse ldrs over 2f out: drvn and wknd over 1f out* **4/1**[2]

25- **6** *3 ½* **Moscow Ballet (IRE)**[206] 5665 3-8-11 ................................... JPSpencer 5 95
(APO'Brien, Ire) *trckd ldrs: rdn along over 3f out: drvn 2f out and sn wknd* **5/1**[3]

510- **7** *5* **Mutawaffer**[201] 5731 3-8-11 99.................................................. RHills 8 86
(BWHills) *in tch: rdn along 4f out: sn wknd* **33/1**

3-50 **8** *5* **Barbajuan (IRE)**[11] 1764 3-8-11 110..................................... PRobinson 4 77
(NACallaghan) *lw: led 2f: cl up tl rdn along over 4f out and sn wknd* **33/1**

1134 **9** *5* **Skidmark**[21] 1538 3-8-11 102................................................ RHughes 10 68
(DRCElsworth) *a rr* **25/1**

1- **10** *1 ¼* **Oman Gulf (USA)**[298] 3411 3-8-11 ........................................ MHills 2 66
(BWHills) *cl up: led after 2f: pushed along and hdd over 4f out: sn rdn and wknd* **25/1**

2m 15.69s (6.25) **Going Correction** +0.875s/f (Soft) **10** Ran SP% **111.7**
Speed ratings: **110,109,107,106,102 99,95,91,87,86**CSF £48.15 TOTE £6.30: £2.30, £2.40, £1.40; EX 53.60 Trifecta £125.60 Pool: £1680.90. 9.50 winning tickets..
**Owner** Ballymacoll Stud **Bred** Ballymacoll Stud **Trained** Newmarket, Suffolk
■ Stewards Enquiry : L Dettori four-day ban: used whip with excessive frequency, without regard to stride pattern and without giving colt time to respond (May 23-26)

**FOCUS**
A fair renewal of this Derby trial, but only an average time for a three-year-old Group Two at this stage of the season. The runners came up the centre of the track in the home straight.
**NOTEBOOK**
**North Light(IRE)** produced a taking display to put himself firmly into the Derby picture. Kicked for home with three to run, he responded in fine style, maintaining the gallop and winning a shade more easily than the margin suggests, as Fallon eased him a little close home after looking over the wrong shoulder and failing to notice the runner-up. Sure to relish the step up to a mile and a half, he should find plenty more improvement between now and Epsom.
**Rule Of Law(USA)**, who was handled by David Loder at two, was without the visor for this seasonal bow but did have his tongue tied. A lazy individual, he took time to pick up before responding to some fairly vigorous driving, and was keeping on strongly at the line. Faster ground will suit him and he looks a worthy second string to Snow Ridge for Epsom, but a sobering statistic is that no horse beaten in the Dante has ever won the Derby.
**Let The Lion Roar** was at the back of the field turning in, but he swept past most of his rivals on the outside once in the straight. The effort flattened out in the last furlong and a half and, like a number of Sadler's Wells' stock, he showed an awkward head carriage. A step up to 12 furlongs will suit him.
**Top Seed(IRE)** finished slightly further behind Let The Lion Roar than he had at Newbury, but this was another solid effort. He may need to travel abroad if he is to add to his single win to date.
**Andean**, impressive in a mile maiden on fast ground, was taking a huge step up in class and tackling a longer trip in different conditions. He appeared not to see it out, having raced a little keenly, but it may be premature to write him off.
**Moscow Ballet(IRE)**, who became warm at the start, did not get home in the dead ground.
**Mutawaffer** weakened steadily in the home straight and does not look up to this class. A half-brother to smart sprinter Munjiz, he might not have stayed, although there is stamina in his pedigree too as his dam is a half-sister to Melbourne Cup winner At Talaq.
**Barbajuan(IRE)** has run three disappointing races now this season and connections must be scratching their heads.
**Skidmark**, who became warm at the start, was always trailing. He has yet to prove himself on turf.
**Oman Gulf(USA)** fractured a cannonbone after his winning debut last July. He used up too much energy in an early duel for the lead with Barbajuan and weakened tamely in the home straight.

## 2044 BANK OF SCOTLAND CORPORATE BANKING HAMBLETON RATED STKS (H'CAP) (LISTED RACE) 7f 205y
**3:00** (3:02) (A) (0-110,110) 4-Y-0+ **£17,400** (£6,600; £3,300; £1,500) **Stalls** Low

Form RPR
40-1 **1** **Autumn Glory (IRE)**[47] 1114 4-8-7 **96** oh2 SDrowne 12 109+
(GWragg) *trckd ldrs. hdwy 3f out: rdn to ld ins last: styd on wl* **9/2**[1]
440- **2** *2* **Duck Row (USA)**[193] 5872 9-9-5 **108** SSanders 5 116
(JARToller) *trckd ldrs: hdwy 3f out: rdn to ld over 1f out: drvn and hdd ins last: kpt on* **25/1**
06-2 **3** *hd* **Mine (IRE)**[25] 1469 6-8-10 **99** (v) TQuinn 11 107
(JDBethell) *hld up towards rr: hdwy 3f out: ev ch ent last: sn rdn and nt qckn* **12/1**
4-01 **4** *shd* **Blue Spinnaker (IRE)**[11] 1773 5-8-9 **98** JPSpencer 17 105+
(MWEasterby) *hld up in rr: gd hdwy on outer over 2f out: rdn over 1f out: styd on strly ins last: n earest fin* **10/1**
-015 **5** *shd* **El Coto**[11] 1758 4-8-13 **102** WSupple 4 109
(BAMcmahon) *lw: in tch: hdwy 3f out: rirdden to chse ldrs over 1f out: drvn and wknd ins last* **7/1**[2]
40-0 **6** *5* **Pentecost**[46] 1125 5-8-9 **98** KFallon 10 94
(AMBalding) *bhd: hdwy 3f out: rdn and kpt on fnl 2f: nreest fin* **14/1**
033- **7** *3* **Play That Tune**[244] 4844 4-8-7 **96** JFanning 9 85
(MJohnston) *chsd ldr: rdn and ev ch 2f out: sn drvn and wknd* **20/1**
26-0 **8** *2* **Convent Girl (IRE)**[46] 1125 4-8-7 **96** oh1 RHavlin 15 80
(MrsPNDutfield) *s.i.s: bhd tl styd on fnl 3f* **50/1**
-010 **9** *½* **Pablo**[18] 1621 5-9-0 **103** (p) MHills 6 86
(BWHills) *in tch: hdwy to chse ldrs 3f out: rdn over 2f out and sn wknd* **12/1**
1/1- **10** *shd* **Prince Tum Tum (USA)**[389] 1118 4-9-2 **105** MJKinane 18 88
(JLDunlop) *bhd tl sme late hdwy* **16/1**
12-3 **11** *1 ¾* **King's County (IRE)**[25] 1456 6-8-8 **96** oh1 ow1 RHughes 13 76
(LMCumani) *lw: in tch: effrt over 3f out: rdn over 2f out and sn btn* **7/1**[2]
04- **12** *5* **Atavus**[200] 5737 7-8-8 **97** JMackay 2 64
(GGMargarson) *led: rdn along over 2f out: hdd & wknd wl over 1f out* **25/1**
14-0 **13** *3* **Calcutta**[29] 1385 8-8-10 **99** RHills 7 59
(BWHills) *in tch: rdn along 3f out: wknd fnl 2f* **25/1**
3-40 **14** *5* **Cote Quest (USA)**[13] 1741 4-8-7 **96** oh4 MartinDwyer 3 45
(SCWilliams) *bhd fr 1/2-way* **40/1**
06-6 **15** *8* **Jazz Messenger (FR)**[18] 1623 4-8-7 **96** oh1 EAhern 14 26
(GAButler) *in tch: effrt over 3f out: sn rdn along and wknd: eased fnl 2f* **8/1**[3]
30-0 **16** *6* **Millennium Force**[11] 1758 6-9-7 **110** CCatlin 1 27
(MRChannon) *a rr* **50/1**
113- **17** *13* **Excellento (USA)**[312] 3013 4-8-13 **102** LDettori 19 —
(SaeedBinSuroor) *racd wd: chsd ldrs: rdn along 4f out and sn wknd* **10/1**
1m 40.75s (3.01) **Going Correction** +0.875s/f (Soft) **17 Ran SP% 123.1**
Speed ratings: **119,117,116,116,116 111,108,106,106,106 104,99,96,91,83 77,64**CSF £128.01 CT £1284.96 TOTE £6.10: £1.70, £4.30, £2.20, £2.50; EX 187.50 Trifecta £1334.20 Pool: £3570.45. 1.90 winning tickets..
**Owner** Mollers Racing **Bred** Margaret Conlon **Trained** Newmarket, Suffolk
**FOCUS**
An oustanding time for a race of its type, and this is sure to prove excellent handicap form. The runners again came up the centre of the track in the home straight and the first five home finished clear.
**NOTEBOOK**
**Autumn Glory(IRE)** landed a tidy gamble. He went up a stone for winning the Spring Mile, but that was nothing like enough to anchor him as he scored a shade comfortably. He did not like the tacky ground according to his trainer and, as this was only the fifth run of his life, he may not have stopped improving yet.
**Duck Row(USA)**, whose owner the Duke of Devonshire died recently, was runner-up in this race in 2002 on his last appearance in a handicap. He will continue to give a good account of himself in minor pattern company but winning opportunities may be hard to come by.
**Mine(IRE)**, with the visor refitted, ran a sound race. He is well suited by big-field handicaps such as this but may need dropping a few pounds.
**Blue Spinnaker(IRE)** went up 8lb for his Thirsk win but may not have stopped improving. Drawn wide, he made good progress on the outside in the straight and, after momentarily appearing to hang fire, finished well.
**El Coto** was back in handicap company off a mark 8lb higher than when winning the Newbury Spring Cup. Just edged out of the placings, he remains at the top of his game.
**Pentecost** ran a decent race but could not get within striking distance of the first five. He does not win too often and is best on faster ground.
**Play That Tune**, placed in Listed company for Henry Cecil last season, ran well for a long way on this seasonal debut but shaped as if a drop back to seven furlongs is required.
**Convent Girl(IRE)** missed the break, and was amongst the stragglers until picking up well in the latter stages and staying on through beaten horses.
**Pablo** had ground conditions to suit, but after improving on to the heels of the leaders his response when brought under pressure was rather disappointing.
**King's County(IRE)** had run well at Newbury, and this was a lacklustre effort off a pound higher mark. His stable is not firing yet, however.
**Atavus** was 13lb lower than when last running in a handicap nearly two years ago. After setting a brisk pace, he was headed below the distance and faded out of the picture. This trip is too far for him and he is better on a faster surface.
**Calcutta** *Official explanation: jockey said horse was unsuited by the ground*
**Cote Quest(USA)** *Official explanation: trainer said filly was found to be in season*
**Jazz Messenger(FR)** *Official explanation: jockey said gelding lost its action*
**Excellento(USA)**, trained last season by David Loder, had to use up energy early on to take up a prominent position from his wide draw and he weakened tamely once into the home straight. Nevertheless, he has grown into a fine-looking four-year-old and he is surely capable of better than this. *Official explanation: jockey said colt was unsuited by the ground*

## 2045 EUROPEAN BREEDERS FUND MAIDEN STKS 6f 3y
**3:35** (3:35) (D) 2-Y-0 **£4,894** (£1,506; £753; £376) **Stalls** High

Form RPR
**1** **Pivotal Flame** 2-9-0 SSanders 6 84
(BAMcmahon) *w'like: scope: hld up: hdwy 1/2-way: effrt to chal on outer whn rdr dropped reins over 1f out: sn led: rdn and edgd rt ins* **14/1**
**2** *¾* **Crimson Sun (USA)** 2-9-0 LDettori 5 82
(SaeedBinSuroor) *w'like: scope: bit bkwd: keen: trckd ldrs: effrt 2f out: rdn to chal 1f out: kpt on wl fnl f* **7/2**[2]
**3** *½* **Capable Guest (IRE)** 2-9-0 TEDurcan 11 81
(MRChannon) *w'like: towards rr: rdn along 1/2-way: edgd lft and hdwy 2f out: styd on wl fnl f: nrst fin* **14/1**
5 **4** *hd* **Fiefdom (IRE)**[25] 1462 2-9-0 JFanning 2 80
(MJohnston) *lw: led: rdn along 2f out: drvn and hdd over 1f out: one pce fnl f* **4/1**[3]
**5** *1 ½* **Amsterdam (IRE)** 2-9-0 JPSpencer 8 76
(APO'Brien, Ire) *w'like: scope: cl up: rdn along 2f out: grad wknd appr last* **3/1**[1]
**6** *shd* **Coleorton Dane** 2-9-0 NCallan 3 75
(KARyan) *w'like: bit bkwd: trckd ldrs: hdwy to chal and ev ch 2f out: sn rdn and wknd over 1f our* **50/1**
3 **7** *1 ¼* **Wilko (USA)**[9] 1826 2-9-0 EAhern 1 71
(JNoseda) *cl up: rdn along 2f out: wknd over 1f out* **7/2**[2]
**8** *hd* **Aire De Mougins (IRE)** 2-9-0 KDarley 7 71
(PCHaslam) *w'like: hld up towards rr: n.m.r 1/2-way: styd on fnl 2f: nrst fin* **25/1**
**9** *10* **Sowerby** 2-9-0 TWilliams 9 41
(MBrittain) *unf: bit bkwd: bhd fr 1/2-way* **66/1**
**10** *6* **Loyalty Lodge (IRE)** 2-9-0 TQuinn 10 23
(JDBethell) *w'like: str: scope: bit bkwd: a rr* **50/1**
**11** *¾* **Lauren Louise** 2-8-9 (t) RWinston 4 16
(NTinkler) *w'like: tall: bit bkwd: prom: rdn along 2f out: sn wknd* **50/1**
1m 18.03s (6.96) **Going Correction** +0.825s/f (Soft) **11 Ran SP% 114.0**
Speed ratings: **86,85,84,84,82 81,80,80,66,58 57**CSF £59.24 TOTE £17.80: £3.10, £2.10, £3.30; EX 85.80.
**Owner** R L Bedding **Bred** Cheveley Park Stud Ltd **Trained** Hopwas, Staffs
**FOCUS**
The best looking field of two-year-olds seen so far this season, and the vast majority of the top juvenile trainers were represented. The winning time was ordinary, but the race will surely produce plenty of future winners.
**NOTEBOOK**
**Pivotal Flame**, a late foal with both speed and stamina in his pedigree, comes from a stable that knows what it takes to get one ready first time up. However, with the likes of Johnston, bin Suroor and Channon represented he was unsurprisingly made a 14/1 shot. He showed more than was expected, and having got into contention stayed on well to hold Crimson Sun despite his jockey momentarily dropping his reins. There should be more to come from this promising colt, and another furlong is sure to bring about further improvement.
**Crimson Sun(USA)** ◆, by Danzig out of the excellent mare Crimplene, who progressed with racing, was the pick of the paddock. He made a most pleasing debut, going forward at the end despite having raced keenly, and leaving the impression he will improve for the experience. He too will get another furlong and should have little trouble winning his maiden.
**Capable Guest(IRE)** ◆, a 130,000gns purchase who is a half-brother to sprint winner Petardia's Magic, looked all at sea for much of the race and his rider seemed to have accepted the fact he was not going to win. However, he finally got the hang of things and finished strongly under tender handling, suggesting he would have won in another half a furlong. With the run under his belt and sure to benefit mentally, he should reverse form with those that finished in front of him were they to meet again.
**Fiefdom(IRE)** ◆, who was typical of his trainer's juveniles on his debut, in that he was too inexperienced to get involved, knew what was required of him today and stuck on well, having given way just over a furlong out. By Singspiel, he can only improve for a stiffer test of stamina and will not be long in winning.
**Amsterdam(IRE)** ◆ has a blend of both speed and stamina in his pedigree, being related to both middle-distance and sprint winners. He showed up well for a long way before tiring late on, and will improve for the outing and seven furlongs.
**Coleorton Dane**, who was very green in the paddock, is bred to be speedy and ran well for one at his price. This looked a decent heat and he should have little trouble winning his maiden.
**Wilko(USA)**, who shaped with promise on heavy ground at Kempton earlier in the month, was expected to improve for this extra furlong, but having raced prominently found little for pressure and folded disappointingly. He is undoubtedly better than this and maybe just found the run coming too soon after his debut.
**Aire De Mougins(IRE)** ◆, who is bred to be effective at two, did not get the clearest of runs through, but stayed on well towards the end and was closing with every stride at the line. Another furlong will suit, but he should be able to win at this trip and pulled ten lengths clear of the remainder.

## 2046 TADCASTER MAIDEN STKS 6f 217y
**4:10** (4:11) (D) 3-Y-0 **£4,933** (£1,518; £759; £379) **Stalls** Low

Form RPR
2 **1** **Soldier's Tale (USA)**[27] 1413 3-9-0 EAhern 5 96
(JNoseda) *lw: trckd ldrs: hdwy 1/2-way: led wl over 1f out: sn pushed clr and styd on wl* **4/9**[1]
6 **2** *5* **Capestar (IRE)**[28] 1400 3-8-9 TQuinn 12 78
(BGPowell) *in tch: hdwy to trckd ldrs 3f out: rdn to chse wnr over 1f out: sn drvn and no imp* **14/1**[3]
**3** *9* **New Order** 3-8-9 RHughes 8 55
(BWHills) *unf: scope: lw: hmpd s: sn in tch: hdwy to chse ldrs 3f out: rdn 2f out and sn one pce* **7/2**[2]
0 **4** *1 ¾* **Peter Paul Rubens (USA)**[9] 1830 3-9-0 KDarley 7 55
(PFICole) *wnt rt s: keen and sn led: clr 1/2-way: rdn along 2f out: sn hdd wknd* **28/1**

0 **5** *1 3/4* **Imtalkinggibberish**[29] [1386] 3-9-0 ........................ SWKelly 9 51
(JRJenkins) *in tch: hdwy to chse ldrs over 2f out: sn rdn and edgd lft and rt: drvn and plugged on same pce* **25/1**
**6** *nk* **Huggin Mac (IRE)** 3-8-2 ........................ SuzanneFrance(7) 4 45
(NBycroft) *leggy: s.i.s and bhd tl sme late hdwy* **100/1**
0- **7** *1 1/2* **Noble Desert (FR)**[135] [6248] 3-8-9 ........................ MartinDwyer 6 41
(RGuest) *towards rr: hdwy 1/2-way: rdn along over 2f out and nvr a factor* **100/1**
2U6- **8** *2* **Olivander**[210] [5572] 3-9-0 80 ........................ LDettori 10 41
(GAButler) *lw: chsd ldrs: rdn along over 3f out and sn wknd* **14/1**[3]
00 **9** *5* **Gustavo**[9] [1820] 3-9-0 ........................ MHills 1 28
(BWHills) *dwlt: sn outpcd and a rr* **50/1**
30- **10** *2 1/2* **Shinko Femme (IRE)**[190] [5916] 3-8-9 62 ........................ WRyan 11 16
(NTinkler) *midfield: rdn along 1/2-way: sn wknd* **66/1**
0- **11** *6* **Albadi**[196] [5825] 3-9-0 ........................ TEDurcan 2 —
(CEBrittain) *bkwd: a rr* **66/1**
**12** *10* **Dee En Ay (IRE)** 3-9-0 ........................ SSanders 3 —
(TDEasterby) *w'like: bit bkwd: prom: rdn along after 2f: sn outpcd and bhd fnl 3f* **66/1**

1m 28.63s (5.32) **Going Correction** +0.825s/f (Soft) **12** Ran SP% **120.5**
Speed ratings: **102,96,86,84,82 81,79,77,71,69 62,50**CSF £8.82 TOTE £1.50: £1.10, £3.00, £1.90; EX 6.90.
**Owner** Syd Belzberg **Bred** Budget Stables Inc **Trained** Newmarket, Suffolk

**FOCUS**
A good display from Soldier's Tale in winning what was admittedly a weak race.

**NOTEBOOK**
**Soldier's Tale(USA)**, a highly encouraging second on his debut at Newmarket, won this modest maiden as he was entitled to and deserves a crack at a better race.
**Capestar(IRE)** confirmed the promise of his Newmarket debut and was the only one to try and go in pursuit of the winner. An ordinary race is hers for the taking.
**New Order** was not disgraced on this racecourse debut and can only improve for a step up in trip.
**Peter Paul Rubens(USA)** raced keenly at the head of affairs before being readily brushed aside by the front three. He will be of more interest when qualified for handicaps.
**Imtalkinggibberish** improved on his debut effort and is another future handicapper.
**Huggin Mac(IRE)** *Official explanation: jockey said filly stumbled and lost its action*
**Olivander** was most disappointing and is one to avoid until showing more.
**Gustavo** needs one more run to qualify for a handicap mark and will improve for further.

## 2047 TOTEEXACTA H'CAP — 1m 5f 197y
4:45 (4:45) (C) (0-90,89) 4-Y-O+ — £11,056 (£3,402; £1,701; £850) Stalls Low

Form — RPR
50-5 **1** **Star Member (IRE)**[9] [1832] 5-9-2 **77** ........................ KFallon 10 92
(APJarvis) *midfield: hdwy on inner over 4f out: effrt wl over 1f out: rdn to ld ins last: sn clr* **14/1**
060/ **2** *3* **Captain Miller**[944] [5226] 8-8-6 **67** ........................ TQuinn 18 78
(NJHenderson) *lw: a.p: hdwy to ld over 2f out and sn clr: rdn over 1f out: hdd ins last and kpt on same pce* **9/1**[3]
0023 **3** *3* **High Point (IRE)**[32] [1329] 6-9-5 **80** ........................ LDettori 7 87
(GPEnright) *hld up: stdy hdwy over 5f out: rdn to chse ldrs over 2f out: sn drvn and one pce* **6/1**[2]
-060 **4** *3 1/2* **Moon Emperor**[32] [1329] 7-9-5 **80** ........................(v) MJKinane 9 82
(JRJenkins) *hld up in rr: hdwy on inner over 3f out: rdn 2f out: kpt on same pce* **25/1**
0313 **5** *1/2* **George Stubbs (USA)**[10] [1785] 6-8-4 **65** ........................ GGibbons 17 66
(MJPolglase) *chsd ldrs: rdn along 3f out: drvn 2f out and grad wknd* **20/1**
-035 **6** *1 1/2* **Nawow**[25] [1457] 4-9-0 **76** ........................ KDalgleish 6 75
(PDCundell) *hld up in rr: hdwy 4f out: rdn along to chse ldrs 2f out: sn drvn and no imp* **12/1**
-504 **7** *3/4* **Sahem (IRE)**[10] [1785] 7-9-1 **76** ........................ RHughes 13 74
(DEddy) *lw: hld up: hdwy on outer over 3f out: rdn to chse ldrs over 2f out: sn drvn and btn* **14/1**
2161 **8** *8* **Jorobaden (FR)**[9] [1832] 4-9-11 **87** 4ex ........................ JQuinn 19 74
(CFWall) *lw: hld up in rr: hdwy over 5f out: in tch and rdn along whn hung lft 2f out: sn btn* **11/2**[1]
04-0 **9** *1 3/4* **Promoter**[25] [1457] 4-9-12 **88** ........................ EAhern 5 73
(JNoseda) *lw: led: rdn along over 3f out: hdd over 2f out and sn wknd* **9/1**[3]
210 **10** *1 3/4* **Gran Dana (IRE)**[16] [1661] 4-9-4 **80** ........................ JFanning 3 62
(MJohnston) *prom: rdn along over 3f out: wknd over 2f out* **20/1**
3-05 **11** *5* **Mana D'Argent (IRE)**[7] [1880] 7-9-7 **89** ........................ WHogg(7) 14 64
(MJohnston) *midfield: hdwy 5f out: rdn along over 3f out and nvr a factor* **16/1**
60-0 **12** *10* **Freedom Now (IRE)**[18] [1615] 6-9-0 **75** ........................ SDrowne 1 36
(MDHammond) *chsd ldrs: rdn along 4f out: sn wknd* **33/1**
60-2 **13** *5* **Highland Games (IRE)**[12] [1744] 4-9-9 **85** ........................ KDarley 11 39
(JGGiven) *midfield: hdwy on outer over 4f out: sn rdn along and nvr a factor* **16/1**
1-00 **14** *3* **Bid For Fame (USA)**[25] [1457] 7-9-5 **80** ........................(p) WRyan 8 30
(NTinkler) *a rr* **33/1**
1-00 **15** *4* **Snow's Ride**[32] [1329] 4-9-3 **79** ........................ MartinDwyer 4 23
(WRMuir) *bhd fr 1/2-way* **50/1**
1-03 **16** *3/4* **Greenwich Meantime**[18] [1615] 4-9-4 **80** ........................ JPSpencer 2 23
(MrsJRRamsden) *hld up in rr: sme hdwy 3f out: sn rdn and btn* **6/1**[2]
11-5 **17** *6* **Tempsford (USA)**[57] [1030] 4-9-12 **88** ........................ SSanders 12 23
(SirMarkPrescott) *cl up: rdn along 4f out: sn wknd* **16/1**
033/ **18** *dist* **Weet For Me**[909] [5731] 8-9-10 **85** ........................ WSupple 20 —
(RHollinshead) *bit bkwd: chsd ldrs: rdn along over 5f out: sn wknd* **100/1**

3m 6.09s (9.69) **Going Correction** +0.875s/f (Soft)
**WFA** 4 from 5yo+ 1lb **18** Ran SP% **124.8**
Speed ratings: **107,105,103,101,101 100,100,95,94,93 90,84,82,80,78 77,74,—**CSF £126.82 CT £857.76 TOTE £18.90: £5.00, £2.20, £2.00, £6.10; EX 167.00 Place 6 £19.90, Place 5 £14.74.
**Owner** Jarvis Associates **Bred** Killeen Castle Stud **Trained** Twyford, Bucks
■ Stewards Enquiry : K Fallon one-day ban: used whip above shoulder height (May 23)

**FOCUS**
A competitive handicap, if not quite up to the usual standard for track. Star Member won comfortably and looks one to have on your side in future.

**NOTEBOOK**
**Star Member(IRE)** ◆ is a pretty consistent performer in this sort of race but was recording his first win since his debut in June 2002. He stays well and looks to have improved from four to five, so can be expected to win again in a higher grade.
**Captain Miller** was having his first start since October 2001 and it was the lack of a previous outing that appeared to foil him, as he looked the most likely winner when going on two out. He can pick up a similar race if going the right way.
**High Point(IRE)** hides nothing from the Handicapper, but is an honest individual who stays well and should continue to pay his way.
**Moon Emperor**, dropped 7lb since his last outing, returned to something like his best, the visor having a better effect than last time.
**George Stubbs(USA)** confirmed Hamilton form with Sahem and ran his race.
**Nawow** plugged on from the rear, but is not a winner.
**Sahem(IRE)** seems to struggle to get this sort of trip and could do with dropping back to a mile and a half.
**Jorobaden(FR)** was the disappointment of the race, hanging under pressure and looking awkward.
**Promoter** has become disappointing and the change in tactics failed to make any difference.
**Gran Dana(IRE)** was not disgraced for one so lightly raced.
**Highland Games(IRE)** *Official explanation: jockey said gelding lost its action*
**Greenwich Meantime** never really got involved and was a disappointment.
T/Jkpt: Not won. T/Plt: £217.60 to a £1 stake. Pool: £111,791.90. 374.90 winning tickets. T/Qpdt: £14.80 to a £1 stake. Pool: £9,142.90. 455.55 winning tickets. JR

2048 - 2050a (Foreign Racing) - See Raceform Interactive

# [1963]LINGFIELD (L-H)
Thursday, May 13

**OFFICIAL GOING: Standard**

## 2051 RADIO MERCURY ROADSHOW APPRENTICE BANDED STKS — 7f (P)
6:00 (6:02) (H) 3-Y-O+ — £1,435 (£410; £205) Stalls Low

Form — RPR
-034 **1** **Ballygriffin Kid**[27] [1443] 4-9-4 40 ........................ RLucey-Butler(3) 1 43
(TPMcgovern) *hld up bhd ldrs: effrt on inner over 1f out: shkn up to ld last 150yds: styd on wl* **5/2**[2]
0-42 **2** *1 1/4* **Sea Jade (IRE)**[9] [1863] 5-9-7 40 ........................ DTudhope 2 40
(JWPayne) *mde most: set slow pce to 3f out: rdn and flashed tail fr over 1f out: hdd and nt qckn last 150yds* **6/4**[1]
3431 **3** *1 1/2* **Rathmullan**[2] [2012] 5-9-8 40 ........................(b) LiamJones(5) 4 42
(EAWheeler) *racd wd: cl up: chal fr 3f out to 2f out: fnd nil over 1f out: kpt on nr fin* **4/1**[3]
0632 **4** *nk* **Newcorr (IRE)**[9] [1861] 5-9-2 35 ........................ MHalford(5) 3 35
(JJBridger) *pressed ldr: chal fr 3f out: ev ch over 1f out: fdd fnl f* **9/2**

1m 28.3s (2.36) **Going Correction** +0.05s/f (Slow) **4** Ran SP% **106.8**
Speed ratings: **88,86,84,84**CSF £6.50 TOTE £3.30; EX 8.30.
**Owner** Tommy Breen **Bred** Tommy Breen **Trained** Lewes, E Sussex
■ Robert Lucey-Butler's first Flat winner.

**FOCUS**
Poor horses, and a modest winning time.

**NOTEBOOK**
**Ballygriffin Kid**, who ran as though he would appreciate the return to seven two outings back, enjoyed a good run up the rail to get up inside the last. He appears suited by patient tactics, and, dropped in like this, his trainer is optimistic he will get a mile.
**Sea Jade(IRE)** looked to hold a strong chance in this grade but she flashed her tail under pressure and might not be the most trustworthy. She is currently in foal to Lujain.
**Rathmullan** has never shown his best here and looks far more comfortable on the Fibresand.
**Newcorr(IRE)**, collared for third inside the last, appreciates a bit of give, so this surface is probably not ideal.

## 2052 BOOK A BOX AT LINGFIELD BANDED STKS — 1m (P)
6:30 (6:30) (H) 3-Y-O+ — £1,435 (£410; £205) Stalls High

Form — RPR
0-60 **1** **Tarkwa**[119] [537] 5-9-7 40 ........................ BDoyle 2 49
(RMHCowell) *trckd ldng pair: pushed along over 3f out: effrt over 1f out: drvn to ld wl ins fnl f: jst hld on* **10/1**
0040 **2** *shd* **Robin Sharp**[3] [1986] 6-9-7 40 ........................(p) JQuinn 3 49
(JAkehurst) *rdn thrght: pressed ldr: led u.p over 2f out: hdd wl ins fnl f: kpt on: jst failed* **5/2**[2]
0063 **3** *5* **Mythical Charm**[28] [1404] 5-9-7 40 ........................ JTate 1 37
(JJBridger) *led: rdn and hdd over 2f out: one pce over 1f out* **9/4**[1]
04-0 **4** *3/4* **Brandywine Bay (IRE)**[37] [1278] 4-9-7 40 ........................(p) GBaker 4 36
(APJones) *s.s: detached in last tl clsd and in tch 3f out: sn rdn: one pce fnl 2f* **5/1**
6-22 **5** *7* **Benjamin (IRE)**[10] [1494] 6-9-7 40 ........................(bt) VSlattery 5 19
(JaneSouthcombe) *chsd ldrs: rdn 3f out: wknd 2f out* **7/2**[3]

1m 41.36s (1.81) **Going Correction** +0.05s/f (Slow) **5** Ran SP% **107.3**
Speed ratings: **92,91,86,86,79**CSF £33.00 TOTE £14.10: £4.70, £1.70; EX 34.80.
**Owner** J B Robinson **Bred** J B Robinson **Trained** Six Mile Bottom, Cambs

**FOCUS**
A moderate winning time, even for a banded stakes.

**NOTEBOOK**
**Tarkwa**, returning from a four-month break, just edged out the eventual runner-up following a lengthy battle up the straight. She stays farther, but her racing days are numbered as she is currently in foal to Classic Cliche.
**Robin Sharp** was ridden along most of the way and saw the mile out well, only being edged out at the finish. The sounder surface appeared to suit.
**Mythical Charm**, in a change of tactics, made the running. She dropped away disappointingly from the turn in though, and one can imagine hold-up tactics being re-employed next time.
**Brandywine Bay(IRE)** was always struggling to go the pace.
**Benjamin(IRE)** is a long-standing maiden but his recent form suggested that he should have run better this.

## 2053 SATURDAY NIGHT RACING HERE STARTS SOON BANDED STKS — 1m 2f (P)
7:00 (7:02) (H) 3-Y-O+ — £1,662 (£475; £237) Stalls Low

Form — RPR
0441 **1** **Kingsdon (IRE)**[14] [1722] 7-9-7 45 ........................(vt) JFEgan 7 62
(TJFitzgerald) *wl plcd: effrt over 2f out: led on inner 1f out: sn pushed clr* **4/1**[1]
0253 **2** *4* **Ryan's Bliss (IRE)**[22] [1545] 4-9-4 45 ........................ RMiles(3) 12 54
(TDMcCarthy) *hld up: prog on outer 1/2-way: effrt to ld over 2f out: hdd and outpcd 1f out* **12/1**
**3** *3* **Fairland (IRE)**[32] [4592] 5-9-0 45 ........................ LSmith(7) 14 48
(SDow) *s.s: racd wd: wl in rr: stdy prog fr 3f out: nudged along and styd on wl fr over 1f out: hopeless task* **50/1**
1133 **4** *1/2* **Mrs Cube**[52] [1079] 5-9-7 45 ........................ PMcCabe 10 47
(PHowling) *t.k.h: hld up in tch: prog to ld 3f out: hdd over 2f out: sn outpcd* **11/1**
1623 **5** *3* **Galey River (USA)**[2] [2015] 5-9-4 45 ........................(p) DCorby(3) 11 42
(JJSheehan) *racd in midfield: hrd rdn over 3f out: one pce and no ch w ldrs* **10/1**
2514 **6** *hd* **Due To Me**[3] [1986] 4-9-7 45 ........................(p) SWhitworth 3 41
(GLMoore) *trckd ldrs: lost pl 1/2-way: rdn 3f out: one pce after* **7/1**[3]
5640 **7** *1* **Our Glenard**[5] [1962] 5-9-0 45 ........................ LTreadwell(7) 2 39
(SLKeightley) *s.s: sn drvn in rr: effrt in midfield 3f out: no prog after* **10/1**

0-00 **8** *nk* **Down To The Woods (USA)**[13] 1754 6-9-2 45................(p) TEaves(5) 8 39
(RDEWoodhouse) *rdn in rr early: sn in midfield: drvn and struggling over 4f out: sn no ch* **20/1**

3011 **9** *1/2* **Iamback**[2] 2015 4-9-13 45........................................ DHolland 6 44
(MissGayKelleway) *trckd ldrs: rdn 3f out: outpcd over 2f out: wknd over 1f out* **11/2**[2]

-224 **10** *1* **Six Pack (IRE)**[8] 1888 6-9-7 45........................................ CCatlin 13 36
(AndrewTurnell) *a in rr: shkn up and no prog over 2f out* **11/1**

44-3 **11** *3* **Mr Fleming**[65] 997 5-9-7 45........................................(b) CLowther 5 30
(DrJDScargill) *t.k.h: led for 2f: led again 4f out to 3f out: sn wknd* **33/1**

0000 **12** *5* **Mandahar (IRE)**[31] 1352 5-9-7 45........................................ JQuinn 1 21
(AWCarroll) *rdn in rr early: a struggling* **25/1**

-513 **13** *nk* **Husky (POL)**[16] 1691 6-9-7 45........................................(p) BDoyle 4 20
(RMHCowell) *led after 2f to 4f out: wknd 3f out: eased* **8/1**

250- **14** *23* **Lost Spirit**[208] 5631 8-9-0 45................................ NataliaGemelova(7) 9 —
(PWHiatt) *reluctant to go to post: chsd ldrs: rdn and lost pl 1/2-way: t.o* **20/1**

2m 7.11s (-0.74) **Going Correction** +0.05s/f (Slow) **14 Ran SP% 119.8**
Speed ratings: **104,100,98,98,95 95,94,94,94,93 90,86,86,68**CSF £48.86 TOTE £6.00: £2.00, £4.80, £31.50; EX 84.50.
**Owner** Mike Browne **Bred** Barronstown Stud **Trained** Norton, N Yorks

**FOCUS**
A decent winning time for the grade of contest.

**NOTEBOOK**
**Kingsdon(IRE)**, who was fairly well supported, has been in good form this spring and followed up his Ayr victory in good style. He is clearly a useful tool in this lowly company and it would not be a surprise to see him turned out again before he is reassessed.
**Ryan's Bliss(IRE)** took it up turning into the straight and made a brave attempt to break her maiden tag, but the in-form winner proved just too strong. She deserves to get off the mark and clearly has the ability to do so in this grade.
**Fairland(IRE)**, making his All-Weather debut, was given an awful lot to do after missing the break. Passing rivals on the outside, he stayed on well without being hard ridden, and is one to note for a similar race.
**Mrs Cube** ran a fair race but appears to have hit a class barrier since moving into 0-45 grade.
**Galey River(USA)** did not find the re-application of cheekpieces bringing about an improved display.
**Iamback** is clearly happier on the Fibresand surface.
**Husky(POL)** *Official explanation: jockey said gelding had hung right*

## 2054 NEW SITE @ LINGFIELD-RACECOURSE.CO.UK TRI-BANDED STKS — 1m 2f (P)
**7:30** (7:32) (H) 3-Y-O — **£1,438** (£411; £205) **Stalls** Low

Form RPR

-502 **1** **Joint Destiny (IRE)**[16] 1695 3-9-0 45........................................ DHolland 4 51
(EJO'Neill) *t.k.h: hld up in last pair: smooth prog over 3f out: led over 1f out: sn drvn clr: kpt on fnl f* **7/2**[2]

0432 **2** *1* **Divina**[7] 1916 3-8-2 35 ow1........................................(v) BReilly(3) 2 40
(SLKeightley) *t.k.h in midfield: lost pl and last 1/2-way: rdn and prog on outer over 2f out: chsd wnr 1f out: clsd but a hld* **11/2**[3]

6040 **3** *3* **Shalati Princess**[11] 1800 3-9-0 45........................................ PMcCabe 7 43
(JCFox) *chsd ldrs: pushed along over 4f out: outpcd over 2f out: kpt on one pce after* **12/1**

4123 **4** *1/2* **Oktis Morilious (IRE)**[20] 1579 3-9-0 45........................................ JQuinn 1 42
(AWCarroll) *racd in midfield: pushed along over 4f out: outpcd over 2f out: styd on fr over 1f out* **2/1**[1]

4230 **5** *2* **Sir Frank Gibson**[71] 957 3-9-0 45........................................ CCatlin 3 39
(MrsJaneGalpin) *chsd ldr to 6f out: lost pl and struggling over 4f out: no ch over 2f out: kpt on fnl f* **9/1**

0325 **6** *shd* **Regency Malaya**[2] 2016 3-9-0 45........................................(bt) SRighton 6 38
(MFHarris) *s.s: t.k.h and hld up tl prog to ld 6f out: hdd & wknd over 1f out* **7/1**

-003 **7** *12* **Lenwade**[14] 1726 3-8-9 40........................................(b[1]) NPollard 8 11
(GGMargarson) *led to 6f out: chsd ldr to over 2f out: sn wknd* **10/1**

6634 **8** *1* **Harbour Princess**[9] 1863 3-8-1 35........................................(v[1]) RMiles(3) 5 4
(MFHarris) *t.k.h: in tch: rdn and struggling over 4f out: sn bhd* **25/1**

2m 9.77s (1.92) **Going Correction** +0.05s/f (Slow) **8 Ran SP% 114.1**
Speed ratings: **94,93,90,90,88 88,79,78**CSF £22.93 TOTE £3.30: £1.10, £1.50, £2.90; EX 19.50.
**Owner** T F Brennan **Bred** Thomas F Brennan **Trained** Newmarket, Suffolk

**FOCUS**
This race was run in a time 2.66sec slower than the contest won by Kingsdon.

**NOTEBOOK**
**Joint Destiny(IRE)** travelled well and handled the step up in trip with little problem. Currently in foal to Tobougg, she is clearly in good form at present and should continue to run well in this grade.
**Divina** had looked sure to appreciate the step up in trip and certainly stayed it well, but the winner got first run on her and went beyond recall. She has the ability to win in this grade.
**Shalati Princess** is fairly slow but she kept on well enough.
**Oktis Morilious(IRE)** looked to hold every chance back over this trip, but he let the winner get first run and did not get the clearest of passages himself. He should still have done better than this, though.

## 2055 COME EVENING RACING 29TH MAY BANDED STKS — 1m 4f (P)
**8:00** (8:00) (H) 4-Y-O+ — **£1,281** (£366; £183) **Stalls** Low

Form RPR

5013 **1** **Buying A Dream (IRE)**[16] 1700 7-9-0 35........................................ CCatlin 7 34
(AndrewTurnell) *settled in last pair: pushed along and prog over 4f out: chsd ldrs 2f out: styd on u.p to ld last 100yds* **11/4**[1]

3541 **2** *3/4* **Adjiram (IRE)**[9] 1861 8-9-6 30........................................(v) JQuinn 6 39
(AWCarroll) *t.k.h: trckd ldr after 2f: led over 4f out: drvn and hdd over 3f out: rallied to ld over 1f out: hdd and no ex last 100yds* **7/1**

-555 **3** *1/2* **Sylvan Twister**[14] 1728 5-9-0 30........................................ JFEgan 10 32
(PMitchell) *dwlt: racd in rr: rdn 5f out: prog u.p 3f out: clsd on ldrs fr 2f out: jst unable to chal* **16/1**

00/0 **4** *1/2* **Italian Counsel (IRE)**[40] 663 7-9-0 30........................................ DHolland 8 31
(LADace) *chsd ldrs: pushed along fr 8f out: effrt u.p over 2f out : kpt on fnl f: nvr able to chal* **11/2**[3]

6346 **5** *2* **Hellbent**[8] 1885 5-9-0 35........................................ VSlattery 2 28
(JAOsborne) *dwlt: t.k.h and hld up in midfield: effrt 3f out: drvn and kpt on one pce fr over 1f out* **7/1**

/0-5 **6** *1 1/4* **Ripcord (IRE)**[119] 539 6-9-0 35........................................ NPollard 5 26
(BRJohnson) *t.k.h: led 1f: styd prom: trckd ldr over 4f out: led gng easily over 3f out: drvn 2f out: hdd & wknd over 1f out* **14/1**

00/0 **7** *10* **Golden Legend (IRE)**[3] 2006 7-8-11 30........................................ RMiles(3) 4 10
(RJPrice) *dwlt: settled in midfield: rdn and outpcd over 3f out: eased whn no ch over 1f out* **20/1**

-006 **8** *3/4* **Bridewell (USA)**[14] 1722 5-8-9 30........................................(p) TEaves(5) 1 9
(FWatson) *rdn in rr after 3f: sn struggling: wl bhd fnl 3f* **14/1**

-006 **9** *14* **Superclean**[20] 1581 4-8-9 30........................................(v) BSwarbrick(5) 3 —
(AWCarroll) *a in rr: str reminders 7f out: sn lost tch: t.o* **33/1**

0321 **10** *shd* **The Last Mohican**[7] 1917 5-9-6 30........................................(p) PMcCabe 9 —
(PHowling) *led after 1f to over 4f out: wknd rapidly: t.o* **7/2**[2]

2m 35.57s (1.33) **Going Correction** +0.05s/f (Slow) **10 Ran SP% 116.2**
Speed ratings: **97,96,96,95,94 93,87,86,77,77**CSF £22.38 TOTE £3.40: £1.40, £3.80, £2.20; EX 21.20.
**Owner** Robinson Webster (holdings) Ltd **Bred** James Kavanagh **Trained** Malton, N Yorks

**FOCUS**
The leaders appeared to go off too quick.

**NOTEBOOK**
**Buying A Dream(IRE)** appreciated the return to Polytrack and the fast pace the leaders set eventually played into his hands. His style of running suggests that a slowly-run tactical affair is the last thing he would want.
**Adjiram(IRE)**, a winner over a mile last time, ran well in defeat but the suspicion is that he went off too fast and did not get home. Slightly less aggressive tactics may pay off next time.
**Sylvan Twister** ran his best race to date thanks to the strong gallop which brought him into contention late on.
**Italian Counsel(IRE)** just kept on under pressure. He is badly handicapped over hurdles but the faster ground of summer will suit him.
**Hellbent**, who is not one to trust, never really got competitive this time.
**Ripcord(IRE)**, having his first start for four months, has been lightly raced in recent years. He looked to do too much in front on this occasion and his finishing position does not reflect an encouraging performance.
**The Last Mohican** blew his chance by doing much too much in front. *Official explanation: jockey said gelding ran too free early on.*

## 2056 LINGFIELD LEISURE CLUB BANDED STKS — 6f (P)
**8:30** (8:30) (H) 3-Y-O+ — **£1,438** (£411; £205) **Stalls** Low

Form RPR

600- **1** **Bronx Bomber**[272] 4141 6-9-0 35........................................(b[1]) CLowther 4 43
(DrJDScargill) *chsd ldrs: rdn 1/2-way: prog 2f out: drvn to ld over 1f out : hanging rt but kpt on fnl f* **13/2**[3]

2215 **2** *1 3/4* **Tiny Tim (IRE)**[8] 1890 6-8-13 35........................................ TBlock(7) 1 44
(AMBalding) *trckd ldrs gng wl: effrt over 1f out: rdn to chse wnr ent fnl f: no imp* **11/10**[1]

000- **3** *5* **Crusty Lily**[363] 1643 8-9-0 30........................................(p) BDoyle 5 23
(RMHCowell) *pressed ldr: rdn to ld over 2f out: hdd over 1f out: fdd fnl f* **7/1**

060- **4** *2* **Mrs Boz**[177] 6022 4-9-0 35........................................ JQuinn 2 17
(AWCarroll) *s.i.s: hld up in last pair: prog over 2f out: rdn and nt qckn over 1f out* **8/1**

00-6 **5** *3 1/2* **Madame Roux**[8] 1890 6-9-0 30........................................ GCarter 7 7
(CDrew) *s.i.s: racd in last pair: rdn and struggling over 2f out* **14/1**

4000 **6** *3/4* **Janes Valentine**[3] 1986 4-8-9 35........................................(v[1]) NChalmers(5) 3 4
(JJBridger) *mde most to over 2f out: wknd rapidly over 1f out* **5/1**[2]

0-00 **7** *3 1/2* **Kafil (USA)**[28] 1403 10-9-0 30........................................(b) JTate 6 —
(JJBridger) *pressed ldrs to 1/2-way: sn wknd* **16/1**

1m 13.1s (0.18) **Going Correction** +0.05s/f (Slow) **7 Ran SP% 113.8**
Speed ratings: **100,97,91,88,83 82,78**CSF £13.99 TOTE £11.70: £2.60, £1.50; EX 22.30 Place 6 £214.46, Place 5 £58.14.
**Owner** R A Dalton **Bred** Jonathan Crisp **Trained** Newmarket, Suffolk

**FOCUS**
The winner is unexposed in this grade and could be capable of better.

**NOTEBOOK**
**Bronx Bomber**, taking a huge drop in trip and grade, and sporting blinkers for the first time, came in for market support on his first start for nine months. He ended a long losing streak for his trainer and this is clearly now his level.
**Tiny Tim(IRE)** had the blinkers left off this time and ran well enough back on his favourite All-Weather surface. He was unlucky to a certain extent in running into the winner, who is unexposed at this level, but he has been beaten a number of times in this grade.
**Crusty Lily**, who has not won for almost five years, was having her first start for a year. She ran as though the outing was needed, weakening from a furlong out.
**Mrs Boz**, well beaten in three maidens, was taking a big drop in class on her return from a six-month absence but did not show much.
**Janes Valentine** set a fair pace in the first-time visor but was beating a retreat before entering the straight.

T/Plt: £564.30 to a £1 stake. Pool: £32,006.30. 41.40 winning tickets. T/Qpdt: £9.50 to a £1 stake. Pool: £3,447.30. 267.55 winning tickets. JN

# 1796 SALISBURY (R-H)
Thursday, May 13

**OFFICIAL GOING: Good (good to firm in places)**

## 2057 "JAMAICA INN AT SALISBURY PLAYHOUSE" MAIDEN STKS (DIV I) — 5f
**1:40** (1:42) (D) 2-Y-O — **£4,663** (£1,435; £717; £358) **Stalls** High

Form RPR

3 **1** **Obe Gold**[5] 1961 2-9-0........................................ TEDurcan 5 79
(MRChannon) *trckd ldrs: chal fr 2f out: rdn to ld wl ins fnl f* **11/2**[2]

0323 **2** *3/4* **Grand Option**[26] 1462 2-8-11........................................ TPQueally(3) 4 76
(BWDuke) *led: rdn 2f out: kpt slt advantage tl hdd and no ex wl ins last* **8/1**

**3** *2* **Angel Sprints** 2-8-9........................................ ADaly 9 63
(LGCottrell) *in tch: edgd rt to rail over 3f out: rdn 2f out: styd on wl fnl f: nt rch ldrs* **50/1**

**4** *shd* **Galeota (IRE)** 2-9-0........................................ PDobbs 2 68
(RHannon) *in tch: pushed along and one pce over 2f out: styd on fnl f but nvr gng pce of ldrs* **4/6**[1]

**5** *3/4* **Empire's Ghodha** 2-8-11........................................ LPKeniry(3) 10 65
(BJMeehan) *chsd ldr: rdn to chal 2f out: no ex ins fnl f* **20/1**

**6** *1/2* **Wood Spirit (IRE)** 2-8-9........................................ RHavlin 1 58
(MrsPNDutfield) *outpcd and rdn 1/2-way: styd on wl fnl f but nt pce to rch ldrs* **50/1**

**7** *1 3/4* **Dartanian** 2-9-0........................................ NCallan 3 56
(PDEvans) *mid-div: rdn and kpt on same pce fr 1/2-way* **66/1**

**8** *3/4* **Heidi's Dash (IRE)** 2-8-9........................................ SDrowne 6 48
(RCharlton) *bhd: sn rdn: nvr gng pce to rch ldrs* **7/1**[3]

**9** *1 3/4* **Black Draft** 2-9-0........................................ MJO'Hara 11 46
(Jean-ReneAuvray) *s.i.s: hmpd on rails over 3f out: swtchd lft to outside over 2f out: nvr nr ldrs* **66/1**


The Form Book, Raceform Ltd, Compton, RG20 6NL

10 *nk* **Don't Tell Trigger (IRE)** 2-8-9 .......... JDSmith 8 39
(JSMoore) *sn outpcd* **33/1**

62.74 secs (1.17) **Going Correction** +0.05s/f (Good) **10** Ran SP% **113.6**
Speed ratings: **92,90,87,87,86 85,82,81,78,78**CSF £42.97 TOTE £6.10: £1.80, £1.80, £7.30; EX 20.70.
**Owner** M Channon **Bred** Mrs M Mason **Trained** West Ilsley, Berks

**FOCUS**
A modest maiden in which the two with previous experience fought out the finish.

**NOTEBOOK**
**Obe Gold** readily improved on his debut effort to score in determined fashion. He handled this quicker ground and, while he does not look one of his stable's leading lights, he should progress further.
**Grand Option** pinged out of the gates and did little wrong, but just found another too good. He set the standard on form and is now looking exposed, but always seems to give his best.
**Angel Sprints** made a pleasing debut. She was distinctly green early on and got the hang of things all too late, but she will come on plenty for the experience and looks capable of winning a similar event.
**Galeota(IRE)** ◆, heavily backed to make a winning debut, was too green to go the pace early on and tended to hang to his right on the outside of the field before running on too late in the final furlong. He will have learnt plenty from this, has the scope to be a useful juvenile and will surely not be long in losing his maiden tag.
**Empire's Ghodha** ran well until his lack of experience told late on. He showed plenty of dash and looks the type to do well in nurseries.
**Wood Spirit(IRE)** ran as though he would come on for the experience and another furlong.
**Heidi's Dash(IRE)**, who cost 140,000gns, was never on terms, but it will be a suprise if she does not leave this form behind when her stable gets into top gear.

## 2058 "JAMAICA INN AT SALISBURY PLAYHOUSE" MAIDEN STKS (DIV II) 5f

**2:10** (2:10) (D) 2-Y-O **£4,647** (£1,430; £715; £357) **Stalls** High

| Form | | | | RPR |
|---|---|---|---|---|
| | **1** | | **Black Velvet** 2-9-0 .......... WSupple 9<br>(MPTregoning) *mde all: drvn and styd on wl fr over 1f out* **5/1**[2] | 86 |
| | **2** | *2* | **Brag (IRE)** 2-8-9 .......... SDrowne 1<br>(RCharlton) *chsd ldrs: wnt 2nd 2f out: rdn and kpt on wl but nt pce of wnr ins last* **8/1**[3] | 73 |
| | **3** | *½* | **Age Of Kings (USA)** 2-9-0 .......... JPMurtagh 4<br>(JHMGosden) *slowly away: rdn in last pl: hdwy over 2f out:swtchd rt and r.o over 1f out: fin wl but nt rch ldrs* **6/5**[1] | 76+ |
| | **4** | *1 ¼* | **Veritable** 2-8-9 .......... PDobbs 7<br>(SKirk) *hdwy to chse ldrs 3f out: rdn and kpt on same pce fnl 2f* **25/1** | 66 |
| 0 | **5** | *1* | **Caly Dancer (IRE)**[24] 1505 2-9-0 .......... NPollard 6<br>(DRCElsworth) *pressed ldrs to 1/2-way: sn rdn: kpt on same pce ins last* **16/1** | 67 |
| 6 | **6** | *3 ½* | **Atsos (IRE)**[10] 1826 2-9-0 .......... DaneO'Neill 3<br>(RHannon) *bhd: hdwy to chse ldrs 1/2-way: wknd over 1f out* **8/1**[3] | 53 |
| | **7** | *1* | **Nanton (USA)** 2-9-0 .......... RLMoore 8<br>(PFICole) *chsd ldrs tl n.m.r on rails 3f out: n.d after* **8/1**[3] | 49 |
| | **8** | *1 ½* | **Inchcape Rock** 2-9-0 .......... RHavlin 5<br>(LGCottrell) *s.i.s: sme hdwy 3f out: wknd fr 2f out* **16/1** | 43 |
| | **9** | *hd* | **Kenwyn** 2-9-0 .......... FNorton 11<br>(MBlanshard) *bhd: hmpd over 3f out: n.d after* **33/1** | 42 |
| 0 | **10** | *1 ¾* | **Pie Corner**[9] 1853 2-8-11 .......... LPKeniry(3) 2<br>(MMadgwick) *chsd wnr to 2f out: wknd rapidly appr fnl f* **100/1** | 35 |

61.97 secs (0.40) **Going Correction** +0.05s/f (Good) **10** Ran SP% **115.0**
Speed ratings: **98,94,94,92,90 84,83,80,80,77**CSF £43.26 TOTE £4.60: £1.70, £1.80, £1.40; EX 39.30.
**Owner** Lady Tennant **Bred** Mrs James Wigan **Trained** Lambourn, Berks

**FOCUS**
The second division of this maiden was significantly faster and the stronger of the pair.

**NOTEBOOK**
**Black Velvet**, a striking newcomer, was quickly away from the gates and showed a great attitude to score readily. An expensive yearling, he was the stable's first juvenile runner and handled this ground well. He is bred to get further and connections cited the Coventry Stakes at Royal Ascot as a possible target.
**Brag(IRE)**, a sharp and precocious juvenile, showed plenty of dash early on and made a pleasing debut. She should come on a fair bit for this outing and looks well suited to this trip.
**Age Of Kings(USA)** ◆, well backed in the ring, lost all chance at the start. He finally stumbled out of the gates and ran very green in the first couple of furlongs, but when the penny dropped he shaped with a good deal of promise and was finishing strongly. It will be a big surprise if he fails to leave this form a long way behind next time, as he looks a potentially smart recruit.
**Veritable**, a half-sister to winning sprinter Sharp Hat, ran as though this will bring on her a fair bit and shaped with promise.
**Caly Dancer(IRE)**, who had run green on his debut at Windsor last time, could not quicken with the leaders when push came to shove and will fare better when eligible for nurseries over further.
**Atsos(IRE)**, as on his debut, was slow to break and looked to use up too much energy in trying to recover. He seemed to handle this quicker ground without a problem.
**Nanton(USA)** showed some early dash, but although he was tight for room on the rail approaching three out, he would not have won. He looks the type to do much better over further in time.

## 2059 WISE CATERING MAIDEN FILLIES' STKS (DIV I) 1m 1f 198y

**2:40** (2:42) (D) 3-Y-0+ **£5,551** (£1,708; £854; £427) **Stalls** High

| Form | | | | RPR |
|---|---|---|---|---|
| 5- | **1** | | **Quiff**[265] 4347 3-8-7 .......... BDoyle 1<br>(SirMichaelStoute) *trckd ldrs: wnt 2nd wl over 1f out: qcknd to ld ins last: comf* **7/2**[2] | 83 |
| 3- | **2** | *1* | **Dawn Surprise (USA)**[202] 5722 3-8-7 .......... KMcEvoy 9<br>(SaeedBinSuroor) *sn trcking ldr: led 2f out: hdd ins fnl f: kpt on but nt pce of wnr* **11/8**[1] | 81 |
| | **3** | *5* | **Feaat** 3-8-7 .......... WSupple 2<br>(JHMGosden) *s.i.s: sn mid-div: rn wd bnd 7f out: hdwy 3f out: edgd lft 2f out: kpt on wl fnl f but no ch w ldrs* **8/1** | 72 |
| 000- | **4** | *1* | **Santa Caterina (IRE)**[202] 5722 3-8-7 .......... DaneO'Neill 3<br>(JLDunlop) *bhd: hdwy 4f out: styng on whn edgd rt 2f out: kpt on fnl f but nvr gng pce of ldrs* **50/1** | 70 |
| 04-5 | **5** | *nk* | **Moonlight Tango (USA)**[16] 1683 3-8-7 76 .......... RHavlin 4<br>(JHMGosden) *sn prom: chsd ldrs over 3f out: sn rdn: styd on same pce fr over 1f out* **10/1** | 69 |
| 0-0 | **6** | *5* | **Crystal Choir**[42] 1224 4-9-8 .......... JPMurtagh 6<br>(NJHenderson) *sn led: hdd 2f out: wknd over 1f out* **50/1** | 60 |
| 02-4 | **7** | *¾* | **Bubbling Fun**[19] 1619 3-8-7 .......... RLMoore 5<br>(EALDunlop) *bhd: sme hdwy 3f out: nvr gng pce to rch ldrs* **40/1** | 58 |
| 0 | **8** | *5* | **Uig**[16] 1683 3-8-7 .......... TEDurcan 7<br>(HSHowe) *t.k.h: rn wd bnd 7f out: hdwy 5f out: styng on whn nt clr run on outside 2f out: sn btn* **100/1** | 49 |
| 0 | **9** | *1 ¼* | **Apron (IRE)**[27] 1440 3-8-7 .......... SDrowne 10<br>(RCharlton) *bhd: hdwy 4f out: chsd ldrs and rdn 3f out: sn wknd* **40/1** | 46 |
| 2- | **10** | *2* | **Force Of Nature (USA)**[323] 2678 4-9-8 .......... PaulEddery 8<br>(HRACecil) *t.k.h: trckd ldrs: rdn and outpcd 3f out: wknd qckly over 2f out* **4/1**[3] | 42 |

2m 8.06s (-0.26) **Going Correction** +0.05s/f (Good)
**WFA** 3 from 4yo 15lb **10** Ran SP% **114.3**
Speed ratings: **103,102,98,97,97 93,92,88,87,85**CSF £8.34 TOTE £4.80: £1.60, £1.30, £2.30; EX 11.30.
**Owner** K Abdulla **Bred** Juddmonte Farms **Trained** Newmarket, Suffolk

**FOCUS**
A fair maiden run at a solid pace and the first two pulled clear. The form looks the stronger of the two divisions.

**NOTEBOOK**
**Quiff** picked up very strongly two out and won this going away. She ran green on her sole juvenile start, but has obviously wintered well, and this beautifully-bred filly looks the type to hold her own at a higher level.
**Dawn Surprise(USA)** ◆ held every chance if good enough, but had no answer to the winner as that rival challenged. However, this run will bring her on and she was clear of the rest, so should not be too long in going one better. She will stay further.
**Feaat** was sluggish at the start and did not handle the bend too well at the seven-furlong marker, but ran on nicely late in the day and posted a fair debut display. She will be sharper next time and looks the type to stay further.
**Santa Caterina(IRE)**, who ran keenly on all three juvenile starts, settled better this time but lacked the pace to trouble the principals over this trip. She is entitled to improve for the run and will be seen to better effect over further.
**Moonlight Tango(USA)** set the standard on form, but did not improve on his last effort. She looks as if she may benefit from a switch to handicap company.
**Force Of Nature(USA)** pulled like the proverbial train early on and was most disappointing. This well-bred filly has now to prove she has trained on from two to three.

## 2060 WISE CATERING MAIDEN FILLIES' STKS (DIV II) 1m 1f 198y

**3:10** (3:13) (D) 3-Y-0+ **£5,551** (£1,708; £854; £427) **Stalls** High

| Form | | | | RPR |
|---|---|---|---|---|
| 2- | **1** | | **Well Known**[251] 4709 3-8-7 .......... SDrowne 5<br>(RCharlton) *reluctant to post: sn led: 2l clr and gng wl appr fnl f: eased fnl 100yds: drvn last strides and jst hld on* **11/8**[1] | 80+ |
| 0 | **2** | *hd* | **Anna Pallida**[26] 1461 3-8-4 .......... TPQueally(3) 9<br>(PWHarris) *trckd wnr 3f: styd prom: wnt 2nd again 3f out: rdn and one pce over 1f out: r.o strly as wnr eased nr fin: jst failed* **7/2**[2] | 76 |
| | **3** | *nk* | **Goslar** 3-8-7 .......... DaneO'Neill 8<br>(HCandy) *s.i.s: bhd: hdwy over 2f out: swtchd lft and str run fr over 1f out: fin wl* **16/1** | 75 |
| 0- | **4** | *¾* | **Wou Oodd**[271] 4185 3-8-7 .......... TEDurcan 3<br>(MRChannon) *s.i.s: bhd: hdwy fr 3f out: str run fnl f: kpt on cl home* **33/1** | 74 |
| 26- | **5** | *4* | **Garryurra**[202] 5722 3-8-7 .......... BDoyle 7<br>(SirMichaelStoute) *in tch: rdn and hdwy over 2f out: kpt on same pce appr fnl f* **7/2**[2] | 66 |
| -6 | **6** | *1 ¾* | **Lebenstanz**[54] 1059 4-9-5 .......... NMackay(3) 4<br>(LMCumani) *in tch: dropped rr 5f out: rdn 3f out: styd on one pce fnl 2f* **10/1**[3] | 63 |
| 0 | **7** | *nk* | **Twelve Bar Blues**[17] 1674 3-8-7 .......... RHavlin 6<br>(JHMGosden) *chsd ldrs: pushed along over 4f out: no imp on ldrs fnl 2f* **25/1** | 62 |
| 0 | **8** | *nk* | **Spot In Time**[69] 969 4-9-8 .......... RPrice 2<br>(JPearce) *chsd wnr 7f to 3f out: wknd over 2f out* **100/1** | 62? |
| 0 | **9** | *28* | **Highfluting**[75] 916 3-8-7 .......... DKinsella 1<br>(RMFlower) *a bhd: lost tch fnl 4f* **100/1** | 9 |

2m 10.53s (2.21) **Going Correction** +0.05s/f (Good)
**WFA** 3 from 4yo 15lb **9** Ran SP% **110.3**
Speed ratings: **93,92,92,92,88 87,87,86,64**CSF £5.64 TOTE £1.70: £1.20, £1.30, £2.50; EX 6.70.
**Owner** K Abdulla **Bred** Juddmonte Farms **Trained** Beckhampton, Wilts

**FOCUS**
The weaker of the two divisions and it produced a time 2.47 seconds slower than the first division.

**NOTEBOOK**
**Well Known** dictated a stop-start gallop and made all, being value for more than the winning margin, as she was eased before the runner-up came again at the line. This sister to the yard's classy Trade Fair has proved temperamental in both her outings to date, but she is clearly useful and should go on to better things.
**Anna Pallida** looked held by the winner with a furlong to run, but rallied to challenge as that rival was eased and only just failed. This was a big improvement on her debut and she appreciated the extra two furlongs on this occasion.
**Goslar**, making a belated debut, ran green in the early stages, but really flew home when the penny dropped. She will get farther and on this evidence, looks to have a future.
**Wou Oodd** gave herself a fair bit to do after a tardy start, but shaped with promise and has obviously improved from two to three. She is another who should have little trouble staying further.
**Garryurra** looked to have a chance on the form of her two juvenile outings, but could not quicken under pressure and looks one paced. She may do better now she qualifies for handicaps however.

## 2061 "RACING WELFARE KEN CAREY LIFETIME IN RACING" CLAIMING STKS 6f 212y

**3:45** (3:46) (E) 3-Y-0 **£3,536** (£1,088; £544; £272) **Stalls** High

| Form | | | | RPR |
|---|---|---|---|---|
| -040 | **1** | | **Whiplash (IRE)**[3] 1997 3-8-5 59 .......... RLMoore 15<br>(RHannon) *trckd ldrs on rail: rdn over 2f out: led jst ins fnl f: shkn up and hld on wl* **16/1** | 54 |
| 6016 | **2** | *½* | **Joy And Pain**[44] 1184 3-9-2 58 .......... TPQueally(3) 13<br>(GLMoore) *hld up mid-div: hdwy on rails and nt clr run over 2f out: swtchd lft sn after and str run ins last: nt rch wnr* **16/1** | 67 |
| 1012 | **3** | *1 ½* | **Lady Mo**[19] 1627 3-9-0 65 .......... NCallan 10<br>(KARyan) *chsd ldrs: chal 2f out: led over 1f out: hdd jst ins last: styd on one pce* **4/1**[1] | 58 |
| 0-33 | **4** | *1 ¾* | **City General (IRE)**[36] 1296 3-8-4 56 .......... (p) DerekNolan(7) 11<br>(JSMoore) *sn led: rdn over 2f out: hdd appr fnl f: wknd ins last* **12/1** | 50 |
| 0-00 | **5** | *6* | **The Footballresult**[89] 766 3-8-2 58 .......... JoannaBadger 14<br>(MrsGHarvey) *bhd: drvn along 1/2-way: styd on fr over 1f out: nt a danger* **50/1** | 26 |
| -030 | **6** | *nk* | **Arfinnit (IRE)**[10] 1841 3-9-1 70 .......... TEDurcan 8<br>(MRChannon) *in tch: rdn and effrt over 2f out: nvr gng pce to rch ldrs: wknd over 1f out* **6/1**[2] | 38 |
| 0- | **7** | *2* | **Cloud Catcher (IRE)**[418] 758 3-8-2 .......... SRighton 12<br>(IAWood) *s.i.s: bhd: rdn and hdwy over 3f out: nvr rchd ldrs: wknd fnl 2f* **33/1** | 20 |
| 0-50 | **8** | *1* | **Deign To Dance (IRE)**[26] 1464 3-8-12 70 .......... (p) WSupple 3<br>(JGPortman) *in tch: chsd ldrs and rdn 1/2-way: wknd qckly 2f out* **8/1**[3] | 27 |
| 50 | **9** | *½* | **Farnborough (USA)**[43] 1202 3-9-5 .......... NPollard 4<br>(DRCElsworth) *a in rr* **20/1** | 33 |

-366 **10** *nk* **Marksgold (IRE)**[9] 1854 3-8-7 60 ... SDrowne 7 20
(PFICole) *chsd ldrs tl rdn and wknd qckly fr 3f out* **12/1**

043 **11** *4* **Rocket (IRE)**[9] 1854 3-8-11 ... DaneO'Neill 9 14
(RHannon) *chsd ldrs: rdn 3f out: sn btn* **6/1[2]**

4060 **12** *1* **Livia (IRE)**[7] 1908 3-8-3 50 ... (p) RMiles(3) 1 6
(JGPortman) *chsd ldrs: rdn and effrt 3f out: sn btn* **50/1**

0-00 **13** *5* **Spring Dancer**[38] 1270 3-9-0 58 ... JPMurtagh 5 1
(BGPowell) *chsd ldrs tl wknd over 2f out* **20/1**

-004 **14** *3 1/2* **City Affair**[85] 817 3-8-11 60 ... VSlattery 2 —
(MrsLCJewell) *a in rr* **14/1**

1m 28.96s (-0.04) **Going Correction** +0.05s/f (Good) **14** Ran SP% **109.9**
Speed ratings: **102,101,99,97,90 90,88,87,86,86 81,80,74,70**CSF £193.37 TOTE £24.20: £5.00, £3.90, £1.60; EX 79.90.Lady Mo was claimed by G. G. Margarson for £12,000; Whiplash (IRE) was claimed by Ken Cunningham-Brown for £5,000.
**Owner** Dr Thomas & Mrs Thelma Wade **Bred** Mrs Mary McGrath **Trained** East Everleigh, Wilts

**FOCUS**
A weak race lacking any strength in depth. A high draw proved an advantage and the first four were clear.

**NOTEBOOK**
**Whiplash(IRE)** was all out at the finish to get off the mark at the ninth attempt. He was given a fair ride on this occasion and was aided by his draw, so would be no good thing to follow up. *Official explanation: trainer said, regarding the improved form shown, colt seemed better suited by today's faster ground and drop in class*
**Joy And Pain**, badly in at the weights with the winner, did not get the best of runs approaching two out and that looked to cost him victory.
**Lady Mo** had every chance if good enough, but although she put up another brave display, she failed to translate her recent All-Weather form on to the turf.
**City General(IRE)**, backed at long odds in the betting ring, could find no more in the last furlong having set the pace for most of the way. He ran up to form.
**Arfinnit(IRE)** could not quicken when push came to shove and is a frustrating character.

## 2062 PORTWAY FILLIES' RATED STKS (H'CAP) 1m 4f
**4:20** (4:20) (C ) (0-95,90) 4-Y-0+ **£8,473** (£3,214; £1,607; £730) **Stalls** High

Form RPR

23-2 **1** **Desert Royalty (IRE)**[17] 1671 4-8-13 **82** ... WSupple 2 94
(EALDunlop) *hld up rr but in tch: hdwy on outside over 2f out: str run to ld jst ins fnl f: styd on wl* **5/2[1]**

0-51 **2** *1 3/4* **Tawny Way**[17] 1671 4-9-0 **83** ... SDrowne 7 92
(WJarvis) *hld up in tch: hdwy 3f out: slt led ins fnl 2f: hdd jst ins last: styd on same pce* **9/2[2]**

110- **3** *3* **Pongee**[266] 4321 4-9-1 **87** ... NMackay(3) 9 91
(LMCumani) *stdd rr: pushed along 4f out: hdwy on rails over 2f out: kpt on fnl f but nvr gng pce to rch ldrs* **15/2**

0-04 **4** *2 1/2* **Desert Island Disc**[17] 1671 7-8-7 **76** ... RLMoore 10 76
(JJBridger) *chsd ldrs: rdn to ld ins fnl 3f: hdd ins fnl 2f: wknd fnl f* **13/2[3]**

05-0 **5** *1 1/4* **Largo (IRE)**[12] 1768 4-9-7 **90** ... KMcEvoy 8 88
(JLDunlop) *trckd ldrs: shkn up 3f out: fdd over 1f out* **12/1**

00-0 **6** *1/2* **Ribbons And Bows (IRE)**[38] 1272 4-8-6 **75** ... SWhitworth 4 72
(CACyzer) *bhd: reminders 6f out and 5f out: styd on fr over 1f out but nvr a danger* **25/1**

0101 **7** *1 1/4* **Tight Squeeze**[41] 1232 7-8-11 **80** ... CCatlin 1 75
(PWHiatt) *in tch: chsd ldrs fr 7f out: wknd ins fnl 2f* **8/1**

0-00 **8** *3/4* **Claradotnet**[16] 1684 4-8-6 **75** ... TEDurcan 5 69
(MRChannon) *bhd: styd on fnl 2f: nvr nr ldrs* **33/1**

-205 **9** *1 1/2* **Doris Souter (IRE)**[43] 1203 4-8-4 **73** oh3 ... RSmith 6 65
(RHannon) *led tl hdd ins fnl 3f: styd pressing ldrs tl wknd rapidly wl over 1f out* **12/1**

1030 **10** *3 1/2* **Maystock**[16] 1684 4-8-5 **77** ... (v) TPQueally(3) 3 63
(GAButler) *trckd ldr after 3f: chal fr 4f out: stl ev ch over 2f out: sn wknd* **14/1**

2m 35.29s (-1.06) **Going Correction** +0.05s/f (Good) **10** Ran SP% **111.8**
Speed ratings: **105,103,101,100,99 99,98,97,96,94**CSF £12.52 CT £70.48 TOTE £2.20: £1.10, £2.20, £2.80; EX 5.30.
**Owner** Mrs Janice Quy **Bred** Miss Karyn Flannery **Trained** Newmarket, Suffolk

**FOCUS**
A fair fillies' handicap run at a sound pace and the winner reversed recent form with the runner-up on 1lb better terms.

**NOTEBOOK**
**Desert Royalty(IRE)** cosily reversed recent form with the runner-up and gained a deserved success. She is a most consistent handicapper, and although she is effective at shorter, she looks best suited by being held up over this trip. Unlikely to go up too much in the weights for this, she can score again before the Handicapper gets his way.
**Tawny Way** came there with every chance two out, but could not quicken and failed to confirm recent form with the winner over this longer trip.She looked to get this trip, but reverting to ten furlongs will be of benefit and she may still have more to offer at that trip.
**Pongee**, last seen when unplaced in the Galtres Stakes, made a pleasing comeback form her 266-day absence and is entitled to improve on this.
**Desert Island Disc** ran her race, but look in need of a drop in the weights.

## 2063 DUTTON GREGORY H'CAP 6f
**4:55** (4:55) (E ) (0-75,75) 3-Y-0 **£3,757** (£1,156; £578; £289) **Stalls** High

Form RPR

-413 **1** **Bridgewater Boys**[90] 758 3-8-8 **62** ... (b) NCallan 9 73
(KARyan) *trckd ldrs: led wl over 1f out: drvn and hld on wl fnl f* **9/1[3]**

6-01 **2** *1/2* **Cornwallis**[9] 1854 3-8-2 **61** 6ex ... HayleyTurner(5) 4 70
(JSKing) *mid-div: hdwy on outside over 2f out: str run fr over 1f out: fin wl but no imp nr fin* **14/1**

6-06 **3** *1 1/2* **Dr Synn**[13] 1749 3-8-8 **65** ... SHitchcott(3) 5 70
(JAkehurst) *bhd: rdn and gd hdwy on outside fnl 2f: fin wl but nt rch ldrs* **20/1**

60-0 **4** *shd* **Estihlal**[37] 1288 3-8-6 **60** ... WSupple 14 64
(EALDunlop) *n.m.r after 1f and bhd: hdwy over 2f out: styd on fnl f but nvr gng pce of ldrs* **14/1**

4133 **5** *1/2* **Kryssa**[35] 1312 3-8-6 **60** ... RLMoore 17 63
(GLMoore) *bhd: hdwy fr 2f out: rdn and kpt on fnl f: one pce cl home* **7/2[2]**

600- **6** *2 1/2* **Moscow Times**[166] 6090 3-9-3 **71** ... JPMurtagh 13 66
(DRCElsworth) *in tch: pushed along 2f out: nt pce of ldrs and outpcd fnl f* **5/2[1]**

653 **7** *hd* **Simpsons Mount (IRE)**[41] 1228 3-9-1 **69** ... DSweeney 12 64
(RMFlower) *bhd: stdy hdwy over 2f out: kpt on ins last but nt pce to trble ldrs* **25/1**

005- **8** *shd* **Signor Panettiere**[201] 5751 3-8-13 **67** ... PDobbs 18 61
(RHannon) *chsd ldrs: rdn over 2f out: wknd appr fnl f* **12/1**

0611 **9** *nk* **Melaina**[7] 1907 3-8-2 **61** 6ex ... (p) PMakin(5) 1 54
(MSSaunders) *sn pressing ldrs: led over 3f out: hdd wl over 1f out: wknd ins last* **12/1**

5030 **10** *1/2* **Instinct**[38] 1270 3-8-8 **62** ... DaneO'Neill 11 54
(RHannon) *s.i.s: bhd: kpt on fr over 1f out but nt a danger* **14/1**

430- **11** *3 1/2* **One Upmanship**[210] 5590 3-9-1 **69** ... (p) KMcEvoy 8 50
(JGPortman) *trckd ldrs: rdn over 2f out: wknd qckly over 1f out* **33/1**

52-0 **12** *1 1/4* **Disco Diva**[48] 1119 3-9-0 **68** ... FNorton 7 46
(MBlanshard) *bhd tl mod late prog* **25/1**

000- **13** *1/2* **Bahama Belle**[220] 5424 3-8-8 **62** ... TEDurcan 16 38
(HSHowe) *sn bhd* **50/1**

610- **14** *shd* **Bertocelli**[187] 5950 3-9-7 **75** ... NPollard 15 51
(GGMargarson) *chsd ldrs: rdn 3f out: wknd 2f out* **20/1**

66-0 **15** *2 1/2* **Red Sovereign**[15] 1702 3-9-1 **72** ... TPQueally(3) 3 40
(IAWood) *w ldr: led after 2f: hdd over 3f out: sn wknd* **25/1**

00-4 **16** *1* **Jinksonthehouse**[9] 1854 3-8-6 **60** ... ADaly 2 25
(MDIUsher) *sn outpcd* **40/1**

0430 **17** *3* **Kuringai**[33] 1333 3-9-3 **71** ... OUrbina 10 27
(BWDuke) *led 2f: wknd qckly over 2f out* **14/1**

1m 14.63s (-0.31) **Going Correction** +0.05s/f (Good) **17** Ran SP% **131.2**
Speed ratings: **104,103,101,101,100 97,96,96,96,95 91,89,88,88,85 83,79**CSF £124.20 CT £2505.52 TOTE £12.10: £2.50, £3.70, £3.90, £6.00; EX 79.50.
**Owner** Bishopthorpe Racing **Bred** Southill Stud **Trained** Hambleton, N Yorks

**FOCUS**
A handicap full of unexposed types, run at a solid pace, but only modest form.

**NOTEBOOK**
**Bridgewater Boys**, progressive on the All-Weather during the winter, showed a game attitiude inside the final furlong to score. This was by far his best effort on turf to date and he is a likeable, consistent individual.
**Cornwallis**, winner of a claimer nine days previously, finished best of all, but found the winner had gone beyond recall. This was a solid effort and she should continue to pay her way at this level.
**Dr Synn** got going all too late, but showed markedly improved form on this handicap debut and should find a small race off his current mark.
**Estihlal**, making her handicap debut, was another who took her time to get into full stride, but ran her best race to date.
**Kryssa** ran on again from off the pace, but is becoming frustrating and needs everything to fall right.
**Moscow Times**, seriously well backed throughout the day, never really looked like landing the support on this handicap bow. However, he got excited at the start, and as he is evidently considered better than his current mark, he may be worth another chance. *Official explanation: trainer said gelding sweated up badly at the start*
**Kuringai** *Official explanation: jockey said said colt lost its action two furlongs out.*

## 2064 TRYON H'CAP 6f 212y
**5:25** (5:26) (D ) (0-80,79) 3-Y-0+ **£5,980** (£1,840; £920; £460) **Stalls** High

Form RPR

00-2 **1** **Goodenough Mover**[41] 1230 8-8-10 **67** ... HayleyTurner(5) 19 78
(JSKing) *mde all: rdn 2f out: hld on gamely thrght fnl f* **5/1[1]**

6244 **2** *1/2* **And Toto Too**[41] 1229 4-9-0 **66** ... (b) NCallan 5 76
(PDEvans) *trckd ldrs: rdn over 2f out: r.o wl fnl f: gng on cl home* **12/1**

4133 **3** *hd* **Chateau Nicol**[10] 1840 5-9-11 **77** ... (v) JPMurtagh 14 86
(BGPowell) *chsd ldrs: wnt 2nd over 1f out: sn hrd drvn: nt qckn ins last: lost 2nd last strides* **5/1[1]**

006- **4** *shd* **Resonate (IRE)**[163] 6119 6-9-5 **71** ... DaneO'Neill 12 80
(AGNewcombe) *bhd: hdwy on outside fr 2f out: hrd drvn and str run fnl f: fin wl* **14/1**

40-0 **5** *hd* **Little Venice (IRE)**[31] 1354 4-9-7 **76** ... LisaJones(3) 8 85
(CFWall) *mid-div: hdwy and hmpd over 2f out: r.o wl fnl f: gng on cl home* **16/1**

0000 **6** *1 1/4* **Ephesus**[10] 1845 4-9-13 **79** ... (v) WSupple 17 84
(MissGayKelleway) *bhd: hdwy fr 2f out: styng on whn nt clr run ins last and again last half f: nt rcvr* **16/1**

1303 **7** *nk* **Danielle's Lad**[20] 1598 8-9-2 **71** ... (b) TPQueally(3) 13 76
(BPalling) *chsd ldrs: rdn over 2f out: styd on same pce ins last* **16/1**

-022 **8** *3 1/2* **Michelle Ma Belle (IRE)**[36] 1294 4-9-9 **75** ... RLMoore 1 71
(SKirk) *mid-div: gd hdwy over 2f out: chsd ldrs and hung bdly rt ins fnl 2f: nt run on fnl f: eased* **9/1[3]**

20-0 **9** *1 3/4* **Night Kiss (FR)**[10] 1828 4-8-12 **64** ... RSmith 7 55
(RHannon) *bhd: stl plenty to do 2f out: r.o wl fnl f but nt a danger* **16/1**

0-00 **10** *hd* **Kew The Music**[19] 1608 4-8-10 **62** ... TEDurcan 11 53
(MRChannon) *bhd tl sme hdwy fr over 1f out* **16/1**

2002 **11** *1 3/4* **Mistral Sky**[42] 1225 5-9-2 **68** ... (v) SDrowne 15 54
(MrsStefLiddiard) *chsd ldrs: wkng whn bmpd over 1f out* **13/2[2]**

000/ **12** *1/2* **Threezedzz**[39] 5097 6-8-13 **65** ... RHavlin 3 50
(MrsPNDutfield) *s.i.s: bhd: rdn and effrt 3f out: nvr rchd ldrs* **40/1**

50-0 **13** *3/4* **Coranglais**[12] 1772 4-9-7 **73** ... SCarson 4 56
(JMBradley) *in tch: chsd to chse ldrs 1/2-way: wknd ins fnl 2f* **50/1**

40-0 **14** *nk* **Oh Boy (IRE)**[38] 1275 4-8-13 **65** ... PDobbs 10 47
(RHannon) *chsd ldrs 4f* **33/1**

00-0 **15** *1 3/4* **Compton Arrow (IRE)**[9] 1873 8-8-8 **63** ... SHitchcott(3) 9 40
(AWCarroll) *a outpcd* **50/1**

-045 **16** *5* **Point Calimere (IRE)**[19] 1602 3-9-0 **78** ... KMcEvoy 20 42
(CREgerton) *sn bhd: no ch whn hmpd over 2f out* **25/1**

50-0 **17** *1 3/4* **Craic Sa Ceili (IRE)**[15] 1708 4-9-1 **72** ... (p) PMakin(5) 18 32
(MSSaunders) *in tch whn n.m.r on rails 4f out: wknd over 2f out* **12/1**

30-0 **18** *5* **Secret Formula**[30] 1385 4-9-10 **79** ... LPKeniry(3) 16 26
(SKirk) *chsd ldrs over 3f* **33/1**

20-0 **19** *1 3/4* **Bi Polar**[12] 1765 4-9-10 **76** ... NPollard 6 18
(DRCElsworth) *chsd ldrs: rdn 3f out: wknd rapidly over 2f out* **14/1**

1m 28.35s (-0.65) **Going Correction** +0.05s/f (Good)
**WFA** 3 from 4yo+ 12lb **19** Ran SP% **130.9**
Speed ratings: **105,104,104,104,103 102,102,98,96,95 93,93,92,92,90 84,82,76,74**CSF £64.71 CT £337.22 TOTE £6.60: £1.80, £5.20, £2.40, £5.00; EX 70.60 Place 6 £30.14, Place 5 £5.30.
**Owner** D Goodenough Removals & Transport **Bred** G Foster **Trained** Broad Hinton, Wilts

**FOCUS**
A fair handicap run at a sound pace and the top five home finished in a heap behind the winner.

**NOTEBOOK**
**Goodenough Mover** showed the benefit of his recent comeback effort on the Polytrack to make all in game style. He was very much aided by his high draw on this occasion, but shows he retains all his ability at the age of eight.
**And Toto Too**did not enjoy the best of runs just in behind the leaders, but ran a nice race and did the best of those drawn in single figures.
**Chateau Nicol** ran respectably under top weight, but although he is a consistent performer, is the type who flatters to deceive off the bridle.
**Resonate(IRE)**, off for 163 days prior to this, looked ring-rusty in the early stages, but picked up strongly in the final stages to finish best of all. He will come on a good deal for this outing.
**Little Venice(IRE)** was another doing all of his best work late on and appreciated this slight step up in trip.
**Michelle Ma Belle(IRE)** *Official explanation: jockey said filly hung badly right handed*

T/Plt: £17.10 to a £1 stake. Pool: £22,458.35. 956.45 winning tickets. T/Qpdt: £4.30 to a £1 stake. Pool: £2,313.90. 395.60 winning tickets. ST

## 2041 YORK (L-H)
### Thursday, May 13

**OFFICIAL GOING: Good to soft (good in places)**
The ground was reckoned to be holding and cut up against the running rail hence the jockeys came down the centre.
Wind: Slt across Weather: Fine and Sunny

## 2065 LANGLEYS SOLICITORS RATED STKS (H'CAP) 6f 3y
**1:30** (1:31) (B) (0-105,103) 4-Y-0+ **£12,818** (£4,862; £2,431; £1,105) **Stalls** High

Form RPR

2556 **1** **Quito (IRE)**[12] [1758] 7-9-7 **103** ....(b) ACulhane 12 117
(DWChapman) *hld up: gd hdwy 2f out: str run to ld ins last: sn clr* **12/1**

10-0 **2** *3* **Tom Tun**[12] [1759] 9-8-11 **93** ....(b) DeanMcKeown 10 98
(JBalding) *disuted ld tl led 1/2-way: rdn clr wl over 1f out: hdd and nt qckn ins last* **25/1**

03-0 **3** *1 3/4* **Marsad (IRE)**[12] [1765] 10-8-7 **89** oh1 .... PDoe 4 89
(JAkehurst) *dwlt: bhd and swtchd rt 1/2-way: gd hdwy 2f out: rdn and hung lft over 1f out and ins last: kpt on same pce* **14/1**

0-40 **4** *3/4* **Indian Spark**[31] [1353] 10-8-13 **95** .... KFallon 5 93
(JSGoldie) *lw: hdwy over 2f out: rdn to chse ldrs over 1f out: sn drvn and one pce* **8/1**

5251 **5** *2 1/2* **Chappel Cresent (IRE)**[6] [1927] 4-8-8 **90** 3ex .... ANicholls 9 80
(DNicholls) *disp ld: pushed along 1/2-way: rdn 2f out and sn wknd* **4/1**[1]

-024 **6** *1/2* **Halmahera (IRE)**[5] [1955] 9-9-6 **102** ....(b) RWinston 6 91
(KARyan) *trckd ldrs: effrt 2f out: sn rdn and btn* **12/1**

-520 **7** *hd* **Cd Flyer (IRE)**[12] [1765] 7-8-3 **89** oh4 ow1 .... TEaves(5) 8 78
(BEllison) *midfield: hdwy 1/2-way: rdn to chse ldrs 2f out: sn drvn and one pce* **12/1**

0-63 **8** *2* **Mazepa (IRE)**[11] [1789] 4-8-13 **95** .... LDettori 14 77
(NACallaghan) *trckd ldrs: effrt 2f out: rdn and edgd rt over 1f out: sn wknd* **7/1**[3]

-010 **9** *4* **Proud Boast**[16] [1685] 6-8-11 **93** .... KDarley 3 63
(DNicholls) *outpcd and pushed along in rr 1/2-way: nvr a factor* **16/1**

352- **10** *3 1/2* **Pivotal Point**[195] [5854] 4-8-9 **91** .... SSanders 7 50
(PJMakin) *lw: plld hrd: cl up tl wknd qckly over 2f out* **11/2**[2]

630- **11** *1 1/4* **Mutawaqed (IRE)**[201] [5761] 6-8-7 **89** oh3 ....(t) EAhern 15 45
(MAMagnusson) *b.hind: in tch: effrt on outer 2f out rdn and ch whn hmpd and squeezed out over 1f out* **14/1**

2-00 **12** *2 1/2* **Pomfret Lad**[6] [1923] 6-9-4 **100** .... AlexGreaves 1 48
(DNicholls) *cl up: rdn along over 2f out: sn wknd* **50/1**

06-6 **13** *hd* **Dazzling Bay**[26] [1471] 4-9-7 **103** .... JFEgan 13 51
(TDEasterby) *in tch: rdn along 1/2-way: sn wknd* **25/1**

6-34 **14** *5* **Circuit Dancer (IRE)**[12] [1759] 4-8-10 **92** .... JCarroll 11 25
(ABerry) *rrd s and v.s.a: a bhd* **25/1**

1m 13.71s (2.64) **Going Correction** +0.65s/f (Yiel) **14** Ran SP% **114.8**
Speed ratings: **108,104,101,100,97 96,96,93,88,83 82,78,78,71**CSF £282.86 CT £4291.79 TOTE £16.00: £4.30, £5.30, £5.10; EX 378.40 TRIFECTA Not won. Pool of £1918.80 rolled over to Newbury 2.30 Friday..
**Owner** Michael Hill **Bred** Sheikh Mohammed Bin Rashid Al Maktoum **Trained** Stillington, N Yorks
■ Stewards Enquiry : P Doe caution: careless riding

**FOCUS**
A decent, competitive sprint run at a fair pace for the grade. Quito showed a level of form that will seldom be bettered in handicaps this year.

**NOTEBOOK**
**Quito(IRE)**, 11lb higher than when he won the Ayr Gold Cup and 2lb higher than when runner-up in the Lincoln, showed himself better than ever and he is a great credit to his trainer.
**Tom Tun**, suited by the soft ground, led them a merry dance but had no answer to the winner's finishing burst. At nine he seems better than ever.
**Marsad(IRE)**, who has not won for over two years, persisted in hanging left and his rider seemed slow changing his whip hand.
**Indian Spark**, on his toes beforehand, has a good record at York and showed a return to his best.
**Chappel Cresent(IRE)**, taken on for the lead, was nowhere near as effective over this sorter trip on this totally different track.
**Halmahera(IRE)** ran better than at Beverley but still did not exactly sparkle.
**Pivotal Point** looked backward in his coat and was far too keen on his return. He will do a lot better in due course.

## 2066 SHARP MINDS BETFAIR RATED STKS (H'CAP) 1m 2f 88y
**2:00** (2:02) (B) (0-105,105) 4-Y-0+ **£13,247** (£5,024; £2,512; £1,142) **Stalls** Low

Form RPR

-060 **1** **Vintage Premium**[54] [1062] 7-9-0 **98** .... PHanagan 7 109
(RAFahey) *mde all: rdn and qcknd over 2f out: drvn and edgd lft ins last: kpt on gamely* **16/1**

10-3 **2** *nk* **Shahzan House (IRE)**[22] [1540] 5-8-10 **94** .... PRobinson 5 105
(MAJarvis) *lw: trckd ldrs gng wl: hdwy 3f out: chal wl over 1f out: sn rdn and ev ch tl drvn and nt qckn nr fin* **6/1**[2]

-002 **3** *1* **Dumaran (IRE)**[33] [1328] 6-8-8 **92** .... KFallon 10 101
(WJMusson) *hld up in tch: hdwy over 2f out: swtchd rt and rdn to chal 1f out: sn drvn and kpt on same pce* **4/1**[1]

5-44 **4** *nk* **Bagan (FR)**[12] [1768] 5-8-4 **88** oh2 .... WRyan 12 96
(HRACecil) *bhd: hdwy 4f out: rdn over 2f out: styd on wl fnl f: nrst fin* **15/2**

0-03 **5** *3/4* **Jabaar (USA)**[10] [1821] 6-8-4 **88** oh1 .... ANicholls 3 95
(DNicholls) *midfield: hdwy on inner over 3f out: rdn and ev ch over 1f out: drvn and one pce ins last* **12/1**

30-6 **6** *1 3/4* **Cripsey Brook**[12] [1773] 6-8-4 **88** oh2 .... KimTinkler 2 92
(DonEnricoIncisa) *a.p: rdn along over 2f out: wknd appr last* **25/1**

00-2 **7** *6* **Always Esteemed (IRE)**[19] [1623] 4-8-13 **97** .... MartinDwyer 4 90
(GWragg) *trckd ldrs: effrt 3f out: rdn 2f out and sn wknd* **6/1**[2]

6-00 **8** *5* **St Pancras (IRE)**[12] [1762] 4-8-4 **88** .... EAhern 14 72
(NACallaghan) *lw: bhd: sme hdwy over 3f out: nvr a factor* **14/1**

40-0 **9** *2 1/2* **Prince Nureyev (IRE)**[33] [1328] 4-8-11 **95** .... JPSpencer 11 75
(BRMillman) *bhd: effrt and sme hdwy 3f out: nvr a factor* **16/1**

0-61 **10** *1 1/2* **Telemachus**[10] [1821] 4-8-5 **89** 3ex .... MFenton 8 66
(JGGiven) *chsd ldrs: rdn along over 3f out: sn wknd* **13/2**[3]

35-0 **11** *3* **Barrissimo (IRE)**[12] [1762] 4-8-8 **92** .... MJKinane 1 64
(WJMusson) *trckd ldrs on inner: hdwy 4f out: rdn along 3f out and sn wknd* **33/1**

0-00 **12** *hd* **Gala Sunday (USA)**[12] [1762] 4-8-4 **88** oh1 .... DaleGibson 13 59
(MWEasterby) *a rr* **66/1**

6-04 **13** *6* **Middlemarch (IRE)**[10] [1849] 4-9-7 **105** .... JFEgan 9 65
(JSGoldie) *nvr a factor* **25/1**

32/0 **14** *hd* **Sir George Turner**[19] [1622] 5-9-6 **104** .... KDalgleish 6 64
(MJohnston) *swtg: cl up: rdn along over 3f out: sn wknd* **25/1**

2m 13.99s (4.55) **Going Correction** +0.65s/f (Yiel) **14** Ran SP% **115.8**
Speed ratings: **107,106,105,105,105 103,98,94,92,91 89,89,84,84**CSF £99.43 CT £465.55 TOTE £18.90: £4.20, £2.40, £2.10; EX 141.80 Trifecta £611.00 Pool of £5,680.04 - 6.60 winning units..
**Owner** J C Parsons **Bred** D Shirley **Trained** Musley Bank, N Yorks

**FOCUS**
A sound gallop and a competitive handicap that should throw up plenty of future winners.

**NOTEBOOK**
**Vintage Premium**, who won the John Smith's Cup here two seasons ago from a 3lb higher mark, looked back to his very best beforehand. Suited by getting his toe in, he proved supremely game and thoroughly deserved this seventh career win.
**Shahzan House(IRE)**, who looked in tip-top shape beforehand, looked to have the winner covered but when his hand was played he came off just second best. He deserves to go one better.
**Dumaran(IRE)**, 2lb higher, looked in peak condition and was heavily backed. He gave the first two start and, hard as he tried, he could not peg them back.
**Bagan(FR)** ◆, who won here in August from an 8lb lower mark, was not on his best behaviour in the paddock. Settled off the pace and given plenty to do, he put in some sterling late work and is one to note for a good-class handicap over a bit further in the coming weeks.
**Jabaar(USA)** turned the tables on Telemachus compared to Doncaster and this robust-type looks right back to his best. He will surely put an end to his lengthy losing sequence soon.
**Cripsey Brook**, who improved over a stone and won six times last year, was 2lb out of the handicap and would have preferred quicker ground. Further success seems likely to come his way this time.
**Always Esteemed(IRE)**, 2lb higher, looked very fit and impressed going to post but he did not seem to fully see out the extended trip.
**Middlemarch(IRE)** *Official explanation: trainer said colt was unsuited by the ground.*

## 2067 EMIRATES AIRLINE YORKSHIRE CUP (GROUP 2) 1m 5f 197y
**2:30** (2:32) (A) 4-Y-0+ **£81,200** (£30,800; £15,400; £7,000) **Stalls** Low

Form RPR

42-3 **1** **Millenary**[15] [1703] 7-8-13 117 ....(b) TQuinn 1 121
(JLDunlop) *hld up in tch: smooth hdwy 4f out: cl up over 2f out: effrt and qcknd to ld ent last: sn clr* **9/2**[2]

24-1 **2** *3* **Alcazar (IRE)**[43] [1212] 9-8-10 118 .... MFenton 2 114
(HMorrison) *b.hind: lw: trckd ldrs: smooth hdwy 4f out: led wl over 1f out: rdn and hdd ent last: nt match pce of wnr* **7/1**[3]

1/06 **3** *4* **Jelani (IRE)**[11] [1792] 5-8-10 106 .... MJKinane 7 108
(AndrewTurnell) *cl up: led after 2f tl 1 1/2-way: cl up tl led again over 2f out: sn rdn and hdd wl over 1f out: drvn and kpt on same pce* **16/1**

116- **4** *2* **Mr Dinos (IRE)**[221] [5401] 5-9-1 122 .... KFallon 5 110
(PFICole) *b. b.hind: hld up in rr: hdwy over 4f out: rdn along wl over 2f out: sn drvn and no imp fr wl over 1f out* **4/1**[1]

0200 **5** *7* **Dutch Gold (USA)**[26] [1455] 4-8-9 111 ....(b[1]) DHolland 4 96
(CEBrittain) *prom: led 1/2-way: rdn along and hdd over 2f out: sn wknd* **50/1**

00-0 **6** *3 1/2* **Maktub (ITY)**[15] [1703] 5-8-10 .... PRobinson 10 91
(MAJarvis) *hld up: hdwy 1/2-way: rdn along over 3f out: sn wknd* **16/1**

325- **7** *6* **Highest (IRE)**[327] [2555] 5-8-10 .... LDettori 3 82
(SaeedBinSuroor) *bkwd: hld up: hdwy 5f out: rdn along over 3f out and sn btn* **4/1**[1]

43-6 **8** *12* **Salsalino**[26] [1455] 4-8-9 107 .... RHughes 9 66
(AKing) *swtg: racd wd: led 2f: prom tl riddne along over 4f out and sn wknd* **7/1**[3]

131- **9** *dist* **Shanty Star (IRE)**[328] [2518] 4-8-9 105 .... KDarley 8 —
(MJohnston) *trckd ldrs: tl rdn alonga nd wknd qckly 4f out: sn bhd* **8/1**

U0-P **P** **Morozov (USA)**[15] [1703] 5-8-10 .... IMongan 6 —
(CNAllen) *in tch: rdn along over 4f out: wkng whn hung lft over 2f out: b ehind whn p.u wl over 1f out* **50/1**

3m 1.61s (5.21) **Going Correction** +0.65s/f (Yiel)
**WFA** 4 from 5yo+ 1lb **10** Ran SP% **110.0**
Speed ratings: **111,109,107,105,101 99,96,89,—,—**CSF £33.28 TOTE £5.40: £1.80, £2.90, £4.90; EX 42.70 Trifecta £471.90 Pool of £2,127.08 - 3.20 winning units..
**Owner** L Neil Jones **Bred** Abergwaun Farms **Trained** Arundel, W Sussex
■ Millenary was the first seven-year-old to triumph since the race started in 1927.

**FOCUS**
A tactical race with a stop-start gallop and a modest winning time for a Group Two, but the winner could be named some way out.

**NOTEBOOK**
**Millenary**, who really took the eye beforehand, had the blinkers back on. Running over his optimum trip and with the ground in his favour, the 2000 St Leger winner travelled hard on the steel, and when given the office had this won in a matter of strides.
**Alcazar(IRE)**, sweating and upset in the paddock, likes to get his toe in and ran right up to his best even though in the end no match.
**Jelani(IRE)**, fourth in the 2002 Derby before injury put him on the sidelines, looked very fit but is an edgy type who needs handling with kid gloves. Regaining the lead halfway up the straight, in the end he did not see out the trip anyway near as well as the first two.
**Mr Dinos(IRE)**, who looked supremely well, was very keen to get on with it beforehand. In the race itself he ran rustily, on-and-off the bridle, but another outing will put him spot on for a repeat bid in the Ascot Gold Cup, as the extended trip there plays to his strengths.
**Dutch Gold(USA)**, in first-time blinkers, was quite keen and went on, but the ground and the trip proved his downfall.
**Maktub(ITY)** looked in good nick but because of the steady pace he pulled much too hard. A fast-run mile and a half might suit him a lot better.
**Highest(IRE)**, absent since disappointing in a visor at Royal Ascot last year, took the eye in the paddock but never looked like repeating the sort of form that saw him finish runner-up in the 2002 St Leger.
**Shanty Star(IRE)**, absent since taking the Queen's Vase at Royal Ascot last year, is a rangy, good-topped grey. Even allowing for the ground being softer than he prefers it was an abject return. It will be back to the drawing board now. *Official explanation: trainer was unable to offer any explanation for poor form shown*
**Morozov(USA)** *Official explanation: jockey said horse lost his action*

## 2068 MICHAEL SEELY MEMORIAL GLASGOW STKS (LISTED RACE) (C&G) 1m 2f 88y
**3:00** (3:01) (A) 3-Y-O **£18,600** (£6,600; £3,300; £1,500) **Stalls** Low

Form RPR

1 **1** **Day Flight**[11] [1800] 3-8-11 .... RHughes 1 113+
(JHMGosden) *lw: w'like: trckd ldr: led 4f out: pushed clr fnl 2f: unchal* **5/2**[2]

1-3 **2** *20* **Mac Regal (IRE)**[27] [1439] 3-8-11 .... LDettori 4 77
(MGQuinlan) *lw: cl up on outer: rdn along and outpcd 4f out: styd on u.p fnl 2f: no ch w wnr* **20/1**

\- **3** *4* **Go For Gold (IRE)**[326] [2612] 3-8-11 .... JPSpencer 2 70
(APO'Brien, Ire) *leggy: led: rdn along and heded 4f out: drvn 2f out and sn outpcd* **11/2**[3]

1-4 **4** *6* **Fort Dignity (USA)**[26] [1459] 3-8-11 **108** ........ KFallon 3 59
(SirMichaelStoute) *lw: hld up in tch: niggled along 1/2-way: rdn over 3f out: drvn and btn over 2f out* **4/6**[1]

2m 15.39s (5.95) **Going Correction** +0.65s/f (Yiel) **4** Ran SP% **108.7**
Speed ratings: **102,86,82,78**CSF £28.42 TOTE £3.80; EX 36.80.
**Owner** K Abdulla **Bred** Juddmonte Farms **Trained** Manton, Wilts

**FOCUS**
A disappointing turn out number-wise and just a steady pace, resulting in an ordinary time. Day Flight was most impressive, but might not have beaten much.

**NOTEBOOK**
**Day Flight** did not impress at all going down, but came back a lot better. He went clear in a matter of strides, winning by a huge margin by Flat race standards, and is clearly a smart colt. His action suggests he appreciates give underfoot and the flatter track the better, so the Irish Derby or Royal Ascot look better bets track-wise than Epsom.
**Mac Regal(IRE)**, who did not impress with his attitude at Newbury, finished a fraction further behind the winner here than he did behind the Dante third Let The Lion Roar there.
**Go For Gold(IRE)**, a half-brother to the St Leger winner Milan, scrambled home in a maiden at Gowran in June on his one outing at two. A tall type, he was taken to post early and set just a steady gallop. He dropped out in a matter of strides and was most disappointing.
**Fort Dignity(USA)**, who continually swished his tail in the paddock, was taken to post very gingerly. Taking a fierce grip, he was the first to come under pressure and, never happy, dropped right away. The trip and the ground were not solely to blame, and he has a lot to prove now.
*Official explanation: trainer was unable to offer any explanation for poor form shown*

## 2069 SHARP MINDS BETFAIR STKS (H'CAP) 7f 205y
**3:35** (3:36) (C ) (0-95,82) 3-Y-O **£10,965** (£3,374; £1,687; £843) **Stalls** Low

Form RPR

-325 **1** **Oddsmaker (IRE)**[7] [1899] 3-9-2 **77** ........ DeanMcKeown 8 88
(PDEvans) *a.p: cl up over 2f out: rdn to ld ent last: kpt on* **9/1**

041 **2** *1* **Inchloss (IRE)**[13] [1749] 3-8-12 **73** ........ GGibbons 3 82
(BAMcmahon) *lw: chsd ldrs: hdwy 3f out: rdn along 2f out: kpt on u.p ins last* **10/1**

1141 **3** *1/2* **Barathea Dreams (IRE)**[20] [1585] 3-9-4 **79** ........ MartinDwyer 1 87
(JSMoore) *led: rdn along 2f out: drvn and hdd ent last: kpt on same pce* **5/2**[1]

0-03 **4** *2 1/2* **Freak Occurence (IRE)**[10] [1831] 3-9-7 **82** ........ DHolland 6 84
(MissECLavelle) *in tch: lost pl and towards rr 1/2-way: hdwy 3f out: rdn 2f out: sn drvn and no imp* **6/1**[2]

-000 **5** *3* **Poppys Footprint (IRE)**[19] [1614] 3-9-0 **75** ........ PFessey 4 70
(KARyan) *towards rr: hdwy on inner over 3f out: chsd ldrs 2f out: sn rdn and kpt on same pce fnl 2f* **33/1**

246- **6** *hd* **Charlotte Vale**[261] [4479] 3-8-7 **68** ........ ACulhane 9 63
(MDHammond) *bhd: hdwy 3f out: styd on fnl 2f: nrst fin* **50/1**

663- **7** *nk* **Aperitif**[183] [5977] 3-9-0 **75** ........ RHills 11 69
(WJHaggas) *unruly stalls: dwlt and towards rr: hdwy 3f out: rdn along 2f out: nrst fin* **14/1**

-015 **8** *1 3/4* **Cotosol**[10] [1841] 3-9-2 **77** ........ IMongan 15 67
(BAMcmahon) *in tch: hdwy to chse ldrs over 2f out: sn rdn and wknd wl over 1f out* **20/1**

64-2 **9** *2* **Rondelet (IRE)**[24] [1506] 3-9-2 **77** ........ SSanders 10 62
(RMBeckett) *in tch: rdn along 3f out: hung lft and wknd 2f out* **10/1**

11-0 **10** *5* **Breathing Sun (IRE)**[28] [1414] 3-9-3 **78** ........(t) KFallon 7 52
(WJMusson) *dwlt: a rr* **7/1**[3]

1201 **11** *11* **Play Master (IRE)**[24] [1506] 3-8-13 **74** ........ WRyan 5 23
(DHaydnJones) *prom: rdn along over 3f out: sn wknd* **12/1**

4115 **12** *2 1/2* **Certifiable**[20] [1585] 3-8-12 **73** ........ ANicholls 13 16
(AndrewReid) *midfield: hdwy on outer over 3f out: rdn and btn 2f out* **25/1**

015- **13** *4* **Swift Sailing (USA)**[266] [4327] 3-9-5 **80** ........ MHills 14 14
(BWHills) *a rr* **20/1**

2-25 **14** *5* **Gjovic**[33] [1322] 3-9-3 **78** ........(b[1]) KDarley 12 —
(BJMeehan) *in tch: rdn along 3f out: sn wknd* **25/1**

1m 41.4s (3.66) **Going Correction** +0.65s/f (Yiel) **14** Ran SP% **120.0**
Speed ratings: **107,106,105,103,100 99,99,97,95,90 79,77,73,68**CSF £86.57 CT £303.96 TOTE £12.00: £3.70, £2.40, £1.80; EX 122.10.
**Owner** D Maloney **Bred** Margaret Conlon **Trained** Pandy, Gwent

**FOCUS**
A race run at a fair tempo, but it was crucial to be close to the pace and very few got into it.

**NOTEBOOK**
**Oddsmaker(IRE)** was dropping back from 12 furlongs and found this trip much more to his liking. Always stalking the leader, he found plenty when asked to go and win his race and looks progressive, but this was a contest where racing close to the pace was a major advantage.
**Inchloss(IRE)**, a winner over six furlongs last time and making his handicap debut, was never too far away but still deserves credit as being the only one to get amongst the two front runners. He has scope for further improvement.
**Barathea Dreams(IRE)**, raised 6lb for his Sandown victory, established his normal position out in front. The track favouring horses with his style of running probably enabled him to hang on for as long as he did, but this was still a decent effort.
**Freak Occurence(IRE)** ran a nice race and was coming home as well as any. He could be interesting over ten furlongs.
**Poppys Footprint(IRE)** is being given a chance by the Handicapper and ran as well as could be expected given the way the track was suiting front runners. This does look her best trip.
**Charlotte Vale** ◆, still a maiden, ran especially well considering the way the track was riding and did not give the impression she was bothered by this longer trip. She is one to keep an eye on.
**Breathing Sun(IRE)** did not improve for the reapplication of the tongue tie, but in his defence he was trying to achieve the impossible in coming from off the pace and this was the first time he had encountered soft ground.
**Gjovic** *Official explanation: jockey said colt ran too free in the early stages and was unsuited by the dead ground.*

## 2070 SWISSCOM EUROSPOT STKS (H'CAP) 1m 3f 198y
**4:10** (4:11) (D ) (0-85,85) 3-Y-O **£6,610** (£2,034; £1,017; £508) **Stalls** Low

Form RPR

02-3 **1** **Cutting Crew (USA)**[20] [1588] 3-9-3 **81** ........ MartinDwyer 8 96
(PWHarris) *mde all: rdn over 1f out and styd on strly* **9/1**

4-12 **2** *4* **Absolutelythebest (IRE)**[28] [1416] 3-9-0 **78** ........ EAhern 3 87?
(EALDunlop) *lw: scope: midfield: hdwy 5f out: rdn to chse ldrs over 2f out: drvn and ev ch over 1f out: kpt on same pce ins last* **8/1**[3]

5521 **3** *1 3/4* **Nessen Dorma (IRE)**[10] [1823] 3-9-1 **79** 5ex........ MFenton 7 85
(JGGiven) *cl up tl lost pl after 2f: behind and rdn along 1/2-way: swtchd wd and hdwy over 3f out: kpt on u.p fnl 2f* **20/1**

51 **4** *nk* **Dallool**[19] [1605] 3-9-1 **79** ........ PRobinson 1 85
(MAJarvis) *trckd ldrs: hdwy 3f out: sn chsng wnr: rdn wl over 1f out: drvn and wknd ins last* **10/3**[2]

3522 **5** *5* **Gavroche (IRE)**[10] [1831] 3-8-6 **73** ........ J-PGuillambert[(3)] 9 71
(CADwyer) *midfield: hdwy to chse ldrs over 4f out: rdn over 2f out and grad wknd* **33/1**

13 **6** *3* **Jomacomi**[17] [1672] 3-9-3 **81** ........ JFanning 11 75
(MJohnston) *prom: rdn along over 3f out and sn wknd* **14/1**

4-60 **7** *1 3/4* **Royal Distant (USA)**[21] [1558] 3-8-12 **76** ........ DaleGibson 2 67
(MWEasterby) *midfield: hdwy on inner to chse ldrs 3f out: 2f out and grad wknd* **50/1**

1 **8** *9* **Master Wells (IRE)**[15] [1713] 3-9-7 **85** ........ LDettori 4 63
(JDBethell) *s.i.s and bhd: effrt and sme hdwy 3f out: sn rdn and nvr a factor* **16/1**

140- **9** *nk* **Saida Lenasera (FR)**[237] [5033] 3-8-12 **76** ........ ACulhane 5 53
(MrsPSly) *a towards rr* **100/1**

60-4 **10** *4* **Scarrabus (IRE)**[31] [1356] 3-8-11 **75** ........ TQuinn 10 46
(BGPowell) *stdd s: a rr* **100/1**

1-01 **11** *26* **Anousa (IRE)**[10] [1831] 3-9-4 **82** 5ex........(v) KFallon 6 14
(PHowling) *a rr* **12/1**

45-3 **12** *20* **Glide**[31] [1365] 3-8-7 **71** ........ KDarley 14 —
(RCharlton) *midfield: gd hdwy on outer to chse ldrs 1/2-way: rdn along over 3f out and sn wknd* **9/1**

41-2 **13** *6* **Asiatic**[7] [1899] 3-9-2 **80** ........ KDalgleish 13 —
(MJohnston) *prom: niggled along 1/2-way: rdn over 3f out and sn wknd* **11/4**[1]

304 **14** *dist* **Border Saint**[30] [1387] 3-9-1 **79** ........ IMongan 12 —
(MLWBell) *chsd ldrs: rdn along 4f out: sn wknd* **25/1**

2m 35.57s (6.71) **Going Correction** +0.65s/f (Yiel) **14** Ran SP% **116.6**
Speed ratings: **103,100,99,98,95 93,92,86,86,83 66,52,48,**—CSF £72.42 CT £1402.31 TOTE £9.70: £2.70, £4.90; EX 58.50.
**Owner** Mrs P W Harris **Bred** P W Harris **Trained** Ringshall, Bucks
■ Stewards Enquiry : E Ahern five-day ban: used whip with excessive frequency (May 24-28)

**FOCUS**
Another race run at a fair pace and again there was a bias towards those that raced prominently. The field finished well strung out.

**NOTEBOOK**
**Cutting Crew(USA)** ◆, a maiden coming into this, was in the ideal position out in front given the way the track was riding. Very brave down the home straight, this longer trip proved ideal and he was pulling away again at the line. The best of him may yet to be seen.
**Absolutelythebest(IRE)**, raised 5lb for getting beaten last time, did his best to get on terms with the winner down the home straight, but found him too strong. This was a decent effort nonetheless and he still remains open to improvement on turf.
**Nessen Dorma(IRE)**, carrying a 5lb penalty for his Doncaster win, ran a very strange race. After holding a prominent position early, he came off the bridle at halfway and dropped back, appearing likely to finish in rear, but he picked up again in the straight and was staying on throughout the last couple of furlongs. A step back up in trip looks necessary.
**Dallool**, having only his third start and making his handicap debut, tried to launch a challenge racing down the home straight but his efforts to get on terms eventually took their toll. There is still room for improvement.
**Gavroche(IRE)** ran with credit, but he seemed to find this trip in the conditions a shade too far. He does not have the scope of some of those that finished ahead of him, but will find easier opportunities than this.
**Jomacomi** showed up for a long way before finding it all too much. He still has scope for improvement as he did not race as a juvenile and this was only his third-ever start, but he does not look particularly well handicapped at present.
**Master Wells(IRE)**, winner of a slowly run heavy-ground Pontefract maiden on his only previous start, looked extremely badly handicapped judged on that. Giving away ground at the start was the last thing he needed and he never got into the race. Its seems as though he is going to need a lot of help from the Handicapper.
**Anousa(IRE)**, trying an extra three furlongs following his Kempton victory and carrying a 5lb penalty, was out the back the whole way and is surely better than this.
**Glide** kept wide in search of better ground, tended to carry his head to one side and never looked at all happy.
**Asiatic** was hugely disappointing considering he was in a good position early, and perhaps this came too quickly after his promising Chester reappearance. *Official explanation: trainer was unable to offer any explanation for poor form shown*
**Border Saint** *Official explanation: jockey said gelding had lost his action.*

## 2071 CONSTANT SECURITY MAIDEN FILLIES' STKS 5f 3y
**4:45** (4:47) (D ) 2-Y-O **£4,875** (£1,500; £750; £375) **Stalls** High

Form RPR

2 **1** **Dance Away**[29] [1399] 2-8-11 ........ JMackay 4 91+
(MLWBell) *cl up: led wl over 1f out: qcknd clr ent last: easily* **9/2**[3]

**2** *4* **Mizz Tee (IRE)** 2-8-8 ........ DAllan[(3)] 8 75+
(TDEasterby) *chsd ldrs: effrt 2f out: swtchd lft and rdn over 1f out: styd on wl fnl f* **16/1**

**3** *nk* **Nufoos** 2-8-11 ........ RHills 1 74+
(MJohnston) *w'like: scope: cl up: ev ch 2f out: sn rdn and one pce appr last* **11/2**

32 **4** *2* **Smiddy Hill**[14] [1717] 2-8-11 ........ RFfrench 6 66
(RBastiman) *led: rdn along 2f out: sn hdd & wknd appr last* **25/1**

2 **5** *3 1/2* **Alexander Capetown (IRE)**[10] [1839] 2-8-11 ........ MHills 3 52
(BWHills) *towards rr: pushed along and hdwy 2f out: sn rdn and no imp* **4/1**[2]

**6** *1* **Tesary** 2-8-11 ........ EAhern 7 48
(EALDunlop) *bkwd: in tch: rdn along over 2f out: sn wknd* **12/1**

**7** *2 1/2* **Burton Ash** 2-8-11 ........ MFenton 10 38
(JGGiven) *w'like: bhd fr 1/2-way* **25/1**

**8** *1* **Deputy Of Wood (USA)** 2-8-11 ........ KFallon 5 34
(PFICole) *trckd ldrs: shkn up 1/2-way: sn rdn and wknd* **9/4**[1]

6 **9** *1 1/4* **Melandre**[12] [1769] 2-8-11 ........ TWilliams 9 29
(MBrittain) *chsd ldrs:rdn over 2f out: grad wknd* **50/1**

45 **10** *11* **Next Time (IRE)**[32] [1340] 2-8-11 ........ LDettori 2 —
(MJPolglase) *swvd bdly lft s: a rr* **16/1**

61.34 secs (2.60) **Going Correction** +0.65s/f (Yiel) **10** Ran SP% **113.4**
Speed ratings: **105,98,98,94,89 87,83,82,80,62**CSF £69.11 TOTE £5.60: £1.70, £3.40, £2.00; EX 77.80 Place 6 £1,668.70, Place 5 £163.98.
**Owner** Cheveley Park Stud **Bred** Cheveley Park Stud Ltd **Trained** Newmarket, Suffolk

**FOCUS**
A truly run race and a cracking winning time for a race of its type at this stage of the season. Winners should come out of it.

**NOTEBOOK**
**Dance Away** ◆, all the better for her Newmarket debut, absolutely powered away from her rivals and had no problem with the softer conditions. She should be able to handle a step up in class now and looks very much an out-and-out sprinter.
**Mizz Tee(IRE)** ◆, a 15,000gns half-sister to Zaraglen, made a debut full of promise. Although well beaten by the winner, she was still going forward at the line and should looks sure to improve. Her pedigree also suggests she will appreciate further.
**Nufoos** ◆, who fetched 100,000gns as a foal and is a half-sister to the triple juvenile winner Valiant Romeo, showed good early pace and stayed on again after losing her pitch at halfway. She is likely to be hard to beat next time.

**Smiddy Hill** had the edge in experience and again showed good early pace, but this softer ground appeared to find her out and she lost two places in the last half-furlong. She has the ability to win a race and should find easier opportunities than this.
**Alexander Capetown(IRE)** did not really improve from her debut, but ran as though she may need an extra furlong now.
**Tesary**, a half-sister to the useful handicapper Baldour, is likely to do better in time.
**Deputy Of Wood(USA)**, a $220,000 half-sister to a couple of Graded winners in the US, was well backed to make a winning debut but was one of the first beaten. She is obviously thought capable of better, and perhaps a sounder surface will bring about some improvement.
T/Jkpt: Not won. T/Plt: £2,011.80 to a £1 stake. Pool: £111,892.40. 40.60 winning tickets.
T/Qpdt: £61.40 to a £1 stake. Pool: £9,195.30. 110.70 winning tickets. JR

## 1922 LONGCHAMP (R-H)
### Thursday, May 13

**OFFICIAL GOING: Very soft**

### 2072a PRIX DE GUICHE (GROUP 3) (COLTS) 1m 1f 55y
**1:20** (1:21) 3-Y-O **£25,704** (£10,282; £7,711; £5,141)

RPR

1 **Mister Sacha (FR)**[27] 3-9-2 ........ IMendizabal 3 108
(J-CRouget, France) *held up in 5th to straight, switched out & good headway over 1f out, driven to lead 150y out, ran on well* 1

2 1 ½ **Red Tune (FR)**[23] [1536] 3-9-2 ........ OPeslier 1 105
(MmeCHead-Maarek, France) *always close up, racing in 3rd to straight, ridden & every chance inside final f, ran on same pace* 3

3 1 **Charmo (FR)**[13] 3-9-2 ........ SPasquier 7 103
(PDemercastel, France) *raced in 4th to straight, headway on outside well over 1f out, every chance 150y out, one pace*

4 5 **Joursanvault (FR)**[8] [1898] 3-9-2 ........ CSoumillon 4 94
(ADeRoyer-Dupre, France) *led to 150y out, weakened quickly*

5 1 ½ **Marnhac (FR)**[32] [1350] 3-9-2 ........ C-PLemaire 6 91
(PKhozian, France) *held up in rear, last straight, some headway on outside from well over 1f out, beaten approaching final f*

6 ¾ **Advice**[17] 3-9-2 ........ GaryStevens 5 90
(AFabre, France) *reluctant to load, raced in 6th to straight, never a factor* 2

7 6 **Larionov (IRE)**[23] [1536] 3-9-2 ........ DBoeuf 2 79
(ELellouche, France) *tracked leader to straight, ridden 2f out, weakened quickly, eased final f*

1m 57.8s **Going Correction** +0.575s/f (Yiel) 7 Ran SP% **122.9**
Speed ratings: **114,112,111,107,106 105,100.**
**Owner** Lagardere Family **Bred** Snc Lagardere Elevage **Trained** France

**NOTEBOOK**
**Mister Sacha(FR)**, shut in early in the straight, saw daylight one and a half furlongs out. The colt accelerated impressively after a couple of taps from his jockey and he then outclassed the field. He is now unbeaten in three races this season and goes on to the Prix Jean-Prat. Definitely one for the notebook.
**Red Tune(FR)**, racing on the rail and never far from the leader, he was extracted to challenge halfway up the straight and ran on well but he didn't have the same acceleration as the winner. This colt looks progressive and is capable of winning a similar race
**Charmo(FR)** was the first to attack the longtime leader at the furlong pole but he couldn't quicken with the winner and runner-up. It was a decent effort from this rank outsider.

### 2073a PRIX HOCQUART (GROUP 2) (C&F) 1m 4f
**2:20** (2:20) 3-Y-O **£42,148** (£16,268; £7,765; £5,176)

RPR

1 **Lord Du Sud (FR)**[34] 3-9-2 ........ ELegrix 1 111
(J-CRouget, France) *close 3rd to straight, led on rails 2f out, driven out* 3

2 ¾ **Prospect Park**[39] [1260] 3-9-2 ........ OPeslier 6 110
(CLaffon-Parias, France) *restrained in rear, last straight, headway on outside from 2f out, chased winner final f, nearest at finish* 1

3 3 **Cherry Mix (FR)**[32] [1350] 3-9-2 ........ GaryStevens 5 105
(AFabre, France) *raced in 4th to straight, stayed on at one pace final 2f, took 3rd 100y out*

4 1 ½ **Malevitch (IRE)**[32] [1350] 3-9-2 ........ DBoeuf 2 103
(ELellouche, France) *set steady pace, led til edged left & headed 2f out, one pace*

5 5 **King Of Cry (FR)** 3-9-2 ........ CNora 4 96
(RMartin-Sanchez, Spain) *raced in 5th to straight, ridden & beaten well over 1f out*

6 5 **Fast And Furious (FR)**[32] [1350] 3-9-2 ........ IMendizabal 3 88
(J-CRouget, France) *tracked leader to straight, soon beaten* 2

2m 35.9s **Going Correction** +0.575s/f (Yiel) 6 Ran SP% **103.3**
Speed ratings: **117,116,114,113,110 106.**
**Owner** Mme B Hermelin **Bred** Alexandre Guerni **Trained** France

**NOTEBOOK**
**Lord Du Sud(FR)** stayed on strongly and definitely acts well on testing ground. Now unbeaten in four races he's improving with every outing and has now earned a tilt at the Prix du Jockey- Club.
**Prospect Park** was outpaced when things quickened up in the straight and then stayed on progressively as the race came to an end. Ridden closer to the pace he might have troubled the winner a little more. He is still on target for the Jockey-Club.
**Cherry Mix(FR)** ran free early on before settling in fourth position and appeared unbalanced halfway up the straight, before he then ran on again up the far rail.

## 1929 HAMILTON (R-H)
### Friday, May 14

**OFFICIAL GOING: Good to soft (good in places)**

### 2074 SKY BET WATCH & BET PRESS RED MAIDEN AUCTION STKS (QUALIFIER FOR HAMILTON PARK 2YO SERIES) 6f 5y
**6:20** (6:20) (E) 2-Y-O **£3,867** (£1,190; £595; £297) **Stalls** High

Form RPR

3 1 **Alsu (IRE)**[17] [1686] 2-8-4 ........ MartinDwyer 2 66
(AMBalding) *w ldrs: led 1/2-way: clr appr fnl f: edgd lft ins last: r.o* **7/4**[2]

2 1 ¾ **Trickshot** 2-8-2 ........ DaleGibson 5 59
(TDEasterby) *s.i.s and sn wl bhd: gd hdwy over 1f out: r.o: no ch w wnr* **25/1**[3]

2 3 nk **Exit Smiling**[18] [1658] 2-8-9 ........ RFfrench 7 65
(MJohnston) *cl up: rdn 1/2-way: one pce fr over 1f out* **4/6**[1]

4 shd **Melvino** 2-8-3 ........ PMakin(5) 6 64
(TDBarron) *led to 1/2-way: sn rdn: kpt on same pce fnl f* **25/1**[3]

0 5 nk **Dramatic Review (IRE)**[30] [1390] 2-8-5 ........ LEnstone(3) 3 63
(PCHaslam) *sn outpcd: hdwy over 1f out: kpt on: nrst fin* **33/1**

0 6 6 **Ahaz**[17] [1686] 2-8-2 ........ BSwarbrick(5) 4 44
(IAWood) *in tch 2f: sn outpcd* **50/1**

7 5 **Fransiscan** 2-8-0 ........ RoryMoore(7) 1 29
(PCHaslam) *sn outpcd: no ch fr 1/2-way* **33/1**

1m 15.97s (2.87) **Going Correction** +0.125s/f (Good) 7 Ran SP% **111.9**
Speed ratings: **85,82,82,82,81 73,67**CSF £35.59 TOTE £2.80: £1.70, £4.80; EX 19.60.
**Owner** Columbus Costa del Sol **Bred** Gaucho Ltd **Trained** Kingsclere, Hants

**FOCUS**
With the first five home covered by just over two lengths, this bare form is nothing out of the ordinary and the time was slow, but the winner is a well regarded type who may well be capable of better and there were a couple of other promising performances.

**NOTEBOOK**
**Alsu(IRE)** confirmed debut promise over this extra furlong and won with a bit more in hand than the official margin suggests. Life will be tougher under a penalty, but it will be no surprise to see her fare better again.
**Trickshot**, the second foal of a five-furlong winner, is not much to look at at this stage but showed more than enough, despite running green, on this racecourse debut to suggest she can win a small race.
**Exit Smiling**, up in trip, again ran creditably and, although off the bridle a long way out, stuck to his task in a manner that suggested a further step up in trip on a more galloping course may be the answer.
**Melvino**, who is related to a couple of juvenile winners, showed more than enough, despite looking in need of the race, to suggest he will be winning races in due course. He has plenty of physical scope and is one to keep an eye on.
**Dramatic Review(IRE)**, who still looked in need of the race, has plenty of scope for improvement and fared a good deal better than on his debut. A stiffer test of stamina will suit and he looks the type to win races over further in due course.
**Ahaz** looked fit and in tremendous condition but again offered no immediate encouragement.
**Fransiscan**, the first foal of a dam who won over middle distances, is not very big and was soundly beaten on this debut outing.

### 2075 MCGRATTAN PILING H'CAP 6f 5y
**6:50** (6:50) (C) (0-95,87) 3-Y-O **£9,326** (£3,537; £1,768; £804) **Stalls** High

Form RPR

01-0 1 **Bo McGinty (IRE)**[9] [1881] 3-8-10 **79** ........ THamilton(3) 5 84
(RAFahey) *chsd ldrs: rdn to ld over 1f out: kpt on fnl f: hld on wl* **11/4**[1]

-005 2 shd **Lets Get It On (IRE)**[20] [1614] 3-8-9 **75** ........ RWinston 2 80
(JJQuinn) *hld up: gd hdwy over 1f out: kpt on wl: jst hld* **11/1**

00-0 3 4 **Louisiade (IRE)**[27] [1473] 3-8-2 **68** ........ DaleGibson 3 61
(TDEasterby) *hld up: hdwy over 1f out: kpt on: no imp* **20/1**

0-06 4 ¾ **George The Best (IRE)**[13] [1760] 3-8-9 **75** ........ ACulhane 11 66
(MDHammond) *midfield: effrt 2f out: one pce fnl f* **11/2**[3]

002- 5 1 ¼ **Fiore Di Bosco (IRE)**[220] [5434] 3-8-11 **82** ........ PMakin(5) 8 69
(TDBarron) *hld up: rdn whn n.m.r wl over 1f out: no imp fnl f* **20/1**

334- 6 ½ **Sweet Cando (IRE)**[168] [6083] 3-7-12 **64** ........ RFfrench 1 50
(MissLAPerratt) *racd centre: effrt over 2f out: nt pce to chal* **40/1**

-304 7 ½ **A Little Bit Yarie**[18] [1659] 3-9-0 **80** ........ (v[1]) DarrenWilliams 9 64
(KRBurke) *led and clr tl hdd & wknd over 1f out* **8/1**

21-0 8 2 ½ **Granato (GER)**[31] [1388] 3-9-7 **87** ........ MartinDwyer 4 64
(ACStewart) *midfield: effrt over 2f out: btn ent fnl f* **7/2**[2]

9 4 **Madra Rua (IRE)**[202] [5759] 3-7-12 **64** oh1 ........ PFessey 10 29
(MissLAPerratt) *chsd ldrs tl wknd fr 2f out* **33/1**

13-6 10 6 **Vademecum**[22] [1558] 3-9-0 **80** ........ FLynch 7 27
(BSmart) *hld up: rdn 1/2-way: n.d* **11/2**[3]

1-60 11 5 **Attacca**[13] [1760] 3-8-9 **75** ........ (b[1]) JFanning 6 7
(JRWeymes) *bhd centre: drvn 1/2-way: nvr on terms* **33/1**

1m 13.29s (0.19) **Going Correction** +0.125s/f (Good) 11 Ran SP% **116.9**
Speed ratings: **103,102,97,96,94 94,93,90,84,76 70**CSF £31.35 CT £510.18 TOTE £3.60: £1.70, £3.10, £8.70; EX 64.90.
**Owner** Paddy McGinty & Bo Turnbull **Bred** Stephen Breen **Trained** Musley Bank, N Yorks

**FOCUS**
A fair handicap in which the field raced centre to far side, but the winner and second did well to pull so far clear of the remainder and both appeal as types to win more races in the coming weeks.

**NOTEBOOK**
**Bo McGinty(IRE)** ◆, who was not totally disgraced from a poor draw on softer ground on his reappearance, turned in a much-improved display and showed the right attitude. The way he travelled through the race suggested there may be more to come, and he may be able to hold his own in a more competitive race after reassessment.
**Lets Get It On(IRE)** ◆ has improved with every outing this term and ran a career-best race in defeat. She deserves extra credit as this course favours those racing up with the pace and, although she will be up in the weights for this, is more than capable of winning a similar race in the near future.
**Louisiade(IRE)** fared a good deal better than on his reappearance and, although a stiffer test of stamina over this trip may have helped, he would not be one to write off in less competitive company from his current mark just yet.
**George The Best(IRE)** had the best of the draw and was not disgraced, but did not really leave the impression that he was a winner waiting to happen.
**Fiore Di Bosco(IRE)** was not disgraced after meeting trouble on her reappearance run but, although entitled to strip fitter for it, does look a shade high in the weights at present.
**Sweet Cando(IRE)** fared a bit better than the bare result after racing in the centre from her low draw and, with her stable among the winners of late, would not be one to write off just yet.
**A Little Bit Yarie** pulled too hard in the first-time visor and on his first run over this trip and did not get home. He looks vulnerable from this mark but will be suited by the return to five furlongs.
**Granato(GER)** was again disappointing and, although he looks plenty high enough in the weights and may not have been suited by this track, he has a bit to prove at present.
**Vademecum** *Official explanation: trainer said gelding had mucus in its nostrils*

### 2076 SAFFIE JOSEPH & SONS BRAVEHEART RATED STKS (H'CAP) (LISTED RACE) 1m 4f 17y
**7:25** (7:25) (A) (0-110,109) 4-Y-O+ **£20,300** (£7,700; £3,850; £1,750) **Stalls** Low

Form RPR

03-0 1 **Collier Hill**[9] [1880] 6-8-8 **96** ........ RWinston 4 107
(GASwinbank) *hld up: hdwy whn n.m.r wl over 2f out: effrt over 1f out: led ins fnl f: hld on wl* **9/1**

0601 2 nk **Vintage Premium**[1] [2066] 7-8-13 **101** 3ex ........ THamilton 6 112
(RAFahey) *led to over 2f out: rallied and ev ch ins fnl f: kpt on gamely: jst hld* **8/1**

50-2 3 2 ½ **Bourgeois**[38] [1286] 7-8-7 **95** ........ FLynch 10 102
(TDEasterby) *midfield: pushed along 1/2-way: effrt over 2f out: one pce ins fnl f* **9/2**[1]

-005 4 1 **Perfect Storm**[13] [1768] 5-8-7 **95** oh4 ........ FNorton 12 101
(MBlanshard) *hld up: hdwy to ld over 2f out: edgd rt: hdd and no ex ins fnl f* **10/1**

502- **5** *10* **Sun Bird (IRE)**[209] 5639 6-9-1 **103** ACulhane 3 94
(RAllan) *hld up: pushed along over 2f out: kpt on fnl f: n.d* **16/1**
25/2 **6** *1 ¼* **Grampian**[20] 1618 5-9-0 **102** MFenton 11 91
(JGGiven) *chsd ldrs: effrt and edgd lft over 2f out: no ex over 1f out* **10/1**
461- **7** *1 ¼* **Desert Quest (IRE)**[214] 5550 4-8-7 **95** oh6 (v) MartinDwyer 7 82
(AMBalding) *midfield: rdn whn nt clr run over 2f out: sn rdn and btn* **25/1**
520- **8** *½* **Fight Your Corner**[330] 2481 5-9-7 **109** (t) KMcEvoy 9 95
(SaeedBinSuroor) *chsd ldrs: effrt whn carried sltly rt over 2f out: sn btn* **6/1**[2]
4052 **9** *6* **Bonecrusher**[23] 1540 5-9-5 **107** TPQueally 2 84
(DRLoder) *hld up: effrt whn bdly hmpd over 2f out: nt rcvr* **9/2**[1]
31/4 **10** *2* **Legal Approach**[20] 1618 5-9-7 **109** RFfrench 8 83
(MJohnston) *in tch tl rdn and wknd over 3f out* **25/1**
265 **11** *11* **Easter Ogil (IRE)**[24] 1522 9-8-7 **95** oh40 PMakin 1 53
(JaneSouthcombe) *bhd: rdn 1/2-way: nvr on terms* **200/1**
151- **12** *16* **Morson Boy (USA)**[308] 3188 4-8-11 **99** JFanning 5 33
(MJohnston) *trckd ldr: rdn 4f out: outpcd whn bdly hmpd over 2f out: virtually p.u* **7/1**[3]

2m 37.13s (-2.07) **Going Correction** +0.20s/f (Good) **12** Ran SP% **116.5**
Speed ratings: **114,113,112,111,104 103,103,102,98,97 90,79**CSF £76.66 CT £370.00 TOTE £11.10: £3.40, £5.00, £2.00; EX 103.90.
**Owner** R H Hall & Ashley Young **Bred** George Strawbridge **Trained** Melsonby, N Yorks
■ Stewards Enquiry : F Norton two-day ban: careless riding (May 25,26)

**FOCUS**
A competitive handicap in which the pace was sound and the time was good, but it proved a very messy race and the final placings of a couple of these is best ignored. Nevertheless a gutsy performance from Collier Hill, who likes it here and turned in a career-best effort.

**NOTEBOOK**
**Collier Hill**, who did not stay two and a quarter miles last time, proved well suited by the return to this track and trip and turned in a career-best effort. He is a useful performer around this trip on good and softer ground.
**Vintage Premium**, who broke a long losing run at York the previous day, ran equally as well over this longer trip under his penalty and again showed the right attitude under pressure. He is vulnerable to progressive sorts from his mark, but should continue to go well now he has found his feet again.
**Bourgeois**, 6lb higher than when placed in this race last year, lost very little in defeat but is another vulnerable from his current mark and his wins on the Flat are few and far between these days.
**Perfect Storm ◆**, 4lb out of the handicap, shaped as though better than the bare result, as he made up plenty of ground in a fairly short space of time then had little to offer in the closing stages. He is one to keep an eye on.
**Sun Bird(IRE)**, who turned in a career-best effort when second in last year's Cesarewitch on his latest start, shaped as though retaining a fair bit of his ability over a trip a fair bit short of his optimum. Life will not be easy in handicaps from this mark, but he will be much better suited by a much stiffer test of stamina.
**Grampian** ran creditably back in handicap company with very few excuses other than that he may well continue to look vulnerable from his current mark in this sort of company.
**Desert Quest(IRE)** should have been suited by the return to this trip on this first start for new connections but did not show enough to suggest he will be winning from his current mark in competitive handicaps in the near future.
**Fight Your Corner**, tried in a tongue-tie and back in trip for this first start since last June, looked in tremendous condition but was edgy in the preliminaries and ran below his best. He may not be the easiest to place successfully.
**Bonecrusher**, upped in trip, did not get the chance to show whether he stayed and is worth another chance over it. *Official explanation: jockey said gelding suffered interference below the 3f marker*
**Morson Boy(USA)**, a progressive sort last year, looked fit enough to do himself justice on this reappearance run. He was the worst sufferer in the trouble and, although looking held at the time, is not one to write off just yet.

## 2077 LUDDON CONSTRUCTION MAIDEN STKS 1m 1f 36y
**7:55** (7:57) (D) 3-Y-O+ **£6,240** (£1,920; £960; £480) **Stalls** High

Form RPR
5-22 **1** **Never Will**[12] 1794 3-8-9 JFanning 4 84
(MJohnston) *mde all: rdn 2f out: hld on wl* **8/11**[1]
043- **2** *1* **Reservoir (IRE)**[191] 5925 3-8-9 77 MartinDwyer 1 82
(WJHaggas) *chsd ldrs: rdn and outpcd 2f out: kpt on fnl f* **11/2**[3]
2 **3** *¾* **Backgammon**[16] 1713 3-8-6 TPQueally(3) 5 81
(DRLoder) *dwlt: sn prom: smooth hdwy and ch 2f out: sn rdn: one pce fnl f* **11/4**[2]
33 **4** *3* **Into The Shadows**[12] 1786 4-8-13 TEaves(5) 3 70
(MrsMReveley) *hld up: shkn up 3f out: kpt on: nvr nrr* **20/1**
4 **5** *8* **Caymans Gift**[12] 1786 4-9-4 PMulrennan(5) 6 59
(ACWhillans) *in tch to over 3f out: sn btn* **50/1**
000- **6** *15* **Kintore**[238] 5029 3-8-9 MFenton 7 29
(JSGoldie) *chsd ldrs tl wknd fr 3f out* **100/1**
- **7** *9* **Howards Rocket** 3-8-9 RWinston 2 11
(ISemple) *s.i.s: n.d* **33/1**

2m 1.35s (1.75) **Going Correction** +0.20s/f (Good)
**WFA** 3 from 4yo 14lb **7** Ran SP% **110.6**
Speed ratings: **100,99,98,95,88 75,67**CSF £4.79 TOTE £1.70: £1.10, £3.10; EX 4.80.
**Owner** Maktoum Al Maktoum **Bred** Gainsborough Stud Management Ltd **Trained** Middleham Moor, N Yorks

**FOCUS**
Not the most competitive of maidens and the winner, who was allowed the run of the race, did not have to improve too much to get off the mark. He will be of interest in handicap company.

**NOTEBOOK**
**Never Will**, a progressive performer, very much had the rub of things and did not have to improve too much to get off the mark. He will be interesting in ordinary handicap company around this trip.
**Reservoir(IRE)** is a consistent sort who shaped as though retaining all his ability on this reappearance run, and on this evidence will not be inconvenienced by the step up to a mile and a quarter. He looks sure to win a similar race away from progressive sorts.
**Backgammon** ran creditably dropped in trip in these less testing conditions, but left the impression that the step up to middle distances and ordinary handicap company would be in his favour.
**Into The Shadows ◆**, dropped a fair way in trip for this third and qualifying run for a handicap mark, showed more than enough to suggest she can win an ordinary race in handicap company when returned to middle distances.
**Caymans Gift** was again well beaten and is likely to continue to look vulnerable in this grade.
**Kintore** is from an in-form stable but his future surely lies in low-grade handicap company.

## 2078 SKY VEGAS LIVE ON CHANNEL 295 H'CAP (QUALIFIER FOR TOTE BOOKMAKERS HANDICAP SERIES FINAL) 1m 65y
**8:30** (8:31) (E) (0-75,72) 3-Y-O+ **£4,371** (£1,345; £672; £336) **Stalls** High

Form RPR
00-5 **1** **Jordans Elect**[18] 1660 4-9-0 **65** TEaves(5) 11 74
(ISemple) *w ldr: led ent fnl f: edgd lft: drvn out* **7/1**[2]
0002 **2** *¾* **Meelup (IRE)**[11] 2343 4-8-8 **57** (p) LEnstone(3) 13 64
(JaneSouthcombe) *led to ent fnl f: rallied: hld towards fin* **16/1**
00-0 **3** *nk* **Mount Pekan (IRE)**[30] 1393 4-8-0 **46** FNorton 4 52
(JSGoldie) *plld hrd: stdd rr: gd hdwy centre over 1f out: r.o wl fnl f* **20/1**
0603 **4** *2* **Bailieborough (IRE)**[10] 1868 5-9-7 **67** AlexGreaves 7 69
(DNicholls) *hld up midfield: effrt whn nt clr run over 2f to over 1f out: r.o fnl f* **14/1**
3250 **5** *½* **Sarraaf (IRE)**[14] 1746 8-9-11 **71** ACulhane 12 72
(ISemple) *prom: drvn over 2f out: kpt on same pce fnl f* **7/1**[2]
60-0 **6** *shd* **Wuxi Venture**[6] 1962 9-9-3 **66** THamilton(3) 6 67
(RAFahey) *in tch on outside: effrt over 2f out: edgd rt: no imp over 1f out* **8/1**[3]
3010 **7** *hd* **Pharoah's Gold (IRE)**[10] 1875 6-8-8 **54** (v) DarrenWilliams 5 54
(DShaw) *hld up: hdwy over 1f out: n.m.r ins fnl f: nvr rchd ldrs* **10/1**
-006 **8** *1 ½* **Clann A Cougar**[10] 1857 4-8-12 **63** (b) BSwarbrick(5) 14 60
(IAWood) *chsd ldrs tl wknd over 1f out* **14/1**
/5-0 **9** *1* **Late Arrival**[20] 1620 7-8-1 **47** DaleGibson 10 42
(MDHammond) *trckd ldrs: rdn over 3f out: wknd over 1f out* **66/1**
06-0 **10** *1* **Gifted Flame**[30] 1393 5-9-0 **65** PMakin(5) 9 58
(TDBarron) *hld up: rdn 3f out: n.d* **8/1**[3]
5-02 **11** *1 ¼* **Anthemion (IRE)**[12] 1783 7-9-0 **60** RFfrench 8 51
(MrsJCMcgregor) *prom tl rdn and wknd fr 2f out* **9/1**
06-0 **12** *shd* **Basinet**[20] 1620 6-8-10 **56** RWinston 3 46
(JJQuinn) *hld up: rdn 3f out: n.d* **16/1**
0311 **13** *nk* **Ace Coming**[7] 1932 3-8-3 **67** 6ex (b) PMulrennan(5) 1 57
(DEddy) *hld up: rdn over 2f out: sn btn* **7/2**[1]
-300 **14** *3 ½* **Creskeld (IRE)**[28] 1451 5-9-12 **72** FLynch 2 54
(BSmart) *sn chsng ldrs: wknd 2f out: eased* **25/1**

1m 50.88s (1.58) **Going Correction** +0.20s/f (Good)
**WFA** 3 from 4yo+ 13lb **14** Ran SP% **123.7**
Speed ratings: **100,99,98,96,96 96,96,94,93,92 91,91,91,87**CSF £115.09 CT £2217.73 TOTE £9.70: £3.10, £8.60, £5.80; EX 87.10.
**Owner** Ian Crawford **Bred** James Thom And Sons **Trained** Carluke, S Lanarks

**FOCUS**
A run-of-the-mill handicap in which the pace was fair and the whole field raced centre to stands' side in the straight. Those racing up with the pace had the edge so the third home may be a bit better than the bare form.

**NOTEBOOK**
**Jordans Elect** had the run of the race from his favourable draw and elected to put his best foot forward but, given his record, would be no certainty to put it all in next time.
**Meelup(IRE)** ran creditably from a favourable draw but, given his record is one of inconsistency and that he did have the run of the race, he may not be one to get too heavily involved with at shortish odds next time.
**Mount Pekan(IRE)**, from a stable among the winners, shaped well given how the race unfolded but, given he looks far from straightforward and, with his record, he may not be one to be lumping on at shortish odds.
**Bailieborough(IRE) ◆**, who did not get the best of runs, again shaped as though coming to hand and is more than capable of winning a race around this trip from his current mark in the near future.
**Sarraaf(IRE)** was well drawn and had conditions and the trip to suit and, although not disgraced, remains one to place minimal faith in.
**Wuxi Venture** may be a bit better than the bare form as he saw plenty of daylight on the outside of the field and, with his stable starting to hit top gear, would not be one to write off just yet.
**Ace Coming** was well supported but was a long way below his recent best from the worst draw and on very different ground conditions.

## 2079 CMPE GLASGOW CLASSIFIED STKS 5f 4y
**9:05** (9:06) (E) 3-Y-O+ **£3,802** (£1,170; £585; £292) **Stalls** High

Form RPR
0204 **1** **The Fisio**[24] 1518 4-9-8 70 (v) MartinDwyer 6 80
(AMBalding) *w ldr: led 1/2-way: hld on wl fnl f* **4/1**[2]
0410 **2** *½* **Frascati**[6] 1956 4-9-6 71 FLynch 3 76
(ABerry) *trckd ldrs: effrt over 2f out: kpt on fnl f* **12/1**
-500 **3** *nk* **Chairman Bobby**[6] 1974 6-9-1 69 RoryMoore(7) 8 77
(DWBarker) *led to 1/2-way: rallied: kpt on same pce ins fnl f* **4/1**[2]
210- **4** *nk* **Twice Upon A Time**[209] 5634 5-9-8 73 ACulhane 7 76
(BSmart) *hld up in tch: effrt over 1f out: r.o u.p fnl f* **9/2**[3]
40-0 **5** *hd* **Vigorous (IRE)**[11] 1825 4-9-8 73 AlexGreaves 4 75?
(DNicholls) *trckd ldrs: effrt over 1f out: nt qckn fnl f* **10/1**
0-32 **6** *2 ½* **Roxanne Mill**[7] 1937 6-9-4 74 BSwarbrick(5) 2 67
(JMBradley) *in tch: effrt 2f out: rdn and veered lft over 1f out: sn one pce* **3/1**[1]
600- **7** *nk* **Marshallspark (IRE)**[199] 5820 5-9-5 70 THamilton(3) 1 65
(RAFahey) *hld up in tch: rdn 2f out: no imp over 1f out* **20/1**
-000 **8** *6* **Regal Song (IRE)**[48] 1131 8-9-8 68 (b) RWinston 5 44
(TJEtherington) *hung rt and sn outpcd: nvr on terms* **10/1**

61.06 secs (-0.20) **Going Correction** +0.125s/f (Good) **8** Ran SP% **113.8**
Speed ratings: **106,105,104,104,103 99,99,89**CSF £49.43 TOTE £5.40: £1.70, £2.20, £1.80; EX 39.00 Place 6 £249.29, Place 5 £94.30.
**Owner** D H Caslon **Bred** E Duggan And D Churchman **Trained** Kingsclere, Hants
■ Stewards Enquiry : Rory Moore two-day ban: used whip with excessive frequency (May 25,26)

**FOCUS**
A tightly-knit conditions stakes run at a fair pace, and once again those that raced up with the pace had the edge.

**NOTEBOOK**
**The Fisio**, a fair performer on his day, had the run of the race that suits his style of racing and showed the right attitude to prevail. He should continue to give a good account.
**Frascati**, who floundered on bad ground from a poor draw last time, confirmed that running to be all wrong and is capable of winning another small race from her current mark.
**Chairman Bobby** had a little bit to find at the weights, but confirmed his latest and rare poor effort to be all wrong with a creditable run. However, this consistent sort is likely to look plenty high enough when returned to handicaps.
**Twice Upon A Time**, who goes well for Tony Culhane, confirmed she retains most of her ability but Hamilton would not be the best course to suit her come-from-behind style of racing. She is likely to win races this term.
**Vigorous(IRE) ◆** shaped a good deal better than her reappearance run, and will be one to note in handicaps from her current mark when her stable really starts to get into top gear.
**Roxanne Mill** looked to have solid claims at these weights but, although not disgraced, she did not look the easiest of rides and, given she has not won a race since August 2002, remains one to tread carefully with.
**Marshallspark(IRE)** was anything but disgraced over an inadequate trip on his reappearance and, given that his stable is back among the winners, will be one to keep an eye on granted a stiffer test in the near future.
T/Plt: £377.60 to a £1 stake. Pool: £46,094.00. 89.10 winning tickets. T/Qpdt: £33.70 to a £1 stake. Pool: £3,731.00. 81.90 winning tickets. RY

## 1455 NEWBURY (L-H)

Friday, May 14

**OFFICIAL GOING: Good (good to soft in places)**

### 2080 CANTOR SPORT CARNARVON STKS (LISTED RACE) 6f 8y
1:30 (1:31) (A) 3-Y-O £17,400 (£6,600; £3,300; £1,500) Stalls High

| Form | | | | RPR |
|---|---|---|---|---|
| 41-3 | 1 | | **So Will I**[27] 1459 3-8-11 109 RHills 8 (MPTregoning) *lw: bhd: pushed along over 3f out: swtchd to outside and hdwy over 2f out: str run to ld last half f: r.o wl* **15/8**[1] | 104+ |
| 2-54 | 2 | 1 | **Mac Love**[16] 1706 3-8-11 102 GCarter 5 (JAkehurst) *in tch: hdwy over 1f out: str run ins fnl f: fin wl but nt rch wnr* **40/1** | 101 |
| 12-4 | 3 | hd | **Nights Cross (IRE)**[34] 1323 3-9-1 104 ACulhane 4 (MRChannon) *lw: swtchd rt s: bhd: hdwy: swtchd lft and nt clr run over 1f out: swtchd rt and hmpd ins last: fin wl: nt rcvr* **20/1** | 104+ |
| 611- | 4 | ½ | **Rum Shot**[206] 5697 3-8-11 97 DaneO'Neill 2 (HCandy) *lw: chsd ldrs: rdn 2f out: led ins last: hdd and nt qckn last half f* **8/1** | 99 |
| 204- | 5 | 1 | **Botanical (USA)**[263] 4462 3-8-11 (t) LDettori 7 (SaeedBinSuroor) *trckd ldrs: led ins fnl 2f: sn rdn: hdd ins last: wknd nr fin* **14/1** | 96 |
| 11-2 | 6 | hd | **La Cucaracha**[17] 1685 3-8-6 99 MHills 9 (BWHills) *h.d.w: lw: hld up in tch: nt clr run 2f out: swtchd rt and hmpd over 1f out: stl no room thrght fnl f: nt rcvr* **3/1**[2] | 90+ |
| 2-11 | 7 | 2 | **Sevillano**[18] 1659 3-8-11 106 TEDurcan 3 (PDCundell) *sn chsng ldr: rdn 2f out: wknd fnl f* **6/1**[3] | 89 |
| 5-23 | 8 | 7 | **Crafty Fancy (IRE)**[16] 1706 3-8-6 93 TQuinn 11 (DJSFfrenchDavis) *in tch: rdn 3f out: swtchd lft and wknd fr 2f out* **40/1** | 63 |
| 05-1 | 9 | 2½ | **If Paradise**[34] 1323 3-9-1 105 RHughes 10 (RHannon) *lw: led tl hdd ins fnl 2f: wkng whn hmpd on rails over 1f out* **14/1** | 65 |
| 03- | 10 | 25 | **Innclassic (IRE)**[197] 5835 3-8-6 EAhern 6 (BJMeehan) *chsd ldrs tl wknd 2f out* **100/1** | — |
| 0-50 | 11 | 10 | **Venables (USA)**[30] 1396 3-9-1 104 (t) JPMurtagh 1 (RHannon) *sn bhd: lost tch and eased fnl 2f* **33/1** | — |

1m 13.73s (-0.64) **Going Correction** +0.075s/f (Good) 11 Ran SP% **112.1**
Speed ratings: **107,105,105,104,103 103,100,91,87,54 41**CSF £96.05 TOTE £2.80: £1.30, £8.50, £3.00; EX 138.60.
**Owner** Hamdan Al Maktoum **Bred** Mrs M Campbell-Andenaes **Trained** Lambourn, Berks
■ Stewards Enquiry : M Hills four-day ban: careless riding (May 25-28)

**FOCUS**
A decent sprint run at a solid pace, but the result can not be taken at face value as several horses suffered trouble in running.

**NOTEBOOK**
**So Will I**, despite looking to have it all to do from off the pace, picked up strongly approaching the final furlong to win a touch cosily in the end. This drop back to six furlongs was not sure to suit, but he was aided by a decent early gallop and he confirmed the promise of his third in the Greenham last month. A tilt at the Jersey Stakes back over seven furlongs is now very much on the cards.
**Mac Love** put in his best run for current connections and posted a welcome return to form. This display eased fears that he had failed to train on from his juvenile campaign, and he appreciated this better ground.
**Nights Cross(IRE)** can be considered unlucky. He was full of running when encountering serious traffic problems and finished best of all. This confirmed he has trained on and is best on a quick surface, but he will not be easy to place off his current mark.
**Rum Shot** made a pleasing comeback and only tired out of contention late on. He will come on plenty for this and could have a decent prize in him this year.
**Botanical(USA)** had the run of the race, but got tired inside the final furlong on this return from a 263-day layoff. He too is entitled to come on for the outing.
**La Cucaracha** was another to suffer serious traffic problems. She looked to be full of running on the rail, but had nowhere to go on several occasions and can be considered a lot better than the bare form suggests. She is pure speed and looks sure to win more races.
**Sevillano**, who had looked smart when dominating small fields the last twice, was found out by this step up in class and had no excuse.
**Innclassic(IRE)** *Official explanation: jockey said filly lost its action*
**Venables(USA)** *Official explanation: jockey said colt had a breathing problem*

### 2081 SWETTENHAM STUD FILLIES' TRIAL STKS (LISTED RACE) 1m 2f 6y
2:00 (2:01) (A) 3-Y-O £17,400 (£6,600; £3,300; £1,500) Stalls Centre

| Form | | | | RPR |
|---|---|---|---|---|
| 61-3 | 1 | | **Rave Reviews (IRE)**[12] 1793 3-8-9 81 KDarley 2 (JLDunlop) *lw: trckd ldrs: wnt 2nd over 2f out: drvn to chal over 1f out: slt ld ins last: hld on wl u.p* **7/1** | 105 |
| 61-2 | 2 | ¾ | **Sahool**[12] 1793 3-8-9 86 RHills 4 (MPTregoning) *lw: trckd ldr: chal 4f out: sn led: rdn 2f out: hdd ins last: styd on gamely tl no ex cl home* **4/1**[2] | 104 |
| 21-3 | 3 | 2½ | **Crystal Curling (IRE)**[9] 1879 3-8-9 MHills 7 (BWHills) *t.k.h: hld up rr but in tch: hdwy and n.m.r over 2f out: sn rdn: styd on same pce appr fnl f* **9/2**[3] | 99 |
| 1 | 4 | 2 | **Winds Of March (IRE)**[28] 1440 3-8-9 95 LDettori 5 (JHMGosden) *lw: chsd ldrs: rdn and edgd lft over 2f out: sn no imp: wknd appr fnl f* **5/4**[1] | 95 |
| 0-36 | 5 | 3 | **Ithaca (USA)**[9] 1879 3-8-9 102 RHughes 1 (HRACecil) *hld up rr but in tch: rdn and effrt over 2f out: n.d and wknd sn after* **16/1** | 90 |
| 6 | 6 | 6 | **Fire Finch**[36] 1311 3-8-9 TEDurcan 3 (MRChannon) *a in rr and n.d* **100/1** | 78? |
| 4-1 | 7 | 8 | **Pont Allaire (IRE)**[14] 1753 3-8-9 79 DaneO'Neill 6 (HCandy) *led tl hdd ins fnl 4f: wknd over 2f out* **12/1** | 63 |

2m 9.16s (0.45) **Going Correction** +0.075s/f (Good) 7 Ran SP% **109.7**
Speed ratings: **101,100,98,96,94 89,83**CSF £32.01 TOTE £9.00: £3.40, £2.30; EX 19.40.
**Owner** Prince A A Faisal **Bred** Quay Bldst The Luma Wells Syndicate And H King **Trained** Arundel, W Sussex

**FOCUS**
A fair pace to this fillies' Listed event and the first two pulled clear at the finish.

**NOTEBOOK**
**Rave Reviews(IRE)** stayed on strongly inside the last furlong to score a game success. She reversed recent Pretty Polly form with the runner-up and gave a strong impression that she will be even better over further, with the Ribblesdale at Royal Ascot a realistic target.
**Sahool** did not give up and ran a brave race. She ran close to the form of her second in the Pretty Polly last time, but narrowly failed to confirm the form with the winner. Likely to be suited by further, she too is likely to be aimed at the Ribblesdale.
**Crystal Curling(IRE)**, third last time out in the Cheshire Oaks, ran too keen in the early stages and could not find a change of gear late on. That said, this was another fair effort and she should not be long in winning a race, although any hopes of Group-race success look optimistic at this stage.
**Winds Of March(IRE)** looked a big threat to all approaching two out, but quickly came under pressure and could only keep on at the one pace from there on. She was reported to have been in season and it would be a suprise if she failed to leave this well behind in due course. *Official explanation: trainer said filly was in season*
**Ithaca(USA)** looks to be going the wrong way and has become most frustrating.
**Pont Allaire(IRE)** *Official explanation: trainer had no explanation for the poor form shown*

### 2082 SCOTTISH EQUITABLE/JOCKEYS ASSOCIATION OF GREAT BRITAIN STKS (H'CAP) 6f 8y
2:30 (2:30) (D) (0-85,85) 3-Y-O £6,188 (£1,904; £952; £476) Stalls High

| Form | | | | RPR |
|---|---|---|---|---|
| 46-0 | 1 | | **Wyatt Earp (IRE)**[31] 1388 3-8-10 74 JPMurtagh 9 (JARToller) *stdd s: hld up in tch: rdn and hdwy fr 2f out: led ins fnl f: hld on all out* **12/1** | 78 |
| 1-5 | 2 | nk | **Missus Links (USA)**[27] 1464 3-8-6 70 RHills 6 (RHannon) *led: rdn over 2f out: kpt slt advantage tl hdd ins fnl f: kpt on wl: no ex last strides* **6/1**[3] | 74 |
| 35-1 | 3 | shd | **Primo Way**[24] 1530 3-9-2 80 MHills 8 (BWHills) *lw: in tch: hdwy to trck ldrs and nt clr run over 1f out: swtchd rt jst ins last: fin strly* **7/2**[2] | 83+ |
| 40- | 4 | hd | **Delphie Queen (IRE)**[215] 5519 3-9-3 81 RHughes 10 (SKirk) *trckd ldrs: rdn 2f out: nt clr run 1f out and jst ins last: rallied and r.o wl cl home* **20/1** | 84+ |
| 3104 | 5 | hd | **Instant Recall (IRE)**[9] 1881 3-9-0 78 LDettori 4 (BJMeehan) *bhd: racd on outside: pushed along and hung lft fr over 2f out: r.o fnl f: gng on cl home* **10/3**[1] | 80 |
| 1-60 | 6 | 1 | **After The Show**[17] 1689 3-8-5 68 ow1 TEDurcan 2 (JRJenkins) *t.k.h: chsd ldrs: rdn over 2f out: effrt over 1f out:outpcd wl ins last* **25/1** | 68 |
| 314- | 7 | 1½ | **Jimmy Ryan (IRE)**[210] 5613 3-9-3 84 J-PGuillambert[(3)] 3 (TDMcCarthy) *t.k.h: sn w ldr: stl ev ch 1f out: wknd wl ins last* **16/1** | 79 |
| 012- | 8 | ¾ | **I Won't Dance (IRE)**[213] 5562 3-9-4 82 RSmith 5 (RHannon) *s.i.s: t.k.h in rr: pushed along over 2f out: styng on ins last whn checked fnl 100yds: nt rcvr* **25/1** | 74 |
| 1-31 | 9 | 3½ | **Kabreet**[107] 619 3-9-7 85 DaneO'Neill 7 (EALDunlop) *bkwd: hld up in rr: hdwy on outside to chse ldrs 2f out: hit over hd w whip and wknd over 1f out* **7/1** | 67 |
| 1105 | 10 | ½ | **Peruvian Style (IRE)**[13] 1760 3-8-12 76 KDarley 1 (NPLittmoden) *chsd ldrs: rdn over 2f out: wknd fnl f* **10/1** | 56 |
| 04-3 | 11 | 5 | **Hilites (IRE)**[11] 1829 3-8-12 83 DerekNolan[(7)] 11 (JSMoore) *s.i.s: bhd: rdn and effrt over 2f out: nvr rchd ldrs and sn wknd* **12/1** | 48 |

1m 13.96s (-0.41) **Going Correction** +0.075s/f (Good) 11 Ran SP% **114.9**
Speed ratings: **105,104,104,104,103 102,100,99,94,94 87**CSF £78.28 CT £306.22 TOTE £14.50: £3.20, £2.10, £2.00; EX 119.90 Trifecta £675.40 Pool of £7,229.74 - 7.60 winning units.
**Owner** Byculla Thoroughbreds **Bred** J W Parker And Keith Wills **Trained** Newmarket, Suffolk

**FOCUS**
A rough race, and the first five home were very tightly bunched at the finish. The pace was fair.

**NOTEBOOK**
**Wyatt Earp(IRE)** responded well to pressure to gamely score all out. This was his first-ever success and he could still have more to offer over this trip.
**Missus Links(USA)** had the run of the race and was only just denied. This showed she had come on plenty for her seasonal reappearance and she is a winner waiting to happen at this distance, but this looks as good as she is.
**Primo Way** ◆ has to go down as an unlucky loser. He was given a nightmare ride from off the pace, finding plenty of trouble, and really flew once he was in the clear, but the line came just too soon. He is much better than the bare form.
**Delphie Queen(IRE)**, making her debut for new connections, was another who can be considered unlucky as she had to wait for a gap to open on the rail before she could unleash her challenge. She was not beaten at all far and has obviously improved from two to three.
**Instant Recall(IRE)** ran a solid race, but had his chance if good enough and was inclined to hang to his left on this occasion. *Official explanation: jockey said colt hung left-handed throughout*

### 2083 SANCTUARY GROUP FILLIES' CONDITIONS STKS 5f 34y
3:00 (3:00) (C) 2-Y-O £7,516 (£2,851; £1,425; £648) Stalls High

| Form | | | | RPR |
|---|---|---|---|---|
| 1 | 1 | | **Siena Gold**[30] 1399 2-8-11 LDettori 2 (BJMeehan) *lw: trckd ldr: chal fr 1/2-way: drvn to ld appr fnl f: sn in commmand: readily* **30/100**[1] | 93+ |
| | 2 | 1 | **Indiannie Star** 2-8-5 TEDurcan 4 (MRChannon) *leggy: lw: chsd ldrs: rdn over 2f out: rn to chse wnr ins last but no imp* **25/1** | 83+ |
| 511 | 3 | 1 | **Polly Alexander (IRE)**[20] 1616 2-8-11 KDarley 5 (MJWallace) *led: rdn 2f out: hdd appr fnl f: outpcd ins last* **10/1**[3] | 85 |
| | 4 | nk | **Spirit Of Chester (IRE)** 2-8-5 RHavlin 1 (MrsPNDutfield) *leggy: s.i.s: bhd: rdn 1/2-way: kpt on fnl f but nvr gng pce to rch ldrs* **25/1** | 78 |
| | 5 | 2½ | **Bentley's Bush (IRE)** 2-8-5 RSmith 3 (RHannon) *lenghty: str: scope: v.s.a: in tch 1/2-way: sn rdn: kpt on ins fnl f but nvr a danger* **33/1** | 68 |
| | 6 | 1 | **Unreal** 2-8-5 MHills 6 (BWHills) *str: scope: hld up in tch: trckd ldrs 2f out: sn pushed along: wknd fnl f* **6/1**[2] | 64 |

63.03 secs (0.38) **Going Correction** +0.075s/f (Good) 6 Ran SP% **110.9**
Speed ratings: **99,97,95,95,91 89**CSF £12.35 TOTE £1.30: £1.02, £7.10; EX 6.50.
**Owner** N Attenborough & Mrs L Mann **Bred** Limestone Stud **Trained** Upper Lambourn, Berks

**FOCUS**
This fillies' stakes was run at a solid gallop and the field were strung out behind the winner.

**NOTEBOOK**
**Siena Gold** was rather more workmanlike than on her debut, but again showed plenty of speed. She was always holding on and reportedly only does just enough, so the Queen Mary remains the target. She would need to improve again, but her trainer knows what it takes to win the race.
**Indiannie Star**, a good-looking filly, made a very promising debut. She was really moving late on, having run green early, and looks a certainty for a maiden over this trip.
**Polly Alexander(IRE)**, stepping up in class, ran her race and was far from disgraced under her penalties. She looks all speed.
**Spirit Of Chester(IRE)** walked out of the stalls and gave herself way too much to do, but caught the eye staying on well late on. She will be sharper next time and looks in need of six furlongs.
**Bentley's Bush(IRE)** was another who lost all chance at the start. She did pick up late on and will have learnt plenty from this.
**Unreal** ran distinctly green and quickly tired out of it entering the final two furlongs. She will improve for this, but on this evidence does not look anything special.

## 2084 TKP SURFACING H'CAP — 1m 2f 6y
3:35 (3:35) (D) (0-80,78) 3-Y-0+ — £6,370 (£1,960; £980; £490) Stalls Centre

Form — RPR

312- **1** **Hawridge Prince**[221] [5425] 4-9-10 **76** ... SCarson 12 — 89
(LGCottrell) *lw: trckd ldrs: chal 3f out: led 2f out: drvn over 1f out: pushed out and styd on wl fnl f* **12/1**

54-0 **2** 1 3/4 **Shredded (USA)**[4] [2000] 4-9-9 **75** ... RHavlin 5 — 84
(JHMGosden) *swtg: chsd ldrs: rdn over 2f out: styd on wl fnl f to take 2nd last strides but no imp on wnr* **25/1**

6522 **3** hd **Dickie Deadeye**[16] [1715] 7-7-13 **56** ... RThomas(5) 16 — 65
(GBBalding) *prom: wnt 2nd 7f out: led ins fnl 4f:rdn and narrowly hdd 2f out: styd pressing wnr:outpcd fnl f: lost 2nd cl home* **14/1**

0-64 **4** 1 3/4 **Todlea (IRE)**[20] [1624] 4-9-7 **73** ... JPMurtagh 2 — 79
(JAOsborne) *hld up in tch: drvn along 3f out: styd on wl fr over 1f out: kpt on ins last* **14/1**

4-40 **5** 1/2 **Dream Magic**[20] [1604] 6-9-11 **77** ... SWhitworth 15 — 82
(MJRyan) *chsd ldrs: rdn over 2f out: kpt on same pce fr over 1f out* **12/1**

-204 **6** 1 3/4 **J R Stevenson (USA)**[16] [1708] 8-9-10 **76** ... LDettori 8 — 77
(MWigham) *lw: hld up mid-div: rdn and effrt fr 3f out: styd on fr over 1f out but nvr gng pce to rch ldrs* **7/1**[2]

0002 **7** nk **Briareus**[11] [1821] 4-9-12 **78** ... KDarley 7 — 79
(AMBalding) *sn led: hdd after 2f: styd chsng ldrs: rdn 3f out: wknd over 1f out* **7/1**[2]

0642 **8** nk **Invitation**[4] [2000] 6-9-4 **70** ... RSmith 13 — 70
(ACharlton) *bhd: hdwy on outside fr 3f out: hrd drvn and kpt on fnl 2f: nt rch ldrs* **8/1**[3]

4430 **9** hd **Barry Island**[13] [1762] 5-9-12 **78** ... KFallon 3 — 78
(DRCElsworth) *hld up in rr: hdwy over 4f out: n.m.r 3f out: kpt on fnl 2f but n.d* **11/2**[1]

1220 **10** 3 **Classic Role**[23] [1540] 5-9-11 **77** ... (v) RHughes 9 — 71
(RIngram) *hld up in tch: trckd ldrs gng wl appr fnl 2f: shkn up and wknd appr fnl f* **11/1**

46-4 **11** nk **Lady McNair**[39] [1272] 4-9-10 **76** ... TEDurcan 11 — 70
(PDCundell) *lw: bhd: pushed along and sme hdwy fnl 2f: nt a danger* **14/1**

-006 **12** 3 1/2 **Traveller's Tale**[36] [1308] 5-9-2 **68** ... DKinsella 4 — 55
(PGMurphy) *in tch: rdn 3f out: wknd fr 2f out* **16/1**

110- **13** 1 3/4 **Factual Lad**[270] [4247] 6-9-2 **68** ... TQuinn 17 — 52
(BRMillman) *pushed along to ld after 2f: hdd ins fnl 4f: wknd qckly ins fnl 2f* **50/1**

006- **14** nk **Major Blade (GER)**[336] [2320] 6-8-9 **61** ... RHills 18 — 44
(BGPowell) *bhd: sme hdwy on outside over 3f out: nvr a danger and sn bhd* **50/1**

41-0 **15** nk **Best Flight**[11] [1821] 4-9-6 **72** ... MHills 1 — 54
(BWHills) *mid-div: hdwy and n.m.r on rails over 3f out: n.d after* **16/1**

56-0 **16** 2 1/2 **Den'S-Joy**[4] [2000] 8-7-9 **52** ... DFox(5) 6 — 30
(VSmith) *a in rr* **33/1**

054- **17** 1 1/4 **Aragon's Boy**[295] [3534] 4-9-5 **71** ... DaneO'Neill 10 — 46
(HCandy) *n.d* **33/1**

000 **18** 10 **Huxley (IRE)**[16] [1708] 5-9-11 **77** ... PMcCabe 19 — 33
(MGQuinlan) *slowly away: bhd most of way* **50/1**

20-0 **19** 29 **Royal Trigger**[39] [1272] 4-9-4 **70** ... (t) EAhern 14 — —
(IanWilliams) *lw: chsd ldrs tl rdn 5f out: sn wknd* **50/1**

2m 9.77s (1.06) **Going Correction** +0.075s/f (Good) **19 Ran SP% 124.6**
Speed ratings: **98,96,96,95,94 93,93,92,92,90 89,87,85,85,85 83,82,74,51**CSF £296.67 CT £4190.24 TOTE £16.20: £3.90, £5.50, £2.90, £4.70; EX 648.10.
**Owner** Eric Gadsden **Bred** Downclose Stud **Trained** Dulford, Devon

**FOCUS**
A competitive handicap run to suit those racing prominently, but the final time was modest.

**NOTEBOOK**
**Hawridge Prince** ran on well under pressure, having hit the front two out, and scored readily on this comeback from a 221-day break. He is entitled to come on again for this and should not go up too much in the weights, but had quite a hard race on this occasion.
**Shredded(USA)** improved on his latest effort four days previously and stayed on as if he would appreciate further. He remains a maiden, but looks to be coming to hand and can be placed to advantage off this mark before too long.
**Dickie Deadeye** ran another fair race on this step up in class, but gave the impression he may be worth a try over further. The drying ground was probably against him, but he is a very hard horse to win with.
**Todlea(IRE)** ran with credit over a trip that looks to just stretch him. He was staying on in the straight, but the leaders had gone beyond recall.
**Invitation**, a fair second over this trip last time, failed to reproduce that form, but was among the few staying on from off the pace at the end.
**Barry Island** found himself with nowhere to go at a crucial stage and can be considered a lot better than the bare form. He is frustrating to follow, but is threatening to win at this level and should not be written off just yet.
**Royal Trigger** *Official explanation: jockey said gelding lost its action*

## 2085 DICKIE GASKELL MAIDEN STKS — 1m 2f 6y
4:10 (4:14) (D) 3-Y-0 — £6,240 (£1,920; £960; £480) Stalls Centre

Form — RPR

**1** **Remaadd (USA)** 3-9-0 ... KDarley 15 — 93
(MPTregoning) *str: scope: bkwd: sn in tch: led 2f out: drvn out ins last* **5/1**[2]

0 **2** 1 3/4 **Massif Centrale**[12] [1800] 3-9-0 ... JPMurtagh 5 — 90
(DRCElsworth) *bhd: swtchd rt to outside and hdwy over 3f out: styd on to chse wnr over 1f out: kpt on but one pce ins last* **10/3**[1]

**3** 4 **Haadef** 3-9-0 ... RHills 17 — 82
(JHMGosden) *str: bkwd: green: bhd and sn pushed along: swtchd rt to outside and hdwy over 2f out: kpt on wl fnl f: nt rch ldrs* **8/1**

**4** shd **Double Aspect (IRE)** 3-9-0 ... SWhitworth 13 — 82
(SirMichaelStoute) *tall: scope: s.i.s: bhd: stdy hdwy fr 3f out: kpt on wl fr over 1f out but nvr a danger* **33/1**

56- **5** 3 1/2 **Present Oriented (USA)**[225] [5335] 3-9-0 ... PDoe 10 — 76
(HRACecil) *prom: chsd ldr 7f out: chal 4f out: led over 3f out: rdn and hdd 2f out: wknd appr fnl f* **14/1**

0 **6** 1 1/4 **Kaska (IRE)**[30] [1395] 3-8-9 ... MHills 16 — 68
(BWHills) *lw: chsd ldrs: rdn over 2f out: wknd appr fnl f* **12/1**

**7** 3 **Dune Raider (USA)** 3-9-0 ... RHavlin 4 — 67
(SirMichaelStoute) *rangy: lw: mid-div: hdwy over 2f out: nt clr run ins last but nvr gng pce to rch ldrs* **10/1**

54- **8** 6 **Fu Fighter**[200] [5792] 3-9-0 ... EAhern 8 — 56
(JAOsborne) *sn led: hdd over 3f out: wknd qckly and hmpd over 2f out* **33/1**

**9** 3/4 **Golden Key** 3-9-0 ... KFallon 3 — 55
(SirMichaelStoute) *chsd ldrs: rdn 3f out: wknd and hung lft over 2f out* **8/1**

**10** 6 **Sinistra** 3-8-9 ... TQuinn 11 — 38
(HRACecil) *b.hind: scope: chsd ldrs: rdn over 3f out: sn wknd* **14/1**

**11** 1/2 **Gift Voucher (IRE)** 3-9-0 ... SCarson 2 — 42
(SirMichaelStoute) *leggy: bkwd: scope: nvr bttr than mid-div* **25/1**

0- **12** 6 **Purr**[189] [5940] 3-9-0 ... TEDurcan 9 — 31
(JLDunlop) *a in rr* **50/1**

0 **13** nk **Tumbaga (USA)**[30] [1395] 3-9-0 ... RHughes 6 — 30
(RCharlton) *chsd ldr 3f: styd prom: wknd fr 3f out* **6/1**[3]

00- **14** 3/4 **Plovers Lane (IRE)**[219] [5449] 3-9-0 ... DaneO'Neill 1 — 29
(MPTregoning) *rdn 4f out: a bhd* **100/1**

0-0 **15** 1/2 **Ocean Rock**[56] [1050] 3-9-0 ... PMcCabe 14 — 28
(CAHorgan) *bhd: sme hdwy 4f out: sn wknd* **100/1**

0 **16** 4 **High View (USA)**[11] [1827] 3-9-0 ... RSmith 18 — 20
(FJordan) *a in rr* **100/1**

000- **17** 14 **True Patriot**[232] [5177] 3-9-0 ... DKinsella 19 — —
(PMitchell) *bhd: rn wd and and lost tch bnd 4f out* **100/1**

2m 8.95s (0.24) **Going Correction** +0.075s/f (Good) **17 Ran SP% 122.0**
Speed ratings: **102,100,97,97,94 93,91,86,85,80 80,75,75,74,74 71,60**CSF £20.09 TOTE £7.50: £2.60, £2.40, £3.30; EX 27.30 Place 6 £188.19, Place 5 £75.10.
**Owner** Sheikh Ahmed Al Maktoum **Bred** Darley **Trained** Lambourn, Berks

**FOCUS**
A strung-out finish and difficult form to weigh up, but there were some promising types behind the useful-looking winner.

**NOTEBOOK**
**Remaadd(USA)**, an imposing newcomer, made a winning debut in good style. He was handy throughout and got every yard of this trip, enjoying the underfoot conditions. He possesses a lot of scope and could eventually prove a smart performer.
**Massif Centrale** ◆ showed the benefit of his debut and, despite never looking a serious threat to the winner, was clear of the rest. He stands over a lot of ground and promises to stay further than this. A maiden, at least, is well within his grasp.
**Haadef** ran distinctly green in the early stages, but the further he went the better he looked, and this backward colt will improve plenty for this experience.
**Double Aspect(IRE)**, a half-brother to the very smart Inglenook, was sluggish at the start and took his time to find his full stride, but shaped nicely late in the straight and is another who should improve a fair bit from this outing.
**Present Oriented(USA)** looked to be going well when he hit the front just over three out, but soon came under pressure and looked one paced thereafter. He is now eligible for handicaps and can be placed to advantage in that sphere.
**Kaska(IRE)** came to join the leading group two out and looked to be travelling as well as any, but found disappointingly little off the bridle. She is not the first to have let down the Wood Ditton form.
**Dune Raider(USA)** *Official explanation: jockey said colt was short of room in the closing stages*
**Gift Voucher(IRE)** *Official explanation: jockey said colt had a breathing problem*
T/Jkpt: Not won. T/Plt: £227.50 to a £1 stake. Pool: £76,559.50. 245.60 winning tickets. T/Qpdt: £44.80 to a £1 stake. Pool: £4,314.10. 71.20 winning tickets. ST

# 1941 NOTTINGHAM (L-H)
Friday, May 14

**OFFICIAL GOING: Good to soft**
Race 2 hand timed.
Wind: Almost Nil Weather: Fine

## 2086 EUROPEAN BREEDERS FUND NOVICE STKS — 6f 15y
2:20 (2:20) (D) 2-Y-0 — £4,823 (£1,484; £742; £371) Stalls Low

Form — RPR

21 **1** **Goodricke**[20] [1607] 2-8-13 ... TPQueally(3) 4 — 89+
(DRLoder) *stdd s: hld up: hdwy over 2f out: shkn up to ld over 1f out: sn clr* **4/9**[1]

4 **2** 3 **Stedfast McStaunch (IRE)**[11] [1826] 2-8-9 ... LPKeniry(3) 1 — 76
(BJMeehan) *chsd ldrs: outpcd 2f out: styd on to go 2nd ins last* **22/1**

52 **3** 1 1/4 **Lincolneurocruiser**[16] [1709] 2-8-5 ... JDO'Reilly(7) 7 — 72
(JO'Reilly) *carried rt s: sn chsng ldrs: outpcd 2f out: kpt on fnl f* **12/1**[3]

61 **4** shd **King's Gait**[16] [1709] 2-9-2 ... DAllan(3) 3 — 79
(TDEasterby) *w ldrs: ev ch over 2f out: wknd ins last* **25/1**

22 **5** 3 1/2 **Dante's Diamond (IRE)**[29] [1415] 2-8-12 ... SWKelly 6 — 61
(FJordan) *swvd rt s: led tl over 1f out: sn wknd* **5/1**[2]

021 **6** 5 **Im Spartacus**[19] [1638] 2-9-2 ... DNolan(3) 5 — 53
(IAWood) *trckd ldrs: lost pl over 2f out: eased ins last* **25/1**

216 **7** 5 **Norcroft**[16] [1707] 2-9-5 ... PDobbs 2 — 38
(NACallaghan) *s.i.s: outpcd over 2f out: sn bhd* **12/1**[3]

1m 17.78s (2.98) **Going Correction** +0.375s/f (Good) **7 Ran SP% 113.3**
Speed ratings: **95,91,89,89,84 77,71**CSF £15.48 TOTE £1.40: £1.10, £8.60; EX 13.10.
**Owner** Sheikh Mohammed **Bred** Red House Stud **Trained** Newmarket, Suffolk

**FOCUS**
Three Valleys took this race last year and we may have seen another smart sort in Goodricke. Although this did not tell us a great deal as there were excuses for some of those in behind.

**NOTEBOOK**
**Goodricke**, considered a Royal Ascot possible after getting off the mark over five furlongs at Leicester on his previous start, was heavily backed to follow up over this extra furlong and justified the market confidence with a comfortable victory. This did not tell us how good he is, but if he goes to Ascot he must be respected, for his stable has plenty of other talented juveniles against which to gauge this one's talents.
**Stedfast McStaunch(IRE)** shaped well on his debut over five furlongs behind another Royal Ascot possible in Turnkey, and confirmed the promise with a good effort. A slight worry would have to be that he appeared to hit a flat spot when asked to quicken, but faster ground should sort out that problem out and this was still a good run in the circumstances. It will be most disappointing if he does not find a maiden.
**Lincolneurocruiser**, who has shown promise in maiden company over five furlongs, including when runner-up to today's fourth on his previous start, was stuck on the outside after being carried to the right soon after the start and never really looked like going with the winner.
**King's Gait** found this tougher than the Pontefract maiden he won on his previous start and may not have been suited by this step up in trip.
**Dante's Diamond(IRE)** had today's third and fourth behind when runner-up at Ripon on his latest outing, but proved disappointing this time. Six furlongs on this sort of ground may have been asking a bit much of him and he will find things easier in maidens.
**Im Spartacus** did not appear to handle the ground.
**Norcroft** again showed a disliking for this sort of ground.

## 2087 WEST BROMWICH ALBION FOOTBALL CLUB MEDIAN AUCTION MAIDEN STKS — 6f 15y
2:50 (2:51) (E) 2-Y-0 — £3,715 (£1,143; £571; £285) Stalls Low

Form — RPR

**1** **Royal Alchemist** 2-8-9 ... ADaly 6 — 79
(MDIUsher) *s.i.s: bhd: gd hdwy on outer over 1f out: str run to ld last 100yds* **25/1**



The Form Book, Raceform Ltd, Compton, RG20 6NL

523 **2** *3* **The Crooked Ring**$^{9}$ [1882] 2-9-0 ............ SWKelly 10 75
(PDEvans) *stdd s: hld up: hdwy on outer 2f out: led jst ins fnl f: nt qckn* **2/1**$^{1}$

**3** *1* **English Fellow** 2-9-0 ............ JCarroll 2 72
(BAMcmahon) *sn trcking ldrs: n.m.r 2f out: kpt on ins last* **9/2**$^{2}$

**4** *¾* **Doctor Hilary** 2-9-0 ............ IMongan 9 70
(MLWBell) *s.i.s: hdwy 3f out: led over 1f out: hdd jst ins last: sn fdd* **5/1**$^{3}$

5 **5** *1 ¾* **Lady Misha**$^{32}$ [1364] 2-8-6 ............ DAllan$^{(3)}$ 7 60
(JeddO'Keeffe) *chsd ldrs: edgd lft and led 2f out: sn hdd: wknd fnl f* **9/1**

**6** *1 ¼* **Malinsa Blue (IRE)** 2-8-9 ............ DeanMcKeown 1 56
(JAGlover) *sn trcking ldrs: nt clr run 2f out: kpt on fnl f* **20/1**

0 **7** *1* **Grand Welcome (IRE)**$^{17}$ [1686] 2-9-0 ............ PDobbs 5 58
(CTinkler) *led early: chsd ldrs: wknd 2f out* **33/1**

**8** *shd* **Truckle** 2-9-0 ............ KDalgleish 4 57
(MJohnston) *dwlt: sn led: hdd 2f out: wknd appr fnl f* **15/2**

06 **9** *1 ¼* **Miss Good Time**$^{10}$ [1865] 2-8-9 ............ JBramhill 11 49
(JGGiven) *swtchd lft after s: outpcd and drvn along over 3f out: nvr on terms* **20/1**

0 **10** *1 ¾* **Countrywide Sun**$^{29}$ [1412] 2-9-0 ............ VSlattery 3 48
(NPLittmoden) *w ldrs: wknd over 1f out* **22/1**

**11** *1 ¾* **Tyson Returns** 2-8-11 ............ DNolan$^{(3)}$ 8 43
(PABlockley) *s.i.s: sn in tch: wknd 2f out* **14/1**

1m 18.9s (4.10) **Going Correction** +0.375s/f (Good) **11** Ran SP% **117.3**
Speed ratings: **87,83,81,80,78 76,75,75,73,71 68**CSF £70.71 TOTE £30.60: £5.20, £1.30, £2.30; EX 108.80.
**Owner** The Ridgeway Partnership **Bred** B Minty **Trained** Upper Lambourn, Berks

**FOCUS**
Those with previous experience had shown just ordinary form but ran their races, and the newcomers are ones to take from this contest. This race was hand timed.

**NOTEBOOK**
**Royal Alchemist**, a half-sister to mile three-year-old winner Swift Alchemist out of a seven-furlong winner, was slowly away, but was given plenty of time to find her stride under a good ride from Daly and, when switched out for a run, she picked up nicely. There should be plenty of improvement in her and she will be worthy of respect in a higher grade.
**The Crooked Ring** appeared to stay this extra furlong, but is not progressing and is one to oppose in the long run.
**English Fellow**, a 9,000gns yearling, out of a six-furlong two-year-old winner, hails from a stable with some nice juveniles in their care and made a pleasing debut. He took a while to pick up and did not get the clearest of runs when trying to do so, but will improve and should find a maiden.
**Doctor Hilary**, an 88,000gns half-brother to a five-furlong two-year-old winner out of a ten-furlong scorer, travelled strongly and looked like posing a big threat at one point. However, he tired a little in the ground and dropped out of contention. He is open to plenty of improvement.
**Lady Misha**, up a furlong in trip, again offered some encouragement.
**Malinsa Blue(IRE)**, a 20,000euros half-sister to a one mile-six Listed winner and seven-furlong two-year-old scorer, hinted at ability, running better than her finishing position suggests after not getting a clear run.

## 2088 CLUMBER PARK (S) H'CAP — 1m 54y
**3:25** (3:25) (F) (0-55,52) 3-Y-O **£2,898** (£828; £414) **Stalls** High

Form RPR

-545 **1** **Flying Spud**$^{11}$ [1844] 3-8-11 **47** ............ ADaly 6 54
(JLSpearing) *trckd ldrs: led over 1f out: rdn out* **9/2**$^{3}$

4622 **2** *1 ¼* **Biscar Two (IRE)**$^{18}$ [1667] 3-8-13 **49** ............(v$^{1}$) VHalliday 1 53
(RMWhitaker) *sn in tch: outpcd over 2f out: styd on appr fnl f: tk 2nd last 75yds* **5/2**$^{1}$

0-06 **3** *1 ¾* **Faraway Echo**$^{18}$ [1678] 3-8-11 **52** ............(v$^{1}$) HayleyTurner$^{(5)}$ 4 53
(MLWBell) *trckd ldrs: wnt 2nd 4f out: led on bit over 2f out: hdd over 1f out: nt qckn* **4/1**$^{2}$

6-56 **4** *4* **Weaver Spell**$^{17}$ [1701] 3-8-0 **43** oh8 ............ AMullen$^{(7)}$ 7 35
(JRNorton) *hld up in rr: hrd drvn over 4f out: kpt on fnl f* **25/1**

3340 **5** *3 ½* **Princess Ismene**$^{27}$ [1465] 3-8-11 **50** ............(b) DNolan$^{(3)}$ 3 35
(PABlockley) *hld up: effrt on outside over 3f out: nvr nr ldrs* **4/1**$^{2}$

05-5 **6** *nk* **David's Girl**$^{17}$ [1695] 3-8-9 **45** ............ DMcGaffin 2 29
(DMorris) *sn chsng ldrs: lost pl over 2f out* **10/1**

2666 **7** *3 ½* **Brother Cadfael**$^{10}$ [1864] 3-8-7 **43** oh3 ............ DeanMcKeown 8 20
(JohnAHarris) *hld up in rr: effrt 4f out: lost pl over 2f out* **10/1**

00-5 **8** *17* **Shanghai Surprise**$^{15}$ [1736] 3-9-2 **52** ............(b) PDobbs 5 —
(JBalding) *led tl over 2f out: sn lost pl and bhd* **20/1**

1m 49.6s (3.20) **Going Correction** +0.325s/f (Good) **8** Ran SP% **113.5**
Speed ratings: **97,95,94,90,86 86,82,65**CSF £15.94 CT £47.87 TOTE £6.40: £1.80, £1.10, £2.00; EX 12.60.There was no bid for the winner.
**Owner** M Bishop **Bred** M P Bishop **Trained** Kinnersley, Worcs

**FOCUS**
A weak seller and the only one to take from the race looks to be the winner.

**NOTEBOOK**
**Flying Spud** showed little in four runs on Fibresand, but has improved since switching to turf and ran his best race to date to get off the mark. The form is probably not worth a great deal, but he did the job nicely and a follow up in similar company cannot be ruled out.
**Biscar Two(IRE)**, dropped in grade and fitted with a visor for the first time, was slowly away and could only muster the one pace late on. He may stay further, but not for the first time did not look an easy ride and is not one to place much faith in.
**Faraway Echo**, another with a visor on for the first time, was stepping up in trip and returning to turf. She did not see out her race and is another to be wary of.
**Weaver Spell**, stepping out of banded company and up in trip, stayed on all too late and may get even further.
**Princess Ismene** was never a threat.

## 2089 BROWNE JACOBSON CLASSIFIED STKS — 1m 54y
**4:00** (4:00) (C ) 3-Y-O **£10,192** (£3,136; £1,568; £784) **Stalls** High

Form RPR

1-30 **1** **Cimyla (IRE)**$^{29}$ [1414] 3-9-2 83 ............ GBaker 6 90
(CFWall) *hld up: hdwy over 2f out: edgd lft over 1f out: r.o to ld nr fin* **5/1**$^{3}$

41-0 **2** *½* **Secretary General (IRE)**$^{12}$ [1795] 3-9-5 88 ............ CCatlin 3 92
(PFICole) *led after 1f: qckndd over 3f out: edgd rt over 2f out: hdd nr fin* **15/8**$^{1}$

13- **3** *6* **Fort**$^{240}$ [4992] 3-9-7 90 ............ KDalgleish 2 81
(MJohnston) *sn trckd ldrs: chal over 4f out: wknd over 1f out* **12/1**

40-0 **4** *½* **Baileys Dancer**$^{21}$ [1585] 3-8-13 85 ............ SChin 7 72
(MJohnston) *led 1f: outpcd and lost pl over 3f out: kpt on fnl f* **16/1**

10-5 **5** *3* **Glebe Garden**$^{16}$ [1704] 3-9-3 89 ............ IMongan 5 70
(MLWBell) *trckd ldrs: effrt over 3f out: lost pl over 1f out* **7/2**$^{2}$

05-2 **6** *2* **Cusco (IRE)**$^{11}$ [1829] 3-9-1 87 ............ PDobbs 4 64
(RHannon) *trckd ldrs: wknd over 2f out* **7/2**$^{2}$

01-0 **7** *4* **Zerlina (USA)**$^{34}$ [1327] 3-8-7 86 ............ PGallagher$^{(7)}$ 1 54
(RHannon) *unruls ss: s.i.s: hld up in last: edgd rt 3f out: fnd nthing* **18/1**

1m 47.43s (1.03) **Going Correction** +0.325s/f (Good) **7** Ran SP% **114.7**
Speed ratings: **107,106,100,100,97 95,91**CSF £14.94 TOTE £6.60: £2.70, £1.20; EX 18.70.
**Owner** Peter Botham **Bred** Dr D G St John And Mrs Sherry Collier **Trained** Newmarket, Suffolk

**FOCUS**
A tight classified event with just 8lb separating these on adjusted official figures. Despite that, the front two pulled clear and some of those in behind have it to prove.

**NOTEBOOK**
**Cimyla(IRE)** had the most to find at the weights but that did not stop him. He lost his action at Newmarket on his latest outing, but had previously picked up a fair Polytrack maiden and finished third to the much-improved pair African Dream and Red Lancer on his reappearance. He did well to come from so far off the gallop and slip up the runner-up's inside to gain a narrow success. Things will be tougher when he is reassessed, but he is still progressing.
**Secretary General(IRE)** shaped well on his reappearance in a handicap at Newmarket and came close to bettering that with a win. When Fort dropped away he was in front for long enough and proved unable to resist the winner's late challenge, but he was clear of the remainder and it will be disappointing if he is not found an opportunity.
**Fort**comes from a stable which has been in mixed form lately, but this one had no easy task under top weight and was entitled to need this first run in 240 days.
**Baileys Dancer** dropped out tamely on her reappearance at Sandown and, although this was a little better, she still has something to prove.
**Glebe Garden** travelled strongly, but failed to find much and was most disappointing.
**Cusco(IRE)** won her maiden over a mile, but ran well over six furlongs on her previous outing and this step back up in trip may not have suited.

## 2090 COLWICK PARK MAIDEN STKS — 1m 6f 15y
**4:35** (4:35) (D ) 3-Y-O+ **£4,192** (£1,290; £645; £161) **Stalls** Low

Form RPR

22 **1** **Twofan (USA)**$^{13}$ [1761] 3-8-6 ............ SChin 1 62+
(MJohnston) *mde all: shkn up over 2f out: styd on wl: readily* **8/13**$^{1}$

30-2 **2** *2* **Sadler's Pride (IRE)**$^{18}$ [1662] 4-9-12 72 ............ JCarroll 8 59+
(AndrewTurnell) *t.k.h: hdwy 7f out: kpt on fnl 2f: no imp* **5/1**$^{3}$

**3** *1 ¼* **Watchful Witness**$^{56}$ 4-9-12 ............ DSweeney 10 57
(DrJRJNaylor) *sn chsng ldrs: styd on same pce fnl 2f* **50/1**

0-5 **4** *5* **Brough Supreme**$^{18}$ [1674] 3-8-6 ............ PDobbs 5 50
(HMorrison) *mid-div: effrt over 3f out: sn chsng ldrs: wknd over 1f out* **4/1**$^{2}$

**4** *dht* **Wodhill Hope** 4-9-7 ............ DMcGaffin 9 45
(DMorris) *hld up: hdwy over 4f out: kpt on fnl 2f: nvr nr to chal* **66/1**

2 **6** *1 ¾* **Indian Chase**$^{23}$ [1547] 7-9-6 ............(v) LucyRussell$^{(7)}$ 11 48?
(DrJRJNaylor) *sn trcking ldrs: t.k.h: wknd 2f out* **20/1**

**7** *5* **Great Gidding** 3-8-6 ............ CCatlin 4 41
(HMorrison) *mid-div: outpcd 6f out: sn lost pl: bhd fnl 2f* **28/1**

000- **8** *½* **Pattern Man**$^{179}$ [6012] 3-8-6 ............ JBramhill 2 40
(JRNorton) *chsd ldrs: lost pl 3f out* **100/1**

00 **9** *½* **Court Emperor**$^{20}$ [1612] 4-9-12 ............ GBaker 3 39
(RJPrice) *hld up in rr: hdwy on outside over 4f out: lost pl over 2f out* **100/1**

**10** *25* **Meadow Hawk (USA)**$^{384}$ [1240] 4-9-12 ............ MHenry 7 4
(IanWilliams) *chsd ldrs: lost pl over 2f out: sn bhd and eased* **20/1**

3m 15.15s (7.95) **Going Correction** +0.325s/f (Good)
**WFA** 3 from 4yo 21lb 4 from 7yo 1lb **10** Ran SP% **117.0**
Speed ratings: **90,88,88,85,85 84,81,81,80,66**CSF £3.77 TOTE £1.80: £1.10, £1.20, £8.50; EX 3.30.
**Owner** A Al-Rostamani **Bred** A Lakin And Sons **Trained** Middleham Moor, N Yorks

**FOCUS**
Just a weak maiden and a slow winning time, but Twofan did what he had to and should progress.

**NOTEBOOK**
**Twofan(USA)** had shown promise on his two previous starts over ten furlongs and was able to confirm that on this step up in trip. He will probably need to improve when he goes handicapping, but is the type to progress and he could well follow up.
**Sadler's Pride(IRE)** confirmed his recent Hamilton effort was no fluke with another solid performance. However, he may just keep finding one too good in maidens and a handicap mark of 72 makes things difficult.
**Watchful Witness** did not show much on one start on the Flat in France, but he has since won over hurdles for Gary Moore. Making his debut for new connections and returned to the Flat, he ran a reasonable race and might find his level when handicapped.
**Brough Supreme**, stepping up in trip, was never a threat to the principals and his future now lies in the hands of the Handicapper.
**Wodhill Hope** hinted at ability on this racecourse debut.

## 2091 WOLLATON PARK CLASSIFIED STKS — 6f 15y
**5:05** (5:08) (E) 3-Y-O+ **£3,701** (£1,139; £569; £284) **Stalls** Low

Form RPR

0-00 **1** **Antonio Canova**$^{25}$ [1500] 8-9-4 70 ............ TWilliams 6 86
(BobJones) *racd far side: hld up: hdwy over 2f out: styd on wl to ld last 100yds* **33/1**

5-00 **2** *2 ½* **Under My Spell**$^{27}$ [1464] 3-8-5 70 ............ SChin 2 75
(PDEvans) *racd far side: chsd ldrs: styd on to take 2nd nr fin* **14/1**

0-11 **3** *nk* **Maddie's A Jem**$^{24}$ [1518] 4-9-6 75 ............ SWKelly 15 79
(JRJenkins) *racd stands' side: trckd ldrs: led that gp over 2f out: styd on ins last* **4/1**$^{1}$

-605 **4** *hd* **Full Spate**$^{10}$ [1873] 9-9-4 68 ............ KDalgleish 13 77
(JMBradley) *racd stands' side: hld up: hdwy to chse ldrs over 2f out: kpt on wl fnl f* **14/1**

00-0 **5** *1* **Merlin's Dancer**$^{11}$ [1825] 4-9-9 75 ............ ANicholls 5 79
(DNicholls) *led far side: clr that side over 2f out: hdd 100yds out: wknd* **25/1**

1500 **6** *2* **Time N Time Again**$^{7}$ [1927] 6-9-8 74 ............(p) DeanMcKeown 10 72
(EJAlston) *racd towards far side: chsd ldrs: kpt on same pce fnl 2f* **14/1**

3-65 **7** *3* **Dorchester**$^{20}$ [1608] 7-9-8 74 ............ GCarter 9 63
(WJMusson) *racd far side: bhd tl sme hdwy fnl 2f* **13/2**$^{2}$

0102 **8** *3* **Ask The Clerk (IRE)**$^{16}$ [1702] 3-8-11 73 ............ JoannaBadger 16 53
(VSmith) *racd stands' side: chsd ldrs: weakend fnl 2f* **8/1**$^{3}$

36-6 **9** *nk* **Among Friends (IRE)**$^{37}$ [1294] 4-9-4 70 ............ IMongan 12 49
(BPalling) *led stands' side tl over 2f out: wknd over 1f out* **40/1**

024- **10** *¾* **Cape St Vincent**$^{207}$ [5681] 4-9-6 72 ............ PDobbs 11 48
(HMorrison) *racd stands' side: chsd ldrs: lost pl 2f out* **9/1**

-003 **11** *1* **Waterside (IRE)**$^{10}$ [1873] 5-9-4 68 ............ JCarroll 14 43
(JWHills) *racd stands' side: chsd ldrs: lost pl over 2f out* **10/1**

0060 **12** *shd* **Cashel Mead**$^{20}$ [1608] 4-9-3 72 ............ ADaly 8 42
(JLSpearing) *racd far side: mid-div: hdwy over 2f out: sn lost pl* **12/1**

0-03 **13** *3 ½* **Free Wheelin (IRE)**$^{20}$ [1603] 4-9-6 72 ............ CCatlin 4 35
(WJarvis) *racd far side: hld up: hdwy over 2f out: lost pl over 1f out* **14/1**

334- **14** *½* **Monte Mayor Lad (IRE)**$^{175}$ [6039] 4-9-1 70 ............ DAllan$^{(3)}$ 7 31
(DHaydnJones) *racd far side: sn bhd and drvn along* **50/1**

04-4 **15** *½* **Sewmuch Character**$^{20}$ [1603] 5-9-4 70 ............ DSweeney 3 30
(MBlanshard) *racd far side: hdwy over 2f out: sn lost pl* **9/1**

0455 **16** *hd* **Hard To Catch (IRE)**[36] 1313 6-8-11 69.......................... MHoward(7) 1 29
(DKIvory) *racd far side: chsd ldrs: lost pl over 2f out* **20/1**

1m 16.49s (1.69) **Going Correction** +0.375s/f (Good)
**WFA** 3 from 4yo+ 10lb **16** Ran SP% **123.8**
Speed ratings: **103,99,99,99,97 95,91,87,86,85 84,84,79,78,78 77**CSF £432.62 TOTE £36.60: £6.30, £5.90, £2.60; EX 2296.10 Place 6 £16.06, Place 5 £11.96.
**Owner** The Antonio Canova Partnership **Bred** Mrs W J Hall **Trained** Wickhambrook, Suffolk

**FOCUS**
A tricky sprint with just 6lb separating the entire field on the adjusted official figures. If that was not enough, the field split into two groups, with the far side just coming out on top.

**NOTEBOOK**
**Antonio Canova**, last successful in 2001 off a mark of 85, had just one run last year and had shown little in two starts this term. However, he has tumbled in the weights as a result and was dropping into a Class E for the first time since 2000. One could not back him with any confidence to follow up, but it will interesting to see if he can build on this as he is well handicapped on the best of his form.
**Under My Spell** chased the winner home on the far side. She has not won since making a successful debut in a juvenile seller here last season, but this offered plenty of encouragement.
**Maddie's A Jem**, chasing the hat-trick after a couple of wins in similar company, can be considered a little unlucky for she won her race on the possibly disadvantaged stands' side. She clearly remains on good terms with herself and should continue to go well in similar company.
**Full Spate** ran respectably behind Maddie's A Jem on the stands' side and is running into a bit of form.
**Merlin's Dancer** offered plenty of encouragement in trying to burn off his rivals on the far side.
T/Plt: £13.00 to a £1 stake. Pool: £23,825.00. 1,328.25 winning tickets. T/Qpdt: £6.90 to a £1 stake. Pool: £1,629.50. 173.90 winning tickets. WG

## [1371]YARMOUTH (L-H)
### Friday, May 14

**OFFICIAL GOING: Good to firm**

## 2092 BETFRED.COM NOW ONLINE (S) STKS — 1m 2f 21y
**2:10** (2:10) (G ) 3-4-Y-0 **£2,569** (£734; £367) **Stalls** Low

Form RPR
-000 **1** **Estimate**[108] 614 4-9-2 62.............................................(v) PaulEddery 10 42
(JohnAHarris) *s.i.s: sn chsng ldrs: led over 3f out: r.o: eased nr fin* **10/1**
00-0 **2** *1* **Romeo's Day**[7] 1946 3-8-5 54 ow2.................................. SHitchcott(3) 1 47
(MRChannon) *chsd ldrs: rdn over 2f out: styd on* **6/1**[3]
-003 **3** *2* **Fitz The Bill (IRE)**[15] 1727 4-9-2 30..................................(b) JMackay 4 36
(NBKing) *hld up: hdwy over 3f out: rdn to chse wnr over 2f out tl no ex ins fnl f* **20/1**
36-0 **4** *10* **Stylish Sunrise (IRE)**[49] 1120 3-8-6 70.............................. DHolland 9 22
(MLWBell) *prom: rdn over 4f out: wknd over 2f out* **7/2**[1]
2015 **5** *2 1/2* **Regulated (IRE)**[29] 1422 3-8-12 69................................ SSanders 7 23
(JAOsborne) *slowly in to stride: sn chsng ldrs: rdn over 2f out: nt run on* **7/2**[1]
4166 **6** *2* **Shatin Special**[75] 937 4-9-1 51...........................(p) DeanWilliams(7) 11 14
(GCHChung) *led 1f: chsd ldrs tl wknd 2f out* **12/1**
00-5 **7** *3/4* **Warif (USA)**[6] 1959 3-8-6 ................................................ BDoyle 8 12
(EJO'Neill) *dwlt: rcvrd to ld after 1f: hdd over 3f out: wknd 2f out* **20/1**
**8** *5* **Dovedon Lass** 3-8-1 ................................................ JQuinn 5 —
(PJMcbride) *s.s: a bhd* **40/1**
44-0 **9** *23* **Good Loser (IRE)**[30] 1389 4-9-7 60....................................(t) MTebbutt 3 —
(CRDore) *s.s: a bhd* **4/1**[2]
00 **10** *6* **Byrd Island**[32] 1371 3-8-1 ................................................ JFEgan 6 —
(DMorris) *hld up: rdn over 3f out: sn wknd* **25/1**

2m 9.51s (1.54) **Going Correction** +0.10s/f (Good)
**WFA** 3 from 4yo 15lb **10** Ran SP% **111.3**
Speed ratings: **97,96,94,86,84 83,82,78,60,55**CSF £61.90 TOTE £13.80: £2.20, £2.80, £2.60; EX 89.50.The winner was bought in for 6,000gns.
**Owner** Mrs A E Harris **Bred** Saeed Manana **Trained** Eastwell, Leics

**FOCUS**
An ordinary seller run at just a fair pace

**NOTEBOOK**
**Estimate**, a long-standing maiden, took advantage of the drop in class to register her first success. She won nicely enough and should be capable of following up in similar company.
**Romeo's Day** looks to have found his level and shaped as though he may stay further still.
**Fitz The Bill(IRE)** ran as well as could be expected on these terms, but it will have to be a poor contest if she is to get her head in front.
**Stylish Sunrise(IRE)** did not move that well to post and is clearly of limited ability.
**Regulated(IRE)** looked a far from easy ride and is one to have reservations about. *Official explanation: trainer's representative had no explanation for the poor form shown*
**Good Loser(IRE)** *Official explanation: jockey said gelding finished lame*

## 2093 LORD NELSON - ROYAL NAVY MAIDEN STKS — 1m 3f 101y
**2:40** (2:41) (D ) 3-Y-O **£3,532** (£1,087; £543; £271) **Stalls** Low

Form RPR
4 **1** **Modesta (IRE)**[28] 1440 3-8-9 ........................................ WRyan 6 84+
(HRACecil) *hld up: hdwy over 3f out: rdn to chse ldr over 2f out: edgd lft over 1f out: styd on to ld wl ins fnl f* **7/2**[2]
4- **2** *1* **New Morning (IRE)**[213] 5556 3-8-9 ........................................ PRobinson 8 82+
(MAJarvis) *trckd ldrs: racd keenly: led over 2f out: rdn and hdd wl ins fnl f* **8/11**[1]
6 **3** *5* **Talwandi (IRE)**[20] 1612 3-9-0 ........................................ BDoyle 5 79
(SirMichaelStoute) *chsd ldrs: rdn and hung lft 2f out: sn outpcd* **16/1**
**4** *2 1/2* **Shongweni (IRE)** 3-9-0 ........................................ SSanders 1 75
(PJMcbride) *hld up: r.o ins fnl f: nvr nrr* **100/1**
00- **5** *shd* **Fort Churchill (IRE)**[195] 5867 3-9-0 ........................................ NCallan 10 75
(MHTompkins) *hld up: hdwy and hung lft fr over 2f out: n.d* **100/1**
0-2 **6** *6* **Sunset Mirage (USA)**[20] 1612 3-8-9 ........................................ WSupple 7 60
(EALDunlop) *w ldr: rdn and ev ch over 2f out: wknd over 1f out* **13/2**[3]
0 **7** *4* **Miss Merenda**[12] 1794 3-8-9 ........................................ JMackay 3 54
(DECantillon) *hld up: rdn 1/2-way: a in rr* **66/1**
30-4 **8** *1* **Vamose (IRE)**[19] 1641 3-9-0 69........................................ DHolland 4 57
(MissGayKelleway) *mde most 8f: wknd wl over 1f out* **16/1**
0-5 **9** *3 1/2* **Cleaver**[32] 1356 3-9-0 ........................................ MTebbutt 2 52
(WJarvis) *plld hrd and prom: wknd over 2f out* **25/1**
**10** *dist* **Glanworth (IRE)** 3-9-0 ........................................ AMackay 9 —
(NACallaghan) *dwlt: sn pushed along in rr: bhd fr 1/2-way* **80/1**

2m 26.32s (-1.08) **Going Correction** +0.10s/f (Good) **10** Ran SP% **113.8**
Speed ratings: **107,106,102,100,100 96,93,92,90,—**CSF £6.12 TOTE £3.40: £1.30, £1.10, £2.80; EX 8.20.
**Owner** K Abdulla **Bred** Juddmonte Farms **Trained** Newmarket, Suffolk

**FOCUS**
The front pair apart there probably was not much strength in depth, but it was run at a sound pace.

**NOTEBOOK**
**Modesta(IRE)** confirmed the promise shown on her debut, but it did take a while for the penny to drop. There is still plenty of improvement in her, especially as she looks as though she will stay further.
**New Morning(IRE)** looked as though the race would do her good and any amount of improvement can be expected.
**Talwandi(IRE)** still looked a bit on the green side, but he is learning and should do better when he goes handicapping.
**Shongweni(IRE)**, a half-brother to ten-furlong juvenile winner Penbuck, did not shape too badly on this debut and looks capable of some improvement.
**Fort Churchill(IRE)** will at least have more options open to him now in handicaps.
**Sunset Mirage(USA)** looked to find this trip beyond her.

## 2094 BETFRED SPRINT SERIES (QUALIFIER) (HANDICAP STKS) — 6f 3y
**3:10** (3:10) (D ) (0-85,85) 3-Y-0+ **£5,434** (£1,672; £836; £418) **Stalls** High

Form RPR
3-04 **1** **Pinchbeck**[11] 1825 5-9-5 76..........................................(p) PRobinson 11 85
(MAJarvis) *chsd ldrs: r.o to ld wl ins fnl f* **9/2**[1]
10-0 **2** *1/2* **Prince Hector**[25] 1504 5-9-7 78.......................................... SDrowne 13 86
(WJHaggas) *hld up: r.o wl ins fnl f: nt rch wnr* **9/1**
-000 **3** *shd* **Armagnac**[11] 1825 6-9-6 77.......................................... JQuinn 2 84
(MABuckley) *hld up: hdwy over 1f out: ev ch ins fnl f: r.o* **11/2**[2]
0-40 **4** *1 3/4* **Mr Malarkey (IRE)**[13] 1765 4-9-8 79..........................(b) TGMcLaughlin 7 81
(MrsCADunnett) *led: rdn and hung lft fr over 1f out: hdd wl ins fnl f* **9/2**[1]
-160 **5** *1* **Dusty Dazzler (IRE)**[17] 1685 4-9-9 85.......................... AQuinn(5) 12 84
(WGMTurner) *chsd ldrs: rdn over 1f out: no ex ins fnl f* **9/1**
1-05 **6** *1 3/4* **Willhewiz**[28] 1454 4-10-0 85.......................................... JFEgan 10 79
(CADwyer) *w ldr: rdn and ev ch over 1f out: wknd ins fnl f* **15/2**[3]
000- **7** *hd* **Complication**[199] 5811 4-8-7 67..........................(b) LisaJones(3) 5 60
(JARToller) *chsd ldrs: rdn over 1f out: wknd fnl f* **33/1**
0-00 **8** *1/2* **Musical Fair**[11] 1825 4-9-6 77.......................................... DHolland 8 69
(JAGlover) *hld up: rdn over 1f out: no imp* **10/1**
-010 **9** *3 1/2* **Pedro Jack (IRE)**[11] 1824 7-8-12 72.......................... SHitchcott(3) 3 53
(MABuckley) *s.i.s: hld up: rdn over 2f out: n.d* **22/1**
0000 **10** *hd* **Gone'N'Dunnett (IRE)**[24] 1516 5-7-13 59 oh5 ow4.............. RMiles(3) 4 40
(MrsCADunnett) *prom over 4f* **25/1**
000- **11** *shd* **Mandarin Spirit (IRE)**[207] 5681 4-9-6 77.......................... SSanders 9 57
(GCHChung) *s.i.s: hld up: n.d* **25/1**
0010 **12** *1 1/4* **Warden Warren**[7] 1927 6-8-12 72..........................(p) BReilly(3) 6 49
(MrsCADunnett) *hld up: pushed along 1/2-way: a in rr* **16/1**
0166 **13** *2 1/2* **A Teen**[25] 1504 6-8-5 62.......................................... PaulEddery 1 31
(PHowling) *hld up: a in rr* **14/1**

1m 13.49s (-0.11) **Going Correction** +0.10s/f (Good) **13** Ran SP% **120.1**
Speed ratings: **104,103,103,100,99 97,96,96,91,91 91,89,86**CSF £43.15 CT £239.72 TOTE £4.50: £2.20, £6.00, £2.10; EX 58.50.
**Owner** T G Warner **Bred** Red House Stud **Trained** Newmarket, Suffolk

**FOCUS**
A competitive handicap run at a fair clip.

**NOTEBOOK**
**Pinchbeck**, with the cheekpieces back on, got away with it this time on ground which would have been quick enough for him.
**Prince Hector**, over a trip arguably short of his best, could have been an unlucky loser, for had he got a run when he wanted, would surely have scored.
**Armagnac**, who has never won before June, shaped nicely and is not badly treated on the best of his form.
**Mr Malarkey(IRE)**, as he had done on his seasonal debut at Leicester, hung his chance away. He is a quirky customer, but does have plenty of ability.
**Dusty Dazzler(IRE)** turned in a sound enough effort under her big weight, but she does appear to reserve her best for the Polytrack.
**Willhewiz**, who has yet to win a handicap, showed plenty of pace, despite not wearing his usual visor.
**Complication**, who raced more towards the centre of the track, is sure to strip fitter for the outing.

## 2095 SALTWELL SIGNS MAIDEN AUCTION STKS (DIV I) — 6f 3y
**3:45** (3:48) (F ) 2-Y-O **£2,926** (£836; £418) **Stalls** High

Form RPR
**1** **Highland Cascade** 2-8-2 .......................................... JTate 4 68
(JMPEustace) *chsd ldrs: rdn to ld over 1f out: r.o* **16/1**
**2** *1/2* **Active Asset (IRE)** 2-8-11 .......................................... SHitchcott(3) 12 78
(MRChannon) *chsd ldrs: led over 2f out: rdn and hdd over 1f out: r.o* **7/4**[1]
**3** *1/2* **Kanad** 2-8-11 ..........................................(t) WSupple 11 74
(BHanbury) *hld up in tch: plld hrd: rdn and ev ch fr over 1f out: rn green: r.o* **10/1**
0 **4** *1 1/2* **Haroldini (IRE)**[17] 1686 2-8-7 .......................................... DHolland 10 65
(MrsPNDutfield) *led over 3f: rdn and ev ch over 1f out: styd on same pce* **7/2**[2]
5 **5** *3 1/2* **Silver Visage (IRE)**[32] 1374 2-8-6 .......................................... BReilly(3) 8 57
(MissJFeilden) *prom: pushed along 1/2-way: wknd fnl f* **12/1**
0 **6** *2* **Be Bop Aloha**[18] 1670 2-7-13 .......................................... LisaJones(3) 9 44
(IAWood) *s.i.s: sn prom: hmpd 2f out: sn wknd* **25/1**
4 **7** *shd* **Dane's Rock (IRE)**[39] 1264 2-8-9 .......................................... NPollard 6 50
(PCHaslam) *chsd ldrs: rdn and ev ch whn hung lft 2f out: sn wknd* **10/1**
**8** *3/4* **Lady Susanne (IRE)** 2-8-4 .......................................... JFEgan 7 43
(CADwyer) *s.s: outpcd* **16/1**
**9** *1* **Cry Of The Wolf** 2-8-2 .......................................... StevenHarrison(7) 3 45
(NPLittmoden) *dwlt: outpcd* **33/1**
353 **10** *nk* **Dustini (IRE)**[10] 1853 2-8-9 ..........................................(p) AQuinn(5) 5 49
(WGMTurner) *chsd ldrs: rdn 1/2-way: wknd over 1f out* **8/1**[3]
**11** *3 1/2* **Davala** 2-8-7 .......................................... WRyan 2 32
(ADSmith) *dwlt: outpcd* **50/1**

1m 16.09s (2.49) **Going Correction** +0.10s/f (Good) **11** Ran SP% **116.1**
Speed ratings: **87,86,85,83,79 76,76,75,73,73 68**CSF £41.40 TOTE £26.50: £3.70, £1.30, £3.70; EX 41.80.
**Owner** J M Ratcliffe **Bred** J M And J M Ratcliffe Racehorse Transport Ltd **Trained** Newmarket, Suffolk

**FOCUS**
These did not look a great bunch, and this was the slower of the two divisions.

**NOTEBOOK**
**Highland Cascade**, from the same family as Compton Bolter,was one of the nicer ones in the paddock. She probably did not beat a great deal, but she is open to improvement and looks a likely type for nurseries.
**Active Asset(IRE)**, a half-brother to mile winner Laatansa, is a lightly-made colt. While he is sure to benefit from the experience, he would not have as much improvement in him as some.

**Kanad** a half-brother to winning miler Bold State, is quite a late foal and is very much on the leg at present. He travelled well through the race, but was very green when push came to shove, and he should be capable of plenty of improvement with this experience under his belt.
**Haroldini(IRE)** had the benefit of an outing and tried to burn off his rivals. However, he lacked a change of gear at the business end and may need a stiffer test later on in the season. *Official explanation: jockey said gelding hung left until halfway*
**Silver Visage(IRE)** looks the sort to do better in nurseries.
**Lady Suesanne(IRE)** *Official explanation: jockey said gelding hung left throughout*

## 2096 SALTWELL SIGNS MAIDEN AUCTION STKS (DIV II) 6f 3y
**4:20** (4:21) (F) 2-Y-O **£2,926** (£836; £418) **Stalls** High

| Form | | | | | RPR |
|---|---|---|---|---|---|
| 4 | **1** | | **Alta Petens**[25] 1498 2-8-2 (MLWBell) *w ldr: led over 4f out: rdn clr fnl f* 9/4[1] | JMackay 6 | 73+ |
| 6 | **2** | 5 | **Megell (IRE)**[25] 1498 2-7-13 (MGQuinlan) *w ldrs: rdn over 1f out: sn outpcd* 3/1[2] | LisaJones(3) 5 | 58 |
| 46 | **3** | 5 | **Gryskirk**[29] 1412 2-8-9 (PWD'Arcy) *chsd ldrs: rdn and wknd over 1f out* 14/1 | PaulEddery 11 | 50 |
| | **4** | 2 ½ | **Fong Shui** 2-8-9 (PJMakin) *s.i.s: hdwy over 4f out: swtchd lft over 2f out: wknd over 1f out* 14/1 | SSanders 7 | 43 |
| 0 | **5** | ¾ | **Clinet (IRE)**[18] 1670 2-8-2 (PMPhelan) *led: hdd over 4f out: wknd over 1f out* 13/2 | JQuinn 10 | 33 |
| 0 | **6** | 1 ¼ | **Faithisflying**[21] 1589 2-8-7 (CADwyer) *prom over 3f* 66/1 | NCallan 8 | 35 |
| | **7** | nk | **Lord Normacote** 2-8-11 (CADwyer) *dwlt: outpcd* 50/1 | SDrowne 9 | 38 |
| 0 | **8** | ½ | **Fair Along (GER)**[25] 1505 2-8-9 (WJarvis) *chsd ldrs over 3f* 16/1 | MTebbutt 4 | 34 |
| | **9** | 2 | **Ugly Sister (USA)** 2-8-4 (GCBravery) *in tch: sn pushed along: wknd 1/2-way* 33/1 | JFEgan 2 | 23 |
| | **10** | hd | **Pacific Star (IRE)** 2-9-0 (EALDunlop) *hld up: wknd 1/2-way* 4/1[3] | WSupple 1 | 33 |
| | **11** | 12 | **Kerry's Blade (IRE)** 2-8-9 (PCHaslam) *dwlt: outpcd* 33/1 | NPollard 3 | — |

1m 14.94s (1.34) **Going Correction** +0.10s/f (Good) **11** Ran SP% **117.7**
Speed ratings: **95,88,81,78,77 75,75,74,71,71 55**CSF £8.71 TOTE £2.80: £1.60, £1.70, £3.00; EX 11.90.
**Owner** Joy And Valentine Feerick **Bred** Joy And Valentine Feerick **Trained** Newmarket, Suffolk

**FOCUS**
This looked the better of the two divisions and that was reflected in the time, which was over a second quicker.

**NOTEBOOK**
**Alta Petens** was much better suited by this quicker surface and shoed a nice turn of foot to go clear. While she will need placing with care, she should be capable of adding to this.
**Megell(IRE)** had clearly learnt from her debut and got closer to the winner than she did on her debut. While she is no great shakes, she should be capable of winning a small race somewhere.
**Gryskirk** at least jumped out of the stalls on terms this time and gave himself a chance. However, he was easily shaken off by the fillies and it looks as though his future lies in nurseries.
**Fong Shui**, a half-brother to juvenile winner Insubordinate, is sure to have learnt plenty from this.
**Clinet(IRE)** showed plenty of pace from her high draw, but dropped away tamely when push came to shove.
**Fair Along(GER)** *Official explanation: jockey said colt had breathing problem*
**Pacific Star(IRE)** never went a yard and will need to find plenty of improvement if he is to score.

## 2097 HKB WILTSHIRES LEGAL SERVICES CLASSIFIED STKS 7f 3y
**4:50** (4:53) (E) 3-Y-O **£3,630** (£1,117; £558; £279) **Stalls** High

| Form | | | | | RPR |
|---|---|---|---|---|---|
| 500- | **1** | | **Sforzando**[223] 5362 3-8-8 65 (JARToller) *hld up: hdwy over 1f out: led ins fnl f: r.o* 25/1 | LisaJones(3) 10 | 74 |
| 20-0 | **2** | 1 | **Speedbird (USA)**[30] 1400 3-9-2 70 (GWragg) *hld up in tch: led over 1f out: hdd ins fnl f: styd on* 15/2 | JFEgan 5 | 76 |
| 23-6 | **3** | 1 ½ | **Dandouce**[11] 1841 3-9-2 70 (PWChapple-Hyam) *chsd ldrs: rdn and ev ch over 1f out: styd on same pce* 5/1[2] | BDoyle 13 | 72 |
| 602- | **4** | 3 | **Best Desert (IRE)**[224] 5339 3-9-0 65 (JRBest) *chsd ldrs: rdn and ev ch over 1f out: wknd ins fnl f* 20/1 | NPollard 2 | 62 |
| 51-0 | **5** | 2 ½ | **Aesculus (USA)**[20] 1613 3-8-13 70 (LMCumani) *chsd ldrs: n.m.r and outpcd over 2f out: styd on ins fnl f* 25/1 | NMackay(3) 4 | 58 |
| 50-2 | **6** | hd | **River Of Babylon**[32] 1370 3-8-11 64 (MLWBell) *mde most over 5f: sn wknd* 9/2[1] | JMackay 16 | 52 |
| 50-5 | **7** | 4 | **Canadian Storm**[10] 1869 3-9-5 70 (MHTompkins) *s.i.s: hld up: effrt 2f out: nvr trbld ldrs* 33/1 | PRobinson 12 | 50 |
| 033 | **8** | shd | **Green Falcon**[83] 846 3-9-1 66 (JWHills) *s.i.s: sn prom: wknd over 1f out* 11/2[3] | DHolland 14 | 46 |
| 0-45 | **9** | hd | **King Of Knight (IRE)**[20] 1613 3-9-4 69 (GProdromou) *chsd ldrs over 5f* 20/1 | OUrbina 1 | 48 |
| 00-1 | **10** | 1 | **Hasayis**[37] 1301 3-9-2 70 (JLDunlop) *hld up in tch: rdn over 2f out: wknd over 1f out* 11/2[3] | WSupple 11 | 44 |
| 600- | **11** | 1 ¾ | **Carla Moon**[231] 5190 3-8-11 65 (CFWall) *hld up: a in rr* 33/1 | WRyan 6 | 34 |
| 6-44 | **12** | 6 | **Orchestration (IRE)**[90] 774 3-9-1 69 (JWUnett) *prom: rdn 1/2-way: wknd 2f out* 33/1 | SHitchcott(3) 7 | 25 |
| 324- | **13** | hd | **New York (IRE)**[168] 6082 3-9-2 70 (WJHaggas) *prom over 5f* 20/1 | SDrowne 9 | 23 |
| 0360 | **14** | 2 ½ | **Fools Entire**[44] 1214 3-9-1 66 (JAGilbert) *chsd ldrs over 5f* 14/1 | JQuinn 3 | 15 |
| 2100 | **15** | 1 ¼ | **Global Achiever**[14] 1742 3-9-0 65 (GCHChung) *chsd ldrs: rdn over 2f out: sn wknd* 66/1 | TGMcLaughlin 17 | 11 |
| -000 | **16** | 10 | **Dellagio (IRE)**[16] 1702 3-9-3 68 (CADwyer) *w ldrs 4f: wknd 2f out* 40/1 | SSanders 8 | — |
| 0-56 | **17** | 7 | **Fubos**[114] 580 3-9-1 66 (JulianPoulton) *prom 4f: eased* 66/1 | (v) NCallan 15 | — |

1m 27.54s (1.04) **Going Correction** +0.10s/f (Good) **17** Ran SP% **120.3**
Speed ratings: **98,96,95,91,88 88,84,83,83,82 80,73,73,70,69 57,49**CSF £177.90 TOTE £35.50: £7.70, £2.20, £2.80; EX 150.60.
**Owner** P C J Dalby **Bred** M E Wates **Trained** Newmarket, Suffolk

**FOCUS**
A fair, quite competitive, contest with several of these open to improvement.

**NOTEBOOK**
**Sforzando** was unexposed coming into this and has clearly gone the right way over the winter. She is open to improvement, especially as it looks as though she will stay a bit further still. *Official explanation: trainer's representative had no explanation for the improved form shown*
**Speedbird(USA)** had shown enough as a juvenile to suggest she is up to winning a race, and at least this confirmed she has trained on. Connections can be relied upon to find her an opening.
**Dandouce** handled this faster surface well and can gain compensation before too long.
**Best Desert(IRE)** raced widest of all in the latter stages and just got tired. He will certainly be sharper with this outing under his belt.
**Aesculus(USA)**, from a yard that has yet to hit top form, did not shape too badly having lost her pitch and will almost certainly be capable of better as she steps up in trip.
**River Of Babylon** had a fitness advantage over several of her rivals, but found precious little off the bridle, having travelled well.
**Fubos** *Official explanation: jockey said gelding had stumbled throughout; vet said gelding was lame*

## 2098 HOWARDS HOLDINGS FILLIES' H'CAP 6f 3y
**5:20** (5:25) (F) (0-55,61) 3-Y-O+ **£3,017** (£862; £431) **Stalls** High

| Form | | | | | RPR |
|---|---|---|---|---|---|
| 40-2 | **1** | | **Princess Galadriel**[8] 1907 3-8-4 **50** (JRBest) *racd far side: hld up: hdwy u.p over 1f out: r.o to ld wl ins fnl f* 10/1 | NPollard 15 | 64 |
| 012- | **2** | 1 ½ | **Come Away With Me (IRE)**[308] 3181 4-9-2 **52** (MABuckley) *racd far side: w ldr tl led over 1f out: edgd rt and hdd wl ins fnl f* 6/1[1] | JQuinn 12 | 61 |
| 0-06 | **3** | 1 ¼ | **Vendors Mistake (IRE)**[116] 561 3-8-2 **48** (AndrewReid) *led far side over 5f: styd on same pce ins fnl f* 40/1 | JFEgan 17 | 53 |
| 430- | **4** | shd | **Mannora**[239] 5025 4-9-3 **53** (PHowling) *racd far side: hld up in tch: rdn over 1f out: styd on* 8/1[3] | SDrowne 14 | 58 |
| 100- | **5** | shd | **Emmervale**[206] 5688 5-9-0 **50** (RMHCowell) *racd far side: chsd ldrs: rdn over 1f out: styd on* 50/1 | (v) BDoyle 11 | 55 |
| 4220 | **6** | 1 ½ | **Ranny**[32] 1373 4-8-8 **49** (DrJDScargill) *racd far side: chsd ldrs: rdn over 1f out: styd on same pce* 12/1 | NChalmers(5) 4 | 49 |
| 3041 | **7** | ¾ | **Pickle**[8] 1908 3-9-1 **61** 6ex (SCWilliams) *racd far side: chsd ldrs: rdn over 1f out: styd on same pce* 6/1[1] | DHolland 6 | 59 |
| 6430 | **8** | 2 | **Docklands Blue (IRE)**[37] 1300 3-7-13 **52** (NPLittmoden) *s.i.s and bmpd s: swtchd to r far side and sn outpcd: r.o ins fnl f: nvr nrr* 25/1 | (b[1]) StevenHarrison(7) 20 | 44 |
| 040- | **9** | nk | **Caerphilly Gal**[203] 5728 4-9-2 **55** (PLGilligan) *racd far side: chsd ldrs: rdn over 1f out: wknd ins fnl f* 20/1 | RMiles(3) 3 | 46 |
| 000- | **10** | 1 ¾ | **Essex Star (IRE)**[221] 5415 3-8-4 **53** (MissJFeilden) *racd far side: hld up: n.d* 50/1 | BReilly(3) 10 | 39 |
| 06 | **11** | ½ | **Princess Bankes**[27] 1476 3-8-2 **55** (MissGayKelleway) *racd stands' side: outpcd: styd on appr fnl f* 33/1 | DeanWilliams(7) 19 | 39 |
| 00-3 | **12** | shd | **Red Leicester**[11] 1824 4-9-0 **50** (JAGlover) *racd far side: chsd ldrs over 5f* 14/1 | WRyan 9 | 34 |
| 0041 | **13** | ½ | **Pardon Moi**[4] 1985 3-8-2 **51** 6ex (MrsCADunnett) *racd far side: prom: outpcd 4f out: r.o ins fnl f* 14/1 | LisaJones(3) 1 | 33 |
| 4400 | **14** | 1 ¼ | **Inching**[46] 1178 4-8-7 **48** (RMHCowell) *racd stands' side: chsd ldrs over 3f* 10/1 | (t) AQuinn(5) 18 | 27 |
| 556 | **15** | 6 | **Joans Jewel**[51] 1096 3-8-8 **54** (GGMargarson) *racd far side: prom over 3f* 7/1[2] | JTate 16 | 15 |
| -306 | **16** | 2 | **Anisette**[18] 1676 3-8-7 **53** ow1 (JulianPoulton) *racd far side: prom over 3f* 50/1 | (v[1]) NCallan 13 | 8 |
| 065- | **17** | ½ | **Scarlett Breeze**[190] 5931 3-8-7 **53** (JWHills) *racd far side: chsd ldrs 4f* 10/1 | PRobinson 2 | 6 |
| 020- | **18** | ½ | **Cut Ridge (IRE)**[214] 5546 5-8-11 **47** (JSWainwright) *racd far side: hld up: wknd over 2f out* 20/1 | WSupple 8 | — |
| 3366 | **19** | 2 ½ | **Cloudless (USA)**[10] 1855 4-9-0 **53** (JWUnett) *racd far side: a in rr* 12/1 | SHitchcott(3) 5 | — |
| 000- | **20** | 26 | **Gunnhildr (IRE)**[167] 6100 4-9-4 **54** (PJMakin) *racd far side: prom to 1/2-way: eased* 40/1 | SSanders 7 | — |

1m 14.52s (0.92) **Going Correction** +0.10s/f (Good)
**WFA** 3 from 4yo+ 10lb **20** Ran SP% **135.2**
Speed ratings: **97,95,93,93,93 91,90,87,87,84 84,83,83,81,73 70,70,69,66,31**CSF £67.89 CT £2384.99 TOTE £12.70: £2.10, £2.70, £9.60, £2.30; EX 71.60.
**Owner** Mrs Pam Akhurst **Bred** N J And Mrs Hubbard **Trained** Hucking, Kent

**FOCUS**
This was no better than a seller, but the time was respectable for the grade.

**NOTEBOOK**
**Princess Galadriel** took advantage of this easier task to win with something to spare. While she is nothing out of the ordinary, she should be capable of scoring again.
**Come Away With Me(IRE)**, who is open to more improvement than most of her rivals, is sure to strip sharper having not been seen since last July.
**Vendors Mistake(IRE)**, having her first outing on turf, showed plenty of pace before lack of condition took its toll. She can be expected to strip sharper next time.
**Mannora** shaped as though this trip was a little on the sharp side for her.
**Emmervale** ran a solid race on this return to action and is just as effective over an extra furlong.
**Ranny** is better suited to an extra furlong.
**Essex Star(IRE)** *Official explanation: jockey said filly was kicked at the start*

## 2099 CUSTOM KITCHENS STAND CLASSIFIED STKS 7f 3y
**5:50** (5:52) (F) 4-Y-O+ **£2,905** (£830; £415) **Stalls** High

| Form | | | | | RPR |
|---|---|---|---|---|---|
| 1150 | **1** | | **Warlingham (IRE)**[84] 834 6-9-0 57 (PHowling) *hld up: hdwy over 2f out: led over 1f out: rdn out* 5/2[2] | SSanders 4 | 65 |
| -006 | **2** | nk | **Cryfield**[20] 1620 7-9-0 58 (NTinkler) *chsd ldrs: rdn and ev ch ins fnl f: r.o* 15/8[1] | KimTinkler 1 | 64 |
| 2030 | **3** | ½ | **Aguila Loco (IRE)**[21] 1595 5-9-0 56 (MrsStefLiddiard) *led over 5f: r.o* 4/1[3] | (p) SDrowne 2 | 63 |
| 0-00 | **4** | 11 | **Tuscan Treaty**[10] 1857 4-8-11 57 (TTClement) *chsd ldrs over 5f* 11/2 | JMackay 5 | 30 |
| 0-00 | **5** | 2 | **Tata Naka**[11] 1820 4-8-8 45 (MrsCADunnett) *chsd ldr over 4f: sn wknd* 16/1 | LisaJones(3) 3 | 25 |

1m 26.9s (0.40) **Going Correction** +0.10s/f (Good) **5** Ran SP% **104.6**
Speed ratings: **101,100,100,87,85**CSF £6.78 TOTE £3.10: £1.70, £1.10; EX 5.40 Place 6 £112.67, Place 5 £15.58.
**Owner** David Andrew Brown **Bred** Paul Hyland **Trained** Newmarket, Suffolk

**FOCUS**
An ordinary contest, but run at a fair pace.

**NOTEBOOK**
**Warlingham(IRE)** got first run on the runner-up, and that proved vital in the end.
**Cryfield**, who stays further than this, may have done better had he a little more use made of him.
**Aguila Loco(IRE)** has been a bit in and out of late, but he kept battling away here.
**Tuscan Treaty** dropped away tamely and is clearly out of sorts at present.
T/Plt: £174.60 to a £1 stake. Pool: £27,670.00. 115.65 winning tickets. T/Qpdt: £33.20 to a £1 stake. Pool: £2,176.50. 48.40 winning tickets. CR

2100 - 2101a (Foreign Racing) - See Raceform Interactive

## 1377 CORK (R-H)

Friday, May 14

**OFFICIAL GOING: Good to firm (firm in places)**

### 2102a IRISH STALLION FARMS EUROPEAN BREEDERS FUND BLUE WIND STKS (GROUP 3) (F&M) 1m 2f 50y

**7:20** (7:21) 3-Y-0+ **£41,197** (£12,042; £5,704; £1,901)

RPR

1 **Hazarista (IRE)**[12] 1807 3-8-9 FMBerry 4 104
(JohnMOxx, Ire) *chsd ldrs: 5th into st: rdn to chal in 2nd 2f out: led under 1f out: sn clr: comf* **7/1**

2 2 **Cache Creek (IRE)**[33] 1347 6-9-10 93 JAHeffernan 6 100
(PHughes, Ire) *mid-div: rdn in 6th fr early st: 5th 2f out: kpt on wl into 2nd ins fnl f: no threat to wnr* **10/1**

3 1 1/2 **Felicity (IRE)**[12] 1790 4-9-10 PShanahan 9 97
(JHMGosden) *attempted to make all: chal and strly pressed fr over 2f out: hdd under 1f out: sn no ex* **5/1**[3]

4 1 **Livadiya (IRE)**[5] 1982 8-9-10 109 JPSpencer 7 95
(HRogers, Ire) *hld up in rr: rdn and prog into 5th 2f out: 4th and kpt on same pce fr over 1f out* **9/4**[2]

5 2 1/2 **Mrs Mason (IRE)**[19] 1646 3-8-9 87 DPMcDonogh 2 91
(KevinPrendergast, Ire) *trckd ldrs: 3rd into st: rdn and kpt on same pce fr over 1 1/2f out* **10/1**

6 3/4 **Lisieux Orchid (IRE)**[27] 1480 3-8-9 PJSmullen 3 89
(DKWeld, Ire) *hld up towards rr: 8th and rdn fr early st: kpt on same pce fr under 2f out* **10/1**

7 nk **Zarafsha (IRE)**[20] 1635 3-8-9 MJKinane 5 89
(JohnMOxx, Ire) *trckd ldr in 2nd: rdn and wknd fr over 2f out* **2/1**[1]

8 2 1/2 **Turn Back Time (IRE)**[12] 1815 4-9-10 89 KJManning 8 84
(JSBolger, Ire) *trckd ldrs: 4th fr early st: rdn whn bdly hmpd over 2f out: no imp after* **20/1**

9 10 **Wensum Dancer**[13] 1155 7-9-10 78 (t) AJNolan 1 65
(FTierney, Ire) *towards rr thrght: rdn and no imp st* **33/1**

2m 9.80s
**WFA** 3 from 4yo+ 15lb **9** Ran SP% **128.2**
Speed ratings: CSF £82.54 TOTE £11.80: £1.90, £4.30, £2.30; DF 644.30.
**Owner** H H Aga Khan **Bred** H H Aga Khan's Studs S C **Trained** Currabeg, Co Kildare

**FOCUS**
A Group Three race in name only.

**NOTEBOOK**
**Hazarista(IRE)**, supplemented earlier in the week but very much the stable's second string on jockey arrangements, handled the fast ground better than her opponents and won easily. A winner of a very average looking maiden at Gowran on her previous start, she seems much improved, even taking the face value of the form. She will stay farther but the key to her appears to be fast ground.
**Cache Creek(IRE)** is a 93-rated handicapper whose last win was gained off 80 a year ago. She ran on inside the last without threatening.
**Felicity(IRE)** went off in front but was readily outpaced once headed by the winner.
**Livadiya(IRE)**, easy in the market, never looked comfortable on the ground despite having won on it last season.
**Mrs Mason(IRE)** had no real business in this line-up but still was not disgraced.
**Zarafsha(IRE)** ran second but was weakening when involved in a skirmish with Turn Back Time early in the straight. Her jockey reported that she did not like the ground and was changing her legs throughout. *Official explanation: jockey said filly changed its legs throughout and did not like the good to firm ground*

2103 - 2106a (Foreign Racing) - See Raceform Interactive

## 2080 NEWBURY (L-H)

Saturday, May 15

**OFFICIAL GOING: Good (good to soft in places)**

### 2107 LONDON PADDY POWER GOLD CUP (HANDICAP STKS) 1m 3f 5y

**1:35** (1:36) (C) (0-95,93) 3-Y-0 **£11,536** (£4,375; £2,187; £994) **Stalls** Low

Form RPR

431- 1 **Pukka (IRE)**[168] 6091 3-8-7 78 ow1 LDettori 8 93
(LMCumani) *lw: in tch: hdwy 3f out: led appr fnl 2f: drvn and styd on wl fnl f* **11/1**

414- 2 1 1/4 **Maraahel (IRE)**[208] 5674 3-9-7 **93** RHills 1 105+
(SirMichaelStoute) *h.d.w: lw: s.i.s: sn in tch: hmpd ins fnl 4f:swtchd rt and hdwy over 2f out: wnt 2nd over 1f out: kpt on: nt rch wnr* **16/1**

0-61 3 2 **Frank Sonata**[4] 2018 3-9-6 **92** 4ex JPMurtagh 3 101
(MGQuinlan) *chsd ldrs: led ins fnl 3f: hdd appr fnl 2f: styd on same pce u.p fr over 1f out* **11/2**[1]

34-1 4 3 **Bukit Fraser (IRE)**[33] 1356 3-9-0 **86** KFallon 6 90
(PFICole) *lw: nudged along in rr early: sn hld up but in tch: rdn 3f out: styd on fr over 1f out but nvr gng pce of ldrs* **10/1**[3]

52-4 5 1 1/4 **Mocca (IRE)**[30] 1414 3-8-4 **76** MartinDwyer 5 78
(DJCoakley) *led 1f: styd w ldr tl led again 4f out: hdd ins fnl 3f: wknd ins fnl 2f* **10/1**[3]

20-1 6 4 **Maganda (IRE)**[21] 1619 3-8-12 **84** PRobinson 10 80
(MAJarvis) *bhd: rdn and hdwy fr 3f out: effrt over 2f out: nvr rchd ldrs and wknd sn after* **11/1**

5-1 7 13 **Vinando**[26] 1508 3-8-12 **84** SDrowne 11 59
(CREgerton) *chsd ldrs: rdn 3f out: wknd qckly fr 2f out* **8/1**[2]

2-04 8 4 **Gravardlax**[18] 1683 3-8-13 **85** (b[1]) MHills 2 53
(BJMeehan) *slt ld after 1f: hdd 4f out: wknd ins fnl 3f* **40/1**

62-4 9 11 **Le Tiss (IRE)**[49] 1134 3-8-9 **81** TEDurcan 4 32
(MRChannon) *a in rr: lost tch fr over 2f out* **25/1**

-311 10 1/2 **Another Choice (IRE)**[18] 1688 3-8-7 **78** ow1 (t) DHolland 7 29
(NPLittmoden) *hld up in rr: sme hdwy on outside 3f out: nvr rchd ldrs and sn wknd* **12/1**

2m 20.0s (-2.81) **Going Correction** -0.10s/f (Good) **10** Ran SP% **81.2**
Speed ratings: **106,105,103,101,100 97,88,85,77,76** CSF £80.48 CT £313.30 TOTE £7.60: £2.50, £3.70, £1.70; EX 115.50 Trifecta £347.50 Part won. Pool of £489.34 - 0.50 winning units..

**Owner** Fittocks Stud **Bred** Fittocks Stud **Trained** Newmarket, Suffolk
■ Stewards Enquiry : R Hills two-day ban: careless riding (May 26,27)

**FOCUS**
A strong three-year-old handicap run at a reasonable pace. The first two should go on again from here. Swagger stick (13/8 fav) was withdrawn on vet's advice. Rule 4 35p in the £.

**NOTEBOOK**
**Pukka(IRE)** ◆ progressed with every run last year and showed he is still improving with a nice performance. His stable is beginning to hit form and this one looks worth following.
**Maraahel(IRE)**, third in a mile Listed race on his final start at two, ran a reasonable race under top weight on this first start in 208 days. He did not get the clearest of runs, but had long enough to get to the winner if good enough. There should be more to come.
**Frank Sonata** caused a bit of a surprise when scoring at 33/1 at York four days previously, and was unable to follow up under his 4lb penalty over this extra furlong on faster ground.
**Bukit Fraser(IRE)**, off the mark in a maiden over this trip at Kempton on his reappearance, proved a little disappointing on this switch into handicap company. He got stuck in behind horses and never really got one continuous run when it mattered.
**Mocca(IRE)** had no chance with the principals and may need her sights lowered a little.
**Maganda(IRE)** *Official explanation: jockey said colt was hanging left*
**Another Choice(IRE)** *Official explanation: trainer said colt was hanging right throughout*

### 2108 PADDY POWER STKS (REGISTERED AS THE ASTON PARK STAKES) (LISTED RACE) 1m 5f 61y

**2:05** (2:12) (A) 4-Y-0+ **£17,400** (£6,600; £3,300; £1,500) **Stalls** Low

Form RPR

2-02 1 **The Whistling Teal**[8] 1925 8-8-12 107 DHolland 2 114
(GWragg) *lw: hld up rr but in tch: hdwy 4f out: led over 2f out: pushed clr fnl f: comf* **5/4**[1]

34-0 2 4 **Delsarte (USA)**[49] 1144 4-8-12 (t) LDettori 6 109
(SaeedBinSuroor) *hld up rr but in tch: hdwy to ld appr fnl 3f: rdn and hdd over 2f out: outpcd by wnr over 1f out:hld on for 2nd* **9/4**[2]

06-0 3 1/2 **Gulf (IRE)**[35] 1329 5-8-12 97 JPMurtagh 4 108
(DRCElsworth) *swtg: hld up in rr: hdwy fr 3f out: drvn and styd on fr 2f out: kpt on ins last and clsng on 2nd: no ch w wnr* **33/1**

55-0 4 3 **Savannah Bay**[17] 1703 5-8-12 111 (b) RHughes 5 104
(BJMeehan) *chsd ldrs: rdn over 2f out and no imp: wknd fnl f* **10/1**

15-0 5 8 **Distinction (IRE)**[28] 1455 5-8-12 107 KFallon 8 93
(SirMichaelStoute) *trckd ldrs: led 1m out: rdn and hdd appr fnl 3f: wknd fr 2f out* **6/1**[3]

603- 6 5 **Gold Medallist**[226] 5330 4-9-1 102 DaneO'Neill 7 89
(DRCElsworth) *bhd: rdn 3f out: n.d and sn dropped away* **14/1**

-405 7 2 1/2 **Forest Magic (IRE)**[8] 1925 4-8-12 100 PaulEddery 3 82
(PWD'Arcy) *lw: sn led: hdd 1m out: styd chsng ldr tl n.m.r ins fnl 4f: wknd 3f out* **33/1**

10-0 8 dist **Yawmi**[21] 1622 4-9-1 109 RHills 1 —
(BWHills) *chsd ldrs: rdn and wknd rapidly 4f out: t.o* **25/1**

2m 48.97s (-2.02) **Going Correction** -0.10s/f (Good) **8** Ran SP% **115.0**
Speed ratings: **102,99,99,97,92 89,87,**—CSF £4.09 TOTE £2.20: £1.10, £1.50, £5.70; EX 5.80 Trifecta £179.90 Pool of £1,317.67 - 5.20 winning units..
**Owner** Mrs F A Veasey **Bred** Mrs F A Veasey **Trained** Newmarket, Suffolk

**FOCUS**
The Whistling Teal did what he had to, but it is hard to know what to make of the form, with 97-rated Gulf in third, confirmed stayer Savannah Bay fourth and the others all below form. They appeared to go a good pace, but the time was moderate for the grade.

**NOTEBOOK**
**The Whistling Teal** failed to win a race in four runs last season, but is in fine form this time around and ran out a most decisive winner. One could pick holes in the form, but he is a really tough sort who will surely continue to go well at this sort of level.
**Delsarte(USA)**, well held in the Dubai Sheema Classic on his debut for Godolphin, had a tongue-tie fitted on this return to England and was returning to the grade in which he gained his last success. However, he was no match for the winner and had just a length in hand of 97-rated Gulf.
**Gulf(IRE)** does most of his racing over further in lower-class races, so it was a surprise to see him run so well. The strong pace clearly suited and he will be one to keep an eye on when he steps back up in trip.
**Savannah Bay** is better over further, but this will have provided him with a much-needed confidence boost after being tailed off in awful ground at Ascot on his previous start. He is one to keep an eye on when he steps back up in trip.
**Distinction(IRE)** again failed to perform.
**Gold Medallist** was never going.
**Forest Magic(IRE)** may have had a little bit too much use made of him early.
**Yawmi** *Official explanation: trainer said colt finished distressed*

### 2109 JUDDMONTE LOCKINGE STKS (GROUP 1) 1m (S)

**2:40** (2:44) (A) 4-Y-0+ **£116,000** (£44,000; £22,000; £10,000) **Stalls** Centre

Form RPR

125- 1 **Russian Rhythm (USA)**[210] 5641 4-8-11 117 KFallon 3 118
(SirMichaelStoute) *lw: hld up mid-div: hdwy 2f out: str run fr over 1f out: led fnl 100yds: gamely* **3/1**[1]

10-0 2 1/2 **Salselon**[21] 1621 5-9-0 113 (b) JPMurtagh 8 120
(LMCumani) *hld up in rr: rapid hdwy on far side fr 2f out: str chal ins fnl f: no ex fnl 100yds* **66/1**

60-4 3 nk **Norse Dancer (IRE)**[21] 1621 4-9-0 117 TQuinn 14 119
(DRCElsworth) *hld up in rr: rapid hdwy fr 2f out to led ins fnl f: hdd and founf no ex fnl 100yds* **10/1**

05-1 4 1 **Firebreak**[49] 1142 5-9-0 (t) KMcEvoy 10 117
(SaeedBinSuroor) *tracked ldrs: led ins fnl 3f: hdd ins fnl f: styd on same pce* **16/1**

5-31 5 1 **Hurricane Alan (IRE)**[21] 1621 4-9-0 116 PDobbs 15 114
(RHannon) *hld up in tch:rdn over 2f out: kpt on fnl f but nt pce to rch ldrs* **14/1**

10-3 6 3/4 **Ikhtyar (IRE)**[17] 1705 4-9-0 117 RHills 12 113
(JHMGosden) *lw: in tch: hdwy 3f out: rdn to press ldrs ins fnl 2f: outpcd fnl f* **11/2**[3]

3360 7 1/2 **Checkit (IRE)**[21] 1621 4-9-0 112 TEDurcan 6 112
(MRChannon) *hld up in rr: hdwy: n.m.r and swtchd lft ins fnl 2f: kpt on ins last but nvr gng pce to rch ldrs* **25/1**

00-0 8 1 1/2 **Refuse To Bend (IRE)**[49] 1146 4-9-0 (t) LDettori 9 108
(SaeedBinSuroor) *chsd ldrs: rdn over 2f out: sn one pce* **5/1**[2]

00-5 9 3/4 **Indian Haven**[21] 1621 4-9-0 114 DHolland 1 106
(PWD'Arcy) *pressed ldrs: stl upsides and rdn over 2f out: wknd fnl f* **20/1**

5561 10 3/4 **Quito (IRE)**[2] 2065 7-9-0 103 (b) ACulhane 4 105
(DWChapman) *s.i.s: bhd: kpt on fr over 1f out but nvr in contention* **25/1**

0212 11 shd **Gateman**[21] 1621 7-9-0 115 KDalgleish 7 104
(MJohnston) *led 2f: styd pressing ldrs: rdn 3f out: wknd fr ins fnl 2f* **16/1**

3-4 12 1/2 **Krataios (FR)**[14] 1780 4-9-0 OPeslier 11 103
(CLaffon-Parias, France) *tall: str: lw: bhd: rdn 3f out: nvr in contention* **25/1**

121- 13 5 **With Reason (USA)**[233] 5168 6-9-0 (t) RHughes 13 92
(SaeedBinSuroor) *pressed ldrs: rdn 3f out: wknd 2f out* **25/1**

210- 14 15 **Desert Deer**[333] 2445 6-9-0 114 KDarley 2 57
(JHMGosden) *slt ld after 2f: hdd ins fnl fnl 3f: wknd qckly over 1f out: wnt lame on line and dismntd: dead.* **16/1**

05-1 **15** *6* **Tout Seul (IRE)**[21] [1610] 4-9-0 113........................................ SCarson 5 43
(RFJohnsonHoughton) *chsd ldrs: rdn over 2f out: sn btn: no ch whn bdly hmpd on line* **12/1**

1m 37.0s (-3.83) **Going Correction** -0.10s/f (Good) **15** Ran SP% **119.8**
Speed ratings: **115,114,114,113,112 111,110,109,108,107 107,107,102,87,81**CSF £267.34 TOTE £3.40: £1.80, £20.60, £3.20; EX 519.60 Trifecta £2611.80 Part won. Pool of £3,678.70 - 0.90 winning units..
**Owner** Cheveley Park Stud **Bred** Brushwood Stable **Trained** Newmarket, Suffolk

**FOCUS**
A competitive renewal of the Lockinge, featuring three Guineas winners from 2003, but some of the principals had questions to answer. The pace was decent for the grade. Russian Rhythm confirmed herself an exceptional filly without quite reproducing last year's Coronation Stakes or Queen Elizabeth II form.

**NOTEBOOK**
**Russian Rhythm(USA)**, a Group One winner against her own sex three times last season, had to prove she could do it against the boys and did not disappoint. Always going really nicely, she picked up well when switched out for a run and saw off challengers on both sides in very game fashion. She is likely to face tougher tasks this term, but she is an exceptional filly and versatile one with regards to trip. She has any number of options and Royal Ascot will surely be next, where the Queen Anne or Prince of Wales's Stakes are obvious targets.
**Salselon** had never won at higher than Group Three level in Italy and showed little on his debut for Luca Cumani at Sandown. However, back up in grade with blinkers re-fitted, he ran a blinder and would have gone even closer had he not lost his concentration and pricked his ears in the closing stages. He does not have that much to find to make his mark at this level and, if his trainer can keep him focused, he could be in for a big season.
**Norse Dancer(IRE)** ran several fine races in defeat last term, including when third in the Guineas, fourth in the Derby and third in the Sussex Stakes. However, he has not won since his two-year-old days and again showed himself to be a very hard ride. He quickened up smartly and looked all over the winner inside the final furlong, but appeared to accept defeat rather easily and could not even manage second. There is a big one in him, but he is a nightmare to predict.
**Firebreak** looked good when gaining his second Godolphin Mile success on the dirt at Nad Al Sheba on his previous outing and ran a cracker on this return to turf, faring best of those to race on the pace.
**Hurricane Alan(IRE)**, back to winning form in the Betfred Mile at Sandown on his previous outing, falls just short of this level and did not look to have any excuses.
**Ikhtyar(IRE)** was very easy to back and looked to need his reappearance at Ascot. With the benefit of that run, he was all the rage this time but did not deliver. He lacked a change of pace and may be better suited by ten furlongs.
**Refuse To Bend(IRE)** has won only a Group 3 at Leopardstown - admittedly smart form - since the 2000 Guineas and looks badly flattered by that victory.
**Desert Deer**, making his debut for John Gosden, sadly fractured his near-hind fetlock and later had to be put down.

## 2110 PADDYPOWER.COM STKS (H'CAP) 1m 4f 5y
3:10 (3:15) (C) (0-100,96) 3-Y-0+ **£17,400** (£6,600; £3,300; £1,500) **Stalls** Low

Form RPR

234 **1** **Swift Tango (IRE)**[39] [1286] 4-9-6 **90**........................................ LDettori 17 103
(EALDunlop) *lw: hld up in rr: n.m.r on rails over 2f out: swtchd rt and gd hdwy sn after: squeezed through 1f out: led wl ins last: all* **16/1**

3241 **2** *shd* **Cold Turkey**[24] [1539] 4-9-1 **85**........................................ SWhitworth 10 98
(GLMoore) *hld up rr: stl plenty to do whn swtchd off rails to outside over 2f out: str run over 1f out: chal wl ins last: jst failed* **9/2**[1]

40-1 **3** *1* **Red Fort (IRE)**[21] [1604] 4-9-10 **94**........................................ PRobinson 7 105+
(MAJarvis) *trckd ldrs: led ins fnl 3f: rdn and kpt on wl fr over 1f out: hdd and no ex wl ins last* **8/1**

1-00 **4** *2 ½* **Turbo (IRE)**[35] [1328] 5-9-9 **93**........................................(p) SDrowne 5 100
(GBBalding) *hld up in rr: hdwy over 2f out: kpt to chse ldrs over 1f out: outpcd ins last* **16/1**

16-0 **5** *1 ½* **Mephisto (IRE)**[31] [1401] 5-9-2 **86**........................................ DHolland 6 91+
(LMCumani) *chsd ldrs: led ins fnl 4f: hdd ins fnl 3f: wknd fnl f* **10/1**

12-0 **6** *2* **Laggan Bay (IRE)**[13] [1801] 4-8-4 **77** ow2........................................ LPKeniry(3) 14 78
(JCFox) *swtg: hld up in rr: stdy hdwy on outside fr 3f out: kpt on same pce fnl f* **25/1**

0-45 **7** *hd* **Flotta**[31] [1401] 5-9-2 **86**........................................ ACulhane 18 87
(MRChannon) *bhd: hdwy 6f out: rdn and styd on fnl 2f: nvr gng pce to rch ldrs* **7/1**[3]

0603 **8** *¾* **Lion Hunter (USA)**[19] [1671] 5-9-3 **87**........................................ RHughes 19 87
(MissECLavelle) *hld up mid-div: hdwy on outside 3f out: rdn 2f out: wknd fnl f* **16/1**

14-0 **9** *½* **Wunderwood (USA)**[31] [1401] 5-9-6 **90**........................................ TQuinn 15 89
(LadyHerries) *chsd ldrs: rdn 3f out: wknd fnl f* **6/1**[2]

115/ **10** *6* **Manorson (IRE)**[731] [1449] 5-9-11 **95**........................................ MartinDwyer 16 84
(MAMagnusson) *trckd ldr: chal fr over 4f out tl over 3f out: wknd fr 2f out* **33/1**

203- **11** *1* **Defining**[273] [4187] 5-9-11 **95**........................................ JPMurtagh 2 83
(JRFanshawe) *behund: hdwy 6f out: rdn to chse ldrs 3f out: wknd 2f out* **16/1**

0520 **12** *6* **General**[19] [1661] 7-8-2 **72**........................................ SCarson 8 50
(NPLittmoden) *bhd: hdwy fr 4f out to chse ldrs 3f out: wknd over 2f out* **33/1**

631/ **13** *5* **Thundering Surf**[697] [2227] 7-9-9 **93**........................................ PDobbs 13 63
(JRJenkins) *hld up mid-div: trckd ldrs 3f out: wknd over 2f out* **33/1**

10-0 **14** *3 ½* **Harcourt (USA)**[24] [1540] 4-9-2 **86**........................................ KFallon 3 51
(PFICole) *chsd ldrs tl wknd ins fnl 3f* **12/1**

10-0 **15** *4* **Financial Future**[14] [1768] 4-9-12 **96**........................................ JFanning 9 54
(MJohnston) *chsd ldrs 9f* **33/1**

21/- **16** *¾* **Valiant Effort**[656] [3425] 5-8-5 **75**........................................ KMcEvoy 11 32
(MMeade) *bkwd: sn led: hdd ins fnl 4f: wknd ins fnl 3f* **100/1**

41-5 **17** *2* **Wiggy Smith**[19] [1671] 5-8-10 **80**........................................ DaneO'Neill 1 34
(HCandy) *mid-div: effrt 5f out: sn wknd* **6/1**[2]

2m 32.63s (-3.66) **Going Correction** -0.10s/f (Good) **17** Ran SP% **127.3**
Speed ratings: **108,107,107,105,104 103,103,102,102,98 97,93,90,87,85 84,83**CSF £85.15 CT £648.92 TOTE £16.00: £2.60, £1.40, £2.20, £3.60; EX 88.40 Trifecta £260.80 Pool of £1,946.90 - 5.30 winning units.
**Owner** Khalifa Sultan **Bred** Killeen Castle Stud **Trained** Newmarket, Suffolk

**FOCUS**
A competitive handicap run at a good gallop. Solid form.

**NOTEBOOK**
**Swift Tango(IRE)**, surprisingly enough had never previously raced beyond ten furlongs, but he got this mile and a half very well. He had to wait for a gap, but picked up well when in the clear and was always just holding the runner-up's customary late challenge. There could be more to come over this sort of trip. *Official explanation: trainer said, regarding the improved form shown, gelding was better suited by today's faster ground*
**Cold Turkey** has not stopped progressing since winning a Goodwood claimer last October, and this was another tremendous effort off a career-high turf mark. He had to be switched out wide for his run, but at the same time the winner was suffering interference so he cannot really be considered unlucky. There is, however, probably even more to come.
**Red Fort(IRE)** was 6lb higher than when winning at Haydock on his reappearance and ran well again. He is still relatively unexposed.
**Turbo(IRE)** kept on well enough, but lacked the change of pace shown by the front two.
**Mephisto(IRE)** ran better than he did at Newmarket on his reappearance and could be worth keeping an eye on now his stable are beginning to hit form. *Official explanation: jockey said gelding was hanging left in the last furlong*
**Wunderwood(USA)** *Official explanation: jockey said gelding was never travelling*
**Manorson(IRE)** did not run a bad race at all on this first start in 731 days.

## 2111 DAVID WILSON HOMES MAIDEN STKS 6f 8y
3:45 (3:47) (D) 2-Y-O **£5,164** (£1,589; £794; £397) **Stalls** Centre

Form RPR

2 **1** **Iceman**[11] [1853] 2-9-0........................................ LDettori 7 93+
(JHMGosden) *lw: trckd ldrs: led appr fnl 2f: drvn over 1f out: qcknd and kpt on wl fnl f: readily* **5/2**[2]

**2** *2* **Screwdriver** 2-9-0........................................ DaneO'Neill 6 87
(RHannon) *str: scope: lw: trckd ldrs: pushed along over 2f out: styd on fr over 1f out: tk 2nd cl home but no imp on wnr* **66/1**

**3** *nk* **Mushajer** 2-9-0........................................ RHills 4 86
(MPTregoning) *leggy: unf: chsd ldrs: chal over 2f out: sn chsng wnr: outpcd fnl f and lost 2nd cl home* **8/1**

**4** *2 ½* **Witchry** 2-9-0........................................ PRobinson 10 79
(MAJarvis) *bkwd: in tch: hdwy 2f out: chsd ldrs over 1f out: wknd ins fnl f* **5/1**[3]

**5** *1* **Al Garhoud Bridge** 2-9-0........................................ ACulhane 8 76
(MRChannon) *rangy: hld up in rr: hdwy fr 2f out: chsd ldrs over 1f out: sn one pce* **20/1**

**6** *2* **Shaheer (IRE)** 2-8-11........................................ LPKeniry(3) 9 70
(BJMeehan) *w'like: bkwd: bhd: rdn and hdwy 2f out: nvr rchd ldrs: wknd fnl f* **66/1**

**7** *¾* **Perfect Choice (IRE)** 2-9-0........................................ DHolland 13 67
(BJMeehan) *tall: scope: s.i.s: bhd: hdwy over 1f out: kpt on but nvr gng pce to rch ldrs* **11/1**

**8** *1* **League Of Nations (IRE)** 2-9-0........................................ KFallon 3 64
(PFICole) *str: bkwd: chsd ldrs: pushed along 2f out: wknd over 1f out* **10/1**

**9** *½* **Bakke** 2-9-0........................................ SDrowne 12 63
(MPTregoning) *tall: scope: hld up in rr: sme hdwy fr over 1f out but nvr gng pce to rch ldrs* **50/1**

5 **10** *3 ½* **Aberdeen Park**[11] [1853] 2-8-9........................................ JoannaBadger 1 47
(MrsHSweeting) *chsd ldrs: rdn: hung bdly lft and wknd over 1f out* **66/1**

**11** *2 ½* **Rusky Dusky (USA)** 2-9-0........................................ RHughes 5 45
(RHannon) *str: bkwd: hld up mid-div: hdwy 2f out: sn wknd* **20/1**

4 **12** *4* **Art Legend**[35] [1331] 2-9-0........................................ JPMurtagh 2 33
(DRCElsworth) *t.k.h: led tl hdd appr fnl 2f: sn btn* **20/1**

**P** **Bla Shak (IRE)** 2-9-0........................................ MartinDwyer 11 —
(MPTregoning) *lenghty: str: sn pushed along in rr: p.u and dismntd 1/2-way: lame* **9/4**[1]

1m 13.9s (-0.47) **Going Correction** -0.10s/f (Good) **13** Ran SP% **125.3**
Speed ratings: **99,96,95,92,91 88,87,86,85,80 77,72,—**CSF £183.32 TOTE £3.80: £1.50, £5.20, £3.50; EX 111.70.
**Owner** Cheveley Park Stud **Bred** Cheveley Park Stud Ltd **Trained** Manton, Wilts

**FOCUS**
Hard to know what to make of this maiden as the winner was beaten in an ordinary Bath maiden on his debut, yet is considered Royal Ascot material, and many of the newcomers were unfancied in the betting.

**NOTEBOOK**
**Iceman**, only second when sent off 11/8 on his debut at Bath 11 days previously, built on that promise to take what was surely a better maiden in good style. He is considered Royal Ascot class and the Coventry Stakes looks an obvious target.
**Screwdriver**, a 30,000gns half-brother to a seven-furlong two-year-old winner, out of an unraced half-sister to Classic Cliche, was very easy to back but made a most promising debut. He is sure to improve and will stay further.
**Mushajer**, a 78,000gns half-brother to seven winners, offered enough promise to suggest he will have little trouble in finding a maiden.
**Witchry**, a half-brother to successful South African sire Manshood, out of a five-time Group One winner over middle-distances, made a respectable debut.
**Al Garhoud Bridge**, a 40,000euros yearling, half-brother to three two-year-old winners, made a nice debut and should be open to plenty of improvement.
**Bla Shak(IRE)** has clearly been showing something at home for he was sent off favourite for this racecourse debut, but he cracked a bone in his leg and is sadly out for the season.

## 2112 CATRIDGE FARM STUD & MANOR FARM PACKERS FILLIES' H'CAP 7f (S)
4:20 (4:21) (D) (0-80,78) 3-Y-O **£6,318** (£1,944; £972; £486) **Stalls** Centre

Form RPR

01- **1** **Red Sahara (IRE)**[224] [5378] 3-8-13 **70**........................................ KFallon 7 82
(WJHaggas) *lw: h.d.w: scope: stdd s: hld up: hdwy and nt clr ins fnl 3f and again over 1f out: led over 1f out: styd on wl: readily* **13/2**[2]

210- **2** *2* **Go Between**[226] [5334] 3-9-7 **78**........................................ SDrowne 6 85
(EALDunlop) *in tch: hdwy to chse ldrs over 2f out: str chal over 1f out: kpt on but nt pce of wnr ins last* **33/1**

-41 **3** *½* **Andaluza (IRE)**[22] [1597] 3-8-13 **70**........................................ SCarson 10 76
(PDCundell) *in tch: hdwy fr 2f out: kpt on wl ins fnl f: gng on cl home* **25/1**

4-53 **4** *2 ½* **Lyca Ballerina**[12] [1842] 3-8-9 **73**........................................ KMay(7) 19 72
(BWHills) *lw: chsd ldrs: rdn and ev ch fr over 1f out: outpcd ins fnl f* **7/1**[3]

502- **5** *hd* **Here To Me**[191] [5929] 3-9-1 **72**........................................ RHughes 11 70
(RHannon) *a chsng ldrs: rdn 2f out: wknd fnl f* **25/1**

0-00 **6** *1 ½* **Hana Dee**[37] [1309] 3-8-3 **67**........................................ TO'Brien(7) 8 62
(MRChannon) *bhd: hdwy and nt clr run over 1f out: kpt on ins last but nt trble ldrs* **50/1**

-305 **7** *½* **Wavertree Girl (IRE)**[23] [1558] 3-9-4 **75**........................................ JFanning 5 68
(NPLittmoden) *chsd ldrs: rdn to chal over 1f out: wknd fnl f* **25/1**

43-3 **8** *½* **Ela Paparouna**[25] [1530] 3-9-2 **73**........................................ DaneO'Neill 12 65
(HCandy) *hld up in rr: n.m.r 2f out: swtchd lft over 1f out: kpt on ins last but nt a danger* **13/2**[2]

400- **9** *nk* **Filliemou (IRE)**[204] [5734] 3-8-8 **65**........................................ RHills 9 56
(AWCarroll) *bhd: hdwy: n.m.r and carried lft over 1f out: r.o ins last* **50/1**

550- **10** *1* **Nine Red**[215] [5535] 3-8-7 **64**........................................ MHills 17 53
(BWHills) *bhd: styd on wl fr over 1f out: nt trble ldrs* **20/1**

43-0 **11** *hd* **True (IRE)**[26] [1507] 3-9-2 **73**........................................ MartinDwyer 2 61
(MPTregoning) *sn led: hdd over 3f out: led over 2f out: hdd over 1f out and sn btn* **10/1**

44-1 **12** *1 ¼* **Farriers Charm**[19] [1678] 3-8-5 **65**........................................ LPKeniry(3) 15 50
(DJCoakley) *chsd ldrs over 2f out: wknd over 1f out* **25/1**

0-50 **13** *1* **Fadeela (IRE)**[30] [1408] 3-8-13 **70**........................................ PaulEddery 1 52
(PWD'Arcy) *nvr gng pce to trble ldrs* **20/1**

01- **14** 1 3/4 **Blue Daze**[336] 2362 3-9-3 **74** PDobbs 4 52
(RHannon) *chsd ldrs: ev ch ins fnl 2f: wknd fnl f* **25/1**
660- **15** shd **Abington Angel**[179] 6023 3-9-7 **78** LDettori 16 55
(BJMeehan) *nvr gng pce to rch ldrs* **13/2**[2]
524- **16** shd **Cyfrwys (IRE)**[198] 5834 3-9-7 **78** KDarley 3 55
(BPalling) *chsd ldrs: rdn to chal ins fnl 2f: wknd over 1f out* **33/1**
1561 **17** 3 **Generous Gesture (IRE)**[16] 1737 3-9-4 **75** (v) DHolland 20 44
(MLWBell) *w ldrs: led over 3f out tl over 2f out: wknd qckly* **10/1**
200- **18** 4 **Coconut Cookie**[232] 5185 3-9-1 **72** JPMurtagh 14 31
(RHannon) *chsd ldrs 5f* **33/1**
620- **19** 1/2 **Waaedah (USA)**[251] 4750 3-9-7 **78** ACulhane 13 36
(MRChannon) *sn bhd* **33/1**
31-1 **20** 1 3/4 **Beejay**[28] 1464 3-9-4 **75** TQuinn 18 28
(PFICole) *lw: in tch: rdn 1/2-way: wknd fr 2f out* **5/1**[1]

1m 26.17s (-1.05) **Going Correction** -0.10s/f (Good) **20** Ran SP% **131.8**
Speed ratings: **102,99,99,96,96 94,93,93,92,91 91,90,88,86,86 86,83,78,78,76**CSF £215.76 CT £5058.96 TOTE £6.80: £1.60, £9.90, £6.60, £2.60; EX 211.90.
**Owner** Shortgrove Manor Stud **Bred** P Hardy **Trained** Newmarket, Suffolk

**FOCUS**
Probably just an ordinary handicap and there were some hard-luck stories in behind. That said, the winner was still impressive.

**NOTEBOOK**
**Red Sahara(IRE)**, not seen since narrowly landing a Wolverhampton maiden over six furlongs 224 days previously, improved on that form to make a successful handicap debut, winning with some authority. She had to wait for a gap, but picked up really stylishly when in the clear and could well follow up.
**Go Between** made a pleasing reappearance. She travelled really strongly towards the far side of the track, but lacked the winner's change of pace. Given that she won her maiden over six furlongs, a return to that trip may suit.
**Andaluza(IRE)** confirmed the promise she showed when getting off the mark over this trip at Wolverhampton and looks on a reasonable enough mark.
**Lyca Ballerina**, still a maiden, ran respectably on this drop back in trip and return to handicap company, and will find easier opportunities that this one.
**Here To Me**, another still awaiting her first success, ran a respectable first race in 191 days and may find a small race.
**Hana Dee**, dropping back from a mile, would probably have been closer with better luck in running.
**Ela Paparouna** is another who would have been closer with better luck.
**Generous Gesture(IRE)** *Official explanation: jockey said filly was slowly away and hung left-handed*
**Beejay** ran no race at all. *Official explanation: jockey said filly ran flat*

## 2113 PADDY POWER DIAL-A-BET MAIDEN STKS (DIV I) 1m (S)
**4:55** (4:56) (D) 3-Y-O **£5,902** (£1,816; £908; £454) **Stalls** Centre

Form RPR
**1** **Madid (IRE)** 3-9-0 RHills 15 90
(JHMGosden) *str: scope: lw: s.i.s: hld up in rr: smooth hdwy on stands side to ld over 1f out: edgd lft ins last: readily* **7/1**
6 **2** 1 **Grand But One (IRE)**[31] 1395 3-9-0 MHills 9 88
(BWHills) *mde most tl hdd over 1f out: kpt on wl fnl f but nt pce of wnr* **9/1**
5- **3** 2 **Secret Flame**[196] 5868 3-8-9 LDettori 1 79
(WJHaggas) *mid-div: hdwy 2f out: chsd ldrs ins last: edgd lft: nt qckn* **9/2**[2]
0 **4** nk **Principal Witness (IRE)**[28] 1461 3-9-0 MartinDwyer 4 83
(WRMuir) *chsd ldrs: drvn to chal ins fnl 2f tl over 1f out: outpcd ins last* **66/1**
0-5 **5** 3 **Whitsbury Cross**[28] 1461 3-9-0 JPMurtagh 11 76
(DRCElsworth) *lw: sn in tch: chsd ldrs 1/2-way: rdn over 2f out: kpt on same pce ins last* **4/1**[1]
2-4 **6** 1/2 **Sound Of Fleet (USA)**[19] 1674 3-9-0 KFallon 12 75
(PFICole) *b.hind: sn w ldr: chal fr over 5f out tl 2f out: wknd over 1f out* **5/1**[3]
0 **7** 3 **Eizawina Docklands**[13] 1794 3-9-0 (t) KDarley 5 68?
(NPLittmoden) *bhd: hdwy over 2f out: kpt on fr over 1f out but nvr a danger* **66/1**
02-6 **8** nk **Bailaora (IRE)**[12] 1830 3-9-0 79 (b) TQuinn 16 67
(BWDuke) *chsd ldrs: rdn over 2f out: wknd qckly over 1f out* **16/1**
**9** 1/2 **Chica Roca (USA)**[205] 3-8-6 80 LPKeniry(3) 3 61
(BJMeehan) *chsd ldrs tl wknd ins fnl 2f* **50/1**
6-0 **10** 1/2 **Want (USA)**[13] 1794 3-9-0 RHughes 6 65
(JHMGosden) *hld up mid-div: hdwy 3f out: wknd fr 2f out* **12/1**
0 **11** 1 3/4 **Fuel Cell (IRE)**[28] 1461 3-9-0 DaneO'Neill 13 61
(RHannon) *s.i.s: sn rdn in mid-div: n.d* **9/1**
**12** 1/2 **Aljaareh (USA)** 3-9-0 SDrowne 7 60
(MPTregoning) *lengthy: scope: in tch: rdn 3f out: wknd fr 2f out: eased whn no ch fnl f* **8/1**
**13** 2 1/2 **Shaaban (IRE)** 3-9-0 ACulhane 2 54
(MRChannon) *bkwd: s.i.s: a in rr* **16/1**
**14** nk **Solipsist (IRE)** 3-9-0 PDobbs 17 53
(RHannon) *leggy: bhd: effrt 1/2-way: n.d and sn rr* **33/1**
**15** 6 **Wodhill Gold** 3-9-0 OUrbina 10 40
(DMorris) *w'like: nvr bttr than mid-div* **66/1**
0 **16** 3 1/2 **Batchworth Beau**[13] 1796 3-9-0 SCarson 8 31
(EAWheeler) *w ldrs over 4f* **100/1**
5-0 **17** hd **Locator (IRE)**[7] 1972 3-9-0 JTate 14 31
(JMPEustace) *chsd ldrs over 5f* **66/1**

1m 39.7s (-1.13) **Going Correction** -0.10s/f (Good) **17** Ran SP% **129.8**
Speed ratings: **101,100,98,97,94 94,91,90,90,89 88,87,85,84,78 75,75**CSF £71.65 TOTE £8.80: £2.60, £4.00, £2.50; EX 123.60.
**Owner** Hamdan Al Maktoum **Bred** Cranford Stud **Trained** Manton, Wilts

**FOCUS**
The faster of the two divisions and a race that should produce its share of winners. Madid could be pretty smart.

**NOTEBOOK**
**Madid(IRE)** ◆, a 150,000gns purchase, three-parts brother to a seven-furlong Listed winner, made a winning debut with a smart performance. He recovered well from a slow start, travelling really strongly for Hills before finding plenty when asked to go on. There should be much more to come and he could be pretty smart.
**Grand But One(IRE)**, sixth in probably just an ordinary Wood Ditton, ran a solid race in second, pulling clear of all bar the winner. He should win his maiden before too much longer.
**Secret Flame** confirmed the promise she showed on her only start at two in a Newmarket maiden. She never really threatened the winner, but showed enough to suggest she will soon be winning.
**Principal Witness(IRE)** improved on his debut running and looked sure to play a part in the finish until tiring close home. He will progress again and should win a maiden.
**Whitsbury Cross** ran well in a similar race over this course and distance on his reappearance, but proved unable to build on that this time and has to be considered disappointing.
**Sound Of Fleet(USA)**, dropped two furlongs in trip, found little for pressure and was another to disappoint.

## 2114 PADDY POWER DIAL-A-BET MAIDEN STKS (DIV II) 1m (S)
**5:25** (5:27) (D) 3-Y-O **£5,876** (£1,808; £904; £452) **Stalls** Centre

Form RPR
33 **1** **Credit (IRE)**[13] 1794 3-9-0 KFallon 9 79
(RHannon) *lw: in tch: trckd ldrs 3f out: rdn to ld wl ins fnl f: hld on wl cl home* **6/4**[1]
**2** hd **Long Road (USA)** 3-9-0 PRobinson 10 79
(JNoseda) *tall: str: lw: s.i.s: hdwy 3f out: str run fr over 1f out to chal wl ins last: no ex cl home* **12/1**
**3** 1/2 **Silverstein (USA)** 3-9-0 LDettori 6 78
(JHMGosden) *gd sort: str: scope: bkwd: s.i.s: sn rcvrd and in tch: chsd ldrs 1/2-way: drvn to ld over 1f out: hdd and nt qckn wl ins la* **5/1**[2]
**4** 1 1/4 **Different Planet** 3-9-0 TQuinn 4 75
(JWHills) *mid-div: pushed along 2f out:styng on whn n.m.r 1f out and jst ins last: kpt on cl home* **20/1**
0-52 **5** 3/4 **Pizazz**[12] 1827 3-9-0 79 MHills 12 73
(BJMeehan) *chsd ldrs: rdn to chal and edgd rt 1f out: wknd ins fnl f* **6/1**[3]
**6** 1 1/4 **Lost Soldier Three (IRE)** 3-9-0 DHolland 5 70
(LMCumani) *str: mid-div: pushed along 1/2-way: hdwy over 1f out: kpt on fnl f but nt pce to trble ldrs* **12/1**
00- **7** nk **Zuma (IRE)**[242] 4958 3-9-0 PDobbs 15 69
(RHannon) *chsd ldr: chal over 2f out: one pce whn bmpd 1f out and lost position: kpt on again cl home* **33/1**
00-0 **8** nk **My Hope (IRE)**[12] 1830 3-8-9 SDrowne 2 64
(RCharlton) *bhd: hdwy over 2f out: chsd ldrs: swtchd lft and n.m.r over 1f out: outpcd ins last* **33/1**
**9** 1/2 **Gentle Raindrop (IRE)** 3-8-9 MartinDwyer 7 63
(SKirk) *neat: chsd ldrs tl wknd over 1f out* **50/1**
0- **10** 1 **Three Ships**[204] 5723 3-9-0 RHughes 11 65
(BWHills) *led tl hdd over 1f out: bmpd and wknd 1f out* **14/1**
0 **11** hd **Desert Hawk**[13] 1794 3-9-0 DaneO'Neill 3 65
(RHannon) *bhd: drvn and hdwy to chse ldrs 2f out: outpcd over 1f out* **20/1**
000 **12** 5 **Forge Lane (IRE)**[8] 1939 3-9-0 RBrisland 1 53
(GLMoore) *outpcd most of way* **50/1**
**13** 3/4 **Count Boris** 3-9-0 SCarson 14 52
(GBBalding) *leggy: chsd ldrs tl edgd lft and wknd fr 2f out* **50/1**
**14** 18 **King's Minstrel (IRE)** 3-9-0 ACulhane 8 10
(MRChannon) *s.i.s: sn rdn: a outpcd* **14/1**
**15** 1 1/2 **Government (IRE)** 3-9-0 KDarley 13 7
(JHMGosden) *bkwd: slowly away: sn rdn and a bhd* **12/1**

1m 40.31s (-0.52) **Going Correction** -0.10s/f (Good) **15** Ran SP% **128.7**
Speed ratings: **98,97,97,96,95 94,93,93,92,91 91,86,86,68,66**CSF £21.56 TOTE £2.40: £1.30, £4.70, £2.10; EX 32.20 Place 6 £182.81, Place 5 £66.88.
**Owner** Highclere Thoroughbred Racing XV **Bred** G J Cullinan **Trained** East Everleigh, Wilts

**FOCUS**
A reasonable maiden, but it will be disappointing if one or two of these do not progress past the winner in time.

**NOTEBOOK**
**Credit(IRE)** has improved with every run to date, but had to work pretty hard to get off the mark and justify his skinny odds. There will be a few in this race that may progress past him, and his future lies in the hands of the Handicapper.
**Long Road(USA)**, a brother to a ten and 11-furlong winner out of a half-sister to smart miler Duck Row, made a very pleasing debut. He should find a similar race.
**Silverstein(USA)**, a $400,000 purchase, three-parts brother to French Group One juvenile mile winner Way Of Light out of an unraced half-sister to Machiavellian, Coup De Genie and Exit To Nowhere, showed plenty of ability on this debut, overcoming a slow start to hold every chance when it mattered. He should be winning soon enough.
**Different Planet**, a 60,000gns half-brother to six and seven-furlong performer Indian Trail, may just have won this with better luck in running. It will be most disappointing if he does gain compensation soon.
**Pizazz** was put in his place and may struggle in handicaps off his current mark.
T/Plt: £50.90 to a £1 stake. Pool: £99,166.40. 1,419.75 winning tickets. T/Qpdt: £49.20 to a £1 stake. Pool: £3,985.00. 59.90 winning tickets. ST

# 2086 NOTTINGHAM (L-H)
### Saturday, May 15

**OFFICIAL GOING: Good (good to soft in places)**
The going had dried out overnight but was still described as 'a bit on the dead side'. Race 3 hand timed.
Wind: Almost Nil Weather: Fine and Sunny

## 2115 TOTEPOOL CLASSIFIED STKS 6f 15y
**1:50** (1:50) (C) 3-Y-O **£13,812** (£4,250; £2,125; £1,062) **Stalls** Low

Form RPR
-531 **1** **Lake Garda**[10] 1881 3-8-13 91 GGibbons 4 93
(BAMcmahon) *w ldr: t.k.h: rdn over 1f out: r.o to ld post* **11/4**[1]
2231 **2** shd **Morse (IRE)**[7] 1965 3-8-12 88 SSanders 2 92
(JAOsborne) *led: qcknd over 3f out: hrd rdn fnl f: hdd post* **3/1**[2]
-230 **3** 2 **Harry Up**[10] 1883 3-8-12 90 MFenton 3 86
(JGGiven) *sn trcking ldrs: effrt over 2f out: styd on same pce appr fnl f* **10/1**
120- **4** 3 1/2 **Mandobi (IRE)**[226] 5333 3-9-1 93 PMcCabe 6 79
(ACStewart) *hld up: effrt over 2f out: wnt lft: kpt on one pce* **6/1**
161- **5** 1 **Promenade**[322] 2783 3-8-9 89 JMackay 7 70
(MLWBell) *hld up in last: effrt and nt clr run 2f out: nvr nrr* **15/2**
1-00 **6** 3/4 **Mahmoom**[13] 1795 3-8-12 87 CCatlin 1 70
(MRChannon) *chsd ldrs: drvn along over 3f out: lost pl over 1f out* **11/2**[3]
250- **7** 9 **Silver Prelude**[245] 4877 3-8-12 90 DSweeney 5 43
(DKIvory) *chsd ldrs: effrt over 2f out: sn lost pl and bhd* **25/1**

1m 15.55s (0.75) **Going Correction** +0.20s/f (Good) **7** Ran SP% **106.0**
Speed ratings: **103,102,100,95,94 93,81**CSF £9.48 TOTE £2.90: £1.80, £1.80; EX 6.70.
**Owner** J C Fretwell **Bred** Capt J H Wilson **Trained** Hopwas, Staffs
■ Stewards Enquiry : S Sanders two-day ban: used whip with excessive frequency and without allowing sufficient time for response (May 26,27)

**FOCUS**
A decent classified contest run at just a fair pace for the class.

**NOTEBOOK**
**Lake Garda** looked in tip-top shape but, after being taken to post ahead of the rest, he became a bit warm at the start. He had the leader covered and put his head in front right on the line.
**Morse(IRE)** stepped up the gallop from the front just before the halfway mark. Despite his saddle slipping back slightly his rider threw everything at him only to be touched off on the line. He never flinched but may remember this. *Official explanation: jockey said saddle slipped*

**Harry Up**, on his toes beforehand, put a disappointing run last time behind him and the sixth furlong was not a problem.
**Mandobi(IRE)**, a moderate mover, found six furlongs too sharp.
**Promenade**, winner of three of her four starts at two, did not reappear after June. She looked very light and was warm beforehand. She had no luck in running but has something to prove now.
**Mahmoom** did not improve for the drop in trip and his three outings this time have been a let down.

## 2116 TOTESPORT.COM H'CAP 1m 6f 15y

**2:20** (2:20) (D ) (0-80,80) 3-Y-0+ **£8,599** (£2,646; £1,323; £661) **Stalls** Low

Form RPR

0302 **1** **Bucks**[13] [1801] 7-8-11 **70** ........................ MHoward(7) 15 81+
(DKIvory) *trckd ldrs: nt clr run and swtchd rt 2f out: r.o fnl f: led post* **7/1**[2]

046- **2** *shd* **Clarinch Claymore**[192] [5926] 8-8-12 **69** ........................ TEaves(5) 3 80
(JMJefferson) *dwlt: hdwy 8f out: drvn along to chse ldrs 5f out: led over 1f out: jst ct* **16/1**

2210 **3** *1* **Glory Quest (USA)**[51] [1103] 7-8-13 **65** ........................ MFenton 18 75
(MissGayKelleway) *hld up: hdwy on outside 4f out: styd on wl fnl f* **14/1**

-410 **4** *1 3/4* **Crossways**[50] [1122] 6-9-2 **68** ........................ RHavlin 5 75
(PDEvans) *chsd ldrs: ev ch on ins 3f out: styd on ins last* **25/1**

/040 **5** *2* **Bakiri (IRE)**[8] [1928] 6-8-8 **60** ........................ GGibbons 17 64
(AndrewReid) *trckd ldrs: led 3f out tl over 1f out: wknd ins last* **66/1**

5-40 **6** *1 1/4* **Moonshine Beach**[26] [1501] 6-8-3 **60** ........................ (p) PMakin(5) 10 63
(PWHiatt) *sn chsng ldrs: one pce fnl 2f* **16/1**

06-0 **7** *1 3/4* **Party Ploy**[15] [1754] 6-8-8 **60** ........................ VHalliday 4 60
(KRBurke) *led 1f: trckd ldrs: kpt on same pce fnl 2f* **25/1**

3-03 **8** *1 1/4* **Mexican Pete**[8] [1928] 4-9-5 **75** ........................ RMiles(3) 16 73
(PWHiatt) *hld up and bhd: hdwy on outside 4f out: kpt on: nvr rchd ldrs* **9/1**

-506 **9** *3 1/2* **Sonoma (IRE)**[12] [1832] 4-9-1 **68** ........................ JMackay 7 62
(MLWBell) *w ldr: led over 4f out: hdd 3f out: sn wknd* **14/1**

00-0 **10** *shd* **Football Crazy (IRE)**[6] [1539] 5-9-9 **80** ........................ BSwarbrick(5) 9 73
(PBowen) *chsd ldrs: chal 4f out: wknd over 2f out* **10/1**

0-50 **11** *1/2* **Treasure Trail**[12] [1832] 5-9-4 **70** ........................ JDSmith 13 63
(SKirk) *sn bhd: pushed along 1/2-way: nvr a factor* **25/1**

1005 **12** *3/4* **Sun Hill**[13] [1801] 4-9-3 **70** ........................ DSweeney 11 62
(MBlanshard) *rr-div: hdwy over 3f out: sn rdn and btn* **14/1**

1060 **13** *6* **Vanbrugh (FR)**[7] [1973] 4-8-7 **60** ........................ (vt) DaleGibson 8 43
(MissDAMchale) *chsd ldrs: lost pl over 2f out* **50/1**

-000 **14** *1 1/2* **Sahaat**[40] [1272] 6-9-8 **74** ........................ VSlattery 12 55
(JAOsborne) *hld up and a in rr* **50/1**

0-04 **15** *1/2* **Nobratinetta (FR)**[7] [1973] 5-9-9 **75** ........................ (p) RWinston 2 55
(MrsMReveley) *chsd ldrs: pushed along 1/2-way: lost pl over 2f out* **12/1**

13-0 **16** *3 1/2* **Individual Talents (USA)**[24] [1539] 4-9-1 **68** ........................ CCatlin 14 44
(SCWilliams) *in rr: drvn along 4f out* **6/1**[1]

513- **17** *20* **Head To Kerry (IRE)**[216] [5502] 4-9-0 **67** ........................ JFEgan 1 15
(DJSFrenchDavis) *mid-div whn hmpd bnd after 2f: t.o 2f out* **14/1**

241- **18** *dist* **Astyanax (IRE)**[283] [3900] 4-9-7 **74** ........................ SSanders 6 —
(SirMarkPrescott) *led after 1f: drvn along 7f out: hdd over 4f out: sn bhd: wl t.o 2f out: virtually p.u* **15/2**[3]

3m 7.04s (-0.16) **Going Correction** +0.075s/f (Good)
**WFA** 4 from 5yo+ 1lb **18** Ran SP% **120.7**
Speed ratings: **103,102,102,101,100 99,98,97,95,95 95,95,91,90,90 88,77,**—CSF £104.33 CT £1538.88 TOTE £7.40: £2.50, £4.80, £3.10, £12.60; EX 131.40.
**Owner** M Murphy **Bred** Meon Valley Stud **Trained** Radlett, Herts

**FOCUS**
A modest staying handicap run at a sound gallop.

**NOTEBOOK**
**Bucks** took the eye in the paddock and would have been an unlucky loser. Forced to switch to get a run, he put his head in front right on the line.
**Clarinch Claymore**, having his first outing since November, worked hard to get his head in front only to be pipped right on the line.
**Glory Quest(USA)** looked in tip-top shape. He made his ground on the outer once in line for home and was closing down the first two at the line. Four of his six wins have been on the All-Weather, but he seems equally effective on turf.
**Crossways**, absent since March, was putting in his best work at the finish and is worth a try over two miles.
**Bakiri(IRE)** ran easily his best race on his fourth start for his new stable.
**Moonshine Beach**, in first-time cheekpieces, just kept on in his own time. He appreciates a severe test of stamina.
**Party Ploy**
**Individual Talents(USA)** looked very light and was warm beforehand. She never fired at all and the ground was not the sole reason.
**Astyanax(IRE)**, 8lb higher than when winning his final start last year at Yarmouth in August, looked in peak condition but driven along to maintain the lead at halfway dropped back once in line for home and eventually made the finishing line in his own time. This was much too bad to be true.

## 2117 TOTESPORT FILLIES' STKS (REGISTERED AS THE KILVINGTON STAKES) (LISTED RACE) 6f 15y

**2:55** (2:56) (A ) 3-Y-0+ **£23,200** (£8,800; £4,400; £2,000) **Stalls** Low

Form RPR

-023 **1** **Golden Nun**[7] [1964] 4-9-3 100 ........................ (b) RWinston 8 99
(TDEasterby) *dwlt: swtchd lft after s: effrt on inner and nt clr run over 3f out: nt clr run over 1f out: str run ins last: led post* **7/1**

2131 **2** *shd* **Forever Phoenix**[8] [1937] 4-9-3 81 ........................ BDoyle 2 99+
(RMHCowell) *trckd ldrs gng wl: n.m.r over 2f out: qcknd to ld jst ins last: hdd post* **13/2**[3]

04-3 **3** *1 1/2* **Look Here's Carol (IRE)**[12] [1825] 4-9-3 83 ........................ GGibbons 9 94
(BAMcmahon) *w ldrs: led over 1f out tl jst ins last: no ex* **12/1**

20-2 **4** *2 1/2* **Millybaa (USA)**[10] [1893] 4-9-3 100 ........................ SSanders 4 87
(RGuest) *trckd ldrs: effrt over 2f out: kpt on same pce appr fnl f* **7/2**[2]

0-10 **5** *3/4* **Silca's Gift**[13] [1791] 3-8-13 109 ........................ CCatlin 5 90
(MRChannon) *trckd ldr: led over 3f out tl over 1f out: fdd* **11/8**[1]

003- **6** *3* **Indian Steppes (FR)**[249] [4804] 5-9-3 70 ........................ LisaJones 7 75
(JulianPoulton) *hld up: effrt over 2f out: sn chsng ldrs: edgd lft and wknd fnl f* **100/1**

25-4 **7** *1 1/2* **Needles And Pins (IRE)**[30] [1417] 3-8-11 102 ........................ JMackay 3 75
(MLWBell) *w ldrs: outpcd: nt clr run and lost pl over 3f out: swtchd rt and hdwy over 2f out: n.d after* **22/1**

12 **8** *2 1/2* **Petite Rose (IRE)**[30] [1417] 3-8-7 95 ........................ RHavlin 1 63
(JHMGosden) *led tl over 3f out: lost pl 2f out* **12/1**

16-0 **9** *6* **Vermilliann (IRE)**[18] [1685] 3-8-7 93 ........................ RSmith 6 45
(RHannon) *w ldrs: drvn along 3f out: sn lost pl and bhd* **40/1**

1m 15.7s (0.90) **Going Correction** +0.20s/f (Good)
**WFA** 3 from 4yo+ 10lb **9** Ran SP% **113.3**
Speed ratings: **102,101,99,96,95 91,89,86,78**CSF £49.86 TOTE £7.80: £2.20, £2.50, £2.50; EX 47.30.
**Owner** T G & Mrs M E Holdcroft **Bred** Bearstone Stud **Trained** Great Habton, N Yorks

**FOCUS**
A good turnout for this Listed race confined to fillies and mares, though the final time was ordinary. This race was hand timed.

**NOTEBOOK**
**Golden Nun**, fourth last year, was drawn one off the outside. Making her effort against the far rail, she ran into all sorts of traffic problems but her rider was at his most determined and conjured a run out of her inside the last to lead right on the line. She is a tough cookie.
**Forever Phoenix** looked in top trim. She travelled strongly and looked to have it in the bag when going a length up inside the last only to be nailed right on the line. This was a career best effort.
**Look Here's Carol(IRE)**, runner-up a year ago, proved she is every bit as good as ever.
**Millybaa(USA)**, third last year, was not at her very best just ten days after the trip to Ireland.
**Silca's Gift**, who looked as fit as a flea, was dropping back in trip. After showing ahead she faded in disapointing fashion.
**Indian Steppes(FR)**, who had a lot to find, was having her first outing since September. Her two wins have been on the All-Weather.
**Needles And Pins(IRE)** had no luck at all.
**Petite Rose(IRE)** looked very fit indeed but ran poorly, never looking happy on the ground. *Official explanation: jockey said filly would not left herself down on the rough ground*

## 2118 GO RACING IN THE MIDLANDS H'CAP 5f 13y

**3:25** (3:25) (E ) (0-75,74) 3-Y-0+ **£3,740** (£1,151; £575; £287) **Stalls** Low

Form RPR

0-00 **1** **Guns Blazing**[11] [1872] 5-8-9 **58** ........................ (b) MHoward(7) 9 69
(DKIvory) *mde all on far side: clr over 1f out: jst lasted* **25/1**

2431 **2** *1/2* **Savile's Delight (IRE)**[11] [1873] 5-9-12 **68** ........................ JFEgan 17 77
(RBrotherton) *racd stands' side: chsd ldr: led that side ins last: styd on wl nr fin* **8/1**[3]

6000 **3** *1/2* **Prime Recreation**[33] [1368] 7-9-5 **61** ........................ DaleGibson 6 68
(PSFelgate) *chsd wnr: edgd rt fnl 2f: no ex ins last* **20/1**

-000 **4** *1/2* **Brantwood (IRE)**[11] [1872] 4-9-2 **58** ........................ (tp) GGibbons 3 64
(BAMcmahon) *chsd ldrs: kpt on wl fnl f* **8/1**[3]

0205 **5** *hd* **Rafters Music (IRE)**[12] [1824] 9-9-4 **60** ........................ GCarter 2 65
(JulianPoulton) *sn in rr: hdwy 2f out: styd on wl ins last* **18/1**

0023 **6** *hd* **Pulse**[11] [1872] 6-9-7 **63** ........................ (p) SSanders 12 67
(JMBradley) *trckd ldrs: kpt on wl fnl f* **8/1**[3]

3012 **7** *hd* **Dunn Deal (IRE)**[16] [1738] 4-9-4 **65** ........................ BSwarbrick(5) 10 68
(WMBrisbourne) *mid-div: hdwy over 1f out: styd on ins last* **15/2**[2]

-302 **8** *3/4* **Catch The Cat (IRE)**[7] [1956] 5-9-13 **69** ........................ (b) RWinston 16 70
(JSWainwright) *led stands' side gp tl ins last: no ex* **11/2**[1]

200- **9** *2 1/2* **Parkside Pursuit**[222] [5427] 6-9-7 **68** ........................ HayleyTurner(5) 15 60
(JMBradley) *racd stands' side: chsd ldrs: kpt on same pce appr fnl f* **33/1**

3/06 **10** *1 1/4* **El Chaparral (IRE)**[13] [1796] 4-10-0 **70** ........................ DSweeney 11 57
(DKIvory) *sn in rr: sme hdwy fnl 2f: nvr a factor* **25/1**

-100 **11** *hd* **Wainwright (IRE)**[47] [1175] 4-9-3 **62** ........................ DNolan(3) 8 49
(PABlockley) *sn outpcd and in rr* **14/1**

2424 **12** *3/4* **Multahab**[43] [1228] 5-9-7 **63** ........................ CLowther 4 47
(MissGayKelleway) *in tch: rdn 2f out: sn fdd* **14/1**

0061 **13** *nk* **Full Pitch**[11] [1872] 8-10-0 **70** ........................ VSlattery 13 53
(WJenks) *dwlt: a bhd* **11/1**

1522 **14** *nk* **Marinaite**[16] [1737] 3-9-9 **74** ........................ JBramhill 14 56
(SRBowring) *racd stands' side: chsd ldrs: lost pl over 1f out* **11/1**

6040 **15** *nk* **Bahamian Belle**[11] [1855] 4-8-10 **55** ........................ (t) LisaJones(3) 7 36
(PSMcentee) *s.v.s: a bhd* **16/1**

00-0 **16** *1 1/2* **Beyond Calculation (USA)**[14] [1774] 10-9-8 **64** ........................ CCatlin 1 39
(JMBradley) *lost pl after 2f: sn in rr* **25/1**

005/ **17** *8* **Smirfys Night**[651] [3563] 5-9-2 **63** ........................ TEaves(5) 5 9
(DNicholls) *restless in stalls: dwlt: a bhd: eased* **33/1**

62.00 secs (0.20) **Going Correction** +0.20s/f (Good)
**WFA** 3 from 4yo+ 9lb **17** Ran SP% **123.8**
Speed ratings: **106,105,104,103,103 102,102,101,97,95 95,93,93,92,92 90,77**CSF £202.17 CT £4209.93 TOTE £22.90: £4.70, £2.30, £7.00, £1.70; EX 399.70.
**Owner** R D Hartshorn **Bred** Mrs C A R Lockhart **Trained** Radlett, Herts

**FOCUS**
In effect a 0-70 handicap with the runners stretched across the entire width of the track.

**NOTEBOOK**
**Guns Blazing**, with the blinkers back on, kicked clear on the far side but in the end the post came just in time. He really prefers quicker ground.
**Savile's Delight(IRE)**, 4lb higher, was dropping back in trip. He worked hard to get on top on the stands' side and would have collared the winner with a bit further to go. Six probably suits him that bit better.
**Prime Recreation** showed a lot more dash, and would have been even more closely involved in the finish had he not edged right and ended up in no man's land in the centre. *Official explanation: jockey said gelding hung right*
**Brantwood(IRE)** has slid right down the ratings and showed a lot more dash in first-time cheekpieces.
**Rafters Music(IRE)**, beaten in a claimer last time, ran a lot better coming through strongly late on. He really needs a sixth furlong.
**Pulse** as usual travelled strongly and he will be back in the money when he encounters quicker ground than he raced on here.
**Catch The Cat(IRE)** led down the stands' side but he was handicapped by a slipping saddle. He is clearly in very good form. *Official explanation: jockey said saddle slipped*
**Marinaite** *Official explanation: jockey said filly hung left*

## 2119 KONICA EAST CLASSIFIED STKS 1m 54y

**4:00** (4:00) (E ) 3-Y-0+ **£3,750** (£1,154; £577; £288) **Stalls** High

Form RPR

-340 **1** **Brazilian Terrace**[33] [1372] 4-8-12 73 ........................ HayleyTurner(5) 8 80
(MLWBell) *hld up: stdy hdwy over 3f out: styd on to ld last 100yds* **8/1**

30-3 **2** *1 1/4* **Mr Velocity (IRE)**[21] [1624] 4-9-3 70 ........................ SSanders 10 77
(ACStewart) *hld up: effrt over 3f out: nt clr run and swtchd rt 2f out: ev ch ins last: no ex* **5/2**[1]

6450 **3** *nk* **Skibereen (IRE)**[28] [1475] 4-8-10 70 ........................ PPMathers(7) 7 76
(IWMcinnes) *dwlt: hld up: hdwy on outsice over 3f out: led over 1f out: hdd and nt qckn ins last* **28/1**

00-0 **4** *3 1/2* **Madamoiselle Jones**[12] [1821] 4-9-0 64 ........................ DKinsella 5 65
(HSHowe) *led eraly: trckd ldrs: nt clr run over 1f out: kpt on ins last* **12/1**

06-1 **5** *2* **Azreme**[11] [1877] 4-9-3 70 ........................ DSweeney 9 64
(DKIvory) *trckd ldrs: t.k.h: ev ch over 2f out tl wknd fnl f* **4/1**[3]

00-3 **6** *4* **Lady Georgina**[21] [1613] 3-8-2 71 ........................ JMackay 3 52
(JRFanshawe) *sn leed: keen infront: hdd 2f out: sn wknd* **11/4**[2]

-050 **7** *5* **Prince Of Gold**[21] [1620] 4-9-3 67 ........................ DaleGibson 6 43
(RHollinshead) *w ldrs: led 2f out: sn hdd & wknd* **8/1**

1-00 **8** *10* **Bethanys Boy (IRE)**[30] 1418 3-8-6 72 RWinston 1 22
(BEllison) *sn chsng ldrs: rdn over 3f out: wknd over 1f out: sn bhd and eased* **14/1**

1m 45.16s (-1.24) **Going Correction** +0.075s/f (Good)
**WFA** 3 from 4yo+ 13lb **8** Ran SP% **115.3**
Speed ratings: **109,107,107,103,101 97,92,82**CSF £28.63 TOTE £5.40: £3.40, £1.40, £5.40; EX 32.30.
**Owner** Mrs G Rowland-Clark/M L W Bell Racing **Bred** Mount Coote Stud **Trained** Newmarket, Suffolk

**FOCUS**
A competitive classified event and a fair time for the grade.

**NOTEBOOK**
**Brazilian Terrace** showed a return to form under a well judged and tidy ride. She prefers even better ground and is right back to her best.
**Mr Velocity(IRE)** has now been placed six times from eight starts. He does little wrong but just lacks that bit of final dash.
**Skibereen(IRE)**, dropping in trip and without the headgear, ran right up to his best. He has now been placed five times from 12 starts but that first success is proving elusive.
**Madamoiselle Jones**, who had a bit to find, would have finished on the heels of the first three with better luck. She prefers much quicker ground.
**Azreme**, an edgy sort, is a very scratchy mover. He would not settle and in the end did not see the trip out.
**Lady Georgina**, who looked very fit, was quite keen to post. She would not settle in front and in the end dropped right away. She looks her own worst enemy.

## 2120 MIDLANDS RACING - 9 GREAT VENUES - H'CAP (DIV I) 1m 1f 213y
**4:35** (4:37) (E) (0-70,78) 3-Y-0+ **£3,672** (£1,130; £565; £282) **Stalls** Low

Form RPR

1014 **1** **Supreme Salutation**[8] 1935 8-10-1 **78** MHoward(7) 3 87
(DKIvory) *trckd ldrs: t.k.h: led 2f out: hld on wl* **16/1**

0-06 **2** *1* **Graft**[31] 1393 5-9-4 **60** (b1) DaleGibson 2 67
(MWEasterby) *hld up: shkn up and hdwy 5f out: ev ch 2f out: kpt on ins last* **13/2**[2]

0506 **3** *3/4* **Champion Lion (IRE)**[8] 1928 5-9-10 **66** CCatlin 6 71
(MRChannon) *s.i.s: hdwy over 3f out: styd on wl fnl f* **10/3**[1]

62-3 **4** *3/4* **Champain Sands (IRE)**[28] 1479 5-8-10 **57** PMakin(5) 5 61
(WMBrisbourne) *mid-div: hdwy over 3f out: kpt on wl fnl f* **14/1**

4-00 **5** *1 1/2* **Apache Point (IRE)**[26] 1502 7-9-2 **58** KimTinkler 8 59
(NTinkler) *trckd ldrs: t.k.h: led 3f out tl 2f out: wknd fnl f* **28/1**

1421 **6** *1* **Double Ransom**[13] 1783 5-9-3 **59** (b) RWinston 13 58
(MrsLStubbs) *bhd: hdwy 6f out: sn chsng ldrs: one pce fnl 2f* **13/2**[2]

4-24 **7** *nk* **Sir Ninja (IRE)**[25] 1535 7-9-5 **61** ADaly 10 60
(SKirk) *in tch on outer: lost pl over 5f out: hrd rdn 3f out: hung lft: styd on fnl f* **9/1**

0-06 **8** *1* **Mcqueen (IRE)**[25] 1522 4-8-13 **55** GGibbons 4 52
(MrsHDalton) *chsd ldrs: one pce fnl 2f* **16/1**

0-51 **9** *1/2* **Saxe-Coburg (IRE)**[11] 1856 7-9-8 **64** SSanders 1 60
(GAHam) *chsd ldrs: wkng whn n.m.r on ins over 2f out* **9/1**

0003 **10** *1 3/4* **Midshipman**[17] 1715 6-8-13 **62** CHaddon(7) 7 55
(AWCarroll) *hld up in rr: sme hdwy over 2f out: nvr on terms* **28/1**

-504 **11** *3* **Lennel**[19] 1660 6-9-10 **66** VSlattery 11 53
(ABailey) *s.s: a bhd* **11/1**

0-00 **12** *6* **Zeis (IRE)**[50] 1118 4-9-12 **68** (t) JFEgan 12 43
(HMorrison) *chsd ldrs: wknd over 1f out* **8/1**[3]

1-00 **13** *12* **Buscador (USA)**[17] 1715 5-8-8 **55** BSwarbrick(5) 14 8
(WMBrisbourne) *led: clr 6f out: hdd 3f out: edgd lft and sn lost pl: sn bhd* **16/1**

3030 **14** *shd* **New Options**[19] 1665 7-8-10 **52** GCarter 9 —
(WJMusson) *a bhd* **66/1**

2m 10.99s (1.49) **Going Correction** +0.075s/f (Good) **14** Ran SP% **121.9**
Speed ratings: **97,96,95,95,93 93,92,91,91,90 87,82,73,73**CSF £116.59 CT £442.16 TOTE £16.80: £4.70, £2.40, £1.90; EX 256.90.
**Owner** Mrs Karen Graham **Bred** M I Marsh **Trained** Radlett, Herts

**FOCUS**
A modest handicap run at an ordinary pace but completing a 3,535/1 treble for trainer Dean Ivory and his apprentice Mark Howard, ending a losing run of 57 mounts stretching back to last year.

**NOTEBOOK**
**Supreme Salutation**, 10lb higher than his last success, raced with plenty of enthusiasm and held on well to give his trainer and rider a memorable day.
**Graft**, in first-time blinkers, worked his way upsides two furlongs out but he was never really doing enough.
**Champion Lion(IRE)**, slipping to a far more realistic mark, likes to get his toe in and a second career success must now beckon.
**Champain Sands(IRE)**, placed five times in 13 previous starts, was putting in his best work when it was all over and is worth a try over further.
**Apache Point(IRE)**, as usual taken down early and walked to post, is looking to be finding his feet.
**Double Ransom**, 3lb higher, had no excuse.
**Sir Ninja(IRE)** *Official explanation: jockey said gelding was hanging left*
**Zeis(IRE)** *Official explanation: jockey said gelding made a noise*

## 2121 MIDLANDS RACING - 9 GREAT VENUES - H'CAP (DIV II) 1m 1f 213y
**5:05** (5:06) (E) (0-70,68) 3-Y-0+ **£3,662** (£1,127; £563; £281) **Stalls** Low

Form RPR

0-01 **1** **Summer Bounty**[11] 1875 8-9-9 68 RMiles(3) 12 81
(FJordan) *hld up: stdy hdwy over 3f out: led 2f out: r.o wl* **12/1**

540- **2** *1 1/4* **Perfect Punch**[232] 5189 5-9-6 62 SSanders 8 73
(CFWall) *hld up in rr: nt clr run 4f out: swtchd outside over 2f out: wnt 2nd over 1f out: r.o wl* **12/1**

4114 **3** *4* **Jair Ohmsford (IRE)**[39] 1282 5-9-10 66 GCarter 1 69
(WJMusson) *in tch on inner: effrt over 3f out: styd on fnl f* **4/1**[1]

50-0 **4** *hd* **Escalade**[134] 406 7-8-10 57 (p) BSwarbrick(5) 2 60
(WMBrisbourne) *dwlt: hdwy on outside over 3f out: kpt on same pce fnl 2f* **14/1**

/315 **5** *nk* **Calatagan (IRE)**[19] 1661 5-9-2 63 TEaves(5) 6 65
(JMJefferson) *in tch: rdn and outpcd over 2f out: kpt on wl fnl f: fin strly* **5/1**[2]

50-0 **6** *1/2* **Mythical King (IRE)**[3] 2038 7-8-11 53 DSweeney 7 55
(RLee) *chsd ldrs: rdn over 2f out: hung lft: one pce* **15/2**

2600 **7** *2* **Cool Bathwick (IRE)**[11] 1858 5-8-7 49 (b) RHavlin 11 47
(BRMillman) *sn chsng ldrs: one pce fnl 2f* **20/1**

20-0 **8** *3/4* **Burley Firebrand**[33] 1369 4-9-1 57 (v1) DaleGibson 14 53
(JGGiven) *chsd ldrs: drvn along over 4f out: one pce fnl 2f* **33/1**

04 **9** *1* **Welsh Wind (IRE)**[52] 1097 8-9-3 59 (tp) BDoyle 13 53
(MWigham) *hld up in rr: sme hdwy over 3f out: nvr a factor* **9/1**

0006 **10** *hd* **Adalar (IRE)**[53] 1088 4-9-4 67 SJDonohoe(7) 9 61
(PDEvans) *mid-div: effrt on outer over 3f out: nvr a factor* **16/1**

36-4 **11** *1/2* **The Fairy Flag (IRE)**[7] 1962 6-9-3 59 (p) VSlattery 10 52
(ABailey) *w ldrs: chal over 4f out: wknd over 1f out* **20/1**

1320 **12** *nk* **Fortune Point (IRE)**[40] 1272 6-9-4 60 ADaly 5 52
(AWCarroll) *led tl 2f out: sn wknd* **16/1**

-015 **13** *hd* **Archie Babe (IRE)**[39] 1282 8-9-10 66 RWinston 4 58
(JJQuinn) *chsd ldrs: rdn over 2f out: nt clr run over 2f out tl ins fnl f: nt rcvr* **13/2**[3]

050- **14** *19* **No Chance To Dance (IRE)**[231] 5227 4-8-13 55 CCatlin 3 11
(HJCollingridge) *hld up in rr: effrt over 3f out: lost tch over 2f out* **50/1**

2m 10.12s (0.62) **Going Correction** +0.075s/f (Good) **14** Ran SP% **120.0**
Speed ratings: **100,99,95,95,95 95,93,92,92,91 91,91,91,75**CSF £141.69 CT £687.45 TOTE £13.70: £3.70, £4.00, £2.20; EX 206.10.
**Owner** Tim Powell **Bred** Berkshire Equestrian Services Ltd **Trained** Adstone, Northants

**FOCUS**
Another modest event, and an ordinary time for the class.

**NOTEBOOK**
**Summer Bounty**, who looked in tip-top shape, defied a 6lb weight rise in decisive fashion. He is in the form of his life.
**Perfect Punch** ◆, a big sort, was having his first run since September. Anchored towards the back, he met traffic problems before making up many lengths on the winner but the post came far too soon. He looks sure to add to his record this time.
**Jair Ohmsford(IRE)**, well handicapped compared to his All-Weather mark, ran a lot better clearly appreciating the much less testing conditions underfoot.
**Escalade**, with the cheekpieces back on, ran a respectable race but he is proving very hard to win with, his last success was over two years ago.
**Calatagan(IRE)**, back in trip, could not dominate. Tapped for toe he finished with a flourish and would have snatched third spot with a bit further to go.
**Mythical King(IRE)** ran better appreciating this easier test but he hung under pressure and was made to look very one paced.

## 2122 CHILDREN COME RACING FREE APPRENTICE MAIDEN H'CAP 1m 54y
**5:35** (5:37) (G) (0-70,69) 3-Y-0+ **£2,856** (£816; £408) **Stalls** High

Form RPR

0033 **1** **Parnassian**[7] 1969 4-8-11 **56** RThomas(3) 7 67
(GBBalding) *hld up: hdwy and nt clr run 2f out: swtchd rt: edgd lft and styd on wl to ld last 75yds* **10/3**[1]

4-00 **2** *1 1/4* **Madame Marie (IRE)**[8] 1939 4-8-8 **50** LisaJones 13 58
(SDow) *bhd: hdwy on outer 3f out: str run ins fnl f: tk 2nd nr fin* **20/1**

2230 **3** *1 1/2* **Big Bad Burt**[11] 1874 3-8-4 **64** (p) DeanWilliams(5) 10 69
(MissGayKelleway) *trckd ldrs: ev ch and hung lft 2f out: nt qckn fnl f* **7/1**[2]

-044 **4** *1* **Cooden Beach (IRE)**[39] 1278 4-8-3 **48** HayleyTurner(3) 3 50
(MLWBell) *chsd ldr: led over 2f out: edgd lft and hdd wl ins fnl f: no ex* **10/1**

34-6 **5** *hd* **Lorien Hill (IRE)**[26] 1507 3-8-11 **69** AMedeiros(3) 9 71
(BWHills) *sn chsng ldrs: styd on same pce fnl 2f* **8/1**

00-0 **6** *1/2* **Noble Penny**[5] 1993 5-8-3 **50** WHogg(5) 4 51
(MrsKWalton) *chsd ldrs on ins: n.m.r and one pce fnl 2f* **16/1**

-460 **7** *nk* **Shamwari Fire (IRE)**[47] 1165 4-8-1 **48** NataliaGemelova(5) 14 48
(IWMcinnes) *hld up: hdwy over 3f out: one pce whn n.m.r ins last* **16/1**

3-06 **8** *3 1/2* **Artistic Style**[7] 1972 4-9-8 **67** TEaves(3) 2 59
(BEllison) *led tl over 2f out: wknd over 1f out* **10/1**

3300 **9** *1/2* **Zalkani (IRE)**[38] 1298 4-8-11 **53** RMiles 11 44
(BGPowell) *hld up in rr: hdwy on wd outside over 3f out: nvr nr ldrs* **12/1**

0450 **10** *2* **Springalong (USA)**[37] 1308 4-9-2 **63** SJDonohoe(5) 18 49
(PDEvans) *bhd: sme hdwy on outer over 3f out: nvr a factor* **16/1**

5-00 **11** *shd* **Top Achiever (IRE)**[23] 1557 3-8-2 **62** KristinStubbs(5) 12 48
(MrsLStubbs) *unruly s: bhd tl sme hdwy fnl 2f* **14/1**

-000 **12** *1 1/4* **Dexileos (IRE)**[11] 1876 5-8-7 **52** (t) NChalmers(3) 6 35
(ADWPinder) *chsd ldrs: lost pl over 1f out* **25/1**

40-0 **13** *1* **Suerte**[120] 552 4-8-10 **57** PMakin(5) 15 38
(RMHCowell) *a in rr* **25/1**

53-5 **14** *1/2* **Lieuday**[26] 1515 5-8-1 **48** (p) BSwarbrick(5) 1 28
(WMBrisbourne) *sn chsng ldrs: drvn along over 4f out: lost pl over 2f out* **15/2**[3]

0-00 **15** *1* **Rocky Reppin**[29] 1451 4-8-5 **54** (b) KPierrepont(7) 5 31
(JBalding) *s.i.s: t.k.h in rr: sme hdwy on inner 3f out: nvr a factor* **33/1**

400- **16** *3/4* **Lady Redera (IRE)**[242] 4959 3-8-5 **60** BReilly 17 36
(HSHowe) *mi-div: sme hdwy over 3f out: sn lost pl* **14/1**

0/0- **17** *4* **Guardian Spirit**[328] 2605 5-8-4 **53** DawnWatson(7) 16 19
(DShaw) *a bhd* **50/1**

0-50 **18** *20* **Stop The Nonsense (IRE)**[28] 1466 3-7-12 **60** (t) KJackson(7) 8 —
(EJO'Neill) *mid-div: lost pl over 3f out: sn bhd and eased* **33/1**

1m 46.17s (-0.23) **Going Correction** +0.075s/f (Good)
**WFA** 3 from 4yo+ 13lb **18** Ran SP% **135.6**
Speed ratings: **104,102,101,100,100 99,99,95,95,93 93,91,90,90,89 88,84,64**CSF £83.11 CT £478.99 TOTE £3.40: £1.40, £4.70, £1.40, £2.70; EX 73.20 Place 6 £373.97, Place 5 £255.31.
**Owner** Miss B Swire **Bred** Miss B Swire **Trained** Kimpton,Hants

**FOCUS**
A moderate maiden but run at a sound gallop.

**NOTEBOOK**
**Parnassian**, who in the past has often threatened better, overcame difficulties to break his duck at the 22nd attempt. He is clearly not straightforward.
**Madame Marie(IRE)**, a very keen type, sprouted wings inside the last to snatch second spot. She is still a maiden after 11 starts now.
**Big Bad Burt**, in cheekpieces this time, came to win his race but he hung fire and was eventually worried out of it. Quicker ground might help.
**Cooden Beach(IRE)**, fit from the All-Weather, took it up but she moved over to the running rail and seemed to be worried out of it.
**Lorien Hill(IRE)** improved on her initial effort and the mile trip did not seem to be a problem.
**Noble Penny**chased them on the inside but left short of room could keep on in her own time. A mile seems to stretch her to the limit.

T/Plt: £594.60 to a £1 stake. Pool: £45,372.60. 55.70 winning tickets. T/Qpdt: £85.70 to a £1 stake. Pool: £2,075.30. 17.90 winning tickets. WG

# [1913]SOUTHWELL (L-H)

Saturday, May 15

**OFFICIAL GOING: Standard**

There appeared to be an advantage in racing up the centre of the track.

## 2123 SAFFIE JOSEPH H'CAP 6f (F)
**6:00** (6:01) (F ) (0-55,55) 3-Y-0+ **£2,982** (£852; £426) **Stalls** Low

Form RPR

0-04 **1** **Roman Empire**[68] [987] 4-9-0 **50**.....(b) NCallan 5 64
(KARyan) *chsd ldrs: hdwy 2f out: rdn and edgd rt ent last: styd on to ld last 100 yds* **13/2**[2]

6312 **2** *2* **Larky's Lob**[9] [1913] 5-8-8 **51**..... JDO'Reilly[(7)] 13 59
(JO'Reilly) *cl up: led 1/2-way: rdn clr 11/2f out: drvn ins last: hdd & wknd last 100 yds* **9/2**[1]

3326 **3** *1 1/2* **Largs**[25] [1516] 4-8-12 **48**..... JEdmunds 14 52
(JBalding) *in tch: hdwy over 2f out: rdn to chse ldr over 1f out: drvn and one pce ins last* **9/1**

0300 **4** *1* **Speedfit Free (IRE)**[13] [1783] 7-9-0 **50**.....(v) RWinston 8 51
(MissAStokell) *midfield: hdwy 2f out: sn rdn and kpt on fnl f: nrst fin* **12/1**

3010 **5** *nk* **Lucius Verrus (USA)**[11] [1872] 4-9-4 **54**.....(v[1]) DarrenWilliams 2 54
(DShaw) *midfield: hdwy on inner over 2f out: rdn and kpt on appr last: nrst fin* **12/1**

1600 **6** *3/4* **Scary Night (IRE)**[21] [1625] 4-9-1 **54**.....(p) THamilton[(3)] 3 51
(JBalding) *chsd ldng pair: rdn along over 2f out: grad wknd* **10/1**

3061 **7** *hd* **Bulawayo**[47] [1176] 7-8-13 **49**.....(b) GGibbons 4 46
(AndrewReid) *outpcd and bhd 1/2-way: hdwy 2f out: styd on u.p fnl f: nrst fin* **12/1**

0002 **8** *3/4* **The Gambler**[11] [1868] 4-8-5 **48**.....(p) DFentiman[(7)] 15 43
(PaulJohnson) *dwlt and bhd: hdwy to chse ldrs wl over 1f out: sn rdn and no imp* **11/1**

4034 **9** *3/4* **Kennington**[28] [1477] 4-9-5 **55**.....(v) JMackay 12 47
(MrsCADunnett) *led: rdn along and hdd 1/2-way: drvn 2f out and sn wknd* **8/1**[3]

00-0 **10** *4* **Desert Fury**[19] [1681] 7-8-12 **48**..... RFfrench 11 28
(RBastiman) *s.i.s and bhd tl sme late hdwy* **14/1**

5-00 **11** *3 1/2* **Princess Erica**[12] [1824] 4-8-12 **48**.....(p) JBramhill 10 18
(JBalding) *a rr* **25/1**

00/0 **12** *2 1/2* **Louis Georgio**[20] [1642] 5-9-0 **50**..... JFEgan 16 12
(MRHoad) *midfield: pushed along and n.m.r 1/2-way: sn wknd* **33/1**

5-00 **13** *1 1/4* **In Tune**[11] [1856] 4-8-11 **50**.....(b) DCorby[(3)] 7 9
(SCBurrough) *bhd fr 1/2-way* **33/1**

2112 **14** *3 1/2* **Baytown Flyer**[16] [1724] 4-9-2 **52**..... TGMcLaughlin 9 —
(PSMcentee) *chsd ldrs: rdn along over 2f out and sn wknd* **9/1**

0221 **15** *6* **Alastair Smellie**[16] [1724] 8-8-12 **48**.....(v) PMcCabe 1 —
(SLKeightley) *chsd ldrs on inner: rdn along whn n.m.r 1/2-way and sn wknd* **10/1**

1m 15.95s (-0.95) **Going Correction** -0.05s/f (Stan) **15** Ran SP% **128.6**
Speed ratings: **105,102,100,99,98 97,97,96,95,90 85,82,80,75,67**CSF £37.39 CT £280.87 TOTE £6.80: £1.90, £2.50, £3.40; EX 64.10.
**Owner** Yorkshire Racing Syndicates IV **Bred** Mervyn Ayers And Richard Brunger **Trained** Hambleton, N Yorks

■ Stewards Enquiry : J D O'Reilly two-day ban: used whip with excessive frequency and without allowing gelding time to respond (May 26,28)

**FOCUS**
A moderate handicap but run 2.67sec faster than the following juvenile race. The runners came centre to stands' side in the straight.

**NOTEBOOK**
**Roman Empire**, making his debut for Kevin Ryan and having only his second try on this surface, put his stamina to good use to get up in the last half furlong. He looks reasonably treated at present, but his opportunities on sand in the near future are limited.
**Larky's Lob** has been in good form in banded events over course and distance of late, and put up a game effort from his outside draw. The early effort needed to gain a good position on the bend probably cost him in the end, and he deserves compensation.
**Largs**, a maiden whose best recent form has been on this track, was another to put up a sound effort from an outside draw.
**Speedfit Free(IRE)**, who ran over a mile last time, did not arrive on the scene until the race was over and may need another furlong these days.
**Lucius Verrus(USA)** did quite well considering the inside was not the place to be in the straight.
**Scary Night(IRE)** is slipping down the weights but it did not make a difference on this occasion.
**Bulawayo**stays a mile and found this trip too short.

## 2124 DISCOVERY OF CAPE COD (S) STKS 6f (F)
**6:30** (6:30) (G ) 2-Y-0 **£2,513** (£718; £359) **Stalls** Low

Form RPR

523 **1** **Speed Dial Harry (IRE)**[16] [1717] 2-8-12 .....(v[1]) DarrenWilliams 6 62+
(KRBurke) *cl up on outer: led on bit 1/2-way: sn clr: easily* **6/4**[1]

0 **2** *6* **Miller Hill**[7] [1960] 2-8-7 ..... PMulrennan[(5)] 5 38
(MWEasterby) *in tch and sn pushed along: hdwy on inner over 2f out: rdn and styd on appr last: no ch w wnr* **20/1**

030 **3** *1 1/4* **Joshar**[7] [1970] 2-8-7 ..... DaleGibson 7 30
(MWEasterby) *dwlt: sn rdn along in rr: hdwy wl over 1f out: kpt on u.p ins last* **10/1**

54 **4** *hd* **Missed Turn**[7] [1970] 2-8-7 ..... PFessey 2 29
(KARyan) *cl up: rdn along over 2f out and sn wknd* **7/2**[2]

510 **5** *6* **Kissing A Fool**[7] [1970] 2-8-10 ..... LTreadwell[(7)] 4 21
(WGMTurner) *chsd ldrs: rdn along after 2f: sn outpcd and bhd* **10/1**

6 **6** *2* **Shish (IRE)**[5] [2003] 2-8-7 ..... NCallan 3 5
(JAOsborne) *cl up: rdn along 1/2-way: drvn and wknd 2f out* **9/1**[3]

2330 **7** *5* **Nutty Times**[19] [1670] 2-8-7 ..... ADaly 1 —
(WGMTurner) *led: pushed along and hdd 1/2-way: sn rdn and wknd 2f out* **7/2**[2]

1m 18.62s (1.72) **Going Correction** -0.05s/f (Stan) **7** Ran SP% **117.4**
Speed ratings: **87,79,77,77,69 66,59**CSF £36.26 TOTE £2.70: £1.40, £17.20; EX 58.70.Speed Dial Harry was bought in for 15,500gns. Missed Turn was claimed by J. M. P. Eustace for £6000.
**Owner** J C S Wilson **Bred** Brendan Lavery **Trained** Middleham Moor, N Yorks

**FOCUS**
A poor seller run 2.67sec slower than the opening handicap. Speed Dial Harry was entitled to win this easily.

**NOTEBOOK**
**Speed Dial Harry(IRE)**, in a seller for the first time and fitted with a visor, had this won a long way from home and absolutely cantered up. He was retained at the auction but may suffer at the hands of the assessor for the ease of this victory.
**Miller Hill**, who finished last on his debut, looked like doing so again after missing the break. He kept on well up the inside rail in the straight, but what he achieved remains to be seen.
**Joshar**, beaten in claimers on turf prior to this, like her stable companion was keeping on in the latter stages and may be the best guide to the level of the form.
**Missed Turn**'s best effort now in three runs was the only time she encountered turf.
**Nutty Times**, who had experience of the surface, seems to be regressing.

## 2125 MAGUIRE & BATTY MEDIAN AUCTION MAIDEN STKS 5f (F)
**7:00** (7:01) (F ) 2-Y-0 **£3,393** (£1,044; £522; £261) **Stalls** High

Form RPR

**1** **Rosein** 2-8-12 ..... JFanning 11 71
(MrsGSRees) *dwlt: sn cl up: led 2f out: rdn and hung lft ent last: styd on wl* **7/1**

2 **2** *3/4* **Extra Mark**[8] [1930] 2-9-3 ..... NPollard 1 73
(JRBest) *chsd ldrs: effrt wl over 1f out: sn rdn and kpt on ins last* **2/1**[1]

**3** *2 1/2* **Forzeen** 2-9-3 ..... SSanders 5 63
(JAOsborne) *chsd ldng pair: hdwy 2f out: rdn to chal over 1f out and ev ch tl drvn and one pce ins last* **3/1**[2]

04 **4** *2 1/2* **Coleorton Dancer**[11] [1865] 2-9-3 ..... NCallan 3 53
(KARyan) *led: rdn along and hdd 2f out: grad wknd appr last* **5/1**[3]

03 **5** *3* **Eternally**[16] [1735] 2-9-3 .....(p) MHenry 9 41
(RMHCowell) *outpcd and rdn along 1/2-way: styd on appr last: n.d* **25/1**

**6** *1/2* **Pee Jay's Dream** 2-9-3 ..... DaleGibson 2 39
(MWEasterby) *in tch centre: rdn along 1/2-way and sn outpcd* **25/1**

**7** *hd* **Roko** 2-8-12 ..... PMulrennan[(5)] 8 38
(MWEasterby) *dwlt: nvr a factor* **25/1**

5 **8** *3/4* **Uredale (IRE)**[25] [1523] 2-9-3 ..... RFfrench 10 35
(MrsADuffield) *s.i.s: a rr* **33/1**

**9** *10* **Kerny (IRE)** 2-9-3 ..... RWinston 4 —
(JJQuinn) *in tch: rdn along 1/2-way: sn wknd* **12/1**

02 **10** *hd* **Urabande**[16] [1735] 2-8-9 ..... LisaJones[(3)] 7 —
(JulianPoulton) *in tch: rdn along after 2f: sn wknd* **7/1**

**11** *3/4* **Kentucky Bankes** 2-9-3 ..... ADaly 6 —
(WGMTurner) *chsd ldrs: rdn along and edgd lft after 11/2f: sn outpcd and bhd fr 1/2-way* **20/1**

60.02 secs (-0.38) **Going Correction** -0.30s/f (Stan) **11** Ran SP% **126.9**
Speed ratings: **91,89,85,81,77 76,75,74,58,58 57**CSF £21.78 TOTE £9.10: £3.20, £1.10, £1.60; EX 29.60.
**Owner** Tom Murray **Bred** J Gittins And Capt J H Wilson **Trained** Sollom, Lancs

**FOCUS**
A decent-looking juvenile contest for the track, run in a good time. Only the first four were concerned from an early stage.

**NOTEBOOK**
**Rosein**, a Komaite half-sister to the useful Proud Boast, originally had the champion jockey booked. She showed speed to get into the centre of the track from her stand-rail draw and, despite swishing her tail, ran on strongly to score in a good time. She should improve for the run and has more races in her.
**Extra Mark**, who had performed well on easy ground on his debut, ran a good race on this first encounter with sand. Another furlong will be in his favour, and fast ground may also suit him.
**Forzeen ◆**, who is bred to be a two-year-old, ran with plenty of promise on this racecourse debut and should have learnt a fair amount.
**Coleorton Dancer**, making his sand debut on his third outing, again showed speed before fading. He may be one to keep in mind for a nursery on fast ground and a sharp track.
**Urabande**, who ran well in a similar race here last time, was struggling from an early stage against these rivals.

## 2126 MANSFIELD 103.2 H'CAP 2m (F)
**7:30** (7:32) (E ) (0-70,64) 4-Y-0+ **£3,789** (£1,166; £583; £291) **Stalls** Low

Form RPR

140- **1** **Herne Bay (IRE)**[234] [5146] 4-9-2 **56**..... RWinston 8 66
(ABailey) *trckd ldrs: hdwy over 5f out: rdn to ld 2f out: drvn ins last and styd on wl* **10/1**

2202 **2** *2* **Madiba**[7] [1973] 5-9-9 **60**..... JFanning 4 68
(PHowling) *cl up: led 5f out: rdn along and hdd 2f out: drvn and rallied ent last: no ex last 150 yds* **11/4**[1]

4503 **3** *16* **Macaroni Gold (IRE)**[15] [1754] 4-9-10 **64**..... MTebbutt 5 52
(WJarvis) *hld up: hdwy over 3f out: rdn along over 2f out: plugged on: nvr nr ldng pair* **9/2**[2]

/3-4 **4** *2 1/2* **Sportsman (IRE)**[21] [839] 5-8-3 **40**.....(b) DaleGibson 7 25
(MWEasterby) *chsd ldrs: rdn along 4f out: drvn over 2f out and sn outpcd* **16/1**

4444 **5** *shd* **Jamaican Flight (USA)**[26] [1501] 11-8-8 **45**..... JQuinn 11 30
(MrsSLamyman) *led: rdn along and hdd 5f out: sn outpcd: swtchd wd and kpt on towards fin* **7/1**

0160 **6** *2 1/2* **Jungle Lion**[28] [1463] 6-9-1 **52**.....(t) DeanMcKeown 12 34
(JohnAHarris) *in tch: effrt over 4f out: rdn along 3f out and sn btn* **12/1**

/0-3 **7** *6* **Myrtus**[22] [1599] 5-8-1 **45**..... DFentiman[(7)] 6 20
(JRWeymes) *nvr a factor* **40/1**

-013 **8** *17* **Sunnyside Royale (IRE)**[9] [1914] 5-8-12 **49**.....(t) RFfrench 9 —
(RBastiman) *hld up: stdy hdwy over 5f out: rdn to chse ldrs over3f out: sn wknd* **12/1**

0-03 **9** *10* **River Of Fire**[10] [1887] 6-7-5 **35** oh5.....(v) NataliaGemelova[(7)] 3 —
(CNKellett) *cl up: rdn along 1/2-way: wknd 6f out* **16/1**

/4-0 **10** *13* **Migration**[15] [1754] 8-9-4 **55**..... LVickers 2 —
(MPitman) *a rr* **12/1**

4-01 **11** *1 3/4* **Best Port (IRE)**[28] [1463] 8-9-2 **53**..... NCallan 1 —
(JParkes) *in tch on inner: rdn along 6f out: sn outpcd and bhd fnl 3f* **6/1**[3]

**12** *dist* **Tinta**[210] 4-8-12 **55**..... DNolan[(3)] 10 —
(PABlockley) *a rr: lost tch 6f out: t.o fnl 3f* **16/1**

3m 40.0s (-12.40) **Going Correction** -0.05s/f (Stan)
**WFA** 4 from 5yo+ 3lb **12** Ran SP% **123.9**
Speed ratings: **103,102,94,92,92 91,88,79,74,68 67,—**CSF £39.30 CT £149.47 TOTE £13.00: £3.40, £1.80, £1.70; EX 93.50.
**Owner** T R Pearson **Bred** Roland H Alder **Trained** Little Budworth, Cheshire

**FOCUS**
A modest handicap, effectively 0-64, that concerned only two throughout the last half mile.

**NOTEBOOK**
**Herne Bay(IRE)**, having his first run for nearly eights months, was being niggled at halfway but travelled better as the race progressed and had the upper hand from halfway up the straight. He is only modest, but handles fast turf as well as sand and appears to have improved a little over the winter.
**Madiba** again ran his race, but for the fifth time in six races ended up second-best. He seems better without headgear, but it is difficult to believe he is other than a sound Placepot prospect.
**Macaroni Gold(IRE)**, whose only two wins were on this track, did not arrive on the scene until the first two had got away. He made little impression in the straight and may have to be ridden closer to the pace in future.

**Sportsman(IRE)**, who has raced mainly over hurdles of late, was not helped by some scrimmaging down the far side. He is better off in banded races from his current mark.
**Jamaican Flight(USA)** could not dominate but was running on again at the end. He has been running on sand or soft ground of late, and may appreciate a return to a fast surface.
**Jungle Lion**, another that suffered in the scrimmaging when going well, found very little in the straight and was disappointing.
**Best Port(IRE)**, having his first run on sand for 18 months, seems better on a sound surface on turf. *Official explanation: jockey said gelding would not face the kick-back*
**Tinta** *Official explanation: jockey said filly was never travelling*

## 2127 MARGARET SIMPSON'S 50TH BIRTHDAY CLAIMING STKS — 1m 3f (F)
8:00 (8:00) (F) 3-Y-O+ £2,898 (£828; £414) Stalls Low

Form — RPR

2312 **1** **Caspian Dusk**[16] 1736 3-8-2 70 — CHaddon(7) 7 — 65
(WGMTurner) *trckd ldrs: hdwy 5f out: led wl over 2f out and sn rdn clr drvn out* **3/1**[3]

1624 **2** *1 3/4* **Heathers Girl**[22] 1590 5-9-4 54 — PaulEddery 2 — 54
(DHaydnJones) *trckd ldng pair: hdwy 4f out: rdn to chse wnr wl over 1f out: drvn and kpt on ins last* **7/1**

3262 **3** *2 1/2* **Fox Hollow (IRE)**[22] 1600 3-8-2 51 — RMiles(3) 4 — 54
(MJHaynes) *cl up: led 4f out: rdn along and hdd wl over 2f out: grad wknd* **10/1**

1021 **4** *1 1/4* **Platinum Charmer (IRE)**[11] 1867 4-10-0 55 — (p) DarrenWilliams 5 — 58
(KRBurke) *hld up in tch: hdwy 3f out: rdn 2f out and sn no imp* **2/1**[1]

6105 **5** *1* **Game Guru**[25] 1535 5-9-12 70 — (p) DeanMcKeown 6 — 55
(PABlockley) *hld up in tch: effrt 3f out: sn rdn and no imp appr last* **11/4**[2]

130/ **6** *15* **Jazil**[791] 1104 9-9-11 — (t) RWinston 3 — 30
(KAMorgan) *led: rdn along 1/2-way: hdd 4f out and sn wknd* **11/1**

2m 29.17s (0.27) **Going Correction** -0.05s/f (Stan)
**WFA** 3 from 4yo+ 17lb — **6** Ran SP% **114.9**
Speed ratings: **98,96,94,94,93 82**CSF £24.11 TOTE £3.20: £2.50, £3.50; EX 25.50.
**Owner** P Nabavi **Bred** P Nabavi And Mrs M Nabavi **Trained** Sigwells, Somerset

**FOCUS**
A moderate claimer run at a steady pace early and developing into a sprint down the straight.

**NOTEBOOK**
**Caspian Dusk**, who had a good chance based on official ratings, was given a good ride and, kicking off the final bend, established a lead he was never in danger of losing. He handled the step up in trip and, clearly at home on the surface, should continue to go well in this grade.
**Heathers Girl**, who had a difficult task on official ratings, appreciated this longer trip and was doing her best work at the end. Handicaps give her a better chance of adding to her score.
**Fox Hollow(IRE)**, another who had plenty to find on the ratings, was given a positive ride but appeared to not quite see out the trip on this surface. A return to Wolverhampton's nine furlongs will be in his favour.
**Platinum Charmer(IRE)** had his chance and there was no excuse on account of trip or surface. In fact he ran close to official ratings with the runner-up.
**Game Guru** was held up at the back, but that was the wrong place to be the way the contest was run.

## 2128 FLIGHT OF THE 1ST BRITISH TURBOJET H'CAP — 1m (F)
8:30 (8:31) (F) (0-55,60) 3-Y-O+ £2,982 (£852; £426) Stalls Low

Form — RPR

0451 **1** **Yenaled**[7] 1962 7-9-5 **60** — DonnaCaldwell(7) 12 — 76
(KARyan) *sn outpcd and bhd: hdwy on inner 3f out: rdn to chal over 1f out: styd on wl to ld ins last* **6/1**[3]

0406 **2** *3* **Spy Gun (USA)**[25] 1531 4-9-4 **52** — SSanders 6 — 62
(TWall) *chsd ldrs: hdwy to ld wl over 1f out: rdn ent last: sn hdd and nt qckn* **9/2**[1]

5143 **3** *3 1/2* **Kenny The Truth (IRE)**[22] 1582 5-9-2 **50** — (t) ADaly 9 — 53
(MrsJCandlish) *in rr and rdn along 1/2-way: wd st: gd hdwy wl over 1f out: styd on ins last: nrst fin* **6/1**[3]

3364 **4** *1 1/2* **Call Of The Wild**[5] 2007 4-9-0 **51** — (b[1]) THamilton(3) 14 — 51
(RAFahey) *dwlt and sn rdn along in rr: wd st: hdwy u.p 2f out: styd on ins last: nrst fin* **12/1**

0140 **5** *3/4* **Sorbiesharry (IRE)**[28] 1479 5-9-2 **50** — (p) RFitzpatrick 7 — 49
(MrsNMacauley) *midfield: hdwy 3f out: rdn along 2f out: drvn and one pce appr last* **12/1**

-011 **6** *shd* **Saros (IRE)**[9] 1916 3-8-9 **56** ow1 — FLynch 11 — 54
(BSmart) *cl up: led 3f out: rdn and hdd wl over 1f out: drvn ent last and sn wknd* **11/2**[2]

3603 **7** *shd* **Xaloc Bay (IRE)**[21] 1629 6-9-6 **54** — DarrenWilliams 13 — 52
(BPJBaugh) *cl up: rdn along over 3f out and sn wknd* **14/1**

0220 **8** *nk* **Wilson Bluebottle (IRE)**[28] 1479 5-9-1 **49** — (b) DaleGibson 8 — 47
(MWEasterby) *in tch: rdn along to chse ldrs 3f out: drvn 2f out and sn no imp* **20/1**

1050 **9** *4* **Printsmith (IRE)**[5] 1993 7-9-0 **48** — JBramhill 4 — 38
(JRNorton) *nvr a factor* **20/1**

0206 **10** *3/4* **Hoh's Back**[11] 1868 5-9-0 **51** — (p) LisaJones(3) 5 — 39
(PaulJohnson) *chsd ldrs: rdn along 3f out and sn wknd* **10/1**

600- **11** *13* **Night Market**[196] 5881 6-8-12 **46** oh1 — RWinston 10 — 8
(NWilson) *led: rdn along and hdd 3f out: sn wknd* **10/1**

0500 **12** *4* **Bennanabaa**[37] 1310 5-9-4 **55** — (t) DCorby(3) 1 — 9
(SCBurrough) *nvr nr ldrs* **50/1**

1-01 **13** *2* **Waterpark**[5] 1992 6-9-6 **54** 6ex — PFessey 3 — 4
(RCraggs) *midfield: effrt and hdwy 1/2-way: sn rdn and wknd wl over 2f out* **6/1**[3]

0-00 **14** *1 1/4* **Kedross (IRE)**[19] 1676 3-8-4 **51** — JQuinn 15 — —
(JJay) *a rr* **33/1**

0 **15** *6* **Mystery Solved (USA)**[40] 1263 4-8-9 **46** oh1 — DNolan(3) 2 — —
(PABlockley) *a rr* **25/1**

1m 43.61s (-0.99) **Going Correction** -0.05s/f (Stan)
**WFA** 3 from 4yo+ 13lb — **15** Ran SP% **134.9**
Speed ratings: **103,100,96,95,94 94,94,93,89,89 76,72,70,68,62**CSF £34.98 CT £186.62 TOTE £7.20: £3.00, £2.50, £3.10; EX 80.50 Place 6 £61.30, Place 5 £30.01.
**Owner** The Fishermen **Bred** R S A Urquhart **Trained** Hambleton, N Yorks

**FOCUS**
A moderate handicap run at a good gallop in which the principals tended to come from off the pace.

**NOTEBOOK**
**Yenaled** was given a confident ride by his apprentice partner, being last of all going into the bend and then cutting through the field to win comfortably in the end. He has rediscovered the form that he showed in the winter of 2001/02 and, having won an amateurs' race last time, clearly goes well for an inexperienced rider.
**Spy Gun(USA)**, the subject of a gamble, was restive in the stalls but ran a fine race, faring best of those that raced up with the early pace. He looks capable of gaining compensation for supporters before long.
**Kenny The Truth(IRE)**, who has gone up in the weights after some decent efforts in banded company, came from well back to finish best of all. He is usually ridden more prominently, but appeared unable to go the early gallop.
**Call Of The Wild** was another running on at the end after missing the break and being outpaced.
**Sorbiesharry(IRE)** ran well enough, but seems more effective around Wolverhampton.
**Saros(IRE)**, who has improved in banded company this spring, had taken a hike in the weights as a result. He made a bid for home early in the straight, but the strong early gallop meant he had nothing in reserve. His current mark looks about right judged on this effort.
**Xaloc Bay(IRE)** was another that seemed to run his race.
**Waterpark** *Official explanation: jockey said mare was never travelling*
**Mystery Solved(USA)** *Official explanation: jockey said filly hung right*
T/Plt: £62.50 to a £1 stake. Pool: £30,302.50. 353.65 winning tickets. T/Qpdt: £13.40 to a £1 stake. Pool: £2,060.50. 113.10 winning tickets. JR

# 1970 THIRSK (L-H)
Saturday, May 15

**OFFICIAL GOING: Good to firm**

## 2129 EUROPEAN BREEDERS FUND CARLTON MINIOTT NOVICE FILLIES' STKS — 5f
2:15 (2:16) (D) 2-Y-O £5,577 (£1,716; £858; £429) Stalls High

Form — RPR

**1** **Miss Meggy** 2-8-7 — DAllan(3) 8 — 86
(TDEasterby) *dwlt: sn in tch: hdwy over 1f out: rdn to ld ins fnl f: edgd lft: r.o* **20/1**

12 **2** *1 1/4* **Bright Moll**[8] 1943 2-8-12 — IMongan 1 — 83
(MLWBell) *trckd ldrs: chal 2f out: sn rdn: ev ch ent fnl f: no ex ins last* **15/8**[1]

21 **3** *1 1/2* **World At My Feet**[14] 1769 2-9-3 — JQuinn 9 — 82
(NBycroft) *cl up: slt ld wl over 1f out: rdn and hdd ins last: no ex* **3/1**[2]

**4** *2 1/2* **Colonial Girl (IRE)** 2-8-10 — WSupple 3 — 65
(TDEasterby) *dwlt: rr div: drvn along 2f out: r.o fnl f: nvr able to chal* **25/1**

4 **5** *nk* **Elisha (IRE)**[19] 1670 2-8-10 — SWKelly 5 — 64
(DMSimcock) *cl up: rdn over 1f out: wknd ins last* **16/1**

1 **6** *1* **Handsome Lady**[16] 1717 2-8-10 — NCallan 4 — 60
(ISemple) *trckd ldrs: rdn wl over 1f out: sn btn* **3/1**[2]

**7** *1* **African Breeze** 2-8-10 — DeanMcKeown 10 — 56
(RMWhitaker) *s.s: sn rr div but in tch: n.d* **25/1**

0 **8** *1* **Serene Pearl (IRE)**[30] 1415 2-8-10 — NPollard 2 — 52
(GMMoore) *rr div: rdn 2f out: sn btn* **100/1**

01 **9** *3/4* **Flossytoo**[21] 1601 2-8-10 — JDO'Reilly(7) 6 — 56
(JO'Reilly) *dwlt: sn led: hung lft u.p and hdd wl over 1f out: fdd* **9/1**[3]

**10** *dist* **Amanderica (IRE)** 2-8-3 — AndrewWebb(7) 7 — —
(MCChapman) *s.s: sn t.o* **100/1**

59.84 secs (-0.06) **Going Correction** -0.175s/f (Firm) — **10** Ran SP% **115.1**
Speed ratings: **93,91,88,84,84 82,80,79,78,—**CSF £55.54 TOTE £23.40: £4.10, £1.50, £1.60; EX 82.80.
**Owner** David W Armstrong **Bred** Trickledown Stud **Trained** Great Habton, N Yorks

**FOCUS**
An average juvenile fillies' novice race that was run at a fair pace.

**NOTEBOOK**
**Miss Meggy** overcame a sluggish start to score on her debut. This daughter of Pivotal showed a willing turn of foot on this occasion and is entitled to improve on this display.
**Bright Moll**, having her third outing, set the standard on form and held every chance if good enough. She went on the ground, but she may be better with some cut.
**World At My Feet** ran her race, but was always looking held under top weight. She had won nicely over course and distance last time and may do better once the nurseries begin.
**Colonial Girl(IRE)** was staying on late in the day, having been slow to break, and will improve plenty on this debut display.
**Handsome Lady**, a decisive winner on her debut last time, was forced to race with no cover and was beaten some way out, finding nothing under pressure. This was a disappointing effort as she escaped a penalty for winning last time, and now has it all to prove.

## 2130 SALLY WALPOLE 30TH BIRTHDAY H'CAP — 5f
2:50 (2:52) (D) (0-80,77) 3-Y-O+ £5,746 (£1,768; £884; £442) Stalls High

Form — RPR

2503 **1** **Polish Emperor (USA)**[20] 1642 4-9-5 **70** — (e[1]) NCallan 17 — 88
(PWHarris) *racd stands side: mde most: hrd pressed and rdn ent fnl f: fnd ex ins last* **9/1**

-005 **2** *1* **Online Investor**[12] 1825 5-9-0 **65** — AlexGreaves 18 — 79
(DNicholls) *trckd ldrs stands side: disp ld ent fnl f: no ex u.p ins last* **9/2**[1]

00-6 **3** *3 1/2* **Brigadore**[14] 1774 5-8-13 **67** — THamilton(3) 19 — 67
(JRWeymes) *prom stands side: kpt on u.p fr over 1f out: no imp on first 2 ins last* **8/1**[3]

011- **4** *1 1/4* **Raccoon (IRE)**[241] 4990 4-9-6 **74** — TPQueally(3) 6 — 69
(TDBarron) *trckd far side ldrs: rdn 2f out: kpt on to ld gp clsng stages: no imp on stands side ldrs* **13/2**[2]

0010 **5** *1/2* **Chico Guapo (IRE)**[3] 2041 4-9-12 **77** — IMongan 4 — 70
(JAGlover) *led far side gp: rdn 2f out: kpt on: no ex ins last* **13/2**[2]

-051 **6** *1/2* **Erracht**[20] 1642 6-9-0 **65** — GBaker 13 — 56
(MrsHSweeting) *chsd stands side ldrs: rdn 2f out: no hdwy* **10/1**

00-0 **7** *shd* **Kangarilla Road**[50] 1113 5-9-5 **70** — DeanMcKeown 1 — 61
(MrsJRRamsden) *in tch far side: hdwy wl over 1f out: kpt on fnl f: n.d* **18/1**

0-00 **8** *nk* **Tommy Smith**[14] 1774 6-9-7 **72** — (b) DMcGaffin 3 — 61
(JSWainwright) *prom far side: rdn 2f out: no ex* **14/1**

0-00 **9** *hd* **Whistler**[14] 1774 7-9-10 **75** — (p) DarrenWilliams 5 — 64
(JMBradley) *chsd far side ldrs: rdn 2f out: no hdwy* **25/1**

6355 **10** *1 3/4* **Amanda's Lad (IRE)**[12] 1820 4-9-0 **65** — NPollard 8 — 47
(MCChapman) *chsd fare side ldrs: rdn 2f out: no hdwy* **66/1**

0-00 **11** *1/2* **John O'Groats (IRE)**[14] 1774 6-9-7 **72** — SWKelly 20 — 52
(MDods) *racd stands side: dwlt: towards rr: kpt on fnl 2f: n.d* **40/1**

000- **12** *shd* **Charlie Parkes**[218] 5472 6-9-12 **77** — WSupple 10 — 56
(EJAlston) *cl up far side: rdn 2f out: fdd* **14/1**

50-0 **13** *shd* **Candleriggs (IRE)**[7] 1956 8-8-10 **68** — LTreadwell(7) 7 — 47
(DNicholls) *sn rr div far side: n.d* **33/1**

00-0 **14** *2* **Sir Sandrovitch (IRE)**[7] 1956 8-8-7 **58** — (p) GParkin 15 — 29
(RAFahey) *sn rr div stands side: n.d* **20/1**

00-0 **15** *nk* **Ballybunion (IRE)**[13] 1787 5-9-0 **65** — ANicholls 9 — 35
(DNicholls) *s.i.s: a towards rr far side* **28/1**

L-00 **16** *1/2* **Time To Remember (IRE)**[7] 1974 6-8-13 **64** — JCarroll 2 — 32
(DNicholls) *sn towards rr far side* **50/1**

420- **17** *1* **Strensall**[155] 6170 7-9-12 **77** — RFitzpatrick 14 — 41
(REBarr) *dwlt: a rr div stands side* **33/1**

0001 **18** *2 ½* **Cash**[11] 1870 6-8-5 **59**...(p) LEnstone(3) 12 13
(PaulJohnson) *chsd stands side ldrs: rdn 2f out: sn wknd* **18/1**

0000 **19** *16* **African Spur (IRE)**[7] 1974 4-8-4 **62** ow4...(t) DTudhope(7) 16 —
(DCarroll) *racd stands side: rel to r and v.s.a: a wl bhd: t.o* **66/1**

000- **U** **Elvington Boy**[240] 5007 7-9-9 **74**... TLucas 11 —
(MWEasterby) *rrd bdly and uns rdr leaving stalls* **25/1**

58.43 secs (-1.47) **Going Correction** -0.175s/f (Firm) **20** Ran SP% **128.1**
Speed ratings: **104,102,96,94,94 93,93,92,92,89 88,88,88,85,84 83,82,78,52,—**CSF £45.51 CT £276.18 TOTE £11.70: £2.80, £2.30, £2.90, £2.30; EX 55.40.
**Owner** Edrich, Graves, Harris **Bred** Chevington Stud **Trained** Ringshall, Bucks

**FOCUS**
A fair sprint which saw those drawn high fill the first three places.

**NOTEBOOK**
**Polish Emperor(USA)**, racing in an eye-shield for the first time, was quickly away and showed a good attitude to make most of the running. He was aided by his high draw, but his form on the All-Weather entitled him to run well in this and he went well on this ground. It was a first win since going in at Wolverhampton last November and a first win on turf since his maiden in 2002.
**Online Investor** ran his best race for some time and is clearly on a winning mark at present. He was another who was helped by his high draw and he has not won since his sole success back in 2001 but, on this evidence, could soon go one better.
**Brigadore** could not quicken late on with the first two, but again ran his race and deserves to get his head in front. He likes this quick ground.
**Raccoon(IRE)** won the battle on the far side and made a promising return from his eight-month break. This lightly-raced individual has clearly had problems, but he is a progressive sprinter and he should not be long in scoring again. He would probably have won if he had raced on the stands' side.
**Chico Guapo(IRE)** was again quickly away and posted another fair effort, but does look vunerable late on. He may be capable of winning again of this mark when all goes his way.
**Time To Remember(IRE)** *Official explanation: jockey said gelding hung right-handed throughout*
**Cash** *Official explanation: trainer's representative said gelding finished lame*
**African Spur(IRE)** *Official explanation: trainer said gelding spread a plate*

## 2131 RECTANGLE GROUP H'CAP 5f
**3:20** (3:21) (C) (0-100,98) 3-Y-O **£9,821** (£3,022; £1,511; £755) **Stalls** High

Form RPR

0-10 **1** **Benbaun (IRE)**[10] 1881 3-8-7 **87**...(v) DCorby(3) 2 99
(MJWallace) *mde all: rdn 2f out: r.o wl* **14/1**

05-4 **2** *1 ¼* **Lualua**[14] 1760 3-7-12 **75**... PFessey 10 82
(TDBarron) *dwlt: hld up: drvn along and hdwy 2f out: wnt 2nd ins fnl f: r.o: no imp on wnr* **22/1**

5-10 **3** *¾* **Johnny Parkes**[10] 1883 3-8-6 **83**... IMongan 13 87
(MrsJRRamsden) *prom: rdn 2f out: r.o fnl f* **15/2**

1-6 **4** *nk* **Two Step Kid (USA)**[32] 1384 3-8-11 **88**... EAhern 9 91
(JNoseda) *chsd ldrs: ch and rdn over 1f out: no ex ins last* **9/4**[1]

410- **5** *1 ½* **Traytonic**[203] 5740 3-9-7 **98**... FLynch 4 95
(HJCyzer) *bhd: drvn along over 1f out: r.o strly ins last: nvr able to chal* **14/1**

2211 **6** *½* **Mr Wolf**[14] 1775 3-8-2 **79**... ANicholls 1 74
(DWBarker) *cl up: rdn and ch over 1f out: fdd ins last* **10/1**

61-0 **7** *shd* **Tribute (IRE)**[10] 1883 3-8-2 **82** ow3... TPQueally(3) 11 76
(DRLoder) *slowly away: towards rr: drvn along and hdwy over 1f out: no further prog fnl f* **6/1**[3]

36-0 **8** *1 ½* **Who's Winning (IRE)**[32] 1388 3-7-9 **75** oh2... JFMcDonald(3) 14 63
(CADwyer) *nvr bttr than mid-div* **25/1**

46-2 **9** *½* **Celtic Thunder**[19] 1659 3-8-4 **84**... DAllan(3) 7 70
(TJEtherington) *chsd ldrs: rdn 2f out: fading whn hmpd ins fnl f* **11/2**[2]

211- **10** *nk* **Paradise Isle**[227] 5302 3-8-13 **90**... GBaker 3 75
(CFWall) *slowly away: hld up in rr: effrt over 1f out: rdn and no hdwy fnl f* **14/1**

340- **11** *1 ¼* **Self Belief**[278] 4052 3-7-7 **75** oh8... DFox(5) 12 55
(MCChapman) *prom tl rdn and wknd 2f out* **100/1**

61-0 **12** *shd* **Divine Spirit**[10] 1883 3-8-6 **83**... WSupple 5 63
(MDods) *nvr bttr than mid-div* **25/1**

312- **13** *2* **Fyodor (IRE)**[243] 4943 3-8-8 **85**... SWKelly 8 57
(WJHaggas) *midfield tl wknd 2f out* **12/1**

164- **14** *2 ½* **Molly Moon (IRE)**[263] 4480 3-8-12 **89**... FNorton 6 51
(MBlanshard) *mid-div tl wknd 2f out* **40/1**

58.33 secs (-1.57) **Going Correction** -0.175s/f (Firm) **14** Ran SP% **124.5**
Speed ratings: **105,103,101,101,98 98,97,95,94,94 92,92,88,84**CSF £303.35 CT £2571.00 TOTE £18.20: £3.60, £6.50, £2.60; EX 334.40.
**Owner** Ransley, Skidmore, Birks **Bred** Dr T A Ryan **Trained** Newmarket, Suffolk
■ Stewards Enquiry : A Nicholls one-day ban: failed to keep straight from stalls (May 26)
D Corby one-day ban: failed to keep straight from stalls (May 26)

**FOCUS**
A decent sprint handicap which again saw those racing on the stands' side at an advantage.

**NOTEBOOK**
**Benbaun(IRE)** pinged out of the gates and made a decisive move to bag the favoured stands'-side rail to make all. This return to the minimum trip on better ground worked the oracle.
**Lualua**, who had a 7lb pull with the winner for a three-length beating last time, ran very much to his mark. He can go one better in this grade, but had the best draw on this occasion.
**Johnny Parkes** ran a much-improved race back on this fast ground and he too can score off this mark when things go his way.
**Two Step Kid(USA)** struggled to go the pace on this drop in trip, but had to race down the centre on this occasion and is worth another chance when upped to six furlongs.
**Traytonic** ran as though this will bring him on and he lost little in defeat.

## 2132 TOTEEXACTA H'CAP 6f
**3:55** (3:57) (C) (0-95,92) 4-Y-O+ **£9,997** (£3,076; £1,538; £769) **Stalls** High

Form RPR

-140 **1** **Celtic Mill**[14] 1765 6-9-0 **84**... LEnstone(3) 2 98
(DWBarker) *racd far side: mde virtually all: rdn over 1f out: hrd pressed fnl f: fnd ex clsng stages* **10/1**[3]

3-16 **2** *¾* **Mine Behind**[19] 1663 4-8-11 **78**... NPollard 1 90
(JRBest) *trckd first 2 far side: rdn to chal ent fnl f: ev ch ins last: no ex clsng stages* **16/1**

0-20 **3** *3* **Hiccups**[12] 1825 4-9-0 **81**...(p) IMongan 19 84
(MrsJRRamsden) *s.i.s: sn trcking ldrs stands side: rdn 2f out: kpt on u.p to ld gp ins fnl f: nt trble first 2* **7/1**[2]

6342 **4** *½* **Ellens Academy (IRE)**[14] 1765 9-8-13 **80**... WSupple 14 81
(EJAlston) *sn trcking ldrs stands side: led gp wl over 1f out: kpt on same pce ins last* **4/1**[1]

4-00 **5** *½* **Inter Vision (USA)**[26] 1500 4-9-2 **86**... ABeech(3) 4 86
(ADickman) *chsd ldrs far side: kpt on fnl f: nvr able to chal* **33/1**

30-0 **6** *shd* **Million Percent**[12] 1825 5-9-1 **82**... DarrenWilliams 12 81
(KRBurke) *midfield stands side: hdwy 2f out: disp gp ld and rdn fnl f: no ex clsng stages* **16/1**

310- **7** *hd* **Lafi (IRE)**[231] 5210 5-9-4 **92**... LTreadwell(7) 16 91
(DNicholls) *rr div stands side: nt clr run 2f out: hdwy over 1f out: kpt on fnl f: n.d* **16/1**

021- **8** *hd* **Cd Europe (IRE)**[194] 5908 6-9-11 **92**... NCallan 7 90
(KARyan) *bhd far side: kpt on fr over 1f out: n.d* **11/1**

-440 **9** *nk* **Viewforth**[14] 1765 6-8-8 **75**...(b) JCarroll 3 72
(ISemple) *chsd wnr far side: rdn 2f out: sn btn* **14/1**

60-0 **10** *2 ½* **Seafield Towers**[34] 1343 4-8-8 **78**...(p) NMackay(3) 10 68
(MissLAPerratt) *led stands side gp tl hdd wl over 1f out: fdd* **33/1**

0-00 **11** *1 ¼* **Obe One**[14] 1765 4-8-5 **72**... FNorton 13 58
(ABerry) *racd stands side: dwlt: sn midfield: rdn 2f out: no hdwy* **33/1**

-000 **12** *½* **True Night**[14] 1772 7-8-9 **76**... PMQuinn 18 61
(DNicholls) *racd stands side: towards rr most of way* **25/1**

00-0 **13** *nk* **Ragamuffin**[12] 1825 6-8-3 **73**... DAllan(3) 20 57
(TDEasterby) *racd stands side: midfield: drvn along 1/2-way: no hdwy* **14/1**

00-0 **14** *½* **Banjo Bay (IRE)**[8] 1927 6-9-3 **84**... AlexGreaves 8 66
(DNicholls) *racd stands side: prom tl rdn and wknd over 1f out* **16/1**

50-0 **15** *¾* **Najeebon (FR)**[14] 1765 5-9-3 **87**... SHitchcott(3) 11 67
(MRChannon) *towards rr stands side: sn drvn along: n.d* **7/1**[2]

0-04 **16** *½* **Paddywack (IRE)**[7] 1956 7-8-0 **67**...(b) JQuinn 6 45
(DWChapman) *racd far side: dwlt: a towards rr* **11/1**

-500 **17** *1 ½* **Awarding**[57] 1051 4-8-4 **78**... LucyRussell(7) 5 52
(DrJRJNaylor) *racd far side: dwlt: chsd ldrs tl wknd 2f out* **50/1**

000- **18** *1 ¼* **Prince Dayjur (USA)**[322] 2797 5-8-12 **79**... EAhern 15 49
(MJWallace) *prom stands side tl wknd over 2f out* **14/1**

1100 **19** *1* **No Time (IRE)**[34] 1343 4-9-11 **92**... TGMcLaughlin 17 59
(MJPolglase) *cl up stands side tl wknd 2f out* **20/1**

1m 11.03s (-1.47) **Going Correction** -0.175s/f (Firm) **19** Ran SP% **133.7**
Speed ratings: **102,101,97,96,95 95,95,95,94,91 89,88,88,87,86 86,84,82,81**CSF £161.55 CT £1258.50 TOTE £14.60: £4.80, £3.90, £2.50, £1.60; EX 178.90.
**Owner** P Asquith **Bred** P Asquith **Trained** Scorton, N Yorks
■ Stewards Enquiry : N Mackay one-day ban: careless riding (May 26)

**FOCUS**
Low numbers were favoured for this sprint, which reversed the trend set previously on the card.

**NOTEBOOK**
**Celtic Mill** put a poor display last time firmly behind him with a brave front-running display. Things went his way on this occasion and, although he is capable of holding his form, he is no good thing to follow-up.
**Mine Behind** markedly improved on his latest effort, but could not peg back the winner under maximum pressure late on.
**Hiccups** can be rated slightly better than the bare form would indicate. He had to endure traffic problems on this occasion, but cosily won the battle on the stands' side.
**Ellens Academy(IRE)** ran his race with no excuses, but again showed enough to suggest his winning turn is not too far off.
**Najeebon(FR)** was never a threat form his middle draw and has now proved disappointing in two outings this year.

## 2133 GRAPES GREAT HABTON MAIDEN STKS 1m 4f
**4:30** (4:31) (D ) 3-Y-0+ **£5,681** (£1,748; £874; £437) **Stalls** Low

Form RPR

40-3 **1** **Portrait Of A Lady (IRE)**[25] 1521 3-8-0 74... JQuinn 8 73
(HRACecil) *trckd ldrs: rdn to ld appr fnl f: styd on u.p: jst hld on* **11/2**[3]

60-2 **2** *shd* **Sunny Lady (FR)**[33] 1356 3-7-11 73... NMackay(3) 2 73
(EALDunlop) *in tch: drvn along over 2f out: styd on wl u.p fnl f: jst failed* **11/2**[3]

**3** *¾* **Sunday City (JPN)** 3-8-2... TPQueally(3) 7 77
(DRLoder) *in tch: effrt 3f out: sn rdn: styd on u.p fnl f* **11/4**[1]

3 **4** *1 ½* **Cumbria**[21] 1605 3-8-0... ANicholls 9 69
(MJohnston) *w ldr: slt ld and rdn 2f out: hdd appr fnl f: no ex* **10/3**[2]

-066 **5** *1* **Hathlen (IRE)**[17] 1714 3-8-5 76... RLappin 4 73
(MRChannon) *led tl rdn and hdd 2f out: wknd appr fnl f* **11/2**[3]

3-0 **6** *5* **Victory Lap (GER)**[13] 1800 3-8-2 ow5... SHitchcott(3) 11 65
(MRChannon) *hld up: hdwy into midfield 4f out: rdn 3 out: no further prog* **14/1**

2/ **7** *9* **Awwal Marra (USA)**[650] 3579 4-9-5... DeanMcKeown 10 45
(EWTuer) *hld up: effrt 4f out: no hdwy* **25/1**

**8** *2 ½* **Jidiya (IRE)**[37] 5800 5-9-10... IMongan 12 46
(SGollings) *slowly away: sn chsng ldrs: drvn along 4f out: wknd 3 out* **33/1**

50-6 **9** *1* **Ashtaroute (USA)**[66] 432 4-8-12 49... AndrewWebb(7) 1 40
(MCChapman) *sn bhd* **50/1**

0-3 **10** *2 ½* **Dawn Air (USA)**[14] 1770 3-8-0... PFessey 13 36
(KARyan) *sn bhd* **20/1**

**11** *1 ¼* **I'm A Dark Horse** 3-8-5... GParkin 5 39
(KARyan) *slowly away: a bhd* **50/1**

00- **12** *2 ½* **Zameel (IRE)**[190] 5940 3-8-2... DAllan(3) 6 35
(JeddO'Keeffe) *in tch tl wknd 5f out* **100/1**

005- **13** *dist* **Lagosta (SAF)**[195] 3607 4-9-10 46... NPollard 3 —
(GMMoore) *chsd ldrs tl wknd 5f out: t.o* **50/1**

2m 34.72s (-0.48) **Going Correction** +0.10s/f (Good)
**WFA** 3 from 4yo+ 19lb **13** Ran SP% **121.0**
Speed ratings: **105,104,104,103,102 99,93,91,91,89 88,86,—**CSF £34.35 TOTE £6.20: £2.20, £2.50, £2.00; EX 28.20.
**Owner** J Shack **Bred** Pat Garvey **Trained** Newmarket, Suffolk

**FOCUS**
An ordinary maiden run at a good pace for the grade, and producing a thrilling finish.

**NOTEBOOK**
**Portrait Of A Lady(IRE)** only narrowly scored a vital success for breeding purposes, but deserves credit for sticking to her task late on. She showed enough last time to suggest a win was not far off, but this looks as good as she is and she could stuggle off her mark in handicaps.
**Sunny Lady(FR)** was only just denied and looks well up to winning a similar race. She looks as though she will stay further and went well on this ground.
**Sunday City(JPN)** made a satisfactory debut. He was beaten through lack of experience and looks well up to winning a similar event.
**Cumbria** had the run of the race, but could not improve on her debut effort on this quicker ground.
**Hathlen(IRE)** ran another frustrating race and has yet to prove he has trained on from two to three.

## 2134 SUN INN NORMANBY H'CAP 1m
**5:00** (5:00) (D ) (0-80,80) 3-Y-0 **£5,785** (£1,780; £890; £445) **Stalls** Low

Form RPR

0-33 **1** **Mystical Girl (USA)**[7] 1957 3-9-2 **75**... SChin 8 92+
(MJohnston) *cl up: led over 2f out: qcknd clr fnl f: easily* **5/1**[1]

40-5 **2** *2* **La Persiana**[33] 1371 3-8-13 **72**... JQuinn 11 84
(WJarvis) *midfield: hdwy over 2f out: wnt 2nd jst ins fnl f: r.o wl: no imp on wnr* **11/1**

0-43 **3** 3 **Burley Flame**[14] 1771 3-8-13 **72** .... MFenton 3 78
(JGGiven) *mde most tl rdn and hdd over 2f out: styd on* **10/1**

-220 **4** 1 **Oh Golly Gosh**[13] 1794 3-9-0 **76** ....(p) J-PGuillambert(3) 4 79
(NPLittmoden) *in tch: hdwy to chse ldrs over 2f out: kpt on: no further prog* **25/1**

01-0 **5** shd **Hezaam (USA)**[30] 1408 3-9-4 **77** .... WSupple 7 80
(JLDunlop) *hld up: rdn 3f out: kpt on wl fnl f: nvr able to chal* **8/1**[3]

35-0 **6** 1 ½ **Double Vodka (IRE)**[15] 1755 3-8-2 **64** .... DAllan(3) 1 64
(MrsJRRamsden) *slowly away: hld up: hdwy over 2f out: rdn over 1 out: kpt on: nvr able to chal* **25/1**

0-04 **7** nk **Auroville**[15] 1755 3-8-7 **66** .... IMongan 14 65
(MLWBell) *midfield: hdwy to chse ldrs over 2f out: sn rdn: no further prog* **16/1**

13-0 **8** 1 ½ **The Violin Player (USA)**[35] 1322 3-9-7 **80** .... MTebbutt 18 75
(WJarvis) *sn bhd: styd on fnl 3f: n.d* **50/1**

1-4 **9** 2 **Catherine Howard**[30] 1418 3-8-12 **74** .... SHitchcott(3) 12 65
(MRChannon) *chsd ldrs: rdn 3f out: wknd 2f out* **9/1**

5542 **10** 1 ¼ **On The Waterfront**[20] 1641 3-8-8 **67** .... JCarroll 15 55
(JWHills) *sn bhd: kpt on fnl 3f: n.d* **14/1**

2-10 **11** ¾ **Show No Fear**[12] 1831 3-8-12 **71** .... WRyan 6 57
(HRACecil) *hld up: effrt 3f out: sn rdn and btn* **7/1**[2]

-144 **12** 1 **Honest Injun**[12] 1831 3-9-4 **77** .... EAhern 17 61
(BWHills) *hld up midfield: hmpd and lost pl after 1f: rdn over 2f out: styng on same pce whn hmpd jst ins fnl f* **14/1**

1413 **13** 3 **Dispol Veleta**[30] 1418 3-8-6 **68** .... NMackay(3) 10 45
(TDBarron) *prom: rdn 3f out: wknd 2f out* **7/1**[2]

214- **14** 2 **Stevedore (IRE)**[216] 5503 3-9-3 **79** .... JFMcDonald(3) 5 51
(BJMeehan) *in tch tl wknd 4f out* **20/1**

5143 **15** 2 ½ **Norwegian**[72] 959 3-8-3 **65** ....(v) TPQueally(3) 13 32
(DRLoder) *in tch: rdn 3f out: wknd 2f out* **10/1**

24-0 **16** nk **Named At Dinner**[23] 1559 3-8-11 **73** .... ABeech(3) 9 39
(MrsADuffield) *prom tl wknd 4f out* **66/1**

0-00 **17** 8 **Lady Sunset (IRE)**[33] 1362 3-8-1 **60** .... FNorton 16 —
(KARyan) *bhd fr 1/2-way* **66/1**

320- **18** dist **Hearthstead Dream**[194] 5906 3-8-13 **72** .... ANicholls 2 —
(MJohnston) *sn bhd: t.o and eased fnl 2f* **40/1**

1m 38.9s (-0.80) **Going Correction** +0.10s/f (Good) **18** Ran SP% **128.3**
Speed ratings: **108,106,103,102,101 100,100,98,96,95 94,93,90,88,86 85,77,**—CSF £58.34 CT £567.24 TOTE £6.50: £2.20, £3.60, £2.90, £4.10; EX 148.60.
**Owner** T T Bloodstocks **Bred** Simon Tindall **Trained** Middleham Moor, N Yorks

**FOCUS**
A modest handicap which produced an easy winner and a decent time for the grade.

**NOTEBOOK**
**Mystical Girl(USA)** ◆ moved to the front just over two out travelling sweetly and won this comfortably in the end. She was raised 3lb for her third place last time, but it proved no barrier and she looks a progressive filly.

**La Persiana**, making her handicap debut, ran on to be a clear second but found the winner gone beyond recall. This was her best display yet and she may be even better over further. *Official explanation: jockey said filly hung left-handed in the closing stages*

**Burley Flame** could not quicken when challenged for the lead two out, but stuck to his task well enough late on. He may be better when reverting to shorter.

**Oh Golly Gosh** made good headway to join the pace two out but, not for the first time, did not look the most willing under pressure and could only muster the one pace.

**Honest Injun** had a nightmare run throughout and can be rated much better than the bare form would suggest.

**Hearthstead Dream** *Official explanation: jockey said gelding was never travelling*

## 2135 BOLTBY CLASSIFIED STKS 1m
5:30 (5:31) (D) 3-Y-O **£5,577** (£1,716; £858; £429) **Stalls** Low

Form RPR

4-40 **1** **Attune**[17] 1704 3-8-6 80 .... JFMcDonald(3) 6 81
(BJMeehan) *prom: effrt over 2f out: styd on u.p to ld ins fnl f: all out* **9/1**

16- **2** hd **Alekhine (IRE)**[190] 5944 3-9-1 83 .... EAhern 4 87
(PWHarris) *s.i.s: hld up in tch: effrt over 2f out: styd on u.p to chal ins fnl f: styd on* **11/2**[3]

615- **3** shd **Alshawameq (IRE)**[206] 5708 3-8-13 81 .... WSupple 8 85
(JLDunlop) *trckd ldrs: led over 1f out: rdn and hdd ins fnl f: styd on* **13/2**

052- **4** 1 ¼ **Major Effort (USA)**[234] 5144 3-8-12 80 .... FLynch 5 81
(SirMichaelStoute) *hld up in tch: effrt over 2f out: styd on u.p fnl f: nvr able to chal* **3/1**[2]

04-0 **5** 2 **Sweet Reply**[30] 1408 3-8-6 78 .... LEnstone(3) 3 73
(IAWood) *led tl rdn and hdd 2f out: fdd fnl f* **22/1**

1 **6** nk **Davorin (JPN)**[32] 1386 3-8-12 83 .... TPQueally(3) 7 79
(DRLoder) *s.i.s: sn cl up: slt ld 2f out: rdn and hdd over 1 out: fdd fnl f* **7/4**[1]

4120 **7** nk **Heversham (IRE)**[49] 1134 3-8-12 80 .... SWKelly 1 75
(WJHaggas) *trckd ldrs: effrt over 2f out: kpt on same pce* **9/1**

1m 41.28s (1.58) **Going Correction** +0.10s/f (Good) 7 Ran SP% **114.4**
Speed ratings: **96,95,95,94,92 92,91**CSF £56.81 TOTE £13.50: £3.00, £3.00; EX 54.70 Place 6 £158.46 , Place 5 £100.98.
**Owner** Wyck Hall Stud **Bred** Wyck Hall Stud Ltd **Trained** Upper Lambourn, Berks

**FOCUS**
A decent classified contest run at a moderate pace, that developed into a sprint three out. The form looks suspect.

**NOTEBOOK**
**Attune** gamely ran on under pressure to score all-out. This was her first success and she was suited by this quick surface, but is no good thing to follow-up in a more competitive race.

**Alekhine(IRE)** was not suited by being held up off this slow gallop and did very well in the circumstances. He can win off this mark and will be seen to better effect when faced with a stiffer test.

**Alshawameq(IRE)** had every chance if good enough, but could not find any more when challenged inside the final 100 yards. He can improve on this seasonal reappearance.

**Major Effort(USA)** was another unsuited by being held up off the slow gallop. He is entitled to come on for this seasonal reappearance and is capable of better.

**Davorin(JPN)** was not helped by a sluggish start, and may have used up too much energy in rushing up to the lead, but had every chance if good enough and proved disappointing. He may be worth another chance in a more truly-run race.

T/Plt: £136.80 to a £1 stake. Pool: £38,242.25. 204.00 winning tickets. T/Qpdt: £30.50 to a £1 stake. Pool: £2,112.80. 51.20 winning tickets. JF

2136 - 2137a (Foreign Racing) - See Raceform Interactive

# 1805 SAN SIRO (R-H)
Saturday, May 15

**OFFICIAL GOING: Good**

## 2138a PREMIO PAOLO MEZZANOTTE (GROUP 3) (F&M) 1m 2f
3:20 (3:35) 4-Y-O+ **£36,396** (£17,473; £9,959; £4,979)

RPR

**1** **Deva (GER)** 5-8-9 .... KKerekes 8 100
(DRonge, Germany) *held up in rear, headway to lead 100y out, ran on well*

**2** 1 **Jacira (FR)**[208] 5684 5-8-9 .... JHorcajada 14 98
(MDelcher-Sanchez, Spain) *led to 100y out, just held on for 2nd*

**3** nse **Vale Mantovani**[202] 5781 4-8-9 .... MEsposito 6 98
(VCaruso, Italy) *held up in rear, headway on outside from 2f out, finished well*

**4** nse **Morbidezza (GER)**[41] 4-8-9 .... IRossi 4 98
(MTrinker, Germany) *raced in 6th, stayed on under pressure final 1 1/2f*

**5** ½ **Miss Nashwan (IRE)**[14] 1776 4-8-12 .... MBelli 9 100
(MGrassi, Italy) *raced in 4th, ridden 1 1/2f out, stayed on*

**6** ½ **Aguilera (GER)**[244] 4-8-9 ....(b) GBietolini 13 96
(RSuerland, Germany) *midfield, stayed on final 2f*

**7** nse **Dan Grey (IRE)**[202] 5781 4-8-9 .... SMulas 3 96
(BGrizzetti, Italy) *raced in 5th on inside, effort 2f out, one pace*

**7** dht **Arlecchina (GER)**[14] 1776 4-8-9 .... FMBerry 7 96
(UStoltefuss, Germany) *last to over 2f out, stayed on final f, nearest finish*

**9** nk **Holy Moon (IRE)**[274] 4172 4-8-9 .... EBotti 2 96
(A&GBotti, Italy) *held up in 13th, no room 2f out til inside final f, unlucky*

**10** 1 **Mity Dancer (GER)**[33] 4-8-9 .... LHammer-Hansen 11 94
(DKRichardson, Germany) *never a factor*

**11** nk **Antique Rose (GER)**[209] 4-8-9 .... WMongil 12 93
(HSteinmetz, Germany) *never a factor*

**12** 4 **Supereva (IRE)** 4-8-9 .... MDemuro 5 86
(BGrizzetti, Italy) *raced in 2nd til weakened over 1 1/2f out*

**13** 1 ½ **Wigman (USA)**[566] 4-8-9 .... MMonteriso 1 84
(VValiani, Italy) *always in rear*

**14** 1 **Biographie**[13] 4-8-9 .... MTellini 10 82
(EBorromeo, Italy) *always in rear*

2m 5.70s **14** Ran
Speed ratings: .
**Owner** Gestut Park Wiedingen **Bred** H Von Finck **Trained** Germany

# PIMLICO (L-H)
Saturday, May 15

**OFFICIAL GOING: Fast**

## 2139a PREAKNESS STKS (GRADE 1) 1m 1f 110y(D)
11:15 (11:25) 3-Y-O **£363,128** (£111,732; £55,866; £27,933)

RPR

**1** **Smarty Jones (USA)**[14] 1781 3-9-0 .... ShaneElliott 7 131
(JohnCServis, U.S.A) *raced in 2nd til led over 2f out, ridden clear, impressive* **7/10**[1]

**2** 11 ½ **Rock Hard Ten (USA)**[42] 3-9-0 .... GaryStevens 10 111
(JOrman, U.S.A) *raced in 7th, headway to go 2nd just under 1 1/2f out, kept on but no chance with winner* **69/10**

**3** 2 **Eddington (USA)**[35] 3-9-0 .... JDBailey 9 107
(MHennig, U.S.A) *raced in 6th, 8th 2 1/2f out, steady headway final 2f to take 3rd close home* **132/10**

**4** hd **Lion Heart (USA)**[14] 1781 3-9-0 .... MESmith 1 107
(PLBiancone, U.S.A) *led til headed over 2f out, one pace, lost 3rd close home* **49/10**[2]

**5** hd **Imperialism (USA)**[14] 1781 3-9-0 .... KDesormeaux 8 106
(KristinMulhall, U.S.A) *raced in 3rd or 4th, ridden and one pace final 1 1/2f out* **66/10**[3]

**6** 1 **Sir Shackleton (USA)** 3-9-0 .... RBejarano 6 105
(NZito, U.S.A) *raced in 5th, ridden and no impression 1 1/2f out* **375/10**

**7** ¾ **Borrego (USA)**[14] 1781 3-9-0 ....(b) VEspinoza 2 103
(CBGreely, U.S.A) *raced in 8th, never a factor* **128/10**

**8** 5 ½ **Little Matth Man (USA)**[35] 3-9-0 ....(b) RMigliore 3 94
(MCiresa, U.S.A) *last to over 2f out, never a factor* **45/1**

**9** 2 **Song Of The Sword (USA)**[14] 1781 3-9-0 ....(b) JChavez 5 90
(JenniferLeigh-Pedersen, U.S.A) *close up til weakened over 2f out* **51/1**

**10** 3 ½ **Water Cannon (USA)** 3-9-0 ....(b) RFogelsonger 11 84
(LindaAlbert, U.S.A) *raced in 9th, always in rear* **40/1**

1m 55.59s **10** Ran SP% **125.0**
Speed ratings: .
**Owner** Someday Farm **Bred** Someday Farm **Trained** USA

**NOTEBOOK**
**Smarty Jones(USA)**, in search of the second leg having won the Kentucky Derby, hit the front two and destroyed his rivals, running right away to win with any amount in hand. This was a hugely impressive performance and he now heads to the Belmont with outstanding claims of becoming the first horse to complete the Triple Crown since Affirmed.

# 1614 RIPON (R-H)
Sunday, May 16

**OFFICIAL GOING: Good (good to firm in places)**
Wind: slt hlf against Weather: fine & sunny

## 2140 SKYBET.COM WOODEN SPOON CHARITY (S) STKS 6f
2:00 (2:03) (F) 2-Y-O **£3,900** (£1,200; £600; £300) **Stalls** Low

Form RPR

0402 **1** **Goldhill Prince**[6] 2003 2-8-7 ....(p) CHaddon(7) 9 55
(WGMTurner) *w ldrs on outer: led 2f out: edgd lft: kpt on wl* **9/4**[2]

03 **2** 2 ½ **Stan's Girl**[22] 1601 2-8-6 .... SHitchcott(3) 3 43
(MRChannon) *led: rdn 1f out: hdd 2f out: nt qckn ins last* **5/4**[1]

**3** 3 ½ **Cois Na Tine Eile** 2-8-9 .... NCallan 6 32
(KARyan) *w'like: s.i.s: hdwy 1/2-way: wnt 3rd 1f out: eased ins last* **12/1**



The Form Book, Raceform Ltd, Compton, RG20 6NL

50 **4** 1/2 **Bowland Bride (IRE)**[8] 1970 2-8-2 .................... PPMathers(7) 4 31
(ABerry) *sn chsng ldrs: kpt on fnl f* **40/1**
05 **5** 2 **Steal The Thunder**[20] 1658 2-9-0 .................... FLynch 5 30
(ABerry) *w ldrs on outer: edgd lft and fdd fnl 2f* **9/1**[3]
**6** 3/4 **Riverweld** 2-9-0 .................... NicolaTopper 2 27
(GMMoore) *chsd ldrs: reminder 1/2-way: one pce* **50/1**
**7** 4 **Sabo Prince** 2-9-0 .................... SCarson 11 15
(JMBradley) *s.i.s: bhd tl sme hdwy fnl 2f* **33/1**
0 **8** 9 **La Bella Rosa (IRE)**[8] 1961 2-8-2 .................... (v[1]) AReilly(7) 12 —
(JSWainwright) *chsd ldrs on wd outside: wknd over 2f out* **80/1**
**9** 2 1/2 **Lady Indiana (IRE)** 2-8-9 .................... RWinston 7 —
(JSWainwright) *s.i.s: a bhd* **14/1**
**10** 1 **Singhalongtasveer** 2-9-0 .................... JBramhill 10 —
(WStorey) *s.s: a bhd* **66/1**
00 **11** hd **Ryans Lil Ol Gal**[17] 1735 2-8-9 .................... JMcAuley 8 —
(ABCoogan) *in tch: lost pl over 2f out: sn bhd* **80/1**

1m 15.04s (2.14) **Going Correction** -0.05s/f (Good) **11** Ran SP% **110.9**
Speed ratings: **83,79,75,74,71 70,65,53,50,48 48**CSF £4.83 TOTE £4.10: £1.40, £1.10, £2.80; EX 6.00.Goldhill Prince was bought in for 3,600gns. Stan's Girl was claimed by Ian Wood for £6,000.
**Owner** Gold Hill Racing **Bred** N D Fisher **Trained** Sigwells, Somerset

**FOCUS**
A very moderate contest unlikely to yield many future winners and a modest time, even for a seller.

**NOTEBOOK**
**Goldhill Prince**, the most experienced in the field, saw the extra furlong out well enough but he has little in the way of scope and will probably need to stick to a modest level if he is to win again.
**Stan's Girl**, dropped into a seller for the first time, showed plenty of speed from the front but did not seem to enjoy the undulating track and faster ground.
**Cois Na Tine Eile**, a good-bodied half-sister to a couple of winners including Pix Me Up, showed a small amount of ability and is likely to turn out the best of these in the long run.
**Bowland Bride(IRE)**, unplaced in a couple of claimers, was up a furlong and did not fail through lack of stamina, but looks modest and is not progressing.
**Steal The Thunder** did not improve for the drop in grade or extra furlong.

## 2141 GIVING FOR SIGHT MAIDEN STKS 6f
**2:30** (2:33) (D ) 2-Y-O **£5,200** (£1,600; £800; £400) **Stalls** Low

Form RPR
**1** **Hearthstead Wings** 2-9-0 .................... JFanning 4 83+
(MJohnston) *rangy: scope: chsd ldrs: led over 1f out: edgd lft: wnt clr ins last: readily* **8/1**[3]
2 **2** 4 **Distinctly Game**[14] 1782 2-9-0 .................... NCallan 8 71
(KARyan) *ld tl over 1f out: styd on: no ch w wnr* **1/1**[1]
3 **3** 2 1/2 **Twice Nightly**[15] 1769 2-9-0 .................... TQuinn 1 64
(JDBethell) *neat: chsd ldrs: effrt over 2f out: kpt on same pce* **9/2**[2]
**4** hd **Dahteer (IRE)** 2-9-0 .................... CCatlin 11 63
(MRChannon) *w'like: chsd ldrs: effrt over 2f out: kpt on same pce* **11/1**
**5** 3 **Kilmovee** 2-8-9 .................... KDarley 6 49
(NTinkler) *cmpt: s.i.s: styd on fnl 2f: nvr nr ldrs* **12/1**
**6** 1 1/2 **Wolds Dancer** 2-8-6 .................... DAllan(3) 9 44
(TDEasterby) *lenghty: unf: s.i.s: hdwy and swtchd rt over 2f out: styd on fnl f* **16/1**
**7** 3 **Ellis Cave** 2-9-0 .................... RWinston 12 40+
(JJQuinn) *racd far side: hdwy to ld that gp after 2f: kpt on fnl 2f: no ch w stands' side* **16/1**
**8** 1 1/4 **Eskdale (IRE)** 2-8-11 .................... DNolan(3) 10 37
(RFFisher) *chsd ldrs: wknd over 2f out* **50/1**
**9** 3/4 **Dancing Deano (IRE)** 2-9-0 .................... VHalliday 13 34
(RMWhitaker) *s.i.s: swtchd lft after s: bhd tl kpt on fnl 2f* **66/1**
06 **10** 1 1/4 **Whistling Along**[16] 1751 2-9-0 .................... SCarson 5 31
(JMBradley) *rr-div: sme hdwy over 2f out: nvr on terms* **100/1**
0 **11** 8 **Metolica**[17] 1735 2-8-9 .................... RFitzpatrick 18 —
(CSmith) *racd far side: outpcd fr 1/2-way* **80/1**
0 **12** 1/2 **Timmy**[8] 1960 2-9-0 .................... GParkin 3 —
(MESowersby) *sn bhd* **50/1**
5 **13** shd **Northern Revoque (IRE)**[13] 1819 2-8-2 .................... PPMathers(7) 14 —
(ABerry) *chsd ldrs: lost pl over 2f out* **100/1**
**14** 1 1/4 **Frogs' Gift (IRE)** 2-8-9 .................... NicolaTopper 16 —
(GMMoore) *racd far side: led that gp 2f: swtchd lft and wandered: bhd fnl 2f* **66/1**
65 **15** shd **Lane Marshal**[18] 1709 2-8-9 .................... TEaves(5) 15 —
(MESowersby) *racd far side: bhd fr 1/2-way* **50/1**
05 **16** 9 **Aza Wish (IRE)**[11] 1882 2-8-9 .................... SRighton 17 —
(MsDeborahJEvans) *unruly in stalls: rrd s: swtchd lft after s: a last* **33/1**

1m 13.14s (0.24) **Going Correction** -0.05s/f (Good) **16** Ran SP% **122.1**
Speed ratings: **96,90,87,87,83 81,77,75,74,72 62,61,61,59,59 47**CSF £15.89 TOTE £9.00: £2.60, £1.10, £1.30; EX 16.20.
**Owner** Hearthstead Homes Ltd **Bred** M P B Bloodstock Ltd **Trained** Middleham Moor, N Yorks

**FOCUS**
A fair maiden for the track won by a potentially useful sort. The time was 1.9 seconds faster than the seller.

**NOTEBOOK**
**Hearthstead Wings**, a half-brother to a couple of winners out of a dam who won at Listed level and was placed in Group company, came away from his rivals to win in great style and it will be a surprise if he does not go on to much better things.
**Distinctly Game**, well backed to confirm the promise of his Hamilton debut over this extra furlong, probably did improve on that but was unfortunate to come up against a potentially useful prospect.
**Twice Nightly** ran another creditable race over this extra furlong and should be up to winning an ordinary maiden.
**Dahteer(IRE)**, out of a half-sister to the top-class middle-distance performer Morshdi, showed some encouragement on this debut especially as he was drawn out in no-man's land. Improvement can be expected.
**Kilmovee ◆**, sold for 25,000gns as a two-year-old, is out of a half-sister to Bannister. She took a while to realise what was required, but seemed to get the hang of things as the race progressed. Her yard do not have many debut winners, so this was encouraging for the future.

## 2142 MIDDLEHAM TRAINERS ASSOCIATION H'CAP 1m 2f
**3:00** (3:03) (D ) (0-85,84) 3-Y-0+ **£6,388** (£1,965; £982; £491) **Stalls** High

Form RPR
2460 **1** **Intricate Web (IRE)**[22] 1604 8-9-1 **74** .................... DAllan(3) 7 83
(EJAlston) *bhd: pushed along over 4f out: hdwy and n.m.r over 2f out: rdn and squeezed through on inner ent last: sn led and r.o* **20/1**
310- **2** 1/2 **Shamara (IRE)**[179] 6035 4-9-11 **81** .................... SSanders 17 89
(CFWall) *trckd ldrs: hdwy over 2f out: rdn to ld over 1f out: drvn and hdd ins last: kpt on* **7/1**[3]
10-0 **3** 1/2 **Stallone**[13] 1821 7-8-13 **72** .................... THamilton(3) 8 79
(NWilson) *behind: hdwy on inner over 2f out: swtchd lft ent last and fin wl* **50/1**
425- **4** nk **Nevada Desert (IRE)**[260] 4578 4-9-1 **71** .................... MHills 19 78
(RMWhitaker) *led: pushed along and hdd 4f out: led again and hung bdly lft 2f out: sn hdd and drvn: one pce ins last* **16/1**
03-0 **5** 3 1/2 **Leighton (IRE)**[36] 1321 4-9-10 **80** .................... (p) TQuinn 9 80
(JDBethell) *in tch gng wl: nt clr run over 2f out: swtchd lft and rdn over 1f out: sn drvn and one pce* **25/1**
34-2 **6** 1 **Petrula**[10] 1903 5-9-11 **81** .................... (b) NCallan 18 79
(KARyan) *in tch: hdwy 3f out: n.m.r over 2f out: sn rdn and no imp appr last* **9/2**[1]
5-00 **7** 3/4 **Takes Tutu (USA)**[15] 1773 5-9-6 **76** .................... DarrenWilliams 12 73
(KRBurke) *midfield: hdwy3f out: rdn and kpt on same pce fnl 2f* **28/1**
0-42 **8** hd **Grey Clouds**[16] 1752 4-8-13 **69** .................... KDarley 14 65
(TDEasterby) *trckd ldrs: hdwy to chal 4f out and ev ch tl rdn and wknd wl over 1f out* **13/2**[2]
01-0 **9** 1 **Anglo Saxon (USA)**[41] 1273 4-9-11 **84** .................... TPQueally(3) 15 78
(DRLoder) *in tch: hdwy 3f out: rdn along and no imp fnl 2f* **12/1**
0-00 **10** 3 **Everest (IRE)**[15] 1762 7-9-13 **83** .................... RWinston 20 72
(BEllison) *bhd tl sme late hdwy* **10/1**
50-6 **11** 3 **Low Cloud**[10] 1903 4-9-6 **76** .................... AlexGreaves 6 59
(DNicholls) *towards rr: hdwy on outer 3f out: sn rdn: edgd rt and wknd* **33/1**
-005 **12** 1/2 **Compton Dragon (USA)**[13] 1821 5-9-5 **75** .................... JFanning 10 57
(DNicholls) *nvr nr ldrs* **16/1**
-000 **13** 1 1/2 **Broadway Score (USA)**[13] 1821 6-9-5 **80** .................... PMulrennan(5) 2 59
(MWEasterby) *nvr a factor* **25/1**
0455 **14** 1 1/2 **Silvaline**[25] 1540 5-9-4 **74** .................... KFallon 13 50
(TKeddy) *in tch: hdwy to trck ldrs 4f out: effrt 2f out: sn rdn and btn* **9/2**[1]
50-0 **15** 3/4 **Movie King (IRE)**[9] 1928 5-8-12 **68** .................... JQuinn 1 43
(SGollings) *cl up: rdn along 4f out: sn wknd* **25/1**
0-00 **16** 4 **Island Light (USA)**[13] 1821 4-9-5 **80** .................... TEaves(5) 11 47
(MrsMReveley) *s.i.s and bhd: hdwy over 4f out: rdn along to chse ldrs 3f out: sn wknd* **50/1**
40-0 **17** 3/4 **Rifleman (IRE)**[46] 1199 4-9-8 **78** .................... GDuffield 4 44
(MrsADuffield) *a rr* **33/1**
160- **18** 1 1/4 **Bond May Day**[266] 4407 4-9-2 **72** .................... FLynch 16 35
(BSmart) *cl up: led 4f out: rdn and hdd 2f out: sn wknd* **25/1**
00 **19** dist **Arawan (IRE)**[13] 1821 4-9-7 **77** .................... DaleGibson 5 —
(MWEasterby) *a rr* **80/1**

2m 4.24s (-3.76) **Going Correction** -0.225s/f (Firm) **19** Ran SP% **125.4**
Speed ratings: **106,105,105,104,102 101,100,100,99,97 95,94,93,92,91 88,87,86,—**CSF £141.42 CT £6849.35 TOTE £26.10: £4.20, £2.60, £14.40, £4.00; EX 517.20.
**Owner** Morris, Oliver, Pierce **Bred** Moyglare Stud Farm Ltd **Trained** Longton, Lancs

**FOCUS**
A fair handicap run at a solid pace and although high numbers were favoured, the first and third were drawn low.

**NOTEBOOK**
**Intricate Web(IRE)** picked up strongly under pressure to score a first win on turf since October 2002. He won twice on the Fibresand during the winter, but his two efforts on turf prior to this were below par and this was a welcome return to form. No doubt he will face a rise in the weights for this, but it was a solid effort from his wide draw.
**Shamara(IRE)** held every chance inside the final furlong, but her lack of fitness told and she could only find the one pace under her big weight. This was a solid reappearance, she remains relatively unexposed and she deserves credit for this display.
**Stallone** put in a much improved effort from his single-figure stall and was finishing strongly late on. He can be considered slightly better than the bare form.
**Nevada Desert(IRE)**, off for 260 days previously, was given a positive ride from his decent draw and only found his lack of a recent run telling inside the final two furlongs. He hung when tired late on, but will improve physically for the outing and although he has only won once in 16 attempts, he can get closer next time.
**Leighton(IRE)** stepped up on his latest effort and appreciated this quicker ground. He seemed to concentrate better for the application of cheekpieces and did not have the luck in running on this occasion, but is the type who needs all to fall right in his races.
**Petrula** could not repeat the form that saw him finish second at Chester last time on this quicker ground, and failed to capitalise on his favoured high draw.
**Takes Tutu(USA)**
**Grey Clouds** found disappointingly little under pressure and ran below par.
**Silvaline** could never land a blow and ultimately proved disappointing. *Official explanation: jockey said the gelding slipped on the bend*
**Bond May Day** *Official explanation: jockey said the filly suffered interference in running*

## 2143 TOTEPLACEPOT FILLIES' RATED STKS (H'CAP) 6f
**3:30** (3:31) (C ) (0-95,90) 3-Y-0+ **£11,014** (£4,177; £2,088; £949) **Stalls** Low

Form RPR
463- **1** **Enchanted**[202] 5791 5-9-8 **88** .................... WRyan 3 97
(NACallaghan) *trckd ldrs stands side: hdwy over 2f out: qcknd to ld over 1f out: sn rdn and styd on strly* **8/1**[2]
01-5 **2** 2 1/2 **Enchantment**[14] 1797 3-8-4 **79** .................... CCatlin 5 81
(JMBradley) *cl up stands side: led 2f out: sn rdn: hdd over 1f out and nt qckn* **8/1**[2]
500- **3** hd **Bandit Queen**[196] 5888 4-9-5 **85** .................... PRobinson 12 86
(WJarvis) *cl up far side: rdn to ld far side gp over 1f out and ev ch tl rdn and nt qckn ins last* **22/1**
10-4 **4** 1 **Twice Upon A Time**[2] 2079 5-8-7 **73** .................... FLynch 8 71
(BSmart) *dwlt and swtchd to stands rail: bhd tl hdwy 2f out: sn rdn and kpt on ins last: nrst fin* **10/1**[3]
0300 **5** nk **Sierra Vista**[4] 2041 4-8-9 **78** .................... (p) LEnstone(3) 16 75
(DWBarker) *led far side gp: riddne along 2f out: hdd over 1f out and kpt on same pce* **8/1**[2]
22-0 **6** 1 **Dispol Katie**[15] 1774 3-8-8 **83** .................... KDarley 2 77
(TDBarron) *chsd ldrs stand side: rdn 2f out: kpt on same pce* **6/1**[1]
0-00 **6** dht **Gaelic Princess**[57] 1065 4-9-7 **87** .................... RWinston 14 81
(AGNewcombe) *chsd ldrs far side: rdn along 2f out: kpt on same pce* **16/1**
-552 **8** 1 **Simianna**[9] 1923 5-9-10 **90** .................... GDuffield 11 81
(ABerry) *in tch centre: rdn along 2f out: no imp appr last* **6/1**[1]
-000 **9** 5 **Safranine (IRE)**[82] 876 7-8-7 **73** oh3 .................... AnnStokell 6 49
(MissAStokell) *a rr* **33/1**
405- **10** 1/2 **Linden's Lady**[243] 4969 4-8-0 **73** oh1 .................... DFentiman(7) 15 48
(JRWeymes) *cl up far side: rdn alon g over 2f out: sn wknd* **33/1**
400- **11** nk **College Queen**[191] 5941 6-8-7 **73** oh6 .................... JQuinn 1 47
(SGollings) *overal ldr stands side: rdn along and hdd 2f out: sn wknd* **33/1**
-000 **12** 2 **Flashing Blade**[19] 1685 4-8-12 **78** .................... (t) SSanders 10 46
(BAMcmahon) *chsd ldrs stands side: rdn along 2f out sn wknd* **14/1**
0-40 **13** 3 1/2 **Consensus (IRE)**[8] 1956 5-8-13 **79** .................... TWilliams 13 36
(MBrittain) *swtchd to r stands side: c hased ldrs tl rdn and wknd 2f out* **8/1**[2]

1-00 **14** *1 ¾* **Riva Royale**[8] [1964] 4-9-1 **84** .......... TPQueally(3) 9 36
(IAWood) *chsd ldrs stands side: rdn along over 2f out: sn wknd* **20/1**
00-0 **15** *8* **Bollin Janet**[27] [1500] 4-8-8 **74** .......... (b1) KFallon 7 2
(TDEasterby) *in tch stands side: rdn along over 2f out and sn btn* **10/1**3
1m 11.44s (-1.46) **Going Correction** -0.05s/f (Good)
**WFA** 3 from 4yo+ 9lb **15** Ran SP% **121.7**
Speed ratings: **107,103,103,102,101 100,100,99,92,91 91,88,83,81,70**CSF £66.29 CT £1381.56 TOTE £10.60: £3.30, £2.40, £8.10; EX 28.70 Trifecta £1579.30 Part won. Pool: £2,224.48. 0.30 winning tickets..
**Owner** Norcroft Park Stud **Bred** Norcroft Park Stud, Miss J Nicholls And A J Hol **Trained** Newmarket, Suffolk
■ Stewards Enquiry : K Darley three-day ban: failed to ride out for sixth place outright (May 27-29)

**FOCUS**
A decent sprint which saw the field split into two groups and those on the stands' side emerged on top. The time was solid for the grade.

**NOTEBOOK**
**Enchanted ◆**, off for 202 days prior to this, showed a fair turn of foot to lead over a furlong from home and stayed on to win readily. She rather lost her form last year, but has dropped a bit in the weights and has obviously matured during the winter. She will come on again for the run and could be progressive.
**Enchantment** showed the benefit of her recent comeback outing and lost little in defeat. This was a fair effort against her elders and she can soon make amends, especially when reverting to the minimum trip.
**Bandit Queen** won the race on the far side and went down fighting. This was a pleasing effort after a her 196-day absence and she is one to keep an eye on for a similar event.
**Twice Upon A Time**, a trademark slow starter, again blew the break and stayed on all too late in the day. This was still a solid effort, as she had been beaten into fourth on her seasonal reappearance only two days previously.
**Sierra Vista** ran with credit on the far side and did improve on her latest effort just four days previously, but is a very difficult horse to catch right.
**Dispol Katie** could not find much under pressure when asked to quicken entering the final two furlongs. She will again come on physically for this outing and is not one to be writing off just yet.
**Simianna** was not aided by racing down the centre, but failed to run up to the form of her last outing at Chester. She is an inconsistent mare.

## 2144 TRUE TEMPER MAIDEN STKS (DIV I) 1m 1f
4:05 (4:06) (D) 3-Y-O £4,804 (£1,478; £739; £369) **Stalls** High

Form RPR
4-0 **1** **Aqualung**[19] [1683] 3-9-0 .......... MHills 13 90
(BWHills) *t.k.h in front: qcknd 3f out: styd on wl: unchal* **9/1**3
3 **2** *4* **Marbush (IRE)**[32] [1395] 3-9-0 .......... PRobinson 2 82
(MAJarvis) *lw: tk v t.k.h: trckd wnr: effrt over 2f out: hung rt over 1f out: no imp* **7/4**2
3-2 **3** *1 ¼* **Magnetic Pole**[19] [1683] 3-9-0 .......... KFallon 6 80
(SirMichaelStoute) *lw: trckd ldrs: effrt and clr 3rd 3f out: styd on same pce* **4/5**1
**4** *11* **Protective** 3-9-0 .......... MFenton 10 58
(JGGiven) *in tch: outpcd 3f out: kpt on fnl f* **66/1**
0-5 **5** *1* **Snowed Under**[24] [1557] 3-9-0 .......... CCatlin 8 56
(JDBethell) *in rr: effrt 4f out: kpt on fnl f* **66/1**
**6** *3* **Kalamansi (IRE)** 3-8-9 .......... SWKelly 4 45
(NACallaghan) *neat: bhd: sme hdwy 2f out: nvr a factor* **50/1**
000- **7** *5* **Quay Walloper**[232] [5221] 3-9-0 .......... DarrenWilliams 9 40
(JRNorton) *chsd ldrs: lost pl over 3f out* **100/1**
5 **8** *nk* **Blue Nun**[26] [1524] 3-8-9 .......... GDuffield 5 34
(MrsADuffield) *reminders after s: sn chsng ldrs: lost pl over 2f out* **125/1**
**9** *1 ½* **Belshazzar (USA)** 3-9-0 .......... DaleGibson 1 36
(TPTate) *unruly in stalls: s.i.s: a bhd* **100/1**
**10** *¾* **Dalmarnock (IRE)** 3-9-0 .......... FLynch 3 34
(BSmart) *mid-div: lost pl over 3f out* **100/1**
**11** *3 ½* **Tornado Bay (IRE)** 3-8-6 .......... TPQueally(3) 7 22
(IAWood) *s.s: bhd fnl 3f* **100/1**
60- **12** *dist* **Celtic Solitude (IRE)**[173] [6069] 3-8-9 .......... KDarley 12 —
(MrsMReveley) *bhd and pushed along 4f out: eased over 2f out: t.o* **100/1**
1m 51.54s (-2.31) **Going Correction** -0.225s/f (Firm) **12** Ran SP% **112.6**
Speed ratings: **101,97,96,86,85 83,78,78,76,76 73,**—CSF £24.28 TOTE £7.90: £3.70, £1.10, £1.02; EX 24.40.
**Owner** K Abdulla **Bred** Juddmonte Farms **Trained** Lambourn, Berks

**FOCUS**
With nine of the 12 runners starting at 50/1 or longer, this was not the most competitive of maidens and the front three in the market finished well clear of the others, but in the wrong order.

**NOTEBOOK**
**Aqualung** again made the running and took a good hold in front, but this track very much suits front runners and he never looked to be in much danger. He is improving, but these tactics may not always prove so effective elsewhere.
**Marbush(IRE)**, representing the form of the Wood Ditton which has yet to produce a subsequent winner, did not help his chances by taking far too keen a hold and could not stop the winner from running away from him. A strongly-run race should see him in a better light.
**Magnetic Pole** was rather disappointing and there seemed no obvious excuse. It may be he needs a much greater test of stamina and it will be interesting to see what handicap marks he gets.
**Protective**, a half-brother to five winners, was well beaten, but still did best of the newcomers and may be capable of improving on this.
**Snowed Under** looks a stayer and now qualifies for a handicap mark.
**Celtic Solitude(IRE)** *Official explanation: jockey said the filly lost her action*

## 2145 TRUE TEMPER MAIDEN STKS (DIV II) 1m 1f
4:35 (4:36) (D) 3-Y-O £4,795 (£1,475; £737; £368) **Stalls** High

Form RPR
3 **1** **Yaahomm**[30] [1442] 3-8-11 .......... TPQueally(3) 11 76
(DRLoder) *lw: wnt bdly lft s: sn cl up: effrt 2f out and sn rdn: drvn ins last and styd on to ld nr fin* **11/10**1
-322 **2** *nk* **My Paris**[15] [1771] 3-9-0 73 .......... NCallan 1 75
(KARyan) *mde most: rdn along 2f out: drvn and edgd rt and lft ins last: hdd and no ex nr fin* **7/2**2
**3** *7* **Always Waining (IRE)** 3-9-0 .......... JFanning 2 61
(MJohnston) *in tch on outer: hdwy 3f out: rdn along 2f out: kpt on same pce* **7/1**3
0-00 **4** *5* **Unprecedented (IRE)**[33] [1386] 3-9-0 50 .......... (v1) JQuinn 8 51
(TTClement) *chsd ldrs: rdn long 3f out: drvn and outpcd fnl 2f* **50/1**
0 **5** *5* **Jalousie Dream**[22] [1619] 3-8-9 .......... SWKelly 6 36
(GMMoore) *in tch: rdn along 4f out: outpcd fnl 3f* **100/1**
00- **6** *4* **Redmarley (IRE)**[192] [5934] 3-9-0 .......... MFenton 10 33
(JGGiven) *hmpd s: a towards rr* **20/1**
**7** *½* **Eagle Feathers** 3-8-6 .......... DAllan(3) 9 27
(TDEasterby) *hmpd s: a towards rr* **16/1**
**8** *nk* **Manhattan Jack** 3-9-0 .......... RWinston 3 31
(GASwinbank) *a rr* **25/1**
4-0 **9** *1 ¾* **Saharan Song (IRE)**[29] [1461] 3-8-9 .......... MHills 4 23
(BWHills) *chsd ldrs: rdn along over 3f out: sn wknd* **7/1**3
**10** *15* **Dont Tell Simon** 3-8-9 .......... TEaves(5) 12 —
(MESowersby) *s.i.s: bhd whn rn v wd home turn* **66/1**
03 **11** *7* **Clouds Of Gold (IRE)**[18] [1711] 3-8-9 .......... PMQuinn 5 —
(JSWainwright) *plld hrd: chsd ldrs tl rn v wd home turn and sn wl b ehind* **25/1**
0-0 **12** *23* **Mikes Mate**[15] [1771] 3-8-11 .......... DNolan(3) 7 —
(CJTeague) *s.i.s: a bhd: t.o* **150/1**
1m 54.39s (0.54) **Going Correction** -0.225s/f (Firm) **12** Ran SP% **118.3**
Speed ratings: **88,87,81,77,72 69,68,68,66,53 47,26**CSF £4.44 TOTE £2.10: £1.02, £1.50, £2.80; EX 5.00.
**Owner** Sheikh Ahmed Al Maktoum **Bred** Darley **Trained** Newmarket, Suffolk

**FOCUS**
A modest winning time, 2.85 seconds slower than the first division, and the first two pulled well clear at the finish.

**NOTEBOOK**
**Yaahomm**, who looked very fit in the preliminaries, made hard work of landing the spoils, but duly lost his maiden tag at the second attempt. This drop in trip was probably not ideal, but the quick ground suited and he had the best of the draw.
**My Paris** paid late on for using up plenty of energy in the early stages to get to the lead from his low draw and over this longer trip. He was clear of the rest and deserves to get his head in front, as he always gives his best.
**Always Waining(IRE)** made a satisfactory debut and was a clear third. Like most of his stable's debutants, he will come on considerably for this and improve with more racing.
**Unprecedented(IRE)** showed a bit more enthusiasm racing in the visor for the first time, but he looks only plating-class.
**Manhattan Jack** *Official explanation: jockey said the gelding slipped on the bend*
**Saharan Song(IRE)** ran a poor race and has now disappointed in two starts this term.
**Dont Tell Simon** *Official explanation: jockey said the gelding hung badly left handed on the bend leaving the back straight*
**Clouds Of Gold(IRE)** *Official explanation: jockey said the filly hung badly left handed on the bend turning into the straight*

## 2146 GARDEN RACECOURSE H'CAP 1m 4f 60y
5:05 (5:06) (E) (0-75,75) 3-Y-O £6,271 (£1,929; £964; £482) **Stalls** High

Form RPR
3362 **1** **Siegfrieds Night (IRE)**[13] [1823] 3-7-13 **58** .......... DFox(5) 12 66
(MCChapman) *trckd ldrs: styd on to ld 1f out: kpt on wl* **11/2**3
45-1 **2** *2* **Meadaaf (IRE)**[21] [1640] 3-9-7 **75** .......... KFallon 4 80
(ACStewart) *trckd ldrs: led 3f out: rdn and hung rt over 1f out: sn hdd and unable qckn* **7/2**2
00-5 **3** *2 ½* **Havetoavit (USA)**[15] [1770] 3-8-6 **60** .......... TQuinn 9 61
(JDBethell) *led: qcknd over 3f out: sn hdd: styd on same pce appr fnl f* **12/1**
0-02 **4** *1 ¾* **Romeo's Day**[2] [2092] 3-7-13 **53** ow1 .......... CCatlin 5 51
(MRChannon) *trckd ldrs: hung rt and outpcd over 2f out: styd on fnl f* **14/1**
4-22 **5** *1* **Gold Card**[9] [1933] 3-8-12 **66** .......... RWinston 3 63
(JRWeymes) *s.i.s: hdwy to chse ldrs 7f out: ev ch over 3f out: one pce fnl 2f* **14/1**
05-6 **6** *shd* **Alaloof (USA)**[19] [1688] 3-8-13 **67** .......... RHills 1 63
(JLDunlop) *hld up: hdwy to chse ldrs over 3f out: sn rdn: one pce* **10/3**1
3-02 **7** *2 ½* **Bargain Hunt (IRE)**[14] [1784] 3-7-12 **52** oh2 .......... JBramhill 13 44
(WStorey) *a chsng ldrs: one pce fnl 3f* **33/1**
-054 **8** *2 ½* **The King Of Rock**[24] [1559] 3-8-2 **56** .......... JQuinn 10 44
(AGNewcombe) *hld up in rr: hdwy on ins 3f out: sn rdn: nvr nr ldrs* **7/1**
0-06 **9** *4* **Northern Spirit**[9] [1947] 3-7-12 **52** oh2 .......... PFessey 6 34
(KARyan) *rr-div: drvn along 4f out: nvr on terms* **50/1**
50-0 **10** *1* **Classic Event (IRE)**[46] [1201] 3-8-9 **63** .......... KDarley 15 43
(TDEasterby) *s.s: sme hdwy on outside 4f out: nvr a factor* **10/1**
40-0 **11** *1 ¼* **Our Kid**[24] [1559] 3-8-5 **62** .......... (b1) DAllan(3) 2 40
(TDEasterby) *s.s: nvr on terms* **40/1**
-053 **12** *6* **Tancred Imp**[14] [1784] 3-7-12 **52** oh7 .......... RFfrench 8 21
(DWBarker) *prom: lost pl 3f out* **66/1**
60-0 **13** *3* **Desert Daisy (IRE)**[38] [1309] 3-8-5 **62** .......... TPQueally(3) 14 26
(IAWood) *chsd ldrs: wknd over 3f out: sn bhd* **50/1**
0-00 **14** *shd* **Calomeria**[30] [1440] 3-8-12 **66** .......... SSanders 7 30
(RMBeckett) *rn in snatches: mid-div: rdn and lost pl over 3f out* **50/1**
06-6 **15** *2 ½* **Canni Thinkaar (IRE)**[21] [1640] 3-8-13 **67** .......... NCallan 11 27
(PWHarris) *mid-div: drvn along 4f out: sn lost pl* **16/1**
2m 37.35s (-2.55) **Going Correction** -0.225s/f (Firm) **15** Ran SP% **121.9**
Speed ratings: **99,97,96,94,94 94,92,90,88,87 86,82,80,80,78**CSF £24.27 CT £229.60 TOTE £7.20: £1.80, £2.40, £2.90; EX 32.00 Place 6 £34.80, Place 5 £29.79.
**Owner** K D Blanch **Bred** Barronstown Stud And Orpendale **Trained** Market Rasen, Lincs

**FOCUS**
A competitive if modest handicap run at just a fair pace.

**NOTEBOOK**
**Siegfrieds Night(IRE)**, dropping back from 14 furlongs, showed a smart turn of foot to gain his first ever win on turf. He looks a natural middle-distance handicapper, so did remarkably well to win over six furlongs at the start of the year.
**Meadaaf(IRE)**, stepping up in trip, looked awkward in front in the latter stages and had the race snatched from him. He probably needs a flatter track.
**Havetoavit(USA)**, a maiden, did his best to steal this from the front and ran with credit, but this track's suitability to front-runners may flatter him somewhat.
**Romeo's Day**, beaten in a seller just two days earlier, was up in trip and ran as though he would get even further, but it will still be a poor race he gets off the mark in.
**Gold Card**, making his handicap debut after having been placed three times in maidens, did not achieve a lot and needs to drop a few pounds.
**Alaloof(USA)** did not improve for the step up in trip and was disappointing in view of her promising comeback. She may be worth one more chance on a more conventional track.
**Canni Thinkaar(IRE)** *Official explanation: jockey said the gelding lost his action*
T/Jkpt: Not won. T/Plt: £32.50 to a £1 stake. Pool: £51,679.70. 1,158.35 winning tickets. T/Qpdt: £32.70 to a £1 stake. Pool: £1,823.60. 41.20 winning tickets. WG

2147 - 2154a (Foreign Racing) - See Raceform Interactive

## 1776 CAPANNELLE (R-H)

Sunday, May 16

**OFFICIAL GOING: Good to soft**

### 2155a PREMIO PRESIDENTE DELLA REPUBBLICA SIS (GROUP 1) 1m 2f

4:55 (5:00) 4-Y-0+ £213,380 (£105,458; £60,915; £30,458)

| | | | RPR |
|---|---|---|---|
| 1 | | **Altieri**[182] 6008 6-9-2 ... MEsposito 6 *(VCaruso, Italy) held up, racing in 3rd, slightly hampered approaching final f, led inside final f, quickened clear, ridden out* | 117 |
| 2 | 3 | **Vespone (IRE)**[14] 1804 4-9-2 ... KMcEvoy 7 *(SaeedBinSuroor) led after 1f, set strong pace, hung sharply left approaching final f, ridden & ducked right inside final f, headed 150yds o* | 112 |
| 3 | 2 | **Nonno Carlo (IRE)**[357] 1857 4-9-2 ... MBelli 2 *(MGrassi, Italy) tracked leader, challenged 2f out, hanging left from over 1f out, one pace* | 109 |
| 4 | nk | **Le Vie Dei Colori**[21] 4-9-2 ... DVargiu 1 *(RBrogi, Italy) held up in 4th, kept on but never able to challenge* | 108 |
| 5 | 2 ½ | **Duca D'Atri (IRE)**[21] 5-9-2 ... (b) GBietolini 5 *(ARenzoni, Italy) last to straight, never a factor* | 104 |
| 6 | 3 | **Quel Del Giaz (IRE)**[182] 6008 5-9-2 ... MPasquale 4 *(FCamici, Italy) 6th straight, no headway* | 99 |
| 7 | 2 | **Blu For Life (IRE)**[182] 6008 7-9-2 ... MMimmocchi 3 *(RMimmocchi, Italy) 5th straight, beaten 2f out* | 95 |

1m 58.7s 7 Ran

Speed ratings:

**Owner** Scuderia Incolinx **Bred** Azienda Agricola Loreto Luciani **Trained** Italy

**NOTEBOOK**

**Altieri** is a ten-furlong specialist and improved upon his solid third behind Rakti in this race last year. Hitting the front a furlong out, he clocked a quick time and his future targets include the Eclipse Stakes, in which his trainer saddled Misil to be touched off by Opera House in 1993.

**Vespone(IRE)** went off at a good pace, but did himself no favours in hanging all over the place when getting tired with a furlong to run. This obviously did not help his cause, but whether he would have beat the cosy winner is open to question.

## KRANJI (L-H)

Sunday, May 16

**OFFICIAL GOING: Good**

### 2156a SINGAPORE AIRLINES INTERNATIONAL CUP (GROUP 1) 1m 2f

1:30 (1:31) 3-Y-0+ £523,026 (£197,368; £98,684; £49,342)

| | | | | RPR |
|---|---|---|---|---|
| 1 | | **Epalo (GER)**[246] 5-9-0 ... AStarke 16 *(ASchutz, Germany) led after 1f, quickened entering straight, ridden clear over 1f out, unchallenged* | 64/10[3] | 120 |
| 2 | 5 | **Surveyor (SAF)**[50] 1146 4-9-0 ... (b) BVorster 5 *(MFDeKock, South Africa) raced in 2nd, 4th and soon ridden straight, stayed on to take 2nd from over 1f out* | 126/10 | 111 |
| 3 | ¾ | **Bowman's Crossing (IRE)**[21] 1657 5-9-0 ... MJKinane 13 *(DOughton, Hong Kong) mid-division towards outside, 8th straight, ridden and ran on from 1 1/2f out to take 3rd inside final furlong* | 54/10[2] | 110 |
| 4 | 2 ½ | **Ain't Here (AUS)**[21] 1657 4-9-0 ... GMosse 4 *(DHayes, Hong Kong) held up, finished strongly from over 1f out to take 4th on line* | 23/1 | 105 |
| 5 | shd | **Moon Shadow (AUS)**[436] 6-9-0 ... CraigCarmody 2 *(DBaertschiger, Singapore) mid-division, 6th and ridden straight, stayed on under pressure to take 4th inside final furlong til lost place on line* | 30/1 | 105 |
| 6 | nk | **Imperial Dancer**[29] 1455 6-9-0 ... TEDurcan 9 *(MRChannon) towards rear, pushed along approaching straight, carried slightly wide entering straight, effort 2f out, stayed on closing* | 3/1[1] | 105 |
| 7 | 1 | **Sarrasin (FR)**[71] 980 5-9-0 ... MBlancpain 7 *(CLaffon-Parias, France) close 3rd, pushed along and 2nd on rail straight, ridden 2f out, one pace and lost 2nd over 1f out* | 25/1 | 103 |
| 8 | ¾ | **Superior Star (AUS)**[155] 4-8-11 ... JLTaylor 8 *(LLaxon, Singapore) behind, some late headway but never dangerous* | 21/1 | 99 |
| 9 | nk | **Gruntled**[210] 5670 5-9-0 ... DBeadman 6 *(JEHammond, France) towards rear, ridden & stayed on from 1 1/2f out* | 126/10 | 101 |
| 10 | 4 | **Lord Of The Pines (AUS)**[1233] 9-9-0 ... KBSoo 3 *(JMeagher, Singapore) mid-division, 5th straight, soon driven and beaten* | 50/1 | 94 |
| 11 | nk | **Paolini (GER)**[21] 1657 7-9-0 ... EPedroza 10 *(AWohler, Germany) mid-division, 7th and ridden in centre straight, ran on til weakened 1f out* | 96/10 | 94 |
| 12 | hd | **Blizz Bless (ARG)**[414] 862 7-9-0 ... JGeroudis 11 *(PShaw, Singapore) in touch til ridden and one pace from approaching straight* | 66/1 | 93 |
| 13 | 1 ½ | **Exaggerate (NZ)** 5-9-0 ... (b) JPatton 1 *(JMeagher, Singapore) towards rear, pushed along entering straight, never dangerous* | 116/10 | 91 |
| 14 | ½ | **Physique (AUS)**[69] 5-9-0 ... (b) NRawiller 15 *(LTreloar, Australia)* | 116/10 | 90 |
| 15 | dist | **Muscle Man (NZ)** 5-9-0 ... JSaimee 12 *(CLeck, Singapore) towards rear, beaten approaching straight* | 154/10 | — |
| P | | **Confluence (NZ)**[436] 8-8-11 ... OChavez 14 *(FNathan, Malaysia) behind, last half-way, pulled up* | 166/10 | — |

2m 2.60s 16 Ran SP% 125.2

Speed ratings: .

**Owner** Gary A Tanaka **Bred** *unknown **Trained** Germany

**NOTEBOOK**

**Epalo(GER)** ran out a most impressive winner of this valuable contest, coming away to win by a cosy five lengths. He is a consistent performer, sure to score more success in this sort of company, and the Arlington Million is his main target.

**Imperial Dancer** struggled to go the early pace and was carried wide turning into the straight. He seems to lack the pace for this sort of test these days and is better at farther.

## 1802 COLOGNE (R-H)

Sunday, May 16

**OFFICIAL GOING: Good**

### 2157a SCHWARZGOLD-RENNEN (DIANA-TRIAL - DEUTSCHER STUTEN-PREIS) (GROUP 3) 1m 3f

3:05 (3:15) 3-Y-0 £22,535 (£7,042; £3,521; £2,113)

| | | | RPR |
|---|---|---|---|
| 1 | | **Amarette (GER)** 3-9-0 ... ASuborics 2 *(ASchutz, Germany) in touch, 4th and shaken up straight, ran on in centre to challenge over 1 1/2f out, stayed on to lead 100 yards out, pushe* | 98 |
| 2 | 1 ¾ | **Saldentigerin (GER)**[217] 5531 3-9-0 ... FilipMinarik 11 *(PSchiergen, Germany) soon clear leader, pushed along over 2f out, ran on til headed 100 yards out* 1 | 95 |
| 3 | 1 ¾ | **Vallera (GER)**[226] 5353 3-9-0 ... ABoschert 1 *(UOstmann, Germany) raced in 3rd, stayed on steadily under pressure from over 1 1/2f out* 2 | 92 |
| 4 | 3 ½ | **Sword Roche (GER)** 3-9-0 ... J-PCarvalho 6 *(MarioHofer, Germany) towards rear, stayed on strongly from over 2f out to take 4th inside final furlong* | 86 |
| 5 | 2 ½ | **Iduna (GER)** 3-9-0 ... NRichter 10 *(WHickst, Germany) raced in 2nd, pushed along over 2f out, ridden 1 1/2f out, one pace* | 82 |
| 6 | 1 | **Top Call (GER)** 3-9-0 ... THellier 5 *(ASchutz, Germany) behind, 10th straight, some late headway but never dangerous* | 80 |
| 7 | shd | **Estefania (GER)**[34] 3-9-0 ... AHelfenbein 9 *(PRau, Germany) mid-division, never a factor* | 80 |
| 8 | 2 ½ | **Dalicia (GER)** 3-9-0 ... ADeVries 3 *(PRau, Germany) mid-division, never threatened* | 76 |
| 9 | 4 | **Ustilla (GER)** 3-9-0 ... WMongil 7 *(HBlume, Germany) raced in 4th, 5th straight, one pace from 2f out* 3 | 70 |
| 10 | 3 | **Song Of Night (GER)**[191] 3-9-0 ... LHammer-Hansen 8 *(HSteinmetz, Germany) mid-division, effort over 2f out, never a threat* | 65 |
| 11 | 14 | **Wellvita (GER)**[226] 5353 3-9-0 ... FJohansson 4 *(WidoNeuroth, Norway) behind, effort over 3f out, never dangerous* | 42 |

2m 17.19s 11 Ran SP% 133.0

Speed ratings: .

**Owner** Gestut Schlenderhan **Bred** Gestut Schlenderhan **Trained** Germany

### 2158a MEHL-MULHENS-RENNEN (GROUP 2) (C&F) 1m

4:10 (4:25) 3-Y-0 £70,423 (£26,761; £12,676; £6,338)

| | | | RPR |
|---|---|---|---|
| 1 | | **Brunel (IRE)**[32] 1396 3-9-2 ... DHolland 8 *(WJHaggas) made all, moved to middle entering straight, ran on well, cleverly* 1 | 115 |
| 2 | ½ | **Lazio (GER)**[267] 3-9-2 ... ADeVries 5 *(ATrybuhl, Germany) always prominent, 3rd straight, ran on under pressure to take 2nd last strides* | 114 |
| 3 | hd | **Assiun (GER)**[28] 3-9-2 ... ASuborics 4 *(PSchiergen, Germany) raced in 3rd, went 2nd entering straight, hard ridden & every chance 1f out, lost 2nd last strides* 2 | 114 |
| 4 | 2 | **Pepperstorm (GER)**[210] 5660 3-9-2 ... ABoschert 3 *(UOstmann, Germany) mid-division, 6th straight, stayed on to take 4th close home* 3 | 109 |
| 5 | ½ | **Omikron (IRE)**[28] 3-9-2 ... J-PCarvalho 10 *(MarioHofer, Germany) dwelt, 7th straight, some headway 2f out, never near to challenge* | 108 |
| 6 | ½ | **Bischoff's Boy (GER)**[28] 3-9-2 ... J-LSilverio 6 *(NSauer, Germany) tracked leader, 3rd straight, remained alone on far rail, weakened over 1f out* | 107 |
| 7 | ½ | **Matrix (GER)**[225] 3-9-2 ... IFerguson 2 *(WBaltromei, Germany) hampered on turn over 3f out, 8th straight, always behind* | 106 |
| 8 | nk | **Mokabra (IRE)**[13] 1847 3-9-2 ... ACulhane 1 *(MRChannon) held up, 5th on inside straight, soon beaten* | 105 |
| 9 | 15 | **Vicomte (GER)** 3-9-2 ... WMongil 9 *(MTrybuhl) last and ran wide straight, soon well behind* | 70 |

1m 36.3s 9 Ran SP% 131.0

Speed ratings: .

**Owner** Highclere Thoroughbred Racing X **Bred** Philip Brady **Trained** Newmarket, Suffolk

**NOTEBOOK**

**Brunel(IRE)**, whose rider set a pace to suit himself, made every yard for a comfortable success. His trainer considers the colt as good as his 2002 winner of this race Dupont, and a tilt at the St James's Palace Stakes is now on the cards.

**Mokabra(IRE)** looks like he is going to be difficult to place this term.

## 2072 LONGCHAMP (R-H)

Sunday, May 16

**OFFICIAL GOING: Good to firm**

### 2159a PRIX LUPIN (GROUP 1) (3YO COLTS & FILLIES) 1m 2f 110y

2:15 (2:15) 3-Y-0 £80,479 (£32,197; £16,099; £8,042)

| | | | | RPR |
|---|---|---|---|---|
| 1 | | **Voix Du Nord (FR)**[35] 1350 3-9-2 ... DBoeuf 5 *(DSmaga, France) held up last to straight but always close up, driven to challenge distance, narrow lead 150y to 100y out, led line, all out* | 15/8[2] | 115 |
| 2 | nse | **Millemix (FR)**[21] 1654 3-9-2 ... C-PLemaire 2 *(MmeCHead-Maarek, France) held up in close 4th to straight, led just over 1 1/2f out to 150y out, slight lead under pressure from 100y out, caught on* | 13/8[1] | 115 |
| 3 | 2 | **Valixir (IRE)**[26] 1536 3-9-2 ... GaryStevens 3 *(AFabre, France) tracked leader from 6f out, led 2f out to just over 1 1/2f out, no extra from distance* | 5/2[3] | 112 |
| 4 | 6 | **Esperanto (IRE)**[21] 1654 3-9-2 ... (b) JPSpencer 1 *(APO'Brien, Ire) led 2f, 3rd straight, bumped by leader well over 2f out, ridden & found little 2f out, eased when beaten* | 10/1 | 101 |

5 *15* **Alcinos (FR)**[35] 1350 3-9-2 (b) SPasquier 4 76
(DSmaga, France) *led after 2f with rider continually looking over his shoulder, quickened well over 3f out, headed and weakened 2f out* **100/1**

2m 8.50s **Going Correction** -0.35s/f (Firm) **5** Ran SP% **111.5**
Speed ratings: **110,109,108,104,93.**
**Owner** Baron T Van Zuylen De Nyevelt **Bred** Baron Thierry Van Zuylen De Nyevelt **Trained** France

**NOTEBOOK**
**Voix Du Nord(FR)**, dropped out early on, joined battle with the runner-up inside the final furlong. It was anybody's guess but the colt just had his nose in front at the right time. Considering the setback he had after the Noailles, it was a major training feat to bring him back to win a Group One event in such a short time. Some improvement must be expected after this outing and he now goes for the Prix du Jockey-Club.
**Millemix(FR)**, who looked extremely well beforehand, was probably just ahead a stride before the post and a stride after but not at the crucial moment. It was a two-horse race from one out and he lost nothing in defeat, and connections plan to take on the winner again in the Jockey-Club.
**Valixir(IRE)** ran very free early on. He held the lead for a short time early in the straight but did not go through with his effort, his rider later expressing the view that the ground was a disadvantage.
**Esperanto(IRE)** wore blinkers for the first time but they did not do much good. He was always well up, but was a beaten force early in the straight and the ground again could have been the reason for this disappointing run.

## 2160a GAINSBOROUGH POULE D'ESSAI DES POULICHES (GROUP 1) (FILLIES) 1m

**2:50** (2:49) 3-Y-O **£140,838** (£56,345; £28,173; £14,074)

RPR

1 **Torrestrella (IRE)**[35] 1349 3-9-0 OPeslier 5 115
(FRohaut, France) *tracked leader til led just over 2f out, driven out* **12/1**

2 *1 1/2* **Grey Lilas (IRE)**[21] 1652 3-9-0 GaryStevens 1 111
(AFabre, France) *raced in 3rd to straight, ridden & every chance 1 1/2f out, no extra inside final f* **9/4**[1]

3 *2* **Miss Mambo (USA)**[20] 3-9-0 CSoumillon 13 107
(ELibaud, France) *always in touch, close 8th straight on outside, stayed on to take 3rd close home* **6/1**[3]

4 *nk* **Via Milano (FR)**[21] 1652 3-9-0 TThulliez 11 107
(MmeJLaurent-JoyeRossi, France) *mid-division, 7th straight, headway over 2f out, 3rd 1f out, no extra close home* **25/1**

5 *snk* **Nyramba**[29] 1458 3-9-0 IMendizabal 4 106
(JHMGosden) *always in touch, 6th straight, disputed 4th 2f out, ran on same pace under pressure* **10/1**

6 *shd* **Cairns (UAE)**[14] 1791 3-9-0 TGillet 12 106
(SaeedBinSuroor) *last to 2f out, good headway final 1 1/2f, finished well* **16/1**

7 *hd* **Dalna (FR)**[21] 1652 3-9-0 C-PLemaire 10 106
(MmeCHead-Maarek, France) *held up, 10th straight, headway on outside from 2f out, ran on under pressure, nearest at finish* **16/1**

8 *1 1/2* **Cattiva Generosa**[20] 3-9-0 TJarnet 3 102
(RGibson, France) *tracked leaders, 4th straight, one pace final 1 1/2f* **40/1**

9 *1* **Carry On Katie (USA)**[14] 1791 3-9-0 LDettori 2 100
(SaeedBinSuroor) *led to just over 2f out, weakened final f* **7/2**[2]

10 *nk* **Rumba Loca (IRE)**[15] 1778 3-9-0 MDemuro 9 100
(BGrizzetti, Italy) *12th straight, never a factor* **14/1**

11 *nk* **Tulipe Royale (FR)**[20] 3-9-0 ELegrix 8 99
(MmeNRossio, France) *9th straight, effort under pressure 2f out, soon one pace* **40/1**

12 *2* **Grandes Illusions (FR)**[21] 1652 3-9-0 DBoeuf 6 95
(DSmaga, France) *prominent, 5th on inside straight, weakened over 1f out* **25/1**

13 *1 1/2* **Royal Tigress (USA)**[28] 1485 3-9-0 JPSpencer 7 92
(APO'Brien, Ire) *held up in rear, 11th straight, ridden 2f out, soon beaten* **10/1**

1m 35.7s **Going Correction** -0.35s/f (Firm) **13** Ran SP% **124.2**
Speed ratings: **115,113,111,111,111 110,110,109,108,107 107,105,104.**
**Owner** B Bargues **Bred** Francois Montauban **Trained** France

**NOTEBOOK**
**Torrestrella(IRE)** was given an enterprising ride by her jockey, who ensured she was smartly away and settled in second place in a race that went at a fair pace from the start. She kicked on early in the straight and then joined battle with the runner-up, who was dominated inside the final furlong. Wisely supplemented into this Classic, she will now go on to the Prix de Diane.
**Grey Lilas(IRE)**, who was also smartly away, joined the eventual winner a furlong and a half out but was one-paced as the race came to an end. Connections felt she did not stretch out on the firmish ground. She is in the Coronation Stakes at Ascot but could go instead for the Prix de Sandringham.
**Miss Mambo(USA)** broke well from her outside draw and settled in behind the leading group. She appeared a little outpaced early in the straight but ran on again close home. The effort of ensuring a good position soon after the start might have played a role and the draw was blamed for her defeat. This was a decent performance but she is still not a Group winner so there are many options still open.
**Via Milano(FR)** was not really seen until the latter part of this fastly-run Classic. She quickened well from a furlong and a half out and only missed third place by a neck. The Sandringham is also on the cards for her.
**Nyramba** put up a good performance. She raced in mid-division for much of the event and stayed on well throughout the final stages.
**Cairns(UAE)**, held up in last, still had an enormous task on her hands at the entrance to the straight. From 300 yards out, though, she began to quicken, and finished best of all. Had she been put into the race earlier she might well have finished in the frame. This performance augurs well for the future.
**Carry On Katie(USA)** was smartly into her stride and soon taking the field along at a proper gallop. She kept the advantage until early in the straight and then dropped out of contention. Her rider reported that the filly ran a bit flat.

## 2161a GAINSBOROUGH POULE D'ESSAI DES POULAINS (GROUP 1) (COLTS) 1m

**3:30** (3:29) 3-Y-O **£140,838** (£56,345; £28,173; £14,074)

RPR

1 **American Post**[21] 1653 3-9-2 RHughes 4 113+
(MmeCHead-Maarek, France) *raced in 3rd to straight, ridden & every chance inside final f, left in front 50y out, driven out* **4/11**[1]

2 *1/2* **Diamond Green (FR)**[21] 1653 3-9-2 GaryStevens 6 112+
(AFabre, France) *hld up in 6th to str, got through on rail 1 1/2f out, ev ch whn slightly hmpd ins fnl f, rallied cl hme* **6/1**[2]

3 *nk* **Byron**[240] 5038 3-9-2 LDettori 2 111
(SaeedBinSuroor) *first to show, tracked leader to straight, led well over 1f out to inside final f, ran on* **8/1**[3]

4 *1/2* **Ershaad (USA)**[35] 3-9-2 TGillet 7 110
(JEHammond, France) *held up in rear to straight, headway from over 1f out, finished well* **33/1**

5 *nk* **Antonius Pius (USA)**[21] 1653 3-9-2 JPSpencer 3 119+
(APO'Brien, Ire) *5th str, 6th & looking for room fr 2f out, fnd gap dist, led ins fnl f, went sharply rt & hit rails 75y out, not recover* **9/1**

6 *1 1/2* **Newton (IRE)**[13] 1847 3-9-2 (b) PJScallan 1 106
(APO'Brien, Ire) *led to well over 1f out* **50/1**

7 *2 1/2* **Sunday Doubt (USA)**[21] 3-9-2 OPeslier 5 100
(MmeCHead-Maarek, France) *restrained start, soon racing in 4th, beaten over 1f out* **33/1**

1m 36.5s **Going Correction** -0.35s/f (Firm) **7** Ran SP% **116.6**
Speed ratings: **111,110,110,109,109 107,105.**
**Owner** K Abdulla **Bred** Juddmonte Farms **Trained** France
■ Stewards Enquiry : J P Spencer six-day ban (May 25-30)

**NOTEBOOK**
**American Post** was never far from the lead on the outside. He made a forward move early in the straight to lead one out, but could do nothing when Antonius Pius burst through at the furlong pole and would have been well held had that rival not thrown the race away. Connections felt the ground was on the lively side for him. A tilt at the Vodafone Derby has been put on hold and he definitely appears to need some cut in the ground.
**Diamond Green(FR)** was again unlucky. He raced in sixth position on the rail in the early stages and made a forward move one and a half furlongs out, but was then seriously hampered well inside the final furlong. He still managed to finish second and a tilt at the St James' Palace Stakes at Ascot has not been ruled out.
**Byron**, always close up, joined battle with American Post at the furlong and a half marker and was staying on when hampered towards the end.
**Ershaad(USA)** raced in last position and then made up a considerable amount of ground inside the last furlong and a half. He might have finished even closer if brought with a run up the centre of the track and is certainly one to follow in the future.
**Antonius Pius(USA)** had this race at his mercy having quickened impressively to lead at the furlong marker, but some 60 yards from the post he veered violently to the right and hit the running rail, at the same time interfering with Diamond Green and Byron. He eventually finished fifth and the Stewards suspended Jamie Spencer for six days for not doing his utmost to keep the colt straight.

## 2162a PRIX DE SAINT-GEORGES (GROUP 3) 5f (S)

**4:00** (4:07) 3-Y-O+ **£25,704** (£10,282; £7,711; £5,141)

RPR

1 **The Trader (IRE)**[154] 6186 6-9-2 (b) JPSpencer 5 118
(MBlanshard) *slowly into stride, headway from halfway, led inside final f, ran on well* 3

2 *2* **The Tatling (IRE)**[154] 6186 7-9-7 LDettori 3 116
(JMBradley) *soon close up on rails, led well over 1f out to inside final f, ran on one pace*

3 *1 1/2* **Patavellian (IRE)**[224] 5402 6-9-11 (b) SDrowne 1 114
(RCharlton) *led rails group, overall leader over 2f out, headed well over 1f out, one pace* 1

4 *1* **Chineur (FR)**[16] 1756 3-8-8 ELegrix 8 102
(MDelzangles, France) *tracked leaders on outside, kept on same pace final 1 1/2f*

5 *snk* **Rue La Fayette (SWE)**[20] 1682 4-8-11 TGillet 10 96
(FReuterskiold, Sweden) *walked to start, always prominent on outside, every chance well over 1f out, one pace*

6 *1* **Dobby Road (FR)**[20] 1682 5-9-0 IMendizabal 4 96
(MlleVDissaux, France) *always in touch, one pace final 2f*

7 *nk* **Much Faster (IRE)**[227] 5332 3-8-12 TThulliez 2 101
(PBary, France) *raced on rails, never able to challenge* 2

8 *snk* **Melkior (FR)**[20] 1682 7-9-2 C-PLemaire 12 96
(TLallie, France) *outpaced til staying on final 2f, never nearer*

9 *shd* **Meliksah (IRE)**[20] 1682 10-9-0 CSoumillon 7 94
(WBaltromei, Germany) *always outpaced*

10 *3* **Sweet Salsa (FR)**[16] 1756 3-8-3 DBonilla 9 80
(YDeNicolay, France) *burst out of stalls, delaying start, slowly into stride, always outpaced*

11 *1 1/2* **Swedish Shave (FR)**[20] 1682 6-9-7 TJarnet 6 84
(RGibson, France) *chased leaders 3f*

12 *3* **St Paul House**[357] 1855 6-9-0 PAragoni 11 67
(OCamuffo, Italy) *led to over 2f out, weakened quickly well over 1f out*

56.80 secs **Going Correction** -0.15s/f (Firm)
**WFA** 3 from 4yo+ 8lb **12** Ran SP% **124.5**
Speed ratings: **113,109,107,105,105 103,103,103,103,98 95,91.**
**Owner** Mrs C J Ward **Bred** Lady Bland **Trained** Upper Lambourn, Berks

**NOTEBOOK**
**The Trader(IRE)**, behind early, was brought with a perfectly timed late run from halfway. He quickened from one out and went on to win in good style with something in hand. He will probably come back for the Prix du Gros-Chene at Chantilly.
**The Tatling(IRE)**, in mid-division early, he made a forward move one and a half out and led at the furlong marker. He was then unable to hold off the winner's late run, but was conceding four and a half pounds.
**Patavellian(IRE)** raced just behind the leading group early on. He had a slight lead 300 yards out and then stayed on at the same pace. He now goes to Royal Ascot for one of the big sprints, but the main target is another crack at the Abbaye. He was conceding 9lb to the winner and was beaten three and a half lengths, so it was a pretty fine effort.
**Chineur(FR)** was well away and raced just behind the leaders early on. He made his effort from two out, but could not quicken with the front three.

# MIJAS (L-H)

Sunday, May 16

**OFFICIAL GOING: Standard**

## 2163a GRAN PREMIO DE ANDALUCIA - MIJAS CUP (ALL-WEATHER) 1m 4f

**1:15** (12:00) 4-Y-O+ **£35,915** (£14,366; £7,183; £3,592)

RPR

1 **Adopted Hero (IRE)**[45] 5386 4-9-0 SWhitworth 14 —
(GLMoore) *in touch and always going well, smooth headway to lead 3f out, easily 17-10F*

2 *3 3/4* **Luth High (FR)**[154] 4-9-0 JCJarcovsky 6 —
(FBedouret, Spain) *finished 3rd, placed 2nd*

3 *7 1/2* **Oceaninternational (USA)** 4-9-0 JohnFortune 16 —
(PHaley, Spain) *finished 2nd, placed 3rd*

4 *3/4* **Lake Lover (ARG)** 4-8-11 JEJarcovsky 11 —
(PDiaz, Spain)

5 nk **Red-Bull (SPA)**[189] 8-9-0 .......... RDosRamos 9 —
(ORodriguez, Spain)
6 3 1/2 **Bawsian**[736] 1346 9-9-0 .......... JDekeyser 13 —
(JLEyre, Spain)
7 2 1/4 **Mejhar (IRE)**[323] 2809 4-9-0 .......... ACreighton 18 —
(EJCreighton, Spain)
8 **Mister Quicksand (USA)**[28] 5-9-0 .......... AMackay 5 —
(JBrown, New Zealand)
9 **Turturilla (IRE)**[728] 1531 5-8-10 .......... FGonzalez 7 —
(RMartin, Spain)
10 **Strasbourg (USA)**[154] 7-9-0 .......... JMSanchez 3 —
(JMSanchez, Spain)
11 **Mortadelo (IRE)**[175] 5-9-0 .......... JCLopera 8 —
(EJCreighton, Spain)
12 **Alisar (IRE)**[354] 1933 4-9-0 .......... MrSCreighton 2 —
(EJCreighton, Spain)
13 **Mr Fast (ARG)** 7-9-0 .......... DeanMcKeown 17 —
(PHaley, Spain)
14 **Whitcomb (USA)**[28] 4-9-0 .......... JMackay 20 —
(JBrown, New Zealand)
15 **Hathaal (IRE)**[28] 5-9-0 .......... ECreighton 19 —
(EJCreighton, Spain)
16 **Denominado (ARG)**[28] 5-9-0 .......... DDelgado 12 —
(GBindella, Spain)
17 **Anbari**[525] 7-9-0 .......... PFredericks 15 —
(CBjorling, Sweden)
18 **Quirinale (USA)**[229] 4-9-0 .......... FJiminez 4 —
(EOlgado-Guillen, Spain)

2m 38.13s **18** Ran
Speed ratings: .
**Owner** N J Jones, Phil Collins **Bred** Swettenham Stud **Trained** Woodingdean, E Sussex

**NOTEBOOK**
**Adopted Hero(IRE)** travelled sweetly throughout and, hitting the front with three furlongs to run, won as he pleased.

# 1853 BATH (L-H)
## Monday, May 17
**OFFICIAL GOING: Good to firm (firm in places)**

## 2164 BATH ALES HOP POLE EBF NOVICE STKS 5f 11y
**2:10** (2:11) (D) 2-Y-O **£4,104** (£1,263; £631; £315) **Stalls** Low

Form RPR
1 **Russian General (IRE)** 2-8-12 .......... TQuinn 5 51+
(PFICole) *w ldr tl slt advantage 3f out: rdn 2f out: hung lft u.p appr fnl f: pushed out cl home* **4/11**[1]
2 1 1/2 **Dreamer's Lass** 2-8-7 .......... SCarson 8 40
(JMBradley) *in tch: rdn and outpcd over 2f out: rallied and styd on fnl f to take 2nd last stride: no imp on wnr* **14/1**
6 3 nk **Troublesome Gerri**[13] 1853 2-8-4 .......... LPKeniry(3) 2 39
(SCBurrough) *led tl narrowly hdd 3f out: styd pressing wnr and stl ev ch over 1f out: outpcd ins last and lost 2nd last strides* **25/1**
0 4 2 **Make It Happen Now**[13] 1853 2-8-7 .......... EAhern 6 31
(SCBurrough) *chsd ldrs: rdn: hung lft and wknd fnl f* **20/1**
5 2 **Dorn Hill** 2-8-8 ow1 .......... VSlattery 3 24
(MrsMaryHambro) *v.s.a: v green: 12 l bhd 3f out: styd on fr over 1f out: nt rch ldrs* **10/1**[2]
6 6 **Dominer (IRE)** 2-8-12 .......... CCatlin 7 —
(JMBradley) *in tch: hung rt and wknd over 2f out* **11/1**[3]

65.47 secs (2.97) **Going Correction** 0.0s/f (Good) **6** Ran SP% **106.0**
Speed ratings: **76,73,73,69,66 57**CSF £5.50 TOTE £1.30: £1.10, £2.40; EX 5.50.
**Owner** The Blandford Partnership **Bred** Redmondstown Stud **Trained** Whatcombe, Oxon

**FOCUS**
A race weakened significantly after the withdrawal of the likely market leaders Tournedos and Canton and the winning time was pedestrian.

**NOTEBOOK**
**Russian General(IRE)**, a 55,000euros purchase, is a half-brother to an eight-furlong winner out of a five- to seven-furlong two-year-old winner, was not very impressive in beating an ordinary bunch and could struggle to follow up.
**Dreamer's Lass**, a half-sister to three two-year-old winners, out of a six-furlong juvenile scorer, took an age to pick up and never really looked like getting to the winner.
**Troublesome Gerri** offered encouragement over this course and distance on her debut and again ran with credit, showing plenty of early pace. However, she will need to improve to win a similar race.
**Make It Happen Now** was unable to reverse recent placings with her stablemate Troublesome Gerri, and is another who will need to improve.
**Dorn Hill**, a half-sister to a six-furlong three-year-old winner, and a ten-furlong scorer, was badly outpaced early on, but finished to good effect and will stay further.
**Dominer(IRE)** weakened tamely.

## 2165 BATH ALES SPA MEDIAN AUCTION MAIDEN STKS 5f 11y
**2:40** (2:41) (F) 3-4-Y-0 **£2,975** (£850; £425) **Stalls** Low

Form RPR
0302 1 **Nanna (IRE)**[24] 1596 3-8-8 48 .......... JMackay 6 62
(RHollinshead) *mde all: drvn and styd on wl fnl f* **22/1**
3442 2 1 **Boavista (IRE)**[23] 1625 4-8-12 54 ow3 .......... SJDonohoe(7) 1 61
(PDEvans) *chsd wnr thrght: rdn fr 2f out: no imp ins last* **10/1**
3-3 3 nk **General Feeling (IRE)**[11] 1906 3-8-13 .......... PDobbs 12 62
(SKirk) *mid-div: hdwy 2f out: swtchd lft and styd on wl fnl f: nt rch ldrs* **11/2**[3]
022- 4 3/4 **Spearious (IRE)**[231] 5277 3-8-13 70 .......... (t) SDrowne 9 59
(BRMillman) *chsd ldrs: rdn over 2f out: styd on same pce fnl f* **9/2**[1]
6530 5 1 1/4 **Simpsons Mount (IRE)**[4] 2063 3-8-13 69 .......... DSweeney 13 55
(RMFlower) *bhd: rdn and hdwy fr 2f out: hung lft and r.o fnl f* **14/1**
5262 6 nk **Laconia (IRE)**[20] 1689 3-8-8 73 .......... MartinDwyer 15 49
(JSMoore) *chsd ldrs: rdn 2f out: outpcd fnl f* **5/1**[2]
-00 7 1 1/2 **Red Monarch (IRE)**[9] 1975 3-8-10 .......... DNolan(3) 14 48
(PABlockley) *bhd: rdn and styd on fnl 2f: nt pce to rch ldrs* **66/1**
8 nk **Arian's Lad** 3-8-13 .......... SSanders 5 47
(BPalling) *in tch: hdwaay to chse ldrs 1/2-way: wknd fnl f: eased cl home* **50/1**
9 nk **Dance To The Blues (IRE)** 3-8-8 .......... CCatlin 2 41
(BDeHaan) *bhd: n.m.r on rails 3f out: styd on wl fr over 1f out: gng on cl home* **7/1**
0000 10 2 **Philly Dee**[26] 1546 3-8-5 49 .......... LisaJones(3) 7 34
(NEBerry) *fly-jmpd stalls: bhd: hdwy fr 2f out: kpt on fnl f but nt a danger* **66/1**
0- 11 1/2 **Humility**[264] 4495 3-8-8 .......... KFallon 4 32
(CACyzer) *chsd ldrs tl wknd fnl f* **9/1**
0- 12 2 1/2 **Even Hotter**[322] 2854 3-8-8 .......... TQuinn 8 23
(DWPArbuthnot) *chsd ldrs 3f: wknd over 1f out* **33/1**
0305 13 shd **Somethingabouther**[69] 1000 4-9-2 48 .......... BDoyle 17 23
(PWHiatt) *a outpcd on outside* **66/1**
0600 14 1/2 **Beau Jazz**[20] 1689 3-8-13 55 .......... SRighton 11 26
(WDeBest-Turner) *early spd: bhd fr 1/2-way* **66/1**
546- 15 1 1/2 **Lyrical Lady**[154] 6191 3-8-8 57 .......... EAhern 10 16
(MrsAJBowlby) *s.i.s: outpcd* **50/1**
0 16 3 **Weir's Annie**[10] 1942 3-8-9 ow1 .......... DaneO'Neill 3 6
(HCandy) *sn chsng ldrs: wknd ins fnl 2f* **5/1**[2]
17 5 **Lord Zinc** 3-8-10 .......... SHitchcott(3) 16 —
(DWPArbuthnot) *slowly away: a wl bhd* **66/1**

61.94 secs (-0.56) **Going Correction** 0.0s/f (Good)
**WFA** 3 from 4yo 8lb **17** Ran SP% **123.8**
Speed ratings: **104,102,101,100,98 98,95,95,94,91 90,86,86,85,83 78,70**CSF £223.11 TOTE £29.60: £6.60, £3.20, £2.20; EX 159.90.
**Owner** Mrs G A Weetman **Bred** Mark Clarke **Trained** Upper Longdon, Staffs

**FOCUS**
A weak maiden in which it proved hard to come from off the pace.

**NOTEBOOK**
**Nanna(IRE)** had never previously run on turf and was beaten in a Fibresand claimer on her previous start but, switched to the grass, she gained a straightforward success. However, she is likely to struggle to follow up when reassessed.
**Boavista(IRE)** had 6lb in hand over the winner at the weights, but is a most frustrating sort and found that one too strong.
**General Feeling(IRE)** posted another respectable effort, but again shaped as though another furlong will suit. He is now qualified for a handicap mark.
**Spearious(IRE)**, fitted with a tongue-tie for this first run in 231 days, failed to confirm the promise he showed at two and has it all to prove now.
**Simpsons Mount(IRE)** could not pick up for hanging to his left and looks harshly treated off a mark of 69.
**Laconia(IRE)**, switched back to maiden company, did not run to form and has to be considered disappointing.
**Dance To The Blues(IRE)**, out a five-furlong All-Weather winner, was quite well backed, but got no luck in running and has to be considered unlucky not to have finished closer.
**Humility** *Official explanation: jockey said the filly lost her action*
**Weir's Annie** has not progressed from her debut running.

## 2166 BATH ALES RARE HARE H'CAP 5f 161y
**3:10** (3:11) (F) (0-55,55) 3-Y-O+ **£3,444** (£984; £492) **Stalls** Low

Form RPR
60-0 1 **High Ridge**[13] 1873 5-9-4 55 .......... (p) DaneO'Neill 11 68
(JMBradley) *stdd s: bhd: rapid hdwy on outside fr 2f out: str run: edgd lft and led wl ins last: hld on wl* **33/1**
0226 2 hd **Illusive (IRE)**[45] 1230 7-9-4 55 .......... (b) TQuinn 13 67
(MWigham) *hld up in rr: gd hdwy 2f out: qcknd to chse ldrs 1f out: str chal wl ins fnl f: no ex last strides* **12/1**
1120 3 2 **Attorney**[18] 1738 6-8-13 50 .......... (v) KFallon 6 56
(DShaw) *held up mid-div: stdy hdwy fr 2f out: chsd ldrs ins last: outpcd nr fin* **8/1**
0-03 4 1 1/2 **Davids Mark**[27] 1516 4-9-3 54 .......... SSanders 8 55
(JRJenkins) *sn led: rdn 2f out: styd on wl tl hdd and outpcd wl ins last* **6/1**[1]
2106 5 nk **Double M**[35] 1368 7-8-10 47 .......... (v) RHughes 1 47
(MrsLRichards) *stdd in tch: hdwy: nt clr run and hmpd 1f out: r.o ins last but nt rcvr* **6/1**[1]
1460 6 nk **Long Weekend (IRE)**[27] 1516 6-8-2 46 .......... (v) DawnWatson(7) 3 45
(DShaw) *bhd: hrd drvn fr 1/2-way: r.o wl appr fnl f: gng on cl home* **16/1**
014- 7 1/2 **Pascali**[217] 5546 4-9-4 55 .......... SDrowne 5 52
(HMorrison) *hld up in tch on rails: smooth hdwy to trck ldrs whn hmpd jst ins fnl f: nt rcvr* **13/2**[2]
0-00 8 3/4 **Jagged (IRE)**[13] 1873 4-9-3 54 .......... GBaker 10 49
(MrsHSweeting) *chsd ldr: rdn 2f out: wknd fnl f* **16/1**
0410 9 nk **Bali-Star**[10] 1941 9-8-9 46 .......... PDobbs 15 40
(RJHodges) *racd on outside: rr: rdn 3f out: kpt on fnl f but n.d* **33/1**
3314 10 shd **Mayzin (IRE)**[45] 1230 4-9-4 55 .......... (p) DSweeney 18 48
(RMFlower) *sn pressing ldrs: wknd appr fnl f* **15/2**[3]
0000 11 1 1/2 **Ridicule**[13] 1873 5-9-4 55 .......... (vt) EAhern 12 43
(JGPortman) *chsd ldrs: rdn 2f out: edgd lft: bmpd and wknd 1f out* **14/1**
66-0 12 shd **Run On**[10] 1941 6-8-13 53 .......... DNolan(3) 7 41
(DGBridgwater) *chsd ldrs tl wknd fnl f* **40/1**
0000 13 shd **Arabian Knight (IRE)**[11] 1909 4-9-4 55 .......... MartinDwyer 14 43
(RJHodges) *bhd: sme hdwy fnl f: n.d* **16/1**
0003 14 nk **Shady Deal**[7] 1994 8-8-12 49 .......... CCatlin 9 36
(JMBradley) *in tch: rdn and effrt 2f out: wknd fnl f* **14/1**
5-40 15 1 1/4 **Pompey Chimes**[40] 1295 4-9-4 55 .......... SCarson 17 38
(GBBalding) *racd on outside: a outpcd* **33/1**
0-00 16 2 **Danifah (IRE)**[39] 1312 3-8-5 51 .......... JoannaBadger 16 27
(PDEvans) *sn chsng ldrs: rdn 1/2-way: wknd 2f out* **16/1**
02-0 17 1 3/4 **Brave Chief**[133] 438 3-8-7 53 .......... BDoyle 2 23
(JAPickering) *chsd ldrs 3f* **50/1**
U3-0 18 3 **Royal Supremacy (IRE)**[13] 1855 3-8-6 52 .......... SRighton 4 12
(JMBradley) *chsd ldrs 3f* **50/1**

1m 10.94s (-0.20) **Going Correction** 0.0s/f (Good)
**WFA** 3 from 4yo+ 9lb **18** Ran SP% **124.5**
Speed ratings: **101,100,98,96,95 95,94,93,93,93 91,90,90,90,88 86,83,79**CSF £382.30 CT £3575.95 TOTE £58.50: £8.30, £3.30, £2.30, £1.20; EX 476.80.
**Owner** James Leisure Ltd **Bred** Buckram Thoroughbred Enterprises Inc **Trained** Sedbury, Gloucs
■ Stewards Enquiry : Dane O'Neill two-day ban: careless riding (May 28,29)

**FOCUS**
A competitive sprint handicap run at a good pace and the principals came from off the speed.

**NOTEBOOK**
**High Ridge** made his debut over a mile and a half for Henry Cecil back in 2002, but is quite clearly a sprinter and, racing over a trip this short for the first time, gained his first ever success. Appreciating the strong pace, he picked up really well when switched to the outside and there appeared little fluke about this success.
**Illusive(IRE)**, without success since 2001, has almost forgotten how to win but there was little wrong with this effort. He picked up well enough, but the winner just too strong.
**Attorney** gets on well with Fallon and appeared to run his race, finishing to good effect but proving no match for the front two.
**Davids Mark** has not won for over a year, but this was a decent effort considering he tried to make all and the first three home came from off the pace.

**Double M** is nicely handicapped on turf and would have gone close with better luck in running.
**Pascali** is another who would have would have been closer with better luck in running.

## 2167 BATH ALES BARNSTORMER FILLIES' H'CAP 1m 5f 22y

3:40 (3:40) (E) (0-75,69) 3-Y-0+ £3,809 (£1,172; £586; £293) Stalls Low

Form RPR

4542 **1** **Anyhow (IRE)**[10] 1940 7-8-13 **61** DNolan(3) 6 68
(MissKMGeorge) *hld up rr: hdwy fr 3f out: hrd rdn and styd on gamely fnl f to ld last stride* **5/1**[3]

2213 **2** *shd* **Fleeting Moon**[70] 981 4-9-4 **63** MartinDwyer 10 70
(AMBalding) *in tch: chsd ldrs over 2f out: hrd rdn and str chal appr fnl f: led cl home: ct last stride* **12/1**

-520 **3** *½* **Sashay**[27] 1534 6-8-0 **45** JMackay 1 51
(RHollinshead) *led tl hdd jst ins fnl 3f: rallied to ld again jst ins last hdd and no ex cl home* **9/1**

-332 **4** *shd* **Compton Eclaire (IRE)**[7] 2004 4-8-10 **55** (v) EAhern 5 61
(GAButler) *hld up in tch: outpcd and pushed along over 2f out: swtchd rt and goof hdwy over 1f out: fin wl: gng on cl home* **8/1**

-022 **5** *½* **Classic Millennium**[23] 1630 6-8-10 **58** LisaJones(3) 7 63
(WJMusson) *hdwy to chse ldrs 9f out: outpcd over 2f out: rallied and r.o wl fnl f: nt rch ldrs* **9/2**[2]

01-2 **6** *1 ¼* **Calamintha**[17] 1754 4-9-5 **64** KFallon 2 68
(MCPipe) *chsd ldr to 6f out: outpcd over 2f out: rallied to chal appr fnl f: outpcd ins last* **3/1**[1]

31-0 **7** *nk* **Beechy Bank (IRE)**[131] 467 6-9-10 **69** VSlattery 3 72
(MrsMaryHambro) *chsd ldrs: wnt 2nd 6f out: led ins fnl 3f: hdd jst ins last: hung lft and sn wknd* **16/1**

-605 **8** *1* **Aoninch**[40] 1297 4-9-0 **59** RHavlin 11 61
(MrsPNDutfield) *hld up in rr: hdwy on outside 3f out: kpt on fnl 2f but nt pce to rch ldrs* **15/2**

3430 **9** *2 ½* **Anniversary Guest (IRE)**[18] 1728 5-7-9 **43** oh3 JFMcDonald(3) 4 41
(MrsLucindaFeatherstone) *t.k.h: hld up in rr: hdwy 6f out: rdn ins fnl 3f: sn one pce* **25/1**

0300 **10** *9* **Miss Koen (IRE)**[30] 1463 5-8-6 **51** (t) CCatlin 8 37
(DLWilliams) *hld up in rr: hdwy over 3f out: sn rdn and btn* **25/1**

2m 53.97s (2.67) **Going Correction** -0.075s/f (Good) **10** Ran SP% **114.0**
Speed ratings: **88,87,87,87,87 86,86,85,84,78**CSF £61.81 CT £518.48 TOTE £6.10: £2.00, £2.40, £3.10; EX 89.40.
**Owner** Stableline **Bred** The Duke Of Marlborough **Trained** Higher Easington, Devon
■ Stewards Enquiry : Martin Dwyer one-day ban: used whip from above shoulder height (May 28)

**FOCUS**
Quite a competitive fillies' handicap, but the pace was just ordinary and the winning time was very slow.

**NOTEBOOK**
**Anyhow(IRE)**, 2lb higher than when winning over a mile and a half on the Polytrack earlier in the year, and 8lb higher than when last successful on turf, benefited from a good waiting ride from Nolan to gain a narrow victory. She should not go up too much in the weights for this and should continue to go well in similar company.
**Fleeting Moon** did not appear to get two miles on her previous start but, returned to a more suitable trip and racing on turf for the first time, this was much better.
**Sashay** posted a good effort over a trip short of her optimum, keeping on well when headed.
**Compton Eclaire(IRE)** again shaped as though a return to two miles will suit.
**Classic Millennium** ran respectably on her return to turf and should pay her way again this season.
**Calamintha** was quite keen on ground that would have been plenty fast enough for her.

## 2168 BATHALES.COM MEDIAN AUCTION MAIDEN STKS 1m 2f 46y

4:10 (4:12) (E) 3-Y-0 £3,555 (£1,094; £547; £273) Stalls Low

Form RPR

324- **1** **Cause Celebre (IRE)**[219] 5489 3-8-9 **78** RHills 2 75
(BWHills) *mde virtually all: shkn up over 1f out: r.o wl: readily* **2/1**[1]

2 **2** *1 ¾* **Charleston**[14] 1830 3-9-0 RHughes 7 76
(JHMGosden) *chsd ldrs: wnt 2nd over 2f out: styd on u.p but no imp on wnr over 1f out: readily hld ins last but clr 2nd* **5/2**[2]

600- **3** *3 ½* **Velvet Waters**[251] 4794 3-8-9 **59** SCarson 13 65
(RFJohnsonHoughton) *chsd wnr after 2f: rdn 3f out: no imp and lost 2nd over 2f out: sn no ch w ldrs: hld on for 3rd* **33/1**

003- **4** *nk* **Man At Arms (IRE)**[206] 5726 3-9-0 **69** PDobbs 6 69
(RHannon) *bhd: stl plenty to do fr 3f out: drvn and styd on wl fr 2f out: rapid hdwy ins last: fin strly* **5/1**[3]

0 **5** *3* **Lucky Arthur (IRE)**[9] 1967 3-8-9 DSweeney 5 58
(JGMO'Shea) *s.i.s: bhd: hdwy 5f out: styd on fnl 2f but nvr gng pce to rch ldrs* **50/1**

520- **6** *3* **Avesomeofthat (IRE)**[217] 5551 3-9-0 **74** RHavlin 17 58
(MrsPNDutfield) *chsd ldrs: rdn 3f: wknd over 2f out* **20/1**

05 **7** *shd* **Nounou**[24] 1597 3-9-0 CCatlin 16 57
(DJDaly) *chsd ldr 2f: styd chsng ldrs: wknd over 2f out* **33/1**

4500 **8** *1* **Looks The Business (IRE)**[33] 1392 3-8-7 **65** CHaddon(7) 11 56
(WGMTurner) *chsd ldrs tl wknd over 2f out* **11/1**

000- **9** *1 ¼* **Autumn Flyer (IRE)**[215] 5572 3-9-0 RSmith 9 53
(CGCox) *in tch: bhd fnl 3f* **25/1**

0-50 **10** *7* **Rumour Mill (IRE)**[30] 1465 3-8-10 **50** ow1 MSavage(5) 12 41
(NEBerry) *mid-div: rdn 4f out: wknd 3f out* **100/1**

0 **11** *4* **Open Book**[15] 1800 3-8-9 SDrowne 4 27
(HMorrison) *stdd s: rdn over 3f out: a bhd* **28/1**

0000 **12** *¾* **Steppenwolf**[10] 1946 3-9-0 **40** SRighton 3 31
(WDeBest-Turner) *a in rr* **100/1**

**13** *2* **Silken John (IRE)** 3-9-0 EAhern 10 27
(JGPortman) *a in rr* **25/1**

0 **14** *6* **Dorset (USA)**[33] 1395 3-8-9 MartinDwyer 8 11
(AMBalding) *in tch 5f: sn bhd* **20/1**

**15** *2* **Sovereign Girl** 3-8-9 SSanders 1 7
(BNDoran) *s.i.s: sn rcvrd and in tch: wknd 4f out* **100/1**

00 **16** *26* **Highfluting**[4] 2060 3-8-9 DKinsella 15 —
(RMFlower) *a in rr* **100/1**

2m 8.98s (-2.02) **Going Correction** -0.075s/f (Good) **16** Ran SP% **119.4**
Speed ratings: **105,103,100,100,98 95,95,94,93,88 85,84,82,78,76 55**CSF £5.67 TOTE £3.60: £1.10, £1.20, £8.30; EX 5.50.
**Owner** The Hon Mrs J M Corbett & C Wright **Bred** Epona Bloodstock Ltd **Trained** Lambourn, Berks

**FOCUS**
Not a very competitive maiden, but a fair time for the grade.

**NOTEBOOK**
**Cause Celebre(IRE)** showed promise at up to a mile as a juvenile and, granted an easy lead on this step up in trip and first run in 219 days, found plenty under pressure to see off all challengers. However, she will need to improve to follow up off a mark of 78.
**Charleston**, runner-up in just an ordinary maiden on heavy ground first time up, had every chance but proved unable to peg back the winner. There is a minor race to be one with him.
**Velvet Waters**, racing for the first time in 251 days and stepping up from a mile, was no match for the front two and will find things easier in handicaps.
**Man At Arms(IRE)**, stepping up in trip from a mile, did little to justify his rating of 69 on this first start in 206 days.
**Lucky Arthur(IRE)** should find things easier when handicapped, possibly over further.

## 2169 BATH ALES SALAMANDER CLASSIFIED STKS 1m 2f 46y

4:40 (4:44) (E) 3-Y-0 £3,425 (£1,054; £527; £263) Stalls Low

Form RPR

4-15 **1** **Etmaam**[32] 1418 3-9-3 **75** RHills 14 80
(MJohnston) *hld up in rr: hdwy on outside fr 3f out: rapid hdwy fr 2f out: str run ins last to ld last stride* **9/2**[2]

03-0 **2** *shd* **Albinus**[30] 1461 3-8-13 **71** (b[1]) MartinDwyer 9 76
(AMBalding) *in tch: trckd ldrs and rn wd bnd over 5f out: hdwy over 2f out: str run to ld last half f: ct last stride* **8/1**

6003 **3** *1 ½* **Desert Image (IRE)**[20] 1688 3-8-9 **69** DCorby(3) 11 72
(CTinkler) *hld up in rr: rapid hdwy fr 2f out: styd on wl fnl f but nt pce to chal* **7/1**[3]

315- **4** *hd* **Kythia (IRE)**[210] 5671 3-8-11 **72** MFenton 13 71
(HMorrison) *hld up in rr: hdwy on outside over 2f out: styd on wl to chse ldrs ins last: nt qckn nr fin* **18/1**

31-3 **5** *1 ¼* **Kristal's Dream (IRE)**[22] 1640 3-8-13 **74** TQuinn 4 70
(JLDunlop) *led after 2f: kpt narrow advantage and rdn over 2f out: hdd last half f: eased whn hld cl home* **4/1**[1]

-544 **6** *1* **Slavonic (USA)**[22] 1640 3-9-0 **72** (b) RHughes 2 69
(JHMGosden) *hld up in tch: nt clr run 2f out: gng wl whn nt clr run on rails 1f out and thrght fnl f: nt rcvr* **10/1**

6-23 **7** *shd* **Sailmaker (IRE)**[14] 1827 3-9-3 **75** SDrowne 3 72
(RCharlton) *chsd ldrs: n.m.r and rdn 2f out: one pce fnl f* **9/2**[2]

040 **8** *1 ¾* **Master Mahogany**[20] 1683 3-8-12 **69** VSlattery 6 64
(RJHodges) *s.i.s: sn in tch: rdn and one pce over 2f out: styd on again fnl f but nt a danger* **25/1**

3-50 **9** *2* **Principessa**[20] 1683 3-8-9 **69** KFallon 5 57
(BPalling) *chsd ldrs tl lost position 4f out: rdn and sme hdwy over 2f out: sn one pce* **16/1**

50-4 **10** *¾* **Morag**[23] 1613 3-8-9 **70** SCarson 12 56
(IAWood) *chsd ldrs tl wknd fr 2f out* **20/1**

-300 **11** *½* **Charlie Tango (IRE)**[9] 1957 3-8-9 **67** SHitchcott(3) 1 58
(MRChannon) *hld up mid-div: pushed along 7f out: sme hdwy 3f out: wknd ins fnl 2f* **16/1**

03-4 **12** *3* **Maria Bonita (IRE)**[27] 1532 3-8-9 **70** SSanders 7 49
(RMBeckett) *led 2f: chsed ldr and chal 6f out to 3f out: wknd qckly over 2f out* **50/1**

46-0 **13** *6* **Reign Of Fire (IRE)**[28] 1507 3-8-6 **64** LPKeniry(3) 8 38
(BJMeehan) *in tch tl wknd over 2f out* **100/1**

2m 9.03s (-1.97) **Going Correction** -0.075s/f (Good) **13** Ran SP% **117.7**
Speed ratings: **104,103,102,102,101 100,100,99,97,97 96,94,89**CSF £38.42 TOTE £4.90: £2.40, £3.40, £4.00; EX 56.10.
**Owner** Hamdan Al Maktoum **Bred** Hawkers Stud **Trained** Middleham Moor, N Yorks

**FOCUS**
With just 4lb separating these on official figures, this was a competitive classified event. The winning time was fair for the grade and the first two showed improved form.

**NOTEBOOK**
**Etmaam** got going too late on his handicap debut over a mile at Ripon on his previous start. Stepped up two furlongs in trip, he again took a while to pick, but eventually hit full stride and got up on the line. He should get even further, but does not appeal as an obvious one to follow up.
**Albinus** hinted at ability in maidens, but looked on a stiff enough mark for this first venture outside of this grade. With the blinkers on for the first time, he ran a most encouraging race and it will be disappointing if he does not win a similar contest.
**Desert Image(IRE)** ran another solid race and shaped as though he may stay a little further.
**Kythia(IRE)** made a respectable reappearance and should improve for the outing. However, she looks on a high enough mark.
**Kristal's Dream(IRE)** appeared to have every chance, but proved unable to quicken against the rail and has something to prove.
**Slavonic(USA)**, with blinkers replacing a visor, got no luck in running and could have finished a lot closer.
**Sailmaker(IRE)** proved disappointing on this step up from a mile.

## 2170 BATH ALES GEM BITTER H'CAP 1m 5y

5:10 (5:12) (E) (0-70,68) 3-Y-0+ £4,004 (£1,232; £616; £308) Stalls Low

Form RPR

0-00 **1** **Voice Mail**[26] 1542 5-9-10 **68** LPKeniry(3) 11 77
(AMBalding) *hld up in rr: hdwy and nt clr run over 2f out: swtchd rt to outside and rapid hdwy ins last: led last strides* **17/2**

146 **2** *nk* **Zafarshah (IRE)**[47] 1204 5-9-7 **62** KFallon 9 70
(PDEvans) *trckd ldrs: drvn to chal ins last: led cl home: ct last strides* **7/2**[1]

3352 **3** *shd* **Sangiovese**[16] 1757 5-9-11 **66** SDrowne 8 74
(HMorrison) *sn led:styd on wl whn strly chal fr over 3f out: stl hld advantage ins last: hdd and no ex cl home* **4/1**[2]

0-00 **4** *1 ¼* **Bishopstone Man**[23] 1624 7-9-6 **68** CCavanagh(7) 10 73
(HCandy) *t.k.h: early: trckd ldrs: n.m.r on rails appr fnl f: nt clr run ins last: nt rcvr and one pce* **11/1**

-646 **5** *½* **Phred**[9] 1969 4-9-8 **63** SCarson 13 67
(RFJohnsonHoughton) *sn chsng ldr: str chal over 3f out tl over 1f out: wknd ins last* **11/1**

0503 **6** *½* **Realism (FR)**[16] 1757 4-9-6 **61** BDoyle 12 64
(PWHiatt) *chsd ldrs: rdn fr 3f out: wknd ins fnl f* **14/1**

0000 **7** *1* **Daimajin (IRE)**[7] 2007 5-8-11 **55** DNolan(3) 6 56
(MrsLucindaFeatherstone) *bhd: rdn 3f out: hdwy over 2f out: nvr gng pce to rch ldrs* **66/1**

6303 **8** *hd* **Quantum Leap**[47] 1204 7-9-7 **65** LisaJones(3) 15 65
(SDow) *bhd: pushed along and hung lft 3f out: styd on wl fr over 1f out but n.d* **12/1**

0-44 **9** *shd* **Mobo-Baco**[13] 1857 7-9-2 **57** MartinDwyer 3 57
(RJHodges) *bhd: rdn and kpt on fr 3f out: nvr gng pce to rch ldrs* **7/1**[3]

-503 **10** *nk* **Ember Days**[13] 1857 5-9-6 **61** (p) VSlattery 4 60
(JLSpearing) *behund: rdn over 3f out: mod hdwy 2f out: nvr nr ldrs* **25/1**

012U **11** *2* **The Gaikwar (IRE)**[13] 1875 5-9-8 **68** (b) MSavage(5) 1 63
(NEBerry) *chsd ldrs tl wknd over 2f out* **11/1**

0336 **12** *nk* **Spindor (USA)**[5] 2030 5-9-7 **62** (p) RHughes 2 56
(JAOsborne) *s.i.s: a in rr* **12/1**

1m 40.8s (-0.20) **Going Correction** -0.075s/f (Good) **12** Ran SP% **117.6**
Speed ratings: **98,97,97,96,95 95,94,94,94,93 91,91**CSF £37.93 CT £140.38 TOTE £8.60: £3.70, £3.20, £1.90; EX 58.50 Place 6 £221.49, Place 5 £187.28.
**Owner** Roger Parry **Bred** G Coull **Trained** Kingsclere, Hants

**FOCUS**
A modest but competitive handicap. The winning time was modest for the grade.

**NOTEBOOK**
**Voice Mail**, just a pound higher than when last successful in June 2003, had to be switched out wide for a run but flew home when in the clear and got up virtually on the line. He has never followed up, but his stable are at least in good form.
**Zafarshah(IRE)**, returning from a short 47-day break, has never won off a mark this high but only just failed. There should be a similar race in him.
**Sangiovese** ran a cracker from the front and, only 3lb higher than when gaining his only success to date, he should continue to go well in similar events.
**Bishopstone Man** has been given a bit of a chance by the handicapper and may well have won with a clear run.
**Phred** had conditions to suit and ran respectably.
T/Plt: £153.20 to a £1 stake. Pool: £34,538.30. 164.50 winning tickets. T/Qpdt: £32.60 to a £1 stake. Pool: £2,045.90. 46.40 winning tickets. ST

# [1865] MUSSELBURGH (R-H)
Monday, May 17

**OFFICIAL GOING: Good to firm (firm in places)**

## 2171 BUDWEISER APPRENTICE H'CAP — 2m
6:20 (6:20) (F) (0-55,51) 4-Y-0+ — £2,912 (£832; £416) Stalls Low

Form — RPR
5610 **1** **Galandora**[9] [1958] 4-8-3 **47** ... LucyRussell(7) 7 — 56
(DrJRJNaylor) *hld up: stdy hdwy 4f out: rdn over 1f out: styd on to ld ins last* — 6/1
6660 **2** *1* **Joely Green**[22] [1644] 7-8-3 **45** ... (b) StevenHarrison(7) 3 — 53
(NPLittmoden) *hld up in rr: hdwy on outer 4f out: swtchd wd and led 2f out: sn rdn: hdd and nt qckn ins last* — 9/2[2]
0-60 **3** *5* **Repulse Bay (IRE)**[15] [1785] 6-8-9 **51** ... JCurrie(7) 6 — 53
(JSGoldie) *trckd ldrs: hdwy 3f out: rdn wl over 1f out and sn one pce* 13/2
44/6 **4** *1* **Western Bluebird (IRE)**[13] [1866] 6-8-7 **45** ... (b[1]) PMulrennan(3) 4 — 46
(MissKateMilligan) *led: rdn along 3f out: hdd 2f out and grad wknd* 16/1
00-4 **5** *hd* **Sea Cove**[32] [1426] 4-8-1 **45** ... AMullen(7) 8 — 45
(JMJefferson) *chsd ldr: hdwy 4f out: rdn and hung bdly lft over 2f out: sn wknd* — 5/1[3]
0-03 **6** *1 3/4* **Dormy Two (IRE)**[13] [1866] 4-8-8 **48** ... (p) TEaves(3) 1 — 46
(JSWainwright) *hld up in rr: hdwy 4f out: rdn along 3f out: edgd rt and bmpd 2f out: sn btn* — 7/1
60-3 **7** *hd* **Haystacks (IRE)**[18] [1721] 8-8-7 **40** oh2 ... (p) LEnstone 2 — 40
(JamesMoffatt) *trckd ldrs: gng wl: shkn up and outpcd 3f out: rdn and hmpd 2f out: no ch after* — 4/1[1]
465U **8** *2* **Cadwallader (USA)**[20] [1693] 4-8-5 **42** oh2 ... THamilton 5 — 38
(PBurgoyne) *trckd ldrs: hdwy 5f out: rdn along 3f out: hmpd and wknd 2f out* — 14/1

3m 35.4s (1.70) **Going Correction** +0.175s/f (Good)
**WFA** 4 from 6yo+ 2lb — **8 Ran SP% 107.5**
Speed ratings: **102,101,99,98,98 97,97,96**CSF £29.06 CT £154.54 TOTE £7.50: £1.60, £2.10, £1.80; EX 24.10.
**Owner** Michael Olpin **Bred** Trevor Calver **Trained** Shrewton, Wilts
■ Stewards Enquiry : J Currie two-day ban: careless riding (May 28,29)
A Mullen one-day ban: careless riding (May 28)

**FOCUS**
A very moderate staying handicap run at a sound gallop, in which the principals came from the back.

**NOTEBOOK**
**Galandora**, who failed to handle the mud last time, goes well for her apprentice rider and, despite again taking a keen hold, had enough left at the finish to prevail. She found the faster surface no problem and looks capable of winning again at a similar modest level.
**Joely Green** is well suited by a fast surface and, with the blinkers re-applied, ran his best race since last summer. He is on a good mark on his old form.
**Repulse Bay(IRE)**, another to have dropped in the weights, was also down in grade and had his chance before fading. He has yet to prove he stays this far.
**Western Bluebird(IRE)**, who has raced mostly over hurdles of late, was fitted with blinkers for the first time and made much of the running. A return to sellers or summer jumping may provide his best chance of a win.
**Sea Cove**, who ran well in a similar grade on the All-Weather last time, wandered under pressure on this fast ground and may be better returned to the more forgiving Fibresand surface.
**Haystacks(IRE)** is more effective over hurdles or in banded company.

## 2172 JOHN SMITH'S EXTRA SMOOTH H'CAP — 7f 30y
6:50 (6:52) (E) (0-70,67) 3-Y-0+ — £4,260 (£1,311; £655; £327) Stalls Low

Form — RPR
0-00 **1** **Border Artist**[31] [1451] 5-9-5 **59** ... ANicholls 5 — 71
(DNicholls) *midfield: hdwy 3f out: led wl over 1f out: sn rdn and styd on wl fnl f* — 4/1[1]
05-1 **2** *nk* **Kirkby's Treasure**[36] [1345] 6-9-4 **58** ... FNorton 2 — 69
(ABerry) *bhd: hdwy over 2f out: rdn to chse wnr over 1f out: drvn and styd on wl fnl f* — 9/1
436- **3** *2* **Killala (IRE)**[205] [5742] 4-9-6 **65** ... TEaves(5) 9 — 71
(ISemple) *chsd ldrs: rdn along 2f out: drvn over 1f out: kpt on u.p fnl f* — 16/1
-600 **4** *shd* **Coustou (IRE)**[9] [1974] 4-9-5 **59** ... PFessey 8 — 65
(ARDicken) *in tch: hdwy 3f out: rdn along 2f out: swtchd lft over 1f out and kpt on ins last* — 33/1
00/3 **5** *1 1/4* **Sea Mark**[42] [1265] 8-9-7 **61** ... RWinston 4 — 63
(BEllison) *hld up: hdwy 1/2-way: rdn along 2f out: sn drvn and no imp appr last* — 11/2[2]
-400 **6** *3/4* **Mon Secret (IRE)**[13] [1868] 6-9-1 **55** ... FLynch 11 — 55
(BSmart) *towards rr: hdwy 3f out: rdn along 2f out and kpt on: nrst fin* — 10/1
-100 **7** *shd* **Smith N Allan Oils**[13] [1868] 5-9-2 **59** ... (p) LEnstone(3) 7 — 59
(MDods) *midfield: hdwy 3f out: rdn along and btn 2f out* — 16/1
5300 **8** *1/2* **Barzak (IRE)**[23] [1620] 4-9-3 **57** ... (t) JBramhill 1 — 56
(SRBowring) *bhd: hdwy on outer over 2f out: edgd rt over 1f out: kpt on ins last: nrst fin* — 14/1
5205 **9** *3/4* **Dispol Peto**[24] [1595] 4-9-3 **57** ... (p) DeanMcKeown 12 — 53
(IanEmmerson) *led: rdn along 3f out: sn hdd & wknd* — 25/1
000- **10** *1/2* **Jedeydd**[337] [2390] 7-9-7 **61** ... (t) DaleGibson 3 — 56
(MDods) *a rr* — 33/1
0006 **11** *1 1/2* **Tally (IRE)**[13] [1876] 4-9-0 **54** ... KDalgleish 6 — 45
(MJPolglase) *chsd ldrs: hdwy 4f out: rdn to ld 2 1/2f out: hdd wl over 1f out and sn wknd* — 14/1
514- **12** *1 1/2* **Roman Maze**[163] [6135] 4-9-13 **67** ... NPollard 14 — 54
(WMBrisbourne) *dwlt: sn pushed along to chse ldrs: rdn 3f out and sn wknd* — 8/1[3]
0-02 **13** *3/4* **Xanadu**[15] [1787] 8-8-8 **53** ... (p) PMulrennan(5) 13 — 38
(MissLAPerratt) *cl up on inner: effrt over 2f out: sn rdn and btn* — 12/1
-502 **14** *1 1/4* **Bella Beguine**[21] [1680] 5-9-1 **55** ... (v) GDuffield 10 — 37
(ABailey) *cl up: rdn along 1/2-way: sn wknd* — 16/1

1m 30.48s (0.95) **Going Correction** +0.175s/f (Good) — **14 Ran SP% 114.0**
Speed ratings: **101,100,98,98,96 95,95,95,94,93 92,90,89,88**CSF £35.97 CT £522.40 TOTE £5.00: £2.00, £3.80, £4.60; EX 53.50.
**Owner** F F Racing Services Partnership V **Bred** Chippenham Lodge Stud Ltd **Trained** Sessay, N Yorks

**FOCUS**
A moderate handicap run at a just a fair pace, and dominated by two with good course records.

**NOTEBOOK**
**Border Artist** loves this track and retained his unbeaten course and distance record with a determined success. He was also repeating last year's win in this race from a 3lb higher mark and should not go up much for this. He will always be worthy of consideration on this track.
**Kirkby's Treasure**, another who goes well on this track, was 3lb higher for his success here last time. His wins prior to that were on soft ground, but he is just as effective on this ground these days.
**Killala(IRE)** is a consistent sort and is well suited by a turning seven furlongs. She could do with dropping another couple of pounds.
**Coustou(IRE)** has dropped 20lb since last autumn and would be interesting if returned to a switchback track.
**Sea Mark** put up another decent effort on this second outing following a year and nine months off. He will appreciate another furlong or more on the Flat, but could also go summer jumping.

## 2173 GORDONS GIN MAIDEN AUCTION STKS — 5f
7:20 (7:26) (F) 2-Y-0 — £3,380 (£1,040; £520; £260) Stalls Low

Form — RPR
**1** **Polly Perkins (IRE)** 2-8-9 ... KDarley 6 — 72+
(NPLittmoden) *trckd ldrs: hdwy 1/2-way: rdn to ld ent last: edgd lft and kpt on* — 4/1[1]
**2** *1 1/2* **Sweet Royale** 2-8-7 ... RWinston 1 — 64
(MissLAPerratt) *cl up: led after 1f: rdn along over 1f out: hdd ent last: n.m.r and swtchd rt ins last: one pce* — 9/1
**3** *nk* **Katie Boo (IRE)** 2-8-5 ... FNorton 2 — 61
(ABerry) *chsd ldrs: effrt and nt clr run over 1f out: swtchd rt ent last and fin strly* — 7/1
5 **4** *nk* **Lady Hopeful (IRE)**[13] [1865] 2-8-2 ... THamilton(3) 5 — 60
(RPElliott) *chsd ldrs stands rail: rdn along 2f out: one pce appr last* 5/1[3]
**5** *1/2* **Alcharinga (IRE)** 2-8-5 ... TEaves(5) 7 — 63
(TJEtherington) *led 1f: cl up tl rdn along 2f out and one pce appr last* 25/1
2 **6** *1/2* **Skippit John**[9] [1961] 2-8-8 ... DeanMcKeown 8 — 59
(RonaldThompson) *wnt rt s: sn cl up: rdn along 2f out and sn wknd* 9/2[2]
04 **7** *2* **Lord John**[33] [1390] 2-8-8 ... DaleGibson 3 — 51
(MWEasterby) *dwlt: sn rdn along in rr: n.d* — 9/2[2]
0 **8** *1/2* **Namking**[13] [1865] 2-8-5 ... PMulrennan(3) 4 — 51
(CWThornton) *broke wl: sn outpcd and bhd tl sme late hdwy* — 12/1

61.96 secs (1.56) **Going Correction** +0.025s/f (Good) — **8 Ran SP% 107.1**
Speed ratings: **88,85,85,84,83 83,79,79**CSF £34.67 TOTE £3.90: £1.70, £3.90, £2.20; EX 42.50.
**Owner** Miss Vanessa Church **Bred** David John Brown **Trained** Newmarket, Suffolk

**FOCUS**
A moderate time for this juvenile contest, being 1.77sec slower than the later seller.

**NOTEBOOK**
**Polly Perkins(IRE)**, by a sprinter and with plenty of speedy types on the dam's side, was supported on this racecourse debut and did all that was required. She can be placed to supplement this success.
**Sweet Royale** ◆, another speedily-bred sort, made the best of her rail draw despite drifting out on the elbow. She was a little short of room late on, and that meant she did not have as hard a race as she could have. She looks capable of picking up a similar race.
**Katie Boo(IRE)**, another sprinting-bred filly, was short of room on the rail just past halfway, but picked up nicely when pulled out late on to finish best of all. She is another who should find a winning opportunity.
**Lady Hopeful(IRE)** ran a similar race to her debut over course and distance, finishing in the same position. She gives a line to the form.
**Alcharinga(IRE)** showed ability but will be better in time over further.
**Skippit John** did not go on from his debut on this much faster surface. *Official explanation: jockey said the gelding was unsuited by the fast ground*
**Lord John** missed the break and never got competitive. *Official explanation: jockey said the colt reared up in the stalls and lost ground at the start*

## 2174 COURVOISIER V.S.O.P. H'CAP — 1m 4f
7:50 (7:51) (E) (0-75,72) 3-Y-0+ — £5,460 (£1,680; £840; £420) Stalls High

Form — RPR
-060 **1** **Rajam**[41] [1287] 6-9-11 **69** ... (v[1]) AlexGreaves 10 — 81
(DNicholls) *trckd ldr: led over 3f out: rdn wl over 1f out: hdd ins last: rallied to ld nr fin* — 22/1
5-40 **2** *nk* **Easibet Dot Net**[44] [1245] 4-9-0 **58** ... (p) RWinston 3 — 70
(ISemple) *trckd ldng pair: hdwy 3f out: rdn to ld ins last: put hd in air and nt run on: hdd nr fin* — 10/1
1050 **3** *3* **Call Me Sunshine**[41] [1282] 4-9-2 **60** ... GFaulkner 9 — 67
(PCHaslam) *hld up in rr: stdy hdwy over 4f out: rdn over 2f out: kpt on same pce appr last* — 25/1
0022 **4** *hd* **Oldenway**[47] [1213] 5-9-11 **72** ... THamilton(3) 7 — 78
(RAFahey) *hld up in tch: hdwy 4f out: chsd ldrs over 2f out: sn rdn and no imp* — 4/1[2]
0-43 **5** *2 1/2* **King's Envoy (USA)**[17] [1747] 5-9-7 **65** ... DMcGaffin 5 — 67
(MrsJCMcgregor) *in tch: hdwy over 3f out: rdn along to chse ldrs 2f out: sn drvn and wknd over 1f out* — 14/1
6-65 **6** *1/2* **Tbm Can**[15] [1785] 5-9-4 **62** ... NPollard 8 — 64
(WMBrisbourne) *hld up in tch: effrt and n.m.r over 2f out: sn rdn and no imp* — 7/2[1]
00-5 **7** *5* **Untidy Daughter**[25] [1560] 5-8-4 **53** ow1 ... (b) TEaves(5) 1 — 47
(BEllison) *hld up and bhd: hdwy on inner over 4f out: sn rdn along and n.d* — 7/1[3]
10-0 **8** *2* **Border Terrier (IRE)**[27] [1527] 6-8-9 **53** ... KDarley 2 — 43
(MDHammond) *hld up: hdwy 4f out: sn rdn along and wknd* — 14/1
5-00 **9** *5* **Piste Bleu (FR)**[41] [1282] 4-8-2 **53** ... DFentiman(7) 6 — 35
(RFord) *hld up in rr: swtchd wd and hdwy 3f out: sn rdn and wknd* — 25/1
10/2 **10** *17* **Plutocrat**[19] [1316] 8-9-13 **71** ... (v[1]) KDalgleish 4 — 26
(LLungo) *led: rdn along and hdd over 3f out: sn wknd* — 7/2[1]

2m 41.46s (3.44) **Going Correction** +0.175s/f (Good) — **10 Ran SP% 111.4**
Speed ratings: **95,94,92,92,91 90,87,86,82,71**CSF £211.52 CT £5333.17 TOTE £24.10: £3.70, £3.50, £5.50; EX 408.50.

**Owner** A A Bloodstock Ltd **Bred** Shadwell Estate Company Limited **Trained** Sessay, N Yorks

**FOCUS**

A moderate winning time for the grade, and the form looks worth treating with some caution.

**NOTEBOOK**

**Rajam**, who had not won since scoring twice for Alex Stewart in 2001, was 21lb lower than when gaining the last of those victories. Fitted with a visor for the first time, he cruised to the front early in the straight and then came again under a spirited ride to regain the lead close home. He is no certainty to follow up, and much depends on the visor having the same effect next time.

**Easibet Dot Net** ran his best race for a while, but did not go through with his effort on this fast surface. He is not one to have faith in, but the more forgiving Fibresand may suit him better.

**Call Me Sunshine** has not run on ground this fast since her juvenile days. This was her best effort since winning on Fibresand early in the year and she seems suited by having a break between races.

**Oldenway**, who has had a break since running two good races in six days early in the turf season, was returning to this longer trip but looks more effective at ten furlongs.

**King's Envoy(USA)**, another stepping back up in trip, has yet to prove he stays this far.

**Tbm Can** is struggling to return to his good form of last summer off his current mark.

**Plutocrat**, who has a good record on this track, both on the Flat and over hurdles, appeared to run too free in the first-time visor and was a spent force early in the straight. *Official explanation: trainer said gelding bled from the nose*

## 2175 ARTHUR MCKAY BUILDING SERVICES (S) STKS — 5f

**8:20** (8:23) (G) 3-Y-O+ — **£2,933** (£838; £419) **Stalls** Low

Form — RPR

0-10 **1** **American Cousin**[41] [1283] 9-9-9 58 ANicholls 3 — 65
(DNicholls) *pushed along towards rr: swtchd rt and hdwy 1/2-way: cl up over 1f out: shkn up to ld ins last: sn clr* **7/2**[2]

3060 **2** *3* **Vijay (IRE)**[15] [1787] 5-9-4 57 (v[1]) RWinston 8 — 48
(ISemple) *cl up: led 11/2f out: sn jnd and rdn: hdd and drvn ins last: nt qckn* **3/1**[1]

4434 **3** *2* **Best Lead**[13] [1870] 5-9-2 52 (b) DFentiman(7) 1 — 45
(IanEmmerson) *dwlt and stmbld s: sn pushed along and in tch: rdn and hung rt wl over 1f out: one pce* **3/1**[1]

0003 **4** *4* **Roan Raider (USA)**[13] [1870] 4-9-1 47 (v) THamilton(3) 5 — 24
(MJPolglase) *in tch: rdn along 2f out: sn btn* **6/1**[3]

00-0 **5** *2* **Robwillcall**[13] [1870] 4-8-13 49 FNorton 4 — 11
(ABerry) *cl up: rdn along 2f out: sn drvn and wknd* **15/2**

00-4 **6** *1* **Attila The Hun**[77] [944] 5-8-13 40 (v) TEaves(5) 9 — 12
(FWatson) *dwlt: sn led on wd outside: rdn along 2f out: sn hdd & wknd* **50/1**

0100 **7** *nk* **Caronte (IRE)**[20] [1699] 4-9-9 40 (b) JBramhill 2 — 16
(SRBowring) *cl up: rdn 2f out: sn wknd* **25/1**

000- **8** *5* **Rhinefield Boy**[252] [4770] 3-8-10 KDarley 6 — —
(JSGoldie) *chse ldrs: rdn 2out and sn wknd* **20/1**

00-0 **9** *5* **Out Of Tune**[41] [1279] 4-9-4 40 GFaulkner 7 — —
(MrsLBNormile) *dwlt and squeezed out s: a bhd* **66/1**

60.19 secs (-0.21) **Going Correction** +0.025s/f (Good)
**WFA** 3 from 4yo+ 8lb — **9** Ran SP% **110.3**
Speed ratings: **102,97,94,87,84 82,82,74,66**CSF £13.15 TOTE £3.10: £1.30, £1.70, £1.40; EX 12.40.The winner was bought in for 7,500gns
**Owner** Middleham Park Racing Xiv **Bred** J W Parker And K Wills **Trained** Sessay, N Yorks

**FOCUS**

Just a run-of-the-mill seller, but the pace was good.

**NOTEBOOK**

**American Cousin**, who failed to handle the conditions at Pontefract last time, was much more at home on this surface and galloped on strongly to complete a hat-trick on the night for his trainer. He is not badly treated off his current mark.

**Vijay(IRE)**, who won on this ground in Ireland, was encountering it for the first time since joining current connections and ran his race without being able to handle the winner. He can win a similar race this summer.

**Best Lead** possibly lost his chance when stumbling at the start, but has given the impression that another furlong may be to his advantage.

**Roan Raider(USA)** could not confirm recent course placings with the third on 5lb worse terms.

**Attila The Hun** *Official explanation: jockey said the gelding hung right throughout*

## 2176 EDINBURGH EVENING NEWS H'CAP — 1m

**8:50** (8:51) (F) (0-55,55) 3-Y-O — **£2,947** (£842; £421) **Stalls** Low

Form — RPR

00-6 **1** **Son Of Thunder (IRE)**[13] [1869] 3-8-11 **50** LEnstone(3) 5 — 54
(MDods) *hld up: n.m.r 1/2-way: hdwy over 2f out: rdn over 1f out: styd on to ld ins last: kpt on* **10/1**

2200 **2** *½* **Sonderborg**[23] [1611] 3-9-5 **55** (e[1]) DaleGibson 4 — 58
(MissAMNewton-Smith) *in tch: pushed along 1/2-way: rdn wl over 2f out: drvn and ch ins last: no ex last 100 yds* **13/2**

03-0 **3** *½* **Welsh Empress**[30] [1467] 3-9-0 **50** FLynch 7 — 52
(PLGilligan) *dwlt and bhd: hdwy on outer 3f out: rdn to chal over 1f out and ev ch tl drvn and no ex wl ins last* **6/1**[3]

00-4 **4** *2½* **Breezit (USA)**[30] [1467] 3-9-3 **53** JBramhill 1 — 49
(SRBowring) *hld up: hdwy over 3f out: led 2f out: sn rdn: hdd & wknd ins last* **7/2**[1]

-024 **5** *4* **Abrogate (IRE)**[90] [802] 3-8-13 **49** GFaulkner 8 — 36
(PCHaslam) *trckd ldrs on inner: effrt over 2f out and ch tl rdn and wknd appr last* **4/1**[2]

00-6 **6** *2* **Mr Moon**[32] [1425] 3-8-10 **46** oh11 KDalgleish 9 — 28
(MDHammond) *led: rdn along 3f out: hdd 2f out and grad wknd* **25/1**

-P02 **7** *2½* **Argent**[9] [1959] 3-9-3 **53** RWinston 2 — 30
(MissLAPerratt) *dwlt: sn chsng ldrs: hdwy to chal 3f out and ev ch tl d riven wl over 1f out and sn wknd* **9/1**

-065 **8** *shd* **Dante's Devine (IRE)**[40] [1301] 3-9-4 **54** GDuffield 6 — 30
(ABailey) *cl up: rdn along 3f out: sn wknd* **7/2**[1]

1m 42.94s (0.24) **Going Correction** +0.175s/f (Good) — **8** Ran SP% **115.0**
Speed ratings: **105,104,104,101,97 95,93,92**CSF £73.15 CT £427.43 TOTE £13.30: £3.40, £2.50, £2.80; EX 60.50 Place 6 £985.10, Place 5 £397.16.
**Owner** Russ Mould **Bred** Sentinel Bloodstock And B Stewart **Trained** Piercebridge, Co Durham

**FOCUS**

A moderate contest and the form looks weak, but a decent winning time for the grade.

**NOTEBOOK**

**Son Of Thunder(IRE)** ◆, making his handicap debut, appeared to score with a little in hand. He looks the sort that will benefit from having got his head in front and, although the form is nothing special, should not go up much from a decent starting point handicap-wise. *Official explanation: trainer said, regarding the improved form shown, gelding was a nervous type who had benefited from the drop in class on this occasion*

**Sonderborg**, better known as an All-Weather performer, had the eyeshield, in which he was narrowly beaten twice earlier in the year, refitted. He ran his race and is capable of picking up a small contest off his current mark, although he remains a maiden after 15 attempts.

**Welsh Empress**, whose best effort was in a seller, tends to raise doubts about the form but ran close to her official mark with the runner-up.

**Breezit(USA)**, given a similar ride to the last time, again appeared to find this trip too far and a drop to seven using similar tactics might work the oracle. *Official explanation: jockey said the filly hung right throughout*

**Abrogate(IRE)** will be better off back in selling company.

**Argent** *Official explanation: jockey said the gelding lost his action*

**Dante's Devine(IRE)** was being pushed along on the turn for home and was disappointing. *Official explanation: jockey said the gelding was unsuited by the track*

T/Plt: £992.00 to a £1 stake. Pool: £37,917.10. 27.90 winning tickets. T/Qpdt: £267.90 to a £1 stake. Pool: £2,715.40. 7.50 winning tickets. JR

# 1996 WINDSOR (R-H)

### Monday, May 17

**OFFICIAL GOING: Good to firm**

Wind: almost nil Weather: sunny & warm

## 2177 COPTHORNE HOTEL SLOUGH/WINDSOR EBF MAIDEN FILLIES' STKS — 5f 10y

**6:05** (6:07) (D) 2-Y-O — **£5,330** (£1,640; £820; £410) **Stalls** High

Form — RPR

**1** **Salsa Brava (IRE)** 2-8-8 J-PGuillambert(3) 12 — 72
(NPLittmoden) *cl up: rdn to ld jst over 1f out: kpt on wl fnl f* **16/1**

**2** *1¼* **Godsend** 2-8-11 DaneO'Neill 8 — 67
(RHannon) *towards rr: shkn up and prog fr 2f out: r.o to chse wnr ins fnl f: no imp* **7/1**

42 **3** *shd* **Ruby's Dream**[7] [1984] 2-8-11 RLMoore 17 — 67
(JMBradley) *racd against nr side rail: chsd ldrs: rdn 2f out: styd on wl fnl f* **11/2**[2]

42 **4** *2½* **Mauro (IRE)**[17] [1751] 2-8-11 JQuinn 10 — 57
(PMPhelan) *racd freely: led to jst over 1f out: fdd fnl f* **20/1**

**5** *nk* **Touch Of Silk (IRE)** 2-8-11 MHills 2 — 56
(BWHills) *chsd ldrs: pushed along 2f out: styd on same pce fr over 1f out* **16/1**

5 **6** *½* **Limonia (GER)**[13] [1871] 2-8-4 MHoward(7) 3 — 54
(DKIvory) *dwlt: racd on outer: sn on terms: cl up over 1f out: fdd* **33/1**

0 **7** *shd* **Aspen Ridge (IRE)**[21] [1670] 2-8-11 JFEgan 18 — 53
(CTinkler) *cl up: rdn 2f out: fdd fnl f* **6/1**[3]

**8** *1½* **Stephanie's Mind** 2-8-11 IMongan 4 — 47
(CNAllen) *rn green and wl in rr: pushed along after 2f: prog over 1f out: nrst fin* **12/1**

5 **9** *hd* **Ivana Illyich (IRE)**[14] [1839] 2-8-11 JDSmith 9 — 47
(SKirk) *t.k.h in midfield: shkn up and rn green 2f out: no prog* **25/1**

**10** *¾* **Romantic Gift** 2-8-11 JTate 14 — 44
(JMPEustace) *s.s: rcvrd into midfield after 2f: no prog over 1f out* **5/1**[1]

**11** *1¼* **Encanto (IRE)** 2-8-4 DerekNolan(7) 19 — 39
(JSMoore) *s.s: wl in rr: modest prog fnl f* **33/1**

4 **12** *nk* **Ms Polly Garter**[13] [1853] 2-8-11 SWhitworth 5 — 37
(JMBradley) *pressed ldrs tl wknd jst over 1f out* **66/1**

**13** *nk* **Diktatit** 2-8-11 TEDurcan 7 — 36
(MRChannon) *dwlt: hanging and rn green: a towards rr* **12/1**

056 **14** *shd* **Misty Princess**[14] [1839] 2-8-8 JFMcDonald(3) 13 — 36
(MJPolglase) *a struggling and towards rr* **40/1**

**15** *½* **Island Swing (IRE)** 2-8-6 HayleyTurner(5) 15 — 34
(JLSpearing) *dwlt: outpcd: nvr on terms* **50/1**

0 **16** *1* **Royal Accolade**[14] [1839] 2-8-11 (t) JMackay 11 — 30
(BHanbury) *chsd ldrs over 3f: eased whn btn fnl f* **10/1**

**17** *1* **Blue Line** 2-8-11 GBaker 1 — 26
(MMadgwick) *dwlt: rn green and a bhd* **100/1**

**18** *nk* **Orpen Annie (IRE)** 2-8-8 BReilly(3) 16 — 25
(MissJFeilden) *nvr on terms w ldrs: hanging bdly lft and wknd over 1f out* **40/1**

**19** *7* **Divani (IRE)** 2-8-11 LDettori 6 — —
(BJMeehan) *racd in midfield to 1/2-way: sn wknd: eased over 1f out* **12/1**

60.96 secs (-0.24) **Going Correction** -0.10s/f (Good) — **19** Ran SP% **126.6**
Speed ratings: **97,95,94,90,90 89,89,87,86,85 83,83,82,82,81 79,78,77,66**CSF £117.04 TOTE £35.60: £8.10, £2.90, £2.90; EX 906.90.
**Owner** Miss Vanessa Church **Bred** Crone Stud Farms Ltd **Trained** Newmarket, Suffolk

**FOCUS**

Probably not a great maiden, but a fair time for the type of race.

**NOTEBOOK**

**Salsa Brava(IRE)** is from a stable not noted for its first-time-out winners, but she did not go unbacked here, having been available at three figures on the exchanges earlier in the day. Always close to the pace, she picked up well when asked to go and win her race, and although this was probably not a strong heat, she looks open to improvement, and the Hilary Needler at Beverley is the next target.

**Godsend** took a while to get the hang of things but when she finally figured out what was required she finished really well on the outside. The run should bring her on and she should be able to find a similar maiden.

**Ruby's Dream** was tackling much quicker ground than she had encountered on her previous two starts, and came home strongly on the stands'-side rail. She finished nicely clear of the rest, but remains vulnerable to something with a bit more potential.

**Mauro(IRE)**, who may have found the drying ground against her, hung left off the favoured stands'-side rail from a furlong out.

**Touch Of Silk(IRE)** did not do too badly from her poor draw and is entitled to benefit from the outing.

**Limonia(GER)** improved on her debut outing and ran a fair race given that she was poorly drawn and stuck out wide in the straight.

**Stephanie's Mind**, another trying to defy a bad draw, ran as though the experience was needed. She should benefit for the run.

**Romantic Gift** was well supported but gave away the advantage of her favourable stalls position with a slow start.

**Encanto(IRE)** *Official explanation: trainer said the filly was unsuited by the good to firm ground*

**Divani(IRE)** *Official explanation: jockey said the filly hung left*

## 2178 SMITH & MILTON CLAIMING STKS — 6f

**6:35** (6:38) (F) 3-Y-O+ — **£3,073** (£878; £439) **Stalls** High

Form — RPR

0504 **1** **I Wish**[13] [1855] 6-8-13 56 GBaker 11 — 64
(MMadgwick) *dwlt: sn rcvrd to trck ldrs: gng easily 2f out: effrt over 1f out: r.o fnl f to ld last stride* **10/1**

5015 **2** *shd* **Effective**[30] [1477] 4-9-8 62 KFallon 2 — 73
(APJarvis) *towards rr: prog on outer over 2f out: hrd rdn to ld jst over 1f out: hdd last stride* **9/1**

-360 **3** *2* **Ivy Moon**[91] [787] 4-8-2 50 RThomas(5) 13 — 52
(BJLlewellyn) *s.i.s: towards rr: plenty to do 2f out: nt clr run over 1f out: swtchd and r.o wl fnl f: nrst fin* **40/1**

6104 **4** ½ **Bells Beach (IRE)**18 [1739] 6-8-9 45 MHills 9 52
(PHowling) *racd in midfield: stdy prog over 2f out: rdn and ev ch jst over 1f out: styd on same pce* **14/1**

60-3 **5** ½ **Tender (IRE)**39 [1319] 4-8-9 57 CCatlin 12 51
(DJDaly) *mde most to 1/2-way: outpcd over 1f out: styd on again ins fnl f* **7/1**[2]

0303 **6** 1 **Aguila Loco (IRE)**3 [2099] 5-9-8 56 (p) SDrowne 17 61
(MrsStefLiddiard) *trckd ldrs: rdn and cl up over 1f out: hanging and fnd nil* **7/1**[2]

3446 **7** shd **Threat**7 [1988] 8-8-9 45 BReilly(3) 3 50
(JMBradley) *prog and prom after 2f: led 1/2-way to jst over 1f out: fdd* **25/1**

0440 **8** 1 ¾ **Port St Charles (IRE)**28 [1504] 7-9-2 66 JQuinn 15 49
(PRChamings) *hld up bhd ldrs against nr side rail: nt clr run over 2f out to over 1f out: one pce after* **6/1**[1]

-050 **9** nk **Rileys Dream**13 [1855] 5-8-7 45 RHavlin 7 39
(BJLlewellyn) *chsd ldrs: cl up whn hung lft over 2f out: n.d fnl f* **50/1**

4610 **10** shd **Flying Faisal (USA)**13 [1859] 6-8-12 47 (b) RLMoore 16 44
(JMBradley) *racd towards rr: shkn up 2f out: no prog tl kpt on ins fnl f* **16/1**

0600 **11** 1 **Sabana (IRE)**7 [1994] 6-9-2 45 (b) SWhitworth 4 45
(JMBradley) *s.s: wl bhd: rdn and styd on fr over 1f out: no ch* **50/1**

0003 **12** ¾ **Pheckless**48 [1185] 5-9-8 58 DaneO'Neill 8 49
(JMBradley) *hld up towards rr: rdn 2f out: no prog* **12/1**

0366 **13** ½ **Tickle**27 [1518] 6-8-7 54 (t) DSweeney 6 32
(PJMakin) *w ldrs: ev ch 2f out: wknd over 1f out* **25/1**

006- **14** nk **Lake Verdi (IRE)**283 [3952] 5-9-8 60 (t) SSanders 18 46
(BHanbury) *w ldrs to 1/2-way: grad wknd fron 2f out* **8/1**[3]

0000 **15** ½ **Naughty Girl (IRE)**13 [1855] 4-8-9 65 (v) JoannaBadger 5 32
(PDEvans) *racd on wd outside: prog and wl in tch 1/2-way: wknd over 1f out* **12/1**

4000 **16** ½ **King's Ballet (USA)**13 [1872] 6-8-9 52 (v1) JFMcDonald(3) 1 33
(PRChamings) *racd on outer: nvr beyond midfield: wknd u.p 2f out* **33/1**

003- **17** 4 **Mac's Talisman (IRE)**214 [5600] 4-9-10 67 MTebbutt 14 33
(VSmith) *in rr whn lost action after 2f: wl bhd after* **10/1**

**18** 7 **Heres Harry**8 4-9-2 JDSmith 10 4
(MissJacquelineSDoyle) *rrd s: a wl bhd* **100/1**

1m 12.6s (-1.27) **Going Correction** -0.10s/f (Good) **18** Ran SP% **124.5**
Speed ratings: **104,103,101,100,99 98,98,96,95,95 94,93,92,92,91 90,85,76** CT £11.70 TOTE £3.20: £3.20, £12.20, £; EX77.40 1.Port St Charles was claimed by C R Dore for £7,000. Tender was claimed by Stef Liddiard for £6,000. Effective was the
**Owner** Mrs Gail Gaisford **Bred** J M T Gaisford **Trained** Denmead, Hants

**FOCUS**
An average claimer, though the runner-up, who can gain compensation, would surely have won with a better draw.

**NOTEBOOK**
**I Wish** ran well at Bath on her previous start and had a fair draw on this drop in grade. She travelled well and just got the better of the runner-up in a driving finish, but had their stalls positions been switched the result would surely have been different.
**Effective** ran a blinder from a poor stall position and would surely have won had he been gifted a high draw. He has yet to win on turf but on this effort a similar heat is well within his abilities.
**Ivy Moon**, beaten in banded grade last time, looked sure to struggle on this drop back in trip despite her high draw. Sure enough, she was doing her best work at the finish.
**Bells Beach(IRE)**, who had a successful spring on the Polytrack, had a bit to find with most of these at the weights. She ran a respectable race in the citrcumstances.
**Tender(IRE)** showed plenty of pace and a drop back to five may help.
**Aguila Loco(IRE)** ran well enough from his good draw, but he has proved himself a difficult horse to win with.
**Port St Charles(IRE)** is another who finds winning difficult, but he looked to have a good deal in his favour here, not least the draw. He got little luck in running, but he is not one to make too many excuses for. *Official explanation: jockey said the gelding suffered interference in running*
**Mac's Talisman(IRE)** *Official explanation: jockey said the colt stumbled twice during the race*

## 2179 ADDLESHAW GODDARD H'CAP — 1m 3f 135y
**7:05** (7:06) (D) (0-85,83) 3-Y-O — **£5,638** (£1,735; £867; £433) **Stalls** Low

Form / RPR

0231 **1** **Tudor Bell (IRE)**10 [1933] 3-8-13 **75** DSweeney 10 81
(JGMO'Shea) *led after 1f: mde rest: rdn and hrd pressed fr over 2f out: styd on wl fnl f* **4/1**[1]

0-00 **2** nk **Coventina (IRE)**32 [1416] 3-9-4 **80** TQuinn 4 85
(JLDunlop) *trckd ldrs: effrt to chal over 2f out: ev ch fnl 2f: styd on but hld last 50y* **6/1**[2]

45-0 **3** hd **Schapiro (USA)**14 [1831] 3-8-13 **75** LDettori 8 80
(JHMGosden) *rousted along to chse wnr after 1f: drvn to chal over 2f out: ev ch over 1f out: hanging lft and nt qckn ins fnl f* **7/1**[3]

46-0 **4** 1 ¾ **Horner (USA)**31 [1437] 3-9-4 **80** SSanders 5 82
(PFICole) *hld up in last pair: prog over 3f out: chsd ldrs over 2f out: styd on fnl f: nvr able to chal* **8/1**

2314 **5** shd **Vantage (IRE)**23 [1609] 3-9-1 **80** J-PGuillambert(3) 3 82
(NPLittmoden) *settled in midfield: prog 4f out: rdn to chal over 2f out: ev ch after: wknd last 150y* **4/1**[1]

30-0 **6** 6 **Nick The Silver**46 [1222] 3-8-3 **65** SCarson 6 57
(GBBalding) *hld up in last: rdn 4f out: struggling and btn over 2f out* **14/1**

03-6 **7** hd **Mustang Ali (IRE)**30 [1466] 3-8-11 **73** PDobbs 1 65
(SKirk) *racd in midfield: forced wd bnd 5f out: rdn and wknd 2f out* **20/1**

30-0 **8** 15 **Wilfred (IRE)**28 [1509] 3-8-8 **70** EAhern 9 38
(JonjoO'Neill) *led for 1f: steadily lost pl fr 1/2-way: wknd 3f out: t.o* **10/1**

00-3 **9** 1 **Hoh Nelson**32 [1419] 3-8-8 **70** RLMoore 7 36
(HMorrison) *chsd ldrs: rdn 4f out: wknd rapidly over 2f out: t.o* **7/1**[3]

2m 30.04s (-0.06) **Going Correction** -0.10s/f (Good) **9** Ran SP% **110.9**
Speed ratings: **96,95,95,94,94 90,90,80,79**CSF £26.05 CT £153.93 TOTE £4.20: £2.00, £2.00, £2.00; EX 52.80.
**Owner** K W Bell & Son Ltd **Bred** Michael Byrne **Trained** Elton, Gloucs
■ Stewards Enquiry : T Quinn four-day ban: used whip with excessive frequency and without giving filly time to respond (May 28-31)
D Sweeney four-day ban: used whip with excessive frequency (May 28-31)

**FOCUS**
A modest time for the grade and a tight finish, and this form is probably not up to the usual standard for this track.

**NOTEBOOK**
**Tudor Bell(IRE)**, proven at the trip, did not set a break-neck pace in front and had plenty in reserve to hold off persistent challengers in the straight. The fact that his rider bagged and kept the rail in the final two furlongs must have helped.
**Coventina(IRE)**, who has only been dropped 2lb for two below-par efforts on easier ground, ran a better race back on fast ground. She still looks high enough in the weights, though.
**Schapiro(USA)** made no show in heavy ground at Kempton on his return and this faster surface appeared to suit. He did not altogether convince with his attitude, however.
**Horner(USA)** never really landed a blow, but he saw the longer trip out well and should be capable of better. Whether he is handicapped to win is another matter, though.
**Vantage(IRE)** settled better this time and had every chance, albeit on the wide outside. He may need some help from the Handicapper.
**Hoh Nelson** *Official explanation: jockey said the colt was unsuited by the good to firm ground*

## 2180 COURT HOUSE CLINICS CONDITIONS STKS — 5f 10y
**7:35** (7:35) (B) 2-Y-O — **£12,151** (£4,609; £2,304; £1,047) **Stalls** High

Form / RPR

11 **1** **Blue Dakota (IRE)**7 [1996] 2-9-3 EAhern 6 100+
(JNoseda) *mde all: drew clr wl over 1f out: easily* **2/9**[1]

13 **2** 2 ½ **Beaver Patrol (IRE)**12 [1878] 2-9-0 SCarson 2 87
(RFJohnsonHoughton) *chsd wnr: rdn bef 1/2-way: kpt on but no imp fr over 1f out* **7/1**[2]

3 **3** 5 **Speed Of Sound**15 [1798] 2-8-6 MartinDwyer 4 59
(AMBalding) *bmpd s: chsd ldng pair: shkn up 1/2-way: outpacd over 1f out* **14/1**[3]

01 **4** 6 **Sea Hunter**15 [1782] 2-9-0 TEDurcan 3 43
(MRChannon) *bmpd s: outpcd and sn wl bhd* **20/1**

**5** 1 **Courageously** 2-8-8 KFallon 1 33
(PFICole) *outpcd and rn green: a wl bhd* **20/1**

3013 **6** 6 **Little Wizzy**7 [1996] 2-8-9 JoannaBadger 5 —
(PDEvans) *bmpd s: outpcd and wl bhd: wknd over 1f out* **66/1**

60.32 secs (-0.88) **Going Correction** -0.10s/f (Good) **6** Ran SP% **112.0**
Speed ratings: **103,99,91,81,79** **70**CSF £2.21 TOTE £1.40: £1.02, £2.40; EX 2.00.
**Owner** A F Nolan, Mrs J M Ryan, Mrs P Duffin **Bred** Michael O'Donnell **Trained** Newmarket, Suffolk
■ Stewards Enquiry : S Carson one-day ban: failed to keep straight from stalls (May 28)

**FOCUS**
Another impressive performance from the speedy Blue Dakota.

**NOTEBOOK**
**Blue Dakota(IRE)**, a taking individual, gave weight to his rivals and put up a professional performance to win again with the minimum of fuss. He will surely go off a short price for the Norfolk Stakes on the back of this, but he sets the standard on what we have seen so far, and it will take a good one to beat him at the Royal meeting.
**Beaver Patrol(IRE)**, who did not get the run of the race at Chester, ran well in defeat but never held out much hope of beating the winner. He will win more races on this evidence and should appreciate a step up to six furlongs.
**Speed Of Sound** was the only other one who could keep tabs on the leader in the early stages, but she was never going quick enough to land a blow. This was still a pleasing step up on the form she showed in contrasting conditions at Salisbury on her debut, though.
**Sea Hunter** won a weak race at Hamilton last time and could never go the pace in this better grade.

## 2181 UFJ INTERNATIONAL PLC H'CAP — 5f 10y
**8:05** (8:06) (D) (0-85,85) 3-Y-O — **£5,622** (£1,730; £865; £432) **Stalls** High

Form / RPR

-422 **1** **Green Manalishi**12 [1883] 3-9-3 **81** TQuinn 7 93+
(DWPArbuthnot) *t.k.h: hld up bhd ldrs: effrt to ld over 1f out: hung lft but in command fnl f* **4/1**[2]

13-3 **2** 1 ¼ **Intriguing Glimpse**11 [1907] 3-8-7 **71** SSanders 1 78
(MissBSanders) *s.i.s: hld up in last trio: prog on outer 2f out: drvn to chse wnr ins fnl f: r.o but a hld* **20/1**

00-2 **3** 1 ¾ **Borzoi Maestro**13 [1854] 3-8-9 **73** ADaly 2 74
(JLSpearing) *s.i.s: t.k.h and hld up: prog and cl up over 1f out: sn rdn and nt qckn* **20/1**

2-05 **4** nk **Dolce Piccata**14 [1829] 3-9-4 **85** JFMcDonald(3) 9 85
(BJMeehan) *pressed ldrs: lost pl and rdn 2f out: hanging over 1f out: r.o again last 100y* **14/1**

1130 **5** nk **Tag Team (IRE)**34 [1388] 3-8-8 **72** MartinDwyer 13 71
(AMBalding) *led to 1/2-way: one pce u.p fr over 1f out* **3/1**[1]

0-00 **6** ½ **Alchera**19 [1702] 3-8-6 **70** (b) SCarson 4 67
(RFJohnsonHoughton) *s.i.s: t.k.h and sn prom: led 1/2-way to over 1f out: wknd ins fnl f* **14/1**

00-0 **7** hd **Mirasol Princess**21 [1673] 3-9-0 **78** IMongan 6 74
(DKIvory) *s.i.s: hld up towards rr: rdn 2f out: one pce and no imp* **9/1**

4615 **8** hd **Crewes Miss Isle**11 [1907] 3-8-3 **67** SWhitworth 12 62
(AGNewcombe) *dwlt: hld up towards rr: shkn up and effrt over 1f out: no prog fnl f* **10/1**

31-5 **9** 1 ¼ **Fiddle Me Blue**30 [1473] 3-8-13 **77** SDrowne 5 68
(HMorrison) *t.k.h: hld up towards rr: rdn 2f out: wknd over 1f out* **9/2**[3]

4431 **10** 1 ¼ **Scottish Exile (IRE)**15 [1788] 3-8-1 **68** (v) LisaJones(3) 11 54
(KRBurke) *pressed ldr for 2f: lost pl and struggling over 2f out* **10/1**

1400 **11** nk **Cheeky Chi (IRE)**5 [2033] 3-8-2 **66** JQuinn 8 51
(PSMcentee) *dwlt: hld up in last trio: rdn and no prog 2f out* **33/1**

16-0 **12** hd **Bahamian Breeze**21 [1673] 3-8-12 **76** (v1) EAhern 10 61
(JNoseda) *dwlt: hld up in last: nudged along 2f out: no prog* **14/1**

60.46 secs (-0.74) **Going Correction** -0.10s/f (Good) **12** Ran SP% **123.8**
Speed ratings: **101,99,96,95,95 94,94,93,91,89 89,89**CSF £88.12 CT £1487.59 TOTE £4.90: £2.00, £5.50, £4.80; EX 138.20.
**Owner** Derrick C Broomfield **Bred** E Aldridge **Trained** Upper Lambourn, Berks

**FOCUS**
A fair sprint and there looks to be more to come from the winner.

**NOTEBOOK**
**Green Manalishi**, pipped at Chester, defied a 3lb higher mark in good style, quickening up well to take up the running inside the last. There looks to be more to come from him and his trainer now plans to send him to Epsom for the Dash.
**Intriguing Glimpse** ran well given that she had the worst stall position to deal with and was forced to challenge widest of all. Granted fast ground and luck with the draw, she looks handicapped to win.
**Borzoi Maestro** usually likes to set the pace but that was always going to be difficult from his low draw. Instead, his rider opted to hold him up on this occasion, and although he raced keenly, he came there to have every chance inside the last.
**Dolce Piccata** ran a better race with the ground having come in her favour. She probably remains a little too high in the handicap at present, though.
**Tag Team(IRE)** showed plenty of early speed, but he edged off the rail in the straight and failed to get home. He has yet to run up to the best of his All-Weather form on turf. *Official explanation: jockey said the colt hung left*
**Alchera** is feasibly treated at present and this was a better effort back on faster ground.
**Mirasol Princess** held a decent chance at the weights based on her course and distance win back in September, but she never got competitive on this occasion after a slow start.
**Bahamian Breeze**, visored for the first time, was never in contention, but at least this effort should help bring his mark down a bit.

## 2182 E-TRINSIC PERFORMANCE CHALLENGE MAIDEN FILLIES' STKS 1m 67y

8:35 (8:37) (D) 3-Y-O+ £4,433 (£1,364; £682; £341) Stalls High

| Form | | | | RPR |
|---|---|---|---|---|
| 4 | 1 | | **Diamond Lodge**[33] 1395 3-8-9 ... SWKelly 17<br>(JNoseda) *sn trckd ldrs: gng easily 3f out: swtchd lft 2f out: effrt to ld ent fnl f: r.o wl: comf* **11/4**[1] | 78 |
| 43 | 2 | 1 1/4 | **Pinching (IRE)**[17] 1753 3-8-9 ... (v[1]) WRyan 3<br>(HRACecil) *hld up in midfield: stdy prog on outer over 3f out: shakn up to chal over 1f out and rdr dropped whip: styd on: a hld* **8/1**[3] | 75 |
| 2-3 | 3 | 1 1/4 | **Kali**[48] 1189 3-8-9 ... DSweeney 2<br>(RCharlton) *cl up: effrt to ld 2f out: hdd and one pce ent fnl f* **12/1** | 72 |
| 02- | 4 | 1 | **Tenny's Gold (IRE)**[196] 5911 3-8-9 ... MHills 9<br>(BWHills) *led for 2f: styd pressing ldr: ev ch 2f out: one pce after* **8/1**[3] | 70 |
| 02 | 5 | 1 | **Sharp Needle**[17] 1747 3-8-9 ... EAhern 16<br>(JNoseda) *prom: rdn over 2f out: kpt on same pce fnl 2f* **11/1** | 67 |
| 0 | 6 | 3/4 | **Sea Of Gold**[33] 1400 3-8-9 ... RLMoore 12<br>(HJCyzer) *chsd ldrs: pushed along over 3f out: unable to chal 2f out: styd on* **100/1** | 66 |
| 0- | 7 | shd | **Bonsai (IRE)**[224] 5422 3-8-9 ... MTebbutt 15<br>(RTPhillips) *walked to post and mounted at s: dwlt: wl in rr: pushed along 3f out: rn green but styd on steadily fnl 2f: nrst fin* **100/1** | 65 |
| 03- | 8 | 5 | **Adaptable**[217] 5539 3-8-9 ... DaneO'Neill 13<br>(HCandy) *led after 2f to 2f out: wknd over 1f out* **9/1** | 54 |
| | 9 | 3 | **Palabelle (IRE)** 3-8-9 ... MartinDwyer 18<br>(PWHarris) *wl in rr: rdn 4f out: no prog tl r.o last 150y: fin wl* **16/1** | 47 |
| 4 | 10 | nk | **Lillianna (IRE)**[17] 1753 3-8-9 ... PaulEddery 1<br>(HRACecil) *racd in midfield: rdn 3f out: no imp ldrs 2f: sn wknd* **33/1** | 46 |
| 5- | 11 | 1 | **Torchlight (USA)**[340] 2306 4-9-7 ... LDettori 8<br>(JHMGosden) *pressed ldrs: rdn over 3f out: wknd 2f out: eased* **4/1**[2] | 44 |
| 0- | 12 | shd | **Golden Drift**[170] 6090 3-8-9 ... DHolland 6<br>(GWragg) *a in rr: rdn and struggling 4f out* **16/1** | 44 |
| | 13 | 2 1/2 | **Land Army (IRE)** 3-8-6 ... BReilly(3) 10<br>(MissJFeilden) *racd in midfield: pushed along 4f out: wknd over 2f out* **100/1** | 38 |
| 0- | 14 | nk | **Eva Jean**[205] 5754 3-8-9 ... SDrowne 11<br>(HMorrison) *t.k.h: prom: rdn over 3f out: wknd over 2f out: eased* **14/1** | 37 |
| | 15 | 1/2 | **Lady Taverner** 3-8-9 ... GCarter 7<br>(HJCyzer) *b: dwlt: a wl bhd* **66/1** | 36 |
| | 16 | 3 1/2 | **Agouti** 3-8-9 ... TQuinn 5<br>(DWPArbuthnot) *a wl bhd* **50/1** | 28 |
| | 17 | 3 | **Favourable** 3-8-6 ... LPKeniry(3) 14<br>(BJMeehan) *s.s: a wl bhd* **66/1** | 21 |
| | P | | **Tytherley** 3-8-6 ... JFMcDonald(3) 4<br>(JRBoyle) *in rr whn nrly rn off crse bnd 6f out: nrly rn off crse bnd 5f out: t.o and p.u over 3f out* **100/1** | — |

1m 45.78s (0.18) **Going Correction** -0.10s/f (Good)
**WFA** 3 from 4yo 12lb **18** Ran SP% **125.2**
Speed ratings: **95,93,92,91,90 89,89,84,81,81 80,80,77,77,76 73,70,**—CSF £24.80 TOTE £4.40: £2.20, £3.20, £2.40; EX 38.20 Place 6 £282.58, Place 5 £87.60.
**Owner** Mrs J Harris **Bred** Chippenham Lodge Stud Ltd **Trained** Newmarket, Suffolk

**FOCUS**
Not a strong maiden on paper, but they went fast early and a modest winning time for the grade suggests that they paid for that effort in the closing stages.

**NOTEBOOK**
**Diamond Lodge** had run with promise in the Wood Ditton on her debut, but that form had taken a few knocks since. She travelled well in this lesser contest, though, and responded well when asked to go and win her race. She looks likely to stay ten furlongs on this evidence.
**Pinching(IRE)**, visored for the first time, ran a fair race in defeat, but in this sort of grade she is always going to look vulnerable to something with a bit more potential.
**Kali** got worked up beforehand but did little wrong in the race itself. Bagging the favoured stands'-side rail in the straight, she did not see out the trip as well as the front two, but this was another solid effort, and she is now eligible for a mark.
**Tenny's Gold(IRE)** is out of a mare who won over a mile six and it could be that she will need farther than this in handicap company.
**Sharp Needle**, who had not looked in need of this drop back in trip on her last outing at Musselburgh, is another now eligible for a mark.
**Sea Of Gold**, a half-sister to four winners out of a mare who was a multiple scorer over middle-distances, showed a lot more this time than she had on her debut, and handicaps beckon for her too after one more run.
**Bonsai(IRE)** does not look the most straightforward, but she should benefit from a step up in distance.
**Palabelle(IRE)** struggled to go the early pace but was putting in some decent work at the finish. A half-sister to five winners over distances of between six furlongs and two miles, she looks sure to leave this effort behind in due course.
**Torchlight(USA)** weakened out of contention in a manner which suggested that there was something amiss. *Official explanation: jockey said the filly hung left*
**Tytherley** *Official explanation: jockey said the filly cocked her jaw*
T/Jkpt: £278,821.81 to a £1 stake. Pool: £589,060.31. 1.50 winning tickets. T/Plt: £73.10 to a £1 stake. Pool: £74,429.35. 742.50 winning tickets. T/Qpdt: £8.70 to a £1 stake. Pool: £3,171.00. 268.60 winning tickets. JN

# 2012 WOLVERHAMPTON (A.W) (L-H)

Monday, May 17

**OFFICIAL GOING: Standard**
There was a bias against those that raced close to the inside rail and it paid to be brought wide into the home straight.
Wind: slt hlf bhd Weather: fine & sunny

## 2183 ENABLED DAY AT DUNSTALL PARK BANDED STKS 5f (F)

2:30 (2:30) (H) 3-Y-0+ £1,442 (£412; £206) Stalls Low

| Form | | | | RPR |
|---|---|---|---|---|
| 0233 | 1 | | **Levelled**[12] 1890 10-9-3 35 ... ACulhane 9<br>(DWChapman) *hld up in mid-div: gd hdwy over 1f out: fin strly to ld nr fin* **10/1** | 49 |
| 0226 | 2 | nk | **Cleveland Way**[11] 1915 4-8-10 40 ... (v) DTudhope(7) 7<br>(DCarroll) *a.p: led 1/2-way: riddden over 1f out: kpt on: hdd nr fin* **4/1**[1] | 48 |
| 5040 | 3 | 5 | **Bells Boy's**[48] 1191 5-9-3 40 ... (p) NCallan 8<br>(KARyan) *a in tch: chsd ldr 1/2-way: rdn and wknd fnl f* **11/1** | 30 |
| 00/0 | 4 | 1 1/4 | **Bright Mist**[24] 1584 5-9-3 40 ... PDoe 2<br>(BPalling) *s.i.s: and wl in rr tl hdwy on wd outside over 1f out: kpt on nvr nrr* **33/1** | 26 |
| 5334 | 5 | 1 1/4 | **Sotonian (HOL)**[18] 1724 11-8-12 40 ... StephanieHollinshead(5) 12<br>(PSFelgate) *a mid-div and nt pce to chal ins fnl 2f* **8/1**[3] | 21 |
| 0230 | 6 | shd | **Avit (IRE)**[13] 1859 4-9-3 40 ... JFEgan 10<br>(PLGilligan) *chsd ldrs tl wknd over 1f out* **8/1**[3] | 21 |
| -044 | 7 | 1 | **Minirina**[12] 1886 4-9-3 35 ... RFitzpatrick 5<br>(CSmith) *led to 1/2-way: rdn and wknd wl over 1f out* **33/1** | 17 |
| -003 | 8 | 1 | **Travellers Joy**[12] 1886 4-9-0 40 ... TPQueally(3) 3<br>(RJHodges) *in tch whn hmpd over 3f out: no ch after* **9/1** | 13 |
| -0U5 | 9 | 1/2 | **Mandy's Collection**[6] 2012 5-9-3 40 ... (p) SWhitworth 11<br>(AGNewcombe) *a outpcd in rr* **12/1** | 12 |
| 0-00 | 10 | 3/4 | **Back In Spirit**[109] 626 4-9-3 40 ... (t) GGibbons 6<br>(BAMcmahon) *s.i.s: outpce thrght* **6/1**[2] | 9 |
| 5155 | 11 | 3 1/2 | **Tuscan Dream**[12] 1886 9-8-12 40 ... PBradley(5) 1<br>(ABerry) *prom on ins whn bdly hmpd over 3f out: no ch after* **16/1** | — |
| 4102 | 12 | 14 | **White O' Morn**[12] 1886 5-9-3 40 ... (p) DHolland 4<br>(JWUnett) *rein broke sn after s: wnt bdly lft overe 3f out and brought home in own time* **4/1**[1] | — |

62.37 secs (-0.43) **Going Correction** -0.125s/f (Stan) **12** Ran SP% **123.4**
Speed ratings: **98,97,89,87,85 85,83,82,81,80 74,52**CSF £51.84 TOTE £10.10: £4.00, £4.40, £3.00; EX 52.90.
**Owner** David W Chapman **Bred** J F Watson **Trained** Stillington, N Yorks

**FOCUS**
A fairly competitive race of its type run at a good pace, but only two mattered in the second half of the contest. Again those that raced away from the inside rail appeared to have an advantage.

**NOTEBOOK**
**Levelled**, back over the minimum trip, has been running well at this level recently and came late down the centre of the track to register his first win for well over four years. This victory owes much to his experienced rider using the track bias to his advantage.
**Cleveland Way**, back to the minimum trip for the first time in four outings, did most things right and looked to have established a significant advantage turning for home, but he edged left into the slower ground under a right-hand drive and had the race snatched from him.
**Bells Boy's** is not short of early speed, but he is a weak finisher and that was again the case despite the drop back to the minimum trip.
**Bright Mist** ◆ ran a remarkable race. Tailed off on her recent return following a break of 22 months, the same fate looked likely here at halfway as she was well detached and hanging badly right on the home bend, but she picked up to some effect once into the straight and flew home to snatch fourth. She had shown ability in a couple of Class D seven-furlong maidens here a couple of years ago and could be very interesting over that sort of trip at this level.
**Sotonian(HOL)** ran his usual sort of race, but has become an incredibly hard horse to win with.
**Travellers Joy** ran into trouble leaving the back straight and had no chance after that.
**Tuscan Dream** showed good pace from his inside draw and tried to reach the bend in front, but he was completely wiped out by the errant White O' Morn and that was his chance gone.
**White O' Morn** had the misfortune of a rein breaking soon after the start and, with the steering gone, she hung badly left and caused serious problems to a couple of rivals on her inside starting the home turn. This run can be safely ignored. *Official explanation: jockey said mare's rein had come away from the bridle*

## 2184 WINNING POST SPECIAL AT DUNSTALL PARK BANDED STKS 1m 1f 79y(F)

3:00 (3:00) (H) 3-Y-0+ £1,442 (£412; £206) Stalls Low

| Form | | | | RPR |
|---|---|---|---|---|
| 2023 | 1 | | **Moyne Pleasure (IRE)**[11] 1917 6-9-7 35 ... (p) DHolland 1<br>(PaulJohnson) *mde all: qcknd 4f out: rdn 2f out: drew wl clr fnl f* **6/4**[1] | 47 |
| 0-52 | 2 | 9 | **Ben Kenobi**[6] 2017 6-9-7 30 ... RFfrench 5<br>(MrsPFord) *chsd wnr thrght: rdn over 2f out: no hdwy after and wknd ins fnl f* **9/4**[2] | 29 |
| /0-4 | 3 | 2 1/2 | **Classical Waltz (IRE)**[12] 1885 6-9-0 30 ... DTudhope(7) 6<br>(JJSheehan) *bhd early: hdwy 6f out: sn rdn: chsd first 2 fnl 2f* **14/1** | 24 |
| 02/ | 4 | 7 | **Royal Exposure (IRE)**[1316] 4877 7-9-7 30 ... PaulEddery 3<br>(MWigham) *s.i.s: rdn and struggling fr over 4f out* **7/1** | 10 |
| 5534 | 5 | 1 | **Second Generation (IRE)**[12] 1890 7-9-4 30 ... TPQueally(3) 2<br>(RJHodges) *chsd ldrs tl wknd qckly over 2f out* **7/2**[3] | 8 |
| 00-0 | 6 | 21 | **Diagon Alley (IRE)**[70] 989 4-9-2 30 ... PBradley(5) 4<br>(KWHogg) *slowly away: sn struggling wl in rr* **25/1** | — |

2m 2.49s (-0.51) **Going Correction** -0.125s/f (Stan) **6** Ran SP% **116.0**
Speed ratings: **97,89,86,80,79 61**CSF £5.41 TOTE £2.60: £1.10, £1.50; EX 2.70.
**Owner** P And Mrs D M Johnson **Bred** Castlemartin Stud **Trained** White-le-Head, Co Durham

**FOCUS**
A moderate and uncompetitive event though the pace was sound.

**NOTEBOOK**
**Moyne Pleasure(IRE)**, officially rated higher than his five opponents, would have eaten these on his form of a couple of year ago and was backed to do just that. Bounced out from the stalls, he always looked comfortable in front and when asked to quicken he disposed of his rivals with disdain. He will not find many opportunities like this.
**Ben Kenobi** had given the impression he would be suited by a return to this sort of trip, but after stalking the winner for much of the way he capitulated rather tamely. It is now back to the drawing board.
**Classical Waltz(IRE)** never looked like winning and finished further behind Moyne Pleasure than he did in an amateur riders' event here last time.
**Royal Exposure(IRE)**, whose only two previous outings came in 2000, showed nothing on his return.
**Second Generation(IRE)** was trying beyond seven furlongs for the first time and failed to stay.

## 2185 NORWAY'S INDEPENDENCE DAY BANDED STKS 1m 100y(F)

3:30 (3:30) (H) 3-Y-0+ £1,445 (£413; £206) Stalls Low

| Form | | | | RPR |
|---|---|---|---|---|
| 30-5 | 1 | | **Super Dominion**[12] 1888 7-8-11 40 ... (p) StephanieHollinshead(5) 10<br>(RHollinshead) *a.p: led 4f out: rdn clr ent fnl f* **3/1**[1] | 50 |
| 0316 | 2 | 4 | **Amethyst Rock**[11] 1918 6-9-2 40 ... JFEgan 4<br>(PLGilligan) *led: hdd 5f out:: wnt 2nd again over 1f out: kpt on but no ch w wnr* **3/1**[1] | 42 |
| 0040 | 3 | 3/4 | **Roving Vixen (IRE)**[7] 1987 3-8-4 40 ... (b[1]) ADaly 6<br>(JLSpearing) *rrd s: wl bhd tl hdwy over 2f out: styd on after nvr nrr* **10/1**[3] | 40 |
| 1606 | 4 | nk | **Dafa**[18] 1728 8-8-13 40 ... (p) TPQueally(3) 3<br>(BJCurley) *wl in rr: hdwy past weakeneing horses over 2f out: styd on wl after: nvr nrr* **3/1**[1] | 39 |
| 4313 | 5 | 1 1/2 | **Rathmullan**[4] 2051 5-9-1 40 ... (b) LiamJones(7) 2<br>(EAWheeler) *trckd early ldr: rdn over 3f out: kpt on one pce after* **10/1**[3] | 42 |
| /04- | 6 | hd | **Tomsk (IRE)**[166] 2521 4-8-9 40 ... PPMathers(7) 9<br>(ABerry) *mid-div: rdn over 2f out: one pce after* **20/1** | 36 |
| 0-00 | 7 | 8 | **Rovella**[10] 1946 3-8-4 40 ... GGibbons 7<br>(MrsHDalton) *prom to 1/2-way* **16/1** | 19 |
| 0-30 | 8 | nk | **Moonlight Song (IRE)**[7] 1992 7-9-2 40 ... PaulEddery 8<br>(JohnAHarris) *trckd ldrs: led 5f out: hdd 4f out: wknd wl over 1f out* **7/1**[2] | 18 |
| -000 | 9 | 1 1/4 | **Miss Ocean Monarch**[12] 1885 4-9-2 30 ... ACulhane 1<br>(DWChapman) *a outpcd in rr* **12/1** | 16 |



The Form Book, Raceform Ltd, Compton, RG20 6NL

00-0 **10** 3 ½ **Forest Queen**$^{70}$ [994] 7-8-11 30 ........ PBradley$^{(5)}$ 5 8
(KWHogg) *sn struggling in rr* **50/1**

1m 51.79s (0.70) **Going Correction** -0.125s/f (Stan)
**WFA** 3 from 4yo+ 12lb **10** Ran SP% **126.0**
Speed ratings: **91,87,86,85,84 84,76,75,74,71**CSF £12.34 TOTE £4.20: £1.20, £1.20, £3.90; EX 23.90.
**Owner** Mrs Norman Hill **Bred** Norman Hill Plant Hire Ltd **Trained** Upper Longdon, Staffs

**FOCUS**
A moderate winning time, even for a banded stakes.

**NOTEBOOK**
**Super Dominion**, who has winning form on this track and has been successful off a mark of 60 in his time, showed the benefit of his recent pipe-opener here and bounded away from his rivals for a clear-cut victory. Even though opportunities at this level have now probably ended, he could still handle a rise in class.
**Amethyst Rock**, so disappointing at Southwell last time, made the early running tight against the inside rail, but he came off the bridle down the back straight and looked likely to drop right out. Once pulled out a little wider, he got his second wind and ran on again to take second without ever posing a threat to the winner. His best trip is still rather a mystery, but he does look to need further than this.
**Roving Vixen(IRE)** lost a good six lengths when jumping up in the air as the stalls opened, so did well to get into the money. She is not without hope at this level.
**Dafa** found the drop back to a mile against him.
**Rathmullan** has never shown much over this trip.

## 2186 MIX BUSINESS WITH PLEASURE AT DUNSTALL PARK BANDED STKS 2m 46y(F)
4:00 (4:00) (H) 4-Y-0+ £1,445 (£413; £206) Stalls Low

Form RPR
64-2 **1** **Prince Of The Wood (IRE)**$^{20}$ [1693] 4-8-12 45 ........ DHolland 3 56
(ABailey) *hld up towards rr: hdwy 7f out: led 5f out: mde rest and in command fnl f* **3/1**$^{3}$
5-14 **2** 1 ¾ **My Legal Eagle (IRE)**$^{7}$ [2004] 10-8-11 45 ........ RMiles$^{(3)}$ 6 54
(RJPrice) *hld up: stdy hdwy to trck wnr 4f out: rdn 2f out: kpt on but no imp fnl f* **4/1**
0-00 **3** 11 **Fairy Wind (GER)**$^{99}$ [715] 7-8-11 45 ........ TPQueally$^{(3)}$ 4 41
(BJCurley) *chsd ldr: led over 1m out: hdd 5f out: rdn over 3f out: sn struggling to keep in tch and wknd 2f out* **9/4**$^{1}$
-415 **4** 24 **Mercurious (IRE)**$^{24}$ [1593] 4-8-12 45 ........ ACulhane 5 12
(JMackie) *trckd ldr 1/2-way: rdn over 4f out: and wknd sn after* **5/2**$^{2}$
2504 **5** 4 **Unleaded**$^{28}$ [1512] 4-8-12 35 ........ PDoe 1 7
(JAkehurst) *trckd ldrs: rdn 7f out: sn struggling in rr* **14/1**
/056 **6** dist **Oulton Broad**$^{8}$ [789] 8-9-0 30 ........(p) SWKelly 2 —
(FJordan) *hld up: lost tch 7f out: t.o* **14/1**
43-6 **7** dist **Ton-Chee**$^{70}$ [992] 5-8-9 30 ........ PBradley$^{(5)}$ 7 —
(KWHogg) *s.i.s but sn led: hdd over 1m out: sn lost tch: t.o* **33/1**

3m 38.63s (-3.67) **Going Correction** -0.125s/f (Stan)
**WFA** 4 from 5yo+ 2lb **7** Ran SP% **120.6**
Speed ratings: **104,103,97,85,83** —,—CSF £16.66 TOTE £5.00: £2.60, £2.50; EX 14.90.
**Owner** The Four Of Us **Bred** William J Hamilton **Trained** Little Budworth, Cheshire

**FOCUS**
A proper test of stamina and a good winning time for a race of its type.

**NOTEBOOK**
**Prince Of The Wood(IRE)** ran well over this trip at Lingfield, but seemed to appreciate the return to this more testing surface and, with the runner-up on his tail throughout the last half-mile, it was staying power that gained him the day. He can win again at this level if given the chance.
**My Legal Eagle(IRE)** looked a big threat to all when moving closer racing down the back straight on the final circuit, but despite several attempts to get on top he found the winner far too determined.
**Fairy Wind(GER)**, backed off the boards, was trying two miles for the first time and did not see it out.
**Mercurious(IRE)** was very disappointing considering how well she saw the trip out when winning on her last visit here.
**Unleaded** has gone off the boil in the last couple of months.
**Oulton Broad** *Official explanation: trainer's representative said the mare had a breathing problem*

## 2187 RACING FOR ALL AT DUNSTALL PARK TRI-BANDED STKS 6f (F)
4:30 (4:30) (H) 3-Y-0 £1,438 (£411; £205) Stalls Low

Form RPR
00-0 **1** **Sam The Sorcerer**$^{10}$ [1942] 3-9-0 45 ........ DarrenWilliams 1 43
(JRNorton) *prom on ins: wnt 2nd 1/2-way and drifted to outside st: edgd rt appr fnl f: r.o wl to ld fnl 50yds* **12/1**
0-03 **2** 1 **Dress Pearl**$^{25}$ [1571] 3-8-4 35 ........(b$^{1}$) GGibbons 6 30
(RPElliott) *in tch: outpcd 1/2-way: fin fast fnl f to go 2nd cl home* **7/1**
0000 **3** nk **Mitzi Caspar**$^{15}$ [1794] 3-8-5 30 ow1 ........ RPrice 7 30
(PLGilligan) *towards rr: hdwy on outside over 2f out: styd on strly fnl f: nvr nrr* **10/1**
-065 **4** hd **Niteowl Express (IRE)**$^{31}$ [1447] 3-8-6 40 ........(b$^{1}$) DAllan$^{(3)}$ 4 34
(JO'Reilly) *led after 1f: rdn and hdd fnl 50yds: no ex* **4/1**$^{1}$
00-0 **5** 1 **Be My Alibi (IRE)**$^{11}$ [1908] 3-8-9 40 ........ SWKelly 2 31
(WMBrisbourne) *chsd ldrs: rdn and nt qckn fnl f* **6/1**$^{3}$
4255 **6** ¾ **Heathyards Joy**$^{7}$ [1985] 3-7-13 35 ........ StephanieHollinshead$^{(5)}$ 5 23
(RHollinshead) *in tch: rdn over 2f out: fdd ent fnl f* **6/1**$^{3}$
0056 **7** 10 **Dandy Jim**$^{5}$ [2037] 3-8-1 30 ........(b$^{1}$) RMiles$^{(3)}$ 9 —
(DWChapman) *slowly away: a struggling in rr* **7/1**
0402 **8** 1 **Indrani**$^{7}$ [1985] 3-8-9 40 ........ PaulEddery 8 —
(JohnAHarris) *racd wd: outpcd and nvr on terms* **5/1**$^{2}$
-054 **9** 9 **Anatom**$^{7}$ [1985] 3-8-2 35 ow1 ........(vt$^{1}$) TPQueally$^{(3)}$ 3 —
(PSMcentee) *led tl hdd after 1f: wknd 1/2-way* **8/1**

1m 16.39s (0.59) **Going Correction** -0.125s/f (Stan) **9** Ran SP% **118.1**
Speed ratings: **91,89,89,89,87 86,73,72,60**CSF £95.04 TOTE £15.80: £2.60, £1.90, £4.80; EX 168.20.
**Owner** Tim Simcox & Exors of Mrs P Farrow **Bred** E A R Morgans **Trained** High Hoyland, S Yorks

**FOCUS**
A moderate contest and it was noticeable that the runners gave the inside rail a wide berth.

**NOTEBOOK**
**Sam The Sorcerer**, no closer than ninth in four previous attempts, was dropping considerably in class. After racing towards the inside of the field early, he really found his stride when switched to the outside in the straight and came with a strong run to land the spoils. This was a bad race, but he does have a little bit of scope. *Official explanation: trainer said, regarding the improved form shown, gelding was big and weak as a two-year-old and had benefited from today's drop in class*
**Dress Pearl**, blinkered for the first time, came home strongly after losing her pitch but her best trip is proving something of a mystery.
**Mitzi Caspar**, well beaten in her four previous starts over a mile, was dropping considerably in class as well as in trip and was doing her best work late. She looks worth a try over seven in this company.
**Niteowl Express(IRE)**, dropping back from a mile and blinkered for the first time, made a bold bid to make every yard and looked to be holding all the aces turning for home. Still in front well inside the last furlong, the wheels then came off completely and she lost three places in the last 50 yards. It will be a real challenge to find her best trip.
**Be My Alibi(IRE)** has become very disappointing after showing a little promise in maiden company a year ago and this drop in trip did not bring about much improvement.

## 2188 SPONSOR A RACE AT DUNSTALL PARK BANDED STKS 7f (F)
5:00 (5:00) (H) 3-Y-0+ £1,435 (£410; £205) Stalls High

Form RPR
1003 **1** **Marabar**$^{9}$ [1956] 6-9-5 45 ........(b) ACulhane 2 53
(DWChapman) *trckd ldr: led 3f out: strly rdn over 1f out: kpt up to work and in command fnl f* **2/1**$^{2}$
3312 **2** 2 ½ **Neutral Night (IRE)**$^{6}$ [2012] 4-9-5 45 ........(v) DHolland 5 47
(RBrotherton) *chsd ldrs: outpcd over 2f out: c wd into staight: kpt on to go 2nd ins fnl f* **6/5**$^{1}$
2316 **3** 1 **Shirley Oaks (IRE)**$^{7}$ [1986] 6-9-0 45 ........ NChalmers$^{(5)}$ 6 44
(MissZCDavison) *hld up in tch: outpcd 1/2-way: styd on to go 3rd wl ins fnl f* **4/1**$^{3}$
0-02 **4** ½ **My Girl Pearl (IRE)**$^{12}$ [1889] 4-9-0 40 ........ PMakin$^{(5)}$ 1 43
(MSSaunders) *led tl hdd 3f out: rdn over 1f out: one pce and fdd ins fnl f* **8/1**
0550 **5** 8 **Young Dynasty**$^{10}$ [1939] 4-8-12 45 ........(b) LiamJones$^{(7)}$ 3 22
(EAWheeler) *plld hrd: a in rr* **28/1**
-030 **6** dist **Gwazi**$^{33}$ [1389] 4-9-5 40 ........(t) DarrenWilliams 4 —
(MissDAMchale) *slowly away: sn wl bhd: t.o 1/2-way: virtually p.u over 2f out* **20/1**

1m 29.72s (-0.60) **Going Correction** -0.125s/f (Stan) **6** Ran SP% **118.1**
Speed ratings: **98,95,94,93,84** —CSF £5.14 TOTE £3.10: £1.70, £1.10; EX 6.20 Place 6 £139.34, Place 5 £44.20.
**Owner** Miss N F Thesiger **Bred** Mrs M T Dawson **Trained** Stillington, N Yorks

**FOCUS**
A modest contest, but at least the pace was sound.

**NOTEBOOK**
**Marabar**, third off a mark of 63 in a Class D handicap on turf at Beverley in her most recent start, is rated much lower on sand and had never shown much over this trip in the past, but she found a race she could win on sand and had the race in safe keeping turning for home. It seems likely that she will be handicapped out of races like this once reassessed, so connections will be keen to strike whilst the iron is hot.
**Neutral Night(IRE)** ran her race and stayed on to finish second at a respectful distance, but the winner proved far too good.
**Shirley Oaks(IRE)** has been running consistently well on Polytrack of late, but two previous tries here do not match up and she was always struggling to make much impression.
**My Girl Pearl(IRE)** ran to a similar level of form with Neutral Night compared to their meeting here 12 days earlier.
**Gwazi** walked out of the stalls and was tailed off when pulled up on the home turn. He had reportedly lost his action. *Official explanation: jockey said the gelding lost his action*
T/Plt: £95.70 to a £1 stake. Pool: £20,938.95. 159.60 winning tickets. T/Qpdt: £32.10 to a £1 stake. Pool: £1,421.00. 32.70 winning tickets. JS

2189 - 2192a (Foreign Racing) - See Raceform Interactive

# 1952 CHANTILLY (R-H)
Monday, May 17

**OFFICIAL GOING: Good**

## 2193a PRIX D'ANGERVILLE (LISTED) (FILLIES) 7f
2:20 (2:20) 3-Y-0 £15,845 (£6,338; £4,754; £3,169)

RPR
**1** **Baqah (IRE)**$^{17}$ [1756] 3-8-12 ........ DBonilla 7 109
(FHead, France) **1**
**2** 1 ½ **Dolma (FR)**$^{17}$ [1756] 3-9-2 ........ C-PLemaire 3 109
(NClement, France)
**3** 2 **Secret Melody (FR)**$^{221}$ 3-8-12 ........ MAndrouin 1 100
(H-APantall, France)
**4** 1 ½ **Bits Of Paradise (FR)**$^{31}$ 3-8-12 ........ GaryStevens 10 97
(AFabre, France)
**5** ¾ **Tolzey (USA)**$^{270}$ [4322] 3-8-12 ........ TJarnet 4 95
(H-APantall, France)
**6** nk **Kunda (IRE)**$^{199}$ [5851] 3-8-12 ........ ELegrix 11 94
(RHannon) *pushed along from start but soon towards rear, 8th straight, ridden 2f out, stayed on one pace under pressure*
**7** 1 **Fastidia**$^{17}$ [1756] 3-8-12 ........ DBoeuf 5 92
(ELellouche, France)
**8** nk **Vulnerable**$^{33}$ 3-8-12 ........ RonanThomas 2 91
(MmeCHead-Maarek, France)
**9** ¾ **Delta**$^{13}$ 3-8-12 ........ TThulliez 6 89
(PBary, France)
**10** 2 ½ **Haskilclara (FR)**$^{22}$ [1652] 3-8-12 ........ CSoumillon 9 83
(YDeNicolay, France)
**11** **Wakired (USA)**$^{33}$ 3-8-12 ........ OPeslier 8 83
(MmeCHead-Maarek, France)

1m 25.7s **11** Ran SP% **18.5**
Speed ratings: .
**Owner** Hamdan Al Maktoum **Bred** Shadwell Estate Company Limited **Trained** France

**NOTEBOOK**
**Kunda(IRE)**, struggled early but was doing her best work at the finish. Her rider felt she would not let herself down on the fast ground.

# 1955 BEVERLEY (R-H)
Tuesday, May 18

**OFFICIAL GOING: Good to firm**
The ground was described as 'fast side of good but rough against the far-side running rail'. The times were slow because of quite a brisk head-on wind.
Wind: mod hlf against Weather: fine & sunny

## 2194 NEW FIXTURE NEXT MONDAY (S) STKS 5f
2:20 (2:20) (F) 2-Y-0 £3,396 (£1,045; £522; £261) Stalls High

Form RPR
66 **1** **Mytton's Dream**$^{13}$ [1884] 2-8-3 ........ TPQueally$^{(3)}$ 6 53
(ABailey) *hmpd s: bhd: hdwy 2f out: swtchd lft and pushed wd jst ins last: r.o to ld last 50 yds* **5/1**$^{2}$

00 **2** 1½ **Keresforth**$^{10}$ [1970] 2-8-11 ....................(b$^{1}$) WSupple 4 52
(TDEasterby) *chsd ldrs: rdn over 2f out: styd on on ins to ld jst ins last: hdd and no ex last 50yds* **18/1**

0 **3** 3½ **Concert Time**$^{53}$ [1115] 2-8-6 .................... RFitzpatrick 1 33
(PTMidgley) *sn outpcd and bhd: hdwy and wnt rt over 1f out: kpt on* **50/1**

526 **4** ¾ **Emma's Venture**$^{22}$ [1666] 2-8-6 .................... GDuffield 9 30
(MWEasterby) *swvd lft s: in tch: swtchd rt over 1f out: kpt on* **6/1**$^{3}$

60 **5** 1 **Our Louis**$^{26}$ [1556] 2-8-6 .................... EAhern 10 26
(JSWainwright) *led: hung lft and hdd jst ins fnl f: sn wknd* **16/1**

3016 **6** 2 **Why Harry**$^{10}$ [1970] 2-9-2 .................... KDarley 11 28
(JJQuinn) *chsd ldrs: rdn 2f out: one pce whn sltly hmpd ins last* **11/8**$^{1}$

**7** ¾ **Hollingwood Soul** 2-8-6 .................... DeanMcKeown 5 15
(RonaldThompson) *hmpd s: bhd tl sme hdwy fnl 2f* **20/1**

02 **8** 8 **Miller Hill**$^{3}$ [2124] 2-8-6 .................... PMulrennan$^{(5)}$ 3 —
(MWEasterby) *dwlt: sn outpcd and bhd* **9/1**

44 **9** 5 **Alice King (IRE)**$^{22}$ [1666] 2-7-13 .................... CHaddon$^{(7)}$ 2 —
(WGMTurner) *chsd ldrs: lost pl 2f out: sn bhd* **14/1**

0 **10** 1¾ **Ruby Rebel**$^{34}$ [1390] 2-8-6 .................... GParkin 7 —
(PTMidgley) *swvd lft s: a bhd* **50/1**

04 **U** **Fold Walk**$^{26}$ [1556] 2-8-6 .................... GGibbons 8 —
(MWEasterby) *swvd rt and bmpd s: sn uns rdr* **12/1**

67.16 secs (3.16) **Going Correction** +0.425s/f (Yiel) **11** Ran SP% **117.2**
Speed ratings: **91,88,83,81,80 77,75,63,55,52** — CT £6.30 TOTE £1.80: £6.70, £13.50, £; EX245.70 1.Mytton's Dream was bought in for 10,000gns. Concert Time was claimed by Conor Dore for £6,000. Keresforth was claimed by Ian Wood for £6,00
**Owner** Gordon Mytton **Bred** D R Tucker **Trained** Little Budworth, Cheshire

**FOCUS**
This is weak form, even by selling standards.

**NOTEBOOK**
**Mytton's Dream**, dropped in class and running on much quicker ground, took a bump at the start. Forced to switch and knocked out of her stride just inside the last, she showed the right sort of spirit to win going away in the end. Her heart is certainly in the right place and connections had to dig deep to retain her.
**Keresforth**, in first-time blinkers, worked his way to the front against the far-side rail but had no answer when the winner swept by him near the line. He was claimed.
**Concert Time**, worst drawm, improved on her initial effort and did enough to attract a claim.
**Emma's Venture**, in a seller this time rather than a claimer, seemed happier on this much quicker ground but a sixth furlong looks needed now.
**Our Louis** again showed bags of toe, but after looking likely to take some pegging back she emptied in a matter of strides and showed signs of distress, hanging left.
**Why Harry** did not impress at all going to post and became somewhat upset in the stalls. He was in trouble soon after halfway and his chance had gone when impeded just inside the last. He does not want the ground as quick as this. *Official explanation: trainer said gelding was unsuited by today's faster ground.*

## 2195 JOCKEYS LOFT FOR GREAT FOOD MAIDEN STKS — 7f 100y
2:55 (2:56) (D) 3-Y-O — **£4,251** (£1,308; £654; £327) **Stalls** High

Form RPR

00- **1** **Ali Deo**$^{215}$ [5590] 3-9-0 .................... PRobinson 12 72
(WJHaggas) *unruly gng to s: ld eraly: trckd ldr: effrt over 1f out: styd on to ld last 75yds* **7/2**$^{2}$

02 **2** ¾ **Star Magnitude (USA)**$^{15}$ [1820] 3-9-0 .................... KDarley 3 70
(JHMGosden) *trckd ldrs: drvn along over 3f out: styd on wl towards fin* **1/1**$^{1}$

0 **3** shd **Hawaajes**$^{16}$ [1794] 3-9-0 .................... WSupple 13 70
(BHanbury) *reminders after s: sn led: qcknd over 3f out: hdd and no ex wl ins last* **11/2**$^{3}$

U00 **4** ½ **Vibe**$^{15}$ [1820] 3-9-0 .................... RFfrench 8 69
(MJohnston) *chsd ldrs: outpcd over 2f out: styd on strly ins last* **25/1**

0-0 **5** 2 **Grey Boy (GER)**$^{11}$ [1939] 3-9-0 .................... GDuffield 1 64
(GCBravery) *sn chsng ldrs on outer: one pce fnl 2f* **40/1**

**6** 2 **Remonstrate (IRE)** 3-9-0 .................... GGibbons 4 59
(TDEasterby) *stdd and swtchd lft s: in rr tl kpt on fnl 2f* **25/1**

00 **7** shd **Ghantoot**$^{18}$ [1749] 3-8-11 .................... NMackay$^{(3)}$ 6 58
(LMCumani) *in tch: outpcd over 2f out: n.d after* **16/1**

**8** 5 **Chisel** 3-9-0 .................... KDalgleish 11 46
(MJohnston) *sn chsng ldrs: outpcd 3f out: wknd over 1f out* **8/1**

00- **9** 4 **Knot In Doubt (IRE)**$^{346}$ [2184] 3-9-0 .................... IMongan 5 36
(JAGlover) *a in rr* **66/1**

00- **10** 1½ **Ballin Rouge**$^{230}$ [5295] 3-8-9 .................... EAhern 7 27
(TJFitzgerald) *sn last* **50/1**

1m 34.31s (0.01) **Going Correction** -0.025s/f (Good) **10** Ran SP% **118.2**
Speed ratings: **98,97,97,96,94 91,91,86,81,79**CSF £7.18 TOTE £5.30: £1.50, £1.10, £1.60; EX 8.50.
**Owner** Mrs J Dye **Bred** A J And Mrs Dye **Trained** Newmarket, Suffolk

**FOCUS**
A modest maiden run at just a steady pace to halfway. The time was poor as a result and the form may not prove solid.

**NOTEBOOK**
**Ali Deo**, fitted with a cross noseband, was in a stew and a real handful beforehand. Skilfully settled on the heels of the leader, in the end he did just enough. With him it is going to be a case of mind games.
**Star Magnitude(USA)**, very warm, was tapped for toe when the pace increased turning in. He only really found his stride inside the last and needs a bit further and easier ground.
**Hawaajes**, best drawn, was having only his second start. Put about his job leaving the stalls, he was given a fine tactical ride from the front. Winding up the gallop coming off the home turn, in the end he was just found lacking.
**Vibe**, unplaced in three previous starts, is still learning. He really picked up the bit late on and will improve further especially in handicap company over further.
**Grey Boy(GER)**, unplaced in two previous starts, ran better and is now qualified to ply his trade in handicap company.
**Remonstrate(IRE)**, a backward newcomer who stands over plenty of ground, made a pleasing debut and there should be better to come in due course.
**Chisel**, a rangy, backward newcomer, showed some ability and will do better when fitter, probably on easier ground.

## 2196 PETER HOLMES "LIFETIME IN RACING" RATED STKS (H'CAP) — 1m 100y
3:25 (3:25) (C) (0-95,94) 3-Y-O+ — **£8,497** (£3,223; £1,611; £732) **Stalls** High

Form RPR

2-06 **1** **Flighty Fellow (IRE)**$^{42}$ [1284] 4-9-6 **90** .................... WSupple 8 99
(TDEasterby) *chsd ldrs: styd on to ld jst ins fnl f: kpt on wl* **10/1**

-050 **2** 1¾ **Ace Of Hearts**$^{24}$ [1623] 5-8-10 **80** oh1 .................... GDuffield 10 85
(CFWall) *sn chsng ldrs on outer: styd on to take 2nd wl ins last* **5/1**$^{2}$

140- **3** nk **Ice Palace**$^{215}$ [5589] 4-9-10 **94** .................... EAhern 6 99
(JRFanshawe) *trckd ldrs: effrt on outside over 2f out: styd on strly ins last: tk 3rd nr line* **4/1**$^{1}$

3-00 **4** ½ **Irony (IRE)**$^{24}$ [1623] 5-9-3 **87** .................... KDarley 2 91
(AMBalding) *led tl jst ins fnl f: no ex* **8/1**

00-6 **5** hd **Star Sensation (IRE)**$^{31}$ [1456] 4-9-2 **86** .................... IMongan 9 89
(PWHarris) *hld up: effrt over 2f out: hung lft over 1f out: kpt on ins last* **11/2**$^{3}$

10-0 **6** ¾ **Stretton (IRE)**$^{12}$ [1903] 6-8-10 **80** .................... PRobinson 1 82
(JDBethell) *sn bhd: hdwy on ins 2f out: kpt on ins last* **20/1**

2000 **7** ½ **The Bonus King**$^{15}$ [1845] 4-8-10 **80** .................... KDalgleish 7 81
(MJohnston) *chsd ldrs: chal 3f out: fdd appr fnl f* **14/1**

20-2 **8** 2 **Vicious Warrior**$^{17}$ [1773] 5-9-2 **86** .................... DeanMcKeown 4 82
(RMWhitaker) *trckd ldrs: keeping on one pce whn sltly hmpd wl over 1f out* **17/2**

0202 **9** 7 **Dawn Piper (USA)**$^{15}$ [1840] 4-8-10 **83** ....................(v) TPQueally$^{(3)}$ 3 65
(DRLoder) *trckd ldrs: t.k.h: rdn to chal 3f out: wandered and hung rt over 1f out: sn lost pl: eased* **10/1**

110- **10** 5 **Spuradich (IRE)**$^{241}$ [5074] 4-9-6 **93** .................... NMackay$^{(3)}$ 5 64
(LMCumani) *rr div: effrt on outside over 3f out: rdn and hung rt 2f out: sn lost pl: eased* **7/1**

1m 45.15s (-2.15) **Going Correction** -0.025s/f (Good) **10** Ran SP% **115.8**
Speed ratings: **109,107,106,106,106 105,105,103,96,91**CSF £58.99 CT £236.26 TOTE £7.00: £1.90, £2.70, £1.70; EX 72.30.
**Owner** David W Armstrong **Bred** F Hinojosa **Trained** Great Habton, N Yorks

**FOCUS**
A competitive handicap run at a sound pace. The form should prove sound.

**NOTEBOOK**
**Flighty Fellow(IRE)**, with the headgear again left off, looks to have finally grown up and, given a good ride, scored in decisive fashion. He should continue to give a good account of himself at this level.
**Ace Of Hearts**, loaded last, had the best of the draw but found himself racing on the outside. He stuck on in willing fashion but never looked like seriously troubling the winner. He hasn't won since July 2002 but seems to do little wrong.
**Ice Palace ◆**, who looked very fit, was taken to post quietly. She found herself in a poor tactical position on the outer once in line for home but made up many lengths in the final furlong and finished best of all. A fast-run race suits her and there are surely good prizes to be won with her this time.
**Irony(IRE)**, drawn one off the outside, did well to adopt his usual front-running role but he could find no extra inside the last. He is rated to the very limit.
**Star Sensation(IRE)**, a keen type, is suited by a turning track. She is not the most straightforward of rides and needs everything to fall just right.
**Stretton(IRE)**, worst drawn, made ground on the inner and kept on steadily without his rider being too hard. He will improve again for the outing and a mile and a quarter seems to suit him better.
**Vicious Warrior** *Official explanation: jockey said gelding had suffered interference in running.*
**Spuradich(IRE)** looks to have done extra well from three to four and will no doubt be making his mark again in due course over further.

## 2197 RAPID LAD H'CAP — 1m 1f 207y
4:00 (4:00) (E) (0-75,75) 3-Y-O — **£4,728** (£1,455; £727; £363) **Stalls** High

Form RPR

-415 **1** **Goblin**$^{21}$ [1688] 3-8-8 **62** .................... GDuffield 10 74
(DECantillon) *hld up towards rr: n.m.r on inner 6f out: hdwy on ins and nt clr run 2f out: r.o wl to ld jst ins fnl f* **7/2**$^{1}$

40-6 **2** 1½ **Fitting Guest (IRE)**$^{29}$ [1508] 3-8-11 **65** .................... PRobinson 1 74
(GGMargarson) *led: qcknd over 2f out: hdd jst ins last: no ex* **14/1**

020- **3** 3 **Ma Yahab**$^{194}$ [5932] 3-9-0 **71** .................... NMackay$^{(3)}$ 8 74
(LMCumani) *mid-div: nt clr run over 2f out: swtchd lft over 1f out: styd on* **8/1**$^{3}$

43-0 **4** ½ **Red Birr (IRE)**$^{52}$ [1129] 3-9-7 **75** .................... KDarley 9 78
(AMBalding) *trckd ldrs: effrt over 2f out: styd on same pce* **8/1**$^{3}$

-424 **5** ¾ **Athollbrose (USA)**$^{15}$ [1843] 3-8-2 **56** .................... GGibbons 5 57
(TDEasterby) *chsd ldrs: rdn and edgd lft 2f out: fdd appr fnl f* **10/1**

6000 **6** 1 **Infidelity (IRE)**$^{12}$ [1899] 3-8-8 **62** .................... DKinsella 7 61
(ABailey) *in rr: hdwy on inner 2f out: wknd ins last* **33/1**

20-6 **7** 2½ **Badr (USA)**$^{18}$ [1747] 3-9-1 **69** .................... RFfrench 3 63
(MJohnston) *sn trcking ldrs: pushed along over 4f out: lost pl over 1f out* **11/1**

30-6 **8** 3½ **Sharaab (USA)**$^{35}$ [1382] 3-9-7 **75** ....................(t) WSupple 4 63
(BHanbury) *w ldrs: chal over 2f out: wknd over 1f out* **7/1**$^{2}$

430- **9** 2½ **Gaiety Girl (USA)**$^{206}$ [5744] 3-8-11 **65** .................... PDoe 6 48
(TDEasterby) *s.i.s: effrt on out over 2f out: sn rdn: hung rt and wknd* **20/1**

-660 **10** 2½ **Orion Express**$^{10}$ [1957] 3-8-4 **63** .................... PMulrennan$^{(5)}$ 2 41
(MWEasterby) *trckd ldrs: rdn and lost pl over 2f out* **14/1**

4222 **11** 6 **Late Opposition**$^{8}$ [1998] 3-8-13 **67** .................... EAhern 11 34
(EALDunlop) *s.i.s: hdwy on outside over 3f out: lost pl 2f out: eased* **7/2**$^{1}$

2m 5.34s (-1.86) **Going Correction** -0.025s/f (Good) **11** Ran SP% **117.6**
Speed ratings: **106,104,102,102,101 100,98,95,93,91 87**CSF £57.05 CT £371.18 TOTE £4.60: £1.50, £3.60, £3.10; EX 82.80.
**Owner** Mrs E M Clarke **Bred** G W Turner And Miss S J Turner **Trained** Carlton, Cambs

**FOCUS**
A fair handicap and a very smart winning time for the grade.

**NOTEBOOK**
**Goblin**, well backed, did really well after meeting all sorts of traffic problems and never leaving the inside. He was right on top at the finish and his veteran rider's nerve is as good as ever.
**Fitting Guest(IRE)**, on his handicap bow, was given a fine tactical ride. He stretched them from the front but he left a gap on his inside and the winner said thankyou very much.
**Ma Yahab**, making his handicap bow, looked in good trim and he seems suited by quick ground. Meeting trouble twice, he was staying on nicely at the finish and can do better over a bit further.
**Red Birr(IRE)**, a weak-looking type, is finding his feet and will be suited by a step up to a mile and a quarter.
**Athollbrose(USA)**, who ran over a mile five last time, found this company too tough.
**Late Opposition**, who has a pronounced knee action, was dropping back in trip and was well below his best on this much quicker ground. *Official explanation: jockey said colt was unsuited by the going.*

## 2198 COLIN STAMFORD IS OUR PAINTER MAIDEN FILLIES' STKS — 1m 1f 207y
4:35 (4:35) (D) 3-Y-O+ — **£4,225** (£1,300; £650; £325) **Stalls** High

Form RPR

0-0 **1** **Portmanteau**$^{29}$ [1507] 3-8-10 .................... FLynch 6 83
(SirMichaelStoute) *w ldrs: ld over 2f out: clr 1f out: pushed out* **8/1**

0- **2** 2½ **Tarandot (IRE)**$^{259}$ [4644] 3-8-10 .................... AMcCarthy 4 78
(GGMargarson) *rr-div: hdwy 3f out: wnt 2nd 1f out: styd on wl* **16/1**

52 **3** 6 **Tree Tops**$^{18}$ [1753] 3-8-10 .................... KDarley 1 67
(JHMGosden) *trckd ldrs: effrt over 2f out: wnt 2nd over 1f out: sn fdd* **15/8**$^{1}$

26 **4** 2½ **High School**$^{28}$ [1521] 3-8-7 .................... ABeech$^{(3)}$ 12 62
(DRLoder) *hld up in rr: hdwy on ins whn bmpd over 3f out: kpt on fnl 2f: nvr nr ldrs* **4/1**$^{3}$

00 **5** *4* **Dareneur (IRE)**[15] 1842 4-9-5 .......... PMakin(5) 9 55
(WMBrisbourne) *chsd ldrs: effrt over 2f out: wknd over 1f out* **66/1**

06 **6** *2 1/2* **Paula**[17] 1770 4-9-10 .......... GGibbons 5 50
(MDods) *hld up in rr: hdwy on outside over 4f out: edgd rt and lost pl over 2f out* **100/1**

6- **7** *shd* **Rainbow Colours (IRE)**[202] 5825 3-8-10 .......... GDuffield 11 50
(JRFanshawe) *led tl over 2f out: lost pl over 1f out* **9/1**

5-0 **8** *1 3/4* **Sweet Repose (USA)**[33] 1420 3-8-10 .......... EAhern 10 46
(EALDunlop) *in tch: effrt over 2f out: sn rdn and btn* **20/1**

5-2 **9** *2 1/2* **Calonnog (IRE)**[17] 1770 4-9-10 .......... PaulEddery 8 42
(HRACecil) *in rr: sn pushed along: nvr on terms* **7/2**[2]

0 **10** *6* **Pointed (IRE)**[15] 1820 3-8-10 .......... RFfrench 2 30
(TDEasterby) *mid-div: lost pl over 3f out: sn bhd* **33/1**

4-0 **11** *1 3/4* **Adees Dancer**[26] 1557 3-8-10 .......... DMcGaffin 3 27
(BSmart) *hld up in rr: hung bdly lft bnd over 3f out: sn bhd* **20/1**

2m 5.78s (-1.42) **Going Correction** -0.025s/f (Good)
**WFA** 3 from 4yo 14lb **11** Ran SP% **118.9**
Speed ratings: **104,102,97,95,92 90,89,88,86,81 80**CSF £118.30 TOTE £10.60: £3.30, £5.80, £1.20; EX 254.40.
**Owner** Maktoum Al Maktoum **Bred** Newgate Stud Co **Trained** Newmarket, Suffolk

**FOCUS**
An ordinary maiden run at a sound pace and the first two came clear.

**NOTEBOOK**
**Portmanteau**, on the leg, proved suited by the step up in trip and better ground. She had this won the minute she hit the front and connections will be hoping for a realistic handicap mark.
**Tarandot(IRE)**, who had just one outing at two, stayed on really well in pursuit of the winner and can do better, especially over further.
**Tree Tops**, worst drawn, didn't take the eye in the paddock and, after showing clear second over a furlong out, she found very little.
**High School**, having her first outing on fast ground, took a hefty bump on the home turn. She stayed on in her own time and this sister to In The Wings may be capable of better over further now she is qualified for handicaps.
**Dareneur(IRE)**, who showed modest form in bumpers, had shown little in two starts proper on the Flat. At least this now qualifies her for low-grade handicaps.
**Sweet Repose(USA)** *Official explanation: jockey said filly was unsuited by the going.*
**Calonnog(IRE)** never went from start to finish and seemed totally unsuited by this track.

## 2199 COME RACING AT BEVERLEY H'CAP — 1m 4f 16y
**5:05** (5:06) (F) (0-55,55) 3-Y-O **£3,503** (£1,078; £539; £269) **Stalls** High

Form RPR

-445 **1** **Prairie Sun (GER)**[15] 1823 3-9-0 **55** .......... GDuffield 12 58
(MrsADuffield) *led 1f: led 8f out: rdn clr 1f out: jst hld on* **8/1**[3]

-032 **2** *3/4* **Danefonique (IRE)**[31] 1465 3-8-13 **54** .......... RFitzpatrick 8 55
(DCarroll) *rea-div: hdwy over 4f out: wnt 2nd over 1f out: styd on ins last* **8/1**[3]

2101 **3** *shd* **Ceasar (IRE)**[29] 1499 3-9-0 **55** .......... GFaulkner 5 56
(PABlockley) *hld up: hdwy over 3f out: nt clr run over 2f out tl over 1f out: swtchd lft: styd on strly towards fin* **8/1**[3]

00-0 **4** *2* **Winslow Boy (USA)**[11] 1466 3-9-0 **55** .......... KDarley 14 53
(CFWall) *s.i.s: bhd tl styd on fnl 2f* **14/1**

-025 **5** *1 1/2* **Holly Walk**[11] 1947 3-8-5 **46** .......... (b) GGibbons 3 42
(MDods) *t.k.h: led after 1f: rn wd paddock bnd: hdd 8f out: kpt on same pce fnl 2f* **14/1**

015- **6** *nk* **Xpressions**[231] 5290 3-8-9 **50** .......... GParkin 1 45
(RAFahey) *bhd and drvn along 4f out: hdwy whn nt clr run over 1f out: swtchd lft and kpt on* **16/1**

0052 **7** *nk* **Avertaine**[28] 1529 3-8-12 **53** .......... PDoe 6 48
(GLMoore) *sn chsng ldrs: wemt 2md 2f out: sn rdn and hung rt: wknd appr fnl f* **10/1**

0-05 **8** *hd* **Nafferton Heights (IRE)**[26] 1559 3-8-3 **49** .......... PMulrennan(5) 4 43
(MWEasterby) *t.k.h: trckd ldrs: outpcd and nt clr run over 2f out: kpt on same pce* **3/1**[1]

30-6 **9** *hd* **Spring Breeze**[36] 1360 3-8-12 **53** .......... (p) FLynch 2 47
(MDods) *hld up and bhd: sme hdwy over 2f out: nvr a factor* **16/1**

0-25 **10** *1 3/4* **Bollin Annabel**[20] 1713 3-8-11 **55** .......... NMackay(3) 13 46
(TDEasterby) *in tch: effrt over 3f out: wknd 2f out* **13/2**[2]

4003 **11** *1/2* **Bonjour Bond (IRE)**[10] 1959 3-8-13 **54** .......... (b) DMcGaffin 9 44
(BSmart) *chsd ldrs: wknd over 2f out* **16/1**

6-03 **12** *2 1/2* **Calara Hills**[15] 1843 3-8-3 **49** .......... PMakin(5) 11 35
(WMBrisbourne) *chsd ldrs: lost pl 4f out* **12/1**

4031 **13** *21* **Ciacole**[10] 1959 3-8-9 **50** .......... DeanMcKeown 10 3
(RonaldThompson) *mid-div: effrt over 3f out: lost pl over 2f out: eased* **12/1**

2m 41.83s (2.53) **Going Correction** -0.025s/f (Good) **13** Ran SP% **127.1**
Speed ratings: **90,89,89,88,87 86,86,86,86,85 84,83,69**CSF £75.41 CT £547.57 TOTE £9.00: £3.50, £3.30, £1.20; EX 121.00 Place 6 £134.15, Place 5 £19.79.
**Owner** Miss Helen Wynne **Bred** Gestut Isarland **Trained** Constable Burton, N Yorks
■ Stewards Enquiry : P Mulrennan two-day ban: careless riding (May 29,30)

**FOCUS**
A seller in all but name and a modest winning time, with the winner dropping anchor in front.

**NOTEBOOK**
**Prairie Sun(GER)**, unplaced in six previous starts, was dropping in trip and racing on much quicker ground. Given a canny ride from the front, she was sent three lengths clear a furlong out but in the end did just enough.
**Danefonique(IRE)** proved suited by the step up in trip and was closing the winner down at the line.
**Ceasar(IRE)**, having his first outing for his new connections, was all dressed up on the inner with nowhere to go. Forced to wait for a gap, when switched he came home to real effect and must be accounted an unlucky loser.
**Winslow Boy(USA)**, on his handicap bow, made a sluggish start and only warmed to his work late on. He looks essentially a stayer.
**Holly Walk**, dropped in trip, took a fierce hold in front and as a result had difficulty making the turn into the back straight. In the circumstances she kept on amazingly well up the final hill.
**Xpressions**, who won a seller at two, was last of all turning in. After meeting trouble and being forced to switch, he was staying on when it was all over. A seller or bottom-grade handicap over a mile six will give him an opportunity.
**Nafferton Heights(IRE)**, stepping up in trip and encountering much quicker ground, didn't settle and his lack of basic speed saw him finding trouble on the inside.
**Ciacole** *Official explanation: jockey said filly had lost its action*
T/Plt: £317.40 to a £1 stake. Pool: £25,962.95. 59.70 winning tickets. T/Qpdt: £47.70 to a £1 stake. Pool: £2,079.40. 32.20 winning tickets. WG

# GOODWOOD (R-H)
Tuesday, May 18

**OFFICIAL GOING: Good**
Wind: almost nil Weather: sunny & warm

## 2200 MARRIOTT GOODWOOD PARK HOTEL CONDITIONS STKS — 7f
**2:10** (2:11) (C ) 3-Y-0+ **£8,444** (£3,203; £1,601; £728) **Stalls** High

Form RPR

001- **1** **Naahy**[220] 5488 4-8-12 103 .......... SHitchcott(3) 2 108
(MRChannon) *swtg: mde all: shkn up over 1f out: wl in command fnl f: pushed out* **5/1**[2]

5-45 **2** *1 3/4* **Suggestive**[33] 1409 6-9-10 107 .......... (b) MHills 5 112+
(WJHaggas) *lw: hld up in last: shkn up wl over 1f out: hanging rt and no prog tl r.o fnl f to take 2nd last 50yds: no ch w wnr* **6/1**[3]

301- **3** *3/4* **Court Masterpiece**[290] 3782 4-9-12 106 .......... JPMurtagh 4 112
(EALDunlop) *t.k.h early: hld up in tch: effrt 2f out: shkn up to chse wnr 1f out: no imp: lost 2nd last 50yds* **8/1**

61-0 **4** *hd* **State City (USA)**[52] 1145 5-9-1 110 .......... (t) LDettori 6 100
(SaeedBinSuroor) *prom: chsd wnr 3f out to 1f out: one pce fnl f* **6/1**[3]

0/0- **5** *shd* **Maghanim**[397] 1097 4-9-1 102 .......... TQuinn 7 100
(JLDunlop) *hld up in tch: effrt and cl up on inner 2f out: hanging rt and nt qckn over 1f out: one pce after* **12/1**

1- **6** *5* **Mustajed**[356] 1912 3-8-6 .......... RHills 3 89
(MPTregoning) *racd on outer: in tch: pushed along and nt qckn over 2f out: wknd over 1f out* **6/4**[1]

31-0 **7** *9* **Caveral**[20] 1704 3-8-1 88 .......... MartinDwyer 1 61
(RHannon) *b.hind: t.k.h: chsd wnr to 3f out: wknd over 2f out* **20/1**

1m 26.24s (-1.79) **Going Correction** +0.025s/f (Good)
**WFA** 3 from 4yo+ 11lb **7** Ran SP% **108.8**
Speed ratings: **111,109,108,107,107 102,91**CSF £31.03 TOTE £5.20: £2.10, £3.00; EX 25.80.
**Owner** Kuwait Racing Syndicate **Bred** Red House Stud **Trained** West Ilsley, Berks
■ Stewards Enquiry : T Quinn caution: used whip down the shoulder in the forehand position

**FOCUS**
Quite a competitive race that should work out at a higher level, as some of these ran well off the back long lay-offs and should improve. The time was also creditable for the grade.

**NOTEBOOK**
**Naahy**, having his first run since chipping a bone in a knee, showed himself as good as ever with a fine effort from the front. A really tough sort, there is more to come and he is considered Listed class at least by connections, who also feel he now settles well enough to get a mile.
**Suggestive** appreciated this step up in trip and drop in class and ran respectably. He took a while to pick up and an all-round stronger gallop may have suited better.
**Court Masterpiece**, successful in a Listed race (working out well) over a mile here on his previous start 290 days previously, looked as though the run would bring him on and made a satisfactory return to action. This was a good run at the weights, but he will need to find a bit more in pattern races.
**State City(USA)**, the winner of the 2003 Group One Golden Shaheen on dirt, was below form on this first run in Britain and second run on turf. He may need a really strongly-run race to be seen at his best.
**Maghanim**, whose only appearance last season came when last in the Craven, ran respectably on what was his first start in 397 days. He did hang a little under pressure, but it did not look too serious and he should go on from this.
**Mustajed**, winner of a pretty ordinary five-furlong Newbury maiden on his only start last term (356 days previoisly), has been entered in the St James's Palace and the Eclipse. Facing a stiff task but backed as if defeat was out of the question, he ran a shocker, finding nothing when pulled out wide for a run.

## 2201 MITSUBISHI DIAMOND VISION STKS (H'CAP) — 1m
**2:40** (2:45) (C ) (0-100,98) 4-Y-0+ **£10,010** (£3,080; £1,540; £770) **Stalls** High

Form RPR

000- **1** **Highland Reel**[141] 5753 7-9-1 **85** .......... TQuinn 6 96
(DRCElsworth) *hld up in rr: prog on wd outside 2f out: drvn and str run fnl f: edgd rt but led last 50yds* **40/1**

4-00 **2** *1/2* **Amandus (USA)**[24] 1623 4-9-10 **94** .......... KFallon 17 104
(DRLoder) *lw: hld up bhd ldrs: effrt and swtchd lft over 1f out: drvn to ld last 150yds: hdd and hld fnl 50yds* **7/1**[1]

0002 **3** *shd* **Nashaab (USA)**[11] 1927 7-9-4 **88** .......... RHavlin 15 98
(PDEvans) *hld up in rr: effrt and n.m.r 2f out: prog over 1f out: r.o wl fnl f: nrst fin* **8/1**[2]

110- **4** *shd* **Able Baker Charlie (IRE)**[227] 5365 5-9-7 **91** .......... JPMurtagh 9 100
(JRFanshawe) *trckd ldrs: shkn up 2f out: ev ch over 1f out: unable qck: r.o again ins fnl f* **8/1**[2]

04-0 **5** *nk* **Finished Article (IRE)**[31] 1456 7-9-6 **90** .......... DaneO'Neill 8 99
(DRCElsworth) *hld up wl in rr: stl one fr last over 1f out: str run on outer fnl f: too much to do* **10/1**[3]

6-05 **6** *3/4* **Alrafid (IRE)**[17] 1762 5-9-1 **85** .......... RLMoore 2 92
(GLMoore) *racd on outer: hld up wl in rr: stl plenty to do whn swtchd ins over 1f out: gd prog fnl f: no ex last 50yds* **16/1**

22-0 **7** *nk* **Impeller (IRE)**[31] 1456 5-9-3 **87** .......... SDrowne 14 93
(WRMuir) *hld up in midfield: nt clr run over 2f out and over 1f out: styd on fnl f: unable to chal* **8/1**[2]

30-0 **8** *1 1/4* **Sri Diamond**[15] 1828 4-8-8 **78** .......... JFEgan 19 81
(SKirk) *swtg: sn pressed ldr: drvn to ld wl over 1f out: hdd & wknd last 150yds* **20/1**

34-0 **9** *2* **Welcome Stranger**[43] 1273 4-8-8 **78** .......... JTate 16 77
(JMPEustace) *s.v.s: last tl over 2f out: prog on inner fr 2f out: styng on whn nt clr run last 100yds: nt rcvr* **20/1**

00-0 **10** *nk* **Omaha City (IRE)**[45] 1241 10-8-2 **72** .......... JQuinn 12 70
(BGubby) *swtg: racd in midfield: effrt on outer 3f out: hanging rt and no prog 2f out: one pce after* **20/1**

3-00 **11** *nk* **Penny Cross**[17] 1773 4-9-2 **86** .......... RHills 5 83
(JGGiven) *led to wl over 1f out: wknd fnl f* **40/1**

-005 **12** *1 1/4* **Desert Opal**[15] 1828 4-9-8 **92** .......... (v[1]) RHughes 10 87
(JHMGosden) *prom: rdn 2f out: fnd nil and sn btn* **7/1**[1]

41-0 **13** *hd* **Spanish Don**[31] 1456 6-9-2 **86** .......... TEDurcan 11 80
(DRCElsworth) *lw: chsd ldrs: rdn and no prog over 2f out: n.d over 1f out* **20/1**

635- **14** *1/2* **Captain Saif**[275] 4210 4-9-8 **92** .......... PDobbs 18 85
(RHannon) *bit bkwd: dwlt: racd in rr on inner: effrt 2f out: keeping on one pce and no ch whn hmpd last 100yds* **33/1**

30-0 **15** *1 1/2* **Hit's Only Money (IRE)**[36] 1367 4-9-10 **97** .......... DNolan(3) 3 86
(PABlockley) *hld up and swtchd to r on inner: effrt over 2f out: no prog over 1f out* **33/1**

24-0 **16** *1/2* **Quiet Storm (IRE)**[17] 1767 4-10-0 **98** .......... DHolland 7 86
(GWragg) *prom: hrd rdn over 2f out: losing pl whn bmpd over 1f out* **16/1**

0-40 **17** *5* **Our Teddy (IRE)**[52] [1125] 4-9-6 **90** .......... MartinDwyer 4 67
(AMBalding) *racd on outer: in tch: rdn over 3f out: sn struggling* **33/1**

034- **18** *6* **Cal Mac**[24] [5749] 5-8-5 **78** ow1 .......... SHitchcott(3) 1 41
(RMHCowell) *t.k.h: hld up: rdn and wknd 3f out* **66/1**

1m 39.75s (-0.52) **Going Correction** +0.025s/f (Good) **18** Ran SP% **113.4**
Speed ratings: **103,102,102,102,102 101,100,99,97,97 97,95,95,95,93 93,88,82**CSF £238.16 CT £2222.39 TOTE £69.40: £9.80, £2.30, £2.00, £2.30; EX 1108.90 TRIFECTA Not won..

**Owner** Sir Gordon Brunton **Bred** Sir Gordon Brunton **Trained** Whitsbury, Hants

**FOCUS**
A really competitive handicap run at a decent enough pace, but there were the usual hard-luck stories.

**NOTEBOOK**
**Highland Reel**, 1lb higher than when successful at Salisbury nearly a year previously, is thought to have been freshened up by a couple of spins over hurdles. This was a good effort considering he had to be switched out widest of all with his challenge, but his overall record does not inspire much confidence of a follow up.
**Amandus(USA)** is progressing with racing this season and posted his best effort of the campaign so far.
**Nashaab(USA)** goes well in these big-field handicaps, especially round here. He did not get the best of luck in running and could be considered a little unlucky, but he quite simply does not win anymore.
**Able Baker Charlie(IRE)** progressed well last season and did not run too badly in the Cambridgeshire on his final start of that campaign. This was a pleasing reappearance and he should be sharper for it.
**Finished Article(IRE)**, 8lb higher than when last successful, got stuck in behind horses towards the rear in the straight and, although flying when in the clear, got going too late.
**Alrafid(IRE)** finished to good effect and appears in fine form.
**Impeller(IRE)** goes well round here and would have gone close with better luck. *Official explanation: jockey said gelding had lost a fore shoe.*
**Welcome Stranger** lost his chance with a slow start, but better luck in running would have seen him go closer.
**Desert Opal** may not have been suited by the fitting of a visor, but the excuses for his efforts this season are already stacking up.

## 2202 TOTESPORT STKS (HERITAGE H'CAP) 1m 1f
**3:15** (3:19) (B ) (0-105,97) 3-Y-O **£43,500** (£16,500; £8,250; £3,750) **Stalls** Low

Form RPR

3-13 **1** **Gatwick (IRE)**[32] [1437] 3-8-11 **87** .......... TQuinn 11 99
(MRChannon) *racd towards rr: pushed along over 2f out: gd prog on outer to ld over 1f out: drvn and in command last 150yds* **9/4**[1]

-611 **2** *1 1/4* **Dancing Lyra**[16] [1799] 3-8-11 **87** .......... KFallon 4 96
(JWHills) *prog into midfield over 3f out: rdn and effrt over 2f out: unable qck over 1f out: styd on to take 2nd last 100yds: no imp* **10/1**[3]

1-13 **3** *1/2* **Mutafanen**[27] [1538] 3-9-7 **97** .......... RHills 2 105
(EALDunlop) *hld up wl in rr: prog on outer fr over 2f out: r.o to press wnr jst over 1f out to last 100yds: kpt on* **12/1**

3613 **4** *hd* **Royal Warrant**[80] [913] 3-8-7 **83** .......... MartinDwyer 15 91
(AMBalding) *prom: rdn and effrt 2f out: cl up over 1f out: styd on same pce fnl f* **14/1**

0-00 **5** *hd* **Tranquil Sky**[16] [1795] 3-8-2 **83** .......... DFox(5) 12 90+
(NACallaghan) *swtg: s.s: hld up wl in rr: prog and nt clr run over 2f out: nt clr run over 1f out: r.o fnl f: nrst fin* **33/1**

-421 **6** *3/4* **Woody Valentine (USA)**[20] [1712] 3-8-4 **80** .......... SChin 16 86+
(MJohnston) *trckd ldrs: cl up whn nt clr run 2f out and lost pl: r.o again fnl f: nt rcvr* **15/2**[2]

1312 **7** *shd* **Tiger Tiger (FR)**[16] [1799] 3-8-9 **85** .......... JFEgan 6 91
(JamiePoulton) *lw: wl in rr: pushed along over 3f out: prog on outer fr 2f out: chsd ldrs u.p 1f out: one pce fnl f* **25/1**

20-5 **8** *2* **Desert Dreamer (IRE)**[12] [1900] 3-9-3 **93** .......... MHills 3 95
(BWHills) *hld up wl in rr: prog on wd outside over 2f out: promising run over 1f out: wknd ins fnl f* **10/1**[3]

1-33 **9** *1* **Momtic (IRE)**[25] [1585] 3-8-4 **80** .......... JQuinn 10 80
(WJarvis) *trckd ldrs: effrt and nt clr run over 2f out and over 1f out: styd on same pce: nt rcvr* **12/1**

25-4 **10** *1/2* **Sew'N'So Character (IRE)**[12] [1900] 3-9-6 **96** .......... FNorton 19 95
(MBlanshard) *trckd ldrs: cl up on inner over 2f out: nowhere to go tl ins fnl f: r.o nr fin: nt rcvr* **16/1**

05-3 **11** *nk* **Pagan Magic (USA)**[10] [1967] 3-7-10 **75** .......... LisaJones(3) 13 73
(JARToller) *lw: hld up in rr: effrt over 2f out: hanging rt and no imp on ldrs* **16/1**

-221 **12** *5* **Never Will**[4] [2077] 3-9-4 **94** 6ex .......... JFanning 1 82
(MJohnston) *lw: disp ld to over 1f out: wknd* **16/1**

1313 **13** *nk* **Hatch**[18] [1745] 3-9-0 **90** .......... DHolland 14 77
(RMHCowell) *pressed ldng pair: rdn 3f out: wknd over 1f out* **16/1**

6-10 **14** *1 1/4* **Fancy Foxtrot**[16] [1795] 3-9-0 **90** .......... RHughes 18 75
(BJMeehan) *disp ld to over 1f out: wknd* **16/1**

1426 **15** *3/4* **Blue Empire (IRE)**[76] [955] 3-7-13 **75** .......... JBramhill 8 58
(PABlockley) *s.i.s: a in rr: rdn and struggling 3f out* **25/1**

2-21 **16** *1 1/4* **Instructor**[46] [1227] 3-8-3 **79** .......... RLMoore 5 60
(RHannon) *prom: rdn over 2f out: losing pl and btn whn squeezed out jst over 1f out* **25/1**

120- **17** *4* **Zweibrucken (IRE)**[206] [5750] 3-8-7 **83** .......... PDobbs 17 56
(SKirk) *trckd ldrs: rdn over 2f out: wknd wl over 1f out* **50/1**

41-0 **18** *nk* **Salisbury Plain**[15] [1831] 3-8-4 **80** .......... TEDurcan 9 52
(DRLoder) *b: lw: a towards rr: rdn on outer over 3f out: sn wknd* **33/1**

1m 55.1s (-1.76) **Going Correction** +0.025s/f (Good) **18** Ran SP% **129.2**
Speed ratings: **108,106,106,106,106 105,105,103,102,102 101,97,97,96,95 94,90,90**CSF £23.81 CT £251.44 TOTE £3.40: £1.10, £2.30, £3.80, £3.40; EX 24.70 Trifecta £743.50 Pool £2,094.44 - 2.00 winning units..

**Owner** W H Ponsonby **Bred** M J Dargan **Trained** West Ilsley, Berks

**FOCUS**
A good handicap in which the leaders appeared to go off a little too fast. Once again, not many horses got a trouble-free run.

**NOTEBOOK**
**Gatwick(IRE)**, third to the subsequent Group winners African Dream and Red Lancer in what has turned out a red-hot mile handicap at Newbury on his previous start, confirmed that promise over this extra furlong. He did not appear to be doing that much when sent to the front and remains open to plenty of improvement.
**Dancing Lyra**, this season, is finally showing the sort of ability he hinted at as a juvenile. Dropped a furlong in trip, he posted a good effort from his low stall and should continue to run well in similar company, especially over further.
**Mutafanen** was below form in a conditions race on soft ground at Epsom on his previous start, but bounced back to the sort of form he showed when hacking up on his reappearance off a mark of 84 at Doncaster. There could yet be more to come from him.
**Royal Warrant**, racing beyond a mile for the first time, fared best of those to race on the pace and would appear to still be progressing.
**Tranquil Sky** ◆ had shown little on his two previous starts this term but, nibbled at in the betting, he would have gone very close to winning this with better luck in running. It will be most disappointing if does not gain compensation.
**Woody Valentine(USA)** found himself in a poor position in the straight and got no luck when looking for a run. He did well to keep plugging on and finish so close and looks a real tough sort.
**Desert Dreamer(IRE)** was forced wider than anything with his run and is better than this.
**Momtic(IRE)** got stopped in his run at a vital stage. *Official explanation: jockey said colt slipped on the bend.*
**Sew'N'So Character(IRE)** got no run and can be rated much better than the bare form.
**Hatch** *Official explanation: jockey said colt had hung left.*

## 2203 LETHEBY & CHRISTOPHER PREDOMINATE STKS (LISTED RACE) (C&G) 1m 3f
**3:45** (3:52) (A ) 3-Y-O **£17,400** (£6,600; £3,300; £1,500) **Stalls** Low

Form RPR

1-5 **1** **Manyana (IRE)**[32] [1439] 3-8-8 **100** .......... (t) MartinDwyer 3 108
(MPTregoning) *lw: hld up in 5th: rdn and prog over 2f out: hanging rt over 1f out: drvn to ld last 100yds: jst hld on* **10/1**

-063 **2** *hd* **Crocodile Dundee (IRE)**[17] [1766] 3-8-8 **96** .......... JFEgan 4 108
(JamiePoulton) *racd in 4th: prog 4f out: drvn to ld narrowly 3f out: hdd u.p last 100yds: rallied nr fin* **25/1**

2221 **3** *2 1/2* **Red Lancer**[12] [1901] 3-9-0 **110** .......... RMiles 6 110
(RJPrice) *settled in 5th: effrt 3f out: rdn and unable qck 2f out: styd on ins fnl f* **10/3**[3]

36-2 **4** *1/2* **Happy Crusader (IRE)**[15] [1822] 3-8-8 **104** .......... KFallon 1 103
(PFICole) *led: set slow pl tl kicked on over 4f out: narrowly hdd 3f out: styd w ldr tl ent fnl f: fdd* **3/1**[2]

12-2 **5** *5* **Mutahayya (IRE)**[38] [1330] 3-8-8 **105** .......... RHills 7 95
(JLDunlop) *lw: hld up in last: effrt 3f out: swtchd ins 2f out: no imp on ldrs: wknd ins fnl f* **2/1**[1]

5-16 **6** *5* **Graham Island**[12] [1901] 3-8-8 **84** .......... DHolland 5 87
(GWragg) *lw: racd in 3rd tl chsd ldr 5f out to 4f out: rdn and wandered 3f out: wkng whn hmpd 2f out* **7/1**

103- **7** *1 3/4* **Zouave (IRE)**[242] [5039] 3-8-8 **92** .......... MHills 2 84
(BJMeehan) *chsd ldr to 5f out: wknd over 3f out* **33/1**

2m 28.01s (1.90) **Going Correction** +0.025s/f (Good) **7** Ran SP% **109.8**
Speed ratings: **94,93,92,91,88 84,83**CSF £184.81 TOTE £12.50: £4.90, £5.60; EX 192.00.

**Owner** Sheikh Mohammed **Bred** C H Wacker Iii **Trained** Lambourn, Berks

**FOCUS**
A weak renewal of the Predominate Stakes and the winning time was pedestrian thanks to a very steady early gallop.

**NOTEBOOK**
**Manyana(IRE)** was reported to have swallowed his tongue when a mile behind Let The Lion Roar at Newbury on his reappearance. With the offending appendage tied down for the first time, he posted a career best effort. This was not a very strong race and he will struggle to follow up at Royal Ascot in the King Edward VII Stakes.
**Crocodile Dundee(IRE)** got a good lead off Happy Crusader and, that one apart, probably enjoyed the best trip. He was four lengths behind Hazyview on his previous start and gives a good guide to the strength of the form.
**Red Lancer**, successful in the Chester Vase on his previous start, ran respectably under his penalty on ground faster than ideal. The ease of his Chester win flatters him to a certain extent, but he can be given another chance at a similar level back on a soft surface.
**Happy Crusader(IRE)** got an easy lead and set just a steady pace. However, he found little under pressure and did not appear to stay.
**Mutahayya(IRE)**, runner-up in a weak Easter Stakes at Kempton on his reappearance, was below form on this first run beyond a mile. The slow pace may not have suited him, but there is no way of knowing if stayed as he never looked like picking up.

## 2204 CASCO MAIDEN STKS 1m
**4:20** (4:21) (D ) 3-Y-O **£5,577** (£1,716; £858; £429) **Stalls** High

Form RPR

25- **1** **Dubois**[232] [5278] 3-9-0 .......... (vt[1]) RHills 7 81
(SaeedBinSuroor) *lw: dwlt: sn led and set str pce: hung lft fr 2f out: rdn and kpt on wl fnl f* **9/4**[1]

0-6 **2** *1 1/4* **Gold Mask (USA)**[35] [1386] 3-9-0 .......... DHolland 10 78
(JHMGosden) *chsd wnr: rdn 3f out: effrt and ch 1f out: hld ins fnl f* **5/2**[2]

6 **3** *1 3/4* **Lucayan Legend (IRE)**[15] [1827] 3-9-0 .......... KFallon 9 74
(RHannon) *w'like: sn pushed along in midfield: effrt over 3f out: chsd ldng pair over 2f out: kpt on same pce* **13/2**

00 **4** *3* **Starmix**[10] [1967] 3-9-0 .......... TQuinn 4 67
(PFICole) *hld up in last: pushed along over 3f out: sme prog over 2f out: one pce over 1f out* **40/1**

**5** *1/2* **Ridge Boy (IRE)** 3-9-0 .......... PDobbs 6 66
(RHannon) *racd in midfield: pushed along 4f out: rn green and struggling 3f out: kpt on fr over 1f out* **33/1**

0 **6** *3* **High Frequency (IRE)**[34] [1395] 3-9-0 .......... MartinDwyer 3 59
(WRMuir) *disp 2nd pl to 3f out: steadily wknd* **25/1**

**7** *1/2* **Zilmy (IRE)** 3-9-0 .......... JPMurtagh 8 58
(PWHarris) *w'like: bit bkwd: dwlt: hld up: prog over 3f out: no imp ldrs 2f out: wknd fnl f: eased* **4/1**[3]

- **8** *1/2* **Innocent Rebel (USA)** 3-9-0 .......... TEDurcan 2 57
(EALDunlop) *unf: a in last trio and wl off the pce: shkn up and no prog 3f out* **12/1**

00-0 **9** *2* **Bahama Reef (IRE)**[55] [1096] 3-9-0 **63** .......... JQuinn 1 52
(BGubby) *swtg: nvr beyond midfield: rdn and struggling over 3f out* **50/1**

6- **10** *hd* **Blaise Wood (USA)**[319] [2963] 3-9-0 .......... RLMoore 5 52
(GLMoore) *bit bkwd: a in last trio: rdn and struggling 3f out* **40/1**

1m 39.9s (-0.37) **Going Correction** +0.025s/f (Good) **10** Ran SP% **114.0**
Speed ratings: **102,100,99,96,95 92,92,91,89,89**CSF £7.45 TOTE £2.90: £1.30, £1.60, £1.80; EX 7.30.

**Owner** Godolphin **Bred** Cheveley Park Stud Ltd **Trained** Newmarket, Suffolk

**FOCUS**
A pretty ordinary maiden by Goodwood standards, although the time was reasonable.

**NOTEBOOK**
**Dubois** hails from a stable with plenty of better three-year-olds in their care, but proved good enough to take this maiden. With a tongue-tie and visor fitted for the first time, he did not look the most straightforward and was noted hanging left under pressure, but he was always going to hold on. He looks no better than a handicapper.
**Gold Mask(USA)**, stepping up from seven furlongs, did not appear good enough. There is a small race to be won with him.
**Lucayan Legend(IRE)** showed the benefit of his debut running and would appear to be going the right way.
**Starmix**, who made his debut over a mile and a half, appeared to run his best race to date dropped back to a mile, but will need to improve to win a similar event. He is now qualified for handicaps and it will be interesting to see what mark he gets after two poor previous efforts.
**Ridge Boy(IRE)**, out of a seven-furlong winner, did not appear at home on this track, but that may have been exaggerated by his inexperience.

**Zilmy(IRE)**, out of a winner over a mile, was quite well backed but did not show that much.

## 2205 AVTRADE MAIDEN AUCTION STKS 5f
4:55 (4:56) (D) 2-Y-O £4,797 (£1,476; £738; £369) Stalls Low

Form RPR
1 **Gortumblo** 2-8-7 TQuinn 8 84
(DJSFfrenchDavis) *w'like: racd on outer: pressed ldrs: rdn 2f out: led over 1f out: drvn out* **25/1**
2 2 1 1/4 **Asian Tiger (IRE)**[7] 2024 2-8-10 RHughes 7 82
(RHannon) *lw: mde most: wandered u.p and hdd over 1f out: one pce* **1/1**[1]
5 3 nk **Empire's Ghodha**[5] 2057 2-8-9 KFallon 3 80
(BJMeehan) *w ldr: rdn and ev ch over 1f out: one pce* **9/2**[3]
4 2 **Ragged Glory (IRE)** 2-8-9 PDobbs 6 72
(RHannon) *w'like: bit bkwd: dwlt: sn in tch: outpcd 2f out: kpt on ins fnl f* **33/1**
5 shd **Shujune Al Hawaa (IRE)** 2-8-5 TEDurcan 5 67
(MRChannon) *unf: bit bkwd: rn green: chsd ldrs: outpcd 2f out: one pce after* **14/1**
34 6 hd **Withering Lady (IRE)**[21] 1686 2-8-2 JQuinn 1 64
(MrsPNDutfield) *in tch: effrt 1/2-way: sn outpcd: one pce after* **10/1**
64 7 1 1/4 **Detonate**[20] 1707 2-8-7 DHolland 2 64
(IAWood) *t.k.h: hld up in last: hmpd 1/2-way: effrt over 1f out: no prog fnl f* **10/3**[2]
8 2 1/2 **In Dream'S (IRE)** 2-8-10 MartinDwyer 4 57
(BGubby) *w'like: bit bkwd: spd 2f: sn lost pl and btn* **50/1**

60.55 secs (1.50) **Going Correction** +0.175s/f (Good) **8 Ran SP% 115.8**
Speed ratings: **95,93,92,89,89 88,86,82**CSF £51.05 TOTE £42.00: £4.10, £1.20, £1.10; EX 121.50.
**Owner** K Corrigan **Bred** London Thoroughbred Services Ltd **Trained** Lambourn, Berks

**FOCUS**
Probably not that bad a maiden and it should produce some winners.

**NOTEBOOK**
**Gortumblo**, an 8,000gns yearling, out of a mile winner, did not go off unsupported and knew his job. There should be more to come and it will be disappointing if he does not get competitive in a higher grade.
**Asian Tiger(IRE)**, runner-up on his debut in what was probably just an ordinary York maiden, does not appear to have progressed from that. He clearly has the ability to win a similar race, but could just be the type to keep finding one too good and does not appeal as one to take a short price about.
**Empire's Ghodha** again offered encouragement and appears to be improving. He should find an ordinary maiden.
**Ragged Glory(IRE)**, a 25,000gns yearling, out of an unraced half-sister to top-class sprinter Pivotal, was unfancied in the betting but offered plenty of promise. He should go on from this.
**Shujune Al Hawaa(IRE)**, a 35,000gns yearling, out of a half-sister to several winners, proved easy to back but was another to offer some encouragement.
**Detonate** had shaped with promise on his two previous starts, but raced keenly under heavy restraint and proved disappointing. He is better than this.

## 2206 SINGLETON STKS (H'CAP) 7f
5:30 (5:34) (C) (0-90,90) 4-Y-O+ £9,964 (£3,066; £1,533; £766) Stalls High

Form RPR
4140 1 **Taranaki**[10] 1968 6-9-3 **82** LisaJones(3) 13 93
(PDCundell) *lw: racd in midfield: prog 2f out: swtchd lft over 1f out: r.o to ld fnl 150yds: sn clr* **9/1**[3]
0-00 2 2 **Material Witness (IRE)**[10] 1968 7-9-7 **83** MartinDwyer 11 89
(WRMuir) *led: kpt on wl whn pressed over 1f out: hdd and outpcd last 150yds* **16/1**
2220 3 3/4 **Just Fly**[20] 1708 4-9-2 **78** PDobbs 16 82
(SKirk) *settled in rr: prog 2f out: swtchd lft 1f out: r.o fnl f: nrst fin* **12/1**
5430 4 nk **Fruit Of Glory**[17] 1765 5-10-0 **90** DHolland 12 93
(JRJenkins) *lw: trckd ldrs: effrt on inner 2f out: pressed ldr 1f out: one pce fnl f* **11/2**[1]
210- 5 nk **Last Appointment (USA)**[250] 4846 4-9-4 **80** JTate 8 82
(JMPEustace) *bit bkwd: mostly chsd ldr: rdn 2f out: cl up 1f out: nt qckn after* **14/1**
3006 6 1/2 **Greenwood**[45] 1241 6-9-1 **77** JFEgan 7 78
(PGMurphy) *settled wl in rr: prog 2f out: rdn and nt clr run briefly over 1f out: r.o ins fnl f: nrst fin* **33/1**
1-30 7 shd **Perfect Portrait**[28] 1531 4-8-11 **73** (v[1]) KFallon 1 73
(DRLoder) *dropped into last pair fr outside draw: sme prog into midfield 2f out: drvn and styd on fnl f: nvr able to chal* **14/1**
4036 8 hd **Digital**[11] 1927 7-9-9 **88** SHitchcott(3) 4 88
(MRChannon) *dropped into last pair fr outside draw: effrt and rdn over 2f out: styd on fr over 1f out: nvr able to chal* **6/1**[2]
0111 9 1 1/4 **Stoic Leader (IRE)**[11] 1929 4-9-4 **80** JFanning 15 77
(RFFisher) *lw: pressed ldrs: rdn and cl up over 1f out: wkng whn squeezed out nr fin* **11/2**[1]
0124 10 3 **Flint River**[11] 1927 6-8-12 **74** RHughes 3 63
(HMorrison) *lw: racd in midfield: rdn over 2f out: no prog* **14/1**
216- 11 1 1/4 **Gift Horse**[276] 4188 4-9-6 **82** JPMurtagh 9 68
(JRFanshawe) *bit bkwd: chsd ldrs: rdn over 2f out: wknd over 1f out* **14/1**
010- 12 1 1/4 **Polar Impact**[121] 5-8-10 **72** TEDurcan 10 54
(GLMoore) *bit bkwd: t.k.h: hld up in rr: rdn wl over 2f out: no prog and sn btn* **10/1**
1201 13 2 1/2 **Just A Glimmer**[15] 1840 4-9-8 **84** FNorton 6 60
(LGCottrell) *chsd ldrs: rdn wl over 2f out: wknd wl over 1f out* **14/1**
5062 14 3/4 **Oakley Rambo**[10] 1968 5-9-4 **80** RLMoore 2 54
(RHannon) *a in rr: shkn up and no prog wl over 2f out* **10/1**
000- 15 nk **Yeoman Lad**[206] 5756 4-9-0 **76** SWhitworth 14 49
(AMBalding) *hld up wl in rr: rdn 3f out: sn btn* **20/1**
10-0 16 6 **Ile Michel**[88] 837 7-9-6 **85** RMiles(3) 5 43
(JGMO'Shea) *chsd ldrs: rdn and wknd 3f out* **33/1**

1m 26.91s (-1.12) **Going Correction** +0.025s/f (Good) **16 Ran SP% 130.8**
Speed ratings: **107,104,103,103,103 102,102,102,100,97 95,94,91,90,90 83**CSF £152.93 CT £1110.88 TOTE £14.00: £3.40, £4.50, £4.80, £2.00; EX 191.10 Place 6 £841.67, Place 5 £179.24.
**Owner** Eric Evers **Bred** E D Evers **Trained** Compton, Berks

**FOCUS**
This had the look of a tight handicap, but Taranaki made it look easy when in full stride.

**NOTEBOOK**
**Taranaki** had never previously won off a mark this high, but showed himself as good as ever with one of the more straightforward wins you will see on this course in a big-field handicap.
**Material Witness(IRE)** ran his best race of the season so far, but the winner was in a different league. Although he has done most of his winning over seven furlongs, six may just suit better.
*Official explanation: jockey said gelding had lost a front shoe.*
**Just Fly** got going all too late and is generally quite a frustrating sort.
**Fruit Of Glory** has been running well enough without winning and has never won before June.
**Last Appointment(USA)** ran better than he did on his handicap debut 250 days previously and should be better for the run.
**Greenwood** has not won for over a year, but would have been closer with better luck.
**Perfect Portrait**, with a visor on for the first time, ran as well as could have been expected from the lowest stall of all.
**Digital** had no easy task from stall four and could never really get into it.
**Stoic Leader(IRE)** did not look to have any excuses, but has been kept busy lately.
T/Jkpt: Not won. T/Plt: £469.00 to a £1 stake. Pool: £79,582.85. 123.85 winning tickets. T/Qpdt: £110.00 to a £1 stake. Pool: £4,247.60. 28.55 winning tickets. JN

# 1607 LEICESTER (R-H)
Tuesday, May 18

**OFFICIAL GOING: Good to firm**
Wind: slt bhd Weather: warm & sunny

## 2207 FENWICK OF LEICESTER H'CAP 7f 9y
6:15 (6:15) (D) (0-80,80) 3-Y-O £5,850 (£1,800; £900; £450) Stalls Low

Form RPR
3-32 1 **Warden Complex**[41] 1293 3-9-2 **75** OUrbina 6 84
(JRFanshawe) *hld up: hdwy and hung rt over 1f out: led ins fnl f: r.o wl* **11/2**[3]
6-64 2 1 3/4 **Midnight Ballard (USA)**[10] 1975 3-9-4 **77** SCarson 16 81
(RFJohnsonHoughton) *chsd ldrs: led 3f out: rdn and hdd ins fnl f: unable qck* **16/1**
16-0 3 1 1/2 **Go Solo**[52] 1129 3-8-11 **77** KMay(7) 5 77
(BWHills) *chsd ldrs: rdn over 1f out: styd on* **7/1**
300- 4 1/2 **Boule D'Or (IRE)**[215] 5592 3-9-2 **75** NDay 13 74
(RIngram) *chsd ldrs: rdn and ev ch over 1f out: styd on same pce ins fnl f* **16/1**
1 5 1/2 **Night Air (IRE)**[17] 1771 3-8-12 **74** TPQueally(3) 15 72
(DRLoder) *s.i.s: sn prom: rdn over 1f out: no ex* **6/1**
06-0 6 2 **Beautiful Noise**[18] 1755 3-7-12 **60** JFMcDonald(3) 7 52
(DMorris) *prom: rdn over 2f out: wknd fnl f* **16/1**
2100 7 1/2 **Hazewind**[15] 1841 3-8-0 **59** ow1 (t) CCatlin 4 50
(PDEvans) *chsd ldrs: rdn over 2f out: wknd fnl f* **25/1**
-102 8 nk **Key Partners (IRE)**[7] 2019 3-8-8 **70** DNolan(3) 2 60
(PABlockley) *hld up: rdn over 2f out: nvr trbld ldrs* **5/1**[2]
30-0 9 shd **Mr Belvedere**[48] 1214 3-8-9 **68** ADaly 1 58
(RHannon) *hld up: rdn over 2f out: n.d* **33/1**
3-20 10 nk **Trench Coat (USA)**[14] 1869 3-8-11 **70** WRyan 9 59
(AMBalding) *led 4f: wknd and eased fnl f* **20/1**
3-04 11 3 **Spin King (IRE)**[16] 1795 3-9-7 **80** IMongan 8 61
(MLWBell) *chsd ldrs: rdn over 2f out: hung rt over 1f out: sn wknd and eased* **7/2**[1]
60-0 12 nk **Lupine Howl**[17] 1760 3-7-13 **58** JMackay 12 39
(BAMcmahon) *chsd ldrs: n.m.r and lost pl 5f out: n.d after* **50/1**
24-0 13 hd **Danish Monarch**[24] 1613 3-8-12 **71** DSweeney 11 51
(ADWPinder) *hld up: effrt over 2f out: sn btn* **40/1**
-000 14 11 **Burkees Graw (IRE)**[56] 1089 3-7-11 **61** oh10 ow4 RThomas(5) 3 12
(MrsSLamyman) *plld hrd and prom: rdn 1/2-way: wknd over 2f out* **66/1**
05-0 15 2 1/2 **Perfect Hindsight (IRE)**[43] 1270 3-8-1 **60** RSmith 14 5
(CGCox) *prom: rdn over 2f out: sn wknd* **20/1**
3-00 P **Thadea (IRE)**[15] 1841 3-8-1 **60** MHenry 10 —
(JGGiven) *hld up: p.u and dismntd 1/2-way* **25/1**

1m 24.68s (-1.42) **Going Correction** -0.225s/f (Firm) **16 Ran SP% 124.8**
Speed ratings: **99,97,95,94,94 91,91,90,90,90 87,86,86,73,71** —CSF £83.15 CT £666.48 TOTE £8.00: £1.80, £3.30, £3.00, £2.90; EX 90.90.
**Owner** Park Farm Racing **Bred** Park Farm Racing **Trained** Newmarket, Suffolk

**FOCUS**
A fair handicap run at a fair pace and the field came home strung out behind the winner. The form looks sound.

**NOTEBOOK**
**Warden Complex**, making his handicap debut, produced a fair turn of foot to win going away. He enjoyed the ground on this occasion and won in the style of a progressive individual.
**Midnight Ballard(USA)** ran his race and improved for this switch back to seven furlongs, but had no answer to the winner's late challenge. He can find a similar race.
**Go Solo** held every chance if good enough, but could not quicken late on. He improved on his latest effort and is a genuine sort.
**Boule D'Or(IRE)** ran very much as if this seasonal return was needed. He was produced to win his race over a furlong from home, but could not quicken and will improve a fair bit for the outing.
**Night Air(IRE)** did not help his chances with a sluggish start and was soon ridden to join the leaders. He only scraped home when winning on his debut last time and, on this evidence, may struggle off his current mark in handicaps.
**Key Partners(IRE)** failed to reproduce his decent effort at York last time and, as he is due to go up 14lb in the future, is likely to struggle in handicap company in the future.
**Spin King(IRE)**, popular in the betting ring, never looked like justifying his position at the head of the market. He was inclined to hang under pressure and this has to go down as a disappointment.
*Official explanation: jockey said colt hung right on the good to firm ground.*

## 2208 BBC RADIO LEICESTER MAIDEN STKS 5f 2y
6:45 (6:46) (D) 2-Y-O £5,499 (£1,692; £846; £423) Stalls Low

Form RPR
6 1 **Chateau Istana**[29] 1505 2-8-11 TPQueally(3) 4 95
(NPLittmoden) *chsd ldr: led and hung rt over 1f out: r.o wl* **11/2**
42 2 4 **Chiselled (IRE)**[18] 1743 2-9-0 DarrenWilliams 11 79
(KRBurke) *wnt rt s: sn led: rdn and hdd over 1f out: sn outpcd* **10/3**[1]
5 3 nk **Marching Song**[32] 1436 2-9-0 RSmith 3 78
(RHannon) *s.i.s: sn pushed along in rr: hdwy over 1f out: nt trble ldrs* **7/2**[2]
6240 4 1 1/4 **Gogetter Girl**[15] 1839 2-8-9 NCallan 6 68
(JGallagher) *chsd ldrs: sn pushed along: rdn over 1f out: no ex* **20/1**
5 3 1/2 **Insignia (IRE)** 2-9-0 RHavlin 8 59
(JHMGosden) *dwlt: outpcd: r.o ins fnl f: nvr nrr* **4/1**[3]
6 2 1/2 **Dove Cottage (IRE)** 2-9-0 IMongan 10 49
(WSKittow) *prom: rdn 1/2-way: hung lft and wknd fr over 1f out* **25/1**
7 1 1/4 **Dhefaaf (IRE)** 2-9-0 WSupple 2 44
(BHanbury) *s.i.s: outpcd* **16/1**
4 8 1 **Mrs Kepple**[11] 1930 2-8-9 KDalgleish 5 35
(MJohnston) *broke wl: chsd ldrs: rdn 1/2-way: wknd wl over 1f out* **16/1**
23 9 1/2 **On The Waterline (IRE)**[13] 1884 2-8-9 SDrowne 7 33
(PDEvans) *unruly stalls: chsd ldrs: rdn 1/2-way: wknd wl over 1f out* **15/2**

10 5 **Tip Toes (IRE)** 2-8-9 ........ CCatlin 9 13
(MRChannon) *s.i.s: outpcd* **33/1**

59.86 secs (-1.07) **Going Correction** -0.225s/f (Firm) **10** Ran SP% **115.8**
Speed ratings: **99,92,92,90,84 80,78,76,76,68**CSF £23.39 TOTE £8.90: £2.00, £1.50, £2.20; EX 52.60.
**Owner** Ivan Allan **Bred** High Bramley Grange Stud Ltd **Trained** Newmarket, Suffolk

**FOCUS**
A useful winning time to what may turn out to be a fair maiden.

**NOTEBOOK**
**Chateau Istana** showed the benefit of his debut and won comfortably in the end, despite wandering about through greenness when hitting the front. This scopey colt showed a good turn of foot to settle the issue and confirmed the excellent current well-being of his stable's juveniles. He has a future.
**Chiselled(IRE)** pinged out of the gates and showed good early speed to lead until the winner swept past. He has a maiden contest within his grasp and he may be worth a try over another furlong.
**Marching Song**, as on his debut, was slowly away and stayed on all too late in the day. He needs to improve from the gates, but has ability and should be capable of losing his maiden tag.
**Gogetter Girl** found little under pressure having been up with the pace for a long way. She is now totally exposed.
**Insignia(IRE)**, a 250,000gns purchase, lost all chance at the start and ran green from that point on. He will improve, but this was still a disappointing introduction.
**Dove Cottage(IRE)** *Official explanation: jockey said colt hung left in the final two furlongs.*

## 2209 E.A.S. WINDOWS ANNIVERSARY (S) STKS — 7f 9y
**7:15** (7:15) (G) 3-Y-O+ **£3,010** (£860; £430) **Stalls** Low

Form RPR
0-00 **1** **Kelseas Kolby (IRE)**[10] 1971 4-9-7 53 ........(v) IMongan 4 61
(JAGlover) *hld up in tch: led and wandered fr over 1f out: rdn out* **6/1**[3]
0020 **2** 2 **Jonny Ebeneezer**[14] 1877 5-9-7 63 ........ BDoyle 10 56
(RMHCowell) *chsd ldrs: rdn and ev ch over 1f out: styd on same pce ins fnl f* **9/2**[2]
6500 **3** ½ **Wodhill Be**[20] 1710 4-9-2 45 ........ MTebbutt 13 49
(DMorris) *hld up: hdwy and hung rt over 1f out: styd on same pce ins fnl f* **25/1**
0055 **4** 1 **Love's Design (IRE)**[54] 810 7-9-2 45 ........ AQuinn(5) 3 52
(MissSJWilton) *s.s: hdwy over 2f out: one pce fnl f* **12/1**
466- **5** nk **Waterline Blue (IRE)**[210] 5697 3-8-10 76 ........(t) NCallan 9 51
(PDEvans) *a.p: rdn over 1f out: no ex* **7/2**[1]
6 **6** 6 **My Country Club**[28] 1533 7-9-7 53 ........ DaneO'Neill 11 35
(AGJuckes) *s.i.s: hld up: hdwy 3f out: wknd over 1f out* **11/1**
6000 **7** 3½ **Zak Facta (IRE)**[10] 1971 4-9-7 47 ........(v) CCogan 5 25
(MissDAMchale) *chsd ldrs: rdn 1/2-way: hung rt and wknd over 1f out* **14/1**
0653 **8** 1¾ **Happy Camper (IRE)**[8] 1986 4-9-7 45 ........ DSweeney 6 20
(MRHoad) *w ldrs: rdn and ev ch over 2f out: wknd over 1f out* **10/1**
00- **9** 1½ **Kallista's Pride**[185] 6005 4-9-2 ........ JoannaBadger 15 11
(MRBosley) *chsd ldrs: racd keenly: ev ch over 2f out: wknd over 1f out* **33/1**
0004 **10** 3 **Roy McAvoy (IRE)**[21] 1691 6-9-7 40 ........ GBaker 2 8
(MrsGHarvey) *dwlt: outpcd* **16/1**
0-04 **11** 1¼ **Fine Frenzy (IRE)**[22] 1680 4-8-9 45 ........(p) MHoward(7) 7 —
(MissSJWilton) *chsd ldrs: led over 2f out: hdd & wknd over 1f out* **7/1**
00-0 **12** 1¼ **Laggan Minstrel (IRE)**[40] 667 6-9-7 52 ........(p) RHavlin 14 —
(BJLlewellyn) *mde most over 4f: sn wknd* **25/1**
00-0 **13** 12 **Toddeano**[2] 1076 8-9-7 ........(t) VSlattery 1 —
(GFierro) *s.s: outpcd* **50/1**

1m 25.81s (-0.29) **Going Correction** -0.225s/f (Firm)
**WFA** 3 from 4yo+ 11lb **13** Ran SP% **117.4**
Speed ratings: **92,89,89,88,87 80,76,74,73,69 68,66,53**CSF £31.29 TOTE £5.80: £2.20, £1.40, £5.90; EX 13.70.Kelseas Kolby was sold to Brooklands Racing for 3,000gns.
**Owner** J A Glover **Bred** J F O'Malley **Trained** Carburton, Notts
■ Stewards Enquiry : G Baker one-day ban: used whip when out of contention (May 29)

**FOCUS**
A modest time, even for a seller, and the form is poor.

**NOTEBOOK**
**Kelseas Kolby(IRE)** appreciated this drop in grade and won readily, despite wandering about under pressure. This is his level and he was sold for 3,000gns at the subsequent auction to Paul Blockley.
**Jonny Ebeneezer** looked to have a solid chance at the weights, but again ran a frustrating race. He is a very hard horse to catch right.
**Wodhill Be** improved for this better ground and ran arguably her best race to date, but her proximity at the finish does very little for the form. This lightly-raced filly looks bound for Banded racing.
**Love's Design(IRE)**, reverting from a brief hurdles campaign, did not help his chances with a sluggish start, yet still ran a sound race at these weights and will find easier oppotunites in this grade.
**Waterline Blue(IRE)**, making his three-year-old debut and racing in the tongue tie for the first time, found disappointingly little under pressure and will have left connections scratching their heads after this tame effort.

## 2210 RECTANGLE GROUP H'CAP — 1m 1f 218y
**7:45** (7:45) (D) (0-85,84) 4-Y-O+ **£5,668** (£1,744; £872; £436) **Stalls** High

Form RPR
2-1 **1** **Fine Palette**[10] 1967 4-9-8 79 ........ WRyan 3 92
(HRACecil) *hld up: hdwy and hung rt fr over 2f out: led 1f out: rdn out* **7/1**[3]
000- **2** 2½ **Frontier**[7] 5935 7-8-9 66 ........ RHavlin 8 74
(BJLlewellyn) *led 1f: chsd ldr: led over 2f out: rdn and hdd 1f out: styng on same pce whn hmpd wl ins fnl f* **15/2**
0300 **3** 1½ **Northside Lodge (IRE)**[12] 1903 6-9-6 77 ........ DHolland 7 82
(PWHarris) *hld up: rdn over 3f out: hdwy and hung rt 2f out: styd on to 2nd post* **11/4**[1]
4215 **4** nk **Say What You See (IRE)**[40] 1308 4-9-0 71 ........ EAhern 14 76
(JWHills) *s.i.s: rcvrd to ld after 1f: rdn and hdd over 2f out: no ex ins fnl f* **11/2**[2]
11-0 **5** nk **Coup De Chance (IRE)**[60] 1054 4-9-10 84 ........(b) DNolan(3) 1 88
(PABlockley) *hld up: hdwy and nt clr run over 2f out: r.o ins fnl f : nt rch ldrs* **18/1**
660- **6** 1¼ **Piri Piri (IRE)**[223] 5452 4-8-9 66 ........ SSanders 5 68
(PJMcbride) *hld up: hdwy over 2f out: rdn over 1f out: styng on same pce whn n.m.r ins fnl f* **20/1**
0060 **7** 2 **Adalar (IRE)**[3] 2121 4-8-10 67 ........ SDrowne 12 65
(PDEvans) *chsd ldrs: rdn over 3f out: wknd over 1f out* **25/1**
1010 **8** 1¼ **Tight Squeeze**[5] 2062 7-9-9 80 ........ BDoyle 10 75
(PWHiatt) *hld up: effrt over 2f out: sn wknd* **9/1**
0-00 **9** shd **Prairie Wolf**[15] 1821 8-9-9 80 ........ IMongan 4 75
(MLWBell) *hld up: n.d* **14/1**
14/ **10** 2 **Hors La Loi (FR)**[40] 3925 8-9-3 74 ........ CCatlin 6 65
(IanWilliams) *hld up: a in rr* **50/1**
01-0 **11** 1 **Tetou (IRE)**[11] 1940 4-8-9 69 ........ JFMcDonald(3) 13 59
(BJMeehan) *chsd ldrs over 7f* **33/1**
000/ **12** 1¾ **Ursa Major**[585] 5196 10-7-12 55 oh3 ........ MHenry 11 41
(TKeddy) *chsd ldrs: rdn over 3f out: hmpd and wknd 2f out* **66/1**
2-24 **13** 3 **Khanjar (USA)**[18] 1746 4-9-1 75 ........(v) TPQueally(3) 9 56
(DRLoder) *rel to r: awlasy bhd* **14/1**
2120 **14** 10 **Hip Hop Harry**[17] 1768 4-9-11 82 ........(v) KFallon 2 44
(EALDunlop) *hld up: rdn over 4f out: sn wknd* **7/1**[3]

2m 5.37s (-3.03) **Going Correction** -0.225s/f (Firm) **14** Ran SP% **122.4**
Speed ratings: **103,101,99,99,99 98,96,95,95,94 93,91,89,81**CSF £56.85 CT £183.46 TOTE £6.90: £2.50, £3.00, £1.50; EX 110.30.
**Owner** Mrs Angela Scott **Bred** Addison Racing Ltd Inc **Trained** Newmarket, Suffolk
■ Stewards Enquiry : W Ryan one-day ban: careless riding (May 29)

**FOCUS**
A decent gallop to this fair handicap which produced a ready winner.

**NOTEBOOK**
**Fine Palette** ◆ readily followed up on his maiden success last time, despite looking uneasy on this much faster ground. He enjoyed the decent early gallop, will improve when getting his toe into the ground and looks progressive.
**Frontier**, reverting from a winless hurdles campaign, ran a solid race and can be considered slightly better than the bare form, as the winner hung across him late on. He would not have won however and can expect a rise in the weights for this effort.
**Northside Lodge(IRE)**, the gamble of the race, took time to hit full stride and had to endure a troubled passage, but never really looked like scoring. He had his conditions on this occasion and looked well handicapped, but is becoming frustrating.
**Say What You See(IRE)** was rushed up to lead after a sluggish start and that proved costly, as he could not find a change of pace when headed over two out. He is on a winning mark and is not one to write off just yet.
**Coup De Chance(IRE)**, in great form last year, ran better than on her seasonal reappearance in March and should be rated better than the bare form, as she did not get the best of runs around two out. She is a tricky ride, but looks to be coming to herself and is one to note when hitting top form.

## 2211 FIRST AID MAIDEN STKS — 5f 218y
**8:15** (8:16) (D) 3-Y-O **£5,642** (£1,736; £868; £434) **Stalls** Low

Form RPR
4-52 **1** **Alderney Race (USA)**[16] 1796 3-9-0 84 ........ SDrowne 1 89
(RCharlton) *trckd ldrs: led over 1f out: r.o wl* **9/4**[1]
0-3 **2** 5 **Majorca**[33] 1413 3-9-0 ........ KFallon 9 74
(JHMGosden) *s.i.s: hdwy over 3f out: rdn to ld wl over 1f out: sn hdd and outpcd* **9/4**[1]
000 **3** 4 **Adorata (GER)**[18] 1749 3-8-9 ........ OUrbina 18 57
(JJay) *w ldrs: rdn over 2f out: ev ch over 1f out: sn wknd* **66/1**
**4** shd **Laska (IRE)** 3-8-6 ........ DCorby(3) 10 57
(MJWallace) *chsd ldrs: rdn 1/2-way: sn outpcd: styd on ins fnl f* **50/1**
-022 **5** ½ **Get To The Point**[6] 2029 3-9-0 72 ........ DHolland 19 60
(PWD'Arcy) *chsd ldrs: rdn and ev ch over 1f out: sn wknd* **8/1**[3]
000 **6** 1 **Half A Handful**[28] 1530 3-9-0 ........ RHavlin 12 57
(MJWallace) *s.i.s: hld up: outpcd 1/2-way: styng on whn hmpd ins fnl f: nvr trble ldrs* **66/1**
4 **7** ¾ **Called Up**[18] 1749 3-9-0 ........ DSweeney 16 55
(HCandy) *hld up: effrt over 1f out: n.d* **25/1**
**8** ¾ **Zameyla (IRE)** 3-8-9 ........ PRobinson 17 48
(MAJarvis) *s.i.s: hdwy over 4f out: wknd and eased over 1f out* **8/1**[3]
62- **9** ¾ **Willofcourse**[318] 2993 3-9-0 ........ DaneO'Neill 2 50
(HCandy) *mde most over 4f: sn edgd rt: wknd fnl f* **7/1**[2]
**10** ¾ **Chatshow (USA)**[292] 3-9-0 ........ PDoe 3 48
(LADace) *w ldrs over 4f: sn wknd* **25/1**
2-0 **11** 1¼ **Pink Supreme**[53] 1111 3-8-6 ........(t) TPQueally(3) 5 39
(IAWood) *hld up in tch: rdn and wknd over 1f out* **25/1**
**12** 1 **Petrion** 3-8-9 ........ CLowther 14 36
(RGuest) *s.i.s: outpcd* **50/1**
00-0 **13** 2½ **Ravel (IRE)**[17] 1771 3-9-0 ........ IMongan 20 34
(MLWBell) *s.i.s: sn chsng ldrs: rdn over 2f out: wknd over 1f out* **50/1**
0 **14** 1¾ **Flying With Eagles**[6] 2029 3-9-0 ........ GBaker 8 29
(JJay) *s.s: outpcd* **100/1**
00- **15** 2½ **Shifty Night (IRE)**[329] 2648 3-8-9 ........ CCatlin 11 16
(MrsCADunnett) *chsd ldrs over 3f* **100/1**

1m 11.56s (-1.84) **Going Correction** -0.225s/f (Firm) **15** Ran SP% **118.6**
Speed ratings: **103,96,91,90,90 88,87,86,85,84 83,81,78,76,72**CSF £5.83 TOTE £3.40: £1.30, £1.20, £27.00; EX 7.90.
**Owner** Britton House Stud Ltd **Bred** Britton House Stud Inc **Trained** Beckhampton, Wilts

**FOCUS**
An average maiden lacking any strength in depth, but the first two home were clear of the rest.

**NOTEBOOK**
**Alderney Race(USA)** got off the mark at the fourth attempt in decisive fashion. He relished this return to a quick surface and showed a neat turn of foot to settle the issue over a frulong from home. Although he may not have beaten much on this occasion, he could only win as he did and has more to offer in handicaps over this trip.
**Majorca** ◆ was not helped by being left at the start and stayed on as though this sprint trip was against him. He is capable of better and should be given another chance back over further, especially as he is now eligible for handicaps.
**Adorata(GER)** ran her best race to date, but was outclassed by the front two. She looks worth a try in handicap company.
**Laska(IRE)** made a satisfactory debut and ran on well enough having run green and been outpaced at halfway. She is bred to sprint and is entitled to improve for this experience.
**Zameyla(IRE)** *Official explanation: jockey said, regarding the running and riding, his orders were to get across from a wide draw and obtain the best possible placing without being too hard on filly but filly hung early in the early stages, stumbled and lost her action when asked for an effort in the final furlong, and became very leg weary, this being her first run*

## 2212 CARIBBEAN EVENING H'CAP — 1m 3f 183y
**8:45** (8:45) (E) (0-70,66) 4-Y-O+ **£3,669** (£1,129; £564; £282) **Stalls** High

Form RPR
16-6 **1** **Field Spark**[31] 1463 4-8-12 54 ........(p) DHolland 6 67
(JAGlover) *hld up: hdwy over 2f out: rdn to ld over 1f out: hung lft: r.o* **6/1**[2]
22-4 **2** nk **Reminiscent (IRE)**[71] 666 5-8-13 55 ........(v) SCarson 11 68
(RFJohnsonHoughton) *s.i.s: hld up: hdwy over 2f out: rdn over 1f out: r.o* **16/1**
-250 **3** 2 **Man The Gate**[16] 1801 5-9-0 56 ........ SSanders 9 65
(PDCundell) *hld up: hdwy over 2f out: rdn and ev ch over 1f out: styd on same pce* **9/2**[1]

1212 **4** 2 ½ **Great View (IRE)**[14] 1858 5-9-6 **65**....(v) DCorby(3) 15 70
(MrsALMKing) *w ldr tl led over 2f out: rdn and hdd over 1f out: no ex ins fnl f* **9/2**[1]

353- **5** 1 **Trusted Mole (IRE)**[331] 2610 6-8-10 **52**.... KFallon 5 56
(WMBrisbourne) *s.i.s: hld up: pushed along 4f out: hdwy u.p over 1f out: no imp towards fin* **7/1**[3]

-000 **6** ¾ **Forest Tune (IRE)**[6] 2032 6-9-3 **59**.... WSupple 17 62
(BHanbury) *chsd ldrs: rdn over 2f out: wknd ins fnl f* **25/1**

-665 **7** 6 **Most-Saucy**[6] 2032 8-9-6 **62**.... EAhern 12 55
(IAWood) *hld up: hdwy 5f out: rdn over 1f out: sn wknd* **9/1**

3302 **8** shd **Lazzaz**[84] 867 6-8-7 **49**.... MHenry 1 42
(PWHiatt) *chsd ldrs: rdn over 2f out: wknd over 1f out* **14/1**

40-5 **9** 2 **Little Englander**[20] 1715 4-9-3 **59**.... DaneO'Neill 16 49
(HCandy) *prom: rdn over 3f out: hung rt and wknd over 1f out* **33/1**

1300 **10** ½ **Madhahir (IRE)**[10] 1958 4-9-1 **60**.... TPQueally(3) 19 49
(CADwyer) *prom: rdn and n.m.r 3f out: wknd over 1f out* **25/1**

2005 **11** shd **Fight The Feeling**[52] 1136 6-8-9 **51**.... ADaly 13 40
(JWUnett) *hld up: nvr nrr* **33/1**

340- **12** 4 **Red River Rebel**[213] 5635 6-9-2 **58**.... DarrenWilliams 18 40
(JRNorton) *led over 9f: wknd over 1f out* **33/1**

004 **13** 2 ½ **Logger Rhythm (USA)**[17] 1770 4-9-4 **60**.... MFenton 14 38
(RDickin) *chsd ldrs: rdn 1/2-way: wknd over 2f out* **22/1**

0-00 **14** 6 **Go Classic**[52] 1135 4-9-6 **62**.... CCatlin 8 31
(AMHales) *hld up: bhd fr 1/2-way* **50/1**

05-0 **15** dist **St Jerome**[18] 1754 4-9-1 **57**.... NCallan 7 —
(NPLittmoden) *hld up in tch: wknd over 3f out* **33/1**

5-04 **P** **Ipsa Loquitur**[24] 1611 4-9-2 **58**.... SDrowne 3 —
(SCWilliams) *chsd ldrs: lost pl 1/2-way: sn t.o: p.u over 1f out* **7/1**[3]

2m 31.31s (-3.37) **Going Correction** -0.225s/f (Firm) **16** Ran SP% **124.0**
Speed ratings: **102,101,100,98,98 97,93,93,92,91 91,89,87,83,—** —CSF £89.91 CT £483.86 TOTE £11.10: £2.50, £4.70, £1.60, £1.80; EX 178.00 Place 6 £37.61, Place 5 £9.35.
**Owner** G Taylor & J P Burton **Bred** F Hinojosa **Trained** Carburton, Notts

**FOCUS**
A moderate handicap which was run to suit those held up off the decent gallop. The form looks sound enough.

**NOTEBOOK**
**Field Spark**, dropping back to a more suitable trip, ran on strongly to lead late on to win this all out. He showed the benefit of his recent comeback effort and could well follow up on this, as he is still well treated on his old form.
**Reminiscent(IRE)**, reverting from a brief hurdles campaign, finished best of all and was only just denied. He was caught napping at the start and that probably cost him, but he is on a long losing run and finds it hard to get his head in front.
**Man The Gate**, who has gained both his wins at this venue, ran his race and had every chance. He is a bit one-paced in a finish and is another who often runs his race with a habit of finding a couple too good.
**Great View(IRE)** did best of those to run up with the pace, but had little left in the tank when the challengers loomed up approaching the final furlong. The Handicapper may have got his measure on this evidence, but this was another sound effort.
**Trusted Mole(IRE)**, having his first start since June 2003, ran very much as though this outing was needed and he will improve a fair bit for the run.
**St Jerome** *Official explanation: jockey said gelding was unsuited to the track*
**Ipsa Loquitur** *Official explanation: trainer said filly had atrial fibrillation.*
T/Plt: £56.60 to a £1 stake. Pool: £42,374.45. 545.90 winning tickets. T/Qpdt: £7.80 to a £1 stake. Pool: £3,537.60. 333.00 winning tickets. CR

## 1990 REDCAR (L-H)
Tuesday, May 18

**OFFICIAL GOING: Firm (good to firm in places)**

### 2213 EUROPEAN BREEDERS FUND MEDIAN AUCTION MAIDEN FILLIES' STKS 6f
**2:00** (2:01) (F) 2-Y-0 **£3,643** (£1,041; £520) **Stalls** Centre

Form RPR

32 **1** **Umniya (IRE)**[7] 2023 2-8-11.... ACulhane 9 77+
(MRChannon) *cl up: led over out: r.o u.p* **4/5**[1]

**2** 2 ½ **Taras Treasure (IRE)** 2-8-11.... RWinston 2 68
(JJQuinn) *sn chsng ldrs: rdn to chse wnr fnl f: no imp ins last* **14/1**

2 **3** 3 ½ **Tagula Bay (IRE)**[10] 1960 2-8-8.... DAllan(3) 12 57
(TDEasterby) *cl up: led over 3f out: rdn and hdd over 1f out: no ex* **9/2**[2]

**4** nk **Knock Bridge (IRE)** 2-8-11.... SSanders 10 56
(MJWallace) *trckd ldrs: rdn and ev ch over 1f out: kpt on same pce* **6/1**[3]

**5** hd **Missperon (IRE)** 2-8-11.... NCallan 7 55
(KARyan) *chsd ldrs: rdn 2f out: kpt on same pce* **20/1**

**6** 2 **Underthemistletoe (IRE)** 2-8-11.... FLynch 11 49
(BSmart) *s.i.s: sn in tch: rdn and swished tail over 1f out: wknd fnl f* **33/1**

0 **7** 1 ¼ **Kashmar Flight**[15] 1839 2-8-4.... AMullen(7) 3 45
(TDEasterby) *s.s and swvd lft: rr div tl styd on appr fnl f: n.d* **33/1**

**8** ½ **Falcon Goer (USA)** 2-8-11.... KimTinkler 13 43
(NTinkler) *dwlt: rr div tl styd on appr fnl f: n.d* **66/1**

**9** ¾ **Dorn Dancer (IRE)** 2-8-8.... LEnstone(3) 4 41
(DWBarker) *s.i.s: sn midfield: rdn 2f out: sn btn* **33/1**

**10** 1 ¾ **Three Pennies** 2-8-11.... SWKelly 5 35
(MDods) *s.i.s: a rr div* **50/1**

**11** 1 ½ **Canary Dancer** 2-8-11.... GFaulkner 8 30
(PCHaslam) *s.i.s: sn midfield: rdn 2f out: sn btn* **66/1**

0 **12** 2 ½ **Fantastic Star**[36] 1364 2-8-11.... MFenton 1 22
(JGGiven) *led tl hdd over 3f out: wknd over 2f out* **66/1**

**13** 2 **Live In Hope** 2-8-11.... NPollard 6 16
(JeddO'Keeffe) *sn rr div* **100/1**

1m 11.82s (0.12) **Going Correction** -0.125s/f (Firm) **13** Ran SP% **115.7**
Speed ratings: **94,90,86,85,85 82,81,80,79,77 75,71,69**CSF £12.19 TOTE £1.80: £1.10, £2.00, £1.50; EX 9.90.
**Owner** Kuwait Racing Syndicate **Bred** Knockainey Stud **Trained** West Ilsley, Berks

**FOCUS**
An ordinary fillies' maiden, but a decent pace and a good winning time for the grade. There should be more to come from the front pair.

**NOTEBOOK**
**Umniya(IRE)** ♦, who had the best form going into this, had no problem with the faster ground and won this with a bit in hand. She should be able to hold her own in better company and the way she was pulling away at the finish suggests she will stay further than this in time.
**Taras Treasure(IRE)** ♦, a 48,000euros half-sister to the three-time two-year-old winner Soonest, ran a blinder on this debut. She was not given at all a hard time in the last furlong when it was obvious the winner had her measure, but she pulled right away from the others and should not take long in going one better.
**Tagula Bay(IRE)**, on totally different ground compared to her debut and up a furlong, was given a positive ride but found the front pair far too good. It is more likely that she was beaten by two much better fillies rather than she failed to see out the trip and she should still be able to find an ordinary maiden.
**Knock Bridge(IRE)**, a 5,500gns half-sister to the nine-furlong winner Twilight Breeze, was never far away and never stopped trying. She will eventually get further and improvement can be expected.
**Missperon(IRE)**, an 18,000gns half-sister to five winners including Lagoon and Muchtarak, was the subject of some market support at long odds and she showed enough on this debut to suggest the money was not completely misplaced.
**Fantastic Star** *Official explanation: jockey said filly became unbalanced in the last two furlongs.*

### 2214 WILTON CLAIMING STKS 1m 3f
**2:30** (2:31) (F) 3-Y-0+ **£2,919** (£834; £417) **Stalls** Low

Form RPR

00-2 **1** **Arms Acrossthesea**[14] 1867 5-9-1 50.... AMullen(7) 1 56
(ACWhillans) *hld up: hdwy 3f out: drvn to ld over 1f out: styd on* **13/2**

0214 **2** 1 ½ **Platinum Charmer (IRE)**[3] 2127 4-9-12 55....(p) DarrenWilliams 5 58
(KRBurke) *trckd ldrs: chal gng wl 2f out: rdn over 1f out: chsd wnr fnl f: styd on: no imp* **5/2**[1]

00-1 **3** 3 ½ **Righty Ho**[19] 1721 10-9-6 45.... RWinston 2 46
(WHTinning) *mde most tl rdn and hdd over 1f out: no ex* **7/2**[2]

03-5 **4** ¾ **Merlins Profit**[19] 1720 4-9-3 40.... LEnstone(3) 4 45
(MDods) *hld up: hdwy u.p 3f out: ch 2f out: kpt on same pce* **12/1**

000/ **5** 8 **Percy-Verance (IRE)**[84] 4044 6-9-10.... MFenton 6 36
(JJQuinn) *hld up in rr: drvn along and outpcd over 4f out: styd on fnl 2f: n.d* **16/1**

404- **6** shd **Double Blade**[150] 3997 9-9-10 45.... ACulhane 3 36
(NWilson) *trckd ldrs: effrt over 2f out: sn beateb* **9/1**

60-5 **7** 1 ¾ **Erupt**[13] 1885 11-9-0 45.... TEaves(5) 10 28
(REBarr) *hld up in rr: effrt 4f out: no real hdwy* **25/1**

0003 **8** 6 **Mikasa (IRE)**[14] 1867 4-9-8 40.... SSanders 8 22
(RFFisher) *w ldr: wkng whn stmbld wl over 1f out: no ch whn eased fnl f* **14/1**

4600 **9** 2 ½ **Turftanzer (GER)**[20] 1715 5-9-5 35....(t) KimTinkler 9 15
(DonEnricoIncisa) *in tch to 1/2-way: sn bhd* **50/1**

4010 **10** dist **Fortunes Favourite**[6] 2038 4-9-3 45.... SWKelly 7 —
(GMMoore) *slowly away: sn in tch: wknd over 3f out: bhd and eased fnl f: t.o* **11/2**[3]

2m 20.82s (-0.18) **Going Correction** 0.0s/f (Good) **10** Ran SP% **115.6**
Speed ratings: **100,98,96,95,90 89,88,84,82,—**CSF £22.85 TOTE £8.20: £2.70, £1.10, £1.30; EX 17.00.Arms Acrossthesea was claimed by John Balding for £8,000.
**Owner** Play Fair Partnership **Bred** Miss Mandy Jane Barber **Trained** Newmill-On-Slitrig, Borders

**FOCUS**
An poor claimer contested by some exposed and moderate performers.

**NOTEBOOK**
**Arms Acrossthesea**, one of those better in on adjusted official ratings, was 6lb better off with Platinum Charmer for a three-length beating at Musselburgh earlier this month but, more importantly, that was his first outing for eight months so he was likely to come on for it. Brought with a sustained run on the outside before outbattling the favourite, he is in good form at the moment and now joins John Balding after being claimed for £8,000.
**Platinum Charmer(IRE)**, marginally best in on adjusted official ratings, looked to be cruising all over his rivals racing down the home straight, but he did not find as much off the bridle as had looked likely and the winner proved far too strong.
**Righty Ho**, who would have found this trip the bare minimum for him, was given a positive ride to compensate but was still done for foot in the latter stages.
**Merlins Profit**, who had a bit to find at the weights, did not run badly under the circumstances, but he is still a maiden and his ideal trip is still to be established.
**Double Blade**, back on the Flat after a successful winter campaign over jumps, was nonetheless racing for the first time in five months and may have needed it, but it is more likely he lacks the necessary pace over this sort of trip on the level these days and is not getting any younger.
**Mikasa(IRE)** *Official explanation: jockey said gelding lost its action*
**Fortunes Favourite**, one of those best in on adjusted official ratings, ran too badly to be true. *Official explanation: jockey said filly was unsuited by the fast going.*

### 2215 MARSKE H'CAP 7f
**3:05** (3:05) (D) (0-80,80) 3-Y-0+ **£6,532** (£2,010; £1,005; £502) **Stalls** Centre

Form RPR

0-00 **1** **Sawwaah (IRE)**[18] 1746 7-9-12 **78**.... AlexGreaves 13 88
(DNicholls) *midfield: hdwy 2f out: led ent fnl f: hung lft u.p: styd on* **20/1**

2103 **2** ¾ **Whippasnapper**[11] 1929 4-8-13 **65**.... NPollard 12 73
(JRBest) *midfield: drvn along and sme hdwy over 2f out: styd on wl u.p fnl f: nt rch wnr* **8/1**[3]

6040 **3** nk **Pride Of Kinloch**[14] 1875 4-8-5 **57**.... JMcAuley 9 64
(JHetherton) *trckd ldrs: hdwy to ld 2f out: rdn and hdd ent fnl f: styd on* **66/1**

0-22 **4** 1 ¼ **Annijaz**[8] 1992 7-8-2 **57**.... BReilly(3) 20 61
(JMBradley) *swtchd towards far side sn after s: towards rr: hdwy u.p over 2f out: chsd ldrs fnl f: no further prog* **10/1**

0006 **5** 2 **Branston Tiger**[15] 1825 5-9-4 **70**.... MFenton 1 68
(JGGiven) *in tch: rdn over 2f out: kpt on fnl f* **20/1**

00-4 **6** shd **Cashneem (IRE)**[14] 1877 6-8-8 **60**.... SWKelly 16 58
(WMBrisbourne) *midfield: rdn 3f out: kpt on fnl f. nvr able to chal* **14/1**

5-00 **7** shd **Iberus (GER)**[15] 1821 6-9-3 **74**....(p) TEaves(5) 14 72
(SGollings) *sn towards rr and drvn along: hdwy over 1f out: styd on strly fnl f: nrst fin* **33/1**

-006 **8** hd **Go Tech**[17] 1772 4-9-10 **79**.... DAllan(3) 2 76+
(TDEasterby) *towards rr: drvn along and hdwy over 2f out: midfield and styng on whn hmpd appr fnl f: nt rcvr* **5/1**[1]

-000 **9** ¾ **Tre Colline**[22] 1665 5-8-13 **65**.... KimTinkler 18 60
(NTinkler) *sn towards rr: kpt on fnl 2f: n.d* **20/1**

1142 **10** ½ **Up Tempo (IRE)**[24] 1603 6-9-11 **77**....(b) NCallan 11 71+
(KARyan) *trckd ldrs: nt clr run fr over 2f out tl ins fnl f: nvr able to chal* **7/1**[2]

10-2 **11** ¾ **Queen Charlotte (IRE)**[40] 1315 5-9-2 **68**.... RWinston 7 60
(MrsKWalton) *cl up tl wknd over 1f out* **14/1**

-050 **12** shd **Atlantic Quest (USA)**[15] 1821 5-10-0 **80**.... JCarroll 19 72
(GAHarker) *sn wl bhd: styd on fr over 1f out: n.d* **12/1**

0-00 **13** ¾ **One Way Ticket**[14] 1877 4-8-5 **60**....(p) LEnstone(3) 8 50
(JMBradley) *led tl hdd 1/2-way: wknd 2f out* **25/1**

0205 **14** ½ **Flying Edge (IRE)**[16] 1787 4-8-8 **60**.... ANicholls 6 48
(EJAlston) *prom: rdn 3f out: sn btn* **10/1**

2501 **15** ¾ **My Bayard**[25] 1595 5-8-7 **59**.... PFessey 5 45
(JO'Reilly) *cl up: led 1/2-way tl rdn and hdd 2f out: sn wknd* **20/1**

1643 **16** nk **Weet Watchers**[34] 1389 4-8-8 **60**.... ACulhane 10 45
(DNicholls) *prom: effrt 2f out: sn rdn and wknd* **16/1**

6000 **17** *shd* **Bond Playboy**[29] 1500 4-9-1 **67** ........ SSanders 15 52
(BSmart) *rr div fr 1/2-way* **25/1**
2060 **18** *nk* **Oases**[12] 1909 5-8-6 **58** ........ DarrenWilliams 17 42
(DShaw) *s.s: sme hdwy u.p 1/2-way: wknd 2f out* **40/1**
-000 **19** *10* **Riska King**[11] 1927 4-9-4 **73** ........ THamilton(3) 3 30
(RAFahey) *s.s: a wl bhd* **20/1**

1m 23.4s (-1.50) **Going Correction** -0.125s/f (Firm) **19** Ran SP% **123.7**
Speed ratings: **103,102,101,100,98 97,97,97,96,96 95,95,94,93,92 92,92,92,80**CSF £152.84 CT £10046.69 TOTE £25.40: £6.90, £2.40, £13.10, £2.50; EX 291.10.
**Owner** Fayzad Thoroughbred Limited **Bred** Shadwell Estate Company Limited **Trained** Sessay, N Yorks

**FOCUS**
A competitive handicap run at an even pace, but quite a rough race with a few hard-luck stories. Those drawn in double figures provided seven of the first ten home, but the way the race panned out there did not seem to be any great track bias.

**NOTEBOOK**
**Sawwaah(IRE)** ◆, back on fast ground for the first time since winning on it last summer, was always travelling well and stayed on dourly to score despite hanging left under pressure in the last furlong. This was a fair effort over a trip that would have been on the sharp side and, with his stable now clicking into gear, he could well add to this.
**Whippasnapper** has been racing mostly over shorter of late, but he has won over this trip on Polytrack and the way he stayed on here suggests he can win over it on turf too.
**Pride Of Kinloch** ran her best race for some time under a positive ride and on ground probably faster than ideal. She continues to drop down the handicap, but has flattered to deceive in the past and remains a maiden after 16 attempts.
**Annijaz**, despite starting from the highest stall, ended up making her challenge on the far side. She did little wrong and was only just held, but she had been raised 3lb for getting beaten last time, so is not exactly well handicapped just now.
**Branston Tiger** ran a fair race over on the far side of the track and has become very well handicapped, but he is still to win beyond six furlongs.
**Cashneem(IRE)**, back on his ideal ground, ran with credit and should find an ordinary handicap over this trip.
**Iberus(GER)** ◆ is becoming very well handicapped and was noted finishing very strongly over a trip that would have been far too short. He is one to watch out for like a hawk when stepped back up to middle distances.
**Go Tech** ran into traffic problems when staying on and would have been several places closer otherwise. He looks nicely handicapped at present and is still one to keep an eye on for a similar event.
**Up Tempo(IRE)** endured a nightmare passage throughout the last quarter-mile and this effort can be safely ignored. *Official explanation: jockey said he had no luck in running.*
**Atlantic Quest(USA)** *Official explanation: jockey said gelding was outpaced in the early part of the race.*
**My Bayard** *Official explanation: jockey said gelding was unsuited by the fast ground.*
**Riska King** *Official explanation: jockey said gelding sat down in the stalls and was slow away.*

## 2216 WHITBY H'CAP 1m 2f
**3:35** (3:37) (E ) (0-75,75) 3-Y-0+ **£3,688** (£1,135; £567; £283) **Stalls** Low

Form RPR
-013 **1** **Olivia Rose (IRE)**[11] 1944 5-9-4 **65** ........ SSanders 6 74
(JPearce) *settled midfield: smooth hdwy to ld over 1f out: pushed out ins last* **6/1**[2]
3335 **2** *½* **Trouble Mountain (USA)**[11] 1928 7-9-6 **67** ........(b) DaleGibson 14 75
(MWEasterby) *hld up: drvn along and hdwy over 2f out: chsd wnr fnl f: styd on: no imp* **11/2**[1]
00-6 **3** *3 ½* **Michaels Dream (IRE)**[10] 568 5-7-12 **45** oh5........(v) JMcAuley 10 46
(JHetherton) *prom: rdn 3f out: ch 2 out: kpt on same pce* **20/1**
000- **4** *nk* **Sir Night (IRE)**[12] 5705 4-8-6 **53** ........ NPollard 15 54
(JeddO'Keeffe) *towards rr: hdwy u.p over 1f out: styd on fnl f: nvr able to chal* **10/1**
000- **5** *¾* **Stepastray**[174] 5373 7-8-1 **48** ........ CCogan 17 47
(REBarr) *towards rr: hdwy u.p 3f out: kpt on fnl f: nvr able to chal* **33/1**
006- **6** *1 ¾* **Market Avenue**[203] 5821 5-8-12 **62** ........ THamilton(3) 2 58
(RAFahey) *hld up: hdwy whn nt clr run over 2f out and over 1f out: styd on fnl f: nvr able to chal* **8/1**[3]
-041 **7** *nk* **Jimmy Byrne (IRE)**[22] 1669 4-9-6 **72** ........ TEaves(5) 11 68
(BEllison) *midfield: rdn 3f out: no hdwy* **10/1**
0-00 **8** *1 ¼* **Uno Mente**[11] 1931 5-8-11 **58** ........ KimTinkler 13 51
(DonEnricoIncisa) *towards rr: styd on fr over 2f out: n.d* **40/1**
1- **9** *1 ¼* **Trance (IRE)**[167] 6126 4-10-0 **75** ........ PFessey 9 66
(TDBarron) *bhd: sme hdwy whn nt clr run wl over 1f out: n.d* **22/1**
5663 **10** *¾* **East Riding**[14] 1876 4-8-0 **47** ow2........ AnnStokell 4 36
(MissAStokell) *midfield: outpcd over 2f out: n.d* **33/1**
/05- **11** *1 ½* **Lara Bay**[351] 2049 4-9-3 **64** ........ ACulhane 8 50
(AMBalding) *prom: rdn 3f out: wknd 2f out* **14/1**
0-04 **12** *2 ½* **Escalade**[3] 2121 7-8-10 **57** ........(p) SWKelly 5 39
(WMBrisbourne) *midfield: rdn 3f out: in tch whn nt clr run appr fnl f* **10/1**
0-00 **13** *shd* **The Loose Screw (IRE)**[28] 1527 6-7-5 **45** ........ DFentiman(7) 16 27
(GMMoore) *led after 3f tl rdn and hdd over 1f out: sn wknd* **50/1**
0-00 **14** *1 ¼* **Every Note Counts**[34] 1393 4-9-6 **67** ........ RWinston 12 46
(JJQuinn) *prom: ev ch and rdn 3f out: wknd 2f out* **12/1**
5315 **15** *nk* **Jake Black (IRE)**[14] 1856 4-8-5 **59** ........ DTudhope(7) 3 38
(JJQuinn) *trcking ldrs whn hmpd 5f out and over 4f out: in tch whn hmpd over 2f out and over 1f out: nt rcvr* **8/1**[3]
560/ **16** *dist* **Nifty Roy**[582] 5225 4-8-0 **54** ow9........ PPMathers(7) 1 —
(KWHogg) *led 3f: cl up whn stmbld 5f out: wknd qckly: t.o* **100/1**

2m 5.95s (-0.85) **Going Correction** 0.0s/f (Good) **16** Ran SP% **113.9**
Speed ratings: **103,102,99,99,98 97,97,96,95,94 93,91,91,90,90** —CSF £33.39 CT £616.48 TOTE £5.00: £1.90, £1.30, £3.20, £2.60; EX 15.70.
**Owner** A Watford **Bred** Dermot Cantillon **Trained** Newmarket, Suffolk

**FOCUS**
A fairly competitive handicap run at an even pace.

**NOTEBOOK**
**Olivia Rose(IRE)** is at the top of her game at present and this was her best effort for a couple of years. Always cantering, she quickly found a couple of lengths when pushed into the lead and that was enough to hold off the runner-up's late flourish. Her versatility with regards the ground will continue to stand her in good stead and she can win again in her current mood.
**Trouble Mountain(USA)**, not for the first time, was doing all his best work late and was cutting into the winner's advantage at the line, but is flattered by the margin. Considering his ability, his strike-rate is modest and he has spent this year finding different ways of getting himself beat.
**Michaels Dream(IRE)**, fit from hurdling, ran with great credit from 5lb out of the handicap, especially as he could have done with an extra quarter-mile.
**Sir Night(IRE)**, another fit from hurdling, ran with credit under his ideal conditions.
**Stepastray**, off since November, stayed on in the latter stages but a record of one win from 55 Flat starts is a worry.
**Market Avenue** ◆ experienced a nightmare passage between the two- and one-furlong markers and ran on in most eye-catching style once extracted. With her stable just getting back into full swing, she is well worth keeping an eye on. *Official explanation: jockey said he had no luck in running.*
**Uno Mente** *Official explanation: jockey said mare lost a front shoe.*
**Trance(IRE)** *Official explanation: jockey said gelding was unsuited by the fast ground.*
**Jake Black(IRE)** got murdered on several occasions on the inside in the second half of the contest and this effort can be completely ignored.

## 2217 CAPTAIN COOK RATING RELATED MAIDEN STKS 7f
**4:10** (4:11) (E ) 3-Y-0+ **£3,454** (£1,063; £531; £265) **Stalls** Centre

Form RPR
450- **1** **Perle D'Or (IRE)**[213] 5642 3-8-8 **70** ........ ACulhane 4 67
(WJHaggas) *hld up: drvn along over 2f out: styd on wl u.p to ld cl home* **11/4**[2]
053 **2** *nk* **Ballinger Express**[46] 1227 4-9-0 **64** ........(b[1]) NChalmers(5) 3 66
(AMBalding) *dwlt: trckd ldrs: slt ld 2f out tl rdn and hdd ent fnl f: disp ld wl ins last: no ex cl home* **22/1**
2035 **3** *nk* **Pawan (IRE)**[22] 1665 4-9-8 **61** ........ AnnStokell 5 68
(MissAStokell) *mde most tl hdd 2f out: rdn to ld again ent fnl f: hdd cl home* **10/1**
33-6 **4** *1 ½* **Flash Ram**[48] 1209 3-8-8 **70** ........ DAllan(3) 9 64
(TDEasterby) *drvn along in rr 1/2-way: styd on fnl 2f: nvr able to chal* **33/1**
0-43 **5** *nk* **Sessay**[13] 1881 3-8-11 **69** ........ ANicholls 11 64
(DNicholls) *prom: ch and rdn over 1f out: no ex ins last* **2/1**[1]
22-0 **6** *nk* **Nicholas Nickelby**[14] 1877 4-9-5 **60** ........ THamilton(3) 2 63
(MJPolglase) *cl up: rdn and ev ch over 1f out: no ex ins last* **50/1**
40-5 **7** *2 ½* **Tyzack (IRE)**[41] 1303 3-8-11 **69** ........ MFenton 10 56
(JGGiven) *prom: rdn 2f out: fdd* **15/2**[3]
30-5 **8** *nk* **Oeuf A La Neige**[10] 1975 4-9-8 **67** ........ SSanders 1 55
(GCHChung) *in tch: rdn 2f out: sn btn* **10/1**
-403 **9** *2* **Little Eye (IRE)**[90] 816 3-8-11 **66** ........ NPollard 7 50
(JRBest) *wnt lft s: hld up: effrt 2f out: sn rdn: no hdwy* **8/1**
54-4 **10** *¾* **Aliba (IRE)**[25] 1597 3-8-11 **66** ........ RWinston 8 48
(BSmart) *dwlt: hld up: sme hdwy 3f out: wknd 2 out* **25/1**
04-0 **11** *25* **Spartan Spear**[18] 1749 3-8-11 **68** ........ JEdmunds 6 —
(JBalding) *bmpd s: bhd fr 1/2-way: t.o* **50/1**

1m 23.74s (-1.16) **Going Correction** -0.125s/f (Firm)
**WFA** 3 from 4yo 11lb **11** Ran SP% **116.1**
Speed ratings: **101,100,100,98,98 97,95,94,92,91 63**CSF £67.85 TOTE £4.30: £1.60, £3.60, £3.10; EX 64.70.
**Owner** The Perle d'Or Partnership **Bred** J Bowdren **Trained** Newmarket, Suffolk

**FOCUS**
A moderate maiden for horses rated 70 or lower and it is not likely to produce many future winners.

**NOTEBOOK**
**Perle D'Or(IRE)**, not seen since finishing last of ten in the Group Two Rockfel Stakes at Newmarket last October, did not look like winning for most of the contest as she was off the bridle and hanging, but she eventually found her stride and got up for a last-gasp victory. On this evidence she is nothing special.
**Ballinger Express**, blinkered for the first time and making her debut on grass, was up there from the off, but no sooner had she got the better of Pawan than the winner mugged her near the line. She may be better off in handicap company off her proper mark.
**Pawan(IRE)**, who has already finished runner-up four times, was given a positive ride and after regaining the lead it looked as though he would end his rider's winnerless run stretching back 2,988 days, but the two fillies arrived late to spoil the party.
**Flash Ram**, racing beyond the minimum trip for the first time, did not fail through lack of stamina but was just not good enough.
**Sessay** does not seem to be progressing, but would probably have preferred easier ground. *Official explanation: jockey said gelding was unsuited by the fast ground.*

## 2218 SALTBURN CLASSIFIED STKS 1m
**4:45** (4:46) (E ) 3-Y-0+ **£3,562** (£1,096; £548; £274) **Stalls** Centre

Form RPR
-123 **1** **Samuel Charles**[6] 2030 6-9-2 **63** ........ SWKelly 2 71
(WMBrisbourne) *sn led: rdn and hdd ins fnl f: rallied to ld cl home* **15/2**
-204 **2** *shd* **Efidium**[14] 1868 6-8-9 **64** ........ SuzanneFrance(7) 8 71
(NBycroft) *hld up: hdwy 2f out: slt ld ins fnl f: hdd cl home* **7/1**[3]
0-00 **3** *¾* **Eastern Hope (IRE)**[36] 1358 5-9-2 **63** ........(b) MFenton 10 69
(MrsLStubbs) *slowly away: bhd: hdwy into midfield over 1f out: r.o wl u.p fnl f: nvr able to chal* **14/1**
1160 **4** *shd* **Steely Dan**[24] 1624 5-9-4 **67** ........ NPollard 1 71
(JRBest) *hld up: hdwy 2f out: ev ch and rdn ins fnl f: no ex clsng stages* **8/1**
0-00 **5** *1* **Blaeberry**[31] 1466 3-8-1 **57** ........ ANicholls 4 64?
(PLGilligan) *chsd ldrs: rdn 2f out: kpt on fnl f* **25/1**
-030 **6** *1 ¼* **Reap**[17] 1757 6-9-4 **67** ........ SSanders 9 66
(JPearce) *cl up: rdn and ev ch over 1f out: fdd ins last* **11/2**[2]
-060 **7** *hd* **Artistic Style**[3] 2122 4-8-13 **67** ........ TEaves(5) 3 65
(BEllison) *stdd s: hld up: rdn over 2f out: kpt on fnl f: nvr able to chal* **50/1**
6034 **8** *1* **Bailieborough (IRE)**[4] 2078 5-9-5 **68** ........ AlexGreaves 6 64
(DNicholls) *trckd ldrs: rdn over 2f out: wknd appr fnl f* **9/2**[1]
6-04 **9** *3 ½* **Newcorp Lad**[22] 1669 4-9-6 **69** ........ ACulhane 7 57
(MrsGSRees) *in tch: rdn 3f out: wknd over 1f out* **10/1**
0260 **10** *5* **Hov**[15] 1845 4-9-7 **70** ........ RWinston 5 46
(JJQuinn) *in tch: rdn over 2f out: wknd over 1f out* **15/2**
1-04 **11** *½* **Duelling Banjos**[22] 1675 5-9-2 **65** ........ GCarter 12 40
(JAkehurst) *prom early: bhd fr 1/2-way* **8/1**
00-5 **12** *19* **Give Him Credit (USA)**[33] 1423 4-9-2 **65** ........(b) JCarroll 11 —
(MrsADuffield) *keen: hmpd after 1f: hld up in tch: rdn 3f out: sn btn: bhd and eased fnl f: t.o* **66/1**

1m 36.9s (-0.80) **Going Correction** -0.125s/f (Firm)
**WFA** 3 from 4yo+ 12lb **12** Ran SP% **114.9**
Speed ratings: **99,98,98,98,97 95,95,94,91,86 85,66**CSF £56.60 TOTE £12.30: £2.90, £3.00, £7.00; EX 75.70.
**Owner** J F Thomas **Bred** Sheikh Mohammed Obaid Al Maktoum **Trained** Great Ness, Shropshire

**FOCUS**
A modest event, though a tight one on adjusted official figures. The field migrated towards the stands side of the track.

**NOTEBOOK**
**Samuel Charles**, given a positive ride, bagged pole position against the stands rail and despite showing his trademark head-carriage, battled on well to run out a narrow winner. This is as good as he is.
**Efidium** came with his effort down the centre of the track and looked like scoring, but the winner found an extra burst near the line and snatched the race from him. He goes well for his regular pilot and the combination should find further success.

**Eastern Hope(IRE)**, 17lb lower than at this stage last season, ran on late to put up his best performance for some time. Easier ground would suit him better and he is not without hope. *Official explanation: jockey said gelding stood on the gate and missed the break.*
**Steely Dan** ran with credit, but he has a much lower mark on turf than on sand for a reason.
**Blaeberry**, unplaced in four previous starts, was not totally disgraced against her elders although her proximity at the end does not enhance the form.
**Bailieborough(IRE)** seemed to have a lot going for him so excuses are hard to find for this disappointing effort.
**Give Him Credit(USA)** *Official explanation: jockey said gelding lost its action.*

## 2219 HORSERACE BETTING LEVY BOARD H'CAP — 6f

**5:15** (5:15) (E) (0-75,72) 3-Y-O+ — **£3,659** (£1,126; £563; £281) **Stalls** Centre

Form — RPR

100- **1** **Playful Dane (IRE)**[209] 5706 7-8-2 **55** .......... DFentiman(7) 18 — 64
(WSCunningham) *cl up: led 1/2-way: r.o u.p fnl f: all out* — **20/1**

-000 **2** *hd* **One Last Time**[16] 1783 4-8-13 **59** .......... PFessey 14 — 67
(RBastiman) *midfield: hdwy over 2f out: rdn over 1f out: r.o u.p fnl f to go 2nd cl home: jst hld* — **33/1**

26-0 **3** *3/4* **Compton Plume**[10] 1975 4-8-9 **55** .......... VHalliday 12 — 61
(WHTinning) *prom: rdn 2f out: ev ch ent fnl f: kpt on u.p ins last* — **20/1**

0-00 **4** *nk* **Silver Chime**[18] 1750 4-9-7 **67** .......... MFenton 1 — 72
(DMSimcock) *led tl hdd 1/2-way: rdn 2f out: ev ch 1 out: kpt on u.p* — **25/1**

0-00 **5** *hd* **Certa Cito**[36] 1361 4-8-7 **56** .......... DAllan(3) 2 — 61
(TDEasterby) *dwlt: hld up: hdwy 1/2-way: rdn and ch ent fnl f: kpt on* — **12/1**

6054 **6** *1 3/4* **Full Spate**[4] 2091 9-9-4 **67** .......... LEnstone(3) 16 — 66
(JMBradley) *rr div: hdwy 2f out: r.o u.p fnl f: nvr able to chal* — **11/2**[2]

0-00 **7** *1* **Zuhair**[10] 1974 11-9-3 **70** .......... LTreadwell(7) 9 — 66
(DNicholls) *dwlt: rr div: drvn along 1/2-way: kpt on fr over 1f out: n.d* — **14/1**

/0-3 **8** *nk* **Fenwicks Pride (IRE)**[11] 1941 6-8-6 **55** .......... (v) THamilton(3) 17 — 51
(RAFahey) *prom: rdn 2f out: wknd fnl f* — **7/1**[3]

4653 **9** *1 1/4* **Dark Champion**[10] 1975 4-9-4 **64** .......... JCarroll 4 — 56
(REBarr) *chsd ldrs: rdn 2f out: wknd appr fnl f* — **20/1**

0005 **10** *nk* **Pagan Storm (USA)**[10] 1974 4-8-12 **65** .......... KristinStubbs(7) 8 — 56
(MrsLStubbs) *nvr bttr than mid-div* — **16/1**

U550 **11** *shd* **Ronnie From Donny (IRE)**[28] 1526 4-9-7 **67** .......... RWinston 15 — 58
(BEllison) *towards rr most of way* — **12/1**

-001 **12** *nk* **Pays D'Amour (IRE)**[15] 1824 7-9-8 **68** .......... AlexGreaves 10 — 58
(DNicholls) *midfield: rdn 2f out: sn btn* — **5/1**[1]

42-0 **13** *1 3/4* **Tuscan Flyer**[11] 1929 6-9-4 **64** .......... DaleGibson 5 — 48
(RBastiman) *chsd ldrs tl wknd appr fnl f* — **16/1**

0002 **14** *3 1/2* **Type One (IRE)**[15] 1824 6-9-5 **72** .......... DTudhope(7) 7 — 46
(JJQuinn) *in tch: rdn over 2f out: wknd over 1f out* — **9/1**

0000 **15** *2* **Drury Lane (IRE)**[22] 1665 4-9-0 **60** .......... (b) ACulhane 11 — 28
(DWChapman) *towards rr most of way* — **8/1**

200- **16** *5* **Zap Attack**[238] 5133 4-9-8 **68** .......... NPollard 20 — 21
(JParkes) *racd alone stands rails: prom to 1/2-way: sn wknd* — **25/1**

1m 10.3s (-1.40) **Going Correction** -0.125s/f (Firm) — **16** Ran SP% **124.4**
Speed ratings: **104,103,102,102,102 99,98,98,96,95 95,95,93,88,85 79**CSF £541.93 CT £12575.09 TOTE £33.90: £5.80, £9.20, £5.50, £9.20; EX 805.30 Place 6 £150.01, Place 5 £123.54.
**Owner** Ann And David Bell **Bred** Omicida Syndicate **Trained** Hutton Rudby, N Yorks

**FOCUS**
A modest handicap run at a fair pace, and a bunch finish. The majority of the field raced down the centre for much of the race and the only one to race on the stands side finished last.

**NOTEBOOK**
**Playful Dane(IRE)**, with conditions in his favour for this first start since October, took over at halfway and managed to dourly hang on to the line with late challengers arriving aplenty. He has been hobdayed since last season and it seems to have done the trick.
**One Last Time ◆**, now officially rated 30lb lower than at this stage last year when in the care of Richard Hannon, was running over this shorter trip for the first time since then and performed much better. Any improvement on this would give him a great chance off this sort of mark.
**Compton Plume**, up there from the start, kept on trying his hardest but is without a win after 21 attempts.
**Silver Chime** is back on a winning mark and did not perform badly under a positive ride from her draw.
**Certa Cito** has been very much out of form since showing ability in her first two starts of last year, but this was more like it.
**Full Spate**, back on his favoured fast ground, was doing his best work late but could never quite get on terms with the front quintet. His stable is just starting to click into gear and an opportunity will surely be found.
**Pays D'Amour(IRE)**, who bounced back to form with victory in a Doncaster claimer last time, should have been suited by these conditions but was very disappointing on this return to handicap company.
**Drury Lane(IRE)** *Official explanation: jockey said gelding lost its action.*
T/Plt: £145.90 to a £1 stake. Pool: £23,694.45. 118.55 winning tickets. T/Qpdt: £61.80 to a £1 stake. Pool: £1,562.10. 18.70 winning tickets. JF

# 2200 GOODWOOD (R-H)

## Wednesday, May 19

**OFFICIAL GOING: Good to firm**
Weather: fine & warm

## 2220 M-REAL CONDITIONS STKS — 1m 4f

**2:10** (2:12) (B) 4-Y-O+ — **£9,883** (£3,748; £1,874; £852) **Stalls** Low

Form — RPR

5- **1** **Papineau**[353] 2044 4-8-9 103 .......... (t) KMcEvoy 12 — 111
(SaeedBinSuroor) *lw: hld up: hdwy over 2f out: short of room and swtchd left over 1f out: str run to ld ins fnl f and wnt clr* — **8/1**[3]

52-5 **2** *2 1/2* **Songlark**[18] 1767 4-8-9 107 .......... (vt) TEDurcan 14 — 107
(SaeedBinSuroor) *trckd ldrs: led wl over 1f out: rdn and hdd ins fnl f: nt pce of wnr* — **25/1**

/1-6 **3** *3/4* **Persian Majesty (IRE)**[25] 1622 4-9-5 108 .......... JPMurtagh 13 — 116
(PWHarris) *always prom: rdn over 1f out: kpt on to fin* — **10/1**

00-4 **4** *1/2* **Persian Lightning (IRE)**[18] 1767 5-8-9 102 .......... MJKinane 6 — 105
(JLDunlop) *in tch: hdwy 6f out: short of room on ins over 3f out and again whn swtchd lft 2f out: r.o u.p* — **7/1**[2]

0-02 **5** *3* **Tizzy May (FR)**[18] 1762 4-8-9 98 .......... DaneO'Neill 4 — 100
(RHannon) *in rr tl hdwy over 2f out: r.o fnl f: nvr nrr* — **33/1**

3000 **6** *1 3/4* **Corriolanus (GER)**[28] 1540 4-8-9 100 .......... DHolland 5 — 97
(PMitchell) *trckd ldr to 2f out: wknd fnl f* — **100/1**

50-0 **7** *1 3/4* **Tuning Fork**[37] 1355 4-8-9 98 .......... TQuinn 7 — 95
(JAkehurst) *led tl hdd wl over 1f out: sn btn* — **66/1**

0-55 **8** *1 3/4* **Pugin (IRE)**[32] 1455 6-8-9 105 .......... KFallon 2 — 92
(DRLoder) *s.i.s: nvr on terms* — **11/2**[1]

12-6 **9** *1 1/2* **Hambleden**[13] 1902 7-8-9 101 .......... PRobinson 10 — 89
(MAJarvis) *trckd ldrs tl wknd wl over 1f out: eased* — **7/1**[2]

5-02 **10** *1/2* **Private Charter**[18] 1767 4-8-9 110 .......... MHills 3 — 89
(BWHills) *in tch tl wknd stedily ins fnl 2f* — **11/2**[1]

00-0 **11** *3* **Ulundi**[123] 558 9-8-9 107 .......... RHughes 8 — 84
(PRWebber) *hld up: a bhd* — **20/1**

3-60 **12** *5* **Salsalino**[6] 2067 4-8-9 107 .......... KDarley 11 — 76
(AKing) *in rr: rdn over 3f out: nvr on terms* — **7/1**[2]

1600 **13** *3/4* **Rawyaan**[12] 1925 5-9-5 112 .......... (b) RHills 9 — 85
(JHMGosden) *v.s.a: a bhd* — **14/1**

0455 **14** *5* **Bourgainville**[13] 1902 6-8-9 105 .......... MartinDwyer 1 — 67
(AMBalding) *prom tl rdn and wknd over 3f out* — **14/1**

2m 34.33s (-4.60) **Going Correction** -0.025s/f (Good) — **14** Ran SP% **115.8**
Speed ratings: **114,112,111,111,109 108,107,106,105,104 102,99,98,95**CSF £199.32 TOTE £8.10: £2.60, £7.30, £4.20; EX 272.20 Trifecta £1224.10 Part won. Pool of £1,724.11 - 0.80 winning units..
**Owner** Godolphin **Bred** Exors Of The Late Peter Winfield **Trained** Newmarket, Suffolk

**FOCUS**
A very smart winning time for the grade, but this looked a Pattern-class field and the form looks very strong. It resulted in a one-two for Godolphin, but third-placed Persian Majesty deserves a deal of credit too..

**NOTEBOOK**
**Papineau ◆**, not seen since picking up a knee injury in last year's French Derby when with Andre Fabre, made the perfect start for Godolphin. Tucked away amongst traffic passing the two-furlong marker, he then made a dramatic switch to his left before producing a very impressive turn of foot to leave his rivals for dead. He looks a very useful recruit for the boys in blue and should have no trouble winning in Group company if remaining sound.
**Songlark** was much more organised than at Newmarket and ran well under a positive ride, but he had no answer to his stable-companion's turn of foot. Although he was Group class in France, he is proving hard to place for his current connections.
**Persian Majesty(IRE)**, trying this trip for the first time, had to carry a whopping 10lb penalty against a smart field due to his victory in a Listed event last season. He wasn't beaten through lack of stamina and emerges much the best horse at the weights. He can hold his own in Group company
**Persian Lightning(IRE)**, who is not an easy ride, got the strong pace he needs but his style of running does require some luck and he did not enjoy the clearest of passages. Having said that, he was by no means unlucky and is probably a better horse over ten furlongs.
**Tizzy May(FR)**, trying this trip for the first time, ran well at the weights but his rating is making him hard to place.
**Corriolanus(GER)**, encountering fast ground for the first time, ran very well under a positive ride but is proving very hard to place.
**Tuning Fork** was responsible for the fast pace and ultimately paid for it. He is nothing like the horse that finished runner-up in last year's Dante.
**Pugin(IRE)** was down in class, but never looked happy and probably found the trip inadequate and the ground too quick.
**Private Charter** faded rather tamely, and there seemed no valid excuse.

## 2221 NORMANDIE STUD LUPE STKS (LISTED RACE) (FILLIES) — 1m 1f 192y

**2:40** (2:46) (A) 3-Y-O — **£17,400** (£6,600; £3,300; £1,500) **Stalls** Low

Form — RPR

11-3 **1** **Halicardia**[39] 1327 3-8-8 97 .......... DHolland 6 — 102
(PWHarris) *hld up towards rr: hdwy 4f out: rn green ins fnl 3f: rallied u.p to ld cl home* — **7/2**[1]

1-40 **2** *nk* **Spotlight**[17] 1791 3-8-11 101 .......... MJKinane 4 — 104
(JLDunlop) *in tch: hdwy to ld 3f out: rdn over 1f out: r.o: hdd cl home* — **9/2**[2]

11- **3** *6* **Carini**[210] 5708 3-8-8 .......... DaneO'Neill 3 — 90
(HCandy) *led after 1f tl over 7f out: rdn and outpcd 3f out: kpt on to go 3rd ins fnl f* — **11/2**[3]

115- **4** *2 1/2* **Madaeh (USA)**[228] 5363 3-8-8 94 .......... RHills 1 — 85
(JLDunlop) *in tch: led 7f out: hdd 3f out: wknd steadily fr over 1f out* — **11/2**[3]

01-1 **5** *3* **Shady Reflection (USA)**[21] 1704 3-8-11 91 .......... KFallon 7 — 82
(JHMGosden) *b: lw: in tch tl wknd over 2f out* — **11/2**[3]

01-0 **6** *2 1/2* **Deraasaat**[14] 1879 3-8-8 93 .......... WSupple 5 — 74
(EALDunlop) *led for 1f: in tch tl wknd over 3f out* — **12/1**

21- **7** *26* **Al Sifaat**[261] 4623 3-8-8 90 .......... (t) KMcEvoy 2 — 25
(SaeedBinSuroor) *plld hrd: hld up in rr: rn wd on bnd over 3f out: c home in own time: t.o* — **6/1**

2m 7.13s (-0.55) **Going Correction** -0.025s/f (Good) — **7** Ran SP% **108.5**
Speed ratings: **101,100,95,93,91 89,68**CSF £17.20 TOTE £4.00: £2.20, £2.20; EX 17.40.
**Owner** Persistent Partners **Bred** C R Mason **Trained** Ringshall, Bucks

**FOCUS**
Supposedly a trial for the Oaks, but nowhere near that level of form and unlikely to have any bearing on it. The winning time was ordinary for the class.

**NOTEBOOK**
**Halicardia** appreciated the longer trip and faster ground. Coming from a long way back to deliver her challenge inside the last two furlongs, she hung all over the place and looked to be shirking the issue but was gathered together for a successful last-gasp lunge. It would be hard to blame greenness for her antics as this was her fifth start and it is more likely she is just a bit quirky. At this stage the Ribblesdale would look a better option than the Oaks.
**Spotlight**, more relaxed in the preliminaries than when 16th in the Guineas, appeared to have made a race-winning move when sent into the lead passing the three-furlong marker and never stopped galloping, but was nailed near the line. She seemed to stay the longer trip, but does not have the scope of one or two of the others.
**Carini**, off since October, was left behind by the front pair over the final couple of furlongs. It is too early to say whether she stayed this trip or not, but she may be capable of better with this outing under her belt.
**Madaeh(USA)**, another making her seasonal reappearance and stepping up three furlongs in trip, was given a positive ride but gradually dropped away after losing the lead. She may have needed it, but has still to prove she stays this far.
**Shady Reflection(USA)** has gained both of her wins with cut in the ground and she did not look at all happy on this surface.
**Deraasaat** disappointed for the second time and may not have trained on.
**Al Sifaat** pulled her chance away. *Official explanation: jockey said filly had run too free*

## 2222 VODAFONE "DASH" TRIAL STKS (H'CAP) — 5f

**3:15** (3:18) (B) (0-110,105) 3-Y-O+ — **£12,093** (£4,587; £2,293; £1,042) **Stalls** Low

Form — RPR

-500 **1** **Whitbarrow (IRE)**[7] 2041 5-8-11 **90** .......... RLMoore 11 — 101
(JMBradley) *racd on outside: steday prog to chal 2f out: led jst ins fnl f: r.o wl* — **9/1**

113- **2** *3/4* **Texas Gold**[151] 6225 6-8-8 **87** .......... SDrowne 7 — 95
(WRMuir) *always in tch: prom fr 1/2-way: ev ch ent fnl f: nt qckn ins fnl f* — **8/1**

00-0 **3** *1 1/2* **Roses Of Spring**[12] 1937 6-8-4 **83** .......... (p) EAhern 10 — 86
(RMHCowell) *a.p: led 2f out: hdd jst ins fnl f: no ex fnl 100yds* — **14/1**

0-54 **4** *1* **Corridor Creeper (FR)**[7] 2041 7-8-11 **90**............................(p) CCatlin 2 89
(JMBradley) *a.p stands side: rdn over 1f out: kpt on one pce* **9/2**[1]
5-50 **5** *shd* **Little Edward**[33] 1438 6-9-4 **97**.................................... JPMurtagh 1 96
(BGPowell) *racd stands side: led after 2f: hdd 2f out: one pce fnl f* **7/1**[3]
001- **6** *1* **Malapropism**[196] 5924 4-8-2 **88**........................................ BO'Neill(7) 4 83
(MRChannon) *slowly away: rdn and hdwy whn short of room over 1f out: no chane after* **16/1**
6-00 **7** *nk* **Dubaian Gift**[18] 1763 5-9-10 **103**.................................... MartinDwyer 9 97
(AMBalding) *prom tl rdn and wknd wl over 1f out* **7/1**[3]
-613 **8** *½* **Turibius**[49] 1205 5-8-1 **80** ow1................................................ JFEgan 6 72
(TEPowell) *spd to 1/2-way* **7/1**[3]
0020 **9** *½* **Peruvian Chief (IRE)**[18] 1763 7-9-3 **96**..............................(v) DHolland 8 87
(NPLittmoden) *spd for 3f* **11/2**[2]
0-00 **10** *1 ¾* **Repertory**[18] 1763 11-9-9 **105**...................................... RMiles(3) 5 89
(MSSaunders) *led for 2f: wknd wl over 1f out* **16/1**
1300 **11** *nk* **Further Outlook (USA)**[12] 1923 10-8-2 **84**...................... TPQueally(3) 3 67
(DKIvory) *spd early: struggling in rr fr 1/2-way* **25/1**

58.39 secs (-0.66) **Going Correction** +0.05s/f (Good) **11** Ran SP% **114.5**
Speed ratings: **107,105,103,101,101 100,99,98,97,95 94**CSF £76.94 CT £1000.44 TOTE £11.40: £3.50, £2.20, £4.20 Trifecta £2817.50 Pool of £6,746.18 - 1.70 winning units.
**Owner** Seasons Holidays **Bred** James Burns And A Moynan **Trained** Sedbury, Gloucs

**FOCUS**
A competitive handicap run at a brisk pace, and the first three home all raced down the centre of the track. A race that looks sure to have a bearing on Epsom's Vodafone Dash.

**NOTEBOOK**
**Whitbarrow(IRE)** ◆, absolutely thrown in on his old form, raced widest of all and showed decent finishing pace to get up and score. The change of scenery and return to faster ground both played their parts in this return to form and he would look an obvious candidate for the Vodafone Dash itself on Derby Day, granted suitable conditions and a favourable draw. *Official explanation: trainer said, regarding the improved form shown, gelding had been setter suited by having a clear run today, having been covered up at York previously*
**Texas Gold** ◆, one of the most consistent sprint handicappers around, ran a cracker on this first start since December and only just lost out. Equally effective over an extra furlong, he should enjoy plenty more success during the season.
**Roses Of Spring** ◆ likes to hear her feet rattle and ran a fine race down the centre of the track under a positive ride. She is in foal to Kyllachy and considering mares in her condition have been known to thrive, another victory before she goes off to the paddocks is a definite possibility.
**Corridor Creeper(FR)** ◆ did best of those that raced next to the stands' rails but, for the second race in a row, did not enjoy the best of the track bias. With his stable running into form it would be no surprise to see him on the scoresheet when more favourably drawn.
**Little Edward** ◆ was racing under his ideal conditions and showed decent pace against the stands' rail. Although eventually overhauled, this effort may have been better than it looks because that part of the track was probably not the place to be.
**Malapropism**, racing for the first time in five months, gave himself plenty to do after a tardy start and did well to finish as close as he did. He will have to have improved to overcome a 5lb higher mark than he ended last season on, but that is not impossible.

## 2223 CHICHESTER FESTIVAL THEATRE MAIDEN FILLIES' STKS 7f
**3:45** (3:49) (D) 3-Y-O £5,512 (£1,696; £848; £424) **Stalls** High

Form RPR
0- **1** **Another Faux Pas (IRE)**[329] 2676 3-8-11 ........................ RLMoore 1 79
(RHannon) *bit bkwd: in rr: rdn and hdwy 2f out: str run fnl f to ld last strides* **100/1**
00-3 **2** *nk* **All Quiet**[7] 2029 3-8-11 .................................................. RHughes 10 78
(RHannon) *s.i.s: sn in tch mid-div: hdwy 3f out: rdn to ld ins fnl f: hdd last strides* **25/1**
3-50 **3** *1* **Halabaloo (IRE)**[21] 1704 3-8-11 78.................................... DHolland 9 75
(GWragg) *lw: a.p: rdn and kpt on fnl f* **4/1**[3]
040- **4** *1* **Indiana Blues**[230] 5332 3-8-11 93............................... MartinDwyer 11 73
(AMBalding) *led tl hdd & wknd ins fnl f* **10/3**[2]
**5** *1* **Cut Short (USA)** 3-8-11 ................................................ JPMurtagh 6 70
(JHMGosden) *unf: scope: bit bkwd: bhd tl rdn and styd on ins fnl 2f: nvr nrr* **12/1**
3- **6** *1 ½* **Girl Warrior (USA)**[200] 5868 3-8-11 ...................................... KDarley 4 66
(PFICole) *towards rr: r.o one pce ins fnl 2f* **8/1**
0 **7** *3* **Tipsy Lady**[17] 1796 3-8-11 .................................................. TQuinn 5 58
(DRCElsworth) *b: slowly away: effrt on ins 3f out: wknd ent fnl f* **25/1**
**8** *½* **San Lorenzo (UAE)** 3-8-11 ............................................ TEDurcan 3 56
(MRChannon) *leggy: unf: in tch: rdn 2f out: wknd fnl f* **10/1**
6 **9** *1* **Scrunch**[53] 1133 3-8-11 .......................................................... KFallon 7 54
(BJMeehan) *trckd ldrs: tl hung bdly lft and wknd ins fnl 2f* **25/1**
0-2 **10** *½* **Noora (IRE)**[13] 1904 3-8-11 .................................................. RHills 8 52
(MPTregoning) *t.k.h: bhd fnl 3f* **9/4**[1]
**11** *3* **Bonnetts (IRE)** 3-8-11 ...................................................... DaneO'Neill 12 44
(HCandy) *w'like: bit bkwd: s.i.s: rdn over 3f out: a in rr* **33/1**
00 **12** *1 ¼* **Dulcimer**[17] 1796 3-8-11 .................................................. SDrowne 2 41
(GBBalding) *a bhd* **100/1**

1m 28.15s (0.12) **Going Correction** -0.025s/f (Good) **12** Ran SP% **118.2**
Speed ratings: **98,97,96,95,94 92,89,88,87,86 83,81**CSF £1667.21 TOTE £51.00: £9.70, £4.30, £1.80; EX 470.60.
**Owner** Jubert Family **Bred** Stonethorn Stud Farms Ltd **Trained** East Everleigh, Wilts

**FOCUS**
An ordinary maiden, weakened by the favourite blowing her chance in the stalls.

**NOTEBOOK**
**Another Faux Pas(IRE)**, whose pedigree suggested a longer trip would suit, came from well off the pace to snatch this from her stable companion near the line. This was a surprise to the trainer, and as such she should improve for the run. Her future, however, is in the hands of the Handicapper.
**All Quiet**, who missed the break, moved to the front looking all over the winner but had the prize snatched away close home. She seems to be progressing and may find a suitable opportunity in a handicap.
**Halabaloo(IRE)**, dropping back in trip, appreciated this much faster surface and ran her race. She appears to appreciate an easy track.
**Indiana Blues**, whose last run was in the Cheveley Park, made the running but did not look entirely happy on the track and probably did too much in front. A return to six furlongs with her would not be a surprise.
**Cut Short(USA)**, a sister to high-class juvenile Daggers Drawn, who won on this track, was representing a trainer with a good record here with his three-year-olds. She looked in need of both the run and experience but stayed on well without threatening the principals, and looks sure to come on for the outing.
**Girl Warrior(USA)** shapes as though she will be suited by farther.
**San Lorenzo(UAE)**, out of a half-sister to Starborough, Our Aristotle and Ballingarry, was the subject of market support and showed enough to suggest she will make her mark in time.
**Scrunch** *Official explanation: jockey said filly had hung badly left in the last 2f*
**Noora(IRE)** was sent off a pretty short price for this based on her Chester form, which did not look particularly strong and was on easier ground. She had every chance before fading tamely over the last couple of furlongs, but considering the awful state she got herself into in the stalls it may be best to forgive her this. *Official explanation: jockey said filly had lost her action*

## 2224 BAKER TILLY TROPHY STKS (H'CAP) 7f
**4:20** (4:23) (C) (0-100,97) 3-Y-O £10,400 (£3,200; £1,600; £800) **Stalls** High

Form RPR
1130 **1** **Secret Place**[34] 1408 3-8-6 **82**............................................ EAhern 13 96
(EALDunlop) *lw: trckd ldrs: led wl over 1f out: qcknd clr* **6/1**
5-41 **2** *3* **Dr Thong**[16] 1820 3-8-2 **78**................................................ RLMoore 6 84
(PFICole) *t.k.h: a.p: tk narrow ld over 2f out: edgd rt and hdd wl over 1f out: r.o fnl f but outpcd* **5/1**[3]
1-03 **3** *nk* **Jedburgh**[17] 1795 3-9-7 **97**............................................... MJKinane 4 102
(JLDunlop) *hld up: hdwy over 3f out but n.m.r and tk several positions: rn to chse first 2 fnl f* **9/4**[1]
040- **4** *2* **Lord Links (IRE)**[252] 4814 3-8-10 **86**.................................... RHughes 5 86
(RHannon) *slowly away: hdwy 2f out: r.o one pce fnl f* **33/1**
1-60 **5** *nk* **Bravo Maestro (USA)**[46] 1239 3-9-5 **95**.................................. TQuinn 7 94
(DWPArbuthnot) *b.hind: t.k.h: trckd ldr: disp ld over 2f out tl bmpd 2f out: wknd fnl f* **7/1**
-000 **6** *2 ½* **Distant Connection (IRE)**[13] 1900 3-7-12 **74** oh2.................. JQuinn 11 67
(APJarvis) *t.k.h in rr: short of room over 3f out: nvr nr to chal* **16/1**
3-00 **7** *1* **Compton's Eleven**[17] 1797 3-8-11 **87**.................................. TEDurcan 1 77
(MRChannon) *mid-div: no hdwy ins fnl 3f* **33/1**
-005 **8** *½* **Treasure House (IRE)**[21] 1706 3-8-12 **88**.............................. DHolland 3 77
(BJMeehan) *in tch for over 4f* **25/1**
2-60 **9** *shd* **Anuvasteel**[17] 1795 3-7-9 **76**............................................... DFox(5) 8 65
(NACallaghan) *in tch on ins tl wknd 2f out* **4/1**[2]
666- **10** *4* **Hoh Bleu Dee**[221] 5483 3-8-12 **88**................................... MartinDwyer 10 66
(SKirk) *sn in rr and styd there* **33/1**
10-6 **11** *3* **Our Gamble (IRE)**[16] 1829 3-8-10 **86**................................ DaneO'Neill 12 56
(RHannon) *led tl hdd over 2f out: wknd qckly* **33/1**
112- **12** *1 ¾* **King Carnival (USA)**[283] 4018 3-9-5 **95**.................................. PDobbs 2 61
(RHannon) *lw: a in rr* **25/1**

1m 26.19s (-1.84) **Going Correction** -0.025s/f (Good) **12** Ran SP% **119.6**
Speed ratings: **109,105,105,102,102 99,98,98,97,93 89,87**CSF £33.55 CT £87.50 TOTE £8.60: £2.50, £1.70, £1.60; EX 28.80.
**Owner** Khalifa Sultan **Bred** Whitsbury Manor Stud **Trained** Newmarket, Suffolk

**FOCUS**
A strong-looking handicap and a smart winning time for the class. The first two both look progressive.

**NOTEBOOK**
**Secret Place**, 2lb lower than when unlucky in running at Newmarket, looked well handicapped beforehand and had the best of the draw. Having tracked the pace next to the rail, he quickened clear for an easy win. Everything went right this time but he does look a progressive sort, and this trip looks his ideal.
**Dr Thong** lookeed on a fair enough mark beforehand and ran a solid race on this quicker ground. He may have been unlucky to run into a better-handicapped rival.
**Jedburgh** was well supported but was slightly disappointing. Although he did not get the best of runs in the straight, he took a while to pick up, and it appeared that this trip on this sharp track was an inadequate test. He should be more at home back on a more galloping track.
**Lord Links(IRE)** shaped well on his seasonal reappearance and handicap debut, running on well at the end without ever having been close enough to get competitive. On this evidence there is a race to be won with him off this sort of mark.
**Bravo Maestro(USA)** had no excuse as he raced in the perfect position throughout.
**Distant Connection(IRE)**, who is still a maiden, performed with credit from 2lb out of the handicap.
**Compton's Eleven** never really got competitive from his poor draw.
**Treasure House(IRE)** *Official explanation: jockey said colt had hung right*
**Anuvasteel** is relatively exposed but came in for plenty of support following an encouraging run at Newmarket. He never looked likely to justify it, and there was no obvious excuse.

## 2225 DELTA INTERNATIONAL EBF MAIDEN STKS 6f
**4:55** (4:56) (D) 2-Y-O £4,771 (£1,468; £734; £367) **Stalls** Low

Form RPR
**1** **Henrik** 2-9-0 ............................................................ TEDurcan 5 84+
(MRChannon) *leggy: trckd ldr: led appr fnl f: drvn out: jst hld on* **5/1**[3]
**2** *shd* **Qadar (IRE)** 2-9-0 ..................................................................(t) RHills 1 84+
(MPTregoning) *w'like: scope: bit bkwd: chsd ldrs on ins: short of room and swtchd rt over 1f out: strly rdn to press wnr fnl 50yds: jst f* **6/4**[1]
2 **3** *1 ¼* **Chalison (IRE)**[30] 1505 2-9-0 ............................................ RHughes 4 80
(RHannon) *led: rdn over 1f out: hdd appr fnl f: r.o one pce* **5/2**[2]
**4** *4* **Silver Wraith (IRE)** 2-9-0 ................................................ JPMurtagh 2 68+
(NACallaghan) *w'like: in tch tl rdn and wknd wl over 1f out* **14/1**
**5** *3 ½* **Safendonseabiscuit** 2-9-0 .................................................. PDobbs 3 58
(SKirk) *leggy: scope: slowly away: sn trckd ldrs: rdn over 2f out: wknd over 1f out* **14/1**
**6** *1 ¾* **Part Time Love** 2-9-0 ...................................................... CCatlin 6 52
(MRChannon) *leggy: neat: outpcd thrght* **16/1**
**7** *hd* **Wise Dennis** 2-9-0 .......................................................... DHolland 7 52
(APJarvis) *leggy: slowly away: sn tch on outside: rdn and wknd 2f out* **16/1**

1m 13.54s (0.70) **Going Correction** +0.05s/f (Good) **7** Ran SP% **110.3**
Speed ratings: **97,96,95,89,85 82,82**CSF £12.01 TOTE £5.40: £3.00, £1.90; EX 15.00.
**Owner** John Breslin **Bred** Jeremy Green And Sons **Trained** West Ilsley, Berks

**FOCUS**
This looked a decent maiden, with the first three, including promising Windsor second Chalison, pulling nicely clear.

**NOTEBOOK**
**Henrik**, a half-brother to juvenile winners Bishop's Lake and Spritzeria, cost 100,000gns as a yearling. He may have got first run on the favourite, but he found more when challenged and looks a useful sprinting juvenile in the making.
**Qadar(IRE)** ◆, whose dam is closely related to top-class sprinter Sheikh Albadou, is a half-brother to juvenile winners Ikan, To The Woods and Valjarv. A 250,000gns purchase, he was all the rage beforehand and travelled well in the race itself. Switched out wide to challenge, he failed to pick the leader up as well as his rider expected and ended up getting to the line just too late. He should be a good thing to win his maiden next time, and looks a bright prospect.
**Chalison(IRE)** set a decent standard, as his Windsor effort looked solid form. Setting out to make all, he made it a proper test and the fact that the first three pulled clear suggests the form is strong. He will not always run into two such smart rivals.
**Silver Wraith(IRE)** cost 180,000gns as a yearling and shaped with promise on this debut. Not knocked about in a lost cause inside the last, he nevertheless came clear of the fifth, and will have learnt a lot from this. He should progress with racing and have no trouble winning his maiden.
**Safendonseabiscuit** did not perform too badly in what was a strong heat, especially as he is a colt who, on breeding, should do better in time.

## 2226 CUCUMBER STKS (H'CAP) 1m
5:30 (5:32) (D ) (0-80,80) 3-Y-O+ £5,811 (£1,788; £894; £447) Stalls High

Form RPR
0006 1 Ephesus[6] 2064 4-9-10 76....(v) WSupple 17 83
(MissGayKelleway) *a in tch on ins: hrd rdn and pressed for ld ins fnl 2f: jst hld on* 4/1[1]
500- 2 shd Pango[189] 5976 5-9-5 71.... PDobbs 11 78+
(HMorrison) *hld up in mid-div: hdwy whn short of room 2f out: swtchd lft: stong run fnl f: jst failed* 10/1[3]
3030 3 hd Quantum Leap[2] 2170 7-8-13 65....(v) DHolland 7 71
(SDow) *t.k.h: hld up: hdwy 3f out: pressed wnr fnl 2f tl lost 2nd pl cl home* 11/1
266 4 ½ Priors Dale[88] 846 4-9-0 66.... DaneO'Neill 9 71
(KBell) *bhd tl hdwy over 2f out: r.o: nvr nrr* 25/1
1040 5 1¾ Mad Carew (USA)[28] 1540 5-9-10 76.... SWhitworth 18 77
(GLMoore) *hld up: hdwy whn short of room fr over 2f out tl over 1f out: r.o fnl f* 12/1
22-0 6 3 Spirit's Awakening[23] 1675 5-8-6 58.... JQuinn 8 52
(JAkehurst) *trckd ldrs: effrt and ev ch 2f out: wknd fnl f* 20/1
-140 7 ¾ Miss Pebbles (IRE)[9] 2000 4-9-2 68.... NPollard 20 60
(BRJohnson) *prom: rdn 3f out: kpt on but no hdwy after* 14/1
-001 8 nk Lockstock (IRE)[15] 1857 6-9-3 72....(p) RMiles(3) 19 64
(MSSaunders) *led after 2f: hdd over 2f out: stl prom whn bmpd over 1f out: sn wknd* 10/1[3]
2010 9 nk Caroubier (IRE)[23] 1671 4-9-10 76.... TEDurcan 15 67
(JGallagher) *s.i.s and wl in rr tl mde some hdwy ins fnl 2f* 16/1
0000 10 hd Agilis (IRE)[7] 2030 4-8-7 59....(b) CCatlin 4 50
(JamiePoulton) *hld up: a towards rr* 40/1
40-0 11 hd Poppyline[47] 1229 4-8-3 55.... MartinDwyer 10 45
(WRMuir) *in rr: effort over 2f out: nvr on terms* 33/1
0500 12 ¾ Rebate[25] 1624 4-8-12 64.... RHughes 6 52
(RHannon) *in rr but in tch whn short of room fr over 2f out: nvr got into r* 25/1
1152 13 ¾ Amnesty[15] 1857 5-8-10 62....(be) RLMoore 16 49
(GLMoore) *in rr tl hdwy on ins over 3f out: wknd wl over 1f out* 8/1[2]
/0-0 14 hd Night Driver (IRE)[15] 1857 5-8-7 59.... RBrisland 14 45
(GLMoore) *wl in rr: effrt on ins over 2f out: sn btn* 33/1
-220 15 nk Blue Trojan (IRE)[21] 1708 4-9-12 78.... EAhern 12 63
(SKirk) *mid-div: rdn 3f out: wknd over 2f out* 12/1
0122 16 8 Best Before (IRE)[16] 1845 4-8-13 65.... SDrowne 3 32
(PDEvans) *trckd ldrs: rdn over 3f out: wknd qckly* 10/1[3]
3030 17 12 Danielle's Lad[6] 2064 8-9-5 71....(b) TQuinn 13 10
(BPalling) *prom tl rdn over 2f out: wknd rapidly* 14/1
1110 18 5 Stoic Leader (IRE)[1] 2206 4-9-11 80.... DNolan(3) 1 8
(RFFisher) *led for 2f: styd prom tl wknd over 3f out* 16/1

1m 39.75s (-0.52) **Going Correction** -0.025s/f (Good) **18** Ran SP% **128.0**
Speed ratings: **101,100,100,100,98 95,94,94,94,93 93,92,92,92,91 83,71,66**CSF £40.21 CT £440.17 TOTE £6.60: £2.60, £3.50, £2.40, £8.20; EX 70.90 Place 6 £1,342.18, Place 5 £150.25.
**Owner** Ionian Partnership **Bred** Slatch Farm Stud **Trained** Newmarket, Suffolk

**FOCUS**
An ordinary handicap and plenty of trouble in running, but solid enough form.

**NOTEBOOK**
**Ephesus** did not get much luck in running at Salisbury on his previous start but enjoyed a perfect trip on this occasion, with Lockstock kindly moving off the rail to let him through at just the right time. He just held on in a tight finish in the end, and on this evidence he could cope with a drop back to seven furlongs.
**Pango**, whose style of running will always make him vulnerable to a troubled run around this sort of track, was in behind the eventual winner early in the straight, but did not get the fine run his rival enjoyed. Switched wide, he flew in the closing stages, but the line came just too soon. He is clearly on a winning mark at present.
**Quantum Leap**, who had the visor back on, had every chance to go by the eventual winner during a final-furlong duel, but appeared to decline the opportunity.
**Priors Dale** was still last two and a half furlongs out but passed the majority of the field on the outside in the closing stages. He looks handicapped to get off the mark on a more galloping track.
**Mad Carew(USA)** looked high enough in the weights and was racing without headgear, but ran really well. He did not get much of a run and would probably have made the frame with a clear passage. *Official explanation: jockey said, regarding the running and riding, his orders were to capitalise on a good draw but he was outpaced early, had been short of room 2f out and hung left, adding that he said to trainer on dismounting he believed gelding was not moving right behind; trainer added that gelding has often worn headgear in the past - quirky and has a tendency to hang left - and confirmed gelding finished stiff behind*
**Spirit's Awakening** was soon well placed and had his chance.
**Miss Pebbles(IRE)** had a good draw and no excuse.
**Lockstock(IRE)**, 7lb higher, had every chance from his good draw but the ground was a lot quicker here than it was at Bath.
**Caroubier(IRE)** is another whose style of running makes it difficult for him around this sort of track. He ran a lot better than the bare facts suggest.
**Rebate** got no run at all and this performance is best forgotten. *Official explanation: jockey said gelding suffered interference in running in the last 2f*
**Danielle's Lad** *Official explanation: jockey said gelding hung left and stopped quickly*
T/Jkpt: Not won. T/Plt: £1,941.50 to a £1 stake. Pool: £89,762.85. 33.75 winning tickets. T/Qpdt: £79.80 to a £1 stake. Pool: £5,253.10. 48.70 winning tickets. JS

# 2123 SOUTHWELL (L-H)
Wednesday, May 19

**OFFICIAL GOING: Standard**

## 2227 ROYAL BANK OF SCOTLAND BANDED STKS 6f (F)
2:20 (2:20) (H ) 4-Y-O+ £1,449 (£414; £207) Stalls Low

Form RPR
2262 1 Cleveland Way[2] 2183 4-8-5 40....(v) DTudhope(7) 10 51
(DCarroll) *chsd ldrs: led over 2f out: rdn out* 9/2[2]
0031 2 1¼ Marabar[2] 2188 6-9-4 45....(b) ACulhane 8 53
(DWChapman) *chsd ldrs: ev ch 2f out: styd on same pce ins fnl f* 11/4[1]
0245 3 1 Mr Uppity[22] 1696 5-8-5 40....(e) MHalford(7) 7 44
(JulianPoulton) *s.i.s: sn prom: outpcd 1/2-way: hdwy over 1f out: r.o* 28/1
6000 4 2 Pilgrim Princess (IRE)[29] 1526 6-8-9 45....(p) DAllan(3) 2 38
(EJAlston) *mde most over 3f: styd on same pce appr fnl f* 6/1[3]
5005 5 2 Lake Eyre (IRE)[13] 1913 5-8-12 45.... JEdmunds 6 32
(JBalding) *chsd ldrs: rdn over 2f out: wknd over 1f out* 12/1
0264 6 shd Finger Of Fate[8] 2012 4-8-12 40....(b) RFitzpatrick 1 32
(MJPolglase) *s.i.s: outpcd over 3f out: nt clr run over 1f out: styd on ins fnl f:nt trble ldrs* 8/1
0002 7 3 Ejay[9] 1988 5-8-9 45.... LisaJones(3) 3 23
(JulianPoulton) *sn outpcd* 7/1
2306 8 3½ Avit (IRE)[2] 2183 4-8-12 40.... GFaulkner 4 12
(PLGilligan) *w ldr over 3f: wknd over 1f out* 25/1
0-34 9 1 Pirlie Hill[20] 1719 4-8-12 45.... RWinston 5 9
(MissLAPerratt) *s.i.s: sn chsng ldrs: wknd over 1f out* 7/1
000- 10 7 Miss Ceylon[242] 5070 4-8-12 45.... DaleGibson 9 —
(SPGriffiths) *s.i.s: sn outpcd* 50/1

1m 16.8s (-0.10) **Going Correction** -0.025s/f (Stan) **10** Ran SP% **112.2**
Speed ratings: **99,97,96,93,90 90,86,81,80,71**CSF £16.21 TOTE £5.90: £1.80, £1.40, £5.60; EX 10.70.
**Owner** The Boot & Shoe Ackworth Partnership **Bred** Miss L Pearson **Trained** Warthill, N Yorks

**FOCUS**
Quite a competitive race for the grade with the winner not winning out of turn. There didn't appear to be any draw bias throughout the day.

**NOTEBOOK**
**Cleveland Way** gained reward for some consistent efforts of late and looked to run up to his best. This was his 13th outing since the turn of the year and it will be interesting to see whether connections give him a break, and bring him back in the autumn, or give him an outing or two on turf.
**Marabar** made a bold bid to follow up her win two days earlier, but the concession of 13lb to the winner proved just beyond her. However, she remains in good form and with her ability to handle any ground on turf should find another opening.
**Mr Uppity**, a long-standing maiden, again showed that all is not lost with him just yet, although he is clearly a tricky ride.
**Pilgrim Princess(IRE)**, taking a drop in class, showed a bit more sparkle than of late, but is clearly still below her best. *Official explanation: trainer said mare bled from the nose*
**Lake Eyre(IRE)** has had plenty of chances in the past, and had no excuses here, even at this level.
**Finger Of Fate** has been beaten over a variety of trips, including seven furlongs, but he shaped here as though that really ought to be his optimum.

## 2228 SPANISH PREMIER PROPERTIES AMATEUR RIDERS' (S) STKS 1m 3f (F)
2:50 (2:50) (H ) 4-Y-O+ £1,442 (£412; £206) Stalls Low

Form RPR
-002 1 Romil Star (GER)[8] 1866 7-10-11 65....(v) MrSDobson(3) 4 68
(KRBurke) *chsd ldrs: led over 4f out: sn clr: easily* 4/6[1]
4340 2 13 El Pedro[22] 1698 5-10-7 40.... MrJoshuaHarris(7) 2 47
(NEBerry) *s.i.s: sn prom: chsd wnr over 3f out: sn rdn and no imp* 9/1[3]
5000 3 5 Morris Dancing (USA)[14] 1885 5-10-11 30....(v[1]) MrEDehdashti(3) 9 39
(BPJBaugh) *led over 6f: wknd over 3f out* 33/1
0-04 4 5 Littleton Valar (IRE)[11] 1617 4-11-0 30....(be) KJMercer 8 31
(JRWeymes) *s.i.s: hld up: n.d* 12/1
5145 5 nk Misty Man (USA)[9] 1987 6-10-12 45....(b) MissFionaBrown(7) 3 36
(MissJFeilden) *sn pushed along and prom: wknd 5f out* 6/1[2]
6 13 Miss Danbys[11] 9-10-9.... MrNickyTinkler 6 5
(JMJefferson) *s.i.s: hdwy over 5f out: sn rdn: eased fnl 2f: sddle slipped* 14/1
00-0 7 nk Regal Repose[28] 1547 4-10-2 50.... MrGTumelty(7) 5 4
(AJChamberlain) *unruly stalls: prom over 6f* 40/1
/066 8 ½ Te Anau[30] 1493 7-10-2 30.... MsAmyBoeder(7) 7 3
(WJMusson) *prom to 1/2-way* 50/1
0333 9 9 Dundonald[14] 1885 5-10-11 35....(bt) MrLNewnes(3) 1 —
(MAppleby) *w ldr 4f: wknd over 5f out* 14/1

2m 30.63s (1.73) **Going Correction** -0.025s/f (Stan) **9** Ran SP% **112.6**
Speed ratings: **92,82,78,75,75 65,65,65,58**CSF £7.00 TOTE £1.80: £1.02, £1.60, £7.30; EX 8.10.The winner was bought in for 6,600gns.
**Owner** Mrs Elaine M Burke **Bred** J H A Baggen **Trained** Middleham Moor, N Yorks
■ Stewards Enquiry : Mr E Dehdashti four-day ban: used whip with excessive frequency (Jun 1,2,4,8)

**FOCUS**
No strength in depth here with the winner outclassing his rivals.

**NOTEBOOK**
**Romil Star(GER)** didn't need to be at his best to beat some disappointing rivals.
**El Pedro** faced a hopeless task with the winner on these terms.
**Morris Dancing(USA)**, sharpened up by the first-time visor, was easily shaken off turning for home.
**Misty Man(USA)** looked in a mood, for he didn't want to go out onto the track and then spat the dummy out before leaving the back straight.\n\x\x straight.
**Miss Danbys** *Official explanation: jockey said saddle slipped*
**Regal Repose** *Official explanation: trainer said filly was found to have been in season*
**Dundonald** *Official explanation: jockey said gelding had hung right-handed*

## 2229 FASTHANDLE LIMITED BUILDING LAND PURCHASE BANDED STKS 7f (F)
3:25 (3:26) (H ) 3-Y-O+ £1,452 (£415; £207) Stalls Low

Form RPR
00-1 1 Bronx Bomber[6] 2056 6-9-10 35....(b) CLowther 5 51
(DrJDScargill) *trckd ldrs: led 3f out: sn rdn and hdd: rallied u.p to ld ins fnl f: styd on wl* 7/2[1]
2152 2 4 Tiny Tim (IRE)[6] 2056 6-8-11 35.... TBlock(7) 8 35
(AMBalding) *trckd ldrs: led over 2f out: sn rdn: hdd & wknd ins fnl f* 7/2[1]
3000 3 5 Westmead Etoile[9] 1986 4-9-4 35....(vt) SWKelly 4 22
(JRJenkins) *chsd ldrs over 4f* 11/2[3]
-030 4 3½ Optimum Night[14] 1888 5-9-4 35....(p) RWinston 3 13
(PDNiven) *s.i.s: sn pushed along and prom: wknd over 3f out* 9/1
3321 5 hd Countrywide Girl (IRE)[8] 2017 5-9-10 35.... FNorton 6 18
(ABerry) *w ldr 4f: hung lft and wknd over 1f out* 9/2[2]
0000 6 2½ Meticulous[16] 1824 6-9-4 30.... LVickers 2 5
(MCChapman) *outpcd* 25/1
0000 7 11 Magic Eagle[10] 1197 7-9-4 35.... GParkin 10 —
(PTMidgley) *mde most 4f: wknd over 2f out* 11/1
-000 8 6 Samba Beat[57] 1091 5-9-4 35.... DeanMcKeown 7 —
(RFMarvin) *s.s: outpcd* 20/1
/00- 9 2½ Sea Tern[265] 4535 4-9-4 35.... SRighton 9 —
(DGBridgwater) *s.s: outpcd* 16/1
000- 10 11 Lill's Star Lad[298] 3602 6-9-4 30.... ANicholls 1 —
(PRWood) *sn outpcd* 66/1

1m 31.43s (0.63) **Going Correction** -0.025s/f (Stan) **10** Ran SP% **112.3**
Speed ratings: **95,90,84,80,80 77,65,58,55,42**CSF £14.44 TOTE £5.80: £1.70, £1.20, £3.10; EX 10.90.
**Owner** R A Dalton **Bred** Jonathan Crisp **Trained** Newmarket, Suffolk
■ Stewards Enquiry : C Lowther one-day ban: used whip with excessive frequency (May 30)

**FOCUS**
With three recent winners taking part this looked fairly competitive for the grade, but the field finished well strung out.

**NOTEBOOK**
**Bronx Bomber** looks to have been transformed by the blinkers and confirmed the Lingfield form with the runner-up on 12lb worse terms. He proved well suited by this trip and looks to be on the upgrade.
**Tiny Tim(IRE)**, 12lbs better off with the winner for under two lengths on their running at Lingfield, travelled much the better of the pair here until his stamina gave way in the closing stages. He looks better suited to the faster Polytrack surface.
**Westmead Etoile** had the visor back on here instead of the blinkers, but to no avail.
**Optimum Night** didn't look to improve much for the first-time cheekpieces.
**Countrywide Girl(IRE)** looked below her best and was already on the retreat when hanging badly in the last couple of furlongs. *Official explanation: jockey said mare had lost her action*
**Lill's Star Lad** *Official explanation: jockey said gelding was never travelling*

## 2230 NSPCC FULL STOP BANDED STKS — 1m 6f (F)
**4:00** (4:00) (H) 4-Y-O+ — £1,442 (£412; £206) Stalls Low

Form — RPR
6234 **1** **Berkeley Heights**[22] [1698] 4-8-12 40 — NCallan 1 — 46
(MrsJCandlish) *s.i.s: sn pushed along in rr: hdwy 5f out: rdn to ld over 2f out: styd on* — **3/1**[1]
6324 **2** *1* **Dora Corbino**[9] [1989] 4-8-12 40 — ACulhane 7 — 45
(RHollinshead) *led over 3f: remained handy: led 5f out: rdn and hdd over 2f out: styd on u.p* — **9/2**[3]
3210 **3** *1* **Seraph**[20] [1728] 4-8-12 40 — (p) DeanMcKeown 6 — 43
(JohnAHarris) *chsd ldrs: rdn and ev ch fr over 2f out: no ex ins fnl f* — **10/3**[2]
3-00 **4** *5* **Staff Nurse (IRE)**[34] [1426] 4-8-12 40 — KimTinkler 2 — 37
(DonEnricoIncisa) *trckd ldrs: plld hrd: dropped rr over 10f out: n.d after* — **9/1**
3350 **5** *5* **Western Command (GER)**[14] [1888] 8-8-12 35 — JoannaBadger 8 — 30
(MrsNMacauley) *chsd ldrs over 10f* — **10/1**
0410 **6** *6* **Rhetoric (IRE)**[9] [1987] 5-8-7 40 — BSwarbrick(5) 3 — 23
(DGBridgwater) *plld hrd and prom: rdn and wknd over 3f out* — **11/2**
060/ **7** *11* **Sorrento King**[4] [2855] 7-8-12 30 — (t) RHavlin 4 — 8
(CNKellett) *hld up: bhd fnl 7f* — **20/1**
0-00 **8** *8* **Maravedi (IRE)**[20] [1723] 4-8-12 40 — (v) FNorton 5 — —
(SLKeightley) *hld up: hdwy to ld over 10f out: hdd 5f out: wkng whn n.m.r over 3f out* — **14/1**

3m 11.32s (1.62) **Going Correction** -0.025s/f (Stan) — **8** Ran SP% **112.2**
Speed ratings: **94,93,92,90,87 83,77,72**CSF £16.05 TOTE £3.30: £1.10, £1.30, £2.30; EX 12.50.
**Owner** A J Cartlich **Bred** P T Tellwright **Trained** Basford, Staffs

**FOCUS**
Not a strong race, but the front three had been in good form of late.
**NOTEBOOK**
**Berkeley Heights** was never on the bridle, but she has stamina in abundance and in the end that enabled her to get off the mark.
**Dora Corbino** isn't very quick, but she is all heart and never stopped trying. She deserves to find one of these contests.
**Seraph** bounced back from a poor effort last time, and seemed to get this trip well enough.
**Staff Nurse(IRE)** did herself no favours by being too keen early on.
**Western Command(GER)** was taking a keen interest and looked to be enjoying himself until the pace picked up, but his little legs were unable to respond.

## 2231 SOUTHWELL SPONSORSHIP BANDED STKS — 1m (F)
**4:35** (4:36) (H) 3-Y-O+ — £1,449 (£414; £207) Stalls Low

Form — RPR
5652 **1** **Ballyrush (IRE)**[8] [2015] 4-9-0 45 — (b) RKeogh(7) 7 — 50
(KRBurke) *a.p: led 3f out: clr whn hung lft over 1f out: eased nr fin* — **4/1**[2]
6421 **2** *3* **Dalriath**[13] [1918] 5-9-0 40 — AndrewWebb(7) 5 — 44
(MCChapman) *hld up: hdwy 3f out: chsd wnr and hung lft over 1f out: no imp* — **3/1**[1]
0-00 **3** *6* **Mexican (USA)**[20] [1720] 5-9-7 40 — (v) DarrenWilliams 3 — 32
(MDHammond) *s.i.s: sn chsng ldrs: hung lft and wknd 2f out* — **14/1**
2520 **4** *4* **Tee Jay Kassidy**[9] [1986] 4-9-0 40 — MHalford(7) 2 — 24
(JulianPoulton) *hld up: hdwy 1/2-way: rdn and wknd over 1f out* — **8/1**
000- **5** *nk* **Fabuloso**[232] [5288] 3-8-9 45 — MTebbutt 8 — 23
(VSmith) *chsd ldrs: led over 3f out: sn hdd: wknd 2f out* — **6/1**
0113 **6** *15* **Cumbrian Princess**[30] [1494] 7-9-7 45 — DSweeney 1 — —
(MBlanshard) *sn outpcd: hdwy over 3f out: wknd over 2f out* — **11/2**[3]
4443 **7** *3 1/2* **Bretton**[8] [2014] 3-8-4 45 — (b) StephanieHollinshead(5) 6 — —
(RHollinshead) *led: hung rt over 4f out: hdd: hmpd and wknd over 3f out* — **9/1**
5003 **8** *11* **Sunset Blues (FR)**[34] [1407] 4-9-7 40 — (be) ACulhane 4 — —
(KOCunningham-Brown) *chsd ldrs: hung rt over 3f out: sn wknd* — **7/1**

1m 44.65s (0.05) **Going Correction** -0.025s/f (Stan)
**WFA** 3 from 4yo+ 12lb — **8** Ran SP% **114.9**
Speed ratings: **98,95,89,85,84 69,66,55**CSF £16.54 TOTE £5.00: £1.80, £1.60, £5.20; EX 16.70.
**Owner** Mrs B Keogh **Bred** Brian Killeen **Trained** Middleham Moor, N Yorks

**FOCUS**
Some iffy customers on show and it will be a surprise if many winners come out of this race.
**NOTEBOOK**
**Ballyrush(IRE)** at last found a race he could win, but with so many of his rivals looking less than keen, this took little winning.
**Dalriath** came into this in good form and had already proven herself over course and distance. However, she just met one too good on the day.
**Mexican(USA)**, a winning chaser, is a poor performer on the level.
**Tee Jay Kassidy** dropped away tamely and has yet to prove he truly stays this far.
**Fabuloso** was entitled to need this after a break, but she will need to find plenty if she is to get her head in front.
**Cumbrian Princess**, who had been in good form on the Polytrack, hardly went a yard here.
**Sunset Blues(FR)** *Official explanation: jockey said gelding had hung right-handed*

## 2232 ENTERTAIN WITH RACING AT SOUTHWELL TRI-BANDED STKS — 7f (F)
**5:10** (5:13) (H) 3-Y-O — £1,445 (£413; £206) Stalls Low

Form — RPR
-000 **1** **Tsarbuck**[16] [1827] 3-9-0 45 — GFaulkner 9 — 64
(RMHCowell) *chsd ldrs: led over 2f out: rdn clr over 1f out* — **9/2**[2]
0003 **2** *5* **Mitzi Caspar**[2] [2187] 3-8-4 30 — RPrice 5 — 41
(PLGilligan) *led over 4f: styd on same pce appr fnl f* — **15/2**
0423 **3** *2* **Monkey Or Me (IRE)**[26] [1594] 3-8-4 35 — RFitzpatrick 6 — 36
(PTMidgley) *hld up: styd on u.p fnl 2f: n.d* — **7/2**[1]
40-5 **4** *nk* **Campbells Lad**[26] [1596] 3-9-0 45 — FNorton 7 — 45?
(ABerry) *prom: rdn 1/2-way: styd on same pce fnl 2f* — **12/1**
0660 **5** *5* **Bookiesindexdotcom**[16] [1844] 3-9-0 45 — (v) SWKelly 3 — 33
(JRJenkins) *chsd ldrs: rdn over 2f out: wknd over 1f out* — **6/1**
5000 **6** *3 1/2* **Numpty (IRE)**[23] [1667] 3-8-9 40 — (t) KimTinkler 8 — 19
(NTinkler) *s.i.s: sn prom: wknd 3f out* — **10/1**
0-40 **7** *5* **Beaver Diva**[17] [1784] 3-7-13 30 — BSwarbrick(5) 10 — —
(WMBrisbourne) *hld up: plld hrd: hung rt over 4f out: sn bhd* — **16/1**
0560 **8** *7* **Dandy Jim**[2] [2187] 3-8-4 30 — (b) JBramhill 4 — —
(DWChapman) *s.s: outpcd: effrt 1/2-way: sn wknd* — **25/1**
0-01 **9** *2* **Sam The Sorcerer**[2] [2187] 3-9-6 45 6ex — DarrenWilliams 2 — —
(JRNorton) *chsd ldrs over 4f* — **5/1**[3]
0-60 **10** *2* **Tapleon**[20] [1719] 3-8-4 40 — TEaves(5) 1 — —
(CJTeague) *prom: lost pl over 4f out: bhd fr 1/2-way* — **66/1**

1m 30.53s (-0.27) **Going Correction** -0.025s/f (Stan) — **10** Ran SP% **111.1**
Speed ratings: **100,94,92,91,85 81,76,68,65,63**CSF £36.08 TOTE £6.00: £2.60, £1.10, £1.90; EX 46.20 Place 6 £6.47, Place 5 £3.74.
**Owner** S P Shore **Bred** Genesis Green Stud Ltd **Trained** Six Mile Bottom, Cambs

**FOCUS**
Another less than competitive contest, but it was run in a fair time for the grade.
**NOTEBOOK**
**Tsarbuck**, tackling this surface for the first time, turned in an improved effort. Lightly raced, there should be plenty to come from him.
**Mitzi Caspar** had more use made of her here and didn't quite see this trip out as well as she might have. While she is no great shakes, she isn't without a little ability.
**Monkey Or Me(IRE)** was doing his best work late on and clearly found this an insufficient test.
**Campbells Lad** may well have still needed this to put an edge on him, but he will have to find plenty of improvement if he is to score.
**Bookiesindexdotcom** has clearly gone the wrong way and is one to treat with caution.
**Numpty(IRE)** *Official explanation: jockey said gelding suffered interference leaving the stalls*
**Beaver Diva** *Official explanation: jockey said filly hung right-handed throughout*
T/Plt: £8.10 to a £1 stake. Pool: £20,720.05. 1,853.45 winning tickets. T/Qpdt: £5.90 to a £1 stake. Pool: £1,262.90. 156.30 winning tickets. CR

2233 - (Foreign Racing) - See Raceform Interactive

# 1819 DONCASTER (L-H)
### Thursday, May 20

**OFFICIAL GOING: Good to firm (firm in places)**
The going was described as 'firm with jar'.
Wind: mod, hlf bhd Weather: fine & sunny

## 2234 SKY BET PRESS RED TO BET NOW MAIDEN AUCTION STKS — 6f
**6:20** (6:22) (E) 2-Y-O — £3,591 (£1,105; £552; £276) Stalls High

Form — RPR
5 **1** **Indibraun (IRE)**[52] [1170] 2-8-7 — GFaulkner 13 — 71
(PCHaslam) *mde all racing against stands' side: shkn up and edgd lft over 1f out: styd on wl* — **7/2**[1]
5 **2** *1 1/2* **Rockburst**[31] [1498] 2-8-2 — ANicholls 8 — 62
(KRBurke) *sn trcking ldrs: t.k.h: wnt 2nd 1f out: no imp* — **8/1**
**3** *2* **Mr Kalandi (IRE)** 2-8-9 — PaulEddery 14 — 63
(PWD'Arcy) *leggy: unf: scope: sn chsng ldrs: kpt on same pce appr fnl f* — **12/1**
6 **4** *1 1/4* **Mimi Mouse**[34] [1449] 2-8-1 — DAllan(3) 7 — 54
(TDEasterby) *chsd ldrs: one pce fnl 2f* — **8/1**
**5** *1 3/4* **Satin Rose** 2-8-2 — JMackay 12 — 47
(TDEasterby) *leggy: scope: swvd rt s: bhd: hdwy 2f out: styd on ins last* — **33/1**
5 **6** *1 1/2* **Piddies Pride (IRE)**[19] [1769] 2-8-2 — GDuffield 1 — 42
(IAWood) *chsd ldrs on outside: wknd over 1f out* — **16/1**
**7** *2 1/2* **Shingle Street (IRE)** 2-8-9 — PRobinson 11 — 42
(MHTompkins) *neat: bhd: hdwy over 2f out: rn green and hung lft over 1f out: sn fdd* — **15/2**[3]
**8** *1* **Bond City (IRE)** 2-8-9 — FLynch 2 — 39
(BSmart) *cmpt: unf: w ldrs on outside: lost pl over 1f out* — **9/1**
**9** *nk* **Saint Clements (USA)** 2-8-11 — RFfrench 5 — 40
(MJohnston) *rangy: lw: sn chsng ldrs: edgd lft and wknd over 1f out* **6/1**[2]
6 **10** *1/2* **Mirage Prince (IRE)**[36] [1390] 2-8-7 — CCatlin 4 — 34
(WMBrisbourne) *chsd ldrs: lost pl over 1f out* — **25/1**
**11** *3 1/2* **Zarova (IRE)** 2-9-0 — ACulhane 3 — 31
(MWEasterby) *rangy: unf: scope: dwlt: sn chsng ldrs on outer: hung lft and lost pl over 1f out* — **16/1**
**12** *hd* **Hamburg Springer (IRE)** 2-8-4 — JFMcDonald(3) 9 — 23
(MJPolglase) *leggy: unf: dwlt: plld v hrd: sn chsng ldrs: lost pl over 2f out* — **33/1**
**13** *5* **Belton** 2-8-7 — DeanMcKeown 10 — 8
(RonaldThompson) *lengthy: unf: s.v.s: a wl bhd* — **33/1**
**14** *1 1/2* **Dishdasha (IRE)** 2-8-9 — GGibbons 6 — 6
(TDEasterby) *cmpt: s.s: bmpd after 1f: sn bhd* — **16/1**

1m 13.63s (-0.65) **Going Correction** -0.30s/f (Firm) — **14** Ran SP% **118.5**
Speed ratings: **92,90,87,85,83 81,78,76,76,75 70,70,64,62**CSF £28.93 TOTE £4.80: £2.00, £2.50, £3.60; EX 49.60.
**Owner** D Browne **Bred** Tally-Ho Stud **Trained** Middleham Moor, N Yorks
■ Stewards Enquiry : C Catlin two-day ban: careless riding (Jun 2,3)

**FOCUS**
A race in which there was not much evidence to go on, and probably only average form behind the winner. It paid to race close to the stands' rail
**NOTEBOOK**
**Indibraun(IRE)**, whose debut effort at Newcastle has been well advertised since, knew his job this time. Allowed to stride out after hanging away from the fence when sent about his business he was right on top at the line. He should improve again.
**Rockburst** took a fierce grip. He went in pursuit of the winner but was never going to be anything but second best.
**Mr Kalandi(IRE)**, a March foal, is up in the air and narrow. He ran a pleasing first race and will be better suited by seven furlongs.
**Mimi Mouse** improved a good deal on her debut effort.
**Satin Rose**, an April foal, in on the leg and has a pronounced knee action. After losing ground at the start she picked up in encouraging fashion late on. This will have taught her plenty.
**Shingle Street(IRE)** *Official explanation: jockey said colt hung both ways*
**Bond City(IRE)** *Official explanation: jockey said gelding hung left-handed*
**Saint Clements(USA)**a March foal, stands over plenty of ground and was easily the paddock pick. He looked really well, but after showing speed rolled towards the centre and weakened. He looks capable of a fair bit better.
**Belton** *Official explanation: jockey said colt missed the break, did not act on the frirm ground and hung both ways*

## 2235 SOUTH YORKSHIRE TIMES STKS (H'CAP) — 1m 4f
**6:50** (6:51) (E) (0-75,70) 3-Y-O+ — £3,552 (£1,093; £546; £273) Stalls Low

Form — RPR
-000 **1** **Maritime Blues**[26] [1611] 4-8-12 58 — ACulhane 9 — 69
(JGGiven) *lw: chsd ldrs: drvn along 5f out: styd on to ld over 2f out: rdn clr fnl f* — **11/2**[2]

050- **2** *5* **Swynford Pleasure**[197] 5928 8-8-4 **53** DAllan(3) 3 56
(JHetherton) *hld up: hdwy on ins 4f out: nt clr run over 2f out: wnt 2nd 1f out: no ch w wnr* **14/1**

0-63 **3** *2½* **Michaels Dream (IRE)**[2] 2216 5-7-12 **44** oh4 JMcAuley 8 43
(JHetherton) *chsd ldrs: one pce fnl 2f* **15/2**

0/00 **4** *¾* **Perestroika (IRE)**[56] 1103 6-8-9 **60** TEaves(5) 4 58
(BEllison) *hld up in rr: effrt 4f out: sn rdn: kpt on fnl 2f* **28/1**

56-0 **5** *shd* **Distant Cousin**[50] 1203 7-9-4 **64** (v) DHolland 7 62
(MABuckley) *chsd ldrs: one pce fnl 2f* **7/1**[3]

33-4 **6** *shd* **Merrymaker**[8] 2032 4-8-13 **59** (b) GBaker 10 56
(WMBrisbourne) *s.s: hdwy to chse ldrs 7f out: one pce fnl 2f* **7/1**[3]

4-00 **7** *5* **Kirov King (IRE)**[17] 1832 4-9-10 **70** PRobinson 2 59
(BGPowell) *trckd ldrs: t.k.h: effrt 3f out: lost pl over 1f out* **11/2**[2]

00-0 **8** *1¼* **Liberty Seeker (FR)**[31] 1503 5-8-11 **60** (p) SHitchcott(3) 5 47
(PDNiven) *bhd: sme hdwy on outside 4f out: nvr on terms* **14/1**

004- **9** *nk* **Night Sight (USA)**[224] 5463 7-9-7 **67** CCatlin 11 54
(MrsSLamyman) *bit bkwd: trckd ldrs: t.k.h: led over 3f out: hdd over 2f out: wknd over 1f out* **8/1**

3440 **10** *3½* **Jadeeron**[26] 1615 5-9-1 **64** (p) LisaJones(3) 6 45
(MissDAMchale) *hld up in mid-field: effrt 3f out: edgd lft and lost pl over 1f out* **5/1**[1]

50-3 **11** *dist* **Inmom (IRE)**[13] 1945 3-7-12 **61** JBramhill 1 —
(SRBowring) *set mod pce: hdd over 3f out: sn lost pl and bhd: eased: t.o* **33/1**

2m 35.02s (-0.68) **Going Correction** +0.025s/f (Good) **11** Ran SP% **115.0**
**WFA** 3 from 4yo+ 17lb
Speed ratings: **103,99,98,97,97 97,94,93,93,90** —CSF £77.99 CT £578.93 TOTE £7.30: £2.60, £3.90, £2.70; EX 114.90.
**Owner** Downlands Racing **Bred** Downlands Racing **Trained** Willoughton, Lincs

**FOCUS**
A 0-70 handicap run at just a steady pace until starting the home turn. Many of the runners had question marks over them and the form is not strong.

**NOTEBOOK**
**Maritime Blues ◆**, dropped 7lb after two runs on unsuitable ground, really took the eye beforehand. He took time to warm to his task but in the end won by a decisive margin. Connections will be keen to get him out under a penalty before he is reassessed.
**Swynford Pleasure**, having her first run since November, is at her best at this time of the year - she is a real summer mare. She made her effort on the inner and after meeting traffic problems stayed on in willing fashion to finish clear second best.
**Michaels Dream(IRE)**, making a quick return and stepping up in distance, last tasted success in October 2002.
**Perestroika(IRE)**, out of sorts in two previous outings this year, was having his first run since March. Anchored in the rear he kept on in his own time and needs a longer trip.
**Distant Cousin**, having his first outing since March, looked in good trim. He is suited by further nowadays, and overdue a change of luck after finishing runner-up four times last year.
**Merrymaker**, with the blinkers back on, gave away ground at the start and when called on for his effort on the wide outside always looked to be saving a bit for himself.
**Kirov King(IRE)**, a winner twice over this trip on fast ground in Ireland, was down 8lb after two outings this time. Well backed, he was very keen to post and in the race itself all he wanted to do was fight his rider before tending to hang right and drop right away. *Official explanation: jockey said colt hung right-handed*
**Jadeeron**, dropping back in trip, came off a straight line and, never a threat, dropped right out. He was found to be lame afterwards. *Official explanation: vet said gelding finished lame*

## 2236 LAKESIDE VILLAGE MEDIAN AUCTION MAIDEN STKS 6f
7:20 (7:21) (E) 3-4-Y-O £3,581 (£1,102; £551; £275) Stalls High

Form RPR

40-5 **1** **Neon Blue**[19] 1775 3-8-9 68 MHills 12 71
(RMWhitaker) *racd stands' side: chsd ldrs: led over 1f out: kpt on wl* **9/2**[2]

0-63 **2** *1* **Kensington (IRE)**[13] 1942 3-8-9 67 JCarroll 10 68
(RGuest) *racd stands' side: trckd ldrs: ev ch jst ins last: no ex nr fin* **15/2**

00 **3** *nk* **Fair Options**[8] 2029 3-8-9 GCarter 7 67
(HJCyzer) *s.i.s: swtchd rt and racd stands' side: bhd tl edgd lft and hdwy over 1f out: styd on wl ins last* **14/1**

3550 **4** *shd* **Amanda's Lad (IRE)**[5] 2130 4-9-4 65 LVickers 9 67?
(MCChapman) *swtchd rt after s and racd stands' side: led that gp tl over 1f out: kpt on wl* **33/1**

4-55 **5** *½* **Isaz**[18] 1796 4-9-4 73 DSweeney 13 65
(HCandy) *racd stands' side: chsd ldrs: styd on fnl f* **4/1**[1]

06-5 **6** *¾* **True Magic**[33] 1472 3-8-4 65 PRobinson 1 58
(JDBethell) *led on far side: kpt on wl fnl f: no ex ins last* **16/1**

5- **7** *nk* **Truman**[245] 5022 3-8-9 SSanders 16 62
(JARToller) *racd stands' side: mid-div: styd on appr fnl f* **7/1**[3]

6 **8** *shd* **Irusan (IRE)**[17] 1820 4-8-11 LeanneKershaw(7) 2 62?
(JeddO'Keeffe) *racd far side: chsd ldr: kpt on wl fnl f* **66/1**

000- **9** *8* **Alfelma (IRE)**[300] 3577 4-8-13 47 ANicholls 19 33
(PRWood) *racd stands' side: chsd ldrs: wknd over 1f out* **100/1**

56-3 **10** *1½* **Soviet Sceptre (IRE)**[20] 1749 3-8-9 73 KDarley 3 33
(GAButler) *racd far side: chsd ldrs: rdn 2f out: sn btn* **4/1**[1]

**11** *1* **Raetihi** 3-8-6 ow2 NCallan 15 27
(ASenior) *racd stands' side: mid-div: lost pl over 1f out* **66/1**

00-0 **12** *nk* **Quintillion**[52] 1169 3-8-4 TEaves(5) 20 29
(TJEtherington) *racd stands' side: mid-div: hung lft and lost pl 2f out* **50/1**

**13** *1½* **Parliament Act (IRE)** 3-8-9 (t) GGibbons 4 25
(BAMcmahon) *racd far side: chsd ldrs: lost pl 2f out* **25/1**

00 **14** *¾* **Radlett Lady**[14] 1906 3-8-4 CCatlin 6 18
(DKIvory) *racd far side: sn outpcd and in rr* **50/1**

**15** *hd* **Judda** 3-8-9 DeanMcKeown 17 22
(RFMarvin) *s.s: racd stands' side: wl bhd tl sme hdwy fnl 2f* **66/1**

0/0- **16** *shd* **Feed The Meter (IRE)**[382] 1368 4-8-13 JMackay 14 17
(TTClement) *racd stands' side: mid-div: lost pl over 2f out* **66/1**

**17** *1¼* **Lord Of The Fens**[26] 4-9-4 GBaker 11 18
(CNKellett) *s.s: racd stands' side: a wl bhd* **100/1**

6- **18** *1½* **Tikitano (IRE)**[388] 1260 3-8-4 RFfrench 5 9
(DKIvory) *racd far side: in rr: bhd fnl 2f* **25/1**

**19** *¾* **Barholm Charlie** 3-8-9 JBramhill 18 11
(MABuckley) *racd stands' side: chsd ldrs: lost pl over 2f out* **33/1**

1m 13.74s (-0.54) **Going Correction** -0.30s/f (Firm) **19** Ran SP% **120.4**
**WFA** 3 from 4yo 9lb
Speed ratings: **91,89,89,89,88 87,87,86,76,74 72,72,70,69,69 69,67,65,64**CSF £33.73 TOTE £7.00: £2.20, £2.00, £8.60; EX 25.40.
**Owner** Country Lane Partnership **Bred** R And Mrs Watson And Mrs A J Ralli **Trained** Scarcroft, W Yorks

**FOCUS**
A very modest sprint maiden and a very moderate winning time for the grade.

**NOTEBOOK**
**Neon Blue**, placed in four of his 10 previous starts, had a good chance on official figures and broke his duck despite the very firm ground.
**Kensington(IRE)**, fitted with a cross noseband, looked very fit indeed. He was almost upsides just inside the last but then only just held on to second.
**Fair Options ◆**, having his third start, still looked to be carrying plenty of condition. Switched to race with the stands' side group he was out of contact until picking up in good style coming to the last. He finished with quite a flourish and will be interesting in handicap company over seven furlongs plus.
**Amanda's Lad(IRE)**, having his 45th start, keeps giving a good account of himself without ever looking like breaking his duck.
**Isaz**, on the leg and narrow, appreciated the better ground and is worth a try over seven.
**True Magic**, one of six to stick to the far side, led that group throughout but inside the last she looked to be feeling the lack of company and leaned towards the stands' side group. *Official explanation: jockey said filly hung right-handed in the closing stages*
**Truman**, who was taking on plenty on his sole backend outing at two, is a keen-type. He stayed on late in the day and looks capable of better in due course.
**Irusan(IRE)**, having just his second outing, finished clear second best on the far side. He needs another outing before he can run in handicaps.
**Soviet Sceptre(IRE)**, taken to post early, never looked happy on the very firm ground. *Official explanation: trainer's representative said colt was unsuited by the firm ground*

## 2237 STONEACRE GROUP CLASSIFIED STKS 1m (S)
7:50 (7:51) (D) 3-Y-O+ £5,687 (£1,750; £875; £437) Stalls High

Form RPR

0000 **1** **Mystic Man (FR)**[19] 1773 6-9-4 82 NCallan 7 92
(KARyan) *trckd ldrs: led over 1f out: r.o strly* **16/1**

136- **2** *2½* **Langford**[227] 5416 4-9-2 79 GDuffield 12 84
(MHTompkins) *trckd ldrs: qcknd to ld over 2f out: hdd over 1f out: styd on same pce* **16/1**

5356 **3** *nk* **Weet A Head (IRE)**[9] 2018 3-8-4 80 WSupple 2 83
(RHollinshead) *chsd ldrs: effrt 3f out: styd on same pce appr fnl f* **16/1**

05-0 **4** *hd* **Devant (NZ)**[17] 1828 4-9-2 83 PRobinson 6 83
(MAJarvis) *rr-div: hdwy and swtchd lft over 1f out: kpt on same pce* **7/1**

4-00 **5** *3* **Tedstale (USA)**[19] 1773 6-9-1 82 (b) DAllan(3) 5 78
(TDEasterby) *rr-div: drvn along and hdwy over 4f out: nvr rchd ldrs* **20/1**

0240 **6** *nk* **Linning Wine (IRE)**[14] 1903 8-9-4 82 KDarley 8 77
(BGPowell) *bhd: nt clr run over 2f out tl over 1f out: swtchd lft: styd on* **9/2**[2]

5-00 **7** *2* **Atlantic Ace**[19] 1773 7-9-2 78 FLynch 3 71
(BSmart) *dwlt: swtchd rt after s: bhd: sme hdwy over 2f out: nvr on terms* **33/1**

/43- **8** *½* **Morning After**[311] 3267 4-8-13 78 OUrbina 16 67
(JRFanshawe) *chsd ldrs: lost pl over 1f out* **14/1**

3100 **9** *¾* **Topton (IRE)**[22] 1708 10-9-2 78 (b) RWinston 15 68
(PHowling) *s.i.s: bhd tl sme hdwy fnl 2f* **14/1**

216- **10** *6* **Obrigado (USA)**[236] 5217 4-9-2 80 DHolland 4 54
(WJHaggas) *swtg: w ldrs: t.k.h: lost pl over 1f out: eased ins last* **7/2**[1]

0300 **11** *1¼* **Kentucky King (USA)**[17] 1845 4-9-3 81 ACulhane 9 52
(PWHiatt) *a in rr* **20/1**

2-01 **12** *¾* **Love In Seattle (IRE)**[20] 1746 4-9-2 80 KDalgleish 10 49
(MJohnston) *led 2f: chsd ldrs: lost pl 2f out* **5/1**[3]

05-0 **13** *¾* **Johannian**[17] 1845 6-9-2 79 SCarson 13 48
(JMBradley) *w ldrs: led after 2f tl hdd & wknd over 2f out* **33/1**

0-00 **14** *9* **Blue Patrick**[14] 1903 4-9-2 80 TGMcLaughlin 1 27
(JMPEustace) *sn chsng ldrs on outside: lost pl over 1f out: eased* **66/1**

1m 37.79s (-3.81) **Going Correction** -0.30s/f (Firm) **14** Ran SP% **117.4**
**WFA** 3 from 4yo+ 12lb
Speed ratings: **107,104,104,104,101 100,98,98,97,91 90,89,88,79**CSF £229.05 TOTE £21.50: £7.80, £3.80, £3.90; EX 323.60.
**Owner** R J H Limited **Bred** Gainsborough Stud Management Ltd **Trained** Hambleton, N Yorks

**FOCUS**
A tight-knit classified stakes with just 6lb covering the entire field on official figures, but in the end a clear-cut winner.

**NOTEBOOK**
**Mystic Man(FR)** is ideally suited by getting cover in a strongly-run race and found his form with a vengeance. *Official explanation: trainer said, regarding the improved form shown, gelding was better suited by the drop in class and having a clear run in the race*
**Langford**, absent since October, went on and stepped up the pace but in the end the winner was simply too quick for him. This trip is his bare minimum.
**Weet A Head(IRE)**, drawn one off the outside, had the least chance on official figures.
**Devant(NZ)**, much happier on this quick surface, switched violently left and ended up making her finishing effort towards the centre. Suited by a straight track she is happiest making the running.
**Tedstale(USA)**, with the blinkers back on, was soon making hard work of it but stayed on in his own time. This was marginally more encouraging.
**Linning Wine(IRE)** had no luck at all and with a clear passage might well have finished second best.
**Topton(IRE)** *Official explanation: trainer said gelding was unsuited by the firm ground*
**Obrigado(USA)**, progressive in just four outing at three, was awash with sweat at the start. He took a fierce grip before tending to hang, looking unhappy on the very firm ground. Hopefully he will bounce back. *Official explanation: jockey said gelding hung left on the firm ground*
**Love In Seattle(IRE)** reverted to type, dropping right out when called on for a serious effort.

## 2238 HATFIELDS CHRYSLER CROSSFIRE FILLIES' H'CAP 6f
8:20 (8:20) (D) (0-80,79) 3-Y-O+ £5,736 (£1,765; £882; £441) Stalls High

Form RPR

01-2 **1** **Mis Chicaf (IRE)**[19] 1775 3-8-10 **70** RWinston 10 83
(JSWainwright) *led on stands' side rail: qcknd over 2f out: r.o wl: readily* **9/2**[1]

223- **2** *1½* **Favour**[201] 5875 4-9-6 **71** IMongan 8 79
(MrsJRRamsden) *t.k.h: hdwy over 2f out: styd on to go 2nd last 75yds: no real imp* **13/2**[3]

-400 **3** *1¾* **Consensus (IRE)**[4] 2143 5-10-0 **79** TWilliams 9 82
(MBrittain) *chsd ldrs: hung lft and kpt on same pce fnl f* **9/2**[1]

-000 **4** *1½* **Princess Erica**[5] 2123 4-8-0 **51** oh1 ow2 (p) FNorton 5 49
(JBalding) *chsd ldrs: kpt on same pce fnl 2f* **33/1**

10-5 **5** *¾* **Bint Royal (IRE)**[26] 1625 6-8-9 **60** (p) DHolland 6 56
(MissVHaigh) *chsd ldrs: outpcd over 2f out: kpt on fnl f* **8/1**

2-03 **6** *nk* **Just One Smile (IRE)**[10] 1992 4-8-8 **62** DAllan(3) 2 57
(TDEasterby) *s.i.s: swtchd rt after s: hdwy on ins and nt clr run over 1f out: swtchd lft: kpt on* **9/2**[1]

3003 **7** *2* **Playful Spirit**[45] 1262 5-7-12 **49** oh2 (v) JBramhill 4 38
(JBalding) *swtchd rt after s: sn chsng ldrs: outpcd fnl 2f* **12/1**

00-5 **8** *3½* **Bowling Along**[20] 1750 3-7-12 **58** RFfrench 7 37
(MESowersby) *n.m.r and lost pl over 4f out: nvr on terms after* **25/1**

30-5 **9** *¾* **Tapau (IRE)**[30] 1518 6-9-6 **71** SCarson 3 47
(JMBradley) *chsd ldrs: lost pl over 1f out* **11/1**

135- **10** *23* **Officer's Pink**[197] [5924] 4-9-5 **70**.............................................(t) KDarley 1 —
(PFICole) *chsd ldrs on outer: hung lft and lost pl 2f out: heavily eased* **6/1**[2]

1m 12.04s (-2.24) **Going Correction** -0.30s/f (Firm)
**WFA** 3 from 4yo+ 9lb **10** Ran SP% **116.1**
Speed ratings: **102,100,97,95,94 94,91,86,85,55**CSF £33.53 CT £126.41 TOTE £6.00: £1.70, £2.80, £2.10; EX 25.50.
**Owner** Anthony D Copley **Bred** Mrs E Thompson **Trained** Kennythorpe, N Yorks

**FOCUS**
A fair handicap, and a fine tactical ride by Robert Winston on the winner.

**NOTEBOOK**
**Mis Chicaf(IRE)**, who looked very fit, had the plum stands' side draw. Her rider dropped anchor in front before going for home and she was never in any real danger. This was her trainer's first success since she scored at Beverley in September.
**Favour**, a fiery-type, took a fierce grip as a result of the winner slowing the pace from the front. She stuck on to take second spot well inside the last and has the ability to go one better when everything falls into place.
**Consensus(IRE)**, making a quick reappearance and conceding weight all round, ran much better but looks weighted to the hilt.
**Princess Erica** ran her best race for her present yard on her fourth outing this term. She has slipped to a lenient mark if her trainer, who is a dab hand with sprinters, can get her mind right.
**Bint Royal(IRE)** found this an insufficient test, especially the way the winner was ridden. Seven suits her better nowadays.
**Just One Smile(IRE)**, drawn one off the outside, missed the break slightly and was switched to race towards the stands' side rail. She met traffic problems and was never in the hunt. A true-run seven would suit her better.
**Tapau(IRE)** *Official explanation: trainer said mare was unsuited by the firm ground*
**Officer's Pink**, worst drawn, hung and looked most unhappy before being virtually pulled up. Her rider reported that she had gurgled. *Official explanation: jockey said filly had a breathing problem*

## 2239 SKY VEGAS LIVE ON CHANNEL 295 H'CAP — 7f
**8:50** (8:51) (D ) (0-85,82) 3-Y-O **£5,898** (£1,815; £907; £453) **Stalls** High

Form RPR
0-12 **1** **Kamanda Laugh**[17] [1841] 3-9-2 **77**............................................... MHills 2 85
(BWHills) *trckd ldrs: led over 1f out: jst hld on* **7/4**[1]
00-0 **2** *nk* **Reidies Choice**[26] [1614] 3-8-11 **72**............................................... ACulhane 3 79
(JGGiven) *s.i.s: swtchd rt after s: nt clr run on ins over 2f out: styd on wl fnl f: jst failed* **14/1**
0005 **3** *nk* **Poppys Footprint (IRE)**[7] [2069] 3-9-0 **75**................................ NCallan 6 81
(KARyan) *s.i.s: edgd rt after s: hdwy and n.m.r 2f out: styd on strly fnl f: no ex nr fin* **9/1**
1-00 **4** *1* **Outer Hebrides**[18] [1795] 3-8-13 **77**.................................... TPQueally(3) 4 80
(DRLoder) *trckd ldrs: edgd rt and kpt on same pce appr fnl f* **7/1**[3]
00-2 **5** *3 1/2* **Times Review (USA)**[19] [1760] 3-9-6 **81**................................. KDarley 12 75
(TDEasterby) *led: qcknd 3f out: hdd over 1f out: fdd* **11/2**[2]
2400 **6** *1 1/2* **Western Roots**[40] [1322] 3-9-2 **77**............................................ SSanders 9 67
(PFICole) *in tch: outpcd over 3f out: kpt on fnl f* **12/1**
000- **7** *1* **Sky Galaxy (USA)**[220] [5535] 3-9-7 **82**................................... DHolland 10 69
(EALDunlop) *trckd ldrs: effrt over 2f out: kpt on same pce* **12/1**
5-10 **8** *2* **Capetown Girl**[26] [1606] 3-8-12 **73**......................................... GFaulkner 11 55
(KRBurke) *trckd ldrs: outpcd over 2f out: n.d after* **14/1**
2-04 **9** *7* **Kingsmaite**[28] [1558] 3-8-9 **70**................................................... JBramhill 7 33
(SRBowring) *t.k.h: trckd ldrs n.m.r over 5f out: lost pl over 1f out* **18/1**
6000 **10** *1 3/4* **Mr Midasman (IRE)**[12] [1957] 3-8-2 **63**.................................... JMackay 5 21
(RHollinshead) *s.i.s: hdwy on outer to chse ldrs over 2f out: sn lost pl* **25/1**
300- **11** *1* **Nesnaas (USA)**[246] [4997] 3-8-11 **72**...................................... WSupple 8 27
(BHanbury) *w ldr: lost pl 2f out* **20/1**
04-0 **12** *9* **Commander Bond**[19] [1775] 3-8-11 **72**...................................... FLynch 1 3
(BSmart) *t.k.h on wd outside: hdwy to chse ldrs 5f out: lost pl 2f out: sn bhd and eased* **33/1**

1m 24.99s (-2.82) **Going Correction** -0.30s/f (Firm) **12** Ran SP% **119.8**
Speed ratings: **104,103,103,102,98 96,95,93,85,83 81,71**CSF £28.67 CT £183.95 TOTE £2.50: £1.40, £3.20, £2.40; EX 43.30 Place 6 £601.21, Place 5 £256.61.
**Owner** John Sillett **Bred** Miss K Rausing **Trained** Lambourn, Berks
■ Stewards Enquiry : T P Queally one-day ban: failed to keep straight from stalls (May 31)

**FOCUS**
Not a strong pace, yet the second and third came from behind. The winner is improving.

**NOTEBOOK**
**Kamanda Laugh**, racing on totally different ground from a 4lb higher mark, took what looked a decisive advantage but in the end it was a desperate thing.
**Reidies Choice**, who seemed to go the wrong way at two, was switched after the start to overcame an outside draw. He found his passage blocked but picked up in fine style inside the last and would have made it in three more strides. He definitely has the ability to make amends from this sort of mark.
**Poppys Footprint(IRE)**, who had a mid-field draw to overcome, was left short of room at a crucial stage. She stayed on in good style and this trip and this ground suit her. She deserves to regain the winning thread.
**Outer Hebrides**, with the headgear left off, edged in from his outside draw, getting in the way of Kingsmark. Down 6lb after two outings this time, he still looks over-rated.
**Times Review(USA)** stepped up the pace from the front but in the end did not get home over this extended trip. American-bred, he is well worth another try on the All-Weather round a bend.
**Western Roots**, absent for six weeks, was racing on totally different ground and found this an insufficient test.
T/Plt: £1,692.40 to a £1 stake. Pool: £45,441.70. 19.60 winning tickets. T/Qpdt: £307.00 to a £1 stake. Pool: £3,194.60. 7.70 winning tickets. WG

# 2220 GOODWOOD (R-H)
### Thursday, May 20

**OFFICIAL GOING: Good to firm**
Wind: almost nil Weather: fine becoming cloudy, heavy rain race 7

## 2240 SUNSEEKER STKS (RATED STAKES) (H'CAP) — 1m 6f
**2:10** (2:13) (B ) (0-100,100) 4-Y-0+ **£12,852** (£4,875; £2,437; £1,108) **Stalls** High

Form RPR
14-0 **1** **Barolo**[33] [1455] 5-9-5 **98**....................................................... MartinDwyer 12 112
(PWHarris) *trckd ldr to 6f out: styd cl up: rdn and effrt to ld over 2f out: drew clr wl over 1f out: r.o wl* **7/1**[3]
00-0 **2** *5* **Archduke Ferdinand (FR)**[15] [1880] 6-8-7 **86**.......................... SSanders 10 93
(PFICole) *t.k.h: trckd ldrs: effrt 3f out: drvn to chse wnr wl over 1f out: no imp* **20/1**
330- **3** *nk* **Romany Prince**[215] [5639] 5-9-7 **100**...................................... DaneO'Neill 13 107
(DRCElsworth) *t.k.h: hld up: prog into midfield gng wl enough 3f out: shkn up and nt qckn over 2f out: r.o fnl f: nvr nrr* **14/1**
2412 **4** *1/2* **Cold Turkey**[5] [2110] 4-8-6 **85**................................................. SWhitworth 2 91+
(GLMoore) *hld up in last: stdy prog over 3f out: chsng ldrs whn nt clr run over 1f out tl ins fnl f: r.o: no ch* **11/4**[1]
13-6 **5** *1/2* **Reveillez**[40] [1329] 5-8-13 **92**................................................. JPMurtagh 3 97
(JRFanshawe) *swtg: mde most to over 2f out: sn outpcd* **7/1**[3]
-023 **6** *hd* **Gold Ring**[9] [2022] 4-8-8 **87**.................................................... SDrowne 4 92
(GBBalding) *lw: trckd ldrs: rdn 3f out: one pce fnl 2f* **13/2**[2]
61-4 **7** *5* **Cara Fantasy (IRE)**[40] [1326] 4-8-4 **83** oh3................................ WSupple 8 81
(JLDunlop) *s.s: sn rcvrd and prom: chsd ldr 6f out: rdn and upsides 3f out: btn 2f out: wknd rapidly fnl f* **20/1**
211- **8** *2* **Escayola (IRE)**[197] [5926] 4-8-9 **88**........................................(v) TQuinn 1 83
(WJHaggas) *settled towards rr: shkn up 3f out: edgd rt and one pce over 1f out: nvr on terms* **10/1**
64-0 **9** *nk* **Almizan (IRE)**[15] [1880] 4-8-7 **86**.......................................... TEDurcan 7 81
(MRChannon) *t.k.h: hld up in midfield: rdn and lost pl over 3f out: struggling after* **8/1**
6-00 **10** *10* **Wait For The Will (USA)**[19] [1768] 8-8-7 **86**........................ RLMoore 6 67
(GLMoore) *hld up in midfield: shkn up 3f out: sn lost pl and btn: wknd 2f out* **20/1**
-023 **11** *nk* **King Flyer (IRE)**[33] [1457] 8-8-6 **83** oh3 ow2.......................... DHolland 5 65
(MissJFeilden) *hld up in rr: effrt 6f out: rr again and btn 3f out: wknd* **20/1**
04-0 **S** **Theatre (USA)**[18] [1801] 5-8-4 **83** oh3.......................................... PDoe 9 —
(JamiePoulton) *hld up: slipped up bnd after 2f* **20/1**

3m 4.27s (0.52) **Going Correction** +0.05s/f (Good) **12** Ran SP% **115.7**
Speed ratings: **100,97,96,96,96 96,93,92,92,86 86,—**CSF £141.34 CT £1878.04 TOTE £7.90: £2.40, £6.90, £5.70; EX 194.00 Trifecta £1631.70 Pool of £2,298.27 - 0.40 winning units..
**Owner** Mrs P W Harris **Bred** Pendley Farm **Trained** Ringshall, Bucks

**FOCUS**
A decent handicap, and a Listed class performance from the winner, but the gallop was stop-start and did not suit those held up off the pace.

**NOTEBOOK**
**Barolo**, who had the riderless Theatre for company when kicking clear in the straight, stayed on right to the line to score decisively. He enjoyed the fast ground much better than the soft he encountered in a Group Three on his reappearance, and this was a classy performance. He will probably have to step up to Listed company now but is still progressing and could well have a decent prize in him.
**Archduke Ferdinand(FR)**, wearing a net muzzle and warm beforehand, was not helped by the stop-start gallop in the first half of the race, as he ran keenly until the turn for home, but stayed on well for pressure in the straight and ran his best race for some time. He has looked regressive since his victory in the Northumberland Plate in 2001, but as a result has slipped to a favourable mark.
**Romany Prince**, who looked fit for this reappearance, stayed on strongly from off the pace late in the straight and posted a fair comeback effort under top-weight. He was unsuited by being held up off the steady early gallop and although he has a habit of finishing too late, he is entitled to build on this.
**Cold Turkey** had nowhere to go when seemingly full of running and making a strong challenge just over a furlong from home. Held up in last place for most of the way, he was another to be unsuited by the stop-start gallop and he would have been second with a clear run. The problem is he is due to go up 5lb in the future and those who back him, must know he needs all to fall right in his races, despite the fact he is a most progressive performer.
**Reveillez** was responsible for setting the steady early pace and may not have been suited by such tactics. That said, he had an easy lead and proved slightly disappointing, suggesting he could do with a drop in the weights.
**Gold Ring** held every chance, but was unable to quicken on this fast ground and would have been seen to better effect with a stronger gallop.
**Escayola(IRE)**, off for 197-days previously, travelled nicely until coming under pressure about three out and is capable of improving on the bare form, with this run under his belt.
**Theatre(USA)** was up very quickly after his slip on the and 'won' the race riderless.

## 2241 PETERS FAIRLINE FESTIVAL STKS (LISTED RACE) — 1m 1f 192y
**2:40** (2:48) (A ) 4-Y-0+ **£17,400** (£6,600; £3,300; £1,500) **Stalls** Low

Form RPR
1-54 **1** **Alkaadhem**[33] [1456] 4-8-12 102.................................................. RHills 8 114
(MPTregoning) *lw: hld up in midfield: clsd to trck ldrs 3f out: gng easily 2f out: effrt to ld ent fnl f: rdn out to hold on nr fin* **10/3**[2]
0503 **2** *nk* **Compton Bolter (IRE)**[13] [1925] 7-9-1 108.............................. RHughes 9 116
(GAButler) *trckd ldrs: gng easily 3f out: effrt to ld over 1f out: drvn and hdd ent fnl f: kpt on wl: jst hld* **16/1**
110- **3** *1/2* **Big Bad Bob (IRE)**[242] [5109] 4-9-4 112................................. JPMurtagh 5 118
(JLDunlop) *chsd ldrs: stmbld bnd 5f out: effrt to chal over 2f out: sn rdn and nt qckn: kpt on wl again fnl f* **7/1**
4-10 **4** *3/4* **Sublimity (FR)**[26] [1621] 4-9-1 110...........................................(t) KFallon 7 114
(SirMichaelStoute) *hld up in rr: outpcd and shkn up 3f out: drvn and styd on wl fnl 2f: nvr able to chal* **9/2**[3]
2-30 **5** *1 3/4* **Island House (IRE)**[26] [1622] 8-8-12 111.................................. DHolland 3 107
(GWragg) *lw: hld up in rr: outpcd and rdn 3f out: styd on wl fr over 1f out: no imp last 75yds* **15/2**
3420 **6** *3 1/2* **Anani (USA)**[33] [1455] 4-9-1 106................................................ EAhern 10 104
(EALDunlop) *led for 2f: trckd ldr: led again over 2f out to over 1f out: wknd fnl f* **12/1**
200- **7** *3* **Foodbroker Founder**[293] [3745] 4-8-12 103................................ TQuinn 6 95
(DRCElsworth) *racd in midfield: outpcd and rdn 3f out: no ch after* **33/1**
-640 **8** *6* **Lago D'Orta (IRE)**[14] [1902] 4-9-1 104................................. DaneO'Neill 4 87
(CGCox) *s.s: a towards rr: rdn over 3f out: no prog* **33/1**
62-2 **9** *5* **Parasol (IRE)**[14] [1902] 5-8-12 114..........................................(v) TPQueally 1 74
(DRLoder) *led after 2f and set str pce: slipped bdly bnd 5f out: rdn over 3f out: hdd & wknd over 2f out* **5/2**[1]
2/16 **10** *3 1/2* **Wake (USA)**[36] [1397] 4-8-12 90................................................. SDrowne 2 67
(BJMeehan) *hld up in rr: brief effrt over 4f out: sn wknd* **66/1**

2m 6.13s (-1.55) **Going Correction** +0.05s/f (Good) **10** Ran SP% **115.0**
Speed ratings: **108,107,107,106,105 102,100,95,91,88**CSF £53.25 TOTE £4.50: £1.80, £3.90, £1.60; EX 69.40 Trifecta £283.70 Pool of £1,798.54 - 4.50 winning units.
**Owner** Hamdan Al Maktoum **Bred** Meon Valley Stud **Trained** Lambourn, Berks

**FOCUS**
A decent field for this Listed event and it was run at a solid gallop. A good effort from the winner and solid enough form from the placed horses.

**NOTEBOOK**
**Alkaadhem** put behind him two unlucky runs in handicaps and won in the style of a decent horse. He was travelling particularly sweetly just over two out, and although he only won a neck, he was value for more than that as his rider was keen not to hit the front too soon. This dispelled fears he may be a "nearly horse" and he looks capable of holding his own at a higher level. The major prizes at Royal Ascot are not ruled out.
**Compton Bolter(IRE)** ran a solid race in defeat over trip short of his best. He improved for this fast ground and there was a lot to like about the manner in which he rallied, having been headed late on. Despite his age, he retains all the ability to win a similar race at least this year.

**Big Bad Bob(IRE)** was unable to adopt his preferred front-running role and stumbled on the bend at halfway, so deserves credit for finishing third under a penalty after a 242-day layoff. His penalty will not make life easy, but he is a talented horse who is entitled to come on for this and should win races this year.

**Sublimity(FR)** put a below par run at Sandown behind him with a creditable effort on this better ground but got going too late and had to be angled out for a run, which cost him a bit of momentum. Much more settled at the start on this occasion, he can be considered better than the bare form and has another Listed prize in him at the least.

**Island House(IRE)**, who had previously won this event twice and been touched off another occasion, looked as though he may get involved in the finish when hitting full stride approaching the final furlong, but was flattening out in the closing stages.

**Parasol(IRE)** pulled himself into a clear lead early on and ran far too keenly, then lost his confidence after stumbling badly on the bend five out. He can be excused this, but is far from strightforward and not one to place too much faith in. *Official explanation: jockey said horse slipped badly on the final bend and lost its confidence thereafter*

## 2242 EXCEL SCHRODERS LONDON BOAT SHOW EBF CONQUEROR STKS (LISTED RACE) (F&M) 1m

**3:15** (3:18) (A) 3-Y-O+ **£17,400** (£6,600; £3,300; £1,500) **Stalls** High

Form RPR

-012 **1** **Gonfilia (GER)**[12] [1964] 4-9-6 100..........(t) KMcEvoy 4 105
(SaeedBinSuroor) *led for 2f: led again over 2f out: shkn up and 2l clr over 1f out: pushed out fnl f* **9/4**[2]

3-1 **2** *3/4* **Classical Dancer**[31] [1507] 3-8-5 84.......... TQuinn 2 100
(HCandy) *hld up: effrt over 2f out: drvn and hanging rt over 1f out: r.o to chse wnr last 100yds: clsng at fin but a hld* **9/1**

1-20 **3** *1* **Incheni (IRE)**[18] [1791] 3-8-5 103.......... SDrowne 3 98
(GWragg) *hld up: rdn 3f out: no prog tl r.o over 1f out: tk 3rd nr fin* **8/1**[3]

-400 **4** *nk* **Cote Quest (USA)**[8] [2044] 4-9-3 92.......... MartinDwyer 8 97
(SCWilliams) *lw: wl in tch: rdn to chse wnr 2f out: no imp 1f out: one pce fnl f* **33/1**

0-00 **5** *4* **Starbeck (IRE)**[12] [1964] 6-9-3 88.......... PMcCabe 7 88
(PHowling) *s.s: t.k.h and hld up in last: rdn 3f out: hung lft over 1f out: n.d* **40/1**

621- **6** *2 1/2* **Chic**[222] [5482] 4-9-6 97.......... KFallon 5 85
(SirMichaelStoute) *trckd ldrs: rdn to chal over 2f out: wknd over 1f out* **6/4**[1]

5/0 **7** *3 1/2* **Ianina (IRE)**[19] [1776] 4-9-3.......... JPMurtagh 6 74
(RRohne, Germany) *pushed into ld after 2f: hdd & wknd over 2f out* **25/1**

42-5 **8** *10* **Zietory**[18] [1790] 4-9-6 102.......... DHolland 1 54
(PFICole) *hld up in last pair: rdn and struggling 3f out: sn bhd* **8/1**[3]

1m 39.06s (-1.21) **Going Correction** +0.05s/f (Good)
**WFA** 3 from 4yo+ 12lb **8** Ran **SP%** **112.2**
Speed ratings: **108,107,106,105,101 99,95,85**CSF £21.39 TOTE £3.30: £1.30, £1.80, £1.80; EX 22.00 Trifecta £72.90 Pool of £1,683.99 - 16.39 winning units.
**Owner** Godolphin **Bred** Gestut Auenquelle **Trained** Newmarket, Suffolk

**FOCUS**
A fair Listed contest for fillies and mares, run at a solid pace. Much improved form from the second.

**NOTEBOOK**
**Gonfilia(GER)**, warm in the paddock, got back into the winning groove under a well-judged ride. She caught a tartar last time at Lingfield on soft ground, but found these conditions much more to her liking and duly showed her true form. A Group Three over this trip is the aim, and it is probably feasible granted the right conditions.

**Classical Dancer ◆**, had a very stiff task, as the 15lb she received from the winner was merely weight-for-age. She finished fast, having taken her time to hit full stride and not getting the best of runs entering the final furlong, and ran most promisingly. She handles most types of ground and can go one better at this level, perhaps over further.

**Incheni(IRE)**, outclassed on the 1000 Guineas last time, went some way to erasing the memory that disappointemt with a sound run in third. She had no problems with the trip and is still lighty raced and so open to further improvement. However, she still has to improve a bundle to justify her Group One entry in the Coronation Stakes.

**Cote Quest(USA)** ran a much improved race on ground that did not look to suit. She made good headway two out, but hung to her left on account of the quick ground, and could not quicken from that point onwards. This was her best effort to date for her current connections and she will be seen to better effect when able to get her toe into the ground.

**Starbeck(IRE)** again ran a frustrating race. She has the talent, but is quirky.

**Chic** held every chance over two out, but found very little under pressure and folded tamely. This has to rate a disappointment, but she may well improve plenty for this seasonal return and prove capable of much better in due course.

**Zietory** *Official explanation: trainer said filly was unsuited by the good to firm ground*

## 2243 DE NOVO RAYMARINE MAIDEN FILLIES' STKS 1m 1f

**3:45** (3:52) (D) 3-Y-O **£5,499** (£1,692; £846; £423) **Stalls** Low

Form RPR

36 **1** **Springtime Romance (USA)**[37] [1387] 3-8-11.......... KFallon 9 74
(EALDunlop) *lw; chsd ldrs: prog to ld narrowly jst over 2f out: hrd pressed after: hrd rdn and hld on fnl f* **10/3**[1]

36- **2** *hd* **Al Shuua**[255] [4777] 3-8-11.......... DHolland 11 74
(CEBrittain) *trckd ldr 1f: styd prom: effrt to chal over 2f out: w wnr and ev ch fr 2f out: jst hld nr fin* **14/1**

0- **3** *2 1/2* **Golden Island (IRE)**[201] [5868] 3-8-11.......... RHills 5 69
(JWHills) *lw: hld up in last: plenty to do whn snatched up over 3f out and sn swtchd lft: gd prog fnl 2f: clsng at fin: improve* **8/1**[3]

6 **4** *1 1/2* **Miss Monica (IRE)**[17] [1842] 3-8-11.......... WRyan 14 66
(HRACecil) *racd in midfield: rdn and prog over 2f out: chsd ldng pair over 1f out: kpt on but no imp: lost 3rd last 100yds* **10/1**

303- **5** *2* **Appetina**[219] [5556] 3-8-11 77.......... MFenton 10 62
(JGGiven) *led at decent pce: hdd jst over 2f out and hmpd on inner sn after: fdd u.p* **11/2**[2]

5 **6** *6* **Cultured**[10] [2001] 3-8-11.......... EAhern 3 50
(MrsAJBowlby) *racd in midfield: pushed along 3f out: sn outpcd and btn* **12/1**

50 **7** *1/2* **Olympias (IRE)**[30] [1521] 3-8-11.......... SDrowne 8 49
(HMorrison) *a towards rr: rdn over 3f out: sn struggling* **33/1**

00 **8** *nk* **Cool Clear Water (USA)**[45] [1271] 3-8-11.......... WSupple 6 48
(BJMeehan) *chsd ldr after 1f to wl over 2f out: sn wknd* **50/1**

**9** *9* **Topple** 3-8-11.......... DaneO'Neill 2 30
(HCandy) *unf: s.i.s and pushed along early: a in rr: rdn and btn over 3f out* **25/1**

**10** *7* **Ruggtah** 3-8-11.......... TEDurcan 13 16
(MRChannon) *leggy bit bkwd: a in rr: rdn over 3f out: sn wknd* **11/1**

**11** *4* **Prairie Oyster** 3-8-11.......... JPMurtagh 12 8
(DRCElsworth) *w'like: scope: a in rr: rdn over 3f out: sn wknd* **16/1**

0 **12** *5* **Collada (IRE)**[31] [1507] 3-8-11.......... RHughes 7 —
(JHMGosden) *prom tl wknd 4f out* **14/1**

1m 55.9s (-0.96) **Going Correction** +0.05s/f (Good) **12** Ran **SP%** **102.7**
Speed ratings: **106,105,103,102,100 95,94,94,86,80 76,72**CSF £37.36 TOTE £3.60: £1.60, £5.20, £2.70; EX 65.30.
**Owner** Maktoum Al Maktoum **Bred** Gainsborough Farm Llc **Trained** Newmarket, Suffolk

**FOCUS**
A decent time for the type of contest, but uneven form. Judged through the fifth, the first four have all improved.

**NOTEBOOK**
**Springtime Romance(USA)** appreciated this drop in trip to lose her maiden tag at the third time of asking, but made hard work of doing so. She came there looking all over the winner approaching two out, but idled in front and got very close to the runner-up several times before sticking her head out on the line. She is likely to start life in handicaps off a mark of about 80 and still has more improvement in her.

**Al Shuua ◆** made a very pleasing return from a 255-day absence and was only just denied. She has obviously trained on well from two to three and looks a ready-made winner of a similar event, but also now has the option of handicaps.

**Golden Island(IRE) ◆** picked up strongly late on, having been set a fair bit to do, and was finishing best of all. If she had started her run earlier, this Ribblesdale entry would have gone close, and she is entitled to improve plenty for the outing.

**Miss Monica(IRE)** held every chance if good enough in the straight, but could only muster the one pace under pressure and never looked like picking up the leaders.

**Appetina** was being ridden when she got hampered on the rail about two furlongs out, but kept on well enough and made a satisfactory comeback. She will be sharper for the experience and is not one to write off just yet.

**Cultured**

## 2244 MOTOR BOAT & YACHTING CENTENARY H'CAP 1m 3f

**4:20** (4:24) (D) (0-85,86) 3-Y-O **£5,551** (£1,708; £854; £427) **Stalls** Low

Form RPR

1-00 **1** **Watamu (IRE)**[17] [1831] 3-9-0 **78**.......... SSanders 12 92
(PJMakin) *lw: chsd ldr: clsd to chal 2f out: rdn to ld jst over 1f out: drvn out* **12/1**

-331 **2** *1 1/4* **Mystical Girl (USA)**[5] [2134] 3-9-2 **80** 5ex.......... SChin 9 92
(MJohnston) *led: drew 4l clr over 4f out: pressed but gng wl 2f out: hdd jst over 1f out: rdn and kpt on same pce fnl f* **11/4**[2]

21-4 **3** *2 1/2* **Camrose**[27] [1588] 3-9-5 **83**.......... TQuinn 11 91
(JLDunlop) *racd in midfield: prog on inner 3f out: cl up and ch 2f out: one pce over 1f out* **7/2**[3]

0-41 **4** *3* **Obay**[34] [1450] 3-9-7 **85**.......... KFallon 2 88
(EALDunlop) *chsd ldrs: rdn over 2f out: one pce and no imp over 1f out* **7/1**

425- **5** *1 1/4* **Mommkin**[209] [5722] 3-8-13 **77**.......... TEDurcan 6 78
(MRChannon) *swtg: racd in midfield: rdn 3f out: kpt on one pce: n.d* **20/1**

2-31 **6** *1* **Cutting Crew (USA)**[7] [2070] 3-9-8 **86** 5ex.......... MartinDwyer 10 86
(PWHarris) *lw: hld up in rr: rdn and nt qckn 3f out: struggling after: kpt on fnl f* **5/2**[1]

3340 **7** *12* **Lord Of The Sea (IRE)**[61] [1064] 3-8-6 **70**.......... PDoe 1 50
(JamiePoulton) *racd in midfield: drvn and effrt 3f out: wknd 2f out* **20/1**

3436 **8** *hd* **Ground Patrol**[45] [1271] 3-8-5 **69** ow1.......... SDrowne 8 49
(AMBalding) *lw: dwlt: a in rr: rdn over 3f out: no prog and sn btn* **16/1**

1-00 **9** *shd* **Laawaris (USA)**[17] [1831] 3-9-2 **80**.......... SWKelly 5 60
(JAOsborne) *s.s: a in rr: rdn and struggling over 3f out* **33/1**

200- **10** *13* **Carlburg (IRE)**[255] [4776] 3-8-7 **71**.......... EAhern 4 30
(CEBrittain) *trckd ldrs to over 3f out: wkng whn n.m.r over 2f out: t.o* **33/1**

2m 25.8s (-0.31) **Going Correction** +0.05s/f (Good) **10** Ran **SP%** **118.9**
Speed ratings: **103,102,100,98,97 96,87,87,87,78**CSF £44.15 CT £144.10 TOTE £14.80: £3.50, £1.60, £1.40; EX 59.90.
**Owner** R A Henley **Bred** Crandon Park Stud **Trained** Ogbourne Maisey, Wilts

**FOCUS**
A fair three-year-old handicap run at a steady gallop that did not suit those racing off the pace.

**NOTEBOOK**
**Watamu(IRE) ◆**, popular in the betting ring, stayed on strongly when hitting the front approaching the last furlong and won with a bit in hand. He had looked useful when landing his maiden on his second start last term, but had failed to improve on that in two outings this year and this was much more like his true form. More improvement is expected and he could well follow up. *Official explanation: trainer said, regarding the improved form shown, colt was better suited by today's good to firm ground*

**Mystical Girl(USA)**, still 4lb ahead of the Handicapper despite her penalty for winning last time, looked to going sweetly on the bridle two out, but found less than expected and was well held in the end by the winner. This was still a decent effort and she was clear of the rest, so to write her off would be unwise.

**Camrose** held every chance in the straight, but failed to find a chance of gear on this ground. This was not a bad effort and a similar race is within his compass when reverting to softer ground.

**Obay**, a facile winner of a maiden on testing ground last time, was not suited by the steady early gallop and may not have enjoyed this faster grond. He still has more improvement to come and was far from disgraced.

**Mommkin** making her handicap debut, was another who did not look happy off the modest gallop and lost momentum in having to switch wide to make her challenge. She can do better when faced with a stiffer test.

**Cutting Crew(USA)** was the disappointment of the race. He was still officially 5lb well-in despite his penalty for winning at York, but found nil under pressure and this effort will have left connections scratching thier heads.

## 2245 FINNING POWER EBF MAIDEN FILLIES' STKS 6f

**4:55** (4:56) (D) 2-Y-O **£4,797** (£1,476; £738; £369) **Stalls** Low

Form RPR

**1** **Baltic Dip (IRE)** 2-8-11.......... RHughes 1 81
(RHannon) *w'like: scope: racd against nr side rail: mde virtually all: jnd 2f out: rdn over 1f out: styd on wl: won on the nod* **3/1**[2]

**2** *shd* **Park Romance (IRE)** 2-8-11.......... KFallon 2 81
(BJMeehan) *w'like: scope: trckd ldrs: jnd wnr 2f out: edgd rt over 1f out: disp ld fnl f: pipped on the post* **5/2**[1]

**3** *2 1/2* **Shivaree** 2-8-11.......... TEDurcan 5 74
(MRChannon) *w'like: trckd ldrs: effrt to chal over 2f out: one pce jst over 1f out* **4/1**[3]

**4** *6* **Marianis** 2-8-11.......... RLMoore 6 56
(JGPortman) *unf: s.i.s: outpcd and pushed along: lost tch 2f out: kpt on fnl f* **7/1**

**5** *1/2* **Some Night (IRE)** 2-8-11.......... JPMurtagh 3 54
(JHMGosden) *w'like: str: bit bkwd: racd in 5th: outpcd and rdn 2f out: no ch after* **9/2**

0 **6** *8* **Mystery Maid (IRE)**[23] [1686] 2-8-11.......... SDrowne 4 30
(HSHowe) *w wnr to over 2f out: wknd* **25/1**

1m 13.34s (0.50) **Going Correction** +0.05s/f (Good) **6** Ran **SP%** **108.1**
Speed ratings: **98,97,94,86,85 75**CSF £10.05 TOTE £4.20: £2.50, £1.70; EX 13.40.

**Owner** Thurloe Thoroughbreds Viii **Bred** S And S Hubbard Rodwell **Trained** East Everleigh, Wilts

**FOCUS**

A decent looking maiden with all bar one of the runners making their debuts. The field came home strung out behind the first two.

**NOTEBOOK**

**Baltic Dip(IRE)** showed a game attitude to score on the rail in a bobbing finish. She was smart from the gates and showed plenty of toe for a juvenile who could have been expected to need a stiffer test on breeding. This was a taking debut, and as she had not come in her coat yet, significant improvement can be expected. A tilt at the Albany Stakes at Royal Ascot is now on the cards.

**Park Romance(IRE)**, a good-bodied individual, made a very pleasing debut and only failed by the most narrow of margins. She showed plenty of pace, but spoilt her chance by running green under pressure late on. She looks to have a bright future.

**Shivaree ◆**, an athletic, quite attractive sort, failed to quicken with the front two inside the final furlong, but was clear of the rest and shaped with promise. She will know a lot more next time and should have no trouble in landing a similar race.

**Marianis** fell out of the gates and ran distinctly green until halway, when she picked up well enough. Her stable's juveniles often need their debut outings and she may do better over another furlong.

**Some Night(IRE)**, who did not look fully wound up for this racecourse bow, was struggling to go the pace from halfway and was not given a hard time when her chance had gone. She should leave this form behind in due course but is no superstar.

## 2246 AVON INFLATABLES APPRENTICE STKS (H'CAP) 5f

**5:30** (5:33) (E) (0-70,68) 3-Y-O+ **£3,916** (£1,205; £602; £301) **Stalls** Low

Form RPR

00-0 **1** **Parkside Pursuit**[5] 2118 6-9-7 **68**........ CJDavies(5) 1 78
(JMBradley) *hld up nr side gp: prog 1/2-way: hung bdly rt fr wl over 1f out: led 1f out: drvn out* **50/1**

3332 **2** *nk* **Aintnecessarilyso**[16] 1859 6-7-12 **45**........ MHalford(5) 14 54
(NEBerry) *hld up rr of centre gp: prog 2f out: str chal ins fnl f: jst hld* **10/1**

-001 **3** *nk* **Guns Blazing**[5] 2118 5-9-4 **65** 7ex........(b) MHoward(5) 18 73
(DKIvory) *disp ld in centre: overall ldr 1/2-way to 1f out: unable qck nr fin* **5/1**[1]

030- **4** *¾* **Redwood Star**[202] 5849 4-9-1 **57**........(e) DFox 13 62
(PLGilligan) *pressed ldrs in centre: rdn over 1f out: chal ins fnl f: no imp last 50yds* **12/1**

1065 **5** *nk* **Double M**[3] 2166 7-8-5 **47**........(v) RThomas 10 51+
(MrsLRichards) *hld up in centre: effrt 2f out: running on whn hmpd jst ins fnl f: swtchd rt and r.o wl nr fin* **8/1**[3]

0236 **6** *nk* **Pulse**[5] 2118 6-9-7 **63**........(p) AQuinn 11 66
(JMBradley) *pressed ldrs in centre: rdn and unable qck over 1f out: styd on again ins fnl f* **6/1**[2]

3020 **7** *nk* **Henry Tun**[27] 1584 6-7-7 **40**........(p) DFentiman(5) 5 42
(NEBerry) *prom nr side: hung rt fr 2f out: ev ch 1f out: carried rt after: hld whn hmpd last 100yds* **33/1**

0040 **8** *nk* **Panjandrum**[16] 1872 6-8-13 **55**........ MSavage 12 56
(NEBerry) *hld up in centre: rdn 2f out: kpt on fnl f: nvr able to chal* **20/1**

35-4 **9** *shd* **Cerulean Rose**[13] 1937 5-9-7 **68**........ LiamJones(5) 4 68
(AWCarroll) *s.i.s: racd nr side: swtchd to centre 1/2-way to chse ldrs: swtchd lft again fnl f: kpt on* **5/1**[1]

0311 **10** *1* **Maromito (IRE)**[23] 1699 7-8-8 **55**........ DTudhope(5) 17 52+
(RBastiman) *pressed ldrs in centre: rdn and ev ch jst over 1f out: hld whn hmpd last 50yds and lost several pls* **5/1**[1]

0000 **11** *3* **Firecat**[14] 1909 5-7-12 **40** oh5........ HayleyTurner 6 26
(APJones) *disp ld nr side gp but nt on terms: btn over 1f out* **50/1**

000- **12** *shd* **Loch Inch**[241] 5129 7-9-1 **57**........(b) NChalmers 3 43
(JMBradley) *bit bkwd: chsd ldrs nr side: nt on terms and no prog over 1f out* **40/1**

1256 **13** *¾* **Crafty Politician (USA)**[16] 1859 7-7-12 **45**........(b) StevenHarrison(5) 8 28
(GLMoore) *w nr side ldrs for 3f: sn btn* **50/1**

0516 **14** *shd* **Erracht**[5] 2130 6-9-6 **65**........ BSwarbrick(3) 2 48
(MrsHSweeting) *spd nr side to 1/2-way: sn btn* **20/1**

145- **15** *hd* **Indian Bazaar (IRE)**[239] 5156 8-8-5 **50**........ PMakin(3) 16 32
(NEBerry) *disp overall ld in centre to 1/2-way: wknd over 1f out* **14/1**

-500 **16** *¾* **Goodwood Prince**[26] 1608 4-8-13 **62**........(v1) JCoffill-Brown(7) 9 41
(SDow) *w nr side ldrs to 1/2-way: sn struggling* **33/1**

0010 **17** *1 ¼* **Arogant Prince**[21] 1738 7-8-13 **60**........(b) SaleemGolam(5) 7 35
(JPearce) *prom nr side: swtchd to far side 1/2-way: hung rt and nt on terms after* **25/1**

0400 **18** *14* **Bahamian Belle**[5] 2118 4-8-8 **55**........(b) DeanWilliams(5) 15 —
(PSMcentee) *rel to r: a t.o* **33/1**

58.94 secs (-0.11) **Going Correction** +0.05s/f (Good) **18 Ran SP% 129.4**

Speed ratings: **102,101,101,99,99 98,98,97,97,96 91,91,90,89,89 88,86,63**CSF £482.86 CT £3054.13 TOTE £51.20: £8.30, £2.70, £2.20, £3.50; EX 580.20 Place 6 £136.79, Place 5 £28.28.

**Owner** J M Bradley **Bred** J K Keegan **Trained** Sedbury, Gloucs

■ Stewards Enquiry : C J Davies two-day ban: careless riding (May 31, Jun 1)

M Savage three-day ban: excessive use of the whip (May 31-Jun 2)

**FOCUS**

A moderate aprrentices' sprint in which the winner hung dramatically across the track and hampered rivals. The form looks highly suspect.

**NOTEBOOK**

**Parkside Pursuit**, warm beforehand, hung dramatically to his right across the track under maximum pressure, but still had enough guts to hold on and score.

**Aintnecessarilyso**, placed in Banded events the last twice, ran a solid race off his light weight and showed he is in good heart at present, but will go up in the weights for this, making life a lot tougher.

**Guns Blazing** was again quickly away and stuck to his task gamely, but could not quite follow up his Nottingham win under his 7lb penalty. Nevertheless, he should continue to pay his way.

**Redwood Star** was not helped by the winner hanging and ran a sound race on this return from a 202-day break. She has always run well at this venue in the past and is one to bear in mind when returning for a similar event.

**Double M** was the chief sufferer by the winner's antics. He was just starting to wind up and lost momentum, but recovered well and finished strongly, so has to be considered unlucky.

**Pulse** ran his race, but on this evidence may need a drop in the weights before he is winning again.

**Henry Tun** got checked by the winner, but was under pressure at the time.

**Cerulean Rose** was sluggish at the start, but picked well enough at halfway and came out best of those to stay on the stands' side.

**Maromito(IRE)** can be considered better than the bare form, as he too suffered quite badly when the winner hung across the track. He managed to translate his form in All-Weather Banded events over to the turf and is in great nick at present.

T/Jkpt: Not won. T/Plt: £334.20 to a £1 stake. Pool: £91,747.75. 200.40 winning tickets. T/Qpdt: £10.70 to a £1 stake. Pool: £6,080.60. 420.35 winning tickets. JN

# 2035 NEWCASTLE (L-H)

Thursday, May 20

**OFFICIAL GOING: Good to firm (good in places)**

## 2247 SALTWELL SIGNS NOVICE STKS 5f

**2:20** (2:21) (D) 2-Y-O **£3,536** (£1,088; £544; £272) **Stalls** Centre

Form RPR

1 **1** **Royal Island (IRE)**[12] 1961 2-9-2........ KDalgleish 3 83+
(MJohnston) *mde all: drvn along appr fnl f: eased clsng stages* **1/6**[1]

21 **2** *2* **Unlimited**[21] 1735 2-9-0........ GDuffield 5 69
(MrsADuffield) *a chsng wnr: drvn along 1/2-way: kpt on: no imp* **8/1**[2]

**3** *5* **Regal Lustre** 2-8-7........ RWinston 4 42
(JRWeymes) *dwlt: sn chsng first 2: drvn along 1/2-way: sn btn* **25/1**

**4** *hd* **Gracie's Gift (IRE)** 2-8-12........ GFaulkner 1 46
(PCHaslam) *sn bhd: drvn along 1/2-way: n.d* **10/1**[3]

60.60 secs (-0.93) **Going Correction** -0.175s/f (Firm) **4 Ran SP% 109.7**

Speed ratings: **100,96,88,88**CSF £3.25 TOTE £1.50: £1.10, £1.20; EX 4.10.

**Owner** Markus Graff **Bred** Mrs Bill O'Neill **Trained** Middleham Moor, N Yorks

**FOCUS**

All four runners went to the far side and the order never changed throughout the contest. The time was decent for the grade, but it was one-way traffic, the winner looking a useful prospect in beating the other runner with previous experience in the style his odds suggested he should

**NOTEBOOK**

**Royal Island(IRE) ◆**, on very different ground compared to his Beverley debut, made every yard and was not hard pressed to hold off the runner-up. He may now head back to Beverley for the Brian Yeardley Continental Two-Year-Old Trophy at the beginning of next month, a race his stable took last year.

**Unlimited**, both of whose efforts to date have been on Fibresand, did his very best to get on terms with the winner but was always being held. He should find a race on turf in less exalted company.

**Regal Lustre**, an 11,500gns sister to Caerphilly Gal and half-sister to three other winners, faced a stiff task for this debut and ran green throughout the contest. She ultimately found the two previous winners far too good, but should have benefited from the experience and her next outing should tell us more.

**Gracie's Gift(IRE)**, an 8,000gns two-year-old out of a half-sister to two winners, was always being taken off her feet but should have learnt something from this.

## 2248 CULTURE 10 CLAIMING STKS 6f

**2:50** (2:54) (F) 2-Y-O **£3,087** (£882; £441) **Stalls** Centre

Form RPR

50 **1** **Ronnies Lad**[21] 1735 2-8-7........ DarrenWilliams 5 53
(JRNorton) *prom early: drvn along in midfield 1/2-way: swtchd rt over 1f out: rapid hdwy u.p fnl f: led cl home* **33/1**

633 **2** *nk* **Straffan (IRE)**[10] 2003 2-8-8........ JCarroll 4 53
(EJO'Neill) *led: rdn fnl f: hdd cl home* **6/1**[2]

0303 **3** *2 ½* **Joshar**[5] 2124 2-8-4........ DaleGibson 12 42
(MWEasterby) *chsd ldrs: rdn and ch over 1f out: no ex ins last* **11/1**

2366 **4** *shd* **Turtle Magic (IRE)**[10] 2002 2-8-1........ CHaddon(7) 11 45
(WGMTurner) *sn trcking ldrs: ch and rdn over 1f out: no ex ins last* **2/1**[1]

306 **5** *1 ¾* **Procrastinate (IRE)**[8] 2035 2-8-6........ PPMathers(7) 10 45
(RFFisher) *slowly away: sn prom: ev ch and rdn over 1f out: no ex ins last* **7/1**[3]

45 **6** *½* **Mount Ephram (IRE)**[8] 2035 2-8-8........ PBradley(5) 1 43
(RFFisher) *towards rr: nt clr run over 2f out: hdwy whn hmpd 2f out: styd on wl fnl f: nvr able to chal* **9/1**

**7** *3 ½* **Lojo** 2-8-5........ THamilton(3) 3 28
(RPElliott) *slowly away: rr div tl styd on fnl 2f: n.d* **16/1**

0 **8** *2* **Fransiscan**[6] 2074 2-9-1........ GFaulkner 8 29
(PCHaslam) *midfield: rdn 2f out: no hdwy* **20/1**

**9** *5* **Samalan** 2-8-9........ GDuffield 2 8
(JParkes) *sn drvn along: a rr div* **33/1**

05 **10** *1 ¼* **Frisby Ridge (IRE)**[28] 1556 2-8-8........(b1) KDalgleish 9 —
(TDEasterby) *dwlt: sn prom: rdn and wknd over 2f out: bhd whn eased ins fnl f* **10/1**

04U **11** *5* **Fold Walk**[2] 2194 2-8-3........ PMulrennan(5) 6 —
(MWEasterby) *dwlt: a towards rr: bhd whn eased ins fnl f* **12/1**

505 **12** *7* **Voice Of An Angel (IRE)**[10] 2003 2-8-8........ FNorton 7 —
(ABerry) *nvr bttr than mid-div: bhd whn eased ins fnl f* **12/1**

1m 15.52s (0.48) **Going Correction** -0.175s/f (Firm) **12 Ran SP% 119.5**

Speed ratings: **89,88,85,85,82 82,77,74,68,66 59,50**CSF £219.39 TOTE £46.10: £3.90, £2.30, £2.40; EX 375.50.Ronnies Lad was claimed by G L Moore for £7,000.

**Owner** The Matthewman Partnership **Bred** Mrs G E Cutler And P Cutler **Trained** High Hoyland, S Yorks

**FOCUS**

A modest claimer and once again the field raced far side. Weak form.

**NOTEBOOK**

**Ronnies Lad**, who had shown very little in two outings on Fibresand, was effectively taking a drop in grade. It is more likely that the switch to fast ground on turf and the extra furlong contributed to this improved effort though, as he won this by outstaying his rivals. He was subsequently claimed by Gary Moore for £7,000.

**Straffan(IRE)** was given a positive ride over this extra furlong and did nothing wrong, but had the race snatched from her in the dying strides. She should be able to find a similarly modest event.

**Joshar** probably ran to form, but she lacks both pace and scope and it will be a very poor race she wins.

**Turtle Magic(IRE)** was technically dropping in grade, though some of her previous races have been little better than this. She did not always have much room to play with against the far rail in the final couple of furlongs, but neither was she seriously inconvenienced and the extra furlong did not bring about much improvement. She looks exposed now.

**Procrastinate(IRE)**, down in class, had every chance but was made to look slow in the latter stages.

**Mount Ephram(IRE) ◆**, whose two previous starts have been on heavy ground, did not enjoy much of a run and was staying on late on this faster surface. He is worth keeping in mind for a similarly modest event over an extra furlong. *Official explanation: jockey said gelding hung left throughout*

**Voice Of An Angel(IRE)** *Official explanation: jockey said filly was unsuited by the fast ground*

## 2249 PUTTER & FLUTTER H'CAP 2m 19y

**3:25** (3:25) (E) (0-70,70) 4-Y-O+ **£4,104** (£1,263; £631; £315) **Stalls** Centre

Form RPR

244- **1** **Red Sun**[19] 3203 7-8-6 **48**........(t) RWinston 6 67+
(JMackie) *mde all: qcknd over 5f out: clr over 2 out: unchal* **10/3**[1]

240- **2** *5* **Academy (IRE)**[176] 6079 9-9-0 **56**........ CCatlin 8 62
(AndrewTurnell) *hld up: drvn along 4f out: styd on u.p to go 2nd appr fnl f: no ch w wnr* **5/1**[3]

003 **3** *1¼* **Berrywhite (IRE)**[24] [1668] 6-7-12 **40** JMackay 4 44
(CGrant) *prom: drvn along 5f out: wnt 2nd over 3f out: sn rdn: no imp on wnr* **8/1**

0-10 **4** *hd* **Green 'N' Gold**[31] [1501] 4-8-13 **57** KDarley 5 61
(MDHammond) *hld up: drvn along and hdwy 3f out: styd on u.p fnl 2f: nt clr run cl home: nvr able to chal* **11/2**

05/0 **5** *4* **Almnadia (IRE)**[35] [1173] 5-8-8 **50** (p) IMongan 2 49
(SGollings) *prom: drvn along 5f out: wknd over 2 out* **4/1**[2]

030- **6** *2½* **Royal Castle (IRE)**[104] [5817] 10-8-4 **46** RFfrench 1 42
(MrsKWalton) *midfield: outpcd and dropped rr over 4f out: n.d after* **7/1**

0-40 **7** *4* **Autumn Fantasy (USA)**[12] [1973] 5-8-13 **60** TEaves(5) 3 51
(BEllison) *prom: drvn along 5f out: wknd over 2f out* **16/1**

00-0 **8** *5* **Dance Light (IRE)**[117] [603] 5-9-6 **62** TGMcLaughlin 7 47
(TTClement) *hld up: hdwy 4f out: disp 2nd and rdn 2f out: wknd qckly* **8/1**

0630 **9** *9* **Marino Mou (IRE)**[16] [1866] 4-8-1 **45** AMcCarthy 10 19
(MissDMountain) *hld up: hdwy into midfield 7f out: rdn 4f out: sn btn* **20/1**

3m 34.26s (-0.77) **Going Correction** 0.0s/f (Good)
**WFA** 4 from 5yo+ 2lb **9** Ran SP% **120.5**
Speed ratings: **101,98,97,97,95 94,92,90,85**CSF £21.19 CT £126.73 TOTE £3.60: £1.20, £2.70, £2.30; EX 13.20.
**Owner** Bulls Head Racing Club **Bred** Paul L Coe **Trained** Church Broughton, Derbys
■ Stewards Enquiry : C Catlin two-day ban: careless riding (May 31, Jun 1)

**FOCUS**
An ordinary staying handicap, but a fair pace and an impressive winner.

**NOTEBOOK**
**Red Sun**, better known as a useful hurdler, runs only rarely on the Flat these days and was racing on the level for the first time in ten months. He was thrown in if he ever showed anything like his hurdles form and, given his usual positive ride, ran his rivals into the ground. In this form he would be very interesting under a penalty.
**Academy(IRE)** off since November, came from well off the pace to snatch second place but was never in the same parish as the winner. He should come on for this and is becoming well handicapped.
**Berrywhite(IRE)**, trying this trip for the first time on the Flat, kept battling away and was not disgraced but would have preferred softer ground.
**Green 'N' Gold**, given a patient ride, kept staying on but could never land an effective blow, though he would have finished third had he not been intimidated by the runner-up in the last few strides. He is another that would have preferred more cut.
**Almnadia(IRE)**, who seems to need three miles over hurdles these days, was making a fleeting appearance on the Flat and was completely done for foot down the home straight.
**Royal Castle(IRE)** is a versatile sort, though inconsistent these days and getting a bit long in the tooth for this game.
**Dance Light(IRE)** *Official explanation: trainer said mare was found to be in season*

## 2250 NORTHUMBERLAND PLATE THREE DAY FESTIVAL MEDIAN AUCTION MAIDEN STKS 1m 2f 32y
**4:00** (4:03) (E) 3-Y-O **£3,526** (£1,085; £542; £271) **Stalls** High

Form RPR

**1** **What's Up Doc (IRE)**[202] [5858] 3-9-0 82 KDalgleish 5 85+
(MJohnston) *mde all: hung lft fr over 2f out: unchal* **4/5**[1]

622- **2** *5* **Atlantic City**[216] [5620] 3-9-0 71 KDarley 2 69
(WJHaggas) *prom: wnt 2nd 4f out: chsd wnr after: rdn 2f out: styd on: no imp* **11/4**[2]

0-40 **3** *12* **Dancing Bear**[33] [1466] 3-9-0 62 NPollard 4 46
(JulianPoulton) *in tch: rdn 3f out: sn outpcd by first 2* **11/1**

**4** *2* **Aston Lad** 3-9-0 DarrenWilliams 3 42
(MDHammond) *hld up: effrt over 3f out: sn rdn and btn* **25/1**

46 **5** *6* **Empress Eugenie (FR)**[22] [1713] 3-8-9 JCarroll 6 26
(JMPEustace) *cl up: rdn over 3f out: sn btn* **7/1**[3]

0 **6** *hd* **Milly Golightly**[12] [1972] 3-8-6 LEnstone(3) 1 25
(MDods) *hld up: drvn along 4f out: no hdwy* **50/1**

**P** **Matrimony** 3-9-0 (t) IMongan 7 —
(EALDunlop) *s.i.s: sn drvn along in rr: lost tch over 2f out: p.u and dismntd over 1f out* **14/1**

2m 11.17s (-0.43) **Going Correction** 0.0s/f (Good) **7** Ran SP% **115.5**
Speed ratings: **101,97,87,85,81 80,**—CSF £3.25 TOTE £1.50: £1.10, £2.20; EX 4.10.
**Owner** James Monaghan **Bred** James J Monaghan **Trained** Middleham Moor, N Yorks

**FOCUS**
An uncompetitive maiden run at only a fair pace. The market got it right.

**NOTEBOOK**
**What's Up Doc(IRE)**, up in trip after having raced three times in Ireland last season, made every yard and only had to be nudged out to hold off the runner-up despite hanging towards the inside rail down the home straight. He was entitled to win this the way he did on official ratings and his handicap mark looks by no means lenient, but on the other hand he may prefer easier ground than he encountered here and he still has scope for improvement.
**Atlantic City** was the only one within a street of the winner racing down the home straight, but with 11lb to find on official ratings could never get on terms. All of his races so far have been on fast ground, but his action suggests he does not want it.
**Dancing Bear** had a lot to find on official ratings and was beaten accordingly. He probably needs a much greater test of stamina than this and would also be better off in handicap company.
**Aston Lad**, a half-brother to the winning stayer Green 'N' Gold and also related to winners over hurdles and fences, was exposed for foot on this debut and it would be no surprise to see him over hurdles in the autumn.
**Empress Eugenie(FR)** disappointed for a second time since making such an encouraging debut at Windsor, a race that is working out well otherwise, and now has plenty of questions to answer.
**Matrimony** *Official explanation: jockey said colt had a breathing problem*

## 2251 BBC RADIO NEWCASTLE H'CAP 1m 3y(S)
**4:30** (4:30) (E) (0-70,70) 3-Y-O **£4,052** (£1,247; £623; £311) **Stalls** Centre

Form RPR

00-0 **1** **Ego Trip**[24] [1667] 3-8-1 **50** DaleGibson 6 55
(MWEasterby) *towards rr and pushed along 1/2-way: hdwy u.p 2f out: nt clr run and swtchd rt wl ins fnl f: led clsng stages* **20/1**

00-0 **2** *1* **Charlie Bear**[38] [1365] 3-9-4 **67** JCarroll 12 70
(EALDunlop) *mde most tl rdn and hdd clsng stages* **9/1**

4102 **3** *¾* **Time To Relax (IRE)**[13] [1932] 3-9-3 **66** KDalgleish 3 67
(JJQuinn) *midfield: hdwy u.p over 2f out: disputing 2nd and no ex whn bmpd wl ins fnl f* **6/1**[3]

3604 **4** *hd* **Rare Coincidence**[13] [1932] 3-9-4 **67** (p) JFEgan 14 68
(RFFisher) *prom: ev ch and rdn 2f out: disputing 2nd and no ex whn bmpd wl ins fnl f* **12/1**

06-6 **5** *1¾* **Futoo (IRE)**[12] [1957] 3-8-12 **61** NPollard 7 58
(GMMoore) *in tch: hdwy to chse ldrs 2f out: sn rdn: no further prog fnl f* **12/1**

5-23 **6** *2* **Joshua's Gold (IRE)**[16] [1869] 3-8-9 **58** RFitzpatrick 4 50
(DCarroll) *hld up: hdwy u.p 2f out: kpt on fnl f: nvr able to chal* **13/2**

6-61 **7** *3* **Dance To My Tune**[8] [2037] 3-8-6 **60** 6ex PMulrennan(5) 13 45
(MWEasterby) *dwlt: hld up: sme hdwy 3f out: kpt on same pce fnl 2f: n.d* **13/2**

000- **8** *1¼* **Cobalt Blue (IRE)**[198] [5916] 3-8-6 **55** KDarley 10 37
(WJHaggas) *midfield: rdn over 2f out: no hdwy* **4/1**[1]

-204 **9** *5* **Vrisaki (IRE)**[14] [1908] 3-8-4 **53** (p) TWilliams 8 24
(MissDMountain) *cl up whn hmpd after 2f: hung rt 5f out: wknd over 2f out* **33/1**

030- **10** *nk* **Restart (IRE)**[159] [6173] 3-8-11 **63** LEnstone(3) 11 33
(PCHaslam) *hld up: rdn 1/2-way: no hdwy* **25/1**

0-00 **11** *1¼* **Dark Day Blues (IRE)**[12] [1957] 3-9-3 **66** DarrenWilliams 9 33
(MDHammond) *hld up in tch: effrt 3f out: sn rdn and btn* **25/1**

0-20 **12** *3½* **Reedsman (IRE)**[38] [1363] 3-8-1 **50** FNorton 5 9
(RCGuest) *a rr div* **25/1**

50-0 **13** *7* **Shebaan**[36] [1400] 3-8-6 **55** AMcCarthy 2 —
(PSMcentee) *s.i.s: a bhd* **50/1**

6631 **14** *12* **Premier Dream (USA)**[16] [1874] 3-9-7 **70** JFanning 1 —
(MJohnston) *cl up early: in tch tl wknd 3f out: t.o* **5/1**[2]

1m 41.68s (0.48) **Going Correction** -0.175s/f (Firm) **14** Ran SP% **124.2**
Speed ratings: **90,89,88,88,86 84,81,80,75,74 73,70,63,51**CSF £183.70 CT £1264.50 TOTE £28.30: £5.20, £3.30, £2.70; EX 335.00.
**Owner** K Hodgson & Mrs J Hodgson **Bred** K And Mrs Hodgson **Trained** Sheriff Hutton, N Yorks

**FOCUS**
A modest pace and a very slow time for the grade. Again the whole field raced far side.

**NOTEBOOK**
**Ego Trip**, all the better for his reappearance here, seemed to appreciate the faster ground and came from a long way back to snatch the race from the fire. He had been given a chance by the Handicapper and this was not a great race.
**Charlie Bear**, unplaced in all four of his previous outings, was given a positive ride on this drop back from ten furlongs and looked the likely winner until the winner produced his whirlwind finish.
**Time To Relax(IRE)** had every chance, but was found wanting for pace in the closing stages and would probably have preferred a stronger gallop over this trip.
**Rare Coincidence** was back over a more suitable trip, but is yet to show his improved Fibresand form back on turf and looks plenty high enough in the handicap.
**Futoo(IRE)**ran another fair race, but even with the modest pace is yet to conclusively prove he stays this trip.
**Joshua's Gold(IRE)** ran another fair race, but as a result is not going to get any help from the Handicapper.
**Cobalt Blue(IRE)**, making his seasonal reappearance, started favourite despite having finished no closer than tenth in four previous outings. He never looked like justifying his position in the market.
**Vrisaki(IRE)** *Official explanation: jockey said colt hung badly right throughout*
**Dark Day Blues(IRE)** *Official explanation: jockey said colt was unsuited by the fast going*
**Premier Dream(USA)** ran too badly to be true, though this was his first try on fast ground.

## 2252 SHIELDS GAZETTE FILLIES' H'CAP 5f
**5:05** (5:06) (E) (0-75,74) 3-Y-O+ **£3,799** (£1,169; £584; £292) **Stalls** Centre

Form RPR

3000 **1** **Lady Protector**[16] [1870] 5-7-13 **45** DaleGibson 12 57
(JBalding) *hld up stands side: effrt 2f out: r.o wl u.p to ld ins fnl f* **14/1**

-000 **2** *1½* **Musical Fair**[6] [2094] 4-10-0 **74** SCarson 14 81
(JAGlover) *trckd ldr stands side: led jst ins fnl f: sn hdd: r.o* **10/1**

2200 **3** *½* **Lady Pekan**[13] [1937] 5-9-1 **61** (b) TGMcLaughlin 10 66
(PSMcentee) *racd stands side: led tl hdd jst ins fnl f: r.o* **14/1**

00-0 **4** *shd* **Roman Mistress (IRE)**[12] [1974] 4-9-6 **66** KDalgleish 7 71
(TDEasterby) *hld up far side: rdn 1/2-way: r.o wl u.p fnl f to ld gp cl home: nt trble stands side ldrs* **8/1**[3]

-626 **5** *shd* **Karminskey Park**[12] [1956] 5-9-2 **62** RWinston 4 66
(TJEtherington) *slowly away: bhd far side: hdwy 2f out: r.o wl to dispute gp ld wl ins fnl f: no ex clsng stages* **3/1**[1]

00-0 **6** *½* **College Queen**[4] [2143] 6-9-7 **67** (p) IMongan 3 70
(SGollings) *cl up far side: led gp over 1f out: no ex ins last* **11/1**

-406 **7** *½* **College Maid (IRE)**[16] [1870] 7-8-2 **48** (b) JFEgan 6 49
(JSGoldie) *in tch far side: kpt on same pce fnl f* **8/1**[3]

-044 **8** *½* **Tancred Times**[18] [1787] 9-8-7 **56** LEnstone(3) 2 55
(DWBarker) *led far side gp tl hdd over 1f out: no ex ins last* **7/1**[2]

600- **9** *1* **Bettys Pride**[274] [4276] 5-9-2 **62** DarrenWilliams 1 57
(MDods) *trckd ldrs far side: effrt whn nt clr run over 1f out: no hdwy fnl f* **20/1**

15-0 **10** *1¾* **Mystery Pips**[16] [1870] 4-8-5 **51** (v) KimTinkler 11 40
(NTinkler) *in tch stands side: hung lft 1/2-way: wknd appr fnl f* **20/1**

0-43 **11** *½* **Obe Bold (IRE)**[21] [1737] 3-8-6 **60** FNorton 13 47
(ABerry) *prom stands side tl wknd over 1f out* **14/1**

0005 **12** *4* **Tamarella (IRE)**[42] [1319] 4-8-10 **56** AMcCarthy 5 29
(GGMargarson) *prom far side tl wknd 2f out* **16/1**

000- **13** *2½* **Blues Princess**[233] [5286] 4-8-7 **56** THamilton(3) 9 20
(RAFahey) *racd far side: bhd fr 1/2-way* **7/1**[2]

59.98 secs (-1.55) **Going Correction** -0.175s/f (Firm)
**WFA** 3 from 4yo+ 8lb **13** Ran SP% **125.1**
Speed ratings: **105,102,101,101,101 100,99,99,97,94 93,87,83**CSF £154.00 CT £1285.95 TOTE £14.80: £4.30, £4.90, £4.50; EX 223.00 Place 6 £378.87, Place 5 £304.58.
**Owner** Simon Mapletoft Racing II **Bred** P J Wightman **Trained** Scrooby, Notts

**FOCUS**
A modest fillies' handicap, but a decent pace. Eight of the runners went far side, but the five who elected to come stands' side provided the first three home.

**NOTEBOOK**
**Lady Protector**, runner-up behind Karminskey Park in this race last year off a 3lb higher mark, is rather in-and-out but she can motor when on song and, held up in the stands' side group, came with a devastating late run to eventually win going away. The draw played a big part in this result though, and her profile does not suggest a follow-up is likely.
**Musical Fair**, under her ideal conditions and, as it turned out, with the draw in her favour came with a well-timed run on the stands' side, but the winner was finishing even quicker and she could do nothing about it. The Handicapper is just beginning to give her a chance, but she is still 3lb above her highest winning mark.
**Lady Pekan** showed good speed on the stands' side and managed to hang on until the closing stages. As things turned out she was well drawn so this effort may flatter her a bit, but she still has the ability to win a small race.
**Roman Mistress(IRE)** ◆ put up her best performance for a while and came through to 'win' the race on the far side. She is brilliantly handicapped at present and is worth bearing in mind.
**Karminskey Park**, winner of this race last year off a 1lb lower mark, would have appreciated easier ground than this and as things turned out, was also drawn on the wrong side. Those factors, combined with a very tardy start, something she has done before, proved too much of a handicap for her to overcome.
**College Queen** is probably better over six furlongs and needs to drop a bit further in the handicap.
**College Maid(IRE)** continues to freefall down the handicap, but did not offer much encouragement.
**Tancred Times** showed good speed over on the far side of the track, but was not drawn to advantage this time.

T/Plt: £88.00 to a £1 stake. Pool: £22,115.00. 183.25 winning tickets. T/Qpdt: £37.20 to a £1 stake. Pool: £2,162.30. 43.00 winning tickets. JF

# 1717 AYR (L-H)

Friday, May 21

**OFFICIAL GOING: Good to firm**

Wind: light, half against Weather: cloudy/bright

## 2256 DM HALL MEDIAN AUCTION MAIDEN STKS 6f

2:20 (2:24) (E) 2-Y-O £3,666 (£1,128; £564; £282) Stalls High

Form RPR

4 1 **Doctor Hilary**[7] [2087] 2-9-0 JMackay 7 67+
(MLWBell) *mde all: edgd lft ins fnl f: pushed out* **4/7**[1]

0 2 2 1/2 **Mac Cois Na Tine**[10] [2024] 2-9-0 GParkin 3 60
(KARyan) *dwlt: sn pushed in tch: effrt over 2f out: kpt on fnl f: no ch w wnr* **13/2**[3]

43 3 shd **Aunty Euro (IRE)**[44] [1299] 2-8-9 JCarroll 4 54
(EJO'Neill) *chsd ldrs: rdn over 2f out: kpt on same pce fnl f* **12/1**

05 4 1 1/4 **No Commission (IRE)**[19] [1782] 2-9-0 JFEgan 6 55
(RFFisher) *plld hrd: trckd ldrs: rdn over 2f out: one pce fnl f* **100/1**

5 1 1/4 **Sound And Vision (IRE)** 2-9-0 FLynch 2 52
(MDods) *sn outpcd: hdwy over 1f out: no imp fnl f* **14/1**

6 2 **Ballycroy Girl (IRE)** 2-8-9 RWinston 1 41
(ABailey) *dwlt: rdn 1/2-way: n.d* **20/1**

7 2 **Toss The Caber (IRE)** 2-9-0 KDarley 5 40
(MRChannon) *cl up: rdn and hung lft fr 1/2-way: wknd over 1f out: eased whn btn fnl f* **5/1**[2]

1m 13.49s (-0.23) **Going Correction** -0.40s/f (Firm) **7 Ran SP% 113.8**

Speed ratings: **85,81,81,79,78 75,72**CSF £4.90 TOTE £1.40: £1.10, £4.10; EX 3.80.

**Owner** H E Sheikh Rashid Bin Mohammed **Bred** The Lavington Stud **Trained** Newmarket, Suffolk

**FOCUS**

An ordinary bunch on looks and just modest form for a race run in a slow time. The winner had the rub of things next to the stands side rail.

**NOTEBOOK**

**Doctor Hilary**, who looked in good shape, had the run of the race next to the stands'-side rail and did not have to improve to get off the mark at the second attempt. Although this bare form is only ordinary, he may be capable of better and will stay further.

**Mac Cois Na Tine** bettered his debut effort over this longer trip and shaped as though an even stiffer test would be in his favour. He may be capable of better but his future may lie in ordinary handicap company.

**Aunty Euro(IRE)**, having her first run over six furlongs and her first run on a sound surface, ran creditably but is likely to remain vulnerable in similar company. She should stay seven furlongs.

**No Commission(IRE)**, up in trip and on this first run on fast ground, turned in his best effort yet but will struggle to win a maiden.

**Sound And Vision(IRE)**, related to a couple of winners abroad, looked in need of the race but hinted at ability on this racecourse debut, and looks the type to do better over further in modest handicaps in due course.

**Ballycroy Girl(IRE)**, a half-sister to turf and multiple sand winner Blonde En Blonde, achieved little on this racecourse debut.

**Toss The Caber(IRE)**, a half-brother to winning miler Celtic Heroine, was easy to back and ran as though ill-at-ease on the fast ground on this racecourse debut. He may do better granted an easier surface. *Official explanation: jockey said colt hung left handed throughout*

## 2257 KIDZPLAY MAIDEN STKS 1m 2f

2:55 (2:55) (D) 3-Y-O+ £5,512 (£1,696; £848; £424) Stalls Low

Form RPR

33-3 1 **Tannoor (USA)**[39] [1356] 3-8-11 77 KDarley 1 79+
(MAJarvis) *mde all: shkn up over 1f out: comf* **2/5**[1]

3-44 2 2 1/2 **Miss Adelaide (IRE)**[48] [1250] 3-8-6 77 ACulhane 2 66
(BWHills) *trckd ldrs: wnt 2nd over 2f out: effrt and shkn up over 1f out: no ex ins fnl f* **9/4**[2]

3 10 **African Sunset (IRE)**[76] [3026] 4-9-11 RWinston 4 52
(JHowardJohnson) *chsd wnr tl outpcd over 2f out* **40/1**[3]

0 4 1 1/4 **Columbian Emerald (IRE)**[21] [1747] 3-8-6 TEaves(5) 6 50
(TJEtherington) *prom tl outpcd fnl 3f* **100/1**

5 1 3/4 **Sharabad (FR)**[9] 6-9-11 JFEgan 5 46
(MrsLBNormile) *in tch tl wknd fr 3f out* **100/1**

/00- 6 6 **Lord Lahar**[492] [310] 5-9-4 TO'Brien(7) 3 35
(MRChannon) *hld up: rdn 4f out: sn btn* **50/1**

2m 8.29s (-3.90) **Going Correction** -0.40s/f (Firm)

**WFA** 3 from 4yo+ 14lb **6 Ran SP% 108.6**

Speed ratings: **99,97,89,88,86 81**CSF £1.41 TOTE £1.40: £1.10, £1.10; EX 1.60.

**Owner** Sheikh Ahmed Al Maktoum **Bred** N M Lotz And K Bruce Kline **Trained** Newmarket, Suffolk

**FOCUS**

An uncompetitive event run at just a fair pace and one in which the form horses came to the fore.

**NOTEBOOK**

**Tannoor(USA)**, back on a sound surface and back in trip, had the run of the race and did not have to improve to get off the mark. He will find life much tougher back in handicaps from his current mark.

**Miss Adelaide(IRE)**, up in trip and back on fast ground for the first time this year, ran better, but she does not look so good as last year and her official mark of 77 flatters her.

**African Sunset(IRE)**, back on the Flat and having his first start for new connections, looks flattered by his proximity and will be seen to better effect in low-grade handicaps in due course.

**Columbian Emerald(IRE)** was again well beaten and will continue to struggle in this grade.

**Sharabad(FR)** did not progress over hurdles and offered no immediate promise on this Flat debut.

**Lord Lahar**, back over a longer trip, again achieved little.

## 2258 DAWN CONSTRUCTION STKS (H'CAP) 1m 2f

3:25 (3:25) (C) (0-95,95) 3-Y-O+ £8,607 (£3,264; £1,632; £742) Stalls Low

Form RPR

412- 1 **Arcalis**[251] [4879] 4-9-7 **88** RWinston 8 100+
(JHowardJohnson) *hld up in tch: hdwy to ld 2f out: r.o strly* **4/1**[1]

0224 2 2 **Oldenway**[4] [2174] 5-8-2 **72** THamilton(3) 6 79
(RAFahey) *cl up: ev ch tl over 1f out: one pce fnl f* **6/1**[3]

1560 3 1 1/4 **Blue Sky Thinking (IRE)**[55] [1125] 5-10-0 **95** DarrenWilliams 4 100
(KRBurke) *hld up in tch: n.m.r over 2f out: swtchd and effrt over 1f out: hung lft: no imp fnl f* **9/2**[2]

10-0 4 1 1/4 **Millagros (IRE)**[14] [1931] 4-8-11 **78** JCarroll 5 80
(ISemple) *bhd tl styd on fr 2f out: nvr rchd ldrs* **20/1**

-622 5 1/2 **Tony Tie**[21] [1746] 8-8-9 **76** JFEgan 3 77
(JSGoldie) *trckd ldrs tl rdn and outpcd over 1f out* **7/1**

-035 6 1 **Jabaar (USA)**[8] [2066] 6-9-6 **87** (v1) AlexGreaves 1 86
(DNicholls) *keen: chsd ldrs tl wknd over 1f out* **9/2**[2]

011- 7 8 **Kirkham Abbey**[217] [5622] 4-7-12 **65** (v) MHenry 2 49
(MAJarvis) *led to 2f out: sn wknd* **4/1**[1]

501- 8 16 **Devine Light (IRE)**[209] [5748] 4-7-12 **65** PFessey 7 19
(BMactaggart) *prom to 1/2-way: sn lost tch* **100/1**

2m 5.68s (-6.51) **Going Correction** -0.40s/f (Firm) **8 Ran SP% 108.9**

Speed ratings: **110,108,107,106,106 105,98,86**CSF £25.39 CT £98.95 TOTE £5.30: £1.80, £2.10, £2.90; EX 45.30.

**Owner** Andrea & Graham Wylie **Bred** P E Clinton **Trained** Crook, Co Durham

**FOCUS**

A fair quality contest but lack of a decent gallop means this bare form may not prove entirely reliable. However the winner looks an improved sort and may be capable of better granted a stiffer test of stamina.

**NOTEBOOK**

**Arcalis ◆**, had conditions to suit for this reappearance run and first start for new connections and turned in an improved effort. A more strongly-run race would have suited him even better and he looks one to keep on the right side this term.

**Oldenway**, from a stable that is back among the winners, ran creditably but had the run of the race. He should continue to give a good account over middle distances on a sound surface.

**Blue Sky Thinking(IRE)** was far from disgraced given this race was not really run to suit, but the way he was hanging to his left in the straight suggested this ground was plenty quick enough. He will be of more interest when guaranteed a generous pace.

**Millagros(IRE)** is a bit better than the bare form, as she did well to come from so far back in a race run at just a steady gallop. A stronger pace will suit, but her record suggests she may not be one to place maximum faith in.

**Tony Tie**, from a stable that has been going well, was not disgraced but may be ideally suited by a more strongly-run race around a mile. He is a consistent sort though, and should continue to give a good account.

**Jabaar(USA)**, who shaped as though coming to hand at York last time, was keen to post and in the race in the first-time visor. He has not won for some time, but may be worth another chance in a more strongly-run race.

**Kirkham Abbey**, a progressive sort with a good strike rate last year, was up in grade but had conditions to suit and the run of the race on this reappearance. He dropped out tamely but, given his record last year, would not be one to write off yet.

## 2259 BIGGART BAILLIE CLASSIFIED STKS 1m

4:00 (4:00) (F) 3-Y-O £3,346 (£956; £478) Stalls Low

Form RPR

6104 1 **Showtime Annie**[25] [1678] 3-8-9 58 JFanning 8 57
(ABailey) *trckd ldrs: led 2f out: pushed out: edgd rt towards fin* **8/1**

-452 2 1 **Graceful Air (IRE)**[17] [1869] 3-8-11 62 RWinston 5 57
(JRWeymes) *cl up: effrt and ev ch fr over 2f out: one pce wl ins fnl f* **6/1**[2]

-454 3 shd **One 'N' Only (IRE)**[19] [1784] 3-8-9 55 RFfrench 4 54
(MissLAPerratt) *midfield: effrt over 1f out: styng on whn n.m.r nr fin* **25/1**

56-0 4 1 3/4 **Colloseum**[40] [1342] 3-8-7 59 TEaves(5) 2 53
(TJEtherington) *keen: prom: effrt over 2f out: kpt on same pce fnl f* **16/1**

00-6 5 1/2 **Kalishka (IRE)**[29] [1557] 3-9-1 63 KDarley 6 55
(AndrewTurnell) *hld up: hdwy centre over 1f out: kpt on: nvr rchd ldrs* **9/2**[1]

3-60 6 3/4 **Menai Straights**[37] [1392] 3-9-1 63 JFEgan 1 54
(RFFisher) *prom: effrt over 2f out: one pce over 1f out* **9/1**

-000 7 nk **The Stick**[17] [1874] 3-8-9 57 RLappin 3 47
(MRChannon) *s.i.s: sn midfield: effrt over 2f out: wknd over 1f out* **14/1**

666 8 1 1/2 **Indi Ano Star (IRE)**[31] [1528] 3-8-7 62 DTudhope(7) 7 48
(DCarroll) *bhd: rdn and hung lft over 3f out: kpt on: nvr rchd ldrs* **14/1**

54-6 9 1 1/4 **Balwearie (IRE)**[25] [1659] 3-9-1 63 (p) JCarroll 10 47
(MissLAPerratt) *hld up: hdwy centre over 1f out: no imp ins fnl f* **20/1**

204- 10 3 **Violet Avenue**[272] [4380] 3-8-11 62 SChin 13 36
(JGGiven) *cl up tl rdn and wknd over 1f out* **20/1**

2566 11 hd **Come What July (IRE)**[25] [1669] 3-9-0 65 (b) LEnstone(3) 9 41
(RGuest) *in tch tl rdn and wknd over 2f out* **13/2**[3]

2-66 12 3 1/2 **Chase The Rainbow**[19] [1784] 3-8-9 59 FLynch 12 25
(ABerry) *led to 2f out: wknd* **50/1**

3000 13 shd **Munaawesh (USA)**[17] [1874] 3-9-2 64 ACulhane 11 32
(DWChapman) *midfield: rdn over 3f out: sn btn* **7/1**

0-P0 14 2 **Grande Terre (IRE)**[20] [1761] 3-9-0 65 JMackay 14 25
(JGGiven) *bhd: lost tch fr 1/2-way* **20/1**

1m 41.25s (-1.87) **Going Correction** -0.40s/f (Firm) **14 Ran SP% 118.7**

Speed ratings: **93,92,91,90,89 88,88,87,85,82 82,79,79,77**CSF £50.28 TOTE £9.50: £2.90, £1.70, £7.90; EX 63.30.

**Owner** Showtime Ice Cream Concessionaire **Bred** S And R Ewart **Trained** Little Budworth, Cheshire

**FOCUS**

A fair gallop, but a weak race that is unlikely to be throwing up too many winners. As is usually the case at this course, those racing close to the pace held the edge.

**NOTEBOOK**

**Showtime Annie**, back on turf and back up in trip, had the run of the race and showed the right attitude to notch her second win from her last four starts, but she will find life tougher after reassessment.

**Graceful Air(IRE)**, back on a sound surface and tackling this trip for the first time, had a decent chance at the weights and ran creditably, but she is fully exposed.

**One 'N' Only(IRE)** ran well in the face of a stiffish task, but her proximity confirms this form is only modest at best. She is exposed but may well be worth another try over a bit further. *Official explanation: jockey said filly drifted left as the winner drifted right before winning post and he had to stop riding to avoid clipping heels*

**Colloseum**, upped in trip on only this fourth start, was not disgraced but will have to settle better if he is to progress.

**Kalishka(IRE)**, back on a sound surface, fared the best of those that were dropped out but shaped as though the step up to a mile and a quarter would suit.

**Menai Straights**, back on a sound surface, ran his best race of the year for a stable that has been among the winners, but he will have to improve again to win a handicap from his current mark.

## 2260 "STRIP THE WILLOW" H'CAP 7f 50y

4:30 (4:33) (F) (0-55,55) 3-Y-O+ £3,626 (£1,036; £518) Stalls Low

Form RPR

0-02 1 **Downland (IRE)**[11] [1994] 8-9-0 **50** KDarley 6 67
(NTinkler) *trckd ldrs: led over 1f out: pushed out* **6/1**[1]

00-0 2 nk **Francis Flute**[19] [1783] 6-8-6 **47** PMulrennan(5) 13 63
(BMactaggart) *in tch: effrt and edgd lft over 2f out: ev ch over 1f out: r.o fnl f* **14/1**

5-04 3 1 1/2 **Jubilee Street (IRE)**[18] [1824] 5-8-13 **52** ABeech(3) 14 64
(MrsADuffield) *bhd tl hdwy 2f out: r.o fnl f* **12/1**

0-00 4 1 1/2 **Mr Bountiful (IRE)**[13] [1971] 6-9-4 **54** (p) FLynch 8 62
(MDods) *hld up: hdwy 2f out: kpt on fnl f: no imp* **14/1**

5550 5 1/2 **Waltzing Wizard**[13] [1971] 5-9-3 **53** JFanning 16 60
(ABerry) *hld up: hdwy 2f out: no ex wl ins fnl f* **14/1**

0-16 6 1 **Zhitomir**[11] [1993] 6-8-12 **51** LEnstone(3) 3 55
(MDods) *prom: outpcd over 2f out: rallied fnl f: no imp* **7/1**[2]

00-0 7 3 **Yorkshire Blue**[21] [1748] 5-8-12 **48** JFEgan 18 44
(JSGoldie) *bhd tl hdwy centre over 1f out: n.d* **12/1**

/0-3 **8** 1 **Joshuas Boy (IRE)**[22] 1719 4-8-10 **46** oh1 (p) GParkin 4 39
(KARyan) *chsd ldrs: effrt over 2f out: wknd fnl f* **33/1**

-605 **9** 2 **Old Bailey (USA)**[17] 1868 4-8-10 **46** oh1 (b) PFessey 2 34
(TDBarron) *keen: w ldrs tl wknd over 1f out* **8/1**[3]

1423 **10** ½ **Silver Mascot**[31] 1533 5-9-0 **55** TEaves(5) 7 41
(ISemple) *led after 2f to over 1f out: wknd* **10/1**

0010 **11** ½ **Redoubtable (USA)**[14] 1941 13-9-0 **50** ACulhane 17 35
(DWChapman) *hld up: effrt over 2f out: sn no imp* **25/1**

2302 **12** *nk* **Luke After Me (IRE)**[13] 1971 4-9-4 **54** RWinston 12 38
(GASwinbank) *hld up midfield: no room and hmpd over 2f out: nt rcvr* **6/1**[1]

6-00 **13** 7 **Environmentalist**[19] 1787 5-8-10 **46** oh1 (t) DMcGaffin 9 11
(DANolan) *missed break: nvr on terms* **100/1**

-600 **14** *nk* **Andreyev (IRE)**[11] 1994 10-8-3 **46** oh6 JCurrie(7) 15 10
(JSGoldie) *dwlt: nvr on terms* **50/1**

5020 **15** ½ **Legal Set (IRE)**[19] 1787 8-9-2 **52** AnnStokell 11 15
(MissAStokell) *in tch on outside tl wknd over 2f out* **25/1**

0-00 **16** 1 **Square Dancer**[14] 1929 8-8-10 **46** oh11 (t) JMcAuley 5 6
(DANolan) *led 2f: wkng whn hmpd over 2f out* **100/1**

500- **17** 5 **Procreate (IRE)**[420] 839 4-8-10 **46** SChin 1 —
(MissAMWinters, Ire) *bolted to post: keen: chsd ldrs tl wknd over 2f out* **8/1**[3]

0-04 **18** 20 **Howards Dream (IRE)**[22] 1722 6-8-10 **46** oh16 (t) JMackay 10 —
(DANolan) *a bhd* **66/1**

1m 28.98s (-3.49) **Going Correction** -0.40s/f (Firm) **18** Ran SP% **123.8**
Speed ratings: **103,102,100,99,98 97,94,92,90,90 89,89,81,80,80 79,73,50**CSF £86.17 CT £1021.97 TOTE £7.30: £2.50, £3.40, £2.40, £3.40; EX 154.10.
**Owner** A Graham **Bred** Yeomanstown Stud **Trained** Langton, N Yorks
■ Stewards Enquiry : P Mulrennan one-day ban: careless riding (Jun 1)

**FOCUS**
A low-grade handicap but one run at a decent gallop. The form should stand up at a modest level.

**NOTEBOOK**
**Downland(IRE)** has slipped a long way down the handicap and confirmed his recent return to form back on this much faster surface. He won with a bit in hand, but his record suggests he would not be an obvious one to follow up.
**Francis Flute** fared much better than on his reappearance from his double-figure draw but, although capable of winning a race from his current mark, his record suggests he is not guaranteed to reproduce this next time.
**Jubilee Street(IRE)** ran creditably for a stable that has been going well and may be a bit better than the bare form, as he was moderately drawn and fared the best of those coming from off the pace. He looks worth another try over a mile.
**Mr Bountiful(IRE)**, a seven-furlong specialist, had the race run to suit but is the type that needs things to fall just right. He remains one to tread carefully with.
**Waltzing Wizard** was not disgraced from his wide draw. He is fairly consistent, but his losing run stretches back to August 2002.
**Zhitomir** was not disgraced from his favourable draw on this sound surface but is another that needs things to fall just right.
**Yorkshire Blue ◆**, having his second run for his in-form yard, looks a bit better than the bare form, as he had the worst of the draw and attempted to make ground in the centre of the course. He is on a fair mark and is one to keep an eye on.

## 2261 DUKE OF PERTH H'CAP 6f
5:05 (5:06) (D) (0-85,82) 3-Y-O+ **£5,629** (£1,732; £866; £433) **Stalls** High

Form RPR

3234 **1** **Highland Warrior**[14] 1929 5-8-9 **66** JFEgan 8 78
(JSGoldie) *dwlt: hld up midfield: hdwy to ld appr fnl fg: drvn out* **6/1**[3]

-162 **2** ¾ **Mine Behind**[6] 2132 4-9-7 **78** NPollard 6 88
(JRBest) *cl up: led on bit wl over 1f out: hdd appr last: r.o* **4/1**[1]

0-00 **3** 2 **Snow Bunting**[39] 1373 6-7-5 **55** oh5 LeanneKershaw(7) 10 59
(JeddO'Keeffe) *bhd: hdwy over 1f out: r.o fnl f: nt rch first two* **20/1**

0001 **4** *shd* **Friar Tuck**[19] 1787 9-7-12 **55** RFfrench 12 58
(MissLAPerratt) *prom: effrt over 2f out: one pce fnl f* **7/1**

00-0 **5** 2 **Undeterred**[39] 1361 8-9-6 **77** KDarley 9 74
(TDBarron) *bhd: rdn 1/2-way: hdwy over 1f out: nrst fin* **10/1**

0003 **6** 1¾ **Armagnac**[7] 2094 6-9-3 **74** ACulhane 4 66
(MABuckley) *dwlt: hld up in tch centre: effrt over 2f out: no imp fnl f* **5/1**[2]

040- **7** 3 **Machinist (IRE)**[286] 3995 4-9-11 **82** AlexGreaves 13 65
(DNicholls) *prom: no room fr over 2f to over 1f out: nt rcvr* **50/1**

60-0 **8** *shd* **Kings College Boy**[13] 1974 4-8-2 **61** ow1 THamilton(3) 14 45
(RAFahey) *led tl hung lft and hdd wl over 1f out: sn btn* **25/1**

-020 **9** 1¾ **Xanadu**[4] 2172 8-7-12 **55** oh2 (p) PFessey 11 33
(MissLAPerratt) *chsd ldrs: outpcd 2f out: n.d after* **20/1**

1/-1 **10** 2½ **Zoom Zoom**[27] 1603 4-9-6 **77** RWinston 3 47
(MrsLStubbs) *disp ld tl wknd over 1f out* **9/1**

0353 **11** ½ **Pawan (IRE)**[3] 2217 4-8-4 **61** AnnStokell 2 30
(MissAStokell) *spd centre to 2f out: wknd* **14/1**

-010 **12** 1¼ **Grey Cossack**[13] 1956 7-9-9 **80** GParkin 5 45
(PTMidgley) *in tch tl wknd fr over 2f out* **20/1**

00-0 **13** 1½ **Nemo Fugat (IRE)**[53] 1175 5-8-9 **66** JCarroll 1 26
(DNicholls) *racd centre: wknd fr 1/2-way* **33/1**

-000 **14** 7 **John O'Groats (IRE)**[6] 2130 6-9-1 **72** (p) FLynch 7 11
(MDods) *prom centre to 1/2-way: sn btn* **14/1**

1m 10.72s (-3.00) **Going Correction** -0.40s/f (Firm) **14** Ran SP% **114.1**
Speed ratings: **104,103,100,100,97 95,91,91,88,85 84,83,81,71**CSF £25.32 CT £449.02 TOTE £6.60: £2.60, £2.00, £4.80; EX 38.80 Place 6 £34.29, Place 5 £26.47.
**Owner** Frank & Annette Brady **Bred** Rowcliffe Stud **Trained** Uplawmoor, E Renfrews

**FOCUS**
A run of the mill sprint in which the pace was sound and those racing towards the stands side held the edge over those that raced in the centre. The form should stand up at a similar level.

**NOTEBOOK**
**Highland Warrior**, who has been running well at up to seven furlongs this year, is from an in-form yard and notched his third win at this course. He goes on most ground and should continue to give a good account.
**Mine Behind**, who ran well from a good draw at Thirsk, ran to a similar level from a moderate one this time and, given the way he went through the race, could well pick up a similar event in the near future.
**Snow Bunting**, back in trip, settled better in this more strongly-run race and ran creditably from 5lb out of the handicap, but again showed just why he is such a hard horse to win with.
**Friar Tuck**, 5lb higher than at Hamilton, did nothing wrong under suitable conditions but remains one to tread carefully with.
**Undeterred**, back on a sound surface, shaped better than on his reappearance. He may not be the most straightforward, but is one to keep an eye on.
**Armagnac** shaped a bit better than the bare form as he did the best of those that raced in the centre group. He looks capable of landing a similar event in the near future.
**Machinist(IRE)**, having his first start for David Nicholls, got no chance to show what he was capable of and this bare form is best ignored.
**Kings College Boy** *Official explanation: jockey said gelding hung left handed throughout*
**Zoom Zoom** will almost certainly be better suited by easier ground and is not one to write off yet.
*Official explanation: jockey said colt was unsuited by the fast ground*
**Pawan(IRE)** *Official explanation: jockey said gelding hung right handed in final 2f*
T/Plt: £78.60 to a £1 stake. Pool: £30,298.10. 281.25 winning tickets. T/Qpdt: £34.20 to a £1 stake. Pool: £1,705.50. 36.80 winning tickets. RY

# 2164 BATH (L-H)
Friday, May 21

**OFFICIAL GOING: Firm**

## 2262 BATHWICK TYRES LADY RIDERS' H'CAP 1m 2f 46y
6:05 (6:07) (F) (0-70,73) 4-Y-O+ **£3,395** (£970; £485) **Stalls** Low

Form RPR

-001 **1** **Voice Mail**[4] 2170 5-11-0 **73** 5ex MissMSowerby(5) 4 81
(AMBalding) *s.i.s and bhd: bmpd fter 3f: stl plenty to do 3f out: gd hdwy fr 2f out: led ins last: readily* **9/2**[2]

3431 **2** 1¾ **He Who Dares (IRE)**[13] 1969 6-10-9 **63** MrsSBosley 11 68
(AWCarroll) *s.i.s and bhd: hdwy over 2f out: chsd ldr ins finsl f: kpt on same pce u.p* **9/2**[2]

-510 **3** 2 **Saxe-Coburg (IRE)**[6] 2120 7-10-10 **64** MissSBrotherton 5 65
(GAHam) *stdd rr after 3f: hdwy 3f out: chsd ldrs appr fnl f: sn one pce* **10/1**

0-02 **4** *hd* **Holly Rose**[9] 2034 5-9-12 **52** (p) MsCWilliams 6 52
(DECantillon) *chsd ldrs: wnt 2nd 3f out: rdn 2f out: outpcd inside fnl f* **3/1**[1]

00-6 **5** ½ **Rainstorm**[25] 1681 9-9-2 **45** MrsSOwen(3) 7 45
(WMBrisbourne) *prom: led 5f out: rdn 2f out: hdd & wknd ins fnl f* **11/1**

5115 **6** 5 **Landescent (IRE)**[35] 1181 4-9-7 **50** MrsSMoore(3) 2 40
(MissKMGeorge) *led tl hdd 5f out: hung rt and wknd fr 2f out* **12/1**

5040 **7** 3½ **Top Of The Class (IRE)**[31] 1535 7-9-13 **56** (v) MissEFolkes(3) 3 39
(PDEvans) *chsd ldrs tl wknd 2f out* **14/1**

000- **8** *shd* **Senior Minister**[278] 4220 6-10-4 **63** MrsMarieKing(5) 9 46
(PWHiatt) *chsd ldrs: plld hrd: rdn: hung rt and wknd over 2f out* **40/1**

20-0 **9** 5 **Larking About (USA)**[13] 1962 4-10-1 **62** MsAmyBoeder(7) 1 36
(WJMusson) *s.i.s: bhd most of way* **50/1**

6530 **10** *shd* **Chakra**[10] 2017 10-8-9 **40** MissFayeBramley(5) 8 14
(CJGray) *chsd ldrs over 6f* **50/1**

3411 **P** **Absolute Utopia (USA)**[24] 1687 11-10-9 **63** MissEJJones 12 —
(JLSpearing) *p.u and dismntd after 3f* **11/2**[3]

2m 11.07s (0.07) **Going Correction** +0.10s/f (Good) **11** Ran SP% **114.9**
Speed ratings: **103,101,100,99,99 95,92,92,88,88** —CSF £24.21 CT £189.16 TOTE £5.70: £2.60, £2.60, £3.50; EX 28.60.
**Owner** Roger Parry **Bred** G Coull **Trained** Kingsclere, Hants

**FOCUS**
The second win of the week for Voice Mail, who is in hot form at present, but a weakish affair..

**NOTEBOOK**
**Voice Mail** came from a long way back to win going away, following up his win earlier in the week. He is clearly thriving and there is every chance of him completing the hat-trick if turned out quickly, but he is likely to struggle when reassessed.
**He Who Dares(IRE)** came from a similar position to the winner, but did not have the legs to go with Voice Mail. He remains in good form.
**Saxe-Coburg(IRE)** seems to be at his best with some cut in the ground and these fast conditions would not have played to his strengths.
**Holly Rose** is back down to a winning mark, but she had her chance and was not up to it on the day.
**Rainstorm** went for it early and was always going to leave himself vulnerable.
**Absolute Utopia(USA)**evidently went wrong and the run is best ignored.

## 2263 E B F / CHLOE TWO YEARS ON MAIDEN STKS 5f 161y
6:35 (6:40) (D) 2-Y-O **£4,400** (£1,354; £677; £338) **Stalls** Low

Form RPR

**1** **Hoh Hoh Hoh** 2-9-0 MartinDwyer 1 87+
(AMBalding) *t.k.h: trckd ldrs: n.m.r and edgd rt ins fnl 2f: qcknd to ld appr fnl f: sn clr: easily* **5/2**[1]

5 **2** 7 **Come Good**[11] 1996 2-9-0 DaneO'Neill 7 59
(RHannon) *chsd ldrs: chalng whn bmpd ins fnl 2f: chsd wnr fnl f but no ch* **11/4**[2]

0 **3** 5 **Agilete**[17] 1853 2-9-0 SDrowne 5 41
(LGCottrell) *trckd ldr: led appr fnl 2f: sn rdn: hdd appr fnl f: wknd ins last* **7/2**[3]

**4** 4 **Master Joseph** 2-9-0 CCatlin 8 27
(MRChannon) *sn outpcd and wl bhd: styd on fr 2f out but n.d* **5/1**

54 **5** 2½ **Iam Foreverblowing**[19] 1798 2-8-6 LPKeniry(3) 3 13
(SCBurrough) *led tl hdd appr fnl 2f: wknd rapidly* **9/1**

6 **6** 2 **Dominer (IRE)**[4] 2164 2-9-0 SCarson 6 11
(JMBradley) *chsd ldrs to 1/2-way: wknd rapidly* **33/1**

**7** ¾ **Sarah Brown (IRE)** 2-8-6 TPQueally(3) 2 4
(IAWood) *a bhd* **14/1**

1m 10.58s (-0.56) **Going Correction** -0.225s/f (Firm) **7** Ran SP% **113.7**
Speed ratings: **94,84,78,72,69 66,65**CSF £9.56 TOTE £3.50: £2.20, £1.70; EX 11.40.
**Owner** D F Allport **Bred** D R Botterill **Trained** Kingsclere, Hants

**FOCUS**
A most impressive performance from Hoh Hoh Hoh, who injected a deadly turn of pace a furlong out and is now Royal Ascot bound.

**NOTEBOOK**
**Hoh Hoh Hoh**, bred to be speedy, simply blitzed his rivals, quickening up most impressively to run right away from his field. Admittedly this was not a strong race, but the manner in which he did it entitles him to go to Royal Ascot, with his trainer reporting he will be entered in the Norfolk, Coventry and Windsor Castle Stakes.
**Come Good** improved on his debut effort on this better ground and beat the remainder well enough. He has a small race in him.
**Agilete** has a similar profile to the second and he too can win races.
**Master Joseph** will appreciate another furlong in time and should come on for the experience.

## 2264 TOTEEXACTA CLASSIFIED STKS 5f 11y
7:05 (7:07) (D) 3-Y-O **£6,643** (£2,044; £1,022; £511) **Stalls** Low

Form RPR

1-52 **1** **Enchantment**[5] 2143 3-8-13 **79** CCatlin 4 91
(JMBradley) *mde all: drvn clr fnl f* **9/4**[1]

0-06 **2** 2½ **Bathwick Bill (USA)**[19] 1797 3-9-2 **80** GBaker 3 85
(BRMillman) *chsd ldrs: hung lft on rail fr 3f out: chsd wnr ins fnl 2f: kpt on but no imp* **5/1**[3]

3-00 **3** 5 **Shielaligh**[38] 1388 3-8-13 **80** (t) DHolland 6 64
(MissGayKelleway) *in tch: pushed along fr 3f out: kpt on fr over 1f out to take 3rd ins last but no ch w ldrs* **5/1**[3]

0-00 **4** ½ **Mirasol Princess**[4] 2181 3-8-13 78 DaneO'Neill 2 62
(DKIvory) *outpcd and sn pushed along: styd on fnl f but n.d* **12/1**
40-0 **5** *shd* **Catch The Wind**[16] 1881 3-8-10 79 TPQueally(3) 7 62
(IAWood) *sn chsng wnr: rdn 3f out: wknd fnl f* **16/1**
-240 **6** ½ **Trick Cyclist**[32] 1504 3-9-2 78 MartinDwyer 9 63
(AMBalding) *outpcd and sn drvn along: styd on fr over 1f out but nvr gng pce to rch ldrs* **3/1**[2]
431- **7** *5* **Corps De Ballet (IRE)**[206] 5812 3-9-2 83 SSanders 5 45
(JLDunlop) *chsd ldrs tl wknd 2f out* **11/2**
0- **8** *1* **Solved (USA)**[229] 5394 3-8-10 79 DNolan(3) 1 38
(PABlockley) *early spd: n.m.r on rails and wknd qckly 3f out* **25/1**

60.16 secs (-2.34) **Going Correction** -0.225s/f (Firm) **8 Ran SP% 121.9**
Speed ratings: **109,105,97,96,96 95,87,85**CSF £15.17 TOTE £3.20: £1.20, £2.50, £1.80; EX 18.50.
**Owner** Ms A M Williams **Bred** Downclose Stud **Trained** Sedbury, Gloucs
■ Stewards Enquiry : T P Queally four-day ban: failed to ride out for fourth place (Jun 1-4)

**FOCUS**
A tight little classified event, with only 5lb separating the field. The first two finished clear in a good time.

**NOTEBOOK**
**Enchantment** ◆ has speed to burn and has been crying out for a drop back to this trip. She does stay further and was always going to be terribly difficult to pass once bagging the lead. There is more to come from her.
**Bathwick Bill(USA)** appreciates this quick ground and stayed on well for a clear second without proving any match for the winner. He is back to last year's best and his winning turn will not be far away.
**Shielaligh** ran well without proving a match for the front two.
**Mirasol Princess** has yet to hit top form this season, but is not far off.
**Catch The Wind** showed good early speed before weakening, her rider dropping his hands close home and costing her fourth spot.
**Trick Cyclist** was never going the pace.

## 2265 CHARLES SAUNDERS FOODSERVICE CLAIMING STKS 5f 11y
7:35 (7:35) (F) 3-Y-O £3,164 (£904; £452) Stalls Low

Form RPR
0-40 **1** **Jinksonthehouse**[8] 2063 3-7-11 57 HayleyTurner(5) 7 58
(MDIUsher) *in tch: hdwy on outside 3f out: chal 2f out: led 1f out: hrd drvn: hung lft and r.o wl* **10/1**
-340 **2** 1¼ **Only If I Laugh**[31] 1517 3-8-2 70 (b) JFMcDonald(3) 5 56
(BJMeehan) *bmpd s: hdwy to trck ldrs 1/2-way: drvn to chal over 1f out: kpt on ins last but nt pce wnr* **7/4**[1]
636- **3** *shd* **Blue Moon Hitman (IRE)**[146] 6246 3-8-11 55 DHolland 3 62?
(RBrotherton) *trckd ldrs: led ins fnl 2f: hdd 1f out: kpt on same pce u.p* **10/1**
1605 **4** *3* **Cut And Dried**[9] 2033 3-9-5 68 MartinDwyer 6 59
(DMSimcock) *sn rdn and outpcd: styd on fnl f but nvr gng pce to trble ldrs* **11/4**[2]
4403 **5** 2½ **Rehia**[9] 2033 3-8-4 53 SWhitworth 2 35
(JWHills) *w ldr: led over 3f out: hdd ins fnl 2f: wknd qckly over 1f out* **7/2**[3]
4003 **6** ½ **Parallel Lines (IRE)**[22] 1725 3-8-5 46 (b) EAhern 4 34
(PDEvans) *bmpd s: rdn to chse ldrs over 3f out: wknd over 2f out* **14/1**
0-00 **7** *9* **Cinnamon Ridge (IRE)**[9] 2029 3-8-4 ow2 (b) LPKeniry(3) 1 —
(BJMeehan) *sn led: hdd over 3f out: sn wknd* **16/1**

61.78 secs (-0.72) **Going Correction** -0.225s/f (Firm) **7 Ran SP% 116.0**
Speed ratings: **96,94,93,89,85 84,69**CSF £28.83 TOTE £15.70: £8.30, £1.40; EX 92.90.Only If I Laugh (no.4) was claimed by P A Blockley for £5,000.
**Owner** Midweek Racing **Bred** Midweek Racing Club **Trained** Upper Lambourn, Berks

**FOCUS**
Favourite Only If I Laugh was well below form and the third looks the best guide to the race. Jinkonthehouse ended up winning a shade cosily.

**NOTEBOOK**
**Jinksonthehouse** had plenty to find with the favourite on official ratings but proved much too strong and won with a little in hand, despite hanging under pressure.
**Only If I Laugh** was easily best in on official figures, but could not make it tell and was a long way below his best again. He may be worth risking back over further.
**Blue Moon Hitman(IRE)** regularly places, but remains winless. *Official explanation: jockey said colt was hanging right in the closing stages.*
**Cut And Dried** was giving away plenty of weight but was well below recent Brighton form and never threatened.
**Rehia** faced a stiff task.

## 2266 CAUDA EQUINA H'CAP 5f 161y
8:05 (8:05) (E) (0-75,72) 3-Y-O £4,299 (£1,323; £661; £330) Stalls Low

Form RPR
1305 **1** **Tag Team (IRE)**[4] 2181 3-9-7 **72** MartinDwyer 7 81
(AMBalding) *mde virtually all: hrd rdn and styd on wl whn strly chal fr ins fnl f* **7/4**[1]
05-0 **2** *hd* **Signor Panettiere**[8] 2063 3-9-2 **67** PDobbs 1 75
(RHannon) *hld up in tch: squeezed through on rails 1f out and str chal ins last tl no ex last strides* **9/2**[2]
40-0 **3** *3* **Melody King**[46] 1270 3-9-2 **67** (b) SDrowne 9 64
(PDEvans) *w wnr: rdn ins fnl 3f: wknd ins fnl f* **14/1**
-050 **4** ¾ **Barabella (IRE)**[17] 1855 3-8-6 **60** JFMcDonald(3) 3 54
(RJHodges) *s.i.s: rdn over 2f out: hung lft u.p over 1f out: kpt on ins last* **7/1**
0306 **5** ½ **Arfinnit (IRE)**[8] 2061 3-8-9 **67** (v) TDean(7) 8 60
(MRChannon) *s.i.s: sn rcvrd: trckd ldrs 3f out: wknd fnl f* **13/2**
50-0 **6** 3½ **Nebraska City**[48] 1243 3-8-13 **64** DaneO'Neill 6 44
(BGubby) *a outpcd* **16/1**
-630 **7** *4* **Off Beat (USA)**[46] 1270 3-9-7 **72** (b) SCarson 5 38
(RFJohnsonHoughton) *chsd ldrs: rdn over 3f out: wknd over 2f out* **11/2**[3]
505- **8** *1* **Jailbird**[207] 5785 3-8-7 **58** SSanders 4 20
(RMBeckett) *chsd ldrs: rdn and wknd fr 1/2-way* **14/1**

1m 11.12s (-0.02) **Going Correction** -0.225s/f (Firm) **8 Ran SP% 115.0**
Speed ratings: **91,90,86,85,85 80,75,73**CSF £9.67 CT £81.98 TOTE £2.80: £1.20, £1.20, £4.10; EX 8.90.
**Owner** Magic Moments **Bred** Miss Sally Hodgins **Trained** Kingsclere, Hants

**FOCUS**
A fair handicap but a poor time, fractionally slower than the juvenile event earlier on the card.

**NOTEBOOK**
**Tag Team(IRE)** made almost every yard and dug deep to hold the challenge of Signor Panettiere in the closing stages, showing a good attitude in the process. He was well treated on his All Weather form.
**Signor Panettiere** ran his best race for a while and may be nearing a win.
**Melody King** was not discredited in third and may appreciate a return to further.
**Barabella(IRE)** plugged on, having been a bit tardy at the gate, and did not look at ease on the ground.

## 2267 WEATHERBYS BANK MEDIAN AUCTION MAIDEN STKS 1m 5y
8:35 (8:35) (F) 3-Y-O £3,437 (£982; £491) Stalls Low

Form RPR
4 **1** **Our Jaffa (IRE)**[34] 1466 3-8-9 JPMurtagh 1 70
(DJDaly) *s.i.s: hld up and sn in tch: swtchd rt to outer 2f out: qcknd to ld ins fnl f: readily* **10/3**[2]
0 **2** 1¼ **Vamp**[35] 1441 3-8-9 SSanders 11 67
(RMBeckett) *hld up in rr: hdwy on outside over 2f out: drvn to chse wnr wl ins last but no imp* **5/1**[3]
**3** *1* **Magic Merlin** 3-9-0 DHolland 9 70
(PWHarris) *chsd ldrs: led over 1f out: hdd ins last and kpt on same pce* **3/1**[1]
0-02 **4** 1¾ **Delightfully**[25] 1679 3-8-9 69 MartinDwyer 6 61
(BWHills) *chsd ldr after 2f: led over 2f out: sn rdn: hdd over 1f out: wknd ins last* **5/1**[3]
00-2 **5** *nk* **Dark Raider (IRE)**[14] 1945 3-8-6 63 DCorby(3) 3 60
(APJones) *chsd ldrs: rdn and outpcd over 2f out: kpt on again fnl f* **10/1**
55-3 **6** ¾ **Carry On Doc**[28] 1597 3-9-0 73 SWhitworth 7 64
(JWHills) *sn led: hdd over 2f out: wknd ins fnl f* **7/1**
000- **7** *1* **Iphigenia (IRE)**[178] 6069 3-8-6 50 RMiles(3) 5 56
(PWHiatt) *chsd ldrs tl wknd 2f out* **66/1**
53-0 **8** *2* **My Michelle**[46] 1270 3-8-9 72 EAhern 8 52
(BPalling) *nvr gng pce to rch ldrs* **16/1**
00-0 **9** ½ **Pleasure Seeker**[19] 1796 3-8-9 ADaly 4 51
(MDIUsher) *s.i.s: a in rr* **20/1**
0-0 **10** 3½ **Seagold**[25] 1674 3-8-9 SDrowne 10 42
(CFWall) *in tch: rdn 3f out: sn wknd* **40/1**
000 **11** *5* **Harry Came Home**[19] 1800 3-8-11 LPKeniry(3) 2 36
(JCFox) *a bhd* **66/1**

1m 42.66s (1.66) **Going Correction** +0.10s/f (Good) **11 Ran SP% 119.1**
Speed ratings: **95,93,92,91,90 89,88,86,86,82 77**CSF £20.21 TOTE £4.00: £2.10, £2.70, £1.30; EX 23.50 Place 6 £13.84, Place 5 £5.03..
**Owner** Miss A H Marshall **Bred** Hamwood Stud **Trained** Newmarket, Suffolk

**FOCUS**
The proximity of the exposed Iphigenia (officially rated only 50) in seventh confirms this is just an ordinary maiden.

**NOTEBOOK**
**Our Jaffa(IRE)** improved on her debut effort and ended up winning with something to spare after a change of pace settled the matter around a furlong out.
**Vamp** improved for this step up to a mile and will improve again for a bit further again.
**Magic Merlin** made a promising debut and can pick up a small race.
**Delightfully** is likely to find life easier in handicaps.
**Dark Raider(IRE)** is another going to be seen to better effect in handicaps.
**Carry On Doc** does not look up to winning a standard maiden and will also find it easier in handicaps.
T/Plt: £42.90 to a £1 stake. Pool: £39,405.15. 669.15 winning tickets. T/Qpdt: £8.50 to a £1 stake. Pool: £2,848.10. 245.60 winning tickets. ST

# 1757 HAYDOCK (L-H)
### Friday, May 21

**OFFICIAL GOING: Good to firm**
Wind: 1/2 behind Weather: overcast

## 2268 STELLA MOLONY MAIDEN AUCTION STKS 5f
2:00 (2:05) (E) 2-Y-O £3,692 (£1,136; £568; £284) Stalls Centre

Form RPR
3 **1** **Beckermet (IRE)**[19] 1782 2-8-2 PBradley(5) 5 73
(RFFisher) *dwlt: trckd ldrs: rdn 2f out: r.o to ld wl ins fnl f* **8/1**[3]
3 **2** *shd* **Space Shuttle**[18] 1819 2-8-4 DAllan(3) 2 73
(TDEasterby) *w ldrs: rdn over 2f out: ev ch wl ins fnl f: r.o u.p* **6/4**[1]
03 **3** *hd* **Gifted Gamble**[25] 1658 2-8-7 (b[1]) NCallan 10 72
(KARyan) *dwlt and carried lft s: sn prom: led 3f out: hdd wl ins fnl f* **12/1**
2630 **4** 1½ **I'm Aimee**[16] 1878 2-8-2 GDuffield 11 61
(PDEvans) *wnt lft s: led: hdd 3f out: cl 4th and rdn whn n.m.r ins fnl f: styd on same pce* **11/4**[2]
**5** *1* **Amphitheatre (IRE)** 2-8-7 SCarson 1 62
(RFJohnsonHoughton) *midfield: rdn over 2f out: kpt on fnl f: nt pce to chal* **20/1**
00 **6** *10* **Morning World**[17] 1865 2-8-9 KDalgleish 6 24
(JRWeymes) *trckd ldrs: rdn over 2f out: wknd over 1f out* **66/1**
**7** *hd* **Bold Minstrel (IRE)** 2-8-7 FNorton 4 21
(MQuinn) *a outpcd* **8/1**[3]
**8** *2* **Dan's Heir** 2-8-7 GFaulkner 9 —
(PCHaslam) *slowly away and hmpd s: a outpcd* **33/1**
**9** 1½ **Courtintime** 2-8-2 JQuinn 3 —
(TDEasterby) *dwlt: midfield: rdn over 2f out: sn wknd* **33/1**
**10** *2* **Oldstead Flyer (IRE)** 2-8-7 RFitzpatrick 7 —
(DCarroll) *s.s: towards rr: sn pushed along: nvr on terms* **50/1**
**11** *3* **Countrywide Dream (IRE)** 2-8-7 DHolland 8 —
(ABerry) *dwlt and wnt rt s: a outpcd* **20/1**

60.72 secs (-1.35) **Going Correction** -0.325s/f (Firm) **11 Ran SP% 115.4**
Speed ratings: **97,96,96,94,92 76,76,73,70,67 62**CSF £18.73 TOTE £10.90: £3.10, £1.10, £2.00; EX 19.20.
**Owner** Great Head House Estates Limited **Bred** Fritz Von Ball Moss **Trained** Ulverston, Cumbria

**FOCUS**
A modest maiden and just average form.

**NOTEBOOK**
**Beckermet(IRE)** had run too freely on his debut at Musselburgh but settled better this time. She just got up in a close finish and shapes as though she will appreciate a step up to six.
**Space Shuttle**, whose debut form looked the strongest coming into the race, may have found the faster ground against him. He stayed on well, though, and is another likely to benefit from a step up to six.
**Gifted Gamble** raced prominently in the first-time blinkers but was cut down in the closing stages. This was a modest event and he will always be vulnerable to something with a bit more potential.
**I'm Aimee** showed pace, but she failed to get home despite the quicker ground.
**Amphitheatre(IRE)**, a half-brother to three winners, did best of the newcomers and pulled nicely clear of the rest.
**Bold Minstrel(IRE)** came in for some support but disappointed his followers on his debut.

## 2269 PERFORMANCE CAR HIRE H'CAP 6f
2:35 (2:37) (D) (0-85,81) 3-Y-O £6,077 (£1,870; £935; £467) Stalls Centre

Form RPR
4131 **1** **Bridgewater Boys**[8] 2063 3-8-7 67 5ex (b) NCallan 3 76
(KARyan) *in tch: rdn and hdwy 2f out: led ins fnl f: r.o* **10/1**

| Form | Pos | Dist | Horse | Jockey | RPR |
|---|---|---|---|---|---|
| 10-4 | 2 | shd | **Flipando (IRE)**$^{23}$ [1702] 3-9-1 **75** (TDBarron) *midfield: pushed along 3f out: hdwy 2f out: ev ch ins fnl f: r.o u.p* **7/1** | DHolland 2 | 83 |
| 40-4 | 3 | hd | **Delphie Queen (IRE)**$^{7}$ [2082] 3-9-7 **81** (SKirk) *hld up: rdn and hdwy wl over 1f out: edgd lft ins fnl f and sn swtchd rt: r.o strly cl home: nrst fin* **11/2**$^{2}$ | RHughes 11 | 89 |
| 16-2 | 4 | hd | **Red Romeo**$^{27}$ [1614] 3-9-1 **75** (GASwinbank) *led: rdn 2f out: edgd lft and sn hdd ins fnl f: nt qckn cl home* **7/1** | DaleGibson 9 | 82 |
| 1-53 | 5 | nk | **Treasure Cay**$^{20}$ [1775] 3-9-1 **75** (PWD'Arcy) *s.s: in rr: rdn 2f out: hdwy over 1f out: ch ins fnl f: hld cl home* **14/1** | (bt$^{1}$) PaulEddery 5 | 81 |
| 5113 | 6 | 3 ½ | **He's A Rocket (IRE)**$^{14}$ [1934] 3-8-3 **63** (KRBurke) *w ldrs: rdn 2f out: edgd rt 1f out: no ex ins fnl f* **12/1** | (b) JQuinn 10 | 59 |
| 0052 | 7 | ½ | **Lets Get It On (IRE)**$^{7}$ [2075] 3-9-1 **75** (JJQuinn) *chsd ldrs: rdn over 2f out: forced to go rt 1f out: no ex ins fnl f* **13/2**$^{3}$ | KDalgleish 12 | 69 |
| 0-10 | 8 | ¾ | **Commando Scott (IRE)**$^{16}$ [1881] 3-8-11 **76** (ABerry) *prom: rdn 2f out: wknd ins fnl f* **33/1** | PBradley$^{(5)}$ 4 | 68 |
| 21-5 | 9 | 2 | **Ace Club**$^{16}$ [1881] 3-8-13 **73** (WJHaggas) *racd keenly: in tch: rdn over 2f out: wknd over 1f out* **9/2**$^{1}$ | MHills 7 | 59 |
| 0-30 | 10 | nk | **Stormy Nature (IRE)**$^{23}$ [1702] 3-9-1 **75** (PWHarris) *prom: rdn 2f out: wknd ins fnl f* **16/1** | EAhern 1 | 60 |
| 006- | 11 | nk | **Mind Alert**$^{235}$ [5273] 3-8-9 **72** (TDEasterby) *prom tl rdn and wknd over 1f out* **50/1** | DAllan$^{(3)}$ 6 | 56 |
| 000- | 12 | 1 | **Shamrock Tea**$^{184}$ [6029] 3-7-7 **60** (RAFahey) *in tch: rdn and wknd 2f out* **25/1** | NataliaGemelova$^{(7)}$ 8 | 41 |
| 100- | 13 | 13 | **Orpenberry (IRE)**$^{277}$ [4242] 3-8-12 **72** (JBalding) *a bhd* **40/1** | JEdmunds 13 | 14 |

1m 12.87s (-2.02) **Going Correction** -0.325s/f (Firm) **13** Ran SP% **112.4**
Speed ratings: **100,99,99,99,98 94,93,92,89,89 89,87,70**CSF £71.31 CT £438.00 TOTE £11.20: £3.40, £3.00, £1.90; EX 74.00.
**Owner** Bishopthorpe Racing **Bred** Southill Stud **Trained** Hambleton, N Yorks

**FOCUS**
This looked a competitive heat on paper with a few in-form performers taking on lightly raced, unexposed types open to improvement. The first five finished clear, and the form should work out.

**NOTEBOOK**
**Bridgewater Boys** has been in cracking form of late and a 5lb penalty for his Salisbury victory was not enough to stop him notching his third win in his last four starts. A progressive three-year-old, he has the stamina for seven.
**Flipando(IRE)** showed the benefit of his reappearance outing at Ascot and came close to opening his account for the year. He clearly acts on this faster surface just as well.
**Delphie Queen(IRE)** ran another promising race, but her style of running suggests she will be seen to best effect on a stiffer track.
**Red Romeo**, first home on the wrong side at Ripon last time, once again showed plenty of pace for one who has won over seven furlongs.
**Treasure Cay** was slowly away but finished to good effect. He still gives the impression that he needs to drop a pound or two.
**He's A Rocket(IRE)** is probably happier over five furlongs.
**Lets Get It On(IRE)** was racing on ground quicker than she has encountered so far this term.
**Ace Club**, who may have been flattered at Chester when running on through beaten horses, was tackling quicker ground on this occasion.
**Stormy Nature(IRE)** *Official explanation: jockey said filly had hung left*
**Orpenberry(IRE)** *Official explanation: vet said filly was in season*

## 2270 HAYDOCK PARK ANNUAL BADGEHOLDERS MAIDEN STKS — 1m 30y
**3:05** (3:06) (D) 3-Y-O — **£6,019** (£1,852; £926; £463) **Stalls** Low

| Form | Pos | Dist | Horse | Jockey | RPR |
|---|---|---|---|---|---|
| 2-34 | 1 | | **Brindisi**$^{19}$ [1793] 3-8-9 89 (BWHills) *trckd ldrs: 2f out: r.o* **2/5**$^{1}$ | MHills 5 | 70+ |
| 0-0 | 2 | 1 ½ | **Adaikali (IRE)**$^{20}$ [1771] 3-9-0 (SirMichaelStoute) *in tch: hdwy over 2f out: rdn to go 2nd over 1f out: hung lft ins f: styd on: nt trble wnr* **14/1** | BDoyle 3 | 72 |
| | 3 | 2 | **Nordwind (IRE)** 3-9-0 (PWHarris) *s.s: bhd: pushed along 4f out: hdwy over 2f out: rn green and hung lft ins fnl f: kpt on: nt trble ldrs* **10/1**$^{2}$ | DHolland 1 | 67 |
| 3 | 4 | 1 ¾ | **Foolish Groom**$^{41}$ [1325] 3-9-0 (RHollinshead) *towards rr: rdn 4f out: outpcd over 2f out: styd on fnl f* **16/1** | DaleGibson 10 | 63 |
| | 5 | shd | **First Counsel** 3-9-0 (MAJarvis) *hld up: effrt 2f out: one pce ins fnl f* **12/1**$^{3}$ | PRobinson 7 | 63 |
| 6 | 6 | 2 | **Acuzio**$^{20}$ [1761] 3-8-9 (WMBrisbourne) *in tch: rdn and hdwy over 2f out: wknd ins fnl f* **100/1** | BSwarbrick$^{(5)}$ 8 | 58 |
| 0-6 | 7 | 1 | **Moscow Blue**$^{30}$ [1541] 3-9-0 (JHMGosden) *prom: rdn and ev ch 2f out: wknd over 1f out: btn whn n.m.r ins fnl f* **12/1**$^{3}$ | RHughes 9 | 56 |
| | 8 | 4 | **Desert Leader (IRE)** 3-9-0 (BAMcmahon) *s.v.s: bhd: rdn 4f out: hdwy 2f out: wknd over 1f out* **40/1** | GGibbons 2 | 47 |
| 000- | 9 | ½ | **Calculaite**$^{165}$ [6142] 3-8-11 (MrsGSRees) *led: rdn and hdd 2f out: sn wknd* **100/1** | NMackay$^{(3)}$ 6 | 46 |

1m 42.17s (-3.38) **Going Correction** -0.325s/f (Firm) **9** Ran SP% **112.9**
Speed ratings: **103,101,99,97,97 95,94,90,90**CSF £7.21 TOTE £1.40: £1.10, £3.10, £2.20; EX 7.40.
**Owner** M H Dixon **Bred** Exors Of The Late R D Hollingsworth **Trained** Lambourn, Berks

**FOCUS**
An uncompetitive maiden in which Brindisi did not need to run anywhere near her Pretty Polly form.

**NOTEBOOK**
**Brindisi** stood out beforehand on her Listed-grade form behind Oaks fancy Ouija Board at Newmarket, and had little trouble beating an average bunch with ease. This trip looked more suitable, although she did not have to run up to her best to win here.
**Adaikali(IRE)** ran on well enough for second despite hanging under pressure. He is now eligible for a mark, and while on breeding one would not assume that he will improve for a step up in trip, his style of running gives some hope in that direction.
**Nordwind(IRE)** shaped with promise on his debut, staying on from the rear despite running green. He is a half-brother to several winners in Germany and the stayer Numitas, and looks to have a future. *Official explanation: jockey said colt persistently hung left in the final 2f*
**Foolish Groom** came home well, building on the promise of his debut. He looks to need farther.
**First Counsel**, making his debut, is a half-brother to a couple of moderate older winners over distances between six and ten furlongs.
**Moscow Blue** once again disappointed, the fast ground failing to bring about improvement.
**Desert Leader(IRE)** *Official explanation: jockey said colt sat down in the stalls and was slowly away*

## 2271 GOLBORNE RATED STKS (H'CAP) — 1m 30y
**3:40** (3:42) (C) (0-90,86) 4-Y-O+ — **£10,151** (£3,123; £1,561; £780) **Stalls** Low

| Form | Pos | Dist | Horse | Jockey | RPR |
|---|---|---|---|---|---|
| 2200 | 1 | | **Blue Trojan (IRE)**$^{2}$ [2226] 4-8-13 **78** (SKirk) *led 1f: remained prom: led 1f out: sn edgd lft: r.o: eased cl home* **14/1** | FNorton 1 | 89+ |
| -034 | 2 | 1 ¼ | **Young Mr Grace (IRE)**$^{20}$ [1772] 4-8-6 **74** (TDEasterby) *chsd ldr: led 2f out: hdd 1f out: nt qckn towards fin* **14/1** | DAllan$^{(3)}$ 2 | 82 |
| 4601 | 3 | ¾ | **Intricate Web (IRE)**$^{5}$ [2142] 8-8-12 **77** 3ex (EJAlston) *hld up: nt clr run over 2f out: rdn and hdwy over 1f out: r.o ins fnl f* **10/1** | JQuinn 8 | 83+ |
| 1-01 | 4 | nk | **Flowerdrum (USA)**$^{39}$ [1372] 4-9-4 **83** (WJHaggas) *midfield: rdn over 2f out: hdwy over 1f out: edgd lft ins fnl f: kpt on* **5/1**$^{2}$ | RHughes 12 | 89 |
| 113- | 5 | hd | **Ettrick Water**$^{236}$ [5252] 5-9-7 **86** (LMCumani) *led after 1f: rdn and hdd 2f out: no ex ins fnl f* **9/2**$^{1}$ | (v) DHolland 10 | 91 |
| 3010 | 6 | hd | **Harry Potter (GER)**$^{20}$ [1772] 5-8-6 **71** (KRBurke) *in tch: rdn and hdwy over 2f out: hung lft after: one pce cl home* **16/1** | (v) DSweeney 9 | 76 |
| -100 | 7 | 1 ½ | **Uhoomagoo**$^{20}$ [1773] 6-9-2 **81** (KARyan) *hld up: rdn over 3f out: hdwy over 2f out: keeping on whn nt clr run ins fnl f: sn eased* **9/1** | (b) NCallan 3 | 82 |
| 042- | 8 | ¾ | **Sheriff's Deputy**$^{214}$ [5683] 4-8-7 **72** (JWUnett) *hld up: rdn 2f out: nvr able to chal* **25/1** | SWKelly 11 | 72 |
| 4-04 | 9 | nk | **Cherished Number**$^{20}$ [1773] 5-9-0 **79** (ISemple) *hld up: rdn over 3f out: nvr able to chal* **10/1** | KDalgleish 4 | 78 |
| 0-06 | 10 | nk | **Namroud (USA)**$^{48}$ [1246] 5-9-7 **86** (RAFahey) *chsd ldrs: rdn 2f out: wkng whn n.m.r ins fnl f: sn eased* **11/2**$^{3}$ | EAhern 6 | 84 |
| 26-3 | 11 | 3 ½ | **Qualitair Wings**$^{20}$ [1772] 5-8-8 **73** (JHetherton) *s.s: rdn over 2f out: a bhd* **12/1** | GDuffield 7 | 63 |
| 60-0 | 12 | 1 | **Band**$^{23}$ [1708] 4-8-7 **72** (BAMcmahon) *midfield: hdwy over 3f out: sn rdn: wknd fnl f* **33/1** | GGibbons 5 | 60 |

1m 41.24s (-4.31) **Going Correction** -0.325s/f (Firm) **12** Ran SP% **112.1**
Speed ratings: **108,106,106,105,105 105,103,103,102,102 98,97**CSF £185.67 CT £2060.60 TOTE £21.70: £8.70, £4.90, £2.80; EX 203.20 Trifecta £3706.60 Part won. Pool £5,220.61 - 0.90 winning units..
**Owner** The Ex Katy Boys **Bred** Patrick Cassidy **Trained** Upper Lambourn, Berks

**FOCUS**
The betting suggested this was a tight handicap and the form looks sound.

**NOTEBOOK**
**Blue Trojan(IRE)** had failed to act around Goodwood earlier in the week according to his trainer, and found this fairer track far more to his liking. He won cosily and should be capable of building on this. *Official explanation: trainer said, regarding the improved form shown, gelding had met trouble in running at Goodwood last time*
**Young Mr Grace(IRE)** is on a fair mark at present and ran another sound race. He appeared to see out this longer trip well enough.
**Intricate Web(IRE)**, a winner over ten furlongs last time, had to wait for a split to appear and finished all too late. He will appreciate a return to farther.
**Flowerdrum(USA)**, terribly weak in the market, was poorly drawn and had a 7lb higher mark to overcome. She had every chance.
**Ettrick Water**, popular in the market, crossed over to make the runnning, but the way he tired in the closing stages suggests he needed this reappearance outing.
**Harry Potter(GER)** was racing on ground he would have found plenty quick enough.
**Namroud(USA)** was down to a 1lb lower mark than when last successful, but he was beaten a fair way out and has questions to answer now. *Official explanation: jockey said gelding had been unsuited by the ground*

## 2272 GEORGE FORMBY CENTENARY STKS (H'CAP) — 1m 2f 120y
**4:10** (4:10) (E) (0-75,75) 4-Y-O+ — **£3,770** (£1,160; £580; £290) **Stalls** High

| Form | Pos | Dist | Horse | Jockey | RPR |
|---|---|---|---|---|---|
| 50-4 | 1 | | **Smart John**$^{14}$ [1944] 4-8-13 **60** (WMBrisbourne) *in tch: rdn and hdwy over 2f out: led over 1f out: rdn out* **10/1** | SWKelly 2 | 67 |
| 0050 | 2 | 1 | **Nuzzle**$^{14}$ [1940] 4-8-0 **47** (MQuinn) *chsd ldr: rdn to ld over 2f out: stl ev ch ins fnl f: styd on* **14/1** | FNorton 10 | 52 |
| -050 | 3 | nk | **Rotuma (IRE)**$^{25}$ [1660] 5-9-1 **62** (MDods) *chsd ldrs: rdn 4f out: clsd over 2f out: kpt on ins fnl f* **11/2**$^{2}$ | (b) EAhern 7 | 67 |
| 4012 | 4 | shd | **Lawood (IRE)**$^{34}$ [1470] 4-10-0 **75** (KARyan) *hld up: hdwy over 2f out: rdn over 2f out: kpt on ins fnl f* **9/2**$^{1}$ | NCallan 4 | 80 |
| 0050 | 5 | ½ | **Compton Dragon (USA)**$^{5}$ [2142] 5-10-0 **75** (DNicholls) *hld up: rdn and hdwy over 1f out: kpt on ins fnl f* **9/1** | ANicholls 11 | 79 |
| 044- | 6 | 5 | **Glen Vale Walk (IRE)**$^{307}$ [3393] 7-7-11 **47** (MrsGSRees) *s.s: hld up: hdwy over 4f out: rdn 2f out: eased whn btn ins fnl f* **16/1** | (b) NMackay$^{(3)}$ 3 | 42 |
| 00-4 | 7 | 3 ½ | **Sir Night (IRE)**$^{3}$ [2216] 4-8-6 **53** (JeddO'Keeffe) *midfield: rdn over 3f out: no imp* **9/2**$^{1}$ | DHolland 8 | 42 |
| 1500 | 8 | 1 ¾ | **Mi Odds**$^{57}$ [1109] 8-9-6 **67** (MrsNMacauley) *midfield: lost pl 5f out: n.d after* **8/1**$^{3}$ | PRobinson 6 | 53 |
| 224- | 9 | ½ | **Iftikhar (USA)**$^{270}$ [4463] 5-9-2 **63** (WMBrisbourne) *s.s: hld up: rdn 4f out: nvr on terms* **20/1** | KDalgleish 5 | 48 |
| -054 | 10 | nk | **Libre**$^{23}$ [1715] 4-9-3 **64** (RCGuest) *prom: rdn over 2f out: wknd over 1f out* **8/1**$^{3}$ | (p) DeanMcKeown 9 | 49 |
| 000- | 11 | 6 | **Luxor**$^{224}$ [5468] 7-7-7 **45** oh5 (WMBrisbourne) *led: rdn and hdd over 2f out: sn wknd* **20/1** | (p) BSwarbrick$^{(5)}$ 1 | 20 |

2m 15.04s (-2.69) **Going Correction** -0.325s/f (Firm) **11** Ran SP% **115.1**
Speed ratings: **96,95,95,94,94 90,88,87,86,86 82**CSF £138.44 CT £843.91 TOTE £11.40: £3.00, £3.30, £3.10; EX 159.90.
**Owner** Mr & Mrs D J Smart **Bred** D J And Mrs K D Smart **Trained** Great Ness, Shropshire

**FOCUS**
A modest heat, but the leader set a decent pace up front.

**NOTEBOOK**
**Smart John** returned to his best and finally got off the mark at the ninth attempt, but on only his second start for his present stable. He had got tired in bad ground on his reappearance at Nottingham but showed the benefit of that outing here, keeping on gamely when rivals came to challenge.
**Nuzzle** is undeniably well handicapped on a lot of the form she showed last season, but the fact that she took 23 races to get off the mark, and has not won in her six starts since, makes one question her will to win.
**Rotuma(IRE)**, down to a 2lb higher mark than when last successful, appears to go on any ground and posted an encouraging effort.
**Lawood(IRE)** kept on well and looks worth trying over a mile and a half again.
**Compton Dragon(USA)**, a smart performer a couple of years ago, ran a respectable race but probably still needs to drop a pound or two before he will be winning again.
**Glen Vale Walk(IRE)** could probably have finished right behind the leading group of five had he not been eased inside the last.

**Sir Night(IRE)** may have found this race coming too quickly after his effort at Redcar three days earlier.
**Mi Odds** *Official explanation: jockey said gelding had been unsuited by the ground*

## 2273 CRANKWOOD MAIDEN STKS — 1m 3f 200y
**4:45** (4:49) (D ) 3-Y-O+ — **£5,668** (£1,744; £872; £436) **Stalls** High

| Form | Pos | Dist | Horse | Jockey | RPR |
|---|---|---|---|---|---|
| 26 | 1 | | **Strike**[19] 1800 3-8-9 (JHMGosden) *s.i.s: hld up: hdwy over 4f out: led over 1f out: rdn out* **2/1**[1] | RHughes 5 | 79 |
| 2 | 2 | ¾ | **Woolly Back (IRE)**[27] 1605 3-8-9 (RHollinshead) *racd keenly: chsd ldrs: rdn and nt qckn 3f out: r.o cl home* **11/2** | DaleGibson 9 | 78 |
| 02 | 3 | nk | **Stocking Island**[27] 1619 3-8-4 (BHanbury) *racd keenly: prom: led 4f out: rdn 3f out: hdd over 1f out: no ex cl home* **3/1**[2] | GDuffield 3 | 73 |
| | 4 | 1½ | **Pope's Hill (IRE)**[215] 3-8-9 (LMCumani) *midfield: pushed along most of way: lost pl over 4f out: rdr dropped whip ent fnl f: styd on wl: nrst fin* **7/2**[3] | DHolland 1 | 75 |
| 5- | 5 | 5 | **Double Turn**[334] 2600 4-9-12 (WMBrisbourne) *sn led: hdd 4f out: sn rdn: wknd over 1f out* **50/1** | KDalgleish 2 | 67 |
| 360- | 6 | ¾ | **Turner**[219] 5578 3-8-9 73 (WMBrisbourne) *hld up: hdwy over 3f out: rdn over 2f out: nvr trbld ldrs* **20/1** | SWKelly 7 | 66 |
| 00- | 7 | 11 | **Heart Springs**[209] 5755 4-9-7 (DrJRJNaylor) *sn prom: rdn and wknd over 3f out* **100/1** | DSweeney 8 | 43 |
| 2-5 | 8 | 12 | **Kelbrook**[13] 1972 5-9-12 (ABailey) *s.s: a bhd* **16/1** | VSlattery 4 | 29 |
| 05 | 9 | 28 | **Ba Clubman (IRE)**[15] 1912 4-9-12 (SCWilliams) *chsd ldrs tl wknd 5f out* **50/1** | (p) BDoyle 6 | — |

2m 33.22s (-1.94) **Going Correction** -0.325s/f (Firm)
**WFA** 3 from 4yo+ 17lb — **9** Ran SP% **111.5**
Speed ratings: **93,92,92,91,87 87,80,72,53**CSF £12.64 TOTE £2.50: £1.50, £1.20, £1.60; EX 11.70.
**Owner** Duke Of Devonshire **Bred** Side Hill Stud **Trained** Manton, Wilts

**FOCUS**
An average maiden and a slow time.. The winner was below his debut form.

**NOTEBOOK**
**Strike**, who may not have handled the ground at Salisbury when sent off favourite but beaten a fair way by his stablemate Day Flight, was not impressive but did see the trip out well. This was just an ordinary maiden and connections will be hoping for a lenient mark from the Handicapper.
**Woolly Back(IRE)** stayed on well to finish runner-up again, despite the ground being much faster than when he was last here. He will stay farther than this.
**Stocking Island** is a keen-going sort and is likely to do better when she can employ her front-running tactics around a sharp track.
**Pope's Hill(IRE)** came home well on his British debut, despite his rider dropping his whip. A half-brother to three winners, he should command plenty of respect once he is eligible for handicaps.
**Double Turn** was soon brushed aside when the principals came to challenge. He looked one-paced.
**Turner**, making his debut for his new stable, looked an awkward ride and clearly has his own ideas about the game.
**Heart Springs** *Official explanation: jockey said filly slipped on the home bend and subsequently lost her action*
**Ba Clubman(IRE)** *Official explanation: jockey said gelding hung right up the straight*

## 2274 MONKS HEATH APPRENTICE H'CAP — 5f
**5:15** (5:15) (E ) (0-75,75) 3-Y-O+ — **£3,939** (£1,212; £606; £303) **Stalls** Centre

| Form | Pos | Dist | Horse | Jockey | RPR |
|---|---|---|---|---|---|
| 0620 | 1 | | **Byo (IRE)**[14] 1937 6-9-3 **69** (MQuinn) *a.p: rdn 2f out: led narrowly 1f out: r.o u.p* **9/1** | KMay(5) 8 | 77 |
| 0-52 | 2 | hd | **Valiant Romeo**[17] 1870 4-8-2 **54** (RBastiman) *led: rdn 2f out: hdd narrowly 1f out: r.o u.p* **9/2**[1] | (v) SaleemGolam(5) 9 | 61 |
| -000 | 3 | ½ | **Whistler**[6] 2130 7-9-9 **75** (JMBradley) *hld up: hdwy over 1f out: sn rdn: ev ch ins fnl f: nt qckn* **13/2**[3] | (p) CJDavies(5) 3 | 80 |
| 2055 | 4 | hd | **Malahide Express (IRE)**[17] 1870 4-8-5 **55** (EJAlston) *chsd ldrs: rdn over 1f out: ev ch ins fnl f: nt qckn* **8/1** | JDO'Reilly(3) 2 | 59 |
| 0120 | 5 | ½ | **Dunn Deal (IRE)**[6] 2118 4-9-4 **65** (WMBrisbourne) *broke wl: towards rr after 1f: rdn 2f out: hdwy over 1f out: styd on ins fnl f* **6/1**[2] | BSwarbrick 4 | 67 |
| 5-05 | 6 | 1¾ | **Boanerges (IRE)**[17] 1872 7-8-10 **57** (JMBradley) *hld up: rdn and hdwy 2f out: kpt on ins fnl f* **15/2** | PMakin 6 | 52 |
| 0-00 | 7 | 1 | **Beyond Calculation (USA)**[6] 2118 10-9-3 **64** (JMBradley) *midfield: rdn 3f out: nt pce to chal* **20/1** | LTreadwell 5 | 55 |
| 006- | 8 | nk | **Loughlorien (IRE)**[220] 5561 5-8-7 **54** (RAFahey) *midfield: rdn over 2f out: nvr trbld ldrs* **9/1** | NataliaGemelova 7 | 44 |
| -004 | 9 | 3 | **Quicks The Word**[17] 1872 4-8-13 **63** (CWThornton) *midfield: rdn 3f out: wknd over 1f out* **11/1** | (b) DFentiman(3) 10 | 41 |
| 0060 | 10 | 1 | **Telepathic (IRE)**[14] 1929 4-9-3 **64** (ABerry) *hld up: hdwy 2f out: sn rdn: wknd 1f out* **25/1** | PPMathers 1 | 38 |
| -000 | 11 | ½ | **Tommy Smith**[6] 2130 6-9-11 **72** (JSWainwright) *chsd ldrs: rdn over 2f out: wknd over 1f out* **8/1** | (b) SJDonohoe 11 | 44 |

59.86 secs (-2.21) **Going Correction** -0.325s/f (Firm) — **11** Ran SP% **116.7**
Speed ratings: **104,103,102,102,101 98,97,96,92,90 89**CSF £48.88 CT £290.42 TOTE £16.50: £4.50, £2.60, £2.50; EX 191.20 Place 6 £194.38, Place 5 £111.59.
**Owner** J G Dooley **Bred** E Johnston **Trained** Sparsholt, Oxon

**FOCUS**
A tight handicap, but ordinary form.

**NOTEBOOK**
**Byo(IRE)** did not run too well last time but his two previous efforts on ground much softer than he would ideally like suggested he was up to winning off this sort of mark, although his poor strike-rate will always be a concern when considering a win-only bet.
**Valiant Romeo** had the visor back on and showed plenty of dash to cut out the running for the majority of the race. He only went down narrowly and his turn is close.
**Whistler**, drawn on the wrong side at Thirsk last time, ran as though he is hitting form. He is slipping in the ratings and can take advantage before too long.
**Malahide Express(IRE)** ran another decent race but has a terrible strike-rate.
**Dunn Deal(IRE)** could not pick up as well on this quicker surface.
**Boanerges(IRE)** should have done a bit better than this, as the ground was in his favour this time.
T/Jkpt: £50,414.20 to a £1 stake. Pool: £71,006.00. 1.00 winning ticket. T/Plt: £322.70 to a £1 stake. Pool: £43,594.85. 98.60 winning tickets. T/Qpdt: £60.60 to a £1 stake. Pool: £2,481.50. 30.30 winning tickets. DO

# [1789]NEWMARKET (R-H)
Friday, May 21

**OFFICIAL GOING: Good to firm**

## 2275 POSTTS VODAFONE TOP-UP VOUCHER MAIDEN FILLIES' STKS — 6f
**2:10** (2:16) (D ) 2-Y-O — **£4,745** (£1,460; £730; £365) **Stalls** High

| Form | Pos | Dist | Horse | Jockey | RPR |
|---|---|---|---|---|---|
| | 1 | | **Heres The Plan (IRE)** 2-8-11 (MGQuinlan) *neat: trckd ldrs: edgd lft ins fnl f: r.o to ld post* **25/1** | PMcCabe 9 | 73 |
| | 2 | shd | **Beautiful Mover (USA)** 2-8-11 (JWHills) *cmpt: bkwd: dwlt: hld up: hdwy 1/2-way: led over 1f out: rdn and edgd rt ins fnl f: hdd post* **5/1**[3] | RHills 7 | 73 |
| | 3 | 1½ | **Catch A Star** 2-8-11 (NACallaghan) *leggy: scope: w ldrs: rdn to ld 2f out: hdd over 1f out: unable qck ins fnl f* **7/2**[2] | JPMurtagh 10 | 68 |
| | 4 | ½ | **Thunder Calling (USA)** 2-8-11 (PFICole) *w'like: chsd ldrs: rdn and ev ch over 1f out: styng on same pce whn n.m.r ins fnl f* **3/1**[1] | KFallon 4 | 67 |
| | 5 | nk | **Aberdovey** 2-8-11 (MLWBell) *lt-fr:leggy: chsd ldrs: nt clr run over 1f out: styd on* **10/1** | IMongan 6 | 66 |
| 53 | 6 | 2 | **Baileys Applause**[11] 2002 2-8-11 (CADwyer) *b.hind: hld up: hdwy and nt clr run over 1f out: nt trble ldrs* **14/1** | SDrowne 1 | 60 |
| | 7 | 2½ | **Moon Mischief (IRE)** 2-8-11 (NPLittmoden) *w'like: led after 1f: rdn and hdd 2f out: wknd fnl f* **7/1** | TGMcLaughlin 11 | 53 |
| | 8 | 5 | **Ladruca** 2-8-11 (RHannon) *lt-fr: leggy: scope: sn outpcd* **10/1** | RLMoore 2 | 38 |
| | 9 | nk | **Jay (IRE)** 2-8-11 (NACallaghan) *b.bkwd: w'like: scope: s.s: outpcd* **25/1** | WRyan 5 | 37 |
| | 10 | 3½ | **Time For You** 2-8-11 (PJMcbride) *w'like: led 1f: wknd over 2f out* **33/1** | SSanders 8 | 26 |

1m 15.93s (2.84) **Going Correction** +0.40s/f (Good) — **10** Ran SP% **111.9**
Speed ratings: **97,96,94,94,93 91,87,81,80,76**CSF £137.79 TOTE £31.50: £5.70, £1.40, £1.60; EX 206.90.
**Owner** Liam Mulryan **Bred** Yeomanstown Stud **Trained** Newmarket, Suffolk

**FOCUS**
This didn't look the strongest of fillies races to be held here and was slowly run.

**NOTEBOOK**
**Heres The Plan(IRE)**, a half-sister to a couple of juvenile winners, is an early foal. Bred to stay seven furlongs, the race was hardly run to suit, but the hill brought her stamina into play and, despite going to her left, just wore down the runner-up.
**Beautiful Mover(USA)** ◆, a half-sister to three U.S sprint winners, is well named, for she really does cover the ground. One of the nicer ones in the paddock, she can only go one way.
**Catch A Star**, a 180,000 guineas yearling, is out of a mare that won in the U.S.A. There is plenty of stamina on the dam's side and she will be suited by a stiffer test than she faced here.
**Thunder Calling(USA)**, a half-sister to five winners, is quite a late foal and had only just passed her second birthday. She is sure to do better as she gets stronger.
**Aberdovey**, who is out of a mare that won as a juvenile, did not have the best of runs and can be expected to improve on this effort.
**Baileys Applause** had looked ordinary in her two outings so far, but she did not shape too badly after having to be switched for a run. This effort should ensure she starts her nursery career on a favourable mark.

## 2276 ROBINSONS MERCEDES-BENZ A-ONDITIONS RACE CLASS C — 1m
**2:45** (2:45) (C ) 3-Y-O — **£8,398** (£3,185; £1,592; £724) **Stalls** High

| Form | Pos | Dist | Horse | Jockey | RPR |
|---|---|---|---|---|---|
| 16- | 1 | | **Almuraad (IRE)**[237] 5208 3-8-12 (SirMichaelStoute) *lw: a.p: chsd ldr over 2f out: rdn to ld over 1f out: r.o* **11/10**[1] | RHills 6 | 109 |
| 13-0 | 2 | ½ | **Mukafeh (USA)**[34] 1459 3-8-12 100 (JLDunlop) *led: rdn and hdd over 1f out: r.o* **7/1**[3] | WSupple 3 | 107 |
| 02-5 | 3 | 4 | **Bayeux (USA)**[20] 1766 3-8-12 112 (SaeedBinSuroor) *lw: chsd ldr over 5f: outpcd over 1f out* **7/2**[2] | (t) KMcEvoy 5 | 98 |
| 2-32 | 4 | shd | **Psychiatrist**[36] 1411 3-9-2 102 (RHannon) *trckd ldrs: rdn over 2f out: styd on same pce appr fnl f* **7/1**[3] | RLMoore 4 | 102 |
| 01- | 5 | nk | **Coy (IRE)**[212] 5700 3-8-7 (SirMichaelStoute) *wnt lft s and s.s: sn prom: pushed along 1/2-way: outpcd over 2f out: styd on ins fnl f* **9/1** | KFallon 2 | 92 |
| 53-0 | 6 | 11 | **Naaddey**[36] 1411 3-8-12 92 (MRChannon) *s.s and hmpd s: sn given reminders: effrt 1/2-way: wknd wl over 2f out* **33/1** | (v) TEDurcan 1 | 72 |

1m 39.75s (0.35) **Going Correction** +0.40s/f (Good) — **6** Ran SP% **107.8**
Speed ratings: **114,113,109,109,109 98**CSF £8.55 TOTE £2.10: £1.30, £4.00; EX 10.20.
**Owner** Hamdan Al Maktoum **Bred** 6c Stallions Ltd **Trained** Newmarket, Suffolk

**FOCUS**
Quite a competitive contest for the grade run in a fast time and was probably worthy of Listed status.

**NOTEBOOK**
**Almuraad(IRE)** took a while to get the better of the owner's second-string, but the experience will not be lost on him and he can leave this effort behind in due course, especially over a bit further.
**Mukafeh(USA)**, carrying the second colours, had an easy time of things up front, but battled on bravely when headed. He proved well suited by this step up in trip, and looks up to winning a similar contest.
**Bayeux(USA)**, again with the tongue tie on, failed to deliver. He looks to have something to prove now.
**Psychiatrist** had a stiff task on these terms and, although he handles a fast surface, may be better with some give underfoot.
**Coy(IRE)**, who was mounted on the track, still looked on the green side and can only improve for this outing.
**Naaddey** looks to be going the wrong way.

## 2277 ROBINSONS MERCEDES-BENZ SLK STKS (H'CAP) — 1m 4f
**3:15** (3:18) (C ) (0-90,84) 3-Y-O+ — **£9,412** (£2,896; £1,448; £724) **Stalls** Centre

| Form | Pos | Dist | Horse | Jockey | RPR |
|---|---|---|---|---|---|
| 00-5 | 1 | | **Astrocharm (IRE)**[21] 1746 5-9-0 **73** (MHTompkins) *lw: hld up: hdwy over 2f out: led over 1f out: rdn out* **11/1** | RHills 1 | 82 |
| 6-00 | 2 | 1¼ | **Dovedon Hero**[20] 1768 4-9-4 **77** (PJMcbride) *lw: s.s: hld up: hdwy over 1f out: r.o* **7/1**[3] | (b) SSanders 7 | 84 |
| 103- | 3 | nk | **Valance (IRE)**[191] 5368 4-9-3 **76** (CREgerton) *lw: hld up: hdwy over 2f out: rdn and ev ch over 1f out: styd on same pce* **6/1**[2] | SDrowne 6 | 83 |

/01- **4** *2* **Stealing Beauty (IRE)**[217] 5609 4-9-3 **76** JPMurtagh 8 79
(LMCumani) *h.d.w: chsd ldrs: hmpd over 2f out: styd on same pce fnl f* **8/1**

0-06 **5** *2* **Ravenglass (USA)**[34] 1457 5-9-8 **81** RHavlin 3 81
(JGMO'Shea) *chsd ldr: led over 2f out: rdn and hdd over 1f out: wknd ins fnl f* **6/1**[2]

-360 **6** *nk* **Sir Haydn**[11] 2000 4-8-11 **70** WRyan 4 70
(JRJenkins) *hld up: hdwy over 2f out: rdn and ev ch over 1f out: wknd ins fnl f* **10/1**

10-3 **7** *6* **Prairie Falcon (IRE)**[37] 1401 10-9-6 **84** AMedeiros(5) 5 74
(BWHills) *led over 9f: wknd fnl f* **4/1**[1]

3-00 **8** *dist* **Individual Talents (USA)**[6] 2116 4-8-9 **68** KFallon 2 —
(SCWilliams) *lw: chsd ldrs: ev ch over 2f out: wknd and eased over 1f out* **4/1**[1]

2m 37.53s (4.07) **Going Correction** +0.40s/f (Good) **8** Ran SP% **109.6**
Speed ratings: **102,101,100,99,98 94,94,—**CSF £77.83 CT £470.49 TOTE £12.50: £3.00, £2.10, £2.80; EX 64.90.
**Owner** Mystic Meg Limited **Bred** Miss D J Merson **Trained** Newmarket, Suffolk

**FOCUS**
Not a strong 0-90 with the top weight rated just 84. The pace was only steady.

**NOTEBOOK**
**Astrocharm(IRE)**, who had failed in two previous attempts over this trip, had the blinkers left off and was ridden with a bit more patience. With only a steady pace being set it did not put too much emphasis on stamina.
**Dovedon Hero**, with the blinkers back on, turned in his best effort of the season to date. While he is not the most consistent animal in training, he is now back down to a winning mark.
**Valance(IRE)** ◆ turned in a sound first run of the season over a trip which is a little short of his best. A stronger pace would have suited him much better, but with this run under his belt can be found an opening.
**Stealing Beauty(IRE)** lacked the experience of her rivals, but was far from disgraced on this venture into handicap company. Messed around when Valance made his move, she never really got back into the action, but the experience will not be lost on her and she should find compensation before too long.
**Ravenglass(USA)** stays much further than this and would not have been suited by the steady pace. He is not badly treated on his best form and, granted a stiffer test, can get back to winning ways.
**Sir Haydn** again gave the impression that this trip just stretches him.
**Prairie Falcon(IRE)**, who set a right gallop over course and distance last time, went just a steady pace this time which was newly played to his strengths.
**Individual Talents(USA)** again turned in a poor effort and looks to have plenty to prove at present.
*Official explanation: trainer said filly was reluctant to race when under pressure in the closing stages of the race*

## 2278 ESSEX AND SUFFOLK CHAMBER OF COMMERCE CLASSIFIED STKS 1m 2f
**3:50** (3:51) (D) 3-Y-O+ **£5,408** (£1,664; £832; £416) **Stalls** High

Form RPR

524- **1** **Trueno (IRE)**[257] 4754 5-9-0 80 TPQueally(3) 1 89
(LMCumani) *lw: chsd ldrs: led over 1f out: rdn out* **15/2**

206- **2** *1* **Solo Flight**[231] 5349 7-9-8 85 SDrowne 8 92
(HMorrison) *lw: hld up: swtchd lft and hdwy over 1f out: r.o* **7/1**[3]

15/0 **3** *¾* **Ken's Dream**[25] 1671 5-9-3 77 PMcCabe 7 86?
(MsAEEmbiricos) *lw: hld up: plld hrd: hdwy over 1f out: styd on* **33/1**

50-6 **4** *hd* **Barking Mad (USA)**[25] 1671 6-9-6 83 KFallon 5 88
(MLWBell) *swtg: lw: led: clr 7f out: rdn and hdd over 1f out: no ex ins fnl f* **7/2**[2]

0 **5** *5* **Tresor Secret (FR)**[20] 1762 4-9-3 80 RLMoore 9 76
(NACallaghan) *hld up: rdn over 3f out: swished tail: n.d* **12/1**

162- **6** *1 ¼* **James Caird (IRE)**[210] 5724 4-9-5 82 RHills 2 75
(MHTompkins) *chsd ldr: rdn over 2f out: wknd fnl f* **3/1**[1]

2200 **7** *2* **Te Quiero**[15] 1954 6-9-3 80 (t) MFenton 4 70
(MissGayKelleway) *lw: b. chsd ldrs over 8f* **12/1**

0153 **8** *8* **Jools**[14] 1938 6-9-3 80 TQuinn 3 54
(DKIvory) *b. prom: rdn over 3f out: wknd over 1f out* **8/1**

1- **9** *7* **Ultimata**[361] 1865 4-9-2 82 JPMurtagh 6 40
(JRFanshawe) *lw: hld up: wknd over 2f out* **10/1**

2m 9.05s (3.36) **Going Correction** +0.40s/f (Good) **9** Ran SP% **110.0**
Speed ratings: **102,101,100,100,96 95,93,87,81**CSF £54.48 TOTE £10.70: £3.30, £3.10, £4.50; EX 73.00.
**Owner** Mrs Liz Jones **Bred** Tanner Investments Co Ltd **Trained** Newmarket, Suffolk

**FOCUS**
A competitive contest with just 6lbs covering the field on official figures. The pace was only steady.

**NOTEBOOK**
**Trueno(IRE)**, who had been campaigned over longer trips, was ridden accordingly over this shorter trip. Always in the right place, he got first run on his rivals going into the dip, a tactic which was to win him the race.
**Solo Flight** did not have the strong pace he needs at this trip, but he turned in a solid effort on this first start for new connections. Although he is not the easiest of animals to win with, he certainly has the ability if everything falls right for him.
**Ken's Dream** had a little to find on these terms and was far from disgraced. A little too keen early on, a stronger pace would have suited him much better.
**Barking Mad(USA)** was running into a slight headwind, which would not have been ideal for a front-runner.
**Tresor Secret(FR)**, the winner of a couple of handicaps in France on easier ground than he faced here, looked a moody customer and gave a few hefty swishes of his tail when asked to go about his business.
**James Caird(IRE)**, a progressive performer last autumn, ran as though he just needed this outing.
**Ultimata** *Official explanation: trainer said he had no explanation for poor form shown.*

## 2279 ROBINSONS MERCEDES-BENZ M-TAKES (H'CAP) CLASS D 1m
**4:20** (4:20) (D) (0-80,78) 3-Y-O+ **£5,746** (£1,768; £884; £442) **Stalls** High

Form RPR

00-4 **1** **Tiber Tiger (IRE)**[46] 1275 4-9-8 **74** (b) TGMcLaughlin 7 86
(NPLittmoden) *s.s: hld up: hdwy over 1f out: rdn to ld ins fnl f: r.o* **8/1**[3]

0-11 **2** *1 ½* **Harrison Point (USA)**[62] 1066 4-9-12 **78** KFallon 9 87
(PWChapple-Hyam) *lw: trckd ldrs: led over 1f out: hdd and unable qck ins fnl f* **3/1**[1]

0331 **3** *2 ½* **Parnassian**[6] 2122 4-7-13 **56** RThomas(5) 5 59
(GBBalding) *hld up: outpcd: over 2f out: r.o ins fnl f: nt rch ldrs* **3/1**[1]

52-0 **4** *shd* **Habshan (USA)**[39] 1371 4-9-4 **70** JPMurtagh 1 73
(NAGraham) *lw: sn led: rdn and hdd over 1f out: styd on same pce* **25/1**

231- **5** *½* **Leoballero**[207] 5793 4-9-12 **78** MTebbutt 4 80
(DJDaly) *lw: trckd ldrs: rdn and ev ch over 1f out: no ex ins fnl f* **12/1**

0005 **6** *¾* **Dash For Cover (IRE)**[9] 2030 4-8-12 **64** RLMoore 6 64
(RHannon) *chsd ldrs: rdn and ev ch over 1f out: no ex* **16/1**

5100 **7** *2 ½* **Lygeton Lad**[13] 1969 6-9-6 **72** (t) MFenton 3 66
(MissGayKelleway) *lw: hld up: plld hrd: rdn over 1f out: n.d* **5/1**[2]

55-0 **8** *½* **Island Rapture**[27] 1623 4-9-8 **77** LisaJones(3) 2 70
(JARToller) *chsd ldr tl wknd over 1f out* **8/1**[3]

-450 **9** *¾* **Must Be Magic**[58] 1097 7-8-9 **61** (v) SSanders 8 52
(HJCollingridge) *hld up: rdn over 2f out: wknd over 1f out* **16/1**

1m 41.67s (2.27) **Going Correction** +0.40s/f (Good) **9** Ran SP% **112.2**
Speed ratings: **104,102,100,99,99 98,96,95,94**CSF £31.07 CT £88.51 TOTE £8.40: £1.80, £1.30, £1.60; EX 26.40.
**Owner** Mark Harniman **Bred** N Hartery **Trained** Newmarket, Suffolk

**FOCUS**
Not a strong handicap run at an ordinary pace.

**NOTEBOOK**
**Tiber Tiger(IRE)**, from a yard in much better form now, showed a nice turn of foot to score readily. However, with some of his rivals not performing as well as they might, it may pay not to get too carried away with this pefomance.
**Harrison Point(USA)** ◆ probably did a little too much too soon, and was unable to fend off the late challenge of the winner. Ridden with a little more restraint, we may have seen a different result.
**Parnassian**, unpenalised for winning an apprentice race earlier in the week, was caught out when the pace lifted and only picked up when the race was all but over. He deserves another chance.
**Habshan(USA)**, tackling handicappers for the first time, was not disgraced and looks to have a little race in him.
**Leoballero**, without the tongue tie he wore last season, travelled well for much of the trip before lack of a recent outing found him out. He will strip sharper next time.
**Dash For Cover(IRE)** has yet to prove he truly stays this far.

## 2280 ROBINSONS MERCEDES-BENZ S-TAKES (MAIDEN) CLASS D 1m 2f
**4:55** (4:56) (D) 3-Y-O **£5,512** (£1,696; £848; £424) **Stalls** High

Form RPR

2-4 **1** **Silent Hawk (IRE)**[19] 1794 3-9-0 (t) KMcEvoy 5 84
(SaeedBinSuroor) *lw: led: hdd over 7f out: styd w ldr: led over 1f out: edgd lft: rdn and edgd rt ins fnl f: r.o* **10/11**[1]

02 **2** *2* **Anna Pallida**[8] 2060 3-8-9 TQuinn 6 75
(PWHarris) *lw: w ldr: led over 7f out: rdn and hdd over 1f out: styd on same pce* **7/2**[2]

**3** *4* **Daze** 3-8-9 KFallon 2 68
(SirMichaelStoute) *gd sort: bkwd: chsd ldrs: outpcd fnl 2f: eased ins fnl f* **7/1**[3]

5- **4** *3 ½* **On Every Street**[223] 5489 3-9-0 (v[1]) WRyan 4 66
(HRACecil) *h.d.w: chsd ldrs: rdn over 3f out: wknd over 2f out* **9/1**

4 **5** *8* **Race The Ace**[27] 1612 3-9-0 JPMurtagh 1 51
(JLDunlop) *dwlt: hld up: wknd over 3f out* **9/1**

6- **6** *6* **Wavertree Spirit**[261] 4665 3-9-0 TGMcLaughlin 3 39
(NPLittmoden) *hld up: wknd over 3f out* **20/1**

2m 8.83s (3.14) **Going Correction** +0.40s/f (Good) **6** Ran SP% **111.9**
Speed ratings: **103,101,98,95,89 84**CSF £4.26 TOTE £2.10: £1.20, £1.80; EX 4.80 Place 6 £69.31, Place 5 £33.71.
**Owner** Godolphin **Bred** Gainsborough Stud Management Ltd **Trained** Newmarket, Suffolk

**FOCUS**
The way this was run hardly put the emphasis on stamina.

**NOTEBOOK**
**Silent Hawk(IRE)** did not look that keen, going first one way and then the other, but he had enough class to see him through.
**Anna Pallida** did not do anything wrong, she just met one too good on the day. As she is a half-sister to Group One-winner Sulk, connections will be hoping to score with her sooner, rather than later.
**Daze**, a half-sister to 12-furlong winner Fraternize, shaped with plenty of promise for the future, under a considerate ride.
**On Every Street** did not show a great deal in the first-time visor.
**Race The Ace** would not have been suited to the steady pace, over what is surely an inadequate trip.
T/Plt: £268.90 to a £1 stake. Pool: £43,937.60. 119.25 winning tickets. T/Qpdt: £25.50 to a £1 stake. Pool: £3,028.30. 87.70 winning tickets. CR

# 1702 ASCOT (R-H)
## Saturday, May 22

**OFFICIAL GOING: Good to firm**
The stands' rail was off limits, owing to a false rail 10 yards or so out, and high numbers had a clear advantage in big fields on the straight course.
Wind: It across Weather: fine & sunny

## 2281 FIRST NATIONAL STKS (H'CAP) 1m 2f
**1:45** (1:47) (C) (0-90,90) 3-Y-O **£9,850** (£3,031; £1,515; £757) **Stalls** High

Form RPR

-010 **1** **Mudawin (IRE)**[20] 1795 3-9-7 **90** SWhitworth 4 101
(MPTregoning) *lw: s.i.s: hld up in rr: stdy prog on outer fr 4f out: rdn to ld 1f out: styd on wl and sn clr* **11/1**

3-23 **2** *3 ½* **Ganymede**[36] 1450 3-8-11 **80** MFenton 10 84
(MLWBell) *chsd ldr 1f: styd prom in chsng gp: rdn and cl up 2f out: unable qck over 1f out: styd on to take 2nd nr fin* **16/1**

160- **3** *½* **Spring Goddess (IRE)**[215] 5674 3-8-13 **82** NCallan 2 85
(APJarvis) *hld up in rr: rdn and prog over 2f out: styd on fnl f to take 3rd nr fin* **50/1**

1-04 **4** *nk* **Golden Grace**[11] 2018 3-9-5 **88** JFEgan 6 90
(EALDunlop) *lw: s.i.s: t.k.h and sn prom: effrt 3f out: led wl over 1f out to 1f out: no ch w wnr: wknd nr fin* **5/1**[1]

16- **5** *hd* **Shalaya (IRE)**[203] 5874 3-9-4 **87** BDoyle 3 89
(SirMichaelStoute) *t.k.h: trckd clr ldr after 1f: clsd to ld over 2f out: hdd wl over 1f out: wknd nr fin* **10/1**

35-3 **6** *¾* **Rio De Jumeirah**[14] 1963 3-8-9 **78** DHolland 11 79?
(CEBrittain) *hld up towards rr: prog over 2f out: nt clr run and swtchd lft over 1f out: kpt on: no ch* **16/1**

031 **7** *nk* **Iktitaf (IRE)**[15] 1926 3-9-4 **87** WSupple 8 87
(JHMGosden) *wl in tch: rdn 3f out: cl up 2f out: one pce and btn over 1f out* **13/2**[2]

6-1 **8** *2 ½* **First Centurion**[19] 1827 3-9-4 **87** TQuinn 5 82
(JWHills) *lw: hld up in last: rdn over 3f out: stmbld bnd sn after: styd on wl fr over 1f out: nvr rchd ldrs* **5/1**[1]

0-04 **9** *¾* **Baileys Dancer**[8] 2089 3-8-12 **81** SChin 12 75
(MJohnston) *trckd ldrs: rdn and lost pl wl over 3f out: one pce and struggling after* **8/1**[3]

63-1 **10** *nk* **Incursion**[12] 2001 3-9-1 **84** VSlattery 13 77
(AKing) *lw: hld up wl in rr: rdn 4f out: no prog and btn 3f out* **17/2**

61-0 **11** 3 ½ **Top Spec (IRE)**[11] 2018 3-9-2 **85** ........ RLMoore 1 72
(RHannon) *rousted along early: racd on outer and sn chsd ldrs: rdn 3f out: wknd wl over 1f out* **16/1**

435- **12** 4 **Stanley Crane (USA)**[214] 5694 3-8-9 **78** ........ (t) OUrbina 7 57
(BHanbury) *b. racd freely: led and sn clr: wknd and hdd over 2f out: eased* **50/1**

0-21 **13** shd **Magic Amigo**[16] 1911 3-8-5 **74** ........ FNorton 14 53
(JRJenkins) *a towards rr: rdn and struggling 4f out* **33/1**

6-10 **14** 21 **Gretna**[40] 1357 3-8-13 **82** ........ GCarter 9 21
(JLDunlop) *midfield tl dropped qckly to last over 5f out: sn t.o* **25/1**

2m 9.01s (0.28) **Going Correction** -0.10s/f (Good) **14** Ran SP% **114.1**
Speed ratings: **94,91,90,90,90 89,89,87,86,86 83,80,80,63**CSF £161.31 CT £8083.58 TOTE £12.40: £3.90, £4.50, £11.40; EX 191.50.
**Owner** Hamdan Al Maktoum **Bred** Shadwell Estate Company Limited **Trained** Lambourn, Berks

**FOCUS**
A competitive three-year-old handicap, won in great style by Mudawin, who looked Listed class in powering home clear. The winning time was pedestrian for the grade, however.

**NOTEBOOK**
**Mudawin(IRE)** left a disappointing effort at Newmarket behind, winning in style after showing a good change of pace to take it up around the furlong marker. With a couple of the main contenders running below form for one reason or another the form should be treated with caution, but he is undoubtedly a progressive colt and may be the type for the King George V Handicap at the Royal Meeting over an extra couple of furlongs next month, as he will get further.
**Ganymede**, who is still a maiden, improved on all previous form on this handicap debut and ran out best of the bunch in the scrap for second. He will be suited by the return to further.
**Spring Goddess(IRE)** ◆, making her seasonal debut, gave connections plenty of reason for optimism with this running-on third. This was her first try at the trip and she was edging nearer with every stride. There is more to come from her.
**Golden Grace** has yet to prove this trip suits as his sole win to date came over seven furlongs. On this evidence a return to shorter will help.
**Shalaya(IRE)** did herself no favours by racing keenly on this seasonal debut and had nothing left when it mattered. She was not beaten far in the end though and should improve.
**Rio De Jumeirah**, a distant third in the Lingfield Oaks Trial, was more at home in this company and slightly unlucky not to finish closer as she had to be switched after not receiving the clearest of runs.
**Iktitaf(IRE)** was disappointing, finding little having been bang there two out. His maiden win came on easy going and maybe softer ground suits.
**First Centurion**, whose maiden win at Kempton came on heavy ground, never looked at home on this faster surface and failed to let himself down. He will become of interest again when there is a little cut in the ground.

## 2282 RITZ CLUB LONDON CONDITIONS STKS (F&M) 7f
**2:15** (2:17) (B) 4-Y-O+ **£11,948** (£4,532; £2,266; £1,030) **Stalls** Low

Form RPR

63-1 **1** **Enchanted**[6] 2143 5-8-5 88 ........ FNorton 4 97
(NACallaghan) *lw: t.k.h: hld up in rr: plld out and prog wl over 1f out: led ent fnl f: rdn clr* **10/11**[1]

42-4 **2** 2 **Blaise Castle (USA)**[14] 1964 4-8-5 90 ........ RLMoore 2 92
(GAButler) *trckd ldrs: rdn over 2f out: effrt to chal 1f out: chsd wnr after: no imp* **4/1**[2]

0-60 **3** 2 ½ **Dame De Noche**[15] 1927 4-8-9 88 ........ MFenton 3 89
(JGGiven) *lw: led: rdn 2f out: hdd ent fnl f: wkng nr fin* **7/1**[3]

-005 **4** 1 **Starbeck (IRE)**[2] 2242 6-8-6 89 ow1 ........ NCallan 5 84
(PHowling) *lw: b. s.s: t.k.h: hld up in last: rdn over 2f out: styd on fnl f: no ch* **9/1**

0-04 **5** ½ **Madamoiselle Jones**[7] 2119 4-8-5 64 ........ WSupple 7 81?
(HSHowe) *prom: rdn over 2f out: wknd 1f out* **33/1**

55-5 **6** 2 ½ **High Finance (IRE)**[44] 1317 4-8-9 79 ........ TQuinn 6 79
(JWHills) *t.k.h: hld up in rr: effrt 2f out: no prog over 1f out: sn wknd* **12/1**

0-35 **7** ¾ **Tender (IRE)**[5] 2178 4-8-5 57 ........ JFEgan 1 73?
(MrsStefLiddiard) *t.k.h: trckd ldr: rdn over 2f out: wknd over 1f out* **66/1**

1m 27.13s (-2.54) **Going Correction** -0.10s/f (Good) **7** Ran SP% **107.0**
Speed ratings: **110,107,104,103,103 100,99**CSF £3.94 TOTE £1.80: £1.20, £3.00; EX 5.40.
**Owner** Norcroft Park Stud **Bred** Norcroft Park Stud, Miss J Nicholls And A J Hol **Trained** Newmarket, Suffolk

**FOCUS**
This was won in great style by the improving Enchanted, but the fifth and the seventh are both moderate and hold the form down.

**NOTEBOOK**
**Enchanted** ◆ is a filly on a roll and flew home once being asked to go and win her race. Effective at 6f and 7f, she has not finished winning yet and looks worth another try at Listed level
**Blaise Castle(USA)**, who has been competing at Group and Listed level of late, ran well in this lesser event on ground that would probably have been a little quick, but could not match the winner.
**Dame De Noche** left herself vulnerable to something with a turn of foot in making the running, and was readily brushed aside by the front pair from inside the furlong.
**Starbeck(IRE)** ran respectably, but may have found this coming too soon after her run at Goodwood in the week.
**High Finance(IRE)**, despite being poorly in at the weights, looked a big threat at one stage, but she folded close home and came back a little sore. *Official explanation: vet said filly was lame.*

## 2283 TOTESPORT VICTORIA CUP (HERITAGE H'CAP) 7f
**2:45** (2:48) (B) (0-110,102) 4-Y-O+ **£34,800** (£13,200; £6,600; £3,000) **Stalls** Low

Form RPR

6-23 **1** **Mine (IRE)**[10] 2044 6-9-7 **99** ........ (v) TQuinn 16 113
(JDBethell) *lw: hld up in rr far side: prog wl over 1f out: swept into ld last 150y: sn in command: rdn out* **5/1**[1]

5-44 **2** ¾ **Greenslades**[21] 1765 5-8-13 **91** ........ SCarson 20 103
(PJMakin) *lw: trckd far side ldrs: effrt over 1f out: prog to chse wnr ins fnl f: r.o but a hld* **10/1**

1001 **3** 1 ¼ **Vortex**[16] 1954 5-9-5 **97** ........ (t) NCordrey 6 106
(MissGayKelleway) *b.hind: trckd nr side ldr: led gp 2f out: r.o wl fr over 1f out: hld by ldng pair far side* **16/1**

34-0 **4** hd **Camp Commander (IRE)**[14] 1968 5-9-2 **94** ........ (t) BDoyle 12 102
(CEBrittain) *dwlt: racd on outer of nr side gp and hld up: prog over 2f out: racd alone in centre fnl 2f: ch 1f out: r.o* **16/1**

-305 **5** 2 **Kool (IRE)**[14] 1968 5-9-0 **92** ........ SChin 13 95
(PFICole) *pressed ldng pair far side: rdn to chal 2f out: one pce fnl f* **16/1**

4-0 **6** shd **Atavus**[10] 2044 7-9-3 **95** ........ AMcCarthy 18 98
(GGMargarson) *led far side gp: overall ldr 2f out: hdd & wknd last 150yds* **25/1**

-000 **7** 1 **Audience**[19] 1828 4-9-0 **92** ........ (p) MFenton 14 92
(JAkehurst) *lw: hld up in rr far side: rdn and effrt 2f out: nt qckn and edgd lft over 1f out: one pce after* **20/1**

-000 **8** 1 **Master Robbie**[21] 1765 5-8-12 **90** ........ RLappin 15 88
(MRChannon) *hld up in rr far side: effrt 2f out: drvn and one pce over 1f out* **12/1**

0155 **9** 1 ¼ **El Coto**[10] 2044 4-9-7 **102** ........ BReilly[(3)] 8 96
(BAMcmahon) *trckd nr side ldrs: hrd rdn over 2f out: outpcd and btn over 1f out* **11/1**

4-00 **10** hd **Calcutta**[10] 2044 8-8-13 **98** ........ KMay[(7)] 3 92
(BWHills) *hld up towards rr nr side: shkn up and nt qckn 2f out: sn outpcd: kpt on fnl f* **33/1**

0-22 **11** ½ **Hidden Dragon (USA)**[49] 1242 5-9-5 **100** ........ DNolan[(3)] 4 93
(PABlockley) *b. pressed nr side ldrs: chsd gp ldr briefly wl over 1f out: sn fdd* **20/1**

110- **12** nk **Vindication**[205] 5838 4-9-1 **93** ........ (t) OUrbina 19 85
(JRFanshawe) *trckd ldrs far side: rdn and cl up over 1f out: wknd fnl f* **25/1**

30-4 **13** 1 **Selective**[35] 1469 5-9-8 **100** ........ DHolland 11 89
(ACStewart) *trckd nr side ldrs: cl up but nt clr run 2f out: wknd over 1f out* **8/1**[3]

-000 **14** 4 **Fantasy Believer**[21] 1765 6-8-12 **90** ........ FNorton 10 69
(JJQuinn) *trckd nr side ldrs: cl enough 2f out: sn wknd* **50/1**

**15** shd **Maksad (IRE)**[35] 4-9-3 **95** ........ WSupple 7 74
(JEHammond, France) *strong: lw: hld up in last pair nr side: nt clr run over 2f out: wknd over 1f out* **6/1**[2]

35-0 **16** ½ **Captain Saif**[4] 2201 4-9-0 **92** ........ (b) RLMoore 2 69
(RHannon) *dwlt: hld up in midfield nr side: nt clr run over 2f out: wknd over 1f out* **25/1**

54-0 **17** 1 ¼ **Crafty Calling (USA)**[20] 1789 4-8-13 **94** ........ (t) LPKeniry[(3)] 17 68
(PFICole) *pressed far side ldr to 2f out: wknd rapidly* **33/1**

0560 **18** 2 ½ **Will He Wish**[21] 1758 8-9-3 **95** ........ NCallan 5 62
(SGollings) *led nr side gp to 2f out: wknd rapidly* **33/1**

6001 **19** 10 **Golden Chalice (IRE)**[14] 1968 5-8-13 **91** ........ JFEgan 1 32
(AMBalding) *lw: dwlt: sn chsd nr side ldrs: wknd rapidly 2f out* **16/1**

125- **20** ¾ **Into The Breeze (IRE)**[266] 4570 4-9-3 **95** ........ SWhitworth 9 35
(JWHills) *hld up rr of nr side gp: wknd 2f out: sn bhd* **33/1**

1m 26.7s (-2.97) **Going Correction** -0.10s/f (Good) **20** Ran SP% **125.5**
Speed ratings: **112,111,109,109,107 107,105,104,103,103 102,102,101,96,96 95,94,91,80,79**CSF £46.27 CT £785.72 TOTE £5.60: £2.10, £3.20, £3.20, £4.30; EX 64.80 Trifecta £1888.20 Part won. Pool of £2,659.00 - 0.80 winning units..
**Owner** M J Dawson **Bred** David John Brown **Trained** Middleham Moor, N Yorks
■ This race was switched from its traditional date at the end of April and controversially limited to 20 runners.
■ Stewards Enquiry : B Doyle two-day ban: excessive use of the whip (Jun 2-3)

**FOCUS**
An ultra competitive handicap. A high draw was a big advantage as they raced in two groups and six of the first eight raced far-side. Career-best form from Mine, who is a regular in these top handicaps.

**NOTEBOOK**
**Mine(IRE)**, who is a battle-hardened and experienced handicapper, was winning his first race for practically a year off his highest-ever mark. He was drawn on what turned out to be the right side and, having crept into contention, burst through to lead in the final furlong before running on well. Connections are keen to come back here for the Royal Hunt Cup before have another crack at the Bunbury Cup, a race he won two years ago.
**Greenslades**, who was subject of a change of tactics, as he is usually up helping to force the pace. He came through to challenge the winner in the final furlong, but was never going to get to him. He continues to run well in defeat and as a result he creeps up the handicap.
**Vortex**, winner of a Listed race on the sand in Sweden on his most recent outing, ran a mighty race on the 'wrong' side, pulling around five and a half lengths clear of his nearest pursuer. His target is the Royal Hunt Cup, a race in which he would have a major chance in this sort of form, and connections are keen to book Dettori for the ride.
**Camp Commander(IRE)**, winner of this race last season off an 11lb higher mark, came alone down the centre of the track with his challenge and finished with purpose, without ever looking likely to quite get there. This was a fine effort, but he will not be easy to win with as there are not that many 'big' handicaps over seven furlongs around, a trip he seems best over.
**Kool(IRE)** was entitled to run well on his Lingfield running, form which has worked out well, and he duly did, just lacking the pace of others when it mattered. There is a suspicion that softer ground suits better, and he can pocket a nice prize when getting it.
**Atavus** ran a good race from the front on the far side, but is always going to leave himself vulnerable.
**Audience** kept on through beaten horses and was never really going the pace in this competitive event.
**Master Robbie**, a tough and progressive handicapper last season, is slipping down the weights and showed further signs of returning to form.
**El Coto** was slightly disappointing and probably needs to drop a few pounds before he is winning again.
**Maksad(IRE)**, representing trainer John Hammond, who has an excellent record with his British raiders, particularly at this course, did not get the clearest of runs, but that made no difference to his performance and softer ground suits better.
**Golden Chalice(IRE)** *Official explanation: jockey said said gelding was unsuited by the good to firm ground.*
**Into The Breeze(IRE)** *Official explanation: vet said gelding was lame on the right fore.*

## 2284 BRUNSWICK GROUP FILLIES' H'CAP 1m (S)
**3:20** (3:22) (D) (0-80,80) 3-Y-O+ **£7,117** (£2,190; £1,095; £547) **Stalls** Low

Form RPR

1-05 **1** **Enchanted Princess**[18] 1857 4-9-1 **67** ........ (b[1]) DHolland 15 79
(WJHaggas) *lw: hld up in rr far side: prog 2f out: rdn to ld last 150yds: hung lft but sn clr* **12/1**

10-0 **2** 1 ½ **Pink Sapphire (IRE)**[42] 1333 3-8-5 **69** ........ OUrbina 13 78
(DRCElsworth) *b.hind: mde most on far side: overall ldr and 2l clr 2f out: hdd and one pce last 150yds* **33/1**

0-61 **3** 2 ½ **Citrine Spirit (IRE)**[15] 1945 3-8-10 **74** ........ FNorton 6 77
(JHMGosden) *led nr side gp thrght: clr of rest fnl f: r.o but nt on terms w ldng pair far side* **9/1**[2]

221- **4** 2 **Florida Heart**[246] 5033 3-8-9 **76** ........ LPKeniry[(3)] 11 74
(AMBalding) *LW: hld up in rr far side: effrt whn nt clr run wl over 2f out: prog 2f out: chsd ldrs 1f out: one pce after* **12/1**

1400 **5** nk **Miss Pebbles (IRE)**[3] 2226 4-9-1 **67** ........ (v[1]) NPollard 5 65
(BRJohnson) *trckd nr side ldrs: rdn to chse ldr over 1f out: styd on fnl f* **12/1**

4410 **6** hd **Spark Up**[22] 1752 4-8-13 **65** ........ (b) TQuinn 19 62
(JWUnett) *prom far side: chsd ldr over 2f out to over 1f out: fdd ins fnl f* **25/1**

0633 **7** 3 **Mythical Charm**[9] 2052 5-8-3 **55** ........ (t) JTate 1 45
(JJBridger) *pressed nr side ldr to over 2f out: lost pl: kpt on again fnl f* **20/1**

-002 **8** hd **Cheese 'n Biscuits**[15] 1938 4-9-10 **76** ........ RLMoore 18 66
(GLMoore) *hld up in rr far side: rdn over 2f out: one pce and nvr able to chal* **7/1**[1]

06-0 **9** 1 3/4 **Tuscarora (IRE)**[22] 1750 5-8-3 **55** ow1 PDoe 16 41
(AWCarroll) *hld up far side: prog to press ldrs over 2f out: wknd jst over 1f out* **14/1**

0-00 **10** *hd* **Night Kiss (FR)**[9] 2064 4-8-10 **62** RSmith 3 47
(RHannon) *in tch nr side: rdn in last pair over 2f out: one pce after* **10/1**[3]

0-04 **11** 2 **Miss Grace**[15] 1940 4-8-2 **57** DCorby(3) 8 38
(JJSheehan) *squeezed out s: sn in tch nr side: hrd rdn over 2f out: btn over 1f out* **14/1**

123- **12** *hd* **Strategy**[269] 4499 4-10-0 **80** SWhitworth 4 60
(PRWebber) *hld up nr side: rdn to chse ldr over 2f out to over 1f out: wknd* **25/1**

115- **13** *shd* **Music Maid (IRE)**[249] 4962 6-8-10 **62** NCallan 20 42
(HSHowe) *pressed far side ldrs to over 2f out: sn wknd* **16/1**

0220 **14** 4 **Michelle Ma Belle (IRE)**[9] 2064 4-9-9 **75** ADaly 2 46
(SKirk) *cl up nr side: rdn and hanging bdly rt over 2f out: sn wknd* **14/1**

0-1 **15** 3/4 **Dreaming Of You (IRE)**[19] 1842 3-8-11 **75** BDoyle 14 44
(SirMichaelStoute) *rr of far side gp: rdn and no reponse over 4f out: brief effrt over 2f out: heavily eased whn btn fnl f* **7/1**[1]

04-4 **16** 1 1/4 **Keeper's Lodge (IRE)**[16] 1904 3-8-8 **72** WSupple 17 38
(BAMcmahon) *a in rr far side: rdn and struggling 3f out* **40/1**

51-0 **17** 1 1/4 **In The Pink (IRE)**[18] 1877 4-8-13 **65** RLappin 10 28
(MRChannon) *towards rr far side: rdn and wandered over 2f out: wknd* **20/1**

0 **18** 1/2 **Faith Healer (IRE)**[22] 1755 3-7-12 **62** oh2 (p) AMcCarthy 12 24
(VSmith) *racd far side: a in rr: struggling over 2f out* **50/1**

210- **19** *nk* **Helderberg (USA)**[68] 5943 4-9-4 **70** MFenton 7 32
(BSRothwell) *h.d.w: b.bkwd: wnt rt s: racd far side: a in rr: last of gp and wkng over 2f out* **40/1**

0-60 **20** 9 **Margalita (IRE)**[33] 1504 4-9-6 **72** (bt) JFEgan 9 13
(PMitchell) *pressed far side ldr to wl over 2f out: wknd rapidly: sddle slipped* **25/1**

1m 40.83s (-1.09) **Going Correction** -0.10s/f (Good)
**WFA** 3 from 4yo+ 12lb **20** Ran SP% **123.9**
Speed ratings: **101,99,97,95,94 94,91,91,89,89 87,87,87,83,82 81,79,79,79,70**CSF £374.34 CT £3785.84 TOTE £11.30: £2.80, £6.80, £2.70, £4.30; EX 282.10.
**Owner** Mrs Susan J Jensen **Bred** Highclere Stud Ltd And John Warren **Trained** Newmarket, Suffolk

**FOCUS**
Those drawn high again came out on top in what looked a weakish handicap for the track.

**NOTEBOOK**
**Enchanted Princess**, sporting first-time blinkers, made her move over a furlong out and came through strongly to win going away, despite hanging left. She is currently in foal to Dr Fong and will not be racing for much longer, but if the blinkers have the same effect again she could pick up another race.
**Pink Sapphire(IRE)**, well held on her seasonal debut on softish ground, appreciated this step up to a mile and only found the one too good. She will be of interest in a less competitive race where her positive tactics will be easier to pull off.
**Citrine Spirit(IRE)** left her maiden form behind with a solid third, winning the stands'-side race. She is going the right way.
**Florida Heart** ran a nice race on this seasonal debut, running on for fourth having been denied a clear run two out.
**Miss Pebbles(IRE)** ran well in the first-time visor and will be suited by a return to a mile and a quarter.
**Spark Up** had every chance on the far side and was not disgraced.
**Michelle Ma Belle(IRE)** *Official explanation: jockey said filly had hung right handed.*
**Dreaming Of You(IRE)** was always going to face a stiff task for one so lightly raced, this being only her third-ever start having won her maiden last time, and she never looked up to the task.
**Margalita(IRE)** *Official explanation: jockey said filly lost her action.*

## 2285 BONUSPRINT.COM H'CAP — 2m 45y
3:55 (3:57) (D) (0-85,86) 4-Y-0+ **£8,323** (£2,561; £1,280; £640) **Stalls** High

Form RPR

22-0 **1** **Land 'n Stars**[19] 1832 4-8-13 **72** PDoe 14 87
(JamiePoulton) *lw: cl up in chsng gp: prog over 3f out: chsd ldr over 2f out: rdn to ld wl over 1f out: sn clr* **66/1**

113- **2** 5 **Got One Too (FR)**[28] 1826 7-9-1 **72** DHolland 9 81
(NJHenderson) *pushed up to ld after 1f and sn wl clr: breather and c bk to field over 4f out: kicked on again 3f out: hdd wl over 1f out:* **7/2**[1]

6-06 **3** 3/4 **Mostarsil (USA)**[20] 1801 6-8-11 **68** (p) RLMoore 5 76
(GLMoore) *prom in chsng gp: rdn and unable qck over 3f out: styd on again fnl 2f* **7/1**[2]

0-51 **4** 1 3/4 **Star Member (IRE)**[10] 2047 5-10-1 **86** NCallan 10 92
(APJarvis) *lw: hld up in midfield: gng easily but outpcd over 3f out: rdn and styd on fr 2f out: nt rch ldrs* **8/1**[3]

00-0 **5** 2 1/2 **Don Fernando**[45] 1302 5-9-7 **78** JFEgan 6 81
(MCPipe) *hld up in rr: prog u.p 3f out: one pce fnl 2f: n.d* **20/1**

3-50 **6** 1 3/4 **Kristensen**[17] 1880 5-9-10 **81** (p) BDoyle 12 82
(DEddy) *racd in midfield: rdn over 3f out: no imp ldrs after* **10/1**

-640 **7** *hd* **San Hernando**[20] 1801 4-8-12 **71** TQuinn 3 72
(DRCElsworth) *hld up in last pair: rdn 4f out: styd on fnl 2f: no ch* **8/1**[3]

5-00 **8** 1 **Establishment**[21] 1768 7-9-6 **77** SWhitworth 7 76
(CACyzer) *lw: hld up in rr: rdn 4f out: one pce and no imp on ldrs* **8/1**[3]

2022 **9** *shd* **Madiba**[7] 2126 5-8-3 **60** SCarson 2 59
(PHowling) *prom in chsng gp: chsd ldr wl over 3f out to over 2f out: wknd* **16/1**

56-0 **10** 1 1/4 **Stoop To Conquer**[20] 1801 4-8-9 **68** GCarter 11 66
(JLDunlop) *hld up in last pair: rdn and struggling 4f out* **14/1**

**11** 2 1/2 **Simply Honest (IRE)**[15] 1951 9-8-1 **58** FNorton 8 53
(AJMartin, Ire) *lw: strong: racd in midfield: rdn whn n.m.r over 3f out: no prog over 2f out: wknd* **7/1**[2]

002- **12** 3 1/2 **Domenico (IRE)**[163] 3285 6-9-3 **74** WSupple 1 65
(JRJenkins) *b.bkwd: prom in chsng gp tl wknd u.p fr over 3f out* **66/1**

21P/ **13** 26 **Grand Fromage (IRE)**[661] 3475 6-8-13 **70** VSlattery 4 29
(AKing) *bkwd: a towards rr: rdn and wknd 4f out: t.o* **33/1**

15-0 **14** 8 **Skye's Folly (USA)**[14] 1973 4-9-5 **78** MFenton 13 28
(JGGiven) *led for 1f: chsd clr ldr to wl over 3f out: wknd rapidly: t.o* **16/1**

3m 31.23s (-3.61) **Going Correction** -0.10s/f (Good)
**WFA** 4 from 5yo+ 2lb **14** Ran SP% **118.8**
Speed ratings: **105,102,102,101,100 99,99,98,98,97 96,94,81,77**CSF £280.88 CT £1885.25 TOTE £62.90: £12.80, £1.40, £3.40; EX 289.70.
**Owner** Kenneth Wilkinson **Bred** C A Cyzer **Trained** Telscombe, E Sussex

**FOCUS**
There was a bias towards those that raced up with the pace, and those who were held up struggled to get into it. Fair form despite the tactical nature.

**NOTEBOOK**
**Land 'n Stars**, still a maiden coming into the race, is related to Establishment and improved on all previous form on his first try at the trip, springing a huge surprise in the process. There was a bias towards racing up with the pace, but connections are considering races like the Ascot Stakes and Cesarewitch.
**Got One Too(FR)**, who has been in reasonable form over fences, was given a good tactical ride by Holland and looked to have nicked it at one stage, but he understandably got weary late on and had no answer to the winner. He is on a winning mark at present and can pick up a race in his turn.
**Mostarsil(USA)** is currently only 3lb higher than when last scoring, and it would come as no surprise to see him back to winning ways in the coming weeks.
**Star Member(IRE)**, a stylish winner at York on his most recent outing, fared best of those coming from off the pace, but was left with too much to do.
**Don Fernando** has not won on the Flat since his debut and is not one to place total faith in, albeit he ran well.
**San Hernando** plugged on from the rear without threatening.
**Establishment** has not been at his best this season.
**Madiba** *Official explanation: trainer said gelding was unsuited by the good to firm ground.*

## 2286 WYNDHAM MAIDEN STKS — 7f
4:30 (4:30) (D) 3-Y-0 **£6,825** (£2,100; £1,050; £525) **Stalls** Low

Form RPR

04 **1** **Peter Paul Rubens (USA)**[10] 2046 3-9-0 DHolland 7 95
(PFICole) *lw: t.k.h: mde all: jnd and pushed along over 2f out: drew clr over 1f out: r.o wl* **14/1**

3-23 **2** 5 **Red Top (IRE)**[24] 1704 3-8-9 **87** RLMoore 6 77
(RHannon) *lw: sn trckd wnr: effrt to chal and upsides over 2f out: rdn and found nil wl over 1f out: btn after* **10/11**[1]

2- **3** 1 **Awesome Love (USA)**[313] 3259 3-9-0 SChin 8 79
(MJohnston) *trckd ldrs: rdn and outpcd 2f out: one pce after* **3/1**[2]

4-0 **4** 2 **Latif (USA)**[35] 1461 3-9-0 (t) WSupple 4 74
(JHMGosden) *b.hind: t.k.h early: trckd ldrs: outpcd 2f out: shkn up briefly over 1f out: nt qckn* **10/1**[3]

0 **5** 1 3/4 **Gentle Raindrop (IRE)**[7] 2114 3-8-9 JFEgan 2 64
(SKirk) *sn pushed along in rr: a struggling: kpt on fnl 2f* **10/1**[3]

**6** 3 **Pine Bay** 3-8-9 MFenton 3 56
(BGubby) *wl grwn: strong: b.bkwd: dwlt: racd in last: effrt but no ch whn hung rt wl over 1f out : no prog after* **66/1**

06- **7** 1 1/2 **First Dawn**[243] 5119 3-8-9 RLappin 9 53
(MRChannon) *hld up in tch: rdn and outpcd over 2f out: wknd* **25/1**

**8** 11 **Nikiforos** 3-9-0 TQuinn 1 29
(JWHills) *lengthy: strong: scope: a in rr: rdn over 3f out: wknd over 2f out* **25/1**

0-0 **9** 5 **Albadi**[10] 2046 3-9-0 BDoyle 5 16
(CEBrittain) *b.bkwd: prom 4f: wknd rapidly* **50/1**

1m 27.37s (-2.30) **Going Correction** -0.10s/f (Good) **9** Ran SP% **113.4**
Speed ratings: **109,103,102,99,97 94,92,80,74**CSF £26.36 TOTE £20.10: £3.50, £1.30, £1.10; EX 50.30 Place 6 £314.20, Place 5 £20.70.
**Owner** Richard Green (fine Paintings) **Bred** Mueller Farm **Trained** Whatcombe, Oxon

**FOCUS**
A decent time for the grade of contest, and good maiden form from the winner.

**NOTEBOOK**
**Peter Paul Rubens(USA)**, whose two previous runs had been on a soft surface, raced keenly, but improved dramatically on this faster surface and came right away to win easily, having led throughout. Given he beat an 87-rated filly it is unlikely the handicapper is going to be kind.
**Red Top(IRE)** has had her chances and found little, having come there to throw down her challenge approaching the two pole. She is not one to follow.
**Awesome Love(USA)**, a promising second on his debut last season over six, lacked the pace to challenge and will appreciate a mile plus.
**Latif(USA)** is now qualified for handicaps and will be capable of better in that sphere.
**Gentle Raindrop(IRE)** needs one more run to qualify for handicaps.
T/Plt: £421.60 to a £1 stake. Pool: £74,013.90. 128.15 winning tickets. T/Qpdt: £28.80 to a £1 stake. Pool: £4,639.30. 119.00 winning tickets. JN

# 2256 AYR (L-H)
Saturday, May 22

**OFFICIAL GOING: Firm (good to firm in places)**
Wind: breezy, half-across Weather: hot, sunny

## 2287 DOBBIE ELECTRICAL H'CAP — 1m 5f 13y
1:00 (1:00) (E) (0-70,75) 4-Y-0+ **£2,324** (£2,324; £547; £273) **Stalls** Low

Form RPR

2316 **1** *dht* **Toni Alcala**[14] 1973 5-9-5 **66** PMulrennan(5) 7 74
(RFFisher) *hld up in tch: hdwy over 2f out: disp ld wl ins last: jst hld on* **7/2**[1]

300- **1** **Cosmic Case**[9] 5928 9-8-3 **45** ANicholls 4 53
(JSGoldie) *hld up in tch: effrt over 2f out: hdwy to dispute ld wl ins last: jst hld on* **11/2**

0601 **3** 1 **Rajam**[5] 2174 6-10-5 **75** 6ex (v) AlexGreaves 2 82
(DNicholls) *keen: cl up: led over 1f out to wl ins last: one pce whn n.m.r cl home* **5/1**[3]

-000 **4** 1 1/2 **Magic Charm**[103] 727 6-7-5 **40** LeanneKershaw(7) 8 45
(JeddO'Keeffe) *trckd ldrs: led over 3f to over 1f out: one pce ins fnl f* **20/1**

00-5 **5** *shd* **Exalted (IRE)**[26] 1668 11-8-12 **54** DaleGibson 3 58
(TAKCuthbert) *chsd ldrs: drvn 3f out: rallied: r.o fnl f* **8/1**

-000 **6** 7 **Forever My Lord**[55] 919 6-8-4 **49** J-PGuillambert(3) 1 44
(JRBest) *led to over 3f out: wknd over 1f out* **4/1**[2]

0450 **7** *nk* **Astromancer (USA)**[18] 1866 4-8-7 **49** (b[1]) MHenry 5 43
(MHTompkins) *hld up: rdn over 3f out: sn btn* **7/1**

000- **8** 24 **Alafdal (USA)**[221] 5568 4-9-12 **68** KRenwick 6 29
(RAllan) *keen: hld up in tch: rdn over 3f out: sn wknd* **25/1**

2m 50.23s (-5.62) **Going Correction** -0.45s/f (Firm) **8** Ran SP% **106.5**
Speed ratings: **99,99,98,97,97 93,92,78** TRIFECTA W: TA 1.9, CC 2.7; Pl: TA 1.10, CC 1.70, 2.80; Ex: TA/CC 7.5, CC/TA 8.0; CSF: TA/CC 9.8, CC/TA 10.78; Tri: TA/CC/R 38.6, CC/TA/R 41.
**Owner** The Cosmic Cases **Bred** V H Rowe **Trained** Uplawmoor, E Renfrews
■ Stewards Enquiry : P Mulrennan caution: careless riding

**FOCUS**
A run-of-the-mill handicap run at only a fair gallop, but the form should prove reliable at an ordinary level.

**NOTEBOOK**
**Cosmic Case**, from an in-form stable, had slipped to an attractive mark and confirmed the promise shown over hurdles last time. She should not be going up too much for this, and will remain of interest in similar company on fast ground when a good gallop looks likely.
**Toni Alcala**, from an in-form stable, has been running much more consistently of late and once again put his best foot forward over a trip that is arguably his optimum. He seems well suited by a sound surface.

**Rajam**, under a penalty for his Musselburgh success, had the run of the race and ran at least as well with the visor on again and the interference suffered in the closing stages made little difference to the result. He may look vulnerable in a more competitive handicap from his current mark, though.
**Magic Charm**, back on turf on her favoured fast ground and on her first start for new connections, ran creditably but did have the run of the race to a larger extent than the first two home. Her record is one of inconsistency, but she is capable of winning again from her current mark.
**Exalted(IRE)** ◆ ran well enough on ground quicker than ideal to suggest he will be one to be interested in for the near future if the ground is on the soft side. The mile and five amateur riders' handicap at Hamilton next month, that he has won in two of the last three years, looks an obvious target if he gets his ground.
**Forever My Lord**, back on the Flat, is from a stable that has been among the winners of late but was below his best on this first run for nearly two months.

## 2288 AYR RACECOURSE IN BLOOM (S) STKS 6f
**1:35** (1:35) (G) 2-Y-O **£2,520** (£720; £360) **Stalls** High

Form RPR
4021 **1** **Goldhill Prince**[6] [2140] 2-8-10 (p) CHaddon(7) 2 56
(WGMTurner) *mde all: drew clr fr 2f out: easily* **1/7**[1]
00 **2** *5* **Houdini Bay (IRE)**[12] [2003] 2-8-3 THamilton(3) 1 30
(RPElliott) *chsd ldrs: wnt 2nd 2f out: no imp* **25/1**
**3** *7* **Tonight (IRE)** 2-8-11 FLynch 4 14
(WMBrisbourne) *outpcd: sme late hdwy: nvr on terms* **12/1**[2]
504 **4** *¾* **Bowland Bride (IRE)**[6] [2140] 2-7-13 PPMathers(7) 5 7
(ABerry) *chsd wnr to 2f out: sn btn* **14/1**[3]
1m 13.39s (-0.33) **Going Correction** -0.45s/f (Firm) 4 Ran SP% **105.7**
Speed ratings: **84,77,68,67**CSF £4.83 TOTE £1.20; EX 12.30.The winner was bought in for 4,500gns.
**Owner** Gold Hill Racing **Bred** N D Fisher **Trained** Sigwells, Somerset

**FOCUS**
The withdrawal of Mytton's Dream meant this was a very straightforward task for Goldhill Prince, who did not have to improve to run out the easy winner of a poor race.

**NOTEBOOK**
**Goldhill Prince**, an improved performer of late, did not have to progress to beat three poor rivals with plenty in hand but may be one to take on back in a more competitive event next time.
**Houdini Bay(IRE)** was not totally disgraced on her first start over this trip but this form amounts to little and she is likely to continue to look vulnerable.
**Tonight(IRE)**, the first foal of an unraced half-sister to a sprint winner, looked in need of the race and was green on this racecourse debut and achieved little.
**Bowland Bride(IRE)** was beaten a lot further by the winner than at Ripon and looks of very limited ability.

## 2289 AYRSHIRE SHOP FRONTS MEDIAN AUCTION MAIDEN STKS 7f 50y
**2:10** (2:10) (F) 3-Y-O **£3,038** (£868; £434) **Stalls** Low

Form RPR
502- **1** **West Highland Way (IRE)**[207] [5822] 3-8-9 80 TEaves(5) 4 80
(ISemple) *cl up: led 2f out: rdn out* **2/1**[2]
2204 **2** *2 ½* **Oh Golly Gosh**[7] [2134] 3-8-11 74 (p) J-PGuillambert(3) 1 73
(NPLittmoden) *prom: effrt and chsd wnr over 1f out: kpt on fnl f* **6/4**[1]
04 **3** *3* **My Pension (IRE)**[15] [1939] 3-9-0 JCarroll 2 65
(PHowling) *cl up: led over 3f to 2f out: one pce* **9/4**[3]
44 **4** *24* **Queen Lucia (IRE)**[22] [1747] 3-8-9 DaleGibson 3 —
(JGGiven) *led to over 3f out: sn lost tch* **16/1**
1m 29.46s (-3.01) **Going Correction** -0.45s/f (Firm) 4 Ran SP% **110.0**
Speed ratings: **99,96,92,65**CSF £5.49 TOTE £2.50; EX 3.90.
**Owner** Laumar Racing **Bred** J And Mrs J Peel **Trained** Carluke, S Lanarks

**FOCUS**
Another uncompetitive race in which the gallop was only fair at best but, although West Highland Way has plenty of scope and appeals as the type to win more races. However, neither he or the second are particularly well handicapped at present.

**NOTEBOOK**
**West Highland Way(IRE)** ◆, who looked in tremendous shape, was easy to back but did not have to improve to win an uncompetitive race. Life will be tougher in handicaps from his current mark but he has plenty of physical scope, is in good hands and should prove equally effective over a mile. He appeals as the type to win more races.
**Oh Golly Gosh**, an exposed performer, was well supported and ran creditably over this shorter trip but did not find as much off the bridle as had looked likely for a long way and does not look one to place too much faith in.
**My Pension(IRE)** having his first run on a sound surface, did not really have the chance the betting suggested and, although not disgraced after having the run of the race, is likely to be seen to better effect in low-grade handicaps.
**Queen Lucia(IRE)**, who had shown ability on her previous starts on good ground, was soundly beaten back in trip on her first run on very fast ground. She may well need easier ground.

## 2290 ROBERT DUNN PLANT HIRE MEDIAN AUCTION MAIDEN FILLIES' STKS 6f
**2:40** (2:41) (E) 3-4-Y-O **£3,487** (£1,073; £536; £268) **Stalls** High

Form RPR
0-30 **1** **Cefira (USA)**[37] [1413] 3-8-10 67 MHenry 1 66
(MHTompkins) *trckd ldrs: led 2f out: rdn out* **5/2**[2]
-340 **2** *1 ½* **Pirlie Hill**[3] [2227] 4-9-5 45 JCarroll 2 61?
(MissLAPerratt) *prom: effrt and ev ch 2f out: r.o same pce ins fnl f* **12/1**
22-0 **3** *1* **Champagne Cracker**[12] [1991] 3-8-5 63 TEaves(5) 5 58
(MissLAPerratt) *trckd ldrs: effrt 2f out: one pce fnl f* **11/1**
3050 **4** *½* **Wavertree Girl (IRE)**[7] [2112] 3-8-7 72 J-PGuillambert(3) 6 57
(NPLittmoden) *in tch: effrt 2f out: no imp fnl f* **6/5**[1]
004- **5** *3 ½* **Amber Fox (IRE)**[215] [5676] 3-8-10 54 FLynch 3 46
(ABerry) *led to 2f out: sn wknd* **8/1**[3]
**6** *12* **Answer Do** 4-8-12 KGhunowa(7) 4 10
(MJPolglase) *outpcd and flashed tail thrght* **25/1**
1m 12.22s (-1.50) **Going Correction** -0.45s/f (Firm)
**WFA** 3 from 4yo 9lb 6 Ran SP% **105.0**
Speed ratings: **92,90,88,88,83 67**CSF £25.94 TOTE £3.20: £2.60, £4.60; EX 25.80.
**Owner** Mrs Jane Bailey **Bred** Edwin Cleveland **Trained** Newmarket, Suffolk

**FOCUS**
Another uncompetitive event and, with the market leader disappointing once again, this race did not take a great deal of winning. The proximity of the runner-up confirms this bare form is best treated with caution.

**NOTEBOOK**
**Cefira(USA)**, in a much less competitive race than last time, had to be firmly pushed out to beat a rival rated 22lb her inferior and, as such, she may not be easy to place in handicap company from her current mark of 67.
**Pirlie Hill**, much more relaxed in the paddock than at this course at the end of last month, looked in tremendous shape and ran well in the face of a stiff task. She should prove equally effective over five furlongs, but her immediate future depends on how the Handicapper reacts to this seemingly improved performance.
**Champagne Cracker** seemed much happier back on a sound surface and looks worth a try over a bit further but, although not disgraced, this race has a dubious look to it and her current rating of 63 means she may struggle in handicaps.
**Wavertree Girl(IRE)**, the pick on ratings, is from an in-form stable but was not suited by the drop back to sprinting. Although the return to further will help, she is a disappointing type who is not going to be easy to place successfully.
**Amber Fox(IRE)**, exposed as modest, looked up against it at the weights for this reappearance but, although having the run of the race next to the stands' rail, did not show enough to suggest she will be of interest in the near future.
**Answer Do**, who is related to a couple of winners, has plenty of size and scope but, although looking badly in need of the race, showed nothing on this racecourse debut.

## 2291 LIKIT PRODUCTS H'CAP 7f 50y
**3:15** (3:15) (D) (0-80,79) 3-Y-O+ **£5,557** (£1,710; £855; £427) **Stalls** Low

Form RPR
000- **1** **Flur Na H Alba**[73] [5515] 5-9-8 79 (p) TEaves(5) 2 91
(ISemple) *keen: mde virtually all: rdn and hld on wl fnl f* **7/1**[3]
1231 **2** *¾* **Samuel Charles**[4] [2218] 6-8-13 70 6ex PMakin(5) 4 80
(WMBrisbourne) *sn trcking ldrs: effrt over 2f out: edgd lft and carried hd high: kpt on fnl f: hld cl home* **4/1**[1]
-050 **3** *¾* **Sea Storm (IRE)**[21] [1773] 6-9-8 79 PMulrennan(5) 8 87
(DRMacleod) *prom: rdn over 2f out: r.o fnl f: nrst fin* **8/1**
0000 **4** *½* **True Night**[7] [2132] 7-9-1 74 LTreadwell(7) 9 81
(DNicholls) *taken early to post: hld up: effrt over 2f out: hung lft: r.o fnl f* **12/1**
06-6 **5** *nk* **Albashoosh**[15] [1929] 6-8-13 65 AlexGreaves 10 71
(DNicholls) *keen: prom: stdy hdwy over 2f out: edgd lft: r.o same pce fnl f* **8/1**
54-0 **6** *1* **Ballyhurry (USA)**[41] [1345] 7-9-4 73 THamilton(3) 6 76
(JSGoldie) *midfield: effrt over 2f out: one pce fnl f* **7/1**[3]
305- **7** *½* **Wood Dalling (USA)**[302] [3581] 6-7-13 58 ow2 PPMathers(7) 3 60
(RAllan) *dwlt: bhd tl styd on fnl f: n.d* **50/1**
512- **8** *2* **Pop Up Again**[218] [5626] 4-9-9 75 FLynch 12 72
(GASwinbank) *hld up: rdn over 2f out: n.d* **8/1**
3004 **9** *2 ½* **Speedfit Free (IRE)**[7] [2123] 7-7-12 50 oh2 (v) AnnStokell 1 40
(MissAStokell) *disp ld to 1/2-way: wknd over 1f out* **33/1**
0050 **10** *2 ½* **Pagan Storm (USA)**[4] [2219] 4-8-6 65 KristinStubbs(7) 7 49
(MrsLStubbs) *a bhd* **20/1**
0052 **11** *6* **Online Investor**[7] [2130] 5-9-3 69 ANicholls 11 37
(DNicholls) *hld up: effrt over 2f out: edgd lft: wknd over 1f out* **6/1**[2]
6 **12** *16* **Caribe (FR)**[35] [1469] 5-8-13 65 JCarroll 5 —
(ABerry) *trckd ldrs tl wknd fr over 2f out* **50/1**
1m 28.52s (-3.95) **Going Correction** -0.45s/f (Firm) 12 Ran SP% **111.9**
Speed ratings: **104,103,102,101,101 100,99,97,94,91 84,66**CSF £31.87 CT £229.36 TOTE £8.20: £2.90, £1.20, £3.20; EX 64.20.
**Owner** The Mathieson Partnership **Bred** The Mathieson Partnership **Trained** Carluke, S Lanarks

**FOCUS**
A fair handicap on paper but not many were in top form and the lack of early pace suited those ridden prominently and, consequently, this bare form looks unreliable.

**NOTEBOOK**
**Flur Na H Alba**, soundly beaten on his hurdles debut last time, looked in good shape and ran right up to his best to win his second race over course and distance. However, given his inconsistency and the fact he very much had the run of the race, he may well be one to field against at short odds next time.
**Samuel Charles**, one of the very few that came into this race in any sort of form, ran well in this better grade under his penalty, despite again looking less than straightforward under pressure. He should continue to give a good account.
**Sea Storm(IRE)**, who is back on a fair mark, had conditions to suit and ran creditably, but left the impression that a stiffer test of stamina over this trip would have suited. He should continue to give a good account.
**True Night** may not be straightforward but had conditions to suit and fared the best of those that came from off the pace, so looks better than the bare form. With his stable starting to hit form, he is one to keep an eye on from this mark, especially when a stronger gallop looks likely. *Official explanation: jockey said gelding hung left handed in the straight*
**Albashoosh** ◆, back on a potentially favourable mark, again shaped as though retaining plenty of ability for his current yard and may also be a bit better than the bare form, as he failed to settle from his high draw and was not knocked about. He is capable of winning races around this trip.
**Ballyhurry(USA)**, from a stable that has been going well of late, likes it here and fared better than on his reappearance, but is another in this race that would have been much better suited by an end-to-end gallop. He is not one to write off.
**Wood Dalling(USA)** did well to finish as close as he did given his position at halfway on this first run since last July, and his new connections are likely to place him to best advantage in due course.
**Pop Up Again** *Official explanation: jockey said filly did not handle the bends.*
**Online Investor**, who had run creditably over five furlongs last time, was below that level over this longer trip in a much more steadily-run race, and this effort is best overlooked. *Official explanation: jockey said gelding ran too free.*
**Caribe(FR)** *Official explanation: jockey said horse lost its action.*

## 2292 LABURNAM CLASSIFIED STKS 7f 50y
**3:45** (3:45) (F) 3-Y-O+ **£3,206** (£916; £458) **Stalls** Low

Form RPR
0013 **1** **She's Our Lass (IRE)**[35] [1467] 3-8-3 60 RFitzpatrick 6 67
(DCarroll) *trckd ldrs: rdn to ld over 1f out: styd on strly* **4/1**[2]
1032 **2** *1 ¾* **Whippasnapper**[4] [2215] 4-9-5 65 J-PGuillambert(3) 9 70
(JRBest) *hld up in tch: hdwy to chse wnr over 1f out: r.o fnl f* **11/4**[1]
6004 **3** *1 ½* **Coustou (IRE)**[5] [2172] 4-8-12 59 TEaves(5) 1 61
(ARDicken) *trckd ldrs: effrt over 2f out: kpt on same pce fnl f* **10/1**
3020 **4** *hd* **Luke After Me (IRE)**[1] [2260] 4-9-3 54 FLynch 3 61
(GASwinbank) *dwlt: hld up: effrt whn nt clr run over 2f to over 1f out: r.o: nrst fin* **5/1**[3]
00-3 **5** *1* **Golden Spectrum (IRE)**[20] [1787] 5-9-3 58 AlexGreaves 2 58
(DNicholls) *trckd ldrs: rdn whn n.m.r briefly over 2f out: one pce fnl f* **6/1**
-000 **6** *hd* **Time To Remember (IRE)**[7] [2130] 6-9-3 60 ANicholls 5 57
(DNicholls) *keen: led to over 1f out: no ex* **12/1**
0-40 **7** *shd* **Regent's Secret (USA)**[18] [1868] 4-9-3 65 PMulrennan(5) 7 62
(JSGoldie) *hld up: hdwy on ins 2f out: no imp fnl f* **10/1**
4000 **8** *5* **Ellen Mooney**[15] [1931] 5-8-11 57 (b) THamilton(3) 8 41
(RPElliott) *hld up in tch: reminders over 3f out: btn 2f out* **20/1**
0200 **9** *2 ½* **Legal Set (IRE)**[1] [2260] 8-9-3 52 AnnStokell 4 38
(MissAStokell) *cl up tl wknd fr 2f out* **40/1**
1m 28.68s (-3.79) **Going Correction** -0.45s/f (Firm)
**WFA** 3 from 4yo+ 11lb 9 Ran SP% **110.7**
Speed ratings: **103,101,99,99,97 97,97,91,89**CSF £14.37 TOTE £4.70: £1.70, £1.40, £3.00; EX 14.20 Place 6 £54.84, Place 5 £32.48.
**Owner** We-Know Partnership **Bred** Illuminatus Investments **Trained** Warthill, N Yorks

**FOCUS**
An modest contest run at only a fair pace and once again suited those ridden close to the pace. The form is fairly sound.

**NOTEBOOK**
**She's Our Lass(IRE)** extended her run of creditable efforts and, although ideally placed throughout, she showed the right attitude and, as she is equally effective over a mile, should continue to give a good account.
**Whippasnapper**, a versatile and reliable sort, may have been suited by a stronger gallop but ran his race and there is no reason why he should not continue to give a good account.
**Coustou(IRE)**, who has slipped a fair way in the weights, had the run of the race but was anything but disgraced. He shaped as though a more strongly-run race would have been in his favour.
**Luke After Me(IRE)** for the second time in successive days at this course, failed to get anything like a clear run and was not knocked about. He is better than the bare form again but he has yet to win a race and his style of racing means things have to fall just right.
**Golden Spectrum(IRE)** looked sure to be suited by the return to this trip after a pleasing debut run for current connections at Hamilton last time but is another from this race that would have been better suited by a stronger pace. He is not one to write off yet, despite his lengthy losing run.
**Time To Remember(IRE)** looked in good shape but pulled too hard at the head of affairs and not surprisingly had little to offer when tackled in the closing stages. The return to six will suit, though and he is one to keep an eye on from his current mark.
T/Plt: £57.70 to a £1 stake. Pool: £25,031.15. 316.40 winning tickets. T/Qpdt: £86.70 to a £1 stake. Pool: £1,417.90. 12.10 winning tickets. RY

# [2268]HAYDOCK (L-H)

## Saturday, May 22

**OFFICIAL GOING: Good to firm**
The going was described as 'firm but no jar'.
Wind: slight, 1/2 against Weather: fine

## 2293 OPTION HYGIENE H'CAP 5f

**1:30** (1:32) (B) (0-105,96) 3-Y-0+ **£14,092** (£4,336; £2,168; £1,084) **Stalls** Centre

Form RPR

11-4 **1** **Raccoon (IRE)**[7] 2130 4-8-6 **74**........(v[1]) KDarley 8 97+
(TDBarron) *racd far side: chsd ldrs: edgd rt and led overall over 1f out: r.o strly* **5/1**[2]

006- **2** *3* **Connect**[219] 5593 7-9-4 **86**........(b) GDuffield 7 93
(MHTompkins) *racd far side: bhd: hdwy over 1f out: styd on wl ins last* **12/1**

0-00 **3** *3/4* **Seafield Towers**[7] 2132 4-8-6 **77**........(p) NMackay[(3)] 1 81
(MissLAPerratt) *racd far side: w ldrs: nt qckn appr fnl f* **20/1**

-404 **4** *nk* **Indian Spark**[9] 2065 10-9-11 **93**........ TEDurcan 13 96
(JSGoldie) *racd stands' side: sn bhd: styd on fnl 2f: nt rch ldrs* **12/1**

00-0 **5** *hd* **Talbot Avenue**[15] 1923 6-8-12 **80**........ SRighton 12 82
(MMullineaux) *racd stands' side: bhd tl styd on fnl 2f: kpt on wl ins last* **28/1**

00-0 **6** *1/2* **Absent Friends**[14] 1955 7-9-13 **95**........ JEdmunds 11 95
(JBalding) *racd stands' side: w ldrs: led that gp 2f out: kpt on same pce* **33/1**

-055 **7** *1/2* **Matty Tun**[10] 2041 5-9-11 **93**........ RHughes 15 92
(JBalding) *slwoly into stride: racd stands' side: kpt on fnl 2f: nt rch ldrs* **11/2**[3]

0450 **8** *2 1/2* **Prince Of Blues (IRE)**[10] 2041 6-7-5 **66** oh2........(p) PVarley[(7)] 2 56
(MMullineaux) *led on far side tl over 1f out: fdd* **40/1**

0105 **9** *nk* **Chico Guapo (IRE)**[7] 2130 4-8-5 **76**........ TPQueally[(3)] 5 65
(JAGlover) *racd far side: w ldrs: wknd appr fnl f* **12/1**

2-15 **10** *shd* **Foursquare (IRE)**[17] 1883 3-9-2 **92**........ DeanMcKeown 14 80
(JMackie) *led stands' side tl 2f out: fdd* **9/1**

00-0 **11** *1 1/4* **Charlie Parkes**[7] 2130 6-8-2 **73**........ DAllan[(3)] 4 57
(EJAlston) *racd far side: chsd ldrs: wknd over 1f out* **16/1**

05-0 **12** *3 1/2* **Salviati (USA)**[10] 2041 7-9-7 **89**........ KDalgleish 10 60
(JMBradley) *s.s: racd far side: a bhd* **16/1**

060- **13** *2* **Atlantic Viking (IRE)**[255] 4815 9-10-0 **96**........ SWKelly 6 60
(DNicholls) *racd far side: mid-div: lost pl 2f out* **50/1**

1213 **14** *shd* **Maktavish**[15] 1923 5-9-3 **85**........(p) RWinston 9 49
(ISemple) *racd stands' side: w ldr: lost pl over 1f out: eased* **4/1**[1]

0600 **15** *1/2* **Palawan**[15] 1923 8-9-0 **82**........ MartinDwyer 3 44
(AMBalding) *racd far side: chsd ldrs: lost pl over 1f out* **25/1**

60.67 secs (-1.40) **Going Correction** -0.175s/f (Firm)
**WFA** 3 from 4yo+ 8lb **15** Ran SP% **116.3**
Speed ratings: **104,99,98,97,97 96,95,91,91,90 88,83,80,80,79**CSF £55.65 CT £1130.07 TOTE £5.30: £2.00, £4.40, £5.60; EX 70.80.
**Owner** P D Savill **Bred** P D Savill **Trained** Maunby, N Yorks
■ Stewards Enquiry : N Mackay two-day ban: used whip above shoulder height (Jun 2-3)

**FOCUS**
In effect a 0-96 handicap but nonetheless competitive, and run at break-neck early pace. The form looks solid.

**NOTEBOOK**
**Raccoon(IRE)** ◆, lit up beforehand by the first-time visor, wandered in front but still scored in most decisive fashion. He is a sprinter very much on the up, and well worth keeping on the right side.
**Connect**, 10lb higher than his last win a year ago, did not look at his very best on his return to action. He stayed on in good style from off the pace to snatch second spot near the line.
**Seafield Towers**returned to form, showing all his old speed and keeping on in willing fashion under a vigorous ride.
**Indian Spark**, bidding for his third success in this race, did not impress going to post. He kept on in willing fashion and these days prefers either easier ground or a sixth furlong.
**Talbot Avenue**, who won from a 5lb higher mark at York last July, raced virtually alone down the stands'-side rail. He was putting in his best work at the finish and looks on the way back.
**Absent Friends** went head to head with Maktavish and kept on surprisingly well. He looks right back to his best.
**Matty Tun**, drawn 15 of 15, had nothing on his right side and blew it leaving the stalls.
**Maktavish**, on ground plenty fast enough for him, did not enjoy an uncontested lead and decided this was not his day. He will bounce back. *Official explanation: trainer's representative said gelding can disappoint when unable to make the running*

## 2294 DAVE JONES FOR MORTGAGES STKS (REGISTERED AS THE SANDY LANE STAKES) (LISTED RACE) 6f

**2:00** (2:01) (A) 3-Y-0 **£17,400** (£6,600; £3,300; £1,500) **Stalls** Centre

Form RPR

3-41 **1** **Moss Vale (IRE)**[17] 1883 3-8-11 **106**........ KDarley 9 115
(BWHills) *lw: wnt lft after s: t.k.h: led after 2f out: shkn up over 1f out: qcknd clr: readily* **5/2**[2]

41-3 **2** *3* **Boogie Street**[21] 1763 3-9-0 **107**........(t) RHughes 4 109
(RHannon) *trckd ldrs: effrt 2f out: styd on to go 2nd ins last: no imp* **11/2**[3]

20-1 **3** *3* **High Voltage**[28] 1614 3-8-11 **99**........(t) DarrenWilliams 3 97
(KRBurke) *led 2f: chsd ldrs: nt qckn appr fnl f* **16/1**

3-00 **4** *shd* **Fast Heart**[10] 2041 3-8-11 **99**........(t) JFMcDonald 1 97
(BJMeehan) *chsd ldrs: kpt on same pce fnl 2f* **40/1**

-150 **5** *2 1/2* **Local Poet**[17] 1883 3-8-11 **92**........ GGibbons 2 90
(BAMcmahon) *chsd ldrs: wknd fnl f* **28/1**

1-60 **6** *3 1/2* **Nero's Return (IRE)**[35] 1459 3-9-0 **105**........ KDalgleish 8 82
(MJohnston) *sltly hmpd sn after s: rdn and hung lft over 2f out: nvr a factor* **16/1**

13-1 **7** *2* **Millbag (IRE)**[24] 1706 3-9-0 **107**........ TEDurcan 6 76
(MRChannon) *sltly hmpd sn after s: sn chsng ldrs: rdn over 2f out: lost pl over 1f out* **7/4**[1]

00-4 **8** *1 1/4* **Embassy Lord**[17] 1883 3-8-11 **80**........(b) JDO'Reilly 5 69
(JO'Reilly) *sn outpcd: wandered and lost pl over 2f out* **140/1**

11-4 **9** *2 1/2* **Rum Shot**[8] 2080 3-8-11 **97**........ DSweeney 7 62
(HCandy) *hmpd sn after s: sn chsng ldrs: rdn over 2f out: sn lost pl* **7/1**

1m 12.11s (-2.78) **Going Correction** -0.175s/f (Firm) **9** Ran SP% **111.2**
Speed ratings: **111,107,103,102,99 94,92,90,87**CSF £15.63 TOTE £3.90: £1.80, £2.00, £2.50; EX 17.40.
**Owner** John C Grant **Bred** Derek Veitch **Trained** Lambourn, Berks

**FOCUS**
A good renewal despite a coming together at the start, and an impressive winner who should take high rank in time. Despite a couple running below expectations the form looks sound.

**NOTEBOOK**
**Moss Vale(IRE)** ◆ looked in outstanding condition. He leaned left coming out of the stalls, impeding the three on his immediate inside. Taking a keen grip, he quickened up in fine style and was right on top at the finish. Still on the up, he has the makings of a high-class sprinter.
**Boogie Street**, a big type, looked in top trim. He kept on in good style to take second spot inside the last but the winner was much too good. This sixth furlong seemed to suit him.
**High Voltage**, inclined to get warm beforehand, had something to find with the first two on official figures.
**Fast Heart** ran better but will be hard to place.
**Local Poet** had plenty to find and was simply not up to it.
**Nero's Return(IRE)** took a bump at the start but even so this was another lifeless display.
**Millbag(IRE)** took a bump at the start but that was not enough to account for this poor display. This was simply too bad to be true.
**Rum Shot**, making a quick reappearance, was well below par after collecting a bump leaving the stalls.

## 2295 TOTESPORT SILVER BOWL (HERITAGE H'CAP) 1m 30y

**2:30** (2:31) (B) (0-110,103) 3-Y-0 **£52,200** (£19,800; £9,900; £4,500) **Stalls** Low

Form RPR

-131 **1** **Gatwick (IRE)**[4] 2202 3-8-10 **95** 8ex........ SHitchcott[(3)] 17 109+
(MRChannon) *dwlt: bhd: hdwy over 3f out: nt clr run over 1f out: str run to ld ins fnl f: r.o wl* **11/2**[2]

0340 **2** *1 3/4* **Makfool (FR)**[16] 1900 3-8-8 **90**........ TEDurcan 10 100
(MRChannon) *chsd ldrs: led over 1f out tl ins last: no ex* **40/1**

-142 **3** *shd* **Zonus**[16] 1900 3-8-5 **87**........ KDarley 12 97+
(BWHills) *dwlt: bhd: hdwy over 2f out: nt clr run and swtchd outside over 1f out: hung lft and carried hd high: fin wl* **5/2**[1]

3120 **4** *shd* **Appalachian Trail (IRE)**[16] 1900 3-8-4 **86**........ GDuffield 2 96
(ISemple) *chsd ldrs: edgd lft over 1f out: kpt on wl ins fnl f* **12/1**

1-11 **5** *2* **Oasis Star (IRE)**[16] 1900 3-8-4 **86**........ MartinDwyer 11 91
(PWHarris) *chsd ldrs: effrt over 2f out: styd on same pce* **6/1**[3]

-034 **6** *nk* **Freak Occurence (IRE)**[9] 2069 3-7-11 **82**........ JFMcDonald[(3)] 4 86
(MissECLavelle) *chsd ldrs: kpt on same pce fnl 2f* **25/1**

32-2 **7** *1/2* **Capped For Victory (USA)**[14] 1972 3-8-1 **88**........ BSwarbrick[(5)] 3 91
(SirMichaelStoute) *led after 1f: qckmd over 4f out: hdd over 1f out: one pce* **12/1**

1-02 **8** *1/2* **Secretary General (IRE)**[8] 2089 3-8-5 **92**........ RThomas[(5)] 5 94
(PFICole) *rr-div: nt clr run 3f out: styd on fnl f* **12/1**

55-5 **9** *1* **Asia Winds (IRE)**[11] 2020 3-8-11 **93**........ WRyan 15 93
(BWHills) *s.i.s: hdwy whn nt clr run over 2f out tl over 1f out: styd on ins last* **25/1**

5-00 **10** *hd* **Overdrawn (IRE)**[20] 1795 3-8-10 **92**........ SWKelly 8 91
(JAOsborne) *mid-div: kpt on fnl 3f: nvr rchd ldrs* **12/1**

61-0 **11** *3 1/2* **Benny The Ball (USA)**[37] 1408 3-8-1 **83**........ JBramhill 1 74
(NPLittmoden) *trckd ldrs: chal over 2f out: wknd over 1f out* **50/1**

-030 **12** *nk* **Parkview Love (USA)**[11] 2019 3-9-7 **103**........ KDalgleish 18 93
(MJohnston) *chsd ldrs on outside: lost pl over 4f out* **66/1**

4-00 **13** *shd* **Convince (USA)**[11] 2019 3-8-5 **87**........ DeanMcKeown 7 77
(MABuckley) *hld up in rr: nvr a factor* **50/1**

-420 **14** *1/2* **Star Pupil**[14] 1965 3-7-12 **83**........ FPFerris[(3)] 13 72
(AMBalding) *hld up in rr: effrt on ins whn nt clr run over 3f out and over 1f out: saddle slipped* **40/1**

22-6 **15** *1 3/4* **Colour Wheel**[29] 1585 3-8-8 **90**........(t) RHughes 6 75
(RCharlton) *led 1f: chsd ldrs: lost pl over 1f out* **20/1**

4-40 **16** *shd* **White Hawk**[16] 1900 3-8-10 **95**........ TPQueally[(3)] 14 80
(DRLoder) *hld up: a in rr* **50/1**

2360 **17** *2* **Bahiano (IRE)**[11] 2019 3-8-9 **98**........ DeanWilliams[(7)] 16 78
(CEBrittain) *chsd ldrs: lost pl over 2f out* **33/1**

0-00 **18** *3* **Spanish Ace**[38] 1396 3-9-2 **98**........ DSweeney 9 71
(AMBalding) *alwys in rr* **66/1**

1m 41.73s (-3.82) **Going Correction** -0.175s/f (Firm) **18** Ran SP% **118.2**
Speed ratings: **112,110,110,110,108 107,107,106,105,105 102,101,101,101,99 99,97,94**CSF £217.05 CT £705.37 TOTE £5.20: £2.30, £10.10, £1.10, £2.70; EX 250.10 Trifecta £520.80 Pool of £2,421.02 - 3.30 winning units.
**Owner** W H Ponsonby **Bred** M J Dargan **Trained** West Ilsley, Berks

**FOCUS**
A highly competitive 0-103 handicap, but a messy race. The early pace was not strong, but the overall time was good and the form looks particularly sound.

**NOTEBOOK**
**Gatwick(IRE)**, making a quick reappearance under a stiff penalty, was drawn wide and a tardy start left him with a lot to do. He met traffic problems and was left with nowhere to go at one stage, but finished with a real flourish to snatch the prize out of the fire. This was a smart effort, all the more so in view of the problems he encountered, and he looks well capable of holding his own in better company, especially when stepping up to ten furlongs or more. He has not finished improving yet.
**Makfool(FR)**, much better suited by this more galloping track, kept out of trouble but, after showing ahead, had no answer to his stablemate's devastating late burst.
**Zonus**, 4lb higher, had it all to do after a tardy start. He ran into traffic problems but, eventually making his way to the outside, finished strongly despite carrying his head high and on one side. He has plenty of ability but needs everything to fall just right.
**Appalachian Trail(IRE)** ran well in this company but, possibly feeling the fast ground, came off a straight line, getting in the way of the winner.
**Oasis Star(IRE)**, 5lb higher, lost her unbeaten record but even so she ran with plenty of credit in what was a much tougher event than Chester.

**Freak Occurence(IRE)** is a model of consistency but is paying the price with an unchanged handicap mark.
**Capped For Victory(USA)**, dropped 12lb after Thirsk, had the run of the race, quickening the pace from the front once in line for home. It seems this is as good as he is now.
**Secretary General(IRE)**, 5lb higher, met traffic problems trying to come from way off the pace. In the circumstances he did as well as could be expected.
**Asia Winds(IRE)** ◆, happier on this much quicker ground, met severe traffic problems. Staying on in fine style at the finish, she deserves to find a nice handicap.
**Convince(USA)** *Official explanation: jockey said gelding did not handle the bend*
**Star Pupil** appreciated this step up in trip but enjoyed no luck in running on the inside and his rider eventually accepted it, his saddle having slipped. He is much better than the bare form. *Official explanation: jockey said saddle slipped*

## 2296 EBF BOLLIN MAIDEN FILLIES' STKS — 6f
**3:05** (3:07) (D) 2-Y-O — **£5,369** (£1,652; £826; £413) **Stalls** Centre

Form — RPR
22 **1** **Sapphire Dream**[17] 1878 2-8-11 ........ RWinston 6 77
(ABailey) *mde all: shkn up over 1f out: r.o wl* **10/11**[1]
**2** *1 ¾* **Mytton's Bell (IRE)** 2-8-11 ........ JBramhill 4 72
(ABailey) *cmpt: trckd ldrs: effrt 2f out: styd on same pce* **33/1**
**3** *hd* **Easy Feeling (IRE)** 2-8-11 ........ RHughes 7 71
(RHannon) *w'like: lengthy: chsd ldrs: effrt over 1f out: wnt lft ins last: no imp* **6/1**[3]
**4** *1 ¼* **Wasalat (USA)** 2-8-11 ........ TEDurcan 5 67
(MRChannon) *w'like: compt: s.i.s: sn trcking ldrs: effrt 2f out: sn rdn and outpcd: styd on wl ins last: improve* **5/1**[2]
**5** *4* **Sweet Marguerite** 2-8-8 ........ DAllan(3) 8 55
(TDEasterby) *leggy: unf: scope: bit bkwd: sn chsng ldrs: drvn along over 3f out: edgd lft and lost pl over 1f out* **14/1**
0 **6** *shd* **Don't Tell Trigger (IRE)**[9] 2057 2-8-11 ........ JDSmith 2 55
(JSMoore) *trckd ldrs: effrt over 2f out: lost pl over 1f out* **25/1**
4 **7** *3 ½* **Make Us Flush**[28] 1601 2-8-6 ........ PBradley(5) 3 45
(ABerry) *trckd ldrs: effrt over 2f out: lost pl over 1f out* **20/1**
**8** *hd* **Sukuma (IRE)** 2-8-11 ........ MartinDwyer 1 44
(AMBalding) *leggy: unf: dwlt: lost pl 2f out* **10/1**
0 **9** *20* **Gloria Nimbus**[28] 1601 2-8-11 ........ SRighton 9 —
(MMullineaux) *swvd rt s: t.k.h: sn trcking ldrs: lost pl over 2f out: sn bhd and eased* **66/1**

1m 14.84s (-0.05) **Going Correction** -0.175s/f (Firm) **9** Ran SP% **112.1**
Speed ratings: **93,90,90,88,83 83,78,78,51**CSF £44.82 TOTE £1.80: £1.10, £6.20, £1.60; EX 44.80.
**Owner** P T Tellwright **Bred** P T Tellwright **Trained** Little Budworth, Cheshire

**FOCUS**
Just an ordinary maiden with the winner dictating things from the front and running up to previous form.

**NOTEBOOK**
**Sapphire Dream**, the most experienced in the field, was happy to sit in front. When shaken up she lengthened her stride and took this with the minimum of fuss, paying a complement to her Chester conqueror.
**Mytton's Bell(IRE)**, a March foal, is a close-coupled sort. She kept close tabs on the winner and in the end she did just enough to follow her stablemate home.
**Easy Feeling(IRE)** ◆, long in the back, made a pleasing bow and, but for coming off a straight line, would have secured second spot. The experience will have done her a world of good.
**Wasalat(USA)** ◆, a likeable, medium-sized filly, was very inexperienced. She stayed on in fine style late on and is sure to improve and win a race or two when stepped up in trip.
**Sweet Marguerite**, a February foal, looks as if she needs more time yet. She showed that she does possess some ability.

## 2297 EBF JOAN WESTBROOK PINNACLE STKS (LISTED RACE) (F&M) — 1m 3f 200y
**3:35** (3:35) (A) 4-Y-O+ — **£23,200** (£8,800; £4,400; £2,000) **Stalls** High

Form — RPR
10-3 **1** **Pongee**[9] 2062 4-8-11 87 ........ TEDurcan 1 96
(LMCumani) *trckd ldr: led over 1f out: styd on strly* **3/1**[2]
3-21 **2** *2 ½* **Desert Royalty (IRE)**[9] 2062 4-8-11 82 ........ RHughes 2 92
(EALDunlop) *hld up on heels of ldrs: effrt and n.m.r 2f out: sn rdn: styd on to go 2nd ins last: no imp* **5/2**[1]
13-0 **3** *2* **Chantress**[20] 1790 4-8-11 92 ........(p) MartinDwyer 6 89
(MrsJRRamsden) *trckd ldrs: chal over 3f out: styd on same pce appr fnl f* **15/2**
5-03 **4** *shd* **Felicity (IRE)**[8] 2102 4-8-11 97 ........ RHavlin 3 89
(JHMGosden) *led: qcknd 4f out: hdd over 1f out: kpt on one pce* **9/2**
20-5 **5** *shd* **Thingmebob**[10] 2042 4-8-11 104 ........ GDuffield 5 88
(MHTompkins) *t.k.h: trckd ldrs: effrt 3f out: one pce fnl 2f* **10/3**[3]
-235 **6** *17* **Transcendantale (FR)**[22] 1752 6-8-11 47 ........ TPQueally 4 61?
(MrsSLamyman) *wl in tch: rdn over 3f out: lost pl over 2f out: eased* **100/1**
50 **7** *dist* **My Little Sophia**[19] 1842 4-8-11 ........ SWKelly 7 —
(MMullineaux) *swtchd lft after s: a last: t.o 3f out* **200/1**

2m 32.16s (-3.00) **Going Correction** -0.175s/f (Firm) **7** Ran SP% **108.1**
Speed ratings: **103,101,100,99,99 88,—**CSF £9.66 TOTE £4.30: £1.70, £1.70; EX 11.20.
**Owner** Fittocks Stud **Bred** Fittocks Stud **Trained** Newmarket, Suffolk

**FOCUS**
A Listed race for fillies and mares but not a great contest and the gallop only stepped up once in line for home.

**NOTEBOOK**
**Pongee** looked in very good trim and in the end won going away. No doubt her summer target will be a repeat bid in the Galtres Stakes at York in August, a Listed race her trainer has dominated.
**Desert Royalty(IRE)**, meeting the winner on 5lb worse terms, travelled supremely well but in the end she was very much second best.
**Chantress** ran a lot better and if anything seemed suited by the step up in distance.
**Felicity(IRE)**, a big filly, stepped up the pace from the front but in the end was simply not good enough.
**Thingmebob**, rated 17lb ahead of the winner, is not in the same sort of form she showed last summner. She looks as though she will appreciate some sun on her back.
**Transcendantale(FR)** was rewarded for just turning up.

## 2298 MTB GROUP MAIDEN STKS — 1m 2f 120y
**4:10** (4:13) (D) 3-Y-O — **£5,707** (£1,756; £878; £439) **Stalls** High

Form — RPR
3 **1** **Nunki (USA)**[28] 1612 3-9-0 ........ WRyan 5 85
(HRACecil) *trckd ldrs: styd on to ld jst ins fnl f: hld on nr fin* **11/4**[2]
0 **2** *hd* **Idealistic (IRE)**[26] 1674 3-8-9 ........ MartinDwyer 6 80
(LMCumani) *trckd ldrs: pushed along over 4f out: led over 1f out tl jst ins last: rallied: jst hld* **16/1**
3 **3** *4* **Always Waining (IRE)**[6] 2145 3-9-0 ........ KDalgleish 8 78+
(MJohnston) *set mod pce for 2f: hung rt bnd over 5f out: led and hung lft over 2f out: hdd over 1f out: wl hld whn eased ins last* **7/1**
-250 **4** *3* **Gjovic**[9] 2069 3-8-11 75 ........ JFMcDonald(3) 4 73
(BJMeehan) *hld up: hdwy on ins over 4f out: kpt on one pce fnl 2f* **4/1**[3]
0-54 **5** *1 ¾* **Mouftari (USA)**[15] 1926 3-9-0 84 ........ KDarley 9 70
(BWHills) *trckd ldrs: led over 3f out tl over 2f out: wknd over 1f out* **5/2**[1]
0-3 **6** *2* **Mungo Jerry (GER)**[21] 1761 3-9-0 ........ GDuffield 10 67
(JGGiven) *t.k.h: trckd ldrs: rdn and wknd over 2f out* **10/1**
4 **7** *7* **Protective**[6] 2144 3-9-0 ........ TEDurcan 7 55
(JGGiven) *s.i.s: drvn along and lost pl 3f out: sn bhd* **20/1**
0-0 **8** *8* **Phoenix Eye**[15] 1926 3-9-0 ........ SWKelly 3 41
(MMullineaux) *led after 2f: qcknd over 5f out: hdd over 3f out: lost pl over 2f out: sn bhd* **100/1**
**9** *½* **Twilight Years** 3-8-11 ........ DAllan(3) 1 40
(TDEasterby) *big: rangy: bkwd: s.v.s: a bhd: lost tch over 2f out* **40/1**
0-00 **10** *5* **Mad Maurice**[15] 1939 3-8-11 ........(p) TPQueally(3) 2 32
(BJCurley) *hld up in rr: hdwy to chse ldrs 4f out: wknd over 2f out: sn bhd and eased* **40/1**

2m 15.19s (-2.54) **Going Correction** -0.175s/f (Firm) **10** Ran SP% **113.3**
Speed ratings: **102,101,98,96,95 94,88,83,82,79**CSF £42.06 TOTE £2.70: £1.80, £3.00, £2.30; EX 52.10.
**Owner** Niarchos Family **Bred** Flaxman Holdings Ltd **Trained** Newmarket, Suffolk
■ Stewards Enquiry : Martin Dwyer one-day ban: used whip from above shoulder height (Jun 2)

**FOCUS**
A decent maiden run at a steady gallop but the first two in the end pulling clear.

**NOTEBOOK**
**Nunki(USA)**, still carrying condition, showed a good attitude but in the end it was a close call. This will have taught him plenty and his future prospects rely on being given a realistic handicap mark.
**Idealistic(IRE)** ◆, who has a pronounced knee action, improved a good deal on her initial effort and went down guns blazing. She will improve again and deserves to find a race.
**Always Waining(IRE)** had difficulty handling the turn. He showed in inexperience in front and, when nailed by the first two, he was sensibly given as easy time as possible. He will improve again and should find a race.
**Gjovic**, with the blinkers left off, was settled towards the rear. Staying on in his own time late on, a much stronger gallop would have suited him better. Even so he does not look the most straightforward individual.
**Mouftari(USA)**, very warm at the start, went on and stepped up the pace but in the end he was nowhere near good enough. He will struggle in handicap company from a rating of 84.
**Mungo Jerry(GER)** would not settle and could have done with a much stronger early pace.
**Twilight Years** *Official explanation: jockey said gelding hung left*

## 2299 MARY PAGE BIRTHDAY H'CAP — 1m 6f
**4:40** (4:40) (E) (0-75,75) 4-Y-O+ — **£3,640** (£1,120; £560; £280) **Stalls** Low

Form — RPR
5322 **1** **Nakwa (IRE)**[20] 1785 6-8-13 63 ........ DAllan(3) 9 73
(EJAlston) *led tl 9f out: led 4f out: styd on wl: clr 1f out: eased towards fin* **7/2**[1]
0056 **2** *5* **Northern Nymph**[14] 1958 5-9-0 66 ........ StephanieHollinshead(5) 4 69
(RHollinshead) *hld up in rr: hdwy on outside over 3f out: kpt on to take 2nd ins last: no ch w wnr* **6/1**[3]
300- **3** *1 ¼* **Once (FR)**[346] 2278 4-10-0 75 ........ SWKelly 2 76
(JAOsborne) *chsd ldng pair: effrt over 3f out: kpt on one pce fnl 2f* **11/1**
430- **4** *1 ¼* **Fantastico (IRE)**[9] 5463 4-9-3 64 ........ KDalgleish 6 64
(MrsKWalton) *in tch: effrt over 3f out: kpt on ins last* **20/1**
3102 **5** *¾* **Bramantino (IRE)**[49] 1245 4-8-11 58 ........(b) GParkin 7 56
(RAFahey) *trckd ldng pair: effrt 4f out: one pce fnl 2f* **7/1**
-000 **6** *2 ½* **Claradotnet**[9] 2062 4-9-9 70 ........ TEDurcan 5 65
(MRChannon) *hld up in rr: hdwy over 3f out: nvr nr ldrs* **8/1**
-603 **7** *3* **Repulse Bay (IRE)**[5] 2171 6-8-1 51 ........ NMackay(3) 10 42
(JSGoldie) *chsd ldrs: lost pl 4f out: nvr a factor after* **11/2**[2]
-220 **8** *2* **Vicars Destiny**[13] 1615 6-9-8 69 ........(p) GDuffield 3 57
(MrsSLamyman) *hld up in rr: pushed along over 6g out: sme hdwy over 3f out: nvr on terms* **6/1**[3]
020- **9** *4* **Circus Maximus (USA)**[19] 3655 7-8-11 58 ........(b) KDarley 1 40
(IanWilliams) *hld up in rr: pushed alobg over 6g out: nvr a factor* **12/1**
0600 **10** *7* **Vanbrugh (FR)**[7] 2116 4-8-8 55 ........(vt) DarrenWilliams 8 28
(MissDAMchale) *t.k.h: trckd ldr: led 9f out tl 4f out: hung lft and lost pl 3f out: eased* **16/1**

3m 2.63s (-3.52) **Going Correction** -0.175s/f (Firm) **10** Ran SP% **116.5**
Speed ratings: **103,100,99,98,98 96,95,94,91,87**CSF £24.15 CT £209.83 TOTE £3.20: £2.00, £1.80, £4.50; EX 42.20 Place 6 £56.30, Place 5 £15.33.
**Owner** Alan Dick **Bred** Teviot Stud **Trained** Longton, Lancs

**FOCUS**
A moderate handicap but a decent pace for this grade, with the winner prominent throughout.

**NOTEBOOK**
**Nakwa(IRE)**, suited by the strong pace, regained the lead once in line for home and kept up the gallop with real gusto. He never looked like being challenged and at the line was able to ease down. This stiffer test clearly brought out the very best in him.
**Northern Nymph**, a stone better off with winner compared with their running here three outings ago, wanted nothing to do with the fast and furious pace. He stayed on down the wide outside to secure second spot inside the last.
**Once(FR)**, absent for almost a year and having just his eighth career start, looked to be carrying condition. He kept tabs on the two pacesetters and deserves credit for the way he kept going all the way to the line.
**Fantastico(IRE)**, fit from hurdling, appreciated the return to the Flat and if anything looks likely to appreciate an even stiffer test.
**Bramantino(IRE)**, who finished ahead of the winner at Newcastle, was having his first outing for seven weeks after an enforced abscence. He ran as if it was just needed.
**Claradotnet** had no chance the way she was ridden, sitting way off the pace with her stamina unproven.
T/Plt: £45.60 to a £1 stake. Pool: £55,753.65. 891.40 winning tickets. T/Qpdt: £6.50 to a £1 stake. Pool: £2,540.80. 285.70 winning tickets. WG

# 1984 KEMPTON (R-H)
Saturday, May 22

**OFFICIAL GOING: Good to firm (good in places)**

## 2300 NEW FIXTURE MAIDEN AUCTION STKS — 6f
**6:05** (6:06) (E) 2-Y-O — **£3,562** (£1,096; £548; £274) **Stalls** Low

Form — RPR
**1** **Aastral Magic** 2-8-2 ........ RLMoore 16 69
(RHannon) *leggy: lt-fr: bhd: gd hdwy over 1f out: rdn to ld wl ins fnl f* **20/1**
6 **2** *nk* **Shaheer (IRE)**[7] 2111 2-8-6 ........ LPKeniry(3) 1 75
(BJMeehan) *a in tch: rdn over 1f out: r.o wl to go 2nd nr fin* **4/1**[2]
0 **3** *¾* **Flying Pass**[19] 1826 2-8-9 ........ TQuinn 6 73
(DJSFfrenchDavis) *a.p: led over 2f out: r.o: hdd wl ins fnl f* **20/1**

4 1/2 **Ridder** 2-8-10 ........ DHolland 14 72
(DJCoakley) *neat: a.p: rdn ent fnl f: no ex fnl 100yds: promising* **20/1**

5 2 **Cloann (IRE)** 2-8-2 ........ RSmith 12 58
(RHannon) *neat: slowly away: hdwy 2f out: r.o wl fnl f: nvr nrr* **33/1**

4 6 3 1/2 **Zendaro**[23] 1735 2-8-8 ........ WSupple 8 54
(WMBrisbourne) *w ldrs: rdn over 1f out: wknd ins last* **12/1**

7 *hd* **Whatatodo** 2-7-11 ........ HayleyTurner(5) 17 47
(MLWBell) *lt-fr: b.bkwd: racd on outside: bhd tl mde sme late hdwy* **25/1**

8 1 3/4 **Missed A Beat** 2-8-3 ........ FNorton 19 43
(MBlanshard) *neat: b.bkwd: slowly away: nvr nr to chal* **9/1**[3]

9 *hd* **King Of Fire** 2-8-7 ........ SCarson 7 46
(MissBSanders) *neat: b.bkwd: nvr bttr than mid-div* **66/1**

10 3/4 **Mister Aziz (IRE)** 2-8-8 ........ JTate 11 45
(JMPEustace) *neat: bkwd: chsd ldrs tl rdn and wknd appr fnl f* **16/1**

11 *hd* **Fly To Dubai (IRE)** 2-8-8 ........ JQuinn 4 44
(EJO'Neill) *neat: in tch tl rdn and wknd 2f out* **7/2**[1]

12 1/2 **Spaced (IRE)** 2-8-10 ........ RHughes 5 45
(RHannon) *neat: in rr: mde som late hdwy* **9/1**[3]

13 2 **Young Thomas (IRE)** 2-8-8 ........ MFenton 3 37
(MLWBell) *lt-fr: a outpcd in rr* **14/1**

14 1 1/4 **Mill By The Stream** 2-8-9 ........ NCallan 18 34
(APJarvis) *neat: lw: mid-div: racd wd: in tch to 1/2-way* **20/1**

15 *nk* **Don Pele (IRE)** 2-8-9 ........ JFEgan 13 33
(SKirk) *neat: bkwd: prom tl rdn and wknd wl over 1f out* **10/1**

0 16 *nk* **Amalgam (IRE)**[18] 1853 2-8-2 ........ DKinsella 10 25
(MrsPNDutfield) *a bhd* **66/1**

0 17 3 **Big Bambo (IRE)**[47] 1269 2-8-7 ........ RHavlin 2 21
(MrsPNDutfield) *lw: led tl hdd over 2f out: wknd qckly* **100/1**

18 4 **Pips Pearl (IRE)** 2-8-0 ........ RMiles(3) 20 —
(MrsPNDutfield) *unf: drawn wd: sn bhd* **33/1**

19 10 **Smart Dawn** 2-8-4 ........ SChin 9 —
(CTinkler) *neat: in rr whn hmpd over 3f out: little ch after* **33/1**

1m 13.89s (0.82) **Going Correction** -0.125s/f (Firm) **19** Ran SP% **127.2**
Speed ratings: **89,88,87,86,84 79,79,77,76,75 75,74,72,70,70 69,65,60,47**CSF £91.06 TOTE £22.90: £8.80, £2.10, £7.40; EX 162.30.

**Owner** Green Pastures Partnership **Bred** Green Pastures Farm **Trained** East Everleigh, Wilts

**FOCUS**

A largely unprepossessing bunch on looks and pedigreee and almost certainly ordinary maiden for the track. They all raced towards the stands'-side rail.

**NOTEBOOK**

**Aastral Magic**, who is closely related to the stable's Jersey Stakes winner Lots Of Magic, was retained cheaply at the sales. Nothing much was expected by the stable judging by her starting price, and this did not look a great maiden, but she is likely to be kept on the go throughout the summer and should give her owners plenty of fun.

**Shaheer(IRE)**, coltish beforehand, had the benefit of a previous run under his belt and was taking on lesser opposition here. He kept on well next to the rail and this half-brother to a couple of winners should be capable of winning a similarly average maiden.

**Flying Pass**, always behind on his previous visit here in bad ground, appreciated the improved conditions and showed plenty of pace.

**Ridder**, whose dam won over seven furlongs at two, is likely to benefit from an extra furlong in time. This was not a bad effort on his debut for he came there looking like a winner inside the final furlong, only to flatten out in the closing stages. *Official explanation: jockey said colt was hanging left.*

**Cloann(IRE)**, a half-sister to a mile juvenile winner and to useful dual-purpose performer Silver Groom, kept on well upthe rail without being knocked about. This was a pleasing introduction and she should do better over farther.

**Zendaro**, another with the benefit of a previous run, had little excuse.

**Fly To Dubai(IRE)**, who was popular in the market, is bred to better in time over farther.

**Spaced(IRE)**, a half-brother to fair juvenile winner Menas Gold, stayed on steadily without ever getting into contention. He was given a very kind introduction here and should be capable of better in time.

**Don Pele(IRE)** *Official explanation: jockey said colt lost its action in the closing stages.*

## 2301 FULLER'S LONDON PRIDE MAIDEN STKS 7f (J)

**6:35** (6:35) (D ) 3-Y-O **£5,642** (£1,736; £868; £434) **Stalls** High

Form RPR

34-3 1 **Kind (IRE)**[38] 1400 3-8-9 80 ........ RHughes 9 77
(RCharlton) *b.hind: t.k.h: sn led and wnt clr: kpt up to work ins fnl 2f: unchal* **4/5**[1]

0-43 2 6 **Farewell Gift**[20] 1796 3-9-0 84 ........ RLMoore 4 65
(RHannon) *racd in 3rd: rdn to go 2nd over 1f out: kpt on but no ch w wnr* **2/1**[2]

24- 3 3/4 **Tropical Storm (IRE)**[213] 5700 3-9-0 ........ EAhern 5 63
(JNoseda) *swtg: racd in 4th: short of room over 2f out: kpt on one pce ins fnl 2f* **14/1**

00-0 4 1/2 **Snow Joke (IRE)**[40] 1366 3-8-9 57 ........ RHavlin 8 57
(MrsPNDutfield) *slowly away: styd on one pce fnl 2f* **100/1**

004 5 2 **Mr Hullabalou (IRE)**[20] 1796 3-9-0 79 ........ NDay 7 57
(RIngram) *b.hind: chsd wnr tl rdn and wknd over 1f out* **10/1**[3]

6 7 **Pure Imagination (IRE)** 3-9-0 ........ SCarson 2 38
(JMBradley) *w'like: a struggling in rr* **66/1**

7 3/4 **Iltravitore (IRE)** 3-9-0 ........ NPollard 6 36
(DRCElsworth) *unf: scope: slowly away: a bhd* **40/1**

8 29 **Sylvaticus (IRE)** 3-9-0 ........ RSmith 3 —
(RHannon) *w'like: scope: a wl bhd: t.o fnl 3f* **66/1**

1m 26.25s (-1.02) **Going Correction** 0.0s/f (Good) **8** Ran SP% **111.1**
Speed ratings: **105,98,97,96,94 86,85,52**CSF £2.33 TOTE £1.70: £1.02, £1.30, £2.40; EX 3.40.

**Owner** K Abdulla **Bred** Juddmonte Farms **Trained** Beckhampton, Wilts

**FOCUS**

An uncompetitive maiden, dominated throughout by Kind, who probably ran to previous form.

**NOTEBOOK**

**Kind(IRE)** was fractious beforehand and raced keenly in the contest itself, but she had far too many guns for this opposition and ran out a clear winner. If she is to progress to a higher level, though, she is going to have to learn to settle.

**Farewell Gift**, officially rated 4lb superior to the winner, had previously raced exclusively over six furlongs. He never got in a blow at the winner and looks overrated on the balance of his form. *Official explanation: jockey said colt was hanging right handed throughout.*

**Tropical Storm(IRE)**, who was on edge beforehand and did himself himself no good, did not pick up that well when asked to go in pursuit of the winner. However, he is now eligible for a mark, and he will have stronger chances in handicap company.

**Snow Joke(IRE)** is exposed as a moderate performer.

**Mr Hullabalou(IRE)** looks flattered by his current handicap mark of 79.

## 2302 SHARP MINDS BETFAIR H'CAP 1m 2f (J)

**7:05** (7:08) (E ) (0-70,69) 3-Y-O+ **£3,649** (£1,123; £561; £280) **Stalls** High

Form RPR

00-3 1 **Giunchiglio**[50] 1232 5-9-7 **62** ........ KFallon 9 71
(WMBrisbourne) *hld up in mid-div: hdwy 3f out: led over 1f out: strly rdn: all out* **7/1**[2]

204/ 2 3/4 **Swellmova**[603] 4917 5-8-12 **58** ........ AQuinn(5) 6 66
(JRBoyle) *trckd ldr: led briefly wl over 1f out: kpt on gamely* **14/1**

5132 3 3/4 **Blazing The Trail (IRE)**[15] 1944 4-9-12 **67** ........ SWhitworth 2 74
(JWHills) *hld up towards rr: rdn and hdwy 2f out: r.o wl* **9/1**[3]

0055 4 *hd* **Karaoke (IRE)**[15] 1944 4-9-10 **65** ........ JFEgan 4 71
(SKirk) *hld up: rdn and hdwy over 2f out: one pce fnl f* **10/1**

222- 5 *shd* **Qabas (USA)**[40] 5748 4-10-0 **69** ........ RHughes 1 75
(PRWebber) *hld up in rr: str hdwy on outside fnl 2f: nvr nrr; sddle slipped* **16/1**

0-00 6 5 **Castaigne (FR)**[115] 623 5-9-2 **57** ........ RHavlin 14 54
(BWDuke) *hld up in rr: hdwy over 2f out: hdwy over 2f out: sn one pce* **25/1**

-405 7 *nk* **Lyrical Way**[60] 1085 5-9-7 **62** ........(b) FNorton 17 58
(PRChamings) *bhd: rdn and hdwy over 2f out: one pce fnl f* **16/1**

0-20 8 2 **Castaway Queen (IRE)**[15] 1940 5-9-7 **62** ........(b1) EAhern 5 54
(WRMuir) *mid-div: hdwy 4f out: wknd appr fnl f* **16/1**

553- 9 1 **Billy Bathwick (IRE)**[223] 5500 7-9-3 **58** ........ DHolland 10 48
(JMBradley) *trckd ldrs: rdn over 2f out: wknd over 1f out* **10/1**

-020 10 1/2 **Catch The Fox**[12] 1986 4-8-4 **45** ........ JTate 19 34
(JJBridger) *lw: in rr: effrt over 2f out: sn btn* **33/1**

00-3 11 *hd* **Bluegrass Boy**[44] 1308 4-9-8 **63** ........ SCarson 11 52
(GBBalding) *b. slowly away: sme hdwy 3ft out: wknd 2f out* **10/1**

0213 12 5 **Icannshift (IRE)**[18] 1856 4-9-0 **55** ........ RLMoore 8 34
(SDow) *led tl hdd wl over 1f out: wknd qckly* **6/1**[1]

5-00 13 8 **Bosco (IRE)**[26] 1672 3-8-7 **62** ........(b1) PDobbs 3 26
(RHannon) *prom tl wknd 3f out* **25/1**

00-0 14 3/4 **Havantadoubt (IRE)**[32] 1522 4-9-5 **60** ........ GBaker 13 23
(MRBosley) *swtg: a in rr* **25/1**

06-0 15 8 **Major Blade (GER)**[8] 2084 6-9-3 **58** ........ DSweeney 12 6
(BGPowell) *mid-div: rdn and wknd over 2f out* **33/1**

30-0 16 8 **Haribini**[15] 1940 4-8-2 **48** ow3........ NChalmers(5) 15 —
(JJBridger) *slowly away: a bhd* **40/1**

00-0 P **Seal Of Office**[26] 1675 5-9-8 **63** ........ CCatlin 18 —
(AMHales) *prom tl wknd qckly 6f out: p.u over 3f out: dismntd* **25/1**

2m 6.70s (0.56) **Going Correction** 0.0s/f (Good)
**WFA** 3 from 4yo+ 14lb **17** Ran SP% **112.1**
Speed ratings: **97,96,95,95,95 91,91,89,88,88 88,84,77,77,70 64,**—CSF £75.71 CT £664.09 TOTE £6.00: £2.30, £4.30, £1.70, £3.00; EX 184.70.

**Owner** Nev Jones **Bred** Red House Stud **Trained** Great Ness, Shropshire

**FOCUS**

An ordinary handicap in which the leaders probably went off too fast, as the hold-up performers largely dominated at the finish. The winning time was modest, but the form is sound enough for the grade.

**NOTEBOOK**

**Giunchiglio**, having his second start for his new stable and with Fallon taking over in the saddle, had to be driven right out to get off the mark at the 14th attempt. This win should do his confidence some good.

**Swellmova**, who has had a fractured knee screwed, was having his first start for 603 days. He did by far the best of those who raced prominently and, given the decent pace, to finish second was a great effort. This lightly-raced gelding clearly has the ability to win a race off this sort of mark, although he may need a break after this big effort as there is always the chance that he could bounce if turned out again quickly.

**Blazing The Trail(IRE)** had the race run to suit and stayed on well to place again. He is a consistent animal.

**Karaoke(IRE)** has dropped 9lb in the handicap since his first run on turf this season thanks to being campaigned on unsuitably soft ground. This was more like his form, and he looks primed to strike soon.

**Qabas(USA)**, who has been in action over timber lately, was disappointing last term, finishing runner-up on no fewer than five of his eight starts. This was a promising effort under top weight, especially as his rider later reported that his saddle had slipped, but we have been here before and he remains a maiden. *Official explanation: jockey said saddle slipped*

**Icannshift(IRE)** dropped away tamely after setting a decent pace. He is probably happier dominating a smaller field at a pace that suits himself. *Official explanation: trainer was unable to offer any explanation for poor form shown*

**Seal Of Office** *Official explanation: jockey said gelding bled from the nose.*

## 2303 HAPPY BIRTHDAY DON CHADWICK H'CAP 5f

**7:35** (7:39) (D ) (0-80,79) 3-Y-O+ **£5,512** (£1,696; £848; £424) **Stalls** Low

Form RPR

-160 1 **Devise (IRE)**[21] 1765 5-9-8 **76** ........ RMiles(3) 1 87
(MSSaunders) *mid-div: short of room and swtchd lft 2f out: str run on rails to ld appr fnl f: drvn out* **10/1**

2406 2 3/4 **Blue Knight (IRE)**[31] 1537 5-9-7 **72** ........ KFallon 11 80
(APJarvis) *lw: towards rr: gd hdwy over 1f out: wnt 2nd last strides* **7/1**[2]

5000 3 *nk* **Seven No Trumps**[15] 1937 7-9-11 **76** ........ RLMoore 13 83
(JMBradley) *mid-div: hdwy to chse wnr fnl f tl lost 2nd last strides* **12/1**

0-00 4 1 3/4 **Hollow Jo**[28] 1608 4-9-4 **69** ........ RHughes 4 69
(JRJenkins) *lw: towards rr: short of room and swtchd lft wl over 1f out: r.o wl fnl f: nvr nrr* **8/1**[3]

500- 5 3/4 **Yorkies Boy**[268] 4536 9-8-5 **56** ........ CCatlin 6 53
(JMBradley) *b. a.p: kpt on one pce fnl f* **25/1**

1430 6 1/2 **Playtime Blue**[18] 1872 4-8-11 **62** ........ GBaker 12 57
(MrsHSweeting) *lw: prom: ev ch 1f out: one pce fnl f* **12/1**

023- 7 1 **Snow Wolf**[213] 5700 3-9-6 **79** ........ DaneO'Neill 7 70
(JMBradley) *lw: in rr: effrt over 1f out: kpt on fnl f* **16/1**

2441 8 *hd* **If By Chance**[14] 1974 6-9-9 **74** ........(b) DHolland 5 64
(RCraggs) *hld up: hdwy whn hmpd over 1f out: no ch after* **9/2**[1]

0003 9 *nk* **Prime Recreation**[7] 2118 7-8-8 **62** ........ LPKeniry(3) 2 51
(PSFelgate) *b. lw: prom: led 3f out: tl hdd appr fnl f: one pce after* **10/1**

4550 10 1 **Hard To Catch (IRE)**[8] 2091 6-8-8 **66** ........(b) MHoward(7) 14 51
(DKIvory) *b. prom on outside tl one pce fnl f* **12/1**

-000 11 *shd* **Beauvrai**[21] 1765 4-9-8 **73** ........ MTebbutt 10 57
(VSmith) *lw: slowly away: hdwy whn hmpd over 1f out: nt rcvr* **8/1**[3]

5000 12 *nk* **Goodwood Prince**[2] 2246 4-8-11 **62** ........ TQuinn 3 45
(SDow) *stdd s: effrt over 1f out: nvr on terms* **14/1**

060- 13 2 **Formalise**[261] 4688 4-9-3 **68** ........ SCarson 9 43
(GBBalding) *prom tl wknd over 1f out* **20/1**

220- **14** 1 1/2 **Tomthevic**[261] 4688 6-8-9 **60** ........ MFenton 8 29
(MrsPSly) *led tl hdd 3f out: wknd over 1f out* **20/1**

59.51 secs (-1.70) **Going Correction** -0.125s/f (Firm)
**WFA** 3 from 4yo+ 8lb **14** Ran SP% **120.1**
Speed ratings: **108,106,106,103,102 101,99,99,99,97 97,96,93,91**CSF £75.92 CT £882.95 TOTE £16.20: £5.20, £3.00, £7.00; EX 145.80.
**Owner** D Naylor **Bred** Clody Norton And Mrs Con Collins **Trained** Haydon, Somerset

**FOCUS**
Just a fair sprint handicap, with the main players coming from off the pace.

**NOTEBOOK**
**Devise(IRE)**, stepping back down to his best trip having cut little ice over six furlongs on his last two starts, looked as though he was going to run into trouble when waiting for a gap to appear a quarter mile out, but as soon as an avenue opened up next to the rail he quickened up in good style to take it.
**Blue Knight(IRE)**, who has a poor strike-rate and has done his winning over farther, stayed on well but the bird had flown. He is clearly in form and a return to six furlongs may be the answer.
**Seven No Trumps** had the headgear left off and ran a better race on this faster ground, but his winning days are hard to predict.
**Hollow Jo** ◆ struggled when rated in the 70s but is becoming more realistically handicapped again and is clearly running back into form. Although dropping back in trip, he was more patiently ridden than usual and finished in eye-catching fashion. He is very well suited by this quicker ground and looks poised to strike again, possibly back over a bit further.
**Yorkies Boy** has not won for three years but has plummeted in the weights as a result. This was not a bad reappearance.
**Playtime Blue** was disappointing, especially as the ground appeared to have come in his favour.
**Snow Wolf**, who was previously with Marcus Tregoning, was the only three-year-old in the field and was not disgraced on his reappearance. He will be interesting back amongst his own age group.
**If By Chance** was a surprising favourite given that each of his seven wins have come over six furlongs.
**Prime Recreation** *Official explanation: jockey said gelding was hanging right handed throughout.*
**Beauvrai** got blocked in his run and hampered. This run can be forgotten and he remains on a mark which can be exploited.

## 2304 RECTANGLE GROUP CLASSIFIED STKS — 1m (J)
**8:05** (8:08) (E) 3-Y-O+ **£3,591** (£1,105; £552; £276) **Stalls** High

Form / RPR

23-1 **1** **Salinor**[26] 1675 4-9-8 75 ........ KFallon 1 89+
(ACStewart) *lw: hld up: gd hdwy on outside 2f out: led ins fnl f: eased last strides* **1/1**[1]

-540 **2** *nk* **Climate (IRE)**[24] 1708 5-9-7 74 ........(v) DSweeney 13 84
(JRBoyle) *lw: hld up: hdwy whn short of room over 2f out: swtchd lft: r.o u.p to go 2nd wl ins fnl f* **14/1**

06-2 **3** 1 1/2 **Analyze (FR)**[10] 2030 6-9-6 73 ........ RLMoore 5 80
(BGPowell) *lw: prom: ev ch ent fnl f: no ex fnl 50yds* **15/2**[2]

0561 **4** *1* **Scottish River (USA)**[12] 2000 5-9-5 77 ........ HayleyTurner(5) 2 81
(MDIUsher) *lw: slowly away: sn mid-div: outpcd 2f out: r.o fnl f* **12/1**

20-6 **5** *hd* **Summer Shades**[29] 1598 6-9-0 70 ........ TQuinn 9 71
(WMBrisbourne) *led tl hdd & wknd ins fnl f* **16/1**

526- **6** *1* **Wizard Looking**[186] 6023 3-8-6 71 ........(t) PDobbs 12 72
(RHannon) *trckd ldrs: rdn 2f out: one pce fnl f* **33/1**

05-0 **7** *hd* **Anna Walhaan (IRE)**[19] 1845 5-9-6 73 ........ CCatlin 7 74
(IanWilliams) *lw: in rr: hdwy 2f out: one pce fnl f* **20/1**

-006 **8** *1* **Aimee's Delight**[22] 1746 4-9-4 74 ........ MFenton 11 70
(JGGiven) *hld up: hdwy over 2f out: swtchd lft sn after: one pce fnl f* **12/1**

-000 **9** 1/2 **Cartronageeraghlad (IRE)**[19] 1841 3-8-10 75 ........(b) DaneO'Neill 6 73
(JAOsborne) *a in rr* **25/1**

1604 **10** *nk* **Steely Dan**[4] 2218 5-9-3 67 ........ NPollard 3 67
(JRBest) *lw: a in rr* **11/1**[3]

0-00 **11** *shd* **Boundless Prospect (USA)**[112] 647 5-9-5 72 ........ EAhern 8 69
(JWHills) *stdd s: in rr tl hdwy over 2f out: short of room over 1f out and eased whn no ch ins* **20/1**

0-01 **12** *5* **Muyassir (IRE)**[129] 525 9-9-3 63 ........ JQuinn 4 55
(MissBSanders) *lw: trckd ldr: wkng whn hmpd over 1f out: eased* **16/1**

1m 40.68s (1.06) **Going Correction** 0.0s/f (Good)
**WFA** 3 from 4yo+ 12lb **12** Ran SP% **120.2**
Speed ratings: **94,93,92,91,91 90,89,88,88,88 87,82**CSF £15.87 TOTE £2.00: £1.20, £4.10, £3.10; EX 21.70.
**Owner** M J C Hawkes & A Goddard **Bred** D P Martin **Trained** Newmarket, Suffolk

**FOCUS**
A tight race on the ratings. The winning time was very slow for the grade, but the hot favourite won a shade cosily, and the form looks solid as the first six were close to their recent best.

**NOTEBOOK**
**Salinor** was the only one they wanted to know in the market and he did not disappoint. Picking up in good style, he only had to be pushed out to score cosily, and continues on an upward curve.
**Climate(IRE)** appreciated the quicker ground and bounced back to form. He has dropped to a fair mark and might be able to nick a race back in handicap company.
**Analyze(FR)**, who ran another solid race, has done all his winning over ten furlongs.
**Scottish River(USA)** had more to do than at Windsor and the drying ground was probably not in his favour, so he ran a respectable race in the circumstances. *Official explanation: jockey said gelding was hanging left in the final furlong.*
**Summer Shades** ran a decent race from the front but looks high in the weights at present.
**Wizard Looking**, making his seasonal reappearance, has yet to fully convince over this trip.
**Cartronageeraghlad(IRE)** *Official explanation: jockey said gelding suffered interference in running*

## 2305 SHARP MINDS BETFAIR STKS (H'CAP) — 1m 4f
**8:35** (8:45) (D) (0-80,78) 3-Y-O+ **£7,020** (£2,160; £1,080; £540) **Stalls** High

Form / RPR

431- **1** **Ocean Avenue (IRE)**[290] 3884 5-9-10 **76** ........ DHolland 6 91
(CAHorgan) *mde all: rdn 2f out: r.o wl: clr fnl f* **9/2**[2]

60/2 **2** 3 1/2 **Captain Miller**[10] 2047 8-9-4 **70** ........ TQuinn 9 79
(NJHenderson) *lw: sn trckd wnr: tried to cl 2f out: no imp ins fnl 2f* **7/2**[1]

4300 **3** 1 1/4 **Barry Island**[8] 2084 5-9-11 **77** ........ DaneO'Neill 3 84
(DRCElsworth) *s.i.s: hld up: hdwy 3f out: kpt on but no ch w first 2 ins fnl 2f* **7/1**[3]

0002 **4** *nk* **Danakil**[10] 2032 9-9-4 **70** ........ RLMoore 2 77
(SDow) *b. towards rr: hdwy 3f out: swtchd rt over 2f out: rdn and kpt on one pce* **9/2**[2]

0-05 **5** 2 1/2 **Silver Prophet (IRE)**[12] 2000 5-9-7 **73** ........ GBaker 4 76
(MRBosley) *in rr: hdwy to chse ldrs 6f out: rdn over 2f out: one pce after* **20/1**

000- **6** *5* **Honor Rouge (IRE)**[249] 4976 5-9-5 **74** ........ DNolan(3) 13 69
(DGBridgwater) *a abt same pl: no hdwy ins fnl 3f* **25/1**

4300 **7** *1* **Ezz Elkheil**[31] 1539 5-9-6 **72** ........ RHughes 14 65
(JRJenkins) *plld hrd: trckd ldrs: rdn over 3f out: wknd 2f out* **7/1**[3]

4-00 **8** *nk* **Stolen Hours (USA)**[20] 1801 4-9-4 **70** ........ GCarter 8 62
(JAkehurst) *hld up in rr: nvr on terms* **50/1**

0-00 **9** *1* **Persian King (IRE)**[31] 1539 7-9-12 **78** ........ VSlattery 10 69
(JABOld) *a towards rr* **33/1**

05/ **10** *4* **Deferlant (FR)**[49] 4669 7-9-4 **70** ........(v) EAhern 11 54
(KBell) *sn in rr and nvr on terms* **25/1**

1030 **11** *7* **So Vital**[21] 1768 4-9-4 **70** ........(p) JQuinn 12 43
(JPearce) *hld up: a in rr* **25/1**

6-00 **12** *5* **Komati River**[18] 1858 5-8-0 **52** oh5 ow2 ........ CCatlin 5 17
(JAkehurst) *t.k.h: sn chsd ldrs: rdn over 3f out: wknd qckly over 2f out* **50/1**

3-10 **13** *11* **Squirtle Turtle**[106] 693 4-9-2 **68** ........(bt) KFallon 7 16
(PFICole) *lw: slowly away: sn prom: wknd wl over 2f out and sn eased* **11/1**

2m 34.27s (-0.73) **Going Correction** +0.075s/f (Good) **13** Ran SP% **115.1**
Speed ratings: **105,102,101,101,99 96,95,95,95,92 87,84,77**CSF £17.29 CT £94.34 TOTE £5.00: £1.90, £2.20, £2.20; EX 18.40 Place 6 £83.26, Place 5 £22.14.
**Owner** A Kinghorn **Bred** Steve Starkey **Trained** Ogbourne Maisey, Wilts

**FOCUS**
A fair handicap run at a decent gallop. The first two were in those positions throughout.

**NOTEBOOK**
**Ocean Avenue(IRE)** came in for good market support on his seasonal reappearance and was allowed to dictate his own pace in front. He came home clear of the runner-up, with the rest nicely strung out, suggesting the form is solid, and a return to a mile six will not cause him any problem.
**Captain Miller**, 3lb higher, ran a solid race but could not pick the winner up on this faster ground. He too stays farther than this, and should be able to score off this sort of mark.
**Barry Island**, who has still to win a race on turf, appreciated the step up in trip, but he was given too much to do having been held up at the rear, and the first two had flown by the time he got going.
**Danakil** is fairly handicapped and had his ideal conditions. He too was given a lot to do from the back of the field, though.
**Silver Prophet(IRE)** was another who never really got into it having been held up at the back for most of the race.
**Ezz Elkheil**, who has a poor strike-rate, proved difficult to settle.
**Squirtle Turtle** *Official explanation: jockey said gelding was unable to dominate.*
T/Plt: £45.10 to a £1 stake. Pool: £38,442.70. 622.05 winning tickets. T/Qpdt: £17.00 to a £1 stake. Pool: £3,113.10. 135.20 winning tickets. JS

# 2275 NEWMARKET (R-H)
### Saturday, May 22

**OFFICIAL GOING: Good to firm**

## 2306 NEWMARKET COUNTRYSIDE RACEDAY H'CAP — 1m
**1:50** (1:53) (C) (0-90,85) 3-Y-O **£9,763** (£3,004; £1,502; £751) **Stalls** High

Form / RPR

1-05 **1** **Red Spell (IRE)**[36] 1437 3-8-13 **77** ........ PaulEddery 3 83
(RHannon) *lw: sn chsng ldr: rdn to ld over 1f out: r.o gamely* **10/1**

1-26 **2** *shd* **Lets Roll**[29] 1588 3-8-6 **70** ........ TWilliams 8 76
(CWThornton) *chsd ldrs: n.m.r and lost pl over 6f out: hdwy and nt clr run over 1f out: hmpd ins fnl f: r.o* **12/1**

2-21 **3** *hd* **Maclean**[22] 1747 3-8-12 **76** ........ KFallon 1 82
(SirMichaelStoute) *lw: chsd ldrs: rdn over 2f out: r.o* **9/2**[1]

1-24 **4** *nk* **Solar Power (IRE)**[24] 1704 3-9-6 **84** ........ EAhern 4 89
(JRFanshawe) *lw: chsd ldrs: rdn and ev ch ins fnl f: unable qck nr fin* **5/1**[2]

30-1 **5** *nk* **Apex**[19] 1841 3-9-0 **78** ........ DaneO'Neill 10 82
(EALDunlop) *hld up: hdwy over 2f out: rdn over 1f out: r.o* **10/1**

00-3 **6** *nk* **Mr Jack Daniells (IRE)**[19] 1841 3-8-6 **73** ........ RMiles(3) 12 77
(WRMuir) *hld up: nt clr run over 1f out: r.o: nt rch ldrs* **8/1**[3]

13- **7** *nk* **Sweet Indulgence (IRE)**[273] 4383 3-9-6 **84** ........ KMcEvoy 14 87
(DrJDScargill) *chsd ldrs: hmpd over 1f out: r.o* **25/1**

0-00 **8** *nk* **Motu (IRE)**[24] 1702 3-8-8 **72** ........ PRobinson 13 74
(JLDunlop) *hld up in tch: rdn over 2f out: nt clr run ins fnl f: styd on* **20/1**

31-0 **9** 3/4 **Muhaymin (USA)**[37] 1414 3-9-7 **85** ........ RHills 7 86
(JLDunlop) *led over 6f: edgd rt: no ex ins fnl f* **16/1**

46-4 **10** *hd* **Fine Silver (IRE)**[11] 2019 3-9-5 **83** ........ JQuinn 6 83
(PFICole) *lw: hld up in tch: hmpd and outpcd over 2f out: r.o ins fnl f: nt rch ldrs* **10/1**

-503 **11** 1 1/4 **Panshir (FR)**[19] 1820 3-8-9 **73** ........ MHills 9 70
(CFWall) *s.i.s: hld up: hdwy over 1f out: one pce ins fnl f* **12/1**

-414 **12** *1* **Just Tim (IRE)**[29] 1585 3-8-12 **76** ........ PDobbs 11 71
(RHannon) *b. prom: rdn over 2f out: styd on same pce appr fnl f* **12/1**

006 **13** *20* **Hana Dee**[7] 2112 3-8-1 **65** ........ CCatlin 5 14
(MRChannon) *hld up: bhd fnl 3f* **25/1**

25- **14** *2* **Sanbonah (USA)**[214] 5698 3-8-5 **72** ........ LisaJones(3) 2 16
(NACallaghan) *chsd ldrs over 5f* **25/1**

1m 38.97s (-0.43) **Going Correction** 0.0s/f (Good) **14** Ran SP% **118.5**
Speed ratings: **102,101,101,101,101 100,100,100,99,99 98,97,77,75**CSF £116.11 CT £628.19 TOTE £17.10: £5.00, £3.70, £1.60; EX 74.70.
**Owner** Mrs John Lee **Bred** Tom Darcy And Vincent McCarthy **Trained** East Everleigh, Wilts

**FOCUS**
A competitive handicap run at a fair pace and a triumph for the Handicapper. Several hard-luck stories however.

**NOTEBOOK**
**Red Spell(IRE)** confirmed himself an improving performer with a gutsy win here. His trainer may send him to Royal Ascot for the Britannia Handicap but, while that may be flying a bit high, there is no doubt there are more races to be won with him.
**Lets Roll** ◆ had all sorts of traffic problems and did well to finish as close as he did. A strongly-run mile suits him well, and he should have little difficulty gaining compensation.
**Maclean** found things happening a shade too quickly for him here, but he stuck well enough to his task and granted a stiffer test, can get back to winning ways.
**Solar Power(IRE)** looked the likely winner entering the final furlong, but just lacked a change of gear near the finish. However, there was no disgrace in this effort.
**Apex**, 5lb higher than when winning at Warwick, handled this much faster surface well and looks to be on the upgrade.
**Mr Jack Daniells(IRE)** ◆, like so many in this event, had no luck in running and is one to keep an eye on in the near future.
**Sweet Indulgence(IRE)** ◆ turned in a cracking effort, for he was all but put over the rails in the dip. He should have no trouble paying his way this term.
**Motu(IRE)** looked better suited to this faster ground and just about stayed this longer trip, although seven-furlongs could prove to be his optimum distance.
**Fine Silver(IRE)** ◆ messed around on more than one occasion, did plenty of running in the closing stages and can be rated as finishing up with the placed horses at least.
**Panshir(FR)** flaterred briefly on the outside before his run petered out. He will find easier tasks than he faced here.

## 2307 HAVEN AND BRITISH HOLIDAYS FAIRWAY STKS (LISTED RACE) 1m 2f

2:20 (2:21) (A) 3-Y-O £17,400 (£6,600; £3,300; £1,500) Stalls High

Form RPR

1112 **1** **Hazyview**[14] 1966 3-9-3 103 ........ EAhern 4 110
(NACallaghan) *lw: chsd ldrs: rdn over 2f out: led 1f out: styd on wl* **11/2**[3]

10-1 **2** 1 3/4 **Duke Of Venice (USA)**[19] 1822 3-8-12 109 ........ (t) KMcEvoy 1 102
(SaeedBinSuroor) *sn chsng ldr: led over 2f out: hdd 1f out: unable qck* **10/11**[1]

34-2 **3** 2 1/2 **Castleton**[15] 1939 3-8-12 100 ........ KFallon 2 97
(HJCyzer) *lw: a.p: rdn and ev ch 2f out: sn edgd lft: styd on same pce fnl f* **10/1**

1-4 **4** 3/4 **Si Si Amiga (IRE)**[17] 1879 3-8-7 92 ........ MHills 3 91
(BWHills) *lw: led over 7f: no ex fnl f* **18/1**

21 **5** 3/4 **Rehearsal**[20] 1794 3-8-12 94 ........ PRobinson 6 94
(CGCox) *hld up: effrt over 2f out: sn btn* **7/2**[2]

1-0 **6** 17 **Jath**[20] 1791 3-8-7 85 ........ RHills 5 57
(JulianPoulton) *hld up: wknd over 2f out* **40/1**

2m 4.42s (-1.27) **Going Correction** 0.0s/f (Good) **6** Ran SP% **106.8**
Speed ratings: **105,103,101,101,100 86**CSF £9.91 TOTE £5.00: £2.10, £1.40; EX 10.10.
**Owner** T Mohan **Bred** N E Poole **Trained** Newmarket, Suffolk

**FOCUS**
A decent little contest, but the pace was only a fair one. The runner-up was probably below his best, but the others give the form a solid look.

**NOTEBOOK**
**Hazyview** bounced back on this quicker ground to confirm himself a more than useful performer. Ridden with a little more restraint than of late, he showed a nice turn of foot to win a little more cosily than the verdict suggests, showing improved form yet again. He should be at least as effective over 12 furlongs on the right ground and will have a wide range of opportunites this summer, at home and abroad.
**Duke Of Venice(USA)** should really have beaten the winner on these terms. Whether this trip just proved beyond him, or the winner is fast improving, one cannot be sure.
**Castleton** was far from disgraced, on ground which could well have been fast enough for him. A maiden should be a formality.
**Si Si Amiga(IRE)**, tackling the boys for the first time, was not disgraced and should do better as the season goes on.
**Rehearsal**, whose maiden win here was given a boost by both the runner-up and third, settled much better this time, but failed to pick up. Although a shade disappointing, it is too soon to be writing him off. *Official explanation: jockey said colt shortened his stride running down into the dip.*

## 2308 CHEVELEY PARK STUD KING CHARLES II STKS (LISTED RACE) 7f

2:50 (2:51) (A) 3-Y-O £17,400 (£6,600; £3,300; £1,500) Stalls High

Form RPR

0-22 **1** **Fokine (USA)**[35] 1459 3-8-12 114 ........ MHills 4 110
(BWHills) *lw: trckd ldr: led over 1f out: drvn out* **4/1**[3]

11-3 **2** nk **Peak To Creek**[37] 1410 3-9-5 111 ........ EAhern 8 116
(JNoseda) *lw: hld up: hdwy over 1f out: sn ev ch: r.o* **7/1**

310- **3** 3/4 **Cartography (IRE)**[224] 5480 3-8-12 104 ........ KMcEvoy 2 107
(SaeedBinSuroor) *h.d.w: led over 5f: styd on* **14/1**

124- **4** 4 **Auditorium**[232] 5348 3-9-2 113 ........ KFallon 6 101
(SirMichaelStoute) *hld up: outpcd 1/2-way: styd on ins fnl f* **7/2**[2]

1 **5** 2 **Saint Etienne (IRE)**[94] 816 3-8-7 ........ PRobinson 3 86
(AMBalding) *prom: racd keenly: wknd over 1f out* **14/1**

12-1 **6** nk **Iqte Saab (USA)**[39] 1384 3-8-12 104 ........ RHills 1 91
(JLDunlop) *trckd ldrs: racd keenly: wknd over 1f out* **11/8**[1]

3-22 **7** 2 **Moonlight Man**[24] 1706 3-8-12 105 ........ DaneO'Neill 7 85
(RHannon) *lw: chsd ldrs over 5f* **20/1**

140- **8** 2 1/2 **Sgt Pepper (IRE)**[196] 5962 3-9-2 100 ........ PDobbs 5 83
(RHannon) *s.i.s: a bhd* **50/1**

1m 24.58s (-1.89) **Going Correction** 0.0s/f (Good) **8** Ran SP% **116.9**
Speed ratings: **110,109,108,104,101 101,99,96**CSF £32.69 TOTE £5.30: £1.90, £2.00, £3.80; EX 22.20.
**Owner** Sangster Family **Bred** Swettenham Stud **Trained** Lambourn, Berks

**FOCUS**
A good renewal and probably up to Group 3 class. It was run at a good pace.

**NOTEBOOK**
**Fokine(USA)** ◆ showed his true colours on this quicker surface, and kept finding more to hold off the persistent runner-up. He is a real battler and looks sure to give a good account in the Jersey Stakes at the Royal meeting, his next intended target.
**Peak To Creek** ◆ ran a cracking race under his Group Three penalty on his favoured fast surface. A smart colt with a useful turn of foot, he is equally at home over six furlongs and should have plenty of opportunities this summer, including in the Jersey Stakes, should he take that route, where he will again cross swords with the winner.
**Cartography(IRE)** appeared to stay this longer trip, but six furlongs could prove his optimum.
**Auditorium** has taken time to come to himself this term and still looked as though the race would do him good. He was not given a hard time and looks sure to leave this effort behind in due course.
**Saint Etienne(IRE)**, the only filly in the field, lacked the experience of her rivals and did herself no favours by pulling too hard. Highly-regarded, she should do better in time. *Official explanation: jockey said colt was very keen early on*
**Iqte Saab(USA)** was most disappointing and dropped away tamely. He did himself no favours by taking quite a keen hold early on, and he looks to have something to prove now. *Official explanation: trainer's representative said colt ran too free early on and could not get cover; trainer said gelding was suffering from a tracheal infection.*

## 2309 CORAL SPRINT (H'CAP) 6f

3:25 (3:27) (C) (0-100,97) 3-Y-O £26,000 (£8,000; £4,000; £2,000) Stalls High

Form RPR

-221 **1** **Buy On The Red**[10] 2029 3-7-12 77 ........ RMiles(3) 2 87
(WRMuir) *racd centre: chsd ldrs: led that gp over 1f out: sn hung rt: r.o* **10/1**

420- **2** 3/4 **Big Bradford**[192] 5979 3-8-9 85 ........ (v1) DKinsella 6 93
(PGMurphy) *plld hrd: led centre over 4f: hmpd 1f out: r.o* **66/1**

-515 **3** 1 **Molcon (IRE)**[14] 1965 3-8-5 81 ........ PRobinson 3 86
(NACallaghan) *racd centre: hld up in tch: rdn over 1f out: r.o* **20/1**

2-13 **4** 2 **Bygone Days**[11] 2019 3-8-9 85 ........ KFallon 16 84
(WJHaggas) *lw: racd far side: chsd ldrs: rdn over 1f out: led that gp wl ins fnl f: no ch w centre gp* **9/2**[1]

221- **5** nk **Partners In Jazz (USA)**[236] 5273 3-8-12 88 ........ EAhern 14 86
(TDBarron) *mde most far side tl wl ins fnl f: no ex* **9/1**[3]

0-44 **6** 1 1/4 **Vienna's Boy (IRE)**[14] 1965 3-8-10 86 ........ PDobbs 18 80
(RHannon) *racd far side: sn chsng ldrs: rdn over 1f out: styd on same pce* **20/1**

21-1 **7** 1/2 **Spliff**[20] 1797 3-9-5 95 ........ DaneO'Neill 19 88
(HCandy) *racd far side: hld up: hdwy 2f out: styd on same pce ins fnl f* **5/1**[2]

2312 **8** hd **Morse (IRE)**[7] 2115 3-9-1 91 ........ CCatlin 7 83
(JAOsborne) *racd centre: chsd ldrs: rdn over 1f out: sn outpcd* **20/1**

33-0 **9** shd **Imperial Echo (USA)**[22] 1745 3-8-7 83 ........ PFessey 9 75
(TDBarron) *racd far side: hld up: effrt over 1f out: nvr trbld ldrs* **33/1**

-000 **10** 1 **Valjarv (IRE)**[20] 1791 3-9-5 95 ........ TGMcLaughlin 17 84
(NPLittmoden) *racd far side: hld up: sme hdwy over 1f out: n.d* **33/1**

33-6 **11** shd **Danesmead (IRE)**[11] 2019 3-9-5 95 ........ KMcEvoy 1 84
(TDEasterby) *racd centre: hld up: n.d* **16/1**

52-0 **12** hd **Swinbrook (USA)**[37] 1413 3-8-4 83 ........ LisaJones(3) 10 71
(JARToller) *racd far side: chsd ldrs: rdn over 1f out: wknd ins fnl f* **50/1**

-513 **13** 3/4 **Distant Times**[28] 1614 3-8-3 79 ........ RFfrench 11 65
(TDEasterby) *racd far side: hld up: hdwy over 1f out: wknd ins fnl f* **16/1**

10-5 **14** 1/2 **Traytonic**[7] 2131 3-9-2 97 ........ NChalmers(5) 5 81
(HJCyzer) *racd far side: s.i.s: hld up: nt clr run over 1f out: n.d* **12/1**

-310 **15** 1 **Kabreet**[8] 2082 3-8-6 82 ........ RHills 4 63
(EALDunlop) *racd centre: w ldr over 4f: sn wknd* **20/1**

15-2 **16** 1 3/4 **Danzig River (IRE)**[39] 1388 3-9-6 96 ........ MHills 15 72
(BWHills) *lw: racd far side: chsd ldrs over 4f* **9/2**[1]

1-00 **17** 3/4 **Divine Spirit**[7] 2131 3-8-6 82 ........ PaulEddery 13 56
(MDods) *racd far side: chsd ldrs over 4f* **66/1**

10-1 **18** 5 **Saristar**[39] 1388 3-8-8 84 ........ JQuinn 8 43
(PFICole) *b.hind: racd far side: w ldrs to 1/2-way: wknd wl over 1f out* **10/1**

1m 11.68s (-1.41) **Going Correction** 0.0s/f (Good) **18** Ran SP% **130.5**
Speed ratings: **109,108,106,104,103 101,101,101,100,99 99,99,98,97,96 93,92,86**CSF £590.10 CT £6469.77 TOTE £16.90: £3.30, £17.80, £4.90, £1.90; EX 1613.30 TRIFECTA Not won..
**Owner** R Haim **Bred** J Gittins And Capt J H Wilson **Trained** Lambourn, Berks

**FOCUS**
A competitive sprint run at a good pace in a decent time with the field splitting into two. The first three home raced up the centre of the course. This is usually a strong handicap and the form looks sound enough.

**NOTEBOOK**
**Buy On The Red**, tackling handicappers for the first time, handles a fast surface well and confirmed himself a progressive performer. Future plans include the Balmoral Handicap at Royal Ascot, a race connections won two years ago with Zargus.
**Big Bradford** proved difficult to settle in the early stages, but he battled on well at the business end, despite the winner hanging into him. The visor, instead of the usual blinkers, appears to have sharpened him up and he ought to score if reproducing this.
**Molcon(IRE)** still looks to be on the upgrade and, with his abilty to handle most types of ground, should have no trouble adding to his tally.
**Bygone Days** came out best of those to race on the far side and, as this was only his fifth outing, is still open to improvement.
**Partners In Jazz(USA)** showed plenty of pace on this return to action and is one to keep in mind for a similar contest.
**Vienna's Boy(IRE)** is beginning to slide down the handicap, and was far from disgraced.
**Danzig River(IRE)** dropped away tamely and is better than he showed here.

## 2310 PERSIMMON HOMES EBF MAIDEN STKS 6f

4:00 (4:02) (D) 2-Y-O £4,715 (£1,451; £725; £362) Stalls High

Form RPR

0 **1** **Destinate (IRE)**[37] 1412 2-9-0 ........ PDobbs 1 81
(RHannon) *led over 3f: rdn to ld wl ins fnl f: r.o* **16/1**

**2** 3/4 **Juantorena** 2-9-0 ........ IMongan 8 79
(MLWBell) *w'like: b.bkwd: w ldrs: led over 2f out: hung lft 1f out: hdd wl ins fnl f* **8/1**[3]

3 **3** hd **Capable Guest (IRE)**[10] 2045 2-9-0 ........ CCatlin 7 78
(MRChannon) *w ldrs: rdn over 1f out: r.o* **4/5**[1]

**4** 1 **Darko Karim** 2-9-0 ........ KFallon 5 75
(DRLoder) *w'like: w ldrs: rdn over 1f out: styng on same pce whn n.m.r ins fnl f* **4/1**[2]

**5** 5 **Arc Of Light (IRE)** 2-9-0 ........ MHills 6 60
(BWHills) *lt-fr: leggy: scope: s.s: hld up: plld hrd: wknd 2f out* **12/1**

**6** 2 1/2 **Desert Lover (IRE)** 2-9-0 ........ EAhern 3 53
(JNoseda) *neat: scope: lw: s.i.s: plld hrd and sn prom: wknd 2f out* **8/1**[3]

04 **7** 3/4 **Our Choice (IRE)**[26] 1658 2-9-0 ........ TGMcLaughlin 4 50
(NPLittmoden) *started slowly, always behind* **20/1**

0 **8** 3/4 **Cry Of The Wolf**[8] 2095 2-9-0 ........ DaneO'Neill 2 48
(NPLittmoden) *chased leaders over 3f* **28/1**

1m 14.42s (1.33) **Going Correction** 0.0s/f (Good) **8** Ran SP% **119.6**
Speed ratings: **91,90,89,88,81 78,77,76**CSF £141.28 TOTE £34.00: £4.20, £1.90, £1.10; EX 82.20.
**Owner** Michael Pescod & Justin Dowley **Bred** Yeomanstown Stud **Trained** East Everleigh, Wilts

**FOCUS**
This did not look the strongest of maidens for the course. The pace was only steady.

**NOTEBOOK**
**Destinate(IRE)**, a half-brother to 12-furlong winner Fiza, had clearly learnt from his debut and appreciated this quicker surface. He will stay further in time.
**Juantorena**, a late foal, is a half-brother to Millybaa. He is a good mover who can only get better as he gets stronger. *Official explanation: jockey said colt hung left.*
**Capable Guest(IRE)** again took a while for the penny to drop and looks sure to appreciate a seventh furlong.
**Darko Karim**, a half-brother to Group Two winner Hanami, shaped with plenty of promise and is sure to have learnt plenty from the experience.
**Arc Of Light(IRE)**, a late foal, is a half-brother to the useful Rainbow Ways and Storm Seeker. A backward type, he looks sure to do better later on in the season.
**Desert Lover(IRE)**, from the same family as the useful performers Crystal Hearted, Solar Crystal and State Crystal, should benefit from the experience.

## 2311 COUNTRYSIDE ALLIANCE MAIDEN STKS 1m

4:35 (4:35) (D) 3-Y-O £5,629 (£1,732; £866; £433) Stalls High

Form RPR

**1** **Moon Dazzle (USA)** 3-8-9 ........ RHills 8 86
(WJHaggas) *lt-fr: neat: hld up in tch: led 1f out: r.o* **12/1**

2 **2** 3 **Long Road (USA)**[7] 2114 3-9-0 ........ EAhern 10 84
(JNoseda) *lw: trckd ldrs: led over 1f out: sn hdd and unable qck* **5/4**[1]

0- **3** 4 **Arrgatt (IRE)**[232] 5345 3-9-0 ........ KMcEvoy 12 75
(MAJarvis) *lw: led over 6f: wknd ins fnl f* **22/1**

42- **4** 5 **Telefonica (USA)**[213] 5701 3-8-9 ........ KFallon 13 59
(SirMichaelStoute) *lw: w ldr: rdn and ev ch over 1f out: sn wknd* **7/2**[2]

0-0 **5** 3/4 **Viola Da Braccio (IRE)**[19] 1842 3-8-9 ........ DaneO'Neill 6 57
(DJDaly) *prom 6f* **66/1**

**6** 8 **Lady Lexie** 3-8-9 ........ IMongan 2 39
(RGuest) *w'like: bkwd: s.i.s: hld up: n.d* **33/1**

0 **7** 1 **King's Minstrel (IRE)**[7] 2114 3-9-0 ........ CCatlin 7 41
(MRChannon) *dwlt: outpcd* **40/1**

0 **8** *1 ¾* **Antigua Bay (IRE)**[38] [1400] 3-8-6 .................................... LisaJones(3) 5 32
(JARToller) *hld up: effrt over 3f out: sn wknd* **4/1**[3]
**9** *nk* **Cayman Calypso (IRE)** 3-9-0 ...................................... PRobinson 11 37
(MAJarvis) *leggy: scope: prom over 5f* **10/1**
**10** *¾* **Bold Phoenix (IRE)** 3-9-0 .................................................. JMcAuley 4 35
(ACStewart) *cmpt: bkwd: prom: rdn 1/2-way: wknd over 2f out* **33/1**
00 **11** *5* **Suspicious Minds**[20] [1794] 3-8-9 ............................................. MHills 1 18
(GCBravery) *hld up: a in rr* **50/1**
00 **12** *1* **Eizawina Docklands**[7] [2113] 3-9-0 .............................(t) TGMcLaughlin 3 21
(NPLittmoden) *s.i.s: a in rr* **50/1**
**13** *28* **Karashinko (IRE)** 3-9-0 ................................................... CLowther 9 —
(RGuest) *leggy: scope: sn outpcd* **33/1**

1m 38.51s (-0.89) **Going Correction** 0.0s/f (Good) **13** Ran SP% **124.5**
Speed ratings: **104,101,97,92,91 83,82,80,80,79 74,73,45**CSF £27.18 TOTE £16.90: £2.60, £1.50, £4.70; EX 28.90.
**Owner** Wentworth Racing (pty) Ltd **Bred** Wentworth Racing **Trained** Newmarket, Suffolk

**FOCUS**

A decent maiden but probably not that much strength in depth here outside the first four, although it was run at a sound pace.

**NOTEBOOK**

**Moon Dazzle(USA)** ◆, a half-sister to German 2000 Guineas winner Dupont, showed a nice turn of foot, having travelled well, and is clearly a smart filly.
**Long Road(USA)** ◆ did nothing wrong and was probably a little unlucky to run into an above average filly.
**Arrgatt(IRE)** knew a bit more this time and showed plenty of speed until lack of a recent outing took its toll in the closing stages. He looks capable of winning a small maiden before going handicapping.
**Telefonica(USA)** ran as though the outing as needed, but will have more opportunities now he is qualified for handicaps.
**Viola Da Braccio(IRE)**, a half-sister to Wuxi Venture and Winning Venture, showed her first signs of ability and will be easier to place now she is eligible for handicaps.
**Antigua Bay(IRE)**, who shaped with plenty of promise on her debut, was never really going on this faster ground.

## 2312 NGK SPARK PLUGS/FMI MAIDEN STKS — 1m 4f

**5:10** (5:11) (D) 3-Y-O **£5,421** (£1,668; £834; £417) **Stalls** Centre

Form RPR
4-23 **1** **Larkwing (IRE)**[15] [1926] 3-9-0 85 ........................................ KFallon 1 77
(GWragg) *hld up in tch: shkn up to ld over 1f out: styd on* **8/13**[1]
4-4 **2** *1 ¾* **Turnstile**[36] [1442] 3-9-0 ............................................................ PDobbs 3 74
(RHannon) *lw: chsd ldr: rdn and ev ch over 1f out: styd on same pce* **10/1**[3]
4 **3** *½* **Water Taxi**[20] [1800] 3-9-0 ................................................ DaneO'Neill 5 73
(RCharlton) *lw: chsd ldrs: rdn and nt clr run over 1f out: swtchd lft: styd on same pce ins fnl f* **10/3**[2]
0 **4** *hd* **Honeymooning**[12] [2001] 3-8-9 ............................................ PaulEddery 6 68
(HRACecil) *hld up: hdwy over 2f out: rdn over 1f out: no ex ins fnl f* **12/1**
06- **5** *2 ½* **Ivy League Star (IRE)**[196] [5948] 3-8-9 ...................................... MHills 4 64
(BWHills) *h.d.w: led: rdn and hdd over 1f out: wknd ins fnl f* **20/1**
0 **6** *dist* **Glanworth (IRE)**[8] [2093] 3-8-11 .................................... LisaJones(3) 2 —
(NACallaghan) *chsd ldrs over 8f* **66/1**
**7** *dist* **Flamingo Palace** 3-9-0 ................................................ TGMcLaughlin 7 —
(PJMcbride) *wl grwn: lw: hld up: wknd 5f out* **40/1**

2m 34.98s (1.52) **Going Correction** 0.0s/f (Good) **7** Ran SP% **110.5**
Speed ratings: **94,92,92,92,90** —,—CSF £7.18 TOTE £1.60: £1.20, £3.10; EX 7.00 Place 6 £70.24, Place 5 £28.11.
**Owner** Mollers Racing **Bred** Airlie Stud **Trained** Newmarket, Suffolk

**FOCUS**

A fair maiden but a modest time for the grade, and the winner likely to be better in a stronger-run race.

**NOTEBOOK**

**Larkwing(IRE)**, with a handicap mark of 85, was entitled to win this, but he made hard work of it and probably was not suited by the steady pace. He handled this faster ground well enough and is capable of better than he showed here.
**Turnstile** will at least have more options open to him now he is eligible for handicaps, but will have done himself no favours by finishing on the heels of an 85-rated rival.
**Water Taxi**, out of a mare that won over this trip, handled this faster surface well enough and may have done a little \n\x\x better had he not had to switch for a run. He lacks a change of gear and looks as though he will appreciate a bit further.
**Honeymooning** is going the right way, but this steady pace was not in her favour and improvement can be expected when she gets a stiffer test.
**Ivy League Star(IRE)** ran as though the outing was needed and can step up on this when going handicapping.
CR

2313 - (Foreign Racing) - See Raceform Interactive

# 1846 CURRAGH (R-H)

Saturday, May 22

**OFFICIAL GOING: Good to firm (good in places in straight)**

## 2314a ISABEL MORRIS MARBLE HILL STKS (LISTED) — 5f

**2:45** (2:47) 2-Y-O **£26,590** (£5,759; £5,759; £1,266)

RPR
**1** **Russian Blue (IRE)**[19] [1846] 2-9-0 ....................................... JPSpencer 2 98
(APO'Brien, Ire) *mde all: rdn and kpt on wl fnl f: comf* **1/5**[1]
**2** *1* **L'Altro Mondo (IRE)**[48] [1251] 2-9-0 ......................................... TPO'Shea 3 94
(MHalford, Ire) *trckd ldrs: 2nd 1/2-way: rdn to chal over 1f out: no imp ins fnl f* **12/1**[3]
**2** *dht* **Kay Two (IRE)**[37] [1428] 2-9-0 ............................................. PJSmullen 4 94
(MsFMCrowley, Ire) *hld up: impr into 3rd and rdn 2f out: kpt on u.p fnl f* **20/1**
**4** *4* **Joyce (IRE)**[37] [1428] 2-9-0 .............................................. JAHeffernan 1 78
(APO'Brien, Ire) *cl up in 2nd: rdn and wknd 1/2-way: eased ins fnl f* **5/1**[2]

61.30 secs **Going Correction** -0.25s/f (Firm) **4** Ran SP% **112.5**
Speed ratings: **91,89,89,83** TOTE £1.30.
**Owner** Exors of the late R E Sangster **Bred** Swettenham Stud **Trained** Ballydoyle, Co Tipperary

**FOCUS**

There was no significant improvement on his previous effort, but the winner looks to be the stable leading hope for the Coventry.

**NOTEBOOK**

**Russian Blue(IRE)** had little difficulty in keeping his unbeaten record, making all. There was no time recorded but video playback suggested it was on par with his last success here. The Coventry is his mentioned Ascot target.
**L'Altro Mondo(IRE)** finished ten lengths behind the winner here in March. He ran on gamely inside the last but is flattered by his proximity at the finish.
**Kay Two(IRE)** had finished second to Joyce in a heavy-ground maiden at Tipperary and stepped up on that performance, forcing a dead heat for second place close home.
**Joyce(IRE)** was impressive on his debut win but ran as though something was amiss here, being eased inside the last.

## 2315a BOYLESPORTS IRISH 2,000 GUINEAS (GROUP 1) (ENTIRE COLTS & FILLIES) — 1m

**3:20** (3:21) 3-Y-O **£164,225** (£54,366; £26,197; £9,295)

RPR
**1** **Bachelor Duke (USA)**[21] [1764] 3-9-0 ................................... SSanders 8 120
(JARToller) *hld up in 6th: 5th and swtchd to outer 2f out: chal 1f out: led 100 yds out: styd on wl* **12/1**
**2** *1* **Azamour (IRE)**[21] [1764] 3-9-0 118.......................................... MJKinane 5 118
(JohnMOxx, Ire) *trckd ldrs on far rail: 3rd 1/2-way: 4th under 2f out: impr to ld under 1f out: hdd 100 yds out* **6/4**[1]
**3** *½* **Grey Swallow (IRE)**[21] [1764] 3-9-0 118.................................... PJSmullen 3 116
(DKWeld, Ire) *trckd ldrs in 4th: 3rd and rdn over 1 1/2 f out: chal 1f out: kpt on u.p* **2/1**[2]
**4** *1 ½* **Leitrim House**[19] [1847] 3-9-0 .............................................. SDrowne 2 113
(BJMeehan) *cl up in 2nd: rdn under 3f out: disp ld 2f out: slt advantage under 1f out: sn hdd and no ex* **5/1**[3]
**5** *3* **Grand Reward (USA)**[19] [1847] 3-9-0 111.......................... JPSpencer 6 106
(APO'Brien, Ire) *led: rdn and jnd 2f out: hdd under 1f out: sn no ex* **14/1**
**6** *1 ½* **Newton (IRE)**[6] [2161] 3-9-0 106....................................(b) PJScallan 4 103
(APO'Brien, Ire) *chsd ldrs: 5th 1/2-way: 6th and no ex fr 2f out* **50/1**
**7** *4 ½* **Amarula Ridge (IRE)**[34] [1487] 3-9-0 100...................... DPMcDonogh 1 92
(KevinPrendergast, Ire) *hld up: 6th 1/2-way: wknd over 2f out* **50/1**
**8** *¾* **Hayburn Street (IRE)**[62] [1074] 3-9-0 ................................ PShanahan 7 91?
(DKWeld, Ire) *s.i.s and a in rr: lost tch over 2f out* **200/1**

1m 40.0s **Going Correction** -0.025s/f (Good) **8** Ran SP% **108.8**
Speed ratings: **113,112,111,110,107 105,101,100**CSF £27.69 TOTE £22.70: £3.10, £1.10, £1.20; DF 47.50.
**Owner** Exors of the late Duke of Devonshire **Bred** Airlie Stud **Trained** Newmarket, Suffolk

**FOCUS**

An up-to-standard renewal of this Classic with the seventh, third and fourth from Newmarket filling the first three places

**NOTEBOOK**

**Bachelor Duke(USA)** was possibly suited by the steady early pace here and was settled in the rear. Switched for his effort over a furlong and a half down, he hesitated momentarily but then produced a sustained run on the outer that saw him lead under pressure inside the last half furlong. He picked up well but it would be difficult to say that he actually quickened. He would be vulnerable to the runner-up in the St James's Palace if they meet again.
**Azamour(IRE)** was able to go with the pace this time. In front just inside the last, he could not quicken a second time when the winner came at him. A stronger pace may have suited better and it is too early yet to write him off.
**Grey Swallow(IRE)** looked hard trained. He had every chance a furlong out but failed to quicken. An extra two furlongs might help but the Epsom Derby is not an option now. The Prix Jean Prat or the Irish Derby are under consideration
**Leitrim House** was unable to dictate this time despite the apparent lack of pace and could not quicken when asked early inside the last. There will be plenty of other opportunities for him.
**Grand Reward(USA)** rather surprisingly was asked to make the running. He punctured quickly early inside the last.
**Newton(IRE)** is a bit of an enigma at the moment.
**Amarula Ridge(IRE)** was outclassed and looked uncomfortable on the ground.
**Hayburn Street(IRE)** could not go the pace but was not disgraced for a once-raced maiden.

## 2316a WEATHERBYS IRELAND GREENLANDS STKS (GROUP 3) — 6f

**3:55** (3:57) 3-Y-O+ **£36,619** (£10,704; £5,070; £1,690)

RPR
**1** **The Kiddykid (IRE)**[37] [1409] 4-9-6 .................................... JPSpencer 9 114
(PDEvans) *trckd ldrs in 3rd: impr into 2nd over 1 1/2f out: rdn to ld 1f out: kpt on wl u.p: all out* **12/1**
**2** *hd* **Arakan (USA)**[11] [2021] 4-9-6 ........................................... GaryStevens 3 113
(SirMichaelStoute) *hld up: 6th and hdwy 2 1/2f out: 2nd and kpt on wl ins fnl f: jst failed* **4/5**[1]
**3** *1 ½* **Ringmoor Down**[25] [1685] 5-9-3 ........................................ JPMurtagh 4 106
(DWPArbuthnot) *hld up towards rr: 8th over 1f out: r.o wl wout troubling wnr* **10/1**[3]
**4** *1 ½* **Hanabad (IRE)**[223] [5523] 4-9-6 109........................................ MJKinane 2 104
(JohnMOxx, Ire) *chsd ldrs: 4th and drvn along 1/2-way: 3rd and chal over 1f out: no ex ins fnl f* **7/2**[2]
**5** *nk* **Orientor**[11] [2021] 6-9-9 ......................................................... SSanders 6 107
(JSGoldie) *hld up in rr: hdwy on outer 2f out: 4th 1f out: sn no ex* **16/1**
**6** *1 ½* **Osterhase (IRE)**[62] [1068] 5-9-6 106......................................(b) FMBerry 5 99
(JEMulhern, Ire) *broke wl: sn led: rdn 2f out: hdd 1f out: wknd* **14/1**
**7** *4* **Favourite Nation (IRE)**[244] [5104] 3-8-11 98..................... PJSmullen 10 87
(DKWeld, Ire) *chsd ldrs: 6th 1/2-way: 5th 1 1/2f out: sn no ex* **14/1**
**8** *3* **One Won One (USA)**[13] [1982] 10-9-6 102......................... KJManning 8 78
(MsJoannaMorgan, Ire) *chsd ldrs on outer: 8th and drvn along 1/2-way: wknd over 2f out* **20/1**
**9** *2 ½* **Blue Crush (IRE)**[40] [1379] 3-8-8 101..............................(t) NGMcCullagh 7 68
(EdwardLynam, Ire) *broke wl: settled 2nd: wknd fr 2f out: eased* **16/1**
**10** *hd* **Sun Slash (IRE)**[17] [1893] 4-9-3 98........................................ PShanahan 1 67
(MsJoannaMorgan, Ire) *chsd ldrs in 4th: wknd 2 1/2f out: eased 1 1/2f out* **33/1**

1m 11.8s **Going Correction** -0.25s/f (Firm)
**WFA** 3 from 4yo+ 9lb **10** Ran SP% **127.4**
Speed ratings: **109,108,106,104,104 102,97,93,89,89**CSF £24.09 TOTE £23.80: £3.90, £1.10, £2.50; DF 51.40.
**Owner** Mrs Claire Massey **Bred** Knocklong House Stud **Trained** Pandy, Gwent

**FOCUS**

A fairly run-of-the mill Group Three sprint dominated by the British raiders.

**NOTEBOOK**

**The Kiddykid(IRE)** put his Newmarket effort behind Arakan well behind him, going on a furlong down and always looking likely to hold on. He coped well with the fast ground.
**Arakan(USA)** looked to have been given too much to do, although he narrowed the deficit down to a head on the line. He needs the extra furlong.
**Ringmoor Down** came through strongly at the end from an impossible position a furlong down.
**Hanabad(IRE)** needed this first run of the season badly.
**Orientor** had a stiff task at these weights and acquitted himself well on ground a bit firmer than he really likes.
**Osterhase(IRE)** stepped up from his handicap effort back in March and will get his turn soon.

## 2318a RIDGEWOOD PEARL STKS (GROUP 2) (F&M) 1m
4:55 (4:56) 4-Y-0+ £56,760 (£17,394; £8,239; £2,746)

RPR

1 **Soviet Song (IRE)**[28] 1621 4-8-11 JPMurtagh 4 118
(JRFanshawe) *trckd ldrs in 3rd: smooth hdwy over 2f out: qcknd into ld 1 1/2f out: clr fnl f: easily* **11/10**[1]

2 6 **Livadiya (IRE)**[8] 2102 8-8-11 107 MJKinane 5 104
(HRogers, Ire) *settled in rr: prog 2f out: mod 2nd and kpt on wl fnl f* **14/1**

3 3 **Hanami**[231] 5364 4-9-0 SSanders 2 100
(JARToller) *trckd ldrs in 4th: impr into 3rd and rdn 2f out: no imp fr over 1f out* **8/1**[3]

4 2 1/2 **Echoes In Eternity (IRE)**[20] 1790 4-9-0 (t) JPSpencer 3 95
(SaeedBinSuroor) *led: rdn and strly pressed 2f out: hdd 1 1/2f out: wknd* **7/4**[2]

5 25 **Hymn Of Love (IRE)**[251] 4913 4-8-11 101 (b) PJSmullen 1 34
(DKWeld, Ire) *cl up in 2nd: wknd qckly 2f out: eased fnl f* **12/1**

1m 39.5s **Going Correction** -0.025s/f (Good) 5 Ran SP% 109.5
Speed ratings: **115,109,106,103,78**CSF £15.96 TOTE £1.70: £1.10, £3.20; DF 13.40.
**Owner** Elite Racing Club **Bred** Elite Racing Club **Trained** Newmarket, Suffolk

**FOCUS**
A nice confidence booster for Soviet Song.

**NOTEBOOK**
**Soviet Song(IRE)** had plenty going for her here under the conditions and sprinted clear a furlong and a half out for an unchallenged win. The Queen Anne or the Windsor Forest are her Ascot options.
**Livadiya(IRE)** finds it hard to win in her own class but, ridden for second place here, gained her first Group 2 placing.
**Hanami** was totally outpaced over the last furlong and a half.
**Echoes In Eternity(IRE)** was ridden from the front but was struggling in the straight before being readily outpaced when he winner went on.
**Hymn Of Love(IRE)** *Official explanation: jockey said filly lost her action and dropped out quickly*

2319 - (Foreign Racing) - See Raceform Interactive

# BADEN-BADEN (L-H)
Saturday, May 22

**OFFICIAL GOING: Good**

## 2320a BETTY BARCLAY-RENNEN (GROUP 3) 2m
3:25 (3:30) 4-Y-0+ £26,761 (£12,676; £5,634; £3,169)

RPR

1 **Darasim (IRE)**[24] 1703 6-9-2 (v) JFanning 3 110
(MJohnston) *made all, ridden out* 2

2 1 1/2 **Bailamos (GER)**[21] 1779 4-8-12 ASuborics 7 106
(PSchiergen, Germany) *raced in 4th, 3rd straight, went 2nd over 1 1/2f out, kept on but not threaten winner*

3 2 1/2 **King Of Boxmeer (GER)**[20] 1802 5-8-12 (b) IFerguson 2 102
(WBaltromei, Germany) *last til slipped though on inside to go 6th entering straight, stayed on final 1 1/2f*

4 1 1/2 **Liquido (GER)**[21] 1779 5-8-12 ABoschert 1 100
(HSteinmetz, Germany) *held up in 7th, 5th straight, ridden and one pace final 2f* 3

5 1 3/4 **Western Devil (IRE)**[21] 1779 4-8-12 AStarke 4 100
(ASchutz, Germany) *raced in 5th, came wide and 7th straight, never a factor*

6 3 **Levirat (GER)**[20] 1802 5-8-12 J-PCarvalho 6 95
(MarioHofer, Germany) *raced in 3rd, 2nd straight, weakened over 1 1/2f out*

7 nk **Salutare (IRE)**[12] 4-8-5 CStefan 8 90
(JEPease, France) *raced in 6th, last on outside straight, soon ridden and no impression*

8 13 **Dusky Warbler**[24] 1703 5-8-12 JMackay 5 82
(MLWBell) *pressed leader, 4th and weakening straight, eased final f* 1

3m 21.59s
**WFA** 4 from 5yo+ 2lb 8 Ran SP% 131.4
Speed ratings: .
**Owner** Markus Graff **Bred** His Highness The Aga Khan's Studs S C **Trained** Middleham Moor, N Yorks

**NOTEBOOK**
**Darasim(IRE)**, returning to a faster surface, took this race in decisive fashion and would have scored by at least another length if he had not been eased in the last strides. He is likely to take his chance in the Ascot Gold Cup next.
**Dusky Warbler** finished well ahead of the winner at Ascot last time, but disappointed on this occasion. He raced very\n\x\x keenly on the outside of Darasim in the early stages and found nothing in the straight. Perhaps an autumn campaign on testing ground may get the best out of him.

# 2029 BRIGHTON (L-H)
Sunday, May 23

**OFFICIAL GOING: Good to firm (firm in places)**
Wind: almost nil Weather: sunny spells

## 2321 EBF/HARDINGS BAR AND CATERING SERVICES NOVICE MEDIAN AUCTION STKS 5f 213y
2:20 (2:20) (E) 2-Y-0 £3,711 (£1,142; £571; £285) Stalls Low

Form RPR

1 1 **Brecon Beacon**[12] 2024 2-9-6 SDrowne 5 70
(PFICole) *chsd ldr: led 2f out: hrd rdn: hld on wl* **4/9**[1]

6 2 shd **Queen's Glory (IRE)**[13] 1984 2-8-7 JQuinn 1 57
(WRMuir) *trckd ldng pair: plld out and effrt 2f out: str chal fnl f: r.o* **25/1**

0 3 1 1/4 **Bridge Place**[57] 1130 2-8-12 DaneO'Neill 4 57
(BJMeehan) *in tch: rdn 1/2-way: nt handle trck and wandered fnl 2f: wnt 3rd 1f out: kpt on* **7/2**[2]

5413 4 5 **Zimbali**[23] 1751 2-8-7 SCarson 2 35
(JMBradley) *led tl 2f out: no ex over 1f out* **8/1**[3]

0 5 7 **Sabo Prince**[7] 2140 2-8-12 CCatlin 3 15
(JMBradley) *t.k.h: in tch: rdn over 2f out: sn wknd* **50/1**

1m 11.51s (1.41) **Going Correction** +0.175s/f (Good) 5 Ran SP% 108.4
Speed ratings: **97,96,95,88,79**CSF £13.04 TOTE £1.40: £1.10, £5.60; EX 14.60.
**Owner** Elite Racing Club **Bred** Elite Racing Club **Trained** Whatcombe, Oxon

**FOCUS**
Just a weak race, although the winner did not act on the track and may be a little better than this effort suggests.

**NOTEBOOK**
**Brecon Beacon**, who justified favouritism in just an ordinary maiden at York on his debut, had to work much harder to follow up under his penalty and was reportedly not suited by the track. Even allowing for that, he would be one to take on in stronger contest.
**Queen's Glory(IRE)** improved on the form she showed on her debut in a heavy ground-maiden at Kempton, pushing the winner all the way to the line. She should find a maiden.
**Bridge Place** ran too green on his debut in a fair Kempton maiden 57 days ago, but this was better. He kept on well for pressure, but could never quite get to the winner and did not appear to handle the track as well as some of the others.
**Zimbali** should do better returned to five.
**Sabo Prince**, beaten in a seller on his debut, did not do much better this time.

## 2322 MISHON MACKAY (S) STKS 6f 209y
2:50 (2:54) (G) 3-Y-0+ £2,590 (£740; £370) Stalls Low

Form RPR

0202 1 **Jonny Ebeneezer**[5] 2209 5-9-6 63 BDoyle 2 70
(RMHCowell) *uns rdr and wnt to s rdrless: rrd s: hld up in midfield: effrt 2f out: hrd rdn 1f out: r.o to ld last 50 yds* **5/2**[1]

54-0 2 nk **Ziet D'Alsace (FR)**[11] 2030 4-9-1 52 IMongan 8 64
(AWCarroll) *trckd ldrs: led 2f out: hrd rdn fnl f: hdd fnl 50 yds: kpt on* **9/2**[3]

-334 3 5 **City General (IRE)**[10] 2061 3-8-2 55 (p) DerekNolan(7) 9 56
(JSMoore) *towards rr and wd: hrd rdn and hdwy over 1f out: edgd bdly lft: one pce fnl f* **3/1**[2]

0000 4 2 1/2 **Espada (IRE)**[27] 1675 8-9-6 58 SWKelly 10 50
(JAOsborne) *led 2f: w ldr tl outpcd fnl 2f* **5/1**

4460 5 nk **Threat**[6] 2178 8-9-6 45 CCatlin 3 49
(JMBradley) *w ldr: led after 2f tl 2f out: wknd fnl f* **16/1**

0000 6 2 **Easily Averted (IRE)**[11] 2033 3-8-9 59 (p) ADaly 7 44
(PButler) *s.i.s: hld up and bhd: hdwy on rail 2f out: hrd rdn over 1f out: no ex* **20/1**

000- 7 5 **Cafe Americano**[209] 5787 4-9-6 49 TQuinn 6 31
(DWPArbuthnot) *hld up towards rr: effrt over 2f out: wknd over 1f out* **16/1**

0455 8 1 1/4 **Polar Haze**[24] 1739 7-9-12 40 (v) JQuinn 1 33
(JPearce) *prom 2f: n.d fnl 3f* **16/1**

6100 9 1/2 **Flying Faisal (USA)**[6] 2178 6-9-12 47 (b) SCarson 4 32
(JMBradley) *prom: jnd ldrs over 3f out: wknd 2f out* **16/1**

0004 10 dist **Costa Del Sol (IRE)**[97] 790 3-8-9 45 JTate 5 —
(JJBridger) *sn wl bhd: t.o fr 1/2-way* **25/1**

1m 23.41s (0.81) **Going Correction** +0.175s/f (Good)
**WFA** 3 from 4yo+ 11lb 10 Ran SP% 120.6
Speed ratings: **102,101,95,93,92 90,84,83,82,—**CSF £14.58 TOTE £3.20: £1.80, £2.30, £1.20; EX 31.40.The winner was bought in for 5,000 guineas.
**Owner** Mrs J M Penney **Bred** John Purcell **Trained** Six Mile Bottom, Cambs

**FOCUS**
Just an ordinary seller won by Jonny Ebeneezer, who was best off at the weights. They went a decent enough pace, but the form may not be that reliable.

**NOTEBOOK**
**Jonny Ebeneezer** is nowhere near as good as he was and is much better suited by a softer surface. Add to that, he got loose beforehand and things did not look good. However, class told and he ran out a narrow winner.
**Ziet D'Alsace(FR)**, dropped a furlong in trip, settled better this time and was just denied. He was clear of the remainder and looks up to winning a similar contest in the coming weeks.
**City General(IRE)** is a regular in these type of events and ran his race.
**Espada(IRE)** is on the downgrade and was well held.
**Threat** is on a long losing run and has never won beyond six furlongs.

## 2323 DONATELLOS FAMILY RACEDAY SUNDAY 6TH JUNE MAIDEN STKS 1m 3f 196y
3:20 (3:24) (D) 3-Y-0+ £3,789 (£1,166; £583; £291) Stalls High

Form RPR

63 1 **Talwandi (IRE)**[9] 2093 3-8-10 BDoyle 6 84
(SirMichaelStoute) *trckd ldrs: squeezed through 3f out: led 1f out: flashed tail: rdn to hold on fnl f* **6/4**[1]

0-22 2 hd **Sunny Lady (FR)**[8] 2133 3-8-5 73 EAhern 1 78
(EALDunlop) *chsd ldr: ev ch fnl f: r.o* **2/1**[2]

3-43 3 2 **Al Beedaa (USA)**[20] 1823 3-8-5 73 TQuinn 7 75
(JLDunlop) *led: hrd rdn: flashed tail and hdd 1f out: one pce* **3/1**[3]

0 4 14 **Oh So Hardy**[27] 1674 3-8-5 CCatlin 5 53
(MAAllen) *in rr: rdn and outpcd 5f out: n.d after: wnt remote 4th 1f out* **66/1**

00 5 2 **Twelve Bar Blues**[10] 2060 3-8-5 FNorton 9 49
(JHMGosden) *dwlt: sn chsng ldrs: wknd over 2f out* **10/1**

0-00 6 21 **Salford Rocket**[17] 1911 4-9-13 SSanders 4 21
(GCHChung) *in tch tl wknd 3f out* **33/1**

000 7 dist **Highfluting**[6] 2168 3-8-5 DKinsella 2 —
(RMFlower) *sn bhd: t.o fnl 4f* **100/1**

2m 33.61s (1.51) **Going Correction** +0.175s/f (Good)
**WFA** 3 from 4yo+ 17lb 7 Ran SP% 112.8
Speed ratings: **101,100,99,90,88 74,—**CSF £4.63 TOTE £2.80: £1.70, £1.50; EX 5.40.
**Owner** H H Aga Khan **Bred** His Highness The Aga Khan's Studs S C **Trained** Newmarket, Suffolk

**FOCUS**
A fair but uncompetitive maiden that is unlikely to produce many future winners outside the front three.

**NOTEBOOK**
**Talwandi(IRE)** was able to confirm the promise he showed on his two previous starts, but only just. He travelled well enough, but flashed his tail under pressure and took an age to get on top. He does not appeal as one to follow.
**Sunny Lady(FR)** again found one too good. There is a small race in her, but she is not one to take a short price about.
**Al Beedaa(USA)**, third in a mile-six handicap on her previous start, was disappointing returned to maidens and was another to flash her tail.
**Oh So Hardy** was again well held and will find things easier when handicapped.

## 2324 SOUTHERN FM CHALLENGE CUP H'CAP 1m 1f 209y
3:50 (3:54) (F) (0-55,55) 3-Y-0+ £3,101 (£886; £443) Stalls High

Form RPR

1243 1 **Our Destiny**[11] 2031 6-9-3 51 IMongan 4 59
(AWCarroll) *hld up towards rr: hmpd after 1f: hdwy whn hmpd and swtchd rt over 1f out: r.o to ld fnl 75 yds* **10/1**[3]

3-00 2 1/2 **Kernel Dowery (IRE)**[29] 1611 4-9-6 54 (e[1]) TQuinn 12 61
(PWHarris) *led: hrd rdn over 1f out: hdd fnl 75 yds: kpt on* **5/1**[1]

0-03 3 1/2 **Fantasy Crusader**[11] 2034 5-8-13 47 (p) JQuinn 18 53
(JAGilbert) *w ldrs: hrd rdn and ev ch 1f out: kpt on* **10/1**[3]

3 **4** *shd* **Fairland (IRE)**[10] 2053 5-8-7 **48** oh1 ow2 ........ LSmith(7) 11 54
(SDow) *bhd: wd st: gd hdwy fnl 2f: nrst fin* **25/1**

3043 **5** *nk* **Theatre Lady (IRE)**[24] 1723 6-8-12 **46** ........ SDrowne 15 51
(PDEvans) *t.k.h: in tch: drvn to chse ldrs over 1f out: kpt on* **12/1**

0050 **6** *shd* **Even Easier**[45] 1309 3-8-7 **55** ........ SWhitworth 10 60?
(GLMoore) *in tch: effrt 2f out: ev ch ins fnl f: one pce* **10/1**[3]

-002 **7** *2* **Gran Clicquot**[24] 1723 9-8-12 **46** oh1 ........ CCatlin 13 47
(GPEnright) *chsd ldrs: one pce appr fnl f* **14/1**

4200 **8** *nk* **Burgundy**[11] 2034 7-9-7 **55** ........ (b) EAhern 7 56
(PMitchell) *hld up: hdwy into midfield after 3f: effrt on rail whn n.m.r 2f out: drvn to chse ldrs over 1f out: one pce* **11/1**

1063 **9** *1* **Private Benjamin**[11] 2032 4-9-1 **49** ........ FNorton 2 48+
(JamiePoulton) *prom: ev ch over 1f out: hld whn n.m.r ins fnl f: eased* **5/1**[1]

1334 **10** *1 1/4* **Mrs Cube**[10] 2053 5-8-12 **46** oh1 ........ SSanders 1 43+
(PHowling) *chsd ldrs tl no ex 1f out: eased whn btn* **16/1**

0205 **11** *3/4* **Private Seal**[32] 1545 9-8-5 **46** oh1 ........ (t) MHalford(7) 19 41
(JulianPoulton) *towards rr: effrt over 2f out: nvr rchd ldrs* **33/1**

00-0 **12** *3/4* **Don Argento**[41] 1366 3-7-9 **46** oh1 ........ FPFerris(3) 14 40
(MrsAJBowlby) *plld hrd towards rr: effrt and hung lft 2f out: n.d* **25/1**

00-0 **13** *3/4* **Pearl Of York (DEN)**[36] 1466 3-8-4 **55** ........ TPQueally(3) 3 47
(RGuest) *mid-div: no hdwy fnl 2f* **33/1**

6600 **14** *hd* **Piquet**[84] 929 6-8-12 **46** oh1 ........ JTate 9 38
(JJBridger) *prom tl wknd over 1f out* **20/1**

000- **15** *1 1/2* **Lysander's Quest (IRE)**[277] 4285 6-8-12 **46** oh6 ........ NDay 6 35
(RIngram) *bhd: rdn over 2f out: nvr trbld ldrs* **33/1**

6665 **16** *2 1/2* **Figura**[16] 1940 6-9-1 **49** ........ DaneO'Neill 8 33
(RIngram) *in rr: effrt over 2f out: nvr able to chal* **7/1**[2]

-006 **17** *shd* **Fife And Drum (USA)**[11] 2034 7-8-11 **48** ........ (p) BReilly(3) 5 32
(MissJFeilden) *mid-div tl eased over 1f out* **14/1**

5-50 **18** *7* **Venetian Romance (IRE)**[20] 1844 3-8-2 **50** ........ (p) GHannon 16 21
(APJones) *mid-div tl wknd over 2f out* **33/1**

0500 **19** *1/2* **Coolfore Jade (IRE)**[57] 1136 4-8-10 **49** ........ MSavage(5) 17 19
(NEBerry) *mid-div: effrt and hrd rdn 3f out: sn wknd* **25/1**

2m 3.81s (1.27) **Going Correction** +0.175s/f (Good)
**WFA** 3 from 4yo+ 14lb **19** Ran SP% **136.4**
Speed ratings: **101,100,100,100,99 99,98,97,97,96 95,94,94,94,93 91,90,85,84**CSF £59.10 CT £536.81 TOTE £8.60: £2.20, £1.90, £3.70, £6.80; EX 75.50.
**Owner** Dennis Deacon **Bred** D A And Mrs Hicks **Trained** Wixford, Warwicks

**FOCUS**
Quite a competitive handicap for the grade that should work out at a similar level.

**NOTEBOOK**
**Our Destiny** gained his first win in a handicap since January 2003 and first win on turf since July 2000. Things did not really go his way - he had to come from a fair way back and got stopped in his run - so this was a good effort considering.
**Kernel Dowery(IRE)**, with eye-shields on instead of cheekpieces, did nothing wrong. He is still a maiden, but will surely find a similar race before too much longer.
**Fantasy Crusader**, back on a winning mark and with the cheekpieces re-fitted, appeared to run his race and should continue to go well in similar events.
**Fairland(IRE)** holds the form down a little for he was beaten in a banded race on his previous start. He came widest of all into the straight and kept on under his inexperienced rider.
**Theatre Lady(IRE)** had conditions to suit and can have no excuses.
**Private Benjamin** proved disappointing and may not have been suited by this slight drop in trip.

## 2325 EBONY ROOM BRIGHTON MARINA 1ST ANNIVERSARY (H'CAP) STKS — 6f 209y
**4:20** (4:20) (E ) (0-70,60) 3-Y-0+ **£4,163** (£1,281; £640; £320) **Stalls** Low

Form RPR

40-6 **1** **A Woman In Love**[51] 1229 5-9-8 **58** ........ SDrowne 8 68
(MissBSanders) *plld hrd in midfield: hdwy 2f out: led ins fnl f: rdn out* **4/1**[1]

0003 **2** *1 1/4* **Londoner (USA)**[53] 1207 6-9-3 **53** ........ TQuinn 1 60
(SDow) *led: rdn and hdd ins fnl f: nt qckn* **8/1**

0131 **3** *1* **Alafzar (IRE)**[85] 918 6-9-9 **59** ........ (bt) EAhern 6 63
(PDEvans) *sn chsng ldr: ev ch 1f out: one pce* **5/1**[3]

5520 **4** *hd* **Temper Tantrum**[92] 847 6-9-7 **60** ........ (p) J-PGuillambert(3) 4 64
(AndrewReid) *hld up in midfield: effrt and nt clr run 2f out: styd on fnl f* **5/1**[3]

0065 **5** *1* **Zinging**[19] 1863 5-8-0 **36** ow1 ........ FNorton 10 37
(JJBridger) *chsd ldrs: hrd rdn 2f out: one pce* **16/1**

0460 **6** *1 1/4* **Gun Salute**[33] 1516 4-8-11 **47** ........ SWhitworth 2 45
(GLMoore) *hld up in rr: nt clr run over 1f out: eased outside: nrst fin* **9/1**

0000 **7** *shd* **Agilis (IRE)**[4] 2226 4-9-2 **55** ........ (b) RMiles(3) 9 53
(JamiePoulton) *in tch: nt clr run 2f out tl over 1f out: nt fully rcvr* **10/1**

-516 **8** *3/4* **Doctor Dennis (IRE)**[70] 1018 7-8-13 **49** ........ (v) NPollard 5 45
(JPearce) *plld hrd towards rr: rdn 2f out: nvr able to chal* **14/1**

00-0 **9** *1* **Elsinora**[80] 959 3-8-10 **57** ........ PDobbs 3 50
(HMorrison) *prom tl wknd over 1f out* **33/1**

1501 **10** *hd* **Warlingham (IRE)**[9] 2099 6-9-8 **58** ........ SSanders 7 50
(PHowling) *plld hrd in rr: rdn over 2f out: n.d* **9/2**[2]

1m 23.84s (1.24) **Going Correction** +0.175s/f (Good)
**WFA** 3 from 4yo+ 11lb **10** Ran SP% **117.2**
Speed ratings: **99,97,96,96,95 93,93,92,91,91**CSF £36.53 CT £168.06 TOTE £6.00: £1.60, £2.20, £2.90; EX 33.70.
**Owner** High & Dry Racing **Bred** Stratford Place Stud **Trained** Epsom, Surrey
■ Stewards Enquiry : S Drowne caution: used whip down the shoulder in the forehand position

**FOCUS**
A moderate handicap lacking strength, run at a pretty ordinary pace.

**NOTEBOOK**
**A Woman In Love**, 7lb higher than when last successful, had conditions to suit and scored a decisive success. She wins in her turn, but has never followed up.
**Londoner(USA)** is nowhere near as good as he was, but appears to have found his level and posted a pleasing effort on his first start in 53 days.
**Alafzar(IRE)**, 10lb lower than when last winning on turf, and 3lb higher than when winning on the Polytrack on his previous start, ran a solid race.
**Temper Tantrum** proved a little disappointing during the All-Weather season, but this was a respectable return from 92 days off.
**Zinging** does not win very often and has not won on turf since 2001.
**Agilis(IRE)** *Official explanation: jockey said gelding hung left throughout.*
**Warlingham(IRE)** was keen early and found nothing under pressure.

## 2326 BET365 CALL 08000 322365 H'CAP — 5f 59y
**4:50** (4:50) (E ) (0-75,71) 3-Y-0 **£4,410** (£1,357; £678; £339) **Stalls** Low

Form RPR

0051 **1** **Imperium**[11] 2033 3-9-5 **69** ........ FNorton 9 76
(MrsStefLiddiard) *dwlt: in tch: led over 1f out: wnt bdly lft: rdn out* **4/1**[2]

3-32 **2** *hd* **Intriguing Glimpse**[6] 2181 3-9-7 **71** ........ SSanders 3 77
(MissBSanders) *hdwy 2f out: str chal fnl f: r.o* **1/1**[1]

60-3 **3** *3 1/2* **Miss Madame (IRE)**[27] 1678 3-8-8 **61** ........ TPQueally(3) 7 53
(RGuest) *led tl over 1f out: one pce* **9/1**

0000 **4** *1* **Dellagio (IRE)**[9] 2097 3-8-10 **60** ........ SDrowne 6 48
(CADwyer) *towards rr tl rdn and styd on fnl 2f* **8/1**

310- **5** *2* **Mouseman**[233] 5340 3-8-10 **60** ........ IMongan 8 40
(CNKellett) *pressed ldr: disputing cl 2nd and ev ch whn bdly hmpd 1f out: nt rcvr* **20/1**

0060 **6** *1 1/4* **Sussex Style (IRE)**[50] 1243 3-8-3 **53** ........ DKinsella 2 28
(RMFlower) *bhd: rdn 2f out: nvr trbld ldrs* **33/1**

4236 **7** *nk* **Alizar (IRE)**[11] 2033 3-8-8 **58** ........ TQuinn 5 32
(SDow) *chsd ldrs: disputing cl 2nd and ev ch whn hmpd 1f out: nt rcvr: 6th and wl btn whn eased fnl 100 yds* **13/2**[3]

4000 **8** *2 1/2* **Cheeky Chi (IRE)**[6] 2181 3-9-0 **64** ........ SWKelly 1 28
(PSMcentee) *dwlt: sn chsng ldrs: wknd 2f out* **16/1**

63.35 secs (1.08) **Going Correction** +0.175s/f (Good) **8** Ran SP% **118.0**
Speed ratings: **98,97,92,90,87 85,84,80**CSF £8.67 CT £33.99 TOTE £5.40: £1.70, £1.10, £2.20; EX 9.50 Place 6 £7.84, Place 5 £5.71.
**Owner** The Cross Keys Racing Club **Bred** Mrs H B Raw **Trained** Great Shefford, Berks
■ Stewards Enquiry : F Norton one-day ban: careless riding (Jun 3)

**FOCUS**
Just a modest sprint handicap domiated by in-form horses.

**NOTEBOOK**
**Imperium** followed up his recent course and distance success off a 4lb higher mark. He is clearly going the right way, but had little in hand and may be one to take on next time.
**Intriguing Glimpse** is not doing anything wrong and her turn is not far off.
**Miss Madame(IRE)** showed good early speed on this first run over five furlongs, but lacked a change of pace.
**Dellagio(IRE)**, dropping back from seven furlongs, was nibbled at in the betting and did not run too badly. Another furlong may suit better.
**Mouseman**, with the blinkers left off, may have been closer had he not been hampered.
**Alizar(IRE)** lost all chance when hampered at the furlong pole.
T/Plt: £9.70 to a £1 stake. Pool: £36,416.65. 2,732.80 winning tickets. T/Qpdt: £8.50 to a £1 stake. Pool: £2,134.80. 184.50 winning tickets. LM

# 2313 CURRAGH (R-H)
Sunday, May 23

**OFFICIAL GOING: Good to firm**

## 2329a TATTERSALLS GOLD CUP (GROUP 1) — 1m 2f 110y
**3:05** (3:07) 4-Y-0+ **£113,521** (£34,788; £16,478; £5,492)

RPR

**1** **Powerscourt**[253] 4898 4-9-0 117 ........ JPSpencer 3 122+
(APO'Brien, Ire) *mde all: qcknd clr 2f out: styd on wl: easily* **10/3**[2]

**2** *6* **Livadiya (IRE)**[1] 2318 8-8-11 107 ........ JAHeffernan 2 108
(HRogers, Ire) *hld up in rr: 5th and rdn 2f out: kpt on wl u.p to go mod 2nd wl ins fnl f* **16/1**

**3** *1/2* **Nysaean (IRE)**[20] 1849 5-9-0 ........ MJKinane 1 110
(RHannon) *trckd ldrs in 4th: 3rd and rdn under 2f out: mod 2nd briefly 1f out: sn no ex* **9/10**[1]

**4** *1/2* **Napper Tandy (IRE)**[28] 1647 4-9-0 109 ........ (b) KJManning 5 109
(JSBolger, Ire) *plld hrd early: settled 3rd: rdn early st: kpt on same pce u.p* **8/1**

**5** *1 1/2* **Naheef (IRE)**[78] 979 5-9-0 ........ (bt[1]) KMcEvoy 7 106
(SaeedBinSuroor) *cl 2nd: rdn and outpcd ent st: no ex ins fnl f: eased* **6/1**[3]

**6** *4 1/2* **Private Charter**[4] 2220 4-9-0 ........ MHills 4 98
(BWHills) *hld up in tch: cl 5th appr st: wknd 2f out* **16/1**

2m 11.0s **6** Ran SP% **112.9**
Speed ratings: CSF £48.59 TOTE £4.00: £1.90, £4.20; DF 68.50.
**Owner** Mrs John Magnier **Bred** Juddmonte Farms **Trained** Ballydoyle, Co Tipperary

**NOTEBOOK**
**Powerscourt** was impressive in a Group 1 greatly weakened by the absence of Sulamani. He travelled particularly strongly in front throughout and was unchallenged over the last quarter mile. He showed a good attitude as well and it could be that he has matured greatly since last season when he appeared to need distance to overcome lack of pace. He looks very interesting although this was really just a Group 1 in name only.
**Livadiya(IRE)** turned out for the second time in 24 hours and with similar tactics employed, this 8 y-o mare managed to earn Group 1 black type as well as a healthy slice of the prize money.
**Nysaean(IRE)** was disappointing on ground a bit to fast for him. He was struggling two furlongs out and found nothing inside the last.
**Napper Tandy(IRE)** proved difficult to settle and could make no impression on the winner in the straight.
**Naheef(IRE)** ran second but was done with turning for home and eased inside the last.
**Private Charter** could not find anything after being close up to the straight.

## 2330a BOYLESPORTS IRISH 1,000 GUINEAS (GROUP 1) (FILLIES) — 1m
**3:40** (3:42) 3-Y-0 **£158,591** (£54,366; £26,197; £9,295)

RPR

**1** **Attraction**[21] 1791 3-9-0 ........ KDarley 5 116
(MJohnston) *mde virtually all: rdn and strly pressed over 1f out: kpt on wl: comf* **2/1**[1]

**2** *1* **Alexander Goldrun (IRE)**[14] 1980 3-9-0 106 ........ KJManning 12 114
(JSBolger, Ire) *a.p: 2nd fr 3f out: rdn to chal under 2f out: no imp ins fnl f: kpt on wl* **8/1**

**3** *2* **Illustrious Miss (USA)**[15] 1964 3-9-0 ........ KFallon 6 109
(DRLoder) *hld up: 7th 1 1/2f out: kpt on wl fnl f* **9/2**[3]

**4** *1* **Kinnaird (IRE)**[255] 4840 3-9-0 ........ MJKinane 9 107
(PCHaslam) *trckd ldrs: impr into 3rd 2 1/2f out: kpt on same pce u.p* **16/1**

**5** *1/2* **Secret Charm (IRE)**[21] 1791 3-9-0 ........ MHills 15 106
(BWHills) *trckd ldrs: impr into 3rd over 2f out: sn rdn and no imp* **4/1**[2]

**6** *1 1/2* **Necklace**[21] 1791 3-9-0 108 ........ JAHeffernan 8 102
(APO'Brien, Ire) *trckd ldrs: 5th 1/2-way: 4th over 1f out: sn no ex* **16/1**

**7** *1 1/2* **Majestic Desert**[21] 1791 3-9-0 ........ TEDurcan 7 99
(MRChannon) *chsd ldrs: 6th 1 1/2f out: kpt on same pce* **12/1**

**8** *5* **Misty Heights**[14] 1980 3-9-0 105 ........ (b[1]) PJSmullen 13 87
(DKWeld, Ire) *hld up: 7th and rdn under 2f out: no imp* **20/1**

**9** *2* **Last Love (IRE)**[35] 1484 3-9-0 ........ JPSpencer 1 83
(APO'Brien, Ire) *hld up in tch: effrt and no imp fr 2 1/2f out* **20/1**

**10** *1/2* **Kisses For Me (IRE)**[21] 1793 3-9-0 ........ PCosgrave 3 82
(APO'Brien, Ire) *cl up early: rdn and wknd 1/2-way* **100/1**



The Form Book, Raceform Ltd, Compton, RG20 6NL

11 2 ½ **Takrice**[35] 1485 3-9-0 104 .............................. WSupple 10 76
(KevinPrendergast, Ire) *towards rr: no imp fr 3f out* **66/1**

12 2 **Follow (USA)**[211] 5762 3-9-0 92 .............................. CO'Donoghue 14 71
(APO'Brien, Ire) *nvr a factor: trailing fr over 2f out* **100/1**

13 3 **Miss Childrey (IRE)**[14] 1980 3-9-0 104 .............................. PShanahan 11 64
(FrancisEnnis, Ire) *cl up early: racd alone on far rail: wknd fr 3f out* **100/1**

14 2 **Queen Of Palms (IRE)**[18] 1897 3-9-0 .............................. DPMcDonogh 4 60
(KevinPrendergast, Ire) *a bhd: wknd over 2f out* **33/1**

15 6 **Lucky (IRE)**[14] 1980 3-9-0 103 .............................. PJScallan 2 46
(APO'Brien, Ire) *a in rr: eased 2f out* **40/1**

1m 37.6s **Going Correction** -0.325s/f (Firm) **15** Ran SP% **121.5**
Speed ratings: **113,112,110,109,108 107,105,100,98,98 95,93,90,88,82**CSF £17.55 TOTE £2.70: £1.50, £1.80, £2.20; DF 15.60.
**Owner** Duke Of Roxburghe **Bred** Floors Farming **Trained** Middleham Moor, N Yorks

**NOTEBOOK**
**Attraction** made racing history by becoming the first filly to win both the Newmarket and Curragh 1,000 Guineas and she did it in some style; making most of the running and appearing to have something in hand. She had so many of the field struggling with two furlongs to run and the expected challengers just did not materialise. Her unbeaten record can stand for a while yet with Ascot's Coronation Stakes the next objective. But she appears to have the speed for sprinting too.
**Alexander Goldrun(IRE)** continues to thrive and this was easily her career best on ground that might have been a bit lively for her.
**Illustrious Miss(USA)** kept on strongly without ever holding out any serious hopes of troubling the winner.
**Kinnaird(IRE)** ran well on her reappearance but was a one paced third from over two furlongs down.
**Secret Charm(IRE)** did not improve on her luckless Newmarket effort behind the winner.
**Necklace** was one to get a bit closer than at Newmarket and might go a bit further than a mile.
**Majestic Desert** was not capable of making any impression over the last furlong and a half.
**Last Love(IRE)** was not quickly away but managed to flatter briefly two furlongs down before weakening.
**Takrice** *Official explanation: vet said filly was coughing after race*

## 2333a AIRLE STUD GALLINULE STKS (GROUP 3) 1m 2f
**5:15** (5:16) 3-Y-O **£36,676** (£10,760; £5,126; £1,746)

RPR

1 **Meath (IRE)**[14] 1982 3-9-0 106 .............................. JPSpencer 3 106
(APO'Brien, Ire) *mde all: rdn early st: styd on wl u.p fnl f* **11/8**[2]

2 1 ½ **Cairdeas (IRE)**[18] 1894 3-9-0 .............................. PJSmullen 5 103
(DKWeld, Ire) *settled 4th: hdwy 2f out: 3rd and rdn over 1f out: kpt on u.p* **4/5**[1]

3 nk **Barati (IRE)**[14] 1979 3-9-0 .............................. MJKinane 6 103
(JohnMOxx, Ire) *chsd ldrs in 3rd: pushed along ent st: 2nd briefly 1f out: sn no ex* **9/1**[3]

4 1 ½ **Danelissima (IRE)**[35] 1485 3-8-11 97 ..............................(b) KJManning 1 97
(JSBolger, Ire) *hld up in rr: kpt on u.p fr 2f out* **16/1**

5 nk **Lord Admiral (USA)**[21] 1810 3-9-0 95 .............................. FMBerry 4 99
(CharlesO'Brien, Ire) *trckd ldrs in 2nd: rdn over 2f out: no ex over 1f out* **20/1**

2m 10.9s **Going Correction** +0.325s/f (Good) **5** Ran SP% **118.3**
Speed ratings: **107,105,105,104,104**CSF £3.10 TOTE £2.50: £1.20, £1.30; DF 3.80.
**Owner** Mrs John Magnier **Bred** Sweetman Bloodstock **Trained** Ballydoyle, Co Tipperary

**NOTEBOOK**
**Meath(IRE)** had an easy task on paper over a hyped rival and made all to win in workmanlike style. He could go to Epsom with Yeats but would still appear to have plenty to find. The ground did not bother him.
**Cairdeas(IRE)**, with a win in a very ordinary Naas maiden to his credit, had been the subject of some long-odds speculation for the Epsom Derby. That bubble burst here and his sights are now set on the Curragh equivalent. He looked pretty one paced under pressure.
**Barati(IRE)** , five lengths last behind Yeats in the Derby Trial at Leopardstown two weeks previously, could not quicken when asked and needs further.
**Danelissima(IRE)** had plenty to do on these terms and was not disgraced.
**Lord Admiral(USA)** was beaten a similar distance when second to Tarakala at Gowran but was a trailing third behind Yeats in a Group Three back in April.

2334 - (Foreign Racing) - See Raceform Interactive

# [2320] BADEN-BADEN (L-H)
Sunday, May 23

**OFFICIAL GOING: Good**

## 2335a SCHERPING-RENNEN (LISTED) 6f
**2:10** (2:12) 3-Y-O **£13,380** (£5,282; £2,465; £1,408)

RPR

1 **Fulminant (IRE)**[217] 5660 3-9-2 .............................. ASuborics 11 101
(WKujath, Germany)

2 ¾ **Directa Star (GER)** 3-9-0 .............................. JPalik 4 97
(AndreasLowe, Germany)

3 nse **At Once (GER)**[232] 3-8-5 .............................. AHelfenbein 8 88
(FrauEMader, Germany)

4 2 ½ **Petardias Magic (IRE)**[15] 1965 3-9-2 .............................. JFanning 3 91
(EJO'Neill) *always in touch, 4th straight, effort 2f out, ran on til no extra final f (5/2F)* 1

5 nk **Momou Sy (GER)** 3-8-7 .............................. NRichter 6 81
(AndreasLowe, Germany)

6 hd **Koonunga Hill (GER)** 3-8-12 .............................. MTimpelan 5 86
(MarioHofer, Germany)

7 nse **Aristaios (GER)**[261] 4711 3-9-2 .............................. THellier 9 89
(BruceHellier, Germany)

7 dht **Donatello (GER)**[261] 4711 3-8-12 .............................. IFerguson 7 85
(WBaltromei, Germany)

9 1 ¼ **Tennessee Master (GER)** 3-8-12 .............................. J-PCarvalho 10 82
(MarioHofer, Germany)

10 6 **Twice Royal (IRE)**[255] 4855 3-8-12 .............................. AStarke 12 64
(USuter, Germany)

11 13 **Mandoline (GER)** 3-8-5 .............................. JBojko 2 18
(MRolke, Germany)

68.75 secs **11** Ran SP% **28.6**
Speed ratings: .
**Owner** Stall Zorbas **Bred** Dr Klaus Schulte **Trained** Germany

**NOTEBOOK**
**Petardias Magic(IRE)**, sent off favourite, raced close behind a line of three disputing the lead. He went third with two furlongs to run but was safely held at the distance and only just hung on for fourth.

## 2336a CAPGEMINI BADENER MEILE (GROUP 3) 1m
**3:25** (3:27) 3-Y-O+ **£26,761** (£10,563; £5,634; £3,169)

RPR

1 **Bear King (GER)**[224] 5530 7-9-3 .............................. NRichter 3 112
(CSprengel, Germany) *mid-division, 5th straight, switched outside well over 1f out, stayed on to lead 150yds out, driven out* 2

2 1 ¼ **Horeion Directa (GER)**[210] 5779 5-9-3 .............................. JPalik 8 109
(AndreasLowe, Germany) *led 1f, tracked leader to straight, led approaching final f to 150yds out, ran on same pace*

3 hd **Madresal (GER)**[294] 3821 5-9-1 .............................. THellier 6 107
(PSchiergen, Germany) *held up, 6th straight, followed winner on outside, stayed on to just miss 2nd* 1

4 2 **Up And Away (GER)**[224] 5525 10-9-5 .............................. LHammer-Hansen 5 107
(FrauEMader, Germany) *always close up, 4th straight, outpaced well over 1f out, rallied to regain 4th closing stages*

5 ¾ **Sambaprinz (GER)**[210] 5779 5-9-1 .............................. ASuborics 9 102
(HHorwart, Germany) *broke well, settled in 3rd to straight, hard ridden & every chance over 1f out, no extra final f*

6 shd **Arlecchina (GER)**[8] 2138 4-8-12 .............................. AStarke 7 98
(UStoltefuss, Germany) *last straight, stayed on final 1 1/2f, nearest at finish*

7 ¾ **Capital Secret (USA)**[17] 1954 7-9-5 .............................. MTimpelan 2 104
(MarioHofer, Germany) *8th straight, never a factor*

8 ¾ **Gonpardo (GER)** 3-8-2 .............................. J-PCarvalho 4 97
(MarioHofer, Germany) *7th straight, never a factor* 3

9 ¾ **Medici (GER)**[189] 6007 4-9-5 .............................. AHelfenbein 1 101
(MarioHofer, Germany) *led after 1f til headed approaching final f, gradually faded*

1m 38.96s
**WFA** 3 from 4yo+ 12lb **9** Ran SP% **130.3**
Speed ratings: .
**Owner** R Wusk **Bred** Gestut Rietberg **Trained** Germany

# [2233] LONGCHAMP (R-H)
Sunday, May 23

**OFFICIAL GOING: Good**

## 2337a PRIX VICOMTESSE VIGIER (GROUP 2) 1m 7f 110y
**2:20** (2:21) 4-Y-O+ **£42,148** (£16,268; £7,764; £5,176)

RPR

1 **Forestier (FR)**[31] 1578 4-8-12 .............................. C-PLemaire 5 111
(EDanel, France) *raced in 3rd, driven to lead approaching straight, ridden and ran on gamely when pressed final 1 1/2f, driven out*

2 nk **Westerner**[31] 1578 5-9-2 .............................. DBoeuf 2 113
(ELellouche, France) *hld up, headway straight, pushed along to challenge 2f out, every chance 1 1/2f out, ridden and no extra inside final f* 1

3 ¾ **Clear Thinking**[38] 1435 4-8-12 .............................. GaryStevens 1 110
(AFabre, France) *raced in 4th, disputing 3rd straight, pushed along 2f out, stayed on final furlong to take 3rd* 3

4 1 ½ **Le Carre (USA)**[31] 1578 6-8-12 .............................. CSoumillon 6 106
(ADeRoyer-Dupre, France) *led, headed approaching straight, 2nd and ridden straight, kept on at one pace* 2

5 2 **Clety (FR)**[13] 8-8-12 .............................. TThulliez 4 104
(FDoumen, France) *raced in 2nd, pushed along and disputing 3rd straight, beaten 1 1/2f out*

6 nse **Idaho Quest**[31] 1578 7-8-12 .............................. OPeslier 3 104
(H-APantall, France) *raced in last, never dangerous*

3m 29.9s **Going Correction** -0.075s/f (Good)
**WFA** 4 from 5yo+ 1lb **6** Ran SP% **114.7**
Speed ratings: **86,85,85,84,83 83.**
**Owner** Mme R-J Wattinne **Bred** Mme Rene Wattinne **Trained** France

**NOTEBOOK**
**Forestier(FR)** quickened well in the straight and ran out a game winner, battling back well when headed a furlong out. He is improving and, not going to be hurried, his trainer is thinking about aiming him at the Goodwood Cup later in the year.
**Westerner** was pulled out to make a challenge at the two furlong marker and pushed up well enough, but the winner was just too strong. He has to be considered disappointing and connections felt he might have found the ground a little too fast.
**Clear Thinking** did not get the best of runs, but made excellent progress when in the clear and was catching the winner and runner-up at the post.
**Le Carre(USA)** could only find the one pace when headed. He is better on soft ground.

## 2338a PRIX SAINT-ALARY (GROUP 1) (FILLIES) 1m 2f
**2:55** (2:56) 3-Y-O **£80,479** (£32,197; £16,099; £8,042)

RPR

1 **Ask For The Moon (FR)**[44] 1320 3-9-0 .............................. IMendizabal 2 110
(J-CRouget, France) *disputed 3rd, 4th straight, pushed along 2f out, headway to challenge 1 1/2f out, led 150 yards out, driven out* **1/1**[1]

2 nk **Asti (IRE)**[21] 1803 3-9-0 .............................. DBoeuf 5 109
(ELellouche, France) *2nd and pulled early, pushed along entering straight, pressing leader 1 1/2f out, outpaced approaching final f but rallied* **11/4**[2]

3 ½ **Agata (FR)**[42] 1349 3-9-0 .............................. DBonilla 7 108
(YDeNicolay, France) *raced in 5th, ridden and finished well from 1 1/2f out to take 3rd close home* **16/1**

4 1 ½ **Super Lina (FR)**[44] 1320 3-9-0 .............................. CSoumillon 4 105
(YDeNicolay, France) *led, pressed 1 1/2f out, ran on til headed 150 yards out, kept on* **14/1**

5 nk **Ometsz (IRE)**[23] 3-9-0 .............................. GaryStevens 1 105
(RodCollet, France) *raced in 6th on inside, pushed along and headway 1 1/2f out, no extra inside final furlong* **25/1**

6 ¾ **Australie (IRE)**[31] 3-9-0 .............................. TJarnet 3 103
(RGibson, France) *disputed 3rd, 3rd straight, pushed along on outside 1 1/2f out, unable to quicken under pressure final stages* **12/1**

7 ½ **Green Swallow (FR)**[21] [1803] 3-9-0 ........................................ TGillet 6 102
(PDemercastel, France) *raced in last and not settle early, effort 2f out, no impression* **5/1**[3]

2m 5.10s **Going Correction** -0.075s/f (Good) 7 Ran SP% **117.4**
Speed ratings: **109,108,108,107,106 106,105.**
**Owner** J-P Dubois **Bred** Mme Gilles Forien & Jean Francois Gribomont **Trained** France

**NOTEBOOK**
**Ask For The Moon(FR)** raced a little freely early on, but picked up well when it mattered. She is probably value for more than the winning margin for she idled when she hit the front. Unbeaten in four races this season, she now goes for the Prix de Diane Hermes.
**Asti(IRE)** has to be considered a little unlucky for she was slightly hampered a furlong out and seemed to lose her momentum. She rallied and finished best of all, but could not get to the winner. Plans are still for her to run in the Diane.
**Agata(FR)** arrived late on the scene after being outpaced early in the straight and was staying on well at the death. She will be better suited the slightly longer trip in the Diane.
**Super Lina(FR)** lacked a change of pace.

## 2339a PRX D'ISPAHAN (GROUP 1) 1m 1f 55y
**3:30** (3:31) 4-Y-0+ **£80,479** (£32,197; £16,099; £8,042)

RPR

1 **Prince Kirk (FR)**[224] [5530] 4-9-2 ....................................(b) MMonteriso 3 121
(EBorromeo, Italy) *held up, last straight, ridden and headway over 1 1/2f out, ran on to lead 100 yards out, jinked right close home, kept on* **25/1**

2 ½ **Six Perfections (FR)**[211] [5769] 4-8-13 ................................ TThulliez 2 117
(PBary, France) *held up, 4th straight, headway 1 1/2f out to lead 1f out, headed 100 yards out, kept on* **8/11**[1]

3 2½ **Checkit (IRE)**[8] [2109] 4-9-2 ............................................ SHitchcott 1 115
(MRChannon) *led, ridden 2f out, headed 1f out, kept on* **20/1**

4 1½ **Sunstrach (IRE)**[29] [1622] 6-9-2 ........................................ JPMurtagh 4 112
(LMCumani) *raced in 3rd, ridden over 1 1/2f out, unable to quicken* **10/1**[3]

5 4 **Nebraska Tornado (USA)**[259] [4761] 4-8-13 ................. GaryStevens 5 101
(AFabre, France) *reluctant to load, raced in 2nd, pressing leader in straight til weakened from over 1f out* **13/8**[2]

1m 52.0s **Going Correction** -0.075s/f (Good) 5 Ran SP% **113.7**
Speed ratings: **113,112,110,109,105.**
**Owner** Scuderia Pieffegi **Bred** Srl So Li Ca **Trained** Italy

**NOTEBOOK**
**Prince Kirk(FR)**, with blinkers on for the first time, was given a fine ride by his jockey. He looked to have plenty to do at the entrance to the straight, but quickened well a furlong and a half out. The only moments worry was when he appeared to slip and brushed the running rail close home. His trainer will now consider the Eclipse and Arlington Million.
**Six Perfections(FR)** looked well in the paddock and moved to the start in good style. However, she found the winner too strong late on and connections feel she may be better over a mile. Her next target could be the Queen Anne at Royal Ascot.
**Checkit(IRE)** posted a decent effort from the front under a fine ride by his young jockey.
**Sunstrach(IRE)** did not have things go his way. He was boxed in when things quickened up in the straight and could never recover to pose a threat. Murtagh felt that softer ground would have been an advantage.

# 2138 SAN SIRO (R-H)
### Sunday, May 23

**OFFICIAL GOING: Good**

## 2340a COPPA D'ORO (LISTED) 1m 7f
**2:20** (2:26) 3-Y-0+ **£24,648** (£10,845; £5,915; £2,958)

RPR

1 **Swing Wing**[18] [1880] 5-9-7 ................................................ DHolland 7 109
(PFICole) *held up in 3rd to straight, led 2f out, ridden out (34/100F)* 1

2 ½ **Around Alone**[336] [2623] 7-9-7 ........................................... MEsposito 4 109
(MGasparini, Italy)

3 8 **Il Bimbo De Oro**[203] [5903] 5-9-7 ........................................ LPanici 6 101
(MCiciarelli, Italy)

4 3 **Sammiyo (IRE)**[203] [5903] 4-9-10 ........................................ EBotti 5 102
(AZucchegni, Italy)

5 ¾ **Entusiasmo (ITY)**[21] [1805] 3-7-12 ...................................... MBelli 1 95
(JHeloury, Italy)

6 dist **Fano Adriano (IRE)**[210] [5780] 3-8-2 .................................. MDemuro 2 —
(BGrizzetti, Italy)

7 1 **Carlo Bank (IRE)**[728] [1676] 8-9-7 ....................................... DVargiu 3 —
(GRomano, Italy)

3m 11.7s
**WFA** 3 from 4yo 21lb 4 from 5yo+ 1lb 7 Ran SP% **74.6**
Speed ratings: .
**Owner** Sir Martyn Arbib **Bred** Martyn Arbib **Trained** Whatcombe, Oxon

**NOTEBOOK**
**Swing Wing**, never far behind an erratic leader, was given more of a fight than expected in the final furlong but saw it out well. His next target is the Group 2 Premio Carlo d'Alessio at the Capannelle, Rome.

## 2341a OAKS D'ITALIA (GROUP 1) (FILLIES) 1m 3f
**3:50** (4:09) 3-Y-0 **£251,127** (£133,768; £79,789; £39,894)

RPR

1 **Menhoubah (USA)**[18] [1879] 3-8-12 ....................................(p) DHolland 1 102
(CEBrittain) *wore cheek pieces, raced in 3rd to straight, led approaching final f, ridden out, ran on well* **207/100**[2]

2 1¼ **Step Danzer (IRE)** 3-8-12 ................................................... EBotti 4 100
(ABotti, Italy) *mid-division, 6th straight, headway on rails over 2f out, every chance approaching final f, ran on one pace* **20/1**

3 1¾ **Loriana (IRE)** 3-8-12 ........................................................ GTemperini 3 97
(RBrogi, Italy) *in rear to straight, 9th 2f out, switched outside, stayed on well from over 1f out, nearest at finish* **132/10**

4 ½ **Rumba Loca (IRE)**[7] [2160] 3-8-12 ..................................... MDemuro 7 96+
(BGrizzetti, Italy) *dwelt, last straight, headway over 3f out, slightly hampered over 2f out, every chance well over 1f out, one pace* **58/10**[3]

5 ¾ **Tamarillo**[57] [1143] 3-8-12 ................................................. MFenton 6 95
(MLWBell) *tracked leader, led 2f out to approaching final f, one pace* **13/10**[1]

6 ¾ **Kayak**[66] [1048] 3-8-12 ....................................................... DVargiu 12 94
(PBary, France) *8th straight, headway 3f out, one pace final 2f* **123/10**

7 8 **Indian Filly** 3-8-12 ............................................................ LPanici 5 81
(MCicarelli, Italy) *always in mid-division, beaten well over 1f out* **50/1**

8 ½ **Shoko**[22] [1778] 3-8-12 ...................................................... GBietolini 10 80
(BGrizzetti, Italy) *in touch to over 2f out* **58/10**[3]

9 3 **Lotta (GER)** 3-8-12 ............................................................. EPedroza 8 76
(AWohler, Germany) *always towards rear* **69/10**

10 1½ **Oligarchica (GER)**[21] [1805] 3-8-12 ...................................... MEsposito 11 73
(RRohne, Germany) *prominent, 4th straight, weakened 3f out* **11/1**

11 4 **Bond Deal (IRE)**[22] [1778] 3-8-12 .......................................... FJovine 9 67
(LRiccardi, Italy) *led to 2f out* **51/1**

2m 15.1s 11 Ran SP% **149.7**
Speed ratings: .
**Owner** Saeed Manana **Bred** Woodlynn Farm Inc And Elliot Horowitz **Trained** Newmarket, Suffolk

**NOTEBOOK**
**Menhoubah(USA)**, winning for the first time in five attempts this year, was never worse than third. She is stoutly bred and should find further opportunities at this sort of trip.
**Step Danzer(IRE)** got a perfect run up the inside and kept on creditably.
**Loriana(IRE)**, still with only two behind her a quarter of a mile from home, moved to the outside and finished well. She could have been second with a better run.
**Rumba Loca(IRE)**, down the field in the Poule d'Essai des Pouliches only seven days earlier, lost five lengths at the start. She was still last entering the straight but made up her ground on the rails until baulked by the weakening Oligarchica. She recovered to have every chance inside the final two furlongs but reached the limit of her stamina soon after.
**Tamarillo**, back with Michael Bell after a winter in Dubai, grabbed a narrow lead inside the final quarter-mile but could only keep on at her own pace once headed by the winner.

# LES LANDES
### Monday, May 3

**OFFICIAL GOING: Good to soft**

## 2342a BRADY & GALLAGHER H'CAP SPRINT 5f 100y
**3:05** (12:00) 3-Y-0+ **£1,260** (£525; £315)

RPR

1 **Master Rattle**[14] [1515] 5-10-10 ........................................... KRenwick 3 —
(JaneSouthcombe) 1

2 3 **Johayro**[280] [3827] 11-9-11 ................................................. VSlattery 1 —
(MrsJLLeBrocq, Jersey) 3

3 5 **Unveil**[252] 6-9-12 .............................................................. RStudholme 5 —
(MrsAMalzard, Jersey) 2

1m 11.0s 3 Ran SP% **98.3**
Speed ratings: .
**Owner** Mark Savill **Bred** Mrs R D Peacock **Trained** Combe St Nicholas, Somerset

## 2343a JERSEY GUINEAS 1m 100y
**3:40** (12:00) 3-Y-0+ **£1,590** (£662; £398)

RPR

1 **Catcando (IRE)**[252] 6-10-0 ............................................... AProcter 7 —
(JSOArthur, Jersey) 2

2 3 **Meelup (IRE)**[7] [1675] 4-10-0 .............................................. VSlattery 6 —
(JaneSouthcombe) 1

3 4 **Minnie's Mystery (FR)**[281] [3828] 6-9-11 .............................. KBradshaw 4 —
(CMccready, Jersey) 2

1m 56.0s 3 Ran SP% **107.1**
Speed ratings: .
**Owner** D M Ahler **Bred** Mrs Jill M Harley **Trained** Jersey

## 2344a GEOFFREY EDWARDS MEMORIAL H'CAP 1m 4f
**4:15** (12:00) 3-Y-0+ **£1,260** (£525; £315)

RPR

1 **Khuzdar (IRE)**[90] [661] 5-9-13 ............................................ PJBrennan 3 —
(MrsAMalzard, Jersey) 1

2 2 **Bold Enough**[364] 11-8-11 .................................................. JonjoFowle 7 —
(JSOArthur, Jersey)

3 1 **Palala River**[267] [4475] 11-10-7 ......................................... RStudholme 1 —
(MrsAMalzard, Jersey) 3

6 1 **Giko**[18] [1402] 10-10-2 ........................................................ AJones 8 —
(JaneSouthcombe) 2

2m 58.0s 4 Ran SP% **92.7**
Speed ratings: .
**Owner** Mrs Y Burnett, Mrs H Hamilton & Hopeless Punters G **Bred** P J B O'Callaghan **Trained** Jersey

# 2194 BEVERLEY (R-H)
### Monday, May 24

**OFFICIAL GOING: Good to firm (firm in places)**
18mm of water had been put on the track since the meeting six days earlier. The jockeys said it was good, fast ground and less rough after being rolled.
Wind: moderate, half-against Weather: fine

## 2345 WINDMILL BANDED STKS 1m 100y
**2:30** (2:30) (H) 3-Y-0+ **£1,470** (£420; £210) **Stalls High**

Form RPR

6366 1 **Sennen Cove**[25] [1718] 5-9-2 40.........................................(t) RFfrench 8 45
(RBastiman) *sn chsng ldrs: effrt on outer over 3f out: led over 1f out: kpt on* **15/2**

0000 2 1½ **Miss Ocean Monarch**[7] [2185] 4-9-2 40 ................................. ANicholls 9 42
(DWChapman) *hld up towards rr: hdwy on outer over 3f out: edgd rt and wnt 2nd appr fnl f: no real imp* **4/1**[1]

0/5- 3 1¾ **Little Task**[18] [2424] 6-9-2 30 ............................................. RWinston 7 38
(JSWainwright) *s.s: bhd and pushed along: hdwy 3f out: kpt on to take 3rd nr fin* **8/1**

0231 4 1¾ **Moyne Pleasure (IRE)**[7] [2184] 6-9-8 40 ..........................(p) IMongan 4 41
(PaulJohnson) *led tl over 1f out: fdd ins last* **4/1**[1]

0304 5 3 **Optimum Night**[5] [2229] 5-9-2 35 .........................................(p) GParkin 6 28
(PDNiven) *chsd ldrs: one pce fnl 2f* **16/1**

060- 6 1 **Miss Lehman**[202] [5914] 6-8-11 40 ...................................... TEaves(5) 5 26
(MrsMReveley) *plld v hrd: sn trcking ldrs: one pce fnl 2f* **25/1**

5024 **7** 3/4 **Sea Ya Maite**[38] 1444 10-9-2 40...(t) JBramhill 10 25
(SRBowring) *t.k.h in rr: pushed along over 5f out: sme hdwy on wd outside over 3f out: nvr on terms* **7/1**3

4322 **8** 2 1/2 **Divina**[11] 2054 3-7-11 40...(v) DFentiman(7) 3 19
(SLKeightley) *dwlt: sn trcking ldrs: lost pl over 2f out* **5/1**2

0534 **9** nk **All On My Own (USA)**[14] 1987 9-9-4 35 ow2...(b) LVickers 2 21
(IWMcinnes) *dwlt: a in rr* **12/1**

/00- **10** 4 **Dalyan (IRE)**[284] 4105 7-9-2 30... PFessey 1 10
(AJLockwood) *chsd ldrs: pushed along 5f out: lost pl over 2f out* **33/1**

1m 47.22s (-0.08) **Going Correction** -0.15s/f (Firm)
**WFA** 3 from 4yo+ 12lb **10** Ran SP% **112.4**
Speed ratings: **94,92,90,89,86 85,84,81,81,77**CSF £36.15 TOTE £8.50: £2.40, £2.00, £2.20; EX 48.90.
**Owner** Border Rail & Plant Limited **Bred** Fonthill Stud **Trained** Cowthorpe, N Yorks
■ Stewards Enquiry : R Ffrench two-day ban: careless riding (Jun 6,7)

**FOCUS**
A poor affair, but the form look solid for the grade.

**NOTEBOOK**
**Sennen Cove** made it 29th time lucky in a dire contest.
**Miss Ocean Monarch** ran her best race so far this year.
**Little Task**, recently in action under National Hunt rules, last won on the Flat over three years ago. He found this trip much too sharp but was staying on in good style when it was all over.
**Moyne Pleasure(IRE)** again adopted front-running tactics, but he didn't truly see this slightly shorter trip out on this much stiffer track.
**Optimum Night**, placed once in seven previous starts, probably ran right up to his limited best.
**Miss Lehman**, half asleep in the paddock, was the opposite in the race, pulling much too hard for her own good.

## 2346 BEVERLEY CONSERVATIVE CLUB MAIDEN CLAIMING STKS 7f 100y
3:00 (3:00) (H) 3-Y-O+ **£1,508** (£431; £215) **Stalls High**

Form RPR

4600 **1** **Shamwari Fire (IRE)**[9] 2122 4-9-5 46... RFfrench 13 56
(IWMcinnes) *mid-div: hdwy over 2f out: edgd rt and wnt 2nd over 1f out: led post* **11/2**2

35-6 **2** shd **Time To Regret**[19] 1888 4-9-5 53... RWinston 14 56
(JJQuinn) *trckd ldrs: smooth hdwy on ins to ld over 2f out: hrd rdn fnl f: jst ct* **11/4**1

5/ **3** 2 **Seyed (IRE)**[723] 1783 4-9-5 ... MTebbutt 11 51
(VSmith) *bhd: hdwy on wd outside 3f out: hung bdly rt: kpt on same pce fnl f* **7/1**

/00- **4** 2 1/2 **Niteowl Dream**[364] 1867 4-8-7 58... JDO'Reilly(7) 10 40
(JO'Reilly) *hld up and bhd: hdwy on ins and nt clr run 2f out: swtchd lft 1f out: fin wl* **25/1**

3400 **5** 1/2 **Knight To Remember (IRE)**[12] 2040 3-8-8 45... GFaulkner 5 44
(KRBurke) *led tl over 2f out: fdd ins last* **20/1**

640- **6** hd **Delightful Gift**[298] 3733 4-9-0 48... TWilliams 9 38
(MBrittain) *chsd ldrs: one pce fnl 2f* **25/1**

0-00 **7** 1/2 **Smart Minister**[14] 1993 4-9-5 49... PFessey 7 42
(JJQuinn) *mid-div: hdwy on outer over 2f out: kpt on: nvr rchd ldrs* **6/1**3

2556 **8** 1 1/4 **Heathyards Joy**[7] 2187 3-8-3 35... DaleGibson 6 34
(RHollinshead) *mid-div: hdwy to chse ldrs over 2f out: one pce* **20/1**

0-05 **9** 1 1/2 **Soleil D'Hiver**[118] 615 3-7-9 40... RoryMoore(7) 8 29
(PCHaslam) *mid-div: effrt on wd outside over 2f out: nvr nr ldrs* **20/1**

00 **10** hd **Welcome Archie**[14] 1994 4-9-2 ... ANicholls 15 31
(JSHaldane) *s.i.s: hdwy on inner over 2f out: one pce whn hmpd ins last* **40/1**

**11** nk **Cottam Karminski** 3-8-3 ... PMQuinn 12 29
(JSWainwright) *s.i.s: sme hdwy 2f out: nvr on terms* **25/1**

/400 **12** 7 **Bettys Valentine**[25] 1718 4-8-9 30... TEaves(5) 3 11
(DWBarker) *chsd ldrs: lost pl over 2f out* **50/1**

-200 **13** 2 **Good Timing**[105] 726 6-9-5 45... LVickers 4 11
(JHetherton) *mid-div: drvn along over 3f out: lost pl over 2f out* **25/1**

-360 **14** 14 **Compton Princess**[21] 1824 4-8-13 40...(b[1]) JMackay 2 —
(MrsADuffield) *keen on wd outside: hdwy over 3f out: sn chsng ldrs: lost pl and hmpd 2f out: sn bhd and eased* **16/1**

32L5 **L** **Spinning Dove**[51] 1241 4-9-0 65... IMongan 1 —
(NAGraham) *ref to r: tk no part* **6/1**3

1m 32.98s (-1.32) **Going Correction** -0.15s/f (Firm)
**WFA** 3 from 4yo+ 11lb **15** Ran SP% **123.1**
Speed ratings: **101,100,98,95,95 94,94,92,91,91 90,82,80,64,**—CSF £18.12 TOTE £7.90: £2.50, £1.70, £2.90; EX 32.20.Seyed was claimed by N Wilson for £5,000
**Owner** Ivy House Racing **Bred** Mrs P M Kalman **Trained** Catwick, E Yorks
■ Stewards Enquiry : R Ffrench two-day ban: careless riding (Jun 6-7)

**FOCUS**
A poor claimer but a fair pace, and the draw was a major factor.

**NOTEBOOK**
**Shamwari Fire(IRE)** made it 21st time lucky but he had to switch to get a run and it was only right on the line that he put his head in front.
**Time To Regret**, on his toes in the paddock, had a favourable draw and looked sure to break his duck at the 13th attempt when taking it up travelling smoothly, but he began to tread water inside the last and was just caught.
**Seyed(IRE)**, who cost 180,000gns as a yearling, showed little in one outing at two for David Loder. Making his effort on the wide outside turning in, all he wanted to do was hang right.
**Niteowl Dream**, having her first outing for a year, was very free to post. Making ground from the rear, she encountered severe traffic problems otherwise she might well have finished on the heels of the first two. The question is though, will she run as well next time?
**Knight To Remember(IRE)**, drawn four from the outside, was very warm beforehand. He had run over five furlongs on Turf on his previous start, and after making the running his stamina seemed to give out altogether inside the last.
**Spinning Dove**wouldn't leave the shelter of the stalls and a repeat will see her banned.

## 2347 BEAVER BANDED STKS 1m 4f 16y
3:30 (3:30) (H) 3-Y-O+ **£1,491** (£426; £213) **Stalls High**

Form RPR

10-6 **1** **Life Is Beautiful (IRE)**[32] 1560 5-9-8 45... RWinston 9 53
(WHTinning) *hld up in mid-div: hdwy and nt clr run over 3f out and over 2f out: swtchd ins: wnt 2nd over 1f out: led jst ins fnl f* **6/4**1

6400 **2** 1 3/4 **Stage Two (IRE)**[14] 1989 3-8-5 40... RFfrench 13 50
(MJohnston) *hld up in rr: stdy hdwy on ins 5f out: led over 2f out: hdd jst ins last: no ex* **15/2**

3242 **3** 4 **Dora Corbino**[5] 2230 4-9-3 40... StephanieHollinshead(5) 12 44
(RHollinshead) *a chsng ldrs: kpt on same pce fnl 2f* **9/1**

3402 **4** 2 1/2 **El Pedro**[5] 2228 5-9-3 40... MSavage(5) 2 40
(NEBerry) *chsd ldrs travelling comf: effrt over 2f out: one pce* **7/1**3

043U **5** nk **Upthedale (IRE)**[14] 1995 3-7-12 40... DFentiman(7) 11 39
(JRWeymes) *bhd: hdwy and hrd rdn over 2f out: styd on fnl f* **33/1**

2510 **6** 1 1/2 **Dash Of Magic**[32] 1560 6-9-8 45... MTebbutt 7 37
(JHetherton) *s.s: hdwy on wd outsider over 3f out: kpt on: nvr rchd ldrs* **6/1**2

0-25 **7** 3 **Let It Be**[17] 1946 3-8-5 45... ANicholls 1 32
(MrsMReveley) *hld up in rr: hdwy over 3f out: sn chsng ldrs: fdd over 1f out* **14/1**

-000 **8** 2 **Rovella**[7] 2185 3-8-5 40... DaleGibson 10 29
(MrsHDalton) *in tch: rdn over 2f out: hung rt and sn wknd* **50/1**

-003 **9** 3 **Dances With Angels (IRE)**[20] 1862 4-9-8 40... IMongan 4 24
(MrsALMKing) *bhd: reminders on outer 7f out: sn chsng ldrs: wknd over 2f out* **16/1**

50-0 **10** 2 1/2 **Quinn**[55] 1193 4-9-8 40... GFaulkner 5 20
(CWFairhurst) *rr-div: sme hdwy over 3f out: sn rdn and no imp* **50/1**

0-56 **11** 1 3/4 **Cezzaro (IRE)**[27] 1697 6-9-8 45... JBramhill 3 17
(SRBowring) *w ldrs: lost pl over 1f out* **16/1**

65/- **12** 5 **Hibernate (IRE)**[657] 3644 10-9-3 45... TEaves(5) 8 9
(CJTeague) *led tl over 2f out: sn lost pl* **22/1**

404- **13** 29 **Sea Of Happiness**[247] 5065 4-9-8 45... PFessey 6 —
(CGrant) *chsd ldrs: lost pl over 4f out: bhd and eased 2f out* **40/1**

2m 38.26s (-1.04) **Going Correction** -0.15s/f (Firm)
**WFA** 3 from 4yo+ 17lb **13** Ran SP% **120.6**
Speed ratings: **97,95,93,91,91 90,88,86,84,83 82,78,59**CSF £12.34 TOTE £2.30: £1.10, £2.20, £2.80; EX 14.50.
**Owner** W H & Mrs J A Tinning **Bred** Azienda Agricola Loreto Luciani **Trained** Thornton-le-Clay, N Yorks

**FOCUS**
A very moderate event won by a course specialist and the form looks fair for the grade.

**NOTEBOOK**
**Life Is Beautiful(IRE)**, much better drawn this time, recorded her fourth course and distance win. She is a credit to her small yard.
**Stage Two(IRE)**, bred in the purple, is a good-looking individual who stood head and shoulders above his rivals in the paddock. Breeding and looks count for nothing though if the raw talent is missing, and after making the running his stride shortened noticeably inside the last. This was nevertheless easily his best effort so far on his sixth career start.
**Dora Corbino** has been running better of late but this trip is her bare minimum.
**El Pedro** travelled strongly but didn't seem to quite see it out. On a track as stiff as this 10 furlongs might be far as he wants to go.
**Upthedale(IRE)** seemed suited by the step up in trip and if anything will appreciate an even stiffer test.
**Dash Of Magic**, twice a winner here, gave away ground at the start and then took the by-pass route. She deserves credit for this effort.
**Dances With Angels(IRE)** *Official explanation: jockey said filly hung right-handed throughout*
**Sea Of Happiness** *Official explanation: vet said gelding lost a shoe*

## 2348 DOG AND DUCK, WALKINGTON, BANDED STKS 1m 1f 207y
4:00 (4:01) (H) 3-Y-O+ **£1,501** (£429; £214) **Stalls High**

Form RPR

3346 **1** **Larad (IRE)**[18] 1908 3-8-2 45 ow1...(b) DerekNolan(7) 9 52
(JSMoore) *trckd ldrs: led over 1f out: styd on* **5/1**3

3-54 **2** 1 1/2 **Merlins Profit**[6] 2214 4-9-3 40... TEaves(5) 5 48
(MDods) *hld up and bhd: pushed along 6f out: hdwy to chse ldrs over 2f out: kpt on to take 2nd nr line* **8/1**

0-13 **3** nk **Righty Ho**[6] 2214 10-9-8 45... RWinston 7 47
(WHTinning) *mid-div: effrt on outer over 3f out: edgd rt and wnt 2nd over 1f out: kpt on same pce* **5/2**1

6400 **4** 1 3/4 **Our Glenard**[11] 2053 5-9-1 45... DFentiman(7) 11 44
(SLKeightley) *s.s: hld up in rr: hdwy over 3f out: kpt on fnl 2f* **7/1**

006 **5** 6 **Archenko**[22] 1786 4-9-3 45... PBradley(5) 1 33
(ABerry) *led tl over 1f out: fdd ins last* **33/1**

/0-0 **6** 3 1/2 **Sunridge Fairy (IRE)**[29] 1233 5-9-8 35... PFessey 2 26
(AJLockwood) *sn in rr and pushed along: nvr on terms* **33/1**

-601 **7** 5 **Tarkwa**[11] 2052 5-9-8 45... GFaulkner 10 17
(RMHCowell) *chsd ldrs: lost pl over 1f out* **3/1**2

6302 **8** 2 **Desires Destiny**[18] 1918 6-9-8 45... TWilliams 3 13
(MBrittain) *trckd ldrs: t.k.h: hdwy on wd outside over 4f out: lost pl and eased over 1f out* **10/1**

0-06 **9** 1 3/4 **Delta Lady**[18] 1916 3-8-8 45... RFfrench 8 9
(RBastiman) *trckd ldrs: t.k.h: lost pl over 2f out* **16/1**

05-0 **10** dist **Rileys Rocket**[84] 945 5-9-8 40... JMackay 6 —
(RHollinshead) *trckd ldrs: hung bdly lft bnd over 4f out: sn lost pl and bhd: eased* **25/1**

2m 6.29s (-0.91) **Going Correction** -0.15s/f (Firm)
**WFA** 3 from 4yo+ 14lb **10** Ran SP% **118.6**
Speed ratings: **97,95,95,94,89 86,82,80,79,**—CSF £44.49 TOTE £7.20: £1.70, £2.80, £1.60; EX 64.00.
**Owner** A P Crook **Bred** Mrs E Thompson **Trained** East Garston, Berks

**FOCUS**
Another poor race, in which the form looks average for the grade.

**NOTEBOOK**
**Larad(IRE)**, much happier on this much faster ground, scored in decisive fashion.
**Merlins Profit**, a maiden after 12 starts, struggled to keep up but stayed on to snatch second spot near the line. He will apppreciate a much stiffer test.
**Righty Ho** likes it round here but, in his 11th year, his powers are starting to wane.
**Our Glenard**, taken to post early, seemed to be anchored a degree or two too many leaving the stalls. He stayed on up the final hill but never looked like doing enough to take a real hand.
**Archenko**, unplaced in three previous starts, had run over two furlongs further last time. He made the running but the needle was on empty just inside the last.
**Tarkwa**, reportedly in foal, dropped out in most disappointing fashion.
**Desires Destiny** *Official explanation: jockey said mare had lost her action*
**Rileys Rocket** *Official explanation: jockey said mare had bolted to the start*

## 2349 EAGER BEAVER TRI-BANDED STKS 1m 100y
4:30 (4:31) (H) 3-Y-O **£1,484** (£424; £212) **Stalls High**

Form RPR

3123 **1** **Roman The Park (IRE)**[18] 1916 3-8-9 40... PMQuinn 11 45
(TDEasterby) *trckd ldrs: led 2f out: styd on: readily* **5/1**3

0534 **2** 1 1/4 **Given A Chance**[17] 1946 3-9-0 45... RWinston 3 47
(MrsSLamyman) *bhd: hdwy over 2f out: styd on wl ins last* **17/2**

0-00 **3** nk **Delcienne**[21] 1844 3-8-11 45... ABeech(3) 5 46
(GGMargarson) *hld up in rr: hdwy on ins over 3f out: kpt on ins last* **16/1**

4233 **4** nk **Monkey Or Me (IRE)**[5] 2232 3-8-4 35... RFitzpatrick 13 36
(PTMidgley) *rr-div: hdwy 3f out: sn chsng ldrs: one pce appr fnl f* **9/2**2

0001 **5** 2 **Tsarbuck**[5] 2232 3-9-6 45 6ex... GFaulkner 12 48
(RMHCowell) *led tl 2f out: wknd ins last* **10/3**1

065 **6** 1 1/4 **Cunning Pursuit**[17] 1942 3-9-0 45... IMongan 1 39
(MLWBell) *swvd lft ss: hld up on outer: hdwy over 2f out: kpt on: nvr rchd ldrs* **10/1**

0-00 **7** *3/4* **Queens Square**[25] 1737 3-8-9 45 ........ TEaves(5) 9 37
(NTinkler) *in tch: effrt over 2f out: one pce* **20/1**

5201 **8** *1 3/4* **A Bit Of Fun**[13] 2016 3-9-0 45 ........ RFfrench 6 34
(JJQuinn) *w ldrs: wknd over 1f out* **7/1**

00-0 **9** *hd* **Johnny Alljays (IRE)**[28] 1667 3-8-7 45 ........ DerekNolan(7) 2 33
(JSMoore) *bhd: hdwy over 2f out: nt clr run over 1f out: nvr on terms* **25/1**

5344 **10** *9* **Platinum Chief**[13] 2016 3-8-9 45 ........ PBradley(5) 7 14
(ABerry) *chsd ldrs: rdn over 2f out: wandered and sn wknd* **14/1**

0000 **11** *2* **Peace Treaty (IRE)**[97] 808 3-8-4 35 ........ JBramhill 4 —
(SRBowring) *chsd ldrs: hung rt and lost pl over 2f out* **66/1**

00-0 **12** *3* **Major Project (IRE)**[97] 808 3-7-11 30 ........ RoryMoore(7) 10 —
(PCHaslam) *hld up and detached in last: a bhd* **50/1**

5600 **13** *22* **Dandy Jim**[5] 2232 3-8-4 30 ........(b) ANicholls 8 —
(DWChapman) *plld v hrd: sn trcking ldrs: jnd ldrs on outside 4f out: sn lost pl and bhd: t.o* **25/1**

1m 48.31s (1.01) **Going Correction** -0.15s/f (Firm) **13** Ran SP% **118.5**
Speed ratings: **88,86,86,86,84 82,82,80,80,71 69,66,44**CSF £43.92 TOTE £5.80: £1.90, £3.20, £7.00; EX 49.20.

**Owner** Middleham Park Racing Ii **Bred** Dermot Brennan **Trained** Great Habton, N Yorks

**FOCUS**
A modest winning time, even for a tri-banded stakes, and the overall form is poor.

**NOTEBOOK**
**Roman The Park(IRE)**, in good form of late on the All-Weather, took this in most convincing fashion, giving her rider his first winner for 252 days.
**Given A Chance**, drawn just three from the outside, really found his stride inside the last and will be suited by a return to further.
**Delcienne** ran much better and seemed suited by the fast ground. Given a patient ride, in the end she enjoyed a dream run up the inner.
**Monkey Or Me(IRE)**, on his toes beforehand, was stepping up in trip but did not fail through lack of stamina.
**Tsarbuck**, drawn one off the inside, had a 6lb penalty to carry but it was the extended trip that proved his downfall.
**Cunning Pursuit**came out of the stalls sideways and damaged his rider's ankle.
**Platinum Chief** *Official explanation: jockey said saddle slipped*
**Dandy Jim** *Official explanation: jockey said colt had run too free in the early stages*

## 2350 ROSE AND CROWN BANDED STKS 5f
5:00 (5:01) (H ) 3-Y-O+ **£1,501** (£429; £214) **Stalls** High

Form RPR

000- **1** **Molotov**[249] 5025 4-9-3 45 ........ RFfrench 18 48
(IWMcinnes) *w ldr: led over 1f out: hld on towards fin* **16/1**

0-00 **2** *3/4* **Fairgame Man**[20] 1870 6-9-3 45 ........(p) GParkin 8 45
(JSWainwright) *chsd ldrs: styd on ins last* **14/1**

6042 **3** *shd* **Law Maker**[33] 1546 4-9-3 40 ........(v) JBramhill 19 45
(MABuckley) *led tl over 1f out: styd on same pce ins last* **8/1**[3]

1020 **4** *hd* **White O' Morn**[7] 2183 5-9-3 40 ........(p) ANicholls 10 44
(JWUnett) *mid-divsion: hdwy on outside 2f out: str run ins last* **33/1**

0554 **5** *1/2* **Lydia's Look (IRE)**[35] 1497 7-8-10 45 ........ KristinStubbs(7) 13 42
(TJEtherington) *mid-div: hdwy on inner and nt clr run over 1f out: styd on ins last* **10/1**

0200 **6** *1/2* **Henry Tun**[4] 2246 6-8-12 40 ........(p) MSavage(5) 11 41
(NEBerry) *in tch: kpt on wl appr last* **10/1**

-055 **7** *1/2* **Smart Danny**[28] 1676 3-8-9 45 ........ RWinston 16 39
(JJQuinn) *swvd lft s: sn chsng ldrs: kpt on same pce fnl 2f* **5/1**[1]

0043 **8** *1* **So Sober (IRE)**[20] 1859 6-8-10 45 ........ DerekNolan(7) 5 35
(DShaw) *swvd lft s: rr-div: hdwy over 1f out: nvr rchd ldrs* **25/1**

20-0 **9** *hd* **Cut Ridge (IRE)**[10] 2098 5-8-12 45 ........ PBradley(5) 9 35
(JSWainwright) *mid-divsion: effrt on ins and nt clr run over 2f out tl over 1f out: nt rcvr* **33/1**

1600 **10** *nk* **Ace-Ma-Vahra**[17] 1941 6-9-0 45 ........(b) ABeech(3) 4 33
(SRBowring) *hmpd s: bhd tl hdwy over 1f out: nvr nrr* **50/1**

0-46 **11** *1 1/4* **Attila The Hun**[7] 2175 5-9-3 40 ........(p) MTebbutt 2 29
(FWatson) *rr-div: hdwy on outside 2f out: nvr nrr* **66/1**

20-5 **12** *hd* **Petana**[25] 1719 4-9-3 45 ........(b) JoannaBadger 12 28
(MDods) *in tch: outpcd fnl 2f* **20/1**

2646 **13** *shd* **Finger Of Fate**[5] 2227 4-9-0 45 ........(b) JFMcDonald(3) 20 28
(MJPolglase) *chsd ldrs: outpcd fnl 2f* **5/1**[1]

60-5 **14** *shd* **Diamond Ring**[31] 1584 5-9-3 45 ........ ADaly 15 28
(MrsJCandlish) *hmpd s: bhd: sme hdwy whn hmpd over 1f out* **11/1**

/000 **15** *2 1/2* **Lady Double U**[26] 1711 4-9-3 45 ........ PMQuinn 6 19
(TDEasterby) *swvd lft s: nvr bttr than mid-div* **50/1**

0-00 **16** *nk* **Proud Western (USA)**[20] 1870 6-8-12 45 ........(t) TEaves(5) 7 17
(BEllison) *s.i.s: a bhd* **14/1**

4000 **17** *1* **Inching**[10] 2098 4-9-3 45 ........(t) GFaulkner 17 14
(RMHCowell) *w ldrs over 3f: sn lost pl* **7/1**[2]

00-0 **18** *3* **Prince Pyramus**[16] 1956 6-9-3 45 ........ JMackay 3 3
(CGrant) *a bhd* **40/1**

-005 **19** *1* **Stavros (IRE)**[12] 2040 4-9-3 45 ........ DMcGaffin 14 —
(JSWainwright) *bmpd s: chsd ldrs: lost pl over 1f out: eased* **33/1**

00-6 **20** *6* **Pay Time**[14] 1991 5-8-10 40 ........ RoryMoore(7) 1 —
(REBarr) *in tch on outside: lost pl over 1f out: eased* **66/1**

63.69 secs (-0.31) **Going Correction** -0.15s/f (Firm)
**WFA** 3 from 4yo+ 8lb **20** Ran SP% **129.5**
Speed ratings: **96,94,94,94,93 92,91,90,90,89 87,87,87,86,82 82,80,76,74,64**CSF £215.02 TOTE £22.00: £5.40, £8.50, £4.00; EX 998.40 Place 6 £141.40, Place 5 £55.92.

**Owner** Ivy House Racing **Bred** Guy Reed And Mrs A H Daniels **Trained** Catwick, E Yorks

■ A 938/1 treble for Royston Ffrench and an across-the-card treble for local trainer Ian McInnes.

**FOCUS**
The draw, as is often the case, was a major factor in the result and the runner-up deserves credit for finishing where he did.

**NOTEBOOK**
**Molotov**, who has had trouble with his joints, was ideally drawn on his first outing since September and he did just enough to contribute to a memorable day for his local handler.
**Fairgame Man**, with the cheekpieces on, deserves credit for finishing second best from a single-figure draw.
**Law Maker**, back on turf, had an ideal draw and connections will have been encouraged the way he fought back when headed.
**White O' Morn**, whose 10 previous starts were on the All-Weather, did amazingly well considering she made her effort towards the wide outside on a track where high numbers enjoy a significant advantage.
**Lydia's Look(IRE)**, happy to be back on turf, had a poor run against the far side rail. She is clearly in good heart.
**Henry Tun** again gave a good account of himself but this is as good as he is in his 12th year.
**Smart Danny**, unplaced in five previous starts, lacks the experience needed in a big field like this. All the family have improved with age.
**Cut Ridge(IRE)**, beaten a long way on her reappearance just 10 days earlier, had a nightmare passage and never saw daylight trying for a run up the far side.

**Finger Of Fate** had the plum draw but lacked the basic speed to capitalise on it. His one win was on the firm but over seven.
T/Plt: £469.90 to a £1 stake. Pool: £30,775.95. 47.80 winning tickets. T/Qpdt: £33.90 to a £1 stake. Pool: £2,503.70. 54.55 winning tickets. WG

# CARLISLE (R-H)
Monday, May 24

**OFFICIAL GOING: Firm**
Wind: breezy, across Weather: sunny

## 2351 VIACOM OUTDOOR RATING RELATED MAIDEN STKS 5f 193y
2:20 (2:20) (F ) 3-Y-O **£3,262** (£932; £466) **Stalls** High

Form RPR

0-04 **1** **Estihlal**[11] 2063 3-8-11 60 ........ WSupple 13 69
(EALDunlop) *hld up: hdwy 1/2-way: led over 1f out: pushed out* **6/4**[1]

-000 **2** *2 1/2* **Fox Covert (IRE)**[12] 2036 3-9-0 59 ........(v1) FLynch 8 64
(DWBarker) *led tl hdd over 1f out: kpt on same pce* **14/1**

40-4 **3** *4* **Open Mind**[22] 1788 3-8-11 52 ........ FNorton 12 49
(EJAlston) *sn rdn along in tch: effrt 1/2-way: no imp over 1f out* **12/1**

0-00 **4** *1 1/4* **Beamsley Beacon**[28] 1667 3-9-0 49 ........(b) KDarley 9 48
(GMMoore) *chsd ldrs: sn rdn along: hung rt 1/2-way: no ex fr 2f out* **40/1**

03-3 **5** *1/2* **Willjojo**[54] 1196 3-8-8 57 ........(v) THamilton(3) 3 44
(RAFahey) *racd wd in tch: effrt over 2f out: outpcd over 1f out* **7/1**[2]

0-60 **6** *shd* **Killerby Nicko**[54] 1196 3-8-11 57 ........ DAllan(3) 2 46
(TDEasterby) *sn outpcd: hdwy on ins 2f out: nt pce to chal* **25/1**

0603 **7** *1 1/4* **Lord Baskerville**[22] 1788 3-9-0 57 ........ DarrenWilliams 11 43
(WStorey) *midfield: rdn 1/2-way: n.d* **8/1**[3]

0-20 **8** *1 1/2* **Boris The Spider**[16] 1975 3-9-0 58 ........ ACulhane 4 38
(MDHammond) *sn wl bhd: sme late hdwy: n.d* **14/1**

0-00 **9** *3/4* **Lupine Howl**[6] 2207 3-9-0 58 ........(p) GGibbons 7 36
(BAMcmahon) *in tch 2f: sn rdn and lost pl: n.d after* **25/1**

55-0 **10** *7* **Red Rocky**[139] 452 3-8-11 55 ........ JCarroll 6 12
(RHollinshead) *sn outpcd: nvr on terms* **66/1**

-000 **11** *3 1/2* **Lady Sunset (IRE)**[9] 2134 3-8-4 55 ........(p) DonnaCaldwell(7) 5 1
(KARyan) *in tch to over 2f out: sn wknd* **33/1**

50-0 **12** *5* **Joey Perhaps**[24] 1755 3-9-0 60 ........ JFanning 14 —
(JRBest) *chsd ldrs to over 2f out: sn rdn and wknd* **12/1**

30-0 **13** *11* **Shinko Femme (IRE)**[12] 2046 3-8-11 60 ........ KimTinkler 10 —
(NTinkler) *s.v.s: t.o thrght* **9/1**

1m 12.8s (-1.40) **Going Correction** -0.15s/f (Firm) **13** Ran SP% **116.9**
Speed ratings: **103,99,94,92,92 91,90,88,87,77 73,66,51**CSF £22.52 TOTE £2.00: £1.10, £3.80, £2.80; EX 20.00.

**Owner** Hamdan Al Maktoum **Bred** Shadwell Estate Company **Trained** Newmarket, Suffolk

**FOCUS**
A poor contest, but a fair time for a race of its type even allowing for the fast ground. The draw played its part with two of the three highest stalls making the frame.

**NOTEBOOK**
**Estihlal**, on fast ground for the first time, appreciated the stiff track and pulled right away for a comfortable and confidence-boosting victory. A return to further back in modest handicap company could see her add to this.
**Fox Covert(IRE)** made a bold bid to make all, but found the winner far too strong. He is totally exposed, but his best form has been on this sort of ground and if he is to get off the mark then it is likely to be under similar conditions.
**Open Mind** ended up well beaten by the front pair and may need to drop even further in grade to break her duck.
**Beamsley Beacon**, who was badly in at the weights with all of his rivals, emerges with some credit back over this shorter trip especially as he was all at sea on the very fast ground. His best performance to date came over this trip on Fibresand.
**Willjojo**, who has been beaten in a seller, did best of those drawn low but was found wanting for pace even at the end of this stiff six. He is exposed, but does still look worth a try over further.
**Shinko Femme(IRE)** lost all chance by standing still as the stalls opened. *Official explanation: jockey said filly was very slowly away from the stalls.*

## 2352 VIACOM OUTDOOR MEDIAN AUCTION MAIDEN STKS 5f
2:50 (2:53) (E ) 2-Y-O **£3,835** (£1,180; £590; £295) **Stalls** High

Form RPR

**1** **Carte Royale** 2-9-0 ........ SChin 14 87+
(MJohnston) *chsd ldrs: shkn up and led over 1f out: rn green: kpt on strly* **5/1**[2]

**2** *2* **Tagula Sunrise (IRE)** 2-8-6 ........ THamilton(3) 12 74
(RAFahey) *led to over 1f out: kpt on fnl f* **9/1**

**3** *1 1/2* **Jerry's Girl (IRE)** 2-8-6 ........ RMiles(3) 10 68
(MissLAPerratt) *outpcd tl hdwy centre over 1f out: nrst fin* **25/1**

3 **4** *2* **English Fellow**[10] 2087 2-9-0 ........ GGibbons 2 65
(BAMcmahon) *chsd ldrs: rdn thrght: kpt on same pce over 1f out* **5/1**[2]

33 **5** *1 3/4* **Monsieur Mirasol**[24] 1743 2-9-0 ........ WSupple 7 58
(KARyan) *hld up midfield: effrt over 2f out: no imp over 1f out* **4/1**[1]

45 **6** *1/2* **Glasson Lodge**[35] 1505 2-8-9 ........ DarrenWilliams 5 51
(PDEvans) *racd wd in midfield: rdn and no imp fr 2f out* **6/1**[3]

30 **7** *1* **Almaty Express**[12] 2035 2-8-9 ........ RThomas(5) 4 52
(MTodhunter) *chsd ldrs tl rdn and outpcd over 1f out* **16/1**

35 **8** *hd* **Paris Bell**[16] 1961 2-8-11 ........ DAllan(3) 9 51
(TDEasterby) *keen: in tch ins tl outpcd over 1f out* **7/1**

**9** *1 3/4* **Hymn Of Victory (IRE)** 2-9-0 ........ JFanning 3 44
(TJEtherington) *cl up tl rdn and outpcd fr over 1f out* **28/1**

**10** *nk* **Tillingborn Dancer (IRE)** 2-9-0 ........ ACulhane 8 43
(MDHammond) *sn outpcd: nvr rchd ldrs* **20/1**

**11** *3* **Mossmann Gorge** 2-9-0 ........ KDarley 11 31
(GASwinbank) *s.s: nvr on terms* **12/1**

**12** *9* **Black Combe Lady (IRE)** 2-8-9 ........ FNorton 6 —
(ABerry) *sn outpcd: no ch fr 1/2-way* **25/1**

**13** *dist* **Antley Court (IRE)** 2-9-0 ........ JCarroll 1 —
(ABerry) *s.v.s: t.o thrght* **33/1**

61.24 secs (-0.26) **Going Correction** -0.15s/f (Firm) **13** Ran SP% **122.5**
Speed ratings: **96,92,90,87,84 83,82,81,78,78 73,59,—**CSF £47.18 TOTE £4.70: £1.30, £3.00, £8.20; EX 55.10.

**Owner** Mr & Mrs Heywood & Mr & Mrs Bovingdon **Bred** Cheveley Park Stud Ltd **Trained** Middleham Moor, N Yorks

**FOCUS**
An ordinary maiden in which the first three came from the four highest stalls, but possibly more to come from the front three who were all making their debuts. The form is difficult to assess.

**NOTEBOOK**
**Carte Royale ◆**, a 22,000gns yearling out of a dual winner over this trip, won this nicely despite running green and holding his head high as if not enjoying the fast ground. Improvement is likely in any case and he looks a useful recruit.

**Tagula Sunrise(IRE)** ◆, a 35,000gns sister to Pacific Paddy and half-sister to Lord Links, showed good speed from the gate and did not fall in a heap once headed by the winner. She should come on for this.
**Jerry's Girl(IRE)** ◆, first foal of an unraced half-sister to Cheshire Oaks winner Abury and fair performer Forest Shadow, saw plenty of daylight on the outside and was outpaced until taking off coming to the furlong pole. She finished to some purpose and there are races to be won with her over further.
**English Fellow** did not seem to improve for the furlong-shorter trip and much faster ground, but still did best of those drawn low.
**Monsieur Mirasol** had the edge in experience on those in front of him so this was a below-par effort, but perhaps the very fast ground and stiff track were not to his liking.
**Glasson Lodge** does not seem to be progressing.
**Antley Court(IRE)** *Official explanation: jockey said colt lost its action*

## 2353 MARK PETERSEN RACEGOERS CLUB H'CAP 5f
**3:20** (3:20) (E) (0-70,63) 3-Y-O £3,770 (£1,160; £580; £290) **Stalls** High

Form RPR
10-6 **1** **Feu Duty (IRE)**[24] 1742 3-9-4 **60** JFanning 7 68
(TJEtherington) *mde all: edgd lft and drew clr fr over 1f out* **6/1**[3]
0-00 **2** 4 **Leopard Creek**[24] 1750 3-8-10 **55** (p) DAllan(3) 1 48
(MrsJRRamsden) *bhd: rdn 1/2-way: kpt on fnl f: no ch w wnr* **8/1**
0035 **3** shd **Blue Power (IRE)**[34] 1517 3-9-0 **56** DarrenWilliams 5 49
(KRBurke) *plld hrd: chsd ldrs: effrt over 1f out: one pce* **7/2**[2]
600- **4** 1 **Thornaby Green**[209] 5824 3-9-7 **63** KDarley 4 52
(TDBarron) *chsd ldrs tl rdn and no ex fr over 1f out* **10/3**[1]
05-2 **5** hd **Westborough (IRE)**[12] 2040 3-8-13 **55** KimTinkler 2 44
(NTinkler) *hld up: rdn over 2f out: no imp over 1f out* **7/2**[2]
6360 **6** 1 ¾ **Lavish Times**[17] 1934 3-8-8 **50** (b) FNorton 6 32
(ABerry) *chsd ldrs tl wknd over 1f out* **7/1**
0 **7** 3 **Madra Rua (IRE)**[10] 2075 3-9-4 **60** (p) WSupple 3 32
(MissLAPerratt) *chsd ldrs on outside tl wknd fr 2f out* **10/1**

60.99 secs (-0.51) **Going Correction** -0.15s/f (Firm) 7 Ran SP% **114.5**
Speed ratings: **98,91,91,89,89 86,81**CSF £51.62 TOTE £7.70: £3.60, £6.10; EX 88.60.
**Owner** Miss M Greenwood, A Watson, K Hart **Bred** Christy McDonnell **Trained** Norton, N Yorks

**FOCUS**
A modest handicap and a one-horse race, but the time was nothing special and there are questions over the form.
**NOTEBOOK**
**Feu Duty(IRE)**, with a rail to run against, bounced out of the stalls and made every yard to win with ease. She does tend to hang, but has plenty of speed and may be capable of a bit more.
**Leopard Creek**, dropped 7lb since her previous start and fitted with cheekpieces, was slow to get into stride and trailed the field early, but stayed on late in the day to reach her first ever placing. She may be capable of better over further.
**Blue Power(IRE)** raced prominently for a long way, but the winner left him for dead over the final couple of furlongs. His best form is on Fibresand so he might not have appreciated the ground this fast.
**Thornaby Green**, racing under his ideal conditions, is steadily dropping down the handicap and was entitled to need this first run in seven months.
**Westborough(IRE)** may have found this coming too quick after his promising return in the Newcastle quagmire.

## 2354 AZURE CLAIMING STKS 1m 3f 206y
**3:50** (3:50) (F) 3-Y-O+ £2,982 (£852; £426) **Stalls** Low

Form RPR
0020 **1** **Quarry Island (IRE)**[20] 1856 3-7-7 40 BSwarbrick(5) 1 51
(PDEvans) *mde all: rdn and hld on wl fnl 2f* **14/1**
-030 **2** shd **Spitting Image (IRE)**[22] 1785 4-9-8 61 ACulhane 2 55
(MrsMReveley) *cl up: rdn and ev ch over 2f out: one pce whn blkd ins fnl f: fin 3rd: plcd 2nd* **11/8**[1]
20-0 **3** 1 ½ **Hearthstead Dream**[9] 2134 3-8-3 69 SChin 3 53
(MJohnston) *chsd ldrs: nt clr run on ins fr over 2f out: squeezed through and r.o wl ins fnl f: r.o: fin 2nd: disq: plcd 3rd* **3/1**[3]
2142 **4** 1 ¼ **Platinum Charmer (IRE)**[6] 2214 4-9-13 55 (p) DarrenWilliams 4 58
(KRBurke) *keen: trckd ldrs: effrt and ev ch over 1f out: no ex ins last* **7/4**[2]

2m 32.36s (-0.04) **Going Correction** -0.15s/f (Firm)
**WFA** 3 from 4yo 17lb 4 Ran SP% **110.1**
Speed ratings: **94,92,93,92**CSF £34.02 TOTE £17.60; EX 38.50.Hearthstead Dream was claimed by John O'Shea for £5,000. Quarry Island was claimed by P G Airey for £5,000
**Owner** G E Amey **Bred** Golden Vale Stud **Trained** Pandy, Gwent
■ Stewards Enquiry : S Chin two-day ban: careless riding (Jun 6,7)

**FOCUS**
A moderate pace and modest winning time, but still a rough race despite the small field and the form looks dubious.
**NOTEBOOK**
**Quarry Island(IRE)**, badly in with her three rivals on adjusted official ratings, was allowed a soft lead and that enabled her to keep enough in reserve to score. This form is suspect though and she will do well to follow up.
**Spitting Image(IRE)** needs a greater test of stamina than this, so the modest pace was not in her favour. She could never quite get on terms with the winner, but managed to hold Hearthstead Dream in a pocket as she tried to do so and the interference she suffered as that rival was pulled out probably cost her second. She was subsequently promoted a place in the Stewards' Room.
**Hearthstead Dream**, best in on official ratings and stepping up half a mile in trip, managed to get himself trapped in a pocket in a four-horse race. He had been off the bridle for some time when trying to force his way out and getting into a barging match with Spitting Image, so it is unlikely he would have won, but he did improve his position with the manoeuvre and was rightly put back a place.
**Platinum Charmer(IRE)** had a lot to find with a couple of his rivals on adjusted official ratings and could never land a blow.

## 2355 ALTHAM BUILDERS MERCHANT FILLIES' H'CAP 1m 1f 61y
**4:20** (4:20) (E) (0-70,68) 3-Y-O £3,737 (£1,150; £575; £287) **Stalls** High

Form RPR
0-26 **1** **Sunset Mirage (USA)**[10] 2093 3-9-7 **68** WSupple 5 73
(EALDunlop) *trckd ldrs: led over 1f out: rdn out* **7/2**[1]
4-41 **2** nk **Ivory Coast (IRE)**[117] 622 3-8-9 **59** RMiles(3) 3 64
(WRMuir) *in tch: hdwy 2f out: rdn and kpt on fnl f: jst hld* **5/1**[3]
00-1 **3** 1 ½ **Night Frolic**[21] 1830 3-9-5 **66** KDarley 6 68
(JWHills) *prom: rdn and hung lft over 2f out: r.o fnl f: nrst fin* **5/1**[3]
50-2 **4** nk **Rabitatit (IRE)**[46] 1309 3-8-11 **63** BSwarbrick(5) 4 64
(JGMO'Shea) *led to over 1f out: kpt on same pce* **9/2**[2]
046- **5** 1 **Fairlie**[292] 3888 3-9-6 **67** ACulhane 7 66
(MrsJRRamsden) *in tch: effrt 2f out: no imp fnl f* **7/1**
00-0 **6** shd **Dame Nova (IRE)**[38] 1453 3-8-0 **47** CCogan 1 46
(PCHaslam) *hld up: outpcd 3f out: r.o fnl f: n.d* **16/1**
-402 **7** 13 **Pay Attention**[17] 1946 3-8-7 **57** DAllan(3) 2 30
(TDEasterby) *chsd ldrs tl wknd over 2f out: eased whn no ch fnl f* **7/2**[1]

1m 56.98s (-1.05) **Going Correction** -0.15s/f (Firm) 7 Ran SP% **114.3**
Speed ratings: **98,97,96,96,95 95,83**CSF £21.18 TOTE £4.80: £3.20, £2.70; EX 30.70.
**Owner** Maktoum Al Maktoum **Bred** Gainsborough Farm Llc **Trained** Newmarket, Suffolk

**FOCUS**
A modest race but the form is fair for the grade.
**NOTEBOOK**
**Sunset Mirage(USA)**, making her handicap debut, appreciated the return to a shorter trip and won with a little in hand despite the narrow margin. Despite this victory, she may prefer more give underfoot.
**Ivory Coast(IRE)** ◆, making her debut on turf after five runs on sand and returning from a four-month break, kept staying on and although probably a little flattered by the margin, ran well enough to suggest she can find a race on grass.
**Night Frolic** ◆, making her handicap debut and trying her longest trip to date, could not have encountered conditions more different to when winning at Kempton, but she certainly did not fail through lack of stamina as she was doing all her best work late. She should be winning again back on a more forgiving surface.
**Rabitatit(IRE)**, stepping up in trip, was not ridden as though stamina was going to be an issue but in the end it probably was.
**Fairlie**, stepping up more than two furlongs in trip, was entitled to need this first run in nine months and is likely to be a different proposition with this outing under her belt.
**Pay Attention**, raised 6lb for getting beaten last time, dropped out rather tamely and probably found the ground too quick. *Official explanation: jockey said filly was unsuited by the firm ground.*

## 2356 VIACOM OUTDOOR APPRENTICE H'CAP 7f 200y
**4:50** (4:54) (F) (0-55,55) 3-Y-O+ £3,108 (£888; £444) **Stalls** High

Form RPR
-630 **1** **Zawrak (IRE)**[78] 650 5-9-4 **55** NataliaGemelova(3) 16 67
(IWMcinnes) *unruly bef s: hld up: hdwy to ld over 1f out: edgd rt: r.o strly* **8/1**
0405 **2** 2 **Shifty**[14] 1993 5-8-11 **48** LTreadwell(3) 7 55
(DNicholls) *dwlt: hld up: hdwy and ev ch over 1f out: r.o fnl f* **11/2**[3]
065- **3** ¾ **We'll Meet Again**[244] 5136 4-9-5 **53** PMulrennan 14 58
(MWEasterby) *hld up: hdwy over 2f out: r.o fnl f* **12/1**
4-10 **4** 1 ½ **Heathyards Pride**[47] 1305 4-8-9 **50** HFellows(7) 5 51
(RHollinshead) *in tch: rdn over 2f out: r.o fnl f* **20/1**
-003 **5** ½ **Encounter**[14] 1993 8-8-13 **47** THamilton 17 47
(JHetherton) *chsd ldrs gng wl: effrt and ch 2f out: sn rdn and nt qckn* **4/1**[1]
0435 **6** 3 **Theatre Lady (IRE)**[1] 2324 6-8-7 **46** MHoward(5) 18 39
(PDEvans) *cl up: rdn over 2f out: outpcd over 1f out* **9/2**[2]
5-00 **7** 3 **Late Arrival**[10] 2078 7-8-7 **46** oh1 DTudhope(5) 2 31
(MDHammond) *bhd: nt clr run over 2f out: styng on but no imp whn hmpd ins fnl f: n.d* **16/1**
00-0 **8** ½ **Willhego**[18] 1906 3-8-6 **52** J-PGuillambert 9 36
(JRBest) *s.i.s: nvr rchd ldrs* **14/1**
0-00 **9** ¾ **Blue Venture (IRE)**[16] 1962 4-8-12 **53** DWakenshaw(7) 3 35
(PCHaslam) *prom tl outpcd fr 2f out* **16/1**
06-0 **10** nk **Bolshevik (IRE)**[26] 1711 3-8-4 **50** DAllan 10 31
(TDEasterby) *led to over 1f out: sn btn* **16/1**
065- **11** 5 **Zouche**[217] 5683 4-8-11 **48** BSwarbrick(3) 15 17
(WMBrisbourne) *in tch tl wknd fr 2f out* **8/1**
0-66 **12** nk **Mr Moon**[7] 2176 3-7-11 **46** oh11 LeanneKershaw(3) 12 14
(MDHammond) *a bhd* **25/1**
60/0 **13** 18 **Nifty Roy**[6] 2216 4-8-7 **46** oh1 KGhunowa(5) 11 —
(KWHogg) *chsd ldrs tl wknd over 3f out* **66/1**
0-00 **U** **Poppyline**[5] 2226 4-9-7 **55** RMiles 1 —
(WRMuir) *cocked jaw and uns rdr s* **9/1**

1m 38.88s (-1.12) **Going Correction** -0.15s/f (Firm)
**WFA** 3 from 4yo+ 12lb 14 Ran SP% **127.9**
Speed ratings: **99,97,96,94,94 91,88,87,87,86 81,81,63,—**CSF £53.97 CT £560.16 TOTE £14.20: £4.20, £2.90, £5.10; EX 148.60 Place 6 £7,106.34, Place 5 £3,914.10.
**Owner** New Century Windows Ltd **Bred** Shadwell Estate Company Limited **Trained** Catwick, E Yorks

**FOCUS**
A modest apprentice handicap run at a sound pace.
**NOTEBOOK**
**Zawrak(IRE)**, whose only outing since January was when pulled up over hurdles, unshipped his rider during his first attempt at being loaded into the stalls but was fine in the race itself. Given a patient ride, he got stronger as the race progressed and, as he stays further than this, was not going to stop after hitting the front.
**Shifty** ◆, back on his favoured surface, ran his best race for a while and is gradually coming to hand. He is now 10lb below his last winning mark.
**We'll Meet Again** ◆, 1lb below his last winning mark, ran very well on his first start in seven months, especially as he is best over an easy seven.
**Heathyards Pride** ◆, tackling his shortest trip to date, was doing his best work over the last couple of furlongs and will appreciate a return to further or a slower surface.
**Encounter** had every chance, but did not find much off the bridle. His strike rate in recent seasons does not make him an ideal betting proposition.
**Theatre Lady(IRE)** was done for toe over the last couple of furlongs and even the stiff track did not compensate for the inadequate trip.
**Late Arrival** got into all sorts of trouble over the last couple of furlongs and even though he would not have made the frame, would have finished several lengths closer. He is gradually getting it together after his long layoff and is not completely without hope.
T/Plt: £11,869.60 to a £1 stake. Pool: £24,389.60. 1.50 winning tickets. T/Qpdt: £1,298.30 to a £1 stake. Pool: £1,754.50. 0.80 winning tickets. RY

# 2207 LEICESTER (R-H)
Monday, May 24

**OFFICIAL GOING: Good to firm**
Wind: mod bhd Weather: warm & sunny

## 2357 HUNT STAFF BENEFIT SOCIETY MAIDEN STKS 1m 3f 183y
**2:10** (2:10) (D) 3-Y-O £5,551 (£1,708; £854; £427) **Stalls** High

Form RPR
4-2 **1** **New Morning (IRE)**[10] 2093 3-8-9 PRobinson 6 62+
(MAJarvis) *mde virtually all: clr fnl 4f: canter* **1/16**[1]
0- **2** 11 **Devito (FR)**[265] 4638 3-9-0 VSlattery 7 50
(AKing) *prom: rdn over 4f out: sn outpcd: wnt remote 2nd ins fnl f* **66/1**
0 **3** 1 ¾ **Great Gidding**[10] 2090 3-9-0 SDrowne 8 47
(HMorrison) *chsd wnr: rdn over 4f out: sn outpcd* **50/1**[3]
0- **4** 1 **Greek Star**[244] 5139 3-8-9 PMakin(5) 4 45
(KAMorgan) *hld up: sme hdwy over 2f out: n.d* **25/1**[2]
-000 **5** 14 **Kedross (IRE)**[9] 2128 3-8-9 58 OUrbina 1 18
(JJay) *hld up: a in rr* **50/1**[3]

0 **6** *1 1/4* **Sovereign Girl**[7] 2168 3-8-9 ........ SSanders 5 16
(BNDoran) *s.i.s: hld up: wknd over 4f out* **150/1**
0- **7** *7* **Tout Les Sous**[200] 5932 3-9-0 ........ SWKelly 2 10
(Jean-ReneAuvray) *s.s: hdwy to chse ldrs 10f out: wknd over 3f out* **150/1**
45 **8** *shd* **Ses Seline**[17] 1945 3-8-9 ........ PaulEddery 3 5
(JohnAHarris) *prom: lost pl over 6f out: sn bhd* **66/1**
2m 33.24s (-1.44) **Going Correction** -0.15s/f (Firm) **8** Ran SP% **106.2**
Speed ratings: **98,90,89,88,79 78,74,73**CSF £7.18 TOTE £1.10: £1.02, £5.30, £1.80; EX 7.10.
**Owner** N R A Springer **Bred** Ballymacoll Stud Farm Ltd **Trained** Newmarket, Suffolk
**FOCUS**
A weak maiden and, the winner apart, these were probably a moderate bunch.
**NOTEBOOK**
**New Morning(IRE)** had a nice confidence-booster and never had to get out of second gear to beat some moderate opposition. She has plenty of improvement in her and will hold her own in better company.
**Devito(FR)** achieved little in finishing runner-up.
**Great Gidding** tried to mix it with the winner before that effort took its toll and cost him second spot.
**Greek Star** stayed on from the back without ever looking likely to take a hand.

## 2358 QUORN HUNT CONDITIONS STKS 7f 9y
**2:40** (2:40) (D) 3-Y-O+ **£6,553** (£2,325; £1,162; £528) **Stalls** Low

Form RPR
30-3 **1** **Mister Links (IRE)**[23] 1759 4-9-4 104 ........ KMcEvoy 1 107
(SaeedBinSuroor) *mde all: rdn clr fnl f* **4/6**[1]
314/ **2** *6* **St Andrews (IRE)**[590] 5207 4-9-4 ........ PRobinson 2 91
(MAJarvis) *trckd wnr: outpcd fnl f* **12/1**[3]
210- **3** *5* **Colisay**[341] 2460 5-9-4 103 ........ DHolland 4 78
(ACStewart) *chsd ldrs tl wknd over 1f out* **13/8**[2]
0020 **4** *12* **Mistral Sky**[11] 2064 5-9-4 67 ........(v) SDrowne 3 47
(MrsStefLiddiard) *chsd ldrs over 4f* **50/1**
1m 23.33s (-2.77) **Going Correction** -0.15s/f (Firm) **4** Ran SP% **107.7**
Speed ratings: **109,102,96,82**CSF £8.69 TOTE £1.70; EX 4.40.
**Owner** Godolphin **Bred** T Ward **Trained** Newmarket, Suffolk
**FOCUS**
With the runner-up and third looking likely to benefit from the run, this probably didn't take as much winning as it should have. The form is therefore questionable, although it was soundly run.
**NOTEBOOK**
**Mister Links(IRE)**, who had done his winning when there had been plenty of give underfoot, handled this fast ground well. He looks the type to improve again and is one to keep on the right side of.
**St Andrews(IRE)** looked to be carrying condition on this return to action and wasn't knocked around when his chance had gone. A winner over a mile last year, he can regain the winning thread when stepping back up in trip.
**Colisay**, off the track for nearly a year, looked as though the outing would do him good.
**Mistral Sky** was simply outclassed.

## 2359 FERNIE HUNT (S) STKS 5f 218y
**3:10** (3:10) (G) 3-5-Y-O **£2,982** (£852; £426) **Stalls** Low

Form RPR
0500 **1** **Rileys Dream**[7] 2178 5-8-7 45 ........ RHavlin 2 38
(BJLlewellyn) *hld up: hdwy 2f: rdn to ld ins fnl f: r.o* **7/1**[3]
0000 **2** *1/2* **Frenchmans Lodge**[14] 1988 4-9-2 35 ........(b) PDoe 4 46
(JMBradley) *hld up: hdwy 2f: rdn and ev ch ins fnl f: styd on* **50/1**
0000 **3** *1 1/4* **Tappit (IRE)**[20] 1877 5-9-10 57 ........(p) DHolland 1 50
(JMBradley) *chsd ldr: rdn to ld over 1f out: hdd and unable qck ins fnl f* **13/2**[2]
560- **4** *1* **Charlieismydarling**[161] 6191 3-8-3 55 ........ MartinDwyer 5 35
(JAOsborne) *hld up: pushed along 1/2-way: hdwy over 1f out: nt rch ldrs* **10/1**
0-30 **5** *1 1/2* **Red Leicester**[10] 2098 4-8-11 48 ........(v[1]) DeanMcKeown 14 29
(JAGlover) *led over 4f: wknd ins fnl f* **7/1**[3]
-000 **6** *hd* **Zambezi River**[17] 1939 5-9-4 ow1 ........ CJDavies[(7)] 13 43
(JMBradley) *s.i.s: hdwy over 1f out: nt clr run ins fnl f : nt trble ldrs* **40/1**
-000 **7** *1/2* **Dr Fox (IRE)**[12] 2040 3-8-2 47 ........(p) PMakin[(5)] 3 32
(KAMorgan) *sn outpcd: styd on ins fnl f: n.d* **20/1**
034- **8** *shd* **Mickledor (FR)**[258] 4792 4-9-2 47 ........(v) LEnstone[(3)] 11 35
(MDods) *slowly itno stride: sn pushed along in rr: hdwy u.p over 2f out: wknd ins fnl f* **14/1**
6613 **9** *1/2* **Welsh Whisper**[13] 2017 5-8-7 45 ........ NChalmers[(5)] 12 26
(SABrookshaw) *hld up: effrt over 2f out: no imp appr fnl f* **15/2**
0034 **10** *2* **Roan Raider (USA)**[7] 2175 4-9-10 47 ........(v) KFallon 8 32
(MJPolglase) *chsd ldrs: rdn over 2f out: wknd and eased ins fnl f* **10/1**
5600 **11** *2* **Back At De Front (IRE)**[37] 1464 3-9-1 67 ........ CCatlin 10 26
(NEBerry) *prom 4f* **8/1**
-000 **12** *9* **Simply Red**[32] 1571 3-8-11 40 ........ VSlattery 7 —
(RBrotherton) *chsd ldrs over 3f* **33/1**
-000 **13** *2* **Queen Of Bulgaria (IRE)**[24] 1750 3-8-10 56 ........ JQuinn 6 —
(JPearce) *chsd ldrs over 3f* **6/1**[1]
00-0 **14** *16* **Jacks Delight**[97] 807 4-8-12 ........ SSanders 15 —
(BDLeavy) *bhd fr 1/2-way* **50/1**
1m 13.62s (0.22) **Going Correction** -0.15s/f (Firm)
**WFA** 3 from 4yo+ 9lb **14** Ran SP% **114.4**
Speed ratings: **92,91,89,88,86 86,85,85,84,81 79,67,64,43**CSF £329.29 TOTE £10.50: £3.50, £9.80, £2.50; EX 453.50.The winner was bought in for 4,400gns
**Owner** Greg Robinson And A N Jay **Bred** R Olley **Trained** Fochriw, Caerphilly
**FOCUS**
A poor seller in which the leaders looked to go off plenty quick enough and the first two places were filled by horses coming from off the pace. The first four home all had a low-figure draw.
**NOTEBOOK**
**Rileys Dream**, although a winner off a mark of 59 last year, lacks consistency. This is clearly her grade now, but she couldn't be relied upon to reproduce this effort.
**Frenchmans Lodge** is a poor performer, but this was one of his better efforts.
**Tappit(IRE)**, proven on a faster surface, had his chance, but is an infrequent winner nowadays.
**Charlieismydarling** was doing his best work in the closing stages and is well worth a try at further.
**Red Leicester** set a fast pace in the first-time visor, but paid for her effort late on and didn't get home.
**Zambezi River** was always struggling after missing the break, but showed enough to suggest he is up to winning a similar contest.
**Roan Raider(USA)** *Official explanation: jockey said gelding was unsuited by the good to firm ground.*
**Jacks Delight** *Official explanation: jockey said gelding had lost his action.*

## 2360 PYTCHLEY HUNT MAIDEN STKS 5f 218y
**3:40** (3:40) (D) 2-Y-O **£5,616** (£1,728; £864; £432) **Stalls** Low

Form RPR
3 **1** **Nufoos**[11] 2071 2-8-9 ........ RHills 3 81+
(MJohnston) *mde all: shkn up over 1f out: r.o* **5/6**[1]
**2** *2* **Satchem (IRE)** 2-9-0 ........ KFallon 4 79+
(DRLoder) *a.p: rdn to chse wnr over 1f out: no imp* **11/10**[2]
**3** *5* **Hawridge King** 2-9-0 ........ MFenton 2 62
(WSKittow) *w wnr over 3f: hung lft and wknd over 1f out* **66/1**
**4** *7* **Yours Sincerely (IRE)** 2-8-11 ........ DNolan[(3)] 7 37
(PABlockley) *chsd ldrs: rdn over 2f out: wknd wl over 1f out* **40/1**[3]
**5** *1 1/2* **Gavioli (IRE)** 2-9-0 ........ CCatlin 1 32
(JMBradley) *dwlt: outpcd* **50/1**
6 **6** *2 1/2* **Taipan Tommy (IRE)**[18] 1905 2-9-0 ........ JFEgan 6 23
(SDow) *plld hrd and prom: wknd wl over 1f out* **40/1**[3]
**7** *11* **Flying Tara** 2-8-9 ........ PaulEddery 5 —
(JohnAHarris) *s.i.s: outpcd* **100/1**
1m 12.26s (-1.14) **Going Correction** -0.15s/f (Firm) **7** Ran SP% **111.5**
Speed ratings: **101,98,91,82,80 77,62**CSF £1.88 TOTE £1.80: £1.10, £1.10; EX 2.50.
**Owner** Hamdan Al Maktoum **Bred** R And Mrs Watson And Mrs A J Ralli **Trained** Middleham Moor, N Yorks
**FOCUS**
The front pair apart the rest are probably an ordinary bunch. This was run at a fair pace.
**NOTEBOOK**
**Nufoos** had the edge in experience and just knew too much for the runner-up. She handled this faster surface well enough and should be capable of scoring again.
**Satchem(IRE)**, a 100,000 guineas yearling, wore a rug for stalls entry. He can only improve for the experience and will be hard to beat in an ordinary maiden next time.
**Hawridge King** showed plenty of pace, on ground which looked to be plenty quick enough for him.
**Yours Sincerely(IRE)** is out of a mare that won over seven furlongs as a three-year-old, and is likely to be seen to better effect when facing a stiffer test.

## 2361 BELVOIR HUNT H'CAP 1m 1f 218y
**4:10** (4:11) (D) (0-80,77) 3-Y-O **£5,785** (£1,780; £890; £445) **Stalls** High

Form RPR
2-46 **1** **Sound Of Fleet (USA)**[9] 2113 3-9-7 77 ........ KFallon 2 86
(PFICole) *a.p: chsd ldr 3f out: rdn to ld over 1f out: edgd rt ins fnl f: r.o* **11/2**[3]
3221 **2** *1 3/4* **Man Of Letters (UAE)**[20] 1869 3-9-6 76 ........ KDalgleish 8 82
(MJohnston) *sn chsng ldrs: led over 3f out: rdn and hdd over 1f out: swtchd lft ins fnl f: styd on same pce* **6/4**[1]
06-0 **3** *2 1/2* **Wake Up Henry**[20] 1874 3-7-13 58 ........ NMackay[(3)] 11 59
(RCharlton) *chsd ldrs: rdn over 2f out: styd on same pce fnl f* **25/1**
6036 **4** *1/2* **Anduril**[14] 1997 3-8-12 68 ........ JTate 12 68
(JMPEustace) *s.i.s: hld up: hdwy over 2f out: styd on* **14/1**
0-60 **5** *1 1/4* **Laabbij (USA)**[14] 2001 3-9-6 76 ........ MartinDwyer 9 74
(MPTregoning) *s.i.s: hld up: outpcd over 3f out: styd on ins fnl f: nt trble ldrs* **9/2**[2]
-100 **6** *nk* **Show No Fear**[9] 2134 3-9-0 70 ........ WRyan 4 67
(HRACecil) *hld up: hdwy over 3f out: styd on same pce appr fnl f* **12/1**
600- **7** *nk* **Dhehdaah**[199] 5939 3-8-9 65 ........ RHills 10 62
(NAGraham) *hld up in tch: rdn over 2f out: styd on same pce* **40/1**
30-0 **8** *3* **Mr Independent (IRE)**[24] 1755 3-8-7 63 ........ PRobinson 5 54
(EALDunlop) *hld up: rdn over 3f out: n.d* **12/1**
044- **9** *5* **Penny Stall**[215] 5710 3-8-6 62 ........ SSanders 6 44
(JLDunlop) *hld up: rdn 1/2-way: a in rr* **8/1**
30-0 **10** *11* **Chubbes**[12] 2030 3-9-1 71 ........(v) TQuinn 7 32
(MCPipe) *led and sn clr: rdn and hdd over 3f out: wknd wl over 1f out* **16/1**
2m 5.48s (-2.92) **Going Correction** -0.15s/f (Firm) **10** Ran SP% **118.9**
Speed ratings: **105,103,101,101,100 99,99,97,93,84**CSF £14.39 CT £196.37 TOTE £7.30: £2.80, £1.10, £7.10; EX 14.70 Trifecta £177.70 Pool £976.64, 3.90 winning units.
**Owner** Meyrick, Smith, Landis & Cole **Bred** Mrs Alice Du Pont Mills **Trained** Whatcombe, Oxon
**FOCUS**
An ordinary handicap, but full of unexposed sorts, and there was plenty of pace on. The form should work out.
**NOTEBOOK**
**Sound Of Fleet(USA)**, tackling handicappers for the first time, turned in a workmanlike display and should be capable of adding to this.
**Man Of Letters(UAE)** appeared to stay this trip well enough, but he just met one too good on the day.
**Wake Up Henry**, tackling his fastest surface to date, showed a bit more here, but while he is no great shakes he should be capable of finding a small event.
**Anduril** looked much happier on this faster surface and found this trip well within his compass.
**Laabbij(USA)**, tackling handicap company for the first time, shaped as though a stiffer test would suit.
**Show No Fear** may need a softer surface to show his best.
**Mr Independent(IRE)** *Official explanation: jockey said gelding hung to the right throughout.*
**Penny Stall** *Official explanation: trainer said filly was unsuited by the good to firm ground*

## 2362 SUSIE AND JIM CELEBRATION CLAIMING STKS 1m 9y
**4:40** (4:40) (F) 3-Y-O+ **£3,503** (£1,078; £539; £269) **Stalls** High

Form RPR
50-0 **1** **Ben Hur**[40] 1393 5-9-10 56 ........ SWKelly 6 68
(WMBrisbourne) *w ldr tl led 5f out: rdn out* **7/2**[2]
2-06 **2** *1* **Nicholas Nickelby**[6] 2217 4-9-10 60 ........ TQuinn 8 66
(MJPolglase) *plld hrd: led 3f: rdn and ev ch over 1f out: styd on same pce ins f* **11/2**[3]
0454 **3** *1 1/4* **Tinian**[13] 2013 6-9-2 50 ........ KDalgleish 9 55
(KRBurke) *hld up: hdwy over 1f out: nt clr run ins fnl f: r.o* **8/1**
-001 **4** *1/2* **Kelseas Kolby (IRE)**[6] 2209 4-8-13 53 ........(v) DNolan[(3)] 5 54
(PABlockley) *hld up: hdwy over 2f out: rdn: hung lft and rt fr over 1f out: nt run on* **2/1**[1]
3343 **5** *6* **City General (IRE)**[1] 2322 3-8-8 55 ........(p) JDSmith 1 44
(JSMoore) *hld up: rdn over 3f out: n.d* **8/1**
-000 **6** *3 1/2* **Thumamah (IRE)**[30] 1606 5-9-3 49 ........(t) JFEgan 4 33
(BPJBaugh) *hld up: hdwy over 3f out: wknd over 1f out* **20/1**
60-0 **7** *1/2* **Bijou Dancer**[28] 1675 4-9-6 56 ........ GBaker 3 35
(MRBosley) *chsd ldrs over 8f* **11/1**
**8** *5* **Irish Chapel (IRE)**[714] 8-9-5 ........ NChalmers[(5)] 7 27
(HEHaynes) *s.s: hdwy 6f out: rdn and wknd 3f out* **100/1**


The Form Book, Raceform Ltd, Compton, RG20 6NL

650- **9** *10* **Relative Hero (IRE)**[157] 6211 4-9-5 62 .......... AQuinn(5) 2 4
(MissSJWilton) *hld up: hdwy over 3f out: wknd 2f out* **14/1**

1m 42.4s (-0.20) **Going Correction** -0.15s/f (Firm)
**WFA** 3 from 4yo+ 12lb **9** Ran SP% **113.9**
Speed ratings: **95,94,92,92,86 82,82,77,67**CSF £22.78 TOTE £5.80: £1.40, £1.50, £2.40; EX 25.40.
**Owner** D C Rutter & H Clewlow **Bred** Blue Blood Investments **Trained** Great Ness, Shropshire

**FOCUS**
A moderate event, but it was run at a fair pace, and the winner is well treated on hi old form.

**NOTEBOOK**
**Ben Hur**, unlike some of his rivals, didn't mind a battle and proved far too resolute for some dodgy rivals. A winner off 60 in a maiden handicap on Fibresand last year, he had struggled since, but this drop in grade did the trick and with his proven ability to handle fast ground he should be able to add to this at this level.
**Nicholas Nickelby** did himself no favours by taking a keen hold early on. He does have a little ability, but will need to learn to settle.
**Tinian** got going far too late and doesn't look one to trust implicitly.
**Kelseas Kolby(IRE)** looked a thorough pig, even allowing for the fact that this trip may have been beyond his best.

## 2363 SANDICLIFFE MOTOR GROUP FILLIES' H'CAP 1m 3f 183y
**5:10** (5:11) (E) (0-70,61) 3-Y-O+ **£4,085** (£1,257; £628; £314) **Stalls** Low

Form RPR
05-0 **1** **Selebela**[24] 1755 3-8-1 **58** .......... NMackay(3) 5 81+
(LMCumani) *trckd ldrs: racd keenly: led over 3f out: clr fnl f* **6/1**
0041 **2** *8* **Banningham Blaze**[12] 2031 4-8-10 **50** .......... SHitchcott(3) 6 56
(AWCarroll) *s.i.s: hld up: hdwy to chse wnr over 2f out: rdn and hung rt over 1f out: sn wknd* **9/4**[1]
6650 **3** *1 1/2* **Most-Saucy**[6] 2212 8-9-7 **61** .......... DNolan(3) 1 65
(IAWood) *hld up: hdwy over 2f out: hung rt and wknd over 1f out* **11/2**
5520 **4** *4* **Free Style (GER)**[20] 1858 4-8-13 **50** .......... GBaker 4 47
(MrsHSweeting) *chsd ldrs 10f* **7/1**
00-0 **5** *8* **Science Academy (USA)**[14] 1998 3-8-4 **58** .......... TQuinn 7 42
(PFICole) *chsd ldrs over 9f* **4/1**[2]
5000 **6** *13* **Margery Daw (IRE)**[12] 2032 4-9-9 **60** .......... TGMcLaughlin 3 24
(PSMcentee) *sn led: hdd over 3f out: wknd over 2f out* **33/1**
50-2 **7** *26* **Cantemerle (IRE)**[12] 2038 4-9-4 **55** .......... SWKelly 2 —
(WMBrisbourne) *hld up in tch: wknd over 3f out* **5/1**[3]

2m 31.45s (-3.23) **Going Correction** -0.15s/f (Firm)
**WFA** 3 from 4yo+ 17lb **7** Ran SP% **112.5**
Speed ratings: **104,98,97,95,89 81,63**CSF £19.29 TOTE £5.20: £2.60, £1.30; EX 12.80 Place 6 £15.36, Place 5 £15.19.
**Owner** Scuderia Rencati Srl **Bred** Fittocks Stud **Trained** Newmarket, Suffolk

**FOCUS**
A 0-61 in effect, but it was run at a fair pace for the grade and the winner drew right away from her older rivals.

**NOTEBOOK**
**Selebela** showed her true colours on this step up in trip, won with a ton in hand and is at the right end of the handicap to follow up.
**Banningham Blaze** came into this in fair form having won a seller last time and was unlucky to run into a well-treated, unexposed rival.
**Most-Saucy** flattered briefly on the outside of the field, but she still looks below her best at present.
**Free Style(GER)**, the winner of a Banded race on the Polytrack, found this too competitive.
T/Plt: £27.10 to a £1 stake. Pool: £21,479.95. 577.35 winning tickets. T/Qpdt: £13.00 to a £1 stake. Pool: £1,757.20. 99.50 winning tickets. CR

# 2129 THIRSK (L-H)
### Monday, May 24

**OFFICIAL GOING: Firm**

## 2364 MILLY'S FILLIES' (S) STKS 6f
**6:30** (6:30) (E) 2-Y-O **£3,575** (£1,100; £550; £275) **Stalls** High

Form RPR
5044 **1** **Bowland Bride (IRE)**[2] 2288 2-8-2 .......... PPMathers(7) 10 48
(ABerry) *trckd ldrs gng wl: swtchd lft and hdwy to ld appr last: sn rdn and kpt on* **14/1**
**2** *1* **Mermaid's Cry** 2-8-6 .......... TPQueally(3) 6 45
(JAGlover) *dwlt and bmpd s: sn in tch: hdwy and nt clr run wl over 1f out: swtchd lft and chsd wnr ins last: kpt on* **8/1**
**3** *2 1/2* **Shuchbaa** 2-8-9 .......... PFessey 13 38
(KARyan) *s.i.s and bhd: hdwy 1/2-way: swtchd lft and styd on appr last: nrst fin* **7/1**
3033 **4** *nk* **Joshar**[4] 2248 2-8-9 .......... DaleGibson 8 37
(MWEasterby) *cl up: rdn 2f out and ev ch tl drvn and one pce appr last* **6/1**[3]
050 **5** *shd* **Frisby Ridge (IRE)**[4] 2248 2-8-9 .......... GGibbons 5 37
(TDEasterby) *cl up: rdn 2f out and ev ch tl drvn and one pce appr last* **10/1**
03 **6** *1 1/4* **Concert Time**[6] 2194 2-8-4 .......... RThomas(5) 7 33
(CRDore) *in tch: hdwy 2f out: sn rdn and kpt on same pce* **5/1**[2]
**7** *3/4* **Diction (IRE)** 2-8-9 .......... DarrenWilliams 4 31
(KRBurke) *dwlt and bhd: hdwy 2f out: sn rdn and swtchd lft: no imp appr last* **6/1**[3]
5264 **8** *2* **Emma's Venture**[6] 2194 2-8-9 .......... KDarley 11 25
(MWEasterby) *led: rdn along 2f out: drvn and hdd over 1f out: sn wknd* **7/2**[1]
0 **9** *1 3/4* **Hollingwood Soul**[6] 2194 2-8-9 .......... DeanMcKeown 1 19
(RonaldThompson) *a rr* **14/1**
00 **10** *9* **Ruby Rebel**[6] 2194 2-8-9 .......... (b[1]) RFitzpatrick 9 —
(PTMidgley) *towards rr and sn pushed along: sme hdwy 1/2-way: rdn and hung bdly lft 2f out and wknd* **50/1**
00 **11** *2* **Boracay Beauty**[16] 1970 2-8-2 .......... DFentiman(7) 3 —
(JRWeymes) *chsd ldrs: rdn along 1/2-way: sn wknd* **25/1**

1m 14.82s (2.32) **Going Correction** -0.25s/f (Firm) **11** Ran SP% **119.3**
Speed ratings: **74,72,69,68,68 67,66,63,61,49 46**CSF £123.26 TOTE £18.90: £5.90, £4.90, £2.80; EX 395.10.There was no bid for the winner. Mermaid's Cry was claimed by R Brotherton for £6,000
**Owner** A B Parr **Bred** Miss Roberta Dowley **Trained** Cockerham, Lancs

**FOCUS**
A weak juvenile seller which produced an extremely slow time, even for a contest like this.

**NOTEBOOK**
**Bowland Bride(IRE)** put her previous experience to good use and duly lost her maiden tag at the fifth time of asking. She travelled well on the firm ground and could be called the winner entering the last furlong, but this was a poor event and it is hard to see her following up at a higher level. *Official explanation: trainer said, regarding the improved form shown, filly was unsuited by trying to dispute lead with better class 2yos at Ayr whereas she was not asked for an effort until 2f out on this occasion*
**Mermaid's Cry** has to be considered unlucky on this racecourse debut. She lost ground at the start, did not get any sort of run when trying to challenge over one out and the winner had flown by the time she was in the clear. This daughter of Danzero is entitled to improve and looks the one to take out of the race.
**Shuchbaa** was another to blow the start and ran distinctly green on this debut. However, she shaped with a degree of promise late on, finishing nicely, and handled this firm ground.
**Joshar** ran her race, but looked to be feeling this firm surface late on. She is fully exposed, but would have preferred an easier surface.
**Frisby Ridge(IRE)** was another who looked to be feeling the firm ground late on, but improved on her latest effort, with the blinkers left off this time.
**Concert Time** ran below the form of her latest outing on this debut for her new connections. *Official explanation: trainer said saddle slipped.*
**Diction(IRE)** ran too green through the early stages and, although she is entitled to come on for this experience, it was a disappointing debut display. *Official explanation: jockey said filly was unsuited by the fast ground.*
**Emma's Venture**, popular in the betting ring, quickly tried to capitalise on her high draw and held every chance, but came under heavy pressure over a furlong from home and dropped out tamely.

## 2365 HERRIOT HAPPENING H'CAP 1m 4f
**7:00** (7:00) (C) (0-100,95) 3-Y-O+ **£9,490** (£2,920; £1,460; £730) **Stalls** Low

Form RPR
0-23 **1** **Bourgeois**[10] 2076 7-9-10 **95** .......... RWinston 3 104
(TDEasterby) *chsd ldrs: hdwy 3f out: rdn to chal wl over 1f out: drvn ins last: styd on to ld nr line* **4/1**[1]
0-20 **2** *nk* **Highland Games (IRE)**[12] 2047 4-9-0 **85** .......... KDarley 7 93
(JGGiven) *hld up in rr: gd hdwy 4f out: led over 2f out: sn rdn: drvn ins last: hdd and no ex nr line* **7/1**
4-11 **3** *1/2* **Court Of Appeal**[17] 1928 7-8-9 **85** .......... (t) TEaves(5) 1 92
(BEllison) *hld up in tch: swtchd outside and hdwy 3f out: rdn wl over 1f out: drvn and styd on u.p ins last* **9/2**[2]
103 **4** *nk* **Glory Quest (USA)**[9] 2116 7-7-6 **70** oh2 ow1 .......... DeanWilliams(7) 8 77
(MissGayKelleway) *chsd ldng pair: hdwy and cl up over 4f out: ev ch over 2f out: sn rdn: drvn and nt qckn ins last* **10/1**
00-0 **5** *hd* **Sporting Gesture**[13] 2022 7-8-3 **74** .......... DaleGibson 4 81
(MWEasterby) *in tch: hdwy over 4f out: rdn to chse ldrs on inner over 2f out: drvn and kpt on ins last* **11/2**[3]
10-0 **6** *6* **Sovereign Dreamer (USA)**[13] 2022 4-8-9 **80** .......... (t) JBramhill 9 77
(PFICole) *set str pce: rdn along over 3f out: hdd over 2f out and sn wknd* **18/1**
00-0 **7** *2* **Double Obsession**[13] 2022 4-9-7 **92** .......... SChin 2 86
(MJohnston) *chsd ldrs: rdn along and lost pl over 5f out: sn drvn and bhd fnl 3f* **9/1**
00-0 **8** *3* **Annambo**[40] 1401 4-8-9 **83** .......... (v) TPQueally(3) 5 72
(DRLoder) *chsd ldr: rdn along 4f out: wknd 3f out* **9/2**[2]
03-0 **9** *hd* **Derwent (USA)**[21] 1821 5-8-9 **80** .......... WSupple 6 69
(JDBethell) *in tch: rdn along over 3f out: sn btn* **25/1**

2m 32.47s (-2.73) **Going Correction** -0.175s/f (Firm) **9** Ran SP% **112.4**
Speed ratings: **102,101,101,101,101 97,95,93,93**CSF £31.05 CT £128.54 TOTE £4.70: £1.50, £3.10, £1.40; EX 38.90.
**Owner** C H Stevens **Bred** Juddmonte Farms **Trained** Great Habton, N Yorks

**FOCUS**
A decent, competitive handicap run at a frenetic early gallop.

**NOTEBOOK**
**Bourgeois** responded gamely to pressure late on and narrowly justified favouritism. His latest effort in a Listed event over the trip gave him an obvious chance in this, and he is clearly in good nick at present, but will have to improve to follow up at a higher level.
**Highland Games(IRE)** looked like scoring when hitting the front two out, but could not quite last home. This was his true form, and while this looks about as good as he is, he can make amends in a similar event on this ground.
**Court Of Appeal** failed to land the hat-trick off this 7lb higher mark for winning last time, but was far from disgraced in defeat. He is in the form of his life at present.
**Glory Quest(USA)** paid for chasing the frenetic early gallop and tired late on, but ran another brave race and faced a stiff task at the weights.
**Sporting Gesture** ran very much as this outing would bring him on again physically and he should improve next time out.
**Annambo** helped set the frantic early pace and had nothing left to give when push came to shove three out. He is better than this.

## 2366 SKYBET PRESS RED - BET NOW CLASSIFIED STKS 7f
**7:30** (7:30) (D) 3-Y-O+ **£5,499** (£1,692; £846; £423) **Stalls** Low

Form RPR
0500 **1** **Atlantic Quest (USA)**[6] 2215 5-8-12 80 .......... (p) PMulrennan(5) 9 89
(GAHarker) *trckd ldrs: hdwy 3f out: swtchd lft and effrt 2f out: rdn ent last: styd on to ld last 100 yds* **9/2**[2]
31-0 **2** *nk* **King Harson**[23] 1772 5-9-5 82 .......... (v) JFanning 8 90
(JDBethell) *led: rdn 2f out: drvn ins last: hdd and nt qckn last 100 yds* **7/1**
-001 **3** *1* **Sawwaah (IRE)**[6] 2215 7-9-9 78 .......... AlexGreaves 7 91
(DNicholls) *in tch: hdwy to chse ldrs 2f out: rdn and ev ch whn edgd lft 1f out: kpt on u.p ins last* **8/1**
0645 **4** *3* **H Harrison (IRE)**[17] 1927 4-8-10 78 .......... PPMathers(7) 3 78
(IWMcinnes) *chsd ldr: effrt and ev ch 3f out: sn rdn and wknd wl over 1f out* **3/1**[1]
4-35 **5** *1/2* **Endless Summer**[28] 1673 7-9-3 80 .......... (t) FLynch 4 76
(KRBurke) *chsd ldrs: effrt on inner 3f out: rdn 2f out and hld whn n.m.r wlver out* **13/2**
10-0 **6** *shd* **Wessex (USA)**[23] 1772 4-9-6 83 .......... DeanMcKeown 1 79
(JamesMoffatt) *dwlt: towards rr: hdwy 3f out: nt clr run 2f out:s witched outside and styd on fnl f: nrst fin* **33/1**
420 **7** *3/4* **Fiveoclock Express (IRE)**[16] 1968 4-9-1 81 .......... (v) TPQueally(3) 5 75
(MissGayKelleway) *chsd ldrs: rdn over 2f out: sn one pce* **7/1**
4314 **8** *1/2* **What-A-Dancer (IRE)**[46] 1317 7-9-3 77 .......... RWinston 6 73
(GASwinbank) *hld up in rr: hdwy on inner 3f out: n.m.r 2f out and over 1f out: sn no imp* **11/2**[3]
0000 **9** *3* **Safranine (IRE)**[8] 2143 7-9-0 70 .......... AnnStokell 2 62
(MissAStokell) *prom: rdn along over 2f out: sn wandered and wknd* **50/1**
0-50 **10** *7* **Silver Seeker (USA)**[51] 1246 4-9-2 84 .......... (p) TEaves(5) 10 51
(ISemple) *s.i.s: a rr* **20/1**

1m 24.46s (-2.64) **Going Correction** -0.175s/f (Firm) **10** Ran SP% **117.7**
Speed ratings: **108,107,106,103,102 102,101,100,97,89**CSF £35.65 TOTE £6.20: £1.70, £3.70, £2.60; EX 39.00.

**Owner** A Polignone **Bred** Bemark N V & Bon Marche **Trained** Wensley, N Yorks

**FOCUS**

A decent handicap run at a reasonable gallop. A high draw proved advantageous but the form looks sound.

**NOTEBOOK**

**Atlantic Quest(USA)** put his proven stamina to good use late on to score all-out. The re-application of cheekpieces seemed to help him concentrate better this time and he acted well on this quick ground.

**King Harson** tried to make all and was only just denied. He set a decent clip throughout and stuck to his task well under pressure, but could find no more when challenged. This was a big improvement on his seasonal reappearance over course and distance.

**Sawwaah(IRE)** held every chance if good enough, but edged left under maximum pressure and could not quicken thereafter. He was not disgraced however, and seems to have come to himself now.

**H Harrison(IRE)** was produced to win his race three out, but found only the one pace under pressure and may have been feeling this firm ground. He is on a fair mark at present and could improve for an easier surface.

**Endless Summer** did not get the best of runs on the rail, but did not shape as though this step up in trip was to his advantage. He is capable of better. *Official explanation: jockey said gelding had a breathing problem.*

**Wessex(USA)** missed the break and suffered traffic problems throughout. He can be rated slightly better than the bare form.

**What-A-Dancer(IRE)** did not quicken from off the pace as expected and was disappointing. He would have been better suited by a stronger early pace. *Official explanation: jockey said gelding had no luck in running.*

## 2367 CARLETON FURNITURE GROUP MAIDEN STKS — 7f

**8:00** (8:00) (D) 3-Y-O+ — **£5,512** (£1,696; £848; £424) **Stalls** Low

Form — RPR

26- **1** **Mutamared (USA)**[216] 5693 4-9-11 ..... WSupple 6 — 87
(MPTregoning) *plld hrd: in tch: hdwy 3f out: rdn to ld over 1f out: hung lft ent last: sn clr* **3/1**[2]

32-5 **2** *5* **Wychbury (USA)**[12] 2029 3-9-0 77 ..... KDarley 3 — 74
(MJWallace) *led: rdn along 2f out: hdd over 1f out: drvn and kpt on same pce* **6/5**[1]

/0-0 **3** *1* **Blue Mariner**[16] 1972 4-9-11 ..... JFanning 12 — 71
(PWHarris) *chsd ldr: effrt 3f out: rdn to chal 2f out and ev ch tl drvn and one pce appr last* **16/1**

**4** *3/4* **Swainsworld (USA)** 3-8-11 ..... DAllan(3) 7 — 69
(TDEasterby) *hld up in tch: hdwy 3f out: rdn to chse ldrs wl over 1f out: no imp fnl f* **40/1**

63-3 **5** *7* **Island Spell**[18] 1904 3-8-9 75 ..... PFessey 8 — 45
(CGrant) *chsd ldng pair: effrt 3f out: rdn over 2f out and grad wknd* **8/1**[3]

00-0 **6** *2 1/2* **Koodoo**[16] 1972 3-9-0 62 ..... VHalliday 1 — 43
(ACrook) *midfield: hdwy 1/2-way: rdn wl over 2f out and sn no imp* **66/1**

**7** *1 1/4* **Kentucky Express** 3-9-0 ..... RWinston 9 — 40
(TDEasterby) *s.i.s and bhd: hdwy into midfield over 3f out: sn rdn along and n.d* **25/1**

**8** *1 1/2* **Pure Vintage (IRE)** 3-8-11 ..... THamilton(3) 5 — 36
(RAFahey) *s.i.s and bhd: stmbld bdly bnd after 2f and rn green: hdwy over 2f out: styd on fnl f: nrst fin* **16/1**

045- **9** *shd* **Missie**[230] 5433 4-9-6 50 ..... FLynch 2 — 31
(GASwinbank) *chsd ldrs on inner: rdn along 3f out: sn wknd* **50/1**

04 **10** *shd* **Akiramenai (USA)**[14] 1991 4-9-3 ..... TPQueally(3) 4 — 30
(MrsLStubbs) *in tch: rdn along 3f out: sn wknd* **20/1**

5-6 **11** *1 1/4* **Ballyboro (IRE)**[18] 1904 3-8-6 ..... DCorby(3) 11 — 27
(MJWallace) *midfield pushed along over 3f out: sn wknd* **50/1**

30 **12** *8* **Mister Regent**[16] 1975 3-9-0 ..... NCallan 10 — —
(KARyan) *s.i.s: a rr* **11/1**

1m 25.21s (-1.89) **Going Correction** -0.175s/f (Firm)
**WFA** 3 from 4yo 11lb — 12 Ran SP% 118.1
Speed ratings: **103,97,96,95,87 84,83,81,81,81 79,70**CSF £6.45 TOTE £4.00: £1.40, £1.30, £3.00; EX 6.50.

**Owner** Hamdan Al Maktoum **Bred** E J Hudson Jr, Irrevocable Trust & Kilroy T'Bred **Trained** Lambourn, Berks

**FOCUS**

An ordinary maiden that saw the field well strung out behind the winner at the finish.

**NOTEBOOK**

**Mutamared(USA)** ran very keenly in the early parts, but as the race progressed he settled nicely and produced a telling turn of foot to settle the issue over a furlong from home. He was value for more than the official winning margin and, although he is a headstrong individual, may be able to score in handicap company.

**Wychbury(USA)** dictated the pace as he pleased, but had no answer to the winner as that rival swept past approaching the final furlong. He stuck to his task once headed and may be worth a chance over further, but this looks as good as he is.

**Blue Mariner** showed the benefit of his seasonal reappearance last time with an improved display, but was made to look very one-paced in the straight. He may benefit from a switch to handicaps now.

**Swainsworld(USA)** got the hang of things the further he went and hinted at ability late on. This was a satisfactory debut and he pulled clear of the rest.

**Kentucky Express** *Official explanation: jockey said colt hung right in last furlong.*

**Pure Vintage(IRE)**, making his racecourse debut, walked out of the stalls and then almost fell when colliding with the rail early on. He ran on late, despite still looking green, and is better than the bare form would suggest.

## 2368 CALVERTS CARPETS H'CAP — 1m

**8:30** (8:32) (E) (0-70,70) 3-Y-O+ — **£3,740** (£1,151; £575; £287) **Stalls** Low

Form — RPR

-060 **1** **Acomb**[23] 1757 4-9-6 62 ..... KDarley 5 — 74
(MWEasterby) *mde all: qcknd clr 2f out: rdn out* **5/1**[1]

02-3 **2** *2* **Rymer's Rascal**[26] 1710 12-8-7 49 ..... WSupple 3 — 56
(EJAlston) *midfield: hdwy 3f out:s witched outside and rdn to chse wnr ins last: kpt on* **16/1**

2042 **3** *1 1/4* **Efidium**[6] 2218 6-9-8 64 ..... GFaulkner 10 — 68
(NBycroft) *midfield: hdwy 3f out: rdn wl over 1f out: drvn ent last and kpt on same pce* **6/1**[2]

0062 **4** *hd* **Cryfield**[10] 2099 7-9-1 57 ..... KimTinkler 1 — 61
(NTinkler) *in tch on inner: hdwy over 2f out: sn rdn and kpt on ent last* **15/2**

4503 **5** *shd* **Skibereen (IRE)**[9] 2119 4-9-6 69 ..... PPMathers(7) 13 — 72
(IWMcinnes) *s.i.s and bhd: hdwy over out:rdn over 1f out: styd on wl fnl f: nrst fin* **7/1**

000- **6** *3/4* **Alchemist Master**[223] 5561 5-8-13 55 ..... DeanMcKeown 6 — 57
(RMWhitaker) *chsd ldrs: rdn along over 2f out: kpt on same pce* **20/1**

-001 **7** *1/2* **Border Artist**[7] 2172 5-9-9 65 6ex ..... ANicholls 4 — 66
(DNicholls) *trckd ldrs: hdwy over 2f out: rdn wl over 1f out and grad wknd* **13/2**[3]

1000 **8** *1* **Smith N Allan Oils**[7] 2172 5-9-3 59 ..... (p) FLynch 15 — 57
(MDods) *stdd and swtchd lft s: bhd tl hdwy over 3f out: rdn 2f out: nrst fin* **20/1**

000- **9** *5* **Aries (GER)**[249] 5016 4-9-11 70 ..... DCorby(3) 2 — 57
(MJWallace) *midfield: effrt 3f out: sn rdn along and no imp fnl 2f* **14/1**

04-5 **10** *2* **Oscar Pepper (USA)**[23] 1757 7-9-2 63 ..... PMakin(5) 17 — 45
(TDBarron) *in tch: pushed along and outpcd 3f out: styd on u.p fnl f* **11/1**

6000 **11** *nk* **Soft Mist (IRE)**[16] 1962 4-8-12 54 ..... RWinston 16 — 35
(JJQuinn) *bhd tl sme late hdwy* **66/1**

0-51 **12** *3/4* **Jordans Elect**[10] 2078 4-9-8 69 ..... TEaves(5) 12 — 49
(ISemple) *cl up: rdn along 3f out: wknd 2f out* **9/1**

204- **13** *1 1/4* **Northern Games**[205] 5878 5-8-10 59 ..... CWilliams(7) 7 — 36
(KARyan) *chsd ldrs: rdn along 3f out: sn wknd* **50/1**

64-6 **14** *2* **Scramble (USA)**[16] 1971 6-8-7 52 ..... (t) THamilton(3) 11 — 24
(BEllison) *a rr* **16/1**

1-00 **15** *nk* **Buthaina (IRE)**[14] 1992 4-9-7 63 ..... JFanning 8 — 35
(THCaldwell) *a rr* **40/1**

5-00 **16** *3/4* **General Smith**[20] 1868 5-8-8 55 ..... PMulrennan(5) 14 — 25
(GAHarker) *cl up: rdn along 3f out: wknd over 2f out* **80/1**

54-0 **17** *nk* **Outward (USA)**[16] 1972 4-9-6 62 ..... RFfrench 9 — 31
(RBastiman) *s.i.s: a rr* **100/1**

0-00 **18** *1 1/2* **Mehmaas**[14] 1993 8-8-9 51 ..... (v) CCogan 18 — 17
(REBarr) *in tch on outer: rdn along 1/2-way: sn wknd* **66/1**

1m 37.69s (-2.01) **Going Correction** -0.175s/f (Firm) — 18 Ran SP% 124.4
Speed ratings: **103,101,99,99,99 98,98,97,92,90 89,89,87,85,85 84,84,83**CSF £82.09 CT £518.35 TOTE £5.60: £2.10, £3.00, £1.70, £2.10; EX 100.50.

**Owner** Giles W Pritchard-Gordon **Bred** D F Spence And M W Easterby **Trained** Sheriff Hutton, N Yorks

**FOCUS**

A moderate handicap which saw those drawn low at an advantage. The winner looks progressive.

**NOTEBOOK**

**Acomb** was quickly into the lead and capitalised on his decent draw, before showing a smart turn of foot to win his race approaching two out. This marked a welcome return to form and he relished this faster ground, but the form looks poor and he may struggle with another rise in the weights.

**Rymer's Rascal**, up in class and dropping in trip, stayed on best of all behind the winner from his favoured low draw. He has begun the current campaign in good style and handled this faster ground without fuss.

**Efidium**, narrowly pipped last time in a classified event, ran another sound race, but could only muster the one pace under presuure in the straight. He has improved of late since racing on this quick ground.

**Cryfield** ran his race, but did not improve as expected for this step up in trip and was not suited by way the race was run.

**Skibereen(IRE)** would have finished closer but for a sluggish start, as he was staying on well in the straight. This was a fair effort form his poor draw and he is better than the bare form, but he is a fiendishly hard horse to win with.

**Border Artist** proved disappointing. He never looked like following up his latest win seven days previously under his 6lb penalty.

**Jordans Elect**, up 4lb for winning last time, failed to land a blow from his high draw.

## 2369 BUCK INN, THORNTON WATLASS, FILLIES' H'CAP — 5f

**9:00** (9:00) (D) (0-80,80) 3-Y-O+ — **£5,525** (£1,700; £850; £425) **Stalls** High

Form — RPR

0002 **1** **Musical Fair**[4] 2252 4-9-11 73 ..... RWinston 9 — 86+
(JAGlover) *trckd ldrs: effrt and nt clr run over 1f out: swtchd lft and rdn to ld ins last: edgd lft and styd on* **13/8**[1]

2-22 **2** *1 1/4* **Baron Rhodes**[22] 1788 3-8-11 72 ..... TEaves(5) 11 — 80
(JSWainwright) *cl up: ev ch over 1f out: sn rdn and nt qckn wl ins last* **7/1**

4102 **3** *hd* **Frascati**[10] 2079 4-9-8 70 ..... FLynch 8 — 77
(ABerry) *led: rdn along wl over 1f out: edgd lft and drvn ent last: sn hdd and no ex* **10/1**

00-0 **4** *3* **Bettys Pride**[4] 2252 5-9-0 62 ..... DarrenWilliams 5 — 57
(MDods) *s.i.s: hdwy 2f out: sn rdn and kpt on ins last: nrst fin* **14/1**

505- **5** *nk* **Sharoura**[182] 6062 8-8-11 62 ..... THamilton(3) 10 — 56
(RAFahey) *hld up: hdwy 2f out: kpt on ins last: nrst fin* **14/1**

0-04 **6** *1* **Roman Mistress (IRE)**[4] 2252 4-9-4 66 ..... KDalgleish 1 — 56
(TDEasterby) *cl up pnr 2f out: wknd over 1f out* **6/1**[3]

5-00 **7** *3* **Mystery Pips**[4] 2252 4-8-3 51 ..... (v) KimTinkler 6 — 29
(NTinkler) *chsd ldrs to 1/2-way: grad wknd* **33/1**

0-05 **8** *1* **Vigorous (IRE)**[10] 2079 4-9-8 70 ..... AlexGreaves 7 — 44
(DNicholls) *chsd ldrs: pushed along 2f out: sn wknd* **5/1**[2]

100- **9** *1 1/4* **Rewayaat**[240] 5226 3-9-10 80 ..... WSupple 2 — 49
(BHanbury) *in tch: hdwy on outer 1/2-way: sn rdn and wknd* **14/1**

0060 **10** *13* **Mesmerised**[13] 2017 4-7-13 47 oh11 ow1 ..... AnnStokell 3 — —
(MissAStokell) *sn outpcd and bhd* **100/1**

57.79 secs (-2.11) **Going Correction** -0.25s/f (Firm)
**WFA** 3 from 4yo+ 8lb — 10 Ran SP% 114.6
Speed ratings: **106,104,103,98,98 96,92,90,88,67**CSF £13.04 CT £85.84 TOTE £2.70: £1.40, £1.70, £1.90; EX 18.30 Place 6 £128.48, Place 5 £15.89.

**Owner** P And S Partnership **Bred** Mrs J Glover **Trained** Carburton, Notts

■ Stewards Enquiry : K Dalgleish one-day ban: failed to keep straight from stalls (Jun 6)

**FOCUS**

A modest sprint run at a fair pace. The high numbers had an advantage and the bare form is unexceptional.

**NOTEBOOK**

**Musical Fair**, despite having to be switched to challenge entering the final furlong, readily justified favouritism. She had gone close at Newcastle last time and this effort confirmed she is in great heart at present, so she looks one to follow up on this, granted fast ground.

**Baron Rhodes** ran right up to form, but again found one too good. She is versatile as regards ground and has been reliable of late, so deserves to gain compensation.

**Frascati** set the pace, but quickly came under pressure and had nothing left when challenged. She has been in fair form of late and can be placed to advantage under similar conditions before long.

**Bettys Pride** lost ground at the start, so ran well in the circumstances. This was an improvement on her seasonal reappearance just four days previously.

**Sharoura**

**Roman Mistress(IRE)** found little off the bridle and proved disappointing.

**Vigorous(IRE)** never looked happy and has not shown much in three starts now this season.

T/Plt: £258.30 to a £1 stake. Pool: £43,548.15. 123.05 winning tickets. T/Qpdt: £9.00 to a £1 stake. Pool: £3,877.20. 315.50 winning tickets. JR

# 2177 WINDSOR (R-H)

## Monday, May 24

**OFFICIAL GOING: Good to firm**

The ground had been watered and the regular bias towards those racing next to the stands' rail in the straight was not as evident.

Wind: almost nil Weather: fine but cloudy

## 2370 ALLEN & OVERY LLP EBF NOVICE STKS 5f 10y

**6:15** (6:16) (D ) 2-Y-O **£5,122** (£1,576; £788; £394) **Stalls** High

Form RPR

1 **Pike Bishop (IRE)** 2-8-12 .......... SDrowne 3 87+
(RCharlton) *t.k.h: in tch: carried lft into centre of crse 1/2-way: effrt 2f out: led jst over 1f out: r.o wl* **8/1**

53 2 1 ³/₄ **Empire's Ghodha**[6] 2205 2-8-12 .......... KFallon 4 80
(BJMeehan) *pressed ldng pair: hung lft into centre wl over 2f out: sn rdn: styd on to chse wnr ins fnl f: no imp* **11/2**[3]

215 3 *hd* **Monashee Prince (IRE)**[19] 1878 2-9-2 .......... NPollard 7 83
(JRBest) *mde most: rdn 2f out: hdd jst over 1f out: one pce* **7/2**[1]

14 4 ½ **High Chart**[13] 2023 2-8-9 .......... AMcCarthy 2 74
(GGMargarson) *in tch: carried lft into centre of crse 1/2-way: rdn and effrt 2f out: one pce fnl f* **11/2**[3]

22 5 *shd* **Asian Tiger (IRE)**[6] 2205 2-8-12 .......... DHolland 8 77
(RHannon) *sn pressed ldr: rdn 2f out: unable qck and lost pl over 1f out: kpt on fnl f* **7/2**[1]

6 2 ½ **Rubyanne (IRE)** 2-8-7 .......... TEDurcan 1 62+
(MJWallace) *dwlt and rrd s: lost 10l: rcvrd after 1f: prog to chal wl over 1f out: ev ch: wknd and eased ins fnl f* **5/1**[2]

7 3 **Archie Glenn** 2-8-12 .......... PMcCabe 5 55
(MrsPNDutfield) *dwlt: t.k.h: in tch tl wknd 2f out* **50/1**

8 *hd* **Lord Elrond** 2-8-12 .......... JQuinn 6 54
(PWChapple-Hyam) *in tch tl wknd 2f out* **16/1**

61.27 secs (0.07) **Going Correction** -0.20s/f (Firm) **8** Ran SP% **110.8**

Speed ratings: **91,88,87,87,86 82,78,77**CSF £48.06 TOTE £9.50: £2.10, £2.00, £1.30; EX 67.40.

**Owner** Michael Pescod **Bred** J Hanly **Trained** Beckhampton, Wilts

**FOCUS**

A fair race in which the previously unraced pair of Pike Bishop and Rubyanne look the ones to take out of the race. The form looks solid.

**NOTEBOOK**

**Pike Bishop(IRE)**, a half-brother to useful German two-year-old Medina and to six-furlong juvenile winners Contact and Motu, was nibbled at in the market and, despite being carried towards the centre in the straight, did well to get the better of four horses with previous racecourse experience. It will be disappointing if he cannot build on this promising start to his career, and he could be up to running at Royal Ascot.

**Empire's Ghodha** carried the eventual first and fourth wide in the straight, but while this manoeuvre would normally have caused all three to be at a disadvantage, on this day the ground up the centre of the track did not appear to be riding slower. *Official explanation: jockey said colt hung left.*

**Monashee Prince(IRE)**, who had to give weight all round, ran a solid race but, under his penalty, will always be vulnerable to a juvenile with more potential.

**High Chart**, who was not at a disadvantage racing down the centre of the track, looks to have been overrated by her trainer based on her performances on her final two starts.

**Asian Tiger(IRE)** had every chance but did not even come out on top of the group which raced towards the stands' side. He is becoming disappointing.

**Rubyanne(IRE)** ◆, who was the subject of plenty of support on her debut, reared up as the stalls opened and lost many lengths. She still looked to hold a big chance a furlong out, though, and that is probably a good indication that she would have gone close had she broken on terms. She clearly has the ability to win a maiden. *Official explanation: jockey said filly reared up as stalls opened.*

## 2371 FINSPREADS H'CAP 1m 67y

**6:45** (6:46) (E ) (0-70,70) 3-Y-O **£3,659** (£1,126; £563; £281) **Stalls** High

Form RPR

0-60 1 **Balearic Star (IRE)**[21] 1831 3-9-3 66 .......... KFallon 7 74
(BRMillman) *hld up: prog into midfield 5f out: rdn and effrt 2f out: drvn to ld ent fnl f: styd on* **5/1**[3]

0301 2 ½ **Foley Prince**[14] 1997 3-9-6 69 .......... SDrowne 12 76+
(MrsStefLiddiard) *trckd ldrs: nt clr run 2f out to over 1f out: rdn to chal ins fnl f: kpt on but a hld* **4/1**[2]

-005 3 *nk* **Habanero**[14] 1997 3-9-3 66 .......... RLMoore 8 72
(RHannon) *pressed ldr: led over 2f out tl ent fnl f: kpt on same pce* **6/1**

3-63 4 *nk* **Dandouce**[10] 2097 3-9-5 68 .......... BDoyle 3 73
(PWChapple-Hyam) *cl up: rdn to press ldr 2f out: ev ch 1f out: one pce* **7/2**[1]

400- 5 ½ **Dami (USA)**[233] 5362 3-9-5 68 .......... DHolland 11 72
(CEBrittain) *t.k.h: trckd ldrs: nt handle bnd 6f out and dropped to rr : rdn 4f out: prog and swtchd lft 2f out: styd on: nvr nrr* **10/1**

0-20 6 5 **Landucci**[14] 1997 3-9-3 66 .......... MHills 6 59
(JWHills) *wl plcd: rdn to chal 2f out: wknd 1f out* **10/1**

40-0 7 *nk* **Rajayoga**[39] 1422 3-8-6 62 .......... SaleemGolam[(7)] 10 54
(MHTompkins) *hld up: nt handle bnd 6f out and dropped to rr: rdn and effrt on outer 3f out: nvr rchd ldrs: kpt on* **50/1**

0-40 8 1 ¼ **Morag**[7] 2169 3-9-4 70 .......... LEnstone[(3)] 5 59
(IAWood) *hld up in midfield: forced wd bnd over 5f out: effrt on outer and rdn 3f out: wknd over 1f out* **16/1**

3-06 9 ½ **Gabana (IRE)**[46] 1309 3-9-4 67 .......... SSanders 4 55
(CFWall) *hld up: hmpd bnd 6f out: wl in rr and rdn 4f out: sme prog 3f out: fdd over 1f out* **8/1**

-000 10 1 **Sworn To Secrecy**[30] 1627 3-9-1 64 .......... PDobbs 13 50
(SKirk) *trckd ldrs: cl up whn nt clr run over 2f out: wknd over 1f out* **33/1**

40-0 11 1 ¼ **Washbrook**[24] 1755 3-8-12 61 .......... CCatlin 9 44
(AndrewTurnell) *t.k.h: hld up in midfield: nt handle bnd 6f out and dropped to rr: rdn 4f out: no prog over 2f out* **20/1**

00-0 12 4 **Dreaming Waters**[17] 1940 3-8-11 60 .......... SCarson 14 34
(RFJohnsonHoughton) *mde most to over 2f out: wknd rapidly* **50/1**

3-00 13 *shd* **Among Dreams**[21] 1841 3-9-0 63 .......... DaneO'Neill 1 36
(AGNewcombe) *dwlt: hld up: hmpd bnd 6f out: nvr a factor* **33/1**

40-4 14 5 **Stiletto Lady (IRE)**[14] 2005 3-8-12 61 .......... MFenton 2 23
(JGGiven) *hanging lft thrght: nt handle bnd 6f out and again over 4f out: wl bhd after* **16/1**

1m 45.48s (-0.12) **Going Correction** +0.025s/f (Good) **14** Ran SP% **128.8**

Speed ratings: **101,100,100,99,99 94,94,92,92,91 90,86,86,81**CSF £26.06 CT £129.61 TOTE £6.30: £2.40, £2.00, £2.00; EX 25.70.

**Owner** G W Dormer **Bred** William Shaughnessy **Trained** Kentisbeare, Devon

**FOCUS**

Just a modest heat but the first five came nicely clear.

**NOTEBOOK**

**Balearic Star(IRE)** was racing off a 4lb lower mark than when making a promising reappearance at Nottingham and could be excused his lesser effort in heavy ground last time. Brought home under a strong ride from the Champion, he once again suggested that farther will suit. *Official explanation: trainer said, regarding the improved form shown, colt had benefited from the good to firm ground on this occasion*

**Foley Prince**, 4lb higher for his win in soft ground here last time, handles this quicker surface just as well. This was a sound effort but things are not going to get any easier off an even higher mark.

**Habanero** looked likely to be swamped approaching the furlong marker, but he kept on remarkably well next to the stands' side. He looked much happier on this quicker ground.

**Dandouce**, backed into favouritism, had every chance and saw this longer trip out well enough. She is nothing special, though.

**Dami(USA)** ◆, who hails from a stable struggling for winners at present, was putting in her best work in the closing stages, as befits her middle-distance pedigree. She will surely do a lot better when stepped up in trip and looks worth bearing in mind. *Official explanation: jockey said filly had trouble handling the first bend*

**Landucci** could not get as close to Habanero as he had on his previous visit here, despite racing on identical terms.

**Stiletto Lady(IRE)** *Official explanation: jockey said filly was unsuited by the track.*

## 2372 FRENCH HORN CLASSIFIED STKS 6f

**7:15** (7:16) (C ) 3-Y-0+ **£9,431** (£2,902; £1,451; £725) **Stalls** High

Form RPR

1-00 1 **Caveral**[6] 2200 3-8-5 88 .......... RLMoore 1 101
(RHannon) *hld up: prog 1/2-way: rdn to ld jst over 1f out: styd on strly* **15/2**

4304 2 3 **Fruit Of Glory**[6] 2206 5-9-0 90 .......... DHolland 5 92
(JRJenkins) *led: rdn and edgd lft over 1f out: sn hdd: nt qckn fnl f* **5/4**[1]

23-0 3 2 ½ **King's Caprice**[22] 1797 3-8-8 87 .......... SCarson 2 88
(GBBalding) *s.i.s: hld up: effrt 1/2-way: outpcd 2f out: one pce after* **14/1**

-244 4 1 **Fromsong (IRE)**[23] 1763 6-9-8 95 .......... SDrowne 3 90
(BRMillman) *hld up: smooth prog 1/2-way: cl up 2f out: rdn and fnd nil over 1f out: wknd fnl f* **10/3**[2]

-630 5 *dist* **Mazepa (IRE)**[11] 2065 4-9-8 95 .......... KFallon 4 —
(NACallaghan) *rdn to press ldr to 1/2-way: sn wknd: eased and t.o* **7/2**[3]

1m 11.55s (-2.32) **Going Correction** -0.20s/f (Firm)

**WFA** 3 from 4yo+ 9lb **5** Ran SP% **108.2**

Speed ratings: **107,103,99,98,—**CSF £16.95 TOTE £8.10: £3.40, £1.10; EX 12.60.

**Owner** A L Stalder **Bred** Gainsborough Stud Management Ltd **Trained** East Everleigh, Wilts

**FOCUS**

A fairly tight race on the adjusted official ratings. The pace was sound and the form looks reliable enough.

**NOTEBOOK**

**Caveral**, whose disappointing run at Goodwood could not be explained by her trainer, bounced back in style, running out a clear winner against her elders. She landed a decent gamble for her connections in the process and the drop back to six looked in her favour as she travelled well before quickening clear.

**Fruit Of Glory**, favoured by the weights and with the ground in her favour, ran with credit and was just unfortunate to run into a three-year-old showing improved form.

**King's Caprice** struggled to go the pace on this quicker ground and could be worth a try over another furlong.

**Fromsong(IRE)**, who raced more prominently when winning this race last season, travelled like a winner for a long way but found disappointingly little under pressure. He is difficult to place off his current mark.

**Mazepa(IRE)** failed to run his race and clearly there was something amiss.

## 2373 TELECTRONICS SYSTEM LEISURE STKS (LISTED RACE) 6f

**7:45** (7:46) (A ) 3-Y-0+ **£17,400** (£6,600; £3,300; £1,500) **Stalls** High

Form RPR

1401 1 **Celtic Mill**[9] 2132 6-9-1 91 .......... LEnstone 1 111
(DWBarker) *mde all: rdn and clr 1f out: wandered fnl f: kpt on wl* **16/1**

0-30 2 1 ¼ **Ashdown Express (IRE)**[13] 2021 5-9-8 111 .......... SSanders 3 114+
(CFWall) *hld up in last trio: plld out and prog wl over 1f out: chsd wnr ins fnl f: clsd but nvr able to chal* **7/2**[2]

1-26 3 2 **La Cucaracha**[10] 2080 3-8-1 99 .......... MartinDwyer 5 96
(BWHills) *mostly chsd wnr: rdn to chal 2f out: wandered and nt qckn over 1f out: one pce after* **9/2**[3]

05-0 4 1 ¾ **Country Reel (USA)**[13] 2021 4-9-1 107 .......... (vt) KMcEvoy 8 96
(SaeedBinSuroor) *prom: rdn and nt qckn 2f out: one pce after* **7/1**

000- 5 *hd* **Twilight Blues (IRE)**[219] 5638 5-9-1 114 .......... DHolland 7 95
(BJMeehan) *chsd ldrs: rdn over 2f out: one pce and no imp ldrs* **2/1**[1]

0030 6 ½ **Miss George**[16] 1964 6-8-10 82 .......... DaneO'Neill 6 89
(DKIvory) *dwlt: hld up in last: effrt jst over 1f out: kpt on fnl f: no ch* **25/1**

0-40 7 7 **Stormont (IRE)**[74] 1004 4-9-11 .......... JQuinn 9 83
(HJCollingridge) *a in rr: shkn up and no prog over 2f out: wknd over 1f out* **50/1**

00-6 8 1 ¾ **Baltic King**[23] 1763 4-9-1 104 .......... (t) SDrowne 2 68
(HMorrison) *chsd ldrs: rdn 2f out: no prog: wknd and eased fnl f* **10/1**

5-60 9 5 **Bonus (IRE)**[13] 2021 4-9-8 105 .......... RHughes 4 60
(RHannon) *chsd ldrs: rdn 2f out: wknd and eased over 1f out* **8/1**

1m 10.91s (-2.96) **Going Correction** -0.20s/f (Firm)

**WFA** 3 from 4yo+ 9lb **9** Ran SP% **118.1**

Speed ratings: **111,109,106,104,104 103,94,91,85**CSF £73.12 TOTE £18.50: £3.60, £1.50, £2.20; EX 73.00.

**Owner** P Asquith **Bred** P Asquith **Trained** Scorton, N Yorks

**FOCUS**

A fairly competitive Listed race, with Celtic Mill making a successful leap from handicap company. The form looks up to scratch for the grade.

**NOTEBOOK**

**Celtic Mill** had it all to do at the weights in this company, but he came here at the top of his game and was sure to have his own way in front. Making every yard, he went on to win in good style, and small-field conditions races, in which he can dominate, look sure to provide him with more success in the future.

**Ashdown Express(IRE)** usually runs well but finds winning a touch challenging. The winner got first run on him and, although he was closing that rival down at the finish, he was never going to catch him.

**La Cucaracha**, although unlucky in running last time, looked to have more to do on this occasion against her elders. Well positioned throughout, she had no excuse.

**Country Reel(USA)** did not achieve much in a light campaign last term and his performances this season suggest he will remain difficult to place.

**Twilight Blues(IRE)** was best in by some margin on adjusted figures and had run well fresh in the past, so it was no surprise to see him well supported beforehand. He struggled to go the pace, though, and failed to pick up when required. This was disappointing.

**Miss George** was worst in at the weights and is the type who needs the leaders to go off too fast and stop in front.

**Bonus(IRE)** continues to run way below his best. *Official explanation: trainer was unable to offer any explanation for poor form shown.*

## 2374 RUINART CHAMPAGNE MAIDEN STKS 1m 2f 7y
**8:15** (8:17) (D) 3-Y-O **£4,498** (£1,384; £692; £346) **Stalls** Low

| Form | | | | RPR |
|---|---|---|---|---|
| 5 | 1 | | **Motive (FR)**[21] [1830] 3-9-0 ........ KFallon 19<br>(SirMichaelStoute) *prom: effrt over 3f out: hung lft over 2f out: narrow ld 1f out: drvn and jst hld on* **3/1**[2] | 73 |
| 2-5 | 2 | *shd* | **Coming Again (IRE)**[41] [1382] 3-9-0 ........ MHills 11<br>(BWHills) *led for 2f: chsd ldr after: chal over 2f out: ev ch after : drifted lft ins fnl f: jst pipped* **7/4**[1] | 73 |
| 00 | 3 | *1 1/2* | **Uig**[11] [2059] 3-8-9 ........ DKinsella 18<br>(HSHowe) *led after 2f: pushed along 2f out: hdd 1f out: edgd lft and styd on same pce* **100/1** | 65 |
| | 4 | *2 1/2* | **Plummet (USA)** 3-8-9 ........ RHughes 14<br>(JHMGosden) *wl plcd: effrt on outer 3f out: ev ch over 1f out: fdd fnl f* **10/1** | 60 |
| 02 | 5 | *3* | **Nietzsche (IRE)**[28] [1674] 3-9-0 ........ SWKelly 10<br>(JNoseda) *trckd ldrs: rdn over 3f out: hanging lft over 2f out: nt qckn and btn fr over 1f out* **7/2**[3] | 60 |
| | 6 | *3 1/2* | **Double Dagger Lady (USA)** 3-8-9 ........ DHolland 16<br>(JNoseda) *dwlt: wl in rr: sme prog into midfield 4f out: pushed along and kpt on one pce fnl 2f* **8/1** | 48 |
| | 7 | *1* | **Shastye (IRE)** 3-8-9 ........ RHavlin 3<br>(JHMGosden) *wl in rr: shkn up over 3f out: kpt on same pce fnl 2f: n.d* **25/1** | 46 |
| 05 | 8 | *shd* | **Lucky Arthur (IRE)**[7] [2168] 3-8-9 ........ DSweeney 17<br>(JGMO'Shea) *racd in midfield: shuffled along over 2f out: grad fdd* **40/1** | 46 |
| 00 | 9 | *1 3/4* | **High View (USA)**[10] [2085] 3-9-0 ........ GBaker 13<br>(FJordan) *prom: rdn 4f out: stl chsng ldrs 2f out: wknd* **66/1** | 47 |
| 00 | 10 | *2 1/2* | **Open Book**[7] [2168] 3-8-9 ........ SDrowne 12<br>(HMorrison) *racd in midfield: rdn over 3f out: no prog and btn over 2f out* **100/1** | 38 |
| | 11 | *hd* | **Stylish Dancer** 3-8-9 ........ JQuinn 20<br>(MBlanshard) *s.s: wl in rr: modest prog fnl 2f: n.d* **50/1** | 37 |
| | 12 | *nk* | **Charnwood Pride (IRE)** 3-9-0 ........(t) MFenton 2<br>(PWHarris) *a wl in rr* **25/1** | 42 |
| | 13 | *1/2* | **Pearnickity** 3-8-9 ........ PDoe 8<br>(AWCarroll) *dwlt: wl bhd: last 1/2-way: nvr a factor* **100/1** | 36 |
| 00 | 14 | *1/2* | **Silencio (IRE)**[14] [2001] 3-9-0 ........ VSlattery 9<br>(AKing) *racd in midfield: rdn 4f out: sn struggling* **50/1** | 40 |
| 0 | 15 | *2* | **Magic Verse**[22] [1794] 3-8-9 ........ CLowther 4<br>(RGuest) *racd in midfield: shkn up 3f out: wknd 2f out* **66/1** | 31 |
| 6 | 16 | *14* | **Kalamansi (IRE)**[8] [2144] 3-8-9 ........ WRyan 7<br>(NACallaghan) *a wl in rr: wl bhd fnl 2f* **40/1** | 4 |
| | 17 | *10* | **Imtouchingwood** 3-8-9 ........ DaneO'Neill 6<br>(PRHedger) *moved bdly to post: dwlt: a wl bhd: t.o* **66/1** | — |
| 000 | 18 | *3/4* | **Second User**[14] [2001] 3-9-0 ........ SSanders 5<br>(JRJenkins) *chsd ldrs to 1/2-way: wknd: t.o* **100/1** | — |

2m 10.47s (2.17) **Going Correction** +0.025s/f (Good) **18 Ran SP% 128.7**
Speed ratings: **92,91,90,88,86 83,82,82,81,79 79,78,78,78,76 65,57,56**CSF £8.46 TOTE £4.20: £1.80, £1.30, £28.40; EX 9.50.
**Owner** Highclere Thoroughbred Racing X **Bred** Darley Stud Management **Trained** Newmarket, Suffolk

**FOCUS**
A very slow time for a contest of this grade and it may be wise to be wary about the form.

**NOTEBOOK**
**Motive(FR)** had run a promising race on his debut at Kempton when the ground was probably too soft for him. With the benefit of that experience, and this quicker surface proving more suitable, he came home a narrow winner. Well bred, he looks likely to stay another two furlongs.
**Coming Again(IRE)** set a decent standard on the form he had shown on his two previous starts, and only went down narrowly. His Derby and King Edward VII entries look optimistic on this evidence, but he should win his maiden.
**Uig** benefited from setting a pretty moderate gallop, but she kept on well to secure the minor placing. This effort qualifies her for a mark and, for her connections' sake, it is to be hoped that the Handicapper does not burden her with an unrealistic rating on the basis of this run.
**Plummet(USA)**, a half-sister to a dual winning juvenile in Japan and a winning three-year-old miler in France, was the better fancied of the Gosden pair according to the market. Challenging widest of all in the straight, she ran with plenty of promise and can be expected to build on this.
**Nietzsche(IRE)** ran another fair race and the door to handicaps is now open to connections.
**Double Dagger Lady(USA)**, a half-sister to a winner in America, was not knocked about and stayed on in good style on her debut. She should be capable of improving on this in time.
**Shastye(IRE)**, a well-bred half-sister to Arc winner Sagamix, Group One ten-furlong juvenile scorer Sagacity and Group Two 12-furlong winner Sage Et Jolie, was poorly drawn on her debut. She was noted staying on in the closing stages and is another who should be capable of better in time.

## 2375 SAFFIE JOSEPH H'CAP 1m 3f 135y
**8:45** (8:47) (F) (0-55,55) 3-Y-O+ **£3,129** (£894; £447) **Stalls** Low

| Form | | | | RPR |
|---|---|---|---|---|
| 2422 | 1 | | **Diamond Orchid (IRE)**[20] [1856] 4-9-4 **49**........(v) KFallon 18<br>(PDEvans) *settled midfield: shkn up 4f out: prog over 2f out: drvn to ld 1f out: edgd lft but hld on* **4/1**[1] | 59 |
| -361 | 2 | *1/2* | **Make My Hay**[14] [1989] 5-9-1 **46**........ TEDurcan 14<br>(JGallagher) *hld up towards rr: prog 3f out: rdn to chal 1f out: ev ch: jst hld nr fin* **8/1**[3] | 55 |
| -524 | 3 | *3* | **Vanilla Moon**[110] [676] 4-9-3 **48**........(v) WRyan 12<br>(JRJenkins) *led after 3f to 6f out: led again 4f out: drvn and hdd 1f out: one pce* **25/1** | 52 |
| 0-32 | 4 | *2 1/2* | **Shape Up (IRE)**[18] [1910] 4-9-5 **50**........(b) PDoe 20<br>(TKeddy) *sn trckd ldrs: prog over 3f out: shkn up to chal 2f out: ev ch 1f out: nt qckn* **10/1** | 50 |
| 5530 | 5 | *1 1/4* | **Summer Special**[12] [2038] 4-9-0 **48**........ LEnstone[(3)] 7<br>(DWBarker) *s.i.s: hld up towards rr: effrt over 3f out: styd on u.p fnl 2f: nvr able to chal* **14/1** | 46 |
| /120 | 6 | *hd* | **Lissahanelodge**[29] [1644] 5-9-1 **46**........ SWhitworth 10<br>(PRHedger) *dwlt: hld up in last pair: gd prog on wd outside fr 3f out: chsd ldrs 1f out: no ex* **10/1** | 44 |
| 6000 | 7 | *5* | **Cool Bathwick (IRE)**[9] [2121] 5-9-2 **47**........(p) SDrowne 1<br>(BRMillman) *t.k.h: led 1f: styd prom: rdn and wknd over 2f out* **14/1** | 37 |
| 30-0 | 8 | *3/4* | **Dubonai (IRE)**[12] [2038] 4-9-6 **51**........(t) CCatlin 9<br>(AndrewTurnell) *settled towards rr: prog 3f out: hrd rdn and chsd ldrs 2f out: wknd over 1f out* **12/1** | 40 |
| 1666 | 9 | *1 1/2* | **Shatin Special**[10] [2092] 4-9-2 **47**........(p) JQuinn 8<br>(GCHChung) *racd towards rr: rdn and prog 3f out: no imp 2f out: wknd* **33/1** | 33 |
| 6-00 | 10 | *6* | **Den'S-Joy**[10] [2084] 8-9-5 **50**........ MartinDwyer 11<br>(VSmith) *s.s: racd in last pair: gd prog on wd outside 3f out: wknd over 1f out* **14/1** | 27 |
| 3556 | 11 | *1 1/4* | **Alisa (IRE)**[17] [1940] 4-9-7 **55**........(t) LisaJones[(3)] 17<br>(BICase) *chsd ldrs: wknd over 2f out* **25/1** | 30 |
| -060 | 12 | *2* | **Mcqueen (IRE)**[9] [2120] 4-9-7 **52**........ JFEgan 6<br>(MrsHDalton) *prom tl wknd over 2f out* **14/1** | 24 |
| 6312 | 13 | *1 1/2* | **Montosari**[27] [1691] 5-9-9 **54**........ DHolland 16<br>(PMitchell) *plld hrd: prom: wknd 3f out* **11/2**[2] | 23 |
| 415- | 14 | *1/2* | **Gregorian (IRE)**[13] [3276] 7-9-6 **51**........ DSweeney 5<br>(JGMO'Shea) *led after 1f to after 3f: wknd 3f out* **20/1** | 19 |
| 6004 | 15 | *nk* | **On Guard**[13] [2015] 6-9-3 **48**........ DKinsella 19<br>(PGMurphy) *hld up in rr: rdn and no prog over 3f out: sn btn* **16/1** | 16 |
| 6033 | 16 | *3/4* | **Salford Flyer**[20] [1858] 8-8-13 **49**........(b) AQuinn[(5)] 2<br>(JaneSouthcombe) *plld hrd: led after 6f to 4f out: sn wknd* **20/1** | 16 |
| -000 | 17 | *2 1/2* | **Cantrip**[12] [2032] 4-9-4 **49**........ SSanders 13<br>(MissBSanders) *cl up: wkng whn n.m.r over 2f out: eased* **10/1** | 12 |
| 00-6 | 18 | *20* | **Roaming Vagabond (IRE)**[17] [1933] 3-8-7 **55**........ NPollard 15<br>(NACallaghan) *a in rr: rdn and wknd 4f out: t.o* **14/1** | — |

2m 29.98s (-0.12) **Going Correction** +0.025s/f (Good)
**WFA** 3 from 4yo+ 17lb **18 Ran SP% 140.8**
Speed ratings: **101,100,98,97,96 96,92,92,91,87 86,85,84,83,83 83,81,68**CSF £37.50 CT £778.87 TOTE £4.00: £1.70, £2.10, £8.40, £3.60; EX 26.80 Place 6 £66.58, Place 5 £31.58.
**Owner** Diamond Racing Ltd **Bred** Eamon O'Mahony **Trained** Pandy, Gwent

**FOCUS**
A moderate race for the track, but the first two have run up to their best.

**NOTEBOOK**
**Diamond Orchid(IRE)**, in good form over hurdles of late, had run well on soft ground on her return to the Flat on her previous outing, despite being without the visor. The headgear was back on here, though, and the Champion had been booked to do the shoving. All went to plan.
**Make My Hay**, who got off the mark at the 22nd attempt last time out in banded grade, enjoyed the decent pace, but his performance emphasises the moderate nature of the contest.
**Vanilla Moon**, who cut out much of the running, has had plenty of chances.
**Shape Up(IRE)** finished placed for the sixth time in his career but is still seeking that elusive first victory.
**Summer Special** enjoyed the better ground but he too is a long-standing maiden.
**Lissahanelodge**, comparatively lightly raced, showed a bit more sparkle than he had at Brighton.
**Mcqueen(IRE)** *Official explanation: jockey said gelding lost his action in the closing stages.*
T/Jkpt: Not won. T/Plt: £40.80 to a £1 stake. Pool: £61,142.55. 1,091.50 winning tickets. T/Qpdt: £6.60 to a £1 stake. Pool: £3,886.60. 433.10 winning tickets. JN

# 2051 LINGFIELD (L-H)
### Tuesday, May 25

**OFFICIAL GOING: Turf course - good to firm; all-weather course - standard**
Wind: nil Weather: fine

## 2376 LINGFIELD LEISURE CLUB MEDIAN AUCTION MAIDEN STKS 5f
**2:20** (2:20) (F) 2-Y-O **£3,031** (£866; £433) **Stalls** High

| Form | | | | RPR |
|---|---|---|---|---|
| 2 | 1 | | **Indiannie Star**[11] [2083] 2-8-9 ........ TEDurcan 7<br>(MRChannon) *trckd ldrs: led 2f out: hrd rdn fnl f: kpt on* **2/5**[1] | 77 |
| | 2 | *1 1/4* | **Kwame** 2-8-9 ........ SWKelly 6<br>(MissECLavelle) *w'like: leggy: in tch in rr: prog 1/2-way: effrt to chse wnr 1f out: kpt on but a hld* **66/1** | 72 |
| 33 | 3 | *nk* | **Edge Fund**[36] [1505] 2-9-0 ........ SSanders 1<br>(BRMillman) *racd on outer: pressed ldrs: hanging lft 1/2-way: drvn and effrt to dispute 2nd 1f out: kpt on* **7/1**[2] | 76 |
| | 4 | *hd* | **Turks Wood (IRE)** 2-8-11 ........ FPFerris[(3)] 3<br>(MHTompkins) *w'like: str: bit bkwd: s.s: wl in rr: drvn and r.o wl fr jst over 1f out: gaining fast at fin* **33/1** | 75 |
| 0 | 5 | *1/2* | **Russian Rocket (IRE)**[15] [1984] 2-8-9 ........ HayleyTurner[(5)] 2<br>(MrsCADunnett) *dwlt: rcvrd to chse ldrs on outer over 3f out: rdn 2f out: kpt on same pce* **66/1** | 73 |
| | 6 | *1 3/4* | **Ride Safari** 2-9-0 ........ PDoe 9<br>(PWinkworth) *w'like: v s.i.s: last and wl bhd tl styd on wl fnl f: nvr nrr* **40/1** | 66 |
| 6304 | 7 | *1/2* | **I'm Aimee**[4] [2268] 2-8-9 ........ SCarson 4<br>(PDEvans) *w ldrs tl wknd over 1f out* **12/1**[3] | 59 |
| 0 | 8 | *nk* | **Black Draft**[12] [2057] 2-8-11 ........ TPQueally[(3)] 11<br>(Jean-ReneAuvray) *prom: pressed wnr 2f out to 1f out: wknd* **50/1** | 63 |
| 4 | 9 | *1/2* | **Perianth (IRE)**[15] [1996] 2-9-0 ........ SDrowne 5<br>(BJMeehan) *chsd ldrs: rdn 2f out: grad wknd* **12/1**[3] | 61 |
| | 10 | *2 1/2* | **Kempsey** 2-9-0 ........ JTate 12<br>(JJBridger) *w'like: outpcd and bhd after 2f: nvr on terms after* **50/1** | 51 |
| | 11 | *shd* | **Hallucinate** 2-9-0 ........ RLMoore 10<br>(RHannon) *w'like: scope: dwlt: outpcd and a bhd* **20/1** | 50 |
| 34 | 12 | *1* | **Majestical (IRE)**[30] [1638] 2-8-11 ........ RMiles[(3)] 8<br>(WRMuir) *mde most to 2f out: wknd rapidly* **20/1** | 46 |

59.90 secs (1.03) **Going Correction** -0.05s/f (Good) **12 Ran SP% 121.1**
Speed ratings: **89,87,86,86,85 82,81,81,80,76 76,74**CSF £65.79 TOTE £1.40: £1.02, £20.10, £2.40; EX 133.20.
**Owner** Timberhill Racing Partnership **Bred** Timber Hill Racing Partnership **Trained** West Ilsley, Berks

**FOCUS**
An uncompetitive, somewhat messy, heat with the winner not improving on her debut and the rest finishing in a heap.

**NOTEBOOK**
**Indiannie Star**, runner-up in a decent event at Newbury on her debut, appeared to have a simple task in this lower grade and did it easily enough. She has plenty of speed and the National Stakes at Sandown is now on the agenda.
**Kwame**, whose dam won over a mile at two, is bred to appreciate a bit farther this year.
**Edge Fund**, finishing third for the third time running, ran another solid race, but he looks likely to continue to meet one or two too good in this grade.
**Turks Wood(IRE)**, a half-brother to winners in Sweden and Turkey, looked in need of the run and experience, but he was putting in good work at the finish and looks open to improvement.
**Russian Rocket(IRE)**, who made little impression in heavy ground at Kempton on his debut, ran a better race with that experience behind him.
**Perianth(IRE)** came in for some support in the market and was not knocked about once his chance had gone. He should be capable of better than he showed here.
**Majestical(IRE)** *Official explanation: trainer said colt lost a left fore shoe.*

## 2377 FIRST TITLE CLASSIFIED STKS 7f
**2:50** (2:52) (E) 3-Y-O **£3,688** (£1,135; £567; £283) **Stalls** High

| Form | | | | RPR |
|---|---|---|---|---|
| 0-36 | 1 | | **Lady Georgina**[10] [2119] 3-8-13 **70**........ OUrbina 16<br>(JRFanshawe) *cl up gng wl: effrt to ld over 1f out: sn rdn clr* **8/1**[2] | 76 |

02-4 **2** 3 1/2 **Best Desert (IRE)**[11] 2097 3-8-11 65 .................................... NPollard 12 65
(JRBest) *racd in midfield: pushed along 1/2-way: effrt u.p 2f out: chsd wnr ins fnl f: no imp* **6/1**[1]

02-5 **3** 1/2 **Here To Me**[10] 2112 3-8-13 70 .................................... PDobbs 13 66
(RHannon) *lw: hld up in midfield: prog over 2f out: sn drvn: styd on to dispute 2nd ins fnl f: no ch w wnr* **6/1**[1]

2303 **4** 1 1/4 **Big Bad Burt**[10] 2122 3-8-11 63 .................................... (tp) SSanders 3 60
(MissGayKelleway) *b.hind: lw: prom: rdn over 2f out: nt qckn over 1f out: one pce after* **8/1**[2]

-500 **5** hd **Deign To Dance (IRE)**[12] 2061 3-8-8 64 .................................... TEDurcan 5 57
(JGPortman) *racd on outer: towards rr: shkn up over 2f out: no prog tl kpt on fnl f: nrst fin* **25/1**

3-00 **6** 1/2 **Kitley**[15] 1997 3-8-11 63 .................................... SWhitworth 2 58
(BGPowell) *settled in rr: shuffled along fr over 2f out: kpt on steadily: nvr nr ldrs* **14/1**

1-00 **7** nk **Chorus Beauty**[21] 1874 3-8-8 61 .................................... SDrowne 9 55
(GWragg) *pressed ldrs: rdn over 2f out: one pce fnl 2f* **20/1**

353- **8** 3/4 **Piccleyes**[179] 6082 3-8-11 65 .................................... RLMoore 4 56
(RHannon) *pressed ldr: led 3f out to over 1f out: wknd ins fnl f* **20/1**

1000 **9** hd **Hazewind**[7] 2207 3-8-11 58 .................................... (vt[1]) SCarson 14 55
(PDEvans) *settled in rr: shkn up over 2f out: kpt on one pce fr over 1f out: n.d* **12/1**

24-0 **10** 3/4 **New York (IRE)**[11] 2097 3-8-11 68 .................................... (t) SWKelly 8 53
(WJHaggas) *b.hind: led to 3f out: shkn up over 2f out: wknd 1f out* **20/1**

-052 **11** shd **Indian Edge**[18] 1942 3-8-11 65 .................................... DKinsella 15 53
(BPalling) *lw: dwlt: hld up in rr: swtchd fr ins to wd outside over 2f out: no real prog after* **8/1**[2]

0-40 **12** nk **Velocitas**[35] 1530 3-8-8 58 .................................... TPQueally[(3)] 11 52
(HJCollingridge) *hld up in rr: nt clr run over 2f out: sn rdn and no prog* **9/1**[3]

050- **13** 3/4 **Yashin (IRE)**[291] 3965 3-8-8 65 .................................... FPFerris[(3)] 17 50
(MHTompkins) *cl up: swtchd rt over 2f out: nt clr run fr over 1f out: eased* **20/1**

004- **14** 5 **Red Contact (USA)**[157] 6219 3-9-0 68 .................................... RSmith 6 39
(ACharlton) *a in rr: rdn and no prog whn bmpd over 2f out* **33/1**

5500 **15** 5 **Star Fern**[18] 1939 3-8-11 55 .................................... TQuinn 10 23
(JAkehurst) *a in rr: rdn and no prog wl over 2f out* **50/1**

05-0 **16** 12 **Dream Of Dubai (IRE)**[91] 869 3-8-8 62 .................................... GGibbons 7 —
(PMitchell) *t.k.h: hld up: losing pl whn stmbld over 2f out: eased* **20/1**

1m 23.36s (-0.85) **Going Correction** -0.05s/f (Good) **16** Ran SP% **118.8**
Speed ratings: **102,98,97,96,95 95,94,94,93,92 92,92,91,85,80 66**CSF £46.32 TOTE £6.70: £2.70, £2.00, £1.90; EX 39.90.
**Owner** Byerley Turf **Bred** Khorshed And Ian Deane And Eamonn Phelan **Trained** Newmarket, Suffolk

**FOCUS**
A competitive race judged by the betting, but a runaway winner. The draw favoured those berthed high but the form looks fair.

**NOTEBOOK**
**Lady Georgina**, well drawn, settled better this time and travelled well throughout on this quicker surface. She picked up in good style to go clear and can progress again if she continues to be amenable to restraint.
**Best Desert(IRE)**, also well drawn, came out of the pack to take second but was never a threat to the winner. He should remain competitive off his current mark back in handicap company.
**Here To Me**, despite remaining a maiden, does not look too badly rated, and she could be worth looking out for in a fillies'-only handicap.
**Big Bad Burt**, whose ideal trip remains something of a mystery, did best of those drawn in single figures.
**Deign To Dance(IRE)**, who had the cheekpieces left off this time, was running on at the finish. She is another whose ideal trip remains a question.
**Kitley** appreciated the quicker conditions but the drop back in trip was not in her favour.
**Dream Of Dubai(IRE)** *Official explanation: jockey said filly had lost her action.*

## 2378 LINGFIELD PARK H'CAP 7f

**3:20** (3:21) (D) (0-85,84) 3-Y-O **£5,768** (£1,775; £887; £443) **Stalls** High

Form RPR

0-00 **1** **Flip Flop And Fly (IRE)**[23] 1797 3-9-2 **79** .................................... RLMoore 10 88
(SKirk) *hld up wl in rr: gd prog 2f out: rdn to ld last 150y: sn in command* **25/1**

-160 **2** 1 1/2 **Free Trip**[19] 1900 3-9-6 **83** .................................... RHavlin 2 88
(JHMGosden) *racd far side: led rival and clr fr 3f out: ev ch w nr side ldrs 1f out: r.o* **8/1**

0162 **3** 1 1/2 **Joy And Pain**[12] 2061 3-8-2 **68** ow3 .................................... TPQueally[(3)] 12 69
(GLMoore) *trckd ldrs: rdn to chal over 1f out: ev ch ent fnl f: unable qck* **15/2**[3]

-421 **4** 3/4 **Mission Man**[18] 1942 3-9-5 **82** .................................... PDobbs 8 81
(RHannon) *lw: pressed ldr to 1/2-way: styd cl up: rdn over 2f out: kpt on one pce* **7/1**[2]

32-5 **5** hd **Handsome Cross (IRE)**[22] 1840 3-9-7 **84** .................................... SDrowne 9 82
(HMorrison) *lw: mde most tl hdd and no ex last 150yds* **8/1**

2-60 **6** 1 **Bailaora (IRE)**[10] 2113 3-8-12 **75** .................................... (b) SSanders 11 71
(BWDuke) *racd in midfield: rdn 3f out: effrt to chse ldrs over 1f out: no prog fnl f* **20/1**

-006 **7** 2 **Rise**[19] 1907 3-7-12 **61** oh1 .................................... (b) DKinsella 5 51
(AndrewReid) *b: b.hind: racd wd: nt on terms w ldrs: urged along 2f out: kpt on fnl f: no ch* **25/1**

2310 **8** 1 1/4 **Finders Keepers**[27] 1702 3-9-0 **77** .................................... TQuinn 3 64
(EALDunlop) *lw: racd on outer: sn trckd ldrs gng wl: pressed ldr 3f out: rdn over 1f out: sn wknd* **7/1**[2]

5212 **9** 1 3/4 **Jomus**[70] 1029 3-8-2 **65** .................................... CCogan 13 47
(LMontagueHall) *s.s: last and detached fr remainder: modest late prog* **10/1**

2-00 **10** nk **Disco Diva**[12] 2063 3-7-12 **66** .................................... RThomas[(5)] 15 47
(MBlanshard) *a towards rr: rdn and struggling 3f out* **25/1**

15-0 **11** hd **Swift Sailing (USA)**[12] 2069 3-9-0 **77** .................................... (b[1]) TEDurcan 4 58
(BWHills) *chsd ldrs: rdn 4f out: nvr on terms after* **25/1**

00-0 **12** 1 1/4 **One Alone**[138] 482 3-7-13 **62** oh16 ow1 .................................... MHenry 6 40
(Jean-ReneAuvray) *a towards rr: rdn and struggling 3f out* **66/1**

5310 **13** 1 1/4 **St Savarin (FR)**[19] 1900 3-8-11 **74** .................................... NPollard 1 48
(JRBest) *racd far side: chsd rival: lost tch fr 3f out* **14/1**

10-0 **14** 1 1/2 **Bertocelli**[12] 2063 3-8-10 **73** .................................... JMackay 14 43
(GGMargarson) *chsd ldrs: rdn over 3f out: wknd over 2f out* **12/1**

-642 **15** 3 **Midnight Ballard (USA)**[7] 2207 3-9-0 **77** .................................... SCarson 7 39
(RFJohnsonHoughton) *lw: prom: ev ch 3f out: sn wknd rapidly* **4/1**[1]

1m 23.16s (-1.05) **Going Correction** -0.05s/f (Good) **15** Ran SP% **124.1**
Speed ratings: **104,102,100,99,99 98,96,94,92,92 90,90,89,87,84**CSF £205.28 CT £1717.64 TOTE £15.20: £4.10, £3.80, £2.80; EX 181.90.
**Owner** Mike Browne **Bred** Ronnie Boland **Trained** Upper Lambourn, Berks

■ Stewards Enquiry : R Thomas two-day ban: careless riding (Jun 6-7)

**FOCUS**
The majority of the field came down the stands' side but the eventual runner-up raced next to the far-side rail, with St Savarin for company. The form looks reliable.

**NOTEBOOK**
**Flip Flop And Fly(IRE)**, third in a Listed race as a juvenile, had lost his form subsequently and dropped a fair way in the handicap as a result. He came from way off the pace, but there looked no fluke about it as the leaders did not die in front. *Official explanation: trainer had no explanation for the improved form shown*
**Free Trip** ◆ had an impossible draw at Chester last time and was berthed on the wrong side again this time. Nevertheless, he finished well clear of his only companion on the far side and was not beaten far in second. Granted some luck with the draw, he looks primed to score again in the very near future.
**Joy And Pain** ran a good race when badly in at the weights in a claimer last time and, having been raised 10lb in the interim, ran a blinder off his new mark.
**Mission Man**, who had an easy task last time, had quicker ground and an extra furlong to cope with on this occasion. He continues to look held by the Handicapper.
**Handsome Cross(IRE)** once again shaped as though this trip stretches his stamina.
**Finders Keepers** is not one to trust and is a dream horse for in-running layers.
**Midnight Ballard(USA)** was very disappointing and his rider's excuse that the colt did not handle the good to firm ground does not tally with his mount's decent previous form on a quick surface. *Official explanation: jockey said colt was unsuited by the good to firm ground*

## 2379 SATURDAY NIGHT AT LINGFIELD ON 29TH MAY CLAIMING STKS 7f

**3:50** (3:51) (E) 3-Y-O+ **£3,464** (£1,066; £533; £266) **Stalls** High

Form RPR

5310 **1** **Lady Piste (IRE)**[60] 1121 3-7-11 61 .................................... (vt) FPFerris[(3)] 7 57
(PDEvans) *cl up: effrt over 2f out: rdn to ld over 1f out: sn clr: pushed out* **9/2**[2]

2023 **2** 3 **Cargo**[19] 1913 5-8-11 48 .................................... (tp) RMiles[(3)] 1 52
(BAPearce) *pressed ldr gng wl: led over 2f out: shkn up and fnd nil wl over 1f out: sn hdd and btn* **7/1**[3]

00-4 **3** nk **A One (IRE)**[28] 1692 5-9-4 51 .................................... DSweeney 8 55
(BPalling) *led to over 2f out: sn rdn and outpcd: kpt on fnl f* **20/1**

2522 **4** 1/2 **Fayr Firenze (IRE)**[21] 1864 3-8-3 45 .................................... SRighton 3 50
(MFHarris) *in rr and pushed along after 2f: effrt u.p 2f out: styd on fnl f: n.d* **16/1**

3603 **5** 1 3/4 **Ivy Moon**[8] 2178 4-8-4 50 .................................... RThomas[(5)] 9 40
(BJLlewellyn) *b: b.hind: in rr and pushed along after 2f: effrt u.p to chse ldrs 2f out: no imp over 1f out* **11/4**[1]

0610 **6** 1 **Bulawayo**[10] 2123 7-9-0 49 .................................... (b) GGibbons 2 42
(AndrewReid) *b: b.hind: chsd ldrs: rdn 3f out: steadily fdd fnl 2f* **7/1**[3]

500 **7** 1 **Farnborough (USA)**[12] 2061 3-8-13 59 .................................... TQuinn 6 50
(DRCElsworth) *racd in last pair and outpcd after 2f: shuffled along 3f out: one pce and nvr rchd ldrs* **12/1**

0-00 **8** 16 **Mac The Knife (IRE)**[23] 1797 3-8-13 79 .................................... PDobbs 4 6
(RHannon) *s.s: a in last pair and nvr gng wl: wl bhd fnl 2f* **7/1**[3]

13-0 **9** 14 **Phrenologist**[140] 448 4-9-10 65 .................................... SSanders 5 —
(AndrewReid) *b: b.hind: prom to 1/2-way: wknd rapidly: eased 2f out: t.o* **8/1**

1m 23.67s (-0.54) **Going Correction** -0.05s/f (Good)
**WFA** 3 from 4yo+ 11lb **9** Ran SP% **111.8**
Speed ratings: **101,97,97,96,94 93,92,74,58**CSF £34.29 TOTE £5.80: £1.60, £1.70, £6.40; EX 45.10.Lady Piste was claimed by George Margarson for £6,000.
**Owner** Mrs S J Lawrence **Bred** Mrs M Fox **Trained** Pandy, Gwent

**FOCUS**
A modest claimer but run at a fair gallop.

**NOTEBOOK**
**Lady Piste(IRE)**, second best in at the weights, was rated 11lb higher the last time she raced on turf. She ran out a clear winner in the end but this was not a strong heat.
**Cargo** has been running with credit in banded grade of late and ran a good race at the weights, but his strike-rate is poor.
**A One(IRE)** was another who ran a creditable race at the weights. She would ideally have preferred a bit of cut in the ground.
**Fayr Firenze(IRE)**, who was without the headgear on this occasion, looks tripless.
**Ivy Moon** looked sure to appreciate the return to seven furlongs and it was disappointing to see her unable to pick up at the business end.
**Mac The Knife(IRE)** *Official explanation: jockey said colt had a breathing problem.*
**Phrenologist** *Official explanation: jockey said gelding was unsuited by the good to firm ground.*

## 2380 FURLONGS AND FAIRWAYS AT LINGFIELD PARK H'CAP 6f

**4:20** (4:21) (F) (0-55,55) 3-Y-O **£3,038** (£868; £434) **Stalls** High

Form RPR

6-44 **1** **Cherokee Nation**[32] 1600 3-8-12 **53** .................................... TQuinn 17 60
(PWD'Arcy) *trckd ldrs: coaxed along and effrt to ld over 1f out: pushed out* **5/1**[1]

0-01 **2** 3/4 **Yamato Pink**[26] 1725 3-8-9 **50** .................................... GBaker 15 55
(MrsHSweeting) *hld up in midfield: effrt 2f out: prog to chse wnr ent fnl f: hanging and nt qckn* **11/1**

06-5 **3** nk **Miss Judgement (IRE)**[57] 1169 3-8-8 **52** .................................... RMiles[(3)] 4 56
(WRMuir) *racd on outer in midfield: rdn 2f out: styd on wl fnl f: nrst fin* **16/1**

0410 **4** nk **Pardon Moi**[11] 2098 3-8-2 **48** .................................... HayleyTurner[(5)] 8 51
(MrsCADunnett) *racd on outer: trckd ldrs: effrt 2f out: cl up 1f out: unable qck* **20/1**

05-0 **5** 3/4 **Dubaian Mist**[122] 597 3-8-7 **53** .................................... NChalmers[(5)] 2 54
(AMBalding) *sn trckd across to chase ldrs: rdn and cl up over 1f out: hld whn n.m.r last strides* **25/1**

06-0 **6** 1 1/4 **Maluti**[28] 1689 3-8-9 **50** .................................... JMackay 14 47
(RGuest) *lw: prom: rdn to chal over 1f out: ev ch ent fnl f: btn whn hmpd last 50yds* **5/1**[1]

5560 **7** 2 1/2 **Joans Jewel**[11] 2098 3-8-10 **51** .................................... JTate 3 41
(GGMargarson) *b.hind: wl in rr: pushed along 1/2-way: kpt on fnl f: no ch* **25/1**

4503 **8** shd **Black Oval**[35] 1517 3-9-0 **55** .................................... RLMoore 10 44
(SDow) *b.hind: lw: chsd ldrs: outpcd and rdn over 2f out: one pce after* **13/2**[2]

0036 **9** nk **Parallel Lines (IRE)**[4] 2265 3-8-6 **47** ow1 .................................... (b) SDrowne 11 35
(PDEvans) *led: 2l clr over 2f out: hdd & wknd over 1f out* **20/1**

2650 **10** nk **Mister Completely (IRE)**[56] 1184 3-8-8 **49** .................................... NPollard 6 37
(JRBest) *swtchd to r against rail: hld up in rr: shkn up 2f out: no real prog* **10/1**[3]

0-60 **11** 3/4 **I Wish I Knew**[48] 1300 3-8-6 **50** .................................... TPQueally[(3)] 5 35
(DJCoakley) *wl in rr: reminder bef 1/2-way: kpt on fnl f: n.d* **16/1**

0500 **12** hd **Jaolins**[21] 1854 3-8-7 **48** .................................... RHavlin 12 33
(PGMurphy) *sn chsd ldrs: wknd 2f out* **14/1**

65-0 **13** ¾ **Scarlett Breeze**[11] 2098 3-8-10 **51**.................................... SWhitworth 7 33
(JWHills) *stdd s: hld up wl in rr: nudged along and nt clr run 2f out : nvr nr ldrs* **25/1**

-444 **14** 1½ **Bold Wolf**[29] 1676 3-8-11 **52**.......................................................... ADaly 13 30
(JLSpearing) *pressed ldr to over 2f out: wknd* **13/2**[2]

0606 **15** 1 **Sussex Style (IRE)**[2] 2326 3-8-12 **53**.................................. DSweeney 9 28
(RMFlower) *t.k.h: hld up in midfield: wknd wl over 1f out* **12/1**

6004 **16** 4 **Jasmine Pearl (IRE)**[26] 1725 3-8-5 **49**.............................. DCorby(3) 16 12
(TMJones) *b: chsd ldrs: wknd 2f out: eased fnl f* **14/1**

1m 11.83s (0.18) **Going Correction** -0.05s/f (Good) **16** Ran SP% **131.3**
Speed ratings: **96,95,94,94,93 91,88,88,87,87 86,86,85,83,81 76**CSF £60.00 CT £872.07 TOTE £7.40: £2.80, £3.10, £6.60, £4.00; EX 66.90.

**Owner** Walt Sylvester **Bred** Miss Paula Sylvester And W Sylvester **Trained** Newmarket, Suffolk

**FOCUS**
A moderate contest but the form is fairly solid for the grade. The whole field came stands' side.

**NOTEBOOK**
**Cherokee Nation**, taking a dramatic drop in trip having run too freely over farther, had a good draw and only had to be pushed out to score, although given his previous behaviour he might not be one with which much force can be used.

**Yamato Pink**, also nicely drawn, had more to do than when winning in banded grade last time and did not run at all badly. The return to sprinting has seen an improvement in her form, although the way she was hanging inside the last suggests softer ground may suit.

**Miss Judgement(IRE)**, returning to handicap company, did well to stay on from her poor draw on the outside. She does not look too badly handicapped on this effort.

**Pardon Moi** was stuck out wide for much of the race, which was a disadvantage.

**Dubaian Mist**, dropping in trip on her handicap debut, was poorly drawn and did not get the best of runs. She is probably better than this bare form implies.

**Maluti** was well drawn and was expected to appreciate the return to six furlongs. This was only an average performance in the circumstances.

**Scarlett Breeze**, whose rider was not the busiest, ran her best race to date on her handicap debut on easy ground. She is better than she showed here and could be one to be interested in when the heavens open.

**Jasmine Pearl(IRE)** *Official explanation: vet said filly lost a shoe and was lame*

## 2381 LADBROKES.COM AMATEUR RIDERS' H'CAP 1m 4f (P)
4:50 (4:50) (E) (0-75,71) 4-Y-O+ **£3,552** (£1,093; £546; £273) **Stalls** Low

Form RPR

0024 **1** **Danakil**[3] 2305 9-10-6 **63**........................................... MrDHutchison(7) 10 79
(SDow) *hld up in rr: gd prog over 3f out: led over 2f out: sn clr: pushed out* **9/2**[2]

-040 **2** 5 **Pay The Silver**[13] 2030 6-9-11 **54**.................................(p) GBartley(7) 8 63+
(IAWood) *hld up: prog over 4f out: nt clr run over 3f out and lost pl: effrt and nt clr run 2f out: chsd wnr last 150yds: no imp* **12/1**

251 **3** 1½ **Bank On Him**[13] 2034 9-10-7 **62**..................................... MrJJones(5) 13 68
(GLMoore) *hld up in rr: prog over 3f out: chsd wnr over 2f out: no imp: lost 2nd last 150yds* **11/2**[3]

2-42 **4** hd **Reminiscent (IRE)**[7] 2212 5-11-1 **65**..........................(v) MsCWilliams 5 71
(RFJohnsonHoughton) *hld up towards rr: swtchd to wd outside and prog 3f out: rdn to chse ldng pair 2f out: no imp* **4/1**[1]

4-60 **5** 1½ **Compton Aviator**[21] 1858 8-10-3 **53**..............................(t) MrsSBosley 3 57
(AWCarroll) *dwlt: hld up in last pair: rdn and effrt over 2f out: one pce and no ch w ldrs* **9/1**

050- **6** 5 **Optimaite**[133] 4976 7-11-2 **71**.................................(t) MissMSowerby(5) 9 67
(BRMillman) *s.s: hld up in last pair: effrt on outer 3f out: no prog fr 2f out* **20/1**

0400 **7** ½ **Top Of The Class (IRE)**[4] 2262 7-9-1 **40**.................(v) MissEFolkes(3) 1 35
(PDEvans) *midfield: lost pl and rr over 2f out: n.d after* **16/1**

0-06 **8** 5 **Ribbons And Bows (IRE)**[12] 2062 4-11-6 **70**..............(b[1]) MrSWalker 4 58
(CACyzer) *midfield: prog to chse ldrs 4f out: sn rdn: lost pl and struggling 3f out* **14/1**

0/-1 **9** 1 **Lago Di Como**[19] 1914 7-10-5 **60**..........................(t) MrsCThompson(5) 2 46
(MrsPTownsley) *led and sn clr: hdd over 2f out: bmpd along and wknd* **12/1**

3-60 **10** 1½ **Light Brigade**[40] 1426 5-9-11 **50** ow5.................. MissJoannaRees(3) 11 34
(JMPEustace) *chsd ldrs: lost pl and btn over 3f out* **6/1**

0 **11** 4 **One Of Them**[15] 2000 5-10-4 **57**...............................(b) MrsSMoore(3) 6 35
(JSMoore) *chsd clr ldr to over 3f out: sn wknd* **50/1**

05-0 **12** nk **Lara Bay**[7] 2216 4-10-7 **64**........................................ MrSGoswell(7) 12 42
(AMBalding) *chsd ldng pair: wnt 2nd wl over 3f out: wknd wl over 2f out* **33/1**

0262 **13** 10 **Paso Doble**[88] 903 6-10-4 **61**......................................... MrJMillman(7) 7 24
(BRMillman) *midfield tl lost pl and struggling 1/2-way: last and losing tch 4f out* **20/1**

2m 36.35s (2.11) **Going Correction** +0.275s/f (Slow) **13** Ran SP% **120.2**
Speed ratings: **103,99,98,98,97 94,93,90,89,88 86,86,79**CSF £55.30 CT £309.18 TOTE £6.90: £2.00, £2.70, £2.70; EX 32.30 Place 6 £288.14, Place 5 £233.23.

**Owner** The Danakilists **Bred** Juddmonte Farms **Trained** Epsom, Surrey
■ This was Dan Hutchinson's first winner.

**FOCUS**
A modest race in which not many could be seriously fancied.

**NOTEBOOK**
**Danakil** ran well despite having been given too much to do at Kempton three days earlier, and made amends in style. Presumably connections will be keen to get him out again under a penalty following this wide-margin success.

**Pay The Silver** is currently fairly handicapped on sand and turf. He got little luck in running on this occasion and, given his record, is one to note when next running on a switchback track.

**Bank On Him**, who rarely races beyond a mile and a quarter, did not quite see the trip out.

**Reminiscent(IRE)** had to challenge wide around the turn and never really got in a blow over a trip which is probably short of his best.

**Compton Aviator** ran a better race back on Polytrack but he is a desperately difficult horse to win with.

**Light Brigade** was sent off a surprisingly short price for what he has achieved.

T/Jkpt: Not won. T/Plt: £122.10 to a £1 stake. Pool: £36,481.90. 218.00 winning tickets. T/Qpdt: £99.80 to a £1 stake. Pool: £1,835.59. 13.60 winning tickets. JN

# 2115 NOTTINGHAM (L-H)
## Tuesday, May 25

**OFFICIAL GOING: Good to firm**
There appeared a bias towards those racing prominently over the sprint trips. This probably had a lot to do with the quality of the horses racing.
Wind: slt across Weather: cloudy

## 2382 QUICKSILVER-SLOTZ MEDIAN AUCTION MAIDEN STKS 5f 13y
2:30 (2:31) (H) 2-Y-O **£1,655** (£473; £236) **Stalls** High

Form RPR

502 **1** **Town House**[20] 1882 2-8-9 ........................................................ JFEgan 5 70
(BPJBaugh) *broke wl: mde all: crossed to stands' rail after 1f: clr whn rdn over 1f out: drvn out* **20/1**

3 **2** ¾ **Kanad**[11] 2095 2-9-0 ..................................................................(t) RHills 14 72
(BHanbury) *hld up mid-div: rdn and hdwy over 1f out: swtchd lft ins fnl f: r.o towards fin* **8/1**[3]

2 **3** hd **Laconicos (IRE)**[54] 1219 2-9-0 ............................................... KFallon 13 71
(DRLoder) *a.p: rdn 2f out: kpt on same pce ins fnl f* **4/9**[1]

423 **4** 1½ **Ruby's Dream**[8] 2177 2-8-9 .............................................. DaneO'Neill 11 60
(JMBradley) *s.i.s: sn prom: rdn and chsd wnr 2f out: one pce* **6/1**[2]

**5** 1 **Zolash (IRE)** 2-8-7 ........................................................ DerekNolan(7) 8 61
(JSMoore) *s.i.s: outpcd: hdwy on stands' rail fnl f: nrst fin* **66/1**

0 **6** hd **Desert Buzz (IRE)**[17] 1960 2-9-0 ........................................... JQuinn 2 60
(JHetherton) *hld up in tch: rdn over 2f out: one pce* **66/1**

00 **7** 1¼ **Fair Along (GER)**[11] 2096 2-9-0 ........................................... MTebbutt 6 55
(WJarvis) *hld up mid-div: styng on whn nt clr run briefly ins fnl f: n.d* **80/1**

0463 **8** 1 **Wizzskilad**[15] 1984 2-8-7 ............................................... AmyBaker(7) 9 51
(MrsPNDutfield) *mid-div: rdn and no hdwy fnl 2f* **50/1**

2 **9** 1½ **Dreamer's Lass**[8] 2164 2-8-9 .............................................. CCatlin 10 40
(JMBradley) *chsd ldrs over 2f* **33/1**

0 **10** 1¾ **Sherbourne**[15] 1984 2-8-9 ............................................... PaulEddery 3 33
(MGQuinlan) *s.i.s: sn chsng ldrs: wknd over 2f out* **14/1**

06 **11** hd **Faithisflying**[11] 2096 2-9-0 .............................................. NCallan 4 37
(CADwyer) *outpcd* **66/1**

**12** ½ **Debs Broughton** 2-8-9 ...................................................... GCarter 12 30
(WJMusson) *s.i.s: outpcd* **50/1**

5 **13** 5 **Belle Largesse**[29] 1666 2-8-9 ......................................... JMcAuley 7 10
(CBBBooth) *chsd wnr tl jst over 2f out: wknd over 1f out* **100/1**

60.95 secs (-0.85) **Going Correction** -0.25s/f (Firm) **13** Ran SP% **119.6**
Speed ratings: **96,94,94,92,90 90,88,86,84,81 81,80,72**CSF £164.88 TOTE £24.20: £3.90, £2.20, £1.02; EX 131.40.

**Owner** J H Chrimes **Bred** J H Chrimes **Trained** Audley, Staffs

**FOCUS**
Just a modest maiden, though the time was good for the grade and the form is fair. With the favourite running below form and the runner-up very unlucky in-running, the winner is slightly flattered by this success.

**NOTEBOOK**
**Town House** is progressing with every run, and was able to confirm the promise she had shown when runner-up in a soft-ground Chester maiden on this much faster surface. The bare form does flatter her a little and she may struggle to follow up in a higher grade.

**Kanad**, beaten just a length on his debut in a modest six-furlong Yarmouth maiden, was not suited by this drop in trip. He lacked the pace to take advantage of his draw against the rail and, when finally hitting full stride, he had to be switched out wide for a run. With a clearer passage he would have got up and it will be disappointing if he does not find a maiden, especially back over further.

**Laconicos(IRE)**, runner-up on his debut behind a fair sort at Leicester 54 days previously, proved most disappointing. He never really travelled that well and proved unable to pick up - his rider reported he lost his action. Given the length of time he had off, there may have been a problem and he has it all to prove now. *Official explanation: jockey said colt had lost its action*

**Ruby's Dream** continues in reasonable but, at the same time, continues to find a few too good. She is a reasonable guide to the strength of the form.

**Zolash(IRE)**, out of an unraced half-sister to a smart two-year-old sprinter, caught the eye on this racecourse debut. He missed the break and was outpaced early on, but kept on nicely and will have learnt from this.

**Faithisflying** *Official explanation: jockey said colt hung left throughout*

## 2383 QUICKSILVER GAMING CENTRES (S) STKS 6f 15y
3:00 (3:01) (H) 3-Y-O+ **£1,519** (£434; £217) **Stalls** High

Form RPR

0400 **1** **Danakim**[28] 1699 7-9-3 35.............................................. DFentiman(7) 7 54
(JRWeymes) *mde all: rdn over 2f out: edgd lft over 1f out: drvn out* **33/1**

0023 **2** 2½ **Valazar (USA)**[28] 1696 5-9-5 45........................................... KFallon 17 42
(DWChapman) *w wnr: rdn and ev ch whn edgd lft over 1f out: nt qckn ins fnl f* **9/2**[2]

0030 **3** nk **Only One Legend (IRE)**[23] 1787 6-9-5 55........................(b) NCallan 10 41
(KARyan) *outpcd: hdwy over 1f out: r.o under stands' rail ins fnl f: nrst fin* **7/2**[1]

4605 **4** ¾ **Threat**[2] 2322 8-9-2 45............................................(b) LPKeniry(3) 16 38
(JMBradley) *dwlt: sn chsng ldrs: kpt on same pce fnl f* **8/1**[3]

0340 **5** ¾ **Roan Raider (USA)**[1] 2359 4-8-12 47..............................(v) KGhunowa(7) 8 36
(MJPolglase) *mid-div: rdn over 2f out: kpt on same pce fnl f* **20/1**

2453 **6** ½ **Mr Uppity**[6] 2227 5-8-12 40...........................................(e) MHalford(7) 15 35
(JulianPoulton) *chsd ldrs: one pce fnl 2f* **16/1**

0030 **7** hd **Shady Deal**[8] 2166 8-9-5 47................................................... CCatlin 12 34
(JMBradley) *outpcd: hdwy fnl f: nvr nrr* **20/1**

**8** 2 **Osla** 3-8-8 ow3................................................................ DaneO'Neill 1 26
(HCandy) *racd far side: outpcd tl hdwy 1f out: r.o* **14/1**

0502 **9** 1¼ **Jalouhar**[30] 1639 4-9-5 49..............................................(p) MTebbutt 11 24
(BPJBaugh) *bhd fnl 2f* **12/1**

0004 **10** shd **Princess Erica**[5] 2238 4-9-0 45......................................(p) JEdmunds 2 19
(JBalding) *racd far side: prom: one pce fnl 2f* **8/1**[3]

0-56 **11** ½ **Travelling Times**[141] 436 5-9-2 49..............................(b) LEnstone(3) 3 22
(JSWainwright) *led far side 3f: one pce* **12/1**

0/00 **12** ½ **Louis Georgio**[10] 2123 5-9-5 45............................................... JFEgan 6 21
(MRHoad) *outpcd* **33/1**

1000 **13** 1¼ **Flying Faisal (USA)**[2] 2322 6-9-3 47............................(b) CJDavies(7) 5 22
(JMBradley) *racd far side: edgd rt over 2f out: sn struggling* **22/1**

6606 **14** 1½ **Lone Piper**[30] 1639 9-8-12 40.......................................... HazelBoyd(7) 14 13
(JMBradley) *a bhd* **20/1**

00-0 **15** 5 **Alfelma (IRE)**[5] 2236 4-8-7 47........................................... DTudhope(7) 9 —
(PRWood) *dwlt: sn mid-div: hung lft over 3f out: bhd fnl 2f* **66/1**

0132 **P** **Mizhar (USA)**[14] 2013 8-9-7 52......................(p) SHitchcott(3) 13 —
(JJQuinn) *a bhd: p.u and dismntd ins fnl f* **8/1**[3]

1m 13.31s (-1.49) **Going Correction** -0.25s/f (Firm)
**WFA** 3 from 4yo+ 9lb **16** Ran SP% **127.7**
Speed ratings: **99,95,95,94,93 92,92,89,88,87 87,86,84,82,76** —CSF £172.79 TOTE £41.00: £14.70, £1.50, £1.30; EX 266.70.The winner was bought in for 4,200gns. Osla was claimed by Roy Brotherton for £4,000.
**Owner** Miss K Buckle **Bred** R T And Mrs Watson **Trained** Middleham Moor, N Yorks
■ Stewards Enquiry : D Fentiman one-day ban: failed to keep straight from stalls (Jun 6)

**FOCUS**
A poor but competitive enough seller in which all bar four of the runners raced towards the stands'-side rail. Those who opted to race on the far side had no chance.

**NOTEBOOK**
**Danakim**, without a win on turf since scoring over this course and distance in May 2002, had conditions in his favour for this switch from the All-Weather and, despite drifting out to the centre of the course under pressure, ran out a clear-cut winner. He should continue to go well at this sort of level.
**Valazar(USA)**, in good form in banded company on Fibresand recently, posted another respectable effort returned to turf.
**Only One Legend(IRE)**, with blinkers replacing cheekpieces, was the best off at the weights, but is a very hard horse to win with, and never looked like getting to the winner. He did best of those coming from off the pace, but is not one to place much faith in.
**Threat**, without a win since May 2002, failed to improve for the re-fitting of blinkers.
**Roan Raider(USA)** ran better than he did in a similar race the previous day.
**Osla**, a 500gns purchase whose dam was placed over six furlongs on her only start, did best of those on the far side of the track, despite starting slowly, and offered plenty of encouragement.
**Mizhar(USA)** *Official explanation: vet said gelding bled from the nose*

## 2384 QUICKSILVER-SLOTZ LEADERS BANDED STKS 6f 15y
3:30 (3:31) (H) 3-Y-0+ **£1,508** (£431; £215) **Stalls** High

Form RPR
3345 **1** **Sotonian (HOL)**[8] 2183 11-9-0 40.................... StephanieHollinshead(5) 9 39
(PSFelgate) *a.p: rdn 2f out: r.o to ld last strides* **14/1**
0001 **2** *nk* **Master Rattle**[22] 2342 5-9-2 40.......................... LEnstone(3) 15 38
(JaneSouthcombe) *chsd ldr: rdn over 1f out: ev ch ins fnl f: r.o* **9/1**
0403 **3** *shd* **Bells Boy's**[8] 2183 5-9-5 40..............................(p) NCallan 11 38
(KARyan) *led: rdn over 1f out: hdd last strides* **17/2**
4550 **4** *½* **Polar Haze**[2] 2322 7-9-5 40..............................(b) JQuinn 8 37
(JPearce) *chsd ldrs: rdn over 1f out: ev ch ins fnl f: nt qckn* **6/1**[2]
-000 **5** *nk* **Moonglade (USA)**[32] 1591 4-9-5 30..............................(b[1]) JMcAuley 13 36
(MissJFeilden) *s.i.s: sn prom: rdn over 2f out: one pce fnl f* **50/1**
0030 **6** *shd* **Travellers Joy**[8] 2183 4-9-0 40.............................. MSavage(5) 12 35
(RJHodges) *pushed along after 2f: rdn and hdwy 2f out: one pce fnl f* **8/1**[3]
4210 **7** *1 ½* **Grand View**[26] 1719 8-9-5 40..............................(p) KFallon 5 31
(JRWeymes) *sn outpcd: hdwy fnl f: nt rchd ldrs* **3/1**[1]
0000 **8** *hd* **Gruff**[49] 1283 5-9-5 30.............................. RFitzpatrick 10 30
(PTMidgley) *s.i.s: outpcd: hdwy over 1f out: no imp fnl f* **66/1**
0330 **9** *nk* **Eternal Bloom**[19] 1913 6-8-12 40.............................. DTudhope(7) 7 29
(MBrittain) *chsd ldrs tl wknd over 1f out* **14/1**
6-03 **10** *1 ¾* **Miss Faye**[21] 1860 4-9-5 30..............................(p) DaneO'Neill 16 24
(JMBradley) *s.s: n.d* **25/1**
00/0 **11** *nk* **Frederick James**[17] 1969 10-9-0 35.............................. BSwarbrick(5) 14 23
(HEHaynes) *sn outpcd* **33/1**
4646 **12** *nk* **Vlasta Weiner**[86] 932 4-9-5 40..............................(b) CCatlin 4 22
(JMBradley) *mid-div: rdn over 2f out: sn bhd* **10/1**
00-3 **13** *1 ¼* **Crusty Lily**[12] 2056 8-9-2 35..............................(p) LPKeniry(3) 6 19
(RMHCowell) *dwlt: a bhd* **12/1**
4000 **14** *8* **Yellow River (USE)**[17] 1969 4-9-2 40..............................(b[1]) SHitchcott(3) 2 —
(RCurtis) *s.i.s: sn mid-div: bhd fnl 2f* **11/1**
0/00 **15** *18* **Our Sion**[13] 2029 4-9-5 35.............................. VSlattery 1 —
(RBrotherton) *sn outpcd: t.o* **66/1**
-000 **16** *10* **My Wild Rover**[13] 2040 4-9-5 30..............................(vt[1]) JFEgan 3 —
(KAMorgan) *chsd ldrs over 2f: eased whn no ch over 1f out: t.o* **50/1**

1m 14.63s (-0.17) **Going Correction** -0.25s/f (Firm) **16** Ran SP% **123.1**
Speed ratings: **91,90,90,89,89 89,87,87,86,84 83,83,81,71,47 33**CSF £130.83 TOTE £21.50: £3.90, £2.20, £2.50; EX 247.90.
**Owner** F Dean **Bred** Stal De Kraal **Trained** Grimston, Leics

**FOCUS**
A modest winning time, but a competitive sprint for the grade in which it proved hard to come from off the pace. The form is poor.

**NOTEBOOK**
**Sotonian(HOL)** had not won since August 2001, but had been in fair form on the All-Weather and this switch back to turf did the trick. It is hard to see him following up.
**Master Rattle** appeared to have lost his way recently, but a success in Jersey has clearly boosted his confidence as this was his best effort in this country for a little while.
**Bells Boy's** looked to have every chance against the rail and appeared to run his race. However, he remains a maiden after 25 starts.
**Polar Haze** did not do a great deal wrong, but he has only ever won on the Fibresand at Southwell.
**Moonglade(USA)**, with the tongue-tie off and the blinkers on for the first time, ran one of his better races but cannot be trusted to build on this.
**Grand View** was never really going the pace and may be worth over try over seven furlongs.

## 2385 BRYDONS NOSE BAGGERS BANDED STKS 1m 6f 15y
4:00 (4:01) (H) 4-Y-0+ **£1,662** (£475; £237) **Stalls** Low

Form RPR
-001 **1** **Court One**[32] 1593 6-8-11 45.............................. JFMcDonald(3) 6 50
(RJPrice) *s.i.s: hld up: hdwy over 5f out: rdn over 3f out: styd on to ld last strides* **9/1**
-351 **2** *nk* **Toledo Sun**[15] 2004 4-9-0 45.............................. JoannaBadger 15 50
(VSmith) *a.p: rdn to ld over 3f out: hdd last strides* **7/2**[1]
2054 **3** *1* **Paradise Valley**[13] 2031 4-9-0 45..............................(t) JQuinn 8 48
(MrsStefLiddiard) *hld up: rdn over 3f out: hdwy over 2f out: styd on ins fnl f* **9/1**
0041 **4** *2* **Royale Pearl**[26] 1728 4-9-0 45.............................. DaneO'Neill 4 45
(RIngram) *hld up mid-div: rdn and hdwy on ins over 2f out: styd on ins fnl f* **12/1**
4300 **5** *1* **Anniversary Guest (IRE)**[8] 2167 5-8-11 40.................... DNolan(3) 12 44
(MrsLucindaFeatherstone) *a.p: rdn over 3f out: plld out over 2f out: one pce fnl f* **14/1**
00-0 **6** *hd* **Promote**[92] 855 8-8-11 40.............................. SHitchcott(3) 5 44
(MsAEEmbiricos) *hld up: hdwy over 6f out: rdn over 3f out: wknd ins fnl f* **40/1**
-051 **7** *1 ¼* **Fletcher**[28] 1693 10-9-0 45.............................. KFallon 11 42
(HMorrison) *hld up mid-div: rdn over 3f out: no hdwy fnl 2f* **5/1**[3]
1622 **8** *nk* **Doctor John**[28] 1698 7-9-0 45..............................(p) CCatlin 13 42
(AndrewTurnell) *prom tl rdn and wknd over 2f out* **9/2**[2]
**9** *¾* **Watership Down (IRE)**[21] 1398 7-9-0 45.............................. VSlattery 3 40
(BGPowell) *a bhd* **33/1**
0-00 **10** *1 ¼* **Annakita**[28] 1693 4-9-0 45.............................. GCarter 9 39
(WJMusson) *a bhd* **20/1**
03-2 **11** *shd* **Quest On Air**[36] 1492 5-9-0 45.............................. WRyan 2 39
(JRJenkins) *chsd ldr: rdn to ld briefly 4f out: wknd fnl f* **11/1**
0030 **12** *8* **Dances With Angels (IRE)**[1] 2347 4-9-0 40.............................. NCallan 14 27
(MrsALMKing) *hld up mid-div: hdwy over 5f out: rdn over 3f out: nt clr run briefly over 2f out: sn wknd* **12/1**
65U0 **13** *13* **Cadwallader (USA)**[8] 2171 4-8-11 40.............................. LPKeniry(3) 1 9
(PBurgoyne) *led: rdn and hdd 4f out: sn wknd* **28/1**

3m 5.30s (-1.90) **Going Correction** -0.25s/f (Firm) **13** Ran SP% **121.0**
Speed ratings: **95,94,94,93,92 92,91,91,91,90 90,85,78**CSF £39.48 TOTE £10.20: £3.10, £2.00, £4.90; EX 67.50.
**Owner** Derek & Cheryl Holder **Bred** Mrs C R Holder **Trained** Ullingswick, H'fords

**FOCUS**
In the context of banded company, this was not that bad a race.

**NOTEBOOK**
**Court One**, off the mark on his first run in this grade at Warwick on his previous start, followed up with a narrow victory. He travelled nicely, but took a while to pick up when switched out for a run and he promises to improve again for a step up to two miles.
**Toledo Sun** was very game when picking up a similar race at Wolverhampton on his previous start and again gave it everything. The winner was just too strong in the closing stages.
**Paradise Valley**, stepped back up in trip, ran respectably but is quite simply a hard horse to win with and not worth following.
**Royale Pearl**, off the mark over a mile five on the Polytrack on her previous start, failed to build on that success.
**Anniversary Guest(IRE)** raced very keenly early on and this was probably a reasonable effort in the circumstances.
**Fletcher** was not on a going day. *Official explanation: jockey said gelding suffered interferene in the early stages and subsequently lost interest*
**Cadwallader(USA)** *Official explanation: jockey said gelding had breathing problems*

## 2386 LAWRENCES LONDON MARAUDERS APPRENTICE BANDED STKS 1m 1f 213y
4:30 (4:30) (H) 3-Y-0+ **£1,477** (£422; £211) **Stalls** Low

Form RPR
/5-3 **1** **Little Task**[1] 2345 6-9-2 30.............................. AReilly(5) 6 41
(JSWainwright) *s.i.s: hld up and bhd: rdn and hdwy over 3f out: r.o to ld last strides* **4/1**[2]
300- **2** *hd* **Eddies Jewel**[197] 5973 4-9-2 35.............................. RKeogh(5) 13 41
(HAlexander) *chsd ldrs: rdn over 3f out: led 2f out: hdd last strides* **16/1**
-054 **3** *2* **Paradise Garden (USA)**[19] 1918 7-9-0 30.............................. RKennemore(7) 3 37
(PLClinton) *hld up and bhd: hdwy 3f out: r.o ins fnl f* **8/1**
-030 **4** *¾* **River Of Fire**[10] 2126 6-9-7 30..............................(v) WHogg 2 36
(CNKellett) *hld up mid-div: hdwy 5f out: rdn to ld over 2f out: sn hdd: one pce fnl f* **9/1**
0550 **5** *½* **Ipledgeallegiance (USA)**[26] 1721 8-9-7 35.............................. CHaddon 1 35
(DWChapman) *hld up and bhd: hdwy on ins over 5f out: rdn over 3f out: no ex ins fnl f* **3/1**[1]
0/60 **6** *3* **Galaxy Fallon**[63] 1094 6-9-4 30.............................. AMullen(3) 9 29
(MDods) *hld up and bhd: hdwy on ins over 3f out: wknd fnl f* **20/1**
-044 **7** *½* **Littleton Valar (IRE)**[6] 2228 4-9-7 30.............................. DFentiman 14 28
(JRWeymes) *hld up and bhd: rdn and hdwy over 3f out: one pce fnl 2f* **5/1**[3]
0-06 **8** *2 ½* **Boozy Douz**[14] 2017 4-9-2 30.............................. BO'Neill(5) 10 23
(HSHowe) *no hdwy fnl 3f* **40/1**
0-43 **9** *1* **Classical Waltz (IRE)**[8] 2184 6-9-4 30.............................. KMay(3) 7 22
(JJSheehan) *hmpd and lost pl after 1f: hdwy 3f out: wknd 2f out* **16/1**
0-00 **10** *3 ½* **Diva Dancer**[51] 783 4-9-7 35..............................(b[1]) MHoward 8 15
(JHetherton) *chsd ldrs tl wknd over 2f out* **20/1**
3005 **11** *¾* **Platinum Boy (IRE)**[28] 1691 4-9-7 35..............................(p) DeanWilliams 11 13
(MWellings) *led 1f: chsd ldr: led over 3f out tl over 2f out: sn wknd* **20/1**
/366 **12** *12* **Dancing Dolphin (IRE)**[15] 1987 5-9-2 30.............................. MHalford(5) 4 —
(JulianPoulton) *prom tl wknd 2f out* **12/1**
00-0 **13** *nk* **Lill's Star Lad**[6] 2229 6-9-2 30.............................. StevenHarrison(5) 15 —
(PRWood) *a bhd* **80/1**
00-0 **14** *6* **Sea Tern**[6] 2229 4-9-7 35.............................. DerekNolan 5 —
(DGBridgwater) *prom: rdn whn hung rt and rn wd bnd over 4f out: sn lost pl* **25/1**
00-0 **15** *13* **Lawgiver (IRE)**[35] 1532 3-8-7 35..............................(p) DTudhope 12 —
(TJFitzgerald) *led after 1f: rdn and hdd over 3f out: wknd qckly* **33/1**

2m 10.07s (0.57) **Going Correction** -0.25s/f (Firm)
**WFA** 3 from 4yo+ 14lb **15** Ran SP% **127.0**
Speed ratings: **87,86,85,84,84 81,81,79,78,75 75,65,65,60,50**CSF £63.83 TOTE £5.00: £2.60, £3.20, £2.70; EX 147.40.
**Owner** Keith Jackson **Bred** Stetchworth Park Stud Ltd **Trained** Kennythorpe, N Yorks

**FOCUS**
A dreadful affair, run in a slow time.

**NOTEBOOK**
**Little Task** is better known as a hurdler/chaser these days, but he offered encouragement when third in similar company at Beverley the previous day and proved able to build on that promise to gain his first win on the level since 2000. If kept to this code, he would appeal as one to oppose next time.
**Eddies Jewel**, racing beyond a mile for the first time, and with the headgear left off on his debut for new connections, did nothing wrong and was just denied. Given that this was his first run in 197 days, he should improve and looks up to winning a similar race.
**Paradise Garden(USA)**, with the visor left off this time, ran respectably returned to turf and stepped back up in trip. However, he last won in July 2001 and has just two wins to his name in 36 career starts.
**River Of Fire** does most of his racing at around two miles these days (the trip he last won over) so this was a good effort over a trip surely on the short side these days.
**Ipledgeallegiance(USA)** is a regular in these type of events, but remains on a long losing run.
**Platinum Boy(IRE)** *Official explanation: trainer said gelding lost a front shoe in the race and was lame the following morning.*

## 2387 WALDRONS WAIFS & STRAYS BANDED STKS 1m 54y
5:00 (5:00) (H) 4-Y-0+ **£1,508** (£431; £215) **Stalls** Low

Form RPR
2400 **1** **My Maite (IRE)**[63] 1088 5-9-0 45..............................(bt) NDay 11 50
(RIngram) *hld up: hdwy over 3f out: rdn whn edgd lft and bmpd over 2f out: swtchd rt over 1f out: r.o u.p to ld post* **13/2**[3]
20-0 **2** *shd* **Gemini Lady**[15] 1993 4-9-0 45.............................. JFEgan 8 50
(MrsGSRees) *plld hrd towards rr: swtchd rt over 3f out: rdn and hdwy whn edgd lft 2f out: led 1f out: hdd post* **14/1**
4222 **3** *nk* **Tojoneski**[15] 1986 5-9-0 45..............................(p) RFfrench 15 49
(IWMcinnes) *a.p: led 4f out: rdn over 2f out: hdd 1f out: r.o* **4/1**[2]

0034 **4** ½ **Lucefer (IRE)**[13] 2034 6-9-0 45 KFallon 7 48
(GCHChung) *hld up mid-div: rdn and hdwy whn n.m.r over 2f out: ev ch ins fnl f: nt qckn* **7/2**[1]

6510 **5** 1¼ **Chickasaw Trail**[15] 1987 6-8-9 45 StephanieHollinshead(5) 10 45
(RHollinshead) *hld up and bhd: hdwy over 3f out: sn rdn: kpt on ins fnl f* **16/1**

0066 **6** 2½ **Peartree House (IRE)**[20] 1889 10-8-11 45 SHitchcott(3) 18 40
(DWChapman) *hld up and bhd: hdwy over 3f out: sn rdn: one pce fnl f* **10/1**

-000 **7** ½ **Parisian Playboy**[21] 1876 4-9-0 45 JQuinn 2 38
(JeddO'Keeffe) *led: hdd 4f out: rdn over 2f out: wknd fnl f* **14/1**

0-30 **8** nk **Seejay**[21] 1856 4-9-0 45 CCatlin 1 38
(MAAllen) *hld up and bhd: rdn over 2f out: hdwy over 1f out: nvr trbld ldrs* **25/1**

1433 **9** 1¾ **Kenny The Truth (IRE)**[10] 2128 5-9-0 45 (t) PMQuinn 9 34
(MrsJCandlish) *hld up and bhd: rdn over 3f out: swtchd rt over 1f out: nvr nrr* **7/1**

0341 **10** 1 **Ballygriffin Kid**[12] 2051 4-9-0 45 DaneO'Neill 13 31
(TPMcgovern) *t.k.h towards rr: rdn over 2f out: hdwy over 1f out: n.d* **16/1**

-225 **11** 1¾ **Benjamin (IRE)**[12] 2052 6-8-11 45 (bt) LEnstone(3) 16 27
(JaneSouthcombe) *plld hrd: prom: rdn whn edgd rt and bmpd over 2f out: sn wknd* **25/1**

6521 **12** shd **Ballyrush (IRE)**[6] 2231 4-8-13 45 (b) RKeogh(7) 4 33
(KRBurke) *hld up: hdwy on ins over 4f out: rdn over 2f out: wknd over 1f out* **7/1**

5140 **13** 1¼ **Over To You Bert**[19] 1582 5-9-0 45 VSlattery 14 24
(RJHodges) *plld hrd: prom: rdn over 3f out: wknd over 2f out* **25/1**

0550 **14** 2½ **Indian Warrior**[15] 1986 8-8-9 45 (b) BSwarbrick(5) 5 18
(JJay) *hld up mid-div: rdn over 3f out: bhd fnl 2f* **25/1**

0005 **15** 1¼ **Ellamyte**[14] 2017 4-8-11 45 DNolan(3) 3 16
(DGBridgwater) *prom: rdn over 3f out: wknd over 2f out* **50/1**

0-60 **16** hd **Landofheartsdesire (IRE)**[138] 474 5-9-0 45 (v) DMcGaffin 17 15
(JSWainwright) *stdd s: a bhd* **33/1**

00-0 **17** 1¾ **Ace In The Hole**[43] 1369 4-8-11 45 (p) JFMcDonald(3) 12 11
(FJordan) *prom: rdn over 4f out: wknd over 3f out* **66/1**

4400 **P** **Taiyo**[52] 1244 4-9-0 45 NCallan 6 —
(JWPayne) *hld up in tch: stmbld and sddle slipped over 2f out: p.u ins fnl f* **16/1**

1m 43.65s (-2.75) **Going Correction** -0.25s/f (Firm) **18** Ran SP% **142.4**
Speed ratings: **103,102,102,102,100 98,97,97,95,94 93,92,91,89,87 87,86,**—CSF £103.24 TOTE £9.20: £2.00, £3.90, £2.80; EX 131.90 Place 6 £244.01, Place 5 £198.61.
**Owner** The Stargazers 2nd Xi **Bred** S Gollogly **Trained** Epsom, Surrey
■ Stewards Enquiry : N Day one-day ban: careless riding (Jun 6)

**FOCUS**
A fair time for a banded stakes and the form looks sound.

**NOTEBOOK**
**My Maite(IRE)** had just one win to his name in his previous 30 starts and had never previously won on the turf. However, dropped two furlongs in trip and with the blinkers replacing a visor, he bounced right back to form.
**Gemini Lady**, an inconsistent maiden, posted one of her better efforts and a repeat of this would probably be enough to pick up a similar race.
**Tojoneski**, hailing from a yard in fine form, is not running too badly himself and is up to winning a similar race.
**Lucefer(IRE)**, down two furlongs in trip and dropped into banded company, appeared to have his ideal conditions and can have no excuses.
**Chickasaw Trail**, back on more suitable ground and dropped back to the trip she won over, did not run badly.
**Taiyo** did not look out of it when meeting trouble. *Official explanation: jockey said filly stumbled causing saddle to slip*
T/Plt: £475.00 to a £1 stake. Pool: £30,455.10. 46.80 winning tickets. T/Qpdt: £113.80 to a £1 stake. Pool: £1,323.30. 8.60 winning tickets. KH

## 2140 RIPON (R-H)

### Tuesday, May 25

**OFFICIAL GOING: Good to firm**

## 2388 EBF SPA WELTER MAIDEN STKS 5f

**2:10** (2:11) (D) 2-Y-O £5,590 (£1,720; £860; £430) **Stalls** Low

Form RPR

2 **1** **Mizz Tee (IRE)**[12] 2071 2-8-6 DAllan(3) 10 75
(TDEasterby) *cl up: pushed along 2f out: rdn over 1f ou styd on to ld ins last* **5/4**[1]

**2** ¾ **Hanseatic League (USA)** 2-9-0 JFanning 6 77
(MJohnston) *qckly away and led: rdn along wl over 1f out: hdd and no ex ins last* **11/4**[2]

**3** 1½ **Strathtay** 2-8-9 GFaulkner 4 66
(PCHaslam) *in tch: hdwy 2f out: styd on ent last: nrst fin* **16/1**

05 **4** 1¼ **Ashes (IRE)**[14] 2023 2-8-9 KDalgleish 8 61
(KRBurke) *wemt lft s: sn cl up: evey ch 2f out: sn rdn and wknd appr last* **25/1**

**5** ½ **High Petergate (IRE)** 2-8-9 DaleGibson 3 59
(MWEasterby) *midfield: rdn along 2f out: kpt on ins last: nrst fin* **33/1**

**6** hd **Rich Albi** 2-9-0 WSupple 9 63
(TDEasterby) *chsd ldrs: rdn along 2f out: wandered and lost action over 1f out: kpt on ins last* **16/1**

**7** 1½ **High Minded** 2-9-0 DarrenWilliams 5 57
(KRBurke) *s.i.s and bhd: hdwy and swtchd lft to stands rail 1/2-way: shkn up and n.m.r over 1f out: kpt on ins last* **16/1**

**8** ½ **Saffa Garden (IRE)** 2-8-9 DHolland 7 50
(CEBrittain) *bmpd s: sn chsng ldrs: rdn along 2f out and kpt on same pce* **8/1**[3]

**9** 3½ **Mill End Chateau** 2-8-9 PMulrennan(5) 12 41
(MWEasterby) *chaased ldrs: rdn along 2f out: sn wknd* **50/1**

**10** 16 **Mist Opportunity (IRE)** 2-9-0 KDarley 2 —
(PCHaslam) *sn outpcd and bhd* **20/1**

**11** 13 **Mickey Boggitt** 2-9-0 JCarroll 1 —
(ABerry) *s.i.s: a rr* **25/1**

**12** 19 **Highbury Lass** 2-8-9 ACulhane 11 —
(PCHaslam) *s.i.s: a rr* **66/1**

61.72 secs (1.52) **Going Correction** +0.05s/f (Good) **12** Ran SP% **118.7**
Speed ratings: **89,87,85,83,82 82,79,79,73,47 27,**—CSF £4.01 TOTE £2.30: £1.10, £1.40, £6.60; EX 4.90.
**Owner** Salifix **Bred** Dr Dean Harron **Trained** Great Habton, N Yorks

**FOCUS**
Just a fair maiden with only two having raced before, although the time was moderate.

**NOTEBOOK**
**Mizz Tee(IRE)**, who made such a promising debut in a race at York that is beginning to work out well, fulfilled that to some extent by taking this maiden. She should get another furlong and can win again.
**Hanseatic League(USA)** ◆, a speedily-bred newcomer, made the running but could not hold off the more experienced winner. He is sure to come on for the outing and should not take long to get off the mark.
**Strathtay** ◆, but a speedy sire out of a juvenile winner, made a promising debut and ran as if she will appreciate another furlong at least. She is another to keep on the right side of.
**Ashes(IRE)**, dropped back to five having been well beaten in a decent fillies event on easy ground at York, ran much better. However, this improved effort does raise a slight question over the value of the form.
**High Petergate(IRE)**, another with plenty of speed in the family, is from a yard whose juveniles usually improve with experience, and as such this was a decent introductory run.
**Rich Albi**, a stable companion of the winner, is related to a couple of juvenile winners and by a speedy sire. He showed signs of greenness and did well to finish as close as he did.

## 2389 MARKINGTON CLAIMING STKS 6f

**2:40** (2:40) (F) 3-Y-O £3,255 (£930; £465) **Stalls** Low

Form RPR

3065 **1** **Arfinnit (IRE)**[4] 2266 3-8-11 64 (v) ACulhane 2 64
(MRChannon) *cl up: led over 2f out: sn rdn and kpt on wl fnl f* **3/1**[1]

-430 **2** 1½ **Obe Bold (IRE)**[5] 2252 3-8-4 60 JCarroll 4 53
(ABerry) *trckd ldrs: effrt 2f out: sn rdn and kpt on ins last* **9/2**[3]

-060 **3** shd **Wares Home (IRE)**[36] 1506 3-9-3 67 (v[1]) DarrenWilliams 1 65
(KRBurke) *led: rdn along and hdd over 2f out: sn drvn and one pce ins last* **5/1**

15-0 **4** 3 **Maunby Raver**[139] 462 3-9-7 65 GFaulkner 5 60
(PCHaslam) *chsd ldrs: rdn along over 2f out: drvn and wknd ent last* **4/1**[2]

1020 **5** 7 **Could She Be Magic (IRE)**[13] 2036 3-8-2 55 (b) DaleGibson 6 20
(TDEasterby) *chsd ldrs: rdn along 1/2-way: wknd 2f out* **3/1**[1]

-000 **6** 14 **Wilheheckaslike**[28] 1699 3-8-3 35 (vt) JBramhill 3 —
(WStorey) *sn outpcd and bhd fr 1/2-way* **33/1**

1m 13.75s (0.85) **Going Correction** +0.05s/f (Good) **6** Ran SP% **107.8**
Speed ratings: **96,94,93,89,80 61**CSF £15.28 TOTE £2.90: £1.50, £2.00; EX 10.90.
**Owner** Tim Corby **Bred** Robert De Vere Hunt **Trained** West Ilsley, Berks

**FOCUS**
A modest claimer and an ordinary time.

**NOTEBOOK**
**Arfinnit(IRE)**, a lazy sort who ran better on faster ground in a first-time visor the week before, was helped by the drop in grade. He did not have an easy task on official ratings, and may suffer a little in the handicap as a result.
**Obe Bold(IRE)**, who has been struggling this season after some good efforts as a juvenile, ran a little better but was entitled to do so based on the weights and official ratings.
**Wares Home(IRE)**, who has been struggling of late, appreciated the return to a shorter trip ansd sounder surface.
**Maunby Raver**, both of whose wins have been on Fibresand, had a difficult task at the weights on his first run for 20 weeks and did not fare badly.

## 2390 BLACK SHEEP BREWERY H'CAP 1m 2f

**3:10** (3:11) (E) (0-70,70) 3-Y-O £4,309 (£1,326; £663; £331) **Stalls** High

Form RPR

0-20 **1** **Daggers Canyon**[38] 1467 3-8-6 **58** LisaJones(3) 6 66
(JulianPoulton) *led 3f: cl up tl led again over 2f out: rdn over 1f out: kpt on wl fnl f* **33/1**

0-62 **2** ½ **Fitting Guest (IRE)**[7] 2197 3-9-2 **65** PRobinson 5 72
(GGMargarson) *trckd ldrs: hdwy 3f out: rdn to chse wnr wl over 1f out: sn drvn: edgd rt and ev ch: kpt on* **3/1**[1]

0-03 **3** 1½ **Wing Collar**[15] 1995 3-9-2 **65** WSupple 9 69+
(TDEasterby) *towards rr: hdwy 3f out: rdn wl over 1f out: styd on ins last: nrst fin* **14/1**

54-0 **4** nk **Redi (ITY)**[52] 1241 3-9-4 **67** DHolland 12 71
(LMCumani) *in tch: hdwy on inner 3f out: rdn to chse ldrs 2f out: drvn and one pce ent last* **7/2**[2]

0044 **5** 3 **Heartbeat**[41] 1389 3-7-12 **47** DaleGibson 14 45
(PJMcbride) *midfield: hdwy on inner 3f out: kpt on wl fnl 2f: nrst fin* **22/1**

1526 **6** nk **Always Flying (USA)**[18] 1932 3-9-7 **70** KDalgleish 8 67
(MJohnston) *cl up: led after 3f: rdn along 3f out and sn hdd: drvn and one pce fnl 2f* **9/1**

0-00 **7** ½ **Planters Punch (IRE)**[28] 1683 3-8-13 **62** MartinDwyer 1 58
(RHannon) *bhd tl styd on fnl 2f: nt rch ldrs* **20/1**

6222 **8** 1¼ **Biscar Two (IRE)**[11] 2088 3-8-0 **49** JBramhill 11 43
(RMWhitaker) *bhd: rdn along over 3f out: styd on u.p fnl 2f: nvr a factor* **8/1**

-003 **9** 1 **Strangely Brown (IRE)**[18] 1946 3-8-3 **55** BReilly(3) 10 47
(SCWilliams) *keen: trckd ldrs: stmbld bdly home turn: effrt 3f out: rdn along 2f out and sn wknd* **7/1**[3]

4130 **10** 2 **Dispol Veleta**[10] 2134 3-9-4 **67** KDarley 13 55
(TDBarron) *hld up: hdwy over 3f out: rdn and btn 2f out* **8/1**

456- **11** 2½ **Euippe**[238] 5284 3-9-1 **64** MFenton 2 48
(JGGiven) *a rr* **33/1**

20-0 **12** 9 **Pearl Pride (USA)**[15] 1995 3-9-7 **70** JFanning 7 36
(MJohnston) *chsd ldrs: rdn along 3f out: grad wknd* **25/1**

05-0 **13** nk **Storm Clouds**[24] 1771 3-8-1 **53** ow1 DAllan(3) 4 19
(TDEasterby) *a rr* **40/1**

062- **14** 7 **Acca Larentia (IRE)**[221] 5621 3-8-8 **57** VHalliday 15 10
(RMWhitaker) *in tch: rdn along over 4f out: sn lost pl and bhd fnl 2f* **50/1**

6-60 **15** 26 **Raheed (IRE)**[33] 1559 3-9-2 **65** ACulhane 3 —
(EALDunlop) *a bhd: t.o fnl 3f* **25/1**

2m 7.28s (-0.72) **Going Correction** +0.05s/f (Good) **15** Ran SP% **125.7**
Speed ratings: **104,103,102,102,99 99,99,98,97,95 93,86,86,80,59**CSF £126.09 CT £1538.54 TOTE £30.80: £6.50, £1.80, £2.40; EX 295.00.
**Owner** S M Kemp **Bred** Ellis Stud Partnership **Trained** Kentford, Suffolk

**FOCUS**
A moderate handicap featuring a number of unexposed sorts, but run at a fair gallop and the form looks fairly solid.

**NOTEBOOK**
**Daggers Canyon** adopted positive tactics on this return to a longer trip and they paid off. He seems to take after his dam's side and may get further in time.
**Fitting Guest(IRE)**, who was ridden from the front last time, was not made quite as much use of but seemed to run his race and looks to have a similar race in him. He may appreciate another couple of furlongs.
**Wing Collar** ran a similar race to his previous outing, finishing well from off the pace. He looks as if a return to 12 furlongs will be in his favour.

**Redi(ITY)**, stepping up in trip, seems to be gradually finding his feet and is the sort that his trainer does well with.
**Heartbeat** has finished well on the two occasions she has been ridden from behind, but did not get home when ridden prominently. She is slipping in the weights and may eventually find an opportunity in banded races.
**Always Flying(USA)** seems happier on a sound surface, but was run out of it after being up with the pace from the start.
**Pearl Pride(USA)** *Official explanation: jockey said filly got tired and failed to get the trip.*

## 2391 NICK WILMOT-SMITH MEMORIAL H'CAP — 6f
**3:40** (3:41) (C) (0-95,88) 3-Y-0+ — **£9,100** (£3,451; £1,725; £784) **Stalls** Low

Form — RPR

-100 **1** — **Steel Blue**[24] 1765 4-9-11 **85** ........ ACulhane 10 — 94
(RMWhitaker) *mde most far side and sn overall ldr: rdn along over 1f out: drvn and styd on wl fnl f* — **10/1**

1046 **2** 1½ **Johnston's Diamond (IRE)**[18] 1923 6-10-0 **88** ........ WSupple 9 — 93
(EJAlston) *cl up far side: effrt 2f out: sn rdn and ev ch tl drvn and nt qckn ins laast* — **8/1**

5006 **3** 1½ **Time N Time Again**[11] 2091 6-8-7 **70** ........(p) DAllan(3) 12 — 70
(EJAlston) *chsd ldrs far side: rdn along over 2f out: kpt on under fnl f* — **12/1**

5043 **4** ¾ **Romany Nights (IRE)**[31] 1608 4-9-2 **76** ........(v) DHolland 4 — 74
(JWUnett) *trckd ldr stands side: swtchd lft and hdwy over 1f out: rdn ld that gp ent last: kpt on: no ch w far side* — **7/2**[1]

045- **5** ¾ **Blythe Spirit**[213] 5747 5-8-12 **75** ........ THamilton(3) 1 — 71
(RAFahey) *led stands side gp: rdn along 2f out: edgd rt and hdd ent last: one pce* — **7/1**[3]

-000 **6** 1½ **Obe One**[10] 2132 4-8-9 **69** ........ JCarroll 8 — 60
(ABerry) *chsd ldrs far side: effrt over 2f out and ev ch tl rdn and wknd appr last* — **16/1**

0-05 **7** ¾ **Undeterred**[4] 2261 8-9-3 **77** ........ KDarley 2 — 66
(TDBarron) *trckd ldrs stands side: effrt and n.m.r wl over 1f out: swtchd rt and rdn ent last: no imp* — **4/1**[2]

0036 **8** 1 **Armagnac**[4] 2261 6-9-5 **79** ........ MartinDwyer 11 — 65
(MABuckley) *swtchd lft s: bhd stands side: hdwy over 2f out: rdn and wknd wl over 1f out* — **7/1**[3]

00-0 **9** 2 **Extinguisher**[57] 1175 5-8-6 **66** ........ ANicholls 5 — 46
(DNicholls) *chsd ldrs stands side: rdn along 1/2-way: wknd 2f out* — **16/1**

02-5 **10** 2 **Fiore Di Bosco (IRE)**[11] 2075 3-8-6 **80** ........ PMakin(5) 7 — 54
(TDBarron) *c hased ldrs stands side: rdn 2f out and sn wknd* — **20/1**

1000 **11** nk **Wainwright (IRE)**[10] 2118 4-8-0 **60** ........ JBramhill 6 — 33
(PABlockley) *chsd ldrs stands side: rdn along over 2f out and sn wknd* — **33/1**

1m 12.11s (-0.79) **Going Correction** +0.05s/f (Good) — **11** Ran SP% **114.6**
**WFA** 3 from 4yo+ 9lb
Speed ratings: **107,105,103,102,101 99,98,96,94,91 90**CSF £85.35 CT £684.81 TOTE £10.30: £4.00, £3.40, £2.80; EX 102.60 TRIFECTA Not won..
**Owner** Country Lane Partnership **Bred** R T And Mrs Watson **Trained** Scarcroft, W Yorks

**FOCUS**
A competitive sprint run in a reasonable time for the grade, but dominated by those that switched to race on the far side. The race should throw up some winners.

**NOTEBOOK**
**Steel Blue**, who had disappointed in two outings since making all at the Lincoln meeting, made the switch to the faster ground on the far rail and, getting an uncontested lead, was always in command. He is a difficult horse to beat when things fall right for him, but will not find things easy from his revised mark.
**Johnston's Diamond(IRE)** is a consistent sort at this level but, although he handles a fast surface, he does seem to appreciate a little cut in the ground.
**Time N Time Again**, who was in good form on the All-Weather early in the year, is gradually slipping to a mark that reflects his ability on turf.
**Romany Nights(IRE)** does not have a great strike-rate for one of his ability, but did nothing wrong this time and came out best of those racing on the stands' side. His last win was just over a year ago, but the signs are that his turn is not far away.
**Blythe Spirit**, who raced without the eyeshield this time, stays further and the best use was made of his stamina on this drop in trip. A slight drop in grade may see him winning again.
**Obe One**, needs a sharp five furlongs and fast ground to be seen at his best, and is certainly on a winning mark if he gets those conditions.
**Undeterred** is gradually running into form and we can expect to see the best of him later in the summer.

## 2392 GRANTLEY MAIDEN STKS — 1m
**4:10** (4:40) (D) 3-Y-0 — **£4,881** (£1,502; £751; £375) **Stalls** High

Form — RPR

63 **1** — **Lucayan Legend (IRE)**[7] 2204 3-9-0 ........ MartinDwyer 4 — 82
(RHannon) *chsd ldrs: hdwy 3f out: rdn to ld over 1f out: styd on* — **10/1**[3]

62 **2** 1¼ **Grand But One (IRE)**[10] 2113 3-9-0 ........ ACulhane 12 — 79
(BWHills) *cl up: led wl over 2f out: sn rdn: drvn and hdd over 1f out: kpt on* — **4/7**[1]

**3** 5 **Murbaat (IRE)** 3-9-0 ........ PMcCabe 11 — 68
(ACStewart) *bhd: swtchd outside and hdwy 2f out: rdn and edgd rt ins last: nrst fin* — **40/1**

0- **4** nk **Bluetoria**[318] 3208 3-8-9 ........ JFanning 3 — 62
(JAGlover) *bhd: gd hdwy 4f out: styd on fnl 2f: nrst fin* — **100/1**

5- **5** 7 **Soviet Treat (IRE)**[254] 4911 3-8-9 95 ........ KDalgleish 10 — 46
(MJohnston) *led: rdn along 3f out: sn hdd and grad wknd* — **7/2**[2]

-000 **6** 5 **Red Monarch (IRE)**[8] 2165 3-9-0 ........ DeanMcKeown 14 — 39
(PABlockley) *in tch: rdn along 4f out: drvn 3f out and sn wknd* — **66/1**

-004 **7** nk **Unprecedented (IRE)**[9] 2145 3-9-0 50........(v) WSupple 1 — 39
(TTClement) *chsd ldrs: rdn over 3f out: sn wknd* — **100/1**

032- **8** 5 **Fanling Lady**[232] 5414 3-8-9 74 ........ ANicholls 5 — 22
(DNicholls) *chsd ldrs: rdn along over 3f out: sn wknd* — **20/1**

50 **9** 6 **Nod's Star**[22] 1820 3-8-9 ........ DaleGibson 2 — —
(MissJACamacho) *a bhd* — **66/1**

50 **10** 1¾ **Blue Nun**[9] 2144 3-8-9 ........ JCarroll 8 — —
(MrsADuffield) *a rr* — **100/1**

000 **11** 1¼ **Ghantoot**[7] 2195 3-9-0 ........ KDarley 6 — —
(LMCumani) *in tch: rdn along over 4f out: sn wknd* — **25/1**

40 **12** 1¾ **Estepona**[24] 1771 3-9-0 ........ GParkin 7 — —
(MissJACamacho) *a bhd* — **66/1**

1m 40.56s (-0.54) **Going Correction** +0.05s/f (Good) — **12** Ran SP% **113.5**
Speed ratings: **104,102,97,97,90 85,85,80,74,72 71,69**CSF £14.48 TOTE £10.00: £1.90, £1.10, £6.20; EX 22.80.
**Owner** Lucayan Stud **Bred** Bernard Cooke **Trained** East Everleigh, Wilts
■ The race was delayed for half an hour due to swans on the track and the need to sand the home turn.

**FOCUS**
A fair maiden with little strength in depth on paper and mixed form, but the first two came clear.

**NOTEBOOK**
**Lucayan Legend(IRE)** is progressing with racing, and got off the mark with a performance that suggests there is more to come. A lot will depend on what mark the Handicapper gives him.
**Grand But One(IRE)**, again had to play second fiddle, despite pulling well clear of the remainder. He also qualifies for handicaps now, and will no doubt be placed to score before long.
**Murbaat(IRE)**, a debutant with a stamina-laden pedigree, was doing his best work at the finish and, although his half-brother was best around this trip, he looks certain to appreciate a good deal further in time. *Official explanation: jockey said colt was hanging*
**Bluetoria**, who missed the break and was tailed off on her only previous appearance 12 months ago, produced a much more encouraging effort and should appreciate another couple of furlongs in time.
**Soviet Treat(IRE)**, making her debut for current connections, was somewhat disappointing and her official rating looks on the high side judged on this performance.
**Nod's Star** *Official explanation: jockey said filly was never travelling*
**Ghantoot** *Official explanation: jockey said colt was never travelling*
**Estepona** *Official explanation: jockey said gelding was never travelling*

## 2393 GALPHAY CLASSIFIED STKS — 1m 2f
**4:40** (5:01) (E) 3-Y-0+ — **£4,104** (£1,263; £631; £315) **Stalls** High

Form — RPR

1-34 **1** — **Polar Jem**[15] 2000 4-9-3 73 ........ AMcCarthy 6 — 82
(GGMargarson) *mde all: rdn 2f out: styd on strly* — **6/1**

4-21 **2** 4 **Aleron (IRE)**[13] 2039 6-9-5 72 ........ KDarley 3 — 76
(JJQuinn) *chsd ldrs: rdn along: n.m.r and outpcd wl over 2f out: styd on ins last* — **11/4**[1]

54-5 **3** nk **Stateroom (USA)**[101] 768 6-9-2 72........(b) LisaJones(3) 7 — 76
(JARToller) *trckd ldrs: hdwy on inner over 3f out: rdn over 2f out: drvn and kpt on fnl f* — **7/1**

0-03 **4** ½ **Stallone**[9] 2142 7-9-5 72 ........ RWinston 4 — 75
(NWilson) *hld up: hdwy 4f out: rdn to chse wnr wl over 1f out: drvn and wknd ins last* — **10/3**[2]

0410 **5** 5 **Jimmy Byrne (IRE)**[7] 2216 4-9-0 72 ........ TEaves(5) 2 — 65
(BEllison) *cl up: rdn along 3f out: drvn and wknd fnl 2f* — **25/1**

531- **6** 2½ **Opening Ceremony (USA)**[210] 5823 5-8-11 68........ THamilton(3) 1 — 56
(RAFahey) *cl up: rdn along 3f out: drvn 2f out and sn wknd* — **8/1**

120 **7** 1½ **Megan's Magic**[18] 1931 4-9-0 69 ........ JBramhill 5 — 53
(WStorey) *s.i.s: hdwy on outer 3f out: rdn to chse ldrs over 2f out: sn wknd* — **4/1**[3]

2m 6.87s (-1.13) **Going Correction** +0.05s/f (Good) — **7** Ran SP% **111.5**
Speed ratings: **106,102,102,102,98 96,94**CSF £21.68 TOTE £6.40: £3.00, £1.80; EX 21.30.
**Owner** Norcroft Park Stud **Bred** Norcroft Park Stud **Trained** Newmarket, Suffolk

**FOCUS**
A competitive classified event on paper run at in a fair time and producing a decisive winner who looks to have improved.

**NOTEBOOK**
**Polar Jem**, getting her favoured ground for the first time this season, set off in front and, quickening halfway up the straight, was always going to hold on.
**Aleron(IRE)**, whose last win came on heavy ground in first-time cheekpieces, acts on this surface but could not quicken as well as the winner. He possibly needs a softer surface to blunt his rivals' speed.
**Stateroom(USA)**, having his first run since February, had his ground and ran quite well. He should be better for the outing. he has yet to prove he truly stays this trip.
**Stallone**, who stays further than this, probably did not have the race run to suit.
**Megan's Magic**, whose form this season has been at shorter trips on easy ground, was again slowly away but could never get in a blow on this faster surface.

## 2394 STUDLEY ROYAL H'CAP — 1m 4f 60y
**5:10** (5:23) (E) (0-75,71) 3-Y-0+ — **£4,095** (£1,260; £630; £315) **Stalls** High

Form — RPR

3-02 **1** — **Albinus**[8] 2169 3-8-11 **71** ........(b) MartinDwyer 1 — 86
(AMBalding) *mde all: rn wd bnd 6f out and on home turn: qcknd 3f out: rdn wl over 1f out and styd on strly* — **9/4**[1]

60-3 **2** 6 **Santiburi Lad (IRE)**[17] 1962 7-8-8 **54** ........ THamilton(3) 4 — 59
(NWilson) *keen: trckd ldrs: hdwy on outer 3f out: rdn to chse wnr over 1f out: sn drvn and one pce* — **12/1**

6-05 **3** hd **Distant Cousin**[5] 2235 7-9-7 **64**........(v) JFanning 3 — 69
(MABuckley) *trckd ldrs: hdwy 4f out: rdn 2f out: kpt on same pce* — **10/1**

3352 **4** 2½ **Trouble Mountain (USA)**[7] 2216 7-9-10 **67**........(b) KDarley 5 — 68
(MWEasterby) *hld up in tch: hdwy 4f out: rdn to chse ldrs over 2f out: sn drvn and one pce* — **7/2**[3]

6-61 **5** hd **Field Spark**[7] 2212 4-9-3 **60** 6ex........(p) DHolland 7 — 60
(JAGlover) *hld up in rr: effrt and sme hdwy 3f out: rdn 2f out and sn no imp* — **5/2**[2]

00-1 **6** 10 **Royal Melbourne (IRE)**[13] 2038 4-8-12 **55** ........ RWinston 6 — 39
(MissJACamacho) *prom: chsd wnr 1/2-way: rdn along 3f out: wknd 2f out* — **7/1**

2m 42.24s (2.34) **Going Correction** +0.05s/f (Good) — **6** Ran SP% **110.8**
**WFA** 3 from 4yo+ 17lb
Speed ratings: **94,90,89,88,88 81**CSF £27.21 TOTE £2.60: £1.60, £4.90; EX 41.80 Place 6 £93.46, Place 5 £73.81.
**Owner** Miss K Rausing **Bred** Miss K Rausing **Trained** Kingsclere, Hants

**FOCUS**
A modest handicap run at a very steady early pace, and resulting in a runaway winner that was allowed to dominate.

**NOTEBOOK**
**Albinus**, touch off last time, again had the blinkers fitted and, despite running wide on the bends, came right away from his older rivals in the straight. As a half-brother to Alborada and Albanova among others, he is likely to continue to improve.
**Santiburi Lad(IRE)**, trying his longest trip on the Flat to-date, seemed to run his race but may not have got home. He is one to look out for if dropped back to ten furlongs, especially at Redcar, where he has a fair record.
**Distant Cousin** has not won on turf for two years, but is not getting any help from the Handicapper following a series of decent efforts last season.
**Trouble Mountain(USA)** is proving notoriously difficult to win with, and the blinkers have made little difference. His best chance of winning is if he gets a fast early pace and those in front stop, but generally he is a better place than win bet.
**Field Spark**, who had the race run to suit last time, had a 6lb penalty and did not get the good gallop he needs this time. *Official explanation: jockey said gelding hung left*
T/Plt: £174.30 to a £1 stake. Pool: £32,561.40. 136.30 winning tickets. T/Qpdt: £71.50 to a £1 stake. Pool: £1,546.00. 16.00 winning tickets. JR

# [2240] GOODWOOD (R-H)

Wednesday, May 26

**OFFICIAL GOING: Straight course - good; round course - good to firm**

## 2395 SOLENT SKY - HOME OF THE SPITFIRE (S) STKS (H'CAP) 1m 3f

**6:10** (6:11) (F) (0-55,55) 3-Y-O **£3,386** (£1,042; £521; £260) **Stalls** Low

Form RPR

06-3 **1** **Garston Star**[31] [1643] 3-8-6 **52**.......................................... MartinDwyer 7 59
(JSMoore) *mde all: rdn and styd on fnl 3f: r.o wl fnl f: readily* **6/1**[3]

1234 **2** *2* **Oktis Morilious (IRE)**[13] [2054] 3-7-11 **46** oh1.............. JFMcDonald(3) 6 50
(AWCarroll) *lw: chsd ldrs: rdn 3f out: styd on to chse wnr appr fnl f: sn no imp* **7/2**[1]

0-6 **3** *5* **Mr Strowger**[23] [1844] 3-8-1 **47**.......................................... RLMoore 2 43
(ACharlton) *lw: chsd wnr: rdn 3f out: no imp fnl 2f and lost 2nd over 1f out* **7/2**[1]

3405 **4** *nk* **Princess Ismene**[12] [2088] 3-7-12 **47**.........................(b) FPFerris(3) 4 42
(PABlockley) *in tch: rdn 3f out: swtchd lft over 2f out and sn outpcd* **8/1**

-000 **5** *4* **Spring Dancer**[13] [2061] 3-8-7 **53**.......................................... TQuinn 8 42
(BGPowell) *v.s.a: in tch after 4f: hdwy on outside fr 4f out: nvr gng pce to rch ldrs and wknd 2f out* **13/2**

-000 **6** *3 ½* **Grist Mist (IRE)**[16] [1998] 3-8-9 **55**.......................................(t) RHavlin 3 38
(MrsPNDutfield) *sn in tch: rdn and effrt over 3f out: nvr rchd ldrs and wknd over 2f out* **14/1**

5451 **7** *3 ½* **Flying Spud**[12] [2088] 3-8-4 **50**.......................................... ADaly 5 28
(JLSpearing) *broke wl: stdd rr after 2f: rdn over 3f out and sn btn* **5/1**[2]

00-0 **8** *17* **True Patriot**[12] [2085] 3-8-7 **53**.......................................(b[1]) JFEgan 9 —
(PMitchell) *a bhd: no ch fr over 3f out* **20/1**

-000 **9** *3 ½* **Altares**[65] [1080] 3-8-0 **46** oh11.......................................... CCatlin 1 —
(PHowling) *b. a bhd: lost tch fr over 3f out* **33/1**

2m 28.35s (2.24) **Going Correction** -0.025s/f (Good) **9** Ran SP% **114.2**
Speed ratings: **90,88,84,84,81 79,76,64,61**CSF £26.97 CT £84.36 TOTE £4.10: £2.00, £1.40, £1.60; EX 17.60.There was no bid for the winner.
**Owner** East Garston Racing **Bred** Mrs P Lewis **Trained** East Garston, Berks

**FOCUS**
Ordinary stuff, but a sound performance from Garston Star who led throughout for a comfy success, albeit in a modest time.

**NOTEBOOK**
**Garston Star**, a decent third in a better race last time, had the run of it from the front and found what was required to run out a comfy winner. He is capable of winning again, but strikes as the type to do well in the juvenile hurdle division later in the year.
**Oktis Morilious(IRE)**, whose sole success to date came at banded level, ran well in defeat and pulled five lengths clear of the third.
**Mr Strowger** improved on previous form for this step up in trip and has a poor race in him.
**Princess Ismene** ran another fair race without being good enough.
**Spring Dancer**, who lost ground at the start, looked likely to play a hand in the finish with half a mile to run, but failed to make any further progress and was held two out.

## 2396 GOODWOOD FLYING SCHOOL MAIDEN AUCTION STKS 5f

**6:40** (6:42) (E) 2-Y-O **£4,075** (£1,254; £627; £313) **Stalls** Low

Form RPR

45 **1** **Elisha (IRE)**[11] [2129] 2-8-4 .......................................... CCatlin 6 67
(DMSimcock) *mde all: drvn and styd on wl fnl f* **8/1**[3]

05 **2** *1 ½* **Clinet (IRE)**[12] [2096] 2-8-2 .......................................... JFEgan 7 59
(PMPhelan) *s.i.s: sn rcvrd: hdwy 2f out: styd on wl to chse wnr fnl f but no imp* **16/1**

**3** *1 ¾* **Elsie Wagg (USA)** 2-8-9 .......................................... KFallon 8 59
(MJWallace) *unf: chsd ldrs: wnt 2nd over 3f out: sn rdn: no imp on wnr and lost 2nd fnl f* **10/3**[2]

**4** *2 ½* **Blue Marble** 2-8-13 .......................................... DHolland 11 53
(CEBrittain) *leggy: cmpt: sn trcking ldrs: pushed along and effrt ins fnl 2f: styd on same pce fnl f* **12/1**

3232 **5** *1 ½* **Grand Option**[13] [2057] 2-8-6 .......................................... TPQueally(3) 4 43
(BWDuke) *chsd ldr tl over 3f out: rdn over 2f out: wknd fnl f* **3/1**[1]

4 **6** *½* **Ragged Glory (IRE)**[8] [2205] 2-8-13 .......................................... PDobbs 3 45
(RHannon) *lw: sn trcking ldrs: n.m.r on rails 3f out: sn pushed along and outpcd: styd on again fnl f but nt a danger* **3/1**[1]

**7** *3* **Tight Circle** 2-8-2 .......................................... JMackay 9 22
(MrsGHarvey) *leggy: unf: wnt rt s: sn chsng ldrs: rdn over 2f out: wknd over 1f out* **50/1**

**8** *hd* **Chek Oi** 2-8-13 .......................................... MartinDwyer 2 32
(WRMuir) *w'like: b.bkwd: sn outpcd* **16/1**

**9** *nk* **Secret Diva (IRE)** 2-7-13 .......................................... JFMcDonald(3) 1 20
(MrsPNDutfield) *w'like: sn outpcd* **40/1**

**10** *¾* **Lily Lenat** 2-8-4 .......................................... TQuinn 10 20
(JRBoyle) *w'like: b.bkwd: wnt rt s: s.i.s: outpcd* **25/1**

**11** *nk* **Lakesdale (IRE)** 2-8-5 ow1.......................................... TEDurcan 5 18
(MRChannon) *leggy: neat: s.i.s: outpcd* **16/1**

59.39 secs (0.34) **Going Correction** -0.025s/f (Good) **11** Ran SP% **117.8**
Speed ratings: **96,93,90,86,84 83,78,78,78,76 76**CSF £125.58 TOTE £11.00: £2.90, £4.00, £1.70; EX 111.00.
**Owner** Good Connection Ii **Bred** Miss Carmel O'Brien **Trained** Newmarket, Suffolk
■ A first winner for trainer David Simcock.

**FOCUS**
Nothing more than an average juvenile maiden and the form is mixed.

**NOTEBOOK**
**Elisha(IRE)** had looked pretty exposed in two previous outings, but found this improvement in form from somewhere and ran right away with it in the final furlong. Nurseries look set to provide her with the best chance of winning again.
**Clinet(IRE)**, a disappointment last time over six, was unable to reverse Windsor form with the winner, but did more than enough to suggest he can pick up a small race.
**Elsie Wagg(USA)** showed plenty on this racecourse debut and can land an ordinary maiden.
**Blue Marble**, who is bred to ideally want a bit further, showed up well for three parts of the race before being tapped for speed late on. This son of Fraam will improve for an extra furlong and may turn out to be the best of this bunch.
**Grand Option** is well exposed and continues to struggle to find an opening.
**Ragged Glory(IRE)** went the wrong way from his promising debut run and may now be more of a type for nurseries later on in the season.

## 2397 WOODWARD AT GOODWOOD 60TH BIRTHDAY STKS (H'CAP) 1m 4f

**7:10** (7:12) (C) (0-95,91) 3-Y-O **£9,486** (£2,919; £1,459; £729) **Stalls** Low

Form RPR

64-0 **1** **Admiral (IRE)**[39] [1461] 3-8-6 **76**.......................................... KFallon 2 84
(SirMichaelStoute) *lw: hld up: trckd ldrs: qcknd to ld over 2f out: pushed along and kpt finding ex whn strly chal last half f: readily* **9/2**[3]

-001 **2** *nk* **Watamu (IRE)**[6] [2244] 3-8-13 **83** 5ex.......................................... DHolland 5 91
(PJMakin) *lw: in tch: hdwy 3f out: rdn over 2f out: edgd lft over 1f out: str run to chal last half f but a jst hld by wnr* **6/4**[1]

22-1 **3** *1 ½* **Destination Dubai (USA)**[25] [1761] 3-9-7 **91**.....................(v) KMcEvoy 4 97
(SaeedBinSuroor) *lw: led 3f: styd w ldr tl slt ld again 6f out: hdd over 2f out: kpt on wl tl outpcd ins fnl f* **6/1**

P0-4 **4** *1 ¾* **Akritas**[20] [1899] 3-9-4 **88**.......................................... TQuinn 1 91
(PFICole) *lw: bhd: hdwy: nt clr run and swtchd lft ins fnl 3f: kpt on fnl 2f but nvr gng pce to trble ldrs* **15/2**

5112 **5** *15* **Bill Bennett (FR)**[19] [1947] 3-8-7 **77**.......................................... OUrbina 6 56
(JJay) **20/1**

-122 **6** *16* **Absolutelythebest (IRE)**[13] [2070] 3-8-12 **82**.......................... WSupple 3 35
(EALDunlop) *hrd drvn s and reluctant: sn chsng ldr: jinked and led after 3f: hdd 6f out: styd w ldr tl wknd fr 3f out* **4/1**[2]

2m 37.2s (-1.73) **Going Correction** -0.025s/f (Good) **6** Ran SP% **109.0**
Speed ratings: **104,103,102,101,91 80**CSF £11.02 TOTE £5.90: £2.60, £1.40; EX 14.60.
**Owner** Highclere Thoroughbred Racing XI **Bred** R Lee **Trained** Newmarket, Suffolk

**FOCUS**
A good three-year-old handicap dominated in the closing stages by progressive pair Admiral and Watamu and the form looks strong.

**NOTEBOOK**
**Admiral(IRE)**, who ran in a couple of decent maidens last season, finished eighth in a hot one won by Mudawin at Newbury on his seasonal reappearance and showed improved form for this step into handicap company. He won with a little more in hand than it looked, his jockey reporting he was dossing around in front, and is the type for a competitive handicap at the Royal Meeting, possibly the King George V.
**Watamu(IRE)**, a cosy winner at the course last week, went close in trying to defy a 5lb penalty, but was just edged out of it by the winner. He is the type to keep improving, but he will need to if he is to win good races.
**Destination Dubai(USA)**, who struggled to land short odds when winning his maiden at Haydock, was not totally disgraced on this handicap debut, but is going to be hard to place off his mark.
**Akritas** has shaped as though a mile-six plus will help on both starts this season and does not have a change of pace, so was given a poor ride in the circumstances, being held up off the pace. He should improve when granted a greater test.
**Absolutelythebest(IRE)**appeared far from enthusiastic about the game, looking reluctant to race and receiving a couple of reminders early to get to the lead. He is one to leave alone. *Official explanation: jockey said colt slipped on the first bend and lost a shoe.*

## 2398 ON THE HOUSE STKS (LISTED RACE) 1m

**7:45** (7:46) (A) 3-Y-O+ **£17,850** (£6,600; £3,300; £1,500) **Stalls** High

Form RPR

02-2 **1** **Kalaman (IRE)**[42] [1397] 4-9-5 116.......................................... KFallon 5 112
(SirMichaelStoute) *lw: trckd ldrs: drvn and str run to ld last half f: kpt on wl* **2/5**[1]

631- **2** *¾* **Imtiyaz (USA)**[245] [5155] 5-9-8 109.......................................(t) WSupple 2 113
(SaeedBinSuroor) *sn led: rdn and styd on wl whn chal fr 2f out: hdd and nt ex last half f* **7/2**[2]

40-3 **3** *nk* **Vanderlin**[53] [1242] 5-9-8 105.......................................... MartinDwyer 4 112
(AMBalding) *lw: sn trcking ldr: rdn to chal fr 2f out: upsides over 1f out: fnd no ex u.p ins last* **20/1**

2100 **4** *5* **Grand Passion (IRE)**[20] [1902] 4-9-5 103.......................................... SDrowne 3 98
(GWragg) *hld up in rr: sme hdwy 3f out: nvr gng pce to rch ldrs and wknd ins fnl 2f* **16/1**[3]

6-50 **5** *7* **Kings Point (IRE)**[39] [1459] 3-8-12 104.......................................... DaneO'Neill 1 87
(RHannon) *t.k.h: chsd ldrs: rdn 3f out: sn btn* **20/1**

1m 38.51s (-1.76) **Going Correction** -0.025s/f (Good)
**WFA** 3 from 4yo+ 12lb **5** Ran SP% **109.1**
Speed ratings: **107,106,105,100,93**CSF £2.02 TOTE £1.30: £1.10, £1.40; EX 1.90.
**Owner** H H Aga Khan **Bred** His Highness The Aga Khan's Studs S C **Trained** Newmarket, Suffolk

**FOCUS**
An ordinary time for this Listed contest won by Kalaman who continues to fail to live up to his reputation, but the form is decent for the grade.

**NOTEBOOK**
**Kalaman(IRE)**, reportedly in need of the run when a costly failure to many on his seasonal reappearance, faced a lesser bunch, but again failed to impress, winning nowhere near as easily as his previous form and official rating entitled him to. Being a big horse, it is possible he was still in need of it a little, but he has done nothing to date to suggest he is worthy of stepping back up to the highest level.
**Imtiyaz(USA)** was 10lb badly in with Kalaman at the weights and ran mighty well on what was his seasonal debut. His trainer has a good record at improving older horses and there should be more to come from him.
**Vanderlin** was a stone wrong' with the favourite and recorded arguably his best-ever effort, being beaten under a length.
**Grand Passion(IRE)** appears to have lost his form and never looked like getting into it.
**Kings Point(IRE)** has not shown enough thus far to suggest he as trained on.

## 2399 GOODWOOD AERODROME STKS (H'CAP) 6f

**8:15** (8:18) (D) (0-80,80) 3-Y-O+ **£5,616** (£1,728; £864; £432) **Stalls** Low

Form RPR

0-00 **1** **Idle Power (IRE)**[19] [1927] 6-9-4 **70**.............................(p) MartinDwyer 14 84
(JRBoyle) *trckd ldrs: drvn and styd on strly to ld wl ins last* **13/2**[2]

111- **2** *nk* **Devon Flame**[314] [3350] 5-8-11 **66**.......................................... JFMcDonald(3) 11 79
(RJHodges) *t.k.h: trckd ldr tl led appr fnl 2f: kpt on u.p tl hdd and no ex wl ins last* **8/1**

0655 **3** *¾* **Double M**[6] [2246] 7-7-10 **53** oh3 ow3.............................(v) RThomas(5) 16 64
(MrsLRichards) *lw: in tch: hdwy over 1f out: styd on wl fnl f but nt pce of ldrs cl home* **7/1**[3]

0546 **4** *1* **Full Spate**[8] [2219] 9-9-3 **69**.......................................... RLMoore 2 77+
(JMBradley) *lw: s.i.s: bhd: hdwy 2f out: r.o fnl f but nvr gng pce to rch ldrs* **10/1**

0006 **5** *shd* **Firework**[20] [1909] 6-8-9 **61**.......................................(p) TQuinn 10 68
(JAkehurst) *led tl hdd appr fnl 2f: styd w ldrs tl outpcd ins last* **16/1**

1203 **6** *nk* **Attorney**[9] [2166] 6-7-7 **50**.......................................(v) HayleyTurner(5) 9 57
(DShaw) *b. hld up mid-div: rdn and hdwy over 1f out: r.o ins last but no imp on ldrs* **16/1**

36-0 **7** *1 ¼* **Nivernais**[37] [1504] 5-10-0 **80**.......................................... DaneO'Neill 7 83
(HCandy) *bhd: rdn and gd hdwy over 1f out: nt qckn ins last* **9/1**

0-00 **8** *2 ½* **Coranglais**[13] [2064] 4-9-3 **69**.......................................... CCatlin 8 64
(JMBradley) *in tch: rdn and hdwy 2f out: wknd ins fnl f* **25/1**

4606 **9** ½ **Long Weekend (IRE)**[9] 2166 6-7-12 **50** oh4....................(v) JMackay 12 44
(DShaw) *lw: s.i.s: rdn and sme hdwy 1/2-way: wknd fnl f* **25/1**
5305 **10** 1¼ **Simpsons Mount (IRE)**[9] 2165 3-8-5 **66**............................ DSweeney 5 56
(RMFlower) *s.i.s: bhd: sme hdwy over 2f out: nvr gng pce to rch ldrs and wknd fnl f* **33/1**
4062 **11** ¾ **Blue Knight (IRE)**[4] 2303 5-9-6 **72**.......................................... KFallon 4 60
(APJarvis) *lw: bhd: rdn 3f out: nvr gong pce to rch ldrs* **10/3**[1]
-050 **12** ¾ **B A Highflyer**[22] 1857 4-8-11 **63**.......................................... TEDurcan 6 49
(MRChannon) *racd stands side and a outpcd* **20/1**
00-0 **13** *hd* **Ben Lomand**[57] 1185 4-9-8 **74**.......................................... PDobbs 13 59
(BWDuke) *s.i.s: sn in tch: rdn over 2f out: sn wknd* **33/1**
2400 **14** ½ **Currency**[95] 847 7-9-12 **78**.......................................... DHolland 1 61
(JMBradley) *b. swtg: racd stands side: a outpcd* **16/1**
2-00 **15** *nk* **Stokesies Wish**[37] 1504 4-8-12 **64**.......................................... SDrowne 15 47
(JLSpearing) *lw: pressed ldrs 4f: wknd over 1f out* **20/1**
1660 **16** 2 **A Teen**[12] 2094 6-8-5 **60**.......................................... LisaJones(3) 3 37
(PHowling) *b.hind: swtg: a outpcd* **25/1**

1m 11.81s (-1.03) **Going Correction** -0.025s/f (Good)
**WFA** 3 from 4yo+ 9lb **16** Ran SP% **123.7**
Speed ratings: **105,104,103,102,102 101,100,96,96,94 93,92,92,91,91 88**CSF £52.79 CT £292.57 TOTE £9.40: £2.70, £1.70, £2.30, £3.10; EX 83.20.
**Owner** The Idle B's **Bred** Mountarmstrong Stud **Trained** Epsom, Surrey

**FOCUS**
A fair but competitive sprint handicap where it paid to be drawn high. The winner has dropped a long way in the handicap.

**NOTEBOOK**
**Idle Power(IRE)**, 11lb lower than when last winning back in 2002, finally had everything go his way and having sat on the heels of the leaders, ran on strongly to edge out Devon Flame. He is to be targeted at a race on Derby Day at Epsom, but needs to go back up the ratings in order to get in, so will reappear at Brighton later in the week.
**Devon Flame**, a highly progressive sprinter towards the end of last season, winning his final three outings, was having only his eighth ever start on a racecourse and first of the season. Despite this he looked fit, but the lack of match practice may have told close home as he was caught by Idle Power. He remains progressive.
**Double M** ran on without ever looking likely to trouble the front pair and continues to pay his way.
**Full Spate** fared best of those drawn low and did well given he was slowly away.
**Firework** never faced an easy task in trying to make all the running and unsurprisingly lacked the pace of the principals when it mattered.
**Attorney** ran his usual race, staying on through beaten horses.
**Nivernais** hinted a return to winning ways is not far off, performing creditably under top-weight.
**Blue Knight(IRE)** was reported to have finished lame and the run should be ignored *Official explanation: vet said gelding was lame.*

## 2400 AVIATION INDUSTRIES STKS (H'CAP) 1m 1f
**8:45** (8:50) (D ) (0-80,79) 3-Y-O **£5,681** (£1,748; £874; £437) **Stalls** High

Form RPR
00-4 **1** **Boule D'Or (IRE)**[8] 2207 3-9-3 **75**.......................................... NDay 9 84
(RIngram) *lw: hld up in rr: hdwy and hmpd over 2f out: hdwy and nt clr run 1f out: swtchd lft and qckd wl to ld nr fin: readily* **5/1**[1]
0000 **2** 1 **Cartronageeraghlad (IRE)**[4] 2304 3-9-0 **75**................. TPQueally(3) 10 82
(JAOsborne) *hld up in rr: hdwy over 2f out: str run to chal fnl f: outpcd by wnr nr fin* **12/1**
6-00 **3** *nk* **Wild Pitch**[16] 2001 3-8-2 **60**.......................................... RLMoore 12 66
(PMitchell) *bhd: gd hdwy on rails over 3f out: swtchd lft and led over 1f out: hdd and outpcd nr fin* **20/1**
5120 **4** 4 **Phluke**[23] 1841 3-9-1 **73**.......................................... SCarson 5 71
(RFJohnsonHoughton) *lw: chsd ldr: led over 3f out: sn rdn: hdd over 1f out: wknd ins last* **11/1**
31-6 **5** 3½ **The Way We Were**[37] 1506 3-9-3 **75**.......................................... KFallon 1 66
(TGMills) *sn led: hdd over 3f out: wknd fr 2f out* **10/1**
0400 **6** *hd* **Master Mahogany**[9] 2169 3-8-11 **69**.......................................... VSlattery 6 60
(RJHodges) *in tch: hdwy and n.m.r 3f out: kpt on but nvr gng pce to trble ldrs* **25/1**
105- **7** ¾ **Uncle John**[165] 6172 3-8-9 **67**.......................................... JFEgan 7 57
(SKirk) *b.bkwd: bhd: kpt on fnl 2f but n.d* **33/1**
032 **8** 1 **Beauchamp Star**[23] 1842 3-9-2 **74**.......................................... DHolland 2 62
(GAButler) *lw: stmbld stalls: sn rcvrd and mid-div: rdn over 2f out: hung rt and sn wknd* **6/1**[2]
0-02 **9** ½ **Smoothly Does It**[16] 1997 3-8-9 **67**.......................................... TEDurcan 13 54
(MrsAJBowlby) *s.i.s: bhd: hdwy and nt clr run 3f out: swtchd rt and sn rdn: nvr nr ldrs* **5/1**[1]
126 **10** 1 **Chasing The Dream (IRE)**[24] 1799 3-9-0 **72**................ MartinDwyer 14 57
(AMBalding) *lw: chsd ldrs: rdn over 2f out: wknd fnl f* **15/2**[3]
-063 **11** 15 **Dumnoni**[37] 1506 3-9-7 **79**.......................................... NCallan 4 34
(JulianPoulton) *chsd ldrs: rdn 3f out: hung lft and rt and sn btn* **9/1**
-422 **12** 4 **Knickyknackienoo**[20] 1908 3-7-12 **56**.......................................... CCatlin 3 3
(AGNewcombe) *plld hrd: sme hdwy whn nt clr run 3f out: sn btn* **10/1**
0-00 **13** 24 **Mr Independent (IRE)**[2] 2361 3-8-5 **63**.............................(v[1]) WSupple 8 —
(EALDunlop) *chsd ldrs: rdn: bmpd and lost action ins fnl 3f: sn wknd* **16/1**

1m 56.26s (-0.60) **Going Correction** -0.025s/f (Good) **13** Ran SP% **121.0**
Speed ratings: **101,100,99,96,93 93,92,91,91,90 76,73,51**CSF £64.86 CT £789.62 TOTE £7.90: £2.70, £10.20, £13.30; EX 188.60 Place 6 £57.57, Place 5 £35.96.
**Owner** Friends and Family **Bred** Major K R Thompson **Trained** Epsom, Surrey

**FOCUS**
Only an ordinary handicap, but a good winner in Boule D'Or who showed a nice change of gear to settle it and is fairly treated on his old form.

**NOTEBOOK**
**Boule D'Or(IRE)**, who made a pleasing seasonal reappearance when fourth at Leicester, appreciated the extra quarter mile and showed a good change of pace to come through and take it up late on, having had a blocked passage on a couple of occasions. This was a good effort and he should progress again.
**Cartronageeraghlad(IRE)** left a few disappointing efforts behind with a running-on second, but the winner always had the legs of him. This at least saw a return to form. *Official explanation: jockey said gelding suffered interference in running.*
**Wild Pitch**, a handicap debutant, improved on his form in maidens and will improve again for another step up in trip. He pulled four lengths clear of the fourth and has a handicap in him.
**Phluke** ran his race, but could not repel some less exposed types.
**The Way We Were**, although a bit disappointing, is only lightly raced and capable of better.
**Master Mahogany** is ideally in need of at least another furlong and can pick up a small race in time.
**Uncle John** made a pleasing start to the campaign and is entitled to improve.
**Beauchamp Star** did not enjoy the best of times, stumbling leaving the stalls and hanging under pressure.
**Smoothly Does It** was denied a clear run through and never got into it.
**Chasing The Dream(IRE)** is becoming a bit disappointing.
T/Jkpt: Not won. T/Plt: £125.50 to a £1 stake. Pool: £53,897.65. 313.35 winning tickets. T/Qpdt: £31.10 to a £1 stake. Pool: £3,730.20. 88.60 winning tickets. ST

# 2376 LINGFIELD (L-H)
### Wednesday, May 26

**OFFICIAL GOING: Turf course - good to firm (firm in places); all-weather course - standard**

## 2401 COME RACING AT LINGFIELD MAIDEN STKS 1m 1f
**2:25** (2:27) (D ) 3-Y-O **£3,838** (£1,181; £590; £295) **Stalls** Low

Form RPR
**1** **Hasaiyda (IRE)** 3-8-9 .......................................... KFallon 8 73
(SirMichaelStoute) *lw: b.hind: cmpt: strong: scope: s.i.s: stdy hdwy 1/2-way: wnt 2nd overe 1f out: led 1f out: pushed out* **3/1**[2]
3553 **2** 2½ **Resplendent King (USA)**[35] 1541 3-9-0 65.......................... IMongan 3 73
(TGMills) *lw: led: rdn 3f out: hdd 1f out: one pce fnl f* **11/2**[3]
00 **3** 4 **Fuel Cell (IRE)**[11] 2113 3-9-0 .......................................... DaneO'Neill 7 65
(RHannon) *lw: a.p: rdn over 2f out: one pce after* **6/1**
0- **4** *nk* **Michabo (IRE)**[305] 3592 3-9-0 .......................................... TQuinn 2 64
(DRCElsworth) *b.bkwd: plld hrd: trckd ldrs: rdn over 2f out: no further hdwy* **14/1**
**5** ½ **Shuheb** 3-8-9 .......................................... DHolland 5 58
(CEBrittain) *neat: t.k.h: hld up in tch: rdn over 2f out: one pce after* **11/1**
00-0 **6** 2 **Young Love**[16] 2001 3-8-9 .......................................... SDrowne 4 54
(MissECLavelle) *hld up: struggling 1/2-way: nvr on terms* **20/1**
000- **7** *nk* **Tell The Trees**[226] 5549 3-8-6 .......................................... TPQueally(3) 6 54
(RMBeckett) *trckd ldr for 2f: wknd over 2f out* **66/1**
**8** 6 **Safa Park** 3-9-0 .......................................... KMcEvoy 1 47
(SaeedBinSuroor) *rangy: bkwd: slowly away: in rr whn rdn 3f out: hung lft ins fnl 2f and nvr on terms* **9/4**[1]

1m 56.13s (0.84) **Going Correction** +0.175s/f (Good) **8** Ran SP% **106.7**
Speed ratings: **103,100,97,96,96 94,94,89**CSF £17.05 TOTE £3.40: £1.20, £1.70, £2.30; EX 19.10.
**Owner** H H Aga Khan **Bred** His Highness The Aga Khan's Studs S C **Trained** Newmarket, Suffolk

**FOCUS**
An ordinary maiden run at just an average pace in which the betting was dominated by two newcomers from big yards. Whilst one performed, the other did not and the form as it stands is modest, though the winner is entitled to improve.

**NOTEBOOK**
**Hasaiyda(IRE)**, a half-sister to three winners including Hasanpour out of a Listed winner in Ireland, lost ground at the start and did not look happy on this tricky track at various stages, but still had enough ability to win with a degree of comfort. The form does not add up to much, but she should improve and will be suited by a more conventional track.
**Resplendent King(USA)**, who is comparatively exposed, tried to make his experience count under a positive ride and managed to fight off all bar the winner. His rating of 65 is the benchmark to the value of the form.
**Fuel Cell(IRE)** ran as though needing much further than this. He now qualifies for handicaps and in finishing four lengths behind a horse rated 65, his mark will not be very high.
**Michabo(IRE)**, not seen since his debut over six furlongs ten months ago, did not help his chances by pulling hard but does not look anything out of the ordinary in any case.
**Shuheb**, whose dam is a half-sister to the St Leger winner Shantou, may be capable of some improvement when tackling further.
**Safa Park**, a half-brother to several winners including smart performers Ozone Layer, Amusing Time and Musalsal, walked out of the stalls and trailed the field the whole way. Connections will be hoping that the fast ground and tricky track were to blame for this dismal display. *Official explanation: trainer's representative said colt may have been unsuited by the fast ground*

## 2402 FAMILY CELEBRATIONS AT LINGFIELD PARK H'CAP 1m 3f 106y
**3:00** (3:03) (F ) (0-55,55) 3-Y-O **£2,996** (£856; £428) **Stalls** High

Form RPR
00-5 **1** **Vicario**[20] 1911 3-9-0 **50**.......................................... IMongan 3 61
(MLWBell) *hld up in rr: stmbld on bnd over 3f out: rdn and sn mde hdwy: squeezed through to ld ent fnl f: rdn out* **10/1**
0-00 **2** 4 **Regal Performer (IRE)**[29] 1683 3-9-4 **54**.............................. PDobbs 7 59
(SKirk) *s.i.s: hld up in rr: rdn and hdwy 3f out: chsd wnre fnl f* **16/1**
-024 **3** 3½ **Romeo's Day**[10] 2146 3-9-2 **52**.......................................... TEDurcan 4 51
(MRChannon) *lw: towards rr: hdwy 1/2-way: rdn and ev ch 2f out: kpt on one pce* **7/2**[1]
2055 **4** 1¼ **Jackie Kiely**[23] 1843 3-9-2 **52**.......................................... RLMoore 14 49
(TGMills) *trckd ldrs: led 2f out: hdd ent fnl f: sn wknd* **7/1**[3]
0-00 **5** ¾ **Rinneen (IRE)**[16] 1998 3-9-1 **51**..................................(v[1]) DaneO'Neill 10 47
(RHannon) *slowly away and wl in rr tl rdn and styd on past btn horses ins fnl 2f* **12/1**
0-04 **6** ½ **Winslow Boy (USA)**[8] 2199 3-9-5 **55**.............................. GBaker 8 50
(CFWall) *in tch: rdn and wkng whn bmpd over 1f out* **6/1**[2]
2040 **7** *hd* **Vrisaki (IRE)**[6] 2251 3-9-3 **53**.......................................... AMcCarthy 13 48
(MissDMountain) *lw: trckd ldr after 2f: led 4f out: hdd 2f out: wknd appr fnl f* **20/1**
6-60 **8** *nk* **El Magnifico**[119] 622 3-8-12 **48**.......................................... KFallon 11 43
(PDCundell) *in tch: ev ch 2f out: weakenbing whn hmpd appr fnl f* **8/1**
0-66 **9** 9 **Saucy**[49] 1304 3-8-11 **50**..................................(b[1]) JFMcDonald(3) 6 30
(BJMeehan) *t.k.h: trckd ldr for 2f: wknd over 2f out* **20/1**
050 **10** 1¾ **Clare Galway**[67] 1064 3-8-11 **50**.............................. J-PGuillambert(3) 12 27
(TDMccarthy) *mid-div: rdn over 2f out: sn wknd* **25/1**
0-60 **11** 2½ **Donastrela (IRE)**[37] 1507 3-9-3 **53**.............................. MartinDwyer 5 26
(AMBalding) *a struggling in rr* **16/1**
-000 **12** 1½ **Littlestar (FR)**[16] 1998 3-9-2 **52**..................................(b) TQuinn 9 23
(JLDunlop) *led tl hdd 4f out: wknd over 2f out* **16/1**
0000 **13** 2 **Well Knit**[19] 1946 3-9-0 **50**.......................................... JFEgan 1 18
(PWD'Arcy) *lw: mid-div: rdn 1/2-way: wknd over 2f out* **12/1**
-606 **14** *dist* **Unintentional**[19] 1946 3-9-2 **52**.......................................... DHolland 2 —
(RBrotherton) *in tch tl wknd 5f out: eased over 2f out: t.o* **10/1**

2m 32.04s (2.52) **Going Correction** +0.175s/f (Good) **14** Ran SP% **124.7**
Speed ratings: **97,94,91,90,90 89,89,89,82,81 79,78,77,—**CSF £161.45 CT £684.42 TOTE £12.30: £4.30, £8.00, £1.40; EX 301.10.
**Owner** T Redman, P Philips & P Coe **Bred** Mrs A Yearley **Trained** Newmarket, Suffolk

**FOCUS**
A very modest handicap run at an even pace and something of a rough race, but improved efforts from the first two.

**NOTEBOOK**
**Vicario** managed to score despite losing his footing on the home bend and also caused problems for a few when barging his way through approaching the furlong pole. Nonetheless he won in good style and was obviously on a very favourable mark for this handicap debut. The longer trip and fast ground for the first time probably helped, but the Handicapper is likely to take a dim view so it may be wise to turn him out again quickly under a penalty. *Official explanation: trainer's representative said gelding had benefited from the step up in trip and good to firm ground on this occasion*

**Regal Performer(IRE)**, no closer than ninth in four previous outings, like the winner put up an improved effort on his handicap debut off a modest mark over a longer trip. He could nick a modest handicap if repeating this.
**Romeo's Day**, beaten in a seller last time, had a clear run and had every chance but was just not good enough. He looks woefully one paced.
**Jackie Kiely** was given a more positive ride this time, but did not quite see out the trip as a result.
**Rinneen(IRE)**, visored for the first time, ran exactly the same sort of race as in her two previous outings this season, staying on strongly from a hopeless position to reach her final placing. She looks well worth trying over further.
**Winslow Boy(USA)**, was never far away and still had a small chance of making the frame when getting hampered over a furlong from home.
**Vrisaki(IRE)**, given a positive ride on this big step up in trip, was already on the retreat when getting a nudge from the winner over a furlong from home.
**El Magnifico**, off since January, has slipped to a plater's mark but, although he was probably the worst sufferer at the end of the concertina effect caused by the winner over a furlong from home, he would only have been placed at best otherwise.
**Unintentional** *Official explanation: jockey said filly slipped on the first bend.*

## 2403 DORMANSLAND FILLIES' H'CAP 1m 2f
**3:35** (3:36) (D) (0-85,80) 3-Y-O+ **£5,460** (£1,680; £840; £420) **Stalls** Low

Form RPR
45-1 **1** **Heneseys Leg**[23] [1845] 4-8-12 **65**.................................... LisaJones(3) 6 74
(JohnBerry) *a in tch: trckd ldr 1/2-way: led 2f out: pushed clr fnl f* **6/1**
6-40 **2** *1 3/4* **Lady McNair**[12] [2084] 4-9-10 **74**.................................... KFallon 4 80
(PDCundell) *lw: hld up in rr: rdn over 2f out: kpt on u.p to chse wnr ins fnl f* **5/1**[3]
2050 **3** *1* **Doris Souter (IRE)**[13] [2062] 4-9-6 **70**.................................... RLMoore 3 74
(RHannon) *lw: b.hind: trckd ldr to 1/2-way: one pce ins fnl 2f* **6/1**
-025 **4** *1* **Lara Falana**[63] [1097] 6-9-2 **66**.................................... TQuinn 7 68
(MissBSanders) *lw: hld up in rr: hdwy whn short of room over 2f out: no imp after* **9/2**[2]
1 **5** *1/2* **Fling**[36] [1532] 3-9-2 **80**.................................... DaneO'Neill 1 81
(JRFanshawe) *w.w: rdn 3f out: no hdwy after* **2/1**[1]
0100 **6** *1 1/2* **Tight Squeeze**[8] [2210] 7-10-0 **78**.................................... KMcEvoy 2 76
(PWHiatt) *mid-div: hdwy on outside over 3f out: wknd over 1f out* **12/1**
20-0 **7** *1/2* **Jubilee Treat (USA)**[44] [1372] 4-9-12 **76**.................................... DHolland 5 73
(GWragg) *led tl hdd 2f out: wknd qckly* **10/1**

2m 11.65s (2.05) **Going Correction** +0.175s/f (Good)
**WFA** 3 from 4yo+ 14lb **7** Ran **SP% 113.5**
Speed ratings: **98,96,95,95,94 93,93**CSF £35.06 TOTE £5.90: £1.90, £3.70; EX 38.10.
**Owner** Peter J Skinner **Bred** J W Ford **Trained** Newmarket, Suffolk

**FOCUS**
An ordinary pace for this fillies' handicap, but the winner looks progressive.

**NOTEBOOK**
**Heneseys Leg**, back under her ideal conditions having scored over a mile in soft ground last time, maintained her perfect record for the season despite racing off a 5lb higher mark. She was always holding the runner-up in the closing stages and seems to be improving.
**Lady McNair** ◆ looked as though she might provide a stern challenge to the winner inside the last furlong, but that rival kept pulling out more. The Handicapper has taken a long time to forgive her for her successful juvenile campaign, but this was her best effort for some time so it would not be a surprise to see her hit the target again before too long.
**Doris Souter(IRE)**, who has gained both her previous wins under these conditions, had every chance but is still 5lb higher than for her last win.
**Lara Falana** ◆, given a patient ride, found her path blocked when making her effort down the home straight and was not exactly given a hard time when it became obvious she was not going to win. She is well handicapped on grass just now and is worth keeping an eye on.
**Fling**, winner of a soft-ground Southwell maiden on her only previous start, ran a strange sort of race under these very different conditions. Dropping herself out to last racing down the home straight, she did not consent to run on until the race was over, but it would be harsh to condemn her so soon and she should be given another chance back on easier ground on a more conventional track.

## 2404 MARSH GREEN CLAIMING STKS 6f (P)
**4:10** (4:11) (F) 3-Y-O+ **£2,975** (£850; £425) **Stalls** Low

Form RPR
1044 **1** **Bells Beach (IRE)**[9] [2178] 6-8-9 53.................................... KFallon 1 59
(PHowling) *lw: a in tch: hdwy to go 2nd wl over 1f out: led ent fnl f: rdn out* **5/1**[3]
3322 **2** *1 1/4* **Aintnecessarilyso**[6] [2246] 6-9-3 58.................................... MSavage(5) 8 68
(NEBerry) *s.i.s: sn in tch: hdwy u.p over 1f out: r.o to chse wnr ins fnl f* **9/1**
0030 **3** *shd* **Waterside (IRE)**[12] [2091] 5-9-12 82.................................... SWhitworth 9 72
(JWHills) *lw: hld up: gd hdwy whn short of room over 1f out: r.o wl whn got clar run ins fnl f* **3/1**[1]
06-0 **4** *1* **Lake Verdi (IRE)**[9] [2178] 5-9-4 60.................................... (t) DHolland 5 61
(BHanbury) *led tl rdn and hdd ent fnl f: kpt on one pce* **16/1**
0-00 **5** *1* **Bahama Reef (IRE)**[8] [2204] 3-8-10 63 ow1.................................... DaneO'Neill 7 59
(BGubby) *chsd ldrs tl rdn and wknd ins fnl f* **33/1**
0-61 **6** *1* **Boisdale (IRE)**[20] [1913] 6-8-13 53.................................... LTreadwell(7) 4 57
(SLKeightley) *chsd ldr tl rdn and wknd appr fnl f* **16/1**
4120 **7** *hd* **Kilmeena Star**[16] [1988] 6-8-12 54.................................... (b) RLMoore 3 48
(JCFox) *chsd ldrs: rdn 1/2-way: wknd wl over 1f out* **12/1**
3036 **8** *1/2* **Aguila Loco (IRE)**[9] [2178] 5-9-6 56.................................... (p) SDrowne 11 55
(MrsStefLiddiard) *in tch tl rdn and wknd ins fnl 2f* **12/1**
2262 **9** *3/4* **Illusive (IRE)**[9] [2166] 7-9-12 60.................................... (b) TQuinn 2 59
(MWigham) *in tch: rdn 2f out: sn wknd* **9/2**[2]
03-0 **10** *1 3/4* **Mac's Talisman (IRE)**[9] [2178] 4-9-10 67.................................... MTebbutt 6 51
(VSmith) *b.bkwd: a bhd* **33/1**
66-5 **11** *2* **Waterline Blue (IRE)**[8] [2209] 3-8-5 76.................................... (t) RHavlin 12 35
(PDEvans) *outpcd thrght* **10/1**
-000 **12** *3 1/2* **Arctic Burst (USA)**[25] [1765] 4-9-12 78.................................... (v) DarrenWilliams 10 37
(DShaw) *lw: c over to ins fr wd draw: a bhd and eased ins fnl f* **20/1**

1m 13.67s (0.75) **Going Correction** +0.225s/f (Slow)
**WFA** 3 from 4yo+ 9lb **12** Ran **SP% 116.7**
Speed ratings: **104,102,102,100,99 98,97,97,96,93 91,86**CSF £47.62 TOTE £5.10: £1.70, £2.80, £1.80; EX 48.60.Waterside was claimed by Nigel Shields for £12,000.
**Owner** Richard Berenson **Bred** Philip Mahon **Trained** Newmarket, Suffolk

**FOCUS**
A fair pace for this claimer but the form is modest.

**NOTEBOOK**
**Bells Beach(IRE)** had quite a bit to find with some of her rivals on adjusted official ratings, but all three of her previous wins this season have been over this course and distance, and she scored again under a power-packed ride from the champion.
**Aintnecessarilyso**, whose All-Weather mark has recently risen by a whopping 7lb for getting beaten on grass, was still one of those worst in on adjusted official ratings despite that, so this staying-on effort was all the more creditable. The problem is that he has only managed one win in the past three years despite running regularly.
**Waterside(IRE)**, one of those best in at the weights, was taking a big drop in class compared with his most recent starts on this surface, but his come-from-behind style does rely on luck in running over sprint trips and on this occasion he did not get any.
**Lake Verdi(IRE)**, given a positive ride on this sand debut, had something to find at the weights and ran with credit, but is without a win for three years.
**Bahama Reef(IRE)**, still a maiden, showed up for a while over this shorter trip but looks to be on the decline.
**Illusive(IRE)** is on a very long losing run, but still had the form to have run better than this. In his defence, he was one of those worst in at the weights.
**Waterline Blue(IRE)** was best in on adjusted official figures, but is running well below his rating at present and this switch to sand made no difference.

## 2405 PLAY A ROUND AT LINGFIELD GOLF CLUB (S) STKS 5f (P)
**4:45** (4:46) (G) 2-Y-O **£2,534** (£724; £362) **Stalls** High

Form RPR
20 **1** **Story Of One (IRE)**[18] [1960] 2-8-11.................................... DHolland 3 59
(NPLittmoden) *lw: a.p: chsd ldr 1/2-way: rdn to ld ins fnl f: drvn out* **7/2**[3]
440 **2** *1 1/4* **Alice King (IRE)**[8] [2194] 2-7-13.................................... CHaddon(7) 4 49
(WGMTurner) *s.i.s: sn in tch: kpt on to go 2nd ins fnl f* **33/1**
254 **3** *3/4* **Lady Erica**[16] [2003] 2-8-6.................................... DarrenWilliams 9 46
(KRBurke) *lw: led rdn over 1f out: hdd and no ex ins fnl f* **10/3**[2]
66 **4** *nk* **Shish (IRE)**[11] [2124] 2-8-6.................................... SWKelly 5 45
(JAOsborne) *outpcd in rr: r.o past btn horses fnl f: nvr nrr* **25/1**
316 **5** *hd* **Smokincanon**[25] [1769] 2-8-11.................................... AQuinn(5) 7 54
(WGMTurner) *lw: prom: rdn over 1f out: wknd ins fnl f* **13/8**[1]
**6** *shd* **Jonny Fox'S (IRE)** 2-8-11.................................... DSweeney 1 49
(JRBoyle) *leggy: outpcd tl rapid hdwy on outside over 2f out: wknd fnl f* **16/1**
60 **7** *3/4* **Bamboozled**[16] [1984] 2-8-6.................................... (v[1]) SDrowne 6 41
(PDEvans) *swtg: trckd ldr to 1/2-way: prom tl wknd fnl f* **8/1**
0 **8** *hd* **Diatonic**[61] [1115] 2-8-8.................................... LisaJones(3) 8 45
(WJMusson) *s.i.s: outpcd thrght* **25/1**
0 **9** *hd* **Faithfull Girl (IRE)**[50] [1276] 2-8-2 ow1.................................... NChalmers(5) 10 40
(MissZCDavison) *outpcd thrght* **40/1**
00 **10** *1 1/4* **She's My Dream (IRE)**[44] [1374] 2-7-13.................................... DerekNolan(7) 2 34
(JSMoore) *outpcd: a bhd* **50/1**

63.12 secs (3.34) **Going Correction** +0.225s/f (Slow) **10** Ran **SP% 115.4**
Speed ratings: **82,80,78,78,78 77,76,76,76,74**CSF £117.06 TOTE £4.40: £2.20, £12.10, £2.00; EX 69.50.The winner was bought in for 6,000gns. Jonny Fox's was claimed by J Gallagher for £6,000.
**Owner** Richard Green (fine Paintings) **Bred** David Bean And Eugene Matthews **Trained** Newmarket, Suffolk

**FOCUS**
A poor time, even for a race of its type, suggesting these are not very good.

**NOTEBOOK**
**Story Of One(IRE)** found this more to his liking than the stiff Beverley five in heavy ground and responded well to pressure to score, but the slow winning time raises severe questions over the value of the form.
**Alice King(IRE)** stayed on late and may appreciate an extra furlong, but this is still very modest form.
**Lady Erica** managed to get across from her wide draw in front and made much of the running, but still did not get home and is looking a short runner.
**Shish(IRE)** did not appear to stay six last time but seemed to find this trip inadequate, an enigma her trainer will do well to solve.
**Smokincanon**, the only previous winner in the field, had gained his victory over this course and distance but, on this occasion, he was unable to get to the front and did not perform so well as a result.

## 2406 DUNSDALE H'CAP 1m (P)
**5:20** (5:23) (E) (0-70,70) 3-Y-O+ **£3,513** (£1,081; £540; £270) **Stalls** High

Form RPR
5402 **1** **Climate (IRE)**[4] [2304] 5-9-12 **68**.................................... (v) DSweeney 7 79
(JRBoyle) *w.w in tch: smooth prog to go 2nd over 1f out: led ins fnl f: r.o strly* **7/2**[1]
0-00 **2** *2* **Omaha City (IRE)**[8] [2201] 10-10-0 **70**.................................... MTebbutt 6 76
(BGubby) *a.p: led over 2f out: rdn and hdd ins fnl f: nt pce of wnr* **20/1**
5000 **3** *1 1/2* **Rebate**[7] [2226] 4-9-13 **69**.................................... PDobbs 5 72
(RHannon) *led tl hdd over 2f out: chsd ldr tl over 1f out: kpt on one pce* **12/1**
654- **4** *nk* **Royal Advocate**[321] [3124] 4-9-7 **63**.................................... SWhitworth 4 65
(JWHills) *lw: t.k.h: a in tch: r.o fnl f* **16/1**
0331 **5** *1/2* **Free Option (IRE)**[37] [1496] 9-9-2 **65**.................................... LauraPike(7) 2 66
(WJMusson) *hld up in rr: hdwy on ins whn short of room ins fnl f: nvr nr to chal* **10/1**
21-6 **6** *1 3/4* **Didnt Tell My Wife**[22] [1877] 5-9-5 **64**.................................... LisaJones(3) 3 61
(CFWall) *lw: in tch: rdn 2f out: sn btn* **4/1**[2]
-346 **7** *shd* **College Delinquent (IRE)**[19] [1935] 5-9-9 **65**.................................... (t) DaneO'Neill 9 62
(KBell) *b.hind: slowly away: a bhd* **13/2**[3]
462 **8** *hd* **Zafarshah (IRE)**[9] [2170] 5-9-6 **62**.................................... SDrowne 11 58
(PDEvans) *hld up in tch: wknd over 1f out* **7/2**[1]
3360 **9** *3/4* **Spindor (USA)**[9] [2170] 5-9-5 **61**.................................... (b) SWKelly 8 56
(JAOsborne) *a bhd* **14/1**
5000 **10** *3 1/2* **Estimation**[19] [1935] 4-9-8 **64**.................................... IMongan 12 51
(RMHCowell) *chsd ldrs: rdn 2f out: sn wknd* **20/1**
3220 **11** *1/2* **Quiet Reading (USA)**[22] [1875] 7-9-6 **67**.................................... (v) HayleyTurner(5) 10 52
(MRBosley) *lw: sn trckd ldr: rdn and wknd over 2f out* **14/1**

1m 40.57s (1.02) **Going Correction** +0.225s/f (Slow) **11** Ran **SP% 123.3**
Speed ratings: **103,101,99,99,98 96,96,96,95,92 91**CSF £80.02 CT £768.48 TOTE £4.40: £1.50, £6.30, £3.70; EX 84.40 Place 6 £206.71, Place 5 £106.88.
**Owner** Inside Track Racing Club **Bred** Mrs A Naughton **Trained** Epsom, Surrey

**FOCUS**
A competitive little handicap. The early pace was very moderate, but they quickened up appreciably over the last three furlongs.

**NOTEBOOK**
**Climate(IRE)**, who ran so well in a classified stakes on turf just four days earlier, is rated 6lb lower on sand. He was always going well behind the leaders and found a decent turn of foot to score despite a rather ungainly head carriage.
**Omaha City(IRE)** ran much better than when beaten out of sight in a classified stakes here last month in his only previous attempt on sand and, even at his age, looks worth another try.
**Rebate**, given a positive ride, was done for foot after trying to quicken things up from the front three furlongs from home. His two previous tries on this surface were over ten furlongs and the way he did not fold completely after being headed does suggest he needs a stiffer test than this on Polytrack.
**Royal Advocate** ◆, a maiden making his handicap debut and racing on sand for the first time, made a pleasing return after a ten-month break and is one to watch out for from now on.

**Free Option(IRE)**, winner of a claimer here last time, is not an easy horse to predict. Given a patient ride, he was still last approaching the furlong pole, but was staying on against the inside rail when running into a dead end in the closing stages.
**Didnt Tell My Wife** did not help his chances by pulling hard and that was as much of a problem as being 4lb higher than for his course-and-distance victory in November.
**College Delinquent(IRE)** compromised his chances by pulling too hard here last time and on this occasion he handicapped himself with a very tardy start. He looks a very hard ride.
**Zafarshah(IRE)** ran moderately on this return to sand and still looks held off this mark.
T/Plt: £266.60 to a £1 stake. Pool: £32,442.35. 88.80 winning tickets. T/Qpdt: £40.30 to a £1 stake. Pool: £2,440.00. 44.80 winning tickets. JS

## [2388] RIPON (R-H)
### Wednesday, May 26

**OFFICIAL GOING: Good to firm**

## 2407 LISHMAN SIDWELL CAMPBELL & PRICE CLASSIFIED STKS — 6f
**6:25** (6:25) (E) 4-Y-0+ — **£4,056** (£1,248; £624; £312) **Stalls** Low

Form — RPR

0-05 **1** **Merlin's Dancer**[12] 2091 4-9-0 72 ... AlexGreaves 6 — 88
(DNicholls) *cl up stands side: led after 1f: qckndclr wl over 1f out: kpt on wl* **5/1**[2]

5003 **2** 3 ½ **Chairman Bobby**[12] 2079 6-8-9 70 ... LEnstone(3) 9 — 76
(DWBarker) *racd alone far side: a.p: rdn wl over 1f out: kpt on. no ch w wnr* **15/2**[3]

1621 **3** hd **Prince Aaron (IRE)**[68] 1051 4-9-0 72 ... GCarter 7 — 77
(CNAllen) *trckd ldrs stands side: effrt to chse wnr 2f out: sn rdn and no imp* **4/1**[1]

0-30 **4** 3 **Val De Maal (IRE)**[18] 1968 4-8-13 71 ... RFfrench 8 — 67
(GCHChung) *cl up: rdn along 1/2-way: grad wknd* **14/1**

0-00 **5** nk **Ragamuffin**[11] 2132 6-8-12 70 ... KDarley 1 — 65
(TDEasterby) *in tch stands side: effrt 2f out: swtchd rt and rdn wl over 1f out: no imp* **10/1**

05-0 **6** 1 ½ **Linden's Lady**[10] 2143 4-8-11 72 ... RWinston 5 — 60
(JRWeymes) *cl up stands side: rdn along 1/2-way: sn wknd* **11/1**

0063 **7** nk **Time N Time Again**[1] 2391 6-8-12 70 ... (p) JQuinn 2 — 60
(EJAlston) *led stands side 1f: cl up tl rdn along 2f out and sn wknd* **5/1**[2]

60-2 **8** 7 **Hartshead**[18] 1974 5-8-12 68 ... BDoyle 3 — 39
(GASwinbank) *dwlt: a towards rr stands side* **4/1**[1]

240- **9** 15 **Blessingindisguise**[183] 6063 11-8-7 49 ... (b) PMulrennan(5) 4 — —
(MWEasterby) *s.i.s a rr stands side* **33/1**

1m 11.52s (-1.38) **Going Correction** -0.05s/f (Good) — **9** Ran SP% **112.1**
Speed ratings: **107,102,102,98,97 95,95,85,65**CSF £40.48 TOTE £6.30: £1.80, £2.60, £2.50; EX 52.90.
**Owner** Chalfont Foodhalls Ltd **Bred** Cheveley Park Stud Ltd **Trained** Sessay, N Yorks

**FOCUS**
A tight race on the ratings and in the betting, but a clear winner. The winner looks improved for his new yard.

**NOTEBOOK**
**Merlin's Dancer** showed his old sparkle at Nottingham last time on ground too soft, and conditions were much more to his liking on this occasion. Making much of the running, he came clear for a comfortable win, although he did return with a cut on his off-fore.
**Chairman Bobby**, who likes to make the running, made a beeline for the far side and raced alone throughout. He was probably racing on the quicker ground, but he had to cover so much more ground in getting there that the advantage probably balanced out in the end.
**Prince Aaron(IRE)**, a much-improved performer on the All-Weather over the winter, has returned to the turf rated 22lb higher than when he last ran on grass in August. He should come on for his first run in two months.
**Val De Maal(IRE)** had conditions to suit and ran a solid enough race.
**Ragamuffin** is struggling to recapture his best form.
**Time N Time Again** may have found the race coming too soon after his third-placed effort here less than 24 hours earlier.
**Hartshead** was disappointing, failing to land a blow after a missing the break. He may need easier ground. *Official explanation: jockey said gelding was unsuited by the track.*

## 2408 "RIPON SPRING FESTIVAL" (S) H'CAP — 1m 4f 60y
**6:55** (6:56) (F) (0-55,55) 4-5-Y-0 — **£3,276** (£936; £468) **Stalls** High

Form — RPR

-000 **1** **Piste Bleu (FR)**[9] 2174 4-8-12 53 ... PHanagan 9 — 61
(RFord) *hld up: hdwy on inner 3f out: swtchd lft and led appr last: sn drvn and styd on gamely* **7/1**[3]

000- **2** 1 **Fairy Monarch (IRE)**[251] 5015 5-8-5 46 ... (p) RFitzpatrick 6 — 52
(PTMidgley) *hld up: stdy hdwy over 3f out: rdn to challenge over 1f out: drvn ins last and ev ch tl no ex last 50 yds* **16/1**

6-00 **3** 1 ¼ **Margold (IRE)**[127] 568 4-8-9 50 ... ACulhane 10 — 54
(RHollinshead) *trckd ldr: led 4f out: rdn over 2f out: drvn and hdd over 1f out: kpt on same pce* **11/1**

-000 **4** 5 **Blue Venture (IRE)**[2] 2356 4-8-12 53 ... GFaulkner 1 — 49
(PCHaslam) *hld up and bhd: hdwy whn n.m.r 3f out: swtchd outside and rdn wl over 1f out: kpt on ins last: nrst fin* **8/1**

003- **5** hd **Karyon (IRE)**[32] 5542 4-8-6 47 oh6 ow1 ... RWinston 13 — 43
(MissKateMilligan) *chsd ldrs on inner: hdwy over 3f out: rdn 2f out: drvn and wknd wl over 1f out* **20/1**

00-6 **6** ½ **Grady**[33] 1582 5-8-0 46 oh6 ... BSwarbrick(5) 5 — 41
(WMBrisbourne) *hld up and bhd: hdwy 4f out: rdden over 2f out: kpt on u.p fnl f: nrst fin* **9/1**

6-00 **7** 1 ½ **Lord Of Methley**[28] 1710 5-8-7 48 ... VHalliday 12 — 41
(RMWhitaker) *trckd ldrs: effrt over 3f out: sn rdn along and wknd 2f out* **6/1**[2]

6660 **8** shd **Shatin Special**[2] 2375 4-8-6 47 ... (p) RFfrench 2 — 40
(GCHChung) *hld up in rr: hdwy on outer 4f out: rdn wl over 2f out and sn wknd* **17/2**

2103 **9** 1 ¾ **Seraph**[7] 2230 4-8-4 48 oh6 ow2 ... (p) TEaves(3) 7 — 38
(JohnAHarris) *in tch: hdwy o ver 3f out: rdn over 2f out and sn wknd* **9/2**[1]

6040 **10** 2 **Balalaika Tune (IRE)**[22] 1866 5-8-5 46 oh11 ... JBramhill 3 — 33
(WStorey) *prom: hdwy to chal 3f out: sn rdn and wknd fnl 2f* **16/1**

3-44 **11** 2 **Sportsman (IRE)**[11] 2126 5-8-5 46 oh11 ... (b) DaleGibson 11 — 30
(MWEasterby) *s.i.s: a rr* **10/1**

6000 **12** 7 **Turftanzer (GER)**[8] 2214 5-8-5 46 oh11 ... (t) KimTinkler 4 — 18
(DonEnricoIncisa) *chsd ldrs: rdn along 4f out: wkng whn hmpd 3f out: sn bhd* **33/1**

/0-0 **13** 24 **Diligent Lad**[24] 1786 4-8-11 55 ... LEnstone(3) 8 — —
(DWBarker) *t.k.h: sn led: rdn along over 4f out: sn hdd & wknd* **33/1**

2m 39.35s (-0.55) **Going Correction** -0.05s/f (Good) — **13** Ran SP% **116.4**
Speed ratings: **99,98,97,94,94 93,92,92,91,90 88,84,68**CSF £108.16 CT £1210.65 TOTE £8.90: £3.30, £5.00, £3.50; EX 138.40.There was no bid for the winner.
**Owner** M Dunlevy & N Morgan **Bred** Scea Prairies **Trained** Little Budworth, Cheshire
■ Stewards Enquiry : L Enstone two-day ban: careless riding (Jun 6,7)

**FOCUS**
A poor handicap and the form is ordinary.

**NOTEBOOK**
**Piste Bleu(FR)**, whose only previous success came off a 2lb lower mark, was taking a drop in grade. With conditions to suit, she responded well to pressure, but she does not appeal as the type to repeat the trick against stronger opposition.
**Fairy Monarch(IRE)** had plenty to prove on his seasonal reappearance over this longer trip. He saw it out well in this grade though, and hopefully he can now build on this modest promise.
**Margold(IRE)**, off the track since January, is one-paced so her rider kicked her for home early in the straight. The tactic did not work but she finished a creditable third.
**Blue Venture(IRE)**, for whom the step up in trip was an unknown, saw it out surprisingly well after meeting trouble in running.
**Karyon(IRE)** did not get home on her return to the Flat and first try at this trip.
**Lord Of Methley** was without the headgear which he wore for both his successes last season.
**Seraph** found this a tougher assignment than the banded races he has been running in, and he is still a maiden on turf.

## 2409 RIPON FARM SERVICES H'CAP — 2m
**7:25** (7:25) (D) (0-80,80) 4-Y-0+ — **£5,421** (£1,668; £834; £417) **Stalls** Low

Form — RPR

5-26 **1** **Tiyoun (IRE)**[24] 1785 6-9-8 74 ... ACulhane 8 — 88
(JeddO'Keeffe) *hld up in tch: hdwy over 4f out: chsd wnr 3f out: rdn 2f out and styd on wl to ld ins last* **11/2**[3]

44-1 **2** 1 **Red Sun**[6] 2249 7-8-2 54 6ex ... (t) PHanagan 2 — 67
(JMackie) *led: qcknd clr 5f out: rdn along 3f out: drvn over 1f out: hdd and no ex ins last* **15/8**[1]

-406 **3** 12 **Moonshine Beach**[11] 2116 6-8-1 58 ... (p) PMakin(5) 6 — 56
(PWHiatt) *chsd ldrs: rdn along 3f out: drvn and one pce fnl 2f* **13/2**

0-05 **4** ¾ **Sono**[18] 1973 7-9-1 70 ... (p) DAllan(3) 7 — 68
(PDNiven) *hld up: hdwy 4f out: rdn along 3f out: kpt on u.p appr last: n.d* **20/1**

3135 **5** 4 **George Stubbs (USA)**[14] 2047 6-8-11 63 ... KDarley 5 — 56
(MJPolglase) *hld up in tch: pushed along 4f out: rdn to chse ldrs 3f out: sn drvn and btn* **10/3**[2]

0-00 **6** 10 **Freedom Now (IRE)**[14] 2047 6-9-6 72 ... KDalgleish 4 — 53
(MDHammond) *hld up and bhd: hdwy on outer 4f out: rdn along 3f out and sn wknd* **14/1**

31-0 **7** dist **Rouge Blanc (USA)**[22] 1866 4-8-0 54 ... (t) JQuinn 9 — —
(GAHarker) *chsd ldrs: rdn along over 4f out: wknd over 3f out* **12/1**

-400 **8** 5 **Autumn Fantasy (USA)**[6] 2249 5-8-8 60 ... JCarroll 3 — —
(BEllison) *a rr* **33/1**

33/0 **9** 2 ½ **Weet For Me**[14] 2047 8-10-0 80 ... RWinston 1 — —
(RHollinshead) *chsd ldr: rdn along over 4f out: sn wknd* **25/1**

3m 27.81s (-5.69) **Going Correction** -0.05s/f (Good)
**WFA** 4 from 5yo+ 2lb — **9** Ran SP% **112.5**
Speed ratings: **112,111,105,105,103 98,—,—,—**CSF £15.37 CT £67.02 TOTE £7.20: £2.00, £1.40, £2.00; EX 16.50.
**Owner** Miss Sharon Long **Bred** Illuminatus Investments **Trained** Middleham Moor, N Yorks

**FOCUS**
A fair handicap with the first two clear and a very smart time indeed for the grade.

**NOTEBOOK**
**Tiyoun(IRE)** defied those who doubted his stamina over this trip and got the better of the favourite inside the last. This was his first win for almost three years, but the time was good and, provided the Handicapper does not clobber him, further success looks likely.
**Red Sun**, under a 6lb penalty, tried to make all, as he had when successful at Newcastle last time, and had most of them in trouble when kicking on with over half a mile to run. He was eventually caught but both he and the winner finished a mile clear of the rest, and the quick time confirms the impression that he ran to form.
**Moonshine Beach** stays forever and is not badly handicapped, but he could not hold a candle to the front two.
**Sono** still seeks that elusive first win in this country.
**George Stubbs(USA)** has never won on ground this quick.
**Autumn Fantasy(USA)** *Official explanation: jockey said horse had a breathing problem*

## 2410 COCKED HAT FARM FOODS H'CAP — 1m
**8:00** (8:00) (C) (0-90,88) 3-Y-0+ — **£9,030** (£3,425; £1,712; £778) **Stalls** High

Form — RPR

36-2 **1** **Langford**[6] 2237 4-9-11 79 ... PRobinson 7 — 93
(MHTompkins) *mde all: rdn clr over 1f out: styd on wl* **9/2**[1]

-660 **2** 2 **Distant Country (USA)**[25] 1772 5-9-3 71 ... (p) JQuinn 9 — 80
(MrsJRRamsden) *hld up in rr: hdwy 3f out: pushed along and nt clr run wl over 1f out: rdn and n.m.r ins last: styd on nr fin* **13/2**[2]

0001 **3** shd **Mystic Man (FR)**[6] 2237 6-10-1 88 6ex ... PMulrennan(5) 3 — 97
(KARyan) *hld up towards rr: smooth hdwy on outer 3f out: chal wl over 1f out: sn rdn and nt qckn ent last* **13/2**[2]

204- **4** shd **Blonde Streak (USA)**[217] 5709 4-9-4 77 ... PMakin(5) 12 — 86
(TDBarron) *in tch: hdwy over 3f out: rdn along to chse ldrs and n.m.r 2f out and ins last: kpt on* **9/1**

25-4 **5** hd **Nevada Desert (IRE)**[10] 2142 4-9-3 71 ... DeanMcKeown 5 — 79
(RMWhitaker) *trckd ldrs: hdwy 3f out and sn ev ch: rdn 2f out and wknd appr last* **7/1**[3]

-040 **6** 1 ¼ **Cherished Number**[5] 2271 5-9-11 79 ... (v[1]) RWinston 14 — 85
(ISemple) *hld up: hdwy on outer 3f out: sn rdn along and kpt on same pce fnl 2f* **13/2**[2]

02-0 **7** 2 ½ **Adobe**[23] 1845 9-8-10 69 ... BSwarbrick(5) 4 — 69
(WMBrisbourne) *towards rr: stdy hdwy 1/2-way: rdn to chse ldrs 2f out: sn drvn and one pce appr last* **16/1**

500- **8** 2 **Juste Pour L'Amour**[252] 5001 4-9-8 76 ... BDoyle 6 — 71
(PLGilligan) *cl up: rdn along over 3f out: wknd over 2f out* **33/1**

0-20 **9** 2 **Queen Charlotte (IRE)**[8] 2215 5-9-0 68 ... JFanning 2 — 59
(MrsKWalton) *prom: hdwy to chal 4f out and ev ch tl rdn and wknd 2f out* **22/1**

0060 **10** 1 ½ **Aimee's Delight**[4] 2304 4-9-6 74 ... MFenton 13 — 61
(JGGiven) *chsd ldrs: rdn along 3f out: wknd 2f out* **12/1**

0/35 **11** hd **Sea Mark**[9] 2172 8-8-4 61 ... TEaves(3) 11 — 48
(BEllison) *in tch: rdn along 3f out: sn outpcd* **10/1**

0-04 **12** 6 **Unicorn Reward (IRE)**[50] 1284 4-9-10 78 ... ACulhane 1 — 51
(MDHammond) *a bhd* **25/1**

6-U0 L **Tagula Blue (IRE)**[23] 1840 4-9-10 78 (t) KDarley 8 —
(JAGlover) *swvd bdly lft s: tk no part* **16/1**

1m 39.43s (-1.67) **Going Correction** -0.05s/f (Good) **13** Ran SP% **120.4**
Speed ratings: **106,104,103,103,103 102,99,97,95,94 94,88,**—CSF £31.99 CT £199.80 TOTE £4.90: £2.70, £3.00, £2.60; EX 52.00 Trifecta £531.50 Pool of £2,769.89 - 3.70 winning tickets.
**Owner** Marlborough Electronics **Bred** Summertree Stud **Trained** Newmarket, Suffolk

**FOCUS**
A good, competitive handicap run in a fair overall time in which the consistent winner dictated the pace. The form looks sound.

**NOTEBOOK**
**Langford**, with the master tactician on board, dictated the gallop and, after kicking clear inside the two, was never in danger. He is a consistent performer, but may well have improved a little this season and both his wins have been gained from the front.
**Distant Country(USA)** ◆ has been struggling a little this season, but a combination of a drop in the weights and the return to faster ground and waiting tactics produced an improved performance. He did not get a clear passage and looks capable of getting his head in front soon, especially if turned out again before he is re-assesssed.
**Mystic Man(FR)**, who beat Langford last week, was unable to confirm the form under a 6lb penalty. He seemed to have every chance and should continue to give his running once re-assessed.
**Blonde Streak(USA)**, having her first run since the autumn, goes well fresh and ran her race. She is a summer performer and should be able to pick up a decent handicap again this season.
**Nevada Desert(IRE)** ran another decent race on this track, but his record suggests that he is best suited by a stiffer track.
**Cherished Number**, another that is best during the summer, did not find much improvement in the first-time visor, but may be helped by a drop in grade.

## 2411 BLACK SHEEP BREWERY H'CAP — 6f
**8:30** (8:32) (E) (0-70,69) 3-Y-O **£4,280** (£1,317; £658; £329) **Stalls** Low

Form RPR

3-00 **1** **Party Princess (IRE)**[14] 2036 3-8-9 57 DeanMcKeown 8 68
(JAGlover) *swtchd to far side:cl up tl led and overall ldr over 3f out: rdn clr over 1f out: kpt on wl* **5/1**[3]

2120 **2** 2 ½ **Piccolo Prince**[21] 1881 3-9-6 68 JQuinn 4 71
(EJAlston) *cl up stands side: rdn wl over 1f out: led that gp ins last: no ch w wnr* **9/2**[2]

0-21 **3** *hd* **Princess Galadriel**[12] 2098 3-8-9 57 NPollard 10 59
(JRBest) *chsd ldrs far side and sn rdn along: drvn 2f out: styd on u.p ent last* **7/2**[1]

0-16 **4** *3* **Tizzy's Law**[25] 1775 3-9-7 69 JBramhill 2 62
(MABuckley) *led stands side gp: rdn along 2f out: hdd & wknd ins last* **12/1**

600- **5** *hd* **Caribbean Blue**[229] 5470 3-8-4 52 RFfrench 6 45
(RMWhitaker) *bhd stands side: rdn and hdwy 2f out: styd on u.p ins last: nrst fin* **14/1**

040- **6** *1 ¾* **Delusion**[233] 5415 3-9-0 65 DAllan[(3)] 11 53
(TDEasterby) *led far side over 2f: cl up tl rdn along and wknd over 2f out* **25/1**

120- **7** *shd* **Weet An Haul**[151] 6242 3-8-7 55 PHanagan 9 42
(PABlockley) *chsd ldrs far side: rdn along over 2f out: sn wknd* **14/1**

6-50 **8** *¾* **Loveisdangerous**[19] 1934 3-8-2 50 KimTinkler 7 35
(DonEnricoIncisa) *prom far side: riddne along 1/2-way: sn wknd* **16/1**

0-14 **9** *1 ¾* **Game Flora**[19] 1941 3-8-7 58 TEaves[(3)] 1 38
(MESowersby) *cl up stands side: riddne along over 2f out and sn wknd* **14/1**

-005 **10** *nk* **Reversionary**[14] 2036 3-8-2 50 (b) DaleGibson 12 29
(MWEasterby) *dwlt: a rr far side* **8/1**

00-6 **11** *3* **Saratoga Splendour (USA)**[53] 1250 3-7-8 49 LeanneKershaw[(7)] 13 19
(JeddO'Keeffe) *in tch far side: rdn along 1/2-way: sn wknd* **50/1**

0-06 **12** *3 ½* **Compton Micky**[40] 1453 3-8-12 60 JEdmunds 5 19
(JBalding) *chsd ldrs stands side to 1/2-way: sn outpcd and bhd* **22/1**

5-60 **13** *5* **The Warley Warrior**[18] 1975 3-8-4 57 ow6 (b) PMulrennan[(5)] 3 1
(MWEasterby) *dwlt and swtchd to r far side: a bhd* **20/1**

1m 13.23s (0.33) **Going Correction** -0.05s/f (Good) **13** Ran SP% **116.7**
Speed ratings: **95,91,91,87,87 84,84,83,81,80 76,72,65**CSF £25.64 CT £92.20 TOTE £6.70: £2.60, £2.10, £1.80; EX 20.40.
**Owner** Derrick Bloy **Bred** Hardys Of Kilkeel Ltd **Trained** Carburton, Notts
■ Stewards Enquiry : Dean McKeown one-day ban: failed to keep straight from stalls (Jun 6)
P Hanagan 28-day ban (takes into account previous offences and deferred ban): failed to keep straight from stalls (Jun 29-Jul 26)

**FOCUS**
An ordinary sprint in which the field split, but apart from the winner there was not much between the two groups. The winner looks improved and is likely to do better.

**NOTEBOOK**
**Party Princess(IRE)**, appreciated the return to a fast surface after running twice on soft, and won this with something in hand. She is likely to go up a fair amount for this, but at least starts from a moderate mark, and a quick reappearance may be on the cards.
**Piccolo Prince**, whose good early-season form was on sand and an easy surface, seemed to run his race on this drop in grade but may have met an improver in the winner.
**Princess Galadriel**, up in grade and off a 7lb higher mark, had to work hard to keep tabs on the leaders, but ran on nicely and may not have finished improving yet.
**Tizzy's Law**, having only her fourth run, was encountering a fast surface for the first time this season. The form of her previous races this year is working out, and she is one to bear in mind when she gets an easy surface once again.
**Caribbean Blue**having her first outing of the season and making her handicap debut from a plater's mark, ran a fair race without ever seriously threatening and looks one to bear in mind. However, a word of caution is that she did not progress from her initial run last season.
**Game Flora** *Official explanation: trainer said filly was unsuited by the ground*

## 2412 ACCOUNTANT ONLINE MAIDEN STKS — 1m 2f
**9:00** (9:01) (D) 3-Y-O+ **£4,862** (£1,496; £748; £374) **Stalls** High

Form RPR

**1** **Mutasallil (USA)**[454] 4-9-10 (t) JCarroll 3 82
(SaeedBinSuroor) *trckd ldrs: hdwy 3f out: rdn to ld over 1f out: drvn ins last and kpt on* **5/1**

2-2 **2** *½* **Seven Year Itch (IRE)**[18] 1967 4-9-10 (b[1]) KDarley 4 81
(MPTregoning) *led 1f: cl up tl led again 4f out: rdn over 2f out: drvn and hdd over 1f out: kpt on u.p fnl f* **6/4**[1]

0-4 **3** *8* **Wou Oodd**[13] 2060 3-8-5 ACulhane 2 61
(MRChannon) *trckd ldrs: hdwy 4f out: rdn to chse ldng pair 3f out: sn drvn and no imp* **7/2**[3]

0 **4** *2* **Belshazzar (USA)**[10] 2144 3-8-10 JEdmunds 7 62
(TPTate) *prom: rdn along over 3f out: sn drvn and outpcd* **100/1**

0 **5** *nk* **Manhattan Jack**[10] 2145 3-8-10 RWinston 6 61
(GASwinbank) *dwlt: sn chsng ldrs: rdn along over 4f out: drvn and outpcd fnl 3f* **66/1**

**6** *shd* **Roman Forum** 3-8-10 WRyan 8 61
(HRACecil) *sn pushed along towards rr: rdn along 3f out: drvn and hdwy fnl 2f* **5/2**[2]

**7** *21* **Cutthroat**[25] 4-9-10 DaleGibson 5 21
(TPTate) *s.i.s: a bhd* **66/1**

4- **8** *8* **Blue Viking (IRE)**[315] 3299 3-8-3 DFentiman[(7)] 1 6
(JRWeymes) *cl up: led after 1f: rdn along and hdd 4f out: sn wknd and bhd* **80/1**

2m 6.97s (-1.03) **Going Correction** -0.05s/f (Good)
**WFA** 3 from 4yo 14lb **8** Ran SP% **112.7**
Speed ratings: **102,101,95,93,93 93,76,70**CSF £12.62 TOTE £6.40: £1.80, £1.10, £1.40; EX 19.50 Place 6 £28.66, Place 5 £15.00.
**Owner** Godolphin **Bred** Shadwell Farm Llc **Trained** Newmarket, Suffolk

**FOCUS**
An ordinary maiden, with the possible exception of the first two, and the time was nothing special.

**NOTEBOOK**
**Mutasallil(USA)**, absent for 15 months since making his debut on dirt in Dubai, justified the decision to persevere with him by just outbattling the determined runner-up. He should be able to make his mark in handicaps if the Handicapper gives him a reasonable mark.
**Seven Year Itch(IRE)**, who has not looked an easy ride in two previous outings, was fitted with blinkers for the first time and gave the winner a fight. Although he has been runner-up in all three outings now, he has the ability to win a race at around this trip if the blinkers have the same effect next time.
**Wou Oodd** again showed ability without proving a threat to the older colts that beat her. She now qualifies for a handicap mark and should not be too badly treated.
**Belshazzar(USA)** showed much more than on his debut earlier in the month. He is another who will be seen to best advantage in handicaps.
**Roman Forum**, a full-brother to Wince and half-brother to Ulundi, was making his debut but has a long way to go if he is to live up to his pedigree.
T/Plt: £52.60 to a £1 stake. Pool: £39,340.55. 545.50 winning tickets. T/Qpdt: £3.80 to a £1 stake. Pool: £3,120.20. 607.60 winning tickets. JR

# 1976 LEOPARDSTOWN (L-H)
### Wednesday, May 26
**OFFICIAL GOING: Good to firm (good in straight)**

## 2416a SAVAL BEG STKS (LISTED RACE) — 1m 6f
**8:00** (8:01) 3-Y-O+ **£22,922** (£6,725; £3,204; £1,091)

RPR

**1** **Windermere (IRE)**[73] 2040 5-9-9 107 JPMurtagh 1 113
(TMWalsh, Ire) *mde all: sn wl clr: unassailable ld fr 1/2-way: tired fr over 1f out: eased nr fin* **14/1**

**2** *4 ½* **Vinnie Roe (IRE)**[213] 5782 6-10-2 119 (b) PJSmullen 5 114
(DKWeld, Ire) *hld up: remote 4th 1/2-way: remote 2nd early st: kpt on wl: no ch w wnr* **1/2**[1]

**3** *3* **My Renee (USA)**[243] 5184 4-9-9 103 NGMcCullagh 3 103
(MJGrassick, Ire) *hld up: remote last 5f out: remote 5th into st: kpt on* **7/1**[2]

**4** *½* **Holy Orders (IRE)**[27] 5921 7-9-12 107 (b) DJCondon 2 105
(WPMullins, Ire) *s.i.s and hld up: remote 4th 2f out: kpt on* **7/1**[2]

**5** *10* **Jade Quest (IRE)**[24] 1814 4-9-12 100 FMBerry 4 91
(CharlesO'Brien, Ire) *remote 2nd: rdn and wknd appr st* **11/1**[3]

**6** *6* **Darabanka (IRE)**[19] 1948 3-8-0 CatherineGannon 6 76
(JohnMOxx, Ire) *remote 3rd: wknd fr 3f out* **7/1**[2]

3m 2.20s **Going Correction** +0.10s/f (Good)
**WFA** 3 from 4yo+ 20lb **6** Ran SP% **119.2**
Speed ratings: **114,111,109,109,103 100**CSF £23.50 TOTE £12.10: £3.40, £1.30; DF 22.80.
**Owner** W Hennessy **Bred** Hascombe & Valiant Studs **Trained** Kill, Co Kildare

**FOCUS**
All the riders, with the exception of Murtagh, were asked to explain their riding.

**NOTEBOOK**
**Windermere(IRE)**, successful over hurdles in February but having his first Irish Flat start, was allowed an uncontested early lead that had built up to over 30 lengths before halfway. He was getting a bit weary towards the end but his rider still eased him down. Ascot's Queen Alexandra Stakes is an option.
**Vinnie Roe(IRE)** was not asked to go the winner's early sprint pace but stayed on commendably and the Ascot Gold Cup remains the target. He will have derived benefit from this.
**My Renee(USA)** stayed on without ever threatening to make any impact.
**Holy Orders(IRE)** kept on in the straight after being well in arrears throughout.
**Jade Quest(IRE)** ran his race in second place but dropped right out in the straight.
**Darabanka(IRE)**, the only three-year-old in the line-up, ran a moderate third until fading before the straight.

2417 - 2418a (Foreign Racing) - See Raceform Interactive

# 2287 AYR (L-H)
### Thursday, May 27
**OFFICIAL GOING: Good to firm (firm in places)**

## 2419 ARRAN RATING RELATED MAIDEN STKS — 1m 1f 20y
**2:30** (2:30) (E) 3-Y-O **£3,594** (£1,106; £553; £276) **Stalls** Low

Form RPR

33-0 **1** **Another Bottle (IRE)**[61] 1129 3-9-0 70 DaleGibson 2 82+
(TPTate) *keen: trckd ldrs: shkn up to ld over 1f out: edgd rt and drew clr ins last: eased cl home* **11/8**[1]

0-44 **2** *5* **Little Bob**[19] 1972 3-9-0 70 TQuinn 1 67
(JDBethell) *hld up in tch: hdwy over 2f out: rdn and no imp over 1f: kpt on fnl f: no ch w wnr* **8/1**[3]

3000 **3** *nk* **Charlie Tango (IRE)**[10] 2169 3-9-0 67 TEDurcan 3 66
(MRChannon) *trckd ldr: effrt over 2f out: one pce fnl f* **9/1**

6-60 **4** *shd* **La Petite Chinoise**[65] 1086 3-8-11 66 RWinston 4 63
(RGuest) *chsd ldrs: drvn and outpcd 2f out: kpt on fnl f* **16/1**

3-34 **5** *shd* **Nukhbah (USA)**[24] 1842 3-8-11 70 FLynch 5 63
(LadyHerries) *led to over 1f out: outpcd wl ins last* **13/8**[2]

1m 54.75s (0.54) **Going Correction** -0.45s/f (Firm) **5** Ran SP% **107.2**
Speed ratings: **92,87,87,87,87**CSF £11.63 TOTE £1.90: £1.10, £2.70; EX 5.70.
**Owner** J Hanson **Bred** Killeen Castle Stud **Trained** Tadcaster, N Yorks

**FOCUS**
A fair event, but the winner apart, this was pretty ordinary stuff and the remainder do not appeal as worth following given they virtually finished on top of each other.

**NOTEBOOK**
**Another Bottle(IRE)**, racing beyond a mile for the first time, was able to confirm the promise he showed in maiden and most recently handicap company. This was not that strong a race, but he was an easy winner and should be competitive back in handicaps if not raised too much for this success.
**Little Bob** had shown ability in similar company and promised to be suited by this step up from a mile, but he did not achieve a great deal in coming out on top in a bunch finish for second. His rating of 70 appears to flatter him.
**Charlie Tango(IRE)** is proving quite frustrating.
**La Petite Chinoise**, with the blinkers left off this time, did not prove that this step up from seven furlongs suited.
**Nukhbah(USA)** was below form and this represented a step backwards.

## 2420 EUROPEAN BREEDERS FUND CROSSHILL CLASSIFIED STKS 1m
3:00 (3:01) (C ) 3-Y-0 £8,921 (£3,165; £1,582; £719) Stalls Low

Form RPR
6-40 **1** **Fine Silver (IRE)**[5] 2306 3-8-11 **83** ........ TQuinn 2 88
(PFICole) *chsd ldrs: outpcd over 3f out: rallied over 1f out: styd on to ld towards fin* **2/1**[2]
1-21 **2** *hd* **Celtic Heroine (IRE)**[20] 1931 3-8-12 **89** ........ PRobinson 1 89
(MAJarvis) *in tch: smooth hdwy to ld over 1f out: rdn and r.o fnl f: hdd cl home* **11/8**[1]
15- **3** *4* **Mbosi (USA)**[251] 5039 3-8-12 **86** ........ JFanning 3 79
(MJohnston) *led to over 2f out: rallied and ev ch over 1f out: outpcd ins last* **10/1**
1-0 **4** *3* **Oman Gulf (USA)**[15] 2043 3-8-13 **87** ........ ACulhane 4 73
(BWHills) *keen: cl up: led over 2f to over 1f out: sn rdn and btn* **3/1**[3]

1m 38.44s (-4.68) **Going Correction** -0.45s/f (Firm) **4** Ran SP% **109.5**
Speed ratings: **105,104,100,97**CSF £5.22 TOTE £3.10; EX 4.80.
**Owner** Siv Corporation **Bred** Mount Coote Stud **Trained** Whatcombe, Oxon

**FOCUS**
A decent event despite there being just the four runners, but an informative race with the winner seemingly improving..

**NOTEBOOK**
**Fine Silver(IRE)** was unlucky at Newmarket on his previous start, but had no problems this time. He took a while to pick having been a little outpaced when things quickened, but always looked like getting there. He should stay further and will be worthy of respect in similar company.
**Celtic Heroine(IRE)** had previously shown her best turf form on good to soft ground but, back on much faster ground, she ran her race and should continue to go well in similar company.
**Mbosi(USA)**, last in a good Newbury conditions race off the back of a debut win on his final start of 2003, made an encouraging reappearance. He was entitled to get tired close home and should come on for the run.
**Oman Gulf(USA)** looked promising when winning his maiden over six furlongs at Newmarket last July, but was not seen again that season. Last in the Dante on his reappearance, he was dropped in both grade and trip this time, but again failed to beat a rival home. He looks one to avoid for the time being.

## 2421 MACDONALDS SOLICITORS H'CAP 7f 50y
3:30 (3:30) (D ) (0-80,80) 3-Y-O+ £5,525 (£1,700; £850; £425) Stalls Low

Form RPR
0-00 **1** **Yorkshire Blue**[6] 2260 5-7-9 **50** oh2 ........ NMackay[(3)] 4 61
(JSGoldie) *keen: chsd ldrs: led 2f out: drvn out* **9/2**[2]
0000 **2** *½* **The Bonus King**[9] 2196 4-9-7 **80** ........ AElliott[(7)] 2 89
(MJohnston) *w ldrs: pushed along 2f out: r.o fnl f* **8/1**
50-0 **3** *½* **Scotland The Brave**[20] 1931 4-9-1 **67** ........ TQuinn 5 75
(JDBethell) *led 2f: led briefly over 2f out: rdn and r.o fnl f* **12/1**
5505 **4** *½* **Waltzing Wizard**[6] 2260 5-8-1 **53** ........ JFanning 8 60
(ABerry) *hld up: effrt 2f out: r.o fnl f* **6/1**
14-0 **5** *nk* **Roman Maze**[10] 2172 4-9-1 **67** ........ SWKelly 3 73
(WMBrisbourne) *s.i.s: hdwy over 2f out: chsng ldrs over 1f out: no imp wl ins last* **8/1**
0014 **6** *¾* **Friar Tuck**[6] 2261 9-8-3 **55** ........ RFfrench 1 59
(MissLAPerratt) *keen: prom tl rdn and no ex over 1f out* **12/1**
0503 **7** *hd* **Sea Storm (IRE)**[5] 2291 6-9-8 **79** ........ PMulrennan[(5)] 9 83
(DRMacleod) *hld up in tch on outside: rdn and no imp over 2f out: edgd lft and r.o fnl f: no imp* **3/1**[1]
0000 **8** *7* **John O'Groats (IRE)**[6] 2261 6-9-1 **67** ........ FLynch 6 52
(MDods) *hld up: rdr over 2f out: nt pce to chal* **33/1**
0040 **9** *½* **Speedfit Free (IRE)**[5] 2291 7-8-1 **53** oh2 ow3 ........(v) AnnStokell 10 37
(MissAStokell) *keen: led after 2f to over 2f out: edgd lft and sn btn* **50/1**
-036 **10** *1 ¾* **Just One Smile (IRE)**[7] 2238 4-8-7 **62** ........ DAllan[(3)] 7 41
(TDEasterby) *prom: rdn over 2f out: sn btn* **5/1**[3]

1m 28.85s (-3.62) **Going Correction** -0.45s/f (Firm) **10** Ran SP% **116.6**
Speed ratings: **102,101,100,100,99 99,98,90,90,88**CSF £40.43 CT £406.12 TOTE £5.60: £3.40, £5.50, £3.90; EX 72.20 Trifecta £993.40 Pool: £1,399.20. 0.40 winning tickets..
**Owner** John Mc C Hodge **Bred** R T And Mrs Watson **Trained** Uplawmoor, E Renfrews

**FOCUS**
A competitive enough handicap and the form looks fairly sound, but probably not a very strong race for the grade.

**NOTEBOOK**
**Yorkshire Blue** confirmed the promise he showed over this course and distance on his previous start. The Jim Goldie yard would appear to know the key to him and a follow-up cannot be ruled out.
**The Bonus King** has not won since his two-year-old days and had been below form in recent months, but this represented a return to form and he probably would have won had he been ridden by a more experienced jockey - Elliott lacked strength in the finish. However, given his overall record, he cannot be backed with any confidence to build on this next time.
**Scotland The Brave** has not really progressed since making a winning debut last season, but this effort offered some encouragement.
**Waltzing Wizard** has not won since August 2002, but is running into a bit of form and this was another promising effort.
**Roman Maze** ran better than he did on his previous start, but never really looked like getting to the principals.
**Sea Storm(IRE)** has been fitted with cheekpieces for his last two wins, but they have been left off lately. He is well handicapped on some of his form, but is proving quite frustrating.
**John O'Groats(IRE)** *Official explanation: jockey said gelding ran too free and then hung left in the straight*
**Speedfit Free(IRE)** *Official explanation: jockey said gelding ran too free*
**Just One Smile(IRE)** appeared to have conditions in her favour, but she ran no race at all.

## 2422 EUROPEAN BREEDERS FUND AYR MAIDEN STKS 6f
4:00 (4:00) (D ) 2-Y-0 £5,473 (£1,684; £842; £421) Stalls High

Form RPR
**1** **Leo's Lucky Star (USA)** 2-9-0 ........ JFanning 3 67+
(MJohnston) *pressed ldr: led 1/2-way: clr whn hung lft into centre of trck appr fnl f: r.o strly: readily* **1/2**[1]
**2** *3* **Sunset Strip** 2-9-0 ........ TEDurcan 1 58+
(MRChannon) *chsd ldrs: effrt and chsd wnr over 1f out: kpt on: no imp* **9/4**[2]
**3** *¾* **General Max (IRE)** 2-9-0 ........ VHalliday 6 55
(ACrook) *in tch: sn outpcd: hdwy over 1f out: kpt on wl* **33/1**
05 **4** *1 ¾* **Kristikhab (IRE)**[20] 1930 2-9-0 ........ FLynch 2 50
(ABerry) *led to 1/2-way: wknd over 1f out* **25/1**[3]
**5** *5* **Web Racer (IRE)** 2-8-9 ........ RWinston 5 30
(JRWeymes) *sn outpcd: nvr on terms* **33/1**
**6** *11* **Royal Flynn** 2-8-11 ........ LEnstone[(3)] 4 —
(MDods) *sn wl bhd* **40/1**

1m 11.06s (-2.66) **Going Correction** -0.525s/f (Hard) **6** Ran SP% **109.6**
Speed ratings: **96,92,91,88,82 67**CSF £1.66 TOTE £1.40: £1.10, £1.40; EX 1.70.
**Owner** Mrs S J Brookhouse **Bred** Manganaro Llc **Trained** Middleham Moor, N Yorks

**FOCUS**
A maiden won last year by subsequent Group winner Clifden and we may have seen another smart performer in Leo's Lucky Star, who can do a lot better in time.

**NOTEBOOK**
**Leo's Lucky Star(USA)**, a $200,000 yearling, half-brother the hugely talented, but often disappointing Leo's Luckyman, was very well backed to make a winning debut and justified the support with a promising success. A slight concern would be that he carried his head to the right in the early stages before hanging to the left under pressure. This may have been through greenness, but his half-brother was not always straightforward and the quirks could run in the family. Whatever the case, his potential is there for all to see and he will be worthy of respect in a much higher grade.
**Sunset Strip**, a 52,000gns foal, half-brother to four winners, out of an unraced half-sister to several performers in the US, was no match for the winner, but showed plenty of ability and should find a maiden.
**General Max(IRE)**, bought for 23,000gns as a two-year-old, is a half-brother to a six to seven-furlong winner. This was a pleasing debut and, given normal improvement, he should win a maiden.
**Kristikhab(IRE)** showed the benefit of his experience against a field of newcomers and is flattered to get so close.
**Web Racer(IRE)**, a 3,000gns yearling, half-sister to a winning juvenile, showed little immediate promise.

## 2423 17TH JUNE IS LADIES NIGHT H'CAP 5f
4:30 (4:30) (E ) (0-70,69) 3-Y-O+ £3,653 (£1,124; £562; £281) Stalls High

Form RPR
0-01 **1** **Parkside Pursuit**[7] 2246 6-9-2 **65** ........ CJDavies[(7)] 14 78
(JMBradley) *hld up in tch stands side: hdwy to ld that gp ent fnl f: r.o wl* **4/1**[2]
0-00 **2** *1* **Kangarilla Road**[12] 2130 5-9-10 **66** ........ TQuinn 5 75
(MrsJRRamsden) *prom far side: rdn to ld that gp ins fnl f: r.o: nt rch stands side ldr* **3/1**[1]
0060 **3** *½* **Tally (IRE)**[10] 2172 4-8-12 **54** ........ JFanning 15 62
(MJPolglase) *led stands rail to ent fnl f: kpt on towards fin* **25/1**
2340 **4** *nk* **Soaked**[19] 1956 11-9-3 **59** ........(b) ACulhane 2 66
(DWChapman) *led far side to ins fnl f: one pce* **20/1**
3402 **5** *shd* **Pirlie Hill**[5] 2290 4-8-3 **45** ........ RFfrench 16 51
(MissLAPerratt) *prom: effrt whn nt clr run over 1f out to ins fnl f: kpt on* **16/1**
0-63 **6** *½* **Brigadore**[12] 2130 5-9-7 **66** ........ THamilton[(3)] 6 70
(JRWeymes) *chsd far side ldrs tl rdn and nt qckn fnl f* **7/1**[3]
4060 **7** *hd* **College Maid (IRE)**[7] 2252 7-7-13 **48** ........(v[1]) JCurrie[(7)] 10 52
(JSGoldie) *cl up stands side: ev ch that gp over 1f out: one pce* **12/1**
1015 **8** *¾* **Blueberry Rhyme**[20] 1929 5-9-1 **60** ........(v) DNolan[(3)] 9 61
(PABlockley) *prom on outer of stands side gp: rdn and no ex appr fnl f* **25/1**
0602 **9** *2* **Vijay (IRE)**[10] 2175 5-8-8 **57** ........ AMullen[(7)] 12 51
(ISemple) *prom stands side to over 1f out: sn btn* **16/1**
0200 **10** *¾* **Xanadu**[6] 2261 8-8-11 **53** ........(p) RWinston 13 44
(MissLAPerratt) *spd stands side tl wknd appr fnl f* **16/1**
00-5 **11** *nk* **Sea Fern**[31] 1664 3-8-3 **53** ........ PHanagan 7 43
(DEddy) *sn outpcd far side: nvr on terms* **33/1**
-005 **12** *¾* **Peters Choice**[27] 1742 3-9-2 **69** ........ TEaves[(3)] 4 56
(ISemple) *chsd far side ldrs tl wknd over 1f out* **25/1**
0000 **13** *1* **Percy Douglas**[23] 1872 4-8-8 **50** ........(v) AnnStokell 11 34
(MissAStokell) *dwlt: chsd main gp stands side: outpcd fr 2f out* **66/1**
1205 **14** *½* **Dunn Deal (IRE)**[6] 2274 4-9-9 **65** ........ TEDurcan 8 47
(WMBrisbourne) *racd far side: sn outpcd: nvr on terms* **10/1**
-003 **15** *2 ½* **Snow Bunting**[6] 2261 6-8-1 **50** ........ LeanneKershaw[(7)] 3 23
(JeddO'Keeffe) *sn outpcd far side* **7/1**[3]
000- **16** *3 ½* **Northern Svengali (IRE)**[163] 5272 8-7-12 **40** ........(t) JMcAuley 1 —
(DANolan) *rrd s: a bhd far side* **66/1**

57.67 secs (-2.76) **Going Correction** -0.525s/f (Hard) **16** Ran SP% **126.7**
**WFA** 3 from 4yo+ 8lb
Speed ratings: **101,99,98,98,97 97,96,95,92,91 90,89,87,87,83 77**CSF £15.73 CT £289.54 TOTE £5.20: £1.90, £2.10, £5.60, £3.40; EX 27.60.
**Owner** J M Bradley **Bred** J K Keegan **Trained** Sedbury, Gloucs

**FOCUS**
A modest, but competitive sprint dominated by the best handicapped horses. The field split into two groups, but there appeared no obvious bias.

**NOTEBOOK**
**Parkside Pursuit ◆**, a shock 50/1 from what appeared to be an unfavouable draw at Goodwood on his previous start, followed up in most decisive fashion. He has won three on the bounce before (the third off a mark of 67) and he will be hard to oppose in his bid for the hat-trick.
**Kangarilla Road** has not won since 2002, but this effort would suggest he is about to end that run. He came out best of those on the far side and should soon gain compensation in a similar race.
**Tally(IRE)** ran a promising race over a trip short of his best (he has only ever won over six furlongs).
**Soaked** ran his race, but is on quite a long losing run.
**Pirlie Hill**, still a maiden, probably would have been a little closer with better luck.

## 2424 HANSEL FOUNDATION H'CAP 1m 2f
5:00 (5:00) (D ) (0-80,80) 3-Y-O+ £5,473 (£1,684; £842; £421) Stalls Low

Form RPR
1300 **1** **Hiawatha (IRE)**[84] 961 5-9-2 **71** ........ DNolan[(3)] 2 80
(PABlockley) *mde all: rdn over 2f out: carried rt ins fnl f: hld on wl* **9/1**
2-34 **2** *½* **Champain Sands (IRE)**[12] 2120 5-8-0 **57** ........ BSwarbrick[(5)] 1 65
(WMBrisbourne) *trckd ldrs: rdn to chal over 1f out: hung rt ins last: kpt on* **4/1**[1]
-402 **3** *shd* **Easibet Dot Net**[10] 2174 4-8-6 **58** ........(b[1]) RWinston 3 66
(ISemple) *cl up: effrt over 2f out: carried rt ins last: kpt on* **5/1**[2]
3-05 **4** *2 ½* **Leighton (IRE)**[11] 2142 4-10-0 **80** ........ TQuinn 7 83
(JDBethell) *hld up last: effrt over 2f out: r.o fnl f: no imp* **4/1**[1]

00-0 **5** ½ **Skiddaw Jones**[25] 1783 4-8-0 52 ........ RFfrench 5 54
(MissLAPerratt) *chsd ldrs tl rdn and one pce over 1f out* **12/1**

2446 **6** ½ **Sting Like A Bee (IRE)**[31] 1660 5-7-9 50 oh1 ........ NMackay(3) 6 51
(JSGoldie) *hld up in tch: effrt 2f out: sn no imp* **4/1**[1]

5040 **7** 1¼ **Lennel**[12] 2120 6-9-0 66 ........ (b) TEDurcan 4 65
(ABailey) *hld up in tch: rdn over 2f out: btn over 1f out* **6/1**[3]

2m 11.64s (-0.55) **Going Correction** -0.45s/f (Firm) **7** Ran SP% **108.6**
Speed ratings: **84,83,83,81,81 80,79**CSF £40.15 TOTE £9.30: £2.30, £4.70; EX 51.80 Place 6 £110.68, Place 5 £58.46.
**Owner** Nigel Shields **Bred** Kilcarn Stud **Trained** Southwell, Notts

**FOCUS**
Quite a competitive handicap, but the early pace was just steady and therefore the form may not be that sound.

**NOTEBOOK**
**Hiawatha(IRE)**, successful twice in claiming company over nine furlongs during the All-Weather season, showed himself just as effective on turf off the back of an 84-day break. Despite leading at just a steady pace, he could never quite get away from his rivals and had to work pretty hard in the straight. He is no sure thing to follow up, but should continue to go well in similar company.
**Champain Sands(IRE)** is still a maiden, but he has been in good form since joining his current connections and they look sure to find a race for him before too much longer. *Official explanation: jockey said gelding hung right-handed in the final 2f*
**Easibet Dot Net** was a little keen in first-time blinkers, but still had very chance in the straight and may have won this had he not kept ducking in behind the eventual winner when put under pressure. He is one to avoid.
**Leighton(IRE)** ran well in cheekpieces on his previous start, but they were left off this time and he was well held. He was settled in last for much of the way and a stronger pace would have suited.
**Skiddaw Jones** had conditions to suit, but has not won for nearly a year.
**Sting Like A Bee(IRE)** did not put up much of a show and is beginning to frustrate.
T/Plt: £431.70 to a £1 stake. Pool: £32,266.05. 54.55 winning tickets. T/Qpdt: £33.10 to a £1 stake. Pool: £2,220.00. 49.50 winning tickets. RY

# 2262 BATH (L-H)
## Thursday, May 27

**OFFICIAL GOING: Firm**
The course had endured a recent dry spell and the ground was described as firm.

## 2425 EUROPEAN BREEDERS FUND MAIDEN FILLIES' STKS 1m 5y
2:20 (2:20) (D) 3-Y-O £6,929 (£2,132; £1,066; £533) Stalls Low

Form RPR

3- **1** **Peeress**[208] 5869 3-8-11 ........ KFallon 3 68+
(SirMichaelStoute) *s.i.s: sn rcvrd to trck ldrs and t.k.h: led wl over 1f out: edgd lft ins last: kpt on wl: comf* **10/11**[1]

6- **2** 1½ **Grand Apollo**[279] 4347 3-8-11 ........ FNorton 5 65+
(JHMGosden) *s.i.s: bhd: hdwy on rails fr 3f out: styng on whn nt clr run ins last: swtchd rt: fin strly* **20/1**

0-32 **3** 1¼ **All Quiet**[8] 2223 3-8-11 67 ........ RHughes 9 62+
(RHannon) *led: kpt on wl whn strly chal fr over 3f out: hdd wl over 1f out: bdly hmpd ins last: nt rcvr and lost 2nd* **3/1**[2]

3-6 **4** 1 **Girl Warrior (USA)**[8] 2223 3-8-11 ........ SDrowne 10 60+
(PFICole) *chsd ldrs: rdn over 2f out: kpt on same pce appr fnl f* **12/1**

00-0 **5** 1¼ **Iphigenia (IRE)**[6] 2267 3-8-8 50 ........ RMiles(3) 11 57
(PWHiatt) *sn in tch: drvn to chse ldrs appr 3f out: one pce fnl 2f* **66/1**

005- **6** ¾ **La Professoressa (IRE)**[234] 5421 3-8-11 66 ........ RHavlin 4 55
(MrsPNDutfield) *mid-div: rdn 3f out: styd on fnl 2f but nvr gng pce to rch ldrs* **50/1**

0 **7** ½ **Palabelle (IRE)**[10] 2182 3-8-11 ........ MartinDwyer 6 54
(PWHarris) *chsd ldrs: rdn over 2f out: sn outpcd* **10/1**[3]

66 **8** 1¼ **Fire Finch**[13] 2081 3-8-8 ........ SHitchcott(3) 1 51
(MRChannon) *s.i.s: bhd: rdn over 2f out and n.d* **20/1**

2505 **9** ½ **Hsi Wang Mu (IRE)**[37] 1529 3-8-11 47 ........ JFEgan 7 50
(RBrotherton) *in tch: rdn 3f out: wknd 2f out* **100/1**

0- **10** 1¼ **Fatayaat (IRE)**[216] 5735 3-8-11 ........ WSupple 8 47
(BWHills) *trckd ldr: chal over 4f out: stl ev ch ins fnl 2f: wknd qckly over 1f out* **11/1**

-0 **11** 14 **Kerristina**[24] 1842 3-8-11 ........ CCatlin 2 15
(DJSFrenchDavis) *a bhd: lost tch fr over 2f out* **100/1**

1m 41.59s (0.59) **Going Correction** -0.15s/f (Firm) **11** Ran SP% **117.5**
Speed ratings: **91,89,88,87,86 85,84,83,83,81 67**CSF £28.61 TOTE £1.80: £1.10, £4.50, £1.20; EX 21.00.
**Owner** Cheveley Park Stud **Bred** Cheveley Park Stud Ltd **Trained** Newmarket, Suffolk
■ Stewards Enquiry : K Fallon caution: careless riding

**FOCUS**
An interesting maiden featuring some unexposed three-year-old fillies, but it was run at just a moderate pace and suited those that raced prominently and the first four may be better than the bare form.

**NOTEBOOK**
**Peeress** , off for 208 days prior to this, confirmed the promise of her sole juvenile outing to win with a bit up her sleeve, and there was a lot to like about the way she quickened up approaching the final furlong to score. Value for more than the official winning margin, as she still looked green when in the lead, she handled this much faster ground and it will be interesting to see where her connections aim her next.
**Grand Apollo** did the best of those to be held up off the gallop and shaped with promise late on, finishing best of all. She looks to have come on in leaps and bounds over the winter, and with further improvement expected for this experience, she should have little difficulty in losing her maiden tag.
**All Quiet** set the pace until challenged on the turn for home, but could not match the turn of foot shown by the winner late on. Tight for room on the rail when the winner wandered about in front, she can be rated slightly better than the bare form. She saw out this extra furlong well enough and may be worth a switch to handicaps.
**Girl Warrior(USA)** was keeping on at the one pace late on, but was not beaten far and will surely fare better now she is eligible for handicaps.
**Fatayaat(IRE)** dropped out tamely when the tempo increased two out. She has it all to prove now, but is entitled to improve on this return from a 216-day break.

## 2426 BETFRED.COM IN-RUNNING CLASSIFIED CLAIMING STKS 1m 5y
2:50 (2:50) (F) 3-Y-O+ £3,101 (£886; £443) Stalls Low

Form RPR

6110 **1** **Doctored**[21] 1909 3-8-10 60 ........ (p) BReilly(3) 12 66
(BAPearce) *chsd ldrs: rdn over 3f out: styd on to take narrow lded ins: fnl f: hld on all out* **16/1**

0130 **2** hd **Marnie**[54] 1244 7-9-4 51 ........ CCatlin 2 59
(JAkehurst) *chsd ldrs:rdn over 2f out: led appr fnl f: narrowly hdd ins last: styd pressing wnr: no ex last strides* **7/1**[3]

0220 **3** nk **Lord Chamberlain**[85] 953 11-9-11 53 ........ (b) RLMoore 8 65
(JMBradley) *mid-div: hdwy 3f out: styd on wl to chse ldrs ins fnl 2f: kpt on ins last: no ex cl home* **11/1**

0004 **4** 1¾ **Espada (IRE)**[4] 2322 8-9-1 58 ........ (b[1]) MartinDwyer 7 51
(JAOsborne) *led: sn clr: rdn over 2f out: hdd appr fnl f: outpcd ins last* **10/1**

0000 **5** shd **Go Green**[20] 1926 3-7-13 59 ........ FPFerris(3) 3 50
(PDEvans) *bhd: hdwy on ins over 3f out: styd on fr over 1f out: nt rch ldrs ins last* **12/1**

4540 **6** nk **Muqtadi (IRE)**[17] 1986 6-8-8 45 ........ KMay(7) 9 50
(MQuinn) *bhd: hdwy over 2f out: r.o wl fnl f: gng on cl home* **8/1**

0060 **7** 1½ **Eva Peron (IRE)**[15] 2034 4-8-5 45 ........ (p) CHaddon(7) 5 44
(WGMTurner) *in tch: rdn 3f out: styd on fnl 2f but nt trble ldrs* **20/1**

00-0 **8** 3½ **Leitrim Rock (IRE)**[18] 1369 4-9-1 52 ........ SWhitworth 16 39
(AGNewcombe) *v.s.a: bhd: rdn over 3f out: styd on wl fr over 1f out but nvr nr ldrs* **28/1**

-440 **9** 1½ **Mobo-Baco**[10] 2170 7-9-7 57 ........ SDrowne 15 41
(RJHodges) *mid-div: rdn and c wd bnd 3f out: nvr nr ldrs* **7/2**[1]

0-50 **10** ½ **Dark Shah (IRE)**[64] 1098 4-8-12 55 ........ (p) LPKeniry(3) 1 34
(DMSimcock) *mid-div: rdn over 3f out: n.d* **10/1**

000- **11** ½ **Legion Of Honour (IRE)**[350] 2308 5-9-6 60 ........ AQuinn(5) 13 43
(MissSJWilton) *a in rr* **50/1**

4-02 **12** ¾ **Ziet D'Alsace (FR)**[4] 2322 4-9-4 52 ........ IMongan 4 34
(AWCarroll) *chsd ldrs: rdn 3f out: wknd qckly ins fnl 2f* **6/1**[2]

2300 **13** 8 **Emperor Cat (IRE)**[74] 1025 3-8-5 54 ........ (b) DeanMcKeown 6 15
(PABlockley) *a bhd* **33/1**

06-0 **14** 7 **Toberoe Commotion (IRE)**[45] 594 6-9-1 45 ........ (b) RHavlin 11 —
(BJLlewellyn) *a in rr* **66/1**

6032 **15** 4 **Chandelier**[17] 2006 4-9-0 45 ........ (p) MSavage(5) 10 —
(MSSaunders) *s.i.s: a bhd* **20/1**

206- **16** 15 **Buchanan Street (IRE)**[166] 6172 3-8-7 56 ........ (b) KFallon 14 —
(NACallaghan) *a bhd* **10/1**

1m 40.14s (-0.86) **Going Correction** -0.15s/f (Firm)
**WFA** 3 from 4yo+ 12lb **16** Ran SP% **128.7**
Speed ratings: **98,97,97,95,95 95,93,90,88,88 87,87,79,72,68 53**CSF £122.39 TOTE £10.20: £3.00, £2.80, £3.80; EX 129.30.Doctored was claimed by P D Evans for £10,000.
**Owner** T M J Keep **Bred** Wickfield Farm Partnership **Trained** Newchapel, Surrey

**FOCUS**
A weak event that was run at a decent clip and the field was well strung out at the finish. The form is modest.

**NOTEBOOK**
**Doctored** showed a game attitude to hang on close home, relishing the step back up to this trip and a return to fast ground. He has been in good heart of late and, although he was best in at the weights and looked to be running on empty at the end, it was a good effort from his wide draw and he can remain handy at this level.
**Marnie** was only just denied and ran up to form on this drop in class. She often runs well over this course and distance and is always a threat at this level, but is hard to win with.
**Lord Chamberlain** was finishing best of all from off the pace and can be considered a little unlucky. He ran a game race at the weights, enjoyed the drop in grade and has now run with credit on all three outings over course and distance.
**Espada(IRE)** was lit up by the first-time blinkers and paid for setting the frenetic gallop. In the circumstances, he did well to hang on for fourth.
**Go Green** was handy throughout and ran her best race to date, but could only find the one pace under pressure and was well held.
**Mobo-Baco**, last seen in the winner's enclosure when winning this event last year, was well backed to repeat the feat. However, he was not helped by his wide draw and never looked like landing the odds. *Official explanation: jockey said gelding lost its action*
**Toberoe Commotion(IRE)** *Official explanation: jockey said gelding had a breathing problem*
**Chandelier** *Official explanation: jockey said gelding lost its action*
**Buchanan Street(IRE)** *Official explanation: jockey said colt had a breathing problem*

## 2427 BETFRED.COM NOW ONLINE MEDIAN AUCTION MAIDEN FILLIES' STKS 5f 11y
3:20 (3:21) (F) 2-Y-O £2,989 (£854; £427) Stalls Low

Form RPR

**1** **Don't Tell Mum (IRE)** 2-8-11 ........ RHughes 7 86
(RHannon) *sn w ldrs: led appr fnl 2f: narrowly hdd ins last: rdn and rallied to ld again cl home* **10/1**

**2** hd **Roodeye** 2-8-11 ........ KFallon 1 85
(RFJohnsonHoughton) *slt ld tl hdd appr fnl 2f: styd pressing wnr and led again ins last: hdd and no ex cl home* **4/1**[2]

3 **3** 1½ **Angel Sprints**[14] 2057 2-8-11 ........ ADaly 2 79
(LGCottrell) *pressed ldrs: rdn 2f out: one pce appr fnl f* **9/2**[3]

2 **4** 4 **Brag (IRE)**[14] 2058 2-8-11 ........ SDrowne 8 63
(RCharlton) *sn pressing ldrs: swtchd rt over 2f out: shkn up and btn over 1f out* **8/11**[1]

**5** 3 **Madam Caversfield** 2-8-11 ........ PDobbs 4 51
(RHannon) *slowly away: bhd and sn pushed along: kpt on fr over 1f out: fin wl but nvr a danger* **33/1**

40 **6** 6 **Ms Polly Garter**[10] 2177 2-8-11 ........ RLMoore 3 27
(JMBradley) *chsd ldrs: rdn over 3f out: sn wknd* **25/1**

000 **7** 1¼ **Muestra (IRE)**[17] 1984 2-8-11 ........ RHavlin 5 22
(MrsPNDutfield) *sn rdn: outpcd and bhd* **100/1**

**8** 2 **Indian Pearl (IRE)** 2-8-7 ow1 ........ MSavage(5) 6 —
(RJHodges) *wnt rt s: rdn 3f out and sn bhd* **66/1**

60.83 secs (-1.67) **Going Correction** -0.15s/f (Firm) **8** Ran SP% **114.4**
Speed ratings: **107,106,104,97,93 83,81,78**CSF £48.21 TOTE £6.80: £2.30, £1.60, £1.60; EX 32.40.
**Owner** Mrs Teresa M Moriarty **Bred** Pier House Stud **Trained** East Everleigh, Wilts

**FOCUS**
An exceptional winning time for the grade, providing a cracking finsih between two newcomers. The form look strong and it could prove to be an above-average maiden.

**NOTEBOOK**
**Don't Tell Mum(IRE)**, who played up in the stalls beforehand, pinged out from her wide draw and travelled sweetly on the pace, before hitting the front over two out. She was headed by the runner-up late on, but rallied gamely to get back up close home. This was a most pleasing debut effort, she added to her stable's decent strike rate with two-year-olds at the track, and could prove smart.
**Roodeye** ◆, a speedily-bred juvenile, was only just denied a winning start. She showed plenty of early dash and did little wrong in defeat, but could not shake off the winner late on. She had the benefit of the rail on this occasion, but will come on for the experience and looks a ready-made winner of a similar event.
**Angel Sprints** held every chance if good enough and probably ran up to the form of her debut effort at Salisbury last time. She is the benchmark for the form and looks the type to fare better when the nurseries begin.

**Brag(IRE)** failed to confirm the promise of her debut effort. She was on her toes in the paddock, ran keenly this time and may be capable of better, but has it all to prove now. *Official explanation: jockey said filly was unsuited by the firm ground*

**Madam Caversfield** ran distinctly green and was unable to go the pace early on, but shaped with a degree of promise in the straight and should know more next time.

## 2428 BETFRED SPRINT SERIES (QUALIFIER) (A FILLIES' H'CAP) 5f 161y

**3:50** (3:50) (E ) (0-75,67) 3-Y-O+ **£4,478** (£1,378; £689; £344) **Stalls** Low

Form RPR

4422 **1** **Boavista (IRE)**[10] 2165 4-8-13 **54**.............................. RHavlin 9 68
(PDEvans) *mde all: drvn out fnl f* **11/2**[3]

0-64 **2** *1 3/4* **Glencoe Solas (IRE)**[21] 1909 4-9-10 **65**......................(b[1]) PDobbs 5 73
(SKirk) *trckd ldrs: drvn to chse wnr fnl f: sn no imp* **11/2**[3]

1-05 **3** *1* **Aesculus (USA)**[13] 2097 3-9-3 **67**.............................. KFallon 3 71?
(LMCumani) *bhd and pushed along 3f out: swtchd rt to outside over 1f out and styd on wl: nt rch ldrs* **6/1**

0024 **4** *3/4* **Lily Of The Guild (IRE)**[64] 1098 5-8-13 **54**...................... IMongan 7 55
(WSKittow) *missed break: t.k.h: and sn in tch: rdn over 2f: one pce fnl f* **6/1**

0-00 **5** *nk* **Yomalo (IRE)**[23] 1855 4-9-7 **65**.............................. RMiles(3) 1 65
(RGuest) *bhd and outpcd: hdwy on rails fr 2f out:styng on whn hmpd and hung lft ins last: swtchd rt: fin wl: nt rch ldrs* **4/1**[1]

3021 **6** *3/4* **Nanna (IRE)**[10] 2165 3-8-4 **54** 6ex.............................. JMackay 6 52
(RHollinshead) *s.i.s: sn rcvrd and chsd wnr over 3f out: rdn 2f out: wknd fnl f* **5/1**[2]

-224 **7** *1 1/2* **Annijaz**[9] 2215 7-9-2 **57**.............................. RLMoore 2 49
(JMBradley) *a in rr: rdn 1/2-way: nvr gng pce to rch ldrs* **6/1**

-422 **8** *3 1/2* **Sea Jade (IRE)**[14] 2051 5-8-4 **45**.............................. JFEgan 4 25
(JWPayne) *chsd wnr tl over 3f out: wknd qckly over 2f out* **11/1**

69.42 secs (-1.72) **Going Correction** -0.15s/f (Firm)
**WFA** 3 from 4yo+ 9lb **8** Ran **SP% 118.6**
Speed ratings: **105,102,101,100,99 98,96,92**CSF £37.06 CT £191.53 TOTE £6.70: £1.90, £2.50, £1.90; EX 57.90.
**Owner** D Healy **Bred** Martyn J McEnery **Trained** Pandy, Gwent

**FOCUS**
A wide open and competitive fillies' sprint handicap that was run at a sound pace suggesting the form is solid.

**NOTEBOOK**
**Boavista(IRE)** gained a most deserved first success at the 23rd time of asking. She found herself in front early on, due to the lack of pace, but quickly took advantage and never really looked like being caught in the straight. She readily reversed recent course form with Nanna on these revised terms, and although she may struggle with a rise in the weights, she would be of interest if turned out under penalty in the meantime.
**Glencoe Solas(IRE)** ran a fair race in defeat and improved for this faster ground, plus the application of first-time blinkers.
**Aesculus(USA)** ran a moody race and got going all too late in the day, having looked reluctant early on. She has ability, but is clearly temperamental.
**Lily Of The Guild(IRE)** did not look all that suited by this drop in trip and lacked a change of gears.
**Yomalo(IRE)** stayed on in the closing stages having raced lazily in the early parts, and has now disappointed in three outings this term.
**Nanna(IRE)**, who improved for the switch to turf when making all at this track last time, had every chance if good enough, but failed to confirm the form with the winner under a 6lb penalty.

## 2429 BETFRED IN SHOPS, ON PHONE & ONLINE H'CAP 2m 1f 34y

**4:20** (4:20) (E ) (0-70,68) 4-Y-O+ **£3,643** (£1,121; £420; £420) **Stalls** Low

Form RPR

-500 **1** **Treasure Trail**[12] 2116 5-9-9 **65**.............................. JFEgan 6 76
(SKirk) *hld up in rr: rdn over 3f out: swtchd rt to outside over 2f out: strong run to ld 1f out: kpt on wl* **6/1**

4453 **2** *1 1/2* **Delta Force**[32] 1644 5-8-7 **49**.............................. DeanMcKeown 4 58
(PABlockley) *chsd ldrs: chal 3f out: led over 2f out: hdd 1f out: kpt on same pce* **5/1**[3]

06-0 **3** *1* **Noble Calling (FR)**[29] 602 7-8-10 **52**.............................. SDrowne 5 60
(RJHodges) *hld up in rr: hdwy whn squeezed and n.m.r 2f out: kpt on ins last: but nvr gng pce to rch ldrs* **6/1**

**3** *dht* **Donald (POL)**[340] 4-8-12 **56**.............................. RHughes 7 64
(MPitman) *hld up in rr: stdy hdwy over 2f out: sn edgd lft: rdn to chse ldrs over 1f out: nt qckn ins last* **8/1**

-061 **5** *1 1/2* **Sariba**[36] 1547 5-7-7 **40**.............................. HayleyTurner(5) 2 46
(ACharlton) *chsd ldr to 3f out: rdn: n.m.r and lost position wl over 1f out: swtchd rt and r.o again ins last* **9/2**[2]

5203 **6** *2* **Sashay**[10] 2167 6-8-3 **45**.............................. JMackay 3 49
(RHollinshead) *in tch: hdwy 7f out: rdn to chse ldrs 4f out: outpcd 2f out: styd on again fnl f* **10/3**[1]

43-5 **7** *1* **Henry Island (IRE)**[37] 1520 11-9-12 **68**.............................. CCatlin 8 71
(MrsAJBowlby) *chsd ldrs: t.k.h: rdn over 2f out: wknd over 1f out* **15/2**

66-0 **8** *1/2* **North Point (IRE)**[15] 2032 6-8-6 **51**......................(b[1]) RMiles(3) 1 53
(RCurtis) *led tl hdd over 2f out: sn btn* **16/1**

3m 47.88s (-1.72) **Going Correction** -0.15s/f (Firm)
**WFA** 4 from 5yo+ 2lb **8** Ran **SP% 115.3**
Speed ratings: **98,97,96,96,96 95,94,94**CSF £36.23 TOTE £7.70: £2.90, £1.50; EX 41.30 TRIFECTA Pl: Donald 1.30, Noble Calling 1.30; Tri: Treasure Trail/Delta Force/Donald 121.00, Treasure Trail/Delta Force/Noble Calling 94.13.
**Owner** T Neill & Mrs John Lee **Bred** R G Percival And R Kent **Trained** Upper Lambourn, Berks
■ Stewards Enquiry : J Mackay caution: used whip down the shoulder in the forehand position

**FOCUS**
A moderate staying handicap run at only a steady pace and the form not sure to work out.

**NOTEBOOK**
**Treasure Trail**, settled in last place for most of the way, was suited by the running of the race and showed a fair turn of foot to hit the front and settle the issue just over a furlong from home. He has tumbled in the weights as a result of losing his form on the level, but has been hurdling over the winter and has clearly come to himself of late. *Official explanation: trainer said, regarding the improved form shown, gelding was suited by not being bustled along in the early stages today*
**Delta Force**, who proved easy to back in the betting ring, paid late on for running too freely for the first half of the race, but lost little in defeat over this longer trip. He can be placed to advantage off this lowly turf mark.
**Noble Calling(FR)**, a winner over hurdles latest, was another doing all of his best work late in the day and put up an improved display without ever looking like winning.
**Donald(POL)** ◆ looks the one to take out of the race. He was still on the bridle two out and looked to be going like the winner, but understandably tired on this return from a 340-day absence. This was a pleasing British debut and he should improve on this.
**Sariba** can be rated slightly better than the bare form as she did not enjoy the best of runs when making her challenge.
**Sashay**, the popular favourite, proved disappointing and had no obvious excuses.

## 2430 BETFRED.COM EARLY PRICES FROM 9 A.M. H'CAP 1m 2f 46y

**4:50** (4:52) (E) (0-70,73) 3-Y-O+ **£3,633** (£1,118; £559; £279) **Stalls** Low

Form RPR

4-04 **1** **Nantucket Sound (USA)**[17] 1997 3-8-11 **67**.............................. KFallon 8 76
(MCPipe) *sn pushed along: hdwy and drvn 5f out: rdn again 3f out: r.o to ld and edgd lft 1f out: kpt on wl u.p* **5/2**[1]

0554 **2** *nk* **Karaoke (IRE)**[5] 2302 4-9-9 **65**.............................. JFEgan 2 74+
(SKirk) *bhd: hdwy and nt clr run 2f out: swtchd rt and hdwy to chse wnr jst ins fnl f: hld cl home* **9/2**[2]

0011 **3** *1* **Voice Mail**[6] 2262 5-10-0 **73** 5ex.............................. LPKeniry(3) 4 80+
(AMBalding) *hld up in rr: stdy hdwy fr 2f out: qckning whn nt clr run 1f out: swtchd rt: fin strly but nt rcvr* **5/2**[1]

3000 **4** *1/2* **Skylarker (USA)**[17] 2000 6-10-0 **70**.............................. IMongan 5 76
(WSKittow) *chsd ldrs: led 6f out: rdn over 2f out: hdd 1f out and sn outpcd* **9/1**[3]

2120 **5** *7* **Wanna Shout**[20] 1940 6-8-13 **58**.............................. LisaJones(3) 11 51
(RDickin) *bhd: hdwy on outside fr 3f out: drvn to chse ldrs ins fnl 2f: wknd fnl f* **20/1**

0502 **6** *4* **Nuzzle**[6] 2272 4-8-5 **47**.............................. FNorton 3 32
(MQuinn) *chsd ldrs: rdn: n.m.r and wknd qckly 1f out* **10/1**

-006 **7** *4* **Castaigne (FR)**[5] 2302 5-9-1 **57**.............................. RHavlin 7 35
(BWDuke) *chsd ldrs: rdn over 2f out: wknd over 1f out* **20/1**

53-0 **8** *3/4* **Billy Bathwick (IRE)**[5] 2302 7-9-2 **58**.............................. RLMoore 9 34
(JMBradley) *chsd ldrs tl wknd 2f out* **14/1**

000- **9** *1 1/4* **Wood Street (IRE)**[28] 2363 5-9-2 **58**.............................. VSlattery 6 32
(RJBaker) *a in rr* **66/1**

10-0 **10** *3* **Factual Lad**[13] 2084 6-9-12 **68**.............................. GBaker 10 36
(BRMillman) *led tl hdd 6f out: wknd over 2f out* **20/1**

4322 **11** *1 1/4* **Mr Whizz**[9] 1987 7-7-13 **41** ow1..............................(p) CCatlin 12 7
(APJones) *a in rr* **22/1**

0500 **12** *2* **Bowing**[52] 1272 4-9-4 **60**.............................. DKinsella 1 22
(PGMurphy) *w ldr after 2f: wknd rapidly 5f out* **40/1**

2m 7.22s (-3.78) **Going Correction** -0.15s/f (Firm)
**WFA** 3 from 4yo+ 14lb **12** Ran **SP% 123.6**
Speed ratings: **109,108,107,107,101 98,95,94,93,91 90,88**CSF £13.04 CT £32.22 TOTE £4.90: £2.10, £1.80, £1.60; EX 25.40 Place 6 £70.40, Place 6 £56.18.
**Owner** T M Hely-Hutchinson **Bred** Janus Bloodstock Inc **Trained** Nicholashayne, Devon

**FOCUS**
A modest handicap that produced a very fast time for the grade and the first four were clear, which suggests the form is sound.

**NOTEBOOK**
**Nantucket Sound(USA)**, who disappointed when well-backed at Windsor last time, needed all of his rider's strength and persistence to score a first-ever success on this much faster ground. He is a tricky ride, but remains lightly raced and can build on this.
**Karaoke(IRE)** only just went down and ran another solid race on ground he clearly needs to be seen at his best. He deserves to get his head in front.
**Voice Mail** has to be considered slightly unlucky on this attempt to land the quick-fire course hat-trick. He was still full of running behind the leaders with a furlong to run, but found nowhere to go and lost momentum when having to be switched to challenge thereafter.
**Skylarker(USA)** improved on recent efforts for this faster ground, but held every chance if good enough and could do with a further drop in the weights. He was clear of the rest.
**Factual Lad** *Official explanation: jockey said gelding lost its action*
T/Jkpt: Not won. T/Plt: £112.70 to a £1 stake. Pool: £42,821.00. 277.15 winning tickets. T/Qpdt: £28.60 to a £1 stake. Pool: £2,844.60. 73.60 winning tickets. ST

2431 - 2437a (Foreign Racing) - See Raceform Interactive

2337

# LONGCHAMP (R-H)

Thursday, May 27

**OFFICIAL GOING: Good to soft**

## 2438a PRIX DU PALAIS-ROYAL (GROUP 3) 7f

**2:20** (2:22) 3-Y-O+ **£25,704** (£10,282; £7,711; £5,141)

RPR

**1** **Puppeteer**[28] 1741 4-9-4 .............................. CSoumillon 8 109
(ADeRoyer-Dupre, France) *hld up, progress on outside over 2f out, rdn to chal over 1f out, led 100y out, drvn out* 1

**2** *nk* **Saratan (IRE)**[26] 1780 7-9-4 ..............................(b) ELegrix 2 108
(MDelzangles, France) *hld up, pushed along over 1 1/2f out, rdn & ran on to chal ins fnl f, tk 2nd cl hme*

**3** *nk* **Crystal Castle (USA)**[28] 1741 6-9-4 .............................. TGillet 1 107
(JEHammond, France) *mid-div on rail, effort & hdwy 1 1/2f out, ev ch ins fnl f, kpt on*

**4** *nk* **Charming Groom (FR)**[28] 1741 5-9-4 .............................. OPeslier 4 106
(FHead, France) *disp ld tl tk clr advantage over 3f out, pushed along over 1 1/2f out, hdd 100yds out, kpt on* 2

**5** *1 1/2* **Rockets 'n Rollers (IRE)**[17] 1999 4-9-4 .............................. DaneO'Neill 6 103
(RHannon) *mid-div, disp 3rd str, effort to chase ldrs 2f out, ran on til no ex ins fnl f*

**6** *1/2* **Indian Haven**[12] 2109 4-9-4 .............................. DHolland 9 101
(PWD'Arcy) *raced towards rr, pushed along 1 1/2f out, nvr threatened* 3

**7** *nse* **The Wise Lady (FR)**[28] 1741 4-9-1 .............................. FSpanu 3 98
(MNigge, France) *prom, cl up disp 4th str, pushed along & ran on from 1 1/2f out til one pce ins fnl f*

**8** *2* **Blanche (FR)**[51] 1291 5-9-3 .............................. C-PLemaire 5 95
(JRossi, France) *prom til pushed along & one pace 1 1/2f out*

**9** *8* **Key To Pleasure (GER)**[242] 5261 4-9-4 .............................. ASuborics 7 76
(MarioHofer, Germany) *towards rr early, prog to disp 3rd str, pushed along over 1 1/2f out, one pace*

**10** *2* **Fabuleux River (FR)**[28] 1741 4-9-4 ..............................(b) YBarberot 10 71
(NMadamet, France) *disp ld tl 2nd over 3f out, pushed along 2f out, wknd*

1m 19.8s **Going Correction** -0.10s/f (Good) **10** Ran **SP% 120.9**
Speed ratings: **113,112,112,111,110 109,109,107,98,95.**
**Owner** 6c Racing Ltd **Bred** Cheveley Park Stud Ltd **Trained** France

**NOTEBOOK**
**Puppeteer** looks a progressive performer and this quicker ground saw him in a better light. He deserved his first Group success and was suited by this truly-run race. Connections are now looking for a Group Two race over a similar distance in Europe.
**Saratan(IRE)** was also held up and literally followed the winner throughout the final stages. He was given every possible chance and a tilt at the Prix de La Porte Maillot is now on the cards.
**Crystal Castle(USA)** was putting in his best work at the finish. He now looks back to his best and has been entered in both the Golden Jubilee at Ascot and the July Cup.
**Charming Groom(FR)** set a fast early pace. He was still well there one out but just ran out of steam in the final stages.

**Rockets 'n Rollers(IRE)**, who failed to see out the mile last time, was happier back over this trip, but was taking on better opposition. He quickened from one and a half out and looked dangerous until his stride shortened in the closing stages.
**Indian Haven** found the ground too fast according to his rider. He made up some late ground inside the last furlong but never really got in a blow on this occasion.

# 2321 BRIGHTON (L-H)

Friday, May 28

**OFFICIAL GOING: Firm**

Wind: Hazy, sunny Weather: Fresh, hlf across

## 2439 EBF/YELL LTD MEDIAN AUCTION MAIDEN STKS 5f 213y
2:10 (2:11) (E) 2-Y-O £3,406 (£1,048; £524; £262) Stalls Low

Form RPR

4 **1** **Dahteer (IRE)**[12] 2141 2-9-0 ........ TEDurcan 1 80
(MRChannon) *led after 1f: edgd rt ins fnl f: rdn out* **11/4**[2]

4 **2** 1 ¾ **Silver Wraith (IRE)**[9] 2225 2-9-0 ........ JPMurtagh 5 78+
(NACallaghan) *chsd ldrs: swtchd lft over 4f out: chal and hung lft fr 2f out: eased whn hld last 50 yds* **13/8**[1]

42 **3** ½ **Stedfast McStaunch (IRE)**[14] 2086 2-8-11 ........ LPKeniry(3) 4 73
(BJMeehan) *chsd ldrs: sltly hmpd over 4f out: swtchd lft and effrt 2f out: sn hld by ldng pair: styd on nr fin* **9/2**[3]

02 **4** 3 ½ **Alright My Son (IRE)**[18] 1996 2-9-0 ........ RLMoore 3 62
(RHannon) *led 1f: w ldrs tl no ex fnl 2f* **11/2**

**5** 6 **Ransacker** 2-9-0 ........ PDobbs 8 44
(CEBrittain) *s.s: rdn along and bhd: nvr nr to chal* **25/1**

20 **6** 5 **Colonel Bilko (IRE)**[41] 1462 2-9-0 ........(b[1]) SDrowne 7 28
(BRMillman) *hung rt thrght: w ldrs 4f* **14/1**

5 **7** 2 **Tipsy Lillie**[18] 1984 2-8-9 ........ NPollard 6 17
(JulianPoulton) *sn outpcd: towards rr whn hmpd over 4f out: bhd fnl 2f* **33/1**

00 **8** 8 **Faithfull Girl (IRE)**[2] 2405 2-8-6 ........ FPFerris(3) 2 —
(MissZCDavison) *sn outpcd: towards rr whn hmpd over 4f out: no ch fnl 2f* **100/1**

1m 10.26s (0.16) **Going Correction** -0.075s/f (Good) **8 Ran SP% 112.8**
Speed ratings: **95,92,92,87,79 72,70,59**CSF £7.35 TOTE £3.70: £1.20, £1.10, £1.80; EX 8.40.
**Owner** Sheikh Ahmed Al Maktoum **Bred** Darley **Trained** West Ilsley, Berks
■ Stewards Enquiry : J P Murtagh caution: careless riding

**FOCUS**
A medium tempo which quickened soon after halfway and this looks strong juvenile form for the track.

**NOTEBOOK**
**Dahteer(IRE)** did not look entirely comfortable on the track but had the rail to help him, despite showing a tendency to edge away from it in the straight. This confirmed the promise of his debut, and there is more to come.
**Silver Wraith(IRE)** became hopelessly unbalanced on the camber and proved almost unrideable in the final furlong. He will find a race on a more conventional track. *Official explanation: jockey said colt hung left in the last 2 furlongs.*
**Stedfast McStaunch(IRE)** gets this trip really well and shapes as if he will stay farther. In the meantime, a routine maiden over six furlongs is there for the taking.
**Alright My Son(IRE)** has early speed but became unbalanced, drifting up the camber on this notoriously tricky course. Five furlongs on a straight, flat, course would suit him better at present.
**Ransacker** blew it at the start, but the experience of this first outing will help. His dam won over this course.
**Colonel Bilko(IRE)** was wearing blinkers for the first time, but he still hung dreadfully from the outset and raced too freely into the bargain.
**Tipsy Lillie** *Official explanation: jockey said filly was struck into and lost her action.*

## 2440 BETFRED SPRINT SERIES (QUALIFIER) (A H'CAP) 5f 59y
2:40 (2:40) (D) (0-80,78) 3-Y-0+ £5,421 (£1,668; £834; £417) Stalls Low

Form RPR

5500 **1** **Hard To Catch (IRE)**[6] 2303 6-8-11 66........(b) MSavage(5) 8 77
(DKIvory) *outpcd towards rr: hrd rdn and hdwy over 1f out: drvn to ld fnl 100 yds: sn clr* **5/1**[1]

1000 **2** 1 ½ **Yorkie**[33] 1642 5-8-3 53........ JFEgan 3 59
(PABlockley) *prom: hrd rdn 2f out: led 1f out: hdd and one pce fnl 100 yds* **7/1**

2-04 **3** 1 ¼ **Jayanjay**[123] 607 5-10-0 78........ SSanders 5 80
(MissBSanders) *chsd ldrs: one pce appr fnl f* **5/1**[1]

4400 **4** ¾ **Port St Charles (IRE)**[11] 2178 7-8-11 66........ RThomas(5) 4 65
(CRDore) *sn bhd: hrd rdn and hdwy over 1f out: hung lft: swtchd rt ins fnl f: fin wl* **20/1**

2003 **5** nk **Lady Pekan**[8] 2252 5-8-8 61........(b) FPFerris(3) 1 59
(PSMcentee) *broke wl: led tl 1f out: no ex* **7/1**

0013 **6** ½ **Guns Blazing**[8] 2246 5-8-5 62........(b) MHoward(7) 10 58
(DKIvory) *chsd ldr: rdn and ev ch over 1f out: no ex fnl f* **11/2**[2]

6201 **7** ¾ **Byo (IRE)**[7] 2274 6-9-5 69........ JPMurtagh 9 62
(MQuinn) *a abt same pl: hrd rdn wl over 1f out: nvr able to chal* **6/1**[3]

-350 **8** 2 **Tender (IRE)**[6] 2282 4-8-7 57........ SDrowne 7 43
(MrsStefLiddiard) *sn outpcd in rr* **12/1**

00-0 **9** ½ **Loch Inch**[8] 2246 7-8-7 57........(b) RLMoore 6 41
(JMBradley) *plld hrd: in tch over 3f* **20/1**

-000 **10** 6 **Beyond Calculation (USA)**[7] 2274 10-8-10 60........(p) TEDurcan 2 23
(JMBradley) *chsd ldrs: hmpd on rail and snatched up after 1f: nt rcvr: bhd whn eased over 1f out* **10/1**

61.46 secs (-0.81) **Going Correction** -0.075s/f (Good) **10 Ran SP% 114.3**
Speed ratings: **103,100,98,97,96 96,94,91,90,81**CSF £38.94 CT £185.30 TOTE £6.80: £2.40, £2.30, £2.40; EX 58.90.
**Owner** Mrs Karen Graham **Bred** Flan Hannon **Trained** Radlett, Herts

**FOCUS**
An ordinary handicap but a solid gallop all the way.

**NOTEBOOK**
**Hard To Catch(IRE)** goes well on the track but the early tempo had him at full stretch. However, he looked better the further he went, and by the finish he was well on top.
**Yorkie** bounced back to form with a fine effort. He showed speed throughout and is worth noting if running here again from a good draw.
**Jayanjay** ran well, despite being off the track for nearly four months. He goes well on switchback courses and is a good weight carrier in races like this.
**Port St Charles(IRE)** showed a return to form on a track that was not ideal, and over a trip short of his best. If he reproduces this effort under more favourable conditions, he is handicapped to win.
**Lady Pekan** blazed a trail but slightly overdid it and did not quite get up the final hill. She deserves to win again and has every chance of doing so.
**Guns Blazing** paid the penalty for taking on the leader, but his natural pace will give him plenty more chances.
**Byo(IRE)** finds five furlongs on fast ground here a bit on the sharp side, and it was again his inability to go the early pace that proved his downfall.
**Beyond Calculation(USA)** was effectively put out of the race by an early incident. He tends to win during the summer months, and his trainer will find him more good opportunities despite the advance of time.

## 2441 WEATHERBYS BANK RATED STKS (H'CAP) 6f 209y
3:10 (3:10) (D) (0-85,82) 4-Y-O+ £4,737 (£1,796; £898; £408) Stalls Low

Form RPR

-001 **1** **Idle Power (IRE)**[2] 2399 6-8-12 73 3ex........(p) JPMurtagh 6 86
(JRBoyle) *dwlt: sn chsng ldrs: drvn to ld over 1f out: all out* **6/4**[1]

0066 **2** hd **Greenwood**[10] 2206 6-9-2 77........ SDrowne 7 89
(PGMurphy) *hdwy 2f out: str chal fnl f: hrd rdn: r.o* **4/1**[2]

300- **3** 7 **Concubine (IRE)**[260] 4852 5-8-4 65 oh5........ RLMoore 2 59
(JRBoyle) *outpcd in rr: styd on to take mod 3rd ins fnl f* **9/1**

2020 **4** 1 ¾ **Dawn Piper (USA)**[10] 2196 4-9-4 82........(v) TPQueally(3) 5 71
(DRLoder) *chsd ldr tl over 2f out: wknd over 1f out* **9/2**[3]

00-0 **5** 2 ½ **Mandarin Spirit (IRE)**[14] 2094 4-9-0 75........(b) SSanders 3 58
(GCHChung) *led tl over 1f out: sn wknd* **15/2**

0000 **6** 7 **Agilis (IRE)**[5] 2325 4-8-4 65 oh10........(b) JFEgan 4 30
(JamiePoulton) *chsd ldrs 4f* **16/1**

2350 **7** nk **Single Track Mind**[18] 1986 6-8-4 65 oh20........ MHenry 1 29
(JRBoyle) *outpcd: sn wl bhd* **50/1**

1m 21.09s (-1.51) **Going Correction** -0.075s/f (Good) **7 Ran SP% 107.8**
Speed ratings: **105,104,96,94,91 83,83**CSF £6.58 TOTE £2.50: £1.40, £2.50; EX 7.10.
**Owner** The Idle B's **Bred** Mountarmstrong Stud **Trained** Epsom, Surrey

**FOCUS**
A fair handicap, although not that competitive race, but a strong gallop, with the field soon stretched out.

**NOTEBOOK**
**Idle Power(IRE)** only just managed to overcome a 3lb penalty for his win at Goodwood two days earlier. However, he has won off much higher marks in the past and, now he is such good form again, he should be capable of handling a further rise.
**Greenwood** is back at the top of his game and can certainly win off this mark, so his connections will be hoping he is not raised too much for the narrow defeat.
**Concubine(IRE)** ran satisfactorily on this first appearance since September considering she was out of the handicap. However, she has only one career win to her name.
**Dawn Piper(USA)** chased the tearaway leader and suffered a similar fate.
**Mandarin Spirit(IRE)** went off plenty fast enough, leaving nothing for the final climb.
**Agilis(IRE)** has now been reported as having hung left on this track twice running. In addition, he was 10lb out of the handicap. *Official explanation: jockey said gelding had hung left.*
**Single Track Mind** *Official explanation: jockey said gelding did not handle the track.*

## 2442 BRIGHTON SQUARE FILLIES' H'CAP 1m 1f 209y
3:40 (3:41) (E) (0-75,68) 3-Y-O £3,779 (£1,163; £581; £290) Stalls High

Form RPR

00-4 **1** **Prenup (IRE)**[18] 1998 3-8-11 58........ JPMurtagh 7 69
(LMCumani) *trckd ldr: led 5f out: hrd rdn over 1f out: hld on wl* **5/2**[1]

0-05 **2** nk **Wee Dinns (IRE)**[28] 1755 3-9-6 67........ JFEgan 1 78
(SKirk) *cl up: drvn to chse wnr 2f out: str chal fnl f: r.o* **13/2**

261- **3** 4 **Munaawashat (IRE)**[311] 3479 3-9-7 68........ RHills 2 71
(MJohnston) *dwlt: hld up in rr: swtchd v wd ent st: hdwy over 2f out: hung lft: one pce* **9/2**[2]

2-40 **4** nk **Bubbling Fun**[15] 2059 3-9-4 65........ SDrowne 3 67
(EALDunlop) *t.k.h: in tch: drvn and outpcd over 3f out: rallied over 1f out: no ex fnl f* **20/1**

5-50 **5** 1 **Dolly Wotnot (IRE)**[18] 1998 3-9-0 64........ TPQueally(3) 6 65
(NPLittmoden) *hld up in rr: effrt 3f out: hrd rdn and carried lft fr 2f out: no imp* **12/1**

00-3 **6** 2 **Velvet Waters**[11] 2168 3-8-12 59........ SSanders 4 56
(RFJohnsonHoughton) *led 5f: hrd rdn and btn 2f out* **5/1**[3]

524- **7** 13 **Tardis**[246] 5175 3-9-3 64........ IMongan 8 36
(MLWBell) *chsd ldng pair: cl 3rd and rdn whn hmpd 2f out: sn btn* **9/1**

0445 **8** 3 **Mambina (USA)**[18] 1998 3-9-4 65........ TEDurcan 5 31
(MRChannon) *t.k.h: cl up: rdn 4f out: wknd 2f out* **6/1**

2m 1.59s (-0.95) **Going Correction** -0.075s/f (Good) **8 Ran SP% 113.5**
Speed ratings: **100,99,96,96,95 93,83,81**CSF £18.85 CT £68.13 TOTE £2.90: £1.30, £2.50, £1.70; EX 20.30.
**Owner** Fittocks Stud **Bred** Fittocks Stud Ltd **Trained** Newmarket, Suffolk

**FOCUS**
A moderate handicap run at only a fair pace until the tempo wound up turning down into the straight. The form looks sound enough.

**NOTEBOOK**
**Prenup(IRE)** was in the right position to quicken up the pace inside the last half-mile, and that undoubtedly helped her. However, she is relatively unexposed.
**Wee Dinns(IRE)** gave the winner a tough battle. She got the trip well and can win a similar event.
**Munaawashat(IRE)**, whose rider is unlikely to enjoy watching the video of this race, could hardly have made her effort wider without ending up in the car park, and the fact the she then hung the other way only added to her problems. This was a satisfactory seasonal debut but, ideally, she needs a rail on her left side.
**Bubbling Fun** made a fair handicap debut, but she races keenly and looks as if she will be suited by a stronger pace.
**Dolly Wotnot(IRE)** continues to run with credit. The hanging Munaawashat carried her left-handed across the track and, while she would not have troubled the first two, that hindered her efforts to reach the first three for the first time in her career.
**Velvet Waters** failed to live up the promise of her seasonal debut, but the way this race was run did not suit her. She should be at home over a truly-run a mile and a half.
**Mambina(USA)** *Official explanation: jokcey said filly did not handle the track.*

## 2443 PLEASURE PALACE RACING LADY RIDERS SERIES CLAIMING STKS 1m 3f 196y
4:10 (4:11) (F) 4-Y-O+ £2,884 (£824; £412) Stalls High

Form RPR

-600 **1** **Golden Boot**[26] 1785 5-10-3 63........(v) MissVCottrill(7) 6 69
(ABailey) *s.s: wl bhd and patiently rdn tl smooth hdwy in centre over 1f out: led ins fnl f: rdn clr* **5/2**[2]

0412 **2** 4 **Banningham Blaze**[4] 2363 4-10-3 50........(v) MrsSBosley 5 56
(AWCarroll) *sn bhd: rdn and hdwy over 2f out: chsd ldr over 1f out: one pce fnl f* **3/1**[3]

0006 **3** shd **Margery Daw (IRE)**[4] 2363 4-9-10 60........ MissJCDuncan(5) 1 54
(PSMcentee) *led: sn 10 l clr: wknd and hdd ins fnl f* **20/1**

0021 **4** 3 **Romil Star (GER)**[9] 2228 7-10-6 50........(b) MsCWilliams 3 54
(KRBurke) *remote 3rd to 1/2-way: 20 l 5th ent st: styd on fnl f* **9/2**

4102 **5** 2 **Chocolate Boy (IRE)**[16] 2031 5-10-1 60........(b) MissHGrissell(5) 2 51
(GLMoore) *chsd clr ldr and 20 l clr of rest: wknd and lost 2nd over 1f out* **9/4**[1]

6000 **6** *8* **Piquet**[5] 2324 6-10-5 45 ow3................................ MissDonnaHandley(7) 4 44
(JJBridger) *plld hrd and bhd: wnt remote 3rd 1/2-way: btn over 2f out* **50/1**

2m 33.53s (1.43) **Going Correction** -0.075s/f (Good) **6** Ran SP% **109.2**
Speed ratings: **92,89,89,87,85 80**CSF £9.80 TOTE £3.90: £2.00, £1.20; EX 11.80.
**Owner** Peter G Freeman **Bred** R S Cockerill (farms) Ltd **Trained** Little Budworth, Cheshire
■ Stewards Enquiry : Miss V Cottrill £80 fine: passport irregularity

**FOCUS**
Just a moderate race, but with Margery Daw tearing off ten lengths ahead of Chocolate Boy, and the others another 20 lengths adrift, this was a bizarre race to watch. However, the two leaders eventually ran themselves into the ground.

**NOTEBOOK**
**Golden Boot**, given an ice-cool ride, was produced with impeccable timing despite still being last, 15 lengths behind the leader, at the two-furlong pole. The fast pace played into his hands, but his rider knew exactly what she was doing.
**Banningham Blaze**, given a tidy ride, ran her usual game race but was beaten on merit.
**Margery Daw(IRE)** nearly nicked it from the front despite setting a strong pace. She held on for a remarkably long time but, predictably, the final hill found her out.
**Romil Star(GER)**, not ideally suited by the combination of trip, pace and fast ground, was soon struggling and only began to recover too late.
**Chocolate Boy(IRE)** paid the price for being the only one to chase the fast tempo set by Margery Daw.
**Piquet** was held up to get the trip but is likely to be more effective being allowed to stride out over shorter distances.

## 2444 RENDEZVOUS CASINO CLASSIFIED STKS 5f 213y
4:40 (4:40) (E) 3-Y-O £3,360 (£1,034; £517; £258) Stalls Low

Form RPR

0-23 **1** **Borzoi Maestro**[11] 2181 3-9-0 73..................................(p) SSanders 6 79
(JLSpearing) *t.k.h: chsd ldrs: led over 1f out: edgd lft: hrd rdn fnl f: hld on wl* **4/1**[2]

010- **2** *nk* **Sweet Pickle**[216] 5751 3-8-5 70.......................................... TPQueally(3) 3 72
(DJCoakley) *racd freely: led tl over 1f out: hrd rdn: kpt on wl* **25/1**

1020 **3** *1 1/4* **Ask The Clerk (IRE)**[14] 2091 3-9-0 73.................................. MTebbutt 9 74
(VSmith) *mid-div: rdn and hdwy over 1f out: kpt on* **9/1**

-214 **4** *1/2* **Shrink**[27] 1775 3-8-8 69.................................................... IMongan 1 67
(MLWBell) *chsd ldrs: rdn over 2f out: kpt on fnl f* **7/2**[1]

2-1 **5** *shd* **Place Cowboy (IRE)**[58] 1200 3-9-2 75.......................................... SWKelly 7 75
(JAOsborne) *towards rr: effrt over 2f out: carried hd high: r.o fnl 100 yds* **5/1**

04-4 **6** *1 1/4* **Fair Compton**[16] 2029 3-8-8 65................................................ PDobbs 8 63
(RHannon) *prom: ev ch 2f out: one pce appr fnl f* **12/1**

210- **7** *1 1/4* **Averlline**[204] 5931 3-8-11 73.............................................. DKinsella 5 62
(BDeHaan) *hld up in rr: hrd rdn 2f out: hung lft: 7th and sme hdwy whn snatched up nr fin* **14/1**

30-0 **8** *nk* **One Upmanship**[15] 2063 3-8-11 68...................................(e[1]) RLMoore 2 61
(JGPortman) *towards rr: outpcd and bhd 2f out: swtchd outside 1f out: styd on* **16/1**

0225 **9** *1* **Get To The Point**[10] 2211 3-8-13 72.................................. JPMurtagh 10 60
(PWD'Arcy) *s.i.s: hld up in rr: shkn up 2f out: swtchd lft over 1f out: n.d* **9/2**[3]

4300 **10** *3 1/2* **Kuringai**[15] 2063 3-8-6 69........................................................ AQuinn(5) 4 48
(BWDuke) *prom 4f* **12/1**

69.75 secs (-0.35) **Going Correction** -0.075s/f (Good) **10** Ran SP% **118.9**
Speed ratings: **99,98,96,96,96 94,92,92,91,86**CSF £98.91 TOTE £4.80: £1.60, £5.40, £2.40; EX 145.20 Place 6 £25.38, Place 5 £21.71.
**Owner** The Square Milers **Bred** B A Beale & Bbb Computer Services Ltd **Trained** Kinnersley, Worcs

**FOCUS**
A tight sprint in which only 5lb separated the runners on official adjusted ratings and the form has a solid look. They went a medium sprint pace early on, with the final charge developing soon after halfway.

**NOTEBOOK**
**Borzoi Maestro** got away on level terms this time and the early pace was not strong enough to stop him being too keen. However, he looks an improved performer this season.
**Sweet Pickle** was too fresh early on and had to be restrained in front. However, the way she battled back after being headed suggests she will have a good season.
**Ask The Clerk(IRE)** is well exposed but he seems to go on any ground and this was one of his better efforts.
**Shrink** saw her race out well despite being slightly caught for speed two furlongs from home. She gets this trip well and should win again.
**Place Cowboy(IRE)** did not look comfortable as he hit the climb in the last two furlongs, but he was going on well at the finish and only just missed third place. He would stay seven furlongs.
**Fair Compton** travelled noticeably well and has the speed to cope with a return to five furlongs.
**Averlline** found things happening a bit too fast on this seasonal debut. On ground as fast as this over a sharp track, an extra furlong would help.
**Get To The Point** was again badly drawn and never had the position to get competitive. However, he should be kept in mind in similar company.
T/Plt: £32.50 to a £1 stake. Pool: £32,736.45. 734.35 winning tickets. T/Qpdt: £12.00 to a £1 stake. Pool: £1,957.10. 120.60 winning tickets. LM

# 1709 PONTEFRACT (L-H)
Friday, May 28

**OFFICIAL GOING: Good to firm**
There was drizzle during the evening and race times suggest the ground was on the fast side of good. The inside rail was moved out by about five yards.

## 2445 BUTTERCROSS CLAIMING STKS 1m 4y
6:35 (6:35) (E) 4-Y-O+ £3,731 (£1,148; £574; £287) Stalls Low

Form RPR

0340 **1** **Bailieborough (IRE)**[10] 2218 5-9-2 68...........................(v) AlexGreaves 2 70
(DNicholls) *hld up in tch: hdwy over 3f out: led over 1f out: sn clr* **11/10**[1]

-600 **2** *5* **Countykat (IRE)**[16] 2039 4-8-9 68................................ DonnaBashton(7) 3 59
(KRBurke) *trckd ldrs: hdwy on inner an d n.m.r over 2f out: swtchd rt and led briefly over 1f out: sn hdd: kpt on same pce* **7/2**[2]

**3** *3* **Good Time Bobby**[396] 7-8-8 ................................................ DAllan(3) 5 47
(JO'Reilly) *s.i.s and bhd: hdwy over 2f out: kpt on appr last: n.d* **16/1**

/004 **4** *6* **Lord Conyers (IRE)**[30] 1710 5-8-1 40..............................(p) PHanagan 4 23
(BEllison) *chsd ldrs: rdn along 3f out: wknd 2f out* **15/2**

2625 **5** *hd* **Dancing King (IRE)**[18] 2007 8-8-2 48 ow1........................... PMakin(5) 1 29
(PWHiatt) *led: rdn along 3f out: hdd over 1f out and wknd qckly* **4/1**[3]

000/ **6** *13* **Holderness Girl**[19] 1965 11-8-1 30........................................ RFfrench 6 —
(MESowersby) *chsd ldr: rdn along 3f out: wkng whn hmpd 2f out and sn b ehind* **50/1**

1m 45.19s (-0.41) **Going Correction** -0.025s/f (Good) **6** Ran SP% **109.4**
Speed ratings: **101,96,93,87,86** —CSF £4.87 TOTE £2.10: £1.40, £2.70; EX 5.40.
**Owner** Middleham Park Racing Xviii **Bred** Churchtown Stud **Trained** Sessay, N Yorks
■ Stewards Enquiry : Donna Bashton two-day ban: careless riding (Jun 8-9)

**FOCUS**
A modest claimer in which only a couple had a realistic chance at the weights and they finished first and second. The pace was solid enough, but the form is difficult to assess overall.

**NOTEBOOK**
**Bailieborough(IRE)**, with the the visor back on, was suited by the decent gallop. Given a patient ride, when asked to go and win his race he found more than enough to sweep past some modest rivals. He has never won a handicap and this looks to be his level.
**Countykat(IRE)**, marginally best in on adjusted official ratings, was just getting the better of the pace-setter when the favourite ranged alongside and that was the end of that. He was rated 90 when returning to these shores last summer, which shows just how much he has gone backwards.
**Good Time Bobby**, who has been placed over hurdles, was making his Flat debut following a break of 13 months. He never offered a serious threat, but appears to retain some ability and this should have put an edge on him for a return to timber.
**Lord Conyers(IRE)**, a modest plater, had plenty on at the weights and ran accordingly.
**Dancing King(IRE)** established his usual position out in front, but merely set the race up for others and was easily picked off. This stiff mile seemed to find him out. *Official explanation: jockey said gelding slipped on the bend and lost his action.*

## 2446 MSK FILLIES' H'CAP 1m 2f 6y
7:05 (7:05) (E) (0-70,70) 3-Y-O+ £5,603 (£1,724; £862; £431) Stalls Low

Form RPR

-420 **1** **Grey Clouds**[12] 2142 4-9-13 **69**................................................ WSupple 3 76
(TDEasterby) *hld up in midfield: stdy hdwy 4f out: swtchd rt wl over 1f out rdn to ld ent last: styd on wl* **11/2**[3]

0131 **2** *1 3/4* **Olivia Rose (IRE)**[10] 2216 5-10-0 **70** 5ex.................................. JQuinn 6 74
(JPearce) *hld up in tch: hdwy on inner 4f out: led wl over 1f out: rdn and hdd ent last: kpt on u.p* **5/1**[2]

0-50 **3** *2* **Untidy Daughter**[11] 2174 5-8-7 **52**........................................(p) TEaves(3) 2 52
(BEllison) *hld up and bhd: hdwy on inner 2f out: swtchd rt and rdn over 1f out: kpt on ins last: nrst fin* **14/1**

200- **4** *shd* **Dreams Forgotten (IRE)**[353] 2256 4-9-1 **57**..................... AMcCarthy 4 57
(GGMargarson) *led: rdn along over 2f out: hdd wl over 1f out and grad wknd appr last* **40/1**

4210 **5** *3/4* **Got To Be Cash**[16] 2034 5-8-7 **52**.......................................... DAllan(3) 5 50
(WMBrisbourne) *hld up and bhd: hdwy 2f out: swtchd lft and rdn over 1f out: kpt on in inslast: n earest fin* **11/1**

00 **6** *3/4* **Zan Lo (IRE)**[16] 2039 4-9-2 **58**............................................ PHanagan 7 55
(BSRothwell) *bhd: hdwy on inner 2f out: sn rdn and kpt on ins last: nrst fin* **40/1**

3004 **7** *1* **Dance Party (IRE)**[51] 1297 4-9-7 **63**......................................(p) KFallon 9 58
(AMBalding) *trckd ldrs: hdwy 4f out: pushed along over 2f out: rdn and wkng whn n.m.r over 1f out* **11/2**[3]

0-30 **8** *nk* **Odabella (IRE)**[21] 1931 4-9-9 **68**.................................... LisaJones(3) 12 62
(JohnBerry) *bhd: hdwy 2f out: swtchd outside and styd on wl fnl f: nrst fin* **9/1**

2356 **9** *3* **Transcendantale (FR)**[6] 2297 6-8-5 **47**.............................. JFanning 11 36
(MrsSLamyman) *in tch: rdn along 4f out: wknd over 2f out* **14/1**

0006 **10** *shd* **Infidelity (IRE)**[10] 2197 3-8-6 **62**......................................... CCatlin 10 50
(ABailey) *chsd ldrs on outer: rdn along over 2f out: drvn and wknd wl over 1f out* **14/1**

6630 **11** *2* **East Riding**[10] 2216 4-8-3 **45**.............................................. AnnStokell 8 30
(MissAStokell) *chsd ldr: rdn along over 3f out: wknd over 2f out* **50/1**

0001 **12** *5* **Estimate**[14] 2092 4-9-6 **62**...............................................(v) PaulEddery 13 37
(JohnAHarris) *in tch on outer: rdn along over 3f out: sn wknd* **14/1**

-024 **13** *7* **Holly Rose**[7] 2262 5-8-7 **54**........................................(p) HayleyTurner(5) 1 16
(DECantillon) *hld up in rr: hdwy and in tch over 4f out: rdn and wedakened over 3f out* **9/2**[1]

2m 14.3s (0.39) **Going Correction** -0.025s/f (Good)
**WFA** 3 from 4yo+ 14lb **13** Ran SP% **117.5**
Speed ratings: **97,95,94,93,93 92,91,91,89,89 87,83,78**CSF £32.17 CT £369.11 TOTE £6.70: £1.90, £2.10, £3.40; EX 22.90.
**Owner** Vintage Partners **Bred** Gleadhill House Stud Ltd **Trained** Great Habton, N Yorks
■ Stewards Enquiry : W Supple two-day ban: careless riding (Jun 8-9)

**FOCUS**
A fairly competitive fillies' handicap, though the pace was ordinary. The first two are not particularly well treated.

**NOTEBOOK**
**Grey Clouds** put her disappointing Ripon effort behind her on a track more suited to closers. She was a little fortunate to get a dream run against the inside rail on the home turn, but when pulled out for her effort she grasped the opportunity with both hands.
**Olivia Rose(IRE)**, carrying a 5lb penalty for her Redcar victory, enjoyed the run of the race and did nothing wrong at all. Her rider even took a glance over his right shoulder passing the furlong pole so well was the mare travelling, but he would have been horrified by what he saw.
**Untidy Daughter**, better known as a hurdler and still a maiden on the Flat, stayed on well in the short home straight to snatch third place. Things did not pan out for her over a longer trip last time, but on this evidence she looks worth another try.
**Dreams Forgotten(IRE)**, a maiden trying her longest trip to date and reappearing after a break of 11 months, was given a positive ride and ran well at a huge price. Lack of peak fitness may have found her out rather than lack of stamina and she looks worth another go at the trip.
**Got To Be Cash** is a very hard horse to win with and is 7lb above her winning mark, but she was a bit unlucky here as she had to sit and suffer behind a wall of horses passing the furlong pole, and by the time she got out the principals had gone beyond recall. She would probably have finished third otherwise.
**Zan Lo(IRE)** ◆ had the whole field in front of her turning for home, but when switched inside stayed on in encouraging fashion up the home straight. This was her best effort since arriving from the French Provinces and the faster ground may have been the reason. She is one to watch out for under similar conditions.
**Odabella(IRE)** ◆ was noted staying on at the death and is from a stable well capable of placing their horses to advantage. *Official explanation: trainer said mare was not suited by the firm ground and was sore in her back.*
**Transcendantale(FR)** *Official explanation: jockey said mare was struck into.*
**Holly Rose** ought to have had no problem with the conditions, but failed to perform. *Official explanation: trainer was unable to offer any explanation for poor form shown.*

## 2447 YOUNGSTERS CONDITIONS STKS 6f
7:35 (7:35) (C) 2-Y-O £9,210 (£3,493; £1,746; £794) Stalls Low

Form RPR

**1** **Tony James (IRE)** 2-8-8 .......................................................... DHolland 5 95+
(CEBrittain) *cl up: led wl over 1f out: pushed out* **6/1**

12 **2** *1* **Dario Gee Gee (IRE)**[45] 1383 2-8-13 ........................ NCallan 6 94
(KARyan) *keen: trckd ldrs on outer: hdwy 2f out and sn ev ch: rdn and edgd lft ent last: sn drvn and nt qckn* **6/4**[1]

1 **3** *6* **Society Music (IRE)**[39] 1498 2-8-5 ........................ LEnstone(3) 4 71
(MDods) *trckd ldrs: effrt over 2f out: sn rdn and one pce fr over 1f out* **10/3**[3]

51 **4** *shd* **Indibraun (IRE)**[8] 2234 2-8-13 ........................ GFaulkner 3 76
(PCHaslam) *led: rdn along over 2f out: hdd wl overf 1f out and sn wknd* **3/1**[2]

**5** *11* **Forest Viking (IRE)** 2-8-5 ........................ TEaves(3) 2 38
(JSWainwright) *s.i.s: a rr* **50/1**

**6** *7* **Midnight In Moscow (IRE)** 2-8-1 ........................ RoryMoore(7) 1 17
(PCHaslam) *trckd ldrs: effrt on inner whn jinked and hit rail over 2f out: nt rcvr* **25/1**

1m 17.82s (0.52) **Going Correction** -0.025s/f (Good) **6** Ran SP% **108.2**
Speed ratings: **95,93,85,85,70 61**CSF £14.38 TOTE £7.80: £2.90, £1.20; EX 19.50.
**Owner** A J Richards **Bred** Ewar Stud Farms **Trained** Newmarket, Suffolk

**FOCUS**
A very interesting juvenile event. The time was only fair, but the winner was not all out to score and the form looks strong.

**NOTEBOOK**
**Tony James(IRE)**, a 22,000euros yearling out of a half-sister to several winners including Ben Ewar, was thrown in at the deep end for this debut but passed with flying colours. He looked sure to be swallowed up by the favourite a furlong from home, but he found extra and his rider never had to get serious with him. The winning time was only fair, but beating previous winners on your debut is always a smart effort and he should go on to better things.
**Dario Gee Gee(IRE)**, up a furlong in trip and on fast ground for the first time, came with what looked to be a race-winning challenge on the outside soon after turning for home, but he found the winner had more up his sleeve and he was comfortably held, though he did pull a long way clear of the rest. Time may show he faced an impossible task in trying to concede weight to a decent sort.
**Society Music(IRE)**, on very different ground to when making a winning debut here last month, was completely left behind by the front pair in the home straight. There was a question mark over her on the ground, but it is more likely she was just outclassed. *Official explanation: jockey said filly was unsuited by the ground.*
**Indibraun(IRE)** tried the same tactics that worked so well for him at Doncaster, but on this stiffer track and against much better opposition he was very quickly found out.
**Forest Viking(IRE)**, a half-brother to two winners in Japan, faced a tall order on this debut and showed little.
**Midnight In Moscow(IRE)**, who fetched 27,000gns as a two-year-old, is a half-brother to a couple of winners abroad. He ended up well beaten on this debut, but that was partly due to getting into a real tangle on the home turn. He may prove himself a bit better than this, and his American pedigree could make him interesting on sand.

## 2448 SKY BET PRESS RED TO BET H'CAP — 1m 4y
**8:05** (8:05) (D ) (0-85,85) 3-Y-O **£10,712** (£3,296; £1,648; £824) **Stalls** Low

Form RPR

1- **1** **Penrith (FR)**[227] 5563 3-9-7 **85** ........................ JFanning 3 90
(MJohnston) *trckd ldrs on inner: pushed along and outpcd 3f out: gd hdwy on inner 2f out: rdn to ld ins last: drvn and kpt on gamely* **11/2**[3]

-005 **2** *shd* **Tranquil Sky**[10] 2202 3-9-5 **83** ........................ KFallon 5 88
(NACallaghan) *in tch: hdwy to trck ldrs over 3f out: effrt on outer over 1f out and sn ev ch: rdn and hung lft ins last: kpt on* **5/2**[1]

16-2 **3** *1* **Alekhine (IRE)**[13] 2135 3-9-7 **85** ........................ PHanagan 4 88
(PWHarris) *s.i.s and bhd: hdwy 3f out: swtchd rt over 1f out and sn rdn: styd on strly ins last: nrst fin* **10/1**

3563 **4** *2 1/2* **Weet A Head (IRE)**[8] 2237 3-8-13 **77** ........................ WSupple 6 74+
(RHollinshead) *tacked ldrs: hdwy to chal over 2f out: rdn over 1f out and ev ch whn hmpd and squeezed out ins last* **16/1**

3222 **5** *1 1/4* **My Paris**[12] 2145 3-8-9 **73** ........................ NCallan 11 67
(KARyan) *trckd ldng pair: effrt over 2f out and ev ch tl rdn and btn whn n.m.r ins last* **16/1**

-316 **6** *1/2* **Granston (IRE)**[26] 1795 3-9-0 **78** ........................ PRobinson 1 71
(JDBethell) *cl up: rdn along over 2f out: drvn and edgd lft over 1f out: hld whn hmpd ins last* **4/1**[2]

0-02 **7** *1* **Reidies Choice**[8] 2239 3-8-8 **72** ........................ MFenton 7 63
(JGGiven) *hld up in rr: hdwy on outer over 2f out: sn rdn and kpt on same pce appr last* **10/1**

1200 **8** *shd* **Mount Vettore**[26] 1795 3-9-2 **80** ........................ DHolland 2 70
(MrsJRRamsden) *hld up and bhd tl sme late hdwy* **8/1**

1200 **9** *3 1/2* **Heversham (IRE)**[13] 2135 3-9-0 **78** ........................ ACulhane 10 60
(WJHaggas) *led: rdn along over 2f out: edgd rt over 1f out: hdd ent fnl f: wknd whn n.m.r ins last* **33/1**

0412 **10** *5* **Inchloss (IRE)**[15] 2069 3-8-13 **77** ........................ JQuinn 9 48
(BAMcmahon) *in tch: effrt on outer 2f out: sn rdn and btn* **12/1**

1563 **11** *5* **Wings Of Morning (IRE)**[44] 1392 3-8-3 **67** ........................ JBramhill 8 26
(PABlockley) *chsd ldrs: rdn along over 3f out: sn wknd* **50/1**

1m 44.04s (-1.56) **Going Correction** -0.025s/f (Good) **11** Ran SP% **117.6**
Speed ratings: **106,105,104,102,101 100,99,99,96,91 86**CSF £19.56 CT £136.16 TOTE £4.60: £2.60, £2.10, £3.90; EX 14.40.
**Owner** Sheikh Mohammed **Bred** Gilles Forien And Mme Gilles Forien **Trained** Middleham Moor, N Yorks
■ Stewards Enquiry : K Fallon caution: careless riding

**FOCUS**
A competitive handicap producing a thrilling finish and a decent winning time for the grade. The form looks reasonably solid.

**NOTEBOOK**
**Penrith(FR)**, off since making a winning debut at Leicester last October, did not look likely to figure approaching the home bend, but once in line for home a gap appeared on the inside rail as the leader started to hang and he was quickly through it. The courage he then showed to hold off the favourite was typical of one from the yard and with only two outings under his belt there seems no reason why he should not continue to improve.
**Tranquil Sky**, backed to gain compensation for his rather unlucky effort at Goodwood despite the shorter trip, was off the bridle turning for home, but kept responding. He then started to hang left inside the last furlong, despite the best efforts of the champion, and arguably lost more ground by doing so than he was beaten by.
**Alekhine(IRE)** ◆, making his handicap debut, was slowly away and then trailed the field for much of the contest, but he really found his feet up the final climb and did very well to finish so close. He is very much one to watch out for when stepped up to ten furlongs.
**Weet A Head(IRE)**, who is gradually sliding down the handicap, was never far away and was right in there pitching when badly hampered by the runner-up inside the last furlong. He would have been placed at least.
**My Paris** is still a maiden, but ran another decent race under a positive ride and it is only a matter of time before things fall right for him.
**Granston(IRE)** ran another sound race of his new mark, especially as he suffered in the chain reaction caused by the runner-up and can be rated a few lengths better than his finishing position.
**Reidies Choice** did not improve for the longer trip on a stiff track.
**Mount Vettore** *Official explanation: jockey said gelding hung right handed.*
**Heversham(IRE)** made the running as usual, but was already dropping away when getting caught up in the melee inside the last furlong.

## 2449 ST JOHN AMBULANCE H'CAP — 1m 4f 8y
**8:35** (8:35) (E ) (0-70,67) 3-Y-O+ **£5,018** (£1,544; £772; £386) **Stalls** Low

Form RPR

-316 **1** **Red Forest (IRE)**[24] 1858 5-8-8 **48** ........................ (t) DaleGibson 4 61
(JMackie) *hld up in tch on inner: hdwy 3f out: chal wl over 1f out and ev ch: drvn ins last: rallied wl ld last 100 yds* **9/1**

04-0 **2** *2* **Night Sight (USA)**[8] 2235 7-9-13 **67** ........................ KFallon 6 77
(MrsSLamyman) *hld up in rr: gd hdwy 4f out: led wl over 1f out: rdn and edgd lft ent last: sn drvn: hdd and no ex last 100 yds* **10/1**

2-40 **3** *5* **Blackthorn**[28] 1754 5-9-4 **58** ........................ DHolland 7 60
(MrsJRRamsden) *behind: rdn along 1/2-way: hdwy on inner 3f out: hmpd and swtchd rt over 1f out: styd on wl fnl f: nrst fin* **6/1**[3]

40-0 **4** *3* **Red River Rebel**[10] 2212 6-9-4 **58** ........................ DarrenWilliams 11 55
(JRNorton) *chsd ldr: led wl over 2f out: rdn and hdd wl over 1f out: drvn and one pce appr last* **25/1**

50-2 **5** *1 1/4* **Swynford Pleasure**[8] 2235 8-8-10 **53** ........................ DAllan(3) 2 48
(JHetherton) *hld up: hdwy over 3f out: rdn 2f out: drvn over 1f out and sn no imp* **11/2**[2]

60-0 **6** *nk* **Commemoration Day (IRE)**[20] 1972 3-8-7 **64** ........................ RWinston 1 59
(JGGiven) *in tch: pushed along over 4f out: rdn and wkng whn hmpd over 3f out: bhd after* **8/1**

1025 **7** *shd* **Bramantino (IRE)**[6] 2299 4-9-4 **58** ........................ (b) PHanagan 5 52
(RAFahey) *chsd ldrs: rdn along over 3f out: sn wknd* **10/1**

140- **8** *6* **Tasneef (USA)**[151] 5500 5-9-6 **63** ........................ J-PGuillambert(3) 10 48
(TDMccarthy) *plld hrd: sn led: rdn along and hdd wl over 2f out: grad wknd* **40/1**

0001 **9** *3/4* **Maritime Blues**[8] 2235 4-9-9 **63** 5ex ........................ MFenton 8 47
(JGGiven) *chsd ldrs: rdn along 4f out: sn btn* **9/2**[1]

1211 **10** *2 1/2* **Isa'Af (IRE)**[28] 1754 5-9-5 **64** ........................ PMakin(5) 9 44
(PWHiatt) *towards rr: effrt over 3f out: sn rdn and no hdwy* **9/2**[1]

-633 **11** *10* **Michaels Dream (IRE)**[8] 2235 5-8-0 **40** ........................ (b) JMcAuley 3 4
(JHetherton) *a rr* **16/1**

2m 39.35s (-0.70) **Going Correction** -0.025s/f (Good)
**WFA** 3 from 4yo+ 17lb **11** Ran SP% **117.5**
Speed ratings: **101,99,96,94,93 93,93,89,88,87 80**CSF £95.61 CT £588.54 TOTE £12.30: £3.60, £2.20, £2.90; EX 94.00.
**Owner** P Riley **Bred** Olympic B'Stock Ltd, Freynestown B'Stock And B Hi **Trained** Church Broughton, Derbys

**FOCUS**
An ordinary handicap in which a few paid for taking a keen hold in front and it suited those coming from off the pace. The form looks sound, however.

**NOTEBOOK**
**Red Forest(IRE)**, whose rider was content to take a pull after half a mile having started off on terms, got stronger as the race progressed. He looked sure to be beaten when the runner-up ranged alongside a furlong from home, but found much more than that rival off the bridle and this stiff 12 furlongs appeared to suit him perfectly.
**Night Sight(USA)**, given a patient ride, looked sure to end his long losing run under the champion jockey when brought with his effort in the short home straight, but he found disappointingly little under pressure. He is 9lb below his last winning mark, but has also become very expensive to follow.
**Blackthorn** ◆, not for the first time this year, ran an eye-catching race under conditions that suit and he is well handicapped at present. He is one to watch out for when the market speaks in his favour. *Official explanation: jockey said gelding hung right handed in the closing stages.*
**Red River Rebel** was unable to get to the front until rounding the home bend, and then had little with which to resist the closers, but he still did best of those that raced up with the pace from the off. He is worth keeping in mind if returned to his beloved Beverley.
**Swynford Pleasure** was a little disappointing, but is well handicapped if rediscovering her best form.
**Commemoration Day(IRE)**, making his handicap debut and stepping up half a mile in trip, did not perform as though the longer distance was what he needed.
**Tasneef(USA)**, back on the Flat after three runs over hurdles and racing for the first time since December, did too much too soon and eventually paid for it.
**Maritime Blues** was beaten too far from home for the 5lb penalty for his Doncaster victory to have been the only reason. *Official explanation: trainer was unable to offer any explanation for poor form shown.*
**Isa'Af(IRE)** ran poorly and a whopping 9lb rise for his two victories last month appear to have undone him.

## 2450 BARBICAN MAIDEN STKS — 6f
**9:05** (9:05) (D ) 3-Y-O **£5,616** (£1,728; £864; £432) **Stalls** Low

Form RPR

3-23 **1** **Emtilaak**[43] 1420 3-9-0 78 ........................ WSupple 5 81+
(BHanbury) *trckd ldr: led 1/2-way: clr wl over 1f out: easily* **13/8**[1]

30- **2** *5* **Wrenlane**[296] 3887 3-9-0 ........................ PHanagan 4 62
(RAFahey) *towards rr: hdwy 3f out: pushed along 2f out: styd on ins last: no ch w wnr* **16/1**

50 **3** *nk* **Four Kings**[38] 1530 3-9-0 ........................ (t) JTate 3 61
(JMPEustace) *hld up in rr: hdwy on inner over 2f out: rdn over 1f out: kpt on ins last nrst fin* **9/1**

4 **4** *hd* **Laska (IRE)**[10] 2211 3-8-9 ........................ KFallon 6 56
(MJWallace) *hld up: hdwy 3f out: rdn to chse wnr over 1f out: hung bdly lft ins last and sn wknd* **10/3**[3]

3- **5** *6* **Firebird Rising (USA)**[379] 1618 3-8-9 ........................ DHolland 7 38
(TDBarron) *chsd ldrs: shkn up over 2f out: btn and eased over 1f out* **5/2**[2]

00-0 **6** *6* **Grey Orchid**[20] 1972 3-8-6 ........................ TEaves(3) 1 20
(TJEtherington) *led: rdn along and hdd 1/2-way: wknd 2f out* **50/1**

**7** *2* **Estoille** 3-8-9 ........................ JQuinn 2 14
(MrsSLamyman) *chsd ldrs: rdn along over 2f out: sn wknd* **50/1**

1m 16.17s (-1.13) **Going Correction** -0.025s/f (Good) **7** Ran SP% **109.5**
Speed ratings: **106,99,98,98,90 82,80**CSF £26.66 TOTE £2.70: £1.50, £4.50; EX 37.00 Place 6 £83.14, Place 5 £68.32.
**Owner** Hamdan Al Maktoum **Bred** Shadwell Estate Company Limited **Trained** Newmarket, Suffolk

**FOCUS**
An uncompetitive maiden in which less than half the field had a realistic chance, but a decent time for the grade.

**NOTEBOOK**
**Emtilaak** found the drop back in trip just what he needed, and he treated this modest field with contempt. Whether he has truly turned the corner remains to be seen, though and it will be interesting to see where he goes next, especially as his handicap mark does not look in any way lenient.
**Wrenlane**performed well enough if beaten pointless by the winner, but this was his first start in nine months and he now qualifies for a handicap mark.
**Four Kings** may not have achieved that much in finishing third, but this was still his best effort so far and he also now qualifies for a mark.

**Laska(IRE)** did not seem to improve much from her promising Leicester debut, but the way she hung late on suggests there may have been other reasons for this slightly below-par effort.
**Firebird Rising(USA)**, not seen since a promising debut at York a year ago, raced prominently until turning into the home straight. She may then have blown up and if she has retained any ability then her current handler will find it.
T/Plt: £84.50 to a £1 stake. Pool: £50,933.75. 439.60 winning tickets. T/Qpdt: £31.00 to a £1 stake. Pool: £2,848.10. 67.90 winning tickets. JR

## 2183 WOLVERHAMPTON (A.W) (L-H)

Friday, May 28

**OFFICIAL GOING: Standard**
Wind: slt across Weather: light rain

### 2451 PETER GENT - NIGHTFREIGHT FILLIES' H'CAP 7f (F)
**2:30** (2:31) (F) (0-55,55) 3-Y-0+ **£2,947** (£842; £421) **Stalls** High

Form RPR
-030 **1** **Miskina**[21] 1932 3-8-2 **55** ... BSwarbrick(5) 7 62
(WMBrisbourne) *hld up mid-div: hdwy over 3f out: rdn over 2f out: r.o to ld nr fin* **11/2**[3]
3263 **2** *nk* **Largs**[13] 2123 4-8-10 **47** ... JEdmunds 11 53
(JBalding) *hld up: hdwy over 4f out: led over 2f out: sn rdn: hdd nr fin* **5/1**[2]
6402 **3** *1* **Dasar**[39] 1515 4-8-4 **48** ...(v) DTudhope(7) 10 51
(MBrittain) *w ldrs: rdn and ev ch over 2f out: r.o one pce fnl f* **7/1**
40-5 **4** *2 ½* **Hilarious (IRE)**[24] 1875 4-8-12 **49** ... GBaker 9 46
(BRMillman) *prom: lost pl 4f out: sn rdn: rallied over 1f out: kpt on same pce fnl f* **13/2**
6000 **5** *3 ½* **Ace-Ma-Vahra**[4] 2350 6-8-10 **47** ... JBramhill 8 35
(SRBowring) *led: rdn and hdd over 2f out: wknd fnl f* **20/1**
2451 **6** *½* **Maggie's Pet**[32] 1681 7-8-13 **50** ...(t) SWhitworth 3 37
(KBell) *chsd ldrs: rdn over 3f out: no hdwy fnl 2f* **7/2**[1]
0005 **7** *2* **Kedross (IRE)**[4] 2357 3-7-9 **50** ow4 ... CHaddon(7) 12 31
(JJay) *s.s: nvr nr ldrs* **25/1**
**8** *2* **Red Melodica (USA)**[26] 1818 4-9-4 **55** ... RWinston 6 31
(JJQuinn) *hld up and bhd: hdwy on outside over 3f out: sn rdn: wknd over 1f out* **25/1**
3660 **9** *1 ¾* **Cloudless (USA)**[14] 2098 4-9-3 **54** ... GGibbons 5 26
(JWUnett) *w ldrs: rdn and ev ch over 2f out: sn wknd* **7/1**
060 **10** *1 ¼* **Princess Bankes**[14] 2098 3-7-9 **50** ... DeanWilliams(7) 1 18
(MissGayKelleway) *sn outpcd* **12/1**
066- **11** *5* **Duncanbil (IRE)**[172] 6141 3-7-13 **54** ow1 ... DerekNolan(7) 4 9
(RFFisher) *prom: rdn over 4f out: sn wknd* **12/1**
-006 **12** *nk* **Satsu (IRE)**[32] 1667 3-8-4 **52** ... MFenton 2 7
(JGGiven) *outpcd* **10/1**

1m 31.14s (0.82) **Going Correction** 0.0s/f (Stan)
**WFA** 3 from 4yo+ 11lb **12** Ran SP% **129.5**
Speed ratings: **95,94,93,90,86 86,83,81,79,78 72,72**CSF £35.67 CT £203.82 TOTE £9.00: £2.00, £2.20, £4.00; EX 57.30.
**Owner** The Blacktoffee Partnership **Bred** Darley **Trained** Great Ness, Shropshire

**FOCUS**
A poor affair with the top weight rated only 55 and overall the form is banded level.

**NOTEBOOK**
**Miskina**, 2lb lower than when a fair third over the stretch mile here last month, needed every yard of this trip.
**Largs** could not quite hold the winner on this return back up to seven.
**Dasar** turned in another sound effort wearing the visor in this slightly higher grade.
**Hilarious(IRE)** appeared to find this distance on the short side on her All-Weather debut.

### 2452 D A CONSTABLE LTD LIABILITY UNDERWRITERS CLAIMING STKS 1m 4f (F)
**3:00** (3:00) (F) 3-Y-0 **£2,905** (£830; £415) **Stalls** Low

Form RPR
2500 **1** **Bold Blade**[34] 1613 3-9-1 70 ...(b) GGibbons 1 71+
(MJPolglase) *mde all: pushed clr 3f out: rdn wl over 1f out: eased ins fnl f* **8/1**
0-00 **2** *9* **Spectested (IRE)**[21] 1947 3-8-2 56 ...(p) JFMcDonald(3) 5 47
(BJMeehan) *s.i.s: hld up: rdn over 6f out: hdwy over 5f out: chsd wnr 2f out: no imp* **10/1**
3121 **3** *3 ½* **Caspian Dusk**[13] 2127 3-8-12 70 ... CHaddon(7) 3 56
(WGMTurner) *hld up: rdn and hdwy over 4f out: chsd wnr briefly over 2f out: wknd 1f out* **6/5**[1]
6301 **4** *10* **Pepe (IRE)**[29] 1740 3-8-9 57 ... StephanieHollinshead(5) 7 36
(RHollinshead) *w wnr tl rdn over 3f out: wknd over 2f out* **2/1**[2]
2305 **5** *16* **Sir Frank Gibson**[15] 2054 3-8-9 45 ... SWhitworth 6 7
(MrsJaneGalpin) *hld up: rdn over 6f out: wl bhd fnl 4f* **16/1**
0-00 **6** *dist* **Our Kid**[12] 2146 3-8-11 62 ...(b) RWinston 4 —
(TDEasterby) *dwlt: wl bhd fnl 5f: t.o* **7/1**[3]
0 **7** *dist* **Tornado Bay (IRE)**[12] 2144 3-7-13 ... BSwarbrick(5) 2 —
(IAWood) *hld up: rdn over 6f out: sn struggling: t.o* **50/1**

2m 42.3s (120.50) **Going Correction** 0.0s/f (Stan) **7** Ran SP% **119.3**
Speed ratings: **98,92,89,83,72** —,—CSF £85.35 TOTE £11.20: £4.10, £3.50; EX 121.80.Spectested was claimed by A. W. Carroll for £5,000
**Owner** Paul J Dixon **Bred** J W Ford **Trained** Southwell, Notts

**FOCUS**
An uncompetitive claimer and the form is modest.

**NOTEBOOK**
**Bold Blade**, who has changed stables, was stepping up in distance for this return to the sand after disappointing on turf. Given a good tactical ride from the front, he was given a breather by Gibbons with a circuit to go.
**Spectested(IRE)** could not live with the winner but was subsequently claimed by Tony Carroll for £5,000.
**Caspian Dusk** may have got found out by the extra furlong in the separate race for second.
**Tornado Bay(IRE)** *Official explanation: jockey said filly had lost its action.*

### 2453 EUROPEAN BREEDERS FUND MAIDEN STKS 6f (F)
**3:30** (3:31) (D) 2-Y-0 **£4,046** (£1,245; £622; £311) **Stalls** Low

Form RPR
352 **1** **Windy Prospect**[24] 1865 2-8-11 ... DNolan(3) 7 79
(PABlockley) *led after 1f: rdn 2f out: r.o wl* **9/4**[2]
22 **2** *1 ½* **Distinctly Game**[12] 2141 2-9-0 ... JCarroll 10 75
(KARyan) *a.p: jnd wnr 2f out: rdn over 1f out: nt qckn ins fnl f* **7/4**[1]
2 **3** *5* **Mytton's Bell (IRE)**[6] 2296 2-8-9 ... JBramhill 6 55
(ABailey) *a.p: rdn over 2f out: one pce* **4/1**[3]
**4** *10* **Zantero** 2-8-11 ... THamilton(3) 3 30
(RPElliott) *s.s: gd hdwy on outside 3f out: no further prog fnl 2f* **33/1**
0 **5** *1 ¼* **League Of Nations (IRE)**[13] 2111 2-9-0 ... ACulhane 11 26
(PFICole) *outpcd: rdn and hdwy over 3f out: no imp fnl 2f* **4/1**[3]
**6** *1* **Kalika (IRE)** 2-8-9 ... GGibbons 8 18
(MsDeborahJEvans) *chsd ldrs: rdn over 4f out: wknd over 2f out* **25/1**
05 **7** *1 ¾* **Dramatic Review (IRE)**[14] 2074 2-9-0 ... GFaulkner 5 18
(PCHaslam) *chsd ldrs: rdn over 3f out: sn wknd* **16/1**
**8** *1 ¼* **Zando** 2-8-7 ... RoryMoore(7) 1 14
(PCHaslam) *outpcd* **25/1**
0 **9** *3* **Ellenare (IRE)**[30] 1709 2-8-4 ... BSwarbrick(5) 4 —
(MsDeborahJEvans) *outpcd* **50/1**
545 **10** *2* **Iam Foreverblowing**[7] 2263 2-8-6 ... DCorby(3) 9 —
(SCBurrough) *led 1f: w wnr tl wknd over 2f out* **33/1**
2 **11** *1 ½* **Mas O Menos (IRE)**[18] 1990 2-9-0 ... DeanMcKeown 2 —
(MsDeborahJEvans) *bhd fnl 4f* **20/1**

1m 16.04s (0.24) **Going Correction** 0.0s/f (Stan) **11** Ran SP% **133.3**
Speed ratings: **98,96,89,76,74 73,70,69,65,62 60**CSF £7.16 TOTE £5.00: £1.10, £1.60, £1.20; EX 6.90.
**Owner** bellhouseracing.com **Bred** T J Cooper **Trained** Southwell, Notts
■ Stewards Enquiry : D Nolan two-day ban: used whip with excessive force (Jun 8-9)

**FOCUS**
The nature of the surface meant this was a stiff test for juveniles at this stage of their career. The form is difficult to assess and caution is advised.

**NOTEBOOK**
**Windy Prospect** got the extra furlong well on such a demanding surface but his rider was given a two-day ban for using his whip with excessive force.
**Distinctly Game** again did nothing wrong on his All-Weather debut but his frustrating run of seconds continued.
**Mytton's Bell(IRE)** was unable to really build on her Haydock debut and could not go with the two principals in the home straight.
**Zantero** probably burst himself in trying to recover from a very tardy start. He should be better for the experience.

### 2454 WOLVERHAMPTON & DUDLEY BREWERIES (S) STKS 1m 100y(F)
**4:00** (4:01) (G) 3-Y-0+ **£2,611** (£746; £373) **Stalls** Low

Form RPR
0402 **1** **Frank's Quest (IRE)**[18] 2007 4-9-4 53 ... SHitchcott(3) 6 56
(PBurgoyne) *hld up in tch: hdwy over 3f out: rdn over 2f out: led wl over 1f out: all out* **5/1**[3]
0/0- **2** *hd* **Celtic Thatcher**[498] 319 6-9-7 ...(v) GGibbons 9 56
(NPLittmoden) *stmbld after s: sn rdn along: hdwy over 3f out: edgd rt wl over 1f out: kpt on towards fin* **11/4**[1]
0403 **3** *3 ½* **Roving Vixen (IRE)**[11] 2185 3-8-1 35 ...(b) RMiles(3) 3 43
(JLSpearing) *led early: prom: led 3f out: sn rdn: hdd wl over 1f out: hung rt and wknd fnl f* **7/1**
0553 **4** *¾* **Kanz Wood (USA)**[17] 2013 8-9-7 45 ... ADaly 5 47
(AWCarroll) *s.s: sn wl bhd: hdwy over 3f out: one pce fnl f* **10/1**
0- **5** *8* **Fred's First**[195] 6002 3-8-9 ... MFenton 4 30
(BPalling) *sn wl bhd: hdwy over 1f out: nvr nr ldrs* **33/1**
6030 **6** *2 ½* **Xaloc Bay (IRE)**[13] 2128 6-9-12 53 ... DarrenWilliams 13 30
(BPJBaugh) *sn led: rdn and hdd 3f out: wknd 2f out* **11/2**
66 **7** *hd* **My Country Club**[10] 2209 7-9-2 53 ... NChalmers(5) 11 24
(AGJuckes) *chsd ldrs: rdn over 3f out: sn wknd* **25/1**
00-0 **8** *4* **Mr Loverman (IRE)**[29] 1723 4-9-7 40 ... RFitzpatrick 7 16
(MissVHaigh) *rdr slow to remove blindfold: s.v.s: a wl bhd* **50/1**
3061 **9** *nk* **Forty Forte**[17] 2013 8-9-7 52 ...(tp) BSwarbrick(5) 10 20
(MissSJWilton) *mid-div: sn rdn along: short-lived effrt over 4f out* **10/1**
0030 **10** *10* **Mikasa (IRE)**[10] 2214 4-9-4 40 ...(p) DNolan(3) 12 —
(RFFisher) *w ldr: rdn over 3f out: wknd over 2f out: sddle slipped* **25/1**
34-0 **11** *½* **Cal Mac**[10] 2201 5-9-7 77 ... RWinston 8 —
(RMHCowell) *prom: eased whn btn over 2f out* **4/1**[2]
0-0 **12** *7* **Cloud Catcher (IRE)**[15] 2061 3-8-1 ... JFMcDonald(3) 1 —
(IAWood) *sn bhd* **16/1**
45-0 **13** *16* **Banners Flying (IRE)**[43] 1424 4-9-7 70 ... ACulhane 2 —
(DWChapman) *s.i.s: sn wl bhd: t.o* **12/1**

1m 51.43s (0.34) **Going Correction** 0.0s/f (Stan)
**WFA** 3 from 4yo+ 12lb **13** Ran SP% **135.6**
Speed ratings: **98,97,94,93,85 83,82,78,78,68 68,61,45**CSF £21.31 TOTE £6.80: £2.20, £1.50, £2.90; EX 28.90.Frank's Quest was bought in for 7,500gns.
**Owner** Fun & Fantasy & Andrew Haynes Racing Ltd **Bred** Rathasker Stud **Trained** Collingbourne Ducis, Wilts

**FOCUS**
They went a good clip in this run-of-the-mill seller, but the form is poor.

**NOTEBOOK**
**Frank's Quest(IRE)** just managed to hold on over a slightly shorter distance on this return to selling company.
**Celtic Thatcher**, off course since January 2003, was taking a big drop in class. He would have been 25lb worse off with the winner in a handicap.
**Roving Vixen(IRE)** has improved since being fitted with blinkers but had a tough task at the weights.
**Kanz Wood(USA)** gave himself far too much to do after a poor start.
**Mikasa(IRE)** *Official explanation: jockey said saddle slipped.*
**Cal Mac** was allowed to come home in his own time after his rider had looked down as if something was amiss. Winston subsequently reported that his mount was hanging left. *Official explanation: jockey said gelding hung to the left.*

### 2455 LADBROKES.COM H'CAP 6f (F)
**4:30** (4:32) (E) (0-75,73) 3-Y-0+ **£3,760** (£1,157; £578; £289) **Stalls** Low

Form RPR
24-0 **1** **Cape St Vincent**[14] 2091 4-9-11 **70** ...(v1) ACulhane 12 88
(HMorrison) *chsd ldrs: chal 2f out: rdn over 1f out: led wl ins fnl f: r.o* **5/1**[3]
0023 **2** *nk* **Another Glimpse**[21] 1937 6-9-11 **73** ...(t) RMiles(3) 4 90
(MissBSanders) *hld up: hdwy over 3f out: led wl over 1f out: sn rdn: hdd wl ins fnl f: nt qckn* **9/2**[2]
-040 **3** *5* **Xpres Digital**[25] 1841 3-9-5 **73** ...(t) JBramhill 9 75
(SRBowring) *a.p: rdn and one pce fnl 2f* **14/1**
3511 **4** *1 ¼* **Gilded Cove**[41] 1474 4-9-0 **64** ... StephanieHollinshead(5) 3 62
(RHollinshead) *s.i.s: hdwy on outside over 1f out: nvr nrr* **14/1**
6060 **5** *½* **Parker**[24] 1857 7-8-11 **59** ...(b) SHitchcott(3) 7 56
(BPalling) *prom tl wknd over 2f out* **12/1**
0000 **6** *½* **Gone'N'Dunnett (IRE)**[14] 2094 5-9-5 **64** ...(p) DarrenWilliams 1 59
(MrsCADunnett) *led 1f: prom: rdn over 2f out: wknd fnl f* **14/1**
1000 **7** *hd* **Global Achiever**[14] 2097 3-8-8 **69** ... DeanWilliams(7) 10 64
(GCHChung) *led after 1f: rdn and hdd wl over 1f out: wknd fnl f* **14/1**
1010 **8** *2 ½* **Blakeshall Quest**[28] 1750 4-9-12 **71** ...(v) RWinston 5 58
(RBrotherton) *prom tl wknd over 2f out* **8/1**
0200 **9** *½* **St Ivian**[46] 1368 4-9-8 **67** ...(p) RFitzpatrick 8 53
(MrsNMacauley) *bhd fnl 3f* **12/1**

3104 **10** *1* **Italian Mist (FR)**[29] 1738 5-9-9 **68**........................................(e) BDoyle 11 51
(JulianPoulton) *a bhd* **4/1**[1]

0-46 **11** *7* **Teehee (IRE)**[43] 1424 6-9-5 **64**........................................(b) MFenton 6 26
(BPalling) *bhd tl hdwy on ins over 2f out: sn wknd* **20/1**

0610 **12** *½* **Full Pitch**[13] 2118 8-9-2 **68**........................................ KirbyHarris(7) 13 28
(WJenks) *outpcd* **20/1**

0004 **13** *½* **Noble Locks (IRE)**[34] 1625 6-9-6 **65**........................................ JoannaBadger 2 24
(JWUnett) *a bhd* **8/1**

1m 14.34s (-1.46) **Going Correction** 0.0s/f (Stan)
**WFA** 3 from 4yo+ 9lb **13** Ran SP% **136.3**
Speed ratings: **109,108,101,100,99 98,98,95,94,93 84,83,82**CSF £32.10 CT £325.08 TOTE £5.40: £2.80, £2.20, £6.90; EX 43.50.
**Owner** Barbara Jamet and Templeton Stud **Bred** Miss C A Green **Trained** East Ilsley, Berks

**FOCUS**
JUst a fair handicap, but plenty of pace on and a good time for the grade. The first two were clear and open to improvement on the surface.

**NOTEBOOK**
**Cape St Vincent** was suited by a strongly-run race and, travelling well in the first-time visor, overcame the outside draw.
**Another Glimpse** back up to six, had no problem handling the Fibresand surface and lost little in defeat.
**Xpres Digital** could not go with the two main protagonists on this drop back to six.
**Gilded Cove** could never recover from an indifferent start in this better company.
**Parker** was reverting to six for the first time since winning a Redcar last August.

## 2456 WINNING POST SPECIAL AT DUNSTALL PARK H'CAP 1m 1f 79y(F)
**5:00** (5:00) (F ) (0-55,56) 3-Y-0+ **£2,996** (£856; £428) **Stalls** Low

Form RPR

0-21 **1** **Arms Acrossthesea**[10] 2214 5-9-9 **56** 6ex........................ JEdmunds 11 66
(JBalding) *hld up: hdwy 4f out: rdn to ld over 1f out: r.o wl* **9/1**

3644 **2** *2* **Call Of The Wild**[13] 2128 4-9-0 **50**........................(p) THamilton(3) 8 56
(RAFahey) *hld up: hdwy over 5f out: wnt 2nd over 3f out: rdn and ev ch over 1f out: nt qckn ins fnl f* **9/2**[3]

5-15 **3** *3* **Vandenberghe**[16] 2034 5-9-5 **52**........................................ VSlattery 5 52
(JAOsborne) *hld up and bhd: rdn and hdwy over 3f out: styd on ins fnl f* **7/2**[1]

0-51 **4** *¾* **Super Dominion**[11] 2185 7-8-8 **46** 6ex.......(p) StephanieHollinshead(5) 12 45
(RHollinshead) *hld up: hdwy 6f out: led over 4f out: clr whn rdn 3f out: hdd over 1f out: wknd fnl f* **9/2**[3]

-003 **5** *7* **Arjay**[18] 2007 6-9-1 **48**........................................ JCarroll 6 33
(AndrewTurnell) *mid-div: lost pl 4f out: hdwy over 1f out: n.d* **10/1**

0-05 **6** *1¾* **Encore Royale**[22] 1910 4-9-0 **47**........................................ OUrbina 9 28
(JJay) *s.v.s: hdwy on outside over 4f out: wknd over 2f out* **16/1**

6640 **7** *5* **Royaltea**[76] 1012 3-8-5 **51**........................................ JoannaBadger 7 22
(MsDeborahJEvans) *prom tl wknd 4f out* **33/1**

3011 **8** *3* **Rocinante (IRE)**[18] 1993 4-9-6 **53**........................................ RWinston 13 18
(JJQuinn) *sn chsng ldrs: rdn over 3f out: wknd over 2f out* **4/1**[2]

0110 **9** *8* **Iamback**[15] 2053 4-9-1 **55**........................................ DeanWilliams(7) 1 4
(MissGayKelleway) *w ldrs tl rdn and wknd over 3f out* **7/1**

00-0 **10** *9* **Furniture Factors (IRE)**[30] 1715 4-9-3 **50**................(p) DeanMcKeown 3 —
(RonaldThompson) *led: hdd 6f out: wknd over 4f out* **40/1**

0000 **11** *½* **Zak Facta (IRE)**[10] 2209 4-8-11 **47**........................(v) SHitchcott(3) 4 —
(MissDAMchale) *w ldr: led 6f out tl over 4f out: sn wknd* **16/1**

0-00 **12** *3* **Suerte**[13] 2122 4-9-2 **49**........................................(p) BDoyle 2 —
(RMHCowell) *a bhd* **12/1**

2m 3.74s (0.74) **Going Correction** 0.0s/f (Stan)
**WFA** 3 from 4yo+ 13lb **12** Ran SP% **135.0**
Speed ratings: **96,94,91,90,84 83,78,76,68,60 60,57**CSF £56.37 CT £181.19 TOTE £10.80: £4.60, £1.90, £1.90; EX 109.80 Place 6 £407.39, Place 5 £163.40.
**Owner** J Carter **Bred** Miss Mandy Jane Barber **Trained** Scrooby, Notts

**FOCUS**
An ordinary handicap in which the top-weighted winner was only racing off 56 despite his penalty. The field was well strung out and the form looks sound for the grade.

**NOTEBOOK**
**Arms Acrossthesea** was having his first run on sand for over two years and appeared to defy his penalty with something in hand.
**Call Of The Wild** is a frustrating sort who is still in search of that elusive first victory.
**Vandenberghe**, 4lb higher than when successful over course and distance two outings ago, again got going too late.
**Super Dominion** did not get away with going for home so soon over a slightly longer trip in this stronger company.
T/Plt: £215.90 to a £1 stake. Pool: £26,272.95. 88.80 winning tickets. T/Qpdt: £13.70 to a £1 stake. Pool: £2,631.40. 141.50 winning tickets. KH

# 2065 YORK (L-H)
Friday, May 28

**OFFICIAL GOING: Good to firm**
A one-day fixture transferred from Catterick. The ground was described as 'lightning fast but with a good cover of grass'.
Wind: fresh hlf bhd Weather: overcast

## 2457 SPORTINGOPTIONS.CO.UK 08702 070707 H'CAP 6f 3y
**2:20** (2:22) (E ) (0-70,76) 3-Y-0 **£3,906** (£1,202; £601; £300) **Stalls** Centre

Form RPR

1-21 **1** **Mis Chicaf (IRE)**[8] 2238 3-9-13 **76** 6ex........................................ KFallon 16 94
(JSWainwright) *trckd ldr: led 3f out: pushed clr fnl f* **11/4**[1]

1311 **2** *7* **Bridgewater Boys**[7] 2269 3-9-10 **73** 6ex........................................(b) NCallan 6 70
(KARyan) *swvd lft s: bhd: hdwy over 2f out: styd on wl to go 2nd wl ins last* **5/1**[2]

0002 **3** *1* **Fox Covert (IRE)**[4] 2351 3-8-7 **59**........................................(v) LEnstone(3) 10 53
(DWBarker) *swvd lft s: led tl 3f out: edgd lft over 1f out: kpt on* **7/1**[3]

0-20 **4** *½* **Volaticus (IRE)**[42] 1453 3-8-11 **60**........................................ ANicholls 7 53
(DNicholls) *chsd ldrs: carried lft fnl f: kpt on* **14/1**

6-00 **5** *shd* **Go Yellow**[23] 1881 3-9-0 **70**........................................ SJDonohoe(7) 1 62
(PDEvans) *in tch on far side: carried lft and styd on fnl f* **16/1**

30-5 **6** *1* **Turkish Delight**[29] 1737 3-9-2 **65**........................................ WSupple 8 54
(JBalding) *bmpd s: hdwy over 2f out: styd on fnl f* **25/1**

1030 **7** *½* **Garnock Venture (IRE)**[21] 1934 3-8-6 **55**........................(b) FNorton 15 43
(ABerry) *chsd ldrs: kpt on same pce fnl 2f* **33/1**

0-50 **8** *2* **Bowling Along**[8] 2238 3-8-6 **58**........................................ TEaves(3) 5 40
(MESowersby) *hmpd s: bhd tl kpt on wl fnl 2f* **50/1**

-606 **9** *3* **Killerby Nicko**[4] 2351 3-8-5 **57**........................................ DAllan(3) 11 30
(TDEasterby) *chsd ldrs: outpcd fnl 2f* **33/1**

-055 **10** *¾* **Musiotal**[21] 1934 3-7-10 **48**........................................ NMackay(3) 12 18
(JSGoldie) *s.i.s: bhd tl kpt on fnl 2f* **9/1**

-305 **11** *1¼* **Uhuru Peak**[58] 1200 3-8-8 **62**........................................ PMulrennan(5) 14 29
(MWEasterby) *bhd: sme hdwy over 2f out: nvr on terms* **20/1**

2-00 **12** *1½* **Gasparini (IRE)**[25] 1820 3-9-1 **64**........................................ DHolland 4 26
(TDEasterby) *mid-div: drvn along 3f out: nvr on terms* **25/1**

0-00 **13** *½* **Shinko Femme (IRE)**[4] 2351 3-8-11 **60**........................................ WRyan 2 21
(NTinkler) *s.s: bhd tl sme hdwy fnl 2f* **20/1**

402- **14** *1½* **Fitzwarren**[213] 5824 3-9-6 **69**........................................(v) CCatlin 3 25
(NBycroft) *chsd ldrs 4f: sn wknd* **25/1**

0050 **15** *1¾* **Reversionary**[2] 2411 3-8-1 **50**........................................ DaleGibson 13 1
(MWEasterby) *sn outpcd and in rr* **25/1**

-405 **16** *1* **Lady Of The Links (IRE)**[16] 2037 3-8-0 **49**........................(v) KimTinkler 18 —
(NTinkler) *chsd ldrs towards stands' side: outpcd over 2f out: sn lost pl* **33/1**

2-33 **17** *5* **El Palmar**[16] 2040 3-9-0 **68**........................................ PMakin(5) 19 1
(TDBarron) *racd stands' side: bhd fr 1/2-way* **16/1**

3600 **18** *2½* **Fools Entire**[14] 2097 3-9-0 **63**........................................ JQuinn 17 —
(JAGilbert) *sn bhd* **33/1**

4-00 **19** *3½* **Named At Dinner**[13] 2134 3-9-5 **68**........................................ JFanning 20 —
(MrsADuffield) *racd towards stands' side: bhd fnl 3f* **66/1**

1m 11.43s (0.36) **Going Correction** +0.15s/f (Good) **19** Ran SP% **124.4**
Speed ratings: **103,93,92,91,91 90,89,86,82,81 80,78,77,75,73 71,65,61,57**CSF £12.02 CT £94.19 TOTE £3.10: £1.50, £1.80, £1.80, £3.80; EX 12.80.
**Owner** Anthony D Copley **Bred** Mrs E Thompson **Trained** Kennythorpe, N Yorks

**FOCUS**
In effect a 0-76 handicap and a wide-margin winner, suggesting it is worth taking a positive view of the form. The best ground seemed to be up the middle away from both rails.

**NOTEBOOK**
**Mis Chicaf(IRE)** looked in tip-top condition and made light of her 6lb penalty. She will shoot up in the ratings after this, but at least her revised mark will ensure her place in the William Hill Gold Cup line-up here in two weeks time. The sixth furlong that day should not be a problem.
**Bridgewater Boys**, taken to post early, lost several lengths at the start. He ran really well under his penalty staying on in determined fashion to snatch second place. He looks a reformed character.
**Fox Covert(IRE)**with the visor on again, swerved leaving the stalls. He showed bags of toe to take them along but he came off a straight line getting in the way of the fourth and fifth. It is not hard to see why he is still a maiden after 16 starts now.
**Volaticus(IRE)**, making his handicap debut, gave a good account of himself and was not helped by the third carrying him off a straight line. He is still inexperienced.
**Go Yellow**, dropped 5lb after two outings this time, ran much better suited by the quick ground. Considering he ended up racing on the slower far side rail this was a highly creditable effort.
**Turkish Delight**, happy to be back on turf, did well considering she collected a hefty bump at the start.
**Musiotal** *Official explanation: jockey said colt was unsuited by the ground.*
**Fools Entire** *Official explanation: jockey said gelding was switching his legs and never moving well throughout.*

## 2458 SPORTINGOPTIONS.CO.UK COMMISSION CUTTERS MAIDEN AUCTION FILLIES' STKS 5f 3y
**2:50** (2:53) (F ) 2-Y-0 **£3,136** (£896; £448) **Stalls** Centre

Form RPR

324 **1** **Smiddy Hill**[15] 2071 2-8-4........................................ RFfrench 7 81
(RBastiman) *mde all: shkn up and wnt clr 1f out: rdn out* **5/2**[1]

3 **2** *5* **Katie Boo (IRE)**[11] 2173 2-8-4........................................ FNorton 15 64
(ABerry) *chsd ldrs towards stands' side: kpt on wl ins last: tk 2nd nr line* **9/2**[3]

4 **3** *nk* **Lady Dan (IRE)**[20] 1961 2-8-4........................................ TLucas 11 62
(MWEasterby) *chsd ldrs: styd on wl fnl f* **25/1**

60 **4** *¾* **Melandre**[15] 2071 2-8-4........................................ TWilliams 10 60
(MBrittain) *unruly leaving paddock: chsd ldrs: kpt on same pce fnl 2f* **50/1**

23 **5** *½* **Tagula Bay (IRE)**[10] 2213 2-8-4........................................ WSupple 2 58
(TDEasterby) *trckd ldrs: effrt 2f out: nt qckn fnl f* **7/2**[2]

2404 **6** *1* **Gogetter Girl**[10] 2208 2-8-4........................................ JQuinn 4 55
(JGallagher) *chsd ldrs: one pce fnl 2f* **15/2**

**7** *1¼* **Ochil Hills Dancer (IRE)** 2-8-5 ow1........................................ LEnstone(3) 9 54
(ACrook) *leggy: chsd ldrs: outpcd over 2f out: edgd lft and kpt on fnl f* **20/1**

6 **8** *5* **Justenjoy Yourself**[59] 1183 2-7-13........................................ HayleyTurner(5) 1 33
(CADwyer) *in tch: outpcd over 3f out: n.d after* **33/1**

**9** *nk* **Miss Jellybean (IRE)** 2-8-7........................................ KimTinkler 14 35
(NTinkler) *leggy: scope: dwlt: sn chsng ldrs towards stands' side: wknd over 1f out* **25/1**

**10** *½* **Tomobel** 2-8-4........................................ PRobinson 12 30
(MHTompkins) *w'like: bit bkwd: s.i.s: bhd tl sme hdwy fnl 2f: nvr nrr* **12/1**

**11** *5* **Marian's Gift** 2-8-4........................................ DaleGibson 5 12
(MWEasterby) *leggy: unf: s.i.s: a outpcd and in rr* **33/1**

**12** *4* **First Rhapsody (IRE)** 2-8-2 ow1........................................ TEaves(3) 13 —
(TJEtherington) *leggy: chsd ldrs: outpcd and lost pl over 2f out* **33/1**

60 **13** *nk* **Kilkenny Kitten (IRE)**[56] 1234 2-8-4........................................(t) ANicholls 3 —
(NTinkler) *chsd ldrs: lost pl over 2f out* **50/1**

**14** *3* **Lanas Turn** 2-8-1........................................ DAllan(3) 8 —
(TDEasterby) *leggy: scope: s.v.s: a bhd* **20/1**

02 **15** *11* **Danehill Fairy (IRE)**[32] 1666 2-8-4........................................(b) JFanning 6 —
(MrsADuffield) *got loose in paddock: rrd s: a wl bhd* **33/1**

59.25 secs (0.51) **Going Correction** +0.15s/f (Good) **15** Ran SP% **121.3**
Speed ratings: **101,93,92,91,90 88,86,78,78,77 69,63,62,57,40**CSF £11.63 TOTE £3.60: £1.80, £1.70, £6.50; EX 12.20.
**Owner** I B Barker **Bred** I B Barker **Trained** Cowthorpe, N Yorks

**FOCUS**
A very smart winning time for a race of its type. The winner is clearly very speedy but overall it was a maiden auction fillies' race lacking any strength in depth.

**NOTEBOOK**
**Smiddy Hill**, a creditable fourth in a much stronger race here two weeks ago, made this look simple and when popped the question she came right away. She is all speed and bounces off fast ground.
**Katie Boo(IRE)**, probably racing on the slower ground, stuck to her guns and snatched second spot near the line. A sixth furlong will not come amiss.
**Lady Dan(IRE)** improved on this totally different ground. She will improve again especially if given a chance to tackle six furlongs.
**Melandre**, about ten lengths behind the winner here two weeks earlier, gave problems leaving the paddock.
**Tagula Bay(IRE)**travelled strongly but having run over six on her previous start it was disconcerting to see her tie up near the line.
**Gogetter Girl** was having her sixth start and the much faster ground did not seem to bother her.
**Ochil Hills Dancer(IRE)**, an April foal, stayed on again towards the finish and this will have taught this breeze-up purchase plenty.

**Kilkenny Kitten(IRE)** *Official explanation: jockey said filly hung right handed from approximately two and a half furlongs out.*
**Danehill Fairy(IRE)** *Official explanation: jockey said filly reared as stalls opened.*

## 2459 SPORTINGOPTIONS.CO.UK 2ND ANNIVERSARY H'CAP 6f 217y
**3:20** (3:23) (D) (0-80,77) 3-Y-O+ **£5,882** (£1,810; £905; £452) **Stalls** Low

Form RPR
0423 **1** **Efidium**[4] 2368 6-9-0 **64** CCatlin 10 76
(NBycroft) *bhd: gd hdwy on outer over 2f out: styd on wl to ld last 100yds* **9/1**[3]
020- **2** *2 ½* **Magic Amour**[204] 5937 6-8-10 **60** PRobinson 9 66
(IanWilliams) *lw: led tl over 2f out: led over 1f out: hdd and no ex ins last* **16/1**
2505 **3** *shd* **Sarraaf (IRE)**[14] 2078 8-9-6 **70** KFallon 13 75
(JSGoldie) *chsd ldrs on outside: kpt on wl fnl 2f* **10/1**
-600 **4** *½* **Kareeb (FR)**[39] 1504 7-9-12 **76** GCarter 3 80
(WJMusson) *sn trcking ldrs: effrt over 2f out: ev ch over 1f out: kpt on same pce* **8/1**[2]
5500 **5** *nk* **Ronnie From Donny (IRE)**[10] 2219 4-9-0 **67** TEaves(3) 11 70
(BEllison) *hld up towards rr: nt clr run over 2f out: swtchd rt over 1f out: styd on wl ins last* **33/1**
0500 **6** *hd* **Prince Of Gold**[13] 2119 4-9-0 **64** WSupple 12 67
(RHollinshead) *chsd ldrs on outside: nt clr run over 2f out: kpt on ins last* **16/1**
0403 **7** *1 ¼* **Pride Of Kinloch**[10] 2215 4-8-7 **57** KMcEvoy 4 56
(JHetherton) *w ldr: led over 2f out tl over 1f out: one pce* **12/1**
00-0 **8** *1 ½* **Jedeydd**[11] 2172 7-8-8 **61** (t) LEnstone(3) 8 56
(MDods) *hld up in rr: hdwy over 2f out: sn chsng ldrs: one pce whn eased wl ins last* **33/1**
23-2 **9** *shd* **Favour**[8] 2238 4-9-7 **71** DHolland 14 66
(MrsJRRamsden) *sn trcking ldrs: effrt 2f out: kpt on same pce* **7/2**[1]
5540 **10** *hd* **Pas De Surprise**[32] 1681 6-8-5 **55** SChin 15 50
(PDEvans) *in rr: hdwy on wd outside over 2f out: styd on ins last* **33/1**
1420 **11** *½* **Up Tempo (IRE)**[10] 2215 6-9-13 **77** (b) NCallan 16 70
(KARyan) *sn in rr and pushed along: hmpd over 4f out: edgd lft and kpt on fnl f: nvr on terms* **14/1**
5003 **12** *2* **No Grouse**[50] 1317 4-9-9 **73** PHanagan 7 61
(RAFahey) *mid-div: effrt over 2f out: fdd over 1f out* **10/1**
4062 **13** *2 ½* **Spy Gun (USA)**[13] 2128 4-8-0 **50** RFfrench 2 32
(TWall) *in tch: rdn over 2f out: sn btn* **11/1**
1313 **14** *3 ½* **Alafzar (IRE)**[5] 2325 6-8-9 **59** (v) RHavlin 6 32
(PDEvans) *swtg: chsd ldrs: lost pl over 1f out: eased* **8/1**[2]
0000 **15** *½* **Tre Colline**[10] 2215 5-9-1 **65** (v[1]) KimTinkler 5 36
(NTinkler) *racd towards far side: w ldrs: lost pl over 2f out* **25/1**
-000 **16** *1 ¼* **Mehmaas**[4] 2368 8-8-1 **51** (v) CCogan 1 19
(REBarr) *racd towards far side: in tch: lost pl over 2f out* **33/1**

1m 24.18s (0.87) **Going Correction** +0.15s/f (Good) **16** Ran SP% **122.7**
Speed ratings: **101,98,98,97,97 96,95,93,93,93 92,90,87,83,83 81**CSF £138.28 CT £1458.35 TOTE £11.00: £2.00, £2.70, £2.30, £2.30; EX 181.30.
**Owner** Hambleton Racing Partnership **Bred** T Umpleby **Trained** Brandsby, N Yorks

**FOCUS**
A fair handicap and the form looks sound.

**NOTEBOOK**
**Efidium** is as tough as old boots and sweeping down the outside in the end won going away. He should continue to give a good account of himself.
**Magic Amour** took the eye beforehand on his first outing since November. Taken on for the lead, he stuck to his task but had no answer to the winner's finishing burst.
**Sarraaf(IRE)**, ridden by Kieren Fallon for the first time, chased the leaders and appreciated the open spaces towards the outer.
**Kareeb(FR)**, back on the type of surface he appreciates, travelled strongly but possibly saw a little more daylight than he prefers. He looks a winner just waiting to happen.
**Ronnie From Donny(IRE)** did well to finish so close after an unhappy passage. His three career wins have been on the All-Weather.
**Prince Of Gold** ran better than of late and dropping back in trip was putting in all his best work at the finish after running out of racing room.
**Pride Of Kinloch**, a maiden after 16 starts, did well taking on the pacesetter but found lacking in the final furlong racing on the slightly slower part of the track.
**Favour**, stepping up in trip, saw plenty of daylight towards the outer and when push came to shove the response was very limited.
**Spy Gun(USA)** *Official explanation: trainer said gelding bled internally after scoping.*
**Alafzar(IRE)**, very warm behind the stalls, ran without the declared tongue strap when it could not be refitted. *Official explanation: trainer said gelding ran without a tongue strap as it could not be refitted.*

## 2460 VAL GREAVES - A LIFETIME IN RACING MAIDEN STKS 1m 3f 198y
**3:50** (3:51) (D) 3-Y-O+ **£3,594** (£1,106; £553; £276) **Stalls** Low

Form RPR
0-2 **1** **Tarandot (IRE)**[10] 2198 3-8-3 AMcCarthy 2 77
(GGMargarson) *trckd ldrs: wnt 2nd over 2f out: styd on to ld last 150yds* **6/4**[1]
2-0 **2** *¾* **Force Of Nature (USA)**[15] 2059 4-9-6 WRyan 5 76
(HRACecil) *led: qcknd over 5f out: rdn and edgd lft over 1f out: hdd and no ex ins last* **7/2**[3]
2 **3** *1 ½* **Light Of Morn**[38] 1521 3-8-5 ow2 DHolland 3 76
(RGuest) *sn trcking ldr: effrt over 2f out: kpt on same pce appr fnl f* **2/1**[2]
3 **4** *20* **Watchful Witness**[14] 2090 4-9-4 LucyRussell(7) 4 47
(DrJRJNaylor) *trckd ldrs: t.k.h: effrt over 3f out: lost pl over 2f out* **12/1**
**5** *1* **Daring Games** 3-8-3 PHanagan 6 40
(BEllison) *cmpt: s.i.s: last and pushed along 8f out: rn green: lost pl over 3f out: sn bhd* **33/1**
**6** *20* **Grey Samurai**[20] 4-9-8 LEnstone(3) 1 13
(PTMidgley) *dwlt: sn trcking ldrs: drvn along over 4f out: lost pl over 3f out: sn bhd* **100/1**

2m 35.2s (6.34) **Going Correction** +0.575s/f (Yiel)
**WFA** 3 from 4yo 17lb **6** Ran SP% **107.2**
Speed ratings: **101,100,99,86,85 72**CSF £6.43 TOTE £2.70: £1.60, £2.00; EX 9.30.
**Owner** Norcroft Park Stud **Bred** Bjorn E Nielsen **Trained** Newmarket, Suffolk

**FOCUS**
A modest maiden run at no pace until starting the home turn, but the winner looks to have some potential and will improve again especially over further and the form is fairly solid.

**NOTEBOOK**
**Tarandot(IRE)** went in pursuit of the leader but it was only late on that she came out on top. She will improve again especially if given a truer-test. In time she will get much further.
**Force Of Nature(USA)**, who pulled hard when last of ten on her return two weeks earlier, is a moderate mover. She had her own way in front and started to wind up the pace starting the final turn. Edging left under pressure at the line she was definitely second best.
**Light Of Morn**, whose dam won the Yorkshire Oaks, continually swished her tail in the paddock. She kept on in her own time in pursuit of the first two and still looks inexperienced.
**Watchful Witness**, a poor mover, took a fierce hold but fell in a heap when the race began in earnest.

## 2461 SARAH LUNN MEMORIAL STKS (H'CAP) 6f 3y
**4:20** (4:23) (D) (0-85,85) 3-Y-O+ **£6,435** (£1,980; £990; £495) **Stalls** Centre

Form RPR
-660 **1** **Pax**[27] 1774 7-9-0 **78** LTreadwell(7) 11 92
(DNicholls) *chsd ldrs: styd on to ld jst ins last: hld on wl* **7/1**[1]
0434 **2** *1* **Romany Nights (IRE)**[3] 2391 4-9-5 **76** (v) DHolland 1 87
(JWUnett) *chsd ldrs: styd on to go 2nd last 75yds: kpt on same pce* **8/1**[2]
-040 **3** *1* **Paddywack (IRE)**[13] 2132 7-8-7 **64** (b) JQuinn 14 72
(DWChapman) *w ldr: led over 2f out: hdd jst ins last: no ex* **25/1**
0000 **4** *1 ¼* **Winthorpe (IRE)**[25] 1825 4-9-1 **72** KDalgleish 8 76
(JJQuinn) *sn chsng ldrs: kpt on wl fnl f* **50/1**
0-05 **5** *½* **Talbot Avenue**[6] 2293 6-9-9 **80** SRighton 15 83
(MMullineaux) *t.k.h: trckd ldrs: nt clr run and swtchd rt on to stands' side rail 2f out: styd on ins last* **8/1**[2]
000- **6** *shd* **Bollin Edward**[213] 5811 5-8-3 **63** DAllan(3) 6 65
(TDEasterby) *mid-div: hdwy 2f out: styd on ins last* **20/1**
4400 **7** *shd* **Viewforth**[13] 2132 6-9-2 **73** KFallon 16 75
(JSGoldie) *chsd ldrs: nt qckn appr fnl f* **9/1**[3]
10-4 **8** *shd* **Native Title**[21] 1923 6-9-12 **83** ANicholls 4 85
(DNicholls) *swvd lft s: hdwy 2f out: chsng ldrs over 1f out: fdd ins last* **9/1**[3]
0-00 **9** *1 ¼* **Extinguisher**[3] 2391 5-8-9 **66** WSupple 9 64
(DNicholls) *led tl over 2f out: wknd over 1f out* **25/1**
-355 **10** *¾* **Endless Summer**[4] 2366 7-9-9 **80** PRobinson 7 76
(KRBurke) *sn bhd: sme hdwy 2f out: nvr on terms* **8/1**[2]
-000 **11** *nk* **Zuhair**[10] 2219 11-8-13 **70** FNorton 3 65
(DNicholls) *sn bhd: hdwy over 1f out: eased wl ins last* **33/1**
0100 **12** *1 ¼* **Pedro Jack (IRE)**[14] 2094 7-8-10 **67** JFanning 5 58
(MABuckley) *mid-div: effrt over 2f out: no imp* **66/1**
-044 **13** *3* **Blackheath (IRE)**[32] 1673 8-9-9 **80** AlexGreaves 20 62
(DNicholls) *rr-div: sme hewady on stands' side rail over 2f out: sn n.m.r: nvr a factor* **16/1**
032 **14** *2 ½* **Lord Of The East**[21] 1929 5-8-7 **67** LisaJones(3) 18 42
(DNicholls) *chsd ldrs: edgd lft and wknd 2f out* **10/1**
00-0 **15** *3* **Marshallspark (IRE)**[14] 2079 5-8-10 **67** PHanagan 10 33
(RAFahey) *sn in rr* **20/1**
-101 **16** *hd* **American Cousin**[11] 2175 9-8-7 **64** 6ex PMQuinn 2 29
(DNicholls) *mid-div: effrt on wd outsode over 2f out: wknd over 1f out* **25/1**
05-0 **17** *¾* **Proud Native (IRE)**[16] 2041 10-10-0 **85** NCallan 12 48
(DNicholls) *sn in rr* **33/1**
6-00 **18** *1 ½* **Colemanstown**[42] 1452 4-8-10 **70** TEaves(3) 19 28
(BEllison) *racd stands' side: sn in rr* **33/1**
0032 **19** *2* **Chairman Bobby**[2] 2407 6-8-10 **70** LEnstone(3) 17 22
(DWBarker) *chsd ldrs towards stands' side: lost pl 2f out* **11/1**
4003 **20** *½* **Consensus (IRE)**[8] 2238 5-9-8 **79** TWilliams 13 30
(MBrittain) *chsd ldrs: wkng whn n.m.r over 2f out: eased towards fin* **16/1**

1m 11.85s (0.78) **Going Correction** +0.15s/f (Good) **20** Ran SP% **128.4**
Speed ratings: **100,98,97,95,95 94,94,94,92,91 91,89,85,82,78 78,77,75,72,71**CSF £54.71 CT £1394.65 TOTE £7.40: £2.30, £3.00, £5.30, £10.00; EX 90.60 TRIFECTA Not won..
**Owner** D Nicholls **Bred** Bloomsbury Stud **Trained** Sessay, N Yorks
■ Stewards Enquiry : S Righton caution: careless riding

**FOCUS**
A competitive sprint but a modest time for the grade, 0.42 seconds slower than the earlier lower-grade handicap for three-year-olds. David Nicholls saddled eight in a race run in memory of his former assistant trainer.

**NOTEBOOK**
**Pax**, just 1lb higher than for his last win, had the trip and the ground in his favour and recorded a poignant victory, as Sarah Lunn, whom this race commemorated, owned a leg in him before her death in a car accident last October.
**Romany Nights(IRE)**, making a quick reappearance, stuck on to claim second spot but he looks weighted to the hilt.
**Paddywack(IRE)**, who has slipped to a lenient mark, showed a lot more dash than usual and was only worn down over the final 150 yards.
**Winthorpe(IRE)**, who had the fast ground he likes, ran much better. His three wins were over the minimum trip.
**Talbot Avenue** took a fierce grip. He hung right and ended up on the slower ground against the stands' side rail. He finished to some effect and things will surely fall into place for him before much longer. *Official explanation: jockey said gelding hung right handed from three furlongs out.*
**Bollin Edward**, who has just one career win to his credit, ran really well on his return and deserves to add to his record this time round.
**Native Title** was playing catch-up after fluffing his lines at the start and the exertions took their toll late on. He is clearly in top form.
**Endless Summer** *Official explanation: jockey said gelding stumbled leaving the stalls.*
**Zuhair** shaped as if on the way back and six of this veteran's last seven wins have been at Goodwood.
**Marshallspark(IRE)** *Official explanation: jockey said gelding stumbled leaving the stalls.*
**Chairman Bobby** *Official explanation: jockey said race came too soon for the gelding.*
**Consensus(IRE)** *Official explanation: jockey said mare swallowed her tongue and was eased; trainer said mare had a sore back after the race.*

## 2462 SPORTINGOPTIONS.CO.UK MAX 3% APPRENTICE H'CAP 1m 5f 197y
**4:50** (4:50) (F) (0-55,54) 4-Y-O+ **£3,094** (£884; £442) **Stalls** Low

Form RPR
-142 **1** **My Legal Eagle (IRE)**[11] 2186 10-8-10 **45** HayleyTurner 9 49
(RJPrice) *hld up: hdwy 3f out: sn rdn: styd on wl ins last: led nr fin* **5/1**[1]
6101 **2** *½* **Galandora**[11] 2171 4-8-13 **53** 6ex LucyRussell(5) 5 56
(DrJRJNaylor) *hld up: hdwy over 2f out: sn chsng ldrs: styd on wl ins last: no ex nr fin* **7/1**[2]
4500 **3** *hd* **Astromancer (USA)**[6] 2287 4-8-9 **49** SaleemGolam(5) 12 52
(MHTompkins) *sn trcking ldrs: styd on and ev ch ins last: no ex nr line* **7/1**[2]
4-21 **4** *nk* **Prince Of The Wood (IRE)**[11] 2186 4-8-13 **51** 6ex (p) PMakin(3) 1 54
(ABailey) *set str pce: edgd rt fr over 2f out: hdd and no ex cl home* **5/1**[1]
000/ **5** *1 ½* **Kristineau**[19] 4908 6-8-10 **48** (t) PPMathers(3) 6 48
(MrsDianneSayer) *sn trcking ldrs: chal on ins over 2f out: fdd last 75yds* **14/1**
5020 **6** *4* **Smarter Charter**[18] 1987 11-8-7 **45** oh15 KristinStubbs(3) 3 40
(MrsLStubbs) *s.v.s: hdwy on ins 3f out: kpt on same pce* **25/1**
040 **7** *1 ¼* **Sarn**[20] 1971 5-8-3 **45** PVarley(7) 8 38
(MMullineaux) *in rr: sn pushed along: dropped bk last over 4f out: sme hdwy fnl 2f: nvr a factor* **25/1**

6-05 **8** *hd* **Mr Fortywinks (IRE)**[24] 1866 10-8-10 **50**................. SuzanneFrance(5) 4 43
(BEllison) *in tch: outpcd over 4f out: n.d after* **8/1**[3]
00-0 **9** *8* **Bulgaria Moon**[32] 1668 4-8-10 **45** oh5................. PBradley 11 27
(CGrant) *sn chsng ldrs: drvn along over 5f out: lost pl 3f out* **50/1**
0040 **10** *14* **Washington Pink (IRE)**[24] 1867 5-8-5 **45** oh5................. MHalford(5) 7 7
(CGrant) *rr-div: lost pl over 3f out* **16/1**
4/64 **11** *5* **Western Bluebird (IRE)**[11] 2171 6-8-7 **45**........(b) LeanneKershaw(3) 10 —
(MissKateMilligan) *chsd ldrs: outpcd over 4f out: lost pl 3f out* **16/1**
-000 **12** *2 1/2* **The Loose Screw (IRE)**[10] 2216 6-8-5 **45**..................... DFentiman(5) 2 —
(GMMoore) *w ldr: lost pl over 3f out: sn bhd* **16/1**
1-00 **13** *3/4* **Rouge Blanc (USA)**[2] 2409 4-9-5 **54**........................(bt[1]) PMulrennan 13 5
(GAHarker) *hld up in rr: hdwy on outside over 5f out: lost pl 3f out* **14/1**
600 **P** **Illicium (IRE)**[26] 1786 5-8-10 **45** oh5..................................... DFox 14 —
(MrsMReveley) *hld up in rr: p.u over 5f out: lame* **20/1**

3m 2.54s (6.14) **Going Correction** +0.575s/f (Yiel) **14** Ran SP% **114.8**
Speed ratings: **105,104,104,104,103 101,100,100,95,87 85,83,83,**—CSF £34.62 CT £244.68 TOTE £4.40: £1.70, £1.90, £2.80; EX 17.70 Place 6 £51.88, Place 5 £42.65.
**Owner** E G Bevan **Bred** G J Freyne **Trained** Ullingswick, H'fords

**FOCUS**
A fair time for the grade, a 0-54 handicap probably the lowest ever rated race run on the Knavesmire and the form is nothing out of the ordinary.

**NOTEBOOK**
**My Legal Eagle(IRE)** looked to be going nowhere until suddenly picking up the bit and swooping between horses to put his head in front right on the line.
**Galandora**, under her penalty, was making no impact on the leader until staying on inside the last. She really needs two miles.
**Astromancer(USA)**, with the blinkers left off, is still a maiden after 16 starts now but here she did nothing at all wrong and in the end just missed out.
**Prince Of The Wood(IRE)**, in first-time cheekpieces, set a sound gallop. Tending to edge left towards the centre, in the end he was just edged out.
**Kristineau**, in good form in novice hurdles for her new yard, was having her first outing on the Flat since September 2001. In a truly-run contest, this trip looked to stretch her stamina to the very limit.
**Smarter Charter**, 15lb out of the handicap, stood still when the stalls opened and was far from disgraced. However he seems to have lost the winning habit.
T/Jkpt: £14,229.20 to a £1 stake. Pool: £70,144.00. 3.50 winning tickets. T/Plt: £69.30 to a £1 stake. Pool: £71,714.40. 754.60 winning tickets. T/Qpdt: £28.00 to a £1 stake. Pool: £3,208.50. 84.70 winning tickets. WG

2463 - 2465a (Foreign Racing) - See Raceform Interactive

## 2335 BADEN-BADEN (L-H)
### Friday, May 28

**OFFICIAL GOING: Good**

## 2466a BENAZET-RENNEN (GROUP 3) 6f
**3:25** (3:33) 3-Y-O+ **£26,761** (£10,563; £5,634; £3,169)

RPR
**1** **Lucky Strike**[268] 4674 6-9-6 ........................................ ADeVries 2 111
(ATrybuhl, Germany) *soon led, hung & came very wide to stands side straight, ridden 1 1/2f out ran on, driven out* 1
**2** *2* **Topkamp**[229] 5528 4-9-2 ........................................ ASuborics 9 101
(MLWBell) *prominent, went 2nd after 1 1/2f, ridden 2f out, ran on but not reach winner* 3
**3** *4 1/2* **Sacho (GER)**[222] 5664 6-9-6 ........................................ AHelfenbein 1 92
(WKujath, Germany) *prominent, pushed along 2f out, ridden and went 3rd 1 1/2f out, stayed on to hold 3rd*
**4** *nk* **Capricho (IRE)**[62] 1126 7-9-6 ........................................ PDoe 5 91
(JAkehurst) *in touch, 4th straight, ridden 1 1/2f out, disputed 3rd 150 yards out, kept on* 2
**5** *1/2* **Areias (GER)**[77] 6-9-6 ........................................ AStarke 8 89
(ATrybuhl, Germany) *raced in last, ridden and ran on from 2f out, stayed on to line at one pace*
**6** *3/4* **Just Sing A Song**[201] 5964 5-9-2 ........................................ KKerekes 7 83
(JHeidenreich, Germany) *mid-division, pushed along entering straight, never in challenging position*
**7** *4 1/2* **Gold Type (IRE)**[201] 5964 5-9-6 ........................................(b) JPalik 3 73
(KWoodburn) *mid-division on rail, pushed along straight, soon ridden, one pace final furlong*
**8** *1/2* **Call Me Big (GER)**[268] 4674 6-9-6 ........................................ THellier 10 72
(EGroschel, Germany) *mid-division, ridden 2f out, some brief headway but soon one pace*
**9** *7* **Fiepes Shuffle (GER)**[194] 6009 4-9-6 ..............................(b) J-PCarvalho 6 51
(MarioHofer, Germany) *prominent til under pressure approaching straight, soon ridden and beaten*
**10** *13* **Best Smiling (GER)**[201] 5964 4-9-2 ....................(b) LHammer-Hansen 4 8
(FrauEMader, Germany) *prominent, pushed along approaching straight, weakened*

67.94 secs **10** Ran SP% **133.1**
Speed ratings: .
**Owner** Stall Lucky Stables International **Bred** Red House Stud **Trained** Germany

**NOTEBOOK**
**Lucky Strike** will be kept to straight courses for the time being and his main target is the Prix Maurice de Gheest, at Deauville in August, in which he was fifth last year.
**Topkamp**, who is in foal to Cadeaux Genereaux, likes this ground and ran a blinder on her reappearance. She was running on at the finish and a Group Three at Leopardstown is now on the agenda.
**Capricho(IRE)** was run out of third in the closing stages but this was still a more promising performance.

## 2234 DONCASTER (L-H)
### Saturday, May 29

**OFFICIAL GOING: Good to firm (firm in places in straight)**
With quite a fresh headwind it favoured horses coming from off the pace.
Wind: Fresh against Weather: Sunny

## 2467 SKYBET.COM CLASSIFIED STKS 6f
**1:50** (1:51) (D) 3-Y-O+ **£5,508** (£1,695; £847; £423) **Stalls** High

Form RPR
-203 **1** **Hiccups**[14] 2132 4-9-2 80........................................(p) RWinston 5 89
(MrsJRRamsden) *unruly stalls: s.s: hld up in tch: nt clr run wl over 1f out: led ins fnl f: edgd rt: rdn out* **4/1**[2]
0-06 **2** *1/2* **Million Percent**[14] 2132 5-9-2 80........................................ KFallon 7 88+
(KRBurke) *chsd ldrs: nt clr run over 1f out: r.o ins fnl f: nt rch wnr* **3/1**[1]
0-00 **3** *1 1/2* **Banjo Bay (IRE)**[14] 2132 6-8-11 82........................................ LTreadwell(5) 6 85
(DNicholls) *chsd ldrs: rdn to ld 1f out: hdd and unable qck ins fnl f* **16/1**
3424 **4** *hd* **Ellens Academy (IRE)**[14] 2132 9-9-2 80........................................ RHills 2 82
(EJAlston) *s.s: hld up: hdwy over 1f out: r.o* **4/1**[2]
2-00 **5** *1 1/4* **Smirfys Systems**[22] 1927 5-8-11 78........................................ BSwarbrick(5) 3 79
(WMBrisbourne) *s.s: sn chsng ldrs: rdn over 1f out: styd on same pce ins fnl f* **14/1**
-404 **6** *3 1/2* **Mr Malarkey (IRE)**[15] 2094 4-9-2 78........................................(b) MHills 8 68
(MrsCADunnett) *sn led: rdn and hdd 1f out: btn whn n.m.r ins fnl f* **7/1**
-056 **7** *1 3/4* **Willhewiz**[15] 2094 4-9-1 82........................................(b[1]) J-PGuillambert(3) 4 65
(CADwyer) *w ldr 4f: wknd fnl f* **16/1**
-002 **8** *hd* **Material Witness (IRE)**[11] 2206 7-9-6 84........................................ MFenton 1 66
(WRMuir) *w ldrs: lost pl over 3f out: wknd wl over 1f out* **11/2**[3]

1m 13.22s (-1.06) **Going Correction** -0.075s/f (Good) **8** Ran SP% **111.3**
Speed ratings: **104,103,101,101,99 94,92,92**CSF £15.50 TOTE £4.10: £1.20, £1.90, £4.90; EX 14.20.
**Owner** J M & Mrs E E Ranson **Bred** Mrs Susan Corbett **Trained** Sandhutton, N Yorks

**FOCUS**
With just 2lbs covering the field on official ratings this was a competitive contest, run at a sound pace.

**NOTEBOOK**
**Hiccups**, a strong-travelling type, got first run on the runner-up and that made the difference. While he is effective over this trip, he has plenty of pace and is just as at home over the minimum.
**Million Percent**, closely matched with the winner on their running at Thirsk last time, did not have much luck in running. This was a good effort considering, and he can be found another opening before too long.
**Banjo Bay(IRE)** has struggled with the Handicapper since winning this time last year, but there was more promise in this effort and, now he has slipped to a more realistic mark, can be found an opening.
**Ellens Academy(IRE)** is running well enough at present and may have done better still had he not launched his effort down the outside of the field.
**Smirfys Systems**, back on his favoured fast surface, turned in a solid effort and looks to be returning to form. *Official explanation: jockey said gelding hung right–handed in closing stages.*
**Mr Malarkey(IRE)** had the stands'-side rail to help and showed plenty of pace, without hanging as he had done recently. However, with quite a strong headwind it was not a day for front-running.

## 2468 LAKESIDE MEDIAN AUCTION MAIDEN STKS 5f
**2:25** (2:25) (E) 3-Y-O **£3,464** (£1,066; £533; £266) **Stalls** High

Form RPR
2 **1** **Catherine Wheel**[43] 1453 3-8-9 ........................................ KFallon 2 66
(JRFanshawe) *hld up: hdwy over 1f out: rdn to ld nr fin* **1/3**[1]
5-4 **2** *nk* **Ex Mill Lady**[23] 1906 3-8-9 ........................................ NCallan 9 65
(JohnBerry) *led: rdn over 1f out: edgd lft and hdd nr fin* **16/1**[3]
32-4 **3** *nk* **Fishlake Flyer (IRE)**[47] 1362 3-8-9 66........................................ MFenton 1 64
(JGGiven) *chsd ldrs: rdn and ev ch fr over 1f out: r.o* **8/1**[2]
**4** *1/2* **Harrington Bates** 3-9-0 ........................................ DeanMcKeown 6 67
(RMWhitaker) *s.i.s: sn chsng ldrs: running on whn nt clr run wl ins fnl f* **8/1**[2]
P0-0 **5** *1* **From The North (IRE)**[21] 1975 3-8-6 ..............................(v[1]) ABeech(3) 4 58
(ADickman) *hld up: swtchd lft and hdwy over 1f out: styd on* **100/1**
00-0 **6** *1 3/4* **New Day Dawning**[29] 1749 3-8-9 48........................................ JFanning 7 52
(CSmith) *hld up: hdwy and hmpd over 1f out: styd on same pce* **100/1**
0-43 **7** *3/4* **Open Mind**[5] 2351 3-8-9 52........................................ RHills 3 49
(EJAlston) *prom: hmpd and outpcd 1/2-way: rdn over 1f out: no ex* **22/1**
0-50 **8** *2 1/2* **Shanghai Surprise**[15] 2088 3-9-0 45........................................(b) EAhern 5 45
(JBalding) *w ldr 3f: hmpd and wknd over 1f out* **100/1**

61.34 secs (-0.08) **Going Correction** -0.075s/f (Good) **8** Ran SP% **110.4**
Speed ratings: **97,96,96,95,93 90,89,85**CSF £6.45 TOTE £1.40: £1.10, £3.00, £1.40; EX 9.70.
**Owner** Cheveley Park Stud **Bred** Cheveley Park Stud Ltd **Trained** Newmarket, Suffolk

**FOCUS**
With the third rated just 66 this was probably just an ordinary maiden, but the winner was not at her best over this trip and can leave this effort behind.

**NOTEBOOK**
**Catherine Wheel**, facing different conditions to thoset she encountered on her debut, took a while to get on top. This trip on fast ground did not see her at her best, and she can leave this effort well behind in due course.
**Ex Mill Lady** looked to find a bit of improvement for tackling her fastest surface to date. She will have more options open to her now in handicaps.
**Fishlake Flyer(IRE)** looked exposed coming into this, although she did little wrong at the business end.
**Harrington Bates ◆**, out of a winning sprinter, did not enjoy the best of runs and looked an unlucky loser. He can be found compensation at this level.
**From The North(IRE)** shaped better on the fastest ground she has encountered to date, in the first-time visor. Related to a couple of seven-furlong winners, she may be capable of better when she steps up in trip.
**New Day Dawning** would certainly have finished closer had she not been messed around. Yet to tackle selling company, that is where her future lies.

## 2469 SKY VEGAS LIVE ON CHANNEL 295 H'CAP 7f
**2:55** (2:58) (C) (0-100,98) 3-Y-O+ **£9,958** (£3,064; £1,532; £766) **Stalls** High

Form RPR
1000 **1** **Uhoomagoo**[8] 2271 6-8-8 **80**........................................(b) NCallan 1 97
(KARyan) *hld up: hdwy over 2f out: led 1f out: rdn clr* **7/1**[3]
4-60 **2** *3* **Flying Express**[35] 1623 4-8-12 **84**........................................ MHills 9 93
(BWHills) *chsd ldrs: led over 1f out: sn hdd and outpcd* **7/2**[2]
-600 **3** *1* **Jay Gee's Choice**[26] 1828 4-9-0 **86**........................................ CCatlin 6 93
(MRChannon) *hmpd s: chsd ldrs: rdn over 1f out: styd on same pce* **10/1**
3140 **4** *1/2* **What-A-Dancer (IRE)**[5] 2366 7-8-5 **77**........................................ RWinston 11 82
(GASwinbank) *hld up: hmpd wl over 3f out: nt clr run over 2f out: hdwy over 1f out: styd on same pce ins fnl f* **10/1**
20-0 **5** *1/2* **Manaar (IRE)**[46] 1385 4-8-13 **85**........................................ EAhern 8 89
(JNoseda) *hld up in tch: outpcd over 2f out: styd on fnl f* **9/1**
0-02 **6** *1 3/4* **Prince Hector**[15] 2094 5-8-8 **80**........................................ KFallon 2 79
(WJHaggas) *hld up: pushed along 4f out: hdwy over 1f out: edgd lft and no ex ins fnl f* **11/4**[1]
-000 **7** *3 1/2* **Penny Cross**[11] 2201 4-8-12 **84**........................................ MFenton 10 74
(JGGiven) *chsd ldrs: stmbld wl over 3f out: wknd over 1f out* **22/1**
000- **8** *3 1/2* **Pieter Brueghel (USA)**[273] 4570 5-9-0 **86**........................................ RHills 4 67
(DNicholls) *led over 5f: sn wknd* **50/1**
0-00 **9** *nk* **Hit's Only Money (IRE)**[11] 2201 4-9-9 **95**................. DeanMcKeown 7 75
(PABlockley) *mid-div: pushed along 1/2-way: wknd wl over 1f out* **16/1**
-220 **10** *1/2* **Hidden Dragon (USA)**[7] 2283 5-9-12 **98**........................................ KMcEvoy 3 77
(PABlockley) *chsd ldrs: hung lft over 2f out: wknd over 1f out* **14/1**

1-02 **11** *5* **King Harson**[5] [2366] 5-8-10 **82**...............................(v) JFanning 5 48
(JDBethell) *wnt rt s: sn chsng ldr: wknd wl over 1f out* **8/1**

1m 24.86s (-2.95) **Going Correction** -0.075s/f (Good) **11** Ran SP% **119.5**
Speed ratings: **113,109,108,107,107 105,101,97,96,96 90**CSF £32.24 CT £255.23 TOTE £8.30: £2.30, £2.40, £3.00; EX 45.90 Trifecta £364.90 Pool £1,284.86, 2.50 winning units.
**Owner** J Duddy & T Fawcett **Bred** C R Mason And Mrs N T Pope **Trained** Hambleton, N Yorks
■ Stewards Enquiry : K McEvoy caution: allowed gelding to coast home with no assistance

**FOCUS**
This looked a competive handicap on paper and was run at a fast pace. The second anf third are well-treated and could be a bit better than this.

**NOTEBOOK**
**Uhoomagoo** had the strongly-run race he needs and, despite having had plenty of racing, looks as good as ever. The Royal Hunt Cup is his next intended target and while he is sure to find life more difficult in that, he should at least get the sound pace he needs.
**Flying Express** is beginning to slip down the handicap and showed a bit more than of late. This fast ground suits him well and, although he has not won since his juvenile days, still retains ability.
**Jay Gee's Choice**, who struggled in the face of some stiff tasks last term, is beginning to get some respite from the Handicapper.
**What-A-Dancer(IRE)** did not get the run of the race, but he is a hold-up horse who is always going to need luck in running.
**Manaar(IRE)** did not get the best of runs and, by the time he got going again, the leaders had flown. At home on a fast surface, he should not be difficult to place.
**Prince Hector** was not helped by having to make his ground up out wide and deserves another chance.
**King Harson** *Official explanation: jockey said gelding had stumbled on leaving the stalls.*

## 2470 EUROPEAN BREEDERS FUND ZETLAND MAIDEN STKS 6f
**3:30** (3:31) (D) 2-Y-O £4,790 (£1,474; £737; £368) **Stalls** High

Form RPR
2 **1** **Crimson Sun (USA)**[17] [2045] 2-9-0 ............................ KMcEvoy 3 79
(SaeedBinSuroor) *mde all: hung lft over 1f out: rdn out* **8/11**[1]
3 **2** *1 1/2* **Adoration**[18] [2024] 2-9-0 ............................ JFanning 4 75
(MJohnston) *chsd ldrs: rdn over 2f out: sn edgd lft: styd on ins fnl f* **9/2**[2]
5 **3** *hd* **Safendonseabiscuit**[10] [2225] 2-9-0 ............................ EAhern 5 74
(SKirk) *chsd ldrs: rdn over 1f out: styd on same pce ins fnl f* **11/1**[3]
**4** *3/4* **Miss Rosie** 2-8-9 ............................ RWinston 8 67
(TDEasterby) *s.i.s: hld up: hmpd over 4f out: hdwy and hung lft over 1f out: r.o* **25/1**
0 **5** *hd* **Profit's Reality (IRE)**[17] [2035] 2-9-0 ............................ DeanMcKeown 1 71
(PABlockley) *prom: rdn over 2f out: no ex ins fnl f* **66/1**
**6** *1/2* **Tom Forest** 2-9-0 ............................ VHalliday 9 70
(ACrook) *chsd ldrs: lost pl over 4f out: hdwy over 1f out: styd on* **28/1**
**7** *1 1/2* **Mighty Empire (IRE)** 2-9-0 ............................ RHills 10 65
(MHTompkins) *chsd ldrs: rdn over 1f out: wknd ins fnl f* **50/1**
0 **8** *19* **Belton**[9] [2234] 2-9-0 ............................ NCallan 6 8
(RonaldThompson) *prom: lost pl over 4f out: wknd over 2f out* **100/1**
0 **9** *1* **Robury**[31] [1709] 2-8-7 ............................ JDO'Reilly[(7)] 2 5
(EJAlston) *chsd ldrs over 3f* **100/1**
**10** *3/4* **Country Rambler (USA)** 2-9-0 ............................ MHills 7 —
(BWHills) *s.s: bhd: wknd over 2f out* **9/2**[2]

1m 15.02s (0.74) **Going Correction** -0.075s/f (Good) **10** Ran SP% **115.3**
Speed ratings: **92,90,89,88,88 87,85,60,59,58**CSF £3.99 TOTE £1.80: £1.10, £1.70, £2.90; EX 3.70.
**Owner** Godolphin **Bred** Darley **Trained** Newmarket, Suffolk

**FOCUS**
This has been won by some useful performers in the past, but with just over three lengths covering the first six home this probably wasn't that strong a maiden. However, conditions were not ideal for front-runners, so the winner deserves plenty of credit.

**NOTEBOOK**
**Crimson Sun(USA)** still looked a little green in front, but he is still learning and it would come as no surprise if he was to leave this effort behind. Connections have said they intend to give him an entry in the Coventry Stakes.
**Adoration** ◆ was on and off the bridle throughout, but he stuck well to his task and shaped as though a little further would not come amiss.
**Safendonseabiscuit** had clearly learnt from his debut, but his future looks to lie in handicaps.
**Miss Rosie**, out of a mare that won over hurdles, is not short of pace, although she will be suited by further in time.
**Profit's Reality(IRE)**, a brother to seven-furlong winner Key Partners, stepped up on his debut and can be found an opening when going handicapping.
**Tom Forest**, a half-brother to winning miler Forum Finale, can improve for the experience and will be suited by a stiffer test.
**Belton** *Official explanation: jockey said colt was unsuited by the firm ground.*

## 2471 MEADOWHALL H'CAP 1m 4f
**4:05** (4:05) (D) (0-85,80) 3-Y-O+ £5,606 (£1,725; £862; £431) **Stalls** Low

Form RPR
00-0 **1** **Lucky Leo**[35] [1611] 4-8-9 **64**............................ CCatlin 8 75
(IanWilliams) *hld up: hdwy 3f out: rdn to ld 1f out: r.o* **25/1**
-030 **2** *nk* **Mexican Pete**[14] [2116] 4-9-5 **74**............................ EAhern 2 85
(PWHiatt) *chsd ldrs: led over 1f out: sn rdn and hdd: r.o* **7/1**
30-4 **3** *1 3/4* **Crathorne (IRE)**[18] [2022] 4-9-11 **80**............................(p) KMcEvoy 4 88
(JDBethell) *hld up: hdwy over 2f out: rdn and ev ch over 1f out: unable qck ins fnl f* **9/2**[2]
20-2 **4** *10* **Carrowdore (IRE)**[82] [984] 4-8-13 **68**............................(p) DeanMcKeown 7 60
(CNAllen) *chsd ldrs: rdn over 2f out: hung lft and wknd wl over 1f out* **10/1**
2214 **5** *2 1/2* **Dissident (GER)**[26] [1832] 6-9-1 **77**............................(v) LTreadwell[(7)] 9 65
(DFlood) *chsd ldrs: led over 2f out: hdd & wknd over 1f out* **5/1**[3]
3-00 **6** *3* **Jeepstar**[22] [1928] 4-9-6 **75**............................ GGibbons 3 58
(TDEasterby) *led over 9f: wknd over 1f out* **13/2**
0-51 **7** *5* **Astrocharm (IRE)**[8] [2277] 5-9-7 **76**............................ RHills 6 51
(MHTompkins) *hld up: rdn and wknd over 2f out* **7/2**[1]
40-0 **8** *shd* **Mr Lear (USA)**[22] [1928] 5-8-12 **70**............................ THamilton[(3)] 5 45
(RAFahey) *w ldr over 9f: wknd qckly* **16/1**
100/ **9** *6* **Triphenia (IRE)**[669] [3461] 6-9-6 **75**............................ KFallon 1 41
(MLWBell) *hld up: rdn over 2f out: sn wknd* **8/1**

2m 33.55s (-2.15) **Going Correction** -0.075s/f (Good) **9** Ran SP% **112.8**
Speed ratings: **104,103,102,95,94 92,88,88,84**CSF £185.13 CT £941.44 TOTE £26.80: £4.40, £2.00, £2.30; EX 297.40.
**Owner** B and S Vaughan **Bred** J K And Mrs Keegan **Trained** Portway, Warwicks

**FOCUS**
With two of the runners going off rather quickly, this suited those coming from off the pace. The front three pulled nicely clear.

**NOTEBOOK**
**Lucky Leo**, who was racing off his lowest mark since going handicapping, has taken a while to get his act together. This step up in trip, along with the fast ground, proved ideal and he is certainly at the right end of the handicap to take advantage.
**Mexican Pete** did not go down without a fight and, although he is 8lb higher than when last successful, still looks more than capable of scoring if granted his favoured fast ground.
**Crathorne(IRE)** had the strong pace he needs and looked to run close to his best.
**Carrowdore(IRE)** ran as though the race was needed.
**Dissident(GER)** having travelled to the front going well, stopped very quickly and may not have enjoyed this faster surface.
**Jeepstar**, with Mr Lear for company, was never allowed a free role up front and dropped away tamely when headed.
**Astrocharm(IRE)** looked some way below her best and was beaten too far out for stamina to have been an issue. *Official explanation: trainer was unable to offer any explanation for poor form shown.*

## 2472 MERLIN LAND ROVER H'CAP 1m 2f 60y
**4:40** (4:41) (D) (0-85,83) 3-Y-O £5,850 (£1,800; £900; £450) **Stalls** Low

Form RPR
5225 **1** **Gavroche (IRE)**[16] [2070] 3-8-8 **73**............................ J-PGuillambert[(3)] 8 85
(CADwyer) *s.i.s: hld up: hdwy and swtchd rt over 1f out: r.o to ld last strides* **11/1**
-151 **2** *hd* **Etmaam**[12] [2169] 3-9-4 **80**............................ RHills 4 92
(MJohnston) *hld up: hdwy over 2f out: led over 1f out: sn hdd: rallied to ld wl ins fnl f: hdd last strides* **6/4**[1]
4-21 **3** *1* **Sunisa (IRE)**[42] [1476] 3-9-0 **76**............................ MHills 3 86
(BWHills) *hld up: hdwy over 2f out: led over 1f out: hdd wl ins fnl f* **8/1**[3]
00-2 **4** *5* **Strider**[35] [1628] 3-9-2 **78**............................ KFallon 2 79
(SirMichaelStoute) *chsd ldrs: rdn and ev ch over 1f out: wknd ins fnl f* **7/2**[2]
6624 **5** *1 3/4* **Zaffeu**[31] [1714] 3-8-8 **70**............................ JFanning 6 67
(NPLittmoden) *s.i.s: hld up: hdwy over 3f out: n.m.r and dropped rr over 2f out: nt rcvr* **11/1**
40-0 **6** *1/2* **Saida Lenasera (FR)**[16] [2070] 3-8-7 **72**............................ THamilton[(3)] 9 68
(MrsPSly) *chsd ldr: led over 2f out: hdd & wknd over 1f out* **33/1**
0330 **7** *1 1/4* **Green Falcon**[15] [2097] 3-8-1 **63**............................ CCatlin 1 57
(JWHills) *prom: rdn and nt clr run over 2f out: wknd over 1f out* **10/1**
1-0 **8** *1* **Rendezvous Point (USA)**[27] [1793] 3-9-1 **77**............................ KMcEvoy 7 69
(JHMGosden) *chsd ldrs: rdn and ev ch 2f out: wkng whn n.m.r over 1f out* **10/1**
-600 **9** *13* **Royal Distant (USA)**[16] [2070] 3-8-12 **74**............................ DaleGibson 11 41
(MWEasterby) *led 8f: sn wknd* **16/1**

2m 10.39s (-1.37) **Going Correction** -0.075s/f (Good) **9** Ran SP% **117.0**
Speed ratings: **102,101,101,97,95 95,94,93,83**CSF £28.31 CT £147.12 TOTE £16.20: £3.10, £1.10, £1.40; EX 63.20.
**Owner** J L Guillambert **Bred** John O'Connor **Trained** Newmarket, Suffolk

**FOCUS**
This was run at a fair pace and as in the earlier race it suited those coming from off the pace.

**NOTEBOOK**
**Gavroche(IRE)** ◆ looked to turn an an improved display and there appeared no fluke about it. Ridden with plenty of confidence, he was produced as late as possible and may even have won with a little in hand. This trip, on fast ground proved ideal and it would come as no surprise if he was to follow up.
**Etmaam** ◆ looks to be going the right way and was only just denied here. He may have done better had he been held onto a little longer.
**Sunisa(IRE)** stepped up on her All-Weather victory and looks to be an improving filly.
**Strider**, tackling handicappers for the first time, had no excuses.
**Zaffeu** was still travelling well within himself when squeezed out going to the two-furlong pole. It was too early to say whether he would have won or not, but he is certainly worth another chance.

## 2473 CANTLEY APPRENTICE H'CAP 7f
**5:15** (5:15) (E) (0-70,70) 4-Y-O+ £3,591 (£1,105; £552; £276) **Stalls** High

Form RPR
-043 **1** **Jubilee Street (IRE)**[8] [2260] 5-8-10 **52**............................ SaleemGolam 11 64
(MrsADuffield) *hld up: hdwy over 2f out: rdn to ld and hung rt over 1f out: r.o* **9/2**[1]
0-06 **2** *2 1/2* **Noble Penny**[14] [2122] 5-8-1 **48**............................ AElliott[(5)] 17 54
(MrsKWalton) *s.i.s: hld up: hdwy and nt clr run over 1f out: r.o* **15/2**[2]
00-0 **3** *1/2* **Beneking**[25] [1876] 4-8-8 **55**............................ HFellows[(5)] 16 59
(RHollinshead) *hld up: hdwy over 1f out: styd on same pce ins fnl f* **12/1**
0100 **4** *1 1/2* **Warden Warren**[15] [2094] 6-9-13 **69**............................(p) StevenHarrison 14 69
(MrsCADunnett) *mid-div: hdwy over 2f out: no ex fnl f* **10/1**[3]
0010 **5** *2 1/2* **Open Handed (IRE)**[35] [1620] 4-9-1 **57**............................(t) AMullen 6 51
(BEllison) *s.i.s: hld up: hdwy over 1f out: wknd ins fnl f* **25/1**
03-6 **6** *shd* **Indian Steppes (FR)**[14] [2117] 5-10-0 **70**............................ MHalford 7 64
(JulianPoulton) *trckd ldrs: rdn and n.m.r over 1f out: sn wknd* **10/1**[3]
0340 **7** *hd* **Kennington**[14] [2123] 4-8-12 **54**............................(v) LauraPike 13 47
(MrsCADunnett) *chsd ldrs: led 1/2-way: hdd over 1f out: wknd ins fnl f* **20/1**
304- **8** *hd* **Tedsdale Mac**[204] [5945] 5-8-10 **52**............................(p) SuzanneFrance 15 45
(NBycroft) *prom: rdn over 2f out: btn whn n.m.r ins fnl f* **11/1**
3135 **9** *5* **Rathmullan**[12] [2185] 5-7-12 **40**............................(b) LiamJones 10 20
(EAWheeler) *chsd ldrs 4f* **20/1**
-000 **10** *1* **Mutabari (USA)**[7] [1888] 10-7-7 **40** oh5............................ AmyMyatt[(5)] 1 17
(JLSpearing) *dwlt: outpcd* **50/1**
660/ **11** *3/4* **Stone Crest (IRE)**[964] [5173] 6-7-12 **40** oh10............................ SYourston 8 15
(THCaldwell) *led to 1/2-way: wkng whn n.m.r over 1f out* **100/1**
0-55 **12** *1* **Bint Royal (IRE)**[9] [2238] 6-9-2 **58**............................(p) DawnWatson 18 30
(MissVHaigh) *prom: rdn over 2f out: sn wknd* **9/2**[1]
-420 **13** *nk* **Super Canyon**[59] [1204] 6-8-9 **56**............................ KirstyMilczarek[(5)] 12 28
(JPearce) *mid-div: wknd over 2f out* **16/1**
140- **14** *1 3/4* **Alpine Hideaway (IRE)**[265] [4751] 11-8-7 **49**............................ AReilly 5 16
(JSWainwright) *w ldrs to 1/2-way: wknd wl over 1f out* **33/1**
001- **15** *1/2* **Boing Boing (IRE)**[14] [5126] 4-9-0 **56**............................ BO'Neill 9 22
(MissSJWilton) *bhd fr 1/2-way* **14/1**
4106 **16** *nk* **Spark Up**[7] [2284] 4-9-7 **63**............................(b) KGhunowa 2 28
(JWUnett) *s.s: hdwy over 2f out: wknd over 1f out* **16/1**
-000 **17** *3 1/2* **Rocky Reppin**[14] [2122] 4-8-4 **51**............................ KPierrepont[(5)] 3 7
(JBalding) *chsd ldrs over 4f* **66/1**
000 **18** *2 1/2* **Indian Shores**[88] [951] 5-8-6 **53**............................ PVarley[(5)] 4 2
(MMullineaux) *chsd ldrs 5f* **33/1**

1m 26.3s (-1.51) **Going Correction** -0.075s/f (Good) **18** Ran SP% **124.5**
Speed ratings: **105,102,101,99,97 96,96,96,90,89 88,87,87,85,84 84,80,77**CSF £33.49 CT £393.43 TOTE £5.60: £1.90, £2.90, £3.50, £2.80; EX 56.80 Place 6 £26.56, Place 5 £14.53.
**Owner** D W Holdsworth & J A McMahon **Bred** My Firebird Syndicate **Trained** Constable Burton, N Yorks
■ Stewards Enquiry : Saleem Golam caution: careless riding

**FOCUS**
An ordinary handicap, but run at a fair pace for the grade with the hold-up horses coming out best. The form looks sound.

**NOTEBOOK**
**Jubilee Street(IRE)**, who had been in better form of late had his optimum conditions, and despite drifting to his right when going on, never looked in any danger after. He clearly goes well for an apprentice, having won both times in this grade.
**Noble Penny** had plenty to do and deserves plenty of credit for getting as close as she did.
**Beneking** is not the most consistent of animals, but there was not much wrong with this effort.
**Warden Warren** did not shape too badly considering he always had plenty of company around him.
**Open Handed(IRE)** did not run too badly considering the ground would have been faster than ideal.
**Indian Steppes(FR)** may still have need this and was not disgraced under her big weight.
T/Plt: £26.70 to a £1 stake. Pool: £57,945.40. 1,578.75 winning tickets. T/Qpdt: £16.70 to a £1 stake. Pool: £3,591.40. 158.20 winning tickets. CR

## 2300 KEMPTON (R-H)
### Saturday, May 29

**OFFICIAL GOING: Good to firm**
This was a day in which it proved difficult to come from off the pace.

## 2474 TOTESPORT H'CAP — 1m 2f (J)
**1:35** (1:37) (C) (0-90,88) 3-Y-0+ **£9,759** (£3,003; £1,501; £750) **Stalls** High

Form RPR
-341 **1** **Polar Jem**[4] 2393 4-9-3 **79** 6ex AMcCarthy 1 89
(GGMargarson) *mde all: rdn and qcknd over 2f out: hld on wl fnl f* **12/1**
5542 **2** *1 ½* **Karaoke (IRE)**[2] 2430 4-8-3 **65** RLMoore 6 73
(SKirk) *hld up in rr: gd hdwy over 2f out: str run to chse wnr over 1f out: kpt on wl but no imp on wnr cl home* **13/2**[2]
-644 **3** *nk* **Todlea (IRE)**[15] 2084 4-8-10 **72** RHughes 4 79
(JAOsborne) *chsd ldrs: rdn over 2f out and qcknd to disp 2nd over 1f out: kpt on but no imp on wnr* **10/1**
5233 **4** *2* **Street Life (IRE)**[19] 2000 6-8-12 **74** GCarter 16 77
(WJMusson) *bhd: hdwy fr 2f out: kpt on fr over 1f out: nt rch ldrs* **16/1**
3003 **5** *1 ¾* **Northside Lodge (IRE)**[11] 2210 6-9-1 **77** MartinDwyer 2 77
(PWHarris) *lw: disp 2nd tl chsd wnr over 3f out: sn rdn: wknd fnl f* **8/1**
4550 **6** *½* **Silvaline**[13] 2142 5-8-12 **74** PDoe 8 73
(TKeddy) *hld up in rr: stready hdwy fr 2f out: styng on whn hmpd ins last: rallied and kpt on again cl home* **25/1**
4020 **7** *nk* **Arry Dash**[38] 1540 4-9-10 **86** TEDurcan 3 84
(MRChannon) *lw: in tch: rdn and outpcd 3f out: kpt on again fnl f* **14/1**
-044 **8** *nk* **Desert Island Disc**[16] 2062 7-8-10 **75** JFMcDonald(3) 10 73
(JJBridger) *hld up mid-div: rdn 3f out: kpt on fnl 2f: nt trble ldrs* **16/1**
0-26 **9** *1* **Lilli Marlane**[22] 1931 4-8-10 **72** (b[1]) PDobbs 7 68
(NACallaghan) *bhd: kpt on fnl 2f but nvr rchd ldrs* **7/1**[3]
-000 **10** *½* **Prairie Wolf**[11] 2210 8-9-2 **78** IMongan 13 73
(MLWBell) *disp 2nd tl over 3f out: wknd fr 2f out* **14/1**
-011 **11** *¾* **Summer Bounty**[14] 2121 8-8-11 **76** RMiles(3) 11 70
(FJordan) *s.i.s: bhd most of way* **16/1**
131- **12** *1 ¼* **Windy Britain**[171] 6162 5-9-12 **88** DHolland 5 79
(LMCumani) *chsd ldrs tl wknd 2f out* **11/2**[1]
2310 **13** *¾* **Rasid (USA)**[28] 1768 6-8-13 **75** SDrowne 15 65
(CADwyer) *b. hind: in tch: rdn 3f out: wknd 2f out* **50/1**
0100 **14** *1 ¼* **Caroubier (IRE)**[10] 2226 4-9-0 **76** JQuinn 12 63
(JGallagher) *a in rr* **16/1**
6225 **15** *2* **Tony Tie**[8] 2258 8-8-13 **75** JFEgan 9 59
(JSGoldie) *t.k.h: chsd ldrs over 6f* **20/1**

2m 5.57s (-0.57) **Going Correction** +0.125s/f (Good) **15** Ran SP% **116.5**
Speed ratings: **107,105,105,103,102 102,101,101,100,100 99,98,98,97,95**CSF £82.69 CT £818.09 TOTE £12.10: £4.10, £2.20, £3.50; EX 85.30 Trifecta £600.90 Part won. Pool £846.34 - 0.10 winning units..
**Owner** Norcroft Park Stud **Bred** Norcroft Park Stud **Trained** Newmarket, Suffolk

**FOCUS**
Quite a well contested handicap in which the winner enjoyed the run of the race.

**NOTEBOOK**
**Polar Jem** replicated her all-the-way win at Ripon under a 6lb penalty. Quickening early in the home straight, she was eased off once the race was in the bag, allowing the second and third to reduce the winning margin. She is improving and this looks the way to ride her.
**Karaoke(IRE)** ran his third good race in the space of eight days, but the filly had taken first run on both him and the eventual third. He is weighted to win at present.
**Todlea(IRE)**, 11lb lower than when running at Royal Ascot last year, had no problem with this fast ground and just lost out after a good tussle for second.
**Street Life(IRE)** made headway in the last quarter-mile without landing a blow, on a day when it proved difficult to come from off the pace. Without a win for nearly two years, he has done all his winning in easy ground.
**Northside Lodge(IRE)**, 6lb lower than at the start of the turf season, is certainly well enough handicapped, but he is proving difficult to win with.
**Silvaline** would have finished closer to the placed horses than he did had he not met with problems inside the last.
**Lilli Marlane**, back at ten furlongs and blinkered for the first time, never got into this after a slow start but was doing her best work at the finish.
**Summer Bounty** *Official explanation: jockey said gelding was never travelling.*
**Windy Britain** was unable to reproduce the sort of form that she was in before Christmas and might have needed this reappearance.
**Tony Tie** *Official explanation: jockey said gelding ran too free early on.*

## 2475 FAVOURITES RACING ACHILLES STKS (LISTED RACE) — 5f
**2:05** (2:07) (A) 3-Y-0+ **£17,400** (£6,600; £3,300; £1,500) **Stalls** Centre

Form RPR
1-32 **1** **Boogie Street**[7] 2294 3-8-13 107 (t) RHughes 10 115
(RHannon) *wnt rt s: sn rcvrd to trck ldrs: led over 1f out: hld on wl* **4/1**[2]
130- **2** *1* **Lochridge**[237] 5402 5-9-2 106 MartinDwyer 5 106
(AMBalding) *lw: chsd ldrs: rdn and outpcd 1/2-way: hdwy over 1f out: kpt on wl to chse wnr ins last: nt qckn nr fin* **9/2**[3]
40-2 **3** *½* **The Tatling (IRE)**[13] 2162 7-9-10 112 DHolland 8 113
(JMBradley) *hld up in tch: nt much much room ins fnl 2f: rdn and hdwy to chse ldrs fnl f: gng on cl home* **2/1**[1]
2444 **4** *1 ¼* **Fromsong (IRE)**[5] 2372 6-9-3 95 TEDurcan 6 101
(BRMillman) *lw: hld up in tch: hdwy 1/2-way: chsd ldrs fnl f: one pce ins last* **25/1**
-606 **5** *shd* **Colonel Cotton (IRE)**[21] 1955 5-9-7 103 PRobinson 3 105
(NACallaghan) *lw: stdd s: hld up: rdn: swtchd rt and hdwy over 1f out: kpt on ins last: nt rch ldrs* **12/1**
124- **6** *¾* **Bali Royal**[226] 5593 6-9-2 104 RMiles 8 97
(MSSaunders) *w ldrs: led over 3f out: hdd over 1f out: wknd ins last* **10/1**
0200 **7** *shd* **Peruvian Chief (IRE)**[10] 2222 7-9-3 96 (v) GCarter 7 98
(NPLittmoden) *lw: bhd: rdn 1/2-way: edgd rt u.p over 1f out: nvr gng pce to rch ldrs* **20/1**
-505 **8** *1 ¼* **Little Edward**[10] 2222 6-9-3 97 JPMurtagh 2 93
(BGPowell) *pressed ldrs: rdn 1/2-way: wknd ins fnl f* **20/1**
00-6 **9** *1* **Border Subject**[27] 1789 7-9-3 105 (b[1]) SDrowne 4 89
(RCharlton) *swtg: sn led: hdd over 3f out: styd pressing ldrs tl squeezed and wknd jst ins fnl f* **12/1**
000- **10** *6* **Boleyn Castle (USA)**[238] 5357 7-9-3 96 SWKelly 1 68
(PSMcentee) *s.i.s: sn rcvrd to chse ldrs: wknd fr 2f out* **33/1**

58.96 secs (-2.25) **Going Correction** -0.25s/f (Firm)
**WFA** 3 from 5yo+ 8lb **10** Ran SP% **112.3**
Speed ratings: **108,106,105,103,103 102,102,100,98,88**CSF £20.10 TOTE £5.30: £1.80, £2.30, £1.20; EX 25.50.
**Owner** Hippodrome Racing **Bred** Raffin Bloodstock **Trained** East Everleigh, Wilts
■ Stewards Enquiry : R Miles £150 fine: went into stall 8 when drawn in stall 9

**FOCUS**
This is useful Listed form, and the winner produced a Group-class performance. Due to a mix-up The Tatling started from stall 9 and Bali Royal from stall 8.

**NOTEBOOK**
**Boogie Street** went right at the start, having been playing with his tongue tie in the stalls according to his rider, but quickly recovered and went on to win in good style. Paying a compliment to his Haydock conqueror Moss Vale, he appreciated the return to five furlongs and this was a very useful performance against his elders. He goes for the King's Stand Stakes now where fast ground will help his cause.
**Lochridge** made a highly encouraging start to her fourth season on the track. This was only the second run over five furlongs of her life and the return to six will suit this mare, who could well have more improvement in her.
**The Tatling(IRE)** faced a stiff task under his Group-race penalty and had no real excuses. He had a fine season last year, but won only twice from 16 starts and it may be a similar story this time round.
**Fromsong(IRE)**, fourth in this event in 2001 and runner-up a year later, handled the ground but might have preferred a bit of give. *Official explanation: vet said gelding lost a shoe.*
**Colonel Cotton(IRE)**, who wins infrequently, has a style of running not really suited to flat tracks such as this.
**Bali Royal** was withdrawn at the start on her intended reappearance at Cork last month, having pulled off two of her shoes. Starting from the wrong stall here, incurring a fine for her rider, she faded after showing her customary dash. She has never won first time out.
**Border Subject**, blinkered for the first time, showed bags of pace to lead some speed merchants on his first-ever run over the minimum trip. He was already beginning to struggle when squeezed out entering the final furlong.

## 2476 BYRNE GROUP HERON STKS (LISTED RACE) — 1m (J)
**2:40** (2:40) (A) 3-Y-0 **£17,400** (£6,600; £3,300; £1,500) **Stalls** High

Form RPR
4-42 **1** **Tahreeb (FR)**[28] 1766 3-8-12 108 MartinDwyer 5 110
(MPTregoning) *trckd ldr: led wl over 2f out: rdn and styd on wl whn chal thrght fnl f* **3/1**[3]
204- **2** *nk* **Leicester Square (IRE)**[245] 5208 3-8-12 107 (t) LDettori 4 109
(SaeedBinSuroor) *h.d.w: hld up in tch: hdwy over 2f out: chsd wnr and edgd lft over 1f out: chal ins last: carried hd high: nt go by* **9/4**[1]
220- **3** *3* **Orcadian**[231] 5485 3-8-12 103 JTate 6 102
(JMPEustace) *sn led: hdd wl over 2f out: outpcd appr fnl f* **16/1**
44-5 **4** *nk* **Azarole (IRE)**[45] 1396 3-8-12 108 JPMurtagh 3 101
(JRFanshawe) *chsd ldrs: rdn over 2f out: sn one pce: kpt on again ins last but nt a danger* **11/4**[2]
4-50 **5** *1* **Kelucia (IRE)**[27] 1791 3-8-7 100 JFEgan 1 94
(JSGoldie) *hld up in rr: swtchd rt 2f out: continually flashed tail whn rdn but kpt on ins fnl f: nvr a danger* **14/1**
01- **6** *hd* **Resplendent One (IRE)**[267] 4706 3-8-12 RMiles 7 99
(TGMills) *hld up in rr: shkn up and kpt on fr over 1f out: nt trble ldrs* **20/1**
-500 **7** *2 ½* **Barbajuan (IRE)**[17] 2043 3-9-3 102 PRobinson 8 98?
(NACallaghan) *chsd ldrs: rdn over 2f out: sn wknd* **20/1**
1-6 **8** *¾* **Mustajed**[11] 2200 3-8-12 (v[1]) WSupple 2 91
(MPTregoning) *chsd ldrs tl wknd qckly 2f out* **14/1**

1m 37.76s (-1.86) **Going Correction** +0.125s/f (Good) **8** Ran SP% **111.2**
Speed ratings: **114,113,110,110,109 109,106,105**CSF £9.56 TOTE £4.60: £1.20, £1.10, £3.50; EX 13.20.
**Owner** Sheikh Ahmed Al Maktoum **Bred** S C E A Haras De Bois Carrouges **Trained** Lambourn, Berks
■ Stewards Enquiry : L Dettori one-day ban: used whip in an incorrect place (Jun 9)

**FOCUS**
A very smart time for the type of race and fair form for the grade.

**NOTEBOOK**
**Tahreeb(FR)** went on early in the straight and battled on much too bravely for the somewhat reluctant favourite. He is worth another try over ten furlongs, although he did not convince everyone he stayed that trip at Newmarket when chasing home Hazyview.
**Leicester Square(IRE)**, trained at two by Mark Johnston, wore a tongue strap like a lot of Godolphin's runners this season. Challenging on the outside, he got to the winner's quarters but put his head in the air and would not go by. Ten furlongs may suit him better but he looks one to be wary of.
**Orcadian**, who has been gelded over the winter, made a decent return to action. All his runs have been on fast ground and he clearly goes well on it, but it would still be interesting to see how he handled some cut.
**Azarole(IRE)**, who finished only half a length behind Tahreeb in the Free Handicap on the same terms, has reportedly been sidelined with a heel problem since. He seemed to hang fire a little before keeping on and this was slightly disappointing.
**Kelucia(IRE)** kept on from the rear in the straight despite several flashes of the tail. She is clearly held in some regard by her trainer but is not going to be easy to place.
**Resplendent One(IRE)**, who lacked the experience of most of these, became rather warm down at the start. He did not settle in the first part of the race, but was keeping on in the latter stages and this run should bring him on.
**Barbajuan(IRE)**, who was conceding weight all round, continues to disappoint.
**Mustajed**, a stablemate of the winner, ran a second poor race since returning to the track after splitting a pastern. The first-time visor brought about no improvement.

## 2477 TOTETRIFECTA WOKINGHAM TRIAL H'CAP — 6f
**3:15** (3:17) (C) (0-90,88) 3-Y-0+ **£12,760** (£4,840; £2,420; £1,100) **Stalls** Centre

Form RPR
6213 **1** **Prince Aaron (IRE)**[3] 2407 4-8-11 **72** GCarter 17 91
(CNAllen) *racd far side: trckd ldrs: led overall ins fnl 2f: drvn clr ins last* **7/1**[2]
0004 **2** *2 ½* **True Night**[7] 2291 7-8-13 **74** TEDurcan 20 85
(DNicholls) *racd far side: in tch: hdwy 2f out: chsd wnr ins last: no imp ins last* **14/1**



The Form Book, Raceform Ltd, Compton, RG20 6NL

-000 **3** 2 1/2 **One Way Ticket**[11] 2215 4-7-7 59 oh2....................(p) HayleyTurner(5) 16 63
(JMBradley) *trckd ldrs far side: led that gp over 3f out: hdd ins fnl 2f: kpt on same pce ins last* **25/1**

30-0 **4** 3/4 **Mutawaqed (IRE)**[16] 2065 6-9-10 85................................(t) JPMurtagh 6 86
(MAMagnusson) *b.hind: lw: racd stands side: bhd: hdwy and rdn fr 2f out: styd on wl to ld that gp ins fnl f but nvr gng pce of far side* **10/1**[3]

-002 **5** shd **Loyal Tycoon (IRE)**[26] 1825 6-9-6 81 ................................ LDettori 14 82
(DNicholls) *racd far side: in tch: rdn 3f out: hdwy 2f out: styd on fnl f but nt rch ldrs* **5/1**[1]

0003 **6** nk **Seven No Trumps**[7] 2303 7-9-2 77.....................................(p) RLMoore 8 77
(JMBradley) *racd stands side: led that gp over 2f out: tl ins fnl f but nvr gng pce of far side* **20/1**

4312 **7** 1/2 **Savile's Delight (IRE)**[14] 2118 5-8-9 70................................ JFEgan 4 69
(RBrotherton) *sn led stands side gp: hdd over 2f out: one pce fnl f* **14/1**

3-03 **8** hd **Marsad (IRE)**[16] 2065 10-9-13 88.......................................... PDoe 10 86
(JAkehurst) *chsd ldrs stands side: rdn 2f out: kpt on same pce appr fnl f* **12/1**

6004 **9** nk **Marker**[21] 1968 4-9-8 83................................................................ RHavlin 9 80
(GBBalding) *racd stands side: hdwy over 1f out: r.o wl fnl f but nvr gng pce of far side* **20/1**

16-0 **10** 1/2 **Canterloupe (IRE)**[141] 486 6-9-3 78....................................(t) DHolland 5 74
(PJMakin) *chsd ldrs stands side: rdn 1/2-way: one pce ins last* **25/1**

001- **11** 3/4 **Thurlestone Rock**[250] 5120 4-9-0 78.......................... JFMcDonald(3) 19 71
(BJMeehan) *bkwd: led far side 1f: styd chsng ldrs tl wknd ins last* **20/1**

4343 **12** nk **Zarzu**[51] 1313 5-8-13 74.................................................................. JBramhill 7 66
(CRDore) *chsd ldrs stands side: rdn over 2f out: wknd fnl f* **20/1**

243- **13** 1/2 **Danehill Stroller (IRE)**[241] 5310 4-9-10 88.................... LisaJones(3) 13 79
(RMBeckett) *s.i.s: sn in tch: rdn over 2f out: wknd fnl f* **25/1**

040- **14** nk **Hey Presto**[255] 4990 4-8-13 74............................................ PRobinson 15 64
(CGCox) *bkwd: led far side after 1f: hdd over 3f out: wknd over 1f out* **20/1**

-421 **15** 2 1/2 **Kingscross**[26] 1825 6-9-4 79............................................................. JQuinn 2 62
(MBlanshard) *swtg: s.i.s: racd stands side: sme hdwy 2f out: n.d* **10/1**[3]

0-00 **16** shd **Najeebon (FR)**[14] 2132 5-9-7 85.................................... SHitchcott(3) 12 67
(MRChannon) *racd far side: bhd: rdn 3f out: n.d* **12/1**

234- **17** 1 1/2 **Domirati**[241] 5310 4-9-4 79.......................................................... SDrowne 11 57
(RCharlton) *chsd ldrs far side 4f* **12/1**

6130 **18** 4 **Turibius**[10] 2222 5-9-4 79........................................................... RHughes 1 45
(TEPowell) *racd stands side: outpcd most of way* **16/1**

-006 **19** 2 1/2 **Gaelic Princess**[13] 2143 4-9-10 85.................................... SWhitworth 3 43
(AGNewcombe) *racd stands side: rdn and effrt over 2f out: sn wknd* **33/1**

1m 10.28s (-2.79) **Going Correction** -0.25s/f (Firm) 19 Ran SP% **127.9**
Speed ratings: **108,104,101,100,100 99,99,98,98,97 96,96,95,95,92 91,89,84,81**CSF £86.92 CT £1436.98 TOTE £8.00: £1.70, £4.20, £9.00, £3.00; EX 105.90 Trifecta £1236.30 Pool £5,746.23, 3.30 winning units..
**Owner** Black Star Racing **Bred** Peter Charles And J R Bamforth **Trained** Newmarket, Suffolk

**FOCUS**
The field split into two groups in this competitive sprint with the far side holding the advantage, although the winner would have won from either flank and the form looks sound.

**NOTEBOOK**
**Prince Aaron(IRE)**, beaten off a mark of 50 on his final turf start of last season, has made great strides on sand since and stepped up on his run in a messy race at Ripon. Scoring so comfortably that he would have won had he been drawn on the other side, he picks up an 8lb penalty for the Wokingham but that still leaves him unlikely to get in. He has a big handicap in him at some point this season, however.
**True Night**, who has not won over this trip since the second run of his life, was weak in the market. No match for the winner, he still ran well and is certainly well handicapped at present.
**One Way Ticket**, well treated on his form in the early part of last season, ran a good race from 2lb out of the handicap. He has been racing too freely over seven furlongs and benefited from this drop in trip.
**Mutawaqed(IRE)**, runner-up in this event a year ago when 9lb lower, stayed on late to come out on top of his group although he was some way adrift of the first three on the far side. He has no problem with fast ground but probably prefers some cut.
**Loyal Tycoon(IRE)** raced in the favoured far-side group and this was a shade disappointing after his good run last time. However, he will still be interesting if going for the handicap at Epsom on Derby day which he won last year off a mark of 84.
**Seven No Trumps**, with the cheekpieces back on, finished second of the ten to race up the stands' side. He has run with credit on each of his visits to Kempton this year.
**Savile's Delight(IRE)**, back at six furlongs, ran respectably but was found out by the step up in grade, having been contesting Class E races.
**Marker** was 12lb lower than at the end of last season and connections will have been pleased enough with this effort.
**Hey Presto**, who has slipped to an attractive mark, was rather keen on this return to action and faded after showing early dash. *Official explanation: jockey said gelding ran too freely early on.*
**Turibius** *Official explanation: jockey said gelding was never travelling.*

## 2478 PLATINUM SECURITY CONDITIONS STKS 6f
**3:50** (3:51) (C ) 2-Y-O **£7,290** (£2,765; £1,382; £628) **Stalls** Centre

Form RPR
132 **1** **Beaver Patrol (IRE)**[12] 2180 2-9-0 ................................ SCarson 6 98
(RFJohnsonHoughton) *lw: trckd ldrs: rdn and styd on wl u.p ins fnl f to ld last stride* **1/1**[1]

41 **2** hd **Doctor Hilary**[8] 2256 2-8-10 ........................................ JMackay 5 93
(MLWBell) *lw: led: rdn and kpt on wl fnl f: hdd last stride* **7/1**[3]

321 **3** 3/4 **Umniya (IRE)**[11] 2213 2-8-5 ............................................ TEDurcan 2 86
(MRChannon) *chsd ldrs: rdn over 1f out: kpt on ins last: nt qckn nr fin* **7/2**[2]

**4** 7 **Banknote** 2-8-7 ................................................................ MartinDwyer 1 67
(AMBalding) *bkwd: s.i.s: sn in tch: rdn: swtchd rt and effrt fr 2f out: nvr gng pce of ldrs and wknd ins last* **7/1**[3]

0216 **5** 2 **Im Spartacus**[15] 2086 2-9-0 ............................................ IMongan 3 68
(IAWood) *chsd ldrs tl wknd 2f out* **25/1**

**6** nk **Bibi Helen** 2-7-11 ................................................................ DFox(5) 7 55
(NACallaghan) *w'like: s.i.s: a outpcd in rr* **50/1**

**7** 1 1/4 **Doctor's Cave** 2-8-7 .............................................................. DHolland 4 57
(CEBrittain) *str: bkwd: sn rdn: outpcd and bhd* **14/1**

1m 13.06s (-0.01) **Going Correction** -0.25s/f (Firm) 7 Ran SP% **109.7**
Speed ratings: **90,89,88,79,76 76,74**CSF £7.91 TOTE £1.90: £1.40, £3.10; EX 8.30.
**Owner** G C Stevens **Bred** Kevin B Lynch **Trained** Blewbury, Oxon

**FOCUS**
A modest winning time for a race of this class. Only the first three ever counted and the form looks good enough.

**NOTEBOOK**
**Beaver Patrol(IRE)**, no match for the classy Blue Dakota at Windsor, was tackling six furlongs for the first time and needed all the extra yardage to wear down the leader. He is set to go to the Royal meeting now, but is likely to find someting too good for him there.
**Doctor Hilary** travelled well in front and was the last to come off the bridle, but having seen off the filly he was nailed right on the line. He has a lot of natural pace and he might be worth a try at the minimum trip.
**Umniya(IRE)** ran a solid race but had to concede defeat in the last 50 yards. She finished well clear of the remainder.
**Banknote** is a half-brother to Double Brandy who won at six and eight furlongs, and to bumper and hurdles winner Brandy Snap. He was beaten a long way in the end by three previous winners, but is entitled to improve with the experience behind him.
**Im Spartacus**, penalised like the eventual winner, was rather disappointing and the ground could not be put forward as an excuse this time. He may improve when tackling seven furlongs.

## 2479 BJORN AGAIN HERE WEDNESDAY JUNE 2ND MAIDEN STKS 1m (J)
**4:25** (4:26) (D ) 3-Y-O **£5,720** (£1,760; £880; £440) **Stalls** High

Form RPR
62 **1** **Capestar (IRE)**[17] 2046 3-8-10 ow1.................................... JPMurtagh 9 77
(BGPowell) *sn trcking ldr: chal over 2f out tl drvn to ld appr fnl f: r.o wl* **9/4**[1]

**2** 1/2 **Serre Chevalier (IRE)** 3-9-0 ........................................ MartinDwyer 8 80
(PWHarris) *w'like: lenghty: hld up in tch: hdwy over 2f out: drvn to press wnr ins last: pushed but no ex nr fin* **20/1**

00-0 **3** 1 **Zuma (IRE)**[14] 2114 3-9-0 ................................................ DHolland 13 78
(RHannon) *s.i.s: sn in tch: rdn 4f out: outpcd 3f out: rallied over 1f out: styd on wl cl home* **5/1**[3]

324- **4** nk **Zwadi (IRE)**[263] 4805 3-8-9 75.......................................... SWhitworth 12 72
(HCandy) *sn led: rdn over 2f out and kpt narrow ld tl hdd appr fnl f: wknd cl home* **20/1**

00 **5** 2 1/2 **Tumbaga (USA)**[15] 2085 3-9-0 ............................................(t) RHughes 1 71
(RCharlton) *wnt lft s: sn prom and racd on outside: outpcd bnd 3f out: kpt on again fnl 2f: one pce ins last* **7/1**

4- **6** 1/2 **Pre Eminance (IRE)**[210] 5867 3-9-0 .................................... SDrowne 5 70
(CREgerton) *lw: chsd ldrs: rdn over 2f out: wknd fnl f* **6/1**

0 **7** 1/2 **Shaaban (IRE)**[14] 2113 3-9-0 ............................................ TEDurcan 6 69
(MRChannon) *swtg: s.i.s: sn rcvrd but in rr: hdwy over 2f out: styd on u.p fnl f but nvr nr ldrs* **25/1**

523- **8** 3/4 **Hunter's Valley**[225] 5614 3-8-9 80.......................................... PDobbs 10 62
(RHannon) *bkwd: bhd: pushed along 3f out: kpt on fr over 1f out but n.d* **12/1**

03- **9** nk **Chigorin**[229] 5547 3-9-0 .......................................................... JTate 2 67
(JMPEustace) *racd on outside: sme hdwy fnl 2f but n.d* **25/1**

0 **10** 1 **Killmorey**[27] 1794 3-9-0 ............................................................ JQuinn 4 64
(SCWilliams) *lw: s.i.s: hld up: kpt on wl fnl f but nvr a danger* **66/1**

25- **11** 4 **Powerful Parrish (USA)**[230] 5531 3-8-9 .............................. LDettori 3 50
(PFICole) *swtg: in tch: rdn 3f out: sn btn* **9/2**[2]

0- **12** 7 **Karma Chamelian (USA)**[359] 2127 3-8-6 .................... LisaJones(3) 7 34
(JWHills) *chsd ldrs tl wknd over 2f out* **50/1**

000- **13** 18 **Court Chancellor**[241] 5313 3-9-0 ........................................ RLMoore 11 —
(PMitchell) *a in rr* **100/1**

1m 40.39s (0.77) **Going Correction** +0.125s/f (Good) 13 Ran SP% **121.8**
Speed ratings: **101,100,99,99,96 96,95,94,94,93 89,82,64**CSF £56.84 TOTE £3.70: £1.30, £4.70, £2.20; EX 66.90.
**Owner** D & J Newell **Bred** Park Place International Ltd **Trained** Morestead, Hants

**FOCUS**
This was an ordinary maiden for Kempton although the form looks solid enough.

**NOTEBOOK**
**Capestar(IRE)**, always in the first two, went on early in the straight and proved game in holding off the runner-up's challenge. This was her first run at a mile and she saw it out well.
**Serre Chevalier(IRE)** ♦, from the yard successful in this race a year ago, threw down a strong challenge but could not get past the tenacious filly. Sure to come on for the run, he should have no problem going one better and looks the type to make a nice handicapper.
**Zuma(IRE)** was slightly hampered on the approach to the home straight and the leaders got away from him, but he was keeping on late. Handicaps over farther look where his future lies.
**Zwadi(IRE)**, trained at two by Barry Hills, made the running but, having been collared, faded as if this trip stretched her.
**Tumbaga(USA)**, fitted with a tongue strap for this return to a mile, is now eligible for handicaps.
**Pre Eminance(IRE)**, who showed promise in a backend maiden on easy ground, needs one more run for a mark.
**Shaaban(IRE)**, as on his recent debut, was slowly away, but he shaped with a little promise this time.
**Killmorey** was again slow to find his stride, but he did make modest late progress and is the type to improve over farther.

## 2480 WEDNESDAY EVENING SERIES H'CAP 2m
**4:55** (4:55) (D) (0-85,80) 3-Y-O+ **£5,486** (£1,688; £844; £422) **Stalls** High

Form RPR
/06- **1** **Quedex**[14] 893 8-8-5 60.................................................... RMiles(3) 6 71
(RJPrice) *hld up in rr: racd on outside: stdy hdwy over 2f out: str run to ld 1f out: readily* **8/1**[3]

4-0S **2** 1 1/2 **Theatre (USA)**[9] 2240 5-10-0 80.............................................. PDoe 7 89
(JamiePoulton) *in tch: rdn and lost pl 7f out: sn rcvrd: chsd ldr 4f out: led ins fnl 3f: hdd 1f out: styd on same pce* **8/1**[3]

0233 **3** 1 **High Point (IRE)**[17] 2047 6-9-11 80............................ SHitchcott(3) 9 88
(GPEnright) *in tch: hrd drvn over 2f out: styd on ins fnl f but nt rch ldrs* **4/1**[1]

0300 **4** nk **Sudden Flight (IRE)**[19] 2000 7-8-13 65................................ RHavlin 10 73+
(PDEvans) *chsd ldrs: styng on whn hmpd and lost pl 2f out:rallied and r.o again fnl f: kpt on cl home* **25/1**

5121 **5** 5 **Malarkey**[42] 1457 7-9-10 76.............................................. SDrowne 2 78
(MrsStefLiddiard) *hld up in rr: hdwy on rails 3f out: chsd ldr 2f out: wknd fnl f* **4/1**[1]

5001 **6** 3 **Treasure Trail**[2] 2429 5-9-4 70 5ex........................................ JFEgan 3 68
(SKirk) *hld up in rr: hdwy 7f out: rdn and edgd rt 2f out: wknd over 1f out* **9/2**[2]

360- **7** 3 **Peak Park (USA)**[227] 5576 4-7-9 52 oh4........................ LisaJones(3) 8 46
(JARToller) *t.k.h in rr: mod hdwy fnl 2f* **25/1**

13-0 **8** 1/2 **Head To Kerry (IRE)**[14] 2116 4-8-11 65.............................. RHughes 4 59
(DJSFfrenchDavis) *t.k.h: chsd ldrs: disp 2nd 10f out: wknd fr 2f out* **8/1**[3]

-000 **9** 13 **Snow's Ride**[17] 2047 4-9-7 75............................................(b[1]) DHolland 1 53
(WRMuir) *led after 1f: hdd ins fnl 3f: wknd qckly over 2f out* **25/1**

-112 **10** 25 **Linens Flame**[26] 1832 5-9-9 75.......................................... JPMurtagh 5 23
(BGPowell) *led 1f: styd chsng ldr tl wknd rapidly 3f out: eased fnl 2f* **8/1**[3]

3m 30.53s (0.17) **Going Correction** +0.125s/f (Good)
**WFA** 4 from 5yo+ 2lb 10 Ran SP% **114.2**
Speed ratings: **104,103,102,102,100 98,97,96,90,77**CSF £66.90 CT £292.14 TOTE £9.10: £2.50, £2.50, £2.00; EX 61.80 Place 6 £58.66, Place 5 £12.46.
**Owner** Fox And Cub Partnership **Bred** Leo Van Hijkoop **Trained** Ullingswick, H'fords

**FOCUS**
A fair handicap run at a decent pace, and this looks sound form.
**NOTEBOOK**
**Quedex** gained his last win on the Flat over this course and distance back in 2000 when trained by Ed James, and was 20lb lower here. Successful in his last two outings over hurdles, he came with a sweeping run to score a shade readily and can be placed to advantage again while in this sort of form.
**Theatre(USA)**, rousted along past halfway to recover his pitch, slipped up the inner to lead early in the home straight but was worn down. This was a decent effort under his big weight.
**High Point(IRE)** stayed on over this more suitable trip but could not get to the first two. He is a particularly consistent individual who goes well at this track.
**Sudden Flight(IRE)** was tackling two miles for the first time and seemed to stay. He might even have finished second had he not lost momentum when making ground two furlongs out, although he would probably not have troubled the winner.
**Malarkey**, racing from a 6lb higher mark, was briefly short of room on the home turn before giving chase to the leader. He was still third entering the final furlong, but faded quite quickly in the last 100 yards.
**Treasure Trail**, under a 5lb penalty, never really looked like supplementing his win at Bath two days earlier.
**Linens Flame** *Official explanation: jockey said gelding hung right throughout.*
T/Plt: £87.70 to a £1 stake. Pool: £81,703.75. 679.20 winning tickets. T/Qpdt: £25.50 to a £1 stake. Pool: £3,930.30. 114.05 winning tickets. ST

## 2401 LINGFIELD (L-H)
### Saturday, May 29

**OFFICIAL GOING: Turf course - good to firm (firm in places); all-weather course - standard**
On the turf course there seemed to be an advantage to those that raced away from the stands' rail.
Wind: Nil Weather: Fine

### 2481 EUROPEAN BREEDERS FUND MAIDEN FILLIES' STKS — 6f
**6:05** (6:08) (D) 2-Y-O — **£5,801** (£1,785; £892; £446) **Stalls** High

| Form | Pos | Dist | Horse / Trainer / Comment | Jockey | RPR |
|---|---|---|---|---|---|
| | **1** | | **Masa (USA)** 2-8-11 (SaeedBinSuroor) *gd sort: w'like: bkwd: mde all: pushed clr wl over 1f out: easily* **4/1**[1] | LDettori 5 | 80+ |
| 6 | **2** | 5 | **Tesary**[16] 2071 2-8-11 (EALDunlop) *prom: rdn over 2f out: chsd wnr over 1f out: no imp* **7/1**[3] | TEDurcan 11 | 65 |
| 0 | **3** | nk | **Stephanie's Mind**[12] 2177 2-8-11 (CNAllen) *prom: drvn 1/2-way: styd on same pce fnl 2f: no ch w wnr* **8/1** | IMongan 9 | 64 |
| 50 | **4** | nk | **Ivana Illyich (IRE)**[12] 2177 2-8-11 (SKirk) *prom: rdn wl over 2f out: styd on same pce fr over 1f out* **20/1** | JFEgan 13 | 63 |
| | **5** | 1 1/2 | **Kissing Lights (IRE)** 2-8-11 (MLWBell) *unf: chsd wnr to over 1f out: wknd ins fnl f* **10/1** | JMackay 4 | 59 |
| | **6** | 1 | **Extreme Beauty (USA)** 2-8-11 (CEBrittain) *w'like: bkwd: racd in midfield: outpcd 1/2-way: kpt on fr over 1f out: n.d* **16/1** | DHolland 10 | 56 |
| | **7** | 3/4 | **Gone Fishing (IRE)** 2-8-11 (MAJarvis) *leggy: scope: lw: s.i.s: chsd ldng gp: outpcd and shkn up over 2f out: one pce after* **9/2**[2] | PRobinson 8 | 53 |
| 0 | **8** | nk | **Romantic Gift**[12] 2177 2-8-11 (JMPEustace) *chsd ldrs: rdn over 2f out: one pce after* **12/1** | JTate 6 | 53 |
| | **9** | 1 1/4 | **Rock Chick** 2-8-11 (JHMGosden) *w'like: scope: racd towards rr: outpcd and pushed along over 3f out: kpt on steadily fr over 1f out* **9/1** | JPMurtagh 3 | 49 |
| | **10** | 3/4 | **County Clare** 2-8-11 (AMBalding) *w'like: bkwd: dwlt: outpcd and rn green: nvr on terms: kpt on fnl f* **7/1**[3] | MartinDwyer 12 | 47 |
| | **11** | 1 | **Imperial Miss (IRE)** 2-8-11 (BWDuke) *neat: s.s: outpcd and wl bhd: kpt on fr over 1f out* **66/1** | SCarson 7 | 44 |
| | **12** | 11 | **Rosiella** 2-8-11 (MBlanshard) *leggy: uns rdr bef s: dwlt: outpcd and a bhd* **100/1** | JQuinn 2 | — |
| | **13** | 10 | **Just Beware** 2-8-6 (MissZCDavison) *w'like: s.s: outpcd: sn t.o* **100/1** | NChalmers(5) 1 | — |

1m 10.61s (-1.04) **Going Correction** -0.20s/f (Firm) **13** Ran **SP% 115.2**
Speed ratings: **98,91,90,90,88 87,86,85,84,83 81,67,53**CSF £30.00 TOTE £4.60: £2.90, £2.40, £2.10; EX 22.10.
**Owner** Godolphin **Bred** Diamond A Racing Corp **Trained** Newmarket, Suffolk
**FOCUS**
A decent pace and a very smart time for the type of race. Very few got into it but the winner was impressive.
**NOTEBOOK**
**Masa(USA)** ◆, a $95,000 yearling out of a winning half-sister to dual Italian classic-winner Miss Gris, certainly knew her job at the first time of asking. Bouncing out of the gates, she set the pace and gradually forged further and further clear in the latter stages. We will be hearing a lot more of her.
**Tesary** improved from her debut effort over this extra furlong and faster ground. Always in pursuit of the winner, she was made to look ordinary by that rival but should have little difficulty in winning an ordinary maiden.
**Stephanie's Mind**, always close to the pace, appreciated the extra furlong and put up an improved display in what was probably a hot maiden for the track.
**Ivana Illyich(IRE)** ran her best race to date over this extra furlong, but had more experience than the front trio and is unlikely to progress much from this.
**Kissing Lights(IRE)**, who cost 110,000gns as a yearling, is out of a winning half-sister to Raise A Grand. She did hint at some ability and is likely to improve for the experience.
**Extreme Beauty(USA)**, a $15,000 yearling whose dam was a Listed winner in Ireland, showed some promise for the future but also gave the impression she found this an inadequate test.
**Gone Fishing(IRE)**, a 110,000euros full-sister to New Trumps, gave the impression that she will improve with racing.

### 2482 MID SUSSEX TIMBER 75TH ANNIVERSARY FILLIES' H'CAP — 5f
**6:40** (6:40) (E) (0-70,66) 3-Y-O+ — **£3,493** (£1,075; £537; £268) **Stalls** High

| Form | Pos | Dist | Horse / Trainer / Comment | Jockey | RPR |
|---|---|---|---|---|---|
| 0001 | **1** | | **Lady Protector**[9] 2252 5-8-12 **52** (JBalding) *chsd ldrs on outer: rdn 2f out: styd on wl fnl f to ld last strides* **8/1** | DHolland 6 | 59 |
| 0000 | **2** | nk | **Inching**[5] 2350 4-8-5 **45** (RMHCowell) *racd in centre: mostly pressed ldr: drvn to ld wl ins fnl f: hdd last strides* **33/1** | MartinDwyer 4 | 51 |
| 0035 | **3** | hd | **Lady Pekan**[1] 2440 5-9-7 **61** (b) (PSMcentee) *racd in centre: mde most: drvn 2f out: hdd and unable qck wl ins fnl f* **10/1** | TGMcLaughlin 2 | 66 |
| 0-36 | **4** | 1/2 | **Comeraincomeshine (IRE)**[51] 1312 3-8-9 **60** (TGMills) *racd towards nr side: w ldrs: rdn over 2f out: kpt on same pce fnl f* **16/1** | RMiles(3) 11 | 63 |
| 5041 | **5** | 3/4 | **I Wish**[12] 2178 6-9-2 **56** (MMadgwick) *hld up in rr: pushed along 1/2-way: effrt but unable qck over 1f out: styd on fnl f* **4/1**[1] | LDettori 14 | 56 |
| 3422 | **6** | shd | **Princess Kai (IRE)**[17] 2033 3-8-6 **57** (b) (RIngram) *lw: racd in centre: towards rr: rdn over 2f out: styd on wl fnl f* **16/1** | SHitchcott(3) 1 | 57 |
| 0050 | **7** | shd | **Tamarella (IRE)**[9] 2252 4-8-12 **52** (v[1]) (GGMargarson) *racd centre: pressed ldrs: kpt on one pce u.p fnl f* **25/1** | AMcCarthy 3 | 51 |
| 0030 | **8** | nk | **Playful Spirit**[9] 2238 5-8-7 **46** ow1 (v) (JBalding) *towards rr: shuffled along 2f out: kpt on fnl f: nt rch ldrs* **16/1** | JEdmunds 7 | 45 |
| 063- | **9** | nk | **Minimum Bid**[292] 4039 3-8-8 **56** (MissBSanders) *stdd s: began on nr side but racd in centre bef 1/2-way: wl bhd: nudged along and styd on wl fr over 1f out: gaining at fin* **25/1** | JQuinn 13 | 53 |
| 4221 | **10** | 1 1/4 | **Boavista (IRE)**[2] 2428 4-9-5 **66** 7ex (PDEvans) *racd nr side: prom: rdn over 2f out: fdd fnl f* **6/1**[3] | SJDonohoe(7) 9 | 58 |
| 5160 | **11** | 1/2 | **Erracht**[9] 2246 6-9-5 **64** (MrsHSweeting) *racd nr side: prom: rdn over 2f out: wknd fnl f* **20/1** | NChalmers(5) 5 | 54 |
| 30-4 | **12** | 1 | **Redwood Star**[9] 2246 4-9-3 **57** (e) (PLGilligan) *prom nr side: rdn over 2f out: wknd over 1f out* **9/2**[2] | JFEgan 15 | 43 |
| 4000 | **13** | 3/4 | **Bahamian Belle**[9] 2246 4-9-0 **54** (t) (PSMcentee) *lw: s.i.s: t.k.h and hld up in rr: rdn and no prog 2f out* **50/1** | SWKelly 10 | 37 |
| 1253 | **14** | 3/4 | **Empress Josephine**[30] 1738 4-9-2 **56** (v) (JRJenkins) *racd nr side: chsd ldrs: squeezed out 1/2-way: no ch after* **25/1** | TEDurcan 12 | 36 |
| 05-0 | **15** | 1/2 | **Ryan's Quest (IRE)**[57] 1228 5-8-5 **45** (TDMccarthy) *chsd ldrs: nt clr run 2f out: btn and eased after* **25/1** | PDoe 8 | 23 |

57.63 secs (-1.24) **Going Correction** -0.20s/f (Firm)
**WFA** 3 from 4yo+ 8lb **15** Ran **SP% 115.4**
Speed ratings: **101,100,100,99,98 98,97,97,96,94 94,92,91,90,89**CSF £249.30 CT £2638.79 TOTE £9.00: £2.70, £10.60, £4.70; EX 553.10.
**Owner** Simon Mapletoft Racing II **Bred** P J Wightman **Trained** Scrooby, Notts
**FOCUS**
A typically competitive if modest race of its type and a blanket finish. Those that raced down the centre of the track appeared to hold a major advantage and those that raced nearside can be given the benefit of the doubt.
**NOTEBOOK**
**Lady Protector**, up 7lb for her Newcastle victory, is in the form of her life at present and the style of her win was exactly the same, coming with a devastating late run on the favoured side of the track to get up near the line. She has found consistency and improvement from somewhere, and in this mood you would not bet against her completing the hat-trick.
**Inching**, who has not been in the best of form of late, returned to her best and can be considered unlucky not to have finally got off the mark at the 25th attempt. No sooner had she got the better of a protracted battle with Lady Pekan than the winner came and mugged them both.
**Lady Pekan**, making a quick reappearance after finishing unplaced at Brighton the previous day, showed her usual decent speed down the centre of the track and was only just denied, though she was probably racing on a faster strip.
**Comeraincomeshine(IRE)** ◆ did best of those that race more towards the stands' side, though she did hang left under pressure in the closing stages and may not have been totally at home on the ground. She is still a maiden, but is also more lightly raced than most of these and may be capable of some improvement, especially on easier ground.
**I Wish** was not helped by the drop in trip, nor by having to race on the slower stands' side. She did not get going until it was far too late, but this was still a fair effort under the circumstances.
**Princess Kai(IRE)** was always struggling to go the pace, but did make some late progress down the same strip of ground as the winner.
**Minimum Bid** ◆, racing for the first time in nine months and making her handicap debut, was the real eye-catcher of the race. Switched to race down the centre of the track from her high draw after a furlong, she was completely tailed off at halfway but, with her rider doing very little, she took off in the second half of the contest and finished full of running. This did not look good at all. *Official explanation: jockey said, regarding the running and riding, on the way to post he realised filly was very sensitive on the left side of her mouth, adding that filly jumped awkwardly and began to hang badly left; vet confirmed filly had a sore mouth caused by an ulcer*

### 2483 DEREK BURRIDGE RACING & GOLF TROPHIES H'CAP — 7f
**7:10** (7:10) (E) (0-75,70) 3-Y-O+ — **£4,013** (£1,235; £617; £308) **Stalls** High

| Form | Pos | Dist | Horse / Trainer / Comment | Jockey | RPR |
|---|---|---|---|---|---|
| 0303 | **1** | | **Quantum Leap**[10] 2226 7-9-6 **66** (v) (SDow) *mde virtually all: shkn up 2f out: drew clr fnl f* **8/1**[3] | RLMoore 12 | 79 |
| 0-21 | **2** | 2 1/2 | **Goodenough Mover**[16] 2064 8-9-4 **69** (JSKing) *w ldrs: rdn over 2f out: w wnr 1f out: sn no ex* **5/1**[1] | HayleyTurner(5) 14 | 75 |
| 0204 | **3** | 1/2 | **Mistral Sky**[5] 2358 5-9-7 **67** (p) (MrsStefLiddiard) *chsd ldrs: plld out and rdn over 2f out: styd on fr over 1f out to take 3rd nr fin* **16/1** | JFEgan 11 | 72 |
| 2442 | **4** | 3/4 | **And Toto Too**[16] 2064 4-9-0 **67** (b) (PDEvans) *midfield: rdn 3f out: prog on inner 2f out: styd on fnl f: nrst fin* **5/1**[1] | SJDonohoe(7) 17 | 70 |
| 0200 | **5** | shd | **Captain Darling (IRE)**[17] 2030 4-9-3 **63** (v[1]) (RMHCowell) *trckd ldrs: rdn wl over 2f out: one pce fr over 1f out* **14/1** | EAhern 4 | 66 |
| 4133 | **6** | 1 | **Adantino**[90] 928 5-8-8 **54** (b) (BRMillman) *chsd ldrs: rdn and prog over 2f out: chsd ldng pair briefly over 1f out: wknd fnl f* **14/1** | SDrowne 9 | 54 |
| 6-15 | **7** | 1/2 | **Azreme**[14] 2119 4-9-3 **70** (DKIvory) *b.hind: trckd ldrs gng wl: rdn over 2f out: sn nt qckn and btn* **14/1** | MHoward(7) 16 | 69 |
| 3140 | **8** | nk | **Mayzin (IRE)**[12] 2166 4-8-7 **53** (p) (RMFlower) *lw: dwlt: t.k.h and sn prom: wknd wl over 1f out* **12/1** | TEDurcan 15 | 51 |
| 6040 | **9** | 1 1/2 | **Steely Dan**[7] 2304 5-9-5 **65** (JRBest) *lw: hld up wl in rr: effrt 3f out: kpt on fr over 1f out: n.d* **13/2**[2] | LDettori 3 | 59 |
| 60-0 | **10** | 3/4 | **Logistical**[25] 1877 4-9-5 **65** (ADWPinder) *b.near: b.hind: wl in rr: off the pce and no ch over 2f out: modest late prog* **20/1** | SWhitworth 2 | 57 |
| 0-20 | **11** | 3/4 | **Treetops Hotel (IRE)**[17] 2030 5-8-6 **57** (BRJohnson) *hld up in last and wl off the pce: effrt over 2f out: carried hd high and no ch* **33/1** | NChalmers(5) 1 | 47 |
| /060 | **12** | 2 1/2 | **El Chaparral (IRE)**[14] 2118 4-9-3 **66** (p) (DKIvory) *rrd s: in tch: rdn 3f out: fnd nil and sn btn: eased fnl f* **33/1** | RMiles(3) 8 | 50 |
| -200 | **13** | 1/2 | **Power Bird (IRE)**[108] 745 4-9-2 **62** (BRJohnson) *a wl in rr and off the pce: struggling 3f out* **20/1** | JPMurtagh 7 | 45 |
| 0-00 | **14** | 4 | **Compton Arrow (IRE)**[16] 2064 8-8-13 **59** (AWCarroll) *wl in rr: effrt and sme prog on inner 3f out: hanging rt 2f out: wknd and eased* **33/1** | IMongan 5 | 31 |
| 000- | **15** | 2 1/2 | **Old Harry**[230] 5509 4-8-5 **54** ow2 (PCRitchens) *dwlt: plld hrd and hld up wl in rr: wknd over 2f out* **33/1** | LPKeniry(3) 6 | 20 |

222- **16** *8* **Franksalot (IRE)**[240] [5326] 4-9-5 **65**........................................ JQuinn 13 10
(MissBSanders) *w ldrs to 1/2-way: sn lost pl and eased: t.o* **16/1**

1m 22.06s (-2.15) **Going Correction** -0.20s/f (Firm) **16** Ran SP% **118.5**
Speed ratings: **104,101,100,99,99 98,97,97,95,94 94,91,90,86,83 74**CSF £41.98 CT £620.33 TOTE £10.20: £1.80, £1.90, £5.90, £2.30; EX 67.10.

**Owner** Mrs M E O'Shea **Bred** L C And Mrs A E Sigsworth **Trained** Epsom, Surrey

**FOCUS**
With the whole field migrating over to the stands' side, the track bias was not as pronounced as in the previous race, but it was still noticeable that those who raced furthest from the stands' rail appeared to come home stronger. The front pair dominated from the off and very few got into it, but the form looks sound enough.

**NOTEBOOK**
**Quantum Leap** was always up with the pace and when asked to go and win his race, did not shirk the issue this time. The drop back to seven did not seem to bother him at all.
**Goodenough Mover**, up 2lb from his Salisbury win, ran very well considering he did not enjoy an uncontested lead and was racing closer to the stands' rail than the winner. He seems to have lost none of his gusto and his rider gets on really well with him.
**Mistral Sky**, wearing cheekpieces rather than a visor, took a while to respond to pressure but eventually came home in good style. He is not badly handicapped at present.
**And Toto Too** ran another solid race and can be given some extra credit as she never left the stands' rail and that may have been a handicap at this meeting.
**Captain Darling(IRE)**, visored for the first time, ran better on this return to seven but is not the easiest to win with.
**Adantino** may have just needed this first run since February, but is still looking for his first win on turf after 20 attempts.
**Azreme** travelled well, but found little off the bridle and this ground was almost certainly too quick for him.

## 2484 RAPPORTEUR H'CAP 1m 2f (P)
7:45 (7:46) (F) (0-55,55) 3-Y-O **£3,024** (£864; £432) **Stalls** Low

Form RPR
6-51 **1** **Incisor**[34] [1643] 3-8-11 **52**........................................ PDobbs 7 63
(SKirk) *swtg: trckd ldrs gng wl: prog over 2f out: shkn up to ld jst ins fnl f: comf* **7/2**[1]
0-00 **2** *2 ½* **Willhego**[5] [2356] 3-8-11 **52**........................................ MartinDwyer 10 58
(JRBest) *sn led: rdn 2f out: hdd jst ins fnl f: no ch w wnr* **20/1**
0-24 **3** *1 ½* **Ask The Driver**[33] [1667] 3-8-13 **54**........................................ SWhitworth 11 57
(DJSFfrenchDavis) *n.m.r s and dropped to last: prog on outer fr 3f out: drvn and styd on to take 3rd nr fin* **6/1**[2]
0500 **4** *½* **Clare Galway**[3] [2402] 3-8-6 **50**........................................ RMiles(3) 6 52
(TDMccarthy) *trckd ldrs: rdn over 2f out: one pce fr over 1f out* **12/1**
-660 **5** *2* **Saucy**[3] [2402] 3-8-6 **50**........................................(b) JFMcDonald(3) 13 48
(BJMeehan) *chsd ldr to over 1f out: wknd* **25/1**
0520 **6** *1 ¼* **Avertaine**[11] [2199] 3-8-11 **52**........................................ RLMoore 12 48
(GLMoore) *hld up in rr: rdn 3f out: sme prog u.p 2f out: nvr rchd ldrs* **8/1**[3]
-060 **7** *shd* **Lady Stripes**[73] [1038] 3-8-11 **52**........................................ TEDurcan 1 48
(MJWallace) *prom: rdn and cl up whn hmpd on inner 2f out: no ch after* **12/1**
3-40 **8** *2 ½* **Nafferton Girl (IRE)**[36] [1600] 3-8-9 **50**........................................ SWKelly 8 41
(JAOsborne) *chsd ldrs: hrd rdn wl over 2f out: wknd over 1f out* **20/1**
6500 **9** *shd* **Mister Completely (IRE)**[4] [2380] 3-8-8 **49**........................................ IMongan 5 40
(JRBest) *settled in rr: rdn over 4f out: struggling after* **10/1**
04-5 **10** *hd* **Sharplaw Destiny (IRE)**[33] [1678] 3-8-12 **53**........................................ SDrowne 2 43
(WJHaggas) *towards rr: rdn over 4f out: no prog* **10/1**
6040 **11** *½* **Mystic Moon**[22] [1946] 3-8-13 **54**........................................ DHolland 4 43
(JRJenkins) *chsd ldrs: rdn over 3f out: wknd 2f out* **20/1**
00-5 **12** *¾* **Daydream Dancer**[47] [1370] 3-8-12 **53**........................................ PRobinson 14 41
(CGCox) *a towards rr: rdn and no prog 4f out* **9/1**
00-6 **13** *1 ¾* **Adeeba (IRE)**[35] [1628] 3-9-0 **55**........................................ WSupple 9 40
(EALDunlop) *a wl in rr: rdn 4f out: no prog* **25/1**
600 **14** *4* **Sunset Dreamer (USA)**[47] [1352] 3-8-11 **52**........................................ EAhern 3 29
(PMitchell) *a towards rr: rdn over 4f out: wknd 3f out* **10/1**

2m 7.99s (0.14) **Going Correction** 0.0s/f (Stan) **14** Ran SP% **122.3**
Speed ratings: **99,97,95,95,93 92,92,90,90,90 90,89,88,84**CSF £83.88 CT £414.23 TOTE £3.90: £1.70, £7.10, £2.20; EX 391.10.

**Owner** R Gander **Bred** J Godfrey **Trained** Upper Lambourn, Berks

**FOCUS**
A very poor handicap, but the pace was sound enough and the form looks likely to work out.

**NOTEBOOK**
**Incisor** transferred his recent improvement on turf on to the Polytrack. Always going well, his only worry was whether the gaps would appear in time for him, but fortunately they did and, despite having to take evasive action when the runner-up started to hang, he quickened up nicely when asked. This was a bad race, but he does seem to be improving.
**Willhego**, who had finished no closer than eighth in five previous outings, improved over this longer trip on his Polytrack debut. Making a bold bid to lead all the way, he quickened the tempo on the turn for home, but then started to hang right under pressure and found the winner's late rush too much for him.
**Ask The Driver** is a slow starter at the best of times and when he did get his start right, like he did here, he then runs out of room and is knocked to the back of the field. He did make up a lot of ground over the last three furlongs though, and is obviously not completely without ability.
**Clare Galway** ran alright, but is still to really confirm early promise.
**Saucy**, making her sand debut, was always in the front two and deserves some credit for hanging in there for as long as she did, because she took a good hold early.
**Avertaine** made some late progress, but may be better suited by a slower surface than this.
**Lady Stripes** was already getting the worst of it when quite badly bumped on the inside turning for home. Connections seem to be struggling to find her best trip.

## 2485 MOTT MACDONALD (S) STKS 1m 4f (P)
8:20 (8:20) (G ) 3-Y-O **£2,562** (£732; £366) **Stalls** Low

Form RPR
6-56 **1** **Peruvian Breeze (IRE)**[33] [1662] 3-8-12 59........................................ EAhern 2 66
(NPLittmoden) *lw: trckd ldr: rdn to chal 2f out: kpt on to ld last 100yds* **4/1**[3]
4500 **2** *½* **Another Con (IRE)**[32] [1688] 3-8-13 66........................................(p) RHavlin 3 66
(MrsPNDutfield) *led: clr w wnr over 2f out: rdn over 1f out: edgd rt and fnd nil: hdd and hld last 100yds* **10/3**[2]
5660 **3** *5* **Come What July (IRE)**[8] [2259] 3-9-4 73........................................(v[1]) DHolland 5 63
(RGuest) *mostly trckd ldng pair: outpcd and hrd rdn over 2f out: no rspnse and no imp* **9/4**[1]
0506 **4** *7* **Frambo (IRE)**[40] [1499] 3-8-7 45........................................(tp) RLMoore 9 41
(JGPortman) *hld up in midfield: rdn over 3f out: sn outpcd and btn* **20/1**
3660 **5** *6* **Marksgold (IRE)**[16] [2061] 3-8-12 57........................................ SDrowne 8 36
(PFICole) *hld up: hrd rdn over 4f out: sn wl btn* **12/1**
0-60 **6** *4* **Signora Panettiera (FR)**[40] [1499] 3-8-4 58........................................ SHitchcott(3) 6 25
(MRChannon) *trckd ldrs: hrd rdn over 3f out: sn wknd* **6/1**
-000 **7** *1 ¾* **Once Around (IRE)**[27] [1800] 3-8-9 51........................................ RMiles(3) 4 27
(TGMills) *hld up in last pair: outpcd and rdn over 3f out: no prog and sn bhd* **14/1**
0-50 **8** *2 ½* **Warif (USA)**[15] [2092] 3-8-12 53........................................(b[1]) BDoyle 1 23
(EJO'Neill) *lw: t.k.h: prom briefly: in last pair and rdn over 3f out: sn bhd* **16/1**

2m 35.53s (1.29) **Going Correction** 0.0s/f (Stan) **8** Ran SP% **113.1**
Speed ratings: **95,94,91,86,82 80,78,77**CSF £17.35 TOTE £5.00: £1.70, £1.30, £1.50; EX 17.80.The winer was bought in for 6,400gns. Another Con was claimed by D C Patrick for £6,000.

**Owner** M C S D Racing Ltd **Bred** Charles Flynn **Trained** Newmarket, Suffolk

**FOCUS**
A very weak seller run at an ordinary pace. The front pair dominated from the start and the form looks decent enough for the grade.

**NOTEBOOK**
**Peruvian Breeze(IRE)**, badly in with a couple at the weights, had never previously been placed but he was taking a huge step down in class. He always had the leader in his sights, but it needed all his rider's strength to get him past in an all-out duel to the line.
**Another Con(IRE)**, winner of a 0-to-70 handicap here in February, was another in a seller for the first time. Meeting the winner on 6lb better terms than she would have been in a handicap, she made a bold bid to make all and certainly did not go down without a fight. She ought to be up to winning another modest contest on this surface.
**Come What July(IRE)**, best in at the weights, travelled well enough but he had to switch off the inside to see daylight racing down the false straight, and the time he took to do so enabled the front pair to scamper clear. There was no way back from there.
**Frambo(IRE)**, placed in claiming company on sand during the winter, had plenty on at the weights and was soundly beaten by the market principals.
**Signora Panettiera(FR)**, making her sand debut, looks to have gone the wrong way as she was off the bridle and going nowhere from some way out.

## 2486 MUSIC AFTER RACING MAIDEN STKS 1m 2f (P)
8:50 (8:52) (D ) 3-Y-O **£3,994** (£1,229; £614; £307) **Stalls** Low

Form RPR
34 **1** **Swainson (USA)**[21] [1967] 3-9-0........................................ DHolland 6 77
(PMitchell) *mde virtually all: set stdy pce tl kicked on wl over 1f out: drvn out fnl f* **9/4**[2]
2-0 **2** *½* **St Francis Wood (USA)**[45] [1398] 3-8-9........................................ EAhern 10 71
(JNoseda) *t.k.h: cl up: trckd wnr gng easily over 2f out: shkn up to chal ins fnl f: nt qckn: too much to do* **13/8**[1]
**3** *2 ½* **Supamach (IRE)** 3-8-9........................................ SDrowne 3 66
(PFICole) *unf: cl up: effrt over 2f out: rdn and ch 1f out: one pce after* **10/1**[3]
-0 **4** *3* **Innocent Rebel (USA)**[11] [2204] 3-9-0........................................ TEDurcan 8 66
(EALDunlop) *t.k.h: cl up: shkn up and effrt over 2f out: one pce over 1f out* **12/1**
04 **5** *3* **Maidstone Midas (IRE)**[21] [1966] 3-9-0........................................ BDoyle 9 60
(WSKittow) *pressed wnr to over 2f out: fdd over 1f out* **50/1**
0 **6** *¾* **Pins 'n Needles (IRE)**[59] [1202] 3-8-9........................................ JFEgan 4 53
(CACyzer) *t.k.h: cl up: shkn up over 2f out: one pce after* **20/1**
**7** *1 ¾* **Johnny Rook (IRE)** 3-9-0........................................ IMongan 12 55
(EALDunlop) *w'like: bkwd: lenghty: rn green in rr: pushed along over 4f out: lost tch over 2f out: kpt on fnl f* **14/1**
0- **8** *1 ½* **Bee Dees Legacy**[293] [4016] 3-9-0........................................ RBrisland 2 52?
(GLMoore) *a in rr: pushed along and struggling 3f out* **50/1**
**9** *hd* **Sailorman** 3-9-0........................................ MartinDwyer 7 52
(GAButler) *unf: lw: b.hind: mounted on crse and uns rdr: rn green in midfield: outpcd wl over 2f out: sn btn* **10/1**[3]
**10** *1 ¼* **Breaking The Rule (IRE)** 3-8-9........................................ RLMoore 5 44
(PRWebber) *midfield: pushed along 4f out: chsd ldr over 2f out: sn wknd* **33/1**
0 **11** *7* **Crimson Star (IRE)**[22] [1945] 3-8-6........................................ RMiles(3) 1 31
(CTinkler) *prom: n.m.r on inner after 2f: wknd wl over 2f out* **20/1**
**12** *1* **Surface To Air** 3-9-0........................................ RHavlin 11 34
(MrsPNDutfield) *leggy: unf: s.s and early reminder: racd in last: rdn and no prog 4f out* **66/1**
**13** *dist* **Amazonic** 3-8-9........................................ RPrice 14 —
(TTClement) *w'like: racd wd: midfield: wknd 4f out: t.o* **100/1**

2m 8.65s (0.80) **Going Correction** 0.0s/f (Stan) **13** Ran SP% **120.3**
Speed ratings: **96,95,93,91,88 88,86,85,85,84 78,78,—**CSF £5.87 TOTE £3.30: £1.20, £1.30, £4.10; EX 8.20 Place 6 £49.69, Place 5 £21.75.

**Owner** Richard J Cohen **Bred** Palides Investments N V Inc **Trained** Epsom, Surrey

**FOCUS**
A two-horse race according to the market and so it proved. The first two home were in the front three throughout and very few got into it. The winning time was moderate for the grade and there was little promise outside the front trio.

**NOTEBOOK**
**Swainson(USA)**, who has at least already shown ability on turf and Polytrack, was given a virtuoso Holland front-running ride. He looked sure to be swallowed up by the favourite turning for home, but refused to give in and ultimately ground out an ultra-game victory. The best of him is still to be seen, probably over further.
**St Francis Wood(USA)** was taking a massive step down in class after finishing last in the Nell Gwyn, but she did not help herself over this longer trip by pulling too hard early and seeing too much daylight on the outside. Despite that, she still seemed to be cruising turning for home, but when asked to go and win her race there was not very much left in the locker. She is still lightly raced, but does not look as good as connections obviously thought she would be. *Official explanation: jockey said filly ran too freely.*
**Supamach(IRE)**, a half-sister to Swellmova out of a winning half-sister to a couple of Group One winners, ran with credit on this belated debut if never able to offer a threat to the front pair. She was pulled out of her intended debut due to the fast ground, so she may need a slower surface than this.
**Innocent Rebel(USA)** ran better than on his debut 11 days earlier, but will need to improve again is he is to win a race.
**Maidstone Midas(IRE)** was effectively taking a big step down in class after running in the Derby Trial here earlier in the month, but he was beaten half the track there and this is more a measure of his true ability. He split the two market principals for much of the way before fading over the last couple of furlongs.
**Pins 'n Needles(IRE)** *Official explanation: jockey said filly ran too keen.*
**Crimson Star(IRE)** *Official explanation: jockey said filly did not get the 1m2f trip*

T/Plt: £39.80 to a £1 stake. Pool: £38,057.15. 697.95 winning tickets. T/Qpdt: £2.30 to a £1 stake. Pool: £3,123.20. 997.10 winning tickets. JN

# $^{2171}$MUSSELBURGH (R-H)

Saturday, May 29

**OFFICIAL GOING: Good to firm (firm in places)**

## 2487 ONE MAIDEN STKS — 1m

1:45 (1:46) (D) 3-Y-0+ **£4,745** (£1,460; £730; £365) **Stalls Low**

Form — RPR

32 **1** **Marbush (IRE)**$^{13}$ [2144] 3-8-12 .............. SSanders 6 82
(MAJarvis) *trckd ldr: hdwy over 2f out: rdn to ld wl over 1f out: wandered ent last and drvn out* **Evs$^{1}$**

2-3 **2** ¾ **Awesome Love (USA)**$^{7}$ [2286] 3-8-12 .............. KDalgleish 4 80
(MJohnston) *led: pushed along over 2f out: hdd wl over 1f out and sn rdn: drvn and rallied ins last: kpt on* **Evs$^{1}$**

-606 **3** 11 **Menai Straights**$^{8}$ [2259] 3-8-12 62.............. FNorton 2 55
(RFFisher) *prom:rdn along 3f out: wknd fnl 2f* **33/1$^{2}$**

0500 **4** nk **Lucky Largo (IRE)**$^{27}$ [1783] 4-9-10 53..............(b) DMcGaffin 7 54
(MissLAPerratt) *chsd ldrs: rdn along over 3f out: sn btn* **66/1**

0 **5** ½ **Young Warrior (IRE)**$^{61}$ [1174] 3-8-12 .............. ANicholls 5 53
(DNicholls) *bhd fr 1/2-way* **100/1**

45 **6** 5 **Caymans Gift**$^{15}$ [2077] 4-9-7 .............. TEaves$^{(3)}$ 1 42
(ACWhillans) *a rr* **50/1$^{3}$**

000- **7** dist **Taili**$^{290}$ [4076] 3-8-7 .............. JMcAuley 3 —
(DANolan) *sn bhd: t.o fnl 3f* **100/1**

1m 40.15s (-2.55) **Going Correction** -0.225s/f (Firm)

**WFA** 3 from 4yo 12lb **7 Ran SP% 108.4**

Speed ratings: **103,102,91,90,90 85,**—CSF £2.02 TOTE £2.00: £1.02, £1.50; EX 1.90.

**Owner** Sheikh Ahmed Al Maktoum **Bred** Stratford Place Stud And Watership Down Stud **Trained** Newmarket, Suffolk

**FOCUS**

A modest maiden, run at just a steady gallop, which saw joint favourites pull miles clear of the rest. The form is fair for the grade.

**NOTEBOOK**

**Marbush(IRE)**, who had shaped with promise on his two previous outings, lost his maiden tag in workmanlike fashion. He was again keen early on and ran green when hitting the front approaching one out, so this strong colt should build on this with more experience and stay further, granted he learns to settle.

**Awesome Love(USA)** had every chance if good enough, but could not get back to the winner when he was headed, try as he may. He certainly has the ability to get off the mark.

**Menai Straights** was totally outclassed by the front pair and did not look to improve on recent efforts.

## 2488 VICTOR CHANDLER SCOTTISH SPRINT CUP (HERITAGE H'CAP) — 5f

2:20 (2:21) (B) (0-105,96) 3-Y-0+ **£29,000** (£11,000; £5,500; £2,500) **Stalls Low**

Form — RPR

1-41 **1** **Raccoon (IRE)**$^{7}$ [2293] 4-8-12 **84**..............(v) SSanders 1 100
(TDBarron) *mde all: rdn wl over 1f out: stayued on wl fnl f* **11/4$^{1}$**

-544 **2** ¾ **Corridor Creeper (FR)**$^{10}$ [2222] 7-9-3 **89**..............(p) RFfrench 4 102
(JMBradley) *trckd ldrsm: hdwy over 2f out: rdn to chal wl over 1f out and ev ch tl rdn andnt qckn wl ins last* **10/1**

0121 **3** 1¼ **Magic Glade**$^{48}$ [1343] 5-8-10 **87**.............. RThomas$^{(5)}$ 10 96
(CRDore) *a.p: effrt over 1f out: sn rdn and nt qckn ins last* **6/1$^{2}$**

06-2 **4** nk **Connect**$^{7}$ [2293] 7-8-12 **87**..............(b) FPFerris$^{(3)}$ 13 94
(MHTompkins) *midfield: n.m.r and swtchd rt over 1f out: styd on wl fnl f* **16/1**

-003 **5** nk **Vita Spericolata (IRE)**$^{21}$ [1955] 7-8-13 **85**..............(v) PHanagan 8 91
(JSWainwright) *cl up: ev ch 2f out: sn rdn and wknd appr last* **20/1**

5520 **6** ½ **Simianna**$^{13}$ [2143] 5-9-4 **90**..............(p) FNorton 7 95
(ABerry) *towards rr and sn rdn along: hdwy over 1f out: styd on strly ins last: nrst fin* **33/1**

5001 **7** nk **Whitbarrow (IRE)**$^{10}$ [2222] 5-9-10 **96**.............. KDalgleish 3 99
(JMBradley) *in tch stands rail: hdwy 2f out: sn rdn and no imp* **12/1**

1622 **8** ½ **Mine Behind**$^{8}$ [2261] 4-8-10 **82**..............(p) NPollard 12 84
(JRBest) *chsd ldrs rdn wl over 1f out: kpt on same pce* **10/1**

4221 **9** 1¼ **Green Manalishi**$^{12}$ [2181] 3-8-8 **88**.............. JCarroll 2 85
(DWPArbuthnot) *pushed along and outpcd stands ide: rdn 1/2-way: nvr rch ldrs* **8/1$^{3}$**

6331 **10** ½ **Moayed**$^{28}$ [1765] 5-8-12 **87**..............(bt) TPQueally$^{(3)}$ 6 82
(NPLittmoden) *dwlt: sn outpcd and bhd tl sme late hdwy* **14/1**

-501 **11** shd **River Falcon**$^{17}$ [2041] 4-8-9 **84**.............. NMackay$^{(3)}$ 14 79
(JSGoldie) *chsd ldrs: rdn along 2f out: drvn and wknd appr last* **16/1**

-001 **12** shd **Ptarmigan Ridge**$^{22}$ [1923] 8-8-11 **86**.............. TEaves$^{(3)}$ 5 81
(MissLAPerratt) *chsd ldrs: rdn 2f out: wknd over 1f out* **33/1**

0-06 **13** nk **Absent Friends**$^{7}$ [2293] 7-9-1 **94**.............. PPMathers$^{(7)}$ 9 88
(JBalding) *midfield: rdn along 1/2-way: no hdwy* **28/1**

-003 **14** shd **Seafield Towers**$^{7}$ [2293] 4-8-2 **77**..............(p) DAllan$^{(3)}$ 11 70
(MissLAPerratt) *sn outpcd and a rr* **33/1**

01-6 **15** nk **Malapropism**$^{10}$ [2222] 4-9-1 **87**.............. ACulhane 15 79
(MRChannon) *racd wd: in tch tl rdn along and wknd over 1f out* **20/1**

5-00 **16** 1¾ **Salviati (USA)**$^{7}$ [2293] 7-9-1 **87**.............. DarrenWilliams 16 73
(JMBradley) *dwlt: towards rr: sme hdwy 1/2-way: sn rdn and wknd* **66/1**

0-03 **17** ¾ **Roses Of Spring**$^{10}$ [2222] 6-8-8 **85** ow2..............(p) AQuinn$^{(5)}$ 17 68
(RMHCowell) *racd wd: a rr* **40/1**

57.81 secs (-2.59) **Going Correction** -0.225s/f (Firm)

**WFA** 3 from 4yo+ 8lb **17 Ran SP% 122.1**

Speed ratings: **111,109,107,107,106 106,105,104,102,101 101,101,101,101,100 97,96**CSF £26.47 CT £164.40 TOTE £3.10: £1.70, £2.20, £2.40, £3.20; EX 38.80 Trifecta £157.00 Pool £1,946.20, 8.80 winning units.

**Owner** P D Savill **Bred** P D Savill **Trained** Maunby, N Yorks

■ Stewards Enquiry : F P Ferris caution: careless riding

**FOCUS**

A decent handicap sprint run at a good gallop and a low draw proved advantageous, but this looks strong form.

**NOTEBOOK**

**Raccoon(IRE)** pinged out of the gates and made the most of his favoured low draw to make all in grand style. He is still relatively lightly raced, has plenty of early speed, and the manner in which he defied a 10lb penalty for winning last time was most pleasing.

**Corridor Creeper(FR)** could not get to the winner, try as he might, late on, but again ran with credit and has to be considered unlucky to have met the winner, despite his favoured low draw.

**Magic Glade** could not find any more late on after showing good early pace to get involved from his double-figure draw. This was a decent effort off his current mark and his winning turn may not be far off.

**Connect** ran a much improved race and deserves a lot of credit, as he had a difficult draw. He looks to be coming back to somewhere near top form.

**Vita Spericolata(IRE)** could find no more entering the final furlong having raced on the pace from the start. She again showed her liking for this fast ground and is the type to pop up when least expected. *Official explanation: jockey said mare hung left.*

**Simianna** looked to get outpaced early on, but was finishing best of all. This was another fair effort on ground that was plenty fast enough.

**Green Manalishi**, a decent winner at Windosr last time, was disappointing. He was never really going the pace on this first try against his elders and could not capitalise on his low draw.

## 2489 SANTINI (S) STKS — 5f

2:50 (2:51) (E) 2-Y-0 **£6,734** (£2,072; £1,036; £518) **Stalls Low**

Form — RPR

54 **1** **Theatre Of Dreams**$^{24}$ [1884] 2-8-11 .............. ANicholls 9 72+
(DNicholls) *cl up: led 2fout: edgd lft and sn clr* **13/8$^{1}$**

4 **2** 3½ **Knock Bridge (IRE)**$^{11}$ [2213] 2-8-3 .............. DCorby$^{(3)}$ 1 53
(MJWallace) *in tch: hdwy 2f out: rdn to chse wnr over 1f out: no imp* **5/2$^{2}$**

50 **3** 1¾ **Chilali (IRE)**$^{19}$ [2002] 2-8-6 .............. FNorton 3 46
(ABerry) *led: rdn along and hdd 2f out: edgd rt and one pce wl over 1f out* **25/1**

4 **4** 2 **Gracie's Gift (IRE)**$^{9}$ [2247] 2-8-8 .............. LEnstone$^{(3)}$ 4 43
(PCHaslam) *prom: rdn along 1/2-way: swtchd rt and one pce wl over 1f out* **12/1**

112 **5** nk **Little Biscuit (IRE)**$^{21}$ [1970] 2-8-11 .............. DarrenWilliams 2 42
(KRBurke) *towards rr: rdn along 1/2-way: sme late hdwy* **4/1$^{3}$**

40 **6** nk **Dane's Rock (IRE)**$^{15}$ [2095] 2-8-11 ..............(v$^{1}$) GFaulkner 5 41
(PCHaslam) *chsd ldrs: rdn along 1/2-way: sn wknd* **25/1**

4 **7** ¾ **Chicago Nights (IRE)**$^{35}$ [1616] 2-7-13 .............. RoryMoore$^{(7)}$ 8 33
(PCHaslam) *cl up: rdn along 1/2-way: wknd wl over 1f out* **25/1**

055 **8** 1 **Steal The Thunder**$^{13}$ [2140] 2-8-11 .............. FLynch 6 34
(ABerry) *a rr* **50/1**

**P** **Shatin Leader** 2-8-3 .............. NMackay$^{(3)}$ 7 —
(MissLAPerratt) *hmpd s and slowly away: sn wl outpcd: bhd whn hung bdly rt 1/2-way: taile doff whn p.u and dismntd 1f out* **28/1**

59.73 secs (-0.67) **Going Correction** -0.225s/f (Firm) **9 Ran SP% 111.3**

Speed ratings: **96,90,87,84,83 83,82,80,**—CSF £5.05 TOTE £2.30: £1.10, £1.50, £6.30; EX 6.60.The winner was bought in for 22,000gns. Knock Bridge was claimed by Diamond Racing Ltd for £20,000.

**Owner** D Nicholls **Bred** D J And Mrs Deer **Trained** Sessay, N Yorks

**FOCUS**

A weak heat but run at a fair pace and the winner looks above average for the grade.

**NOTEBOOK**

**Theatre Of Dreams**, down in grade, put up his best display to date and won readily. He showed a liking for this ground, has plenty of speed and looks up to holding his own at a much higher level. Connections bought him back in for 22,000gns.

**Knock Bridge(IRE)** was put in his place by the winner, but showed more than enough to suggest he should be winning in this grade before long.

**Chilali(IRE)** pinged out to grab the lead and showed plenty of early toe. She could not go with the winner and tired late on, but could score in the grade over the trip. *Official explanation: jockey said filly hung right throughout*

**Little Biscuit(IRE)** looked to have an obvious chance on his previous form, but was never going on this occasion and proved disappointing.

**Shatin Leader** *Official explanation: jockey said, regarding the running and riding, filly was very green and became upset by the preliminaries and the large crowd; trainer said filly had done plenty of fast work and was disappointing here*

## 2490 VICTOR CHANDLER SPRINT TROPHY H'CAP — 5f

3:25 (3:25) (D) 3-Y-0+ **£10,081** (£3,102; £1,551; £775) **Stalls Low**

Form — RPR

3020 **1** **Catch The Cat (IRE)**$^{14}$ [2118] 5-9-3 **69**..............(b) GParkin 12 79
(JSWainwright) *cl up: rdn to ld 1f out: hdd ins last: sn drvn and rallied to ld last 50 yds* **16/1**

20-0 **2** shd **Strensall**$^{14}$ [2130] 7-9-10 **76**.............. RFitzpatrick 4 86
(REBarr) *trckd ldrs: hdwy over 1f out: rdn to ld ins last: sn drvn: hdd and no ex last 50 yds* **25/1**

-326 **3** nk **Roxanne Mill**$^{15}$ [2079] 6-9-9 **75**.............. PHanagan 8 84
(JMBradley) *led: rdn along 2f out: hdd 1f out: drvn and kpt on ins last* **20/1**

0006 **4** nk **Obe One**$^{4}$ [2391] 4-9-3 **69**.............. FNorton 1 77
(ABerry) *chsd ldrs: rdn along over 1f out: swtchd rt and n.m.r ins last: kpt on* **8/1$^{3}$**

0520 **5** shd **Online Investor**$^{7}$ [2291] 5-9-3 **69**.............. AlexGreaves 11 76
(DNicholls) *chsdldrs:hdwy 2f out: rdn a ev ch 1f out: drvn and nt qckn ins last* **13/2$^{2}$**

2341 **6** nk **Highland Warrior**$^{8}$ [2261] 5-9-4 **73**.............. NMackay$^{(3)}$ 10 79
(JSGoldie) *s.i.s and bhd: sn s witched to stands rail: hdwy and nt clr run over 1f out: styd on ins last: nrst fin* **10/1**

0003 **7** ½ **Whistler**$^{8}$ [2274] 7-9-9 **75**..............(p) SSanders 2 80
(JMBradley) *in tch stands side: hdwy over 1f out: styng on whn nt clr run ent last: kpt on* **6/1$^{1}$**

1023 **8** shd **Frascati**$^{5}$ [2369] 4-9-4 **70**.............. ACulhane 13 74
(ABerry) *in tch: hdwy 2f out: rdn and ev ch on outer out: one pce ins last* **20/1**

-011 **9** 1¼ **Parkside Pursuit**$^{2}$ [2423] 6-9-4 **77** 6ex.............. CJDavies$^{(7)}$ 3 77
(JMBradley) *rrd s and bhd: hdwy 2f out: sn rdn and no imp* **6/1$^{1}$**

5-00 **10** ¾ **Izmail (IRE)**$^{28}$ [1774] 5-9-3 **69**.............. KDalgleish 15 66
(DNicholls) *chsd ldrs: effrt and ch 2f out: sn rdn and wknd appr last* **33/1**

0-00 **11** 1 **Ballybunion (IRE)**$^{14}$ [2130] 5-8-10 **62**.............. ANicholls 14 55
(DNicholls) *dwlt: a rr* **33/1**

-636 **12** 1½ **Brigadore**$^{2}$ [2423] 5-8-7 **66**.............. DFentiman$^{(7)}$ 17 54
(JRWeymes) *racd wd: in tch tl rdn along and wknd 2f out* **25/1**

-002 **13** nk **Kangarilla Road**$^{2}$ [2423] 5-8-11 **66**.............. TPQueally$^{(3)}$ 16 53
(MrsJRRamsden) *keen: in tch on outer: rdn 2f out and sn wknd* **6/1$^{1}$**

0-44 **14** ¾ **Twice Upon A Time**$^{13}$ [2143] 5-9-6 **72**.............. FLynch 6 56
(BSmart) *dwlt: a rr* **12/1**

4410 **15** 3 **If By Chance**$^{7}$ [2303] 6-9-5 **74**..............(b) TEaves$^{(3)}$ 5 47
(RCraggs) *chsd ldrs: rdn over 2f out: sn wknd* **16/1**

58.93 secs (-1.47) **Going Correction** -0.225s/f (Firm)

**WFA** 3 from 4yo+ 8lb **15 Ran SP% 118.9**

Speed ratings: **102,101,101,100,100 100,99,99,97,96 94,92,91,90,85**CSF £375.90 CT £7918.95 TOTE £14.90: £5.20, £6.40, £7.20; EX 349.60.

**Owner** T W Heseltine **Bred** Mrs Jill M Harley **Trained** Kennythorpe, N Yorks

**FOCUS**

A competitive sprint but a modest time for the class of race and the first six home were closely bunched at the finish. Some caution is advised but the form should work out.

**NOTEBOOK**

**Catch The Cat(IRE)** did very well to overcome a bad draw and showed guts to repel the challengers near the line. His explosive early pace won him the day on this occasion, and it was a deserved victory for this genuine sprinter.

**Strensall** did everything right, but just failed. He had plenty in his favour and is clearly back in good heart at present.
**Roxanne Mill** made a bold bid from the front, but could not quite hold off the challengers inside the final furlong.
**Obe One** was staying on well at the end, having met trouble inside the last, and deserves credit. He may be seen to better effect back over another furlong.
**Online Investor** ran a fair race from his wide draw and he continues to suggest that a well overdue success is not far off.
**Whistler** met trouble when finishing fast late in the day. He may have been better served by a more positive ride this time, as he had a plum draw.
**Parkside Pursuit**, chasing the hat-trick, was unable to go the early gallop and ran very much as though he is now in the Handicapper's grip off this new mark. *Official explanation: jockey said gelding reared in the stalls and missed the break.*

## 2491 SHERATON GRAND CUP (A H'CAP) 1m 6f
**4:00** (4:03) (D) (0-85,85) 3-Y-0+ **£13,572** (£4,176; £2,088; £1,044) **Stalls** High

Form RPR
540- **1** **Jack Dawson (IRE)**[9] 4713 7-9-0 **71** .......... FNorton 6 82
(JohnBerry) *hld up in rr: hdwy over 2f out: swtchd outside over 2f out: rdn to ld over 1f out and sn hung rt: drvn out* **7/2**[1]
-506 **2** *2* **Kristensen**[7] 2285 5-9-8 **79** .......... (p) PHanagan 11 88
(DEddy) *in tch: hdwy on inner 3f out: rdn and ch ent last: sn drvn: n.m.r and no ex* **8/1**[3]
3161 **3** *3* **Toni Alcala**[7] 2287 5-8-9 **69** ow1 .......... DNolan(3) 12 74
(RFFisher) *trckd ldrs: hdwy on inner 3f out: rdn along and n.m.r over 1f out: kpt on same pce ins last* **14/1**
-450 **4** *½* **Flotta**[14] 2110 5-10-0 **85** .......... ACulhane 2 90
(MRChannon) *trckd ldrs: oushed along and lost pl 3f out: drvn 2f out: styd on again fnl f* **7/2**[1]
0-10 **5** *½* **Tandava (IRE)**[27] 1785 6-8-12 **72** .......... (p) TPQueally(3) 1 76
(ISemple) *led: rdn along over 2f out: sn hdd and grad wknd* **16/1**
0510 **6** *½* **Gargoyle Girl**[17] 2038 7-8-0 **60** .......... NMackay(3) 4 64
(JSGoldie) *hld up and bhd: hdwy over 2f out: swtchd rt and rdn wl over 1f out: nrst fin* **20/1**
6013 **7** *½* **Rajam**[7] 2287 6-9-4 **75** .......... (v) AlexGreaves 5 78
(DNicholls) *prom: effrt to ld 2f out: sn rdn and hdd over 1f out: grad wknd* **20/1**
/004 **8** *4* **Perestroika (IRE)**[9] 2235 6-8-3 **60** .......... RFfrench 3 58
(BEllison) *hld up: a rr* **12/1**
0003 **9** *hd* **Riyadh**[21] 1973 6-8-13 **70** .......... (b) KDalgleish 9 68
(MJohnston) *slowly in to stride and behin d: hdwy to chse ldrs 1/2-way: rdn along over 3f out and sn wknd* **13/2**[2]
00-5 **10** *1 ½* **Sea Plume**[39] 1521 5-9-3 **74** .......... SSanders 7 70
(LadyHerries) *chsd ldr: rdn along 3f out: wkng whn hmpd wl over 1f out* **33/1**
50-0 **11** *3* **Recount (FR)**[38] 1540 4-9-6 **77** .......... NPollard 8 70
(JRBest) *midfield: rdn along over 3f out: sn wknd* **16/1**
46-2 **12** *5* **Clarinch Claymore**[14] 2116 8-8-13 **73** .......... TEaves(3) 10 60
(JMJefferson) *in tch: rdn along over 5f out: wknd over 3f out* **14/1**

3m 1.87s (-3.73) **Going Correction** -0.225s/f (Firm) **12** Ran SP% **114.1**
Speed ratings: **101,99,98,97,97 97,97,94,94,93 92,89**CSF £29.18 CT £345.92 TOTE £3.40: £1.60, £2.90, £3.90; EX 28.50.
**Owner** The Premier Cru **Bred** P C Green **Trained** Newmarket, Suffolk
■ Stewards Enquiry : F Norton caution: careless riding

**FOCUS**
A fair staying handicap run only at a modest pace, but sound straightforward form.

**NOTEBOOK**
**Jack Dawson(IRE)**, last seen winning over hurdles, stayed on strongly in the straight to record a second win in this event. He won two years ago off a 3lb lower mark when the race was over further, and is in great heart at present.
**Kristensen** put up a much-improved display on this drop in trip. He has benefitted from a drop in the weights, and although he has not won since 2002, he can be placed to advantage off this mark.
**Toni Alcala** could not go with the front two late on and was well held, but still ran up to his best off this current mark.
**Flotta** ran in snatches and was staying on again in the straight all too late in the day.
**Tandava(IRE)** had the run of the race, but dropped out when challenged entering the final two furlongs. The cheekpieces seemed to make little diffference on this occasion.

## 2492 VCPOKER.COM H'CAP 7f 30y
**4:30** (4:31) (D) (0-85,72) 3-Y-0+ **£6,734** (£2,072; £1,036; £518) **Stalls** Low

Form RPR
5-12 **1** **Kirkby's Treasure**[12] 2172 6-9-0 **62** .......... FLynch 1 70
(ABerry) *hld up and bhd: hdwy on outer 2f out: rdn to ld and edgd lft ent last: drvn and styd on* **7/1**
3530 **2** *½* **Pawan (IRE)**[8] 2261 4-8-13 **61** .......... AnnStokell 6 68
(MissAStokell) *trckd ldrs: hdwy 3f out: rdn to chal and eev ch over 1f out tl no ex ins last* **20/1**
-600 **3** *1 ¼* **Night Wolf (IRE)**[17] 2030 4-9-4 **66** .......... ACulhane 2 70
(MRChannon) *hld up in tch: hdwy over 2f out: rdn to ld and hung rt over 1f out: drvn and hdd ent last: one pce* **8/1**
4-06 **4** *1 ½* **Ballyhurry (USA)**[7] 2291 7-9-7 **72** .......... NMackay(3) 4 72
(JSGoldie) *hld up and bhd: hdwy over 2f out: rdn to chse ldrs whn n ot clr run over 1f out: kpt on* **5/1**[3]
36-3 **5** *2 ½* **Killala (IRE)**[12] 2172 4-9-0 **65** .......... TEaves(3) 3 58
(ISemple) *prom: effrt to chal over 2f out: rdn and evc hance whn carried rt over 1f out: sn wknd* **8/1**
6-65 **6** *½* **Albashoosh**[7] 2291 6-9-2 **64** .......... AlexGreaves 7 56
(DNicholls) *trckd ldr: hdwy to ld over 2f out: sn rdn: hdd over 1f out and sn wknd* **7/2**[2]
0322 **7** *hd* **Whippasnapper**[7] 2292 4-9-5 **67** .......... NPollard 9 59
(JRBest) *chsd ldrs: rdn along over 2f out: sn wknd* **3/1**[1]
0000 **8** *4* **Riska King**[11] 2215 4-9-8 **70** .......... PHanagan 5 51
(RAFahey) *a rr* **16/1**
-020 **9** *17* **Locombe Hill (IRE)**[40] 1502 8-9-0 **62** .......... ANicholls 8 —
(DNicholls) *led: rdn along 3f out: sn hdd & wknd* **14/1**

1m 27.97s (-1.56) **Going Correction** -0.225s/f (Firm) **9** Ran SP% **115.9**
Speed ratings: **99,98,97,95,92 91,91,87,67**CSF £133.10 CT £1147.20 TOTE £10.10: £2.20, £5.70, £3.00; EX 130.00.
**Owner** Kirkby Lonsdale Racing **Bred** Mrs J M Berry **Trained** Cockerham, Lancs
■ Stewards Enquiry : A Culhane caution: careless riding

**FOCUS**
A weak handicap that saw a modest time for the grade and the form is only ordinary.

**NOTEBOOK**
**Kirkby's Treasure**, 7lb higher then when winning over course and distance in April, responded well to pressure in the final furlong to score readily. He clearly loves this track and is improving this season.
**Pawan(IRE)** stepped up on his recent form and held every chance if good enough. He remains a maiden after 13 outings, but seems genuine and can go one better in a similar event.
**Night Wolf(IRE)**, dropping back form a mile, was produced to win his race approaching the last furlong, but hung when in the lead and threw his chance away.
**Ballyhurry(USA)** would have finished closer but for meeting trouble late in the day and can be rated better than the bare form.
**Albashoosh** ran another flat race and has not shown any signs of capitalising on his declining handicap mark this term.
**Whippasnapper** proved disappointing and was soon beaten. *Official explanation: jockey said gelding ran flat.*
**Locombe Hill(IRE)** *Official explanation: jockey said gelding ran flat.*

## 2493 AKD 15 YEARS AT THE TOP OF IT CLASSIFIED STKS 1m
**5:05** (5:05) (D) 3-Y-0+ **£5,421** (£1,668; £834; £417) **Stalls** Low

Form RPR
5030 **1** **Sea Storm (IRE)**[2] 2421 6-9-4 79 .......... (p) TPQueally(3) 6 87
(DRMacleod) *cl up: led 3f out: rdn over 1f out: hit rail ins last: drvn out* **10/1**
-000 **2** *1* **Takes Tutu (USA)**[13] 2142 5-9-3 73 .......... (b) DarrenWilliams 4 81
(KRBurke) *trckd ldrs: hdwy to chal wl over 1f out: sn rdn and ev ch tl drvn and no ex wl ins last* **7/1**
5-00 **3** *1 ¼* **Johannian**[9] 2237 6-9-3 74 .......... RFfrench 7 78
(JMBradley) *held up twrds rr: rdn to chse leasders wl over 1f out: kpt ons ame pce ins last* **33/1**
0-04 **4** *¾* **Millagros (IRE)**[8] 2258 4-9-1 76 .......... JCarroll 2 74
(ISemple) *s.i.s and bhd: hdwy on outer wl over 2f out: rdn and edgd rt over 1f out: sn no imp* **11/2**[3]
0342 **5** *¾* **Young Mr Grace (IRE)**[8] 2271 4-9-0 74 .......... DAllan(3) 1 74
(TDEasterby) *chsd ldrs: rdn along wl over 2f out: drvn and wknd wl over 1f out* **7/2**[1]
-000 **6** *3 ½* **Atlantic Ace**[9] 2237 7-9-4 76 .......... FLynch 9 67
(BSmart) *s.i.s and bhd: hdwy 3f out: rdn to chse ldrs wl over 1f out: sn btn* **9/1**
-010 **7** *5* **Love In Seattle (IRE)**[9] 2237 4-9-7 79 .......... KDalgleish 8 59
(MJohnston) *led: rdn along and hdd 3f out: sn drvn and wknd* **7/1**
3-14 **8** *3* **Brief Goodbye**[26] 1821 4-9-4 76 .......... FNorton 5 49
(JohnBerry) *in tch: rdn along 3f out: wknd 2f out* **9/2**[2]
10-5 **9** *6* **Rudood (USA)**[119] 647 4-9-6 78 .......... SSanders 3 37
(LadyHerries) *hld up in tch: hdwy 3f out: rdn 2f out and sn wknd* **6/1**

1m 38.8s (-3.90) **Going Correction** -0.225s/f (Firm) course record **9** Ran SP% **117.1**
Speed ratings: **110,109,107,107,106 102,97,94,88**CSF £78.94 TOTE £10.40: £3.20, £2.30, £9.80; EX 101.20 Place 6 £523.51, Place 5 £522.63.
**Owner** Maurice W Chapman **Bred** Dan Daly **Trained** Lauder, Borders
■ A first winner for trainer David MacLeod.

**FOCUS**
A tight event and a smart time for a grade of its type and the form looks sound.

**NOTEBOOK**
**Sea Storm(IRE)** ◆, despite veering into the rail late on, ran on well for pressure to score. He put a poor show last time well behind him with this effort, and the cheekpieces do make a difference. On this evidence, he can follow-up.
**Takes Tutu(USA)** showed he may be about to hit form with an improved effort on this drop back to a mile and with the blinkers back on. He could be dangerously well-handicapped if able to maintain this mood.
**Johannian** is not the force of old and did look one paced late on, but has plummeted in the weights and can find a similar event in which to end his losing run.
**Millagros(IRE)** was not helped by a sluggish start and had to come wide in the straight in order to throw down a challenge. Although she is slightly better than the bare form, she is quirky and not one to trust.
**Young Mr Grace(IRE)** came into this on the back of a solid run last time, but could not reproduce that form and disappointed. He may be worth another chance, as he is on a favourable mark and may be better over shorter.
**Rudood(USA)** *Official explanation: jockey said gelding was unsuited by the fast ground.*
T/Plt: £511.80 to a £1 stake. Pool: £48,552.95. 69.25 winning tickets. T/Qpdt: £207.70 to a £1 stake. Pool: £1,824.80. 6.50 winning tickets. JR

2494 - 2497a (Foreign Racing) - See Raceform Interactive

# [1158]LIMERICK (R-H)
Saturday, May 29

**OFFICIAL GOING: Firm**

## 2498a MARTIN MOLONY STKS (LISTED RACE) 1m 4f
**8:00** (8:02) 3-Y-0+ **£22,922** (£6,725; £3,204; £1,091)**Stalls** Far side

RPR
**1** **Mkuzi**[62] 1156 5-9-12 108 .......... MJKinane 2 113
(JohnMOxx, Ire) *settled 2nd: smooth prog 4f out: led ent st: qcknd clr: styd on wl fnl f* **9/4**[2]
**2** *3* **Ivowen (USA)**[6] 2331 4-9-6 101 .......... PJSmullen 1 102
(DKWeld, Ire) *chsd ldrs in 4th: pushed along 4f out: 3rd and rdn early st: no imp whn hmpd under 1 1/2f out* **5/2**[3]
**3** *3* **Tarakala (IRE)**[27] 1810 3-8-3 98 .......... CatherineGannon 3 97
(JohnMOxx, Ire) *trckd ldrs in 3rd: 2nd and rdn early st: edgd lft 1 1/2f out: no imp fnl f* **7/4**[1]
**4** *1* **Royal Devotion (IRE)**[215] 5806 4-9-6 98 .......... TPO'Shea 6 96
(MHalford, Ire) *hld up: 5th and in tch 3f out: no imp early st: kpt on fnl f* **8/1**
**5** *8* **Imoya (IRE)**[27] 1814 5-9-6 96 .......... PCosgrave 5 83
(EndaKelly, Ire) *led: attempted to hang lft ent bk st: clr appr 1/2-way: rdn 4f out: hdd ent st: sn wknd* **9/1**
**6** *2 ½* **Raggtime Toon (IRE)**[6] 2331 4-9-6 79 .......... MCHussey 4 79
(TimothyDoyle, Ire) *hld up in rr: in tch and effrt over 3f out: wknd st* **33/1**

2m 35.5s
**WFA** 3 from 4yo+ 17lb **6** Ran SP% **119.8**
Speed ratings: CSF £9.10 TOTE £4.20: £2.50, £1.80; DF 12.00.
**Owner** Sheikh Mohammed **Bred** Sheikh Mohammed Bin Rashid Al Maktoum **Trained** Currabeg, Co Kildare
■ Stewards Enquiry : Catherine Gannon four-day ban: careless riding (Jun 7-10)

**NOTEBOOK**
**Mkuzi** went on early in the straight, quickening nicely to dispel stamina doubts.
**Ivowen(USA)** would not have beaten the winner but might have finished second but for being badly hampered.
**Tarakala(IRE)**, surprisingly preferred to her winning stable-companion in the market, was not making any impression when edging over onto Ivowen over a furlong out. She was subsequently demoted to third place with her jockey getting a 4-day ban.
**Royal Devotion(IRE)** ran well enough in this class on ground possibly a bit too fast for her.

2499 - 2500a (Foreign Racing) - See Raceform Interactive

# 2306 NEWMARKET (R-H)

Sunday, May 30

**OFFICIAL GOING: Good to firm**

All six winners were never too far off the pace and hold-up horses appeared to be at a disadvantage.

Wind: Fresh half-behind. Weather: Cloudy with sunny spells.

## 2501 WIN £1,000'S NIGHTLY AT BRECKLAND BINGO LADIES H'CAP (FOR LADY AMATEUR RIDERS) 1m 4f

**2:05** (2:06) (E ) (0-70,71) 3-Y-O+ **£3,630** (£1,117; £558; £279) **Stalls** Centre

| Form | Pos | Btn | Horse / Comment | SP | RPR |
|---|---|---|---|---|---|
| -324 | 1 | | **Shape Up (IRE)**[6] 2375 4-9-8 **50**...(b) MissLynseyHanna 13 (TKeddy) *a.p: jnd ldr over 2f out: led on bit over 1f out: shkn up and r.o wl* | **14/1** | 61 |
| 5-05 | 2 | 3 | **Royal Axminster**[39] 1543 9-8-7 **40**... MissAWallace(5) 15 (MrsPNDutfield) *led: hdd over 1f out: outpcd ins fnl f* | **16/1** | 46 |
| 4151 | 3 | 1 1/4 | **Goblin**[12] 2197 3-9-12 **71**... MissEJJones 20 (DECantillon) *b.hind: hld up: hdwy over 4f out: rdn and ev ch over 1f out: styng on same pce whn n.m.r towards fin* | **5/1**[2] | 75 |
| 6330 | 4 | hd | **Michaels Dream (IRE)**[2] 2449 5-9-3 **45**...(b) MrsSBosley 9 (JHetherton) *lw: chsd ldrs: rdn over 2f out: styd on same pce appr fnl f* | **14/1** | 49 |
| 400/ | 5 | 3/4 | **Greyfield (IRE)**[488] 4635 8-9-8 **55**... MissDawnRankin(5) 8 (KBishop) *lw: s.i.s: swtchd rt sn after s: hld up: hdwy over 3f out: rdn over 1f out: styd on same pce* | **33/1** | 58 |
| 2503 | 6 | 5 | **Man The Gate**[12] 2212 5-9-7 **56**... MissCNosworthy(7) 4 (PDCundell) *hld up: hdwy over 4f out: rdn and wknd over 1f out* | **5/1**[2] | 51 |
| 16/0 | 7 | nk | **Reviewer (IRE)**[64] 679 6-10-9 **70**... MissVSturgis(5) 7 (MMeade) *lw: hld up: swtchd lft and hdwy over 2f out: nt rch ldrs* | **20/1** | 64 |
| 400/ | 8 | 1/2 | **King Halling**[585] 5441 5-10-2 **65**... CarolineHurley(7) 17 (RFord) *chsd ldrs over 9f* | **40/1** | 59 |
| 600- | 9 | 1 1/2 | **Wizard Of The West**[125] 1058 4-9-9 **56**... MsDGoad(5) 2 (MissSheenaWest) *chsd ldrs: rdn over 2f out: wknd over 1f out* | **50/1** | 47 |
| 2124 | 10 | nk | **Great View (IRE)**[12] 2212 5-10-8 **64**...(v) MsCWilliams 14 (MrsALMKing) *hld up: hdwy over 4f out: rdn and wknd over 1f out* | **7/2**[1] | 55 |
| 325- | 11 | 1 | **Shalbeblue (IRE)**[243] 5012 7-9-5 **50**...(b) MissLEllison(3) 11 (BEllison) *hld up in tch: wknd 2f out* | **20/1** | 39 |
| 0510 | 12 | 3 | **Fletcher**[5] 2385 10-9-0 **45**... MissLJHarwood(3) 1 (HMorrison) *lw: hld up: effrt over 3f out: wknd over 2f out* | **14/1** | 29 |
| 0-00 | 13 | 1 3/4 | **Larking About (USA)**[9] 2262 4-9-8 **57**... MsAmyBoeder(7) 12 (WJMusson) *hld up and bhd: n.d* | **33/1** | 38 |
| -062 | 14 | shd | **Graft**[15] 2120 5-10-6 **62**... MissSBrotherton 5 (MWEasterby) *hld up: hdwy over 4f out: wknd over 2f out* | **8/1**[3] | 43 |
| 0004 | 15 | 6 | **Magic Charm**[8] 2287 6-8-5 **40**... MissJWaring(7) 16 (JeddO'Keeffe) *lw: s.s: a bhd* | **16/1** | 12 |
| 0063 | 16 | 3 1/2 | **Margery Daw (IRE)**[2] 2443 4-9-13 **60**... MissJCDuncan(5) 6 (PSMcentee) *chsd ldr tl wknd over 2f out* | **25/1** | 26 |
| 00-0 | 17 | 26 | **Little Sky**[41] 1492 7-8-12 **45**... MissJoeyEllis(5) 10 (DMullarkey) *hld up: a in rr* | **33/1** | — |
| /000 | 18 | 19 | **Trusted Instinct (IRE)**[55] 1275 4-10-8 **67**...(t) MrsEmmaLittmoden(3) 18 (CADwyer) *lw: hld up: effrt over 5f out: sn wknd* | **40/1** | — |

2m 32.18s (-1.28) **Going Correction** -0.175s/f (Firm)

**WFA** 3 from 4yo+ 17lb **18 Ran SP% 127.5**

Speed ratings: **97,95,94,94,93 90,90,89,88,88 87,85,84,84,80 78,60,48**CSF £204.15 CT £1298.88 TOTE £15.50: £3.20, £3.00, £1.80, £2.40; EX 300.80.

**Owner** Andrew Duffield **Bred** Gainsborough Stud Management Ltd **Trained** Newmarket, Suffolk

**FOCUS**

Just a moderate handicap.

**NOTEBOOK**

**Shape Up(IRE)** finally got his head in front at the 19th attempt. It is surprising it took him so long to win a race given the way he did this and he would be interesting if turned out under a penalty.

**Royal Axminster**, beaten in a banded race on his previous start, does not win very often and was no match for the winner.

**Goblin** ran well on this first run beyond ten furlongs, but found a 9lb rise in the weights for his recent Beverley success enough to stop him.

**Michaels Dream(IRE)** is well handicapped on some of his form and had conditions to suit, but he remains without a win since 2002.

**Greyfield(IRE)**, having his first run in 488 days, and his first run on the Flat in 992 days, ran a cracker and should improve for the outing.

**Great View(IRE)** usually goes well in these type of races, but is high enough in the weights and was below form.

## 2502 PLAY AT BRECKLAND BINGO BRANDON MAIDEN STKS 5f

**2:35** (2:37) (D) 2-Y-O **£4,774** (£1,469; £734; £367) **Stalls** Low

| Form | Pos | Btn | Horse / Comment | SP | RPR |
|---|---|---|---|---|---|
| 5 | 1 | | **Skywards**[19] 2024 2-9-0... LDettori 7 (SaeedBinSuroor) *lw: mde all: shkn up over 1f out: qcknd clr* | **4/1**[2] | 90+ |
| 6 | 2 | 5 | **Komac**[19] 2024 2-9-0... SSanders 10 (BAMcmahon) *lw: chsd wnr: rdn over 1f out: sn outpcd* | **16/1** | 70 |
| 4 | 3 | 1 1/2 | **Witchry**[17] 2111 2-9-0... PRobinson 6 (MAJarvis) *lw: chsd ldrs: rdn over 1f out: sn outpcd* | **4/6**[1] | 64 |
| | 4 | 2 1/2 | **Diamond Hombre (USA)** 2-9-0... MHills 9 (JWHills) *leggy: scope: slowly into stride: sn prom: wknd over 1f out* | **14/1** | 54 |
| | 5 | hd | **Town End Tom** 2-9-0... MFenton 1 (DMSimcock) *neat: s.i.s: sn chsng ldrs: wknd over 1f out* | **50/1** | 53 |
| | 6 | shd | **Hedingham Knight (IRE)** 2-9-0... DaneO'Neill 3 (NACallaghan) *leggy: scope: b.hind: lw: s.i.s: outpcd: styd on ins fnl f: nvr nrr* | **25/1** | 53 |
| | 7 | 2 | **Cool Panic (IRE)** 2-9-0... DHolland 5 (MLWBell) *cmpt: s.i.s: sn prom: wknd over 1f out* | **15/2**[3] | 45 |
| | 8 | 4 | **Lowestoft Playboy** 2-8-11... TPQueally(3) 8 (MrsCADunnett) *neat: s.s: outpcd* | **33/1** | 29 |
| | 9 | 1 3/4 | **Lighthorne Lad** 2-9-0... SKelly 4 (JRJenkins) *w'like: scope: sn outpcd* | **80/1** | 22 |
| | 10 | 11 | **Whatsheworth** 2-9-0... PMcCabe 2 (PSMcentee) *w'like: s.i.s: outpcd* | **66/1** | — |

59.30 secs (-1.11) **Going Correction** -0.175s/f (Firm) **10 Ran SP% 115.8**

Speed ratings: **101,93,90,86,86 86,82,76,73,56**CSF £59.05 TOTE £4.00: £1.60, £3.50, £1.10; EX 53.30.

**Owner** Godolphin **Bred** Gainsborough Stud Management Ltd **Trained** Newmarket, Suffolk

**FOCUS**

Probably not a great maiden by Newmarket standards, but Skywards was impressive and could be off to Royal Ascot.

**NOTEBOOK**

**Skywards**, a well-held fifth on his debut in a York maiden that had not really been working out that well, showed the benefit of that run to score an impressive success. He is likely to be sent to Royal Ascot and a race like the Norfolk looks a logical target.

**Komac** was only a length behind Skywards at York on his debut, but was no match for that one this time around. There is a maiden in him.

**Witchry**, a promising fourth in what was probably just an ordinary six-furlong Newbury maiden on his debut, did not appear suited by this drop in trip. A return to six should suit and it will be disappointing if he does not find a maiden, but he is not one to take too short a price about. *Official explanation: jockey said colt was very coltish.*

**Diamond Hombre(USA)**, a $105,000 yearling, half-brother to a seven-furlong two-year-old winner, out of a six-furlong juvenile scorer who was later a high-class sprinter, made a satisfactory debut and should improve.

**Town End Tom**, out of a five- to seven-furlong winner, including over six furlongs at two, made a promising debut and can be expected to come on for this.

## 2503 BRECKLANDBINGO.CO.UK H'CAP 7f

**3:10** (3:10) (B ) (0-105,95) 3-Y-O+ **£13,780** (£4,240; £2,120; £1,060) **Stalls** Low

| Form | Pos | Btn | Horse / Comment | SP | RPR |
|---|---|---|---|---|---|
| 0000 | 1 | | **Master Robbie**[8] 2283 5-9-0 **88**... SHitchcott(3) 10 (MRChannon) *lw: chsd ldrs: rdn to ld 1f out: r.o* | **8/1**[3] | 99 |
| 16-0 | 2 | 1/2 | **Obrigado (USA)**[10] 2237 4-8-9 **80**... RHills 13 (WJHaggas) *lw: racd alone: jnd main gp and led 5f out: rdn and hdd 1f out: r.o* | **20/1** | 90 |
| 2-30 | 3 | nk | **King's County (IRE)**[18] 2044 6-9-10 **95**... DHolland 2 (LMCumani) *prom: outpcd over 2f out: rdn and nt clr run over 1f out: r.o* | **5/2**[1] | 104 |
| 00-0 | 4 | 1 | **Juste Pour L'Amour**[4] 2410 4-8-5 **76**... JFEgan 8 (PLGilligan) *lw: chsd ldrs: rdn over 2f out: styd on same pce fnl f* | **33/1** | 82 |
| 1401 | 5 | 1/2 | **Taranaki**[12] 2206 6-9-3 **88**... SSanders 1 (PDCundell) *chsd ldrs: nt clr run over 1f out: styd on same pce* | **8/1**[3] | 93 |
| 10-0 | 6 | hd | **Vindication**[8] 2283 4-9-7 **92**...(t) LDettori 6 (JRFanshawe) *hld up in tch: rdn over 1f out: no ex ins fnl f* | **9/1** | 97 |
| 3-11 | 7 | 1 | **Enchanted**[8] 2282 5-9-10 **95**... KFallon 5 (NACallaghan) *lw: hld up: hdwy over 1f out: one pce ins fnl f* | **4/1**[2] | 97 |
| -030 | 8 | 1 | **Marshman (IRE)**[22] 1968 5-8-12 **90**... SaleemGolam(7) 3 (MHTompkins) *s.i.s: hld up: styd on ins fnl f: nvr trbld ldrs* | **16/1** | 89 |
| 3-43 | 9 | 3 1/2 | **Wing Commander**[54] 1286 5-9-5 **93**... THamilton(3) 9 (RAFahey) *hld up: rdn over 2f out: sn wknd* | **10/1** | 83 |
| 3-00 | 10 | 1 1/2 | **Hurricane Floyd (IRE)**[27] 1828 6-8-12 **86**... TPQueally(3) 12 (DRLoder) *s.i.s: hld up: rdn and wknd 2f out* | **11/1** | 72 |
| 0006 | 11 | 8 | **Prince Cyrano**[22] 1968 5-8-5 **76**... GCarter 11 (WJMusson) *hld up: wknd 2f out* | **20/1** | 42 |

1m 24.31s (-2.16) **Going Correction** -0.175s/f (Firm) **11 Ran SP% 116.6**

Speed ratings: **105,104,104,102,102 102,101,99,95,94 85**CSF £157.23 CT £523.83 TOTE £7.20: £2.00, £4.30, £1.40; EX 117.90 Trifecta £1185.00 Pool £2,837.50 - 1.70 winning units..

**Owner** Alec Tuckerman **Bred** A And Mrs Tuckerman **Trained** West Ilsley, Berks

**FOCUS**

A really competitive handicap and the form is sound. It proved hard to come from off the pace.

**NOTEBOOK**

**Master Robbie** was 2lb lower than when last successful and, with conditions ideal, he ran out a narrow winner. He should continue to go well in similar company over seven furlongs on fast ground.

**Obrigado(USA)** sweated up badly before disappointing at Doncaster on his reappearance but, despite getting quite warm once again, this was a better effort.

**King's County(IRE)** was well backed on this drop in grade, but found a couple too strong. He did not get the clearest of runs, but cannot really be considered unlucky.

**Juste Pour L'Amour** is back on a winning mark and ran well. In this sort of form he may well be able to end a losing run stretching back to 2002.

**Taranaki** looked good when winning at Goodwood on his previous start, but a 6lb rise in the weights was enough to stop him.

**Vindication** did best of those who came from off the pace.

**Enchanted** could not really get into it from off the pace and a stronger gallop may have suited better.

## 2504 PLAY AT BRECKLAND BINGO THETFORD CLASSIFIED STKS 1m

**3:45** (3:46) (D) 3-Y-O+ **£6,747** (£2,076; £1,038; £519) **Stalls** Low

| Form | Pos | Btn | Horse / Comment | SP | RPR |
|---|---|---|---|---|---|
| 0502 | 1 | | **Ace Of Hearts**[12] 2196 5-9-3 80... SSanders 7 (CFWall) *chsd ldr: led over 1f out: edgd lft ins fnl f: rdn out* | **9/2**[3] | 90 |
| -000 | 2 | 1 1/2 | **St Pancras (IRE)**[17] 2066 4-9-7 84... EAhern 2 (NACallaghan) *lw: sn rdn to ld: hdd over 1f out: styd on same pce ins fnl f* | **10/3**[2] | 91 |
| 321- | 3 | 1 3/4 | **Unscrupulous**[333] 2904 5-9-3 80... LDettori 6 (JRFanshawe) *hld up: plld hrd: hdwy over 1f out: nt rch ldrs* | **2/1**[1] | 83 |
| 1000 | 4 | 2 | **Topton (IRE)**[10] 2237 10-9-3 76...(b) KFallon 3 (PHowling) *lw: hld up: hdwy over 1f out: styd on same pce ins fnl f* | **16/1** | 78 |
| 4200 | 5 | 2 1/2 | **Fiveoclock Express (IRE)**[6] 2366 4-9-4 81... DHolland 5 (MissGayKelleway) *lw: chsd ldrs: rdn over 1f out: sn wknd* | **20/1** | 73 |
| 243- | 6 | nk | **Honorine (IRE)**[256] 4993 4-9-0 80... PRobinson 8 (JWPayne) *hld up: hdwy over 1f out: sn wknd* | **10/1** | 68 |
| 0-41 | 7 | 1 1/2 | **Tiber Tiger (IRE)**[9] 2279 4-9-3 80...(b) TGMcLaughlin 1 (NPLittmoden) *trckd ldrs: rdn 2f out: wknd fnl f* | **5/1** | 68 |

1m 36.32s (-3.08) **Going Correction** -0.175s/f (Firm) **7 Ran SP% 111.0**

Speed ratings: **108,106,104,102,100 99,98**CSF £18.63 TOTE £5.60: £2.40, £2.30; EX 28.10.

**Owner** Lady Stuttaford & W G Bovill **Bred** Whitsbury Manor Stud **Trained** Newmarket, Suffolk

**FOCUS**

Quite a competitive classified event (there was just 3lb separating five of the seven runners at the weights), but once again it proved hard to come from off the pace.

**NOTEBOOK**

**Ace Of Hearts** had not won since July 2002, but he got the ideal trip compared to some and made no mistake.

**St Pancras(IRE)** has not won since making a winning debut back in 2002, but he would appear to have found his mark now and offered some promise. However, he did not look straightforward, needing a couple of reminders from Ahern just to get to the front soon after the start.

**Unscrupulous**, well backed to defy a 333-day lay-off, was not suited by racing from off the pace and was given plenty to do by Dettori. He can be given another chance.

**Topton(IRE)** was the worst off at the weights and would have been suited by a stronger pace. A good effort in the circumstances.

**Fiveoclock Express(IRE)** had the visor left off this time and can have no excuses. He would appear much better suited by Fibresand.

**Tiber Tiger(IRE)** did not appear harshly treated by a 6lb rise for his recent course and distance success, but ran poorly.



The Form Book, Raceform Ltd, Compton, RG20 6NL

## 2505 PLAY BINGO AT BURY ST EDMUNDS MAIDEN STKS — 7f
4:20 (4:22) (D) 3-Y-O — £5,577 (£1,716; £858; £429) Stalls Low

Form — RPR
0 **1** **Aricia (IRE)**$^{46}$ [1400] 3-8-9 .................... KFallon 13 — 88
(JHMGosden) *s.i.s: sn chsng ldrs: led 3f out: pushed clr over 1f out* **11/8**$^{1}$
0 **2** 5 **Zameyla (IRE)**$^{12}$ [2211] 3-8-9 .................... PRobinson 14 — 75
(MAJarvis) *chsd ldrs: rdn over 1f out: styd on same pce* **11/1**
2-00 **3** ¾ **Great Exhibition (USA)**$^{27}$ [1827] 3-9-0 85 ....................(t) LDettori 18 — 78
(SaeedBinSuroor) *lw: led: hdd 3f out: rdn over 1f out: no ex* **5/2**$^{2}$
00- **4** 6 **Barons Spy (IRE)**$^{205}$ [5939] 3-9-0 .................... MHills 3 — 62
(AWCarroll) *hld up: hdwy 1/2-way: hung rt and wknd over 1f out* **50/1**
0-60 **5** hd **Sharaab (USA)**$^{12}$ [2197] 3-9-0 74 ....................(t) RHills 16 — 62
(BHanbury) *lw: chsd ldrs over 4f* **11/2**$^{3}$
**6** 3 ½ **Polar Sun** 3-9-0 .................... EAhern 9 — 53
(JRFanshawe) *w'like: s.i.s: hld up: nvr trbld ldrs* **16/1**
06- **7** nk **Moon Legend (USA)**$^{239}$ [5367] 3-8-9 .................... DHolland 19 — 47
(WJarvis) *prom 5f* **20/1**
**8** 1 ¼ **Eijaaz (IRE)** 3-9-0 .................... WSupple 12 — 49
(ACStewart) *gd sort: s.s: hdwy 5f out: wknd 2f out* **20/1**
0 **9** 2 ½ **Petrion**$^{12}$ [2211] 3-8-9 .................... SSanders 6 — 37
(RGuest) *hld up: n.d* **100/1**
0-0 **10** nk **Rawalpindi**$^{40}$ [1519] 3-8-11 .................... LisaJones(3) 1 — 41
(JARToller) *n.d* **66/1**
0 **11** 5 **Judda**$^{10}$ [2236] 3-9-0 .................... TGMcLaughlin 2 — 28
(RFMarvin) *s.i.s: outpcd* **100/1**
60 **12** nk **Kalamansi (IRE)**$^{6}$ [2374] 3-8-4 .................... DFox(5) 11 — 23
(NACallaghan) *s.s: outpcd* **66/1**
**13** ¾ **Mary Carleton** 3-8-9 .................... BDoyle 8 — 21
(RMHCowell) *leggy: scope: s.s: outpcd* **66/1**
6-0 **14** 6 **Tikitano (IRE)**$^{10}$ [2236] 3-8-9 .................... CCatlin 17 — 5
(DKIvory) *chsd ldrs 4f* **40/1**
00 **15** ¾ **Miss St Albans**$^{24}$ [1912] 3-8-9 .................... RPrice 15 — 3
(TTClement) *prom to 1/2-way* **100/1**
**16** 4 **Electras Dream (IRE)** 3-8-4 .................... HayleyTurner(5) 10 — —
(MrsCADunnett) *neat: bkwd: mid-div: wknd 1/2-way* **66/1**

1m 24.18s (-2.29) **Going Correction** -0.175s/f (Firm) **16** Ran SP% **123.1**
Speed ratings: **106,100,99,92,92 88,88,86,83,83 77,77,76,69,68 64**CSF £17.69 TOTE £2.40: £1.50, £2.30, £1.70; EX 19.70.
**Owner** George Strawbridge **Bred** George Strawbridge **Trained** Manton, Wilts

**FOCUS**
Not that strong a maiden, but a good performance from the Royal Ascot entrant Aricia. The field came down the middle of the track.

**NOTEBOOK**
**Aricia(IRE)** shaped well in a more competitive maiden than this one on her debut over course and distance and, with the benefit of that experience, ran out a ready winner. She travelled really strongly for Fallon and found plenty when asked, suggesting she will be up to holding her own in a higher grade. It is hard to know just how good she could be, but a Coronation Stakes entry suggests she is held in some regard.
**Zameyla(IRE)** doubled in price and was well held in an ordinary Leicester maiden on her debut, but this represents improved form and she should continue to go the right way. *Official explanation: jockey said filly changed legs and became unbalanced.*
**Great Exhibition(USA)** was bogged down by heavy ground at Kempton on his previous start and the decent ground this time appeared to suit. His rating of 85 may flatter him, but he should find a maiden.
**Barons Spy(IRE)** showed ability on both his starts at two and again offered promise. However, the handicapper may have to be quite harsh on him given his proximity.
**Sharaab(USA)**, well beaten in a handicap off a mark of 75 over a mile and a quarter on his previous start, ran respectably.

## 2506 WINNERSBINGO.CO.UK FILLIES' H'CAP — 6f
4:50 (4:52) (D) (0-85,86) 3-Y-0+ — £6,838 (£2,104; £1,052; £526) Stalls Low

Form — RPR
-004 **1** **Silver Chime**$^{12}$ [2219] 4-8-10 67 .................... MFenton 8 — 76
(DMSimcock) *mde all: rdn over 1f out: r.o gamely* **7/1**
-642 **2** hd **Glencoe Solas (IRE)**$^{3}$ [2428] 4-8-8 65 ....................(b) PDobbs 6 — 73
(SKirk) *lw: chsd ldrs: rdn and ev ch fr over 1f out: r.o* **4/1**$^{1}$
-550 **3** shd **Bint Royal (IRE)**$^{1}$ [2473] 6-7-13 59 ow1 ....................(p) RMiles(3) 4 — 67
(MissVHaigh) *b.off fore: hld up: hung lft and r.o wl ins fnl f* **9/1**
00-3 **4** 2 **Bandit Queen**$^{14}$ [2143] 4-10-1 86 .................... PRobinson 5 — 88
(WJarvis) *lw: prom: rdn and hung rt fr over 1f out: r.o* **11/2**$^{3}$
-113 **5** shd **Maddie's A Jem**$^{16}$ [2091] 4-9-4 75 .................... SWKelly 2 — 77
(JRJenkins) *lw: hld up in tch: rdn and ev ch fr over 1f out: unable qck wl ins fnl f* **5/1**$^{2}$
00-0 **6** shd **Complication**$^{16}$ [2094] 4-8-3 63 ....................(b) LisaJones(3) 10 — 64
(JARToller) *chsd ldrs: outpcd 2f out: styd on ins fnl f* **8/1**
-500 **7** 1 ¼ **Fadeela (IRE)**$^{15}$ [2112] 3-8-1 67 .................... CCatlin 11 — 65
(PWD'Arcy) *prom: rdn over 1f out: no ex* **10/1**
/31- **8** nk **Sparkling Jewel**$^{368}$ [1916] 4-9-6 77 .................... RLMoore 1 — 74
(RHannon) *hld up: rdn and hung lft over 1f out: nvr trbld ldrs* **7/1**
0000 **9** ½ **Flashing Blade**$^{14}$ [2143] 4-9-3 74 ....................(tp) SSanders 3 — 69
(BAMcmahon) *lw: chsd ldrs: rdn 1/2-way: styd on same pce appr fnl f* **25/1**
0000 **10** nk **Safranine (IRE)**$^{6}$ [2366] 7-8-10 67 .................... AnnStokell 7 — 61
(MissAStokell) *s.s: a in rr* **33/1**
-005 **11** 5 **Tata Naka**$^{16}$ [2099] 4-7-7 55 oh15 ....................(v$^{1}$) HayleyTurner(5) 9 — 34
(MrsCADunnett) *chsd ldrs over 3f* **66/1**

1m 12.25s (-0.84) **Going Correction** -0.175s/f (Firm)
**WFA** 3 from 4yo+ 9lb **11** Ran SP% **115.5**
Speed ratings: **98,97,97,94,94 94,93,92,91,91 84**CSF £33.98 CT £256.13 TOTE £10.30: £2.90, £1.50, £2.70; EX 52.70 Place 6 £119.56, Place 5 £82.40.
**Owner** Tick Tock Partnership **Bred** Littleton Stud **Trained** Newmarket, Suffolk

**FOCUS**
An ordinary but competitive sprint handicap in which the field raced towards the middle of the track.

**NOTEBOOK**
**Silver Chime** confirmed the promise she showed at Redcar on her previous start, running out a particularly determined winner. A rise in the weights for this could be enough to stop her.
**Glencoe Solas(IRE)** is back on a fair mark and running well. She was only just denied and it will be disappointing if she does not end a year-long losing run.
**Bint Royal(IRE)** had not run very well at Doncaster the previous day but, down a furlong in trip, she would have won but for hanging badly left under pressure. A good effort to come from so far off the pace. *Official explanation: jockey said mare hung left.*
**Bandit Queen**, a good third in a race that has worked out really well on her previous start, did not build on that and has to be considered a little disappointing.
**Maddie's A Jem** may just be in the Handicapper's grip.

T/Jkpt: Not won. T/Plt: £78.80 to a £1 stake. Pool: £66,932.35. 619.55 winning tickets. T/Qpdt: £14.80 to a £1 stake. Pool: £3,642.10. 182.10 winning tickets. CR

2507 - (Foreign Racing) - See Raceform Interactive

# 2466 BADEN-BADEN (L-H)
Sunday, May 30

**OFFICIAL GOING: Good**

## 2508a GROSSER MERCEDES-BENZ PREIS (GROUP 2) — 1m 3f
3:25 (3:43) 4-Y-0+ — £57,746 (£23,329; £11,268; £6,338)

RPR
**1** **Touch Of Land (FR)**$^{28}$ [1804] 4-8-12 .................... C-PLemaire 4 — 116
(H-APantall, France) *tracked leaders on inside, 3rd straight, switched right and headway 1 1/2f out, ridden 1f out, led 100y out, driven out* 3
**2** ¾ **Rotteck (GER)**$^{238}$ [5400] 4-8-12 .................... JPalik 3 — 115
(HSteguweit, Germany) *mid division, 4th straight, stayed on under pressure final 2f to take 2nd close home*
**3** hd **Scott's View**$^{35}$ [1657] 5-8-12 .................... SChin 10 — 114
(MJohnston) *always prominent, 2nd pressing leader entering straight, led 1 1/2f out, headed and no extra 100y out, lost 2nd close home* 1
**4** 1 ¼ **Olaso (GER)**$^{28}$ [1802] 5-9-1 .................... THellier 14 — 115
(PVovcenko, Germany) *raced in 6th, stayed on at same pace down outside final 2f* 2
**5** nk **Senex (GER)**$^{28}$ [1802] 4-8-12 .................... ADeVries 12 — 112
(HBlume, Germany) *held up, 8th straight, ridden over 2f out, kept on*
**6** 1 ¼ **Winning Dash (GER)**$^{56}$ [1259] 4-8-12 .................... AHelfenbein 11 — 110
(WKujath, Germany) *close up on outside, 5th straight, one pace final 2f*
**7** 1 ¼ **Soldier Hollow**$^{56}$ [1259] 4-8-12 .................... FilipMinarik 2 — 108
(PSchiergen, Germany) *held up in rear, last straight, never a factor*
**8** ¾ **El Dessert (GER)**$^{210}$ [5901] 5-8-12 .................... ABoschert 5 — 107
(MarioHofer, Germany) *held up in rear, 9th straight, never a factor*
**9** 3 **King Of Boxmeer (GER)**$^{8}$ [2320] 5-8-12 .................... IFerguson 1 — 102
(WBaltromei, Germany) *towards rear, 7th straight, soon ridden and beaten*
**10** ¾ **Tuning Fork**$^{11}$ [2220] 4-8-12 .................... JQuinn 6 — 101?
(JAkehurst) *led to 1 1/2f out, weakened*

2m 18.42s **10** Ran SP% **131.8**
Speed ratings: .
**Owner** Gary A Tanaka **Bred** Unknown **Trained** France

**NOTEBOOK**
**Touch Of Land(FR)**, out of his class when sixth in the Ganay, was a clever winner here and could enjoy a successful European season at around one and a half miles. His immediate targets may well be across the Atlantic however.
**Scott's View** would have benefited from a stronger pace and was done for speed in the final furlong. He was odds-on here and should soon find a similar opportunity.
**Tuning Fork** set a moderate pace and dropped out as soon as he was headed. He had done little in recent appearances to earn his place in this company.

# 2155 CAPANNELLE (R-H)
Sunday, May 30

**OFFICIAL GOING: Good**

## 2510a DERBY ITALIANO (GROUP 1) (C&F) — 1m 4f
4:20 (4:28) 3-Y-0 — £425,662 (£221,007; £130,437; £65,218)

RPR
**1** **Groom Tesse**$^{217}$ [5780] 3-9-2 ....................(b) DVargiu 12 — 116
(LCamici, Italy) *mid division, headway on outside to challenge well over 1f out, led distance, ran on well* **10/1**
**2** 2 ½ **Dayano (GER)**$^{21}$ 3-9-2 .................... EPedroza 5 — 113
(AWohler, Germany) *pulled hard early, always close up, 5th straight, led well over 2f out to distance, kept on same pace* **8/1**$^{3}$
**3** 3 **Privy Seal (IRE)**$^{24}$ [1901] 3-9-2 ....................(v) JPMurtagh 14 — 108
(JHMGosden) *always in touch, 6th straight, 3rd when slightly hampered well over 1f out, one pace* **5/1**$^{2}$
**4** 1 ¼ **Distant Way (USA)**$^{168}$ [6189] 3-9-2 .................... MPasquale 16 — 106
(LBrogi, Italy) *mid division, stayed on final 2f, never reached leaders* **9/1**
**5** ½ **Bravo Tazio (IRE)**$^{29}$ [1777] 3-9-2 .................... EBotti 15 — 105
(A&GBotti, Italy) *last early, mid division halfway, headway over 3f out, no extra final f* **9/1**
**6** 1 ½ **Putra Sas (IRE)**$^{23}$ [1924] 3-9-2 .................... SDrowne 7 — 103
(PFICole) *prominent, 4th straight, one pace final 2f* **5/1**$^{2}$
**7** ½ **Kaypen (IRE)**$^{231}$ [5529] 3-9-2 .................... SMulas 6 — 102
(BGrizzetti, Italy) *prominent, 3rd straight, effort on inside, still 4th approaching final f, no extra* **66/1**
**8** ½ **Whilly (IRE)**$^{29}$ [1777] 3-9-2 .................... GaryStevens 10 — 102
(BGrizzetti, Italy) *first to show pulling hard, settled behind leader to straight, led well over 3f out to well over 2f out, gradually faded* **16/1**
**9** nse **Sa Fem Zifulum (IRE)** 3-9-2 .................... FJovine 2 — 102
(LCamici, Italy) *always midfield* **33/1**
**10** 1 **Apeiron (GER)**$^{35}$ [1656] 3-9-2 .................... J-PCarvalho 1 — 100
(MarioHofer, Germany) *7th straight, beaten over 2f out* **4/1**$^{1}$
**11** 1 ½ **Domdemil (IRE)**$^{217}$ [5780] 3-9-2 ....................(b) MJKinane 9 — 98
(A&GBotti, Italy) *soon led, headed well over 3f out* **14/1**
**12** 4 **Boysun (IRE)**$^{217}$ [5780] 3-9-2 .................... GBietolini 4 — 92
(LauraGrizzetti, Italy) *towards rear, effort on inside over 3f out, soon beaten* **25/1**
**13** 2 **Ceprin (IRE)**$^{29}$ [1777] 3-9-2 .................... IRossi 13 — 89
(A&GBotti, Italy) *always in rear* **11/1**
**14** 2 **Mac Regal (IRE)**$^{17}$ [2068] 3-9-2 .................... APolli 3 — 86
(MGQuinlan) *prominent, 8th straight, weakened over 3f out* **25/1**
**15** 1 **Larofino (GER)**$^{289}$ [4170] 3-9-2 .................... MEsposito 11 — 84
(RMonaco, Italy) *always in rear* **50/1**

2m 27.68s **15** Ran SP% **128.5**
Speed ratings: .
**Owner** Scuderia L3c **Bred** Azienda Agricola Rosati Colarieti **Trained** Italy

**NOTEBOOK**
**Groom Tesse** had won a Group Three with blinkers on last October, but had not worn them in two runs this spring, including when second to Distant Way. The blinkers were back on for this classic and he had no trouble with his first attempt at this trip. He is unlikely to be seen again until the autumn, but has now demonstrated his talent on both good and testing conditions.

**Privy Seal(IRE)** was sent off favourite, but only by a fraction from three others. He ran an honest race, but was not quite good enough and this trip may be beyond him. Though slightly hampered by the runner-up inside the final two furlongs, he would not have finished much closer.
**Putra Sas(IRE)** was close up until being left behind in the final quarter-mile. He is stoutly-bred on his dam's side but appeared not to stay.
**Mac Regal(IRE)** kept in touch by coming tight round the rail on the final turn, but did not last long once in the straight.

# 1579 CHEPSTOW (L-H)

Monday, May 31

**OFFICIAL GOING: Good to firm (good in places)**

A high draw again proved an advantage on the straight course.
Wind: nil Weather: raining race 3 onwards

## 2513 PETE SMITH CARSALES@WYVERN-CARSALES.CO.UK MAIDEN STKS — 1m 4f 23y

2:15 (2:15) (D) 3-Y-O — **£3,614** (£1,112; £556; £278) **Stalls** Low

Form — RPR

33 **1** **Always Waining (IRE)**[9] 2298 3-9-0 ... KDalgleish 3 — 83
(MJohnston) *sn led: rdn over 2f out: r.o wl* **11/4**[2]

6-04 **2** *1* **Horner (USA)**[14] 2179 3-9-0 80 ... RLMoore 6 — 81
(PFICole) *hld up in tch: rdn over 3f out: styd on ins fnl f* **5/2**[1]

0 **3** *½* **Forged (IRE)**[34] 1683 3-8-11 ... NMackay(3) 8 — 80
(LMCumani) *s.i.s: hld up: hdwy over 3f out: rdn over 2f out: swtchd lft ins fnl f: styd on* **33/1**

0-3 **4** *2½* **Blaze Of Colour**[33] 1713 3-8-9 ... BDoyle 7 — 71
(SirMichaelStoute) *a.p: rdn over 3f out: no ex ins fnl f* **3/1**[3]

42-0 **5** *nk* **Song Of Vala**[65] 1134 3-9-0 80 ... SWhitworth 1 — 76
(RCharlton) *led early: chsd wnr: rdn and ev ch 2f out: wknd ins fnl f* **9/1**

2 **6** *10* **On Cloud Nine**[62] 1186 3-8-4 ... HayleyTurner(5) 2 — 55
(MLWBell) *t.k.h: rdn over 3f out: sn struggling* **7/1**

0 **7** *2* **Bayou Princess**[25] 1911 3-8-9 ... AMcCarthy 4 — 52
(BDeHaan) *a in rr: wl bhd fnl 5f* **100/1**

00-0 **8** *5* **Plovers Lane (IRE)**[17] 2085 3-9-0 ... (p) ADaly 5 — 49
(MPTregoning) *a in rr: wl bhd fnl 5f* **33/1**

2m 38.72s (0.22) **Going Correction** 0.0s/f (Good) — **8** Ran SP% **109.6**
Speed ratings: **99,98,98,96,96 89,88,84**CSF £9.11 TOTE £4.00: £1.20, £1.20, £8.40; EX 13.00.
**Owner** The Always Trying Partnership **Bred** Barouche Stud Ireland Ltd **Trained** Middleham Moor, N Yorks

**FOCUS**
A fair maiden, run in a time over two and a half seconds slower than the handicap 35 minutes later.

**NOTEBOOK**
**Always Waining(IRE)** is progressing with experience. Making much of the running, he was suited by the step up in trip and will get a bit farther yet.
**Horner(USA)**, back in maiden company, stayed on in game fashion but could not peg back the winner. With an official rating of 80 he is a good measure of the form's worth.
**Forged(IRE)**, made an inauspicious debut, finishing last of 20, and was again slow to find his stride, but he showed ability this time. This longer trip suited him and he should do better once handicapped, with softer ground likely to suit.
**Blaze Of Colour**, stepping up in trip and racing on better ground, ran respectably and is now eligible for handicaps.
**Song Of Vala** appeared not to get home over this extra quarter-mile. Rated 80 like the runner-up, he may need to be dropped a few pounds if he is to make his mark in handicaps.
**On Cloud Nine** was too keen for her own good and did not progress from her debut effort.

## 2514 EUROPEAN BREEDERS FUND FILLIES' H'CAP — 1m 4f 23y

2:50 (2:50) (D) (0-80,76) 3-Y-O+ — **£6,760** (£2,080; £1,040; £520) **Stalls** Low

Form — RPR

00-6 **1** **Tidal**[27] 1856 5-8-2 55 ... RThomas(5) 9 — 66
(AWCarroll) *chsd ldr: led 2f out: sn rdn: r.o* **16/1**

31-1 **2** *1* **Wasted Talent (IRE)**[20] 1684 4-9-10 72 ... (v[1]) RLMoore 1 — 81
(JGPortman) *led: rdn and hdd 2f out: ev ch ins fnl f: no ex towards fin* **5/1**[2]

0-31 **3** *shd* **Portrait Of A Lady (IRE)**[16] 2133 3-8-9 74 ... PaulEddery 6 — 83
(HRACecil) *hld up: hdwy over 4f out: swtchd rt 3f out: rdn over 2f out: kpt on same pce ins fnl f* **6/1**[3]

4-55 **4** *2* **Moonlight Tango (USA)**[18] 2059 3-8-7 72 ... SWhitworth 7 — 78
(JHMGosden) *hld up and bhd: hdwy on ins over 4f out: sn rdn: one pce fnl f* **6/1**[3]

5421 **5** *10* **Anyhow (IRE)**[14] 2167 7-9-0 62 ... KDalgleish 8 — 52
(MissKMGeorge) *hld up and bhd: hdwy over 5f out: rdn over 3f out: wknd over 2f out* **6/1**[3]

3324 **6** *3½* **Compton Eclaire (IRE)**[14] 2167 4-8-7 55 ... (v) SWKelly 3 — 39
(GAButler) *s.i.s: a bhd* **8/1**

01-4 **7** *1¼* **Stealing Beauty (IRE)**[10] 2277 4-9-11 76 ... NMackay(3) 10 — 58
(LMCumani) *prom: rdn over 3f out: wknd over 2f out* **4/1**[1]

4000 **8** *5* **Top Of The Class (IRE)**[6] 2381 7-8-6 54 ... (v) JoannaBadger 4 — 28
(PDEvans) *hld up and bhd: hdwy 5f out: sn rdn: wknd over 3f out* **18/1**

43/5 **9** *hd* **Castanet**[41] 1534 5-7-12 46 oh2 ... AMcCarthy 2 — 20
(AEPrice) *prom 6f* **16/1**

26-5 **10** *25* **Garryurra**[18] 2060 3-8-9 74 ... BDoyle 5 — 8
(SirMichaelStoute) *hld up: lost pl after 5f: bhd whn rdn over 4f out: eased whn no ch over 1f out* **14/1**

2m 36.14s (-2.36) **Going Correction** 0.0s/f (Good)
**WFA** 3 from 4yo+ 17lb — **10** Ran SP% **114.3**
Speed ratings: **107,106,106,104,98 95,95,91,91,74**CSF £92.35 CT £542.55 TOTE £23.60: £5.20, £2.30, £1.80; EX 224.00.
**Owner** Mrs B Quinn **Bred** Wyck Hall Stud Ltd **Trained** Wixford, Warwicks

**FOCUS**
This was run at a good pace, resulting in a time over two and a half seconds faster than the opening maiden. Few got into it.

**NOTEBOOK**
**Tidal**, from a yard in form, was tackling this trip for the first time since finishing sixth in this event a year ago. She is well handicapped at present having begun last season, when in the care of Brian Meehan, with an official rating of 77.
**Wasted Talent(IRE)**, a winner again over hurdles since her last run on the Flat, wore a visor instead of her usual cheekpieces. She only gave best in the last 50 yards and should continue to run well.
**Portrait Of A Lady(IRE)** won a weak maiden at Thirsk and the handicapper did not put her up for that. She shaped as if she will get a little farther than this.
**Moonlight Tango(USA)** was tackling a longer trip for this handicap debut. This looks as good as she is and but she should do better back against her own age group.
**Stealing Beauty(IRE)** did not enjoy the run of the race on her reappearance but there seemed no excuses this time. *Official explanation: trainer was unable to offer any explanation for poor form shown.*
**Garryurra** *Official explanation: jockey said his saddle slipped.*

## 2515 BRITISH RACING SCHOOL (S) STKS — 6f 16y

3:25 (3:26) (G) 2-Y-O — **£2,527** (£722; £361) **Stalls** High

Form — RPR

06 **1** **Don't Tell Trigger (IRE)**[9] 2296 2-8-6 ... JDSmith 7 — 59
(JSMoore) *mde all: rdn over 2f out: edgd lft jst over 1f out: r.o wl* **11/4**[2]

0 **2** *2* **Lakesdale (IRE)**[5] 2396 2-8-6 ... RLMoore 6 — 53
(MRChannon) *sn outpcd: hdwy over 3f out: chsd wnr fnl f: swtchd rt: no imp* **13/2**[3]

456 **3** *2* **Glasson Lodge**[7] 2352 2-8-7 ow1 ... SWKelly 2 — 48
(PDEvans) *a.p: rdn over 3f out: one pce fnl 2f* **5/4**[1]

0 **4** *2½* **Princely Vale (IRE)**[38] 1589 2-8-4 ... BO'Neill(7) 4 — 45
(WGMTurner) *sn chsng ldrs: swtchd to stands' rail over 4f out: rdn over 2f out: wknd ins fnl f* **10/1**

**5** *3* **Royal Cozyfire (IRE)** 2-8-11 ... KDalgleish 1 — 36
(BPalling) *s.i.s: jnd ldrs 4f out: ev ch over 2f out: sn rdn and edgd lft: wknd fnl f* **8/1**

0 **6** *5* **Kentucky Bankes**[16] 2125 2-8-11 ... ADaly 5 — 21
(WGMTurner) *w wnr tl rdn and hung lft over 3f out: wknd over 2f out* **25/1**

000 **7** *6* **She's My Dream (IRE)**[5] 2405 2-8-6 ... SWhitworth 3 — —
(JSMoore) *s.i.s: outpcd* **33/1**

1m 14.46s (2.26) **Going Correction** +0.20s/f (Good) — **7** Ran SP% **111.4**
Speed ratings: **92,89,86,83,79 72,64**CSF £19.63 TOTE £4.30: £1.80, £3.20; EX 21.90.The winner was bought in for 5,200gns. Lakesdale was claimed by C J Gray for £6,000.
**Owner** Bigwigs Bloodstock Racing Club V **Bred** Park Place International Ltd **Trained** East Garston, Berks

**FOCUS**
This appeared a reasonable race of its type. They were well spread out at the line.

**NOTEBOOK**
**Don't Tell Trigger(IRE)**, dropped in class, made best use of her draw against the stands' rail. She will stay farther and will switch to nurseries soon.
**Lakesdale(IRE)**, who made her debut only five days earlier, was dropping to the bottom grade and stepping up a furlong. She probably needs seven already.
**Glasson Lodge** was rather disappointing on this first run in a seller, but she was not ideally drawn on what is a tricky course.
**Princely Vale(IRE)**, a 30,000gns yearling, knew a bit more on this second outing but this looks his grade.
**Kentucky Bankes** *Official explanation: jockey said colt was hanging left handed.*

## 2516 WESTERN DAILY PRESS CLUB CLASSIFIED STKS — 1m 14y

4:00 (4:00) (D) 3-Y-O+ — **£5,473** (£1,684; £842; £421) **Stalls** High

Form — RPR

140 **1** **Just Tim (IRE)**[9] 2306 3-8-5 74 ... RLMoore 3 — 83
(RHannon) *hld up in tch: rdn over 3f out: led jst over 1f out: r.o wl* **9/2**[3]

30-4 **2** *2½* **Leaping Brave (IRE)**[28] 1841 3-8-6 76 ... AMcCarthy 1 — 78
(BRMillman) *led over 1f: w ldr: rdn to ld again 2f out: hdd jst over 1f out: nt qckn* **13/2**

00-1 **3** *½* **Ali Deo**[13] 2195 3-8-7 77 ... SWKelly 6 — 78
(WJHaggas) *w ldr: led over 6f out: rdn and hdd 2f out: sn edgd lft: one pce fnl f* **11/2**

0002 **4** *1* **The Bonus King**[4] 2421 4-8-12 77 ... AElliott(7) 7 — 76
(MJohnston) *a.p: sltly outpcd over 2f out: edgd lft over 1f out: kpt on same pce fnl f* **5/2**[1]

0-06 **5** *½* **Certain Justice (USA)**[28] 1840 6-9-0 77 ... NDeSouza(5) 5 — 74
(PFICole) *hld up: hdwy over 4f out: rdn 3f out: one pce fnl 2f* **9/1**

0620 **6** *4* **Oakley Rambo**[13] 2206 5-9-1 80 ... PGallagher(7) 4 — 68
(RHannon) *hld up: hdwy 4f out: rdn 3f out: wknd 2f out* **4/1**[2]

05 **7** *14* **Tresor Secret (FR)**[10] 2278 4-9-3 75 ... (b[1]) KDalgleish 2 — 31
(NACallaghan) *a in rr: lost tch 3f out* **14/1**

1m 36.79s (0.89) **Going Correction** +0.20s/f (Good)
**WFA** 3 from 4yo+ 12lb — **7** Ran SP% **112.1**
Speed ratings: **103,100,100,99,98 94,80**CSF £31.82 TOTE £4.80: £2.90, £2.80; EX 27.30.
**Owner** D J Walker **Bred** Mrs S Joint **Trained** East Everleigh, Wilts

**FOCUS**
The field was closely matched on official figures and the three-year-olds emerged on top.

**NOTEBOOK**
**Just Tim(IRE)** has been found wanting in decent handicaps on his last two starts and faced an easier task here. He seemed to benefit from being held up off the pace and settled better.
**Leaping Brave(IRE)**, always in the first two, had no problem with the extra furlong. He has run well here before more than once.
**Ali Deo** behaved much better than he had at Beverley. He saw out this slightly longer trip and remains relatively unexposed.
**The Bonus King** has not won since taking the Woodcote Stakes on Derby day two years ago and is likely to remain difficult to place. Stronger handling should suit him.
**Certain Justice(USA)**, the first ride in Britain for his jockey, who has ridden 30 winners in Brazil, disappointed on ground that was faster than he would have liked. He has only won once in the last four years and has not worn blinkers since that victory in August 2002.
**Tresor Secret(FR)** *Official explanation: jockey said gelding would not face the blinkers.*

## 2517 BRITISHHORSERACING.COM INFORMATION STAND MAIDEN STKS — 1m 14y

4:35 (4:38) (D) 3-Y-O+ — **£3,799** (£1,169; £584; £292) **Stalls** High

Form — RPR

3 **1** **Magic Merlin**[10] 2267 3-8-12 ... BDoyle 15 — 76
(PWHarris) *t.k.h: a.p: led 3f out: pushed along over 1f out: r.o wl* **15/8**[1]

4-20 **2** *¾* **Rondelet (IRE)**[18] 2069 3-8-12 76 ... MTebbutt 3 — 74
(RMBeckett) *hld up and bhd: rdn and hdwy over 2f out: chsd wnr over 1f out: kpt on* **9/2**[2]

**3** *2* **Minority Report** 4-9-7 ... NMackay(3) 4 — 69
(LMCumani) *s.s: hdwy over 2f out: r.o fnl f: bttr for r* **10/1**

00 **4** *2* **Masked (IRE)**[23] 1967 3-8-12 ... NDay 6 — 65
(JWHills) *s.s: hdwy over 1f out: kpt on fnl f: nrst fin* **25/1**

260- **5** *nk* **Blaina**[192] 6039 4-9-0 75 ... RThomas(5) 7 — 59
(DRCElsworth) *wnt lft s: t.k.h mid-div: hdwy over 3f out: rdn over 2f out: one pce fnl f* **7/1**[3]

5 **6** *¾* **Ridge Boy (IRE)**[13] 2204 3-8-12 ... RLMoore 11 — 62
(RHannon) *s.i.s: sn prom: rdn over 3f out: one pce fnl 2f* **9/2**[2]

06 **7** *1* **High Frequency (IRE)**[13] 2204 3-8-12 ... KDalgleish 17 — 60
(WRMuir) *w ldrs: rdn and wknd 2f out* **8/1**

5-0 **8** *nk* **Chambray (IRE)**[53] 1311 3-8-0 ... TBlock(7) 5 — 54
(AMBalding) *hld up mid-div: rdn over 2f out: no hdwy* **50/1**

0 **9** *1¾* **Cotton Easter**[45] 1441 3-8-7 ... PaulEddery 1 — 50
(MrsAJBowlby) *nvr nrr* **66/1**

| | | | | |
|---|---|---|---|---|
| | **10** *nk* | **Ink In Gold (IRE)** 3-8-9 ........ DNolan(3) 16 | 55 |
| | | (PABlockley) *s.s: sn mid-div: rdn over 3f out: wknd fnl f* **25/1** | |
| 05- | **11** *shd* | **Total Force (IRE)**[242] 5325 3-8-5 ........ PGallagher(7) 2 | 54 |
| | | (RHannon) *hld up and bhd: rdn over 3f out: hdwy on outside over 2f out: wknd ins fnl f* **33/1** | |
| -455 | **12** *2 1/2* | **Rood Boy (IRE)**[42] 1506 3-8-7 55 ........ HayleyTurner(5) 14 | 49 |
| | | (JSKing) *led: rdn and hdd 3f out: wknd over 1f out* **16/1** | |
| 500- | **13** *2* | **Sweet Az**[252] 5115 4-9-5 39 ........ SWhitworth 10 | 39 |
| | | (SCBurrough) *prom tl wknd over 2f out* **100/1** | |
| 6-00 | **14** *3/4* | **Nina Fontenail (FR)**[27] 1856 3-8-7 45 ow3 ........ ABeech(3) 9 | 40 |
| | | (NJHawke) *prom 5f* **100/1** | |
| 0 | **15** *16* | **Chatshow (USA)**[13] 2211 3-8-12 ........ AMcCarthy 12 | 6 |
| | | (LADace) *dwlt: t.k.h: sn in tch: rdn and wknd over 2f out: t.o* **100/1** | |
| 00 | **16** *13* | **Spector (IRE)**[24] 1939 4-9-7 ........ DCorby(3) 8 | — |
| | | (JJSheehan) *bhd: rdn over 6f out: t.o fnl 4f* **66/1** | |
| 0 | **17** *shd* | **Lord Of The Fens**[11] 2236 4-9-10 ........ SWKelly 13 | — |
| | | (CNKellett) *uns rdr and bolted bef s: dwlt: sn chsng ldrs: wknd over 3f out: t.o* **100/1** | |

1m 37.1s (-7.07) **Going Correction** +0.20s/f (Good)
**WFA** 3 from 4yo 12lb **17** Ran SP% **129.3**
Speed ratings: **102,101,99,97,96 96,95,94,93,92 92,90,88,87,71 58,58**CSF £10.01 TOTE £2.70: £1.30, £2.70, £3.30; EX 14.80.
**Owner** The Magic Circle **Bred** T R Lock **Trained** Ringshall, Bucks

**FOCUS**
A fair maiden, run in a slightly slower time than the previous classified stakes.

**NOTEBOOK**
**Magic Merlin**, showing the benefit of his debut experience, settled better here. He made full use of a favourable draw and scored a shade comfortably.
**Rondelet(IRE)**, back in maiden company, ran a sound race from his moderate draw. He ideally needs faster ground.
**Minority Report**, making a belated racecourse debut, was not given a hard time and seems sure to improve for the experience. His dam, winner of the Listed Firth Of Clyde Stakes, never ran beyond six furlongs, but he looks as if he will stay farther.
**Masked(IRE)**, having his third run, did not shape as if the drop back from ten furlongs was the answer.
**Blaina**, who was a beaten favourite on her previous three runs, again showed that she is less than straightforward.
**Ridge Boy(IRE)** was unable to build on his debut promise. Both his runs so far have come on undulating tracks.
**Chatshow(USA)** *Official explanation: jockey said gelding had a breathing problem.*

## 2518 BET365 08000 322 365 FILLIES' STKS (H'CAP) 6f 16y
**5:10** (5:10) (E) (0-75,75) 3-Y-O **£4,221** (£1,299; £649; £324) **Stalls** High

| Form | | | RPR |
|---|---|---|---|
| 50-6 | **1** | **Verkhotina**[49] 1366 3-9-4 72 ........ BDoyle 11 | 85 |
| | | (RCharlton) *hld up: hdwy on stands' rail over 2f out: rdn to ld wl over 1f out: sn edgd lft: readily* **5/1**[2] | |
| -002 | **2** *3 1/2* | **Under My Spell**[17] 2091 3-9-2 70 ........ SWKelly 2 | 72 |
| | | (PDEvans) *chsd ldrs: rdn over 1f out: kpt on ins fnl f: no ch w wnr* **9/2**[1] | |
| 4-00 | **3** *shd* | **Urban Rose**[28] 1841 3-8-7 64 ........ DCorby(3) 12 | 66 |
| | | (JWUnett) *a.p: rdn 2f out: one pce fnl f* **8/1** | |
| 0-60 | **4** *1 3/4* | **La Vie Est Belle**[26] 1881 3-9-5 73 ........ AMcCarthy 4 | 69 |
| | | (BRMillman) *w ldrs: ev ch 2f out: one pce* **8/1** | |
| 6110 | **5** *1 3/4* | **Melaina**[18] 2063 3-8-9 66 ........ (p) ABeech(3) 8 | 57 |
| | | (MSSaunders) *led: rdn and hdd 2f out: wknd fnl f* **12/1** | |
| 2360 | **6** *shd* | **Alizar (IRE)**[8] 2326 3-8-4 58 ........ RLMoore 6 | 49 |
| | | (SDow) *hld up: hdwy 2f out: swtchd lft over 1f out: eased whn btn wl ins fnl f* **14/1** | |
| -401 | **7** *3/4* | **Jinksonthehouse**[10] 2265 3-8-1 60 ........ HayleyTurner(5) 7 | 49 |
| | | (MDIUsher) *w ldrs: rdn and ev ch 2f out: wknd ins fnl f* **10/1** | |
| -000 | **8** *1 3/4* | **Danifah (IRE)**[14] 2166 3-7-12 52 oh5 ........ JoannaBadger 1 | 35 |
| | | (PDEvans) *chsd ldrs on outside: rdn over 3f out: wknd over 1f out* **22/1** | |
| 6150 | **9** *4* | **Crewes Miss Isle**[14] 2181 3-8-10 64 ........ SWhitworth 3 | 35 |
| | | (AGNewcombe) *a bhd* **7/1**[3] | |
| 46-0 | **10** *3 1/2* | **Lyrical Lady**[14] 2165 3-7-11 56 ow3 ........ (b[1]) RThomas(5) 9 | 17 |
| | | (MrsAJBowlby) *s.i.s: outpcd* **50/1** | |
| 40-0 | **11** *1 1/4* | **Ninah**[28] 1841 3-9-0 68 ........ KDalgleish 10 | 25 |
| | | (JMBradley) *w ldrs: rdn 3f out: sn wknd* **10/1** | |
| 1-10 | **12** *2* | **Beejay**[16] 2112 3-9-2 75 ........ NDeSouza(5) 5 | 26 |
| | | (PFICole) *s.i.s and wnt lft: a bhd* **8/1** | |

1m 13.2s (1.00) **Going Correction** +0.20s/f (Good) **12** Ran SP% **119.5**
Speed ratings: **101,96,96,93,91 91,90,88,82,78 76,73**CSF £28.01 CT £183.23 TOTE £8.20: £2.40, £2.10, £3.70; EX 27.50 Place 6 £139.36, Place 5 £81.57..
**Owner** A E Oppenheimer **Bred** Hascombe And Valiant Studs **Trained** Beckhampton, Wilts

**FOCUS**
A fair handicap in which a high draw proved an advantage.

**NOTEBOOK**
**Verkhotina** was well drawn and put some previous disappointments behind her to score nicely. She looks a sprinter and this appears the way to ride her. Sure to go up a fair bit for this, she would be interesting under a penalty. *Official explanation: trainer's representative said filly had benefited from the good to firm ground on this occasion*
**Under My Spell** put in a good effort from her low-numbered stall, splitting two fillies drawn high. She was third in the listed National Stakes at Sandown a year ago and is capable of winning from her current mark.
**Urban Rose**, who was found out by soft ground at Warwick, ran better here albeit from the plum draw.
**La Vie Est Belle** was done no favours by the draw for the second successive outing.
**Melaina** got to the front but was unable to dominate. She seems held by the handicapper.
T/Plt: £423.60 to a £1 stake. Pool: £29,627.70. 51.05 winning tickets. T/Qpdt: £26.30 to a £1 stake. Pool: £1,878.00. 52.70 winning tickets. KH

# [2357]LEICESTER (R-H)
Monday, May 31

**OFFICIAL GOING: Good to firm (firm in places)**
Wind: fresh bhd Weather: warm & sunny

## 2519 MRS B A SPENCER MEDIAN AUCTION MAIDEN STKS 1m 9y
**1:55** (1:57) (F) 3-Y-O **£3,610** (£1,111; £555; £277) **Stalls** High

| Form | | | RPR |
|---|---|---|---|
| 5-3 | **1** | **Tableau (USA)**[66] 1111 3-9-0 ........ RHughes 3 | 78 |
| | | (BWHills) *mde all: shkn up over 1f out: r.o: eased nr fin* **9/4**[1] | |
| 04 | **2** *1/2* | **Principal Witness (IRE)**[16] 2113 3-9-0 ........ SSanders 9 | 76 |
| | | (WRMuir) *a.p: rdn and nt clr run over 1f out: r.o: nt rch wnr* **3/1**[3] | |
| 35-0 | **3** *1 3/4* | **Master Theo (USA)**[29] 1794 3-9-0 77 ........ JQuinn 7 | 72 |
| | | (HJCollingridge) *chsd wnr: rdn over 1f out: styd on same pce ins fnl f* **12/1** | |
| 4 | **4** *3 1/2* | **Different Planet**[16] 2114 3-9-0 ........ EAhern 4 | 64 |
| | | (JWHills) *chsd ldrs: rdn over 2f out: styd on same pce appr fnl f* **5/2**[2] | |
| | **5** *nk* | **Dan Di Canio (IRE)** 3-9-0 ........ PDoe 12 | 64 |
| | | (PWHarris) *s.i.s: hld up: styd on fnl 2f: nt trble ldrs* **33/1** | |
| 500- | **6** *3/4* | **Kentmere (IRE)**[211] 5887 3-9-0 71 ........ (t) SCarson 2 | 62 |
| | | (WJHaggas) *chsd ldrs: outpcd over 3f out: styd on ins fnl f* **20/1** | |
| 0- | **7** *shd* | **Fifth Column (USA)**[251] 5137 3-9-0 ........ OUrbina 10 | 62 |
| | | (JRFanshawe) *prom over 6f* **14/1** | |
| | **8** *1/2* | **After Lent (IRE)** 3-9-0 ........ JBramhill 15 | 61 |
| | | (PABlockley) *hld up: hdwy over 2f out: wknd over 1f out* **100/1** | |
| 02- | **9** *3* | **Super King**[232] 5511 3-9-0 ........ WSupple 6 | 54 |
| | | (NBycroft) *prom over 5f* **14/1** | |
| 0 | **10** *1 1/2* | **Chisel**[13] 2195 3-9-0 ........ RFfrench 14 | 50 |
| | | (MJohnston) *hld up in tch: rdn 1/2-way: wknd over 2f out* **33/1** | |
| 55 | **11** *6* | **Knight Of Hearts (IRE)**[37] 1628 3-9-0 ........ PMcCabe 13 | 36 |
| | | (REPeacock) *hld up: a in rr* **150/1** | |
| | **12** *dist* | **Zalebe** 3-8-9 ........ RPrice 5 | — |
| | | (JPearce) *a in rr* **50/1** | |

1m 40.53s (-2.07) **Going Correction** -0.15s/f (Firm) **12** Ran SP% **119.6**
Speed ratings: **104,103,101,98,97 97,97,96,93,92 86,—**CSF £8.86 TOTE £3.10: £1.60, £1.20, £3.70; EX 17.40.
**Owner** K Abdulla **Bred** Juddmonte Farms Inc **Trained** Lambourn, Berks

**FOCUS**
A decent time for the grade. Tableau had the form to win and did so comfortably.

**NOTEBOOK**
**Tableau(USA)**, third behind useful stable companion Zonus on his seasonal debut back in March, was given a simple ride from the front and found what was required to run out a cosy winner. There should be more to come and with connections expecting slightly easier ground to suit, will soon be making his mark at handicap level.
**Principal Witness(IRE)**, who had shown promise in two decent Newbury maidens prior to this, was maybe a little unlucky not to get a tad closer to the winner, but the result would have been the same. He should have little trouble landing a similar event if asked to.
**Master Theo(USA)** made his seasonal reappearance - a staying-on seventh of 24 - in a decent Newmarket maiden that has produced winners and, although comfortably held, did not completely let the form down.
**Different Planet**, a highly encouraging fourth at Newbury on his debut, did not run up to scratch and failed to progress for that run. His stable seem to have taken a dip in form having started the season well and he is better than this.
**Dan Di Canio(IRE)** saw his race out well on this racecourse debut having been tardy at the start and normal improvement should see him going close next time.
**Kentmere(IRE)** is well exposed, but was at least finishing with purpose on this debut for the Haggas yard.

## 2520 GERALDINE HAUKE (S) STKS 1m 1f 218y
**2:25** (2:25) (G) 3-5-Y-O **£2,954** (£844; £422) **Stalls** High

| Form | | | RPR |
|---|---|---|---|
| 0155 | **1** | **Regulated (IRE)**[17] 2092 3-8-12 65 ........ DaneO'Neill 9 | 60 |
| | | (DBFeek) *hld up: hdwy over 2f out: rdn and hung rt over 1f out: r.o to ld wl ins fnl f* **5/1**[2] | |
| 0- | **2** *1 1/4* | **Labelled With Love**[319] 3345 4-9-0 ........ LTreadwell(7) 10 | 53 |
| | | (WGMTurner) *s.i.s: plld hrd and sn prom: led 3f out: clr over 1f out: rdn and hdd wl ins fnl f* **40/1** | |
| 6-04 | **3** *2 1/2* | **Stylish Sunrise (IRE)**[17] 2092 3-8-7 65 ........ (t) EAhern 5 | 48 |
| | | (MLWBell) *hld up: hdwy 1/2-way: outpcd over 2f out: styd on u.p appr fnl f* **5/1**[2] | |
| | **4** *1/2* | **Uncle Batty**[57] 4-9-7 ........ RFfrench 4 | 47 |
| | | (GAHarker) *s.i.s: hld up: hdwy over 1f out: nt rch ldrs* **10/1** | |
| | **5** *3/4* | **Ali Bruce**[18] 4-9-7 ........ TGMcLaughlin 11 | 46 |
| | | (DECantillon) *trckd ldrs: racd keenly: rdn over 2f out: styd on same pce appr fnl f* **7/2**[1] | |
| 4 | **6** *1 1/2* | **Enna (POL)**[41] 1533 5-8-11 51 ........ BSwarbrick(5) 8 | 38 |
| | | (AGJuckes) *chsd ldr: rdn and ev ch over 2f out: wknd over 1f out* **15/2** | |
| 0033 | **7** *6* | **Fitz The Bill (IRE)**[17] 2092 4-9-2 42 ........ (b) SSanders 1 | 26 |
| | | (NBKing) *hld up: hdwy 1/2-way: rdn and wknd over 1f out* **11/2**[3] | |
| 50-0 | **8** *1 1/2* | **Relative Hero (IRE)**[7] 2362 4-9-2 62 ........ (p) AQuinn(5) 7 | 28 |
| | | (MissSJWilton) *prom: rdn over 2f out: wknd over 1f out* **8/1** | |
| 00-0 | **9** *11* | **Buckenham Stone**[41] 1519 5-9-2 ........ JQuinn 2 | 3 |
| | | (JPearce) *hld up: bhd fr 1/2-way* **33/1** | |
| 0/4 | **10** *1 3/4* | **First Class Girl**[144] 471 5-9-2 ........ GCarter 3 | — |
| | | (CBBBooth) *hld up: bhd fr 1/2-way* **50/1** | |
| U/0- | **11** *2 1/2* | **Wafani**[353] 2344 5-9-7 ........ (b) GGibbons 12 | — |
| | | (WJMusson) *sn led: hdd & wknd 3f out* **40/1** | |
| 0600 | **12** *1 1/4* | **Mesmerised**[7] 2369 4-9-2 35 ........ (p) AnnStokell 6 | — |
| | | (MissAStokell) *hld up: bhd fr 4f* **25/1** | |
| 0 | **13** *dist* | **Jem's Law**[56] 1274 5-8-9 ........ (v) JJeffrey(7) 13 | — |
| | | (JRJenkins) *s.i.s: sn prom: wknd 1/2-way* **66/1** | |

2m 7.11s (-1.29) **Going Correction** -0.15s/f (Firm)
**WFA** 3 from 4yo+ 14lb **13** Ran SP% **118.0**
Speed ratings: **99,98,96,95,95 93,89,87,79,77 75,74,—** CT £6.50 TOTE £2.50: £6.00, £3.10, £; EX170.90 1.The winner was bought in for 7,000gns. Enna was claimed by Stef Liddiard for £6,000; Uncle Batty was claimed by Graham S
**Owner** D R Hunnisett **Bred** Churchtown House Stud **Trained** Brightling, E Sussex

**FOCUS**
This looked a weak race of its type.

**NOTEBOOK**
**Regulated(IRE)**, disappointing without excuse latest, showed his true form and came home with over a length to spare despite lugging to his right. This was his first start for the Feek yard and maybe a change of scenery did the trick. He was bought in for 7,000gns.
**Labelled With Love** left his well-beaten debut running behind on this seasonal debut, pulling hard and going clear a furlong out before his early exertions told late on. This was a good effort and the drop back to a mile should see him winning in the near future.
**Stylish Sunrise(IRE)** failed to confirm Yarmouth form with the winner, but was at least running on towards the finish.
**Uncle Batty**, who has been running in bumpers, shaped as though a stiffer test of stamina will suit.
**Ali Bruce**, another who has been competing in bumpers, was supported down from 12/1 in the ring but could only stay on at the one pace. He is another sure to be suited by further.
**Enna(POL)**
**Wafani** *Official explanation: jockey said gelding tired rapidly from two out.*
**Jem's Law** *Official explanation: trainer said mare lost her action.*

## 2521 NEW STREET CHAMBERS FILLIES' H'CAP 1m 9y
**3:00** (3:00) (D) (0-85,80) 3-Y-O+ **£6,831** (£2,102; £1,051; £525) **Stalls** High

| Form | | | RPR |
|---|---|---|---|
| -045 | **1** | **Madamoiselle Jones**[9] 2282 4-8-8 64 ........ DKinsella 6 | 75 |
| | | (HSHowe) *mde all: rdn over 1f out: r.o* **20/1** | |

0-65 **2** *nk* **Summer Shades**[9] 2304 6-8-8 **69** .... BSwarbrick(5) 8 79
(WMBrisbourne) *chsd ldrs: rdn and hung rt over 1f out: ev ch ins fnl f: styd on* **9/1**

4330 **3** *1 ¾* **Oh So Rosie (IRE)**[23] 1969 4-8-2 **58** .... SCarson 7 64
(JSMoore) *hld up in tch: outpcd over 2f out: styd on u.p fnl f* **20/1**

04-4 **4** *½* **Blonde Streak (USA)**[5] 2410 4-9-7 **77** .... RHughes 5 82
(TDBarron) *hld up in tch: rdn over 2f out: styd on* **5/1**[3]

265- **5** *½* **Sharp Secret (IRE)**[207] 5937 6-7-13 **55** .... JQuinn 4 59
(JARToller) *chsd ldrs: rdn over 2f out: styd on same pce fnl f* **14/1**

01-1 **6** *1* **Red Sahara (IRE)**[16] 2112 3-8-10 **78** .... SSanders 9 79
(WJHaggas) *trckd ldr: racd keenly: rdn over 2f out: no ex fnl f* **11/8**[1]

5-04 **7** *1 ½* **Devant (NZ)**[11] 2237 4-9-10 **80** .... MHenry 2 78
(MAJarvis) *sn pushed along in rr: hdwy over 1f out: styng on same pce whn n.m.r ins fnl f* **9/2**[2]

4424 **8** *½* **And Toto Too**[2] 2483 4-8-11 **67** .... (b) DaneO'Neill 3 64
(PDEvans) *hld up: rdn over 3f out: n.d* **8/1**

0-00 **9** *12* **Craic Sa Ceili (IRE)**[18] 2064 4-8-12 **68** .... TGMcLaughlin 1 37
(MSSaunders) *hld up: bhd fnl 3f* **33/1**

1m 40.24s (-2.36) **Going Correction** -0.15s/f (Firm) **9** Ran SP% **117.2**
**WFA** 3 from 4yo+ 12lb
Speed ratings: **105,104,102,102,101 100,99,98,86**CSF £185.49 CT £3632.31 TOTE £19.70: £3.10, £3.10, £4.70; EX 126.10.
**Owner** Horses Away Racing Club **Bred** Mill House Stud **Trained** Oakford, Devon

**FOCUS**
An ordinary handiacp, producing a deserved success for Madamoiselle Jones who has a great attitude and appreciated the return to handicap company.

**NOTEBOOK**
**Madamoiselle Jones**, outclassed, although not entirely disgraced in a conditions event at Ascot on her most recent outing, appreciated the return to this company and led throughout for a game win.
**Summer Shades** came there with every chance, but could not get past the plucky winner. This was a good effort.
**Oh So Rosie(IRE)** ran on from the rear without ever really threatening and appreciated the return to this faster surface.
**Blonde Streak(USA)** has shaped promisingly on both starts this season. Her winning turn should not be far away.
**Sharp Secret(IRE)** made a pleasing seasonal reappearance and is entitled to improve for the blow out.
**Red Sahara(IRE)**, winner of a competitive handicap at Newbury, proved most disappointing off an 8lb higher mark.
**And Toto Too** *Official explanation: jockey said filly lost her action.*

## 2522 FOXY'S LUCKY PEG & CONCRETE SHUFFLE MEDIAN AUCTION MAIDEN STKS — 5f 2y

**3:35** (3:37) (E) 2-Y-O — **£4,153** (£1,278; £639; £319) **Stalls** Low

Form — RPR

**1** **Safari Sunset (IRE)** 2-9-0 .... PDoe 5 87
(PWinkworth) *chsd ldrs: led over 1f out: edgd rt ins fnl f: rdn out* **20/1**

**2** *1* **Drum Dance (IRE)** 2-9-0 .... SCarson 17 84
(RFJohnsonHoughton) *chsd ldrs: rdn and ev ch fr over 1f out: unable qck towards fin* **7/1**

532 **3** *1 ¼* **Empire's Ghodha**[7] 2370 2-8-11 .... (b[1]) JFMcDonald(3) 12 79
(BJMeehan) *w ldrs: led 1/2-way: edgd rt and hdd over 1f out: styd on same pce* **6/1**[2]

**4** *2* **Loaderfun (IRE)** 2-9-0 .... DaneO'Neill 15 72
(HCandy) *sn outpcd: hdwy over 1f out: nt rch ldrs* **14/1**

225 **5** *hd* **Dante's Diamond (IRE)**[17] 2086 2-9-0 .... GBaker 10 71
(FJordan) *led to 1/2-way: hung rt outpcd over 1f out* **13/2**[3]

**6** *½* **Belly Dancer (IRE)** 2-8-9 .... JQuinn 2 65
(PFICole) *chsd ldrs: rdn 1/2-way: styd on same pce fnl 2f* **4/1**[1]

4 **7** *3* **Melvino**[17] 2074 2-8-9 .... PMakin(5) 16 59
(TDBarron) *prom 3f* **16/1**

2 **8** *1 ¼* **Bogaz (IRE)**[24] 1936 2-9-0 .... SSanders 6 55
(RMBeckett) *prom to 1/2-way* **8/1**

5 **9** *½* **Alcharinga (IRE)**[14] 2173 2-9-0 .... DKinsella 7 53
(TJEtherington) *prom to 1/2-way* **33/1**

**10** *2 ½* **Three Strikes (IRE)** 2-8-9 .... OUrbina 9 39
(JRFanshawe) *mid-div: sme hdwy 1/2-way: sn wknd* **10/1**

5 **11** *½* **Cloann (IRE)**[9] 2300 2-8-9 .... RHughes 11 38
(RHannon) *chsd ldrs 3f* **10/1**

**12** *1 ¼* **Monash Lad (IRE)** 2-8-7 .... SaleemGolam(7) 13 38
(MHTompkins) *s.s: outpcd* **50/1**

5 **13** *nk* **Dorn Hill**[14] 2164 2-8-4 .... BSwarbrick(5) 1 32
(MrsMaryHambro) *sn outpcd* **50/1**

**14** *½* **Tit For Tat** 2-8-9 .... RFfrench 8 30
(MJohnston) *dwlt: outpcd* **10/1**

**15** *nk* **Balthasar** 2-9-0 .... JBramhill 18 34
(PABlockley) *sn outpcd* **66/1**

**16** *½* **Indian Smoke** 2-8-11 .... LEnstone(3) 14 33
(JAPickering) *s.i.s: outpcd fnl 3f* **100/1**

**17** *4* **Sastre (IRE)** 2-8-9 .... EAhern 3 14
(PMPhelan) *s.s: outpcd* **66/1**

**18** *3 ½* **Hidden Jewel** 2-9-0 .... WSupple 4 —
(BAMcmahon) *sn outpcd* **33/1**

58.99 secs (-1.94) **Going Correction** -0.45s/f (Firm) **18** Ran SP% **129.6**
Speed ratings: **97,95,93,90,89 89,84,82,81,77 76,74,74,73,72 72,65,60**CSF £156.25 TOTE £31.50: £8.20, £4.10, £3.10; EX 457.40.
**Owner** P Winkworth **Bred** Aidan Fogarty **Trained** Chiddingfold, Surrey

**FOCUS**
This looked decent maiden form and the race is likely to produce winners.

**NOTEBOOK**
**Safari Sunset(IRE)**, by a speedy sire, knew his job on this racecourse debut and ran on strongly once hitting the front to deny the well-touted runner up. He was a rare Flat winner for the yard, let alone juvenile debutant, and is clearly useful. There should be more to come.
**Drum Dance(IRE)** ◆, well regarded by connections who have already introduced a couple of decent juveniles, showed up well for a long way before finding the winner too speedy late on. This was a promising effort and he should have little trouble winning his maiden.
**Empire's Ghodha** is well exposed and the first-time blinkers failed to bring around much improvement.
**Loaderfun(IRE)** made a pleasing debut and is in the right hands to win a similar race.
**Dante's Diamond(IRE)** may find life easier once being able to run in nurseries as he will continue to be vulnerable in this type of contest.
**Belly Dancer(IRE)** was well fancied for this racecourse debut, but found the five furlongs too sharp. He will be capable of better in time.
**Bogaz(IRE)** failed to show any progression from his good debut effort and is another going to be better suited to nurseries.
**Cloann(IRE)** *Official explanation: jockey said filly slipped shortly after the start.*
**Sastre(IRE)** *Official explanation: jockey said filly was left in the stalls and slowly away.*

## 2523 JUNE HALL CLAIMING STKS — 5f 2y

**4:10** (4:11) (F) 2-Y-O — **£3,376** (£1,039; £519; £259) **Stalls** Low

Form — RPR

1 **1** **Key Secret**[21] 2003 2-8-13 .... JFMcDonald(3) 5 63
(MDIUsher) *chsd ldr: led over 1f out: edgd lft ins fnl f: rdn out* **9/2**[3]

04 **2** *1 ¼* **Haroldini (IRE)**[17] 2095 2-8-12 .... BSwarbrick(5) 6 60
(MrsPNDutfield) *hld up: outpcd 3f out: hdwy and swtchd lft fnl f: r.o nr fin* **9/4**[1]

5163 **3** *½* **Von Wessex**[23] 1970 2-8-6 .... CHaddon(7) 1 54
(WGMTurner) *led and hung rt: rdn and hdd over 1f out: unable qck ins fnl f* **10/3**[2]

55 **4** *¾* **Beverley Beau**[32] 1717 2-8-13 .... DaneO'Neill 7 51
(MrsLStubbs) *plld hrd and prom: outpcd 1/2-way: rallied over 1f out: styd on same pce ins fnl f* **10/1**

264 **5** *4* **General Nuisance (IRE)**[21] 1984 2-8-6 .... DerekNolan(7) 2 37
(JSMoore) *s.i.s: sn chsng ldrs: rdn and wknd wl over 1f out* **10/3**[2]

060 **6** *3 ½* **Faithisflying**[6] 2382 2-8-9 .... SSanders 4 21
(CADwyer) *bhd fr 1/2-way* **16/1**

60.40 secs (-0.53) **Going Correction** -0.45s/f (Firm) **6** Ran SP% **110.1**
Speed ratings: **86,84,83,82,75 70**CSF £14.44 TOTE £5.00: £3.00, £2.10; EX 18.40.The winner was claimed by Michael Bell for £14,000.
**Owner** I Sheward **Bred** Barry Minty **Trained** Upper Lambourn, Berks

**FOCUS**
A modest time, even for a contest like this, although the form should prove fairly reliable.

**NOTEBOOK**
**Key Secret**, winner of a claimer on her debut at Wolverhampton, was good enough to follow up on this turf debut. She was claimed for 14,000gns by Michael Bell after the race.
**Haroldini(IRE)** ◆ ideally wants another furlong and will be winning in this grade when getting it.
**Von Wessex** can be used as a form guide for this sort of event as he usually runs his race.
**Beverley Beau** left himself vulnerable in the finish as a result of pulling hard early and will be winning when learning to relax.
**General Nuisance(IRE)** is a poor animal and will need to find a dire race to lose his maiden tag.
**Faithisflying** *Official explanation: jockey said colt hung to the left.*

## 2524 JEANETTE BRASSIL H'CAP — 5f 218y

**4:45** (4:46) (E) (0-75,75) 3-Y-O+ — **£5,629** (£1,732; £866; £433) **Stalls** Low

Form — RPR

-101 **1** **Caustic Wit (IRE)**[25] 1909 6-8-8 **60** .... (p) PMakin(5) 10 73
(MSSaunders) *chsd ldrs: led 1/2-way: rdn and hdd over 1f out: rallied to ld ins fnl f: r.o* **8/1**

0003 **2** *nk* **One Way Ticket**[2] 2477 4-8-10 **57** .... (p) RFfrench 15 69
(JMBradley) *w ldrs: rdn to ld over 1f out: hdd ins fnl f: kpt on* **10/3**[1]

0004 **3** *3 ½* **Brantwood (IRE)**[16] 2118 4-8-11 **58** .... (t) WSupple 8 60
(BAMcmahon) *chsd ldrs: outpcd over 3f out: hdwy over 2f out: styd on* **9/1**

53-0 **4** *nk* **Charlottebutterfly**[27] 1855 4-8-8 **58** .... JFMcDonald(3) 1 59
(TTClement) *sn pushed along in rr: hdwy over 2f out: nt rch ldrs* **20/1**

4001 **5** *shd* **Danakim**[6] 2383 7-7-5 **42** 7ex oh3 .... DFentiman(7) 3 45
(JRWeymes) *led to 1/2-way: sn hung rt: styd on same pce appr fnl f* **5/1**[3]

0400 **6** *1 ½* **Speedfit Free (IRE)**[4] 2421 7-8-2 **49** ow2 .... (p) AnnStokell 12 45
(MissAStokell) *sn outpcd: sme hdwy over 1f out: n.d* **25/1**

34-0 **7** *1 ¼* **Monte Mayor Lad (IRE)**[17] 2091 4-9-3 **64** .... (b) DKinsella 11 56
(DHaydnJones) *s.i.s: hdwy over 3f out: wknd 2f out* **20/1**

00-0 **8** *1* **Toppling**[146] 453 6-8-6 **58** .... BSwarbrick(5) 2 47
(JMBradley) *w ldr to 1/2-way: wknd wl over 1f out* **18/1**

-004 **9** *3 ½* **Hollow Jo**[9] 2303 4-9-7 **68** .... GGibbons 14 47
(JRJenkins) *chsd ldr: rdn over 2f out: sn wknd* **7/2**[2]

-000 **10** *shd* **Super Song**[35] 1451 4-9-2 **70** .... (t) SJDonohoe(7) 6 48
(PDEvans) *s.i.s: a in rr* **33/1**

300- **11** *1 ½* **Baby Barry**[174] 6151 7-8-10 **57** .... (v) JQuinn 9 31
(MrsGSRees) *s.i.s: sn chsng ldrs: wknd 1/2-way* **16/1**

-343 **12** *6* **Wonky Donkey**[35] 1676 3-7-12 **54** .... (t) MHenry 13 10
(SCWilliams) *in tch: hmpd and lost pl over 4f out: sn bhd* **8/1**

1m 11.11s (-2.29) **Going Correction** -0.45s/f (Firm)
**WFA** 3 from 4yo+ 9lb **12** Ran SP% **121.6**
Speed ratings: **97,96,91,91,91 89,87,86,81,81 79,71**CSF £33.99 CT £257.52 TOTE £9.20: £3.10, £1.60, £3.20; EX 44.60.
**Owner** Mrs Sandra Jones **Bred** Gainsborough Stud Management Ltd **Trained** Haydon, Somerset

**FOCUS**
Ordinary stuff, but the winner is in great heart at present and still looks feasibly handicapped.

**NOTEBOOK**
**Caustic Wit(IRE)**, a winner in soft ground at Folkestone earlier in the month, proved too strong and willing for the second and defied a 4lb higher mark. He should continue to run well and still looks feasibly weighted given he won off a mark of 92 back in 2000.
**One Way Ticket** did nothing wrong in defeat but found the winner too strong on the day. He has run well the last twice over six furlongs and wants a step back up to seven - the distance of his sole victory to date.
**Brantwood(IRE)** is still without a win since his debut back in 2002 and remains frustrating.
**Charlottebutterfly** kept on without threatening and remains progressive.
**Danakim**, a winner in selling company latest, ran his race from the front but did himself no favours in hanging right.
**Hollow Jo** shaped with plenty of promise over five last time so it was disappointing the step back up to a more suitable trip did not bring about further progress. *Official explanation: jockey said gelding was unsuited by today's good to firm (firm in places) ground.*
**Wonky Donkey** *Official explanation: jockey said gelding lost his action and appeared unsuited by the going - good to firm (firm in places).*

## 2525 STEVEN ABRAHAM APPRENTICE H'CAP — 1m 3f 183y

**5:15** (5:15) (F) (0-55,54) 4-Y-O+ — **£3,493** (£1,075; £537; £268) **Stalls** High

Form — RPR

53-5 **1** **Trusted Mole (IRE)**[13] 2212 6-8-12 **52** .... BSwarbrick 7 59
(WMBrisbourne) *trckd ldrs: led over 4f out: rdn out* **11/4**[1]

300/ **2** *¾* **Cracow (IRE)**[631] 4481 7-8-5 **45** .... PMakin 4 51
(AMHales) *hld up in tch: rdn and ev ch fr over 1f out: styd on* **16/1**

44-6 **3** *nk* **Glen Vale Walk (IRE)**[10] 2272 7-8-2 **45** .... (b) CHaddon(3) 2 50
(MrsGSRees) *plld hrd and prom: rdn over 2f out: r.o* **8/1**

5-20 **4** *nk* **Tom Bell (IRE)**[44] 1463 4-8-7 **47** .... PPMathers 1 52
(JGMO'Shea) *hld up: hdwy 5f out: rdn over 1f out: r.o* **15/2**[3]

0206 **5** *1 ¾* **Smarter Charter**[3] 2462 11-8-5 **45** oh15 .... KristinStubbs 6 47
(MrsLStubbs) *hld up: hdwy over 2f out: no imp ins fnl f* **10/1**

0001 **6** *nk* **Piste Bleu (FR)**[5] 2408 4-8-6 **51** 6ex .... AMullen(5) 11 53
(RFord) *chsd ldr: rdn and ev ch over 1f out: no ex ins fnl f* **10/3**[2]

1200 **7** *4* **Aveiro (IRE)**[35] 1668 8-8-4 **47** .... DeanWilliams(3) 13 42
(MissGayKelleway) *hld up: rdn over 4f out: n.d* **9/1**

00-6 **8** *6* **Lord Lahar**[10] 2257 5-7-12 **45** .... TO'Brien(7) 12 31
(MRChannon) *plld hrd and prom: wknd over 2f out* **33/1**

050/ **9** *2 1/2* **Pertino**[5] [4503] 8-8-6 **53**....................(p) CWilliams(7) 9 35
(JMJefferson) *hld up: plld hrd: hdwy 5f out: wknd over 3f out* **16/1**

000- **10** *11* **Sherzabad (IRE)**[118] [5359] 7-8-1 **46** oh1 ow1.............. SaleemGolam(5) 3 10
(MissIECraig) *s.i.s: a in rr* **20/1**

50-0 **11** *dist* **Lost Spirit**[18] [2053] 8-8-0 **45** oh5.................... StevenHarrison(5) 5 —
(PWHiatt) *led: hdd & wknd over 4f out: virtually p.u fnl 2f* **16/1**

2m 35.35s (0.67) **Going Correction** -0.15s/f (Firm) **11** Ran SP% **117.1**
Speed ratings: **91,90,90,90,88 88,86,82,80,73** —CSF £48.78 CT £319.48 TOTE £3.20: £1.70, £4.20, £2.60; EX 83.50 Place 6 £650.19, Place 5 £408.37..
**Owner** P G Evans & David Manning Associates **Bred** Patrick Joseph O'Brien **Trained** Great Ness, Shropshire

**FOCUS**
A very slow time for the grade and this looks weak form.

**NOTEBOOK**
**Trusted Mole(IRE)** made a pleasing seasonal debut at the course last time and progressed enough to take this off the same mark. His stable are in decent form at present and he may be capable of winning again, although he was held off higher marks last year.
**Cracow(IRE)**, 14th in the 2000 Derby, was having his first run for 631 days and ran a stormer. His current rating is vastly lower than a couple of years ago and if going the right way from this is up to winning a similar event.
**Glen Vale Walk(IRE)** ran pleasingly and could pick up a small race if learning to settle a little better.
**Tom Bell(IRE)** kept on without posing a threat.
**Piste Bleu(FR)** had every chance but may have found the run coming too soon after her win five days earlier.
**Lost Spirit** *Official explanation: trainer said gelding had a breathing problem.*
T/Plt: £726.00 to a £1 stake. Pool: £25,609.90. 25.75 winning tickets. T/Qpdt: £55.70 to a £1 stake. Pool: £1,528.70. 20.30 winning tickets. CR

## 2213 REDCAR (L-H)
### Monday, May 31

**OFFICIAL GOING: Good to firm (firm in places)**

## 2526 ENTER TODAY'S RACECARD COMPETITION NOVICE AUCTION STKS 5f
**2:00** (2:01) (E) 2-Y-O **£3,503** (£1,078; £539; £269) **Stalls** Centre

Form RPR

412 **1** **Bold Marc (IRE)**[30] [1769] 2-8-13 .................... DarrenWilliams 2 86+
(KRBurke) *trckd ldrs: hdwy 2f out: shkn up to ld over 1f out: edgd lft and qcknd clr* **13/8**[1]

1 **2** *1 3/4* **Melalchrist**[23] [1960] 2-8-13 .................... RWinston 5 77
(JJQuinn) *cl up: rdn 2f out: led briefly over 1f out: kpt on* **9/2**[3]

0 **3** *2 1/2* **Ryedane (IRE)**[19] [2035] 2-8-6 .................... DAllan(3) 1 63
(TDEasterby) *cl up: ev ch 2f out: sn rdn and wknd appr last* **28/1**

2153 **4** *3/4* **Monashee Prince (IRE)**[7] [2370] 2-9-1 .................... NPollard 3 66
(JRBest) *led: rdn along 2f out: drvn and hdd over 1f out* **7/4**[2]

**5** *nk* **Jun Fan (USA)** 2-8-6 .................... TEaves(3) 4 59
(BEllison) *s.i.s and bhd: hdwy 2f out: kpt on ins last* **16/1**

50 **6** *1 1/2* **Uredale (IRE)**[16] [2125] 2-8-9 .................... JCarroll 6 53
(MrsADuffield) *chsd ldrs: rdn along 2f out: sn wknd* **50/1**

**7** *4* **Kimberley Hall** 2-8-4 ow2.................... DeanMcKeown 7 32
(JAGlover) *wnt rt s: sn chsng ldrs on outer: rdn along 1/2-way: sn wknd* **16/1**

59.52 secs (0.82) **Going Correction** -0.05s/f (Good) **7** Ran SP% **109.8**
Speed ratings: **91,88,84,83,82 80,73**CSF £8.63 TOTE £2.40: £1.80, £2.30; EX 6.80.
**Owner** Market Avenue Racing Club 1 **Bred** Eamon D Delany **Trained** Middleham Moor, N Yorks

**FOCUS**
An ordinary pace for this novice auction event, but a fluent winner and the form should prove reliable.

**NOTEBOOK**
**Bold Marc(IRE)**, who had the ground in his favour, got a nice lead from the two leaders and travelled extremely well. Once unleashed, he showed a smart turn of foot to score and should enjoy further success when conditions are in his favour.
**Melalchrist**, on totally different ground compared to his winning debut, was never far away and though swamped by the winner's turn of foot, still deserves some credit for hanging on to second because he had taken a keen hold early.
**Ryedane(IRE)**, on much faster ground than on his debut, did well to finish right amongst the three previous winners and will find an opening at some point.
**Monashee Prince(IRE)** as usual made the running, but not for the first time he finished his race rather weakly. *Official explanation: jockey said colt was unsuited by the going.*
**Jun Fan(USA)**, a 13,000gns yearling who is related to several winners in Australia, had a lot on against previous winners on this debut, but acquitted himself with credit and should come on for the experience.

## 2527 TOTESPORT ZETLAND GOLD CUP (HERITAGE H'CAP) 1m 2f
**2:35** (2:36) (B ) (0-105,102) 3-Y-O+ **£32,500** (£10,000; £5,000; £2,500) **Stalls** Low

Form RPR

-014 **1** **Blue Spinnaker (IRE)**[19] [2044] 5-9-2 **98**.................... PMulrennan(5) 1 111+
(MWEasterby) *hld up towards rr: hdwy on inner over 3f out: nt clr run 2f out: swtchd rt over 1f out: str run ent last: led nr line* **5/1**[2]

62-6 **2** *nk* **James Caird (IRE)**[10] [2278] 4-8-2 **82**.................... FPFerris(3) 4 90
(MHTompkins) *hld up towards rr: hdwy on outer 3f out: rdn to ld over 1f out: drvn and hung lft ins last: hdd and nt qckn nr line* **10/1**

5-03 **3** *shd* **Crow Wood**[25] [1903] 5-9-1 **92**.................... NPollard 7 100
(JGGiven) *trckd ldrs: swtchd rt and hdwy 2f out: rdn and ev ch ins last: kpt on* **11/1**

04-1 **4** *nk* **Zero Tolerance (IRE)**[51] [1321] 4-8-13 **90**.................... DHolland 2 97
(TDBarron) *hld up in midfield: hdwy on inner 3f out: effrt 2f out: cl up whn n.m.r over 1f out: sn rdn and styd on nr fin* **4/1**[1]

0-20 **5** *shd* **Vicious Warrior**[13] [2196] 5-8-8 **85**.................... DeanMcKeown 14 92
(RMWhitaker) *chsd ldr: hdwy to ld 2 1/2f out: sn rdn: hdd over 1f out and grad wknd* **20/1**

150- **6** *1 1/4* **Millafonic**[240] [5365] 4-9-4 **95**.................... ACulhane 9 100
(LMCumani) *hld up in rr: hdwy 3f out: rdn along 2f out: styd on ins last: nrst fin* **11/1**

0-66 **7** *1/2* **Cripsey Brook**[18] [2066] 6-8-9 **86**.................... KimTinkler 12 90
(DonEnricoIncisa) *in tch: hdwy 3f out: rdn 2f out: kpt on same pce* **11/1**

2/00 **8** *1 1/2* **Sir George Turner**[18] [2066] 5-9-9 **100**.................... JFanning 3 101
(MJohnston) *chsd ldrs on inner: rdn along 3f out: drvn and wknd over 1f out* **25/1**

0-06 **9** *shd* **Stretton (IRE)**[13] [2196] 6-8-2 **79**.................... JMackay 5 80
(JDBethell) *hld up in rr: hdwy 3f out: rdn along 2f out and no imp* **8/1**[3]

-610 **10** *2* **Telemachus**[18] [2066] 4-8-13 **90**.................... FLynch 10 87
(JGGiven) *chsd ldrs whn hmpd and squeezed out after 1f: a rr* **25/1**

000- **11** *2* **Castleshane (IRE)**[9] [5468] 7-8-12 **89**.................... RWinston 11 82
(SGollings) *led: rdn along 3f out: sn hdd anmd wkng whn hmpd 2f out* **25/1**

0-00 **12** *nk* **Ulundi**[12] [2220] 9-9-11 **102**.................... PHanagan 8 95
(PRWebber) *in tch: hdwy to chse ldrs 3f out: sn rdn and wknd* **28/1**

4550 **13** *nk* **Bourgainville**[12] [2220] 6-9-6 **102**.................... NChalmers(5) 15 94
(AMBalding) *chsd ldrs: rdn along 3f out: sn wknd* **16/1**

0-20 **14** *nk* **Always Esteemed (IRE)**[18] [2066] 4-9-6 **97**.................... JCarroll 17 89
(GWragg) *hld up in rr: gd hdwy on outer 3f out: rdn and edgd lft wl over 1f out: sn wknd* **16/1**

61-0 **15** *1/2* **Pagan Sky (IRE)**[30] [1762] 5-8-6 **86**.................... LisaJones(3) 13 77
(JARToller) *midfield: effrt 3f out: sn rdn and btn* **16/1**

2m 4.13s (-2.67) **Going Correction** -0.05s/f (Good) **15** Ran SP% **119.3**
Speed ratings: **108,107,107,107,107 106,105,104,104,103 101,101,101,100,100**CSF £49.02 CT £532.96 TOTE £6.00: £2.90, £3.10, £4.10; EX 56.80 Trifecta £249.20 Pool £1,860.70 - 5.30 winning units..
**Owner** G Sparkes G Hart S Curtis & T Dewhirst **Bred** M3 Elevage And Haras D'Etreham **Trained** Sheriff Hutton, N Yorks

**FOCUS**
An ultra-competitive renewal of this famous old race, but not run at a breakneck pace resulting in traffic problems for some and a bunch finish. This is strong handicap form

**NOTEBOOK**
**Blue Spinnaker(IRE)**, whose stamina was unproven coming into this, was content to be dropped out from his rails draw. He travelled well, stalking the favourite Zero Tolerance for much of the way, but it looked as though he was never going to get a run. However, that rival being switched to the inside a furlong from home provided him with the gap he needed and he swooped through it to get up near the line. This was a fine effort by both horse and rider.
**James Caird(IRE)**, all the better for his reappearance effort, had conditions in his favour and ran a blinder. He had to come wide in order to get a run down the home straight, but despite hanging left he hit the front looking the likely winner well over a furlong from home, only to have the race snatched from him. He deserves compensation.
**Crow Wood** ran a cracker and was coming back for more at the line. This was an especially fine effort considering he was off a 13lb higher mark than when filling the same position in this last year, but this effort means he is unlikely to get any respite.
**Zero Tolerance(IRE)** did not see much daylight down the home straight, but once switched to the inside rail ran on strongly to snatch fourth. He cannot be considered unlucky though, as the winner endured a similar trip and came from further back. His previous wins came on soft ground or a slow Fibresand surface, but this does show he can act on fast ground.
**Vicious Warrior** ran a fine race from his high draw and, after losing three places in the last half-furlong, was still only beaten a length by the winner at the line. He is still 3lb higher than for his last win, despite that being 21 months ago, and efforts like this will not help.
**Millafonic** ◆, not seen since finishing down the field in last season's Cambridgeshire, stayed on well despite not getting the clearest of runs and should be placed to advantage before too long.
**Telemachus** got into a spot of bother soon after the start and never really recovered from it.
**Bourgainville** took a keen hold on the outside and ultimately paid for it.
**Always Esteemed(IRE)** could never get any cover from his outside draw and saw too much daylight as a result. A mid-race effort came to little, but he can be forgiven this to a certain extent.

## 2528 GO RACING IN YORKSHIRE ON BANK HOLIDAY (S) STKS 7f
**3:10** (3:11) (F ) 3-5-Y-O **£2,989** (£854; £427) **Stalls** Centre

Form RPR

**1** **Sedge (USA)**[8] 4-9-7 .................... RFitzpatrick 3 62
(PTMidgley) *towards rr and rdn along 1/2-way: hdwy 2f out: swtchd rt and styd on wl ins last to ld on line* **66/1**

-500 **2** *hd* **Silver Seeker (USA)**[7] [2366] 4-9-7 84.................... DHolland 11 61
(ISemple) *a cl up: effrt 2f out: rdn to ld ent last: sn drvn and hdd on line* **5/1**[1]

0-00 **3** *1 1/2* **Tantric**[75] [1039] 5-9-0 60.................... JDO'Reilly(7) 1 57
(JO'Reilly) *chsd ldrs: hdwy on outer 1/2-way: rdn to to ld 2f out: hdd ent last and one pce* **10/1**

5-62 **4** *1/2* **Time To Regret**[7] [2346] 4-9-7 53.................... RWinston 6 56
(JJQuinn) *chsd ldrs: hdwy 2f out: sn rdn and edgd lft over 1f out: one pce* **6/1**[2]

6430 **5** *2* **Weet Watchers**[13] [2215] 4-9-12 56.................... AlexGreaves 8 56
(DNicholls) *led: rdn along and hdd 2f out: grad wknd* **9/1**

0000 **6** *1 1/4* **Wainwright (IRE)**[6] [2391] 4-9-12 60.................... (p) GParkin 14 53
(PABlockley) *chsd ldrs: rdn along 2f out: wknd appr last* **10/1**

0540 **7** *hd* **Libre**[6] [2272] 4-9-7 61.................... (p) DeanMcKeown 13 47
(RCGuest) *bhd: hdwy over 2f out: sn rdn and kpt on in side last: nrst fin* **6/1**[2]

0541 **8** *1/2* **Cayman Breeze**[98] [858] 4-9-12 60.................... ACulhane 5 51
(JMBradley) *bhd tl sme late hdwy* **5/1**[1]

3600 **9** *2 1/2* **Compton Princess**[7] [2346] 4-9-2 39.................... JMackay 12 34
(MrsADuffield) *keen: dwlt and hmpd s: a rr* **33/1**

00-0 **10** *1/2* **Efimac**[28] [1824] 4-8-9 43.................... SuzanneFrance(7) 15 33
(NBycroft) *in tch: rdn along 1/2-way: sn btn* **28/1**

-004 **11** *8* **Beamsley Beacon**[7] [2351] 3-8-10 49.................... (p) NPollard 7 17
(GMMoore) *bhd fr 1/2-way* **14/1**

30-0 **12** *4* **Looking Down**[49] [1358] 4-9-2 67.................... GFaulkner 10 2
(PCHaslam) *s.i.s: hdwy to chse ldrs 1/2-way: rdn along and wknd over 2f out* **15/2**[3]

400- **13** *6* **Matriarchal**[174] [6153] 4-9-2 34.................... KimTinkler 2 —
(DonEnricoIncisa) *a rr* **100/1**

00-0 **14** *1 3/4* **Due Diligence (IRE)**[31] [1748] 5-9-7 45.................... JFanning 9 —
(CWFairhurst) *chsd ldrs: rdn along 1/2-way: sn wknd* **25/1**

1m 24.48s (-0.42) **Going Correction** -0.05s/f (Good) **14** Ran SP% **121.2**
**WFA** 3 from 4yo+ 11lb
Speed ratings: **100,99,98,97,95 93,93,92,90,89 80,75,68,66**CSF £370.68 TOTE £135.90: £36.00, £1.90, £3.60; EX 1633.50.There was no bid for the winner.
**Owner** Peter Mee **Bred** Twin Creeks Farm **Trained** Westow, N Yorks

**FOCUS**
A shock result to this modest seller. The pace was solid enough for a race of its type.

**NOTEBOOK**
**Sedge(USA)**, making his debut on the Flat after finishing down the field in two bumpers, came from off the pace to nail the joint-favourite on the line and cause a real shock. At least he was unexposed compared to his rivals and there seemed no fluke about it.
**Silver Seeker(USA)**, who had upwards of 12lb in hand of his rivals on adjusted official ratings, was taking a massive step down in class and still could not win. On the other hand he was given a positive ride and was only beaten by an unexposed sort, so he could probably win a similar race.
**Tantric**, bounced back to form after a couple of modest efforts on sand and had every chance, but despite plenty of assistance from the saddle was just held. He probably prefers a stiffer seven than this.
**Time To Regret**, still a maiden, had plenty on at the weights and ran as well as could be expected.
**Weet Watchers** was given a positive ride and ran a good deal better than on his first start for his new yard. He should be placed to advantage, but may prefer a bit more cut.
**Cayman Breeze** was well backed to make a winning debut for his new yard, but never got into it and ran as if he needs even further.

**Due Diligence(IRE)** *Official explanation: jockey said gelding had lost his action.*

## 2529 CARLSBERG LAGER H'CAP — 1m 3f

3:45 (3:45) (D) (0-80,77) 3-Y-O — £5,996 (£1,845; £922; £461) Stalls Low

Form — RPR

01-4 **1** **Zeitgeist (IRE)**[35] [1672] 3-9-7 77 ... DHolland 2 87
(LMCumani) *trckd ldrs: hdwy 3f out: rdn to ld wl over 1f out: styd on* **6/4**[1]

23-4 **2** 2 **Silverhay**[23] [1957] 3-8-12 68 ... PHanagan 5 75
(TDBarron) *cl up: led 3f out: sn rdn: drvn and hdd wl over 1f out: kpt on same pce* **13/8**[2]

540- **3** ¾ **Sand And Stars (IRE)**[230] [5556] 3-8-10 69 ... FPFerris(3) 1 74
(MHTompkins) *keen: trckd ldrs: effrt 3f out: rdn over 2f out and kpt on same pce* **20/1**

6-50 **4** hd **Rutters Rebel (IRE)**[25] [1899] 3-9-2 72 ... RWinston 6 77
(GASwinbank) *bhd: hdwy over 3f out: rdn 2f out: kpt on same pce appr last* **14/1**

0-60 **5** 5 **Badr (USA)**[13] [2197] 3-8-9 65 ... JFanning 4 62
(MJohnston) *led: rdn along over 3f out: sn hdd and drvn: wknd wl over 1f out* **9/1**

0-16 **6** 3 **Marine City (JPN)**[25] [1899] 3-9-5 75 ... ACulhane 3 67
(MAJarvis) *chsd ldrs: rdn along 3f out: drvn and wknd 2f out* **15/2**[3]

2m 19.26s (-1.74) **Going Correction** -0.05s/f (Good) 6 Ran SP% **111.3**
Speed ratings: **104,102,102,101,98 96**CSF £4.13 TOTE £2.20: £1.20, £1.30; EX 3.40.
**Owner** L Marinopoulos **Bred** Sir Eric Parker **Trained** Newmarket, Suffolk

**FOCUS**
Only a modest pace for this handicap, although the form looks fairly strong. Two horses dominated the market and they filled the first two places without finishing as far clear as they had seemed likely to.

**NOTEBOOK**
**Zeitgeist(IRE)** did not really have the race run to suit and he was being shoved along from some way out, but he got stronger as the contest progressed and was well on top at the line. A stronger gallop and a greater test of stamina will bring out the best in him.
**Silverhay**, stepping up markedly in trip, had every chance but did not see the distance out as well as the winner. He should be able to break his duck in a similar contest over a bit shorter.
**Sand And Stars(IRE)**, returning from an eight-month break, making her handicap debut and stepping up three furlongs in trip, may have done too much too soon but should come on for the run.
**Rutters Rebel(IRE)** would definitely have preferred a stronger gallop. *Official explanation: jockey said gelding hung left all the way.*
**Badr(USA)** was able to lead at his own pace, yet still put in another disappointing effort.

## 2530 STOKESLEY MEDIAN AUCTION MAIDEN STKS — 6f

4:20 (4:23) (E) 3-Y-O — £3,474 (£1,069; £534; £267) Stalls Centre

Form — RPR

23-0 **1** **Snow Wolf**[9] [2303] 3-9-0 76 ... DHolland 1 76
(JMBradley) *mde all: rdn wl over 1f out: styd on wl* **10/11**[1]

03-2 **2** 2½ **Flying Bantam (IRE)**[23] [1975] 3-9-0 71 ... PHanagan 5 69
(RAFahey) *cl up: effrt 2f out: sn rdn and kpt on* **6/4**[2]

**3** 2½ **Otago (IRE)** 3-9-0 ... NPollard 6 61
(JRBest) *trckd ldrs: hdwy to chse ldng pair 2f out: sn rdn and one pce appr last* **14/1**[3]

- **4** shd **Key Factor** 3-8-4 ... PMulrennan(5) 4 56
(MWEasterby) *dwlt: in rr: hdwy over 2f out: rdn over 1f out: kpt on ins last: nrst fin* **20/1**

000- **5** 7 **Borodinsky**[205] [5947] 3-8-11 ... TEaves(3) 3 40
(REBarr) *chsd ldrs: rdn along 1/2-way: sn wknd* **50/1**

4-60 **6** 8 **Balwearie (IRE)**[10] [2259] 3-9-0 62 ... (p) JCarroll 2 16
(MissLAPerratt) *chsd ldrs: rdn along 1/2-way: sn wknd* **16/1**

1m 11.41s (-0.29) **Going Correction** -0.05s/f (Good) 6 Ran SP% **111.7**
Speed ratings: **99,95,92,92,82 72**CSF £2.44 TOTE £1.90: £1.10, £1.20; EX 2.30.
**Owner** E A Hayward **Bred** Mrs S Thomson Jones **Trained** Sedbury, Gloucs

**FOCUS**
An uncompetitive maiden dominated by the front two in the market, but a fair time for the grade.

**NOTEBOOK**
**Snow Wolf**, who showed ability against his elders in a 0 to 80 handicap last time, would have bolted on his way to post given half a chance but fortunately he did not, though he did get very warm. His rider wisely let him stride on leaving the stalls and he was never really in much danger. Considering he had plenty in hand on official ratings, he should not go up for this.
**Flying Bantam(IRE)** keeps on finding one too good, but he had 5lb to find with the winner on official ratings and so probably ran to form.
**Otago(IRE)**, who fetched 30,000gns as a two-year-old, has speed in his pedigree and emerged best of the newcomers, although what she actually achieved must be open to question.
**Key Factor** is another with speed in her pedigree, but she ran as though she will get further than this and should do better in time.

## 2531 REDCAR H'CAP — 1m 6f 19y

4:55 (4:55) (E) (0-70,61) 3-Y-O+ — £3,474 (£1,069; £534; £267) Stalls Low

Form — RPR

-010 **1** **Best Port (IRE)**[16] [2126] 8-9-2 58 ... MLawson(5) 2 67
(JParkes) *hld up in rr: smooth hdwy over 2f out: led in bit over 1f out: sn clr* **9/2**[2]

6-00 **2** 5 **Party Ploy**[16] [2116] 6-9-6 57 ... DarrenWilliams 4 59
(KRBurke) *hld up in tch: hdwy 4f out: led wl over 2f out: sn rdn and hdd over 1f out: one pce* **7/2**[1]

2314 **3** ½ **Next Flight (IRE)**[19] [2038] 5-9-1 52 ... DHolland 1 53
(REBarr) *led to 1/2-way: cl up and rdn to ld again over 3f out: drvn and hdd wl over 2f out: kpt on same pce* **9/2**[2]

0303 **4** ½ **Spitting Image (IRE)**[7] [2354] 4-9-10 61 ... ACulhane 3 62
(MrsMReveley) *trckd ldrs: hdwy on outer over 3f out and sn ev ch: rdn 2f out and sn one pce* **5/1**[3]

4-40 **5** 5 **Morvern (IRE)**[59] [1238] 4-8-11 48 ... JFanning 7 42
(JGGiven) *prom: effrt and ev ch 3f out: sn rdn and wknd* **12/1**

5/05 **6** 4 **Almnadia (IRE)**[11] [2249] 5-8-11 48 ... (p) RWinston 6 36
(SGollings) *trckd ldrs: hdwy to ld 1/2-way: rdn along whn bumped and hdd over 3f out: sn wknd* **9/1**

0503 **7** 4 **Call Me Sunshine**[14] [2174] 4-9-8 59 ... GFaulkner 8 41
(PCHaslam) *hld up: hdwy 4f out: rdn along 3f out and sn btn* **8/1**

-104 **8** 15 **Green 'N' Gold**[11] [2249] 4-9-6 57 ... PHanagan 5 18
(MDHammond) *chsd ldrs: hdwy and cl up 5f out: rdn and wknd 4f out* **9/1**

00-5 **9** 11 **Tioga Gold (IRE)**[25] [1914] 5-7-12 35 ... JMackay 9 —
(LRJames) *a bhd: t.o fnl 4f* **33/1**

3m 3.03s (-1.97) **Going Correction** -0.05s/f (Good) 9 Ran SP% **117.0**
Speed ratings: **103,100,99,99,96 94,92,83,77**CSF £20.96 CT £75.25 TOTE £6.40: £2.30, £2.20, £1.90; EX 20.10 Place 6 £21.52 Place 5 £11.61..
**Owner** M Wormald **Bred** Lord Harrington **Trained** Upper Helmsley, N Yorks

**FOCUS**
A modest handicap, run at a sound pace.

**NOTEBOOK**
**Best Port(IRE)** loves it here and stays extremely well, so all he needed was a decent pace and he got that. He could be called the winner some way out and when asked to go and win his race, found more than enough. This was the highest mark he has ever won off.
**Party Ploy**, still 3lb higher than for his last win, had every chance, but he is yet to win over this trip and was basically outstayed.
**Next Flight(IRE)**, given a positive ride, had every chance but was done for foot over the last couple of furlongs. He may be better on softer ground.
**Spitting Image(IRE)** likes this ground, but still appears to need a greater test of stamina than this. She remains a maiden after 20 attempts.
**Morvern(IRE)** is steadily dropping down the handicap, but did not progress much with the visor left off.
**Almnadia(IRE)** found this a totally insufficient test and was already feeling the pinch when meeting interference three furlongs from home.
**Green 'N' Gold** is a much better horse on soft ground and so can be forgiven this. *Official explanation: jockey said filly was unsuited by the going.*
T/Plt: £30.40 to a £1 stake. Pool: £37,553.15. 899.40 winning tickets. T/Qpdt: £8.20 to a £1 stake. Pool: £2,344.20. 209.60 winning tickets. JR

# 1621 SANDOWN (R-H)

Monday, May 31

**OFFICIAL GOING: Good to firm (firm in places on sprint course)**
Wind: nil Weather: sunny & warm

## 2532 BONUSPRINT.COM NATIONAL STKS (LISTED RACE) — 5f 6y

1:45 (1:53) (A) 2-Y-O — £14,500 (£5,500; £2,750; £1,250) Stalls High

Form — RPR

1 **1** **Polly Perkins (IRE)**[14] [2173] 2-8-7 ... KDarley 2 93
(NPLittmoden) *s.s: racd in last pair: effrt on outer and bmpd over 1f out: drvn and r.o to ld last 100yds: sn clr* **25/1**

21 **2** 1½ **Moscow Music**[24] [1936] 2-9-1 ... SDrowne 1 96
(MGQuinlan) *lw: trckd ldrs: effrt over 1f out: drvn to chal ins fnl f: outpcd by wnr last 100yds* **9/1**[3]

1 **3** nk **Bunditten (IRE)**[72] [1060] 2-8-12 ... JFEgan 5 92
(AndrewReid) *b: b.hind: mde most: rdn 2f out: hdd and one pce last 100yds* **33/1**

332 **4** 1 **Alpaga Le Jomage (IRE)**[26] [1884] 2-8-12 ... KFallon 3 88
(BJMeehan) *pressed ldr: rdn 2f out: ev ch ent fnl f: one pce* **20/1**

13 **5** nk **Next Time Around (IRE)**[48] [1383] 2-9-3 ... MFenton 6 92
(MrsLStubbs) *lw: hanging rt thrght: in rr: styd on fnl f: nt rch ldrs* **20/1**

21 **6** shd **Indiannie Star**[6] [2376] 2-8-7 ... TEDurcan 7 82
(MRChannon) *trckd ldrs gng easily: plld out and bmpd wnr over 1f out: sn rdn and nt qckn* **8/1**[2]

01 **7** ½ **Celtic Spa (IRE)**[24] [1943] 2-8-7 ... RHavlin 4 80
(MrsPNDutfield) *s.v.s and lost 5l: hanging rt thrght: hmpd over 3f out: effrt to chse ldrs 1f out: wknd ins fnl f* **33/1**

11 **8** 3 **Prince Charming**[33] [1707] 2-9-3 ... LDettori 8 80
(JHMGosden) *lw: trckd ldrs: rdn 1/2-way: nt qckn over 1f out: btn whn squeezed out ins fnl f* **4/11**[1]

61.65 secs (-0.54) **Going Correction** -0.05s/f (Good) 8 Ran SP% **113.7**
Speed ratings: **102,99,99,97,97 96,96,91**CSF £203.04 TOTE £17.70: £3.50, £1.30, £5.70; EX 175.80.
**Owner** Miss Vanessa Church **Bred** David John Brown **Trained** Newmarket, Suffolk
■ Stewards Enquiry : T E Durcan two-day ban: careless riding (Jun 11,12)

**FOCUS**
Maybe not the strongest of Listed races, but very competitive nonetheless.

**NOTEBOOK**
**Polly Perkins(IRE)**, who justified favouritism when making a winning debut at Musselburgh, followed up with a decisive success. She had to overcome getting bumped at a crucial stage and is a really tough sort, but she may just find a couple too good in the Queen Mary, her next target.
**Moscow Music**, who won his maiden at Lingfield despite the soft ground, ran a cracker on this step up in grade, but the winner was just too strong. He should get six furlongs and there could be a similar race in him, possibly abroad.
**Bunditten(IRE)** had not been seen since making a winning debut in the first juvenile contest of the season, a race that has not really worked out. Racing for the first time in 72 days, she showed plenty of speed and would be of interest for a similar contest on more of a speed track.
**Alpaga Le Jomage(IRE)** was disappointing in a maiden at Chester on his previous start, but this faster surface suited better and he ran a fine race. He should win his maiden before stepping back up in grade.
**Next Time Around(IRE)** ran very respectably, but has not really progressed as well as one might have expected from his Brocklesby success and he could struggle to add to that under his penalty. Not for the first time, he was noted to be hanging. *Official explanation: jockey said colt had hung badly right throughout.*
**Indiannie Star** can be rated better than the bare form, for she took quite a bump when switched out for her run and could not recover.
**Celtic Spa(IRE)** lost her chance with a slow start. *Official explanation: jockey said filly hung right handed throughout.*
**Prince Charming**, successful on his first two starts, was far too short to complete the hat-trick on this step up in grade and ran as though something was amiss. He is better than this, but how much is anyone's guess. *Official explanation: jockey said colt hung badly right handed throughout.*

## 2533 BONUSPRINT.COM HENRY II STKS (GROUP 2) — 2m 78y

2:20 (2:23) (A) 4-Y-O+ — £63,220 (£23,980; £11,990; £5,450) Stalls High

Form — RPR

5-1 **1** **Papineau**[12] [2220] 4-8-12 111 ... (t) LDettori 2 117
(SaeedBinSuroor) *gd sort: lw: prom: trckd ldr over 2f out: pushed into ld wl over 1f out: edgd rt fnl f: kpt on* **9/4**[2]

16-4 **2** 1½ **Mr Dinos (IRE)**[18] [2067] 5-9-5 122 ... KFallon 7 120
(PFICole) *lw: prom: rdn and outpcd 3f out: rallied to chse wnr ent fnl f: styng on whn n.m.r and snatched up 100yds out* **2/1**[1]

401- **3** 1½ **New South Wales**[206] [5942] 4-8-12 105 ... (t) KMcEvoy 5 113
(SaeedBinSuroor) *lw: led for 1f: trckd ldr: led again wl over 2f out: hdd wl over 1f out: one pce after* **20/1**

0-21 **4** ¾ **Risk Seeker**[33] [1703] 4-8-12 ... DBoeuf 9 112
(ELellouche, France) *settled in midfield: effrt over 2f out: chsd ldrs over 1f out: no imp ins fnl f* **4/1**[3]

-30P **5** 2 **Hilbre Island**[33] [1703] 4-8-12 110 ... MHills 4 110
(BJMeehan) *lw: hld up in last trio: rdn 4f out: effrt u.p over 2f out: one pce and no imp* **66/1**

1-02 **6** 1¼ **Misternando**[26] [1880] 4-8-12 105 ... SHitchcott 3 108
(MRChannon) *in tch: rdn 4f out: no imp ldrs over 2f out: one pce after* **8/1**

01/5 **7** shd **Royal Rebel**[33] [1703] 8-9-0 112 ... JPMurtagh 8 108
(MJohnston) *midfield: rdn 4f out: sn outpcd and dropped to last pair: no ch after: kpt on ins fnl f* **20/1**



The Form Book, Raceform Ltd, Compton, RG20 6NL

5-04 **8** 2 1/2 **Savannah Bay**[16] 2108 5-9-0 111........................................(b) TEDurcan 1 105
(BJMeehan) *rousted along to ld after 1f: hdd wl over 2f out: wknd over 1f out* **33/1**

31-0 **P** **Shanty Star (IRE)**[18] 2067 4-8-12 105........................................ KDarley 10 —
(MJohnston) *s.s: a last: rdn 4f out: wknd 3f out: t.o whn p.u and dismunted jst bef fin* **16/1**

3m 34.17s (-4.06) **Going Correction** -0.05s/f (Good)
**WFA** 4 from 5yo+ 2lb **9** Ran SP% **115.1**
Speed ratings: **108,107,106,106,105 104,104,103,—**CSF £6.77 TOTE £3.40: £1.50, £1.60, £5.00; EX 7.70.
**Owner** Godolphin **Bred** Exors Of The Late Peter Winfield **Trained** Newmarket, Suffolk
■ Stewards Enquiry : L Dettori two-day ban: careless riding (Jun 11,12)

**FOCUS**
A competitive renewal of the Henry II Stakes that provided us with some clues for the forthcoming Ascot Gold Cup, but there was no end-to-end gallop on and the time was modest for a Group Two.

**NOTEBOOK**
**Papineau**, a clear-cut winner of a good conditions race on his debut for Godolphin over a mile and a half at Goodwood, coped well with the step up both in class and trip. He is flattered by the winning margin as the runner-up had to be snatched up at a vital stage, but he is progressing and is well worth his place in the Ascot Gold Cup field. His stamina for the two and a half-mile trip rather than his ability will be a question mark there.
**Mr Dinos(IRE)** was disappointing on his reappearance in the Yorkshire Cup, but he was well backed to return to form and ran better. He would have been closer had the winner not cut across him close home, but it did not affect the result. This should put him spot on for a repeat bid in the Gold Cup.
**New South Wales** never really fulfilled his potential in four runs last year, but this run offered plenty of promise. He lacked the change of pace shown by his stablemate, but kept on and could well run a big race in the Gold Cup.
**Risk Seeker**, a runaway winner of the Sagaro Stakes on awful ground at Ascot on his previous start, ran respectably but was not good enough on this surface.
**Hilbre Island** appreciated this better ground, but never really threatened the principals.
**Misternando** deserved another crack at Group company given the way he has improved in handicaps, but he was a little disappointing. He travelled better than he sometimes does and that may actually have played against him. He can be given another chance.
**Royal Rebel** did not show a great deal, but the Gold Cup is his aim and a third success in that very race cannot be ruled out.
**Shanty Star(IRE)** showed nothing in the Yorkshire Cup on his return from nearly a year off on his previous start and again ran as though something is troubling him. He is one to avoid, but do not be surprised if Johnston nurses him back.

## 2534 DOUBLEPRINT H'CAP 1m 14y
2:55 (2:58) (B ) (0-105,102) 3-Y-0+ **£15,413** (£5,846; £2,923; £1,328) **Stalls** High

Form RPR

0-63 **1** **Putra Kuantan**[30] 1762 4-9-3 **94**........................................ PRobinson 13 109
(MAJarvis) *lw: led for 1f: trckd ldr: led again wl over 1f out: 3l clr and wl in command fnl f: drvn out* **5/2**[1]

2-00 **2** 2 **Impeller (IRE)**[13] 2201 5-8-10 **87**........................................ SDrowne 6 97
(WRMuir) *lw: t.k.h: hld up bhd ldrs: effrt over 2f out: chsd wnr over 1f out: no imp: jst hld on for 2nd* **13/2**[2]

4-05 **3** *nk* **Finished Article (IRE)**[13] 2201 7-8-13 **90**........................................ KDarley 9 99
(DRCElsworth) *lw: hld up in rr: rdn over 2f out: prog wl over 1f out: styd on fnl f* **15/2**[3]

2001 **4** 1/2 **Blue Trojan (IRE)**[10] 2271 4-8-7 **84**........................................ JFEgan 2 92
(SKirk) *racd on outer in midfield: rdn wl over 2f out: prog to chse ldrs over 1f out: styd on same pce* **9/1**

-400 **5** *nk* **Our Teddy (IRE)**[13] 2201 4-8-10 **87**........................................(b[1]) MartinDwyer 3 94
(AMBalding) *dwlt: racd wl in rr: rdn over 2f out: prog over 1f out: styd on wl fnl f: nrst fin* **33/1**

1110 **6** *hd* **Consonant (IRE)**[25] 1903 7-8-13 **90**........................................ KFallon 8 97
(DGBridgwater) *prom: rdn over 2f out: styd on same pce u.p fr over 1f out* **16/1**

12-0 **7** 1 **King Carnival (USA)**[12] 2224 3-8-3 **92**........................................ RSmith 4 97
(RHannon) *t.k.h: hld up towards rr: effrt over 2f out: hanging rt over 1f out: shuffled along and kpt on* **66/1**

-000 **8** *hd* **Calcutta**[9] 2283 8-9-5 **96**........................................ MHills 1 100
(BWHills) *hld up in last trio: effrt on outer over 2f out: chsd ldrs over 1f out: one pce after* **12/1**

13-0 **9** 1 1/4 **Excellento (USA)**[19] 2044 4-9-11 **102**........................................ LDettori 7 103
(SaeedBinSuroor) *led after 1f: shkn up and hdd wl over 1f out: wknd and eased ins fnl f* **10/1**

10-0 **10** *hd* **Chinkara**[44] 1456 4-8-12 **92**........................................ LPKeniry[(3)] 11 93
(BJMeehan) *hld up towards rr: effrt over 2f out: hanging rt fnl 2f: no real prog* **16/1**

00-1 **11** *nk* **Highland Reel**[13] 2201 7-8-10 **87**........................................ JPMurtagh 10 87
(DRCElsworth) *hld up in last pair: rdn and no prog wl over 2f out: n.d after* **14/1**

6-00 **12** 2 **Convent Girl (IRE)**[19] 2044 4-9-3 **94**........................................ RHavlin 5 90
(MrsPNDutfield) *lw: dwlt: sn prom: wknd wl over 1f out* **12/1**

140- **13** *shd* **Binanti**[255] 5041 4-9-0 **91**........................................ MFenton 12 86
(PRChamings) *hld up in midfield: rdn and wkng whn n.m.r on inner wl over 1f out* **33/1**

-011 **14** 3 **Lifted Way**[24] 1935 5-8-3 **80**........................................ KMcEvoy 14 68
(PRChamings) *lw: stmbld s: sn pressed ldrs: wknd 2f out* **9/1**

1m 41.99s (-1.93) **Going Correction** -0.05s/f (Good)
**WFA** 3 from 4yo+ 12lb **14** Ran SP% **124.0**
Speed ratings: **107,105,104,104,103 103,102,102,101,101 100,98,98,95**CSF £17.89 CT £116.54 TOTE £3.20: £1.90, £2.40, £2.90; EX 27.40 Trifecta £128.20 Pool £2,312.37 - 12.80 winning units..
**Owner** H R H Sultan Ahmad Shah **Bred** John Warren **Trained** Newmarket, Suffolk

**FOCUS**
Traditionally the Whitsun Cup, this looked like quite a competitive handicap, but Putra Kuantan ran out a clear-cut winner.

**NOTEBOOK**
**Putra Kuantan** had never previously run over a trip shorter than ten furlongs, but he was well supported and absolutely bolted up. He must go very close in the Royal Hunt Cup in which he will carry a penalty for this success.
**Impeller(IRE)**, 4lb higher than when last successful, can have no excuses this time, the winner was just far too good.
**Finished Article(IRE)** was again doing his best work at the finish and is surely worth another chance over ten furlongs.
**Blue Trojan(IRE)**, 6lb higher than when scoring at Haydock on his previous start, did not look to have any excuses.
**Our Teddy(IRE)** ran better in the first-time blinkers and would appear to be coming to hand.
**Lifted Way** *Official explanation: jockey said horse ran too freely early on.*

## 2535 BONUSPRINT EUROPEAN BREEDERS FUND MAIDEN FILLIES' STKS 5f 6y
3:30 (3:32) (D ) 2-Y-0 **£4,875** (£1,500; £750; £375) **Stalls** High

Form RPR

**1** **Jewel In The Sand (IRE)** 2-8-11........................................ PDobbs 3 80
(RHannon) *neat: lw: pressed ldr: led over 1f out: edgd rt u.p ins fnl f: styd on wl* **9/1**

5 **2** 3/4 **Touch Of Silk (IRE)**[14] 2177 2-8-11........................................ MHills 5 77
(BWHills) *trckd ldrs: effrt on inner over 1f out: pressed wnr ins fnl f: hld last 75yds* **7/2**[2]

**3** 2 **Liwa's Lake (USA)** 2-8-11........................................ LDettori 4 69
(SaeedBinSuroor) *rangy: scope: led: shkn up and hdd over 1f out: hld whn squeezed out last 150yds* **5/4**[1]

0 **4** 2 1/2 **Heidi's Dash (IRE)**[18] 2057 2-8-11........................................ SDrowne 2 59
(RCharlton) *chsd ldrs: drvn 2f out: fdd over 1f out* **5/1**[3]

**5** 1/2 **Xeeran** 2-8-11........................................ PRobinson 7 57
(MAJarvis) *leggy: scope: s.i.s: t.k.h and hld up: rdn 2f out: wknd fnl f* **11/2**

0 **6** 7 **Chutney Mary (IRE)**[35] 1670 2-8-11........................................ KDarley 6 29
(JGPortman) *dwlt: a last: hung bdly lft fr 1/2-way: bhd over 1f out* **25/1**

62.36 secs (0.17) **Going Correction** -0.05s/f (Good) **6** Ran SP% **112.6**
Speed ratings: **96,94,91,87,86 75**CSF £40.16 TOTE £9.70: £3.40, £1.90; EX 27.90.
**Owner** Sand Associates **Bred** Gerrardstown House Stud **Trained** East Everleigh, Wilts

**FOCUS**
Hard to know what to make of this maiden as only two of the six runners had previous experience (both appeared to post improved performances), but it was probably a reasonable contest.

**NOTEBOOK**
**Jewel In The Sand(IRE)** is a 65,000euros yearling, half-sister to a six-furlong Listed winner in Germany, and to a five-furlong juvenile winner, out of a useful six-furlong two-year-old scorer. She made a very pleasing debut, showing the right attitude when challenged by the eventual runner-up, but still shaping as though there is plenty of room for improvement. She could now head to Royal Ascot for the six-furlong Albany Stakes and will be worthy of respect.
**Touch Of Silk(IRE)** shaped well on her debut from a poor draw at Windsor and ran another encouraging race. She travelled as well as anything and held every chance when in the clear, but the winner was just too good. There is a similar race in her.
**Liwa's Lake(USA)**, a $300,000 purchase, out of a half-sister to a Grade One winner, made a respectable debut. She proved no match for the front two close home, but should progress and go a couple of places better before too much longer.
**Heidi's Dash(IRE)** stepped up on the form she showed on her debut and would appear to be going the right way.
**Xeeran**, a 60,000gns yearling, half-sister to dual five-furlong two-year-old winner Autumn Pearl, out of a five-furlong winner, raced too keenly to do herself justice and is probably capable of much better.
**Chutney Mary(IRE)** *Official explanation: jockey said filly hung badly left handed.*

## 2536 TRIPLEPRINT H'CAP 7f 16y
4:05 (4:05) (D ) (0-80,79) 3-Y-0 **£5,759** (£1,772; £886; £443) **Stalls** High

Form RPR

0006 **1** **Distant Connection (IRE)**[12] 2224 3-8-12 **70**........................................ KMcEvoy 8 77
(APJarvis) *lw: pressed ldr: drvn to chal 2f out: led 1f out: jst hld on* **6/1**

-525 **2** *shd* **Pizazz**[16] 2114 3-9-7 **79**........................................ MHills 2 86
(BJMeehan) *hld up in rr: plenty to do 2f out: rdn and gd prog jst over 1f out: styd on strly nr fin: jst failed* **10/1**

600- **3** 1 1/4 **Love Triangle (IRE)**[232] 5503 3-9-4 **79**........................................ LPKeniry[(3)] 4 82
(DRCElsworth) *bit bkwd: prom: rdn to chal 2f out: unable qck over 1f out: kpt on* **14/1**

0-02 **4** *nk* **Pink Sapphire (IRE)**[9] 2284 3-9-1 **73**........................................ JPMurtagh 6 76
(DRCElsworth) *swtg: b.hind: chsd ldrs: rdn over 2f out: unable qck over 1f out: kpt on ins fnl f* **9/2**[2]

1-52 **5** *hd* **Missus Links (USA)**[17] 2082 3-8-13 **71**........................................ KDarley 12 73
(RHannon) *lw: led: hrd pressed fr over 2f out: hdd 1f out: fdd nr fin* **5/1**[3]

050- **6** 3/4 **Kinbrace**[269] 4705 3-8-3 **61**........................................ MartinDwyer 1 61
(MPTregoning) *dwlt: hld up in last trio: pushed along on wd outside 3f out: styd on fr over 1f out: nvr nrr* **10/1**

-120 **7** *hd* **Whitgift Rock**[47] 1392 3-9-3 **75**........................................ JFEgan 13 75
(SDow) *lw: chsd ldrs: drvn over 2f out: unable qck wl over 1f out: one pce after* **14/1**

-413 **8** *nk* **Andaluza (IRE)**[16] 2112 3-9-0 **72**........................................ KFallon 10 71
(PDCundell) *racd in midfield: drvn 3f out: one pce and nvr rchd ldrs* **10/3**[1]

50-0 **9** 1 3/4 **Nine Red**[16] 2112 3-7-10 **61**........................................ KMay[(7)] 5 55
(BWHills) *hld up in last trio: pushed along over 2f out: kpt on one pce: no ch* **16/1**

26-6 **10** *shd* **Wizard Looking**[9] 2304 3-8-11 **69**........................................(t) PDobbs 9 63
(RHannon) *hld up in rr: effrt on inner and nt clr run 3f out: n.d after: kpt on* **20/1**

0000 **11** *hd* **Sworn To Secrecy**[7] 2371 3-8-6 **64**........................................(b[1]) SDrowne 7 58
(SKirk) *hld up in rr: sme prog 3f out: no imp ldrs over 1f out* **33/1**

05-6 **12** 2 1/2 **La Professoressa (IRE)**[4] 2425 3-8-8 **66**........................................ RHavlin 3 53
(MrsPNDutfield) *racd in midfield: drvn wl over 2f out: nt qckn u.p wl over 1f out: fdd* **33/1**

1m 29.98s (-1.11) **Going Correction** -0.05s/f (Good) **12** Ran SP% **120.3**
Speed ratings: **104,103,102,102,101 101,100,100,98,98 98,95**CSF £64.33 CT £820.36 TOTE £7.40: £2.30, £3.70, £4.20; EX 91.50.
**Owner** Mrs Ann Jarvis **Bred** Mrs C F Van Straubenzee And Partners **Trained** Twyford, Bucks

**FOCUS**
A competitive enough handicap, but probably just ordinary form.

**NOTEBOOK**
**Distant Connection(IRE)** ran well from out of the handicap in a similar event at Goodwood on his previous start and confirmed that to gain his first ever success at the tenth attempt. There was nothing in it at the line, but he appears capable of further progression.
**Pizazz** was disappointing in a maiden at Newbury on his previous start, but this was a better effort. He clearly has the ability to win a race and it will be disappointing if he is not found an opportunity.
**Love Triangle(IRE)**, racing for the first time in 232 days, looked as though the run would bring him on a little so this was an encouraging return.
**Pink Sapphire(IRE)** ran a solid race, but shaped as though she may be better over another furlong. She fared best of the fillies.
**Missus Links(USA)** appeared to be found out by this step up from six furlongs.

## 2537 BONUSPRINT H'CAP 1m 2f 7y
4:40 (4:40) (D ) (0-80,80) 4-Y-0+ **£5,733** (£1,764; £882; £441) **Stalls** High

Form RPR

521- **1** **Faayej (IRE)**[281] 4403 4-9-12 **78**........................................ RHills 14 86
(SirMichaelStoute) *lw: settled in midfield: smooth prog over 2f out: led ent fnl f: shkn up and edgd rt: styd on wl* **6/1**[2]

0314 **2** 1/2 **True Companion**[24] 1928 5-9-2 **71**........................................ J-PGuillambert[(3)] 7 78
(NPLittmoden) *hld up towards rr: rdn over 2f out: prog over 1f out: styd on wl fnl f to take 2nd nr fin* **12/1**

2130 **3** *nk* **Icannshift (IRE)**[9] [2302] 4-7-13 **54** .................... RMiles(3) 5 61
(SDow) *led and set gd pce: rdn 2f out: hdd ent fnl f: kpt on wl* **25/1**

-402 **4** *nk* **Lady McNair**[5] [2403] 4-9-8 **74** .................... KFallon 12 80
(PDCundell) *trckd ldrs: rdn wl over 2f out: n.m.r on inner over 1f out: styd on but nvr able to chal* **9/2**[1]

214- **5** *nk* **Tender Falcon**[284] [4311] 4-9-1 **67** .................... JPMurtagh 4 72
(RJHodges) *pressed ldr: drvn fr wl over 2f out: unable qck wl over 1f out: kpt on again ins fnl f* **20/1**

6050 **6** *nk* **Aoninch**[14] [2167] 4-8-5 **57** ow1 .................... RHavlin 3 62
(MrsPNDutfield) *stdd s: hld up in last and wl off the pce: prog on outer over 2f out: rdn and styd on fr over 1f out: nrst fin* **20/1**

51-0 **7** *nk* **Best Be Going (IRE)**[44] [1460] 4-9-10 **76** .................... TEDurcan 6 80
(PWHarris) *lw: chsd ldrs: rdn over 2f out: effrt u.p over 1f out: styd on same pce fnl f* **9/1**

3003 **8** *2* **Barry Island**[9] [2305] 5-9-11 **77** .................... KDarley 11 77
(DRCElsworth) *hld up wl in rr and wl off the pce: effrt 3f out: prog to chse ldrs over 1f out: no imp after* **7/1**[3]

4-00 **9** *3½* **Welcome Stranger**[13] [2201] 4-9-11 **77** .................... JTate 8 71
(JMPEustace) *chsd ldrs: hrd rdn 3f out: wknd over 1f out* **12/1**

1323 **10** *3* **Blazing The Trail (IRE)**[9] [2302] 4-9-1 **67** .................... MHills 2 55
(JWHills) *settled wl in rr and wl off the pce: shkn up and sme prog into midfield 2f out: fdd over 1f out* **7/1**[3]

00-0 **11** *1¼* **Deewaar (IRE)**[27] [1856] 4-7-7 **50** oh3 .................... DFox(5) 13 36
(JCFox) *b: settled wl in rr and wl off the pce: rdn 3f out: no prog fnl 2f* **100/1**

2500 **12** *nk* **Learned Lad (FR)**[24] [1935] 6-8-4 **56** .................... JFEgan 9 41
(JamiePoulton) *hld up wl in rr and wl off the pce: rdn and no prog 3f out* **16/1**

-405 **13** *1½* **Dream Magic**[17] [2084] 6-9-11 **77** .................... MartinDwyer 1 59
(MJRyan) *pressed ldng pair: rdn over 3f out: wknd 2f out* **7/1**[3]

1530 **14** *nk* **Jools**[10] [2278] 6-9-7 **80** .................... MHoward(7) 10 62
(DKIvory) *b.hind: settled towards rr: shkn up 3f out: sn struggling* **16/1**

-000 **15** *2* **Kirov King (IRE)**[11] [2235] 4-9-1 **70** .................... LPKeniry(3) 15 48
(BGPowell) *racd in midfield: rdn over 3f out: wknd 2f out* **25/1**

2m 8.34s (-1.84) **Going Correction** -0.05s/f (Good) **15** Ran SP% **125.3**
Speed ratings: **105,104,104,104,103 103,103,101,99,96 95,95,94,93,92**CSF £73.66 CT £1713.93 TOTE £5.30: £3.90, £3.40, £4.30; EX 91.80 Place 6 £1,426.65, Place 5 £161.72..
**Owner** Hamdan Al Maktoum **Bred** Orpendale And Dr M V O'Brien **Trained** Newmarket, Suffolk
■ Stewards Enquiry : R Hills one-day ban: careless riding (Jun 11)

**FOCUS**
A competitive handicap in which the first seven home finished on top of each other.

**NOTEBOOK**
**Faayej(IRE)** did not really impress when winning his maiden at Beverley on his final start at three, but his current connections kept hold of him for a reason and he repaid the faith with a narrow success. There should be more to come.
**True Companion**, dropped back from a mile and a half, finished to good effect and shaped as though worth another try over further.
**Icannshift(IRE)** ran a game race from the front and has a handicap mark that allows him to race in a much lower class - he would be interesting dropped in grade.
**Lady McNair** did not have much room against the rail when looking to make her challenge and probably would have finished closer with a clearer passage. She has not won since her two-year-old days.
**Tender Falcon** made a pleasing return to action off the back of a 284-day break. He should be sharper next time.
**Aoninch** made a lot of late ground from the back of the field over this shorter trip.
T/Jkpt: Not won. T/Plt: £2,010.80 to a £1 stake. Pool: £91,314.15. 33.15 winning tickets. T/Qpdt: £122.00 to a £1 stake. Pool: £6,611.50. 40.10 winning tickets. JN

## MUNICH (L-H)
Monday, May 31

**OFFICIAL GOING: Good**

### 2541a WWW.PFERDEWETTEN.DE BAVARIAN CLASSIC (GROUP 3) 1m 2f
**3:45** (3:59) 3-Y-O **£24,648** (£9,859; £4,930; £2,817)

RPR

**1** **Fight Club (GER)** 3-9-2 .................... AStarke 1 111
(ASchutz, Germany) *mid-division, 5th straight, challenged 1 1/2f out, ridden to lead over 1f out, ran on strongly* 1

**2** *1½* **Egerton (GER)**[36] [1656] 3-9-2 .................... AHelfenbein 2 108
(PRau, Germany) *in touch, 3rd straight, ridden to lead over 1 1/2f out, ran on til headed over 1f out, kept on*

**3** *1½* **Gentle Tiger (GER)** 3-9-2 .................... ASuborics 7 105
(PSchiergen, Germany) *mid-division, ridden 1 1/2f out on outside, stayed on to take 3rd inside final furlong* 3

**4** *1¼* **Delsun (IRE)**[43] 3-9-2 .................... ADeVries 4 103
(MarioHofer, Germany) *in touch, 4th straight, effort 1 1/2f out, kept on same pace*

**5** *3* **Eleazar (GER)**[36] [1656] 3-9-2 .................... WMongil 3 98
(HBlume, Germany) *mid-divison, pushed along 2f out, unable to quicken*

**6** *1¼* **Siberion (GER)**[36] [1656] 3-9-2 .................... PJSmullen 6 96
(MarioHofer, Germany) *raced in close 2nd, led over 2f out to over 1 1/2f out, no extra once headed*

**7** *10* **Genios (GER)**[36] [1656] 3-9-2 .................... LHammer-Hansen 5 78
(DrABolte, Germany) *raced in rear, never dangerous*

**8** *8* **Next Society (GER)** 3-9-2 .................... THellier 8 64
(ASchutz, Germany) *led, headed over 2f out, soon weakened* 2

2m 11.64s **8** Ran SP% **127.4**
Speed ratings:
**Owner** W H Sport International **Bred** Gestut Karlshof **Trained** Germany

## 2028 SAINT-CLOUD (L-H)
Monday, May 31

**OFFICIAL GOING: Good to soft**

### 2543a PRIX CORRIDA (GROUP 2) (F&M) 1m 2f 110y
**2:50** (2:50) 4-Y-O+ **£42,148** (£16,268; £7,764; £5,176)

RPR

**1** **Actrice (IRE)**[24] [1952] 4-8-9 .................... OPeslier 10 109
(ELellouche, France) *held up in last, progress in centre 2f out, ridden to lead over 1f out, ran on well* 2

**2** *1½* **Visorama (IRE)**[24] [1952] 4-8-11 .................... CSoumillon 9 108
(AFabre, France) *held up in 9th, 8th straight, driven and headway 2f out in centre to dispute lead 1 1/2f out, stayed on final furlong to ta* 1

**3** *½* **Pride (FR)**[24] [1952] 4-8-11 .................... DBonilla 8 107
(ADeRoyer-Dupre, France) *raced in 8th, 9th straight, progress 2f out, ridden and pressing leaders over 1f out, kept on* 2

**4** *nk* **Whortleberry (FR)**[25] [1922] 4-8-13 .................... TGillet 6 109
(FRohaut, France) *mid-division, disputing 6th straight, ridden and ran on from 1 1/2f out to dispute 3rd inside final furlong, no extra final*

**5** *5* **Maredsous (FR)**[25] [1922] 4-8-9 .................... IMendizabal 2 96
(DSepulchre, France) *in touch, disputing 4th straight, effort to press leaders 2f out, one pace from over 1f out*

**6** *nse* **Monturani (IRE)**[51] [1332] 5-8-9 .................... TJarnet 5 96
(GWragg) *in touch, close 3rd straight, ridden and every chance over 1 1/2f out, no extra from over 1f out*

**7** *nk* **Samando (FR)**[24] [1952] 4-8-9 .................... C-PLemaire 1 95
(FDoumen, France) *in touch on rail, disputing 4th straight, effort and ran on to lead over 1 1/2f out, headed over 1f out, one pace*

**8** *2½* **Smala Tica (FR)**[25] 4-8-9 .................... TThulliez 3 91
(ELibaud, France) *mid-division, disputing 6th straight, never in challenging position*

**9** *2* **Silence Is Golden**[29] [1790] 5-8-9 .................... MJKinane 4 87
(BJMeehan) *raced in close 2nd, led approaching straight til ridden and headed over 2f out, soon one pace*

**10** *4* **Russian Hill**[24] [1952] 4-8-9 .................... GaryStevens 7 80
(AFabre, France) *led, headed approaching straight, led again over 2f out to over 1 1/2f out, weakened* 3

2m 13.5s **Going Correction** -0.275s/f (Firm) **10** Ran SP% **121.0**
Speed ratings: **115,113,113,113,109 109,109,107,106,103.**
**Owner** Ecurie Wildenstein **Bred** Dayton Investments Ltd **Trained** France

**NOTEBOOK**
**Actrice(IRE)**, not given a brilliant ride in her previous race, made amends on this occasion. Waiting tactics were employed before she came with a run up the centre of the track. Leading inside the final furlong, she was going away at the end. The Nassau Stakes and the Prix d'Astarte will now be looked at for this filly who excels on good ground.
**Visorama(IRE)** made progress from a furlong and a half out but could never get to within striking distance of the winner. She is improving as the season moves forward.
**Pride(FR)** did not have the luckiest of runs. Her forward move came from two out but she had to change direction when making her challenge. She took third place in the final few strides.
**Whortleberry(FR)** was tucked in just behind the leading group and took advantage for a short time 300 yards from the post. She was then one-paced but battled on well. She needs softer ground and a longer distance really, and her main target is the Prix Vermeille in September.
**Monturani(IRE)**, never far from the leaders, was very one-paced in the final stages having been given every possible chance.
**Silence Is Golden**, one of the early leaders, ran out of steam halfway up the straight and her jockey felt the filly ran a bit flat.

## 2519 LEICESTER (R-H)
Tuesday, June 1

**OFFICIAL GOING: Good (good to firm in places)**
The overnight rain saw the ground easing slightly and the rain continued to drizzle throughout the morning.
Wind: fresh bhd Weather: drizzle, rain after race 4

### 2544 EBF WOLVEY MAIDEN FILLIES' STKS 5f 2y
**2:30** (2:32) (D) 2-Y-O **£5,590** (£1,720; £860; £430) **Stalls** Low

Form RPR

**1** **Sharplaw Star** 2-8-11 .................... MHills 7 81+
(WJHaggas) *trckd ldrs: led over 1f out: r.o wl* **7/4**[1]

**2** *2½* **Molly Marie (IRE)** 2-8-11 .................... TQuinn 1 72
(TDEasterby) *a.p: swtchd rt over 1f out: styd on* **9/1**

3 **3** *nk* **Easy Feeling (IRE)**[10] [2296] 2-8-11 .................... RLMoore 3 71
(RHannon) *a.p: chsd ldr 1/2-way: led over 1f out: sn hdd: no ex ins fnl f* **3/1**[3]

3 **4** *2* **Elsie Wagg (USA)**[6] [2396] 2-8-11 .................... KFallon 6 64
(MJWallace) *sn led: rdn and hdd over 1f out: sn btn* **5/2**[2]

**5** *12* **Miss Cotswold Lady** 2-8-11 .................... JQuinn 2 22
(AWCarroll) *sn outpcd* **66/1**

**6** *5* **Dancing Moonlight (IRE)** 2-8-11 .................... RFitzpatrick 4 5
(MrsNMacauley) *s.s: outpcd* **80/1**

2 **7** *1½* **Mermaid's Cry**[8] [2364] 2-8-11 .................... JFEgan 5 —
(RBrotherton) *chsd ldr to 1/2-way: wknd qckly* **33/1**

61.07 secs (0.14) **Going Correction** 0.0s/f (Good) **7** Ran SP% **105.6**
Speed ratings: **98,94,93,90,71 63,60**CSF £15.11 TOTE £2.40: £1.60, £3.80; EX 15.60.
**Owner** Miss Tina Miller **Bred** Angmering Park Stud **Trained** Newmarket, Suffolk

**FOCUS**
Fairly strong fillies' maiden forn, and a good time for the grade.

**NOTEBOOK**
**Sharplaw Star**, who cost 92,000gns as a yearling, was well backed to open her account at the first time of asking, and duly landed the odds in great style. She clearly knew her job, as she was smartly away and forced to race wide of the pack, before displaying a smart turn of foot to settle the issue approaching the final furlong. She is being considered for Royal Ascot and there would be worse outsiders in the Queen Mary.
**Molly Marie(IRE)** ◆ took her time to get going but shaped promisingly late on and grabbed second close home. This was a pleasing debut effort and, as most of her stable's juveniles improve considerably for their first run, she looks a certain winner of a similar event. She should stay another furlong.
**Easy Feeling(IRE)**, a fair third over six furlongs on her debut at Haydock, held every chance but paid for trying to go with the winner late on. The drop back to the minimum trip may not have totally suited and this lengthy filly should come on again for the experience.
**Elsie Wagg(USA)** pinged out of the gates and bagged the rail, showing plenty of early speed, but found little under pressure and eventually finished well beaten. On this evidence, she looks only modest.
**Mermaid's Cry** *Official explanation: jockey said filly hung to the right.*

### 2545 HATHERN CLAIMING STKS 1m 9y
**3:00** (3:00) (F) 3-Y-O **£3,367** (£1,036; £518; £259) **Stalls** High

Form RPR

4006 **1** **Western Roots**[12] [2239] 3-9-10 74 .................... TQuinn 8 81
(PFICole) *hld up in tch: led over 1f out: edgd lft ins fnl f: rdn out* **5/2**[1]

0-02 **2** *nk* **Hearthstead Dream**[8] [2354] 3-8-8 69 .................... DSweeney 4 64
(JGMO'Shea) *hld up: hdwy over 2f out: rdn and ev ch ins fnl f: nt run on* **12/1**

6006 **3** *7* **Kings Rock**[20] 2036 3-9-4 58 PFessey 5 58
(KARyan) *hld up: rdn 1/2-way: hdwy and hung rt over 1f out: nvr trbld ldrs* **5/1**[3]

100- **4** *2 1/2* **Papeete (GER)**[250] 5175 3-9-5 73 KFallon 1 53
(WJHaggas) *dwlt: sn pushed along in rr: hdwy over 1f out: wknd fnl f* **7/2**[2]

5-00 **5** *1 1/4* **Red Rocky**[8] 2351 3-8-5 55 MartinDwyer 6 37
(RHollinshead) *led 2f: remained handy: led 2f out: sn hdd: wknd fnl f* **66/1**

06-0 **6** *1 1/2* **Erte**[38] 1613 3-9-0 62 KDarley 10 42
(MRChannon) *w ldr: led 6f out: rdn and hdd 2f out: wknd fnl f* **14/1**

0-00 **7** *3/4* **Compassion (IRE)**[20] 2029 3-8-1 58 (p) AMcCarthy 3 27
(GCHChung) *hld up: hdwy 1/2-way: wknd over 1f out* **40/1**

0-00 **8** *nk* **Cashema (IRE)**[25] 1946 3-8-9 52 (p) RHavlin 9 35
(MrsPNDutfield) *chsd ldrs: n.m.r and wknd over 1f out* **33/1**

0-00 **9** *3 1/2* **Desert Daisy (IRE)**[16] 2146 3-7-13 59 JQuinn 7 17
(IAWood) *chsd ldr tl wknd over 1f out* **6/1**

0-00 **10** *3 1/2* **Mr Belvedere**[14] 2207 3-9-0 65 (b) DaneO'Neill 2 24
(RHannon) *prom 6f* **7/1**

1m 42.89s (0.29) **Going Correction** 0.0s/f (Good) **10** Ran SP% **115.5**
Speed ratings: **98,97,90,88,86 85,84,84,80,77**CSF £33.69 TOTE £3.50: £1.40, £3.10, £1.30; EX 28.80.Hearthstead Dream was subject to a friendly claim of £7,000. Western Roots was claimed by K. Morgan for £15,000.
**Owner** David Murrell **Bred** Stratford Place Stud **Trained** Whatcombe, Oxon

**FOCUS**
A modest claimer, but it was run at a fair pace and the first two were clear of the rest at the finish.

**NOTEBOOK**
**Western Roots**, taking a big drop in grade, looked all over the winner having joined the leaders on the bridle two out, but had to dig deep late on to repel the runner-up. He enjoyed the decent early gallop, the extra furlong was in his favour and this was his best effort to date on turf.
**Hearthstead Dream**, down in trip, was held up early on and took time to find his full stride in the straight. He came through to make the winner pull out all the stops, and this was a pleasing debut for his new connections, although his tendency to carry his head a bit high was slightly worrying. He is not well handicapped at present.
**Kings Rock** ran on late in the day, but failed to improve for this quicker ground and the extra furlong. He has not progressed as once looked likely and remains a maiden after 11 outings.
**Papeete(GER)** proved disappointing on this three-year-old debut, given that she was down in grade, but she should improve physically for the outing and was not given a hard time in the straight.
**Desert Daisy(IRE)**

## 2546 "SHEFF WILSON" LIFETIME IN RACING H'CAP 1m 3f 183y
**3:30** (3:31) (E) (0-70,67) 3-Y-O **£4,299** (£1,323; £661; £330) **Stalls** High

Form RPR

5-01 **1** **Selebela**[8] 2363 3-9-3 63 5ex JPMurtagh 15 76+
(LMCumani) *chsd ldrs: led over 2f out: sn clr: eased ins fnl f* **10/11**[1]

6-12 **2** *7* **Ilwadod**[20] 2037 3-8-10 56 KDarley 1 58
(MRChannon) *hld up: hdwy 7f out: outpcd over 4f out: hdwy over 2f out: wnt 2nd over 1f out: no ch w wnr* **11/2**[2]

3621 **3** *2* **Siegfrieds Night (IRE)**[16] 2146 3-9-1 66 DFox(5) 12 65
(MCChapman) *hld up: hdwy over 3f out: nvr trbld ldrs* **9/1**

0-50 **4** *1/2* **Canadian Storm**[18] 2097 3-9-0 60 DHolland 4 58
(MHTompkins) *hld up: plld hrd: hdwy to ld 8f out: rdn and hdd over 2f out: wknd over 1f out* **25/1**

0322 **5** *hd* **Danefonique (IRE)**[14] 2199 3-8-11 57 RFitzpatrick 7 55
(DCarroll) *s.i.s: hld up: styd on fnl 2f: nvr trbld ldrs* **25/1**

0030 **6** *1 3/4* **Darn Good**[50] 1365 3-9-6 66 (b[1]) RLMoore 13 61
(RHannon) *chsd ldrs over 9f* **33/1**

360- **7** *1* **Chanfron**[245] 5290 3-9-5 65 AMcCarthy 8 58
(BRMillman) *prom over 9f* **80/1**

-021 **8** *hd* **True To Yourself (USA)**[21] 2014 3-8-1 47 JQuinn 5 40
(JGGiven) *hld up: rdn over 4f out: n.d* **20/1**

0445 **9** *2 1/2* **Heartbeat**[7] 2390 3-7-12 47 FPFerris(3) 2 36
(PJMcbride) *s.i.s: hld up: a in rr* **20/1**

00-4 **10** *1* **Verasi**[29] 1830 3-9-7 67 SDrowne 3 55
(RCharlton) *chsd ldrs over 9f* **8/1**[3]

-600 **11** *1/2* **El Magnifico**[6] 2402 3-7-13 48 (v[1]) LisaJones(3) 6 35
(PDCundell) *led 4f: wknd 2f out* **50/1**

0-20 **12** *3 1/2* **Waltzing Beau**[129] 598 3-8-13 59 TQuinn 17 40
(BGPowell) *hld up: rdn over 4f out: n.d* **66/1**

0513 **13** *9* **Three Welshmen**[26] 1908 3-8-11 57 SSanders 10 24
(BRMillman) *hld up: rdn over 4f out: a in rr* **25/1**

00 **14** *5* **Faith Healer (IRE)**[10] 2284 3-8-9 55 (p) JoannaBadger 11 14
(VSmith) *bhd fr 1/2-way* **80/1**

0-40 **15** *2* **Cadeaux Rouge (IRE)**[25] 1947 3-9-0 60 RHavlin 14 16
(MrsPNDutfield) *prom over 8f* **50/1**

2m 33.04s (-1.64) **Going Correction** 0.0s/f (Good) **15** Ran SP% **120.8**
Speed ratings: **105,100,99,98,98 97,96,96,94,94 93,91,85,82,80**CSF £4.66 CT £30.19 TOTE £1.90: £1.10, £3.40, £2.70; EX 10.30.
**Owner** Scuderia Rencati Srl **Bred** Fittocks Stud **Trained** Newmarket, Suffolk

**FOCUS**
This moderate handicap was run at a stop-start early gallop and the field was fairly strung out from an early stage.

**NOTEBOOK**
**Selebela**, who routed her opposition when getting off the mark in a poor handicap over course and distance eight days previously, repeated that feat in almost identical fashion, easily defying a 5lb penalty. She will take a hike in the weights for this, but is still unexposed and it could pay to follow her this summer in middle-distance handicaps.
**Ilwadod** ran on to take a clear second, but held no chance with the winner. He again ran quite green through the early stages and may have found the ground a touch on the quick side, but he got the trip well enough and remains open to further improvement.
**Siegfrieds Night(IRE)** ran on late and again gave his all, but the 8lb rise for winning last time looked to find him out.
**Canadian Storm** ran his best race to date and was still travelling well at the head of affairs over two out, but quickly fell in a hole over this much longer trip. He will be seen to a better effect when dropped to around a mile.
**Danefonique(IRE)** stayed on at the one pace in the straight having been held up to get the trip on this step up in grade. She may improve when eased in distance, but is hard to win with.

## 2547 FOREST H'CAP 1m 1f 218y
**4:00** (4:00) (E) (0-70,65) 3-Y-O+ **£4,280** (£1,317; £658; £329) **Stalls** High

Form RPR

-000 **1** **Planters Punch (IRE)**[7] 2390 3-8-8 62 KFallon 5 73
(RHannon) *hld up in tch: pushed along 1/2-way: led over 1f out: edgd lft ins fnl f: rdn out* **9/2**[2]

0-00 **2** *3* **Movie King (IRE)**[16] 2142 5-9-10 65 (p) DHolland 11 70
(SGollings) *led and sn clr: rdn and hdd over 1f out: styd on same pce* **13/2**

11-0 **3** *1/2* **Kirkham Abbey**[11] 2258 4-9-10 65 (v) KDarley 12 69
(MAJarvis) *a.p: rdn to chse ldr over 2f out: styd on same pce fnl f* **7/2**[1]

-211 **4** *1 1/4* **Arms Acrossthesea**[4] 2456 5-9-4 59 5ex JEdmunds 7 61
(JBalding) *hld up: hdwy over 3f out: rdn over 1f out: styd on same pce* **11/2**[3]

00-0 **5** *3 1/2* **Danebank (IRE)**[28] 1856 4-8-7 48 GCarter 10 43
(JMackie) *hld up: styd on appr fnl f: nvr nrr* **14/1**

4050 **6** *shd* **Lyrical Way**[10] 2302 5-9-5 60 (b) SDrowne 8 55
(PRChamings) *chsd ldrs: rdn over 3f out: wknd over 1f out* **7/1**

000- **7** *3* **Lucky Archer**[221] 5082 11-8-13 54 RLMoore 2 43
(IanWilliams) *hld up: nvr nrr* **33/1**

0-50 **8** *1 1/4* **Little Englander**[14] 2212 4-9-0 55 DaneO'Neill 1 42
(HCandy) *hld up: rdn 1/2-way: n.d* **10/1**

**9** *1 3/4* **Sachsenwalzer (GER)**[7] 6-8-12 53 MartinDwyer 9 36
(CGrant) *chsd ldr tl wknd over 2f out* **20/1**

0-30 **10** *hd* **Kyle Of Lochalsh**[125] 623 4-9-2 57 AMcCarthy 3 40
(GGMargarson) *hld up: a in rr* **16/1**

5-00 **11** *5* **Rileys Rocket**[8] 2348 5-8-2 43 ow3 PaulEddery 6 17
(RHollinshead) *dwlt: hld up: plld hrd: a bhd* **66/1**

2m 7.73s (-0.67) **Going Correction** 0.0s/f (Good)
**WFA** 3 from 4yo+ 13lb **11** Ran SP% **112.5**
Speed ratings: **102,99,99,98,95 95,92,91,90,90 86**CSF £31.59 CT £111.97 TOTE £6.20: £2.30, £3.60, £1.50; EX 66.10.
**Owner** Lucayan Stud **Bred** Miss Sarah Thompson **Trained** East Everleigh, Wilts

**FOCUS**
A moderate contest that was run at a solid gallop courtesy of the clear early leader Movie King.

**NOTEBOOK**
**Planters Punch(IRE)** responded well to strong pressure approaching the home turn to join the leaders and in the end won going away. This was by far his best effort to date, and he looks suited by this trip, but prospered from a vintage ride from the champion on this occasion. *Official explanation: trainer said, regarding the improved form shown, the race was run to suit*
**Movie King(IRE)** was granted a clear lead early on but came back to the field and looked a sitting duck approaching two out, so he deserves credit for battling back to regain second close home. This was his best effort of the current campaign and he looks to be coming back into form.
**Kirkham Abbey** held every chance if good enough but could not find the change of gears to go with the winner. He was made to look one-paced, but this was still an improved effort, and he can find a small race.
**Arms Acrossthesea** could not get to the leaders in the straight and may have found this race coming a bit too quick after his success at Wolverhampton four days earlier.

## 2548 LEICESTER RACECOURSE CONFERENCE CENTRE FILLIES' CONDITIONS STKS 7f 9y
**4:30** (4:30) (C) 3-Y-O **£8,537** (£3,238; £1,619; £736) **Stalls** Low

Form RPR

21 **1** **Lucky Spin**[25] 1939 3-8-9 90 RLMoore 6 90
(RHannon) *mde all: shkn up over 1f out: r.o* **1/1**[1]

01-5 **2** *1 1/4* **Coy (IRE)**[11] 2276 3-8-9 92 KFallon 7 87
(SirMichaelStoute) *Slowly into stride: sn chsng ldrs: pushed along 1/2-way: outpcd over 2f out: styd on ins fnl f: nt trble wnr* **3/1**[2]

16- **3** *3/4* **Surf The Net**[227] 5642 3-8-9 DaneO'Neill 4 85
(RHannon) *chsd ldrs: rdn over 2f out: one pce fnl f* **10/1**

10-0 **4** *nk* **Totally Yours (IRE)**[48] 1398 3-8-7 90 MartinDwyer 8 82
(WRMuir) *chsd wnr: rdn over 2f out: no ex ins fnl f* **11/2**[3]

12-0 **5** *7* **Nephetriti Way (IRE)**[34] 1704 3-8-9 87 SDrowne 1 66
(PRChamings) *prom: rdn over 2f out: wknd over 1f out* **8/1**

-660 **6** *3* **Chase The Rainbow**[11] 2259 3-8-3 55 ow1 PBradley(5) 2 57?
(ABerry) *hld up: rdn 3f out: wknd 2f out* **150/1**

1m 26.1s **Going Correction** 0.0s/f (Good) **6** Ran SP% **111.2**
Speed ratings: **100,98,97,97,89 85**CSF £4.11 TOTE £1.60: £1.10, £2.00; EX 4.60.
**Owner** George C Scudder **Bred** Roland Hope **Trained** East Everleigh, Wilts

**FOCUS**
An interesting little fillies' classified event, but it developed into a tactical affair and the form may be unreliable.

**NOTEBOOK**
**Lucky Spin ◆** had looked potentially smart when hacking up in her maiden at Lingfield last time, and confirmed that was no fluke with this cosy success in much better company. Granted she had the run of the race and enjoyed the ease in the ground, but she could only win as she did and looks progressive, with a Listed event surely within her compass.
**Coy(IRE)** was unsuited by the tactical nature of this race and lacked the turn of foot to go with the winner as the tempo increased entering the final furlong. This was an improved effort and she looks sure to be placed to advantage this summer.
**Surf The Net**, last seen finishing sixth in the Group Two Rockfel Stakes last October, posted a pleasing seasonal reappearance and is entitled to improve plenty for this outing. She has clearly trained on from two to three.
**Totally Yours(IRE)**, who has some decent juvenile form last year, was another not totally suited by the way the race was run, but still held every chance if good enough. She improved on her reappearance in the Nell Gwyn and seemed to stay the trip this time.
**Nephetriti Way(IRE)** dropped out quickly when things quickened up inside the last two furlongs. She has yet to prove that she has trained on this year, but is not one to write off just yet.

## 2549 CORONATION CLASSIFIED STKS 5f 218y
**5:00** (5:00) (D) 3-Y-O **£5,609** (£1,726; £863; £431) **Stalls** Low

Form RPR

0-25 **1** **Times Review (USA)**[12] 2239 3-8-12 81 KDarley 4 86
(TDEasterby) *chsd ldrs: rdn over 1f out: r.o to ld post* **4/1**[2]

050- **2** *shd* **Chance For Romance**[214] 5851 3-8-11 83 MartinDwyer 5 85
(WRMuir) *chsd ldrs: led over 2f out: rdn and hdd post* **12/1**

4-30 **3** *1/2* **Hilites (IRE)**[18] 2082 3-8-10 82 SWhitworth 9 82
(JSMoore) *hld up: hdwy over 1f out: r.o* **20/1**

-446 **4** *1 3/4* **Vienna's Boy (IRE)**[10] 2309 3-9-1 84 DaneO'Neill 3 82
(RHannon) *w ldr: plld hrd: led 1/2-way: sn hdd: styd on same pce ins fnl f* **5/2**[1]

-054 **5** *3/4* **Dolce Piccata**[15] 2181 3-8-12 84 TQuinn 8 77
(BJMeehan) *hld up in tch: bmpd and outpcd over 3f out: hdwy and nt clr run over 1f out: nt trbld ldrs* **8/1**

12-0 **6** *3/4* **Fyodor (IRE)**[17] 2131 3-9-1 84 MHills 7 77
(WJHaggas) *hld up: hdwy over 1f out: no ex ins fnl f* **11/2**[3]

3-63 **7** *2* **Baylaw Star**[36] 1659 3-8-11 75 JEdmunds 6 67
(JBalding) *chsd ldrs over 4f* **20/1**

4302 **8** *1 1/2* **Obe Bold (IRE)**[7] 2389 3-8-3 57 PBradley(5) 10 60
(ABerry) *chsd ldrs: rdn 1/2-way: wknd over 1f out* **100/1**

1-00 **9** *3 1/2* **Benny The Ball (USA)**[10] 2295 3-8-8 80 J-PGuillambert(3) 2 52
(NPLittmoden) *s.i.s: hdwy over 3f out: wknd over 1f out* **6/1**

011- **10** *10* **Little Ridge (IRE)**[208] 5931 3-9-0 83 ow3.......................... LFletcher(3) 1 28
(HMorrison) *led to 1/2-way: wknd 2f out* **8/1**
1m 14.04s (0.64) **Going Correction** 0.0s/f (Good) **10** Ran SP% **118.7**
Speed ratings: **95,94,94,91,90 89,87,85,80,67**CSF £50.66 TOTE £6.80: £1.70, £3.20, £4.70; EX 85.30 Place 6 £19.68, Place 5 £9.78.
**Owner** Times Of Wigan **Bred** Charger 6 Ventures **Trained** Great Habton, N Yorks

**FOCUS**
A tight and competitive classified event that saw the first three pull clear at the finish.

**NOTEBOOK**
**Times Review(USA)** relished this drop back to six furlongs and knuckled down well in the closing stages to post a narrow success. He had looked a non-stayer over seven last time, but found these conditions much more to his liking and this was his true form.
**Chance For Romance** looked the most likely winner two out, but was soon under pressure and could not repel the winner close home. This was a most pleasing return from her 214-day absence and she should improve a great deal for the outing.
**Hilites(IRE)** struggled to go the early pace but picked up strongly under maximum pressure late on and was not beaten far. She put a poor run last time well and truly behind her and should find a race before long.
**Vienna's Boy(IRE)**, popular in the betting ring, held every chance but could not quicken with the front three late on.
**Dolce Piccata** did not get the best of runs when trying to challenge in the final furlong and can be rated slightly better than the bare form. *Official explanation: jockey said he suffered interference shortly after the start.*
**Fyodor(IRE)** was still travelling sweetly two out, but found disappointingly little off the bridle and was well held at the finish. He has a lot to prove now.
T/Plt: £48.10 to a £1 stake. Pool: £36,556.55. 554.55 winning tickets. T/Qpdt: £4.00 to a £1 stake. Pool: £2,661.70. 482.40 winning tickets. CR

## 2526 REDCAR (L-H)
Tuesday, June 1

**OFFICIAL GOING: Firm (good to firm in places)**
Wind: almost nil Weather: steady rain

### 2550 EUROPEAN BREEDERS FUND MEDIAN AUCTION MAIDEN FILLIES' STKS — 6f
**2:15** (2:17) (E) 2-Y-O **£3,987** (£1,227; £613; £306) **Stalls** Centre

Form RPR
5 **1** **Aberdovey**[11] 2275 2-8-11 .................................... JMackay 2 73
(MLWBell) *chsd ldrs: led over 1f out: hld on wl* **5/2[1]**
**2** *shd* **Arabian Dancer** 2-8-11 .................................... TEDurcan 5 73
(MRChannon) *dwlt: hld up: hdwy over 2f out: rdn and r.o strly fnl f: jst failed* **7/2[3]**
5 **3** *hd* **Missperon (IRE)**[14] 2213 2-8-11 .................................... NCallan 6 72
(KARyan) *led to appr fnl f: rallied: jst hld* **12/1**
0 **4** *1 1/4* **Burton Ash**[19] 2071 2-8-11 .................................... MFenton 4 68
(JGGiven) *cl up: rdn over 2f out: kpt on same pce ins fnl f* **14/1**
3 **5** *hd* **Jane Jubilee (IRE)**[22] 1990 2-8-11 .................................... RFfrench 10 68
(MJohnston) *trckd ldrs: effrt and ev ch 2f out: kpt on same pce fnl f* **20/1**
2 **6** *shd* **Taras Treasure (IRE)**[14] 2213 2-8-11 .................................... RWinston 1 67
(JJQuinn) *keen: hld up: effrt and drifted lft over 1f out: kpt on fnl f* **11/4[2]**
6 **7** *2* **Wolds Dancer**[16] 2141 2-8-8 .................................... DAllan(3) 9 61
(TDEasterby) *hld up: hdwy 1/2-way: rdn and no imp over 1f out* **20/1**
050 **8** *1 1/4* **Aza Wish (IRE)**[16] 2141 2-8-11 .................................... SRighton 8 58
(MsDeborahJEvans) *bhd: outpcd 1/2-way: sme late hdwy: nvr on terms* **66/1**
5 **9** *hd* **Kilmovee**[16] 2141 2-8-11 .................................... ACulhane 7 57
(NTinkler) *disp ld to 2f out: sn rdn and outpcd* **12/1**
55 **10** *1/2* **Lady Misha**[18] 2087 2-8-11 .................................... PHanagan 11 56
(JeddO'Keeffe) *prom tl rdn and wknd over 1f out* **25/1**
**11** *nk* **Elliebow** 2-8-11 .................................... FLynch 12 55
(TDEasterby) *s.i.s: n.d* **50/1**
**12** *1 1/4* **Spectrum Of Light** 2-8-11 .................................... DeanMcKeown 3 51
(CWFairhurst) *in tch to 2f out: sn rdn and wknd* **100/1**
1m 12.69s (0.99) **Going Correction** +0.025s/f (Good) **12** Ran SP% **117.3**
Speed ratings: **94,93,93,91,91 91,88,87,86,86 85,84**CSF £10.41 TOTE £3.50: £1.40, £2.90, £4.70; EX 12.10.
**Owner** Usk Valley Stud **Bred** Usk Valley Stud **Trained** Newmarket, Suffolk

**FOCUS**
Not a strong maiden, especially given that Taras Treasure was below form, but it was competitive and should produce some winners in similar events.

**NOTEBOOK**
**Aberdovey** shaped well on her debut in a fair Newmarket maiden and found this easier. She would appear to be going the right way and looks capable of improvement, but things will be tougher under a penalty.
**Arabian Dancer**, one of the stable's cheaper two-year-olds at 3,000gns, is out of a middle-distance winner in France. Despite the stamina influence in her pedigree, she showed herself effective over a sprint trip and was just denied. She is going to want further in time, but looks up to winning a maiden over this trip given normal improvement.
**Missperon(IRE)** offered some promise on her debut in a similar event over this course and distance and, with the benefit of that experience, was just denied. She may just have the pace to prove effective over five furlongs and a minor maiden should come her way.
**Burton Ash** found this easier than the York maiden she made her debut in (well beaten) and would appear to be progressing.
**Jane Jubilee(IRE)**, last of three on her debut over five furlongs, showed more this time and is in good hands.
**Taras Treasure(IRE)** ran a most encouraging race on her debut in a course and distance maiden, but she failed to reproduce that form and was disappointing. She has already shown she is better than this, but has a little bit to prove now.
**Elliebow** *Official explanation: jockey said filly missed the break.*

### 2551 LEVY BOARD H'CAP — 1m 1f
**2:45** (2:45) (E) (0-70,70) 3-Y-0+ **£3,571** (£1,099; £549; £274) **Stalls** Low

Form RPR
U002 **1** **Archirondel**[22] 1993 6-8-6 **48** ow1.......................... ACulhane 5 61
(MDHammond) *hld up: hdwy centre to ld over 1f out: edgd lft: drvn out* **4/1[1]**
0-60 **2** *2* **Scriptorium**[57] 1271 3-8-1 **58**.......................... NMackay(3) 11 67
(LMCumani) *chsd ldrs: effrt and chal fr over 2f out: kpt on fnl f* **13/2[3]**
0035 **3** *2 1/2* **Arjay**[4] 2456 6-8-6 **48**.......................... JCarroll 4 52
(AndrewTurnell) *hld up: hdwy centre 2f out: kpt on: nt rch first two* **16/1**
-005 **4** *3/4* **Apache Point (IRE)**[17] 2120 7-9-1 **57**.......................... KimTinkler 13 60
(NTinkler) *trckd ldrs: effrt over 2f out: one pce over 1f out* **5/1[2]**
10-0 **5** *nk* **Helderberg (USA)**[10] 2284 4-9-11 **67**.......................... MFenton 9 69
(BSRothwell) *midfield: effrt and prom over 2f out: one pce over 1f out* **33/1**
4-50 **6** *1 1/2* **Oscar Pepper (USA)**[8] 2368 7-9-7 **63**.......................... GFaulkner 1 62
(TDBarron) *prom on ins: outpcd over 3f out: kpt on fnl f: no imp* **5/1[2]**
01-0 **7** *2* **Merdiff**[57] 1265 5-9-4 **60**.......................... SWKelly 14 55
(WMBrisbourne) *cl up: effrt and ev ch over 2f out: wknd over 1f out* **8/1**
6-00 **8** *1/2* **Basinet**[18] 2078 6-8-12 **54**.......................... (p) RWinston 15 48
(JJQuinn) *s.i.s: bhd tl kpt on fnl f: n.d* **12/1**
-000 **9** *1* **Buscador (USA)**[17] 2120 5-8-6 **53**.......................... BSwarbrick(5) 8 45
(WMBrisbourne) *keen: cl up: led 3f to over 1f out: sn btn* **16/1**
-000 **10** *2* **Cryptogam**[103] 824 4-8-4 **49** ow2.......................... TEaves(3) 6 37
(MESowersby) *bhd: drvn over 3f out: nt pce to chal* **100/1**
50-0 **11** *1 1/4* **Ash Laddie (IRE)**[29] 1820 4-8-13 **58**.......................... DAllan(3) 7 43
(EJAlston) *bhd: rdn 1/2-way: nvr on terms* **100/1**
2200 **12** *1 1/2* **Wilson Bluebottle (IRE)**[17] 2128 5-8-3 **45**.......................... (b) DaleGibson 12 27
(MWEasterby) *led to 3f out: sn rdn and wknd* **11/1**
00-5 **13** *1* **Stepastray**[14] 2216 7-8-4 **46**.......................... CCogan 2 26
(REBarr) *keen in midfield: rdn and wknd over 3f out* **16/1**
000 **14** *21* **Arawan (IRE)**[16] 2142 4-10-0 **70**.......................... TLucas 3 8
(MWEasterby) *a bhd: lost tch fr 1/2-way* **50/1**
066 **15** *10* **Paula**[14] 2198 4-8-8 **53**.......................... (v[1]) LEnstone(3) 10 —
(MDods) *racd wd in rr: rdn over 3f out: sn btn* **66/1**
1m 51.7s (-1.70) **Going Correction** +0.025s/f (Good)
**WFA** 3 from 4yo+ 12lb **15** Ran SP% **119.8**
Speed ratings: **108,106,104,103,103 101,99,99,98,96 95,94,93,74,65**CSF £28.67 CT £387.03 TOTE £5.40: £1.50, £4.20, £5.30; EX 51.30.
**Owner** The Archi Partnership **Bred** Jerry Sung **Trained** Middleham, N Yorks

**FOCUS**
Just a moderate handicap, but they went a good pace and the time was smart for the grade.

**NOTEBOOK**
**Archirondel** was racing off a mark 12lb lower than when last winning in June 2002 and ended his losing run in good style. This will have provided him with a welcome confidence boost and it would be no surprise to see him follow up.
**Scriptorium** ran his best race to date on this handicap debut and showed enough to suggest his current mark can be exploited.
**Arjay** has tumbled in the weights since gaining his last success, but he is most frustrating and never really looked like going with the winner.
**Apache Point(IRE)** is on a nice mark and is running into a bit of form.
**Helderberg(USA)** offered plenty of encouragement and should go on from this.
**Oscar Pepper(USA)** did not run to his best and has to be considered a little disappointing.

### 2552 CONSTANT SECURITY SPRINT STKS (H'CAP) — 5f
**3:15** (3:17) (C) (0-90,89) 3-Y-0 **£10,452** (£3,216; £1,608; £804) **Stalls** Centre

Form RPR
-521 **1** **Enchantment**[11] 2264 3-9-3 **85**.......................... RFfrench 1 96+
(JMBradley) *trckd ldr: led over 1f out: sn clr* **5/2[1]**
6-56 **2** *2 1/2* **True Magic**[12] 2236 3-7-9 **66** oh4.......................... NMackay(3) 3 67
(JDBethell) *hld up: hdwy over 1f out: kpt on fnl f: no ch w wnr* **25/1**
-000 **3** *shd* **Divine Spirit**[10] 2309 3-8-12 **80**.......................... FLynch 8 81
(MDods) *hld up: hdwy over 1f out: r.o: nrst fin* **66/1**
2303 **4** *hd* **Harry Up**[17] 2115 3-9-7 **89**.......................... MFenton 10 89
(JGGiven) *bhd: hdwy over 1f out: kpt on fnl f* **7/1**
6-20 **5** *nk* **Celtic Thunder**[17] 2131 3-9-2 **84**.......................... RWinston 5 83
(TJEtherington) *chsd ldrs: rdn and edgd lft 2f out: one pce fnl f* **10/1**
16-0 **6** *2 1/2* **Tyne**[45] 1473 3-9-1 **83**.......................... PHanagan 11 73
(TDBarron) *prom tl rdn and outpcd fr 2f out* **9/1**
-103 **7** *nk* **Johnny Parkes**[17] 2131 3-9-1 **83**.......................... ACulhane 9 72
(MrsJRRamsden) *hld up midfield: effrt over 2f out: btn fnl f* **6/1[3]**
50-0 **8** *1* **Silver Prelude**[17] 2115 3-9-5 **87**.......................... NCallan 2 72
(DKIvory) *led to over 1f out: sn btn* **25/1**
-231 **9** *shd* **Borzoi Maestro**[4] 2444 3-8-10 **78** 6ex.......................... (p) ADaly 6 63
(JLSpearing) *hld up: rdn over 2f out: n.d* **17/2**
61-5 **10** *3* **Promenade**[17] 2115 3-9-4 **86**.......................... JMackay 4 60
(MLWBell) *chsd ldrs tl wknd fr 2f out* **11/2[2]**
0-06 **11** *1 1/2* **Sir Ernest (IRE)**[27] 1883 3-8-7 **75**.......................... GGibbons 7 44
(MJPolglase) *chsd ldrs to 1/2-way: sn rdn and btn* **20/1**
57.69 secs (-1.01) **Going Correction** +0.025s/f (Good) **11** Ran SP% **114.3**
Speed ratings: **109,105,104,104,104 100,99,97,97,93 90**CSF £77.00 CT £3286.06 TOTE £4.70: £1.30, £7.80, £11.90; EX 123.30 Trifecta £909.90 Part won. Pool of £1,281.60 - 0.60 winning units..
**Owner** Ms A M Williams **Bred** Downclose Stud **Trained** Sedbury, Gloucs

**FOCUS**
Probably just an ordinary sprint featuring some badly handicapped three-year-olds suffering off the back of successful juvenile campaigns, but that cannot be said of the winner Enchantment, who is progressing.

**NOTEBOOK**
**Enchantment** ◆ followed up her recent Bath success with another emphatic victory. She has speed to burn and could make up into a Listed-class performer.
**True Magic**, still a maiden, ran well on this drop back from six furlongs but she was never going to get to the winner. She was due to be dropped 4lb before this.
**Divine Spirit** ◆ ran his best race of the season so far and could be ready to strike. He is on a nice mark and, given that he has gained both his previous wins in cheekpieces, it would be most interesting if the headgear is re-fitted next time.
**Harry Up** appeared to have conditions to suit, but he never really landed a blow and may continue to struggle.
**Celtic Thunder** ran respectably and, take out the well-handicapped winner, he was not beaten far at all.
**Johnny Parkes** did not run his race and has to be considered disappointing.
**Silver Prelude** tried to go with Enchantment and that was not a good idea.
**Promenade** has got it all to prove after this showing.

### 2553 GREAT VALUE YORKSHIRE SEASON TICKET CLASSIFIED STKS — 7f
**3:45** (3:46) (E) 3-Y-0+ **£3,376** (£1,039; £519; £259) **Stalls** Centre

Form RPR
1004 **1** **Warden Warren**[3] 2473 6-8-11 69.......................... (p) BReilly(3) 1 79
(MrsCADunnett) *chsd ldrs: rdn over 2f out: led ins fnl f: r.o wl* **10/3[3]**
2312 **2** *3* **Samuel Charles**[10] 2291 6-9-2 72.......................... SWKelly 3 73+
(WMBrisbourne) *led 1f: led over 2f out: edgd lft: hdd ins fnl f: one pce* **5/2[1]**
220- **3** *6* **Bandos**[255] 5063 4-9-5 75.......................... (t) PHanagan 2 61
(ISemple) *missed break: keen and led after 1f: hdd over 2f out: sn wknd* **11/4[2]**
-300 **4** *1* **Perfect Portrait**[14] 2206 4-9-2 72.......................... (v) DRMcCabe 4 55
(DRLoder) *keen: trckd ldrs: rdn over 2f out: fnd nthing and sn btn* **11/4[2]**
1m 24.75s (-0.15) **Going Correction** +0.025s/f (Good) **4** Ran SP% **105.0**
Speed ratings: **101,97,90,89**CSF £10.96 TOTE £2.80; EX 9.80.
**Owner** Annwell Inn Syndicate **Bred** R G Percival **Trained** Hingham, Norfolk
■ Stewards Enquiry : B Reilly one-day ban: used whip with excessive frequency (Jun 12)

**FOCUS**
A funny race and not one to pay too much attention to with regards future contests. Bandos fell out of the stalls, but was rushed up to lead at quite a fast pace and not surprisingly dropped out, while Samuel Charles and Perfect Portrait did not look straightforward.
**NOTEBOOK**
**Warden Warren** loves to have plenty of space in his races and this small field suited him ideally. So too did the decent pace, and he came through for a pretty straightforward success.
**Samuel Charles** carried his head awkwardly to the right for much of the way and was no match for the winner when it mattered.
**Bandos** missed the break and needed quite a bit of pressure to get to the front. Given that this was his first run in 255 days, he was entitled to get tired, especially given he went quite fast, but he carried his head high and his attitude did not impress. *Official explanation: jockey said gelding missed the break.*
**Perfect Portrait** found nothing under pressure and looks one to avoid.

## 2554 REDCARRACING.CO.UK MAIDEN H'CAP — 1m 6f 19y
**4:15** (4:17) (F) (0-55,54) 3-Y-O — **£2,975** (£850; £425) **Stalls** Low

Form — RPR
3343 **1** **Nocatee (IRE)**[25] 1947 3-9-6 **52**........(p) GFaulkner 1 — 58
*(PCHaslam) trckd ldrs: effrt and swtchd over 3f out: edgd lft and led over 1f out: hld on wl* **7/1**
0-60 **2** *hd* **Spring Breeze**[14] 2199 3-9-2 **51**........(p) LEnstone(3) 16 — 57
*(MDods) keen: prom: effrt over 3f out: swtchd over 1f out: kpt on wl: jst hld* **16/1**
-060 **3** *½* **Northern Spirit**[16] 2146 3-9-0 **46**........(p) NCallan 7 — 51
*(KARyan) cl up: led over 3f to over 1f out: rallied: hld towards fin* **20/1**
-250 **4** *2* **Bollin Annabel**[14] 2199 3-9-4 **53**........ DAllan(3) 4 — 55
*(TDEasterby) hld up: effrt over 3f out: rdn and kpt on fnl f: no imp* **16/1**
-032 **5** *7* **Savannah River (IRE)**[29] 1843 3-8-13 **45**........(t) PHanagan 15 — 37
*(CWThornton) bhd: hdwy and prom 3f out: outpcd fr 2f out* **10/1**
-032 **6** *1 ¾* **Royal Upstart**[21] 2016 3-8-3 **40**........(b) BSwarbrick(5) 2 — 30
*(WMBrisbourne) in tch tl outpcd 3f out: n.d after* **25/1**
5240 **7** *nk* **Valiant Air (IRE)**[25] 1947 3-8-10 **42**........ RWinston 5 — 32
*(JRWeymes) prom: ev ch over 3f out: wknd over 1f out* **10/1**
4002 **8** *1 ¼* **Stage Two (IRE)**[8] 2347 3-8-8 **40**........(v¹) RFrench 9 — 28
*(MJohnston) prom on outside tl wknd over 3f out* **11/2**²
-050 **9** *7* **Nafferton Heights (IRE)**[14] 2199 3-9-1 **47**........ DaleGibson 3 — 25
*(MWEasterby) keen: led to over 3f out: sn btn* **6/1**³
43U5 **10** *3* **Upthedale (IRE)**[8] 2347 3-8-0 **39**........ DFentiman(7) 6 — 13
*(JRWeymes) a bhd* **25/1**
0243 **11** *hd* **Romeo's Day**[6] 2402 3-9-6 **52**........ TEDurcan 11 — 26
*(MRChannon) hld up: hdwy into midfield 1/2-way: rdn and wknd over 3f out* **5/1**¹
00-0 **12** *3 ½* **Quay Walloper**[16] 2144 3-9-4 **50**........ DarrenWilliams 12 — 19
*(JRNorton) in tch to 1/2-way: sn rdn and btn* **25/1**
60-0 **13** *3* **Celtic Solitude (IRE)**[16] 2144 3-9-0 **46**........ ACulhane 14 — 10
*(MrsMReveley) hld up: rdn and edgd lft 4f out: sn btn* **33/1**
0006 **14** *9* **Baroque**[24] 1959 3-8-2 **34** oh14........ JBramhill 10 — —
*(CSmith) bhd: rdn over 4f out: nvr on terms* **100/1**

3m 6.86s (1.86) **Going Correction** +0.025s/f (Good) — **14** Ran SP% **109.0**
Speed ratings: **95,94,94,93,89 88,88,87,83,81 81,79,78,72**CSF £83.28 CT £1560.82 TOTE £8.00: £3.70, £6.80, £6.20; EX 177.70.
**Owner** Middleham Park Racing & Middleham Turf **Bred** Major W R Paton-Smith **Trained** Middleham Moor, N Yorks

**FOCUS**
A very weak race that is unlikely to produce many winners outside of banded company.
**NOTEBOOK**
**Nocatee(IRE)** ran well on his return from nearly three months off the track at Nottingham on his previous outing and, with the cheekpieces re-fitted, progressed from that run to gain his first win. There could be more to come.
**Spring Breeze** appreciated this step up in trip and was just held. There could find a similar race.
**Northern Spirit** had cheekpieces on for the first time and, back up in trip, he ran a promising race.
**Bollin Annabel** ran respectably, faring best of the fillies, but things will be harder back in normal handicaps.
**Stage Two(IRE)** did not appear to take to the fitting of a visor.
**Nafferton Heights(IRE)** should have appreciated this step up in trip, but he was disappointing.
**Romeo's Day**, stepped up from a mile and a half, ran poorly and has been a beaten favourite on his last two starts.

## 2555 KIRKLEATHAM MAIDEN STKS — 1m 2f
**4:45** (4:46) (D) 3-Y-O+ — **£3,552** (£1,093; £546; £273) **Stalls** Low

Form — RPR
3 **1** **Feaat**[19] 2059 3-8-6........ JCarroll 5 — 79
*(JHMGosden) cl up: effrt to chal over 2f out: led ins fnl f: styd on* **4/6**¹
0-3 **2** *¾* **Arrgatt (IRE)**[10] 2311 3-8-11........ NCallan 1 — 83
*(MAJarvis) led: jnd and rdn over 2f out: hdd ins fnl f: kpt on: hld cl home* **5/2**²
00 **3** *19* **Pointed (IRE)**[14] 2198 3-8-6........ RWinston 4 — 42
*(TDEasterby) trckd ldrs tl rdn and outpcd fr 3f out* **100/1**
000- **4** *¾* **River Line (USA)**[248] 5221 3-8-11........ DeanMcKeown 9 — 45
*(CWFairhurst) hld up: shkn up over 3f out: n.d* **33/1**
**5** *3 ½* **Swahili Dancer (USA)** 3-8-8........ NMackay(3) 7 — 39
*(LMCumani) hld up: rdn and outpcd over 4f out: n.d after* **7/1**³
000- **6** *shd* **Bay Solitaire**[248] 5221 3-8-8........ DAllan(3) 2 — 39
*(TDEasterby) rrd s: keen in tch: rdn and wknd fr 4f out* **50/1**
0 **7** *17* **Dont Tell Simon**[16] 2145 3-8-8........ TEaves(3) 6 — 6
*(MESowersby) bhd: rdn 5f out: sn btn* **100/1**
**8** *shd* **Indibar (IRE)** 3-8-11........ ANicholls 8 — 6
*(AndrewTurnell) prom tl rdn and wknd over 4f out* **16/1**

2m 7.15s (0.35) **Going Correction** +0.025s/f (Good)
**WFA** 3 from 4yo 13lb — **8** Ran SP% **113.8**
Speed ratings: **99,98,83,82,79 79,66,66**CSF £2.45 TOTE £1.60: £1.02, £1.10, £15.40; EX 2.20.
**Owner** Hamdan Al Maktoum **Bred** Glebe Stud And Mrs F Woodd **Trained** Manton, Wilts

**FOCUS**
A race that lacked strength in depth, and the front two had this race to themselves after the Luca Cumani horse lost his position on the home turn.
**NOTEBOOK**
**Feaat** had to work pretty hard to get the better of the runner-up and confirm the promise of her debut effort, but she is open to further improvement. Her future lies in the hands of the Handicapper.
**Arrgatt(IRE)** is progressing and made the favourite work quite hard. He was well clear of the remainder and looks up to winning a similar contest.
**Pointed(IRE)** should find things easier now she is qualified for a handicap mark.
**Swahili Dancer(USA)**, a 40,000gns purchase, half-brother to the useful ten-furlong filly Design Perfection, lost his place badly on the home turn and his chance went at the same time. He is likely to come into his own when handicapped.
**Bay Solitaire** *Official explanation: jockey said gelding lost its action.*

## 2556 REDCAR AMATEUR RIDERS' MAIDEN H'CAP — 6f
**5:15** (5:16) (G) (0-55,55) 3-Y-O+ — **£2,688** (£768; £384) **Stalls** Centre

Form — RPR
00-0 **1** *½* **Desert Arc (IRE)**[51] 1345 6-10-7 **55**........ MrCDavies(7) 6 — 63
*(WMBrisbourne) hld up: hdwy over 1f out: r.o strly fnl f: fin 2nd, ½l: awrdd r* **14/1**
00-0 **2** *nk* **Orangino**[25] 1929 6-9-7 **39**........ MissRDavidson(5) 10 — 47
*(JSHaldane) prom: effrt 2f out: ev ch ins fnl f: kpt on: fin 3rd, ½l & nk: plcd 2nd* **33/1**
0-03 **3** *2* **Lord Wishingwell (IRE)**[22] 1985 3-9-0 **38**.....(v) MissKellyHarrison(3) 12 — 40
*(JSWainwright) w ldrs: rdn over 2f out: r.o fnl f: fin 4th, ½l, nk & 2l: plcd 3rd* **33/1**
-004 **4** *1* **Royal Nite Owl**[35] 1701 3-9-8 **46** ow6........ MrSDobson(3) 8 — 45
*(JO'Reilly) led to 1/2-way: cl up: rdn and nt qckn fnl f: fin 5th: plcd 4th* **50/1**
0002 **5** *1* **Frenchmans Lodge**[8] 2359 4-9-8 **35**........(b) MissEJJones 18 — 29
*(JMBradley) cl up: led 1/2-way to ent fnl f: edgd lft and sn no ex: fin 6th: plcd 5th* **6/1**³
6066 **6** *¾* **Frimley's Mattery**[22] 1994 4-9-11 **45**........ MissVBarr(7) 7 — 39
*(REBarr) prom: rdn and edgd lft over 1f out: no ex: fin 7th, plcd 6th* **25/1**
0000 **7** *¾* **Lady Double U**[8] 2350 4-10-4 **45**........ MissAElsey 5 — 37
*(TDEasterby) bhd: hdwy over 1f out: r.o fnl f: nrst fin: fin 8th, plcd 7th* **50/1**
0000 **8** *nk* **Valuable Gift**[56] 1283 7-9-1 **35** oh5........(p) GBartley(7) 2 — 26
*(RCGuest) chsd far side ldrs tl outpcd over 1f out: fin 9th, plcd 8th* **33/1**
0040 **9** *nk* **Princess Erica**[7] 2383 4-10-4 **45**........(p) MissLynseyHanna 13 — 35
*(JBalding) chsd ldrs: rdn and one pce wl over 1f out: fin 10th, plcd 9th* **10/1**
-002 **10** *2* **Leopard Creek**[8] 2353 3-10-6 **55**........(p) MissSBrotherton 1 — 39
*(MrsJRRamsden) cl up tl outpcd over 1f out* **10/1**
3-06 **11** *1* **Chantry Falls (IRE)**[22] 2007 4-10-7 **48**........ MsCWilliams 19 — 29
*(JGGiven) racd stands rail: n.d* **16/1**
000- **12** *nk* **Fizzy Lizzy**[256] 5047 4-9-5 **39**........ MissJWaring(7) 9 — 19
*(JeddO'Keeffe) chsd ldrs to over 2f out: sn btn* **50/1**
34-0 **13** *shd* **Mickledor (FR)**[8] 2359 4-10-3 **47**........(b) MissLEllison(3) 4 — 27
*(MDods) s.i.s: sn prom: rdn and wknd fr 2f out* **33/1**
4033 **14** *3 ½* **Bells Boy's**[7] 2384 5-9-10 **37**........(p) MissNCarberry 3 — 6
*(KARyan) cl up far side tl wknd fr 2f out* **3/1**¹
-200 **15** *hd* **Reedsman (IRE)**[12] 2251 3-9-11 **46**........(v¹) MrsSBosley 14 — 15
*(RCGuest) midfield: rdn 1/2-way: sn btn* **25/1**
000/ **16** *1 ¼* **Charlatan (IRE)**[50] 5808 6-9-3 **35** oh5........ MissJCDuncan(5) 16 — —
*(MrsCADunnett) in tch 2f: sn lost pl* **33/1**
-000 **17** *2* **Queens Square**[8] 2349 3-9-3 **45**........ MissARothery(7) 11 — 4
*(NTinkler) prom to 1/2-way: sn lost pl* **50/1**
030 **18** *1 ¾* **Clouds Of Gold (IRE)**[16] 2145 3-9-10 **50**........ MrPCallaghan(5) 17 — 4
*(JSWainwright) sn bhd towards stands side* **25/1**
6-03 **D** **Compton Plume**[14] 2219 4-11-0 **55**........ MrNickyTinkler 15 — 65
*(WHTinning) chsd ldrs: rdn to ld ins fnl f: lost weight cloth: kpt on wl: fin first, disq: weighed in 2lb light* **4/1**²

1m 13.42s (1.72) **Going Correction** +0.025s/f (Good)
**WFA** 3 from 4yo+ 8lb — **19** Ran SP% **124.1**
Speed ratings: **88,87,85,83,82 81,80,80,79,77 75,75,75,70,70 68,66,63,89**CSF £423.34 CT £20128.31 TOTE £29.00: £4.30, £12.80, £3.30, £6.00; EX 501.10 Place 6 £321.16, Place 5 £196.22.
**Owner** Steve Roberts **Bred** D J And Mrs Deer **Trained** Great Ness, Shropshire

**FOCUS**
A weak maiden handicap that would have been won by Compton Plume, had he not been disqualified for losing a weight cloth close home.
**NOTEBOOK**
**Desert Arc(IRE)** would still be a maiden had Compton Plume's saddle stayed intact. Things will be tougher back in normal handicaps.
**Orangino** has been tried over all sorts of trips on all sorts of ground, but these conditions appeared to suit and he was only pegged back by the promoted winner near the line.
**Lord Wishingwell(IRE)**, beaten in banded company on heavy ground on his previous start, handled this faster surface well enough and ran respectably.
**Royal Nite Owl** had never previously run over a trip this short, but he showed plenty of speed.
**Bells Boy's** made it 26 straight defeats and is not one to trust.
**Compton Plume** looked all set to win his first race at the 22nd attempt, but he lost a pad and a weight cloth close home, and therefore had the race taken off him in the Stewards' room.
T/Plt: £535.50 to a £1 stake. Pool: £42,110.70. 57.40 winning tickets. T/Qpdt: £104.70 to a £1 stake. Pool: £2,703.60. 19.10 winning tickets. RY

# 2532 SANDOWN (R-H)
### Tuesday, June 1

**OFFICIAL GOING: Good to soft (good in places)**
Wind: lt against Weather: overcast & drizzly

## 2557 SHARP MINDS BETFAIR: BEST ODDS CLASSIFIED STKS — 1m 14y
**6:15** (6:19) (D) 3-Y-O — **£5,603** (£1,724; £862; £431) **Stalls** High

Form — RPR
3312 **1** **Mystical Girl (USA)**[12] 2244 3-9-2 85........ SChin 8 — 95+
*(MJohnston) sn led: drew 3l clr wl over 1f out: rdn fnl f: kpt on* **2/1**¹
41 **2** *1 ¼* **Diamond Lodge**[15] 2182 3-8-11 79........ EAhern 10 — 84
*(JNoseda) lw: dwlt and rousted along in rr early: effrt 3f out: drvn and prog to chse wnr over 1f out: clsd ins fnl f: a hld* **9/2**²
0346 **3** *1 ¼* **Freak Occurence (IRE)**[10] 2295 3-9-1 81........ SDrowne 9 — 85
*(MissECLavelle) racd in midfield: rdn wl over 2f out: no prog tl styd on fr over 1f out: nrst fin* **6/1**³
0-40 **4** *¾* **Saffron Fox**[39] 1588 3-9-0 83........ LDettori 1 — 82
*(JGPortman) racd on outer: chsd ldrs: rdn over 3f out: lost pl and struggling over 2f out: styd on again fnl f* **14/1**
5-00 **5** *shd* **Winners Delight**[50] 1357 3-8-11 80........ RMiles(3) 13 — 82
*(APJarvis) dwlt: racd in last pair: c wd bnd over 3f out: prog over 2f out: rdn and hanging rt over 1f out: styd on* **25/1**
66-0 **6** *3 ½* **Hoh Bleu Dee**[13] 2224 3-9-4 84........ JFEgan 3 — 79
*(SKirk) racd towards rr: rdn 3f out: no prog and struggling 2f out: one pce after* **33/1**
14-0 **7** *2* **Stevedore (IRE)**[17] 2134 3-8-11 77........ LPKeniry(3) 4 — 71
*(BJMeehan) in rr: rdn 3f out: no prog and btn 2f out* **66/1**
-000 **8** *nk* **Compton's Eleven**[13] 2224 3-9-0 83........ SHitchcott(3) 5 — 73
*(MRChannon) hld up in rr: effrt on inner and nt clr run over 2f out: nt qckn and no prog over 1f out* **33/1**
-0U5 **9** *½* **Mister Saif (USA)**[21] 2019 3-9-5 85........ RHughes 7 — 74
*(RHannon) lw: prom: rdn wl over 2f out: hanging and nt qckn wl over 1f out: wknd* **14/1**

1-06 **10** *nk* **Jath**[10] 2307 3-9-2 85 ........ NPollard 11 70
(JulianPoulton) *chsd wnr after 3f to over 1f out: wknd* **20/1**

0-1 **11** *2* **Another Faux Pas (IRE)**[13] 2223 3-8-11 79 ........ RLMoore 2 61
(RHannon) *settled in last pair: shkn up 3f out: nt clr run over 2f out: no prog after* **14/1**

52-4 **12** *1 1/2* **Major Effort (USA)**[17] 2135 3-9-0 80 ........ KFallon 12 61
(SirMichaelStoute) *lw: trckd ldrs: rdn 3f out: sn lost pl and struggling* **13/2**

-401 **13** *1/2* **Attune**[17] 2135 3-8-11 80 ........ DHolland 6 57
(BJMeehan) *chsd wnr for 3f: wknd 2f out* **20/1**

1m 46.76s (2.84) **Going Correction** +0.425s/f (Yiel) **13** Ran SP% **119.9**
Speed ratings: **102,100,99,98,98 95,93,92,92,92 90,88,88**CSF £9.29 TOTE £2.80: £1.30, £2.10, £2.80; EX 10.10.
**Owner** T T Bloodstocks **Bred** Simon Tindall **Trained** Middleham Moor, N Yorks

**FOCUS**

A tight contest on the ratings, but in reality few could be seriously fancied. The form looks solid.

**NOTEBOOK**

**Mystical Girl(USA)** had not quite seen out the trip last time and the drop back to a mile always looked likely to suit. Making every yard, she had to be kept up to her work in the closing stages, but was always holding her rivals. She should continue to run well between a mile and ten furlongs.

**Diamond Lodge** won just a fair maiden at Windsor and this looked an improved effort. Once again she ran as though a step up to ten furlongs will be within her compass.

**Freak Occurence(IRE)** enjoys a little ease in the ground and continues to run to a consistent level. He once again ran his race.

**Saffron Fox** benefited from the easing of the ground as all her best form has been with cut.

**Winners Delight**, having his first outing since being banned from racing under the non-triers' rule, kept on well enough, although he did hang right under pressure.

**Hoh Bleu Dee** has yet to recapture his best form this season.

**Major Effort(USA)** may not have found the easing ground suiting him.

**Attune** *Official explanation: jockey said filly was unsuited by the good to soft ground.*

## 2558 SHARP MINDS CALL 0870 90 80 121 H'CAP — 1m 2f 7y

**6:45** (6:48) (C) (0-90,85) 3-Y-O **£10,010** (£3,080; £1,540; £770) **Stalls** High

Form RPR

002- **1** **Odiham**[212] 5886 3-9-0 78 ........ SDrowne 10 93
(HMorrison) *racd in midfield: swtchd lft and effrt 2f out: rdn to ld jst ins fnl f: styd on strly* **14/1**

2213 **2** *2* **Keelung (USA)**[30] 1799 3-9-7 85 ........ PRobinson 7 96
(MAJarvis) *lw: hld up in last pair: brought towards nr side st: prog 3f out: led over 1f out: wandered and hdd jst ins fnl f: nt qckn* **7/1**

2-14 **3** *1* **Settlement Craic (IRE)**[47] 1416 3-9-4 85 ........ RMiles(3) 6 95
(TGMills) *hld up in last pair: rdn and effrt over 2f out: styd on wl fr over 1f out: nrst fin* **12/1**

-330 **4** *2 1/2* **Momtic (IRE)**[14] 2202 3-9-2 80 ........ JPMurtagh 11 85
(WJarvis) *swtg: prom: rdn over 2f out: effrt to chal and ev ch over 1f out: fdd ins fnl f* **9/2[2]**

2212 **5** *4* **Man Of Letters (UAE)**[8] 2361 3-8-12 76 ........ KDalgleish 9 74
(MJohnston) *prom: chsd ldr over 3f out: rdn and losing pl whn squeezed out over 1f out: no ch after* **5/1[3]**

-213 **6** *2* **Maclean**[10] 2306 3-8-13 77 ........ KFallon 2 71
(SirMichaelStoute) *trckd ldrs: effrt 3f out: cl up u.p over 1f out: hanging and wknd* **9/4[1]**

1-60 **7** *6* **Mr Tambourine Man (IRE)**[30] 1799 3-9-2 80 ........ SSanders 5 63
(PFICole) *swtg: racd in midfield: rdn 3f out: no prog 2f out: sn wknd* **25/1**

010 **8** *1* **Anousa (IRE)**[19] 2070 3-9-5 83 ........(v) JFanning 1 65
(PHowling) *lw: settled in rr: rdn and effrt 3f out: struggling and btn 2f out* **25/1**

0003 **9** *nk* **Charlie Tango (IRE)**[5] 2419 3-7-8 65 ........ TDean(7) 8 46
(MRChannon) *dwlt: a towards rr: rdn 3f out: wknd 2f out* **25/1**

25-1 **10** *6* **Dubois**[14] 2204 3-9-4 82 ........(vt) LDettori 3 52
(SaeedBinSuroor) *led: gng easily over 2f out: hdd & wknd rapidly over 1f out* **11/2**

5-36 **11** *2 1/2* **Rio De Jumeirah**[10] 2281 3-9-0 78 ........ DHolland 4 44
(CEBrittain) *chsd ldr to over 3f out: sn wknd* **25/1**

2m 13.61s (3.43) **Going Correction** +0.425s/f (Yiel) **11** Ran SP% **123.2**
Speed ratings: **103,101,100,98,95 93,89,88,87,83 81**CSF £108.54 CT £1209.81 TOTE £21.20: £4.60, £2.00, £3.10; EX 199.00.
**Owner** Odiham Partnership **Bred** Glebe Stud **Trained** East Ilsley, Berks

**FOCUS**

A decent gallop on here and the principals came from off the pace. The field finished well strung out and the form looks fairly strong.

**NOTEBOOK**

**Odiham**, making his seasonal reappearance and handicap debut, came through from off the pace and won fairly cosily in the end. Clearly the step up in trip suited and it is unlikely that another two furlongs will cause him any bother. The King George V Handicap at Royal Ascot could be on the agenda now.

**Keelung(USA)**, who no doubt appreciated the rain, was brought towards the centre of the track in search of quicker ground. The tactic appeared to have worked as he hit the front approaching the last, but the colt threw his chance away by wandering under pressure.

**Settlement Craic(IRE)** stayed on well from the back of the field but shaped as though he would have preferred another two furlongs. A return to a mile and a half should bring its dividends. *Official explanation: jockey said colt was unsuited by the good to soft ground.*

**Momtic(IRE)** did best of those who raced towards the head of affairs and in the circumstances performed with credit.

**Man Of Letters(UAE)** was another who probably paid for racing up with the strong pace.

**Maclean** had looked likely to be suited by the step up to this trip but it is possible that the easing of the ground scuppered his chance. He deserves another chance on a quicker surface.

**Dubois** set a decent gallop which played into the hands of those coming from behind. He did, however, drop out very tamely, and is clearly not one of his stable's stars.

## 2559 BETFAIR.COM BRIGADIER GERARD STKS (GROUP 3) — 1m 2f 7y

**7:15** (7:19) (A) 4-Y-O+ **£29,000** (£11,000; £5,500; £2,500) **Stalls** High

Form RPR

-011 **1** **Bandari (IRE)**[26] 1902 5-8-10 114 ........ WSupple 3 123
(MJohnston) *trckd ldr: led 1/2-way: drvn and jnd 2f out: battled on wl to gain upper hand cl home* **7/2[2]**

0-36 **2** *nk* **Ikhtyar (IRE)**[17] 2109 4-8-10 113 ........ RHills 5 122
(JHMGosden) *lw: racd in midfield: stdy prog 3f out: jnd wnr 2f out: rdn and edgd lft over 1f out: no ex nr fin* **7/2[2]**

3-34 **3** *7* **Sunstrach (IRE)**[9] 2339 6-8-10 112 ........ JPMurtagh 6 110
(LMCumani) *lw: racd in midfield: rdn and effrt 3f out: no ch w ldng pair fr wl over 1f out: kpt on* **10/1**

5213 **4** *2 1/2* **Nysaean (IRE)**[9] 2329 5-8-13 114 ........ RHughes 2 108
(RHannon) *lw: prom: trckd wnr over 4f out: chal 3f out: ev ch 2f out: hrd rdn and fdd* **12/1**

103- **5** *3 1/2* **Comfy (USA)**[300] 3885 5-8-10 113 ........ KFallon 1 99
(SirMichaelStoute) *taken steadily to post: t.k.h: hld up in last pair: rdn over 3f out: sn struggling and bhd: kpt on fr over 1f out* **12/1**

330- **6** *1* **Kaieteur (USA)**[227] 5641 5-8-10 117 ........ DHolland 8 97
(BJMeehan) *swtg: hld up in rr: rdn over 3f out: sn struggling: modest prog 2f out: sn no hdwy* **7/1[3]**

141- **7** *6* **Lateen Sails**[310] 3632 4-8-13 114 ........(t) LDettori 7 89
(SaeedBinSuroor) *lw: t.k.h: trckd ldrs: rdn 3f out: sn wknd* **3/1[1]**

650 **8** *21* **Easter Ogil (IRE)**[18] 2076 9-8-10 55 ........ NPollard 9 49
(JaneSouthcombe) *dwlt: racd in last: lost tch over 3f out: t.o* **200/1**

-010 **9** *5* **Chancellor (IRE)**[30] 1804 6-8-13 112 ........ SSanders 4 43
(JLDunlop) *led to 1/2-way: wknd over 3f out: eased: t.o* **20/1**

2m 10.65s (0.47) **Going Correction** +0.425s/f (Yiel) **9** Ran SP% **111.7**
Speed ratings: **115,114,109,107,104 103,98,81,77**CSF £15.39 TOTE £4.40: £1.90, £2.10, £1.90; EX 15.60.
**Owner** Hamdan Al Maktoum **Bred** Rathasker Stud **Trained** Middleham Moor, N Yorks

**FOCUS**

A strong renewal, with the first two, who came clear, showing better form than many Group One winners. The winning time was a fair one for a Group Three given the conditions.

**NOTEBOOK**

**Bandari(IRE)**, who has been in cracking form this term, responded well to pressure to get the better of his owner's other representative in a protracted duel. This ten-furlong trip now seems to be ideal for him and, while things will be a lot tougher back in Group One company, this performance suggests he has every chance of running well in races such as the Prince of Wales's Stakes and Eclipse.

**Ikhtyar(IRE)** , the choice of Richard Hills, travelled well into contention but could not get past his battle-hardened rival in a duel which lasted a quarter mile. He was not given a forceful ride, though, and hopefully that kindness will repay connections in some of the big summer races to come. However, fast ground is considered unsuitable for him.

**Sunstrach(IRE)** was making a fairly quick reappearance after his recent fourth in a French Group One. The ground had come in his favour and he appeared to run his race.

**Nysaean(IRE)**, third in an Irish Group One last time, could not live with the first two as they settled down to battle it out. This was a fair effort but once again showed up his limitations.

**Comfy(USA)** has had his problems and is lightly raced for a five-year-old, but connections clearly retain some faith in him. This was not a bad reappearance effort, especially as the ground was probably soft enough.

**Kaieteur(USA)** had his ideal conditions but he was taking on race-fit rivals on his reappearance and that proved too much. He should come on for the outing, though.

**Lateen Sails** raced too keenly and failed to give his running. These conditions should have brought out the best in him and he deserves another chance to prove this run all wrong. *Official explanation: trainer said colt was very fresh and appeared to be too keen early on.*

## 2560 SHARP MINDS BETFAIR H'CAP — 1m 14y

**7:50** (7:55) (D) (0-80,80) 3-Y-O+ **£5,603** (£1,724; £862; £431) **Stalls** High

Form RPR

0601 **1** **Acomb**[8] 2368 4-9-1 67 5ex ........ KFallon 9 85+
(MWEasterby) *prom: led 3f out: sn clr: in n.d fnl 2f: eased nr fin* **3/1[1]**

5-00 **2** *5* **Anna Walhaan (IRE)**[10] 2304 5-9-4 70 ........ TQuinn 2 78
(IanWilliams) *s.i.s: hld up in rr: shkn up 3f out: prog over 1f out : styd on wl to take 2nd last strides* **10/1**

2-06 **3** *nk* **Spirit's Awakening**[13] 2226 5-8-4 56 ........ JQuinn 3 63
(JAkehurst) *racd in midfield: rdn 3f out: prog 2f out: disp 2nd ins fnl f: no ch w wnr* **8/1**

0212 **4** *1/2* **Fen Gypsy**[28] 1876 6-8-8 60 ........ RHavlin 11 66
(PDEvans) *trckd ldrs: rdn to chse wnr over 2f out: no imp: lost 2 pls nr fin* **9/1**

0-00 **5** *3 1/2* **Oh Boy (IRE)**[19] 2064 4-8-8 60 ........ RLMoore 12 59
(RHannon) *lw: hld up in midfield: effrt 3f out: rdn and nt qckn 2f out: n.d over 1f out* **20/1**

0-00 **6** *1/2* **Sri Diamond**[14] 2201 4-9-10 76 ........ JFEgan 6 74
(SKirk) *trckd ldrs: rdn over 2f out: nt qckn and sn btn* **7/1[3]**

10-3 **7** *hd* **Crail**[34] 1708 4-9-6 72 ........ GBaker 1 69
(CFWall) *s.i.s: hld up in detached last pair: shkn up 3f out: no prog tl styd on fr over 1f out* **7/1[3]**

-210 **8** *hd* **Instructor**[14] 2202 3-9-0 77 ........ RHughes 10 74
(RHannon) *pressed ldr to 3f out: sn rdn: fdd fnl 2f* **12/1**

0060 **9** *6* **Invader**[108] 775 8-10-0 80 ........(bt) SDrowne 4 64
(CEBrittain) *trckd ldrs: rdn 3f out: wknd 2f out* **20/1**

0022 **10** *1/2* **Meelup (IRE)**[18] 2078 4-8-7 59 ........(p) NPollard 13 42
(JaneSouthcombe) *led to 3f out: sn wknd* **20/1**

-003 **11** *5* **Eastern Hope (IRE)**[14] 2218 5-8-11 63 ........(b) DHolland 7 36
(MrsLStubbs) *dwlt: hld up in rr: hrd rdn over 2f out: wknd over 1f out* **5/1[2]**

0-00 **12** *14* **Night Driver (IRE)**[13] 2226 5-8-3 55 ........ RBrisland 5 —
(GLMoore) *s.i.s: hld up in last: rdn 3f out: sn t.o* **50/1**

1m 45.54s (1.62) **Going Correction** +0.425s/f (Yiel)
**WFA** 3 from 4yo+ 11lb **12** Ran SP% **120.8**
Speed ratings: **108,103,102,102,98 98,98,97,91,91 86,72**CSF £32.91 CT £228.84 TOTE £3.90: £1.90, £3.20, £2.80; EX 32.00.
**Owner** Giles W Pritchard-Gordon **Bred** D F Spence And M W Easterby **Trained** Sheriff Hutton, N Yorks

**FOCUS**

A standard handicap but the winner is in fine form at present and ran away with the race.

**NOTEBOOK**

**Acomb** made light of his 5lb penalty to run out a clear winner. He appears to handle easy ground just as well as a quicker surface, and should continue to run well while in this form. He will, however, take a pretty big hike in the weights for his recent success, and things will be a lot tougher off his revised mark.

**Anna Walhaan(IRE)** has dropped a long way in the handicap over the last two years and ran his best race for a good while, but he remains winless for two years.

**Spirit's Awakening**, who looks on a fair mark judged on last year's form, ran a more promising race, and quicker ground should see him in a better light.

**Fen Gypsy** runs well with cut in the ground and looked booked for second until weakening well inside the last.

**Oh Boy(IRE)**, another 5lb lower, ran his best race of the campaign, although his tendency to flash his tail under pressure was slightly worrying.

**Sri Diamond**, who disappointed when well drawn at Goodwood last time, only ran a fair race.

## 2561 BET "IN RUNNING" AT BETFAIR H'CAP — 1m 6f

**8:20** (8:23) (D) (0-80,80) 3-Y-O **£5,486** (£1,688; £844; £422) **Stalls** Low

Form RPR

-110 **1** **Golden Quest**[47] 1416 3-9-5 78 ........ JFanning 10 85
(MJohnston) *trckd ldrs: effrt to ld wl over 2f out: drvn and wandered fnl 2f: hrd pressed fnl f: kpt on wl* **13/2[3]**

5-01 **2** *3/4* **Considine (USA)**[34] 1714 3-8-8 67 ........ JTate 6 73
(JMPEustace) *led to 10f out: trckd ldrs after: rdn over 2f out: effrt to chal ins fnl f: hld nr fin* **12/1**

5213 **3** ½ **Nessen Dorma (IRE)**[19] 2070 3-9-7 **80** MFenton 5 85
(JGGiven) *prom: led 8f out to over 5f out: drvn to chal again 2f out: ev ch ins fnl f: styd on* **5/1**[2]

-331 **4** ½ **Bumptious**[30] 1786 3-9-2 **75** PRobinson 2 79
(MHTompkins) *settled in rr: prog 3f out: drvn to press ldrs fnl f: kpt on but a hld* **5/1**[2]

54-0 **5** *hd* **Fu Fighter**[18] 2085 3-8-13 **72** EAhern 13 76
(JAOsborne) *prom: led over 5f out: 3l clr 4f out: rdn and hdd wl over 2f out: kpt on to chal again fnl f: no ex nr fin* **25/1**

0665 **6** 1 ½ **Hathlen (IRE)**[17] 2133 3-8-11 **73** SHitchcott(3) 14 75
(MRChannon) *lw: hld up in tch: rdn and effrt 3f out: chsd ldrs 2f out: hanging lft and no imp: kpt on* **20/1**

1125 **7** ¾ **Bill Bennett (FR)**[6] 2397 3-9-4 **77** GBaker 9 78
(JJay) *settled towards rr: rdn and effrt 3 out: kpt on fnl 2f: nvr able to rch ldrs* **14/1**

6-11 **8** 15 **Fleetfoot Mac**[22] 1998 3-8-6 **65** KFallon 12 47
(PDEvans) *prog to ld 10f out: hdd 8f out: rdn and btn 3f out: eased over 1f out* **4/1**[1]

4-42 **9** 1 ¾ **Turnstile**[10] 2312 3-9-1 **74** PDobbs 11 53
(RHannon) *trckd ldrs tl wknd u.p over 2f out* **5/1**[2]

6-10 **10** 1 ¼ **Liquidate**[47] 1416 3-8-7 **66** SDrowne 7 44
(HMorrison) *hld up in rr: rdn 3f out: sn struggling* **10/1**

2-05 **11** 3 ½ **Blue Hills**[30] 1786 3-8-11 **70** KDalgleish 3 43
(MJohnston) *a in rr: rdn and no prog 3f out* **33/1**

3m 11.88s (7.51) **Going Correction** +0.425s/f (Yiel) **11** Ran SP% **118.3**
Speed ratings: **95,94,94,94,93 93,92,84,83,82 80**CSF £80.02 CT £426.12 TOTE £9.00: £2.80, £3.30, £1.90; EX 294.90.
**Owner** Syndicate 2002 **Bred** Fittocks Stud **Trained** Middleham Moor, N Yorks
■ Stewards Enquiry : E Ahern one-day ban: used whip in an incorrect place (Jun 12)

**FOCUS**
A competitive affair producing a tight finish, but a modest time for the grade.

**NOTEBOOK**
**Golden Quest**, despite being a dual winner over a mile and a half on the All-Weather, had shaped as though finding the trip too short on his return to the turf. This longer distance suited and he rallied well when challenged in the final quarter mile. There is more to come from him as he looks a typical Johnston improver.
**Considine(USA)**, a winner in heavy ground on his previous start, no doubt welcomed the rain which had eased the surface. Having made much of the running, he came back for more after being headed, and stamina clearly looks his forte.
**Nessen Dorma(IRE)**, who has yet to race on ground quicker than good, appreciated the return to this longer trip having found a mile and a half too short at York last time.
**Bumptious** was not sure to be suited by the step up in trip and appeared to be ridden to get it. In the event he saw it out well.
**Fu Fighter**, who kicked clear leaving the back straight, kept battling away after being headed. He got the longer trip alright on this handicap debut, and there is better to come from him.
**Fleetfoot Mac** found a 6lb higher mark and a longer trip finding him out in this better grade.

## 2562 SHARP MINDS BETFAIR MAIDEN STKS 1m 2f 7y
8:50 (8:57) (D ) 3-Y-0+ £5,772 (£1,776; £888; £444) Stalls High

Form RPR

3 **1** **Haadef**[18] 2085 3-8-11 RHills 9 86
(JHMGosden) *lw: settled midfield: prog over 2f out: shkn up to ld ent fnl f: pushed out: comf* **1/1**[1]

**2** 1 ¼ **Elmustanser** 3-8-11 (t) LDettori 3 84
(SaeedBinSuroor) *leggy: unf: prom: shkn up to chal over 1f out: w wnr ent fnl f: r.o but hld last 100yds* **5/1**[2]

**3** 3 **Shambar (IRE)**[768] 5-9-10 JPMurtagh 2 78
(PRChamings) *t.k.h: mostly trckd ldr: led 3f out: drvn and hdd ent fnl f: one pce* **20/1**

2- **4** *shd* **Maid To Treasure (IRE)**[213] 5868 3-8-6 TQuinn 14 73
(JLDunlop) *bit bkwd: racd in midfield: outpcd 3f out: shkn up and styd on wl fr over 1f out: nrst fin* **5/1**[2]

0- **5** 4 **Shooting Lodge (IRE)**[267] 4777 3-8-6 KFallon 1 66
(SirMichaelStoute) *trckd ldrs: shkn up over 2f out: outpcd fnl 2f* **12/1**

0/0- **6** 2 **Secret Jewel (FR)**[421] 956 4-9-5 SSanders 15 62
(LadyHerries) *bit bkwd: dwlt: racd towards rr: shuffled along 3f out: wandered but kpt on fnl 2f: nvr nrr* **66/1**

**7** ¾ **Enhancer**[59] 6-9-10 JFEgan 10 66
(MrsLCJewell) *racd keenly bhd ldrs: rdn and effrt over 2f out: no imp: wknd fnl f* **66/1**

0- **8** ½ **Song Of The Sea**[266] 4803 3-8-6 SWhitworth 12 60
(JWHills) *dwlt: wl in rr: bhd 3f out: r.o fr over 1f out: nvr nrr* **66/1**

0-0 **9** ½ **Bonsai (IRE)**[15] 2182 3-8-6 EAhern 8 59
(RTPhillips) *prom: rdn over 2f out: wknd over 1f out* **33/1**

00- **10** 1 **My Sunshine (IRE)**[306] 3719 3-8-6 PRobinson 7 57
(BWHills) *trckd ldrs: shkn up over 2f out: wknd over 1f out* **20/1**

0-32 **11** 3 **Midshipman Easy (USA)**[22] 2001 3-8-11 77 DHolland 13 57
(PWHarris) *led to 3f out: steadily wknd* **15/2**[3]

26 **12** 3 **Indian Chase**[18] 2090 7-9-3 (v) LucyRussell(7) 11 51?
(DrJRJNaylor) *dwlt: a towards rr: struggling 3f out* **100/1**

0-00 **13** 7 **Ocean Rock**[18] 2085 3-8-11 PMcCabe 6 39
(CAHorgan) *s.v.s: a wl in rr* **100/1**

000 **14** *shd* **Alianna (FR)**[63] 1189 3-8-6 RLMoore 5 34
(SDow) *a in rr: bhd fnl 3f* **100/1**

**15** 22 **Delfinia** 3-8-7 ow1 SDrowne 16 —
(HSHowe) *w'like: bit bkwd: a in rr: bhd 3f out: t.o* **100/1**

0-0B **16** 3 **Good Article (IRE)**[26] 1912 3-8-8 (e) DCorby(3) 4 —
(APJones) *racd keenly: trckd ldrs: wknd 4f out: t.o* **100/1**

2m 14.82s (4.64) **Going Correction** +0.425s/f (Yiel) **16** Ran SP% **124.7**
**WFA** 3 from 4yo+ 13lb
Speed ratings: **98,97,94,94,91 89,89,88,88,87 85,82,77,77,59 57**CSF £5.80 TOTE £1.90: £1.10, £2.10, £4.40; EX 9.00 Place 6 £156.19, Place 5 £118.96.
**Owner** Hamdan Al Maktoum **Bred** Shadwell Estate Company Limited **Trained** Manton, Wilts

**FOCUS**
A fair maiden, and there is a lot more to come from the first two.

**NOTEBOOK**
**Haadef ◆**, who had run an eye-catching race on his debut, won this with a bit more in hand than the official margin would suggest, as he had to wait for a run a quarter-mile out before making up his ground easily. The conditions were not a worry for this son of Sadler's Wells and he will get farther than this. Indeed, his connections intend to step him straight up to two miles for the Queen's Vase at Royal Ascot, and that test of stamina could well be the making of him.
**Elmustanser ◆**, a brother to Dubai World Cup winner Almutawakel and 1000 Guineas runner-up Muwakleh, would probably not have been suited by the easy ground so in the circumstances this was a good effort. He should have no trouble at all winning his maiden.
**Shambar(IRE)**, an Aga Khan cast-off previously trained in France, was having his first outing for more than two years. He was the only one to upset market expectations and clearly retains a fair amount of ability. He could be an interesting one for handicaps after one more run.
**Maid To Treasure(IRE)**, who was down in the paper as a likely non-runner had there been no rain, had conditions turn in her favour. She shaped as though likely to appreciate a sterner test of stamina.
**Shooting Lodge(IRE)** is a half-sister to seven winners, including useful middle-distance performer Sinntara and smart hurdler Mistinguett, the dam of Misternando. She will be of more interest once she is qualified to run in handicaps.
**Secret Jewel(FR)** was entitled to need this run on her reappearance, having been off the track for 421 days. Handicaps are now open to her.
**Song Of The Sea** will need a stiffer test once eligible for handicaps.
T/Jkpt: Not won. T/Plt: £158.60 to a £1 stake. Pool: £86,982.25. 400.25 winning tickets. T/Qpdt: £10.50 to a £1 stake. Pool: £5,351.80. 375.80 winning tickets. JN

2563 - 2566a (Foreign Racing) - See Raceform Interactive

# 2345 BEVERLEY (R-H)
Wednesday, June 2

**OFFICIAL GOING: Good to firm (firm in back straight)**
After 5mm of rain and 18mm of water put in the track over the previous eight days the ground was described as 'near perfect, just on the quick side of good'.
Wind: Mod. 1/2 behind. Weather: Fine.

## 2567 BIG SCREEN IS HERE TONIGHT STKS (H'CAP) 1m 4f 16y
6:35 (6:35) (E ) (0-70,69) 3-Y-O £3,952 (£1,216; £608; £304) Stalls High

Form RPR

006- **1** **Zalda**[223] 5716 3-8-11 **59** RWinston 4 65
(RCharlton) *trckd ldr: effrt over 2f out: styd on to ld last 100yds* **14/1**

0-53 **2** 1 ¼ **Havetoavit (USA)**[17] 2146 3-8-12 **60** TQuinn 2 64
(JDBethell) *led: hdd and no ex ins last* **9/2**[2]

0-51 **3** ¾ **Vicario**[7] 2402 3-8-5 **56** 6ex DAllan(3) 1 59
(MLWBell) *sn bhd and pushed along: hdwy whn bmpd over 2f out: hung rt and styd on: swtchd lft wl ins last* **13/8**[1]

00-3 **4** 6 **Dunlea Dancer**[41] 1559 3-8-8 **56** JFanning 6 49
(MJohnston) *chsd ldrs: wknd over 1f out* **9/2**[2]

3-06 **5** 1 **Victory Lap (GER)**[18] 2133 3-9-5 **67** TEDurcan 3 59
(MRChannon) *hld up: hdwy 5f out: rdn and edgd lft over 2f out: sn wknd* **11/1**

15-6 **6** *nk* **Xpressions**[15] 2199 3-8-2 **50** PHanagan 8 41
(RAFahey) *sn chsng ldrs: drvn along over 4f out: lost pl 2f out* **11/2**[3]

00-6 **7** 28 **Redmarley (IRE)**[17] 2145 3-8-11 **59** MFenton 7 5
(JGGiven) *bhd and pushed along 8f out: t.o 3f out* **25/1**

004 **8** 6 **Moonshaft (USA)**[35] 1713 3-9-7 **69** EAhern 5 6
(EALDunlop) *hld up: hdwy on outside over 6f out: sn chsng ldrs: wknd over 2f out: eased* **12/1**

2m 36.0s (-3.30) **Going Correction** -0.175s/f (Firm) **8** Ran SP% **116.4**
Speed ratings: **104,103,102,98,98 97,79,75**CSF £76.99 CT £160.50 TOTE £13.40: £4.50, £1.70, £1.10; EX 122.90.
**Owner** D J Deer **Bred** D J And Mrs Deer **Trained** Beckhampton, Wilts

**FOCUS**
A fair time for the grade but the form looks modest.

**NOTEBOOK**
**Zalda**, who showed little in three backend outings at two, was warm and on her toes beforehand. She gained the upper hand late in the day and will be better suited by an even stiffer test. *Official explanation: trainer's representative said, regarding the improved form shown, filly had strengthened up during the winter and had benefited from the step up in trip on this occasion*
**Havetoavit(USA)**, a keen type who likes to dominate, found the winner just too strong inside the last.
**Vicario**, who is not that big, was soon struggling. Collecting a bump once in line for home, he stayed on all the way to the line despite looking unhappy on the fastish ground.
**Dunlea Dancer**, fitted with a cross noseband, was in the right position throughout but he did not improve for the step up in trip.
**Victory Lap(GER)** was in the end well beaten on her handicap debut.
**Xpressions** gained his one win at two in selling company.
**Redmarley(IRE)** *Official explanation: jockey said gelding was never travelling*
**Moonshaft(USA)**, making his handicap bow under a stiffish mark, dropped right out. *Official explanation: jockey said colt lost its action*

## 2568 HILARY NEEDLER TROPHY (LISTED RACE) (FILLIES) 5f
7:05 (7:07) (A ) 2-Y-O £14,500 (£5,500; £2,750; £1,250) Stalls High

Form RPR

1 **1** **Miss Meggy**[18] 2129 2-8-11 DAllan 1 87+
(TDEasterby) *dwlt: bhd: hdwy on outer over 1f out: r.o wl to ld nr fin* **16/1**

2 **2** *nk* **Tagula Sunrise (IRE)**[9] 2352 2-8-8 PHanagan 10 83
(RAFahey) *trckd ldrs: sltly hmpd after 1f: styd on to ld 150yds out: hdd and no ex nr fin* **10/1**

31 **3** *nk* **Mary Read**[33] 1743 2-8-8 FLynch 5 82
(BSmart) *led: edgd rt after 1f: hdd jst ins fnl f: no ex* **25/1**

0 **4** ½ **African Breeze**[18] 2129 2-8-8 DeanMcKeown 14 80+
(RMWhitaker) *hmpd sn after star: mid-div: hdwy on inner 2f out: styd on wl fnl f* **28/1**

21 **5** *hd* **Mizz Tee (IRE)**[8] 2388 2-8-11 WSupple 15 82+
(TDEasterby) *s.s: gd hdwy on wd outside over 1f out: fin strly* **2/1**[1]

221 **6** ½ **Sapphire Dream**[11] 2296 2-8-11 TEDurcan 11 81
(ABailey) *chsd ldrs: drvn along over 2f out: edgd rt over 1f out: kpt on* **5/2**[2]

1 **7** 1 ½ **Rosein**[18] 2125 2-8-8 JFanning 9 72
(MrsGSRees) *sn chsng ldrs: nt clr run over 1f out: kpt on ins last* **8/1**[3]

341 **8** ½ **Tiviski (IRE)**[28] 1884 2-8-11 EAhern 13 74
(EJAlston) *hmpd sn after s: chsd ldrs: edgd lft and outpcd over 1f out* **9/1**

54 **9** 2 **Tantien**[21] 2035 2-8-8 NCallan 7 64
(JohnAHarris) *sn bhd: sme late hdwy* **100/1**

16 **10** *hd* **Handsome Lady**[18] 2129 2-8-8 TQuinn 8 63
(ISemple) *chsd ldrs: wknd over 1f out* **10/1**

11 **11** ¾ **Nova Tor (IRE)**[25] 1970 2-8-8 JCarroll 12 60
(NPLittmoden) *swtchd rt after s: w ldr: edgd lft and wknd 1f out* **16/1**

010 **12** *dist* **Flossytoo**[18] 2129 2-8-11 JDO'Reilly 6 —
(JO'Reilly) *dwlt: hdwy on outside whn sddle slipped 2f out: sn virtually p.u: t.o* **33/1**

63.66 secs (-0.34) **Going Correction** -0.075s/f (Good) **12** Ran SP% **124.2**
Speed ratings: **99,98,98,97,96 96,93,92,89,89 88,—**CSF £169.53 TOTE £20.00: £4.00, £3.10, £4.60; EX 233.80.
**Owner** David W Armstrong **Bred** Trickledown Stud **Trained** Great Habton, N Yorks

**FOCUS**
Horses drawn 2, 3 and 4 were withdrawn withs vets' certificates. The winner came from stall one in a Listed race which went to Attraction 12 months earlier. It was a messy race this time and the standard falls some way short of last year's race.

**NOTEBOOK**

**Miss Meggy**, a lazy walker, showed her inexperience when making a tardy start. She came sweeping through on the outside to show ahead near the line, and will improve again.

**Tagula Sunrise(IRE)** still does not look 100% fit. Tightened up at the end of the first furlong, she worked hard to get her head in front only to have the valuable prize pinched from under her nose near the line. She is a ready-made winner of a maiden race.

**Mary Read** is all speed, but after getting in the way of the runner-up at the end of the first furlong she was worn down in the closing stages.

**African Breeze**, well beaten first time behind tonight's winner at Thirsk, was left short of room on the inner early on. Sticking to the far-side rail, she put in some sterling work and deserves to find a race.

**Mizz Tee(IRE)** ◆, drawn best, was on her knees coming out of the stalls. With just two behind her over a furlong out, she finished with a real flourish on the wide outside. She looked the best filly on view and deserves rich compensation. *Official explanation: jockey said filly slipped coming out of the stalls*

**Sapphire Dream** gave a good account of herself, but she rolled towards the fence over a furlong out, getting in the way of Rosein.

**Rosein**, a good-quartered filly, looked to be carrying loads of condition. She never really had the run of the race and is well worth another chance.

**Handsome Lady** *Official explanation: jockey said filly had lost her action*

**Flossytoo** *Official explanation: jockey said saddle slipped*

## 2569 SKY BET PRESS RED TO BET NOW H'CAP — 7f 100y

**7:35** (7:35) (D) (0-80,80) 3-Y-O — **£6,906** (£2,125; £1,062; £531) **Stalls** High

Form — RPR

-433 **1** **Burley Flame**[18] 2134 3-8-13 **72** ........ MFenton 7 82
(JGGiven) *trckd ldr: sltly hmpd bnd 6f out: styd on to ld last 100yds* **8/1**

4-01 **2** *nk* **Doctorate**[43] 1519 3-9-7 **80** ........ EAhern 6 89
(EALDunlop) *trckd ldr: led over 1f out tl ins last: no ex* **11/2**[3]

21 **3** *2* **Snap**[25] 1975 3-9-0 **73** ........ JFanning 3 77
(MJohnston) *trckd ldrs: effrt over 2f out: edgd rt over 1f out: kpt on same pce* **7/4**[1]

0053 **4** *nk* **Poppys Footprint (IRE)**[13] 2239 3-9-4 **77** ........ NCallan 5 81
(KARyan) *trckd ldrs: effrt over 3f out: keeping on same pce whn n.m.r over 1f out* **7/2**[2]

51-0 **5** *4* **Misaro (GER)**[25] 1956 3-9-0 **76** ........ DNolan(3) 1 70
(PABlockley) *led: edgd rt bnd 6f out: hdd over 1f out: edgd rt and wknd fnl f* **25/1**

-454 **6** *½* **Trojan Flight**[21] 2036 3-8-7 **66** ........ (p) ACulhane 4 58
(MrsJRRamsden) *hld up towards rr: sn t.k.h: hdwy on inner over 2f out: no imp whn n.m.r ins last* **8/1**

0-51 **7** *hd* **Neon Blue**[13] 2236 3-8-9 **68** ........ MHills 8 60
(RMWhitaker) *hld up: outpcd over 3f out: sme hdwy 2f out: sn wknd* **7/1**

520- **8** *7* **Eboracum (IRE)**[212] 5906 3-8-3 **65** ........ DAllan(3) 2 39
(TDEasterby) *hld up in rr: drvn along on outer over 3f out: sn lost pl* **25/1**

1m 32.31s (-1.99) **Going Correction** -0.175s/f (Firm) — **8** Ran SP% **116.4**
Speed ratings: **104,103,101,101,96 95,95,87**CSF £52.18 CT £111.71 TOTE £9.60: £3.00, £2.10, £1.40; EX 92.90.
**Owner** Burley Appliances Ltd **Bred** Miss D Fleming **Trained** Willoughton, Lincs

**FOCUS**
Fair form, with the winner giving a boost to Mythical Girl's Thirsk race.

**NOTEBOOK**

**Burley Flame** proved very willing and gained the upper hand late in the day. He clearly has the right attitude.

**Doctorate**, on his handicap debut, travelled strongly and only missed out near the line. The experience will not be lost on him. *Official explanation: jockey said colt failed to handle the bend*

**Snap**, stepping up in trip on his handicap bow, came off a straight line and never really looked like picking up. Still inexperienced, he can do better, possibly over further on a more galloping track.

**Poppys Footprint(IRE)**, 2lb higher, was only keeping on in her own time when tightened up coming to the final furlong.

**Misaro(GER)**, suited by this totally different ground, had his own way in front but he didn't see it out. A slight drop back in trip and easier ground will aid his cause.

**Trojan Flight**, a headstrong sort, was only half doing it when running out of racing room on the inner inside the last. He looks anything but straightforward.

## 2570 BRIAN YEARDLEY CONTINENTAL TWO YEAR OLD TROPHY (CONDITIONS STKS) — 5f

**8:10** (8:12) (B) 2-Y-O — **£11,669** (£4,426; £2,213; £1,006) **Stalls** High

Form — RPR

**1** **Bolton Hall (IRE)** 2-8-6 ........ PHanagan 6 83
(RAFahey) *w'like: rangy: sn chsng ldrs: hrd rdn and edgd lft appr fnl f: wnt lft and led nr fin* **10/1**

1 **2** *nk* **Tournedos (IRE)**[47] 1436 2-8-13 ........ TEDurcan 4 89
(MRChannon) *trckd ldr: slt ld 1f out: hdd and no ex nr fin* **6/4**[1]

1 **3** *nk* **Midnight Tycoon**[26] 1930 2-8-11 ........ FLynch 8 86
(BSmart) *led: edgd lft and qcknd 2f out: hdd 1f out: no ex ins last* **2/1**[2]

12 **4** *1 ¾* **Bigalos Bandit**[30] 1819 2-8-13 ........ RWinston 3 82
(JJQuinn) *trckd ldrs: ev ch and rdn whn hmpd 1f out: nt rcvr* **7/2**[3]

**5** *9* **Waggledance (IRE)** 2-8-6 ........ JCarroll 2 43
(JSWainwright) *rangy: unf: s.s: hdwy over 2f out: lost pl over 1f out* **25/1**

**6** *2 ½* **Den Perry** 2-8-6 ........ PBradley 1 35
(ABerry) *w'like: cmpt: unruly in stalls: sn outpcd and bhd* **40/1**

650 **7** *8* **Lane Marshal**[17] 2141 2-8-9 ........ TEaves 5 10
(MESowersby) *hung rt thrght: sn wl outpcd and bhd* **100/1**

63.43 secs (-0.57) **Going Correction** -0.075s/f (Good) — **7** Ran SP% **111.9**
Speed ratings: **101,100,100,97,82 78,66**CSF £24.57 TOTE £11.20: £3.10, £1.20; EX 33.30.
**Owner** J J Staunton **Bred** M Duffy **Trained** Musley Bank, N Yorks

**FOCUS**
The time was respectable for the grade, 0.23 seconds faster than the Hilary Needler, and this is strong form. Unbeaten Joseph Henry, backed as if defeat was out of the question, had to be withdrawn after playing up and injuring himself in the saddling box.

**NOTEBOOK**

**Bolton Hall(IRE)**, a February foal, was not unfancied on his debut. He never flinched under a punishing ride first time but his rider seemed fortunate to escape censure.

**Tournedos(IRE)**, who defeated the subsequent National Stakes runner-up Moscow Music when successful on his debut at Newbury, travelled strongly but had no excuse, just getting edged out near the line.

**Midnight Tycoon** sat in front, only quickening the pace with two furlongs left to run. He came off the inside, leaving the door open for the winner, and missed out near the line.

**Bigalos Bandit** was bang on terms when knocked sideways a furlong out but the impression was that he was only fourth best anyway.

**Waggledance(IRE)**, an April foal, was thrown in at the deep end first time but he was far from disgraced. He looks the type who needs more time yet.

**Den Perry**, an April foal, played up in the stalls and was soon out of contention, but was still handsomely rewarded just for making up the numbers.

## 2571 WEATHERBYS INSURANCE H'CAP — 1m 100y

**8:40** (8:40) (E) (0-75,72) 3-Y-O — **£4,728** (£1,455; £727; £363) **Stalls** High

Form — RPR

1212 **1** **Riley Boys (IRE)**[25] 1957 3-9-6 **71** ........ MFenton 5 79
(JGGiven) *led: qcknd over 2f out: hld on wl towards fin* **7/4**[1]

5-06 **2** *½* **Double Vodka (IRE)**[18] 2134 3-8-11 **62** ........ ACulhane 9 69
(MrsJRRamsden) *hld up: hmpd over 3f out: hdwy on ins 2f out: hrd rdn and nt qckn ins last* **6/1**[3]

5-20 **3** *½* **Fossgate**[25] 1957 3-9-6 **71** ........ TQuinn 3 77?
(JDBethell) *w wnr: hung rt 1f out: nt qckn ins last* **8/1**

4245 **4** *1 ¾* **Athollbrose (USA)**[15] 2197 3-8-4 **55** ........ WSupple 7 57
(TDEasterby) *sn chsng ldrs: effrt over 2f out: kpt on same pce fnl f* **8/1**

-040 **5** *½* **Auroville**[18] 2134 3-9-0 **65** ........ TEDurcan 4 66
(MLWBell) *hld up: hdwy and nt clr run 2f out: swtchd rt: kpt on fnl f* **6/1**[3]

5342 **6** *¾* **Given A Chance**[9] 2349 3-7-10 **52** oh6 ow3 ........ RThomas(5) 8 51?
(MrsSLamyman) *sn trcking ldrs: effrt and nt clr run 2f out: swtchd lft: kpt on fnl f* **14/1**

1000 **7** *1 ½* **Glendale**[25] 1957 3-8-8 **59** ........ (p) NCallan 2 55
(CADwyer) *trckd ldrs: quite keen: rdn and wknd over 1f out* **16/1**

4260 **8** *4* **Blue Empire (IRE)**[15] 2202 3-9-4 **72** ........ DNolan(3) 6 60
(PABlockley) *stdd s: hld up: hdwy on outer over 2f out: wknd over 1f out* **20/1**

0-24 **9** *3 ½* **Rabitatit (IRE)**[9] 2355 3-8-9 **63** ........ RMiles(3) 1 43
(JGMO'Shea) *hld up: hdwy on outer over 4f out: rdn and wknd 2f out* **11/2**[2]

1m 46.66s (-0.64) **Going Correction** -0.175s/f (Firm) — **9** Ran SP% **119.9**
Speed ratings: **96,95,95,93,92 92,90,86,83**CSF £13.11 CT £70.19 TOTE £2.70: £1.50, £1.80, £2.70; EX 15.90.
**Owner** Paul Riley **Bred** P J Makin **Trained** Willoughton, Lincs

**FOCUS**
Just a steady gallop until once in line for home. The form looks fair, but the proximity of the sixth from out of the handicap is a concern.

**NOTEBOOK**

**Riley Boys(IRE)**, given his own way in front, steadily wound up the pace and showed real grit. The much quicker ground was not a problem.

**Double Vodka(IRE)**, 2lb lower, was chopped off on the inner on the home turn. Sticking to the rail, the gap was there inside the last but he was just held.

**Fossgate**, suited by this much quicker ground, sat upsides in a race run at a moderate pace. He tended to hang under pressure and still looks to have something to learn.

**Athollbrose(USA)**, dropping back in trip, could have done with a much stronger gallop.

**Auroville**, closely matched with tonight's winner on Nottingham running, didn't have the best of luck but does not seem to be progressing as much as him. He might appreciate slightly easier ground.

**Given A Chance**, a maiden after 13 starts was running from out of the handica. He had a messy passage and is worth a try over a bit further.

**Rabitatit(IRE)**, warm beforehand, was much too keen to post and was well below her best. *Official explanation: jockey said gelding ran flat*

## 2572 NEXT MEETING IS WEDNESDAY 9 JUNE MAIDEN FILLIES' STKS — 7f 100y

**9:10** (9:10) (D) 3-Y-O+ — **£4,160** (£1,280; £640; £320) **Stalls** High

Form — RPR

4-65 **1** **Lorien Hill (IRE)**[18] 2122 3-8-9 67 ........ MHills 2 74
(BWHills) *trckd ldrs: styd on to ld jst ins last: r.o wl: readily* **15/8**[1]

26-0 **2** *2* **Vas Y Carla (USA)**[51] 1372 3-8-9 80 ........ TEDurcan 1 69
(DRLoder) *hld up: hdwy on outer 3f out: styd on ins last: tk 2nd nr fin* **4/1**[3]

0 **3** *¾* **Khafayif (USA)**[49] 1400 3-8-9 ........ WSupple 6 67
(BHanbury) *trckd ldrs: led over 1f out: hdd jst ins last: nt qckn* **9/2**

4522 **4** *3* **Graceful Air (IRE)**[12] 2259 3-8-9 62 ........ RWinston 5 60
(JRWeymes) *w ldr: led over 5f out: shkn up 2f out: sn hdd: one pce* **11/4**[2]

00- **5** *2* **Neqaawi**[251] 5172 3-8-2 ........ (t) CharlotteKerton(7) 4 55
(BHanbury) *plld hrd: led tl over 5f out: outpcd and hung rt over 1f out* **33/1**

00 **6** *2 ½* **Wedowannagiveuthat (IRE)**[30] 1820 3-8-6 ........ DAllan(3) 3 48
(TDEasterby) *hld up towards rr: effrt 3f out: no imp* **25/1**

6 **7** *1 ½* **Huggin Mac (IRE)**[21] 2046 3-8-2 ........ SuzanneFrance(7) 7 45
(NBycroft) *dwlt: hdwy on outside over 4f out: lost pl 2f out* **20/1**

0 **8** *4* **Cottam Karminski**[9] 2346 3-8-9 ........ PMQuinn 8 35
(JSWainwright) *dwlt: hld up in rr: hdwy on ins over 2f out: lost pl over 1f out* **50/1**

1m 34.26s (-0.04) **Going Correction** -0.175s/f (Firm) — **8** Ran SP% **113.1**
Speed ratings: **93,90,89,86,84 81,79,75**CSF £9.15 TOTE £2.90: £1.50, £1.40, £1.90; EX 11.50 Place 6 £66.87, Place 5 £47.00.
**Owner** D M James **Bred** Quay Bloodstock And Swettenham Stud **Trained** Lambourn, Berks

**FOCUS**
A fair maiden, but they went no pace at all until in line for home resulting in a slow winning time for the class of contest.

**NOTEBOOK**

**Lorien Hill(IRE)** is going the right way and took this in decisive fashion in the end. She will be suited by a step in trip when she reverts to handicap company.

**Vas Y Carla(USA)** may not be 100% straightforward. She has the ability to find a race and if she does she will be a valuable broodmare.

**Khafayif(USA)**, an excitable type, improved on her debut effort but she was treading water inside the last.

**Graceful Air(IRE)**, a maiden after 13 previous starts, was given a good ride in what was a tactical affair but she was still not nearly good enough.

**Neqaawi**, who showed little in two starts at two, wouldn't settle as a result of the modest pace, then hung late on. She looks as if she needs a little more time yet.

**Wedowannagiveuthat(IRE)**, owned by the Fastest Finger Partnership, is unlikely to make them millionaires even though she is now qualified for a handicap mark.

T/Plt: £62.30 to a £1 stake. Pool: £44,744.15. 523.75 winning tickets. T/Qpdt: £3.00 to a £1 stake. Pool: £4,110.20. 983.55 winning tickets. WG

# 2474 KEMPTON (R-H)

Wednesday, June 2

**OFFICIAL GOING: Good (good to firm in places)**

## 2573 WEDNESDAY NIGHT IS NIGHT APPRENTICE H'CAP — 1m 1f (R)

**6:20** (6:22) (E) (0-70,65) 3-Y-O+ — **£3,610** (£1,111; £555; £277) **Stalls** High

Form — RPR

2641 **1** **Unsuited**[23] 1987 5-8-9 **50** ........ NataliaGemelova 12 63+
(JELong) *bhd: stl plenty to do over 2f out: rapid hdwy on rails to ld over 1f out: sn clr: readily* **12/1**

5030 **2** 5 **Ember Days**[16] 2170 5-9-1 **59**....(p) RLucey-Butler(3) 6 62
(JLSpearing) *bhd: pushed along and styd on fr 2f out: r.o fnl f to take 2nd last strides but no ch w wnr* **20/1**

-040 **3** hd **Miss Grace**[11] 2284 4-8-8 **54**.... BO'Neill(5) 11 57
(JJSheehan) *b: bhd: hdwy on outside fr 2f out: r.o fnl f but nt pce to trble wnr: lost 2nd last strides* **20/1**

0200 **4** 1 **Catch The Fox**[11] 2302 4-7-11 **43**.... LucyRussell(5) 4 44
(JJBridger) *chsd ldrs: rdn over 2f out: styd on one pce fr over 1f out* **33/1**

5400 **5** 1 **Pas De Surprise**[5] 2459 6-9-0 **55**.... SJDonohoe 2 54
(PDEvans) *mid-div: hdwy fr 2f out: kpt on fnl f but nt pce to trble ldrs* **14/1**

1303 **6** ½ **Icannshift (IRE)**[2] 2537 4-8-6 **54**.... LSmith(7) 14 52
(SDow) *chsd ldr tl led over 4f out: hdd over 1f out: sn wknd* **9/2**[2]

6235 **7** 1 ¾ **Galey River (USA)**[20] 2053 5-7-9 **41**.... LiamJones(5) 15 35
(JJSheehan) *mid-div: rdn 3f out: styd on fr over 1f out: nt trble ldrs* **16/1**

0344 **8** ¾ **Lucefer (IRE)**[8] 2387 6-8-1 **45**.... SaleemGolam(3) 13 38
(GCHChung) *lw: bhd: sme hdwy fnl 2f: n.d* **10/1**

0056 **9** 1 ¼ **Dash For Cover (IRE)**[12] 2279 4-9-6 **61**.... PGallagher 8 51
(RHannon) *bhd: nvr bttr then mid-div* **16/1**

000- **10** hd **Expected Bonus (USA)**[282] 4439 5-8-9 **55**....(b) KGhunowa(5) 10 45
(SCWilliams) *b: led tl hdd over 4f out: styd chsng ldr tl wl over 1f out: wknd fnl f* **7/2**[1]

6330 **11** nk **Mythical Charm**[11] 2284 5-8-9 **53**....(t) MHoward(3) 9 42
(JJBridger) *in tch: rdn to chse ldrs over 3f out: wknd over 1f out* **12/1**

0-31 **12** 7 **Giunchiglio**[11] 2302 5-9-9 **64**.... BSwarbrick 1 39
(WMBrisbourne) *lw: bhd: effrt 3f out: n.d* **7/1**[3]

0-06 **13** 3 ½ **Crystal Choir**[20] 2059 4-9-7 **65**.... WHogg(3) 7 33
(NJHenderson) *chsd ldrs: rdn: hung lft and wknd fr 2f out* **16/1**

4500 **14** 2 **Must Be Magic**[12] 2279 7-9-4 **59**....(v) NicolPolli 5 23
(HJCollingridge) *chsd ldrs tl wknd 2f out* **10/1**

L-00 **R** **Silver Louie (IRE)**[57] 1278 4-7-13 **45**.... TBlock(5) 3 —
(GBBalding) *ref to r* **66/1**

1m 54.96s (0.63) **Going Correction** +0.175s/f (Good) **15** Ran SP% **124.7**
Speed ratings: **104,99,99,98,97 97,95,94,93,93 93,87,84,82,**—CSF £243.03 CT £4819.40 TOTE £17.70: £4.80, £13.30, £5.70; EX 1744.70.
**Owner** Amaroni Racing **Bred** Lawn Stud **Trained** Woldingham, Surrey

**FOCUS**
A weak handicap, but the winner is progressing and certainly the one to take from the race.

**NOTEBOOK**
**Unsuited** was let off very lightly by the Handicapper for her 17-length success on heavy ground in banded company and followed up in good style. She is progressing and could well complete the hat-trick - she will be very hard to beat if turned out before she is reassessed, as she will escape a penalty.
**Ember Days** did not appear to do a great deal wrong, but she was no match whatsoever for the winner.
**Miss Grace** has tumbled in the weights recently and this was a respectable effort.
**Catch The Fox** is still a maiden and did not shape like a winner waiting to happen.
**Pas De Surprise** is only 1lb higher than when last successful, but he was not at his best.
**Icannshift(IRE)** looked sure to be suited by this drop in class, but he was disappointing and this race may have come too soon for him.
**Expected Bonus(USA)** was rated 100 at his peak and, 45lb lower now, things looked interesting when the money came for him. However, he never looked like landing the gamble and would therefore have to be considered disappointing. That said, he has surely been showing something at home and is worth keeping an eye on.

## 2574 HH ASSOCIATES EBF MEDIAN AUCTION MAIDEN STKS 5f
**6:50** (6:52) (E) 2-Y-O **£3,454** (£1,063; £531; £265) **Stalls** Low

Form RPR

**1** **Soar** 2-8-9 .... JPMurtagh 8 89+
(JRFanshawe) *unf: leggy: trckd ldr: led ins fnl 2f: c clr ins last: comf* **9/2**[2]

**2** 3 **Safsoof (USA)** 2-9-0 .... LDettori 7 78+
(SaeedBinSuroor) *w'like: scope: lw: sn led: shkn up and hdd ins fnl 2f: no ch w wnr fnl f but kpt on wl for 2nd* **8/11**[1]

5 **3** 1 ½ **Feminist (IRE)**[31] 1798 2-8-9 .... KFallon 4 67
(MRChannon) *chsd ldrs: pushed along over 2f out: sn one pce* **13/2**[3]

0 **4** 1 **Lily Lenat**[7] 2396 2-8-9 .... DSweeney 1 63
(JRBoyle) *s.i.s: outpcd: hdwy over 1f out: kpt on ins last but nt trble ldrs* **20/1**

**5** ¾ **Transvestite (IRE)** 2-9-0 .... RLMoore 3 65
(JWHills) *unf: scope: sn outpcd and pushed along in rr: hdwy fnl f but nvr gng pce to rch ldrs* **20/1**

**6** 3 ½ **Anfield Dream** 2-9-0 .... CLowther 5 51
(JRJenkins) *w'like: bit bkwd: chsd ldrs: rdn 1/2-way: edgd rt and wknd over 1f out* **33/1**

0 **7** 5 **Higgys Prince**[40] 1589 2-9-0 .... DaneO'Neill 6 31
(DFlood) *unruly ent stalls: outpcd* **50/1**

4 **8** shd **Josear**[27] 1905 2-9-0 .... AMcCarthy 2 31
(SCWilliams) *in tch 3f* **14/1**

60.87 secs (-0.34) **Going Correction** -0.10s/f (Good) **8** Ran SP% **110.5**
Speed ratings: **98,93,90,89,88 82,74,74**CSF £7.54 TOTE £5.90: £1.50, £1.10, £1.50; EX 8.90.
**Owner** Cheveley Park Stud **Bred** Cheveley Park Stud Ltd **Trained** Newmarket, Suffolk

**FOCUS**
Not that competitive a maiden, but there were some nice types in the line-up and it could be significant that Soar's trainer James Fanshawe introduced Soviet Song to win her maiden at this very course. A fair winning time for the grade.

**NOTEBOOK**
**Soar** is a half-sister to a dual five-furlong juvenile winner, and to the smart sprinter Feet So Fast, out of a useful sprinter who won three times at two. She was a big drifter on course, but did everything right on the track and created a good impression. She is a real sharp sort, but there should be more to come and she deserves to take her chance in the Queen Mary.
**Safsoof(USA)**, a $275,000 purchase, out of an unraced half-sister to the Group-class two-year-old Pearl Of Love, showed plenty of speed, but was no match for the winner. He is likely to improve on this and win a maiden.
**Feminist(IRE)**, a long way behind Lady Filly on her debut in a Salisbury conditions race, would appear to have progressed from that and should find a maiden.
**Lily Lenat** appeared to improve on her debut running and is going the right way.
**Transvestite(IRE)** , a 27,000gns yearling, half-brother a couple of three-year-old sprint winners, out of a full-sister to the top-class sprinter Hever Golf Rose, was too inexperienced to ever get competitive and looks capable of much better.

## 2575 PEMBERTON GREENISH REDFERN H'CAP 7f (J)
**7:20** (7:20) (C) (0-90,90) 4-Y-O+ **£9,600** (£2,954; £1,477; £738) **Stalls** High

Form RPR

13-5 **1** **Ettrick Water**[12] 2271 5-9-10 **86**....(v) DHolland 4 99
(LMCumani) *lw: mde virtually all: rdn ins fnl 2f: styd on wl fnl f: readily* **11/2**[2]

16-0 **2** 1 **Gift Horse**[15] 2206 4-9-4 **80**.... JPMurtagh 10 90
(JRFanshawe) *in tch: hdwy 2f out: str run to chse wnr 1f out: fnd no ex u.p ins last* **20/1**

3055 **3** 1 ¾ **Kool (IRE)**[11] 2283 5-10-0 **90**.... SSanders 11 96
(PFICole) *lw: bhd: hdwy on rails over 2f out: chsd ldrs over 1f out: nt qckn u.p ins last* **5/1**[1]

1333 **4** ¾ **Chateau Nicol**[20] 2064 5-9-2 **78**....(v) LDettori 2 82
(BGPowell) *stdd s and swtchd rt: bhd: hdwy fr 2f out: str run ins last: nt rch ldrs* **9/1**

-231 **5** 2 ½ **Soyuz (IRE)**[26] 1938 4-9-11 **87**.... PRobinson 13 84
(MAJarvis) *in tch: pushed along 3f out: chsd ldrs 2f out: wknd ins fnl f* **6/1**[3]

3031 **6** nk **Quantum Leap**[4] 2483 7-8-10 **72** 6ex....(v) RLMoore 3 69
(SDow) *lw: chsd wnr: rdn over 2f out: wknd fnl f* **11/1**

0-00 **7** 1 **Craiova (IRE)**[46] 1456 5-9-11 **87**.... RHills 8 81
(BWHills) *chsd ldrs: hung lft u.p fr 2f out and sn wknd* **10/1**

0360 **8** nk **Digital**[15] 2206 7-9-8 **87**.... SHitchcott(3) 7 80
(MRChannon) *behind: hdwy and nt clr run 2f out and appr fnl f: nvr gng pce to rch ldrs* **9/1**

1240 **9** nk **Flint River**[15] 2206 6-8-11 **73**.... RHughes 9 65
(HMorrison) *chsd ldrs: wnt 2nd briefly appr fnl 2f: wknd qckly ins fnl f* **12/1**

-000 **10** ½ **Yakimov (USA)**[12] 1828 5-9-10 **86**.... DaneO'Neill 1 77
(DJWintle) *a in rr* **50/1**

0020 **11** 7 **Cheese 'n Biscuits**[11] 2284 4-8-13 **75**....(p) KFallon 12 48
(GLMoore) *bhd most of way* **8/1**

2203 **12** 5 **Just Fly**[15] 2206 4-9-2 **78**.... JFEgan 6 38
(SKirk) *chsd ldrs tl wknd ins over 1f out and eased whn no ch* **9/1**

4005 **13** 1 ¾ **Terraquin (IRE)**[35] 1708 4-8-12 **74**.... JTate 5 29
(JJBridger) *b: prom 4f* **33/1**

1m 27.28s (0.01) **Going Correction** +0.175s/f (Good) **13** Ran SP% **122.2**
Speed ratings: **106,104,102,102,99 98,97,97,96,96 88,82,80**CSF £115.89 CT £615.12 TOTE £7.00: £3.30, £4.60, £2.10; EX 102.30 Trifecta £1445.90 Part won. Pool of £2,036.53 - 0.90 winning units..
**Owner** Mrs E H Vestey **Bred** Wickfield Farm Partnership **Trained** Newmarket, Suffolk

**FOCUS**
Quite a competitive handicap, and the form looks solid.

**NOTEBOOK**
**Ettrick Water** got tired on his reappearance when sent off favourite for a similar event at Haydock but, with the benefit of that run, he showed improved form. He would appear progressive and looks capable of adding to this.
**Gift Horse** stepped up on the form he showed on his reappearance at Goodwood. He is lightly raced and open to further improvement, possibly back over a mile.
**Kool(IRE)**, 2lb lower than when last winning in August 2002, has had his problems since then but is in good heart again now and posted another decent effort. There could be similar race in him whilst he is in this sort of form.
**Chateau Nicol** continues in good form, but has proved a little bit frustrating since gaining his last win.
**Soyuz(IRE)** would have preferred softer ground. *Official explanation: jockey said gelding was unsuited by the fast ground*
**Digital** did not get the clearest of runs. He is beginning to look pretty well handicapped and is one to keep an eye on.
**Just Fly** *Official explanation: jockey said gelding was distressed*

## 2576 WILLIAMHILLPOKER.COM CLASSIFIED STKS 6f
**7:55** (7:57) (D) 3-Y-O **£5,525** (£1,700; £850; £425) **Stalls** Low

Form RPR

4-31 **1** **Kind (IRE)**[11] 2301 3-8-10 82.... RHughes 9 85
(RCharlton) *lw: wnt rt s:rcvrd to press ldr:slt ld ins fnl 3f drvn and qcknd over 1f out: pushed along and hld on wl cl home* **10/11**[1]

2-00 **2** hd **Swinbrook (USA)**[11] 2309 3-8-11 80.... SSanders 4 85
(JARToller) *hmpd after 1f: hdwy 3f out and swtchd rt: str run fnl f to press wnr cl home: jst failed* **11/1**

-432 **3** hd **Farewell Gift**[11] 2301 3-8-11 80.... KFallon 1 84
(RHannon) *lw: chsd ldrs tl n.m.r after 1f: outpcd 1/2-way: styd on wl u.p fnl f: fin wl* **7/1**[3]

1045 **4** ¾ **Instant Recall (IRE)**[19] 2082 3-8-11 78.... DHolland 3 82
(BJMeehan) *bmpd s: outpcd and bhd: swtchd rt to outside 3f out: rapid hdwy over 1f out: str run ins last: kpt on cl home* **5/1**[2]

26-0 **5** 5 **Trotters Bottom**[70] 1099 3-8-11 79.... JFEgan 6 67
(AndrewReid) *b: b.hind: chsd ldrs: n.m.r after 1f: styd chsng ldrs: rdn 3f out: wknd fnl f* **25/1**

2-55 **6** ¾ **Handsome Cross (IRE)**[8] 2378 3-9-1 84.... SDrowne 8 69
(HMorrison) *lw: c lft to stands rail sn after s: sn led: hdd ins fnl 3f: wknd over 1f out* **5/1**[2]

0045 **7** ½ **Mr Hullabalou (IRE)**[11] 2301 3-8-11 77.... NDay 2 63
(RIngram) *b.hind: tight for room in rr after 1f:nvr gng pce to rch ldrs* **66/1**

100- **8** 5 **Binnion Bay (IRE)**[203] 5979 3-9-1 84.... RSmith 5 52
(RHannon) *a outpcd* **50/1**

0-60 **9** 1 ¾ **Our Gamble (IRE)**[14] 2224 3-8-10 82.... DaneO'Neill 7 42
(RHannon) *early spd: bhd fr 1/2-way* **20/1**

1m 13.07s **Going Correction** -0.10s/f (Good) **9** Ran SP% **118.6**
Speed ratings: **96,95,95,94,87 86,86,79,77**CSF £12.62 TOTE £1.90: £1.50, £3.20, £1.10; EX 19.50.
**Owner** K Abdulla **Bred** Juddmonte Farms **Trained** Beckhampton, Wilts
■ Stewards Enquiry : S Drowne three-day ban: careless riding (Jun 15-17)

**FOCUS**
Just 6lb separated the whole field on official figures and this was a very tight classified event. The time, however, was only modest for the grade.

**NOTEBOOK**
**Kind(IRE)**, off the mark over seven furlongs on her previous start, showed bags of pace on this drop in trip and followed up narrowly. She should not be too harshly treated for this and there should be more to come.
**Swinbrook(USA)** is still looking for his first win, but ran right up to his best and was just held - things may have been even closer had he not been hampered soon after the start. He should be winning soon and a maiden may provide him with the best opportunity.
**Farewell Gift** has to be considered a little unlucky as he did not get the clearest of runs and hit full stride all too late.
**Instant Recall(IRE)** finished to good effect in the centre of the track and may be proved better back over seven furlongs.
**Handsome Cross(IRE)** shaped as though a return to this sort of trip would suit when fifth at Lingfield (turf) on his previous start, but this was disappointing.

## 2577 WILLIAMHILLCASINO.COM FILLIES' H'CAP 7f (J)
8:25 (8:29) (E) (0-75,75) 3-Y-O £3,610 (£1,111; £555; £277) Stalls High

Form RPR
1335 1 Kryssa[20] 2063 3-8-5 59 PRobinson 12 68
(GLMoore) sn in tch: trckd ldrs 3f out: gd hdwy fr 2f out to chse wnr jst ins last: r.o gamely to ld nr fin 11/2[2]
2-33 2 nk Kali[16] 2182 3-9-4 72 DSweeney 2 80
(RCharlton) bhd: hdwy on outside over 2f out: qcknd to ld 1f out: hdd and no ex nr fin 8/1[3]
0410 3 2 Pickle[19] 2098 3-8-8 62 SSanders 11 65
(SCWilliams) bhd: hdwy 2f out: kpt on wl fnl f but nt pce of ldrs 11/1
2-53 4 shd Here To Me[8] 2377 3-9-2 70 RHughes 8 73
(RHannon) chsd ldrs: rdn over 2f out: nt qckn fnl f 14/1
0-20 5 1 1/4 Thara'A (IRE)[33] 1753 3-9-1 69 SDrowne 1 69
(EALDunlop) b: stdd s and swtchd rt: hdwy and hmpd 2f out: nt clr run appr fnl f: fin strly 20/1
3-30 6 shd Ela Paparouna[18] 2112 3-9-3 71 DaneO'Neill 3 70
(HCandy) bhd: racd on outside: stl plenty to do 2f out: r.o wl fnl f: gng on cl home 9/1
504- 7 1 United Spirit (IRE)[186] 6097 3-8-6 60 KFallon 5 57
(MAMagnusson) chsd ldrs tl outpcd 3f out: rdn and rallied fr 2f out: kpt on ins last 12/1
0-04 8 3/4 Snow Joke (IRE)[11] 2301 3-8-6 60 RHavlin 10 55
(MrsPNDutfield) in tch: hdwy 3f out: kpt on same pce appr fnl f 50/1
-634 9 3/4 Dandouce[9] 2371 3-9-0 68 (b[1]) RLMoore 17 61
(PWChapple-Hyam) sn led: rdn over 2f out: hdd & wknd 1f out 4/1[1]
40-0 10 1 Sahara Storm (IRE)[61] 1229 3-9-4 72 DHolland 13 62
(LMCumani) chsd ldr: rdn over 2f out: wknd qckly fnl f 14/1
06-0 11 1 First Dawn[11] 2286 3-8-13 70 SHitchcott[(3)] 6 58
(MRChannon) bhd: sme hdwy fr over 1f out: nt a danger 25/1
5030 12 nk Black Oval[8] 2380 3-7-12 55 LisaJones[(3)] 14 42
(SDow) b.hind: sn in tch: rdn over 2f out: wknd over 1f out 25/1
0123 13 2 1/2 Lady Mo[20] 2061 3-8-9 63 AMcCarthy 15 43
(GGMargarson) bhd most of way 11/1
-060 14 shd Man Crazy (IRE)[46] 1464 3-8-11 65 MTebbutt 7 45
(RMBeckett) racd on outside: chsd ldrs 4f 50/1
-000 15 1 Just One Look[32] 1760 3-9-0 68 JPMurtagh 4 45
(MBlanshard) a in rr 33/1
0 16 1 3/4 Chica Roca (USA)[18] 2113 3-9-7 75 LDettori 9 48
(BJMeehan) chsd ldrs tl wknd 2f out 16/1
2230 17 6 Archerfield (IRE)[55] 1309 3-8-12 66 RHills 16 23
(JWHills) chsd ldrs: rdn 3f out: wknd qckly appr fnl 2f 14/1

1m 27.84s (0.57) **Going Correction** +0.175s/f (Good) 17 Ran SP% 126.1
Speed ratings: **103,102,100,100,98 98,97,96,95,94 93,93,90,90,89 87,80**CSF £46.70 CT £496.69 TOTE £6.70: £2.30, £2.40, £3.50, £2.90; EX 50.90.
**Owner** D J Deer **Bred** D J And Mrs Deer **Trained** Woodingdean, E Sussex

**FOCUS**
A really competitive fillies' handicap and they went a strong pace. The winning time was fair for the grade.

**NOTEBOOK**
**Kryssa** was ideally suited by the strong pace and came through for a game success. She is a real tough sort and there could yet be more to come.
**Kali**, racing over a trip this short for the first time on her handicap debut, did nothing wrong and was clear of the remainder. She is a maiden, but should find a race.
**Pickle** appreciated this step back up to seven furlongs, but was no match for the front two.
**Here To Me** is running well enough, but appears to lack a decisive change of pace and remains without a win in 11 starts.
**Thara'A(IRE)**, dropped a furlong in trip for this handicap debut, did not get much luck in running and would have been much closer with a clearer passage. She is lightly-raced, but appears capable of progression.
**Ela Paparouna** got going all too late and is capable of better.
**Dandouce** was very keen and went off too fast.

## 2578 BE A WEDNESDAY WINNER H'CAP 1m 4f
8:55 (8:56) (D) (0-85,84) 3-Y-O £5,642 (£1,736; £868; £434) Stalls High

Form RPR
5-30 1 Pagan Magic (USA)[15] 2202 3-8-8 74 LisaJones[(3)] 8 78
(JARToller) in tch: rdn 3f out: drvn to ld ins fnl 2f: hld on all out 6/1[3]
2-40 2 3/4 Le Tiss (IRE)[18] 2107 3-8-12 78 SHitchcott[(3)] 5 81
(MRChannon) hld up in rr: hdwy over 2f out: styd on u.p to chse wnr ins last: no ex nr fin 20/1
3-60 3 1/2 Mustang Ali (IRE)[16] 2179 3-8-5 68 JFEgan 1 70
(SKirk) bhd: hdwy 4f out: styd on whn carried bdly lft ins fnl 2f: rallied: edgd rt and str run ins last: fin wl 25/1
5-03 4 nk Schapiro (USA)[16] 2179 3-9-0 77 (b[1]) LDettori 4 79
(JHMGosden) tardy stalls: bhd: gd hdwy fr 2f out: styd on wl fnl f but no impresson on ldrs cl home 10/1
0-53 5 1 1/4 Peak Of Perfection (IRE)[37] 1679 3-8-10 73 PRobinson 9 73
(MAJarvis) sn led: rdn and edgd lft 2f out: sn hdd: styd on same pce fnl f 9/1
1 6 1 3/4 What's Up Doc (IRE)[13] 2250 3-9-5 82 KDalgleish 3 79
(MJohnston) lw: sn chsng ldr: rdn and hung bdly lft fr 2f out: nt rcvr 7/2[2]
4-14 7 1 3/4 Bukit Fraser (IRE)[18] 2107 3-9-7 84 DHolland 6 78
(PFICole) chsd ldrs: rdn over 2f out: sn edgd lft u.p: wknd sn after 15/8[1]
056- 8 2 1/2 Lawaaheb (IRE)[232] 5565 3-8-7 70 RHills 2 60
(JLDunlop) bhd: t.k.h: hdwy on ins to chse ldrs over 2f out:wknd over 1f out 7/1
20-6 9 13 Avesomeofthat (IRE)[16] 2168 3-8-9 72 RHavlin 7 41
(MrsPNDutfield) chsd ldrs: rdn 4f out: wknd fr 3f out 33/1

2m 37.32s (2.32) **Going Correction** +0.175s/f (Good) 9 Ran SP% 114.4
Speed ratings: **99,98,98,97,97 95,94,93,84**CSF £115.04 CT £2752.96 TOTE £8.30: £2.00, £4.80, £3.60; EX 187.40 Place 6 £616.43, Place 5 £49.32.
**Owner** The Gap Partnership **Bred** W Lazy T Ltd **Trained** Newmarket, Suffolk

**FOCUS**
The early pace was just steady and there was something of a sprint to the line. The field were spread out all over the track in the straight.

**NOTEBOOK**
**Pagan Magic(USA)**, racing over a trip this far for the first time, found this easier than the Goodwood handicap he contested behind Gatwick on his previous start and probably benefited from the steady early pace. He had nothing in hand at the finish and, while he is lightly raced and therefore open to some improvement, he may just struggle to follow up.
**Le Tiss(IRE)**, back on a winning mark, ran his best race of the season so far and could be worth keeping in mind for similar events now he has found his form.
**Mustang Ali(IRE)** raced wider than anything in the straight, right against the stands'-side rail, and was just held. He is still a maiden, but his stable are in form and a similar event may come his way.
**Schapiro(USA)**, in blinkers for the first time, kept on for pressure, but never really looked like getting there and would have preferred a stronger pace.
**Peak Of Perfection(IRE)** tried to make every yard and got an easy enough lead, but he was outpaced in the straight. *Official explanation: jockey said gelding hung badly left througout*
**What's Up Doc(IRE)** got off the mark in good style at Newcastle on his previous start, but was well held on this handicap debut and may be harshly treated off a mark of 82.
**Bukit Fraser(IRE)** was a little disappointing on his handicap debut at Newbury and again failed to impress. He is another who may have benefited from a better gallop.
T/Jkpt: £34,382.80 to a £1 stake. Pool: £48,426.50. 0.50 winning tickets. T/Plt: £1,854.80 to a £1 stake. Pool: £60,601.50. 23.85 winning tickets. T/Qpdt: £121.20 to a £1 stake. Pool: £5,012.70. 30.60 winning tickets. ST

# 2247 NEWCASTLE (L-H)
Wednesday, June 2

**OFFICIAL GOING: Good**
Wind: lt hlf bhd Weather: cloudy but bright

## 2579 ST JAMES SECURITY MAIDEN STKS 5f
2:30 (2:31) (D) 2-Y-O £3,623 (£1,115; £557; £278) Stalls High

Form RPR
1 Council Member (USA) 2-9-0 KMcEvoy 8 91+
(SaeedBinSuroor) mde virtually all: shkn up and kpt on strly fnl f 7/2[2]
2 2 1/2 Juantorena[11] 2310 2-9-0 KDarley 6 89+
(MLWBell) disp ld: rdn 2f out: kpt on fnl f: hld cl home 1/2[1]
0 3 6 Prospect Court[22] 2024 2-9-0 SChin 10 68
(JDBethell) trckd ldrs tl rdn and one pce fr 2f out 33/1
4 1/2 Sentiero Rosso (USA) 2-8-11 TEaves[(3)] 7 67
(BEllison) sn outpcd: hdwy 2f out: no imp fnl f 9/1[3]
0 5 shd Hymn Of Victory (IRE)[9] 2352 2-9-0 MFenton 9 66
(TJEtherington) trckd ldrs: rdn 1/2-way: sn one pce 100/1
6 1 1/2 Mozafin 2-9-0 TEDurcan 5 61
(MRChannon) rn green in rr: pushed along 1/2-way: nvr rchd ldrs 16/1
7 1 3/4 Davy Crockett 2-9-0 PFessey 2 55
(MrsJRRamsden) outpcd: sme hdwy over 1f out: nvr on terms 100/1
5 8 3 Misty Miller[51] 1359 2-9-0 RWinston 1 44
(TDEasterby) wnt bdly lft s: swtchd rt and hld up: hdwy whn nt clr run over 2f out: sn outpcd 33/1
9 9 Forpetesake 2-9-0 (v[1]) ACulhane 3 —
(MrsJRRamsden) sn outpcd: nvr on terms 66/1
06 10 2 Hiats[51] 1359 2-8-7 JDO'Reilly[(7)] 4 —
(JO'Reilly) trckd ldrs tl edgd lft and wknd fr 2f out 200/1

60.14 secs (-1.39) **Going Correction** -0.425s/f (Firm) 10 Ran SP% 114.6
Speed ratings: **94,93,83,82,82 80,77,72,58,55**CSF £5.44 TOTE £4.60: £1.10, £1.10, £9.90; EX 6.20.
**Owner** Godolphin **Bred** Dean Greenwood Llc **Trained** Newmarket, Suffolk

**FOCUS**
An ordinary bunch on looks but a reasonable gallop and the form looks likely to stand up at a similar level. The first two did well to pull clear of the remainder and both look nice prospects.

**NOTEBOOK**
**Council Member(USA)** ◆, who cost $800,000 and is related to a top-class US juvenile, had the rail to help and created a favourable impression on this racecourse debut. He is likely to win more races, especially when upped to six furlongs.
**Juantorena**, back in trip, ran to a similar level as on his debut and pulled well clear of the remainder in the closing stages. He again showed enough to suggest a similar race can be found.
**Prospect Court** bettered his debut effort on this first run on a sound surface and shaped as though the step up to six furlongs would suit. He looks capable of winning an ordinary race in due course.
**Sentiero Rosso(USA)**, who cost 30,000 euros and is the second foal of a dual 6f winner, shaped as though the race would do him good and was far from disgraced on this racecourse debut. He can win a minor event in due course over six furlongs.
**Hymn Of Victory(IRE)** bettered his debut effort and once again shaped as though a stiffer test of stamina would be in his favour. He will be seen to better effect in low-grade handicaps in due course.
**Mozafin**, the first foal of a dam who won over a mile and three furlongs at three years, was easy to back and shaped as though in need of this debut run. He is another that should fare better in due course.
**Davy Crockett**, a cheap purchase but one with a bit of speed in his pedigree, hinted at ability but looks more of a long term prospect.
**Misty Miller** shaped as though a bit better than the bare form and may well improve on this in ordinary nursery company in due course.
**Hiats** *Official explanation: jockey said colt hung left-handed in the final 2f*

## 2580 GOSFORTH DECORATING & BUILDING SERVICES H'CAP 1m (R)
3:00 (3:02) (E) (0-75,71) 3-Y-O+ £4,192 (£1,290; £645; £322) Stalls Low

Form RPR
3434 1 Goodbye Mr Bond[23] 1993 4-8-7 52 KDarley 4 65
(EJAlston) in tch: effrt and ev ch over 1f out: led ins fnl f: rdn out 9/4[1]
0-23 2 1 1/4 Top Dirham[47] 1451 6-9-12 71 DaleGibson 10 81
(MWEasterby) hld up: niggled 1/2-way: hdwy to ld over 1f out: hdd ins fnl f: kpt on 9/4[1]
101- 3 3/4 Mallard (IRE)[231] 5573 6-9-5 64 MFenton 2 72
(JGGiven) chsd ldrs: led over 2f out to over 1f out: one pce fnl f 8/1[3]
0-02 4 1 Francis Flute[12] 2260 6-8-3 53 ow2 PMulrennan[(5)] 6 59
(BMactaggart) keen: hld up midfield: hdwy over 1f out: no imp fnl f 6/1[2]
0-00 5 nk Nemo Fugat (IRE)[12] 2261 5-9-3 62 ANicholls 5 67
(DNicholls) s.i.s: hld up: hdwy on ins whn n.m.r and swtchd rt 2f out: r.o fnl f 25/1
0035 6 1 1/2 Encounter[9] 2356 8-8-1 49 ow2 DAllan[(3)] 1 51
(JHetherton) hld up: hdwy on ins to chse ldrs 2f out: no ex fnl f 9/1
2060 7 10 Hoh's Back[18] 2128 5-9-1 63 (p) LEnstone[(3)] 7 42
(PaulJohnson) slt ld to over 2f out: wknd over 1f out 20/1
00-0 8 shd Wahoo Sam (USA)[47] 1452 4-9-1 65 PMakin[(5)] 3 44
(TDBarron) disp ld to over 2f out: wknd over 1f out 40/1
-050 9 10 Hula Ballew[31] 1783 4-8-11 56 RWinston 9 12
(MDods) prom tl rdn and wknd over 2f out 20/1
-020 10 11 Anthemion (IRE)[19] 2078 7-9-1 60 DMcGaffin 8 —
(MrsJCMcgregor) in tch: rdn 1/2-way: sn n.d 25/1

1m 43.36s (-0.12) **Going Correction** +0.175s/f (Good) 10 Ran SP% 116.6
Speed ratings: **107,105,105,104,103 102,92,92,82,71**CSF £6.22 CT £33.72 TOTE £3.00: £1.80, £1.10, £2.30; EX 7.30.
**Owner** Peter J Davies **Bred** Michael Ng **Trained** Longton, Lancs

**FOCUS**
A run-of-the-mill handicap but a race run at just a fair pace and the runner-up, who fared the best of those held up, may be a bit better than the bare form.

**NOTEBOOK**

**Goodbye Mr Bond**, who had not had the best of luck previously this term, had the run of the race and elected to put his best foot forward over arguably his optimum trip. He should continue to give a good account.

**Top Dirham ◆**, back on a sound surface, ran to a similar level as his latest start back on this sound surface, but may be a bit better than the bare form as he fared the best of those held up. He is capable of winning again from this mark but would ideally prefer a stronger gallop.

**Mallard(IRE)**, 10lb lower on turf than on sand, had the run of the race but showed more than enough on this reappearance outing to suggest he can win more races this term on grass.

**Francis Flute**, from the Ayr race that has already thrown up a couple of winners, was not disgraced, especially as he was not really ridden to best advantage in a steadily-run race. His strike rate is only modest but he is capable of winning from his current mark.

**Nemo Fugat(IRE)**, who has tumbled in the weights since his last win nearly two years ago, was far from disgraced given the way this race panned out and looks the type that will be placed to best advantage by his very capable handler.

**Encounter**, who has not won for over a year, was not disgraced but remains one to tread carefully with.

## 2581 BETFRED SPRINT SERIES (QUALIFIER) (A H'CAP) 6f

3:30 (3:36) (D) (0-85,73) 3-Y-O+ £5,421 (£1,668; £834; £417) Stalls High

Form RPR

0603 **1** **Tally (IRE)**[6] 2423 4-7-10 **50** RThomas(5) 6 62
(MJPolglase) *prom: rdn over 2f out: led ins fnl f: hld on wl* **5/1**[3]

0030 **2** *shd* **Snow Bunting**[6] 2423 6-8-6 **55** MFenton 5 67
(JeddO'Keeffe) *bhd: n.m.r over 2f out: hdwy over 1f out: r.o wl: jst hld* **14/1**

0-10 **3** *1 1/2* **Ulysees (IRE)**[31] 1787 5-9-7 **70** RWinston 12 77
(ISemple) *trckd ldrs on ins: rdn over 2f out: kpt on wl fnl f* **7/1**

0146 **4** *shd* **Friar Tuck**[6] 2421 9-8-6 **55** DMcGaffin 9 62
(MissLAPerratt) *chsd ldrs: led over 1f out to ins fnl f: no ex towards fin* **25/1**

6602 **5** *nk* **Distant Country (USA)**[7] 2410 5-9-8 **71** (p) ACulhane 2 77
(MrsJRRamsden) *hld up: hdwy over 1f out: r.o fnl f: nrst fin* **4/1**[2]

5464 **6** *1/2* **Full Spate**[7] 2399 9-9-5 **68** DarrenWilliams 8 73
(JMBradley) *missed break: hld up: stdy hdwy 1/2-way: rdn and nt qckn appr fnl f* **8/1**

3416 **7** *nk* **Highland Warrior**[4] 2490 5-9-10 **73** TEDurcan 10 77
(JSGoldie) *hld up: nt clr run fr 1/2-way: nt rcvr* **11/4**[1]

4025 **8** *1 3/4* **Pirlie Hill**[6] 2423 4-8-1 **50** PFessey 1 48
(MissLAPerratt) *in tch: effrt wd over 1f out: btn ins fnl f* **33/1**

0-00 **9** *1 1/4* **William's Well**[25] 1974 10-8-12 **61** (b) DaleGibson 4 56
(MWEasterby) *chsd ldrs tl rdn and wknd over 1f out* **25/1**

2000 **10** *1* **Legal Set (IRE)**[11] 2292 8-8-0 **49** (t) AnnStokell 11 41
(MissAStokell) *led to over 1f out: wknd ins fnl f* **50/1**

-005 **11** *2 1/2* **Ragamuffin**[7] 2407 6-9-7 **70** KDarley 3 54
(TDEasterby) *hld up: rdn over 2f out: sn btn* **10/1**

-000 **12** *3/4* **Colemanstown**[5] 2461 4-9-4 **70** TEaves(3) 7 52
(BEllison) *cl up tl wknd fr 2f out* **50/1**

1m 13.14s (-1.90) **Going Correction** -0.425s/f (Firm) **12** Ran SP% **117.3**
Speed ratings: **95,94,92,92,92 91,91,88,87,85 82,81**CSF £67.32 CT £496.83 TOTE £6.90: £2.10, £4.40, £2.80; EX 98.80.

**Owner** General Sir Geoffrey Howlett **Bred** D Twomey **Trained** Southwell, Notts

**FOCUS**

An ordinary handicap run at just a fair pace (time modest) and one in which the whole field raced towards the stands' side.

**NOTEBOOK**

**Tally(IRE)** got first run and confirmed recent Ayr promise back over this more suitable trip. He should not be going up too much for this win but his record suggests he is not one to place maximum faith in.

**Snow Bunting** is not the most reliable, but elected to put his best foot forward and may be a bit better than this bare form as he fared the best of those that came from off the pace. His record suggests he is not sure to repeat this next time.

**Ulysees(IRE)**, who had the run of the race against the stands' rail, could have done with a stronger overall gallop but gave it his best shot and, on this evidence, looks well worth another try over seven furlongs.

**Friar Tuck** is not particularly consistent and, although he had the run of the race and ran creditably, would be by no means certain to reproduce this next time.

**Distant Country(USA)** is the sort that needs things to fall just right, but showed clear signs of a return to form over a trip short of his optimum and will be one to keep an eye on back over seven furlongs when it looks as though there will be plenty of pace on.

**Full Spate** was not disgraced after losing ground at the start and, given the way he travelled for much of the way, will be one to keep an eye on in the near future.

**Highland Warrior ◆**, anything but disgraced over a quick five furlongs last time, shaped as though a good deal better than the bare result and is one to keep an eye on over this trip, especially if returned to Ayr, the scene of his three course victories. *Official explanation: jockey said horse was continually denied a run*

## 2582 RECTANGLE CLAIMING STKS 5f

4:00 (4:00) (F) 3-Y-O+ £3,101 (£886; £443) Stalls High

Form RPR

3404 **1** **Soaked**[6] 2423 11-8-10 59 (b) ACulhane 9 61
(DWChapman) *mde all: rdn over 1f out: r.o strly* **3/1**[1]

1010 **2** *2* **American Cousin**[5] 2461 9-9-2 64 ANicholls 4 60
(DNicholls) *bhd: rdn 1/2-way: hdwy over 1f out: kpt on: nt rch wnr* **9/2**[3]

4343 **3** *1* **Best Lead**[16] 2175 5-8-9 52 (b) DFentiman(7) 7 56
(IanEmmerson) *cl up: effrt 1/2-way: one pce over 1f out* **14/1**

4164 **4** *1* **Miss Wizz**[36] 1699 4-7-12 37 (p) RoryMoore(7) 10 42
(WStorey) *in tch: rdn 1/2-way: no imp fnl f* **50/1**

-20L **5** *shd* **Joyce's Choice**[29] 1870 5-8-12 53 GParkin 6 48
(JSWainwright) *cl up tl rdn and no ex over 1f out* **25/1**

0-01 **6** *1/2* **Dizzy In The Head**[23] 1994 5-8-13 65 (e) JDO'Reilly(7) 3 54
(JO'Reilly) *prom tl rdn and outpcd over 1f out* **5/1**

3-00 **7** *3/4* **Flying Tackle**[65] 1171 6-8-13 49 LEnstone(3) 5 48
(MDods) *in tch: effrt wl over 1f out: one pce* **33/1**

5-00 **8** *hd* **Proud Native (IRE)**[5] 2461 10-9-12 85 KDarley 1 57
(DNicholls) *bhd: rdn 1/2-way: nvr rchd ldrs* **7/2**[2]

0003 **9** *shd* **Tappit (IRE)**[9] 2359 5-9-0 57 (b[1]) DarrenWilliams 2 45
(JMBradley) *racd wd: in tch tl rdn and outpcd over 1f out* **8/1**

**10** *1/2* **Needwood Bucolic (IRE)**[41] 6-8-5 DTudhope(7) 8 41
(RAllan) *in tch tl wknd fr 2f out* **100/1**

60.05 secs (-1.48) **Going Correction** -0.425s/f (Firm) **10** Ran SP% **109.6**
Speed ratings: **94,90,89,87,87 86,85,85,84,84**CSF £15.00 TOTE £4.20: £1.50, £1.80, £5.10; EX 15.10.Dizzy In The Head was claimed by Paul Johnson for £10,000.

**Owner** David W Chapman **Bred** Stetchworth Park Stud Ltd **Trained** Stillington, N Yorks

**FOCUS**

The usual mixed bag for this type of event, but a muddling race both pace- and form-wise and one in which the winner was given the perfect waiting-in-front ride by Tony Culhane.

**NOTEBOOK**

**Soaked**, another on this card to advertise his latest Ayr race, had a good chance at the weights under ideal conditions and more than confirmed that return to form after being allowed to dominate. He is capable in this grade on his day but he is by no means certain to be allowed the same rope next time.

**American Cousin** had conditons to suit and a good chance at the weights, and ran another solid race in a race that did not really play to his strengths. He should continue to give a good account for his in-form stable.

**Best Lead** was not disgraced in the face of a stiff task and, although he is not a regular winner, is a fairly consistent sort on turf and sand who looks worth another try over six furlongs.

**Miss Wizz**, who has yet to win on turf, was not disgraced in the face of a stiffish task but shaped as though the return to six furlongs would be in her favour. She is not the most reliable around, though.

**Joyce's Choice**, who refused to race on his previous start, jumped off on terms this time and was not disgraced in the face of a stiffish task, but is not one to place any faith in.

**Dizzy In The Head**, back in trip and on much quicker ground, was below his recent win and looks better suited by further and softer ground.

**Proud Native(IRE)**, the clear pick of the weights, was a long way below his best and has not come to himself as yet this season.

## 2583 NITEX.CO.UK H'CAP 1m 2f 32y

4:30 (4:31) (E) (0-75,75) 3-Y-O+ £3,926 (£1,208; £604; £302) Stalls High

Form RPR

0503 **1** **Rotuma (IRE)**[12] 2272 5-8-12 **62** (b) LEnstone(3) 7 71
(MDods) *prom: led over 2f out: hld on wl fnl f* **4/1**[3]

0505 **2** *3/4* **Compton Dragon (USA)**[12] 2272 5-9-12 **73** (v[1]) ANicholls 6 81
(DNicholls) *hld up: hdwy over 2f out: r.o fnl f: nt rch wnr* **10/1**

20-3 **3** *nk* **Ma Yahab**[15] 2197 3-8-12 **72** KDarley 8 79
(LMCumani) *chsd ldr: ev ch over 2f out: hld wl fnl f* **2/1**[1]

1-0 **4** *1* **Trance (IRE)**[15] 2216 4-9-9 **75** PMakin(5) 11 80
(TDBarron) *prom: effrt over 2f out: one pce fnl f* **25/1**

1344 **5** *nk* **Disabuse**[67] 1136 4-8-3 **50** DaleGibson 3 55
(MWEasterby) *chsd ldrs: drvn and outpcd over 2f out: kpt on fnl f* **3/1**[2]

2314 **6** *1 1/2* **Moyne Pleasure (IRE)**[9] 2345 6-7-5 **45** oh3 (p) DFentiman(7) 10 47
(PaulJohnson) *hld up outside: effrt over 2f out: kpt on fnl f: no imp* **20/1**

11-0 **7** *3/4* **Silvertown**[65] 1172 9-9-2 **68** PMulrennan(5) 4 69
(LLungo) *keen in rr: effrt over 2f out: nt pce to chal* **10/1**

0-05 **8** *5* **Skiddaw Jones**[6] 2424 4-8-5 **52** GParkin 1 44
(MissLAPerratt) *prom tl rdn and wknd fr 2f out* **25/1**

-435 **9** *1 1/4* **King's Envoy (USA)**[16] 2174 5-9-3 **64** DMcGaffin 9 53
(MrsJCMcgregor) *bhd: rdn and effrt 3f out: n.d* **20/1**

-000 **10** *3/4* **Wahchi (IRE)**[22] 2022 5-9-11 **72** TLucas 2 60
(GPKelly) *led to over 2f out: sn rdn and btn* **50/1**

2m 14.99s (3.39) **Going Correction** +0.175s/f (Good)
**WFA** 3 from 4yo+ 13lb **10** Ran SP% **115.7**
Speed ratings: **93,92,92,91,91 89,89,85,84,83**CSF £38.53 CT £102.13 TOTE £5.80: £2.00, £2.70, £1.10; EX 45.60.

**Owner** Denton Hall Racing Ltd **Bred** Sean Twomey **Trained** Piercebridge, Co Durham

**FOCUS**

An ordinary event with a couple of interesting performances down the field, but a steady early gallop resulted in a very moderate time for the grade and means this bare form is not entirely trustworthy.

**NOTEBOOK**

**Rotuma(IRE)** fully confirmed recent promise over his optimum trip and, although he had the run of the race, should not be going up too much for this win and should continue to give a good account in a similar grade.

**Compton Dragon(USA)** has not won for over two years but shaped well in the first-time visor in a race that was run to suit those ridden prominently. He is better than the bare form and undoubtedly well treated, but it remains to be seen whether this is reproduced next time.

**Ma Yahab**, the most unexposed in the field, had the run of the race and arguably ran his best race to date. He looks capable of winning a similar event around this trip.

**Trance(IRE)**, who did not move particularly well to post, ran creditably for a stable that is back among the winners but may be happier on an easier surface.

**Disabuse**, having his first start for just over two months, was anything but disgraced given that a stiffer test of stamina would have been in his favour and he is one to keep an eye out for in similar company in the near future.

**Moyne Pleasure(IRE)** looks a bit better than the bare form and would prefer a stronger gallop over this trip but, although it is a long time since his last win on turf, he would be of interest back in banded company.

**Silvertown ◆**, having his first run for over two months, was not really seen to best effect in a race that suited those ridden prominently, but he should be spot-on now for a second tilt at the Cumberland Plate over a mile and a half later this month. *Official explanation: jockeys said, regarding the running and riding, his orders were to settle gelding early, adding that gelding pulled hard early on and hit a flat spot turning into the home straight before staying on at one pace; trainer confirmed orders, adding that gelding does not run for vigorous use of the whip*

## 2584 JUMBRELLA APPRENTICE CLASSIFIED STKS 1m 4f 93y

5:00 (5:00) (G) 3-Y-O+ £2,548 (£728; £364) Stalls Low

Form RPR

-400 **1** **Illeana (GER)**[23] 1998 3-8-3 58 PMakin 8 63
(WRMuir) *hld up: effrt 2f out: kpt on wl fnl f to ld cl home* **8/1**

0405 **2** *nk* **Bakiri (IRE)**[18] 2116 6-9-7 59 RoryMoore 5 66
(AndrewReid) *prom: rdn over 2f out: led appr fnl f: kpt on: hdd cl home* **13/2**

-403 **3** *3/4* **Blackthorn**[5] 2449 5-9-2 58 AMullen(5) 7 65
(MrsJRRamsden) *hld up: hdwy over 2f out: r.o fnl f* **3/1**[1]

3150 **4** *2 1/2* **Jake Black (IRE)**[15] 2216 4-9-4 59 DTudhope(3) 3 61
(JJQuinn) *keen: led to appr fnl f: one pce whn n.m.r wl ins fnl f* **11/2**[3]

-225 **5** *1 1/4* **Gold Card**[17] 2146 3-8-6 63 DFentiman(3) 1 62
(JRWeymes) *in tch: outpcd over 3f out: rallied over 1f out: no imp fnl f* **15/2**

3000 **6** *3* **Madhahir (IRE)**[15] 2212 4-9-7 57 StephanieHollinshead 6 54
(CADwyer) *pressed wnr: ev ch over 2f out: wknd appr fnl f* **11/1**

4451 **7** *1 3/4* **Prairie Sun (GER)**[15] 2199 3-8-0 59 DeanWilliams(3) 2 48
(MrsADuffield) *trckd ldrs tl wknd fr 2f out* **9/2**[2]

1424 **8** *8* **Platinum Charmer (IRE)**[9] 2354 4-9-0 56 (p) SBushby(7) 4 38
(KRBurke) *hld up in tch: effrt over 4f out: wknd 3f out* **9/1**

2m 45.52s (2.22) **Going Correction** +0.175s/f (Good)
**WFA** 3 from 4yo+ 15lb **8** Ran SP% **113.1**
Speed ratings: **99,98,98,96,95 93,92,87**CSF £57.26 TOTE £10.80: £2.40, £3.50, £1.40; EX 71.30 Place 6 £18.34, Place 5 £15.86.

**Owner** Foursome Thoroughbreds **Bred** Graf And Grafin Von Stauffenberg **Trained** Lambourn, Berks

■ Stewards Enquiry : A Mullen one-day ban: careless riding (Jul 6)

**FOCUS**

Just an ordinary gallop to a modest finale but the winner did well to come from off the pace.

**NOTEBOOK**

**Ileana(GER)**, soundly beaten on soft last time, ran his best race to date back on fast ground and looks a bit better than the bare form as he did well to come from off just a modest early pace. Although this was not much of a race he is only lightly raced and may be capable of improvement.
**Bakiri(IRE)**, back in trip, had the run of the race and ran right up to his best for his current stable. He is best on a sound surface and may be able to win a similar event.
**Blackthorn** is best around this trip on a sound surface but, like many from this stable, really needs a decent gallop given his style of racing, and consequently may be a bit better than this bare form.
**Jake Black(IRE)** had the run of the race, but will ideally have to settle better than he did here if he is to prove equally effective over this longer trip.
**Gold Card**, who still looks high enough in the weights, was another from this race to shape as though he would be better suited by a stiffer test of stamina over this trip.
**Madhahir(IRE)** had the run of the race, but did not get home this time and remains a disappointing sort who is not one to place too much faith in.
T/Plt: £27.00 to a £1 stake. Pool: £32,168.90. 868.30 winning tickets. T/Qpdt: £21.40 to a £1 stake. Pool: £1,951.60. 67.35 winning tickets. RY

# 2382 NOTTINGHAM (L-H)

## Wednesday, June 2

**OFFICIAL GOING: Good to firm (good in places)**
Wind: slt bhd Weather: cloudy

## 2585 EUROPEAN BREEDERS FUND MAIDEN FILLIES' STKS — 5f 13y

2:10 (2:11) (D) 2-Y-O — £5,005 (£1,540; £770; £385) Stalls High

| Form | Pos | Btn | Horse | Jockey | RPR |
|---|---|---|---|---|---|
| | 1 | | **Gloved Hand** 2-8-11 | KFallon 11 | 87+ |
| | | | (JGGiven) *leggy: a.p: rdn over 2f out: edgd lft and led ins fnl f: r.o* | **20/1** | |
| 3 | 2 | hd | **Castelletto**[26] 1943 2-8-11 | GGibbons 2 | 86 |
| | | | (BAMcmahon) *w ldr: led 2f out: sn rdn: hdd ins fnl f: r.o* | **16/1** | |
| 4 | 3 | 7 | **Colonial Girl (IRE)**[18] 2129 2-8-11 | WSupple 8 | 62 |
| | | | (TDEasterby) *hld up in tch: rdn over 2f out: kpt on same pce fnl f* | **9/1** | |
| 33 | 4 | ¾ | **Speed Of Sound**[16] 2180 2-8-11 | MHills 4 | 59 |
| | | | (AMBalding) *led: rdn and hdd 2f out: wknd fnl f* | **9/4**[1] | |
| | 5 | 1 ½ | **Dubai Escapade (USA)** 2-8-11 | LDettori 1 | 54 |
| | | | (SaeedBinSuroor) *a.p: rdn 2f out: wknd fnl f* | **11/4**[2] | |
| | 6 | ½ | **Nella Fantasia (IRE)** 2-8-11 | SSanders 10 | 52 |
| | | | (GCBravery) *chsd ldrs: sn rdn along: wknd over 1f out* | **12/1** | |
| 56 | 7 | 1 ¼ | **Limonia (GER)**[16] 2177 2-8-4 | MHoward(7) 5 | 48 |
| | | | (DKIvory) *t.k.h early: in tch: rdn over 2f out: sn wknd* | **16/1** | |
| | 8 | 5 | **Encouragement** 2-8-11 | RHughes 6 | 30 |
| | | | (RHannon) *s.i.s: sn outpcd* | **13/2**[3] | |
| | 9 | 1 ¼ | **Great Opinions (USA)** 2-8-11 | JPMurtagh 9 | 26 |
| | | | (JHMGosden) *s.i.s: outpcd* | **12/1** | |
| | 10 | 1 ½ | **Frantic** 2-8-11 | TQuinn 7 | 21 |
| | | | (TDEasterby) *s.s: a in rr* | **40/1** | |
| | 11 | 7 | **Beeches Theatre (IRE)** 2-8-11 | JFEgan 3 | — |
| | | | (RBrotherton) *s.i.s: sn outpcd* | **100/1** | |

60.51 secs (-1.29) **Going Correction** -0.10s/f (Good) — 11 Ran SP% **116.1**
Speed ratings: **106,105,94,93,90 90,88,80,78,75 64**CSF £298.68 TOTE £24.90: £5.80, £4.40, £1.60; EX 793.00.
**Owner** Mrs M V Chaworth-Musters **Bred** Mrs M Chaworth Musters **Trained** Willoughton, Lincs

**FOCUS**
A decent-looking maiden with the first pair coming clear and a cracking winning time for the grade of contest, 1.56 seconds faster than the maiden for older horses half an hour later.

**NOTEBOOK**

**Gloved Hand ◆**, out of a half-sister to Definite Article, Salford Express and Derby contender Salford City, put up a terrific performance on her debut. She was always close to the pace and picked up nicely to beat the runner-up a shade comfortably. She recorded a very good time and her jockey rates her the best filly he has ridden this season. She is likely to go straight to the Queen Mary at Royal Ascot, and looks a major contender judged on this performance.
**Castelletto ◆** improved considerably on her debut here on soft ground, and was the only one to give the winner a race in the last quarter-mile. She will have no difficulty winning a similar contest.
**Colonial Girl(IRE)**, who ran with promise on her debut behind a stable companion who went on to win the Listed Hilary Needler later in the day, stayed on steadily despite having no chance with the first two. She should be capable of winning an ordinary maiden, possibly over a longer trip.
**Speed Of Sound**, the most experienced in the field, set the pace but was brushed aside by the principals. However, she ran up to previous efforts against such as Blue Dakota, which adds to the impression that this was a strong race.
**Dubai Escapade(USA)**, a $2m two-year-old from a high-class US family, showed up throughout but could not pick up with the principals. The experience will not be lost on her.
**Nella Fantasia(IRE)**, from a decent family, could never go the pace on this debut and will appreciate further in time.
**Encouragement** *Official explanation: jockey said filly had lost her action*

## 2586 HBLB MEDIAN AUCTION MAIDEN STKS — 5f 13y

2:40 (2:41) (E) 3-5-Y-O — £3,604 (£1,109; £554; £277) Stalls High

| Form | Pos | Btn | Horse | Jockey | RPR |
|---|---|---|---|---|---|
| -305 | 1 | | **Red Leicester**[9] 2359 4-9-2 48 | (v) DeanMcKeown 1 | 62 |
| | | | (JAGlover) *racd alone far side: mde all: rdn over 1f out: drvn out* | **9/1** | |
| 2626 | 2 | 1 ¼ | **Laconia (IRE)**[16] 2165 3-8-2 72 | DerekNolan(7) 3 | 58 |
| | | | (JSMoore) *a.p: led stands' side 2f out: edgd lft ins fnl f: kpt on* | **11/4**[1] | |
| 0 | 3 | 1 | **Dance To The Blues (IRE)**[16] 2165 3-8-9 | PDobbs 7 | 54 |
| | | | (BDeHaan) *a.p: rdn 2f out: r.o one pce fnl f* | **8/1** | |
| 50-0 | 4 | nk | **Lady Justice**[33] 1750 4-9-2 65 | KFallon 4 | 53 |
| | | | (WJarvis) *hdwy over 1f out: kpt on ins fnl f* | **13/2**[3] | |
| 0 | 5 | 1 ¾ | **Dane Rhapsody (IRE)**[128] 606 3-8-9 | SSanders 9 | 47 |
| | | | (BPalling) *hld up: rdn over 2f out: hdwy fnl f: nt rch ldrs* | **40/1** | |
| 6 | 6 | 1 | **Intavac Boy**[25] 1975 3-9-0 | JPMurtagh 13 | 48 |
| | | | (CWThornton) *s.i.s: outpcd: hdwy fnl f: nrst fin* | **9/2**[2] | |
| 0423 | 7 | 1 | **Law Maker**[9] 2350 4-9-7 40 | (v) JBramhill 8 | 44 |
| | | | (MABuckley) *led stands' side 3f: wknd over 1f out* | **8/1** | |
| 0 | 8 | nk | **Parliament Act (IRE)**[13] 2236 3-9-0 | (t) GGibbons 11 | 43 |
| | | | (BAMcmahon) *prom tl wknd over 1f out* | **33/1** | |
| 0- | 9 | ½ | **Themesofgreen**[245] 5313 3-8-7 | LHarman(7) 12 | 41 |
| | | | (MRChannon) *s.i.s: nvr nrr* | **20/1** | |
| 0 | 10 | ½ | **Radmore Spirit**[106] 811 4-9-2 | JFEgan 14 | 35 |
| | | | (JWUnett) *sn outpcd: nvr nr ldrs* | **100/1** | |
| 400 | 11 | ½ | **Cedric Coverwell**[31] 1796 4-9-0 51 | MHoward(7) 15 | 38 |
| | | | (DKIvory) *prom: hung lft over 3f out: wknd over 1f out* | **20/1** | |
| 0 | 12 | shd | **Arian's Lad**[16] 2165 3-9-0 | DSweeney 10 | 37 |
| | | | (BPalling) *prom over 3f* | **14/1** | |
| 00 | 13 | 8 | **Weir's Annie**[16] 2165 3-8-9 | DaneO'Neill 6 | 4 |
| | | | (HCandy) *prom over 3f* | **14/1** | |
| 0 | 14 | 2 ½ | **Barholm Charlie**[13] 2236 3-9-0 | JFanning 2 | — |
| | | | (MABuckley) *bhd fnl 3f* | **100/1** | |
| 00 | 15 | 5 | **Sapphire Sky**[27] 1906 3-8-6 | RMiles(3) 5 | — |
| | | | (DKIvory) *chsd ldrs over 3f* | **50/1** | |

62.07 secs (0.27) **Going Correction** -0.10s/f (Good)
**WFA** 3 from 4yo 7lb — 15 Ran SP% **122.6**
Speed ratings: **93,91,89,88,86 84,82,82,81,80 80,79,67,63,55**CSF £32.45 TOTE £10.10: £2.90, £1.30, £3.30; EX 58.50.
**Owner** Philip A Jarvis **Bred** Mrs A C Bromley **Trained** Carburton, Notts

**FOCUS**
A moderate maiden and a very poor time for the grade of contest.

**NOTEBOOK**

**Red Leicester**, who was beaten in a seller at Nottingham last time out, made the switch from the outside stall to the far rail and it proved decisive. The time was slow for the grade of race and it is hard to see her following up.
**Laconia(IRE)** had a sound chance on official ratings and again appeared to run her race, doing best of those that chose the centre to stands'-side route. She edged across towards the winner in the closing stages and may have found this ground a little fast for her, but until she gets her head in front is one to be cautious with.
**Dance To The Blues(IRE)** finished a length closer to the runner-up than she had on her racecourse debut, but at least has scope for improvement and will be better off once qualified for handicaps.
**Lady Justice**, who has had her problems and as a consequence has had very little racing, proved she still possesses a modest level of ability and may yet find a small race in order to increase her stud value.
**Dane Rhapsody(IRE)**, who showed speed on her sole previous run at Wolverhampton in January, adopted different tactics on this turf debut. She was keeping on steadily and the run should bring her on.
**Intavac Boy** ran a similar race to his debut, being slowly away and then running on at the finish. He will be better off in handicaps, but needs to learn to start more quickly.
**Themesofgreen** *Official explanation: jockey said saddle slipped*

## 2587 CLIFF SMITH 70TH BIRTHDAY CELEBRATION FILLIES H'CAP — 1m 54y

3:10 (3:13) (D) (0-80,79) 3-Y-O — £5,980 (£1,840; £920; £460) Stalls Low

| Form | Pos | Btn | Horse | Jockey | RPR |
|---|---|---|---|---|---|
| 41 | 1 | | **Our Jaffa (IRE)**[12] 2267 3-9-5 77 | JPMurtagh 3 | 86+ |
| | | | (DJDaly) *hld up in tch: rdn to ld 2f out: drvn out* | **4/1**[2] | |
| 006 | 2 | 1 | **Pella**[23] 2001 3-8-0 58 | FNorton 7 | 65 |
| | | | (MBlanshard) *dwlt: bhd tl hdwy 2f out: r.o wl ins fnl f: nt rch wnr* | **50/1** | |
| 5220 | 3 | 1 ¼ | **Marinaite**[18] 2118 3-9-1 73 | JBramhill 8 | 77 |
| | | | (SRBowring) *led: rdn and hdd 2f out: no ex ins fnl f* | **25/1** | |
| 1-40 | 4 | nk | **Catherine Howard**[18] 2134 3-8-13 71 | KFallon 11 | 74 |
| | | | (MRChannon) *hld up mid-div: hdwy over 3f out: rdn over 2f out: kpt on ins fnl f* | **9/1** | |
| 5221 | 5 | nk | **Charmatic (IRE)**[25] 1957 3-8-7 65 | DeanMcKeown 5 | 68 |
| | | | (JAGlover) *s.i.s: sn prom: n.m.r on ins jst over 2f out: sn rdn: one pce fnl f* | **5/1**[3] | |
| 0-00 | 6 | 5 | **Susiedil (IRE)**[23] 1997 3-7-13 60 | RMiles(3) 6 | 51 |
| | | | (PWHarris) *bhd: hdwy 2f out: hung lft over 1f out: sn wknd* | **20/1** | |
| 0-02 | 7 | 3 | **Speedbird (USA)**[19] 2097 3-9-0 72 | JFEgan 12 | 56 |
| | | | (GWragg) *hld up in tch: rdn over 2f out: sn wknd* | **11/2** | |
| 0-00 | 8 | 2 | **Magical Mimi**[31] 1795 3-8-7 72 | LeanneKershaw(7) 4 | 52 |
| | | | (JeddO'Keeffe) *nvr nr ldrs* | **66/1** | |
| -613 | 9 | ½ | **Citrine Spirit (IRE)**[11] 2284 3-9-2 74 | LDettori 14 | 52 |
| | | | (JHMGosden) *w ldr: rdn and wknd over 2f out* | **3/1**[1] | |
| 00-0 | 10 | ¾ | **Sky Galaxy (USA)**[13] 2239 3-9-7 79 | WSupple 15 | 56 |
| | | | (EALDunlop) *hld up: hdwy over 3f out: rdn over 2f out: sn wknd* | **50/1** | |
| 00-0 | 11 | 1 | **Coconut Cookie**[18] 2112 3-8-11 69 | PDobbs 13 | 43 |
| | | | (RHannon) *a bhd* | **50/1** | |
| -040 | 12 | shd | **Baileys Dancer**[11] 2281 3-9-6 78 | JFanning 1 | 52 |
| | | | (MJohnston) *prom: rdn over 3f out: sn wknd* | **8/1** | |
| 60-0 | 13 | 2 ½ | **Abington Angel**[18] 2112 3-9-3 75 | MHills 9 | 43 |
| | | | (BJMeehan) *a bhd* | **50/1** | |
| 50-0 | P | | **Molinia**[23] 1997 3-8-1 62 | JFMcDonald(3) 10 | — |
| | | | (RMBeckett) *iron broke sn after s: sn p.u* | **66/1** | |

1m 45.34s (-1.06) **Going Correction** -0.025s/f (Good) — 14 Ran SP% **117.6**
Speed ratings: **104,103,101,101,101 96,93,91,90,89 88,88,86,**—CSF £201.97 CT £4362.29 TOTE £5.40: £1.80, £17.00, £14.90; EX 232.80.
**Owner** Miss A H Marshall **Bred** Hamwood Stud **Trained** Newmarket, Suffolk

**FOCUS**
A fair handicap run 0.76sec slower than the following conditions race. The first five drew away.

**NOTEBOOK**

**Our Jaffa(IRE)** looks to be on the upgrade and followed up her maiden victory by scoring with more in hand than the official margin indicates. She should not go up a great deal for this and the hat-trick is possible if she is not aimed too high.
**Pella**, dropped in trip for her handicap debut, had to overcome a tardy start on this occasion before finishing best of all. She looks well handicapped and may well go up a few pounds for this, so it will be no surprise to see her turning out before she is re-assessed.
**Marinaite**, returning to a mile for the first time since her debut, seemed to handle this faster surface and did not drop away after being headed by the winner. She looks capable of winning a similar race over this trip.
**Catherine Howard**, who won her maiden over six furlongs, has now been beaten three times over this trip and, although she appears to get it, may be better at shorter.
**Charmatic(IRE)**, encountering a fast surface for the first time, was another to miss the break. She got to the rail in the straight but never saw much daylight and failed to pick up. She may not appreciate it this quick.
**Speedbird(USA)** *Official explanation: jockey said filly did not stride out on the firm ground*
**Citrine Spirit(IRE)**, who handled similar ground at Ascot last time, made a quick start from her high draw but did not really settle. She dropped away quickly in the straight as though she had had a problem. *Official explanation: jockey said filly was unsuited by the firm ground*
**Abington Angel** *Official explanation: jockey said filly was never travelling*
**Molinia** *Official explanation: jockey said a stirrup pin came loose*

## 2588 ILLUMA - THE DAWN OF A NEW ERA CONDITIONS STKS — 1m 54y

3:40 (3:40) (C) 3-Y-O+ — £12,296 (£4,664; £2,332; £1,060) Stalls Low

| Form | Pos | Btn | Horse | Jockey | RPR |
|---|---|---|---|---|---|
| -501 | 1 | | **Shot To Fame (USA)**[30] 1828 5-9-1 101 | JPMurtagh 5 | 106 |
| | | | (PWHarris) *mde all: rdn over 2f out: drvn out* | **15/8**[2] | |
| 2 | 2 | 1 ½ | **Ancient World (USA)**[23] 1999 4-9-7 100 | LDettori 1 | 109+ |
| | | | (SaeedBinSuroor) *chsd wnr: rdn and ev ch 2f out: nt qckn ins fnl f* | **4/6**[1] | |
| /0-5 | 3 | nk | **Maghanim**[15] 2200 4-9-1 98 | RHills 2 | 102 |
| | | | (JLDunlop) *t.k.h: prom: ev ch 2f out: sn rdn: nt qckn fnl f* | **8/1**[3] | |
| 00-0 | 4 | hd | **Narrative (IRE)**[26] 1925 6-9-1 106 | KFallon 4 | 101 |
| | | | (DRLoder) *t.k.h: in tch: rdn 3f out: styd on towards fin* | **20/1** | |
| 620- | 5 | 21 | **Sophrano (IRE)**[175] 6161 4-8-8 63 | SYourston(7) 6 | 53 |
| | | | (PABlockley) *a bhd: t.o fnl 4f* | **150/1** | |
| 5020 | 6 | 20 | **Jalouhar**[8] 2383 4-9-4 47 | NCallan 3 | 10 |
| | | | (BPJBaugh) *a bhd: t.o fnl 3f* | **250/1** | |

1m 44.1s (-2.30) **Going Correction** -0.025s/f (Good) — 6 Ran SP% **111.7**
Speed ratings: **110,108,108,108,87 67**CSF £3.42 TOTE £3.40: £1.80, £1.10; EX 7.00.



The Form Book, Raceform Ltd, Compton, RG20 6NL

**Owner** The Conquistadors **Bred** Eric Puerari **Trained** Ringshall, Bucks

**FOCUS**

A decent conditions race run in a respectable time for the grade of contest.

**NOTEBOOK**

**Shot To Fame(USA)**, who won the Jubilee Handicap last time on totally different going, once again dictated the gallop and picked up well from halfway up the straight. Having been raised 12lb for his previous victory he is likely to go up a few more pounds, and handicap opportunities are going to be rare for him from now on.

**Ancient World(USA)**, runner-up in a Listed race on his debut for Godolphin and a Queen Anne entry, followed the winner throughout but could not pick up as well as that rival. He won his races on France on a soft surface, and may be better returning there as he is unlikely to get those conditions in the next couple of months.

**Maghanim**, a market drifter, moved up halfway up the straight looking the likely winner. However, once asked to go on the response was limited. Given his problems it was a reasonable effort, but he will not be easy to place.

**Narrative(IRE)**, a front-runner and former pacemaker who has been racing over much longer trips, was surprisingly held up over this trip and again failed to settle. He was keeping on at the finish and presumably the idea is to get him to relax in order to get the best out of him.

**Jalouhar** *Official explanation: jockey said gelding lost its action in the closing stages*

## 2589 BYRON H'CAP — 6f 15y

**4:10** (4:10) (D) (0-85,83) 3-Y-O — **£5,801** (£1,785; £892; £446) **Stalls** High

Form / RPR

31-0 **1** **Corps De Ballet (IRE)**[12] 2264 3-9-7 **83** ... SSanders 11 — 90
(JLDunlop) *mde all stands' side: rdn 2f out: r.o wl* **33/1**

-163 **2** ¾ **Presto Shinko (IRE)**[25] 1965 3-9-1 **77** ... RHughes 4 — 82
(RHannon) *led far side: rdn clr 2f out: r.o* **6/1**[3]

5-42 **3** ¾ **Lualua**[18] 2131 3-9-1 **77** ... KFallon 10 — 80
(TDBarron) *dwlt: chsd wnr stands' side: ev ch 2f out: nt qckn fnl f* **4/1**[2]

-000 **4** 2 **Bright Sun (IRE)**[22] 2019 3-9-2 **78** ... KimTinkler 1 — 75
(NTinkler) *chsd ldr far side over 2f: wnt 2nd again 1f out: one pce* **11/1**

-040 **5** ½ **Kingsmaite**[13] 2239 3-8-4 **66** ... JBramhill 5 — 61
(SRBowring) *chsd ldr far side over 3f out to 1f out: no ex* **40/1**

5-13 **6** 2½ **Primo Way**[19] 2082 3-9-5 **81** ... MHills 2 — 69
(BWHills) *chsd ldrs far side: lost pl over 3f out: rallied over 1f out: nt rch ldrs* **13/8**[1]

14-0 **7** 5 **Jimmy Ryan (IRE)**[19] 2082 3-9-4 **83** ... J-PGuillambert(3) 3 — 56
(TDMccarthy) *s.s: hdwy far side over 2f out: wknd over 1f out* **13/2**

0-03 **8** 1¾ **Louisiade (IRE)**[19] 2075 3-8-5 **67** ... WSupple 7 — 34
(TDEasterby) *hld up far side: wknd over 1f out* **9/1**

2250 **9** ¾ **Get To The Point**[5] 2444 3-8-10 **72** ... JPMurtagh 8 — 37
(PWD'Arcy) *outpcd far side* **14/1**

-003 **10** 2½ **Shielaligh**[12] 2264 3-9-1 **77** ... (t) LDettori 6 — 35
(MissGayKelleway) *hld up in tch far side: wknd over 1f out* **12/1**

00-0 **11** 7 **Orpenberry (IRE)**[12] 2269 3-8-6 **68** ... JEdmunds 9 — —
(JBalding) *outpcd stands' side* **66/1**

1m 13.97s (-0.83) **Going Correction** -0.10s/f (Good) — **11** Ran SP% **125.3**
Speed ratings: **101,100,99,96,95 92,85,83,82,79 69**CSF £233.04 CT £1011.06 TOTE £39.90: £7.50, £2.60, £2.10; EX 302.80.
**Owner** Mrs P G M Jamison **Bred** David Jamison Bloodstock **Trained** Arundel, W Sussex

**FOCUS**

Only three came stands' side but two of them finished first and third.

**NOTEBOOK**

**Corps De Ballet(IRE)** had clearly benefited from her pipe-opener and, with the draw advantage playing in her favour, made every yard on the stands' side. The extra furlong suited her and, as a lightly-raced filly, there should be better to come. *Official explanation: trainer said, regarding the improved form shown, filly was better suited by the good to firm ground and appreciated the extra furlong*

**Presto Shinko(IRE)** came clear of his rivals on the far side. He has not had the best of luck this season and this performance once again suggested that there is a race to be won with him off this sort of mark.

**Lualua**, 2lb higher and back up to six furlongs, had a good battle with the winner up the stands' side but eventually had to accept defeat. He should continue to run well at this level but looks only fairly handicapped.

**Bright Sun(IRE)**, who has dropped 8lb since the beginning of the season, had ground and trip in his favour for the first time this year. Granted a little more leniency, he could soon be winning again.

**Kingsmaite**, a winner over a mile towards the end of last year, found this an inadequate test.

**Primo Way**, an unlucky loser at Newbury last time, never really got competitive on this quicker ground, and he has questions to answer now.

## 2590 WATSON FOTHERGILL H'CAP — 1m 6f 15y

**4:40** (4:42) (E) (0-70,69) 3-Y-O+ — **£3,750** (£1,154; £577; £288) **Stalls** Low

Form / RPR

1421 **1** **My Legal Eagle (IRE)**[5] 2462 10-8-1 **45** ... RMiles(3) 12 — 54
(RJPrice) *hld up: hdwy over 3f out: rdn to ld 1f out: r.o wl* **3/1**[1]

4104 **2** 1¾ **Crossways**[18] 2116 6-10-0 **69** ... RHavlin 11 — 76
(PDEvans) *hld up in tch: led 3f out to 1f out: nt qckn* **9/1**

5103 **3** 7 **Saxe-Coburg (IRE)**[12] 2262 7-9-7 **62** ... SSanders 13 — 59
(GAHam) *hld up: hdwy over 3f out: one pce fnl 2f* **16/1**

-000 **4** nk **Snifia (IRE)**[29] 1857 4-9-0 **55** ... ADaly 14 — 51
(GAHam) *stdd s: hld up and bhd: hdwy over 2f out: sn rdn: one pce* **40/1**

04-0 **5** 1½ **Purdey**[29] 1858 4-8-4 **45** ... DKinsella 4 — 39
(HMorrison) *hld up and bhd: rdn over 2f out: hdwy over 1f out: nvr nrr* **20/1**

0050 **6** 1½ **Fight The Feeling**[15] 2212 6-8-6 **47** ... GGibbons 16 — 39
(JWUnett) *hld up in tch: rdn over 2f out: wknd over 1f out* **25/1**

5-00 **7** ½ **Lunar Lord**[36] 1687 8-8-12 **53** ... RPrice 15 — 44
(DBurchell) *hld up towards rr: hdwy over 2f out: rdn over 1f out: sn no imp* **25/1**

0031 **8** 1½ **Only For Sue**[29] 1858 5-9-5 **60** ... (b) NCallan 7 — 49
(WSKittow) *plld hrd: prom tl wknd over 2f out* **10/1**

0000 **9** nk **Cool Bathwick (IRE)**[9] 2375 5-8-6 **47** ... (b) FNorton 3 — 36
(BRMillman) *hld up mid-div: rdn over 3f out: no hdwy fnl 2f* **33/1**

50-0 **10** ½ **Caliban (IRE)**[23] 2004 6-8-5 **46** ... RFitzpatrick 17 — 34
(IanWilliams) *hld up mid-div: rdn and short-lived effrt over 3f out* **20/1**

0220 **11** 5 **Madiba**[11] 2285 5-9-5 **60** ... KFallon 2 — 41
(PHowling) *hld up and bhd: hdwy on ins whn n.m.r wl over 1f out: n.d after* **5/1**[3]

5060 **12** 3 **Sonoma (IRE)**[18] 2116 4-9-11 **66** ... MHills 8 — 43
(MLWBell) *sn led: hdd 3f out: wknd over 1f out* **12/1**

6000 **13** ¾ **Vanbrugh (FR)**[11] 2299 4-8-10 **51** ... (vt) PDobbs 5 — 27
(MissDAMchale) *hld up in tch: rdn over 4f out: sn wknd* **40/1**

40-1 **14** 3½ **Herne Bay (IRE)**[18] 2126 4-9-0 **62** ... DerekNolan(7) 1 — 33
(ABailey) *hld up: hmpd on ins bnd after 3f: sn bhd* **12/1**

-053 **15** 4 **Distant Cousin**[8] 2394 7-9-6 **61** ... (v) JBramhill 18 — 26
(MABuckley) *plld hrd: prom: led 7f out to 3f out: sn wknd* **12/1**

0-10 **16** ½ **Etching (USA)**[25] 1973 4-9-5 **60** ... JPMurtagh 10 — 25
(JRFanshawe) *led early: prom: rdn 4f out: wknd qckly 2f out* **9/2**[2]

5-00 **17** dist **St Jerome**[15] 2212 4-8-11 **55** ... J-PGuillambert(3) 9 — —
(NPLittmoden) *hld up and bhd: rdn over 6f out: t.o* **33/1**

3m 6.61s (-0.59) **Going Correction** -0.025s/f (Good) — **17** Ran SP% **135.9**
Speed ratings: **100,99,95,94,93 93,92,91,91,91 88,86,86,84,82 81,**—CSF £30.77 CT £406.89 TOTE £4.00: £1.50, £1.90, £3.50, £7.90; EX 49.90.
**Owner** E G Bevan **Bred** G J Freyne **Trained** Ullingswick, H'fords

**FOCUS**

For some reason a high draw often proves an advantage over this trip, and the double-figure stalls dominated.

**NOTEBOOK**

**My Legal Eagle(IRE)**, who was able to race off the same mark as when successful in an apprentices' event at York last time, stays well and confirmed his recent good form with another success. This was not a strong event and things will be tougher off a higher mark, but he should continue to give a good account.

**Crossways** has returned in good form and made a bold bid under top weight, but he found the well-treated winner just too strong. He pulled clear of the rest, though, and would have chances off this sort of mark in similar company.

**Saxe-Coburg(IRE)** did not run at all badly but the evidence suggests that he is too highly handicapped at present.

**Snifia(IRE)** found the step up in trip bringing about improvement and ran her best race of the year so far.

**Purdey** did not perform badly given her low draw and the excuses. *Official explanation: jockey said filly had lost a front shoe and lost her action*

**Caliban(IRE)** *Official explanation: jockey said gelding lost its action*

**Etching(USA)** had conditions in her favour but failed to give her running. *Official explanation: jockey said filly ran flat*

**St Jerome** *Official explanation: jockey said gelding lost its action*

## 2591 TELETEXT RACING "HANDS AND HEELS" APPRENTICE H'CAP — 1m 1f 213y

**5:10** (5:10) (F) (0-75,75) 3-Y-O+ — **£3,087** (£882; £441) **Stalls** Low

Form / RPR

5036 **1** **Realism (FR)**[16] 2170 4-8-13 **60** ... StevenHarrison 8 — 70
(PWHiatt) *a.p: rdn over 2f out: led ins fnl f: r.o* **14/1**

2154 **2** nk **Say What You See (IRE)**[15] 2210 4-9-7 **71** ... HGemberlu(3) 7 — 80
(JWHills) *w ldr: rdn 3f out: led wl over 1f out tl ins fnl f: r.o* **11/4**[2]

6664 **3** 4 **First Maite**[104] 825 11-7-12 **50** ... MNem(5) 6 — 51
(SRBowring) *hld up: rdn and hdwy over 2f out: wknd ins fnl f* **16/1**

0002 **4** ¾ **Cartronageeraghlad (IRE)**[7] 2400 3-8-12 **72** ... KMay 1 — 72
(JAOsborne) *bhd tl hdwy over 1f out: styd on ins fnl f* **3/1**[3]

440- **5** ¾ **Aswan (IRE)**[403] 1220 6-9-3 **64** ... AReilly 5 — 63
(SRBowring) *led: rdn over 3f out: hdd wl over 1f out: wknd ins fnl f* **25/1**

-300 **6** nk **Kylkenny**[46] 1460 9-9-9 **75** ... (t) RJKilloran(5) 4 — 73
(HMorrison) *prom: rdn and lost pl over 2f out: rallied over 1f out: no ex ins fnl f* **8/1**

40-2 **7** 4 **Perfect Punch**[18] 2121 5-9-3 **67** ... SO'Hara(3) 2 — 57
(CFWall) *prom: rdn over 3f out: wknd over 2f out* **7/4**[1]

2050 **8** 5 **Private Seal**[10] 2324 9-7-9 **45** oh4 ... (t) MHalford(3) 3 — 26
(JulianPoulton) *a in rr* **33/1**

2m 10.84s (1.34) **Going Correction** -0.025s/f (Good)
**WFA** 3 from 4yo+ 13lb — **8** Ran SP% **118.5**
Speed ratings: **93,92,89,88,88 88,84,80**CSF £54.55 CT £646.88 TOTE £15.80: £3.30, £1.40, £4.90; EX 62.30 Place 6 £603.33, Place 5 £57.44.
**Owner** Miss Maria McKinney **Bred** Darley Stud Management Co Ltd **Trained** Hook Norton, Oxon

**FOCUS**

A modest winning time for the grade.

**NOTEBOOK**

**Realism(FR)** was not sure to appreciate the step up to this trip, but he got it well and this should open up new opportunities for him.

**Say What You See(IRE)** ran another solid race and only went down narrowly. He has not worn any headgear for a while and it might be worth considering putting the visor back on, as his shock maiden win came with headgear being applied for the first time.

**First Maite** is undoubtedly well handicapped, but it appears that his years are catching up with him.

**Cartronageeraghlad(IRE)**, stepping up in trip once more, was again staying on when it was all over. A stronger pace would have suited him.

**Aswan(IRE)** is ideally suited by a shorter trip than this, and so this was not a bad reappearance effort in the circumstances.

**Perfect Punch** is happier coming from behind off a stronger pace.

T/Plt: £524.20 to a £1 stake. Pool: £34,398.55. 47.90 winning tickets. T/Qpdt: £25.40 to a £1 stake. Pool: £2,891.80. 84.20 winning tickets. KH

# 2092 YARMOUTH (L-H)

### Wednesday, June 2

**OFFICIAL GOING: Firm (good to firm in places)**

Wind: fresh bhd Weather: cloudy

## 2592 EUROPEAN BREEDERS FUND/VAUXHALL HOLIDAY PARK NOVICE STKS — 6f 3y

**2:20** (2:21) (D) 2-Y-O — **£4,784** (£1,472; £736; £368) **Stalls** High

Form / RPR

30 **1** **Wilko (USA)**[21] 2045 2-8-12 ... EAhern 5 — 85+
(JNoseda) *broke wl: plld hrd: stdd sn after s: hdwy over 1f out: led ins fnl f: r.o wl* **7/2**[3]

1 **2** 1 **Dance Anthem**[29] 1865 2-9-2 ... PMcCabe 3 — 86
(MGQuinlan) *hld up: hdwy over 1f out: ev ch whn hung rt ins fnl f: kpt on* **11/4**[2]

5231 **3** 2½ **Speed Dial Harry (IRE)**[18] 2124 2-8-12 ... (b[1]) GFaulkner 2 — 75
(KRBurke) *led 5f out: edgd lft: hdd and no ex ins fnl f* **20/1**

5 **4** nk **Emerald Penang (IRE)**[62] 1219 2-8-12 ... SWhitworth 7 — 74
(PWChapple-Hyam) *led 1f: remained handy: rdn over 2f out: hmpd and no ex ins fnl f* **80/1**

4 **5** ¾ **Simplify**[47] 1436 2-8-12 ... DHolland 6 — 71
(DRLoder) *sn pushed along and prom: nt clr run and hmpd over 1f out: styd on same pce* **2/1**[1]

1 **6** 2 **Striking Endeavour**[27] 1905 2-9-2 ... SDrowne 4 — 69
(GCBravery) *chsd ldrs: rdn over 2f out: nt clr run over 1f out: wknd ins fnl f* **9/2**

**7** 16 **Parsley's Return** 2-8-12 ... WRyan 1 — 17
(NACallaghan) *s.i.s: outpcd* **33/1**

1m 11.87s (-1.73) **Going Correction** -0.40s/f (Firm) — **7** Ran SP% **109.3**
Speed ratings: **95,93,90,89,88 86,64**CSF £12.22 TOTE £4.90: £2.60, £1.60; EX 15.30.
**Owner** Mrs Susan Roy **Bred** Ro Parra **Trained** Newmarket, Suffolk
■ Stewards Enquiry : P McCabe caution: careless riding

**FOCUS**
An interesting little novice event and the pace was solid.
**NOTEBOOK**
**Wilko(USA)**, who may have found the race coming too soon when disappointing at York last time, seemed to improve significantly for this first try on fast ground. His rider was keen to rein him back soon after the start, but the colt got stronger as the race progressed and he showed a decent turn of foot to come between horses to lead. He was well on top at the line and now heads for Royal Ascot.
**Dance Anthem** , tackling faster ground, was the only one to go with the winner in the closing stages and put up a good performance in trying to concede 4lb to his rival.
**Speed Dial Harry(IRE)**, bought in for 15,500gns after winning a Southwell seller last month, was blinkered for the first time and was allowed to bowl along in front in these very different conditions. He had no answer to the front pair inside the last furlong, but there should still be another race in him at a more realistic level.
**Emerald Penang(IRE)** ran better than he did when last of five on his debut. He moved to his current yard after that and could progress again from this performance.
**Simplify**, who should have been suited by this longer trip, was hampered when making his effort but did not exactly take off when eventually in the clear, and he is now looking a very expensive purchase.
**Striking Endeavour** was on totally different ground to his winning debut and did not perform.

## 2593 EXPRESS CAFES (S) STKS 6f 3y
**2:50** (2:51) (G) 2-Y-O **£2,541** (£726; £363) **Stalls** High

Form RPR
6 **1** **Part Time Love**[14] 2225 2-8-8 .......... SHitchcott(3) 1 52
(MRChannon) *outpcd: hdwy over 2f out: rdn to ld and hung rt over 1f out: drvn out* **11/10**[1]
4134 **2** *2 1/2* **Zimbali**[10] 2321 2-8-12 .......... RFfrench 4 46
(JMBradley) *trckd ldrs: rdn and ev ch over 1f out: styd on same pce* **9/2**[3]
201 **3** *shd* **Story Of One (IRE)**[7] 2405 2-9-3 .......... DHolland 2 50
(NPLittmoden) *led over 4f: no ex ins fnl f* **2/1**[2]
3 **4** *3/4* **Petite Elle**[67] 1137 2-8-6 ..........(v[1]) JQuinn 6 37
(PJMcbride) *prom: hung lft and outpcd over 1f out: styd on ins fnl f* **22/1**
4402 **5** *3 1/2* **Alice King (IRE)**[7] 2405 2-7-13 .......... CHaddon(7) 3 26
(WGMTurner) *chsd ldrs: rdn and ev ch over 1f out: wknd ins fnl f* **10/1**
1m 14.15s (0.55) **Going Correction** -0.40s/f (Firm) **5** Ran SP% **112.6**
Speed ratings: **80,76,76,75,70**CSF £6.76 TOTE £1.90: £1.10, £2.40; EX 7.40.The winner was bought for 20,000gns by Jane Chapple-Hyam.
**Owner** Graeme Love **Bred** Hellwood Stud Farm **Trained** West Ilsley, Berks
**FOCUS**
A very modest time, even for a juvenile seller, being 2.28 seconds slower than the opening juvenile novice event.
**NOTEBOOK**
**Part Time Love**, taking a huge drop in class after finishing sixth in a Goodwood maiden last month, was brought with his effort down the centre of the track and eventually ran out a clear-cut winner. He was bought for 20,000gns at the subsequent auction, but may not be easy to place from now on.
**Zimbali**, well beaten in better company after winning a Regional maiden auction event at Warwick in April, did not seem to fail through lack of stamina and stayed on to snatch second place on the line.
**Story Of One(IRE)** ran creditably under his penalty over this extra furlong.
**Petite Elle**, not seen since finishing third of four in a Wolverhampton seller back in March, probably ran better in the first-time visor if again only beating one home.
**Alice King(IRE)**, 6lb better off with Story Of One for a beating of just over a length at Lingfield last week, was on her toes beforehand and failed to perform.

## 2594 RCA/BHB SPONSORSHIP DAY H'CAP 1m 2f 21y
**3:20** (3:21) (F) (0-55,57) 4-Y-0+ **£3,507** (£1,002; £501) **Stalls** Low

Form RPR
-002 **1** **Kernel Dowery (IRE)**[10] 2324 4-9-5 **54**..........(e) DHolland 3 64
(PWHarris) *chsd ldrs: led over 3f out: rdn out* **11/4**[1]
4543 **2** *1/2* **Tinian**[9] 2362 6-9-1 **50**.......... GFaulkner 13 59
(KRBurke) *hld up: hdwy over 4f out: rdn and ev ch fr over 2f out: no ex ins fnl f* **25/1**
2000 **3** *shd* **Burgundy**[10] 2324 7-9-6 **55**..........(b) OUrbina 14 64
(PMitchell) *hld up: hdwy over 1f out: hung lft: r.o* **14/1**
4000 **4** *3 1/2* **Sammy's Shuffle**[21] 2034 9-8-12 **47**..........(b) PDoe 11 49
(JamiePoulton) *hld up in tch: rdn over 2f out: styd on same pce fnl f* **50/1**
3000 **5** *1 1/4* **Zalkani (IRE)**[18] 2122 4-9-2 **51**.......... VSlattery 8 51
(BGPowell) *s.i.s: hld up: hdwy over 1f out: nt rch ldrs* **20/1**
411- **6** *nk* **Rojabaa**[183] 5717 5-8-11 **53**.......... LTreadwell(7) 5 52
(WGMTurner) *hld up: hdwy over 2f out: edgd lft: nt rch ldrs* **8/1**
00/0 **7** *3/4* **Ursa Major**[15] 2210 10-9-1 **50**.......... SDrowne 1 48
(TKeddy) *w ldrs: rdn over 3f out: styd on same pce appr fnl f* **14/1**
6650 **8** *1* **Figura**[10] 2324 6-9-0 **49**.......... PRobinson 4 45
(RIngram) *hld up: styd on appr fnl f: nvr nrr* **8/1**
2431 **9** *3/4* **Our Destiny**[10] 2324 6-9-5 **57** 6ex.......... SHitchcott(3) 10 52
(AWCarroll) *chsd ldrs: rdn over 2f out: wknd over 1f out* **6/1**[3]
-033 **10** *1 3/4* **Fantasy Crusader**[10] 2324 5-8-12 **47**..........(p) JQuinn 6 38
(JAGilbert) *prom: n.m.r and lost pl over 2f out: n.d after* **5/1**[2]
-000 **11** *1/2* **Den'S-Joy**[9] 2375 8-8-12 **50**.......... LPKeniry(3) 16 40
(VSmith) *s.s: a in rr* **18/1**
0060 **12** *5* **Fife And Drum (USA)**[10] 2324 7-8-10 **48**..........(p) BReilly(3) 15 29
(MissJFeilden) *mde most over 6f: wknd over 1f out* **28/1**
00 **13** *5* **Acola (FR)**[26] 1940 4-9-5 **54**..........(p) WRyan 12 25
(RMHCowell) *prom: rdn over 3f out: wknd over 1f out* **50/1**
3340 **14** *1* **Mrs Cube**[10] 2324 5-8-10 **45**.......... SWhitworth 9 14
(PHowling) *dwlt: hld up: rdn over 3f out: a in rr* **28/1**
55-0 **15** *5* **French Risk (IRE)**[39] 1630 4-8-10 **45**.......... SWKelly 7 5
(WMBrisbourne) *hld up: rdn over 4f out: wknd over 3f out* **25/1**
100- **16** *4* **Stars At Midnight**[303] 3830 4-9-0 **49**.......... RFfrench 2 1
(JMBradley) *hld up in tch: wknd over 2f out* **50/1**
2m 7.65s (-0.32) **Going Correction** +0.05s/f (Good) **16** Ran SP% **123.7**
Speed ratings: **103,102,102,99,98 98,97,97,96,95 94,90,86,85,81 78**CSF £85.61 CT £844.20 TOTE £3.40: £1.50, £2.80, £2.70, £7.00; EX 70.90.
**Owner** The Treasure Hunters **Bred** A Lyons Bloodstock **Trained** Ringshall, Bucks
■ Stewards Enquiry : S Drowne two-day ban: careless riding (Jun 13,14)
**FOCUS**
A race run at a fair pace with Fife And Drum and Our Destiny disputing the lead for much of the way.
**NOTEBOOK**
**Kernel Dowery(IRE)** was getting off the mark at the 17th attempt, but he had shown himself to be in form with a close second at Brighton in his most recent start and he won this in good style. He could be interesting under a penalty as he was already due to go up 2lb even before this.
**Tinian** is not the easiest of rides, but he ran much better back over a longer trip despite not looking totally at home on the fast ground in the closing stages.
**Burgundy** is a difficult horse to catch right, but he is very well handicapped on his best form and put in a strong finish that was always going to be too late. He cannot be relied on to run so well next time though.
**Sammy's Shuffle** ran his best race for some time under conditions that suit.
**Zalkani(IRE)** not for the first time hinted at ability despite not seeing much daylight in the home straight.
**Rojabaa** ◆ shaped with some promise on this first run for 183 days.
**Ursa Major** ran much better than on his recent reappearance following a 19-month layoff.
**Our Destiny**, under a 6lb penalty for his recent Brighton win, helped force the early pace but dropped away tamely.
**Fantasy Crusader** never threatened, but he did not enjoy a trouble-free passage so should be given the benefit of the doubt.
**Den'S-Joy** *Official explanation: jockey said mare was very slowly away from the stalls*
**Mrs Cube** *Official explanation: jockey said mare slipped on the bend*

## 2595 PKF ACCOUNTANCY SERVICES H'CAP 1m 3f 101y
**3:50** (3:50) (E ) (0-70,69) 3-Y-0+ **£3,789** (£1,166; £583; £291) **Stalls** Low

Form RPR
0-00 **1** **Duc's Dream**[63] 1198 6-9-0 **53**.......... JMackay 3 61
(DMorris) *a.p: rdn to ld nr fin* **4/1**[2]
60-6 **2** *hd* **Piri Piri (IRE)**[15] 2210 4-9-12 **65**.......... SWhitworth 9 73
(PJMcbride) *hld up: plld hrd: hdwy over 3f out: rdn to ld over 1f out: hdd nr fin* **7/1**
00-5 **3** *1 1/4* **Fort Churchill (IRE)**[19] 2093 3-9-2 **69**.......... PRobinson 8 75
(MHTompkins) *led: hdd after 1f: led 8f out: rdn and hdd over 1f out: styd on same pce* **7/1**
3-46 **4** *1 1/4* **Merrymaker**[13] 2235 4-9-2 **55**.......... SWKelly 6 59
(WMBrisbourne) *hld up: rdn over 3f out: styd on appr fnl f: nt rch ldrs* **6/1**[3]
00-5 **5** *1 1/2* **Dami (USA)**[9] 2371 3-9-1 **68**.......... DHolland 5 70
(CEBrittain) *mid-div: pushed along 1/2-way: outpcd over 3f out: styd on ins fnl f* **10/3**[1]
3-20 **6** *5* **Quest On Air**[8] 2385 5-8-3 **45** ow1.......... DCorby(3) 10 39
(JRJenkins) *chsd ldrs: rdn over 2f out: wknd over 1f out* **10/1**
5021 **7** *3* **Joint Destiny (IRE)**[20] 2054 3-7-13 **52**.......... JQuinn 1 41
(EJO'Neill) *hld up: hdwy over 3f out: rdn and wknd over 1f out* **12/1**
0304 **8** *1 1/2* **River Of Fire**[8] 2386 6-7-5 **37** oh7..........(v) CHaddon(7) 2 23
(CNKellett) *chsd ldrs: led 9f out: hdd 8f out: wknd over 2f out* **25/1**
0030 **9** *hd* **Midshipman**[18] 2120 6-9-7 **60**..........(vt) WRyan 7 46
(AWCarroll) *led after 1f: hdd 9f out: remained handy: rdn and ev ch 2f out: sn wknd* **28/1**
1-40 **10** *2 1/2* **Grand Wizard**[31] 1801 4-10-0 **67**..........(t) MTebbutt 4 49
(WJarvis) *hld up in tch: rdn over 2f out: wknd over 1f out* **9/1**
2m 27.55s (0.15) **Going Correction** +0.05s/f (Good)
**WFA** 3 from 4yo+ 14lb **10** Ran SP% **116.4**
Speed ratings: **101,100,99,99,97 94,92,91,90,89**CSF £32.19 CT £190.93 TOTE £5.50: £2.20, £3.40, £2.60; EX 36.20.
**Owner** Mrs S I Parry **Bred** I W Parry **Trained** Newmarket, Suffolk
**FOCUS**
Not a particularly strong early gallop with several keen to get a lead.
**NOTEBOOK**
**Duc's Dream** has not been in great form in recent months, but as a result he had dropped to a mark 2lb lower than when winning over course and distance on similar ground last September. He goes well on this track and was brought with a strong late run to get up virtually on the line.
**Piri Piri(IRE)** appeared to have the race in the bag when finally getting the better of Fort Churchill, only to have it snatched from her. She is 2lb lower than for her last win and should be spot-on after this.
**Fort Churchill(IRE)**, making his handicap debut, tried to wind things up from the front but may not have been seen to best advantage by being forced to make his own running and the ground may also not have suited. He is probably capable of better when getting a lead and the maiden he ran in here last time is working out particularly well, but he will need to improve as he is already set to go up 5lb. *Official explanation: jockey said gelding was unsuited by the frim ground*
**Merrymaker** was noted staying on nicely towards the end and this was certainly his best effort since joining his current yard.
**Dami(USA)**, stepping up significantly in trip, tended to run in snatches. She saw a lot of daylight on the wide outside in the home straight, but did not fail through lack of stamina and finished well clear of the others. *Official explanation: jockey said filly ran in snatches*

## 2596 RACING AHEAD MAGAZINE MAIDEN STKS 7f 3y
**4:20** (4:23) (D ) 3-Y-0+ **£3,412** (£1,050; £525; £262) **Stalls** High

Form RPR
34-4 **1** **Royal Prince**[56] 1295 3-8-11 77.......... DHolland 9 78
(JRFanshawe) *trckd ldrs: led over 1f out: r.o wl* **8/11**[1]
**2** *2 1/2* **Mr Mistral** 5-9-7 .......... SDrowne 2 72
(GWragg) *hld up: hdwy over 1f out: r.o: no ch w wnr* **20/1**
052- **3** *shd* **River Nurey (IRE)**[221] 5741 3-8-11 72.......... PRobinson 10 71
(BWHills) *chsd ldr: rdn over 1f out: styd on same pce* **9/2**[2]
**4** *hd* **Kabeer**[51] 6-9-7 .......... DRMcCabe 4 71?
(PSMcentee) *sn led: rdn and hdd over 1f out: no ex ins fnl f* **66/1**
35-0 **5** *6* **Stanley Crane (USA)**[11] 2281 3-8-11 75..........(t) SWKelly 11 55
(BHanbury) *chsd ldrs: rdn over 2f out: sn outpcd* **10/1**
**6** *hd* **Cronkyvoddy** 3-8-11 ..........(t) JQuinn 1 55
(MissGayKelleway) *s.s: bhd tl styd on ins fnl f: nvr nrr* **66/1**
62- **7** *2 1/2* **Ice Dragon**[267] 4803 3-8-6 .......... MHenry 3 43
(MHTompkins) *chsd ldrs over 5f* **14/1**
350- **8** *3/4* **King Of Music (USA)**[205] 5968 3-8-11 72.......... OUrbina 14 46
(GProdromou) *mid-div: rdn over 2f out: no imp* **28/1**
000- **9** *hd* **Arran**[202] 5988 4-9-7 .......... GCarter 6 46
(VSmith) *s.s: outpcd: nvr nrr* **100/1**
400- **10** *1/2* **Boogie Magic**[168] 6205 4-8-13 68.......... BReilly(3) 7 39
(CNAllen) *chsd ldrs over 4f* **66/1**
**11** *3* **White Sail** 3-8-6 .......... WRyan 13 32
(HRACecil) *sn outpcd* **8/1**[3]
3 **12** *1 1/2* **Otago (IRE)**[2] 2530 3-8-11 .......... NPollard 5 33
(JRBest) *mid-div: rdn 1/2-way: sn wknd* **25/1**
00 **13** *5* **Flying With Eagles**[15] 2211 3-8-4 .......... CHaddon(7) 8 20
(JJay) *outpcd* **100/1**
000- **14** *shd* **Absolutely Fab (IRE)**[312] 3600 3-8-1 35.......... HayleyTurner(5) 12 14
(MrsCADunnett) *mid-div: sn pushed along: wknd 1/2-way* **100/1**
1m 22.65s (-3.85) **Going Correction** -0.40s/f (Firm)
**WFA** 3 from 4yo+ 10lb **14** Ran SP% **122.5**
Speed ratings: **106,103,103,102,95 95,92,92,91,91 87,86,80,80**CSF £24.75 TOTE £1.90: £1.10, £5.80, £2.10; EX 24.60.
**Owner** Abdulla Buhaleeba **Bred** Snailwell Stud Co Ltd **Trained** Newmarket, Suffolk
**FOCUS**
A modest maiden lacking in strength in depth and only limited encouragement amongst the beaten horses, though the pace was decent.

**NOTEBOOK**

**Royal Prince** has shown ability in all three of his starts before this and had little difficulty in running right away from a modest field. Whether he will be effective outside this level remains to be seen, but at least he is going the right way.

**Mr Mistral**, whose dam was a winner over this trip for the same yard, was making a belated debut and stayed on from well back to snatch second place. He has already been gelded, but does appear to have a little ability.

**River Nurey(IRE)**, not seen since narrowly beaten in a decent Doncaster nursery last October, was always near the front but was made to look very one-paced in the latter stages. He may have needed this, but is obviously nothing special.

**Kabeer**, comfortably beaten in two bumpers before this, made much of the running on this Flat debut but the fact that he only narrowly lost out for second advertises the value of the form outside the winner.

**Stanley Crane(USA)**, given a much more patient ride than at Ascot, did not show a great deal.

**Cronkyvoddy** ◆ probably did well to reach his final position considering how much ground he lost at the start. From the same family as Assessor, he is likely to need further than this and is not totally without hope.

**Arran** *Official explanation: jockey said gelding was unsuited by the firm ground*

## 2597 GRAYS DRY LINING H'CAP — 1m 3y

4:50 (4:51) (F) (0-55,55) 3-Y-0+ — £3,542 (£1,012; £506) Stalls High

Form — RPR

/024 **1** **Prime Offer**[63] 1207 8-9-12 **53** ..... OUrbina 11 67
(JJay) *mde all: rdn out* **16/1**

6U36 **2** *3* **Brilliantrio**[64] 1191 6-9-10 **51** ..... LVickers 12 58
(MCChapman) *hld up: hdwy 1/2-way: rdn over 1f out: styd on same pce* **40/1**

-00U **3** *1 1/4* **Poppyline**[9] 2356 4-9-12 **53** ..... SDrowne 16 57
(WRMuir) *hld up: hdwy 1/2-way: hung lft over 2f out: styd on* **20/1**

2203 **4** *1 1/4* **Lord Chamberlain**[6] 2426 11-9-5 **53** ..... (b) CJDavies(7) 14 54
(JMBradley) *s.i.s: hld up: hdwy over 2f out: styd on* **9/1**

3546 **5** *nk* **Miss Peaches**[51] 1373 6-9-5 **46** ..... PRobinson 7 47
(GGMargarson) *broke wl: lost pl 6f out: r.o ins fnl f: nvr nr to chal* **14/1**

0-00 **6** *1/2* **Desert Fury**[18] 2123 7-9-3 **44** ..... RFfrench 2 43
(RBastiman) *mid-div: hdwy over 2f out: rdn over 1f out: styd on same pce* **10/1**

0523 **7** *1/2* **Balerno**[33] 1748 5-9-10 **51** ..... GCarter 6 49
(RIngram) *mid-div: hdwy over 2f out: sn rdn: no imp fnl f* **13/2**[1]

6413 **8** *shd* **My Lilli (IRE)**[26] 1940 4-9-8 **49** ..... JMackay 10 47
(PMitchell) *chsd ldrs: rdn over 2f out: wknd ins fnl f* **7/1**[2]

3-60 **9** *1* **Kindness**[29] 1875 4-9-9 **50** ..... SWhitworth 17 46
(ADWPinder) *hld up: rdn over 2f out: sn edgd lft: nvr trbld ldrs* **50/1**

50-0 **10** *nk* **No Chance To Dance (IRE)**[18] 2121 4-9-9 **50** ..... (t) NPollard 8 45
(HJCollingridge) *s.i.s: nvr nrr* **66/1**

0045 **11** *3/4* **Classic Vision**[25] 1971 4-9-12 **53** ..... (p) DHolland 20 46
(WJHaggas) *chsd ldrs: rdn over 2f out: wknd fnl f* **9/1**

-020 **12** *1 1/4* **Ziet D'Alsace (FR)**[6] 2426 4-9-11 **52** ..... WRyan 3 42
(AWCarroll) *chsd ldrs: rdn over 2f out: wknd ins fnl f* **14/1**

-000 **13** *3* **Sabalara (IRE)**[23] 1992 4-10-0 **55** ..... (e[1]) SCarson 15 39
(PWHarris) *prom over 6f* **25/1**

6104 **14** *3* **Ballare (IRE)**[43] 1531 5-9-6 **47** ..... TWilliams 19 24
(BobJones) *hld up: rdn over 3f out: n.d* **8/1**[3]

0-20 **15** *1 1/4* **Halcyon Magic**[26] 1941 6-9-2 **50** ..... (b) LauraPike(7) 5 24
(MissJFeilden) *mid-div: wknd 2f out* **16/1**

1525 **16** *1* **Titian Lass**[60] 1244 5-9-4 **48** ..... (b) LPKeniry(3) 1 19
(CEBrittain) *hld up: effrt over 3f out: sn wknd* **16/1**

06-0 **17** *3/4* **Rubaiyat (IRE)**[30] 1827 3-9-3 **55** ..... JQuinn 4 25
(GWragg) *prom 6f* **40/1**

400P **18** *4* **Taiyo**[8] 2387 4-9-4 **45** ..... SWKelly 9 6
(JWPayne) *prom over 5f* **50/1**

0666 **19** *1/2* **Peartree House (IRE)**[8] 2387 10-9-4 **45** ..... GFaulkner 13 4
(DWChapman) *chsd ldrs over 5f* **25/1**

0444 **20** *6* **Cooden Beach (IRE)**[18] 2122 4-9-0 **46** ..... HayleyTurner(5) 18 —
(MLWBell) *hld up: rdn over 3f out: sn wknd* **9/1**

1m 35.95s (-3.75) **Going Correction** -0.40s/f (Firm)
**WFA** 3 from 4yo+ 11lb — **20 Ran SP% 129.8**
Speed ratings: **102,99,97,96,96 95,95,95,94,93 93,91,88,85,84 83,82,78,78,72**CSF £581.54 CT £12150.40 TOTE £21.20: £6.30, £15.00, £6.80, £1.90; EX 1049.50.
**Owner** Miss K A Bartlett **Bred** Cheveley Park Stud Ltd **Trained** Newmarket, Suffolk

**FOCUS**

A competitive, if modest handicap on paper though the pace was decent.

**NOTEBOOK**

**Prime Offer** bounced out of the stalls and made every yard. Better know as a sand performer these days, he had only appeared once on turf before this since the autumn of 2001, but was racing off a 10lb lower mark than for his only win on grass.

**Brilliantrio** has been notable for ejecting her jockey on occasions when she feels like it, but she showed here that she can run when she wants to. Whether she will reproduce this next time though is anybody's guess.

**Poppyline** stayed on well to finish third. She likes this ground and has ability, but remains a maiden after 21 attempts.

**Lord Chamberlain** continues to belie his years and ran another sound race under conditions that suit.

**Miss Peaches** made up a lot of late ground and may be worth a try over further, but she has only a single banded stakes success to her name.

**Desert Fury**, backed at long odds despite a losing run stretching back three years, was not totally disgraced.

**Balerno**, whose only win in 30 previous attempts came in a banded contest on Polytrack, never threatened to land a blow.

**Classic Vision** *Official explanation: jockey said filly had hung*

## 2598 RACING WELFARE "ARTHUR TAYLOR" LIFETIME IN RACING AMATEUR RIDERS' H'CAP — 7f 3y

5:20 (5:20) (F) (0-70,66) 3-Y-0+ — £3,332 (£952; £476) Stalls High

Form — RPR

0-46 **1** **Cashneem (IRE)**[15] 2215 6-10-6 **58** ..... MrCDavies(7) 5 69
(WMBrisbourne) *s.i.s: sn chsng ldrs: led over 1f out: rdn out* **3/1**[1]

0032 **2** *3/4* **Londoner (USA)**[10] 2325 6-10-3 **53** ..... MrDHutchison(5) 9 62
(SDow) *chsd ldrs: hung lft over 4f out: rdn over 2f out: r.o* **3/1**[1]

2-00 **3** *1/2* **Tuscan Flyer**[15] 2219 6-10-12 **62** ..... MissRBastiman(5) 8 70
(RBastiman) *chsd ldrs: rdn and ev ch over 1f out: styd on* **16/1**

5503 **4** *shd* **Bint Royal (IRE)**[3] 2506 6-10-8 **58** ..... (p) MissVHaigh(5) 3 65
(MissVHaigh) *mid-div: hdwy over 2f out: rdn and ev ch over 1f out: styd on same pce* **3/1**[1]

6600 **5** *1 1/4* **Horizontal (USA)**[29] 1875 4-10-10 **55** ..... (t) MrRHFowler 6 59
(VSmith) *s.i.s: sn prom: outpcd 1/2-way: r.o ins fnl f* **10/1**[3]

5030 **6** *1/2* **Feast Of Romance**[43] 1516 7-10-2 **47** ..... (b) MlleA-SPacault 7 50
(CNAllen) *mde most over 5f: no ex* **16/1**

0000 **7** *4* **Dexileos (IRE)**[18] 2122 5-10-2 **47** ..... (t) MrsSBosley 4 39
(ADWPinder) *sn outpcd* **33/1**

-660 **8** *2* **Prince Du Soleil (FR)**[57] 1277 8-8-13 **37** ow2 ..... MrNSoares(7) 10 24
(JRJenkins) *sn outpcd* **33/1**

0011 **9** *1* **Somerset West (IRE)**[25] 1969 4-11-2 **66** ..... MissJFerguson(5) 1 51
(JRBest) *w ldrs: rdn and ev ch 2f out: wknd over 1f out* **5/1**[2]

1m 25.11s (-1.39) **Going Correction** -0.40s/f (Firm)
**WFA** 3 from 4yo+ 10lb — **9 Ran SP% 118.4**
Speed ratings: **91,90,89,89,88 87,82,80,79**CSF £12.12 CT £121.46 TOTE £3.30: £2.10, £1.50, £4.30; EX 17.00 Place 6 £119.37, Place 5 £54.14.
**Owner** Law Abiding Citizens **Bred** Mrs Teresa Bergin **Trained** Great Ness, Shropshire

**FOCUS**

An ordinary amateur riders' handicap run at a fair pace.

**NOTEBOOK**

**Cashneem(IRE)** loves this fast ground and, particularly well handled by his pilot, saw his race out in good style. He was racing off a mark just 1lb higher than for his last win and depending on how he comes out of this, may turn out again quickly.

**Londoner(USA)** came into this in fair form and stayed on to snatch second, but he has not won for 20 months and he is already due to go up 2lb, so things will not get any easier.

**Tuscan Flyer** ran his best race of the season so far, but all his wins have been at the minimum trip and he is still 2lb above his last winning mark.

**Bint Royal(IRE)**, 1lb below her last winning mark on turf, had every chance and kept on to the line under an animated finish from her rider.

**Horizontal(USA)**, no closer than fifth in five previous attempts, tended to run in snatches.

**Feast Of Romance** set the early pace, but did not get home. He looks better when held up for a late run.

**Somerset West(IRE)**, bidding for a hat-trick off a 3lb higher mark, was rather awkward leaving his outside stall and then took a good hold. He may also not have been helped by being taken on for the early lead and eventually dropped tamely away.

T/Plt: £150.60 to a £1 stake. Pool: £27,043.45. 131.05 winning tickets. T/Qpdt: £22.90 to a £1 stake. Pool: £1,809.60. 58.40 winning tickets. CR

2602 - (Foreign Racing) - See Raceform Interactive

# 2413 LEOPARDSTOWN (L-H)

Wednesday, June 2

**OFFICIAL GOING: Good**

## 2603a GLENCAIRN STKS (LISTED RACE) — 1m

7:30 (7:32) 4-Y-0+ — £22,922 (£6,725; £3,204; £1,091)

RPR

**1** **Abunawwas (IRE)**[28] 1893 4-9-5 109 ..... DPMcDonogh 3 111
(KevinPrendergast, Ire) *towards rr: prog 3f out: 5th travelling wl ent st: rdn to ld under 1 1/2f out: kpt on wl u.p fnl f* **8/1**

**2** *nk* **Napper Tandy (IRE)**[10] 2329 4-9-3 109 ..... (b) KJManning 1 108
(JSBolger, Ire) *settled 3rd: impr to ld early st: hdd under 1 1/2f out: rallied 1f out: kpt on wl u.p* **6/1**[3]

**3** *hd* **Fearn Royal (IRE)**[193] 5958 5-8-11 91 ..... CO'Donoghue 7 102?
(PeterCasey, Ire) *broke wl: settled towards rr: 9th appr st: impr into 4th over 1f out: kpt on wl nr fin* **20/1**

**4** *shd* **Latino Magic (IRE)**[30] 1849 4-9-3 104 ..... RMBurke 2 108
(RJOsborne, Ire) *trckd ldrs in 4th: 3rd and rdn early st: drifted rt ins fnl f: kpt on wl* **7/1**

**5** *1 1/2* **One Won One (USA)**[11] 2316 10-9-0 102 ..... PShanahan 5 101
(MsJoannaMorgan, Ire) *trckd ldrs in 6th: 5th and kpt on fnl f* **16/1**

**6** *nk* **Mr Houdini (IRE)**[35] 5958 7-9-3 ..... TPO'Shea 9 103
(MrsJohnHarrington, Ire) *hld up in rr: last into st: impr into 6th 1f out: kpt on* **14/1**

**7** *3* **Livadiya (IRE)**[10] 2329 8-9-0 107 ..... JAHeffernan 11 94
(HRogers, Ire) *towards rr: 10th ent st: no imp fr 1 1/2f out* **11/2**[2]

**8** *4* **Twiggy's Sister (IRE)**[24] 1982 6-8-11 100 ..... JPSpencer 6 81
(DermotMurphy, Ire) *hld up in tch: no ex early st* **12/1**

**9** *2 1/2* **D'Anjou**[24] 1982 7-9-5 112 ..... MJKinane 10 84
(JohnMOxx, Ire) *trckd ldrs: 5th 1/2-way: wknd early st* **7/2**[1]

**10** *6* **Beau Cheval (IRE)**[7] 2415 5-8-11 80 ..... (b) DMGrant 8 62
(HRogers, Ire) *led: rdn 3f out: hdd & wknd early st* **40/1**

**11** *11* **Multazem (USA)**[24] 1982 4-9-0 108 ..... (b) PJSmullen 4 40
(DKWeld, Ire) *settled 2nd: rdn to chal early st: eased 1 1/2f out: virtually p.u ins fnl f* **7/2**[1]

1m 40.5s **Going Correction** -0.15s/f (Firm) — **11 Ran SP% 125.2**
Speed ratings: **113,112,112,112,110 110,107,103,101,95 84**CSF £59.20 TOTE £12.10: £2.70, £2.30, £21.80; DF 125.20.
**Owner** Hamdan Al Maktoum **Bred** Airlie Stud **Trained** Friarstown, Co Kildare

**NOTEBOOK**

**Abunawwas(IRE)** showed his undoubted turn of foot here but was committed a bit earlier than usual. This was his first success over a mile and he appeared to see the trip out well. Some give in the ground is essential and he will possibly go pot hunting in France although there is an opportunity for him here in a week's time.

**Napper Tandy(IRE)** is possibly more effective over further but despite the level of his form is proving difficult to win with. He did nothing wrong here though.

**Fearn Royal(IRE)** ran a career best. She got a flyer out of the stalls but had only two behind her turning for home. She finished well to snatch third place close home.

**Latino Magic(IRE)** did not have the pace to keep out of trouble, he hung right inside the last and lost third place in the last few strides but it was a surprise when his jockey objected, unsuccessfully, to the runner-up for alleged interference.

**One Won One(USA)** is hardly on the decline considering his age.

**Livadiya(IRE)** did not run anywhere near her Curragh form of ten days previously.

**D'Anjou** quit early in the straight.

**Multazem(USA)** was found to be suffering from a "respiratory abnormality". *Official explanation: vet said colt was found to have a respiratory abnormality*

# 2340 SAN SIRO (R-H)

Wednesday, June 2

**OFFICIAL GOING: Good to firm**

## 2607a PREMIO STRADELLA (F&M) — 1m 4f

2:20 (2:23) 3-Y-0+ — £8,803 (£3,873; £2,113; £1,056)

RPR

**1** **Landinium (ITY)**[21] 2042 5-9-0 ..... CColombi 1 —
(CFWall) *raced in 3rd & always going well, progress to track leader straight, led 1 1/2f out, easily 58-100F*

2 *6* **Entusiasmo (ITY)**$^{10}$ [2340] 3-8-7 ........ GBietolini 6 —
(JHeloury, Italy)
3 *7* **Musical Score**$^{31}$ 5-9-11 ........ MEsposito 2 —
(MGonnelli, Italy)
4 *4* **Blu Fasliyeva (IRE)**$^{368}$ 3-7-13 ........ APolli 4 —
(VCaruso, Italy)
5 *dist* **Jamnica (ITY)**$^{381}$ [1705] 4-9-0 ........ DVargiu 3 —
(LD'Auria, Italy)

2m 29.6s
**WFA** 3 from 4yo+ 15lb **5** Ran
Speed ratings: .
**Owner** Ettore Landi **Bred** Urbano Aletti **Trained** Newmarket, Suffolk

**NOTEBOOK**
**Landinium(ITY)** has been contesting better events back in England of late and this represented a simple task. She did not let her supporters down and coasted home with six lengths in hand.

## 2608a PREMIO EMILIO TURATI (GROUP 2) 1m
**3:50** (4:17) 3-Y-O+ **£52,817** (£23,239; £12,676; £6,338)

RPR

1 **Marbye (IRE)**$^{32}$ [1776] 4-9-3 ........ MDemuro 4 112
(BGrizzetti, Italy) *soon led, quickened approaching final furlong, ran on well* 2
2 *3 ½* **Honey Bunny** 4-9-6 ........ MEsposito 5 108
(VCaruso, Italy) *always close up, tracked winner after 3f, ridden & got to within 1/2l two furlongs out, kept on same pace from over 1f out*
3 *1 ¼* **Lindholm (GER)**$^{45}$ 5-9-6 ........ KKerekes 7 106
(WernerGlanz, Germany) *held up, 6th straight, reached 3rd 2f out, one pace* 3
4 *shd* **Giovane Imperatore**$^{59}$ 6-9-6 ........ MTellini 2 105
(LBrogi, Italy) *first to show, 3rd straight, one pace final 2f*
5 *nk* **Eagle Rise (IRE)**$^{194}$ [6044] 4-9-6 ........ ASuborics 1 105
(ASchutz, Germany) *held up in rear, last straight, headway on outside 3f out, 4th 2f out, kept on one pace* 1
6 *¾* **Golden Devious (IRE)**$^{295}$ [4065] 4-9-6 ........ DVargiu 3 103
(LD'Auria, Italy) *in touch, 4th straight, beaten over 2f out*
7 *8* **Caluki**$^{27}$ [1954] 7-9-6 ........ MMonteriso 6 87
(LCamici, Italy) *5th straight, beaten over 2f out*

1m 40.1s **7** Ran **SP% 131.1**
Speed ratings: .
**Owner** Teruya Yoshida **Bred** Curtasse Snc **Trained** Italy

# 2513 CHEPSTOW (L-H)
Thursday, June 3
**OFFICIAL GOING: Good (good to firm in places)**

## 2609 WENDY FAIR MARKETS MAIDEN AUCTION STKS 6f 16y
**2:30** (2:31) (E) 2-Y-O **£3,591** (£1,105; £552; £276) **Stalls** High

Form RPR

1 **Caesar Beware (IRE)** 2-8-11 ........ DaneO'Neill 14 97+
(HCandy) *trckd ldrs: shkn up 2f out: qcknd to ld jst ins fnl f: sn clr: easily* **7/2**$^{1}$
0 2 *3* **Don Pele (IRE)**$^{12}$ [2300] 2-8-11 ........ JFEgan 16 88
(SKirk) *chsd ldrs: rdn to ld appr fnl f: hdd jst ins last: sn no ch w wnr but kpt on wl for 2nd* **12/1**
3 *4* **Holbeck Ghyll (IRE)** 2-8-7 ........ LPKeniry$^{(3)}$ 18 75
(AMBalding) *t.k.h: sn led: rdn and hdd appr fnl f: one pce inside last* **5/1**$^{2}$
4 *3 ½* **Musico (IRE)** 2-8-13 ........ SDrowne 12 68
(BRMillman) *mid-div: rdn over 2f out: kpt on fnl f: nt trble ldrs* **25/1**
0 5 *3* **Lady Chef**$^{41}$ [1589] 2-8-2 ........ AMcCarthy 6 48
(BRMillman) *chsd ldrs: hung badly lft to far side 3f out: styd up w ldrs tl outpcd over 1f out* **66/1**
0 6 *1* **Encanto (IRE)**$^{17}$ [2177] 2-8-3 ........ MartinDwyer 7 46
(JSMoore) *chsd ldrs: wknd over 1f out* **20/1**
5 7 *1* **Al Garhoud Bridge**$^{19}$ [2111] 2-8-13 ........ TEDurcan 2 53
(MRChannon) *racd in centre crse: kpt on fr over 1f out: nvr gng pce to rch ldrs* **5/1**$^{2}$
0 8 *½* **Granary Girl**$^{37}$ [1686] 2-8-1 ow2 ........ RMiles$^{(3)}$ 4 42
(BPalling) *s.i.s: sme hdwy fnl f* **40/1**
9 *½* **He's A Star** 2-8-9 ........ RLMoore 5 46
(RHannon) *s.i.s: bhd: sme hdwy fr over 1f out* **20/1**
560 10 *¾* **Joe Ninety (IRE)**$^{28}$ [1905] 2-8-2 ........ DerekNolan$^{(7)}$ 17 43
(JSMoore) *chsd ldrs over 3f* **66/1**
11 *nk* **Alzarma** 2-8-4 ........ BReilly$^{(3)}$ 13 40
(MrsLWilliamson) *chsd ldrs over 3f* **50/1**
62 12 *½* **Shaheer (IRE)**$^{12}$ [2300] 2-8-10 ........ DHolland 3 42
(BJMeehan) *in tch over 3f* **5/1**$^{2}$
0 13 *1 ½* **Champagne Brandy (IRE)**$^{68}$ [1128] 2-8-0 ........ FPFerris$^{(3)}$ 11 30
(PDEvans) *sn outpcd* **66/1**
14 *1* **Barnbrook Empire (IRE)** 2-7-12 ........ RThomas$^{(5)}$ 8 —
(IAWood) *s.i.s: outpcd* **66/1**
40 15 *hd* **Veneer (IRE)**$^{54}$ [1324] 2-8-10 ........ RHughes 15 34
(RHannon) *a outpcd* **25/1**
5 16 *1 ½* **Amphitheatre (IRE)**$^{13}$ [2268] 2-8-7 ........ JQuinn 10 —
(RFJohnsonHoughton) *in tch over 3f* **9/1**$^{3}$
6050 17 *1 ½* **Zachy Boy**$^{24}$ [1984] 2-8-7 ........ EAhern 9 —
(JSMoore) *chsd ldrs over 3f* **66/1**
5 18 *6* **Gavioli (IRE)**$^{10}$ [2360] 2-8-10 ........ SWhitworth 1 —
(JMBradley) *pressed ldrs over 3f* **50/1**

1m 12.67s **Going Correction** +0.25s/f (Good) **18** Ran **SP% 121.0**
Speed ratings: **106,102,96,92,88 86,85,84,84,83 82,81,79,78,78 76,74,66**CSF £40.70 TOTE £4.60: £2.00, £4.00, £2.10; EX 46.50.
**Owner** Mill House Partnership **Bred** Glending Bloodstock **Trained** Wantage, Oxon

**FOCUS**
A very smart time indeed for the grade and a smart winner in Caesar Beware. They finished well strung out and the form looks decent.

**NOTEBOOK**
**Caesar Beware(IRE)**, whose stable were on a 32-day losing streak comng into the race, was strongly supported throughout the course of the day and settled the issue in a matter of strides with a telling burst just over a furlong out. This was an impressive display and he looks worthy of a step up in grade, the St Leger sales race in September being his long-term aim.
**Don Pele(IRE)** ◆ improved on his debut effort, pulling four lengths clear of the third and sticking to the task well. He should have little trouble landing a similar event.
**Holbeck Ghyll(IRE)** ◆ showed plenty of zip on this racecourse debut, racing against the stands' side rail throughout and keeping on at the one pace. The speed he showed suggests he will be fully effective back at five and like the winner, should be up to winning an average maiden.
**Musico(IRE)** shaped with plenty of promise on this racecourse debut, staying on from out of the pack to claim fourth.
**Lady Chef** improved on her debut and ended up far side having hung badly left. This was a pleasing effort. *Official explanation: jockey said filly hung violently left*
**Encanto(IRE)** showed up well until fading and is going the right way. She will win when dropped in grade.
**Al Garhoud Bridge** was never in a challenging position from his low drawn and deserves another chance.
**Shaheer(IRE)** was another who failed to show his true form from a poor draw.
**Amphitheatre(IRE)** *Official explanation: jockey said gelding hung left throughout.*
**Gavioli(IRE)** *Official explanation: trainer said colt had breathing problems*

## 2610 FIFEHEAD GROUP H'CAP 5f 16y
**3:00** (3:00) (E) (0-75,75) 3-Y-O **£3,584** (£1,103; £551; £275) **Stalls** High

Form RPR

3114 1 **Ivory Lace**$^{22}$ [2033] 3-9-7 **70** ........ DSweeney 7 79
(SWoodman) *hld up rr but in tch: gd hdwy over 1f out: led ins last: pushed out* **6/1**
0-03 2 *1 ½* **Melody King**$^{13}$ [2266] 3-9-0 **66** ........ (b) FPFerris$^{(3)}$ 6 70
(PDEvans) *mde most tl rdn and hdd ins fnl f: styd on same pce u.p* **10/1**
0511 3 *3* **Imperium**$^{11}$ [2326] 3-9-12 **75** 6ex ........ SDrowne 8 68
(MrsStefLiddiard) *trckd ldrs: rdn 2f out: effrt over 1f out: no imp and btn fnl f* **9/2**$^{2}$
-006 4 *¾* **Alchera**$^{17}$ [2181] 3-9-5 **68** ........ (b) KFallon 4 59
(RFJohnsonHoughton) *trckd ldrs: rdn: effrt and hung lft over 1f out: wknd ins fnl f* **11/4**$^{1}$
4-46 5 *2 ½* **Fair Compton**$^{6}$ [2444] 3-9-2 **65** ........ DaneO'Neill 3 47
(RHannon) *chsd ldrs: rdn 2f out: wknd fnl f* **12/1**
0-33 6 *1 ¾* **Miss Madame (IRE)**$^{11}$ [2326] 3-8-12 **61** ........ DHolland 2 36
(RGuest) *bhd: rdn 2f out: hung lft and fnd little over 1f out: no ch whn nt clr run ins last* **11/2**$^{3}$
3-00 7 *2 ½* **Pass Go**$^{28}$ [1906] 3-8-11 **60** ........ (t) MartinDwyer 9 26
(GAButler) *s.i.s: a outpcd* **20/1**
4310 8 *nk* **Scottish Exile (IRE)**$^{17}$ [2181] 3-9-5 **68** ........ (v) EAhern 5 33
(KRBurke) *v.s.a and a bhd: sme hdwy fr over 1f out* **8/1**
306- 9 *5* **Ardkeel Lass (IRE)**$^{243}$ [5356] 3-8-10 **66** ........ MHoward$^{(7)}$ 1 13
(DKIvory) *w ldr 3f: sn rdn: wknd appr fnl f* **10/1**

60.78 secs (1.28) **Going Correction** +0.25s/f (Good) **9** Ran **SP% 116.3**
Speed ratings: **99,96,91,90,86 83,79,79,71**CSF £64.41 CT £296.45 TOTE £7.40: £1.90, £3.20, £2.40; EX 39.50.
**Owner** Christopher J Halpin **Bred** D R Tucker **Trained** East Lavant, W Sussex

**FOCUS**
Nothing more than a modest sprint handicap, but the winner is improving.

**NOTEBOOK**
**Ivory Lace**, never quite competitive from a low draw at Brighton, had been in great form prior to that and got back to winning ways. She got a nice tow through from Melody King on the favoured stands' rail and did not shun the invite to nip up that one's inside in the final furlong.
**Melody King**, who clearly goes well at this course - winner here last year - set out to make all on the fence and only found one too good in trying to do so.
**Imperium**, 10lb worse off for about a length advantage over Ivory Lace on Brighton form, unsurprisingly could not confirm the placings, but still ran well in defeat.
**Alchera** is not the easiest of rides and hung under pressure.
**Miss Madame(IRE)** found trouble in the final furlong but was beaten at the time anyhow. *Official explanation: jockey said filly, having been eased in the closing stages to avoid clipping heels, was hanging left throughout*
**Scottish Exile(IRE)** *Official explanation: jockey said filly put her head down as the starting stalls opened and missed the break*

## 2611 BLACKHORSE MOTOR FINANCE MAIDEN STKS 1m 2f 36y
**3:30** (3:31) (D) 3-Y-O+ **£3,571** (£1,099; £549; £274) **Stalls** Low

Form RPR

6 1 **Lost Soldier Three (IRE)**$^{19}$ [2114] 3-8-11 ........ DHolland 10 89
(LMCumani) *s.i.s: t.k.h and chsd ldrs 7f out: shkn up and qcknd to ld over 2f out: c clr fnl f: easily* **5/1**$^{2}$
22 2 *7* **Charleston**$^{17}$ [2168] 3-8-11 ........ RHughes 7 76
(JHMGosden) *sn led: hdd 7f out:styd trcking ldr tl led again over 3f out: hdd over 2f out: no ch w wnr and flashed tailed ins last* **15/8**$^{1}$
53-6 3 *3 ½* **Hashid (IRE)**$^{63}$ [1221] 4-9-10 77 ........ (b) MartinDwyer 5 69
(PCRitchens) *w ldr: led 7f out: hdd over 3f out: outpcd fr 2f out: no ch w ldrs whn veered lft u.p ins last* **33/1**
4 *nk* **Rossall Point** 3-8-11 ........ SDrowne 2 69
(JLDunlop) *hld up in rr: stdy hdwy fnl 2f: gng on cl home but nt a danger* **33/1**
204- 5 *½* **Geller**$^{258}$ [5039] 3-8-11 83 ........ RLMoore 4 68
(RHannon) *broke wl: t.k.h and stdd rr: hdwy over 2f out: styng on but nt trble ldrs whn hmpd on rail ins fnl f* **8/1**$^{3}$
000 6 *1 ½* **Cool Clear Water (USA)**$^{14}$ [2243] 3-8-6 ........ TEDurcan 3 60
(BJMeehan) *sn chsng ldrs: rdn over 3f out: one pce fnl 2f* **25/1**
000 7 *1* **Silencio (IRE)**$^{10}$ [2374] 3-8-11 ........ VSlattery 1 63
(AKing) *bhd: pushed along 3f out: kpt on fr over 1f out: nvr a danger* **50/1**
56-5 8 *12* **Present Oriented (USA)**$^{20}$ [2085] 3-8-11 82 ........ WRyan 6 40
(HRACecil) *bhd most of way* **5/1**$^{2}$
03-0 9 *9* **Adaptable**$^{17}$ [2182] 3-8-6 75 ........ DaneO'Neill 9 18
(HCandy) *sn in tch: wknd fr 3f out* **20/1**
0 10 *3* **Golden Key**$^{20}$ [2085] 3-8-11 ........ KFallon 8 17
(SirMichaelStoute) *t.k.h: in tch: chsd ldrs and pushed along 3f out: wknd qckly over 2f out: eased whn no ch fnl f* **5/1**$^{2}$
11 *dist* **Pridewood Dove**$^{9}$ 5-9-2 ........ RMiles$^{(3)}$ 11 —
(RJPrice) *s.i.s: sn rcvrd to chse ldrs: wknd over 5f out: t.o* **100/1**

2m 11.21s (1.61) **Going Correction** +0.25s/f (Good)
**WFA** 3 from 4yo+ 13lb **11** Ran **SP% 113.3**
Speed ratings: **103,97,94,94,93 92,91,82,75,72** —CSF £13.26 TOTE £6.70: £2.50, £1.10, £6.10; EX 14.10.
**Owner** Sheikh Mohammed Obaid Al Maktoum **Bred** Darley **Trained** Newmarket, Suffolk

**FOCUS**
There were some disappointments down the field, but Lost Soldier Three beat a solid yardstick impressively and the time was faster than the classified stakes later on the card.

**NOTEBOOK**
**Lost Soldier Three(IRE)** improved on his debut effort with an easy success, albeit in ordinary company. An extra couple of furlongs should not bother him and as long as he keeps going the right way - he is reportedly a nervous sort - he should make his mark in handicap company.
**Charleston** has now finished second on all three starts and his overall form is nothing special. He may find life easier handicapping.

**Hashid(IRE)** ran a better race on this second start for new connections, but was still well below last year's best and clearly has his quirks, as he veered left inside the final furlong.
**Rossall Point** made a pleasing debut and will ideally want at least another couple of furlongs.
**Geller** was impeded close home and would have been a little closer with a clear run.
**Cool Clear Water(USA)** can now run in handicaps and should do better in that sphere.
**Silencio(IRE)** is another now eligible for handicapping and will appreciate a mile and a half.
**Present Oriented(USA)** is going the wrong way.
**Golden Key** reportedly lost his action and deserves another chance. *Official explanation: jockey said colt lost its action; vet said colt had a breathing problem*

## 2612 LISTEN TO REAL RADIO 105-106FM CLASSIFIED STKS — 1m 2f 36y
**4:00** (4:01) (D) 3-Y-0+ — **£5,447** (£1,676; £838; £419) **Stalls** Low

Form — RPR
601- **1** **Ski Jump (USA)**[332] [3048] 4-9-5 82 ....(b) RHughes 2 — 89
(RCharlton) *hrd drvn to ld sn after s: rdn over 2f out: styd on wl fr over 1f out: all out* **9/2**[2]
24-1 **2** *1 ½* **Trueno (IRE)**[13] [2278] 5-9-6 83 .... DHolland 1 — 87
(LMCumani) *trckd ldrs: wnt 2nd 3f out: rdn and effrt to cl on wnr over 1f out: kpt on ins last but no imp* **10/11**[1]
1-00 **3** *1 ¼* **Anglo Saxon (USA)**[18] [2142] 4-9-5 82 .... KFallon 3 — 84
(DRLoder) *hld up in tch: hdwy over 2f out: drvn to chse ldrs over 1f out: kpt on same pce ins last* **13/2**[3]
0-00 **4** *2* **Ile Michel**[16] [2206] 7-9-5 82 .... DSweeney 6 — 80
(JGMO'Shea) *hld up in rr: hdwy 2f out: rdn and r.o fnl f but nvr gng pce to rch ldrs* **50/1**
1-00 **5** *4* **Top Spec (IRE)**[12] [2281] 3-8-7 83 .... DaneO'Neill 4 — 73
(RHannon) *drvn early: chsd ldrs 7f out: rdn over 3f out: wknd fr 2f out* **10/1**
5614 **6** *5* **Scottish River (USA)**[12] [2304] 5-8-12 77 .... HayleyTurner(5) 7 — 61
(MDIUsher) *s.i.s: bhd: hdwy on outside 5f out: rdn and effrt 3f out: wknd over 2f out* **14/1**
103 **7** *hd* **Dance World**[31] [1832] 4-9-0 76 .... BReilly(3) 5 — 60
(MissJFeilden) *chsd ldrs tl wknd 3f out* **12/1**
5000 **8** *nk* **Awarding**[19] [2132] 4-8-10 74 ....(t) LucyRussell(7) 8 — 60
(DrJRJNaylor) *plld hrd: chsd wnr 7f out tl over 3f out: sn btn* **100/1**

2m 11.37s (1.77) **Going Correction** +0.25s/f (Good) — **8** Ran SP% **110.3**
**WFA** 3 from 4yo+ 13lb
Speed ratings: **102,100,99,98,95 91,90,90**CSF £8.27 TOTE £3.80: £1.30, £1.10, £1.70; EX 6.80.
**Owner** K Abdulla **Bred** Juddmonte Farms Inc **Trained** Beckhampton, Wilts

**FOCUS**
A tight little event with only 6lb splitting runners on adjusted official ratings.

**NOTEBOOK**
**Ski Jump(USA)** has been gelded since last seen at Bath 332 days previously and dug deep under pressure to fend off the challenge of the second. Blinkers seem to help and he could make his mark in handicaps again, as there may be more to come.
**Trueno(IRE)**, winner of a similar race at Newmarket recently, ran well without proving good enough to get past the winner. He seemed to run his race.
**Anglo Saxon(USA)** showed more encouraging signs than of late and seems to be coming back to form.
**Ile Michel** was trying a longer trip but ran as if he ideally wants even further nowadays.
**Top Spec(IRE)**, the only three-year-old in the line-up, continues out of form.

## 2613 WEATHERBYS INSURANCE H'CAP — 2m 2f
**4:30** (4:31) (D) (0-85,82) 3-Y-0+ — **£5,772** (£1,776; £888; £444) **Stalls** Low

Form — RPR
1-26 **1** **Calamintha**[17] [2167] 4-8-9 63 .... DHolland 13 — 71
(MCPipe) *sn led: rdn and qcknd 4l clr: 4f out: stl 3l clr and rdn over 1f out: hld on all out* **8/1**
0230 **2** *½* **King Flyer (IRE)**[14] [2240] 8-10-0 80 .... SWhitworth 3 — 87
(MissJFeilden) *hld up in rr: hdwy on ins over 2f out: str run fnl f to take 2nd last strides: nt rch wnr* **16/1**
1215 **3** *hd* **Malarkey**[5] [2480] 7-9-10 76 .... SDrowne 4 — 83
(MrsStefLiddiard) *hld up in rr: hdwy fr 3f out: styd on wl to chse wnr wl ins last: no imp and lost 2nd last strides* **9/1**
4-00 **4** *½* **Almizan (IRE)**[14] [2240] 4-10-0 82 .... TEDurcan 9 — 88
(MRChannon) *in tch: wnt prom 7f out: chsd wnr 3f out: styd on fnl f but no imp on wnr: outpcd and lost 2nd nr fin* **16/1**
06-1 **5** *½* **Quedex**[5] [2480] 8-8-10 65 5ex .... RMiles(3) 14 — 71+
(RJPrice) *bhd: hdwy 5f out: styd on u.p on outside fr 3f out: kpt on wl fnl f but nt rch ldrs* **11/4**[1]
4063 **6** *1 ½* **Moonshine Beach**[8] [2409] 6-8-6 58 ....(p) EAhern 10 — 62
(PWHiatt) *in tch: hdwy 10f out: rdn to chse ldrs 3f out but nvr nr wnr: wknd fnl f* **15/2**[3]
-214 **7** *5* **Prince Of The Wood (IRE)**[6] [2462] 4-7-12 52 oh6 ....(p) DKinsella 2 — 51
(ABailey) *chsd ldrs: rdn and swtchd rt over 2f out: no imp and wknd over 1f out* **10/1**
3344 **8** *8* **Ocean Tide**[26] [1958] 7-9-7 73 ....(v) KFallon 8 — 63
(RFord) *chsd ldrs tl wknd fr 3f out* **9/2**[2]
1P/0 **9** *shd* **Grand Fromage (IRE)**[12] [2285] 6-9-1 67 .... VSlattery 1 — 57
(AKing) *nvr bttr than mid-div: no ch fnl 3f* **100/1**
-000 **10** *13* **Establishment**[12] [2285] 7-9-9 75 .... DaneO'Neill 11 — 50
(CACyzer) *bhd: sme hdwy 6f out: sn rdn and bhd again* **14/1**
00-0 **11** *3* **Imtihan (IRE)**[33] [1305] 5-7-9 50 oh1 ....(t) FPFerris(3) 12 — 22
(SCBurrough) *chsd ldrs: rdn 5f out: sn wknd* **16/1**
0/5- **12** *dist* **Laffah (USA)**[27] [2723] 9-8-6 58 ....(b) RLMoore 5 — —
(GLMoore) *a bhd: t.o* **33/1**
-065 **P** **Ravenglass (USA)**[13] [2277] 5-9-13 79 .... RHavlin 6 — —
(JGMO'Shea) *chsd ldr to 3f out: wknd qckly 2f out: p.u and dismntd bef line: lame* **20/1**

4m 2.25s (2.05) **Going Correction** +0.25s/f (Good)
**WFA** 4 from 5yo+ 2lb — **13** Ran SP% **119.8**
Speed ratings: **105,104,104,104,104 103,101,97,97,91 90,—,—**CSF £127.46 CT £1184.71 TOTE £10.40: £3.40, £6.10, £2.80; EX 382.20.
**Owner** David Jenks **Bred** Chieveley Manor Stud **Trained** Nicholashayne, Devon

**FOCUS**
An excellent ride from Darryll Holland on Calamintha who stole a decisive advantage early in the straight and just found enough to hold on. The form is nothing special, but King Flyer is a good guide and gives it a solid look.

**NOTEBOOK**
**Calamintha** was given an astute ride from Holland, who stole a decisive early in the straight and was always just finding enough to cling on. Her best form prior to this had come on softer going and she may be capable of better still back on her favoured surface.
**King Flyer(IRE)** finished well after being held up well in rear, but it was too late.
**Malarkey** came from nearly as far back as the second and was finishing almost as well, but again too late in the day.
**Almizan(IRE)** ran his best race of the season back down in grade and is evidently returning to form.
**Quedex** ran well considering it was a disadvantage to race down the outer in the straight.

## 2614 SAFFIE JOSEPH & SON H'CAP — 7f 16y
**5:00** (5:00) (E) (0-70,69) 3-Y-0+ — **£3,721** (£1,145; £572; £286) **Stalls** High

Form — RPR
-600 **1** **Mister Trickster (IRE)**[24] [1998] 3-8-7 58 .... SRighton 14 — 68
(RDickin) *pressed ldrs: styd on wl u.p to ld cl home* **20/1**
-212 **2** *¾* **Goodenough Mover**[5] [2483] 8-9-9 69 .... HayleyTurner(5) 5 — 77
(JSKing) *trckd ldrs: slt ld 3f out: rdn and kpt on gamely fnl f: ct cl home* **9/2**[3]
0320 **3** *nk* **Middleton Grey**[63] [1225] 6-9-4 62 ....(b) LPKeniry(3) 6 — 69
(AGNewcombe) *s.i.s: bhd: hdwy over 2f out: r.o wl fnl f: kpt on cl home* **12/1**
6465 **4** *1 ¾* **Phred**[17] [2170] 4-9-7 62 .... JQuinn 13 — 65
(RFJohnsonHoughton) *chsd ldrs: rdn 2f out: kpt on same pce u.p fnl f* **7/2**[1]
0-01 **5** *shd* **High Ridge**[17] [2166] 5-9-2 60 ....(p) FPFerris(3) 9 — 62
(JMBradley) *chsd ldrs: rdn over 2f out: one pce fnl f* **12/1**
0654 **6** *shd* **Bought Direct**[38] [1681] 5-8-13 57 .... ABeech(3) 10 — 59
(RJSmith) *bhd: hdwy over 1f out: kpt on ins last: nt rch ldrs* **17/2**
00/0 **7** *½* **Threezedzz**[21] [2064] 6-9-0 62 .... SJDonohoe(7) 1 — 63
(PDEvans) *racd alone far side: wl up w pce on stands side tl no ex ins fnl f* **25/1**
050 **8** *1 ¼* **Nounou**[17] [2168] 3-9-0 65 .... SWhitworth 15 — 63
(DJDaly) *bhd: hdwy 2f out: kpt on fnl f but nvr gng pce to rch ldrs* **16/1**
6-62 **9** *1 ¼* **Blue Quiver (IRE)**[87] [988] 4-9-1 56 .... PaulEddery 7 — 50
(CAHorgan) *pressed ldrs: stl ev ch u.p over 1f out: wknd fnl f* **4/1**[2]
0605 **10** *8* **Parker**[2] [2455] 7-9-4 59 ....(b) DSweeney 4 — 33
(BPalling) *bhd most of way* **25/1**
410- **11** *2* **Five Gold (IRE)**[223] [5734] 3-9-2 67 .... GBaker 12 — 35
(BRMillman) *chsd ldrs 4f* **20/1**
0300 **12** *2 ½* **Instinct**[21] [2063] 3-8-4 61 ow1 .... PGallagher(7) 2 — 24
(RHannon) *a outpcd* **20/1**
40-0 **13** *½* **Caerphilly Gal**[20] [2098] 4-8-10 54 .... RMiles(3) 3 — 15
(PLGilligan) *led tl hdd 3f out: hung lft to centre crse and wknd 2f out* **14/1**
0-00 **14** *10* **Don Argento**[11] [2324] 3-7-12 49 oh4 .... DKinsella 8 — —
(MrsAJBowlby) *sn bhd* **33/1**

1m 24.3s (1.10) **Going Correction** +0.25s/f (Good)
**WFA** 3 from 4yo+ 10lb — **14** Ran SP% **123.8**
Speed ratings: **103,102,101,99,99 99,99,97,96,87 84,81,81,69**CSF £102.41 CT £1199.57 TOTE £23.50: £5.10, £1.20, £3.90; EX 229.40 Place 6 £136.60, Place 5 £13.10.
**Owner** The Tricksters **Bred** Ballyhane Stud **Trained** Atherstone on Stour, Warwicks

**FOCUS**
The winner had the advantage of the stands' rail and his extra stamina came into play late on.

**NOTEBOOK**
**Mister Trickster(IRE)** has been running over middle-distances and that extra stamina came in handy close home as he pulled out a little more to deny the top-weight. He raced against the favoured stands' rail for most of the way so was probably flattered, so he would not be one to back to follow up.
**Goodenough Mover** deserved plenty of credit for his effort under top-weight, as he raced towards the centre of the track. He went down fighting.
**Middleton Grey** stayed on well, having been a bit tardy at the gate, but remains without a win on turf.
**Phred** is better over a mile and was doing all his best work at the end.
**High Ridge**, a winner over five and a half furlongs on his most recent outing, did not find as much as once looked likely and may be better at shorter given the way he travelled.
**Bought Direct** is better at a mile and will be of interest when upped a furlong.
**Threezedzz** went at it alone on the far side and ran well on this second start back from a break.
**Nounou** was staying on at the one pace and can improve at further.
**Parker** *Official explanation: jockey said gelding had a breathing problem*
T/Jkpt: Not won. T/Plt: £136.60 to a £1 stake. Pool of £33,037.20 - 176.45 winning units T/Qpdt: £13.10 to a £1 stake. Pool of £2,427.30 - 137.00 winning units ST

# 2074 HAMILTON (R-H)
### Thursday, June 3

**OFFICIAL GOING: Good to firm (good in places)**
Once again on fast ground at this course in races run at less than a true gallop, those racing close to the pace at distances above 6f held a big advantage.
Wind: lt across Weather: overcast

## 2615 LORD ADVOCATE H'CAP — 1m 5f 9y
**2:10** (2:11) (E) (0-75,72) 4-Y-0+ — **£3,883** (£1,195; £597; £298) **Stalls** High

Form — RPR
-002 **1** **Party Ploy**[3] [2531] 6-8-11 57 .... DarrenWilliams 1 — 66
(KRBurke) *keen: trckd ldr: led 3f out: hld on wl fnl f* **7/2**[1]
2110 **2** *hd* **Isa'Af (IRE)**[6] [2449] 5-8-10 63 .... PPMathers(7) 6 — 72
(PWHiatt) *keen: trckd ldrs: effrt over 2f out: ev ch ins fnl f: edgd lft briefly last 100yds: jst hld* **10/1**[3]
-063 **3** *1 ½* **Millennium Hall**[22] [2038] 5-8-5 54 .... LEnstone(3) 4 — 60
(PMonteith) *keen: prom: effrt over 2f out: one pce fnl f* **12/1**
-105 **4** *1 ½* **Tandava (IRE)**[5] [2491] 6-9-12 72 ....(p) GDuffield 2 — 76
(ISemple) *led to 3f out: one pce over 1f out* **11/1**
1613 **5** *¾* **Toni Alcala**[5] [2491] 5-9-5 68 .... DNolan(3) 10 — 71
(RFFisher) *prom: rdn and outpcd over 2f out: rallied and edgd lft over 1f out: kpt on: no imp* **6/1**[2]
3-51 **6** *1* **Trusted Mole (IRE)**[3] [2525] 6-8-1 52 .... BSwarbrick(5) 9 — 53
(WMBrisbourne) *hld up in tch: rdn and edgd rt over 2f out: no imp over 1f out* **7/2**[1]
00-1 **7** *nk* **Cosmic Case**[12] [2287] 9-8-1 47 .... ANicholls 5 — 48
(JSGoldie) *hld up: rdn over 4f out: sme late hdwy: n.d* **6/1**[2]
0-55 **8** *7* **Exalted (IRE)**[12] [2287] 11-8-8 54 .... DaleGibson 8 — 44
(TAKCuthbert) *hld up: rdn over 3f out: sn btn* **20/1**
30-4 **9** *3* **Fantastico (IRE)**[12] [2299] 4-9-2 62 .... RWinston 7 — 48
(MrsKWalton) *hld up: rdn over 4f out: btn over 2f out* **10/1**[3]

2m 53.87s (0.47) **Going Correction** 0.0s/f (Good) — **9** Ran SP% **112.0**
Speed ratings: **98,97,96,96,95 94,94,90,88**CSF £38.14 CT £370.93 TOTE £4.20: £2.00, £3.00, £3.40; EX 47.80.
**Owner** Ian A McInnes **Bred** I McInnes **Trained** Middleham Moor, N Yorks
■ Stewards Enquiry : Darren Williams one-day ban: careless riding (Jun 14)

**FOCUS**
An ordinary handicap in which the steady gallop gave those racing close to the pace the edge. The form may not be entirely reliable.

**NOTEBOOK**
**Party Ploy**, who signalled a return to form earlier in the week, had the run of the race and confirmed that promise. Although a shade flattered given the way the race unfolded, he showed the right attitude and, as he should not be going up too much for this win, should continue to give a good account around this trip.
**Isa'Af(IRE)**, who ran poorly last time for no apparent reason, left that effort firmly behind him. Although he had the run of the race, he has been progressive this year and will still be of interest around this trip, especially when a better gallop is on the cards.
**Millennium Hall**, back on a sound surface, was another to enjoy the run of the race. He ran creditably and is capable of winning from his current mark, but his record suggests he is not one to place maximum faith in.
**Tandava(IRE)** was allowed the run of the race and ran creditably at a course that favours his style of racing. However, he remains vulnerable from his current mark.
**Toni Alcala** has been in decent heart of late and ran creditably but left the impression that a more galloping course and a stronger pace would have been in his favour. He seems much more consistent this term.
**Trusted Mole(IRE)**, while not disgraced, may be a bit better than the bare form, for he did not appear best suited by this course and this race favoured those racing close to the pace.
**Cosmic Case**, who returned to form at Ayr last time, was not suited by the way this race unfolded and this effort is best ignored.
**Exalted(IRE)** would have preferred softer ground and a stronger pace and is not one to write off yet.

## 2616 YELLOW PAGES 118 24 7 CLAIMING STKS (A QUALIFIER FOR THE HAMILTON PARK 2-Y-O SERIES FINAL) 5f 4y

2:40 (2:42) (E) 2-Y-O £3,883 (£1,195; £597; £298) Stalls Low

| Form | | | Horse | Jockey | RPR |
|---|---|---|---|---|---|
| 0211 | 1 | | **Goldhill Prince**[12] [2288] 2-8-2 (p) | CHaddon(7) 3 | 54 |
| | | | (WGMTurner) *hung rt thrght: w ldr: led 1/2-way: r.o fnl f: jst hld on* | **7/4**[1] | |
| 054 | 2 | shd | **Kristikhab (IRE)**[7] [2422] 2-9-3 | FLynch 4 | 62 |
| | | | (ABerry) *sn rdn in tch: hdwy over 1f out: r.o wl fnl f: jst failed* | **7/1**[3] | |
| 3065 | 3 | 3 1/2 | **Procrastinate (IRE)**[14] [2248] 2-8-0 | PPMathers(7) 7 | 39 |
| | | | (RFFisher) *wnt lft s: sn outpcd: hdwy centre over 1f out: no imp fnl f* | **11/1** | |
| 0 | 4 | 1/2 | **Canary Dancer**[16] [2213] 2-8-12 | GFaulkner 2 | 43 |
| | | | (PCHaslam) *chsd ldng gp: rdn 1/2-way: effrt over 1f out: no imp fnl f* | **14/1** | |
| 6332 | 5 | 5 | **Straffan (IRE)**[14] [2248] 2-8-6 | JCarroll 8 | 19 |
| | | | (EJO'Neill) *cl up tl rdn and one pce over 1f out* | **7/2**[2] | |
| 020 | 6 | 1/2 | **Danehill Fairy (IRE)**[6] [2458] 2-8-2 | GDuffield 5 | 13 |
| | | | (MrsADuffield) *led to 1/2-way: wknd over 1f out* | **33/1** | |
| 00 | 7 | 5 | **Droopys Joel**[54] [1324] 2-8-10 | THamilton(3) 6 | 7 |
| | | | (RPElliott) *chsd ldrs to 1/2-way: sn rdn and wknd* | **33/1** | |
| 6 | 8 | 15 | **City Torque (USA)**[53] [1340] 2-8-4 | PMakin(5) 1 | — |
| | | | (TDBarron) *sn wl bhd: t.o* | **7/2**[2] | |

61.38 secs (0.12) **Going Correction** -0.20s/f (Firm) **8** Ran SP% **114.2**
Speed ratings: **91,90,85,84,76 75,67,43**CSF £14.89 TOTE £2.90: £1.02, £2.90, £3.40; EX 18.50.There was no bid for the winner.
**Owner** Gold Hill Racing **Bred** N D Fisher **Trained** Sigwells, Somerset
■ Stewards Enquiry : F Lynch one-day ban: used whip with excessive frequency (Jun 14)

**FOCUS**
A low-grade event run at a decent pace, and one in which the field raced centre to stands side. Not a race that will be throwing up many winners.

**NOTEBOOK**
**Goldhill Prince**, facing a tougher task than at Ayr, did not look an easy ride but ran right up to his best back over this shorter trip and did show the right attitude late on. A rise in class may find him out but he is a capable performer in this grade.
**Kristikhab(IRE)**, down in grade, turned in his best effort to date and shaped as the return to six furlongs would be in his favour. He looks capable of winning in similar company.
**Procrastinate(IRE)**, down in trip, was not disgraced over a trip that is on the sharp side. A return to six furlongs will suit, but he will have to improve to win a similar event.
**Canary Dancer** bettered his debut effort and, although this form amounts to little, is in good hands. He is one to look out for later in the year on turf or sand given a much stiffer test of stamina.
**Straffan(IRE)** proved unsuited by the drop back to this trip and failed to confirm recent placings with Procrastinate. Six furlongs on a more galloping course may suit but she is now starting to look exposed.
**Danehill Fairy(IRE)** was again well beaten on a sound surface and, although an easier surface may suit better, her form to date is very modest
**City Torque(USA)** attracted a bit of support but was never going. More will be needed before he is worth a bet, but this run is probably best overlooked. *Official explanation: vet said filly finished stiff behind.*

## 2617 BEN RACEDAY MAIDEN AUCTION FILLIES' STKS (QUALIFIER FOR HAMILTON PARK 2YO SERIES FINAL) 6f 5y

3:10 (3:14) (E) 2-Y-O £3,997 (£1,230; £615; £307) Stalls Low

| Form | | | Horse | Jockey | RPR |
|---|---|---|---|---|---|
| 52 | 1 | | **Rockburst**[14] [2234] 2-8-3 | ANicholls 9 | 72 |
| | | | (KRBurke) *mde all: rdn and hld on wl fnl f* | **9/2**[3] | |
| 2242 | 2 | 1 1/4 | **Evanesce**[40] [1616] 2-8-4 ow4 | SHitchcott(3) 4 | 72 |
| | | | (MRChannon) *keen: cl up: effrt and ev ch over 1f out: r.o fnl f* | **7/2**[2] | |
| 6 | 3 | 1/2 | **Almost Perfect (IRE)**[35] [1735] 2-8-2 | PFessey 6 | 66 |
| | | | (TDBarron) *w wnr: rdn over 2f out: r.o fnl f: hld towards fin* | **50/1** | |
| 40 | 4 | nk | **Make Us Flush**[12] [2296] 2-7-13 ow4 | PPMathers(7) 7 | 69 |
| | | | (ABerry) *hld up midfield: hdwy centre over 1f out: r.o fnl f: n.d* | **100/1** | |
| 0 | 5 | 1/2 | **Ochil Hills Dancer (IRE)**[6] [2458] 2-8-6 | VHalliday 8 | 67 |
| | | | (ACrook) *prom: rdn over 2f out: one pce fnl f* | **25/1** | |
| | 6 | 1/2 | **Hill Fairy** 2-8-9 | DaleGibson 3 | 69 |
| | | | (TPTate) *bhd: rdn after 2f: hdwy whn checked over 1f out: r.o fnl f: nrst fin* | **16/1** | |
| 5 | 7 | shd | **Dixie Queen (IRE)**[26] [1960] 2-8-6 ow1 | RWinston 11 | 65 |
| | | | (MDods) *checked after 1f: bhd tl sme late hdwy: n.d* | **14/1** | |
| 3 | 8 | nk | **Strathtay**[9] [2388] 2-8-6 | GFaulkner 12 | 64 |
| | | | (PCHaslam) *trckd ldrs: effrt whn n.m.r briefly over 2f out: sn rdn and one pce over 1f out* | **10/11**[1] | |
| | 9 | 3/4 | **Spinnakers Girl** 2-8-2 | PHanagan 2 | 58 |
| | | | (JRWeymes) *bhd and rdn along: sme late hdwy: nvr rchd ldrs* | **40/1** | |
| 40 | 10 | 5 | **Chicago Nights (IRE)**[5] [2489] 2-7-11 | RoryMoore(7) 5 | 45 |
| | | | (PCHaslam) *s.i.s: sn in tch: rdn and outpcd fr 2f out* | **40/1** | |
| 00 | 11 | 5 | **Comintrue (IRE)**[51] [1383] 2-8-5 ow2 | JCarroll 1 | 31 |
| | | | (EJO'Neill) *bhd centre: rdn 1/2-way: n.d* | **50/1** | |
| | 12 | 4 | **Eminence Gift** 2-8-3 ow2 | THamilton(3) 10 | 20 |
| | | | (RPElliott) *hung rt thrght: towards rr: rdn and wknd fr 1/2-way: eased whn no ch over 1f out* | **50/1** | |

1m 13.83s (0.73) **Going Correction** -0.20s/f (Firm) **12** Ran SP% **120.9**
Speed ratings: **87,85,84,84,83 82,82,82,81,74 68,62**CSF £20.33 TOTE £6.60: £1.30, £1.40, £10.30; EX 13.30.
**Owner** Mrs Sally L Jones **Bred** J A And Mrs Duffy **Trained** Middleham Moor, N Yorks

**FOCUS**
An ordinary event in which the market leader failed to confirm debut promise. Although the pace was sound, those racing prominently were favoured so the bare form is a shade suspect. The whole field tacked over to race centre to far side.

**NOTEBOOK**
**Rockburst** had the run of the race and fully confirmed her latest bit of promise over this trip on similarly fast ground. As she had the run of things she may be vulnerable under a penalty, but she seems genuine and should continue to give a good account.
**Evanesce** is a reliable yardstick who once again gave it her best shot, despite a tendency to race keenly. She should continue to go well around this trip but is starting to look exposed.
**Almost Perfect(IRE)** turned in a much improved effort on this turf debut, despite having the run of the race. She is in good hands and is likely to be placed to effect over further in due course.
**Make Us Flush**, who had only shown modest form, turned in an improved effort and looks a bit better than the bare result as she fared the best of those that came from off the pace and made her ground in the centre. She looks capable of winning a small event in the North this summer.
**Ochil Hills Dancer(IRE)** was not disgraced in the face of a stiffish task and may do better in nurseries in due course, upped to seven furlongs on a more galloping course.
**Hill Fairy** ◆ cost 46,000 euros and has plenty of middle distance winners in her pedigree. She took the eye in the paddock and, despite showing inexperience throughout, did enough to suggest she can leave this well behind in due course when granted a stiffer test at a more galloping track.
**Strathtay**, whose debut form had been franked, had the run of the race but failed by a long chalk to confirm that promise over a trip that should have been ideal. This race may have come a bit quick, though, and she is not one to write off just yet.
**Eminence Gift** *Official explanation: jockey said bit slipped through the filly's mouth as she left the stalls*

## 2618 HAMILTON PARK SERIES H'CAP (A QUALIFIER FOR THE TOTEPOOL HANDICAP SERIES FINAL) 1m 1f 36y

3:40 (3:40) (E) (0-75,75) 3-Y-O+ £4,290 (£1,320; £660; £330) Stalls High

| Form | | | Horse | Jockey | RPR |
|---|---|---|---|---|---|
| -510 | 1 | | **Jordans Elect**[10] [2368] 4-9-5 **69** | TEaves(3) 7 | 82 |
| | | | (ISemple) *cl up: led over 2f out: drvn out* | **8/1** | |
| 0002 | 2 | 2 | **Takes Tutu (USA)**[5] [2493] 5-9-12 **73** (b) | DarrenWilliams 3 | 82 |
| | | | (KRBurke) *hld up in tch: effrt and swtchd rt over 2f out: ev ch over 1f out: no ex ins fnl f* | **7/4**[1] | |
| -506 | 3 | shd | **Oscar Pepper (USA)**[2] [2551] 7-9-2 **63** (v) | RWinston 9 | 72 |
| | | | (TDBarron) *hld up in tch: rdn over 3f out: swtchd centre and hdwy 2f out: kpt on wl fnl f: no imp* | **11/2**[3] | |
| 6044 | 4 | 6 | **Rare Coincidence**[14] [2251] 3-8-9 **71** ow4 (p) | DNolan(3) 2 | 68 |
| | | | (RFFisher) *led to 3f out: wknd over 1f out* | **10/1** | |
| -342 | 5 | 1/2 | **Champain Sands (IRE)**[7] [2424] 5-8-5 **57** | BSwarbrick(5) 1 | 53 |
| | | | (WMBrisbourne) *trckd ldrs: effrt 3f out: wknd over 1f out* | **7/1** | |
| -050 | 6 | 3 | **Skiddaw Jones**[1] [2583] 4-8-5 **52** | JCarroll 5 | 42 |
| | | | (MissLAPerratt) *hld up: outpcd over 4f out: n.d after* | **16/1** | |
| 0-03 | 7 | 1 1/2 | **Mount Pekan (IRE)**[20] [2078] 4-8-0 **47** | PHanagan 6 | 34 |
| | | | (JSGoldie) *plld hrd: prom: rdn whn checked over 2f out: wknd* | **5/1**[2] | |
| 0-00 | 8 | 5 | **Rifleman (IRE)**[18] [2142] 4-10-0 **75** (p) | GDuffield 8 | 52 |
| | | | (MrsADuffield) *cl up tl rdn and wknd over 2f out* | **12/1** | |

1m 57.65s (-1.95) **Going Correction** 0.0s/f (Good)
**WFA** 3 from 4yo+ 12lb **8** Ran SP% **114.7**
Speed ratings: **108,106,106,100,100 97,96,91**CSF £22.54 CT £85.13 TOTE £7.80: £2.90, £1.10, £2.00; EX 25.70.
**Owner** Ian Crawford **Bred** James Thom And Sons **Trained** Carluke, S Lanarks
■ Stewards Enquiry : Darren Williams one-day ban: careless riding (Jun 14)

**FOCUS**
An ordinary handicap featuring mainly disappointing and exposed types. It was run at just a modest gallop and the winner got first run.

**NOTEBOOK**
**Jordans Elect** had the run of the race and showed the right attitude to beat a disappointing type at a course he seems to like. But he did get first run and, as his record is inconsistent, he would not be one to be lumping on next time. *Official explanation: trainer said, regarding the improved form shown, gelding could only stay on at one pace last time because it was badly drawn and as a consequence too much use was made of it in order to get a better position early on; he added that gelding may be unsuited by a sharp track*
**Takes Tutu(USA)** travelled strongly for a long way and once again ran creditably in terms of form. But he again failed to find as much off the bridle as seemed likely and his lengthy losing run means he is one to steer clear of at short odds.
**Oscar Pepper(USA)**, with the visor back on, took more interest in a race that was not really run to suit but, although he may be a bit better than the bare form, he is the type that needs things to fall just right.
**Rare Coincidence** had the run of the race but was below his latest effort at a course that should have suited his style of running. Consistency has never been his strongest suit.
**Champain Sands(IRE)** was a fair way below his recent best and, although the race was not really run to suit, could have been expected to fare a bit better. He has yet to win and looks one to tread carefully with.
**Skiddaw Jones**, turned out quickly, was again below his best and, given his inconsistency, is another from this field to tread carefully with.
**Mount Pekan(IRE)**, who shaped as though better than the bare form last time, has yet to win a race and will struggle to do so until he learns to settle. *Official explanation: jockey said gelding hung left-handed.*

## 2619 HOWARD MCDOWALL MEMORIAL CLASSIFIED STKS 1m 3f 16y

4:10 (4:10) (E) 3-Y-O+ £3,818 (£1,175; £587; £293) Stalls High

| Form | | | Horse | Jockey | RPR |
|---|---|---|---|---|---|
| 5561 | 1 | | **Magic Sting**[24] [1995] 3-8-9 66 | JMackay 5 | 73 |
| | | | (MLWBell) *keen: trckd ldrs: smooth hdwy to ld over 1f out: edgd rt: r.o fnl f* | **5/1** | |
| -034 | 2 | 1 3/4 | **Kid'Z'Play (IRE)**[22] [2039] 8-9-5 64 | TEaves(3) 6 | 69 |
| | | | (JSGoldie) *led: rdn 3f out: hdd over 1f out: swtchd ins last: kpt on* | **9/4**[2] | |
| 0006 | 3 | 3 | **Claradotnet**[12] [2299] 4-9-4 67 | SHitchcott(3) 4 | 63 |
| | | | (MRChannon) *in tch: effrt over 2f out: one pce over 1f out* | **7/2**[3] | |
| 4-23 | 4 | 14 | **Templet (USA)**[38] [1662] 4-9-13 70 | PHanagan 1 | 47 |
| | | | (ISemple) *prom: rdn over 3f out: wknd over 2f out* | **2/1**[1] | |
| 6/-6 | 5 | nk | **Saspys Lad**[47] [1470] 7-9-3 65 | BSwarbrick(5) 3 | 41 |
| | | | (WMBrisbourne) *hld up: rdn over 4f out: sn btn* | **12/1** | |
| -040 | 6 | 30 | **Howards Dream (IRE)**[13] [2260] 6-9-8 30 (t) | JMcAuley 2 | — |
| | | | (DANolan) *cl up tl rdn and wknd over 2f out* | **100/1** | |

2m 25.54s (-0.96) **Going Correction** 0.0s/f (Good)
**WFA** 3 from 4yo+ 14lb **6** Ran SP% **111.7**
Speed ratings: **103,101,99,89,89 67**CSF £16.49 TOTE £5.00: £2.60, £2.00; EX 21.00.
**Owner** Mrs P T Fenwick **Bred** Michael Watt And Exors Of The Late Miss Jemima Joh **Trained** Newmarket, Suffolk

**FOCUS**
A fairly uncompetitive event in which the runner-up was allowed to dictate a modest pace. The winner is on the upgrade, though, and may be able to hold his own in handicap company.

**NOTEBOOK**
**Magic Sting ♦**, back over this longer trip and on much quicker ground than last time, turned in his best effort yet. He handles soft and fast ground, will be suited by a more truly run race and appeals as the type to win again.
**Kid'Z'Play(IRE)**, from an in-form stable, had the run of the race and gave it his best shot at a course that suits his style of racing. Everything fell into place, but he showed his vulnerability to a progressive sort in this type of event.
**Claradotnet** shaped as though a stiffer test of stamina would have been in her favour but, although anything but disgraced, will have to improve to win in handicap company from her current mark.
**Templet(USA)** may have preferred easier ground and a stronger pace but was disappointing on these terms. He will have his work cut out in handicaps from his current mark.
**Saspys Lad**, back on his preferred sound surface, was again well beaten and has plenty to prove at present.
**Howards Dream(IRE)** faced a very stiff task and ran accordingly.

## 2620 RECTANGLE GROUP MAIDEN H'CAP 5f 4y
**4:40** (4:41) (F) (0-55,55) 3-Y-O+ **£3,094** (£884; £442) **Stalls** Low

Form RPR
0250 **1** **Pirlie Hill**[1] 2581 4-9-11 **50** JCarroll 2 61
(MissLAPerratt) *prom stands side: led and overall ldr over 1f out: drifted bdly rt to far rail: kpt on strly* **5/1**[3]
3050 **2** 1 ³/₄ **Somethingabouther**[17] 2165 4-9-6 **45** DarrenWilliams 4 50
(PWHiatt) *prom stands side: effrt and chsd wnr over 1f out: kpt on ins fnl f* **20/1**
500 **3** 3 **Noble Mount**[28] 1906 3-9-9 **55** JMackay 10 49
(RGuest) *hld up far side: effrt 2f out: r.o fnl f: no imp* **8/1**
0-50 **4** ½ **Petana**[10] 2350 4-8-10 **42** (b) NataliaGemelova(7) 7 34
(MDods) *swtchd to far side and bhd: hdwy 2f out: no imp fnl f* **10/1**
-460 **5** 1 **Attila The Hun**[10] 2350 5-8-10 **35** PHanagan 14 24
(FWatson) *trckd far side ldrs: rdn 1/2-way: one pce over 1f out* **4/1**[1]
04-5 **6** 1 ½ **Amber Fox (IRE)**[12] 2290 3-9-8 **54** FLynch 6 37
(ABerry) *led stands side to over 1f out: sn outpcd* **10/1**
52P4 **7** ¾ **Wendy's Girl (IRE)**[27] 1934 3-9-4 **53** THamilton(3) 12 34
(RPElliott) *cl up far side: led that gp over 2f to over 1f out: no ex* **9/2**[2]
0440 **8** 1 ³/₄ **Minirina**[17] 2183 4-8-5 **35** PMakin(5) 1 9
(CSmith) *prom stands side tl outpcd fr 2f out* **25/1**
0-60 **9** nk **Pay Time**[10] 2350 5-8-12 **40** LEnstone(3) 9 13
(REBarr) *led far side to over 2f out: wknd over 1f out* **33/1**
0-05 **10** 2 ½ **Be My Alibi (IRE)**[17] 2187 3-8-3 **42** BSwarbrick(5) 11 —
(WMBrisbourne) *chsd far side ldrs to 1/2-way: sn btn* **7/1**
00-0 **11** 1 ¼ **Rhinefield Boy**[17] 2175 3-8-13 **48** TEaves(3) 3 —
(JSGoldie) *chsd stands side ldrs to 1/2-way: wknd over 1f out* **33/1**
45-0 **12** 4 **Missie**[10] 2367 4-9-11 **50** RWinston 8 —
(GASwinbank) *in tch far side to over 2f out: sn wknd* **16/1**
0-00 **13** 1 ¼ **Forest Queen**[17] 2185 7-8-0 **32** oh10 ow2 PPMathers(7) 13 —
(KWHogg) *bhd far side: lost tch fr 1/2-way* **50/1**

60.30 secs (-0.96) **Going Correction** -0.20s/f (Firm)
**WFA** 3 from 4yo+ 7lb **13** Ran **SP%** **119.0**
Speed ratings: **99,96,91,90,89 86,85,82,82,78 76,69,67**CSF £107.74 CT £819.92 TOTE £6.50: £2.40, £5.60, £2.90; EX 131.90 Place 6 £141.26, Place 5 £46.30.
**Owner** The Hon Miss Heather Galbraith **Bred** Miss Heather Galbraith **Trained** Ayr, Strathclyde

**FOCUS**
A low-grade event, but the pace was sound. The bottom five in the draw raced stands side (remainder far side) but there was no advantage. Pirlie Hill did well to win after hanging badly over to the far rail.

**NOTEBOOK**
**Pirlie Hill**, turned out quickly and down in grade, showed what she was capable of back over this trip and won with more in hand than the official margin suggests. She would be interesting under a penalty but the way she hung from one side of the course to the other sets the alarm bells ringing.
**Somethingabouther** ran creditably but is inconsistent and took her losing run to 28.
**Noble Mount**, one of the least exposed members of the field, ran creditably and shaped as though the return to six furlongs on a more galloping course would be in his favour.
**Petana** is unreliable but was not disgraced.
**Attila The Hun** was not disgraced from a better draw this time without headgear or cheekpieces, but he may have to wait for the return of regional racing to get off the mark.
**Amber Fox(IRE)** did not really improve for the return to five furlongs and will remain one to field against in anything but the worst company in the near future.
T/Plt: £156.30 to a £1 stake. Pool: £31,163.95. 145.50 winning tickets. T/Qpdt: £24.10 to a £1 stake. Pool: £2,602.70. 79.90 winning tickets. RY

# 2293 HAYDOCK (L-H)
### Thursday, June 3

**OFFICIAL GOING: Good to firm (good in places) changing to good to soft after race 3 (3.20)**
Wind: almost nil Weather: wet

## 2621 LITTLEWOODS BET DIRECT MAIDEN STKS 6f
**2:20** (2:22) (D) 3-Y-O+ **£5,882** (£1,810; £905; £452) **Stalls** Centre

Form RPR
03 **1** **Hawaajes**[16] 2195 3-8-13 WSupple 11 76
(BHanbury) *a.p: led ins fnl f: edgd lft: rdn out* **7/1**[3]
0 **2** 1 ¼ **Kentucky Express**[10] 2367 3-8-10 DAllan(3) 9 72
(TDEasterby) *dwlt: midfield: hdwy over 1f out: r.o towards fin* **66/1**
0 **3** ½ **San Lorenzo (UAE)**[15] 2223 3-8-8 ACulhane 8 66
(MRChannon) *led: rdn over 1f out: hdd ins fnl f: no ex cl home* **12/1**
0-32 **4** hd **Majorca**[16] 2211 3-8-13 78 LDettori 7 70
(JHMGosden) *trckd ldrs: rdn 2f out: styd on same pce ins fnl f* **1/1**[1]
00- **5** 2 **Trois Etoiles (IRE)**[215] 5869 3-8-8 MHills 13 59
(JWHills) *in rr: pushed along after 2f: hdwy over 1f out: styd on: nvr able to chal* **66/1**
**6** 7 **Grand Rapide** 3-8-8 KMcEvoy 6 38
(JLSpearing) *hld up bhd: rdn over 1f out: styd on fnl f: nvr nrr* **20/1**
0-0 **7** shd **Light The Dawn (IRE)**[31] 1842 4-9-2 SWKelly 14 38
(WMBrisbourne) *in tch: rdn and wknd over 1f out* **66/1**
**8** ½ **Bunkhouse** 4-9-7 JPMurtagh 12 41
(MissECLavelle) *dwlt: midfield: rdn over 2f out: rn green: nvr trbld ldrs* **33/1**
6 **9** 2 **Grey Gurkha**[22] 2040 3-8-13 RFitzpatrick 17 35
(PTMidgley) *hld up: rdn 2f out: hing lft over 1f out: nvr trbld ldrs* **66/1**
0- **10** 1 **Alpha Zeta**[210] 5930 3-8-13 DeanMcKeown 16 32
(CWThornton) *midfield: rdn and wknd 2f out* **100/1**
40-4 **11** nk **Indiana Blues**[15] 2223 3-8-8 89 KDarley 1 26
(AMBalding) *racd keenly: in tch: rdn and wknd over 2f out* **3/1**[2]
60-0 **12** hd **Designer City (IRE)**[58] 1288 3-8-3 52 PBradley(5) 10 26
(ABerry) *chsd ldrs tl rdn and wknd over 1f out* **66/1**
60 **13** 1 **Irusan (IRE)**[14] 2236 4-9-0 LeanneKershaw(7) 5 28
(JeddO'Keeffe) *prom tl wknd 2f out* **20/1**
**14** ½ **Red Hot Ruby** 3-8-8 GParkin 15 21
(RAFahey) *dwlt: towards rr: rdn 2f out: edgd lft over 1f out: nvr on terms* **33/1**
000- **15** 4 **Luke Sharp**[235] 5511 3-8-13 NCallan 4 14
(KARyan) *cl up tl rdn and wknd over 2f out* **66/1**
**16** 1 **Brain Washed** 3-8-8 SSanders 3 6
(TDEasterby) *s.s: hld up: effrt 2f out: wknd 1f out* **50/1**

1m 13.45s (-1.44) **Going Correction** -0.075s/f (Good)
**WFA** 3 from 4yo 8lb **16** Ran **SP%** **122.5**
Speed ratings: **106,104,103,103,100 91,91,90,87,86 86,85,84,83,78 77**CSF £409.93 TOTE £7.00: £1.90, £18.00, £3.20; EX 391.60.
**Owner** Hamdan Al Maktoum **Bred** Theobalds Stud **Trained** Newmarket, Suffolk

**FOCUS**
With some of the form horses below their best this is a hard race to assess with confidence, but the time was fair and it has been given the benefit of doubt to begin with.

**NOTEBOOK**
**Hawaajes** did not get home over an extended seven furlongs last time and the drop back to sprinting suited him well. This was not a strong maiden, but he won it well and is open to improvement in handicap company.
**Kentucky Express**, a half-brother to three winners over various distances, was keeping on well at the finish and was the only one to bustle up the Arab-owned runners. He left the impression was that he will appreciate a return to farther.
**San Lorenzo(UAE)** showed up well for a long way. The drop back in trip appeared to suit and this was a big improvement on her debut effort.
**Majorca** set a fair standard for the others to aim at but was once again found out. There is a weak maiden to be won with him but he is vulnerable to anything with a bit more potential, and handicaps may be the best route now.
**Trois Etoiles(IRE)**is now eligible to run in handicaps and has shown enough to suggest that she is capable of quite a bit better when stepped up in distance.
**Grand Rapide** has plenty of speed in her pedigree but never really got competitive on this debut.
**Indiana Blues** is becoming disappointing and her current rating flatters her.

## 2622 SKYBET.COM (S) STKS 6f
**2:50** (2:53) (F) 2-Y-O **£3,108** (£888; £444) **Stalls** Centre

Form RPR
0 **1** **Island Swing (IRE)**[17] 2177 2-8-6 SCarson 3 55+
(JLSpearing) *mde all: drvn clr fnl f* **4/1**[1]
406 **2** 5 **Dane's Rock (IRE)**[5] 2489 2-8-11 (b[1]) KDarley 8 45
(PCHaslam) *cl up: rdn to chse wnr 2f out: no imp fnl f* **4/1**[1]
0 **3** 1 ½ **Lojo**[14] 2248 2-8-6 WSupple 4 36
(RPElliott) *trckd ldrs: rdn 2f out: one pce fnl f* **11/2**[2]
3 **4** nk **Tonight (IRE)**[12] 2288 2-8-11 SWKelly 1 40
(WMBrisbourne) *broke wl: lost pl and outpcd after 2f: kpt on one pce fnl f* **12/1**
0 **5** 2 ½ **Diction (IRE)**[10] 2364 2-8-6 KMcEvoy 2 27
(KRBurke) *prom tl rdn and wknd 2f out* **4/1**[1]
**6** 6 **Cash Time** 2-8-6 RFitzpatrick 7 9
(JO'Reilly) *s.i.s: hld up: rdn over 2f out: wknd over 1f out* **20/1**
0441 **7** 2 **Bowland Bride (IRE)**[10] 2364 2-8-6 PBradley(5) 5 8
(ABerry) *trckd ldrs tl rdn and wknd 2f out* **6/1**[3]
**8** 25 **Eternal Sunshine (IRE)** 2-8-6 SChin 6 —
(RPElliott) *prom tl lost pl qckly 3f out: bhd after* **10/1**

1m 17.1s (2.21) **Going Correction** -0.075s/f (Good) **8** Ran **SP%** **111.2**
Speed ratings: **82,75,73,72,69 61,58,25**CSF £18.64 TOTE £5.60: £2.70, £2.00, £1.80; EX 51.30.The winner was bought in for 13,500 guineas.
**Owner** J Spearing **Bred** Tomaju Investments **Trained** Kinnersley, Worcs

**FOCUS**
A very poor time, even for a juvenile seller. Weak form, with no strength in depth.

**NOTEBOOK**
**Island Swing(IRE)**, who was stepping up in trip and taking on much lesser oppostion than she met on her debut in a maiden at Windsor, ran out a clear winner of what was a very modest affair. Subsequently bought in for 13,500gns, she could pay her way in nurseries.
**Dane's Rock(IRE)**, already well beaten in a seller, had blinkers on instead of a visor. He could only chase the winner home at a respectful distance.
**Lojo** appeared to have less to do in this company than when beaten in a claimer on her debut, but she was always struggling to cope with the pace of the first two.
**Tonight(IRE)** once again looked green and has yet to achieve much in two outings.
**Diction(IRE)** was popular enough in the market but failed to justify that confidence.

## 2623 BANK OF SCOTLAND CORPORATE STKS (REGISTERED AS THE JOHN OF GAUNT STAKES) (LISTED RACE) 7f 30y
**3:20** (3:22) (A) 4-Y-O+ **£17,400** (£6,600; £3,300; £1,500) **Stalls** Low

Form RPR
-452 **1** **Suggestive**[16] 2200 6-8-12 107 (b) MHills 5 109
(WJHaggas) *midfield: rdn 2f out: hdwy over 1f out: r.o to ld cl home* **9/2**[2]
-554 **2** ½ **Makhlab (USA)**[33] 1758 4-8-12 105 WSupple 2 108
(BWHills) *chsd ldr: rdn over 1f out: ev ch fnl f: nt qckn cl home* **16/1**
2-10 **3** shd **Three Graces (GER)**[84] 1004 4-8-12 109 (vt) LDettori 8 108
(SaeedBinSuroor) *led: rdn over 1f out: hdd and no ex cl home* **9/2**[2]
0-00 **4** ¾ **Millennium Force**[22] 2044 6-8-12 107 KDarley 10 106
(MRChannon) *s.i.s: bhd: rdn over 2f out: hdwy over 1f out: edgd rt wl ins fnl f: r.o*
01-3 **5** 2 **Court Masterpiece**[16] 2200 4-8-12 106 JPMurtagh 12 101
(EALDunlop) *hld up: hdwy over 2f out: rdn and styd on over 1f out: hung lft ins fnl f: one pce towards fin* **5/1**[3]
5610 **6** ¾ **Quito (IRE)**[19] 2109 7-8-12 111 (b) ACulhane 1 99
(DWChapman) *racd keenly: sn chsd ldrs: rdn 2f out: one pce whn n.m.r wl ins fnl f* **6/1**
054- **7** 4 **Desert Destiny**[287] 4326 4-8-12 107 (v) KMcEvoy 6 88
(SaeedBinSuroor) *hld up: rdn 2f out: edgd rt over 1f out: no imp* **16/1**
1550 **8** 5 **El Coto**[12] 2283 4-8-12 102 SSanders 7 75
(BAMcmahon) *midfield: rdn over 3f out: wknd 2f out* **11/1**
0000 **9** nk **Crimson Silk**[26] 1968 4-8-12 94 (p) PRobinson 3 74
(DHaydnJones) *chsd ldrs tl rdn and wknd over 1f out* **40/1**
5302 **10** 1 **Pawan (IRE)**[5] 2492 4-8-12 61 AnnStokell 9 72?
(MissAStokell) *chsd ldrs tl rdn and wknd over 2f out* **150/1**
5-10 **11** 8 **Tout Seul (IRE)**[19] 2109 4-9-3 110 SCarson 4 56
(RFJohnsonHoughton) *hld up: rdn over 3f out: wknd 2f out* **4/1**[1]

1m 29.57s (-2.59) **Going Correction** -0.075s/f (Good) **11** Ran **SP%** **115.3**
Speed ratings: **111,110,110,109,107 106,101,96,95,94 85**CSF £71.01 TOTE £6.50: £2.20, £4.30, £1.60; EX 106.30.
**Owner** Mrs Barbara Bassett **Bred** Keith Freeman **Trained** Newmarket, Suffolk

**FOCUS**
There was a good pace on here for what looked a competitive affair on paper.

**NOTEBOOK**

**Suggestive** appreciates a strong gallop, and he got that here. He certainly has plenty of ability but he is undoubtedly difficult to catch right, and it is anyone's guess if things will fall as sweetly for him next time.

**Makhlab(USA)** would have probably preferred it had the race taken place an hour or two later, as by then the rain had got into the ground, but he still ran a solid race, eventually overhauling the leader, only to have already been passed by the winner on his outside.

**Three Graces(GER)**, who has an admirable strike-rate, has been gelded since his last outing. He was given a very positive ride by Dettori, who set a proper gallop on him, and it was only well inside the last that he got caught. He stays a mile and there are races to be won with him at this level.

**Millennium Force**, a seven-furlong specialist, finished his race well. The strong pace suited his style of running but ideally he prefers a straight track.

**Court Masterpiece** was entitled to reverse Goodwood form with Suggestive at these weights. He had every chance but lacked the finishing kick of the winner.

**Quito(IRE)** ran a respectable race with the pace suiting his style of running. He would have finished slightly closer had he not run into a little trouble late on.

**Crimson Silk** *Official explanation: jockey said he was unhappy with the gelding's action over the final 2f*

**Tout Seul(IRE)** failed to run his race and something may well have been amiss. *Official explanation: trainer's representative had no explanation for the poor form shown*

## 2624 BETFRED THE BONUS KING H'CAP — 1m 2f 120y

3:50 (3:50) (C) (0-95,90) 3-Y-0+ — **£9,977** (£3,070; £1,535; £767) **Stalls** High

| Form | | | | RPR |
|---|---|---|---|---|
| 0-10 | **1** | | **Ionian Spring (IRE)**[33] 1762 9-9-11 **90** ... RSmith 7<br>(CGCox) *hld up: hdwy over 3f out: led 2f out: rdn over 1f out: all out* **8/1** | 99 |
| 3164 | **2** | *shd* | **Ofaraby**[28] 1903 4-9-7 **86** ... PRobinson 6<br>(MAJarvis) *trckd ldrs: rdn to chse wnr over 1f out: r.o ins fnl f: jst failed* **5/2**[1] | 95 |
| 0020 | **3** | *3 ½* | **Briareus**[20] 2084 4-9-0 **79** ... KDarley 9<br>(AMBalding) *trckd ldrs: rdn over 3f out: styd on same pce fnl f* **13/2** | 82 |
| 60-0 | **4** | *½* | **Freeloader (IRE)**[47] 1460 4-8-9 **74** ... MHills 4<br>(JWHills) *hld up: rdn and hdwy over 1f out: kpt on one pce fnl f* **11/2**[3] | 76 |
| 21- | **5** | *2 ½* | **Baltic Blazer (IRE)**[234] 5554 4-8-11 **76** ... JPMurtagh 2<br>(PWHarris) *midfield: rdn over 3f out: nvr able to chal* **8/1** | 74 |
| 0-25 | **6** | *nk* | **La Sylphide**[23] 2022 7-9-3 **82** ... SWKelly 3<br>(GMMoore) *sn led: rdn over 2f out: sn hdd: wknd fnl f* **11/4**[2] | 79 |
| 13-0 | **7** | *1* | **Liquid Form (IRE)**[31] 1840 4-9-6 **85** ... WSupple 5<br>(BHanbury) *hld up: rdn over 3f out: no imp* **14/1** | 81 |
| 00-4 | **8** | *hd* | **Vicious Prince (IRE)**[47] 1470 5-8-9 **74** ... DeanMcKeown 8<br>(RMWhitaker) *prom: rdn over 2f out: wknd over 1f out* **14/1** | 69 |
| -000 | **9** | *30* | **Island Light (USA)**[18] 2142 4-8-11 **76** ... ACulhane 1<br>(MrsMReveley) *hld up: struggling over 3f out: sn btn* **25/1** | 20 |

2m 18.5s (0.77) **Going Correction** +0.125s/f (Good) — **9** Ran SP% **123.4**

Speed ratings: **102,101,99,99,97 96,96,96,74**CSF £30.40 CT £145.74 TOTE £8.20: £2.10, £1.80, £2.30; EX 38.80 Trifecta £141.60 Pool of 1277.10, 6.40 winning units.

**Owner** Elite Racing Club **Bred** Ballymacoll Stud Farm Ltd **Trained** Lambourn, Berks

**FOCUS**

A reasonable handicap, but the leaders went off too quick, so the time was modest even allowing for the deteriorating ground. The official going was changed before this race.

**NOTEBOOK**

**Ionian Spring(IRE)**, for whom the easing ground was not a worry, needs a good pace to be seen at his best. With the leaders going off too fast in the ground, he came through from the rear and just held on in a tight finish to win off a career-high mark. This was some accomplishment for a nine-year-old.

**Ofaraby**, slightly disappointing from a good draw at Chester last time, was probably thankful for the rain which had fallen. He finished strongly and would have won in another stride, but he is becoming expensive to follow. Indeed, things are unlikely to get any easier, with another rise in the handicap now likely.

**Briareus** is a consistent sort but as a result gets little respite from the Handicapper.

**Freeloader(IRE)**, who has shown his best form on a faster surface, could only stay on at the one pace.

**Baltic Blazer(IRE)**, who was pretty friendless in the market, ran as though this reappearance outing was needed. He is surely capable of better than this.

**La Sylphide** has won on soft ground before so the rain was not a worry, but she did too much in front and paid the price in the closing stages.

## 2625 EBF PRINCESS ROYAL TRUST FOR CARERS UNISYS CLASSIFIED STKS — 6f

4:20 (4:22) (C) 3-Y-0+ — **£8,850** (£3,357; £1,678; £763) **Stalls** Centre

| Form | | | | RPR |
|---|---|---|---|---|
| 0-50 | **1** | | **Traytonic**[12] 2309 3-8-12 95 ... JPMurtagh 5<br>(JRFanshawe) *hld up: rdn and hdwy over 1f out: led ins fnl f: r.o wl* **9/2**[2] | 101+ |
| 1001 | **2** | *2 ½* | **Steel Blue**[9] 2391 4-9-7 85 ... ACulhane 6<br>(RMWhitaker) *led: rdn over 1f out: hdd and no ex ins fnl f* **11/2**[3] | 93 |
| 05-5 | **3** | *5* | **Tedburrow**[26] 1955 12-9-1 90 ... WSupple 2<br>(EJAlston) *in tch: rdn 2f out: one pce ins fnl f* **14/1** | 72 |
| 00-0 | **4** | *2* | **Danecare (IRE)**[20] 2101 4-9-6 95 ... KDarley 11<br>(JGBurns, Ire) *in rr: hdwy 2f out: kpt on: nt pce to chal* **7/1** | 71 |
| 0-00 | **5** | *2 ½* | **Onlytime Will Tell**[68] 1125 6-9-4 93 ... SWKelly 10<br>(DNicholls) *dwlt: hld up: hdwy over 2f out: rdn over 1f out: wknd ins fnl f* **9/2**[2] | 62 |
| 4044 | **6** | *1 ¼* | **Indian Spark**[12] 2293 10-9-3 92 ... KDalgleish 8<br>(JSGoldie) *hld up: rdn over 1f out: no imp* **10/3**[1] | 57 |
| 0206 | **7** | *¾* | **Jalouhar**[1] 2588 4-9-1 47 ... MTebbutt 7<br>(BPJBaugh) *in tch: lost pl over 2f out: n.d after* **200/1** | 53 |
| 0-02 | **8** | *1 ¾* | **Tom Tun**[21] 2065 9-9-5 94 ... (b) DeanMcKeown 3<br>(JBalding) *prom tl rdn and wknd over 1f out* **9/2**[2] | 51 |
| 0600 | **9** | *2 ½* | **Telepathic (IRE)**[13] 2274 4-8-10 62 ... PBradley(5) 12<br>(ABerry) *in tch: rdn 2f out: sn wknd* **200/1** | 40 |
| 4006 | **10** | *7* | **Speedfit Free (IRE)**[3] 2524 7-9-1 47 ... (v) AnnStokell 9<br>(MissAStokell) *towards rr: outpcd over 2f out* **200/1** | 19 |
| 4-00 | **11** | *14* | **Rosselli (USA)**[26] 1955 8-8-8 46 ... CEly(7) 4<br>(ABerry) *prom tl rdn and wknd 3f out* **150/1** | — |
| 0306 | **12** | *1* | **Xaloc Bay (IRE)**[6] 2454 6-9-1 49 ... NCallan 1<br>(BPJBaugh) *trckd ldrs tl rdn and wknd over 2f out* **100/1** | — |

1m 14.36s (-0.53) **Going Correction** +0.125s/f (Good)

**WFA** 3 from 4yo+ 8lb — **12** Ran SP% **115.3**

Speed ratings: **108,104,98,95,92 90,89,87,83,74 55,54**CSF £29.09 TOTE £6.20: £2.30, £2.10, £2.90; EX 46.80.

**Owner** Colin Davey Racing **Bred** Col J L Parkes **Trained** Newmarket, Suffolk

**FOCUS**

A fair race but they were well strung out at the finish and many failed to run up to their best.

**NOTEBOOK**

**Traytonic**, the only three-year-old in the field, ran out a clear winner on his debut for his new stable. His ability to handle easy ground as well as fast will stand him in good stead, and he looks to be worth trying back in Listed grade.

**Steel Blue** likes to have his own way in front and made a brave attempt to make all. This was a solid effort giving weight all round.

**Tedburrow** ran as well as could be expected but must be on the downgrade now and will remain difficult to place off his current mark.

**Danecare(IRE)**, a very useful handicapper in Ireland, appeared to have conditions to suit. He kept on well enough for fourth, but was beaten a long way.

**Onlytime Will Tell** went winless in 2003 and continues to look difficult to place.

**Indian Spark** was another who looked to have plenty in his favour but failed to run up to his best. His best days too are probably behind him now.

**Tom Tun**, the subject of support following the rain, is better than this. He was not the only one to run below form in this contest.

**Xaloc Bay(IRE)** *Official explanation: jockey said gelding was unsuited by the ground*

## 2626 BETFRED IN-SHOPS OR ON-PHONE H'CAP — 6f

4:50 (4:52) (D) (0-85,85) 3-Y-0+ — **£5,707** (£1,756; £878; £439) **Stalls** Centre

| Form | | | | RPR |
|---|---|---|---|---|
| 2000 | **1** | | **Cardinal Venture (IRE)**[27] 1927 6-10-0 **85** ... NCallan 2<br>(KARyan) *mde all: rdn clr over 1f out: sn hung lft: r.o wl* **3/1**[2] | 96 |
| 4342 | **2** | *5* | **Romany Nights (IRE)**[6] 2461 4-9-5 **76** ... (b[1]) SWKelly 7<br>(JWUnett) *trckd ldrs: wnt 2nd 3f out: rdn over 1f out: hung rt and btn ins fnl f* **3/1**[2] | 72 |
| 4500 | **3** | *1 ¾* | **Prince Of Blues (IRE)**[12] 2293 6-8-5 **62** ... (p) WSupple 4<br>(MMullineaux) *in tch: rdn over 1f out: one pce* **16/1** | 53 |
| 5200 | **4** | *1 ½* | **Cd Flyer (IRE)**[21] 2065 7-9-9 **85** ... PMulrennan(5) 3<br>(BEllison) *hld up: hdwy 2f out: rdn over 1f out: one pce ins fnl f* **11/4**[1] | 71 |
| 0100 | **5** | *shd* | **Grey Cossack**[13] 2261 7-8-12 **79** ... RFitzpatrick 1<br>(PTMidgley) *hld up: rdn over 2f out: kpt on ins fnl f: nt pce to chal* **6/1**[3] | 65 |
| 2036 | **6** | *4* | **Attorney**[8] 2399 6-7-12 **55** oh5 ... (v) JoannaBadger 8<br>(DShaw) *hld up: rdn 2f out: no imp* **11/1** | 29 |
| 0020 | **7** | *10* | **Type One (IRE)**[16] 2219 6-8-13 **70** ... (v) KDalgleish 6<br>(JJQuinn) *prom: rdn over 2f out: sn wknd* **16/1** | 14 |

1m 14.76s (-0.13) **Going Correction** +0.125s/f (Good) — **7** Ran SP% **111.1**

Speed ratings: **105,98,96,94,93 88,75**CSF £11.67 CT £112.91 TOTE £4.00: £2.90, £2.10; EX 19.60 Place 6 £200.45, Place 5 £45.32.

**Owner** Tony Fawcett **Bred** Patrick Gleeson **Trained** Hambleton, N Yorks

**FOCUS**

Few got into this, and the winner made all for an authoritative success.

**NOTEBOOK**

**Cardinal Venture(IRE)**, down 2lb, goes on an easy surface and, although dropping back in trip, has never been short of pace. He made every yard and, despite hanging left towards the far-side rail under pressure, was always well clear. The Wokingham could well be on the cards now.

**Romany Nights(IRE)** goes on this ground but is a difficult horse to win with. He had blinkers on this time instead of the usual visor, but he had to settle for a place again.

**Prince Of Blues(IRE)** was unable to make the running with Cardinal Venture in the field.

**Cd Flyer(IRE)** had the ground to suit but he remains on a stiff enough mark. He needs some help from the Handicapper on this evidence.

**Grey Cossack** has won six of his seven races in April or May, but at least he has slipped back into the 70s - he has never won a handicap off a mark in the 80s despite 14 attempts.

T/Plt: £411.30 to a £1 stake. Pool: £43,671.85. 77.50 winning tickets. T/Qpdt: £30.40 to a £1 stake. Pool: £4,012.85. 97.60 winning tickets. DO

# 2557 SANDOWN (R-H)

### Thursday, June 3

**OFFICIAL GOING: Good (good to firm in places on round course)**

Wind: nil Weather: overcast

## 2627 HELICAL BAR MAIDEN AUCTION STKS — 5f 6y

6:20 (6:21) (E) 2-Y-0 — **£4,085** (£1,257; £628; £314) **Stalls** High

| Form | | | | RPR |
|---|---|---|---|---|
| | **1** | | **Kings Quay** 2-8-11 ... DaneO'Neill 3<br>(RHannon) *w'like: lw: dwlt: rcvrd to trck ldrs after 2f: nt clr run over 1f out tl swtchd rt and led ins fnl f: sn in command* **9/2**[3] | 88+ |
| 2 | **2** | *1 ¼* | **Spirit Of France (IRE)**[44] 1523 2-8-11 ... JFanning 8<br>(MJohnston) *lw: pressed ldr: led wl over 1f out: hdd and edgd lft ins fnl f: nt qckn* **7/2**[2] | 84 |
| 05 | **3** | *1 ¾* | **Caly Dancer (IRE)**[21] 2058 2-8-9 ... TQuinn 1<br>(DRCElsworth) *rr of main gp and pushed along over 3f out: effrt over 1f out: styd on wl fnl f to take 3rd nr fin* **33/1** | 76 |
| 22 | **4** | *nk* | **Extra Mark**[19] 2125 2-8-7 ... NPollard 4<br>(JRBest) *trckd ldrs: rdn and ev ch over 1f out: fdd ins fnl f* **6/1** | 73 |
| 3324 | **5** | *2* | **Alpaga Le Jomage (IRE)**[3] 2532 2-8-9 ... (b[1]) LDettori 5<br>(BJMeehan) *led to wl over 1f out: hanging rt and nt qckn fnl f* **3/1**[1] | 68 |
| | **6** | *1 ½* | **Geisha Lady (IRE)** 2-8-2 ... MartinDwyer 7<br>(RMBeckett) *bit bkwd: dwlt: outpcd in last pair: no prog tl kpt on fnl f* **33/1** | 56 |
| | **7** | *1* | **Pitch Up (IRE)** 2-9-0 ... KFallon 2<br>(TGMills) *str: lw: dwlt: hung lft after s and lost all ch: wl bhd to 1/2-way: effrt over 1f out: no ch w ldrs* **7/2**[2] | 64+ |
| | **8** | *7* | **Our Nigel (IRE)** 2-8-7 ... SDrowne 9<br>(MrsPNDutfield) *cmpt: bkwd: pressed ldrs tl wknd wl over 1f out* **50/1** | 33 |

63.25 secs (1.06) **Going Correction** +0.075s/f (Good) — **8** Ran SP% **109.8**

Speed ratings: **94,92,89,88,85 83,81,70**CSF £18.79 TOTE £5.30: £2.20, £1.50, £6.20; EX 13.40.

**Owner** J R May **Bred** Newsells Park Stud Limited **Trained** East Everleigh, Wilts

■ A first-ever runner and winner for the great Montjeu.

**FOCUS**

An ordinary maiden, but a couple of eye-catching performances.

**NOTEBOOK**

**Kings Quay ◆**, a 32,000gns yearling out of the useful Glen Rosie, came from off the pace to make a winning debut despite getting caught in a pocket and having to wait for a gap. Fortunately one appeared next to the inside rail when the early leader faded and he went on to score with more in hand than the margin would suggest. He should stay further and go on to better things.

**Spirit Of France(IRE)**, racing on much faster ground than on his debut, was unable to dominate this time and when he did eventually get the better of the pacemaker he was merely a sitting duck for the winner. He probably ran into a decent sort and it is only a matter of time before he gets off the mark.

**Caly Dancer(IRE)** is progressing slowly with experience and was doing all his best work late. This effort again suggested he needs further.

**Extra Mark**, runner-up in a couple of modest contests, was probably up against better rivals this time. He looks the ideal sort for nurseries later on.

**Alpaga Le Jomage(IRE)**, reappearing quickly after his good effort in Listed company here three days earlier, made the running in the first-time blinkers but was rather easily picked off. This may have come too quick, but as this was already his fifth outing there is also the possibility he is not progressing.
**Pitch Up(IRE)**, a 40,000gns half-brother to a winner in Italy, had no chance after messing up the start completely and is surely better than this.

## 2628 NUMIS SECURITIES H'CAP 5f 6y
**6:50** (6:53) (D) (0-85,82) 3-Y-0+ **£5,551** (£1,708; £854; £427) **Stalls** High

Form RPR
0030 **1** **Whistler**[5] 2490 7-9-4 **75**...(p) RHills 1 86
(JMBradley) *racd in midfield: prog on outer 2f out: shkn up to ld 1f out: pushed out* **5/1**[2]
0050 **2** *1 ½* **Taboor (IRE)**[30] 1872 6-7-9 **55** oh2...(b) LisaJones(3) 9 61
(JWPayne) *swtg: trckd ldrs: effrt on inner to chal 1f out: ev ch: nt qckn* **14/1**
4004 **3** *1* **Port St Charles (IRE)**[6] 2440 7-8-1 **63**... RThomas(5) 4 65
(CRDore) *squeezed out sn after s: racd in last trio after: prog over 1f out: styd on fnl f to take 3rd nr fin* **15/2**
3000 **4** *nk* **Further Outlook (USA)**[15] 2222 10-9-11 **82**... TQuinn 6 83
(DKIvory) *b: b.hind: mde most to 1f out: one pce* **16/1**
/-10 **5** *½* **Zoom Zoom**[13] 2261 4-9-5 **76**... MFenton 5 75
(MrsLStubbs) *lw: racd in midfield: rdn and no prog whn bmpd over 1f out: one pce after* **12/1**
-600 **6** *¾* **Margalita (IRE)**[12] 2284 4-8-12 **69**...(t) JFEgan 8 65
(PMitchell) *lw: sn rdn in last trio: effrt u.p whn bmpd over 1f out: nt clr run sn after: kpt on nr fin* **33/1**
1400 **7** *shd* **Mayzin (IRE)**[5] 2483 4-7-9 **55** oh2...(p) JFMcDonald(3) 10 51
(RMFlower) *w ldrs to 2f out: fdd u.p fnl f* **13/2**[3]
2041 **8** *1 ½* **The Fisio**[20] 2079 4-9-2 **73**...(v) MartinDwyer 7 64
(AMBalding) *w ldrs to 1/2-way: sn lost pl: struggling whn bmpd over 1f out* **5/1**[2]
6-00 **9** *½* **Nivernais**[8] 2399 5-9-9 **80**... DaneO'Neill 3 69
(HCandy) *swvd rt sn after s: a in last trio: shkn up and no prog over 1f out* **4/1**[1]
320- **10** *1 ½* **Wicked Uncle**[209] 5941 5-9-5 **76**...(b) DHolland 2 59
(SGollings) *pressed ldrs: ev ch 2f out: hung rt over 1f out: wknd and wandered after* **10/1**

62.12 secs (-0.07) **Going Correction** +0.075s/f (Good) **10** Ran SP% **110.7**
Speed ratings: **103,100,99,98,97 96,96,93,93,90**CSF £67.92 CT £504.83 TOTE £3.30: £2.00, £3.00, £2.10; EX 74.70.
**Owner** Raymond Tooth **Bred** Raymond Clive Tooth **Trained** Sedbury, Gloucs

**FOCUS**
A competitive little sprint handicap run at a sound pace.

**NOTEBOOK**
**Whistler**, off a 3lb lower mark than for his last win, was kept wide out of trouble from his low draw and was always cantering over his rivals. He found plenty when eventually shaken up and is a useful tool in this grade when things go his way.
**Taboor(IRE)** ◆ has dropped to a very favourable mark and ran his best race for some time. *Official explanation: trainer said gelding ran without tongue-strap, which had come adrift and could not be re-fitted*
**Port St Charles(IRE)** ◆ was unlucky. Squeezed out soon after the start, he was staying on against the inside rail when the door was slammed in his face by the runner-up inside the last furlong, but for which he would probably have finished second. This was an encouraging effort over an inadequate trip and he is another that has slipped to a handy mark, although his style of running does require some luck.
**Further Outlook(USA)** ran his best race since winning in soft ground on his reappearance. He won off much higher marks than this in his heyday, but probably needs to drop a few more pounds now. *Official explanation: jockey said gelding hung right*
**Zoom Zoom** was not disgraced, but needs much softer ground than this.
**Nivernais** was very errant soon after the start and never got competitive after that.
**Wicked Uncle** *Official explanation: jockey said gelding lost its action*

## 2629 IG INDEX 30TH ANNIVERSARY SURREY STKS (LISTED RACE) 7f 16y
**7:20** (7:22) (A) 3-Y-0 **£17,400** (£6,600; £3,300; £1,500) **Stalls** High

Form RPR
1 **1** **Madid (IRE)**[19] 2113 3-8-11 ... RHills 6 111
(JHMGosden) *lw: settled in last: prog 2f out: chsd ldng pair jst over 1f out: styd on strly to ld nr fin* **11/2**[2]
111- **2** *½* **Pastoral Pursuits**[271] 4720 3-9-3 110... SDrowne 4 116
(HMorrison) *settled in 5th: prog over 2f out: rdn to ld jst over 1f out and looked likely wnr: tired ins fnl f: hdd nr fin* **9/1**
1-32 **3** *2 ½* **Peak To Creek**[12] 2308 3-9-3 115... EAhern 5 110
(JNoseda) *lw: settled in 4th: prog on inner to ld wl over 1f out: hdd and nt qckn jst over 1f out* **5/6**[1]
5-24 **4** *6* **Jack Sullivan (USA)**[68] 1143 3-8-11 ... MJKinane 7 88
(GAButler) *pressed ldr: led over 2f out to wl over 1f out: wknd* **20/1**
12-1 **5** *8* **Catstar (USA)**[117] 711 3-8-6 107...(t) KMcEvoy 1 62
(SaeedBinSuroor) *lw: led at fast pce: hdd over 2f out: wknd rapidly over 1f out* **11/2**[2]
3114 **6** *13* **Rosencrans (USA)**[61] 1239 3-9-1 100...(vt) LDettori 2 37
(SaeedBinSuroor) *lw: racd freely: pressed ldng pair 1st 2f: shkn up and wknd over 2f out: t.o* **7/1**[3]

1m 28.73s (-2.36) **Going Correction** 0.0s/f (Good) **6** Ran SP% **112.6**
Speed ratings: **113,112,109,102,93 78**CSF £50.24 TOTE £5.90: £2.30, £3.30; EX 42.70.
**Owner** Hamdan Al Maktoum **Bred** Cranford Stud **Trained** Manton, Wilts

**FOCUS**
A race run at a decent pace and a smart winning time for the grade. Strong form.

**NOTEBOOK**
**Madid(IRE)** ◆, having only his second start, was dropped out early and looked more likely to finish last than first two furlongs from home. Even half a furlong out it seemed unlikely that he would win, but he then found enough to sweep past the leader and eventually score with a degree of comfort. This stiff track probably compensated for the furlong shorter trip and so Ascot should also suit him perfectly if he does line up for the Jersey Stakes.
**Pastoral Pursuits**, who went from strength to strength last season before chipping a bone in his knee, did everything right on this first start in nine months and looked like scoring until nailed near the line. Lack of peak fitness, rather than lack of stamina, is more likely the reason for this defeat and he lost nothing in trying to concede 6lb to such a progressive sort.
**Peak To Creek** had every chance but found the front pair too strong in the last furlong. He is consistent, but his penalty for winning a Group race last term is not helping him in contests like this. There is always the option of bringing him back to sprinting.
**Jack Sullivan(USA)**, nearly seven lengths behind Peak To Creek in last season's Horris Hill, finished a bit closer this time with the help of a 6lb pull. He was entitled to need this first run since March, but his yard remain out of form.
**Catstar(USA)** was responsible for the cracking early pace, but had little chance of maintaining it.
**Rosencrans(USA)**, who was inclined to take a good hold early, may have been racing on turf for the first time but this was still too bad to be true. *Official explanation: jockey said colt had breathing problems*

## 2630 NUMIS SECURITIES FILLIES' RATED STKS (H'CAP) 1m 1f
**7:55** (7:55) (C ) (0-95,95) 4-Y-0+ **£9,256** (£2,848; £1,424; £712) **Stalls** High

Form RPR
3411 **1** **Polar Jem**[5] 2474 4-8-4 **76** 3ex oh2... AMcCarthy 3 87
(GGMargarson) *lw: mde all: shkn up over 1f out: hrd pressed fnl f: pushed out and a holding on* **11/8**[1]
10-2 **2** *nk* **Shamara (IRE)**[18] 2142 4-8-9 **83**... SSanders 2 91
(CFWall) *hld up in tch: chsd wnr 2f out: drvn to chal fnl f: styd on wl but a hld* **9/4**[2]
1-4 **3** *3* **Salagama (IRE)**[27] 1931 4-8-11 **85**... KFallon 1 87
(PFICole) *chsd wnr 2f out: rdn whn n.m.r over 1f out: one pce after* **9/2**[3]
5-00 **4** *1 ¼* **Island Rapture**[13] 2279 4-8-1 **78** oh4... LisaJones(3) 5 78
(JARToller) *hld up in last: rdn and no prog over 2f out: one pce after* **14/1**
33-0 **5** *3* **Play That Tune**[22] 2044 4-9-7 **95**... JFanning 4 89
(MJohnston) *lw: t.k.h: trckd ldrs: cl up 2f out: wknd jst over 1f out* **8/1**

1m 54.68s (-1.43) **Going Correction** 0.0s/f (Good) **5** Ran SP% **108.8**
Speed ratings: **106,105,103,101,99**CSF £4.58 TOTE £1.50: £1.50, £1.80; EX 5.70.
**Owner** Norcroft Park Stud **Bred** Norcroft Park Stud **Trained** Newmarket, Suffolk

**FOCUS**
Only five runners, but a truly run race and the form looks solid.

**NOTEBOOK**
**Polar Jem** was almost forced to run here in her hat-trick bid, as she was able to race off a 3lb lower mark than for her last win and is imminently due to go up 10lb. She completed the task with a game all-the-way victory and looks very much a filly on the up.
**Shamara(IRE)** came on from her reappearance and ran a fine race in defeat. She kept trying to overhaul the winner, but could never quite manage it and would probably have preferred a bit further.
**Salagama(IRE)** was still in there fighting when things got a bit tight for her over a furlong from home, but she did not find much when eventually seeing daylight and it is doubtful it made any difference to the result. This was only her third start and she still has scope for improvement.
**Island Rapture** is slowly dropping down the handicap, but she was up against three progressive fillies here and they proved much too good for her.
**Play That Tune**, more exposed than some of her rivals, looks very high in the handicap now and the longer trip did not help her.

## 2631 BINARYBET.COM H'CAP 1m 6f
**8:25** (8:28) (D ) (0-85,77) 3-Y-0+ **£5,460** (£1,680; £840; £420) **Stalls** Low

Form RPR
4-02 **1** **Shredded (USA)**[20] 2084 4-9-11 **76**... LDettori 7 83
(JHMGosden) *lw: t.k.h: trckd ldng pair: led over 1f out: drvn and kpt on wl fnl f* **5/2**[1]
6420 **2** *¾* **Invitation**[20] 2084 6-9-7 **72**... RHughes 3 78
(ACharlton) *lw: dwlt: racd in last pair tl 6f out: plld out and drvn 2f out: styd on fnl f: tk 2nd last stride* **10/1**
0-30 **3** *shd* **Rome (IRE)**[31] 1832 5-9-0 **65**... DaneO'Neill 6 71
(GPEnright) *lw: chsd ldr to 2f out: chsd wnr over 1f out: drvn and styd on fnl f: a jst hld: lost 2nd last stride* **33/1**
-063 **4** *1* **Mostarsil (USA)**[12] 2285 6-9-3 **68**...(p) RLMoore 2 72
(GLMoore) *racd in midfield: rdn and effrt over 2f out: hanging and nt clr run over 1f out: kpt on fnl f: a hld* **7/2**[2]
131- **5** *¾* **Tilla**[212] 5920 4-8-13 **67**... LFletcher(3) 5 70
(HMorrison) *swtg: bit bkwd: hld up in rr: gng easily 3f out: effrt 2f out: drvn and styng on one pce whn nt clr run nr fin* **7/1**
0604 **6** *¾* **Moon Emperor**[22] 2047 7-9-11 **76**... MJKinane 9 78
(JRJenkins) *lw: settled in last pair: rdn over 3f out: sn outpcd: styd on wl fnl 2f: nrst fin* **6/1**
-000 **7** *5* **Persian King (IRE)**[12] 2305 7-9-5 **70**... VSlattery 8 65
(JABOld) *racd in last pair: rdn 3f out: sn outpcd: n.d after* **33/1**
1120 **8** *2 ½* **Linens Flame**[5] 2480 5-9-10 **75**... DSweeney 11 67
(BGPowell) *led at gd pce to over 1f out: wknd* **20/1**
-030 **9** *9* **Greenwich Meantime**[22] 2047 4-9-12 **77**... KFallon 10 56
(MrsJRRamsden) *hld up in midfield: n.m.r over 2f out: hanging and fnd nil wl over 1f out: wknd and eased* **5/1**[3]
605- **10** *11* **The Varlet**[225] 5703 4-9-7 **72**... SSanders 1 36
(BICase) *prom tl wknd rapidly 2f out* **50/1**

3m 8.11s (3.74) **Going Correction** 0.0s/f (Good) **10** Ran SP% **115.9**
Speed ratings: **89,88,88,87,87 87,84,82,77,71**CSF £27.40 CT £664.33 TOTE £2.30: £1.60, £3.40, £6.70; EX 52.00.
**Owner** George Strawbridge **Bred** L Kessler **Trained** Manton, Wilts

**FOCUS**
Something of a stop/start gallop and a pedestrian winning time for the grade. Muddling form.

**NOTEBOOK**
**Shredded(USA)**, stepping up half a mile in a bid to lose his maiden tag, was always going well, though he had to wait for a gap to appear after turning for home. Once it did, he quickened up well and was then very game as he had several snapping at heels all the way to the line. The slow winning time does put a question mark over the form, but he remains unexposed over this sort of trip.
**Invitation**, a guaranteed stayer, is on a bit of a losing run but this was one of his better recent efforts. He was staying on all the way to the line on ground that would have been plenty fast enough.
**Rome(IRE)**, whose only previous win came in a bumper, has plenty of stamina and it was that which enabled him to get as close as he did. This was only his third race on turf on the Flat and by far his best effort on the surface.
**Mostarsil(USA)** is yet to win beyond 12 furlongs, but he does stay much further and just lacked that vital finishing kick over this trip.
**Tilla** ◆ put up a fine effort after a break of seven months, especially as she did not see much daylight in the home straight. She is one to keep in mind.
**Moon Emperor**, with the visor left off, is not the easiest to predict, but he is freefalling down the handicap and was noted staying on strongly at the line. He would probably have preferred a proper all-round gallop.
**Greenwich Meantime** had every chance against the inside rail starting up the home straight, but then looked an awkward ride over the last couple of furlongs, even for the champion jockey. *Official explanation: jockey said gelding hung badly right-handed in the final 2f.*

## 2632 JUNE MAIDEN STKS 1m 2f 7y
**8:55** (8:58) (D) 3-Y-0 **£5,759** (£1,772; £886; £443) **Stalls** High

Form RPR
24-2 **1** **Buckeye Wonder (USA)**[51] 1382 3-9-0 92... PRobinson 2 86
(MAJarvis) *lw: mde all: hrd pressed fr over 1f out: pushed out and hld on wl nr fin* **8/11**[1]

0-3 **2** *hd* **Golden Island (IRE)**[14] 2243 3-8-9 ........................................ KFallon 3 81
(JWHills) *cl up: chsd wnr 2f out: chal over 1f out: drvn and upsides fnl f: jst hld nr fin* **11/4**[2]

4 **3** *3 ½* **Zangeal**[96] 916 3-9-0 ........................................ JQuinn 1 79
(CFWall) *str: rangy: scope: bit bkwd: h.d.w: t.k.h: hld up towards rr: prog to chal 2f out and ev ch: nt qckn and btn over 1f out* **16/1**

**4** *1 ¾* **Warningcamp (GER)** 3-9-0 ........................................ SSanders 9 76
(LadyHerries) *leggy: bit bkwd: dwlt: hld up: prog to press ldrs 2f out: nt qckn and btn over 1f out* **50/1**

**5** *4* **Qudraat (IRE)** 3-9-0 ........................................ RHills 11 68
(ACStewart) *neat: dwlt: hld up in rr: outpcd over 2f out: shuffled along and kpt on steadily fr over 1f out* **10/1**[3]

6-0 **6** *3 ½* **Blaise Wood (USA)**[16] 2204 3-9-0 ........................................(p) RLMoore 7 61?
(GLMoore) *t.k.h: chsd wnr for 1f: restrained: rdn over 2f out: sn outpcd and btn: fdd* **100/1**

6 **7** *2* **Shazana**[48] 1441 3-8-9 ........................................ MartinDwyer 6 53
(BWHills) *t.k.h: chsd wnr after 1f to 2f out: wknd* **20/1**

6- **8** *½* **Masterman Ready**[220] 5798 3-9-0 ........................................ EAhern 8 57
(PWHarris) *racd in midfield: shkn up and wknd over 2f out* **66/1**

**9** *½* **Encompass (FR)** 3-8-9 ........................................ RHughes 12 51
(HRACecil) *wl-grwn: bit bkwd: trckd ldrs to over 2f out: wknd and eased* **14/1**

**10** *6* **Laugh 'n Cry** 3-8-9 ........................................ DaneO'Neill 5 39
(CACyzer) *bit bkwd: t.k.h early: hld up in last of main gp: wknd over 2f out* **100/1**

0 **11** *3 ½* **Charnwood Pride (IRE)**[10] 2374 3-9-0 ........................................(t) MFenton 10 38
(PWHarris) *chsd ldrs: rdn and wknd 3f out* **100/1**

**12** *nk* **Paint The Lily (IRE)** 3-8-6 ........................................ LisaJones(3) 4 32
(JWHills) *str: s.v.s: a last and bhd* **66/1**

2m 12.27s (2.09) **Going Correction** 0.0s/f (Good) **12 Ran SP% 118.9**
Speed ratings: **91,90,88,86,83 80,79,78,78,73 70,70**CSF £2.62 TOTE £1.90: £1.10, £1.40, £2.60; EX 3.90 Place 6 £139.80, Place 5 £47.62.
**Owner** John W Phillips **Bred** Phillips Racing Partnership **Trained** Newmarket, Suffolk

**FOCUS**
A modest pace and a very moderate winning time for the grade, but a thrilling finish.

**NOTEBOOK**
**Buckeye Wonder(USA)** was given a canny front-running ride, the type Robinson performs so well, but the combination had to dig very deep in order to hold off the persistent runner-up in a dig-dong finish. He still seems to be improving and a handicap mark of 92 looks fair enough.
**Golden Island(IRE)** ◆, stepped up from her reappearance effort over this extra furlong and hardly deserved to lose. She can improve further yet and her turn is merely delayed.
**Zangeal** ran another solid race on this turf debut considering he would have preferred a stronger gallop or longer trip.
**Warningcamp(GER)** ◆, resold for 34,000gns as a yearling, is a half-brother to two winners in Germany. He showed definite signs of ability and should have learnt plenty from this.
**Qudraat(IRE)** ◆, a 230,000gns half-brother to Imoya, was noted staying on nicely at the end and has every chance of starting to pay back his purchase price judged on this effort.
**Blaise Wood(USA)** did not seem to see out this longer trip, but should have a better chance in handicaps rather than contests like this.
**Charnwood Pride(IRE)** *Official explanation: jockey said gelding hung right*
T/Plt: £192.50 to a £1 stake. Pool: £56,412.95. 213.85 winning tickets. T/Qpdt: £28.70 to a £1 stake. Pool: £3,975.10. 102.30 winning tickets. JN

2633 - 2635a (Foreign Racing) - See Raceform Interactive

## 1537 EPSOM (L-H)
### Friday, June 4

**OFFICIAL GOING: Good**
A false rail on the inside of the track extended race distances to such an extent that comparisons with Saturday's times will not be totally accurate.
Wind: lt against Weather: v.overcast, becoming fine

## 2636 VODAFONE TEMPLE STKS (GROUP 2) 5f
**1:45** (1:47) (A) 3-Y-O+ **£63,800** (£24,200; £12,100; £5,500) **Stalls** Far side

Form RPR

00-0 **1** **Night Prospector**[23] 2041 4-9-4 89 ........................................ JPMurtagh 9 106
(JWPayne) *lw: w ldr: rdn to ld 1f out: styd on wl* **33/1**

51-1 **2** *1 ¼* **Autumn Pearl**[32] 1829 3-8-8 93 ........................................ PRobinson 11 98
(MAJarvis) *racd against nr side rail: led to 1f out: one pce u.p* **10/1**

-120 **3** *½* **Bishops Court**[23] 2041 10-9-4 110 ........................................ LDettori 10 100
(MrsJRRamsden) *b: lw: racd against nr side rail: hld up: chsd ldng pair over 1f out: clsng whn nt clr run 100yds out: nt rcvr* **3/1**[1]

3232 **4** *1* **Boston Lodge**[85] 1004 4-9-4 97 ........................................(b) MJKinane 7 96
(GAButler) *lw: pressed ldrs: drvn and outpcd wl over 1f out: kpt on again fnl f* **25/1**

6065 **5** *¾* **Colonel Cotton (IRE)**[6] 2475 5-9-4 103 ........................................(b) DHolland 12 93
(NACallaghan) *racd against nr side rail: hld up in rr: outpcd 2f out: no ch after: styd on fnl f* **9/1**

5-10 **6** *2* **If Paradise**[21] 2080 3-8-11 105 ........................................ RHughes 3 86
(RHannon) *lw: chsd ldrs: rdn 1/2-way: unable qckn over 1f out: hanging rt and fdd fnl f* **12/1**

-000 **7** *1 ¼* **Repertory**[16] 2222 11-9-4 105 ........................................ TGMcLaughlin 4 82
(MSSaunders) *w ldrs to 1/2-way: sn u.p and lost pl* **14/1**

-000 **8** *1* **Dubaian Gift**[16] 2222 5-9-4 103 ........................................ MartinDwyer 6 78
(AMBalding) *b: lw: s.s: sn rcvrd to press ldrs: wknd u.p over 1f out* **14/1**

0-23 **9** *1* **Speed Cop**[38] 1685 4-9-1 99 ........................................ KDarley 5 71
(AMBalding) *b.hind: s.s: sn chsd ldrs: nt clr run over 2f out: hrd rdn and wknd over 1f out* **8/1**[3]

1-60 **10** *4* **Incise**[30] 1883 3-8-8 90 ........................................ KFallon 1 57
(BJMeehan) *s.s: rcvrd to chse ldrs on outer after 2f: hung lft fr wl over 1f out: wknd* **33/1**

4200 **11** *5* **Dragon Flyer (IRE)**[23] 2041 5-9-1 98 ........................................ SDrowne 2 39
(MQuinn) *s.v.s: a wl bhd* **16/1**

1312 **L** **Forever Phoenix**[20] 2117 4-9-1 92 ........................................ EAhern 8 —
(RMHCowell) *lw: facing wrong way s: tk no part* **9/2**[2]

56.10 secs (0.42) **Going Correction** +0.225s/f (Good)
**WFA** 3 from 4yo+ 7lb **12 Ran SP% 110.0**
Speed ratings: **105,103,102,100,99 96,94,92,91,84 76,—**CSF £308.20 TOTE £54.00: £10.10, £2.20, £1.80; EX 338.20 Trifecta £1081.10 Part won. Pool: £1,522.70 - 0.80 winning units..
**Owner** C Cotran **Bred** Miss S N Ralphs **Trained** Newmarket, Suffolk
■ This race, previously run at Sandown Park, was started from the old tape start due to a stalls handlers' dispute.

**FOCUS**
The transfer from Sandown had a decidedly negative effect on the quality of the field assembled for this Group Two, and the ragged flip start, attributed partly to communication difficulties caused by the BBC's helicopter hovering overhead, renders the form suspect. The draw positions are largely irrelevant and the race was hand timed.

**NOTEBOOK**
**Night Prospector**, a useful handicapper at best before this, got the run of the race and kept on well to cause a major surprise in this Group Two. This was a sub-standard renewal, but that will not bother connections. However, he may struggle in future if the Handicapper takes this form at face value.
**Autumn Pearl**, who scored over six furlongs on heavy ground last time, was another to get the run of the race and kept going against the near-side rail once headed. She is progressive and looks capable of winning a Pattern event.
**Bishops Court**, who has generally run well on this track over the years, did so again, but had to switch off the nearside rail to try to deliver a challenge and never looked like making it. He will be winning again soon, and presumably the City Wall Stakes at Chester in July, which he has won for the last two seasons, will be on the agenda.
**Boston Lodge**, who had a rewarding time in Dubai earlier in the year, was taking a big drop in trip on this return to turf and did well to finish so close. A return to a longer trip will suit him and he should be able to pick up a conditions race.
**Colonel Cotton(IRE)**, a hold-up horse, had the favoured rail draw but the way the race panned out did not suit his style of running. Also he still looks high in the weights following a couple of improved efforts last backend.
**If Paradise** did not look at home on the track and ran well in the circumstances.
**Repertory**, not helped by his draw or the flip start, was unable to dominate. This can be forgiven.
**Dubaian Gift**, another front-runner, missed the break. This can be ignored.
**Speed Cop**, like her stable companion, lost her chance at the start.
**Incise** missed the break and looked ill at ease on the track, tending to hang down the slope.
**Dragon Flyer(IRE)** was totally caught out when the tapes went up and had no chance from that point.
**Forever Phoenix**, who was well backed, was facing the wrong way when the tapes went up and was left. She did not expend any energy from that point, and so connections may be able to find an early opportunity for compensation.

## 2637 VODAFONE MILE (H'CAP) 1m 114y
**2:15** (2:17) (B) (0-105,94) 3-Y-O+ **£23,200** (£8,800; £4,400; £2,000) **Stalls** Low

Form RPR

0001 **1** **Uhoomagoo**[6] 2469 6-9-1 85 5ex ........................................(b) NCallan 8 99
(KARyan) *lw: hld up: 11th st: rdn 3f out: gd prog on wd outside 2f out : led last 150yds: sn clr* **7/1**[3]

-056 **2** *3* **Alrafid (IRE)**[17] 2201 5-9-1 85 ........................................ RLMoore 11 93
(GLMoore) *hld up: 9th st: prog on outer over 2f out: rdn to chal 1f out: outpcd by wnr* **7/1**[3]

565- **3** *1 ½* **Definite Guest (IRE)**[250] 5252 6-8-12 82 ........................................ PHanagan 7 87+
(RAFahey) *trckd ldrs: 6th st: n.m.r 3f out to over 2f out: styd on fr over 1f out to take 3rd nr fin* **20/1**

0013 **4** *¾* **Sawwaah (IRE)**[11] 2366 7-8-12 82 ........................................ JFanning 3 85
(DNicholls) *cl up: 4th st: prog to ld over 1f out and edgd lft: hdd & wknd last 150yds* **12/1**

0023 **5** *nk* **Dumaran (IRE)**[22] 2066 6-9-8 92 ........................................(v) KFallon 9 95+
(WJMusson) *lw: s.s: racd in last and nt gng wl: drvn and hanging lft in st: no prog tl styd on ins fnl f* **5/1**[1]

-002 **6** *nk* **Impeller (IRE)**[4] 2534 5-9-3 87 ........................................ SDrowne 5 89
(WRMuir) *restless stalls: wl in tch: 7th st: effrt over 2f out: nt qckn over 1f out: one pce after* **13/2**[2]

-000 **7** *nk* **Convent Girl (IRE)**[4] 2534 4-9-10 94 ........................................ RHavlin 6 95
(MrsPNDutfield) *restless stalls: dwlt: hld up in rr: 10th st: nt clr run 3f out: effrt 2f out: one pce after* **33/1**

3-30 **8** *hd* **Mysterinch**[34] 1762 4-9-8 92 ........................................ JFEgan 10 93
(JeddO'Keeffe) *prom: chsd ldr 1/2-way: rdn to ld over 2f out and edgd lft : hdd and sltly hmpd over 1f out: n.d after* **25/1**

6003 **9** *½* **Jay Gee's Choice**[6] 2469 4-8-13 86 ........................................ SHitchcott(3) 2 86
(MRChannon) *lw: led to 4f out: 3rd and losing pl st: struggling over 2f out: one pce after* **7/1**[3]

223/ **10** *1* **Ocean Of Storms (IRE)**[50] 9-8-10 80 ........................................(t) MartinDwyer 1 78
(ChristianWroe, UAE) *racd in midfield: 8th st: sn lost pl and in rr: no imp ldrs after* **25/1**

0113 **11** *1* **Voice Mail**[8] 2430 5-8-5 78 ........................................ LPKeniry(3) 13 74
(AMBalding) *swtg: dwlt: hld up: 12th st: rdn 3f out: no prog* **16/1**

0014 **12** *shd* **Blue Trojan (IRE)**[4] 2534 4-9-0 84 ........................................ FNorton 4 80
(SKirk) *prom: 5th and losing pl st: struggling fnl 3f* **10/1**

-004 **13** *shd* **Irony (IRE)**[17] 2196 5-9-2 86 ........................................ KDarley 12 81
(AMBalding) *b: pressed ldr: led 4f out: rdn and hdd over 2f out and sltly hmpd: n.d after: eased ins fnl f* **10/1**

1m 44.3s (-1.44) **Going Correction** +0.075s/f (Good) **13 Ran SP% 114.7**
Speed ratings: **109,106,105,104,104 103,103,103,102,102 101,101,100**CSF £50.21 CT £932.65 TOTE £7.70: £3.00, £2.20, £5.70; EX 53.10 Trifecta £1314.70 Part won. Pool: £1,851.80 - 0.40 winning units..
**Owner** J Duddy & T Fawcett **Bred** C R Mason And Mrs N T Pope **Trained** Hambleton, N Yorks
■ Due to an equiopment failure, this race was hand timed and the placings and distances were judged by eye.

**FOCUS**
A competitive 0-105 handicap, even though the top weight was rated just 94. It was run at a sound pace and the principals came from the rear, while those that forced it finished well behind.

**NOTEBOOK**
**Uhoomagoo**, who has always looked better at seven furlongs than this trip in the past, followed up his good win at Doncaster. He again got the fast gallop he requires, and powered down the centre of the track to win going away and record a career-best RPR. He is in blinding form and the Hunt Cup could be next, although he may struggle to make the cut, even with a penalty for this.
**Alrafid(IRE)** ◆ is running well at present and posted another fine effort despite having no chance with the winner. He stays a mile and a quarter but is well suited by nine furlongs, and is one to bear in mind for a race at Goodwood, where he has performed well in the past.
**Definite Guest(IRE)** ◆, having his first run since the autumn, gave the impression this outing will put an edge on him. He will be more at home on a conventional track, and having scored twice in eight days in July last season, may have those races on the agenda again.
**Sawwaah(IRE)** ◆ has found his form of late and, despite being raised 4lb, again performed with credit on this step up in grade. He did best of those that raced up with the pace and can score again at a slightly lower level.
**Dumaran(IRE)**, who won this race on much softer ground two years ago, had the visor back on but lost his chance with a slow start. He hung on the track and did well to finish as close as he did. He can be forgiven this. *Official explanation: jockey said gelding was left in the stalls and hung left in the home straight*
**Impeller(IRE)** was unsettled by the antics of Convent Girl in the adjacent stall and then might have seen a bit too much daylight on the outside. Ultimately, however, he failed to find the necessary change of gear. *Official explanation: jockey said gelding was upset in the stalls and unbalanced in the race.*

**Convent Girl(IRE)** played up in the stalls and was slowly away, so put up a fair effort in the circumstances.

## 2638 VODAFONE ROSE BOWL (H'CAP) 1m 2f 18y
**2:50** (2:52) (B) 4-Y-0+ **£23,200** (£8,800; £4,400; £2,000) **Stalls Low**

Form RPR

0-44 **1** **Persian Lightning (IRE)**$^{16}$ 2220 5-9-2 **102** MJKinane 1 113
(JLDunlop) *settled off the pce: 4th and prog st: led wl over 1f out and sn rdn clr: eased nr fin: jst hld on* **11/2$^{3}$**

61-0 **2** *hd* **Desert Quest (IRE)**$^{21}$ 2076 4-8-3 **89** (b$^{1}$) MartinDwyer 3 100
(AMBalding) *hld up: last and wl bhd st: hanging lft and rdn after: gd prog fr 2f out: clsd on wnr fnl f: jst failed* **20/1**

0-32 **3** *2* **Shahzan House (IRE)**$^{22}$ 2066 5-8-10 **96** (p) PRobinson 7 103
(MAJarvis) *chsd clr ldrs: 3rd and prog st: led over 2f out to wl over 1f out: one pce after* **9/2$^{1}$**

10-3 **4** *1 3/4* **Counsel's Opinion (IRE)**$^{55}$ 1328 7-9-4 **104** SSanders 8 108
(CFWall) *lw: dwlt: hld up in rr: 8th st: rdn and effrt over 2f out: kpt on fr over 1f out: nvr able to chal* **11/2$^{3}$**

5032 **5** *1 1/2* **Compton Bolter (IRE)**$^{15}$ 2241 7-9-10 **110** RHughes 11 111
(GAButler) *hld up off the pce: 9th st: nt clr run briefly 3f out: prog over 2f out: btn whn sltly hmpd over 1f out* **8/1**

-414 **6** *1/2* **Blythe Knight (IRE)**$^{34}$ 1762 4-9-3 **103** LDettori 6 103+
(EALDunlop) *settled off the pce: 7th st: bdly hmpd 3f out: effrt over 2f out: swtchd rt over 1f out: kpt on same pce* **5/1$^{2}$**

0-45 **7** *1 1/4* **Danelor (IRE)**$^{70}$ 1114 6-8-0 **86** PHanagan 5 84
(RAFahey) *chsd ldng pair: wnt 2nd over 4f out and led ent st: hdd over 2f out: fdd* **5/1$^{2}$**

0002 **8** *5* **St Pancras (IRE)**$^{5}$ 2504 4-7-7 **84** (b$^{1}$) DFox$^{(5)}$ 9 73
(NACallaghan) *s.i.s and reminders: sn chsd ldrs: 5th st: swtchd sharply lft 3f out: wknd over 2f out* **14/1**

0-01 **9** *nk* **Guilded Flyer**$^{29}$ 1903 5-8-1 **87** JFEgan 10 76
(WSKittow) *led at breakneck pce: hdd ent st: sn btn* **16/1**

/000 **10** *28* **Sir George Turner**$^{4}$ 2527 5-9-0 **100** JFanning 4 38
(MJohnston) *a in rr: rdn over 5f out: 10th st: wknd: t.o* **33/1**

0-00 **11** *1 1/2* **Rocket Force (USA)**$^{34}$ 1767 4-8-11 **97** (v$^{1}$) KFallon 2 32
(EALDunlop) *lw: pressed ldr at furious pce to over 4f out: 6th and wkng st: hmpd 3f out: t.o* **50/1**

2m 6.36s (-2.34) **Going Correction** +0.075s/f (Good) **11 Ran SP% 115.6**
Speed ratings: **112,111,110,108,107 107,106,102,102,79 78**CSF £109.78 CT £536.31 TOTE £6.20: £2.10, £3.90, £2.00; EX 102.70 Trifecta £902.30 Pool: £2,287.60 - 1.80 winning units.
**Owner** Windflower Overseas Holdings Inc **Bred** Windflower Overseas **Trained** Arundel, W Sussex
■ Stewards Enquiry : D Fox nine-day ban: careless riding (Jun 15-23)

**FOCUS**
Another competitive affair, run at a fast pace. This is classy handicap form, and the winner scored more easily than the margin suggests.

**NOTEBOOK**
**Persian Lightning(IRE)**, who had finished behind two subsequent Group winners in his two runs this season, will now go to Royal Ascot for the Listed handicap in which he was touched off last year.
**Desert Quest(IRE)** ◆, a relatively lightly-raced individual, was fitted with blinkers instead of a visor and appreciated the return to a sound surface. However, he looked ill at ease on the track until picking up so well once meeting the rising ground that he nearly stole the race. He looks one to keep in mind for a good handicap back on a flat track.
**Shahzan House(IRE)**, with cheekpieces on for the first time, acts well on this track but was not good enough, having had every chance. He is creeping up the weights without winning and, although very able, will be difficult to place off this sort of mark. *Official explanation: jockey said horse was unsuited by today's good ground.*
**Counsel's Opinion(IRE)**, running off a career-high mark, put up another good performance without ever looking likely to win. He is genuine and consistent, but probably needs a stiffer track at this trip nowadays, and Royal Ascot offers more than one option for him.
**Compton Bolter(IRE)**, whose stable has been in the doldrums, gave a clear indication last time that he is on the way back, and did well to finish so close having not had the best of luck in running. He may renew rivalry with several of these at Royal Ascot.
**Blythe Knight(IRE)**, who won the City and Suburban on his only previous appearance on the track, acts on this ground but was murdered by the errant St Pancras early in the straight and had no chance thereafter. This effort can be ignored.
**Danelor(IRE)**, runner-up in this last year, has been lighly raced since and possibly needed this first outing for ten weeks. It will have put an edge on him for another tilt at next month's the John Smith's Cup.
**St Pancras(IRE)**overcame a slow start to be on the heels of the leaders turning in. However, his rider then switched inside as the winner pulled out in front of him, causing considerable interference to three of his rivals and earning Fox a nine-day ban.

## 2639 VODAFONE CORONATION CUP (GROUP 1) 1m 4f 10y
**3:30** (3:31) (A) 4-Y-0+ **£145,000** (£55,000; £27,500; £12,500) **Stalls Centre**

Form RPR

3-53 **1** **Warrsan (IRE)**$^{33}$ 1792 6-9-0 117 DHolland 5 124
(CEBrittain) *lw: prom: lost pl 1/2-way and pushed along: 7th st: plld wd and drvn over 2f out: prog to ld jst over 1f out: styd on wl* **7/1**

124- **2** *1 3/4* **Doyen (IRE)**$^{243}$ 5406 4-9-0 121 LDettori 1 121+
(SaeedBinSuroor) *lw: lengthy: settled in midfield: 6th st: effrt whn nt clr run over 2f out and wl over 1f out: rdn to chse wnr last 100yds:* **9/2$^{2}$**

11-4 **3** *shd* **Vallee Enchantee (IRE)**$^{33}$ 1804 4-8-11 DBoeuf 3 121+
(ELellouche, France) *lw: leggy: settled in rr: 8th st: effrt over 2f out: hmpd wl over 1f out: r.o fnl f: nrst fin* **6/1$^{3}$**

212- **4** *shd* **High Accolade**$^{223}$ 5752 4-9-0 116 MartinDwyer 11 121
(MPTregoning) *mostly chsd ldr: drvn to ld jst over 2f out: hdd jst over 1f out: kpt on u.p* **4/1$^{1}$**

3-15 **5** *1 1/2* **Brian Boru**$^{32}$ 1849 4-9-0 (t) JPSpencer 10 119
(APO'Brien, Ire) *swtg: hld up in rr: 9th st: effrt on outer over 2f out: one pce and nvr rchd ldrs* **9/1**

022- **6** *1* **Magistretti (USA)**$^{290}$ 4269 4-9-0 121 JPMurtagh 12 117
(NACallaghan) *sn trckd ldrs: 4th st: rdn and outpcd over 2f out: n.d after: kpt on nr fin* **7/1**

3133 **7** *shd* **Scott's View**$^{5}$ 2508 5-9-0 115 KFallon 4 117
(MJohnston) *prom: rdn over 4f out: 3rd st: led 3f out to jst over 2f out : fdd fnl f* **10/1**

3-14 **8** *1/2* **Dubai Success**$^{33}$ 1792 4-9-0 113 MHills 8 116
(BWHills) *lw: trckd ldrs: 5th st: rdn over 2f out: hanging and nt qckn: wknd fnl f* **25/1**

0-36 **9** *3* **Imperial Dancer**$^{19}$ 2156 6-9-0 117 TEDurcan 6 112
(MRChannon) *lw: hld up in rr: 10th st: sn rdn and no prog* **11/1**

-321 **10** *1 1/4* **Systematic**$^{28}$ 1925 5-9-0 113 KDarley 9 110
(MJohnston) *lw: led at mod pce: kicked on 5f out: hdd 3f out: wkng whn n.m.r 2f out* **10/1**

/00- **11** *6* **Sunny Glenn**$^{195}$ 6051 6-9-0 78 RHavlin 2 101?
(MrsPNDutfield) *dwlt: a last: lost tch 3f out* **100/1**

2m 35.96s (-2.76) **Going Correction** +0.075s/f (Good) **11 Ran SP% 118.8**
Speed ratings: **112,110,110,110,109 109,108,108,106,105 101**CSF £38.96 TOTE £9.60: £2.90, £2.40, £2.40; EX 51.30 Trifecta £224.50 Pool: £4,143.44 - 13.10 winning units.
**Owner** Saeed Manana **Bred** Saeed Manana **Trained** Newmarket, Suffolk
■ Warrsan became only the fifth horse to win this Group One twice.

**FOCUS**
A decent renewal of a Group One that frequently attracts just a handful of runners, although the pace was steady and the time unexceptional for the grade.

**NOTEBOOK**
**Warrsan(IRE)** completed a rare double and improved again on the form he showed 12 months previously, overcoming difficulties in the process. Unable to make the running with Systematic in the field, he looked in trouble when losing his place at the top of the hill. However, he responded well to his rider's urgings, and came with a strong run down the centre of the track to win decisively. He is admirably tough and genuine and a good yardstick to the merits of the young pretenders.
**Doyen(IRE)**, last year's Arc fourth and making his debut for Godolphin, put up a fine effort, as he was denied an opening at a crucial stage. He is entered at Royal Ascot, but may well be at his best with some cut in the ground in the autumn. In the meantime a race like next month's Grand Prix de Saint-Cloud may suit him.
**Vallee Enchantee(IRE)** ◆, as in the Ganay, got into all sorts of trouble in running and was finishing best of all. Her owner was unequivocal in his criticism of the jockey, whom he insists will not be allowed to ride the filly again. He was clearly at fault, in that he failed to take the gaps when they presented themselves, and she would have been a clear second at least had he done so. Compensation awaits.
**High Accolade** ◆, backed down to favourite on this seasonal reappearance, put up a brave show and was just run out of the placings. He was quirky last year but looks to have matured over the winter, as he did nothing wrong on this occasion. He is two from two over the mile and a half at Ascot, and the Hardwicke and King George look obvious targets.
**Brian Boru**, who had a nightmare in the Derby last year, handled the track better this time but still gives the impression that he is much more effective with cut in the ground.
**Magistretti(USA)** had not run since York last August, but looked quite fit and ran a fair race over a trip that may be beyons his best. Presumably the Juddmonte will again be his principal summer target.
**Scott's View**, who has been globetrotting this spring, ran his race but is not quite up to this class.

## 2640 VODAFONE OAKS (GROUP 1) (FILLIES) 1m 4f 10y
**4:10** (4:10) (A) 3-Y-O **£203,000** (£77,000; £38,500; £17,500) **Stalls Centre**

Form RPR

13-1 **1** **Ouija Board**$^{33}$ 1793 3-9-0 110 KFallon 3 124
(EALDunlop) *dwlt: racd in 6th tl 4th and prog st: led over 2f out: shkn up and surged clr fr over 1f out* **7/2**

1 **2** *7* **All Too Beautiful (IRE)**$^{41}$ 1634 3-9-0 JPSpencer 6 113
(APO'Brien, Ire) *rangy: lw: hld up: prog and 3rd st: led 3f out: rdn and hdd over 2f out: wandered w hd in air and no ch w wnr after* **11/4$^{1}$**

13-1 **3** *3 1/2* **Punctilious**$^{24}$ 2020 3-9-0 110 (t) LDettori 2 108
(SaeedBinSuroor) *lw: racd in 3rd tl led 7f out: rdn and hdd 3f out: sn btn: fin tired* **10/3$^{3}$**

0-06 **4** *1 1/2* **Necklace**$^{12}$ 2330 3-9-0 JPMurtagh 5 105
(APO'Brien, Ire) *hld up in last: wnt 6th st: sn outpcd and btn* **10/1**

0-21 **5** *18* **Crystal (IRE)**$^{39}$ 1674 3-9-0 93 MHills 7 76
(BJMeehan) *lw: racd in 4th tl chsd ldr over 4f out: upsides ent st: sn wknd rapidly: t.o* **25/1**

12-2 **6** *4* **Sundrop (JPN)**$^{33}$ 1791 3-9-0 117 KMcEvoy 4 70
(SaeedBinSuroor) *racd freely early: trckd ldr to 7f out: 5th and losing pl st : rdn and hung bdly rt 3f out: t.o* **3/1$^{2}$**

50 **7** *dist* **Kisses For Me (IRE)**$^{12}$ 2330 3-9-0 PJScallan 1 —
(APO'Brien, Ire) *tall: lengthy: led to 7f out: last and wkng st: t.o* **66/1**

2m 35.41s (-3.31) **Going Correction** +0.075s/f (Good) **7 Ran SP% 111.4**
Speed ratings: **114,109,107,106,94 91**,—CSF £12.82 TOTE £4.20: £2.40, £1.90; EX 15.50.
**Owner** Lord Derby **Bred** Stanley Estate And Stud Co **Trained** Newmarket, Suffolk
■ Joint-smallest field since Pretty Polly won in 1904, and success for Lord Derby, whose ancestor owned the first Oaks winner.

**FOCUS**
A small field for this Classic, but the time was good - 0.55sec faster than the preceding Coronation Cup - and Ouija Board put up an outstanding performance in surging impressively clear.

**NOTEBOOK**
**Ouija Board** followed up her easy victory in the Pretty Polly with an even more impressive success in this Classic, dispelling all doubts about her ability to stay. She has provisionally been rated the best Oaks winner of the last decade, her RPR a pound higher than that recorded by Ramruna in 1999, and unless something extra special emerges from the continent she should be able to mop up a series of fillies' Group Ones this summer.
**All Too Beautiful(IRE)**, a full-sister to Derby winner Galileo, came into this with little experience but travelled really well in the race and looked the winner early in the straight. However, she had no answer when the winner swept past, and will need to avoid that rival if she is to pick up a Group One.
**Punctilious**, who won an ordinary Musidora last time, had every chance in the race but appeared outclassed by the first two and did not get home. She ran a little below her York form and will be better back on a more conventional track at around ten furlongs.
**Necklace** showed something of a return to form without ever looking likely to win. A drop in class might help her regain the winning thread, although it will not be easy with her Group One penalty.
**Crystal(IRE)**, taking a big step up in class, was out of her depth. *Official explanation: trainer said filly finished dehydrated and tied up.*
**Sundrop(JPN)**, runner-up in the 1000 Guineas, failed to settle on this step up in trip and was beaten before stamina really became an issue. She then wandered all over the track in the straight. This was not her true running, but a drop back in trip looks likely. *Official explanation: vet said filly had been struck into.*

## 2641 PRINCESS ELIZABETH STKS (SPONSORED BY VODAFONE) (GROUP 3) (F&M) 1m 114y
**4:50** (4:50) (A) 3-Y-O+ **£29,000** (£11,000; £5,500; £2,500) **Stalls Low**

Form RPR

0121 **1** **Gonfilia (GER)**$^{15}$ 2242 4-9-6 102 (t) LDettori 10 104
(SaeedBinSuroor) *lw: mde all: drew clr fr 2f out: comf* **11/10$^{1}$**

52-6 **2** *2 1/2* **Kunda (IRE)**$^{18}$ 2193 3-8-8 96 RHughes 1 99
(RHannon) *b.hind: trckd ldng pair: rdn to chse wnr over 2f out: kpt on but no imp* **20/1**

0-05 **3** *1* **Qasirah (IRE)**$^{30}$ 1879 3-8-8 98 (b) PRobinson 5 97
(MAJarvis) *trckd ldrs: 4th st: effrt over 2f out: chsd ldng pair 1f out: kpt on same pce* **20/1**

11-0 **4** *3/4* **Top Romance (IRE)**$^{51}$ 1398 3-8-8 102 KFallon 7 95
(SirMichaelStoute) *hld up: n.m.r 6f out and lost pl: 7th st: rdn 3f out: hanging lft but kpt on fr over 1f out* **13/2$^{3}$**

1 **5** *3* **Blue Oasis (IRE)**$^{27}$ 1972 3-8-8 77 KDarley 6 89
(RGuest) *dwlt: hld up: 6th st: rdn and no prog wl over 2f out* **20/1**

6 shd **Tizdubai (USA)**[300] 3-8-8 ....................(t) KMcEvoy 8 89
(SaeedBinSuroor) *trckd wnr to over 2f out: shuffled along and edgd rt sn after: fdd over 1f out: eased nr fin* **8/1**

122 7 2 **Glen Innes (IRE)**[24] 2020 3-8-8 101.................... DHolland 2 84
(DRLoder) *hld up in last: rdn and effrt on outer over 2f out: sn no prog: wknd over 1f out* **11/2**[2]

-411 8 6 **Imperialistic (IRE)**[43] 1558 3-8-8 94..................(p) DarrenWilliams 4 72
(KRBurke) *racd in midfield: 5th st: hanging lft and wknd over 2f out* **7/1**

1m 45.61s (-0.13) **Going Correction** +0.075s/f (Good)
**WFA** 3 from 4yo 12lb **8** Ran SP% **114.2**
Speed ratings: **103,100,99,99,96 96,94,89**CSF £29.33 TOTE £2.10: £1.20, £3.20, £4.20; EX 22.00.
**Owner** Godolphin **Bred** Gestut Auenquelle **Trained** Newmarket, Suffolk

**FOCUS**
An ordinary-looking Listed contest run at a modest pace. Gonfilia comfortably outclassed some relatively exposed younger rivals.

**NOTEBOOK**
**Gonfilia(GER)**, who is well suited by making the running, was allowed an uncontested lead and Dettori was able to dictate the pace to suit himself. He opened up a gap halfway up the straight and the filly never looked like being caught. She is a useful tool at around this trip and in this grade, and she may be able to pick up a Group race before the season is out.
**Kunda(IRE)**, a consistent juvenile last season, proved she had trained on, although no match for the winner. She got the trip well enough, but a race like the Oak Tree Stakes at Goodwood in July over seven furlongs might suit her better. *Official explanation: jockey said filly had hung left.*
**Qasirah(IRE)**, dropping back in trip, seemed to run her race but may be worth a try at ten furlongs with the blinkers left off. *Official explanation: jockey said filly was unsuited by the track.*
**Top Romance(IRE)**, who ran in the Nell Gwyn last time, could not confirm those placings with Qasirah but seemed not to handle the track.
**Blue Oasis(IRE)** was taking a big step up in class after her debut win in a maiden and showed improved form.
**Tizdubai(USA)** won both of her races at two in the States, one of them at Grade Two level, but they were on dirt and over shorter distances. This was an inauspicious turf debut, but it is too early to dismiss her.
**Glen Innes(IRE)**, runner-up in the Musidora last time, looked to have a major chance on this drop in grade but, having been held up, was never in contention. She may not have handled the track and is better than this effort suggests. *Official explanation: jockey said filly had hung left.*
**Imperialistic(IRE)**, taking a step up in grade and on faster ground than for her two recent wins, appeared not to handle the track and can be given another chance under more suitable conditions.

## 2642 VODAFONE GROUP SERVICES H'CAP 7f
**5:25** (5:25) (C ) (0-100,100) 3-Y-O **£23,200** (£8,800; £4,400; £2,000) **Stalls** Low

Form RPR

3402 1 **Makfool (FR)**[13] 2295 3-9-0 93.................... TEDurcan 8 103
(MRChannon) *prom: chsd ldr 4f out: rdn to ld 2f out: in command fnl f: drvn out* **9/1**[3]

20-4 2 ¾ **Mandobi (IRE)**[20] 2115 3-8-13 92.................... KFallon 14 100+
(ACStewart) *lw: dwlt: wl in rr: 15th st: rdn and prog on outer fr 3f out: drvn to chse wnr ins fnl f: no imp* **14/1**

-100 3 nk **Fancy Foxtrot**[17] 2202 3-8-8 87.................... MJKinane 11 94
(BJMeehan) *lw: dwlt: plld hrd and hld up: 16th st: gd prog on wd outside over 2f out: kpt on wl fnl f* **40/1**

0U50 4 hd **Mister Saif (USA)**[3] 2557 3-8-6 85.................... PDobbs 4 91
(RHannon) *lw: racd in midfield: 9th st: nt clr run briefly 3f out: prog 2f out: styd on same pce fnl f* **20/1**

1602 5 2 ½ **Free Trip**[10] 2378 3-8-4 83.................... RHavlin 13 83
(JHMGosden) *lw: prom: 4th st: rdn and effrt over 2f out: disp 2nd pl 1f out: wknd ins fnl f* **14/1**

0-50 6 ¾ **Desert Dreamer (IRE)**[17] 2202 3-8-13 92.................... MHills 15 90
(BWHills) *lw: hld up: 12th st: stdy prog on outer over 2f out: chsd ldrs over 1f out: shkn up and fdd fnl f* **8/1**[2]

-001 7 hd **Flip Flop And Fly (IRE)**[10] 2378 3-8-5 84 5ex.................... JFEgan 10 82
(SKirk) *racd in midfield: 10th st: drvn over 2f out: hanging lft after: kpt on one pce* **8/1**[2]

0300 8 1 **Parkview Love (USA)**[13] 2295 3-9-7 100.................... JFanning 12 95
(MJohnston) *chsd ldrs: 7th st: hrd rdn over 2f out: no imp* **25/1**

216 9 1 **Cello**[29] 1900 3-8-3 82.................... RLMoore 5 74
(RHannon) *dwlt: settled in rr: 13th st: effrt on inner and nt clr run briefly over 2f out: one pce after* **12/1**

-000 10 ¾ **Spanish Ace**[13] 2295 3-8-13 92....................(v[1]) MartinDwyer 6 82
(AMBalding) *lw: b: racd freely: led to 2f out: wknd rapidly fnl f* **16/1**

-313 11 nk **Taruskin (IRE)**[33] 1797 3-8-7 86.................... FNorton 9 76
(NACallaghan) *dwlt: wl in rr: 14th and rdn st: nvr a factor* **10/1**

-140 12 shd **Bettalatethannever (IRE)**[50] 1408 3-8-13 92.................... DaneO'Neill 16 81
(SDow) *lw: racd in last and pushed along over 4f out: rdn and effrt 3f out: no real prog* **16/1**

-000 13 1 ½ **Overdrawn (IRE)**[13] 2295 3-8-11 90.................... SWKelly 2 75
(JAOsborne) *racd in midfield: 11th st: hanging lft and no prog over 2f out* **20/1**

4-60 14 nk **Iskander**[24] 2019 3-8-8 87.................... NCallan 7 72
(KARyan) *chsd ldrs: 6th st: rdn and losing pl whn n.m.r 2f out* **40/1**

04-5 15 6 **Botanical (USA)**[21] 2080 3-9-5 98....................(t) LDettori 17 67
(SaeedBinSuroor) *lw: trckd ldrs: 8th st: gng wl enough over 2f out: sn wknd: eased fnl f* **16/1**

1301 16 2 **Secret Place**[16] 2224 3-8-11 90.................... EAhern 3 54
(EALDunlop) *trckd ldrs: 5th st: rdn and effrt 3f out: wknd 2f out: eased* **5/2**[1]

21-0 17 ½ **First Candlelight**[37] 1704 3-8-6 85.................... MFenton 1 48
(JGGiven) *chsd ldr to 4f out: 3rd st: sn wknd* **25/1**

1m 23.39s (-0.56) **Going Correction** +0.075s/f (Good) **17** Ran SP% **130.7**
Speed ratings: **106,105,104,104,101 100,100,99,98,97 97,97,95,94,88 85,85**CSF £125.97 CT £4803.94 TOTE £8.90: £2.30, £3.50, £7.20, £4.80; EX 47.40 Place 6 £132.46, Place 5 £51.58.
**Owner** Sheikh Ahmed Al Maktoum **Bred** Darley Stud Management **Trained** West Ilsley, Berks

**FOCUS**
A competitive handicap run at a fair pace. Decent form.

**NOTEBOOK**
**Makfool(FR)**, who ran well against stable companion Gatwick last time, was given a positive ride on this drop in trip and had enough in reserve to hold on for a deserved victory. This was improved form, but he will not find things easy from his new mark.
**Mandobi(IRE)** ◆, trying his longest trip to date and moderately drawn, missed the break and came from well back to be closest at the finish. He looks capable of finding a similar race and is one to bear in mind.
**Fancy Foxtrot** ran his best race on turf this season, like the runner-up having to come from the back of the field. He is dropping to a more suitable mark.
**Mister Saif(USA)** is fairly exposed but seemed to appreciate this return to a sounder surface. This was his best race yet.
**Free Trip**, again given a positive ride, reversed recent running with Flip Flop And Fly on 5lb better terms.
**Desert Dreamer(IRE)**, dropped in trip, did not appear to get home and has something to prove.
**Flip Flop And Fly(IRE)**, who beat today's fifth last time, could not confirm that form under a penalty but did not look happy on the track.
**Botanical(USA)** *Official explanation: jockey said colt lost its action.*
**Secret Place**, an easy winner last time, seemed to have his chance but dropped away and was eased as if he had a problem. *Official explanation: trainer said gelding ran flat and was unsuited by the track.*
**First Candlelight** *Official explanation: jockey said filly was unsuited by the track.*
T/Jkpt: Not won. T/Plt: £165.10 to a £1 stake. Pool: £138,464.80. 611.90 winning tickets. T/Qpdt: £24.40 to a £1 stake. Pool: £8,096.00. 244.90 winning tickets. JN

# 2395 GOODWOOD (R-H)
Friday, June 4

**OFFICIAL GOING: Good to firm**

## 2643 ELM FARM RESEARCH CENTRE STKS (H'CAP) (FOR AMATEUR RIDERS) 1m 1f
**6:20** (6:26) (F ) (0-70,69) 3-Y-O+ **£3,838** (£1,181; £590; £295) **Stalls** Far side

Form RPR

0020 1 **Gran Clicquot**[12] 2324 9-9-4 45.................... MrJPemberton(7) 9 53
(GPEnright) *trckd ldrs: pressed ldr ins fnl 2f: kpt on grimly to ld cl home* **14/1**

1220 2 hd **Best Before (IRE)**[16] 2226 4-11-0 65.................... MissEFolkes(3) 4 73
(PDEvans) *led: rdn over 1f out: kpt on: hdd cl home* **10/1**

-606 3 1 ½ **Liberty Royal**[44] 1542 5-11-2 64....................(p) MrSWalker 14 69
(PJMakin) *mid-div: hdwy 5f out: ev ch appr fnl f: wknd ins* **7/1**

2513 4 1 ¾ **Bank On Him**[10] 2381 9-9-11 50.................... MrJJones(5) 12 51
(GLMoore) *mid-div: hdwy over 2f out: kpt on one pce fnl f* **7/2**[1]

2620 5 1 ¼ **Paso Doble**[10] 2381 6-10-2 57.................... MrJMillman(7) 15 56
(BRMillman) *hld up: swtchd rt and hdwy over 2f out: nvr pce to chal* **20/1**

0-65 6 shd **Rainstorm**[14] 2262 9-9-7 44.................... MrsSOwen(3) 13 42
(WMBrisbourne) *mid-div: hdwy over 2f out: wknd fnl f* **7/1**

6010 7 2 ½ **Tarkwa**[11] 2348 5-9-10 44.................... MrGArizkorreta 2 37
(RMHCowell) *mid-div: rdn over 2f out: one pce after* **16/1**

3313 8 1 ½ **Parnassian**[14] 2279 4-10-4 59.................... MissJHannaford(7) 6 49
(GBBalding) *a towards rr* **6/1**[3]

00-0 9 ½ **Tintawn Gold (IRE)**[101] 874 4-9-9 50.................... MissRWoodman(7) 10 39
(SWoodman) *prom tl rdn and wknd over 2f out* **25/1**

0402 10 1 ¼ **Pay The Silver**[10] 2381 6-11-0 69....................(p) GBartley(7) 16 56
(IAWood) *hld up: rdn over 3f out: nvr on terms* **4/1**[2]

000- 11 3 ½ **Somayda (IRE)**[230] 5279 9-9-6 47.................... JDoyle(7) 7 27
(MissJacquelineSDoyle) *a in rr* **33/1**

5000 12 5 **Learned Lad (FR)**[4] 2537 6-10-5 56....................(b[1]) MrSDobson(3) 5 26
(JamiePoulton) *mid-div: hdwy 5f out: wknd 2f out* **20/1**

-005 13 nk **Sweet Reflection (IRE)**[38] 1690 4-8-13 40....................(t) MissJPledge(7) 11 9
(WJMusson) *a bhd* **33/1**

00-0 14 1 ½ **Mutared (IRE)**[133] 589 6-10-1 52.................... MrsEmmaLittmoden(3) 3 18
(NPLittmoden) *in rr and nvr on terms* **20/1**

0006 15 1 **Grist Mist (IRE)**[9] 2395 3-9-4 55....................(t) MissAWallace(5) 1 19
(MrsPNDutfield) *plld hrd: racd wd: wknd 3f out* **33/1**

5505 16 8 **Young Dynasty**[18] 2188 4-9-8 45....................(b) MrLNewnes(3) 8 —
(EAWheeler) *prom tl wknd wl over 2f out* **50/1**

1m 59.2s (2.34) **Going Correction** +0.10s/f (Good)
**WFA** 3 from 4yo+ 12lb **16** Ran SP% **132.1**
Speed ratings: **93,92,91,89,88 88,86,85,84,83 80,76,75,74,73 66**CSF £143.91 CT £1132.94 TOTE £21.30: £5.00, £4.10, £3.00, £1.10; EX 240.40.
**Owner** Mrs M Enright **Bred** D L Chown **Trained** Lewes, E Sussex
■ Jay Pemberton's first winner under Rules.

**FOCUS**
The flip-start was a shambles and this is a race to treat with real caution. The runners were made to wait at the start for quite a long time as He Who Dares slipped up and broke his leg on the way down (R4 15p in the £). When the runners were finally let go, some did not stick to their draw (most notably the first two home) and plenty were several lengths behind before they had broken into a gallop. In any case the form is ordinary.

**NOTEBOOK**
**Gran Clicquot** had gained both her previous wins in selling company. She was one of the main beneficiaries of the flip start as her rider was able to gain an ideal position, one that would have been far from guaranteed had there been stalls.
**Best Before(IRE)** probably would have won this had he not been so keen early on. He might as well have been in stall 17 as his rider completely ignored the draw and deserves no credit whatsoever for finishing second.
**Liberty Royal**, with declared cheekpieces on for the first time, ran respectably, but never really looked like getting to the front two.
**Bank On Him** did not appear to do a great deal wrong and could well have been closer had it not been for the ragged start.
**Paso Doble** only has a Wolverhampton claiming win to his name.
**Pay The Silver** was never going the pace and is probably better suited by further these days. The flip-start did not exactly help matters.

## 2644 GREEN & BLACK'S ORGANIC CHOCOLATE EBF MAIDEN STKS 6f
**6:50** (6:50) (D ) 2-Y-O **£4,832** (£1,487; £743; £371) **Stalls** Low

Form RPR

1 **Dubawi (IRE)** 2-9-0 .................... LDettori 3 89+
(SaeedBinSuroor) *s.i.s: swtchd rt and gd hdwy to chal 2f out: rn green but led over 1f out: r.o wl fnl f* **11/4**[2]

2 1 ¼ **Fox** 2-9-0 .................... DHolland 4 85+
(CEBrittain) *a.p: cl 2nd 1/2-way ev ch 1f out: nt pce of wnr* **11/2**[3]

2 3 nk **Qadar (IRE)**[16] 2225 2-9-0 ....................(t) RHills 1 84
(MPTregoning) *led after 1f: rdn and hdd appr fnl f: r.o one pce* **1/2**[1]

600 4 12 **Waterline Lover**[32] 1839 2-8-9 .................... SDrowne 2 43
(PDEvans) *broke wl: led for 1f: wknd wewll over 1f out* **50/1**

5 dist **Buzz Maite** 2-9-0 .................... PDoe 5 —
(PButler) *outpcd thrght: t.o* **50/1**

1m 13.51s (0.67) **Going Correction** +0.10s/f (Good) **5** Ran SP% **112.6**
Speed ratings: **99,97,96,80,—**CSF £17.62 TOTE £3.10: £1.70, £2.30; EX 13.30.
**Owner** Godolphin **Bred** Darley **Trained** Newmarket, Suffolk
■ A first-ever runner and winner for the great, but sadly ill-fated Dubai Millennium.

**FOCUS**
Despite the small field this was a classy maiden, as the third has been adjudged to have repeated his previous good effort.

**NOTEBOOK**
**Dubawi(IRE)**, out of an Italian Oaks winner, was a first-ever runner for the great Dubai Millennium. Last out of the gates, he ran in snatches a little and appeared to be very green when pulled out wide for his run. Despite that, he always looked like getting on top and left the impression he had plenty left. He has bags of potential and could head to Royal Ascot but, while he would obviously command respect there, he may just need to mature mentally.
**Fox**, a half-brother to the Group-class juvenile filly Badminton out of a useful miler, made a most encouraging debut. He is well regarded and should have no trouble winning a maiden before stepping up in class.
**Qadar(IRE)**, an unlucky loser when 6/4 favourite for a course and distance maiden on his debut, had no excuse this time. He probably ran into a couple of pretty smart performers, but would not appear to be progressing as well as one might have expected, and is not one to take a short price about.
**Waterline Lover** showed good early pace, but was left behind as she was entitled to be when it mattered.
**Buzz Maite** showed little.

## 2645 AMBERLEY WORKING MUSEUM MAIDEN STKS — 1m 3f
**7:20** (7:21) (D) 3-Y-O — **£5,538** (£1,704; £852; £426) **Stalls** Low

Form / RPR
43-2 **1** **Reservoir (IRE)**[21] [2077] 3-9-0 80 ... MartinDwyer 2 — 82
(WJHaggas) *a.p: led over 3f out: hld on to narrow advantage u.p ins fnl 3f* **2/1**[2]
-232 **2** ½ **Ganymede**[13] [2281] 3-9-0 81 ... DHolland 7 — 81
(MLWBell) *sn trckd ldr: pressed wnr thrght fnl 3f u.p: no ex fnl 50yds* **5/4**[1]
5-4 **3** 13 **On Every Street**[14] [2280] 3-9-0 ... (v) RHughes 5 — 60
(HRACecil) *led: hdd over 3f out: sn rdn: wknd over 1f out* **6/1**[3]
**4** 2½ **Port 'n Starboard** 3-8-11 ... LisaJones(3) 3 — 56
(CACyzer) *in rr: rdn 2f out: kpt on to go poor 4th ins fnl f* **20/1**
0 **5** 1¾ **Stylish Dancer**[11] [2374] 3-8-9 ... RHavlin 6 — 48
(MBlanshard) *chsd ldrs tl wknd wl over 2f out* **33/1**
0-0 **6** 3 **Purr**[21] [2085] 3-9-0 ... PDoe 4 — 49?
(JLDunlop) *prom: reminders 5f out: wknd 3f out* **22/1**
**7** ¾ **Sharadi (IRE)**[280] [4561] 3-9-0 77 ... MTebbutt 8 — 47
(VSmith) *hld up in rr: sa bhd* **14/1**
000 **8** 6 **Open Book**[11] [2374] 3-8-9 ... SDrowne 1 — 33
(HMorrison) *racd wd: hld up in rr: a bhd* **66/1**

2m 27.21s (1.10) **Going Correction** +0.10s/f (Good) **8 Ran SP% 112.3**
Speed ratings: **100,99,90,88,87 84,84,80**CSF £4.51 TOTE £2.90: £1.20, £1.20, £2.00; EX 5.30.
**Owner** Highclere Thoroughbred Racing XVI **Bred** Lord Rothschild **Trained** Newmarket, Suffolk
■ Stewards Enquiry : Martin Dwyer two-day ban: used whip with excessive frequency and from above shoulder height (Jun 20,21)

**FOCUS**
A fairly decent maiden, but the early pace was just ordinary.

**NOTEBOOK**
**Reservoir(IRE)** confirmed the promise he showed over a shorter distance on his reappearance with a narrow success. He and the second were well clear of the third, but things will be tougher in handicaps.
**Ganymede**, runner-up in a competitive Ascot handicap on his previous start, did not do a great deal wrong switched back into maiden company. However, he just keeps finding one too good and has been a beaten favourite on three of his six starts to date.
**On Every Street** looked to have every chance in the straight, but did not find a great deal under pressure and was left behind by the front two. It can only be hoped the Handicapper is not hard on him now he is qualified for a mark.
**Port 'n Starboard**, a 4,000gns half-brother three moderate winners, did not run badly but is likely to find things easier when handicapped.
**Sharadi(IRE)**, ex-Irish, showed nothing to justify his rating of 77.

## 2646 HILDON STKS (H'CAP) — 7f
**7:55** (7:57) (D) (0-85,85) 3-Y-O+ — **£6,825** (£2,100; £1,050; £525) **Stalls** High

Form / RPR
0020 **1** **Material Witness (IRE)**[6] [2467] 7-9-13 84 ... MartinDwyer 8 — 95
(WRMuir) *mde all: rdn over 1f out: kpt on wl* **9/2**[3]
-112 **2** 1 **Harrison Point (USA)**[14] [2279] 4-9-10 81 ... RHughes 4 — 89
(PWChapple-Hyam) *t.k.h: hld up in rr: hdwy to chse ldr wl over 1f out: no imp ins fnl f* **11/4**[1]
620 **3** 2½ **Zafarshah (IRE)**[9] [2406] 5-8-7 64 ow1 ... SWKelly 5 — 66
(PDEvans) *in rr: rdn and outpcd over 2f out: styd on past btn horses fnl f* **10/1**
0061 **4** 1¼ **Ephesus**[16] [2226] 4-9-7 78 ... (v) KFallon 3 — 76
(MissGayKelleway) *in tch: rdn 2f out: one pce after* **4/1**[2]
-604 **5** shd **Fearby Cross (IRE)**[27] [1969] 8-8-6 66 ... LisaJones(3) 2 — 64
(WJMusson) *in rr: rdn over 2f out: kpt on one pce but nvr on terms* **7/1**
060- **6** 1 **Giocoso (USA)**[209] [5946] 4-10-0 85 ... EAhern 9 — 80
(BPalling) *chsd ldrs: wkng whn short of room over 1f out* **25/1**
10-5 **7** 2 **Last Appointment (USA)**[17] [2206] 4-9-8 79 ... DHolland 7 — 69
(JMPEustace) *trckd wnr: rdn and wknd wl over 1f out* **5/1**

1m 27.22s (-0.81) **Going Correction** +0.10s/f (Good) **7 Ran SP% 107.0**
Speed ratings: **108,106,104,102,102 101,99**CSF £15.04 CT £95.29 TOTE £6.80: £2.60, £2.10; EX 17.00.
**Owner** M J Caddy **Bred** M Henochsberg **Trained** Lambourn, Berks
■ Stewards Enquiry : S Drowne £125 fine: arrived at start without declared cheekpieces

**FOCUS**
Just an ordinary handicap in which Material Witness soon bagged the favoured rail and never looked back. The form is fair for the grade.

**NOTEBOOK**
**Material Witness(IRE)** could not have been backed given the way he ran at Doncaster on his previous start, but this was more like it. He had everything go his way and is not always consistent, but a follow-up cannot be ruled out if he is able to reproduce this level of form next time.
**Harrison Point(USA)** travelled really strongly for Hughes, but although finding enough to pull clear of the remainder, the winner was too strong. He is in fine form, but creeping up the weights all the time.
**Zafarshah(IRE)**, 3lb higher than when last winning on turf, did not appear to have any excuses.
**Ephesus** was not as well dawn as when winning over a mile here on his previous start and was well held. *Official explanation: jockey said gelding lost its action.*
**Fearby Cross(IRE)**, just 1lb higher than when last successful, proved unable to justify significant market support.

## 2647 JOMATI ANNIVERSARY MAIDEN FILLIES' STKS — 1m
**8:30** (8:30) (D) 3-Y-O — **£5,577** (£1,716; £858; £429) **Stalls** High

Form / RPR
5 **1** **Cut Short (USA)**[16] [2223] 3-8-11 ... JPMurtagh 9 — 79
(JHMGosden) *chsd ldr: led over 2f out: r.o strly fnl f* **5/2**[1]
**2** 1½ **Nouveau Riche (IRE)** 3-8-11 ... RLMoore 8 — 75
(HMorrison) *a in tch: hdwy over 1f out to chse wnr ins fnl f: kpt on but no imp* **10/1**
**3** nk **Posteritas (USA)** 3-8-11 ... RHughes 6 — 75
(HRACecil) *in tch: rdn over 2f out and outpcd: styd on fnl f* **9/1**
**4** 1¼ **Merwaha (IRE)** 3-8-11 ... RHills 10 — 72
(MPTregoning) *hld up: hdwy over 2f out: styd on but nvr nr to chal* **10/3**[2]
5- **5** 1¾ **Gwen John (USA)**[261] [4986] 3-8-11 ... SDrowne 1 — 68
(HMorrison) *in tch: one pce ins fnl 2f* **9/2**[3]
52- **6** ½ **Heart's Desire (IRE)**[219] [5831] 3-8-11 ... MHills 2 — 67
(BWHills) *trckd ldrs: rdn over 2f out: wknd fnl f* **9/2**[3]
6 **7** 2½ **Pine Bay**[13] [2286] 3-8-11 ... MFenton 11 — 61
(BGubby) *in tch: rdn over 2f out: wknd over 1f out* **25/1**
5 **8** nk **Prelude**[29] [1904] 3-8-11 ... SWKelly 7 — 60
(WMBrisbourne) *t.k.h: a bhd* **33/1**
40- **9** 5 **Kiniska**[210] [5938] 3-8-11 ... EAhern 5 — 49
(BPalling) *led: hdd over 2f out: wknd qckly* **50/1**
**10** 20 **Satan's Sister** 3-8-6 ... RThomas(5) 4 — —
(AWCarroll) *s.i.s: a bhd: t.o* **50/1**

1m 39.92s (-0.35) **Going Correction** +0.10s/f (Good) **10 Ran SP% 117.8**
Speed ratings: **105,103,103,101,100 99,97,96,91,71**CSF £28.37 TOTE £3.10: £1.50, £1.80, £2.30; EX 30.60.
**Owner** Cliveden Stud **Bred** Cliveden Stud Ltd **Trained** Manton, Wilts

**FOCUS**
With the second, third and fourth home all making their debuts, one cannot be sure how good a maiden this was. However, the time was decent for the grade and it was a contest that should produce some future winners.

**NOTEBOOK**
**Cut Short(USA)** proved able to build on the promise she showed on her debut round here over seven furlongs on this step up to a mile. She is going the right way, but her future, for the time being, would appear to lie in the hands of the Handicapper.
**Nouveau Riche(IRE)**, a 47,000gns yearling, half-sister to the very smart performers Guys And Dolls, Pawn Broker and Blushing Bride, was nibbled at in the betting and made a pleasing debut. She should stay a little further and can pick up a maiden.
**Posteritas(USA)**, out of a smart performer at up to seven furlongs who represented these connections, offered plenty of encouragement on this racecourse debut and, given normal improvement, it will be disappointing if she is not found a race.
**Merwaha(IRE)**, whose dam is out of the top-class US three-year-old Lucky Lucky Lucky, made a satisfactory debut and appears capable of improvement.
**Gwen John(USA)**, a stablemate of the runner-up, ran respectably and should progress.
**Heart's Desire(IRE)** progressed well in couple of runs at two, but this was a somewhat disappointing first run in 219 days. She has a little bit to prove after this.

## 2648 SOIL ASSOCIATION STKS (H'CAP) — 1m 1f 192y
**9:00** (9:04) (D) (0-80,75) 3-Y-O — **£5,655** (£1,740; £870; £435) **Stalls** Low

Form / RPR
464- **1** **Waziri (IRE)**[204] [5986] 3-9-6 74 ... SDrowne 9 — 76
(HMorrison) *slowly away: hdwy over 3f out: wnt 2nd over 2f out: led 1f out: r.o wl* **12/1**
0000 **2** nk **Hazewind**[10] [2377] 3-8-2 56 ... (vt) MartinDwyer 8 — 57
(PDEvans) *led: sn clr: rdn and hdd 1f out: kpt on but no imp ins last* **14/1**
2504 **3** ½ **Gjovic**[13] [2298] 3-9-7 75 ... KFallon 10 — 75
(BJMeehan) *t.k.h: trckd ldrs: kpt on one pce fnl f* **3/1**[2]
5446 **4** ¾ **Slavonic (USA)**[18] [2169] 3-9-5 73 ... (b) RHughes 7 — 72
(JHMGosden) *hld up: hdwy 3f out: swtchd rt over 2f out: styd on one pce after* **4/1**[3]
0-50 **5** shd **Mrs Pankhurst**[37] [1712] 3-9-5 73 ... MHills 3 — 71
(BWHills) *in rr: hdwy on outside over 2f out: nvr nrr* **20/1**
0-40 **6** 1½ **Scarrabus (IRE)**[22] [2070] 3-9-2 70 ... JPMurtagh 4 — 66
(BGPowell) *hld up in rr: hdwy whn nt clr run over 2f out: no imp after* **16/1**
00-3 **7** ½ **Pangloss (IRE)**[46] [1509] 3-9-2 70 ... RLMoore 6 — 65
(GLMoore) *a in rr* **6/1**
1-05 **8** ½ **Hezaam (USA)**[20] [2134] 3-9-7 75 ... RHills 5 — 69
(JLDunlop) *in tch: outpcd over 2f out and nvr on terms after* **11/4**[1]
3400 **9** 1 **Lord Of The Sea (IRE)**[15] [2244] 3-8-13 67 ... PDoe 1 — 59
(JamiePoulton) *in tch tl rdn and wknd appr fnl f* **16/1**
00-0 **10** 12 **Filliemou (IRE)**[20] [2112] 3-8-3 62 ... RThomas(5) 2 — 31
(AWCarroll) *plld hrd: trckd ldr tl wknd qckly over 2f out* **14/1**

2m 10.63s (2.95) **Going Correction** +0.10s/f (Good) **10 Ran SP% 123.5**
Speed ratings: **92,91,91,90,90 89,89,88,87,78**CSF £176.25 CT £644.63 TOTE £14.80: £3.20, £3.50, £1.80; EX 346.60 Place 6 £77.70, Place 5 £37.71.
**Owner** Ashley House Racing **Bred** Ashley House Stud **Trained** East Ilsley, Berks

**FOCUS**
A handicap that was lacking in progressive types. The time was moderate but the form looks sound.

**NOTEBOOK**
**Waziri(IRE)**, who offered some promise in three runs over a mile on Polytrack, appreciated both the switch to handicapping and step up in trip. He is open to more further improvement, especially considering this was his first run in 204 days.
**Hazewind** ran a fine race under a positive ride. He was keen early on and looked all set to drop right out when headed a furlong down, but to his credit he kept on right the way to the line.
**Gjovic** was a little keen under restraint and unable to take advantage of his draw against the rail. He is frustrating, but capable of better than he showed this time.
**Slavonic(USA)** could never really muster the pace to pose a serious threat and is proving hard to win with.
**Mrs Pankhurst** again shaped as though she will stay further.
**Hezaam(USA)** ran respectably at Thirsk on his previous start, but this was a poor effort and represented a step back.
T/Plt: £65.30 to a £1 stake. Pool: £45,756.00. 511.40 winning tickets. T/Qpdt: £12.60 to a £1 stake. Pool: £3,379.50. 197.05 winning tickets. JS

# 2621 HAYDOCK (L-H)
Friday, June 4

**OFFICIAL GOING: Good to soft (good in places)**
Wind: almost nil Weather: overcast; It rail late on

## 2649 PATRICIA THOMPSON SURPRISE BIRTHDAY CELEBRATION H'CAP (FOR LADY AMATEUR RIDERS) — 1m 2f 120y
**6:35** (6:37) (G) (0-70,66) 3-Y-0+ — **£2,744** (£784; £392) **Stalls** High

Form / RPR
0-32 **1** **Santiburi Lad (IRE)**[10] [2394] 7-9-11 54 ... MrsNWilson(5) 6 — 67
(NWilson) *mde all: pushed out* **4/1**[1]
00-6 **2** nk **Inchnadamph**[27] [1962] 4-9-9 47 ... (t) MissAElsey 3 — 59
(TJFitzgerald) *plld hrd: a.p: rdn to chse wnr over 1f out: r.o ins fnl f* **11/1**
5106 **3** 5 **Dash Of Magic**[11] [2347] 6-9-3 41 ... MissSBrotherton 4 — 45
(JHetherton) *hld up: pushed along and hdwy 3f out: styd on fnl f: nt trble ldrs* **7/1**[3]

400 **4** *1* **Sarn**[7] 2462 5-9-0 **45** ............ MissMMullineaux(7) 9 47
(MMullineaux) *hld up: pushed along over 2f out: styd on fr over 1f out: nt trble ldrs* **9/1**

00-5 **5** *1 1/2* **Pension Fund**[27] 1962 10-9-10 **55** ow6 ............ MissJCoward(7) 8 55
(MWEasterby) *hld up: hdwy over 4f out: rdn over 2f out: wknd fnl f* **8/1**

600- **6** *3* **Double Spey**[336] 2672 5-9-3 **46** ow5 ............ MissAArmitage(5) 11 41
(MissKateMilligan) *plld hrd: hld up: pushed along 3f out: keeping on whn nt clr run and hmpd over 1f out: no imp after* **12/1**

3461 **7** *2 1/2* **Larad (IRE)**[11] 2348 3-8-9 **50** 5ex ............ (b) MrsSMoore(3) 2 40
(JSMoore) *prom: rdn 2f out: wknd 1f out* **5/1**[2]

0543 **8** *1* **Paradise Garden (USA)**[10] 2386 7-8-7 **34** oh7... MissKellyHarrison(3) 1 23
(PLClinton) *in tch: hdwy over 4f out: rdn and swtchd rt over 2f out: edgd rt over 1f out: sn wknd* **10/1**

0-00 **9** *hd* **Border Terrier (IRE)**[18] 2174 6-9-12 **50** ............ MsCWilliams 5 38
(MDHammond) *hld up: rdn over 2f out: no imp* **7/1**[3]

0010 **10** *dist* **Margarets Wish**[25] 1987 4-9-0 **43** ............ MissVCottrill(5) 7 —
(TWall) *in tch: sddle sn slipped: wknd over 3f out: t.o* **8/1**

0420 **11** *15* **Crusoe (IRE)**[25] 2007 7-9-13 **51** ............ (b) MissEJJones 12 —
(ASadik) *prom: lost pl qckly over 5f out: bhd after: t.o* **10/1**

2m 20.21s (2.48) **Going Correction** +0.20s/f (Good)
**WFA** 3 from 4yo+ 14lb **11** Ran SP% **128.1**
Speed ratings: **98,97,94,93,92 90,88,87,87,**— —CSF £53.97 CT £315.03 TOTE £5.50: £1.50, £9.00, £2.70; EX 105.10.
**Owner** Mrs Karan Ridley **Bred** Rathbarry Stud **Trained** Malton, N Yorks
■ Stewards Enquiry : Miss Kelly Harrison caution: careless riding

**FOCUS**
An ordinary race run at a steady pace set by the winner.

**NOTEBOOK**
**Santiburi Lad(IRE)** appreciated the return to this trip with an all-the-way success and continues in good heart.
**Inchnadamph** put in a fair effort, offering some encouragement for the future considering he refused to settle early.
**Dash Of Magic** continues in fine form at this level.
**Sarn**, who ran with credit over further recently, did so again without landing a serious blow.
**Pension Fund** struggled in the closing stages with the overweight.
**Double Spey** is not the most straightforward ride, but was keeping on when tightened up approaching the final furlong.
**Larad(IRE)**, a winner on a quick surface, faded on the dead ground.
**Margarets Wish** *Official explanation: jockey said saddle slipped*
**Crusoe(IRE)** *Official explanation: jockey said gelding had ran wide going into the top bend*

## 2650 DEAN MOOR H'CAP 5f
**7:05** (7:05) (E) (0-75,75) 3-Y-O **£3,770** (£1,160; £580; £290) **Stalls** Far side

Form RPR

2-03 **1** **Champagne Cracker**[13] 2290 3-8-6 **60** ............ RFfrench 8 65
(MissLAPerratt) *chsd ldrs: rdn to ld over 1f out: r.o* **16/1**

-060 **2** *2* **Sir Ernest (IRE)**[3] 2552 3-9-7 **75** ............ ACulhane 11 73
(MJPolglase) *led: rdn over 2f out: hdd over 1f out: styd on same pce ins f* **9/1**

-222 **3** *1 1/2* **Baron Rhodes**[11] 2369 3-9-1 **72** ............ TEaves(3) 9 64
(JSWainwright) *wnt lft and nrly uns rdr s: in tch: rdn over 2f out: styd on ins fnl f* **4/1**[1]

-630 **4** *3/4* **Baylaw Star**[3] 2549 3-9-2 **75** ............ PMulrennan(5) 10 65
(JBalding) *a.p: rdn 2f out: no ex ins fnl f* **8/1**

-164 **5** *3/4* **Tizzy's Law**[9] 2411 3-9-1 **69** ............ JBramhill 4 56
(MABuckley) *hmpd s: bhd: hdwy over 2f out: rdn over 1f out: wknd wl ins fnl f* **5/1**[2]

333- **6** *1* **Abelard (IRE)**[261] 4985 3-8-10 **67** ............ THamilton(3) 3 50
(RAFahey) *hmpd s: bhd: rdn along thrght: nt pce to chal* **12/1**

1136 **7** *1 3/4* **He's A Rocket (IRE)**[14] 2269 3-8-9 **63** ............ (b) KDalgleish 7 40
(KRBurke) *chsd ldrs: rdn over 2f out: sn wknd* **5/1**[2]

3020 **8** *2 1/2* **Obe Bold (IRE)**[3] 2549 3-8-8 **57** ow5 ............ JCarroll 5 30
(ABerry) *hmpd s: bhd: rdn 3f out: eased whn btn ins fnl f* **12/1**

0-61 **9** *8* **Feu Duty (IRE)**[11] 2353 3-8-12 **66** 6ex ............ RWinston 6 5
(TJEtherington) *s.i.s: in tch: hdwy over 2f out: rdn and hung lft fr over 1f out: sn wknd: eased ins fnl f* **6/1**[3]

600- **10** *1 1/2* **Sir Loin**[250] 5255 3-8-6 **60** ............ KimTinkler 1 —
(NTinkler) *w.r.s: a wl bhd* **33/1**

63.60 secs (1.53) **Going Correction** +0.30s/f (Good) **10** Ran SP% **112.9**
Speed ratings: **99,95,93,92,91 89,86,82,69,67**CSF £147.40 CT £540.68 TOTE £7.90: £1.90, £4.00, £1.60; EX 227.80.
**Owner** Jim McLaren **Bred** P Baugh **Trained** Ayr, Strathclyde
■ Stewards Enquiry : A Culhane £150 fine: did not line up in correct position for flip-start

**FOCUS**
A flip start was used for this moderate sprint, the result was a very untidy one, with one runner whipping round hampering three others, another contender veering to the left nearly unseating her rider, and the eventual second starting from the wrong draw. Sir Ernest and Baron Rhodes started from each other's stalls, Culhane fined £150.

**NOTEBOOK**
**Champagne Cracker** displayed good pace to break her maiden and show her effectiveness on slow ground.
**Sir Ernest(IRE)** managed to get a flying start but failed to quicken with the winner approaching the final furlong. He is the type who does well on sharpish tracks.
**Baron Rhodes** very nearly parted company with her rider at the start; that considered she performed well.
**Baylaw Star** was found wanting towards the end.
**Tizzy's Law** was caught up in the mess at the start and ran respectably.
**Abelard(IRE)** could never get into the race after being hampered at the start.
**Feu Duty(IRE)** not for the first time hung left in the closing stages, and was ultimately disappointing with the prevailing ground conditions counting against her. *Official explanation: jockey said filly was unsuited by the going*

## 2651 DAVID REILLY'S GETTING HITCHED EBF MAIDEN STKS 6f
**7:35** (7:43) (D) 2-Y-O **£5,856** (£1,802; £901; £450) **Stalls** Centre

Form RPR

**1** **Where With All (IRE)** 2-9-0 ............ KMcEvoy 6 84
(SaeedBinSuroor) *disp ld: def advantage over 1f out: wandered ins fnl 1f r.o* **10/3**[2]

4 **2** *2 1/2* **Wasalat (USA)**[13] 2296 2-8-9 ............ ACulhane 2 71
(MRChannon) *disp ld: rdn 2f out: nt qckn over 1f out* **5/2**[1]

**3** *2 1/2* **African Gift** 2-8-9 ............ TQuinn 10 64
(JGGiven) *trckd ldrs: rdn 3f out: hung lft over 1f out: one pce ins fnl f* **9/1**[3]

**4** *2 1/2* **Wedlock** 2-9-0 ............ WSupple 8 61
(TDEasterby) *dwlt: in tch: rdn 3f out: edgd lft over 1f out: wknd ins fnl f* **33/1**

**5** *1 3/4* **Group Captain** 2-9-0 ............ DeanMcKeown 11 56
(SKirk) *s.s: racd keenly: sn in tch: rdn over 2f out: wknd over 1f out* **20/1**

**6** *1/2* **Pevensey (IRE)** 2-9-0 ............ JCarroll 4 54
(JHMGosden) *dwlt: bhd: hdwy 3f out: sn rdn: wknd fnl f* **10/1**

054 **7** *1 3/4* **No Commission (IRE)**[14] 2256 2-8-11 ............ DNolan(3) 3 49
(RFFisher) *racd keenly: chsd ldrs: rdn 2f out: wknd over 1f out* **33/1**

**8** *shd* **Noodles** 2-9-0 ............ RWinston 5 49
(TDEasterby) *s.s: pushed along over 4f out: a towards rr* **12/1**

**9** *19* **Isitloveyourafter (IRE)** 2-8-6 ............ THamilton(3) 7 —
(RPElliott) *s.s: cl up over 4f out: rdn and wknd over 2f out* **66/1**

0 **10** *dist* **The Terminator (IRE)**[30] 1882 2-8-9 ............ PBradley(5) 1 —
(ABerry) *dwlt: a bhd: eased whn btn over 2f out* **16/1**

1m 17.35s (2.46) **Going Correction** +0.30s/f (Good) **10** Ran SP% **96.5**
Speed ratings: **95,91,88,85,82 82,79,79,54,**—CSF £8.15 TOTE £3.70: £1.90, £1.40, £2.40; EX 7.90.
**Owner** Godolphin **Bred** Kilfrush Stud **Trained** Newmarket, Suffolk
■ Highest Return (9/2) withdrawn (went down in stalls). R4 applies, deduct 15p in the £.

**FOCUS**
Not a great deal of form to work on beforehand, though the winner is a likeable sort, those behind may be nothing special.

**NOTEBOOK**
**Where With All(IRE)** certainly has the scope to go on after this pleasing debut, sharing the work with the runner-up before asserting over a furlong from home to continue the stable's fine run of form with its juveniles. The son of Montjeu, who has a blend of speed and stamina in his pedigree, still has a bit to learn having displayed signs of greeness towards the end.
**Wasalat(USA)** matched strides with the winner for much of the way, coming on for her debut run at this track.
**African Gift**, a March foal related to minor race winners, flattened out towards the end but will come on for this effort.
**Wedlock**, a March foal whose dam won as a youngster, looked green on this debut.
**Group Captain**, a half-brother to middle-distance winning handicapper Scheming, miler Proxima, and six-furlong scorer Verkhotina, raced keenly before fading.
**Pevensey(IRE)**, a full-brother to Group Three winner Steel Princess, will do better in time.
**The Terminator(IRE)** *Official explanation: vet said colt had lost a plate and was found to be sore*

## 2652 RECTANGLE GROUP H'CAP 1m 6f
**8:10** (8:11) (D) (0-85,79) 3-Y-O+ **£5,590** (£1,720; £860; £430) **Stalls** Low

Form RPR

034 **1** **Glory Quest (USA)**[11] 2365 7-8-13 **67** ............ IMongan 7 77
(MissGayKelleway) *chsd ldr: brought wd st over 4f out: rdn to ld over 3f out: clr over 1f out: r.o strly* **2/1**[2]

3221 **2** *8* **Nakwa (IRE)**[13] 2299 6-9-3 **74** ............ DAllan(3) 5 74+
(EJAlston) *led: rdn and hdd over 3f out: eased whn no ex fnl 100 yds* **7/4**[1]

0562 **3** *3 1/2* **Northern Nymph**[13] 2299 5-8-9 **68** ............ StephanieHollinshead(5) 2 63
(RHollinshead) *chsd ldrs: rdn 5f out: wknd over 1f out* **4/1**[3]

0-22 **4** *12* **Sadler's Pride (IRE)**[21] 2090 4-9-4 **72** ............ JCarroll 6 51
(AndrewTurnell) *a bhd: rdn 4f out: eased whn btn over 1f out* **11/2**

3m 6.89s (0.74) **Going Correction** +0.20s/f (Good) **4** Ran SP% **105.1**
Speed ratings: **105,100,98,91**CSF £5.52 TOTE £2.90; EX 4.80.
**Owner** W R B Racing 40 (wrbracing.com) **Bred** Adelphian Ltd And Gainesway Farm **Trained** Newmarket, Suffolk

**FOCUS**
The winner was given an enterprising ride to land an uncompetitive heat, four withdrawals having decimated the field.

**NOTEBOOK**
**Glory Quest(USA)** was brought wide into the straight to race down the centre of the track before running away to record his first win on turf for two years.
**Nakwa(IRE)** stuck to the inside rail but had no answers for the winner off a career-high rating.
**Northern Nymph** was well held approaching the final furlong.

## 2653 CENTROL RECYCLING GROUP MAIDEN STKS 1m 3f 200y
**8:45** (8:47) (D) 3-Y-O+ **£6,097** (£1,876; £938; £469) **Stalls** High

Form RPR

40 **1** **Protective**[13] 2298 3-8-7 ............ WSupple 7 81+
(JGGiven) *midfield: hdwy 4f out: rdn over 2f out: led over 1f out: drew clr ins fnl f: eased cl home* **50/1**

**2** *5* **Historic Place (USA)**[62] 4-9-8 ............ JCarroll 1 71
(GBBalding) *s.s: bhd: rdn and hdwy over 3f out: styd on u.p to snatch 2nd cl home: no ch w wnr* **10/1**

022 **3** *1/2* **Anna Pallida**[14] 2280 3-8-4 81 ow2 ............ TQuinn 12 67
(PWHarris) *led: rdn and hdd over 1f out: wknd ins fnl f* **9/4**[2]

**4** *1 1/2* **Farne Isle**[35] 5-8-12 ............ PMulrennan(5) 5 63
(GAHarker) *s.s: hld up: rdn and hdwy over 2f out: one pce fnl f* **66/1**

052- **5** *5* **Imperial Royale (IRE)**[220] 5816 3-8-7 60 ............ JBramhill 2 61
(PLClinton) *midfield: effrt over 3f out: wknd ins fnl f* **50/1**

22 **6** *3/4* **Woolly Back (IRE)**[14] 2273 3-8-7 ............ DaleGibson 14 59
(RHollinshead) *prom: rdn and ev ch 3f out: wknd over 1f out* **5/1**[3]

**7** *2 1/2* **Molehill** 3-8-2 ............ JMackay 3 51
(JGGiven) *s.i.s: bhd: kpt on fr over 1f out: edgd lft ins fnl f: n.d* **25/1**

0-2 **8** *shd* **Chaplin**[52] 1387 3-8-7 ............ ACulhane 11 55
(BWHills) *trckd ldrs: rdn 3f out: wknd 2f out* **11/10**[1]

**9** *4* **Bravely Does It (USA)** 4-9-8 ............ RWinston 6 49
(WMBrisbourne) *midfield: hdwy over 6f out: rdn 4f out: sn wknd* **50/1**

5-5 **10** *2* **Double Turn**[14] 2273 4-9-3 ............ BSwarbrick(5) 8 46
(WMBrisbourne) *prom: rdn over 4f out: sn wknd* **50/1**

00- **11** *6* **Trofana Falcon**[178] 6153 4-9-8 ............ DeanMcKeown 13 37
(HJCollingridge) *a bhd* **100/1**

6 **12** *16* **Grey Samurai**[7] 2460 4-9-8 ............ RFitzpatrick 9 13
(PTMidgley) *sn bhd* **150/1**

0-00 **13** *20* **Mikes Mate**[19] 2145 3-8-3 ow1 ............ PBradley(5) 4 —
(CJTeague) *in tch: lost pl 5f out: sn bhd* **100/1**

2m 36.68s (1.52) **Going Correction** +0.20s/f (Good)
**WFA** 3 from 4yo+ 15lb **13** Ran SP% **120.0**
Speed ratings: **102,98,98,97,94 93,91,91,89,87 83,73,59**CSF £475.89 TOTE £39.10: £5.80, £2.30, £1.30; EX 607.30.
**Owner** Peter Onslow **Bred** P Onslow **Trained** Willoughton, Lincs

**FOCUS**
A fair maiden run at a sound pace, but the form has an uneven look, although the winner seems improved.

**NOTEBOOK**
**Protective** has been slow to grasp what has been required of him but, stepping up in distance, this son of Hector Protector displayed improvement in form with a convincing win. Having had a few niggling problems in the past, he now looks the sort to go to war with in middle-distance handicaps.
**Historic Place(USA)**, the winner of an Ascot bumper in January, held little chance with the winner towards the finish, but this half-brother to some useful middle-distance performers shaped with promise on this Flat debut.
**Anna Pallida** was quite disappointing, folding inside the final furlong.

**Farne Isle**, a bumper winner, will struggle in this sort of maiden company and will be better served when securing a handicap mark.
**Imperial Royale(IRE)** was beaten in sellers last year and his proximity does not enhance this form.
**Woolly Back(IRE)**, runner-up in his only two races, both over course and distance, should have handled the ground but was below form. He now qualifies for handicaps.
**Molehill** caught the eye making late progress without being over-ridden, and with plenty of stamina in the pedigree will surely improve with distance.
**Chaplin**, runner-up to Percussionist on similar ground at Newmarket, was disappointing and is better than this. *Official explanation: trainer's representative had no explanation for the poor form shown*

## 2654 MTB GROUP MAIDEN STKS 1m 30y
9:15 (9:16) (D) 3-Y-O+ £6,077 (£1,870; £935; £467) Stalls Low

Form RPR
0- **1** **Invasian (IRE)**[249] 5278 3-8-7 WRyan 1 85
(HRACecil) *mde all: r.o wl* **10/1**
5- **2** 2 1/2 **Cantarna (IRE)**[239] 5464 3-8-2 78 RFfrench 16 75
(JMackie) *in tch: lost pl 4f out: rallied over 1f out: r.o to take 2nd ins fnl f: nt trble wnr* **12/1**
5 **3** 2 **First Counsel**[14] 2270 3-8-7 PRobinson 14 76
(MAJarvis) *in tch: rdn and hdwy over 3f out: edgd lft ins fnl f: kpt on* **7/2**[3]
3 **4** 1 3/4 **Nordwind (IRE)**[14] 2270 3-8-7 TQuinn 5 72
(PWHarris) *trckd ldrs: rdn 4f out: wknd over 1f out* **3/1**[2]
34 **5** 1 **Foolish Groom**[14] 2270 3-8-7 DaleGibson 7 70
(RHollinshead) *prom: rdn and ev ch 3f out: hung lft over 1f out: sn wknd* **12/1**
0 **6** 6 **Pure Vintage (IRE)**[11] 2367 3-8-4 THamilton(3) 9 57
(RAFahey) *midfield: rdn over 2f out: no imp* **33/1**
0 **7** 1/2 **Desert Leader (IRE)**[14] 2270 3-8-7 GGibbons 13 56
(BAMcmahon) *dwlt: bhd: rdn over 2f out: kpt on fr over 1f out: n.d* **50/1**
66 **8** 5 **Acuzio**[14] 2270 3-8-2 SWarbrick(5) 8 46
(WMBrisbourne) *in rr: nvr on terms* **50/1**
6 **9** 1/2 **Remonstrate (IRE)**[17] 2195 3-8-7 WSupple 12 45
(TDEasterby) *hld up: rdn 4f out: nvr on terms* **25/1**
**10** 1 **Narciso (GER)** 4-8-13 PMulrennan(5) 4 43
(MWEasterby) *dwlt: in tch: rdn over 3f out: wknd over 2f out* **66/1**
2/ **11** 5 **Successor**[583] 5557 4-9-4 ACulhane 3 32
(BWHills) *dwlt: sn trckd ldrs: rdn over 3f out: wknd over 2f out* **5/2**[1]
**12** 1 3/4 **Rich Chic (IRE)** 3-8-2 JMackay 2 24
(MDHammond) *stdd s: struggling over 4f out: a bhd* **50/1**
000 **13** 1 1/2 **High View (USA)**[11] 2374 3-8-7 DeanMcKeown 6 25
(FJordan) *a bhd* **66/1**
0 **14** 1 1/2 **Tetchy**[32] 1842 4-8-13 JBramhill 10 17
(JGGiven) *s.s: a bhd* **20/1**

1m 45.29s (-0.26) **Going Correction** +0.20s/f (Good)
**WFA** 3 from 4yo 11lb 14 Ran SP% **120.7**
Speed ratings: **109,106,104,102,101 95,95,90,89,88 83,82,80,79**CSF £115.37 TOTE £12.40: £2.50, £2.80, £1.90; EX 66.00 Place 6 £186.31, Place 5 £74.35.
**Owner** Dr Karen Sanderson **Bred** Dr Karen Monica Sanderson **Trained** Newmarket, Suffolk

**FOCUS**
A fair maiden run at a good pace and the form looks solid.

**NOTEBOOK**
**Invasian(IRE)** showed that he is going the right way with this pillar-to-post success, and this half-brother to Lark In The Park should continue to improve
**Cantarna(IRE)** put in some decent work on her British debut, having shown signs of ability in Ireland last year when running against Group-race contenders. This daughter of Ashkalani should be capable of winning at an ordinary level.
**First Counsel** improved from his debut outing and certainly has the ability to land a similar maiden. *Official explanation: jockey said gelding hung left in the home straight*
**Nordwind(IRE)** faded, but it is hoped he can improve with distance.
**Foolish Groom** ran up with the pace before fading and, as last time, finished behind Nordwind. *Official explanation: jockey said gelding hung left in the final 2f*
**Successor** was beaten a long way on his return to active duty, having been absent for the whole of last season with an injured pastern.
T/Plt: £358.20 to a £1 stake. Pool: £53,024.40. 108.05 winning tickets. T/Qpdt: £75.20 to a £1 stake. Pool: £3,091.90. 30.40 winning tickets. DO

# 2364 THIRSK (L-H)
Friday, June 4

**OFFICIAL GOING: Good to firm (good in places)**

## 2655 EUROPEAN BREEDERS FUND NOVICE STKS 5f
2:05 (2:06) (D) 2-Y-O £4,290 (£1,320; £660; £330) Stalls High

Form RPR
31 **1** **Beckermet (IRE)**[14] 2268 2-8-11 PBradley(5) 5 84
(RFFisher) *s.i.s: sn chsng ldrs: rdn 2f out: led ins fnl f: all out* **14/1**
1 **2** 3/4 **Selkirk Storm (IRE)**[23] 2035 2-9-2 DaleGibson 4 81
(MWEasterby) *prom: rdn 2f out: ev ch fnl f: no ex clsng stages* **8/1**[3]
22 **3** hd **Bibury Flyer**[62] 1248 2-8-7 ACulhane 2 72
(MRChannon) *slowly away: hdwy into midfield 1/2-way: drvn along 2f out: styd on wl u.p fnl f: nvr able to chal* **7/2**[2]
3241 **4** 3/4 **Smiddy Hill**[7] 2458 2-8-9 RFfrench 7 71
(RBastiman) *led: rdn over 1f out: hdd ins fnl f: no ex* **4/5**[1]
212 **5** 2 **Unlimited**[15] 2247 2-9-0 GDuffield 6 69
(MrsADuffield) *cl up: hung lft: rdn 2f out: sn btn* **9/1**
410 **6** 3 **Mitchelland**[30] 1878 2-8-11 TEaves(3) 3 59
(JamesMoffatt) *in tch: rdn 2f out: sn btn* **16/1**
**7** 7 **Outrageous Flirt (IRE)** 2-8-7 ow3 ABeech(3) 8 30
(ADickman) *s.i.s: rr: rdn 2f out: no hdwy* **50/1**
**8** 3/4 **Our Kes (IRE)** 2-8-0 PPMathers(7) 1 24
(ABerry) *slowly away: rdn 2f out: sn btn* **100/1**

59.75 secs (-0.15) **Going Correction** -0.10s/f (Good) 8 Ran SP% **114.4**
Speed ratings: **97,95,95,94,91 86,75,73**CSF £119.12 TOTE £13.80: £4.40, £3.10, £1.40; EX 176.80.
**Owner** Great Head House Estates Limited **Bred** Fritz Von Ball Moss **Trained** Ulverston, Cumbria

**FOCUS**
A decent novice for the track and the form looks strong.

**NOTEBOOK**
**Beckermet(IRE)** improved on his Haydock win but may now have to wait for nurseries.
**Selkirk Storm(IRE)**, on totally different ground, almost certainly improved on his Newcastle debut win. In the end just denied, he would not want the ground any quicker.
**Bibury Flyer**, given a nine-week break, appreciated this much quicker ground. But for giving away many lengths at the start, she must have made it third time lucky.
**Smiddy Hill** led them a merry dance, but the watered ground was not in her favour and in the end she did not get home. Quite an exciteable type, this may have come too soon after York.
**Unlimited**, well backed at long odds, was always tending to hang to his left. *Official explanation: jockey said colt hung left throughout.*
**Mitchelland**, who had her trainer with her at the start, had turned over Bibury Flyer on totally different ground at Newcastle.

## 2656 LESLIE PETCH H'CAP 6f
2:40 (2:43) (E) (0-70,69) 3-Y-O+ £3,818 (£1,175; £587; £293) Stalls Far side

Form RPR
2053 **1** **Tayif**[29] 1909 8-9-4 59 (t) SCarson 11 74
(AndrewReid) *racd stands side: mde all: rdn over 1f out: clr ins fnl f* **9/1**[3]
6031 **2** 3 **Tally (IRE)**[2] 2581 4-8-8 56 6ex KGhunowa(7) 5 62
(MJPolglase) *racd far side: hld up: hdwy 1/2-way: styd on u.p to ld gp wl ins fnl f: nt trble wnr* **7/1**[2]
-031 **3** 1/2 **Compton Plume**[3] 2556 4-9-0 55 DaleGibson 6 59
(WHTinning) *cl up far side: led gp 2f out: sn rdn: kpt on same pce fnl f: lost 2nd clsng stages* **11/2**[1]
0000 **4** 1 1/2 **Drury Lane (IRE)**[17] 2219 4-9-3 58 (b) ACulhane 13 58
(DWChapman) *racd stands side: cl up: rdn 2f out: kpt on same pce* **25/1**
00-1 **5** 2 1/2 **Playful Dane (IRE)**[17] 2219 7-8-10 58 DFentiman(7) 17 50
(WSCunningham) *chsd stands side ldrs: rdn 2f out: kpt on same pce* **11/2**[1]
0-50 **6** nk **Oeuf A La Neige**[17] 2217 4-9-8 63 RFfrench 18 54
(GCHChung) *towards rr stands side: drvn along 1/2-way: styd on fnl f: nvr able to chal* **20/1**
5/06 **7** 2 **Brigadier Monty (IRE)**[31] 1872 6-9-2 57 GDuffield 4 42
(MrsSLamyman) *prom far side: rdn to dispute gp ld over 1f out: fdd ins fnl f* **33/1**
0-00 **8** 1 1/4 **Toppling**[4] 2524 6-9-0 58 BReilly(3) 20 39
(JMBradley) *midfield stands side: rdn 1/2-way: no real hdwy* **11/1**
061 **9** shd **Mister Mal (IRE)**[45] 1526 8-8-13 54 (be) VHalliday 10 35
(BEllison) *led far side tl rdn and hdd 2f out: fdd fnl f* **16/1**
0-50 **10** nk **Tapau (IRE)**[15] 2238 6-9-7 69 CJDavies(7) 9 49
(JMBradley) *trckd stands side ldrs: effrt 2f out: sn rdn and btn* **28/1**
4230 **11** 1/2 **Silver Mascot**[14] 2260 5-8-9 53 TEaves(3) 7 32
(ISemple) *midfield far side: sme hdwy u.p 2f out: fdd fnl f* **10/1**
000- **12** 2 **Rum Destiny (IRE)**[213] 5919 5-8-12 53 (v) GParkin 1 26
(JSWainwright) *chsd far side ldrs: hdwy and prom 2f out: wknd appr fnl f* **66/1**
/0-0 **13** 1 1/4 **Hilltime (IRE)**[27] 1974 4-9-7 62 RWinston 12 31
(JJQuinn) *sn rr div stands side: n.d* **40/1**
0500 **14** 1 1/2 **Pagan Storm (USA)**[13] 2291 4-8-12 60 KristinStubbs(7) 16 24
(MrsLStubbs) *chsd stands side ldrs: rdn over 2f out: wknd qckly over 1f out* **33/1**
000- **15** 1 3/4 **Intellibet One**[188] 6095 4-8-12 60 SJDonohoe(7) 8 19
(PDEvans) *racd far side: nvr bttr than mid-div* **33/1**
0-04 **16** 3/4 **Bettys Pride**[11] 2369 5-9-4 59 WSupple 3 16
(MDods) *racd far side: towards rr most of way* **9/1**[3]
0006 **17** 2 **Time To Remember (IRE)**[13] 2292 6-9-3 58 AlexGreaves 2 9
(DNicholls) *racd far side: sn bhd* **10/1**
-000 **18** 24 **General Smith**[11] 2368 5-9-0 55 JCarroll 14 —
(GAHarker) *racd stands side: sn bhd: lost tch over 1f out: t.o* **16/1**

1m 12.0s (-0.50) **Going Correction** -0.10s/f (Good)
**WFA** 3 from 4yo+ 8lb 18 Ran SP% **126.4**
Speed ratings: **99,95,94,92,89 88,85,84,84,83 83,80,78,76,74 73,70,38**CSF £66.16 CT £392.90 TOTE £11.70: £2.30, £2.30, £1.50, £8.80; EX 77.90.
**Owner** A S Reid **Bred** Theakston Stud **Trained** Mill Hill, London NW7
■ A flip start was used owing to a dispute involving stalls handlers.

**FOCUS**
A flip start and they split into two groups. The form is ordinary and there appeared little advantage to either flank.

**NOTEBOOK**
**Tayif**, 2lb lower than his last All-Weather win, broke smartly from the tape start and came right away inside the last. He is clearly in very good form.
**Tally(IRE)**, with a 6lb penalty for his win just two days earlier, was first home on the far side.
**Compton Plume**, seeking swift compensation, gave a good account of himself in this much stronger grade. He really does deserve to lose the maiden tag.
**Drury Lane(IRE)** is tumbling down the ratings and could not be in better hands.
**Playful Dane(IRE)**, 3lb higher, was third best on the stands' side.
**Oeuf A La Neige**, still a maiden, seems better suited by seven.
**Brigadier Monty(IRE)** *Official explanation: jockey said gelding hung right.*
**Time To Remember(IRE)** *Official explanation: jockey said gelding was never travelling.*
**General Smith** *Official explanation: jockey said gelding was never travelling.*

## 2657 BLUE BELL AT KIRBY HILL CLAIMING STKS 7f
3:15 (3:16) (F) 3-Y-O £3,129 (£894; £447) Stalls Low

Form RPR
-330 **1** **El Palmar**[7] 2457 3-8-10 68 PMakin(5) 3 73
(TDBarron) *sn trcking ldrs: smooth hdwy to ld 2f out: r.o wl* **16/1**
3-00 **2** 2 **True (IRE)**[20] 2112 3-8-10 70 WSupple 11 63
(MPTregoning) *hld up midfield: hdwy 3f out: hung lft: wnt 2nd appr fnl f: styd on: no imp on wnr* **2/1**[1]
40-6 **3** 4 **Delusion**[9] 2411 3-8-1 65 DAllan(3) 4 46
(TDEasterby) *prom: rdn and ev ch 2f out: kpt on same pce* **8/1**
0603 **4** 1 1/4 **Wares Home (IRE)**[10] 2389 3-8-12 67 (v) LEnstone(3) 5 54
(KRBurke) *missed break: sn midfield: rdn 2f out: kpt on same pce* **8/1**
-060 **5** hd **Delta Lady**[11] 2348 3-8-0 43 RFfrench 7 39
(RBastiman) *rr div: hdwy and in tch over 2f out: sn rdn: no further prog* **50/1**
0651 **6** 3/4 **Arfinnit (IRE)**[10] 2389 3-9-1 64 (v) ACulhane 1 52
(MRChannon) *mde most tl rdn and hdd 2f out: sn btn* **11/4**[2]
2453 **7** hd **Turf Princess**[23] 2036 3-8-3 56 DFentiman(7) 10 46
(IanEmmerson) *prom: ch over 2f out: sn rdn and btn* **6/1**[3]
45-6 **8** 1 **Salut Saint Cloud**[53] 1363 3-8-5 48 AMcCarthy 8 39
(MissVHaigh) *keen early: sn rr: drvn along 1/2-way: kpt on u.p fnl 2f: n.d* **66/1**
4005 **9** 2 **Knight To Remember (IRE)**[11] 2346 3-8-5 45 RFitzpatrick 13 33
(REBarr) *towards rr: rdn over 2f out: no hdwy* **33/1**
4000 **10** 9 **Hymns And Arias**[29] 1916 3-8-0 43 (p) PFessey 12 —
(RonaldThompson) *s.i.s: a bhd* **50/1**
6-00 **11** 6 **Bolshevik (IRE)**[11] 2356 3-8-6 50 ow1 RWinston 6 —
(TDEasterby) *cl up tl wknd over 2f out: towards rr whn eased appr fnl f:* **50/1**

00-0 **12** *10* **Knot In Doubt (IRE)**[17] 2195 3-8-5 ........................ GDuffield 2 —
(JAGlover) *bhd most of way* **28/1**
1m 28.76s (1.66) **Going Correction** +0.325s/f (Good) **12** Ran SP% **116.2**
Speed ratings: **103,100,96,94,94 93,93,92,89,79 72,61**CSF £45.87 TOTE £17.00: £4.90, £1.30, £2.40; EX 97.50.The winner was claimed by Paul Blockley for £10,000. True was claimed by Sue Lamyman for £10,000.
**Owner** J G Brown **Bred** A C M Spalding **Trained** Maunby, N Yorks

**FOCUS**
A moderate race run at a fair pace for the grade and the first two were both claimed. Although the winner may suffer if the handicapper takes the form at face value.

**NOTEBOOK**
**El Palmar**, stepping up in trip and down in class, travelled strongly but he came off a straight line in front and tended to carry his head high. He was claimed by Paul Blockley.
**True(IRE)**, dropped in class, was flat out turning in. All she wanted to do was hang left, but even so she was claimed by Sue Lamyman. With her it is a mind game. *Official explanation: jockey said filly hung left throughout.*
**Delusion** is only small and this is as good as she is now.
**Wares Home(IRE)**, who made a tardy start, reversed Ripon placings with Arfinnit.
**Delta Lady** had run over ten furlongs on her previous start.
**Arfinnit(IRE)**, drawn one, had his own way in front but he never looked like seeing out the extra furlong.
**Knot In Doubt(IRE)** *Official explanation: jockey said gelding hung right throughout.*

## 2658 ELLERY HILL RATING RELATED MAIDEN STKS (DIV I) 7f
**3:50** (3:51) (F) 3-Y-0+ **£3,059** (£874; £437) **Stalls** Low

Form RPR
30-5 **1** **Carte Noire**[57] 1309 3-8-6 60 ow1 ........................ ACulhane 9 59
(JGPortman) *prom: rdn to ld wl over 1f out: hld on wl u.p fnl f* **11/8**[1]
5504 **2** *½* **Amanda's Lad (IRE)**[15] 2236 4-9-4 60 ........................ WSupple 7 60
(MCChapman) *hld up: keen early: hdwy u.p 2f out: hung lft: wnt 2nd appr appr fnl f: ev ch ins last: no ex* **3/1**[2]
3-50 **3** *2 ½* **Lieuday**[20] 2122 5-9-4 46 ........................(p) GDuffield 3 54
(WMBrisbourne) *s.i.s: rr: hdwy over 1f out: styd on u.p fnl f: nvr able to chal* **9/1**
50-0 **4** *1 ¾* **Esteban**[46] 1502 4-9-4 54 ........................ RWinston 5 49
(JJQuinn) *sn cl up: rdn to ld 2f out: sn hdd: no ex* **12/1**
6660 **5** *1 ¼* **Indi Ano Star (IRE)**[14] 2259 3-8-8 60 ........................ RFitzpatrick 2 46
(DCarroll) *chsd ldrs: drvn along over 2f out: no hdwy* **7/1**[3]
505- **6** *½* **Regal Flight (IRE)**[284] 4466 3-8-8 57 ........................ RFfrench 8 44
(JMBradley) *in tch: drvn along over 2f out: no hdwy* **12/1**
000- **7** *½* **Canlis**[30] 5559 5-8-13 45 ........................ PBradley(5) 1 43
(DWThompson) *midfield: drvn along 3f out: sn btn* **66/1**
-500 **8** *2 ½* **Stop The Nonsense (IRE)**[20] 2122 3-8-8 53 ........................(bt[1]) JCarroll 6 37
(EJO'Neill) *towards rr whn bmpd over 4f out: rdn 3f out: no hdwy* **20/1**
400- **9** *5* **Polar Galaxy**[252] 5191 3-8-5 54 ........................ PFessey 4 21
(CWFairhurst) *mde most tl hdd 2f out: sn wknd* **12/1**
1m 29.29s (2.19) **Going Correction** +0.325s/f (Good)
**WFA** 3 from 4yo+ 10lb **9** Ran SP% **118.9**
Speed ratings: **100,99,96,94,93 92,92,89,83**CSF £5.64 TOTE £1.90: £1.30, £1.10, £2.80; EX 5.40.
**Owner** A H Robinson **Bred** A H And C E Robinson Partnership **Trained** Compton, Berks

**FOCUS**
A moderate race run at just a steady pace and the form looks poor.

**NOTEBOOK**
**Carte Noire** looked to have been found a good opportunity but struggled to get home.
**Amanda's Lad(IRE)**, a longstanding maiden, is running well this year and in the end was just held at bay.
**Lieuday** had plenty to find and seemed to find this trip his bare minimum.
**Esteban** has been tried at up to a mile and a half in the past.
**Indi Ano Star(IRE)** is starting to look fully exposed.
**Regal Flight(IRE)** was having his first outing for his new stable.

## 2659 WEATHERBYS INSURANCE SERVICES H'CAP 1m 4f
**4:35** (4:35) (E) (0-70,61) 3-Y-0+ **£3,594** (£1,106; £553; £276) **Stalls** Low

Form RPR
3161 **1** **Red Forest (IRE)**[7] 2449 5-9-3 54 6ex ........................(t) DaleGibson 5 73+
(JMackie) *keen: in tch: tk clsr order over 4f out: led over 2f out: pushed clr appr fnl f: eased clsng stages* **9/4**[1]
-615 **2** *6* **Field Spark**[10] 2394 4-9-7 58 ........................(p) GDuffield 10 64
(JAGlover) *keen: midfield: hdwy u.p over 2f out: styd on to go 2nd clsng stages: no ch w wnr* **9/2**[2]
4052 **3** *nk* **Bakiri (IRE)**[2] 2584 6-9-1 59 ........................ RoryMoore(7) 7 65
(AndrewReid) *cl up: led 5f out: hdd over 2f out: chsd wnr after: no imp: lost 2nd clsng stages* **5/1**[3]
0-25 **4** *5* **Swynford Pleasure**[7] 2449 8-9-1 55 ........................ DAllan(3) 6 53
(JHetherton) *hld up: hdwy u.p 3f out: no imp on ldrs fnl 2f* **8/1**
-040 **5** *nk* **Escalade**[17] 2216 7-9-6 57 ........................(v[1]) ACulhane 2 54
(WMBrisbourne) *hld up: effrt whn nt clr run briefly over 3f out: styd on fnl 2f: nvr able to chal* **14/1**
0040 **6** *nk* **Magic Charm**[5] 2501 6-7-8 38 ........................ LeanneKershaw(7) 11 35
(JeddO'Keeffe) *led after 1f: hdd 5f out: wknd 2f out* **20/1**
3005 **7** *nk* **Anniversary Guest (IRE)**[10] 2385 5-8-0 37 ........................ RFfrench 4 33
(MrsLucindaFeatherstone) *led 1f: remained prom tl outpcd 4f out: n.d after* **16/1**
6300 **8** *1 ½* **East Riding**[7] 2446 4-8-3 40 ........................ AnnStokell 3 34
(MissAStokell) *keen: midfield: effrt 4f out: no hdwy* **50/1**
4023 **9** *1 ¼* **Easibet Dot Net**[8] 2424 4-9-10 61 ........................(b) RWinston 8 53
(ISemple) *cl up: ev ch 3f out: sn rdn and wknd* **11/2**
006 **10** *5* **Zan Lo (IRE)**[7] 2446 4-9-7 58 ........................ WSupple 1 42
(BSRothwell) *hld up: rdn 4f out: sn btn* **14/1**
220/ **11** *15* **Norma Speakman (IRE)**[595] 5343 4-8-11 48 ........................ PFessey 9 8
(EWTuer) *rr: lost tch fnl 4f: t.o* **100/1**
2m 39.22s (4.02) **Going Correction** +0.325s/f (Good) **11** Ran SP% **119.0**
Speed ratings: **99,95,94,91,91 91,90,89,89,85 75**CSF £12.04 CT £46.82 TOTE £3.10: £1.40, £2.10, £2.60; EX 13.20.
**Owner** P Riley **Bred** Olympic B'Stock Ltd, Freynestown B'Stock And B Hi **Trained** Church Broughton, Derbys

**FOCUS**
In effect a 0-61 handicap and a tactical affair, although the form may be sound enough.

**NOTEBOOK**
**Red Forest(IRE)**, who lay handy in a race run at a very steady pace, raced with plenty of enthusiasm and, after pulling right away, was able to ease up near the line. He is clearly right at the top of his game.
**Field Spark**, 4lb higher than Leicester, was not helped by the lack of pace but he would only have finished second best anyway.
**Bakiri(IRE)**, making a quick reappearance, had the run of the race but was still nowhere near good enough.
**Swynford Pleasure**, at her best at this time of the year, attempted the impossible trying to come from off what was not a strong pace.
**Escalade**, tried in a visor, is on a long losing run and the race was not run to suit him. His stamina was not truly tested.
**Magic Charm**, who dropped anchor in front, seems best suited by much more undulating tracks.

## 2660 ELLERY HILL RATING RELATED MAIDEN STKS (DIV II) 7f
**5:10** (5:10) (F) 3-Y-0+ **£3,052** (£872; £436) **Stalls** Low

Form RPR
060- **1** **Miss Porcia**[227] 5687 3-8-5 59 ........................ AMcCarthy 7 57
(PWChapple-Hyam) *cl up: rdn to ld over 1f out: styd on* **9/2**[3]
05-0 **2** *1 ¼* **Dara Mac**[25] 1993 5-8-11 47 ........................ SuzanneFrance(7) 6 57
(NBycroft) *hld up in rr: hdwy 2f out: rdn appr fnl f: styd on wl ins last to go 2nd clsng stages: nt trble wnr* **40/1**
0204 **3** *1 ¼* **Luke After Me (IRE)**[13] 2292 4-9-4 55 ........................ RWinston 8 54
(GASwinbank) *hld up: hdwy 1/2-way: chsng ldrs and rdn over 1f out: no ex fnl f* **11/4**[1]
00-0 **4** *½* **Ablaj (IRE)**[41] 1613 3-8-8 57 ........................(v[1]) WSupple 4 52
(EALDunlop) *mde most tl rdn and hdd over 1f out: no ex ins last* **3/1**[2]
-060 **5** *¾* **Compton Micky**[9] 2411 3-8-5 60 ........................(p) DAllan(3) 2 51
(JBalding) *keen: trckd ldrs: n.m.r 5f out: chsng ldrs and rdn over 1f out: no ex whn nt clr run clsng stages* **50/1**
2002 **6** *8* **Sonderborg**[18] 2176 3-8-5 58 ........................(be) DaleGibson 1 27
(MissAMNewton-Smith) *dwlt: towards rr whn n.m.r 4f out: sn drvn along: no hdwy* **5/1**
60-2 **7** *nk* **Middleham Park (IRE)**[83] 823 4-9-4 60 ........................ GFaulkner 3 29
(PCHaslam) *keen: trckd ldrs: rdn over 2f out: sn wknd* **8/1**
00-5 **8** *nk* **Caribbean Blue**[9] 2411 3-8-5 52 ........................ RFfrench 5 25
(RMWhitaker) *in tch: drvn along 1/2-way: sn btn* **14/1**
-000 **9** *1 ½* **Military Two Step (IRE)**[23] 2036 3-8-5 58 ........................(p) LEnstone(3) 9 24
(KRBurke) *towards rr: rdn 1/2-way: sn btn* **20/1**
1m 29.13s (2.03) **Going Correction** +0.325s/f (Good)
**WFA** 3 from 4yo+ 10lb **9** Ran SP% **113.5**
Speed ratings: **101,99,98,97,96 87,87,86,85**CSF £164.40 TOTE £5.40: £2.60, £7.40, £1.40; EX 300.10.
**Owner** Charles Alan McKechnie **Bred** C N And Mrs Hart **Trained** Newmarket, Suffolk
■ Stewards Enquiry : R Winston caution: careless riding

**FOCUS**
Another moderate event run at a fair pace but the form looks poor.

**NOTEBOOK**
**Miss Porcia**, with her third trainer on her fifth career start, showed a good attitude and, rated just 59, she should continue to pay her way in modest handicaps. *Official explanation: trainer's representative said, regarding the improved form shown, this was filly's first run from the yard, adding that filly had been working well in recent weeks*
**Dara Mac**, a maiden after 25 starts, would have met the winner on 15lb better terms in a handicap.
**Luke After Me(IRE)** had no excuse this time and is proving hard to win with.
**Ablaj(IRE)**, in a first-time visor, had his own way in front but his attitude does not impress.
**Compton Micky** met trouble in running and was a shade unfortunate not to finish third best.
**Sonderborg** *Official explanation: jockey said filly stumbled shortly after start.*

## 2661 RACING POST APPRENTICE H'CAP 5f
**5:40** (5:41) (G ) (0-55,55) 3-Y-0 **£2,583** (£738; £369) **Stalls** High

Form RPR
46-0 **1** **Icenaslice (IRE)**[28] 1934 3-9-1 **51** ........................ DTudhope(3) 2 74
(JJQuinn) *mde all: drvn clr appr fnl f: comf* **9/2**[2]
0000 **2** *6* **Burkees Graw (IRE)**[17] 2207 3-8-11 **47** ........................ DFentiman(3) 9 49
(MrsSLamyman) *dwlt: hld up: hdwy u.p 2f out: r.o to go 2nd wl ins fnl f: no ch w wnr* **7/1**
-063 **3** *½* **Vendors Mistake (IRE)**[21] 2098 3-9-1 **48** ........................ RoryMoore 1 48
(AndrewReid) *prom in centre: rdn and edgd rt over 1f out: no ex fnl f* **4/1**[1]
50-0 **4** *nk* **Cellino**[80] 1027 3-9-0 **47** ........................ PMakin 5 46
(AndrewTurnell) *chsd ldrs: rdn 2f out: kpt on fnl f* **14/1**
00-0 **5** *shd* **Shamrock Tea**[14] 2269 3-9-8 **55** ........................ NataliaGemelova 6 54
(RAFahey) *in tch: rdn 2f out: kpt on fnl f* **11/2**[3]
0000 **6** *1* **Peace Treaty (IRE)**[11] 2349 3-7-13 **35** ........................ CHaddon(3) 10 30
(SRBowring) *sn rr: sme late hdwy: n.d* **33/1**
-500 **7** *¾* **Shanghai Surprise**[6] 2468 3-8-5 **45** ........................(p) KPierrepont(7) 4 37
(JBalding) *chsd ldrs 3f out: no hdwy* **20/1**
0360 **8** *1* **Parallel Lines (IRE)**[10] 2380 3-8-13 **46** ........................(b) SJDonohoe 8 35
(PDEvans) *prom: rdn 2f out: fdd* **4/1**[1]
66-0 **9** *nk* **Gemini Girl (IRE)**[38] 1689 3-9-7 **54** ........................ MLawson 7 42
(MDHammond) *chsd ldrs: rdn 2f out: fdd* **7/1**
59.93 secs (0.03) **Going Correction** -0.10s/f (Good) **9** Ran SP% **112.9**
Speed ratings: **95,85,84,84,83 82,81,79,79**CSF £35.04 CT £135.14 TOTE £4.90: £2.80, £3.60, £1.90; EX 91.20 Place 6 £33.28, Place 5 £8.86.
**Owner** Miss D A Johnson **Bred** Mrs Roseanne And Paul McEnery **Trained** Settrington, N Yorks

**FOCUS**
A seller in all but name, but the winner was a class above.

**NOTEBOOK**
**Icenaslice(IRE)** proved a totally different proposition on this much faster ground and in the end came clean away. Connections will be keen to turn her out without a penalty before she is reassessed.
**Burkees Graw(IRE)**, suited by a return to the minimum trip and happy to be back on fast ground, has tumbled down the ratings and did just enough to claim a remote second spot.
**Vendors Mistake(IRE)**, drawn one, edged right and like the rest was left for dead by the winner.
**Cellino**, absent for 80 days, was having just her sixth career start.
**Shamrock Tea**, dropped 5lb on his second outing for his new trainer, really needs six and his win was in the soft.
**Peace Treaty(IRE)** is due to race from a 5lb lower mark in future. *Official explanation: jockey said filly stumbled just over one furlong after start.*
**Parallel Lines(IRE)** was on the retreat soon after halfway.
T/Plt: £72.60 to a £1 stake. Pool: £28,322.40. 284.45 winning tickets. T/Qpdt: £6.10 to a £1 stake. Pool: £2,601.25. 314.00 winning tickets. JF

# 2451 WOLVERHAMPTON (A.W) (L-H)
Friday, June 4

**OFFICIAL GOING: Standard**
This was the last meeting to be held at Dunstall Park on Fibresand.
Wind: slt across Weather: cloudy

## 2662 ROOFTOP HOUSING CLAIMING STKS 1m 6f 166y(F)
**1:55** (1:56) (F) 4-Y-0+ **£2,926** (£836; £418) **Stalls** High

Form RPR
0214 **1** **Romil Star (GER)**[7] 2443 7-8-11 65 ........................(v) KDalgleish 2 64
(KRBurke) *hld up: hdwy 6f out: rdn to ld wl over 1f out: sn clr* **5/6**[1]

030- **2** *10* **Desert Quill (IRE)**[236] 5507 4-8-1 50 ............ BSwarbrick(5) 8 46
(WMBrisbourne) *hld up in tch: lost pl over 7f out: hdwy over 5f out: rdn 4f out: wnt 2nd 1f out: no ch w wnr* **16/1**[3]

064- **3** *7* **Gordy's Joy**[24] 4836 4-8-6 35 ............ CCatlin 4 37
(GAHam) *hld up: hdwy after 5f: rdn over 5f out: led over 2f out tl wl over 1f out: wknd fnl f* **66/1**

**4** *½* **Amusement**[400] 8-9-2 ............ DNolan(3) 6 49
(DGBridgwater) *led after 1f tl after 3f: w ldr: led over 4f out: rdn over 3f out: hdd over 2f out: wknd over 1f out* **33/1**

2000 **5** *5* **Aveiro (IRE)**[4] 2525 8-9-5 62 ............ IMongan 3 43
(MissGayKelleway) *led 1f: w ldr: led after 3f: rdn and hdd over 4f out: n.m.r on ins 3f out: sn wknd* **11/8**[2]

0-00 **6** *24* **Regal Repose**[16] 2228 4-8-0 50 ............ AMackay 5 —
(AJChamberlain) *prom: rdn over 6f out: wknd over 4f out: t.o* **80/1**

3 **7** *10* **Good Time Bobby**[7] 2445 7-8-8 ............ JDO'Reilly(7) 1 —
(JO'Reilly) *s.s: a in rr: lost tch over 5f out: t.o* **16/1**[3]

3m 22.99s (1.49) **Going Correction** -0.125s/f (Stan) **7** Ran SP% **114.1**
Speed ratings: **91,85,81,81,79 66,60**CSF £16.11 TOTE £2.10: £1.10, £6.80; EX 17.30.
**Owner** Mrs Elaine M Burke **Bred** J H A Baggen **Trained** Middleham Moor, N Yorks

**FOCUS**
A weak staying claimer and the winner did not need to be at his best to score.

**NOTEBOOK**
**Romil Star(GER)**, back in a visor instead of the blinkers, was well in on official figures. He spreadeagled his field on this return to a longer trip.
**Desert Quill(IRE)** was trying a longer distance on her first outing since leaving David Elsworth.
**Gordy's Joy** had a difficult task judged on official ratings.
**Aveiro(IRE)** may not have been helped by being taken on for the lead, and was already in trouble when briefly short of room leaving the back straight.

## 2663 TOUCHSTONE HOUSING ASSOCIATION H'CAP 5f (F)
**2:30** (2:31) (F) (0-55,54) 3-Y-O+ **£3,003** (£858; £429) **Stalls** Low

Form RPR

3122 **1** **Larky's Lob**[20] 2123 5-9-4 53 ............ JDO'Reilly(7) 13 69
(JO'Reilly) *a.p: led over 3f out: clr 2f out: rdn out* **5/1**[2]

0105 **2** *5* **Lucius Verrus (USA)**[20] 2123 4-9-10 52 ............ (v) SWhitworth 3 50
(DShaw) *mid-div: rdn over 2f out: hdwy over 1f out: r.o ins fnl f: no ch w wnr* **8/1**

1450 **3** *1 ¼* **Star Lad (IRE)**[28] 1941 4-9-5 47 ............ (b) IMongan 11 41
(RBrotherton) *mid-div: rdn over 3f out: hdwy over 2f out: r.o one pce fnl f* **14/1**

-034 **4** *hd* **Davids Mark**[18] 2166 4-9-8 53 ............ DCorby(3) 8 46
(JRJenkins) *chsd ldrs: rdn over 2f out: wnt 2nd wl over 1f out: no ex ins fnl f* **8/1**

-616 **5** *2* **Boisdale (IRE)**[9] 2404 6-9-4 53 ............ LTreadwell(7) 10 39
(SLKeightley) *sn outpcd: hdwy on outside over 1f out: kpt on same pce fnl f* **14/1**

3051 **6** *½* **Red Leicester**[2] 2586 4-9-12 54 6ex ............ (v) DeanMcKeown 7 38
(JAGlover) *prom: rdn over 2f out: wknd ins fnl f* **5/1**[2]

06-0 **7** *1 ¾* **Speed On**[28] 1941 11-9-10 52 ............ DSweeney 9 29
(HCandy) *nvr nr ldrs* **14/1**

0000 **8** *1 ¼* **Blessed Place**[28] 1937 4-9-8 50 ............ CCatlin 6 23
(DJSFfrenchDavis) *w ldr: led after 1f: sn hdd: rdn over 2f out: wknd fnl f* **33/1**

3110 **9** *½* **Maromito (IRE)**[15] 2246 7-9-5 47 ............ KDalgleish 4 18
(RBastiman) *chsd ldrs 2f* **4/1**[1]

00-1 **10** *3 ½* **Molotov**[11] 2350 4-9-9 51 6ex ............ LVickers 1 10
(IWMcinnes) *prom tl rdn and wknd over 2f out* **16/1**

3031 **11** *nk* **Hagley Park**[30] 1886 5-9-2 49 ............ PMulrennan(5) 5 7
(MQuinn) *led 1f: rdn over 3f out: wknd over 2f out* **10/1**

000/ **12** *6* **Dispol Verity**[542] 5871 4-9-2 49 ............ BSwarbrick(5) 12 —
(WMBrisbourne) *sltly hmpd s: outpcd* **33/1**

6006 **13** *22* **Scary Night (IRE)**[20] 2123 4-9-9 51 ............ (p) JEdmunds 2 —
(JBalding) *outpcd: virtually p.u ins fnl f* **7/1**[3]

61.79 secs (-1.01) **Going Correction** -0.125s/f (Stan) **13** Ran SP% **128.9**
Speed ratings: **103,95,93,92,89 88,85,83,83,77 77,67,32**CSF £48.82 CT £562.83 TOTE £6.00: £1.90, £2.80, £5.40; EX 70.90.
**Owner** J O R Racing **Bred** P Balding **Trained** Brierley, S Yorks

**FOCUS**
The time was fair and few got competitive in this weakish sprint handicap. Although the winner looks improved for the drop in trip, the opposition is unreliable.

**NOTEBOOK**
**Larky's Lob**, on his first ever start over the minimum trip, had it sewn up turning for home and only needed to be kept up to his work.
**Lucius Verrus(USA)** found the winner had flown by the time he got going.
**Star Lad(IRE)** seems better suited to six furlongs.
**Davids Mark** ran a lot better than on his only previous outing on Fibresand at Southwell in March last year.
**Boisdale(IRE)** was rather taken off his legs on only his second start over five furlongs.
**Red Leicester**, attempting a quick follow-up, had excuses. *Official explanation: jockey said filly was struck into.*
**Molotov** *Official explanation: jockey said gelding finished distressed.*
**Hagley Park** *Official explanation: jockey said mare hung left in the closing stages.*
**Scary Night(IRE)** *Official explanation: jockey said gelding finished lame.*

## 2664 ST HELENS HOUSING ASSOCIATION (S) STKS 6f (F)
**3:05** (3:05) (G) 3-Y-O+ **£2,625** (£750; £375) **Stalls** Far side

Form RPR

06-4 **1** **Mallia**[25] 1994 11-9-0 46 ............ Laura-JayneCrawford(7) 8 48
(TDBarron) *chsd ldrs: rdn and wnt 2f out: led ins f: jst hld on* **9/1**[3]

4433 **2** *hd* **Indian Music**[24] 2012 7-9-12 38 ............ JBramhill 7 52
(ABerry) *bhd tl hdwy over 2f out: rdn over 1f out: r.o ins fnl f: jst failed* **16/1**

3121 **3** *3* **On The Trail**[36] 1739 7-9-12 56 ............ ANicholls 5 43
(DWChapman) *led: rdn over 1f out: hdd ins fnl f: wknd towards fin* **3/1**[2]

2055 **4** *1* **Rafters Music (IRE)**[20] 2118 9-9-7 66 ............ GCarter 9 35
(JulianPoulton) *mid-div: sn pushed along: rdn and hdwy over 1f out: r.o one pce fnl f* **6/5**[1]

2-00 **5** *½* **Brave Chief**[18] 2166 3-8-13 51 ............ BDoyle 4 34
(JAPickering) *s.i.s: racd wd: hdwy 3f out: kpt on same pce fnl f* **20/1**

050 **6** *shd* **Pips Song (IRE)**[41] 1625 9-9-9 47 ............ RMiles(3) 11 39
(PWHiatt) *prom: rdn over 2f out: wknd 1f out* **14/1**

5 **7** *2 ½* **Plattocrat**[66] 1192 4-9-4 ............ THamilton(3) 6 26
(RPElliott) *chsd ldrs: rdn over 2f out: wknd wl over 1f out* **50/1**

6000 **8** *1* **Back At De Front (IRE)**[11] 2359 3-8-13 58 ............ CCatlin 1 23
(NEBerry) *bhd: rdn over 3f out: n.d* **12/1**

6130 **9** *nk* **Welsh Whisper**[11] 2359 5-9-2 44 ............ NChalmers(5) 3 22
(SABrookshaw) *s.i.s: outpcd* **16/1**

0-00 **10** *3 ½* **Jacks Delight**[11] 2359 4-9-7 ............ (v[1]) LVickers 10 12
(BDLeavy) *chsd ldr tl rdn 2f out: wknd over 1f out* **66/1**

0000 **11** *6* **Zak Facta (IRE)**[7] 2456 4-9-7 45 ............ (v) IMongan 2 —
(MissDAMchale) *bhd fnl 4f* **10/1**

1m 15.7s (-0.10) **Going Correction** -0.125s/f (Stan)
**WFA** 3 from 4yo+ 8lb **11** Ran SP% **123.9**
Speed ratings: **95,94,90,89,88 88,85,83,83,78 70**CSF £147.77 TOTE £12.60: £3.00, £3.00, £1.10; EX 104.70.There was no bid for the winner.
**Owner** Harrowgate Bloodstock Ltd **Bred** B J McAllister **Trained** Maunby, N Yorks
■ A flip start was used due to a dispute involving the stalls handlers

**FOCUS**
A poor seller and not a bad start considering the stalls were not in use because of industrial action. However, the form has a suspect look.

**NOTEBOOK**
**Mallia**, not disgraced on his reappearance at Redcar, just managed to make it ten victories over this course and distance.
**Indian Music** would have been meeting the winner on 13lb better terms in a handicap and could not quite pull it off.
**On The Trail** could not take advantage of the fact that he would have been 5lb and 18lb respectively worse off with the first two in a handicap.
**Rafters Music(IRE)** had a big chance on official ratings and this return to six should also have been in his favour. *Official explanation: jockey said gelding was never travelling.*
**Brave Chief** was one of only two to suffer at the flip start.

## 2665 EXTRACARE CHARITABLE TRUST H'CAP 1m 4f (F)
**3:40** (3:41) (E) (0-70,70) 3-Y-O **£3,770** (£1,160; £580; £290) **Stalls** Low

Form RPR

0402 **1** **Queen's Fantasy**[40] 1643 3-8-7 56 ............ (v) SWhitworth 4 68
(DHaydnJones) *s.i.s: sn prom: led 8f out: rdn and hdd over 2f out: rallied to ld ins fnl f: r.o wl* **14/1**

2223 **2** *3* **Jakarmi**[25] 1997 3-9-4 70 ............ RMiles(3) 8 77
(BPalling) *w ldr: rdn to ld over 2f out: edgd rt wl over 1f out: hdd ins fnl f: no ex* **7/2**[2]

-056 **3** *1 ¼* **Rock Lobster**[25] 1995 3-9-5 68 ............ BDoyle 9 73
(JGGiven) *a.p: rdn and ev ch whn rn wd ent st: one pce fnl f* **11/1**

0146 **4** *1 ¾* **It's Blue Chip**[25] 1998 3-8-13 62 ............ (e) PaulEddery 10 65
(PWD'Arcy) *s.i.s: hld up: hdwy over 5f out: rdn and one pce fnl 2f* **6/1**[3]

-633 **5** *½* **General Flumpa**[25] 1998 3-9-2 65 ............ GBaker 11 67
(CFWall) *hld up and bhd: smooth hdwy over 4f out: rdn 3f out: one pce fnl 2f* **2/1**[1]

031 **6** *16* **Amankila (IRE)**[29] 1912 3-9-5 68 ............ IMongan 1 46
(MLWBell) *hld up and bhd: hdwy 4f out: sn rdn: wknd 3f out* **8/1**

0500 **7** *10* **Amwell Brave**[25] 1997 3-8-13 65 ............ DCorby(3) 6 28
(JRJenkins) *bhd fnl 4f* **16/1**

500- **8** *1 ¾* **Equus (IRE)**[221] 5792 3-8-10 66 ow1 ............ LTreadwell(7) 12 26
(LADace) *hld up: rdn over 5f out: bhd fnl 4f* **40/1**

00-0 **9** *1 ½* **House Of Blues**[38] 1683 3-8-11 60 ............ GGibbons 5 18
(JAOsborne) *prom: rdn 7f out: wknd over 5f out* **25/1**

06-5 **10** *5* **Ivy League Star (IRE)**[13] 2312 3-9-2 65 ............ KDalgleish 7 15
(BWHills) *led 4f: wknd 4f out* **12/1**

1654 **11** *19* **Perfect Balance (IRE)**[25] 1995 3-8-11 60 ............ KimTinkler 2 —
(NTinkler) *a bhd: t.o fnl 4f* **14/1**

0510 **P** **Our Little Rosie**[53] 1365 3-8-11 60 ............ DSweeney 3 —
(MBlanshard) *bhd most of way: t.o whn p.u and dismntd 1f out* **12/1**

2m 39.3s (-2.50) **Going Correction** -0.125s/f (Stan) **12** Ran SP% **130.2**
Speed ratings: **103,101,100,99,98 88,81,80,79,75 63,—**CSF £68.75 CT £596.30 TOTE £15.50: £2.90, £1.90, £4.40; EX 78.60.
**Owner** Mick White **Bred** P A Mason **Trained** Efail Isaf, Rhondda C Taff

**FOCUS**
A moderate but interesting race for the track, but the winner made sure the emphasis was on stamina. The form should stand up on this surface.

**NOTEBOOK**
**Queen's Fantasy** was suited by a return to this trip having shown improved form over ten furlongs at Brighton when fitted with a visor. She should stay further.
**Jakarmi** was ridden as if this longer trip would not be a problem but did eventually just get outstayed by the winner.
**Rock Lobster** did not help his chances by racing wide off the home turn.
**It's Blue Chip** was back on sand having not progressed since springing a surprise at Windsor in April.
**General Flumpa** could not sustain a promising-looking effort.
**Our Little Rosie** *Official explanation: jockey said filly lost her action.*

## 2666 ARENA HOUSING ASSOCIATION H'CAP 7f (F)
**4:25** (4:25) (F) (0-55,54) 3-Y-O+ **£3,038** (£868; £434) **Stalls** High

Form RPR

6050 **1** **Old Bailey (USA)**[14] 2260 4-9-9 54 ............ (v[1]) PMulrennan(5) 7 63
(TDBarron) *hld up: hdwy over 3f out: rdn over 1f out: r.o to ld cl home* **9/2**[2]

0312 **2** *nk* **Marabar**[16] 2227 6-9-10 50 ............ (b) ANicholls 12 58
(DWChapman) *hld up: sn in tch: hdwy 4f out: sn rdn: led 1f out: edgd lft ins fnl f: hdd cl home* **7/1**[3]

5534 **3** *2 ½* **Kanz Wood (USA)**[7] 2454 8-9-2 45 ............ (v[1]) DNolan(3) 5 47
(AWCarroll) *s.i.s: bhd tl hdwy over 1f out: r.o ins fnl f: nrst fin* **8/1**

6106 **4** *nk* **Bulawayo**[10] 2379 7-9-6 49 ............ (b) DCorby(3) 4 50
(AndrewReid) *prom: lost pl over 5f out: rdn 4f out: rallied over 1f out: kpt on ins fnl f* **12/1**

0021 **5** *3* **Turn Around**[25] 2006 4-9-12 52 ............ IMongan 6 45
(BWHills) *led: rdn 3f out: hdd 1f out: wknd* **4/1**[1]

-401 **6** *1 ¾* **Gilly's General (IRE)**[46] 1515 4-9-9 49 ............ GGibbons 11 38
(JWUnett) *w ldr: rdn over 3f out: ev ch over 2f out: wknd wl over 1f out* **16/1**

0300 **7** *2 ½* **New Options**[20] 2120 7-9-10 50 ............ (b) GCarter 10 32
(WJMusson) *bhd: hdwy on outside 3f out: no further progess fnl 2f* **16/1**

2220 **8** *2* **Carlton (IRE)**[27] 1969 10-9-7 52 ............ RThomas(5) 2 29
(CRDore) *prom 3f* **9/2**[2]

-514 **9** *4* **Super Dominion**[7] 2456 7-9-0 45 ............ (p) StephanieHollinshead(5) 3 11
(RHollinshead) *mid-div: rdn 4f out: sn bhd* **10/1**

0-40 **10** *¾* **Puri**[32] 1820 5-9-13 53 ............ BDoyle 1 18
(JGGiven) *a bhd* **12/1**

040- **11** *9* **Tokewanna**[235] 5546 4-9-9 54 ............ BSwarbrick(5) 8 —
(WMBrisbourne) *prom tl wknd over 3f out* **16/1**

-056 **12** *11* **Encore Royale**[7] 2456 4-9-7 47 ............ (b[1]) OUrbina 9 —
(JJay) *rel to r: a t.o* **16/1**

1m 30.14s (-0.18) **Going Correction** -0.125s/f (Stan) **12** Ran SP% **128.0**
Speed ratings: **96,95,92,92,89 87,84,81,77,76 66,53**CSF £39.42 CT £261.78 TOTE £7.40: £2.90, £2.90, £4.10; EX 73.50.
**Owner** J Baggott **Bred** Barbara Hunter **Trained** Maunby, N Yorks

**FOCUS**
A weak handicap with the joint top weights rated only 54. The pace was modest and the form is ordinary.
**NOTEBOOK**
**Old Bailey(USA)**, travelling well in the first-time visor, appreciated the return to Fibresand and made it two out of two over course and distance.
**Marabar**, still thrown in on her turf form, could not quite hold the winner.
**Kanz Wood(USA)**, 10lb lower than when last in a handicap, did not find the fitting of a visor improving his starting.
**Bulawayo** was 3lb higher than when successful in first-time blinkers over course and distance in March.
**Turn Around** put the value of his win in a seller here last time into perspective.
**Carlton(IRE)** *Official explanation: jockey said gelding was never travelling*

## 2667 HOMEZONE HOUSING ASSOCIATION H'CAP — 1m 100y(F)
**5:00** (5:00) (F) (0-55,58) 3-Y-O — **£3,024** (£864; £432) **Stalls** Low

Form — RPR
-511 **1** **Incisor**[6] 2484 3-9-9 **58** 6ex — JDSmith 12 — 78
(SKirk) *hld up: hdwy over 6f out: led over 2f out: sn rdn: edgd lft ins fnl f: rdn out* — **2/1**[2]
00-0 **2** 2 1/2 **Raysoot (IRE)**[49] 1453 3-9-4 **53** — PMcCabe 13 — 68
(ACStewart) *s.i.s: reminders 7f out: gd hdwy on outside over 6f out: led 5f out: rdn over 3f out: hdd over 2f out: no ex ins fnl* — **6/4**[1]
0005 **3** 13 **Spring Dancer**[9] 2395 3-9-1 **53** — RMiles(3) 10 — 40
(BGPowell) *s.i.s: hdwy over 5f out: rdn and wknd over 2f out* — **20/1**
0650 **4** 1 1/2 **Dante's Devine (IRE)**[18] 2176 3-9-3 **52** — OUrbina 1 — 36
(ABailey) *led: hdd 5f out: wknd over 3f out* — **33/1**
006 **5** nk **Purple Rain (IRE)**[35] 1753 3-9-4 **53** — IMongan 3 — 37
(MLWBell) *pushed along: sn wl bhd: hdwy wl over 1f out: nvr nr ldrs* — **10/1**[3]
3060 **6** hd **Anisette**[21] 2098 3-9-0 **49** — GCarter 8 — 32
(JulianPoulton) *chsd ldrs tl wknd over 4f out* — **10/1**[3]
4510 **7** 5 **Flying Spud**[9] 2395 3-9-1 **50** — ADaly 6 — 23
(JLSpearing) *prom: rdn over 5f out: wknd over 4f out* — **12/1**
20-0 **8** 1 **Weet An Haul**[9] 2411 3-9-3 **55** — DNolan(3) 4 — 26
(PABlockley) *chsd ldrs tl rdn and wknd over 3f out* — **14/1**
3-46 **9** 3/4 **Keltic Rainbow (IRE)**[45] 1532 3-9-6 **55** — (v[1]) PaulEddery 9 — 24
(DHaydnJones) *a bhd* — **14/1**
3-00 **10** 6 **Ctesiphon (USA)**[28] 1946 3-9-1 **50** — (b[1]) BDoyle 7 — 6
(JGGiven) *sn rdn along and wl bhd* — **33/1**
-500 **11** 6 **Rumour Mill (IRE)**[18] 2168 3-8-10 **50** — MSavage(5) 11 — —
(NEBerry) *chsd ldrs tl lost pl over 5f out* — **33/1**
3630 **12** nk **Son Of Rembrandt (IRE)**[23] 2029 3-8-10 **52** — MHoward(7) 2 — —
(DKIvory) *a bhd* — **33/1**

1m 49.88s (-1.21) **Going Correction** -0.125s/f (Stan) — **12** Ran SP% **129.1**
Speed ratings: **101,98,85,84,83 83,78,77,76,70 64,64**CSF £5.61 CT £44.41 TOTE £3.80: £1.20, £1.30, £3.90; EX 8.60 Place 6 £157.39, Place 5 £88.18.
**Owner** R Gander **Bred** J Godfrey **Trained** Upper Lambourn, Berks

**FOCUS**
An uncompetitive handicap in which the bookmakers went 10/1 bar two and the market got it spot on. The time was fair and the first two look ahead of the Handicapper.
**NOTEBOOK**
**Incisor** did not have too much difficulty in completing a hat-trick on turf and both All-Weather surfaces in use in this country. He continues in fine form and may not have stopped winning yet.
**Raysoot(IRE)** was a racecourse whisper on this step up in distance but came up against a horse in top form on this sand debut.
**Spring Dancer**, having her first run on this surface, was well beaten by the first two but did not fare that badly after a slow start. Her best form has been at shorter trips
**Dante's Devine(IRE)** *Official explanation: jockey said gelding was hanging right-handed.*
T/Plt: £29.00 to a £1 stake. Pool: £20,199.85. 507.70 winning tickets. T/Qpdt: £14.10 to a £1 stake. Pool: £1,964.90. 102.60 winning tickets. KH

# 2509 CAPANNELLE (R-H)
Friday, June 4

**OFFICIAL GOING: Good**

## 2668a PREMIO ALESSANDRO PERRONE (LISTED) (FILLIES) — 5f 110y
**3:05** (3:08) 2-Y-O — **£24,648** (£10,845; £5,915; £2,958)

RPR
**1** **Tenderlit (USA)** 2-8-11 — DVargiu 4 — 94
(RMenichetti, Italy)
**2** 2 1/2 **Polly Alexander (IRE)**[21] 2083 2-8-11 — FLynch 6 — 85
(MJWallace) *pressed leader, every chance 1f out, one pace, took 2nd close home SP 24-10* — 1
**3** nse **Shalimar (ITY)** 2-8-11 — MPasquale 5 — 85
(LBrogi, Italy)
**4** 3/4 **Golden Sensation (IRE)** 2-8-11 — PBorrelli 7 — 82
(GFratini, Italy)
**5** 4 **Live And Learn (ITY)** 2-8-11 — FJovine 3 — 68
(CCardaioli, Italy)
**6** 1/2 **Lasika** 2-8-11 — SMulas 2 — 66
(BGrizzetti, Italy)
**7** 5 **Seel** 2-8-11 — MMonteriso 1 — 49
(GCollela, Italy)

65.60 secs — **7** Ran SP% **29.4**
Speed ratings: .
**Owner** Scuderia Razza Dell'Olmo **Bred** Foxfield **Trained** Italy

**NOTEBOOK**
**Polly Alexander(IRE)** was taking a theoretical rise in grade and had her chance without proving good enough.

## 2669a PREMIO ALBERTO GIUBILO (LISTED) (C&G) — 5f 110y
**4:05** (4:13) 2-Y-O — **£24,648** (£10,845; £5,915; £2,958)

RPR
**1** **Golden Stravinsky (USA)** 2-8-11 — (t) DVargiu 4 — 87
(GFratini, Italy)
**2** 2 **Catwalk Cleric (IRE)**[30] 1882 2-8-11 — FLynch 8 — 80
(MJWallace) *disputed 4th, headway 1 1/2f out, ran on take 2nd well inside final furlong SP 39-10* — 1
**3** 3/4 **Patapan (USA)** 2-8-11 — GTemperini 5 — 77
(RBrogi, Italy)
**4** 5 **Bold Terms (USA)** 2-8-11 — MPasquale 2 — 60
(APeraino, Italy)
**5** nse **So Vain (ITY)** 2-8-11 — PAragoni 1 — 60
(LRiccardi, Italy)
**6** 2 **Mister Fasliyev (IRE)** 2-8-11 — MMonteriso 3 — 53
(GColella, Italy)
**7** hd **Golden Pyramid (IRE)** 2-8-11 — PBorrelli 7 — 52
(GFratini, Italy)
**8** 1 **Peppone (ITY)** 2-8-11 — LManiezzi 6 — 49
(RMenichetti, Italy)

65.60 secs — **8** Ran SP% **20.4**
Speed ratings: .
**Owner** Scuderia Golden Horse **Bred** Berkshire Stud & Oak Cliff Stable **Trained** Italy

**NOTEBOOK**
**Catwalk Cleric(IRE)** continues to progress along the right lines and shaped here as though an extra furlong will help.

# 2467 DONCASTER (L-H)
Saturday, June 5

**OFFICIAL GOING: Round course - good (good to firm in places); straight course - good to firm (firm in places)**
The going was well watered, almost good but a bit loose on top.
Wind: Mod 1/2 against Weather: Fine

## 2670 TATTENHAM CORNER FILLIES' H'CAP — 6f
**1:50** (1:51) (D) (0-80,77) 4-Y-O+ — **£5,508** (£1,695; £847; £423) **Stalls** Far side

Form — RPR
6422 **1** **Glencoe Solas (IRE)**[6] 2506 4-9-2 **66** — MFenton 3 — 80
(SKirk) *chsd ldrs: led and hung lft over 1f out: hld on wl* — **11/2**[1]
0600 **2** 3/4 **College Maid (IRE)**[9] 2423 7-8-0 **50** oh1 ow2 — (b) CCatlin 5 — 62
(JSGoldie) *in rr: gd hdwy 2f out: nt qckn ins last* — **33/1**
-046 **3** 2 **Roman Mistress (IRE)**[12] 2369 4-8-12 **65** — DAllan(3) 13 — 71
(TDEasterby) *chsd ldr: styd on same pce appr fnl f* — **7/1**[3]
3-66 **4** 3/4 **Indian Steppes (FR)**[7] 2473 5-9-1 **68** — LisaJones(3) 8 — 72
(JulianPoulton) *sn in rr on outside: hdwy over 2f out: nvr rchd ldrs* — **7/1**[3]
0-06 **5** 1/2 **College Queen**[16] 2252 6-8-11 **66** — (b) PMulrennan(5) 4 — 68
(SGollings) *led tl over 1f out: fdd* — **20/1**
1135 **6** 3/4 **Maddie's A Jem**[6] 2506 4-9-11 **75** — SWKelly 12 — 75
(JRJenkins) *chsd ldrs: wknd over 1f out* — **8/1**
5034 **7** 5 **Bint Royal (IRE)**[3] 2598 6-8-6 **56** — (p) JQuinn 11 — 41
(MissVHaigh) *swtg: chsd ldrs: rdn 2f out: sn btn* — **6/1**[2]
35-0 **8** 3/4 **Officer's Pink**[16] 2238 4-9-1 **70** — NDeSouza(5) 7 — 53
(PFICole) *sn bhd and drvn along: nvr on terms* — **25/1**
0532 **9** 1/2 **Ballinger Express**[18] 2217 4-8-9 **64** — (b) NChalmers(5) 6 — 45
(AMBalding) *s.v.s: bhd tl sme hdwy fnl 2f* — **12/1**
02-0 **10** nk **Magic Music (IRE)**[33] 1825 5-9-2 **71** — BSwarbrick(5) 10 — 51
(WMBrisbourne) *trckd ldrs: rdn 2f out: sn wknd* — **11/2**[1]
0300 **11** 2 1/2 **Playful Spirit**[7] 2482 5-7-12 **48** oh3 — (v) JBramhill 2 — 21
(JBalding) *sn in rr* — **40/1**
0030 **12** 18 **Consensus (IRE)**[8] 2461 5-9-13 **77** — TWilliams 1 — —
(MBrittain) *mid-div: rdn and lost pl 2f out: eased* — **20/1**
-005 **13** 1 **Certa Cito**[18] 2219 4-8-6 **56** — JCarroll 9 — —
(TDEasterby) *swtg: s.i.s: a bhd: eased* — **11/1**

1m 13.5s (-0.78) **Going Correction** +0.025s/f (Good) — **13** Ran SP% **115.9**
Speed ratings: **106,105,102,101,100 99,93,92,91,90 87,63,62**CSF £191.98 CT £1324.76 TOTE £5.50: £1.90, £6.70, £3.00; EX 202.80.
**Owner** Eddie Tynan **Bred** E Tynan **Trained** Upper Lambourn, Berks
■ This race had a flip start due to industrial action.

**FOCUS**
An ordinary contest with a flip start, but they largely started from their correct draw. The time was decent but the winner will need to improve to follow up.
**NOTEBOOK**
**Glencoe Solas(IRE)**, who continually swished her tail in the paddock, had the blinkers left off. She tended to hang in front but kept going well enough and was not winning out of turn.
**College Maid(IRE)**, carrying 2lb overweight, returned to her best and was just held at bay.
**Roman Mistress(IRE)**, 10lb lower than her last success, looked at her best yet was a negative on the betting front. Drawn 13 of 13, she raced in isolation early on against the stands' side rail from the flip start.
**Indian Steppes(FR)**, whose two career wins were on the All-Weather, did well coming from off the pace down the outside.
**College Queen**, 4lb higher than her last win, had blinkers on this time and led them a merry dance before fading.
**Maddie's A Jem**, on her toes beforehand, showed a very scratchy action going to post.
**Magic Music(IRE)**, having her first outing for her new trainer, dropped out in a matter of strides. *Official explanation: jockey said mare lost her action.*
**Consensus(IRE)** *Official explanation: jockey said mare lost her action*

## 2671 DONCASTER ROVERS "CHAMPIONS" H'CAP — 1m 4f
**2:20** (2:22) (D) (0-85,85) 4-Y-O+ — **£7,104** (£2,186; £1,093; £546) **Stalls** Low

Form — RPR
1-04 **1** **Trance (IRE)**[3] 2583 4-8-13 **75** — PMakin(5) 4 — 88
(TDBarron) *mid-div: hdwy 4f out: led ins fnl f: hung lft: hld on wl nr fin* — **11/1**
123- **2** nk **Loves Travelling (IRE)**[232] 5608 4-9-0 **74** — NMackay(3) 6 — 87
(LMCumani) *trckd ldng pair: led over 3f out tl ins last: hung lft: no ex nr fin* — **13/2**[3]
4-02 **3** 3 **Night Sight (USA)**[8] 2449 7-8-11 **68** — JQuinn 8 — 76
(MrsSLamyman) *hld up towards rr: nt clr run over 2f out tl over 1f out: r.o: nt rch 1st 2* — **3/1**[1]
-400 **4** 3 **Richemaur (IRE)**[29] 1931 4-9-1 **75** — FPFerris(3) 11 — 78
(MHTompkins) *set str pce: hdd over 3f out: one pce fnl 2f* — **33/1**
6030 **5** shd **Repulse Bay (IRE)**[14] 2299 6-8-0 **57** oh5 ow2 — CCatlin 7 — 60
(JSGoldie) *hld up in rr: hdwy over 3f out: swtchd lft 1f out: styd on* — **20/1**
06-2 **6** 1 1/2 **Solo Flight**[15] 2278 7-10-0 **85** — MFenton 3 — 86
(HMorrison) *t.k.h in mid-div: hdwy to chse ldrs over 3f out: fdd fnl 2f* — **11/2**[2]
0302 **7** 1 **Mexican Pete**[7] 2471 4-9-3 **77** — LisaJones(3) 5 — 76
(PWHiatt) *mid-div: hdwy to chse ldrs 3f out: fdd over 1f out* — **11/2**[2]
-002 **8** 1/2 **Dovedon Hero**[15] 2277 4-9-7 **78** — (b) JMackay 2 — 76
(PJMcbride) *mid-div: n.m.r over 3f out: lost pl 2f out* — **8/1**
162/ **9** 1 1/2 **Coalition**[613] 5011 5-9-6 **77** — SWhitworth 1 — 73
(HCandy) *hld up towards rr: hdwy over 3f out: carried hd high: lost pl over 2f out* — **12/1**



The Form Book, Raceform Ltd, Compton, RG20 6NL

251- **10** *5* **Barman (USA)**[232] 5617 5-9-5 **81** NDeSouza(5) 9 69
(PFICole) *hld up in rr: hdwy on outside over 3f out: hung lft: lost pl over 2f out* **20/1**

0-06 **11** *11* **Sovereign Dreamer (USA)**[12] 2365 4-9-7 **78** (t) JBramhill 10 48
(PFICole) *chsd ldr: lost pl 3f out: sn bhd* **16/1**

2m 35.3s (-0.40) **Going Correction** +0.025s/f (Good) **11** Ran SP% **114.6**
Speed ratings: **102,101,99,97,97 96,96,95,94,91 84**CSF £76.53 CT £270.45 TOTE £14.60: £5.00, £2.40, £1.40; EX 74.80.
**Owner** Nigel Shields **Bred** Forenaghts Stud Co Ltd **Trained** Maunby, N Yorks

**FOCUS**
A fair handicap and a strong early gallop with the winners of this race in each of the last three years again in the line-up. The form looks solid.

**NOTEBOOK**
**Trance(IRE)**, having his second outing in three days, tended to hang into the runner-up and the boy deserves full marks. In the end he did just enough.
**Loves Travelling(IRE)** kept tabs on the two leaders who set a strong pace. He went on and fought back strongly when headed despite a tendency to hang into the running rail. He deserves to go one better.
**Night Sight(USA)**, winner of this two years ago and runner-up 12 months ago, looked back to his very best. He was quite happy to sit off a strong pace then encountered traffic problems. He was unlucky not to give the first two more to do.
**Richemaur(IRE)**, up in trip and with the blinkers left off, set a strong gallop but this trip stretches her to the very limit.
**Repulse Bay(IRE)**, who took this a year ago from in effect a 1lb lower mark, lay out of his ground and though staying on at the finish was never a threat.
**Solo Flight**, who took three years ago, would not settle despite the strong pace.
**Sovereign Dreamer(USA)** *Official explanation: trainer had no explanation for poor form shown.*

## 2672 CARLING EXTRA COLD CONDITIONS STKS 1m 2f 60y
**2:50** (2:51) (C) 3-Y-O+ **£8,720** (£3,307; £1,653; £751) **Stalls** Low

Form RPR

34-0 **1** **Muqbil (USA)**[42] 1622 4-9-2 113 RHills 4 115
(JLDunlop) *hld up: smooth hdwy 3f out: led over 2f out: shkn up appr fnl f: r.o wl* **1/1**[1]

5/26 **2** *5* **Grampian**[22] 2076 5-9-2 100 MFenton 2 105
(JGGiven) *dwlt: hld up: effrt over 3f out: wnt 2nd over 1f out: kpt on same pce fnl f* **7/1**

34-3 **3** *1* **Silver Gilt**[42] 1618 4-9-2 102 JQuinn 7 103
(JHMGosden) *trckd ldrs: effrt 4f out: styd on same pce fnl 2f* **14/1**

0464 **4** *3 1/2* **King's Thought**[30] 1902 5-9-2 98 CCatlin 3 96
(SGollings) *set str pce: hdd over 2f out: one pce* **12/1**

41- **5** *4* **Kingsword (USA)**[248] 5313 3-8-6 BDoyle 6 92
(SirMichaelStoute) *bhd: pushed along 4f out: sme hdwy 3f out: nvr nr ldrs* **5/1**[2]

400- **6** *5* **Shamrock City (IRE)**[266] 4878 7-9-2 93 JMackay 1 79
(PHowling) *trckd ldrs: effrt 4f out: edgd rt and wknd over 2f out* **40/1**

2-53 **7** *5* **Bayeux (USA)**[15] 2276 3-8-4 105 ow1 (t) JCarroll 8 71
(SaeedBinSuroor) *chsd ldr: pushed along over 3f out: lost pl over 2f out* **11/2**[3]

/56- **8** *dist* **Dhabyan (USA)**[389] 1571 4-9-2 98 SWKelly 5 —
(BHanbury) *in rr: lost pl 3f out: sn bhd and eased: t.o* **33/1**

2m 9.86s (-1.90) **Going Correction** +0.025s/f (Good)
**WFA** 3 from 4yo+ 13lb **8** Ran SP% **114.3**
Speed ratings: **108,104,103,100,97 93,89,—**CSF £8.69 TOTE £1.80: £1.20, £2.00, £2.20; EX 7.20.
**Owner** Hamdan Al Maktoum **Bred** Shadwell Farm Llc **Trained** Arundel, W Sussex

**FOCUS**
A decent conditions event and a truly-run race with a winner of some potential getting a confidence booster.

**NOTEBOOK**
**Muqbil(USA)**, who had plenty in hand on official figures, was a lot more settled beforehand. He came there on the bridle and had only to be kept up to his work. This will have done his confidence no end of good and he deserves a crack at something much better.
**Grampian**, much happier on this much flatter, more orthodox track, stayed on to follow the winner home. He is better over a mile and a half.
**Silver Gilt** showed he is back to his best and is well worth a try over much further.
**King's Thought** led them a merry dance but basically he was not up to the task especially on ground quicker than he prefers.
**Kingsword(USA)**, on the leg and narrow, won on his second and last start at two. He never went a yard and never looked like entering the argument.
**Shamrock City(IRE)**, who clearly has had his problems, is happiest these days when able to dominate.
**Bayeux(USA)** looks to have lost the plot for the time being and his smart juvenile form is starting to look history.

## 2673 ALFEA SAN ROSSORE H'CAP 7f
**3:25** (3:25) (D) (0-80,75) 3-Y-O+ **£5,671** (£1,745; £872; £436) **Stalls** High

Form RPR

-001 **1** **Yorkshire Blue**[9] 2421 5-7-12 **52** NMackay(3) 13 65
(JSGoldie) *trckd ldrs: ld over 1f out: hld on wl* **11/2**[2]

112- **2** *1* **Borrego (IRE)**[259] 5077 4-9-9 **74** RHills 4 84
(CEBrittain) *swtg: trckd ldrs: ev ch over 1f out: nt qckn ins last* **13/2**[3]

0-60 **3** *1 3/4* **Low Cloud**[20] 2142 4-9-10 **75** (v[1]) JCarroll 10 81
(DNicholls) *trckd ldrs: n.m.r on ins over 1f out: kpt on wl* **16/1**

-461 **4** *hd* **Cashneem (IRE)**[3] 2598 6-8-10 **64** 6ex DAllan(3) 5 69
(WMBrisbourne) *trckd ldrs: effrt 2f out: kpt on same pce* **9/1**

4231 **5** *2* **Efidium**[8] 2459 6-9-5 **70** CCatlin 7 70
(NBycroft) *swtg: sn trcking ldrs: effrt on outer 3f out: kpt on same pce* **11/2**[2]

4-40 **6** *hd* **Sewmuch Character**[22] 2091 5-9-2 **67** JQuinn 6 67
(MBlanshard) *led: hung lft and hdd over 1f out: one pce* **22/1**

0000 **7** *nk* **Aventura (IRE)**[33] 1840 4-9-7 **75** LFletcher(3) 8 74
(MJPolglase) *chsd ldrs: swtchd rt after 1f: rdn over 2f out: one pce* **18/1**

0302 **8** *1* **Snow Bunting**[3] 2581 6-8-4 **55** ow1 MFenton 3 51
(JeddO'Keeffe) *bhd whn hmpd after 1f: hdwy over 2f out: swtchd lft over 1f out: nvr nr ldrs* **9/2**[1]

0041 **9** *3 1/2* **Warden Warren**[4] 2553 6-9-6 **74** 6ex (p) BReilly(3) 2 61
(MrsCADunnett) *swtchd lft and racd far side: sn w ldrs: wknd jst ins last: eased nr fin* **10/1**

-062 **10** *1/2* **Noble Penny**[7] 2473 5-7-9 **49** LisaJones(3) 1 35
(MrsKWalton) *bhd whn hmpd after 1f: hdwy on outside over 2f out: sn lost pl* **11/1**

-000 **11** *3/4* **Compton Arrow (IRE)**[7] 2483 8-8-4 **55** SRighton 12 39
(AWCarroll) *swtg: hld up in rr: bhd fnl 3f* **50/1**

0222 **U** **Balakiref**[32] 1877 5-8-10 **64** LEnstone(3) 11 —
(MDods) *dwlt: in rr whn uns rdr after 1f* **15/2**

1m 26.91s (-0.90) **Going Correction** +0.025s/f (Good) **12** Ran SP% **118.9**
Speed ratings: **106,104,102,102,100 100,99,98,94,94 93,—**CSF £41.35 CT £553.02 TOTE £5.90: £2.00, £2.40, £7.00; EX 53.10.
**Owner** John Mc C Hodge **Bred** R T And Mrs Watson **Trained** Uplawmoor, E Renfrews
■ Stewards Enquiry : L Fletcher three-day ban (reduced from five on appeal): careless riding (Jun 16-18)

**FOCUS**
In effect a 0-75 handicap. The pace was solid and the form, although ordinary, looks sound enough.

**NOTEBOOK**
**Yorkshire Blue**, who has had a history of foot trouble, wore stick-on shoes. Just 2lb higher he showed a good fighting spirit.
**Borrego(IRE)**, a stone higher than his final success at three, was warm beforehand. He pushed the winner hard all the way and is clearly better than ever.
**Low Cloud**, dropping in trip and with a visor on, was left short of racing room on the inside. This trip is his bare minimum.
**Cashneem(IRE)** had a penalty against better class rivals.
**Efidium**, 6lb higher, was running from a career-high mark.
**Sewmuch Character** ran better than last time but his attitude is not totally convincing.
**Snow Bunting** was in effect put out of the race early on.

## 2674 ERROL TAYLOR MENINGITIS RESEARCH FOUNDATION CHALLENGE MAIDEN AUCTION STKS 6f
**4:00** (4:05) (E) 2-Y-O **£3,601** (£1,108; £554; £277) **Stalls** High

Form RPR

32 **1** **Space Shuttle**[15] 2268 2-8-4 (b[1]) DAllan(3) 12 81
(TDEasterby) *mde all towards stands' side: hld on wl* **11/8**[1]

6 **2** *1* **Malinsa Blue (IRE)**[22] 2087 2-8-2 JQuinn 2 73
(JAGlover) *trckd ldrs: wnt 2nd over 1f out: no ex ins last* **14/1**

5 **3** *6* **Ransacker**[8] 2439 2-8-10 RHills 5 63+
(CEBrittain) *restless in stalls: s.v.s: hdwy on wd outside over 2f out: hung lft: styd on wl ins last* **14/1**

0 **4** *nk* **Aire De Mougins (IRE)**[24] 2045 2-8-10 GFaulkner 6 62
(PCHaslam) *chsd ldrs: one pce appr fnl f* **5/1**[2]

**5** *nk* **Sacred Nuts (IRE)** 2-8-10 JMackay 8 61
(MLWBell) *w'like: lengthy: scope: bit bkwd: s.i.s: sn chsng ldrs: one pce fnl 2f* **14/1**

5 **6** *1* **Sound And Vision (IRE)**[15] 2256 2-8-7 LEnstone(3) 14 58
(MDods) *chsd ldrs: outpcd over 2f out: styd on fnl f* **25/1**

3 **7** *5* **Mr Kalandi (IRE)**[16] 2234 2-8-10 JCarroll 11 43
(PWD'Arcy) *trckd ldrs: rdn along 3f out: lost pl over 1f out* **11/2**[3]

00 **8** *hd* **Fantasy Defender (IRE)**[28] 1961 2-8-7 SWKelly 3 39
(JJQuinn) *chsd ldrs: outpcd after 2f: kpt on fnl f* **66/1**

0 **9** *3/4* **Shingle Street (IRE)**[16] 2234 2-8-4 FPFerris(3) 9 37
(MHTompkins) *chsd ldrs: lost pl over 2f out* **20/1**

0 **10** *hd* **Saint Clements (USA)**[16] 2234 2-8-10 DeanMcKeown 7 40
(MJohnston) *chsd ldrs: lost pl over 1f out* **12/1**

50 **11** *1 1/2* **Tipsy Lillie**[6] 2439 2-7-13 LisaJones(3) 10 27
(JulianPoulton) *chsd ldrs: wknd 2f out* **50/1**

0 **12** *2 1/2* **Ellis Cave**[20] 2141 2-8-10 MFenton 13 28
(JJQuinn) *s.i.s: a bhd* **16/1**

**13** *12* **Slate Grey** 2-8-7 VHalliday 1 —
(KRBurke) *rangy: leggy: unf: s.v.s: a last* **50/1**

1m 14.63s (0.35) **Going Correction** +0.025s/f (Good) **13** Ran SP% **121.8**
Speed ratings: **98,96,88,88,87 86,79,79,78,78 76,73,57**CSF £23.03 TOTE £2.00: £1.10, £4.90, £3.70; EX 32.00.
**Owner** Jennifer Pallister & Jonathan Gill **Bred** Miss S E Hall **Trained** Great Habton, N Yorks

**FOCUS**
Just an ordinary maiden auction race but it was encouraging the way the first two pulled well clear.

**NOTEBOOK**
**Space Shuttle**, beaten by a subsequent winner at Haydock, had blinkers on this time and with the stands' side rail to help was always doing enough.
**Malinsa Blue(IRE)** ◆, still carrying plenty of condition, went in pursuit of the winner and they pulled well clear. She deserves to go one better.
**Ransacker**, who became upset in the stalls, possibly due to the antics of the withdrawn runner next door, walked out of the traps. He made up a deal of ground on the wide outside despite still looking inexperienced. There ought to be even better to come. *Official explanation: jockey said colt missed the break.*
**Aire De Mougins(IRE)** again showed ability but the first two drew right away from him in the final furlong.
**Sacred Nuts(IRE)**, a March foal, is a deep-bodied type who looked very burly. After a tardy start she stayed on iner her own time and should be able to do a fair bit better in due course.
**Sound And Vision(IRE)**, who looked very fit, needs another outing to qualify for nurseries.
**Mr Kalandi(IRE)**, fitted with a cross noseband, did not improve on his initial effort here two weeks earlier.

## 2675 DONCASTER-RACECOURSE.COM MAIDEN STKS 5f
**4:40** (4:43) (D) 3-Y-O+ **£5,573** (£1,715; £857; £428) **Stalls** High

Form RPR

04 **1** **Rene Barbier (IRE)**[29] 1942 3-9-0 DeanMcKeown 12 57
(JAGlover) *chsd ldrs: led over 1f out: wnt rt ins last: hld on towards fin* **8/1**

42 **2** *hd* **Urban Calm**[30] 1906 3-8-9 MHenry 5 51
(RMHCowell) *chsd ldrs: ev ch ins last: no ex nr line* **4/1**[3]

3405 **3** *1 1/4* **Roan Raider (USA)**[11] 2383 4-9-0 45 (v) KGhunowa(7) 9 51
(MJPolglase) *chsd ldrs: nt qckn fnl f* **33/1**

4230 **4** *1* **Law Maker**[3] 2586 4-9-2 43 (v) PMulrennan(5) 1 47
(MABuckley) *chsd ldrs: styd on same pce appr fnl f* **16/1**

0- **5** *shd* **Shibumi**[236] 5541 3-8-9 SWKelly 7 42
(HMorrison) *mid-div: kpt on fnl 2f* **16/1**

**6** *shd* **Millinsky (USA)** 3-8-9 MFenton 2 41
(RGuest) *small: mid-div: hdwy on outside over 2f out: kpt on fnl f* **11/1**

6262 **7** *4* **Laconia (IRE)**[3] 2586 3-8-2 72 DerekNolan(7) 11 25
(JSMoore) *chsd ldrs: wknd appr fnl f* **5/2**[1]

3-5 **8** *1 3/4* **Firebird Rising (USA)**[8] 2450 3-8-4 PMakin(5) 13 18
(TDBarron) *chsd ldrs: rdn over 2f out: lost pl over 1f out* **3/1**[2]

00-0 **9** *1* **Shifty Night (IRE)**[18] 2211 3-8-4 HayleyTurner(5) 4 14
(MrsCADunnett) *in tch: outpcd fnl 2f* **80/1**

4240 **10** *nk* **Multahab**[21] 2118 5-9-7 58 (b[1]) CLowther 8 18
(MissGayKelleway) *led tl hdd & wknd over 1f out* **15/2**

0- **11** *5* **Trinaree (IRE)**[220] 5825 3-9-0 CCatlin 6 —
(SGollings) *s.s: a in rr* **50/1**

0 **12** *2 1/2* **Estoille**[8] 2450 3-8-9 JQuinn 10 —
(MrsSLamyman) *hld up: hdwy over 2f out: wknd over 1f out: eased ins last* **66/1**

0 **13** *17* **Cobalt Runner (IRE)**[112] [764] 3-9-0 ........ BDoyle 14 —
(MissDAMchale) *s.i.s: hung rt and a in rr: eased* **50/1**
0 **14** *11* **Karashinko (IRE)**[14] [2311] 3-9-0 ........ JCarroll 3 —
(RGuest) *s.s: a detached in last* **40/1**
61.81 secs (0.39) **Going Correction** +0.025s/f (Good)
**WFA** 3 from 4yo+ 7lb **14** Ran SP% **128.6**
Speed ratings: **97,96,94,93,92 92,86,83,81,81 73,69,42,24**CSF £41.90 TOTE £12.90: £3.10, £1.90, £8.30; EX 80.80 Place 6 £180.52, Place 5 £55.60..
**Owner** Mrs Janis Macpherson **Bred** Isca Bloodstock **Trained** Carburton, Notts

**FOCUS**
A poor sprint maiden run in a modest time with the exposed third rated just 45, but the winner will improve again.

**NOTEBOOK**
**Rene Barbier(IRE)**, who has had problems with the stalls, wore a rope halter and had his trainer at the start to load him. He dived right onto the stands'-side rail in front, but in the end did just enough. A bit of a baby and backward mentally, he can go on from here.
**Urban Calm**, having only her third outing, improved again and hopefully will start life in handicap company from a realistic mark.
**Roan Raider(USA)**, rated just 45, has now been placed five times from 27 starts.
**Law Maker** still claims the maiden allowance after 20 trips to the races.
**Shibumi**, on her toes beforehand, had just one outing at two and shapes as if she needs a fair bit further.
**Millinsky(USA)**, a half-sister to the stable's Millybaa, is not that big and rather hollow backed. Drawn one from the outside, she showed some promise on her racecourse debut.
**Laconia(IRE)**, taken to post early, had a good draw but, clear top-rated, he ran nowhere near her best.
**Firebird Rising(USA)**, another well drawn, was well below her best for no apparent reason.
**Multahab**, taken to post early, wore first-time blinkers and went off much too fast for his own good.
**Estoille** *Official explanation: jockey said filly had a breathing problem*
**Cobalt Runner(IRE)** *Official explanation: jockey said colt hung right handed; vet said colt was lame in front.*
T/Plt: £296.20 to a £1 stake. Pool: £48,096.45. 118.50 winning tickets. T/Qpdt: £54.00 to a £1 stake. Pool: £2,139.70. 29.30 winning tickets. WG

## 2636 EPSOM (L-H)
### Saturday, June 5

**OFFICIAL GOING: Round course - good (good to firm in places); sprint course - good to firm**
Race times suggest the ground was just on the fast side of good, but the removal of the false rail makes comparison with Friday's times very difficult.
Wind: lt against Weather: fine, but cloudy

### 2676 VODAFONE LIVE! STKS (H'CAP) 1m 2f 18y
**2:00** (2:01) (C) (0-100,90) 3-Y-O **£43,500** (£16,500; £8,250; £3,750) **Stalls** Low

Form RPR
31-3 **1** **Lord Mayor**[25] [2018] 3-9-5 **88** ........ KFallon 1 101
(SirMichaelStoute) *sn shuffled towards rr on inner: 13th st: sme prog 2f out: drvn and hanging lft over 1f out: r.o strly to ld last 75yds* **11/2**[2]
6134 **2** *1 3/4* **Royal Warrant**[18] [2202] 3-9-1 **84** ........ MartinDwyer 14 94
(AMBalding) *lw: prom: 4th st: rdn to chse ldr over 1f out: kpt on but outpcd by wnr last 100yds* **16/1**
3121 **3** *hd* **Mystical Girl (USA)**[4] [2557] 3-9-7 **90** 5ex ........ DHolland 16 100
(MJohnston) *led after 1f: kicked clr wl over 2f out: 4l ahd 1f out: tired and hdd last 75yds* **10/1**
6112 **4** *3* **Dancing Lyra**[18] [2202] 3-9-7 **90** ........ TQuinn 2 94
(JWHills) *s.i.s: hld up in rr: 14th st: effrt but hanging lft 2f out: styd on wl fnl f: no ch w ldrs* **6/1**[3]
21-5 **5** *3/4* **Prime Powered (IRE)**[51] [1414] 3-9-6 **89** ........ RHughes 8 92
(GLMoore) *prom: 5th and rdn st: kpt on one pce fr over 2f out* **20/1**
0-4 **6** *nk* **Malibu (IRE)**[54] [1357] 3-8-7 **76** ........ SSanders 5 78
(SDow) *swtg: hld up in rr: 15th st: effrt on outer and prog over 2f out: hanging lft and kpt on same pce* **33/1**
3120 **7** *1/2* **Tiger Tiger (FR)**[18] [2202] 3-9-2 **85** ........ JFEgan 11 86
(JamiePoulton) *lw: racd in midfield: buffetted abt downhill and 11th st: effrt over 2f out: no imp ldrs* **20/1**
211 **8** *3/4* **Master Marvel (IRE)**[34] [1795] 3-9-6 **89** ........ KDarley 6 89
(MJohnston) *trckd ldrs: nt handle downhill: 7th st: rdn 3f out: unable qck and no prog over 2f out* **7/2**[1]
60-3 **9** *nk* **Spring Goddess (IRE)**[14] [2281] 3-8-13 **82** ........ KMcEvoy 4 81
(APJarvis) *settled in rr: 16th st: rdn 3f out: one pce and no ch w ldrs* **33/1**
30-1 **10** *hd* **Over The Rainbow (IRE)**[77] [1064] 3-9-4 **87** ........ MHills 18 86
(BWHills) *hld up: last st: stl in fnl pair over 2f out: modest late prog* **33/1**
13-3 **11** *shd* **Fort**[22] [2089] 3-9-4 **87** ........ KDalgleish 13 85
(MJohnston) *s.s: wl in rr: 17th st: prog and hung sharply lft over 1f out: styng on whn nt clr run and stmbld sn after: no hope* **33/1**
2-41 **12** *3/4* **Silent Hawk (IRE)**[15] [2280] 3-9-7 **90** ........ (vt[1]) LDettori 10 87
(SaeedBinSuroor) *lw: prom: 3rd st: chsd ldr wl over 2f out to over 1f out: wknd* **11/1**
3145 **13** *1* **Vantage (IRE)**[19] [2179] 3-8-10 **79** ........ (b[1]) EAhern 17 74
(NPLittmoden) *s.i.s: rushed up on outer to chse ldr after 2f: lost 2nd wl over 2f out: wknd over 1f out* **40/1**
3463 **14** *5* **Freak Occurence (IRE)**[4] [2557] 3-8-9 **81** ........ JFMcDonald(3) 7 67
(MissECLavelle) *racd in midfield: keen downhill and n.m.r: 10th st: no prog over 2f out: wknd over 1f out: eased* **16/1**
62-0 **15** *1 1/2* **In Deep**[72] [1108] 3-8-6 **75** ........ DKinsella 9 58
(MrsPNDutfield) *racd on outer: chsd ldrs: 6th st: wkng whn nt clr run over 1f out* **66/1**
6-23 **16** *1/2* **Alekhine (IRE)**[8] [2448] 3-9-4 **87** ........ IMongan 12 69
(PWHarris) *racd on outer: towards rr: 12th st: prog to chse ldrs 2f out: hanging lft and wknd over 1f out* **7/1**
01-0 **17** *16* **Ringsider (IRE)**[30] [1900] 3-8-11 **80** ........ JPSpencer 15 31
(GAButler) *racd in midfield: 9th st: wknd over 2f out: t.o* **40/1**
2042 **18** *1 1/2* **Oh Golly Gosh**[14] [2289] 3-8-5 **74** ........ (p) TEDurcan 3 23
(NPLittmoden) *led for 1f: sn lost pl: 8th and drvn st: wknd over 2f out: t.o* **66/1**
2m 7.08s (-1.62) **Going Correction** -0.075s/f (Good) **18** Ran SP% **122.7**
Speed ratings: **103,101,101,99,98 98,97,97,96,96 96,96,95,91,90 89,76,75**CSF £80.39 CT £871.64 TOTE £7.50: £2.00, £2.90, £2.20, £2.10; EX 116.10 Trifecta £1468.20 Pool £2,274.74 - 1.10 winning units..
**Owner** J M Greetham **Bred** J M Greetham **Trained** Newmarket, Suffolk

**FOCUS**
A good, competitive handicap run at a decent pace and a race from which a decent winner or two should emerge.

**NOTEBOOK**
**Lord Mayor ◆**, third in a decent handicap at York on his reappearance, benefited from a fantastic ride from Fallon to go a couple of places better. He is clearly improving and could now head for the King George V Handicap at Royal Ascot, where the longer trip should show him to even better advantage.
**Royal Warrant**, a real tough sort, ran another fine race. He is improving, but the Handicapper is all too aware of that.
**Mystical Girl(USA)**, whose two previous wins came over a mile, clearly stays further, but having looked all over the winner when kicked into a decisive lead over two furlongs out she she got a little lonely and tired late on. She had no answer to the winner's late burst but is still improving.
**Dancing Lyra**, 3lb higher than when runner-up to Gatwick at Goodwood on his previous start, shaped very much as though he will get a mile and a half and could be aimed at the King George V Handicap at Royal Ascot.
**Prime Powered(IRE)**, off the track for 51 days after making a promising reappearance at Newmarket, again ran respectably and will find easier opportunities.
**Malibu(IRE)** did not help his chance by hanging, but this was still a fair effort.
**Tiger Tiger(FR)** had a roughish passage down the hill and was by no means disgraced.
**Master Marvel(IRE)**, racing beyond nine furlongs for the first time, did not look happy on the track.
**Fort ◆** raced in rear following a slow start but was making good headway and just hitting full stride when squeezed out a furlong from home. He could have finished much closer. *Official explanation: jockey said gelding suffered interference in running.*

### 2677 VODAFONE WOODCOTE STKS (LISTED RACE) 6f
**2:30** (2:32) (A) 2-Y-O **£20,300** (£7,700; £3,850; £1,750) **Stalls** High

Form RPR
2 **1** **Screwdriver**[21] [2111] 2-8-11 ........ RHughes 1 99
(RHannon) *lw: prom: 3rd st: led over 2f out to over 1f out: edgd rt but led again ins fnl f: styd on wl* **7/2**[2]
11 **2** *nk* **Royal Island (IRE)**[16] [2247] 2-9-0 ........ KDalgleish 7 101
(MJohnston) *chsd ldr to 3f out: styd pressing wnr: drvn to ld over 1f out: hdd ins fnl f: kpt on but hld nr fin* **6/5**[1]
1 **3** *4* **Gortumblo**[18] [2205] 2-9-0 ........ TQuinn 5 89
(DJSFfrenchDavis) *outpcd early: 5th st: prog to chse clr ldng pair over 1f out: styd on wl fnl f* **12/1**
31 **4** *3 1/2* **Obe Gold**[23] [2057] 2-9-0 ........ TEDurcan 3 79
(MRChannon) *in rr: 7th st: sn outpcd and struggling: kpt on fr over 1f out* **9/1**
32 **5** *nk* **Adoration**[7] [2470] 2-8-11 ........ KDarley 4 75
(MJohnston) *lw: s.s: nt gng wl and sn t.o in last: no prog tl r.o over 1f out: fin wl* **8/1**[3]
4 **6** *3 1/2* **Blue Marble**[10] [2396] 2-8-11 ........ DHolland 8 64
(CEBrittain) *chsd ldrs: nt handle downhill and 5th st: sn outpcd and btn* **20/1**
450 **7** *1 1/4* **Next Time (IRE)**[23] [2071] 2-8-6 ........ MartinDwyer 2 55
(MJPolglase) *chsd ldng trio: outpcd wl over 2f out: sn wknd* **66/1**
4 **8** *3* **Victoria Peek (IRE)**[31] [1882] 2-8-6 ........ MJKinane 6 46
(DNicholls) *led to over 2f out: wknd rapidly* **12/1**
1m 10.03s (-0.60) **Going Correction** -0.075s/f (Good) **8** Ran SP% **110.4**
Speed ratings: **101,100,95,90,90 85,83,79**CSF £7.45 TOTE £3.30: £1.30, £1.10, £4.60; EX 5.40 Trifecta £53.10 Pool £1,899.56 - 25.36 winning units..
**Owner** Raymond Tooth **Bred** The National Stud Owner Breeders Club Ltd **Trained** East Everleigh, Wilts

**FOCUS**
This looked quite a good renewal of the Woodcote and the first two home look pretty smart. They went quite a gallop.

**NOTEBOOK**
**Screwdriver**, runner-up at 66/1 on his debut in a fair Newbury maiden, improved considerably on that effort. This represented quite a step up in class, but he took it in his stride and got off the mark a shade cosily. There should be even more to come, but his trainer will not be hard on him and could swerve Royal Ascot. That suggests there could well be one or two able deputies in the Hannon camp.
**Royal Island(IRE)**, successful in a couple of uncompetitive events over five furlongs on his first two starts, coped well with the step up in trip and class, but found one just too good at the weights.
**Gortumblo**, off the mark on his debut in a reasonable five-furlong Goodwood maiden, was put firmly in his place, without any real excuse. Nevertheless, he was well clear of the remainder.
**Obe Gold** found this tougher than the Salisbury maiden he landed on his previous start and never showed enough pace to pose a threat.
**Adoration**, who shaped well in maiden company on his first two starts, missed the break and could not go the pace. However, he flew past beaten horses late on, making up an incredible amount of ground to take fifth. It goes without saying he will stay seven furlongs.
**Blue Marble** was taking quite an ambitious step up in class, but was still a little bit disappointing and may not have been suited by the track.
**Next Time(IRE)** was out of her depth.
**Victoria Peek(IRE)** dropped out very quickly and something may have been amiss.

### 2678 VODAFONE DIOMED STKS (GROUP 3) 1m 114y
**3:00** (3:05) (A) 3-Y-O+ **£43,500** (£16,500; £8,250; £3,750) **Stalls** Low

Form RPR
160- **1** **Passing Glance**[174] [6187] 5-9-9 115 ........ MartinDwyer 3 120
(AMBalding) *lw: mde all: 4l clr st: rdn 2f out: kpt on wl fnl f* **20/1**
2005 **2** *1 1/4* **Dutch Gold (USA)**[23] [2067] 4-9-4 110 ........ (b) DHolland 1 112
(CEBrittain) *chsd ldrs: lost pl 1/2-way: 7th and pushed along st: effrt and nt clr run briefly over 2f out: r.o fnl f: tk 2nd post* **33/1**
2120 **3** *hd* **Gateman**[21] [2109] 7-9-7 113 ........ KDalgleish 10 115
(MJohnston) *b.hind: chsd wnr to over 2f out: rallied to chse wnr again 1f out: nt pce to chal: lost 2nd last stride* **8/1**
6003 **4** *1* **Checkit (IRE)**[13] [2339] 4-9-4 112 ........ TEDurcan 8 110
(MRChannon) *chsd ldrs: 5th st: rdn over 2f out: one pce and nvr able to chal* **9/1**
0-33 **5** *nk* **Vanderlin**[10] [2398] 5-9-4 105 ........ KDarley 4 109
(AMBalding) *lw: t.k.h early: prom: 4th st: chsd wnr over 2f out to 1f out: one pce after* **25/1**
020- **6** *1* **Beauchamp Pilot**[294] [4200] 6-9-4 ........ MJKinane 11 107
(GAButler) *b: hld up in last: effrt on outer 3f out: hanging lft but kpt on fnl 2f: nrst fin* **33/1**
11-3 **7** *1 1/2* **Leporello (IRE)**[30] [1902] 4-9-7 114 ........ TQuinn 7 107
(PWHarris) *lw: towards rr: 8th st: rdn and no prog over 2f out: n.d after* **3/1**[1]
-222 **8** *nk* **Vespone (IRE)**[20] [2155] 4-9-4 118 ........ (vt[1]) LDettori 9 103
(SaeedBinSuroor) *stmbld bdly s: rr: 10th st: struggling 3f out: plld out and rdn 2f out: nvr rchd ldrs* **7/2**[2]
40-2 **9** *2* **Duck Row (USA)**[24] [2044] 9-9-4 108 ........ SSanders 5 99
(JARToller) *settled in midfield: 6th st: effrt 3f out: no prog 2f out: wknd* **15/2**

2-20 **10** 3 ½ **Parasol (IRE)**[16] 2241 5-9-4 114......................................(v) JPSpencer 2 92
(DRLoder) *b.hind: prom: 3rd st: hanging lft and fnd nil over 2f out: sn lost pl: wknd over 1f out* **12/1**

-104 **11** 1 ¾ **Sublimity (FR)**[16] 2241 4-9-4 110......................................(t) KFallon 6 88
(SirMichaelStoute) *swtg: dwlt: a wl in rr: 9th st: hrd rdn and no prog over 2f out* **7/1**[3]

1m 42.4s (-3.34) **Going Correction** -0.075s/f (Good) **11** Ran SP% **114.8**
Speed ratings: **111,109,109,108,108 107,106,106,104,101 99**CSF £521.85 TOTE £20.40: £3.90, £5.80, £2.80; EX 316.90 Trifecta £2167.30 Part won. Pool £3,052.66 - 0.90 winning units..
**Owner** Kingsclere Stud And M E Wates **Bred** I A Balding **Trained** Kingsclere, Hants

**FOCUS**
Quite a competitive renewal of the Diomed, and career-best form from Passing Glance, although the first five home were never too far off the pace and there appeared a bias towards those racing prominently.

**NOTEBOOK**
**Passing Glance**, a winner of a handicap off a mark of 89 at this meeting last year, has improved considerably since then and had last been seen in the Hong Kong Mile, albeit below form. Racing for the first time in 174 days, he overcame a stiff penalty under a fine front-running ride from Dwyer. He should go on from this and his main aim is the Sussex Stakes.
**Dutch Gold(USA)** has proved hard to place since winning the Chester Vase over a year ago, but this big drop in trip suited and he ran a cracker to snatch second on the line. His stable really are beginning to fire and he should be able to build on this if his sights are not raised too high, possibly at around ten furlongs.
**Gateman**, bidding to repeat his 2003 win and already having his eighth run of the year, ran a fine race and is as tough as they come. This is his sort of level and he should continue to go well, especially on slightly easier ground.
**Checkit(IRE)**, third of five in a French Group One on his previous start, does not win very often these days but again ran respectably.
**Vanderlin**, a stablemate of the winner, ran really well but may just be better over seven furlongs.
**Beauchamp Pilot** did best of those who raced well off the pace.
**Leporello(IRE)** did not look happy over the shorter trip. It subsequently emerged that he had injured a fetlock.
**Vespone(IRE)** lost his chance when sprawling badly on leaving the stalls and can be forgiven this. *Official explanation: jockey said colt stumbled shortly after start.*
**Parasol(IRE)** travelled well enough, but found nothing and looks one to avoid for the time being. *Official explanation: jockey said horse hung left.*
**Sublimity(FR)** has still to prove he is up to this class, but can be forgiven this effort. He was supposed to be the first down to the start, but got himself in quite a state in the parade ring and ended up being last out.

## 2679 VODAFONE "DASH" STKS (HERITAGE H'CAP) 5f
**3:30** (3:33) (B ) (0-105,97) 3-Y-0+ **£43,500** (£16,500; £8,250; £3,750) **Stalls** High

Form RPR

2-02 **1** **Caribbean Coral**[52] 1391 5-9-5 **92**.......................................... RWinston 8 102
(JJQuinn) *racd nr side: off the pce in midfield after 2f: rdn 1/2-way: str run fnl f to ld last strides* **20/1**

0-60 **2** *shd* **Plateau**[35] 1765 5-8-9 **82**.......................................... MHills 10 92
(DNicholls) *stmbld s: outpcd in centre: last 1/2-way: storming run fr over 1f out: jst failed* **25/1**

10-5 **3** *nk* **Tychy**[35] 1765 5-9-3 **90**.......................................... JPSpencer 2 99
(SCWilliams) *racd towards far side: wl on terms: overall ldr 1/2-way: kpt on wl fnl f: hdd last strides* **20/1**

13-2 **4** *hd* **Texas Gold**[17] 2222 6-9-0 **87**.......................................... MartinDwyer 3 95
(WRMuir) *racd towards far side: pressed ldrs: ev ch ins fnl f: kpt on wl* **16/1**

-302 **5** *shd* **Watching**[24] 2041 7-8-10 **83**.......................................... ANicholls 13 91
(DNicholls) *racd towards nr side: pressed ldrs: drvn and ch ins fnl f: styd on* **16/1**

5442 **6** *hd* **Corridor Creeper (FR)**[7] 2488 7-9-3 **90**..........................(p) DHolland 17 97
(JMBradley) *w ldrs nr side: bmpd after 1f: ev ch ent fnl f: kpt on same pce* **4/1**[2]

0010 **7** *nk* **Whitbarrow (IRE)**[7] 2488 5-9-10 **97** 7ex.......................... DaneO'Neill 1 103
(JMBradley) *lw: racd towards far side: pressed ldr: ev ch 1f out: no ex last 50yds* **25/1**

-055 **8** *nk* **Talbot Avenue**[8] 2461 6-8-7 **80**.......................................... PDobbs 11 84
(MMullineaux) *chsd ldrs: rdn 2f out: styd on fnl f: unable to chal* **33/1**

-303 **9** ½ **Henry Hall (IRE)**[24] 2041 8-9-6 **93**.......................................... KimTinkler 20 95
(NTinkler) *racd against nr side rail: chsd ldrs: bmpd along and nt clr run over 1f out: kpt on one pce fnl f* **12/1**[3]

60-0 **10** 1 ¼ **Atlantic Viking (IRE)**[14] 2293 9-9-9 **96**.......................................... SSanders 12 93
(DNicholls) *s.i.s: outpcd and rdn: swtchd to nr side rail 3f out: styd on fnl f: n.d* **20/1**

6106 **11** *nk* **Cape Royal**[24] 2041 4-9-0 **87**.......................................... LDettori 4 83
(MrsJRRamsden) *racd in centre: pressed ldrs: unable qck over 1f out: fdd* **20/1**

0030 **12** ½ **Seafield Towers**[7] 2488 4-8-5 **78**..........................(p) TEDurcan 6 72
(MissLAPerratt) *racd in centre: outpcd: bhd 2f out: kpt on* **66/1**

2324 **13** *hd* **Boston Lodge**[1] 2636 4-9-10 **97**..........................(b) MJKinane 19 90
(GAButler) *dwlt: outpcd and a in rr* **16/1**

2130 **14** *hd* **Maktavish**[14] 2293 5-8-12 **85**..........................(p) PHanagan 5 78
(ISemple) *racd in centre: pressed ldrs tl wknd over 1f out* **33/1**

1213 **15** ¾ **Magic Glade**[7] 2488 5-8-9 **87**.......................................... RThomas[(5)] 7 77
(CRDore) *b: racd centre: outpcd: nvr a factor* **16/1**

-411 **16** *nk* **Raccoon (IRE)**[7] 2488 4-8-8 **81** 7ex..........................(v) KDarley 9 69
(TDBarron) *prom in centre: drvn 2f out: wknd over 1f out* **3/1**[1]

530- **17** ¾ **Kathology (IRE)**[199] 6030 7-8-11 **84**.......................................... TQuinn 14 69
(DRCElsworth) *swtg: w ldr to 1/2-way: wknd 2f out* **20/1**

013- **18** *hd* **Brave Burt (IRE)**[245] 5357 7-8-10 **83**.......................................... EAhern 18 68
(DNicholls) *b: overall ldr against nr side rail to 1/2-way: wknd* **20/1**

0010 **19** 2 **Ptarmigan Ridge**[7] 2488 8-8-13 **86**.......................................... JPMurtagh 16 63
(MissLAPerratt) *pressed ldrs 3f: wknd* **14/1**

6000 **20** 10 **Palawan**[14] 2293 8-8-6 **82**..........................(b[1]) LPKeniry[(3)] 15 19
(AMBalding) *b: w ldrs for 2f: sn lost pl: t.o* **50/1**

54.86 secs (-0.82) **Going Correction** +0.075s/f (Good) **20** Ran SP% **128.5**
Speed ratings: **109,108,108,108,107 107,107,106,105,103 103,102,102,101,100 100,99,98,95,79**CSF £434.03 CT £9916.58 TOTE £24.10: £3.80, £8.70, £4.70, £2.30; EX 2297.30 TRIFECTA Not won..
**Owner** Dawson, Green, Quinn, Roberts **Bred** P And C Scott **Trained** Settrington, N Yorks

**FOCUS**
As competitive a sprint handicap as you are likely to see and the pace was furious. The usual high-draw bias over 5f failed to apply and they were spread across the track at the finish, the first eight being separated by barely a length.

**NOTEBOOK**
**Caribbean Coral** loves to weave his way through a decent size field off a good gallop and, in the ideal race, he took full advantage. He should continue to go well in similar events and the Wokingham, over another furlong, could be next. He picks up an 8lb penalty.
**Plateau** did not help his chance with a slow start, but was given time by Hills to find his feet and it nearly worked. He flew home, getting a good run considering where he had to come from, and was only just denied. He has not won since 2002, but will surely end that losing run this season.
**Tychy** does most of her racing over further, but she has won over this trip and showed fantastic speed. She was just denied.
**Texas Gold** ran a cracker on his reappearance at Goodwood and this was another fine effort. He looks ready to strike.
**Watching** ran really well again but has not won since 2000.
**Corridor Creeper(FR)** had conditions to suit and was not beaten very far at all.
**Henry Hall(IRE)** would have been closer with a clearer run.
**Maktavish** *Official explanation: jockey said gelding hung right throughout.*
**Magic Glade** *Official explanation: jockey said gelding did not handle the track; vet reported gelding bled from the nose.*
**Raccoon(IRE)** was a blot on the handicap but ran well below form. This was his fourth quick race and the course might not have suited him. *Official explanation: trainer's representative said gelding may have felt effects of racing three times in two weeks.*

## 2680 VODAFONE DERBY STKS (GROUP 1) (ENTIRE COLTS & FILLIES) 1m 4f 10y
**4:20** (4:23) (A ) 3-Y-0 **£788,220** (£298,980; £149,490; £67,950) **Stalls** Centre

Form RPR

21-1 **1** **North Light (IRE)**[24] 2043 3-9-0 115.......................................... KFallon 6 124
(SirMichaelStoute) *lw: trckd ldr: led ent st and kicked on: drvn 2l clr over 2f out: nvr gng to be ct after* **7/2**[1]

13-2 **2** 1 ½ **Rule Of Law (USA)**[24] 2043 3-9-0 114..........................(t) KMcEvoy 11 121
(SaeedBinSuroor) *hld up: last to 5f out: 12th st: hanging lft but prog fr 3f out: styd on wl fnl f to snatch 2nd on post* **20/1**

2-13 **3** *hd* **Let The Lion Roar**[24] 2043 3-9-0 110..........................(v[1]) MJKinane 3 121
(JLDunlop) *dwlt: racd in midfield: lost pl downhill and 11th st: plld out and effrt 2f out: r.o wl fnl f: tk 3rd on post* **14/1**

2-11 **4** *hd* **Percussionist (IRE)**[28] 1966 3-9-0 113.......................................... KDarley 5 121
(JHMGosden) *swtg: prom but sn pushed along: lost pce downhill and 8th st: prog to chse wnr 200yds out: kpt on gamely: lost 2 pls on lin* **7/1**[3]

1-16 **5** 3 **Salford City (IRE)**[35] 1764 3-9-0 115.......................................... JPMurtagh 8 116
(DRCElsworth) *lw: swtg: hld up in last pair: prog and 9th st: hdwy on outer over 2f out: disp 2nd pl 1f out: hung lft and wknd ins fnl f* **8/1**

-111 **6** 1 ½ **American Post**[20] 2161 3-9-0 .......................................... RHughes 13 113
(MmeCHead-Maarek, France) *t.k.h: prom: 4th st: smooth prog to press wnr 3f out: rdn and nt qckn 2f out: wknd ent fnl f* **13/2**[2]

10-2 **7** 1 ¾ **Snow Ridge (IRE)**[35] 1764 3-9-0 120.......................................... LDettori 7 111
(SaeedBinSuroor) *hld up in rr: prog and 7th st: rdn to chse ldrs 2f out: no imp: wknd over 1f out* **7/2**[1]

1121 **8** *hd* **Hazyview**[14] 2307 3-9-0 110.......................................... EAhern 12 110
(NACallaghan) *prom: 3rd and rdn st: styd chsng ldrs tl wknd jst over 1f out* **40/1**

31-1 **9** 1 ½ **Pukka (IRE)**[21] 2107 3-9-0 86.......................................... DHolland 2 108
(LMCumani) *trckd ldrs: 5th and rdn st: no imp over 2f out: wknd over 1f out* **10/1**

1311 **10** 2 ½ **Gatwick (IRE)**[14] 2295 3-9-0 104.......................................... TQuinn 9 104
(MRChannon) *chsd ldrs: 6th st: rdn 3f out: no prog 2f out: grad wknd* **16/1**

02 **11** *nk* **Massif Centrale**[22] 2085 3-9-0 .......................................... DaneO'Neill 10 103
(DRCElsworth) *lw: dwlt: racd on outer: a in rr: 13th st: sn rdn and no prog* **100/1**

2-52 **12** 19 **Coming Again (IRE)**[12] 2374 3-9-0 .......................................... MHills 14 73
(BWHills) *dwlt: sn in midfield: 10th and wkng st: t.o* **80/1**

114- **13** 1 ¼ **Elshadi (IRE)**[238] 5478 3-9-0 96..........................(v[1]) MartinDwyer 4 71
(MPTregoning) *dwlt: t.k.h early: lost pl and rr after 4f: rdn 1/2-way: last and tailing off st* **25/1**

221 **14** 7 **Meath (IRE)**[13] 2333 3-9-0 .......................................... JPSpencer 1 60
(APO'Brien, Ire) *w'like: scope: lw: led tl ent st: wknd: t.o* **16/1**

2m 33.72s (-5.00) **Going Correction** -0.075s/f (Good) **14** Ran SP% **122.2**
Speed ratings: **113,112,111,111,109 108,107,107,106,104 104,91,91,86**CSF £82.97 TOTE £4.50: £1.80, £7.30, £3.20; EX 91.40 Trifecta £698.50 Pool £21,213.28 - 21.56 winning units..
**Owner** Ballymacoll Stud **Bred** Ballymacoll Stud **Trained** Newmarket, Suffolk

■ A second successive Derby for Stoute and Fallon, Fallon having also won the Oaks the previous day.

**FOCUS**
Despite the absence of long-time ante-post favourite Yeats this still looked a typically competitive Derby. It appeared to be run at an even pace throughout, and several of the market leaders were found wanting for stamina. The Dante proved the key, with the first three home there filling the same positions again, but they have all been rated as having improved, North Light provisionally earning an RPR of 124, a touch better than the average for a Derby winner.

**NOTEBOOK**
**North Light(IRE)** had built on the promise he offered at up to a mile as a juvenile when winning the Dante a shade cosily, and improved again to confirm placings with both the second and third, who filled those same positions again. He was among the race's few guaranteed stayers and so was ridden prominently again, showing good tactical speed to hold an ideal position from the start and then pressing on from the entrance to the straight. He galloped strongly all the way to the line without ever looking likely to be caught once American Post had dropped away, and he will be hard to beat in the Irish Derby.
**Rule Of Law(USA)**, half a length behind North Light in the Dante on his reappearance, albeit flattered to get so close, ran a fine race and could even be considered a shade unlucky. Last in the early stages, he had just one behind him turning in and, hanging into the camber in the straight, did not get the clearest of runs. He got going just too late and there should be even more to come on a flatter track.
**Let The Lion Roar**, a beaten favourite when third behind North Light and Rule Of Law in the Dante, had a visor on for the first time. He lost his place down the hill and got going far too late when switched out towards the centre of the track, but he finished so well that John Dunlop fancies he can reverse form with the front two on a flatter track in a race like the Irish Derby. In the longer term the St Leger, won by his half-brother Millenary, is an obvious target.
**Percussionist(IRE)** was flattered by the bare form of his ten-length Lingfield Derby Trial success, but acquitted himself really well in this much tougher contest. His lack of tactical speed saw him struggling to go the pace from an early stage, but he responded well to Darley's urgings and recovered so well that he held second until losing two places close home. He is progressing all the time and will be trained for the St Leger, which ought to suit him ideally.
**Salford City(IRE)**, a slightly disappointing sixth in the 2000 Guineas on his previous start, looked well in the paddock, but was sweating quite badly by the time he got down to the start. In the race itself, he improved to challenge for second a furlong or so out but then failed to get home. He gives the impression he will be ideally suited by around ten furlongs and could be put away now until the Juddmonte International Stakes at York.
**American Post ♦**, a very fortunate winner of the French 2000 Guineas on his previous outing, had never previously raced beyond a mile and simply failed to get home after racing keenly. He was travelling better than anything three furlongs out and lost second only when his stamina ran out a furlong or so from home. Already a triple Group One winner, he is due a short break now but can win yet another major prize over an intermediate trip on his return.

**Snow Ridge(IRE)**, runner-up in the 2000 Guineas on his previous start, was not certain to stay, despite the stamina on his dam's side. He weakened in the final furlong or so after improving from the rear to challenge briefly for second, and is worth another chance back at a shorter trip.
**Hazyview** was supplemented for the race at a cost of £75,000. Ten lengths behind Percussionist on his only previous start beyond ten furlongs, he remains unconvincing at this sort of trip, but was probably not good enough in any case.
**Pukka(IRE)** was sent off a shorter price than for the Newbury handicap (11/1) he won off a mark of 78 on his previous start. He was not good enough, but left the Newbury form far enough behind to blow a highly attractive handicap mark. Connections may now be forced to keep him to Pattern company.
**Gatwick(IRE)**, a supplementary entry, represented top-class handicap form and had shaped in his races at around a mile as if a step up in trip was worth a try. However, the combination of moving up in both class and distance found him out.
**Massif Centrale**, still a maiden and making just his third appearance, ran a very respectable race and can surely be placed to advantage.
**Coming Again(IRE)** was out of his depth and was on the retreat straightening for home.
**Elshadi(IRE)** is evidently well regarded but was too keen in the headgear on this first run in eight months.
**Meath(IRE)**, stablemate of the absent ante-post Derby favourite Yeats, proved a poor substitute and ran a shocker. He may not have stayed, but should have shown more than this.

## 2681 VODAFONE RATED STKS (H'CAP) 1m 4f 10y
5:05 (5:10) (B ) (0-105,104) 4-Y-0+ £23,200 (£8,800; £4,400; £2,000) Stalls Centre

Form RPR
121- **1** **Starry Lodge (IRE)**[259] 5071 4-8-9 **92** ............ KFallon 10 104
(LMCumani) *hld up in rr: prog and 6th st: chsd ldr over 2f out: led over 1f out: sn hrd pressed: drvn out and styd on gamely* **9/2[2]**
341 **2** *hd* **Swift Tango (IRE)**[21] 2110 4-8-13 **96** ............ LDettori 12 108
(EALDunlop) *hld up: 8th st: stdy prog over 2f out: chsd wnr over 1f out: str chal fnl f: jst hld nr fin* **7/2[1]**
020- **3** *1 1/2* **Zibeline (IRE)**[65] 5639 7-8-6 **89** ............ (b) KMcEvoy 3 98
(BEllison) *hld up wl in rr: 12th st: plld out and effrt over 2f out: r.o wl to take 3rd ins fnl f: nt rch ldng pair* **12/1**
60-0 **4** *1* **Anticipating**[78] 1054 4-8-4 **87** oh3 ............ MartinDwyer 8 95
(AMBalding) *racd in midfield: 7th st: rdn over 2f out: styd on same pce* **14/1**
2-06 **5** *nk* **Trust Rule**[35] 1768 4-9-0 **97** ............ MHills 9 104
(BWHills) *trckd ldrs: 5th st: rdn over 2f out: n.m.r 2f out: one pce over 1f out* **15/2[3]**
2145 **6** *nk* **Dissident (GER)**[7] 2471 6-7-11 **87** oh11 ............ (vt) DFentiman(7) 1 94?
(DFlood) *prom: 4th and pushed along st: rdn over 2f out: n.m.r 2f out: one pce after* **33/1**
5-10 **7** *3* **Putra Sandhurst (IRE)**[35] 1767 6-9-7 **104** ............ DHolland 11 106
(MAJarvis) *b: lw: leed to over 9f out: stdd bk into 3rd pl: effrt to ld again 3f out: hdd & wknd over 1f out* **8/1**
0-00 **8** *1 1/4* **Ring Of Destiny**[25] 2022 5-8-6 **89** ............ TQuinn 13 89
(PWHarris) *hld up in rr: 11th st: kpt on same pce over 2f out: n.d* **14/1**
40-0 **9** *14* **Gallery God (FR)**[56] 1328 8-9-1 **98** ............ JPMurtagh 6 76
(SDow) *swtg: led over 9f out and set str pce: hdd 3f out: sn wknd* **11/1**
-025 **10** *3/4* **Tizzy May (FR)**[17] 2220 4-9-1 **98** ............ DaneO'Neill 7 74
(RHannon) *racd in midfield: 9th and rdn st: sn wknd and bhd* **8/1**
15/0 **11** *5* **Manorson (IRE)**[21] 2110 5-8-7 **90** ............ (t) EAhern 2 58
(MAMagnusson) *b: pressed ldr 9f out: rdn and cl 2nd st: sn wknd and bhd* **25/1**
0-00 **12** *17* **Financial Future**[21] 2110 4-8-7 **90** ............ MJKinane 5 31
(MJohnston) *trckd ldrs: 11th and wkng st: sn t.o* **12/1**
050- **13** *dist* **Herodotus**[420] 1021 6-8-4 **87** ............ ANicholls 4 —
(KOCunningham-Brown) *dwlt: a last: t.o st* **66/1**

2m 35.25s (-3.47) **Going Correction** -0.075s/f (Good) **13 Ran SP% 119.7**
Speed ratings: **108,107,106,106,106 105,103,102,93,93 89,78,—**CSF £20.30 CT £180.68 TOTE £3.90: £2.20, £1.90, £4.30; EX 8.90.
**Owner** R C Thompson **Bred** Three Foxes Farm **Trained** Newmarket, Suffolk

**FOCUS**
Quite a good handicap run at a decent pace throughout. The proximity of Dissident from out of the handicap raises a question or two, but it looks strong form overall and the front two are progressing nicely.

**NOTEBOOK**
**Starry Lodge(IRE)**, successful five times in handicap company last term, was 32lb higher than when gaining the first of those wins on this return from a 259 lay-off. Despite that, he proved good enough to carry on where he left off, gamely getting the better of an improver in second. He remains one to keep on your side for the time being.
**Swift Tango(IRE)** improved for the step up to this trip when winning a similar race at Newbury on his previous start and very nearly defied a 6lb rise for that success. He travelled strongly throughout, but was waited with by Dettori and, when finally asked for an effort, was inclined to drift into the camber. This was a fine effort and he is still improving.
**Zibeline(IRE)**, last seen on the Flat when well beaten in the Cesarewitch, had since scored over hurdles at the big Aintree meeting and was racing for the first time since that win. The strong pace was ideal and he ran as well as could have been expected. A return to further will suit.
**Anticipating**, racing for the first time since March, posted a fine effort from 3lb out of the handicap (effectively 10lb higher than when last successful).
**Trust Rule** ran a respectable race, but is quite simply not very well handicapped. *Official explanation: jockey said colt had hung left.*
**Dissident(GER)** ran surprisingly well from 11lb out of the weights.
**Gallery God(FR)** was 4lb lower that when winning this last year but dropped right out after helping force the pace again.

## 2682 VODAFONE STKS (H'CAP) 6f
5:40 (5:42) (C ) (0-100,94) 3-Y-0+ £23,200 (£8,800; £4,400; £2,000) Stalls High

Form RPR
0-40 **1** **Native Title**[8] 2461 6-9-2 **82** ............ PHanagan 1 97
(DNicholls) *trckd ldrs: cl 5th st: effrt to ld over 1f out: drvn clr ins fnl f* **11/1**
0-04 **2** *1 1/2* **Mutawaqed (IRE)**[7] 2477 6-9-4 **84** ............ (t) JPMurtagh 13 95
(MAMagnusson) *b: b.hind: dwlt: last and outpcd: effrt on outer over 2f out: r.o wl fr over 1f out: tk 2nd last strides* **8/1[2]**
10-0 **3** *nk* **Lafi (IRE)**[21] 2132 5-9-11 **91** ............ AlexGreaves 9 101
(DNicholls) *hld up in midfield: 9th st: nt clr run on inner over 2f out: plld out and r.o to press wnr 1f out: no ex: lost 2nd nr post* **14/1**
-043 **4** *3/4* **Jayanjay**[8] 2440 5-8-11 **77** ............ KMcEvoy 11 84
(MissBSanders) *settled towards rr: 11th st: effrt over 2f out: styd on fr over 1f out: nrst fin* **16/1**
2131 **5** *1/2* **Prince Aaron (IRE)**[7] 2477 4-9-1 **81** ............ GCarter 17 87
(CNAllen) *racd wd and towards rr: 13th st: effrt on outer over 2f out: drvn and styd on fr over 1f out: nrst fin* **6/1[1]**
0440 **6** *1/2* **Blackheath (IRE)**[8] 2461 8-8-12 **78** ............ PDobbs 12 82
(DNicholls) *swtg: wl in rr: 14th st: effrt and nt clr run wl over 1f out: styd on fnl f: nrst fin* **25/1**
6220 **7** *nk* **Mine Behind**[7] 2488 4-9-2 **82** ............ NPollard 5 85
(JRBest) *lw: trckd ldrs: 6th st: rdn and effrt 2f out: chsd ldng pair ent fnl f: wknd last 75yds* **10/1[3]**
6601 **8** *1/2* **Pax**[8] 2461 7-8-10 **83** ............ LTreadwell(7) 15 85
(DNicholls) *dwlt: t.k.h and hld up wl in rr: 16th st: styd on fr over 1f out: n.d* **20/1**
0000 **9** *1/2* **Fantasy Believer**[14] 2283 6-9-6 **86** ............ KDalgleish 4 86
(JJQuinn) *trckd ldrs: 8th st: effrt on inner to chse ldng pair 2f out: nt qckn and swtchd rt jst over 1f out: fdd last 100yds* **16/1**
-050 **10** *1 1/4* **Undeterred**[11] 2391 8-8-9 **75** ............ (v) KDarley 3 72
(TDBarron) *lw: s.i.s: wl in rr: 15th st: effrt u.p 2f out: styng on whn hmpd jst ins fnl f* **12/1**
-003 **11** *3/4* **Banjo Bay (IRE)**[7] 2467 6-9-0 **80** ............ DaneO'Neill 2 74
(DNicholls) *mde most to 2f out: wknd fnl f* **14/1**
1-60 **12** *hd* **Malapropism**[7] 2488 4-9-3 **86** ............ SHitchcott(3) 8 80
(MRChannon) *chsd ldrs: 10th st: rdn and hung lft 2f out: no prog after* **25/1**
5031 **13** *3/4* **Polish Emperor (USA)**[21] 2130 4-8-12 **78** ............ (e) NCallan 6 70
(PWHarris) *pressed ldr: drvn to ld 2f out: hdd & wknd over 1f out* **10/1[3]**
0011 **14** *shd* **Idle Power (IRE)**[8] 2441 6-8-11 **77** ............ (p) MartinDwyer 10 68
(JRBoyle) *towards rr: 12th st: rdn and no prog over 2f out* **10/1[3]**
0025 **15** *6* **Loyal Tycoon (IRE)**[7] 2477 6-9-1 **81** ............ ANicholls 7 54
(DNicholls) *trckd ldrs: 7th st: losing pl whn bdly hmpd 2f out and over 1f out: eased* **6/1[1]**
5050 **16** *2 1/2* **Little Edward**[7] 2475 6-10-0 **94** ............ TQuinn 16 60
(BGPowell) *w ldrs: cl 3rd st: wkng whn n.m.r over 1f out: eased* **33/1**
0035 **17** *1* **Vita Spericolata (IRE)**[7] 2488 7-9-4 **84** ............ (v) RWinston 14 47
(JSWainwright) *b: s.i.s: rushed up on outer to join ldrs: cl 4th st: wkng whn hmpd over 1f out: eased* **16/1**

69.04 secs (-1.59) **Going Correction** -0.075s/f (Good) **17 Ran SP% 129.4**
Speed ratings: **107,105,104,103,102 102,101,101,100,98 97,97,96,96,88 85,83**CSF £97.00 CT £1319.74 TOTE £18.30: £6.50, £2.50, £3.70, £3.60; EX 256.20 Place 6 £995.86, Place 5 £390.18..
**Owner** C McKenna **Bred** Mrs W H Gibson Fleming **Trained** Sessay, N Yorks
■ Stewards Enquiry : P Hanagan two-day ban: careless riding (Jun 20-21)

**FOCUS**
Another competitive sprint handicap, but run round a turn so the draw played its part.

**NOTEBOOK**
**Native Title**, 5lb higher than when winning the Ayr Silver Cup last season, made the most of his low draw to grab a good position and run out a decisive winner. He is in the Wokingham and following this career-best effort will command respect if turning up.
**Mutawaqed(IRE)**, third in this last year off a mark of 78, started slowly from his wide draw and came from a mile back to grab second on the line without threatening the winner. He is still 6lb higher than when last successful, but is really finding his form.
**Lafi(IRE)** has done all of his winning over seven furlongs and a mile, but this trip is not a problem and he ran a cracker. Although he cannot really be considered unlucky, he did not get the clearest of runs and looks sure to be placed to advantage by his new trainer.
**Jayanjay** is only 2lb higher than when last winning and this was a reasonable effort.
**Prince Aaron(IRE)** was found out by a wide draw and an 11lb rise in the weights for his recent Kempton victory. *Official explanation: jockey said gelding was unsuited by the track*
**Blackheath(IRE)** would have been closer with better luck.
**Loyal Tycoon(IRE)**, who won this last year, appeared beaten when badly hampered around two out. *Official explanation: jockey said gelding suffered interference approaching the final furlong.*
T/Plt: £1,019.20 to a £1 stake. Pool: £181,083.20. 129.70 winning tickets. T/Qpdt: £293.20 to a £1 stake. Pool: £6,617.00. 16.70 winning tickets. JN

# 2649 HAYDOCK (L-H)
Saturday, June 5

**OFFICIAL GOING: Good (good to soft in places)**
Wind: almost nil Weather: fine

## 2683 SHARP MINDS BETFAIR RATED STKS (H'CAP) 1m 3f 200y
1:35 (1:35) (B ) (0-100,93) 3-Y-O £12,387 (£4,698; £2,349; £1,067) Stalls Far side

Form RPR
-613 **1** **Frank Sonata**[21] 2107 3-9-3 **93** ............ RLMoore 4 107
(MGQuinlan) *hld up: hdwy over 4f out: led over 2f out: r.o* **11/2[3]**
41 **2** *1 3/4* **Modesta (IRE)**[22] 2093 3-8-7 **83** ............ WRyan 5 94
(HRACecil) *in tch: hdwy over 3f out: rdn and edgd lft over 1f out: sn ev ch: nt qckn ins fnl f* **9/2[1]**
4-01 **3** *3* **Admiral (IRE)**[10] 2397 3-8-6 **80** ow2 ............ FLynch 6 88
(SirMichaelStoute) *t.k.h: led after 2f: hdd over 4f out: rdn and ev ch over 2f out: n.m.r over 1f out: kpt on same pce fnl f* **5/1[2]**
514 **4** *2 1/2* **Dallool**[23] 2070 3-8-4 **80** ............ PRobinson 11 82
(MAJarvis) *prom: rdn and outpcd over 2f out: kpt on fnl f* **5/1[2]**
0-44 **5** *2 1/2* **Akritas**[10] 2397 3-8-12 **88** ............ ACulhane 1 86
(PFICole) *led: hdd after 2f: remained prom: led over 4f out: rdn and hdd over 2f out: wknd fnl f* **14/1**
1-53 **6** *1 1/4* **Dumfries**[30] 1899 3-8-4 **80** ............ RHavlin 3 76
(JHMGosden) *midfield: rdn over 3f out: no imp* **16/1**
136 **7** *3/4* **Jomacomi**[23] 2070 3-8-4 **80** ............ RFfrench 8 75
(MJohnston) *midfield: pushed along 6f out: kpt on one pce fr over 4f out: nvr trbld ldrs* **33/1**
10 **8** *1 1/2* **Master Wells (IRE)**[23] 2070 3-8-3 **82** ............ TPQueally(3) 2 75
(JDBethell) *t.k.h: hld up: rdn over 4f out: sme hdwy and edgd lft over 1f out: wknd ins fnl f* **40/1**
241- **9** *8* **Mekuria (JPN)**[235] 5556 3-8-7 **83** ............ JFanning 9 63
(MJohnston) *in tch: rdn over 3f out: wknd over 2f out* **20/1**
24-1 **10** *nk* **Cause Celebre (IRE)**[19] 2168 3-8-2 **78** ............ FNorton 7 57
(BWHills) *in tch: rdn and ev ch over 3f out: wknd 2f out* **14/1**
6-10 **11** *5* **First Centurion**[14] 2281 3-8-9 **85** ............ GDuffield 13 56
(JWHills) *midfield: lost pl over 5f out: n.d after* **16/1**
03-0 **12** *4* **Zouave (IRE)**[18] 2203 3-9-2 **92** ............ SDrowne 10 57
(BJMeehan) *midfield: lost pl 6f out: bhd after* **66/1**
41-4 **13** *1 1/4* **Arkholme**[34] 1799 3-8-4 **80** ............ WSupple 12 43
(WJHaggas) *a bhd* **16/1**

2m 33.0s (-3.96) **Going Correction** +0.05s/f (Good) **13 Ran SP% 109.5**
Speed ratings: **109,107,105,104,102 101,101,100,94,94 91,88,87**CSF £26.56 CT £119.49 TOTE £6.90: £1.90, £1.80, £2.10; EX 14.20.
**Owner** Adams, Flynn, Arnold **Bred** Bishop Wilton Stud **Trained** Newmarket, Suffolk
■ This race was started by a flip start due to a dispute with stalls handlers, and was therefore hand-timed.

**FOCUS**
A decent, competitive handicap featuring several improvers. It was dominated by those at the head of the market and won in style by the top weight. The time was good for the grade and the form should work out.


The Form Book, Raceform Ltd, Compton, RG20 6NL

**NOTEBOOK**
**Frank Sonata** is well suited by some cut in the ground, and trying his longest trip to date, gave weight all round and won with authority. He looks to be still improving and, while there are plenty of good handicaps for him, he may be up to winning in Listed company, possibly abroad, given his favoured conditions.
**Modesta(IRE)**, a half-sister to Oaks winner Reams Of Verse, is still relatively inexperienced and was encountering soft ground for the first time. She ran creditably and, although losing out in a brief struggle with the winner, drew clear of the rest. This was improved form and she should win her share of races.
**Admiral(IRE)** ◆, who won well on fast ground last time, took a keen hold on this easier surface and could not respond when tackled by the principals. He nevertheless ran with credit, and as he will appreciate a return to a sound surface the King George V Handicap at Royal Ascot still looks a reasonable target.
**Dallool** has now run with credit in two decent handicaps since winning his maiden over course and distance. He is still relatively inexperienced, and a slight drop in grade should enable him to get back on the winning trail.
**Akritas**, another who was keen early, stuck to his task once headed but was beaten further by the third than at Goodwood, despite meeting him on better terms.
**Dumfries** again looked less effective on this easy ground, and may improve for a step up in trip and return to the fast ground he won on as a juvenile.

## 2684 SHANK LANE STKS (H'CAP) 2m 45y
**2:05** (2:05) (C) (0-100,99) 4-Y-O+ **£13,877** (£4,270; £2,135; £1,067) **Stalls** Low

| Form | | | | RPR |
|---|---|---|---|---|
| 031/ | **1** | | **Dancing Bay**[35] 2877 7-9-6 **90** WRyan 3<br>(NJHenderson) *hld up in rr: hdwy 4f out: led 2f out: sn hung lft: clr whn flashed tail ins fnl f: styd on wl* **13/2**[2] | 103 |
| 03-4 | **2** | 3 ½ | **Distant Prospect (IRE)**[31] 1880 7-9-6 **90** DSweeney 6<br>(AMBalding) *hld up: hdwy over 3f out: rdn and ev ch 2f out: kpt on same pce ins fnl f* **7/1**[3] | 99 |
| -143 | **3** | 5 | **Sentry (IRE)**[34] 1801 4-9-1 **86** PRobinson 4<br>(JHMGosden) *midfield: hdwy whn nt clr run and swtchd rt over 1f out: styd on ins fnl f: nt trble ldrs* **7/1**[3] | 89+ |
| 0-23 | **4** | ¾ | **Prins Willem (IRE)**[35] 1768 5-9-6 **90** GDuffield 12<br>(JRFanshawe) *midfield: hdwy over 4f out: rdn over 2f out: kpt on one pce* **12/1** | 92 |
| 6-20 | **5** | 1 | **Clarinch Claymore**[7] 2491 8-8-2 **72** RFfrench 2<br>(JMJefferson) *midfield: hdwy 4f out: rdn and ev ch 2f out: wknd fnl f* **20/1** | 73 |
| 1610 | **6** | 2 ½ | **Jorobaden (FR)**[24] 2047 4-9-5 **90** GBaker 14<br>(CFWall) *prom: rdn and ev ch over 2f out: wknd over 1f out* **16/1** | 88 |
| 0-00 | **7** | shd | **Double Obsession**[12] 2365 4-9-2 **90** TPQueally[(3)] 9<br>(MJohnston) *midfield: lost pl 6f out: rdn over 3f out: no imp* **20/1** | 88 |
| 0-00 | **8** | hd | **Random Quest**[31] 1880 6-9-2 **86** RHavlin 5<br>(BJLlewellyn) *hld up: hdwy 4f out: sn rdn: no imp* **12/1** | 84 |
| 0-30 | **9** | ½ | **Prairie Falcon (IRE)**[15] 2277 10-8-9 **84** AMedeiros[(5)] 1<br>(BWHills) *in tch: rdn to ld 3f out: hdd 2f out: wknd over 1f out* **33/1** | 81 |
| 111- | **10** | 3 ½ | **Dorothy's Friend**[271] 4775 4-8-8 **79** SDrowne 10<br>(RCharlton) *hld up: hdwy 6f out: rdn 4f out: sn wknd* **6/1**[1] | 72 |
| 1-06 | **11** | 13 | **Ponderon**[31] 1880 4-9-3 **88** SCarson 8<br>(RFJohnsonHoughton) *prom: rdn 4f out: sn wknd* **13/2**[2] | 65 |
| 51-0 | **12** | ¾ | **Morson Boy (USA)**[22] 2076 4-10-0 **99** JFanning 11<br>(MJohnston) *led: rdn and hdd 3f out: sn wknd* **14/1** | 75 |
| 5-00 | **13** | nk | **Skye's Folly (USA)**[14] 2285 4-8-4 **75** WSupple 7<br>(JGGiven) *close up: rdn to chal over 3f out: nt much whn wkng over 2f out* **33/1** | 51 |
| 0-02 | **14** | dist | **Archduke Ferdinand (FR)**[16] 2240 6-9-2 **86** ACulhane 13<br>(PFICole) *hld up: hdwy 6f out: rdn and wknd over 4f out: t.o* **12/1** | — |

3m 37.2s (-0.70) **Going Correction** +0.05s/f (Good)
**WFA** 4 from 5yo+ 1lb **14** Ran SP% **117.0**
Speed ratings: **103,101,98,98,97 96,96,96,96,94 87,87,87,—**CSF £47.38 CT £327.46 TOTE £5.20: £1.50, £3.40, £2.80; EX 31.30.
**Owner** Elite Racing Club **Bred** Elite Racing Club **Trained** Lambourn, Berks

**FOCUS**
A competitive handicap and sound form. It was run at just a fair gallop but they finished well strung out behind the clear-cut winner.

**NOTEBOOK**
**Dancing Bay**, who had not run on the Flat for nearly two years, has improved with racing over hurdles. Given his ideal underfoot conditions, he transferred that improvement back to the Flat, winning very much as he liked despite hanging across to the far rail once in front. His trainer has done well when running his jumpers in staying races on the Flat in recent seasons, and he could well pick up another race or two with this one.
**Distant Prospect(IRE)** ◆, a former Cesarewitch winner who also scored over hurdles last season, ran well in the Chester Cup last time but appreciated this more galloping track. Although no match for the winner, he came away from the rest and a race such as the Ascot Stakes at the Royal meeting would suit him ideally if there was any give underfoot.
**Sentry(IRE)**, trying his longest trip to date, travelled smoothly but did not pick up as well as the principals. He seemed to get the trip and is one to bear in mind for a decent staying handicap on faster ground.
**Prins Willem(IRE)**, trying this trip for only the second time, had his chance but seemed not to quite get home on ground softer than he prefers. He is creeping up the weights, but may be the sort for a race such as the Ebor later in the season.
**Clarinch Claymore** ran a decent race without quite having the pace in the closing stages. He seems to like Beverley, and is one to watch out for in a staying handicap there this summer.
**Jorobaden(FR)**, who appreciates cut, was ridden more positively than usual on this step up in distance and did not get home. A return to hold-up tactics may help him if trying this trip again.
**Dorothy's Friend**, a progressive stayer last season, was 12lb higher than for his last win and making his seasonal debut. He started favourite but failed to pick up on the ground. His form last year was on good ground or faster, and he deserves a chance to atone on a sound surface.
**Ponderon** has been struggling for form on easy ground this year. He may be better later in the year on a faster surface. *Official explanation: trainer said gelding was stiff behind.*

## 2685 JOSEPH HELER CHEESE CECIL FRAIL STKS (LISTED RACE) (F&M) 6f
**2:35** (2:36) (A) 3-Y-O+ **£17,400** (£6,600; £3,300; £1,500) **Stalls** Centre

| Form | | | | RPR |
|---|---|---|---|---|
| 040- | **1** | | **Tante Rose (IRE)**[231] 5638 4-9-0 107 SDrowne 9<br>(RCharlton) *hld up: hdwy over 1f out: r.o to ld wl ins fnl f* **7/4**[1] | 101 |
| 14-5 | **2** | nk | **Ruby Rocket (IRE)**[49] 1458 3-8-10 105 GDuffield 10<br>(HMorrison) *hld up: hdwy 2f out: rdn to ld over 1f out: hdd wl ins fnl f: r.o* **5/1**[3] | 105 |
| 0231 | **3** | 1 ½ | **Golden Nun**[21] 2117 4-9-4 100 (b) PRobinson 11<br>(TDEasterby) *bhd: hdwy and hung lft over 1f out: r.o ins fnl f: nt qckn towards fin* **9/2**[2] | 100 |
| 030- | **4** | 5 | **Dani Ridge (IRE)**[210] 5953 6-9-0 81 RHavlin 8<br>(EJAlston) *chsd ldrs: rdn over 1f out: wknd fnl f* **80/1** | 81 |
| 5-40 | **5** | nk | **Needles And Pins (IRE)**[21] 2117 3-8-6 97 FLynch 7<br>(MLWBell) *prom: led 3f out: rdn and hdd over 1f out: wknd fnl f* **25/1** | 80 |
| 4-33 | **6** | 1 | **Look Here's Carol (IRE)**[21] 2117 4-9-0 87 GGibbons 5<br>(BAMcmahon) *trckd ldrs: rdn 3f out: wknd over 1f out* **20/1** | 77 |
| 5206 | **7** | 6 | **Simianna**[7] 2488 5-9-0 90 (p) FNorton 3<br>(ABerry) *in tch: rdn over 2f out: wknd over 1f out* **16/1** | 59 |
| 1-40 | **8** | 1 ½ | **Malvern Light**[28] 1964 3-8-6 97 ACulhane 4<br>(WJHaggas) *in tch: rdn 3f out: wknd 2f out* **14/1** | 55 |
| 26-0 | **9** | 3 | **Unshooda**[49] 1458 3-8-6 95 WSupple 1<br>(BWHills) *prom: rdn 2f out: wknd over 1f out* **14/1** | 46 |
| -001 | **10** | 3 | **Caveral**[12] 2372 3-8-6 85 RLMoore 2<br>(RHannon) *hld up: rdn over 2f out: sn btn* **7/1** | 37 |
| 2-42 | **11** | 1 ½ | **Blaise Castle (USA)**[14] 2282 4-9-0 90 (b[1]) TPQueally 6<br>(GAButler) *racd keenly: led: hdd 3f out: sn wknd* **33/1** | 32 |

1m 13.75s (-1.14) **Going Correction** +0.05s/f (Good)
**WFA** 3 from 4yo+ 8lb **11** Ran SP% **115.7**
Speed ratings: **109,108,106,99,99 98,90,88,84,80 78**CSF £9.54 TOTE £2.70: £1.60, £1.60, £2.00; EX 14.10.
**Owner** B E Nielsen **Bred** Addison Racing Ltd Inc **Trained** Beckhampton, Wilts

**FOCUS**
A run-of-the-mill fillies' Listed contest dominated by those at the head of the market, all of whom came from off the pace.

**NOTEBOOK**
**Tante Rose(IRE)** is beautifully bred and cost current connections 350,000gns at the Wafic Said dispersal sale. She clearly goes well fresh, as she won a Group Three first time out last season, and the drop in trip proved no problem in this lower grade. Whether she can go on from this remains to be seen, but she will make a valuable broodmare when she retires.
**Ruby Rocket(IRE)**, encountering an easy surface for the first time on this drop back in trip, travelled well and looked likely to win inside the last before the older filly proved too strong. At the weights she emerges the best horse in the race, and she looks capable of picking up a similar event.
**Golden Nun**, despite the headgear, is a genuine and consistent sort in this grade and again ran her race. By a sire whose stock often prefer cut in the ground, she also handles a fast surface and should pick up more races at this level.
**Dani Ridge(IRE)**, having her first outing since the autumn, had a stiff task on official ratings but ran with plenty of credit, despite being left behind by the front three. Pregnancy clearly suits her, and she can win races and may even earn some black type before retiring to the paddocks.
**Needles And Pins(IRE)**, who won her maiden and was touched off in a Group Three on soft ground as a juvenile, was encountering it for the first time since and ran her best race of the season. She may well have to go abroad again to get her ground this summer and a drop back to five should be in her favour.
**Look Here's Carol(IRE)** finished much further behind Golden Nun than she had at Nottingham, and from her current mark would be better off in handicaps or conditions races.

## 2686 BRIAN DUNN'S BIRTHDAY EBF MAIDEN STKS 5f
**3:10** (3:11) (D) 2-Y-O **£5,183** (£1,595; £797; £398) **Stalls** Centre

| Form | | | | RPR |
|---|---|---|---|---|
| 5 | **1** | | **Piper Lily**[31] 1884 2-8-9 FNorton 4<br>(MBlanshard) *chsd ldrs: rdn 2f out: r.o ins fnl f to ld cl home* **9/1** | 77 |
| 2 | **2** | hd | **Hanseatic League (USA)**[11] 2388 2-9-0 JFanning 9<br>(MJohnston) *led: rdn 2f out: hdd cl home* **1/1**[1] | 81 |
| | **3** | 2 | **Turnaround (GER)** 2-9-0 ACulhane 3<br>(MrsJRRamsden) *hld up: rdn and hdwy over 1f out: styd on ins fnl f: nt rch ldrs* **25/1** | 74 |
| 33 | **4** | 2 ½ | **Easy Feeling (IRE)**[4] 2544 2-8-9 RLMoore 2<br>(RHannon) *prom: rdn and ev ch over 1f out: wknd ins fnl f* **11/4**[2] | 60 |
| 0 | **5** | ½ | **Wonderful Mind**[51] 1415 2-9-0 PRobinson 5<br>(TDEasterby) *racd keenly: prom: rdn over 1f out: wknd fnl f* **15/2**[3] | 64 |
| | **6** | 8 | **Ne Oublie** 2-9-0 DaleGibson 8<br>(JMackie) *s.i.s: sn chsd ldrs: rdn and wknd over 1f out* **20/1** | 36 |
| | **7** | 3 | **Toldo (IRE)** 2-8-9 PBradley[(5)] 1<br>(ABerry) *towards rr: hdwy over 2f out: rdn and wknd over 1f out: sn hung lft* **33/1** | 25 |
| | **8** | 5 | **Fellbeck Fred** 2-8-11 TEaves[(3)] 7<br>(CWThornton) *dwlt: a outpcd* **66/1** | 8 |

62.53 secs (0.46) **Going Correction** +0.05s/f (Good) **8** Ran SP% **111.5**
Speed ratings: **98,97,94,90,89 76,72,64**CSF £17.62 TOTE £8.70: £2.20, £1.10, £4.40; EX 37.50.
**Owner** David Sykes **Bred** D Sykes **Trained** Upper Lambourn, Berks

**FOCUS**
A sound gallop and a maiden that should produce a winner or two.

**NOTEBOOK**
**Piper Lily**, showed the benefit of her run at Chester by proving too strong for the favourite. Although quite diminutive compared with that rival, she stuck her head down and battled her way past him. Her attitude will help her to win more races.
**Hanseatic League(USA)**, as on his debut, set off in front but had to give best to a potentially useful filly. He is probably still a bit weak, and could do with an easy race now to help his confidence.
**Turnaround(GER)** ◆, a half-brother to three German Listed winners, was awkward to load and took a while to learn what was required. However, he was staying on nicely at the finish and will no doubt be placed to win a race before long.
**Easy Feeling(IRE)** has not really progressed from her debut, but was encountering easy ground for the first time and seemed to not get home. A return to faster may help, but she looks the type for nurseries later on.
**Wonderful Mind**, who showed early speed on his debut in April, did the same again and ran with credit. He is another that can make his mark in nurseries.

## 2687 SECURITY GUARD COMPANY 0870 0347333 H'CAP 1m 30y
**3:40** (3:41) (C) (0-95,92) 3-Y-O+ **£10,010** (£3,080; £1,540; £770) **Stalls** Low

| Form | | | | RPR |
|---|---|---|---|---|
| 41-0 | **1** | | **Bishopric**[33] 1821 4-9-10 **88** DSweeney 1<br>(HCandy) *cl up: led over 1f out: rdn out* **12/1** | 100 |
| 00/0 | **2** | 1 ½ | **Prizeman (USA)**[49] 1456 6-10-0 **92** RHavlin 3<br>(GBBalding) *hld up: hdwy 4f out: chsd wnr ins fnl f: styd on* **33/1** | 100 |
| 6013 | **3** | 3 ½ | **Intricate Web (IRE)**[15] 2271 8-9-0 **78** FNorton 8<br>(EJAlston) *in rr: hdwy 3f out: styd on ins fnl f: nt rch ldrs* **9/2**[1] | 78 |
| 0-05 | **4** | 2 ½ | **Nuit Sombre (IRE)**[33] 1845 4-9-1 **79** JFanning 2<br>(MJohnston) *led: rdn and hdd over 1f out: sn wknd* **5/1**[2] | 73 |
| 06-0 | **5** | 1 | **Mezuzah**[60] 1284 4-9-5 **83** SDrowne 10<br>(GWragg) *hld up: rdn over 2f out: kpt on ins fnl f: nt trble ldrs* **10/1** | 75 |
| 0060 | **6** | nk | **Go Tech**[18] 2215 4-9-0 **78** PRobinson 7<br>(TDEasterby) *prom: rdn over 2f out: wknd fnl f* **5/1**[2] | 69 |
| 5006 | **7** | ½ | **Prince Of Gold**[8] 2459 4-7-13 **63** DaleGibson 9<br>(RHollinshead) *towards rr: rdn and hdwy 2f out: wknd ins fnl f* **8/1** | 53 |
| 5506 | **8** | ½ | **Silvaline**[7] 2474 5-8-9 **73** PDoe 4<br>(TKeddy) *midfield: hdwy over 4f out: rdn 3f out: wknd 1f out: eased ins fnl f* **7/1** | 62 |
| 0106 | **9** | 2 ½ | **Harry Potter (GER)**[15] 2271 5-8-7 **71** (b) DarrenWilliams 5<br>(KRBurke) *in tch: rdn over 2f out: wknd over 1f out* **13/2**[3] | 54 |

-000 **10** *9* **Buthaina (IRE)**[12] 2368 4-7-7 **62** oh3 ow2 ........................ SYourston(7) 6 27
(THCaldwell) *prom: rdn over 3f out: wknd over 2f out* **100/1**

1m 45.06s (-0.49) **Going Correction** +0.05s/f (Good) **10** Ran SP% **109.2**
Speed ratings: **104,102,99,96,95 95,94,94,91,82**CSF £310.90 CT £1915.71 TOTE £10.70: £2.70, £6.40, £1.60; EX 381.50.

**Owner** Girsonfield Ltd **Bred** Girsonfield Ltd **Trained** Wantage, Oxon

**FOCUS**

This was run 0.57sec faster than the concluding three-year-old handicap, but the field split into two groups in the straight - the trio on the far rail finished first, second and fourth - and the form looks a bit dubious.

**NOTEBOOK**

**Bishopric**, who was well beaten on his return after nearly a year off at Doncaster having got upset in the stalls, was helped by sticking to the far rail but won quite well in the end. He is lightly raced and could go on from this, given cut in the ground.

**Prizeman(USA)**, having only his second race in nearly three years, got a good lead from Nuit Sombre on the far rail and stayed on for second without ever looking like catching the winner. Connections are likely to have been well pleased with this effort, and his current mark offers him some chance of re-establishing himself..

**Intricate Web(IRE)**, who has held his form well, did clearly best of the group that chose to race up the centre in the straight. He is probably high enough in the weights now, but could well pop up again as he seems best on a faster surface.

**Nuit Sombre(IRE)**, reverting to the front-running tactics that suit him, held the call until the winner went by but then stopped quickly. A summer performer who seems to win his races in pairs, he looked as if he might be on the way back and is on a fair mark.

**Mezuzah** has been struggling for form but has slipped down the handicap as a result. He still needs to show more than he did here before he becomes a betting proposition.

**Go Tech**, who has been running well of late on faster going, was keen early on this rain-softened ground and switching to the centre did not help his cause. *Official explanation: jockey said gelding failed to handle the bend.*

## 2688 HILARY LINDSAY 40TH BIRTHDAY H'CAP — 1m 30y

**4:10** (4:13) (E ) (0-70,70) 3-Y-0 — **£3,952** (£1,216; £608; £304) **Stalls** Low

Form — RPR

6-65 **1** **Futoo (IRE)**[16] 2251 3-8-10 **59** ........................ FLynch 5 64
(GMMoore) *a.p: led over 2f out: all out* **10/1**

52-6 **2** *½* **Miss Eloise**[32] 1874 3-8-0 **56** ........................ AMullen(7) 10 60
(TDEasterby) *midfield: hdwy 4f out: r.o cl home* **8/1**[3]

6-00 **3** *shd* **Ermine Grey**[42] 1613 3-9-7 **70** ........................ (v) PaulEddery 2 74
(DHaydnJones) *trckd ldrs: rdn over 2f out: r.o cl home* **14/1**

5420 **4** *nk* **On The Waterfront**[21] 2134 3-9-3 **66** ........................ GDuffield 3 69
(JWHills) *s.i.s: midfield: hdwy 4f out: ch ins fnl f: styd on* **9/1**

46-6 **5** *1* **Charlotte Vale**[23] 2069 3-9-3 **66** ........................ ACulhane 8 67
(MDHammond) *midfield: rdn and hdwy over 2f out: hung lft ins fnl f: styd on* **6/1**[1]

00-0 **6** *2* **Cobalt Blue (IRE)**[16] 2251 3-8-3 **52** ........................ (b1) GGibbons 11 48
(WJHaggas) *midfield: rdn over 3f out: kpt on one pce* **9/1**

00-1 **7** *6* **Dagola (IRE)**[49] 1467 3-8-13 **62** ........................ RSmith 13 44
(CGCox) *bhd: styd on fnl f: nvr nrr* **13/2**[2]

0-54 **8** *1* **Campbells Lad**[17] 2232 3-7-12 **47** oh5 ........................ PMQuinn 4 27
(ABerry) *s.i.s: hld up: hdwy 3f out: rdn 2f out: wknd fnl f* **66/1**

-400 **9** *2* **Velocitas**[11] 2377 3-8-8 **57** ........................ JFanning 7 32
(HJCollingridge) *prom: rdn 3f out: wknd ins fnl f* **25/1**

4340 **10** *1¾* **Ashstanza**[65] 1222 3-8-9 **58** ........................ PRobinson 1 29
(MAJarvis) *led: rdn and hdd over 2f out: wknd over 1f out* **13/2**[2]

043 **11** *1½* **My Pension (IRE)**[14] 2289 3-9-5 **68** ........................ SDrowne 17 36
(PHowling) *towards rr: rdn over 2f out: nvr trbld ldrs* **12/1**

0-40 **12** *1¼* **Stiletto Lady (IRE)**[12] 2371 3-8-10 **59** ........................ DaleGibson 15 24
(JGGiven) *midfield: pushed along 5f out: wknd 3f out* **20/1**

4-00 **13** *1¼* **Young Patriarch**[24] 2032 3-9-0 **63** ........................ DSweeney 18 25
(BJMeehan) *hld up: rdn over 2f out: no imp* **50/1**

060- **14** *shd* **Schinken Otto (IRE)**[280] 4576 3-8-4 **53** ........................ RFfrench 14 15
(JMJefferson) *prom: rdn over 3f out: sn wknd* **66/1**

3302 **15** *11* **Maybe Someday**[79] 1046 3-8-11 **60** ........................ (p) JEdmunds 12 —
(JBalding) *bhd after 3f* **16/1**

0-00 **16** *8* **Desert Battle (IRE)**[26] 1998 3-8-11 **60** ........................ (b1) FNorton 6 —
(MBlanshard) *racd keenly: trckd ldrs: rdn whn n.m.r over 2f out: sn wknd* **25/1**

00-5 **17** *11* **La Fonteyne**[26] 1991 3-8-6 **58** ........................ TEaves(3) 16 —
(CBBBooth) *a bhd* **50/1**

1m 45.63s (0.08) **Going Correction** +0.05s/f (Good) **17** Ran SP% **120.8**
Speed ratings: **101,100,100,100,99 97,91,90,88,86 84,83,82,82,71 63,52**CSF £81.22 CT £1172.61 TOTE £14.50: £3.80, £1.80, £4.00, £2.80; EX 153.90 Place 6 £79.10, Place 5 £44.01..

**Owner** M K Roddis **Bred** John Bernard O'Connor **Trained** Middleham Moor, N Yorks

**FOCUS**

A modest handicap run 0.57sec slower than the preceding handicap for older horses.

**NOTEBOOK**

**Futoo(IRE)** had dropped back to a winning mark and fulfilled the promise of his recent run at Newcastle with a resolute performance, racing up with the pace from the start, and sticking on bravely to resist a number of challenges. He should not go up much and may have another race in him if this does not leave its mark.

**Miss Eloise**, who is well suited by cut in the ground, did not get the best of passages on the inside and was doing her best work at the finish. She can get off the mark before long if the ground does not turn against her.

**Ermine Grey**, both of whose wins have been on Fibresand, ran well without being able to find a change of gear. He is reasonably handicapped and can find a small race on turf.

**On The Waterfront**, a lightly-raced maiden, seemed to find this slower surface holding him back a little. He is lightly raced and, as his dam was a stayer, he may appreciate the return to a longer trip.

**Charlotte Vale**, dropped in grade, tended to wander off a straight line rather than go forward with purpose. She may respond to the fitting of headgear.

**Cobalt Blue(IRE)**, fitted with first-time blinkers, got closer to the winner than he had at Newcastle but could never land a blow. A drop in grade may be needed.

**Dagola(IRE)** *Official explanation: jockey said gelding was unsuited by the ground.*

T/Plt: £45.00 to a £1 stake. Pool: £63,655.65. 1,031.45 winning tickets. T/Qpdt: £13.10 to a £1 stake. Pool: £2,288.80. 128.50 winning tickets. DO

# 2501 NEWMARKET (R-H)

Saturday, June 5

**OFFICIAL GOING: Good to firm**

Although it was cloudy it was quite warm with a slight breeze, and the ground dried out throughout the day.

Wind: Slight behind. Weather: Cloudy.

## 2689 BOLLINGER CHAMPAGNE CHALLENGE SERIES H'CAP (FOR GENTLEMAN AMATEUR RIDERS) — 1m 4f

**6:30** (6:32) (E ) (0-75,74) 4-Y-0+ — **£3,347** (£1,030; £515; £257) **Stalls** Far side

Form — RPR

3021 **1** **Bucks**[21] 2116 7-11-7 **74** ........................ MrMichaelMurphy(7) 3 86
(DKIvory) *a.p: jnd ldrs over 3f out: edgd rt and led ins fnl f: styd on* **5/1**[2]

0241 **2** *1¾* **Danakil**[11] 2381 9-11-7 **72** ........................ MrDHutchison(5) 6 81
(SDow) *hld up: hdwy 4f out: led over 2f out: hdd and unable qck ins fnl f* **2/1**[1]

02-0 **3** *7* **Domenico (IRE)**[14] 2285 6-11-4 **71** ........................ MrNSoares(7) 7 69
(JRJenkins) *chsd ldrs: led over 3f out: hdd over 2f out: wknd over 1f out* **18/1**

-100 **4** *1* **Squirtle Turtle**[14] 2305 4-11-2 **67** ........................ (b) MrOCole(5) 10 63
(PFICole) *hld up in tch: hmpd and lost pl 3f out: hdwy and hung lft fr over 1f out: nt trble ldrs* **20/1**

0-03 **5** *nk* **Iloveturtle (IRE)**[5] 1698 4-10-3 **54** ........................ MrJMorgan(5) 9 50
(MCChapman) *chsd ldrs: rdn over 2f out: styd on same pce* **14/1**

430/ **6** *3½* **Cyber Santa**[649] 4197 6-9-13 **48** ........................ MrLNewnes(3) 11 38
(JHetherton) *hld up: hdwy 3f out: n.d* **12/1**

0/0- **7** *7* **Ei Ei**[14] 4968 9-9-11 **46** ........................ MrEDehdashti(3) 1 25
(MCChapman) *plld hrd: led after 1f: rdn and hdd over 3f out: wknd over 2f out* **13/2**[3]

-003 **8** *2½* **Fairy Wind (GER)**[19] 2186 7-9-11 **50** ........................ MrDLQueally(7) 8 25
(BJCurley) *chsd ldrs over 8f* **8/1**

3162 **9** *5* **Amethyst Rock**[19] 2185 6-9-8 **47** oh2 ow5 ........................ MrMAHammond(7) 5 14
(PLGilligan) *chsd ldrs over 8f* **20/1**

130- **10** *¾* **Bhutan (IRE)**[435] 835 9-10-0 **51** ow1 ........................ MrJJBest(5) 2 17
(GBBalding) *hld up: effrt over 4f out: a in rr* **14/1**

30/6 **11** *3½* **Jazil**[21] 2127 9-10-9 **60** ........................ (t) MrNPearce(5) 4 20
(KAMorgan) *racd keenly: led 1f: hmpd 10f out: remained handy tl wknd over 3f out* **50/1**

2m 35.3s (1.84) **Going Correction** -0.05s/f (Good) **11** Ran SP% **112.2**
Speed ratings: **91,89,85,84,84 81,77,75,72,71 69**CSF £14.14 CT £161.38 TOTE £6.30: £2.00, £1.40, £3.80; EX 9.80.

**Owner** M Murphy **Bred** Meon Valley Stud **Trained** Radlett, Herts

■ Michael Murphy's first winner.

■ Stewards Enquiry : Mr J J Best £150 fine: failed to line up in position (drawn 2) for flip-start

**FOCUS**

Flip start used, race hand-timed. A modest amateurs' event in which there was only a steady pace, and the two market leaders had the race to themselves in the latter stages. The winner's previous form is working out well.

**NOTEBOOK**

**Bucks**, well handled by his amateur, is in the form of his life at present. He is tough and genuine and should be capable of scoring again.

**Danakil** did little wrong and may have been a shade unlucky to bump into an in-form rival, having pulled well clear of the third.

**Domenico(IRE)** shaped much better, despite the trip being on the sharp side for him.

**Squirtle Turtle**, done no favours as Ei Ei weakened in front of him, stayed on best of all up the hill, but he cannot be described as unlucky.

**Iloveturtle(IRE)** lacks a change of pace and would have been better suited by a stronger gallop.

## 2690 EBF FRANK BUTTERS MAIDEN FILLIES' STKS — 6f

**7:00** (7:03) (D ) 2-Y-O — **£4,735** (£1,457; £728; £364) **Stalls** Low

Form — RPR

2 **1** **Park Romance (IRE)**[16] 2245 2-8-11 ........................ KFallon 4 92
(BJMeehan) *w ldr: led and hung right fr 2f out: r.o wl* **2/1**[1]

5 **2** *1¼* **Bentley's Bush (IRE)**[22] 2083 2-8-11 ........................ RHughes 9 88
(RHannon) *led 4f: rdn over 1f out: styd on same pce ins fnl f* **11/2**[2]

**3** *¾* **Almendrados (IRE)** 2-8-11 ........................ EAhern 1 86
(JNoseda) *chsd ldrs: rdn and edgd rt over 1f out: styd on same pce* **8/1**[3]

**4** *¾* **All For Laura** 2-8-8 ........................ TPQueally(3) 5 84
(DRLoder) *chsd ldrs: rdn over 1f out: styd on same pce* **12/1**

3 **5** *nk* **Catch A Star**[15] 2275 2-8-11 ........................ LDettori 2 83
(NACallaghan) *s.i.s: hld up: pushed along over 2f out: hdwy over 1f out: nt trble ldrs* **2/1**[1]

**6** *5* **Improvise** 2-8-11 ........................ DHolland 6 68
(CEBrittain) *chsd ldrs over 4f* **8/1**[3]

5 **7** *1¼* **Madam Caversfield**[9] 2427 2-8-11 ........................ RLMoore 3 64
(RHannon) *s.i.s: sn pushed along: a in rr* **33/1**

**8** *1¼* **Top Form (IRE)** 2-8-11 ........................ WSupple 8 60
(EALDunlop) *plld hrd and prom: wkng whn hung rt over 1f out* **33/1**

0 **9** *6* **Jay (IRE)**[15] 2275 2-8-11 ........................ WRyan 7 42
(NACallaghan) *s.i.s: a in rr* **100/1**

1m 13.19s (0.10) **Going Correction** -0.05s/f (Good) **9** Ran SP% **118.8**
Speed ratings: **97,95,94,93,92 86,84,82,74**CSF £14.23 TOTE £2.80: £1.70, £1.90, £2.00; EX 21.20.

**Owner** F C T Wilson **Bred** Lodge Park Stud **Trained** Upper Lambourn, Berks

**FOCUS**

Although the time was nothing special, there looked some nice types on show, with the front two having had the benefit of a run, and the form is almost certainly strong for the grade.

**NOTEBOOK**

**Park Romance(IRE)** was well on top in the end, despite still showing signs of greeness. She will stay an extra furlong and there is plenty more to come from her yet.

**Bentley's Bush(IRE)**, out of a mare that stayed ten furlongs, knew a bit more this time and, although well held in the closing stages, showed enough to suggest she can win her maiden.

**Almendrados(IRE)** ◆, a 260,000 guinea yearling, took the eye to post and with improvement to come over a little further, looks to have a bright future.

**All For Laura**, who is out of a mare that won over a mile, did not shape too badly and is sure to be wiser for the experience.

**Catch A Star** was not seen to best effect, being held up in a steadily-run contest.

## 2691 FIFTY YEARS OF TWINNING CLASSIFIED STKS — 1m 4f

**7:30** (7:32) (C ) 3-Y-0+ — **£9,204** (£2,832; £1,416; £708) **Stalls** Centre

Form — RPR

4-00 **1** **Wunderwood (USA)**[21] 2110 5-9-4 **89** ........................ SSanders 5 99
(LadyHerries) *mde all: rdn over 1f out: styd on wl* **11/2**

122- **2** *hd* **Alkaased (USA)**[236] [5543] 4-9-7 93 DHolland 3 102
(LMCumani) *trckd wnr: rdn over 1f out: r.o wl* **7/2**[2]
03-0 **3** *2* **Defining**[21] [2110] 5-9-9 95 OUrbina 6 100
(JRFanshawe) *hld up: hdwy over 1f out: nt rch ldrs* **25/1**
-202 **4** *2* **Highland Games (IRE)**[12] [2365] 4-9-4 87 KFallon 7 92
(JGGiven) *a.p: rdn over 1f out: hung lft and no ex fnl f* **4/1**[3]
2-11 **5** *½* **Fine Palette**[18] [2210] 4-9-4 87 WRyan 4 91
(HRACecil) *hld up: hdwy 3f out: rdn over 1f out: no ex ins fnl f* **9/4**[1]
2-10 **6** *nk* **Arresting**[33] [1832] 4-9-4 85 EAhern 2 91
(JRFanshawe) *trckd ldrs: rdn over 1f out: sn btn* **20/1**
002- **7** *4* **Mamcazma**[211] [5942] 6-9-9 95 MTebbutt 9 90
(DMorris) *hld up in tch: wknd 2f out* **11/1**
/41- **8** *1 ¼* **Urowells (IRE)**[386] [1633] 4-9-6 92 TEDurcan 1 85
(EALDunlop) *hld up in tch: rdn over 2f out: wknd over 1f out* **25/1**
31/0 **9** *10* **Thundering Surf**[21] [2110] 7-9-4 90 RHughes 8 67
(JRJenkins) *broke wl: plld hrd: stdd to rr after 1f: wknd over 2f out* **33/1**

2m 34.07s (0.61) **Going Correction** -0.05s/f (Good) **9** Ran SP% **112.1**
Speed ratings: **95,94,93,92,91 91,89,88,81**CSF £22.99 TOTE £7.10: £2.30, £2.10, £4.00; EX 31.80.
**Owner** Tony Perkins **Bred** Darley Stud Management, L L C **Trained** Angmering, W Sussex

**FOCUS**
A tight classified stakes race with 5lb covering the field on adjusted official ratings. A steadily-run contest which favoured those racing close to the pace, but the form looks sound enough.

**NOTEBOOK**
**Wunderwood(USA)** was given a peach of a ride, and just poached enough of a lead going into the dip to withstand the late flourish of the runner-up.
**Alkaased(USA)** ◆ made a pleasing return to action and, as he stays further than this, should find plenty of opportunities this summer.
**Defining** did well to finish as close as he did, having looked to have come from an impossible position.
**Highland Games(IRE)** looked to run his race and had no excuses.
**Fine Palette** did not stride out at all well to post and, although running well enough, may be better suited to an easier surface.
**Arresting** had no excuses, he just was not good enough on these terms.
**Urowells(IRE)** *Official explanation: jockey said gelding hung left possibly as a result of the good to firm ground*
**Thundering Surf** *Official explanation: jockey said gelding ran too freely early on and was reluctant to let himself down on the Good to Firm ground, when asked for an effort.*

## 2692 NEWMARKET CARNIVAL NIGHT H'CAP — 1m
**8:00** (8:02) (C) (0-95,90) 3-Y-O **£9,646** (£2,968; £1,484; £742) **Stalls** Low

Form RPR
15-3 **1** **Alshawameq (IRE)**[21] [2135] 3-9-0 **83** RHills 9 90
(JLDunlop) *dwlt: hld up: racd centre fr 1/2-way: hdwy over 2f out: r.o to ld nr fin* **20/1**
-051 **2** *hd* **Red Spell (IRE)**[14] [2306] 3-8-10 **79** RHughes 2 86
(RHannon) *chsd ldrs: racd towards stands' side fr 1/2-way: led 3f out: rdn over 1f out: hdd nr fin* **7/1**
0-36 **3** *hd* **Mr Jack Daniells (IRE)**[14] [2306] 3-8-1 **73** RMiles[(3)] 8 79
(WRMuir) *chsd ldrs: racd centre fr 1/2-way: outpcd over 1f out: r.o ins fnl f* **7/2**[1]
1-00 **4** *1* **Granato (GER)**[22] [2075] 3-9-2 **85** LDettori 5 89
(ACStewart) *led: racd centre fr 1/2-way: hdd 3f out: unable qck ins fnl f* **20/1**
-020 **5** *2* **Secretary General (IRE)**[14] [2295] 3-9-7 **90** KFallon 13 89
(PFICole) *chsd ldrs: racd centre fr 1/2-way: rdn and ev ch 2f out: no ex fnl f* **5/1**[2]
021- **6** *2* **Kibryaa (USA)**[266] [4892] 3-8-9 **78** MHenry 7 73
(MAJarvis) *chsd ldrs: racd centre fr 1/2-way: wknd fnl f* **40/1**
0052 **7** *nk* **Tranquil Sky**[8] [2448] 3-9-4 **87** DHolland 3 81
(NACallaghan) *hld up: racd towards stands' side fr 1/2-way: rdn over 2f out: hung lft and wknd ins fnl f* **6/1**[3]
3-00 **8** *2 ½* **The Violin Player (USA)**[21] [2134] 3-8-9 **78** WRyan 4 66
(WJarvis) *s.i.s: hld up: racd towards stands' side fr 1/2-way: hung rt over 2f out: styd on ins fnl f: n.d* **66/1**
2-1 **9** *¾* **Sydney Star**[30] [1904] 3-9-3 **86** MHills 10 72
(BWHills) *hld up in tch: racd centre fr 1/2-way: wknd over 1f out* **5/1**[2]
-301 **10** *6* **Cimyla (IRE)**[22] [2089] 3-9-5 **88** SSanders 11 61
(CFWall) *chsd ldrs: racd centre fr 1/2-way: ev ch 2f out: wknd and eased over 1f out* **9/1**
0-01 **11** *½* **Toparudi**[42] [1613] 3-8-1 **73** FPFerris[(3)] 12 44
(MHTompkins) *s.i.s: sn chsng ldrs: racd centre fr 1/2-way: wknd over 2f out* **40/1**
0-15 **12** *¾* **Apex**[14] [2306] 3-8-9 **78** WSupple 1 48
(EALDunlop) *dwlt: hld up: racd towards stands' side fr 1/2-way: hdwy over 3f out: hung rt and wknd over 1f out* **12/1**
0-16 **13** *1 ¾* **Maganda (IRE)**[21] [2107] 3-9-0 **83** PRobinson 6 49
(MAJarvis) *s.i.s: racd centre fr 1/2-way: wknd over 2f out* **16/1**

1m 37.8s (-1.60) **Going Correction** -0.05s/f (Good) **13** Ran SP% **120.7**
Speed ratings: **106,105,105,104,102 100,100,97,97,91 90,89,88**CSF £146.27 CT £640.58 TOTE £18.90: £3.80, £2.50, £2.20; EX 90.20.
**Owner** Hamdan Al Maktoum **Bred** Shadwell Estate Company Limited **Trained** Arundel, W Sussex

**FOCUS**
A competitive handicap in which the field eventually split into two. The form is not up to the usual standard for the track but appears sound enough.

**NOTEBOOK**
**Alshawameq(IRE)** is not the most straightforward of animals, but he was produced as late as possible and that worked well.
**Red Spell(IRE)** confirmed himself an improved performer, and may have been a little unlucky not to hold on having raced alone for much of the last two furlongs.
**Mr Jack Daniells(IRE)** 2lb better off with the runner-up for having finished just behind him over course and distance at the last meeting, just got a little tapped for toe going into the dip before staying on stoutly up the hill. He may be worth a try over a little further.
**Granato(GER)**, having cut out the running, did not quite see this trip out as well as his rivals.
**Secretary General(IRE)** had every chance and had no excuses. He is proving difficult to place.
**Kibryaa(USA)** showed plenty of pace until lack of a recent outing took its toll in the latter stages. He can be placed to advantage before too long.
**Tranquil Sky** *Official explanation: jockey said filly hung left.*
**Sydney Star** *Official explanation: jockey said filly ran flat.*
**Cimyla(IRE)** *Official explanation: jockey said colt lost his action.*

## 2693 NGK SPARK PLUGS MAIDEN STKS — 1m
**8:30** (8:37) (D) 3-Y-O **£5,642** (£1,736; £868; £434) **Stalls** Low

Form RPR
4-23 **1** **Castleton**[14] [2307] 3-9-0 100 KFallon 1 92+
(HJCyzer) *mde all: clr over 2f out: eased towards fin* **1/2**[1]
**2** *5* **Musicanna** 3-8-9 OUrbina 8 76
(JRFanshawe) *hld up: hdwy over 2f out: wnt 2nd over 1f out: no ch w wnr* **10/1**
**3** *¾* **Red Sail** 3-8-9 JDSmith 9 74
(JRFanshawe) *s.i.s: hld up: hdwy over 1f out: nvr nr to chal* **25/1**
35- **4** *1 ¾* **Flamjica (USA)**[238] [5478] 3-8-6 LisaJones[(3)] 3 70
(JARToller) *chsd ldrs: rdn over 2f out: sn outpcd* **9/1**[3]
0-0 **5** *3 ½* **Golden Drift**[19] [2182] 3-8-9 TEDurcan 6 62
(GWragg) *chsd ldrs: rdn over 2f out: sn outpcd* **40/1**
**6** *6* **Zuri (IRE)** 3-8-9 DHolland 7 48
(LMCumani) *mid-div: shkn up over 2f out: n.d* **13/2**[2]
0-00 **7** *3* **Albadi**[14] [2286] 3-8-11 (b[1]) J-PGuillambert[(3)] 2 46
(CEBrittain) *w wnr over 4f: wknd over 1f out* **50/1**
0 **8** *2 ½* **Hoops And Blades**[72] [1104] 3-9-0 (t) EAhern 4 40
(NPLittmoden) *mid-div: wknd over 2f out* **66/1**
**9** *½* **Mesayan (IRE)** 3-8-7 (t) LauraWells[(7)] 5 39
(ACStewart) *s.s: hld up: a bhd* **40/1**
**10** *1 ¾* **Phone Tapping** 3-9-0 PRobinson 11 35
(MHTompkins) *s.s: a in rr* **33/1**
06 **11** *28* **Glanworth (IRE)**[14] [2312] 3-9-0 FNorton 10 —
(NACallaghan) *sn outpcd* **66/1**

1m 37.87s (-1.53) **Going Correction** -0.05s/f (Good) **11** Ran SP% **115.7**
Speed ratings: **105,100,99,97,94 88,85,82,82,80 52**CSF £5.67 TOTE £1.50: £1.02, £2.70, £5.20; EX 6.30.
**Owner** Mrs Charles Cyzer **Bred** P D Player **Trained** Newmarket, Suffolk

**FOCUS**
A sound enough pace in this modest contest, and the winner did not have to be anywhere near his best to get off the mark.

**NOTEBOOK**
**Castleton**, who got rather warm beforehand, had little more than a piece of work to get off the mark. While he will not find things easy off his current mark, he should be capable of scoring again.
**Musicanna**, a half-sister to several winners, shaped with enough promise, without ever threatening the winner, to suggest she can pay her way in due course.
**Red Sail**, who will stay further in time, should benefit from the experience.
**Flamjica(USA)** will at least have more options open to her now in handicaps.
**Golden Drift** is slow coming to hand and this effort will ensure she starts life off on a favourable mark when going handicapping.
**Hoops And Blades** *Official explanation: jockey said colt was unsuited by the good to firm ground*
**Mesayan(IRE)** *Official explanation: jockey said colt stumbled on leaving the stalls and was slowly away*
**Phone Tapping** *Official explanation: jockey said gelding was unsuited by the good to firm ground*

## 2694 EBF CECIL BOYD ROCHFORT FILLIES' H'CAP — 7f
**9:00** (9:06) (D) (0-85,84) 3-Y-O **£9,054** (£2,786; £1,393; £696) **Stalls** Low

Form RPR
0-43 **1** **Delphie Queen (IRE)**[15] [2269] 3-9-6 **83** JFEgan 10 101
(SKirk) *chsd ldrs: led over 1f out: rdn out* **9/2**[2]
-361 **2** *1 ½* **Lady Georgina**[11] [2377] 3-8-12 **75** OUrbina 7 89
(JRFanshawe) *a.p: nt clr run over 2f out: rdn to chse wnr ins fnl f: styd on same pce* **5/1**[3]
4-05 **3** *3* **Cara Bella**[33] [1842] 3-8-9 **75** TPQueally[(3)] 13 81
(DRLoder) *hld up: hdwy 3f out: rdn and ev ch over 1f out: no ex ins fnl f* **9/1**
0630 **4** *shd* **Dumnoni**[10] [2400] 3-9-1 **78** NCallan 5 84
(JulianPoulton) *plld hrd and prom: rdn over 1f out: no ex* **33/1**
00-1 **5** *nk* **Sforzando**[22] [2097] 3-8-3 **69** LisaJones[(3)] 6 74
(JARToller) *s.s: hdwy 1/2-way: styd on ins fnl f: nt trble ldrs* **10/1**
1-16 **6** *4* **Red Sahara (IRE)**[5] [2521] 3-9-1 **78** MHills 2 73
(WJHaggas) *s.s: swtchd rt over 2f out: styd on ins fnl f: nvr nrr* **11/2**
10-2 **7** *1* **Go Between**[21] [2112] 3-9-4 **81** LDettori 3 73
(EALDunlop) *racd keely: led 5f out: hdd over 1f out: sn btn* **7/1**
500- **8** *1 ½* **Bee Minor**[253] [5185] 3-8-10 **73** RLMoore 12 61
(RHannon) *outpcd: hdwy over 2f out: wknd over 1f out* **66/1**
260- **9** *nk* **Dry Wit (IRE)**[242] [5434] 3-8-2 **65** FNorton 8 53
(RMBeckett) *led 2f: remained handy tl wknd 2f out* **50/1**
60-6 **10** *¾* **Scarlett Rose**[46] [1530] 3-8-5 **68** JQuinn 9 54
(DrJDScargill) *chsd ldrs over 5f* **33/1**
42-4 **11** *3 ½* **Telefonica (USA)**[14] [2311] 3-9-0 **77** KFallon 11 54
(SirMichaelStoute) *mid-div: pushed laong 4f out: hdwy over 2f out: wknd over 1f out* **3/1**[1]
01-0 **12** *4* **Blue Daze**[21] [2112] 3-8-9 **72** RHughes 1 38
(RHannon) *prom 3f* **25/1**

1m 24.77s (-1.70) **Going Correction** -0.05s/f (Good) **12** Ran SP% **120.0**
Speed ratings: **107,105,101,101,101 96,95,93,93,92 88,84**CSF £26.53 CT £200.90 TOTE £6.70: £2.00, £2.30, £3.40; EX 32.40 Place 6 £49.20, Place 5 £30.73.
**Owner** Nicholas Hartery **Bred** Mrs C Hartery **Trained** Upper Lambourn, Berks

**FOCUS**
A fair handicap run at a sound pace and a very decent winning time, The form looks reliable for the grade.

**NOTEBOOK**
**Delphie Queen(IRE)** appreciated this stiffer test and was well on top in the end. There may be more to come from her.
**Lady Georgina** was not disgraced off this 5lb higher mark than when winning at Lingfield, and was a clear second best.
**Cara Bella**, tackling handicappers for the first time, had no excuses and is becoming difficult to place.
**Dumnoni** did herself no favours by taking a fierce grip.
**Sforzando** again shaped as though she will be suited by a little further.
**Red Sahara(IRE)** settled much better this time, but in doing so, never threatened to get competitive.
**Telefonica(USA)**, tackling handicappers for the first time, did not stride out that well to post and was one of the first beaten. *Official explanation: jockey said filly was fractious going to post*

T/Plt: £69.80 to a £1 stake. Pool: £48,097.40. 502.50 winning tickets. T/Qpdt: £14.10 to a £1 stake. Pool: £2,407.10. 126.15 winning tickets. CR

2695-2699a (Foreign Racing) - See Raceform Interactive

## 2193 CHANTILLY (R-H)
Saturday, June 5

**OFFICIAL GOING: Good to soft**

### 2700a PRIX DE ROYAUMONT (GROUP 3) (FILLIES) — 1m 4f
2:50 (2:51) 3-Y-O £25,704 (£10,282; £7,711; £5,141)

RPR

1 **Silverskaya (USA)**[33] 3-9-0 .......... IMendizabal 7 101
(J-CRouget, France) *held up in rear, last straight, ridden 1 1/2f out, ran on steadily down outside to lead 150 yds out, ridden out* 1

2 1 **Kalatuna (FR)**[36] 3-9-0 .......... TThulliez 2 99
(JVanHandenhove, France) *tracked leader in 3rd, led over 1f out til headed 150 yds out, stayed on*

3 1 1/2 **Reverie Solitaire (IRE)**[38] 3-9-0 .......... OPeslier 5 97
(CLaffon-Parias, France) *held up, 5th straight, ridden over 1f out, kept on to take 3rd close home*

4 nk **Super Lina (FR)**[13] 2338 3-9-0 .......... CSoumillon 8 96
(YDeNicolay, France) *raced alone on outside til joined others after 3f, midfield, 4th on outside straight, ridden 1 1/2f out, one pace* 2

5 hd **Risque De Verglas (FR)**[32] 3-9-0 .......... YLerner 3 96
(MmeR-WAllen, France) *raced in 2nd, effort and one pace from over 1 1/2f out* 3

6 1/2 **Pink Palace (IRE)**[25] 2028 3-9-0 .......... SPasquier 4 95
(DSepulchre, France) *held up, 6th straight, never a factor*

7 1 1/2 **Toujours Amour (IRE)**[33] 3-9-0 .......... FXBertras 1 93
(FRohaut, France) *set steady pace til headed over 1f out, weakened*

2m 36.2s **Going Correction** +0.375s/f (Good) **7** Ran SP% **125.0**
Speed ratings: **106,105,104,104,104 103,102.**
**Owner** Earl Champ Gignoux **Bred** M3 Elevage, Pontchartrain Stud & Haras D'Etreham **Trained** France

**NOTEBOOK**
**Silverskaya(USA)** finally won her first Group race in good style. Held up towards the rear early on, she hesitated a little a furlong and a half out, but then quickened impressively as the race came to an end. Her trainer will now aim her at the Prix de Malleret and then the Prix Vermeille.
**Kalatuna(FR)**, backed from 50-1, ran a cracking race. Always well placed, she quickened well in the straight to lead one out, but there was nothing she could do when the winner arrived on the scene.
**Reverie Solitaire(IRE)** was not too lucky a furlong and a half out when going for a gap. She came again on the outside and was putting in her best work at the finish.
**Super Lina(FR)** raced on her own in the early stages and joined the pack with over a mile left to run. Still well there a furlong and a half out, she was one-paced when it mattered and may need softer ground.

## BELMONT PARK (L-H)
Saturday, June 5

**OFFICIAL GOING: Turf course - firm; dirt course - fast**

### 2701a BELMONT STKS (GRADE 1) (DIRT) — 1m 4f (D)
11:38 (11:48) 3-Y-O £335,196 (£111,732; £61,453; £33,520)

RPR

1 **Birdstone (USA)**[35] 1781 3-9-0 .......... EPrado 4 125
(NZito, U.S.A) *always in touch on outside, went 2nd 3f out, hung right distance, driven to lead 70y out, ran on* 36/1

2 1 **Smarty Jones (USA)**[21] 2139 3-9-0 .......... ShaneElliott 9 124
(JohnCServis, U.S.A) *sn pressing ldrs on outside, narrow ld 1m out, clr ldr 3f out, hung rt u.p wl over 1f out, hdd 70y out, one pace* 7/20[1]

3 8 **Royal Assault (USA)**[56] 3-9-0 .......... PDay 6 112
(NZito, U.S.A) *hampered early, soon in mid-division, 5th straight, stayed on same pace, never near first two* 28/1

4 3 **Eddington (USA)**[21] 2139 3-9-0 ..........(b) JDBailey 8 107
(MHennig, U.S.A) *close up on outside til weakening from 3f out* 14/1

5 nse **Rock Hard Ten (USA)**[21] 2139 3-9-0 .......... ASolis 5 107
(JOrman, U.S.A) *prominent, disputed lead 1m out to 3f out, 3rd & beaten straight* 67/10[2]

6 14 **Tap Dancer (USA)** 3-9-0 .......... JCastellano 7 86
(EAllard, U.S.A) *in rear to over 3f out, 6th straight, never a factor* 41/1

7 4 1/4 **Master David (USA)**[14] 3-9-0 .......... JSantos 1 80
(RJFrankel, U.S.A) *always towards rear* 25/1

8 1 **Caiman (USA)** 3-9-0 .......... RADominguez 3 78
(AMedina, U.S.A) *prominent 5f, behind final 5f* 50/1

9 6 1/4 **Purge (USA)**[14] 3-9-0 .......... JRVelazquez 2 69
(TPletcher, U.S.A) *pulled early, led 4f, weakened 3f out* 96/10[3]

2m 27.5s **9** Ran SP% **117.5**
Speed ratings: .
**Owner** Marylou Whitney Stables **Bred** Marylou Whitney Stables **Trained** USA

**NOTEBOOK**
**Birdstone(USA)**, well behind the winner in the Kentucky Derby in sloppy conditions, bypassed the Preakness in favour of this and it paid dividends as he proved too strong for the gallant favourite in the final half furlong.
**Smarty Jones(USA)**, chasing the Triple Crown, was always doing a little too much too soon and had nothing left to offer when the winner came with his strong, late challenge. This was a brave effort nonetheless and he pulled 8 lengths clear of the third.

## 2439 BRIGHTON (L-H)
Sunday, June 6

**OFFICIAL GOING: Firm**

### 2702 EUROPEAN BREEDERS FUND/PIETRO ADDIS & SONS MEDIAN AUCTION MAIDEN STKS — 5f 59y
2:20 (2:20) (F) 2-Y-O £2,905 (£830; £415) Stalls Low

Form RPR

42 1 **Silver Wraith (IRE)**[9] 2439 2-9-0 .......... KFallon 7 87
(NACallaghan) *hld up in tch: hdwy on outside to ld jst ins fnl f: r.o wl* 8/13[1]

05 2 2 1/2 **Russian Rocket (IRE)**[12] 2376 2-8-9 .......... HayleyTurner(5) 5 77
(MrsCADunnett) *trckd ldr: led briefly ent fnl f: nt pce of wnr* 12/1

4234 3 1 1/4 **Ruby's Dream**[12] 2382 2-8-9 .......... RLMoore 3 67
(JMBradley) *chsd ldrs: rdn and ev chand appr fnl f: r.o one pce* 5/1[3]

4 1 1/2 **Talcen Gwyn (IRE)** 2-9-0 .......... JFEgan 1 66
(MFHarris) *chsd ldrs: wknd appr fnl f* 40/1

0 5 1/2 **Blue Line**[20] 2177 2-8-9 .......... GBaker 8 59
(MMadgwick) *outpcd: mde sme hdwy ins fnl 2f* 80/1

62 6 shd **Queen's Glory (IRE)**[14] 2321 2-8-9 .......... JQuinn 4 59
(WRMuir) *led tl rdn and hdd ent fnl f: wknd qckly* 9/2[2]

7 9 **Angela's Girl** 2-8-9 .......... SWhitworth 2 23
(JMBradley) *outpcd thrght* 50/1

8 1 1/4 **Ivory Wolf** 2-9-0 .......... SSanders 9 23
(JLSpearing) *racd wd: outpce thrght* 16/1

05 9 1 3/4 **Sabo Prince**[14] 2321 2-9-0 .......... CCatlin 6 16
(JMBradley) *slowly away: a bhd* 66/1

63.18 secs (0.91) **Going Correction** +0.10s/f (Good) **9** Ran SP% **117.5**
Speed ratings: **96,92,90,87,86 86,72,70,67**CSF £10.15 TOTE £1.80: £1.10, £4.20, £1.50; EX 12.10.
**Owner** M Tabor **Bred** Mrs M Fox **Trained** Newmarket, Suffolk

**FOCUS**
A routine race for the track, but with more to come from the winner. The form looks reasonably solid, and second and third can make their mark in nurseries.

**NOTEBOOK**
**Silver Wraith(IRE)** is not ideally suited by this track, so may improve a bit more in nurseries. *Official explanation: jockey said the colt hung left in the final furlong.*
**Russian Rocket(IRE)** was beaten by a progressive sort and looks a likely type for nurseries.
**Ruby's Dream** is running well without success but should be placed to win a nursery.
**Talcen Gwyn(IRE)** showed some pace from a good draw. A satisfactory debut.
**Blue Line**, not ideally drawn, found the company a bit hot but should be more effective over six furlongs.
**Queen's Glory(IRE)** was rather disappointing. Blazing a trail over this trip did not suit her as well as the race last time.

### 2703 DONATELLO RISTORANTE H'CAP — 6f 209y
2:50 (2:55) (E) (0-70,67) 3-Y-O+ £3,503 (£1,078; £539; £269) Stalls Low

Form RPR

0-61 1 **A Woman In Love**[14] 2325 5-9-11 63 .......... SSanders 2 73
(MissBSanders) *a in tch on ins: r.o strly on far rail to ld ins fnl f* 5/1[1]

5204 2 3/4 **Tee Jay Kassidy**[18] 2231 4-7-5 36 oh1 .......... MHalford(7) 13 44
(JulianPoulton) *racd wd and c over to r alone stands rail strt: str run ins fnl f to take 2nd* 66/1

5146 3 2 1/2 **Due To Me**[24] 2053 4-8-7 45 ..........(p) SWhitworth 12 47
(GLMoore) *nvr out of first 3: rdn appr fnl f: r.o* 40/1

3130 4 nk **Alafzar (IRE)**[9] 2459 6-9-0 59 ..........(bt) SJDonohoe(7) 6 60
(PDEvans) *t.k.h: in tch: kpt on one pce fnl f* 7/1[3]

5010 5 shd **Warlingham (IRE)**[14] 2325 6-9-6 58 .......... KFallon 1 58
(PHowling) *t.k.h: trckd ldr: led over 2f out: rdn and hdd ins fnl f: fdd* 10/1

0655 6 shd **Zinging**[14] 2325 5-7-13 37 oh1 ow1 .......... JQuinn 9 37
(JJBridger) *t.k.h: in rr tl rdn and hdwy over 1f out: r.o: nvr nrr* 25/1

00-3 7 1/2 **Concubine (IRE)**[9] 2441 5-9-8 60 .......... DSweeney 15 59
(JRBoyle) *hld up: hdwy 2f out: hung lft over 1f out and nvr threatened after* 10/1

0360 8 1/2 **Aguila Loco (IRE)**[11] 2404 5-9-3 55 ..........(p) FNorton 10 53
(MrsStefLiddiard) *led: tl hdd over 2f out: wknd ins fnl f* 33/1

2021 9 nk **Jonny Ebeneezer**[14] 2322 5-9-6 58 .......... BDoyle 16 55
(RMHCowell) *hld up: rdn over 2f out: nvr cl enough to chal* 10/1

0105 10 3/4 **Loch Laird**[31] 1909 9-9-0 52 .......... GBaker 3 47
(MMadgwick) *mid-div: short of room on ins 1/2-way: nvr on terms* 20/1

-400 11 3/4 **Morag**[13] 2371 3-9-2 67 .......... TPQueally(3) 4 60
(IAWood) *nvr bttr than mid-div* 25/1

5514 12 nk **Scarrottoo**[29] 1971 6-9-3 55 .......... RLMoore 11 47
(SCWilliams) *s.i.s: a in rr* 6/1[2]

0500 13 1 1/2 **B A Highflyer**[11] 2399 4-9-9 61 .......... CCatlin 7 49
(MRChannon) *chsd ldrs: lost pl after 3f and sn bhd* 12/1

0000 14 nk **Mutabari (USA)**[8] 2473 10-7-9 36 oh1 .......... JFMcDonald(3) 5 23
(JLSpearing) *a struggling in rr* 66/1

00-0 15 6 **Willheconquertoo**[30] 1935 4-9-12 64 ..........(t) JFEgan 8 36
(AndrewReid) *rrd up leaving stalls: sn in tch: rdn and wknd 3f out* 8/1

003 16 1 1/2 **Fair Options**[17] 2236 3-9-3 65 .......... GCarter 14 33
(HJCyzer) *chsd ldrs tl wknd 2f out* 7/1[3]

1m 23.07s (0.47) **Going Correction** +0.10s/f (Good)
**WFA** 3 from 4yo+ 10lb **16** Ran SP% **122.8**
Speed ratings: **101,100,97,96,96 96,96,95,95,94 93,93,91,91,84 82**CSF £365.20 CT £11822.09 TOTE £5.80: £1.20, £10.70, £5.80, £1.60; EX 664.90.
**Owner** High & Dry Racing **Bred** Stratford Place Stud **Trained** Epsom, Surrey

**FOCUS**
A moderate bunch, with the winner clearly putting up the best performance at the weights. This was an ordinary race and the form may not be all it seems.

**NOTEBOOK**
**A Woman In Love** is not straightforward but useful on her day at this level, and has a good turn of foot when she settles. She goes well on the track, and put up a good weight-carrying performance, but her opponents were weak.
**Tee Jay Kassidy** appeared to come wide by accident rather than through inspired tactics, but nearly pulled off a remarkable victory. He lost a shoe in the process and deserves credit, but the form is very moderate. *Official explanation: vet said gelding lost a shoe*
**Due To Me** ran well considering he stays a mile and this is a sharp seven furlongs.
**Alafzar(IRE)**, with the tongue-tie re-fitted, bounced back to form, albeit in a poor race.
**Warlingham(IRE)** lost a shoe in running. This was a fair performance, but no more. *Official explanation: trainer said the gelding was struck into; vet said gelding lost a shoe*
**Zinging** wins rarely and stays farther than this, so it was no surprise to see him arriving too late on the lightning-fast ground.

### 2704 FAT LEO PIZZERIA CLASSIFIED STKS — 6f 209y
3:20 (3:20) (D) 3-Y-O £5,395 (£1,660; £830; £415) Stalls Low

Form RPR

4-05 1 **Sweet Reply**[22] 2135 3-8-5 75 .......... TPQueally(3) 3 76
(IAWood) *trckd ldrs: tk narrow ld 2f out: rdn and maintained advantage to line: all out* 12/1

2-52 2 hd **Wychbury (USA)**[13] 2367 3-8-11 74 .......... KFallon 4 78
(MJWallace) *a in tch: pressed wnr clly thrght fnl 2f* 11/4[2]

U6-0 3 1/2 **Olivander**[25] 2046 3-8-11 75 ..........(b[1]) SSanders 5 77
(GAButler) *wl in rr: rdn 2f out: sme hdwy over 1f out: str burst fnl f: nvr nrr* 12/1

2000 4 1 **Heversham (IRE)**[9] 2448 3-8-11 74 .......... RLMoore 6 75
(WJHaggas) *led for 3f: styd in tch: rdn and kpt on one pce fnl f* 9/1

3-25 5 1/2 **Catalini**[72] 1120 3-8-8 75 .......... SHitchcott(3) 1 73
(MRChannon) *in rr but in tch: kpt on one pce ins fnl 2f* 15/2

5610 **6** *hd* **Generous Gesture (IRE)**[22] 2112 3-8-8 75........................(v) JMackay 8 70
(MLWBell) *plld hrd: led 4f out: hdd 2f out: one pce appr fnl f* **12/1**

12-0 **7** *1 1/4* **I Won't Dance (IRE)**[23] 2082 3-9-2 80........................ PDobbs 7 75
(RHannon) *a in rr* **5/2**[1]

3100 **8** *13* **Finders Keepers**[12] 2378 3-8-11 74........................ EAhern 2 36
(EALDunlop) *stdd s: t.k.h: hdwy on outside 3f out: hung rt and wknd over 1f out: eased* **11/2**[3]

1m 23.16s (0.56) **Going Correction** +0.10s/f (Good) **8** Ran SP% **115.5**
Speed ratings: **100,99,99,98,97 97,95,80**CSF £45.66 TOTE £14.40: £4.00, £1.20, £3.80; EX 56.10.
**Owner** C S Tateson **Bred** C S Tateson **Trained** Upper Lambourn, Berks

**FOCUS**
A race with some useful performers in which the form looks sound, and should yield several winners if they can be found the right opportunities. The winner is highly rated and can progress.

**NOTEBOOK**
**Sweet Reply** hit the front plenty early enough and can do even better if ridden with more restraint.
**Wychbury(USA)** is slightly flattered by his proximity to the winner, who hit the front too soon, but it was a tenacious effort.
**Olivander** stayed the seventh furlong really well and might even get a mile on this evidence. In the right race, he is ready to win.
**Heversham(IRE)** forced the early pace over a trip which is probably his minimum nowadays. He was not speedy enough at the end, but went down fighting.
**Catalini** has the ability to win when everything falls into place.
**Generous Gesture(IRE)** wasted energy by being too headstrong. Though eventually allowed to stride on in front, the damage was largely done over this trip.
**I Won't Dance(IRE)** did not look comfortable on this difficult track. The market support suggests there is better to come.
**Finders Keepers** *Official explanation: jockey said the gelding was too keen early on*

## 2705 TOTEPLACEPOT H'CAP — 1m 1f 209y
3:50 (3:51) (E) (0-70,69) 3-Y-O+ £4,420 (£1,360; £680; £340) Stalls High

Form RPR

0-00 **1** **Factual Lad**[10] 2430 6-9-12 67........................ GBaker 4 75
(BRMillman) *mid-div: hdwy on ins overe 2f out: led over 1f out: r.o wl* **12/1**

0254 **2** *1 1/4* **Lara Falana**[11] 2403 6-9-11 66........................ SSanders 5 72
(MissBSanders) *hld up in rr: hdwy on outside 3f out: r.o wl to go 2nd ins fnl f* **9/2**[2]

0330 **3** *1 1/2* **Fantasy Crusader**[4] 2594 5-8-7 48........................(p) JQuinn 12 51
(JAGilbert) *t.k.h: trcke ldrs: ev ch appr fnl f: one pce after* **11/1**

0035 **4** *1 1/4* **Prince Valentine**[33] 1874 3-8-4 58........................(b[1]) FNorton 11 58
(DBFeek) *led tl rdn and hdd over 1f out: one pce fnl f* **20/1**

2-04 **5** *hd* **Short Change (IRE)**[15] 1858 5-8-4 48 ow1........................ TPQueally(3) 7 48
(AWCarroll) *in tch: rdn over 1f out: fdd fnl f* **6/1**[3]

4001 **6** *shd* **My Maite (IRE)**[12] 2387 5-8-6 47........................(bt) EAhern 9 47
(RIngram) *plld hrd: hld up in rr: hdwy 3f out: sn rdn: no imp fnl f* **6/1**[3]

4500 **7** *1* **Springalong (USA)**[22] 2122 4-8-12 60........................ SJDonohoe(7) 8 58
(PDEvans) *hld up: rdn over 3f out: nvr nr to chal* **25/1**

22-5 **8** *hd* **Qabas (USA)**[15] 2302 4-10-0 69........................ RLMoore 2 67
(PRWebber) *a in rr* **9/2**[2]

0006 **9** *3/4* **Forest Tune (IRE)**[19] 2212 6-8-11 52........................ KFallon 6 48
(BHanbury) *plld hrd: a in rr* **4/1**[1]

0000 **10** *17* **Justice Jones**[27] 2001 3-7-9 52 oh2........................ JFMcDonald(3) 1 16
(JLSpearing) *prom early: dropped out qckly 4f out* **50/1**

0-00 **11** *19* **Bold Ridge (IRE)**[25] 2029 4-8-12 53........................(b[1]) JFEgan 10 —
(SKirk) *hld up: hmpd 7f out: lost tch over 2f out: eaded over 1f out* **12/1**

2m 3.30s (0.76) **Going Correction** +0.10s/f (Good)
**WFA** 3 from 4yo+ 13lb **11** Ran SP% **119.2**
Speed ratings: **100,99,97,96,96 96,95,95,95,81 66**CSF £64.98 CT £626.77 TOTE £17.80: £4.10, £1.50, £2.90; EX 82.00.
**Owner** Tarka Racing **Bred** Wheelersland Stud **Trained** Kentisbeare, Devon

**FOCUS**
A moderate race, won by a course specialist, with the runner-up also doing well. The overall form is ordinary.

**NOTEBOOK**
**Factual Lad** made it two out of two on the course. He should be noted if returning here on fast ground.
**Lara Falana** is running reasonably well at present. She is capable of winning a similar race.
**Fantasy Crusader** put in one of his better efforts but the leading pair outclassed him, even at these weights.
**Prince Valentine** was sharpened up by the blinkers but probably ran a bit too freely as a result, especially over this trip. *Official explanation: jockey said gelding hung right in the closing stages*
**Short Change(IRE)** is getting down to a winning mark but needs to show a little more.
**My Maite(IRE)** pulled his way out of contention and had nothing left for the final climb.
**Qabas(USA)** is not yet in peak form but his position in the market points to the fact that he may be about to stage a revival.
**Forest Tune(IRE)** was too headstong to justify favouritism, but the fact that he led the market suggests he could return to form if settling better.
**Bold Ridge(IRE)** *Official explanation: jockey said gelding lost its action*

## 2706 PINOCCHIO RISTORANTE MEDIAN AUCTION MAIDEN STKS — 7f 214y
4:20 (4:20) (E) 3-4-Y-O £3,464 (£1,066; £533; £266) Stalls Low

Form RPR

2-02 **1** **St Francis Wood (USA)**[8] 2486 3-8-6 90........................ EAhern 7 82
(JNoseda) *sn led: rdn and hdd appr fnl f: rallied gamely to ld again ins fnl f* **1/1**[1]

5- **2** *3/4* **Southern Bazaar (USA)**[289] 4348 3-8-11........................ KFallon 2 86
(BWHills) *chsd wnr: pushed along 3f out: led appr fnl f: carried hd high and hdd ins fnl f: no ex nr fin* **5/4**[2]

334- **3** *12* **Frangipani (IRE)**[294] 4235 3-8-1........................ NDeSouza(5) 5 53
(PFICole) *racd cl 3rd tl rdn over 2f out and sn btn* **10/1**[3]

2-40 **4** *3* **Pregnant Pause (IRE)**[151] 462 3-8-4 64........................ JDWalsh(7) 1 51
(SKirk) *plld hrd and hld up in rr: lost tch 1/2-way* **16/1**

1m 35.04s (0.04) **Going Correction** +0.10s/f (Good) **4** Ran SP% **109.4**
Speed ratings: **103,102,90,87**CSF £2.58 TOTE £1.50; EX 2.90.
**Owner** Sanford R Robertson **Bred** S R Robertson **Trained** Newmarket, Suffolk

**FOCUS**
The first two home were smart performers for the track. Both have underachieved to date and can win again if going the right way.

**NOTEBOOK**
**St Francis Wood(USA)** is a difficult ride, and trying to make all in a small field is unlikely to have played to her strengths. However, if this has helped her confidence, she is capable of much better in a strongly-run contest where she can be covered up.
**Southern Bazaar(USA)** gave the talented, if frustrating, winner a good race. He should be placed to get off the mark.
**Frangipani(IRE)** made an unspectacular seasonal debut, though to be fair the first two home are quite smart.
**Pregnant Pause(IRE)** continues to disappoint. Low grade handicaps are the future on this evidence.

## 2707 GREAT GRANDMA BETTY H'CAP — 5f 213y
4:50 (4:51) (F) (0-55,55) 3-Y-O+ £2,989 (£854; £213) Stalls Low

Form RPR

5160 **1** **Doctor Dennis (IRE)**[14] 2325 7-9-4 47........................(v) SSanders 2 61
(JPearce) *hld up in rr: hdwy 2f out: n.m.r sn after: got clr run ent fnl f: r.o strly to ld cl home* **10/1**

-056 **2** *3/4* **Boanerges (IRE)**[16] 2274 7-9-12 55........................ RLMoore 11 67
(JMBradley) *mid-div: hdwy on outside over 2f out: led 1f out: r.o hdd cl home* **9/1**

00-0 **3** *1 1/4* **Jazzy Millennium**[62] 1268 7-9-10 53........................(b) NCallan 13 61
(BRMillman) *c over to ins and sn trckd ldr: led over 2f out: hdd 1f out: kpt on one pce* **8/1**[3]

3222 **3** *dht* **Aintnecessarilyso**[11] 2404 6-8-13 47........................ MSavage(5) 16 55
(NEBerry) *hld up in rr: hdwy over 1f out: r.o strly fnl f: nvr nrr* **10/1**

3500 **5** *1 3/4* **Tender (IRE)**[9] 2440 4-9-12 55........................ FNorton 10 58
(MrsStefLiddiard) *in tch: swtchd lft over 1f out: gd hdwy on ins whn hmpd ins fnl f: nt rcvr* **20/1**

0006 **6** *hd* **Gone'N'Dunnett (IRE)**[9] 2455 5-9-2 50........................(v) HayleyTurner(5) 12 52
(MrsCADunnett) *a.p: one pce fnl f* **20/1**

-004 **7** *3* **Tuscan Treaty**[23] 2099 4-9-10 53........................(v[1]) BDoyle 3 46
(TTClement) *hld up: n.m.r fr 1/2-way to 2f out: kpt on one pce appr fnl f* **14/1**

0-60 **8** *1/2* **Ela Figura**[33] 1855 4-9-4 50........................ JFMcDonald(3) 6 42
(AWCarroll) *in tch: rdn over 1f out: no hdwy after* **25/1**

00-5 **9** *1/2* **Emmervale**[23] 2098 5-9-7 50........................(v) EAhern 8 40
(RMHCowell) *hld up: rdn 2f out: no further hdwy* **12/1**

000 **10** *1* **Goodwood Prince**[15] 2303 4-9-12 55........................ JFEgan 15 42
(SDow) *racd wd thrght: nvr nr to chal* **16/1**

4606 **11** *3/4* **Gun Salute**[14] 2325 4-9-3 46........................(p) SWhitworth 4 31
(GLMoore) *swtchd to ins after slowly away: a in rr* **7/2**[1]

30-4 **12** *1/2* **Mannora**[23] 2098 4-9-10 53........................ KFallon 5 37
(PHowling) *mid-div: rdn 2f out: sn btn* **5/1**[2]

6-00 **13** *nk* **Run On**[20] 2166 6-9-7 50........................ SRighton 7 33
(DGBridgwater) *a bhd* **25/1**

2015 **14** *3* **Sergeant Slipper**[27] 1994 7-9-3 46........................(v) RFitzpatrick 14 20
(CSmith) *a bhd* **28/1**

6313 **15** *3/4* **Harbour House**[27] 1988 5-9-3 46........................ JQuinn 1 18
(JJBridger) *mid-div whn n.m.r over 1f out: sn btn* **9/1**

0016 **16** *1* **Pleasure Time**[51] 1443 11-9-5 48........................(v) PDobbs 9 17
(CSmith) *led tl hdd over 2f out: wknd sn after* **25/1**

1m 10.5s (0.40) **Going Correction** +0.10s/f (Good) **16** Ran SP% **132.9**
Speed ratings: **101,100,98,98,96 95,91,91,90,89 88,87,87,83,82 80**CSF £96.14 TOTE £11.00: £3.10, £2.40; EX 90.10 Place 6 £221.94, Place 5 £177.13. Pl: JM £2.90, A £2.10. TC: DD/B/JM £406.41, DD/B/A £496.23.
**Owner** Mrs Lydia Pearce **Bred** David Allan **Trained** Newmarket, Suffolk

**FOCUS**
A typical low-grade Brighton handicap and ordinary form, but with a number of horses capable of winning in their turn, particularly around this specialist's track.

**NOTEBOOK**
**Doctor Dennis(IRE)** knows the track well and the fact that he did not get the best of runs may not have been a problem.
**Boanerges(IRE)** had a tricky draw, but a fine effort showed he is ready to win again.
**Jazzy Millennium** crossed over from a wide draw and was unable to dominate. He is hard to beat at his peak on this track, and should be noted if drawn near the inside in future events.
**Aintnecessarilyso** flew home from a bad draw. He is proving expensive to everyone but each-way backers, but his consistency is admirable.
**Tender(IRE)** had a bad run though at the finish, and would have to be considered in a similar race.
**Gone'N'Dunnett(IRE)** ran respectably without being good enough.
**Emmervale** *Official explanation: jockey said the mare did not handle the track*
**Gun Salute** was supported to win, and it would be no surprise to see a much better effort in the near future. *Official explanation: trainer was unable to offer any explanation for the poor run*
T/Plt: £56.60 to a £1 stake. Pool: £44,289.35. 570.45 winning tickets. T/Qpdt: £15.20 to a £1 stake. Pool: £2,075.30. 101.00 winning tickets. JS

2708 - 2710a (Foreign Racing) - See Raceform Interactive

# [2147]GOWRAN PARK (R-H)
Sunday, June 6

**OFFICIAL GOING: Good to firm**

## 2711a IRISH STALLION FARMS EBF VICTOR MCCALMONT MEMORIAL STKS (LISTED) (F&M) — 1m 1f 100y
4:00 (4:02) 3-Y-O+ £32,091 (£9,415; £4,485; £1,528)

RPR

**1** **Misty Heights**[14] 2330 3-8-9 105........................ PJSmullen 12 97
(DKWeld, Ire) *chsd ldrs: 6th into st: rdn to chal in 4th 1 1/2f out: led under 1f out: styd on wl u.p* **2/1**[1]

**2** *1/2* **Leonor Fini (IRE)**[21] 2148 3-8-9 89........................ DPMcDonogh 8 96
(KevinPrendergast, Ire) *mid-div: 7th appr st: rdn fr over 2f out: 6th 1 1/2f out: kpt on wl to go 2nd ins fnl f* **12/1**

**3** *1* **Sand N Sea (IRE)**[15] 2319 3-8-9 87........................ TPO'Shea 5 94
(THogan, Ire) *hld up towards rr: rdn in 7th 1 1/2f out: styd on wl to go 3rd wl ins fnl f* **20/1**

**4** *hd* **Danelissima (IRE)**[14] 2333 3-8-9 97........................(b) KJManning 7 94
(JSBolger, Ire) *trckd ldr in 2nd: dropped to 5th and rdn 1 1/2f out: kpt on same pce u.p* **6/1**[3]

**5** *nk* **Cache Creek (IRE)**[23] 2102 6-9-7 95........................ JAHeffernan 1 93
(PHughes, Ire) *chsd ldrs: impr into 3rd appr st: chal and disp ld fr under 2f out: hdd under 1f out: kpt on same pce u.p* **6/1**[3]

**6** *1/2* **Sissy Slew (USA)**[43] 1634 4-9-7 90........................ NGMcCullagh 6 92
(MJGrassick, Ire) *rr of mid-div: 8th into st: rdn and kpt on wl fr 1 1/2f out* **14/1**

**7** *2* **Rihla (IRE)**[28] 1980 3-8-9 95........................ MJKinane 9 88
(JohnMOxx, Ire) *led sn after 1 f: rdn and strly pressed fr under 2f out: hdd over 1f out: sn no ex* **9/2**[2]

**8** *3/4* **Charmed Forest (IRE)**[5] 2564 3-8-9 85........................ PCosgrave 2 87
(JGBurns, Ire) *chsd ldrs: 5th into st: rdn and kpt on same pce u.p fr 1 1/2f out* **14/1**

**9** *1 1/2* **Happy At Last**[225] 5762 3-8-9 89........................ FMBerry 11 84
(JohnMOxx, Ire) *led early: sn settled 3rd: 4th into st: 3rd fr under 2f out and rdn: sn no ex* **16/1**

**10** *4 1/2* **Avec Plaisir (GER)**[15] 2319 5-9-7 87........................ PShanahan 10 75
(FFlood, Ire) *chsd ldrs: dropped to 10th ent st: sn rdn: no ex fr 2f out* **12/1**

11 *20* **Starrystarrynight (IRE)** 3-8-9 ..................................... CO'Donoghue 3 37
(APO'Brien, Ire) *a towards rr: trailing bef st: sn n.d* **7/1**

**WFA** 3 from 4yo+ 12lb **11** Ran SP% **131.9**
Speed ratings: CSF £33.48 TOTE £2.60: £1.40, £2.90, £3.80; DF 20.50.
**Owner** Lady O'Reilly **Bred** Dr A J O'Reilly & Skymarc Farm **Trained** The Curragh, Co Kildare

2712 - 2717a (Foreign Racing) - See Raceform Interactive

# 2699 CHANTILLY (R-H)
Sunday, June 6

**OFFICIAL GOING: Good to soft**

## 2719a PRIX DU GROS-CHENE (GROUP 2) 5f
**2:10** (2:09) 3-Y-0+ **£42,148** (£16,268; £7,764; £5,176)

RPR

1 **Avonbridge**[36] 1763 4-9-2 ..................................... SDrowne 9 116
(RCharlton) *made all, ridden and ran on from over 1f out, driven out* 2

2 *½* **Porlezza (FR)**[41] 1682 5-9-5 ..................................... CSoumillon 7 117
(YDeNicolay, France) *raced in 2nd, effort to chase leader 1 1/2f out, ran on but not reach winner* 1

3 *nk* **The Trader (IRE)**[21] 2162 6-9-2 .....................................(b) JPSpencer 1 113
(MBlanshard) *raced in last, ridden and progress on outside 1 1/2f out, finished strongly final furlong, nearest at finish* 3

4 *1 ½* **The Tatling (IRE)**[8] 2475 7-9-2 ..................................... DHolland 4 108
(JMBradley) *raced in 5th, pushed along 2f out towards outside, stayed on final furlong to take 4th on line*

5 *shd* **Dobby Road (FR)**[21] 2162 5-8-12 ..................................... FSpanu 3 103
(MlleVDissaux, France) *disputed 6th, pushed along and stayed on to line from over 1f out*

6 *snk* **Chineur (FR)**[21] 2162 3-8-9 ..................................... ELegrix 5 107
(MDelzangles, France) *raced in 4th on outside, pushed along 2f out, went 3rd over 1f out, stayed on at one pace to line*

7 *1 ½* **Millybaa (USA)**[22] 2117 4-8-9 ..................................... LDettori 2 94
(RGuest) *disputed 6th, pushed along over 2f out, outpaced final furlong*

8 *3* **Socks For Glenn**[15] 4-8-12 ..................................... GaryStevens 6 86
(JEPease, France) *raced in 3rd on rail til weakened 2f out*

58.10 secs **Going Correction** -0.05s/f (Good)
**WFA** 3 from 4yo+ 7lb **8** Ran SP% **116.1**
Speed ratings: **115,114,113,111,111 110,108,103.**
**Owner** D J Deer **Bred** D J And Mrs Deer **Trained** Beckhampton, Wilts

**NOTEBOOK**
**Avonbridge**, smartly into his stride, made virtually every yard of the running and fought well when tackled. It was his first Group success and he now heads for Royal Ascot for either the King's Stand or the Golden Jubilee Stakes.
**Porlezza(FR)** raced on the rail behind the winner for much of the race and looked dangerous at the furlong marker, but she could never quite got on terms.
**The Trader(IRE)** looked in trouble at the halfway stage and when he finally got going, it was just too late. He is another who may go to Ascot.
**The Tatling(IRE)** kept on well to post yet another genuine performance.
**Millybaa(USA)** was never really seen with a chance.

## 2720a PRIX DE SANDRINGHAM (GROUP 2) (FILLIES) 1m
**2:45** (2:44) 3-Y-0 **£42,148** (£16,268; £7,764; £5,176)

RPR

1 **Baqah (IRE)**[20] 2193 3-8-11 ..................................... DBonilla 7 109
(FHead, France) *held up, 7th straight, headway 2f out, ridden and pressing leaders 1 1/2f out, ran on under pressure to lead close home* 3

2 *½* **Miss Mambo (USA)**[21] 2160 3-8-11 ..................................... CSoumillon 8 108
(ELibaud, France) *pulled early and prominent, headway to press leaders 2f out, ridden to lead briefly 1f out, kept on under pressure to line* 1

3 *snk* **Dolma (FR)**[20] 2193 3-8-11 ..................................... C-PLemaire 9 108
(NClement, France) *led, pushed along 2f out, headed briefly 1f out, ran on til headed again close home, lost 2nd final strides*

4 *¾* **Super Bobbina (IRE)**[36] 1778 3-8-11 ..................................... GaryStevens 4 106
(IBugattella, Italy) *towards rear, 8th straight, pushed along 2f out, ridden and stayed on to take 4th close home*

5 *hd* **Nyramba**[21] 2160 3-8-11 ..................................... LDettori 1 106
(JHMGosden) *in touch, disputing 4th straight, pushed along 2f over out, ridden 1 1/2f out, no exrea final stages* 2

6 *¾* **Petit Calva (FR)**[42] 1652 3-8-11 ..................................... TJarnet 6 104
(RGibson, France) *prominent, went 2nd after 2f, pushed along 2f out, ridden and weakened 1 1/2f out*

7 *shd* **Bright Abundance (USA)**[245] 5404 3-8-11 ..................................... OPeslier 2 104
(CLaffon-Parias, France) *held up in last, 4 lengths off leader entering straight, pushed along on outside 2f out, stayed on but never a threat*

8 *5* **Zona (ITY)**[36] 1778 3-8-11 ..................................... MEsposito 3 93
(VCaruso, Italy) *mid-division, 6th straight, soon pushed along, never a threat*

9 *1 ½* **Miss Me**[18] 3-8-11 ..................................... IMendizabal 5 90
(J-CRouget, France) *raced in 2nd 2f, disputing 4th on inside straight, pushed along 2f out, ridden and weakened 1 1/2f out*

1m 35.8s **Going Correction** -0.25s/f (Firm) **9** Ran SP% **120.1**
Speed ratings: **115,114,114,113,113 112,112,107,106.**
**Owner** Hamdan Al Maktoum **Bred** Shadwell Estate Company Limited **Trained** France

**NOTEBOOK**
**Baqah(IRE)**, ran freely early on and could have done with a stronger pace, but he proved good enough in any case. A tough and consistent filly, she may now head for either the Falmouth Stakes at Newmarket or the Prix d'Astarte at Deauville.
**Miss Mambo(USA)**, slotted in behind the leaders in this slowly run race, she looked the likely winner when hitting the front, but just found the winner too strong. She will now be given a rest.
**Dolma(FR)** tried make every yard at a very moderate pace and battled well when headed.
**Super Bobbina(IRE)** finished best of all, but a bit too late.
**Nyramba** raced a little keenly and was one paced when it mattered.

## 2721a PRIX JEAN PRAT (GROUP 1) (C&F) 1m 1f
**3:55** (3:55) 3-Y-0 **£80,479** (£32,197; £16,099; £8,042)

RPR

1 **Bago (FR)**[218] 5883 3-9-2 ..................................... TGillet 5 118
(JEPease, France) *raced in 4th, smooth headway from 2f out, led 1 1/2f out, quickened clear over 1f out, ran on strongly, impressive* **1/1**[1]

2 *3* **Cacique (IRE)**[18] 3-9-2 ..................................... GaryStevens 3 112
(AFabre, France) *held up in rear, disputing 6th and pushed along on inside straight, ran on to take 2nd 1f out, no chance with winner* **6/1**

3 *2* **Ershaad (USA)**[21] 2161 3-9-2 ..................................... CSoumillon 7 108
(JEHammond, France) *towards rear, disputing 6th straight, pushed along over 1 1/2f out, ridden and ran on final furlong to take 3rd 100 yards o* **14/1**

4 *¾* **Charmo (FR)**[24] 2072 3-9-2 ..................................... SPasquier 1 107
(PDemercastel, France) *raced in 3rd, pushed along and ran on 2f out, stayed on under pressure to line* **50/1**

5 *nk* **Mister Sacha (FR)**[24] 2072 3-9-2 ..................................... IMendizabal 2 106
(J-CRouget, France) *held up in rear, last straight, headway on outside 2f out, ridden 1 1/2f out, ran on til no extra inside final furlong* **4/1**[2]

6 *2 ½* **Moscow Ballet (IRE)**[25] 2043 3-9-2 ..................................... JPSpencer 6 101
(APO'Brien, Ire) *mid-division, 5th towards outside straight, effort over 1 1/2f out, never dangerous* **10/1**

7 *½* **Pearl Of Love (IRE)**[231] 5665 3-9-2 ..................................... DHolland 8 100
(MJohnston) *close up, led after 3f, pushed along and ran on 2f out til headed 1 1/2f out, one pace final furlong* **5/1**[3]

8 *8* **Alnitak (USA)**[63] 3-9-2 ..................................... C-PLemaire 4 84
(JEPease, France) *led 3f, 2nd straight, lost place 2f out, eased* **150/1**

1m 46.6s **Going Correction** -0.25s/f (Firm) **8** Ran SP% **119.3**
Speed ratings: **112,109,107,106,106 104,103,96.**
**Owner** Niarchos Family **Bred** Famille Niarchos **Trained** France

**NOTEBOOK**
**Bago(FR)** posted an exceptional performance on a reappearance delayed by a virus. Cruising throughout, he was never in danger after quickening to the front and totally outclassed his rivals. He remains unbeaten, and his trainer, who has had the likes of Tikkanen, Spinning World and Act One through his hands, regards him the best he has had by some way. Unfortnately for British racegoers, he is likely to bypass Royal Ascot and wait for the Grand Prix de Paris.
**Cacique(IRE)** made good progress against the far rail and took second place inside the final furlong. He may have been closer had he been ridden more handily, and is certainly a nice colt in the making. One to follow.
**Ershaad(USA)** followed the winner throughout but could not go with that one when things warmed up.
**Charmo(FR)** battled gamely, only to have third place taken off him inside the final furlong.
**Moscow Ballet(IRE)**, who had been among the stable's five-day acceptors for the Derby, had his limitations confirmed.
**Pearl Of Love(IRE)**, forced to miss the 2,000 Guineas owing to a cracked hoof, led into the straight, but was swamped by his rivals one a half out and gradually dropped out of contention. This race will have done him good and he is still marked down for the St James's Palace Stakes.

## 2722a PRIX DU JOCKEY CLUB (GROUP 1) (C&F) 1m 4f
**4:40** (4:42) 3-Y-0 **£442,634** (£177,085; £88,542; £44,232)

RPR

1 **Blue Canari (FR)**[18] 2233 3-9-2 ..................................... TThulliez 10 118
(PBary, France) *held up in rear, pushed along and headway 2f out, ridden 1f out and quickened to challenge 100 yards out, led final stride* **33/1**

2 *hd* **Prospect Park**[24] 2073 3-9-2 ..................................... OPeslier 8 118
(CLaffon-Parias, France) *mid-division, disputing 5th straight, ran on 2f out, ridden to challenge 1 1/2f out, led 100 yards out, ran on, headed fina* **7/1**[3]

3 *½* **Valixir (IRE)**[21] 2159 3-9-2 ..................................... ELegrix 1 117
(AFabre, France) *mid-division, pushed along and closed up 2f out, ridden and ran on 1 1/2f out, stayed on strongly to line, nearest at finis* **15/2**

4 *¾* **Day Flight**[24] 2068 3-9-2 ..................................... RHughes 2 116
(JHMGosden) *prominent, led entering straight, ridden and ran on from 2f out, headed 100 yards out, kept on* **11/4**[1]

5 *2 ½* **Ange Gardien (IRE)**[18] 2233 3-9-2 ..................................... CSoumillon 3 112
(RobertCollet, France) *towards rear, progress approaching straight, driven and closed up briefly 2f out, stayed on under pressure to line* **14/1**

6 *shd* **Lord Du Sud (FR)**[24] 2073 3-9-2 ..................................... IMendizabal 12 112
(J-CRouget, France) *mid-division, disputing 5th straight, stayed on steadily from 1 1/2f out but never in challenging position* **9/2**[2]

7 *shd* **Reefscape**[18] 2233 3-9-2 ..................................... GaryStevens 7 112
(AFabre, France) *towards rear, last towards outside straight, stayed on from 1 1/2f out but never dangerous* **7/1**[3]

8 *¾* **Five Dynasties (USA)**[29] 1966 3-9-2 ..................................... JPSpencer 9 111
(APO'Brien, Ire) *held up, 12th on inside straight, driven 2f out, never threatened* **33/1**

9 *hd* **Top Of The Bill (USA)**[25] 3-9-2 ..................................... TFarina 14 111
(AFabre, France) *prominent, 4th straight, driven and ran on from 2f out til weakened final furlong* **20/1**

10 *¾* **Day Or Night**[42] 1654 3-9-2 ..................................... TGillet 15 109
(JEPease, France) *held up, never dangerous* **16/1**

11 *2* **Manyana (IRE)**[19] 2203 3-9-2 ..................................... MartinDwyer 16 106
(MPTregoning) *towards rear, pushed along approaching straight, never a factor* **20/1**

12 *1 ½* **Delfos (IRE)**[32] 1898 3-9-2 ..................................... LDettori 13 104
(CLaffon-Parias, France) *prominent, 3rd straight, ridden 2f out, one pace from 1 1/2f out* **7/1**[3]

13 *8* **Top Seed (IRE)**[25] 2043 3-9-2 ..................................... TEDurcan 5 92
(MRChannon) *prominent in early stages, pushed along and lost place 4f out, no impression straight* **16/1**

14 *8* **King Of Cry (FR)**[24] 2073 3-9-2 ..................................... CNora 17 80
(RMartin-Sanchez, Spain) *mid-division, never a factor* **100/1**

15 *20* **Yorik**[37] 3-9-2 ..................................... MBlancpain 6 50
(CLaffon-Parias, France) *led, pushed along approaching straight, headed entering straight, soon beaten and eased* **250/1**

2m 25.2s **Going Correction** -0.25s/f (Firm) **15** Ran SP% **129.3**
Speed ratings: **117,116,116,116,114 114,114,113,113,113 111,110,105,100,86.**
**Owner** Ecurie Jean-Louis Bouchard **Bred** Meridian Stud **Trained** France

**NOTEBOOK**
**Blue Canari(FR)** looked as though he was being ridden for a place for much of the race and was last early on. He still appeared to have plenty to do half a furlong out, but got there with a late surge. He has no current engagements and his owner will need to supplement him into races like the Budweiser Irish Derby and the Arc de Triomphe.
**Prospect Park** looked the likely winner at the furlong marker, having been given a very professional ride, but was run out of things in the final few strides. A game effort in defeat.
**Valixir(IRE)** made up a lot of ground in the straight and was battling for the lead a furlong out. He can have no excuses.
**Day Flight** ran a terrific race on ground a little faster than ideal. He will now be rested and has considerable potential, particularly on a softer surface.
**Manyana(IRE)** could not quicken in the straight and appeared to be a little out of his depth.

**Top Seed(IRE)** raced in the centre of the pack in the early part of the race and made no show in the straight.

## HAMBURG (R-H)
Sunday, June 6

**OFFICIAL GOING: Good**

### 2723a PFERDEWETTEN.DE DEUTSCHES STUTEN DERBY-PREIS DER DIANA (FILLIES) 1m 3f
**4:15** (4:22) 3-Y-0 **£124,437** (£49,775; £24,887; £12,662)

RPR

1 **Amarette (GER)**[21] 2157 3-9-2 .......... ASuborics 13 98
(ASchutz, Germany) *always prominent, 2nd straight, led just under 2f out, soon ridden, driven out final f* 2

2 *hd* **La Ina (GER)**[28] 1983 3-9-2 .......... ADeVries 2 97
(ATrybuhl, Germany) *in rear, 14th 4f out, headway on inside to go 7th straight, squeezed through on rail to go 2nd inside final f, stayed on st* 3

3 *1/2* **Saldentigerin (GER)**[21] 2157 3-9-2 .......... TQuinn 15 96
(PSchiergen, Germany) *midfield when slightly hampered first turn, in touch, 5th straight, ridden over 1 1/2f out, stayed on steadily* 1

4 *1 1/4* **La Hermana**[28] 1983 3-9-2 .......... EBotti 6 94
(AWohler, Germany) *close up, 3rd straight, stayed on under pressure final 1 1/2f*

5 *1/2* **Dalicia (GER)**[21] 2157 3-9-2 .......... ABest 7 94
(PRau, Germany) *hampered and dropped to last after 1f, 14th straight, stayed on well down outside under pressure final 2f, nearest finish*

6 *1/2* **Iduna (GER)**[21] 2157 3-9-2 .......... NRichter 8 93
(WHickst, Germany) *in rear, 13th 4f out, 8th on outside straight, headway to chase leaders approaching final f, one pace*

7 *1/2* **Vallera (GER)**[21] 2157 3-9-2 .......... FilipMinarik 12 92
(UOstmann, Germany) *led to just under 2f out, one pace*

8 *2* **Daytona (GER)** 3-9-2 .......... ABoschert 1 89
(FrauABertram, Germany) *held up, 11th 4f out, 9th straight, ridden and one pace final 1 1/2f*

9 *nse* **Cotrina (GER)** 3-9-2 .......... EPedroza 9 89
(AWohler, Germany) *midfield, 10th straight, soon ridden and unable to quicken*

10 *3/4* **Freedom (GER)**[28] 1983 3-9-2 .......... AStarke 16 88
(ASchutz, Germany) *close up, 6th straight, ridden and beaten over 1f out*

11 *1 3/4* **Sword Roche (GER)**[21] 2157 3-9-2 .......... WMongil 11 85
(MarioHofer, Germany) *midfield, 13th straight, no danger after*

12 *1 1/2* **Estefania (GER)**[21] 2157 3-9-2 .......... THellier 4 82
(PRau, Germany) *carried very wide first turn, headway on outside to race in touch, 11th straight, soon beaten*

13 *1* **Ahlefisia**[247] 5353 3-9-2 .......... AGoritz 14 81
(FrauMarionRotering, Germany) *close up, 4th straight, soon weakened*

14 *2* **Give Me Five (GER)** 3-9-2 .......... SChin 3 78
(FrauEMader, Germany) *midfield, 12th straight, soon beaten*

15 *1 3/4* **Song Of Night (GER)**[21] 2157 3-9-2 .......... MTimpelan 10 75
(HSteinmetz, Germany) *towards rear, weakened over 2 1/2f out*

P **Rawhide (GER)** 3-9-2 ..........(b) LHammer-Hansen 5 —
(MarioHofer, Germany) *hampered and saddle slipped after 2f, soon pulled wide and pulled up*

2m 20.24s **16** Ran SP% **130.4**
Speed ratings: .
**Owner** Gestut Schlenderhan **Bred** Gestut Schlenderhan **Trained** Germany

**NOTEBOOK**
**Amarette(GER)**was always up with the pace. Kicking for home passing the two furlong marker, she went a length and a half clear and had just enough in reserve to hold La Ina's late thrust. She is unbeaten after three career starts and should improve again before her next start in the German Derby.
**La Ina(GER)** came from the rear and got a pretty clear passage up the inside, although she had to squeeze through a narrow gap at the furlong pole. The post came a couple of strides too soon for her and she will now head for the USA, where she will be a force in the big turf prizes.
**Saldentigerin(GER)**held a good position entering the home straight, but took time to find her stride and only got into top gear in the closing stages. She may take on the boys in the German Derby, where the extra furlong should be in her favour.

## 1905 FOLKESTONE (R-H)
Monday, June 7

**OFFICIAL GOING: Good to firm (firm in places)**
Wind: nil Weather: sunny & warm

### 2724 SANDGATE H'CAP 5f
**2:20** (2:22) (E) (0-75,72) 3-Y-0+ **£3,484** (£1,072; £536; £268) **Stalls** Low

Form RPR

5001 1 **Hard To Catch (IRE)**[10] 2440 6-9-6 **72** ..........(b) MSavage(5) 12 81
(DKIvory) *s.i.s: racd in last pair far side: prog 2f out: rdn to ld jst ins fnl f: pushed out nr fin* **8/1**

6553 2 *1/2* **Double M**[12] 2399 7-8-7 **54** ow1 ..........(v) NCallan 8 61+
(MrsLRichards) *in tch far side: effrt and nt clr run over 1f out: squeezed through to chse wnr ins fnl f: r.o but a hld* **6/1**[2]

2304 3 *1* **Law Maker**[2] 2675 4-7-13 **46** oh2 ow1 ..........(v) JQuinn 10 50
(MABuckley) *w ldr far side: led over 2f out: hdd and one pce jst ins fnl f* **12/1**

2366 4 *1 1/2* **Pulse**[18] 2246 6-9-1 **62** ..........(p) RLMoore 5 60
(JMBradley) *chsd nr side ldrs: led gp over 1f out: clr of remainder ins fnl f but no ch w far side ldrs* **9/2**[1]

0000 5 *3/4* **Beauvrai**[16] 2303 4-9-8 **69** .......... MTebbutt 3 65
(VSmith) *mounted on crse: dwlt: racd in last pair nr side: prog over 1f out: chsd ldr last 100yds: r.o but no ch* **6/1**[2]

0002 6 *1 3/4* **Inching**[9] 2482 4-8-0 **47** .......... MartinDwyer 9 36
(RMHCowell) *led far side gp to over 2f out: wknd fnl f* **8/1**

4306 7 *hd* **Playtime Blue**[16] 2303 4-9-0 **61** .......... GBaker 6 49
(MrsHSweeting) *led nr side gp to over 1f out: wknd fnl f* **13/2**[3]

6-60 8 *1/2* **Among Friends (IRE)**[24] 2091 4-9-6 **67** ..........(b[1]) TQuinn 4 54
(BPalling) *trckd nr side ldrs: outpcd and btn over 1f out* **16/1**

0000 9 *1/2* **Naughty Girl (IRE)**[21] 2178 4-8-10 **60** ..........(b[1]) FPFerris(3) 1 45
(PDEvans) *racd in last pair nr side and sn pushed along: nvr a factor* **50/1**

45-0 10 *1 1/4* **Indian Bazaar (IRE)**[18] 2246 8-8-0 **50** .......... RMiles(3) 13 30
(NEBerry) *racd far side: in tch: rdn whn hmpd on inner wl over 1f out: no ch after* **20/1**

20-0 11 *1 1/2* **Tomthevic**[16] 2303 6-8-12 **59** .......... MFenton 11 34
(MrsPSly) *chsd far side ldrs: edgd rt and wknd wl over 1f out* **20/1**

0-00 12 *nk* **Loch Inch**[10] 2440 7-8-6 **53** ..........(b) SCarson 7 27
(JMBradley) *pressed nr side ldr to 2f out: wknd* **20/1**

59.31 secs (-1.39) **Going Correction** -0.15s/f (Firm) **12** Ran SP% **112.1**
Speed ratings: **105,104,102,100,99 96,95,95,94,92 89,89**CSF £49.28 CT £569.44 TOTE £11.80: £3.50, £2.10, £4.60; EX 36.50.
**Owner** Mrs Karen Graham **Bred** Flan Hannon **Trained** Radlett, Herts
■ Stewards Enquiry : N Callan caution: careless riding

**FOCUS**
A modest handicap run at a fair gallop. They split into two groups of six, with the first three home racing on the far side.

**NOTEBOOK**
**Hard To Catch(IRE)** defied a 6lb rise for his Brighton victory to score off his highest mark yet. The faster the ground the better for him.
**Double M**, down a furlong in trip, met with trouble but was running on at the end in his usual fashion. He is rather too consistent for his own good.
**Law Maker**, who remains a maiden, is running respectably at present although he was favourably drawn here.
**Pulse**, who is 4lb above his highest winning mark, did best of the sextet who opted to race on the stands' side.
**Beauvrai**, who unseated his rider going to post when appearing to shy at the public address, was slow to break again. He has dropped in the weights and his trainer, who has made a decent start to his career, may be able to exploit that.

### 2725 PILGRIMS HOSPICE RACEDAY ON 25TH JUNE (S) STKS 5f
**2:50** (2:50) (G) 2-Y-0 **£2,506** (£716; £358) **Stalls** Low

Form RPR

002 1 **Keresforth**[20] 2194 2-9-0 ..........(b) NCallan 4 54
(IAWood) *racd nr side: mde all and sn clr of other pair: rdn over 1f out: styd on wl* **11/10**[1]

2 *3 1/2* **Songgaria** 2-8-9 .......... TQuinn 3 37
(BPalling) *restless stalls: racd nr side: sn outpcd by wnr: kpt on fr over 1f out to take 2nd nr fin* **5/2**[2]

664 3 *1 1/2* **Shish (IRE)**[12] 2405 2-8-9 .......... SWKelly 5 32
(JAOsborne) *led far side trio and clr of other pair: no ch w wnr over 1f out: wknd fnl 100yds* **6/1**[3]

4 *3* **Sapphire Princess** 2-8-6 .......... JFMcDonald(3) 6 21
(IAWood) *racd far side: outpcd and sn rdn: kpt on over 1f out: n.d* **10/1**

600 5 *6* **Bamboozled**[12] 2405 2-8-9 ..........(b[1]) JoannaBadger 1 —
(PDEvans) *dwlt: racd nr side: a last of trio and outpcd* **12/1**

0 6 *8* **Whatsheworth**[8] 2502 2-8-11 .......... BReilly(3) 2 —
(PSMcentee) *dwlt and swvd rt s: racd far side: nvr on terms w ldr: wknd 2f out* **25/1**

61.37 secs (0.67) **Going Correction** -0.15s/f (Firm) **6** Ran SP% **111.1**
Speed ratings: **88,82,80,75,65 52**CSF £3.91 TOTE £1.90: £1.10, £2.30; EX 3.90.The winner was bought in for 7,200 guineas. Songgaria was claimed by Mrs Deana Godmon for £6,000.
**Owner** Neardown Stables **Bred** Bearstone Stud **Trained** Upper Lambourn, Berks

**FOCUS**
There was little strength in depth to this seller. The field again split into two equal groups. This time the near flank held the call, but the three to go to the far side had been a little slow to make the move.

**NOTEBOOK**
**Keresforth**, claimed out of Tim Easterby's yard, was smartly away and made all. He appreciated the change of tactics and loved the fast ground.
**Songgaria**, whose dam was a five-furlong winner at two, found her stride in the latter stages and should learn from this introduction.
**Shish(IRE)**, making her turf debut, showed pace on the far side but the near flank was on top.
**Sapphire Princess**, a half-sister to sprint winners Donny Bowling and Game Flora, is a stablemate of the winner. With normal improvement she may be up to winning a similar event.
**Whatsheworth** went over to race on the far side despite being drawn two. The manoeuvre cost him ground and he was soon toiling.

### 2726 TOTEEXACTA H'CAP 6f
**3:20** (3:20) (D) (0-80,82) 3-Y-0 **£8,326** (£2,562; £1,281; £640) **Stalls** Low

Form RPR

3050 1 **Simpsons Mount (IRE)**[12] 2399 3-8-4 **62** .......... RLMoore 2 70
(RMFlower) *racd nr side: trckd ldr: effrt against rail 2f out: led over 1f out: r.o wl fnl f* **20/1**

3-01 2 *1 3/4* **Snow Wolf**[7] 2530 3-9-10 **82** 6ex .......... DaneO'Neill 6 85+
(JMBradley) *led far side gp: hung bdly lft fr 2f out: ended on nr side and hld by wnr ins fnl f* **11/1**

3051 3 *1/2* **Tag Team (IRE)**[17] 2266 3-9-4 **76** .......... MartinDwyer 1 78
(AMBalding) *led nr side gp to over 1f out: edgd rt: unable qck* **11/2**[3]

0203 4 *2 1/2* **Ask The Clerk (IRE)**[10] 2444 3-9-1 **73** .......... MTebbutt 7 67
(VSmith) *racd far side: hld up last of gp: effrt 2f out: one pce fnl f* **9/1**

1-00 5 *shd* **Tribute (IRE)**[23] 2131 3-9-4 **79** .......... TPQueally(3) 8 73
(DRLoder) *racd far side: hld up bhd ldrs: rdn and nt qckn 2f out: one pce after* **9/2**[2]

6-00 6 *hd* **Who's Winning (IRE)**[23] 2131 3-8-9 **70** .......... JFMcDonald(3) 4 63
(CADwyer) *chsd nr side ldr: rdn over 2f out: fdd over 1f out* **16/1**

-441 7 *3* **Cherokee Nation**[13] 2380 3-7-13 **57** .......... JQuinn 9 41
(PWD'Arcy) *chsd far side ldrs: rdn over 2f out: wknd over 1f out* **6/1**

6060 8 *1/2* **Sussex Style (IRE)**[13] 2380 3-7-12 **56** oh6 ..........(t) DKinsella 3 39
(RMFlower) *racd nr side: a last of gp and struggling* **66/1**

-231 9 *5* **Emtilaak**[10] 2450 3-9-6 **78** .......... RHills 5 46
(BHanbury) *dwlt: racd far side: hld up bhd ldrs: rdn over 2f out: sn wknd* **15/8**[1]

1m 11.83s (-1.77) **Going Correction** -0.15s/f (Firm) **9** Ran SP% **113.1**
Speed ratings: **105,102,102,98,98 98,94,93,86**CSF £215.73 CT £1389.72 TOTE £15.80: £3.20, £3.00, £2.10; EX 107.30.
**Owner** C Simpson,Z Mount,T J Lowe,R M Flower **Bred** Thomas Heatrick **Trained** Jevington, E Sussex

**FOCUS**
A fair handicap in which they split into two groups again, but there did not seem much between them. The winner was among the near-side quartet, but Snow Wolf, who initially took the far-side route, would have won had he not hung across the course.

**NOTEBOOK**
**Simpsons Mount(IRE)**, who is very small, was 7lb lower than when making his handicap debut three runs back. Getting away on terms this time, he raced straight and true against the rail and profited from the runner-up's erratic course.
**Snow Wolf**, under a 6lb penalty for his Redcar victory, veered right across the course, but for which he might well have won. He has plenty of dash but is quirky with it. *Official explanation: jockey said the gelding hung left in the final 2f*

**Tag Team(IRE)**, 4lb higher than at Bath, had no problem with the ground but may be better over shorter.
**Ask The Clerk(IRE)**, best of those who raced up the far side throughout, was 7lb higher than when winning over course and distance on easy ground in March.
**Tribute(IRE)** once again looked less than straightforward.
**Emtilaak** failed to pick up at all once coming off the bridle. He is better than this but looks one to be wary of. *Official explanation: trainer was unable to offer any explanation for the poor run*

## 2727 ROSE & CROWN STELLING MINNIS CLASSIFIED STKS 7f (S)
3:50 (3:51) (E) 3-Y-0+ £3,493 (£1,075; £537; £268) Stalls Low

Form RPR
0303 1 **Waterside (IRE)**[12] [2404] 5-9-3 68 RLMoore 6 76
(GLMoore) *racd against far side rail: mde virtually all: shkn up and def advantage over 1f out: styd on wl* 10/3[1]
0-00 2 ¾ **Bi Polar**[25] [2064] 4-9-6 73 DaneO'Neill 1 77
(DRCElsworth) *w wnr: rdn and unable qck 2f out: styd on fnl f: a hld* 5/1[3]
0-00 3 1 ¾ **Bertocelli**[13] [2378] 3-8-7 70 AMcCarthy 7 70
(GGMargarson) *reminder in rr over 5f out: rdn and struggling 1/2-way: effrt u.p 2f out: styd on fnl f* 7/1
450- 4 hd **Spring Jim**[227] [5725] 3-8-9 72 OUrbina 3 71
(JRFanshawe) *s.s: in tch: chsd ldrs 1/2-way: sn rdn and outpcd: kpt on fr over 1f out* 4/1[2]
0-05 5 6 **Mandarin Spirit (IRE)**[10] [2441] 4-9-5 72 (b) SSanders 4 55
(GCHChung) *trckd ldrs: chal 3f out: rdn and unable qck 2f out: wknd rapidly over 1f out* 4/1[2]
0-00 6 4 **Recount (FR)**[9] [2491] 4-9-8 75 NPollard 2 48
(JRBest) *chsd ldrs to 1/2-way: sn rdn and lost tch* 9/1
-441 7 hd **Fizzy Lady**[116] [751] 3-8-1 67 (t) RMiles(3) 5 39
(NEBerry) *outpcd and wl bhd after 2f: nvr on terms after* 12/1

1m 26.18s (-1.62) **Going Correction** -0.15s/f (Firm) 7 Ran SP% 109.9
**WFA** 3 from 4yo+ 10lb
Speed ratings: **103,102,100,99,93 88,88**CSF £18.49 TOTE £4.20: £2.20, £3.70; EX 37.00.
**Owner** Nigel Shields **Bred** Yeomanstown Stud **Trained** Woodingdean, E Sussex

**FOCUS**
A fair handicap, and this time the whole field tacked over to race on the far side.

**NOTEBOOK**
**Waterside(IRE)**, having his first run since being claimed out of John Hills's yard, bagged the rail and the return to front-running tactics paid off. He had no problem with this fast ground.
**Bi Polar** ran his best race of the campaign back in this easier grade. He is currently rated 10lb lower than he was a year ago and may be able to profit back in handicap company.
**Bertocelli** was staying on when it was too late. He did not get home on his one attempt at a mile as a two-year-old, but may be worth another try.
**Spring Jim**, stepped up to seven furlongs on this seasonal debut, appeared to stay but only after hitting a flat spot past halfway. He might do better in handicap company.
**Mandarin Spirit(IRE)** seems best when able to dominate. He was still in third place passing the furlong pole but was already beginning to back-pedal.
**Fizzy Lady** *Official explanation: jockey said the filly was unsuited by the fast ground*

## 2728 TED STANNARD WEDDING PRESENT H'CAP 1m 4f
4:20 (4:20) (F) (0-55,54) 4-Y-0+ £3,052 (£872; £436) Stalls Low

Form RPR
0000 1 **Cantrip**[14] [2375] 4-8-13 45 SSanders 2 53
(MissBSanders) *led tl rn wd bnd over 9f out: chsd clr ldr 7f out: rdn 5f out: clsd over 2f out: drvn to ld 1f out: kpt on* 13/2
03-0 2 1 ¼ **Summer Cherry (USA)**[26] [2032] 7-8-9 41 (t) PDoe 6 47
(JamiePoulton) *t.k.h: prom: led 8f out: sn clr: rdn over 2f out: hdd and no ex 1f out* 14/1
064 3 2 ½ **Ambersong**[44] [1630] 6-8-9 41 IMongan 11 43
(AWCarroll) *rousted along in rr early: rdn and wl off the pce 6f out: prog over 3f out: styd on to take 3rd nr fin* 4/1[1]
-153 4 shd **Vandenberghe**[10] [2456] 5-9-2 48 VSlattery 9 50
(JAOsborne) *settled in midfield: wl off the pce 6f out: rdn and effrt over 3f out: styd on: nvr able to chal* 9/2[2]
5204 5 shd **Free Style (GER)**[14] [2363] 4-8-11 48 NChalmers(5) 10 50
(MrsHSweeting) *midfield: off the pce 6f out: rdn to chse clr ldng trio over 3f out: kpt on: nvr able to chal* 5/1[3]
5000 6 2 ½ **Coolfore Jade (IRE)**[15] [2324] 4-8-10 45 RMiles(3) 8 43
(NEBerry) *chsd ldrs: outpcd 6f out: effrt to chse clr ldng pair 4f out: no imp over 2f out: wknd over 1f out* 14/1
-430 7 ¾ **Classical Waltz (IRE)**[13] [2386] 6-7-13 34 oh4 NMackay(3) 1 31
(JJSheehan) *settled in rr: rdn and wl off the pce over 5f out: one pce and no ch after* 25/1
000- 8 nk **Absinther**[228] [5717] 7-9-0 46 GBaker 4 42
(MRBosley) *stdd s: hld up in last: wl off the pce 1/2-way: effrt over 3f out: no prog 2f out* 12/1
00-0 9 24 **Gabor**[26] [2032] 5-9-8 54 (b) RLMoore 3 12
(GLMoore) *chsd ldrs: rdn over 6f out: sn lost pl: wknd 4f out: t.o* 7/1
000- 10 23 **Estilo**[427] [952] 4-8-2 34 oh4 DKinsella 7 —
(RMFlower) *hld up: rn wd bnd over 9f out: lost pl: last and tailing off over 5f out* 66/1
0-00 11 11 **Silistra**[64] [914] 5-9-4 50 SWKelly 5 —
(MrsLCJewell) *led over 9f out to 8f out: wknd rapidly over 4f out: t.o* 50/1

2m 38.92s (-1.48) **Going Correction** -0.15s/f (Firm) 11 Ran SP% 109.0
Speed ratings: **98,97,95,95,95 93,93,93,77,61 54**CSF £84.56 CT £371.16 TOTE £8.70: £3.30, £3.00, £1.60; EX 82.40.
**Owner** A C Verdie **Bred** A D G Oldrey **Trained** Epsom, Surrey

**FOCUS**
The runner-up made this a decent test of stamina. This was effectively a banded race and the form is weak.

**NOTEBOOK**
**Cantrip** attempted to make all, but that plan went out of the window as she lost the lead when running wide on the first bend. With Sanders alert to the danger as the leader opened up a clear advantage, she responded to pressure to wear him down in game fashion. She was runner-up off 17lb higher last term, when trained by Ralph Beckett, so will still be well treated after this. *Official explanation: trainer said, regarding the improved form shown, filly had been unsuited by being crowded in a large field of runners last time out*
**Summer Cherry(USA)**, well ridden by Doe, soon established a clear lead after going on a mile out, but was caught at the furlong pole. He finished a lot closer to Cantrip than he had on his return from a lengthy absence last time.
**Ambersong** is rated lower on turf than on sand. Staying on late to get the best of a three-way photo for third, he is better over farther.
**Vandenberghe** was stepping up in trip, but again failed to get going until it was too late.
**Free Style(GER)** was keeping on without promising to catch the leading pair over this slightly longer trip.
**Coolfore Jade(IRE)** is best when getting her own way out in front. Going after the leading pair with half a mile to run, she was still in third place approaching the final furlong before weakening.
**Silistra** *Official explanation: jockey said the gelding had a breathing problem*

## 2729 COME TO LADIES NIGHT ON 5TH AUGUST MEDIAN AUCTION MAIDEN STKS 1m 1f 149y
4:50 (4:51) (E) 3-4-Y-0 £3,601 (£1,108; £554; £277) Stalls Low

Form RPR
0-55 1 **Whitsbury Cross**[23] [2113] 3-8-8 77 TQuinn 3 77
(DRCElsworth) *midfield: rdn to chse ldng pair 4f out: styd on wl u.p fr over 1f out: led last stride* 2/1[1]
55 2 shd **Maharaat (USA)**[30] [1967] 3-8-8 (vt[1]) RHills 1 77
(SirMichaelStoute) *jnd ldr over 6f out: disp ld after tl drvn into def advantage 2f out: 2l up 1f out: hdd last stride* 4/1[3]
02 3 1 **Vamp**[17] [2267] 3-8-3 JQuinn 4 70
(RMBeckett) *midfield: rdn over 4f out: effrt u.p over 2f out: clsd fnl f: no ex nr fin* 3/1[2]
000 4 1 ½ **Antigiotto (IRE)**[28] [2001] 3-8-5 NMackay(3) 7 72
(LMCumani) *hld up in rr: prog but outpcd over 3f out: styd on wl fnl 2f: nrst fin* 20/1
03-5 5 5 **Appetina**[18] [2243] 3-8-4 75 ow1 MFenton 13 59
(JGGiven) *led: jnd over 6f out: hdd 2f out: wknd over 1f out* 4/1[3]
0 6 1 ½ **Laurens Girl (IRE)**[66] [1226] 3-8-4 ow1 DRMcCabe 11 56
(MGQuinlan) *t.k.h: hld up in midfield: outpcd 4f out: n.d after: nudged along and kpt on fnl 2f* 66/1
04 7 6 **Lucky Again (IRE)**[32] [1912] 3-8-8 GCarter 5 48
(JLDunlop) *s.i.s: settled in rr: detached in last pair over 3f out: shuffled along and kpt on fnl 2f: nvr nr ldrs* 25/1
03 8 1 **Great Gidding**[14] [2357] 3-8-8 JFEgan 9 46
(HMorrison) *prom tl wknd over 3f out* 50/1
00 9 3 **Miss Merenda**[24] [2093] 3-8-4 ow1 PDoe 10 37
(DECantillon) *a in rr: detached in last pair 4f out: bhd after* 100/1
000 10 8 **Miss St Albans**[8] [2505] 3-8-5 ow5 BReilly(3) 12 26
(TTClement) *prom: rdn 5f out: wknd wl over 3f out* 100/1
6 U **Kilindini**[32] [1911] 3-8-8 SWKelly 6 —
(MissECLavelle) *rrd bdly and uns rdr s* 33/1

2m 3.78s (-1.38) **Going Correction** -0.15s/f (Firm) 11 Ran SP% 115.3
Speed ratings: **99,98,98,96,92 91,86,86,83,77** —CSF £9.53 TOTE £3.40: £1.40, £1.10, £1.50; EX 13.70 Place 6 £101.13, Place 5 £23.77.
**Owner** Mcdowell Racing **Bred** Mrs D O Joly **Trained** Whitsbury, Hants
■ Richard Quinn's 2,000th domestic winner. The first came in 1981, the 1,000th in 1995.

**FOCUS**
A fair maiden for the track, run at an ordinary pace.

**NOTEBOOK**
**Whitsbury Cross**, fifth in two warm maidens earlier this term, ran on well between horses to put his head in front close home. He appreciated this slightly longer trip and will get a bit farther still.
**Maharaat(USA)**, visored for the first time, was led to post by his jockey after refusing to go down. On this more suitable ground, he did nothing wrong in the race but was just touched off.
**Vamp**, tackling a slightly longer trip, threw down a strong challenge to have her chance but the effort just flattened out close home. Now qualified for handicaps, she will be suited by a more galloping track.
**Antigiotto(IRE)** ran his best race to date on this faster surface, and is the type to make his mark in handicap company.
**Appetina**, adopting front-running tactics again, was tightened up slightly just after being headed and was soon on the retreat. She looks to find this trip slightly too far.
**Laurens Girl(IRE)** showed more than she had on her debut on sand and looks to be learning with experience.
T/Plt: £191.50 to a £1 stake. Pool: £34,214.30. 130.40 winning tickets. T/Qpdt: £54.90 to a £1 stake. Pool: £2,381.50. 32.10 winning tickets. JN

# [2445]PONTEFRACT (L-H)
Monday, June 7

**OFFICIAL GOING: Good to firm**

## 2730 ENJOY THE CRAIC MAIDEN AUCTION FILLIES' STKS 6f
6:45 (6:46) (E) 2-Y-0 £4,290 (£1,320; £660; £330) Stalls Low

Form RPR
6 1 **Extreme Beauty (USA)**[9] [2481] 2-8-3 ow1 EAhern 5 67
(CEBrittain) *prom: rdn to ld appr fnl f: r.o wl* 4/1[1]
04 2 3 **Canary Dancer**[4] [2616] 2-8-4 GFaulkner 4 59
(PCHaslam) *mde most tl hdd and rdn appr fnl f: no ex* 33/1
0 3 shd **Whatatodo**[16] [2300] 2-8-2 JMackay 17 56
(MLWBell) *prom: rdn and ch over 1f out: no ex ins last* 18/1
5 4 shd **Sweet Marguerite**[16] [2296] 2-8-2 ow1 DAllan(3) 8 59
(TDEasterby) *cl up: rdn and ev ch over 1f out: no ex ins last* 9/1
5 nk **Flamand (USA)** 2-8-8 KFallon 3 61
(LMCumani) *dwlt: sn midfield: drvn along 2f out: r.o wl clsng stages: nvr able to chal* 9/2[2]
3 6 1 **Lorna Dune**[26] [2035] 2-8-4 PHanagan 11 54
(MrsJRRamsden) *midfield: drvn along and sme hdwy over 1f out: no further prog ins last* 5/1[3]
7 1 **Tequila Sheila (IRE)** 2-8-2 CCatlin 1 49
(KRBurke) *towards rr: hdwy into midfield 2f out: styng on but no imp on ldrs whn nt clr run and hmpd ins fnl f* 14/1
8 5 **Patxaran (IRE)** 2-7-9 RoryMoore(7) 14 34
(PCHaslam) *midfield: rdn 2f out: no hdwy* 33/1
9 1 ¼ **Lara's Girl** 2-8-2 GDuffield 15 30
(IAWood) *dwlt: sn drvn along in rr: styd on fnl 2f: n.d* 25/1
0 10 2 **Live In Hope**[20] [2213] 2-8-2 JFanning 10 24
(JeddO'Keeffe) *prom tl rdn and wknd 2f out* 100/1
0 11 1 **First Rhapsody (IRE)**[10] [2458] 2-8-4 ow5 TEaves(3) 6 26
(TJEtherington) *nvr bttr than mid-div* 100/1
6 12 ½ **Kalika (IRE)**[10] [2453] 2-8-2 GGibbons 12 20
(MsDeborahJEvans) *s.i.s: nvr bttr than mid-div* 66/1
13 nk **Harbour Legend** 2-8-2 JBramhill 7 19
(JGGiven) *dwlt: a rr div* 18/1
14 shd **Scorpio Sally (IRE)** 2-8-2 PMQuinn 9 19
(MDHammond) *chsd ldrs tl wknd over 2f out* 50/1
15 ½ **French Kisses** 2-8-4 DeanMcKeown 2 19
(RonaldThompson) *rrd and slowly away: a rr div* 40/1
2 16 ½ **Trickshot**[24] [2074] 2-8-2 DaleGibson 13 16
(TDEasterby) *sn drvn along: a rr* 5/1[3]

1m 17.47s (0.17) **Going Correction** -0.15s/f (Firm) 16 Ran SP% 116.3
Speed ratings: **92,88,87,87,87 86,84,78,76,73 72,71,71,71,70 69**CSF £144.59 TOTE £5.70: £2.30, £15.60, £3.40; EX 193.20.
**Owner** Dr Ali Ridha **Bred** Peter Vegso Racing Stable **Trained** Newmarket, Suffolk


The Form Book, Raceform Ltd, Compton, RG20 6NL

**FOCUS**
Only an ordinary maiden, run in a moderate time and not a race to go overboard about. However, the winner did it well and deserves a crack at a better race.
**NOTEBOOK**
**Extreme Beauty(USA)**, whose stable appear to have assembled a decent squad of two-years-olds on evidence so far this season, supplemented herself to the list with an authoritative display. A promising sixth on her debut behind a very useful-looking Godolphin runner, she was always going to be suited to this stiffer track and quickened up well before staying on strongly to win going away. She deserves a crack at something better on the evidence of this and will stay at least another furlong.
**Canary Dancer** is improving with racing and found this extra furlong an aid. There should be more to come from her and it will be disappointing if she can not make his mark in nurseries.
**Whatatodo** improved on her debut effort and will be well suited by an extra furlong. She should win her maiden.
**Sweet Marguerite** showed the benefit of her debut and was just run out of a place close home. There should be further improvement in her.
**Flamand(USA)** is bred to be speedy and would have pleased connections with this debut. She was finishing to good effect and should win her maiden.
**Lorna Dune** made a pleasing debut on heavy ground at Newcastle and showed she is effective on this quicker surface.
**Tequila Sheila(IRE)**, whose stable juveniles usually appreciate a run to put them straight, did not receive the clearest of runs through and shaped better than her finishing position suggested. The experience will not be lost on her.
**Trickshot** was never going a yard and failed to run to anything like her debut form when second at Hamilton. *Official explanation: jockey said the filly was unsuited by the ground*

## 2731 TONY BETHELL MEMORIAL H'CAP — 2m 1f 22y
7:15 (7:15) (E) (0-70,69) 4-Y-O+ — £6,971 (£2,145; £1,072; £536) Stalls Low

| Form | | | | | RPR |
|---|---|---|---|---|---|
| 6-00 | 1 | | **Stoop To Conquer**[16] 2285 4-9-9 **66** (JLDunlop) *in tch: hdwy to chse wnr 1/2-way: led 2f out: styd on wl u.p* **15/2**[3] | KFallon 6 | 78 |
| 6135 | 2 | 5 | **Toni Alcala**[4] 2615 5-9-9 **68** (RFFisher) *midfield: hdwy 4f out: styd on u.p to go 2nd ins fnl f: no imp on wnr* **12/1** | LFletcher(3) 2 | 74 |
| 0030 | 3 | 1 1/2 | **Riyadh**[9] 2491 6-9-12 **68** (v) (MJohnston) *midfield: hmpd and lost pl over 6f out: hdwy 4f out: styd on u.p fnl 2f: nvr able to chal* **8/1** | KDalgleish 5 | 72 |
| 200/ | 4 | 3/4 | **Hernandita**[74] 2164 6-9-8 **64** (MissECLavelle) *in tch: rdn and outpcd 3f out: styd on fnl 2f* **16/1** | ACulhane 8 | 68 |
| 2140 | 5 | 1/2 | **Prince Of The Wood (IRE)**[4] 2613 4-8-3 **51** (p) (ABailey) *chsd ldr to 1/2-way: remained prom tl outpcd over 2f out: kpt on fnl f* **12/1** | PMakin(5) 9 | 54 |
| 4-12 | 6 | 3/4 | **Red Sun**[12] 2409 7-9-4 **60** (t) (JMackie) *keen: led after 1f: rdn and hdd 2f out: wknd ins fnl f* **3/1**[1] | PHanagan 12 | 62 |
| 00/5 | 7 | 11 | **Kristineau**[10] 2462 6-8-1 **50** ow3 (t) (MrsDianneSayer) *sn rr div: sme late hdwy: n.d* **25/1** | PPMathers(7) 11 | 40 |
| /4-5 | 8 | 1 3/4 | **Il Cavaliere**[26] 1958 9-9-6 **62** (MrsMReveley) *hld up in rr: sme hdwy 5f out: no further prog fnl 3f* **16/1** | KDarley 1 | 50 |
| 0000 | 9 | 1 | **Vanbrugh (FR)**[5] 2590 4-8-8 **51** (t) (MissDAMchale) *led 1f: chsd ldrs tl wknd 3f out* **50/1** | DarrenWilliams 7 | 38 |
| 2200 | 10 | 3/4 | **Vicars Destiny**[16] 2299 6-9-12 **68** (MrsSLamyman) *chsd ldrs: rdn 4f out: sn wknd* **14/1** | LVickers 13 | 54 |
| 40-2 | 11 | 25 | **Academy (IRE)**[18] 2249 9-9-1 **57** (AndrewTurnell) *in tch: rdn 5f out: sn wknd: t.o* **7/2**[2] | CCatlin 10 | 16 |
| 6602 | 12 | 5 | **Joely Green**[21] 2171 7-8-6 **48** (b) (NPLittmoden) *towards rr: effrt over 5f out: sn btn: t.o* **12/1** | EAhern 4 | 1 |
| 0300 | 13 | 15 | **So Vital**[16] 2305 4-9-6 **63** (JPearce) *a rr: t.o* **50/1** | RPrice 3 | — |

3m 42.55s (-7.95) **Going Correction** -0.15s/f (Firm) — **13** Ran SP% **119.4**
**WFA** 4 from 5yo+ 1lb
Speed ratings: **104,101,100,100,100 100,94,94,93,93 81,79,72**CSF £93.03 CT £744.15 TOTE £8.70: £2.50, £4.20, £2.90; EX 172.50.
**Owner** I H Stewart-Brown & M J Meacock **Bred** I Stewart-Brown And M Meacock **Trained** Arundel, W Sussex
**FOCUS**
A modest race run at a sound pace but ordinary form.
**NOTEBOOK**
**Stoop To Conquer** had yet to really improve as expected for the step up to this sort of trip in several previous tries, but this was the worst handicap he has run in and under an astute ride from Fallon he kicked clear turning for home and was never going to get caught. He had dropped a total of 7lb since October and looks sure to go back up now, but should improve again.
**Toni Alcala** stays well but surprisingly is without a win at this trip. He chased the winner home in hopeless pursuit.
**Riyadh** showed his running last time to be all wrong and stayed on down the outside to claim third.
**Hernandita** raced against the inside rail throughout and stayed on again having been outpaced.
**Prince Of The Wood(IRE)** ran better than at Chepstow and was running on all the way to the line.
**Red Sun** did a bit too much early and left himself vulnerable in the finish. *Official explanation: jockey said the gelding hung right throughout*
**Academy(IRE)** ran a rare bad race and something was presumably not right.

## 2732 TOTEPLACEPOT H'CAP — 1m 2f 6y
7:45 (7:48) (D) (0-80,80) 3-Y-O — £6,955 (£2,140; £1,070; £535) Stalls Low

| Form | | | | | RPR |
|---|---|---|---|---|---|
| 0-02 | 1 | | **Adaikali (IRE)**[17] 2270 3-9-6 **79** (SirMichaelStoute) *in tch: hdwy 3f out: led ins fnl f: drvn out* **9/4**[1] | KFallon 2 | 88 |
| 2410 | 2 | 1 1/4 | **Ile Facile (IRE)**[65] 1239 3-8-8 **67** (t) (NPLittmoden) *hld up midfield: hdwy u.p over 1f out: styd on ins last to go 2nd cl home* **50/1** | EAhern 9 | 74 |
| 5-12 | 3 | nk | **Meadaaf (IRE)**[22] 2146 3-9-6 **79** (ACStewart) *chsd ldrs: drvn along over 3f out: kpt on u.p fnl 2f: no ex fnl f* **4/1**[2] | KDarley 10 | 85 |
| 2215 | 4 | 1/2 | **Charmatic (IRE)**[5] 2587 3-8-6 **65** (JAGlover) *trckd ldr: led 2f out: rdn and hdd ins fnl f: no ex* **12/1** | DeanMcKeown 5 | 70 |
| 3-31 | 5 | 6 | **Tannoor (USA)**[17] 2257 3-9-7 **80** (MAJarvis) *keen: led tl hdd 2f out: wknd fnl f* **6/1**[3] | PRobinson 12 | 74 |
| 30-0 | 6 | 1 1/4 | **Gaiety Girl (USA)**[20] 2197 3-8-2 **64** (TDEasterby) *s.i.s: bhd: styd on fnl 2f: n.d* **50/1** | DAllan(3) 11 | 55 |
| 0-0U | 7 | 3/4 | **Hatch A Plan (IRE)**[44] 1613 3-8-7 **66** (RMBeckett) *midfield: rdn 3f out: no hdwy* **40/1** | GDuffield 1 | 56 |
| 6000 | 8 | 1 | **Royal Distant (USA)**[9] 2472 3-8-13 **72** (MWEasterby) *bhd: drvn along 4f out: styd on fr over 1f out: n.d* **50/1** | DaleGibson 13 | 60 |
| 2000 | 9 | shd | **Mount Vettore**[10] 2448 3-9-5 **78** (MrsJRRamsden) *hld up: hung rt and rdn over 2f out: n.d* **10/1** | KMcEvoy 7 | 66 |
| 10-6 | 10 | 1 1/2 | **Alpine Special (IRE)**[72] 1129 3-8-12 **71** (PCHaslam) *towards rr: sme hdwy 3f out: rdn and btn 2f out* **20/1** | GFaulkner 6 | 56 |
| U004 | 11 | 12 | **Vibe**[20] 2195 3-9-1 **74** (MJohnston) *prom: rdn 4f out: wknd 3f out: lost tch appr fnl f* **10/1** | JFanning 4 | 36 |
| 36-2 | 12 | 6 | **Al Shuua**[18] 2243 3-9-6 **79** (CEBrittain) *in tch: rdn 4f out: wknd 3f out* **7/1** | BDoyle 8 | 30 |

2m 10.27s (-3.64) **Going Correction** -0.15s/f (Firm) — **12** Ran SP% **116.5**
Speed ratings: **108,107,106,106,101 100,99,99,99,97 88,83**CSF £149.52 CT £426.64 TOTE £2.80: £1.50, £7.10, £1.50; EX 211.30 Trifecta £554.30 Pool of £1,249.20 - 1.60 winning units..
**Owner** H H Aga Khan **Bred** His Highness The Aga Khan's Studs S C **Trained** Newmarket, Suffolk
**FOCUS**
A fair handicap but quite what the strength of this form is worth is hard to tell, with the second having competed at banded level. However, Adaikali won with a little in hand in a good time and strikes as the type to keep on improving.
**NOTEBOOK**
**Adaikali(IRE)** gave an improved effort when second to a hot favourite at Haydock and progressed again on this handicap debut. Reportedly still a bit 'colty' beforehand, he still has some learning to do and may yet defy a rise in the weights.
**Ile Facile(IRE)** ran well for one of the rags on this turf debut and is clearly better suited by grass. His sole win to date came in banded company at Lingfield, but he is evidently better than that.
**Meadaaf(IRE)** is better at further and he was never quite going to get there. The return to a mile and a half should see him back to winning ways.
**Charmatic(IRE)** ran with credit on this first try at the distance, but did not truly see it out.
**Tannoor(USA)** raced too keenly for his own good and was a spent force late on.
**Gaiety Girl(USA)** made some late headway from the rear as if to suggest further will help.
**Mount Vettore** got very warm beforehand and remains out of sorts. *Official explanation: jockey said the gelding hung right*
**Vibe** weakened tamely once coming under pressure and either has a physical problem or did not stay.

## 2733 WEATHERBYS BANK PIPALONG STKS (LISTED RACE) (F&M) — 1m 4y
8:15 (8:16) (A) 4-Y-O+ — £20,300 (£7,700; £3,850; £1,750) Stalls Low

| Form | | | | | |
|---|---|---|---|---|---|
| 013- | 1 | | **Chorist**[240] 5481 5-9-2 **111** (WJHaggas) *led after 1f: qcknd 3f out: 3 l clr ins fnl f: eased clsng stages* **4/7**[1] | KFallon 7 | 105 |
| 40-3 | 2 | 1 1/4 | **Ice Palace**[20] 2196 4-8-11 **94** (JRFanshawe) *trckd ldrs: rdn to chse wnr wl over 1f out: styd on: no imp* **5/2**[2] | EAhern 1 | 97 |
| 4-00 | 3 | 5 | **Quiet Storm (IRE)**[20] 2201 4-8-11 **96** (GWragg) *trckd ldrs: ev ch over 2f out: rdn and btn over 1f out* **18/1** | KDarley 5 | 87 |
| 4004 | 4 | 1/2 | **Cote Quest (USA)**[18] 2242 4-8-11 **92** (SCWilliams) *hld up: sme hdwy u.p 2f out: no further prog* **18/1** | PRobinson 8 | 85 |
| 0-03 | 5 | 5 | **Scotland The Brave**[11] 2421 4-8-11 **67** (JDBethell) *led 1f: remained cl up tl wknd over 2f out* **66/1** | KMcEvoy 4 | 75 |
| -051 | 6 | 3/4 | **Enchanted Princess**[16] 2284 4-8-11 **74** (b) (WJHaggas) *hld up: effrt 3f out: sn rdn and btn* **16/1**[3] | ACulhane 3 | 73 |
| 3560 | 7 | 1 1/4 | **Transcendantale (FR)**[10] 2446 6-8-11 **47** (MrsSLamyman) *rr: effrt 3f out: sn rdn and btn* **250/1** | CCatlin 6 | 71? |

1m 43.03s (-2.57) **Going Correction** -0.15s/f (Firm) — **7** Ran SP% **110.5**
Speed ratings: **106,104,99,99,94 93,92**CSF £1.98 TOTE £1.70: £1.40, £1.20; EX 2.60.
**Owner** Cheveley Park Stud **Bred** Cheveley Park Stud Ltd **Trained** Newmarket, Suffolk
**FOCUS**
This was an easy start to the season for Chorist, but the overall form is below Listed level and does not look particularly sound.
**NOTEBOOK**
**Chorist** was rated 15lb superior to all her rivals, and although making her seasonal reappearance over a trip short of her best, proved too strong. Under a good front-running ride, she never saw another rival once taking it up and won a shade cosily. A progressive filly, she should be back winning at Group level before long.
**Ice Palace**, sporting the same colours as the winner, had every chance and ran well, pulling five lengths clear of the third. She too looks progressive.
**Quiet Storm(IRE)** has not been at her best so far this season, and only shaped a little better here.
**Cote Quest(USA)** had little chance at the weights and ran as well as one could have expected.

## 2734 EMERALD ISLE CLASSIFIED STKS — 5f
8:45 (8:45) (E) 3-Y-O+ — £4,134 (£1,272; £636; £318) Stalls Low

| Form | | | | | RPR |
|---|---|---|---|---|---|
| 0000 | 1 | | **Tommy Smith**[17] 2274 6-9-5 67 (b) (JSWainwright) *mde all: rdn over 1f out: r.o wl: eased cl home* **7/1** | DarrenWilliams 2 | 72 |
| 00-0 | 2 | 1 1/2 | **Sholto**[34] 1872 6-8-10 59 (b) (JO'Reilly) *a chsng wnr: rdn over 1f out: r.o: no imp* **6/1**[3] | JDO'Reilly(7) 1 | 65 |
| 6265 | 3 | 3/4 | **Karminskey Park**[18] 2252 5-9-0 62 (TJEtherington) *midfield: drvn along 2f out: r.o wl fnl f: nvr able to chal* **5/1**[2] | JFanning 11 | 59 |
| 1014 | 4 | nk | **Far Note (USA)**[30] 1974 6-9-3 65 (b) (SRBowring) *midfield: hdwy to chse ldrs 2f out: rdn over 1f out: no further prog* **5/1**[2] | JBramhill 5 | 61 |
| 5205 | 5 | 3/4 | **Online Investor**[9] 2490 5-9-7 69 (DNicholls) *dwlt: towards rr: hdwy 1/2-way: chsng ldrs and rdn over 1f out: no further prog ins last* **4/1**[1] | AlexGreaves 8 | 62 |
| 2100 | 6 | 2 | **Mynd**[30] 1956 4-9-3 65 (RMWhitaker) *prom: rdn wl over 1f out: no ex* **7/1** | DeanMcKeown 9 | 51 |
| -000 | 7 | 2 1/2 | **Laurel Dawn**[34] 1870 6-8-10 49 (IWMcinnes) *midfield: rdn 2f out: no hdwy* **40/1** | NataliaGemelova(7) 13 | 42 |
| 4040 | 8 | hd | **Blue Maeve**[104] 875 4-9-3 27 (JHetherton) *prom: rdn 2f out: fdd* **100/1** | GDuffield 12 | 41 |
| 0050 | 9 | shd | **Sugar Cube Treat**[38] 1750 8-9-0 31 (MMullineaux) *sn rr div: n.d* **100/1** | SRighton 10 | 38 |
| 0000 | 10 | 1 1/2 | **John O'Groats (IRE)**[11] 2421 6-9-3 62 (MDods) *sn rr div: n.d* **20/1** | FLynch 4 | 35 |
| 05/0 | 11 | shd | **Smirfys Night**[23] 2118 5-9-3 58 (DNicholls) *chsd ldrs: rdn over 2f out: wknd over 1f out* **50/1** | KDalgleish 6 | 35 |
| 0-51 | 12 | 5 | **Tatweer (IRE)**[26] 2040 4-9-3 60 (v) (DShaw) *sn towards rr: bhd and no ch whn eased wl ins fnl f* **9/1** | KFallon 7 | 17 |
| 6530 | 13 | dist | **Dark Champion**[20] 2219 4-9-3 62 (REBarr) *sddle slipped and sn bhd: virtually p.u* **33/1** | PHanagan 3 | — |

62.89 secs (-0.91) **Going Correction** -0.15s/f (Firm) — **13** Ran SP% **116.7**
Speed ratings: **101,98,97,96,95 92,88,88,88,85 85,77,—**CSF £45.28 TOTE £9.20: £2.80, £2.90, £1.70; EX 28.60.
**Owner** T W Heseltine **Bred** E Smith **Trained** Kennythorpe, N Yorks
**FOCUS**
A contest dominated by the two most recent winners of this race, but the form is ordinary.
**NOTEBOOK**
**Tommy Smith**, successful in this two years ago, was smartly into his stride and had it sewn up turning for home. This was his first win for nearly two years and given he is still on a good mark, he should be up to winning back in handicap company. *Official explanation: trainer said, regarding the improved form shown, his stable had been under a cloud when gelding last ran, adding that gelding was possibly better suited by an uphill track due to injured knees*

**Sholto** last year's winner, stuck to Tommy Smith all the way but was never going to catch him. This was his second start of the season and better should follow.
**Karminskey Park** continues to run well and should find his winning turn not far off.
**Far Note(USA)** was not beaten far and is another in good form at the moment.
**Online Investor** is a frustrating sort and again let those who follow him down.
**Mynd** *Official explanation: jockey said the gelding hung right from 2f out*
**Tatweer(IRE)** scored his sole success to date on heavy ground and ran way below par on this faster surface. *Official explanation: jockey said, regarding the apparent tender ride, his orders were to hold gelding up and arrive as last as possible, adding that he stopped riding the moment he saw the saddle of P Hanagan (Dark Champion) slipping as he thought the rider would fall in front of him*
**Dark Champion** *Official explanation: jockey said saddle slipped.*

## 2735 SHAMROCK AND LEPRECHAUN H'CAP — 6f

**9:15** (9:16) (E) (0-75,75) 3-Y-O+ — **£4,290** (£1,320; £660; £330) **Stalls** Low

Form — RPR

-656 **1** **Albashoosh**[9] 2492 6-9-2 **63** ... AlexGreaves 3 — 80+
(DNicholls) *trckd ldrs: rdn to ld over 1f out: r.o wl: eased cl home* **7/1**[2]

-000 **2** 2 ½ **Blue Patrick**[18] 2237 4-10-0 **75** ... (p) JTate 2 — 84
(JMPEustace) *dwlt: sn midfield: drvn along and hdwy over 1f out: r.o wl u.p to go 2nd clsng stages: no ch w wnr* **20/1**

-000 **3** 1 **Flying Tackle**[5] 2582 6-8-2 **49** ... (p) CCatlin 6 — 55
(MDods) *chsd ldrs: ev ch and rdn 1f out: no ex ins last* **33/1**

00-0 **4** 1 **Midnight Parkes**[30] 1974 5-9-5 **66** ... KDarley 5 — 69
(EJAlston) *cl up: led 2f out: sn rdn and hdd: no ex* **10/1**

00-6 **5** hd **Bollin Edward**[10] 2461 5-8-11 **61** ... DAllan(3) 11 — 63
(TDEasterby) *midfield: drvn along over 2f out: kpt on wl fnl f: nvr able to chal* **3/1**[1]

-021 **6** nk **Downland (IRE)**[17] 2260 8-8-9 **56** ... KimTinkler 10 — 58
(NTinkler) *midfield: sme hdwy u.p over 1f out: kpt on ins last: n.d* **7/1**[2]

2005 **7** 3 **Captain Darling (IRE)**[9] 2483 4-9-1 **62** ... (v) EAhern 12 — 55
(RMHCowell) *midfield: rdn over 1f out: no hdwy* **9/1**[3]

06-0 **8** hd **Loughlorien (IRE)**[17] 2274 5-8-6 **53** ... PHanagan 9 — 45
(RAFahey) *in tch: rdn over 2f out: wknd over 1f out* **16/1**

0-00 **9** hd **Marshallspark (IRE)**[10] 2461 5-9-3 **64** ... GParkin 4 — 55
(RAFahey) *sn towards rr: n.d* **16/1**

0-50 **10** 2 **Palanzo (IRE)**[30] 1974 6-8-13 **67** ... LTreadwell(7) 15 — 52
(DNicholls) *sn towards rr: n.d* **9/1**[3]

5-06 **11** 2 **Linden's Lady**[12] 2407 4-9-6 **67** ... JFanning 8 — 46
(JRWeymes) *led tl hdd 2f out: sn wknd* **25/1**

6060 **12** 2 **Long Weekend (IRE)**[12] 2399 6-7-7 **45** ... (v) BSwarbrick(5) 7 — 18
(DShaw) *slowly away: a rr* **18/1**

06-0 **13** 2 ½ **Smirfys Party**[36] 1787 6-8-7 **54** ... JBramhill 13 — 20
(DNicholls) *s.i.s: a rr div* **33/1**

2621 **14** 9 **Cleveland Way**[19] 2227 4-7-8 **48** ... (v) DFentiman(7) 17 — —
(DCarroll) *midfield tl wknd 2f out* **33/1**

0030 **15** 28 **No Grouse**[10] 2459 4-9-8 **72** ... THamilton(3) 14 — —
(RAFahey) *in tch tl sddle slipped and lost pl 2f out: virtually p.u* **12/1**

1m 15.75s (-1.55) **Going Correction** -0.15s/f (Firm) **15** Ran SP% **121.2**
Speed ratings: **104,100,99,98,97 97,93,93,92,90 87,84,81,69,32**CSF £147.81 CT £2554.73 TOTE £7.50: £2.30, £5.00, £8.00; EX 145.30 Place 6 £249.73, Place 5 £71.80.
**Owner** M J Pipe **Bred** Gainsborough Stud Management Ltd **Trained** Sessay, N Yorks

**FOCUS**
A modest handicap providing a much-needed return to winning ways for Albashoosh who has slipped a long way in the handicap.

**NOTEBOOK**
**Albashoosh ◆** was winning his first race for nearly two years and first for Nicholls. He did it in authoritative fashion as well and it will be most disappointing if he can not supplement it in the coming weeks given he was rated in the mid-80s at one time, and he could have a good handicap in him if working his way back up the ratings with a race like the Ayr Silver Cup being a possible target.
**Blue Patrick** has been a major disappointment this season and had shown nothing in three starts prior. The drop back to this trip seemed to inject some life back into him though and he finished with a strong run to claim second. If building on this he should soon be back in the winner's circle.
**Flying Tackle** has not won since his three-year-old days and does not look set to be ending that barren run anytime soon.
**Midnight Parkes** showed a bit more than of late and is on a good mark if building on this.
**Bollin Edward** was running on without ever getting there from his wide draw and may appreciate more positive tactics.
**Downland(IRE)** was another who never really got involved was runnig on late in the day.
**No Grouse** *Official explanation: jockey said saddle slipped.*
T/Jkpt: £33,653.30 to a £1 stake. Pool: £47,399.12. 1.00 winning ticket. T/Plt: £501.20 to a £1 stake. Pool: £58,154.05. 84.70 winning tickets. T/Qpdt: £63.10 to a £1 stake. Pool: £4,550.70. 53.30 winning tickets. JF

# 2370 WINDSOR (R-H)

Monday, June 7

**OFFICIAL GOING: Good to firm (good in places)**
The stands'-side rail was positioned further out than usual and the bias towards stands'-side runners proved nowhere near as significant.

## 2736 LITTLEWOODS BET DIRECT EBF MEDIAN AUCTION MAIDEN STKS — 6f

**6:30** (6:35) (F) 2-Y-O — **£3,571** (£1,099; £549; £274) **Stalls** High

Form — RPR

**1** **Happy Event** 2-9-0 ... SDrowne 5 — 74
(BRMillman) *bhd: hdwy on outside over 2f out: rdn and r.o wl fnl f: led fnl 75yds* **20/1**

03 **2** ¾ **Bridge Place**[15] 2321 2-9-0 ... (b[1]) LDettori 7 — 72
(BJMeehan) *broke fast and sn slt ld: hdd over 3f out: rdn 2f out:rallied to chal ins last: kpt on wl for 2nd: nt pce of wnr* **7/1**[3]

**3** 1 ¼ **My Princess (IRE)** 2-8-9 ... RLMoore 8 — 63
(NACallaghan) *s.i.s: bhd: hdwy over 2f out: drvn over 1f out: r.o wl finbal f: gng on cl home* **14/1**

**4** hd **Space Maker** 2-9-0 ... DHolland 2 — 67
(MLWBell) *t.k.h: hdwy to ld over 3f out: rdn fnl f: hdd & wknd fnl 75yds* **12/1**

**5** nk **Dry Ice (IRE)** 2-9-0 ... DaneO'Neill 12 — 67
(HCandy) *s.i.s: bhd: swtchd lft over 2f out: sn drvn: kpt wl fnl f but nt rch ldrs* **11/2**[2]

52 **6** 3 ½ **Come Good**[17] 2263 2-9-0 ... RHughes 15 — 56
(RHannon) *broke wl and disp ld 3f: rdn and hung lft 1f out: wknd ins last* **3/1**[1]

**7** shd **Dreemon** 2-9-0 ... RSmith 3 — 56
(BRMillman) *slowly away: hung lft to centre crse: green and bhd 1/2-way: hdwy fr 2f out: r.o wl fnl f: nt rch ldrs* **50/1**

03 **8** nk **Flying Pass**[16] 2300 2-9-0 ... PaulEddery 6 — 55
(DJSFfrenchDavis) *chsd ldrs: styng on same pce whn hmpd jst ins fnl f: nt rcvr* **9/1**

53 **9** 2 ½ **Fortnum**[31] 1936 2-9-0 ... PDobbs 16 — 47
(RHannon) *sn chsng ldrs: rdn over 2f out: styd on one pce* **8/1**

40 **10** 1 ¼ **Perianth (IRE)**[13] 2376 2-9-0 ... NCallan 9 — 44
(BJMeehan) *nvr gng pce to trble ldrs* **25/1**

**11** nk **Makepeace (IRE)** 2-8-11 ... SHitchcott(3) 11 — 43
(MRChannon) *chsd ldrs tl wknd 2f out* **12/1**

00 **12** 2 **Champagne Brandy (IRE)**[4] 2609 2-8-9 ... RWinston 13 — 32
(PDEvans) *in tch over 3f* **66/1**

**13** ½ **Merrymadcap (IRE)** 2-9-0 ... DSweeney 10 — 35
(MBlanshard) *in tch over 3f* **20/1**

**14** 2 **Rowan Lodge (IRE)** 2-8-11 ... FPFerris(3) 17 — 29
(MHTompkins) *sn outpcd* **50/1**

0 **15** ¾ **Archie Glenn**[14] 2370 2-9-0 ... RHavlin 18 — 27
(MrsPNDutfield) *pressed ldrs 3f* **10/1**

1m 13.61s (-0.26) **Going Correction** -0.05s/f (Good) **15** Ran SP% **123.9**
Speed ratings: **99,98,96,96,95 91,90,90,87,85 85,82,81,79,78**CSF £149.82 TOTE £31.70: £7.20, £2.20, £6.40; EX 497.60.
**Owner** Robin Lawson **Bred** R Lawson **Trained** Kentisbeare, Devon

**FOCUS**
A modest juvenile maiden, but strangely, the high draws did not dominate as is usually the case.

**NOTEBOOK**
**Happy Event**, a brother to useful sprinter Maktavish, did well to win on his debut as his trainer believes he is still backward. He got this trip really well, though, and looks to have more stamina than his brother.
**Bridge Place**, who has progressed with every run, ran his best race to date in the first-time blinkers. He might be more of a nursery type, though. *Official explanation: jockey said colt hung left*
**My Princess(IRE)**, a half-sister to a dual seven-furlong winner, is a May foal and looked in need of the experience. She was running on well at the finish, though, and looks capable of improvement.
**Space Maker** travelled easily into the lead but did not see the trip out as well as had looked likely. He will come on for this and looks a ready-made winner of a similar race *Official explanation: jockey said colt hung left*
**Dry Ice(IRE)**, a half-brother to three winners abroad, is bred to need farther than this, and his running appeared to confirm that.
**Come Good** had what appeared a good draw and the benefit of two previous outings under his belt. In the circumstances this was a slightly disappointing performance.
**Fortnum** had never previously run on ground this quick.

## 2737 TOTE SUPPORTS TONIGHT'S CHARITIES CLASSIFIED STKS — 1m 67y

**7:00** (7:01) (E) 3-Y-O+ — **£3,591** (£1,105; £552; £276) **Stalls** High

Form — RPR

-264 **1** **Baker Of Oz**[61] 1294 3-8-6 70 ... RLMoore 1 — 78
(RHannon) *led 1f: drvn to stay chsng ldr tl over 2f out: kpt on strly u.p ins last to ld fnl 100yds* **14/1**

00-2 **2** ¾ **Pango**[19] 2226 5-9-5 72 ... PDobbs 6 — 78
(HMorrison) *trckd ldrs: wnt 2nd over 2f out: led wl over 1f out: sn hrd drvn: hdd and no ex fnl 100yds* **10/11**[1]

1260 **3** 1 ¼ **Chasing The Dream (IRE)**[12] 2400 3-8-3 69 ... JQuinn 3 — 70
(AMBalding) *led after 1f: rdn over 2f out: hdd wl over 1f out: styd pressing fro ld tl no ex fnl 100yds* **12/1**

1201 **4** 1 ¼ **Katiypour (IRE)**[26] 2030 7-9-5 75 ... LisaJones(3) 8 — 75
(MissBSanders) *stdd s: bhd: hdwy and hung rt ins fnl 2f: kpt on ins fnl f but nt pce to rch ldrs* **2/1**[2]

-003 **5** 1 ¾ **Johannian**[9] 2493 6-9-7 74 ... DHolland 2 — 70
(JMBradley) *hld up in rr: hdwy over 2f out: sn rdn to chse ldrs: wknd ins fnl f* **8/1**[3]

6-06 **6** 8 **Cloudingswell**[35] 1843 3-7-12 60 ... NDeSouza(5) 5 — 45
(DLWilliams) *t.k.h: chsd ldrs tl wknd appr fnl 2f* **50/1**

400/ **7** 6 **Lady Jeannie**[511] 3820 7-8-11 48 ... RMiles(3) 7 — 31
(MJHaynes) *s.i.s: bhd and n.d* **66/1**

1m 45.6s **Going Correction** -0.05s/f (Good)
**WFA** 3 from 5yo+ 11lb **7** Ran SP% **114.6**
Speed ratings: **98,97,96,94,93 85,79**CSF £27.62 TOTE £10.10: £3.40, £1.40; EX 15.60.
**Owner** The Mystery Partnership **Bred** M J Worth **Trained** East Everleigh, Wilts

**FOCUS**
No great pace on here and the time was modest, but the form is fair. The first three home were in the first three throughout.

**NOTEBOOK**
**Baker Of Oz** found this quicker ground more in his favour and, with the steady pace ensuring the hold-up horses did not get into it, proved one of the few suited by the way the race was run.
**Pango** had conditions to suit and cruised into the lead looking the likeliest winner, but he found less than expected under pressure and it is probably more than bad luck that he has now finished runner-up seven times, but has only won twice.
**Chasing The Dream(IRE)** looked to have it to do and her rider got the best out of her, making the running at a steady pace before quickening things up turning for home.
**Katiypour(IRE)**, 3lb higher, would have fared better had he raced nearer the pace. As it happened he found himself out of position as the pace quickened.
**Johannian**, over a trip shorter than ideal, was another who found himself unable to peg back the leaders when the pace quickened. The way the race was run did not suit his style of racing.

## 2738 NEWSMITH CAPITAL PARTNERS H'CAP — 1m 2f 7y

**7:30** (7:32) (D) (0-85,82) 3-Y-O+ — **£5,655** (£1,740; £870; £435) **Stalls** Low

Form — RPR

1350 **1** **War Owl (USA)**[28] 2000 7-8-13 **70** ... LisaJones(3) 15 — 79
(IanWilliams) *sn mid-div: hdwy on rails fr 2f out: rdn and str run ins fnl f to ld cl home* **8/1**[3]

040- **2** ½ **Czarina Waltz**[198] 6051 5-10-0 **82** ... GBaker 13 — 90
(CFWall) *trckd ldrs: wnt 2nd 3f out: led wl over 1f out: hrd rdn and kpt on fnl f: hdd cl home* **14/1**

0-64 **3** ½ **Barking Mad (USA)**[17] 2278 6-10-0 **82** ... DHolland 14 — 89
(MLWBell) *led after 1f: rdn over 2f out: hdd wl over 1f out: styd chalng u.p tl no ex wl ins fnl f* **5/1**[2]

5/03 **4** nk **Ken's Dream**[17] 2278 5-9-8 **79** ... SHitchcott(3) 2 — 86
(MsAEEmbiricos) *n.m.r and lost position after 3f: hdwy 3f out:rdn and styd on fnl 2f: chal ins last: no ex nr fin* **12/1**

355- **5** 1 ¾ **Secluded**[269] 4872 4-9-1 **69** ... SSanders 4 — 72
(ACStewart) *s.i.s: bhd: pushed along and hdwy over 2f out: kpt on again ins fnl f: gng on cl home* **8/1**[3]

6443 **6** hd **Todlea (IRE)**[9] 2474 4-9-4 **72** ... LDettori 10 — 75
(JAOsborne) *mid-div: rdn and hdwy over 2f out: swtchd lft over 1f out to chse ldrs: no imp and one pce ins last* **3/1**[1]

3001 **7** ½ **Hiawatha (IRE)**[11] 2424 5-9-4 **75**........................................ DNolan(3) 5 77
(PABlockley) *in tch: hdwy 3f out: hrd drvn to press ldrs ins fnl 2f: wknd ins fnl f* **12/1**

2200 **8** 3 ½ **Classic Role**[24] 2084 5-9-9 **77**........................................(v) NCallan 7 72
(RIngram) *s.i.s: sn rcvrd and mid-div: pushed along 3f out: nvr gng pce to rch ldrs* **12/1**

-000 **9** hd **Stolen Hours (USA)**[16] 2305 4-8-6 **60**........................................ JQuinn 1 55
(JAkehurst) *bhd: kpt on fr over 1f out: nt a danger* **25/1**

0503 **10** 1 **Doris Souter (IRE)**[12] 2403 4-9-2 **70**........................................ RHughes 3 63
(RHannon) *led 1f: stdd rr: swtchd lft to outside 3f out and sn rdn: no imp on ldrs and wknd 2f out* **12/1**

00-0 **11** 8 **Yeoman Lad**[20] 2206 4-9-4 **72**........................................(v¹) SWhitworth 9 50
(AMBalding) *chsd ldrs: rdn 3f out: sn wknd: no ch whn hmpd over 2f out* **20/1**

-300 **12** 1 ½ **Kyle Of Lochalsh**[6] 2547 4-8-3 **57**........................................ AMcCarthy 12 32
(GGMargarson) *chsd ldrs tl wknd qckly over 2f out* **33/1**

50-6 **13** hd **Glimmer Of Light (IRE)**[35] 1821 4-9-8 **76**........................................ RLMoore 6 51
(PWHarris) *in tch: rdn and effrt over 3f out: n.d: sn wknd* **9/1**

030- **14** 14 **Victory Venture (IRE)**[238] 5537 4-9-9 **77**........................................ SWKelly 8 25
(IanWilliams) *chsd ldr after 2f: wknd qckly ins fnl 3f* **33/1**

2m 8.56s (0.26) **Going Correction** -0.05s/f (Good)
**WFA** 3 from 4yo+ 13lb **14** Ran SP% **125.8**
Speed ratings: **96,95,95,94,93 93,93,90,90,89 82,81,81,70**CSF £115.24 CT £628.41 TOTE £10.90: £2.60, £6.40, £2.20; EX 215.00.
**Owner** Mrs Glennie Braune **Bred** Wertheimer Et Frere **Trained** Portway, Warwicks

**FOCUS**
There was a good early pace on here for what was just an average handicap and the form looks solid.

**NOTEBOOK**
**War Owl(USA)** had it to prove off this high a mark on ground this fast, but he likes to come off a strong pace, and that is what he got here. He got a dream run up the stands'-side rail and finished strongly to lead close home, but is likely to struggle again once the Handicapper has had his say.
**Czarina Waltz** has run well fresh in the past and has won off this mark on the All-Weather. This was a sound reappearance and it will be disappointing if she cannot build on this.
**Barking Mad(USA)**, who made almost every yard when successful in this race last year, was back on his last winning mark and attempted to take the race from the front again. This was a brave effort in defeat.
**Ken's Dream** is a keen-going sort and appreciates a strong pace off which he can settle. He had the race run to suit but may have been at a disadvantage challenging widest of all.
**Secluded** made a promising reappearance and looks the type who will appreciate a step up in trip.
**Todlea(IRE)** is running well without reward this year. He had every chance but was unable to raise that extra effort in the closing stages.

## 2739 SUNLEY H'CAP 5f 10y
**8:00** (8:01) (D) (0-85,84) 3-Y-0+ **£6,987** (£2,150; £1,075; £537) **Stalls** High

Form RPR

11-2 **1** **Devon Flame**[12] 2399 5-8-10 **68**........................................ JFMcDonald(3) 5 86+
(RJHodges) *in tch: hdwy and n.m.r 2f out: drvn and str run to ld ins fnl f: r.o wl* **6/1²**

0004 **2** 1 ½ **Further Outlook (USA)**[4] 2628 10-9-13 **82**........................................ DaneO'Neill 4 88
(DKIvory) *chsd ldrs: chal 2f out: led wl over 1f out: hdd ins last: kpt on but nt pce of wnr* **33/1**

000/ **3** 1 **Sunley Sense**[635] 4547 8-9-3 **79**........................................ BO'Neill(7) 6 81
(MRChannon) *mid-div: hdwy 2f out: pressed ldrs appr fnl f: styd on same pce ins last* **50/1**

00-5 **4** nk **Yorkies Boy**[16] 2303 9-7-13 **54**........................................ JQuinn 2 55
(JMBradley) *s.i.s: bhd: hdwy on outside over 1f out: kpt on wl fnl f: nt rch ldrs* **33/1**

0021 **5** shd **Musical Fair**[14] 2369 4-9-9 **78**........................................ RWinston 12 79
(JAGlover) *sn chsng ldrs: rdn and kpt on ins fnl* **7/2¹**

4464 **6** nk **Vienna's Boy (IRE)**[6] 2549 3-9-8 **84**........................................ RLMoore 3 84
(RHannon) *mid-div: hdwy on outside over 1f out: r.o ins last: nt rch ldrs* **8/1**

0043 **7** 1 ¾ **Port St Charles (IRE)**[4] 2628 7-8-8 **63**........................................ SSanders 7 57
(CRDore) *bhd: hdwy appr fnl f: kpt on ins last but nt pce to trble ldrs* **10/1**

0310 **8** nk **Polish Emperor (USA)**[2] 2682 4-9-9 **78**........................................(e) NCallan 8 71
(PWHarris) *chsd ldrs: rdn over 2f out: wknd ins fnl f* **7/2¹**

0353 **9** hd **Lady Pekan**[9] 2482 5-8-4 **62**........................................(b) FPFerris(3) 1 54
(PSMcentee) *pressed ldrs tl led jst ins fnl 2f: hdd over 1f out: wknd ins last* **25/1**

0036 **10** 1 **Seven No Trumps**[9] 2477 7-9-8 **77**........................................ DHolland 10 65
(JMBradley) *bhd: kpt on fr over 1f out but nvr gng pce of ldrs* **7/1³**

0050 **11** ½ **Mr Spliffy (IRE)**[49] 1504 5-7-9 **55**........................................ HayleyTurner(5) 13 41
(MCChapman) *chsd ldrs: n.m.r on rail over 1f out: kpt on same pce ins last* **25/1**

1000 **12** ½ **Its Ecco Boy**[99] 928 6-8-6 **64**........................................ LisaJones(3) 9 49
(PHowling) *bhd: sme hdwy fnl f: nvr a danger* **33/1**

330- **13** 3 **Delegate**[247] 5374 11-8-12 **67**........................................ WRyan 14 41
(NACallaghan) *a outpcd* **20/1**

5000 **14** 2 **Dancing Mystery**[31] 1937 10-9-11 **80**........................................(b) SCarson 15 47
(EAWheeler) *led tl hdd jst ins fnl 2f: sn wknd* **16/1**

59.83 secs (-1.37) **Going Correction** -0.05s/f (Good)
**WFA** 3 from 4yo+ 7lb **14** Ran SP% **120.6**
Speed ratings: **108,105,104,103,103 102,100,99,99,97 96,96,91,88**CSF £197.56 CT £8763.35 TOTE £6.30: £2.50, £7.20, £4.80; EX 114.00.
**Owner** Mrs Angela Tincknell **Bred** W C Tincknell And Mrs A Tincknell **Trained** Charlton Adam, Somerset
■ Stewards Enquiry : F P Ferris one-day ban: failed to keep straight from stalls (Jun 20)

**FOCUS**
A fair handicap but possibly not the strongest form, and once again the high draws were surprisingly eclipsed.

**NOTEBOOK**
**Devon Flame** had no trouble with the drop back in trip and, having travelled well, quickened up well to score. He is a progressive sprinter and, although the Ayr Silver Cup is the long-term aim this season, he can win again before then.
**Further Outlook(USA)** has always run well here and, despite not being at all attractively handicapped, ran a splendid race in defeat.
**Sunley Sense**, returning off a 9lb higher mark than when last seen on the track the best part of two years ago, ran a cracker on his reappearance. He may have had his problems but he clearly retains plenty of ability, and hopefully he can now build on this promising return.
**Yorkies Boy** ran another decent race but he is only plating class these days.
**Musical Fair**, 5lb higher, appeared to be well drawn but, with the rail having been moved out and the advantage nowhere near as significant as usual for the high-drawn horses, she could never quite claw the leaders back.
**Vienna's Boy(IRE)** did not appreciate the drop back to the minimum trip.
**Polish Emperor(USA)** was surprisingly well backed despite being 8lb higher than for his Thirsk win and having his second run in the space of three days.

## 2740 DELOITTE CLAIMING STKS 1m 3f 135y
**8:30** (8:30) (F) 3-Y-0+ **£2,996** (£856; £428) **Stalls** Low

Form RPR

0543 **1** **Paradise Valley**[13] 2385 4-9-5 45........................................(t) SDrowne 7 57
(MrsStefLiddiard) *bhd: styd on fr 3f out: str run u.p fnl f to ld cl home* **8/1**

410/ **2** nk **Cosi Fan Tutte**[557] 5192 6-9-4........................................(vt) DHolland 2 56
(MCPipe) *chsd ldrs: wnt 2nd 4f out: hrd rdn to chal fr 2f out: led jst ins fnl f: hdd cl home* **5/2¹**

0300 **3** ¾ **Rainbow World (IRE)**[63] 1272 4-10-0 65........................................(p) JFEgan 9 64
(AndrewReid) *chsd ldrs: led over 4f out: rdn 3f out: hdd jst ins fnl f: no ex* **12/1**

0-00 **4** 6 **Jack Durrance (IRE)**[27] 1687 4-9-3 55........................................ JFMcDonald(3) 14 47
(GAHam) *bhd: hdwy 3f out: sn rdn and hung lft: styd on same pce fnl 2f* **50/1**

4210 **5** 1 ¾ **Blue Savanna**[12] 1263 4-9-4 45........................................(b) RLMoore 5 42
(JGPortman) *chsd ldrs: rdn over 3f out: one pce fr over 2f out* **10/1**

1551 **6** 1 ¾ **Regulated (IRE)**[7] 2520 3-8-8 65........................................ DaneO'Neill 12 44
(DBFeek) *bhd: pushed along 3f out: mod hdwy fnl 2f* **4/1²**

10-0 **7** 1 ½ **Princess Magdalena**[34] 1857 4-9-3 55........................................ IMongan 4 36
(LGCottrell) *chsd ldrs: rdn 3f out: wknd fr 2f out* **8/1**

5002 **8** ½ **Another Con (IRE)**[9] 2485 3-8-0 58........................................ LisaJones(3) 1 36
(PHowling) *sn led: hdd over 4f out: wknd qckly over 2f out* **7/1³**

2623 **9** 6 **Fox Hollow (IRE)**[23] 2127 3-8-1 38........................................ RMiles(3) 11 27
(MJHaynes) *chsd ldrs: hung lft and wknd fr 3f out* **20/1**

000/ **10** 7 **Real Estate**[413] 5297 10-10-0 52........................................ SWhitworth 16 25
(JSKing) *a in rr* **33/1**

000- **11** 5 **Rare Presence (IRE)**[27] 5692 5-9-5 50........................................(vt) SCarson 6 8
(CPMorlock) *a in rr* **50/1**

**12** 13 **Hickerthriftcastle**[65] 5-9-7........................................ MTebbutt 13 —
(VSmith) *a in rr* **40/1**

00-0 **13** ¾ **Introduction**[85] 1019 3-8-4 45........................................ PaulEddery 15 —
(WJMusson) *a in rr* **20/1**

0-00 **14** 4 **Red Acer (IRE)**[98] 945 3-8-1 25........................................ FPFerris(3) 10 —
(PDEvans) *chsd ldrs: rdn over 5f out: sn wknd* **66/1**

50/6 **15** 13 **Last Rebel (IRE)**[49] 1496 5-9-4 70........................................ RHughes 8 —
(RTPhillips) *mid-div: brief effrt 5f out: sn wknd* **16/1**

2m 30.46s (0.36) **Going Correction** -0.05s/f (Good)
**WFA** 3 from 4yo+ 15lb **15** Ran SP% **126.3**
Speed ratings: **96,95,95,91,90 88,87,87,83,78 75,66,66,63,55** CT £11.00 TOTE £2.90: £1.70, £4.90, £; EX38.10 1.Paradise Valley was the subject of a friendly claim of £6,000. Introduction was claimed by R J Price for £6,000.
**Owner** Valley Fencing **Bred** Brook Stud Ltd **Trained** Great Shefford, Berks

**FOCUS**
A poor race in which stamina won the day.

**NOTEBOOK**
**Paradise Valley**, beaten in banded grade last time, is not much good but he does stay well, and in the end it was his stamina which enabled him to edge out the favourite close home.
**Cosi Fan Tutte**, off the track for 18 months, is clearly not the horse he was, but he still has a race in him judged on this performance. He did too much too soon here and in the end was done for stamina.
**Rainbow World(IRE)**, fitted with cheekpieces on this drop in grade, came clear of the rest of the field and ran a solid race in defeat. Like the runner-up, the fact that he forced the issue eventually played into the hands of the stronger-staying winner.
**Jack Durrance(IRE)** never really got into it, only staying on for a well-beaten fourth place.
**Blue Savanna**, who has disappointed over hurdles since winning on the Polytrack back in March, ran a fair race but he does appear happier on the sand.
**Regulated(IRE)** may have found this race coming too soon only a week after his Leicester success.
**Red Acer(IRE)** *Official explanation: jockey said gelding felt wrong*
**Last Rebel(IRE)** *Official explanation: jockey said gelding lost its action*

## 2741 EBF RETRAINING OF RACEHORSES FILLIES' H'CAP 6f
**9:00** (9:00) (E) (0-75,78) 3-Y-0 **£4,407** (£1,356; £678; £339) **Stalls** High

Form RPR

1464 **1** **Bohola Flyer (IRE)**[32] 1907 3-9-3 **71**........................................ RHughes 6 79
(RHannon) *mid-div: hdwy 2f out: rdn to chal 1f out: styd on u.p to ld ins last: all out* **20/1**

-364 **2** shd **Comeraincomeshine (IRE)**[9] 2482 3-8-3 **60**........................................ RMiles(3) 5 68
(TGMills) *w ldr: led 3f out: c sharply to stands rail over 1f out: hdd ins last: styd on but nt pce of wnr cl home* **14/1**

2-30 **3** 1 **Whistful (IRE)**[32] 1907 3-9-0 **68**........................................ SSanders 2 73
(CFWall) *sn in tch: rdn and hdwy 2f out: drvn to chal 1f out: nt qckn wl ins last* **33/1**

-001 **4** 1 ¼ **Party Princess (IRE)**[12] 2411 3-8-10 **64**........................................ RWinston 4 65
(JAGlover) *bhd: gd hdwy 2f out: drvn to chal 1f out: outpcd ins last* **12/1**

0022 **5** ¾ **Under My Spell**[7] 2518 3-9-2 **70**........................................ SWKelly 8 69
(PDEvans) *in tch: rdn: hdwy and swtchd lft over 1f out: kpt on ins last: nt pce of wnr* **9/1**

0000 **6** shd **Sworn To Secrecy**[7] 2536 3-8-7 **61**........................................(b) JFEgan 7 60
(SKirk) *bhd: hdwy 3f out: rdn to chse ldrs and hung bdly lft wl over 1f out: kpt on but nt rcvr* **25/1**

0060 **7** 1 ½ **Rise**[13] 2378 3-8-3 **57**........................................(b) SCarson 1 51
(AndrewReid) *chsd ldrs: rdn 2f out: wknd fnl f* **33/1**

-003 **8** ¾ **Urban Rose**[7] 2518 3-8-10 **64**........................................ DaneO'Neill 18 56
(JWUnett) *led 3f: styd chsng ldrs tl wknd over 1f out* **14/1**

0-61 **9** shd **Verkhotina**[7] 2518 3-9-10 **78** 6ex........................................ SDrowne 3 70
(RCharlton) *s.i.s: bhd: sme hdwy fr over 1f out: nt a danger* **11/4¹**

2-00 **10** ½ **Pink Supreme**[20] 2211 3-8-13 **70**........................................(t) TPQueally(3) 11 60
(IAWood) *bhd: sme hdwy fr over 1f out: nt rch ldrs* **33/1**

254- **11** ¾ **Sweetest Revenge (IRE)**[160] 6258 3-9-2 **75**........................................ HayleyTurner(5) 9 63
(MDIUsher) *chsd ldrs over 4f* **16/1**

0-56 **12** hd **Turkish Delight**[10] 2457 3-8-8 **62**........................................ NCallan 12 49
(JBalding) *outpcd: sme hdwy whn n.m.r 1/2-way: n.d* **25/1**

4226 **13** ¾ **Princess Kai (IRE)**[9] 2482 3-8-3 **57**........................................(b) SWhitworth 16 42
(RIngram) *chsd ldrs 4f* **25/1**

1-50 **14** nk **Fiddle Me Blue**[21] 2181 3-9-7 **75**........................................ RLMoore 14 59
(HMorrison) *chsd ldrs: wkng whn hmpd over 1f out* **8/1**

-420 **15** 1 ¼ **Gojo (IRE)**[34] 1855 3-9-2 **70**........................................ LDettori 15 50
(BPalling) *early spd* **9/2²**

2144 **16** ½ **Shrink**[10] 2444 3-8-13 **67**........................................(b¹) DHolland 17 46
(MLWBell) *outpcd fr 1/2-way* **11/2³**

03-0 **17** nk **Innclassic (IRE)**[24] 2080 3-9-4 **75**........................................ JFMcDonald(3) 13 53
(BJMeehan) *chsd ldrs over 3f* **33/1**

3606 **18** *3* **Alizar (IRE)**[7] 2518 3-8-3 **57** .................. JQuinn 10 26
(SDow) *in tch to 1/2-way* **50/1**
1m 13.08s (-0.79) **Going Correction** -0.05s/f (Good) **18** Ran SP% **138.3**
Speed ratings: **103,102,101,99,98 98,96,95,95,94 93,93,92,92,90 89,89,85**CSF £282.83 CT £4626.16 TOTE £20.20: £3.90, £3.40, £7.20, £2.70; EX 343.20 Place 6 £1,557,52, Place 5 £297.22.
**Owner** William Durkan **Bred** Swordlestown Stud **Trained** East Everleigh, Wilts
■ Stewards Enquiry : R Miles two-day ban: careless riding (Jun 20,21)

**FOCUS**
A modest race, with the value of the form weakened by the poor performance of the favourite.

**NOTEBOOK**
**Bohola Flyer(IRE)** found this sharp track and quicker ground bringing out the best in her. She lost all chance of winning at Kempton eariler in the season by hanging across the track, but she made no mistake here. She has a progressive profile.
**Comeraincomeshine(IRE)**, first home from what turned out to be a bad draw at Lingfield last time, came with a strong run up the stands'-side rail but was just edged out. She deserves to get off the mark and will surely not be long in doing so.
**Whistful(IRE)** appreciated the quicker conditions having got bogged down in the soft ground at Folkestone last time.
**Party Princess(IRE)** could not deal with a 7lb rise in the handicap.
**Under My Spell**, poorly drawn when runner-up at Chepstow last time, probably needs a stiffer track to be seen at her best. She should not be written off.
**Sworn To Secrecy** did not help her cause by hanging all the way over to the far-side rail in the closing stages. *Official explanation: jockey said filly hung left*
**Verkhotina** had a good draw at Chepstow but still looked a sprinter worth following that day. The 6lb penalty was no excuse and it is more than likely that this race simply came too soon. She deserves the chance to prove this run all wrong.
**Shrink** *Official explanation: jockey said filly ran in snatches*
T/Plt: £2,392.70 to a £1 stake. Pool: £56,050.40. 17.10 winning tickets. T/Qpdt: £702.90 to a £1 stake. Pool: £3,989.90. 4.20 winning tickets. ST

2742 - 2743a (Foreign Racing) - See Raceform Interactive

## 1891 NAAS (L-H)
### Monday, June 7

**OFFICIAL GOING: Good to firm**

## 2744a NAAS SPRINT STKS (LISTED) — 5f
**4:00** (4:15) 3-Y-O+ **£22,922** (£6,725; £3,204; £1,091)

RPR
**1** **Osterhase (IRE)**[16] 2316 5-9-5 104 ..................(b) FMBerry 7 111
(JEMulhern, Ire) *sn prom and led after 1 f: hdd 1/2-way: on terms ins fnl f: styd on wl to gain advantage again cl home* **3/1**[1]
**2** *shd* **Benbaun (IRE)**[23] 2131 3-8-12 ..................(b[1]) DCorby 1 111
(MJWallace) *prom: 2nd tl led fr 1/2-way: rdn and disp ld ins fnl f: no ex and hdd cl home* **6/1**[3]
**3** *2 1/2* **Glocca Morra (IRE)**[239] 5524 6-9-5 102 .................. JPMurtagh 8 101
(WTFarrell, Ire) *s.i.s: impr into 7th fr 2f out: kpt on wl into 3rd 1f out: no threat to ldrs* **7/1**
**4** *2* **Sheer Tenby (IRE)**[24] 2101 7-9-5 99 ..................(bt) JAHeffernan 5 93
(PaulARoche, Ire) *led early: hdd after 1 f: chsd ldrs: rdn in 6th under 2f out: sn no imp: kpt on fr over 1f out* **8/1**
**5** *hd* **Danecare (IRE)**[4] 2625 4-9-5 93 .................. DJCondon 2 92
(JGBurns, Ire) *trckd ldrs: rdn in 4th under 2f out: no imp and kpt on same pce fr 1 1/2f out* **14/1**
**6** *1* **Ulfah (USA)**[29] 1980 3-8-9 90 .................. DPMcDonogh 10 85
(KevinPrendergast, Ire) *chsd ldrs: 6th and kpt on same pce u.p fr 2f out* **14/1**
**7** *1/2* **Marko Jadeo (IRE)**[24] 2101 6-9-5 91 .................. DMGrant 6 86
(PatrickJFlynn, Ire) *trckd ldrs: rdn in 5th 2f out: sn no imp: kpt on same pce fr 1 1/2f out* **25/1**
**8** *1/2* **Tiger Royal (IRE)**[33] 1893 8-9-5 102 ..................(b) PShanahan 3 84
(DKWeld, Ire) *chsd ldrs: rdn and no imp after 1/2-way: eased ins fnl f* **14/1**
**9** *2* **Anna Frid (GER)**[33] 1893 4-9-6 100 .................. PJSmullen 9 77
(DKWeld, Ire) *chsd ldrs: disp 3rd and rdn over 2f out: sn no ex* **10/1**
**10** *1/2* **Symboli West (USA)**[36] 1813 4-9-5 .................. MJKinane 11 74
(JohnMOxx, Ire) *chsd ldrs: rdn and no imp fr 1/2-way* **7/2**[2]
**11** *6* **Prince Monalulu (IRE)**[33] 1893 3-8-12 95 ..................(t) JPSpencer 12 50
(EdwardLynam, Ire) *a towards rr: nvr a factor* **12/1**
**12** *1 1/2* **Maroochydore (IRE)**[29] 1980 3-8-13 100 .................. PCosgrave 13 45
(DavidWachman, Ire) *s.i.s and nvr a threat* **12/1**
**13** *4 1/2* **Blue Crush (IRE)**[16] 2316 3-8-9 99 ..................(b[1]) WMLordan 4 23
(EdwardLynam, Ire) *prom: rdn and wknd fr 1/2-way* **14/1**
58.40 secs **Going Correction** -0.45s/f (Firm)
**WFA** 3 from 4yo+ 7lb **13** Ran SP% **140.1**
Speed ratings: **110,109,105,102,102 100,99,99,99,99 99,99,99**CSF £25.49 TOTE £4.90: £1.90, £1.70, £3.80; DF 29.80.
**Owner** Michael Rosenfeld **Bred** E Kopica & M Rosenfeld **Trained** the Curragh, Co Kildare

**NOTEBOOK**
**Osterhase(IRE)** was soon in front, joined at halfway, he put in a renewed effort close home to settle it on the line.
**Benbaun(IRE)** ran a lot better than his rating and after flattering inside the last was just headed on the line.
**Glocca Morra(IRE)** missed the break but ran on well inside the last. He is hard to place being too high in the better handicaps.
**Sheer Tenby(IRE)**, another handicapper forced into this company, had an Ascot engagement but doesn't travel after this.
**Danecare(IRE)** shaped as if he could be returning to form.
**Ulfah(USA)** also showed a glimmer of ability.
**Symboli West(USA)** never looked comfortable on the ground.

## 2745a SWORDLESTOWN STUD SPRINT STKS (LISTED) (FILLIES) — 6f
**4:30** (4:39) 2-Y-O **£36,676** (£10,760; £5,126; £1,746)

RPR
**1** **Damson (IRE)**[56] 1378 2-8-11 .................. JPSpencer 4 104+
(DavidWachman, Ire) *trckd ldrs: impr to ld travelling wl under 2f out: rdn clr 1f out: eased cl home: comf* **15/8**[2]
**2** *2* **Pictavia (IRE)**[12] 2414 2-8-11 .................. KJManning 1 95
(JSBolger, Ire) *led: jnd and disp ld after 1 1/2 fs: 2nd fr under 2f out: no imp on wnr over 1f out: kpt on same pce fnl f* **11/8**[1]
**3** *1 1/2* **Umniya (IRE)**[9] 2478 2-8-11 .................. TEDurcan 6 91
(MRChannon) *trckd ldrs: mainly 4th: rdn in 3rd and no imp fr 1 1/2f out: kpt on same pce* **7/2**[3]
**4** *3 1/2* **Slip Dance (IRE)**[26] 2048 2-8-11 .................. JAHeffernan 5 80
(EamonTyrrell, Ire) *led and disp and 1 1/2 fs: dropped to 4th and no imp fr over 1 1/2f out: kpt on one pce* **14/1**
**5** *shd* **All Night Dancer (IRE)**[36] 1812 2-8-11 .................. WMLordan 2 80
(DavidWachman, Ire) *chsd ldrs: mainly 5th: rdn and kpt on same pce u.p fr under 2f out* **14/1**
**6** *4* **Yaria (IRE)** 2-8-11 .................. DPMcDonogh 3 68
(KevinPrendergast, Ire) *a bhd and trailing thrght: nvr a danger* **9/1**
1m 10.8s **Going Correction** -0.45s/f (Firm) **6** Ran SP% **122.4**
Speed ratings: **100,97,95,90,90 85**CSF £5.48 TOTE £3.50: £1.70, £1.50; DF 7.30.
**Owner** Mrs John Magnier **Bred** Epona Bloodstock Ltd **Trained** Carrick on Shore, Co Tipperary

**NOTEBOOK**
**Damson(IRE)** looked pretty smart here but might not have had a great deal to beat. Her trainer was keen to play down an ideas of a Queen Mary tilt.
**Pictavia(IRE)** raced prominently throughout but was done for speed by the winner. She needs an extra furlong.
**Umniya(IRE)** came through for third without ever threatening to get on terms with the first pair.
**Slip Dance(IRE)** was not disgraced for a Ballinrobe maiden winner and will appreciate another furlong.

2746 - 2748a (Foreign Racing) - See Raceform Interactive

## 1923 CHESTER (L-H)
### Tuesday, June 8

**OFFICIAL GOING: Good to firm (watered)**
Overwatering rendered the going far softer than the official description suggested. Indeed, times suggest it was riding good to soft.
Wind: almost nil Weather: fine & warm

## 2749 KEMIRA GROW HOW EBF MAIDEN STKS — 5f 16y
**6:20** (6:22) (D) 2-Y-O **£5,343** (£1,644; £822; £411) **Stalls** Low

Form RPR
0 **1** **Dorn Dancer (IRE)**[21] 2213 2-8-6 .................. LEnstone(3) 1 70
(DWBarker) *a.p: led over 2f out: r.o* **16/1**
2 **2** *1/2* **Harvest Warrior**[35] 1871 2-8-11 .................. DAllan(3) 4 73
(TDEasterby) *led: hdd over 2f out: rdn whn n.m.r and outpcd over 1f out: rallied ins fnl f: hld cl home* **8/13**[1]
033 **3** *2 1/2* **Gifted Gamble**[18] 2268 2-9-0 ..................(b) NCallan 8 65
(KARyan) *w ldr: rdn and ev ch over 1f out: no ex ins fnl f* **3/1**[2]
**4** *2 1/2* **Cutlass Gaudy** 2-8-9 .................. StephanieHollinshead(5) 2 56
(RHollinshead) *s.i.s: outpcd: hdwy over 1f out: styd on ins fnl f: nt trble ldrs* **25/1**
**5** *2 1/2* **Menna** 2-8-9 .................. EAhern 9 42
(RHollinshead) *in tch: lost pl 3f out: sn outpcd: kpt on ins fnl f* **25/1**
00 **6** *1/2* **Gloria Nimbus**[17] 2296 2-8-9 .................. SRighton 3 40
(MMullineaux) *racd keenly: chsd ldrs: rdn over 2f out: wknd over 1f out* **100/1**
**7** *1/2* **Oceanico Dot Com (IRE)** 2-8-9 .................. FNorton 6 39
(ABerry) *chsd ldrs: sn rdn along: wknd over 1f out* **20/1**
**8** *1* **Madame Topflight** 2-8-9 .................. GDuffield 5 35
(MrsGSRees) *in tch: rdn over 2f out: wknd over 1f out* **10/1**[3]
**9** *15* **Doughty** 2-9-0 .................. VSlattery 7 —
(DJWintle) *s.i.s: a bhd* **66/1**
64.04 secs (2.06) **Going Correction** +0.40s/f (Good) **9** Ran SP% **116.8**
Speed ratings: **99,98,94,90,86 85,84,83,59**CSF £26.26 TOTE £10.40: £1.90, £1.10, £1.40; EX 22.20.
**Owner** The Ebor Partnership **Bred** Timothy Coughlan **Trained** Scorton, N Yorks

**FOCUS**
Just a modest maiden and the form is ordinary.

**NOTEBOOK**
**Dorn Dancer(IRE)** missed the break on her debut and could never get into the race, but she had clearly learnt plenty from that experience and was quicker off the mark on this occasion. From the best draw, she tracked the leader on the rail before taking up the running just after halfway. She was always holding the favourite, but this does not look strong form and it would not be wise to get carried away.
**Harvest Warrior** was sent off a short price on the back of a promising debut effort, but he was tackling quicker ground on this occasion and, although running on again at the finish, was never quite doing enough. He will be suited by a step up in trip.
**Gifted Gamble** had more racing experience than any other runner in the field but was poorly drawn. His early effort to overcome that disadvantage may have cost him in the end.
**Cutlass Gaudy**, a half-brother to dual course juvenile winner Jimmy Too and three-time winner Princess Efisio, struggled to go the early pace but kept on in good style. He ran best of those making their racecourse debuts.
**Menna** is a half-sister to seven winners, including Jersey Stakes winner Lots Of Magic, and should be suited by farther than this in time.

## 2750 PARK TRAVEL RATED STKS (H'CAP) — 7f 2y
**6:50** (6:50) (C) (0-95,93) 3-Y-O+ **£8,720** (£3,307; £1,653; £751) **Stalls** Low

Form RPR
6454 **1** **H Harrison (IRE)**[15] 2366 4-8-8 **76** .................. RFfrench 1 90
(IWMcinnes) *led early: sn hdd: remained prom: led over 2f out: rdn over 1f out: r.o wl* **15/2**[3]
0-34 **2** *2 1/2* **Bandit Queen**[9] 2506 4-9-4 **86** .................. PRobinson 8 94
(WJarvis) *hld up bhd: nt clr run over 2f out: hdwy and swtchd rt over 1f out: r.o ins fnl f: nt rch wnr* **16/1**
0042 **3** *hd* **True Night**[10] 2477 7-8-9 **77** .................. EAhern 4 84
(DNicholls) *in tch: rdn and nt qckn over 2f out: styd on ins fnl f* **7/4**[1]
-005 **4** *1* **Onlytime Will Tell**[5] 2625 6-9-11 **93** .................. RWinston 2 97
(DNicholls) *in tch: rdn over 2f out: chsd wnr over 1f out tl ins fnl f: no etxra towards fin* **16/1**
4200 **5** *hd* **Up Tempo (IRE)**[11] 2459 6-8-8 **76** ..................(b) NCallan 7 80
(KARyan) *towards rr: pushed along over 4f out: nt clr run under 2f out and again whn hdwy 1f out: styd on ins fnl f* **22/1**
0001 **6** *2 1/2* **Master Robbie**[9] 2503 5-9-6 **91** 3ex .................. SHitchcott(3) 3 88
(MRChannon) *hld up: rdn and hdwy whn nt clr run over 2f out: wknd ins fnl f* **4/1**[2]
-304 **7** *1* **Val De Maal (IRE)**[13] 2407 4-8-1 **76** oh7 .................. DeanWilliams(7) 5 71
(GCHChung) *sn led: rdn and hdd over 2f out: wknd 1f out* **50/1**
-602 **8** *5* **Flying Express**[10] 2469 4-9-3 **85** .................. MHills 9 67
(BWHills) *midfield: effrt on outside 3f out: wknd 2f out* **4/1**[2]
-603 **9** *2* **Dame De Noche**[17] 2282 4-9-6 **88** .................. GDuffield 6 65
(JGGiven) *prom: rdn over 2f out: sn wknd* **9/1**
1m 28.47s (0.18) **Going Correction** +0.40s/f (Good) **9** Ran SP% **116.2**
Speed ratings: **114,111,110,109,109 106,105,99,97**CSF £118.32 CT £304.76 TOTE £9.30: £2.00, £4.00, £1.40; EX 166.70.
**Owner** Ivy House Racing **Bred** Margaret Conlon **Trained** Catwick, E Yorks

**FOCUS**
A decent handicap with a good pace and a very fast time indeed for the grade of contest.
**NOTEBOOK**
**H Harrison(IRE)**, ideally drawn, bagged the rail and travelled well behind the leader for most of the race, before taking it up decisively approaching the quarter-mile pole. A seven-furlong specialist, he struggled off marks in the 80s last year and early this season, so could be vulnerable once reassessed, but he did win this with authority.
**Bandit Queen** had never run over a trip this far before, but she seemed suited by the longer distance. Held up off the pace from her wide draw, she finished well for second, and this performance should open up new opportunities for her.
**True Night**, 1lb higher than when last successful, proved expensive for punters last season, winning only once and being beaten four times at 3-1 or shorter in the summer. He had the race run to suit but just found two too good.
**Onlytime Will Tell** was probably suited by the ground riding easier than the official description, but he continues to look high in the handicap.
**Up Tempo(IRE)** is another who would have been suited by the overwatering which had taken place at the track.
**Master Robbie**, whose style of running is probably not ideal for this track, has never followed up after any one of his nine wins.
**Flying Express** was well backed but could not overcome his poor draw. *Official explanation: jockey said colt was unsuited by the ground.*

## 2751 ERNST & YOUNG CLASSIFIED STKS — 1m 2f 75y
**7:20** (7:21) (D) 3-Y-O — **£5,421** (£1,668; £834; £417) **Stalls** High

Form — RPR
1-35 **1** **Daytime Girl (IRE)**[41] [1714] 3-8-12 76 ... MHills 1 — 76
(BWHills) *mde virtually all: rdn 3f out: r.o* — **5/1**[3]
-210 **2** *2* **Magic Amigo**[17] [2281] 3-9-0 71 ... EAhern 3 — 74
(JRJenkins) *trckd ldrs: rdn to chse wnr 3f out: styd on same pce fnl f* **20/1**
60-6 **3** *2 ½* **Turner**[18] [2273] 3-9-0 73 ... GDuffield 2 — 69
(WMBrisbourne) *hld up in rr: nt clr run over 3f out: over 2f out and whn hdwy over 1f out: styd on ins fnl f: nt trble ldrs* — **40/1**
13-6 **4** *½* **Penzance**[36] [1831] 3-9-3 78 ... JPMurtagh 5 — 72
(JRFanshawe) *in tch: rdn over 2f out: sme hdwy over 1f out: one pce ins fnl f* — **7/2**[1]
25-5 **5** *½* **Mommkin**[19] [2244] 3-8-9 76 ... SHitchcott[(3)] 6 — 66
(MRChannon) *hld up: rdn and hdwy 3f out: one pce fnl f* — **17/2**
5634 **6** *8* **Weet A Head (IRE)**[11] [2448] 3-9-4 79 ... NCallan 8 — 56
(RHollinshead) *chsd ldrs: niggled along 5f out: rdn over 3f out: edgd lft and wknd over 2f out* — **11/2**
1-35 **7** *5* **Kristal's Dream (IRE)**[22] [2169] 3-8-11 74 ... KDarley 4 — 40
(JLDunlop) *prom: rdn 5f out: wknd 2f out: eased ins fnl f* — **7/2**[1]
31 **8** *½* **Yaahomm**[23] [2145] 3-9-1 79 ... TPQueally[(3)] 7 — 46
(DRLoder) *hld up: struggling 5f out: nvr on terms* — **9/2**[2]

2m 15.94s (3.39) **Going Correction** +0.40s/f (Good) — **8** Ran SP% **112.4**
Speed ratings: **102,100,98,98,97 91,87,86**CSF £90.64 TOTE £4.50: £1.40, £3.40, £3.90; EX 111.10.
**Owner** Bonnycastle, Concord Racing, Morton **Bred** Bernard Cooke **Trained** Lambourn, Berks

**FOCUS**
A fair classified contest, and the third race on the trot to fall to the horse in stall one.
**NOTEBOOK**
**Daytime Girl(IRE)**, who ran no sort of race in heavy ground last time, was given a positive ride and was never in any real trouble. She may have been flattered by the way the race was run but, on this evidence, will be worth another try over a mile and a half, as she got this trip really well.
**Magic Amigo** disappointed on fast ground last time and the overwatering meant that the ground was more in his favour. He could struggle while the warm weather persists, though.
**Turner** had a troubled passage. Continually denied a run on the final bend and in the straight itself, he would undoubtedly have finished a lot closer with more luck.
**Penzance** kept on well enough in the straight despite hanging right, but he never landed a blow.
**Mommkin** will probably be better suited by a more galloping track.
**Kristal's Dream(IRE)** may have found the ground easier than ideal. *Official explanation: jockey said filly had a breathing problem.*
**Yaahomm** was representing a trainer struggling for form. *Official explanation: jockey said colt was unsuited by the track.*

## 2752 BANK OF SCOTLAND H'CAP — 1m 2f 75y
**7:50** (7:50) (D) (0-80,80) 3-Y-O+ — **£5,538** (£1,704; £852; £426) **Stalls** High

Form — RPR
00-2 **1** **Frontier**[21] [2210] 7-9-3 69 ... (t) DSweeney 5 — 79
(BJLlewellyn) *trckd ldrs: lost pl over 4f out: swtchd rt and rallied over 2f out: led over 1f out: all out* — **9/2**[1]
5052 **2** *shd* **Compton Dragon (USA)**[6] [2583] 5-9-7 73 ... (v) ANicholls 3 — 83
(DNicholls) *midfield: rdn and hdwy over 2f out: edgd lft 1f out: r.o ins fnl f* — **11/2**[2]
0110 **3** *1* **Summer Bounty**[10] [2474] 8-9-10 76 ... JPMurtagh 8 — 84
(FJordan) *s.i.s: hld up: rdn and hdwy under 2f out: hmpd 1f out: sn swtchd rt: r.o* — **20/1**
3524 **4** *3* **Trouble Mountain (USA)**[14] [2394] 7-9-4 70 ... (b) KDarley 2 — 72
(MWEasterby) *hld up: hdwy whn nt clr run 1f out: sn rdn: styd on: nt trble ldrs* — **6/1**[3]
0400 **5** *1 ½* **Gallant Boy (IRE)**[104] [887] 5-9-5 74 ... (vt) FPFerris[(3)] 9 — 73
(PDEvans) *hld up: rdn and nt clr run over 2f out: styd on ins fnl f* — **16/1**
5031 **6** *½* **Rotuma (IRE)**[6] [2583] 5-8-13 68 6ex ... (b) LEnstone[(3)] 12 — 66
(MDods) *midfield: hdwy over 4f out: riddden over 2f out: carried lft 1f out: sn wknd* — **12/1**
3000 **7** *1* **Ezz Elkheil**[17] [2305] 5-9-1 70 ... TPQueally[(3)] 13 — 67
(JRJenkins) *led: hdd over 4f out: rdn over 2f out: wkng whn n.m.r 1f out* — **25/1**
-040 **8** *5* **Newcorp Lad**[21] [2218] 4-9-0 66 ... GDuffield 4 — 53
(MrsGSRees) *prom: stmbld over 4f out: rdn 2f out: wkng whn n.m.r over 1f out* — **50/1**
-000 **9** *nk* **Everest (IRE)**[23] [2142] 7-10-0 80 ... FNorton 1 — 66
(BEllison) *bhd: nvr trbld ldrs* — **10/1**
5035 **10** *3* **Skibereen (IRE)**[15] [2368] 4-9-3 69 ... RFfrench 10 — 50
(IWMcinnes) *hedl up: effrt 3f out: wknd 2f out* — **16/1**
410- **11** *3* **Rani Two**[255] [5215] 5-9-3 74 ... NChalmers[(5)] 7 — 49
(WMBrisbourne) *midfield: hdwy over 4f out: rdn over 2f out: sn wknd* **14/1**
0124 **12** *½* **Lawood (IRE)**[18] [2272] 4-9-9 75 ... NCallan 11 — 49
(KARyan) *trckd ldrs: rdn over 2f out: wknd over 1f out* — **14/1**
-002 **13** *¾* **Movie King (IRE)**[7] [2547] 5-8-13 65 ... (p) RWinston 6 — 38
(SGollings) *racd keenly: prom: led over 4f out: rdn and hdd over 1f out: sn hmpd whn wkng* — **9/2**[1]

2m 16.04s (3.49) **Going Correction** +0.40s/f (Good) — **13** Ran SP% **118.5**
Speed ratings: **102,101,101,98,97 97,96,92,92,89 87,86,86**CSF £27.39 CT £454.67 TOTE £6.30: £2.70, £2.20, £3.90; EX 43.40.
**Owner** F Jeffers **Bred** Mrs T Stopford-Sackville & London T'Bred Services **Trained** Fochriw, Caerphilly

■ Stewards Enquiry : A Nicholls three-day ban: careless riding (Jun 19-21)
**FOCUS**
A modest handicap.
**NOTEBOOK**
**Frontier ◆**, up 3lb for his excellent Leicester effort, is best with a little cut. He had to be switched wide to come around horses turning into the straight, but quickened up in great style to go clear. He was being pegged back at the end, but his turn of foot should stand him in good stead and he looks worth following while in such good heart.
**Compton Dragon(USA)** is in good form and on a winning mark at the moment. He ran on well to close the winner down and his time is surely near.
**Summer Bounty**, held up well off the pace, put a poor performance in a higher grade race at Kempton behind him and ran well considering he did not enjoy the smoothest of passages.
**Trouble Mountain(USA)**, who is difficult to win with, ran a typical sort of race, staying on without quite doing enough.
**Gallant Boy(IRE)**, having his first outing since February, ran a promising enough race on his reappearance and is well handicapped on last year's form.
**Rotuma(IRE)** did not run too badly given his wide draw.
**Movie King(IRE)**, who did not get his own way in front, prefers quicker ground.

## 2753 EDWARDS HOMES & BRYN THOMAS H'CAP (LADY AMATEUR RIDERS) — 1m 4f 66y
**8:20** (8:20) (E) (0-75,74) 3-Y-O+ — **£3,523** (£1,084; £542; £271) **Stalls** Low

Form — RPR
3241 **1** **Shape Up (IRE)**[9] [2501] 4-9-7 53 3ex ... (b) MissLynseyHanna 7 — 65
(TKeddy) *trckd ldrs: led over 1f out: rdn ins fnl f whn pressed: r.o* — **5/2**[1]
4511 **2** *shd* **Yenaled**[24] [2128] 7-10-3 63 ... MissNCarberry 6 — 75
(KARyan) *hld up: hdwy 3f out: rdn over 1f out: ev ch ins fnl f: r.o* — **11/2**[2]
32-3 **3** *5* **Dick The Taxi**[31] [592] 10-10-7 67 ... MissEJJones 11 — 71
(RJSmith) *led: rdn and hdd over 1f out: wknd ins fnl f* — **8/1**[3]
0400 **4** *shd* **Lennel**[12] [2424] 6-9-13 64 ... (p) MissJoeyEllis[(5)] 9 — 68
(ABailey) *s.s: bhd: hdwy over 1f out: r.o ins fnl f: nrst fin* — **14/1**
500- **5** *1* **Sualda (IRE)**[243] [5463] 5-9-8 59 ... MissVTunnicliffe[(5)] 14 — 61
(RAFahey) *trckd ldrs: lost pl over 2f out: kpt on ins fnl f* — **14/1**
0130 **6** *hd* **Rajam**[10] [2491] 6-10-11 74 ... (v) MissKellyHarrison[(3)] 10 — 76
(DNicholls) *midfield: hdwy over 3f out: rdn over 2f out: wknd ins fnl f* **12/1**
-656 **7** *4* **Rainstorm**[4] [2643] 9-8-9 44 ... MrsSOwen[(3)] 5 — 40
(WMBrisbourne) *s.i.s: bhd: kpt on fnl f: nvr nrr* — **16/1**
004 **8** *hd* **Sarn**[4] [2649] 5-8-4 42 oh1 ow1 ... MissMMullineaux[(7)] 1 — 38
(MMullineaux) *hld up: kpt on fnl f: nvr able to chal* — **16/1**
25-0 **9** *1 ¾* **Shalbeblue (IRE)**[9] [2501] 7-9-1 50 ... (b) MissLEllison[(3)] 4 — 43
(BEllison) *midfield: hdwy over 3f out: rdn and wknd over 1f out* — **20/1**
0600 **10** *5* **Adalar (IRE)**[21] [2210] 4-10-0 63 ... MissEFolkes[(3)] 13 — 48
(PDEvans) *prom: rdn over 2f out: wknd over 1f out* — **50/1**
5305 **11** *4* **Summer Special**[15] [2375] 4-9-1 47 ... MsCWilliams 2 — 25
(DWBarker) *midfield: hdwy over 4f out: rdn over 2f out: sn wknd* — **8/1**[3]
0-66 **12** *hd* **Grady**[13] [2408] 5-8-10 42 oh4 ... MissAElsey 8 — 20
(WMBrisbourne) *midfield: rdn 3f out: wknd 2f out* — **33/1**
600- **13** *4* **Honeystreet (IRE)**[201] [5498] 4-9-9 55 ... MissSBrotherton 3 — 26
(JDFrost) *midfield: wknd 3f out* — **16/1**
-110 **14** *4* **Fleetfoot Mac**[7] [2561] 3-8-13 65 ... MissMSowerby[(5)] 12 — 30
(PDEvans) *prom tl rdn and wknd over 2f out* — **12/1**

2m 48.22s (7.70) **Going Correction** +0.40s/f (Good)
**WFA** 3 from 4yo+ 15lb — **14** Ran SP% **123.5**
Speed ratings: **90,89,86,86,85 85,83,82,81,78 75,75,72,70**CSF £13.75 CT £92.03 TOTE £3.90: £2.00, £2.30, £2.00; EX 14.90.
**Owner** Andrew Duffield **Bred** Gainsborough Stud Management Ltd **Trained** Newmarket, Suffolk

**FOCUS**
A moderate race run at a slow pace, but an exciting finish.
**NOTEBOOK**
**Shape Up(IRE)** enjoyed a dream run on the inside and looked sure to score easily when taking it up, but in the end he was all out to hold on. He does travel well in his races.
**Yenaled**, whose rider got the best out of him, stayed on well to take the race to the wire. He only narrowly failed but confirmed that he is in top form at present, and this longer trip proved no problem at all.
**Dick The Taxi**, back on the Flat after a spell over fences, was only having his third outing of his career on turf. This was not a bad performance but he had his own way in front.
**Lennel**, racing off a 1lb lower mark than for his last win, has never won over a trip this far but, having been held up off the pace, came through to see his race out well.
**Sualda(IRE)** is well handicapped at present and should be all the better for this reappearance outing.
**Rajam** found this ground easier than ideal.

## 2754 SAFFIE JOSEPH & SONS RATED STKS (H'CAP) — 5f 16y
**8:50** (8:50) (D) (0-85,78) 3-Y-O+ — **£4,903** (£1,860; £930; £422) **Stalls** Low

Form — RPR
0650 **1** **Awake**[31] [1956] 7-9-0 70 ... EAhern 3 — 84
(DNicholls) *trckd ldrs gng wl: led over 1f out: r.o wl* — **4/1**[1]
3422 **2** *2 ½* **Romany Nights (IRE)**[5] [2626] 4-9-5 78 ... (b) SHitchcott[(3)] 10 — 83
(JWUnett) *towards rr: rdn 3f out: hdwy over 1f out: r.o ins fnl f: nt rch wnr* — **11/1**
5003 **3** *nk* **Prince Of Blues (IRE)**[5] [2626] 6-7-13 62 ... (p) PVarley[(7)] 9 — 66
(MMullineaux) *in tch: rdn 2f out: hdwy over 1f out: styd on ins fnl f* — **25/1**
34-0 **4** *nk* **Domirati**[10] [2477] 4-9-8 78 ... RWinston 4 — 81
(RCharlton) *trckd ldrs: nt clr run and lost pl over 1f out: swtchd lft ent fnl f: r.o* — **5/1**[2]
-032 **5** *nk* **Melody King**[5] [2610] 3-8-0 66 ... (b) FPFerris[(3)] 1 — 68
(PDEvans) *led: rdn over 2f out: hdd over 1f out: no ex ins fnl f* — **11/2**[3]
000- **6** *1* **Perfect Setting**[283] [4586] 4-8-10 66 ... DSweeney 5 — 64
(PJMakin) *hld up: hdwy 2f out: sn rdn: no ex ins fnl f* — **28/1**
0301 **7** *¾* **Whistler**[5] [2628] 7-9-8 78 3ex ... (p) RFfrench 6 — 74
(JMBradley) *towards rr: rdn 3f out: nvr able to chal* — **4/1**[1]
0064 **8** *½* **Obe One**[10] [2490] 4-8-13 69 ... FNorton 11 — 63
(ABerry) *s.i.s: outpcd: n.m.r ins fnl f: nvr able to chal* — **16/1**
20-0 **9** *2 ½* **Wicked Uncle**[5] [2628] 5-9-6 76 ... (p) KDarley 2 — 61
(SGollings) *w ldrs tl rdn 2f out: wknd over 1f out* — **7/1**
0300 **10** *nk* **Piccled**[31] [1956] 6-9-4 77 ... DAllan[(3)] 7 — 61
(EJAlston) *s.s: bhd: effrt 2f out: no imp* — **20/1**
1050 **11** *8* **Chico Guapo (IRE)**[17] [2293] 4-9-5 75 ... IMongan 8 — 30
(JAGlover) *w ldr tl rdn 2f out: wknd over 1f out* — **12/1**

63.51 secs (1.53) **Going Correction** +0.40s/f (Good)
**WFA** 3 from 4yo+ 7lb — **11** Ran SP% **118.5**
Speed ratings: **103,99,98,98,97 95,94,93,89,89 76**CSF £48.26 CT £998.43 TOTE £5.40: £2.60, £2.70, £6.50; EX 95.40 Place 6 £117.32, Place 5 £103.78.
**Owner** Lucayan Stud & D Nicholls **Bred** Side Hill Stud **Trained** Sessay, N Yorks

**FOCUS**
A fair handicap, run at a decent pace.

**NOTEBOOK**
**Awake**, who had no chance from his draw on his last two starts, had a favourable low box this time and, with the ground easier than advertised, the surface to suit, too. He travelled well throughout, won easily and is clearly well handicapped at present.
**Romany Nights(IRE)** had little chance from his draw but he found the strong pace playing into his hands, and he came from way off the pace to take second. He is not an easy horse to win with, though.
**Prince Of Blues(IRE)**, who is another who finds winning difficult, was also done no favours with the draw.
**Domirati** is a consistent animal, had a decent draw and looked set for a good run. He would certainly have finished second had he not met trouble in running.
**Melody King**, the only three-year-old in the field, tried to make the most of his box draw but was taken on for the lead by Chico Guapo. This was a good effort considering the pace they went.
**Perfect Setting**, who has been lightly raced, was making his seasonal reappearance and shaped encouragingly. He travelled well and was not knocked about once his chance had gone, and there is surely a race in him.
**Whistler**, whose style of running would not be ideally suited to this track, could never get competitive.
T/Plt: £122.70 to a £1 stake. Pool: £63,623.85. 378.50 winning tickets. T/Qpdt: £56.40 to a £1 stake. Pool: £3,226.70. 42.30 winning tickets. DO

## 2550 REDCAR (L-H)
### Tuesday, June 8
**OFFICIAL GOING: Firm (good to firm in places)**

## 2755 MAGNUM (S) STKS — 7f
**2:30** (2:32) (G) 2-Y-O — **£2,947** (£842; £421) **Stalls** Centre

| Form | | | | RPR |
|---|---|---|---|---|
| 36 | 1 | | **Maureen's Lough (IRE)**[40] 1717 2-8-6 ... PFessey 4 *(TDBarron) mde all: drvn out fnl f* **3/1**[2] | 40 |
| 0 | 2 | 1 ½ | **Dan's Heir**[18] 2268 2-8-11 ...(p) GFaulkner 2 *(PCHaslam) trckd wnr: rdn 2f out: styd on fnl f: no imp* **9/4**[1] | 42 |
| 5600 | 3 | 5 | **Joe Ninety (IRE)**[5] 2609 2-8-4 ... DerekNolan(7) 5 *(JSMoore) prom: rdn and outpcd by first 2 over 1f out* **7/2**[3] | 29 |
| 6 | 4 | hd | **Riverweld**[23] 2140 2-8-11 ... FLynch 6 *(GMMoore) prom: rdn over 2f out: kpt on same pce* **4/1** | 29 |
| 0 | 5 | ¾ | **Singhalongtasveer**[23] 2140 2-8-11 ... JBramhill 1 *(WStorey) prom: rdn 2f out: sn btn* **33/1** | 27 |
| 0 | 6 | 9 | **Highbury Lass**[14] 2388 2-7-13 ... RoryMoore(7) 7 *(PCHaslam) dwlt: towards rr: rdn 3f out: lost tch over 1f out* **20/1** | — |
| 0 | 7 | 7 | **Mickey Boggitt**[14] 2388 2-8-11 ... FNorton 3 *(ABerry) bhd and rdn 1/2-way: lost tch over 1f out* **14/1** | — |

1m 26.72s (1.82) **Going Correction** -0.025s/f (Good) 7 Ran SP% **112.4**
Speed ratings: **88,86,80,80,79 69,61**CSF £9.81 TOTE £2.90: £1.90, £2.20; EX 11.30.The winner was bought in for 5,800 guineas.
**Owner** Oghill House Stud **Bred** Paul Hyland **Trained** Maunby, N Yorks
**FOCUS**
A weak juvenile seller run at a slow pace that saw the first two clear at the finish.
**NOTEBOOK**
**Maureen's Lough(IRE)** pinged out of the gates and never looked like getting caught at any stage. She showed the benefit of her previous experience late on and responded well to pressure to pull out more when asked, but this looks about as good as she is, and it is likely she would struggle at a higher level.
**Dan's Heir** took time to hit full stride and was doing all of his best work too late in the day. This experience will not be lost on him and he looks the one to take out of the race, with a similar contest within his compass.
**Joe Ninety(IRE)** ran his best race to date on this drop in grade, but the step up to this trip did not suit as expected, and he looks very one-paced on this evidence.
**Riverweld** again ran a touch green and found the penny dropping all too late in the day. This does not conclusively prove he gets the trip, but he is entitled to come on again for the experience.

## 2756 THE EAST CLEVELAND ADVERTISER H'CAP — 7f
**3:00** (3:01) (E) (0-70,68) 3-Y-O — **£3,935** (£1,211; £605; £302) **Stalls** Centre

| Form | | | | RPR |
|---|---|---|---|---|
| -000 | 1 | | **Dark Day Blues (IRE)**[19] 2251 3-9-2 **63** ... DarrenWilliams 2 *(MDHammond) midfield: hdwy 3f out: rdn to ld 2f out: styd on u.p* **20/1** | 69 |
| 0003 | 2 | 1 ¼ | **Adorata (GER)**[21] 2211 3-9-2 **63** ... OUrbina 6 *(JJay) trckd ldrs: rdn to chse wnr over 1f out: styd on: no imp* **7/1**[2] | 66 |
| 0-00 | 3 | nk | **Washbrook**[15] 2371 3-8-11 **58** ... JCarroll 4 *(AndrewTurnell) hld up: hdwy 3f out: chsng first 2 and styng on whn hmpd ent fnl f: styd on u.p* **22/1** | 60 |
| 6600 | 4 | hd | **Orion Express**[21] 2197 3-8-10 **62** ... PMulrennan(5) 12 *(MWEasterby) s.i.s: towards rr: hdwy 3f out: rdn over 1f out: styd on fnl f: nvr able to chal* **6/1**[1] | 63 |
| 6063 | 5 | ½ | **Menai Straights**[10] 2487 3-8-13 **60** ...(p) FNorton 3 *(RFFisher) cl up: rdn over 2f out: kpt on same pce* **8/1**[3] | 60 |
| 0605 | 6 | ½ | **Compton Micky**[4] 2660 3-8-11 **58** ...(p) JEdmunds 15 *(JBalding) trckd ldrs: keen early: rdn over 2f out: styd on fnl f* **20/1** | 57 |
| 3050 | 7 | 1 | **Uhuru Peak**[11] 2457 3-8-10 **57** ... DaleGibson 7 *(MWEasterby) cl up: rdn over 2f out: fdd fr over 1f out* **16/1** | 53 |
| 4-40 | 8 | shd | **Top Line Dancer (IRE)**[57] 1358 3-9-7 **68** ... KDalgleish 8 *(MJohnston) midfield: rdn 2f out: no real hdwy* **6/1**[1] | 64 |
| 34-6 | 9 | 1 ½ | **Sweet Cando (IRE)**[25] 2075 3-9-1 **62** ... PHanagan 9 *(MissLAPerratt) prom: drvn along 3f out: fdd fnl 2f* **7/1**[2] | 54 |
| -000 | 10 | ½ | **Killoch Place (IRE)**[43] 1667 3-7-7 **45** oh3...(v) BSwarbrick(5) 14 *(JAGlover) cl up: slt ld fr 1/2-way tl hdd 2f out: sn btn* **20/1** | 36 |
| 060 | 11 | 4 | **Hana Dee**[17] 2306 3-9-1 **62** ... ACulhane 13 *(MRChannon) dwlt: a rr div* **9/1** | 42 |
| 6-04 | 12 | 3 ½ | **Colloseum**[18] 2259 3-8-12 **59** ... KMcEvoy 11 *(TJEtherington) slt ld tl hdd 1/2-way: sn wknd* **9/1** | 30 |
| -000 | 13 | hd | **Lupine Howl**[15] 2351 3-8-1 **48** ... SRighton 1 *(BAMcmahon) sn bhd* **25/1** | 19 |
| 305- | 14 | ½ | **Speed Racer**[267] 4933 3-9-1 **62** ... KimTinkler 5 *(DonEnricoIncisa) midfield to 1/2-way: sn bhd* **33/1** | 31 |

1m 25.2s (0.30) **Going Correction** -0.025s/f (Good) 14 Ran SP% **116.0**
Speed ratings: **97,95,95,95,94 93,92,92,90,90 85,81,81,80**CSF £129.72 CT £2698.17 TOTE £22.60: £7.40, £2.40, £9.10; EX 182.80.
**Owner** Mike Newbould **Bred** Derek Iceton **Trained** Middleham, N Yorks
**FOCUS**
A modest affair run at a reasonable pace.

**NOTEBOOK**
**Dark Day Blues(IRE)**, placed off an 8lb higher mark over this trip last year, picked up strongly under pressure to win tidily. This was a big improvement on his recent efforts and he could be capable of following up off a higher mark, now his confidence has been boosted. *Official explanation: trainer said, regarding the improved form shown, gelding had settled better both prior to and during today's race*
**Adorata(GER)** ran a respectable race on this handicap bow and got the trip well. She can be placed to advantage in this grade and has really improved for fast ground of late.
**Washbrook** found traffic problems when finishing with effect from off the pace inside the last furlong. He has to be rated slightly better than the bare form, looks to be coming to himself and is now showing the benefit of a recent slide in the weights.
**Orion Express**, dropping in trip, did himself few favours by missing the break and was staying on all too late. He was well backed for this and could be capable of better.
**Menai Straights** ran a fair race on this drop in trip and responded positively to the cheekpieces.
**Top Line Dancer(IRE)**, well-backed for this handicap debut, failed to improve on his previous efforts and looks a tricky customer.

## 2757 ANDERSON BARROWCLIFF FILLIES' H'CAP — 1m
**3:30** (3:32) (E) (0-70,70) 3-Y-O+ — **£4,277** (£1,316; £658; £329) **Stalls** Centre

| Form | | | | RPR |
|---|---|---|---|---|
| U362 | 1 | | **Brilliantrio**[6] 2597 6-8-4 **51** ... PMakin(5) 6 *(MCChapman) dwlt: hld up: gd hdwy 3f out: rdn to ld 2f out: styd on wl* **7/1** | 63 |
| 3303 | 2 | 2 ½ | **Oh So Rosie (IRE)**[8] 2521 4-8-9 **58** ... DerekNolan(7) 3 *(JSMoore) hld up in rr: hdwy 3f out: chsd wnr fnl f: styd on u.p: no imp* **6/1**[3] | 64 |
| 333- | 3 | 1 ¾ | **Westcourt Dream**[262] 5070 4-8-4 **46** ... DaleGibson 11 *(MWEasterby) trckd ldrs: drvn along and outpcd over 2f out: styd on u.p fnl f* **5/1**[2] | 48 |
| -652 | 4 | shd | **Summer Shades**[8] 2521 6-9-8 **69** ... BSwarbrick(5) 9 *(WMBrisbourne) trckd ldrs: led wl over 2f out: rdn and hdd wl over 1f out: kpt on same pce* **5/2**[1] | 71 |
| 4212 | 5 | 2 | **Dalriath**[13] 2231 5-7-5 **40** oh1 ... CHaddon(7) 12 *(MCChapman) keen: trckd ldrs: rdn over 2f out: kpt on same pce* **9/1** | 37 |
| -000 | 6 | 1 ½ | **Uno Mente**[21] 2216 5-8-13 **55** ... KimTinkler 2 *(DonEnricoIncisa) in tch: reminder 1/2-way: ch and rdn 2f out: fdd* **14/1** | 49 |
| 0600 | 7 | 1 ¼ | **Aimee's Delight**[13] 2410 4-10-0 **70** ... MFenton 8 *(JGGiven) dwlt: towards rr: rdn fnl 2f: n.d* **10/1** | 61 |
| 0005 | 8 | hd | **Celtic Romance**[29] 1992 5-8-7 **49** ... JCarroll 4 *(MrsMReveley) dwlt: hld up: hdwy 1/2-way: ch and rdn 2f out: wknd fnl f* **12/1** | 39 |
| 0002 | 9 | 1 ½ | **Miss Ocean Monarch**[15] 2345 4-7-5 **40** ... DFentiman(7) 1 *(DWChapman) led tl hdd wl over 2f out: sn rdn and wknd* **14/1** | 27 |
| 62-0 | 10 | nk | **Acca Larentia (IRE)**[14] 2390 3-7-8 **52** ... HayleyTurner(5) 5 *(RMWhitaker) prom tl rdn and wknd 3f out* **33/1** | 38 |
| 0000 | 11 | 6 | **Cryptogam**[7] 2551 4-8-4 **49** ow2 ... TEaves(3) 10 *(MESowersby) prom tl rdn and wknd over 3f out* **66/1** | 21 |

1m 37.27s (-0.43) **Going Correction** -0.025s/f (Good)
**WFA** 3 from 4yo+ 11lb 11 Ran SP% **116.6**
Speed ratings: **101,98,96,96,94 93,91,91,90,89 83**CSF £48.23 CT £234.49 TOTE £9.50: £2.90, £2.60, £2.10; EX 60.80.
**Owner** Jack Wilson **Bred** Floors Farming **Trained** Market Rasen, Lincs
**FOCUS**
A modest handicap run at an ordinary gallop.
**NOTEBOOK**
**Brilliantrio**, despite again proving troublesome at the start and missing the break, was always travelling sweetly just off the pace and showed a neat turn of foot to settle the issue two out. This was a pleasing return to form and she was value for more than the official winning margin as she looked to be idling a touch when in the lead, and although she is quirky, she is useful on her day.
**Oh So Rosie(IRE)** stayed on best of all to bag second, but had no chance with the winner. She is a versatile filly, who continues to run consistently without winning.
**Westcourt Dream** ◆ got badly outpaced approaching two out, but picked up well late on under maximum pressure and will strip an awful lot fitter next time. This lightly-raced filly remains one to keep an eye on for a similar event.
**Summer Shades** looked to be going every bit as well as the eventual winner approaching two out, but could not find a change of gear and could only keep on at the one pace. This was, however, another creditable effort.
**Dalriath** ran keen early on and had little left in the tank when push came to shove over two furlongs from home.

## 2758 METHUSELAH MEDIAN AUCTION MAIDEN STKS — 6f
**4:00** (4:03) (E) 2-Y-O — **£3,659** (£1,126; £563; £281) **Stalls** Centre

| Form | | | | RPR |
|---|---|---|---|---|
| 523 | 1 | | **Lincolneurocruiser**[25] 2086 2-8-7 ... JDO'Reilly(7) 4 *(JO'Reilly) mde virtually all: stmbld over 1f out: drifted rt fnl f: hld on wl* **12/1**[3] | 77 |
| | 2 | nk | **Golden Legacy (IRE)** 2-8-9 ... PHanagan 8 *(RAFahey) dwlt: sn in tch: trcking ldrs whn n.m.r 2f out: r.o wl u.p fnl f: jst hld* **14/1** | 71+ |
| 2 | 3 | 1 ¼ | **Beautiful Mover (USA)**[18] 2275 2-8-9 ... DHolland 13 *(JWHills) keen: trckd ldrs: rdn and ev ch ent fnl f: no ex* **4/6**[1] | 67 |
| 34 | 4 | ¾ | **English Fellow**[15] 2352 2-9-0 ... GGibbons 14 *(BAMcmahon) cl up: rdn 2f out: ev ch ent fnl f: no ex ins last* **14/1** | 70 |
| | 5 | 2 ½ | **Kaggamagic** 2-9-0 ... DarrenWilliams 7 *(JRNorton) in tch: drvn along 2f out: no imp on ldrs fnl f* **100/1** | 63 |
| 5 | 6 | nk | **Jun Fan (USA)**[8] 2526 2-9-0 ... KMcEvoy 11 *(BEllison) in tch: rdn and ch over 1f out: no ex fnl f* **14/1** | 62 |
| | 7 | 3 | **Royal Pardon** 2-8-9 ... IMongan 6 *(MLWBell) in tch: outpcd over 2f out: n.d* **20/1** | 48 |
| 06 | 8 | 1 | **Desert Buzz (IRE)**[14] 2382 2-8-11 ... THamilton(3) 3 *(JHetherton) promiunent: rdn over 2f out: wknd over 1f out* **50/1** | 50 |
| | 9 | 1 ½ | **Takhmin (IRE)** 2-9-0 ... RHills 5 *(MJohnston) in tch: hdwy to chse ldrs 1/2-way: rdn and wknd 2f out* **5/1**[2] | 45 |
| 40 | 10 | hd | **Vision Victory (GER)**[31] 1960 2-9-0 ... DaleGibson 12 *(TPTate) sn bhd: n.d* **100/1** | 45 |
| | 11 | ¾ | **Mister Buzz** 2-9-0 ... ACulhane 2 *(MDHammond) sn bhd: n.d* **100/1** | 42 |
| | 12 | ½ | **Speagle (IRE)** 2-9-0 ... JCarroll 1 *(EJO'Neill) s.i.s: a bhd* **100/1** | 41 |
| | 13 | 1 ¼ | **Jessica's Style (IRE)** 2-8-9 ... MFenton 9 *(JGGiven) chsd ldrs to 1/2-way: sn outpcd and bhd* **25/1** | 32 |
| 0 | 14 | 9 | **Countrywide Dream (IRE)**[18] 2268 2-9-0 ... FLynch 10 *(ABerry) slowly away: a bhd* **100/1** | 10 |

1m 11.65s (-0.05) **Going Correction** -0.025s/f (Good) 14 Ran SP% **119.9**
Speed ratings: **99,98,96,95,92 92,88,86,84,84 83,82,81,69**CSF £159.76 TOTE £12.40: £2.70, £5.30, £1.10; EX 345.70.

**Owner** Peter Smith P C Coaches Limited **Bred** David Brown, Slatch Farm Stud And G B Turnbull L **Trained** Brierley, S Yorks

**FOCUS**
An ordinary maiden run at a solid gallop and the form looks decent for the track and grade.

**NOTEBOOK**
**Lincolneurocruiser** was smartly away and responded gamely to pressure late on to repel the runner-up's late thrust. He hung right as if feeling the ground late on, and will be seen to better effect on easier ground and possibly over further.
**Golden Legacy(IRE)** ◆ was flying at the death and would probably have got up in another couple of strides. This was a very pleasing debut display and, if she had not blown the start, the result would probably have been different, so she should have no trouble in losing her maiden tag.
**Beautiful Mover(USA)**, who was just touched off when well backed on her debut at Newmarket last time, was keen early on and covered up behind the leaders. She had every chance if good enough when joining the leaders over one out, but found little of the bridle. This has to rate a disappointment, but she may have found the ground a touch too quick and is worth another chance.
**English Fellow** ran his race, but did not see out the trip as well as the principals. He looks the type to fare much better when the nurseries begin.
**Kaggamagic** made a satisfactory debut and showed good early speed, before finding only the one pace off the bridle.
**Takhmin(IRE)** was smartly away and looked set to take part in the finish, but dropped out tamely when push came to shove. He will benefit from this experience, but does not look one of his stable's leading juveniles.
**Countrywide Dream(IRE)** *Official explanation: jockey said gelding was unsuited by fast ground.*

## 2759 HALF BOTTLE CLAIMING STKS — 2m 4y
4:30 (4:30) (F) 4-Y-0+ — £3,262 (£932; £466) Stalls Low

| Form | | | | | RPR |
|---|---|---|---|---|---|
| 3034 | **1** | | **Spitting Image (IRE)**[8] [2531] 4-8-12 60 ... ACulhane 5 | | 49 |
| | | | (MrsMReveley) *led tl hdd over 6f out: led again 4f out: rdn 2f out: drifted rt fnl f: hld on wl* | **11/4**[2] | |
| 1650 | **2** | *1* | **Red Scorpion (USA)**[31] [1973] 5-8-9 69 ... BSwarbrick(5) 3 | | 49 |
| | | | (WMBrisbourne) *hld up: hdwy 3f out: chsng wnr and rdn 2f out: no imp fnl f* | **11/10**[1] | |
| 014- | **3** | *3/4* | **Lord Lamb**[288] [4456] 12-8-7 70 ow3 ... DHolland 2 | | 41 |
| | | | (MrsMReveley) *in tch: swtchd outside 1/2-way: led over 6f out: hdd 4f out: chsd wnr after: kpt on: no imp* | **11/2**[3] | |
| 0400 | **4** | *3 1/2* | **Balalaika Tune (IRE)**[13] [2408] 5-7-13 35 ... JBramhill 6 | | 29 |
| | | | (WStorey) *hld up: hdwy 3f out: ch and rdn over 1f out: no ex fnl f* | **20/1** | |
| 0033 | **5** | *shd* | **Berrywhite (IRE)**[19] [2249] 6-8-11 40 ... THamilton(3) 1 | | 44 |
| | | | (CGrant) *in tch: effrt 4f out: rdn over 2f out: no imp on ldrs* | **12/1** | |
| 30-6 | **6** | *hd* | **Royal Castle (IRE)**[10] [2249] 10-8-4 44 ow3 ... TEaves(3) 7 | | 36 |
| | | | (MrsKWalton) *prom: rdn 4f out: outpcd 3f out: styd on u.p fnl f* | **10/1** | |
| 0-00 | **7** | *1 1/4* | **Bulgaria Moon**[11] [2462] 4-8-2 35 ow4 ... PBradley(5) 8 | | 36 |
| | | | (CGrant) *prom: rdn 4f out: fdd fr over 2f out* | **100/1** | |
| -000 | **8** | *1 1/4* | **Diva Dancer**[8] [2386] 4-7-5 30 ... (b) DFentiman(7) 9 | | 25 |
| | | | (JHetherton) *rr: rdn 4f out: no hdwy* | **66/1** | |
| 04-0 | **9** | *29* | **Sea Of Happiness**[15] [2347] 4-8-3 41 ... PHanagan 4 | | — |
| | | | (CGrant) *in tch: drvn along 5f out: sn bhd: lost tch and eased fnl f: t.o* | **100/1** | |

3m 31.08s (-0.42) **Going Correction** -0.025s/f (Good) — 9 Ran SP% **114.7**
**WFA** 4 from 5yo+ 1lb
Speed ratings: **100,99,99,97,97 97,96,95,81**CSF £5.98 TOTE £4.40: £1.10, £1.10, £2.00; EX 9.40.There was no bid for the winner.
**Owner** The Mary Reveley Racing Club **Bred** Denis McDonnell **Trained** Lingdale, N Yorks

**FOCUS**
A weak staying event that saw the first three clear of the rest.

**NOTEBOOK**
**Spitting Image(IRE)** proved suited by this step up in trip and won well under a positive ride. This was her first-ever success from 21 outings and she may be able to build on this, as she is unexposed at the distance.
**Red Scorpion(USA)**, dropping in grade, came there with every chance two out, but could not pass the winner, try as he might, and could only keep on at the one pace thereafter.
**Lord Lamb** failed to quicken on this fast ground when holding every chance late on. He always gives his best and deserves credit as he had been off for 288 days prior to this.
**Balalaika Tune(IRE)** ran her race, but her proximity at the death does very little for the form.

## 2760 SALMANAZAR H'CAP — 1m 2f
5:00 (5:02) (F) (0-55,55) 3-Y-O — £3,591 (£1,105; £552; £276) Stalls Low

| Form | | | | | RPR |
|---|---|---|---|---|---|
| 060- | **1** | | **Richtee (IRE)**[275] [4755] 3-9-6 55 ... PHanagan 15 | | 64 |
| | | | (RAFahey) *hld up: hdwy 3f out: styd on wl u.p to ld wl ins fnl f* | **12/1** | |
| 0-00 | **2** | *1* | **Pearl Of York (DEN)**[16] [2324] 3-9-3 52 ... MFenton 4 | | 59 |
| | | | (RGuest) *in tch: hdwy 3f out: rdn to ld over 1f out: hdd wl ins fnl f* | **25/1** | |
| 0-01 | **3** | *1 3/4* | **Ego Trip**[19] [2251] 3-9-4 53 ... DaleGibson 6 | | 56 |
| | | | (MWEasterby) *sn pushed along towards rr: hdwy 4f out: chsng ldrs and rdn ent fnl f: no ex ins last* | **11/4**[1] | |
| 0255 | **4** | *nk* | **Holly Walk**[21] [2199] 3-8-11 46 ... (v[1]) DarrenWilliams 9 | | 49 |
| | | | (MDods) *led tl hdd over 1f out: styd on u.p* | **9/1** | |
| -250 | **5** | *1* | **Let It Be**[15] [2347] 3-8-4 42 ow2 ... TEaves(3) 1 | | 43 |
| | | | (MrsMReveley) *midfield: drvn along and outpcd 3f out: styd on wl fr over 1f out: nvr able to chal* | **14/1** | |
| 4610 | **6** | *1/2* | **Larad (IRE)**[4] [2649] 3-8-6 48 ... (b) DerekNolan(7) 12 | | 48 |
| | | | (JSMoore) *hld up midfield: effrt 3f out: chsng ldrs and rdn over 1f out: no further prog* | **13/2**[3] | |
| -020 | **7** | *1/2* | **Bargain Hunt (IRE)**[23] [2146] 3-8-12 47 ... JBramhill 5 | | 46 |
| | | | (WStorey) *trckd ldr: rdn and ev ch 2f out: fdd* | **12/1** | |
| 0-06 | **8** | *1* | **Koodoo**[15] [2367] 3-9-6 55 ... VHalliday 3 | | 52 |
| | | | (ACrook) *in tch: rdn 3f out: fdd fnl 2f* | **9/1** | |
| -003 | **9** | *3/4* | **Delcienne**[15] [2349] 3-8-6 44 ... ABeech(3) 10 | | 40 |
| | | | (GGMargarson) *midfield: rdn 3f out: no hdwy* | **12/1** | |
| -660 | **10** | *3/4* | **Mr Moon**[15] [2356] 3-8-0 35 ... PMQuinn 11 | | 29 |
| | | | (MDHammond) *s.i.s: hld up: keen early: effrt over 3f out: no hdwy* | **100/1** | |
| 0-00 | **11** | *1 1/4* | **Ravel (IRE)**[21] [2211] 3-8-12 47 ... IMongan 8 | | 39 |
| | | | (MLWBell) *chsd ldrs tl rdn and wknd 3f out* | **11/2**[2] | |
| 0000 | **12** | *7* | **The Stick**[18] [2259] 3-9-6 55 ... ACulhane 7 | | 34 |
| | | | (MRChannon) *midfield tl outpcd and dropped towards rr 1/2-way: n.d* | **14/1** | |
| 040- | **13** | *8* | **Snow Chance (IRE)**[245] [5443] 3-7-11 37 ... BSwarbrick(5) 14 | | — |
| | | | (WMBrisbourne) *sn bhd* | **50/1** | |
| -662 | **14** | *8* | **Middleham Rose**[28] [2014] 3-7-9 37 oh2 ow2 ... RoryMoore(7) 13 | | — |
| | | | (PCHaslam) *prom to 1/2-way: sn bhd* | **20/1** | |

2m 6.37s (-0.43) **Going Correction** -0.025s/f (Good) — 14 Ran SP% **123.4**
Speed ratings: **100,99,97,97,96 96,95,95,94,93 92,87,80,74**CSF £293.54 CT £1072.37 TOTE £13.10: £3.70, £13.40, £1.10; EX 268.60 Place 6 £61.42, Place 5 £40.16.
**Owner** Terence Elsey and Richard Mustill **Bred** Niall Farrell **Trained** Musley Bank, N Yorks

**FOCUS**
A dire contest run at a fair gallop.

**NOTEBOOK**
**Richtee(IRE)**, who showed little promise in three outings as a juvenile last term, produced a fair turn of foot to challenge entering the final furlong and won going away. This proved she has trained on over the winter and she can build on this handicap debut success. *Official explanation: trainer's representative had no explanation for the improved form shown other than that filly had strengthened up over the winter*
**Pearl Of York(DEN)**, dropped 3lb for a poor display on her handicap debut last time, ran by far her best race to date and was a clear second. Granted, she does drag the form down, but she is lightly raced and improved for the extra furlong.
**Ego Trip** held every chance if good enough, but was found out by a combination of this longer trip and a rise in the weights for winning last time.
**Holly Walk**, with the blinkers swapped for the visor on this occasion, tried to make all over this shorter trip, but was found wanting late on. This represented a slight improvement in recent form.
**Larad(IRE)** could not quicken approaching the final furlong when holding every chance.
**Ravel(IRE)**, markedly upped in trip for this handicap bow, again showed little and looks slow. *Official explanation: jockey said colt had a breathing problem*
T/Plt: £137.60 to a £1 stake. Pool: £34,471.35. 182.80 winning tickets. T/Qpdt: £9.30 to a £1 stake. Pool: £3,296.10. 261.30 winning tickets. JF

# 2057 SALISBURY (R-H)
### Tuesday, June 8

**OFFICIAL GOING: Good to firm (firm in places)**
There is often a bias at Salisbury towards those drawn high on the straight track, but that was not apparent at this meeting.

## 2761 EDDIE REAVEY MAIDEN AUCTION STKS — 6f
2:15 (2:16) (E) 2-Y-O — £3,731 (£1,148; £574; £287) Stalls Centre

| Form | | | | | RPR |
|---|---|---|---|---|---|
| 2422 | **1** | | **Evanesce**[5] [2617] 2-8-2 ... CCatlin 6 | | 72 |
| | | | (MRChannon) *lw: mde virtually all: styd on wl u.p fr over 1f out* | **5/1**[3] | |
| | **2** | *shd* | **Polar Dawn** 2-8-2 ... AMcCarthy 9 | | 72 |
| | | | (BRMillman) *leggy: neat: in tch: pushed along and hdwy fr 2f out: str run ins fnl f: fin wl: nt quite get up* | **33/1** | |
| 053 | **3** | *2* | **Caly Dancer (IRE)**[5] [2627] 2-8-10 ... TQuinn 10 | | 74 |
| | | | (DRCElsworth) *chsd ldrs: wnt 2nd over 2f out: sn rdn: no imp fnl f and lost 2nd ins last* | **3/1**[1] | |
| 0 | **4** | *2 1/2* | **Missed A Beat**[17] [2300] 2-8-2 ... JMackay 14 | | 58 |
| | | | (MBlanshard) *chsd ldrs: rdn over 2f out: sn one pce* | **9/2**[2] | |
| | **5** | *3 1/2* | **He's A Diamond** 2-8-11 ... RMiles(3) 8 | | 60 |
| | | | (TGMills) *w'like: bit bkwd: s.i.s: bhd: hdwy on outside and hung rt fr 2f out: kpt on fnl f: nt a danger* | **8/1** | |
| 0 | **6** | *2 1/2* | **Pennestamp (IRE)**[75] [1105] 2-8-7 ... RHavlin 7 | | 45 |
| | | | (MrsPNDutfield) *chsd ldrs: rdn over 2f out: sn btn* | **20/1** | |
| | **7** | *1* | **Kingsgate Bay (IRE)** 2-9-0 ... NPollard 11 | | 49 |
| | | | (JRBest) *unf: bit bkwd: slowly away: bhd: mod hdwy fnl 2f* | **33/1** | |
| | **8** | *nk* | **Mabella (IRE)** 2-8-5 ... SCarson 2 | | 39 |
| | | | (BRMillman) *w'like: bit bkwd: plld hrd and hung lft after s: bhd: no ch whn hung bdly rt 2f out* | **20/1** | |
| 5 | **9** | *2 1/2* | **Zolash (IRE)**[14] [2382] 2-8-7 ... JDSmith 5 | | 34 |
| | | | (JSMoore) *s.i.s: rdn 1/2-way: a bhd* | **9/1** | |
| | **10** | *1 1/4* | **Bee Stinger** 2-8-7 ... SWKelly 1 | | 30 |
| | | | (IAWood) *w'like: bit bkwd: sn prom on outside: hrd drvn to chse ldrs 2f out: sn wknd* | **25/1** | |
| 0 | **11** | *1* | **Davala**[25] [2095] 2-8-7 ... ADaly 13 | | 27 |
| | | | (ADSmith) *a bhd* | **100/1** | |
| 0 | **12** | *1* | **Secret Diva (IRE)**[13] [2396] 2-7-13 ... JFMcDonald(3) 4 | | 19 |
| | | | (MrsPNDutfield) *sn outpcd* | **80/1** | |
| 66 | **13** | *nk* | **Atsos (IRE)**[26] [2058] 2-9-0 ... RHughes 3 | | 30 |
| | | | (RHannon) *sn rdn to press wnr: chal 3f out: wknd over 2f out* | **7/1** | |

1m 14.26s (-0.68) **Going Correction** -0.20s/f (Firm) — 13 Ran SP% **114.9**
Speed ratings: **96,95,93,89,85 81,80,80,76,75 73,72,72**CSF £162.43 TOTE £5.20: £1.70, £7.80, £1.20; EX 201.30.
**Owner** Dave and Gill Hedley **Bred** G Hedley And Mike Channon Bloodstock Limited **Trained** West Ilsley, Berks

**FOCUS**
The bare form of this maiden is just modest but reliable enough, but a few of these should progress past the winner in time.

**NOTEBOOK**
**Evanesce** had been running consistently in similar events and proved good enough to gain a deserved first success. She did well to grab the often-favoured far rail from stall six and was able to put both her experience and race-fitness to good use under a positive ride. Things will be tougher in future and a few of these are likely to progress past her in time, but she is tough and could do well in early-season nurseries.
**Polar Dawn**, a half-sister to a couple of winners, whose dam is out of a half-sister to a high-class juvenile, was allowed to go off unsupported, but made a most encouraging debut. Nicely clear of the remainder, it will be disappointing if she does not improve and pick up a similar race.
**Caly Dancer(IRE)** shaped as though in need of a step up to this trip when third over five furlongs on his previous start, but he proved quite one paced and was disappointing, even allowing for the fact he had to concede 8lb to the front two.
**Missed A Beat**, too green to justify support on her debut at Kempton, was again supported in the market, but can have no excuses this time and has to be considered a little disappointing.
**He's A Diamond**, 25,000gns purchase, first foal, out of a half-sister to a multiple winner in Belgium, was backed at long odds and made an encouraging debut. He was unable to hold a position and never once threatened the principals, but kept on nicely and would appear capable of much better.
**Kingsgate Bay(IRE)** was never a threat to the principals, but was noted keeping on quite well in his own time.
**Atsos(IRE)** *Official explanation: jockey said colt lost its action.*

## 2762 NUMERICA CLAIMING STKS (FOR AMATEUR RIDERS) — 6f 212y
2:45 (2:45) (F) 3-Y-O+ — £3,627 (£1,116; £558; £279) Stalls Centre

| Form | | | | | RPR |
|---|---|---|---|---|---|
| 3163 | **1** | | **Shirley Oaks (IRE)**[22] [2188] 6-10-2 43 ... MissGDGracey-Davison(7) 4 | | 58 |
| | | | (MissZCDavison) *rrd s: sn in tch: swtchd lft 2f out: drvn and hdwy over 1f out: led ins last: pushed out* | **14/1** | |
| -024 | **2** | *1 1/4* | **My Girl Pearl (IRE)**[22] [2188] 4-10-3 50 ... MrLTibbatts(3) 2 | | 52 |
| | | | (MSSaunders) *sn trcking ldrs: led over 2f out: sn rdn: hdd and one pce ins last* | **14/1** | |
| -000 | **3** | *nk* | **Mr Belvedere**[7] [2545] 3-9-11 65 ... (p) MrJJBest(5) 10 | | 57 |
| | | | (RHannon) *led 1f: styd chsng ldrs: rdn: carried hd high and kpt on ins fnl f: no ex nr fin* | **15/2** | |

6205 **4** 1 ½ **Paso Doble**[4] 2643 6-11-0 57 ........ MrJMillman(7) 7 62
(BRMillman) *lw: bhd: rdn over 2f out: r.o fnl f: nt rch ldrs* **6/1**[2]
0000 **5** 1 **Wood Fern (UAE)**[35] 1876 4-10-11 62 ........ MrMWalford(5) 5 54
(MRChannon) *in tch: rdn to chse ldrs over 2f out: wknd ins fnl f* **11/2**[1]
0060 **6** hd **Clann A Cougar**[25] 2078 4-10-6 60 ........ GBartley(7) 12 51
(IAWood) *sn drvn along: styd on u.p fnl 2f: nt rch ldrs* **6/1**[2]
3435 **7** 7 **City General (IRE)**[15] 2362 3-9-13 53 ........(p) MrsSMoore(3) 8 32
(JSMoore) *slt ld after 1f tl hdd over 2f out: sn wknd* **7/1**
-000 **8** 2 **Mac The Knife (IRE)**[14] 2379 3-9-13 70 ........ MrLNewnes(3) 3 27
(RHannon) *bhd: pushed along 3f out: nvr gng pce to rch ldrs* **8/1**
0000 **9** shd **Mutabari (USA)**[2] 2703 10-10-4 35 ........ MrJohnEvans(7) 6 25
(JLSpearing) *slowly away: a bhd* **25/1**
50-0 **10** 1 ½ **Chevronne**[29] 2000 4-11-0 68 ........(p) MrLJefford 1 24
(LGCottrell) *s.i.s: sn rcvrd and disp ld after 2f: wknd qckly 2f out* **13/2**[3]
-005 **11** ½ **The Footballresult**[26] 2061 3-9-13 54 ........ MissEJJones 11 18
(MrsGHarvey) *chsd ldrs 4f* **20/1**
0/00 **12** 1 ¼ **Frederick James**[14] 2384 10-10-11 31 ........ MrJamesWhite(3) 9 20
(HEHaynes) *a bhd* **66/1**

1m 29.09s (0.09) **Going Correction** -0.20s/f (Firm)
**WFA** 3 from 4yo+ 10lb **12** Ran SP% **116.1**
Speed ratings: **91,89,89,87,86 86,78,75,75,74 73,72**CSF £187.67 TOTE £10.30: £2.30, £3.30, £3.00; EX 61.50.There was no bid for the winner.
**Owner** The Secret Circle **Bred** Miss Honora Corridan **Trained** Ashurstwood, W Sussex

**FOCUS**
A very moderate claimer full of disappointing sorts, but they did at least go a good pace.

**NOTEBOOK**
**Shirley Oaks(IRE)**, below her best on Fibresand on her previous start, appreciated the return to turf and proved good enough to score despite having it all to do at the weights. However, with just three wins to her name in 33 career starts, she could not be backed with much confidence to follow up.
**My Girl Pearl(IRE)**, returning to turf after four runs on the All-Weather, did little wrong, but simply had no answer to the winner's late burst. She remains a maiden.
**Mr Belvedere** has been tried in blinkers and a visor, but cheekpieces were tried this time. They did not appear to have the desired effect as he showed an awkward head-carriage under pressure and gave the impression he was not putting it all in.
**Paso Doble** lacked a decisive change of pace. His rider did nothing wrong, but it may just be that he needs stronger handling.
**Wood Fern(UAE)** had every chance but was not good enough on the day and is regressing.
**Clann A Cougar** was unable to take advantage of his draw against the rail after missing the break.
**Chevronne** used too much energy up in trying to recover from a poor start and is probably a little better than the bare form suggests.

## 2763 SOUTH WEST RACING EXPERIENCE STKS (H'CAP) 6f
**3:15** (3:15) (C ) (0-90,89) 3-Y-0+ **£8,792** (£3,335; £1,667; £758) **Stalls** Centre

Form RPR
1011 **1** **Caustic Wit (IRE)**[8] 2524 6-8-2 **66** 6ex ........(p) RMiles(3) 4 81
(MSSaunders) *broke wl: sn led on outside: mde rest: edgd rt to far rail appr fnl f: readily* **8/1**
0-06 **2** 2 **Complication**[9] 2506 4-7-13 **63** ........(b) LisaJones(3) 6 72
(JARToller) *prom: chsd wnr over 1f out: kpt on fnl f but no imp* **12/1**
-000 **3** 2 ½ **Najeebon (FR)**[10] 2477 5-9-8 **83** ........ TEDurcan 2 84
(MRChannon) *lw: bhd: racd on outside: rdn and hung rt fr 2f out: kpt on fr over 1f out: styd on cl home but nt rch ldrs* **8/1**
0110 **4** nk **Parkside Pursuit**[10] 2490 6-8-10 **71** ........ RLMoore 9 71
(JMBradley) *hld up in rr: hdwy and rdn to chse ldrs ins fnl 2f: styd on same pce fnl f* **4/1**[1]
01-0 **5** nk **Thurlestone Rock**[10] 2477 4-8-13 **77** ........ JFMcDonald(3) 10 76
(BJMeehan) *lw: sn pressing ldrs: rdn over 2f out: wknd fnl f* **13/2**[2]
31-0 **6** ¾ **Sparkling Jewel**[9] 2506 4-9-2 **77** ........ DaneO'Neill 12 74
(RHannon) *racd on far rail and pressed ldrs: rdn over 2f out: wknd fnl f* **8/1**
60-0 **7** hd **Formalise**[17] 2303 4-8-4 **65** ........ SCarson 3 61
(GBBalding) *bhd: pushed along on outside over 2f out: r.o ins fnl f but nvr gng pce to rch ldrs* **25/1**
-000 **8** hd **Coranglais**[13] 2399 4-8-4 **65** ........ CCatlin 11 61
(JMBradley) *bhd: hdwy and n.m.r over 1f out: kpt on again ins last* **14/1**
0060 **9** ¾ **Gaelic Princess**[10] 2477 4-9-7 **82** ........ SWhitworth 8 76
(AGNewcombe) *chsd ldrs on far rail tl wknd ins fnl f* **20/1**
40-0 **10** hd **Hey Presto**[10] 2477 4-8-11 **72** ........ RSmith 7 65
(CGCox) *plld hrd: chsd ldrs: rdn 2f out: wknd fnl f* **15/2**[3]
110- **11** 2 ½ **Tahirah**[207] 6000 4-10-0 **89** ........ SSanders 1 74
(RGuest) *bit bkwd: bhd: sme hdwy whn nt clr run over 2f out: n.d after* **11/1**
2-40 **12** 5 **The Best Yet**[66] 1241 6-8-6 **70** ........ DCorby(3) 5 40
(AGNewcombe) *s.i.s: t.k.h: bhd fr 1/2-way* **8/1**

1m 12.86s (-2.08) **Going Correction** -0.20s/f (Firm) **12** Ran SP% **120.8**
Speed ratings: **105,102,99,98,98 97,96,96,95,95 92,85**CSF £102.30 CT £804.44 TOTE £9.50: £2.30, £3.20, £3.40; EX 148.70 Trifecta £1037.90 Part won. Pool of £1,461.86 - 0.50 winning units..
**Owner** Mrs Sandra Jones **Bred** Gainsborough Stud Management Ltd **Trained** Haydon, Somerset

**FOCUS**
Just two of the 12 runners had winning form to their name this season and this was probably not as competitive a sprint handicap as one might have expected.

**NOTEBOOK**
**Caustic Wit(IRE)** continued his fine form, getting the hat-trick up in good style. Despite carrying a 6lb penalty for his recent Leicester success, he was still effectively racing off a mark 26lb lower than his highest winning rating and could defy a further rise in the weights whilst in such good heart. Connections may keep him to similar company rather than go for a big handicap.
**Complication**, nibbled at in the betting, ran her best race of the season so far, but conditions were ideal and it would be unwise to get carried away. Having said that, there should be more to come.
**Najeebon(FR)**, 2lb lower than when last successful, posted a seasonal best and would appear to be coming to himself.
**Parkside Pursuit** had every chance off a mark 6lb lower than when slightly disappointing at Musselburgh on his previous start, but was readily held.
**Thurlestone Rock** lacked a change of speed, but was having just his second run of the campaign and is probably capable of improving.
**The Best Yet**, racing for the first time in 66 days, was too keen.

## 2764 EBF MARGADALE CLASSIFIED STKS 1m 1f 198y
**3:45** (3:45) (C ) 3-Y-0 **£10,645** (£3,777; £1,888; £858) **Stalls** High

Form RPR
10- **1** **Mango Mischief (IRE)**[220] 5874 3-8-11 85 ........ RHughes 4 91
(JLDunlop) *lw: hld up in rr: hdwy on rails and swtchd lft to chse ldr over 2f out: str run fnl f: drvn to ld last strides* **9/1**[3]
1-43 **2** nk **Camrose**[19] 2244 3-9-0 85 ........ TQuinn 2 93
(JLDunlop) *lw: led: kpt on wl whn chal fr 5f out: styd on u.p fnl 2f: hdd and no ex last strides* **9/4**[2]
1-1 **3** 13 **Penrith (FR)**[11] 2448 3-9-5 90 ........ JFanning 3 73
(MJohnston) *lw: sn trcking ldr: chal fr 5f out tl 3f out: sn rdn: wknd qckly over 2f out* **4/7**[1]
04-5 **4** 2 ½ **Geller**[5] 2611 3-9-0 83 ........ RLMoore 1 64
(RHannon) *chsd ldrs tl wknd fr 3f out* **25/1**

2m 6.08s (-2.24) **Going Correction** +0.05s/f (Good) **4** Ran SP% **108.3**
Speed ratings: **110,109,99,97**CSF £28.09 TOTE £6.80; EX 28.20.
**Owner** Antoniades Family **Bred** A G Antoniades **Trained** Arundel, W Sussex

**FOCUS**
With just the four runners, this did not look that competitive an event and with the favourite Penrith below form, that is how it turned out. However, they did go a decent pace and the form of the front two looks reliable, an opinion backed up by the clock, with the winning time smart for the grade.

**NOTEBOOK**
**Mango Mischief(IRE)** was clearly held in high regard last season, for after winning on her debut over seven furlongs here, she was stepped up to Listed company. She showed little that day, but returned to form on this reappearance delayed due to gastric ulcers and narrowly got the better of her stablemate. She should improve and deserves another chance in Listed company - last year's winner of this race, Quiet Storm, went on to gain black type.
**Camrose**, in good form behind useful sorts on both his starts in handicaps this season, set a fair standard and appeared to run his race, but his stablemate was just too good.
**Penrith(FR)** looked to be progressing nicely when winning a competitive handicap off a mark of 85 at Pontefract on his previous start, but he was below form even allowing for this step up from a mile and was reported to have returned lame on his near hind. *Official explanation: vet said colt was lame behind.*
**Geller** may not have been suited by this trip and was out of his depth in any case, but he still has to prove he has trained on.

## 2765 CHAMPAGNE DUVAL-LEROY MAIDEN STKS 6f 212y
**4:15** (4:16) (D ) 3-Y-0 **£6,077** (£1,870; £935; £467) **Stalls** Centre

Form RPR
**1** **Camberwell** 3-8-11 ........ RMiles(3) 10 87
(TGMills) *unf: scope: trckd ldr tl led appr fnl 3f: c clr over 1f out: easily* **12/1**
23-0 **2** 8 **Hunter's Valley**[10] 2479 3-8-9 78 ........ PDobbs 11 61
(RHannon) *lw: led tl hdd over 3f out: styd disputing 2nd tl chsd wnr again fnl f but no ch* **15/8**[1]
6 **3** 2 ½ **Pure Imagination (IRE)**[17] 2301 3-9-0 ........ RLMoore 7 60
(JMBradley) *in tch: hdwy 3f out: disp 2nd 2f out: no chnace w wnr over 1f out and wknd ins last* **40/1**
00-0 **4** ¾ **Bahama Belle**[26] 2063 3-8-9 57 ........ DKinsella 1 53
(HSHowe) *chsd ldrs on outside and t.k.h: one pce fr over 2f out* **16/1**
**5** 2 **Tromp** 3-9-0 ........ SSanders 6 53
(DJCoakley) *w'like: s.i.s: bhd: styd on fr over 2f out: kpt on ins last but nvr a danger* **9/1**
00 **6** nk **Collada (IRE)**[19] 2243 3-8-9 ........ RHavlin 13 47
(JHMGosden) *chsd ldrs: rdn over 2f out: sn btn* **25/1**
**7** ½ **Benny Bathwick (IRE)** 3-9-0 ........ SDrowne 3 50
(BRMillman) *w'like: chsd ldrs 5f* **25/1**
0 **8** 1 ¾ **Iltravitore (IRE)**[17] 2301 3-9-0 ........ TQuinn 4 46
(DRCElsworth) *bhd: mod prog fnl 2f* **14/1**
40 **9** 2 ½ **Called Up**[21] 2211 3-9-0 ........ DaneO'Neill 9 39
(HCandy) *nvr bttr than mid-div* **11/4**[2]
0 **10** 2 ½ **Solipsist (IRE)**[24] 2113 3-9-0 ........ RHughes 5 33
(RHannon) *lw: chsd ldrs: ridcden 3f out: wknd qckly 2f out* **6/1**[3]
000 **11** ½ **Dulcimer**[20] 2223 3-8-4 ........ RThomas(5) 8 27
(GBBalding) *chsd ldrs over 4f* **50/1**
00 **12** ½ **Crimson Star (IRE)**[17] 2486 3-8-9 ........ CCatlin 14 25
(CTinkler) *a bhd* **50/1**
00- **13** 1 **Tartiruga (IRE)**[316] 3646 3-9-0 ........ SCarson 12 28
(LGCottrell) *a in rr* **100/1**
0 **14** 16 **Summer Joy**[62] 1304 3-8-5 ow3 ........ MHoward(7) 2 —
(DKIvory) *sn wl bhd* **66/1**

1m 26.38s (-2.62) **Going Correction** -0.20s/f (Firm) **14** Ran SP% **122.5**
Speed ratings: **106,96,94,93,90 90,89,87,85,82 81,81,79,61**CSF £34.09 TOTE £16.80: £3.60, £1.30, £6.40; EX 40.40.
**Owner** Welcocks Skips Ltd Waste Management **Bred** Fourways Bloodstock **Trained** Headley, Surrey

**FOCUS**
A very weak maiden, but a decent performance from the newcomer Camberwell, who recorded a decent time for the grade.

**NOTEBOOK**
**Camberwell**, a 30,000euros purchase, out of a half-sister to a smart performer in Germany, was not seen out as a two-year-old due to a broken pelvis. It would be silly to get carried away by the winning margin, for the runner-up is a disappointing sort and the remainder are quite simply not that good, but he should progress and will be worthy of respect in a better grade.
**Hunter's Valley** was again disappointing and has done nothing in two runs this season to justify a rating of 78.
**Pure Imagination(IRE)** was well beaten on his only previous start, but this was better and he appears to be going the right way.
**Bahama Belle** ran respectably, but will surely find things easier back in handicaps.
**Tromp**, a 52,00gns purchase, half-brother to six- to eight-furlong winner Border Glen, made no more than a satisfactory debut.
**Collada(IRE)** was well beaten, but is at least now qualified for a handicap mark.
**Called Up** has not gone on from a promising debut effort, but will be worth a look in the market when he makes his handicap debut.
**Solipsist(IRE)** *Official explanation: jockey said colt lost its action.*
**Crimson Star(IRE)** *Official explanation: jockey said filly lost its action.*

## 2766 KNIGHTS & CO H'CAP 6f 212y
**4:45** (4:51) (F ) (0-55,55) 3-Y-0 **£3,744** (£1,152; £576; £288) **Stalls** Centre

Form RPR
0050 **1** **Accendere**[36] 1844 3-9-7 **52** ........ SSanders 3 58
(RMBeckett) *bhd: stdy hdwy fr 3f out: str run to chse ldr jst ins fnl f: led last strides* **12/1**
4362 **2** nk **Turnberry (IRE)**[36] 1844 3-9-10 **55** ........(v) TQuinn 13 60
(JWHills) *trckd ldrs: led ins fnl 3f: hrd drvn fr over 1f out: kpt on: ct last strides* **7/2**[1]
4220 **3** 1 ¼ **Knickyknackienoo**[13] 2400 3-9-10 **55** ........ SWhitworth 9 57
(AGNewcombe) *bmpd s: bhd: hdwy on outside fr 3f out: drvn to press ldrs 2f out: one pce ins last* **9/1**
0506 **4** 1 ¼ **Even Easier**[16] 2324 3-9-10 **55** ........(b[1]) RLMoore 2 54
(GLMoore) *lw: s.i.s: bhd: hdwy on outside over 1f out: fin wl but nt trble ldrs* **8/1**[3]
-012 **5** 2 ½ **Yamato Pink**[14] 2380 3-9-7 **52** ........ GBaker 10 44
(MrsHSweeting) *slowly into struide: sn rcvrd to trck ldrs: rdn over 2f out: wknd fnl f* **8/1**[3]

5-56 **6** 3/4 **David's Girl**[25] 2088 3-8-9 **40** ........ JMackay 15 30
(DMorris) *bhd: hdwy fr 2f out: nt trble ldrs* **33/1**

-600 **7** *hd* **I Wish I Knew**[14] 2380 3-9-0 **45** ........ (v[1]) DaneO'Neill 5 35
(DJCoakley) *led tl hdd ins fnl 3f: wknd over 1f out* **33/1**

60-4 **8** 1/2 **Charlieismydarling**[15] 2359 3-9-6 **51** ........ RHughes 16 39
(JAOsborne) *bhd: hdwy and n.m.r 2f out: swtchd lft over 1f out: styd on but nvr a danger* **8/1**[3]

0-01 **9** *shd* **Pererin**[35] 1864 3-9-3 **48** ........ SWKelly 19 36
(IAWood) *chsd ldrs: n.m.r on ins 3f out: rdn 2f out: wknd over 1f out* **12/1**

0-00 **10** *nk* **Johnny Alljays (IRE)**[15] 2349 3-8-11 **42** ........ (b[1]) JDSmith 11 29
(JSMoore) *bhd: n.m.r and swtchd lft over 2f out: nvr nr ldrs* **50/1**

6606 **11** 1/2 **Chase The Rainbow**[7] 2548 3-9-10 **55** ........ JFanning 14 41
(MissKMGeorge) *chsd ldrs: rdn over 2f out: n.m.r and wknd over 1f out* **25/1**

4-50 **12** 1 1/4 **Sharplaw Destiny (IRE)**[10] 2484 3-9-2 **50** ........ (b[1]) JFMcDonald[(3)] 8 33
(WJHaggas) *wnt lft s: slowly away and bhd: hung rt to far rail 3f out: nvr in contention* **20/1**

-U55 **13** 1/2 **Dalida**[57] 1363 3-9-5 **50** ........ NPollard 12 31
(PCHaslam) *chsd ldrs: rdn 3f out: wknd 2f out* **9/2**[2]

5000 **14** *hd* **Jaolins**[14] 2380 3-8-13 **44** ........ SDrowne 7 25
(PGMurphy) *chsd ldrs over 4f* **25/1**

0050 **15** 1 1/4 **Kedross (IRE)**[11] 2451 3-9-10 **55** ........ (b[1]) CCatlin 17 33
(JJay) *a in rr* **33/1**

0000 **16** *16* **Harry Came Home**[18] 2267 3-8-4 **35** ........ AMcCarthy 1 —
(JCFox) *sn bhd* **80/1**

00-0 **17** 1 1/2 **Miss Tilly**[37] 1796 3-8-10 **46** ........ RThomas[(5)] 18 —
(GBBalding) *sn bhd* **66/1**

6300 **18** *dist* **Son Of Rembrandt (IRE)**[4] 2667 3-9-3 **55** ........ MHoward[(7)] 4 —
(DKIvory) *chsd ldrs early: t.o* **20/1**

1m 28.27s (-0.73) **Going Correction** -0.20s/f (Firm) **18** Ran SP% **129.8**
Speed ratings: **96,95,94,92,89 89,88,88,88,87 87,85,85,85,83 65,63,**—CSF £51.11 CT £435.73 TOTE £16.30: £4.30, £1.50, £1.70, £1.80; EX 89.20.
**Owner** A W A Partnership **Bred** 6c Stallions Ltd **Trained** Lambourn, Berks

**FOCUS**
Only a moderate handicap, but it was competitive enough and the form should work out at a similar level.

**NOTEBOOK**
**Accendere** was most disappointing when a beaten favourite on his handicap debut, but left that form behind to confirm the promise he showed on his third run in maiden company - a run the Stewards looked into. Having not appeared to be going anywhere two out, he picked up well and made the most of the runner-up not doing a great deal in front. Lightly raced, there should be more to come. *Official explanation: trainer said, regarding the improved form shown, gelding had benefited from the good to firm ground*
**Turnberry(IRE)**, runner-up at Warwick on his previous start, again had to settle for minor honours, for once sent to the front, he idled and had little answer to the winner's late burst. There is a race in him, but he is proving frustrating.
**Knickyknackienoo**, too keen from a poor draw at Goodwood on his previous run, posted a better over this shorter trip. However, he remains a maiden.
**Even Easier**, with blinkers on for the first time, found things happening a little too quickly after missing the break on this three-furlong drop in trip.
**Yamato Pink** travelled well, but did not appear to get home and looks better over shorter.
**Son Of Rembrandt(IRE)** *Official explanation: vet said gelding bled from nose.*

## 2767 ALAN BLENCOWE MOTOR RACING H'CAP — 1m 4f
**5:15** (5:19) (E) (0-70,66) 4-Y-0+ **£3,523** (£1,084; £542; £271) **Stalls** High

Form RPR

0630 **1** **Private Benjamin**[16] 2324 4-8-7 **49** ........ PDoe 2 58
(JamiePoulton) *stdd mid-div after 1f: hdwy over 2f out:drvn and r.o wl fnl f: led fnl 50yds* **7/1**[3]

0606 **2** 1/2 **Giko**[36] 2344 10-7-9 **40** oh2 ........ LisaJones[(3)] 10 48
(JaneSouthcombe) *chsd ldrs: led wl over 1f out: styd on u.p: hdd and no ex fnl 50yds* **33/1**

4215 **3** *nk* **Anyhow (IRE)**[8] 2514 7-9-6 **62** ........ JFanning 9 70
(MissKMGeorge) *hld up mid-div: stdy hdwy 2f out: no clr run and swtchd rt appr fnl f: fin wl: nt rcvr* **9/2**[1]

6503 **4** 3/4 **Most-Saucy**[15] 2363 8-9-3 **59** ........ SWKelly 11 65
(IAWood) *s.i.s: bhd: hdwy on outside fr 2f out: str run ins last: nt rch ldrs* **5/1**[2]

-424 **5** 1 1/4 **Reminiscent (IRE)**[14] 2381 5-9-2 **58** ........ (v) SCarson 8 62
(RFJohnsonHoughton) *lw: bhd: hdwy fr 3f out: r.o wl fnl f but nt rch ldrs* **5/1**[2]

022- **6** 1/2 **African Dawn**[44] 1267 6-8-8 **53** ........ (t) LPKeniry[(3)] 4 57
(LGCottrell) *chsd ldrs: rdn over 2f out: wknd fnl f* **14/1**

0060 **7** 1/2 **Traveller's Tale**[25] 2084 5-9-10 **66** ........ DKinsella 6 69?
(PGMurphy) *sn led: rdn and kpt on whn chal fr over 4f out: hdd wl over 1f out and sn wknd* **16/1**

0506 **8** 1/2 **Aoninch**[8] 2537 4-9-0 **56** ........ SWhitworth 5 58
(MrsPNDutfield) *bhd: hdwy on outside fr 3f out: drievn to press ldrs ins fnl 2f: edgd rt and wknd fnl f* **9/2**[1]

010- **9** 2 **Top Trees**[194] 6040 6-8-4 **46** ........ JMackay 3 45
(WSKittow) *sn chsng ldr: chal 5f out tl 3f out: rdn dropped reins 2f out: sn wknd* **33/1**

1033 **10** *hd* **Saxe-Coburg (IRE)**[6] 2590 7-9-3 **62** ........ JFMcDonald[(3)] 1 60
(GAHam) *lw: hld up in rr: hdwy 5f out: styng on one pce whn n.m.r 2f out: eased whn no ch fnl f* **8/1**

40/0 **11** 1 1/4 **Enchanted Ocean (USA)**[68] 1224 5-9-4 **60** ........ RHavlin 7 56
(GBBalding) *mid-div: rdn over 3f out: sn wknd* **16/1**

2m 38.09s (1.74) **Going Correction** +0.05s/f (Good) **11** Ran SP% **117.6**
Speed ratings: **96,95,95,94,94 93,93,93,91,91 90**CSF £209.71 CT £1148.10 TOTE £8.50: £2.90, £6.60, £1.50; EX 334.00 Place 6 £3174.94, Place 5 £1681.60.
**Owner** Mrs J Wotherspoon **Bred** Mrs J Wotherspoon **Trained** Telscombe, E Sussex

**FOCUS**
Just a modest handicap, but they went a stop-start gallop and the winning time was just ordinary.

**NOTEBOOK**
**Private Benjamin** proved disappointing over ten furlongs on his previous start, but this return to the trip he gained his only previous win over suited well. He did not have much in hand at the finish and, given the way the race was run, the bare form of this success cannot be taken too literally.
**Giko** had been in poor form this year, with six straight defeats in banded company followed by a dismal showing in Jersey on his most recent outing, but this was much better. However, he can be relied upon to confirm this next time.
**Anyhow(IRE)**, just 1lb higher than when winning at Bath two starts previously, did not get a clear run when she needed it most and has to be considered very unlucky. She is a regular in these type of events and should continue to go well.
**Most-Saucy**, 5lb lower than when last successful, was given too much to do and did not help her chance by hanging slightly when finally in full stride. She would appear to be hitting form.
**Reminiscent(IRE)** would have benefited from a stronger pace given that his only previous win came over a mile six, but he quite simply does not win very often.
**Aoninch** is on a fair enough mark, but has yet to really find her form.
**Saxe-Coburg(IRE)** *Official explanation: jockey said saddle slipped.*
T/Jkpt: Not won. T/Plt: £460.40 to a £1 stake. Pool: £42,227.70. 66.95 winning tickets. T/Qpdt: £55.10 to a £1 stake. Pool: £2,849.30. 38.20 winning tickets. ST

2772 - (Foreign Racing) - See Raceform Interactive

# 2567 BEVERLEY (R-H)
Wednesday, June 9

**OFFICIAL GOING: Good (good to soft in places)**
After a flash flood and 17mm of rain and hail the previous evening the ground was described as 'just on the soft side of good'.
Wind: slight 1/2 against Weather: Fine and sunny

## 2773 SPORTINGOPTIONS.CO.UK CLAIMING STKS — 5f
**2:20** (2:21) (F) 2-Y-0 **£3,399** (£1,046; £523; £261) **Stalls** High

Form RPR

1633 **1** **Von Wessex**[9] 2523 2-8-8 ........ CHaddon[(7)] 14 52
(WGMTurner) *mde all: hung rt over 1f out: drvn rt out* **15/8**[1]

000 **2** 3/4 **Comintrue (IRE)**[6] 2617 2-8-10 ........ KDarley 10 44
(EJO'Neill) *sn outpcd and pushed along: hdwy over 2f out: swtchd lft over 1f out: styd on wl: nt rch wnr* **12/1**

0206 **3** 1 3/4 **Danehill Fairy (IRE)**[6] 2616 2-8-6 ........ (v[1]) GDuffield 11 34
(MrsADuffield) *swvd rt s: trckd ldrs: pushed lft over 1f out: kpt on wl* **12/1**

440 **4** *shd* **Keepasharplookout (IRE)**[28] 2035 2-8-13 ........ DHolland 2 41
(MrsLStubbs) *mid-div: hdwy over 2f out: kpt on fnl f* **16/1**

0505 **5** 2 **Frisby Ridge (IRE)**[16] 2364 2-8-3 ........ DAllan[(3)] 9 27
(TDEasterby) *reluctant to go to s: chsd ldrs: one pce fnl 2f* **12/1**

020 **6** 2 1/2 **Urabande**[25] 2125 2-8-4 ow1 ........ NPollard 13 16
(JulianPoulton) *chsd ldrs: wknd over 1f out* **13/2**[2]

0653 **7** 1 **Procrastinate (IRE)**[6] 2616 2-8-6 ........ (p) PPMathers[(7)] 5 22
(RFFisher) *swvd lft s: bhd: sme hdwy on wd outside 2f out: nvr nrr* **7/1**[3]

6 **8** *hd* **Jonny Fox'S (IRE)**[14] 2405 2-8-11 ........ NCallan 15 19
(JGallagher) *w wnr: wkng whn sltly hmpd over 1f out* **7/1**[3]

00 **9** 3 **Hollingwood Soul**[16] 2364 2-8-0 ........ JQuinn 7 —
(RonaldThompson) *mid-div: hung rt and lost pl over 1f out* **40/1**

00 **10** 2 1/2 **Timmy**[24] 2141 2-8-4 ow2 ........ TEaves[(3)] 12 —
(MESowersby) *swvd lft s: mid-div: wknd over 1f out* **20/1**

00 **11** 2 **Hunipot**[32] 1961 2-8-2 ........ RFrench 8 —
(MESowersby) *chsd ldrs: lost pl over 1f out* **33/1**

0550 **12** 7 **Steal The Thunder**[11] 2489 2-8-10 ........ (b[1]) FLynch 6 —
(ABerry) *sn bhd: hung lft and eased 3f out* **20/1**

**13** 8 **Tak's Girl** 2-8-10 ........ RFitzpatrick 4 —
(PTMidgley) *leggy: swvd violently lft sn after s: a wl bhd* **40/1**

69.31 secs (5.31) **Going Correction** +0.775s/f (Yiel) **13** Ran SP% **119.4**
Speed ratings: **88,86,84,83,80 76,75,74,69,65 62,51,38**CSF £24.19 TOTE £3.00: £1.40, £3.00, £2.80; EX 33.70.
**Owner** Darren Coombes **Bred** Helshaw Grange Stud Ltd **Trained** Sigwells, Somerset

**FOCUS**
A weak claimer and a high draw was as usual essential.

**NOTEBOOK**
**Von Wessex**, having his seventh start, was carrying bags of condition. He hung right as usual when in front and, three lengths clear a furlong out, was tying up fast on the rain-softened ground near the finish. He is certainly being asked to earn his keep.
**Comintrue(IRE)** soon found herself in a poor position. Forced to pull wide, she stayed on well and was making rapid inroads at the line. Six suits her a lot better.
**Danehill Fairy(IRE)**, in a visor this time, ran much better and seems suited by give underfoot.
**Keepasharplookout(IRE)**, absent for a month with sore shins, appreciated the give underfoot and did well from the worst of the draw. Six will suit him more than this stiff five.
**Frisby Ridge(IRE)**, most reluctant to go to the start, probably ran her best race to date. A return to selling company will give her a better chance.
**Urabande**, on her toes beforehand, matched strides with the winner but faded badly. She seems to be going the wrong way.
**Steal The Thunder** *Official explanation: vet said colt had sore shins.*

## 2774 SPORTINGOPTIONS.CO.UK 08702 070707 H'CAP — 1m 4f 16y
**2:50** (2:50) (E) (0-75,68) 3-Y-0 **£4,208** (£1,295; £647; £323) **Stalls** High

Form RPR

0-41 **1** **Prenup (IRE)**[12] 2442 3-9-1 **62** ........ DHolland 6 82+
(LMCumani) *mde all: drvn clr over 1f out: eased last 50yds* **10/11**[1]

-033 **2** 6 **Wing Collar**[15] 2390 3-9-5 **66** ........ KDarley 1 73
(TDEasterby) *hld up in last: effrt on inner and hmpd over 5f out: hdwy 3f out: wnt 2nd over 1f out: no ch w wnr* **5/2**[2]

00-0 **3** 3 1/2 **Dhehdaah**[16] 2361 3-9-2 **63** ........ RHills 5 64
(NAGraham) *w wnr: drvn along over 3f out: one pce fnl 2f* **10/1**

0325 **4** 4 **Savannah River (IRE)**[8] 2554 3-7-12 **45** ........ (t) PHanagan 2 40
(CWThornton) *chsd ldrs: pushed along over 5f out: hung rt and lost pl over 1f out* **9/1**[3]

0-55 **5** 1 1/4 **Snowed Under**[24] 2144 3-9-4 **65** ........ GDuffield 3 58
(JDBethell) *dwlt: sn chsng ldrs: reminders 6f out: wknd 2f out* **25/1**

055- **6** 25 **Beacon Blue (IRE)**[219] 5906 3-9-7 **68** ........ RFrench 4 21
(MJohnston) *chsd ldrs: rdn over 4f out: sn lost pl and bhd: t.o 2f out* **16/1**

2m 42.36s (3.06) **Going Correction** +0.30s/f (Good) **6** Ran SP% **109.8**
Speed ratings: **101,97,94,92,91 74**CSF £3.13 TOTE £1.60: £1.40, £1.20; EX 3.80.
**Owner** Fittocks Stud **Bred** Fittocks Stud Ltd **Trained** Newmarket, Suffolk

**FOCUS**
A modest handicap and a tactical affair, but a clear-cut winner who is improving fast.

**NOTEBOOK**
**Prenup(IRE)**, who looked very fit, has a daisy-cutting action. She wound it up from the front, and after coming right away won easing right down. Fast ground will suit her even better and she is clearly improving at a rate of knots.
**Wing Collar** was left short of room when trying to improve on the inner starting the home turn. She kept on to finish clear second best, but the winner was much too good.
**Dhehdaah**, stepping up in trip on his handicap debut, looks to lack several gears.
**Savannah River(IRE)** was making hard work of it even before the winner stepped up the pace.
**Snowed Under**, stepping up in trip on his handicap bow, tended to run in snatches and still has a bit to learn.
**Beacon Blue(IRE)**, who does not look to have grown from two to three, showed a very moderate action going to post and ran very badly indeed.

## 2775 SPORTINGOPTIONS MAX 3% RATED STKS (H'CAP) — 1m 1f 207y
**3:20** (3:21) (D) (0-80,80) 4-Y-0+ **£6,116** (£2,319; £1,159; £527) **Stalls** High

Form RPR

2242 **1** **Oldenway**[19] 2258 5-8-13 **72** ........ PHanagan 4 84
(RAFahey) *trckd ldrs: led appr fnl f: jst hld on* **7/2**[1]

4201 **2** *shd* **Grey Clouds**[12] 2446 4-8-13 **75** DAllan(3) 5 87
(TDEasterby) *trckd ldrs: led over 1f out: sn hdd: r.o wl* **5/1**[3]

1312 **3** *2 ½* **Olivia Rose (IRE)**[12] 2446 5-9-0 **73** JQuinn 3 80
(JPearce) *hld up: hdwy on ins over 2f out: styd on same pce appr fnl f* **7/1**

4-32 **4** *1 ¾* **Lauro**[33] 1931 4-8-13 **77** PMulrennan(5) 10 81
(MissJACamacho) *trckd ldrs: effrt on ins to ld 2f out: sn hdd: kpt on one pce* **4/1**[2]

1-40 **5** *10* **Maxilla (IRE)**[30] 2000 4-8-12 **71** DHolland 2 56
(LMCumani) *chsd ldrs: pushed along 6f out: hung rt and lost pl 3f out: n.d after* **11/2**

00-0 **6** *3 ½* **Mister Arjay (USA)**[26] 1773 4-9-0 **76** TEaves(3) 7 54
(BEllison) *w ldrs: drvn along over 3f out: lost pl over 1f out* **16/1**

-000 **7** *½* **Gala Sunday (USA)**[27] 2066 4-9-7 **80** DaleGibson 8 57
(MWEasterby) *led: hung lft and hdd 2f out: sn wknd* **12/1**

3-00 **8** *5* **Derwent (USA)**[16] 2365 5-9-2 **75** (b) GDuffield 1 43
(JDBethell) *hld up: effrt on outer over 3f out: rdn and lost pl 2f out* **25/1**

0000 **9** *10* **Broadway Score (USA)**[24] 2142 6-9-7 **80** TLucas 6 29
(MWEasterby) *chsd ldrs on outer: pushed along 6f out: lost pl over 2f out: sn bhd and eased* **10/1**

P **U** **Harambee (IRE)**[29] 2022 4-9-4 **80** THamilton(3) 9 —
(BSRothwell) *uns rdr leaving stalls* **80/1**

2m 7.87s (0.67) **Going Correction** +0.30s/f (Good) **10** Ran SP% **114.5**

Speed ratings: **109,108,106,105,97 94,94,90,82,—**CSF £20.61 CT £114.93 TOTE £4.40: £1.40, £2.20, £1.80; EX 16.80.

**Owner** J J Staunton **Bred** Snailwell Stud Co Ltd **Trained** Musley Bank, N Yorks

**FOCUS**

A fair handicap run at a sound gallop and a fair time for the grade.

**NOTEBOOK**

**Oldenway**, having only his second outing here, lay handy and in the end did just enough. He would not want the ground any easier.

**Grey Clouds**, 6lb higher, likes it round here and is very genuine. In the end she only just missed out and should continue to give a good account of herself.

**Olivia Rose(IRE)**, meeting Grey Clouds on better terms, rather sat out of her ground and was never going to get in a blow at the first two.

**Lauro**, presented with a big gap on the inner, went on but she was soon going up and down in the same place. This trip stretches her to the limit.

**Maxilla(IRE)** was in trouble a long way out and hanging coming off the home turn, her chance soon disappeared.

**Mister Arjay(USA)**, last seen in action over hurdles, looked at his best but was again well below form.

**Gala Sunday(USA)** made the running but hung away from the running rail presenting Lauro with an inviting opening. His seems to have gone right off the boil.

## 2776 SPORTINGOPTIONS COMMISSION CUTTERS STKS (H'CAP) 7f 100y

3:50 (3:50) (E) (0-70,70) 3-Y-0+ **£4,290** (£1,320; £660; £330) **Stalls** High

Form RPR

0060 **1** **Prince Of Gold**[4] 2687 4-9-7 **63** (p) NCallan 8 74
(RHollinshead) *chsd ldrs: wnt 2nd 1f out: styd on to ld nr fin* **11/1**

00-6 **2** *nk* **Alchemist Master**[16] 2368 5-8-12 **54** DeanMcKeown 10 64
(RMWhitaker) *trckd ldrs: led over 1f out: hunglft and wandered: hdd nr fin* **7/1**[1]

3401 **3** *1 ½* **Bailieborough (IRE)**[12] 2445 5-9-11 **67** (v) AlexGreaves 15 74
(DNicholls) *mid-div: hdwy to chse ldrs over 2f out: styd on same pce fnl f* **7/1**[1]

0-00 **4** *1 ¼* **Jedeydd**[12] 2459 7-9-1 **57** (t) PHanagan 1 60
(MDods) *s.i.s: hdwy over 2f out: kpt on same pce: nvr rchd ldrs* **40/1**

5005 **5** *shd* **Ronnie From Donny (IRE)**[12] 2459 4-9-7 **66** TEaves(3) 16 69
(BEllison) *prom: t.k.h: nt clr run on inner 2f out: swtchd lft: styd on* **8/1**[2]

6001 **6** *nk* **Shamwari Fire (IRE)**[16] 2346 4-8-9 **51** RFfrench 13 53
(IWMcinnes) *trckd ldrs: hmpd after 100yds: one pce fnl 2f* **12/1**

0624 **7** *2* **Cryfield**[16] 2368 7-9-1 **57** KimTinkler 3 54
(NTinkler) *mid-div: effrt on outer 3f out: nvr rchd ldrs* **12/1**

-000 **8** *shd* **Extinguisher**[12] 2461 5-9-6 **62** DRMcCabe 7 59
(DNicholls) *chsd ldrs: one pce fnl 2f* **28/1**

0030 **9** *hd* **Eastern Hope (IRE)**[8] 2560 5-9-7 **63** (b) DHolland 11 60
(MrsLStubbs) *hld up and bhd: hdwy on wd outside over 2f out: nvr nr ldrs* **8/1**[2]

0000 **10** *shd* **Smith N Allan Oils**[16] 2368 5-9-1 **57** (p) DaleGibson 5 53
(MDods) *mid-divsion: hdwy over 3f out: nvr rchd ldrs* **16/1**

54-0 **11** *nk* **Aragon's Boy**[26] 2084 4-10-0 **70** DSweeney 12 66
(HCandy) *led tl hdd & wknd over 1f out* **10/1**

65-3 **12** *5* **We'll Meet Again**[16] 2356 4-8-6 **53** PMulrennan(5) 9 36
(MWEasterby) *hld up towards rr: n.m.r and lost pl over 3f out: nvr a factor* **8/1**[2]

0-01 **13** *12* **Ben Hur**[16] 2362 5-9-6 **62** SWKelly 14 15
(WMBrisbourne) *hdwy on ins whn bdly hmpd after 100yds: in rr after: eased over 1f out* **9/1**[3]

4006 **14** *¾* **Mon Secret (IRE)**[23] 2172 6-8-11 **53** FLynch 6 4
(BSmart) *chsd ldrs: lost pl over 2f out: sn bhd and eased* **20/1**

3000 **15** *24* **Barzak (IRE)**[23] 2172 4-8-13 **55** (t) KDarley 4 —
(SRBowring) *prom: lost pl over 2f out: sn bhd: eased* **25/1**

1m 36.17s (1.87) **Going Correction** +0.30s/f (Good) **15** Ran SP% **121.5**

Speed ratings: **101,100,98,97,97 97,94,94,94,94 93,88,74,73,46**CSF £82.56 CT £604.00 TOTE £12.40: £4.00, £2.30, £3.00; EX 128.10.

**Owner** Horne, Hollinshead, Johnson **Bred** Longdon Stud Ltd **Trained** Upper Longdon, Staffs

■ Stewards Enquiry : Alex Greaves two-day ban: careless riding (Jun 22-23)

D Sweeney five-day ban: careless riding (Jun 20-24)

**FOCUS**

A modest handicap run at a sound gallop.

**NOTEBOOK**

**Prince Of Gold**, in first-time cheekpieces, found this lower grade much more his cup of tea and he nailed the errant leader near the line.

**Alchemist Master**, well handicapped on his All-Weather form, came in for plenty of support. The gamble looked nailed on when he hit the front and went a couple of lengths up, but he lost his way in front and, swishing his tail, was just worried out of it.

**Bailieborough(IRE)**, with the visor on again, ran right up to his best but claimers look a more likely path.

**Jedeydd** is slipping down the ratings and is better suited by quick ground.

**Ronnie From Donny(IRE)**, best drawn, took a fierce grip then ran into traffic problems. The extended trip was not a problem.

**Shamwari Fire(IRE)** was far from disgraced in this higher grade especially as he was almost knocked over in the first furlong.

**Smith N Allan Oils** *Official explanation: jockey said gelding suffered interference in running.*

**Ben Hur** was effectively put out of the contest early on and eventually was simply asked to complete in his own time. This is safely overlooked. *Official explanation: trainer said gelding suffered interference in running.*

## 2777 SPORTINGOPTIONS SUPPORTING RACING MAIDEN STKS 7f 100y

4:20 (4:22) (D) 3-Y-0+ **£5,525** (£1,700; £850; £425) **Stalls** High

Form RPR

-534 **1** **Lyca Ballerina**[25] 2112 3-8-6 **71** RHills 3 76
(BWHills) *trckd ldrs: qcknd to ld over 1f out: r.o wl* **11/4**[2]

2-32 **2** *2 ½* **Awesome Love (USA)**[11] 2487 3-8-11 **83** DHolland 4 75
(MJohnston) *chsd ldrs: ev ch over 1f out: nt qckn* **10/11**[1]

5-03 **3** *1* **Master Theo (USA)**[9] 2519 3-8-11 **77** JQuinn 11 72
(HJCollingridge) *trckd ldrs: nt clr run on inner 2f out: styd on ins last* **5/1**[3]

**4** *1 ½* **Premier Rouge** 3-8-11 KDarley 12 68
(ACStewart) *big: rangy: sn bhd: hdwy over 3f out: styd on fnl 2f* **12/1**

50 **5** *2* **Soviet Spirit**[30] 2001 3-8-6 OUrbina 7 58
(JRFanshawe) *trckd ldrs: nt clr run on inner over 2f out tl over 1f out: kpt on* **16/1**

00 **6** *1 ¾* **Chisel**[9] 2519 3-8-11 RFfrench 8 59?
(MJohnston) *chsd ldrs: wandered 2f out: one pce* **40/1**

**7** *1 ¾* **Scott** 3-8-4 CHaddon(7) 6 55
(JJay) *rangy: unf: s.i.s: hdwy on inner over 2f out: bot clr run over 1f out: nvr on terms* **66/1**

0 **8** *1* **Narciso (GER)**[5] 2654 4-9-7 TLucas 9 52?
(MWEasterby) *s.i.s: sn chsng ldrs: rdn and outpcd 5f out: n.d after* **100/1**

0-00 **9** *1* **Phoenix Eye**[18] 2298 3-8-11 SRighton 5 50?
(MMullineaux) *w ldr: lost pl over 1f out* **100/1**

-4 **10** *¾* **Key Factor**[9] 2530 3-8-4 ow3 PMulrennan(5) 10 46
(MWEasterby) *led tl hdd & wknd over 1f out: eased ins last* **50/1**

**11** *11* **Sonearsofar (IRE)** 4-9-2 MLawson(5) 1 20
(JParkes) *swvd lft s: hdwy on outside over 3f out: lost pl 2f out: sn bhd and eased* **100/1**

1m 36.89s (2.59) **Going Correction** +0.30s/f (Good)

**WFA** 3 from 4yo 10lb **11** Ran SP% **118.2**

Speed ratings: **97,94,93,91,89 87,85,83,82,81 69**CSF £5.58 TOTE £4.30: £1.60, £1.02, £2.10; EX 7.30.

**Owner** Letitia Lucas & R J McCreery **Bred** Stowell Hill Ltd And Mrs C Van Straubenzee **Trained** Lambourn, Berks

**FOCUS**

A fair maiden but just a very steady gallop until straightening up.

**NOTEBOOK**

**Lyca Ballerina** made it 12th time lucky, quickening up in good style and running out a decisive winner in the end.

**Awesome Love(USA)**, who looked at his best, could not match the winner's finishing burst. A stronger gallop will see him going one better.

**Master Theo(USA)**, very warm beforehand, took quite a grip. He ran out of racing room on the inner and was putting in some solid work at the finish. His trainer is struggling to get off the mark.

**Premier Rouge**, a big newcomer, took time to realise what it was all about, but he showed promise staying on nicely late in the day. This will have put him on the right path.

**Soviet Spirit** found herself short of room on the inner and her future depends on a realistic handicap mark.

**Chisel** still looks on the backward side but at least this third outing opens up the handicap route for him.

## 2778 SPORTINGOPTIONS.CO.UK SPONSORING ON FRIDAY FILLIES' H'CAP 5f

4:50 (4:50) (F) (0-55,55) 3-Y-0+ **£4,030** (£1,240; £620; £310) **Stalls** High

Form RPR

5545 **1** **Lydia's Look (IRE)**[16] 2350 7-9-1 **45** TEaves(3) 17 54
(TJEtherington) *chsd ldr: led 2f out: hld on towards fin* **9/2**[1]

0020 **2** *¾* **Leopard Creek**[8] 2556 3-9-3 **54** (p) DAllan(3) 6 60+
(MrsJRRamsden) *swtchd rt after s: hld up: hdwy 2f out: styd on to go 2nd ins last: nt qckn towards fin* **25/1**

4-00 **3** *1 ¾* **Mickledor (FR)**[8] 2556 4-9-4 **45** (p) SWKelly 13 45
(MDods) *mid-div: hmpd over 2f out: hdwy on wd outside 1f out: fin wl* **20/1**

5-30 **4** *nk* **Bond Shakira**[50] 1530 3-9-7 **55** FLynch 18 54
(BSmart) *led: edgd lft and hdd 2f out: drifted lft and styd on fnl f* **7/1**[3]

1644 **5** *nk* **Miss Wizz**[7] 2582 4-8-3 **37** (p) RoryMoore(7) 10 35
(WStorey) *chsd ldrs: swtchd lft over 2f out: edgd rt and styd on fnl f* **14/1**

0206 **6** *shd* **A Bid In Time (IRE)**[33] 1934 3-8-13 **47** NCallan 3 44+
(DShaw) *swtchd rt after s: bhd: hdwy over 1f out: styd on ins last* **25/1**

0-00 **7** *nk* **Efimac**[9] 2528 4-8-9 **43** (b[1]) SuzanneFrance(7) 15 39
(NBycroft) *bmpd s: bhd: hdwy 2f out: styd on ins last* **20/1**

-504 **8** *shd* **Petana**[6] 2620 4-8-13 **40** (b) JoannaBadger 19 36
(MDods) *in tch: hdwy to chse ldrs 2f out: nt qckn appr fnl f* **11/2**[2]

0005 **9** *1 ¾* **Ace-Ma-Vahra**[12] 2451 6-9-2 **43** (b) JBramhill 14 33
(SRBowring) *wnt rt s: hmpd and lost pl after 100yds: hdwy over 1f out: kpt on ins last* **10/1**

0204 **10** *½* **White O' Morn**[16] 2350 5-9-2 **43** (p) GGibbons 5 31
(JWUnett) *mid-div: hdwy over 2f out: nvr rchd ldrs* **20/1**

-000 **11** *2 ½* **Mystery Pips**[16] 2369 4-9-8 **49** (v) KimTinkler 4 28
(NTinkler) *chsd ldrs: fdd appr fnl f* **40/1**

060- **12** *3* **College Hippie**[165] 6243 5-9-2 **48** PMakin(5) 12 16
(JFCoupland) *chsd ldrs: wnt rt after 100yds: wknd over 1f out* **15/2**

6065 **13** *hd* **River Lark (USA)**[30] 1988 5-9-2 **43** (p) RFfrench 7 10
(MABuckley) *chsd ldrs: wknd over 1f out* **12/1**

00-0 **14** *2 ½* **Blues Princess**[20] 2252 4-9-8 **52** THamilton(3) 9 10
(RAFahey) *mid-div: effoer over 2f out: sn wknd* **16/1**

0-06 **15** *2* **Grey Orchid**[12] 2450 3-9-1 **49** GDuffield 8 —
(TJEtherington) *sn outpcd and bhd: nvr on terms* **66/1**

0-06 **16** *½* **New Day Dawning**[11] 2468 3-9-0 **48** RFitzpatrick 11 —
(CSmith) *sn in rr* **33/1**

0-00 **17** *1* **Cut Ridge (IRE)**[16] 2350 5-8-11 **43** PBradley(5) 2 —
(JSWainwright) *rr-div: nvr a factor* **25/1**

0-00 **18** *¾* **Alfelma (IRE)**[15] 2383 4-8-7 **41** NataliaGemelova(7) 1 —
(PRWood) *in tch on wd outside: outpcd over 2f out: sn lost pl* **100/1**

/00- **19** *11* **Comic Times**[382] 1807 4-8-13 **40** SRighton 16 —
(MMullineaux) *chsd ldrs: edgd lft after 100yds: lost pl over 2f out: sn bhd* **33/1**

67.26 secs (3.26) **Going Correction** +0.775s/f (Yiel)

**WFA** 3 from 4yo+ 7lb **19** Ran SP% **123.8**

Speed ratings: **104,102,100,99,99 98,98,98,95,94 90,85,85,81,78 77,75,74,57**CSF £123.47 CT £2130.89 TOTE £4.20: £1.30, £5.40, £6.70, £2.80; EX 174.10 Place 6 £14.64, Place 5 £7.23.

**Owner** Callers And Clerks **Bred** Grange Group **Trained** Norton, N Yorks

■ Stewards Enquiry : T Eaves caution: careless riding

**FOCUS**

In effect a seller in all but name with the top-weight rated just 52 and the draw again critical.

**NOTEBOOK**
**Lydia's Look(IRE)**, who is in foal, looks to be blooming and with a favourable draw recorded her fifth career win.
**Leopard Creek**, drawn six, soon made her way to the far rail. She stayed on really well to hunt up the winner and a win would make her a valuable property at stud.
**Mickledor(FR)**, in cheekpieces this time, returned to form and was unlucky not to seriously trouble the winner.
**Bond Shakira**, suited by the give underfoot, was making her handicap bow. She threw away a favourable draw by edging left and ended up nearer the stands' side rail than the far fence. She looks to have speed to burn and will be better suited by going the other way round.
**Miss Wizz**, rated just 37, was the last to make the cut.
**A Bid In Time(IRE)**, drawn just three from the outside, switched to the far side and stuck on well inside the last. Sellers give her a more realistic chance.
**Ace-Ma-Vahra** *Official explanation: jockey said mare suffered interference in running*
T/Plt: £9.70 to a £1 stake. Pool: £37,642.10. 2,811.00 winning tickets. T/Qpdt: £8.30 to a £1 stake. Pool: £2,639.80. 235.05 winning tickets. WG

## 2615 HAMILTON (R-H)
### Wednesday, June 9

**OFFICIAL GOING: Good to firm**

### 2779 WESTERN SAAB AMATEUR RIDERS' H'CAP — 6f 5y
6:50 (6:53) (E) (0-70,80) 3-Y-O+ — £3,753 (£1,155; £577; £288) Stalls Low

Form — RPR
0-02 **1** **Desert Arc (IRE)**[8] 2556 6-10-9 **62** 7ex ........ MrCDavies(5) 4 — 72
(WMBrisbourne) *sn pushed along towards rr: plenty to do over 1f out: str run fnl f to ld post* **6/1**[3]
-000 **2** *shd* **Bundy**[36] 1877 8-10-10 **61** ........ MrSDobson(3) 7 — 71
(MDods) *sn niggled in rr: hdwy over 1f out: disp ld cl home: jst failed* **14/1**
-016 **3** *hd* **Dizzy In The Head**[7] 2582 5-10-12 **65** ........ (b) MrPEvans(5) 14 — 74
(PaulJohnson) *midfield: effrt and swtchd 1/2-way: led ins fnl f: hdd cl home* **12/1**
6002 **4** *shd* **College Maid (IRE)**[4] 2670 7-9-13 **47** ........ (b) MsCWilliams 6 — 56
(JSGoldie) *chsd ldrs: rdn over 2f out: ev ch over 1f out: nt qckn wl ins fnl f* **5/1**[2]
0200 **5** *1/2* **Locombe Hill (IRE)**[11] 2492 8-10-9 **60** ........ MissKellyHarrison(3) 13 — 68
(DNicholls) *trckd ldrs: rdn over 2f out: kpt on fnl f* **16/1**
2000 **6** *1* **Xanadu**[13] 2423 8-10-3 **51** ........ (p) MissPRobson 11 — 56
(MissLAPerratt) *mde most at str pce tl hdd and no ex ins fnl f* **13/2**
50-2 **7** *shd* **Hebenus**[41] 1720 5-9-6 **45** ........ MissHCuthbert(5) 8 — 49
(TAKCuthbert) *midfield: rdn 1/2-way: kpt on fnl f: nrst fin* **11/1**
0000 **8** *1* **Colemanstown**[7] 2581 4-11-1 **66** ........ MissLEllison(3) 9 — 67
(BEllison) *towards rr: hdwy over 1f out: r.o fnl f* **14/1**
0032 **9** *3* **One Way Ticket**[9] 2524 4-10-9 **57** ........ (p) MissEJJones 1 — 49
(JMBradley) *disp ld tl wknd over 1f out* **10/3**[1]
60 **10** *1 1/2* **Caribe (FR)**[18] 2291 5-10-12 **60** ........ MissSBrotherton 12 — 48
(ABerry) *midfield: outpcd 1/2-way: n.d after* **25/1**
000/ **11** *1 1/4* **Saif Sareea**[610] 5168 4-11-0 **80** ow21 ........ MrGGibson(7) 10 — 53
(KWHogg) *a bhd* **200/1**
233- **12** *2 1/2* **Able Mind**[232] 5693 4-11-0 **69** ........ MrSIrving(7) 3 — 46
(ACWhillans) *a bhd* **25/1**
430- **13** *24* **Unshaken**[146] 5559 10-10-2 **57** ........ MrMMacdonald-Wagstaffe(7) 2 — —
(DANolan) *sn wl bhd* **66/1**

1m 12.42s (-0.68) **Going Correction** -0.275s/f (Firm) **13** Ran SP% **112.3**
Speed ratings: **93,92,92,92,91 90,90,89,85,83 81,78,46**CSF £79.18 CT £996.15 TOTE £7.60: £3.40, £5.20, £2.40; EX 300.90.
**Owner** Steve Roberts **Bred** D J And Mrs Deer **Trained** Great Ness, Shropshire
■ Stewards Enquiry : Miss L Ellison two-day ban: used whip with excessive frequency (Jun 24,25)

**FOCUS**
The early pace was decent and it suited those coming from behind.

**NOTEBOOK**
**Desert Arc(IRE)** was awarded a race at Redcar last week and withdrawn on Monday after unseating his rider on the way to the start. Off a 7lb higher mark he just about got there in time to double up and continues to progress. The fast pace here suited and one could not rule out the hat-trick despite another likely rise.
**Bundy** struggled to go the early pace, but came home strongly and was only just denied. This represented a return to form.
**Dizzy In The Head** was robbed of victory in the dying strides on this debut for the yard and appreciated the return to six.
**College Maid(IRE)**, who returned to form with a second at Doncaster at the weekend but had since come in season, ran another good race and looks to be nearing a win.
**Locombe Hill(IRE)** has not won over this trip for six years, but he was not too far off it here and would be of interest back over further.
**Hebenus**, held in banded company at Ayr towards the end of April, does not do much for the form.
**One Way Ticket** did a bit too much early in the race and was a spent force when the challengers came.

### 2780 REDROW HOMES CHAMPAGNE MAIDEN STKS (QUALIFIER FOR THE HAMILTON PARK 2-Y-O SERIES FINAL) — 6f 5y
7:20 (7:21) (D) 2-Y-O — £5,531 (£1,702; £851; £425) Stalls Low

Form — RPR
**1** **Abraxas Antelope (IRE)** 2-9-0 ........ RWinston 6 — 84+
(JHowardJohnson) *mde all: shkn up and r.o strly fr 2f out* **4/1**
**2** *6* **Arthur Wardle (USA)** 2-9-0 ........ ANicholls 5 — 66
(MLWBell) *sn outpcd: hdwy over 2f out: kpt on fnl f: no ch w wnr* **7/2**[3]
**3** *hd* **Mceldowney** 2-9-0 ........ SChin 2 — 65
(MJohnston) *sn outpcd: hdwy over 1f out: kpt on: no imp fnl f* **10/1**
**4** *2 1/2* **Love Beauty (USA)** 2-9-0 ........ JFanning 4 — 58
(MJohnston) *in tch: outpcd 1/2-way: btn fnl f* **5/2**[1]
**5** *3* **Golband** 2-8-9 ........ JCarroll 3 — 44
(LMCumani) *trckd wnr tl rdn and wknd over 1f out* **3/1**[2]
**6** *6* **Alexia Rose (IRE)** 2-8-9 ........ FNorton 1 — 26
(ABerry) *chsd ldrs: rdn and hung bdly rt fr over 2f out: wknd over 1f out* **25/1**

1m 11.75s (-1.35) **Going Correction** -0.275s/f (Firm) **6** Ran SP% **108.7**
Speed ratings: **98,90,89,86,82 74**CSF £17.01 TOTE £5.90: £2.90, £2.00; EX 30.60.
**Owner** Andrea & Graham Wylie **Bred** Gerry Flannery **Trained** Crook, Co Durham
■ A race won by Mark Johnston for 3 of the last 6 years, but he was out of luck this time.

**FOCUS**
Probably a fair race and a smart performance by Abraxas Antelope, whose impressive debut provided trainer Howard Johnson with his first juvenile winner.

**NOTEBOOK**
**Abraxas Antelope(IRE)**, the first two-year-old runner for connections who have enjoyed high-profile success with jumpers, had been taught his job well and managed to bag the rail. From this point onwards it was one-way traffic and he ran out an emphatic winner. He looks smart, and as connections believe he will appreciate an easier surface he may well be capable of improving significantly on this later in the season.
**Arthur Wardle(USA)** looked as though the experience would do him good and stayed on to claim second, having been outpaced early. He is a relatively late foal and better can be expected in time.
**Mceldowney**, whose stable's two-year-olds usually benefit from a run - they still have several first-time up winners regardless of this - stayed on well for third once getting the hang of things and should win a similar race with normal progression.
**Love Beauty(USA)** ◆, a stablemate of the third, was retained for 90,000gns at auction and expected to go to the Royal meeting if putting in a good performance here. However, he showed distinct signs of greenness and never really got going. Some of the stable better juveniles were beaten on their debut's last season so he can be expected to improve considerably on this.
**Golband** showed speed early, but could not go with the winner when that one quickened and faded late on. She should improve on this, but will need to if she is going to be winning in the near future.
**Alexia Rose(IRE)** flashed her tail in the early stages and then lost all chance when hanging badly right across the course. She probably has ability but does not look straighforward. *Official explanation: jockey said filly hung badly right-handed throughout the race*

### 2781 WALTER SCOTT SAINTS & SINNERS CHALLENGE CUP H'CAP — 1m 65y
7:50 (7:50) (D) (0-85,80) 3-Y-O+ — £6,396 (£1,968; £984; £492) Stalls High

Form — RPR
4341 **1** **Goodbye Mr Bond**[7] 2580 4-8-3 **58** 6ex ........ FNorton 2 — 70
(EJAlston) *prom: outpcd over 3f out: rallied to ld appr fnl f: kpt on strly* **8/1**
2250 **2** *1 1/2* **Tony Tie**[11] 2474 8-9-4 **73** ........ DHolland 9 — 82
(JSGoldie) *trckd ldrs: outpcd over 3f out: rallied over 1f out: kpt on: nt rch wnr* **8/1**
0406 **3** *1/2* **Cherished Number**[14] 2410 5-9-8 **77** ........ (v) RWinston 3 — 84
(ISemple) *trckd ldrs: effrt and ev ch over 1f out: one pce fnl f* **15/2**[3]
5101 **4** *nk* **Jordans Elect**[6] 2618 4-9-3 **75** 6ex ........ LEnstone(3) 11 — 82
(ISemple) *trckd ldrs: effrt over 2f out: one pce fnl f* **11/2**[2]
0022 **5** *1/2* **Takes Tutu (USA)**[6] 2618 5-9-8 **77** ........ (p) DarrenWilliams 8 — 83
(KRBurke) *hld up: hdwy over 2f out: rdn and one pce fnl f* **15/2**[3]
-005 **6** *nk* **Nemo Fugat (IRE)**[7] 2580 5-8-7 **62** ........ JCarroll 10 — 67
(DNicholls) *hld up: rdn over 2f out: kpt on: nt pce to chal* **20/1**
6011 **7** *2 1/2* **Acomb**[8] 2560 4-9-6 **75** 6ex ........ KDarley 5 — 74
(MWEasterby) *plld hrd: led to appr fnl f: sn outpcd* **7/4**[1]
0-06 **8** *1* **Wessex (USA)**[16] 2366 4-9-11 **80** ........ SChin 6 — 77
(JamesMoffatt) *s.i.s: effrt fr rr over 2f out: no imp fnl f* **25/1**
0010 **9** *1 3/4* **Border Artist**[16] 2368 5-8-9 **64** ........ ANicholls 4 — 57
(DNicholls) *hld up: rdn over 2f out: n.d* **20/1**
0100 **10** *1* **Love In Seattle (IRE)**[11] 2493 4-9-9 **78** ........ JFanning 1 — 68
(MJohnston) *w ldr tl rdn and wknd wl over 1f out* **25/1**
300- **11** *5* **Big Smoke (IRE)**[21] 5425 4-9-5 **74** ........ PHanagan 7 — 53
(JHowardJohnson) *towards rr: pushed along 1/2-way: btn 2f out* **100/1**

1m 45.4s (-3.90) **Going Correction** -0.275s/f (Firm) **11** Ran SP% **115.7**
Speed ratings: **108,106,106,105,105 104,102,101,99,98 93**CSF £63.80 CT £511.77 TOTE £8.80: £3.00, £2.80, £2.10; EX 99.10.
**Owner** Peter J Davies **Bred** Michael Ng **Trained** Longton, Lancs

**FOCUS**
Goodbye Mr Bond defied his 6lb penalty for last week's win at Newcastle in good style.

**NOTEBOOK**
**Goodbye Mr Bond** defied his 6lb penalty in decisive fashion and it is unlikely his good recent run has ended here.
**Tony Tie** is an admirable performer, and he finished well to take second.
**Cherished Number** continues to run well in defeat, but needs to drop further in the weights before winning again.
**Jordans Elect** ran well under his 6lb penalty and reversed Thirsk form with Acomb in the process.
**Takes Tutu(USA)** ran pretty much to form with Jordans Elect on their course form latest.
**Nemo Fugat(IRE)** is 24lb lower than when last winning and has suggested then last twice now a return to winning ways may not be far off.
**Acomb** pulled hard early and failed to run to form.
**Wessex(USA)**
**Border Artist** *Official explanation: jockey said gelding never got a run in final two furlongs*

### 2782 SKY BET PRESS RED TO BET NOW H'CAP — 1m 4f 17y
8:20 (8:20) (C) (0-90,83) 3-Y-O+ — £9,065 (£3,438; £1,719; £781) Stalls High

Form — RPR
0633 **1** **Millennium Hall**[6] 2615 5-7-13 **53** ........ PFessey 2 — 63
(PMonteith) *hld up in tch: hdwy to ld over 1f out: pushed out fnl f* **20/1**
1-41 **2** *3/4* **Zeitgeist (IRE)**[9] 2529 3-9-0 **83** 6ex ........ DHolland 4 — 92
(LMCumani) *cl up: chal 4f out: kpt on fnl f: nt pce of wnr* **8/11**[1]
0-62 **3** *1 1/2* **Piri Piri (IRE)**[7] 2595 4-8-11 **65** ........ KDarley 1 — 71
(PJMcbride) *hld up: effrt u.p over 1f out: kpt on fnl f: no imp* **8/1**[3]
1102 **4** *1/2* **Isa'Af (IRE)**[6] 2615 5-8-3 **62** ........ BSwarbrick(5) 8 — 68
(PWHiatt) *trckd ldrs: rdn whn n.m.r 3f out: rdn and one pce over 1f out* **7/1**[2]
06/1 **5** *1/2* **Colorado Falls (IRE)**[26] 1785 6-9-7 **78** ........ LEnstone(3) 5 — 83
(PMonteith) *trckd ldrs: effrt over 2f out: no ex over 1f out* **11/1**
2311 **6** *hd* **Tudor Bell (IRE)**[23] 2179 3-8-9 **78** ........ RWinston 3 — 82
(JGMO'Shea) *cl up: led over 2f to over 1f out: no ex* **10/1**
-504 **7** *5* **Rutters Rebel (IRE)**[9] 2529 3-8-3 **72** ........ DaleGibson 6 — 68
(GASwinbank) *hld up: rdn whn n.m.r briefly 3f out: sn no imp* **14/1**
2100 **8** *5* **Gran Dana (IRE)**[28] 2047 4-9-9 **77** ........ JFanning 7 — 65
(MJohnston) *led to over 2f out: wknd over 1f out* **22/1**

2m 34.86s (-4.34) **Going Correction** -0.275s/f (Firm)
**WFA** 3 from 4yo+ 15lb **8** Ran SP% **114.7**
Speed ratings: **103,102,101,101,100 100,97,94**CSF £35.53 CT £141.94 TOTE £29.60: £4.80, £1.20, £1.70; EX 60.90 Trifecta £561.20 Pool of £1,818.20 - 2.30 winning units.
**Owner** Mrs Elizabeth Ferguson **Bred** Meon Valley Stud **Trained** Rosewell, Midlothian

**FOCUS**
Not much of a race, but a welcome return to winning ways for Millennium Hall.

**NOTEBOOK**
**Millennium Hall** finally returned to winning ways, but it has been a long time coming. He did it nicely in the end, but is hardly one to take a short price about next time.
**Zeitgeist(IRE)** was disappointing on the face if it but actually improved on the form he showed when winning at Redcar. A stiffer test may suit him even better.
**Piri Piri(IRE)** did not really have the race run to suit and did well considering.
**Isa'Af(IRE)** has been in good form and again ran well.

**2783** **TENNENT CALEDONIAN BREWERIES CLAIMING STKS** **1m 3f 16y**
**8:50** (8:50) (E) 3-Y-O **£4,078** (£1,255; £627; £313) **Stalls** High

Form RPR
-022 **1** **Hearthstead Dream**[8] [2545] 3-8-4 65........................(b[1]) BSwarbrick(5) 2 64
(JGMO'Shea) *chsd ldrs: led 2f out: wandered bdly u.p: kpt on fnl f* **6/1**

05 **2** ¾ **Manhattan Jack**[14] [2412] 3-9-3 ............................ RWinston 6 71
(GASwinbank) *hld up: hdwy to dispute ld over 1f out: no ex towards fin* **14/1**

-505 **3** 1½ **Dolly Wotnot (IRE)**[12] [2442] 3-8-9 62........................................ KDarley 1 60
(NPLittmoden) *prom: rdn 4f out: kpt on fnl f: no imp* **3/1**[2]

1365 **4** 3 **Platinum Pirate**[30] [1995] 3-9-0 63...............................(v) DarrenWilliams 3 61
(KRBurke) *keen early: led to 2f out: hung lft: sn outpcd* **6/1**

-043 **5** 1¼ **Stylish Sunrise (IRE)**[9] [2520] 3-8-6 65 ow1.......................(t) DHolland 5 51
(MLWBell) *cl up: effrt over 2f out: ev ch whn bdly hmpd over 1f out: nt rcvr* **9/2**[3]

3-33 **6** 11 **Par Indiana (IRE)**[33] [1933] 3-8-9 60........................................ PHanagan 4 36
(ISemple) *trckd ldrs tl wknd over 2f out* **5/2**[1]

5 **7** 12 **The Fox's Head (IRE)**[38] [1784] 3-8-9 ........................................ JMcAuley 7 17
(BMactaggart) *in tch: rdn over 3f out: sn btn* **33/1**

0 **8** 3½ **Smeorach**[41] [1718] 3-7-13 ............................................................ PFessey 8 1
(JamesMoffatt) *bhd: struggling fr 1/2-way* **66/1**

2m 24.13s (-2.37) **Going Correction** -0.275s/f (Firm) **8** Ran SP% **111.4**
Speed ratings: **97,96,95,93,92 84,75,73**CSF £79.07 TOTE £6.40: £1.80, £3.20, £1.80; EX 71.90.Stylish Sunrise was claimed by Ian Wood for £6,000.

**Owner** Gary Roberts **Bred** G And Mrs Middlebrook **Trained** Elton, Gloucs

■ Stewards Enquiry : B Swarbrick two-day ban: careless riding (Jun 20,21)

**FOCUS**
With the fancied runners disappointing the form is unlikely to add up to much.

**NOTEBOOK**
**Hearthstead Dream** looked less than enthusiastic in a battle at Leicester and the fitting of blinkers appeared to do the trick, although he did still wander under pressure. Nonetheless he pulled out extra under pressure and it may simply have been lack of concentration rather than lack of will at Leicester. He may soon be sent hurdling.

**Manhattan Jack** ran his best race to date on this first try in claiming company and was only run out of it in the final 50 yards. He can pick up a similar event.

**Dolly Wotnot(IRE)** had every chance and was disappointing.

**Platinum Pirate** has been running mainly on a soft surface of late and this fast ground did not help.

**Stylish Sunrise(IRE)** was still in with every chance when badly hampered. This put an end to his race and he was claimed afterwards by Ian Wood for £6,000.

**Par Indiana(IRE)** has been running well in maidens and ran way below form on this first venture into claiming company.

**Smeorach** *Official explanation: jockey said filly was unsuited by fast ground*

**2784** **THISTLE MINING H'CAP** **5f 4y**
**9:20** (9:23) (D) (0-80,75) 3-Y-O+ **£5,707** (£1,756; £878; £439) **Stalls** Low

Form RPR
0554 **1** **Malahide Express (IRE)**[19] [2274] 4-8-0 **55**.................... JDO'Reilly(7) 4 63
(EJAlston) *mde all stands side: rdn and hld on wl fnl f* **11/1**

0320 **2** hd **Chairman Bobby**[12] [2461] 6-9-5 **70**.............................. LEnstone(3) 1 77
(DWBarker) *chsd stands side ldrs: swtchd rt over 1f out: r.o wl fnl f* **10/1**

0-00 **3** nk **Kings College Boy**[19] [2261] 4-8-10 **58**..............................(b) PHanagan 5 64
(RAFahey) *outpcd stands side: hdwy over 1f out: r.o fnl f* **17/2**

4000 **4** shd **Currency**[14] [2399] 7-9-13 **75**................................................ DHolland 6 81
(JMBradley) *hld up in tch stands side: hdwy over 1f out: r.o fnl f: hld cl home* **10/1**

0-00 **5** 1¼ **Aahgowangowan (IRE)**[50] [1525] 5-8-10 **58**......................(t) FLynch 12 59
(MDods) *led far side: kpt on fnl f: nt rch stands side* **7/1**[3]

2501 **6** shd **Pirlie Hill**[6] [2620] 4-8-5 **53** 6ex................................................ JCarroll 3 54
(MissLAPerratt) *prom stands side: effrt over 2f out: edgd rt: one pce fnl f* **11/2**[2]

6020 **7** hd **Vijay (IRE)**[13] [2423] 5-8-7 **55** ow1.......................................(v) RWinston 13 55
(ISemple) *chsd ldrs far side: rdn over 2f out: r.o same pce fnl f* **11/1**

4160 **8** 1¾ **Highland Warrior**[7] [2581] 5-9-11 **73**......................................... KDarley 9 67
(JSGoldie) *missed break: hdwy far side over 2f out: no imp fnl f* **3/1**[1]

0000 **9** 1¾ **Legal Set (IRE)**[7] [2581] 8-8-1 **49**........................................(t) AnnStokell 7 37
(MissAStokell) *sn towards rr far side: rdn 1/2-way: nt pce to chal* **66/1**

00-0 **10** ¾ **Rosie's Result**[50] [1525] 4-8-2 **50**....................................... DaleGibson 10 35
(MTodhunter) *chsd far side ldrs tl rdn and outpcd over 1f out* **33/1**

0-44 **11** ¾ **Elliot's Choice (IRE)**[46] [1602] 3-8-8 **70**.............................. DTudhope(7) 8 52
(DCarroll) *hld up in tch: effrt 1/2-way: btn fnl f* **12/1**

-610 **12** 1 **Feu Duty (IRE)**[5] [2650] 3-8-13 **68**............................................. JFanning 2 47
(TJEtherington) *taken early to post: cl up stands side tl wknd over 1f out* **10/1**

00-0 **13** 7 **Northern Svengali (IRE)**[13] [2423] 8-7-12 **46** oh10.........(tp) JMcAuley 11 —
(DANolan) *chsd far side ldrs tl wknd fr 1/2-way* **100/1**

59.22 secs (-2.04) **Going Correction** -0.275s/f (Firm)
**WFA** 3 from 4yo+ 7lb **13** Ran SP% **120.5**
Speed ratings: **105,104,104,104,102 101,101,98,95,94 93,91,80**CSF £116.91 CT £688.06 TOTE £12.70: £4.00, £4.50, £3.40; EX 66.60 Place 6 £587.39, Place 5 £154.53.

**Owner** The Steady Eddie Partnership **Bred** Yeomanstown Stud **Trained** Longton, Lancs

■ Stewards Enquiry : L Enstone three-day ban: used whip with excessive frequency (Jun 20-22)

**FOCUS**
An ultra competitive event that produced an exciting finish.

**NOTEBOOK**
**Malahide Express(IRE)** led throughout and just found enough to hold on in a blanket finish. This was a welcome return to winning ways.

**Chairman Bobby**, a disappointment when last seen - connections putting it down to the race coming too soon - finished well, but not well enough to get to the winner.

**Kings College Boy**, with blinkers back on, was closing with every stride and may benefit from a return to six furlongs.

**Currency** had his ideal conditions and returned to something like his best.

**Aahgowangowan(IRE)** is better when able to get her toe in.

**Highland Warrior** lost any chance by missing the break. This is best ignored.

T/Plt: £1,575.10 to a £1 stake. Pool: £50,381.95. 23.35 winning tickets. T/Qpdt: £46.60 to a £1 stake. Pool: £4,393.90. 69.70 winning tickets. RY

# [2107]NEWBURY (L-H)
Wednesday, June 9

**OFFICIAL GOING: Good to firm**
There was a major bias towards those that raced down the centre on the straight track. In races 2 and 6 those drawn high faced an impossible task.
Weather: cloudy but warm

**2785** **GREEN ENERGY ENVIRONMENTAL MAIDEN STKS** **6f 8y**
**6:35** (6:36) (D) 3-Y-O **£6,500** (£2,000; £1,000; £500) **Stalls** Centre

Form RPR
0- **1** **Kschessinka (USA)**[249] [5367] 3-8-9 ........................................ MHills 2 81
(WJHaggas) *lw: hld up in rr: swtchd rt to stands side over 2f out: qcknd to ld over 1f out: drvn and hld on wl fnl f* **11/4**[2]

4323 **2** 1¼ **Farewell Gift**[7] [2576] 3-9-0 80........................................ KFallon 10 82
(RHannon) *lw: chsd ldrs: led over 2f out: hdd appr fnl f: kpt on u.p but no imp on wnr* **13/8**[1]

5-0 **3** 3½ **Truman**[20] [2236] 3-9-0 ............................................................ SSanders 3 72
(JARToller) *chsd ldrs: drvn to chal ins fnl 2f: outpcd ins last* **12/1**[3]

3-03 **4** ½ **King's Caprice**[16] [2372] 3-9-0 87........................................ SCarson 6 70
(GBBalding) *t.k.h: chsd ldrs: rdn to chal ins fnl 2f: wknd ins fnl f* **11/4**[2]

0-0 **5** 5 **Even Hotter**[23] [2165] 3-8-9 ........................................................ TQuinn 1 50
(DWPArbuthnot) *outpcd and bhd: styd on fr over 1f out: kpt on wl cl home but nvr a danger* **66/1**

00 **6** shd **Chica Roca (USA)**[7] [2577] 3-8-6 75.................................... LPKeniry(3) 9 50
(BJMeehan) *chsd ldrs: rdn over 2f out: wknd over 1f out* **25/1**

0-0 **7** ¾ **Themesofgreen**[7] [2586] 3-8-7 .............................................. TO'Brien(7) 5 52
(MRChannon) *plld hrd: w ldr tl led over 3f out: hdd over 2f out: wknd over 1f out* **100/1**

**8** 3 **Loveyoulongtime** 3-8-9 ........................................................ SDrowne 7 38
(AMBalding) *bkwd: wl grwn: in tch: pushed along and edgd lft 2f: wknd over 1f out* **33/1**

00 **9** 1 **Batchworth Beau**[25] [2113] 3-9-0 ............................................. ADaly 4 40
(EAWheeler) *led tl hdd over 3f out: wknd 2f out* **100/1**

**10** 6 **Royal Logic** 3-8-9 .............................................................. TEDurcan 8 17
(MRChannon) *bkwd: lengthy: strong: a outpcd in rr* **20/1**

1m 13.56s (-0.81) **Going Correction** -0.125s/f (Firm) **10** Ran SP% **114.1**
Speed ratings: **100,98,93,93,86 86,85,81,79,71**CSF £7.05 TOTE £4.00: £1.40, £1.10, £3.10; EX 8.00.

**Owner** Lael Stable **Bred** John T L Jones Jr And Ashford Stud **Trained** Newmarket, Suffolk

**FOCUS**
A modest contest by Newbury standards, but a couple may be capable of further progress. The field raced down the centre of the track.

**NOTEBOOK**
**Kschessinka(USA)**, who beat only one home in her only start at two, after which she cracked a tibia, was well backed to open her account on this belated reappearance and did so with a degree of comfort. She has obviously improved a good deal since that debut and there should be more to come.

**Farewell Gift** ran right up to his best and was the only one able to keep tabs on the winner. He is exposed in comparison to the winner, but may be better suited by the extra furlong now.

**Truman** ran a decent race on the wide outside and an extra furlong and handicap company could see him off the mark.

**King's Caprice** was inclined to take a good hold early and had little left towards the end. He is becoming exposed and ran moderately in his only previous try on soft ground, but the feeling remains that is what he really needs.

**Even Hotter**has a pedigree that is all speed, but ran as though she requires a greater test of stamina.

**2786** **WEDGEWOOD ESTATES MAIDEN AUCTION FILLIES' STKS** **6f 8y**
**7:05** (7:05) (E) 2-Y-O **£4,761** (£1,465; £732; £366) **Stalls** Centre

Form RPR
**1** **Whazzat** 2-8-9 ................................................................ RHughes 6 87
(BWHills) *lw: lengthy: scope: strong: s.i.s: bhd: stdy hdwy fr 3f out: led 1f out: hdd jst ins: rallied to ld again last strides* **7/1**

**2** nk **Maids Causeway (IRE)** 2-8-9 .................................................. MHills 4 86
(BWHills) *s.i.s: bhd: hdwy over 2f out: qcknd to ld ins fnl f: drvn and kpt on: ct last strides* **16/1**

**3** nk **Cours De La Reine (IRE)** 2-8-9 ............................................ JQuinn 10 85
(PWChapple-Hyam) *lw: lengthy: scope: chsd ldrs: led ins fnl 2f: rdn and hdd 1f out: kpt on u.p ins last* **9/4**[1]

03 **4** ¾ **Stephanie's Mind**[11] [2481] 2-8-4 ........................................ KMcEvoy 2 78
(CNAllen) *chsd ldrs: pressed ldrs over 2f out: stl ev ch jst ins last: outpcd cl home* **5/1**[3]

22 **5** 3½ **Agent Kensington**[34] [1905] 2-8-2 ........................................ RLMoore 9 68+
(RHannon) *chsd ldrs: rdn 2f out: wknd ins fnl f* **9/2**[2]

**6** 1½ **Lady Le Quesne (IRE)** 2-8-5 ow1 ........................................ SDrowne 8 64
(AMBalding) *w'like: mde most tl hdd ins fnl 2f: wknd fnl f* **25/1**

**7** 1¾ **Miss Malone (IRE)** 2-8-6 ........................................................ PDobbs 13 59
(RHannon) *lw: leggy: scope: strong: mid-div: pushed along over 2f out: kpt on fnl f: nt trble ldrs* **33/1**

**8** ½ **You Found Me** 2-8-9 ............................................................... EAhern 17 61
(CTinkler) *b.bkwd: neat: bhd and sn pushed along: kpt on fr over 1f out: styd on cl home* **25/1**

**9** nk **Guinea A Minute (IRE)** 2-8-6 .................................................. TQuinn 15 57
(MLWBell) *w'like: chsd ldrs: rdn over 2f out: wknd fnl f* **11/1**

4 **10** hd **Marianis**[20] [2245] 2-8-4 .......................................................... JMackay 12 54
(JGPortman) *pressed ldrs: rdn over 2f out: wknd fnl f* **11/1**

**11** ½ **Shosolosa (IRE)** 2-8-1 ........................................................ JFMcDonald(3) 18 53
(BJMeehan) *b.bkwd: strong: s.i.s: bhd: kpt on fr over 1f out: nt trble ldrs* **33/1**

06 **12** 1¾ **Mystery Maid (IRE)**[20] [2245] 2-8-2 .......................................... DKinsella 7 46
(HSHowe) *chsd ldrs: rdn 1/2-way: wknd ins fnl 2f* **100/1**

**13** hd **Dara Girl (IRE)** 2-8-4 ................................................................ RHavlin 16 47
(MrsPNDutfield) *lw: neat: bhd: sn rdn and outpcd: styd on fnl f* **66/1**

**14** ¾ **Flying Ridge (IRE)** 2-8-3 ........................................................ LPKeniry(3) 11 47
(AMBalding) *rangy: scope: s.i.s: sn rcvrd to trckd ldrs: wknd over 1f out* **40/1**

0 **15** 1 **Debs Broughton**[15] [2382] 2-7-13 ........................................ LisaJones(3) 3 40
(WJMusson) *pressed ldrs over 3f* **66/1**

**16** ½ **Bazelle** 2-8-6 ................................................................ PaulEddery 14 42
(PWD'Arcy) *bkwd: strong: pressed ldrs over 3f* **50/1**

**17** 3½ **Sirce (IRE)** 2-7-13 ........................................................ FPFerris(3) 5 28
(DJCoakley) *bkwd: strong: wl grwn: sn outpcd in rr* **25/1**

**18** ¾ **Kapaje** 2-8-2 ................................................................ CCatlin 1 25
(MRChannon) *b.bkwd: unf: sn outpcd* **20/1**

19 3 1/2 **Spinning Coin** 2-7-13 ........ RMiles(3) 19 15
(JGPortman) *leggy: unf: slowly away: a bhd* **50/1**

1m 14.33s (-0.04) **Going Correction** -0.125s/f (Firm) **19** Ran SP% **133.2**
Speed ratings: **95,94,94,93,88 86,84,83,83,82 82,79,79,78,77 76,71,70,66**CSF £108.82 TOTE £7.20: £2.70, £4.50, £2.00; EX 87.80.

**Owner** W J Gredley **Bred** Eurostrait Ltd **Trained** Lambourn, Berks

**FOCUS**
A fairly competitive maiden run at a sound pace in which the first four finished clear. Those racing down the centre of the track were favoured.

**NOTEBOOK**
**Whazzat**, a 30,000gns half-sister to Special Envoy, was a springer in the market and showed decent battling qualities to make a winning debut. Her breeding suggests she will be even better suited by a longer trip and she looks to have a future.

**Maids Causeway(IRE)** ◆, out of a half-sister to high-class French performers Vetheuil and Verveine, was brought with a perfectly timed run over on the far side, but her rallying stablemate worried her out of it. It should not take her long to go one better.

**Cours De La Reine(IRE)**, a 30,000gns yearling out of a three-time winner in Ireland, was well backed to make a winning debut. Up there all the way, she was only just outpointed by the Hills pair and should be able to win her maiden soon, possibly over a bit further.

**Stephanie's Mind** had the edge in experience on the front three, but again showed ability under a positive ride, finishing well clear of the others. She has the ability to win an ordinary maiden, but they are getting ever more competitive and she may have more opportunity when nurseries start.

**Agent Kensington** did not see a great deal of daylight, but when she did get out in the clear she did not find much and the front quartet were pulling away from her on the run to the line. She does not seem to be progressing.

**Lady Le Quesne(IRE)**, a 16,000gns half-sister to Space Cowboy plus five winners abroad, out of a dual winner in France, showed good speed for a long way and has obviously inherited some ability.

**Miss Malone(IRE)**, a 32,000euros yearling from the same family as Reel Buddy, was not expected according to the market, so this debut effort was encouraging.

**You Found Me** ◆, a 36,000euros half-sister to three winners including Naughty Nell, is out of a winning half-sister to Compton Bolter. She demonstrated ability herself and deserves extra credit as she did best of those that raced closest to the stands' rail.

## 2787 SUNLEY H'CAP — 1m 5f 61y
7:35 (7:38) (E) (0-75,71) 3-Y-O+ — £4,712 (£1,450; £725; £362) Stalls High

| Form | Pos | Dist | Horse / comment | Jockey | RPR |
|---|---|---|---|---|---|
| 4211 | 1 | | **My Legal Eagle (IRE)**[7] 2590 10-8-5 **52** 6ex — (RJPrice) *hld up in rr: stdy hdwy on outside fr 6f out: led 3f out: pushed along and styd on wl fnl f* **5/1**[1] | RMiles(3) 6 | 61 |
| 1042 | 2 | 1 1/2 | **Crossways**[7] 2590 6-9-11 **69** — (PDEvans) *b. prom: rdn to chse ldrs fr 2f out: wnt 2nd u.p wl ins last but no imp on wnr* **13/2**[2] | RHavlin 4 | 76 |
| 0-24 | 3 | hd | **Carrowdore (IRE)**[11] 2471 4-9-7 **65** — (CNAllen) *chsd ldrs:hdwy and bmpd ins fnl 3f:swtchd lft and hdwy 2f out: chsd wnr and no imp ins last: lost 2nd cl home* **16/1** | (p) IMongan 1 | 72 |
| 6400 | 4 | 1/2 | **San Hernando**[18] 2285 4-9-11 **69** — (DRCElsworth) *lw: hld up in rr: stdy hdwy fr 3f out: chsd ldrs appr fnl f: nt qckn ins last* **13/2**[2] | TQuinn 3 | 75 |
| -055 | 5 | 2 1/2 | **Silver Prophet (IRE)**[18] 2305 5-9-12 **70** — (MRBosley) *s.i.s: bhd: hdwy 3f out: styd on u.p fnl 2f: one pce ins last* **40/1** | GBaker 7 | 73 |
| 1206 | 6 | 1/2 | **Lissahanelodge**[16] 2375 5-7-13 **43** — (PRHedger) *lw: s.i.s: bhd: hdwy over 2f out: kpt on fnl f: nt trble ldrs* **11/1** | CCatlin 9 | 45 |
| 0225 | 7 | nk | **Classic Millennium**[23] 2167 6-8-11 **58** — (WJMusson) *s.i.s: bhd: rdn over 3f out: styd on u.p fnl 2f but nvr gng pce to trble ldrs* **8/1**[3] | LisaJones(3) 11 | 59 |
| -001 | 8 | 9 | **Duc's Dream**[7] 2595 6-9-1 **59** 6ex — (DMorris) *b. lw: broke wl: stdd after 3f: rdn and hdwy 3f out: wknd over 2f out* **20/1** | JMackay 12 | 48 |
| 5/0- | 9 | 8 | **Chivite (IRE)**[23] 259 5-9-9 **67** — (PJHobbs) *in tch: hdwy to trck ldrs 5f out: rdn to chse wnr over 2f out: no imp: wknd over 1f out: eased whn no ch* **5/1**[1] | KFallon 15 | 45 |
| 0-06 | 10 | nk | **Nick The Silver**[23] 2179 3-8-2 **63** ow1 — (GBBalding) *bhd: rdn 3f out and no hdwy* **50/1** | SCarson 2 | 40 |
| 00-P | 11 | 3/4 | **Polanski Mill**[74] 1135 5-9-4 **62** — (CAHorgan) *b. bhd: lost tch and wl bhd 5f out: styd on fnl 2f* **66/1** | PaulEddery 8 | 38 |
| 6/00 | 12 | hd | **Reviewer (IRE)**[10] 2501 6-9-12 **70** — (MMeade) *chsd ldrs tl wknd qckly over 2f out* **20/1** | SDrowne 14 | 46 |
| -000 | 13 | 1/2 | **The Persuader (IRE)**[32] 1958 4-9-13 **71** — (MJohnston) *lw: chsd ldrs tl wknd qckly over 2f out* **8/1**[3] | KDalgleish 5 | 46 |
| 3 | 14 | 14 | **Donald (POL)**[13] 2429 4-8-12 **56** — (MPitman) *lw: chsd ldr tl wknd over 3f out* **10/1** | RHughes 13 | 12 |
| 05/0 | 15 | 3/4 | **Deferlant (FR)**[18] 2305 7-9-2 **60** — (KBell) *sn led: hdd 3f out: sn wknd* **50/1** | (v) EAhern 10 | 15 |

2m 50.88s (-0.11) **Going Correction** +0.075s/f (Good)
**WFA** 3 from 4yo+ 17lb **15** Ran SP% **122.9**
Speed ratings: **103,102,101,101,100 99,99,94,89,88 88,88,88,79,79**CSF £34.73 CT £498.77 TOTE £5.70: £2.30, £2.80, £4.00; EX 28.20.

**Owner** E G Bevan **Bred** G J Freyne **Trained** Ullingswick, H'fords

**FOCUS**
A modest if competitive handicap run at a sound pace.

**NOTEBOOK**
**My Legal Eagle(IRE)** was still on the bridle passing the three-furlong pole whilst most of his rivals were hard at it. He found plenty when finally asked for his effort and completed the hat trick in style. These conditions appear to suit him admirably and his confidence is so high that there is no reason why he cannot win again. He is hardly recognisable as the horse that was beaten in banded company as recently as last month.

**Crossways** was unable to close the gap with My Legal Eagle to any great degree compared to their running at Nottingham ,despite being 7lb better off. This was another sound effort from him though, and he deserves to get his head in front.

**Carrowdore(IRE)** stayed on well against the far rail and is now 2lb lower than for his only previous win.

**San Hernando** is sliding down the handicap and probably ran his best race so far for his current yard, but he could probably do with a bit further.

**Silver Prophet(IRE)** stayed on late, but lacked an effective turn of foot. His best form over hurdles was with cut in the ground.

**Classic Millennium** deserves some credit for reaching her final placing as she gave away a good few lengths at the start.

**Chivite(IRE)** has won five times over hurdles since his last outing on the Flat 17 months ago and was potentially well treated. However, he was one of the first off the bridle and found little. *Official explanation: trainer said gelding lost its action*

## 2788 CITY INDEX FILLIES' H'CAP — 7f (S)
8:05 (8:06) (D) (0-85,84) 3-Y-O+ — £6,279 (£1,932; £966; £483) Stalls Centre

| Form | Pos | Dist | Horse / comment | Jockey | RPR |
|---|---|---|---|---|---|
| 15-0 | 1 | | **Music Maid (IRE)**[18] 2284 6-8-8 **62** — (HSHowe) *hld up in rr: hdwy 2f out: str run to ld 1f out: flashed tail u.p: hld on wl* **9/1** | DKinsella 4 | 72 |
| 4240 | 2 | 1/2 | **And Toto Too**[9] 2521 4-8-13 **67** — (PDEvans) *bhd: hdwy over 2f out: chal over 1f out: kpt on u.p ins last but nt rch wnr* **5/1**[3] | (b) KFallon 1 | 76 |
| 0-05 | 3 | nk | **Little Venice (IRE)**[27] 2064 4-9-8 **76** — (CFWall) *chsd ldrs: rdn to chal over 1f out: styd on u.p ins last but nt qckn nr fin* **10/3**[1] | SSanders 3 | 84 |
| -000 | 4 | 1 | **Riva Royale**[24] 2143 4-9-11 **82** — (IAWood) *sn led: edgd rt fr 2f out: hdd 1f out: one pce ins last* **14/1** | TPQueally(3) 2 | 88 |
| 005- | 5 | hd | **Hot Lips Page (FR)**[249] 5367 3-8-6 **70** — (RHannon) *b: chsd ldrs: rdn and outpcd 1/2-way: kpt on again u.p fnl f* **33/1** | RSmith 5 | 75 |
| 10-0 | 6 | nk | **Danclare (USA)**[56] 1398 3-9-6 **84** — (JHMGosden) *b.bkwd: hld up in tch: n.m.r and lost position 2f out: kpt on again fnl f: gng on cl home* **4/1**[2] | KMcEvoy 6 | 88 |
| -651 | 7 | 1 | **Lorien Hill (IRE)**[7] 2572 3-8-9 **73** 6ex — (BWHills) *lw: chsd ldrs: rdn over 2f out: wknd ins fnl f* **11/2** | MHills 8 | 75 |
| 60-5 | 8 | shd | **Blaina**[9] 2517 4-9-7 **75** — (DRCElsworth) *lw: sn pressing ldr: rdn over 2f out: wknd over 1f out* **16/1** | TQuinn 10 | 76 |
| 05-5 | 9 | 2 | **Calusa Lady (IRE)**[36] 1855 4-7-10 **55** — (GBBalding) *bhd: rdn over 2f out: a outpcd* **10/1** | RThomas(5) 7 | 51 |
| 00-0 | 10 | 6 | **Medusa**[40] 1750 4-8-12 **66** — (DMorris) *sn outpcd* **66/1** | MTebbutt 9 | 47 |

1m 26.21s (-1.01) **Going Correction** -0.125s/f (Firm)
**WFA** 3 from 4yo+ 10lb **10** Ran SP% **111.2**
Speed ratings: **100,99,99,97,97 97,96,96,93,86**CSF £50.83 CT £159.72 TOTE £9.20: £1.90, £1.80, £1.50; EX 36.40.

**Owner** R J Parish **Bred** A W Allen **Trained** Oakford, Devon

**FOCUS**
A fair fillies' handicap in which it was again an advantage to race down the middle of the track.

**NOTEBOOK**
**Music Maid(IRE)**, all the better for her Ascot spin last month, has a good record in fillies' handicaps and, with the trip and ground ideal, was brought with a strong run down the centre of the track. She did not do much in front and flashed her tail, but is probably capable of winning again under her ideal conditions.

**And Toto Too** returned to form following a modest effort and hounded the winner all the way to the line. She has won off a higher mark than this and is running well enough to win again.

**Little Venice(IRE)** just about ran to the pound with And Toto Too on Salisbury running under a positive ride and was coming back again at the finish. She seems to be returning to form.

**Riva Royale** set the pace as usual and did not completely fold once headed. This was her best effort so far this season.

**Hot Lips Page(FR)**, unplaced in three previous starts and making her handicap debut, was not disgraced and ran as though she would appreciate a mile.

**Danclare(USA)**, taking a huge step in class, managed to get herself stuck in traffic and had no time to make up the deficit once out in the clear. She is better than this.

## 2789 RUNDLE & CO CLASSIFIED STKS — 1m (S)
8:35 (8:35) (D) 3-Y-O+ — £5,590 (£1,720; £860; £430) Stalls Centre

| Form | Pos | Dist | Horse / comment | Jockey | RPR |
|---|---|---|---|---|---|
| -140 | 1 | | **Brief Goodbye**[11] 2493 4-9-3 76 — (JohnBerry) *mde all: hrd rdn fnl f: flashed tail: hld on all out* **20/1** | MFenton 8 | 86 |
| -026 | 2 | hd | **Prince Hector**[11] 2469 5-9-3 80 — (WJHaggas) *b.hind: hld up in rr: hdwy over 2f out: drvn and str run fnl f: fin wl: jst failed* **7/2**[1] | KFallon 2 | 86 |
| 0200 | 3 | 1 | **Arry Dash**[11] 2474 4-9-7 84 — (MRChannon) *lw: bhd: rdn and hdwy over 1f out: styd on wl cl home* **8/1** | TEDurcan 4 | 87 |
| 2406 | 4 | shd | **Linning Wine (IRE)**[20] 2237 8-9-5 82 — (BGPowell) *chsd ldrs: wnt 2nd 3f out: hung lft fr 2f out: carried hd high u.p fnl f: nt run on cl home* **4/1**[2] | JPMurtagh 9 | 85 |
| 1-00 | 5 | nk | **Spanish Don**[22] 2201 6-9-4 84 — (DRCElsworth) *lw: chsd ldrs: outpcd 2f out: sn rdn: rallied fnl f and kpt on again cl home* **7/1** | LPKeniry(3) 5 | 86 |
| 0-65 | 6 | 12 | **Star Sensation (IRE)**[22] 2196 4-9-5 85 — (PWHarris) *pitched s: sn rcvrd to trck ldrs: wknd over 1f out* **9/2**[3] | (e[1]) RLMoore 6 | 57 |
| 1 | 7 | 7 | **Dafore**[38] 1796 3-8-11 85 — (RHannon) *lw: s.i.s: bhd: rdn 1/2-way: no rspnse* **4/1**[2] | RHughes 7 | 44 |
| 40-0 | 8 | 3/4 | **Gem Bien (USA)**[39] 1773 6-9-3 80 — (AndrewTurnell) *chsd wnr to 3f out: sn wknd* **33/1** | CCatlin 3 | 37 |

1m 38.96s (-1.87) **Going Correction** -0.125s/f (Firm)
**WFA** 3 from 4yo+ 11lb **8** Ran SP% **111.7**
Speed ratings: **104,103,102,102,102 90,83,82**CSF £84.89 TOTE £24.80: £4.90, £1.30, £2.50; EX 98.30.

**Owner** J McCarthy **Bred** Chippenham Lodge Stud Ltd **Trained** Newmarket, Suffolk

**FOCUS**
A tight classified event run at a sound pace. The field stayed mid-track.

**NOTEBOOK**
**Brief Goodbye** had a bit to find on adjusted official ratings, but he is perfectly suited by these conditions and despite being one of the outsiders, did not go unbacked. He responded really well to a positive ride and was brave at the finish despite a flash of the tail, but beating higher rated rivals will not earn him much sympathy from the Handicapper. *Official explanation: trainer had no explanation for the improved form shown*

**Prince Hector**, back over his best trip, came from off the pace to throw down a serious challenge inside the last furlong. However, despite the champion's best efforts he could never quite get there.

**Arry Dash** ◆ ideally needs an extra quarter-mile these days so it was no surprise to see him doing all his best work late. He is one to watch out for back over ten furlongs.

**Linning Wine(IRE)** had every chance, but tended to hang in behind the winner under pressure and probably found this ground too quick.

**Spanish Don** has shown his best form when coming from off the pace, but this was still an improvement on his two previous outings this season.

**Star Sensation(IRE)** started awkwardly, but was beaten too far for that to have been the only excuse.

**Dafore**, winner of his only previous start, was up two furlongs in trip and taking on some established rivals, but it was the much faster ground that was almost certainly to blame for this modest effort and he should be given another chance when he can get his toe in. *Official explanation: jockey said colt lost its action*

## 2790 SODEXHO PRESTIGE H'CAP 7f (S)

**9:05** (9:06) (E ) (0-75,76) 3-Y-O **£4,537** (£1,396; £698; £349) **Stalls** Centre

Form RPR

5030 **1** **Panshir (FR)**[18] 2306 3-9-4 **72** SSanders 9 86
(CFWall) *lw: hld up in rr: smooth hdwy over 2f out: qckn d to chse ldr 1f out: led last half f: pushed out: readily* **12/1**

0061 **2** 3/4 **Distant Connection (IRE)**[9] 2536 3-9-8 **76** 6ex KMcEvoy 1 88
(APJarvis) *lw: sn led: hdd 3f out: led again ins fnl 2f: hdd last half f: kpt on but a hld by wnr* **8/1**[3]

5-00 **3** 4 **Scientist**[32] 1975 3-9-7 **75** JFortune 7 77
(JHMGosden) *b.bkwd: in tch: hdwy over 2f out: pressed ldrs and rdn wl over 1f out: styd on same pce ins last* **20/1**

0-0P **4** 3 **Molinia**[7] 2587 3-8-8 **62** JQuinn 4 56
(RMBeckett) *s.i.s: sn rcvrd and in tch: chsd ldrs fr 3f out: kpt on same pce appr fnl f* **66/1**

6-06 **5** 1 1/4 **Beautiful Noise**[22] 2207 3-8-0 **57** JFMcDonald[(3)] 6 48
(DMorris) *chsd ldrs: led 3f out: hdd ins fnl 2f: wknd over 1f out* **20/1**

-430 **6** 3/4 **Evaluator (IRE)**[32] 1957 3-9-1 **72** RMiles[(3)] 13 61
(TGMills) *chsd ldrs: rdn over 2f out: wknd over 1f out* **10/1**

-000 **7** 1 **Motu (IRE)**[18] 2306 3-9-3 **71** JPMurtagh 19 57
(JLDunlop) *chsd ldrs: rdn 1/2-way: wknd fr 2f out* **4/1**[2]

-300 **8** 1 1/4 **Torquemada (IRE)**[42] 1702 3-8-6 **60** PDoe 17 43
(WJarvis) *s.i.s: bhd: hdwy over 2f out: rdn and edgd lft 2f out and over 1f out: kpt on ins last: nt a danger* **33/1**

040- **9** 1 1/2 **Blue Java**[182] 6158 3-8-12 **66** SDrowne 20 45
(HMorrison) *in tch: rdn 3f out: wknd fr 2f out* **20/1**

5-00 **10** shd **Swift Sailing (USA)**[15] 2378 3-9-5 **73** MHills 10 52
(BWHills) *chsd ldrs tl wknd 2f out* **40/1**

0-00 **11** 1 1/4 **One Upmanship**[12] 2444 3-8-12 **66** EAhern 2 42
(JGPortman) *chsd ldrs: wknd qckly 2f out* **33/1**

53-0 **12** nk **Piccleyes**[15] 2377 3-8-9 **63** RLMoore 5 38
(RHannon) *in tch: rdn to press ldrs over 2f out: sn wknd* **33/1**

-600 **13** shd **Night Worker**[30] 1997 3-8-3 **57** RSmith 18 32
(RHannon) *in tch: rdn and outpcd 1/2-way: styd on again ins last* **20/1**

400- **14** 1 1/4 **American Duke (USA)**[224] 5829 3-9-2 **70** PaulEddery 14 41
(BJMeehan) *s.i.s: bhd: kpt on fnl 2f but nvr a danger* **66/1**

54-0 **15** 1/2 **Rockley Bay (IRE)**[38] 1796 3-8-11 **65** DSweeney 8 35
(PJMakin) *b.bkwd: in tch: drvn to chse ldrs over 2f out: sn wknd* **33/1**

6-60 **16** 1 1/2 **Wizard Looking**[9] 2536 3-9-1 **69** (t) PDobbs 3 35
(RHannon) *in tch 5f* **28/1**

53-0 **17** nk **Epaminondas (USA)**[42] 1702 3-8-12 **73** PGallagher[(7)] 11 38
(RHannon) *lw: chsd ldrs over 4f* **25/1**

6300 **18** 1/2 **Off Beat (USA)**[19] 2266 3-9-0 **68** (b) SCarson 12 32
(RFJohnsonHoughton) *chsd ldrs 4f* **25/1**

64-0 **19** 7 **Neap Tide**[43] 1688 3-9-7 **75** RHughes 16 21
(JHMGosden) *lw: t.k.h: chsd ldrs to 1/2-way* **9/1**

-053 **20** 1 1/4 **Aesculus (USA)**[13] 2428 3-8-13 **67** KFallon 15 10
(LMCumani) *lw: in tch: rdn 3f out: sn wknd* **3/1**[1]

1m 25.15s (-2.07) **Going Correction** -0.125s/f (Firm) **20** Ran SP% **130.3**
Speed ratings: **106,105,100,97,95 94,93,92,90,90 89,88,88,87,86 84,84,83,75,74**CSF £90.52 CT £1985.82 TOTE £19.00: £3.40, £2.00, £4.10, £20.30; EX 173.50 Place 6 £98.92, Place 5 £69.86.
**Owner** Ettore Landi **Bred** Curtasse S A S **Trained** Newmarket, Suffolk

**FOCUS**
A smart winning time for the grade, more than a second faster than the all-aged fillies' handicap over the same trip. This was another race in which it was crucial to race down the centre of the track.

**NOTEBOOK**
**Panshir(FR)** was a maiden coming into this, but he had threatened to win a race and on this occasion everything went right. Ridden with a lot of confidence, he scythed through the field passing the two-furlong pole and pulled right away along with the runner-up. Now that he has found out how to win, it would be no surprise to see him add to this.
**Distant Connection(IRE)**, under a 6lb penalty for his Sandown win, was given a positive ride out in the middle of the track and though he found the winner too good, he still pulled right away from the others. The track bias helped him, but this was still a good performance under his ideal conditions.
**Scientist ◆**, making his handicap debut, had every chance before being made to look onepaced by the front pair inside the last furlong. There was still a decent margin back to the fourth and he shapes as though a step up to a mile will suit.
**Molinia** ran her best race so far and, though this performance was helped by her racing down the centre of the track, she still deserves credit. Fast ground looks to be the key to her.
**Beautiful Noise** showed up well for a long way under a positive ride but, not for the first time, failed to see out the trip. She may need to drop to six.
**Evaluator(IRE) ◆** may need easier ground, but deserves some credit as he steered a path more towards the stands' side.
**Motu(IRE)** should have been suited by the drop in trip, but even this looked beyond him. In his defence he was not racing on the favoured side of the track and should be given another chance.
**Torquemada(IRE)**, whose best effort to date came on Polytrack, threatened to get into it on the stands' side passing the two-furlong pole, but that was always going to be difficult given the way the track was riding and he also hung under pressure. The extra furlong did not seem to be a problem.
**Aesculus(USA)** *Official explanation: trainer was unable to offer any explanation for poor form shown.*

T/Jkpt: Not won. T/Plt: £323.80 to a £1 stake. Pool: £56,053.00. 126.35 winning tickets. T/Qpdt: £51.50 to a £1 stake. Pool: £3,825.40. 54.95 winning tickets. ST

# 2599 LEOPARDSTOWN (L-H)

Wednesday, June 9

**OFFICIAL GOING: Good to firm**

## 2792a ROCHESTOWN STKS (LISTED RACE) 6f

**6:30** (6:30) 2-Y-O **£22,922** (£6,725; £3,204; £1,091)

RPR

**1** **Man O World (IRE)**[35] 1891 2-9-0 PJSmullen 2 94
(DKWeld, Ire) *settled 2nd: chal st: led over 1f out: strly pressed cl home: all out* **7/4**[2]

**2** hd **Joyce (IRE)**[18] 2314 2-9-0 JPSpencer 4 93
(APO'Brien, Ire) *led: strly pressed 1 1/2f out: hdd over 1f out: rallied u.p* **13/8**[1]

**3** 2 **Clash Of The Ash (USA)**[60] 1334 2-9-0 KJManning 1 87
(JSBolger, Ire) *drvn along early: 4th into st: 3rd and kpt on fr over 1f out* **2/1**[3]

**4** 9 **Tough Enough (IRE)** 2-9-0 DMGrant 3 60
(JohnJosephMurphy, Ire) *chsd ldrs: 3rd u.p ent st: sn wknd* **16/1**

1m 14.1s **Going Correction** -0.05s/f (Good) **4** Ran SP% **113.7**
Speed ratings: **101,100,98,86**CSF £5.29 TOTE £2.90; DF 4.00.
**Owner** L W Heiligbrodt **Bred** Forenaghts Stud **Trained** The Curragh, Co Kildare

**NOTEBOOK**
**Man O World(IRE)** just managed to hold on in a below-par Listed contest which was still run at a fair pace. He is going the right way.
**Joyce(IRE)** handled this faster ground well enough and his renewed effort close home almost saw him back in front again.
**Clash Of The Ash(USA)** was outpaced for most of the way but stayed on well enough inside the last.

## 2793a BALLYCORUS STKS (GROUP 3) 7f

**7:00** (7:00) 3-Y-O+ **£32,042** (£9,366; £4,436; £1,478)

RPR

**1** **Naahy**[22] 2200 4-9-7 SHitchcott 3 109
(MRChannon) *mde all: styd on wl st: comf* **7/4**[1]

**2** 1/2 **Hamairi (IRE)**[20] 2255 3-8-11 96 MJKinane 2 108
(JohnMOxx, Ire) *trckd ldrs in 3rd: 4th early st: 3rd and boxed in 1f out: r.o wl cl home* **13/2**

**3** 1/2 **Latino Magic (IRE)**[7] 2603 4-9-7 104 RMBurke 1 106
(RJOsborne, Ire) *s.i.s: settled 4th: hdwy on outer ent st: 2nd and veered lft 1 1/2f out: edgd lft again under 1f out: sn no ex* **4/1**[3]

**4** 3 1/2 **Rockets 'n Rollers (IRE)**[13] 2438 4-9-7 DaneO'Neill 4 98
(RHannon) *chsd ldr in 2nd: bmpd 1 1/2f out: wkng whn checked over 1f out: no ex* **7/2**[2]

**5** 1/2 **Summer Sunset (IRE)**[31] 1980 3-8-8 95 PJSmullen 6 94
(DKWeld, Ire) *5th thrght: no imp st* **8/1**

**6** 1 1/2 **Avorado (IRE)**[37] 1849 6-9-10 109 KJManning 5 96
(JSBolger, Ire) *dwlt: hld up in rr: no imp st* **7/1**

1m 25.9s **Going Correction** -0.55s/f (Hard)
**WFA** 3 from 4yo+ 10lb **6** Ran SP% **115.5**
Speed ratings: **114,113,112,109,108 107**CSF £14.31 TOTE £2.50: £1.60, £2.30; DF 15.40.
**Owner** Kuwait Racing Syndicate **Bred** Red House Stud **Trained** West Ilsley, Berks
■ Stewards Enquiry : R M Burke one-day ban: careless riding (Jun 16)

**NOTEBOOK**
**Naahy** was given a soft lead and took advantage of it, adopting his usual front-running tactics and was never going to be caught. He remains progressive.
**Hamairi(IRE)** could be considered a bit unlucky, finding himself trapped with nowhere to go inside the last. When he finally got out it was more a case of how far as he was going to get beat rather than could he catch the winner. He is certainly worth another chance.
**Latino Magic(IRE)** did plenty of damage here, going across Rockets 'N Rollers over a furlong out and then leaning on Hamairi inside the last. He ran on well at the end but his rider received a 1 day ban for "improper" riding.
**Avorado(IRE)** missed the kick and took little interest.

## 2796a SILVER STKS (LISTED RACE) 1m 2f

**8:30** (8:30) 3-Y-O+ **£22,922** (£6,725; £3,204; £1,091)

RPR

**1** **Medicinal (IRE)**[31] 1979 3-8-8 105 (b[1]) PJSmullen 2 108
(DKWeld, Ire) *settled 6th: plld hrd to 3f out: 3rd travelling wl ent st: rdn to chal over 1f out: led wl ins fnl f: kpt on wl* **4/1**[2]

**2** 1/2 **Grand Passion (IRE)**[14] 2398 4-9-7 JFEgan 5 107
(GWragg) *cl 2nd: led over 1 1/2f out: sn strly pressed: kpt on wl: hdd wl ins fnl f* **6/1**

**3** 2 **Cobra (IRE)**[226] 5804 3-8-8 JPSpencer 10 103
(APO'Brien, Ire) *settled 4th: 3rd 3f out: chal under 2f out: no ex fnl f* **6/1**

**4** 3 1/2 **Cache Creek (IRE)**[3] 2711 6-9-4 95 JAHeffernan 11 94
(PHughes, Ire) *towards rr: 6th and rdn early st: kpt on u.p fnl f* **10/1**

**5** hd **Napper Tandy (IRE)**[7] 2603 4-9-10 109 KJManning 7 99
(JSBolger, Ire) *hld up: 7th after 1/2-way: rdn and kpt on one pce st* **3/1**[1]

**6** 2 **Lord Admiral (USA)**[17] 2333 3-8-8 100 FMBerry 8 92
(CharlesO'Brien, Ire) *hld up: 8th 4f out: 5th under 2f out: sn no ex* **10/1**

**7** 4 **Liss Ard (IRE)**[17] 2334 3-8-8 90 DMGrant 6 85
(JohnJosephMurphy, Ire) *chsd ldrs: 5th and rdn 3f out: sn no ex* **12/1**

**8** 1 **Akarem**[31] 1977 3-8-8 DPMcDonogh 1 83
(KevinPrendergast, Ire) *a bhd* **10/1**

**9** 4 1/2 **Maralan (IRE)**[14] 2417 3-8-8 77 (b) NGMcCullagh 4 74
(JohnMOxx, Ire) *led: hdd over 1 1/2f out: sn wknd: eased fnl f* **20/1**

**10** 1 1/2 **Ebaziyan (IRE)**[17] 2334 3-8-8 MJKinane 3 72
(JohnMOxx, Ire) *racd in 3rd: rdn and wknd appr st: eased fnl f* **5/1**[3]

2m 3.00s **Going Correction** -0.55s/f (Hard)
**WFA** 3 from 4yo+ 13lb **10** Ran SP% **130.0**
Speed ratings: **107,106,105,102,102 100,97,96,92,91**CSF £32.09 TOTE £2.60: £1.80, £1.90, £2.70; DF 20.30.
**Owner** Ballylinch Stud **Bred** Ballylinch Stud **Trained** The Curragh, Co Kildare

**NOTEBOOK**
**Medicinal(IRE)** wearing first-time blinkers, was very keen. He took control well inside the last and is a progressive colt.
**Grand Passion(IRE)** ran second until leading with less than two furlongs to race. The winner picked him off quite easily but this was a return to form.
**Cobra(IRE)** looked a possibility to cause an upset when launching a challenge two furlongs down but it had petered out early inside the last.
**Cache Creek(IRE)** appeared to run above her best again.
**Napper Tandy(IRE)** flatters in better company but cannot win even when dropped in class. This was disappointing again.
**Ebaziyan(IRE)** lost a hind shoe during the race and is becoming expensive to follow. *Official explanation: trainer said colt lost a hind shoe in running*

2797 - (Foreign Racing) - See Raceform Interactive

# 2702 BRIGHTON (L-H)

Thursday, June 10

**OFFICIAL GOING: Firm**

Wind: It against Weather: mostly fine & sunny

## 2798 PLEASURE PALACE RACING LADY RIDERS' SERIES CLASSIFIED STKS 1m 3f 196y

**6:30** (6:32) (E ) 4-Y-O+ **£3,347** (£1,030; £515; £257) **Stalls** High

Form RPR

02-1 **1** **Flying Spirit (IRE)**[19] 2032 5-10-1 66 MissHayleyMoore[(7)] 2 78
(GLMoore) *prom in chasng gp: led 5f out: pushed clr over 2f out: easily* **4/9**[1]

102- **2** 5 **Needwood Mystic**$^{295}$ [4279] 9-10-3 67 MissLJHarwood$^{(3)}$ 4 68
(MrsAJPerrett) *in tch: outpcd and rdn 5f out: styd on fnl 2f to take 2nd nr fin* **8/1**$^{3}$

4020 **3** ½ **Pay The Silver**$^{6}$ [2643] 6-10-11 69 (p) MsCWilliams 3 72
(IAWood) *in tch: outpcd and rdn 5f out: effrt to chse wnr over 1f out: no imp: lost 2nd nr fin* **5/1**$^{2}$

0506 **4** 4 **Lyrical Way**$^{9}$ [2547] 5-10-7 60 (b) MrsSBosley 5 62
(PRChamings) *in tch: w wnr 5f out to over 2f out: wknd over 1f out* **20/1**

1004 **5** 12 **Squirtle Turtle**$^{5}$ [2689] 4-10-4 67 (b) MrsHClubb$^{(5)}$ 1 45
(PFICole) *racd v wd: sn led and clr: hdd 5f out: btn after* **20/1**

2m 34.1s (2.00) **Going Correction** +0.30s/f (Good) **5** Ran SP% **106.6**
Speed ratings: **105,101,101,98,90**CSF £4.18 TOTE £1.40: £1.02, £3.00; EX 2.80.
**Owner** Richard Green (fine Paintings) **Bred** Sean Madigan **Trained** Woodingdean, E Sussex
■ A winner on her first ride for 16-y-o Hayley Moore, daughter of Gary and sister of Ryan and Jamie.

**FOCUS**
A moderate contest but a decent time for an amateurs' event and the winner is clearly as good as ever.

**NOTEBOOK**
**Flying Spirit(IRE)** had nothing in hand on official ratings, but punters know a good thing when they see one. Very able on tracks like this, he was given a fine ride and bolted up.
**Needwood Mystic** had no chance with the winner and is ideally suited by a longer trip nowadays.
**Pay The Silver** gets this trip on sand. He is worth a try or two at this distance, but was running out of steam near the finish.
**Lyrical Way** has been running over ten furlongs, and did not get home up the final hill.
**Squirtle Turtle**, racing too freely and all over the place, had beaten himself long before the home turn.

## 2799 KARMA BRIGHTON MARINA CLAIMING STKS 5f 213y
**7:00** (7:00) (F) 2-Y-O **£3,017** (£862; £431) **Stalls** Low

Form RPR

2111 **1** **Goldhill Prince**$^{7}$ [2616] 2-8-8 (p) CHaddon$^{(7)}$ 1 56
(WGMTurner) *mde virtually all: rdn clr fr 2f out: idled fnl f: a holding on* **11/4**$^{1}$

501 **2** ½ **Ronnies Lad**$^{21}$ [2248] 2-8-11 (p) RLMoore 2 50
(GLMoore) *in tch: rdn 1/2-way: effrt to chse wnr 1f out: clsd nr fin : a hld* **11/4**$^{1}$

035 **3** 5 **Eternally**$^{26}$ [2125] 2-8-13 (p) EAhern 3 37
(RMHCowell) *w wnr: rdn over 2f out: hung lft and fnd nil: sn btn* **7/1**

3325 **4** 2½ **Straffan (IRE)**$^{7}$ [2616] 2-8-8 SSanders 6 24
(EJO'Neill) *hld up in tch: effrt on outer over 2f out: hanging lft and btn wl over 1f out* **7/2**$^{2}$

2013 **5** 2½ **Story Of One (IRE)**$^{8}$ [2593] 2-9-1 DaneO'Neill 5 23
(NPLittmoden) *t.k.h: trckd ldng pair: rdn over 2f out: immediately lost pl and btn* **5/1**$^{3}$

0 **6** 3 **Itsa Monkey (IRE)**$^{82}$ [1060] 2-8-8 J-PGuillambert$^{(3)}$ 4 10
(NPLittmoden) *a last pair: rdn and struggling over 2f out* **16/1**

1m 13.4s (3.30) **Going Correction** +0.30s/f (Good) **6** Ran SP% **110.6**
Speed ratings: **90,89,82,79,76 72**CSF £10.17 TOTE £3.90: £2.10, £1.70; EX 7.40.The winner was the subject of a friendly claim of £10,000. Ronnies Lad (no.5) was claimed by Andrew Reid for £8,000
**Owner** Gold Hill Racing **Bred** N D Fisher **Trained** Sigwells, Somerset

**FOCUS**
A modest claimer and two runners dominated this; the others were outclassed.

**NOTEBOOK**
**Goldhill Prince** ran straighter this time, and seems to be learning with experience.
**Ronnies Lad** was never quite going to get there, but ran well and continues to look useful at this level.
**Eternally** was flying a bit high against two decent rivals. He has yet to prove he stays six furlongs.
**Straffan(IRE)** was not ideally suited by the track but was outclassed by the leading pair anyway.

## 2800 BET365 CALL 08000 322 365 FILLIES' H'CAP 5f 59y
**7:30** (7:30) (F) (0-55,53) 3-Y-O+ **£2,884** (£824; £412) **Stalls** Low

Form RPR

3060 **1** **Avit (IRE)**$^{22}$ [2227] 4-8-10 **35** JFEgan 6 42
(PLGilligan) *trckd ldrs: effrt 2f out: led over 1f out: drvn and styd on wl* **16/1**

100- **2** nk **Lucky Valentine**$^{223}$ [5849] 4-9-5 **44** (p) RLMoore 9 50
(GLMoore) *racd in midfield: rdn 2f out: prog to chse wnr 1f out: nt qckn and hld nr fin* **10/1**

-600 **3** 1½ **Ela Figura**$^{4}$ [2707] 4-9-11 **50** (p) VSlattery 10 51
(AWCarroll) *hld up in rr: rdn 2f out: prog to press ldng pair ent fnl f: unable qck* **10/1**

0060 **4** 1¾ **Must Be So**$^{31}$ [1985] 3-8-5 **37** (t) ADaly 8 31
(JJBridger) *racd in last: outpcd after 2f: r.o wl u.p fnl f: nrst fin* **25/1**

0300 **5** ½ **Black Oval**$^{8}$ [2577] 3-9-6 **52** DaneO'Neill 4 44
(SDow) *dwlt: sn pushed along in rr: struggling fr 1/2-way: r.o fnl f: n.d* **9/2**$^{2}$

0633 **6** nk **Vendors Mistake (IRE)**$^{6}$ [2661] 3-9-2 **48** SSanders 5 39
(AndrewReid) *pressed ldr: ev ch wl over 1f out: n.m.r sn after and wknd* **5/1**$^{3}$

0026 **7** 1¼ **Inching**$^{3}$ [2724] 4-9-8 **47** EAhern 2 34
(RMHCowell) *prom: ev ch 2f out: nt qckn over 1f out: n.m.r and wknd* **7/2**$^{1}$

0000 **8** ½ **Bahamian Belle**$^{12}$ [2482] 4-9-4 **50** LauraPike$^{(7)}$ 3 35
(PSMcentee) *dwlt: sn in midfield: trckd ldrs on inner 2f out: nowhere to go after: wknd fnl f* **16/1**

0502 **9** 2½ **Somethingabouther**$^{7}$ [2620] 4-9-6 **45** CCatlin 7 21
(PWHiatt) *racd in midfield: rdn and lost pl over 2f out: hanging and no ch after* **9/1**

4035 **10** ¾ **Rehia**$^{20}$ [2265] 3-9-7 **53** SWhitworth 1 26
(JWHills) *mde most to over 1f out: wknd rapidly* **7/1**

64.03 secs (1.76) **Going Correction** +0.30s/f (Good)
**WFA** 3 from 4yo 7lb **10** Ran SP% **113.4**
Speed ratings: **97,96,94,91,90 90,88,87,83,82**CSF £161.49 CT £1679.97 TOTE £19.30: £3.50, £2.10, £3.70; EX 242.20.
**Owner** Treasure Seekers 2000 **Bred** Mrs Isabella Cornwell **Trained** Newmarket, Suffolk
■ Stewards Enquiry : J F Egan one-day ban: used whip with excessive frequency (Jun 19)

**FOCUS**
A good early pace, with the two early leaders fading out of it. However, a mediocre contest, with the winner getting off the mark after 13 losing attempts.

**NOTEBOOK**
**Avit(IRE)**, finally winning at the 14th attempt, was game enough in a driving finish.
**Lucky Valentine** put in a good effort in her first run for seven months, only just being run out of it.
**Ela Figura** ran with credit under her big weight, but was just held by the leading pair.
**Must Be So** ran one of her better races, and a sixth furlong might have made things interesting
**Black Oval** stays farther than this and needed a bit more, especially after missing the break.
**Vendors Mistake(IRE)** chased the pace and probably did a bit too much.
**Inching** could never dominate and eventually faded out of it altogether.
**Bahamian Belle** tried to come with a daring run on the rail but it ended in a cul-de-sac. She can be rated better than this.
**Somethingabouther** *Official explanation: trainer said filly was unsuited by firm ground*

## 2801 G&S MECHANICAL SERVICES (S) STKS 1m 1f 209y
**8:00** (8:01) (G ) 3-5-Y-O **£2,562** (£732; £366) **Stalls** High

Form RPR

-000 **1** **Bosco (IRE)**$^{19}$ [2302] 3-8-5 59 RLMoore 6 45
(RHannon) *racd in last pair: pushed along over 4f out: hanging and reluctant fr 3f out: drvn and kpt on to ld last 100yds: hld on* **11/2**$^{3}$

0554 **2** nk **Jackie Kiely**$^{15}$ [2402] 3-8-5 50 EAhern 4 44+
(TGMills) *trckd ldrs: effrt on ins 2f out: nowhere to go and crashed into rail: renewed effrt to chal last 150yds: jst hld* **11/4**$^{1}$

-500 **3** 1¼ **Bontadini**$^{117}$ [776] 5-9-4 34 SSanders 7 42
(DMorris) *chsd clr ldng pair: pressed ldr over 3f out: rdn and finding little but led 1f out: hdd and btn fnl 100yds* **16/1**

0-00 **4** 5 **Leitrim Rock (IRE)**$^{14}$ [2426] 4-9-4 49 SWhitworth 5 33
(AGNewcombe) *s.s: rcvrd to join chsng gp after 2f: cl up and drvn over 2f out: nt qckn and sn btn* **6/1**

0-2 **5** ¾ **Labelled With Love**$^{10}$ [2520] 4-8-11 LTreadwell$^{(7)}$ 2 31
(WGMTurner) *plld hrd: chsd ldr and clr of rest: led over 3f out: wandering fr 2f out: hdd & wknd rapidly 1f out* **4/1**$^{2}$

6-06 **6** ½ **Erte**$^{9}$ [2545] 3-8-5 62 CCatlin 3 30
(MRChannon) *racd in last pair: drvn 1/2-way: struggling after and no prog* **11/2**$^{3}$

0630 **7** 14 **Margery Daw (IRE)**$^{11}$ [2501] 4-8-6 55 LauraPike$^{(7)}$ 1 —
(PSMcentee) *led at furious pce: hdd & wknd over 3f out* **13/2**

2m 6.22s (3.68) **Going Correction** +0.30s/f (Good)
**WFA** 3 from 4yo+ 13lb **7** Ran SP% **110.9**
Speed ratings: **97,96,95,91,91 90,79** CT £7.60 TOTE £3.00: £2.30, £; EX32.80 1.The winner was sold to Phil McEntee for 5,200gns. Labelled With Love (no.2) was claimed by Jim Boyle for £6,000. Jackie Kiely (no.7) was claime
**Owner** Louis Stalder **Bred** Mrs M O'Callaghan **Trained** East Everleigh, Wilts

**FOCUS**
A poor seller and a suicidal early pace set by Margery Daw, and Labelled With Love ruining his chance by tearing after her. The runner-up was unlucky, but the form is weak.

**NOTEBOOK**
**Bosco(IRE)** showed an awkward head carriage and drifted badly on the camber, but his stamina won the day.
**Jackie Kiely** was lucky not to be brought down on the rail and did remarkably well to rally so bravely.
**Bontadini** ran adequately but did not achieve much in a poor race.
**Leitrim Rock(IRE)** has been out of form and there was not much in this effort despite reaching fourth place.
**Labelled With Love** made the mistake of setting off after the tearaway leader, and it eventually finished him. He can do better at this level.
**Erte** was the first beaten, uncomfortably early in a race of this quality.
**Margery Daw(IRE)** again went too fast.

## 2802 LAURENT PERRIER H'CAP 1m 3f 196y
**8:30** (8:31) (F) (0-70,70) 3-Y-O **£3,386** (£1,042; £521; £260) **Stalls** High

Form RPR

03-4 **1** **Man At Arms (IRE)**$^{24}$ [2168] 3-9-6 **69** RLMoore 4 85
(RHannon) *settled in rr: pushed along 5f out: prog on inner to ld over 2f out : rdn clr* **7/2**$^{1}$

6-31 **2** 8 **Garston Star**$^{15}$ [2395] 3-8-2 **58** ow1 DerekNolan$^{(7)}$ 5 61
(JSMoore) *led at decent pce: edgd rt and hdd over 2f out: sn no ch w wnr: plodded on* **12/1**

5532 **3** 1¾ **Resplendent King (USA)**$^{15}$ [2401] 3-9-7 **70** SSanders 2 70
(TGMills) *chsd ldr to 3f out: sn u.p and one pce* **7/2**$^{1}$

6-03 **4** 5 **Wake Up Henry**$^{17}$ [2361] 3-8-9 **58** SDrowne 6 50
(RCharlton) *trckd ldrs: rdn 3f out: fdd fnl 2f* **7/2**$^{1}$

-006 **5** nk **Persian Dagger (IRE)**$^{33}$ [1967] 3-9-2 **65** GCarter 3 57
(JLDunlop) *settled in rr: pushed along 1/2-way: detached and struggling over 4f out: no ch after: modest late prog* **5/1**$^{2}$

2342 **6** 2½ **Oktis Morilious (IRE)**$^{15}$ [2395] 3-7-9 **47** oh1 JFMcDonald$^{(3)}$ 7 35
(AWCarroll) *wl in tch: rdn 3f out: wknd tamely* **10/1**

-561 **7** nk **Peruvian Breeze (IRE)**$^{12}$ [2485] 3-8-11 **60** EAhern 1 47
(NPLittmoden) *cl up: rdn over 3f out: wknd over 2f out* **8/1**$^{3}$

2m 32.58s (0.48) **Going Correction** +0.30s/f (Good) **7** Ran SP% **111.2**
Speed ratings: **110,104,103,100,99 98,98**CSF £42.81 TOTE £4.90: £3.10, £3.40; EX 46.60.
**Owner** The Waney Racing Group Inc **Bred** John Byrne **Trained** East Everleigh, Wilts

**FOCUS**
A moderate handicap run in a very smart time indeed for the grade. The winner was well suited by the extra distance and should be considered in similar events.

**NOTEBOOK**
**Man At Arms(IRE)** got a lovely run on the rail and looks to have improved for this longer trip. He is progressive.
**Garston Star** had a tough task against the improving winner.
**Resplendent King(USA)** will always find it hard to concede weight to the winner and did as well as could be expected.
**Wake Up Henry** did not prove he stays this trip.
**Persian Dagger(IRE)** was well beaten but can do better when stamina is more in play.
**Oktis Morilious(IRE)** is well exposed and this was a difficult mission.
**Peruvian Breeze(IRE)**, back on turf, failed to finish the race off as he had done on sand last time.

## 2803 RACING'S BIG DAY OUT AUGUST 3RD H'CAP 6f 209y
**9:00** (9:01) (F) (0-55,59) 3-Y-O+ **£3,003** (£858; £429) **Stalls** Low

Form RPR

0322 **1** **Londoner (USA)**$^{8}$ [2598] 6-10-0 **55** RLMoore 3 64
(SDow) *mde all: rdn 2f out: in command over 1f out: styd on wl* **7/2**$^{1}$

0241 **2** 1¼ **Prime Offer**$^{8}$ [2597] 8-10-4 **59** 6ex OUrbina 10 65
(JJay) *prom: drvn to chse wnr over 1f out: rn on but nvr able to chal* **6/1**$^{3}$

006 **3** 1 **Mister Clinton (IRE)**$^{103}$ [918] 7-9-12 **53** DaneO'Neill 4 56
(DKIvory) *racd in midfield: plld out and drvn wl over 1f out: styd on but nvr able to chal* **12/1**

1463 **4** ½ **Due To Me**$^{4}$ [2703] 4-9-4 **45** (p) SWhitworth 5 47
(GLMoore) *racd in rr: rdn over 2f out: no prog tl styd on u.p fnl f* **10/1**

2042 **5** ½ **Tee Jay Kassidy**$^{4}$ [2703] 4-8-1 **35** MHalford$^{(7)}$ 11 36
(JulianPoulton) *dwlt: in tch: c wd in st: no prog over 2f out: kpt on same pce over 1f out* **11/2**$^{2}$

2154 **6** 1½ **Kinsman (IRE)**$^{76}$ [1121] 7-9-9 **53** (b) J-PGuillambert$^{(3)}$ 7 50
(TDMccarthy) *s.s: racd in last: rdn and effrt 3f out: hung fire tl kpt on fnl f* **12/1**

0-05 **7** 3/4 **Iphigenia (IRE)**[14] 2425 3-8-12 **52** RMiles(3) 1 47
(PWHiatt) *trckd ldrs: rdn and effrt on inner 2f out: no imp 1f out: eased* **20/1**

-010 **8** 1 3/4 **Pererin**[2] 2766 3-8-11 **48** (b[1]) SSanders 2 38
(IAWood) *dwlt: racd in rr: last and no ch over 2f out: r.o ins fnl f* **12/1**

0024 **9** 2 **Badou**[31] 1988 4-9-2 **43** EAhern 9 28
(LMontagueHall) *chsd ldrs: cl up over 2f out: sn wknd* **13/2**

3600 **10** 6 **Aguila Loco (IRE)**[4] 2703 5-10-0 **55** (p) SDrowne 8 24
(MrsStefLiddiard) *pressed wnr to over 1f out: wknd and eased* **17/2**

00 **11** 1 **Sekwana (POL)**[14] 645 5-9-4 **45** (bt) VSlattery 12 12
(MissAMNewton-Smith) *racd in midfield: pushed along 1/2-way: wknd over 2f out* **80/1**

1m 24.34s (1.74) **Going Correction** +0.30s/f (Good)
**WFA** 3 from 4yo+ 10lb **11** Ran SP% **113.9**
Speed ratings: **102,100,99,98,98 96,95,93,91,84 83**CSF £22.99 CT £227.62 TOTE £2.90: £1.30, £2.90, £4.80; EX 18.60 Place 6 £130.02, Place 5 £102.77.
**Owner** P McCarthy **Bred** Newgate Stud Farm Inc **Trained** Epsom, Surrey

**FOCUS**
A weak race, but the first two put up creditable weight-carrying performances and the form looks sound.

**NOTEBOOK**
**Londoner(USA)** is useful at this level when everything falls into place, as it did on this occasion.
**Prime Offer** is running nicely at present, and again acquitted himself well.
**Mister Clinton(IRE)** has not shown a great deal lately but the rest seems to have freshened him up. A reproduction of this would give him every chance.
**Due To Me** is very moderate but has done well lately, and again ran with credit.
**Tee Jay Kassidy** showed his last run was not a complete fluke.
**Kinsman(IRE)** does not always get his timing right, and this time he got going too late.
**Iphigenia(IRE)** *Official explanation: jockey said filly did not handle the hill*
T/Plt: £107.10 to a £1 stake. Pool: £37,625.50. 256.30 winning tickets. T/Qpdt: £134.90 to a £1 stake. Pool: £2,553.20. 14.00 winning tickets. JN

# [2785]NEWBURY (L-H)

## Thursday, June 10

**OFFICIAL GOING: Good to firm (firm in places)**

A charity race on the card was won by Catherine Dettori, wife of Frankie, partnering Cristoforo.

## 2804 RECTANGLE GROUP MAIDEN STKS (C&G) 6f 8y

**2:10** (2:11) (D) 2-Y-0 **£5,271** (£1,622; £811; £405) **Stalls** Centre

Form RPR

0 **1** **Perfect Choice (IRE)**[26] 2111 2-8-11 DHolland 3 87
(BJMeehan) *lw: chsd ldrs: chal 2f out: led appr fnl f: rdn and hung rt ins last: kpt on wl* **4/1**[3]

**2** 1 1/4 **Financial Times (USA)** 2-8-11 LDettori 10 83
(SaeedBinSuroor) *leggy: scope: lw: chsd ldrs: rdn to chal appr fnl f: kpt on ins last but nt pce of wnr* **3/1**[2]

**3** shd **Councellor (FR)** 2-8-11 RHughes 11 83
(RHannon) *tall: str: scope: lw: sn led: rdn and hdd over 1f out: styng on one pce whn hmpd ins fnl f and lost 2nd* **5/2**[1]

**4** 5 **Royal Orissa** 2-8-11 PaulEddery 5 68
(DHaydnJones) *w'like: chsd ldrs: edgd lft u.p over 1f out: wknd fnl f* **33/1**

**5** nk **Traianos (USA)** 2-8-11 TQuinn 6 67
(PFICole) *tall: str: scope: bit bkwd: pressed ldrs: stl ev ch 2f out: wknd appr fnl f* **16/1**

**6** 2 **Dream Tonic** 2-8-8 SHitchcott(3) 7 61
(MRChannon) *lengthy: str: scope: bit bkwd: sn pressing ldrs: rdn 2f out: wknd over 1f out* **11/1**

4 **7** 1/2 **Master Joseph**[20] 2263 2-8-11 TEDurcan 4 60
(MRChannon) *lw: in tch: wknd ins fnl 2f* **14/1**

0 **8** 3/4 **Doctor's Cave**[12] 2478 2-8-11 EAhern 2 57
(CEBrittain) *bit bkwd: a outpcd* **25/1**

**9** 1/2 **Wavertree Warrior (IRE)** 2-8-11 WSupple 12 56
(NPLittmoden) *neat: s.i.s: rcvrd into mid-div 1/2-way: wknd 2f out* **16/1**

**10** shd **Liquid Lover (IRE)** 2-8-11 DaneO'Neill 8 56
(RHannon) *str: bkwd: s.i.s: a outpcd* **20/1**

**11** shd **Waatheb (IRE)** 2-8-11 PDobbs 1 55
(RHannon) *w'like: sn outpcd* **33/1**

**12** 3 **Go Mo (IRE)** 2-8-11 JFEgan 9 46
(SKirk) *neat: sn outpcd* **33/1**

1m 14.31s (-0.06) **Going Correction** -0.15s/f (Firm) **12** Ran SP% **117.8**
Speed ratings: **94,92,92,85,85 82,81,80,80,80 79,75**CSF £15.14 TOTE £5.90: £1.80, £1.80, £1.60; EX 20.70.
**Owner** Mrs Susan Roy **Bred** D G Hardisty Bloodstock **Trained** Upper Lambourn, Berks
■ Stewards Enquiry : D Holland one-day ban: careless riding (Jun 21)

**FOCUS**
A fair juvenile maiden in whch very few had previous racecourse experience; the first three came clear and the winner paid a compliment to Icemena's maiden win on the track.

**NOTEBOOK**
**Perfect Choice(IRE)** showed the benefit of his debut here last month, and proved just too strong for his less experienced market rivals. He is related to some decent juveniles and should be able to go on from this. A crack at the Chesham Stakes was mooted afterwards.
**Financial Times(USA)** ◆, from a good American family, looked the part and had every chance in the race. However, he lost little in defeat on this debut and should have no trouble winning his maiden.
**Councellor(FR)** ◆, who cost 140,000euros, was made favourite on this debut. He showed plenty of speed, despite not looking altogether happy on the ground, but was held when crossed by the winner inside the last furlong. He looks the sort to appreciate further and should not be too long in getting off the mark.
**Royal Orissa**, cheaply bought in comparison with the first three, caught the eye running on at the finish. He is related to winners at a mile and ten furlongs and, although by a sprinter, may appreciate a little further.
**Traianos(USA)**, who has a fair amount of stamina in his pedigree, showed a fair amount of promise and is likely to improve with time and distance.
**Dream Tonic**, a half-brother to a juvenile winner, showed some promise on this debut.

## 2805 RENAULT MASTER MAIDEN FILLIES' STKS 1m 2f 6y

**2:45** (2:49) (D) 3-Y-0 **£5,785** (£1,780; £890; £445) **Stalls** High

Form RPR

2- **1** **Nuzooa (USA)**[280] 4691 3-8-11 RHills 9 86
(MPTregoning) *tall: str: lw: trckd ldrs: wnt 2nd over 5f out: led 3f out: drvn clr wl over 1f out: easily* **11/4**[2]

32- **2** 5 **Asaleeb**[230] 5722 3-8-11 WSupple 7 76
(ACStewart) *led 1f: styd chsng ldr tl over 5f out: rdn to chse wnr ins fnl 2f: kpt on wl for 2nd but no ch w easy wnr* **8/1**[3]

5-3 **3** 1 **Secret Flame**[26] 2113 3-8-11 KFallon 8 74
(WJHaggas) *in tch: pushed along and outpcd 3f out: rallied over 1f out to press for 2nd but no ch w wnr: no ex and dropped to 3rd ins* **5/4**[1]

33- **4** 1/2 **Game Dame**[268] 4958 3-8-11 MHills 10 73
(BWHills) *nt grwn: bhd: n.m.r over 3f and ins fnl 3f: kpt on fnl 2f: kpt on wl fnl f but nt rch ldrs* **12/1**

0-25 **5** 2 1/2 **Dark Raider (IRE)**[20] 2267 3-8-8 63 DCorby(3) 12 68
(APJones) *bhd: hdwy 4f out: chsd ldrs and rdn 3f out: wknd over 1f out* **100/1**

**6** hd **Silver Sash (GER)** 3-8-11 TQuinn 5 68
(MLWBell) *leggy: b: s.i.s: bhd: pushed along 3f out: hdwy fr 2f out: kpt on fnl f but nvr a danger* **40/1**

**7** 4 **Burn** 3-8-11 RHughes 4 60
(MLWBell) *unf: b.nr hind: bhd: mod prog fnl 2f* **33/1**

023 **8** hd **Stocking Island**[20] 2273 3-8-11 79 TEDurcan 2 60
(BHanbury) *lw: led after 1f: hdd 3f out: wknd 2f out* **8/1**[3]

**9** 2 1/2 **Alenushka** 3-8-11 DaneO'Neill 6 55
(HCandy) *lengthy: unf: bit bkwd: s.i.s: a bhd* **33/1**

0- **10** 3 **Watership Crystal (IRE)**[222] 5869 3-8-11 LDettori 3 50
(JHMGosden) *h.d.w: bit bkwd: chsd ldrs tl rdn and wknd 3f out* **16/1**

66 **11** 6 **Nassiria**[30] 2020 3-8-11 DHolland 11 38
(CEBrittain) *chsd ldrs tl wknd 3f out* **25/1**

2m 5.82s (-2.89) **Going Correction** -0.10s/f (Good) **11** Ran SP% **120.1**
Speed ratings: **107,103,102,101,99 99,96,96,94,91 87**CSF £24.52 TOTE £3.50: £1.60, £2.90, £1.10; EX 15.70.
**Owner** Hamdan Al Maktoum **Bred** Shadwell Farm Llc **Trained** Lambourn, Berks

**FOCUS**
A fair fillies' maiden and an impressive winner in a very decent time for the grade, over a second quicker than the Listed event.

**NOTEBOOK**
**Nuzooa(USA)**, runner-up in her only previous race last September, appreciated this longer trip and hand this in safe keeping a long way from home. She is nicely bred, looks potentially Pattern class and will get further, and races such as the Lancashire Oaks or Galtres Stakes could be on the agenda.
**Asaleeb**, stepping up in trip, was close up throughout and kept on all the way to the line, without being a match for the winner. She looks a little one paced, but should be able to find a maiden.
**Secret Flame**, a well-backed favourite on this step up in distance, seemed to have every chance halfway up the straight but appeared to not get home. A drop back to a mile should be in her favour.
**Game Dame** finished further behind the winner than on their respective debuts at Newbury, but did not fare too badly on this first outing of the season. She now qualifies for a handicap mark.
**Dark Raider(IRE)** is a consistent and relatively exposed sort, but she appeared to run her race and provides a line to the value of the form. Handicaps should give her her best opportunity of finding a race.
**Silver Sash(GER)**, a half-sister to Shabernak, missed the break on this racecourse debut and then ran green in the straight. On the whole this was not a bad performance and she will be better for the experience and a longer trip.
**Burn** showed signs of ability and should come on for the run.
**Nassiria** *Official explanation: jockey said filly hung right handed in the straight*

## 2806 CANTORODDS.COM STKS H'CAP 1m (S)

**3:15** (3:17) (E) (0-75,80) 3-Y-0+ **£4,543** (£1,398; £699; £349) **Stalls** Centre

Form RPR

-005 **1** **Oh Boy (IRE)**[9] 2560 4-8-13 **60** RSmith 5 74
(RHannon) *lw: trckd ldrs: chal 2f out: rdn to ld 1f out: edgd lft u.p ins last: drvn out* **16/1**

-063 **2** 3/4 **Spirit's Awakening**[9] 2560 5-8-9 **56** CCatlin 3 68
(JAkehurst) *lw: in tch: hdwy fr 2f out: pressed ldrs ins fnl f and hung rt u.p: no ex nr fin* **6/1**[3]

2-04 **3** 2 **Habshan (USA)**[20] 2279 4-9-8 **69** RHughes 10 76
(NAGraham) *hld up in rr: stdy hdwy to ld ins fnl 2f: hdd 1f out: one pce whn hmpd ins last* **13/2**

-050 **4** 1/2 **Cuddles (FR)**[64] 1297 5-8-13 **60** DaneO'Neill 4 66
(KOCunningham-Brown) *bhd: hdwy over 1f out: r.o ins last but nt rch ldrs* **20/1**

401 **5** 1 1/4 **Just Tim (IRE)**[10] 2516 3-9-8 **80** 6ex RLMoore 2 83
(RHannon) *lw: chsd ldrs: rdn over 2f out: wknd fnl f* **6/1**[3]

20-2 **6** 2 **Magic Amour**[7] 2459 6-9-0 **61** DHolland 1 60
(IanWilliams) *lw: led: rdn and hdd ins fnl 2f: sn wknd* **4/1**[1]

0-10 **7** 2 **Iced Diamond (IRE)**[117] 772 5-8-11 **58** TEDurcan 7 52
(WMBrisbourne) *bit bkwd: in tch: rdn over 2f out: sn btn* **16/1**

-010 **8** 5 **Muyassir (IRE)**[19] 2304 9-9-2 **63** SDrowne 9 46
(MissBSanders) *bhd: rdn over 2f out: a outpcd* **16/1**

12-0 **9** 15 **Pop Up Again**[19] 2291 4-10-0 **75** LDettori 8 23
(GASwinbank) *chsd ldrs tl wknd qckly ins fnl 2f* **7/1**

-000 **10** dist **Boundless Prospect (USA)**[19] 2304 5-9-9 **70** MHills 6 —
(JWHills) *net muzzle ct in stalls and virtually lft s: t.o* **9/2**[2]

1m 40.02s (-0.81) **Going Correction** -0.15s/f (Firm)
**WFA** 3 from 4yo+ 11lb **10** Ran SP% **115.0**
Speed ratings: **98,97,95,94,93 91,89,84,69,—**CSF £107.50 CT £712.58 TOTE £23.00: £5.80, £2.30, £3.90; EX 121.70 Trifecta £953.60 Pool £1,611.80 - 1.20 winning units.
**Owner** A F Merritt **Bred** Miss Brid Walsh **Trained** East Everleigh, Wilts
■ Stewards Enquiry : R Smith two-day ban: careless riding (Jun 21-22)

**FOCUS**
A modest sprint for the track, run in a very ordinary time for the grade. The form needs treating with caution.

**NOTEBOOK**
**Oh Boy(IRE)**, a lightly-raced colt, had shown little since running third in a moderate maiden 13 months ago. However, he had slipped in the handicap and the return to fast ground did the trick. The form is nothing special but he does not look badly treated if able to repeat this effort.
**Spirit's Awakening** ran another decent race back on this fast ground, but is not the easiest to win with. Some form of headgear may enable him to take the extra step.
**Habshan(USA)** looked a real threat on only his second try in a handicap, but was weakening out of contention when squeezed up late on. He is lightly raced and still has improvement in him.
**Cuddles(FR)**, best known as a Polytrack performer, has slipped to a fair mark and may be up to winning an ordinary fillies' contest.
**Just Tim(IRE)** seemed to have conditions in his favour but was unable to repeat his Chepstow win under a 6lb penalty.
**Magic Amour** has a tendency to be inconsistent, and apart from his two successive wins last summer tends not to run two races alike. A drop back to seven may be in his favour.
**Pop Up Again** *Official explanation: jockey said filly lost her action*

**Boundless Prospect(USA)**, the subject of a gamble, stood still when the stalls opened, due to getting his net muzzle caught. Supporters will no doubt be looking for an early opportunity to get their money back. *Official explanation: jockey said gelding's net muzzle got caught on the starting stalls mechanism*

## 2807 LORD WEINSTOCK MEMORIAL STKS (REGISTERED AS THE BALLYMACOLL STUD STKS) (LISTED) (FILLIES) 1m 2f 6y

**3:45** (3:45) (A) 3-Y-O **£17,400** (£6,600; £3,300; £1,500) **Stalls** High

Form RPR

-203 **1** **Incheni (IRE)**[21] 2242 3-8-9 101 SDrowne 7 102
(GWragg) *hld up in rr: stdy hdwy on outside over 2f out: qcknd to ld 1f out: drvn out* **9/2**[3]

1-31 **2** 3/4 **Halicardia**[22] 2221 3-8-12 106 DHolland 2 104
(PWHarris) *lw: hld up in rr: hdwy to trck ldrs over 2f out: rdn: swtchd lft and hdwy over 1f out: chsd wnr ins last: no imp* **11/10**[1]

3-12 **3** nk **Classical Dancer**[21] 2242 3-8-9 95 DaneO'Neill 4 100
(HCandy) *in tch: drvn to ld ins fnl 2f: hdd 1f out: styd on same pce u.p* **9/4**[2]

5 **4** 2 1/2 **Shuheb**[15] 2401 3-8-9 TEDurcan 3 96?
(CEBrittain) *chsd ldr 7f out: led 3f out: hdd ins fnl 2f: wknd over 1f out* **100/1**

1-44 **5** 1/2 **Si Si Amiga (IRE)**[19] 2307 3-8-9 92 MHills 1 95
(BWHills) *lw: chsd ldrs: rdn 3f out: wknd over 1f out* **16/1**

1-0 **6** 13 **Proud Tradition (USA)**[36] 1879 3-8-9 80 LDettori 6 70
(JHMGosden) *lw: led: rdn and hdd 3f out: wknd qckly 2f out* **16/1**

2m 6.87s (-1.84) **Going Correction** -0.10s/f (Good) **6** Ran SP% **109.3**
Speed ratings: **103,102,102,100,99 89**CSF £9.38 TOTE £5.00: £1.70, £1.40; EX 10.20.
**Owner** Mrs Emily Oppenheimer Turner **Bred** Hascombe And Valiant Studs **Trained** Newmarket, Suffolk

### FOCUS

An ordinary renewal of this Listed contest, run in only an average time for the grade, over a second slower than the maiden. That said the form looks fairly sound.

### NOTEBOOK

**Incheni(IRE)**, already placed in Group Three and Listed company this season, gained her reward for those efforts and at the same time reversed Goodwood placings with the third on the same terms. She seemed to appreciate the long straight, more galloping track and extra two furlongs.

**Halicardia**, winner of the Lupe Stakes on her reappearance, was covered up then held in briefly when looking for a run. However, she appeared to get out in plenty of time and the penalty for that win probably made the difference.

**Classical Dancer** had the beating of the winner on Goodwood form, but still had something to find on official ratings. She ran her race but gave the impression that this trip was beyond her at this stage.

**Shuheb** was taking a big step up in grade on only her second outing and ran remarkably well. Her breeding suggests she will appreciate a longer trip, and she will have no trouble winning a maiden if this form is to be believed.

**Si Si Amiga(IRE)** had a fair amount to find on official ratings and ran close to her mark on a line through the winner.

## 2808 RENAULT TRAFIC MAIDEN STKS 7f (S)

**4:20** (4:20) (D) 3-Y-O **£5,960** (£1,834; £917; £458) **Stalls** Centre

Form RPR

**1** **Kehaar** 3-9-0 EAhern 8 84
(MAMagnusson) *gd sort: str: lw: trckd ldrs: chal jst ins fnl f: drvn to ld fnl 75yds: readily* **13/2**[3]

5252 **2** 1 1/4 **Pizazz**[10] 2536 3-9-0 79 DHolland 1 81
(BJMeehan) *lw: w ldrs: led over 3f out: rdn fnl f: hdd and no ex fnl 75yds* **10/11**[1]

**3** 3/4 **Deuxieme (IRE)** 3-8-9 SDrowne 4 74?
(RCharlton) *lengthy: scope: lw: s.i.s: bhd: stdy hdwy over 2f out: chsd ldrs and pushed along fnl f: nt qckn ins last* **8/1**

**4** 5 **Corky (IRE)** 3-9-0 RLMoore 9 66
(RHannon) *cmpt: bit bkwd: s.i.s: bhd: pushed along over 2f out: kpt on fnl f but nvr nr ldrs* **33/1**

-323 **5** 3/4 **All Quiet**[14] 2425 3-8-9 78 RHughes 7 59
(RHannon) *chsd ldrs: rdn to chal over 1f out: wknd fnl f* **11/2**[2]

**6** nk **Nazzwah** 3-8-9 TEDurcan 3 58
(MRChannon) *str: scope: bhd: pushed along over 2f out: sme hdwy fr over 1f out: nt a danger* **25/1**

**7** 1 1/4 **Revenir (IRE)** 3-9-0 LDettori 5 60
(ACStewart) *w'like: hld up mid-div: pushed along and hdwy to chse ldrs 3f out: wknd over 1f out* **28/1**

0 **8** 3/4 **Cayman Calypso (IRE)**[19] 2311 3-9-0 KFallon 10 58
(MAJarvis) *chsd ldrs: n.m.r 3f out: styd prom tl wknd qckly over 1f out* **16/1**

0- **9** 3 1/2 **Richie Boy**[223] 5850 3-9-0 MHenry 2 49
(MAJarvis) *hdwy to chse ldrs 1/2-way: sn rdn: wknd fr 2f out* **50/1**

05 **10** hd **Gentle Raindrop (IRE)**[19] 2286 3-8-9 JFEgan 13 43
(SKirk) *s.i.s: sn in tch: rdn over 2f out: sn btn* **16/1**

0 **11** 4 **Black Sabbeth**[38] 1830 3-9-0 CCatlin 11 38
(PJMakin) *bit bkwd: outpcd most of way* **100/1**

00- **12** 5 **So Determined (IRE)**[221] 5886 3-9-0 JFortune 12 25
(GAButler) *sn led: hdd over 3f out: sn btn* **66/1**

1m 25.66s (-1.56) **Going Correction** -0.15s/f (Firm) **12** Ran SP% **118.7**
Speed ratings: **102,100,99,94,93 92,91,90,86,86 81,76**CSF £12.25 TOTE £9.50: £2.70, £1.10, £2.10; EX 15.20.
**Owner** East Wind Racing Ltd **Bred** Watership Down Stud **Trained** Upper Lambourn, Berks

### FOCUS

A fair maiden featuring a number of inexperienced horses in which the first three came clear.

### NOTEBOOK

**Kehaar ◆**, who cost 170,000gns as a yearling, is bred to be a high-class sprinter. He showed signs of his inexperience when asked to go and win his race, but did it well enough in the end. His trainer believes he is the best horse he has had, and he should benefit considerably from the outing.

**Pizazz**, touched off in a handicap last time, was ridden from the front this time but came up against a rival who is potentially very useful. He should win an ordinary maiden.

**Deuxieme(IRE) ◆**, a half-sister to King's County, was slowly away on this debut but picked up nicely in the second half of the race and finished on the heels of the principals with the rest beaten off. She should stay a little further and can win a race before long.

**Corky(IRE)**, a half-brother to the useful sprinter Bonus, missed the break but was getting the hang of things late on. The experience should bring him on.

**All Quiet**, who has been running well in similar maidens, was beaten a fair way on this occasion. Fillies' handicaps may offer her a better chance of success.

**Nazzwah**, another debutante, took a while to get the hang of things but did give some encouragement for the future.

## 2809 FORTIS BANK STKS (H'CAP) 1m 4f 5y

**4:50** (4:50) (D) (0-85,84) 3-Y-O **£5,687** (£1,750; £875; £437) **Stalls** High

Form RPR

-313 **1** **Portrait Of A Lady (IRE)**[10] 2514 3-8-11 74 LDettori 6 85+
(HRACecil) *lw: racd wd early: trckd ldrs: led over 3f out: rdn and kpt on wl appr fnl f* **7/4**[1]

-414 **2** 3 **Obay**[21] 2244 3-9-7 84 KFallon 1 90
(EALDunlop) *trckd ldr: chal fr 1m out tl over 3f out: styd on u.p fr over 1f out: kpt on but no imp ins last* **2/1**[2]

5043 **3** 3 1/2 **Gjovic**[6] 2648 3-8-9 75 JFMcDonald(3) 2 75
(BJMeehan) *chsd ldrs: rdn 4f out: outpcd 3f out: styd on again to take 3rd ins last but n.d* **10/1**

0-41 **4** 1 3/4 **Boule D'Or (IRE)**[15] 2400 3-9-4 81 NDay 5 79
(RIngram) *lw: hld up in rr: hdwy to trck ldrs 6f out: chsd wnr 3f out: rdn and no prog over 2f out: wknd over 1f out* **3/1**[3]

4006 **5** 14 **Master Mahogany**[15] 2400 3-8-3 66 JFEgan 4 41
(RJHodges) *led tl hdd over 3f out: sn btn* **25/1**

660 **6** dist **Fire Finch**[14] 2425 3-8-6 69 TEDurcan 3 —
(MRChannon) *v slowly away and sn reminders: in tch and rdn 6f out: wknd qckly 4f out: t.o* **16/1**

2m 33.57s (-2.72) **Going Correction** -0.10s/f (Good) **6** Ran SP% **113.5**
Speed ratings: **105,103,100,99,90** —CSF £5.69 TOTE £2.40: £1.50, £1.70; EX 5.20.
**Owner** J Shack **Bred** Pat Garvey **Trained** Newmarket, Suffolk

### FOCUS

A fair handicap run at a sound gallop. The winner can rate higher.

### NOTEBOOK

**Portrait Of A Lady(IRE)** has been running well of late but has not suffered at the hands of the assessor. She won this in a manner which suggests she is progressing and, although the Handicapper is now likely to have his say, she may not have finished winning yet.

**Obay**, whose win came with cut in the ground, seemed to handle this surface but could not find an extra gear. He may be helped in that respect by a slower surface.

**Gjovic**, stepping up in trip, settled better but got left behind before running on again. He is capable of running well but is one to be wary of until he gets his act together.

**Boule D'Or(IRE)**, the winner of a similar race at Goodwood, was stepping up three furlongs in trip. He had his chance but faded in the closing stages as if he did not get the trip.

**Fire Finch** *Official explanation: jockey said filly was never travelling*

## 2810 BOLLINGER CHAMPAGNE CHALLENGE SERIES H'CAP (FOR GENTLEMAN AMATEUR RIDERS) 1m 2f 6y

**5:25** (5:25) (E) (0-75,70) 4-Y-0+ **£3,601** (£1,108; £554; £277) **Stalls** High

Form RPR

3523 **1** **Sangiovese**[24] 2170 5-11-6 67 MrJJBest(5) 7 76
(HMorrison) *lw: trckd ldrs: wnt 2nd 4f out: shkn up and slt advantage fr ins fnl 2f: pushed out fnl f* **5/1**[2]

3466 **2** 1 1/2 **Eastborough (IRE)**[29] 2032 5-11-2 58 MrSWalker 8 64
(BGPowell) *swtg: bhd: hdwy on ins fr 5f out: chsd ldrs over 2f out: rdn to go 2nd ins last but nvr gng pce of wnr* **8/1**

3036 **3** 1/2 **Icannshift (IRE)**[8] 2573 4-10-7 54 MrDHutchison(5) 13 59
(SDow) *led tl narrowly hdd ins fnl 2f: styd pressing wnr tl nt qckn ins last* **6/1**[3]

2350 **4** 1 3/4 **Galey River (USA)**[8] 2573 5-9-8 41 MrJPemberton(5) 4 43
(JJSheehan) *chsd ldrs: rdn 3f out: one pce fr over 1f out* **20/1**

1611 **5** 4 **Red Forest (IRE)**[6] 2659 5-10-9 58 5ex (t) MrStephenHarrison(7) 5 52
(JMackie) *chsd ldrs: rdn and outpcd 3f out: styd on again fr over 1f out but n.d* **5/2**[1]

0003 **6** shd **Burgundy**[8] 2594 7-10-8 53 (b) MrLNewnes(3) 12 47
(PMitchell) *racd on outside thrght: c wd into st: kpt on fnl 2f and r.o ins last but nvr a danger* **9/1**

6-03 **7** 2 1/2 **Noble Calling (FR)**[14] 2429 7-10-7 52 MrJamesWhite(3) 11 41
(RJHodges) *bhd: hung rt to centre crse and sme hdwy fr 2f out: n.d* **10/1**

0-30 **8** 3 1/2 **Bluegrass Boy**[19] 2302 4-11-6 62 MrDHDunsdon 3 45
(GBBalding) *s.i.s: bhd: mod prog fr 2f out* **16/1**

-260 **9** 1 1/4 **Lilli Marlane**[12] 2474 4-11-11 70 MrSCallaghan(3) 1 50
(NACallaghan) *lw: s.i.s: bhd: hrd rdn and hdwy 3f out: nvr rch ldrs: wknd 2f out* **7/1**

5026 **10** 5 **Nuzzle**[14] 2430 4-10-1 46 MrSDobson(3) 9 17
(MQuinn) *lw: chsd ldr to 4f out: wknd ins fnl 3f* **20/1**

00-0 **11** 4 **Somayda (IRE)**[6] 2643 9-9-12 47 JDoyle(7) 2 10
(MissJacquelineSDoyle) *b: a in rr* **50/1**

605/ **12** 19 **Seattle Art (USA)**[5] 2329 10-9-3 38 oh3 GBartley(7) 10 —
(DrPPritchard) *s.i.s: a bhd* **100/1**

2m 9.21s (0.50) **Going Correction** -0.10s/f (Good) **12** Ran SP% **120.6**
Speed ratings: **94,92,92,91,87 87,85,82,81,77 74,59**CSF £43.93 CT £250.47 TOTE £6.50: £1.90, £3.00, £1.90; EX 70.80 Place 6 £7.66, Place 5 £6.48.
**Owner** Kentisbeare Quartet **Bred** Jeremy Green And Sons **Trained** East Ilsley, Berks
■ Stewards Enquiry : Mr J J Best seven-day ban: careless riding (Jun 25,28,30, Jul 1,2,10,23)

### FOCUS

A modest amateurs' handicap, effectively a 0-70, run at a moderate gallop and the form is ordinary.

### NOTEBOOK

**Sangiovese** followed up two decent efforts in May with a cosy victory on his return to this trip, having got a good lead from Icannshift. He should not go up too much for this and can be placed to win again. His rider was in hot water with the Stewards for causing interference early in the race.

**Eastborough(IRE)** put up his best effort for a while under his experienced rider, keeping on without ever looking likely to score. He is 8lb below his previous winning turf mark and may have a small race in him at around this trip.

**Icannshift(IRE)** is a game front-runner who handles fast going, but he seems most effective when there is cut in the ground. There are handicaps to be won off his current mark, and he seems to appreciate a right-handed track.

**Galey River(USA)**, a banded-class All-Weather performer, performed with credit in this better grade on turf, given that he was done no favours by the winner early on.

**Red Forest(IRE)** has been in fine form but was 10lb higher than for the first of his two recent wins, and the drop to this shorter trip did not seem to be in his favour.

**Burgundy** was held up at the back as usual, but that was not the place to be the way the race was run. Despite making ground in the straight, he could never land a blow.

T/Jkpt: Not won. T/Plt: £15.40 to a £1 stake. Pool: £45,652.90. 2,158.00 winning tickets. T/Qpdt: £11.90 to a £1 stake. Pool: £2,161.70. 134.10 winning tickets. ST

## [2227]SOUTHWELL (L-H)

Thursday, June 10

**OFFICIAL GOING: Standard**

The going was described as 'slow but dry with less kick-back than usual'.
Wind: Fresh 1/2 behind Weather: Fine and sunny

### 2811 FESTIVAL OF THE FORGOTTEN HERB FILLIES' H'CAP 7f (F)
2:30 (2:31) (F ) (0-55,55) 3-Y-0+ £3,167 (£905; £452) Stalls Low

Form RPR

-005 **1** **Diamond Shannon (IRE)**[34] 1941 3-8-5 **49** DTudhope(7) 13 66
(DCarroll) *chsd ldrs: led over 1f out: sn rdn clr* **6/1**[2]

6001 **2** *5* **Leyaaly**[36] 1885 5-8-6 **38** (p) PMakin(5) 11 42
(BAPearce) *mde most: hdd over 1f out: no ex* **20/1**

00-0 **3** *1 3/4* **Essex Star (IRE)**[27] 2098 3-8-13 **50** GDuffield 14 50
(MissJFeilden) *trckd ldrs on outer: kpt on same pce fnl 2f* **14/1**

-400 **4** *1/2* **Shotley Dancer**[57] 1389 5-8-3 **37** SuzanneFrance(7) 16 35
(NBycroft) *sn bhd: styd on fnl 2f: nt rch ldrs* **40/1**

2240 **5** *nk* **Jessie**[31] 1992 5-8-13 **40** (v[1]) KimTinkler 10 38
(DonEnricoIncisa) *s.i.s: bhd tl kpt on wl fnl 2f: nt rch ldrs* **8/1**

3122 **6** *3/4* **Marabar**[6] 2666 6-9-9 **50** (b) ACulhane 1 46
(DWChapman) *chsd ldrs: kpt on same pce fnl 2f* **7/2**[1]

0/04 **7** *1 1/4* **Bright Mist**[24] 2183 5-8-11 **38** DSweeney 8 31
(BPalling) *chsd ldrs: one pce fnl 2f* **40/1**

3122 **8** *2 1/2* **Neutral Night (IRE)**[24] 2188 4-9-1 **45** (v) FPFerris(3) 6 31
(RBrotherton) *w ldrs: hrd rdn 3f out: wknd fnl 2f* **8/1**

46 **9** *5* **Enna (POL)**[10] 2520 5-9-10 **51** FNorton 15 25
(MrsStefLiddiard) *mi-div: sn drvn along: nvr a factor* **16/1**

-006 **10** *5* **Jessinca**[121] 737 8-8-8 **35** DKinsella 5 —
(APJones) *sn outpcd and bhd* **14/1**

0006 **11** *2* **Thumamah (IRE)**[17] 2362 5-8-10 **37** ow1 (v[1]) MTebbutt 9 —
(BPJBaugh) *chsd ldrs: lost pl over 2f out* **40/1**

0016 **12** *6* **Sandorra**[31] 1992 6-9-1 **47** MLawson(5) 2 —
(MBrittain) *chsd ldrs: lost pl over 2f out* **13/2**[3]

00-4 **13** *2 1/2* **Niteowl Dream**[17] 2346 4-9-7 **55** JDO'Reilly(7) 12 —
(JO'Reilly) *w ldrs: lost pl 3f out: sn bhd* **16/1**

0-00 **14** *2* **Pat's Nemisis (IRE)**[51] 1519 3-7-5 **35** DFentiman(7) 3 —
(BRJohnson) *rrd star: a bhd* **50/1**

-300 **15** *nk* **Moonlight Song (IRE)**[24] 2185 7-8-8 **35** oh1 RFfrench 4 —
(JohnAHarris) *lost pl and bhd over 4f out* **16/1**

0 **16** *14* **Red Melodica (USA)**[13] 2451 4-9-9 **50** RWinston 7 —
(JJQuinn) *sn chsng ldrs: lost pl and heavily eased 2f out: virtually p.u* **14/1**

1m 31.24s (0.44) **Going Correction** +0.125s/f (Slow)
**WFA** 3 from 4yo+ 10lb **16** Ran SP% **123.8**
Speed ratings: **102,96,94,93,93 92,91,88,82,76 74,67,64,62,62 46**CSF £130.91 CT £1064.52 TOTE £6.20: £2.40, £5.40, £4.20, £6.20; EX 172.30.
**Owner** Diamond Racing Ltd **Bred** Mrs A B McDonnell **Trained** Warthill, N Yorks

**FOCUS**
A low-grade fillies' handicap, but an unexposed and decisive winner and the form is sound enough for the level.

**NOTEBOOK**
**Diamond Shannon(IRE)**, having just her fifth start and her first on the All-Weather, started on terms this time and scored with plenty in hand. It was a low-grade handicap but she obviously has some potential. *Official explanation: trainer's representative said, regarding the improved form shown, filly had benefited from racing on an all-weather surface*
**Leyaaly**, dropping back in trip, set a sound pace but in the end was left for dead by the winner.
**Essex Star(IRE)**, having just her sixth start and her first try on the All-Weather, is an excitable-type and was very keen to post. Drawn just three from the outside, she ran with credit and proved suited by the step up in trip.
**Shotley Dancer**, on her toes beforehand, had the worst of the draw. She is still a maiden now after 31 attempts.
**Jessie**, with the tongue strap left off, sported a visor for the first time but it didn't exactly sharpen her up.
**Marabar**, drawn one, was always making hard work of it.
**Thumamah(IRE)** *Official explanation: trainer said mare was found to be stiff following the race*
**Red Melodica(USA)** *Official explanation: jockey said filly lost her action*

### 2812 ST OLIVE OF PALERMO MAIDEN STKS 6f (F)
3:05 (3:05) (D ) 2-Y-O £3,601 (£1,108; £554; £277) Stalls Low

Form RPR

5 **1** **Snookered Again**[33] 1970 2-8-9 PMulrennan(5) 3 66
(MWEasterby) *dwlt: sn drvn along: hdwy and hrd rdn 2f out: styd on to ld jst ins fnl f* **3/1**[1]

6 **2** *1 1/2* **Caitlin (IRE)**[43] 1709 2-8-9 FLynch 4 57
(BSmart) *chsd ldrs: rdn 2f out: styd on ins last* **6/1**[3]

**3** *4* **Lovelorn** 2-9-0 TLucas 10 50
(MWEasterby) *rangy: scope: trckd ldrs on outside: led over 2f out: edgd lft and hdd jst ins last: wknd clsng stages* **20/1**

**4** *2* **Desert Fern (IRE)** 2-8-9 NCallan 11 39
(MsDeborahJEvans) *neat: unf: chsd ldrs: outpcd 2f out: kpt on fnl f* **16/1**

0 **5** *1 1/4* **Brace Of Doves**[57] 1390 2-8-9 PMakin(5) 2 40
(TDBarron) *mde most tl over 2f out: wknd fnl f* **4/1**[2]

0 **6** *1 1/4* **Hidden Jewel**[10] 2522 2-9-0 GGibbons 6 36
(BAMcmahon) *chsd ldrs: drvn along over 3f out: one pce* **33/1**

**7** *3* **Gardasee (GER)** 2-9-0 DaleGibson 9 27
(TPTate) *rangy: scope: hmpd s: sn wl bhd and drvn along: styd on fnl 2f: nvr on terms* **10/1**

500 **8** *1/2* **Tipsy Lillie**[5] 2674 2-8-9 GDuffield 5 21
(JulianPoulton) *chsd ldrs: lost pl over 2f out* **10/1**

0 **9** *3/4* **Tyson Returns**[27] 2087 2-8-11 DNolan(3) 1 23
(PABlockley) *chsd ldrs: ev ch over 2f out: sn wknd* **9/1**

06 **10** *5* **Mindful**[66] 1264 2-9-0 TGMcLaughlin 8 8
(MJPolglase) *swvd rt s: sn chsng ldrs: lost pl over 2f out: eased* **12/1**

20 **11** *5* **Mermaid's Cry**[9] 2544 2-8-6 FPFerris(3) 7 —
(RBrotherton) *swvd rt s: sn bhd and hung rt* **8/1**

1m 19.48s (2.58) **Going Correction** +0.125s/f (Slow) **11** Ran SP% **119.9**
Speed ratings: **87,85,79,77,75 73,69,69,68,61 54**CSF £21.42 TOTE £4.40: £1.10, £1.90, £9.10; EX 18.70.
**Owner** R Edmonds & J Wade **Bred** G C Neate **Trained** Sheriff Hutton, N Yorks

**FOCUS**
A poor event and a slow time for the grade. The form should be treated with caution.

**NOTEBOOK**
**Snookered Again**, on the leg and narrow, had finished fifth in a claimer first time. He made very hard work of it and will appreciate seven on a return to turf.
**Caitlin(IRE)**, a habitual tail swisher, was stuck in the mud on her debut on turf six weeks earlier. She was putting in her best work at the finish, and a seventh furlong will not come amiss.
**Lovelorn**, a February foal, was easily the biggest in the line-up. Drawn wide, he travelled strongly and took it up travelling easily but in the end he didn't see it out anywhere near as well as the winner, a stablemate. He will improve a good deal in time and a drop back to five will not inconvenience him.
**Desert Fern(IRE)**, an April foal, stayed on when it was all over after getting outpaced but she lacks size and scope.
**Brace Of Doves**, gelded after misbehaving in the stalls on his debut, behaved a lot better and will come on for the outing, his first for two months.
**Gardasee(GER)**, a May foal, looks easily the best long-term prospect in the line-up. Knocked over at the start, he was very green but showed some latent ability picking up very late on. He will need time and a trip but will come good one day.

### 2813 RED ROSE FESTIVAL CLASSIFIED CLAIMING STKS 7f (F)
3:35 (3:36) (F ) 3-Y-0+ £3,003 (£858; £429) Stalls Low

Form RPR

0303 **1** **Only One Legend (IRE)**[16] 2383 6-9-3 60 (b) NCallan 5 71
(KARyan) *reminder sn after s: hdwy over 3f out: led over 1f out: styd on* **6/1**[3]

2050 **2** *2 1/2* **Dispol Peto**[24] 2172 4-8-10 57 (p) DTudhope(7) 10 64
(IanEmmerson) *chsd ldrs: kpt on to take 2nd ins last: no imp* **5/1**[1]

0010 **3** *1 1/4* **Pays D'Amour (IRE)**[23] 2219 7-9-11 57 AlexGreaves 8 69
(DNicholls) *chsd ldrs: kpt on same pce appr fnl f* **5/1**[1]

1213 **4** *4* **On The Trail**[6] 2664 7-8-11 56 ACulhane 3 44
(DWChapman) *w ldr: led over 3f out tl over 1f out: wknd ins last* **11/2**[2]

6024 **5** *1* **Air Of Esteem**[35] 1915 8-8-4 43 DFentiman(7) 7 42
(IanEmmerson) *outpcd and lost pl over 3f out: styd on fnl f* **14/1**

0-00 **6** *2 1/2* **Bijou Dancer**[17] 2362 4-8-11 51 (p) GBaker 11 35
(MRBosley) *chsd ldrs on outer: lost pl over 4f out: hrd rdn and wnt lft over 2f out: kpt on fnl f* **20/1**

204- **7** *3/4* **Skylark**[242] 5516 7-8-8 58 KimTinkler 12 30
(DonEnricoIncisa) *sn outpcd and bhd on wd outside: sme hdwy 2f out: nvr a factor* **10/1**

2000 **8** *6* **Power Bird (IRE)**[12] 2483 4-8-13 56 (v[1]) LPKeniry(3) 6 23
(BRJohnson) *chsd ldrs: lost pl over 2f out* **8/1**

3020 **9** *dist* **Maybe Someday**[5] 2688 3-9-1 60 (b) IMongan 1 —
(JBalding) *sn bhd: t.o 2f out* **7/1**

60-0 **10** *1 1/2* **Eastern Dagger**[15] 1502 4-8-11 56 RWinston 4 —
(JRTurner) *s.i.s: bhd whn hung bdly rt bnd over 4f out: sn t.o* **25/1**

0/0- **11** *5* **Miss Noteriety**[276] 4774 4-8-5 25 TEaves(3) 2 —
(CJTeague) *led tl over 3f out: sn lost pl and bhd: t.o 2f out* **100/1**

0-00 **12** *dist* **Mr Loverman (IRE)**[13] 2454 4-9-7 40 GGibbons 9 —
(MissVHaigh) *swvd bdly lft leaving stalls and ref to r: completed in own time: hopelessly t.o* **66/1**

1m 30.92s (0.12) **Going Correction** +0.125s/f (Slow)
**WFA** 3 from 4yo+ 10lb **12** Ran SP% **113.5**
Speed ratings: **104,101,99,95,94 91,90,83,—,— —,—**CSF £33.29 TOTE £8.30: £3.40, £1.70, £2.20; EX 50.20.
**Owner** Sunpak Potatoes **Bred** Rocklow Stud **Trained** Hambleton, N Yorks

**FOCUS**
A modest claimer but a fair time for the grade, although the winner did not need to be at his best to win.

**NOTEBOOK**
**Only One Legend(IRE)**, in blinkers this time, did nothing at all wrong recording his fourth career win but his first at this trip.
**Dispol Peto** stuck on to take second spot but the winner had flown.
**Pays D'Amour(IRE)** had a bit to find with the first two and seems better suited by six on turf.
**On The Trail**, loaded last and walked into the stalls, didn't see out the trip after going on at the halfway mark.
**Air Of Esteem** had something to find and these days seems better suited by a mile.
**Maybe Someday** *Official explanation: jockey said gelding was never travelling*
**Eastern Dagger** *Official explanation: jockey said gelding was never travelling*
**Miss Noteriety** *Official explanation: jockey said filly had a breathing problem*

### 2814 DOREEN PATERSON 1ST TIME RACING H'CAP 1m (F)
4:10 (4:12) (E ) (0-70,70) 3-Y-0+ £3,591 (£1,105; £552; £276) Stalls Low

Form RPR

0000 **1** **Tre Colline**[13] 2459 5-9-7 **60** GBaker 14 80
(NTinkler) *hld up: hdwy 3f out: led on bit over 1f out: smoothly* **11/1**

4200 **2** *7* **Crusoe (IRE)**[6] 2649 7-8-12 **51** (b) IMongan 2 57
(ASadik) *led 2f out: sn hdd: no ch w wnr* **14/1**

2000 **3** *1 1/2* **Yorker (USA)**[40] 1757 6-9-12 **65** NCallan 1 68
(MsDeborahJEvans) *sn led: hdd 2f out: hrd rdn and one pce* **9/1**

0-30 **4** *3* **Inmom (IRE)**[21] 2235 3-8-10 **60** JBramhill 10 57
(SRBowring) *mid-div: hdwy on wd outside over 2f out: styd on fnl f* **12/1**

0600 **5** *1 1/4* **Hoh's Back**[8] 2580 5-8-4 **48** (p) NChalmers(5) 9 43
(PaulJohnson) *s.i.s: sn bhd and pushed along: styd on fnl 2f* **13/2**[2]

3140 **6** *3* **Book Matched**[71] 1214 3-9-6 **70** FLynch 8 59
(BSmart) *chsd ldrs: fdd over 1f out* **11/1**

-460 **7** *nk* **Teehee (IRE)**[13] 2455 6-9-8 **61** (b) DSweeney 5 49
(BPalling) *chsd ldrs: hung lft and wknd over 1f out* **12/1**

13-5 **8** *shd* **Haunt The Zoo**[37] 1861 9-9-3 **59** LFletcher(3) 6 47
(JohnAHarris) *chsd ldrs: rdn 3f out: wknd over 1f out* **16/1**

0000 **9** *hd* **Munaawesh (USA)**[20] 2259 3-8-6 **56** GDuffield 15 43
(DWChapman) *s.i.s: racd wd: sme hdwy 3f out: nvr a factor* **40/1**

4-00 **10** *nk* **Monte Mayor Lad (IRE)**[10] 2524 4-9-11 **64** (p) FNorton 13 51
(DHaydnJones) *racd wd: hld up towards rr: nvr on terms* **12/1**

0444 **11** *5* **Rare Coincidence**[7] 2618 3-9-2 **69** (p) DNolan(3) 12 46
(RFFisher) *chsd ldrs: effrt over 2f out: sn btn* **9/2**[1]

4002 **12** *2 1/2* **Semper Paratus (USA)**[34] 1941 5-9-3 **56** MTebbutt 11 28
(VSmith) *sn bhd* **12/1**

3-03 **13** *11* **Zarin (IRE)**[105] 900 6-9-13 **66** ACulhane 7 16
(DWChapman) *dwlt: lost pl over 3f out: sn bhd* **7/1**[3]

40-6 **14** *12* **Delightful Gift**[17] 2346 4-8-6 **45** TWilliams 4 —
(MBrittain) *led early: chsd ldrs: lost pl over 2f out: sn bhd* **50/1**

3000 **15** *15* **High Cane (USA)**[31] 1992 4-8-13 **52** DarrenWilliams 3 —
(MDHammond) *s.i.s: a bhd: eased 2f out* **28/1**

1m 44.34s (-0.26) **Going Correction** +0.125s/f (Slow)
**WFA** 3 from 4yo+ 11lb **15** Ran SP% **121.8**
Speed ratings: **106,99,97,94,93 90,89,89,89,89 84,81,70,58,43**CSF £155.37 CT £1492.03 TOTE £12.90: £4.30, £2.90, £4.10; EX 180.80.
**Owner** Peter Alderson Mike Gosse Adrian Mornin **Bred** Hesmonds Stud Ltd **Trained** Langton, N Yorks

**FOCUS**
The betting suggested this was open, but Tre Colline was a facile winner. The time was decent for the grade and the winner is unbeaten on the All-Weather.

**NOTEBOOK**

**Tre Colline**, successfull on his only previous outing on the All-Weather, has slipped to a lenient mark. Suited by the step up to a mile, he came there running away and never came off the steel. In this sort of mood he must surely defy a penalty.

**Crusoe(IRE)**, whose last win a year ago came from a 10lb higher mark, showed a return to form but like the rest had no chance with the winner.

**Yorker(USA)**, drawn one, was in the firing line throughout but the winner moved upsides him with a double handful.

**Inmom(IRE)**, having just her fifth start and her first try on the All-Weather, stayed on in good style down the wide outside and will appreciate a return to further.

**Hoh's Back**, much better treated on the All-Weather than on turf, made hard work of it after a sluggish start but was putting in his best work at the finish.

**Rare Coincidence**, back on the All-Weather, was disappointing.

**Delightful Gift** *Official explanation: jockey said filly was unsuited by the all-weather surface*

**High Cane(USA)** *Official explanation: vet said filly finished sore behind*

## 2815 NATIONAL BLACK COW DAY MEDIAN AUCTION MAIDEN STKS 7f (F)

4:40 (4:42) (F) 3-Y-O **£3,038** (£868; £434) **Stalls** Low

Form RPR

0032 **1** **Mitzi Caspar**[22] 2232 3-8-9 37 .......... RPrice 11 52
(PLGilligan) *hdwy over 4f out: sn chsng ldr: hung lft and led over 1f out: styd on* **8/1**

00- **2** *1 ½* **Go Free**[262] 5121 3-9-0 .......... ANicholls 9 53
(AMHales) *chsd ldrs: kpt on same pce fnl f* **22/1**

00 **3** *3* **Petrion**[11] 2505 3-8-9 .......... CLowther 5 41
(RGuest) *chsd ldrs: outpcd and lost pl over 2f out: styd on fnl 2f* **25/1**

3 **4** *½* **Wunderbra (IRE)**[64] 1293 3-8-9 .......... IMongan 12 39
(MLWBell) *trckd ldrs: led over 4f out: hdd over 1f out: wknd ins last* **2/1**[1]

**5** *8* **Too Keen** 3-8-9 .......... PHanagan 10 19
(JMJefferson) *s.i.s: bhd tl styd on appr fnl f* **25/1**

000 **6** *1 ¼* **Flying With Eagles**[8] 2596 3-9-0 .......... GBaker 7 21
(JJay) *sn bhd and drvn along: hung bdly rt bnd over 4f out* **28/1**

00 **7** *hd* **Arian's Lad**[8] 2586 3-9-0 .......... DSweeney 3 21
(BPalling) *w ldrs: lost pl over 2f out* **10/1**

5-25 **8** *2 ½* **Westborough (IRE)**[17] 2353 3-9-0 53 .......... KimTinkler 6 14
(NTinkler) *mde most tl over 4f out: lost pl over 2f out* **4/1**[3]

0-0 **9** *5* **Savannah Sue**[31] 1991 3-8-4 .......... PMulrennan(5) 4 —
(JRNorton) *outpcd and lost pl over 4f out: sn bhd* **80/1**

0 **10** *2 ½* **Osla**[16] 2383 3-8-6 .......... FPFerris(3) 1 —
(RBrotherton) *s.i.s: swtchd to wd outside bnd over 4f out: sn bhd* **16/1**

4-40 **11** *5* **Aliba (IRE)**[23] 2217 3-9-0 62 .......... FLynch 8 —
(BSmart) *w ldrs: lost pl over 3f out: sn bhd and eased* **3/1**[2]

00 **12** *nk* **Judda**[11] 2505 3-9-0 .......... DeanMcKeown 2 —
(RFMarvin) *sn drvn along: lost pl over 4f out: sn bhd* **66/1**

1m 32.82s (2.02) **Going Correction** +0.125s/f (Slow) **12** Ran SP% **122.6**
Speed ratings: **93,91,87,87,78 76,76,73,67,65 59,59**CSF £177.34 TOTE £8.40: £3.00, £15.10, £6.90; EX 474.10.
**Owner** Dr Susan Barnes **Bred** Dr Susan Barnes **Trained** Newmarket, Suffolk

**FOCUS**

A rock bottom maiden, with the winner officially rated just 37 and the 'form' horses running below their best.

**NOTEBOOK**

**Mitzi Caspar** overcame a double figure draw to open her account at the seventh attempt and give her jockey his first domestic winner this year.

**Go Free**, who showed nothing in a couple of outings at two, has changed trainer and wore a cross noseband. At least this now opens up the handicap route.

**Petrion**, unplaced in two previous starts on turf, stayed on in good style after being badly outpaced and will appreciate a mile plus in handicaps.

**Wunderbra(IRE)**, who had two attendants, did not stride out at all going to post. She became very leg weary late on and six with give underfoot looks to suit her.

**Too Keen**, bred to stay on her dam's side, made a satisfactory debut and looks capable of something better in due course.

**Flying With Eagles** would not face the kickback and tried to put himself on the sidelines leaving the backstretch. *Official explanation: jockey said gelding would not face the kick-back*

**Westborough(IRE)** didn't improve at all for the step up in trip on his All-Weather debut.

**Aliba(IRE)** seemed to lose his action completely at the halfway mark and completed in his own time. *Official explanation: jockey said gelding lost its action turning in*

## 2816 HOWLIN' WOLF BIRTHDAY H'CAP 1m 4f (F)

5:15 (5:16) (F) (0-55,50) 4-Y-O+ **£2,996** (£856; £428) **Stalls** Low

Form RPR

1063 **1** **Dash Of Magic**[6] 2649 6-8-12 40 .......... MTebbutt 3 51
(JHetherton) *bhd: hdwy on outside 4f out: styd on wl to ld 1f out* **11/1**

6242 **2** *2* **Heathers Girl**[26] 2127 5-9-8 50 .......... FNorton 7 58
(DHaydnJones) *chsd ldrs: kpt on wl fnl f* **12/1**

6600 **3** *1 ½* **Shatin Special**[15] 2408 4-8-12 40 .......... (p) RFfrench 10 46
(GCHChung) *hdwy to chse ldrs over 5f out: hung lft and led over 1f out: sn hdd and nt qckn* **25/1**

0-40 **4** *nk* **Ela Re**[42] 724 5-8-10 43 .......... RThomas(5) 5 48
(CRDore) *chsd ldrs: outpcd over 3f out: styd on fnl f* **8/1**[3]

0-45 **5** *½* **Sea Cove**[24] 2171 4-9-2 44 .......... PHanagan 15 49
(JMJefferson) *hdwy on outside 7f out: sn drvn along: kpt on fnl f* **11/1**

0 **6** *3 ½* **Dalon (POL)**[35] 1910 5-9-5 50 .......... (b[1]) DAllan(3) 9 49
(DBFeek) *sn prom: one pce fnl 2f* **40/1**

3146 **7** *3* **Moyne Pleasure (IRE)**[8] 2583 6-9-0 45 .......... (p) LFletcher(3) 6 40
(PaulJohnson) *chsd ldrs: led over 5f out: hdd 4f out: fdd appr fnl f* **25/1**

60-2 **8** *½* **Melograno (IRE)**[35] 1914 4-8-13 44 .......... DNolan(3) 11 38
(MarkCampion) *chsd ldrs: led 4f out tl over 1f out: wknd* **25/1**

0636 **9** *1 ½* **Kentucky Bullet (USA)**[47] 1630 8-9-0 45 .......... LPKeniry(3) 16 37
(AGNewcombe) *prom: lost pl over 1f out: eased* **10/1**

6123 **10** *6* **Red Moor (IRE)**[31] 2004 4-9-6 48 .......... ACulhane 1 31
(RHollinshead) *in tch: effrt over 3f out: lost pl over 2f out: fin lame* **4/1**[1]

0-06 **11** *6* **Kalanisha (IRE)**[31] 1989 4-9-0 42 .......... GDuffield 13 16
(NAGraham) *s.i.s: a bhd* **40/1**

0353 **12** *1 ¼* **Arjay**[9] 2551 6-9-3 45 .......... JCarroll 2 17
(AndrewTurnell) *led tl over 5f out: sn btn: heavily eased over 1f out* **14/1**

6262 **13** *7* **Pipssalio (SPA)**[31] 1989 7-9-0 42 .......... (t) PDoe 12 3
(JamiePoulton) *a bhd* **5/1**[2]

00/2 **14** *9* **Cracow (IRE)**[10] 2525 7-8-12 45 .......... PMakin(5) 14 —
(AMHales) *chsd ldrs: lost pl over 3f out: sn bhd and eased* **11/1**

0113 **P** **Eurolink Artemis**[36] 1888 7-8-13 41 .......... (p) NCallan 8 —
(JulianPoulton) *mid-div: drvn along and lost pl over 5f out: t.o whn p.u and dismntd over 2f out* **14/1**

4330 **P** **Kenny The Truth (IRE)**[16] 2387 5-9-7 49 .......... (t) IMongan 4 —
(MrsJCandlish) *t.k.h: chsd ldrs: rdn and lost pl 7f out: t.o over 2f out: p.u and dismntd jst ins last* **11/1**

2m 44.08s (1.98) **Going Correction** +0.125s/f (Slow) **16** Ran SP% **127.6**
Speed ratings: **98,96,95,95,95 92,90,90,89,85 81,80,75,69,—** —CSF £135.58 CT £3245.02 TOTE £9.60: £2.70, £3.80, £4.00, £4.80; EX 147.20 Place 6 £3,413.02, Place 5 £756.52.
**Owner** 21st Century Racing **Bred** Miss Trudy Huggett **Trained** Malton, N Yorks

**FOCUS**

A 0-50 handicap run at a strong early pace. They came home well strung out.

**NOTEBOOK**

**Dash Of Magic**, a winner of two banded races here, came from way off the pace down the wide outside, scoring in most decisive fashion in the end.

**Heathers Girl**, who usually runs in sellers and claimers, found the extended trip no problem.

**Shatin Special**, whose one success was in a banded race, ran easily her best race so far at this track.

**Ela Re**, unplaced in 10 previous start, has won three times over hurdles and was last seen in action at Punchestown. He found this trip too short.

**Sea Cove**, unplaced in six previous starts, is well worth another try over further.

**Dalon(POL)**, a winner three times in Poland, wore blinkers on his second start here and his first on the All-Weather.

**Red Moor(IRE)** dropped out once in line for home and was found to be lame behind afterwards. *Official explanation: trainer said gelding finished lame*

**Eurolink Artemis** *Official explanation: jockey said mare lost its action*

**Kenny The Truth(IRE)** *Official explanation: jockey said gelding had a breathing problem and lost its action*

T/Plt: £10,961.30 to a £1 stake. Pool: £25,526.45. 1.70 winning tickets. T/Qpdt: £502.30 to a £1 stake. Pool: £2,104.60. 3.10 winning tickets. WG

# [2592]YARMOUTH (L-H)

Thursday, June 10

**OFFICIAL GOING: Firm (good to firm in places) changing to firm after race 2 (2:55pm)**

Wind: mod across Weather: warm and sunny

## 2817 EBF NOVICE MEDIAN AUCTION STKS 6f 3y

2:20 (2:21) (E) 2-Y-O **£3,328** (£1,024; £512; £256) **Stalls** High

Form RPR

2 **1** **Satchem (IRE)**[17] 2360 2-8-9 .......... TPQueally(3) 5 79
(DRLoder) *mde all: rdn and hung lft fr over 1f out: r.o* **1/1**[1]

**2** *½* **Captain Hurricane** 2-8-12 .......... JQuinn 1 78
(PWChapple-Hyam) *trckd ldrs: plld hrd: chal 2f out: rdn and hung lft ins fnl f: unable qck nr fin* **6/5**[2]

1 **3** *1 ½* **Highland Cascade**[27] 2095 2-8-11 .......... SSanders 2 72
(JMPEustace) *chsd ldrs: rdn over 2f out: styd on* **10/1**[3]

**4** *11* **Right To Roam (IRE)** 2-8-9 .......... LisaJones(3) 3 40
(JARToller) *s.i.s: outpcd* **25/1**

0 **5** *9* **Parsley's Return**[8] 2592 2-8-12 .......... SWKelly 4 13
(NACallaghan) *broke wl: outpcd fr 1/2-way* **100/1**

1m 13.43s (-0.17) **Going Correction** -0.10s/f (Good) **5** Ran SP% **109.4**
Speed ratings: **97,96,94,79,67**CSF £2.41 TOTE £2.10: £1.10, £1.30; EX 3.20.
**Owner** Lucayan Stud & D D Clee **Bred** K Molloy **Trained** Newmarket, Suffolk

**FOCUS**

A two-horse race according to the betting, and that's the way it panned out. The form is fair for the grade.

**NOTEBOOK**

**Satchem(IRE)** had the benefit of previous racecourse experience and in the end that made the difference. He ended an uncharacteristically lean spell for his trainer, who had gone 29 runners without a winner, and he should stay seven furlongs in time.

**Captain Hurricane**, a well-supported newcomer, travelled strongly on the outside but could not shake off the more experienced Loder runner when push came to shove. This was still a promising debut, though, and he should be able to win a similar race.

**Highland Cascade** won a course and distance maiden last time out but at the time it did not look much to shout about. Her performance here under a penalty, shaping as though farther will suit, suggests it is probably not worth getting too carried away with the form of this race either.

**Right To Roam(IRE)** is bred to be speedy but he was too green to do himself justice on this debut. He can leave this form behind in due course.

## 2818 RACECOURSE VIDEO SERVICES MAIDEN FILLIES' STKS 7f 3y

2:55 (2:56) (D) 3-Y-O **£3,419** (£1,052; £526; £263) **Stalls** High

Form RPR

66 **1** **Keyaki (IRE)**[34] 1939 3-8-11 .......... SSanders 2 74
(CFWall) *chsd ldrs: rdn to ld over 1f out: r.o* **9/2**[2]

02 **2** *nk* **Zameyla (IRE)**[11] 2505 3-8-11 .......... PRobinson 4 73
(MAJarvis) *led 1f: led 1/2-way: hdd over 1f out: r.o* **2/5**[1]

**3** *5* **Chertsey (IRE)** 3-8-11 .......... BDoyle 1 60
(CEBrittain) *chsd ldrs: rdn over 1f out: eased whn btn ins fnl f* **8/1**[3]

0 **4** *6* **Set Alight**[55] 1441 3-8-11 .......... SCarson 5 44
(MissKBBoutflower) *w ldrs: led over 4f out: hdd 1/2-way: wknd over 1f out* **33/1**

00 **5** *3 ½* **Crocolat**[31] 2001 3-8-11 .......... AMackay 3 35
(NACallaghan) *sn outpcd* **33/1**

0 **6** *1 ½* **Mary Carleton**[11] 2505 3-8-11 .......... MFenton 6 31
(RMHCowell) *led 6f out: hdd over 4f out: wknd over 2f out* **80/1**

1m 25.65s (-0.85) **Going Correction** -0.10s/f (Good) **6** Ran SP% **107.8**
Speed ratings: **100,99,93,87,83 81**CSF £6.25 TOTE £5.60: £2.40, £1.02; EX 11.70.
**Owner** Hintlesham SPD Partners **Bred** Rathbarry Stud **Trained** Newmarket, Suffolk

**FOCUS**

Just a modest maiden and there is a doubt about the value of the form.

**NOTEBOOK**

**Keyaki(IRE)**, who had run two fair races on soft ground, found this quicker surface far more suitable and responded well to pressure to get the better of the favourite in a driving finish. Connections will be hoping the Handicapper does not react too harshly to this success.

**Zameyla(IRE)** brought the best form to the table but, having lost her action on her debut and become unbalanced on her next start - both times on fast ground - she still had it to prove on this quick surface. She had every chance but this heavy-topped filly shapes as though she will be happier with some cut underfoot. *Official explanation: jockey said filly was unsuited by the firm ground*

**Chertsey(IRE)**, for whom there was little support in the market beforehand, ran as though this run was needed. Out of a mare who is a half-sister to Dutch Gold, she deserves rating as having finished a bit closer as she was eased right down once her chance of beating the first two had gone.

**Set Alight**, who ran in a decent Newbury maiden first time out, got very warm beforehand. She showed some early speed and will be of more interest once she is eligible for handicaps.

## 2819 DIMASCIO'S ICE CREAMS (S) STKS — 7f 3y
3:25 (3:26) (G) 2-Y-O £2,527 (£722; £361) Stalls High

Form RPR
14 **1** **Lisa Mona Lisa (IRE)**[55] 1449 2-8-11 .......... JQuinn 5 63
(VSmith) *mde all: rdn over 1f out: r.o* **15/8**[1]
02 **2** 3 **Lakesdale (IRE)**[10] 2515 2-8-6 .......... KDarley 6 51
(CJGray) *hld up: hdwy 1/2-way: rdn over 2f out: chsd wnr fnl f: no imp* **5/2**[2]
34 **3** 2 **Tonight (IRE)**[7] 2622 2-8-6 .......... BSwarbrick(5) 2 51
(WMBrisbourne) *plld hrd and prom: rdn 1/2-way: styd on same pce appr fnl f* **16/1**
645 **4** nk **General Nuisance (IRE)**[10] 2523 2-8-4 .......... (p) DerekNolan(7) 4 50
(JSMoore) *chsd wnr: rdn and ev ch wl over 1f out: wknd ins fnl f* **8/1**
**5** 6 **Louise Rayner** 2-8-6 .......... JMackay 1 30
(MLWBell) *s.i.s: outpcd* **3/1**[3]
**6** 1 **Faithful Flash** 2-8-3 .......... TPQueally(3) 3 27
(CADwyer) *sn pushed along and prom: outpcd fr 1/2-way* **22/1**

1m 27.71s (1.21) **Going Correction** -0.10s/f (Good) **6 Ran SP% 109.7**
Speed ratings: **89,85,83,82,76 74** CT £2.30 TOTE £2.40: £1.50, £; EX7.10 1.The winner was bought in for 11,200gns. Lakesdale (no.5) was claimed by Mrs Christine Dunnett for £6,000. Louise Rayner (no.6) was subject to a friendly claim of
**Owner** Stephen Dartnell **Bred** A Geraghty **Trained** Exning, Suffolk

**FOCUS**
Not a bad event of its type, with the seven furlongs placing the emphasis on stamina. The winner is a decent performer in this grade.

**NOTEBOOK**
**Lisa Mona Lisa(IRE)**, stepping back into the bottom grade, was always travelling nicely against the rail and stayed on strongly for an emphatic win. She will not be eligible to run in any more sellers this year, having won two, but ought to pay her way in fast-ground nurseries over this trip or even a mile.
**Lakesdale(IRE)**, claimed out of Mick Channon's yard after finishing second at Chepstow, has been shaping as if this trip would suit but, despite keeping on, was never going to trouble the filly.
**Tonight(IRE)** still showed signs of greenness but appeared to stay the extra furlong. He is eligible for nurseries now.
**General Nuisance(IRE)**, in first-time cheekpieces, was 5lb better off with Lisa Mona Lisa compared with Doncaster in March but, after matching strides with that rival, failed to see out this longer trip.
**Louise Rayner** stood still as the stalls opened and was always fighting a losing battle thereafter. She will know more next time but will need to show plenty of improvement.

## 2820 "ONE" ANGLIA WHERRY LINES FILLIES' H'CAP — 1m 3y
3:55 (3:57) (E) (0-70,70) 3-Y-O £3,906 (£1,202; £601; £300) Stalls High

Form RPR
50-1 **1** **Perle D'Or (IRE)**[23] 2217 3-9-7 **70** .......... KDarley 4 77
(WJHaggas) *hld up in tch: rdn to ld over 1f out: r.o* **4/1**[1]
-213 **2** nk **Princess Galadriel**[15] 2411 3-8-9 **58** .......... NPollard 7 64
(JRBest) *hld up: hdwy over 2f out: rdn over 1f out: r.o* **11/2**[3]
-060 **3** 1 ½ **Gabana (IRE)**[17] 2371 3-9-2 **65** .......... SSanders 10 68
(CFWall) *hld up: hdwy over 2f out: rdn over 1f out: styd on same pce ins fnl f* **9/2**[2]
000 **4** 2 ½ **Faith Healer (IRE)**[9] 2546 3-8-6 **55** .......... (b) JQuinn 1 52
(VSmith) *sn led: rdn and hdd over 1f out: wknd ins fnl f* **40/1**
-005 **5** 1 ¾ **Blaeberry**[23] 2218 3-8-8 **57** .......... MFenton 2 50
(PLGilligan) *chsd ldr over 4f: wknd over 1f out* **11/2**[3]
0114 **6** ¾ **La Puce**[85] 1036 3-9-0 **66** .......... TPQueally(3) 3 57
(MissGayKelleway) *chsd ldrs: rdn over 1f out: wknd ins fnl f* **7/1**
360- **7** 2 ½ **Lady Blade (IRE)**[234] 5671 3-8-12 **64** .......... LisaJones(3) 6 49
(BHanbury) *hld up: hung lft over 1f out: nvr trbld ldrs* **12/1**
24-0 **8** 18 **Tardis**[13] 2442 3-9-1 **64** .......... JMackay 8 8
(MLWBell) *chsd ldrs over 5f* **9/1**
0-00 **9** nk **Pleasure Seeker**[20] 2267 3-8-11 **60** .......... SCarson 5 3
(MDIUsher) *hld up: wknd over 2f out* **33/1**
3-03 **10** 2 ½ **Welsh Empress**[24] 2176 3-8-0 **52** .......... RMiles(3) 9 —
(PLGilligan) *prom: rdn over 3f out: sn wknd* **10/1**

1m 38.9s (-0.80) **Going Correction** -0.10s/f (Good) **10 Ran SP% 113.6**
Speed ratings: **100,99,98,95,93 93,90,72,72,69**CSF £25.20 CT £103.33 TOTE £3.90: £1.70, £2.20, £1.50; EX 15.40.
**Owner** The Perle d'Or Partnership **Bred** J Bowdren **Trained** Newmarket, Suffolk

**FOCUS**
A fairly competitive, if modest fillies' handicap, but the form is solid enough.

**NOTEBOOK**
**Perle D'Or(IRE)** was found the perfect opportunity to build on the promise of her success at Redcar on her reappearance. Clearly at home on a quick surface, she saw this extra furlong out well.
**Princess Galadriel** came with a fast-finishing stands'-side challenge. A winner over six furlongs here last month, there were obvious doubts about her seeing this longer trip out, but she dispelled those concerns in no uncertain manner.
**Gabana(IRE)**, who needs to be held up, ran a fair race, picking up well under pressure but just unable to reach the winner.
**Faith Healer(IRE)**, with the blinkers back on, showed her first piece of worthwhile form since leaving Ireland.
**Blaeberry** was not disgraced on her handicap debut.
**La Puce**, having her first run since March, could not pick up on this fast ground once the race began in earnest.
**Pleasure Seeker** *Official explanation: jockey said filly lost her action and did not appear suited by the firm ground*
**Welsh Empress** *Official explanation: trainer said filly was found to be jarred up*

## 2821 WEATHERBYS INSURANCE H'CAP — 1m 6f 17y
4:30 (4:30) (E) (0-70,67) 3-Y-O £3,770 (£1,160; £580; £290) Stalls Low

Form RPR
-012 **1** **Considine (USA)**[9] 2561 3-9-7 **67** .......... SSanders 1 73
(JMPEustace) *mde all: hrd rdn fnl f: all out* **3/1**[1]
-122 **2** shd **Ilwadod**[9] 2546 3-8-10 **56** .......... KDarley 2 62
(MRChannon) *sn pushed along and bhd: hdwy u.p fr over 2f out: styd on wl: jst failed* **10/3**[2]
6213 **3** 3 **Siegfrieds Night (IRE)**[9] 2546 3-9-6 **66** .......... LVickers 7 68
(MCChapman) *chsd ldrs: rdn over 2f out: styd on same pce fnl f* **8/1**
0-36 **4** 1 ¼ **Velvet Waters**[13] 2442 3-8-13 **59** .......... SCarson 4 59
(RFJohnsonHoughton) *chsd wnr 11f out: rdn and ev ch over 3f out: edgd lft and no ex fnl f* **12/1**
56-0 **5** shd **Euippe**[16] 2390 3-9-2 **62** .......... MFenton 3 62
(JGGiven) *chsd wnr 3f: remained handy: rdn over 2f out: btn whn hmpd 1f out* **33/1**
3225 **6** 9 **Danefonique (IRE)**[9] 2546 3-8-11 **57** .......... RFitzpatrick 6 44
(DCarroll) *hld up: plld hrd: hdwy over 4f out: wknd over 1f out* **9/1**
6-60 **7** 18 **Canni Thinkaar (IRE)**[25] 2146 3-9-6 **66** .......... (e[1]) NPollard 5 28
(PWHarris) *prom: pushed along 10f out: sn lost pl: bhd fnl 6f* **33/1**
0-06 **8** 5 **Frankies Wings (IRE)**[59] 1356 3-8-11 **60** .......... RMiles(3) 8 15
(TGMills) *mid-div: wknd over 5f out* **5/1**[3]
1013 **9** 25 **Ceasar (IRE)**[23] 2199 3-8-13 **59** .......... (p) GFaulkner 9 —
(PABlockley) *hld up: hdwy 6f out: wknd 4f out* **6/1**

3m 1.88s (-3.32) **Going Correction** -0.175s/f (Firm) **9 Ran SP% 113.7**
Speed ratings: **102,101,100,99,99 94,84,81,66**CSF £12.85 CT £69.15 TOTE £3.80: £1.90, £1.20, £3.10; EX 7.20.
**Owner** Elias Haloute **Bred** D Considine **Trained** Newmarket, Suffolk

**FOCUS**
This was run at a sound pace, courtesy of the front-running winner, and only the first two really seemed to see it out. The form appears sound.

**NOTEBOOK**
**Considine(USA)**, who ran well off this mark at Sandown, is a strong galloper and, having fought off several challengers up the long home straight, found the line coming just in time for him. A likeable individual, due to go up 2lb at the weekend, he remains a progressive young stayer.
**Ilwadod** is a stablemate of Misternando, whose winning streak last year started in this event. He appeared to have no chance when last and under pressure turning for home, but he gradually picked up and stayed on strongly inside the last. He would have snatched the race in another stride, and looks the type to improve for a step up to two miles.
**Siegfrieds Night(IRE)** travelled well for a long way but was unable to find a change of gear at the business end. He is a consistent individual and versatile too, having begun the year winning over six furlongs on Fibresand.
**Velvet Waters** also has plenty of stamina in her pedigree but ran as if finding this trip beyond her.
**Euippe** is a half-sister to former high-class stayer and hurdler Midnight Legend, but while she showed more over this longer trip she did not really get home.
**Frankies Wings(IRE)** *Official explanation: jockey said colt was unsuited by the firm ground*
**Ceasar(IRE)** *Official explanation: jockey said gelding lost its action in the home straight*

## 2822 RFC BED-DOWN EXCEL PLUS H'CAP — 1m 3f 101y
5:05 (5:07) (F) (0-55,55) 3-Y-O £3,353 (£958; £479) Stalls Low

Form RPR
-046 **1** **Winslow Boy (USA)**[15] 2402 3-9-6 **53** .......... JQuinn 1 59
(CFWall) *hld up: nt clr run fr over 3f out: hdwy over 1f out: styd on u.p to ld post* **7/2**[1]
0656 **2** shd **Cunning Pursuit**[17] 2349 3-8-10 **43** .......... KDarley 11 49
(MLWBell) *hld up in tch: led 2f out: sn rdn: hdd post* **4/1**[2]
0400 **3** 2 ½ **Vrisaki (IRE)**[15] 2402 3-9-2 **49** .......... AMcCarthy 7 51
(MissDMountain) *chsd ldrs: led over 3f out: hdd 2f out: styd on same pce fnl f* **6/1**
0606 **4** 5 **Anisette**[6] 2667 3-8-13 **49** .......... LisaJones(3) 4 43
(JulianPoulton) *hld up in tch: rdn over 2f out: wknd fnl f* **20/1**
0326 **5** 2 ½ **Royal Upstart**[9] 2554 3-8-2 **40** .......... (b) BSwarbrick(5) 12 30
(WMBrisbourne) *hld up: hdwy over 3f out: rdn and ev ch over 2f out: wknd fnl f* **10/1**
4054 **6** 3 ½ **Princess Ismene**[15] 2395 3-8-12 **45** .......... (b) GFaulkner 10 29
(PABlockley) *s.s: bhd: hdwy u.p over 3f out: wknd over 2f out* **13/2**
4450 **7** hd **Heartbeat**[9] 2546 3-8-9 **45** .......... (b[1]) TPQueally(3) 5 29
(PJMcbride) *prom: rdn and ev ch over 2f out: wknd over 1f out* **11/2**[3]
0000 **8** 5 **La Concha (IRE)**[34] 1947 3-9-5 **52** .......... (v[1]) SWKelly 9 28
(MrsLCJewell) *mde most 8f: wknd 2f out* **33/1**
5-60 **9** 11 **Ballyboro (IRE)**[17] 2367 3-9-7 **54** .......... (v[1]) PRobinson 6 12
(MJWallace) *chsd ldrs 9f* **16/1**
-004 **10** 23 **Maria Maria (IRE)**[34] 1945 3-9-1 **48** .......... RFitzpatrick 2 —
(MrsNMacauley) *hld up: bhd fr 1/2-way* **40/1**
-606 **11** ½ **Signora Panettiera (FR)**[12] 2485 3-9-1 **55** .......... BO'Neill(7) 8 —
(MRChannon) *prom to 1/2-way* **20/1**

2m 27.05s (-0.35) **Going Correction** -0.175s/f (Firm) **11 Ran SP% 115.1**
Speed ratings: **94,93,92,88,86 84,83,80,72,55 55**CSF £16.02 CT £80.45 TOTE £4.60: £1.10, £2.30, £2.80; EX 15.70.
**Owner** Mrs J E Dobie **Bred** Cdc Partnership **Trained** Newmarket, Suffolk

**FOCUS**
A moderate contest, featuring just one previous winner, but it was run at a good pace.

**NOTEBOOK**
**Winslow Boy(USA)** had excuses when beaten at Lingfield last time and, off a 2lb lower mark, returned to the form of his more promising Beverley run. The good pace suited him and he looks sure to stay farther than this.
**Cunning Pursuit** had been beaten in banded grade last time, but that was over a mile and clearly he found that an insufficient test of stamina. He looked sure to score until cut down close home and a similarly weak event could come his way now that he is racing over his correct distance.
**Vrisaki(IRE)** travelled well into the lead but did not see the trip out as well as the first two. Ten furlongs might be his distance.
**Anisette** looked a non-stayer.
**Royal Upstart**, who was one of the more experienced runners in the race, looked very one-paced.
**Princess Ismene** planted in the stalls, missed the break badly and lost eight to ten lengths. All chance went there and then, but to her credit she did stay on late in the day. *Official explanation: jockey said filly planted in the stalls and missed the break*
**Ballyboro(IRE)** *Official explanation: jockey said filly lost her action and made a noise; vet said filly finished lame*
**Maria Maria(IRE)** *Official explanation: jockey said filly finished distressed*

## 2823 SAFFIE JOSEPH & SONS H'CAP — 6f 3y
5:35 (5:39) (F) (0-55,55) 3-Y-O+ £3,451 (£986; £493) Stalls High

Form RPR
0066 **1** **Gone'N'Dunnett (IRE)**[4] 2707 5-9-4 **50** .......... (v) LisaJones(3) 3 63
(MrsCADunnett) *mde all: rdn and hung rt ins fnl f: r.o* **8/1**
3400 **2** 2 ½ **Kennington**[12] 2473 4-9-4 **52** .......... (v) HayleyTurner(5) 14 58
(MrsCADunnett) *bhd: hdwy over 1f out: swtchd lft ins fnl f: r.o: nt rch wnr* **5/1**[2]
1336 **3** hd **Adantino**[12] 2483 5-9-10 **53** .......... (b) KDarley 8 58
(BRMillman) *hld up: hdwy over 1f out: styd on same pce ins fnl f* **4/1**[1]
0306 **4** 2 **Feast Of Romance**[8] 2598 7-9-1 **47** .......... (b) BReilly(3) 12 46
(CNAllen) *hld up: hdwy 1/2-way: rdn over 1f out: styd on* **8/1**
4536 **5** 3 ½ **Mr Uppity**[16] 2383 5-8-11 **40** .......... (e) NPollard 1 28
(JulianPoulton) *racd alone centre: hung rt fr over 1f out: wknd and eased ins fnl f* **16/1**
0000 **6** 2 ½ **African Spur (IRE)**[26] 2130 4-9-12 **55** .......... RFitzpatrick 5 36
(DCarroll) *prom: rdn over 2f out: wknd over 1f out* **6/1**[3]
0-30 **7** ½ **Crusty Lily**[16] 2384 8-8-6 **35** oh5 .......... (p) JMackay 4 14
(RMHCowell) *hld up: nvr trbld ldrs* **25/1**
-500 **8** 1 ¼ **Komena**[129] 654 6-9-4 **47** .......... PRobinson 7 23
(JWPayne) *chsd ldrs over 4f* **14/1**
2340 **9** nk **Off Hire**[66] 1262 8-9-9 **52** .......... (v) MFenton 10 27
(CSmith) *chsd ldrs over 4f* **25/1**
0303 **10** 9 **Polar Force**[46] 1639 4-9-12 **55** .......... SCarson 6 3
(MissKBBoutflower) *prom: lost pl over 4f out: bhd fr 1/2-way* **9/1**


The Form Book, Raceform Ltd, Compton, RG20 6NL

0-50 **11** *5* **Emmervale**[4] 2707 5-9-7 **50**....................(v) BDoyle 9 —
(RMHCowell) *sn outpcd* **14/1**
5-00 **12** *3 1/2* **On The Level**[20] 792 5-9-0 **43**.................... PMcCabe 2 —
(MrsNMacauley) *plld hrd and prom: wknd 1/2-way* **50/1**
5504 **13** *shd* **Polar Haze**[16] 2384 7-8-8 **37**....................(v) JQuinn 11 —
(JPearce) *sn outpcd* **9/1**

1m 13.51s (-0.09) **Going Correction** -0.10s/f (Good) **13** Ran SP% **122.0**
Speed ratings: **96,92,92,89,85 81,81,79,79,67 60,55,55**CSF £47.95 CT £195.81 TOTE £10.40: £2.40, £3.70, £1.50; EX 41.20 Place 6 £2.55, Place 5 £2.44.
**Owner** College Farm Thoroughbreds **Bred** Ocal Bloodstock **Trained** Hingham, Norfolk

**FOCUS**
Good recent form looked thin on the ground for this moderate sprint, with only three horses boasting a win in one of their last seven starts, and it produced a modest time for the grade.

**NOTEBOOK**
**Gone'N'Dunnett(IRE)** had run a fair race at Brighton four days earlier and did not have to improve much on that form to win here. He has shown most of his best form over five furlongs, but he gets an easy six alright provided the ground is quick.
**Kennington** looked to hold a fair chance, albeit based on meagre turf form, as he had not run too badly in a stronger race than this at Doncaster last time. He struggled to go the early pace but came home strongly, as one would expect of a seven-furlong winner.
**Adantino**, surprisingly sent off favourite, is a friend to Placepot punters but win-only backers should know better by now.
**Feast Of Romance** ran a solid race, but his first turf win remains elusive.
**Mr Uppity** hung badly right under pressure and his rider gave up once they were inside the final furlong. He should have finished much closer to the fourth. *Official explanation: jockey said gelding hung right-handed on the firm ground*
**African Spur(IRE)** was taking on much lesser opposition this time and came in for market support. He was disappointing, though. *Official explanation: jockey said saddle slipped*
**Polar Force** *Official explanation: jockey said gelding was found to have fractured a cannon-bone*
**Emmervale** *Official explanation: jockey said mare moved poorly*
**Polar Haze** *Official explanation: jockey said gelding lost its action in the closing stages*
T/Plt: £6.20 to a £1 stake. Pool: £23,460.50. 2,754.15 winning tickets. T/Qpdt: £7.30 to a £1 stake. Pool: £1,203.40. 121.10 winning tickets. CR

## 2609 CHEPSTOW (L-H)
Friday, June 11

**OFFICIAL GOING: Good to firm**
Wind: mod across becoming nil Weather: fine

### 2831 KNIGHT FRANK/EBF NOVICE STKS 6f 16y
6:35 (6:35) (D) 2-Y-O £3,516 (£1,082; £541; £270) Stalls High

Form RPR
41 **1** **Dahteer (IRE)**[14] 2439 2-9-2.................... KFallon 1 84+
(MRChannon) *a.p: rdn over 2f out: led and edgd rt over 1f out: r.o* **4/5**[1]
333 **2** *2 1/2* **Edge Fund**[17] 2376 2-8-12.................... SDrowne 7 73
(BRMillman) *hung lft: led: hdd and rdn over 1f out: one pce* **5/1**[3]
1 **3** *2 1/2* **Observer (IRE)**[65] 1292 2-9-2....................(v[1]) TPQueally[(3)] 6 72
(DRLoder) *w ldr: rdn and ev ch 2f out: wknd fnl f* **9/4**[2]
50 **4** *1 3/4* **Gavioli (IRE)**[8] 2609 2-8-7....................(t) BSwarbrick[(5)] 4 60
(JMBradley) *hld up in tch: rdn and outpcd over 2f out: kpt on ins fnl f* **100/1**
63 **5** *17* **Troublesome Gerri**[25] 2164 2-8-4.................... DCorby[(3)] 2 —
(SCBurrough) *wl bhd fnl 4f* **50/1**
**6** *22* **Just Bonnie** 2-8-9.................... RMiles[(3)] 5 —
(JMBradley) *dwlt: a wl bhd: t.o* **40/1**

1m 12.84s (0.64) **Going Correction** +0.025s/f (Good) **6** Ran SP% **108.4**
Speed ratings: **96,92,89,87,64 35**CSF £4.92 TOTE £1.80: £1.30, £2.30; EX 3.10.
**Owner** Sheikh Ahmed Al Maktoum **Bred** Darley **Trained** West Ilsley, Berks

**FOCUS**
An ordinary event run at a modest pace for the grade. The proximity of the fourth casts slight doubt over the form.

**NOTEBOOK**
**Dahteer(IRE)** was the first of the three main protagonists to come off the bridle. He again showed a tendency to edge right and beat a couple of rivals who are probably not the most straightforward rides.
**Edge Fund** had hung left at Lingfield last time and was inclined to want to come off the stands' rail throughout. Stepping up to six he eventually got well outpointed by the winner.
**Observer(IRE)**, fitted with a visor, did give the impression that there are some doubts about his attitude.
**Gavioli(IRE)** wore a tongue strap having suffered breathing problems last time. This was a significant improvement and another further should help.
**Just Bonnie** *Official explanation: jockey said saddle slipped*

### 2832 GROLSCH PREMIUM LAGER MAIDEN FILLIES' STKS 1m 4f 23y
7:05 (7:07) (D) 3-Y-O £3,633 (£1,118; £559; £279) Stalls Low

Form RPR
3 **1** **Goslar**[29] 2060 3-8-11.................... DaneO'Neill 3 86
(HCandy) *chsd ldr: led 3f out: rdn 2f out: r.o wl* **9/4**[2]
02 **2** *1 3/4* **Idealistic (IRE)**[20] 2298 3-8-11.................... KFallon 7 83
(LMCumani) *chsd ldrs: rdn over 3f out: wnt 2nd over 2f out: edgd lft over 1f out: nt qckn* **2/5**[1]
04 **3** *21* **Oh So Hardy**[19] 2323 3-8-8.................... DCorby[(3)] 1 49
(MAAllen) *prom: rdn over 4f out: wknd 3f out* **50/1**[3]
0 **4** *6* **Delfinia**[10] 2562 3-8-11.................... SDrowne 2 40
(HSHowe) *led: rdn and hdd 3f out: sn wknd* **100/1**
-000 **5** *8* **Nina Fontenail (FR)**[11] 2517 3-8-8 **45**.................... ABeech[(3)] 4 27
(NJHawke) *hld up towards rr: rdn over 5f out: no rspnse* **100/1**
00 **6** *7* **Dorset (USA)**[25] 2168 3-8-6.................... NChalmers[(5)] 6 16
(AMBalding) *rdn over 5f out: a bhd* **50/1**[3]
0 **7** *1/2* **Singitta**[53] 1508 3-8-8.................... RMiles[(3)] 8 15
(BPalling) *a bhd* **50/1**[3]
0 **8** *dist* **Pearnickity**[18] 2374 3-8-11.................... IMongan 5 —
(AWCarroll) *s.i.s: a wl bhd: virtually p.u ins fnl f* **100/1**

2m 39.05s (0.55) **Going Correction** +0.10s/f (Good) **8** Ran SP% **111.1**
Speed ratings: **102,100,86,82,77 72,72,—**CSF £3.35 TOTE £3.30: £1.10, £1.02, £2.90; EX 3.90.
**Owner** Major M G Wyatt **Bred** Dunchurch Lodge Stud Co **Trained** Wantage, Oxon

**FOCUS**
A weak contest but a fair time for the grade in a race that was a match to all intents and purposes, with the bookmakers going 50/1 bar two.

**NOTEBOOK**
**Goslar** built on the promise of her Salisbury debut and relished the extra quarter of a mile. She can go on from here.
**Idealistic(IRE)**, another trying a longer trip, was inclined to lug in behind the winner and may have been feeling the ground.
**Oh So Hardy**, as expected was left well behind by the fron two, but now at least qualifies for a handicap mark.
**Pearnickity** *Official explanation: jockey said filly was unsuited by the track*

### 2833 SKY BET ASTRAC AT CHEPSTOW CLAIMING STKS 7f 16y
7:35 (7:38) (F) 3-Y-O+ £3,164 (£904; £452) Stalls High

Form RPR
0-43 **1** **A One (IRE)**[17] 2379 5-9-2 **51**.................... SSanders 13 61
(BPalling) *mde all: rdn over 2f out: r.o wl* **7/1**[3]
0-00 **2** *hd* **Chevronne**[3] 2762 4-9-6 **68**.................... IMongan 16 64
(LGCottrell) *swtchd lft over 3f out: rdn over 2f out: ev ch fnl f: r.o* **16/1**
6035 **3** *2 1/2* **Ivy Moon**[17] 2379 4-8-9 **45**.................... ADaly 11 47
(BJLlewellyn) *s.i.s: hdwy over 2f out: rdn over 1f out: r.o ins fnl f* **12/1**
2034 **4** *nk* **Lord Chamberlain**[9] 2597 11-9-6 **55**....................(b) DaneO'Neill 8 57
(JMBradley) *hld up: hdwy 2f out: rdn and swtchd lft over 1f out: r.o ins fnl f* **6/1**[2]
2124 **5** *1/2* **Fen Gypsy**[10] 2560 6-9-3 **60**.................... SJDonohoe[(7)] 9 60
(PDEvans) *hld up: hdwy over 3f out: rdn over 1f out: one pce fnl f* **4/1**[1]
-000 **6** *1 3/4* **One Upmanship**[2] 2790 3-9-0 **66**....................(b) KFallon 14 55
(JGPortman) *chsd ldrs: rdn and edgd lft over 1f out: wknd ins fnl f* **15/2**
4400 **7** *6* **Mobo-Baco**[15] 2426 7-9-2 **54**.................... SDrowne 1 32
(RJHodges) *racd alone centre: rdn and no hdwy fnl 2f* **8/1**
-000 **8** *1 1/2* **In Tune**[27] 2123 4-9-0 **40**....................(t) DCorby[(3)] 5 29
(SCBurrough) *s.i.s: rdn over 3f out: hdwy fnl f: nrst fin* **66/1**
0 **9** *shd* **Needwood Bucolic (IRE)**[9] 2582 6-8-13.................... RMiles[(3)] 12 28
(RAllan) *chsd wnr: rdn over 2f out: wknd over 1f out* **33/1**
0-0 **10** *1/2* **Curzon Lodge (IRE)**[156] 463 4-9-11....................(t) TPQueally[(3)] 7 38
(CTinkler) *bhd: styd on fnl f: nrst fin* **50/1**
4016 **11** *1 1/4* **Gilly's General (IRE)**[7] 2666 4-9-2 **49**.................... SWhitworth 10 23
(JWUnett) *prom tl rdn and wknd over 2f out* **20/1**
-000 **12** *hd* **Desert Daisy (IRE)**[10] 2545 3-7-8 **59**....................(v[1]) BSwarbrick[(5)] 15 16
(IAWood) *chsd ldrs: rdn over 3f out: wknd over 2f out* **16/1**
5001 **13** *3/4* **Rileys Dream**[18] 2359 5-8-9 **43**.................... RHavlin 6 14
(BJLlewellyn) *mid-div: rdn over 3f out: short-lived effrt whn edgd lft wl over 1f out* **9/1**
1400 **14** *3/4* **Over To You Bert**[17] 2387 5-8-9 **42**.................... MSavage[(5)] 2 17
(RJHodges) *racd wd tl swtchd rt after 2f: rdn 3f out: no imp whn carried lft over 1f out* **40/1**
5105 **15** *2* **Chickasaw Trail**[17] 2387 6-8-4 **43**.................... StephanieHollinshead[(5)] 3 6
(RHollinshead) *rdn over 3f out: a bhd* **25/1**
000- **16** *3 1/2* **Variety Club**[293] 4370 3-8-0 ow3.................... TBlock[(7)] 4 5
(AMBalding) *a bhd* **25/1**

1m 23.48s (0.28) **Going Correction** +0.025s/f (Good)
**WFA** 3 from 4yo+ 10lb **16** Ran SP% **120.4**
Speed ratings: **99,98,95,95,95 93,86,84,84,83 82,82,81,80,78 74**CSF £104.22 TOTE £7.30: £2.20, £5.90, £3.10; EX 100.40.The winner was claimed by John Manners for £6,000.
**Owner** Albert Yemm **Bred** Humphrey Okeke **Trained** Tredodridge, Vale Of Glamorgan

**FOCUS**
Quantity rather than quality in this modest claimer, but the first two appeared to run to their best.

**NOTEBOOK**
**A One(IRE)** had also made all when landing this race on soft ground two years ago. This was the first time he had scored on ground as quick as this and he was claimed by John Manners for £6,000.
**Chevronne**, who has been struggling to find his best trip, lost nothing in defeat and found that the winner would not be denied.
**Ivy Moon** often loses ground at the start and could not peg back the two principals.
**Lord Chamberlain** definitely wants a mile on ground as quick as this.
**Fen Gypsy** found the combination of a faster surface and a drop back from a mile against him.
**One Upmanship** had the blinkers back on for this drop in class.
**Mobo-Baco** *Official explanation: jockey said gelding lost a shoe during the race*

### 2834 SKY BET ASTRAC RECORD BREAKER H'CAP 7f 16y
8:10 (8:10) (D) (0-80,76) 3-Y-O+ £5,512 (£1,696; £848; £424) Stalls High

Form RPR
2122 **1** **Goodenough Mover**[8] 2614 8-9-3 **70**.................... HayleyTurner[(5)] 5 86
(JSKing) *mde all: rdn 1f out: r.o wl* **4/1**[1]
-500 **2** *3* **Astrac (IRE)**[35] 1941 13-8-0 **48**.................... PMQuinn 10 56
(MrsALMKing) *hld up: hdwy 3f out: rdn to chse wnr over 1f out: no ex ins fnl f* **33/1**
043 **3** *4* **Mistral Sky**[13] 2483 5-9-5 **67**....................(p) SDrowne 7 65
(MrsStefLiddiard) *hld up in tch: lost pl over 4f out: hdwy 2f out: kpt on ins fnl f* **7/1**
0-42 **4** *hd* **Leaping Brave (IRE)**[11] 2516 3-9-4 **76**.................... AMcCarthy 8 73
(BRMillman) *a.p: chsd wnr 3f out tl rdn over 1f out: wknd fnl f* **9/2**[2]
0-00 **5** *1 3/4* **Logistical**[13] 2483 4-9-0 **62**.................... DSweeney 4 55
(ADWPinder) *s.i.s: rdn and hdwy over 2f out: sn no imp* **12/1**
15-0 **6** *hd* **Compton Banker (IRE)**[141] 586 7-9-10 **72**.................... SSanders 9 64
(GAButler) *chsd ldrs: rdn 2f out: wknd fnl f* **8/1**
0010 **7** *3/4* **Lockstock (IRE)**[23] 2226 6-9-7 **72**....................(p) RMiles[(3)] 11 62
(MSSaunders) *a bhd* **8/1**
0-03 **8** *3 1/2* **Beneking**[13] 2473 4-8-0 **55**.................... HFellows[(7)] 6 36
(RHollinshead) *hld up mid-div: rdn and hdwy over 2f out: wknd over 1f out* **12/1**
1304 **9** *8* **Alafzar (IRE)**[5] 2703 6-8-11 **59**....................(vt) KFallon 1 19
(PDEvans) *chsd ldrs: rdn 3f out: sn wknd* **5/1**[3]
4-05 **10** *5* **Jacaranda (IRE)**[56] 1452 4-9-7 **69**.................... DaneO'Neill 3 16
(MrsALMKing) *hld up: sn mid-div: short-lived effrt on outside 3f out* **10/1**
5000 **11** *1/2* **Bennanabaa**[27] 2128 5-7-11 **48**....................(t) JFMcDonald[(3)] 2 —
(SCBurrough) *chsd wnr: rdn over 3f out: wknd over 2f out* **66/1**

1m 22.62s (-0.58) **Going Correction** +0.025s/f (Good)
**WFA** 3 from 4yo+ 10lb **11** Ran SP% **118.5**
Speed ratings: **104,100,96,95,93 93,92,88,79,73 73**CSF £136.93 CT £925.32 TOTE £5.00: £2.00, £4.60, £2.90; EX 170.80.
**Owner** D Goodenough Removals & Transport **Bred** G Foster **Trained** Broad Hinton, Wilts
■ This race commemorated the fact that Astrac has now competed on all 35 Flat courses in Britain, the first horse to do so.

**FOCUS**
An ordinary handicap in which the winner had the run of the race.

**NOTEBOOK**
**Goodenough Mover** got the rail and registered his fourth win at a course which seems to suit his front-running style.
**Astrac(IRE)**, a grand old campaigner, did his best to win a race named after him.
**Mistral Sky**, again in cheekpieces, ran an odd race and eventually came back through to snatch third.
**Leaping Brave(IRE)** surprisingly failed to get home after running well over a mile here last time.

## 2835 SKY BET PRESS RED TO BET NOW H'CAP 1m 2f 36y

8:45 (8:45) (E) (0-70,70) 3-Y-0+ £3,711 (£1,142; £571; £285) Stalls Low

Form RPR

0-61 **1** **Tidal**[11] 2514 5-9-0 **61** 6ex ........................ RThomas(5) 5 81
(AWCarroll) *chsd ldr: led 7f out: clr over 1f out: easily* **5/2**[1]

0361 **2** *8* **Realism (FR)**[9] 2591 4-9-1 **60** ........................ RMiles(3) 11 65
(PWHiatt) *led 3f: chsd wnr: rdn and one pce fnl 2f* **7/2**[2]

3-00 **3** *1/2* **Billy Bathwick (IRE)**[15] 2430 7-9-0 **56** ........................ DaneO'Neill 9 60
(JMBradley) *hld up in tch: hdwy over 3f out: rdn and one pce fnl 2f* **9/1**

0004 **4** *3/4* **Skylarker (USA)**[15] 2430 6-9-9 **70** ........................ MSavage(5) 8 73
(WSKittow) *hld up: hdwy over 4f out: swtchd rt 3f out: sn rdn: wknd 2f out* **13/2**

0002 **5** *1/2* **Hazewind**[7] 2648 3-7-12 **56** ........................(vt) FPFerris(3) 4 58
(PDEvans) *prom: wnt 2nd briefly over 4f out: rdn over 3f out: wknd over 1f out* **11/2**[3]

00-0 **6** *3/4* **Milk And Sultana**[48] 1606 4-8-11 **53** ........................ SDrowne 7 53
(GAHam) *hld up and bhd: hdwy on ins 2f out: nvr nr ldrs* **50/1**

00/5 **7** *3 1/2* **Greyfield (IRE)**[12] 2501 8-8-13 **55** ........................ ADaly 3 49
(KBishop) *hld up and bhd: rdn and sme hdwy 3f out: n.d* **12/1**

-000 **8** *2 1/2* **Lunar Lord**[9] 2590 8-8-11 **53** ........................ RPrice 1 42
(DBurchell) *a bhd* **33/1**

-300 **9** *2 1/2* **Seejay**[17] 2387 4-8-0 **42** ........................ PMQuinn 2 26
(MAAllen) *hld up: rdn over 3f out: no rspnse* **33/1**

0100 **10** *3* **Margarets Wish**[7] 2649 4-7-10 **43** ........................ BSwarbrick(5) 6 21
(TWall) *hld up and bhd: hdwy 5f out: wknd 3f out* **20/1**

00-6 **11** *10* **Mount Benger**[72] 1213 4-9-9 **65** ........................ SSanders 10 24
(RMBeckett) *prom: rdn over 3f out: sn wknd* **16/1**

2m 10.0s (0.40) **Going Correction** +0.10s/f (Good)
**WFA** 3 from 4yo+ 13lb **11** Ran SP% **115.7**
Speed ratings: **102,95,95,94,94 93,90,88,86,84 76**CSF £10.30 CT £66.52 TOTE £3.50: £2.00, £1.80, £2.40; EX 10.90.
**Owner** Mrs B Quinn **Bred** Wyck Hall Stud Ltd **Trained** Wixford, Warwicks

**FOCUS**
A modest contest in which the in-form Tidal routed this field and could rate higher.

**NOTEBOOK**
**Tidal** is on the crest of a wave at the moment and seems likely to still be ahead of the Handicapper on her hat-trick bid.
**Realism(FR)**, set to go up 3lb tomorrow, proved no match for the winner in the final quarter-mile.
**Billy Bathwick(IRE)**, who came into form around this time last year, lost out in the separate race for the runner-up spot.
**Skylarker(USA)** has tumbled down the ratings having not won for almost three years.
**Hazewind** had dominated from the front when narrowly beaten at Goodwood a week ago.
**Milk And Sultana**, ridden to get the trip, gave the impression that there might be better things to come.
**Seejay** *Official explanation: jockey said filly was unsuited by the good to firm ground*

## 2836 SOFRYDD SOCIAL CLUB, CHAIRMAN'S 30TH ANNIVERSARY MAIDEN H'CAP 6f 16y

9:15 (9:16) (E) (0-70,68) 3-Y-0+ £3,926 (£1,208; £604; £302) Stalls High

Form RPR

604- **1** **Millfields Dreams**[291] 4470 5-8-8 **47** ........................ FPFerris(3) 3 65
(RBrotherton) *mde all far side: rdn over 2f out: clr over 1f out: eased towards fin* **33/1**

-005 **2** *6* **Go Yellow**[14] 2457 3-9-3 **68** ........................ SJDonohoe(7) 2 68
(PDEvans) *chsd wnr far side: rdn over 2f out: sn no imp* **18/1**

4-00 **3** *1 1/2* **Danish Monarch**[24] 2207 3-9-8 **66** ........................ DSweeney 20 62
(ADWPinder) *chsd ldrs stands' side: rdn over 2f out: kpt on fnl f* **14/1**

00-0 **4** *hd* **Eight Ellington (IRE)**[65] 1293 3-9-1 **59** ........................ IMongan 18 54
(MissGayKelleway) *hld up stands' side: rdn and hdwy over 2f out: kpt on fnl f* **16/1**

00-0 **5** *shd* **Ligne D'Eau**[44] 1711 3-9-1 **59** ........................ SDrowne 1 54
(PDEvans) *racd far side: sn outpcd: hdwy over 2f out: one pce fnl f* **33/1**

-632 **6** *2 1/2* **Kensington (IRE)**[22] 2236 3-9-8 **66** ........................ SSanders 17 53
(RGuest) *racd stands' side: hld up: rdn 3f out: hdwy wl over 1f out: no imp fnl f* **5/2**[1]

36-3 **7** *shd* **Blue Moon Hitman (IRE)**[21] 2265 3-9-2 **60** ........................ SWhitworth 14 47
(RBrotherton) *led stands' side: rdn 2f out: wknd fnl f* **33/1**

3-00 **8** *nk* **Piccleyes**[2] 2790 3-9-5 **63** ........................(b) DaneO'Neill 15 49
(RHannon) *w ldrs stands' side: rdn 2f out: wknd fnl f* **10/1**

0306 **9** *3/4* **Travellers Joy**[17] 2384 4-7-10 **35** ........................ JFMcDonald(3) 13 19
(RJHodges) *chsd ldrs stands' side: rdn 3f out: sn wknd* **14/1**

0242 **9** *dht* **My Girl Pearl (IRE)**[3] 2762 4-8-11 **50** ........................ RMiles(3) 6 34
(MSSaunders) *hld up centre: nt clr run and swtchd rt wl over 2f out: sn rdn: swtchd lft and hdwy wl over 1f out: one pce fnl f* **8/1**[3]

3-33 **11** *2* **General Feeling (IRE)**[25] 2165 3-9-9 **67** ........................ PDobbs 12 45
(SKirk) *hld up in tch stands' side: rdn and edgd lft over 2f out: wknd ins fnl f* **4/1**[2]

0006 **12** *6* **Zambezi River**[18] 2359 5-8-9 **50** ........................ BSwarbrick(5) 4 10
(JMBradley) *chsd ldrs far side: wknd over 2f out* **25/1**

00-0 **13** *1 1/4* **Sweet Az**[11] 2517 4-8-3 **39** ........................ SRighton 11 —
(SCBurrough) *spd stands' side 2f* **50/1**

6-03 **14** *1* **The Butterfly Boy**[49] 1596 3-8-11 **60** ........................ NDeSouza(5) 16 13
(PFICole) *s.i.s: sn chsng ldrs stands' side: rdn over 3f out: sn wknd* **16/1**

5320 **15** *3/4* **Ballinger Express**[6] 2670 4-9-9 **64** ........................(b) NChalmers(5) 9 15
(AMBalding) *prom stands' side: rdn and wknd over 2f out* **12/1**

6460 **16** *1 3/4* **Vlasta Weiner**[17] 2384 4-7-13 **35** ........................(b) AMcCarthy 10 —
(JMBradley) *racd stands' side: rdn over 3f out: hung lft over 2f out: sn bhd* **50/1**

200- **17** *1* **Stagnite**[243] 5497 4-9-9 **59** ........................ GBaker 7 1
(MrsHSweeting) *s.i.s: racd centre: rdn over 3f out: a bhd* **20/1**

4440 **18** *1 1/4* **Bold Wolf**[17] 2380 3-8-6 **50** ........................ ADaly 5 —
(JLSpearing) *racd centre: a bhd* **33/1**

6-00 **19** *1 1/4* **Lyrical Lady**[11] 2518 3-8-4 **53** ........................(p) RThomas(5) 19 —
(MrsAJBowlby) *s.i.s: racd centre: a bhd* **40/1**

6344 **20** *7* **Mahlstick (IRE)**[45] 1694 6-8-8 **44** ........................ RHavlin 8 —
(DWPArbuthnot) *racd centre: a bhd* **50/1**

1m 11.76s (-0.44) **Going Correction** +0.025s/f (Good)
**WFA** 3 from 4yo+ 8lb **20** Ran SP% **135.5**
Speed ratings: **103,95,93,92,92 89,89,88,86,86 84,76,74,73,72 69,68,66,65,55**CSF £551.44 CT £8594.95 TOTE £64.20: £8.80, £4.60, £3.40, £3.60; EX 442.70 Place 6 £125.70, Place 5 £84.65.
**Owner** Mrs S S Chandler **Bred** T G Price **Trained** Elmley Castle, Worcs

**FOCUS**
A moderate handicap in which he first two came from a quartet that raced on the far side.

**NOTEBOOK**
**Millfields Dreams** caused a big surprise on his belated reappearance and never saw another horse on the far side. Only time will tell if this was a fluke.
**Go Yellow**, given a chance by the Handicapper, was always playing second fiddle in the final quarter-mile.
**Danish Monarch**, another who has dropped to a more realistic mark, won the race on the stands' side but was well beaten by the winner.
**Eight Ellington(IRE)** appeared to benefit from more patient tactics.
**Ligne D'Eau** is shaping as though he needs a longer trip. *Official explanation: jockey said colt did not come down the hill well*
**Kensington(IRE)**, on his handicap debut, never looked likely to send favourite backers home happy.
T/Plt: £127.70 to a £1 stake. Pool: £44,558.95. 254.55 winning tickets. T/Qpdt: £129.60 to a £1 stake. Pool: £2,960.60. 16.90 winning tickets. KH

# 2643 GOODWOOD (R-H)

Friday, June 11

**OFFICIAL GOING: Good (good to firm in places on round course)**

## 2837 EBF CHARLIE NEWMAN - A LIFETIME IN RACING MEDIAN AUCTION MAIDEN FILLIES' STKS 6f

6:20 (6:20) (E) 2-Y-0 £4,667 (£1,436; £718; £359) Stalls Low

Form RPR

**1** **Trempjane** 2-8-11 ........................ RHughes 4 70
(RHannon) *leggy: scope: tall: hld up in tch: pushed along over 3f out: swtchd rt over 2f out: led over 1f out: r.o wl fnl f* **1/1**[1]

**2** *1 1/2* **Gee Bee Em** 2-8-8 ........................ SHitchcott(3) 1 66
(MRChannon) *w'like: bit bkwd: in tch: rdn 2f out: kpt on u.p to chse wner fnl f: no imp* **12/1**

**3** *1 3/4* **Bint Il Sultan (IRE)** 2-8-11 ........................ JPMurtagh 2 60
(EALDunlop) *w'like: t.k.h: prom tl outpcd 2f out: rdn and styd on ins fnl f* **6/1**[3]

**4** *nk* **Classic Guest** 2-8-11 ........................ CCatlin 3 59
(MRChannon) *w'like: leggy: led tl rdn and hdd over 1f out: kpt on one pce* **6/1**[3]

**5** *1/2* **Auwitesweetheart** 2-8-11 ........................ SWKelly 5 58
(BRMillman) *unf: scope: in tch: chal 2f out: rdn and wknd ins fnl f* **12/1**

**6** *5* **Casterossa** 2-8-11 ........................ PaulEddery 6 43
(DHaydnJones) *leggy: broke wl but sn outpcd and a bhd* **4/1**[2]

1m 15.44s (2.60) **Going Correction** +0.20s/f (Good) **6** Ran SP% **114.0**
Speed ratings: **90,88,85,85,84 77**CSF £14.86 TOTE £2.10: £1.70, £2.70; EX 25.10.
**Owner** Mrs W H Gibson Fleming **Bred** Mrs W H Gibson Fleming **Trained** East Everleigh, Wilts

**FOCUS**
Probably nothing more than an ordinary juvenile maiden as the time was pedestrian, but very little to go on.

**NOTEBOOK**
**Trempjane** was backed in the market as though expected to take all the beating and, despite being shoved along before halfway, was on top over a furlong out and just had to be kept up to her work to score readily. This was a nice performance and, with the possibility of a seventh furlong seeing her in an even better light, further progress can be expected.
**Gee Bee Em** was the less fancied of the Channon pair according to the market, but she beat her stable companion comfortably and stayed on to claim second. She will relish another furlong and looks a winner waiting to happen.
**Bint Il Sultan(IRE)** ran a race full of promise, being keen early before finding herself tapped for toe and then running on again. Her stable's juveniles usually benefit from an outing and improvement can be anticipated.
**Classic Guest** showed up well early before being readily brushed aside. She can be expected to improve for this, but will need to if she is to be winning next time.
**Auwitesweetheart** fared a little better than her finishing position may suggest.
**Casterossa** was never really going the gallop, and the fact she was sent off second favourite suggests better can be expected next time.

## 2838 SUN-X UK LEADERBOARD SPORTS CLASSIFIED STKS 7f

6:50 (6:52) (D) 3-Y-0+ £5,421 (£1,668; £834; £417) Stalls High

Form RPR

3612 **1** **Lady Georgina**[6] 2694 3-8-5 75 ow1 ........................ OUrbina 8 82+
(JRFanshawe) *lw: hld up in cl tch: hdwy whn swtchd lft and short of room wl over 1f out: swtchd rt to far rail and drvn out to ld last s* **13/8**[1]

0110 **2** *shd* **Idle Power (IRE)**[6] 2682 6-9-5 77 ........................(p) JPMurtagh 1 83
(JRBoyle) *t.k.h: trckd ldng pair: ev ch ins fnl f and abt to ld whn ct last stride* **6/1**[3]

3122 **3** *nk* **Samuel Charles**[10] 2553 6-9-3 72 ........................ SWKelly 3 80
(WMBrisbourne) *led: rdn over 3f out: r.o gamely fnl f: no ex and hdd by first two cl home* **9/1**

1404 **4** *nk* **What-A-Dancer (IRE)**[13] 2469 7-9-4 76 ........................ TQuinn 7 80
(GASwinbank) *hld up: swtchd lft over 1f out and r.o strly fnl f* **3/1**[2]

0050 **5** *1 1/4* **Terraquin (IRE)**[6] 2575 4-9-3 74 ........................(p) DKinsella 5 76?
(JJBridger) *b: hld up in rr: rdn over 2f out: kpt on one pce fnl f* **25/1**

0316 **6** *2 1/2* **Quantum Leap**[9] 2575 7-9-3 72 ........................(v) PaulEddery 4 70
(SDow) *b.hind: chsd ldng pair tl riden and wknd ent fnl f* **7/1**

6206 **7** *3 1/2* **Oakley Rambo**[11] 2516 5-9-8 80 ........................ RHughes 2 66
(RHannon) *hld up: rdn over 2f out: nt on terms after* **12/1**

1m 29.14s (1.11) **Going Correction** +0.20s/f (Good)
**WFA** 3 from 4yo+ 10lb **7** Ran SP% **111.4**
Speed ratings: **101,100,100,100,98 95,91**CSF £11.24 TOTE £2.50: £1.80, £3.10; EX 11.90.
**Owner** Byerley Turf **Bred** Khorshed And Ian Deane And Eamonn Phelan **Trained** Newmarket, Suffolk

**FOCUS**
A fair classified event , but they went only a modest pace and there was under a length separating the front four at the line, so the form has question marks over it.

**NOTEBOOK**
**Lady Georgina** had strong claims on the back of her second at Newmarket last Saturday and made unnecessarily hard work of it, not getting a clear run and having to squeeze up the inside rail, eventually getting there in the final stride having shown a good change of pace. She is a progressive filly who should be most capable of winning back in handicap company.
**Idle Power(IRE)** would have preferred a stronger gallop and as a result deserves extra credit for his effort. He has hit top form of late and further success should be forthcoming.
**Samuel Charles** enjoyed the run of the race from the front and continued his consistent run of finishing in the first three.
**What-A-Dancer(IRE)** was another who would have been better suited to a stronger gallop and he was doing all his best work at the finish.
**Terraquin(IRE)** showed some signs of a return to form, but there is always the possibility he was flattered by the way the race was run.
**Quantum Leap** did not lead as he likes to and failed to give his running.

## 2839 SOUTHERN DAILY ECHO STKS (H'CAP) 6f
**7:20** (7:20) (D ) (0-80,77) 3-Y-O **£5,408** (£1,664; £832; £416) **Stalls** Low

Form RPR
1632 **1** **Presto Shinko (IRE)**[9] 2589 3-9-7 **77** RHughes 3 89
(RHannon) *lw: hld up: short of room and swtchd rt appr fnl f: got clr run and qckn d wl to ld ins fnl f: won gng away* **5/2**[1]
-041 **2** *1 1/4* **Estihlal**[18] 2351 3-8-8 **64** WSupple 2 72
(EALDunlop) *in tch: swtchd rt and chal 2f out: led over 1f out: rdn and hdd ins last: nt pce of wnr* **7/2**[3]
1 **3** *hd* **Eisteddfod**[36] 1906 3-9-5 **75** TQuinn 8 82
(PFICole) *lw: wnt rt s: sn in tch: rdn over 1f out: r.o one pce fnl f* **9/2**
6-24 **4** *1/2* **Red Romeo**[21] 2269 3-9-5 **75** JPMurtagh 1 81
(GASwinbank) *lw: led tl hdd over 2f out: outpcd but styd on ins fnl f* **3/1**[2]
-500 **5** *3 1/2* **Haydn (USA)**[44] 1702 3-9-3 **73** JFEgan 6 68
(PWChapple-Hyam) *trckd ldrs: rdn over 2f out: wknd over 1f out* **16/1**
6516 **6** *shd* **Arfinnit (IRE)**[7] 2657 3-8-5 **64** (v) SHitchcott[(3)] 7 59
(MRChannon) *led tl hdd over 2f out: hdd over 1f out: wknd* **16/1**
-550 **7** *2 1/2* **Pompey Blue**[108] 868 3-8-10 **66** DHolland 4 54
(PJMcbride) *trckd ldrs tl wknd wl over 1f out* **10/1**
10-0 **8** *7* **Averline**[14] 2444 3-9-0 **70** DKinsella 5 37
(BDeHaan) *in tch tl rdn and wknd wl over 1f out* **20/1**

1m 13.31s (0.47) **Going Correction** +0.20s/f (Good) **8 Ran SP% 119.6**
Speed ratings: **104,102,102,101,96 96,93,83**CSF £12.19 CT £38.17 TOTE £3.90: £1.50, £1.90, £1.40; EX 12.90.
**Owner** Major A M Everett **Bred** Mrs S O'Riordan **Trained** East Everleigh, Wilts

**FOCUS**
A fair handicap but a smart performance from Presto Shinko, who showed a telling turn of foot to settle it instantly. The form has a solid look.

**NOTEBOOK**
**Presto Shinko(IRE)** had to sit and suffer until his gap finally appeared and he did not need a second invitation to take it, quickening up smartly to settle to issue in a matter of strides. This was a smart performance and he is capable of winning something better.
**Estihlal** had every chance but was of no match to the winner. She is going the right way and her winning turn is not far away.
**Eisteddfod** had won his only start prior to this and ran well for one so inexperienced. Given the way he was sticking on at the end the likelihood is than a stiffer test will suit best.
**Red Romeo** has shown plenty over six furlongs this season, but he was tried over a mile at two and it may be that seven proves the happy medium.
**Haydn(USA)** continues to disappoint and faded having shown up well early.
**Pompey Blue** *Official explanation: jockey said filly was unsuited by the good to firm ground*

## 2840 SALLY MILLER MOUNT KILIMANJARO TREK MAIDEN H'CAP 1m 6f
**7:55** (7:55) (E ) (0-75,74) 3-Y-O **£3,770** (£1,160; £580; £290) **Stalls** High

Form RPR
6656 **1** **Hathlen (IRE)**[10] 2561 3-9-3 **73** SHitchcott[(3)] 5 78
(MRChannon) *hld up in mid-div: rdn 3f out: styd on to ld appr fnl f: drvn out* **7/1**
-222 **2** *1* **Sunny Lady (FR)**[19] 2323 3-9-7 **74** DHolland 6 78
(EALDunlop) *trckd ldrs: led 4f out: rdn over 2f out: hdd appr fnl f: kpt on but no imp ins last* **11/4**[1]
5-30 **3** *hd* **Glide**[29] 2070 3-9-3 **70** (v[1]) RHughes 7 74
(RCharlton) *hld up: stdy hdwy fr 5f out: rdn 2f out: styd on fnl f: nvr nrr* **13/2**
4-05 **4** *5* **Fu Fighter**[10] 2561 3-9-5 **72** JPMurtagh 3 69
(JAOsborne) *a.p: chal for ld over 3f out: rdn and wknd appr fnl f* **11/2**
-603 **5** *1 3/4* **Mustang Ali (IRE)**[9] 2578 3-9-1 **68** JFEgan 9 62
(SKirk) *hld up: rdn and hdwy over 3f out: wknd over 1f out* **9/2**[3]
500 **6** *3/4* **Olympias (IRE)**[22] 2243 3-8-7 **60** SWKelly 4 53
(HMorrison) *hld up:: effrt and swtchd rt over 2f out: no ex appr fnl f* **14/1**
0306 **7** *hd* **Darn Good**[10] 2546 3-8-13 **66** (b) RLMoore 2 59
(RHannon) *trckd ldr: rdn over 3f out: wknd wl over 2f out* **20/1**
00-0 **8** *13* **Flying Patriarch**[46] 1674 3-7-9 **51** oh4 (b) LisaJones[(3)] 10 26
(GLMoore) *trckd ldrs tl rdn and wknd wl over 2f out* **33/1**
-200 **9** *1* **Waltzing Beau**[10] 2546 3-8-6 **59** (v[1]) TQuinn 1 32
(BGPowell) *rdn fr s and sn led: hdd 4f out: wknd wl over 2f out* **25/1**
-433 **10** *15* **Al Beedaa (USA)**[19] 2323 3-9-6 **73** (v[1]) WSupple 8 25
(JLDunlop) *hld up: rdn over 3f out: nt run on and sn btn* **4/1**[2]

3m 4.82s (1.07) **Going Correction** +0.20s/f (Good) **10 Ran SP% 124.3**
Speed ratings: **104,103,103,100,99 99,98,91,90,82**CSF £27.87 CT £138.53 TOTE £8.40: £2.30, £1.50, £2.80; EX 22.60.
**Owner** Sheikh Ahmed Al Maktoum **Bred** Darley **Trained** West Ilsley, Berks

**FOCUS**
A weakish race, but a fair time for the grade and a deserved first success for Hathlen.

**NOTEBOOK**
**Hathlen(IRE)** was getting off the mark at the 13th attempt and did it in plucky fashion. He stays really well and kept finding once hitting the front. Although it has taken him time to get his head in front, he has more to offer and the win would have done him good.
**Sunny Lady(FR)** has now finished second on her last four starts but has no problem with her attitude, she just simply keeps finding one too good. She does not seem that well handicapped, but her consistency should eventually be rewarded.
**Glide** showed improved form in the first-time visor and looked a real threat at one stage. His challenge flattened out though, and in the end he had to settle for third.
**Fu Fighter** ran well for a long way and may be best with a slightly easier test.
**Waltzing Beau** *Official explanation: jockey said gelding had run too free early on*
**Al Beedaa(USA)** appeared to resent the first-time blinkers and was tailed off.

## 2841 CRIMBOURNE STUD STALES (H'CAP) 1m 1f 192y
**8:30** (8:31) (D ) (0-85,83) 3-Y-O **£6,776** (£2,085; £1,042; £521) **Stalls** Low

Form RPR
2251 **1** **Gavroche (IRE)**[13] 2472 3-8-13 **78** J-PGuillambert[(3)] 3 85
(CADwyer) *slowly away: in rr tl hdwy 3f out: rdn to ld jst ins fnl f: all out* **5/1**[3]
341 **2** *shd* **Swainson (USA)**[13] 2486 3-9-3 **79** DHolland 4 86
(PMitchell) *sn trckd ldr: led 2f out: hrd rdn and hdd jst ins fnl f: kpt on gamely and pressed wnr to line* **7/2**[1]
-230 **3** *3 1/2* **Sailmaker (IRE)**[25] 2169 3-8-13 **75** (t) RHughes 8 78+
(RCharlton) *hld up: rdn and hdwy 2f out: styd on one pce to take 3rd ins fnl f* **5/1**[3]
1-00 **4** *2 1/2* **Muhaymin (USA)**[20] 2306 3-9-7 **83** WSupple 5 78
(JLDunlop) *lw: led: sn clr: rdn 3f out: hdd 2f out: wknd fnl f* **5/1**[3]
0-43 **5** *1 3/4* **Wou Oodd**[16] 2412 3-9-0 **79** SHitchcott[(3)] 2 71
(MRChannon) *t.k.h: hld up in tch: rdn 3f out: no hdwy appr fnl f* **12/1**
361 **6** *1* **Springtime Romance (USA)**[22] 2243 3-9-4 **80** JPMurtagh 7 70
(EALDunlop) *trckd ldrs tl rdn and wknd 2f out* **4/1**[2]
05-0 **7** *4* **Uncle John**[16] 2400 3-8-3 **65** JFEgan 1 47
(SKirk) *in tch: rdn over 2f out: wknd wl over 1f out* **10/1**
01-0 **8** *2 1/2* **Red Skelton (IRE)**[44] 1712 3-9-1 **77** (t) TQuinn 6 55
(WJHaggas) *lw: a in rr: outpcd and nvr on terms* **14/1**

2m 9.60s (1.92) **Going Correction** +0.20s/f (Good) **8 Ran SP% 115.7**
Speed ratings: **100,99,97,95,93 92,89,87**CSF £23.16 CT £92.02 TOTE £6.30: £1.40, £1.60, £2.40; EX 16.80.
**Owner** J L Guillambert **Bred** John O'Connor **Trained** Newmarket, Suffolk

**FOCUS**
This looked a good handicap and it produced a cracking finish between two progressive colts.

**NOTEBOOK**
**Gavroche(IRE)**, a short-head winner two weeks ago, again just did enough to deny the favourite and is improving fast. He was winning here off a 5lb higher mark and although another rise is likely, one could not rule out him completing the hat-trick.
**Swainson(USA)** still showed signs of greeness going down to post, and it was a similar story in the race itself. He did not go with clear early leader Muhaymin and instead chose to lead the main pack. However, when coming under pressure he did not immediately pick up, and it was only in the final few strides he really got going and was getting back at the winner with every stride. This represented an improvement on his form in maidens and now he has been in a 'proper' race should be able to go on to better things.
**Sailmaker(IRE)** ran on to claim third without ever threatening the front pair, and is worth trying at a mile and a half.
**Muhaymin(USA)** has yet to prove he stays this trip in two attempts now, but his previous try was on his seasonal reappearance when the stable were not at their peak and he may have done too much early here, so it would be foolish to say he does not get it.
**Uncle John** *Official explanation: jockey said gelding lost its action*

## 2842 RAUGHMERE MAIDEN STKS 1m
**9:00** (9:01) (D ) 3-Y-O **£5,486** (£1,688; £844; £422) **Stalls** High

Form RPR
0-62 **1** **Gold Mask (USA)**[24] 2204 3-9-0 78 (v[1]) DHolland 6 79
(JHMGosden) *lw: led after 1f: rdn over 1f out and in command after* **4/5**[1]
0- **2** *1 1/2* **Admiral Compton**[249] 5422 3-9-0 JPMurtagh 9 76
(ACStewart) *in tch: rdn 2f out: kpt on to go 2nd ins fnl f* **10/1**[3]
02-4 **3** *nk* **Tenny's Gold (IRE)**[25] 2182 3-8-9 70 MHills 3 70
(BWHills) *a.p: chsd wnr over 3f out: rdn over 1f out: one pce and lost 2nd ins fnl f* **3/1**[2]
4000 **4** *2 1/2* **Lord Of The Sea (IRE)**[7] 2648 3-9-0 67 PDoe 8 69
(JamiePoulton) *mid-div: kpt on one pce ins fnl 2f* **10/1**[3]
00 **5** *nk* **Desert Hawk**[27] 2114 3-9-0 JFEgan 2 69
(RHannon) *lw: mid-div: kpt on pce fnl 2f* **16/1**
00 **6** *nk* **Miss Inkha**[40] 1794 3-8-9 RLMoore 4 63
(RGuest) *hld up in mid-div: rdn over 3f out: wknd over 1f out* **25/1**
00 **7** *1/2* **Shaaban (IRE)**[13] 2479 3-9-0 CCatlin 7 67
(MRChannon) *lw: hld up: rdn over 2f out: wknd ent fnl f* **12/1**
000- **8** *1 1/2* **Royal Starlet**[280] 4705 3-8-9 WSupple 1 58
(MrsAJPerrett) *in mid-division: rdn ove 2f out: sn btn* **50/1**
0 **9** *20* **Heriot**[39] 1827 3-9-0 (b[1]) TQuinn 5 17
(HCandy) *led for 1f: chsd wnr tl over 3f out: sn wknd* **20/1**
000- **10** *7* **Lola Lola (IRE)**[218] 5929 3-8-9 PaulEddery 10 —
(JLDunlop) *a struggling in rr* **33/1**

1m 41.87s (1.60) **Going Correction** +0.20s/f (Good) **10 Ran SP% 125.8**
Speed ratings: **100,98,98,95,95 95,94,93,73,66**CSF £11.33 TOTE £2.10: £1.10, £2.40, £1.70; EX 14.90 Place 6 £9.41, Place 5 £5.29.
**Owner** W S Farish **Bred** W S Farish **Trained** Manton, Wilts

**FOCUS**
An average maiden and straightforward form.

**NOTEBOOK**
**Gold Mask(USA)** had shown only fair form when second at the course recently and the application of a visor seemed to bring about some improvement. Under a confident ride from the front, he found what he had to to hold Admiral Compton and won a shade cosily. He should be competitive in handicap company, but is always going to be vulnerable to something a bit less exposed.
**Admiral Compton** confirmed the good impression he created on his sole start last year with a staying-on second. He looked an awkward ride under pressure, carrying his head high, but as this was his second-ever start that can still be put down to greenness. He is the one to take from the race and would reverse form were the front pair ever to meet again.
**Tenny's Gold(IRE)** was not beaten far in third but continues to find at least one too good.
**Lord Of The Sea(IRE)** does nothing for the form as he is a maiden after 11 starts.
**Desert Hawk** was not given a hard time of it in fifth, racing wide throughout and staying on down the straight without ever threatening. This run qualified him for a mark and it should be a reasonable one with 67-rated performer ahead of him.
**Miss Inkha** is another now eligible for handicaps and should fare better in that sphere.
JS

# [2627]SANDOWN (R-H)
### Friday, June 11
**OFFICIAL GOING: Good to firm (good in places)**
Wind: mod against Weather: mostly fine & sunny

## 2843 SHARP MINDS BETFAIR CLAIMING STKS 5f 6y
**2:00** (2:01) (E ) 3-Y-0+ **£3,653** (£1,124; £562; £281) **Stalls** High

Form RPR
0560 **1** **Willhewiz**[13] 2467 4-9-8 78 (v) JFEgan 7 86
(CADwyer) *lw: racd against far rail: mde all: rdn and 2l clr over 1f out: styd on wl* **2/1**[1]
00-0 **2** *1 1/2* **Kallista's Pride**[24] 2209 4-8-7 JoannaBadger 8 66
(MRBosley) *chsd ldrs: rdn 2f out: effrt u.p to take 2nd last 100yds: no imp wnr* **66/1**
-000 **3** *3/4* **Proud Native (IRE)**[9] 2582 10-9-8 83 DHolland 4 78
(DNicholls) *b: lw: chsd wnr: pushed along 1/2-way: no imp u.p over 1f out: lost 2nd last 100yds* **4/1**[3]
3550 **4** *hd* **Endless Summer**[14] 2461 7-9-8 78 RHughes 6 77
(KRBurke) *lw: trckd ldrs: rdn 2f out: nt qckn over 1f out: one pce after* **9/4**[2]
0441 **5** *3 1/2* **Bells Beach (IRE)**[16] 2404 6-8-10 45 KFallon 3 53
(PHowling) *lw: racd in midfield: outpcd 2f out: no imp on ldrs after* **13/2**
6003 **6** *1 1/4* **Ela Figura**[1] 2800 4-8-11 50 WRyan 5 49
(AWCarroll) *settled in last pair: effrt but outpcd 2f out: one pce after* **12/1**
0000 **7** *5* **Ridicule**[25] 2166 5-9-1 51 (vt) RLMoore 2 35
(JGPortman) *in tch: rdn 1/2-way: wknd 2f out* **25/1**
0 **8** *19* **Heres Harry**[25] 2178 4-8-11 LPKeniry[(3)] 1 —
(MissJacquelineSDoyle) *last and rdn 3f out: t.o 2f out* **100/1**

62.24 secs (0.05) **Going Correction** +0.025s/f (Good) **8 Ran SP% 111.5**
Speed ratings: **100,97,96,96,90 88,80,50** CT £3.20 TOTE £1.30: £14.30, £1.10, £; EX143.90
1.The winner was claimed by Robert Stronge for £15,000. Endless Summer was claimed by A. W. Carroll for £15,000. Kallista's Pride was claimed by D. S. Ne
**Owner** Mrs C M Goode **Bred** L T And M Foster **Trained** Newmarket, Suffolk

**FOCUS**
Few of these could be given a realistic chance at the weights in this claimer. Apart from the runner-up, the result was as official ratings would suggest and the draw also played its part.
**NOTEBOOK**
**Willhewiz**, drawn one off the far side, utilised his early pace to bag the position next to the rail and was soon bowling along in front. Making every yard, he was unlikely to weaken considering he stays further than this and in the end won with a degree of comfort. His last three victories have been at this level and he is yet to win a handicap despite a slipping mark.
**Kallista's Pride**, well beaten in two Fibresand maidens and a turf seller in her three outings so far, is a very keen sort so a possible reason for this vastly improved effort may have been the drop to the minimum trip for the first time. It will be interesting to see what the Handicapper makes of this performance in finishing amongst three horses all rated 78.
**Proud Native(IRE)**, who has a great record in claimers and also at this track, broke well from the stalls before being restrained in order to get a lead from the eventual winner, but despite holding every chance he did not pick up sufficiently. He is not at the top of game at present and it may be that his best days are now behind him.
**Endless Summer** is a shadow of the horse that won the 2000 Richmond Stakes and has failed to win since returning from a spell in the US last summer. He did not look happy at any stage on this occasion, carrying his head high and finding little for pressure.
**Bells Beach(IRE)** has been in fine form in modest company on Polytrack this year, but had 21lb to find with the principals on adjusted official ratings and was firmly put in her place.

## 2844 SBJ GROUP CLASSIFIED STKS 7f 16y
**2:35** (2:36) (C ) 3-Y-0 **£9,516** (£2,928; £1,464; £732) **Stalls** High

Form RPR
-115 **1** **Oasis Star (IRE)**[20] 2295 3-8-12 86 ... DHolland 2 92
(PWHarris) *lw: trckd ldr: chal and upsides 2f out: drvn ahd last 75yds* **8/13**[1]
U504 **2** *3/4* **Mister Saif (USA)**[7] 2642 3-9-0 85 ... RHughes 5 92
(RHannon) *led: rdn and jnd 2f out: kpt on wl tl no ex last 75yds* **9/2**[2]
341- **3** *2 1/2* **King Of Cashel (IRE)**[261] 5144 3-9-3 88 ... KFallon 4 89
(RHannon) *dwlt: hld up bhd ldrs: hanging rt and nt qckn 2f out: pushed along and kpt on one pce after* **7/1**[3]
3130 **4** *1/2* **Hatch**[24] 2202 3-9-5 90 ... JPMurtagh 3 89
(RMHCowell) *hld up in tch: trckd ldrs over 2f out: nt qckn sn after: edgd lft and one pce over 1f out* **8/1**
2-05 **5** *5* **Nephetriti Way (IRE)**[10] 2548 3-8-13 87 ... SDrowne 1 70
(PRChamings) *in tch: effrt 3f out: wknd 2f out* **25/1**
1m 31.11s (0.02) **Going Correction** +0.025s/f (Good) **5** Ran SP% **107.6**
Speed ratings: **100,99,96,95,90**CSF £3.47 TOTE £1.50: £1.10, £1.80; EX 3.80.
**Owner** R J Creese **Bred** James Gleeson **Trained** Ringshall, Bucks
**FOCUS**
An interesting classified event in which 5lb covered the five runners on adjusted official ratings. The form looks useful.
**NOTEBOOK**
**Oasis Star(IRE)**, who lost her unbeaten record in an ultra-competitive contest at Haydock last time, returned to winning ways but had to dig deep in order to get the better of the runner-up. She still looks a most progressive filly and connections may eventually try and earn some black type with her.
**Mister Saif(USA)**, given a canny front-running ride, was probably helped by being able to dictate from the front as it enabled him to conserve energy for the later stages, and he went down with all guns blazing. He was closely matched with the winner on official figures so he basically ran to form.
**King Of Cashel(IRE)**, reappearing after a nine-month layoff, did not see a great deal of daylight on the inside starting up the home straight and was not given a hard time once it became obvious his chance had gone. He should be all the better for this. *Official explanation: jockey said colt hung right handed*
**Hatch** has proven effective making the running this season, but was switched off out the back this time. He pulled too hard as a result and did not find much once let down.
**Nephetriti Way(IRE)** saw plenty of daylight on the outside and never picked up.

## 2845 SBJ GROUP H'CAP 1m 2f 7y
**3:05** (3:06) (C ) (0-90,83) 3-Y-0+ **£10,244** (£3,152; £1,576; £788) **Stalls** High

Form RPR
/01- **1** **Grooms Affection**[221] 5907 4-9-10 **79** ... JPMurtagh 8 87
(PWHarris) *lw: t.k.h: prom early: restrained into last trio 1/2-way: plenty to do 3f out: prog over 1f out: r.o wl to ld last 50yds* **10/1**
1542 **2** *1 1/4* **Say What You See (IRE)**[9] 2591 4-9-2 **71** ...(v) MHills 3 77
(JWHills) *lw: led at str pce: rdn and 2l clr 2f out: looked likely wnr 1f out : tired and hdd last 50yds* **9/2**[2]
2334 **3** *1/2* **Street Life (IRE)**[13] 2474 6-9-4 **73** ... KFallon 4 78
(WJMusson) *trckd ldrs: hrd rdn 2f out: styng on whn n.m.r wl ins fnl f: nrst fin* **13/2**[3]
21-1 **4** *nk* **Faayej (IRE)**[11] 2537 4-10-0 **83** 5ex ... WSupple 2 87
(SirMichaelStoute) *lw: prom: trckd ldr 1/2-way: rdn and no imp 2f out: tried to cl fnl f: kpt on but lost 2 pls nr fin* **2/1**[1]
0405 **5** *1* **Mad Carew (USA)**[23] 2226 5-9-7 **76** ... RLMoore 1 79
(GLMoore) *hld up in last pair: plenty to do 3f out: shkn up and styd on fnl 2f : nt rch ldrs* **11/1**
2-50 **6** *5* **Qabas (USA)**[5] 2705 4-9-0 **69** ... RHughes 5 62
(PRWebber) *lw: s.s: racd in last pair: plenty to do whn shkn up 3f out: no imp on ldrs* **16/1**
0-04 **7** *5* **Juste Pour L'Amour**[12] 2503 4-9-5 **74** ... DHolland 7 58
(PLGilligan) *t.k.h: trckd ldr to 1/2-way: rdn over 2f out: wknd over 1f out* **12/1**
5422 **8** *6* **Karaoke (IRE)**[13] 2474 4-8-12 **67** ... JFEgan 6 39
(SKirk) *wl in tch: rdn 3f out: wknd 2f out: eased* **9/2**[2]
2m 8.95s (-1.23) **Going Correction** +0.025s/f (Good) **8** Ran SP% **114.0**
Speed ratings: **105,104,103,103,102 98,94,89**CSF £54.09 CT £317.33 TOTE £11.90: £2.60, £1.90, £1.90; EX 78.80.
**Owner** The Racing Grooms **Bred** Newgate Stud Co **Trained** Ringshall, Bucks
**FOCUS**
A competitive handicap even if the top weight was 7lb below the contest's upper ceiling. This was run at a very decent pace and the form looks sound.
**NOTEBOOK**
**Grooms Affection**, who has been very difficult to train, was having only the fourth start of his life and his first since November. He appeared to be going nowhere starting up the home straight, but the leaders may have gone off too quickly and, despite the ground probably being faster than he cares for, he eventually ran past them as though they were standing still. He was very weak in the market so there may very well be even better to come.
**Say What You See(IRE)**, wearing the visor for the first time this season, was responsible for the decent pace and the tactic seemed to have worked as challenger after challenger was beaten off, but there was nothing he could do about the winner. He is running well enough to win a race.
**Street Life(IRE)** had every chance and not enjoying much room in the closing stages made little difference to the result. Even though the ground would have been plenty fast enough, he continues to frustrate and is without a win in two years.
**Faayej(IRE)**, carrying a 5lb penalty for last week's victory over course and distance, could never get past Say What You See despite trying his best, and he lost two places in the last half-furlong.
**Mad Carew(USA)**, 15lb above the mark of his only previous turf win, made up a lot of late ground to finish on the heels of the placed horses.
**Karaoke(IRE)** may have seen too much daylight and was beaten soon after turning for home. *Official explanation: jockey said gelding made a noise*

## 2846 SHARP MINDS BETFAIR EUROPEAN BREEDERS FUND MAIDEN STKS 5f 6y
**3:40** (3:41) (D ) 2-Y-0 **£4,758** (£1,464; £732; £366) **Stalls** High

Form RPR
6 **1** **Spree (IRE)**[40] 1798 2-8-9 ... RHughes 2 93+
(RHannon) *lw: mde all: shkn up and drew rt away fr over 1f out: unchal* **5/1**
2 **2** *6* **Drum Dance (IRE)**[11] 2522 2-9-0 ... SCarson 4 77
(RFJohnsonHoughton) *lw: chsd wnr: rdn and outpcd over 1f out: no ch after* **7/4**[1]
0 **3** *1 3/4* **Pitch Up (IRE)**[8] 2627 2-9-0 ... SDrowne 3 71
(TGMills) *lw: trckd ldrs: outpcd 2f out: no ch after: kpt on* **7/2**[3]
**4** *1* **Annatalia** 2-8-9 ... DHolland 5 62
(BJMeehan) *neat: in tch: effrt over 2f out: sn rdn and outpcd: no ch after* **12/1**
**5** *4* **African Storm (IRE)** 2-9-0 ... JFEgan 6 53
(SKirk) *leggy: scope: racd in last pair: rdn and effrt 1/2-way: wknd over 1f out* **25/1**
**6** *6* **Hornpipe** 2-9-0 ... KFallon 1 32
(SirMichaelStoute) *small: swvd lft s: rn green in last pair: wknd over 1f out* **3/1**[2]
62.39 secs (0.20) **Going Correction** +0.025s/f (Good) **6** Ran SP% **111.8**
Speed ratings: **99,89,86,85,78 69**CSF £14.11 TOTE £7.50: £2.50, £1.60; EX 14.60.
**Owner** A F Merritt **Bred** Cathal Ryan **Trained** East Everleigh, Wilts
**FOCUS**
A couple of interesting newcomers in this maiden up against rivals with proven ability and it was experience that gained the day. The time compared favourably with the earlier claimer for older horses, and the winner could be Listed class.
**NOTEBOOK**
**Spree(IRE)** ◆, who had apparently pulled a shoe around when missing the break and finishing tailed off on her Salisbury debut, was able to get across from her low draw in front this time and gradually forged further and further clear. She is a scopey filly and there looks to be much more to come.
**Drum Dance(IRE)** probably ran to a similar level of form to his Leicester debut and was unfortunate to come up against such a potentially useful sort. He deserves to go one better.
**Pitch Up(IRE)** was more organised than on his debut here the previous week and has the ability to win a race.
**Annatalia**, a 50,000euros filly out of a winning half-sister to Peak To Creek and For Your Eyes Only, showed some ability on this debut and should come on for the experience.
**African Storm(IRE)**, a 110,000euros colt whose winning dam was a half-sister to Pipalong, did not show much on this debut but is likely to be capable of better.
**Hornpipe**, out of the Lowther winner Dance Sequence, was the first juvenile runner of the season for the stable but he was all over the place after swerving left leaving the stalls and has a lot to prove now.

## 2847 MOUSETRAP CHALLENGE CUP H'CAP 1m 14y
**4:15** (4:19) (D ) (0-80,77) 3-Y-0 **£5,603** (£1,724; £862; £431) **Stalls** High

Form RPR
0053 **1** **Habanero**[18] 2371 3-8-10 **66** ... DHolland 8 73
(RHannon) *mde virtually all: hrd rdn over 1f out: jnd ent fnl f: kpt on gamely* **6/1**[1]
3012 **2** *nk* **Foley Prince**[18] 2371 3-9-0 **70** ... SDrowne 9 76
(MrsStefLiddiard) *mostly chsd wnr: rdn over 2f out: chal and upsides 1f out: hld nr fin* **6/1**[1]
6-03 **3** *3/4* **Go Solo**[24] 2207 3-9-7 **77** ... MHills 5 82
(BWHills) *a in ldng trio: rdn 2f out: ev ch ins fnl f: unable qck last 100yds* **7/1**[2]
3-0 **4** *nk* **Aperitif**[29] 2069 3-9-3 **73** ... SWKelly 4 77
(WJHaggas) *hld up in midfield: effrt over 2f out: drvn and styd on fnl f : unable to chal* **10/1**
-251 **5** *shd* **Fit To Fly (IRE)**[85] 1044 3-9-5 **75** ... JFEgan 13 79
(SKirk) *lw: settled towards rr: rdn wl over 2f out: styd on fr over 1f out: nrst fin* **20/1**
03-0 **6** *1* **Chigorin**[13] 2479 3-9-0 **70** ... JPMurtagh 12 71
(JMPEustace) *lw: t.k.h: hld up in last trio: nt clr run fr 3f out to over 1f out: styd on wl fnl f* **12/1**
1200 **7** *1/2* **Whitgift Rock**[11] 2536 3-9-5 **75** ... RLMoore 10 75
(SDow) *trckd ldrs: rdn over 2f out: unable qck over 1f out: one pce after* **7/1**[2]
-522 **8** *nk* **Wychbury (USA)**[5] 2704 3-9-4 **74** ... JFortune 3 74
(MJWallace) *trckd ldrs: rdn 2f out: sn nt qckn: one pce after* **8/1**[3]
41-5 **9** *nk* **Sound Blaster (IRE)**[47] 1640 3-9-1 **74** ... LPKeniry(3) 7 73
(AMBalding) *t.k.h: hld up in rr: rdn over 2f out: hanging and nt qckn wl over 1f out: one pce after* **12/1**
2120 **10** *2 1/2* **Jomus**[17] 2378 3-8-4 **63** ... LisaJones(3) 2 56
(LMontagueHall) *dwlt: t.k.h and hld up in last trio: rdn over 2f out: no prog* **20/1**
-261 **11** *3 1/2* **Sunset Mirage (USA)**[18] 2355 3-9-1 **71** ... WSupple 1 56
(EALDunlop) *t.k.h: hld up wl in rr: effrt on outer 3f out: sn no prog* **14/1**
1-65 **12** *1 1/4* **The Way We Were**[16] 2400 3-9-2 **72** ... KFallon 11 54
(TGMills) *trckd ldrs: lost pl and rdn over 3f out: struggling after* **6/1**[1]
3300 **13** *1 3/4* **Green Falcon**[13] 2472 3-8-4 **60** ...(v1) NDay 6 38
(JWHills) *lw: a towards rr: drvn and effrt on outer 3f out: wknd 2f out* **14/1**
1m 43.11s (-0.81) **Going Correction** +0.025s/f (Good) **13** Ran SP% **126.3**
Speed ratings: **105,104,103,103,103 102,102,101,101,98 95,94,92**CSF £43.10 CT £264.32 TOTE £8.80: £3.00, £2.60, £3.10; EX 26.70.
**Owner** The Waney Racing Group Inc **Bred** Eric Puerari, Oceanic Bloodstock And Haras De Etre **Trained** East Everleigh, Wilts
■ Stewards Enquiry : S W Kelly caution: careless riding
**FOCUS**
A competitive three-year-old handicap run at a very decent pace and a fair time for the grade. The first three were on the front end throughout.
**NOTEBOOK**
**Habanero** ◆, who has been running progressively better with each outing this term, finished just behind the runner-up at Windsor last time and reversed the form on 1lb better terms under a fine front-running ride. He was briefly headed by the runner-up passing the furlong pole, but rallied in splendid style and may be able to win again.
**Foley Prince** had a right battle with the winner from a long way out and has now run three decent races for his current yard. He deserves to get his head back in front and, as he has such a good record at Windsor, he could be especially interesting back there.

**Go Solo** ran a creditable race under top weight and it was only in the dying strides that he was eventually beaten off. He does give the impression that this trip is right on the limit of his stamina and he may be better dropped back to seven.
**Aperitif**, not for the first time gave concern before the off, this time by bolting on the way to the start. Under the circumstances he ran with plenty of credit, especially as he was short of room in the latter stages, but his future prospects very much depend on whether his temperament gets the better of him.
**Fit To Fly(IRE)**, making his handicap debut, ran with credit on this return to turf and seemed to see the trip out well enough.
**Chigorin** ◆ was noted staying on well in the later stages on this handicap debut and could be very interesting over a longer trip.
**The Way We Were** was meant be loaded into the stalls last, but actually went in first and he did not like it. Normally a front-runner, he could never get to the lead and did not run his race as a result, so it is probably best to forgive him this effort. *Official explanation: vet said colt sustained an overreach*

## 2848 ROYAL STAR & GARTER HOME FILLIES' H'CAP 1m 2f 7y
**4:50** (4:53) (E ) (0-75,75) 3-Y-O **£3,939** (£1,212; £606; £303) **Stalls** High

Form RPR
2-45 **1** **Mocca (IRE)**[27] 2107 3-9-7 **75** DHolland 7 90+
(DJCoakley) *lw: led briefly over 8f out: styd cl up: effrt over 2f out: chsd ldr and hmpd over 1f out: hrd rdn and rallied strly to ld* **7/2**[1]
-052 **2** *shd* **Wee Dinns (IRE)**[14] 2442 3-9-2 **70** JFEgan 6 80
(SKirk) *hld up in midfield: prog to ld 2f out: edgd rt over 1f out: 3l clr ent fnl f: hdd last stride* **7/2**[1]
15-4 **3** 2 1/2 **Kythia (IRE)**[25] 2169 3-9-4 **72** SDrowne 12 77
(HMorrison) *lw: hld up in midfield: clsd on ldrs over 2f out: unable qck wl over 1f out: r.o one pce fnl f* **8/1**[3]
235- **4** 2 **Bienvenue**[184] 6158 3-8-13 **67** WSupple 10 68
(MPTregoning) *hld up in midfield: lost pl and in last pair over 3f out: effrt over 2f out: styd on: n.d* **8/1**[3]
40-3 **5** 2 **Sand And Stars (IRE)**[11] 2529 3-8-12 **69** FPFerris(3) 5 67
(MHTompkins) *t.k.h: led to over 8f out: restrained: lost pl over 2f out: sn struggling: kpt on again fnl f* **10/1**
0-04 **6** 1/2 **Ellina**[32] 2001 3-8-13 **67** RPrice 13 64
(JPearce) *hld up in last: rdn 3f out: kpt on fr over 1f out: no ch* **40/1**
0-13 **7** *shd* **Night Frolic**[18] 2355 3-8-12 **66** MHills 4 63
(JWHills) *led after 2f to 2f out: sn outpcd and btn* **8/1**[3]
00-3 **8** 1/2 **Wyoming**[35] 1939 3-8-3 **60** LisaJones(3) 2 56
(JARToller) *racd wd: hld up in rr: effrt 3f out: shuffled along and outpcd 2f out: no ch after* **10/1**
1020 **9** *hd* **Varuni (IRE)**[32] 1998 3-8-8 **62** RLMoore 9 57
(JGPortman) *hld up towards rr: effrt 3f out: wknd over 1f out* **25/1**
-500 **10** 2 **Principessa**[25] 2169 3-8-13 **67** WRyan 1 58
(BPalling) *trckd ldr after 3f to wl over 2f out: sn lost pl and btn* **40/1**
036- **11** 3 1/2 **Cazisa Star (USA)**[263] 5118 3-8-8 **62** SCarson 8 47
(PWHarris) *hld up in midfield: lost pl and wl in rr 3f out: n.d after* **25/1**
3-64 **12** 5 **Girl Warrior (USA)**[15] 2425 3-9-1 **69** KFallon 3 44
(PFICole) *lw: trckd ldrs: effrt to chal over 2f out: sn rdn and wknd: eased* **11/2**[2]

2m 10.43s (0.25) **Going Correction** +0.025s/f (Good) **12** Ran SP% **123.9**
Speed ratings: **100,99,97,96,94 94,94,93,93,92 89,85**CSF £15.06 CT £94.40 TOTE £5.20: £1.90, £1.50, £2.70; EX 17.10 Place 6 £25.52, Place 5 £14.09.
**Owner** Mocca Partnership **Bred** Miss M Noonan **Trained** West Ilsley, Berks
■ Stewards Enquiry : J F Egan caution: careless riding

**FOCUS**
A competitive fillies' handicap featuring several unexposed sorts, but a modest pace with no-one seeming that keen to go on. On a strict form basis the race looks sound.

**NOTEBOOK**
**Mocca(IRE)**, who had finished behind the likes of Hazyview and Pukka in her two previous starts this season, was taking quite a step down in class. Her chance looked to have ended when Wee Dinns came across her and chopped her off a furlong from home, but she soon found her stride again and came with a storming late run to get up on the line. She is value for a good deal more than the official margin.
**Wee Dinns(IRE)**, whose effort behind Prenup at Brighton last time has since been boosted by the winner, looked to have the race won once rushed into a clear lead a furlong from home, at which point she hung right and hampered Mocca, but that rival found a devastating turn of foot to snatch the race from her on the line. She should not remain a maiden for too much longer.
**Kythia(IRE)** confirmed the promise of her reappearance with another solid effort, but may be better suited by further.
**Bienvenue** ◆, making both her handicap and turf debuts after three outings on Polytrack and racing for the first time in six months, was staying on nicely in the latter stages and is worth keeping in mind.
**Sand And Stars(IRE)**, as on her recent reappearance, took a keen hold in front early and was not at all suited by the way the race was run. She is probably capable of much better in a truly-run race.
**Night Frolic** soon found herself in front, probably more by accident than design, but despite setting only an ordinary pace she still did not see out this longer trip.
T/Plt: £42.40 to a £1 stake. Pool: £39,534.30. 680.20 winning tickets. T/Qpdt: £23.40 to a £1 stake. Pool: £2,029.25. 63.90 winning tickets. JN

# 2811 SOUTHWELL (L-H)
Friday, June 11

**OFFICIAL GOING: Standard**
Wind: Slight behind. Weather: Sunny spells.

## 2849 AT THE RACES IS BACK CLAIMING STKS 6f (F)
**2:25** (2:26) (F ) 3-Y-O **£2,912** (£832; £416) **Stalls** Low

Form RPR
0300 **1** **Garnock Venture (IRE)**[14] 2457 3-9-5 54 (b) JFanning 8 73
(ABerry) *w ldr: led 1/2-way: rdn out* **7/1**
3301 **2** 2 **El Palmar**[7] 2657 3-9-1 65 DeanMcKeown 3 63
(PABlockley) *a.p: chsd wnr over 1f out: no ex ins fnl f* **3/1**[1]
3-00 **3** 2 **Innclassic (IRE)**[4] 2741 3-8-7 75 (b[1]) JFMcDonald(3) 6 52
(BJMeehan) *chsd ldrs: rdn over 2f out: styd on same pce fnl f* **6/1**
3-35 **4** 1/2 **Willjojo**[18] 2351 3-8-2 55 PHanagan 5 43
(RAFahey) *chsd ldrs: outpcd over 4f out: styd on ins fnl f* **10/3**[2]
6605 **5** 5 **Bookiesindexdotcom**[23] 2232 3-8-2 41 (v) GGibbons 7 28
(JRJenkins) *sn drvn along in rr: nvr nrr* **20/1**
0040 **6** 3/4 **Beamsley Beacon**[11] 2528 3-8-11 59 (b) NPollard 4 34
(GMMoore) *mde most to 1/2-way: rdn and wknd over 1f out* **16/1**
1500 **7** 3 1/2 **Crewes Miss Isle**[11] 2518 3-8-10 67 SWhitworth 2 23
(AGNewcombe) *sn pushed along in rr: hdwy 1/2-way: wknd over 1f out* **7/2**[3]
0-00 **8** 12 **St George's Girl**[32] 1985 3-7-11 25 ow2 JJeffrey(7) 1 —
(JRJenkins) *dwlt: outpcd* **50/1**

1m 17.45s (0.55) **Going Correction** +0.125s/f (Slow) **8** Ran SP% **109.7**
Speed ratings: **101,98,95,95,88 87,82,66**CSF £25.97 TOTE £6.10: £2.20, £1.40, £3.50; EX 43.70.
**Owner** Robert Aird **Bred** Liam Queally **Trained** Cockerham, Lancs

**FOCUS**
An ordinary claimer and the form has a doubtful appearance.

**NOTEBOOK**
**Garnock Venture(IRE)**, a winner over seven here in March, got to the front despite his outside draw and stayed on willingly. He appears to have improved.
**El Palmar**, having his first run since being claimed from David Barron, carried his head a shade high when coming with his challenge. The drop back from seven furlongs did not look ideal on this Fibresand debut.
**Innclassic(IRE)**, the pick on BHB ratings, was blinkered for the first time. It was also her first run on Fibresand and she appeared to handle the surface.
**Willjojo**, having her second try on Fibresand, kept on having lost her pitch.
**Beamsley Beacon**, wearing blinkers instead of cheekpieces, was still in second place turning for home but edged over to the far rail and was soon beaten.

## 2850 SKY 415, NTL 908, TELEWEST 534 H'CAP 5f (F)
**2:55** (2:55) (E ) (0-70,69) 3-Y-O **£3,406** (£1,048; £524; £262) **Stalls** High

Form RPR
0353 **1** **Blue Power (IRE)**[18] 2353 3-8-10 **58** DSweeney 11 69
(KRBurke) *trckd ldrs: led over 1f out: rdn out* **5/1**[3]
0216 **2** 1 1/4 **Nanna (IRE)**[15] 2428 3-8-3 **51** GDuffield 10 58
(RHollinshead) *chsd ldrs: rdn and ev ch over 1f out: styd on same pce ins fnl f* **9/2**[2]
120 **3** 1 **Sahara Silk (IRE)**[43] 1737 3-9-3 **68** (v) JFMcDonald(3) 6 71
(DShaw) *w ldrs: rdn and ev ch over 1f out: no ex ins fnl f* **7/1**
6-01 **4** 3/4 **Icenaslice (IRE)**[7] 2661 3-8-3 **51** PHanagan 9 52
(JJQuinn) *sn led: hung lft and hdd over 1f out: no ex* **3/1**[1]
3430 **5** 1/2 **Wonky Donkey**[11] 2524 3-8-1 **54** HayleyTurner(5) 1 53
(SCWilliams) *mid-div: hdwy 1/2-way: rdn and hung rt over 1f out: styd on same pce* **8/1**
-005 **6** 3/4 **Brave Chief**[7] 2664 3-8-4 **52** ow1 NPollard 2 48
(JAPickering) *wnt rt s: outpcd: hdwy 1/2-way: no ex fnl f* **33/1**
0354 **7** 2 1/2 **Barras (IRE)**[90] 1008 3-8-9 **57** (v) MFenton 4 44
(MissGayKelleway) *hmpd s: outpcd* **20/1**
-304 **8** *shd* **Bond Shakira**[2] 2778 3-8-7 **55** DMcGaffin 7 42
(BSmart) *sn outpcd* **12/1**
1030 **9** *nk* **Head Of State**[67] 1270 3-8-12 **60** (v) JQuinn 5 46
(RMBeckett) *hmpd s: outpcd* **16/1**
0-00 **10** 1 1/4 **Eastern Pearl**[48] 1602 3-9-7 **69** SWhitworth 3 51
(MissLStubbs) *stmbld and hmpd s: sn chsng ldrs: wknd over 1f out* **25/1**
6065 **11** 5 **Velvet Touch**[36] 1906 3-8-6 **54** (v[1]) GGibbons 8 18
(JRJenkins) *chsd ldrs to 1/2-way* **12/1**

58.83 secs (-1.57) **Going Correction** -0.325s/f (Stan) **11** Ran SP% **116.3**
Speed ratings: **99,97,95,94,93 92,88,88,87,85 77**CSF £26.73 CT £160.85 TOTE £7.60: £1.10, £2.50, £2.10; EX 34.90.
**Owner** F Jeffers **Bred** Farrington Bloodstock **Trained** Middleham Moor, N Yorks
■ Stewards Enquiry : P Hanagan caution: used whip down the filly's shoulder with whip in the forehand position

**FOCUS**
A weakish handicap but fairlyu sound form. The stands' rail looked the place to be.

**NOTEBOOK**
**Blue Power(IRE)** appreciated the return to Fibresand and was 3lb lower than when scoring over track and trip in December. Always travelling well against the stands' rail, he scored a shade comfortably.
**Nanna(IRE)** did nothing wrong on this return to Fibresand and there looked to be no excuses.
**Sahara Silk(IRE)**, who likes it here, was back at the minimum trip on this return from a break.
**Icenaslice(IRE)** was unpenalised for her win in an apprentice race. Having her first run on sand, she was a market drifter. *Official explanation: jockey said filly hung left-handed in the closing stages*
**Wonky Donkey** was drawn in stall one, but drifted across the track and finished up under the stands' rail. He found the drop to the minimum trip against him.
**Brave Chief** was not helped by racing apart from the others down the centre of the track.
**Barras(IRE)** *Official explanation: jockey said he suffered interference shortly after the start*

## 2851 AT THE RACES 9AM TO 1AM EVERY DAY AMATEUR RIDERS' (S) STKS 1m 4f (F)
**3:25** (3:28) (G ) 4-Y-O+ **£2,569** (£734; £367) **Stalls** Low

Form RPR
2141 **1** **Romil Star (GER)**[7] 2662 7-11-2 65 (v) MrSDobson(3) 6 59+
(KRBurke) *trckd ldrs: led over 5f out: clr over 3f out: canter* **2/5**[1]
3505 **2** 6 **Western Command (GER)**[23] 2230 8-11-0 35 (p) MrsMMorris 8 45
(MrsNMacauley) *hld up in tch: chsd wnr over 2f out: no imp* **20/1**
0006 **3** 11 **Coolfore Jade (IRE)**[4] 2728 4-10-7 49 MrJoshuaHarris(7) 5 29
(NEBerry) *prom: jnd wnr 5f out: wknd 3f out* **9/2**[2]
5-00 **4** 1 1/2 **Banners Flying (IRE)**[14] 2454 4-10-7 64 MissRachelClark(7) 2 26
(DWChapman) *led after 1f: hdd over 5f out: wknd over 4f out* **40/1**
0003 **5** 1 3/4 **Morris Dancing (USA)**[23] 2228 5-10-11 32 (v) MrEDehdashti(3) 3 24
(BPJBaugh) *prom over 7f* **50/1**
4006 **6** *nk* **King Priam (IRE)**[45] 1698 9-11-0 30 (p) MissFayeBramley(5) 9 28
(MJPolglase) *w ldrs tl wknd over 4f out* **50/1**
0-00 **7** 10 **Protocol (IRE)**[37] 1501 10-10-9 27 (tp) MrBKing(5) 7 8
(MrsSLamyman) *s.i.s: hld up: a in rr* **14/1**
3210 **8** *hd* **The Last Mohican**[29] 2055 5-10-12 38 MissFGuillambert(7) 1 13
(PHowling) *led 1f: remained handy tl wknd 5f out* **12/1**[3]
**9** 4 **Shameless**[15] 7-10-9 (t) MissDawnRankin(5) 4 2
(HAlexander) *s.s: outpcd* **50/1**

2m 47.19s (5.09) **Going Correction** +0.125s/f (Slow) **9** Ran SP% **117.1**
Speed ratings: **88,84,76,75,74 74,67,67,64**CSF £15.87 TOTE £1.40: £1.10, £3.50, £1.30; EX 7.60.The winner was bought in for 10,500gns.
**Owner** Mrs Elaine M Burke **Bred** J H A Baggen **Trained** Middleham Moor, N Yorks

**FOCUS**
Winner apart, this was a very weak amateurs' seller.

**NOTEBOOK**
**Romil Star(GER)** , who had his visor fitted late by permission of the Stewards, keeps galloping and stays a good bit farther than this. This was nothing more than a cakewalk.
**Western Command(GER)** kept trying, but his losing streak now stands at 45 races.
**Coolfore Jade(IRE)** matched strides with the favourite leaving the back straight but was a spent force with three furlongs to run.
**Banners Flying(IRE)** failed to see out the trip.

## 2852 AT THE RACES DEDICATED RACING CHANNEL MAIDEN STKS 6f (F)

4:00 (4:02) (D ) 2-Y-O £3,838 (£1,181; £590; £295) Stalls Low

Form RPR

5 **1** **Al Qudra (IRE)**[45] 1686 2-8-11 JFMcDonald(3) 8 83
(BJMeehan) *mde virtually all: rdn clr over 1f out* **15/8**[1]

433 **2** 8 **Aunty Euro (IRE)**[21] 2256 2-8-9 JCarroll 6 54
(EJO'Neill) *chsd ldrs: rdn 1/2-way: outpcd fnl 2f* **8/1**

**3** 1 3/4 **Homme Dangereux** 2-9-0 JQuinn 11 54
(CREgerton) *wnt rt s: hdwy and hung rt 1/2-way: outpcd fnl 2f* **20/1**

42 **4** 1/2 **Weet Yer Tern (IRE)**[47] 1638 2-9-0 PHanagan 7 52
(PABlockley) *chsd ldrs: rdn 1/2-way: outpcd fnl 2f* **5/2**[2]

0540 **5** 1 1/4 **No Commission (IRE)**[7] 2651 2-8-11 DNolan(3) 4 49
(RFFisher) *w wnr: rdn and ev ch over 2f out: wknd over 1f out* **12/1**

0 **6** 6 **Oldstead Flyer (IRE)**[21] 2268 2-8-7 DTudhope(7) 10 31
(DCarroll) *dwlt: sn chsng ldrs: wknd over 2f out* **33/1**

00 **7** 6 **Lord Chalfont (IRE)**[43] 1735 2-9-0 GDuffield 9 13
(MJPolglase) *sn drvn along in rr: lost tch fnl 4f* **100/1**

4 **8** 1 3/4 **Monashee Miss**[35] 1943 2-8-9 NPollard 2 —
(JAPickering) *dwlt: outpcd* **50/1**

0560 **9** 1 1/4 **Misty Princess**[25] 2177 2-8-9 GGibbons 5 —
(MJPolglase) *w ldrs to 1/2-way: wknd over 2f out* **14/1**

0542 **10** 27 **Kristikhab (IRE)**[8] 2616 2-9-0 JFanning 1 —
(ABerry) *sn outpcd* **11/2**[3]

1m 17.84s (0.94) **Going Correction** +0.125s/f (Slow) **10** Ran SP% **114.9**
Speed ratings: **98,87,85,84,82 74,66,64,62,26**CSF £16.94 TOTE £2.30: £1.50, £2.10, £5.70; EX 21.20.
**Owner** Abbott Racing Limited **Bred** John Geraghty **Trained** Upper Lambourn, Berks

**FOCUS**
A clear-cut winner of this maiden and this looks strong form for this track.

**NOTEBOOK**
**Al Qudra(IRE)** was always going best and, kept up to his work once in front, he cleared right away. The extra furlong suited him well.
**Aunty Euro(IRE)** stayed on but was no match for the winner, who is by the same sire. This was her first run on Fibresand and she would appear to act on most types of ground.
**Homme Dangereux** is a brother to two-year-old winner Chorus Beauty out of a half-sister to useful middle-distance stayer Rainbow Ways. He was a little green on this debut and will improve for the experience.
**Weet Yer Tern(IRE)** shaped as if in need of farther on this All-Weather bow.
**No Commission(IRE)** again showed pace before fading.
**Kristikhab(IRE)** *Official explanation: jockey said gelding was never travelling and may have been unsuited by the surface*

## 2853 AT THE RACES ON NTL, IRELAND AND CHORUS MEDIAN AUCTION MAIDEN STKS 1m (F)

4:35 (4:36) (E ) 3-Y-O £3,454 (£1,063; £531; £265) Stalls Low

Form RPR

5 **1** **Pass The Port**[39] 1827 3-9-0 JDSmith 6 72
(JRFanshawe) *sn pushed along and prom: chsd ldr over 3f out: led 2f out: rdn clr fnl f* **15/8**[2]

**2** 6 **Senor Set (GER)** 3-8-7 StaceyRenwick(7) 10 60
(PABlockley) *s.s: hdwy over 3f out: hung lft fr over 2f out: nt rch wnr* **66/1**

-222 **3** 1 1/4 **Extra Cover (IRE)**[36] 1911 3-9-0 74 (b[1]) DSweeney 9 57
(RCharlton) *chsd ldrs: led over 4f out: hdd 2f out: nt run on* **5/6**[1]

00 **4** 5 **Magic Verse**[18] 2374 3-8-9 CLowther 8 42
(RGuest) *prom: outpcd over 3f out: n.d after* **66/1**

4-0 **5** 1 3/4 **Blue Viking (IRE)**[16] 2412 3-9-0 PHanagan 12 44
(JRWeymes) *prom: lost pl 5f out: n.d after* **100/1**

24 **6** 3 **Crathes**[38] 1869 3-8-9 MFenton 7 33
(JGGiven) *led over 3f: wknd over 2f out* **9/1**[3]

00- **7** 2 1/2 **Silver Island**[198] 6074 3-9-0 JCarroll 11 33
(RMHCowell) *bhd fr 1/2-way* **100/1**

**8** 10 **Dream Easy** 3-9-0 GDuffield 3 13
(PLGilligan) *s.s: sn drvn along: wknd wl over 3f out* **40/1**

**9** 5 **Sweet At Heart (IRE)** 3-8-9 DeanMcKeown 1 —
(PABlockley) *s.s: outpcd* **66/1**

3456 **10** 5 **Mystic Promise (IRE)**[31] 2016 3-9-0 32 (t) NPollard 13 —
(MrsNMacauley) *chsd ldrs over 4f* **100/1**

6 **11** nk **Cronkyvoddy**[9] 2596 3-9-0 (t) JQuinn 4 —
(MissGayKelleway) *chsd ldrs over 4f* **11/1**

0-0 **12** 5 **Rocky Rambo**[41] 1770 3-8-11 (b[1]) TEaves(3) 5 —
(RDEWoodhouse) *hld up: rdn 1/2-way: sn wknd* **50/1**

**13** nk **Desert Coral (IRE)** 3-8-2 SYourston(7) 2 —
(PABlockley) *s.i.s: outpcd* **66/1**

1m 45.39s (0.79) **Going Correction** +0.125s/f (Slow) **13** Ran SP% **121.0**
Speed ratings: **101,95,93,88,87 84,81,71,66,61 61,56,55**CSF £135.04 TOTE £3.50: £1.30, £14.80, £1.10; EX 144.50.
**Owner** Lancen Farm Partnership **Bred** Meon Valley Stud **Trained** Newmarket, Suffolk

**FOCUS**
A weak maiden and the form looks modest.

**NOTEBOOK**
**Pass The Port**, who had shown ability in the mud on his debut, stayed in the centre down the home straight and came clear for a comfortable victory. This did not take a great deal of winning.
**Senor Set(GER)**, who is related to winners in Germany, was his jockey's first ride as a professional. After a sluggish start, he hung over to the far rail in the home straight, which is not the best place to be, but stayed on to go second inside the final furlong. He will get farther.
**Extra Cover(IRE)** wore blinkers for the first time. He put his head in the air when tackled and would not run on, although he was not helped by racing on a deeper part of the track than the winner. Expensive to follow, he might need holding up instead.
**Magic Verse**, dropped in class for this Fibresand debut, is now eligible for handicaps.
**Blue Viking(IRE)** was keeping on again having lost his pitch. He showed a bit more here and is now handicapped.
**Crathes** did not improve for the step up to a mile but it could be that she failed to handle the surface.
**Silver Island**, who ran twice for Gerard Butler at two, hinted at ability and might be capable of a bit better.
**Cronkyvoddy** *Official explanation: jockey said gelding failed to travel from 4f out*

## 2854 AT THE RACES COMMITTED TO RACING H'CAP 7f (F)

5:10 (5:11) (F ) (0-55,55) 3-Y-O+ £3,038 (£868; £434) Stalls Low

Form RPR

000- **1** **Tancred Miss**[265] 5070 5-8-8 35 TEaves(3) 8 43
(DWBarker) *chsd ldrs: rdn 1/2-way: ev ch over 2f out: nt clr run over 1f out: r.o to ld nr fin* **33/1**

0015 **2** 1/2 **Tsarbuck**[18] 2349 3-9-7 55 JCarroll 13 62
(RMHCowell) *chsd ldrs: led 2f out: hung lft fr over 1f out: hdd nr fin* **8/1**

0000 **3** 1 3/4 **Rocky Reppin**[13] 2473 4-9-1 46 KPierrepont(7) 9 48
(JBalding) *prom: outpcd over 2f out: hdwy over 1f out: r.o* **25/1**

4052 **4** 3/4 **Shifty**[18] 2356 5-9-10 48 JFanning 2 48
(DNicholls) *hld up: hdwy and nt clr run over 1f out: r.o: nt rch ldrs* **7/2**[1]

5-60 **5** 1/2 **Salut Saint Cloud**[7] 2657 3-9-0 48 (v) NPollard 14 47
(MissVHaigh) *sn pushed along and prom: outpcd 1/2-way: hdwy and hung lft over 1f out: r.o* **25/1**

3511 **6** 1 1/2 **Extemporise (IRE)**[32] 1986 4-10-0 52 TGMcLaughlin 4 47
(TTClement) *chsd ldrs: rdn over 2f out: no ex fnl f* **13/2**[3]

0-11 **7** 1 **Bronx Bomber**[23] 2229 6-9-13 51 (b) CLowther 7 44
(DrJDScargill) *w ldr: led over 4f out: hdd 2f out: wknd fnl f* **12/1**

600- **8** nk **Bandbox (IRE)**[232] 5717 9-8-11 35 MFenton 5 27
(MSalaman) *bhd: pushed along 1/2-way: n.d* **25/1**

4023 **9** 2 1/2 **Dasar**[14] 2451 4-9-5 48 (v) MLawson(5) 11 34
(MBrittain) *led over 2f: remained handy tl wknd over 2f out* **12/1**

6504 **10** 1 1/2 **Dante's Devine (IRE)**[7] 2667 3-9-4 52 GDuffield 6 34
(ABailey) *s.i.s: a in rr* **25/1**

6660 **11** 1/2 **Peartree House (IRE)**[9] 2597 10-8-1 32 oh5 DFentiman(7) 15 13
(DWChapman) *s.i.s: hdwy 1/2-way: hung lft and wknd over 1f out* **25/1**

-000 **12** 5 **Rileys Rocket**[10] 2547 5-8-8 32 JQuinn 12 —
(RHollinshead) *a bhd* **33/1**

0000 **13** 1/2 **Gruff**[17] 2384 5-8-8 32 DeanMcKeown 10 —
(PTMidgley) *mid-div: wknd 1/2-way* **28/1**

0116 **14** 14 **Saros (IRE)**[27] 2128 3-9-7 55 DMcGaffin 3 —
(BSmart) *s.s: outpcd* **4/1**[2]

66-0 **15** 17 **Duncanbil (IRE)**[14] 2451 3-8-13 50 DNolan(3) 1 —
(RFFisher) *prom: sn drvn along: lost pl 5f out: bhd fnl 4f* **25/1**

1m 32.64s (1.84) **Going Correction** +0.125s/f (Slow)
**WFA** 3 from 4yo+ 10lb **15** Ran SP% **117.9**
Speed ratings: **94,93,91,90,90 88,87,86,83,82 81,75,75,59,39**CSF £243.25 CT £6587.11 TOTE £47.10: £31.50, £3.30, £17.10; EX 427.00 Place 6 £87.75, Place 5 £45.98.
**Owner** Mrs S J Barker **Bred** D W Barker **Trained** Scorton, N Yorks

**FOCUS**
A weak handicap and moderate time for the grade. The form is very ordinary.

**NOTEBOOK**
**Tancred Miss** stayed on down the centre to strike the front after having to be switched round the eventual runner-up. This was her first run since September and she has reportedly had some back and head problems sorted out since then.
**Tsarbuck** drifted over to the far rail when the pressure was on and was cut down by the mare in the centre of the track. Although he did not really get home on this occasion, seven furlongs does look his best trip.
**Rocky Reppin** had shown very little previously and would appear to have improved for the switch to Fibresand.
**Shifty** was keeping on at the finish having not enjoyed the best of runs. He is weighted to end a lengthy losing sequence.
**Salut Saint Cloud** was quickly off the bridle and found this too sharp.
**Extemporise(IRE)** was unable to complete the hat-trick on this return to sand.
**Bronx Bomber** seems on a high enough mark for his two wins in banded company.
**Saros(IRE)** was always struggling after missing the break. *Official explanation: jockey said colt was very slowly away and would not face the kick-back*
T/Plt: £105.50 to a £1 stake. Pool: £25,969.65. 179.65 winning tickets. T/Qpdt: £11.90 to a £1 stake. Pool: £1,948.10. 120.70 winning tickets. CR

# 2457 YORK (L-H)

## Friday, June 11

**OFFICIAL GOING: Good to firm**
The ground was described as 'very fast but with a good cover of grass'.
Wind: Fresh 1/2 against Weather: Fine

## 2855 BRITESSUNGLASSES & FOX RIVER SOCKS RATED STKS (H'CAP) 1m 5f 197y

2:15 (2:16) (C ) (0-95,87) 4-Y-O+ £9,964 (£3,066; £1,533; £766) Stalls Low

Form RPR

-514 **1** **Star Member (IRE)**[20] 2285 5-9-5 85 KMcEvoy 2 101
(APJarvis) *trckd ldrs: led 2f out: rdn and edgd rt over 1f out: styd on strly to go clr fnl f* **4/1**[2]

11-0 **2** 4 **Escayola (IRE)**[22] 2240 4-9-7 87 (v) TQuinn 6 98+
(WJHaggas) *hld up in rr: hdwy 3f out: chsng wnr and rdn over 1f out: no imp fnl f* **9/2**[3]

-340 **3** 1 3/4 **Thewhirlingdervish (IRE)**[34] 1973 6-8-12 78 KDarley 5 86
(TDEasterby) *hld up: effrt over 3f out: nt clr run over 2f out: styd on u.p: nvr able to chal* **9/1**

4504 **4** nk **Flotta**[13] 2491 5-9-3 83 ACulhane 1 91
(MRChannon) *led: qcknd over 5f out: rdn and hdd 2f out: no ex* **10/3**[1]

0236 **5** 3 1/2 **Gold Ring**[22] 2240 4-9-6 86 RHavlin 4 89
(GBBalding) *in tch: rdn and ch 2f out: fdd* **6/1**

2-00 **6** nk **Gralmano (IRE)**[37] 1880 9-9-3 83 NCallan 3 85
(KARyan) *trckd ldr: drvn along over 3f out: wknd 2f out* **6/1**

-261 **7** 1 3/4 **Tiyoun (IRE)**[16] 2409 6-9-2 82 SSanders 7 82
(JeddO'Keeffe) *sn trcking ldrs: drvn along over 3f out: wknd 2f out* **9/1**

2m 58.76s (2.36) **Going Correction** +0.275s/f (Good) **7** Ran SP% **109.8**
Speed ratings: **104,101,100,100,98 98,97**CSF £20.36 TOTE £4.50: £2.30, £2.70; EX 17.50.
**Owner** Jarvis Associates **Bred** Killeen Castle Stud **Trained** Twyford, Bucks

**FOCUS**
Just a very steady gallop until the final six furlongs for what was in effect a 0-87 handicap. However it was competitive on paper and the form looks sound enough.

**NOTEBOOK**
**Star Member(IRE)**, 8lb higher than when he won here last month, had to angle for an opening and once in front tended to drift right-handed. Better over a mile-six, connections are hoping he gets a run in the Ebor here in August.
**Escayola(IRE)** won five times last year improving over two stone. Essentially a stayer, the modest pace did not play to his strengths and he deserves full credit. He looks sure to add to his record this time.
**Thewhirlingdervish(IRE)**, returning after a seven-week break, showed himself to be back on song. An out-and-out stayer, the lack of pace in the first half of the race was a severe handicap.
**Flotta** had his own way in front. His rider wound up the gallop starting the home turn, but in the end he was still nowhere near good enough. His record of just two career wins from 20 starts now says it all.
**Gold Ring**, who finished ahead of the runner-up at Goodwood three weeks earlier, has now won just once from 20 starts.
**Gralmano(IRE)** kept tabs on the leader but did not really see it out. He is not really firing at present.
**Tiyoun(IRE)** took a keen grip and could have done with a much stronger pace.

## 2856 BATLEYS CHARITY RACEDAY PREMIER CLAIMING STKS 1m 2f 88y
2:45 (2:45) (D) 3-Y-0+ £6,084 (£1,872; £936; £468) Stalls Low

Form RPR

-305 1 Eton (GER)[38] 1867 8-9-3 67 AlexGreaves 2 74
(DNicholls) *mde all: qcknd over 4f out: rdn over 1f out: styd on wl* 9/4[2]

0-00 2 1 1/2 Makulu (IRE)[55] 1457 4-9-7 75 (p) TQuinn 1 75
(BJMeehan) *trckd ldrs: rdn to chse wnr over 2f out: ch ent fnl f: styd on: no imp ins last* 7/1

-004 3 1 1/4 Ile Michel[8] 2612 7-9-3 82 ACulhane 5 69
(JGMO'Shea) *hld up: nt clr run over 3f out: hdwy and in tch over 2f out: styd on u.p but no further prog fnl f* 15/8[1]

/66- 4 10 Tomasino[337] 3123 6-9-5 93 KDarley 3 52
(MrsMReveley) *hld up in tch: hdwy to chse wnr 3f out: sn rdn: wknd over 1f out* 4/1[3]

3 5 nk African Sunset (IRE)[21] 2257 4-9-3 RWinston 4 49
(JHowardJohnson) *trckd wnr: rdn 4f out: wknd 3f out* 14/1

040- 6 dist Curate (USA)[394] 1585 5-9-3 40 (t) NCallan 6 —
(ADickman) *hld up: drvn along over 3f out: sn wknd: lost tch fnl 2f: virtually p.u fnl f* 40/1

2m 14.32s (4.88) **Going Correction** +0.275s/f (Good) 6 Ran SP% 107.2
Speed ratings: **91,89,88,80,80** —CSF £16.09 TOTE £3.10: £1.60, £3.30; EX 22.50.
**Owner** The McCauley Boys **Bred** Gestut Rietberg **Trained** Sessay, N Yorks

**FOCUS**
A modest claimer and a tactical ride from the front by Alex Greaves, resulting in a very slow time indeed for the grade.

**NOTEBOOK**
**Eton(GER)**, who had plenty to find on official figures, sat in front. Sent for home straightening up, he was always doing enough. His rider deserves full marks.
**Makulu(IRE)**, whose three wins have been on the Polytrack, has been bang out of form. He settled better but, after working his way onto the winner's quarters entering the last, he could then find no more.
**Ile Michel** on official figures had 15lb in hand of the winner but it did not work out like that. He has yet to win beyond nine furlongs.
**Tomasino**, rated 24lb ahead of the winner on official figures, had been absent for almost a year with heart and leg problems. He looked fit and well, but after going in pursuit of the winner became very leg-weary. After this he has an awful lot to prove.
**African Sunset(IRE)** looked to have an impossible task and so it proved.
**Curate(USA)**, unplaced in ten previous starts, was having his first outing for a year and virtually pulled up. *Official explanation: jockey said gelding had a breathing problem*

## 2857 SPORTINGOPTIONS.CO.UK RATED STKS (H'CAP) 6f 3y
3:15 (3:15) (B) (0-100,100) 4-Y-0+ £12,423 (£4,712; £2,356; £1,071) Stalls Centre

Form RPR

-340 1 Circuit Dancer (IRE)[29] 2065 4-8-13 92 FLynch 5 101
(ABerry) *slowly away: rr: hdwy over 2f out: r.o wl u.p to ld fnl 75yds: all out* 20/1

-030 2 shd Marsad (IRE)[13] 2477 10-8-7 86 PDoe 9 95
(JAkehurst) *towards rr: hdwy 2f out: chal ins fnl f: r.o u.p: no ex clsng stages* 9/1

6-60 3 3/4 Dazzling Bay[29] 2065 4-9-7 100 SSanders 6 107
(TDEasterby) *w ldr: led 2f out: 2 l clr whn rdn and swvd rt ent fnl f: hdd fnl 75yds: no ex* 6/1[3]

00-0 4 3 Pieter Brueghel (USA)[13] 2469 5-8-7 86 oh4 RWinston 8 84
(DNicholls) *slt ld tl hdd and rdn 2f out: kpt on same pce* 12/1

0012 5 3/4 Steel Blue[8] 2625 4-8-12 91 ACulhane 11 87
(RMWhitaker) *trckd ldrs: rdn 2f out: kpt on same pce* 4/1[1]

0246 6 1/2 Halmahera (IRE)[29] 2065 9-9-7 100 (b) NCallan 1 94
(KARyan) *towards rr: sme hdwy u.p 2f out: no further prog fnl f* 10/1

5010 7 nk River Falcon[13] 2488 4-8-7 86 oh2 KDarley 7 79
(JSGoldie) *stmbld s: sn chsng ldrs: rdn and outpcd 2f out: n.d after* 8/1

0462 8 nk Johnston's Diamond (IRE)[17] 2391 6-8-11 90 KMcEvoy 10 82
(EJAlston) *midfield: rdn 2f out: sn btn* 15/2

312L 9 5 Forever Phoenix[7] 2636 4-8-13 92 EAhern 3 69
(RMHCowell) *chsd ldrs: rdn over 2f out: wknd over 1f out* 9/2[2]

5600 10 2 1/2 Will He Wish[20] 2283 8-8-13 92 KDalgleish 2 62
(SGollings) *dwlt: drvn along in rr 1/2-way: no hdwy* 20/1

1m 11.2s (0.13) **Going Correction** +0.275s/f (Good) 10 Ran SP% 111.7
Speed ratings: **110,109,108,104,103 103,102,102,95,92**CSF £180.90 CT £1203.82 TOTE £25.50: £5.80, £2.90, £1.60; EX 250.90 Trifecta £1557.70 Part won. Pool of £2,194.06 - 0.60 winning tickets..
**Owner** David Fish **Bred** Michael Staunton **Trained** Cockerham, Lancs

**FOCUS**
A good handicap but a fast and furious gallop with the first three all posting season's best efforts.

**NOTEBOOK**
**Circuit Dancer(IRE)**, who has developed problems with the stalls, had the hood removed at the last possible moment. Giving away two or three lengths, he came off just best. He loves fast ground.
**Marsad(IRE)**, runner-up a year ago, has slipped to a lenient mark and in the end only just missed out.
**Dazzling Bay** took the big three-year-old sprint at this meeting last year from a 15lb lower mark. He looked back to his best beforehand and basically threw it away swerving badly. There is another big sprint in him when he is drawn with the running rail on his right-hand side.
**Pieter Brueghel(USA)**, having just his second outing this time, showed bags of toe. He is now 9lb lower than his last win two years ago.
**Steel Blue**travelled strongly on the heels of the leader but, when popped the question, the response was limited. He is happiest when able to dominate.
**Halmahera(IRE)** looked at his very best but this trip is sharp for him now and has last three wins have been in September onwards.
**River Falcon**, 6lb higher than his win here last month, looked in peak condition but blew it stumbling leaving the gates.
**Forever Phoenix** really took the eye beforehand but she was well below par, being unhappy on the very quick ground. *Official explanation: trainer said filly was unsuited by the good to firm ground*

## 2858 M&J SEAFOOD ROUS (S) STKS 6f 3y
3:50 (3:51) (E) 2-Y-0 £4,013 (£1,235; £617; £308) Stalls Centre

Form RPR

01 1 Island Swing (IRE)[8] 2622 2-8-7 ow1 SSanders 7 71
(JLSpearing) *mde all: drew clr over 1f out: drvn out fnl f: styd on wl* 11/4[1]

2 3 1/2 Gold Quay (IRE) 2-8-6 GFaulkner 3 60
(PCHaslam) *cmpt: slowly away: bhd: gd hdwy over 2f out: rdn to chse wnr appr fnl f: styd on wl but no imp* 14/1

50 3 4 Amphitheatre (IRE)[8] 2609 2-8-11 ACulhane 2 53
(RFJohnsonHoughton) *midfield: pushed along over 2f out: hdwy over 1f out: styd on on fnl f: nvr able to chal* 9/2[2]

1125 4 1 3/4 Little Biscuit (IRE)[13] 2489 2-8-6 ANicholls 9 42
(KRBurke) *prom: rdn to chse wnr 2f out: kpt on same pce* 11/2[3]

5 3/4 Magic Genie (IRE) 2-8-6 DaleGibson 1 40
(MWEasterby) *midfield: drvn along 1/2-way: kpt on fnl 2f: n.d* 20/1

0 6 1 3/4 Sowerby[30] 2045 2-8-11 TWilliams 10 40
(MBrittain) *chsd wnr: rdn over 2f out: sn btn* 25/1

0 7 1 Dishdasha (IRE)[22] 2234 2-8-8 DAllan[(3)] 12 37
(TDEasterby) *dwlt: sn chsng ldrs: rdn over 2f out: no hdwy* 33/1

00 8 2 1/2 Diatonic[16] 2405 2-8-11 GCarter 13 29
(WJMusson) *midfield: rdn and no hdwy whn hmpd 2f out* 25/1

0 9 nk Roko[27] 2125 2-8-6 PMulrennan[(5)] 4 28
(MWEasterby) *midfield: drvn along 1/2-way: sn btn* 12/1

6 10 9 Den Perry[5] 2570 2-8-6 PBradley[(5)] 6 —
(ABerry) *sn towards rr* 16/1

3 11 6 Shuchbaa[18] 2364 2-8-6 PFessey 8 —
(KARyan) *slowly away: a bhd* 10/1

0 12 29 Mill End Chateau[17] 2388 2-8-11 RWinston 11 —
(MWEasterby) *chsd ldrs tl wknd over 2f out: eased and lost tch fr over 1f out: t.o* 14/1

0334 13 2 Joshar[18] 2364 2-8-6 KDarley 5 —
(MWEasterby) *bhd: lost tch and eased over 2f out: t.o* 9/1

1m 13.95s (2.88) **Going Correction** +0.275s/f (Good) 13 Ran SP% **121.6**
Speed ratings: **91,86,81,78,77 75,74,70,70,58 50,11,8**CSF £42.76 TOTE £3.90: £1.80, £4.20, £2.60; EX 51.60.The winner was bought in for 28,000 guineas. Gold Quay was claimed by Mr. Nigel Shields for £12,000.
**Owner** J Spearing **Bred** Tomaju Investments **Trained** Kinnersley, Worcs

**FOCUS**
A strong seller with a convincing winner, the first two clear and they both attracted interest afterwards.

**NOTEBOOK**
**Island Swing(IRE)** is not very big but has a willing attitude. Her rider left nothing to chance and connections had to dig deep at the auction. They will be hoping for a realistic nursery mark.
**Gold Quay(IRE)**, a March foal, is a close-coupled type. With two handlers and noisy in the paddock, she recovered from a sluggish start to finish clear second best. She was claimed and is expected to join Nick Littmoden.
**Amphitheatre(IRE)**, who had two handlers in the paddock, had cover this time but he does not look altogether straightfoward.
**Little Biscuit(IRE)**, who is well named, was having her fifth outing and is starting to look fully exposed.
**Magic Genie(IRE)**, a March foal, looks an immature type. She showed some ability on this debut and will be better suited by seven.
**Sowerby**, a March foal, showed more than on his debut and should find a seller.
**Diatonic** *Official explanation: jockey said gelding hung left-handed throughout*
**Den Perry** *Official explanation: jockey said colt was never travelling*
**Mill End Chateau** *Official explanation: jockey said gelding lost its action*
**Joshar** *Official explanation: jockey said filly lost her action*

## 2859 BLACKS - THE PEOPLE FOR PROPERTY STKS (H'CAP) 5f 3y
4:25 (4:28) (C) (0-100,94) 3-Y-0+ £10,328 (£3,178; £1,589; £794) Stalls Centre

Form RPR

3000 1 Piccled[3] 2754 6-8-7 77 DAllan[(3)] 10 90+
(EJAlston) *dwlt: sn trcking ldrs: hdwy to ld appr fnl f: r.o wl* 33/1

0640 2 1 3/4 Obe One[3] 2754 4-8-2 69 FNorton 9 76
(ABerry) *rr: drvn along 1/2-way: hdwy appr fnl f: r.o wl u.p ins last to go 2nd cl home* 10/1

3030 3 shd Henry Hall (IRE)[6] 2679 8-9-13 94 KimTinkler 3 101
(NTinkler) *prom: led briefly over 1f out: kpt on fnl f* 10/1

0-00 4 shd Atlantic Viking (IRE)[6] 2679 9-9-13 94 RWinston 6 100
(DNicholls) *stmbld s: rr: hdwy appr fnl f: r.o wl u.p ins last: nvr able to chal* 16/1

3025 5 nk Watching[6] 2679 7-9-4 85 ANicholls 7 90
(DNicholls) *prom: rdn 2f out: kpt on fnl f* 8/1[3]

0201 6 1 1/2 Catch The Cat (IRE)[13] 2490 5-8-5 72 (b) GParkin 13 72
(JSWainwright) *chsd ldrs: rdn 2f out: no hdwy* 12/1

0-02 7 3/4 Strensall[13] 2490 7-8-10 77 RFitzpatrick 11 74
(REBarr) *in tch: rdn and ch over 1f out: no ex ins last* 14/1

0001 8 hd Tommy Smith[4] 2734 6-8-7 74 7ex (b) DarrenWilliams 2 70
(JSWainwright) *led tl hdd over 1f out: fdd ins last* 7/1[2]

3430 9 1 Zarzu[13] 2477 5-8-7 74 JBramhill 1 67
(CRDore) *nvr bttr than mid-div* 14/1

6-24 10 shd Connect[13] 2488 7-9-6 87 (b) PRobinson 4 79
(MHTompkins) *towards rr most of way* 4/1[1]

0-00 11 1/2 Rectangle (IRE)[56] 1454 4-8-10 77 ACulhane 14 68
(DNicholls) *hld up in tch: effrt 2f out: sn btn* 66/1

2055 12 1/2 Online Investor[4] 2734 5-8-2 69 DRMcCabe 8 58
(DNicholls) *dwlt: a rr* 14/1

2130 13 1 1/2 Magic Glade[6] 2679 5-9-1 87 RThomas[(5)] 5 70
(CRDore) *mid-div: rdn 2f out: sn btn* 8/1[3]

58.75 secs (0.01) **Going Correction** +0.275s/f (Good) 13 Ran SP% **110.9**
Speed ratings: **110,107,107,106,106 104,102,102,100,100 99,99,96**CSF £313.31 CT £3526.88 TOTE £39.10: £7.20, £3.50, £2.30; EX 500.40.
**Owner** The Pain And Heartache Partnership **Bred** The Lavington Stud **Trained** Longton, Lancs

**FOCUS**
In effect a 0-94 handicap run at a scorching pace and the form is sound.

**NOTEBOOK**
**Piccled**, totally unsuited by the heavily watered ground at Chester just three days earlier, took this in good style. With him the flatter the track the better.
**Obe One**, who finished ahead of the winner at Chester, is from a stable getting back into the groove.
**Henry Hall(IRE)**, who won this in 2000, is rated to the hilt but he tries his heart out every time.
**Atlantic Viking(IRE)** blew his chance at the start. He finished with quite a flourish and is clearly right back to his best.
**Watching**, as usual taken to post early, is in good form but he does not appreciate the ground as quick as this.
**Catch The Cat(IRE)**, 3lb higher and in a much better race, was drawn just one from the stands' side.
**Connect** took this a year ago from an 11lb lower mark, but he is not in the same sort of form this time.
**Magic Glade** ran very flat and was found to have burst again. *Official explanation: jockey said gelding had broken a blood vessel*

## 2860 SPORTINGOPTIONS.CO.UK LOW COMMISSION MAIDEN AUCTION STKS 5f 3y
5:00 (5:02) (E) 2-Y-0 £5,070 (£1,560; £780; £390) Stalls Centre

Form RPR

222 1 Distinctly Game[14] 2453 2-8-10 NCallan 5 80
(KARyan) *cl up: led over 1f out: rdn and hdd wl ins fnl f: led again post* 7/4[1]

43 **2** *shd* **Lady Dan (IRE)**[14] 2458 2-8-4 .......... TLucas 10 74
(MWEasterby) *chsd ldrs: r.o u.p fnl f: edgd lft and slt ld wl ins last: hdd post* **10/1**
64 **3** *nk* **Mimi Mouse**[22] 2234 2-8-6 .......... PRobinson 12 75
(TDEasterby) *prom: rdn over 1f out: ev ch ins fnl f: no ex clsng stages* **12/1**
**4** *2* **Dispol Isle (IRE)** 2-8-3 .......... PFessey 13 65
(TDBarron) *leggy: unf: slowly away: sn midfield: hdwy u.p over 1f out: kpt on ins last: nvr able to chal* **50/1**
604 **5** *½* **Melandre**[14] 2458 2-8-4 .......... TWilliams 8 64
(MBrittain) *led tl hdd and rdn over 1f out: no ex* **33/1**
**6** *3½* **Borderlescott** 2-8-11 .......... RFfrench 7 59
(RBastiman) *w'like: cmpt: dwlt: sn midfield: kpt on fnl 2f: n.d* **25/1**
**7** *shd* **Rancho Cucamonga (IRE)** 2-8-5 ow1 .......... KDarley 15 52
(TDBarron) *lengthy: scope: dwlt: sn chsng ldrs: rdn over 1f out: sn btn* **10/1**
**8** *shd* **Skiddaw Wolf** 2-8-3 .......... FNorton 9 50
(BSmart) *lengthy: unf: dwlt: sn in tch: rdn 2f out: no hdwy* **33/1**
3 **9** *1¾* **Llamadas**[38] 1865 2-8-8 .......... LEnstone(3) 3 52
(MDods) *in tch: rdn 2f out: sn btn* **8/1**[2]
0 **10** *nk* **Mill By The Stream**[20] 2300 2-8-11 .......... ANicholls 18 51
(APJarvis) *sn towards rr: kpt on fnl 2f: n.d* **50/1**
0 **11** *½* **Zando**[14] 2453 2-8-10 .......... GFaulkner 17 48
(PCHaslam) *sn bhd: kpt on fnl 2f: n.d* **40/1**
**12** *2* **Kudbeme** 2-8-3 .......... EAhern 6 34
(NBycroft) *cmpt: nvr bttr than mid-div* **40/1**
**13** *hd* **Bust (IRE)** 2-8-9 .......... KDalgleish 11 39
(TDEasterby) *w'like: unf; scope: dwlt: a bhd* **25/1**
6 **14** *½* **Rich Albi**[17] 2388 2-8-10 .......... DAllan(3) 14 42
(TDEasterby) *nvr bttr than mid-div* **8/1**[2]
**15** *shd* **Star Of Kildare (IRE)** 2-8-3 .......... KimTinkler 16 31
(NTinkler) *cmpt: unf: sn bhd* **50/1**
**16** *½* **Open Verdict (IRE)** 2-8-11 .......... KMcEvoy 2 37
(APJarvis) *wl grown: dwlt: towards rr most of way* **16/1**
**17** *½* **Negas (IRE)** 2-8-13 .......... RWinston 4 38
(JHowardJohnson) *w'like: scope: dwlt: sn in tch: wknd wl over 1f out* **9/1**[3]
**18** *2½* **Ben Casey** 2-8-10 .......... FLynch 1 26
(BSmart) *w'like: cmpt: hung rt thrght: bhd fr 1/2-way* **33/1**

59.51 secs (0.77) **Going Correction** +0.275s/f (Good) **18** Ran SP% **127.6**
Speed ratings: **104,103,103,100,99 93,93,93,90,90 89,86,85,85,84 84,83,79**CSF £18.22 TOTE £3.10: £1.70, £3.60, £3.10; EX 25.80 Place 6 £330.01, Place 5 £160.59.
**Owner** Mr & Mrs Julian And Rosie Richer **Bred** J A Forsyth **Trained** Hambleton, N Yorks

**FOCUS**
An excellent winning time for the type of race, just 0.76 seconds slower than the preceding Class C handicap for older horses. The form looks fairly strong.

**NOTEBOOK**
**Distinctly Game**, who looked very fit, made it fourth time lucky but in the end it was a very close call.
**Lady Dan(IRE)** is clearly going the right way, and but for edging left well inside the last she may well have held on. A six furlong nursery now beckons.
**Mimi Mouse**, dropping back in trip, was just found lacking late on. She is clearly going the right way.
**Dispol Isle(IRE)**, born on April Fools Day, is on the leg and narrow. After a sluggish start she picked up in good style late on, and this will have taught her plenty.
**Melandre**, a handful in the paddock and at the stalls, showed bags of toe but her temperament is going to be the problem.
**Borderlescott**, an April foal, was very noisy in the paddock. After a tardy start he was getting the hang of things late on.
**Rancho Cucamonga(IRE)**, an April foal, is a sister to Raccoon. Long in the back, she made a satisfactory debut and will improve in time.
**Star Of Kildare(IRE)** *Official explanation: trainer said he was unable to fit the declared tongue-strap*
**Ben Casey** *Official explanation: jockey said colt had hung right-handed throughout*
T/Jkpt: Not won. T/Plt: £504.90 to a £1 stake. Pool: £63,493.25. 91.80 winning tickets. T/Qpdt: £162.00 to a £1 stake. Pool: £4,620.05. 21.10 winning tickets. JF

2861 - 2867a (Foreign Racing) - See Raceform Interactive

# [2425]BATH (L-H)
Saturday, June 12

**OFFICIAL GOING: Firm (hard in places)**

## 2868 EBF MAINLINE EMPLOYMENT NOVICE STKS 5f 11y
**2:15** (2:16) (D) 2-Y-O **£4,017** (£1,236; £618; £309) **Stalls** Low

Form RPR
421 **1** **Silver Wraith (IRE)**[6] 2702 2-8-11 .......... TPQueally(3) 2 80
(NACallaghan) *racd 3rd: pushed along 2f out: hung lft over 1f out: r.o wl ins fnl f to ld fnl 50yds* **10/3**[3]
1 **2** *½* **Carte Royale**[19] 2352 2-9-2 .......... SChin 1 80
(MJohnston) *led: rdn 2f out: r.o fnl f but hdd fnl 50yds* **10/11**[1]
223 **3** *1¼* **Bibury Flyer**[8] 2655 2-8-6 ow2 .......... SHitchcott(3) 3 69
(MRChannon) *trckd ldr: rdn 2f out: no ex and hld whn sltly hmpd cl home* **3/1**[2]
**4** *10* **My Dream (IRE)** 2-8-3 .......... FNorton 5 27
(RHannon) *slowly away: a last: rdn 1/2-way: wknd ins fnl 2f* **12/1**

62.53 secs (0.03) **Going Correction** 0.0s/f (Good) **4** Ran SP% **108.2**
Speed ratings: **99,98,96,80**CSF £6.88 TOTE £4.70; EX 6.00.
**Owner** M Tabor **Bred** Mrs M Fox **Trained** Newmarket, Suffolk

**FOCUS**
This looks strong novice form despite the small field.

**NOTEBOOK**
**Silver Wraith(IRE)**, who won at Brighton six days earlier despite not acting on the camber, ran on well to get the best of a three-way battle. He goes well on firm ground and another furlong would not come amiss.
**Carte Royale** did not do a lot wrong but was just unable to give away the 5lb. He has had two runs on firm ground now and might appreciate an easier surface.
**Bibury Flyer** ran another decent race and her turn should come, possibly in nursery company.
**My Dream(IRE)** is a full-sister to Craven Stakes winner King's Ironbridge, as well as a half-sister to sprinters Cradle Days and Sister Susan. After missing the break, she could never get in a blow at her experienced rivals, but she may do better in maiden company.

## 2869 GERALD & FREDA BROWN'S GOLDEN WEDDING (S) STKS 5f 161y
**2:45** (2:45) (G) 3-Y-0+ **£2,576** (£736; £368) **Stalls** Low

Form RPR
P-01 **1** **Foley Millennium (IRE)**[33] 1988 6-9-10 49 .......... FNorton 8 64+
(MQuinn) *mde all: clr wl over 1f out: r.o wl* **9/1**
4406 **2** *2* **Juwwi**[56] 1474 10-9-1 62 .......... SHitchcott(3) 6 52
(JMBradley) *hld up in rr: hdwy 2f out: r.o to go 2nd ins fnl f: no ch w wnr* **8/1**
0-50 **3** *½* **Diamond Ring**[19] 2350 5-8-13 40 .......... IMongan 4 45
(MrsJCandlish) *racd mid-div: rdn 2f out: kpt on fnl f* **14/1**
4010 **4** *1¼* **Jinksonthehouse**[12] 2518 3-8-6 60 .......... HayleyTurner(5) 10 47
(MDIUsher) *racd mid-div: rdn 2f out: kpt on one pce* **11/2**[2]
0030 **5** *1¼* **Tappit (IRE)**[10] 2582 5-9-4 54 .......... (p) CCatlin 7 43
(JMBradley) *towards rr: rdn over 2f out: kpt on but nvr nr to chal* **13/2**[3]
0026 **6** *hd* **Frenchmans Lodge**[11] 2556 4-8-13 40 .......... (b) BSwarbrick(5) 12 42
(JMBradley) *in rr: mde sme late hdwy past btn horses ins fnl f* **9/1**
30-0 **7** *1½* **Delegate**[5] 2739 11-9-1 67 .......... TPQueally(3) 11 37
(NACallaghan) *hld up towards rr: rdn 2f out: nvr on terms* **7/2**[1]
2006 **8** *½* **Henry Tun**[19] 2350 6-9-5 41 .......... (p) MSavage(5) 13 42
(NEBerry) *prom tl wknd wl over 1f out* **12/1**
0000 **9** *nk* **Naughty Girl (IRE)**[5] 2724 4-8-13 60 .......... JoannaBadger 1 30
(PDEvans) *promikent on ins tl rdn and wknd 2f out* **10/1**
1200 **10** *8* **Kilmeena Star**[17] 2404 6-9-3 37 .......... (b) DerekNolan(7) 2 17
(JCFox) *slowly away: a bhd* **25/1**
0000 **11** *6* **Hawk**[117] 794 6-9-1 63 .......... LPKeniry(3) 3 —
(PRChamings) *prom to 1/2-way* **11/1**

1m 12.16s (1.02) **Going Correction** 0.0s/f (Good)
**WFA** 3 from 4yo+ 8lb **11** Ran SP% **117.7**
Speed ratings: **93,90,89,88,86 86,84,83,83,72 64**CSF £79.18 TOTE £12.40: £5.10, £2.50, £3.30; EX 135.50.The winner was bought in for 7,200gns.
**Owner** Mrs S G Davies **Bred** Elperefa Bloodstock **Trained** Sparsholt, Oxon

**FOCUS**
A weak race which few got into. Foley Millennium had it sewn up entering the final furlong, but the form horses were not at their best.

**NOTEBOOK**
**Foley Millennium(IRE)** had plenty to find on official ratings but was well treated on old form. A winner in heavy ground last time, he had no problem with these very different conditions and was eased down with his race won in the last half-furlong.
**Juwwi**, who has compiled a long losing run, ran a decent race on his return from a break but is flattered by the margin of defeat as the winner was eased.
**Diamond Ring** is without a win since her second racecourse appearance three years ago.
**Jinksonthehouse** won a poor claimer over the bare five here last month.
**Frenchmans Lodge**, who was poorly drawn, made a little late progress once switched inside.

## 2870 WEATHERBYS INSURANCE CLASSIFIED STKS 1m 3f 144y
**3:20** (3:20) (E) 3-Y-O **£4,251** (£1,308; £654; £327) **Stalls** Low

Form RPR
6245 **1** **Zaffeu**[14] 2472 3-8-8 69 .......... TPQueally(3) 6 74
(NPLittmoden) *hld up in last pl: short of room and swtchd rt over 2f out: rdn wl over 1f out and qcknd on outside to ld ins fnl f* **11/4**[2]
0033 **2** *nk* **Desert Image (IRE)**[26] 2169 3-8-11 73 .......... SHitchcott(3) 5 77
(CTinkler) *trckd ldr: led over 3f out: rdn over 1f out: kpt on but hdd and nt pce of wnr ins fnl f* **11/8**[1]
0-16 **3** *5* **Vengerov**[117] 798 3-8-13 72 .......... IMongan 3 68
(MLWBell) *hld up in 3rd pl: wnt 2nd briefly 2f out: rdn and fdd ins fnl f* **4/1**
4300 **4** *6* **West Country (UAE)**[42] 1760 3-8-11 70 .......... SChin 2 56
(MJohnston) *led tl hdd over 3f out: rdn 2f out: wknd wl over 1f out* **7/2**[3]

2m 30.16s (-0.14) **Going Correction** +0.075s/f (Good) **4** Ran SP% **111.0**
Speed ratings: **103,102,99,95**CSF £7.15 TOTE £4.10; EX 5.30.
**Owner** The Headquarters Partnership Ltd **Bred** Patrick Eddery Ltd **Trained** Newmarket, Suffolk

**FOCUS**
A tight contest in which the winner had a pound to find with the other three on official adjusted ratings. There was no pace on in the first part of the race.

**NOTEBOOK**
**Zaffeu** came with a sweeping run once switched to the outer and scored a shade readily in the end. He looks to be on the upgrade now.
**Desert Image(IRE)** went down fighting and saw out this longer trip, having run over ten furlongs here on his two most recent starts.
**Vengerov**, having his first run on turf this year, had not raced at beyond an extended mile before and he failed to stay.
**West Country(UAE)**, taking a big step up in trip, was able to dictate the pace but did not put up much resistance once headed.

## 2871 TOTEPLACEPOT FILLIES' H'CAP 1m 5y
**3:55** (3:57) (D) (0-85,73) 3-Y-0+ **£6,721** (£2,068; £1,034; £517) **Stalls** Low

Form RPR
3401 **1** **Brazilian Terrace**[28] 2119 4-9-8 73 .......... HayleyTurner(5) 2 82
(MLWBell) *racd in 3rd pl tl wnt 2nd over 3f out: led 2f out: pushed out fnl f* **11/4**[1]
1302 **2** *nk* **Marnie**[16] 2426 7-8-5 51 .......... CCatlin 3 59
(JAkehurst) *hld up in rr: rdn and hdwy over 2f out: hung lft but wnt 2nd ins fnl f: kpt on u.p* **7/2**[3]
0260 **3** *2* **Nuzzle**[2] 2810 4-7-11 46 .......... (v) JFMcDonald(3) 1 50
(MQuinn) *led tl hdd 2f out: lost 2nd and hld whn hmpd ins fnl f* **11/2**
-534 **4** *2* **Here To Me**[10] 2577 3-8-12 69 .......... PDobbs 5 68
(RHannon) *trckd ldr tl over 3f out: sn outpcd and nvr a danger after* **5/1**
3032 **5** *1¾* **Oh So Rosie (IRE)**[4] 2757 4-8-5 58 .......... DerekNolan(7) 4 53
(JSMoore) *hld up in last pl: rdn wl over 2f out and nvr on terms* **10/3**[2]
400- **6** *12* **Stella Marais (IRE)**[224] 5868 3-8-10 67 .......... FNorton 6 34
(PRChamings) *slowly away: plld hrd: lost tch 3f out* **12/1**

1m 40.43s (-0.57) **Going Correction** +0.075s/f (Good)
**WFA** 3 from 4yo+ 11lb **6** Ran SP% **111.7**
Speed ratings: **105,104,102,100,98 86**CSF £12.47 TOTE £3.40: £2.30, £2.60; EX 10.00.
**Owner** Mrs G Rowland-Clark/M L W Bell Racing **Bred** Mount Coote Stud **Trained** Newmarket, Suffolk
■ Stewards Enquiry : C Catlin caution: careless riding

**FOCUS**
A modest handicap that was run at an ordinary pace and the winner did not need to improve to score.

**NOTEBOOK**
**Brazilian Terrace**, with the benefit of the inside rail to race against, held off the runner-up's challenge slightly more easily than the narrow margin suggests. A mile on fast ground is ideal for her.
**Marnie** was free to post and did not settle in the first part of the race. She had every chance but has now been runner-up on her last four visits to Bath.


The Form Book, Raceform Ltd, Compton, RG20 6NL

**Nuzzle** had the visor on for the first time since January. She was unable to get clear of her field and was held in third when tightened up inside the last.
**Here To Me** remains a maiden but the basic ability is there. This trip just stretches her.
**Oh So Rosie(IRE)** did not run badly, but was obliged to mount her effort five deep and could never quite land a blow.
**Stella Marais(IRE)**, making her handicap bow on this seasonal debut, was always at the back of the field after a slow start.

## 2872 WESTERN DAILY PRESS RACECLUB MAIDEN AUCTION STKS 5f 11y
4:30 (4:30) (E) 2-Y-O £3,750 (£1,154; £577; £288) Stalls Low

Form RPR
5323 1 **Empire's Ghodha**[12] 2522 2-8-8 (b) JFMcDonald(3) 8 82
(BJMeehan) *trckd ldr: led 1/2-way: rdn out fnl f* **15/8**[1]
06 2 1 1/4 **Encanto (IRE)**[9] 2609 2-8-2 CCatlin 5 69
(JSMoore) *towards rr but hld up in tch: rdn and hdwy to chse wnr wl over 1f out: kpt on but no imp after* **10/1**
0 3 1 1/2 **Bold Minstrel (IRE)**[22] 2268 2-8-7 FNorton 2 68
(MQuinn) *a.p on ins: rdn and one pce fnl f* **14/1**
3 4 nk **Forzeen**[28] 2125 2-8-6 TPQueally(3) 3 69
(JAOsborne) *racd mid-div: sn pushed along: nvr nr to chal but kpt on fnl f* **9/2**[3]
5 2 **Peopleton Brook** 2-8-7 PDobbs 4 60
(DWPArbuthnot) *plld hrd in rr: effrt over 1f out but nvr on terms* **25/1**
3 6 6 **Mister Bell**[36] 1930 2-8-11 DSweeney 6 42
(JGMO'Shea) *led tl hdd 1/2-way: wknd wl over 1f out* **5/1**
53 7 1 1/2 **Feminist (IRE)**[10] 2574 2-8-6 SHitchcott(3) 7 35
(MRChannon) *prominenet early: sn rdn and wknd 2f out* **3/1**[2]
63.25 secs (0.75) **Going Correction** 0.0s/f (Good) **7** Ran SP% **114.2**
Speed ratings: **94,92,89,89,85 76,73**CSF £21.75 TOTE £3.10: £1.20, £4.60; EX 43.90.
**Owner** Clipper Group Holdings **Bred** Slatch Farm Stud **Trained** Upper Lambourn, Berks

**FOCUS**
A moderate race, with little strength in depth, run in a slower time than the opening juvenile event.

**NOTEBOOK**
**Empire's Ghodha** had begun to look exposed but was found a good opportunity. After quickening to take a grip on the race over a furlong out, he held on well despite edging to his right.
**Encanto(IRE)**, back down to five furlongs, chased the winner through without getting to him. She is eligible for nurseries now.
**Bold Minstrel(IRE)** knew more this time but lacked the pace to make his presence felt.
**Forzeen** shaped as if in need of another furlong.
**Peopleton Brook**, his stable's first two-year-old runner of the campaign, was rather green and should improve.
**Mister Bell** was the subject of market support down from 14/1 but weakened disappointingly.
**Feminist(IRE)** was below par and the firm ground may have been to blame.

## 2873 TOTEQUADPOT RATED STKS (H'CAP) 5f 161y
5:00 (5:00) (D) (0-85,81) 3-Y-O+ £5,990 (£2,272; £1,136; £516) Stalls Low

Form RPR
-015 1 **High Ridge**[9] 2614 5-8-6 **64** oh4 (p) CCatlin 2 78
(JMBradley) *in rr and sn pushed along: hdwy 2f out: rdn to ld ent fnl f: pushed out* **12/1**
1-21 2 1 1/2 **Devon Flame**[5] 2739 5-8-10 **71** 3ex JFMcDonald(3) 3 80
(RJHodges) *trckd ldr: ev ch 2f out tl nt qckn ins fnl f* **8/11**[1]
0320 3 1 3/4 **One Way Ticket**[3] 2779 4-8-1 **64** oh2 (p) HayleyTurner(5) 6 68
(JMBradley) *sn led: rdn and hdd ent fnl f: fdd ins last* **6/1**[3]
215- 4 1 1/4 **Pintle**[297] 4293 4-8-9 **67** SCarson 1 67
(JLSpearing) *prom: rdn 1/2-way: sn outpcd and nvr on terms after* **14/1**
1601 5 1/2 **Devise (IRE)**[21] 2303 5-9-9 **81** TGMcLaughlin 7 80
(MSSaunders) *rrd up leaving stalls: racd wd: rdn 1/2-way: nvr on terms* **4/1**[2]
2010 6 5 **Byo (IRE)**[15] 2440 6-8-11 **72** SHitchcott(3) 4 56
(MQuinn) *in tch tl rdn and wknd wl over 1f out* **14/1**
1m 10.53s (-0.61) **Going Correction** 0.0s/f (Good)
**WFA** 3 from 4yo+ 8lb **6** Ran SP% **113.2**
Speed ratings: **104,102,99,98,97 90**CSF £21.93 TOTE £15.30: £3.30, £1.10; EX 39.10.
**Owner** James Leisure Ltd **Bred** Buckram Thoroughbred Enterprises Inc **Trained** Sedbury, Gloucs

**FOCUS**
A modest handicap and something of a shock, with High Ridge overturning odds-on Devon Flame.

**NOTEBOOK**
**High Ridge**was 4lb out of the handicap and effectively 9lb higher than when scoring over course and distance two starts ago. He appreciated the return to this trip and came between horses to assert.
**Devon Flame**, under a 3lb penalty for his win at Windsor, might have found this run coming too quick. He should be forgiven this.
**One Way Ticket** is running creditably at present but his low strike rate is a concern.
**Pintle** made a satisfactory return to action, although she could be the kind of filly who is hard to place.
**Devise(IRE)**, racing from a 5lb higher mark, reared as the stalls opened and was always racing deepest on the course thereafter.
**Byo(IRE)** was 3lb above his highest winning mark.

## 2874 BATHWICK TYRES LADY RIDERS' H'CAP 2m 2f 34y
5:30 (5:32) (F) (0-55,55) 4-Y-O+ £3,432 (£1,056; £528; £264) Stalls Low

Form RPR
520- 1 **High Drama**[292] 4471 7-9-1 **35** oh1 MissGwenMorris(7) 12 45
(PBowen) *a.p: disp ld 7f out: def advantage over 3f out: pushed out ins fnl 2f* **8/1**
06-6 2 3/4 **Harik**[34] 413 10-9-10 **42** (bt) MissHGrissell(5) 8 51
(GLMoore) *hld up in mid-div: hdwy on outside to chal 2f out: rdn and no imp fnl f* **10/1**
-030 3 1/2 **Noble Calling (FR)**[2] 2810 7-10-8 **52** MissEFolkes(3) 11 61
(RJHodges) *plld hrd in rr: hdwy 4f out: styd on one pce ins fnl f* **5/1**[3]
4-05 4 2 1/2 **Purdey**[10] 2590 4-10-0 **45** MrsSMoore(3) 6 52
(HMorrison) *in tch: styd on one pace fnl 2f* **7/1**
0636 5 nk **Moonshine Beach**[9] 2613 6-10-9 **55** (p) MrsMarieKing(5) 14 61
(PWHiatt) *a prominent: wknd appr fnl f* **9/2**[2]
0615 6 1/2 **Sariba**[16] 2429 5-9-13 **40** MsCWilliams 5 45
(ACharlton) *mde most tl hdd over 3f out: rdn and one pce after* **7/2**[1]
0000 7 3/4 **Vanbrugh (FR)**[5] 2731 4-10-3 **45** (t) MissEJJones 7 51
(MissDAMchale) *hld up: rdn and effot over 2f out: sn btn* **14/1**
6020 8 3 **Joely Green**[5] 2731 7-10-4 **48** (b) MrsEmmaLittmoden(3) 15 50
(NPLittmoden) *mid-div: rdn over 3f out: one pce after* **10/1**
3040 9 5 **River Of Fire**[10] 2595 6-9-3 **35** oh5 (v) MissJoeyEllis(5) 3 32
(CNKellett) *mid-div: pressed ldrs over 5f out: wknd 4f out* **16/1**
5100 10 12 **Fletcher**[13] 2501 10-9-8 **40** (p) MissGDGracey-Davison(5) 1 25
(HMorrison) *hld up in mid-div: hdwy 1/2-way: wknd over 3f out* **11/1**
060- 11 nk **Woodstock Express**[244] 5504 4-9-1 **34** oh6 MissJodieHughes(5) 4 19
(PBowen) *plld hrd: in tch: rdn 7f out: sn btn* **33/1**
605- 12 4 **Cantoris**[38] 5631 4-10-6 **53** (b) MissCStucley(5) 9 34
(CLPopham) *hld up: a struggling in rr* **25/1**
606- 13 12 **Pertemps Sia**[337] 3166 4-9-2 **37** MissJPledge(7) 2 6
(ADSmith) *rrd up s and plld hrd in rr: rapid hdwy to join ldrs after 5f: wknd over 6f out* **33/1**
64-3 14 dist **Gordy's Joy**[8] 2662 4-9-12 **40** MissCO'Neill 13 —
(GAHam) *plld hrd in rr: a bhd: t.o* **25/1**
3m 51.93s (2.33) **Going Correction** +0.075s/f (Good)
**WFA** 4 from 5yo+ 2lb **14** Ran SP% **133.3**
Speed ratings: **97,96,96,95,95 94,94,93,91,85 85,83,78,**—CSF £91.95 CT £458.20 TOTE £12.40: £3.30, £3.80, £2.20; EX 138.00 Place 6 £519.34, Place 5 £100.50.
**Owner** P Bowen **Bred** Bishop's Down Farm **Trained** Letterston, Pembrokes

**FOCUS**
A selling-class ladies' handicap and the form is distinctly moderate.

**NOTEBOOK**
**High Drama**, was having his first run since August, but he has gone well fresh before. He was in command when his rider eased him a shade prematurely going to the line, allowing the second to reduce the margin.
**Harik** won over fences last month but is an infrequent runner on the Flat. He had his chance but edged to his left when held.
**Noble Calling(FR)**, who found ten furlongs too sharp two days earlier, loves ground like this.
**Purdey**, tackling her longest trip to date, saw it out but does lack anything in the way of a gear change.
**Moonshine Beach** is now 8lb lower than at the start of the season.
**Sariba** was able to get the lead but could not dominate in the way that she likes to.
**Gordy's Joy** *Official explanation: jockey said saddle slipped*
T/Plt: £786.30 to a £1 stake. Pool: £37,161.40. 34.50 winning tickets. T/Qpdt: £25.70 to a £1 stake. Pool: £2,530.90. 72.80 winning tickets. JS

# [2544]LEICESTER (R-H)
Saturday, June 12

**OFFICIAL GOING: Good to firm**
As in the previous meeting here it looked to be advantageous to be drawn low in the sprint races.
Wind: Almost nil Weather: Cloudy

## 2875 MERCURY RACE NIGHT FILLIES' H'CAP 5f 218y
6:45 (6:45) (E) (0-75,71) 3-Y-O+ £4,163 (£1,281; £640; £320) Stalls Low

Form RPR
0225 1 **Under My Spell**[5] 2741 3-8-11 **70** SJDonohoe(7) 1 82+
(PDEvans) *sn pushed along in rr: hdwy over 2f out: rdn to ld over 1f out: r.o: eased nr fin* **11/1**
3013 2 1/2 **Amelia (IRE)**[39] 1855 6-8-7 **56** BSwarbrick(5) 5 62
(WMBrisbourne) *chsd ldrs: lost pl over 4f out: hdwy u.p and nt clr run over 1f out: r.o* **6/1**[3]
0050 3 1 **Ace-Ma-Vahra**[3] 2778 6-7-13 **43** (b) JBramhill 8 46
(SRBowring) *hld up: hdwy over 1f out: r.o* **40/1**
0340 4 1 1/2 **Bint Royal (IRE)**[7] 2670 6-9-2 **60** (p) GGibbons 9 58
(MissVHaigh) *chsd ldrs: outpcd over 2f out: r.o ins fnl f* **16/1**
0041 5 1/2 **Silver Chime**[13] 2506 4-9-12 **70** MFenton 4 67
(DMSimcock) *led: hdd over 4f out: rdn over 1f out: styd on same pce* **9/2**[2]
0040 6 3/4 **Tuscan Treaty**[6] 2707 4-8-9 **53** (v) BDoyle 11 47
(TTClement) *s.i.s: hdwy 4f out: rdn over 2f out: no ex fnl f* **20/1**
300- 7 hd **Inch By Inch**[233] 5718 5-9-0 **58** (b) GDuffield 14 52
(PJMakin) *chsd ldrs: led over 4f out: rdn and hdd over 1f out: wkng whn lost action and eased ins fnl f* **25/1**
05-5 8 hd **Sharoura**[19] 2369 8-9-2 **60** PHanagan 6 53
(RAFahey) *hld up: nt clr run over 1f out: r.o: nt rch ldrs* **15/2**
2210 9 shd **Boavista (IRE)**[14] 2482 4-9-2 **60** RHavlin 3 53
(PDEvans) *prom: rdn over 2f out: wknd fnl f* **16/1**
0-40 10 3/4 **Redwood Star**[14] 2482 4-8-12 **56** (e) JFEgan 7 47
(PLGilligan) *chsd ldrs: riddebn and ev ch over 1f out: wknd ins fnl f* **33/1**
0500 11 2 **Tamarella (IRE)**[14] 2482 4-8-7 **51** (v) AMcCarthy 12 36
(GGMargarson) *chsd ldrs: rdn over 2f out: wknd fnl f* **25/1**
0330 12 nk **Blonde En Blonde (IRE)**[85] 1055 4-8-4 **55** (b) StevenHarrison(7) 15 39
(NPLittmoden) *hld up: effrt and n.m.r over 1f out: sn btn* **16/1**
-525 13 2 **Missus Links (USA)**[12] 2536 3-9-5 **71** RHughes 10 49
(RHannon) *stmbld s: sn chsng ldrs: rdn over 2f out: wknd and eased over 1f out* **10/3**[1]
0-04 14 4 **Lady Justice**[10] 2586 4-9-2 **60** (b[1]) KFallon 13 26
(WJarvis) *prom 4f* **16/1**
-000 15 5 **Disco Diva**[18] 2378 3-8-10 **62** DaleGibson 2 13
(MBlanshard) *s.i.s: outpcd* **25/1**
1m 12.43s (-0.97) **Going Correction** -0.15s/f (Firm)
**WFA** 3 from 4yo+ 8lb **15** Ran SP% **120.9**
Speed ratings: **100,99,98,96,95 94,94,93,93,92 90,89,86,81,74**CSF £68.89 CT £2630.32 TOTE £13.90: £4.50, £2.30, £15.20; EX 106.90.
**Owner** J R Salter **Bred** Mrs M Mason **Trained** Pandy, Gwent

**FOCUS**
A moderate contest, but it was run at a fair pace and appeared to favour those drawn low.

**NOTEBOOK**
**Under My Spell** proved well suited to this stiffer course and won with a bit more in hand than the official verdict.
**Amelia(IRE)** is running consistently well at present and may have done better still had she a bit more luck in running.
**Ace-Ma-Vahra** found things happening too quickly for him over this trip, but showed enough to be of interest in similar company when stepping up in trip.
**Bint Royal(IRE)** looks to find this trip on the sharp side nowadays.
**Silver Chime**, just 3lb higher than when successful at Newmarket, had no excuses.
**Sharoura**, well treated on the best of her form, hinted that all is not lost with her just yet. *Official explanation: jockey said mare was unruly in stalls*
**Missus Links(USA)**, who stumbled coming out of the stalls, dropped out and was eased. *Official explanation: jockey said filly stumbled on leaving stalls and was never travelling thereafter*
**Disco Diva** *Official explanation: jockey said filly hung left-handed throughout*

## 2876 SPORT ON MONDAY MAIDEN FILLIES' STKS 5f 218y
7:15 (7:15) (D) 2-Y-O £5,616 (£1,728; £864; £432) Stalls Low

Form RPR
1 **Satin Kiss (USA)** 2-8-11 KMcEvoy 1 78
(SaeedBinSuroor) *led over 4f: rallied to ld ins fnl f: r.o* **11/10**[1]
2 1/2 **Code Orange** 2-8-11 RHavlin 8 76
(JHMGosden) *trckd ldrs: led over 1f out: rdn and hdd ins fnl f: r.o* **9/2**[3]

26 **3** *4* **Azuree (IRE)**[32] 2023 2-8-11 .......... RHughes 5 64
(RHannon) *trckd wnr: rdn over 1f out: eased whn btn ins fnl f* **5/2**[2]
**4** *3* **Night Of Joy (IRE)** 2-8-11 .......... NCallan 2 55
(MAJarvis) *dwlt: hdwy over 3f out: wknd over 1f out* **16/1**
**5** *3/4* **Qawaafil (USA)** 2-8-11 .......... RHills 7 53
(EALDunlop) *s.i.s: sn chsng ldrs: wknd over 1f out* **14/1**
**6** *4* **Liameliss** 2-8-11 .......... RFfrench 3 41
(MAAllen) *s.i.s: sn prom: rdn over 4f out: wknd over 3f out* **50/1**

1m 13.13s (-0.27) **Going Correction** -0.15s/f (Firm) **6** Ran SP% **108.9**
Speed ratings: **95,94,89,85,84 78**CSF £6.05 TOTE £2.10: £1.10, £3.50; EX 5.60.
**Owner** Godolphin **Bred** Darley **Trained** Newmarket, Suffolk

**FOCUS**
Hard to know what to make of this as most of the field were too green to do themselves justice. Although the time was nothing special, the front pair do look above average.

**NOTEBOOK**
**Satin Kiss(USA)**, a sister to four juvenile winners including the Middle Park winner Lujain, looked very professional and seems sure to hold her own in better company.
**Code Orange ◆**, a half-sister to seven-furlong juvenile winner Desert Warning, looks a ready-made winner and will stay further in time.
**Azuree(IRE)** put behind her a dismal display last time and appeared to handle this faster surface well enough. While she is clearly nothing special, she should win a little race somewhere.
**Night Of Joy(IRE)**, a well-related newcomer, found things happening far too quickly for her over this trip and better can be expected as she faces a stiffer test.
**Qawaafil(USA)**, a half-sister to juvenile winner Emran, was too green to do herself justice. However, improvement can be expected and she will be suited by another furlong in time.

## 2877 LEICESTER MERCURY H'CAP — 5f 2y
**7:45** (7:46) (C) (0-90,90) 3-Y-O **£12,412** (£4,708; £2,354; £1,070) **Stalls** Low

Form RPR
132- **1** **Fictional**[231] 5751 3-8-10 **79** .......... GGibbons 9 90
(BAMcmahon) *chsd ldrs: led over 1f out: edgd lft ins fnl f: rdn out* **16/1**
4-1 **2** *nk* **Tony The Tap**[108] 881 3-8-6 **75** .......... KFallon 4 85
(NACallaghan) *hld up: hdwy over 1f out: r.o* **4/1**[1]
2210 **3** *1 1/2* **Green Manalishi**[14] 2488 3-9-5 **88** .......... TQuinn 5 93
(DWPArbuthnot) *trckd ldrs: rdn and unable qck ins fnl f* **4/1**[1]
-150 **4** *1* **Foursquare (IRE)**[21] 2293 3-9-7 **90** .......... NCallan 1 91
(JMackie) *led: hung rt and hdd over 1f out: styd on same pce* **12/1**
33-6 **5** *1 1/4* **Abelard (IRE)**[8] 2650 3-7-12 **67** oh2 .......... PHanagan 7 64
(RAFahey) *outpcd: hdwy over 1f out: r.o* **10/1**
0003 **6** *1* **Divine Spirit**[11] 2552 3-8-11 **80** .......... FLynch 2 73
(MDods) *s.s: outpcd: r.o ins fnl f: nrst fin* **14/1**
2-06 **7** *shd* **Fyodor (IRE)**[11] 2549 3-8-13 **82** .......... JPMurtagh 10 75
(WJHaggas) *chsd ldrs: rdn over 1f out: styd on same pce* **10/1**
-205 **8** *shd* **Celtic Thunder**[11] 2552 3-9-0 **83** .......... JFanning 3 75
(TJEtherington) *w ldr: rdn and ev ch over 1f out: wknd ins fnl f* **12/1**
0-40 **9** *2* **Embassy Lord**[21] 2294 3-8-4 **80** .......... (b) JDO'Reilly(7) 12 65
(JO'Reilly) *s.i.s: outpcd: nvr nrr* **50/1**
-303 **10** *1/2* **Hilites (IRE)**[11] 2549 3-8-13 **82** .......... JFEgan 15 65
(JSMoore) *hld up: effrt 2f out: wknd fnl f* **33/1**
0-00 **11** *1* **Silver Prelude**[11] 2552 3-9-1 **84** .......... ACulhane 6 64
(DKIvory) *chsd ldrs: rdn over 2f out: wknd over 1f out* **33/1**
5113 **12** *1/2* **Imperium**[9] 2610 3-8-6 **74** ow1 .......... MFenton 16 53
(MrsStefLiddiard) *outpcd* **20/1**
4646 **13** *3/4* **Vienna's Boy (IRE)**[5] 2739 3-9-0 **83** .......... RHughes 14 58
(RHannon) *chsd ldrs over 3f* **6/1**[3]
-423 **14** *3/4* **Lualua**[10] 2589 3-8-3 **77** .......... PMakin(5) 8 49
(TDBarron) *s.s: sn chsng ldrs: wknd over 1f out* **11/2**[2]
200- **15** *1 3/4* **Bella Tutrice (IRE)**[226] 5835 3-8-8 **77** .......... GDuffield 11 43
(IAWood) *chsd ldrs: sn drvn along: wknd 1/2-way* **40/1**
6-00 **16** *3* **Vermilliann (IRE)**[28] 2117 3-8-12 **88** .......... PGallagher(7) 13 43
(RHannon) *prom 3f* **50/1**

60.19 secs (-0.74) **Going Correction** -0.15s/f (Firm) **16** Ran SP% **132.8**
Speed ratings: **99,98,96,94,92 90,90,90,87,86 85,84,83,81,79 74**CSF £81.87 CT £325.14 TOTE £20.20: £3.80, £1.90, £1.90, £2.80; EX 230.60.
**Owner** J C Fretwell **Bred** Lady Bland And Dr Susan Barnes **Trained** Hopwas, Staffs

**FOCUS**
A competitive handicap run at an ordinary pace, with the front pair looking progressive sorts beating a pair that give the form solidity.

**NOTEBOOK**
**Fictional ◆** had no problem with the drop in trip and looks capable of holding his own in better company.
**Tony The Tap ◆**, tackling grass for the first time, lacked the experience of his rivals. However, there was much to like about this performance and he should have no trouble getting back to winning ways.
**Green Manalishi** put behind him a below-par effort last time and looked the likely winner going into the latter stages, but he found less than anticipated off the bridle. However, the front pair look progressive types and he must not be written off just yet.
**Foursquare(IRE)** is a pacey colt and tried to make the most of his stands'-side draw but, off the bridle, hung quite badly away.
**Abelard(IRE)** again shaped as though an extra furlong would not come amiss.
**Divine Spirit**, who fell out of the stalls, did well to finish as close as he did. Twice a winner in cheekpieces last term, he has yet to wear the aid this year.

## 2878 SPORTS MERCURY CLASSIFIED STKS — 1m 1f 218y
**8:15** (8:15) (E) 3-Y-O+ **£5,538** (£1,704; £852; £426) **Stalls** High

Form RPR
-622 **1** **Fitting Guest (IRE)**[18] 2390 3-8-4 69 .......... GDuffield 2 78+
(GGMargarson) *led after 1f: rdn clear over 1f out: eased nr fin* **9/4**[2]
0-03 **2** *2* **Blue Mariner**[19] 2367 4-9-3 70 .......... BDoyle 4 74
(PWHarris) *chsd wnr 8f out: rdn over 1f out: styd on same pce* **12/1**
0-04 **3** *1 3/4* **Freeloader (IRE)**[9] 2624 4-9-6 73 .......... RHills 3 74
(JWHills) *plld hrd: led 1f: remained handy: rdn over 1f out: one pce* **7/4**[1]
16-0 **4** *shd* **Colophony (USA)**[32] 1671 4-9-8 75 .......... (t) JPMurtagh 5 76
(KAMorgan) *hld up: plld hrd: outpcd over 2f out: styd on ins fnl f* **9/1**
-002 **5** *4* **Anna Walhaan (IRE)**[11] 2560 5-9-3 70 .......... TQuinn 1 63
(IanWilliams) *plld hrd and prom: wknd over 1f out* **3/1**[3]

2m 8.49s (0.09) **Going Correction** 0.0s/f (Good)
**WFA** 3 from 4yo+ 13lb **5** Ran SP% **109.8**
Speed ratings: **99,97,96,95,92**CSF £24.74 TOTE £4.00: £2.30, £5.20; EX 31.90.
**Owner** John Guest **Bred** Noel McGinn **Trained** Newmarket, Suffolk

**FOCUS**
This was run at a steady pace and the form needs treating with caution.

**NOTEBOOK**
**Fitting Guest(IRE)** got off the mark in good style, but he did have the run of the race with most of his rivals pulling too hard for their own good.
**Blue Mariner** had no excuses on this step up in trip, he just was not good enough.
**Freeloader(IRE)** did himself no favours by refusing to settle.
**Colophony(USA)** was always doing a bit too much early on and was not suited to the steady pace.
**Anna Walhaan(IRE)** pulled far too hard in the early stages and as a consequence did not get home.

## 2879 HARVEY GARDINER MERCURY TIPSTERS TABLE CHAMPION H'CAP — 1m 9y
**8:45** (8:45) (F) (0-55,55) 4-Y-O+ **£4,426** (£1,362; £681; £340) **Stalls** High

Form RPR
0450 **1** **Classic Vision**[10] 2597 4-9-2 **51** .......... (b[1]) RHills 1 59
(WJHaggas) *hld up: hdwy over 2f out: swtchd lft over 1f out: r.o to ld wl ins fnl f: edgd rt nr fin* **16/1**
00-0 **2** *hd* **Canlis**[8] 2658 5-8-10 **45** .......... PHanagan 10 53
(DWThompson) *chsd ldrs: rdn over 3f out: led over 1f out: hdd wl ins fnl f* **33/1**
0-00 **3** *1 3/4* **Dubonai (IRE)**[19] 2375 4-9-0 **49** .......... JPMurtagh 2 53
(AndrewTurnell) *a.p: led over 2f out: rdn and hdd over 1f out: styng on same pce whn n.m.r towards fin* **5/1**[2]
0-00 **4** *2 1/2* **No Chance To Dance (IRE)**[10] 2597 4-8-13 **48** .....(t) DeanMcKeown 14 46
(HJCollingridge) *hld up in tch: rdn over 2f out: one pce fnl f* **25/1**
0-54 **5** *shd* **Hilarious (IRE)**[15] 2451 4-8-12 **47** .......... AMcCarthy 16 45
(BRMillman) *chsd ldr: led over 3f out: hdd over 2f out: wknd ins fnl f* **11/1**
00U3 **6** *1 3/4* **Poppyline**[10] 2597 4-8-13 **53** .......... PMakin(5) 11 47
(WRMuir) *hld up: hdwy over 4f out: outpcd over 2f out: styd on ins fnl f* **13/2**[3]
0-00 **7** *shd* **Zamyatina (IRE)**[35] 1971 5-8-12 **47** .......... JBramhill 15 41
(PLClinton) *hld up in tch: plld hrd: rdn over 2f out: styd on same pce appr fnl f* **33/1**
0356 **8** *shd* **Encounter**[10] 2580 8-8-12 **47** .......... DMcGaffin 5 41
(JHetherton) *unruly stalls: s.s: plld hrd and hdwy 5f out: rdn over 2f out: no ex appr fnl f* **11/1**
6662 **9** *3* **Vermilion Creek**[49] 1606 5-8-13 **53** .......... StephanieHollinshead(5) 9 40
(RHollinshead) *hld up: effrt over 3f out: n.d* **8/1**
0021 **10** *3 1/2* **Archirondel**[11] 2551 6-9-5 **54** .......... ACulhane 3 33
(MDHammond) *hld up: hdwy over 3f out: rdn and hung rt over 2f out: wknd over 1f out* **2/1**[1]
0560 **11** *2* **Encore Royale**[8] 2666 4-8-12 **47** .......... BDoyle 4 21
(JJay) *s.s: a bhd* **40/1**
0-02 **12** *3* **Gemini Lady**[18] 2387 4-8-11 **46** .......... GDuffield 7 13
(MrsGSRees) *hld up: hmpd over 5f out: n.d* **10/1**
0-40 **13** *3* **Niteowl Dream**[2] 2811 4-8-13 **55** .......... JDO'Reilly(7) 13 15
(JO'Reilly) *plld hrd: led over 4f: wknd wl over 1f out* **40/1**
0110 **14** *2 1/2* **Rocinante (IRE)**[15] 2456 4-9-4 **53** .......... MFenton 8 7
(JJQuinn) *hld up: hdwy over 4f out: wknd over 2f out* **11/1**

1m 41.46s (-1.14) **Going Correction** 0.0s/f (Good) **14** Ran SP% **129.0**
Speed ratings: **105,104,103,100,100 98,98,98,95,92 90,87,84,81**CSF £490.83 CT £3098.36 TOTE £19.40: £5.40, £12.20, £3.00; EX 916.40.
**Owner** The Chosen Few Partnership **Bred** R T And Mrs Watson **Trained** Newmarket, Suffolk

**FOCUS**
A very moderate handicap but a fair time for the grade and the winner looks slightly improved.

**NOTEBOOK**
**Classic Vision**, sharpened up by the first-time blinkers, did well to overcome the worst of the draw. However, she still looked to have second thoughts on going about her business.
**Canlis** battled on well enough and showed enough to suggest he can win a similar contest.
**Dubonai(IRE)**, despite the draw, ran well enough over a trip short of his best.
**No Chance To Dance(IRE)** has shown little in five previous outings, and probably did not achieve a great deal in finishing fourth.
**Hilarious(IRE)** could not take advantage of having the best of the draw.
**Poppyline** continues to frustrate and is one to be wary of.
**Archirondel**, even allowing for a poor draw, was somewhat disappointing. *Official explanation: jockey said he was unable to get gelding covered up from an outside draw*

## 2880 SPORTING BLUE H'CAP — 7f 9y
**9:15** (9:16) (D) (0-80,78) 3-Y-O **£7,280** (£2,240; £1,120; £560) **Stalls** Low

Form RPR
4-41 **1** **Royal Prince**[10] 2596 3-9-7 **78** .......... JPMurtagh 8 97
(JRFanshawe) *trckd ldrs: led over 2f out: edgd lft over 1f out: rdn clr ins fnl f: eased nr fin* **8/11**[1]
2121 **2** *5* **Riley Boys (IRE)**[10] 2571 3-9-3 **74** .......... MFenton 5 79
(JGGiven) *w ldrs: rdn and ev ch over 2f out: wknd ins fnl f* **5/1**[3]
-040 **3** *3* **Spin King (IRE)**[25] 2207 3-9-7 **78** .......... DeanMcKeown 6 75
(MLWBell) *mde most over 4f: wknd over 1f out* **7/2**[2]
2-50 **4** *1/2* **Fiore Di Bosco (IRE)**[18] 2391 3-9-0 **76** .......... PMakin(5) 2 72
(TDBarron) *chsd ldrs: rdn and ev ch over 2f out: wknd over 1f out* **16/1**
-200 **5** *1 1/4* **Boris The Spider**[19] 2351 3-7-12 **55** .......... PHanagan 3 48
(MDHammond) *hld up: rdn 1/2-way: n.d* **25/1**
060- **6** *2* **Choristar**[243] 5547 3-8-3 **60** .......... GDuffield 4 47
(WRMuir) *hld up: plld hrd: sn bhd* **40/1**
10-0 **7** *7* **Five Gold (IRE)**[9] 2614 3-8-8 **65** .......... AMcCarthy 7 33
(BRMillman) *s.i.s: sn prom: wknd over 2f out* **25/1**
4-00 **8** *26* **Ticero**[38] 1881 3-9-6 **77** .......... BDoyle 1 —
(CEBrittain) *chsd ldrs over 4f* **33/1**

1m 24.17s (-1.93) **Going Correction** -0.15s/f (Firm) **8** Ran SP% **115.7**
Speed ratings: **105,99,95,95,93 91,83,53**CSF £4.64 CT £8.29 TOTE £1.80: £1.10, £1.90, £2.00; EX 2.70 Place 6 £175.62, Place 5 £43.25.
**Owner** Abdulla Buhaleeba **Bred** Snailwell Stud Co Ltd **Trained** Newmarket, Suffolk

**FOCUS**
This was a reasonable time for the grade and won by a progressive sort who looks well handicapped.

**NOTEBOOK**
**Royal Prince** confirmed himself an improving performer when running right away from this field. On this showing a mile should prove well within his compass.
**Riley Boys(IRE)** looked to find this trip on the sharp side, and paid late on for trying to mix it with the winner.
**Spin King(IRE)** still looks out-of-sorts at present.
**Fiore Di Bosco(IRE)**, back off her winning juvenile mark, found these too hot for her over this trip and looks to need to drop in class.
CR

# [2481]LINGFIELD (L-H)

Saturday, June 12

**OFFICIAL GOING: Turf course - good (good to firm in places); all-weather course - standard**

Wind: nil Weather: cloudy

## 2881 ARABIAN INTERNATIONAL HORSE FESTIVAL H'CAP 1m 2f (P)

**6:30** (6:30) (E) (0-75,74) 3-Y-0+ **£4,280** (£1,317; £658; £329) **Stalls** Low

Form RPR

5060 **1** **Silvaline**[7] 2687 5-9-2 **63** PDoe 3 73
(TKeddy) *s.s: hld up in last trio: gd prog on wd outside fr 4f out: trckd ldr over 2f out: led ins fnl f: drvn out* **7/1**[3]

110- **2** ½ **Golano**[203] 6052 4-9-13 **74** SSanders 6 83
(CFWall) *settled in midfield: prog over 2f out: sn outpcd: drvn and r.o to chse wnr wl ins fnl f: gaining at fin* **15/2**

5134 **3** 1 **Bank On Him**[8] 2643 9-9-1 **62** JQuinn 12 69
(GLMoore) *trckd ldr: led 3f out: kicked on over 2f out: hdd and one pce ins fnl f* **6/1**[2]

2640 **4** nk **Fiddlers Ford (IRE)**[70] 1249 3-8-12 **72** PRobinson 10 79
(JNoseda) *trckd ldrs: outpcd jst over 2f out: hrd rdn and styd on fr over 1f out: unable to chal* **14/1**

3100 **5** 1 ¼ **Rasid (USA)**[14] 2474 6-9-10 **71** DHolland 8 75
(CADwyer) *trckd ldrs: n.m.r and outpcd over 2f out: drvn and styd on same pce fr over 1f out* **16/1**

2542 **6** ¾ **Lara Falana**[6] 2705 6-9-0 **61** RLMoore 5 64
(MissBSanders) *hld up towards rr: n.m.r on inner over 2f out: sn outpcd: swtchd rt over 1f out: kpt on: no ch* **7/1**[3]

0040 **7** 1 ¼ **Dance Party (IRE)**[15] 2446 4-8-10 **62** (p) NChalmers(5) 4 62
(AMBalding) *racd in midfield: outpcd over 2f out: one pce and no imp after* **25/1**

4/ **8** 3 ½ **Saltango (GER)**[283] 5-9-11 **72** DaneO'Neill 7 66
(AMHales) *racd towards rr: rdn wl over 3f out: struggling after* **20/1**

0100 **9** ¾ **Pharoah's Gold (IRE)**[29] 2078 6-8-13 **60** WSupple 1 52
(DShaw) *t.k.h and hld up in last trio: prog on wd outside 3f out: hanging and no imp over 1f out: eased* **33/1**

5612 **10** ½ **Brave Dane (IRE)**[21] 1935 6-9-13 **74** IMongan 2 65
(AWCarroll) *dwlt: hld up in last trio: rousted along and no prog over 3f out: no ch after* **3/1**[1]

0060 **11** ¾ **Forest Tune (IRE)**[6] 2705 6-8-12 **62** LisaJones(3) 9 52
(BHanbury) *led to 3f out: wkng whn n.m.r on inner over 2f out* **25/1**

035- **12** nk **Welcome Signal**[320] 3645 4-9-6 **67** OUrbina 13 56
(JRFanshawe) *racd in midfield: effrt over 2f out: no prog wl over 1f out: eased* **20/1**

3142 **13** 5 **True Companion**[12] 2537 5-9-10 **74** J-PGuillambert(3) 14 54
(NPLittmoden) *racd in midfield: rdn wl over 3f out: sn struggling* **9/1**

00-0 **14** 2 ½ **Aries (GER)**[19] 2368 4-9-4 **68** DCorby(3) 11 43
(MJWallace) *dwlt: a in rr: rdn 4f out: wknd over 2f out* **33/1**

2m 8.87s (1.02) **Going Correction** +0.25s/f (Slow)
**WFA** 3 from 4yo+ 13lb **14** Ran SP% **121.7**
Speed ratings: **105,104,103,103,102 101,100,98,97,97 96,96,92,90**CSF £53.49 CT £338.42 TOTE £8.80: £3.40, £3.60, £2.70; EX 99.90.
**Owner** Andrew Duffield **Bred** P D And Mrs Player **Trained** Newmarket, Suffolk
■ Stewards Enquiry : P Doe two-day ban: careless riding (Jun 23-24)

**FOCUS**
A fair handicap run at no great pace on early, but things quickened up appreciably in the second half of the contest. The preseence of the placed horses give the form a solid look.

**NOTEBOOK**
**Silvaline** had run very well over this course and distance on his last visit here back in March off a 2lb higher mark and is 10lb lower than on grass. He was brought with a perfectly-timed challenge to score, but the problem with him as far as the future is concerned is that he is not very consistent.
**Golano ◆**, who had shown an aptitude for this surface last autumn and was only 2lb higher than for his last win, ran a blinder on this first start in eight months, especially as he may be better suited by an extra quarter-mile these days. He is one to keep in mind.
**Bank On Him** was always in the right place from which to attack and tried to pinch it rounding the home bend, but he was unable to see it through and just looks held off this sort of mark.
**Fiddlers Ford(IRE)** runs consistently on this surface but, not for the first time, was found out for pace where it really mattered.
**Rasid(USA)**, who is not that consistent, ran better than in his last two turf starts, but he was off a 4lb higher mark than when beaten on his last visit here having won on grass in the meantime.
**Lara Falana**, 5lb lower than on turf, does seem to meet more than her fair of share of trouble in running and getting carried back on the home turn left her with too much to do.
**Brave Dane(IRE)**, in such good form both here and over hurdles of late, would probably have preferred a more end-to-end gallop than this, but even allowing for that he ran a stinker.

## 2882 AIHF AT LINGFIELD PARK 13TH JUNE MEDIAN AUCTION MAIDEN STKS 1m 4f (P)

**7:00** (7:02) (E) 3-4-Y-0 **£3,581** (£1,102; £551; £275) **Stalls** Low

Form RPR

-535 **1** **Peak Of Perfection (IRE)**[10] 2578 3-8-9 73 PRobinson 14 73
(MAJarvis) *mde all: set mod pce: drvn over 1f out: hld on nr fin* **4/1**[2]

020 **2** ½ **Champagne Shadow (IRE)**[47] 1672 3-8-9 64 (b) RLMoore 8 72
(GLMoore) *racd in midfield: prog 4f out: chsd ldrs and rdn 3f out: r.o to take 2nd ins fnl f: gaining at fin* **10/1**

4 **3** 1 ¾ **Shongweni (IRE)**[29] 2093 3-8-9 SSanders 4 69
(PJMcbride) *dwlt: hld up towards rr: outpcd over 3f out: drvn and hanging over 2f out: r.o fr over 1f out: nrst fin* **15/2**[3]

222 **4** nk **Charleston**[9] 2611 3-8-9 73 JFortune 10 69
(JHMGosden) *trckd wnr 9f out to over 5f out: styd cl up: rdn over 3f out: one pce fr over 2f out* **9/4**[1]

0 **5** nk **Vicat Cole**[41] 1794 3-8-9 IMongan 13 68
(HJCyzer) *cl up: chsd wnr 3f out: hrd rdn 2f out: hanging and nt look keen over 1f out: lost pl ins fnl f* **100/1**

-024 **6** 1 **Delightfully**[22] 2267 3-7-13 69 AMedeiros(5) 3 62
(BWHills) *trckd ldrs: rdn 3f out: nt qckn over 2f out: one pce after* **12/1**

0500 **7** ½ **Crown Agent (IRE)**[41] 1801 4-9-10 61 DHolland 5 66
(AMBalding) *hld up in rr: prog to trck wnr over 5f out to 3f out: fdd over 1f out* **15/2**[3]

03 **8** 5 **Muslin**[37] 1912 3-8-5 ow1 OUrbina 7 54
(JRFanshawe) *trckd ldrs: outpcd and pushed along over 3f out: no imp after* **8/1**

00-4 **9** 2 **Maximinus**[37] 1911 4-9-10 59 GBaker 12 55
(MMadgwick) *racd in rr: outpcd over 3f out: effrt u.p over 2f out: hanging and no imp* **66/1**

0-0 **10** 11 **Bee Dees Legacy**[14] 2486 3-8-9 RBrisland 15 37
(GLMoore) *dwlt: hld up in last trio: outpcd and pushed along 4f out: nvr nr ldrs after* **100/1**

**11** nk **Pitton Mill** 4-9-3 CHaddon(7) 2 37
(WGMTurner) *sn pushed along in midfield: outpcd 4f out: sn no ch* **66/1**

54- **12** 6 **Fabranese**[308] 3991 4-9-2 LisaJones(3) 11 22
(PHowling) *dwlt: hld up wl in rr: lft bhd fr 4f out: shuffled along and t.o 2f out* **100/1**

0 **13** 10 **Petrolina (IRE)**[36] 1942 3-8-4 JMackay 9 6
(HMorrison) *chsd wnr to 9f out: losing pl whn hmpd 5f out: wknd: t.o* **100/1**

0-00 **14** 2 ½ **Seagold**[22] 2267 3-8-4 JQuinn 1 2
(CFWall) *a towards rr: lost tch over 3f out: eased: t.o* **66/1**

**15** 23 **Triggers Double** 3-8-9 DRMcCabe 6 —
(KBell) *reluctant to go to post: reluctant to enter stalls: s.s: sn rdn and nvr gng wl: t.o* **33/1**

2m 37.88s (3.64) **Going Correction** +0.25s/f (Slow)
**WFA** 3 from 4yo 15lb **15** Ran SP% **113.6**
Speed ratings: **97,96,95,95,95 94,94,90,89,82 81,77,71,69,54**CSF £39.87 TOTE £4.80: £2.30, £2.60, £2.10; EX 30.10.
**Owner** H R H Sultan Ahmad Shah **Bred** Hrh Sultan Ahmad Shah **Trained** Newmarket, Suffolk

**FOCUS**
Only a modest gallop early and the contest basically became a three-furlong sprint. The form does not look that strong.

**NOTEBOOK**
**Peak Of Perfection(IRE)** was given a typically canny front-running ride by his jockey who set his own modest pace and kept enough in reserve to hold off some ordinary opposition. The form does not look great and he seems likely to struggle back in handicap company off this sort of mark.
**Champagne Shadow(IRE)** ran another decent race, just as he did over this trip on his last visit here, but he is exposed and his proximity advertises the strength of the form.
**Shongweni(IRE)**, having only his second-ever start, stayed on nicely in the latter stages and definitely possesses ability. He looks more of a stayer though, so would probably benefit from a stiffer test.
**Charleston**, runner-up in all three of his starts before this, had every chance but the longer trip and switch to sand did not help him and this was his worst effort yet. His handicap mark looks harsh based on this performance.
**Vicat Cole**, stepping up half a mile from this debut on this switch to sand, was right alongside the winner turning for home but he then displayed a rather strange head carriage and did not look to be putting it all in. This was only his second start through, so it may be wise to give him another chance.
**Delightfully** was stepping up half a mile in trip, but lack of pace rather than lack of stamina appeared to be the problem.
**Crown Agent(IRE)** is completely exposed and probably ran to his handicap mark.
**Muslin**, up in trip for this sand debut, ended up well beaten, but her rider was by no means hard on her and she could still be capable of better now that she can be handicapped.

## 2883 ETIHAD AIRWAYS CLASSIFIED STKS 1m (P)

**7:30** (7:32) (F) 3-Y-0+ **£3,031** (£866; £433) **Stalls** High

Form RPR

5005 **1** **Deign To Dance (IRE)**[18] 2377 3-8-5 62 RLMoore 5 64
(JGPortman) *dwlt: hld up wl in rr: prog on inner over 2f out: squeezed through and drvn to ld 1f out: styd on wl* **16/1**

**2** ½ **Millenio (GER)**[83] 4-9-7 64 OUrbina 3 68
(DFlood) *trckd clr ldrs: rdn and effrt over 2f out: prog to chal and ev ch 1f out: pressed wnr after: a hld* **11/2**[3]

-000 **3** 1 **Chorus Beauty**[18] 2377 3-8-6 63 FNorton 11 62
(GWragg) *settled in rr: pushed along 1/2-way: prog over 2f out: drvn to chal 1f out: unable qck* **16/1**

3200 **4** 2 **Fortune Point (IRE)**[16] 2121 6-9-4 61 IMongan 10 58
(AWCarroll) *trckd clr ldrs: prog to ld 2f out: hdd 1f out: nt qckn* **14/1**

54-4 **5** 1 ¾ **Royal Advocate**[17] 2406 4-9-6 63 SWhitworth 1 56
(JWHills) *trckd ldr over 4f out: led briefly over 2f out: sn hrd rdn: fdd over 1f out* **12/1**

4030 **6** nk **Little Eye (IRE)**[25] 2217 3-8-9 63 NPollard 7 56
(JRBest) *sn drvn and struggling in midfield: nvr on terms* **16/1**

6143 **7** shd **Raheel (IRE)**[80] 1097 4-9-3 60 (t) DHolland 8 52
(PMitchell) *s.i.s: hld up in rr: prog on wd outside over 2f out: nt rch ldrs over 1f out: wknd fnl f* **11/2**[3]

00-5 **8** 1 ¼ **Second Warning**[52] 1541 3-8-8 62 DaneO'Neill 6 52
(DJDaly) *s.s: a towards rr: rdn over 2f out: no prog* **25/1**

1-66 **9** 1 ¾ **Didnt Tell My Wife**[17] 2406 5-9-3 63 LisaJones(3) 4 49
(CFWall) *a in rr: rdn and no prog 3f out* **4/1**[1]

-003 **10** 1 **Swift Alchemist**[39] 1877 4-9-2 62 GBaker 2 42
(MrsHSweeting) *chsd ldr to over 4f out: sn u.str.p and nt run on: losing pl whn n.m.r over 2f out* **7/1**

000- **11** 5 **Fulvio (USA)**[165] 6256 4-9-6 63 PDoe 9 35
(JamiePoulton) *chsd ldrs: rdn over 2f out: wknd over 1f out: eased* **25/1**

133- **12** 6 **Florian**[226] 5837 6-9-3 63 RMiles(3) 12 21
(TGMills) *led at str pce to over 2f out: wknd* **5/1**[2]

1m 41.24s (1.69) **Going Correction** +0.25s/f (Slow)
**WFA** 3 from 4yo+ 11lb **12** Ran SP% **119.6**
Speed ratings: **101,100,99,97,95 95,95,94,92,91 86,80**CSF £102.64 TOTE £21.10: £5.30, £2.80, £6.80; EX 268.50.
**Owner** Mrs S J Portman **Bred** Noel O'Callaghan **Trained** Compton, Berks

**FOCUS**
A tight classified event with 3lb covering the whole field and the form is modest. The leaders may have gone off too quick as none of them figured in the finish.

**NOTEBOOK**
**Deign To Dance(IRE)**, one of three horses 3lb well in with the rest of the field on adjusted official ratings, took advantage of a nice gap that presented itself on the inside racing down the home straight to get off the mark at the 11th attempt. She has dropped a fair way in the handicap and this longer trip seemed to help.
**Millenio(GER)**, a winner on sand in his native Germany, was making his British debut and showed enough on this first start in three months to suggest he can win a small race here.
**Chorus Beauty**, another of those 3lb well in at the weights, has struggled in turf handicaps since winning a maiden here in December and ran just a fair race on this return to Polytrack. She is not one of the stable's stars.
**Fortune Point(IRE)**, returning to Polytrack after a couple of outings on turf and a victory over hurdles, managed to get to the front rounding the home bend, but was then done for foot and this trip looks inadequate for him now.
**Royal Advocate**, well adrift of the clear leader for much of the way but clear of the rest, looked to be going best approaching the home bend but, when the cavalry arrived, the response was minimal.
**Little Eye(IRE)** has become very disappointing and is still to get off the mark after 16 attempts.
**Raheel(IRE)** may have just needed this after a three-month break, but could also have done with an extra quarter-mile.

**Didnt Tell My Wife** is still to recapture his best form this year and made no show at all. *Official explanation: jockey said gelding was never travelling*
**Swift Alchemist**, on of those 3lb well in on adjusted official ratings, was unable to get to the front early and eventually had to admit defeat.
**Fulvio(USA)** *Official explanation: jockey said gelding tired rapidly in the closing stages.*
**Florian**, racing for the first time in eight months, is a confirmed front-runner but he went off far too fast and fell in a heap on the home turn.

## 2884 TERRY WEST MEMORIAL FILLIES' MEDIAN AUCTION MAIDEN STKS 5f
**8:00** (8:01) (F) 2-Y-O **£3,311** (£946; £473) **Stalls** High

Form RPR
2 **1** **Kwame**[18] [2376] 2-8-11 ... SWKelly 6 70+
(MissECLavelle) *trckd ldrs: nt clr run and swtchd lft 1f out: drvn and r.o to ld last strides* **7/2**[2]
3 **2** *shd* **Miss Cassia**[59] [1399] 2-8-11 ... PDobbs 7 70
(RHannon) *trckd ldrs gng easily: led over 1f out: drvn fnl f: hdd last strides* **15/8**[1]
04 **3** *3/4* **Lily Lenat**[10] [2574] 2-8-11 ... DSweeney 2 67
(JRBoyle) *racd on outer: trckd ldrs: effrt whn bmpd 1f out: r.o fnl f: a jst hld* **8/1**
**4** *hd* **Right Answer** 2-8-11 ... JQuinn 3 66
(APJarvis) *hld up in tch: nt clr run briefly 2f out and again 1f out: shkn up and r.o ins fnl f: gaining at fin* **6/1**[3]
0 **5** *hd* **Tight Circle**[17] [2396] 2-8-11 ... JMackay 5 66+
(MrsGHarvey) *a.p: hrd rdn to chal 1f out: ev ch: one pce nr fin* **33/1**
**6** *1/2* **Epitomise** 2-8-11 ... SSanders 4 64
(RMBeckett) *outpcd and wl bhd: sme prog over 1f out: r.o wl last 150yds: nrst fin* **14/1**
34 **7** *3/4* **Gaudalpin (IRE)**[59] [1399] 2-8-11 ... SRighton 11 61
(MJAttwater) *led 4f out to over 1f out: wknd ins fnl f* **14/1**
50 **8** *nk* **Aberdeen Park**[28] [2111] 2-8-11 ... GBaker 8 60
(MrsHSweeting) *hld up in tch: effrt on inner whn hmpd over 1f out: kpt on again ins fnl f* **25/1**
**9** *1 1/4* **Saucepot** 2-8-11 ... ADaly 1 56
(MDIUsher) *racd on outer: sn outpcd and bhd: styd on fnl f: n.d* **20/1**
**10** *6* **Apple Of My Eye** 2-8-11 ... WSupple 9 35
(JRJenkins) *dwlt: outpcd and nvr on terms* **20/1**
0 **11** *6* **Beeches Theatre (IRE)**[10] [2585] 2-8-11 ... IMongan 10 14
(RBrotherton) *led for 1f: sn rdn and lost pl: wkng whn n.m.r over 1f out* **100/1**

59.64 secs (0.77) **Going Correction** -0.05s/f (Good) **11** Ran SP% **113.0**
Speed ratings: **91,90,89,89,89 88,87,86,84,74 65**CSF £9.23 TOTE £4.20: £2.20, £1.10, £3.00; EX 8.50.
**Owner** First Impressions Racing Group 2 **Bred** Barry Minty **Trained** Hatherden, Hants
■ Stewards Enquiry : I Mongan two-day ban: careless riding (Jun 23-24)
S W Kelly five-day ban (includes four deferred days): careless riding (Jun 23-27)

**FOCUS**
Not a great maiden with the first eight finishing in a heap and one or two traffic problems and the form is just fair.

**NOTEBOOK**
**Kwame** confirmed the promise of her debut effort on this track. She had to wait a while in order to get a run and gave the third a bump as she was switched out for her effort, but she produced a nice turn of foot to snatch the race and was the winner on merit. An extra furlong would certainly not come amiss.
**Miss Cassia**, given a little break since her promising debut, which is unusual for the yard, travelled really well before hitting the front but she could never break clear. Hanging left under pressure in the closing stages, she had the race snatched from her and does have a small question mark hanging over her.
**Lily Lenat** had every chance when getting a bump from the winner a furlong out, but the way she gathered herself and ran on again suggests she could do with an extra furlong.
**Right Answer ◆**, a 25,000gns yearling out of a winning half-sister to Mind Games, did not enjoy a clear passage at various stages yet still finished right on the heels of the principals. The form may be modest, but she should improve from this and may turn out the best of these.
**Tight Circle** ran a good deal better than on her debut and may have been unlucky not to finish third, as she was momentarily impeded when the runner-up hung across her near the line and that was enough for her to lose two places.
**Epitomise**, a 16,000gns half-sister to Yarrita to Mirasol Princess, took time to find her stride but gradually gasped what was required as the race progressed. She seems to have some ability.
**Gaudalpin(IRE)** made much of the running against the stands' rail, but did not get home and is beginning to look a short runner.

## 2885 HEVER LAKESIDE THEATRE H'CAP 6f
**8:30** (8:32) (F) (0-55,55) 3-Y-O+ **£3,171** (£906; £453) **Stalls** High

Form RPR
5532 **1** **Double M**[5] [2724] 7-9-5 **53** ... (v) RThomas(5) 8 64
(MrsLRichards) *settled towards rr: prog fr 2f out: rdn to ld last 100yds: sn clr* **7/2**[1]
5-00 **2** *1 1/4* **Indian Bazaar (IRE)**[5] [2724] 8-9-4 **50** ... RMiles(3) 4 57
(NEBerry) *mde most: rdn over 1f out: hdd and outpcd last 100yds* **25/1**
0020 **3** *1/2* **Night Cap (IRE)**[54] [1497] 5-8-11 **43** ... J-PGuillambert(3) 16 49
(TDMccarthy) *prom: rdn and cl up over 1f out: styd on same pce fnl f* **14/1**
0344 **4** *2* **Davids Mark**[8] [2663] 4-9-8 **51** ... SSanders 14 51
(JRJenkins) *racd against nr side rail: trckd ldrs: effrt 2f out: drvn and one pce fnl f* **9/1**[3]
0366 **5** *1* **Attorney**[9] [2626] 6-9-6 **49** ... (v) WSupple 3 46
(DShaw) *settled towards rr: rdn over 1f out: kpt on same pce: n.d* **16/1**
2223 **6** *hd* **Aintnecessarilyso**[6] [2707] 6-8-13 **47** ... MSavage(5) 12 43
(NEBerry) *dwlt: racd in rr: rdn over 2f out: kpt on fr over 1f out: n.d* **9/1**[3]
0-54 **7** *3/4* **Yorkies Boy**[5] [2739] 9-9-11 **54** ... RLMoore 13 48
(JMBradley) *racd towards rr: effrt 2f out: styng on whn nt clr run 1f out: no ch* **8/1**[2]
5005 **8** *shd* **Tender (IRE)**[6] [2707] 4-9-12 **55** ... (p) FNorton 19 49
(MrsStefLiddiard) *chsd ldrs: rdn 2f out: no prog over 1f out* **14/1**
0600 **9** *hd* **Long Weekend (IRE)**[5] [2735] 6-8-13 **45** ... JFMcDonald(3) 17 38
(DShaw) *wl in rr and nt gng wl: sme prog 2f out: nvr on terms* **25/1**
0240 **10** *2* **Badou**[2] [2803] 4-9-0 **43** ... (v) CCogan 9 30
(LMontagueHall) *racd in midfield: rdn 1/2-way: no prog over 1f out* **20/1**
6060 **11** *1/2* **Gun Salute**[6] [2707] 4-9-3 **46** ... (b[1]) JFortune 10 32
(GLMoore) *prom: drvn to chse ldr briefly 2f out: wknd over 1f out* **12/1**
0015 **12** *1* **Danakim**[12] [2524] 7-9-0 **50** ... DFentiman(7) 7 33
(JRWeymes) *mostly pressed ldr to 2f out: wknd u.p* **25/1**
0-40 **13** *1 1/2* **Mannora**[6] [2707] 4-9-10 **53** ... JMackay 6 31
(PHowling) *s.s: wl in rr: effrt on outer 2f out: sn no prog* **25/1**
4000 **14** *nk* **Mayzin (IRE)**[9] [2628] 4-9-8 **51** ... (p) DSweeney 18 28
(RMFlower) *s.i.s: a wl in rr* **10/1**
4503 **15** *1/2* **Star Lad (IRE)**[8] [2663] 4-9-3 **46** ... (b) IMongan 5 22
(RBrotherton) *nvr beyond midfield: drvn and struggling over 2f out* **33/1**
-000 **16** *3/4* **Run On**[6] [2707] 6-9-7 **50** ... SRighton 2 23
(DGBridgwater) *racd on outer: outpcd: nvr on terms* **33/1**
1242 **17** *1/2* **Enjoy The Buzz**[96] [990] 5-9-2 **45** ... CCatlin 15 17
(JMBradley) *a wl in rr: rdn and no prog over 2f out* **9/1**[3]
-306 **18** *15* **Second Minister**[77] [1140] 5-9-0 **50** ... (bt) LTreadwell(7) 1 —
(DFlood) *towards rr: wknd over 2f out: t.o* **16/1**

1m 11.01s (-0.64) **Going Correction** -0.05s/f (Good) **18** Ran SP% **131.2**
Speed ratings: **102,100,99,97,95 95,94,94,94,91 90,89,87,86,86 85,84,64**CSF £109.34 CT £1183.18 TOTE £4.30: £1.80, £7.40, £7.10, £2.20; EX 310.20.
**Owner** Bryan Mathieson **Bred** M G Tebbitt **Trained** Funtington, W Sussex

**FOCUS**
A big field and a competitive race, but this was a seller in all but name. The whole field migrated to the stands' side, but very few got into it.

**NOTEBOOK**
**Double M** has lost none of his zest and on this occasion his challenge was timed perfectly. This looks to be his best trip now, but his level of form is well established and a rise in the handicap would leave him vulnerable.
**Indian Bazaar(IRE)**, racing over six furlongs for the first time in well over two and a half years, was suited by the sharp track and after making almost the running had the race snatched from him in the last few strides.
**Night Cap(IRE)**, beaten in banded company in his last two starts, had every chance from the furlong pole but found an extra spurt beyond him. He is yet to win on turf and without a win of any sort in well over two years, so cannot be relied on to repeat this.
**Davids Mark** ran a solid race against the stands' rail, but is another that has become hard to win with despite being 10lb lower than for his last victory.
**Attorney**, who has found his niche in banded company on sand this year, was never seen with a chance despite staying on and is without a win on turf in well over three years.
**Aintnecessarilyso**, a hard horse to win with, needs his effort timing just right but on this occasion he found everything happening too quickly for him.
**Mayzin(IRE)** *Official explanation: trainer said gelding was found to have a large haematoma on its off-fore shoulder on returning home*

## 2886 FIND ALL YOUR WINNERS AT TIPS.TV H'CAP 7f
**9:00** (9:01) (F) (0-55,55) 3-Y-O+ **£3,164** (£904; £452) **Stalls** High

Form RPR
0044 **1** **Espada (IRE)**[16] [2426] 8-9-7 **48** ... (b) SWKelly 7 58
(JAOsborne) *enterprisingly rdn: mde all: 3l clr 3f out: hrd rdn over 1f out: jst lasted* **12/1**
1631 **2** *1/2* **Shirley Oaks (IRE)**[4] [2762] 6-9-3 **49** 6ex ... NChalmers(5) 17 58
(MissZCDavison) *chsd ldrs: rdn over 2f out: effrt over 1f out: chsd wnr ins fnl f: clsng at fin* **13/2**[3]
5140 **3** *nk* **Scarrottoo**[6] [2703] 6-10-0 **55** ... ADaly 3 63
(SCWilliams) *racd on outer: hld up wl in rr: prog over 2f out: drvn and styd on wl fr over 1f out: too much to do* **8/1**
5230 **4** *shd* **Balerno**[10] [2597] 5-9-9 **50** ... NDay 14 58
(RIngram) *hld up in midfield: prog over 2f out: hrd rdn and styd on fr over 1f out: too much to do* **8/1**
0244 **5** *1* **Lily Of The Guild (IRE)**[16] [2428] 5-9-12 **53** ... IMongan 16 58
(WSKittow) *hld up in midfield: prog over 2f out: drvn to chse wnr wl over 1f out: no imp: wknd ins fnl f* **11/2**[1]
3500 **6** *1 1/2* **Single Track Mind**[15] [2441] 6-8-12 **44** ... (p) AQuinn(5) 11 45
(JRBoyle) *settled in midfield: rdn and effrt over 2f out: kpt on fnl f: n.d* **40/1**
-136 **7** *1* **Royal Racer (FR)**[37] [1910] 6-9-9 **50** ... NPollard 9 49
(JRBest) *prom: rdn 3f out: lost pl over 1f out: one pce after* **20/1**
0344 **8** *hd* **Lord Chamberlain**[1] [2833] 11-9-5 **53** ... (b) CJDavies(7) 20 51
(JMBradley) *s.s: racd in last pair: rdn 1/2-way: no prog tl styd on wl fr over 1f out: nrst fin* **10/1**
-200 **9** *hd* **Treetops Hotel (IRE)**[14] [2483] 5-9-13 **54** ... DSweeney 8 52
(BRJohnson) *dwlt: hld up in last pair: nudged along over 2f out: styd on steadily fr over 1f out: nvr nr ldrs* **20/1**
1546 **10** *shd* **Kinsman (IRE)**[2] [2803] 7-9-9 **53** ... (b) J-PGuillambert(3) 6 50
(TDMccarthy) *dwlt: hld up towards rr: effrt over 2f out: one pce and nvr rchd ldrs* **14/1**
2100 **11** *3/4* **Grand View**[18] [2384] 8-8-11 **38** ... (p) JQuinn 5 33
(JRWeymes) *chsd ldrs: rdn and no prog over 2f out: fdd over 1f out* **20/1**
-060 **12** *2* **Chantry Falls (IRE)**[11] [2556] 4-9-4 **45** ... (b[1]) SSanders 1 35
(JGGiven) *racd alone on far side: nvr on terms* **33/1**
1050 **13** *nk* **Loch Laird**[6] [2703] 9-9-11 **52** ... GBaker 4 41
(MMadgwick) *racd on outer: nvr beyond midfield: shuffled along and btn 2f out* **20/1**
2240 **14** *1* **Annijaz**[16] [2428] 7-10-0 **55** ... RLMoore 19 42
(JMBradley) *dwlt: a wl in rr* **6/1**[2]
0005 **15** *1* **Moonglade (USA)**[18] [2384] 4-8-8 **35** ... (b) JMcAuley 18 19
(MissJFeilden) *dwlt: sn chsd wnr: rdn 3f out: wknd wl over 1f out* **33/1**
0000 **16** *2 1/2* **Dr Fox (IRE)**[19] [2359] 3-8-2 **44** ... (p) RThomas(5) 13 22
(KAMorgan) *prom to 1/2-way: sn lost pl and struggling* **50/1**
5000 **17** *5* **Mister Completely (IRE)**[14] [2484] 3-8-10 **47** ... CCatlin 15 12
(JRBest) *dwlt: a in rr: wknd 2f out* **33/1**

1m 24.22s (0.01) **Going Correction** -0.05s/f (Good)
**WFA** 3 from 4yo+ 10lb **17** Ran SP% **120.9**
Speed ratings: **97,96,96,95,94 93,91,91,91,91 90,88,87,86,85 82,77**CSF £75.20 CT £697.29 TOTE £11.30: £2.30, £2.00, £2.90, £1.90; EX 78.80 Place 6 £216.65, Place 5 £87.07.
**Owner** John Livock And Partners **Bred** Pat Beirne **Trained** Upper Lambourn, Berks

**FOCUS**
Another big field for a modest handicap and the pace was only ordinary. The majority of the field raced stands' side though one stayed far side. The form is solid enough for the grade.

**NOTEBOOK**
**Espada(IRE)**, who has plummeted down the handicap, was given another chance in the blinkers and managed to get across to the stands' rail from his low draw in front without causing any interference. The crucial thing was that he settled much better this time and he managed to keep enough in reserve to hold all his rivals at bay. This was a decent tactical ride.
**Shirley Oaks(IRE)** ran a fine race under a 6lb penalty for her Salisbury win and, even though her strike rate is poor, she is running consistently well at the moment.
**Scarrottoo** came from off the pace to snatch third and put up a fair effort under top weight, but he probably needs a stiffer seven than this.
**Balerno** was another to do his best work late on and probably found this sharp seven an inadequate test, but his awful strike rate has to be a concern.
**Lily Of The Guild(IRE)**, without a win for nearly two years, was close enough if good enough a furlong from home, but was beaten soon afterwards.
**Single Track Mind** stayed on to be nearest at the finish, but we have been here before.
**Lord Chamberlain** was always going to find this too sharp and his finishing position was as close as he got.

**Chantry Falls(IRE)**, blinkered for the first time, elected to race alone on the far side from his number one draw. The tactic did not work, but he is still a maiden and out of form this season anyway.
T/Plt: £1,364.60 to a £1 stake. Pool: £38,228.85. 20.45 winning tickets. T/Qpdt: £345.10 to a £1 stake. Pool: £2,658.40. 5.70 winning tickets. JN

# 2843 SANDOWN (R-H)
Saturday, June 12

**OFFICIAL GOING: Good to firm**

## 2887 ROYALTIES GOLD H'CAP — 1m 1f
**1:00** (1:01) (C) (0-90,89) 3-Y-O — **£10,322** (£3,176; £1,588; £794) **Stalls** High

Form — RPR

3010 **1** **Cimyla (IRE)**[7] 2692 3-9-4 **86** ............ GBaker 9 98+
(CFWall) *swtg: hld up in tch: hdwy to ld ins fnl 2f: pushed 3l clr ins fnl f: comf* **12/1**

-262 **2** *2* **Lets Roll**[21] 2306 3-8-3 **71** ............ TWilliams 10 77
(CWThornton) *lw: bhd: hdwy 3f out: nt clr run 2f out: swtchd rt and r.o fnl f to take 2nd last half f but no ch w wnr* **9/2**[2]

-202 **3** *nk* **Rondelet (IRE)**[12] 2517 3-8-8 **76** ............ RLMoore 1 81
(RMBeckett) *s.i.s: bhd: rdn 3f out: hdwy fr 2f out: str run ins fnl f: kpt on wl cl home* **10/1**

0024 **4** *shd* **Cartronageeraghlad (IRE)**[10] 2591 3-8-9 **77** ............ DaneO'Neill 7 82
(JAOsborne) *s.i.s: bhd: gd hdwy on outside fr 2f out: fin wl but nt rch ldrs* **25/1**

1-00 **5** *1 1/2* **Blue Daze**[7] 2694 3-8-0 **68** ............ RSmith 6 70
(RHannon) *lw: t.k.h: chsd ldrs: rdn 2f out: one pce ins fnl f* **50/1**

4216 **6** *1/2* **Woody Valentine (USA)**[25] 2202 3-8-12 **80** ............ KDalgleish 4 81
(MJohnston) *sn w ldr: led after 2f: rdn 3f out: hdd ins fnl 2f: wknd ins fnl f* **7/2**[1]

-601 **7** *1/2* **Balearic Star (IRE)**[19] 2371 3-8-1 **69** ............ AMcCarthy 2 69
(BRMillman) *lw: bhd: hdwy 3f out: sn rdn and one pce: kpt on again fr over 1f out* **9/1**

-213 **8** *1/2* **Sunisa (IRE)**[14] 2472 3-8-10 **78** ............ PRobinson 3 77
(BWHills) *chsd ldrs: rdn 2f out: wknd fnl f* **13/2**

6-03 **9** *1* **Olivander**[6] 2704 3-8-7 **75** ............ (b) SSanders 11 72
(GAButler) *bhd and sn reminders: rdn and kpt on u.p fr over 1f out but n.d* **16/1**

20-0 **10** *hd* **Zweibrucken (IRE)**[25] 2202 3-9-1 **83** ............ JFortune 8 80
(SKirk) *chsd ldrs: rdn 3f out: one pce whn hmpd 2f out:wknd over 1f out* **20/1**

16-5 **11** *1/2* **Shalaya (IRE)**[21] 2281 3-9-5 **87** ............ DHolland 5 83
(SirMichaelStoute) *bhd: rdn and sme hdwy on ins over 2f out: nvr gng pce to rch ldrs and wknd qckly fnl f* **6/1**[3]

1-06 **12** *1/2* **Deraasaat**[24] 2221 3-9-7 **89** ............ WSupple 12 84
(EALDunlop) *led 2f: styd w ldr 4f: rdn and edgd lft 2f out: son btn* **20/1**

1m 54.29s (-1.82) **Going Correction** -0.05s/f (Good) **12** Ran SP% **116.0**
Speed ratings: **106,104,103,103,102 102,101,101,100,100 99,99**CSF £60.90 CT £575.84 TOTE £13.30: £3.60, £1.70, £3.90; EX 87.20.
**Owner** Peter Botham **Bred** Dr D G St John And Mrs Sherry Collier **Trained** Newmarket, Suffolk

**FOCUS**
A competitive handicap where any number could be given a chance beforehand, and it was the change of pace that Cimyla produced over a furlong out that sealed the race. The runner-up gives the form a sound look.

**NOTEBOOK**
**Cimyla(IRE)**, whose two poor runs have come at Newmarket, where he failed to handle the dip and lost his action on both occasions, was running off a 2lb lower mark than last Saturday and, having sat towards the rear for the early part of the race, made good headway to nip up early leader Woody Valentine's inner and quicken well over a furlong and a half out. This was a smart performance and, ignoring the two Newmarket runs, he has a highly-progressive profile.
**Lets Roll**, an unlucky loser at Newmarket when meeting with trouble in running, again failed to get the clearest of passages through and chased the winner unavailingly in the final half furlong. He undoubtedly has a similar race in him, but continues to creep up the handicap.
**Rondelet(IRE)**, out of luck back in maiden company at Chepstow, got much more competitive than on his last handicap outing at York when hanging, and was finishing well having found himself with a bit too much to do after a sluggish start.
**Cartronageeraghlad(IRE)** was another to be tardy at the gate and he was finishing to even better effect than the third. He has found his form again after a slow start to the season and looks well worth trying back over one mile two.
**Blue Daze** ◆ had yet to make a show in two starts this season, but she was trying a new trip and ran well without truly seeing it out. She had been running over seven so maybe a mile will prove ideal, and she remains 6lb lower than at the start of the year.
**Woody Valentine(USA)** seems to be at his best with a little cut in the ground, although he is fully effective on a sound surface. He tried to do it from the front, but was beaten well over a furlong out and faded late on - it being later reported he lost a plate. He is better than this, as we saw with an unlucky sixth behind Gatwick in an ultra competitive Goodwood handicap last month, and a return to easier ground conditions will help to show his true colours. *Official explanation: vet said gelding had lost a plate*
**Balearic Star(IRE)** won a decent handicap at Windsor towards the end of May - the first and second Foley Prince and Habenero confirming the form the previous day - but he could never get involved and just stayed on steadily.
**Sunisa(IRE)** has run two of her better races on the All-Weather and may not want ground conditions too fast. *Official explanation: jockey said filly was unsuited by the ground*
**Olivander** is not the easiest of rides and was being given reminders early in the race. He plugged on down the straight but is one to avoid.
**Shalaya(IRE)** stopped sharply in the final furlong and something may have gone amiss.

## 2888 32RED ONLINE CASINO MAIDEN STKS — 1m 2f 7y
**1:35** (1:37) (D) 3-Y-O — **£5,668** (£1,744; £872; £436) **Stalls** High

Form — RPR

00 **1** **Trew Class**[33] 2001 3-8-9 ............ PRobinson 6 74
(MHTompkins) *lw: trckd ldrs: wnt 2nd 2f out: sn rdn: styd on wl to ld fnl 100yds* **25/1**

60- **2** *1/2* **Meissen**[252] 5363 3-8-9 ............ TQuinn 7 73
(ACStewart) *trckd ldr to 2f out: sn rdn and one pce: rallied and squeezed through ins fnl f to chse wnr cl home* **9/1**

0- **3** *1/2* **Dalisay (IRE)**[253] 5345 3-8-9 ............ JFortune 9 72
(SirMichaelStoute) *b.bkwd: in tch: hdwy 4f out: chsng ldrs and edgd lft u.p appr fnl f: green and styd on ins last* **7/1**[3]

2 **4** *nk* **Line Drawing**[36] 1926 3-9-0 ............ SSanders 2 76
(BWHills) *lw: led: rdn 2f out: hdd and no ex fnl 100yds* **9/4**[2]

0 **5** *1/2* **Rawdon (IRE)**[59] 1395 3-9-0 ............ (v[1]) RHavlin 3 76
(JHMGosden) *bhd: rdn 5f out: hdwy on outside whn pushed lft over 1f out: rdn and hung rt ins last: fnd no ex* **11/1**

**6** *1/2* **Mijdaaf (FR)** 3-9-0 ............ PMcCabe 10 75
(ACStewart) *neat: s.i.s: bhd: hdwy on outside fnl 2f: gng on cl home but nt rch ldrs* **16/1**

0-03 **7** *shd* **Zuma (IRE)**[14] 2479 3-9-0 **80** ............ DHolland 11 74
(RHannon) *lw: hmpd sn after 1f: styd chsng ldrs: rdn 4f out: no ex u.p ins last* **15/8**[1]

0 **8** *14* **Bold Phoenix (IRE)**[21] 2311 3-9-0 ............ JMcAuley 8 48
(ACStewart) *b.bkwd: in tch tl wknd over 3f out* **50/1**

0-4 **9** *3 1/2* **Greek Star**[19] 2357 3-8-9 ............ PMakin(5) 5 41
(KAMorgan) *lw: a in rr* **50/1**

**10** *1 1/4* **Jacobin (USA)** 3-9-0 ............ SWhitworth 4 39
(PJMcbride) *tall: strong: slowly away: a bhd* **50/1**

2m 9.70s (-0.48) **Going Correction** -0.05s/f (Good) **10** Ran SP% **112.0**
Speed ratings: **99,98,98,97,97 97,97,85,83,82**CSF £220.26 TOTE £48.10: £8.40, £2.60, £2.30; EX 408.30.
**Owner** Russell Trew Roofing Ltd **Bred** Aylesfield Farms Stud **Trained** Newmarket, Suffolk

**FOCUS**
Not a strong maiden with the form horses below par and the first three home were the only fillies in the field.

**NOTEBOOK**
**Trew Class** had hinted at ability on her debut at Warwick, but failed to get competitive at Windsor - both runs on soft ground - and this faster surface enabled her to show her true form, although she would not want it much faster. She travelled nicely for most of the way and threw down her challenge from quarter of a mile out, responding well for pressure and nosing ahead well into the final furlong. She will have to go handicapping now and may struggle depending on what sort of mark she gets.
**Meissen** was tried in Listed company on her second and final start at two and seems to have progressed well as a three-year-old. She was just getting going close home and momentarily looked as though she may claim the winner. Like Trew Class her future lies in handicaps.
**Dalisay(IRE)**, a 340,000gns yearling, did not run up to expectations on her sole start at two - albeit in a decent race with Oaks winner Ouija Board in third - but she was always going to make a better three-year-old. She ran well on ground she looked uncomfortable on and, as her breeding suggests, a softer surface will suit better.
**Line Drawing**, a promising second at Chester on his debut, had a soft time of it in front and ultimately disappointed. Despite this he should have little bother finding a poor maiden up north, where his trainer sometimes sends them.
**Rawdon(IRE)** was being ridden a long way from home in the first-time visor and, although running on down the straight, hung right and is not one to trust.
**Mijdaaf(FR)** made a pleasing debut after a tardy start and was edging nearer with every stride at the line.
**Zuma(IRE)** was squeezed up on the rail and hampered early and never looked comfortable thereafter, being niggled for most of the way. He can be given another chance as he had done nothing wrong prior to this and if anything had been progressive.

## 2889 ONE ACCOUNT H'CAP — 5f 6y
**2:10** (2:13) (D) (0-80,77) 3-Y-O — **£5,408** (£1,664; £832; £416) **Stalls** High

Form — RPR

2223 **1** **Baron Rhodes**[8] 2650 3-9-0 **73** ............ TEaves(3) 6 82
(JSWainwright) *trckd ldrs: led jst ins fnl f: hld on all out* **8/1**

-322 **2** *hd* **Intriguing Glimpse**[20] 2326 3-9-4 **74** ............ SSanders 7 82
(MissBSanders) *lw: bhd: rapid hdwy over 1f out: str chal ins fnl f: nt quite get up* **3/1**[1]

-535 **3** *1 1/2* **Treasure Cay**[22] 2269 3-9-5 **75** ............ (t) PaulEddery 2 78
(PWD'Arcy) *s.i.s: bhd: str run fnl f: fin wl but nt rch ldrs* **9/2**[2]

2310 **4** *1 1/4* **Borzoi Maestro**[11] 2552 3-9-7 **77** ............ ADaly 4 75
(JLSpearing) *led tl hdd 2f out: styd chsng ldrs tl nt qckn ins fnl f: wknd fnl 100yds* **16/1**

0501 **5** *hd* **Simpsons Mount (IRE)**[5] 2726 3-8-12 **68** 6ex ............ RLMoore 3 66
(RMFlower) *sn chsng ldrs: led 2f out: hdd jst ins fnl f: wknd fnl 100yds* **8/1**

-004 **6** *1 1/4* **Mirasol Princess**[22] 2264 3-9-6 **76** ............ TQuinn 9 69
(DKIvory) *chsd ldrs: rdn 2f out: wknd ins fnl f* **9/1**

-606 **7** *hd* **After The Show**[29] 2082 3-8-11 **67** ............ WSupple 8 59
(JRJenkins) *bhd: effrt 2f out: n.d and sn outpcd* **13/2**[3]

0004 **8** *nk* **Dellagio (IRE)**[20] 2326 3-8-1 **57** ............ JQuinn 1 48
(CADwyer) *hld up in rr: shkn up and kpt on fnl f but n.d* **12/1**

6304 **9** *6* **Baylaw Star**[8] 2650 3-9-3 **73** ............ DHolland 5 43
(JBalding) *in tch: rdn 2f out: sn wknd* **8/1**

62.09 secs (-0.10) **Going Correction** -0.05s/f (Good) **9** Ran SP% **113.4**
Speed ratings: **98,97,95,93,92 90,90,90,80**CSF £31.65 CT £122.27 TOTE £7.20: £2.20, £1.30, £2.40; EX 19.90.
**Owner** I Barran & P Rhodes **Bred** E Smith **Trained** Kennythorpe, N Yorks

**FOCUS**
A fair race but probably only ordinary form. Two in-form fillies were left to battle it out and it was Baron Rhodes who just found enough to hold Intriguing Glimpse.

**NOTEBOOK**
**Baron Rhodes** had been edging her way up the handicap this season despite not winning - unlucky after nearly unseating rider from a flip start latest - but she got her deserved success and did it bravely, quickening up to come through and lead before just holding off the favourite.
**Intriguing Glimpse** got warm beforehand and that may have proved her undoing. She came with a strong late challenge, but ran out of time.
**Treasure Cay** seemed to appreciate this drop back to five furlongs, but again did himself no favours with a slow start despite the aid of a 'Monty Roberts' rug. He was finishing strongly and seems best suited to a stiff five.
**Borzoi Maestro** showed up well for a long way and only caved in in the final half furlong.
**Simpsons Mount(IRE)** was not disgraced in his bid to follow up Monday's Folkestone win and may have done a bit too much early in the race. *Official explanation: jockey said gelding hung both ways*
**Mirasol Princess** continues to disappoint and never reached a challenging position.
**Dellagio(IRE)** was racing here off a 28lb lower mark than at the start of the season and has to take advantage of his declining mark sooner rather than later. *Official explanation: jockey said colt hung left*
**Baylaw Star** *Official explanation: jockey said colt hung left*

## 2890 PALLETLINE PLC MAIDEN STKS — 7f 16y
**2:40** (2:44) (D) 2-Y-O — **£4,953** (£1,524; £762; £381) **Stalls** High

Form — RPR

**1** **Jalamid (IRE)** 2-9-0 ............ (t) WSupple 13 75
(JHMGosden) *lw: gd sort: strong: led 1f: styd chsng ldrs: wnt 2f 4f out: led jst ins fnl 2f: pushed along and hld on wl fnl f* **5/1**[2]

**2** *hd* **Chapter (IRE)** 2-9-0 ............ JFortune 5 75
(RHannon) *strong: scope: led after 1f: hdd jst ins fnl 2f: styd pressing wnr: rdn ins last: kpt on but no qckn cl home* **8/1**

50 **3** *1 1/2* **Madam Caversfield**[7] 2690 2-8-9 ............ DaneO'Neill 7 66
(RHannon) *chsd ldrs: rdn and kpt on fr over 1f out: one pce ins last* **12/1**

5 **4** *nk* **Group Captain**[8] 2651 2-9-0 RLMoore 3 70
(SKirk) *lw: mid-div: hdwy 3f out: styd on wl fr over 1f out: kpt on ins last but nt pce on ldrs nr fin* **4/1**[1]

**5** *1/2* **Melrose Avenue (USA)** 2-9-0 KDalgleish 9 69
(MJohnston) *tall: scope: chsd ldr 5f out: sn rdn and green: lost position over 3f out: kpt on again fr over 1f out: styd on cl home* **5/1**[2]

0 **6** *2* **Pacific Star (IRE)**[29] 2096 2-9-0 TQuinn 4 64
(EALDunlop) *b.bkwd: bhd: hdwy 3f out: chsd ldrs and rdn 2f out: styd on same pce* **12/1**

463 **7** *1 3/4* **Gryskirk**[29] 2096 2-9-0 PaulEddery 10 59
(PWD'Arcy) *s.i.s: bhd: hdwy on ins over 2f out: kpt on fr over 1f out but nt trble ldrs* **14/1**

**8** *1/2* **Tuvalu (GER)** 2-9-0 PRobinson 11 58
(AMBalding) *b.hind: bkwd: wl grwn: slowly itno stride: bhd and wnt lft after 1f: sn in tch: chsd ldrs 3f out: wknd ins fnl f* **12/1**

**9** *1 3/4* **South O'The Border** 2-9-0 SSanders 1 54
(TGMills) *lengthy: s.i.s: green and bhd: nedver dangerous* **12/1**

**10** *nk* **Moshkil (IRE)** 2-9-0 ADaly 12 53
(MPTregoning) *b.bkwd: strong: hmpd after 1f: in tch: rdn and effrty on rail ins fnl 3f: sn wknd* **6/1**[3]

**11** *1 3/4* **Pocketwood** 2-9-0 MJO'Hara 2 49
(Jean-ReneAuvray) *b.bkwd: w'like: racd on outside: hung lft bnd over 3f out: a bhd* **66/1**

**12** *16* **Kayf Aramis** 2-8-11 LEnstone(3) 6 —
(IAWood) *v.s.a: bhd: no ch whn veered bdly rt ins fnl 3f* **50/1**

1m 33.14s (2.05) **Going Correction** -0.05s/f (Good) **12** Ran SP% **119.6**
Speed ratings: **86,85,84,83,83 80,78,78,76,75 73,55**CSF £45.31 TOTE £5.70: £2.70, £3.00, £4.40; EX 45.80.
**Owner** Hamdan Al Maktoum **Bred** Dr M V O'Brien **Trained** Manton, Wilts

**FOCUS**
A very disappointing time for the type of race, 4.37 seconds slower than the 0-100 handicap for older horses and the form is modest for the track. The front two pulled a length and a half away from the third and enjoyed a good battle.

**NOTEBOOK**
**Jalamid(IRE)**, the most expensive of these at the sales at 300,000gns, was given a positive ride and never raced far off the pace. He hit the front two out having travelled beautifully and, despite running around under pressure and showing distinct signs of greeness on ground that was believed to be on the fast side for him, found enough to hold the persistent challenge of Chapter. This did not look the strongest of maidens for the course, but the winner is entitled to improve for the experience and is well thought of.
**Chapter(IRE)** knew his job better than others - as you would expect from a Hannon juvenile - and was getting back at the winner when the line came. He should win his maiden if going the right way from this.
**Madam Caversfield**, a stablemate to the second, does nothing for the form as she has looked exposed, albeit at shorter. She will not be seen at her best until running in nurseries.
**Group Captain** showed plenty of promise after a slow start on his debut at Haydock and was well supported to confirm that promise. The front two appeared to get awy from him however, and could do no more than stay on.
**Melrose Avenue(USA)** got himself a good early position, but was soon being niggled and showed distinct signs of greeness. He was readily passed in the straight, but showed a good attitude in running on again and pulled two lengths clear of the sixth. He should win his maiden.
**Pacific Star(IRE)** improved on his debut effort and is the type for nurseries.
**Tuvalu(GER)** comes from a stable whose juveniles tend to benefit from a run, and he looks a case in point.
**Moshkil(IRE)** looked in need of the experience and should come on significantly for this.

## 2891 32RED.COM H'CAP 7f 16y
3:15 (3:18) (C ) (0-100,90) 3-Y-0+ **£12,325** (£4,675; £2,337; £1,062) **Stalls** High

Form RPR
3031 **1** **Waterside (IRE)**[5] 2727 5-8-8 **74** 6ex RLMoore 6 84
(GLMoore) *lw: mde virtually all: 4l clr 3f out: hrd drvn fr 2f out: hld on all out* **8/1**

0614 **2** *hd* **Ephesus**[8] 2646 4-8-12 **78** (v) WSupple 8 87
(MissGayKelleway) *bhd: hdwy 2f out: str run to chse wnr ins last: styd on wl: nt quite get up* **10/1**

6020 **3** *1 1/2* **Flying Express**[4] 2750 4-9-5 **85** PRobinson 3 91
(BWHills) *w wnr early: continued in 2nd: rdn over 2f out and no imp: lost 2nd ins fnl f and kpt on same pce* **11/2**[3]

3310 **4** *3/4* **Moayed**[14] 2488 5-9-6 **86** (bt) SSanders 1 90
(NPLittmoden) *lw: s.i.s: bhd: hdwy 2f out: kpt on fr over 1f out but nt rch ldrs* **5/1**[2]

3600 **5** *1* **Digital**[10] 2575 7-9-5 **85** DaneO'Neill 7 86
(MRChannon) *bhd: pushed along over 2f out: kpt on fr over 1f out but nvr gng pce to rch ldrs* **6/1**

40-0 **6** *nk* **Binanti**[12] 2534 4-9-10 **90** JQuinn 5 90
(PRChamings) *b. bhd: hdwy on rails whn nt clr run 2f out: sn one pce* **12/1**

2-00 **7** *4* **King Carnival (USA)**[12] 2534 3-9-0 **90** RSmith 2 80
(RHannon) *chsd ldrs: rdn 3f out: wknd 2f out* **10/1**

12-2 **8** *17* **Borrego (IRE)**[7] 2673 4-8-12 **78** DHolland 4 24
(CEBrittain) *lw: chsd ldrs: rdn 3f out: sn wknd* **9/4**[1]

1m 28.77s (-2.32) **Going Correction** -0.05s/f (Good)
**WFA** 3 from 4yo+ 10lb **8** Ran SP% **114.1**
Speed ratings: **111,110,109,108,107 106,102,82**CSF £82.77 CT £481.64 TOTE £9.20: £2.10, £3.00, £2.30; EX 80.40.
**Owner** Nigel Shields **Bred** Yeomanstown Stud **Trained** Woodingdean, E Sussex

**FOCUS**
A decent handicap and an excellent winning time for the grade, 4.37 seconds faster than the juvenile maiden. Waterside was given a canny ride by Ryan Moore, who stole a decisive advantage early in the straight.

**NOTEBOOK**
**Waterside(IRE)**, who appears to have been revitalised since being claimed and moving to the Moore yard, was given a positive ride in a race where he was allowed an easy lead and he soon found himself clear early in the straight. Despite getting tired, he found enough to cling on up the hill and continue his resurgence to something like his best.
**Ephesus**, not beaten far at Goodwood when reportedly losing his action, came right back to his best and was closing on Waterside with every stride at the finish. He has done well since returning to turf and can continue to pay his way.
**Flying Express** is a frustrating sort who has yet to find a trip that ideally suits despite this being his 13th start. Twice a winner over six furlongs as a juvenile, he has continually struggled since and remains one to leave alone.
**Moayed** was never going the pace dropped to five furlongs at Musselburgh and appreciated this return to seven. He was staying on at the end having been given a bit to do and, although currently 6lb higher than when last winning, his versatility with regard to trip should see him winning again before long.
**Digital** is back down to a winning mark, but continues to struggle to get his head in front.
**Binanti** never had a clear cut at it in the straight and deserves another chance.
**Borrego(IRE)** ran a stinker but, as this may have came too soon after his seasonal reappearance seven days prior, he deserves another chance. *Official explanation: jockey said colt was never travelling*

## 2892 CBFM CONDITIONS STKS 5f 6y
3:50 (3:54) (C ) 3-Y-0 **£9,048** (£3,432; £1,716; £780) **Stalls** High

Form RPR
1012 **1** **Benbaun (IRE)**[5] 2744 3-8-7 93 (v) DCorby(3) 1 99
(MJWallace) *lw: mde all: drvn clr over 1f out: r.o wl* **5/4**[1]

5211 **2** *2* **Enchantment**[11] 2552 3-9-1 85 RLMoore 3 96
(JMBradley) *lw: chsd ldrs wnt 2nd 1/2-way: kpt on u.p fr over 1f out but no imp on wnr* **2/1**[2]

2-06 **3** *3/4* **Oro Verde**[35] 1965 3-8-13 86 DaneO'Neill 4 91
(RHannon) *rr but in tch: hdwy 2f out: kpt on same pce ins fnl f* **16/1**

-600 **4** *shd* **Incise**[8] 2636 3-8-5 90 TQuinn 5 83
(BJMeehan) *rr but in tch: hdwy 1/2-way: one pce fnl f* **17/2**

255- **5** *6* **Changari (USA)**[282] 4692 3-8-8 90 JFortune 6 62
(RCharlton) *a outpcd* **16/1**

306- **6** *5* **Dallaah**[266] 5057 3-8-8 92 PRobinson 2 42
(MAJarvis) *b.bkwd: chsd wnr to 1/2-way: sn wknd* **7/1**[3]

60.80 secs (-1.39) **Going Correction** -0.05s/f (Good) **6** Ran SP% **112.6**
Speed ratings: **109,105,104,104,94 86**CSF £3.97 TOTE £2.10: £1.40, £1.70; EX 3.40.
**Owner** Ransley, Skidmore, Birks **Bred** Dr T A Ryan **Trained** Newmarket, Suffolk

**FOCUS**
A very creditable time for the grade, 1.29 seconds faster than the 0- 80 handicap over the same trip. Two highly progressive sprinters dominated the finish and this looks useful form.

**NOTEBOOK**
**Benbaun(IRE)** ◆, just touched off in Listed company at Naas earlier in the week in the first-time blinkers, escaped penalties for his handicap wins and had the visor back on, so everything was in his favour. He was quickly into his stride and showed bundles of speed, leading Enchantment, who is very quick, and stayed on strongly when challenged by that rival to win comfortably. He remains highly progressive and is likely to return to Ireland for another Listed event on Irish Derby Day.
**Enchantment** ◆ has been on a roll since returning to five furlongs, but she could not lead and had to settle for second best. This was an excellent effort given the winner was in receipt of 8lb, and she too remains highly progressive.
**Oro Verde** ran his best race of the season so far back on his favoured fast ground and off a 5lb lower mark than when starting the season.
**Incise** ran well in defeat and continues to gradually go the right way.
**Changari(USA)** was never going the pace on this seasonal debut over a trip that would be much too sharp for her.
**Dallaah** showed up well early before soon beating a retreat and tiring.

## 2893 32REDPOKER.COM H'CAP 1m 6f
4:25 (4:29) (D ) (0-80,78) 3-Y-0+ **£5,486** (£1,688; £844; £422) **Stalls** Centre

Form RPR
0634 **1** **Mostarsil (USA)**[9] 2631 6-9-2 **68** (p) RLMoore 5 77
(GLMoore) *lw: chsd ldrs: wnt 2nd over 3f out: rdn to ld jst ins fnl f: kpt on wl* **10/3**[1]

000- **2** *3/4* **Mr Ed (IRE)**[209] 4713 6-9-5 **74** DCorby(3) 2 82
(PBowen) *lw: bhd: hdwy on rails over 2f out: str run ins fnl f to take 2nd last stride but no imp on wnr* **12/1**

0001 **3** *shd* **Cantrip**[5] 2728 4-7-12 **50** 5ex JQuinn 6 58
(MissBSanders) *lw: led: rdn over 2f out: hdd ins fnl f: nt pce of wnr and ct for 2nd last stride* **9/1**

0020 **4** *2* **Dovedon Hero**[7] 2671 4-9-12 **78** (b) SSanders 4 83
(PJMcbride) *hld up mid-div: hdwy to trck ldrs over 3f out: sn rdn: kpt on same pce fnl f* **9/1**

-303 **5** *2* **Rome (IRE)**[9] 2631 5-9-0 **66** DaneO'Neill 3 68
(GPEnright) *chsd ldrs: rdn over 2f out: styd on same pce tl wknd ins fnl f* **10/1**

6046 **6** *1 3/4* **Moon Emperor**[9] 2631 7-9-9 **75** DHolland 9 75
(JRJenkins) *lw: bhd: rdn and hdwy fr 2f out: kpt on fnl f but nvr gng pce to rch ldrs* **5/1**[2]

000 **7** *1* **Snow's Ride**[14] 2480 4-8-12 **69** PMakin(5) 8 67
(WRMuir) *bhd: rdn and hdwy fr 2f out: nvr gng pce to rch ldrs* **16/1**

1012 **8** *1/2* **Galandora**[15] 2462 4-7-8 **53** LucyRussell(7) 7 51
(DrJRJNaylor) *bhd: pushed along over 3f out: nvr gng pce to rch ldrs* **9/1**

3-00 **9** *1 1/2* **Head To Kerry (IRE)**[14] 2480 4-8-10 **62** TQuinn 1 58
(DJSFfrenchDavis) *b.bkwd: in tch: hdwy 6f out: wknd appr fnl f* **10/1**

050- **10** *3 1/2* **Cedar Master (IRE)**[13] 3641 7-8-9 **66** (bt) AQuinn(5) 10 57
(JRBoyle) *b.hind: chsd ldr tl over 3f out: sn wknd* **25/1**

011 **11** *15* **Court One**[18] 2385 6-7-12 **53** oh3 ow3 RMiles(3) 11 23
(RJPrice) *swtg: s.i.s: rdn over 4f out: no rspnse and a bhd* **11/2**[3]

3m 2.65s (-1.72) **Going Correction** -0.05s/f (Good) **11** Ran SP% **120.7**
Speed ratings: **102,101,101,100,99 98,97,97,96,94 85**CSF £46.56 CT £339.07 TOTE £4.90: £1.70, £3.60, £2.90; EX 58.00 Place 6 £224.46, Place 5 £78.23.
**Owner** G A Jackman **Bred** Shadwell Farm Inc **Trained** Woodingdean, E Sussex

**FOCUS**
Not the strongest of staying handicaps, but the form is sound if ordinary.

**NOTEBOOK**
**Mostarsil(USA)** has been running well in defeat this season and had everything go his way - he needs a decent pace and plenty of driving to be seen at his best - for a straightforward win off what was his highest-ever winning mark.
**Mr Ed(IRE)** failed to show anything in the first-time blinkers at Haydock on his final start last term and ran much better here with the headgear dispensed, getting up for second in the dying strides.
**Cantrip**, rasied 5lb for winning at Folkestone earlier in the week, was stepping up two furlongs in trip and ran well, just losing out on second.
**Dovedon Hero** ran a better race for this step up in trip but remains hard to win with off his current mark.
**Rome(IRE)** failed to confirm Sandown form with Mostarsil and tired late on.
**Moon Emperor** was disappointing as he is back on a good mark and could never got involved.
**Court One** has won his last two starts in banded company and, although expected to face a much stiffer task, ran too badly to be true. Miles reported he was never travelling. *Official explanation: jockey said gelding was never travelling*
T/Plt: £544.70 to a £1 stake. Pool: £55,412.10. 74.25 winning tickets. T/Qpdt: £30.10 to a £1 stake. Pool: £4,197.80. 103.20 winning tickets. ST

## [2855]YORK (L-H)

### Saturday, June 12

**OFFICIAL GOING: Good to firm**

The ground was described as 'very quick'.

Wind: Moderate 1/2 against Weather: Fine and sunny

### 2894 CADOGAN SILVER SALVER H'CAP — 1m 208y

1:50 (1:51) (B ) (0-105,100) 3-Y-0+ £18,281 (£5,625; £2,812; £1,406) Stalls Low

Form — RPR

0000 **1** — **Krugerrand (USA)**[45] 1708 5-8-5 **77** ........ GCarter 5 — 89
(WJMusson) *swtg: keen: hld up in rr: hdwy 2f out: str run over 1f out: led ins last and sn clr* **14/1**

2-62 **2** 2 1/2 **James Caird (IRE)**[12] 2527 4-8-9 **84** ........ FPFerris(3) 6 — 91
(MHTompkins) *trckd ldrs: effrt and n.m.r over 1f out: swtchd lft and nt clr run ins last: squezed through and styd on nr fin* **7/1**[2]

-205 **3** shd **Vicious Warrior**[12] 2527 5-9-0 **86** ........ DeanMcKeown 11 — 93
(RMWhitaker) *keen: chsd ldrs: hdwy 4f out: rdn along 2f out: styd on ins last* **14/1**

4005 **4** shd **Our Teddy (IRE)**[12] 2534 4-9-1 **87** ........(b) KDarley 3 — 94
(AMBalding) *trckd ldrs on inner: shkn up and outpcd over 2f out: rdn and n.m.r over 1f out: styd on ins last* **8/1**[3]

-040 **5** hd **Middlemarch (IRE)**[30] 2066 4-10-0 **100** ........(p) JFEgan 4 — 106
(JSGoldie) *led: rdn along 4f out: jnd 3f out: hdd ins fnl f: kpt on same pace* **20/1**

**6** hd **Polygonal (FR)**[58] 4-9-3 **89** ........ RHughes 7 — 95
(MrsJRRamsden) *stdd s and bhd: hdwy over 2f out: rdn and kpt on ins last: nrst fin* **14/1**

-660 **7** 1/2 **Cripsey Brook**[12] 2527 6-8-13 **85** ........ KimTinkler 13 — 90
(DonEnricoIncisa) *in rr and sn pushed along: hdwy 2f out: rdn and styd on wl appr last: nrst fin* **20/1**

1106 **8** hd **Consonant (IRE)**[12] 2534 7-9-3 **89** ........ ACulhane 8 — 93
(DGBridgwater) *prom: chsd ldr over 4f out: rdn along 3f out and sn wknd* **12/1**

-060 **9** 3/4 **Stretton (IRE)**[12] 2527 6-8-6 **78** ........ JFanning 9 — 81
(JDBethell) *hld up: hdwy 3f out: effrt and n.m.r over 1f out: kpt on ins last: nrst fin* **10/1**

0301 **10** 3/4 **Sea Storm (IRE)**[14] 2493 6-8-11 **83** ........(p) JPMurtagh 1 — 84
(DRMacleod) *cl up: rdn along 4f out: wknd 3f out* **12/1**

-232 **11** nk **Top Dirham**[10] 2580 6-7-13 **71** ........ DaleGibson 10 — 72
(MWEasterby) *lw: in tch: hdwy over 2f out: rdn and n.m.r wl over 1f out: swtchd rt and styd on inse last* **13/2**[1]

0133 **12** 1 **Intricate Web (IRE)**[7] 2687 8-8-6 **78** ........ GDuffield 14 — 77
(EJAlston) *a rr* **14/1**

65-3 **13** 1/2 **Definite Guest (IRE)**[8] 2637 6-8-10 **82** ........ PHanagan 16 — 80
(RAFahey) *in tch on outer: effrt 3f out: rdn along wl over 1f out and no imp* **8/1**[3]

/15- **14** 1 3/4 **Vicious Knight**[404] 1402 6-10-0 **100** ........ AlexGreaves 15 — 94
(DNicholls) *trckd ldrs: hdwy to chal 3f out and ev ch tl rdn and wknd fnl 2f* **40/1**

-005 **15** nk **Tedstale (USA)**[23] 2237 6-8-8 **80** ........(b) KMcEvoy 2 — 74
(TDEasterby) *midfield on inner pulling hrd: effrt and nt clr run over 2f out: swtchd rt and nt clr run over 1f out: eased ins last* **12/1**

1m 50.99s (1.03) **Going Correction** +0.325s/f (Good) **15** Ran SP% **118.9**

Speed ratings: **108,105,105,105 105,104,104,103,103 103,102,101,100,99**CSF £104.08 CT £1447.77 TOTE £16.90: £3.70, £2.90, £6.50; EX 144.90 Trifecta £766.90 Pool of £2,160.40 - 2 winning tickets.

**Owner** The Square Table II **Bred** T Farmer **Trained** Newmarket, Suffolk

**FOCUS**

A 0-100 handicap run at a steady pace until in line for home and although it is fairly strong form there were several hard luck stories.

**NOTEBOOK**

**Krugerrand(USA)** repeated last year's success from a 2lb lower mark. Warm beforehand as usual, he was last of all with two furlongs left to run but swept down the wide outside and in the end won going away. He is totally unpredictable. *Official explanation: trainer's representative said, regarding the improved form shown, stable had been under a cloud and gelding was possibly suited by the quicker ground here*

**James Caird(IRE)**, 2lb higher, like a few others had a nightmare run. He eventually extricated himself and snatched second spot on the line. He is clearly in very good form.

**Vicious Warrior**, a keen type, is in very good form at present but he has not won since 2002.

**Our Teddy(IRE)**, who looked very fit, was very free to post. With the blinkers on again he was caught flat-footed before running out of room. Staying on at the finish, he does not look the easiest of rides.

**Middlemarch(IRE)**, 5lb lower, had his won way in front but was found lacking in the dash to the line. He still looks a few pounds too high in the ratings.

**Polygonal(FR)**, a French import, was keen under restraint and was last of all into the home straight. He stuck to the inner and never really saw daylight. The ground was plenty quick enough and he needs a stiffer test of stamina.

**Cripsey Brook**, soon struggling, stayed on in good style when it was all over and should soon add to his record.

**Consonant(IRE)** *Official explanation: trainer said gelding had been struck into*

**Stretton(IRE)**, a positive on the betting front, never saw daylight at all. He is clearly considered back to his best, and is on the same mark now as when successful here in October.

**Sea Storm(IRE)** was another who met traffic problems. *Official explanation: jockey said gelding was denied a clear run*

**Top Dirham**, carrying bags of condition, could have done with a much stronger pace. He was caught flat-footed before running out of racing room. There will be another day.

**Tedstale(USA)**, runner-up to Krugerrand from a 4lb higher mark 12 months ago, found himself in a deep, black hole this time and in the end his rider decided this was not their day. *Official explanation: jockey said gelding was denied a clear run*

### 2895 QUEEN MOTHER'S CUP (LADY AMATEUR RIDERS) H'CAP — 1m 3f 198y

2:20 (2:21) (C ) (0-95,95) 3-Y-0+ £10,920 (£3,360; £1,680; £840) Stalls Low

Form — RPR

6-05 **1** — **Mephisto (IRE)**[28] 2110 5-10-5 **86** ........ MrsSCumani 3 — 94
(LMCumani) *hld up in tch: stdy hdwy over 3f out: edgd lft wl over 1f out and appr last: styd on to ld on line* **4/1**[2]

-113 **2** hd **Court Of Appeal**[19] 2365 7-10-5 **86** ........(t) MissLEllison 5 — 93
(BEllison) *a.p: led wl over 2f out: rdn over 1f out: hdd on line* **15/2**

-034 **3** 3/4 **Stallone**[18] 2393 7-9-3 **73** ........ MrsNWilson(3) 1 — 79
(NWilson) *hld up: hdwy 4f out: hmpd wl over 1f out and appr last: swtchd rt and styd on wl fnl f: nrst fin* **12/1**

0-05 **4** nk **Sporting Gesture**[19] 2365 7-9-8 **75** ........ MissSBrotherton 4 — 81
(MWEasterby) *hld up in tch: hdwy 3f out: rdn over 1f out: kpt on same pce ins last* **3/1**[1]

3006 **5** 1/2 **Kylkenny**[10] 2591 9-9-6 **73** ........(t) MrsSBosley 10 — 78
(HMorrison) *in tch: hdwy 4f out: chal over 2f out and ev ch tl rdn and one pce fnl f* **6/1**[3]

15-0 **6** 2 **Kuster**[32] 2022 8-10-4 **91** ........(b) MissFCumani(6) 9 — 93
(LMCumani) *hld up in rr. hdwy on inner and nt clr run over 2f out: swtchd rt wl over 1f out: sn rdn and kpt on: nrest fin ish* **9/1**

56-0 **7** 9 **Rayshan (IRE)**[38] 1880 4-11-0 **95** ........ MissPRobson 2 — 82
(JHowardJohnson) *chsd ldrs: rdn along over 3f out: grad wknd* **20/1**

-450 **8** 1/2 **Danelor (IRE)**[8] 2638 6-10-1 **85** ........ MissVTunnicliffe(3) 6 — 71
(RAFahey) *led and sn clr: rdn along over 3f out: hdd over 2f out and sn wknd* **9/1**

1240 **9** 5 **Lawood (IRE)**[4] 2752 4-9-8 **75** ........ MissNCarberry 7 — 53
(KARyan) *hld up: hdwy 3f out: rdn along whn hmpd wl over 1f out and sn wknd* **10/1**

-062 **10** dist **Nicholas Nickelby**[19] 2362 4-8-7 **63** oh3........ MissFayeBramley(3) 8 — —
(MJPolglase) *chsd ldr: rdn along over 5f out: sn lost pl and bhd* **33/1**

2m 31.52s (2.66) **Going Correction** +0.325s/f (Good) **10** Ran SP% **115.5**

Speed ratings: **104,103,103,103,102 101,95,95,91,**—CSF £33.81 CT £330.84 TOTE £5.20: £2.00, £2.00, £3.10; EX 47.30 Trifecta £559.70 Pool of £1,024.90 - 1.30 winning tickets.

**Owner** Mrs Angie Silver **Bred** Shadwell Estate Company Limited **Trained** Newmarket, Suffolk

**FOCUS**

A strong early gallop but the leaders came back resulting in a bunch finish, and useful form for the grade.

**NOTEBOOK**

**Mephisto(IRE)**, who has comparatively few miles on the clock, again showed a tendency to hang left but, well held together, put his head in front where it matters.

**Court Of Appeal**, 13lb higher than well beaten a year ago, went on and took a decisive lead, but his rider seemed to get more tired than him late on and in the end they just missed out on this prestige event for lady amateur riders.

**Stallone**, who as usual thought twice about being loaded, looked unlucky not to give the first two a lot more to do. He clearly appreciates his trainer's wife's tender handling.

**Sporting Gesture**took this a year ago from a 6lb lower mark. He invariably runs well here but could have done with a stronger pace and never really looked like giving his rider her third success.

**Kylkenny**, a positive on the betting front, was pipped by Sporting Gesture a year ago and here was meeting him on 15lb better terms. He ran easily his best race on turf so far this year, but was still not good enough.

**Kuster**, third last year, was 8lb higher this time. He met traffic problems but, eventually pulled wide, finished best of all under the winning rider's daughter.

**Danelor(IRE)**, taken to post early, raced far too freely in front and gave himself little chance of seeing out this extended trip.

### 2896 DANIEL PRENN ROYAL YORKSHIRE RATED STKS (H'CAP) — 1m 2f 88y

2:50 (2:52) (B ) (0-100,97) 3-Y-0 £12,342 (£4,681; £2,340; £1,064) Stalls Low

Form — RPR

1512 **1** — **Etmaam**[14] 2472 3-8-8 **84** ........ RHills 5 — 91+
(MJohnston) *towards rr: rdn along and edgd lft 3f out: str run on outer over 1f out: styd on strly ins last to ld nr line* **4/1**[2]

51 **2** hd **Motive (FR)**[19] 2374 3-8-10 **86** ........ KFallon 2 — 93
(SirMichaelStoute) *lw: trckd ldng pair: hdwy to ld and hung lft 2f out: rdn ent last: drvn and hdd nr line* **7/2**[1]

5-40 **3** 2 1/2 **Sew'N'So Character (IRE)**[25] 2202 3-9-5 **95** ........ PHanagan 3 — 97
(MBlanshard) *trckd ldrs: hdwy whn n.m.r and swtchd rt 2f out: sn rdn and kpt on same pce fnl f* **9/1**

0-30 **4** 1/2 **Spring Goddess (IRE)**[7] 2676 3-8-6 **82** ........ NCallan 8 — 83
(APJarvis) *hld up: hdwy 4f out: rdn along over 2f out: kpt on same pce* **18/1**

-461 **5** 1 1/4 **Sound Of Fleet (USA)**[19] 2361 3-8-8 **84** ........ KDarley 4 — 83
(PFICole) *chsd ldr: hdwy to ld 3f out: rdn and hdd whn hmpd 2f out: sn drvn and one pce* **4/1**[2]

315- **6** 4 **Lunar Exit (IRE)**[224] 5871 3-9-7 **97** ........ JPMurtagh 7 — 88
(LadyHerries) *a rr* **20/1**

31 **7** 1 **Nunki (USA)**[21] 2298 3-8-11 **87** ........ WRyan 6 — 76
(HRACecil) *chsd ldrs: rdn along over 2f out: sn btn* **8/1**

4-01 **8** 9 **Aqualung**[27] 2144 3-9-2 **92** ........ RHughes 1 — 64
(BWHills) *plld hrd: led: rdn along and hdd 3f out: sn wknd* **5/1**[3]

2m 10.24s (0.80) **Going Correction** +0.325s/f (Good) **8** Ran SP% **110.0**

Speed ratings: **109,108,106,106,105 102,101,94**CSF £16.94 CT £107.52 TOTE £4.70: £1.50, £1.50, £2.30; EX 12.80 Trifecta £432.40 Pool of £1,157.20 - 1.90 winning tickets.

**Owner** Hamdan Al Maktoum **Bred** Hawkers Stud **Trained** Middleham Moor, N Yorks

**FOCUS**

A decent rated stakes and a creditable time for the grade. The form looks useful.

**NOTEBOOK**

**Etmaam** looked to be going nowhere until suddenly finding full stride on the wide outside over a furlong out. He sustained the run to edge ahead near the line.

**Motive(FR)**, a major positive, looks to be thriving. He went on travelling easily best, but in front hung left and onto the running rail. Edged out near the line, this will have taught him plenty on only his third career start. Compensation surely awaits.

**Sew'N'So Character(IRE)**, stepping up in trip, was going nowhere when the runner-up went across his bows. He looks rated to the hilt.

**Spring Goddess(IRE)**, well backed at long odds, was settled off the pace. She stayed on in her own time, and a drop in grade will aid her cause.

**Sound Of Fleet(USA)**, 7lb higher, is a big, keen type. He took it up travelling easily but seems to be one that does not find as much as expected when asked a serious question.

**Lunar Exit(IRE)**, who has started life in handicaps from a stiff mark, missed a beat at the start and never travelled in a straight line.

**Aqualung**, fitted with a cross noseband, was very keen to post and in the race itself would not settle in front. He looks his own worst enemy.

### 2897 WILLIAM HILL TROPHY (HERITAGE H'CAP) — 6f 3y

3:25 (3:26) (B ) (0-105,100) 3-Y-0 £56,104 (£17,263; £8,631; £4,315) Stalls Centre

Form — RPR

1-64 **1** — **Two Step Kid (USA)**[28] 2131 3-8-9 **88** ........ SWKelly 3 — 101
(JNoseda) *cl up: led wl over 2f out: rdn over 1f out and styd on wl* **14/1**

-431 **2** nk **Delphie Queen (IRE)**[7] 2694 3-8-11 **90** ........ JFEgan 8 — 102
(SKirk) *towards rr and pushed along 1/2-way: hdwy 2f out: rdn to chse wnr ins last: kpt on wl* **16/1**

-501 **3** 1 1/2 **Traytonic**[9] 2625 3-9-7 **100** ........ JPMurtagh 16 — 108
(JRFanshawe) *lw: bhd: hdwy 2f out: rdn over 1f out: kpt on strly ins last: nrst fin* **10/1**

-521 **4** shd **Alderney Race (USA)**[25] 2211 3-8-11 **90** ........ SDrowne 4 — 97
(RCharlton) *towards rr and n.m.r whn sltly outpcd 1/2-way: swtchd lft and hdwy 2f out: sn rdn and kpt on wl fnl f* **15/2**[3]

513- **5** nk **Doohulla (USA)**[225] 5851 3-8-10 **89** ........ RHughes 18 — 95
(GAButler) *hld up towards rr: swtchd to stands rail and gd hdwy 2f out: rdn and hung bdly lft ent last: no ex nr fin* **33/1**

0-13 **6** 1½ **High Voltage**[21] 2294 3-9-6 **99**...(t) DarrenWilliams 6 101
(KRBurke) *led: rdn along 1/2-way: sn hdd and kpt on same pce appr last* **25/1**

60-3 **7** 1¾ **Wanchai Lad**[38] 1883 3-8-9 **88**... KDarley 12 85
(DNicholls) *chsd ldrs: rdn wl over 1f out: sn one pce* **8/1**

0203 **8** ½ **Glaramara**[37] 1900 3-9-5 **98**... KFallon 15 93
(ABailey) *dwlt: sn outpcd and bhd: hung bdly lft 1/2-way: rdn to c hase ldrs over 1f out: wknd ins last* **10/1**

5-20 **9** ¾ **Danzig River (IRE)**[21] 2309 3-9-3 **96**... RHills 11 89
(BWHills) *dwlt and towards rr: hdwy 1/2-way: rdn and hung lft wl over 1f out: n.d* **16/1**

32-1 **10** 2½ **Bonne De Fleur**[58] 1417 3-9-4 **97**... FLynch 13 82
(BSmart) *chsd ldrs: rdn along 2f out: grad wknd* **33/1**

1-04 **11** 1½ **Rydal (USA)**[43] 1745 3-8-3 **87**...(b) PMulrennan(5) 5 68
(GAButler) *cl up: rdn along over 2f out: grad wknd* **100/1**

20-2 **12** ½ **Big Bradford**[21] 2309 3-8-11 **90**...(v) DKinsella 17 69
(PGMurphy) *towards rr: hdwy over 2f out: sn rdn and no imp* **12/1**

-004 **13** ¾ **Fast Heart**[21] 2294 3-9-4 **97**...(t) ACulhane 14 74
(BJMeehan) *midfield: rdn along 2f out: hmpd and wknd over 1f out* **40/1**

-251 **14** *hd* **Times Review (USA)**[11] 2549 3-8-6 **85**... PHanagan 20 61
(TDEasterby) *chsd ldrs: rdn along over 2f out: sn wknd* **25/1**

-606 **15** ¾ **Nero's Return (IRE)**[21] 2294 3-9-7 **100**... JFanning 2 74
(MJohnston) *nvr nr ldrs* **50/1**

3034 **16** 1 **Harry Up**[11] 2552 3-8-10 **89**... MFenton 19 60
(JGGiven) *chsd ldrs: rdn along 1/2-way: sn wknd* **20/1**

1505 **17** *shd* **Local Poet**[21] 2294 3-8-13 **92**...(t) GGibbons 9 63
(BAMcmahon) *chsd ldrs: rdn along 1/2-way: sn wknd* **33/1**

-211 **18** 3 **Mis Chicaf (IRE)**[15] 2457 3-8-11 **90**... RWinston 1 52
(JSWainwright) *chsd ldrs: rdn along after 2f out: sn wknd* **5/1**[1]

410- **19** 3½ **Latin Review (IRE)**[280] 4720 3-9-3 **96**... KMcEvoy 7 47
(APJarvis) *swtg: towards rr: hdwy 1/2-way: rdn over 2f out and sn wknd* **66/1**

2-12 **20** 3 **Fun To Ride**[38] 1881 3-9-0 **93**... MHills 10 35
(BWHills) *trckd ldrs pulling hrd: effrt and wandered 1/2-way: sn wknd and eased fnl f* **7/1**[2]

1m 11.94s (0.87) **Going Correction** +0.325s/f (Good) **20** Ran SP% **124.5**
Speed ratings: **107,106,104,104,104 102,99,99,98,94 92,92,91,90,89 88,88,84,79,75**CSF £201.77 CT £2402.42 TOTE £21.60: £4.90, £4.70, £3.10, £3.20; EX 465.80 Trifecta £4009.50 Part won. Pool of £5,647.31 - 0.10 winning ticket..
**Owner** Hesmonds Stud **Bred** D Drazini **Trained** Newmarket, Suffolk

**FOCUS**
A valuable and highly competitive 0-100 sprint handicap, with the winner the only one of the first five to race up with the pace. This race usually provides strong form and has been treated as such again.

**NOTEBOOK**
**Two Step Kid(USA)** had the trip and ground in his favour, and on just his fourth career start gave his trainer a change of luck in Europe's richest three-year-old handicap.
**Delphie Queen(IRE)**, 7lb higher and dropping back in trip, stayed on really well from off the pace and in the end was just held at bay.
**Traytonic** looked a picture. He soon found himself in a poor position and only really found his stride very late in the day. He finished best of all and deserves to find a good prize.
**Alderney Race(USA)**, a bit warm beforehand, was making his handicap bow. Tapped for toe and left short of room soon after halfway he was putting in some solid work late on. The experience will not be lost on him and a seventh furlong will not come amiss.
**Doohulla(USA)**, a progressive juvenile, had the blinkers left off on her return and on her handicap bow. She has an awkward head carriage but stuck on well down the stands' side and the blinkers will make her an easier ride.
**High Voltage** is all speed and a stiff five might suit him better.
**Wanchai Lad**, carrying plenty of condition, was very free to post. Considering he did not settle on the way back he ran with credit. His new trainer will sort him out.
**Glaramara** missed a beat at the start and, hanging left throughout, ended up racing alone on the far-side rail. In the circumstances it was a creditable effort. *Official explanation: jockey said colt hung left-handed throughout*
**Danzig River(IRE)**, much better behaved beforehand, wanted to do nothing but hang left and is clearly not straightforward.
**Mis Chicaf(IRE)**, a stone higher, was brought into the paddock early on and became very stirred up. She was soon pushed along to keep up before dropping right away, and seems to be the type who needs to be fresh and full of herself. *Official explanation: jockey said filly ran flat*
**Fun To Ride**, on this much quicker ground, wanted to nothing but hang left and, on the retreat soon after halfway, in the end her rider drew stumps. She was found to be very sore afterwards. *Official explanation: jockey said filly hung left-handed from halfway*

## 2898 LEONARD SAINER EBF MAIDEN STKS — 6f 3y
**4:00** (4:00) (D) 2-Y-O **£5,772** (£1,776; £888; £444) **Stalls** Centre

Form RPR

**1** **Blues And Royals (USA)** 2-9-0 ... KMcEvoy 9 81+
(SaeedBinSuroor) *gd sort: rangy: wnt rt s: sn trcking ldrs: hdwy to ld wl over 1f out: pushed out* **2/1**[1]

**2** 1¾ **Wise Owl** 2-9-0 ... JFanning 2 76
(MJohnston) *w'like: scope: cl up: ev ch 2f out: sn rdn and kpt on fnl f* **5/1**[3]

**3** ½ **The Duke Of Dixie (USA)** 2-9-0 ... KFallon 7 74
(PFICole) *wl grwn: rangy: outpcd and bhd: rdn over 2f out: styd on appr last: nrst fin* **4/1**[2]

**4** 2 **Malcheek (IRE)** 2-9-0 ... JFEgan 1 68
(TDEasterby) *lengthy: unf: scope: in tch: hdwy to chse ldrs 2f out: sn rdn and kpt on same pce* **25/1**

**5** 1¼ **Venetian King (USA)** 2-9-0 ... PHanagan 4 65
(JHowardJohnson) *w'like: lengthy: scope: stmbld bdly s: sn chsng ldrs: rdn along 2f out and sn no imp* **5/1**[3]

50 **6** 2½ **Misty Miller**[10] 2579 2-8-11 ... DAllan(3) 3 57
(TDEasterby) *led: rdn along over 2f out: hdd wl over 1f out and sn wknd* **20/1**

**7** 5 **Mount Butler (IRE)** 2-9-0 ... MFenton 6 42
(JGGiven) *rangy: sn outpcd and b ehind fr 1/2-way* **25/1**

0 **8** 12 **Toss The Caber (IRE)**[22] 2256 2-9-0 ... KDarley 5 6
(MRChannon) *unruly stalls: cl up tl rdn along and wknd over 2f out* **10/1**

1m 14.3s (3.23) **Going Correction** +0.325s/f (Good) **8** Ran SP% **108.2**
Speed ratings: **91,88,88,85,83 80,73,57**CSF £10.56 TOTE £3.10: £1.40, £1.40, £1.60; EX 7.70.
**Owner** Godolphin **Bred** C A Curtin **Trained** Newmarket, Suffolk

**FOCUS**
No gallop to past halfway resulting in a modest time for the grade. A maiden won by One Cool Cat a year ago and the principals can rate higher.

**NOTEBOOK**
**Blues And Royals(USA)** ◆, an April foal, is a quality colt with what looks a placid temperament. He travelled strongly and in the end had only to be pushed out. Seven furlongs and a mile will suit him even better, and he looks a smart prospect.
**Wise Owl** ◆, a March foal, is bred for stamina rather than speed. A well-made individual, he was noisy in the paddock and his inexperience showed in the middle part of the race. He stuck on well and, sure to improve, looks a useful prospect.
**The Duke Of Dixie(USA)**, a March foal, has plenty of size and scope. With a laboured, pounding action, after getting outpaced he stayed on well down the stands' side in the final furlong. This will have taught him plenty and a seventh furlong will greatly assist him.
**Malcheek(IRE)**, an April foal, is long in the back and was very green going to post. He made a highly satisfactory debut and can only improve.
**Venetian King(USA)**, a February foal, cost 80,000gns at the breeze-up sales. He stumbled at the start but showed ability, soon chasing the leaders. The experience will not be lost on him and much easier targets can be found.
**Misty Miller**, the most experienced in the line-up, ran his best race on his third start showing bags of toe. A five-furlong nursery will give him a much more realistic chance.
**Toss The Caber(IRE)**, on his toes beforehand, moved poorly to post and went berserk in the stalls.

## 2899 CHARLES HENRY MEMORIAL H'CAP — 6f 3y
**4:35** (4:35) (D) (0-80,83) 3-Y-O+ **£7,962** (£2,450; £1,225; £612) **Stalls** Centre

Form RPR

3022 **1** **Cloud Dancer**[110] 861 5-9-5 **71**... GParkin 16 85
(KARyan) *keen: hld up in rr: hdwy 2f out: str run ent last: led last 50 yds* **20/1**

4406 **2** 1 **Blackheath (IRE)**[7] 2682 8-9-11 **77**... AlexGreaves 14 88
(DNicholls) *in tch: smooth hdwy 2f out: chal and carried bdly lft ent last: rdn to ld wl ins last: hdd and nt qckn last 50 yds* **11/1**

4046 **3** ½ **Mr Malarkey (IRE)**[14] 2467 4-9-10 **76**...(b) JPMurtagh 17 86
(MrsCADunnett) *cl up: led over 2f out: rdn and hung bdly lft ent last: hdd and nt qckn wl ins last* **12/1**

0500 **4** 1¾ **Undeterred**[7] 2682 8-9-7 **73**...(v) KDarley 6 77
(TDBarron) *bmpd s and sn in rr: hdwy 2f out: styd on wl fnl f nrst fin* **10/1**

0403 **5** *hd* **Paddywack (IRE)**[15] 2461 7-8-12 **64**...(b) ACulhane 15 68
(DWChapman) *in tch: hdwy to chse ldrs 2f out: sn rdn and one pce ent last* **13/2**[1]

2050 **6** *hd* **Flying Edge (IRE)**[25] 2215 4-8-4 **59**... DAllan(3) 18 62
(EJAlston) *midfield: hdwy to chse ldrs wl over 1f out: sn rdn and one pce appr last* **33/1**

5042 **7** 1½ **Amanda's Lad (IRE)**[8] 2658 4-8-7 **60**... SDrowne 9 59
(MCChapman) *cl up: rdn along over 2f out and grad wknd* **40/1**

2005 **8** *nk* **Up Tempo (IRE)**[4] 2750 6-9-10 **76**...(b) NCallan 11 74
(KARyan) *wnt lft s: midfield tl hdwy 2f out: sn rdn and kpt on same pce: b.b.v* **14/1**

4030 **9** *shd* **Pride Of Kinloch**[15] 2459 4-8-6 **58**... WRyan 8 55
(JHetherton) *chsd ldrs tl squeezed out after 1f: in tch and nt clr run over 2f out and again over 1f out: swtchd lft and styd on: nrst f* **33/1**

00-6 **10** ¾ **Mister Sweets**[35] 1974 5-9-5 **71**... RFitzpatrick 3 66
(DCarroll) *outpcd and bhd tl styd on fnl 2f: nvr a factor* **33/1**

-000 **11** *nk* **Ballybunion (IRE)**[14] 2490 5-8-7 **59**... PMQuinn 7 53
(DNicholls) *wnt lft s: towards rr tl hdwy wl over 1f out: sn rdn and no imp* **25/1**

-003 **12** 1¼ **Tuscan Flyer**[10] 2598 6-8-10 **62**... RFfrench 13 52
(RBastiman) *nvr nr ldrs* **14/1**

45-5 **13** ½ **Blythe Spirit**[18] 2391 5-9-5 **74**...(p) THamilton(3) 1 63
(RAFahey) *led: rdn along and hdd over 2f out: sn wknd* **14/1**

4000 **14** 2 **Viewforth**[15] 2461 6-9-0 **71**...(b) PMulrennan(5) 4 54
(JSGoldie) *chsd ldrs: rdn over 2f out: grad wknd* **10/1**

-600 **15** 6 **Quantica (IRE)**[35] 1974 5-8-10 **62**... KimTinkler 20 27
(NTinkler) *a rr* **66/1**

4541 **16** 1 **H Harrison (IRE)**[4] 2750 4-10-0 **83** 7ex... FPFerris(3) 10 45
(IWMcinnes) *dwlt: a rr* **12/1**

0004 **17** 2½ **Winthorpe (IRE)**[15] 2461 4-9-5 **71**... DarrenWilliams 12 25
(JJQuinn) *plld hrd: chsd ldrs tl lost pl over 2f out* **7/1**[2]

1005 **18** 1¾ **Grey Cossack**[9] 2626 7-9-12 **78**... JCarroll 19 27
(PTMidgley) *swtg: a rr* **33/1**

0312 **19** ¾ **Tally (IRE)**[8] 2656 4-8-5 **57**... JFanning 5 4
(MJPolglase) *in tch: rdn along 1/2-way: sn wknd* **9/1**[3]

-000 **20** 13 **Sir Don (IRE)**[40] 1825 5-8-9 **61**...(v) ANicholls 2 —
(DNicholls) *stmbld bdly s: sn rdn along: bhd fr 1/2-way* **16/1**

1m 12.5s (1.43) **Going Correction** +0.325s/f (Good) **20** Ran SP% **127.9**
Speed ratings: **103,101,101,98,98 98,96,95,95,94 94,92,91,89,81 79,76,74,73,55**CSF £217.74 CT £2788.87 TOTE £17.00: £3.50, £3.20, £3.10, £3.40; EX 523.60.
**Owner** Mrs Gillian Quinn **Bred** Cheveley Park Stud Ltd **Trained** Hambleton, N Yorks

**FOCUS**
A fair handicap with the winner overcoming an absence to score and pretty strong form.

**NOTEBOOK**
**Cloud Dancer**, a leggy mare, was having her first outing since February. She came from well off the pace to get up near the finish. She might be even better over an extra furlong.
**Blackheath(IRE)**, on his toes beforehand, has slipped 8lb down the ratings this year. He travelled easily, but was taken off a straight line by the third and missed out near the line. He deserves imminent compensation.
**Mr Malarkey(IRE)**, who has slipped to a handy mark, was back on song but not for the first time in his career he hung badly left, impeding the runner-up. *Official explanation: jockey said gelding hung left from 2f out*
**Undeterred**, with the visor on again, is back on the same mark as his last win but with him everything needs to fall just right.
**Paddywack(IRE)**, a very tough type, should continue to give a good account of himself.
**Flying Edge(IRE)** put a poor effort last time behind him.
**Up Tempo(IRE)** was found to have bled from the nose. *Official explanation: jockey said gelding had bled from the nose*
**Pride Of Kinloch**, a maiden after 17 starts, had no luck at all over a trip short of her best.
**Mister Sweets**, who has slipped to a handy mark, found this trip too sharp. Both his wins were over seven. *Official explanation: trainer said gelding was found to be coughing after the race*
**Winthorpe(IRE)** took a fierce grip and was found to have been struck into. *Official explanation: jockey said gelding was struck into*
**Sir Don(IRE)** *Official explanation: jockey said gelding hung left from halfway*

## 2900 MICHAEL SOBELL MAIDEN STKS — 7f 205y
**5:05** (5:05) (D) 3-Y-O **£6,493** (£1,998; £999; £499) **Stalls** Low

Form RPR

**1** **Binary Vision (USA)** 3-9-0 ... RHughes 10 91
(JHMGosden) *gd sort: trckd ldrs: smooth hdwy 3f out: led 2f out: qcknd clr appr last* **1/1**[1]

-605 **2** 7 **Sharaab (USA)**[13] 2505 3-9-0 70...(t) RHills 1 75
(BHanbury) *led: rdn along and hdd 3f out: rdn and kpt on fnl 2f: no ch w wnr* **11/1**

5 **3** *shd* **Mikao (IRE)**[41] 1794 3-8-7 ... SaleemGolam(7) 6 75
(MHTompkins) *hld up: hit rail bnd over 5f out: swtchd rt and hdwy 3f out: rdn wl over 1f out: kpt on ins last* **13/2**[2]

3 **4** *1* **Supamach (IRE)**[14] 2486 3-8-9 SDrowne 7 67
(PFICole) *chsd ldrs: rdn along 3f out: kpt on same pce fnl 2f* **12/1**

**5** *1/2* **Hugs Destiny (IRE)** 3-9-0 DeanMcKeown 12 71
(JGGiven) *w'like: scope: chsd ldrs: rdn along and outpcd over 3f out: kpt on u.p fnl 2f* **25/1**

4 **6** *1* **Nistaki (USA)**[53] 1519 3-9-0 KDarley 2 69
(TDEasterby) *chsd ldrs: hdwy to ld 3f out: rdn and hdd 2f out: sn wknd* **10/1**[3]

00-0 **7** *2* **My Sunshine (IRE)**[11] 2562 3-8-9 MHills 11 59
(BWHills) *chsd ldrs: rdn along over 3f out: sn wknd* **16/1**

**8** *3/4* **Team Player** 3-8-11 NMackay(3) 9 63
(LMCumani) *rangy: scope: sn outpcd and bhd: hdwy over 2f out: kpt on ins last: nvr a factor* **10/1**[3]

00-0 **9** *4* **Gallas (IRE)**[35] 1957 3-9-0 61 GParkin 4 53
(JSWainwright) *a rr* **80/1**

04-3 **10** *1 1/4* **Arran Scout (IRE)**[35] 1972 3-9-0 77 JPMurtagh 3 51
(MrsLStubbs) *prom: rdn along 4f out: sn wknd* **10/1**[3]

**11** *5* **Trinity Fair** 3-8-9 JFanning 8 34
(JGGiven) *lt-f: unf: chsd ldrs: rdn along 4f out: sn wknd* **50/1**

02-0 **12** *1* **Super King**[12] 2519 3-9-0 68 DarrenWilliams 13 37
(NBycroft) *a rr* **50/1**

1m 37.76s (0.02) **Going Correction** +0.325s/f (Good) **12 Ran SP% 121.5**
Speed ratings: **112,105,104,103,103 102,100,99,95,94 89,88**CSF £13.54 TOTE £2.30: £1.40, £3.90, £2.30; EX 21.10 Place 6 £280.94, Place 5 £67.54.
**Owner** K Abdulla **Bred** Juddmonte Farms Inc **Trained** Manton, Wilts

**FOCUS**
An outstanding winning time for the type of contest and the winner has the potential to go far, already looking Pattern class, although the form behind is not particularly strong.

**NOTEBOOK**
**Binary Vision(USA)**, with a top-class pedigree, is a good-bodied, keen type. He travelled smoothly and quickened right away inside the last.
**Sharaab(USA)**, who stands over plenty of ground, is a keen type. He was left for dead by the potentially smart winner, and in the end just clung on to second spot.
**Mikao(IRE)**, a lazy walker, lost his pitch when colliding with the running rail on the home turn. Making his way to the outside, he was putting in all his best work at the finish. Still inexperienced, for good measure he put his rider on the deck pulling up.
**Supamach(IRE)**, dropping back in trip after making her debut on the Polytrack two weeks earlier, has a pronounced knee action.
**Hugs Destiny(IRE)**, a half-brother to Hugs Dancer, is a likeable type but he has a short, choppy action. He made a satisfactory debut and will improve a good deal in time and when stepped up in distance.
**Nistaki(USA)**, who has changed stables since his debut in April, travelled very strongly, but after going on he tired badly in the closing stages. He looked short of peak fitness beforehand, and will be very interesting in handicap company with one more outing under his belt.
**Team Player** was very green to post and showed just a moderate action. After getting well behind he picked up in his own time late on. From a fantastic dam-line, he can only improve.
**Arran Scout(IRE)** *Official explanation: jockey said gelding lost its action*
T/Plt: £209.70 to a £1 stake. Pool: £123,619.50. 430.30 winning tickets. T/Qpdt: £25.80 to a £1 stake. Pool: £8,264.90. 236.40 winning tickets. JR

2901 - 2902a (Foreign Racing) - See Raceform Interactive

## 2463 CORK (R-H)
Saturday, June 12

**OFFICIAL GOING: Firm (good to firm in places on chase and sprint courses)**

### 2903a KERRY GROUP BALLYOGAN STKS (GROUP 3) (F&M) 6f
8:00 (8:00) 3-Y-O+ **£36,619** (£10,704; £5,070; £1,690) **Stalls** Far side

RPR

**1** **Golden Nun**[7] 2685 4-9-3 (b) RWinston 1 105
(TDEasterby) *rr: 5th over 2f out: travelling wl and chal 1 1/2f out: rdn to ld over 1f out: styd on wl fnl f* **3/1**[2]

**2** *1 1/2* **Simianna**[7] 2685 5-9-3 (p) DPMcDonogh 2 101
(ABerry) *towards rr: impr into 4th over 2f out: rdn to chal 1 1/2f out: wnt 2nd ins fnl f: kpt on wout troubling wnr* **16/1**

**3** *1* **Topkamp**[15] 2466 4-9-3 JPSpencer 5 98
(MLWBell) *prom: rdn in 5th 1 1/2f out: kpt on same pce into 3rd fnl f* **5/2**[1]

**4** *3/4* **Dowager**[35] 1964 3-8-9 WMLordan 9 95
(RHannon) *chsd ldrs: clsr in 4th 1/2-way: disp ld fr 2f out: hdd over 1f out: kpt on same pce ins fnl f* **6/1**

**5** *3/4* **Sun Slash (IRE)**[21] 2316 4-9-3 95 (p) CatherineGannon 4 93
(MsJoannaMorgan, Ire) *prom: 3rd 1/2-way: almost on terms under 2f out: no ex u.p and kpt on same pce fr over 1f out* **16/1**

**6** *1/2* **Lupine (IRE)**[59] 1255 5-9-3 89 TPO'Shea 8 92
(GWRobinson, Ire) *prom: 5th 1/2-way: rdn and kpt on same pce fr 1 1/2f out* **16/1**

**7** *1/2* **Enchanted**[13] 2503 5-9-3 MJKinane 3 90
(NACallaghan) *mid-div: rdn and kpt on same pce fr over 2f out* **7/1**

**8** *5* **Anna Frid (GER)**[5] 2744 4-9-3 98 PJSmullen 7 75
(DKWeld, Ire) *chsd ldrs: impr to ld briefly sn after 1/2-way: rdn and wknd fr 2f out* **10/1**

**9** *2 1/2* **Miss Childrey (IRE)**[20] 2330 3-8-9 104 JAHeffernan 6 68
(FrancisEnnis, Ire) *sn led: rdn and hdd over 2f out: sn wknd: eased fnl f* **5/1**[3]

67.50 secs
**WFA** 3 from 4yo+ 8lb **9 Ran SP% 123.8**
Speed ratings: CSF £53.70 TOTE £3.00: £1.60, £3.30, £1.30; DF 98.50.
**Owner** T G & Mrs M E Holdcroft **Bred** Bearstone Stud **Trained** Great Habton, N Yorks

**FOCUS**
Another example of the downward spiral in the Irish Pattern with a flag start being employed because of a stalls malfunction. The winning time was a quite amazing 67.5 seconds, but as it was hand-timed it is likely to be inaccurate.

**NOTEBOOK**
**Golden Nun** came through to lead over a furlong out and settled things in a matter of strides. She remains progressive.
**Simianna**, well exposed and rated 14 lb behind the winner, ran on inside the last but was readily held.
**Topkamp**, easy in the market, was never closer than at the finish. This ground might have been a bit fast for her.
**Dowager** was disputing the lead two furlongs out but found herself outpaced when the winner went on.
**Sun Slash(IRE)** ran prominently until finding no more over a furlong out.
**Lupine(IRE)** found this too fast and too sharp.
**Enchanted** did not appear to like the ground and was not a factor from a furlong and a half down.
**Anna Frid(GER)** is below par at the moment.

## 2670 DONCASTER (L-H)
Sunday, June 13

**OFFICIAL GOING: Firm (good to firm in places)**
Wind: Slight against. Weather: Sunny and warm.

### 2904 EBF AMATEUR JOCKEYS ASSOCIATION CHARITY RACEDAY MEDIAN AUCTION MAIDEN STKS 6f
2:20 (2:21) (E) 2-Y-O **£3,649** (£1,123; £561; £280) **Stalls** High

Form RPR

54 **1** **Fiefdom (IRE)**[32] 2045 2-9-0 KDalgleish 17 87
(MJohnston) *led over 4f out: rdn and hung lft fr over 2f out: all out* **10/11**[1]

6 **2** *shd* **Mozafin**[11] 2579 2-9-0 TEDurcan 4 87
(MRChannon) *chsd ldrs: rdn over 1f out: ev ch ins fnl f: r.o* **16/1**

**3** *3* **Queue Up** 2-9-0 MFenton 14 78
(JGGiven) *a.p: rdn over 1f out: styd on same pce* **12/1**

**4** *2 1/2* **Golden Fury** 2-9-0 KDarley 8 70
(JLDunlop) *s.s: hld up: hdwy over 2f out: nt trble ldrs* **13/2**[3]

**5** *3 1/2* **Dover Street** 2-9-0 PaulEddery 12 60
(PWD'Arcy) *dwlt: hld up: swtchd lft over 2f out: styd on ins fnl f: nt rch ldrs* **14/1**

26 **6** *nk* **Skippit John**[27] 2173 2-9-0 DeanMcKeown 5 59
(RonaldThompson) *chsd ldrs over 4f* **25/1**

32 **7** *nk* **Kanad**[19] 2382 2-9-0 (t) RHills 1 58
(BHanbury) *w ldrs: rdn over 2f out: wknd over 1f out* **9/2**[2]

5 **8** *1* **Forest Viking (IRE)**[16] 2447 2-8-11 TEaves(3) 9 55
(JSWainwright) *led: hdd over 4f out: wknd over 1f out* **50/1**

**9** *nk* **Mr Maxim** 2-9-0 VHalliday 7 54
(RMWhitaker) *mid-div: outpcd 3f out: styd on ins fnl f* **50/1**

**10** *3/4* **King Of Blues (IRE)** 2-9-0 EAhern 13 52
(MAMagnusson) *mid-div: dropped rr over 4f out: n.d after* **16/1**

0 **11** *hd* **Slate Grey**[8] 2674 2-9-0 DarrenWilliams 11 51
(KRBurke) *s.s: outpcd: sme hdwy and hung rt over 1f out: sn wknd* **66/1**

0 **12** *nk* **Danehill Angel**[45] 1735 2-8-9 GGibbons 10 45
(MJPolglase) *mid-div: sn drvn along: wkng whn hmpd over 1f out* **50/1**

50 **13** *7* **Northern Revoque (IRE)**[28] 2141 2-8-2 PPMathers(7) 6 24
(ABerry) *hld up: hdwy and hung lft 1/2-way: sn wknd* **100/1**

0 **14** *3* **Eminence Gift**[10] 2617 2-8-6 THamilton(3) 15 15
(RPElliott) *chsd ldrs to 1/2-way* **50/1**

**15** *nk* **Detroit Dancer** 2-9-0 NCallan 16 19
(RonaldThompson) *a in rr* **40/1**

0 **16** *1 1/2* **Lady Indiana (IRE)**[28] 2140 2-8-6 LEnstone(3) 3 —
(JSWainwright) *s.i.s: outpcd* **100/1**

00 **17** *1 3/4* **La Bella Rosa (IRE)**[28] 2140 2-8-2 AReilly(7) 2 —
(JSWainwright) *prom to 1/2-way* **100/1**

1m 14.92s (0.64) **Going Correction** -0.075s/f (Good) **17 Ran SP% 128.6**
Speed ratings: **92,91,87,84,79 79,79,77,77,76 76,75,66,62,61 59,57**CSF £19.63 TOTE £2.20: £1.10, £3.60, £3.10; EX 26.70.
**Owner** Sheikh Mohammed **Bred** Kildaragh Stud **Trained** Middleham Moor, N Yorks

**FOCUS**
A modest juvenile maiden run at a fair pace. The front pair came clear and although their are mixed messages from previous races, the form should hold up.

**NOTEBOOK**
**Fiefdom(IRE)** quickly bounced out of the gates to take advantage of his stands' rail draw and made most to get off the mark at the third attempt. Like many of his yard's juveniles he has improved with each outing and he hung only due to being in front too long on this occasion. Another furlong can only help his progression.
**Mozafin**, who ran distinctly green on his debut, really showed the benefit of that experience and only just went down over this extra furlong. He deserves credit for getting so close from his low draw and, if able to reproduce this form and make the logical improvement, he will be hard to beat in a similar event.
**Queue Up**, half-brother to the yard's useful sprinter Harry Up, made a pleasing debut and showed plenty of early dash before tiring late on. He will come on a fair bit for this and has a sprint maiden well within his compass this year.
**Golden Fury**, the first juvenile runner for the yard this season, was doing all of his best work late on, having looked to find things happening a bit quickly through the first few furlongs on this debut. On pedigree he will have no difficulties staying further and he will be a lot sharper next time.
**Dover Street** was sluggish from the gates and got going all too late on this debut, but shaped with promise nonetheless. He is bred to appreciate further in time.
**Kanad** failed to reproduce the form that saw him placed on his previous two outings and disappointed. Granted he had a poor draw, he will most likely leave this form behind when the nurseries begin.

### 2905 S P BELL PRIVATE CLIENT STOCKBROKERS RATED STKS (H'CAP) 1m (S)
2:50 (2:50) (D) (0-85,84) 3-Y-O+ **£5,736** (£1,765; £882; £441) **Stalls** High

Form RPR

5021 **1** **Ace Of Hearts**[14] 2504 5-9-11 83 SSanders 8 94
(CFWall) *chsd ldrs: led over 1f out: pushed out* **3/1**[2]

6025 **2** *3* **Distant Country (USA)**[11] 2581 5-8-13 71 (p) SWhitworth 2 75
(MrsJRRamsden) *s.i.s: hld up: hdwy over 2f out: chsd wnr fnl f: no imp* **13/2**

5053 **3** *1/2* **Sarraaf (IRE)**[16] 2459 8-8-13 71 KDarley 7 74
(JSGoldie) *hld up in tch: rdn over 2f out: styd on ins fnl f: nt trble ldrs* **12/1**

0030 **4** *hd* **Jay Gee's Choice**[9] 2637 4-9-12 84 TEDurcan 4 87
(MRChannon) *chsd ldrs: rdn over 1f out: styd on same pce* **6/1**

5001 **5** *2 1/2* **Atlantic Quest (USA)**[20] 2366 5-9-5 82 (p) PMulrennan(5) 5 79
(GAHarker) *hld up: effrt over 1f out: n.d* **11/4**[1]

-054 **6** *5* **Nuit Sombre (IRE)**[8] 2687 4-9-4 76 KDalgleish 6 61
(MJohnston) *led over 6f: wknd ins fnl f* **11/2**[3]

4-40 **7** *2 1/2* **Keeper's Lodge (IRE)**[22] 2284 3-8-0 69 FNorton 3 49
(BAMcmahon) *s.i.s: hld up: outpcd fr 1/2-way* **50/1**

1014 **8** *2* **Jordans Elect**[4] 2781 4-8-12 73 TEaves(3) 1 48
(ISemple) *chsd ldrs tl wknd over 1f out* **15/2**

1m 39.22s (-2.38) **Going Correction** -0.075s/f (Good)
**WFA** 3 from 4yo+ 11lb **8 Ran SP% 116.1**
Speed ratings: **108,105,104,104,101 96,94,92**CSF £23.24 CT £206.79 TOTE £4.00: £1.10, £1.80, £2.10; EX 21.50.
**Owner** Lady Stuttaford & W G Bovill **Bred** Whitsbury Manor Stud **Trained** Newmarket, Suffolk

**FOCUS**
A decent, competitive handicap, despite the small field, and the gallop was solid.

**NOTEBOOK**

**Ace Of Hearts** followed up his success 14 days earlier and defied a 3lb rise in the weights with ease. He enjoyed tracking this decent gallop and there was a lot to like about the manner in which he settled the issue when striking the front entering the final furlong. He is thriving at present and won this in the style of an improving handicapper.

**Distant Country(USA)** who ran better than his finishing position suggested over six furlongs last time, showed his true colours back over this more suitable trip, but never looked like reeling in the winner late on.

**Sarraaf(IRE)** ran another frustrating race and although he was running on well towards the finish, looked to be saving plenty for himself. He has talent and often hits the frame, but is a very hard horse to catch right.

**Jay Gee's Choice** ◆ shaped as if the trip stretched him this time. He did well until tiring over one out and it can be no coincidence that his best recent form was on the one occasion he was dropped to seven furlongs.

**Atlantic Quest(USA)** failed to run up to the form of his latest win and put in another frustrating display. He is an inconsistent sort who needs all to fall right in his races.

## 2906 ARENA LEISURE PROUD TO BE AT DONCASTER CLASSIFIED STKS 1m 2f 60y

**3:25** (3:25) (E) 3-Y-O **£3,581** (£1,102; £551; £275) **Stalls** High

| Form | | | | | RPR |
|---|---|---|---|---|---|
| 0-52 | **1** | | **La Persiana**[29] 2134 3-9-0 75 (WJarvis) *a.p: chsd ldr 6f out: led over 3f out: rdn out* **1/1**[1] | WRyan 2 | 81 |
| 2225 | **2** | 1 ¼ | **My Paris**[16] 2448 3-9-1 73 (KARyan) *trckd ldr 4f: rdn over 1f out: styd on* **6/1** | NCallan 1 | 80 |
| 2102 | **3** | 1 ¾ | **Magic Amigo**[5] 2751 3-8-13 71 (JRJenkins) *hld up in tch: rdn over 1f out: hung lft ins fnl f: styd on same pce* **7/2**[2] | KDarley 3 | 75 |
| 0320 | **4** | 1 | **Beauchamp Star**[18] 2400 3-8-11 72 (GAButler) *s.s: hld up in tch: chsd wnr over 2f out: sn rdn and ev ch: btn whn bmpd ins fnl f* **11/2**[3] | EAhern 5 | 71 |
| 150 | **5** | 11 | **Certifiable**[31] 2069 3-8-12 70 (AndrewReid) *led over 6f: wknd wl over 1f out* **8/1** | JFEgan 6 | 52 |
| 6-00 | **6** | dist | **Kalush**[54] 1532 3-8-12 61 (RonaldThompson) *s.s: a bhd* **50/1** | DeanMcKeown 4 | — |

2m 11.33s (-0.43) **Going Correction** -0.075s/f (Good) **6** Ran SP% **115.0**

Speed ratings: **98,97,95,94,86** —CSF £8.06 TOTE £1.70: £1.10, £2.10; EX 5.80.

**Owner** Plantation Stud **Bred** Plantation Stud **Trained** Newmarket, Suffolk

**FOCUS**

A tight classified event run at a good gallop and the form looks sound.

**NOTEBOOK**

**La Persiana** improved over this longer trip and lost her maiden tag at the fifth attempt. She did it well and can be rated better than the bare form, as she idled in front and still had plenty left in the tank when crossing the line. Crucially, this victory will have done wonders for her paddock value, but she may be able to progress further on this in the meantime, back in handicap company.

**My Paris**, who ran another sound race on his handicap debut last time, again found one too good, but saw out the extra distance well enough. He is becoming frustrating, yet always gives his best and certainly deserves to get his head in front.

**Magic Amigo**, turning out quickly after his respectable second at Chester five days previously, ran another sound race on this much faster ground. He is the benchmark for the form.

**Beauchamp Star** improved on her latest effort and proved she can go on this quick surface, however she held every chance yet still looked rather reluctant to go through with her effort.

**Kalush** *Official explanation: jockey said gelding moved poorly throughout race*

## 2907 JOHN GORDON CHEMISTS STKS (H'CAP) 7f

**4:00** (4:01) (C) (0-95,95) 3-Y-O **£9,750** (£3,000; £1,500; £750) **Stalls** High

| Form | | | | | RPR |
|---|---|---|---|---|---|
| -321 | **1** | | **Warden Complex**[26] 2207 3-8-9 **83** (JRFanshawe) *hld up: hdwy and hit over the hd w rivals whip over 2f out: led 1f out: drvn out* **13/8**[1] | OUrbina 4 | 96 |
| 0-42 | **2** | shd | **Flipando (IRE)**[23] 2269 3-8-3 **77** (TDBarron) *w ldrs: led 3f out: rdn and hdd 1f out: r.o* **13/2**[2] | PHanagan 5 | 90 |
| -136 | **3** | ½ | **Primo Way**[11] 2589 3-8-7 **81** (BWHills) *hld up: hdwy over 2f out: rdn and ev ch fr over 1f out: hung lft towards fin: r.o* **10/1** | RHills 1 | 93 |
| 5153 | **4** | 6 | **Molcon (IRE)**[22] 2309 3-8-9 **83** (NACallaghan) *chsd ldrs: hmpd and lost pl over 2f out: n.d* **7/1**[3] | EAhern 7 | 79 |
| 2-00 | **5** | nk | **Mrs Moh (IRE)**[33] 2019 3-8-1 **77** ow1 (TDEasterby) *trckd ldrs: racd keenly: rdn over 2f out: wknd over 1f out* **33/1** | DAllan[(3)] 8 | 73 |
| 144- | **6** | ½ | **Baltic Wave**[308] 4018 3-9-2 **95** (TDBarron) *trckd ldrs: rdn over 2f out: wknd over 1f out* **18/1** | PMakin[(5)] 3 | 89 |
| 3166 | **7** | 1 ¾ | **Granston (IRE)**[16] 2448 3-8-3 **77** (JDBethell) *led 1f: remained handy tl wknd over 1f out* **8/1** | CCatlin 9 | 66 |
| 0000 | **8** | ½ | **Overdrawn (IRE)**[9] 2642 3-8-13 **87** (JAOsborne) *s.i.s: swtchd lft and hdwy over 2f out: n.d* **7/1**[3] | (b[1]) GDuffield 11 | 75 |
| 0534 | **9** | 3 | **Poppys Footprint (IRE)**[11] 2569 3-8-2 **76** (KARyan) *s.i.s: a in rr* **8/1** | PFessey 10 | 56 |
| 4120 | **10** | nk | **Inchloss (IRE)**[16] 2448 3-8-3 **77** (BAMcmahon) *led after 1f: hdd 3f out: wknd wl over 1f out* **25/1** | GGibbons 6 | 57 |

1m 25.65s (-2.16) **Going Correction** -0.075s/f (Good) **10** Ran SP% **119.8**

Speed ratings: **109,108,108,101,101 100,98,97,94,94**CSF £12.82 CT £84.27 TOTE £2.90: £1.10, £2.50, £2.70; EX 16.40.

**Owner** Park Farm Racing **Bred** Park Farm Racing **Trained** Newmarket, Suffolk

■ Stewards Enquiry : P Hanagan one-day ban: used whip with excessive frequency (Jun 24)

**FOCUS**

A smart winning time to this fair handicap and the form looks sound.

**NOTEBOOK**

**Warden Complex** ◆ confirmed the strength of his handicap debut success last time with a neat success off an 8lb higher mark. He is still unexposed, should get a mile and looks a most progressive individual.

**Flipando(IRE)**, back to form in a fair event over six last time, ran a solid race over this extra furlong. He went down fighting on this occasion and should not be long in gaining compensation.

**Primo Way**, desperately disappointing last time when a beaten favourite, proved that running to be all wrong and got this extra furlong well.

**Molcon(IRE)**, although not getting the clearest of runs, failed to reproduce his decent third at Newmarket last time over this longer trip. The ground may well have been a touch too quick on this occasion and he can do better when reverting to shorter. *Official explanation: jockey said gelding hung right*

**Mrs Moh(IRE)** ran her best race of the current campaign, but paid late on for running too freely through the first few furlongs. She has still to prove she has fully trained on this year, but it also may be that she is too high in the ratings at present.

## 2908 JOBS@PERTEMPS MEDIAN AUCTION MAIDEN STKS 6f

**4:30** (4:31) (E) 3-4-Y-O **£3,610** (£1,111; £555; £277) **Stalls** High

| Form | | | | | RPR |
|---|---|---|---|---|---|
| 0- | **1** | | **Khalidia (USA)**[218] 5948 3-8-13 (MAMagnusson) *trckd ldr: rdn to ld wl ins fnl f: r.o* **9/2**[2] | EAhern 6 | 68 |
| 3-22 | **2** | hd | **Flying Bantam (IRE)**[13] 2530 3-8-13 70 (RAFahey) *led: hung lft thrght: rdn and hdd wl ins fnl f* **4/5**[1] | PHanagan 14 | 67 |
| | **3** | 2 | **Bold Bunny** 3-8-8 (SCWilliams) *dwlt: hdwy over 4f out: rdn over 1f out: kpt on* **20/1** | DaleGibson 12 | 56 |
| 00 | **4** | 2 ½ | **Chatshow (USA)**[13] 2517 3-8-13 (LADace) *s.i.s: hld up: hdwy 2f out: nt trble ldrs* **20/1** | ACulhane 8 | 54 |
| 4053 | **5** | 1 | **Roan Raider (USA)**[8] 2675 4-9-4 49 (MJPolglase) *chsd ldrs: rdn over 2f out: wknd fnl f* **8/1**[3] | (p) LFletcher[(3)] 3 | 51 |
| 0- | **6** | 3 | **Comic Tales**[220] 5930 3-8-13 (MMullineaux) *s.i.s: hld up: sme hdwy over 1f out: n.d* **50/1** | SRighton 7 | 42 |
| 0- | **7** | shd | **Wonder Wolf**[300] 4243 3-8-5 (RAFahey) *s.i.s: hld up: styd on ins fnl f: nvr nrr* **20/1** | THamilton[(3)] 13 | 36 |
| 00-0 | **8** | ½ | **Aguilera**[62] 1362 3-8-5 (MDods) *prom over 4f* **50/1** | LEnstone[(3)] 15 | 35 |
| 0 | **9** | 1 ¾ | **Ragazzi (IRE)**[58] 1453 3-8-13 (TDBarron) *plld hrd and prom: dropped rr 5f out: nvr nr to chal* **9/1** | KDarley 9 | 34 |
| 0-00 | **10** | 1 | **Designer City (IRE)**[10] 2621 3-8-3 50 (ABerry) *chsd ldrs over 3f* **20/1** | PBradley[(5)] 4 | 26 |
| 0050 | **11** | 2 ½ | **Blue Emperor (IRE)**[57] 1478 3-8-13 52 (PTMidgley) *sn outpcd* **25/1** | GParkin 2 | 24 |
| 0-0 | **12** | nk | **Trinaree (IRE)**[8] 2675 3-8-13 (SGollings) *chsd ldrs to 1/2-way* **50/1** | CCatlin 1 | 23 |
| 00 | **13** | 5 | **Cottam Karminski**[11] 2572 3-8-8 (JSWainwright) *in rr whn hmpd 5f out: effrt 1/2-way: wknd and eased wl over 1f out* **33/1** | PMQuinn 11 | 3 |
| 00- | **14** | 4 | **Oniz Tiptoes (IRE)**[242] 5572 3-8-10 (JSWainwright) *dwlt: outpcd* **50/1** | TEaves[(3)] 5 | — |

1m 14.36s (0.08) **Going Correction** -0.075s/f (Good)

**WFA** 3 from 4yo 8lb **14** Ran SP% **128.5**

Speed ratings: **96,95,93,89,88 84,84,83,81,79 76,76,69,64**CSF £8.01 TOTE £7.20: £2.40, £1.10, £3.60; EX 11.30.

**Owner** East Wind Racing Ltd **Bred** Dr Hiram Polk & Dr J David Richardson **Trained** Upper Lambourn, Berks

**FOCUS**

A dire contest but the first two came clear.

**NOTEBOOK**

**Khalidia(USA)**, who showed little promise on his sole juvenile outing last year, ran on strongly to collar the runner-up inside the final furlong. He is entitled to improve plenty on this, as he had been off for 218 days previously, and although he beat little on this occasion, he is the type his yard do well with.

**Flying Bantam(IRE)** again found one too good, having done everything right up until he was challenged, and showed a tendency to hang left on this occasion. He was a clear second and does have the talent to lose his maiden tag, but may continue to prove vulnerable to an improver in maiden contests.

**Bold Bunny**, a half-sister to ten-furlong winners among others, made a pleasing debut and would have been closer but for blowing the start. Her lack of a previous run told late on, but she will know more next time.

**Chatshow(USA)** improved a touch for this drop in trip, was staying on well enough late in the day after missing the kick and ran his best race for current connections.

**Roan Raider(USA)** had every chance of filling the frame, until he could find only the one pace under pressure entering the last furlong. He remains a maiden after 28 attempts and does very little for the form.

**Cottam Karminski** *Official explanation: jockey said saddle slipped*

## 2909 LITTLEWOODS BET DIRECT FILLIES' STKS (H'CAP) 5f

**5:00** (5:06) (D) (0-85,85) 3-Y-O+ **£5,573** (£1,715; £857; £428) **Stalls** High

| Form | | | | | RPR |
|---|---|---|---|---|---|
| 0230 | **1** | | **Frascati**[15] 2490 4-8-13 **70** (ABerry) *chsd ldrs: led over 1f out: edgd rt ins fnl f: rdn out* **6/1**[2] | FLynch 11 | 79 |
| 5-40 | **2** | 1 ¼ | **Cerulean Rose**[24] 2246 5-8-10 **67** (AWCarroll) *hld up: hdwy over 1f out: r.o* **5/1**[1] | ACulhane 1 | 72+ |
| 0011 | **3** | ½ | **Lady Protector**[15] 2482 5-7-12 **55** (JBalding) *sn outpcd: hdwy over 1f out: rdn and n.m.r ins fnl f: styd on same pce* **6/1**[2] | DaleGibson 9 | 58 |
| -065 | **4** | 1 | **College Queen**[8] 2670 6-8-8 **65** (SGollings) *chsd ldrs: rdn and ev ch over 1f out: styd on same pce* **12/1** | (p) CCatlin 6 | 64 |
| 000- | **5** | nk | **Le Meridien (IRE)**[270] 4988 6-7-12 **55** (JSWainwright) *hld up: styd on ins fnl f: nvr nrr* **33/1** | PMQuinn 3 | 53 |
| -040 | **6** | 1 ¾ | **Bettys Pride**[9] 2656 5-7-13 **56** (MDods) *s.s: outpcd: styd on ins fnl f: nvr nrr* **11/1** | PHanagan 2 | 48 |
| 30-4 | **7** | nk | **Dani Ridge (IRE)**[8] 2685 6-10-0 **85** (EJAlston) *trckd ldrs: hmpd over 1f out: no ex* **7/1**[3] | EAhern 10 | 76 |
| 3530 | **8** | 1 ¾ | **Lady Pekan**[6] 2739 5-8-5 **62** (PSMcentee) *led 4f out: rdn: hung rt and hdd over 1f out: wknd ins fnl f* **14/1** | (b) JBramhill 7 | 46 |
| 0000 | **9** | nk | **Safranine (IRE)**[14] 2506 7-8-6 **63** (MissAStokell) *chsd ldrs over 3f* **25/1** | (p) AnnStokell 4 | 46 |
| -030 | **10** | 5 | **Roses Of Spring**[15] 2488 6-9-6 **82** (RMHCowell) *chsd ldrs over 3f* **7/1**[3] | (p) PMakin[(5)] 8 | 47 |

60.44 secs (-0.98) **Going Correction** -0.075s/f (Good) **10** Ran SP% **99.7**

Speed ratings: **104,102,101,99,99 96,95,93,92,84**CSF £25.40 CT £101.73 TOTE £6.60: £1.50, £2.60, £1.60; EX 30.70 Place 6 £13.85, Place 5 £8.60.

**Owner** Lord Crawshaw **Bred** Exors Of The Late Lord Crawshaw **Trained** Cockerham, Lancs

**FOCUS**

An ordinary sprint handicap run at a generous pace. The form looks sound enough.

**NOTEBOOK**

**Frascati** was always on the pace from her stands'-rail draw and showed a good attitude to quicken inside the last furlong to score. She had everything go her way on this time and although she is in good heart, it looks about as good as she is.

**Cerulean Rose** ran a decent race from her wide stall and looks to be coming back to herself.

**Lady Protector** confirmed her recent rude health with a valiant effort. She had been raised 10lb for winning the last twice, so deserves credit and would have been a little closer but for traffic problems late on.

**College Queen**, with the blinkers swapped for cheekpieces this time, could not sustain her effort late on, having shown plenty of dash through the early stages.

T/Plt: £7.50 to a £1 stake. Pool: £40,151.15. 3,871.90 winning tickets. T/Qpdt: £2.70 to a £1 stake. Pool: £2,257.20. 599.10 winning tickets. CR



The Form Book, Raceform Ltd, Compton, RG20 6NL

# [2761]SALISBURY (R-H)

Sunday, June 13

**OFFICIAL GOING: Firm (good to firm in places), final 4f - good to firm (firm in places)**

## 2910 AUTECNIQUE ALFA ROMEO RATED STKS (H'CAP) 1m 6f 15y

2:00 (2:00) (C) (0-95,87) 3-Y-O £9,201 (£3,402; £1,701; £773) Stalls Far side

Form RPR

-402 1 **Le Tiss (IRE)**[11] 2578 3-8-6 79 SHitchcott(3) 1 84
*(MRChannon) a in tch: short of room over 2f out: and swtchd lft 2f out: styd on u.p to ld last stride* **10/3**[2]

3116 2 shd **Tudor Bell (IRE)**[4] 2782 3-8-8 78 DSweeney 5 83
*(JGMO'Shea) led tl hdd after 4f: led again over 2f out: hrd rdn and sltly short of room whn hdd last stride* **10/3**[2]

-002 3 nk **Coventina (IRE)**[27] 2179 3-8-12 82 TQuinn 2 87
*(JLDunlop) a in front rnk: ev ch u.p ins fnl 2f tl no ex cl home* **2/1**[1]

1226 4 7 **Absolutelythebest (IRE)**[18] 2397 3-8-12 82 (v[1]) JPMurtagh 4 77
*(EALDunlop) plld hrd in rr tl allowe to come on oustide to ld after 4f: hdd overe 2f out: wknd wl over 1f out* **11/2**[3]

3-00 5 2 ½ **Zouave (IRE)**[8] 2683 3-9-3 87 (b[1]) LDettori 6 78
*(BJMeehan) hld up in last pl: rdn over 3f out and nvr got into r* **7/1**

3m 4.29s (-1.71) **Going Correction** -0.175s/f (Firm) **5 Ran SP% 107.4**
Speed ratings: **97,96,96,92,91**CSF £13.75 TOTE £3.30: £1.70, £2.10; EX 14.00.
**Owner** P Trant **Bred** W Lazy T And Newtown Stud **Trained** West Ilsley, Berks

**FOCUS**
They crawled along for most of the way and it was therefore not a proper test at the trip. The time was moderate as a result.

**NOTEBOOK**
**Le Tiss(IRE)** gave an improved effort when a running-on second at Kempton and, despite not being certain to get this trip on pedigree, finished strongly to snatch it in the shadow of the post, although the slow pace did not make it a proper test. He failed to get a run on the rail from the four- to two-furlong markers and when eventually switched needed every ounce of Sam Hitchcott's strength to get him up in the dying strides. He is a sizeable colt who is going the right way and has more to offer.
**Tudor Bell(IRE)** ran way below form at Hamilton earlier in the week and this was more like the colt. He went down fighting having led at a modest tempo and remains on the up.
**Coventina(IRE)** has come right back to form the last twice, being beaten under half a length on each occasion, and got beat the same distance by Tudor Bell as she had done at Windsor in May, despite being worse off at the weights.
**Absolutelythebest(IRE)** is a wayward character and ran a second bad race in a row.
**Zouave(IRE)** is going the wrong way and the blinkers failed to do anything for him.

## 2911 CHAS H. BAKER MAIDEN FILLIES' STKS 1m

2:30 (2:31) (D) 3-Y-O £6,136 (£1,888; £944; £472) Stalls High

Form RPR

3-2 1 **Dawn Surprise (USA)**[31] 2059 3-8-11 (t) LDettori 10 91+
*(SaeedBinSuroor) mde all: shkn up 2f out: sn clr: easily* **11/10**[1]

3 2 5 **Posteritas (USA)**[9] 2647 3-8-11 RHughes 7 78
*(HRACecil) mid-div: rdn 3f out: styd on to go 2nd to easy wnr wl ins fnl f* **7/2**[2]

2 3 hd **Nouveau Riche (IRE)**[9] 2647 3-8-11 RLMoore 6 78
*(HMorrison) s.i.s: sn mid-div: hdwy to chse wnr over 1f out: no ex and lost 2nd wl ins fnl f* **8/1**

3-02 4 5 **Hunter's Valley**[5] 2765 3-8-11 78 PDobbs 3 66
*(RHannon) trckd ldrs: one pce appr fnl f* **16/1**

6-2 5 ¾ **Grand Apollo**[17] 2425 3-8-11 JFortune 12 64
*(JHMGosden) racd mid-div: no hdwy ins fnl 2f* **6/1**[3]

6 hd **Sudden Impulse** 3-8-11 RSmith 4 64
*(ACharlton) slowly away and in rr tl stdy hdwy ins fnl 2f: nvr nr to chal* **150/1**

7 3 ½ **Medica Boba** 3-8-11 JPMurtagh 11 56
*(HMorrison) a towards rr* **66/1**

24-4 8 nk **Zwadi (IRE)**[15] 2479 3-8-11 75 DaneO'Neill 9 55
*(HCandy) trckd wnr tl wknd qckly over 1f out* **14/1**

00 9 1 **Tipsy Lady**[25] 2223 3-8-11 TQuinn 1 53
*(DRCElsworth) s.i.s: a bhd* **33/1**

-00 10 1 **Kerristina**[17] 2425 3-8-11 SCarson 5 51?
*(DJSFfrenchDavis) outpcd thrght* **100/1**

00 11 hd **Apron (IRE)**[31] 2059 3-8-11 DSweeney 8 50
*(RCharlton) trckd ldrs: rdn and wknd over 2f out* **50/1**

1m 40.3s (-2.67) **Going Correction** -0.175s/f (Firm) **11 Ran SP% 115.8**
Speed ratings: **106,101,100,95,95 94,91,91,90,89 88**CSF £4.68 TOTE £2.40: £1.10, £2.30, £2.70; EX 6.30.
**Owner** Godolphin **Bred** Gainsborough Stud Management Llc **Trained** Newmarket, Suffolk

**FOCUS**
No real strength in depth to this maiden, but Dawn Surprise was an emphatic winner and looks capable of going on to better things. It was a decent winning time for the grade.

**NOTEBOOK**
**Dawn Surprise(USA)** had the best form on offer and was given a simple ride from the front, upping the tempo at the three pole and quickening well to have it sewn up two from home. She reportedly found the mile two trip beyond her on her seasonal debut when second behind the smart Quiff and was much more at home over the mile. There is more to come from her.
**Posteritas(USA)** reversed Goodwood form with Nouveau Riche, but was no match for the winner. She ideally wants further.
**Nouveau Riche(IRE)** was being niggled at over half a mile out and seemed to find the ground a little too quick. She stayed on regardless and will be better on easier going.
**Hunter's Valley** continues to disappoint and remains one to leave well alone.
**Grand Apollo**, although second on firm ground on her reappearance, ran here as though she did not want it and never featured. She is now qualified to run in handicaps and should do better in that sphere.
**Sudden Impulse** made a pleasing start to her career and was keeping on at the one pace.

## 2912 TOTEPLACEPOT H'CAP 5f

3:05 (3:05) (D) (0-85,83) 3-Y-O+ £6,916 (£2,128; £1,064; £532) Stalls High

Form RPR

0000 1 **Dancing Mystery**[6] 2739 10-9-11 80 SCarson 9 90
*(EAWheeler) a in tch on ins: swtchd lft 1f out: str run ins last to ld last stride* **22/1**

3263 2 hd **Roxanne Mill**[15] 2490 6-9-6 75 RLMoore 2 84
*(JMBradley) in tch: rdn to ld over 1f out: r.o: hdd last stride* **5/1**[1]

3010 3 hd **Whistler**[5] 2754 7-9-12 81 (p) MHills 4 89
*(JMBradley) hld up: switched lft to outside 2f out: r.o to chse ldr ins fnl f tl last 2nd last strides* **11/2**[2]

0360 4 ¾ **Seven No Trumps**[6] 2739 7-9-8 77 (p) LDettori 5 82
*(JMBradley) hld up: hdwy over 1f out: r.o fnl f: nvr nrr* **13/2**

3060 5 ½ **Playtime Blue**[6] 2724 4-8-1 61 NChalmers(5) 1 64
*(MrsHSweeting) trckd ldr: led 3f out tl hdd over 1f out: one pce fnl f* **20/1**

30-0 6 nk **Kathology (IRE)**[8] 2679 7-10-0 83 TQuinn 8 85
*(DRCElsworth) led tl hdd 3f out: ev ch tl fdd ins fnl f* **5/1**[1]

0430 7 nk **Port St Charles (IRE)**[6] 2739 7-8-3 63 RThomas(5) 7 64
*(CRDore) s.i.s: sme late hdwy but nvr nr to chal* **7/1**

-000 8 1 ½ **Nivernais**[10] 2628 5-9-8 77 DaneO'Neill 3 72
*(HCandy) trckd ldrs: rdn 2f out: wkng whn hmpd appr fnl f* **5/1**[1]

0502 9 1 **Taboor (IRE)**[10] 2628 6-7-12 56 (b) LisaJones(3) 6 47
*(JWPayne) outpcd thrght* **6/1**[3]

60.43 secs (-1.14) **Going Correction** -0.175s/f (Firm) **9 Ran SP% 114.6**
Speed ratings: **102,101,101,100,99 98,98,96,94**CSF £127.37 CT £707.41 TOTE £26.30: £5.00, £1.60, £2.60; EX 175.70 Trifecta £821.40 Pool of £19,090.73 - 16.50 winning units..
**Owner** Astrod TA Austin Stroud & Co **Bred** Mrs D Price **Trained** Whitchurch-on-Thames, Oxon
■ Stewards Enquiry : S Carson one-day ban: careless riding (Jun 24)

**FOCUS**
A fair handicap in which 'old boy' Dancing Mystery flew home to snatch victory late on having been held up in his run.

**NOTEBOOK**
**Dancing Mystery** bounced right back to form, bursting throught in the final strides to get there in the shadow of the post having had to sit and suffer for most of the journey. He flew home and ended up winning a shade cleverly, but whether he is up to following up is doubtful.
**Roxanne Mill** looked the likely winner when coming through to lead just over a furlong out, but wandered off a straight line and was nailed close home.
**Whistler** could never get involved at Chester and ran a better race.
**Seven No Trumps** is without a win in over two years and ran well on ground that is probably a little fast for him.
**Kathology(IRE)** was disappointing and failed to build on his promising seasonal debut.
**Nivernais** is another who has yet to get it together so far this season.

## 2913 AXMINSTER CARPETS CATHEDRAL STKS (LISTED RACE) 6f

3:35 (3:35) (A) 3-Y-O+ £20,300 (£7,700; £3,850; £1,750) Stalls High

Form RPR

-411 1 **Moss Vale (IRE)**[22] 2294 3-8-13 112 MHills 8 117+
*(BWHills) trckd ldr: led over 2f out: pushed out fnl f but a in command* **4/9**[1]

-542 2 ¾ **Mac Love**[30] 2080 3-8-9 102 GCarter 6 111
*(JAkehurst) a in tch: chsd wnr 2f out: r.o wl fnl f but a hld* **8/1**[2]

-505 3 3 ½ **Kings Point (IRE)**[18] 2398 3-8-9 99 DaneO'Neill 4 101
*(RHannon) hld up: rdn and hdwy to go 3rd ent fnl f but no ch w first 2* **12/1**[3]

24-6 4 3 **Bali Royal**[15] 2475 6-8-12 104 RMiles 5 87
*(MSSaunders) trckd ldrs tl rdn and wknd appr fnl f* **8/1**[2]

0500 5 ¾ **Little Edward**[8] 2682 6-9-3 94 TQuinn 2 89+
*(BGPowell) plld hrd in rr and swtchd over to far side: hdwy 2f out but short of room on rail appr fnl f and nt rcvr* **28/1**

0000 6 2 **Repertory**[9] 2636 11-9-10 102 TGMcLaughlin 3 90
*(MSSaunders) led tl hdd over 2f out: wknd over 1f out* **33/1**

4444 7 ½ **Fromsong (IRE)**[15] 2475 6-9-3 99 RHughes 9 82
*(BRMillman) in mid-div: wknd appr fnl f* **12/1**[3]

8 8 **Live Wire Lucy (USA)**[151] 3-8-4 TPQueally 7 53
*(CTinkler) outpcd thrght* **50/1**

1m 11.85s (-3.09) **Going Correction** -0.175s/f (Firm)
**WFA** 3 from 4yo+ 8lb **8 Ran SP% 115.2**
Speed ratings: **113,112,107,103,102 99,99,88**CSF £4.68 TOTE £1.50: £1.10, £2.20, £2.30; EX 5.00.
**Owner** John C Grant **Bred** Derek Veitch **Trained** Lambourn, Berks

**FOCUS**
A fair Listed sprint that was a clean sweep for the three-year-olds and it was run in a good time. The front pair pulled three and a half lengths clear of Kings Point and are both smart sprinters, but whether Moss Vale proves good enough to take up his entry in the July Cup is open to question.

**NOTEBOOK**
**Moss Vale(IRE)** is a progressive sprinter on a roll and he found plenty under pressure when pressed by Mac Love. Connections have some lofty plans for him, namely a tilt at the July Cup, but he will need to improve dramatically before he can be considered for such a race.
**Mac Love**, an unlucky second behind So Will I in Listed company at Newbury in May, came into this as the clear second choice and he gave the favourite a fright. He travelled beautifully before Moss Vale pulled out more and is right back to his best, if not better.
**Kings Point(IRE)** has been running over further and seemed to appreciate this drop down to six. He unquestionably stays seven furlongs and it might just be the case that he was running against superior opposition rather than over a trip too far.
**Bali Royal** fared best of the older brigade and showed an improvement on her seasonal debut form. She should progress again.
**Little Edward** never really got a clear run and should have been a little closer.
**Live Wire Lucy(USA)** *Official explanation: jockey said filly stumbled coming out of the stalls, became unbalanced and was never travelling thereafter*

## 2914 TOTESPORT.COM "CITY BOWL" (FILLIES' H'CAP) 1m 4f

4:10 (4:10) (D) (0-80,82) 3-Y-O+ £7,098 (£2,184; £1,092; £546) Stalls High

Form RPR

-011 1 **Selebela**[12] 2546 3-9-5 82 JPMurtagh 3 101+
*(LMCumani) mde all: pushed along 2f out: rdn to qckn clr 1f out: comf* **4/6**[1]

2153 2 4 **Anyhow (IRE)**[5] 2767 7-8-10 61 DNolan(3) 5 68
*(MissKMGeorge) hld up: hdwy 3f out: wnt 2nd wl over 1f out: sn rdn and nt pce of wnr* **9/2**[2]

0440 3 2 ½ **Desert Island Disc**[15] 2474 7-9-8 73 JFMcDonald(3) 2 76
*(JJBridger) t.k.h: nvr out of first 3: chsd wnr 2f out tl one pce appr fnl f* **5/1**[3]

-060 4 7 **Ribbons And Bows (IRE)**[19] 2381 4-9-3 65 LDettori 4 57
*(CACyzer) hld up in rr: rdn over 3f out: nvr on terms* **8/1**

5 7 **Latin Queen (IRE)**[359] 2549 4-8-4 55 RMiles(3) 1 36
*(JDFrost) trckd wnr for most of way tl hung rt over 3f out: wknd qckly over 2f out* **50/1**

2m 33.31s (-3.04) **Going Correction** -0.175s/f (Firm)
**WFA** 3 from 4yo+ 15lb **5 Ran SP% 107.9**
Speed ratings: **103,100,98,94,89**CSF £3.81 TOTE £1.50: £1.10, £1.90; EX 3.50.
**Owner** Scuderia Rencati Srl **Bred** Fittocks Stud **Trained** Newmarket, Suffolk

**FOCUS**
Selebela had to do it the hard way and she proved good enough to defy her big rise. She beat some exposed rivals and looks progressive.

NOTEBOOK
**Selebela**, raised a massive 24lb for her two Leicester romps, did it from the front and, having momentarily looked in a little trouble, found more and pulled away to score comfortably. There is no saying how much more improvement there is in her and she could defy a penalty.
**Anyhow(IRE)** rarely runs a bad race and is on a winning mark. She pulled two and a half lengths clear of the third.
**Desert Island Disc** is still 7lb higher than when last successful and needs to drop further in the weights before she is winning again.
**Ribbons And Bows(IRE)** continues out of form and was never competitive.

## 2915 AXMINSTER CARPETS APPRENTICE H'CAP — 1m
**4:40** (4:40) (E) (0-70,70) 3-Y-O — **£3,744** (£1,152; £576; £288) Stalls High

Form — RPR
2140 **1** **Alfridini**[55] [1509] 3-9-7 **70** ... LPKeniry 14 81
(DRCElsworth) *trckd ldr: led over 2f out: rdn out fnl f* **12/1**
0-20 **2** ½ **Captain Marryat**[41] [1827] 3-8-8 **57** ... TPQueally 15 67
(PWHarris) *in tch: short of room and swtchd lft over 2f out: kpt on u.p to chse wnr ins fnl f* **6/1**[3]
003 **3** *1* **Fuel Cell (IRE)**[18] [2401] 3-8-11 **65** ... PGallagher[(5)] 7 73
(RHannon) *hld up: hdwy on ins 2f out: kpt on fnl f* **11/2**[2]
0030 **4** *5* **Charlie Tango (IRE)**[12] [2558] 3-8-13 **62** ... SHitchcott 4 58
(MRChannon) *hld up in mid-div: styd on ins fnl 2f: nvr nr to chal* **8/1**
-404 **5** ¾ **Pregnant Pause (IRE)**[7] [2706] 3-8-8 **64** ... JDWalsh[(7)] 13 58
(SKirk) *hld up: swtchd lft over 1f out: kpt on: nvr nr to chal* **16/1**
4-04 **6** ¾ **Redi (ITY)**[19] [2390] 3-9-5 **68** ... NMackay 12 61
(LMCumani) *mid-div: rdn 2f out: one pce after* **4/1**[1]
5130 **7** *nk* **Three Welshmen**[12] [2546] 3-8-8 **57** ... (b) ABeech 11 49
(BRMillman) *prom: rdn over 2f out: wknd appr fnl f* **20/1**
1623 **8** 3½ **Joy And Pain**[19] [2378] 3-9-1 **67** ... AQuinn[(3)] 5 51
(GLMoore) *prom: rdn over 2f out: kpt on but no imp fnl f* **11/2**[2]
0-00 **9** 2½ **Nine Red**[13] [2536] 3-8-2 **58** ... KMay[(7)] 3 36
(BWHills) *led: hdd over 2f out: wknd over 1f out* **14/1**
-500 **10** *3* **Venetian Romance (IRE)**[21] [2324] 3-7-9 **47** oh2...(p) HayleyTurner[(3)] 10 18
(APJones) *prom tl wknd wl over 1f out* **33/1**
-000 **11** *1* **Bienheureux**[103] [946] 3-7-12 **47** oh7 ... LisaJones 8 16
(WJMusson) *mid-div: rdn and wknd 3f out* **25/1**
00-0 **12** *1* **Court Chancellor**[15] [2479] 3-7-12 **50** ... (v[1]) BSwarbrick[(3)] 2 17
(PMitchell) *swvd lft s: effrt 3f out: sn btn* **66/1**
00-0 **13** *shd* **Lady Redera (IRE)**[29] [2122] 3-7-13 **55** ... BO'Neill[(7)] 6 22
(HSHowe) *a struggling in rr* **33/1**
-006 **14** *4* **Kitley**[19] [2377] 3-8-13 **62** ... RMiles 9 19
(BGPowell) *in cl tch tl wknd qckly 2f out* **7/1**

1m 41.82s (-1.15) **Going Correction** -0.175s/f (Firm) **14 Ran SP% 124.9**
Speed ratings: **98,97,96,91,90 90,89,86,83,80 79,78,78,74**CSF £81.34 CT £467.64 TOTE £17.30: £4.10, £3.60, £3.10; EX 102.30 Place 6 £24.99, Place 5 £8.48.
**Owner** A Heaney **Bred** Miss K Rausing **Trained** Whitsbury, Hants

FOCUS
An ordinary handicap and not a strong race. Thje time was moderate for the grade.

NOTEBOOK
**Alfridini**, beaten out of sight on his turf debut back in April - he had been running well and was a winner on the Polytrack - benefited from a break and showed his true form here, proving his effectiveness on turf in the process.
**Captain Marryat** was unlucky on this handicap debut as he did not get much room up the straight and could not pick up in time when getting out. This was an improved effort.
**Fuel Cell(IRE)** showed improved form on this handicap debut and will stay further.
**Charlie Tango(IRE)** stayed on from his low draw without ever threatening.
**Pregnant Pause(IRE)** left a couple of disappointing efforts behind with this staying-on fifth.
**Kitley** ran as though something was amiss. *Official explanation: jockey said colt ran too free*
T/Jkpt: £12,612.90 to a £1 stake. Pool: £62,176.60. 3.50 winning tickets. T/Plt: £31.80 to a £1 stake. Pool: £41,212.40. 945.05 winning tickets. T/Qpdt: £10.90 to a £1 stake. Pool: £2,207.00. 149.65 winning tickets. JS

2916 - 2922a (Foreign Racing) - See Raceform Interactive

2719
# CHANTILLY (R-H)
Sunday, June 13

**OFFICIAL GOING: Good to soft**

## 2923a PRIX DU CHEMIN DE FER DU NORD (GROUP 3) — 1m
**2:10** (2:10) 4-Y-O+ — **£25,704** (£10,282; £7,711; £5,141)

RPR
**1** **My Risk (FR)**[43] [1780] 5-9-1 ... CSoumillon 1 113
(J-MBeguigne, France) *prominent, 3rd straight, led 1 1/2f out, driven and ran on well when challenged* 1
**2** *hd* **Charming Groom (FR)**[17] [2438] 5-8-12 ... OPeslier 4 110
(FHead, France) *led 3f, 2nd straight, challenged and every chance over 1f out, ran on but held by winner*
**3** 2½ **Star Valley (FR)**[45] [1741] 4-8-12 ... IMendizabal 7 105
(J-CRouget, France) *held up in last, soon pushed along straight, finished well from over 1f out, took 3rd final stride*
**4** *shd* **Puppeteer**[17] [2438] 4-9-1 ... GMosse 2 107
(ADeRoyer-Dupre, France) *held up, disputing 8th straight, pushed along 2f out, ran on in centre 1 1/2f out, lost place last stride* 3
**5** 1½ **Almond Mousse (FR)**[43] [1780] 5-8-8 ... SMaillot 5 97
(RobertCollet, France) *in touch, 7th straight, pushed along 1 1/2f out, stayed on but never in challenging position*
**6** *shd* **Caesarion (IRE)**[59] 5-8-12 ... (b) SPasquier 3 101
(JDeRoualle, France) *in touch, disputing 4th straight, pushed along and ran on over 2f out, stayed on at one pace to line*
**7** *nse* **Putra Pekan**[34] [1999] 6-8-12 ... (b) PRobinson 6 101
(MAJarvis) *prominent, led after 3f, headed 1 1/2f out, one pace final furlong* 1
**8** 2½ **Saratan (IRE)**[17] [2438] 7-8-12 ... ELegrix 10 96
(MDelzangles, France) *mid-division, 6th and pushed along straight, never a threat*
**9** *hd* **Gruntled**[28] [2156] 5-9-1 ... TGillet 8 99
(JEHammond, France) *held up on inner, disputing 8th straight, soon pushed along, never dangerous*
**10** *3* **Art Moderne (USA)**[77] [1163] 4-8-12 ... (b) KFallon 9 90
(ELellouche, France) *prominent, disputing 4th straight, pushed along over 1 1/2f out, unable to quicken* 2

1m 36.1s **Going Correction** -0.20s/f (Firm) **10 Ran SP% 124.2**
Speed ratings: **115,114,112,112,110 110,110,108,107,104.**
**Owner** R Monnier **Bred** R Monnier, D Forsans & D Bougarelle **Trained** France

NOTEBOOK
**My Risk(FR)**, third on the bend, battled it out down the straight with Charming Groom. He was driven out but always had the edge. This was the colt's fourth win and he now heads for the Jacques Le Marois at Deauville. He could run in America at the end of the season.
**Charming Groom(FR)** made a lot of the running and kept on gamely to be beaten only a head. He will be given a break until the autumn.
**Star Valley(FR)** was held up in last position for much of the way. He improved in the straight and accelerated well to take third place from Puppeteer.
**Putra Pekan** refused to settle and pulled his way to the front. When asked to quicken in the straight, he soon showed that he had nothing left. His jockey and trainer both reported that the ground was much too firm and he will now have a\n\x\x break.

## 2924a GRAND PRIX DE CHANTILLY (GROUP 2) — 1m 4f
**3:20** (3:23) 4-Y-0+ — **£42,148** (£16,268; £7,764; £5,176)

RPR
**1** **Policy Maker (IRE)**[70] [1261] 4-9-2 ... KFallon 2 121
(ELellouche, France) *in tch, 5th str, pushed along and headway 1 1/2f out, finished strongly fnl 150yds to ld cl home* 3
**2** *snk* **Fair Mix (IRE)**[42] [1804] 6-8-12 ... OPeslier 4 117
(MRolland, France) *prom and not settle early, hdwy to ld str, pushed along 2f out, rdn and 2l clr fnl f, hdd cl home* 1
**3** *2* **Short Pause**[38] [1922] 5-8-12 ... GaryStevens 7 114
(AFabre, France) *close up, disputing 2nd and pushed along straight, ridden 1 1/2f out, kept on to line* 2
**4** 1½ **Kindjhal (FR)**[38] [1922] 4-8-12 ... DBoeuf 3 112
(ELellouche, France) *towards rr, last half-way but still well in touch, pushed along 1 1/2f out, styd on to take 4th ins fnl f*
**5** ½ **Walkamia (FR)**[38] [1922] 4-8-8 ... ELegrix 5 107
(AFabre, France) *mid-division, 4th straight, pushed along and ran on over 1f out, disputing 2nd 1f out, no extra final stages*
**6** 2½ **Loxias (FR)**[280] [4760] 5-8-12 ... (b) CSoumillon 1 107
(CLaffon-Parias, France) *led til hdd appr str, disp 2nd and pushed along str, driven over 1 1/2f out, one pace fnl f*
**7** ½ **Kalabar**[38] [1922] 4-9-2 ... TThulliez 6 111
(PBary, France) *held up, 6th straight, never in contention* 2

2m 34.9s **Going Correction** +0.025s/f (Good) **7 Ran SP% 116.6**
Speed ratings: **96,95,94,93,93 91,91.**
**Owner** Ecurie Wildenstein **Bred** Dayton Investments Ltd **Trained** France

FOCUS
A very poor time for a Group Two, 2.4 seconds slower than the three-year-old claimer over the same trip.

NOTEBOOK
**Policy Maker(IRE)**, held up in fourth in a race lacking early pace, came up the centre of the track to catch Fair Mix in the last 50 metres. The colt did not hesitate to accelerate when asked, and the jockey reported he had not even needed to\n\x\x pull out the ear plugs, which are a standard part of stable strategy these days. He now goes for the Grand Prix de Saint-Cloud.
**Fair Mix(IRE)** who pulled early, took the lead just before the straight. He looked to have the race in his grasp a furlong out but, though he fought on bravely, was nailed close home. His trainer says the horse has been on the go since last October, so he will now be having a rest and will be brought back in the autumn.
**Short Pause** was outpaced early in the straight but was running on again at the end.
**Kindjhal(FR)**, held up at the back, attempted to make ground in the straight and finished well without being any great threat.

## 2925a PRIX DE DIANE HERMES (GROUP 1) (FILLIES) — 1m 2f 110y
**4:35** (4:39) 3-Y-O — **£201,197** (£80,493; £40,246; £20,106)

RPR
**1** **Latice (IRE)**[42] [1803] 3-9-0 ... CSoumillon 18 116
(J-MBeguigne, France) *hld up in rr, 15th str & moved to outside, hdwy over 2f out, hung rt dist, led 150 yds out, dvn out* **11/4**[1]
**2** ¾ **Millionaia (IRE)**[32] 3-9-0 ... TThulliez 1 115
(ELellouche, France) *mid-div, 8th str, hdwy over 2f out to join ldr 2f out, rdn & ev ch ins fnl f, ran on same pace* **18/1**
**3** ½ **Grey Lilas (IRE)**[28] [2160] 3-9-0 ... GaryStevens 14 114
(AFabre, France) *soon tracking leader, led well over 2f out to 150 yards out, one pace* **8/1**
**4** ¾ **Alexander Goldrun (IRE)**[21] [2330] 3-9-0 ... KManning 4 113
(JSBolger, Ire) *mid-div, hdwy towards ins over 2f out, squeezed through to disp 3rd well over 1f out, one pace fnl f* **13/2**[3]
**5** 1½ **Agata (FR)**[21] [2338] 3-9-0 ... DBoeuf 13 110
(YDeNicolay, France) *hld up in rr, 17th str, moved outside trckng wnr 2f out, ran on under str pressure, nrst at fin* **33/1**
**6** 2½ **Barancella (FR)**[33] [2028] 3-9-0 ... DBonilla 10 106
(FHead, France) *hld up, last str, rdn over 2f out, hdwy on outside fr wl over 1f out, nvr nrr* **25/1**
**7** 1½ **Ask For The Moon (FR)**[21] [2338] 3-9-0 ... IMendizabal 17 104
(J-CRouget, France) *held up towards rear, effort 2f out, kept on same pace from over 1f out* **7/1**
**8** ½ **Dreams Come True (FR)**[89] [1034] 3-9-0 ... (b) C-PLemaire 6 103
(RGibson, France) *mid-division, stayed on same pace final 2 f* **50/1**
**9** ¾ **Asti (IRE)**[21] [2338] 3-9-0 ... KFallon 3 102
(ELellouche, France) *hld up, hdwy on ins ent str, nt clr run over 2f out, squeezed wl over 1f out, sn rdn & one pace* **13/2**[3]
**10** ½ **Steel Princess (IRE)**[33] [2028] 3-9-0 ... TJarnet 16 101
(RGibson, France) *prominent 7f, beaten 2f out* **16/1**
**11** 1½ **Torrestrella (IRE)**[28] [2160] 3-9-0 ... GMosse 12 98
(FRohaut, France) *prominent, 4th straight, ridden 2f out, soon beaten* **9/2**[2]
**12** 2½ **Love And Bubbles (USA)**[33] [2028] 3-9-0 ... SMaillot 11 94
(RobertCollet, France) *prominent, 6th straight, beaten well over 1f out* **33/1**
**13** ½ **Menhoubah (USA)**[21] [2341] 3-9-0 ... DHolland 15 93
(CEBrittain) *prominent, 3rd straight, weakened well over 1f out* **16/1**
**14** *2* **Colony Band (USA)**[63] [1349] 3-9-0 ... OPeslier 7 90
(MmeCHead-Maarek, France) *7th straight, weakened well over 1f out* **16/1**
**15** *5* **Ometsz (IRE)**[21] [2338] 3-9-0 ... ELegrix 9 81
(RodCollet, France) *always towards rear* **50/1**
**16** 1½ **Symphony Of Psalms (USA)**[218] 3-9-0 ... TGillet 5 79
(JEHammond, France) *prominent, 5th straight, weakening when hampered just inside final 2f* **40/1**
**17** *10* **Prairie Flower (IRE)**[13] 3-9-0 ... SCoffigny 8 62
(ELellouche, France) *led to well over 1f out, weakened quickly* **200/1**

2m 7.00s **Going Correction** +0.025s/f (Good) **17 Ran SP% 134.6**
Speed ratings: **113,112,112,111,110 108,107,107,106,106 105,103,103,101,97 96,89.**
**Owner** E Ciampi **Bred** Petra Bloodstock Agency Ltd **Trained** France

**NOTEBOOK**
**Latice(IRE)** broke well from her outside draw but was held up at the back, before being brought with a well-timed run on the outside in the straight to lead inside the final furlong. Her jockey said she is an outstanding filly and could take on the colts, while her trainer thinks she has exceptional acceleration and stays well. She will now rest before being brought back for the Vermeille and the Arc.
**Millionaia(IRE)** accelerated well when asked and battled courageously to the line. This was an outstanding effort considering she was so inexperienced.
**Grey Lilas(IRE)** ran well and was always up with the pace until beaten by the late challenges of Latice and Millionaia. She\n\x\x stayed on well and was given every possible chance by her jockey.
**Alexander Goldrun(IRE)** ran well but was never a threat to the first three. This was her first try beyond one mile and she handled it well.
**Agata(FR)**, in company with the winner towards the rear, tried to follow her through. She was no match for Latice but stayed on under strong pressure to finish ahead of Ask For The Moon and Asti, the pair who had beaten her in the Saint-Alary. Second or third in all her six races, she should have no trouble opening her account over longer trips.
**Barancella(FR)** was supplemented after a Group Three third on only her second appearance, behind two fillies who were among the also-rans here. She stayed on promisingly on the outside to be nearest at the finish. Her maiden win was over a mile and a half and she should prosper at that sort of trip if she remains in France. The catch is that she is now owned by Gary Tanaka and could move to the States at any time.
**Menhoubah(USA)** settled quickly into third position in a truly-run race. She had every chance but had nothing left in the last quarter-mile, fading to be beaten about 14 lengths.

## 2157 COLOGNE (R-H)
Sunday, June 13

**OFFICIAL GOING: Soft**

### 2926a OPPENHEIM-UNION-RENNEN (GROUP 2) — 1m 3f
4:10 (4:27) 3-Y-O — **£42,254** (£16,197; £8,451; £3,521)

RPR
1 — **Malinas (GER)** 3-9-2 ... WMongil 5 111
(PSchiergen, Germany) *mid-division, 5th straight, good headway 3f out in centre, challenged over 1f out, led 1f out, ran on strongly* 2
2 — *1 ¾* **Omikron (IRE)**[28] [2158] 3-9-2 ... ADeVries 3 108
(MarioHofer, Germany) *in touch, 4th straight, headway 2f out, ridden & every chance final f til no extra last 100y*
3 — *1 ¾* **Shirocco (GER)**[29] 3-9-2 ... ASuborics 7 105
(ASchutz, Germany) *led, pushed along 2 1/2f out, headed 1f out, kept on one pace* 1
4 — *¾* **Intendant (GER)**[29] 3-9-2 ... ABoschert 4 104
(FrauABertram, Germany) *prominent, 2nd straight, driven & pressing leader over 2f out, kept on one pace*
5 — *7* **Beau Cadeau (IRE)** 3-9-2 ... THellier 2 93
(PSchiergen, Germany) *always towards rear, stayed on final stages*
6 — *1 ½* **Arkando (GER)** 3-9-2 ... AStarke 6 90
(ASchutz, Germany) *behind, last & pushed along straight, no impression*[3]
7 — *1 ½* **Papini (IRE)**[49] 3-9-2 ... LHammer-Hansen 8 88
(DKRichardson, Germany) *raced in 2nd, 3rd straight, ridden & weakened from 2f out*
8 — *3* **Armand (GER)**[29] 3-9-2 ... (b) SChin 9 83
(PSchiergen, Germany) *held up in rear, never a factor*

2m 18.94s — **8** Ran SP% **133.3**
Speed ratings: .
**Owner** Stiftung Gestut Fahrhof **Bred** Stiftung Gestut Fahrhof **Trained** Germany

## 2798 BRIGHTON (L-H)
Monday, June 14

**OFFICIAL GOING: Firm**
With many coming wide onto what was believed to be faster ground, the runners frequently fanned out across the track, so the form may be unreliable.

### 2927 LLEWELLYN ROK MAIDEN AUCTION STKS — 5f 59y
2:15 (2:16) (F) 2-Y-O — **£2,891** (£826; £413) **Stalls** Low

Form — RPR
4 **1** — **Talcen Gwyn (IRE)**[8] [2702] 2-8-10 ... JFEgan 2 70
(MFHarris) *mde all: edgd rt over 1f out and ins last but a in command* **10/3**[2]
**2** *1 ¾* **Connotation** 2-8-7 ... SSanders 4 61
(PWD'Arcy) *in tch: kpt on to chse wnr over 1f out but no imp ins last* **9/1**
6 **3** *1 ½* **Ride Safari**[20] [2376] 2-8-12 ... PDoe 5 61
(PWinkworth) *s.i.s and in rr tl prog to chse first 2 fnl f* **9/4**[1]
0 **4** *3 ½* **He's A Star**[11] [2609] 2-8-11 ... RLMoore 1 47
(RHannon) *rrd up s: sn chsd wnr: rdn and wknd appr fnl f* **10/3**[2]
626 **5** *1 ¾* **Queen's Glory (IRE)**[8] [2702] 2-8-1 ... RMiles[(3)] 3 34
(WRMuir) *trckd ldrs tl rdn and wknd appr fnl f* **7/2**[3]

64.09 secs (1.82) **Going Correction** +0.175s/f (Good) — **5** Ran SP% **109.1**
Speed ratings: **92,89,86,81,78**CSF £28.50 TOTE £3.80: £2.30, £3.90; EX 32.80.
**Owner** D K Watkins **Bred** Paul Smyth **Trained** Paxford, Gloucs

**FOCUS**
A soft race, typical Brighton maiden auction fare, and no better than a seller.

**NOTEBOOK**
**Talcen Gwyn(IRE)** was deliberately brought wide because his rider believed the inside strip to be slower after watering. Benefiting from the experience gained here last week, he used his speed to good effect.
**Connotation** lacked the experience of the winner but kept on well and will benefit from this. She should stay an extra furlong before long.
**Ride Safari** would be capable of winning a little race like this if he could break on level terms. A sixth furlong would help him recover.
**He's A Star** probably did himself no favours by trying to match the winner for early speed despite rearing at the gate. He lost his action and was not knocked about.
**Queen's Glory(IRE)** stayed near the inside as the winner came wide onto what was believed to be faster ground. She has early speed but her best form was over six furlongs.

### 2928 FRIENDS OF THE ELDERLY CHARITY (S) STKS — 7f 214y
2:45 (2:45) (G) 3-Y-O+ — **£2,541** (£726; £363) **Stalls** Low

Form — RPR
00-0 **1** — **Senior Minister**[24] [2262] 6-9-2 62 ... RMiles[(3)] 2 63
(PWHiatt) *mde all: hung rt and c over to stands side over 1f out: rdn out fnl f* **12/1**
0003 **2** *2* **Mr Belvedere**[6] [2762] 3-8-8 61 ... DaneO'Neill 8 58
(RHannon) *a in tch on far side: styd on fnl f to go 2nd cl home* **5/1**[2]
0014 **3** *nk* **Kelseas Kolby (IRE)**[21] [2362] 4-9-10 55 ... (v) IMongan 5 63
(PABlockley) *hld up in rr: hdwy 3f out: chsd wnr over 2f out tl lost 2nd cl home* **7/1**[3]
00-4 **4** *1* **Papeete (GER)**[13] [2545] 3-8-4 70 ow1 ... (b[1]) TQuinn 6 51
(WJHaggas) *mid-div rdn over 2f out: c centre crse but no imp fnl f* **9/4**[1]
6300 **5** *3 ½* **Margery Daw (IRE)**[4] [2801] 4-9-0 50 ... RLMoore 1 42
(PSMcentee) *in tch tl wknd over 2f out* **15/2**
06-0 **6** *1 ¼* **Buchanan Street (IRE)**[18] [2426] 3-8-8 49 ... SWhitworth 4 44
(NACallaghan) *a outpcd in rr* **33/1**
4-00 **7** *4* **Cal Mac**[17] [2454] 5-9-5 70 ... (p) EAhern 3 35
(RMHCowell) *mid-div: rdn over 3f out: hung lft and wknd wl over 1f out* **5/1**[2]
0503 **8** *6* **Smart Boy Prince (IRE)**[60] [1422] 3-8-13 60 ... SWKelly 7 26
(FJordan) *prom tl hmpd over 4f out: sn lost pl and bhd after* **8/1**
0000 **9** *5* **Trusted Instinct (IRE)**[15] [2501] 4-9-5 62 ... JFEgan 9 10
(CADwyer) *chsd wnr over 3f out tl wknd qckly 2f out: eased ent fnl f* **14/1**

1m 36.61s (1.61) **Going Correction** +0.175s/f (Good)
**WFA** 3 from 4yo+ 11lb — **9** Ran SP% **116.8**
Speed ratings: **98,96,95,94,91 89,85,79,74**CSF £71.68 TOTE £12.30: £4.00, £1.90, £3.60; EX 75.80.There was no bid for the winner. Papeete was claimed by Brooke Sanders for £6,000.
**Owner** Phil Kelly **Bred** Stratford Place Stud **Trained** Hook Norton, Oxon

**FOCUS**
A fair seller, with the winner having been dropped in class.They went a decent pace from the outset, and the placed horses all looked at home in this company, with the third the key to the form.

**NOTEBOOK**
**Senior Minister** came wide through hanging, rather than tactics, but it did him no harm. The drop to selling company was ideal, and this trip suits him better than ten furlongs.
**Mr Belvedere**, with the headgear left off, has yet to win after 13 attempts, but a seller of similar quality is a possibility on this evidence.
**Kelseas Kolby(IRE)** stayed on the inside rail and made a smart move soon after turning for home. He could win a similar seller.
**Papeete(GER)** was best in on official figures. Though unable to capitalise on that, she ran with credit in first-time blinkers and should continue to make her mark in this grade.
**Margery Daw(IRE)** has often raced off in front over longer trips, so it was strange to see her restrained behind the leaders despite the perfect draw. This may have been a missed opportunity.
**Buchanan Street(IRE)**, soon taken off his legs, was staying on a little and should be noted for further signs of ability at this level.
**Cal Mac** *Official explanation: jockey said gelding hung left*
**Smart Boy Prince(IRE)** *Official explanation: jockey said gelding suffered interference at the top of the hill*
**Trusted Instinct(IRE)** *Official explanation: jockey said colt lost its action*

### 2929 TOTESPORT.COM FILLIES' H'CAP — 7f 214y
3:15 (3:15) (E) (0-70,69) 3-Y-O+ — **£3,545** (£1,091; £545; £272) **Stalls** Low

Form — RPR
-611 **1** — **A Woman In Love**[8] [2703] 5-10-2 **69** 6ex ... SSanders 8 82
(MissBSanders) *stdd s: t.k.h and hld up in rr: hdwy over 3f out: led over 1f out: r.o wl* **2/1**[1]
0-55 **2** *1 ¼* **Dami (USA)**[12] [2595] 3-9-4 **68** ... (p) DHolland 1 78
(CEBrittain) *a.p: led over 4f out: rdn and hdd over 1f out: kpt on one pce* **13/2**[3]
-200 **3** *2 ½* **Castaway Queen (IRE)**[23] [2302] 5-9-7 **60** ... (b) BDoyle 6 64
(WRMuir) *in tch: hdwy on outside 2f out: nt qckn fnl f* **8/1**
5064 **4** *2 ½* **Even Easier**[6] [2766] 3-8-5 **55** ... (b) RLMoore 4 54
(GLMoore) *hld up towards rr: hdwy 3f out: pressing ldrs over 1f out: wknd ins last* **5/2**[2]
0100 **5** *shd* **Tarkwa**[10] [2643] 5-8-1 **40** ... MHenry 2 38
(RMHCowell) *prom tl lost pl over 4f out: rdn over 2f out: passed btn horses ins fnl 2f* **16/1**
-006 **6** *6* **Susiedil (IRE)**[12] [2587] 3-8-7 **57** ... EAhern 5 41
(PWHarris) *in tch: rdn over 2f out: wknd over 1f out* **8/1**
0-00 **7** *13* **Coconut Cookie**[12] [2587] 3-9-1 **65** ... PDobbs 7 20
(RHannon) *prom on outside tl rdn and wknd 2f out* **33/1**
6500 **8** *7* **Figura**[12] [2594] 6-8-6 **45** ... (v[1]) NDay 3 —
(RIngram) *sn led: hdd over 4f out: rdn and sn bhd* **12/1**

1m 36.19s (1.19) **Going Correction** +0.175s/f (Good)
**WFA** 3 from 5yo+ 11lb — **8** Ran SP% **114.0**
Speed ratings: **101,99,97,94,94 88,75,68**CSF £15.54 CT £85.42 TOTE £2.90: £1.10, £2.10, £4.10; EX 15.70.
**Owner** High & Dry Racing **Bred** Stratford Place Stud **Trained** Epsom, Surrey

**FOCUS**
An ordinary fillies' handicap but won by a horse in great form and on the upgrade.

**NOTEBOOK**
**A Woman In Love** is on a roll, notching up a hat-trick here, and the track and ground were both ideal. This was her highest-ever handicap mark, but she looks in tremedous heart.
**Dami(USA)** had a tough task against an in-form rival but emerged with credit in the first-time cheekpieces.
**Castaway Queen(IRE)** looks at home over this trip, though she was comfortably held.
**Even Easier** came along the inside, where some believed the ground to be slowest. This was nothing special but she has run well enough on this track in the past to give cause for optimism.
**Tarkwa**, in foal to Classic Cliche, found the trip a bit sharp over this speedy track and on the lightning-fast ground.
**Susiedil(IRE)** might be worth dropping back to her winning trip of seven furlongs.

### 2930 HARDINGS BAR & CATERING SERVICES CLASSIFIED STKS — 1m 1f 209y
3:45 (3:50) (F) 3-Y-O+ — **£2,905** (£830; £415) **Stalls** High

Form — RPR
0021 **1** — **Kernel Dowery (IRE)**[12] [2594] 4-9-3 58 ... (e) DHolland 1 70
(PWHarris) *a in tch: rdn to chse ldr over 2f out: led ins fnl f: r.o wl* **2/1**[1]
1-03 **2** *1 ½* **Kirkham Abbey**[13] [2547] 4-9-8 65 ... (v) MHenry 2 72
(MAJarvis) *a.p: led 4f out: rdn and hdd ins fnl f: nt pce of wnr* **9/2**[3]
0003 **3** *5* **Rebate**[19] [2406] 4-9-5 62 ... PDobbs 3 60
(RHannon) *trckd ldr tl over 2f out: outpcd by first 2 ent fnl f* **7/1**
-602 **4** *½* **Scriptorium**[13] [2551] 3-8-6 61 ow1 ... SSanders 6 59
(LMCumani) *hld up in rr: sme hdwy 3f out: sn rdn: nvr nr to chal* **11/4**[2]
-504 **5** *7* **Canadian Storm**[13] [2546] 3-8-1 60 ... FPFerris[(3)] 5 43
(MHTompkins) *in tch tl rdn and wknd wl over 1f out* **9/1**

1025 **6** *14* **Chocolate Boy (IRE)**[17] [2443] 5-9-3 60........ RLMoore 7 17
(GLMoore) *in rr: sme hdwy over 2f out: eased whn btn ent fnl f* **10/1**

0354 **7** *13* **Prince Valentine**[8] [2705] 3-8-4 58........(b) TQuinn 4 —
(DBFeek) *led tl hdd 4f out: wknd over 2f out* **33/1**

2m 2.52s (-0.02) **Going Correction** +0.175s/f (Good)
**WFA** 3 from 4yo+ 13lb **7 Ran SP% 112.7**
Speed ratings: **107,105,101,101,95 84,74**CSF £11.03 TOTE £3.20: £2.10, £1.60; EX 11.30.
**Owner** The Treasure Hunters **Bred** A Lyons Bloodstock **Trained** Ringshall, Bucks

**FOCUS**
A moderate race of its type, but they went a good pace and the winner is progressive.

**NOTEBOOK**
**Kernel Dowery(IRE)** has got the hang of things now and will be worth considering again in the near future. The eyeshield seems to have done the trick.
**Kirkham Abbey** was 24lb higher than at the start of last season, during which he won five times. He goes well on the track and this was a good effort against an improving rival.
**Rebate** is still looking for only his second win. He ran a fair race but was comfortably seen off.
**Scriptorium** was significantly weak in the betting and looked paceless when the pressure was on. This was a disappointing follow-up to his handicap debut, during which he had shown more than this.
**Canadian Storm** still did not get home despite the drop in trip. He is a keen sort and nine furlongs might be his distance.
**Chocolate Boy(IRE)**, with the headgear left off, ran no race at all. *Official explanation: jockey said gelding lost its action*
**Prince Valentine** *Official explanation: vet said gelding had lost a shoe*

## 2931 BARKING BRICKWORK COMPANY MAIDEN H'CAP — 6f 209y
**4:15** (4:17) (E ) (0-70,66) 3-Y-O — **£3,532** (£1,087; £543; £271) **Stalls** Low

Form RPR

-000 **1** **Albadi**[9] [2693] 3-7-11 **49**........(b) DeanWilliams(7) 2 54
(CEBrittain) *nvr out of first 2: rdn to ld jst ins fnl f: hld on wl* **12/1**

-005 **2** *hd* **Bahama Reef (IRE)**[19] [2404] 3-8-10 **55**........ SCarson 7 59
(BGubby) *trckd ldrs: wnt 2nd over 2f out: led wl over 1f out: hdd jst ins fnl f: kpt on u.p* **12/1**

00-0 **3** *nk* **Growler**[51] [1613] 3-8-11 **56**........ EAhern 4 59
(JLDunlop) *in tch: rdn over 2f out: hdwy over 1f out and kpt on to cl on first 2 nr fin* **20/1**

0-04 **4** *2½* **Ablaj (IRE)**[10] [2660] 3-8-8 **53**........(v) DaneO'Neill 8 50
(EALDunlop) *mid-div: rdn over 2f out: nt qckn fnl f* **4/1**[3]

3622 **5** *1¾* **Turnberry (IRE)**[6] [2766] 3-8-10 **55**........(v) TQuinn 3 47
(JWHills) *in rr: rdn 1/2-way: sme hdwy 2f out: one pce appr fnl f* **15/8**[1]

0000 **6** *½* **Ricky Martan**[41] [1854] 3-8-8 **53**........ SWhitworth 6 44
(GCBravery) *in rr: rdn 4f out: nvr on terms* **33/1**

2500 **7** *4* **Get To The Point**[12] [2589] 3-9-7 **66**........ SSanders 1 46
(PWD'Arcy) *in tch: rdn 3f out: wknd qckly fnl f* **11/4**[2]

6-06 **8** *6* **Blaise Wood (USA)**[11] [2632] 3-9-6 **65**........(b[1]) RLMoore 5 30
(GLMoore) *led: hdd wl over 1f out: wknd rapidly and eased ins fnl f* **8/1**

1m 23.69s (1.09) **Going Correction** +0.175s/f (Good) **8 Ran SP% 115.6**
Speed ratings: **100,99,99,96,94 94,89,82**CSF £143.79 CT £2851.25 TOTE £16.20: £3.80, £3.30, £3.30; EX 112.40.
**Owner** Saeed Manana **Bred** Darley **Trained** Newmarket, Suffolk

**FOCUS**
A poor race with some disappointing types contesting the finish.

**NOTEBOOK**
**Albadi** got into this weak handicap off bottom weight and that proved just enough. *Official explanation: trainer's representative said colt may have benefited from the drop in class on this occasion*
**Bahama Reef(IRE)** was brought wide but wanted to hang back down the camber thereafter. He was only just pipped, but this was a poor race.
**Growler** ran his best race to date but that says as much about the quality of the race as it does about his ability.
**Ablaj(IRE)** is disappointing, a fact that is illustrated by his inability to scrap out the finish of such a poor contest.
**Turnberry(IRE)** has become frustrating and expensive to follow, but this was a poor effort. Seven furlongs normally suits but here it looked too sharp over this track and on such fast ground. *Official explanation: jockey said colt never travelled down the hill*
**Ricky Martan** will need to be dropped even further in class to become competitive.

## 2932 RACECOURSE VIDEO SERVICES H'CAP — 5f 213y
**4:45** (4:45) (F ) (0-55,55) 3-Y-O — **£2,898** (£828; £414) **Stalls** Low

Form RPR

6060 **1** **Alizar (IRE)**[7] [2741] 3-9-8 **55**........ RLMoore 4 61
(SDow) *a.p on ins: rdn to ld ent fnl f: all out* **10/1**

0006 **2** *shd* **Red Monarch (IRE)**[20] [2392] 3-9-5 **52**........ IMongan 3 58
(PABlockley) *led tl hdd over 4f out: led briefly again over 1f out: rallied ins fnl f to press wnr clly nr fin* **3/1**[1]

6-06 **3** *1¼* **Maluti**[20] [2380] 3-9-1 **48**........ SSanders 5 50
(RGuest) *trckd ldrs: rdn over 1f out: r.o fnl f to chse first 2* **4/1**[2]

-520 **4** *2* **Savernake Brave (IRE)**[33] [2033] 3-8-13 **46**........ GBaker 1 42
(MrsHSweeting) *prom: led over 4f out: hdd over 1f out: fdd ins fnl f* **7/1**

0600 **5** *½* **Sussex Style (IRE)**[7] [2726] 3-9-3 **50**........(t) PDobbs 10 44
(RMFlower) *in rr: hdwy over 1f out: nt pce to chal* **33/1**

0001 **6** *shd* **Little Flute**[53] [1571] 3-8-13 **46**........ PDoe 7 40
(TKeddy) *in tch: rdn 1/2-way: one pce appr fnl f* **6/1**[3]

4104 **7** *½* **Pardon Moi**[20] [2380] 3-8-12 **48**........ LisaJones(3) 11 41
(MrsCADunnett) *mid-div: hrd rdn 2f out: no ex appr fnl f* **7/1**

-000 **8** *¾* **Johnny Alljays (IRE)**[6] [2766] 3-8-2 **42**........(b) DerekNolan(7) 2 32
(JSMoore) *towards rr: sme hdwy over 1f out: fdd ins last* **25/1**

3400 **9** *2* **Ashstanza**[9] [2688] 3-9-8 **55**........(b[1]) MHenry 8 39
(MAJarvis) *sn rdn: a in rr* **14/1**

-000 **10** *¾* **Pass Go**[11] [2610] 3-9-5 **55**........(bt[1]) RMiles(3) 12 37
(GAButler) *plld hrd: prom rdn 3f out: hung lft and wknd over 1f out* **16/1**

6000 **11** *2* **I Wish I Knew**[6] [2766] 3-8-12 **45**........(v) DaneO'Neill 6 21
(DJCoakley) *mid-div: sn rdn: wknd 2f out* **12/1**

5-00 **12** *½* **Scarlett Breeze**[20] [2380] 3-9-1 **48**........ SWhitworth 9 23
(JWHills) *prom on outside: rdn 1/2-way: sn wknd* **16/1**

1m 11.81s (1.71) **Going Correction** +0.175s/f (Good) **12 Ran SP% 126.3**
Speed ratings: **95,94,93,90,89 89,89,88,85,84 81,81**CSF £42.72 CT £148.97 TOTE £12.50: £4.00, £1.60, £1.70; EX 55.50 Place 6 £577.51, Place 5 £163.15.
**Owner** The Pink Punters **Bred** Epona Bloodstock Ltd **Trained** Epsom, Surrey

**FOCUS**
A poor contest and the form is modest, with most of the runners out of form in recent races, but they went a decent pace.

**NOTEBOOK**
**Alizar(IRE)** had won three times previously, which gave her a better profile than most of her opponents. She has hinted at a return to form in several recent races and this poor contest was an ideal opportunity.
**Red Monarch(IRE)** was made favourite despite showing little in four previous outings, and the money was nearly on the mark. This was a weak race, but he obviously has ability at this level.
**Maluti** does not have inspiring form figures but has been well-backed in her last two races. She could yet win a race, but it will be a weak one.
**Savernake Brave(IRE)** is well-exposed but showed that he is not wthout ability or pace in this company.
**Sussex Style(IRE)** gets outpaced at this trip and is worth trying over an extra furlong in similarly weak company.
**Little Flute**, winner of a banded race on the sand in April, ran a fair race but lacked pace at the business end.
T/Plt: £494.90 to a £1 stake. Pool: £34,984.85. 51.60 winning tickets. T/Qpdt: £103.50 to a £1 stake. Pool: £3,595.20. 25.70 winning tickets. JS

# 2351 CARLISLE (R-H)
## Monday, June 14
**OFFICIAL GOING: Firm (good to firm in places)**

## 2933 NEWS & STAR NOVICE AUCTION STKS — 5f
**2:30** (2:31) (E ) 2-Y-O — **£3,493** (£1,075; £537; £268) **Stalls** High

Form RPR

32 **1** **Katie Boo (IRE)**[17] [2458] 2-8-4........ FNorton 4 71
(ABerry) *prom: chal 2f out: rdn to ld ins fnl f: r.o* **7/2**[3]

4221 **2** *1½* **Evanesce**[6] [2761] 2-8-7........ SHitchcott(3) 7 72
(MRChannon) *led: hrd pressed fr 2f out: rdn and hdd ins fnl f: no ex* **2/1**[1]

2 **3** *4* **Wise Wager (IRE)**[35] [2002] 2-8-2........ PHanagan 3 50
(RAFahey) *slowly away: hung lft thrght: sn in tch: c stands side over 1f out: no imp on first 2 fnl f* **11/4**[2]

3 **4** *½* **Angelofthenorth**[51] [1616] 2-8-2........ RFfrench 2 48
(JDBethell) *in tch: hdwy u.p to chse ldrs 2f out: hung lft: sn btn* **25/1**

321 **5** *2* **Rightprice Premier (IRE)**[35] [2002] 2-8-10........ NCallan 5 49
(KARyan) *a bhd and sn drvn along: n.d* **4/1**

00 **6** *11* **Serene Pearl (IRE)**[30] [2129] 2-8-7........ KDarley 1 8
(GMMoore) *cl up to 1/2-way: sn wknd: t.o* **40/1**

61.19 secs (-0.31) **Going Correction** -0.225s/f (Firm) **6 Ran SP% 108.5**
Speed ratings: **93,90,84,83,80 62**CSF £10.16 TOTE £3.80: £1.50, £1.50; EX 10.60.
**Owner** The Early Doors Partnership **Bred** Michael McGlynn **Trained** Cockerham, Lancs

**FOCUS**
An average novice event run at a modest pace. The first two came clear and the form, although only fair, looks reliable.

**NOTEBOOK**
**Katie Boo(IRE)**, who had shown ability and improved on each of her two previous outings, put her best foot forward inside the final two furlongs and ran on strongly up the rising ground to score. She was getting weight this time, which aided her cause, but she has done little wrong to date and can only improve for an extra furlong.
**Evanesce** again ran a solid race and was a clear second. Her problem is, that although she is tough and consistent, she is mainly exposed and will remain vulnerable to anything with a turn of foot.
**Wise Wager(IRE)** ran a strange race. She blew the start and, when coming into the home straight, hung badly left and ended up on the stands' side, which cost her a lot of ground. She did very well to finish as close as she did, and is better than the bare form, but has a bit to prove now mentality-wise. *Official explanation: jockey said filly hung left-handed*
**Angelofthenorth** ran well until spoiling any chance of being placed by hanging under pressure. This ground looked plenty fast enough and she can improve with more experience.
**Rightprice Premier(IRE)** failed to run up to the level of her previous three outings on this much quicker going. She is worth a chance when able to get her toe into the ground.

## 2934 SCOTBY MAIDEN STKS — 1m 1f 61y
**3:00** (3:00) (D ) 3-Y-O — **£5,720** (£1,760; £880; £440) **Stalls** High

Form RPR

342- **1** **Little Jimbob**[275] [4893] 3-9-0 70........ PHanagan 7 73
(RAFahey) *keen early: led chsng gp: led 2f out: styd on u.p: all out* **13/2**[3]

2-40 **2** *hd* **Just A Fluke (IRE)**[47] [1712] 3-9-0 77........ KDalgleish 2 73
(MJohnston) *prom chsng gp: rdn to chse wnr over 1f out: styd on u.p: jst hld* **9/4**[2]

3 **3** *3½* **Leg Spinner (IRE)**[63] [1371] 3-9-0........ KDarley 6 66
(MRChannon) *in tch early: drvn along and outpcd 4f out: styd on u.p to go 3rd appr fnl f: no imp on first 2* **11/10**[1]

5-05 **4** *11* **Stanley Crane (USA)**[12] [2596] 3-9-0 70........(t) JCarroll 5 44
(BHanbury) *led: wl clr 1/2-way: wknd and hdd 2f out: sn btn* **9/1**

0 **5** *2½* **I'm A Dark Horse**[30] [2133] 3-9-0........ NCallan 4 39
(KARyan) *slowly away: a rr div: wl bhd fnl 3f* **40/1**

05 **6** *10* **Young Warrior (IRE)**[16] [2487] 3-9-0........ DRMcCabe 3 19
(DNicholls) *a rr div: wl bhd fnl 3f* **66/1**

004- **7** *2½* **The Rip**[314] [3864] 3-8-11 72........ DAllan(3) 1 14
(TDEasterby) *a rr div: wl bhd fnl 3f* **14/1**

1m 53.84s (-4.19) **Going Correction** -0.225s/f (Firm) course record **7 Ran SP% 112.3**
Speed ratings: **109,108,105,95,93 84,82**CSF £20.77 TOTE £6.30: £4.20, £1.10; EX 22.00.
**Owner** Dale Scaffolding Co Ltd **Bred** D R Tucker **Trained** Musley Bank, N Yorks

**FOCUS**
A fair maiden for the track but an extraordinarily fast winning time which beat the five-year-old course record by 1.16 seconds. This meant that the first three home all beat the old record, which is suprising given the calibre of the performers on show.

**NOTEBOOK**
**Little Jimbob** kicked clear two out and looked all over the winner, but fell in a hole late on and in the end was all out to repel the runner-up at the line. It was a combination of the trip and the fact that he had been absent from the track for 275 days previously, that saw him tire dramatically late on, but he proved game and is entitled to improve plenty on this.
**Just A Fluke(IRE)** again showed a tendency to carry his head high under pressure, but did well to get to the winner and go down all guns blazing. He is a talented horse, but a desperately tricky ride, in that he saves plenty for himself. He may do better on a slower surface and will one day lose his maiden tag.
**Leg Spinner(IRE)** stayed on all too late on this occasion. He probably failed to run up to his debut form, but will be seen to a better light over farther and is the type to fare better once handicapped.
**Stanley Crane(USA)** dropped out tamely having set a frenetic pace until two out. He has done this in the past and paid the price, but showed little when ridden more patiently last time and he looks to be going the wrong way.

## 2935 BLACK SHEEP BREWERY H'CAP — 1m 6f 32y
**3:30** (3:30) (D ) (0-80,77) 3-Y-O+ — **£5,538** (£1,704; £852; £426) **Stalls** High

Form RPR

5040 **1** **Sahem (IRE)**[33] [2047] 7-9-10 **73**........ PHanagan 8 85
(DEddy) *mde all: rdn over 2f out: styd on strly* **6/1**[3]

222- **2** *3½* **Most Definitely (IRE)**[299] [4274] 4-8-10 **62**........ DAllan(3) 3 69
(TDEasterby) *hld up: effrt 3f out: rdn to chse wnr ent fnl f: no imp* **9/1**

0300 **3** ½ **Greenwich Meantime**[11] 2631 4-10-0 **77** .......................... LGoncalves 9 83
(MrsJRRamsden) *hld up: effrt 3f out: kpt on fnl fnl f: nvr able to chal* **14/1**

1352 **4** *nk* **Toni Alcala**[7] 2731 5-9-1 **67** .......................................... DNolan(3) 10 73
(RFFisher) *in tch: drvn along 4f out: no imp on ldrs: kpt on u.p fnl f* **5/1**[2]

10/2 **5** *shd* **Magic Combination (IRE)**[36] 1173 11-9-8 **71** .................... WDowling 4 77
(LLungo) *hld up: hdwy 3f out: disp 2nd and rdn appr fnl f: no ex ins last* **16/1**

4532 **6** 1½ **Delta Force**[18] 2429 5-8-1 **50** .......................................... GDuffield 6 54
(PABlockley) *chsd wnr: rdn 3f out: fdd appr fnl f* **7/2**[1]

-006 **7** *hd* **Freedom Now (IRE)**[19] 2409 6-9-6 **69** ................................ ACulhane 2 72
(MDHammond) *hld up: effrt 3f out: sn drvn along: no hdwy* **12/1**

0063 **8** 3 **Claradotnet**[11] 2619 4-8-12 **64** ...................................... SHitchcott(3) 7 63
(MRChannon) *hld up: effrt 4f out: sn rdn: no hdwy* **9/1**

450/ **9** ¾ **Ebinzayd (IRE)**[47] 1548 8-9-9 **77** .............................. PMulrennan(5) 1 75
(LLungo) *prom tl rdn and wknd over 2f out* **8/1**

-000 **10** *dist* **Bid For Fame (USA)**[33] 2047 7-9-13 **76** ............................... KDarley 5 —
(NTinkler) *a bhd: lost tch 4f out: t.o* **6/1**[3]

3m 7.05s (-0.25) **Going Correction** -0.225s/f (Firm) **10** Ran SP% **118.8**
Speed ratings: **91,89,88,88,88 87,87,85,85,**—CSF £60.11 CT £732.57 TOTE £6.40: £2.30, £4.60, £7.00; EX 81.60.
**Owner** Robert Gray **Bred** Barronstown Stud And Orpendale **Trained** Ingoe, Northumberland

**FOCUS**
An average staying handicap that produced very modest winning time for the grade and the form is ordinary.

**NOTEBOOK**
**Sahem(IRE)** ran on strongly to the line, having set a start-stop gallop from the off, and won tidily under a canny ride from Hanagan. Granted he had the run of the race on this occasion, but he has slipped to winning mark of late and has been running slightly better than his recent form figures would suggest, so may go close if turned out under a penalty.
**Most Definitely(IRE)** did the best of those held up off the pace and deserves credit, as this was his first outing for nine months. However, there can be no coincidence that he has now finished second on his last six starts and could be one to avoid for win purposes, despite his big each-way appeal.
**Greenwich Meantime** ran his best race for a while. He had run poorly the last twice, but dropped a few pounds as a result and clearly enjoyed the conditions on this occasion.
**Toni Alcala** stayed on again having been outpaced at a crucial stage, but never looked like scoring. He has been running well so far this season, but although he remains in great heart, he currently looks too high in the weights.
**Delta Force**, who shaped well over two miles last time, dropped out quickly late on over this shorter trip. He settled better on this occasion, but may now need a stiffer test and is not one to write off.
**Bid For Fame(USA)** *Official explanation: jockey said gelding was unsuited by the firm ground*

## 2936 MITCHELL & HEAP H'CAP 5f 193y
**4:00** (4:01) (E ) (0-70,69) 3-Y-0+ **£3,851** (£1,185; £592; £296) **Stalls** High

Form RPR

2300 **1** **Silver Mascot**[10] 2656 5-8-7 **50** ........................................ TEaves(3) 1 61
(ISemple) *trckd ldrs: drvn along 2f out: r.o wl u.p to ld clsng stages* **25/1**

0006 **2** ½ **Xanadu**[5] 2779 8-8-11 **51** ................................................(p) RFfrench 12 60
(MissLAPerratt) *led after 2f tl rdn and hdd clsng stages* **9/1**

-121 **3** *nk* **Kirkby's Treasure**[16] 2492 6-9-12 **66** .................................. KDarley 4 74
(ABerry) *chsd ldrs: drvn along 2f out: r.o u.p and ch ins fnl f: no ex clsng stages* **7/1**[2]

04-0 **4** 1 **Tedsdale Mac**[16] 2473 5-8-10 **50** ........................................ NCallan 6 55
(NBycroft) *towards rr: hdwy over 2f out: r.o wl u.p fnl f: nvr able to chal* **12/1**

0506 **5** 1¼ **Flying Edge (IRE)**[2] 2899 4-9-2 **59** ..................................... DAllan(3) 9 60
(EJAlston) *hld up midfield: hdwy over 2f out: chsd ldrs and rdn ent fnl f: no imp ins last* **8/1**[3]

0-20 **6** ½ **Hartshead**[19] 2407 5-9-9 **68** ......................................... PMulrennan(5) 5 68
(GASwinbank) *hld up: hdwy 2f out: in tch and rdn ent fnl f: no further prog ins last* **16/1**

0-00 **7** ½ **Candleriggs (IRE)**[30] 2130 8-9-9 **63** ................................... ANicholls 15 61
(DNicholls) *midfield: effrt over 2f out: kpt on u.p fr over 1f out: n.d* **16/1**

6561 **8** *nk* **Albashoosh**[7] 2735 6-10-1 **69** 6ex ................................. AlexGreaves 16 66
(DNicholls) *midfield: hdwy to dispute 2nd 2f out: sn rdn: fdd* **11/8**[1]

0501 **9** 4 **Old Bailey (USA)**[10] 2666 4-8-6 **46** .....................................(v) PFessey 3 31
(TDBarron) *towards rr most of way* **12/1**

0-35 **10** 1 **Golden Spectrum (IRE)**[23] 2292 5-9-4 **58** ........................ DRMcCabe 2 40
(DNicholls) *bhd most of way* **33/1**

0000 **11** *hd* **John O'Groats (IRE)**[7] 2734 6-9-8 **62** .............................. RWinston 13 44
(MDods) *midfield: effrt over 2f out: sn btn* **25/1**

0040 **12** 2 **Quicks The Word**[24] 2274 4-9-6 **60** ............................(b) DeanMcKeown 11 36
(CWThornton) *prom tl wknd 2f out* **33/1**

00-0 **13** *shd* **Baby Barry**[14] 2524 7-9-0 **54** ........................................(v) GDuffield 8 30
(MrsGSRees) *midfield: rdn 1/2-way: sn btn* **33/1**

000- **14** 3 **Angel Isa (IRE)**[245] 5540 4-8-10 **50** ..................................... PHanagan 7 17
(RAFahey) *sn bhd* **25/1**

-560 **15** *hd* **Travelling Times**[20] 2383 5-8-5 **45** .................................(b) PMQuinn 14 11
(JSWainwright) *chsd ldrs early: sn drvn along and lost pl: bhd fnl 2f* **25/1**

630- **16** 17 **Whinhill House**[292] 4510 4-8-10 **53** ................................... LEnstone(3) 10 —
(DWBarker) *led 2f: remained cl up tl wknd qckly over 2f out: t.o* **40/1**

1m 11.99s (-2.21) **Going Correction** -0.225s/f (Firm) **16** Ran SP% **129.5**
Speed ratings: **105,104,103,102,100 100,99,99,93,92 92,89,89,85,85 62**CSF £232.91 CT £1846.96 TOTE £41.70: £7.40, £2.10, £2.30, £3.40; EX 524.70.
**Owner** The Ipso Facto Syndicate **Bred** R M West **Trained** Carluke, S Lanarks

**FOCUS**
A modest sprint run at a solid pace, with the first three all showing their form.

**NOTEBOOK**
**Silver Mascot** defied his low draw to win fairly comfortably in the end under a well-judged ride. He had the pace to get across early and really stuck his head out late on, so should be of interest if quickly turned out under a penalty.
**Xanadu** ran a fair race from his inside draw. He had plenty in his favour on this occasion.
**Kirkby's Treasure ◆** deserves a lot of credit for getting as close as he did from his poor draw. This effort confirmed his recent rude health and the rise in the weights for winning last time may not have scuppered a compensation bid next time.
**Tedsdale Mac**, wih the cheekpieces left off this time, ran a solid race and stepped up on his recent efforts. He shaped as if another furlong would not go amiss.
**Flying Edge(IRE)** was a little disappointing. He has slipped to a winning mark of late and his previous race at York gave him good claims in this so, while he was not disgraced, he has a bit to prove next time out.
**Albashoosh** failed to capitalise on his decent draw and ultimately proved very disappointing.
**John O'Groats(IRE)** *Official explanation: jockey said gelding hung left-handed in final furlong*

## 2937 LINSTOCK FILLIES' H'CAP 6f 192y
**4:30** (4:31) (E ) (0-70,67) 3-Y-O **£3,493** (£1,075; £537; £268) **Stalls** High

Form RPR

00-5 **1** **Neqaawi**[12] 2572 3-8-13 **59** ..................................................(t) KDarley 2 71
(BHanbury) *trckd ldr: led 2f out: styd on wl u.p* **7/4**[1]

015 **2** 5 **Friends Hope**[50] 1643 3-8-10 **56** ........................................ GDuffield 1 55
(PABlockley) *dwlt: sn led: hdd 2f out: no ex u.p* **4/1**[3]

3-50 **3** 1¾ **Firebird Rising (USA)**[9] 2675 3-9-2 **67** ............................ PMakin(5) 5 61
(TDBarron) *hld up in tch: effrt over 2f out: rdn over 1f out: no imp on first 2* **5/1**

443- **4** 6 **Micklegate**[223] 5913 3-9-3 **63** ........................................... PHanagan 3 42
(JDBethell) *hld up: effrt 3f out: sn rdn and btn* **11/4**[2]

0-00 **5** 16 **Alice Blackthorn**[44] 1775 3-9-4 **64** .................................. DMcGaffin 4 —
(BSmart) *swvd bdly lft leaving stalls: sn t.o* **8/1**

1m 26.14s (-0.96) **Going Correction** -0.225s/f (Firm) **5** Ran SP% **110.8**
Speed ratings: **96,90,88,81,63**CSF £9.09 TOTE £2.00: £1.40, £3.20; EX 3.90.
**Owner** Hamdan Al Maktoum **Bred** Shadwell Estate Company Limited **Trained** Newmarket, Suffolk

**FOCUS**
A weak handicap and the field came home strung out behind the easy winner, who is open to further improvement.

**NOTEBOOK**
**Neqaawi** was well-backed for this handicap debut and duly landed the odds in good style. She had shown promise on her debut, but had disappointed since and was obviously well-treated off this lowly mark of 59. Entitled to build on this, she beat little this time, but could only win as she did. *Official explanation: trainer said filly had benefited from the drop in class on this occasion*
**Friends Hope**, given a break after flopping on her last outing, was no match for the winner. She did however, shape as though this may bring on her on physically.
**Firebird Rising(USA)** proved easy to back this time and did not obviously improve for the step up in distance.
**Micklegate** did not show much on this first outing since November 2003. She should come on again for the outing, but looked very one-paced late on.

## 2938 HAYTON H'CAP 7f 200y
**5:00** (5:02) (E ) (0-75,75) 3-Y-0+ **£3,753** (£1,155; £577; £288) **Stalls** High

Form RPR

0-00 **1** **Pepper Road**[37] 1971 5-8-1 **48** ........................................ RFfrench 10 60
(RBastiman) *a.p: rdn to ld ins fnl f: r.o* **11/1**

-010 **2** 1 **Ben Hur**[5] 2776 5-9-1 **62** ....................................................... KDarley 8 72
(WMBrisbourne) *led: rdn over 2f out: hdd ins fnl f: no ex* **5/1**[1]

0-00 **3** ¾ **Wahoo Sam (USA)**[12] 2580 4-8-7 **59** ................................ PMakin(5) 6 67
(TDBarron) *in tch: nt clr run 2f out: styd on wl u.p fnl f: nvr able to chal* **28/1**

6-00 **4** ½ **Gifted Flame**[31] 2078 5-9-2 **63** ......................................... PHanagan 5 70
(TDBarron) *dwlt: sn midfield: hdwy over 2f out: disp 2nd and rdn over 1f out: no ex fnl f* **13/2**[3]

-603 **5** 1¼ **Low Cloud**[9] 2673 4-10-0 **75** ..........................................(v) JCarroll 3 79
(DNicholls) *trckd ldrs: ev ch and rdn 2f out: kpt on same pce* **7/1**

2256 **6** *hd* **Active Account (USA)**[44] 1757 7-9-2 **63** ............................ ACulhane 11 66
(MrsHDalton) *towards rr 1/2-way: styd on fnl 2f: n.d* **7/1**

05-0 **7** 1¼ **Wood Dalling (USA)**[23] 2291 6-8-1 **55** ........................ PPMathers(7) 12 56
(ISemple) *hld up: hdwy and in tch over 2f out: sn rdn: no further prog* **7/1**

2-32 **8** 1 **Rymer's Rascal**[21] 2368 12-8-4 **51** .................................... GDuffield 2 49
(EJAlston) *midfield: effrt whn hmpd wl over 1f out: no hdwy after* **8/1**

5054 **9** ½ **Waltzing Wizard**[18] 2421 5-8-5 **52** ...................................... PMQuinn 7 49
(ABerry) *hld up: effrt 3f out: sn rdn and btn* **6/1**[2]

-000 **10** ¾ **Late Arrival**[21] 2356 7-7-12 **45** oh1 ...............................(v) DaleGibson 1 40
(MDHammond) *bhd: effrt 3f out: sn rdn and btn* **25/1**

0000 **11** 1 **Smith N Allan Oils**[5] 2776 5-8-7 **57** ...............................(p) LEnstone(3) 4 50
(MDods) *towards rr: effrt 3f out: sn rdn and btn* **14/1**

6442 **12** ½ **Call Of The Wild**[17] 2456 4-8-4 **54** ow3 ......................(p) THamilton(3) 13 46
(RAFahey) *midfield: rdn 3f out: wknd 2f out* **12/1**

-624 **13** 1¼ **Time To Regret**[14] 2528 4-8-6 **53** ow1 .................................. RWinston 9 42
(JJQuinn) *cl up: rdn over 2f out: wknd over 1f out* **14/1**

1m 37.89s (-2.11) **Going Correction** -0.225s/f (Firm) **13** Ran SP% **129.6**
Speed ratings: **101,100,99,98,97 97,96,95,94,93 92,92,91**CSF £70.78 CT £1564.21 TOTE £11.20: £2.60, £3.20, £10.90; EX 116.00 Place 6 £369.72, Place 5 £212.67.
**Owner** Peter Julian **Bred** Exors Of The Late J G Charlton **Trained** Cowthorpe, N Yorks
■ Stewards Enquiry : P Makin two-day ban: careless riding (Jul 6+1)

**FOCUS**
A moderate handicap run at a fair pace. An inside draw proved an advantage and the form is ordinary.

**NOTEBOOK**
**Pepper Road** was prominent throughout and ran on well to settle the argument inside the final furlong. This was a welcome return to form on a track he has run well at in the past and may well be capable of following-up under a penalty, but it is worth remembering that he had a fair bit in his favour on this occasion. *Official explanation: trainer said, regarding the improved form shown, gelding was suited by today's firm ground*
**Ben Hur** had the run of the race and gave his all, but could not go with the winner late on. His win over a mile on his penultimate start was in a claimer, and the hike in the ratings looks to have taken it's toll, but this was no disgrace.
**Wahoo Sam(USA)** posted a welcome return to form and would have finished closer but for meeting traffic two out. He has tumbled in the weights of late and is clearly in the form to capitalise on that.
**Gifted Flame**, last year's winner of this event off a 2lb higher mark, made a sluggish start and was up against it from then on.
**Low Cloud**, who posted a return to form last time at Doncaster, again ran a sound race, but still looks a little high in the weights at present.
**Waltzing Wizard** again ran below par and is a very difficult horse to predict.
**Smith N Allan Oils** *Official explanation: jockey said gelding ran too keen early on and never got a run*
T/Plt: £951.90 to a £1 stake. Pool: £38,731.30. 29.70 winning tickets. T/Qpdt: £97.00 to a £1 stake. Pool: £2,897.10. 22.10 winning tickets. JF

# 1871 WARWICK (L-H)
Monday, June 14

**OFFICIAL GOING: Firm (good to firm in places)**
Wind: Almost nil. Weather: Hot and sunny.

## 2939 JUHANNUS APPRENTICE H'CAP 1m 2f 188y
**6:45** (6:46) (F ) (0-55,55) 4-Y-0+ **£3,066** (£876; £438) **Stalls** Low

Form RPR

-045 **1** **Short Change (IRE)**[8] 2705 5-8-9 **47** .............................. RThomas(3) 2 54
(AWCarroll) *led over 8f: rallied to ld and edgd rt ins fnl f: r.o* **7/2**[1]

-516 **2** *shd* **Trusted Mole (IRE)**[11] 2615 6-9-3 **55** ............ BSwarbrick(3) 9 62
(WMBrisbourne) *trckd ldrs: rdn over 1f out: edgd lft ins fnl f: r.o* **7/1**

1534 **3** *shd* **Vandenberghe**[7] 2728 5-8-13 **48** ............ TPQueally 7 55
(JAOsborne) *chsd ldrs: nt clr run ins fnl f: r.o* **4/1**[2]

0240 **4** *3/4* **Holly Rose**[17] 2446 5-9-0 **52** ............ (p) HayleyTurner(3) 12 58
(DECantillon) *chsd ldr: led over 2f out: edgd rt and hdd ins fnl f: unable qck towards fin* **11/1**

4-63 **5** *1 1/4* **Glen Vale Walk (IRE)**[14] 2525 7-8-12 **47** ............ (b) NMackay 5 50
(MrsGSRees) *s.i.s: hld up: hdwy over 1f out: nt rch ldrs* **7/1**

4356 **6** *hd* **Theatre Lady (IRE)**[21] 2356 6-8-5 **45** ............ DTudhope(5) 1 48
(PDEvans) *hld up in tch: rdn over 1f out: styd on same pce ins fnl f* **13/2**[3]

-522 **7** *2 1/2* **Ben Kenobi**[28] 2184 6-8-6 **41** ............ DCorby 4 40
(MrsPFord) *hld up: rdn over 2f out: nvr trbld ldrs* **16/1**

2532 **8** *shd* **Ryan's Bliss (IRE)**[32] 2053 4-8-9 **44** ............ J-PGuillambert 3 43
(TDMccarthy) *prom: rdn over 2f out: styd on same pce appr fnl f* **16/1**

0500 **9** *1 3/4* **Private Seal**[12] 2591 9-7-13 **41** ............ (t) MHalford(7) 6 37
(JulianPoulton) *hld up: rdn over 3f out: n.d* **25/1**

34 **10** *1 1/2* **Fairland (IRE)**[22] 2324 5-8-7 **49** ............ LSmith(7) 11 42
(SDow) *s.i.s: hld up: effrt over 3f out: sn wknd* **10/1**

-000 **11** *3/4* **Manikato (USA)**[22] 940 10-8-1 **43** oh10 ow8 ............ KirbyHarris(7) 10 35
(KGWingrove) *prom over 8f* **66/1**

**12** *6* **Regal Fantasy (IRE)**[331] 3436 4-7-12 **40** ............ StaceyRenwick(7) 8 22
(PABlockley) *hld up: wknd over 2f out* **20/1**

2m 18.66s (-0.74) **Going Correction** -0.05s/f (Good) **12** Ran SP% **119.8**
Speed ratings: **100,99,99,99,98 98,96,96,95,94 93,89**CSF £27.88 CT £104.11 TOTE £4.90: £1.40, £2.40, £2.10; EX 34.80.
**Owner** Dennis Deacon **Bred** Tom Radley **Trained** Wixford, Warwicks

**FOCUS**
A moderate, but competitive handicap, although the form is very ordinary. The early pace was just steady and it proved hard to come from off the pace.

**NOTEBOOK**
**Short Change(IRE)** had gained both his previous Flat wins off a mark of 52 and made the most of a 5lb lower rating. He had nothing to spare at the line, but would avoid a penalty if turned out before he is reassessed and a follow up cannot be ruled out.
**Trusted Mole(IRE)**, 3lb higher than when successful at Leicester two starts back, was just denied. He is the type of horse his trainer excels with and he should continue to go well.
**Vandenberghe** does not win very often, but he is in good form and there was nothing wrong with this effort.
**Holly Rose**, well handicapped on some of her form, had conditions to suit and ran respectably.
**Glen Vale Walk(IRE)** did best of those ridden from off the pace.
**Ryan's Bliss(IRE)** *Official explanation: trainer said filly was struck into behind*

## 2940 EBF MAIDEN FILLIES' STKS 5f
**7:15** (7:15) (D) 2-Y-O **£5,469** (£1,683; £841; £420) **Stalls** Low

Form RPR

5 **1** **Kissing Lights (IRE)**[16] 2481 2-8-11 ............ KFallon 2 89
(MLWBell) *chsd ldr tl led over 1f out: sn clr* **10/11**[1]

**2** *5* **Born For Dancing (IRE)** 2-8-11 ............ MHills 1 72
(BWHills) *trckd ldrs: racd keenly: chsd wnr 1f out: styd on same pce* **5/1**[3]

**3** *3* **Vondova** 2-8-11 ............ RHughes 6 61
(RHannon) *hmpd s: effrt over 1f out: nvr trbld ldrs* **12/1**

5 **4** *3/4* **Miss Cotswold Lady**[13] 2544 2-8-11 ............ JQuinn 5 58
(AWCarroll) *wnt rt s: chsd ldrs: rdn over 1f out: wknd ins fnl f* **66/1**

5 **5** *2 1/2* **Xeeran**[14] 2535 2-8-11 ............ PRobinson 4 50
(MAJarvis) *led over 3f: wknd ins fnl f* **2/1**[2]

**6** *6* **Inagh** 2-8-8 ............ DCorby(3) 3 29
(MJWallace) *s.s: outpcd* **33/1**

58.81 secs (-1.39) **Going Correction** -0.40s/f (Firm) **6** Ran SP% **114.5**
Speed ratings: **95,87,82,81,77 67**CSF £6.42 TOTE £1.80: £1.10, £2.90; EX 7.00.
**Owner** M B Hawtin **Bred** Darley **Trained** Newmarket, Suffolk

**FOCUS**
This looked a fair maiden, but Kissing Lights made it look easy and would appear to be an above-average type.

**NOTEBOOK**
**Kissing Lights(IRE)**, a promising fifth in what was probably quite a good six-furlong maiden on her debut at Lingfield, improved on that run on this drop in trip to justify some strong market support. There should be more to some and she may be aimed at a Listed race at Newmarket.
**Born For Dancing(IRE)**, a 45,000euros yearling, half-sister to a winning sprinter, made a satisfactory debut and, given normal improvement, should soon be winning.
**Vondova**, a half-sister to a seven-furlong three-year-old winner, out of an unraced half-sister to a top-class filly in the US, made a respectable debut. She should improve and looks sure to stay further.
**Miss Cotswold Lady** improved on her debut running to post a pleasing effort. She was ultimately well held, but will find easier opportunities.
**Xeeran** found very little under pressure having been quite keen, and again gave the impression she is better than she is showing on the track. *Official explanation: jockey said filly was unsuited by the firm (good to firm in places) ground*

## 2941 PRICEWATERHOUSECOOPERS CLASSIFIED STKS 7f 26y
**7:45** (7:45) (D) 3-Y-O+ **£5,616** (£1,728; £864; £432) **Stalls** Low

Form RPR

3020 **1** **Pawan (IRE)**[11] 2623 4-9-4 63 ............ AnnStokell 1 72
(MissAStokell) *chsd ldr: rdn to ld over 1f out: hdd ins fnl f: rallied to ld post* **13/8**[2]

00-4 **2** *shd* **Barons Spy (IRE)**[15] 2505 3-8-8 66 ............ MHills 3 72
(AWCarroll) *chsd ldrs: rdn over 1f out: hung rt and led ins fnl f: hdd post* **1/1**[1]

20-5 **3** *5* **Sophrano (IRE)**[12] 2588 4-8-11 63 ............ SYourston(7) 5 59
(PABlockley) *led over 5f: wknd ins fnl f* **9/1**[3]

6000 **4** *2* **Telepathic (IRE)**[11] 2625 4-8-13 59 ............ PBradley(5) 4 54
(ABerry) *s.s: hld up: nvr nr to chal* **10/1**

1m 23.92s (-0.98) **Going Correction** -0.05s/f (Good)
**WFA** 3 from 4yo 10lb **4** Ran SP% **107.2**
Speed ratings: **103,102,97,94**CSF £3.58 TOTE £2.70; EX 4.10.
**Owner** Ms Caron Stokell **Bred** Hadi Al Tajir **Trained** Brompton-on-Swale, N Yorks

**FOCUS**
A modest, uncompetitive event, but at least the pace was good.

**NOTEBOOK**
**Pawan(IRE)**, badly outclassed in a Listed race on his previous start, appreciated this drop in grade to end a frustrating run of defeats. This is sure to have boosted his confidence, but he does not appeal as an obvious one to follow up.
**Barons Spy(IRE)** confirmed the promise he showed in maiden company and looks up to winning a similar contest.
**Sophrano(IRE)** went off plenty fast enough, but was not good enough in any case.
**Telepathic(IRE)** lost his chance at the start.

## 2942 WRAGGE & CO FILLIES' H'CAP 6f 21y
**8:15** (8:17) (F) (0-55,55) 3-Y-O **£3,304** (£944; £472) **Stalls** Low

Form RPR

2P40 **1** **Wendy's Girl (IRE)**[11] 2620 3-9-3 **50** ............ (b) SChin 1 64
(RPElliott) *w ldr tl led over 2f out: clr 1f out: rdn out* **9/1**

6-53 **2** *1 1/4* **Miss Judgement (IRE)**[20] 2380 3-9-6 **53** ............ FNorton 11 63
(WRMuir) *led: hdd over 4f out: remained handy: rdn to chse wnr over 1f out: r.o* **13/2**[3]

0125 **3** *2 1/2* **Yamato Pink**[6] 2766 3-9-2 **52** ............ LFletcher(3) 3 55
(MrsHSweeting) *dwlt: outpcd: hdwy over 1f out: hung lft ins fnl f: nt rch ldrs* **5/1**[2]

0000 **4** *shd* **Danifah (IRE)**[14] 2518 3-8-9 **47** ............ BSwarbrick(5) 2 49
(PDEvans) *chsd ldrs: rdn over 2f out: no ex fnl f* **7/1**

44 **5** *1 3/4* **Breezit (USA)**[28] 2176 3-9-5 **52** ............ JBramhill 13 49
(SRBowring) *chsd ldrs: rdn over 2f out: styd on same pce appr fnl f* **15/2**

-430 **6** *1/2* **Open Mind**[16] 2468 3-9-3 **50** ............ TEDurcan 5 46
(EJAlston) *s.i.s: hld up: styd on ins fnl f: nvr nrr* **12/1**

506 **7** *shd* **Indian Lily**[39] 1906 3-9-8 **55** ............ JQuinn 8 50
(CFWall) *prom: rdn over 2f out: edgd lft and wknd over 1f out* **4/1**[1]

-005 **8** *1* **Red Rocky**[13] 2545 3-8-10 **48** ............ (p) StephanieHollinshead(5) 10 40
(RHollinshead) *plld hrd and prom: lost pl over 4f out: n.d after* **40/1**

0000 **9** *1 1/2* **Queen Of Bulgaria (IRE)**[21] 2359 3-9-3 **50** ............ RPrice 9 38
(JPearce) *w ldrs: led over 4f out: hdd over 2f out: wknd fnl f* **20/1**

2030 **10** *1 1/4* **Zonnebeke**[83] 1086 3-9-3 **50** ............ DSweeney 12 34
(KRBurke) *s.i.s: hld up: a in rr* **14/1**

305- **11** *1 3/4* **Berry Racer (IRE)**[236] 5707 3-9-3 **50** ............ TGMcLaughlin 6 29
(NPLittmoden) *prom: over 4f* **25/1**

0-00 **12** *1 1/4* **Moscow Mary**[49] 1676 3-9-1 **55** ............ PGallagher(7) 4 30
(AGNewcombe) *sn pushed along in rr: hung rt over 3f out: sn wknd* **11/1**

05-0 **13** *1 1/2* **Jailbird**[24] 2266 3-9-5 **55** ............ (v[1]) TPQueally(3) 7 26
(RMBeckett) *sn outpcd* **40/1**

1m 10.46s (-1.84) **Going Correction** -0.05s/f (Good) **13** Ran SP% **120.4**
Speed ratings: **110,108,105,104,102 101,101,100,98,96 94,92,90**CSF £64.45 CT £340.27 TOTE £14.30: £3.50, £2.50, £1.30; EX 54.90.
**Owner** E Grayson **Bred** Lars Pearson **Trained** Formby, Lancs

**FOCUS**
Just an ordinary handicap and once again it proved hard to come from off the speed. The time was amazingly fast for the grade, just 1/10 of a second off the course record, and the form look sound.

**NOTEBOOK**
**Wendy's Girl(IRE)**, up a furlong in trip with the blinkers on for only the second time, gained her first win at the 20th attempt. She had proved quite frustrating in the past and, although this may just be the turning point, she will not be one to take a short price about next time.
**Miss Judgement(IRE)** reversed recent Lingfield placings with Yamato Pink under a positive ride, but she was no match for the winner.
**Yamato Pink** should have been suited by this drop back from seven furlongs, but she was unable to get a good position after missing the break and eventually got going too late.
**Danifah(IRE)** has dropped to a very reasonable mark and ran respectably.
**Breezit(USA)** looks worth a try over seven furlongs.
**Indian Lily** was unable to confirm the promise she showed in maiden company and has to be considered disappointing. *Official explanation: jockey said filly did not handle the bend*
**Red Rocky** *Official explanation: jockey said filly had hung until the home straight*

## 2943 COVENTRY EVENING TELEGRAPH H'CAP 1m 22y
**8:45** (8:50) (F) (0-55,61) 3-Y-O+ **£3,822** (£1,092; £546) **Stalls** Low

Form RPR

000- **1** **Hollywood Henry (IRE)**[278] 4825 4-9-13 **54** ............ (p) JQuinn 8 63
(JAkehurst) *hld up: hdwy over 1f out: sn rdn: r.o to ld nr fin* **12/1**

2000 **2** *hd* **Treetops Hotel (IRE)**[2] 2886 5-9-13 **54** ............ DSweeney 1 63
(BRJohnson) *hld up: hdwy 3f out: rdn and ev ch ins fnl f: r.o* **12/1**

2223 **3** *shd* **Tojoneski**[20] 2387 5-9-1 **45** ............ (p) JFMcDonald(3) 16 53
(IWMcinnes) *chsd ldrs: rdn to ld over 1f out: hdd nr fin* **12/1**

3360 **4** *3/4* **Pacific Ocean (ARG)**[55] 1522 5-9-11 **52** ............ (t) FNorton 11 59
(MrsStefLiddiard) *hld up: hdwy over 1f out: r.o* **20/1**

6-00 **5** *1 1/4* **Tuscarora (IRE)**[23] 2284 5-9-11 **52** ............ MHills 15 56
(AWCarroll) *hld up in tch: rdn and ev ch over 1f out: no ex ins fnl f* **7/1**[3]

4-00 **6** *2* **Balmacara**[117] 815 5-9-3 **47** ............ TPQueally(3) 12 46
(MissKBBoutflower) *hld up: hdwy over 1f out: nt rch ldrs* **40/1**

3221 **7** *nk* **Londoner (USA)**[4] 2803 6-10-6 **61** 6ex ............ RHughes 13 59
(SDow) *chsd ldrs: rdn over 1f out: no ex ins fnl f* **7/2**[1]

0016 **8** *shd* **Shamwari Fire (IRE)**[5] 2776 4-9-10 **51** ............ LVickers 2 49
(IWMcinnes) *chsd ldrs: rdn over 2f out: wknd fnl f* **16/1**

-003 **9** *1 1/2* **Dubonai (IRE)**[2] 2879 4-9-8 **49** ............ KFallon 9 44
(AndrewTurnell) *sn outpcd: hdwy over 1f out: nt rch ldrs* **7/2**[1]

0013 **10** *1 1/2* **Bojangles (IRE)**[41] 1875 5-9-4 **48** ............ DNolan(3) 3 39
(RBrotherton) *sn led: rdn and hdd over 1f out: wknd ins fnl f* **9/2**[2]

0004 **11** *nk* **Jamestown**[56] 1511 7-9-3 **47** ............ LFletcher(3) 5 38
(MJPolglase) *hld up: n.d* **33/1**

0-00 **12** *3* **Ash Laddie (IRE)**[13] 2551 4-9-12 **53** ............ (p) TEDurcan 4 37
(EJAlston) *hld up: a in rr* **40/1**

-000 **13** *1* **Zamyatina (IRE)**[2] 2879 5-9-6 **47** ............ JBramhill 7 28
(PLClinton) *prom: rdn over 2f out: wknd over 1f out* **28/1**

1050 **14** *1* **Chickasaw Trail**[3] 2833 6-8-11 **43** ............ (v[1]) StephanieHollinshead(5) 6 22
(RHollinshead) *s.i.s: a in rr* **25/1**

-002 **15** *shd* **Madame Marie (IRE)**[30] 2122 4-9-9 **50** ............ WRyan 17 29
(SDow) *hld up: a in rr* **16/1**

0000 **16** *15* **Blessed Place**[10] 2663 4-9-4 **45** ............ PMcCabe 10 —
(DJSFfrenchDavis) *hld up: plld hrd: hdwy to join ldrs 6f out: wkng whn n.m.r wl over 1f out* **100/1**

0000 **17** *6* **Soft Mist (IRE)**[21] 2368 4-9-5 **51** ............ BSwarbrick(5) 14 —
(JJQuinn) *prom over 4f* **33/1**

1m 38.18s (-1.12) **Going Correction** -0.05s/f (Good) **17** Ran SP% **133.8**
Speed ratings: **103,102,102,101,100 98,98,98,96,95 95,92,91,90,89 74,68**CSF £150.39 CT £1869.53 TOTE £17.80: £2.90, £5.20, £2.50, £5.20; EX 124.10.
**Owner** Lonwin Partnership **Bred** Norelands Bloodstock **Trained** Epsom, Surrey

**FOCUS**
A moderate handicap, but the leaders went off too fast, the form is ordinary as most of these are well exposed.

**NOTEBOOK**
**Hollywood Henry(IRE)**, 21lb lower than when first running in a handicap, had cheekpieces on for the first time and ran out a narrow winner. He is unlikely to go up too much for this and has found his level.
**Treetops Hotel(IRE)**, without a win since September 2001, appeared to appreciate the strong pace on this step back up in trip and was just held.
**Tojoneski** continues in fine heart and, although he keeps finding a couple too good, is not one to give up on just yet.

**Pacific Ocean(ARG)** was another who benefited from the strong pace, but he just got going a little bit too late. A fast-run ten furlongs may be the answer.
**Tuscarora(IRE)** did not look to have any excuses.
**Londoner(USA)** ran a lacklustre race under his 6lb penalty.
**Dubonai(IRE)** could never get into it and should do better back over further.
**Bojangles(IRE)** appeared to do too much in front.
**Blessed Place** gained his only previous win over five furlongs and was far too free over this mile.

## 2944 EVERSHEDS MAIDEN STKS — 1m 4f 134y
9:15 (9:16) (D) 3-Y-0+ — **£3,818** (£1,175; £587; £293) **Stalls** Low

Form — RPR
-042 **1** **Horner (USA)**[14] 2513 3-8-7 80 .......... JQuinn 5 83+
(PFICole) *a.p: led 5f out: clr 3f out: eased ins fnl f* **11/10**[1]
0-0 **2** 7 **Levitator**[49] 1674 3-8-7 .......... KFallon 4 69
(SirMichaelStoute) *chsd ldrs: shkn up over 3f out: sn outpcd* **13/2**[3]
43 **3** *shd* **Water Taxi**[23] 2312 3-8-7 .......... RHughes 2 69
(RCharlton) *sn led: hdd 7f out: outpcd fnl 3f* **15/8**[2]
40- **4** 9 **Four Pence (IRE)**[226] 5870 3-8-7 .......... MHills 3 55
(BWHills) *hld up: effrt over 3f out: sn wknd* **8/1**
3000 **5** *dist* **East Riding**[10] 2659 4-9-5 37 .......... AnnStokell 1 —
(MissAStokell) *plld hrd: sn trcking ldr: led 7f out: hdd 5f out: wknd over 3f out* **100/1**

2m 41.75s (-1.55) **Going Correction** -0.05s/f (Good)
**WFA** 3 from 4yo 17lb — **5 Ran SP% 107.8**
Speed ratings: **102,97,97,92,—**CSF £8.35 TOTE £2.00: £1.30, £2.10; EX 7.10 Place 6 £109.45, Place 5 £63.86.
**Owner** Sir George Meyrick **Bred** Farfellow Farms Ltd **Trained** Whatcombe, Oxon

**FOCUS**
An uncompetitive maiden and a very easy winner.

**NOTEBOOK**
**Horner(USA)** was bound to take all the beating if running anywhere near his rating of 80 and that is the way it turned out. The test will be when he goes handicapping, but on this showing he should hold his own.
**Levitator** was no match whatsoever for the winner, but ran a respectable enough race and is now qualified for a handicap mark.
**Water Taxi** was below the form he showed on his two previous outings and has to be considered very disappointing.
**Four Pence(IRE)** offered promise at up to a mile in two runs as a juvenile but, racing for the first time in 226 days and stepped up in trip, he showed little.
T/Plt: £372.60 to a £1 stake. Pool: £40,380.65. 79.10 winning tickets. T/Qpdt: £65.10 to a £1 stake. Pool: £2,422.30. 27.50 winning tickets. CR

# 2736 WINDSOR (R-H)
Monday, June 14

**OFFICIAL GOING: Good to firm (firm in places)**
Another meeting where it was a big advantage to bag the stands' rail.
Wind: lt bhd Weather: sunny & very warm

## 2945 CHG-MERIDIAN H'CAP — 1m 67y
6:30 (6:31) (E) (0-75,75) 3-Y-0+ — **£3,581** (£1,102; £551; £275) **Stalls** High

Form — RPR
2202 **1** **Best Before (IRE)**[10] 2643 4-8-13 67 .......... SJDonohoe(7) 6 80
(PDEvans) *racd in midfield: nt handle bnd 5f out: effrt 3f out: prog to ld over 1f out: drvn clr* **4/1**[2]
4654 **2** 3 **Phred**[11] 2614 4-9-0 61 .......... SCarson 1 67
(RFJohnsonHoughton) *prom: rdn 3f out: cl up 2f out: sn nt qckn: chsd wnr ins fnl f: no imp* **10/3**[1]
2-00 **3** *hd* **Adobe**[19] 2410 9-9-1 67 .......... MSavage(5) 8 73
(WMBrisbourne) *trckd ldrs: rdn 3f out: swtchd lft over 1f out: drvn and kpt on fnl f* **15/2**
0-00 **4** *nk* **Yeoman Lad**[7] 2738 4-9-8 72 .......... (v) LPKeniry(3) 2 77
(AMBalding) *mostly trckd ldr: drvn 3f out: cl up 2f out: one pce after* **12/1**
0441 **5** *hd* **Espada (IRE)**[2] 2886 8-8-7 54 6ex .......... (b) SWKelly 5 58
(JAOsborne) *led at gd pce: 3l clr 3f out: hdd and no ex over 1f out* **11/2**
-000 **6** 3 ½ **Every Note Counts**[27] 2216 4-9-1 62 .......... TQuinn 3 58
(JJQuinn) *racd in midfield: effrt 3f out: clsng whn squeezed out wl over 1f out: no prog fnl f* **11/1**
000- **7** 1 ¾ **Back In Action**[198] 6089 4-10-0 75 .......... (t) EAhern 4 67
(MAMagnusson) *dwlt: a in last pair: rdn 3f out: no prog* **14/1**
1430 **8** ½ **Raheel (IRE)**[2] 2883 4-8-10 57 .......... (t) DHolland 7 48
(PMitchell) *dwlt: a last: detached and shuffled along over 2f out: no prog* **9/2**[3]

1m 44.46s (-1.14) **Going Correction** -0.10s/f (Good) — **8 Ran SP% 111.1**
Speed ratings: **101,98,97,97,97 93,92,91**CSF £16.68 CT £90.83 TOTE £4.40: £1.20, £1.40, £2.30; EX 16.00.
**Owner** Waterline Racing Club **Bred** Joe Rogers **Trained** Pandy, Gwent
■ Stewards Enquiry : S J Donohoe one-day ban: careless riding (Jun 25)

**FOCUS**
An ordinary handicap run at just a fair pace. One or two did not get the clearest of runs inside the last quarter-mile, but the form backs up early course and distance running.

**NOTEBOOK**
**Best Before(IRE)** deserves extra credit for this victory as he did not handle the loop at all well. He caused a few problems when crossing from the outside to the stands' rail as he came to challenge inside the last two furlongs, but was a clear winner on merit.
**Phred**, back over a more suitable trip, ran a solid race but had no chance with the winner. He is performing better with each run.
**Adobe** ◆ had to switch in order to get a run, but was staying on well at the end. He is returning to form and it should not be long before he scores again provided the ground remains rattling fast.
**Yeoman Lad** ◆, back over a more suitable trip, was never far away and did not see a great deal of daylight in the latter stages, but he never stopped trying. He is sliding down the handicap and is another that seems to be gradually returning to form.
**Espada(IRE)**, under a 6lb penalty for his Lingfield victory 48 hours earlier, attempted the same tactics over this extra furlong but was swamped inside the last two furlongs.
**Every Note Counts** ◆, 15lb lower than at this time last year, was in the process of running a decent race over this shorter trip when completely running out of room approaching the last furlong. He is worth keeping in mind off this sort of mark.
**Raheel(IRE)**, well backed on this return to turf, has never been placed on grass and never looked like justifying the support. *Official explanation: jockey said gelding was unsuited by the Good to Firm ground*

## 2946 KADOOMENT TROPHY (S) STKS — 6f
7:00 (7:01) (G) 2-Y-0 — **£2,884** (£824; £412) **Stalls** High

Form — RPR
50 **1** **Cloann (IRE)**[14] 2522 2-8-6 .......... DaneO'Neill 4 57
(RHannon) *trckd ldr: led after 2f: mde rest: drvn over 1f out: hanging lft and flashed tail: kpt on* **2/1**[1]
00 **2** ¾ **Debs Broughton**[5] 2786 2-8-6 .......... GCarter 2 55
(WJMusson) *in tch: prog 2f out: rdn to chse wnr fnl f: edgd rt: kpt on but a hld* **12/1**
2 **3** 1 **Songgaria**[7] 2725 2-8-6 .......... NPollard 3 52
(JRBest) *prom: pressed wnr over 3f out to 1f out: kpt on one pce u.p* **7/2**[3]
4563 **4** 3 **Glasson Lodge**[14] 2515 2-8-7 ow1 .......... (v[1]) DHolland 7 44
(PDEvans) *led for 2f: outpcd wl over 1f out: kpt on fnl f* **5/2**[2]
0000 **5** 2 ½ **Muestra (IRE)**[18] 2427 2-8-6 .......... RHavlin 6 35
(MrsPNDutfield) *s.i.s: in tch in rr: rdn over 2f out: outpcd and btn over 1f out* **33/1**
0500 **6** ½ **Zachy Boy**[11] 2609 2-8-11 .......... EAhern 5 39
(JSMoore) *trckd ldrs: rdn over 2f out: sn outpcd: n.d after* **16/1**
6643 **7** ½ **Shish (IRE)**[7] 2725 2-8-6 .......... SWKelly 8 32
(JAOsborne) *chsd ldrs: rdn 1/2-way: struggling fnl 2f* **14/1**
6003 **8** *hd* **Joe Ninety (IRE)**[6] 2755 2-8-4 .......... (b[1]) DerekNolan(7) 1 37
(JSMoore) *in tch in rr: hrd rdn 2f out: no prog* **14/1**

1m 14.76s (0.89) **Going Correction** -0.10s/f (Good) — **8 Ran SP% 114.0**
Speed ratings: **90,89,87,83,80 79,79,78** CT £2.90 TOTE £1.30: £3.10, £1.70, £; EX22.50 1.The winner was bought by Swann Racing for 6,000 guineas. Songgaria was claimed by J.S. Wainwright for £6,000. Deb's Broughton was claimed in a friendly sal
**Owner** Dr Michael Dunleavy **Bred** Holborn Trust Co **Trained** East Everleigh, Wilts
■ Stewards Enquiry : G Carter caution: careless riding

**FOCUS**
A poor juvenile seller unlikely to produce many future winners.

**NOTEBOOK**
**Cloann(IRE)**, down in grade, was well supported in the market and, after getting to the front at halfway and bagging the stands' rail, stayed on to break her duck but she showed her resentment of being hit with the whip by swishing her tail. She is obviously not straightforward, but that will be someone else's problem now as she was bought at the subsequent auction for 6,000gns.
**Debs Broughton** was effectively taking a drop in class though she was beaten a mile in a regional maiden on her debut. She showed her first sign of ability, staying on down the centre of the track, but this did not look a good race and she will need to improve again to score. She was the subject of a friendly claim.
**Songgaria**, claimed after finishing runner-up in a similar contest on her debut at Folkestone seven days earlier, was always thereabouts and probably ran to a similar level of form, but will need to find at least as bad a race as this in order to score.
**Glasson Lodge**, more experienced than most, broke well enough but could not hold her place and was struggling soon after halfway. This looks to be as good as she is.
**Muestra(IRE)**, beaten out of sight in four previous starts, was effectively taking a drop in grade but there was little improvement. A couple of the maidens she has been well beaten in were almost as bad as this.

## 2947 GOLD CUP FESTIVAL TROPHY EBF MAIDEN STKS — 5f 10y
7:30 (7:31) (D) 2-Y-0 — **£4,316** (£1,328; £664; £332) **Stalls** High

Form — RPR
**1** **Marajuana** 2-8-4 .......... NChalmers(5) 11 78
(AMBalding) *mde all: hrd pressed fr over 1f out: styd on wl u.p* **8/1**
53 **2** ½ **Marching Song**[27] 2208 2-9-0 .......... JFortune 6 81
(RHannon) *pressed wnr thrght: drvn to chal over 1f out: ev ch ins fnl f: unable qck nr fin* **6/5**[1]
**3** 3 ½ **Diamond Josh** 2-9-0 .......... RHavlin 9 69
(PDEvans) *trckd ldrs: gng wl enough but outpcd wl over 1f out: shuffled along and hanging lft fnl f: kpt on steadily* **33/1**
0 **4** 1 ½ **First Rule**[42] 1826 2-9-0 .......... SSanders 1 64
(CFWall) *towards rr: rdn and prog 2f out: one pce and no imp fnl f* **11/2**[3]
050 **5** ½ **Campeon (IRE)**[45] 1743 2-9-0 .......... RLMoore 4 62
(MJWallace) *settled towards rr: effrt 2f out: hanging fnl f: kpt on* **16/1**
0 **6** ½ **Kempsey**[20] 2376 2-9-0 .......... ADaly 5 60
(JJBridger) *chsd ldng pair: drvn and outpcd fr 2f out: one pce u.p after* **66/1**
**7** *shd* **Phi Phi (IRE)** 2-8-9 .......... LDettori 7 55
(WJHaggas) *dwlt: sn trckd ldrs: edgd lft over 1f out: nt qckn* **4/1**[2]
42 **8** *hd* **Knock Bridge (IRE)**[16] 2489 2-8-9 .......... JoannaBadger 2 54
(PDEvans) *wl in rr: pushed along 1/2-way: nvr a factor: kpt on ins fnl f* **16/1**
**9** 4 **Follow My Lead** 2-8-9 .......... EAhern 3 40
(BWHills) *s.i.s: a wl in rr* **10/1**
40 **10** 5 **Josear**[12] 2574 2-9-0 .......... AMcCarthy 10 27
(SCWilliams) *hld up: no prog whn nt clr run over 1f out: shkn up and wknd* **50/1**
0 **11** *nk* **Lighthorne Lad**[15] 2502 2-9-0 .......... SWKelly 8 26
(JRJenkins) *restless stalls: in tch to 1/2-way: wknd* **66/1**

60.80 secs (-0.40) **Going Correction** -0.10s/f (Good) — **11 Ran SP% 120.7**
Speed ratings: **99,98,92,90,89 88,88,88,81,73 73**CSF £18.29 TOTE £11.70: £2.10, £1.20, £6.50; EX 30.00.
**Owner** Lady C S Cadbury **Bred** Mrs I A Balding **Trained** Kingsclere, Hants
■ Stewards Enquiry : N Chalmers caution: careless riding

**FOCUS**
An ordinary maiden outside the front four, but the time was good, the race is rated through the runner-up, and the first and third are of particular interest.

**NOTEBOOK**
**Marajuana** ◆, a half-sister to Border Music out of a three-time winner, had the plum draw and made full use of it, showing admirable determination to hold off the favourite. She looks a nice prospect.
**Marching Song** had the edge on experience and did everything he could to get past the winner, but found her too determined. He should find an ordinary maiden, but an extra furlong would not come amiss.
**Diamond Josh** ◆, whose dam won over a mile, made a pleasing debut despite running green and a race should be found for him over a bit further.
**First Rule** ran a better race than on his debut on this completely different ground. He looks to be going the right way.
**Campeon(IRE)** finished unplaced for the fourth time, but his pedigree suggests he needs further than this, so he may be capable of a bit better over a longer trip.
**Phi Phi(IRE)**, a half-sister to several winners including Superstar Leo, showed a little ability and should improve for the outing.

## 2948 GOLD CUP TRIPLE WINNER "BLAST OF STORM" H'CAP — 6f

**8:00** (8:01) (D) (0-80,77) 3-Y-0+ **£5,720** (£1,760; £880; £440) **Stalls** High

Form / RPR

0111 **1** **Caustic Wit (IRE)**[6] 2763 6-9-3 **72** 6ex (p) RMiles(3) 10 — 93
(MSSaunders) *prom: led over 3f out: clr 2f out: rdn and hung rt over 1f out: unchal* **4/1**[1]

0151 **2** *3* **High Ridge**[2] 2873 5-9-0 **66** 6ex (p) CCatlin 4 — 78
(JMBradley) *hld up towards rr: prog over 3f out: rdn to chse wnr jst over 1f out: no imp* **8/1**[3]

4646 **3** *1* **Full Spate**[12] 2581 9-9-2 **68** RLMoore 18 — 77
(JMBradley) *chsd ldrs: rdn over 2f out: styd on fr over 1f out: unable to chal* **8/1**[3]

-062 **4** *1/2* **Complication**[6] 2763 4-8-6 **61** (b) LisaJones(3) 14 — 69
(JARToller) *bmpd s: wl in rr: taken to outside and prog 2f out: styd on wl fnl f: nrst fin* **6/1**[2]

4221 **5** *1 3/4* **Glencoe Solas (IRE)**[9] 2670 4-9-6 **72** MFenton 17 — 74
(SKirk) *led to over 3f out: chsd wnr and hanging lft tl jst over 1f out: fdd* **8/1**[3]

-005 **6** *hd* **Yomalo (IRE)**[18] 2428 4-8-12 **64** SSanders 2 — 66
(RGuest) *racd on outer in rr: prog 3f out: chsd ldrs over 1f out: one pce after* **16/1**

0105 **7** *1/2* **Warlingham (IRE)**[8] 2703 6-8-6 **58** JFanning 16 — 58
(PHowling) *chsd ldrs: rdn and nt qckn over 2f out: one pce after* **16/1**

0152 **8** *shd* **Effective**[28] 2178 4-8-12 **64** DHolland 8 — 64
(APJarvis) *a in midfield: rdn and no prog over 2f out* **11/1**

0065 **9** *2* **Firework**[19] 2399 6-8-8 **60** (p) TQuinn 12 — 54
(JAkehurst) *chsd ldrs: rdn over 2f out: wknd over 1f out* **14/1**

6006 **10** *3/4* **Margalita (IRE)**[11] 2628 4-9-2 **68** (t) JFEgan 9 — 60
(PMitchell) *sn rdn in midfield: nvr on terms w ldrs* **40/1**

0002 **11** *shd* **Blue Patrick**[7] 2735 4-9-9 **75** (p) JMackay 6 — 66
(JMPEustace) *hld up wl in rr: effrt 1/2-way: sn rdn and no real prog* **16/1**

3-00 **12** *1 1/2* **Mac's Talisman (IRE)**[19] 2404 4-8-8 **60** MTebbutt 11 — 47
(VSmith) *wl in rr: last 2f out: effrt but no ch whn nt clr run 1f out: kpt on* **50/1**

4505 **13** *1/2* **Madrasee**[38] 1937 6-9-10 **76** CCogan 5 — 61
(LMontagueHall) *a towards rr: rdn and no prog over 2f out* **25/1**

-500 **14** *nk* **Tapau (IRE)**[10] 2656 6-9-0 **66** DaneO'Neill 13 — 50
(JMBradley) *s.s: racd against nr side rail: a wl in rr* **20/1**

635- **15** *shd* **Esatto**[210] 6014 5-9-9 **75** SRighton 3 — 59
(MJAttwater) *dwlt: a struggling in rr* **50/1**

0000 **16** *nk* **Super Song**[14] 2524 4-8-13 **65** (t) JoannaBadger 1 — 48
(PDEvans) *racd on outer: nvr on terms: rdn and no prog over 2f out* **66/1**

1-05 **17** *10* **Thurlestone Rock**[6] 2763 4-9-11 **77** LDettori 15 — 30
(BJMeehan) *wnt lft s: chsd ldr for 2f: wknd 1/2-way: t.o* **9/1**

1m 12.0s (-1.87) **Going Correction** -0.10s/f (Good) **17** Ran SP% **126.7**
Speed ratings: **108,104,102,102,99 99,98,98,95,94 94,92,92,91,91 91,77**CSF £34.07 CT £265.31 TOTE £4.20: £1.90, £3.30, £2.00, £1.80; EX 34.90 Trifecta £380.20 Pool of £1446.14 - 2.70 winning units..

**Owner** Mrs Sandra Jones **Bred** Gainsborough Stud Management Ltd **Trained** Haydon, Somerset

**FOCUS**

A competitive handicap run at a scorching pace and the stands' rail was again the place to be. The form is strong for the grade.

**NOTEBOOK**

**Caustic Wit(IRE)** continues in the form of his life. Breaking well from his middle draw, he travelled really well and gradually migrated to the stands' rail in front before forging right away to complete the four-timer. He was winning this off a 16lb higher mark than when the sequence started and it will be a brave person that thinks it has ended.

**High Ridge**, despite his penalty, was only 2lb higher than when winning at Bath 48 hours earlier due to being out of the handicap there. He ran with great credit considering he was drawn low and made his effort down the centre of the track.

**Full Spate** ◆, well drawn, ran another solid race. He is capable of winning off this mark and still looks about ready to strike.

**Complication**, 8lb better off with Caustic Wit for a two-length beating at Salisbury the previous week, ran another good race off a 2lb lower mark and did especially well as she took a broadside from the horse on her right leaving the stalls.

**Glencoe Solas(IRE)**, raised 6lb for her Doncaster win, broke well enough and tried to make good use of her high draw, but she could do nothing to stop the winner cruising past her, and then hung more and more to her left as the race progressed. *Official explanation: jockey said filly hung left-handed*

**Yomalo(IRE)** ◆, who loves these conditions, ran with credit from her low draw. This effort hinted at a revival and she is worth keeping in mind.

**Thurlestone Rock** was very errant leaving the stalls and, though he showed up for a while, he dropped away quite alarmingly. *Official explanation: jockey said gelding finished distressed*

## 2949 CROP OVER FESTIVAL TROPHY H'CAP — 1m 2f 7y

**8:30** (8:32) (E) (0-75,75) 3-Y-0 **£4,446** (£1,368; £684; £342) **Stalls** Low

Form / RPR

-600 **1** **Mr Tambourine Man (IRE)**[13] 2558 3-9-7 **75** TQuinn 14 — 85+
(PFICole) *hld up: nt clr run bnd 6f out: last 4f out: prog on outer over 2f out: chsd ldr fnl f: hrd rdn to ld last strides* **5/1**[2]

2101 **2** *hd* **Hawkit (USA)**[43] 1784 3-8-13 **74** SJDonohoe(7) 5 — 84
(PDEvans) *trckd ldrs: effrt to ld wl over 1f out: hrd rdn fnl f: hdd last strides* **12/1**

0-00 **3** *2 1/2* **Foxilla (IRE)**[92] 1017 3-7-10 **55** ow3 RThomas(5) 7 — 60
(DRCElsworth) *dwlt: hld up in rr: prog 4f out: chsd ldrs 2f out: hung lft and nt qckn over 1f out* **50/1**

35-0 **4** *1 1/4* **Petite Colleen (IRE)**[63] 1365 3-8-11 **65** DKinsella 11 — 67
(DHaydnJones) *prom: led wl over 3f out: hdd u.p wl over 1f out: one pce* **25/1**

1513 **5** *2 1/2* **Goblin**[15] 2501 3-9-2 **70** SSanders 2 — 68+
(DECantillon) *lost pl after 2f: n.m.r bnd after 4f: effrt 3f out: nvr rchd ldrs* **7/2**[1]

-020 **6** *shd* **Smoothly Does It**[19] 2400 3-8-13 **67** EAhern 8 — 65
(MrsAJBowlby) *sn trckd ldrs: effrt 3f out: drvn and ev ch 2f out: fdd over 1f out* **9/1**

0405 **7** *1 3/4* **Auroville**[12] 2571 3-8-9 **63** IMongan 12 — 57
(MLWBell) *hld up in rr: rdn and prog over 3f out: chsd ldrs u.p over 1f out: no imp* **9/1**

-412 **8** *7* **Ivory Coast (IRE)**[21] 2355 3-8-4 **61** RMiles(3) 10 — 42
(WRMuir) *prom: pressed ldr wl over 3f out to 2f out: wknd rapidly* **7/1**

00-0 **9** *nk* **Autumn Flyer (IRE)**[28] 2168 3-8-11 **65** RSmith 1 — 45
(CGCox) *chsd ldr 3f: nt handle bnd sn after and lost pl: wknd over 2f out* **50/1**

0364 **10** *nk* **Anduril**[21] 2361 3-8-13 **67** (p) JMackay 6 — 47
(JMPEustace) *rrd s: a in rr: rdn and hanging lft over 2f out: wknd* **11/1**

5-60 **11** *shd* **La Professoressa (IRE)**[14] 2536 3-8-8 **62** RHavlin 3 — 42
(MrsPNDutfield) *racd in midfield: rdn and effrt over 3f out: wknd 2f out* **25/1**

056- **12** *5* **Cornish Gold**[202] 6069 3-8-11 **65** DHolland 4 — 35
(NJHenderson) *chsd ldrs: nt handle bnd 6f out: wknd 3f out* **16/1**

5111 **13** *2 1/2* **Incisor**[10] 2667 3-9-1 **69** PDobbs 13 — 34
(SKirk) *lost pl and in rr after 4f: rdn and no prog over 3f out* **11/2**[3]

05-6 **14** *1* **Regal Flight (IRE)**[10] 2658 3-8-0 **54** ow1 CCatlin 9 — 17
(JMBradley) *free to post: racd freely: led to wl over 3f out: wknd rapidly and eased* **50/1**

2m 8.67s (0.37) **Going Correction** -0.10s/f (Good) **14** Ran SP% **122.3**
Speed ratings: **94,93,91,90,88 88,87,81,81,81 81,77,75,74**CSF £62.02 CT £2680.72 TOTE £5.50: £1.90, £3.70, £16.80; EX 87.20.

**Owner** The Hon Mrs J M Corbett & C Wright **Bred** Stratford Place Stud **Trained** Whatcombe, Oxon

**FOCUS**

A modest time and the form is ordinary, but a rough race and the winner should be given extra credit.

**NOTEBOOK**

**Mr Tambourine Man(IRE)** ◆, back on his favoured surface for the first time this season and racing off a 5lb lower mark, can be considered a much more clear-cut winner than the margin would suggest, as he was knocked back to last after getting into real bother on the loop, and was forced to make his effort down the centre of the track.

**Hawkit(USA)** did very little wrong on this return to handicap company and, racing against the favoured stands' rail, only just lost out. He had the run of the race compared to the winner though.

**Foxilla(IRE)** ran by far her best race to date, but the way she hung late on suggests she may not want the ground quite as fast as this.

**Petite Colleen(IRE)** ran much better than on her reappearance and the return to faster ground was definitely the reason for that.

**Goblin** still looks too high in the handicap, but he did not get the run of the race, especially when getting into all sorts of trouble around the loop.

**La Professoressa(IRE)** *Official explanation: jockey said filly coughed on pulling up*

**Cornish Gold** *Official explanation: jockey said filly was unsuited by ground - Good to Firm, Firm in places*

**Incisor**, bidding for a four-timer on this return to turf, ran too badly for the 11lb higher mark to have been the only reason.

## 2950 BARBADOS JAZZ FESTIVAL MAIDEN STKS — 1m 2f 7y

**9:00** (9:02) (D) 3-Y-0+ **£4,407** (£1,356; £678; £339) **Stalls** Low

Form / RPR

**1** **Littleton Telchar (USA)**[13] 2564 4-9-11 BDoyle 3 — 72
(MJRyan) *chsd ldrs: effrt 3f out: rdn to ld wl over 1f out: hrd pressed ins fnl f: all out* **50/1**

**2** *3/4* **Summer Serenade** 3-8-7 LDettori 8 — 66
(LMCumani) *rn green in midfield: effrt 4f out: clsng whn nt clr run 2f out and swtchd lft: chsd wnr over 1f out: chal last 150yds: jst* **2/1**[1]

0-4 **3** *3 1/2* **Michabo (IRE)**[19] 2401 3-8-12 TQuinn 6 — 64
(DRCElsworth) *t.k.h: prom: shkn up and effrt over 2f out: outpcd over 1f out* **10/1**

6 **4** *2 1/2* **Double Dagger Lady (USA)**[21] 2374 3-8-7 EAhern 12 — 54
(JNoseda) *prom: chsd ldr 4f out: led briefly 2f out: fdd over 1f out* **9/2**[3]

3 **5** *1 1/4* **Shambar (IRE)**[13] 2562 5-9-11 JPMurtagh 2 — 57
(PRChamings) *led: rdn and hdd 2f out: eased whn btn fnl f* **5/2**[2]

-66 **6** *5* **Lebenstanz**[32] 2060 4-9-6 SSanders 7 — 42
(LMCumani) *settled in midfield: lost tch w ldrs 1/2-way: nudged along and nvr on terms after* **16/1**

0 **7** *3/4* **Surface To Air**[16] 2486 3-8-12 RHavlin 5 — 46
(MrsPNDutfield) *pushed along and wl in rr: wl bhd 4f out: modest late prog* **66/1**

00-0 **8** *2 1/2* **Heart Springs**[24] 2273 4-9-6 ADaly 10 — 36
(DrJRJNaylor) *rrd s: hld up wl in rr: wl bhd 4f out: shuffled along and no prog after* **50/1**

0 **9** *1 1/4* **Miss Shangri La**[59] 1441 3-8-7 DHolland 11 — 34
(GWragg) *in tch: rdn 4f out: wknd 3f out* **10/1**

0 **10** *3 1/2* **Agouti**[28] 2182 3-8-7 DaneO'Neill 15 — 27
(DWPArbuthnot) *wl in rr: wl bhd 4f out: no prog* **66/1**

0-00 **11** *5* **Doringo**[49] 1674 3-8-12 SCarson 9 — 23
(JLSpearing) *t.k.h: mostly chsd ldr to 4f out: sn wknd* **66/1**

00/0 **12** *2 1/2* **Lake Of Dreams**[51] 1612 5-9-4 LucyRussell(7) 1 — 18
(DrJRJNaylor) *a wl in rr: wl bhd 4f out* **66/1**

**13** *dist* **Baranook (IRE)** 3-8-12 IMongan 14 — —
(PWHarris) *s.s: sn t.o* **10/1**

2m 9.52s (1.22) **Going Correction** -0.10s/f (Good)
**WFA** 3 from 4yo+ 13lb **13** Ran SP% **123.1**
Speed ratings: **91,90,87,85,84 80,80,78,77,74 70,68,**—CSF £154.34 TOTE £113.70: £12.00, £1.50, £2.20; EX 212.60 Place 6 £61.47, Place 5 £36.57.

**Owner** Dr P O'Driscoll **Bred** Morven Stud Ltd **Trained** Newmarket, Suffolk

■ Stewards Enquiry : E Ahern caution: careless riding

**FOCUS**

A poor maiden for the track but a decent pace early, although they may have gone too quick as the front pair came from off the pace and the winning time was nearly a second slower than the preceding handicap.

**NOTEBOOK**

**Littleton Telchar(USA)**, who has changed stables since making his debut in Ireland 13 days earlier, caused a real shock and was definitely a fortunate winner. The way the race was run may make the form a bit suspect too, but this was still a big effort and he obviously has ability.

**Summer Serenade**, a half-sister to Act One, Summer Symphony and Summer Solstice, got outpaced and had to be ridden along from some way out, but would almost certainly have won had she not been squeezed out against the stands' rail when making her effort two furlongs from home, especially given the winning margin.

**Michabo(IRE)**, not for the first time, did his chances little good by pulling too hard early but the fact that he managed to hang on for third suggests he may be capable of better in a strongly-run race. He may do better in handicaps.

**Double Dagger Lady(USA)** was close enough if good enough two furlongs out, but did not appear to get home. She needs one more run for a handicap mark and that is probably where her future lies.

**Shambar(IRE)** almost certainly did too much too soon and may also be suited by easier ground.

**Baranook(IRE)** *Official explanation: jockey said colt was unsuited by the ground - Good to Firm, Firm in places*

T/Jkpt: Not won. Pool of £4,329.50. T/Plt: £98.30 to a £1 stake. Pool: £49,961.05. 371.00 winning tickets. T/Qpdt: £56.00 to a £1 stake. Pool: £2,576.30. 34.00 winning tickets. JN

2951 - 2953a (Foreign Racing) - See Raceform Interactive

2281

# ASCOT (R-H)

Tuesday, June 15

**OFFICIAL GOING: Good to firm**

On the straight cause it was an advantage to be drawn low and those that made an impact from a high draw should be given extra credit.

Wind: fresh hlf against Weather: sunny & warm

## 2954 COVENTRY STKS (GROUP 2) 6f

**2:30** (2:36) (A) 2-Y-O **£40,600** (£15,400; £7,700; £3,500) **Stalls** Low

Form RPR

21 **1** **Iceman**[31] 2111 2-8-12 ........ KFallon 11 109
(JHMGosden) *wl in rr and pushed along over 3f out: prog 2f out: swtchd rt and drvn over 1f out: styd on strly to ld last 75yds* **5/1**[1]

1 **2** ½ **Council Member (USA)**[13] 2579 2-8-12 ........ LDettori 5 107
(SaeedBinSuroor) *lw: w ldrs: shkn up to ld wl over 1f out: drvn fnl f: kpt on wl but hdd last 75yds* **5/1**[1]

33 **3** 1 ¾ **Capable Guest (IRE)**[24] 2310 2-8-12 ........ CCatlin 9 102
(MRChannon) *outpcd in last and wl bhd: stl last and u.p 2f out: swtchd to wd outside over 1f out: styd on strly: nrst fin* **33/1**

1 **4** *nk* **Tony James (IRE)**[18] 2447 2-8-12 ........ DHolland 7 101
(CEBrittain) *w'like: scope: lw: mde most to wl over 1f out: fdd ins fnl f* **13/2**[3]

21 **5** 1 ¾ **Turnkey**[43] 1826 2-8-12 ........ TEDurcan 14 96
(MRChannon) *dwlt: racd in rr on outer: rdn and prog 2f out: ch 1f out: wknd ins fnl f* **7/1**

1 **6** 1 ½ **Berkhamsted (IRE)**[75] 1219 2-8-12 ........ JPMurtagh 8 91
(JAOsborne) *w'like: scope: lw: chsd ldrs: rdn over 2f out: bdly outpcd over 1f out: styd on again last 100yds* **25/1**

**7** *hd* **Oratorio (IRE)**[23] 2327 2-8-12 ........ JPSpencer 6 91
(APO'Brien, Ire) *str: w ldrs: ev ch wl over 1f out: wknd jst over 1f out* **6/1**[2]

122 **8** ½ **Dario Gee Gee (IRE)**[18] 2447 2-8-12 ........ NCallan 3 89
(KARyan) *lw: chsd ldrs: rdn 1/2-way: nt qckn and struggling 2f out: no ch after: kpt on* **33/1**

211 **9** 1 **Goodricke**[32] 2086 2-8-12 ........ TPQueally 4 86
(DRLoder) *lw: trckd ldrs gng wl: rdn 2f out: wknd over 1f out* **14/1**

12 **10** 2 **Dance Anthem**[13] 2592 2-8-12 ........ PMcCabe 12 80
(MGQuinlan) *trckd ldrs: rdn and effrt over 2f out: in tch over 1f out: sn wknd* **50/1**

1321 **11** 1 **Beaver Patrol (IRE)**[17] 2478 2-8-12 ........ SCarson 13 77
(RFJohnsonHoughton) *w ldrs: losing pl u.p whn bmpd jst over 1f out: wknd* **20/1**

1 **12** 1 ½ **Kings Quay**[12] 2627 2-8-12 ........ DaneO'Neill 2 73
(RHannon) *h.d.w: s.i.s: chsd ldrs: u.p and struggling 1/2-way: btn 2f out: eased fnl f* **6/1**[2]

412 **13** 7 **Catwalk Cleric (IRE)**[11] 2669 2-8-12 ........ KDarley 1 52
(MJWallace) *a struggling towards rr: wknd 2f out: eased fnl f* **50/1**

1m 14.83s (-1.16) **Going Correction** -0.025s/f (Good) **13** Ran SP% **112.8**

Speed ratings: **106,105,103,102,100 98,98,97,96,93 92,90,80**CSF £25.24 CT £839.80 TOTE £4.00: £1.60, £1.90, £11.20; EX 18.90 Trifecta £839.80 Pool of £5,086.16 - 4.30 winning units..

**Owner** Cheveley Park Stud **Bred** Cheveley Park Stud Ltd **Trained** Manton, Wilts

**FOCUS**

An average winning time for a juvenile Group Two given the conditions. The winner's rating is well below that awarded to Three Valleys a year ago, but it is in line with other recent winners and the form looks up to scratch. Good efforts from the front pair and some eye-catchers in behind.

**NOTEBOOK**

**Iceman**, whose Newbury victory is working out very well, was taken off his feet early but he got stronger as the race progressed. He had to weave a passage through, but never lost his momentum and was produced with a perfectly-timed effort to score. He is likely to be given a break now before reappearing in the Champagne Stakes at the Doncaster St Leger meeting.

**Council Member(USA)**, stepping up a furlong from his debut, was always up there on the nearside and ran all the way to the line. He should be able to win in Pattern company this season, especially when stepped up again in trip.

**Capable Guest(IRE)** ◆ faced a stiff task for a maiden and his cause looked even more hopeless when he became completely outpaced in the early stages, but he fairly rattled home and when he goes up to seven furlongs he should be winning.

**Tony James(IRE)** tried to make all the running at a decent pace, but just found the task too great at this stage of his career. He is a grand sort and has next year's Kentucky Derby as his long-term target.

**Turnkey**, trying an extra furlong, was on very different ground compared with his Kempton victory. The combination of the widest draw and a slow start made a difficult task near-impossible, and he probably did as well as could be expected. He is still a nice sort for the future, but the feeling remains that he needs an easier surface than this.

**Berkhamsted(IRE)** ◆, given a short break since his winning debut on easy ground at Leicester, tended to run in snatches on this faster surface, but there was nothing wrong with the way he came home and he remains a nice prospect. He should stay further.

**Oratorio(IRE)**, a winner at The Curragh on his debut, had every chance, but was made to look ordinary in the latter stages.

**Dario Gee Gee(IRE)** was a bit out of his depth and finished further behind Tony James than at Pontefract.

**Goodricke** was comfortably held, but all his previous form has been on easy ground. Although nothing special, he is almost certainly capable of winning again under more favourable conditions.

**Beaver Patrol(IRE)**, backed at long odds, was already on the retreat when taking a right buffeting approaching the furlong pole.

**Kings Quay** ran too badly to be true, even allowing for the extra furlong and faster ground.

## 2955 KING'S STAND STKS (GROUP 2) 5f

**3:05** (3:12) (A) 3-Y-O+ **£81,200** (£30,800; £15,400; £7,000) **Stalls** Low

Form RPR

-234 **1** **The Tatling (IRE)**[9] 2719 7-9-2 112........ DHolland 5 119
(JMBradley) *hld up: hdwy over 2f out: rdn over 1f out: led ins fnl f: r.o wl* **8/1**

0/3- **2** 1 ½ **Cape Of Good Hope**[51] 6-9-2 ........ (vt) MJKinane 1 114
(DOughton, Hong Kong) *str: tall: hld up: rdn and hdwy 2f out: ev ch ins fnl f: nt qckn* **13/2**[3]

1-21 **3** *nk* **Frizzante**[45] 1763 5-8-13 111........ JPMurtagh 7 110
(JRFanshawe) *bhd: rdn and hdwy whn nt clr run over 1f out: swtchd lft ins fnl f: fin wl* **9/2**[1]

-613 **4** *nk* **Ringmoor Down**[24] 2316 5-8-13 103........ DaneO'Neill 2 108
(DWPArbuthnot) *s.i.s: hdwy whn nt clr run and swtchd rt over 1f and ins fnl f: r.o* **25/1**

161- **5** *nk* **Majestic Missile (IRE)**[248] 5480 3-8-10 116........ KFallon 13 111
(WJHaggas) *hld up mid-div: hdwy over 2f out: rdn over 1f out: ev ch ins fnl f: no ex* **5/1**[2]

-321 **6** *nk* **Boogie Street**[17] 2475 3-8-10 107........ RHughes 18 110
(RHannon) *b.hind: led: edgd rt to stands' rail over 2f out: hdd 1f out: one pce* **12/1**

4210 **7** *hd* **Bahamian Pirate (USA)**[35] 2021 9-9-2 105........ GaryStevens 11 109
(DNicholls) *s.i.s: hdwy over 1f out: n.m.r ins fnl f: r.o* **50/1**

2-43 **8** *nk* **Nights Cross (IRE)**[32] 2080 3-8-10 105........ TEDurcan 16 108
(MRChannon) *hld up: hdwy on outside over 2f out: sn rdn: one pce fnl f* **50/1**

**9** 1 ¼ **Lydgate (USA)**[46] 4-9-2 ........ (t) LDettori 19 103
(EGHarty, U.S.A) *str: b.hind: hld up towards rr: rdn over 2f out: nvr nr to chal* **16/1**

6-13 **10** *nk* **The Trader (IRE)**[9] 2719 6-9-2 113........ (b) JPSpencer 17 102
(MBlanshard) *lw: s.i.s: hdwy whn n.m.r ins fnl f: nrst fin* **10/1**

2000 **11** *shd* **Dragon Flyer (IRE)**[11] 2636 5-8-13 98........ JAHeffernan 12 99
(MQuinn) *prom: rdn and ev ch over 1f out: wknd fnl f* **100/1**

-400 **12** 1 ½ **Stormont (IRE)**[22] 2373 4-9-5 ........ JQuinn 8 99
(HJCollingridge) *s.i.s: hdwy whn nt clr run over 1f out: nvr nrr* **66/1**

-106 **13** 1 ¼ **If Paradise**[11] 2636 3-8-10 105........ RLMoore 10 93
(RHannon) *chsd ldrs 3f* **100/1**

30-2 **14** *nk* **Lochridge**[17] 2475 5-8-13 106........ KDarley 6 88
(AMBalding) *a bhd* **7/1**

12-0 **15** 1 ¼ **Mornin Reserves**[45] 1763 5-9-2 107........ RWinston 3 86
(ISemple) *prom: rdn over 2f out: wknd over 1f out* **18/1**

0655 **16** ½ **Colonel Cotton (IRE)**[11] 2636 5-9-2 103........ (b) EAhern 4 84
(NACallaghan) *a bhd* **33/1**

6200 **17** *shd* **Smokin Beau**[39] 1923 7-9-2 97........ (b[1]) TGMcLaughlin 14 84
(NPLittmoden) *prom: rdn over 2f out: wknd over 1f out* **100/1**

-230 **18** 4 **Speed Cop**[11] 2636 4-8-13 99........ MHills 9 67
(AMBalding) *chsd ldrs over 2f* **50/1**

0000 **19** 14 **Dubaian Gift**[11] 2636 5-9-2 101........ KMcEvoy 15 19
(AMBalding) *prom tl wknd qckly 2f out: collapsed and died after fin* **66/1**

60.16 secs (-1.77) **Going Correction** -0.025s/f (Good)

**WFA** 3 from 4yo+ 7lb **19** Ran SP% **118.3**

Speed ratings: **113,110,110,109,109 108,108,107,105,105 105,102,100,100,98 97,97,91,68**CSF £53.70 TOTE £11.60: £3.80, £2.00, £2.10; EX 57.90 Trifecta £178.60 Pool of £6,792.75 - 26.99 winning units..

**Owner** Dab Hand Racing **Bred** Patrick J Power **Trained** Sedbury, Gloucs

■ A first Royal Ascot winner in a long career for Milton Bradley.

**FOCUS**

Although a very competitive contest, this did not look the strongest King's Stand. The time was unexceptional for a Group Two under these conditions, but the winner ran up to last year's best form. The first four all had single figure draws.

**NOTEBOOK**

**The Tatling(IRE)** needs a strong pace, so he had the race run to suit and conditions were perfect for him. Once he was pulled out for his effort, he showed his proven turn of foot to score with some comfort and record his biggest win to date. He still seems to be improving even at the age of seven, and it is hard to believe he is the same horse that was getting beaten off a mark of 83 less than two years ago.

**Cape Of Good Hope**, a big gelding who won at Newmarket in 2001 but has been trained in Hong Kong since, has been taking on the best sprinters around the world and ran a fine race in defeat from his plum draw. He gave the impression that the extra furlong of Saturday's Golden Jubilee Stakes would suit him even better.

**Frizzante**, whose trainer was very concerned by the fast ground, ran a blinder nonetheless, finishing strongly against the stands' rail and doing very well to get so close after getting into plenty of trouble. She still looks progressive and can reach the top.

**Ringmoor Down** did really well to finish so close considering her slowish start and the traffic she ran into.

**Majestic Missile(IRE)** faced a stiff task against established older sprinters on this first start in eight months, but he held his place in the market and had every chance until entering the last furlong. The evidence is that he faced a tall order from his draw in any case, and he still has time on his side.

**Boogie Street** showed blinding speed from his high draw and managed to edge across in front to lead the field for half a mile before tiring. He looks well up to this grade.

**Bahamian Pirate(USA)** was far from disgraced. Though he has won on fast ground in the past, he may prefer more cut these days.

**Lydgate(USA)**, trained in the States, was unable to offer a threat from the highest stall over this shorter trip.

**The Trader(IRE)** has usually finished close to The Tatling in their many meetings. On this occasion he was well adrift, though he did not get the clearest of runs. *Official explanation: jockey said gelding stumbled leaving the stalls*

**Stormont(IRE)** *Official explanation: jockey said colt suffered interference in running*

**Lochridge** found everything happening much too quickly for her.

**Dubaian Gift** sadly collapsed and died while being unsaddled in the paddock.

## 2956 ST JAMES'S PALACE STKS (GROUP 1) (ENTIRE COLTS) 1m (R)

**3:45** (3:47) (A) 3-Y-O **£139,896** (£53,064; £26,532; £12,060) **Stalls** High

Form RPR

1-32 **1** **Azamour (IRE)**[24] 2315 3-9-0 ........ MJKinane 1 122
(JohnMOxx, Ire) *lw: trckd ldrs: effrt over 2f out: hrd rdn over 1f out: r.o to ld last 150yds: drvn out* **9/2**[2]

1-42 **2** *nk* **Diamond Green (FR)**[30] 2161 3-9-0 ........ GaryStevens 8 121
(AFabre, France) *w'like: hld up in midfield: effrt over 2f out: rdn and prog over 1f out: chal ent fnl f: r.o but jst hld* **10/1**

0-25 **3** ¾ **Antonius Pius (USA)**[30] 2161 3-9-0 ........ (t) JPSpencer 10 119
(APO'Brien, Ire) *lengthy: hld up in last trio: prog on inner 2f out: swtchd lft over 1f out: cruised up to ldrs: rdn ent fnl f: fnd nil* **7/1**

3-11 **4** *nk* **Haafhd**[45] 1764 3-9-0 124........ RHills 6 119
(BWHills) *trckd ldr: led 2f out: hrd pressed fr over 1f out: hdd and one pce last 150yds* **6/4**[1]

5-11 **5** 1 ½ **Brunel (IRE)**[30] 2158 3-9-0 115........ DHolland 4 115
(WJHaggas) *lw: dwlt: racd in midfield: rdn and unable qck over 2f out: kpt on to press ldrs 1f out: one pce after* **14/1**

-231 **6** *shd* **Castleton**[10] 2693 3-9-0 100........ KFallon 7 115?
(HJCyzer) *lw: led: rdn and hdd 2f out: keeping on wl whn hmpd on inner jst ins fnl f: nt rcvr* **66/1**

4-01 **7** 1 ¼ **Bachelor Duke (USA)**[24] 2315 3-9-0 120........ SSanders 9 112
(JARToller) *t.k.h: hld up in midfield: rdn and nt qckn 3f out: n.d after: kpt on ins fnl f* **6/1**[3]

31-3 **8** 1 ½ **Byron**[30] 2161 3-9-0 111........ (t) LDettori 3 109
(SaeedBinSuroor) *trckd ldrs: rdn 2f out: losing pl whn n.m.r over 1f out: wknd fnl f* **20/1**

11 **9** ½ **Madid (IRE)**[12] 2629 3-9-0 ........ WSupple 5 107
(JHMGosden) *dwlt: racd in last trio: rdn over 3f out: no prog and btn over 2f out: one pce after* **12/1**

31-0 **10** 3 **Pearl Of Love (IRE)**[9] 2721 3-9-0 114........ KDarley 2 101
(MJohnston) *chsd ldrs tl wknd over 2f out* **25/1**

1466 **11** *20* **Newton (IRE)**[24] 2315 3-9-0 ....(v1) PJScallan 11 55
(APO'Brien, Ire) *rel to r and lft 12l: a last: in tch to over 3f out: wknd: t.o*
**100/1**

1m 39.02s (-4.02) **Going Correction** -0.025s/f (Good) **11** Ran SP% **119.5**
Speed ratings: **119,118,117,117,116 116,114,113,112,109 89**CSF £48.04 TOTE £5.50: £1.80, £3.40, £2.90; EX 39.20 Trifecta £230.50 Pool of £10,000.00 - 30.80 winning units..
**Owner** H H Aga Khan **Bred** H H Aga Khan **Trained** Currabeg, Co Kildare

**FOCUS**
A decent renewal and an excellent time, even for a Group One - faster than the Queen Anne despite being run around a bend. Although two horses that could have been expected to lead missed the break, outsider Castleton set a true pace. His proximity at the finish is a concern.

**NOTEBOOK**
**Azamour(IRE)** had the run of the race this time and, produced with a perfectly-timed effort, battled on really well to reverse English and Irish Guineas form with Haafhd and Bachelor Duke respectively. He looks to be progressing and connections are keen to step him up in trip, but that may be put on hold until after a possible tilt at the Sussex Stakes.
**Diamond Green(FR)**, tucked away off the pace, was produced with his effort on the inside a furlong from home, but could not quite match the winner's impetus. This was a smart effort on ground that was probably faster than ideal, and he should be a major player in the big mile races in France later in the season, granted some cut.
**Antonius Pius(USA)**, who threw away certain victory in the French Guineas, travelled better than anything and when he was pulled out it almost looked a question of how far. However, when he was asked for maximum effort the response was very disappointing. The ability is definitely there, but so are the doubts.
**Haafhd**, racing around a bend for the first time, had the run of the race and hit the front soon after turning in, but could not maintain the advantage. This was not his form, and perhaps the ground was faster than ideal.
**Brunel(IRE)** is a much better horse when able to lead, but that plan went out of the window when he missed the break. He did well to get as close as he did, and there are other decent prizes to be won with him.
**Castleton**, taking a massive step up in class, likes to front run and the gods were smiling on him, as for several reasons he found himself enjoying an uncontested lead. He was not completely finished when badly hampered by Diamond Green in the closing stages and this was an absolutely cracking effort. He should be able to win a Pattern race if reproducing this.
**Bachelor Duke(USA)** had everything go his way when winning the Irish 2,000 Guineas, but could not confirm the form and there seemed no obvious excuses.
**Byron**, who split Diamond Green and the unfortunate Antonius Pius in the French Guineas, was already beaten when short of room in the closing stages. He seemed to run to form.
**Madid(IRE)**, who got warm beforehand, was always struggling and probably found this too much of an ask at this stage of his career.
**Pearl Of Love(IRE)** is yet to recapture anything like his two-year-old form. *Official explanation: trainer said colt was bleeding from cracked right fore hoof*

## 2957 QUEEN ANNE STKS (GROUP 1) 1m (S)
4:20 (4:27) (A) 4-Y-O+ **£145,000** (£55,000; £27,500; £12,500) **Stalls** Low

Form RPR
0-00 **1** **Refuse To Bend (IRE)**[31] 2109 4-9-0 115....(t) LDettori 1 123
(SaeedBinSuroor) *lw: trckd ldrs: rdn over 2f out: swtchd rt over 1f out: r.o to ld nr fin* **12/1**
-231 **2** *nk* **Soviet Song (IRE)**[24] 2318 4-8-11 114.... JPMurtagh 3 119
(JRFanshawe) *a.p: rdn to ld 1f out: hdd nr fin* **6/1**[2]
0-02 **3** *3/4* **Salselon**[31] 2109 5-9-0 118....(b) DHolland 9 120
(LMCumani) *hld up and bhd: plld out over 1f out: hdwy fnl f: r.o* **12/1**
61-5 **4** *1* **Nebraska Tornado (USA)**[23] 2339 4-8-11.... GaryStevens 4 115
(AFabre, France) *w'like: leggy: w ldr: led over 3f out to 1f out: nt qckn* **7/1**[3]
330- **5** *1 1/4* **Tillerman**[241] 5638 8-9-0 117.... RHughes 5 115+
(MrsAJPerrett) *dwlt: hld up in rr: nt clr run jst over 2f out: hdwy fnl f: nrst fin* **20/1**
11-2 **6** *3/4* **Six Perfections (FR)**[23] 2339 4-8-11.... TThulliez 12 110
(PBary, France) *lw: hld up: swtchd rt and hdwy whn hung rt over 1f out: one pce fnl f* **5/2**[1]
2-43 **7** *hd* **Bowman's Crossing (IRE)**[30] 2156 5-9-0....(v1) MJKinane 6 113
(DOughton, Hong Kong) *lengthy: hld up mid-div: nt clr run jst over 2f out: rdn and hdwy over 1f out: kpt on same pce fnl f* **33/1**
0034 **8** *1 1/2* **Checkit (IRE)**[10] 2678 4-9-0 112.... TEDurcan 7 109
(MRChannon) *hld up mid-div: hdwy 3f out: sn rdn: wknd ins fnl f* **66/1**
0-51 **9** *nk* **Martillo (GER)**[45] 1780 4-9-0.... WMongil 10 109
(RSuerland, Germany) *h.d.w: hld up and bhd: swtchd rt 2f out: hdwy over 1f out: wknd ins fnl f* **14/1**
-315 **10** *2 1/2* **Hurricane Alan (IRE)**[31] 2109 4-9-0 114.... PDobbs 11 103
(RHannon) *hld up and bhd: nt clr run jst over 2f out: n.d* **25/1**
-541 **11** *1 3/4* **Alkaadhem**[26] 2241 4-9-0 108.... RHills 8 99
(MPTregoning) *lw: prom: rdn over 2f out: wknd over 1f out* **9/1**
-132 **12** *5* **Arakan (USA)**[24] 2316 4-9-0 111.... KFallon 17 88
(SirMichaelStoute) *hld up and bhd: short-lived effrt on outside over 2f out* **16/1**
01-0 **13** *1 1/2* **Just James**[35] 2021 5-9-0 113.... EAhern 16 84
(JNoseda) *a bhd* **33/1**
0-43 **14** *12* **Norse Dancer (IRE)**[31] 2109 4-9-0 117.... TQuinn 14 56
(DRCElsworth) *lw: mid-div: pushed along over 4f out: rdn over 3f out: wknd wl over 1f out* **10/1**
41-0 **15** *7* **Lateen Sails**[14] 2559 4-9-0 114....(t) KMcEvoy 2 40
(SaeedBinSuroor) *led over 3f: rdn and wknd over 1f out* **33/1**
20-6 **16** *24* **Beauchamp Pilot**[10] 2678 6-9-0.... JPSpencer 15 —
(GAButler) *a bhd: eased whn btn over 2f out* **66/1**

1m 39.14s (-2.78) **Going Correction** -0.025s/f (Good) **16** Ran SP% **122.8**
Speed ratings: **112,111,110,109,108 107,107,106,105,103 101,96,95,83,76 52**CSF £33.08 TOTE £12.50: £3.20, £2.70, £4.80; EX 123.50 Trifecta £3057.90 Pool of £8613.89 - 2.00 winning units..
**Owner** Godolphin **Bred** Moyglare Stud Farm Ltd **Trained** Newmarket, Suffolk
■ Stewards Enquiry : L Dettori one-day ban: used whip with excessive frequency (Jun 26)

**FOCUS**
This was not quite up to the standard of recent renewals. They all raced towards the stands' side, but the pace was not great and the winning time was modest for a Group One, slower than the St James's Palace despite being run over a straight mile. The winner looked back to his 2,000 Guineas form but might have struggled if Russian Rhythm had been fit to race.

**NOTEBOOK**
**Refuse To Bend(IRE)**, drawn ideally next to the rail, got a nice tow from his stablemate for much of the race and stayed on well up the rising ground to edge out the filly. Largely disappointing since he won the 2000 Guineas last year, this was a welcome return to form, but he definitely had the race run to suit and would be far from certain to confirm the form.
**Soviet Song(IRE)**, who returned to her best in Ireland last time, ran a blinder in second. Perfectly placed throughout, she 'won' the race between the three well-fancied fillies in the race, coping with the fast ground well, and the Falmouth Stakes at the Newmarket July Meeting looks the obvious target.
**Salselon**, who kicked a stalls handler at the start, was given an awful lot to do by his rider. Held up right at the back of the field on the rail before being switched widest of all, it was not until the furlong marker that he began to be put under pressure, by which time the front two had kicked decisively clear. He came home well for third, and his Lockinge second and this performance suggest that he has the ability to win a Group One over a mile this year.
**Nebraska Tornado(USA)** won two Group Ones last season but both came in slowly-run affairs in which she raced close to the pace. Well positioned throughout on this occasion too, she had little excuse, but this was obviously an improvement on her reappearance effort.
**Tillerman**, who was runner-up in this race last year but was subsequently disqualified, was making his fifth appearance at Royal Ascot. He invariably runs well here, and loves fast ground, but he has always found one or two too strong at the very top level. He finished well from off the pace though, and might have done a bit better had there been a stronger gallop.
**Six Perfections(FR)** was the disappointment of the race. Despite being brought with her challenge, unhindered and at the right time, she just could not find her trademark turn of foot. Her connections later blamed the firm ground, although the stiff mile may also have played a part in her poor performance.
**Bowman's Crossing(IRE)**, a challenger from Hong Kong who finished third in the International Cup in Singapore on his last start, ran a respectable race on his first outing in this country.
**Checkit(IRE)** is not really up to this level so he did not run too badly in the circumstances.
**Martillo(GER)**, successful in a soft-ground French Group Two last time, probably found this rattling surface too quick.
**Alkaadhem** was sent off a shocking price for this Group One race considering what he had actually achieved to date.
**Beauchamp Pilot** *Official explanation: jockey said gelding was unsuited by the good to firm going*

## 2958 ASCOT STKS (H'CAP) 2m 4f
4:55 (5:01) (C) (0-95,95) 4-Y-O+ **£23,200** (£8,800; £4,400; £2,000) **Stalls** High

Form RPR
-000 **1** **Double Obsession**[10] 2684 4-9-2 86....(v) JFEgan 24 104
(MJohnston) *trckd ldr to 6f out: wnt 2nd again over 3f out: led over 2f out and sn clr: rdn out* **25/1**
4-00 **2** *5* **Promoter**[34] 2047 4-9-1 85.... EAhern 28 98
(JNoseda) *t.k.h: trckd ldrs: effrt over 3f out: chsd wnr wl over 1f out: carried hd high but styd on: no imp* **14/1**
234/ **3** *6* **Penny Pictures (IRE)**[24] 3884 5-9-6 87.... GaryStevens 15 94
(MCPipe) *t.k.h: hld up in last trio tl rapid prog fr 10f out: trckd ldr 6f out to over 3f out: one pce u.p* **25/1**
-300 **4** *1* **Redspin (IRE)**[59] 1457 4-7-12 68.... DKinsella 2 74
(JSMoore) *lw: settled wl in rr: stl in last gp over 3f out: c wd st: rapid prog fnl 2f: fin strly* **100/1**
2-01 **5** *1 1/4* **Land 'n Stars**[24] 2285 4-8-9 79.... PDoe 14 84
(JamiePoulton) *trckd ldrs: effrt over 3f out: rdn and outpcd over 2f out: one pce after: eased nr fin* **11/2**[1]
3-26 **6** *nk* **Teresa**[45] 1779 4-8-8 78.... JQuinn 11 82
(JLDunlop) *trckd ldrs: cl enough over 3f out: rdn and outpcd over 2f out: no ch after* **16/1**
0303 **7** *1 1/2* **Riyadh**[8] 2731 6-8-1 68....(v) RFfrench 29 71
(MJohnston) *prom: rdn over 3f out: grad fdd u.p fnl 2f* **14/1**
-004 **8** *1/2* **Almizan (IRE)**[12] 2613 4-8-12 82.... TEDurcan 13 84
(MRChannon) *racd in midfield: effrt 5f out: nt on terms w ldng gp over 3f out: one pce after* **33/1**
/00- **9** *2* **Stance**[19] 5-8-10 77.... RLMoore 16 77
(GLMoore) *lw: in last trio and rdn 12f out: effrt u.p 5f out: nvr on terms: kpt on* **20/1**
0-05 **10** *1 1/4* **Don Fernando**[24] 2285 5-8-9 76.... DHolland 27 75
(MCPipe) *hld up wl in rr: plenty to do over 4f out: plld out and effrt 2f out: no ch* **12/1**[3]
1-12 **11** *1/2* **Wasted Talent (IRE)**[15] 2514 4-8-5 75.... DaneO'Neill 20 74
(JGPortman) *trckd ldng gp: rdn 4f out: no prog: fdd fnl 2f* **25/1**
13-2 **12** *2* **Got One Too (FR)**[24] 2285 7-8-6 73.... MJKinane 25 70
(NJHenderson) *led: clr 8f out: hdd & wknd over 2f out* **11/1**[2]
-006 **13** *1 1/4* **Gralmano (IRE)**[4] 2855 9-9-2 83.... NCallan 6 78
(KARyan) *pressed ldrs: rdn over 5f out: wknd over 2f out* **66/1**
0000 **14** *2* **Establishment**[12] 2613 7-8-3 70.... KMcEvoy 10 63
(CACyzer) *nvr beyond midfield: effrt on inner and n.m.r 4f out: no prog after* **16/1**
00/4 **15** *1 1/4* **Hernandita**[8] 2731 6-7-9 65 oh1.... JFMcDonald(3) 23 57
(MissECLavelle) *chsd ldrs: rdn over 4f out: wknd over 2f out* **66/1**
0- **16** *3* **Amid The Chaos (IRE)**[24] 2319 4-9-4 88....(vt1) PJSmullen 4 77
(DKWeld, Ire) *w'like: racd in midfield: pushed along 5f out: nvr on terms w ldng gp after* **25/1**
14/5 **17** *1 1/4* **Hawadeth**[52] 1329 9-8-12 79....(p) KDarley 22 67
(VRADartnall) *hld up in rr: plenty to do 5f out: no real prog over 3f out* **25/1**
-050 **18** *1 1/2* **Mana D'Argent (IRE)**[34] 2047 7-9-7 88.... JFanning 19 74
(MJohnston) *settled in midfield: plenty to do whn n.m.r 4f out: no prog after* **12/1**[3]
2302 **19** *1 1/4* **King Flyer (IRE)**[12] 2613 8-9-0 81.... SWhitworth 7 66
(MissJFeilden) *wl in rr: last 12f out: nvr a factor* **25/1**
341 **20** *16* **Glory Quest (USA)**[11] 2652 7-8-8 75.... IMongan 21 44
(MissGayKelleway) *chsd ldrs tl wknd rapidly u.p over 3f out* **33/1**
1433 **21** *2* **Sentry (IRE)**[10] 2684 4-9-2 86.... LDettori 1 53
(JHMGosden) *hld up wl in rr: prog fr 6f out: chsd ldng gp over 3f out: wknd over 2f out* **11/1**[2]
00-3 **22** *1/2* **Once (FR)**[24] 2299 4-8-5 75.... SWKelly 26 42
(JAOsborne) *chsd ldng gp: u.p 6f out: sn btn* **66/1**
10-0 **23** *5* **Numitas (GER)**[41] 1880 4-9-5 89.... SSanders 12 51
(PJHobbs) *lw: settled wl in rr: rdn and no prog over 4f out: bhd after* **12/1**[3]
506/ **24** *5* **Chimes At Midnight (USA)**[683] 3591 7-10-0 95....(b) JAHeffernan 18 52
(LukeComer, Ire) *a wl in rr: pushed along and struggling over 4f out: wknd and bhd after* **80/1**
2153 **25** *9* **Malarkey**[12] 2613 7-8-10 77.... KFallon 5 25
(MrsStefLiddiard) *hld up bhd ldng gp: rdn over 6f out: wknd 4f out: t.o* **16/1**
2-03 **26** *1 1/2* **Domenico (IRE)**[10] 2689 6-8-3 70.... WSupple 17 16
(JRJenkins) *swtg: nvr beyond midfield: u.p and wkng 5f out: t.o* **66/1**
200/ **27** *13* **Carlys Quest**[10] 2760 10-9-1 82....(vt) RWinston 3 15
(FerdyMurphy) *settled in rr: no prog 5f out: t.o fnl 3f* **50/1**
4202 **28** *15* **Invitation**[12] 2631 6-8-7 74 ow1.... RHughes 9 —
(ACharlton) *s.i.s: a in rr: wknd 5f out: t.o* **66/1**

320/ **29** *dist* **Xellance (IRE)**[26] 3475 7-8-8 **75** JPSpencer 8 —
(PJHobbs) *pressed ldrs tl wknd rapidly 6f out: t.o last 3f out* **20/1**
4m 20.99s (-3.54) **Going Correction** -0.025s/f (Good)
**WFA** 4 from 5yo+ 3lb **29** Ran SP% **136.2**
Speed ratings: **106,104,101,101,100 100,99,99,98,98 98,97,96,96,95 94,93,93,92,86 85,85,83,81,77 77,72,66,EM**CSF £308.26 CT £8615.92 TOTE £37.00: £11.70, £8.60, £5.80, £58.60; EX 1117.50 Trifecta £4791.70 Part won. Pool: £6,749.00 - 0.50 winning tickets..
**Owner** R W Huggins,R B Huckerby,Atlantic Racing **Bred** Cheveley Park Stud Ltd **Trained** Middleham Moor, N Yorks

**FOCUS**
Despite the extreme distance, a high draw usually offers a big advantage in this race, and the first two home were both drawn in the top six stalls. The time was ordinary for the grade, but the form is strong, with the first two well treated on best from 2003.

**NOTEBOOK**
**Double Obsession** won a couple of mile and a half handicaps here last summer in blinkers and, having had headgear left off for his last three starts, had a visor on this time. He had his stamina to prove over this trip, but his rider always had him well positioned from his high draw and he really saw it out well when he kicked on in the straight. Clearly he has no trouble with fast ground despite his breeding.
**Promoter**, whose form behind Misternando last October appeared to give him a big shout here, was another who was well positioned from his good draw. He did not help his cause by failing to settle, though, and that may have been the reason why he was unable to give the winner a fight in the straight. The Northumberland Plate could now be on the agenda.
**Penny Pictures(IRE)** loves fast ground but the worry with him was this trip, as he struggles to see it out over hurdles. He looked a non-stayer, as he was cruising turning in but failed to pick up in the straight, but with he had raced so keenly early on that that was probably not surprising. It was still a good effort to finish third for a trainer with a fabulous record in this event, and there are races to be won with him on the Flat off this sort of mark.
**Redspin(IRE)** came from well off the pace to finish fourth. The only horse in the field to make the first 12 having been drawn in single figures, there are clearly no stamina worries about him any more.
**Land 'n Stars**, a shock winner but impressive nonetheless last time out, was a well-supported favourite, but he appeared to simply fail the stamina test.
**Teresa**, who ran in a Listed race in Germany last time out, was another who did not truly see out this marathon trip. A drop back to two miles will suit her.
**Riyadh**, who has not won a race since successful in this event two years ago, was able to race off a 20lb lower mark this time around. He had his chance, but he looked unenthusiastic to say the least under pressure.
**Don Fernando**, 5lb lower than when seventh in this race last year, had a great draw but his rider chose to make no use of it. In rear for most of the race, by the time he got going the race was over. The horse is a quirky individual but he was still given too much to do on this occasion.
**Got One Too(FR)**, well drawn, got to the front and dictated. He turned into the straight in front but then his stamina gave out.
**Gralmano(IRE)** *Official explanation: jockey said gelding pulled up lame*
**Mana D'Argent(IRE)** was disappointing at a track where he has such a good record.
**Carlys Quest** *Official explanation: jockey said gelding slipped on the bend and pulled up lame*
**Invitation** *Official explanation: jockey said gelding finished sore*

## 2959 WINDSOR CASTLE STKS (LISTED RACE) 5f
5:30 (5:35) (A) 2-Y-O **£23,200** (£8,800; £4,400; £2,000) **Stalls** Low

Form RPR
61 **1** **Chateau Istana**[28] 2208 2-8-13 TPQueally 7 100
(NPLittmoden) *hld up: rdn over 2f out: hdwy over 1f out: sn hit on hd by rival jockey's whip: hrd rdn to ld ins fnl f: r.o* **12/1**
12 **2** *½* **Tournedos (IRE)**[13] 2570 2-8-13 TEDurcan 12 98
(MRChannon) *hld up: hdwy over 1f out: rdn over 1f out: ev ch ins fnl f: nt qckn cl home* **12/1**
1 **3** *½* **Safari Sunset (IRE)**[15] 2522 2-8-11 PDoe 1 94
(PWinkworth) *a.p: rdn to ld over 1f out: hdd ins fnl f: nt qckn* **12/1**
22 **4** *nk* **Juantorena**[13] 2579 2-8-11 DHolland 5 93
(MLWBell) *lw: w ldrs: rdn and ev ch over 1f out: no ex ins fnl f* **8/1**
010 **5** *1 ½* **Celtic Spa (IRE)**[15] 2532 2-8-6 RLMoore 6 83
(MrsPNDutfield) *hld up mid-div: rdn over 2f out: hdwy over 1f out: kpt on same pce ins fnl f* **66/1**
3 **6** *½* **Age Of Kings (USA)**[33] 2058 2-8-11 JPMurtagh 3 86
(JHMGosden) *leggy: scope: bhd: rdn over 2f out: n.m.r on stands' rail over 1f out: late hdwy: nrst fin* **5/2**[1]
**7** *hd* **Dark Cheetah (USA)**[18] 2464 2-8-13 JPSpencer 13 88
(APO'Brien, Ire) *w'like: str: led: rdn and hdd over 1f out: wkng whn sltly hmpd ins fnl f* **9/2**[2]
3245 **8** *1* **Alpaga Le Jomage (IRE)**[12] 2627 2-8-11 PJSmullen 10 82
(BJMeehan) *prom tl wknd over 1f out* **100/1**
112 **9** *2* **Royal Island (IRE)**[10] 2677 2-8-13 KDarley 14 77
(MJohnston) *w ldrs: rdn and ev ch 2f out: wknd over 1f out* **6/1**[3]
2 **10** *¾* **Safsoof (USA)**[13] 2574 2-8-11 LDettori 4 72
(SaeedBinSuroor) *lw: s.i.s: a bhd* **13/2**
4121 **11** *¾* **Bold Marc (IRE)**[15] 2526 2-8-11 DarrenWilliams 2 70
(KRBurke) *hld up: sn in tch: wknd over 1f out* **20/1**
135 **12** *½* **Next Time Around (IRE)**[15] 2532 2-9-1 RWinston 8 72
(MrsLStubbs) *rdn over 2f out: a bhd* **33/1**
03 **13** *1 ¼* **Prospect Court**[13] 2579 2-8-11 TQuinn 9 64
(JDBethell) *a bhd* **100/1**
13 **14** *6* **Elsie Hart (IRE)**[35] 2023 2-8-8 WSupple 11 40
(TDEasterby) *sn pushed along and bhd* **33/1**
5450 **15** *8* **Iam Foreverblowing**[18] 2453 2-8-6 DCorby 15 10
(SCBurrough) *wl bhd fnl 2f* **200/1**
61.45 secs (-0.48) **Going Correction** -0.025s/f (Good) **15** Ran SP% **123.2**
Speed ratings: **102,101,100,99,97 96,96,94,91,90 89,88,86,76,64**CSF £145.81 TOTE £19.90: £5.30, £4.00, £4.30; EX 209.10 Trifecta £3058.40 Pool of £5,599.89 - 4.30 winning units. Place 6 £3,023.10, Place 5 £1,348.49.
**Owner** Ivan Allan **Bred** High Bramley Grange Stud Ltd **Trained** Newmarket, Suffolk
■ This race had Listed status for the first time.

**FOCUS**
Just a fair time for a juvenile Listed contest and they all finished a bit too close to each other to suggest that it was an exceptional renewal, although the form looks solid enough.

**NOTEBOOK**
**Chateau Istana** did well to overcome being hit by a rival rider's whip and having to challenge wide, and although this did not look a great contest for Royal Ascot, he could improve again when raced over another furlong.
**Tournedos(IRE)**, whose trainer has a fine recent record in this race, was forced to challenge widest of all and comes out of this race with plenty of credit, as he was the only runner able to get into the first six from a double-figure stall.
**Safari Sunset(IRE)** made the most of his stands'-side draw, showing plenty of pace throughout and holding on well for third. He is all speed.
**Juantorena**, whose Newcastle conqueror had boosted the form by running second in the Coventry Stakes earlier on the card, ran a solid race without being quite good enough. His confidence would be boosted with a maiden win.
**Celtic Spa(IRE)**, whose win came against her own sex in soft ground, was not disgraced against the colts on this quicker surface.
**Age Of Kings(USA)** ◆, a well-supported favourite, struggled to go the early pace but was flying at the death without being knocked about. Clearly he needs farther than the minimum trip, and a maiden over six looks his for the taking, before a return to Pattern company. *Official explanation: jockey said colt hung right*
**Dark Cheetah(USA)**, successful at Cork on his debut, showed plenty of pace from his wide draw but had shot his bolt with over a furlong to run.
**Royal Island(IRE)**, back down to the minimum trip, may have found this coming too quick after his big run at Epsom.
**Next Time Around(IRE)** *Official explanation: jockey said colt was unsuited by the good to firm ground*
T/Jkpt: Not won. T/Plt: £4,842.00 to a £1 stake. Pool: £291,185.55. 43.90 winning tickets. T/Qpdt: £1,576.50 to a £1 stake. Pool: £9,161.20. 4.30 winning tickets. JN

# [2655]THIRSK (L-H)
## Tuesday, June 15

**OFFICIAL GOING: Firm**
The going was described as 'lightning fast and a bit rough against the running rail on the round course'.
Wind: fresh 1/2 behind Weather: Overcast but fine.

## 2960 ESK (S) STKS 6f
2:15 (2:16) (E) 2-Y-O **£3,536** (£1,088; £544; £272) **Stalls** High

Form RPR
04 **1** **Princely Vale (IRE)**[15] 2515 2-8-4 (p) CHaddon(7) 9 55
(WGMTurner) *led after 2f: mde rest: rdn 2f out: hld on wl fnl f: all out* **7/2**[2]
03 **2** *nk* **Lojo**[12] 2622 2-8-6 SChin 8 49
(RPElliott) *chsd ldrs: hdwy to chse wnr over 1f out: ev ch and rdn fnl f: no ex clsng stages* **9/2**[3]
2063 **3** *5* **Danehill Fairy (IRE)**[6] 2773 2-8-6 (v) GDuffield 4 34
(MrsADuffield) *led 2f: remained cl up: rdn over 2f out: outpcd by first 2 appr fnl f* **9/1**
0206 **4** *2* **Urabande**[6] 2773 2-8-3 LisaJones(3) 7 28
(JulianPoulton) *cl up: rdn and outpcd 2f out: kpt on fnl f* **13/2**
6530 **5** *1 ¼* **Procrastinate (IRE)**[6] 2773 2-8-11 PRobinson 11 29
(RFFisher) *slowly away: hdwy to chse ldrs after 2f: ev ch 2f out: sn rdn and btn* **3/1**[1]
0 **6** *4* **Forpetesake**[13] 2579 2-8-11 ACulhane 6 17
(MrsJRRamsden) *slowly away: towards rr: kpt on fnl 2f: n.d* **13/2**
**7** *1 ¼* **Paris Tapis** 2-8-6 GParkin 10 9
(KARyan) *lengthy: unf: slowly away: hung lft and racd wd: n.d* **16/1**
**8** *1 ¾* **Xeight Express (IRE)** 2-8-6 JBramhill 3 —
(MABuckley) *neat: sn bhd* **16/1**
000 **9** *13* **Ruby Rebel**[22] 2364 2-8-6 (b) RFitzpatrick 5 —
(PTMidgley) *slowly away: sn midfield: rdn and wknd over 2f out* **66/1**
0 **10** *3* **Eternal Sunshine (IRE)**[12] 2622 2-8-3 THamilton(3) 2 —
(RPElliott) *slowly away: bhd most of way: t.o* **66/1**
1m 12.1s (-0.40) **Going Correction** -0.225s/f (Firm) **10** Ran SP% **116.8**
Speed ratings: **93,92,85,83,81 76,74,72,54,50**CSF £19.76 TOTE £4.80: £2.20, £1.20, £2.30; EX 29.20.The winner was bought in for 6,000 guineas. Lojo was claimed by G.Blum for £6,000.
**Owner** Vale Racing **Bred** Brian Killeen **Trained** Sigwells, Somerset

**FOCUS**
A run-of-the-mill seller, but the winner attracted interest at the auction and the runner-up was claimed.

**NOTEBOOK**
**Princely Vale(IRE)**, with first-time cheekpieces, edged right and in the end did only just enough.
**Lojo**, who is only small, improved again and in the end was only just held. She was claimed.
**Danehill Fairy(IRE)**, in a visor this time, is not that big and the ground was plenty quick enough for her.
**Urabande**, on her toes beforehand, stayed on when it was all over and now will appreciate seven.
**Procrastinate(IRE)** blew it at the start and, after working his way upsides two furlongs out, he seemed to lose his action. *Official explanation: jockey said gelding lost his action*
**Forpetesake**, a poor walker, looked to be carrying plenty of condition. Dropped in class on his second start, he had the visor left off.
**Paris Tapis** *Official explanation: jockey said ground was too firm*

## 2961 MIDDLEHAM MEDIAN AUCTION MAIDEN STKS 7f
2:50 (2:52) (E) 2-Y-O **£3,701** (£1,139; £569; £284) **Stalls** Low

Form RPR
423 **1** **Stedfast McStaunch (IRE)**[18] 2439 2-8-11 LPKeniry(3) 8 76
(BJMeehan) *w ldr: led 2f out: drew clr fnl f: comf* **8/11**[1]
26 **2** *2 ½* **Forfeiter (USA)**[46] 1743 2-9-0 (b[1]) PHanagan 2 70
(TDBarron) *led tl hdd 2f out: styd on: no ch w wnr* **9/2**[2]
**3** *3 ½* **Drax** 2-9-0 DRMcCabe 5 61
(DRLoder) *cmpt: midfield: drvn along 3f out: styd on u.p to go 3rd ent fnl f: no imp on first 2* **6/1**[3]
**4** *1 ½* **King Henrik (USA)** 2-8-11 LEnstone(3) 11 57
(ACrook) *leggy: scope: prom: drvn along 3f out: kpt on same pce* **20/1**
0 **5** *2* **Tit For Tat**[15] 2522 2-8-9 SChin 3 47
(MJohnston) *chsd ldrs: drvn along 3f out: no hdwy* **16/1**
00 **6** *½* **Kashmar Flight**[28] 2213 2-8-2 AMullen(7) 7 46
(TDEasterby) *dwlt: towards rr: rdn 2f out: kpt on fnl f: n.d* **33/1**
**7** *3* **Cava Bien** 2-9-0 MFenton 10 44
(JGGiven) *w'like: leggy: s.i.s: towards rr: rdn whn carried rt and hmpd over 2f out: n.d* **20/1**
**8** *nk* **Bollin Ruth** 2-8-9 DAllan 6 38
(TDEasterby) *leggy: unf: dwlt: a bhd* **25/1**
5 **9** *1* **Web Racer (IRE)**[19] 2422 2-8-2 DFentiman(7) 1 35
(JRWeymes) *in tch: rdn 3f out: fdd* **33/1**
**10** *4* **Paris Heights** 2-9-0 DeanMcKeown 12 30
(RMWhitaker) *unf: scope: s.s: a bhd* **28/1**
0 **11** *2 ½* **Mist Opportunity (IRE)**[21] 2388 2-9-0 GFaulkner 4 24
(PCHaslam) *towards rr: rdn and hung rt 3f out: no hdwy* **50/1**
1m 26.56s (-0.54) **Going Correction** -0.125s/f (Firm) **11** Ran SP% **120.9**
Speed ratings: **98,95,91,89,87 86,83,82,81,77 74**CSF £3.72 TOTE £1.70: £1.10, £1.40, £1.80; EX 6.10.
**Owner** The Comic Strip Heroes **Bred** Mrs Cherry Faeste **Trained** Upper Lambourn, Berks

**FOCUS**
A weak maiden with little strength in depth and, as the betting foretold, a one-sided contest.

**NOTEBOOK**
**Stedfast McStaunch(IRE)**, easily the paddock pick, found this relatively simple and would have won by double the official margin but for being eased. The seventh furlong was right up his treet.

**Forfeiter(USA)**, in first-time blinkers, gave a problem or two in the stalls. Drawn one from the inside, he made the running but he was never going to finish anything but second best.
**Drax**, a February foal, is a close-coupled type who was noisy in the paddock and again in the unsaddling enclosure afterwards. He was flat out to keep tabs on the first two at halfway.
**King Henrik(USA)**, a February foal, is by a 2000 Guineas winner out of a mare that won the 1000 Guineas yet he made just 21,000gns at the breeze-up sale. Noisy in the paddock, he was keen to post and on the way back wanted to do nothing but hang left, as if feeling the very firm ground.
**Tit For Tat**, stepping up in trip, showed a fraction more than she had done on her debut.
**Kashmar Flight**, on her third start, stayed on steadily after a tardy start and can do better now she is qualified for nurseries.
**Cava Bien**, a February foal, was coltish and noisy beforehand.
**Mist Opportunity(IRE)** *Official explanation: jockey said gelding hung violently right coming into the home straight*

## 2962 GO RACING IN YORKSHIRE MAIDEN STKS 7f
**3:25** (3:27) (D) 3-Y-O **£5,460** (£1,680; £840; £420) **Stalls** Low

Form | | | | RPR
-324 **1** | | **Majorca**[12] [2621] 3-9-0 78 ... RHavlin 9 | 81
(JHMGosden) *hld up: gd hdwy over 2f out: led appr fnl f: r.o wl* **9/4**[2]
62- **2** 1 ½ **Taaqaah**[288] [4621] 3-9-0 ... ADaly 6 | 77
(MPTregoning) *led tl hdd 2f out: r.o: no imp on wnr ins last* **8/13**[1]
03- **3** 2 ½ **Mistress Twister**[242] [5623] 3-8-9 ... PHanagan 11 | 66
(TDBarron) *prom: rdn 2f out: kpt on same pce* **14/1**
4 **4** ¾ **Swainsworld (USA)**[22] [2367] 3-9-0 ... DAllan 4 | 69
(TDEasterby) *hld up towards rr: sme hdwy whn nt clr run over 1f out: r.o wl fnl f: nvr able to chal* **20/1**
0-0 **5** 6 **Three Ships**[31] [2114] 3-9-0 ... PRobinson 3 | 53
(BWHills) *s.i.s: sn chsng ldrs: wknd 2f out* **11/1**[3]
**6** nk **Rosie Mac** 3-8-2 ... SuzanneFrance(7) 7 | 47
(NBycroft) *cmpt: unf: cl up: rdn over 2f out: sn btn* **100/1**
00-5 **7** 1 ½ **Borodinsky**[15] [2530] 3-8-11 45 ... TEaves(3) 5 | 48
(REBarr) *midfield: rdn over 2f out: sn btn* **200/1**
06 **8** 2 **Milly Golightly**[26] [2250] 3-8-6 ... LEnstone(3) 2 | 38
(MDods) *prom: rdn over 2f out: wknd over 1f out* **150/1**
00 **9** ½ **Trysting Grove (IRE)**[45] [1771] 3-8-9 ... GParkin 1 | 37
(KARyan) *nvr bttr than mid-div* **66/1**
0 **10** 1 ¼ **Prince Renesis**[42] [1854] 3-8-7 ... NataliaGemelova(7) 8 | 39
(IWMcinnes) *in tch tl wknd over 2f out* **100/1**
-40 **11** dist **Key Factor**[6] [2777] 3-8-4 ... PMulrennan(5) 10 | —
(MWEasterby) *swtg: slowly away: wl bhd whn m v wd bnd 1/2-way: t.o after* **50/1**

1m 25.95s (-1.15) **Going Correction** -0.125s/f (Firm) **11** Ran SP% **119.0**
Speed ratings: **101,99,96,95,88 88,86,84,83,82** —CSF £3.92 TOTE £3.90: £1.10, £1.10, £2.80; EX 4.90.
**Owner** Sheikh Mohammed **Bred** Shadwell Estate Company Limited **Trained** Manton, Wilts

**FOCUS**
Probably a fair maiden by Thirsk standards and the first two have the potential to do even better.
**NOTEBOOK**
**Majorca**, who looked very fit indeed, took a knock at the start. Brought down the outside, in the end he scored in decisive fashion. The extra furlong suited him and he seemed very much at home on the very firm ground.
**Taaqaah**, runner-up on his second and final start at two, is now a gelding. Fitted with a cross noseband and taken very quietly to post, after looking to be travelling easily in front, he was readily picked off by the winner. This will have taken the freshness off him and he will be interesting in a minor handicap.
**Mistress Twister**, who had just two outings last year, is a moderate mover. She edged left under pressure and would not want the ground as quick as this in handicap company.
**Swainsworld(USA)** again showed ability, but will need another outing under his belt before he can ply his trade in handicap company.
**Three Ships**, fitted with a cross noseband, was very keen to post and on the way back hung violently right-handed throughout. *Official explanation: jockey said colt hung right handed throughout*
**Rosie Mac**, an immature-looking newcomer, is a moderate walker and was fitted with a blanket for stalls entry. She did show a glimmer of ability.
**Key Factor** *Official explanation: jockey said filly cocked her jaw leaving the back straight and would not negotiate bend*

## 2963 ANTHONY FAWCETT MEMORIAL FILLIES' H'CAP 1m
**4:00** (4:00) (C) (0-90,82) 3-Y-0+ **£9,373** (£2,884; £1,442; £721) **Stalls** Low

Form | | | | RPR
3-1 **1** | | **Peeress**[19] [2425] 3-9-5 **82** ... BDoyle 7 | 93+
(SirMichaelStoute) *lw: hld up gng wl: effrt 2f out: slt ld ent fnl f: drvn along and hrd pressed ins last: asserted clsng stages* **13/8**[1]
-010 **2** ¾ **Waterpark**[31] [2128] 6-8-4 **56** ... PFessey 6 | 65
(RCraggs) *led: rdn and hdd ent fnl f: styd on: no ex clsng stages* **16/1**
-010 **3** 2 ½ **Raphael (IRE)**[39] [1927] 5-9-13 **79** ... DaleGibson 2 | 82
(TDEasterby) *lw: trckd ldrs: rdn and ch 2f out: kpt on same pce* **3/1**[2]
6524 **4** 3 **Summer Shades**[7] [2757] 6-9-1 **72** ... BSwarbrick(5) 3 | 68
(WMBrisbourne) *hld up gng wl: effrt 2f out: sn rdn and btn* **11/2**
-060 **5** 3 ½ **Linden's Lady**[8] [2735] 4-9-1 **67** ... MFenton 5 | 55
(JRWeymes) *towards rr: sme hdwy over 2f out: no further prog fr over 1f out* **50/1**
1226 **6** ½ **Marabar**[5] [2811] 6-8-9 **61** ... (b) ACulhane 4 | 48
(DWChapman) *prom: rdn over 2f out: fdd* **16/1**
5224 **7** 2 **Graceful Air (IRE)**[13] [2572] 3-7-13 **62** ... PHanagan 1 | 44
(JRWeymes) *hld up in tch: keen early: lost pl and towards rr after 3f: rdn over 1f out: no hdwy* **20/1**
-035 **8** 1 ½ **Scotland The Brave**[8] [2733] 4-9-1 **67** ... PRobinson 8 | 46
(JDBethell) *slowly away: hld up in rr: sme hdwy over 3f out: rdn and btn 2f out* **5/1**[3]

1m 38.15s (-1.55) **Going Correction** -0.125s/f (Firm)
**WFA** 3 from 4yo+ 11lb **8** Ran SP% **113.6**
Speed ratings: **102,101,98,95,92 91,89,88**CSF £30.23 CT £72.96 TOTE £1.70: £1.10, £3.90, £1.40; EX 33.80.
**Owner** Cheveley Park Stud **Bred** Cheveley Park Stud Ltd **Trained** Newmarket, Suffolk

**FOCUS**
In effect a 0-79 fillies' handicap, run at a sound pace.
**NOTEBOOK**
**Peeress ◆**, a sweet-looking filly, travelled strongly but looked to change her legs on the very firm ground. Quickening up nicely late on to put a seal on it, she is still inexperienced and should find further success at this level.
**Waterpark**has won three of her last six starts but as a result has shot up 20lb in the ratings. She had her own way in front but in truth always looked like being picked off by the winner.
**Raphael(IRE)** looked at her very best and ran her usual game race but she now looks rated to the limit, 4lb higher than for her last success.
**Summer Shades**, runner-up a year ago, travelled strongly but when asked a question was disappointing.
**Linden's Lady**, down 6lb in three runs this year, did not totally convince that she has the stamina for a mile. *Official explanation: jockey said filly did not handle bend*
**Marabar** seems slightly off the boil at present.
**Scotland The Brave**, dropped in grade, looked to be carrying not an ounce of surplus flesh and was the first beaten.

## 2964 WHITE SWAN AMPLEFORTH H'CAP 1m 4f
**4:35** (4:36) (D) (0-80,80) 3-Y-0+ **£5,356** (£1,648; £824; £412) **Stalls** Low

Form | | | | RPR
0021 **1** | | **Party Ploy**[12] [2615] 6-8-5 **60** ... LEnstone(3) 1 | 68
(KRBurke) *trckd ldrs: rdn 2f out: styd on wl u.p to ld wl ins fnl f* **5/1**[3]
0523 **2** nk **Bakiri (IRE)**[11] [2659] 6-8-8 **60** ... BDoyle 4 | 68
(AndrewReid) *trckd ldrs: drvn to ld 2f out: styd on wl u.p: hdd wl ins fnl f: no ex* **16/1**
6152 **3** 3 ½ **Field Spark**[11] [2659] 4-8-7 **59** ... (p) GDuffield 2 | 61
(JAGlover) *hld up: drvn along and hdwy 2f out: styd on u.p fnl f: nvr able to chal* **9/2**[2]
0-43 **4** 1 **Crathorne (IRE)**[17] [2471] 4-10-0 **80** ... (p) PRobinson 3 | 80
(JDBethell) *hld up in tch: effrt over 2f out: styd on u.p fnl f: nvr able to chal* **3/1**[1]
0522 **5** 2 ½ **Compton Dragon (USA)**[7] [2752] 5-9-8 **74** ... (v) ANicholls 9 | 70
(DNicholls) *hld up: hdwy u.p and in tch 2f out: no further prog* **7/1**
0010 **6** 3 **Maritime Blues**[18] [2449] 4-8-13 **65** ... MFenton 5 | 57
(JGGiven) *led tl rdn and hdd 2f out: sn btn* **7/1**
60-0 **7** 3 **Bond May Day**[30] [2142] 4-9-4 **70** ... FLynch 6 | 57
(BSmart) *cl up: rdn over 2f out: wknd over 1f out* **20/1**
0-40 **8** 10 **Sir Night (IRE)**[25] [2272] 4-8-0 **52** ... PHanagan 10 | 23
(JeddO'Keeffe) *a bhd: lost tch fnl 2f* **20/1**
-464 **P** | **Merrymaker**[13] [2595] 4-7-12 **55** ... (v) BSwarbrick(5) 7 | —
(WMBrisbourne) *sddle slipped after 4f: p.u* **9/1**

2m 33.7s (-1.50) **Going Correction** -0.125s/f (Firm) **9** Ran SP% **110.3**
Speed ratings: **100,99,97,96,95 93,91,84,—**CSF £72.80 CT £327.37 TOTE £5.90: £2.20, £3.60, £1.50; EX 71.20.
**Owner** Ian A McInnes **Bred** I McInnes **Trained** Middleham Moor, N Yorks

**FOCUS**
A steady gallop resulting in a modest time for the grade.
**NOTEBOOK**
**Party Ploy**, 3lb higher, was happy to be given a lead this time. He showed real battling qualities to get up near the line.
**Bakiri(IRE)** again ran well and just missed out near the line.
**Field Spark** could have done with a much stronger gallop. He tried hard to get on terms with the first two but lacked the pace to land a telling blow. He deserves a change of luck.
**Crathorne(IRE)**, whose only previous win was here at two, keeps running well without hitting the target for a second time.
**Compton Dragon(USA)**, on his toes beforehand, has yet to prove conclusively that he stays this far. All he wanted to do was hang right-handed as the strain was put on his stamina in the last two furlongs. *Official explanation: jockey said gelding hung right handed in final two furlongs*
**Maritime Blues**, 7lb higher than Doncaster, was allowed to set his own pace, but in the dash to the line was readily brushed aside.
**Sir Night(IRE)** *Official explanation: jockey said gelding was never travelling and hung left handed in final two furlongs*
**Merrymaker**, a keen type, was soon effectively out of the contest when his saddle slipped right forward. The lack of a strong gallop would have been against him anyway. *Official explanation: jockey saddle slipped*

## 2965 BARNARD H'CAP 7f
**5:10** (5:10) (E) (0-70,67) 3-Y-0+ **£3,731** (£1,148; £574; £287) **Stalls** Low

Form | | | | RPR
20 **1** | | **Lord Of The East**[18] [2461] 5-9-13 **67** ... DRMcCabe 10 | 78
(DNicholls) *keen: mde all: hrd pressed fnl f: hld on wl u.p* **14/1**
0-62 **2** nk **Alchemist Master**[6] [2776] 5-9-0 **54** ... DeanMcKeown 4 | 64
(RMWhitaker) *lw: trckd ldrs: drvn to chal ent finmal f: ev ch ins last: no ex u.p* **5/2**[1]
0-65 **3** 1 ¾ **Bollin Edward**[8] [2735] 5-9-7 **61** ... DAllan 1 | 67
(TDEasterby) *chsd ldrs: drvn along over 2f out: wnt 3rd over 1f out: kpt on: no imp on first 2* **8/1**[3]
0100 **4** shd **Border Artist**[6] [2781] 5-9-10 **64** ... ANicholls 8 | 69
(DNicholls) *hld up: effrt over 2f out: styd on wl u.p fr over 1f out: nvr able to chal* **8/1**[3]
0216 **5** 2 **Downland (IRE)**[8] [2735] 8-9-2 **56** ... KimTinkler 12 | 56
(NTinkler) *chsd ldrs: drvn along 3f out: kpt on u.p fnl f* **12/1**
5-02 **6** shd **Dara Mac**[11] [2660] 5-8-6 **53** ... SuzanneFrance(7) 9 | 53
(NBycroft) *hld up: hdwy into midfield over 2f out: kpt on u.p fr over 1f out: n.d* **33/1**
0000 **7** 1 ¼ **Smith N Allan Oils**[1] [2938] 5-9-0 **57** ... (p) LEnstone(3) 6 | 54
(MDods) *towards rr: effrt over 2f out: styd on u.p fnl f: n.d* **16/1**
-004 **8** hd **Mr Bountiful (IRE)**[25] [2260] 6-8-13 **53** ... (p) PHanagan 5 | 49
(MDods) *midfield: rdn 2f out: no hdwy* **8/1**[3]
0011 **9** nk **Yorkshire Blue**[10] [2673] 5-9-1 **58** ... NMackay(3) 7 | 53
(JSGoldie) *rr div: sme late hdwy: n.d* **6/1**[2]
2043 **10** ½ **Luke After Me (IRE)**[11] [2660] 4-9-0 **54** ... BDoyle 2 | 48
(GASwinbank) *rr div: hdwy over 2f out: rdn over 1f out: no further prog* **8/1**[3]
0004 **11** 3 ½ **Drury Lane (IRE)**[11] [2656] 4-9-2 **56** ... (b) ACulhane 11 | 41
(DWChapman) *chsd wnr: drvn along over 2f out: fdd fr over 1f out* **14/1**
3550 **12** ¾ **Noble Pursuit**[84] [1090] 7-8-10 **53** ... TEaves(3) 13 | 36
(REBarr) *midfield tl outpcd over 2f out: n.d* **50/1**
04-0 **13** 1 ¾ **Northern Games**[22] [2368] 5-9-3 **57** ... PFessey 14 | 36
(KARyan) *rrd s and slowly away: hdwy and in tch 1/2-way: rdn and wknd 2f out* **33/1**
2000 **14** 1 ½ **St Ivian**[18] [2455] 4-9-6 **60** ... (v) RFitzpatrick 3 | 35
(MrsNMacauley) *rrd in stalls and slowly away: a bhd* **33/1**

1m 24.69s (-2.41) **Going Correction** -0.125s/f (Firm) **14** Ran SP% **125.0**
Speed ratings: **108,107,105,105,103 103,101,101,101,100 96,95,93,92**CSF £49.65 CT £328.60 TOTE £16.90: £4.40, £2.00, £3.00; EX 143.30 Place 6 £16.54, Place 5 £5.54.
**Owner** The Wayward Lads **Bred** Catridge Farm Stud Ltd **Trained** Sessay, N Yorks

**FOCUS**
A modest handicap with plenty wanting to get to the front, resulting in a smart winning time for the class.
**NOTEBOOK**
**Lord Of The East**, who in the past has bolted to post, was led down riderless. He burst out of the stalls and was soon setting a very strong pace and, after looking likely to be swallowed up, in the end proved much the more resolute. He is clearly a nightmare to train and the stable staff deserve full marks.
**Alchemist Master** looked in tip-top trim. He had the leader covered and looked nailed on when pushed upsides entering the last, but in the end he could not be persuaded to put his head in front. He has now lost two consecutive races he ought really to have won.

**Bollin Edward**, who has just one career win, was trying seven furlongs for a second time and did not seem to fail for lack of stamina.
**Border Artist**, 5lb higher than when successful at Musselburgh three outings ago, was returning to a more suitable trip. *Official explanation: jockey said gelding never got a run in final two furlongs*
**Downland(IRE)**, back over his right trip, had a double-figure draw to overcome.
**Dara Mac** has yet to hit the target now in 27 career starts.
**Yorkshire Blue**, 6lb higher, was given a very negative ride and this is best overlooked.
**St Ivian** *Official explanation: jockey said gelding reared leaving stalls*
T/Plt: £9.70 to a £1 stake. Pool: £30,520.60. 2,273.95 winning tickets. T/Qpdt: £7.60 to a £1 stake. Pool: £2,201.70. 212.15 winning tickets. JF

# 2954 ASCOT (R-H)
## Wednesday, June 16

**OFFICIAL GOING: Good to firm (firm in places)**
Wind: almost nil Weather: sunny & v.warm

## 2966 JERSEY STKS (GROUP 3) 7f
**2:30** (2:32) (A) 3-Y-O **£37,700** (£14,300; £7,150; £3,250) **Stalls** Low

Form RPR

210- **1** **Kheleyf (USA)**[257] 5348 3-8-10 108 LDettori 1 113+
(SaeedBinSuroor) *lw: hld up in last trio: gd prog fr over 2f out: shkn up to ld ent fnl f: sn in command* **6/1**[2]

-221 **2** 1 3/4 **Fokine (USA)**[25] 2308 3-8-13 113 MHills 2 111
(BWHills) *hld up towards rr: prog wl over 2f out: shkn up to ld over 1f out: hdd and outpcd jst ins fnl f* **11/2**[1]

10-3 **3** 1/2 **Cartography (IRE)**[25] 2308 3-8-10 106 (t) KMcEvoy 6 107
(SaeedBinSuroor) *trckd ldrs: effrt 2f out: chal and n.m.r jst over 1f out: one pce fnl f* **8/1**[3]

3600 **4** hd **Bahiano (IRE)**[25] 2295 3-8-10 97 DHolland 3 106
(CEBrittain) *lw: s wl in rr: rdn and effrt over 2f out: nt clr run and swtchd rt over 1f out: drvn and kpt on wl fnl f* **50/1**

3-02 **5** 2 1/2 **Mukafeh (USA)**[26] 2276 3-8-10 105 RHills 8 100
(JLDunlop) *mde most to over 1f out: wknd fnl f* **10/1**

2-0 **6** 5 **Favourite Nation (IRE)**[25] 2316 3-8-10 PJSmullen 5 87
(DKWeld, Ire) *w'like: leggy: racd in midfield: hrd rdn over 2f out: outpcd and wl btn over 1f out* **25/1**

-114 **7** 1 1/2 **Leitrim House**[25] 2315 3-9-2 114 MJKinane 11 89
(BJMeehan) *w ldr to 2f out: sn wknd* **6/1**[2]

05 **8** nk **Imtalkinggibberish**[35] 2046 3-8-10 EAhern 4 82?
(JRJenkins) *racd on inner: chsd ldrs: rdn over 2f out: wknd over 1f out* **200/1**

-105 **9** 1 1/4 **Silca's Gift**[32] 2117 3-8-13 109 TEDurcan 15 82
(MRChannon) *racd on outer: trckd ldrs: rdn over 2f out: wknd over 1f out* **20/1**

-324 **10** 1 1/2 **Psychiatrist**[26] 2276 3-8-10 101 RHughes 10 75
(RHannon) *lw: trckd ldrs: pushed along and lost pl 1/2-way: last 2f out: plodded on* **14/1**

40-0 **11** nk **Sgt Pepper (IRE)**[25] 2308 3-8-13 98 JFortune 9 77
(RHannon) *a wl in rr: rdn and struggling 1/2-way: no ch after* **50/1**

24-4 **12** 5 **Auditorium**[25] 2308 3-8-13 113 KFallon 12 64
(SirMichaelStoute) *towards rr: rdn wl over 2f out: no prog and wl btn over 1f out: wknd* **6/1**[2]

2030 **13** shd **Glaramara**[4] 2897 3-8-10 98 RWinston 14 61
(ABailey) *racd on outer: drvn and struggling after 3f: effrt u.p over 2f out: sn wknd* **40/1**

110- **14** 8 **Tashkil (IRE)**[242] 5640 3-8-10 106 WSupple 7 40
(JHMGosden) *chsd ldrs tl wknd rapidly over 2f out* **20/1**

6-25 **15** 7 **Grand Reward (USA)**[25] 2315 3-8-10 JPSpencer 13 22
(APO'Brien, Ire) *trckd ldrs: cl up over 2f out: sn drvn and wknd rapidly* **11/1**

1m 27.35s (-2.32) **Going Correction** +0.05s/f (Good) **15** Ran SP% **113.7**
Speed ratings: **115,113,112,112,109 103,101,101,100,98 98,92,92,83,75**CSF £33.66 TOTE £7.20: £2.40, £2.20, £3.30; EX 40.90 Trifecta £421.50 Pool of £5,461.86 - 9.20 winning units..
**Owner** Godolphin **Bred** Darley **Trained** Newmarket, Suffolk

**FOCUS**
An up-to-standard renewal with an impressive victory for Kheleyf in a very smart winning time for the type of race. The runners raced up the stands' rail and it was dominated by those drawn low, but the second and third ran close to previous form and give the race a sound look.

**NOTEBOOK**
**Kheleyf(USA)** ◆, having his first run since last September's Middle Park Stakes, made light of that absence with an impressive victory. He followed the runner-up through and, once in the clear, brushed that rival aside. His record suggests he goes best fresh, and as his target is the Sussex Stakes at the end of next month, connections should have time to let him down briefly and bring him back for that.
**Fokine(USA)** ◆ is a consistent performer at this level and again ran his race. He had no answer to the winner's challenge but beat the rest well enough and lost little in defeat. Group races at this specialist trip are thin on the ground, but he deserves to win one on his efforts so far this season. The Criterion Stakes at the end of the month is a possibility, and the Hungerford Stakes at Newbury in August looks right up his street.
**Cartography(IRE)**, a stable companion of the winner, ran close to Newmarket form with Fokine despite not getting a straightforward passage. He gives the form a solid look and is another who should be able to win a Pattern race if avoiding those in front of him here.
**Bahiano(IRE)**, who is best known as an All-Weather performer and had a stiff task on official ratings, could not go the early pace but weaved his way through and finished really well. This was his best effort on turf and he should appreciate returning to a mile.
**Mukafeh(USA)**, who finished behind both Fokine and Bahiano in the Greenham, ran close to that form again. He is well suited by making the running, and the fact that he is already proven at a mile increases his options.
**Leitrim House** has been progressive this season, although the form of both his Pattern wins has taken some knocks. He adopted the same tactics as in the Irish Guineas from his wide draw and travelled well enough, but once asked for extra effort found next to nothing. This was disappointing in view of his previous runs.
**Imtalkinggibberish** had an impossible task and appeared to run well. He might do even better back at a slightly shorter distance.
**Silca's Gift** appeared to see too much daylight from her outside stall and can be forgiven this.
**Auditorium**, another drawn high, should have finished in the first six on Newmarket form but, after a brief effort, dropped away. This has to rate as disappointing.
**Glaramara** *Official explanation: jockey said colt hung left handed throughout*

## 2967 WINDSOR FOREST STKS (GROUP 2) (F&M) 1m (S)
**3:05** (3:06) (A) 4-Y-0+ **£81,200** (£30,800; £15,400; £7,000) **Stalls** Low

Form RPR

215- **1** **Favourable Terms**[256] 5364 4-8-12 108 KFallon 4 116
(SirMichaelStoute) *lw: hld up in tch: effrt over 2f out: led over 1f out: rdn clr* **13/2**[2]

2-36 **2** 2 **Monturani (IRE)**[16] 2543 5-8-9 104 DHolland 8 108
(GWragg) *chsd ldrs: led 2f out tl over 1f out: nt qckn* **20/1**

140- **3** 3 1/2 **Soldera (USA)**[256] 5364 4-8-9 103 JPMurtagh 3 100
(JRFanshawe) *chsd ldrs: rdn over 2f out: styd on same pce* **25/1**

3-61 **4** 1 **Actrice (IRE)**[16] 2543 4-8-12 OPeslier 10 101
(ELellouche, France) *leggy: angular: hld up in rr: hdwy and hrd rdn 2f out: one pce* **12/1**

3-41 **5** 1 3/4 **Marbye (IRE)**[14] 2608 4-8-12 (t) MDemuro 1 97
(BGrizzetti, Italy) *w'like: hld up in rr: effrt over 2f out: styd on appr fnl f: nt pce to chal* **10/1**

141 **6** 1 1/4 **Crimson Palace (SAF)**[35] 2042 5-8-9 110 LDettori 6 91
(SaeedBinSuroor) *chsd ldrs: rdn over 2f out: wknd over 1f out* **6/5**[1]

21-6 **7** 1 1/4 **Chic**[27] 2242 4-8-9 97 GaryStevens 2 107+
(SirMichaelStoute) *hld up towards rr: effrt whn bdly hmpd and nrly fell appr fnl 2f: nt rcvr* **16/1**

-112 **8** shd **Beneventa**[35] 2042 4-8-9 110 SSanders 11 88
(JLDunlop) *pressed ldr: led after 3f tl over 2f out: sn wknd* **7/1**[3]

1211 **9** 5 **Gonfilia (GER)**[12] 2641 4-8-9 102 (t) KMcEvoy 9 76
(SaeedBinSuroor) *led 3f: w ldr: led briefly over 2f out: wknd qckly* **8/1**

0054 **10** 5 **Starbeck (IRE)**[25] 2282 6-8-10 88 ow1 PMcCabe 5 66
(PHowling) *b: b.hind: dwlt: t.k.h: bhd fnl 3f* **100/1**

1m 40.37s (-1.55) **Going Correction** +0.05s/f (Good) **10** Ran SP% **114.7**
Speed ratings: **109,107,103,102,100 99,98,98,93,88**CSF £125.10 TOTE £6.10: £1.70, £6.40, £6.70; EX 225.30 Trifecta £1344.00 Pool of £5,678.99 - 3.00 winning units..
**Owner** Maktoum Al Maktoum **Bred** Gainsborough Stud Management Ltd **Trained** Newmarket, Suffolk
■ The inaugural running of this event, one of a series of new or upgraded races for older fillies.

**FOCUS**
An ordinary winning time for the grade, only fractionally faster than the fillies' Listed handicap later on the card. The form looks below Group Two standard.

**NOTEBOOK**
**Favourable Terms**, disappointing in the Sun Chariot Stakes on her final outing last year, ran out a decisive winner in the end. This notably fluent mover might pick up a Group One race this season now that events like the Falmouth Stakes and the Sun Chariot have been upgraded to that level, but whether she can live with the best of the colts is another matter.
**Monturani(IRE)** ran right up to her best and stayed on in pleasing fashion. She is equally at home over ten furlongs but is without a win for two years.
**Soldera(USA)** made a fine return to action and the way she was keeping on up the hill suggests that the step up to ten furlongs is required now.
**Actrice(IRE)**, who finished well ahead of Monturani at Saint-Cloud last time, had to come round the whole field and could never land a blow. All her wins have come at around ten furlongs on an easy surface, and she seemed ill at ease on the ground.
**Marbye(IRE)**, a winner at San Siro in this grade earlier this month, was below form but will remain a force back at home.
**Crimson Palace(SAF)** had ground and trip to suit, but after coming there going really well her response was bitterly disappointing. This had looked an ideal opportunity beforehand. *Official explanation: jockey said mare ran flat*
**Chic** did remarkably well to keep her feet when running into the back of Beneventa at the two pole. This run can be ignored and there should be a pattern race to be won with her this summer provided she gets over this experience. *Official explanation: jockey said filly had clipped heels*
**Beneventa** was beaten too far out for this to have been her true running, although she ran roughly to York form with Crimson Palace.

## 2968 PRINCE OF WALES'S STKS (GROUP 1) 1m 2f
**3:45** (3:47) (A) 4-Y-0+ **£203,000** (£77,000; £38,500; £17,500) **Stalls** High

Form RPR

212- **1** **Rakti**[185] 6188 5-9-0 121 PRobinson 10 129+
(MAJarvis) *h.d.w: plld hrd: racd in 3rd tl trckd ldr 3f out: led wl over 1f out: sn clr: drvn out* **3/1**[2]

13-1 **2** 2 **Powerscourt**[24] 2329 4-9-0 JPSpencer 5 122
(APO'Brien, Ire) *h.d.w: trckd ldrs: effrt 2f out: rdn to chse wnr jst over 1f out: styd on but nvr able to chal* **9/2**[3]

-362 **3** 1/2 **Ikhtyar (IRE)**[15] 2559 4-9-0 113 RHills 3 121
(JHMGosden) *lw: hld up in last pair: prog on wd outside fr over 2f out: r.o to dispute 2nd pl ins fnl f: kpt on same pce after* **8/1**

215- **4** 1 1/2 **Sulamani (IRE)**[235] 5773 5-9-0 125 LDettori 4 118
(SaeedBinSuroor) *hld up towards rr: effrt over 2f out: rdn and unable qck wl over 1f out: hanging rt and no imp ldrs fnl f* **11/4**[1]

1330 **5** nk **Scott's View**[12] 2639 5-9-0 115 SChin 2 118
(MJohnston) *settled in rr: effrt on outer over 2f out: one pce and nvr rchd ldrs* **25/1**

131- **6** 3/4 **Phoenix Reach (IRE)**[241] 5670 4-9-0 115 DHolland 7 116
(AMBalding) *trckd ldr to 3f out: rdn and one pce fr over 2f out* **16/1**

03-5 **7** 2 1/2 **Comfy (USA)**[15] 2559 5-9-0 113 KFallon 11 111
(SirMichaelStoute) *hld up in last pair: rdn wl over 2f out: effrt u.p wl over 1f out: one pce and no imp: eased nr fin* **16/1**

30-6 **8** 2 1/2 **Kaieteur (USA)**[15] 2559 5-9-0 117 MJKinane 9 107
(BJMeehan) *swtg: trckd ldrs: rdn and nt qckn 2f out: wkng whn n.m.r 1f out* **16/1**

0111 **9** 3 **Bandari (IRE)**[15] 2559 5-9-0 114 WSupple 1 101
(MJohnston) *pressed ldrs: rdn over 3f out: wknd over 2f out* **8/1**

6-30 **10** 1 1/4 **Lunar Sovereign (USA)**[81] 1144 5-9-0 110 (t) KMcEvoy 8 99
(SaeedBinSuroor) *lengthy: lw: led to wl over 1f out: wknd* **66/1**

2m 4.95s (-3.78) **Going Correction** +0.05s/f (Good) **10** Ran SP% **115.1**
Speed ratings: **117,115,115,113,113 112,110,108,106,105**CSF £16.74 TOTE £4.50: £1.90, £1.80, £3.10; EX 16.60 Trifecta £171.60 Pool of £8,664.27 - 35.83 winning units..
**Owner** Gary A Tanaka **Bred** Azienda Agricola Rosati Colarieti **Trained** Newmarket, Suffolk

**FOCUS**
A high-class winner, and the sort of time one would expect for a race of this nature, although the form behind is not up to recent renewals.

**NOTEBOOK**
**Rakti**, having his first run since December, went one better than he had in this event twelve months ago. Keen going to post and in the race, he was always well placed and, once striking for home, quickened away and was never going to be caught. Likely to improve on this, he will obviously be a major force in the top ten-furlong races for the remainder of the season, with the BHB's Summer Triple Crown, and its £1 million bonus if he can win the Eclipse and the Juddmonte International, a tempting target.
**Powerscourt**, winner of a substandard Tattersalls Gold Cup, was ridden differently this time. Chasing the winner through without being able to reduce the gap, this was a sound effort and he will not mind a return to twelve furlongs.
**Ikhtyar(IRE)** , drawn low, had to come down the outside with his run and could not quite get past the runner-up. This run confirms that he belongs at this level and Richard Hills will feel his loyalty to the horse has been justified.
**Sulamani(IRE)** missed his intended reappearance in the Tattersalls Gold Cup with a leg problem and was short of peak fitness here. Although he was disappointing, the ground was faster than he would have liked and he will remain a major player on an easy surface over a mile and a half.
*Official explanation: jockey said horse had hung right*

**Scott's View**, with ground and trip to suit, ran as well as he ever has, which underlines his toughness as this was his tenth run of the year already.
**Phoenix Reach(IRE)** underwent minor surgery on an old pastern injury earlier in the year. This trip is short of his best and this was a highly satisfactory return to action.
**Comfy(USA)**, who went steadily to post after parading last, was never able to land a blow. He will remain hard to place.
**Kaieteur(USA)** has disappointed twice now that season and may have to return to the continent to resume winning ways.
**Bandari(IRE)** failed to give his running in this better grade, and it could be that he was not entirely over a hard race at Sandown. The faster ground could also have been a contributory factor.
**Lunar Sovereign(USA)**, winner of the Grade One Man O'War Stakes at Belmont last September, was reduced to pacemaking duties on this British debut for Godolphin.

## 2969 ROYAL HUNT CUP (HERITAGE H'CAP) 1m (S)
4:20 (4:26) (B) 3-Y-0+ £58,000 (£22,000; £11,000; £5,000) Stalls Low

Form RPR
-231 **1** **Mine (IRE)**[25] 2283 6-9-5 **105**.....(v) TQuinn 8 116
(JDBethell) *racd stands side: hdwy over 1f out: r.o to ld last stride* **16/1**
10-4 **2** *hd* **Able Baker Charlie (IRE)**[29] 2201 5-8-5 **91**..... OUrbina 3 102
(JRFanshawe) *lw: hld up in tch stands side: rdn to ld wl ins fnl f: hdd last stride* **14/1**
3-06 **3** *shd* **Zonergem**[20] 706 6-8-4 **90**.....(p) KMcEvoy 23 101
(LadyHerries) *hld up in rr far side: rapid hdwy over 1f out: ev ch nr fin: kpt on* **33/1**
-002 **4** *hd* **Amandus (USA)**[29] 2201 4-8-5 **94**..... TPQueally(3) 29 104
(DRLoder) *chsd ldrs: led far side gp 1f out: ev ch fnl f: kpt on* **20/1**
4-04 **5** *shd* **Camp Commander (IRE)**[25] 2283 5-8-9 **95**.....(t) GaryStevens 31 105
(CEBrittain) *hld up in rr far side: nt clr run 2f out: gd hdwy over 1f out: ev ch nr fin: kpt on* **8/1**[2]
6400 **6** *½* **Lago D'Orta (IRE)**[27] 2241 4-9-0 **100**..... JPSpencer 15 109
(CGCox) *racd stands side: gd hdwy fnl 2f: nrst fin* **66/1**
0504 **7** *shd* **Norton (IRE)**[44] 1828 7-8-5 **91** ow1..... MJKinane 9 100
(TGMills) *prom: led stands side gp over 2f out: hdd and nt qckn wl ins fnl f* **16/1**
0000 **8** *shd* **Audience**[25] 2283 4-8-4 **90**.....(p) RLMoore 30 98
(JAkehurst) *hld up in rr far side: hdwy 2f out: ev ch whn edgd lft ins fnl f: kpt on* **33/1**
0026 **9** *hd* **Impeller (IRE)**[12] 2637 5-8-1 **87**..... JQuinn 5 95
(WRMuir) *chsd ldrs stands side: rdn and kpt on fnl 2f* **66/1**
0013 **10** *nk* **Vortex**[25] 2283 5-8-12 **98**.....(t) LDettori 6 105
(MissGayKelleway) *b.hind: chsd ldrs stands side: one pce fnl f* **9/1**[3]
0011 **11** *¾* **Uhoomagoo**[12] 2637 6-8-1 **87** 7ex.....(b) PFessey 4 93
(KARyan) *racd stands side: styd on fnl 2f: nt rch ldrs* **12/1**
6-21 **12** *shd* **Langford**[21] 2410 4-7-12 **87** 7ex..... FPFerris(3) 26 92
(MHTompkins) *led far side gp and ev ch tl over 1f out: one pce* **66/1**
5500 **13** *¾* **El Coto**[13] 2623 4-9-2 **102**..... SSanders 13 106
(BAMcmahon) *lw: mid-div stands side: no hdwy fnl 2f* **50/1**
-430 **14** *shd* **Wing Commander**[17] 2503 5-8-7 **93**..... PHanagan 24 96
(RAFahey) *prom far side: rdn and kpt on same pce fnl 2f* **40/1**
-631 **15** *1* **Putra Kuantan**[16] 2534 4-9-1 **101** 7ex..... PRobinson 27 102
(MAJarvis) *pressed far side ldr: led briefly over 1f out: no ex fnl f* **14/1**
-053 **16** *1 ½* **Finished Article (IRE)**[16] 2534 7-8-5 **91** ow1..... DaneO'Neill 11 89
(DRCElsworth) *lw: racd stands side: wknd 3f out* **40/1**
4-14 **17** *¾* **Zero Tolerance (IRE)**[16] 2527 4-8-4 **90**..... KDarley 1 86
(TDBarron) *swtg: led stands side gp tl over 2f out: no ex over 1f out* **16/1**
-061 **18** *hd* **Flighty Fellow (IRE)**[29] 2196 4-8-8 **94**..... WSupple 10 89
(TDEasterby) *mid div stands side: outpcd over 2f out: sn btn* **66/1**
0000 **19** *¾* **Calcutta**[16] 2534 8-8-10 **96**..... MHills 32 90
(BWHills) *trckd far side ldrs over 6f* **66/1**
0-35 **20** *1 ¾* **Courageous Duke (USA)**[130] 712 5-8-8 **94** ow1..... OPeslier 2 84
(JNoseda) *dwlt: racd stands side: outpcd final 2f* **50/1**
15-0 **21** *1* **Vicious Knight**[4] 2894 6-9-0 **100**..... RHughes 17 87
(DNicholls) *dwlt: racd stands side: hdwy towards centre over 2f out: no further prog* **80/1**
0-26 **22** *2 ½* **Wizard Of Noz**[116] 852 4-9-4 **104**..... EAhern 22 86
(JNoseda) *chsd ldrs far side over 6f* **33/1**
0-00 **23** *nk* **Chinkara**[16] 2534 4-8-6 **92**..... TEDurcan 28 73
(BJMeehan) *hld up in rr far side: effrt and hung rt 2f out: rdn and no rspnse* **66/1**
11-3 **24** *hd* **Polar Bear**[39] 1968 4-8-4 **90**..... RHills 20 71
(WJHaggas) *lw: in tch far side 6f* **9/1**[3]
0-06 **25** *2 ½* **Pentecost**[35] 2044 5-8-7 **96**..... LPKeniry(3) 16 71
(AMBalding) *mid div: racd stands side: btn 2f out* **25/1**
0-10 **26** *½* **Highland Reel**[16] 2534 7-7-12 **87**..... LisaJones(3) 18 61
(DRCElsworth) *pressed stands side ldr over 5f* **66/1**
6-10 **27** *5* **Evolving Tactics (IRE)**[81] 1146 4-9-10 **110**.....(v[1]) PJSmullen 21 72
(DKWeld, Ire) *in tch far side over 5f* **50/1**
0-11 **28** *¾* **Autumn Glory (IRE)**[35] 2044 4-9-3 **103**..... KFallon 7 63
(GWragg) *lw: hld up in tch stands side: rdn and wknd over 2f out* **11/2**[1]
-303 **29** *3* **King's County (IRE)**[17] 2503 6-8-9 **95**..... DHolland 14 49
(LMCumani) *racd stands side: bhd fr 1/2-way* **16/1**
0000 **30** *½* **Convent Girl (IRE)**[12] 2637 4-8-8 **94**..... RHavlin 12 46
(MrsPNDutfield) *b.hind: prom stands side 5f* **80/1**
00-6 **31** *2* **Shamrock City (IRE)**[11] 2672 7-8-7 **93**..... RWinston 25 41
(PHowling) *b: racd far side: bhd fnl 3f* **100/1**

1m 40.85s (-1.07) **Going Correction** +0.05s/f (Good) **31** Ran SP% **133.1**
Speed ratings: **107,106,106,106,106 105,105,105,105,105 104,104,103,103,102 101,100,100,99,97 96,94,93,93,91** CSF £201.24 CT £7221.57 TOTE £17.40: £3.70, £3.20, £12.70, £6.80; EX 193.30 TRIFECTA Not won..
**Owner** M J Dawson **Bred** David John Brown **Trained** Middleham Moor, N Yorks

### FOCUS
An ultra-competitive handicap as usual in which the field split into two groups, but there was little between them at the end and the form looks typically strong. Considering the class of the race and the big field, the time was ordinary and was the slowest of the three races run over the straight mile.

### NOTEBOOK
**Mine(IRE)**, who loves these big-field handicaps and still seems top be improving, was produced at just the right time and supplemented his Victoria Cup success of last month. Previously thought of as a seven-furlong specialist, this increases his options, but another crack at the Bunbury Cup will not be possible if he goes up at all for this victory.
**Able Baker Charlie(IRE)**, a course and distance winner here last autumn, followed up his promising reappearance with another fine effort. He had a good draw and did nothing wrong, but is not an easy horse to win with and, although sure to take his chance in similar races this summer, his style of running often leads to him finding trouble.
**Zonergem**, seemingly revitalised by a spell over hurdles, had also dropped a couple of pounds in the handicap and ran a fine race, being first home on the far side. He could easily win a good race if he repeats this performance in the future.
**Amandus(USA)** ◆ continued his recent improvement back on this fast ground, and is another who should be a a major contender for the top mile handicaps this summer.
**Camp Commander(IRE)** ◆, 5lb better off with Mine compared with Victoria Cup running, ran right up to that form from his high draw and was keeping on well. He seems to love this track, is effective at seven furlongs and a mile, and is likely to be back here for the valuable handicaps later in the year.
**Lago D'Orta(IRE)** ◆, having his first run in a handicap since last July, ran a fine race from his middle draw and, having dropped to a reasonable mark, is one to keep on the right side from now on.
**Norton(IRE)**, who has not won since taking this race two years ago, was back down to the same mark for the first time since and ran well under the stands' rail. Clearly the ability is still there.
**Audience**, was 6lb better off with Mine compared with Victoria Cup running, and finished a good deal closer. He is another to give the form a solid look.
**Impeller(IRE)**, who is difficult to win with, ran well enough and will be of interest in similar company on a right-handed track. His two wins last season were both over nine furlongs.
**Vortex**, 5lb better off with Mine compared with the Victoria Cup, ran his race and got a little closer.
**Polar Bear** had his chance but his form has been on much easier ground, and he did not appear at home on this surface.
**Autumn Glory(IRE)**, a well-backed favourite, seemed to have every chance at one stage but was another that looked uncomfortable on this faster ground. He should not be written off yet. *Official explanation: jockey said colt lost his action*

## 2970 QUEEN MARY STKS (GROUP 2) (FILLIES) 5f
4:55 (5:01) (A) 2-Y-0 £40,600 (£15,400; £7,700; £3,500) Stalls Low

Form RPR
1 **1** **Damson (IRE)**[9] 2745 2-8-10..... JPSpencer 15 110+
(DavidWachman, Ire) *w'like: lengthy: settled in rr and wl off the pce: rapid prog 2f out: swtchd rt over 1f out: led jst ins fnl f: drvn clr: i* **11/2**[1]
1 **2** *3* **Soar**[14] 2574 2-8-10..... JPMurtagh 16 100
(JRFanshawe) *lw: hld up bhd ldrs: nt clr run over 2f out: effrt wl over 1f out: ev ch ent fnl f: sn no ch w wnr* **11/2**[1]
1 **3** *1 ¼* **Sharplaw Star**[15] 2544 2-8-10..... MHills 17 95
(WJHaggas) *s.i.s: racd on wd outside and in tch: rdn and effrt 2f out: ev ch 1f out: one pce fnl f* **10/1**
13 **4** *1 ¼* **Bunditten (IRE)**[16] 2532 2-8-10..... JFEgan 1 91
(AndrewReid) *b: b.hind: taken to post 20 mins early: led at blazing pce: hdd jst ins fnl f: kpt on* **40/1**
122 **5** *1 ¼* **Bright Moll**[32] 2129 2-8-10..... IMongan 13 87
(MLWBell) *racd in midfield: rdn 1/2-way: no prog over 1f out: kpt on ins fnl f* **40/1**
1 **6** *shd* **Don't Tell Mum (IRE)**[20] 2427 2-8-10..... RHughes 6 86
(RHannon) *lw: pressed ldrs: rdn 2f out: bmpd jst over 1f out: one pce after* **6/1**[2]
111 **7** *shd* **Lady Filly**[45] 1798 2-8-10..... ADaly 7 86
(WGMTurner) *chsd ldr to over 1f out: fdd fnl f* **14/1**
11 **8** *1* **Siena Gold**[33] 2083 2-8-10..... LDettori 3 82
(BJMeehan) *prom tl fdd fr over 1f out* **13/2**[3]
11 **9** *½* **Miss Meggy**[14] 2568 2-8-10..... DAllan 9 81
(TDEasterby) *racd in midfield: rdn 1/2-way: struggling and no prog wl over 1f out* **10/1**
**10** *¾* **Lady Ann Summers (USA)** 2-8-10..... JFortune 12 78
(BJMeehan) *leggy: s.i.s: n.m.r after 100yds: wl bhd tl styd on fnl f* **66/1**
11 **11** *½* **Polly Perkins (IRE)**[16] 2532 2-8-10..... KDarley 10 76
(NPLittmoden) *outpcd and wl in rr after 2f: nvr a factor* **11/1**
144 **12** *nk* **High Chart**[23] 2370 2-8-10..... AMcCarthy 4 75
(GGMargarson) *chsd ldrs: rdn 1/2-way: wknd over 1f out* **100/1**
216 **13** *¾* **Indiannie Star**[16] 2532 2-8-10..... TEDurcan 2 73
(MRChannon) *chsd ldrs: wknd over 1f out* **50/1**
1 **14** *2 ½* **Gloved Hand**[14] 2585 2-8-10..... KFallon 8 64
(JGGiven) *chsd ldrs: rdn 1/2-way: no prog and btn whn squeezed out over 1f out* **7/1**
10 **15** *1* **Tara Tara (IRE)**[42] 1878 2-8-10..... RWinston 14 60
(JJQuinn) *hmpd after 100yds: a struggling in rr after* **50/1**
32 **16** *shd* **Castelletto**[14] 2585 2-8-10..... GGibbons 11 60
(BAMcmahon) *racd on outer in midfield: nt clr run 2f out: wknd* **33/1**
04 **17** *13* **Make It Happen Now**[30] 2164 2-8-10..... LPKeniry 5 15
(SCBurrough) *hmpd after 1f: sn wl bhd: t.o* **150/1**

61.81 secs (-0.12) **Going Correction** +0.05s/f (Good) **17** Ran SP% **119.0**
Speed ratings: **102,97,95,93,91 91,90,89,88,87 86,86,84,80,79 79,58**CSF £32.41 TOTE £7.20: £2.70, £2.60, £4.90; EX 47.50 Trifecta £723.10 Pool of £5,602.22 - 5.50 winning units..
**Owner** Mrs John Magnier & M Tabor **Bred** Epona Bloodstock Ltd **Trained** Carrrick on Shore, Co Tipperary

■ A first Royal Ascot winner for Irish trainer David Wachman.
■ Stewards Enquiry : R Winston one-day ban: careless riding (Jul 20)
J P Spencer caution: careless riding and using whip with whip arm above shoulder height
K Darley two-day ban: careless riding (Jun 28,29)

### FOCUS
A strong-looking renewal on paper and an impressive winner, but just a fair time for the type of race. This event went against the trend with the first three occupying the three outside stalls, but the form looks up to standard and solid enough.

### NOTEBOOK
**Damson(IRE)** ◆, who has already won over six furlongs, was not inconvenienced by the return to five and won going away. She interfered with Don't Tell Mum and in turn Soar when making her run, but it did not affect the result. She is now likely to be rested before an autumn campaign and, with plenty of stamina in her pedigree, should stay further and is the benchmark for contenders aiming for the champion juvenile filly title.
**Soar** ◆, the form of whose Kempton win had not worked out, nevertheless was well backed and, although having no chance with the winner, beat the rest comfortably enough. Out of a mare who won three times at two, she should be able to find more good opportunities.
**Sharplaw Star** ran well considering she missed the break and had to race wide. Having made her debut just 15 days previously, this came early enough in her career, but she should benefit from the experience and is capable of going on to win good races.
**Bunditten(IRE)**, who went to post very early, ran a terrific race from her low draw and set a fierce pace. She reversed National Stakes form with Polly Perkins and looks well up to winning a Pattern race if holding her form.
**Bright Moll**, one of the most experienced in the field, ran creditably. She has won on easy ground and it may be worth giving her a break and bringing her back for an autumn campaign.
**Don't Tell Mum(IRE)**, who was well fancied having put up a good time when winning on her Bath debut, had her chance but was already on the retreat when bumped by the winner.
**Lady Filly**, all of whose three wins were on easy ground, put up a creditable effort on this first encounter with a fast surface. The penalties for her earlier successes may mean she is not be easy to place from now on.
**Siena Gold**, another who came into this unbeaten, showed speed, but was unable to lead and gradually dropped out.
**Gloved Hand** showed up to past halfway, but this race may have come too early for her, and she will appreciate longer trips in time. *Official explanation: jockey said filly suffered interference in running*

## 2971 SANDRINGHAM RATED STKS (H'CAP) (LISTED RACE) (FILLIES) 1m (S)
5:30 (5:37) (A) (0-110,104) 3-Y-O £29,000 (£11,000; £5,500; £2,500) Stalls Low

Form RPR
-212 1 **Celtic Heroine (IRE)**[20] 2420 3-8-7 **90** oh1 KDarley 17 106
(MAJarvis) *dwlt: stdy hdwy 3f out: hit over face by rival's whip 2f out: led 1f out: drvn out* **11/1**[3]
1-52 2 ½ **Coy (IRE)**[15] 2548 3-8-11 **94** KFallon 2 109
(SirMichaelStoute) *prom: led 2f out tl 1f out: hrd rdn: r.o* **11/2**[2]
5- 3 2 **Zosima (USA)**[235] 5768 3-9-7 **104** (t) LDettori 7 117+
(SaeedBinSuroor) *leggy: scope: tall: lengthy: hld up towards rr: nt clr run and eased rt 2f out: styd on wl: nt rch ldng pair* **11/2**[2]
-341 4 2½ **Brindisi**[26] 2270 3-8-12 **95** MHills 14 99
(BWHills) *hld up towards rr: hdwy 3f out: ev ch over 1f out: one pce* **14/1**
0-06 5 1¾ **Danclare (USA)**[7] 2788 3-8-7 **90** oh6 KMcEvoy 4 90
(JHMGosden) *lw: chsd ldrs: rdn and one pce fnl 2f* **11/1**[3]
-053 6 2½ **Qasirah (IRE)**[12] 2641 3-8-12 **95** (b) PRobinson 13 89
(MAJarvis) *dwlt: hld up in rr: hmpd over 2f out: effrt and nt clr run wl over 1f out: nvr rchd ldrs* **16/1**
-232 7 nk **Red Top (IRE)**[25] 2286 3-8-7 **90** oh6 RHughes 19 84
(RHannon) *lw: dwlt: hld up in rr on rail: swtchd wd over 3f out: hdwy over 2f out: no ex over 1f out* **25/1**
16-4 8 1¾ **Doctrine**[67] 1327 3-9-2 **99** JFortune 20 89
(JHMGosden) *mid-div: effrt and short of room over 2f out: no imp* **50/1**
5-26 9 shd **Cusco (IRE)**[33] 2089 3-8-7 **90** oh1 RLMoore 18 80
(RHannon) *lw: towards rr: effrt and hmpd over 2f out: nvr able to chal* **66/1**
-230 10 nk **Crafty Fancy (IRE)**[33] 2080 3-8-10 **93** TQuinn 6 82
(DJSFfrenchDavis) *hld up in midfield: rdn and outpcd 2f out: sn btn* **100/1**
0-63 11 1½ **Bay Tree (IRE)**[36] 2020 3-9-2 **99** TPQueally 8 84
(DRLoder) *hld up in midfield: effrt over 2f out: hrd rdn over 1f out: no imp* **25/1**
1213 12 8 **Mystical Girl (USA)**[11] 2676 3-8-11 **94** SChin 1 61
(MJohnston) *led tl wknd 2f out* **7/2**[1]
040- 13 shd **Buzz Buzz**[279] 4843 3-8-7 **90** oh22 LisaJones 5 57
(CEBrittain) *chsd ldrs 5f* **100/1**
15-4 14 2 **Madaeh (USA)**[28] 2221 3-8-10 **93** RHills 10 55
(JLDunlop) *prom 6f* **25/1**
16-3 15 3 **Surf The Net**[15] 2548 3-8-9 **92** DaneO'Neill 3 47
(RHannon) *dwlt: sn in midfield: wknd over 3f out* **12/1**
0-3 16 5 **Sand N Sea (IRE)**[10] 2711 3-8-7 **90** oh3 WSupple 12 34
(THogan, Ire) *w'like: leggy: mid-div: effrt over 2f out: sn wknd* **33/1**
0-04 17 3½ **Totally Yours (IRE)**[15] 2548 3-8-7 **90** oh1 SSanders 11 26
(WRMuir) *a towards rr* **33/1**
-021 18 4 **St Francis Wood (USA)**[10] 2706 3-8-7 **90** EAhern 16 17
(JNoseda) *t.k.h: w ldr: outpcd and starting to lose pl whn squeezed 2f out: no ch after* **14/1**
3-55 19 9 **Summer Sunset (IRE)**[7] 2793 3-8-12 **95** (b[1]) PJSmullen 9 1
(DKWeld, Ire) *w'like: dwlt: sn in midfield: outpcd whn bmpd over 2f out: n.d after* **16/1**

1m 40.41s (-1.51) **Going Correction** +0.05s/f (Good) 19 Ran SP% **125.3**
Speed ratings: **109,108,106,104,102 99,99,97,97,97 95,87,87,85,82 77,74,70,61**CSF £65.73 CT £390.49 TOTE £15.20: £2.90, £1.70, £1.90, £2.90; EX 94.30 Trifecta £573.10 Pool of £6,619.58 - 8.20 winning units. Place 6 £1,373.13, Place 5 £637.71.
**Owner** P D Savill **Bred** P D Savill **Trained** Newmarket, Suffolk

**FOCUS**
A very good time for the type of race, only marginally slower than the Group Two Windsor Forest, and 0.44 seconds faster than the Royal Hunt Cup. The field bunched towards the stands' side and several met trouble in running, but the form looks very strong for a handicap.

**NOTEBOOK**
**Celtic Heroine(IRE)**, from a 9lb higher mark than when winning at Hamilton two starts back, showed commendable bravery to shrug off an accidental smack across the nose before asserting in the last half-furlong. She confirmed her effectiveness on fast ground and, out of a three-parts sister to Celtic Swing, will be a valuable asset at stud.
**Coy(IRE)**, back over a mile, enjoyed a good run up the rail to lead. She did little wrong but perhaps the winner proved the more resolute. A similar race ought to come her way.
**Zosima(USA)** ◆ won a Grade Three and finished fifth in the Breeders' Cup Juvenile Fillies' when trained in the States by Eoin Harty last year. Having her first run on turf, she was forced to come wide when trapped behind a wall of horses at the quarter-mile pole. With the first two beyond recall she was not knocked about in an effort to catch them, but she came home in taking style and recorded an RPR that puts her within reach of most of the top fillies, bar Attraction. There are clearly nice races to be won with her.
**Brindisi** ran a decent race but was not helped by having to challenge towards the outside. When under pressure she gave the impression that, like her half-brother Fellow Ship, she is not straightforward.
**Danclare(USA)** was a little short of room going to the two pole, but a gap materialised in plenty of time had she been good enough to take advantage.
**Qasirah(IRE)**, a stablemate of the winner, suffered a poor passage and by the time she was in the clear the race was effectively over. She might appreciate a step back up in trip. *Official explanation: jockey said filly was continually denied a run*
**Red Top(IRE)**, drawn out wide, was obliged to come right round the field when making a forward move after being settled on the rail. She was out of the handicap and this was a decent run in the circumstances by a filly who is held in some regard by her trainer.
**Doctrine** did not get much of a run from the worst draw. She probably needs a little farther.
**Mystical Girl(USA)**, raised 4lb for her defeat at Epsom, was back at a mile but, having made the running against the rail, did not put up much of a fight once headed. A busy spell might have left its mark.
**Madaeh(USA)** failed to stay ten furlongs at Goodwood and it was a similar story over this trip.
**Totally Yours(IRE)** *Official explanation: trainer said filly was unsuited by the going - good to firm, firm in places; and was in season.*
T/Jkpt: Not won. T/Plt: £1,662.00 to a £1 stake. Pool: £296,320.97. 130.15 winning tickets. T/Qpdt: £54.50 to a £1 stake. Pool: £18,259.00. 247.90 winning tickets. JN

# 2779 HAMILTON (R-H)
Wednesday, June 16

**OFFICIAL GOING: Good to firm**

## 2972 UNIT GROUP MEDIAN AUCTION MAIDEN STKS (QUALIFIER FOR THE HAMILTON PARK 2-Y-O SERIES FINAL) 6f 5y
2:20 (2:22) (E) 2-Y-O £3,835 (£1,180; £590; £295) Stalls Low

Form RPR
5 1 **Sacred Nuts (IRE)**[11] 2674 2-9-0 JMackay 2 75+
(MLWBell) *dwlt: smooth hdwy on outside 1/2-way: led appr fnl f: kpt on wl* **3/1**[2]
35 2 nk **Jane Jubilee (IRE)**[15] 2550 2-8-9 JFanning 5 69
(MJohnston) *led to appr fnl f: rallied fnl f: kpt on fin* **14/1**
40 3 1¼ **Melvino**[16] 2522 2-8-9 PMakin[(5)] 3 70
(TDBarron) *chsd ldrs: rdn 1/2-way: kpt on wl fnl f* **12/1**
4 5 **Dennick** 2-9-0 GFaulkner 7 55
(PCHaslam) *cl up tl outpcd over 1f out* **25/1**
3 5 4 **My Princess (IRE)**[9] 2736 2-8-9 GDuffield 6 38
(NACallaghan) *chsd ldrs tl wknd over 1f out* **8/11**[1]
3 6 11 **Jerry's Girl (IRE)**[23] 2352 2-8-9 JCarroll 1 —
(MissLAPerratt) *s.i.s and outpcd: nvr on terms* **7/1**[3]
0 7 8 **Black Combe Lady (IRE)**[23] 2352 2-8-2 PPMathers[(7)] 4 —
(ABerry) *outpcd after 2f: t.o* **100/1**

1m 11.88s (-1.22) **Going Correction** -0.25s/f (Firm) 7 Ran SP% **114.6**
Speed ratings: **98,97,95,89,83 69,58**CSF £42.19 TOTE £4.40: £2.30, £5.80; EX 64.30.
**Owner** Fitzroy Thoroughbreds **Bred** John Foley **Trained** Newmarket, Suffolk

**FOCUS**
A decent time for the grade, only 0.42 seconds slower than the 0 to 80 handicap for older horses. A mixed bag on looks but the winner, who has plenty of scope, looks the type to improve again.

**NOTEBOOK**
**Sacred Nuts(IRE)** ◆ confirmed debut promise and may be a bit better than the bare form, as he lost ground at the start and made it up on the outside of the main group. He has plenty of scope and looks the sort to improve again.
**Jane Jubilee(IRE)** had the run of the race and again showed more than enough to suggest she can win an ordinary event in this grade, especially when upped to seven furlongs.
**Melvino**, from a stable in good form, appreciated the return to six furlongs and again showed more than enough to suggest he can win a similar race in due course. He should prove equally effective over seven furlongs.
**Dennick**, the first foal of an unraced half-sister to a couple of winners abroad, took the eye in the paddock, despite looking as though the race would do him good. He hinted at ability on this debut and is likely to do better in due course.
**My Princess(IRE)** failed by a long chalk to confirm debut promise, but she is a tall, leggy filly who may well have been unsuited by the contours of this track. She is worth another chance on a more conventional track.
**Jerry's Girl(IRE)** looked sure to be suited by the step up to this trip after an encouraging debut display, but was a long way below that level and did not look entirely happy on the track. She is capable of a fair bit better. *Official explanation: jockey said filly failed to come down the hill*
**Black Combe Lady(IRE)** again offered no immediate promise.

## 2973 HEALTH MATTERS FOR MEN CLASSIFIED STKS 1m 65y
2:55 (2:55) (E) 3-Y-O £3,932 (£1,210; £605; £302) Stalls High

Form RPR
61-3 1 **Munaawashat (IRE)**[19] 2442 3-8-11 68 JFanning 4 75
(MJohnston) *mde all at stdy pce: pushed along over 2f out: kpt on strly* **9/4**[1]
4204 2 3 **On The Waterfront**[11] 2688 3-8-12 66 GDuffield 1 69
(JWHills) *pressed wnr: effrt and ev ch over 2f out: kpt on same pce fnl f* **11/4**[2]
503 3 ½ **Four Kings**[19] 2450 3-8-11 63 (t) JCarroll 3 67
(JMPEustace) *trckd ldrs: outpcd over 3f out: kpt on fnl f* **14/1**
0316 4 shd **Amankila (IRE)**[12] 2665 3-8-9 66 JMackay 5 65
(MLWBell) *plld hrd: cl up: rdn over 2f out: one pce over 1f out* **7/1**
0221 5 1¼ **Hearthstead Dream**[7] 2783 3-8-12 62 (b) BSwarbrick[(5)] 6 70
(JGMO'Shea) *hld up in tch: rdn over 2f out: nt pce to chal* **14/1**
034 6 nk **Big Bad Burt**[22] 2377 3-8-4 63 (tp) DeanWilliams[(7)] 7 63
(MissGayKelleway) *dwlt: hld up in tch: effrt centre over 2f out: wandered: sn no imp* **11/1**
46-5 7 1¼ **Fairlie**[23] 2355 3-8-8 65 ACulhane 2 57
(MrsJRRamsden) *missed break: hld up: rdn over 2f out: n.d* **9/2**[3]

1m 46.92s (-2.38) **Going Correction** -0.25s/f (Firm) 7 Ran SP% **109.8**
Speed ratings: **101,98,97,97,96 95,94**CSF £7.85 TOTE £2.90: £3.20, £2.50; EX 7.20.
**Owner** Hamdan Al Maktoum **Bred** Shadwell Estate Company Limited **Trained** Middleham Moor, N Yorks

**FOCUS**
An ordinary event in which the winner very much had the rub of things at the head of a steadily-run race and, as a result, the bare form behind the winner looks suspect.

**NOTEBOOK**
**Munaawashat(IRE)**, who shaped as though a bit better than her debut form, very much had the run of the race this time and did not have to improve to get off the mark. She is not very big and may be one to field against in a more competitive race.
**On The Waterfront**, ideally placed in a steadily run race, gave it his best shot and confirmed his recent return to form under these faster conditions. However he is likely to look vulnerable from his current mark in handicaps.
**Four Kings**, stepping up to this trip for the first time, left the impression that a stiffer test of stamina would have been in his favour.
**Amankila(IRE)**, back in trip and racing on a sound surface for the first time, was not disgraced but was another that would have preferred a stiffer test of stamina over this trip.
**Hearthstead Dream**, down in trip and up in grade, was ridden with more restraint than when successful at this course last week and not surprisingly was not seen to best effect.
**Big Bad Burt**, returned to a mile, was again disappointing and did not look an easy ride when put under pressure. He is in capable hands but has yet to win a race and is one to tread carefully with.
**Fairlie** did not get the race run to suit and, although her style of racing means she needs things to fall right, she is not one to write off just yet.

## 2974 HAMISH MACSPORRAN FILLIES' H'CAP 1m 1f 36y
3:30 (3:31) (E) (0-70,68) 3-Y-O+ £3,818 (£1,175; £587; £146) Stalls High

Form RPR
025 1 **Sharp Needle**[30] 2182 3-9-11 **68** SWKelly 4 73
(JNoseda) *prom: smooth hdwy over 2f out: rdn and led 1f out: hld on wl* **5/4**[1]
-240 2 shd **Rabitatit (IRE)**[14] 2571 3-9-0 **62** BSwarbrick[(5)] 7 67
(JGMO'Shea) *led: rdn over 2f out: hdd 1f out: rallied: jst hld* **17/2**
000- 3 ½ **Cyclonic Storm**[232] 5823 5-9-11 **60** THamilton[(3)] 5 64
(RAFahey) *hld up in tch: hdwy and shkn up over 2f out: kpt on fnl f* **5/1**[2]
545- 4 ¾ **Ellovamul**[243] 5608 4-9-1 **52** PMakin[(5)] 1 55
(WMBrisbourne) *trckd ldrs tl rdn and kpt on same pce fnl f* **14/1**
0210 4 dht **Joint Destiny (IRE)**[14] 2595 3-8-6 **49** JCarroll 8 52
(EJO'Neill) *missed break: hdwy on outside to chse ldrs 2f out: one pce fnl f* **10/1**
0060 6 1¼ **Infidelity (IRE)**[19] 2446 3-8-8 **58** (p) DTudhope[(7)] 3 58
(ABailey) *hld up in tch: effrt over 2f out: hung rt and one pce over 1f out* **7/1**[3]
-010 7 7 **Forest Air (IRE)**[37] 1993 4-9-1 **47** DMcGaffin 6 33
(MissLAPerratt) *in tch tl wknd fr 3f out* **14/1**

600 **8** *4* **Kalamansi (IRE)**[17] 2505 3-8-10 **53**........................................ GDuffield 2 31
(NACallaghan) *chsd ldrs to 3f out: wknd* **12/1**

1m 57.85s (-1.75) **Going Correction** -0.25s/f (Firm)
**WFA** 3 from 4yo+ 11lb **8** Ran SP% **114.3**
Speed ratings: **97,96,96,95,95 94,88,84**CSF £12.72 CT £40.66 TOTE £1.50: £1.10, £2.00, £1.50; EX 9.20.
**Owner** Arashan Ali **Bred** Sentinel Bloodstock And Arashan Ali **Trained** Newmarket, Suffolk

**FOCUS**
A modest event in which the pace steadied around halfway. Those racing prominently again held the edge and, as a result, the bare form does not look entirely reliable.

**NOTEBOOK**
**Sharp Needle ◆**, an athletic type, turned in an improved effort on this handicap debut and, given the way she travelled for much of the way and the fact she is unlikely to go up too much for this win, looks the type to win more races.
**Rabitatit(IRE)** is not the most consistent but had the run of the race and showed the right attitude once headed. Whether this is reproduced next time, though, remains to be seen.
**Cyclonic Storm ◆**, who looked as though this reappearance run would do her good, showed more than enough in a race that was not really run to suit to suggest she retains plenty of ability and she is one to keep an eye on from now on.
**Ellovamul** shaped well on this reappearance run, especially as this trip in a less than truly run race would not have been in her favour. It will be no surprise to see her win a modest event this summer.
**Joint Destiny(IRE)** shaped as though a bit better than the bare form as she lost ground at the start and made ground in the centre but her inconsistency means she is not one to be lumping on next time.
**Infidelity(IRE)**, with the cheekpieces on for the first time, did not really have the race run to suit but again did not look an easy ride and continues below her best.
**Forest Air(IRE)** *Official explanation: jockey said filly clipped heels and stumbled*

## 2975 O2 CLAIMING STKS 5f 4y
**4:05** (4:07) (E) 3-Y-O+ **£3,493** (£1,075; £537; £268) **Stalls** Low

Form RPR

0-05 **1** **Robwillcall**[30] 2175 4-8-1 45........................................(p) PPMathers(7) 4 59
(ABerry) *w ldr to 1/2-way: rdn over 1f out: rallied to ld wl ins fnl f: kpt on* **16/1**

4041 **2** *1* **Soaked**[14] 2582 11-8-12 59........................................(b) ACulhane 5 59
(DWChapman) *led: shkn up over 1f out: hdd and no ex towards fin* **5/2**[2]

3433 **3** *½* **Best Lead**[14] 2582 5-8-9 52........................................(b) DTudhope(7) 1 61
(IanEmmerson) *chsd ldrs: effrt 2f out: n.m.r ent fnl f and wl ins last: kpt on* **10/1**

20L5 **4** *¾* **Joyce's Choice**[14] 2582 5-8-12 52........................................ GParkin 9 55
(JSWainwright) *trckd ldrs tl rdn and one pce fnl f* **16/1**

0102 **5** *1¼* **American Cousin**[14] 2582 9-9-3 62........................................ ANicholls 7 55
(DNicholls) *sn outpcd: hdwy centre 2f out: no imp fnl f* **7/4**[1]

0200 **6** *2½* **Vijay (IRE)**[7] 2784 5-8-5 54........................................(p) PMulrennan(5) 2 39
(ISemple) *prom tl rdn and no ex over 1f out* **7/1**[3]

00 **7** *1¼* **Needwood Bucolic (IRE)**[5] 2833 6-8-13 ........................ LEnstone(3) 6 41
(RAllan) *sn outpcd: nvr rchd ldrs* **50/1**

0-00 **8** *½* **Northern Svengali (IRE)**[7] 2784 8-8-5 36........................(tp) CHaddon(7) 3 35
(DANolan) *chsd ldrs to 2f out: sn btn* **100/1**

4000 **9** *2½* **Bettys Valentine**[23] 2346 4-8-5 25........................................ TWilliams 8 19
(DWBarker) *racd wd: rdn and struggling fr 1/2-way* **100/1**

400- **10** *13* **Brevity**[263] 4838 9-8-5 60........................................(v[1]) BSwarbrick(5) 10 —
(JGMO'Shea) *sn outpcd centre: no ch fr 1/2-way* **10/1**

59.75 secs (-1.51) **Going Correction** -0.25s/f (Firm) **10** Ran SP% **111.3**
Speed ratings: **102,100,99,98,96 92,90,89,85,64**CSF £53.43 TOTE £17.40: £3.10, £1.60, £2.60; EX 76.30.Robwillcall was subject to a friendly claim.
**Owner** William Burns **Bred** Norton Grove Stud Ltd **Trained** Cockerham, Lancs

**FOCUS**
A modest race featuring mainly exposed and disappointing types in which the whole field raced centre to stands' side. The pace was sound.

**NOTEBOOK**
**Robwillcall**, from an in-form stable, had conditions to suit and returned to form from out of the blue but, given his overall record, would not be one to be lumping on next time. *Official explanation: trainer said, regarding the improved form shown, stable has now come into form and the re-application of sheepskin cheekpieces may have sharpened her up*
**Soaked** did not get all his own way in the first half of the contest but ran his race. He is not the most consistent but is capable of winning again in this grade, especially when afforded an uncontested lead.
**Best Lead** is a consistent sort who ran again ran creditably, especially as he did not get the best of runs in the closing stages. He should continue to give a good account in low-grade events.
**Joyce's Choice** has not won for nearly three years but, although running creditably, would be by no means certain to reproduce this next time. He remains one to tread carefully with.
**American Cousin**, who won the corresponding race last year, is not the most consistent and was below his recent best after failing to go the early gallop. He is not really the type to be taking short odds about.
**Vijay(IRE)**, with the cheekpieces back on, was not totally disgraced but did not really show enough to suggest he will be back in the winners enclosure in the near future.

## 2976 RAEBURN BRICK H'CAP 6f 5y
**4:40** (4:42) (D) (0-80,78) 3-Y-O+ **£6,357** (£1,956; £978; £489) **Stalls** Low

Form RPR

0000 **1** **Sir Don (IRE)**[4] 2899 5-8-9 **61**........................................(v) ANicholls 2 73
(DNicholls) *swtchd to far side after 2f: cl up: led over 2f out: pushed out* **12/1**

0002 **2** *1¼* **Bundy**[7] 2779 8-8-9 **61**........................................ SWKelly 1 69
(MDods) *racd alone stands side: a.p: rdn and hung rt fr over 1f out: sn chsng wnr: kpt on fnl f* **5/1**[2]

0440 **3** *1* **Tancred Times**[27] 2252 9-8-3 **55**........................................ TWilliams 7 60
(DWBarker) *trckd ldrs: rdn 1/2-way: one pce fnl f* **12/1**

0000 **4** *nk* **Legal Set (IRE)**[7] 2784 8-7-5 **50** oh5........................(t) DFentiman(7) 12 54
(MissAStokell) *midfield: effrt over 2f out: one pce over 1f out* **50/1**

3202 **5** *½* **Chairman Bobby**[7] 2784 6-9-1 **70**........................................ LEnstone(3) 4 73
(DWBarker) *led to over 2f out: one pce over 1f out* **10/3**[1]

612- **6** *1½* **Fonthill Road (IRE)**[355] 2763 4-9-3 **72**........................ THamilton(3) 13 70
(RAFahey) *outpcd tl hdwy over 1f out: nvr nrr* **8/1**

5000 **7** *1* **Sharp Hat**[39] 1956 10-8-10 **62**........................................ ACulhane 5 57
(DWChapman) *w ldrs tl wknd over 1f out* **14/1**

00-0 **8** *¾* **Fort McHenry (IRE)**[78] 1185 4-9-6 **72**........................................ GDuffield 8 65
(NACallaghan) *in tch tl wknd over 2f out* **7/1**

1464 **9** *½* **Friar Tuck**[14] 2581 9-8-5 **57** ow2........................................ JCarroll 10 49
(MissLAPerratt) *sn outpcd: no imp fr 1/2-way* **8/1**

040- **10** *3½* **Haulage Man**[238] 5702 6-8-6 **58**........................................ JFanning 6 39
(DEddy) *in tch to 1/2-way: sn rdn and btn* **6/1**[3]

0050 **11** *1* **Grey Cossack**[4] 2899 7-9-7 **78**........................................ MLawson(5) 3 56
(PTMidgley) *sn outpcd: shortlived effrt 1/2-way: sn btn* **16/1**

1m 11.46s (-1.64) **Going Correction** -0.25s/f (Firm) **11** Ran SP% **118.6**
Speed ratings: **100,98,97,96,95 93,92,91,90,86 84**CSF £71.69 CT £763.32 TOTE £10.00: £3.30, £1.50, £3.70; EX 50.90.
**Owner** Mrs Dian Plant **Bred** C And R O'Brien **Trained** Sessay, N Yorks

**FOCUS**
A run of the mill event in which all the runners bar Bundy (who hung onto the far side late on) had tacked over to the far side after two furlongs. The pace was sound and the form should stand up at a similar level.

**NOTEBOOK**
**Sir Don(IRE)**, from a stable firmly back among the winners, put a series of below-par efforts firmly behind him with a gutsy display. He is not the most consistent, though, and would not be one to be taking short odds about next time.
**Bundy** confirms he is at the top of his game at present and may be a bit better than the bare form as he raced alone for much of the way and hung across the course in the closing stages. He is capable of winning a similar event.
**Tancred Times**, who goes well at this course, confirmed her recent return to form and is one to keep an eye on at a modest level in the near future.
**Legal Set(IRE)**, from a stable among the winners, was well drawn and ran his best race for his current stable but his inconsistency means this is far from certain to be reproduced next time.
**Chairman Bobby** had the run of the race and ran creditably but he has been beaten enough times from similar marks to suggest that the handicapper has him at present.
**Fonthill Road(IRE) ◆**, who won three times from five starts last year, shaped as though retaining plenty of ability on this racecourse debut and is one to keep a close eye on in the near future. *Official explanation: jockey said gelding failed to come down the hill*
**Haulage Man** attracted support but was a long way below his best on this first start since October.

## 2977 DM HALL RATING RELATED MAIDEN STKS 1m 3f 16y
**5:15** (5:16) (E) 3-4-Y-O **£3,558** (£1,095; £547; £273) **Stalls** High

Form RPR

004 **1** **Masked (IRE)**[16] 2517 3-8-8 70........................................ GDuffield 4 71
(JWHills) *hld up in tch: rdn 4f out: rallied to ld over 1f out: r.o wl* **15/8**[2]

-604 **2** *¾* **La Petite Chinoise**[20] 2419 3-8-5 66........................................ JCarroll 3 67
(RGuest) *hld up: hdwy centre and ev ch fr over 1f out: kpt on: hld towards fin* **16/1**[3]

050 **3** *5* **Lucky Arthur (IRE)**[23] 2374 3-8-0 60........................ BSwarbrick(5) 2 59
(JGMO'Shea) *hld up: rdn and hung lft fr 3f out: r.o fnl f: nt rch first two* **20/1**

3-42 **4** *hd* **Silverhay**[16] 2529 3-8-3 69........................................ PMakin(5) 1 62
(TDBarron) *keen early: cl up: led on bit over 3f out: rdn and hdd over 1f out: no ex* **4/5**[1]

0-05 **5** *3½* **Viola Da Braccio (IRE)**[25] 2311 3-8-5 65........................ JFanning 5 53
(DJDaly) *w ldr: led briefly over 3f out: wknd fr 2f out* **16/1**[3]

5-50 **6** *3* **Double Turn**[12] 2653 4-9-7 70........................................ SWKelly 6 51
(WMBrisbourne) *led to over 3f out: wknd* **20/1**

0-35 **7** *shd* **Silver Rhythm**[40] 1933 3-8-5 52........................................ VHalliday 7 48
(KRBurke) *keen early: chsd ldrs to 3f out: wknd* **40/1**

2m 22.32s (-4.18) **Going Correction** -0.25s/f (Firm)
**WFA** 3 from 4yo 13lb **7** Ran SP% **114.1**
Speed ratings: **105,104,100,100,98 95,95**CSF £28.43 TOTE £3.50: £2.40, £5.10; EX 31.60.
**Owner** The Phantom Partnership **Bred** P D Savill **Trained** Upper Lambourn, Berks

**FOCUS**
An uncompetitive event and one run at only a fair overall gallop making the form modest. However, the winner has plenty of physical scope and may be capable of better, especially granted a stiffer test of stamina.

**NOTEBOOK**
**Masked(IRE)** had a good chance at the weights and ran right up to his recent best over the longest trip he has tackled to date. He shapes as though he will stay a mile and a half and he has scope for further improvement.
**La Petite Chinoise**, up in trip, again ran her race and, although she is starting to look exposed, should continue to give a good account in ordinary company up to middle distances.
**Lucky Arthur(IRE)** was not disgraced but did not look the easiest of rides and, although the step up to a mile and a half may help, is likely to continue to look vulnerable in this grade.
**Silverhay** looked the one to beat on recent evidence but proved a disappointment after travelling strongly for a long way and he will have to settle better if he is to progress.
**Viola Da Braccio(IRE)**, upped in trip, did not get home, even in a race run at a less than true gallop and may not be the easiest to place successfully in maiden or handicap company.
**Double Turn**, nibbled at in the market, had the run of the race back on this sound surface but again offered little immediate promise.

## 2978 LANARKSHIRE CHAMBER OF COMMERCE APPRENTICE SERIES H'CAP (ROUND 1) 1m 5f 9y
**5:50** (5:50) (F) (0-55,60) 4-Y-O+ **£3,010** (£860; £430) **Stalls** High

Form RPR

6331 **1** **Millennium Hall**[7] 2782 5-9-11 **60** 6ex........................................ LEnstone 5 69
(PMonteith) *hld up in tch: hdwy to ld over 1f out: r.o wl: eased towards fin* **5/2**[1]

020- **2** *1¼* **Ellway Heights**[251] 5463 7-8-13 **51**........................................ BSwarbrick(3) 9 58
(WMBrisbourne) *keen early: mde most to over 1f out: kpt on ins fnl f* **6/1**

0-10 **3** *1* **Cosmic Case**[13] 2615 9-8-8 **46**........................................ PMulrennan(3) 3 52
(JSGoldie) *hld up: hdwy over 3f out: sn rdn: kpt on fnl f: no imp* **7/2**[2]

-204 **4** *½* **Tom Bell (IRE)**[16] 2525 4-8-8 **48**........................................ PPMathers(5) 6 53
(JGMO'Shea) *in tch: effrt over 2f out: one pce fnl f* **11/2**[3]

5505 **5** *2½* **Ipledgeallegiance (USA)**[22] 2386 8-7-9 **35** oh5........................(b[1]) DFentiman(5) 2 36
(DWChapman) *hld up: drvn over 3f out: kpt on fnl f: n.d* **16/1**

0/50 **6** *2* **Kristineau**[9] 2731 6-8-9 **47**........................................(t) PMakin(3) 10 46
(MrsDianneSayer) *chsd ldrs to 2f out: sn wknd* **9/1**

0406 **7** *5* **Howards Dream (IRE)**[13] 2619 6-7-9 **35** oh5........................(t) CHaddon(5) 8 27
(DANolan) *chsd ldrs tl wknd over 2f out* **33/1**

0005 **8** *1¾* **Aveiro (IRE)**[12] 2662 8-8-5 **45**........................................ DeanWilliams(5) 7 34
(MissGayKelleway) *cl up tl lost pl 3f out: n.d after* **10/1**

-006 **9** *18* **Salford Rocket**[24] 2323 4-7-11 **37** oh5 ow2........................ RoryMoore(5) 1 1
(GCHChung) *w ldrs tl wknd over 3f out* **50/1**

51/ **10** *6* **Congo Man**[1153] 4235 11-9-6 **55**........................................ THamilton 4 11
(DWWhillans) *cl up to 1/2-way: sn lost tch* **33/1**

2m 51.52s (-1.88) **Going Correction** -0.25s/f (Firm) **10** Ran SP% **113.3**
Speed ratings: **95,94,93,93,91 90,87,86,75,71**CSF £16.94 CT £51.25 TOTE £3.60: £2.40, £2.20, £1.90; EX 13.00 Place 6 £148.03, Place 5 £46.57.
**Owner** Mrs Elizabeth Ferguson **Bred** Meon Valley Stud **Trained** Rosewell, Midlothian

**FOCUS**
A moderate pace to an ordinary event resulted in a modest time, even for this grade, but the winner is in good heart and the form looks sound enough.

**NOTEBOOK**
**Millennium Hall** notched his third course success with a fluent win and was value for at least another two lengths. The way he travelled suggested he may be capable of better in the coming weeks.

**Ellway Heights** had the run of the race but shaped as though retaining plenty of ability on this reappearance outing and is likely to be placed to best advantage in the coming weeks.
**Cosmic Case** was not disgraced and may be better than the bare form as this race suited those racing prominently. A strongly run race will see her in a better light.
**Tom Bell(IRE)**, who has yet to win a race, again ran creditably but left the impression that a stiffer test of stamina over this trip would have been to his liking.
**Ipledgeallegiance(USA)** was not disgraced given this race suited those racing prominently but his record suggests he is not really one to be interested in from a punting point of view.
**Kristineau**, back in trip, had the run of the race but did not shape as though a first success was imminent.
T/Plt: £259.80 to a £1 stake. Pool: £23,153.75. 65.05 winning tickets. T/Qpdt: £33.30 to a £1 stake. Pool: £2,044.30. 45.40 winning tickets. RY

# 2407 RIPON (R-H)
## Wednesday, June 16

**OFFICIAL GOING: Good to firm**

## 2979 SKYBET.COM APPRENTICE (S) STKS 6f
6:50 (6:50) (F) 3-4-Y-O £3,248 (£928; £464) Stalls Low

| Form | | | | RPR |
|---|---|---|---|---|
| 4305 | 1 | | **Weet Watchers**[16] 2528 4-9-12 55 MHalford 5<br>(DNicholls) *mde all: rdn 2f out: drew clr appr fnl f* **11/4**[2] | 68 |
| 2060 | 2 | 5 | **Jalouhar**[13] 2625 4-9-7 46 JemmaMarshall 2<br>(BPJBaugh) *trckd ldrs: hdwy to chse wnr 2f out: sn rdn: no imp* **10/1** | 48 |
| 0000 | 3 | 1 3/4 | **Killoch Place (IRE)**[8] 2756 3-8-9 42 (v) JRoberts(5) 1<br>(JAGlover) *prom: kpt on same pce fnl 2f* **9/1** | 43 |
| -000 | 4 | 1 | **Efimac**[7] 2778 4-9-2 40 (b) SuzanneFrance 6<br>(NBycroft) *prom: effrt over 2f out: sn btn* **16/1** | 35 |
| 00-0 | 5 | 5 | **Matriarchal**[16] 2528 4-8-11 34 JaniceWebster(5) 3<br>(DonEnricoIncisa) *sn bhd* **66/1** | 20 |
| -360 | 6 | 8 | **Inistrahull Island (IRE)**[126] 745 4-9-7 56 (b1) MStainton 4<br>(MHTompkins) *dwlt: sn drvn along in rr: wl bhd fnl 2f* **2/1**[1] | 1 |
| /0-0 | 7 | 11 | **Miss Noteriety**[6] 2813 4-8-11 25 (tp) CEly(5) 8<br>(CJTeague) *dwlt: sn prom on outer: wknd qckly over 2f out* **66/1** | — |
| 0404 | L | | **Queen Of Night**[37] 2006 4-9-2 60 AReilly 7<br>(DWChapman) *ref to r: tk no part* **3/1**[3] | — |

1m 12.85s (-0.05) **Going Correction** -0.075s/f (Good) **8** Ran SP% **113.0**
**WFA** 3 from 4yo 7lb
Speed ratings: **97,90,88,86,80 69,54,**—CSF £29.31 TOTE £3.90: £1.10, £3.40, £2.50; EX 26.80.The winner was sold to Ed Weetman for 8,600gns.
**Owner** A A Bloodstock Ltd **Bred** Ed Weetman (haulage And Storage) Ltd **Trained** Sessay, N Yorks

**FOCUS**
A poor seller, weakened further by a fancied horse refusing to race. Not a race that will yield many winners.

**NOTEBOOK**
**Weet Watchers** was given a positive ride on this drop back in trip and that was more than enough for him to see off some pretty poor rivals. He was bought by his original owner for 8,600 guineas at the subsequent auction.
**Jalouhar** faced a more realistic task than in his last two starts, but still was not good enough. One win from 32 starts says it all.
**Killoch Place(IRE)**, who started the season racing over ten furlongs, ran his race on this drop into a seller for the first time, but probably did not achieve much.
**Efimac** had offered a little encouragement in her most recent start, but did not build on it over this extra furlong and continues on the decline.
**Inistrahull Island(IRE)**, best in at the weights of those that actually ran, was not exactly in form when last seen on sand in February and ran a stinker here. *Official explanation: trainer was unable to offer any explanation for poor form shown*
**Queen Of Night**, who had upwards of 9lb in hand on adjusted official ratings, planted herself as the stalls opened and looks to have gone sour.

## 2980 SKY BET JUST PRESS RED TO BET NOVICE MEDIAN AUCTION STKS 5f
7:20 (7:23) (E) 2-Y-O £3,692 (£1,136; £568; £284) Stalls Low

| Form | | | | RPR |
|---|---|---|---|---|
| 1 | 1 | | **Pike Bishop (IRE)**[23] 2370 2-9-6 DHolland 4<br>(RCharlton) *mde all: easily* **2/9**[1] | 99+ |
| 311 | 2 | 3 | **Beckermet (IRE)**[12] 2655 2-9-5 PBradley(5) 6<br>(RFFisher) *trckd wnr: effrt 2f out: no imp: clr 2nd but btn whn eased ins fnl f* **9/2**[2] | 93+ |
| 26 | 3 | 2 1/2 | **Nee Lemon Left**[45] 1782 2-8-7 FNorton 2<br>(ABerry) *chsd ldrs: drvn along 2f out: kpt on: no imp on first 2* **22/1**[3] | 60 |
| 605 | 4 | 4 | **Our Louis**[29] 2194 2-8-4 (p) TEaves(3) 1<br>(JSWainwright) *rr but in tch: drvn along over 2f out: sn btn* **100/1** | 46 |
| 0 | 5 | 1 | **Spectrum Of Light**[15] 2550 2-8-7 DeanMcKeown 3<br>(CWFairhurst) *in tch: drvn along over 2f out: sn btn* **50/1** | 43 |

59.44 secs (-0.76) **Going Correction** -0.075s/f (Good) **5** Ran SP% **111.2**
Speed ratings: **103,98,94,87,86**CSF £1.37 TOTE £1.10: £1.02, £4.90; EX 1.30.
**Owner** Michael Pescod **Bred** J Hanly **Trained** Beckhampton, Wilts

**FOCUS**
An uncompetitive novice, but a very smart time indeed for a race of this type. The winner looks smart and the runner-up is progressing. Both look much better than the bare form.

**NOTEBOOK**
**Pike Bishop(IRE)** was entitled to follow up his Windsor victory and win this easily judging by the market, but he still did it very nicely under a positive ride in a decent time, and he remains a very nice prospect.
**Beckermet(IRE)** did his best to make a race of it with the favourite and even though his rider accepted it plenty earlier enough to exacerbate the winning margin, he was still very much second best.
**Nee Lemon Left** ran her race without being anything like good enough. She may be the type for a modest nursery later on in the season.
**Our Louis** has already been beaten in a seller and two claimers, but did earn a little prize money for connections.
**Spectrum Of Light** has now finished last both times, but her pedigree suggests she needs a much greater test of stamina.

## 2981 NORMAN WELLS MEMORIAL CHALLENGE TROPHY H'CAP 6f
7:50 (7:50) (C) (0-95,85) 3-Y-O £8,607 (£3,264; £1,632; £742) Stalls Low

| Form | | | | RPR |
|---|---|---|---|---|
| 3112 | 1 | | **Bridgewater Boys**[19] 2457 3-8-9 73 (b) RFfrench 3<br>(KARyan) *rr stands side: rdn over 2f out: gd hdwy appr fnl f: led ins last: r.o wl* **13/2**[3] | 85 |
| 1-01 | 2 | 1 1/2 | **Bo McGinty (IRE)**[33] 2075 3-9-7 85 PHanagan 5<br>(RAFahey) *cl up stands side: led 2f out: rdn and hdd ins fnl f: r.o* **6/1**[2] | 92 |
| -510 | 3 | 1 1/4 | **Neon Blue**[14] 2569 3-7-13 68 HayleyTurner(5) 11<br>(RMWhitaker) *chsd far side ldrs: drvn along 1/2-way: r.o u.p to ld gp ins fnl f: nt trble first 2* **16/1** | 71 |
| 3-00 | 4 | 1/2 | **Imperial Echo (USA)**[25] 2309 3-9-2 80 RWinston 1<br>(TDBarron) *trckd ldrs stands side: rdn and ch over 1f out: no ex ins fnl f* **6/1**[2] | 82 |
| 4-16 | 5 | nk | **River Treat (FR)**[47] 1745 3-9-5 83 FNorton 6<br>(GWragg) *trckd ldrs stands side: effrt 2f out: ev ch and rdn ent fnl f: no ex ins last* **14/1** | 84 |
| 2116 | 6 | 1 | **Mr Wolf**[32] 2131 3-8-12 79 TEaves(3) 9<br>(DWBarker) *racd stands side: led tl rdn and hdd 2f out: fdd fnl f* **14/1** | 77 |
| 0545 | 7 | 1/2 | **Dolce Piccata**[15] 2549 3-9-4 82 JBramhill 4<br>(BJMeehan) *trckd ldrs stands side: rdn over 2f out: no hdwy* **14/1** | 78 |
| -006 | 8 | shd | **Mahmoom**[32] 2115 3-9-6 84 (v1) ACulhane 12<br>(MRChannon) *trckd ldr far side: led gp over 1f out: wknd and lost gp ld ins fnl f* **17/2** | 80 |
| -012 | 9 | 3 | **Snow Wolf**[9] 2726 3-9-0 78 DHolland 13<br>(JMBradley) *led far side gp tl hdd over 1f out: sn btn* **4/1**[1] | 65 |
| -600 | 10 | 3 1/2 | **Iskander**[12] 2642 3-9-6 84 NCallan 10<br>(KARyan) *racd far side: rr and drvn along 1/2-way: no hdwy* **12/1** | 61 |
| 5130 | 11 | nk | **Distant Times**[25] 2309 3-9-0 78 (v1) DAllan 8<br>(TDEasterby) *prom stands side: rdn over 2f out: sn wknd* **20/1** | 54 |
| 1202 | 12 | 10 | **Piccolo Prince**[21] 2411 3-8-5 69 JQuinn 7<br>(EJAlston) *racd far side: rr and drvn along 1/2-way: no hdwy: lost tch fnl f* **14/1** | 15 |

1m 11.96s (-0.94) **Going Correction** -0.075s/f (Good) **12** Ran SP% **117.4**
Speed ratings: **103,101,99,98,98 96,96,96,92,87 87,73**CSF £44.83 CT £610.38 TOTE £7.80: £2.10, £2.50, £5.90; EX 43.30.
**Owner** Bishopthorpe Racing **Bred** Southill Stud **Trained** Hambleton, N Yorks

**FOCUS**
A race run at a fair pace and the field split into two with the larger group of seven racing stands' side. Even though one of the far-side group made the frame, it was still the nearside group that was favoured.

**NOTEBOOK**
**Bridgewater Boys**continues in fantastic form, even though for a long time it seemed he would not figure in this, as he was off the bridle and going nowhere at the back of the nearside group. He suddenly engaged turbo charge passing the furlong pole and in the end won going away. He is 11lb higher than when his winning run started, but on this evidence it may not yet have ended.
**Bo McGinty(IRE)** ◆ ran a fine race under a positive ride in the nearside group. He still has a bit of scope and should soon be winning again.
**Neon Blue** ◆, back over his best trip, came through to comfortably beat the other four that raced far side and is one to keep an eye on.
**Imperial Echo(USA)** ◆ ran his best race of the season so far and would not mind an extra furlong.
**River Treat(FR)**, dropping back to six for the first time this season, had every chance but lacked pace where it matters.
**Mr Wolf** was given a very positive ride in the nearside group, but he had to do a lot of running to get across from his draw and that was as big a problem as his inflated handicap mark.
**Dolce Piccata** *Official explanation: jockey said filly became unbalanced on the undulating track*
**Mahmoom**, visored for the first time, showed up prominently in the far side group but did not get home and continues below form this season.
**Snow Wolf** towed the quintet along on the far side for a long way before fading rather tamely. *Official explanation: trainer was unable to offer any explanation for poor form shown*
**Iskander** *Official explanation: jockey said gelding was unsuited by the going*
**Piccolo Prince** for some reason was taken over to race on the far side even though the pair drawn immediately to his right came stands' side. He probably was not good enough anyway and never figured.

## 2982 PRICEWATERHOUSECOOPERS H'CAP 1m 2f
8:20 (8:20) (D) (0-85,82) 3-Y-O+ £5,343 (£1,644; £822; £411) Stalls High

| Form | | | | RPR |
|---|---|---|---|---|
| 3123 | 1 | | **Olivia Rose (IRE)**[7] 2775 5-9-5 73 JQuinn 4<br>(JPearce) *midfield gng wl: tk clsr order over 2f out: swtchd rt 2f out: led ent fnl f: r.o wl* **9/2**[2] | 84 |
| 0606 | 2 | 1 3/4 | **Go Tech**[11] 2687 4-9-8 76 DAllan 7<br>(TDEasterby) *in tch: hdwy 3f out: led wl over 1f out: rdn and hdd ent fnl f: no ex* **14/1** | 84 |
| 1200 | 3 | 2 | **Megan's Magic**[22] 2393 4-9-0 68 JBramhill 11<br>(WStorey) *s.s: hld up in rr: gd hdwy 3f out: chsng first 2 and rdn 1f out: no further prog* **14/1** | 72 |
| 5063 | 4 | hd | **Oscar Pepper (USA)**[13] 2618 7-8-9 63 (v) RWinston 5<br>(TDBarron) *s.i.s: towards rr: hdwy into midfield 4f out: nt clr run over 2f out: styd on u.p fnl 2f: nvr able to chal* **11/1** | 67 |
| -000 | 5 | 1 1/2 | **Dunaskin (IRE)**[36] 2022 4-10-0 82 DHolland 2<br>(DEddy) *led tl rdn and hdd wl over 1f out: kpt on* **7/2**[1] | 83 |
| 0-30 | 6 | 3/4 | **Indian Solitaire (IRE)**[36] 2022 5-9-5 73 (v) PHanagan 3<br>(RAFahey) *hld up: hdwy 4f out: rdn over 2f out: nt clr run wl over 1f out: styd on u.p fnl f: nvr able to chal* **6/1** | 72 |
| 5244 | 7 | 5 | **Trouble Mountain (USA)**[8] 2752 7-9-2 70 (b) RHughes 6<br>(MWEasterby) *hld up towards rr: effrt over 3f out: rdn over 2f out: no hdwy* **11/2**[3] | 60 |
| 0000 | 8 | 1/2 | **Arawan (IRE)**[15] 2551 4-8-11 65 DaleGibson 8<br>(MWEasterby) *prom tl rdn and wknd 2f out* **33/1** | 54 |
| 0035 | 9 | 1/2 | **Johannian**[9] 2737 6-9-6 74 RFfrench 9<br>(JMBradley) *midfield: hdwy over 3f out: ev ch and rdn 2f out: sn wknd* **8/1** | 62 |
| -256 | 10 | 11 | **La Sylphide**[13] 2624 7-9-12 80 KDalgleish 1<br>(GMMoore) *cl up tl rdn and wknd qckly over 2f out* **11/1** | 47 |
| PU | 11 | 16 | **Harambee (IRE)**[7] 2775 4-9-9 80 TEaves(3) 10<br>(BSRothwell) *prom tl wknd qckly 4f out: t.o* **100/1** | 17 |

2m 5.74s (-2.26) **Going Correction** -0.075s/f (Good) **11** Ran SP% **115.1**
Speed ratings: **106,104,103,102,101 101,97,96,96,87 74**CSF £64.44 CT £814.33 TOTE £4.80: £2.00, £4.70, £3.10; EX 47.90.
**Owner** A Watford **Bred** Dermot Cantillon **Trained** Newmarket, Suffolk

**FOCUS**
They went a fair gallop.

**NOTEBOOK**
**Olivia Rose(IRE)** does travel well in her races and did so again this time. She had to wait for a gap to appear, but she picked up in good style when it came. She has been in terrific form this year and appears to go on any ground.
**Go Tech** is well handicapped at present, but he had his stamina to prove at this trip. He saw it out well, though, and this performance opens up new opportunities for him.
**Megan's Magic**, who tends to give away ground at the start, came through from the back of the field for third. The pace cannot be too fast for her.
**Oscar Pepper(USA)** ran a solid enough race over a trip which is probably farther than ideal.
**Dunaskin(IRE)**, running off a mark 1lb lower than when last successful, reverted to front-running tactics at a track where he was won twice last season. He was easily brushed aside, though.
**Indian Solitaire(IRE)** did not get the best of runs, but he was not exactly motoring at the time and remains difficult to win with.

## 2983 H. & C. MOORE MAIDEN STKS — 1m 4f 60y

8:50 (8:52) (D) 3-Y-0+ — £4,849 (£1,492; £746; £373) Stalls High

Form — RPR

5-4 **1** **Act Of The Pace (IRE)**[51] 1662 4-9-5 .......... KDalgleish 1 71
(MJohnston) *cl up: rdn to ld 2f out: styd on u.p* **20/1**[3]

**2** *2* **Mandatum** 3-8-10 .......... DHolland 3 73
(LMCumani) *in tch: outpcd and dropped rr 5f out: rallied over 2f out: styd on to go 2nd ins fnl f: no imp on wnr* **5/2**[2]

4 **3** *2* **Farne Isle**[12] 2653 5-9-5 .......... RWinston 4 65
(GAHarker) *slowly away: hld up: tk clsr order 5f out: rdn 4f out: wnt 2nd briefly appr fnl f: no ex ins last* **20/1**[3]

2-02 **4** *6* **Force Of Nature (USA)**[19] 2460 4-9-5 85.......... RHughes 2 55
(HRACecil) *led tl rdn and hdd 2f out: wknd appr fnl f: bhd and no ch whn eased clsng stages* **4/9**[1]

2m 37.89s (-2.01) **Going Correction** -0.075s/f (Good)
**WFA** 3 from 4yo+ 14lb — **4** Ran SP% **107.3**
Speed ratings: **103,101,100,96**CSF £64.29 TOTE £10.90; EX 23.00.
**Owner** Mrs Joan Keaney **Bred** Mrs Joan Keaney **Trained** Middleham Moor, N Yorks

**FOCUS**
The form here is devalued by a poor show from the favourite, but the first two both shaped like stayers.

**NOTEBOOK**
**Act Of The Pace(IRE)**, for whom there was little support in the market, made the most of the favourite's poor showing and ran out a clear winner. As a half-sister to Yavana's Pace she looks sure to improve with time and longer distances.
**Mandatum**, a half-brother to high-class stayer Boreas, made a pleasing enough debut. He is another who shaped as though he will come into his own when tackling staying trips.
**Farne Isle** was not disgraced and this bumper winner now needs one more run for a handicap mark.
**Force Of Nature(USA)** appeared to have a simple task and got her own way in front to boot. She weakened badly once the tap was turned, though, and she may have a problem. *Official explanation: trainer was unable to offer any explanation for poor form shown*

## 2984 COVERDALE MAIDEN STKS — 6f

9:20 (9:20) (D) 3-Y-0 — £4,420 (£1,360; £680; £340) Stalls Low

Form — RPR

**1** **Doitnow (IRE)** 3-9-0 .......... PHanagan 2 78
(RAFahey) *dwlt: bhd: gd hdwy over 1f out: qcknd to ld jst ins fnl f: sn clr* **20/1**

03 **2** *4* **San Lorenzo (UAE)**[13] 2621 3-8-9 .......... ACulhane 7 61
(MRChannon) *mde most tl hdd jst ins fnl f: styd on: no ch w wnr* **11/4**[3]

02 **3** *1 ½* **Kentucky Express**[13] 2621 3-9-0 .......... RWinston 5 62
(TDEasterby) *dwlt: trckd ldrs: ev ch and rdn appr fnl f: no ex ins last* **15/8**[1]

464- **4** *½* **Troodos Jet**[223] 5929 3-9-0 65.......... FNorton 8 60
(ABerry) *prom: ev ch and rdn appr fnl f: no ex ins last* **16/1**

600- **5** *½* **Hamaasy**[236] 5734 3-9-0 61.......... AlexGreaves 4 59
(DNicholls) *cl up: ev ch and rdn approaqching fnl f: fdd ins last* **50/1**

4 **6** *shd* **Harrington Bates**[18] 2468 3-9-0 .......... DeanMcKeown 1 58
(RMWhitaker) *keen: trckd ldrs: rdn over 1f out: sn btn* **2/1**[2]

50- **7** *1* **Yorke's Folly (USA)**[264] 5197 3-8-9 .......... KDalgleish 6 50
(CWFairhurst) *bhd: rdn over 2f out: kpt on fnl f: n.d* **100/1**

**8** *7* **Bank Games** 3-9-0 .......... DaleGibson 3 34
(MWEasterby) *sn bhd* **100/1**

006 **9** *14* **Chica Roca (USA)**[7] 2785 3-8-9 70.......... (bt[1]) DHolland 9 —
(BJMeehan) *sn bhd: t.o* **20/1**

1m 12.41s (-0.49) **Going Correction** -0.075s/f (Good) — **9** Ran SP% **114.1**
Speed ratings: **100,94,92,92,91 91,89,80,61**CSF £72.00 TOTE £16.70: £2.50, £1.70, £1.40; EX 160.10 Place 6 £116.64, Place 5 £94.26.
**Owner** Hi-Tech Racing Club **Bred** Brian Killeen **Trained** Musley Bank, N Yorks

**FOCUS**
A clear-cut winner, but just an average maiden.

**NOTEBOOK**
**Doitnow(IRE)**, whose dam stays well on the Flat and has won over hurdles, struggled to go the early pace but finished in good style, winning going away. This was not a great maiden but he will be interesting in handicap company.
**San Lorenzo(UAE)**, who set the pace, reversed Haydock form with Kentucky Express but continues to meet one or two too good in maiden company. She is now eligible to run in handicaps, and might have more success in that sphere.
**Kentucky Express** had every chance but was left for dead by the winner and was unable to comfirm form with San Lorenzo, who finished a half length behind him at Haydock last time.
**Troodos Jet** wants easier ground than this and has been exposed in this sort of grade on a number of occasions now.
**Hamaasy**, who was making his seasonal debut, was without the tongue strap he wore on two occasions last season.
**Harrington Bates** was fairly well supported but failed to pick up when the pace quickened and might have been overrated on his debut.
T/Plt: £146.60 to a £1 stake. Pool: £34,240.40. 170.50 winning tickets. T/Qpdt: £63.40 to a £1 stake. Pool: £2,229.80. 26.00 winning tickets. JF

# [2849] SOUTHWELL (L-H)

### Wednesday, June 16

**OFFICIAL GOING: Standard**
60,000 gallons of water were put on the track during the morning. The going was described as 'slow and quite hard work'.
Wind: slt 1/2 behind Weather: Fine and sunny

## 2985 FEAST OF ST QUIRICUS FILLIES' MAIDEN AUCTION STKS — 7f (F)

2:10 (2:15) (F) 2-Y-0 — £2,940 (£840; £420) Stalls Low

Form — RPR

**1** **Simply St Lucia** 2-8-2 .......... CCatlin 6 64
(JRWeymes) *chsd ldrs: led over 4f out: rdn out* **20/1**

54 **2** *3* **Lady Hopeful (IRE)**[30] 2173 2-8-6 .......... DeanMcKeown 16 60
(RPElliott) *sn led: hdd over 4f out: rdn over 1f out: edgd lft and no ex ins fnl f* **5/1**[3]

06 **3** *6* **Be Bop Aloha**[33] 2095 2-8-1 .......... JFMcDonald[(3)] 15 43
(IAWood) *chsd ldrs: rdn 3f out: wknd over 1f out* **14/1**

**4** *½* **Sister Gee (IRE)** 2-7-13 .......... StephanieHollinshead[(5)] 12 42
(RHollinshead) *mid-div: hdwy over 1f out: nvr nrr* **16/1**

0 **5** *6* **Lanas Turn**[19] 2458 2-8-2 .......... PaulEddery 8 25
(TDEasterby) *hmpd s: outpcd: styd on appr fnl f: nvr nrr* **40/1**

5 **6** *shd* **Satin Rose**[27] 2234 2-8-1 .......... AMullen[(7)] 11 31
(TDEasterby) *wnt lft s: outpcd: sme hdwy over 1f out: n.d* **5/2**[1]

0 **7** *3 ½* **Sukuma (IRE)**[25] 2296 2-8-3 .......... NChalmers[(5)] 13 22
(AMBalding) *s.s: hdwy 1/2-way: sn wknd* **4/1**[2]

60 **8** *2* **Kalika (IRE)**[9] 2730 2-8-4 .......... SRighton 7 13
(MsDeborahJEvans) *s.s: outpcd* **40/1**

0 **9** *nk* **Lauren Louise**[35] 2045 2-8-6 .......... (t) KimTinkler 3 14
(NTinkler) *dwlt: hdwy 5f out: wknd 3f out* **25/1**

3 **10** *2 ½* **Cois Na Tine Eile**[31] 2140 2-8-2 .......... DKinsella 1 4
(KARyan) *s.i.s: outpcd* **6/1**

**11** *¾* **Fraambuoyant (IRE)** 2-8-2 .......... RFfrench 5 2
(CWFairhurst) *prom to 1/2-way* **20/1**

0 **12** *1 ½* **Lady Susesanne (IRE)**[33] 2095 2-8-6 .......... FNorton 2 2
(CADwyer) *dwlt: outpcd* **25/1**

6 **13** *7* **Dancing Moonlight (IRE)**[15] 2544 2-8-10 .......... RFitzpatrick 14 —
(MrsNMacauley) *dwlt: sn prom: wknd 3f out: sn hung lft* **40/1**

4 **14** *1* **Desert Fern (IRE)**[6] 2812 2-8-8 ow2.......... NCallan 4 —
(MsDeborahJEvans) *chsd ldrs to 1/2-way* **10/1**

1m 33.08s (2.28) **Going Correction** +0.075s/f (Slow) — **14** Ran SP% **125.7**
Speed ratings: **89,85,78,78,71 71,67,64,64,61 60,59,51,49**CSF £115.12 TOTE £28.70: £4.10, £2.40, £4.80; EX 1098.00.
**Owner** Sporting Occasions Racing No 6 **Bred** Tattersalls Ltd **Trained** Middleham Moor, N Yorks

**FOCUS**
A low-grade fillies' maiden auction race but the winner has some potential.

**NOTEBOOK**
**Simply St Lucia**, a March foal, was one of the bigger fillies in the field. Bought for just 1,400gns. she knew her job and her win was not unexpected. She can go on from here.
**Lady Hopeful(IRE)**, worst drawn, was soon ahead towards the running rail. In the end she found the winner much too strong and a drop back to six will not do her any harm.
**Be Bop Aloha** started on terms this time but did not see out the extra furlong.
**Sister Gee(IRE)**, an April foal, looks immature at present but made a pleasing bow.
**Lanas Turn**, knocked over by her stablemate at the start, picked up late on and can improve again.
**Satin Rose** came out of the stalls sideways and was never on terms. She is surely capable of better than she showed here.
**Sukuma(IRE)** is a narrow type and, very keen to post, her saddle slipped. She was again slowly away and showed next to nothing.
**Cois Na Tine Eile**, carrying bags of condition after a month off since her debut in a seller, never went and would not face the kickback. *Official explanation: jockey said filly would not face the kick back*

## 2986 ST MADONNA OF CARMINE'S DAY CLAIMING STKS — 6f (F)

2:45 (2:46) (F) 3-Y-0 — £3,269 (£934; £467) Stalls Low

Form — RPR

0200 **1** **Obe Bold (IRE)**[12] 2650 3-8-4 54.......... FNorton 5 68
(ABerry) *mde all: rdn clr over 1f out: unchal* **11/8**[1]

0-50 **2** *8* **La Fonteyne**[11] 2688 3-8-2 55.......... JMcAuley 8 42
(CBBBooth) *chsd ldrs: lost pl over 3f out: styd on ins fnl f* **25/1**

3402 **3** *½* **Only If I Laugh**[26] 2265 3-8-9 68.......... DeanMcKeown 6 48
(PABlockley) *hld up: plld hrd: nvr nr to chal* **9/4**[2]

0406 **4** *3 ½* **Beamsley Beacon**[5] 2849 3-8-8 57.......... (v[1]) TEaves[(3)] 1 39
(GMMoore) *chsd ldrs tl wknd 2f out* **14/1**

0050 **5** *nk* **Knight To Remember (IRE)**[12] 2657 3-8-5 43.......... WRyan 9 32
(REBarr) *hld up: n.d* **33/1**

0000 **6** *1 ½* **Back At De Front (IRE)**[12] 2664 3-8-1 55 ow2.......... RMiles[(3)] 3 27
(NEBerry) *s.i.s: n.d* **11/2**[3]

0000 **7** *4* **Philly Dee**[30] 2165 3-7-9 40.......... HayleyTurner[(5)] 4 11
(NEBerry) *chsd wnr tl wknd 2f out* **16/1**

0650 **8** *1* **Velvet Touch**[5] 2850 3-9-0 54.......... SWhitworth 2 22
(JRJenkins) *chsd ldrs 4f* **14/1**

00-0 **9** *24* **Eunice Choice**[119] 816 3-8-2 .......... JFMcDonald[(3)] 7 —
(MJHaynes) *prom: lost pl over 4f out: sn bhd* **66/1**

1m 17.25s (0.35) **Going Correction** +0.075s/f (Slow) — **9** Ran SP% **115.8**
Speed ratings: **100,89,88,84,83 81,76,74,42**CSF £42.92 TOTE £2.40: £1.40, £4.90, £1.10; EX 44.40.Obe Bold was subject to a friendly claim.
**Owner** Alan Berry **Bred** Saud Bin Saad **Trained** Cockerham, Lancs

**FOCUS**
The betting patterns pointed clearly in Obe Bold's favour. The form looks unreliable.

**NOTEBOOK**
**Obe Bold(IRE)** was backed as if defeat was out of the question and so it proved. Her trainer was successful in retaining her in the face of one hostile bid.
**La Fonteyne**, unplaced in four previous starts, snatched second spot on the line and will be better suited by seven.
**Only If I Laugh**, whose last two runs were over five furlongs, had 9lb in hand of the winner on official figures but the market spoke differently. Steadied at the start, he took a remote second place a furlong out but hung right and gave away the runner-up spot near the line. The Stewards asked questions, but basically were told the horse is a tricky ride and that he did not stay. *Official explanation: jockey said, regarding the running and riding, gelding usually runs over 5f and his orders were to ride to get the trip of 6f, adding that gelding has a light mouth and was difficult around the bend, and also hung right when asked to quicken in the home straight before appearing not to stay*
**Beamsley Beacon** had plenty to find and a visor this time made little difference.
**Knight To Remember(IRE)**, a maiden now after 12 starts, had plenty to find.
**Back At De Front(IRE)** had 3lb in hand of the winner on official figures but she is out of form at present.

## 2987 DAVID BROOKFIELD 40TH BIRTHDAY H'CAP — 1m 6f (F)

3:20 (3:20) (E) (0-70,66) 3-Y-0+ — £3,474 (£1,069; £534; £267) Stalls Low

Form — RPR

/005 **1** **Broughtons Flush**[50] 1698 6-8-1 **40**.......... (v) FNorton 5 50
(WJMusson) *hld up in tch: rdn to ld ins fnl f: styd on* **18/1**

3143 **2** *hd* **Next Flight (IRE)**[16] 2531 5-8-6 **45**.......... WRyan 7 55
(REBarr) *chsd ldrs: led over 2f out: rdn over 1f out: hdd ins fnl f: styd on* **9/2**[2]

56-4 **3** *6* **High Policy (IRE)**[132] 684 8-9-6 **64**.......... StephanieHollinshead[(5)] 11 66
(RHollinshead) *hld up: hdwy over 4f out: styd on same pce fnl 2f* **10/1**

-304 **4** *1 ½* **Broughton Melody**[103] 973 5-8-1 **40**.......... CCatlin 4 40
(WJMusson) *chsd ldrs: rdn over 3f out: styd on same pce fnl 2f* **14/1**

/401 **5** *½* **Lucky Judge**[39] 1973 7-8-11 **50**.......... DaleGibson 8 50
(GASwinbank) *sn drvn along in rr: hdwy over 4f out: no imp fnl 2f* **5/1**[3]

4021 **6** *3 ½* **Queen's Fantasy**[12] 2665 3-8-7 **63**.......... (v) PaulEddery 12 58
(DHaydnJones) *s.i.s: hdwy to ld after 2f: rdn and hdd over 2f out : wknd over 1f out* **4/1**[1]

060/ **7** *14* **Al Mabrook (IRE)**[22] 1366 9-7-12 **37** oh7.......... RFfrench 13 14
(NGRichards) *mid-divison: sn pushed along: n.d* **10/1**

-004 **8** *19* **Staff Nurse (IRE)**[28] 2230 4-8-1 **40**.......... KimTinkler 10 —
(DonEnricoIncisa) *bhd fnl 8f* **33/1**

0000 **9** *24* **Vanbrugh (FR)**[4] 2874 4-9-12 **65**.......... (vt) DarrenWilliams 1 —
(MissDAMchale) *chsd ldr: hrd rdn 7f out: sn wknd* **9/1**

00-0 **10** *19* **Equus (IRE)**[12] [2665] 3-8-6 **62**.......... PDoe 6 —
(LADace) *chsd ldrs: lost pl 10f out: sn bhd* **40/1**

04/2 **11** *19* **Turtle Dancer (IRE)**[35] [2039] 6-9-10 **66**.......... TEaves(3) 2 —
(BEllison) *hld up in tch: lost pl over 8f out: sn bhd* **9/1**

0/00 **12** *dist* **Estuary (USA)**[72] [1263] 9-8-8 **50**..........(b1) SHitchcott(3) 3 —
(MsAEEmbiricos) *chsd ldrs 6f* **40/1**

501- **13** *dist* **Swain Davis**[306] [4164] 4-9-10 **63**.......... SWhitworth 9 —
(DJSFfrenchDavis) *prom 8f: virtually p.u over 3f out* **10/1**

3m 9.80s (0.10) **Going Correction** +0.075s/f (Slow)
**WFA** 3 from 4yo+ 17lb **13** Ran SP% **121.9**
Speed ratings: **102,101,98,97,97 95,87,76,62,51 41,—,—**CSF £98.17 CT £879.76 TOTE £19.20: £5.70, £1.30, £3.20; EX 216.70.
**Owner** Broughton Thermal Insulation **Bred** Broughton Bloodstock **Trained** Newmarket, Suffolk

**FOCUS**
A very moderate race and ordinary, if fairly sound, form for the grade.

**NOTEBOOK**
**Broughtons Flush**, whose last success two years ago came from an 8lb higher mark, has now won four times, all on the All-Weather, three of them here. He showed a return to form displaying good battling qualities.
**Next Flight(IRE)** is in good form at present and despite every assistance from the saddle he just missed out. He has just one career win to his credit after 24 starts now.
**High Policy(IRE)**, a winner six times on Fibresand, stayed on in his own time on his first outing since February. Two miles suits him better.
**Broughton Melody**, having only her sixth start, had been absent since March and is presumably difficult to keep right.
**Lucky Judge**, soon detached in last place, moved up leaving the back stretch but, continually hanging left, was never a threat. He would not face the kickback, which is a pity because he is better handicapped than on turf. *Official explanation: jockey said gelding was never travelling because it would not face the kick back*
**Queen's Fantasy**, 7lb higher, was soon in front. Her rider was looking round for dangers leaving the back stretch, but in the end her stamina gave out completely.
**Vanbrugh(FR)** *Official explanation: jockey said gelding had ran flat*
**Turtle Dancer(IRE)** *Official explanation: jockey said gelding would not face the kick back*
**Swain Davis** *Official explanation: jockey said filly was never travelling*

## 2988 SCRUBWOMEN TEA PARTY DAY H'CAP — 1m (F)
3:55 (3:57) (E) (0-75,73) 3-Y-O — **£3,425** (£1,054; £527; £263) **Stalls** Low

Form — RPR

1300 **1** **Dispol Veleta**[22] [2390] 3-9-1 **67**.......... NCallan 8 77
(TDBarron) *hld up in tch: led 2f out: r.o wl* **4/1**[3]

0-00 **2** *2 1/2* **Annie Harvey**[37] [1992] 3-9-4 **70**.......... FLynch 3 75
(BSmart) *led 6f: styd on same pce fnl f* **18/1**

2010 **3** *1* **Play Master (IRE)**[34] [2069] 3-9-7 **73**.......... PaulEddery 4 76
(DHaydnJones) *hld up in tch: rdn over 2f out: styd on same pce fnl f* **5/2**[2]

1510 **4** *3* **Mission Affirmed (USA)**[39] [1957] 3-9-2 **68**.......... DaleGibson 5 65
(TPTate) *chsd ldr: rdn over 2f out: styd on same pce appr fnl f* **7/4**[1]

0000 **5** *5* **Glendale**[14] [2571] 3-8-10 **62**..........(p) JDSmith 6 49
(CADwyer) *sn outpcd: hdwy on outside 3f out: sn rdn and no imp* **12/1**

0-10 **6** *2* **Count Dracula**[65] [1357] 3-8-10 **67**..........(v1) NChalmers(5) 7 50
(AMBalding) *prom: lost pl over 4f out: wknd over 3f out* **10/1**

4360 **7** *10* **Ground Patrol**[27] [2244] 3-9-4 **70**..........(v1) WRyan 2 33
(AMBalding) *dwlt: hdwy to join ldrs over 4f out: n.m.r and wknd 3f out* **10/1**

0000 **8** *9* **Just One Look**[14] [2577] 3-8-13 **65**.......... DSweeney 1 10
(MBlanshard) *chsd ldrs over 4f* **14/1**

1m 45.07s (0.47) **Going Correction** +0.075s/f (Slow) **8** Ran SP% **122.7**
Speed ratings: **100,97,96,93,88 86,76,67**CSF £75.22 CT £223.82 TOTE £6.70: £2.50, £5.10, £1.10; EX 58.70.
**Owner** W B Imison **Bred** B N And Mrs Toye **Trained** Maunby, N Yorks

**FOCUS**
A modest handicap and ordinary but solid form.

**NOTEBOOK**
**Dispol Veleta**, a stone higher than when opening her account here in February, and 3lb higher than Nottingham, was back to her best after two below-par runs on fast ground on turf. She took this in most decisive fashion and there should be even better to come.
**Annie Harvey**, who is not that big, tries hard but hanging right in the end found the winner much too strong. *Official explanation: jockey said filly had hung right*
**Play Master(IRE)**, a very keen type, travels strongly but off the bridle does not find as much as seemed likely. With him the stronger the pace the better.
**Mission Affirmed(USA)**, who accounted for older rivals from a 5lb lower mark here in April, was having his first run over five weeks. Messed about turning in he tired and edged left in the final furlong. He does not handle soft ground on turf and a pair of blinkers might make him a lot sharper.
**Glendale** is not in the best of form at present and he made his effort on the wide outside on the home turn.
**Count Dracula**, in a first time visor, does not look to have a good attitude at all.

## 2989 WOODCHOPPERS JAMBOREE CLASSIFIED STKS — 7f (F)
4:30 (4:32) (F) 3-Y-O+ — **£2,961** (£846; £423) **Stalls** Low

Form — RPR

6002 **1** **Countykat (IRE)**[19] [2445] 4-9-7 64..........(v) DarrenWilliams 10 84+
(KRBurke) *s.i.s: hdwy 1/2-way: led over 1f out: sn clr: eased ins fnl f* **10/1**

4600 **2** *2 1/2* **Teehee (IRE)**[6] [2814] 6-9-1 61..........(b) RMiles(3) 12 69
(BPalling) *trckd ldrs: racd keenly: led over 2f out: rdn and hdd over 1f out: sn outpcd* **50/1**

-041 **3** *1 1/2* **Roman Empire**[32] [2123] 4-9-3 57..........(b) NCallan 5 64+
(KARyan) *sn pushed along in rr: swtchd wd 5f out: hdwy over 1f out: nvr nrr* **2/1**[2]

-150 **4** *4* **Azreme**[18] [2483] 4-9-1 65.......... MHoward(7) 2 59
(DKIvory) *prom: rdn over 2f out: wknd over 1f out* **9/1**[3]

0001 **5** *1* **Tre Colline**[6] [2814] 5-9-9 60.......... GBaker 3 58
(NTinkler) *bhd: nt clr run over 2f out: nvr nr to chal* **6/4**[1]

0003 **6** *3/4* **Yorker (USA)**[6] [2814] 6-9-8 65.......... CCatlin 8 55
(MsDeborahJEvans) *chsd ldrs: rdn over 3f out: wknd over 2f out* **20/1**

-202 **7** *3 1/2* **Zagala**[60] [1477] 4-9-5 65..........(t) FNorton 9 43
(SLKeightley) *led 1f: remained handy tl wknd 2f out* **10/1**

0-51 **8** *2* **Carte Noire**[12] [2658] 3-8-6 60 ow4.......... SHitchcott(3) 6 37
(JGPortman) *prom: rdn over 4f out: hmpd and wknd over 2f out* **25/1**

20-0 **9** *1 1/4* **Eboracum (IRE)**[14] [2569] 3-8-0 62.......... AMullen(7) 11 32
(TDEasterby) *prom: lost pl over 4f out: n.d after* **50/1**

30-5 **10** *1/2* **Megabond**[90] [1047] 3-8-10 62.......... FLynch 4 34
(BSmart) *s.s: outpcd: hdwy u.p over 1f out: wknd and eased fnl f* **10/1**

5010 **11** *3/4* **Old Bailey (USA)**[2] [2936] 4-9-0 59..........(b) TEaves(3) 1 30
(TDBarron) *chsd ldrs over 4f* **20/1**

-000 **12** *5* **Desert Battle (IRE)**[11] [2688] 3-8-8 55..........(b) DaleGibson 7 17
(MBlanshard) *s.i.s: hdwy to ld after 1f: rdn and hdd over 2f out : wknd over 1f out* **66/1**

1m 30.75s (-0.05) **Going Correction** +0.075s/f (Slow)
**WFA** 3 from 4yo+ 9lb **12** Ran SP% **129.4**
Speed ratings: **103,100,98,93,92 91,87,85,84,83 82,77**CSF £455.23 TOTE £13.90: £4.60, £8.20, £1.30; EX 267.90.
**Owner** Bernard Bargh, Jeff Hamer, Steve Henshaw **Bred** Ballyhane Stud **Trained** Middleham Moor, N Yorks

**FOCUS**
A modest handicap but a fair time and the form may well hold up.

**NOTEBOOK**
**Countykat(IRE)** ◆, rated 92 at one time, has taken time to recover after an operation for colic in Dubai last year. Clearly in a good frame of mind beforehand, he made this look very simple and but for being heavily eased would have had at least ten lengths to spare. He is certainly off a lenient mark now if he can reproduce this sort of form.
**Teehee(IRE)**, worst drawn, ran a lot better than of late but the winner was totally different gear.
**Roman Empire** was pulled very wide to race on the outer leaving the back stretch. He really picked up late on and finished with quite a flourish. He looked second best on the day.
**Azreme** has not exactly fired since his win at Warwick on heavy ground in May three outings ago now.
**Tre Colline**, raised 13lb after his facile win here a week earlier, was not in the same mood this time and, never really travelling, was going nowhere when left short of room once in line for home. He would not face the kick-back this time, six days in racing is a long time it seems. *Official explanation: jockey said gelding would not face the kick back*
**Megabond** *Official explanation: jockey said gelding would not face the kick back*

## 2990 TELETEXT RACING "HANDS AND HEELS" APPRENTICE H'CAP — 1m (F)
5:05 (5:09) (F) (0-55,56) 3-Y-O+ — **£2,996** (£856; £428) **Stalls** Low

Form — RPR

4021 **1** **Frank's Quest (IRE)**[19] [2454] 4-9-7 **53**.......... RJKilloran(5) 13 62
(PBurgoyne) *w ldrs: led over 4f out: clr over 1f out: eased nr fin* **13/2**[3]

0051 **2** *3* **Diamond Shannon (IRE)**[6] [2811] 3-9-0 **56** 7ex.. DanielleMcCreery(5) 15 59
(DCarroll) *plld hrd and prom: pushed along over 2f out: styd on* **10/3**[1]

0-50 **3** *1/2* **Erupt**[29] [2214] 11-8-8 **35** oh5.......... LauraPike 14 37
(REBarr) *s.i.s: hdwy 5f out: pushed along over 2f out: styd on* **25/1**

0012 **4** *1/2* **Leyaaly**[6] [2811] 5-8-11 **38**..........(p) LiamJones 7 39
(BAPearce) *s.i.s: hdwy over 4f out: chsd wnr over 3f out: no ex fnl f* **8/1**

6060 **5** *4* **Killerby Nicko**[19] [2457] 3-9-1 **52**.......... AMullen 12 45
(TDEasterby) *led after 1f: hdd over 4f out: wknd over 1f out* **12/1**

5343 **6** *1* **Kanz Wood (USA)**[12] [2666] 8-8-13 **45**..........(v) TDean(5) 9 36
(AWCarroll) *mid-div: hdwy over 3f out: wknd fnl f* **7/1**

0-00 **7** *6* **Buckenham Stone**[16] [2520] 5-8-3 **35** oh5.......... KirstyMilczarek(5) 3 14
(JPearce) *led 1f: wknd over 3f out* **25/1**

1460 **8** *nk* **Moyne Pleasure (IRE)**[6] [2816] 6-9-4 **45**..........(p) StevenHarrison 10 23
(PaulJohnson) *chsd ldrs over 4f* **8/1**

5400 **9** *6* **Libre**[16] [2528] 4-10-0 **55**..........(b) KMay 6 21
(RCGuest) *chsd ldrs over 5f* **10/1**

6005 **10** *2* **Hoh's Back**[6] [2814] 5-9-7 **48**..........(p) LucyRussell 2 10
(PaulJohnson) *s.s: a in rr* **6/1**[2]

060 **11** *2* **Glanworth (IRE)**[11] [2693] 3-7-7 **35** oh5..........(b1) CharlotteKerton(5) 4 —
(NACallaghan) *sn outpcd* **16/1**

60/0 **12** *13* **Stone Crest (IRE)**[18] [2473] 6-8-8 **35** oh5.......... SYourston 8 —
(THCaldwell) *sn outpcd* **50/1**

00/6 **13** *1/2* **Holderness Girl**[16] [2445] 11-8-8 **35** oh10.......... StaceyRenwick 5 —
(MESowersby) *prom: lost pl over 4f out: sn bhd* **66/1**

1m 47.9s (3.30) **Going Correction** +0.075s/f (Slow)
**WFA** 3 from 4yo+ 10lb **13** Ran SP% **119.2**
Speed ratings: **86,83,82,82,78 77,71,70,64,62 60,47,47**CSF £27.47 CT £421.64 TOTE £8.40: £2.50, £2.40, £6.70; EX 35.60 Place 6 £204.54, Place 5 £47.50.
**Owner** Fun & Fantasy & Andrew Haynes Racing Ltd **Bred** Rathasker Stud **Trained** Collingbourne Ducis, Wilts
■ A red letter day for 17-year-old Richard Killoran, aboard his first winner.

**FOCUS**
A pedestrian winning time, 2.83 seconds slower than the earlier handicap and, with the top-weight rated just 55, a seller in all but name.

**NOTEBOOK**
**Frank's Quest(IRE)**, who took a seller last time, travelled strongly and the boy always looked to have things well under control.
**Diamond Shannon(IRE)**, raised 10lb after her clear cut win here a week earlier, had a 7lb penalty to shoulder but had the worst of the draw. After dropping back turning in, she stayed on to claim second spot, but unless her rating is revised she will face even tougher tasks in future.
**Erupt**, 5lb out of the handicap, is a pensioner now but this was a much better effort for his present yard.
**Leyaaly** finished a lot closer to the runner-up this time and is clearly in good heart at present.
**Killerby Nicko**, stepping up in trip, was having just his second try on the All-Weather. A seller looks his cup of tea.
**Kanz Wood(USA)**, with the visor on again, seems marginally better over seven these days.
T/Plt: £284.00 to a £1 stake. Pool: £20,017.90. 51.45 winning tickets. T/Qpdt: £70.20 to a £1 stake. Pool: £1,718.10. 18.10 winning tickets. CR

2991 - 2992a (Foreign Racing) - See Raceform Interactive

# 2742 NAAS (L-H)
Wednesday, June 16

**OFFICIAL GOING: Good to firm (firm in places)**

## 2993a IRISH STALLION FARMS NOBLESSE STKS (GROUP 3) (F&M) — 1m 4f
7:25 (7:28) 3-Y-O+ — **£41,197** (£12,042; £5,704; £1,901)

RPR

**1** **Danelissima (IRE)**[10] [2711] 3-8-9 95..........(b) KJManning 8 102
(JSBolger, Ire) *sn led: hdd 2 1/2f out: rallied 1 1/2f out: regained ld under 1f out: styd on wl* **8/1**

**2** *1/2* **Summitville**[35] [2042] 4-9-12.......... MFenton 1 104
(JGGiven) *settled in rr: 4th and hdwy early st: led under 2f out: hdd under 1f out: kpt on u.p* **4/7**[1]

**3** *2* **Tarakala (IRE)**[18] [2498] 3-8-9 98.......... FMBerry 2 98
(JohnMOxx, Ire) *settled 2nd: rdn appr st: led 2 1/2f out: hdd 2f out: 3rd and no ex fnl f* **5/1**[2]

**4** *2 1/2* **Desert Royalty (IRE)**[25] [2297] 4-9-9.......... JAHeffernan 4 94
(EALDunlop) *trckd ldrs in 4th: 5th over 2f out: kpt on one pced* **8/1**

**5** *1* **Leonor Fini (IRE)**[10] [2711] 3-8-9 97.......... DPMcDonogh 3 92
(KevinPrendergast, Ire) *hld up: 6th and effrt early st: no imp fr 2f out* **7/1**[3]

**6** *3 1/2* **Lisieux Orchid (IRE)**[18] [2500] 3-8-9 86.......... NGMcCullagh 6 87
(DKWeld, Ire) *trckd ldrs in 3rd: rdn appr st: wknd fr 2f out* **12/1**

7 3/4 **Royal Devotion (IRE)**[18] 2498 4-9-9 98 TPO'Shea 5 86
(MHalford, Ire) *chsd ldrs in 5th: wknd appr st* **14/1**

2m 30.4s
**WFA** 3 from 4yo 14lb **7** Ran SP% **129.4**
Speed ratings: CSF £15.12 TOTE £16.20: £4.50, £1.50; DF 28.60.
**Owner** Mrs J S Bolger **Bred** J S Bolger **Trained** Coolcullen, Co Carlow

**FOCUS**
A weak Group Three and of little consequence in the overall Pattern.

**NOTEBOOK**
**Danelissima(IRE)** came good on her fourth outing of the season. This was the first time she had tackled the trip and she stayed on much stronger than the runner-up. She could take her chance in the Irish Oaks but it will be as an outsider.
**Summitville** continues her long losing run and hasn't won since her 2-y-o days. This Epsom Oaks third is clearly not the performer she was although there seems nothing wrong with her attitude. She flattered when getting her head in front with less than two furlongs to race but found nothing under pressure inside the last.
**Tarakala(IRE)** got to the front in the straight but once headed found precious little.
**Desert Royalty(IRE)** had little business in this company and just plodded on for fourth.
**Leonor Fini(IRE)** finished in front of the winner last time but was beaten early in the straight.

2994 - 2995a (Foreign Racing) - See Raceform Interactive

## 2966 ASCOT (R-H)
Thursday, June 17

**OFFICIAL GOING: Good to firm (firm in places) changing to firm after 4.20 (race 4)**
Wind: Almost nil Weather: Overcast

## 2996 NORFOLK STKS (GROUP 3) 5f
**2:30** (2:30) (A) 2-Y-O **£34,800** (£13,200; £6,600; £3,000) **Stalls** Low

Form RPR
111 **1** **Blue Dakota (IRE)**[31] 2180 2-8-12 EAhern 5 106
(JNoseda) *trckd ldr: led over 1f out: edgd lft ins fnl f: drvn out* **5/4**[1]
21 **2** *nk* **Mystical Land (IRE)**[45] 1819 2-8-12 KFallon 4 105
(JHMGosden) *bmpd s: chsd ldrs: drvn to chal fnl f: r.o* **9/1**
51 **3** *1* **Skywards**[18] 2502 2-8-12 LDettori 1 101
(SaeedBinSuroor) *gd sort: broke wl: led tl over 1f out: kpt on wl* **4/1**[2]
**4** *3* **Cougar Cat (USA)**[28] 2253 2-8-12 JPSpencer 10 91
(APO'Brien, Ire) *str: lw: sn pushed along in rr: hdwy 2f out: hrd rdn: hung rt and one pce appr fnl f* **11/2**[3]
3231 **5** *2* **Empire's Ghodha**[5] 2872 2-8-12 (b) PJSmullen 2 84
(BJMeehan) *wnt rt s: prom: hrd rdn 2f out: wknd over 1f out* **66/1**
211 **6** *6* **Dance Night (IRE)**[43] 1878 2-8-12 GGibbons 9 63
(BAMcmahon) *in tch: rdn 1/2-way: sn wknd* **20/1**
3521 **7** *shd* **Windy Prospect**[20] 2453 2-8-12 DHolland 7 63
(PABlockley) *sn outpcd and wl bhd: n.d* **66/1**
3 **8** *1 1/2* **Holbeck Ghyll (IRE)**[14] 2609 2-8-12 KDarley 12 57
(AMBalding) *lw: dwlt: mid-div: outpcd fr 1/2-way* **33/1**
61 **9** *6* **Spree (IRE)**[6] 2846 2-8-9 RHughes 8 33
(RHannon) *lw: wnt rt s: towards rr: lost tch fr 1/2-way* **7/1**

61.97 secs (0.04) **Going Correction** +0.05s/f (Good) **9** Ran SP% **113.0**
Speed ratings: **101,100,98,94,90 81,81,78,69**CSF £12.88 TOTE £2.40: £1.20, £1.60, £1.40; EX 14.00 Trifecta £28.40 Pool of £6,373.36 - 159.00 winning tickets.
**Owner** A F Nolan, Mrs J M Ryan, Mrs P Duffin **Bred** Michael O'Donnell **Trained** Newmarket, Suffolk

**FOCUS**
Not a vintage Norfolk and the time was only ordinary, but Blue Dakota confirmed himself a very speedy juvenile and may well be a bit better than the bare form.

**NOTEBOOK**
**Blue Dakota(IRE)** was many people's idea of the banker of the meeting. Shadowing the leader, he went on travelling easily but began to idle inside the final furlong and needed to be driven out. He is all speed and Ascot's stiff five furlongs tested him, but he showed the right attitude to maintain his unbeaten record. Connections intend making the most of him this year, and he will be kept busy.
**Mystical Land(IRE)**, experiencing quick ground for the first time, looked a big danger going to the final furlong but the winner pulled out that bit more to deny him. The step up to six in something like the July Stakes will surely suit him.
**Skywards** showed plenty of pace to lead the favourite for over three furlongs. Held when that rival edged across him inside the last, he kept on and a sixth furlong should not be a problem.
**Cougar Cat(USA)**, a winner at Tipperary on his debut, was outpaced in the early stages. He improved with a quarter of a mile to run but never appeared to be happy on the ground and was beaten before the furlong pole.
**Empire's Ghodha**, off the mark in a weak event at Bath, ran his best race to date and finished clear of the remainder.
**Dance Night(IRE)**, tackling different underfoot conditions, was found wanting.
**Windy Prospect** was out of his depth, but he did keep on past beaten rivals having looked set to finish a detached last. The return to six furlongs will suit him. *Official explanation: jockey said colt was unsuited by the good to firm, firm in places ground*
**Spree(IRE)** is a well regarded filly, but after leaving the stalls awkwardly was never close enough to get involved. She was not given a hard time when beaten. *Official explanation: jockey said filly was unsuited by the good to firm, firm in places ground*

## 2997 RIBBLESDALE STKS (GROUP 2) (FILLIES) 1m 4f
**3:05** (3:06) (A) 3-Y-O **£75,400** (£28,600; £14,300; £6,500) **Stalls** High

Form RPR
3-13 **1** **Punctilious**[13] 2640 3-8-11 110 (t) LDettori 1 111
(SaeedBinSuroor) *lw: trckd ldr: rdn to chal 2f out: led narrowly 1f out: drew clr last 100yds* **9/2**[2]
1-22 **2** *1 1/2* **Sahool**[34] 2081 3-8-11 103 RHills 3 109
(MPTregoning) *lw: led: rdn and pressed 2f out: narrowly hdd 1f out: kpt on wl tl no ex last 100yds* **7/1**
5-1 **3** *1 1/2* **Quiff**[35] 2059 3-8-11 84 KFallon 5 107
(SirMichaelStoute) *rangy: hld up in last trio: pushed along 5f out: nt clr run wl over 2f out: drvn and styd on fnl 2f to take 3rd nr fin* **7/2**[1]
4-21 **4** *nk* **New Morning (IRE)**[24] 2357 3-8-11 PRobinson 2 106
(MAJarvis) *t.k.h: cl up: chsd ldng pair 3f out: drvn and unable qck over 1f out: fdd and lost 3rd nr fin* **6/1**
0-21 **5** *1* **Hidden Hope**[43] 1879 3-8-11 106 TEDurcan 9 105
(GWragg) *t.k.h: trckd ldng pair to 4f out: cl up and rdn 2f out: one pce after* **11/2**[3]
31 **6** *6* **Feaat**[16] 2555 3-8-11 WSupple 8 95
(JHMGosden) *racd in midfield: rdn 4f out: wknd over 2f out* **33/1**
1-33 **7** *nk* **Crystal Curling (IRE)**[34] 2081 3-8-11 99 MHills 6 94
(BWHills) *t.k.h: hld up in last pair: drvn and effrt over 2f out: hanging and sn btn* **20/1**
412 **8** *5* **Modesta (IRE)**[12] 2683 3-8-11 78 RHughes 7 86
(HRACecil) *hld up and sn last: lost tch 4f out: bhd after* **10/1**
1-31 **9** *1 1/2* **Rave Reviews (IRE)**[34] 2081 3-8-11 105 KDarley 4 84
(JLDunlop) *lw: trckd ldrs: effrt to chse ldng pair 4f out: wknd 3f out* **6/1**

2m 30.12s (-3.44) **Going Correction** +0.05s/f (Good) **9** Ran SP% **113.7**
Speed ratings: **113,112,111,110,110 106,105,102,101**CSF £35.31 TOTE £3.30: £1.40, £2.60, £1.30; EX 35.50 Trifecta £109.10 Pool of £6,396.52 - 41.59 winning units.
**Owner** Godolphin **Bred** Bjorn E Nielsen **Trained** Newmarket, Suffolk

**FOCUS**
Not a strong renewal of the Ribblesdale, but the time was decent and a good winner in Punctilious, who showed no ill effects of her run in the Oaks only 13 days ago previously and was back to her Musidora form. Quiff deserves plenty of credit for her effort, as she came from the back on ground that was way too fast for her.

**NOTEBOOK**
**Punctilious**, evidently none the worse for her Oaks exertions, travelled sweetly on the hind quarters of Sahool for most of the journey and responded well to driving to surge ahead inside the final furlong, her rider reluctant to use the whip as she does not take kindly to it. Epsom was evidently not to her liking, and she clearly stays the trip well. She is now set for a rest.
**Sahool** has now finished second on all three outings this year, running into Ouija Board first time up and then being held by Rave Reviews at Newbury. She had the run of the race from the front and kept finding up the straight without being able to hold off the winner. Her target for later in the season is the Park Hill and she remains progressive.
**Quiff**, winner of her maiden at Salisbury last month, was uncomfortable on the ground and always struggling to get into a rhythm. To make matters worse, she was squeezed up turning in and had to be pulled wide, eventually finishing well for third. She is undoubtedly the one to take from the race and when she gets back on a softer surface she should improve dramatically. Races like the Yorkshire Oaks and Park Hill beckon.
**New Morning(IRE)** was another coming into this on the back of a maiden win and she too ran well until having no more to give from the furlong marker. She lost third only close home and, although by Sadler's Wells, is believed by her trainer to relish this fast ground. She can win at a slightly lesser level.
**Hidden Hope**, winner of the Cheshire Oaks, ran well without proving good enough and may have found the ground a little fast. She will stay further than this and can win again at a lesser level.
**Feaat** finished behind Quiff on her debut and did that filly no favours here in hampering her early in the straight.
**Rave Reviews(IRE)** was the only real disappointment of the race as she had beaten Sahool at Newbury. It looked a simple case of her not handling the ground, and she is much better than this. *Official explanation: jockey said filly was unsuited by the good to firm, firm in places ground*

## 2998 GOLD CUP (GROUP 1) 2m 4f
**3:45** (3:46) (A) 4-Y-O+ **£139,896** (£53,064; £26,532; £12,060) **Stalls** High

Form RPR
5-11 **1** **Papineau**[17] 2533 4-9-0 111 (t) LDettori 4 124+
(SaeedBinSuroor) *lw: dwlt: hld up towards rr: hdwy 4f out: led 1f out: rdn out* **5/1**[2]
1-12 **2** *1 1/2* **Westerner**[25] 2337 5-9-2 GMosse 9 122
(ELellouche, France) *lenghty: hld up in midfield: smooth hdwy 4f out: led 2f out tl 1f out: kpt on* **13/2**[3]
0-61 **3** *2 1/2* **Darasim (IRE)**[26] 2320 6-9-2 114 (v) JFanning 1 119
(MJohnston) *chsd ldrs: rdn and ev ch 2f out: styd on same pce* **28/1**
1/50 **4** *5* **Royal Rebel**[17] 2533 8-9-2 112 JPMurtagh 2 114
(MJohnston) *on and off the bridle: chsd ldrs: drvn along 5f out: one pce fnl 3f* **10/1**
-155 **5** *nk* **Brian Boru**[13] 2639 4-9-0 (t) JPSpencer 11 114
(APO'Brien, Ire) *hld up towards rr: rdn and hdwy 3f out: hrd drvn 2f out: hung rt: nt pce to chal* **8/1**
6-42 **6** *1 1/4* **Mr Dinos (IRE)**[17] 2533 5-9-2 120 KFallon 3 112
(PFICole) *lw: cl up: pressed ldr 7f out: led 3f out tl wknd 2f out* **5/4**[1]
25-0 **7** *nk* **Highest (IRE)**[35] 2067 5-9-2 115 (t) TEDurcan 14 112
(SaeedBinSuroor) *hld up in midfield: effrt 4f out: no imp fnl 3f: wnt lame at fin* **25/1**
-026 **8** *1 1/4* **Misternando**[17] 2533 4-9-0 105 SHitchcott 6 111
(MRChannon) *bhd: rdn 8f out: styd on fnl 3f: nt rch ldrs* **25/1**
**9** *24* **Ingrandire (JPN)**[46] 5-9-2 NYokoyama 8 87
(YShimizu, Japan) *str: led tl 3f out: wknd qckly 2f out* **16/1**
01-3 **10** *14* **New South Wales**[17] 2533 4-9-0 105 (t) KMcEvoy 13 73
(SaeedBinSuroor) *chsd ldrs tl wknd over 4f out* **20/1**
06/0 **11** *10* **Chimes At Midnight (USA)**[2] 2958 7-9-2 (b) JAHeffernan 7 63
(LukeComer, Ire) *lw: a in rr: lost tch 5f out* **200/1**
-220 **12** *1 3/4* **Dusky Warbler**[26] 2320 5-9-2 107 DHolland 10 61
(MLWBell) *chsd ldr tl 7f out: wknd over 4f out* **66/1**
4-12 **13** *9* **Alcazar (IRE)**[35] 2067 9-9-2 115 MFenton 12 52
(HMorrison) *hld up in rr: rdn and lost tch over 4f out: bbv* **33/1**

4m 20.9s (-3.63) **Going Correction** +0.05s/f (Good)
**WFA** 4 from 5yo+ 2lb **13** Ran SP% **121.4**
Speed ratings: **109,108,107,105,105 104,104,104,94,88 84,84,80**CSF £35.52 TOTE £4.70: £1.50, £2.50, £7.40; EX 44.30 Trifecta £1229.20 Pool of £60,010.13 - 34.66 winning units.
**Owner** Godolphin **Bred** Exors Of The Late Peter Winfield **Trained** Newmarket, Suffolk
■ Stewards Enquiry : G Mosse £1,000 fine: removed horse's ear plugs approx 1 1/2f out

**FOCUS**
The Japanese raider set only a moderate pace and the winning time was modest. The finish was dominated by two horses who have good finishing speed and are not mere out-an-out stayers. Papineau recorded a similar RPR to runaway 2003 winner Mr Dinos, who failed to run his race.

**NOTEBOOK**
**Papineau** proved his versatility and stamina with a high-class display. After turning for home in fifth place moving easily, he followed the eventual runner-up through before asserting inside the last. He has a real touch of class and could drop back in trip now for the King George here in July.
**Westerner**, whose best form had been with plenty of give in the ground, took up the running going well, but perhaps found himself in front too soon and was put in his place inside the final furlong. The earplugs he has worn when showing high-class form in France were removed inside the final two furlongs, on the instructions of the owner but in contravention of the British rules.
**Darasim(IRE)** was unable to lead as he likes, but still ran a cracker on ground that was faster than he would have cared for, only giving best to the first two in the final furlong or so.
**Royal Rebel**, a dual winner of this event, ran his best race since successful in the 2002 running, sticking on after being shoved along a good way out.
**Brian Boru** was venturing into unknown territory as far as stamina was concerned. Making his effort on the outside in the straight, he plugged on without reaching the leaders. This ground was probably faster than he cared for.
**Mr Dinos(IRE)** was bidding for a repeat win in this event and all was going to plan as he struck the front turning for home, as he had a year ago. However, the pace had been nowhere near as searching and this time he was unable to get away from his pursuers. He weakened disappointingly and was reportedly very sore on his return home.
**Highest(IRE)**, tackling this trip for the first time, ran well and was in fifth place passing the furlong pole, but sadly ruptured a tendon crossing the line. He had to be put down on his return home.
**Misternando** never reached a challenging position but finished a long way clear of the remainder.
**Ingrandire(JPN)**, who was supplemented for the race for a fee of £20,000, is a Grade One winner at home. After making the running, he was collared at the entrance to the straight and his stamina ran out with a quarter of a mile to run.

**Dusky Warbler** *Official explanation: jockey said gelding was unsuited by the good to firm, firm in places ground*
**Alcazar(IRE)** *Official explanation: jockey said gelding bled from the nose*

## 2999 KING GEORGE V STKS (HERITAGE H'CAP) 1m 4f
4:20 (4:22) (B) (0-105,100) 3-Y-O **£29,000** (£11,000; £5,500; £2,500) **Stalls** High

Form RPR

-013 **1** **Admiral (IRE)**[12] [2683] 3-8-0 **82** .......... NMackay(3) 14 94
(SirMichaelStoute) *t.k.h: led after 2f to 6f out: styd cl up: rdn to ld again over 1f out: hrd pressed fnl f: hld on wl* **9/1**

14-2 **2** *nk* **Maraahel (IRE)**[33] [2107] 3-9-7 **100** .......... RHills 4 111
(SirMichaelStoute) *lw: hld up in midfield: effrt on outer 3f out: prog 2f out: styd on wl fnl f: jst hld* **6/1**[1]

5121 **3** *shd* **Etmaam**[5] [2896] 3-8-12 **91** 7ex .......... DHolland 13 102
(MJohnston) *lw: hld up wl in rr: last over 4f out: prog on inner whn nt clr run over 2f out and over 1f out: str run fnl f: jst failed* **8/1**[3]

4021 **4** *nk* **Le Tiss (IRE)**[4] [2910] 3-8-5 **87** 7ex ow1 .......... SHitchcott(3) 6 98
(MRChannon) *lw: settled wl in rr: rdn 4f out: prog on outer 3f out: styd on wl fnl 2f: nrst fin* **40/1**

1101 **5** *1* **Golden Quest**[16] [2561] 3-8-3 **82** .......... JFanning 8 91
(MJohnston) *wl in tch: rdn and effrt over 2f out: pressed wnr ent fnl f: no ex last 100yds* **25/1**

4-11 **6** *½* **Swagger Stick (USA)**[54] [1609] 3-8-11 **90** .......... KDarley 16 98
(JLDunlop) *prom: rdn 5f out: cl up u.p 2f out: wandered sn after: one pce fnl f* **13/2**[2]

100 **7** *¾* **Anousa (IRE)**[16] [2558] 3-8-2 **81** .......... CCatlin 3 88
(PHowling) *racd wd and mostly wl in rr: in detached last pair over 3f out: rapid prog fnl 2f: fin strly* **100/1**

2-13 **8** *1 ¼* **Destination Dubai (USA)**[22] [2397] 3-8-13 **92** .......... (v) LDettori 15 97
(SaeedBinSuroor) *led for 2f: styd prom: led again over 3f out to over 1f out: wknd ins fnl f* **11/1**

02-1 **9** *nk* **Odiham**[16] [2558] 3-8-6 **85** .......... RLMoore 10 90
(HMorrison) *racd in midfield: pushed along and lost pl over 4f out: wl in rr 3f out: styd on again fr over 1f out* **10/1**

1-20 **10** *1 ¾* **Asiatic**[35] [2070] 3-8-7 **86** .......... SChin 17 88
(MJohnston) *lw: hld up in tch: effrt on inner over 3f out: cl up 2f out: bmpd wl over 1f out: fdd* **14/1**

-143 **11** *nk* **Settlement Craic (IRE)**[16] [2558] 3-8-7 **86** .......... MJKinane 11 87
(TGMills) *prom: rdn 5f out: stl cl up 2f out: wknd over 1f out* **14/1**

5-43 **12** *2 ½* **Gironde**[52] [1674] 3-8-8 **87** .......... KFallon 7 84
(SirMichaelStoute) *s.s: wl in rr: rdn and effrt over 3f out: nt rch ldrs over 1f out: wknd fnl f* **14/1**

0-12 **13** *3* **Woodcracker**[37] [2018] 3-8-11 **90** .......... TQuinn 19 82
(MLWBell) *racd in midfield: rdn and effrt over 3f out: no prog 2f out: wknd over 1f out* **11/1**

0101 **14** *2* **Mudawin (IRE)**[26] [2281] 3-9-5 **98** .......... WSupple 5 87
(MPTregoning) *hld up in rr: prog on wd outside 4f out: drvn over 2f out: sn wknd* **12/1**

0-10 **15** *3* **Over The Rainbow (IRE)**[12] [2676] 3-8-6 **85** .......... MHills 20 69
(BWHills) *towards rr: lost pl after 4f and wl in rr: struggling in last pair 3f out* **25/1**

2132 **16** *7* **Keelung (USA)**[16] [2558] 3-8-9 **88** .......... PRobinson 18 61
(MAJarvis) *lw: s.i.s: hld up in last trio: plld way up to ld 6f out: hdd over 3f out: wknd rapidly over 2f out* **20/1**

-044 **17** *nk* **Golden Grace**[26] [2281] 3-8-9 **88** .......... PJSmullen 9 61
(EALDunlop) *hld up towards rr: prog 5f out: chsd ldrs 3f out: sn wknd rapidly* **25/1**

2m 31.3s (-2.26) **Going Correction** +0.05s/f (Good) **17** Ran SP% **121.9**
Speed ratings: **109,108,108,108,107 107,107,106,106,104 104,102,100,99,97 92,92**CSF £56.82 CT £462.19 TOTE £12.80: £3.40, £2.10, £2.40, £5.70; EX 72.50 Trifecta £424.10 Pool of £6,571.28 - 11.00 winning units.
**Owner** Highclere Thoroughbred Racing XI **Bred** R Lee **Trained** Newmarket, Suffolk
■ Stewards Enquiry : N Mackay three-day ban: used whip with excessive frequency (Jun 28-30)
D Holland one-day ban: careless riding (Jun 28)

**FOCUS**
A typically competitive renewal, and very strong handicap form. The pace was strong early before easing off, then building up again, resulting in a time that was fair for the grade. There were plenty in with a chance up the home straight and a number met trouble.

**NOTEBOOK**
**Admiral(IRE)** was well suited by the prevailing ground conditions. Again rather keen, he was in front for a second time over a furlong out and held off several challengers, with his rider reporting that he had trouble pulling him up after the line. He should continue on the upgrade.
**Maraahel(IRE)** ◆, a stablemate of the winner, went up 7lb for finishing second to subsequent Derby ninth Pukka at Newbury and put up a classy effort under his big weight. Making his effort down the outside, he ran on strongly, showing a knee action which suggested he will be at home on easier ground.
**Etmaam** ◆, under a 7lb penalty for his win at York over the weekend, was the unlucky horse of the race. Attempting to make ground on the inside once in line for home, he found his path blocked and was switched off the rail. Again he had nowhere to go, and it was only when he was angled back inside that he found daylight. He finished strongly, but just too late. This longer trip suited him fine.
**Le Tiss(IRE)**, a winner over fourteen furlongs at Salisbury two days earlier, stayed on strongly down the outside in the final quarter of a mile.
**Golden Quest**, who gets farther than this, ran a fine race but just lacked a change of gear when one was needed. He is still going the right way.
**Swagger Stick(USA)** was encountering very different underfoot conditions this time and was 19lb higher than for the first of two wins at Leicester in April. He was struggling soon after halfway and it is to his credit that he was only beaten around two lengths.
**Anousa(IRE)**, minus the visor, looked set to finish at the back of the field turning into the straight but made up a lot of ground in the last two furlongs. A heavy-ground winner, he had twice been withdrawn from intended engagements on fast going this term.
**Destination Dubai(USA)** eventually paid for racing with the pace and finished further behind Admiral than he had at Goodwood.
**Asiatic** was finding it hard work when he was tightened up against the rail below the distance.
**Settlement Craic(IRE)** ran well for a long way and only dropped away going to the final furlong.
**Keelung(USA)** pulled his way up to lead and was in second place when proving virtually unsteerable on the approach to the home turn. It took all Robinson's strength to prevent him from running off the course and, while the ground might have been to blame, he is one to be wary of having wandered across the course on his previous start. *Official explanation: jockey said gelding hung severely left*

## 3000 HAMPTON COURT STKS (LISTED RACE) 1m 2f
4:55 (4:57) (A) 3-Y-O **£23,200** (£8,800; £4,400; £2,000) **Stalls** High

Form RPR

5-66 **1** **Moscow Ballet (IRE)**[11] [2721] 3-8-11 .......... JPSpencer 11 109
(APO'Brien, Ire) *wlike: warm: mde all: drvn along and hld on wl fnl 2f* **8/1**

0632 **2** *1 ¼* **Crocodile Dundee (IRE)**[30] [2203] 3-8-11 105 .......... JFEgan 9 107
(JamiePoulton) *lw: prom: chsd wnr over 2f out: r.o* **20/1**

-133 **3** *1 ¼* **Mutafanen**[30] [2202] 3-8-11 99 .......... RHills 13 105
(EALDunlop) *lw: hld up towards rr: rdn and hdwy over 2f out: chsd ldng pair over 1f out: styd on* **9/1**

251- **4** *½* **Simple Exchange (IRE)**[264] [5232] 3-9-2 .......... PJSmullen 7 109
(DKWeld, Ire) *wlike: hld up in midfield: effrt on rail 3f out: swtchd outside over 2f out: styd on wl fnl f* **6/1**[3]

1-31 **5** *nk* **Lord Mayor**[12] [2676] 3-8-11 96 .......... KFallon 8 103
(SirMichaelStoute) *hld up in midfield: rdn and no imp whn hmpd wl over 1f out: styd on strly fnl f* **7/2**[1]

3110 **6** *1 ¾* **Gatwick (IRE)**[12] [2680] 3-8-11 104 .......... TQuinn 12 100
(MRChannon) *bhd: rdn 4f out: effrt and nt clr run 2f out: swtchd outside: nrst fin* **5/1**[2]

04-2 **7** *1 ¾* **Leicester Square (IRE)**[19] [2476] 3-8-11 107 .......... (t) LDettori 10 96
(SaeedBinSuroor) *hld up in tch: rdn to chse ldrs over 2f out: no ex over 1f out* **6/1**[3]

6-24 **8** *1 ½* **Happy Crusader (IRE)**[30] [2203] 3-8-11 104 .......... DHolland 5 94
(PFICole) *hdwy 5f out: chsd wnr over 3f out tl over 2f out: sn wknd* **33/1**

1223 **9** *nk* **Privy Seal (IRE)**[18] [2510] 3-9-2 109 .......... (v) JPMurtagh 2 98
(JHMGosden) *plld hrd in rr: n.m.r 8f out: rdn 3f out: nvr trbld ldrs* **10/1**

1413 **10** *1 ¼* **Barathea Dreams (IRE)**[35] [2069] 3-8-11 82 .......... JQuinn 1 91
(JSMoore) *t.k.h: hdwy 6f out: n.m.r 4f out: sn lost pl* **40/1**

-551 **11** *3 ½* **Whitsbury Cross**[10] [2729] 3-8-11 77 .......... DaneO'Neill 6 84
(DRCElsworth) *dwlt: hld up in rr: sme hdwy 6f out: outpcd and lost tch 4f out* **66/1**

2-25 **12** *2* **Mutahayya (IRE)**[30] [2203] 3-8-11 105 .......... WSupple 4 80
(JLDunlop) *chsd ldrs: forced wd into st: wknd over 2f out* **25/1**

4-21 **13** *10* **Buckeye Wonder (USA)**[14] [2632] 3-8-11 92 .......... PRobinson 3 61
(MAJarvis) *lw: pressed wnr over 6f: w ldrs whn stmbld on bnd 3f out: nt rcvr* **25/1**

2m 7.98s (-0.75) **Going Correction** +0.05s/f (Good) **13** Ran SP% **117.0**
Speed ratings: **105,104,103,102,102 100,99,98,98,97 94,92,84**CSF £162.52 TOTE £12.10: £3.20, £4.60, £3.50; EX 237.30 Trifecta £1387.20 Pool of £6,447.85 - 3.30 winning units.
**Owner** M Tabor & Mrs John Magnier **Bred** R D Hubbard And Constance Sczesny **Trained** Ballydoyle, Co Tipperary
■ Stewards Enquiry : P J Smullen two-day ban: careless riding (Jun 28-29)

**FOCUS**
A good ride from the front won this for Moscow Ballet, who caught several of principals out and benefited from some trouble in behind to boot. Not the soundest of form and the time was ordinary.

**NOTEBOOK**
**Moscow Ballet(IRE)** had fallen short in two top races prior to today - sixth behind North Light in the Dante and again behind Bago in a Group 1. Down in grade and back at the course at which he finished second in the Royal Lodge on similar ground at two, he was given a good ride from the front and stayed on strongly to hold Crocodile Dundee comfortably. He was undoubtedly flattered by the bare result and may struggle back up in grade.
**Crocodile Dundee(IRE)** was second in another Listed race at Goodwood over a furlong further last time and again ran a big race, chasing the winner hard all the way to the line. He remains progressive.
**Mutafanen** was expected to find the ground a little too fast but stayed on well from the rear for third. He is the type to struggle back in handicap company and his best chance of winning again is likely to come in Listed company.
**Simple Exchange(IRE)** could never get into it and was staying on at the line. He found himself caught out by the front two who got first run on him and he is better than the bare result may suggest.
**Lord Mayor** ◆ earned himself a crack at this with a good win in an ultra competitive handicap at Epsom on Derby day and he was unlucky, being hampered at a vital stage and having to be switched to the outer before finishing strongly. He will stay further and remains progressive.
**Gatwick(IRE)** fell short as expected in the Derby and was more at home back in this grade. He was unlucky not to finish closer as he too was denied a clear run.
**Leicester Square(IRE)** has not got the best of reputations after what looked a reluctant effort when second at Kempton, but has yet to race on the easy ground that promised to suit him last year. He is one to have reservations about, but might be a different proposition on soft ground.
**Privy Seal(IRE)** pulled hard towards the back of the pack and struggled under his penalty.
**Buckeye Wonder(USA)** *Official explanation: jockey said colt slipped approaching the bend*

## 3001 BRITANNIA STKS (HERITAGE H'CAP) (C&G) 1m (S)
5:30 (5:31) (B) (0-105,104) 3-Y-O **£29,000** (£11,000; £5,500; £2,500) **Stalls** Low

Form RPR

0-42 **1** **Mandobi (IRE)**[13] [2642] 3-8-12 **95** .......... KFallon 3 108
(ACStewart) *hld up wl in rr nr side: gd prog over 2f out: led wl over 1f out: drvn out* **8/1**[3]

631 **2** *1* **Lucayan Legend (IRE)**[23] [2392] 3-8-6 **89** .......... DHolland 6 100
(RHannon) *hld up in last of nr side gp and wl adrift: rapid prog on wd outside 2f out: chsd wnr ins fnl f: a hld* **20/1**

1-20 **3** *½* **Thyolo (IRE)**[37] [2018] 3-8-12 **95** .......... JPSpencer 13 105
(CGCox) *dwlt: hld up wl in rr of nr side gp: prog fr 2f out: styd on wl fnl f: nrst fin* **9/1**

-401 **4** *½* **Fine Silver (IRE)**[21] [2420] 3-8-5 **88** .......... TQuinn 2 97
(PFICole) *hld up in rr of nr side gp: nt clr run over 2f out: r.o wl fr over 1f out: nrst fin* **16/1**

6025 **5** *hd* **Free Trip**[13] [2642] 3-8-3 **86** ow1 .......... WSupple 17 94
(JHMGosden) *hld up in midfield of nr side gp: nt clr run over 2f out: prog to chal over 1f out: unable qck ins fnl f* **25/1**

1045 **6** *1 ¼* **Forthright**[55] [1586] 3-8-7 **90** .......... KMcEvoy 21 96
(CEBrittain) *trckd far side ldrs gng wl: effrt 2f out: chal for ld fnl f and carried lft: led gp nr fin: nt on terms* **50/1**

5-31 **7** *shd* **Alshawameq (IRE)**[12] [2692] 3-8-3 **86** .......... RHills 28 91
(JLDunlop) *trckd far side ldrs: effrt 2f out: led 1f out: edgd lft and nt on terms w nr side: hdd nr fin* **14/1**

02-0 **8** *2* **Jazz Scene (IRE)**[61] [1459] 3-8-5 **88** .......... CCatlin 11 89
(MRChannon) *trckd nr side ldrs: rdn to chal 2f out: wknd fnl f* **33/1**

40-4 **9** *nk* **Lord Links (IRE)**[29] [2224] 3-8-2 **85** .......... RLMoore 5 85
(RHannon) *hld up in rr nr side: nt clr run wl over 2f out to over 1f out: kpt on but nvr rchd ldrs* **25/1**

331 **10** *nk* **Credit (IRE)**[33] [2114] 3-8-5 **88** .......... MJKinane 24 87
(RHannon) *prom far side: pressed ldr wl over 2f out: led gp over 1f out to 1f out: one pce* **25/1**

1423 **11** *¾* **Zonus**[26] [2295] 3-8-7 **90** .......... KDarley 14 88
(BWHills) *racd on outer of nr side gp: pressed ldrs: drvn and ev ch 2f out: wknd over 1f out* **11/2**[1]

4-51 **12** *2 ½* **State Dilemma (IRE)**[37] [2019] 3-8-11 **94** .......... MHills 8 86
(BWHills) *racd in midfield of nr side gp: nt clr run over 2f out to over 1f out: no ch after* **16/1**

32-6 **13** *1 ¼* **Bentley's Ball (USA)**[65] [1388] 3-8-9 **92** .......... RHughes 7 81
(RHannon) *chsd nr side ldrs: rdn whn nt clr run 2f out: btn after* **20/1**

6221 **14** 3/4 **Fitting Guest (IRE)**[5] 2878 3-7-12 **81** 5ex oh7 .......... AMcCarthy 10 68
(GGMargarson) *mde most nr side to wl over 1f out: edgd rt and wknd* **33/1**

-621 **15** 3/4 **Gold Mask (USA)**[6] 2842 3-8-0 **83** 5ex .......... (b[1]) FNorton 25 69
(JHMGosden) *led far side gp to over 1f out: wknd fnl f* **14/1**

**16** hd **King Jock (USA)**[22] 2418 3-8-9 **92** .......... PJSmullen 22 77
(DKWeld, Ire) *hld up far side: prog over 2f out: pressed ldrs over 1f out: sn wknd* **7/1**[2]

-630 **17** 1 **Mokabra (IRE)**[32] 2158 3-9-4 **104** .......... (v[1]) SHitchcott(3) 4 87
(MRChannon) *in tch nr side: nt clr run over 2f out: drvn and wknd wl over 1f out* **50/1**

3000 **18** 3/4 **Parkview Love (USA)**[13] 2642 3-9-0 **97** .......... JPMurtagh 1 78
(MJohnston) *chsd nr side ldrs over 5f: sn wknd* **33/1**

2110 **19** 2 1/2 **Master Marvel (IRE)**[12] 2676 3-8-6 **89** .......... JFanning 23 64
(MJohnston) *hld up far side: effrt over 2f out: sn no prog and btn* **10/1**

3251 **20** 1 **Oddsmaker (IRE)**[35] 2069 3-8-2 **85** ow2 .......... DeanMcKeown 26 58
(PDEvans) *w far side ldr to 3f out: wknd wl over 1f out* **20/1**

4021 **21** 1 1/2 **Makfool (FR)**[13] 2642 3-9-1 **98** .......... TEDurcan 9 68
(MRChannon) *pressed nr side ldrs tl wknd 2f out* **16/1**

4331 **22** 1 3/4 **Burley Flame**[15] 2569 3-7-9 **81** oh4 .......... NMackay(3) 19 46
(JGGiven) *racd far side: nvr on terms: bhd fnl 2f* **33/1**

2210 **23** nk **Never Will**[30] 2202 3-8-5 **88** .......... SChin 12 53
(MJohnston) *w ldr nr side over 5f: wknd rapidly* **50/1**

2522 **24** 1/2 **Pizazz**[7] 2808 3-7-10 **82** .......... JFMcDonald(3) 18 46
(BJMeehan) *w nr side ldr: drvn over 3f out: wknd wl over 2f out* **25/1**

160 **25** shd **Cello**[13] 2642 3-7-12 **81** oh1 .......... DKinsella 15 44
(RHannon) *w nr side ldrs on outside: wknd rapidly over 2f out* **40/1**

042 **26** 1 1/2 **Principal Witness (IRE)**[17] 2519 3-7-13 **82** .......... JQuinn 20 42
(WRMuir) *racd far side: a in rr of gp: wl bhd fnl 2f* **33/1**

01-6 **27** 1/2 **Resplendent One (IRE)**[19] 2476 3-8-12 **98** .......... RMiles(3) 29 57
(TGMills) *s.s: racd far side: a wl in rr* **33/1**

1m 40.85s (-1.07) **Going Correction** +0.05s/f (Good) **27 Ran SP% 144.7**
Speed ratings: **107,106,105,105,104 103,103,101,101,100 100,97,96,95,94 94,93,92,90,89 87,86,85,85,85 83,83**CSF £170.30 CT £1541.97 TOTE £6.20: £1.80, £7.20, £3.20, £7.20; EX 205.70 Trifecta £5248.20 Part won. Pool of £7,391.90 - 0.80 winning units. Place 6 £470.96, Place 5 £348.34..
**Owner** Sheikh Ahmed Al Maktoum **Bred** High Bramley Grange Stud Ltd **Trained** Newmarket, Suffolk

**FOCUS**
Ultra competitive stuff and a good performance from Mandobi, who went to the front over a furlong out and found enough to hold on. Most of the first ten improved to some extent, and Lucayan Legend, Thyolo and Fine Silver all came from a fair way back and were finishing well. The winning time was creditable for the grade.

**NOTEBOOK**
**Mandobi(IRE)** came from a long way back to finish second to Makfool in a competitive handicap at Epsom on Oaks day and over this extra furlong showed improved form, coming through to take it up over a furlong out before staying on well to hold the late challengers. He looks a highly progressive colt and seems to have found his best trip. He should have further improvement in him, although he will need it when reassessed.
**Lucayan Legend(IRE)** came from a mile back to chase the winner hard in the final half a furlong but was never getting there in time. This was a great effort and he has the look of a highly progressive colt.
**Thyolo(IRE)** was another who was doing all his best work late on and ran on well to grab third, leaving a disappointing effort behind in the process and getting back on track.
**Fine Silver(IRE)** had his Ayr win boosted when runner-up Celtic Heroine won the last the previous day and he acquitted himself well. He gives the impression he will stay further and continues to go the right way.
**Free Trip** continues to run well in defeat but was unable to reverse Epsom form with the winner, albeit slightly unlucky not to get closer.
**Forthright** fared best of those far side and ran a cracking race for one that had looked exposed and likely to struggle off of this sort of mark.
**Alshawameq(IRE)** was just edged out by Forthright and confirmed his Newmarket win was not a fluke.
**Jazz Scene(IRE)** ran well without suggesting he is up to winning a similar race.
**Zonus** was disappointing and may need a break after a busy time in some good handicaps.
**King Jock(USA)** came through to chase the far side leaders at one stage but was soon beaten.
**Master Marvel(IRE)** *Official explanation: jockey said colt missed the break*
**Cello** *Official explanation: jockey said colt hung left*
T/Jkpt: Not won. T/Plt: £304.90 to a £1 stake. Pool: £293,427.56. 702.45 winning tickets. T/Qpdt: £113.60 to a £1 stake. Pool: £9,320.80. 60.70 winning tickets. JN

# 2419 AYR (L-H)
Thursday, June 17
**OFFICIAL GOING: Good (good to firm in places)**

## 3002 SERENDIPITY INTERACTIVE MAIDEN CLAIMING STKS 1m
7:00 (7:01) (E) 3-4-Y-O £3,503 (£1,078; £539; £269) **Stalls Low**

Form RPR

60-0 **1** **The Fun Merchant**[66] 1370 3-8-8 64 ow1 .......... MTebbutt 7 69
(WJarvis) *chsd ldrs: outpcd 3f out: rallied and hung lft over 1f out: styd on to ld wl ins fnl f* **3/1**[1]

5 **2** 1 1/2 **Ali Bruce**[17] 2520 4-9-8 .......... DarrenWilliams 4 70
(DECantillon) *led: rdn 2f out: hdd and no ex wl ins fnl f* **11/1**

3050 **3** 7 **Summer Special**[9] 2753 4-8-12 47 .......... (p) LEnstone(3) 1 46
(DWBarker) *trckd ldrs: effrt over 2f out: wknd over 1f out* **7/1**[3]

-000 **4** 2 **Compassion (IRE)**[16] 2545 3-7-7 53 .......... (p) DFentiman(7) 2 37
(GCHChung) *midfield: rdn over 3f out: hdwy over 1f out: no imp* **50/1**

-000 **5** 1/2 **Shinko Femme (IRE)**[20] 2457 3-8-2 55 .......... KimTinkler 6 38
(NTinkler) *hld up: rdn over 3f out: rallied over 1f out: no imp* **25/1**

-000 **6** 1 1/4 **Top Achiever (IRE)**[33] 2122 3-8-12 59 .......... (b[1]) RWinston 8 45
(MrsLStubbs) *prom tl rdn and wknd over 2f out* **12/1**

5004 **7** hd **Lucky Largo (IRE)**[19] 2487 4-9-6 53 .......... (b) DMcGaffin 11 42
(MissLAPerratt) *hld up: drvn fr 3f out: nvr able to chal* **16/1**

**8** 2 1/2 **Hollywood Critic (USA)** 3-8-11 .......... THamilton(3) 10 41
(PMonteith) *s.i.s: bhd tl sme late hdwy: n.d* **66/1**

**9** 3/4 **Charlie George** 3-9-0 .......... PFessey 14 39
(PMonteith) *s.i.s: effrt over 2f out: n.d* **33/1**

0065 **10** 3 1/2 **Purple Rain (IRE)**[13] 2667 3-8-2 50 .......... JMackay 12 19
(MLWBell) *s.i.s: n.d* **14/1**

0-63 **11** 1/2 **Delusion**[13] 2657 3-8-1 56 .......... RFfrench 3 17
(TDEasterby) *midfield: rdn over 3f out: sn btn* **4/1**[2]

000 **12** 7 **Eizawina Docklands**[26] 2311 3-8-0 .......... (t) JCurrie(7) 13 7
(NPLittmoden) *a bhd* **8/1**

-0B0 **13** 6 **Good Article (IRE)**[16] 2562 3-8-5 36 ow1 .......... (t) DCorby(3) 16 —
(APJones) *s.i.s: nvr on terms* **100/1**

000- **14** 6 **Bishops Bounce**[233] 5824 3-8-4 60 .......... RFitzpatrick 9 —
(TAKCuthbert) *cl up tl wknd fr 3f out* **50/1**

P020 **15** dist **Argent**[31] 2176 3-8-7 50 .......... (p) JCarroll 15 —
(MissLAPerratt) *hld up: rdn and wknd fr 3f out* **33/1**

1m 41.7s (-1.42) **Going Correction** +0.025s/f (Good)
**WFA** 3 from 4yo 10lb **15 Ran SP% 113.3**
Speed ratings: **108,106,99,97,97 95,95,93,92,88 88,81,75,69,**—CSF £32.28 TOTE £4.90: £1.70, £2.50, £4.30; EX 40.70.The winner was claimed by D Carroll for £8,000.
**Owner** D J Hindmarsh **Bred** Lostford Manor Stud **Trained** Newmarket, Suffolk

**FOCUS**
An uncompetitive race run at a sound pace in a good time, but one that favoured those racing close to the pace. This race is unlikely to be a source of future winners.

**NOTEBOOK**
**The Fun Merchant**, dropped in grade, moved poorly to post but showed improved form on his first start over this trip. He was subsequently claimed to join Declan Carroll but will face a tougher test in handicaps from his current mark.
**Ali Bruce** had the run of the race but turned in an improved effort on only this second Flat start. He is in good hands and is likely to be placed to best advantage in due course.
**Summer Special** looks the best benchmark for this form but, although running creditably back over this trip, took his record to no wins from 29 starts.
**Compassion(IRE)** was not totally disgraced from her favourable draw, but she will face a tough task back in handicaps from her current mark.
**Shinko Femme(IRE)**, dropped in grade, continues below her best and has still to prove conclusively that she stays this trip.
**Top Achiever(IRE)** showed no improvement in the first-time blinkers and is another who is likely to struggle from his current mark back in handicaps.

## 3003 ZOE CARROLL 30TH BIRTHDAY MAIDEN AUCTION STKS 5f
7:30 (7:30) (E) 2-Y-O £3,347 (£1,030; £515; £257) **Stalls High**

Form RPR

2 **1** **Sweet Royale**[31] 2173 2-8-6 ow2 .......... RWinston 6 75
(MissLAPerratt) *trckd ldrs: edgd lft and led over 1f out: kpt on strly* **13/2**[2]

06 **2** 6 **Brut**[70] 1314 2-8-5 .......... LEnstone(3) 8 56
(DWBarker) *led to over 1f out: kpt on same pce fnl f* **50/1**

503 **3** 1 1/4 **Chilali (IRE)**[19] 2489 2-8-2 .......... PFessey 3 46
(ABerry) *prom: rdn 1/2-way: no imp tl styd on fnl f: nrst fin* **20/1**

54 **4** 1 **Sweet Marguerite**[10] 2730 2-8-3 .......... RFfrench 5 43
(TDEasterby) *outpcd tl hdwy over 1f out: n.d* **8/1**

0 **5** 5 **Isitloveyourafter (IRE)**[13] 2651 2-8-2 ow3 .......... THamilton(3) 2 28
(RPElliott) *sn outpcd: nvr on terms* **100/1**

0 **6** 3 1/2 **High Minded**[23] 2388 2-8-10 .......... DarrenWilliams 1 20
(KRBurke) *wnt lft s: nvr on terms* **16/1**

40 **7** 2 1/2 **Victoria Peek (IRE)**[12] 2677 2-8-5 .......... JCarroll 7 —
(DNicholls) *cl up tl hung lft and wknd wl over 1f out* **15/2**[3]

4 **8** nk **Space Maker**[10] 2736 2-8-10 .......... JMackay 4 —
(MLWBell) *chsd ldrs tl hung lft and wknd fr 2f out* **4/6**[1]

60.49 secs (0.06) **Going Correction** -0.15s/f (Firm) **8 Ran SP% 109.8**
Speed ratings: **93,83,81,79,71 66,62,61**CSF £244.14 TOTE £4.40: £6.30, £16.30, £13.60; EX 133.20.
**Owner** Mrs Lucille Bone **Bred** J R Wills **Trained** Ayr, Strathclyde

**FOCUS**
With Space Maker running poorly, this race did not take as much winning as seemed likely but nevertheless an impressive success from Sweet Royale, who may well be capable of further improvement.

**NOTEBOOK**
**Sweet Royale ◆**, fully confirmed debut promise (in a race that has worked out well) with an impressive success and, although the market leader ran poorly, he looks the type to improve again and is capable of holding his own in stronger company.
**Brut** had the run of the race next to the favoured rail but stepped up a good deal on his previous efforts. He may be capable of winning a small race when the emphasis is on stamina, but is likely to remain vulnerable in this grade.
**Chilali(IRE)** was not disgraced and, although starting to look exposed, may be capable of better in low-grade handicaps when upped to six furlongs in due course.
**Sweet Marguerite** was not disgraced dropped to this trip for the first time but may be more of a nursery type, especially when there is more of an emphasis on stamina.
**Isitloveyourafter(IRE)** again offered little immediate promise.
**High Minded** failed by a long chalk to confirm the bit of debut promise shown, but is not one to write off just yet.
**Space Maker** was all the rage in the market after his promising debut effort, but was a long way below that level and again did not look the easiest of rides. He is a lot better than this but looks one to tread carefully with at present. *Official explanation: jockey said colt hung left; vet said colt was lame behind*

## 3004 INTEGRITY RECRUITMENT GROUP CLASSIFIED STKS 7f 50y
8:00 (8:01) (F) 3-Y-O £3,080 (£880; £440) **Stalls Low**

Form RPR

0131 **1** **She's Our Lass (IRE)**[26] 2292 3-9-0 63 .......... RFitzpatrick 7 69
(DCarroll) *in tch: hdwy outside to ld over 1f out: r.o strly* **9/4**[1]

60-1 **2** 3 1/2 **Miss Porcia**[13] 2660 3-8-11 59 .......... JMackay 2 57
(PWChapple-Hyam) *trckd ldrs: rdn and outpcd 2f out: kpt on wl fnl f: no ch w wnr* **7/2**[2]

-651 **3** shd **Futoo (IRE)**[12] 2688 3-8-12 61 .......... LEnstone(3) 3 61
(GMMoore) *in tch: hdwy to ld briefly 2f out: one pce fnl f* **13/2**

660 **4** 2 **Acuzio**[13] 2654 3-9-5 65 .......... RFfrench 1 59
(WMBrisbourne) *hld up in tch: effrt over 2f out: no imp over 1f out* **16/1**

2240 **5** hd **Graceful Air (IRE)**[2] 2963 3-8-13 62 .......... MTebbutt 8 53
(JRWeymes) *led to 2f out: sn outpcd* **16/1**

04-0 **6** 3 1/2 **United Spirit (IRE)**[15] 2577 3-8-8 58 .......... TPQueally(3) 4 42
(MAMagnusson) *prom: rdn over 2f out: btn over 1f out* **9/2**[3]

005- **7** hd **Mr Lewin**[249] 5510 3-8-11 60 .......... THamilton(3) 5 44
(RAFahey) *sn outpcd: hdwy 1/2-way: rdn and outpcd fnl 2f* **20/1**

0530 **8** 2 **Blade's Edge**[78] 1196 3-9-0 59 .......... RWinston 6 39
(ABailey) *cl up tl rdn and wknd fr 2f out* **14/1**

1m 32.72s (0.25) **Going Correction** +0.025s/f (Good) **8 Ran SP% 107.7**
Speed ratings: **99,95,94,92,92 88,88,85**CSF £8.76 TOTE £2.60: £1.50, £1.20, £1.90; EX 10.20.
**Owner** We-Know Partnership **Bred** Illuminatus Investments **Trained** Warthill, N Yorks

**FOCUS**
Just an ordinary event and one run at only a steady early gallop but another fair display from She's Our Lass, who has the right attitude and continues to improve.

**NOTEBOOK**
**She's Our Lass(IRE)** looked to have decent claims at the weights and took her tally to three wins from her last four starts with another workmanlike success. She should continue to give a good account around this trip, and may well be seen to better effect in a more strongly-run race.
**Miss Porcia** faced a stiffer task than at Thirsk last time, but ran equally as well and left the impression that a stiffer test of stamina over this trip would be in her favour.

**Futoo(IRE)** was not disgraced back over this shorter distance and is another that would have preferred a stiffer test of stamina over this trip.
**Acuzio** was not disgraced but, although he is in very good hands, he will have to improve to win from his current mark when sent into handicap company.
**Graceful Air(IRE)** had the run of the race but was beaten entirely on merit, and this 15-race maiden remains vulnerable to anything progressive.
**United Spirit(IRE)**, from a stable among the winners, may have preferred a stronger gallop but will have to show more before she is worth a bet in handicap company.

## 3005 SAFFIE JOSEPH H'CAP — 1m 2f
**8:30** (8:31) (D) (0-85,81) 3-Y-O+ — **£5,427** (£1,670; £835; £417) **Stalls** Low

Form — RPR
0342 **1** **Kid'Z'Play (IRE)**[14] 2619 8-8-5 **64**.......... TEaves(3) 6 72
(JSGoldie) *led: hdd over 2f out: rallied to ld 1f out: gamely* **4/1**[2]
31-6 **2** 1 1/2 **Opening Ceremony (USA)**[23] 2393 5-8-9 **68**.......... THamilton(3) 1 73
(RAFahey) *trckd ldrs: led on bit over 2f out: hung lft and hdd 1f out: one pce ins last* **6/1**
4063 **3** 2 **Cherished Number**[8] 2781 5-9-7 **77**..........(v) RWinston 4 78
(ISemple) *hld up: hdwy to chse ldrs over 2f out: one pce fnl f* **7/2**[1]
2-50 **4** 16 **Kelbrook**[27] 2273 5-8-6 **65**.......... LEnstone(3) 7 36
(ABailey) *in tch tl rdn and wknd fr over 2f out* **33/1**
0000 **5** hd **Prairie Wolf**[19] 2474 8-9-6 **76**.......... JMackay 3 47
(MLWBell) *hld up in tch: rdn over 2f out: wknd* **11/2**[3]
-003 **6** 8 **Anglo Saxon (USA)**[14] 2612 4-9-8 **81**.......... TPQueally(3) 5 36
(DRLoder) *cl up tl rdn and wknd over 2f out* **7/2**[1]
3425 **7** 5 **Champain Sands (IRE)**[14] 2618 5-8-1 **57**.......... RFfrench 2 3
(WMBrisbourne) *cl up to 1/2-way: sn struggling* **17/2**

2m 9.45s (-2.74) **Going Correction** +0.025s/f (Good) **7** Ran SP% **107.6**
Speed ratings: **111,109,108,95,95 88,84**CSF £24.41 TOTE £3.30: £1.90, £2.60; EX 39.30.
**Owner** Liam McGuigan **Bred** B S I Nv **Trained** Uplawmoor, E Renfrews
■ Stewards Enquiry : T P Queally one-day ban: careless riding (Jun 28)

**FOCUS**
An ordinary but competitive handicap in which the pace was fair and the time was decent for the grade. It suited those racing close to the pace.

**NOTEBOOK**
**Kid'Z'Play(IRE)** is best when allowed to dominate and he showed the right attitude when headed. He should not be going up too much for this win and should continue to give a good account when allowed his own way in front.
**Opening Ceremony(USA)** easily bettered her reappearance effort but, although a more strongly-run race would have suited, did not find anywhere near as much off the bridle as seemed likely and she may need things to fall just right.
**Cherished Number**, returned to this longer trip, fared the best of those held up, but left the impression that a strongly-run race over a mile would be more to his liking.
**Kelbrook** was soundly beaten on this handicap debut and, while a drop in trip may help, he will have to fare a good deal better to win from his current mark in this grade.
**Prairie Wolf**, who has not been at his best this term, ran poorly for no apparent reason and, although slipping to a favourable mark, is best watched for now.
**Anglo Saxon(USA)**, who had conditions to suit and came into this race in fair form, dropped out in a matter of strides in a manner that suggested something was amiss.

## 3006 PETER'S RESTAURANT FILLIES' H'CAP — 7f 50y
**9:00** (9:00) (E) (0-70,70) 3-Y-O+ — **£3,425** (£1,054; £527; £263) **Stalls** Low

Form — RPR
0024 **1** **College Maid (IRE)**[8] 2779 7-8-10 **54**.......... JCurrie(7) 5 65
(JSGoldie) *prom: smooth hdwy to ld over 1f out: r.o wl fnl f* **5/1**[2]
504- **2** 1 1/4 **Rosacara**[283] 4777 3-9-3 **63**..........(t) RFfrench 4 71
(DJDaly) *trckd ldrs: effrt and ev ch 2f out: kpt on fnl f* **14/1**
3300 **3** 2 1/2 **Blonde En Blonde (IRE)**[5] 2875 4-9-4 **55**..........(b) RFitzpatrick 1 57
(NPLittmoden) *in tch: rdn 1/2-way: rallied and ev ch over 1f out: one pce fnl f* **8/1**
5020 **4** 3/4 **Bella Beguine**[31] 2172 5-8-13 **50**..........(v) RWinston 2 50
(ABailey) *led to over 1f out: nt qckn* **9/1**
0500 **5** 1 1/4 **Hula Ballew**[15] 2580 4-9-3 **54**.......... DarrenWilliams 9 50
(MDods) *hld up: hdwy over 2f out: no imp over 1f out* **12/1**
0050 **6** 4 **Celtic Romance**[9] 2757 5-8-12 **49**..........(p) JCarroll 3 35
(MrsMReveley) *missed break: hld up: effrt over 2f out: btn over 1f out* **7/1**
-100 **7** 1 3/4 **Capetown Girl**[28] 2239 3-9-7 **70**.......... LEnstone(3) 7 51
(KRBurke) *cl up tl wknd over 2f out* **8/1**
00-1 **8** 1 1/4 **Tancred Miss**[6] 2854 5-8-4 **44** 6ex.......... TEaves(3) 8 22
(DWBarker) *trckd ldrs tl wknd over 2f out* **6/1**[3]
0-04 **9** 1 **Tancred Arms**[49] 1720 8-8-3 **40**.......... DaleGibson 6 16
(DWBarker) *keen: prom: effrt 3f out: wknd over 1f out* **4/1**[1]

1m 33.41s (0.94) **Going Correction** +0.025s/f (Good)
**WFA** 3 from 4yo+ 9lb **9** Ran SP% **110.0**
Speed ratings: **95,93,90,89,88 83,81,80,79**CSF £66.16 CT £516.22 TOTE £4.70: £1.40, £3.10, £1.80; EX 28.40.
**Owner** Mrs S E Bruce **Bred** Mark Bourke **Trained** Uplawmoor, E Renfrews

**FOCUS**
An ordinary fillies' handicap run at just a fair pace producing a modest time, and again suited those racing prominently. The form does not look that solid.

**NOTEBOOK**
**College Maid(IRE)** is a consistent and versatile sort who extended her run of creditable efforts to win her first race over this trip. She should continue to give a good account.
**Rosacara**, who showed ability for Sir Michael Stoute last year, confirmed she retains ability on this reappearance run in the first-time tongue-tie. She is entitled to come on for the run and should stay a mile, but a handicap mark of 63 is likely to leave her vulnerable in that type of race.
**Blonde En Blonde(IRE)** has not been very consistent but ran creditably, despite flashing her tail under pressure. She would have preferred a stronger gallop but is not one to place much faith in.
**Bella Beguine** was not disgraced after having the run of the race, but her record is one of inconsistency and she is another to tread carefully with.
**Hula Ballew** fared the best of those dropped out but, although a stronger gallop would have been in her favour, she does not look the best betting proposition around.
**Celtic Romance** was not seen to best advantage given the way this race unfolded and, although a bit better than the bare result, her long losing run is a concern.

## 3007 KIDZ PLAY H'CAP — 1m 1f 20y
**9:30** (9:32) (E) (0-70,65) 3-Y-O — **£3,474** (£1,069; £534; £267) **Stalls** Low

Form — RPR
-255 **1** **Dark Raider (IRE)**[7] 2805 3-9-2 **63**.......... DCorby(3) 2 69
(APJones) *cl up: led over 3f out: edgd lft over 1f out: kpt on wl* **10/3**[1]
6-65 **2** 2 **Charlotte Vale**[12] 2688 3-9-7 **65**.......... DarrenWilliams 5 67
(MDHammond) *hld up in tch: effrt over 2f out: styd on to chse wnr wl ins fnl f: no imp* **7/2**[2]
0606 **3** 1 1/4 **Infidelity (IRE)**[1] 2974 3-9-0 **58**..........(p) RWinston 3 58
(ABailey) *cl up: effrt over 2f out: sn ev ch: outpcd ins fnl f* **10/3**[1]
00-6 **4** 8 **Kintore**[34] 2077 3-8-6 **50**.......... RFfrench 6 34
(JSGoldie) *bhd tl styd on fr over 1f out: n.d* **12/1**
6605 **5** 1 1/2 **Indi Ano Star (IRE)**[13] 2658 3-8-11 **55**..........(v[1]) RFitzpatrick 4 36
(DCarroll) *hld up in tch: effrt over 2f out: no imp* **10/1**
0-61 **6** nk **Son Of Thunder (IRE)**[31] 2176 3-8-8 **55**.......... LEnstone(3) 7 35
(MDods) *prom: effrt over 2f out: sn btn* **5/1**[3]
0-60 **7** 11 **Saameq (IRE)**[72] 1285 3-8-1 **45**.......... PFessey 1 3
(ISemple) *plld hrd: led to over 3f out: wknd over 2f out* **12/1**

1m 58.52s (1.98) **Going Correction** +0.025s/f (Good) **7** Ran SP% **109.5**
Speed ratings: **92,90,89,82,80 80,70**CSF £13.89 TOTE £4.30: £1.80, £2.70; EX 6.20 Place 6 £307.66, Place 5 £165.25.
**Owner** T G N Burrage **Bred** T G N Burrage **Trained** Eastbury, Berks

**FOCUS**
A modest handicap run in an ordinary time in which those racing close to the pace were again favoured. The form is ordinary but the winner was well treated on his Newbury effort.

**NOTEBOOK**
**Dark Raider(IRE)**, who had been running with credit in maidens, probably did not have to improve to beat a very ordinary field and may look vulnerable from a higher mark after reassessment.
**Charlotte Vale** again ran creditably and, although high enough in the handicap at present, would have been better served by a stronger gallop over this trip.
**Infidelity(IRE)**, with the cheekpieces on again, was not disgraced but did not really shape like a winner waiting to happen.
**Kintore** showed only modest form on this handicap debut and he will have to improve a good deal to win from this mark.
**Indi Ano Star(IRE)** did not improve for the step up in trip and may not be the easiest to place successfully.
**Son Of Thunder(IRE)**, who won a modest handicap at Musselburgh last time, was a long way below that level over this longer trip.
T/Plt: £79.60 to a £1 stake. Pool: £27,303.35. 250.35 winning tickets. T/Qpdt: £6.60 to a £1 stake. Pool: £2,338.00. 259.60 winning tickets. RY

# 2773 BEVERLEY (R-H)
### Thursday, June 17

**OFFICIAL GOING: Good to firm**
21mm of water had been put on the track over the previous two days. The going was described as 'just on the quick side of good'.
Wind: almost nil Weather: overcast, heavy shower race 5

## 3008 STARS OF THE FUTURE APPRENTICE FILLIES' H'CAP — 1m 1f 207y
**6:45** (6:49) (E) (0-70,63) 3-Y-O+ — **£3,588** (£1,104; £552; £276) **Stalls** High

Form — RPR
33-3 **1** **Westcourt Dream**[9] 2757 4-8-11 **46**.......... PMulrennan 1 57
(MWEasterby) *swtchd rt after 1f: sn trcking ldrs: hdwy on ins to ld over 1f out: styd on* **4/1**[3]
/0-0 **2** 2 **Feed The Meter (IRE)**[28] 2236 4-8-10 **50**.......... SaleemGolam(5) 8 57
(TTClement) *sn chsng ldrs: kpt on to take 2nd ins last: no imp* **12/1**
2105 **3** 1 3/4 **Got To Be Cash**[20] 2446 5-9-3 **52**.......... BSwarbrick 9 56
(WMBrisbourne) *sn chsng ldr: led over 2f out tl over 1f out: kpt on same pce* **10/3**[2]
5600 **4** 4 **Transcendantale (FR)**[10] 2733 6-8-12 **47**.......... RThomas 2 43
(MrsSLamyman) *sn trcking ldrs: effrt 3f out: edgd rt: one pce* **11/2**
0-61 **5** 2 1/2 **Life Is Beautiful (IRE)**[24] 2347 5-8-10 **50**.......... DTudhope(5) 6 42
(WHTinning) *chsd ldrs: effrt 3f out: one pce* **2/1**[1]
20/0 **6** 1 **Norma Speakman (IRE)**[13] 2659 4-8-5 **45**.......... AMullen(5) 10 35
(EWTuer) *s.i.s: bhd: kpt on fnl 3f: nvr on terms* **25/1**
000- **7** nk **Lady Netbetsports (IRE)**[162] 2220 5-9-11 **63**.......... MLawson(3) 3 52
(BSRothwell) *bhd and pushed along: sme hdwy 4f out: nvr on terms* **25/1**
0020 **8** 1 **Miss Ocean Monarch**[9] 2757 4-8-2 **40**.......... CHaddon(3) 5 27
(DWChapman) *uns rdr and rn loose bef s: led: hung lft and hdd over 2f out: lost pl over 1f out* **12/1**
0-00 **9** 8 **Barton Flower**[58] 1528 3-8-0 **50**.......... PPMathers(3) 7 22
(MWEasterby) *sn pushed along: sn chsng ldrs: hung lft and lost pl over 3f out* **25/1**
-000 **10** dist **Tamarina (IRE)**[138] 651 3-8-3 **50**.......... PMakin 4 —
(NEBerry) *chsd ldrs: hung lft thrght: lost pl 7f out: t.o 3f out* **33/1**

2m 6.56s (-0.64) **Going Correction** +0.125s/f (Good)
**WFA** 3 from 4yo+ 12lb **10** Ran SP% **121.7**
Speed ratings: **107,105,104,100,98 98,97,96,90,—**CSF £50.13 CT £181.67 TOTE £3.80: £1.20, £3.40, £1.70; EX 80.50.
**Owner** K Hodgson & Mrs J Hodgson **Bred** Forbes Arms Stud **Trained** Sheriff Hutton, N Yorks

**FOCUS**
A 0-65 handicap, a seller in all but name and run at just a sensible early pace. The form is modest but the winning time was decent for the grade.

**NOTEBOOK**
**Westcourt Dream**, having just her sixth start, appreciated the step up in trip and her rider continues to impress.
**Feed The Meter(IRE)**, unplaced in four previous starts, was warm beforehand on her handicap debut. Judged by this a mile and a half will not come amiss.
**Got To Be Cash**, runner-up last year from a 10lb lower mark, is usually given a more patient ride and her one win was one much easier ground.
**Transcendantale(FR)**, out of her depth her last two starts, is on a losing run now stretching back almost two years.
**Life Is Beautiful(IRE)**, whose last four wins have been here, really needs a mile and a half.
**Norma Speakman(IRE)**, tailed off on her return, would be more at home in selling company.
**Tamarina(IRE)** *Official explanation: jockey said bit slipped through filly's mouth*

## 3009 WELCOME TO OUR WORKS NIGHT OUT MAIDEN AUCTION STKS — 7f 100y
**7:15** (7:15) (E) 2-Y-O — **£3,666** (£1,128; £564; £282) **Stalls** High

Form — RPR
032 **1** **Bridge Place**[10] 2736 2-8-12..........(b) SSanders 3 72
(BJMeehan) *led: qcknd 3f out: hung lft ins last: hld on* **6/4**[1]
3 **2** 1 1/4 **Mceldowney**[8] 2780 2-8-10.......... KDalgleish 9 67
(MJohnston) *s.i.s: hdwy on outsider over 3f out: sn rdn: wnt 2nd 1f out: swtchd rt 75yds out: no real imp* **15/8**[2]
02 **3** 3 **Mac Cois Na Tine**[27] 2256 2-8-10.......... NCallan 1 60
(KARyan) *trckd ldrs: kpt on same pce fnl 2f* **11/2**[3]
6 **4** 1 1/4 **Royal Flynn**[21] 2422 2-8-7.......... PMakin(5) 7 59
(MDods) *chsd ldrs: one pce fnl 2f* **50/1**
56 **5** 1 3/4 **Sound And Vision (IRE)**[12] 2674 2-8-6.......... PMulrennan(5) 6 54
(MDods) *trckd ldrs: wknd fnl f* **12/1**
5 **6** 3/4 **Dusty Dane (IRE)**[42] 1905 2-8-1..........(t) CHaddon(7) 5 49
(WGMTurner) *t.k.h: sn trcking wnr: hung lft over 3f out: lost pl 2f out* **14/1**
60 **7** 9 **Wolds Dancer**[16] 2550 2-8-3.......... PMQuinn 8 23
(TDEasterby) *hld up in rr: pushed along 5f out: lost pl over 2f out: sn bhd* **11/1**

00 8 12 **Countrywide Dream (IRE)**[9] 2758 2-8-2 ....................(p) PPMathers(7) 2 —
(ABerry) *sn bhd: drvn along and rn wd 4f out: sn lost tch* **66/1**
1m 34.85s (0.55) **Going Correction** +0.125s/f (Good) **8** Ran SP% **116.3**
Speed ratings: **101,99,96,94,92 91,81,67**CSF £4.60 TOTE £2.30: £1.10, £1.10, £2.20; EX 3.60.
**Owner** Des O'Rourke & Gallagher Equine Ltd **Bred** Mrs M Gutkin **Trained** Upper Lambourn, Berks

**FOCUS**
A low-grade maiden run at a steady pace until once in line for home, but the winning time was decent for the type of race, but the first two looked slightly improved for the test of stamina.

**NOTEBOOK**
**Bridge Place**, an edgy-type, had his own way in front. Stepping up the gallop coming off the final bend, he again showed a marked tendency to hang left but never really looked like being overhauled.
**Mceldowney**, who stands over plenty of ground, was above himself beforehand. Still very inexperienced, he was getting the worst of the argument when the winner went across his bows, forcing him to switch, inside the last.
**Mac Cois Na Tine**, a rangy type, did not seem to improve on his debut effort for the step up in trip.
**Royal Flynn**, last of six first time, shaped better but he still has a fair way to go if he is to make his mark.
**Sound And Vision(IRE)**, having his third outing, looked very fit and was on his toes beforehand. The extended trip did nothing for him.
**Dusty Dane(IRE)** took a keen hold and looked unsuited by this round track.

## 3010 JAGUAR CENTRE H'CAP 5f
**7:45** (7:45) (E) (0-70,70) 3-Y-0+ **£7,033** (£2,164; £1,082; £541) **Stalls** High

Form RPR
0163 **1** **Dizzy In The Head**[8] 2779 5-9-1 **62**............................(b) NChalmers(5) 19 78
(PaulJohnson) *mde all: qcknd clr over 1f out: r.o wl* **6/1**[2]
2653 **2** 3 **Karminskey Park**[10] 2734 5-9-6 **62**........................................... RHavlin 8 67
(TJEtherington) *chsd ldrs: wnt 2nd 1f out: styd on: no imp* **12/1**
6402 **3** 3 **Obe One**[6] 2859 4-9-13 **69**........................................... ACulhane 4 63
(ABerry) *sn bhd: swtchd rt over 2f out: r.o strly ins last* **14/1**
-522 **4** 3/4 **Valiant Romeo**[27] 2274 4-9-0 **56**....................................(v) SSanders 15 48
(RBastiman) *chsd ldrs: kpt on same pce fnl 2f* **5/1**[1]
0000 **5** nk **Ballybunion (IRE)**[5] 2899 5-9-3 **59**........................................ ANicholls 7 50
(DNicholls) *bhd: swtchd outside over 1f out: fin wl* **16/1**
0-00 **6** shd **Sir Sandrovitch (IRE)**[33] 2130 8-8-12 **54**......................(p) PHanagan 14 44
(RAFahey) *mid-div: hdwy over 1f out: styd on ins last* **5/1**[1]
0144 **7** 3/4 **Far Note (USA)**[10] 2734 6-9-9 **65**.....................................(b) JBramhill 20 53
(SRBowring) *stmbld s: hdwy whn nt clr run 1f out: swtchd lft: r.o* **6/1**[2]
0-04 **8** hd **Midnight Parkes**[10] 2735 5-9-10 **66**.......................................... MHenry 5 53
(EJAlston) *rr-div: kpt on fnl 2f: nvr nr ldrs* **25/1**
/060 **9** 3/4 **Brigadier Monty (IRE)**[13] 2656 6-8-7 **54**........................ RThomas(5) 3 38
(MrsSLamyman) *bhd: sme hdwy 2f out: nvr a factor* **100/1**
0516 **10** nk **Red Leicester**[13] 2663 4-9-0 **56**..........................................(v) NCallan 16 39
(JAGlover) *chsd ldrs: one pce fnl 2f* **20/1**
6-00 **11** hd **Loughlorien (IRE)**[10] 2735 5-8-11 **53**...................................(v) GParkin 1 35
(RAFahey) *bhd: sme hdwy 2f out: nvr a factor* **33/1**
3120 **12** 3/4 **Tally (IRE)**[5] 2899 4-8-8 **57**............................................... MNem(7) 9 37
(MJPolglase) *dwlt: hdwy on ins whn nt clr run 1f out: nvr on terms* **20/1**
2620 **13** 1/2 **Illusive (IRE)**[22] 2404 7-9-3 **59**.........................................(b) WRyan 6 37
(MWigham) *a towards rr* **25/1**
0020 **14** nk **Kangarilla Road**[19] 2490 5-9-12 **68**..................................... SWhitworth 12 45
(MrsJRRamsden) *s.s: sn chsng ldrs: lost pl over 1f out* **12/1**
0062 **15** 1 **Xanadu**[3] 2936 8-8-4 **51**...............................................(p) PMulrennan(5) 18 24
(MissLAPerratt) *chsd ldrs: lost pl over 1f out* **13/2**[3]
0000 **16** 1/2 **John O'Groats (IRE)**[3] 2936 6-9-6 **62**...................................(v[1]) FLynch 10 33
(MDods) *mid-div: nt clr run over 1f out: nvr on terms* **33/1**
0-30 **17** 4 **Count Cougar (USA)**[148] 578 4-9-4 **60**........................... JMcAuley 13 17
(SPGriffiths) *chsd ldrs on outer: lost pl 2f out* **33/1**
0000 **18** 8 **Arctic Burst (USA)**[22] 2404 4-10-0 **70**................................(v) LVickers 11 —
(DShaw) *mid-div: lost pl over 1f out: eased* **40/1**
30-0 **19** nk **Whinhill House**[3] 2936 4-8-11 **53**.......................................... KDalgleish 17 —
(DWBarker) *chsd ldrs: wknd over 1f out: sn bhd and eased* **25/1**
63.11 secs (-0.89) **Going Correction** -0.15s/f (Firm) **19** Ran SP% **136.5**
Speed ratings: **101,96,91,90,89 89,88,88,86,86 86,84,84,83,81 81,74,61,61**CSF £75.07 CT £1041.00 TOTE £8.30: £1.90, £3.10, £2.80, £2.40; EX 153.10.
**Owner** P And Mrs D M Johnson **Bred** Bearstone Stud And T Herbert Jackson **Trained** White-le-Head, Co Durham

**FOCUS**
A modest sprint handicap, and as usual the draw played a major part, although second and third overcame single-figure draws to be involved.

**NOTEBOOK**
**Dizzy In The Head**, who had two handlers in the paddock, had a plum draw and took this in most decisive fashion.
**Karminskey Park** did well considering she had a single-figure draw.
**Obe One**, drawn four, was last of all when switched to the far rail at halfway. He finished strongly to snatch third place but the first two had flown.
**Valiant Romeo**, 2lb higher and with the visor on again, had no excuse.
**Ballybunion(IRE)**, dropped 4lb after York, tends to get behind these days. Switched to the wide outside, he finished with quite a flourish. He looks on the way back and these days may be better suited by six.
**Sir Sandrovitch(IRE)** has won six times in June over the last three seasons. 12lb lower than for his last win, he hinted strongly at an imminent return to form.
**Far Note(USA)**, drawn in pole position, blew his chance at the start then to compound the felony ran into serious traffic problems. *Official explanation: jockey said gelding stumbled badly leaving the stalls and lost all chance*
**Whinhill House** *Official explanation: jockey said gelding tired quickly in the closing stages*

## 3011 LES HART "LIFETIME IN RACING" NOVICE STKS 5f
**8:15** (8:15) (D) 2-Y-0 **£5,508** (£1,695; £847; £423) **Stalls** High

Form RPR
**1** **Imperial Sound** 2-8-8 ........................................................... SSanders 7 85
(TDBarron) *w'like: lengthy: mde all: qcknd over 2f out: forged clr appr fnl f: r.o wl* **5/1**[3]
12 **2** 3 1/2 **Melalchrist**[17] 2526 2-9-2 ................................................ PHanagan 6 81
(JJQuinn) *t.k.h: trckd wnr: wnt rt after 1f: effrt over 2f out: kpt on: no ch w wnr* **7/2**[2]
321 **3** 3/4 **Space Shuttle**[12] 2674 2-9-2 ..................................................(b) DAllan 4 81+
(TDEasterby) *dwlt: hdwy on ins whn hmpd after 1f: rdn and hung lft 2f out: kpt on same pce* **5/4**[1]
50 **4** 5 **Alcharinga (IRE)**[17] 2522 2-8-12 ............................................. RHavlin 3 57
(TJEtherington) *chsd ldrs: wl outpcd fnl 2f* **25/1**
01 **5** 2 **Dorn Dancer (IRE)**[9] 2749 2-9-0 ............................................ FLynch 5 52
(DWBarker) *chsd ldrs: outpcd over 2f out: sn lost pl* **7/2**[2]
**6** 6 **Paula Jo** 2-8-3 ................................................................... PMQuinn 1 20
(JSWainwright) *leggy: unf: scope: sn outpcd and bhd* **40/1**
63.67 secs (-0.33) **Going Correction** -0.15s/f (Firm) **6** Ran SP% **111.8**
Speed ratings: **96,90,89,81,78 68**CSF £22.40 TOTE £5.30: £2.60, £2.20; EX 25.50.
**Owner** J Stephenson **Bred** R Burton **Trained** Maunby, N Yorks

**FOCUS**
A steady pace to halfway but a winning newcomer of some potential.

**NOTEBOOK**
**Imperial Sound** ◆, a March foal, had the plum draw and clearly knew his job. With the second and third getting in each other's way, he came right away and looks a decent prospect.
**Melalchrist** pulled hard early on because of the lack of pace. He stuck on to chase home the winner, but time may show he was facing a stiff task conceding him 8lb.
**Space Shuttle**, dropping back in trip, missed a beat at the start and going for a run up the inner at the end of the first furlong was knocked back by the second. He continually hung left and looked to be giving his rider no great help. His attitude must be questioned after this.
**Alcharinga(IRE)** is struggling to see it out but at least this third outing brings nurseries into play.
**Dorn Dancer(IRE)** was caught flat-footed when the winner stepped up a gear, and she dropped away in a matter of strides. She is surely better than this.

## 3012 WESTWOOD CLASSIFIED STKS 1m 100y
**8:45** (8:45) (E) 3-Y-0+ **£4,108** (£1,264; £632; £316) **Stalls** High

Form RPR
6035 **1** **Low Cloud**[3] 2938 4-9-9 75.......................................................(v) ANicholls 4 81
(DNicholls) *t.k.h in rr: hdwy on outside over 3f out: edgd rt over 2f out: styd on fnl f: led nr fin* **5/1**[3]
1212 **2** hd **Riley Boys (IRE)**[5] 2880 3-8-12 74............................................ MFenton 7 80
(JGGiven) *led: qcknd over 3f out: kpt on: hdd nr fin* **10/11**[1]
40-5 **3** nk **Aswan (IRE)**[15] 2591 6-9-4 64...................................................(t) JBramhill 5 75
(SRBowring) *dwlt: t.k.h in rr: effrt and n.m.r over 2f out: ev ch 1f out: nt qckn wl ins last* **25/1**
0000 **4** 1 1/2 **Riska King**[19] 2492 4-9-4 66.................................................. PHanagan 3 72
(RAFahey) *trckd ldrs: t.k.h: effrt on ins 2f out: kpt on same pce* **12/1**
-404 **5** 3 **Catherine Howard**[15] 2587 3-8-6 71........................................ ACulhane 1 64
(MRChannon) *trckd ldrs: t.k.h: effrt 3f out: n.m.r 2f out: sn lost pl* **3/1**[2]
0-05 **6** 5 **Helderberg (USA)**[16] 2551 4-9-1 66........................................ KDarley 6 52
(BSRothwell) *w wnr: rdn and outpcd whn n.m.r over 2f out: sn btn: eased ins last* **16/1**
1m 48.53s (1.23) **Going Correction** +0.125s/f (Good)
**WFA** 3 from 4yo+ 10lb **6** Ran SP% **111.5**
Speed ratings: **98,97,97,96,93 88**CSF £9.89 TOTE £7.40: £2.70, £1.20; EX 15.10.
**Owner** Maxilead Limited **Bred** Mrs A Rothschild And London Thoroughbred Services **Trained** Sessay, N Yorks

**FOCUS**
A tactical affair and a bit messy. The winning time was therefore modest and the form is ordinary.

**NOTEBOOK**
**Low Cloud**, improved for the fitting of a visor, came there on the outer. He made very hard work of it but put his head in front where it really matters.
**Riley Boys(IRE)** dictated things from the front but in the end just missed out.
**Aswan(IRE)**, who had 6lb to find with the first two on official ratings, was having his second outing in two weeks after over a year off. In the end he was just found lacking.
**Riska King**, who had a bit to find, has been bang out of form but this was a more encouraging effort.
**Catherine Howard**, who had the best chance on official ratings, was already starting to struggle when tightened up. She seemed to drop away in willing fashion and is proving a real disappointment.
**Helderberg(USA)** kept close tabs on the leader but her chance had already gone when tightened up by the winner on her outside with over two furlongs left to run.

## 3013 WORKS NIGHT OUT MEDIAN AUCTION MAIDEN STKS 1m 4f 16y
**9:15** (9:16) (E) 3-Y-0 **£3,536** (£1,088; £544; £272) **Stalls** High

Form RPR
2-2 **1** **Mountain Meadow**[61] 1466 3-9-0 ............................................ KDarley 7 73+
(MrsAJPerrett) *led eraly: trckd ldrs taking t.k.h: effrt and hrd drvn over 3f out: styd on to ld 150yds out: eased nr fin* **1/2**[1]
24 **2** 1 1/2 **Recognise (IRE)**[41] 1933 3-9-0 ........................................ KDalgleish 8 71
(MJohnston) *sn led: set mod pce: rn green and hung lft over 6f out: qcknd over 3f out: edgd lft and hdd jst ins last: no ex* **9/2**[3]
04 **3** 6 **Honeymooning**[26] 2312 3-8-9 ................................................... WRyan 2 56
(HRACecil) *trckd ldr: chal 3f out: nt qckn 1f out: eased ins last* **4/1**[2]
**4** 3 **Chestall** 3-8-7 ................................................................... RKennemore(7) 6 57
(RHollinshead) *tall: unf: t.k.h: in tch: wl outpcd over 2f out* **50/1**
04 **5** 4 **Columbian Emerald (IRE)**[27] 2257 3-9-0 .................................. RHavlin 1 50
(TJEtherington) *chsd ldrs: pushed along over 3f out: lost pl over 1f out* **40/1**
3U50 **6** 6 **Upthedale (IRE)**[16] 2554 3-9-0 35......................................... PHanagan 4 41?
(JRWeymes) *sn in rr: rdn 3f out: nvr a factor* **66/1**
0 **7** 2 1/2 **Twilight Years**[26] 2298 3-9-0 ................................................ FLynch 3 37
(TDEasterby) *dwlt: hld up in rr: effrt on outside 4f out: sn struggling* **40/1**
00- **8** 25 **Weet An Store (IRE)**[213] 6012 3-9-0 ...................................... ACulhane 5 —
(RHollinshead) *in rr: sn pushed along: lost tch over 3f out: t.o 2f out* **50/1**
2m 43.66s (4.36) **Going Correction** +0.125s/f (Good) **8** Ran SP% **115.1**
Speed ratings: **90,89,85,83,80 76,74,58**CSF £3.13 TOTE £1.60: £1.02, £1.20, £1.40; EX 3.60 Place 6 £23.85, Place 5 £7.85.
**Owner** K Abdulla **Bred** Juddmonte Farms **Trained** Pulborough, W Sussex

**FOCUS**
A steady gallop and a moderate winning time, but the form appears sound and the first two have the potential to go on to something better.

**NOTEBOOK**
**Mountain Meadow**, absent for two months with his stable in the doldrums, made hard work of it but was right on top at the finish. Essentially a stayer, the lack of pace and the track were not in his favour.
**Recognise(IRE)**, up in the air and on the weak side, was green to post and his inexperience showed in the back straight. Setting sail for home at the foot of the hill, in the end he had to settle for second spot, clear of the rest. Suited by this much quicker ground, he will improve in time and will surely win races eventually.
**Honeymooning**, who looked very fit, was upsides the leader once in line for home but, clearly only third best, was allowed to take things very easily inside the last.
**Chestall**, a tall, weak newcomer, made a satisfactory bow but the slow pace probably flatters him.
**Columbian Emerald(IRE)**, bred exclusively for speed on his dam's side, had shown next to nothing in two previous starts.
T/Plt: £10.90 to a £1 stake. Pool: £27,140.70. 1,813.00 winning tickets. T/Qpdt: £7.10 to a £1 stake. Pool: £2,057.70. 212.30 winning tickets. WG

# [2979]RIPON (R-H)

Thursday, June 17

**OFFICIAL GOING: Good to firm**

## 3014 E B F LADIES' DAY MAIDEN STKS — 6f

**2:10** (2:11) (D) 2-Y-O **£5,538** (£1,704; £852; £426) **Stalls** Low

Form / RPR

22 **1** **Spirit Of France (IRE)**[14] 2627 2-9-0 ........ KDalgleish 5 84+
(MJohnston) *mde virtually all: rdn wl over 1f out: edgd rt ins last: kpt on* **4/5**[1]

6 **2** *2* **Tom Forest**[19] 2470 2-8-11 ........ LEnstone(3) 2 78
(ACrook) *chsd wnr: sn pushed along and outpcd after 1f: swtchd rt 2f out and sn rdn: styd on wl fnl f* **9/1**[3]

42 **3** *3/4* **Wasalat (USA)**[13] 2651 2-8-9 ........ ACulhane 7 71
(MRChannon) *cl up: rdn and ev ch 2f out: drvn and one pce ent last* **5/2**[2]

**4** *5* **Jazrawy** 2-9-0 ........ SSanders 1 61
(LMCumani) *outpcd in rr: hdwy over 2f out: styd on wl appr last: nrst fin* **20/1**

30 **5** *shd* **Strathtay**[14] 2617 2-8-9 ........ GFaulkner 9 56
(PCHaslam) *wnt rt s: sn cl up and ev ch tl rdn 2f out and sn wknd* **14/1**

0 **6** *1 3/4* **Loyalty Lodge (IRE)**[36] 2045 2-9-0 ........ PHanagan 8 55
(JDBethell) *chsd ldrs: rdn along over 2f out: sn wknd* **100/1**

**7** *1/2* **Tcherina (IRE)** 2-8-9 ........ FLynch 4 49
(TDEasterby) *s.i.s: a rr* **100/1**

4 **8** *nk* **Wedlock**[13] 2651 2-9-0 ........ JFortune 6 53
(TDEasterby) *bhd fr 1/2-way* **20/1**

**9** *1/2* **Mercari** 2-8-6 ........ TEaves(3) 3 47
(GMMoore) *midfield: rdn along and bhd fr 1/2-way* **100/1**

1m 14.01s (1.11) **Going Correction** -0.05s/f (Good) **9** Ran SP% **113.3**
Speed ratings: **90,87,86,79,79 77,76,76,75**CSF £8.58 TOTE £1.80: £1.30, £2.40, £1.10; EX 11.20.

**Owner** A D Spence **Bred** Sunflower International Ltd And Maryl Stud **Trained** Middleham Moor, N Yorks

**FOCUS**
An uncompetitive maiden run in an ordinary time in which the form choices pulled five lengths clear.

**NOTEBOOK**
**Spirit Of France(IRE)** had run well on his two previous starts and this race represented a lesser contest. He won without much trouble, the step up in trip appearing to suit, and he can progress again.
**Tom Forest** found the pace a bit hot early on but saw the trip out well in the end, staying on more strongly than the second favourite. He looks a likely type for nurseries after one more run.
**Wasalat(USA)** could not cope with the winner and lost second late on. She is now eligible for nurseries and might have more success in that sphere.
**Jazrawy**, a half-brother to a juvenile winner in Italy, was green and took a while to get the hang of things, only staying on when the race was all over. He is bred to need a mile plus.
**Strathtay** did not get home this time but she too now qualifies for a mark.

## 3015 ADLER & ALLAN MEDIAN AUCTION MAIDEN STKS — 1m 2f

**2:45** (2:45) (E) 3-Y-O **£3,721** (£1,145; £572; £286) **Stalls** High

Form / RPR

0-6 **1** **Galvanise (USA)**[84] 1104 3-9-0 ........ ACulhane 7 88
(BWHills) *trckd ldrs: hdwy to ld 4f out: rdn along wl over 2f out: drvn over 1f out: kpt on* **11/8**[1]

3 **2** *4* **Murbaat (IRE)**[23] 2392 3-9-0 ........ SSanders 3 80
(ACStewart) *trckd ldrs: rn wd bnd after 4f: hdwy to chal 3f out: sn rdn and ev ch tld riven and one pce approachng last* **6/4**[2]

05 **3** *25* **Jalousie Dream**[32] 2145 3-8-6 ........ TEaves(3) 1 28
(GMMoore) *in tch: effrt 4fout: sn rdn: drvn and outpcd wl over 2f out* **66/1**

0 **4** *hd* **Government (IRE)**[33] 2114 3-9-0 ........(b[1]) JFortune 6 33
(JHMGosden) *keen: led: rdn along and hdd 4f out: sn drvn and outpcd fnl 3f* **16/1**

22-2 **5** *1 3/4* **Atlantic City**[28] 2250 3-9-0 71........(p) SWKelly 2 29
(WJHaggas) *cl up: rdn along over 4f out and sn wknd* **13/2**[3]

4 **6** *2* **Aston Lad**[28] 2250 3-9-0 ........ KDalgleish 8 25
(MDHammond) *s.i.s: a bhd* **66/1**

5 **7** *6* **Jordans Spark**[52] 1662 3-9-0 ........ PHanagan 5 14
(ISemple) *a rr* **20/1**

**8** *dist* **Raybers Magic** 3-8-9 ........ ANicholls 4 —
(JRWeymes) *s.i.s: a bhd* **50/1**

2m 6.17s (-1.83) **Going Correction** -0.05s/f (Good) **8** Ran SP% **111.0**
Speed ratings: **105,101,81,81,80 78,73,—**CSF £3.38 TOTE £2.50: £1.20, £1.10, £9.10; EX 4.90.

**Owner** K Abdulla **Bred** Juddmonte Farms Inc **Trained** Lambourn, Berks

**FOCUS**
Another uncompetitive maiden and the first two in the market had it between them from a long way out. As such the form is not easy to assess.

**NOTEBOOK**
**Galvanise(USA)**, sixth in a Doncaster maiden that has worked out very well on his seasonal reappearance, is bred to need middle distances and duly improved for the step up to ten furlongs. This race lacked any strength in depth, but he won with authority and should command plenty of respect when he moves into handicap company.
**Murbaat(IRE)**, third behind Lucayan Legend, who finished runner-up in the Britannia Handicap later this day, on his debut, is another who appreciated the step up in trip. He was unlucky to come up against another useful rival, but he beat the rest pointless and should find a similar race.
**Jalousie Dream**, having her third outing at the track, was beaten a country mile, but at least she is now eligible for handicaps.
**Government(IRE)** had shown little on his debut and had blinkers on this time. Rather keen in the headgear, he did not get home.
**Atlantic City** has some ability and really should have done better than this in the first-time cheekpieces.
**Jordans Spark** *Official explanation: jockey said colt did not handle the undulating track*

## 3016 TOTAL BUTLER H'CAP — 5f

**3:20** (3:21) (D) (0-80,80) 3-Y-O+ **£5,473** (£1,684; £842; £210) **Stalls** Low

Form / RPR

1000 **1** **Torrent**[44] 1870 9-7-9 50 oh5........(b) LisaJones(3) 6 61
(DWChapman) *qckly away: mde all: rdn wl over 1f out: styd on strly* **20/1**

-003 **2** *1/2* **Kings College Boy**[8] 2784 4-8-6 58........(b) PHanagan 5 67
(RAFahey) *midfield: hdwy over 2f out: sn rdn: drvn and styd on ins last* **11/2**[3]

4035 **3** *3/4* **Paddywack (IRE)**[5] 2899 7-8-12 64........(b) ACulhane 1 70
(DWChapman) *bhd: hdwy 2f out: sn rdn and kpt on ins last: nrst fin* **5/1**[2]

0562 **4** *hd* **Boanerges (IRE)**[11] 2707 7-8-0 55 ........ FPFerris(3) 2 60
(JMBradley) *bhd: hdwy 2f out: sn rdn: kpt on ins last: nrst fin* **9/2**[1]

0400 **4** *dht* **Blue Maeve**[10] 2734 4-7-12 50 oh23 ........ SRighton 7 55
(JHetherton) *sn cl up: rdn along 1/2-way: drvn and one pce ent last* **100/1**

0215 **6** *3/4* **Musical Fair**[10] 2739 4-9-12 78 ........ JFortune 9 80
(JAGlover) *chsd ldrs: rdn 2f out: wknd apprlast* **8/1**

-020 **7** *1* **Strensall**[6] 2859 7-9-11 77 ........ FLynch 3 75
(REBarr) *chsd ldrs: rdn 2f out: grad wknd* **9/1**

-051 **8** *1 3/4* **Merlin's Dancer**[22] 2407 4-10-0 80 ........ ANicholls 12 71
(DNicholls) *racd alone far side: rdn along 1/2-way: no ch w stands side gp* **5/1**[2]

00/3 **9** *1 1/4* **Sunley Sense**[10] 2739 8-9-6 79 ........ BO'Neill(7) 10 65
(MRChannon) *a rr* **14/1**

0-00 **10** *nk* **Bollin Janet**[32] 2143 4-9-6 72 ........ SSanders 8 57
(TDEasterby) *chsd ldrs: rdn over 2f out: sn wknd* **25/1**

0500 **11** *nk* **Mr Spliffy (IRE)**[10] 2739 5-8-3 55 ........ SCarson 4 39
(MCChapman) *dwlt: a rr* **25/1**

0-00 **12** *shd* **Beyond The Clouds (IRE)**[47] 1774 8-9-10 79 ........ TEaves(3) 11 62
(JSWainwright) *a rr* **14/1**

58.96 secs (-1.24) **Going Correction** -0.05s/f (Good) **12** Ran SP% **114.8**
Speed ratings: **107,106,105,104,104 103,101,99,97,96 96,95**CSF £119.09 CT £653.22 TOTE £25.20: £5.80, £1.70, £2.80; EX 125.50.

**Owner** David W Chapman **Bred** Mrs Mary Taylor **Trained** Stillington, N Yorks

■ Stewards Enquiry : Lisa Jones two-day ban: excessive use of the whip (Jun 28-29)

**FOCUS**
An ordinary handicap in which all but one came stands' side and they dominated throughout.

**NOTEBOOK**
**Torrent**, freshened up by a six-week break, made every yard next to the stands'-side rail. Considering he invariably runs in big-field handicaps here, he has a good record at the track, one that now reads 7442191.
**Kings College Boy**, who appears to reserve his best for Hamilton, has a poor strike rate. He needs a strong pace to be seen at his best, and was probably at a disadvantage challenging down the centre of the track.
**Paddywack(IRE)** is running well at present and knocking at the door. He stayed on well from off the pace and a stiffer five furlongs is probably ideal nowadays.
**Blue Maeve**, officially rated just 27, ran a stormer from 23lb out of the handicap. He showed plenty of speed and is clearly much better than the assessor gives him credit for.
**Boanerges(IRE)** was keeping on well at the finish, and a stiffer five furlongs would have seen him in a better light as well.
**Musical Fair** looks to be held by the Handicapper off her new mark.
**Merlin's Dancer** went solo on the far side, but the stands'-side group always had his measure.

## 3017 DEBENHAMS HARROGATE H'CAP — 1m

**3:55** (3:57) (C) (0-90,88) 3-Y-O **£8,607** (£3,264; £1,632; £742) **Stalls** High

Form / RPR

0612 **1** **Distant Connection (IRE)**[8] 2790 3-8-7 74 ........ SSanders 1 79
(APJarvis) *trckd ldr: effrt 3f out: rdn to ld wl over 1f out: drvn ins last: jst hld on* **5/4**[1]

0-1 **2** *hd* **Invasian (IRE)**[13] 2654 3-9-5 86 ........ WRyan 2 91
(HRACecil) *led: rn wd home turn: rdn along over 2f out: hdd wl over 1f out: drvn and rallied ins last: jst failed* **7/2**[3]

210- **3** *1 1/4* **Have Faith (IRE)**[278] 4882 3-9-4 85 ........ JFortune 4 87
(BWHills) *tacked ldng pair: hdwy 3f out: chal 2f out: sn rdn and ev ch tl drvn and one pce ins last* **12/1**

3304 **4** *hd* **Momtic (IRE)**[16] 2558 3-8-13 80 ........ FLynch 3 82
(WJarvis) *hld up: hdwy 4f out: rdn along and outpcd 2f out: drvn and styd on wl fnl f* **3/1**[2]

02-1 **5** *1 1/2* **West Highland Way (IRE)**[26] 2289 3-8-10 80 ........ TEaves(3) 6 78
(ISemple) *biumped s: in tch tl rdn along and outpcd over 2f out: kpt on u.p fnl f* **12/1**

10-0 **6** *29* **Tafaahum (USA)**[46] 1795 3-9-7 88 ........ KDalgleish 5 19
(MJohnston) *hmpd s: sn rdn along and outpcd: bhd fr 1/2-way* **14/1**

1m 39.75s (-1.35) **Going Correction** -0.05s/f (Good) **6** Ran SP% **113.7**
Speed ratings: **104,103,102,102,100 71**CSF £6.08 TOTE £2.40: £1.10, £2.40; EX 5.30.

**Owner** Mrs Ann Jarvis **Bred** Mrs C F Van Straubenzee And Partners **Trained** Twyford, Bucks

**FOCUS**
A fair handicap, but the early gallop was moderate and the form may be suspect with the fourth providing the best guide.

**NOTEBOOK**
**Distant Connection(IRE)**, who came into this in good form, was all out to get up in the dying strides. He was receiving weight from the runner-up, which proved decisive, but this consistent colt may not have finished winning yet and he should improve for a stronger gallop.
**Invasian(IRE)** gave his all in defeat and only went down narrowly. He could not give the weight away to his in-form rival close home, but is improving and is well worth another chance to make amends.
**Have Faith(IRE)** looked to be going as well as any two out, but found her stamina deserting her and may need a return to seven furlongs. This was still a sound effort and she remains unexposed.
**Momtic(IRE)** was the chief sufferer of the modest early pace and will be seen in a much better light when getting a stiffer test, as he finished best of all.
**Tafaahum(USA)** *Official explanation: jockey said colt was never travelling*

## 3018 BEAUMONT ROBINSON INSURANCE LADIES' DERBY H'CAP (LADY AMATEUR RIDERS) — 1m 4f 60y

**4:30** (4:30) (E) (0-70,70) 3-Y-O+ **£3,857** (£1,187; £593; £296) **Stalls** High

Form / RPR

0/0- **1** **Latalomne (USA)**[77] 5821 10-10-9 70 ........ MrsNWilson(5) 4 83
(NWilson) *hld up and bhd: hdwy on inner 3f out: swtchd lft to outer over 2f out: rdn and styd on to ld last 100 yds* **25/1**

00-5 **2** *2* **Sualda (IRE)**[9] 2753 5-9-12 59 ........ MissVTunnicliffe(5) 11 69
(RAFahey) *hld up in midfield: hdwy on inner 3f out: rdn to ld appr last: sn rdn: hdd and nt qckn last 100 yds* **9/2**[1]

0040 **3** *shd* **Sarn**[9] 2753 5-8-6 41 ........ MissMMullineaux(7) 3 51?
(MMullineaux) *hld up and bhd: hdwy on inner 3f out: rdn ent last: kpt on* **33/1**

5-31 **4** *2 1/2* **Little Task**[21] 2386 6-8-7 38 oh1 ........ MissKellyHarrison(3) 7 44
(JSWainwright) *midfield: stdy hdwy 4f out: ev ch 2f out: sn rdn and one pce ent last* **14/1**

020 **5** *1* **Lazzaz**[30] 2212 6-9-0 47 ........ MrsMarieKing(5) 14 51
(PWHiatt) *in tch on inner: swtchd lft and hdwy 3f out: ev ch 2f out: sn rdn and wknd ent last* **11/2**[2]

4105 **6** *3* **Jimmy Byrne (IRE)**[23] 2393 4-10-9 68........(p) MissLEllison(3) 5 68
(BEllison) *hld up: hdwy on outer over 2f out: rdn and edgd rt wl over 1f out: sn wknd* **16/1**

-052 **7** *1/2* **Royal Axminster**[18] 2501 9-8-8 41 ........ MissAWallace(5) 10 40
(MrsPNDutfield) *led: rdn along and hdd 4f out: cl up tl grad wknd appr last* **10/1**

242- **8** *1* **Golden Chance (IRE)**$^{343}$ 3120 7-9-7 **49**.................. MissSBrotherton 2 46
(MWEasterby) *trckd ldrs: swtchd lft and hdwy over 2f out: sn ev ch tl rdn and wknd over 1f out* **10/1**

2-33 **9** *1 1/2* **Dick The Taxi**$^{9}$ 2753 10-10-11 **67**.................. MissEJJones 8 62
(RJSmith) *a rpominent: hdwy to ld over 2f out: sn rdn: hdd & wknd appr last* **8/1**$^{3}$

0620 **10** *5* **Graft**$^{18}$ 2501 5-10-1 **62**..................(b) MrsCThompson$^{(5)}$ 1 49
(MWEasterby) *keen: cl up: led 4f out: rdn and hdd over 2f out: sn wknd* **14/1**

643- **11** *5* **Final Dividend (IRE)**$^{204}$ 6079 8-9-1 **46**.................. MissJoannaRees$^{(3)}$ 9 25
(JMPEustace) *hld up: stdy hdwy to trck ldrs 3f out: rdn 2f out and sn btn* **8/1**$^{3}$

3304 **12** *12* **Michaels Dream (IRE)**$^{18}$ 2501 5-9-2 **44**..................(b) MrsSBosley 12 —
(JHetherton) *a rr* **9/1**

0406 **13** *3* **Magic Charm**$^{13}$ 2659 6-8-3 **38** oh3.................. MissJWaring$^{(7)}$ 6 —
(JeddO'Keeffe) *a bhd: sddle slipped* **40/1**

001- **14** *1/2* **Mischief**$^{302}$ 4279 8-8-5 **38** oh1.................. MissJoeyEllis$^{(5)}$ 13 —
(KBell) *cl up: rdn along over 4f out and sn wknd* **25/1**

4-00 **15** *20* **Outward (USA)**$^{24}$ 2368 4-9-11 **58**.................. MissRBastiman$^{(5)}$ 15 —
(RBastiman) *a rr* **66/1**

2m 39.55s (-0.35) **Going Correction** -0.05s/f (Good) **15** Ran SP% **117.8**
Speed ratings: **99,97,97,95,95 93,92,92,91,87 84,76,74,74,60**CSF £126.48 CT £3756.72 TOTE £31.30: £12.00, £2.20, £9.10; EX 185.30.
**Owner** Alderclad Roofing/k M Everitt **Bred** Gainsborough Farm Inc **Trained** Malton, N Yorks
■ Stewards Enquiry : Mrs N Wilson three-day ban: careless riding (Jun 30, Jul 1,6)

**FOCUS**
A modest event but they went a fair pace and the form is moderate but sound enough.

**NOTEBOOK**
**Latalomne(USA)**, having his first outing for his new stable after leaving Martin Pipe, is better known as a chaser, but he has been a useful performer on the level in the past and loves fast ground. He had the race run to suit and came from well off the pace to score going away.
**Sualda(IRE)**, who goes well for an inexperienced rider, ran with credit on his second start of the season. He is handicapped to win a similar race.
**Sarn** answered any doubts regarding his stamina for this trip.
**Little Task**, successful in banded grade last month, put in a solid performance from 2lb out of the handicap. He is in good heart both on the Flat and over hurdles.
**Lazzaz** is a difficult horse to win with and is still chasing his first victory on turf.
**Jimmy Byrne(IRE)**, with cheekpieces on for the first time, ran a fair race on ground plenty quick enough for him.
**Magic Charm** *Official explanation: jockey said saddle slipped*

## 3019 RICHMOND MEDIAN AUCTION MAIDEN STKS 6f
**5:05** (5:05) (E) 3-4-Y-O **£3,809** (£1,172; £586; £293) **Stalls** Low

Form RPR

-000 **1** **Smart Minister**$^{24}$ 2346 4-9-7 46.................. KDalgleish 8 63
(JJQuinn) *chsd ldrs: hdwy 2f out: rdn to chal and edgd lft over 1f out: led ins last: sn drvn and kpt on* **5/1**$^{3}$

3-64 **2** *nk* **Flash Ram**$^{30}$ 2217 3-9-0 66..................(v$^{1}$) SSanders 7 62
(TDEasterby) *cl up: led 2f out: sn rdn: drvn and hdd ins last: n.m.r: kpt on* **2/1**$^{1}$

0420 **3** *5* **Amanda's Lad (IRE)**$^{5}$ 2899 4-9-7 60.................. LVickers 1 47
(MCChapman) *led: rdn along and hdd 2f out: kpt on same pce* **5/2**$^{2}$

5300 **4** *nk* **Dark Champion**$^{10}$ 2734 4-9-7 62.................. PHanagan 6 46
(REBarr) *chse ldrs: rdn along 2f out: sn drvn and one pce* **11/2**

4-56 **5** *10* **Amber Fox (IRE)**$^{14}$ 2620 3-8-9 52..................(p) FLynch 2 11
(ABerry) *cl up: rdn along 1/2-way: sn wknd* **7/1**

00 **6** *1* **Lord Of The Fens**$^{17}$ 2517 4-9-7.................. SWKelly 4 13
(CNKellett) *wnt rt s: outpcd and bhd fr 1/2-way* **66/1**

000- **7** *6* **I See No Ships**$^{391}$ 1795 4-9-2.................. SRighton 3 —
(MMullineaux) *outpcd and b ehind fr 1/2-way* **66/1**

6000 **8** *11* **Compton Princess**$^{17}$ 2528 4-9-2 37.................. SCarson 5 —
(MrsADuffield) *hmpd s: a bhd* **20/1**

1m 12.87s (-0.03) **Going Correction** -0.05s/f (Good)
**WFA** 3 from 4yo 7lb **8** Ran SP% **114.2**
Speed ratings: **98,97,90,90,77 75,67,53**CSF £15.28 TOTE £8.50: £1.90, £1.50, £1.20; EX 27.80.
**Owner** B Shaw **Bred** Mrs M Shaw **Trained** Settrington, N Yorks

**FOCUS**
A pretty desperate maiden and a moderate time, so the form looks worth treating with caution.

**NOTEBOOK**
**Smart Minister** is a half-brother to the prolific pair Smart Predator and Smart Hostess, and while he is clearly nowhere near as good as them, he did well to beat higher-rated rivals this time.
**Flash Ram**, visored for the first time, had every chance and had the rail to help, but he was just edged out at the finish. He would have had to give the winner 20lb had this been a handicap, so this must go down as a disappointing effort.
**Amanda's Lad(IRE)** has gone 48 races without winning and his current rating flatters him.
**Dark Champion**, another longstanding maiden, has had plenty of chances. *Official explanation: jockey said gelding was unsuited by the undulations in the track*
**Amber Fox(IRE)** did not find the first-time cheekpieces bringing about any improvement.
**Lord Of The Fens** *Official explanation: jockey said gelding was unsuited by the track*

## 3020 LEVY BOARD H'CAP 1m 4f 60y
**5:40** (5:40) (D) (0-80,76) 3-Y-O **£5,473** (£1,684; £842; £421) **Stalls** High

Form RPR

1-3 **1** **Yoshka**$^{54}$ 1609 3-9-7 **76**.................. KDalgleish 3 82
(MJohnston) *in tch: reminders and hdwy 4f out: rdn over 2f out: styd on told and hung rt over 1f out: drvn ins last and styd on wl* **11/4**$^{1}$

1222 **2** *1 1/4* **Ilwadod**$^{7}$ 2821 3-8-5 **60**..................(v$^{1}$) ACulhane 5 64
(MRChannon) *hld up: pushed along in rr 1/2-way: rdn 4f out: hdwy wl over 1f out: drvn and styd on ins last: nrst fin* **7/2**$^{2}$

-513 **3** *1/2* **Vicario**$^{15}$ 2567 3-8-2 **60**.................. FPFerris$^{(3)}$ 7 63
(MLWBell) *trckd ldrs: hdwy 3f out: rdn and ev ch wl over 1f out: drvn and kpt on fnl f* **11/2**$^{3}$

-532 **4** *3 1/2* **Havetoavit (USA)**$^{15}$ 2567 3-8-10 **65**.................. PHanagan 1 63
(JDBethell) *led: rdn along over 3f out: drvn and hdd over 1f out: grad wknd* **12/1**

2133 **5** *1 1/4* **Siegfrieds Night (IRE)**$^{7}$ 2821 3-8-7 **65**.................. LisaJones$^{(3)}$ 6 61
(MCChapman) *trckd ldrs: hdwy to chal 3f out: rdn 2f out and wknd appr last* **13/2**

06-1 **6** *3* **Zalda**$^{15}$ 2567 3-8-11 **66**.................. SWKelly 2 57
(RCharlton) *prom: rdn along over 3 out: drvn 2f out and sn wknd* **6/1**

0-33 **7** *dist* **Ma Yahab**$^{15}$ 2583 3-9-3 **72**.................. SSanders 4 —
(LMCumani) *hld up: rdn along 4f out: wknd wl over 2f out and sn eased* **13/2**

2m 36.98s (-2.92) **Going Correction** -0.05s/f (Good) **7** Ran SP% **112.9**
Speed ratings: **107,106,105,103,102 100,—**CSF £12.17 TOTE £3.30: £2.40, £2.30; EX 9.90
Place 6 £18.54, Place 5 £16.98..

**Owner** Saeed Buhaleeba **Bred** Bloomsbury Stud **Trained** Middleham Moor, N Yorks

**FOCUS**
A fair handicap full of in-form performers run in a decent time and it proved a thorough test at the trip. the form is not outstanding but the winner should go on from this.

**NOTEBOOK**
**Yoshka ◆** got the strong pace he needs at this trip and stayed on best of all. He looks a progressive type, is in the care of a master with this type of animal, and is bound to improve when stepped up in trip. He should be kept on the right side.
**Ilwadod** got a mile six well last time out, and the strong pace over this shorter trip brought his stamina into play. He was finishing second for the fourth time running and deserves a change of luck.
**Vicario** ran well off what was a 10lb higher mark than when successful at Lingfield last month. He is clearly progressing along the right lines.
**Havetoavit(USA)** set a decent pace in front and that played into the hands of those with stronger reserves of stamina. He is still a maiden but should not remain so for long if continuing to run to this level.
**Siegfrieds Night(IRE)** is a consistent animal and his performance suggests the form is solid.
**Zalda**, a shock winner on her reappearance, found attempting to defy a 7lb higher mark too tough.
**Ma Yahab** *Official explanation: jockey said colt was unsuited by the fast ground*
T/Plt: £48.20 to a £1 stake. Pool: £25,001.40. 378.30 winning tickets. T/Qpdt: £34.80 to a £1 stake. Pool: £1,378.40. 29.30 winning tickets. JR

# 2985 SOUTHWELL (L-H)
### Thursday, June 17

**OFFICIAL GOING: Standard**
Wind: Fresh half-behind Weather: Cloudy

## 3021 JAPANESE LILY FESTIVAL MAIDEN AUCTION FILLIES' STKS 5f (F)
**2:20** (2:21) (F) 2-Y-O **£3,367** (£1,036; £518; £259) **Stalls** High

Form RPR

26 **1** **Chilly Cracker**$^{43}$ 1882 2-8-2.................. DaleGibson 1 66
(RHollinshead) *mde all: rdn out* **8/1**

43 **2** *1 1/4* **Colonial Girl (IRE)**$^{15}$ 2585 2-8-6.................. DAllan 5 66
(TDEasterby) *chsd wnr: rdn over 1f out: styd on same pce ins fnl f* **9/4**$^{2}$

0 **3** *nk* **Moon Mischief (IRE)**$^{27}$ 2275 2-8-6.................. JBramhill 2 65
(NPLittmoden) *prom: rdn over 1f out: styd on* **9/2**$^{3}$

6 **4** *1/2* **Belly Dancer (IRE)**$^{17}$ 2522 2-8-5.................. TPQueally$^{(3)}$ 7 65
(PFICole) *s.i.s: sn chsng ldrs: rdn over 1f out: no ex ins fnl f* **13/8**$^{1}$

**5** *8* **Classic Style (IRE)** 2-8-1.................. AMullen$^{(7)}$ 3 37
(TDEasterby) *s.i.s: outpcd* **16/1**

60 **6** *1/2* **Justenjoy Yourself**$^{20}$ 2458 2-7-11.................. HayleyTurner$^{(5)}$ 4 29
(CADwyer) *prom: rdn 1/2-way: wknd over 1f out* **28/1**

**7** *16* **Surrey Downs Girl** 2-8-3 ow1.................. RPrice 8 —
(TTClement) *sn outpcd* **33/1**

59.61 secs (-0.79) **Going Correction** -0.375s/f (Stan) **7** Ran SP% **110.4**
Speed ratings: **91,89,88,87,74 74,48**CSF £24.58 TOTE £6.10: £3.80, £1.70; EX 23.20.
**Owner** John L Marriott **Bred** Henry And Mrs Rosemary Moszkowicz **Trained** Upper Longdon, Staffs

**FOCUS**
This looked only an average juvenile event in which none of the runners had any previous experience of the Fibresand, but the pace was solid.

**NOTEBOOK**
**Chilly Cracker** , who had shown promise on her debut but then failed to handle Chester on her latest outing, settled much better in the lead on this occasion and got off the mark in workmanlike fashion. She has previously only run on easy going and seemed to be enjoying the surface more than the others, which proved decisive.
**Colonial Girl(IRE)** , whose latest effort gave her every chance in this form-wise, was smartly away and held every chance if good enough, but lacked the resolution of the winner from halfway. She looks worth another chance back on turf over another furlong, especially when the nurseries begin.
**Moon Mischief(IRE)** was wide of the pack throughout and looked to be doing her best work at the finish. She is the type to improve with more experience.
**Belly Dancer(IRE)**appeared to be going best of all approaching two out, but again looked green under pressure and failed to find a change of gear late on. The form of her debut has worked out particularly well, with the winner finishing third in the Windsor Castle Stakes, and she can leave this form behind in due course, but is clearly nothing special.
**Classic Style(IRE)** was all at sea from the gates and should come on plenty for the outing.
**Surrey Downs Girl** *Official explanation: vet said filly was lame*

## 3022 PROCESSION OF THE GOLDEN CHARIOT CLAIMING STKS 1m 3f (F)
**2:55** (2:55) (F) 3-Y-O+ **£2,968** (£848; £424) **Stalls** Low

Form RPR

3115 **1** **Pure Mischief (IRE)**$^{36}$ 2039 5-9-7 62.................. BSwarbrick$^{(5)}$ 9 73
(WMBrisbourne) *hld up: hdwy over 3f out: rdn to ld over 1f out: styd on* **11/2**

6110 **2** *1/2* **Maniatis**$^{37}$ 2022 7-9-13 73..................(v) IMongan 6 73
(AndrewReid) *hld up in tch: led 3f out: rdn and hdd over 1f out: styd on* **9/4**$^{1}$

1411 **3** *6* **Romil Star (GER)**$^{6}$ 2851 7-9-10 65..................(v) DSweeney 8 61
(KRBurke) *hld up: hdwy over 3f out: rdn over 1f out: styd on same pce* **3/1**$^{2}$

00-0 **4** *1 1/4* **Big Smoke (IRE)**$^{8}$ 2781 4-9-1 74..................(b) PMulrennan$^{(5)}$ 10 55
(JHowardJohnson) *prom: rdn over 2f out: hung lft and wknd over 1f out* **25/1**

12-0 **5** *nk* **Peruvia (IRE)**$^{48}$ 1752 4-9-3 75..................(vt$^{1}$) GDuffield 5 52
(RMBeckett) *w ldrs: led 8f out: hdd 3f out: wknd over 1f out* **12/1**

453- **6** *15* **Al Azhar**$^{398}$ 1627 10-9-4 68.................. DAllan 2 30
(MDods) *chsd ldrs: rdn over 4f out: wknd over 3f out* **9/1**

1213 **7** *2* **Caspian Dusk**$^{20}$ 2452 3-8-2 65.................. CHaddon$^{(7)}$ 1 31
(WGMTurner) *chsd ldrs: lost pl 7f out: wknd over 3f out* **5/1**$^{3}$

000/ **8** *2* **Worth A Gamble**$^{692}$ 3338 6-8-13 35.................. JDO'Reilly$^{(7)}$ 7 26
(HEHaynes) *chsd ldrs over 7f* **100/1**

0 **9** *28* **Irish Chapel (IRE)**$^{24}$ 2362 8-9-3.................. MSavage$^{(5)}$ 4 —
(HEHaynes) *led 3f: wknd 6f out* **100/1**

0000 **10** *3/4* **Mandahar (IRE)**$^{35}$ 2053 5-9-6 40..................(v$^{1}$) NCallan 3 —
(AWCarroll) *hld up: rdn over 4f out: sn wknd* **50/1**

2m 29.64s (0.74) **Going Correction** +0.15s/f (Slow)
**WFA** 3 from 4yo+ 13lb **10** Ran SP% **113.3**
Speed ratings: **103,102,98,97,97 86,84,83,62,62**CSF £17.50 TOTE £7.40: £2.00, £1.10, £1.60; EX 18.50.The winner was claimed by Mr C. Dore for £14,000.
**Owner** The Cartmel Syndicate **Bred** T F Lacy **Trained** Great Ness, Shropshire

**FOCUS**
An interesting claimer and a fair contest by All-Weather standards, but it was run at a modest early gallop and the front two came clear at in the straight.

**NOTEBOOK**

**Pure Mischief(IRE)**, despite not appearing to have an obvious chance at these weights, made smooth headway to join the pace at the top of the straight and ran on well under pressure to score. This was by far his best effort on the surface, despite the trip appearing to stretch him. Conor Dore claimed him afterwards for £14,000.

**Maniatis** held every chance if good enough, but lacked the turn of foot to go with the winner when challenged in the straight. He did however improve on his only other outing at this venue and was clear in second.

**Romil Star(GER)**, who had won his last two at the course coming into this, found this a much tougher test and seemed to get outpaced when the tempo increased turning for home. Running on again at the finish, he will find easier opportunities in this grade, especially over further.

**Big Smoke(IRE)** ran much better than his previous effort on fast ground last time and appreciated the drop in grade, but never threatened.

**Peruvia(IRE)**, racing in the visor and tongue tie for the first time, dropped in a hole turning for home and again looked a non-stayer over this trip.

**Mandahar(IRE)** *Official explanation: jockey said gelding lost his action*

## 3023 BATTLE OF BUNKER HILL H'CAP — 1m (F)

**3:30** (3:37) (E) (0-70,70) 3-Y-O+ **£3,779** (£1,163; £581; £290) **Stalls** Low

Form RPR

0015 **1** **Tre Colline**[1] 2989 5-9-10 **66** 6ex GBaker 10 82
(NTinkler) *hld up in tch: rdn to ld and edgd lft over 1f out: styd on wl: eased nr fin* **7/2**[1]

0300 **2** *4* **Midshipman**[15] 2595 6-8-13 **55** (vt) IMongan 9 63
(AWCarroll) *chsd ldrs: led over 3f out: rdn and hdd over 1f out: no ex ins fnl f* **9/1**

3-50 **3** *2 1/2* **Haunt The Zoo**[7] 2814 9-9-0 **59** DNolan(3) 6 62
(JohnAHarris) *chsd ldrs: pushed along 1/2-way: edgd lft over 2f out: styd on same pce* **33/1**

2200 **4** *1/2* **Quiet Reading (USA)**[22] 2406 7-9-6 **67** (v) HayleyTurner(5) 2 69
(MRBosley) *outpcd: hdwy over 1f out: nvr nrr* **8/1**[3]

3-40 **5** *2* **Brandy Cove**[63] 1427 7-8-13 **62** MStainton(7) 14 60
(BSmart) *s.s: outpcd: hdwy over 1f out: n.d* **28/1**

0600 **6** *1* **Mcqueen (IRE)**[24] 2375 4-10-0 **70** DSweeney 11 66
(MrsHDalton) *sn outpcd: styd on appr fnl f: nvr nrr* **9/1**

0000 **7** *2* **Estimation**[22] 2406 4-9-0 **61** AQuinn(5) 15 53
(RMHCowell) *chsd ldrs: rdn over 2f out: wknd over 1f out* **16/1**

4013 **8** *hd* **Bailieborough (IRE)**[8] 2776 5-9-11 **67** (v) AlexGreaves 7 59
(DNicholls) *sn outpcd* **10/1**

2002 **9** *1 3/4* **Crusoe (IRE)**[7] 2814 7-8-4 **51** (b) NChalmers(5) 5 39
(ASadik) *bhd fr 1/2-way* **16/1**

1-00 **10** *3* **Merdiff**[16] 2551 5-9-3 **64** BSwarbrick(5) 12 46
(WMBrisbourne) *chsd ldrs: led over 5f: hdd over 3f out: wknd 2f out* **12/1**

0211 **11** *2* **Frank's Quest (IRE)**[1] 2990 4-8-8 **53** LPKeniry(3) 8 31
(PBurgoyne) *prom to 1/2-way* **7/1**[2]

0-00 **12** *5* **Band**[27] 2271 4-9-11 **67** SWhitworth 3 35
(BAMcmahon) *prom 5f* **33/1**

-200 **13** *8* **Trench Coat (USA)**[30] 2207 3-9-1 **67** GDuffield 4 19
(AMBalding) *led: hdd over 5f out: wknd over 3f out: eased* **33/1**

30-5 **14** *7* **Dixie Dancing**[76] 1229 5-9-2 **58** NCallan 13 —
(CACyzer) *prom over 5f* **20/1**

2 **15** *4* **Millenio (GER)**[5] 2883 4-9-8 **64** OUrbina 1 —
(DFlood) *rel to r: a t.o* **8/1**[3]

1m 45.83s (1.23) **Going Correction** +0.15s/f (Slow)
**WFA** 3 from 4yo+ 10lb **15** Ran SP% **122.5**
Speed ratings: **99,95,92,92,90 89,87,86,85,82 80,75,67,60,56**CSF £32.52 CT £893.12 TOTE £3.80: £2.00, £3.70, £12.40; EX 77.50.
**Owner** Peter Alderson Mike Gosse Adrian Mornin **Bred** Hesmonds Stud Ltd **Trained** Langton, N Yorks

**FOCUS**

This moderate handicap was run at a fair clip throughout and the field was well strung out from an early stage as a result. The winner will need to improve off his revised mark, but the runner-up has dropped in the handicap and this was his best effort for a while.

**NOTEBOOK**

**Tre Colline** had to dig deep entering the final furlong to get the better of the runner-up, but won the battle and in the end scored comfortably. He had won with ease over course and distance just a week before, but ran no sort of race at this track 24 hours earlier over seven furlongs. However, over this extra furlong he looked a different animal, and was ridden much more prominently this time. He has to be of interest if turned out under a penalty.

**Midshipman** was the only one to give the winner a race and was well clear in second. He was a force to be reckoned with on this surface in his prime, but has been in decline since. If he can maintain this current mood, he looks very well-treated on his old form and can make amends this summer.

**Haunt The Zoo** ran in snatches, but stayed on again in the straight and improved on her recent form.

**Quiet Reading(USA)** also stepped up on his latest effort over this more suitable course and distance. He is one to keep an eye on for a similar event. *Official explanation: jockey said gelding was struck into*

**Brandy Cove** stayed on late up the far side rail, as has often been the case in the past, and is capable of better.

**Frank's Quest(IRE)**, who escaped a penalty for his convincing success over course and distance in an apprentice race just 24 hours earlier, dropped out tamely after struggling to go the pace early on.

**Trench Coat(USA)** *Official explanation: jockey said saddle slipped*

## 3024 ST HARVEYS DAY (S) H'CAP — 7f (F)

**4:05** (4:10) (G) (0-55,53) 3-Y-O+ **£2,639** (£754; £377) **Stalls** Low

Form RPR

0215 **1** **Turn Around**[13] 2666 4-9-11 **51** IMongan 12 72
(BWHills) *w ldrs: led 3f out: rdn clr 2f out* **3/1**[1]

1064 **2** *7* **Bulawayo**[13] 2666 7-9-3 **48** (b) BSwarbrick(5) 9 52
(AndrewReid) *s.i.s: sn pushed along and prom: outpcd 4f out: styd on appr fnl f* **9/1**

0210 **3** *1* **Jonny Ebeneezer**[11] 2703 5-9-8 **53** AQuinn(5) 16 54
(RMHCowell) *prom: chsd wnr and hung lft over 2f out: styd on same pce* **6/1**[2]

4332 **4** *3 1/2* **Indian Music**[13] 2664 7-9-4 **44** GCarter 6 36
(ABerry) *hld up: hdwy 1/2-way: wknd over 1f out* **8/1**[3]

00-0 **5** *nk* **Bandbox (IRE)**[6] 2854 9-8-9 **35** ADaly 10 27
(MSalaman) *outpcd: hdwy over 1f out: nt trble ldrs* **14/1**

6-41 **6** *nk* **Mallia**[13] 2664 11-8-13 **46** Laura-JayneCrawford(7) 11 37
(TDBarron) *rrd s: outpcd: hdwy over 1f out: nvr nrr* **9/1**

000/ **7** *nk* **Prince Of Aragon**[768] 2103 8-9-3 **43** DSweeney 15 33
(MissSuzySmith) *chsd ldrs over 4f* **50/1**

0516 **8** *nk* **Lord Melbourne (IRE)**[104] 972 5-9-5 **50** NChalmers(5) 13 39
(AGJuckes) *hld up: hdwy 1/2-way: rdn and hung lft over 2f out: nt run on* **14/1**

0303 **9** *1/2* **Headland (USA)**[87] 1076 6-9-6 **51** (be) MSavage(5) 5 39
(DWChapman) *s.s: hdwy 1/2-way: wknd 2f out* **12/1**

3436 **10** *3/4* **Kanz Wood (USA)**[1] 2990 8-9-0 **45** (v) RThomas(5) 3 31
(AWCarroll) *s.s: outpcd* **6/1**[2]

6-00 **11** *3 1/2* **Zietzig (IRE)**[40] 1971 7-9-0 **40** AlexGreaves 8 17
(DNicholls) *w ldrs: led over 4f out: hdd 3f out: wknd 2f out* **14/1**

0160 **12** *6* **Gilly's General (IRE)**[6] 2833 4-9-8 **48** (p) SWhitworth 7 10
(JWUnett) *sn led: hdd over 4f out: wknd 3f out* **20/1**

000- **13** *2* **Cute Cait**[300] 4342 3-9-2 **51** GDuffield 14 8
(MrsGSRees) *sn outpcd* **25/1**

0-00 **14** *8* **Magico**[141] 620 3-8-7 **45** LPKeniry(3) 1 —
(PBurgoyne) *prom to 1/2-way* **50/1**

500 **15** *3 1/2* **My Little Sophia**[26] 2297 4-8-10 **43** (p) PVarley(7) 4 —
(MMullineaux) *sn outpcd* **50/1**

1m 31.07s (0.27) **Going Correction** +0.15s/f (Slow)
**WFA** 3 from 4yo+ 9lb **15** Ran SP% **126.9**
Speed ratings: **104,96,94,90,90 90,89,89,88,88 84,77,74,65,61**CSF £30.33 CT £162.55 TOTE £3.50: £1.60, £3.00, £2.60; EX 38.50.
**Owner** Gryffindor (www.racingtours.co.uk) **Bred** Cheveley Park Stud Ltd **Trained** Lambourn, Berks

**FOCUS**

This weak event was run at a solid early gallop and once again that saw the field well and truly strung out at the finish. The winning time was smart for a seller and the winner could be well treated.

**NOTEBOOK**

**Turn Around**, very popular in the betting ring, set sail for home two out and ran right away with this to land the odds in grand style. He had won a seller at Wolverhampton on his penultimate start, but disappointed in a handicap last time, and this drop back in grade was all he needed to make amends. He was sold for 9,000gns.

**Bulawayo** ran on late from off the pace to bag second, but was never a threat to the winner at any stage.

**Jonny Ebeneezer** is always a force in this grade and ran his race in third, but again did not prove that he is in love with this surface. He was claimed for £6,000.

**Indian Music** was smartly away, but was soon reined back to get the trip and was only running on though tiring horses at the end.

**Bandbox(IRE)**, as is often the case, was unable to go the early pace and just kept on without threatening.

**Kanz Wood(USA)**, unplaced in a handicap at this venue 24 hours earlier, was never a threat over this shorter trip and probably found this coming too quick. He seems a better horse at Wolverhampton.

## 3025 LUDI PISCATARI CLASSIFIED STKS — 6f (F)

**4:40** (4:41) (F) 3-Y-O+ **£3,003** (£858; £429) **Stalls** Low

Form RPR

1034 **1** **Never Without Me**[44] 1873 4-9-2 54 SWhitworth 8 66
(JFCoupland) *a.p: rdn to ld over 1f out: r.o* **14/1**

0043 **2** *3/4* **Brantwood (IRE)**[17] 2524 4-8-13 58 (t) LPKeniry(3) 7 64
(BAMcmahon) *chsd ldr: rdn to ld over 1f out: sn hdd: styd on* **10/1**

0413 **3** *hd* **Roman Empire**[1] 2989 4-9-2 57 (b) NCallan 12 63
(KARyan) *s.i.s: sn prom: rdn over 2f out: r.o* **5/2**[1]

5114 **4** *1 1/2* **Gilded Cove**[20] 2455 4-9-0 63 StephanieHollinshead(5) 1 62
(RHollinshead) *bhd: hdwy over 1f out: nt rch ldrs* **9/1**

1504 **5** *2 1/2* **Azreme**[1] 2989 4-9-0 65 MHoward(7) 2 56
(DKIvory) *s.i.s: bhd: hdwy over 1f out: nt trble ldrs* **9/1**

1221 **6** *2* **Larky's Lob**[13] 2663 5-8-12 63 JDO'Reilly(7) 14 48
(JO'Reilly) *sn led: rdn and hdd over 1f out: wknd ins fnl f* **9/2**[2]

0103 **7** *3 1/2* **Pays D'Amour (IRE)**[7] 2813 7-9-2 57 AlexGreaves 13 35
(DNicholls) *chsd ldrs over 4f* **5/1**[3]

600 **8** *2* **Caribe (FR)**[8] 2779 5-9-2 60 GCarter 10 29
(ABerry) *n.d* **50/1**

310- **9** *shd* **Haze Babybear**[329] 3525 4-8-13 56 GParkin 9 25
(RAFahey) *sn outpcd* **28/1**

50-0 **10** *2 1/2* **Yashin (IRE)**[23] 2377 3-8-9 60 GDuffield 4 21
(MHTompkins) *sn outpcd* **20/1**

-030 **11** *1 1/2* **Free Wheelin (IRE)**[34] 2091 4-9-7 65 IMongan 6 21
(WJarvis) *s.i.s: hdwy 1/2-way: wknd over 1f out* **16/1**

000- **12** *shd* **White Ledger (IRE)**[339] 3273 5-9-0 65 NataliaGemelova(7) 5 21
(RAFahey) *mid-div: wknd 1/2-way* **25/1**

206- **13** *shd* **Moritat (IRE)**[384] 1966 4-8-9 60 SJDonohoe(7) 11 16
(PDEvans) *chsd ldrs over 3f* **10/1**

00-0 **14** *10* **Sugar Snap**[147] 583 4-8-6 35 MHalford(7) 3 —
(CDrew) *n.d* **100/1**

1m 17.43s (0.53) **Going Correction** +0.15s/f (Slow)
**WFA** 3 from 4yo+ 7lb **14** Ran SP% **129.2**
Speed ratings: **102,101,100,98,95 92,88,85,85,81 79,79,79,66**CSF £150.89 TOTE £16.00: £5.70, £3.90, £1.10; EX 234.90.
**Owner** J F Coupland **Bred** Miss Nathalie Lismonde **Trained** Grimsby, Lincs

**FOCUS**

Average fare on offer for this typical All-Weather sprint that was run at a generous early pace, but there were still plenty in with a chance on entering the straight. The level of form is ordinary.

**NOTEBOOK**

**Never Without Me**, making his debut for a new yard, responded gamely to pressure and stuck to his task well when hitting the front entering the final furlong. He enjoyed this switch back to the sand, and the recent change of scenery has clearly sharpened him up.

**Brantwood(IRE)** was quickly rushed up to the lead, helped set the solid pace and went down with all guns blazing. A beaten favourite on his only other outing on this surface, he deserves credit for this display and continues to run consistently well without winning.

**Roman Empire**, a beaten favourite over seven furlongs at this track 24 hours earlier, again ran on strongly over this shorter trip, but never quite looked like getting up. A rise in the weights for winning on this surface in May means the Handicapper looks to have got his measure now.

**Gilded Cove** ran his race in fourth.

**Azreme**, another making a quick reappearance, got going all too late over this shorter trip.

## 3026 EAT ALL OF YOUR VEGETABLES DAY H'CAP — 1m 4f (F)

**5:15** (5:15) (F) (0-55,55) 3-Y-O **£3,304** (£944; £472) **Stalls** Low

Form RPR

5542 **1** **Jackie Kiely**[7] 2801 3-9-5 **50** IMongan 16 60
(PSMcentee) *s.i.s: sn prom: jnd ldr 6f out: led and hung rt over 2f out: hung lft over 1f out: drvn out* **9/2**[2]

0540 **2** *1 1/4* **The King Of Rock**[32] 2146 3-9-0 **45** SWhitworth 5 53
(AGNewcombe) *hld up: hdwy 7f out: outpcd over 2f out: r.o ins fnl f* **10/1**

2554 **3** *1/2* **Holly Walk**[9] 2760 3-9-1 **46** (p) DSweeney 15 53
(MDods) *trckd ldrs: led over 6f out: rdn and hdd over 2f out: outpcd over 1f out: r.o ins fnl f* **12/1**

6-00 **4** *1* **Rubaiyat (IRE)**[15] 2597 3-9-7 **52** RHavlin 8 58
(GWragg) *hld up in tch: rdn to chsd wnr and hung lft over 1f out: no ex ins fnl f* **16/1**

-002 **5** *6* **Pearl Of York (DEN)**[9] 2760 3-9-4 **52** LPKeniry(3) 9 49
(RGuest) *chsd ldrs over 8f* **8/1**
0210 **6** *5* **True To Yourself (USA)**[16] 2546 3-8-12 **43** ADaly 6 32
(JGGiven) *outpcd: hdwy over 3f out: nvr trbld ldrs* **15/2**[3]
500 **7** *5* **Nod's Star**[23] 2392 3-9-2 **47** GParkin 3 29
(MissJACamacho) *bhd: hdwy 6f out: wknd over 3f out* **12/1**
0-00 **8** *19* **Quay Walloper**[16] 2554 3-9-1 **46** JBramhill 7 —
(JRNorton) *outpcd* **33/1**
060 **9** *9* **King Of Meze (IRE)**[106] 956 3-8-9 **40** OUrbina 11 —
(GProdromou) *chsd ldrs 7f* **50/1**
4510 **10** *3* **Prairie Sun (GER)**[15] 2584 3-9-2 **47** GDuffield 4 —
(MrsADuffield) *outpcd* **4/1**[1]
3014 **11** *1 3/4* **Pepe (IRE)**[20] 2452 3-9-5 **55** StephanieHollinshead(5) 12 —
(RHollinshead) *sn led: hdd & wknd over 6f out* **8/1**
6230 **12** *shd* **Fox Hollow (IRE)**[10] 2740 3-9-1 **51** MSavage(5) 13 —
(MJHaynes) *chsd ldrs to 1/2-way* **20/1**
0-00 **13** *5* **Theatre Belle**[47] 1771 3-9-9 **54** DAllan 2 —
(TDEasterby) *chsd ldrs to 1/2-way* **16/1**
0030 **14** *2 1/2* **Strangely Brown (IRE)**[23] 2390 3-9-10 **55** GCarter 1 —
(SCWilliams) *hld up in tch: wknd 1/2-way* **10/1**
0-06 **15** *25* **Dame Nova (IRE)**[24] 2355 3-9-0 **45** GFaulkner 10 —
(PCHaslam) *sn drvn along in rr: lost tch 1/2-way* **12/1**

2m 45.47s (3.37) **Going Correction** +0.15s/f (Slow) **15** Ran SP% **134.9**
Speed ratings: **94,93,92,92,88 84,81,68,62,60 59,59,56,54,37**CSF £54.59 CT £541.38 TOTE £6.10: £2.50, £3.40, £7.30; EX 126.90 Place 6 £119.40, Place 5 £37.16..
**Owner** P S J Croft **Bred** Mrs M Chaworth Musters **Trained** Newmarket, Suffolk

**FOCUS**
A dire contest run at a modest pace and the front four pulled away at the finish. The form is poor but soun enough.

**NOTEBOOK**
**Jackie Kiely**, who looked an unlucky loser in a Brighton seller last time over shorter, won this decisively on his debut for new connections. He was handy for most of the way, joined the pace on the turn for home before kicking into the lead one out, and stuck to his task well close home.
**The King Of Rock** improved for this switch back to the sand and was finishing best of all, but the winner had gone beyond recall. He has yet to win a race, but has the ability to get off the mark at this level on the All-Weather off his current mark.
**Holly Walk** ran on again late, having got outpaced at a crucial stage, but could not match the winner in the battle for the line and was run out of second close home. The cheekpieces seemed to bring about some improvement this time, and it was a respectable display on her All-Weather.
**Rubaiyat(IRE)** did not quite see out this trip, but improved on his latest effort over a mile and was clear of the remainder in fourth.
**Prairie Sun(GER)** *Official explanation: jockey said filly was never travelling*
**Strangely Brown(IRE)** *Official explanation: jockey said gelding was never travelling*
T/Plt: £222.20 to a £1 stake. Pool: £21,877.40. 71.85 winning tickets. T/Qpdt: £60.70 to a £1 stake. Pool: £1,625.10. 19.80 winning tickets. CR

3027 - 3029a (Foreign Racing) - See Raceform Interactive

## 2828 LONGCHAMP (R-H)
Thursday, June 17

**OFFICIAL GOING: Good to soft**

## 3030a LA COUPE (GROUP 3) 1m 2f
**2:20** (2:22) 4-Y-0+ **£25,704** (£10,282; £7,711; £5,141)

RPR
**1** **Aubonne (GER)**[41] 1952 4-8-8 CSoumillon 3 113
(ELibaud, France) *held up, 5th straight, headway to chase clear leader approaching final f, ran on well to lead final 70y* 1
**2** *1 1/2* **Soldier Hollow**[18] 2508 4-8-11 ASuborics 7 113
(PSchiergen, Germany) *held up towards rear, 7th straight, stayed on down outside final 1 1/2f to take 2nd on line*
**3** *snk* **Look Honey (IRE)**[103] 980 4-8-11 (b) YLerner 4 113
(CLerner, France) *held up towards rear, 7th straight, stayed on down outside final 1 1/2f to take 3rd on line*
**4** *hd* **Big Bad Bob (IRE)**[28] 2241 4-8-11 OPeslier 1 113
(JLDunlop) *set str pace: clr after 4f, 8l clear ent str: still 5l clr appr fnl f, hdd 70yds out, lost 2nd on line* 2
**5** *1 1/2* **Nonno Carlo (IRE)**[32] 2155 4-8-11 MBelli 10 110
(MGrassi, Italy) *chased clear leader, 2nd straight, one pace final 2f* 3
**6** *snk* **Bailador (IRE)**[107] 4-8-11 GaryStevens 5 110
(AFabre, France) *held up in rear, 9th straight, stayed on at one pace down inside final 2f*
**7** *nk* **Marshall (FR)**[19] 4-8-11 MBlancpain 9 109
(CLaffon-Parias, France) *held up in 4th, ridden over 1 1/2f out, one pace*
**8** *3/4* **Without Connexion (IRE)**[42] 5-8-11 TThulliez 2 108
(PBary, France) *raced in 3rd, ridden and unable to quicken 1 1/2f out*
**9** *1/2* **Prends Ton Temps (FR)**[19] 7-8-11 DBoeuf 8 107
(DSmaga, France) *held up, 6th straight, one pace final 1 1/2f*
**10** *6* **Kaldushka (FR)**[289] 4650 4-8-8 IMendizabal 6 94
(ELibaud, France) *last straight, always behind*

2m 5.00s **Going Correction** +0.025s/f (Good) **10** Ran SP% **122.6**
Speed ratings: **113,111,111,111,110 110,109,109,108,104**.
**Owner** Mme I Von Schubert **Bred** Gestut Ebbesloh **Trained** France

**NOTEBOOK**
**Aubonne(GER)** looks a progressive type and came from off the strong pace to beat the colts. Her trainer now plans to send her to America for the Beverly D Stakes, before returning for the Prix de l'Opera on Arc weekend.
**Soldier Hollow**, a German challenger, was suited by the way the race was run and put in a personal best.
**Look Honey(IRE)**, blinkered for the first time, was dropped out in the early stages. He was checked when making his challenge and only missed second place by inches. This was a much better performance.
**Big Bad Bob(IRE)** ran a brave race from the front but in the event probably set too strong a pace for his own good. His rider said the gound was too fast for him, which was surprising given that the official going was good to soft.

## 2996 ASCOT (R-H)
Friday, June 18

**OFFICIAL GOING: Firm**
The ground was getting faster by the day and there did not seem to be much difference between the two sides on the straight course.
Wind: slt against Weather: Fine, but cloudy

## 3031 ALBANY STKS (LISTED RACE) (FILLIES) 6f
**2:30** (2:31) (A) 2-Y-O **£23,200** (£8,800; £4,400; £2,000) **Stalls** Low

Form RPR
1 **1** **Jewel In The Sand (IRE)**[18] 2535 2-8-11 RHughes 8 101
(RHannon) *lw: w ldrs for 1f: restrained: lost pl 1/2-way: effrt again wl over 1f out: got through on rail and led ent fnl f: r.o wl* **10/1**
4 **2** *1 1/2* **Spirit Of Chester (IRE)**[35] 2083 2-8-9 RHavlin 1 95
(MrsPNDutfield) *lw: hld up in rr: nt clr run and hmpd over 2f out: squeezed through over 1f out: r.o to chse wnr last 100yds: no imp* **40/1**
1 **3** *1* **Salsa Brava (IRE)**[32] 2177 2-8-11 J-PGuillambert 17 94
(NPLittmoden) *lw: dwlt: wl in rr and nt gng wl: last 1/2-way: drvn and gd prog on wd outside wl over 1f out: ch 1f out: kpt on same pce* **14/1**
2133 **4** *nk* **Umniya (IRE)**[11] 2745 2-8-9 CCatlin 9 91
(MRChannon) *trckd ldrs: effrt over 2f out: led jst over 1f out tl ent fnl f: one pce* **20/1**
21 **5** *1 1/2* **Park Romance (IRE)**[13] 2690 2-8-11 KFallon 4 89
(BJMeehan) *towards rr: rdn over 3f out: effrt on outer 2f out: bmpd sn after : styd on same pce* **6/1**[2]
2 **6** *hd* **Arabian Dancer**[17] 2550 2-8-9 TEDurcan 7 86
(MRChannon) *dwlt: sn trckd ldrs: cl up 2f out: rdn and one pce after* **14/1**
61 **7** *1 1/4* **Extreme Beauty (USA)**[11] 2730 2-8-9 DHolland 2 82
(CEBrittain) *settled towards rr: nt clr run over 2f out to over 1f out: kpt on one pce after: sddle slipped* **33/1**
2 **8** *nk* **Golden Legacy (IRE)**[10] 2758 2-8-9 PHanagan 14 81
(RAFahey) *prom: chal over 2f out: led briefly over 1f out: wknd fnl f* **20/1**
1 **9** *1/2* **Masa (USA)**[20] 2481 2-8-11 LDettori 6 82
(SaeedBinSuroor) *lw;; dwlt: sn trckd ldrs: rdn over 2f out: n.m.r sn after: wknd jst over 1f out* **13/8**[1]
41 **10** *3/4* **Alta Petens**[35] 2096 2-8-9 JMackay 13 78
(MLWBell) *lw: t.k.h: w ldr: led 1/2-way to over 1f out: wknd* **16/1**
31 **11** *3/4* **Nufoos**[25] 2360 2-8-11 RHills 5 77
(MJohnston) *hld up in rr: effrt whn nt clr run and hmpd 2f out: swtchd rt: no ch whn nt clr run jst ins fnl f* **7/1**[3]
011 **12** *nk* **Justaquestion**[38] 2023 2-8-11 GDuffield 3 76
(IAWood) *wl in rr: drvn 1/2-way: nvr a factor* **25/1**
3 **13** *nk* **Cours De La Reine (IRE)**[9] 2786 2-8-9 JQuinn 16 73
(PWChapple-Hyam) *wl in rr: rdn and effrt on outer over 2f out: no imp over 1f out: wknd fnl f* **20/1**
**14** *1* **Chantilly Beauty (FR)**[41] 2-8-9 (p) JPMurtagh 12 70
(RPritchard-Gordon, France) *t.k.h: hld up towards rr: rdn 2f out: fnd nil and sn btn* **25/1**
52 **15** *1/2* **Touch Of Silk (IRE)**[18] 2535 2-8-9 MHills 15 69
(BWHills) *hld up in midfield: cl enough over 2f out: wknd over 1f out* **40/1**
1 **16** *2* **Golden Anthem (USA)**[39] 1984 2-8-9 TQuinn 11 63
(JPearce) *hld up wl in rr: prog on outer over 2f out: chsng ldrs whn bmpd over 1f out: wknd rapidly fnl f* **40/1**
2216 **17** *6* **Sapphire Dream**[16] 2568 2-8-11 PRobinson 10 47
(ABailey) *led to 1/2-way: sn lost pl: wkng whn hmpd over 1f out* **40/1**

1m 16.13s (0.14) **Going Correction** -0.10s/f (Good) **17** Ran SP% **127.9**
Speed ratings: **95,93,91,91,89 89,87,86,86,85 84,83,83,82,81 78,70**CSF £373.68 TOTE £10.00: £2.80, £14.80, £6.20; EX 815.10 TRIFECTA Not won..
**Owner** Sand Associates **Bred** Gerrardstown House Stud **Trained** East Everleigh, Wilts
■ Stewards Enquiry : R Hughes one-day ban: failed to keep straight from stalls (Jun 29); caution: careless riding

**FOCUS**
The third running of this Listed contest, and probably the weakest, even though all but five of the 17 runners were previous winners. It proved to be a rough race with several hard-luck stories and the form may need treating with caution. The winning time was only ordinary for the grade.

**NOTEBOOK**
**Jewel In The Sand(IRE)** ◆, who had shown the right attitude when winning her maiden at the end of last month, displayed the same qualities to win this rough race. Having got a good break she then got trapped on the rail behind the weakening Sapphire Dream. However, she managed to squeeze past that rival and through a gap against the fence to score a shade cosily in the end. She has limited physical scope but clearly enjoys racing and will be a threat to all in the Cherry Hinton at Newmarket .
**Spirit Of Chester(IRE)** ◆, whose debut in a conditions event at Newbury has worked out reasonably well, had clearly learnt a lot from that and overcame traffic problems to hunt up the winner without ever looking likely to score. A maiden should prove a straightforward task, although she may take her chance in a sales race in Ireland later in the month.
**Salsa Brava(IRE)** ◆, drawn on the wide outside, also missed the break slightly. She was running on steadily in the closing stages and this was a good effort in the circumstances. She may renew rivalry with the winner in the Cherry Hinton.
**Umniya(IRE)**, the most experienced filly in the field, is a consistent sort who again ran her race. She was third to the Queen Mary winner Damson on her previous outing and provides a direct line to the relative merit of the form.
**Park Romance(IRE)** ◆ is progressing with her racing and, despite getting a battering in the race, kept on well to the end. She is better than her finishing position suggests.
**Arabian Dancer**, touched off on her debut in a Redcar maiden, seemed to have every chance but again gave the impression that she will appreciate another furlong. She should be able to win at maiden over that trip.
**Extreme Beauty(USA)**, another denied a clear run, was keeping on at the finish and was also inconvenienced by a slipping saddle. *Official explanation: jockey said saddle slipped*
**Golden Legacy(IRE)** ran a fair race from the front despite a wide draw, and is well capable of winning at a lower level.
**Masa(USA)**, a well backed favourite, was upsides the winner at halfway, but appeared to not have the speed, or possibly the experience, to take the gaps when they presented themselves. She may have been intimidated by being squeezed up, or may have found the ground too fast, and can be given a chance to atone.
**Nufoos** tracked the winner on the rail in the early stages, but then appeared to get outpaced before suffering in the general scrimmaging and having to switch, by which point her chance had gone. She can be expected to prove a good deal better than the bare form suggests. *Official explanation: jockey said filly was unlucky in running*
**Cours De La Reine(IRE)** *Official explanation: jockey said filly had hung right handed*
**Chantilly Beauty(FR)** *Official explanation: jockey said filly was unsuited by the firm ground*
**Golden Anthem(USA)** *Official explanation: jockey said filly suffered interference in running*

## 3032 KING EDWARD VII STKS (GROUP 2) (C&G) 1m 4f
3:05 (3:06) (A) 3-Y-O £83,338 (£30,814; £15,407; £7,003) Stalls High

Form RPR

4-30 **1** **Five Dynasties (USA)**[12] 2722 3-8-11 .............................. JPSpencer 7 111
(APO'Brien, Ire) *wl grwn: lw: trckd ldrs gng wl: rdn to ld wl over 1f out: sn edgd rt: r.o wl* **11/4**[1]

14-0 **2** *4* **Elshadi (IRE)**[13] 2680 3-8-11 96.......................................(b) WSupple 6 105
(MPTregoning) *set mod pce: qcknd over 6f out: rdn and hdd wl over 1f out: one pce* **4/1**[3]

43 **3** *3* **Barati (IRE)**[26] 2333 3-8-11 .............................................. MJKinane 2 100
(JohnMOxx, Ire) *hld up: rdn over 5f out: hdwy whn nt clr run and swtchd lft 2f out: wknd 1f out* **3/1**[2]

31 **4** *hd* **Haadef**[17] 2562 3-8-11 .......................................................... RHills 3 99
(JHMGosden) *lw: w ldr: rdn over 3f out: wknd 1f out* **3/1**[2]

-213 **5** *3 ½* **Gold History (USA)**[56] 1586 3-8-11 103.............................. JFanning 4 94
(MJohnston) *hld up: hdwy over 4f out: ev ch 2f out: sn rdn: wknd fnl f* **6/1**

2m 32.26s (-1.30) **Going Correction** -0.10s/f (Good) **5** Ran SP% **111.0**
Speed ratings: **100,97,95,95,92**CSF £13.87 TOTE £4.00: £1.90, £2.90; EX 24.10.
**Owner** Mrs John Magnier & M Tabor **Bred** Pacelco S A & Chelston Stud **Trained** Ballydoyle, Co Tipperary

**FOCUS**
The absence of Rule of Law (vet's certificate) and African Dream (ground) rendered this a below standard Group Two. The winner had been only eighth in the French Derby and the winning time was pedestrian for a such a prestigious contest.

**NOTEBOOK**
**Five Dynasties(USA)** made a winning debut on firm ground in Ireland last year and certainly looked a different animal back on a fast surface. He got the trip far better than the others, and the form is of questionable value, but a tilt at the Irish Derby is a distinct possibility.
**Elshadi(IRE)** put his dismal run in the Derby behind him but was no match for the winner. The intention is to drop him back to a mile and a quarter.
**Barati(IRE)** did not quite get the trip and his trainer confirmed that he is another who will revert to ten furlongs.
**Haadef** was unable to handle both a step up in distance and class on this much quicker ground.
**Gold History(USA)** should not have minded the firm ground but had his stamina limitations exposed after looking a big danger early in the home straight.

## 3033 CORONATION STKS (GROUP 1) (FILLIES) 1m (R)
3:45 (3:45) (A) 3-Y-O £139,823 (£53,036; £26,518; £12,053) Stalls High

Form RPR

1-11 **1** **Attraction**[26] 2330 3-9-0 119........................................... KDarley 10 121+
(MJohnston) *lw: mde all: qcknd clr 2f out: in n.d after: rdn out: impressive* **6/4**[1]

-100 **2** *2 ½* **Majestic Desert**[26] 2330 3-9-0 111................................ TEDurcan 5 113
(MRChannon) *hld up in rr: prog fr 2f out: styd on wl to take 2nd last 100yds: no ch w wnr* **25/1**

11-4 **3** *hd* **Red Bloom**[47] 1791 3-9-0 113.......................................... KFallon 12 113
(SirMichaelStoute) *lw: prom: drvn to chse wnr over 2f out: sn outpcd: kpt on but lost 2nd last 100yds* **10/3**[2]

1 **4** *3 ½* **Moon Dazzle (USA)**[27] 2311 3-9-0 ....................................... RHills 6 105
(WJHaggas) *lw: dwlt: hld up in last pair: prog on inner wl over 1f out: styd on fnl f: nt pce to rch ldrs* **25/1**

11-4 **5** *3 ½* **Kinnaird (IRE)**[26] 2330 3-9-0 107.................................... MJKinane 1 97
(PCHaslam) *racd in midfield: rdn wl over 2f out: sn outpcd: effrt again over 1f out: one pce* **12/1**

-505 **6** *1* **Kelucia (IRE)**[20] 2476 3-9-0 100...................................... WSupple 8 95
(JSGoldie) *racd in midfield: drvn wl over 2f out: sn outpcd: one pce after* **100/1**

310 **7** *nk* **Royal Tigress (USA)**[33] 2160 3-9-0 ............................. JPSpencer 11 94
(APO'Brien, Ire) *leggy: trckd wnr to over 2f out: sn outpcd u.p: wkng whn hmpd ins fnl f* **40/1**

2-1 **8** *1 ½* **Relaxed (USA)**[65] 1400 3-9-0 82..................................... RHughes 3 90
(SirMichaelStoute) *lw: trckd ldrs gng wl: rdn over 2f out: sn btn* **9/1**

1-06 **9** *hd* **Cairns (UAE)**[33] 2160 3-9-0 107...................................... LDettori 7 90
(SaeedBinSuroor) *hld up in last pair: rdn 3f out: one pce and n.d* **7/1**[3]

01 **10** *nk* **Aricia (IRE)**[19] 2505 3-9-0 ........................................... JPMurtagh 2 89
(JHMGosden) *hld up in last trio: rdn 3f out: no prog* **20/1**

1-55 **11** *5* **Secret Charm (IRE)**[26] 2330 3-9-0 112............................. MHills 9 78
(BWHills) *swtg: prom: drvn over 3f out: wknd 2f out* **14/1**

1m 38.54s (-4.50) **Going Correction** -0.10s/f (Good) **11** Ran SP% **115.8**
Speed ratings: **118,115,115,111,108 107,107,105,105,105 100**CSF £51.77 TOTE £2.40: £1.40, £7.10, £1.40; EX 67.00 Trifecta £273.70 Pool: £11,427.36, 29.75 winning units.
**Owner** Duke Of Roxburghe **Bred** Floors Farming **Trained** Middleham Moor, N Yorks
■ A Group One hat-trick for Attraction. Her Guineas double had never been achieved before, and she has raised the bar again.

**FOCUS**
A strong renewal of what is usually a good Group One, with Attraction once again proving herself queen of her generation of fillies with another powerful front-running display. The winning time was a cracking one even for a race of this standard.

**NOTEBOOK**
**Attraction** supplemented her two Classic wins with a devastating display in a time only fractionally outside the track record. Dominant from the start, she had no trouble handling a turn for the first time in a race and confirmed herself outstandingly the best of her age and sex. She is now likely to take on the older fillies in the Falmouth Stakes at Newmarket, and then the colts.
**Majestic Desert**, who won at Newbury early in the season but was below par behind Attraction in both Guineas, looked to be back to her best and got as close to the winner as she has ever done. If she can avoid that rival there are good races to be won with her at around this trip.
**Red Bloom**, who won the Meon Valley Stud Fillies' Mile over course and distance last season, had finished fourth to Attraction in the 1000 Guineas on her return and ran to within a a pound of that form. Connections believe she is capable of better, but she appeared to be taken off her feet early on and will appreciate being stepped up in distance. Her owners have Russian Rhythm in the Sussex Stakes so she may go for the Nassau.
**Moon Dazzle(USA)** ◆, a half-sister to Dupont, was taking a big step up from her debut win in a Newmarket maiden and did really well in the circumstances, finishing clear of the rest although no match for the front three. She probably found this coming too early in her career and is likely to improve a fair amount for the experience.
**Kinnaird(IRE)** finished much further behind Attraction than she had done at the Curragh, and may have found this ground too fast. She confirmed she has trained on and a confidence booster in a slightly lower grade may be on the cards.
**Kelucia(IRE)**, who has been held in Listed company, ran close to her Guineas form with the winner but really needs her sights lowered again.
**Royal Tigress(USA)**, tried to get to the front but had to give best to the winner and was left behind when that rival kicked on straightening up.
**Relaxed(USA)**, whose maiden win in April had worked out quite well, was taking a big step up in class. It proved beyond her, and she will be better off in Listed company for the time being.
**Cairns(UAE)**, who was well backed to improve on her efforts at Newmarket and in the French Guineas, finished further behind, having never got into contention. The ground may well have been unsuitable.
**Secret Charm(IRE)**, who had place credentials on her efforts behind the winner in the English and Irish Guineas, was given a positive ride but dropped out disappointingly. The ground should have not been a problem, so she has something to prove now.

## 3034 WOLFERTON RATED STKS (H'CAP) (LISTED RACE) 1m 2f
4:20 (4:23) (A) (0-110,110) 4-Y-O+ £23,200 (£8,800; £4,400; £2,000) Stalls High

Form RPR

0-13 **1** **Red Fort (IRE)**[34] 2110 4-8-8 **97**....................................... PRobinson 11 118
(MAJarvis) *lw: chsd ldrs: led 2f out: sn qcknd clr: r.o wl* **6/1**[2]

32-1 **2** *8* **Promotion**[48] 1762 4-8-7 **96** oh1........................................ KFallon 10 101
(SirMichaelStoute) *lw: hld up mid-div: rdn over 4f out: hdwy over 3f out: ev ch 2f out: sn outpcd* **2/1**[1]

4146 **3** *1 ¼* **Blythe Knight (IRE)**[14] 2638 4-9-0 **103**............................. LDettori 9 106
(EALDunlop) *hld up: hdwy over 2f out: styd on same pce fnl f* **10/1**

-441 **4** *1 ¼* **Persian Lightning (IRE)**[14] 2638 5-9-4 **107**...................... MJKinane 3 108
(JLDunlop) *hld up and bhd: hdwy over 1f out: nvr nrr* **6/1**[2]

0520 **5** *½* **Bonecrusher**[35] 2076 5-9-4 **107**........................................ TPQueally 16 107
(DRLoder) *hld up mid-div: rdn over 4f out: hdwy over 1f out: one pce fnl f* **16/1**

00-0 **6** *1* **Foodbroker Founder**[29] 2241 4-8-11 **100**.......................... DaneO'Neill 14 98
(DRCElsworth) *hld up: rdn and hdwy on ins over 2f out: swtchd lft wl over 1f out: no further prog* **25/1**

4206 **7** *1 ½* **Anani (USA)**[29] 2241 4-9-1 **104**........................................ JPSpencer 2 99
(EALDunlop) *hld up and bhd: hdwy over 1f out: n.d* **25/1**

50-6 **8** *2* **Millafonic**[18] 2527 4-8-7 **96** oh1....................................... DHolland 8 87
(LMCumani) *nvr nr ldrs* **8/1**[3]

0006 **9** *1 ¼* **Corriolanus (GER)**[30] 2220 4-8-8 **97**.............................. GaryStevens 4 86
(PMitchell) *swtg: plld hrd: sn bhd: sme hdwy whn nt clr run on ins over 1f out: sn eased* **33/1**

0325 **10** *2* **Compton Bolter (IRE)**[14] 2638 7-9-7 **110**......................... RHughes 13 95
(GAButler) *chsd ldrs: wkng whn hmpd wl over 1f out* **16/1**

0-03 **11** *½* **Akshar (IRE)**[46] 1849 5-9-4 **107**.......................................(b) PJSmullen 12 91
(DKWeld, Ire) *s.i.s: a bhd* **12/1**

-000 **12** *6* **Ulundi**[18] 2527 9-8-7 **96** oh1............................................... TQuinn 6 69
(PRWebber) *lw: sn w ldr: rdn and ev ch 2f out: wknd qckly* **25/1**

0000 **13** *12* **Sir George Turner**[14] 2638 5-8-9 **98**..................................(v[1]) JFanning 5 48
(MJohnston) *hld up mid-div: bhd fnl 3f* **50/1**

-000 **14** *7* **Tuning Fork**[19] 2508 4-8-7 **96** oh1......................................(t) JQuinn 1 33
(JAkehurst) *led: hdd 2f out: wknd qckly* **33/1**

2m 4.00s (-4.73) **Going Correction** -0.10s/f (Good) **14** Ran SP% **120.9**
Speed ratings: **114,107,106,105,105 104,103,101,100,99 98,93,84,78**CSF £16.98 CT £123.46 TOTE £7.90: £3.00, £1.30, £2.50; EX 23.00 Trifecta £158.50 Pool £6,698.02, 29.99 w/u.
**Owner** The Red Fort Partnership **Bred** Genesis Green Stud Ltd **Trained** Newmarket, Suffolk
■ Stewards Enquiry : Dane O'Neill caution: careless riding

**FOCUS**
A strong pace after Tuning Fork and Ulundi took each other on for the lead, and top handicap form. The winning time was creditable for a race of its type. The highly impressive Red Fort has been assessed through Promotion's Newmarket win, and he could rate even higher.

**NOTEBOOK**
**Red Fort(IRE)** ◆, reverting to ten furlongs, handled this fast ground well and came off a strong gallop to take the race by storm. The Handicapper is likely to take a dim view of the manner of this victory, and he may be denied the opportunity to race under an 8lb penalty in next month's John Smith's Cup at York as he returned a bit jarred up. However, on this form he can win in better company.
**Promotion**, the gamble of the week so far, was backed as if defeat was out of the question. Sir Michael Stoute thought he found the ground too lively but conceded that he would not have beaten the winner whatever the conditions.
**Blythe Knight(IRE)** ◆, so unlucky at Epsom last time, duly turned around a six-length defeat by Persian Lightning on 5lb better terms. He is another who found conditions quicker than ideal.
**Persian Lightning(IRE)**, raised 5lb, was 9lb higher than when pipped in this race last year. Dropped out from his wide draw, he could never get competitive after finding himself with a lot to do in the home straight.
**Bonecrusher**, again without the visor, ran respectively without ever making his presence felt.
**Foodbroker Founder** has been struggling to find his form since being narrowly beaten over this distance at this meeting last year.
**Compton Bolter(IRE)** *Official explanation: jockey said gelding was unsuited by the firm ground*

## 3035 QUEEN'S VASE (GROUP 3) 2m 45y
4:55 (4:55) (A) 3-Y-O £34,800 (£13,200; £6,600; £3,000) Stalls High

Form RPR

0-12 **1** **Duke Of Venice (USA)**[27] 2307 3-8-11 109...........................(t) LDettori 6 107+
(SaeedBinSuroor) *lw: hld up in midfield: smooth prog over 2f out: pushed into ld over 1f out: sn clr: easily* **9/2**[2]

**2** *6* **Two Miles West (IRE)**[9] 2797 3-8-11 ............................... JPSpencer 8 100
(APO'Brien, Ire) *wklike: lw: trckd ldrs: effrt over 3f out to ld wl over 2f out: rdn and hdd wl over 1f out: sn outpcd* **5/2**[1]

-240 **3** *6* **Top Seed (IRE)**[12] 2722 3-8-11 108.................................... TEDurcan 1 93
(MRChannon) *racd in midfield: rdn 3f out: sn outpcd: kpt on to chse clr ldng pair over 1f out: no imp* **11/2**[3]

3314 **4** *1 ¼* **Bumptious**[17] 2561 3-8-11 75..........................................(b[1]) PRobinson 7 91
(MHTompkins) *settled in rr: last and pushed along 5f out: kpt on u.p fnl 2f: no ch* **33/1**

261 **5** *3* **Strike**[28] 2273 3-8-11 82.....................................................(v[1]) JPMurtagh 10 88
(JHMGosden) *s.s: hld up in rr: rdn 3f out: sn outpcd and btn* **8/1**

2213 **6** *1 ¾* **Red Lancer**[31] 2203 3-9-0 110............................................ RMiles 5 89
(RJPrice) *hld up in rr: prog over 3f out: outpcd and rdn wl over 2f out: hanging rt and btn after* **8/1**

0-21 **7** *1* **Tarandot (IRE)**[21] 2460 3-8-8 87.................................... AMcCarthy 3 81
(GGMargarson) *trckd ldr for 5f: styd cl up: ev ch 3f out: sn outpcd: wknd over 1f out* **11/1**

2133 **8** *½* **Nessen Dorma (IRE)**[17] 2561 3-8-11 81.............................(v[1]) MFenton 4 84
(JGGiven) *lw: rn in snatches: chsd ldr after 5f: drvn 7f out: lost pl and btn 3f out* **16/1**

2165 **9** *17* **Tamarillo**[26] 2341 3-8-8 99............................................... DHolland 9 60
(MLWBell) *t.k.h: hld up: in tch tl wknd over 2f out: eased* **8/1**

-005 **10** *5* **Zouave (IRE)**[5] 2910 3-8-11 87........................................(b) PJSmullen 2 57
(BJMeehan) *led and set brisk pce: hdd wl over 2f out: wknd rapidly* **50/1**

3m 29.14s (-5.70) **Going Correction** -0.10s/f (Good) **10** Ran SP% **114.6**
Speed ratings: **110,107,104,103,101 101,100,100,91,89**CSF £15.81 TOTE £4.30: £1.70, £1.50, £2.60; EX 9.80 Trifecta £115.70 Pool £4,503.20, 27.63 w/u.
**Owner** Godolphin **Bred** Forenaghts Stud **Trained** Newmarket, Suffolk

**FOCUS**
A modest Group Three in which none of the ten runners was proven at the trip. Duke Of Venice won in emphatic style in a time that was fair for the type of race.

**NOTEBOOK**
**Duke Of Venice(USA)** had a sound chance on offical ratings but was taking a big step up in trip, and doubts about his ability to get it, not least from his pedigree, contributed to his starting price. He proved those to be unfounded in exemplary fashion, travelling well throughout and picking up readily once asked for an effort. He now comes into the reckoning for the St Leger, and possibly races such as the Goodwood Cup.
**Two Miles West(IRE)** ◆, a beautifully-bred colt who had made all when scoring on his debut just ten days previously, got a lead this time and went to the front turning in, but was easily brushed aside by the winner. He is clearly open to improvement, may appreciate easier ground and can win a Group race in his home country this season.
**Top Seed(IRE)** had solid form against Derby colts coming into this, but all those efforts were on much easier going. He seemed to travel well, but could not respond when let down. A drop back to a mile and a half and easier ground should enable him to find a winning opportunity, and a race such as the Gordon Stakes at Goodwood may suit him.
**Bumptious**, who was beaten in a 0-80 handicap last time, was tilting at windmills. However, possibly galvanised by the first-time blinkers, he ran above himself, passing beaten rivals in the straight. He will have blown his handicap mark if the assessor takes the form at face value.
**Strike**, who made hard work of winning a maiden on his previous run, was equipped with a visor this time but missed the break and never got into it. He may have found the trip stretching him at this stage of his career, but still improved a little on his maiden form.
**Red Lancer**, who has progressed remarkably since winning on the All-Weather in February, was another taking a big step up in trip. However, the fast ground rather than the distance looked the chief contributor to this below-par effort.

## 3036 BUCKINGHAM PALACE STKS (H'CAP) 7f
**5:30** (5:33) (B ) (0-105,103) 3-Y-0+ **£23,200** (£8,800; £4,400; £2,000) **Stalls** Low

| Form | | | | RPR |
|---|---|---|---|---|
| 21-3 | **1** | | **Unscrupulous**[19] 2504 5-8-5 **80** ........ OUrbina 23<br>(JRFanshawe) *lw: hld up and bhd far side: gd hdwy to ld 1f out: sn edgd rt and qcknd clr* **8/1**[3] | 103 |
| 0-53 | **2** | *5* | **Maghanim**[16] 2588 4-9-7 **96** ........ RHills 30<br>(JLDunlop) *lw: led far side: hdd 1f out: nt pce of wnr* **33/1** | 106 |
| 0423 | **3** | *nk* | **True Night**[10] 2750 7-8-2 **77** ........ JQuinn 29<br>(DNicholls) *hld up far side: hdwy over 2f out: kpt on fnl f* **11/1** | 86 |
| 11-2 | **4** | *3* | **New Seeker**[51] 1705 4-10-0 **103** ........ JPSpencer 1<br>(CGCox) *lw: led stands' side: rdn over 1f out: kpt on* **4/1**[1] | 104 |
| 041 | **5** | *hd* | **Peter Paul Rubens (USA)**[27] 2286 3-8-6 **90** ........ RLMoore 20<br>(PFICole) *a.p in centre: wknd fnl f* **9/1** | 91 |
| 14/2 | **6** | *shd* | **St Andrews (IRE)**[25] 2358 4-9-4 **93** ........ PRobinson 28<br>(MAJarvis) *chsd ldrs far side: wknd fnl f* **16/1** | 94 |
| 0-05 | **7** | *½* | **Manaar (IRE)**[20] 2469 4-8-8 **83** ........ EAhern 26<br>(JNoseda) *lw: hld up mid-div far side: hdwy over 1f out: one pce fnl f* **25/1** | 82 |
| 0250 | **8** | *½* | **Loyal Tycoon (IRE)**[13] 2682 6-8-5 **80** ........ ANicholls 10<br>(DNicholls) *hld up and bhd stands' side: swtchd rt 2f out: hdwy over 1f out: kpt on ins fnl f* **40/1** | 78 |
| -244 | **9** | *½* | **Jack Sullivan (USA)**[15] 2629 3-9-2 **100** ........(t) RHughes 27<br>(GAButler) *racd far side: no hdwy fnl 2f* **50/1** | 97 |
| 0013 | **10** | *nk* | **Mystic Man (FR)**[23] 2410 6-8-13 **88** ........ NCallan 5<br>(KARyan) *hld up mid-div stands' side: rdn and hdwy 2f out: no ex ins fnl f* **10/1** | 84 |
| 5053 | **11** | *hd* | **Kings Point (IRE)**[5] 2913 3-9-1 **99** ........ DaneO'Neill 8<br>(RHannon) *hld up stands' side: nt clr run jst over 2f out: hdwy fnl f: r.o* **25/1** | 94 |
| 6000 | **12** | *1* | **Will He Wish**[7] 2857 8-9-3 **92** ........(b) IMongan 7<br>(SGollings) *hld up in tch stands' side: rdn over 2f out: kpt on same pce fnl f* **66/1** | 85 |
| 0110 | **13** | *shd* | **Uhoomagoo**[2] 2969 6-9-5 **94** ........(b) MFenton 17<br>(KARyan) *racd far side: nvr nrr* **16/1** | 87 |
| -000 | **14** | *2½* | **Hurricane Floyd (IRE)**[19] 2503 6-8-8 **83** ........ GaryStevens 21<br>(DRLoder) *racd far side: n.d* **33/1** | 69 |
| 0140 | **15** | *nk* | **Blue Trojan (IRE)**[14] 2637 4-8-9 **84** ........ JFEgan 25<br>(SKirk) *chsd ldrs far side: rdn 3f out: wknd 2f out* **50/1** | 69 |
| 0134 | **16** | *¾* | **Sawwaah (IRE)**[14] 2637 7-8-9 **84** ........ PDobbs 16<br>(DNicholls) *hld up stands' side: hmpd wl over 1f out: n.d after* **50/1** | 67 |
| 40-0 | **17** | *½* | **Machinist (IRE)**[28] 2261 4-8-2 **80** ........ RMiles(3) 9<br>(DNicholls) *hld up stands' side: nt clr run over 2f out: a bhd* **40/1** | 62 |
| 0030 | **18** | *1¼* | **Banjo Bay (IRE)**[13] 2682 6-8-3 **78** ........ PDoe 2<br>(DNicholls) *prom stands' side: rdn 3f out: wknd 2f out* **50/1** | 57 |
| 0016 | **19** | *1* | **Master Robbie**[10] 2750 5-9-3 **92** ........ TEDurcan 18<br>(MRChannon) *mid-div far side: wknd 2f out* **16/1** | 68 |
| 600- | **20** | *5* | **Sir Edwin Landseer (USA)**[64] 4-8-2 **82** ........ RThomas(5) 4<br>(ChristianWroe, UAE) *prom stands' side: rdn over 2f out: sn wknd* **66/1** | 45 |
| 6004 | **21** | *nk* | **Kareeb (FR)**[21] 2459 7-7-12 **76** ........ LisaJones(3) 13<br>(WJMusson) *hld up mid-div stands' side: hdwy over 2f out: hmpd wl over 1f out: sn wknd* **16/1** | 38 |
| -06 | **22** | *5* | **Atavus**[27] 2283 7-9-4 **93** ........ JMackay 24<br>(GGMargarson) *chsd ldr far side: wknd over 1f out* **20/1** | 42 |
| 5410 | **23** | *1¾* | **H Harrison (IRE)**[6] 2899 4-8-5 **83** 7ex........ TPQueally(3) 22<br>(IWMcinnes) *chsd ldrs far side: rdn and wknd 3f out* **50/1** | 28 |
| 0-40 | **24** | *1* | **Selective**[27] 2283 5-9-8 **97** ........ KFallon 12<br>(ACStewart) *hld up stands' side: hdwy on outside over 2f out: rdn whn hmpd wl over 1f out: sn wknd* **15/2**[2] | 39 |
| -060 | **25** | *1* | **Namroud (USA)**[28] 2271 5-8-10 **85** ........(b[1]) PHanagan 15<br>(RAFahey) *hld up mid-div stands's side: bhd fnl 2f* **33/1** | 25 |
| -020 | **26** | *½* | **King Harson**[20] 2469 5-8-7 **82** ........(v) JFanning 14<br>(JDBethell) *prom stands' side: rdn and wknd 2f out* **66/1** | 20 |
| 6-02 | **27** | *hd* | **Obrigado (USA)**[19] 2503 4-8-7 **82** ........ PJSmullen 11<br>(WJHaggas) *hld up in tch stands side: rdn and wknd qckly 2f out* **16/1** | 20 |
| 2-00 | **28** | *1½* | **Arctic Desert**[66] 1385 4-8-13 **88** ........ MHills 19<br>(AMBalding) *racd centre: a bhd* **50/1** | 22 |

1m 27.41s (-2.26) **Going Correction** -0.10s/f (Good)
**WFA** 3 from 4yo+ 9lb **28** Ran **SP%** **142.1**
Speed ratings: **108,102,101,98,98 98,97,97,96,96 95,94,94,91,91 90,90,88,87,81 81,75,73,72,71 70,70,68**CSF £274.43 CT £3003.71 TOTE £10.40: £2.40, £11.20, £3.40, £1.60; EX 529.70 Trifecta £1709.30 Place 6 £69.31, Place 5 £8.46.
**Owner** Unscrupulous Partners & P Veitch **Bred** Meon Valley Stud **Trained** Newmarket, Suffolk
■ Stewards Enquiry : A Nicholls four-day ban: careless riding (Jun 29-Jul 2)

**FOCUS**
Strong handicap form and an impressive winner. Despite the far side group coming out on top it was probably advantageous to be drawn near either rail. The time was well up to standard for the grade.

**NOTEBOOK**
**Unscrupulous** likes to come from behind off a strong pace and the race could not have panned out better for him. Bursting clear once striking the front, he might be the type for the Bunbury Cup but will not be racing off this sort of mark.
**Maghanim** was trying to concede plenty of weight to the winner and ran a fine race to hold on for second. There will be other days for him.
**True Night** is a summer horse who loves this type of surface. He is knocking on the door and may go for one of the handicaps at Glorious Goodwood which are also very difficult to win.
**New Seeker** ◆ travelled strongly in the lead on the near side and was the first home of that group. A fine effort under a big weight, especially considering he had an interrupted preparation.
**Peter Paul Rubens(USA)** ◆ had nothing to race with in the centre, and this was a first class performance under the circumstances. He is unexposed and still on the upgrade.
**St Andrews(IRE)** seems to be coming to hand after missing all last year with bad fracture to a hind fetlock.
**Loyal Tycoon(IRE)**, ridden to get the trip, was doing his best work in the closing stages after causing interference when switched to get a run.
**Kings Point(IRE)** ◆ was another running on at the death after meeting trouble in running.
**Blue Trojan(IRE)** *Official explanation: jockey said gelding hung left*
T/Jkpt: £27,368.50 to a £1 stake. Pool: £250,557.50. 6.50 winning tickets. T/Plt: £113.80 to a £1 stake. Pool: £285,604.19. 1,831.25 winning tickets. T/Qpdt: £4.30 to a £1 stake. Pool: £18,163.90. 3,121.55 winning tickets. JN

# 3002 AYR (L-H)
Friday, June 18
**OFFICIAL GOING: Good (good to soft in places)**

## 3037 PETER'S RESTAURANT CLAIMING STKS 6f
**2:20** (2:23) (E ) 3-Y-O **£3,386** (£1,042; £521; £260) **Stalls** High

| Form | | | | RPR |
|---|---|---|---|---|
| 5166 | **1** | | **Arfinnit (IRE)**[7] 2839 3-8-13 63........(v) ACulhane 4<br>(MRChannon) *mde all: hld on wl fnl f* **4/5**[1] | 66 |
| -400 | **2** | *½* | **Beaver Diva**[30] 2232 3-7-7 23........ DFentiman(7) 5<br>(WMBrisbourne) *prom: rdn over 2f out: effrt and ev ch fnl f: hld towards fin* **100/1** | 51 |
| 6034 | **3** | *5* | **Wares Home (IRE)**[14] 2657 3-9-1 65........(v) DarrenWilliams 3<br>(KRBurke) *keen: sn cl up: rdn and edgd lft over 1f out: sn outpcd* **6/4**[2] | 51 |
| 6030 | **4** | *7* | **Vaudevire**[44] 1890 3-8-5 23........(b) SChin 1<br>(RPElliott) *prom tl outpcd 1/2-way: n.d after* **66/1** | 20 |
| 0300 | **5** | *½* | **Head Of State**[7] 2850 3-8-12 57........(v) NMackay(3) 2<br>(RMBeckett) *cl up tl wknd over 1f out: eased whn btn ins last* **8/1**[3] | 29 |

1m 13.52s (-0.20) **Going Correction** -0.025s/f (Good) **5** Ran **SP%** **109.1**
Speed ratings: **100,99,92,83,82**CSF £42.89 TOTE £1.60: £1.10, £16.10; EX 28.70.
**Owner** Tim Corby **Bred** Robert De Vere Hunt **Trained** West Ilsley, Berks
■ Stewards Enquiry : N Mackay four-day ban: failed to ride out for fourth place (Jul 1-4)

**FOCUS**
An uncompetitive event in which the winner, who did not have to improve to win, had the run of the race next to the stands side. As the runner up is rated only 23, this form is best treated with caution.

**NOTEBOOK**
**Arfinnit(IRE)**, down in grade, had the run of the race and did not have to be anywhere near his best with his main rival disappointing, to beat a 23-rated rival. He is likely to remain vulnerable back in handicap company.
**Beaver Diva** turned in her best effort dropped in trip but, as her rating is likely to take a big hike after this seemingly improved effort, she is going to be difficult to place successfully.
**Wares Home(IRE)** was closely matched with the winner on recent evidence but was a long way below that level this time and did not look the easiest of rides. The rain may not have helped but he looks one to tread carefully with.
**Vaudevire** faced a very stiff task at the weights and was again soundly beaten.
**Head Of State**'s turf form is a long way removed from the pick of his All-Weather efforts and he was again soundly beaten. He does not look one to place much faith in.

## 3038 UK RACING HERE TODAY H'CAP 6f
**2:55** (2:56) (D ) (0-80,73) 3-Y-0+ **£5,638** (£1,735; £867; £433) **Stalls** High

| Form | | | | RPR |
|---|---|---|---|---|
| -103 | **1** | | **Ulysees (IRE)**[16] 2581 5-9-4 **70**........ TEaves(3) 3<br>(ISemple) *hld up: effrt 2f out: nt clr run and swtchd rt ins fnl f: styd on strly to ld cl home* **11/2**[3] | 77+ |
| 0004 | **2** | *nk* | **Legal Set (IRE)**[2] 2976 8-7-6 **48** oh2 ow1........(t) NataliaGemelova(7) 1<br>(MissAStokell) *prom: hdwy to ld ins fnl f: r.o: hdd towards fin* **20/1** | 54 |
| 0241 | **3** | *hd* | **College Maid (IRE)**[1] 3006 7-8-4 **60** 6ex........ JCurrie(7) 5<br>(JSGoldie) *trckd ldrs: effrt and led over 1f out: hdd ins fnl f: hld towards fin* **13/2** | 65 |
| 1600 | **4** | *2* | **Highland Warrior**[9] 2784 5-9-7 **73**........ NMackay(3) 7<br>(JSGoldie) *missed break: hdwy outside and ev ch over 1f out: one pce ins fnl f* **3/1**[1] | 72 |
| 0033 | **5** | *½* | **Prince Of Blues (IRE)**[10] 2754 6-8-4 **60**........(p) PVarley(7) 9<br>(MMullineaux) *trckd ldrs tl rdn and outpcd over 1f out* **10/1** | 58 |
| -021 | **6** | *nk* | **Desert Arc (IRE)**[9] 2779 6-9-0 **63** 6ex........ SWKelly 8<br>(WMBrisbourne) *in tch: outpaced over 2f out: kpt on fnl f: no imp* **9/2**[2] | 60 |
| 000- | **7** | *hd* | **Fair Spin**[266] 5194 4-9-2 **65**........ ACulhane 10<br>(MDHammond) *hld up: pushed along and sme hdwy over 1f out: nvr rchd ldrs* **25/1** | 61 |
| 4640 | **8** | *¾* | **Friar Tuck**[2] 2976 9-8-6 **55**........ PFessey 11<br>(MissLAPerratt) *hld up: rdn over 2f out: no imp over 1f out* **12/1** | 49 |
| 0-15 | **9** | *1¼* | **Playful Dane (IRE)**[14] 2656 7-8-6 **58**........ LEnstone(3) 4<br>(WSCunningham) *led to over 1f out: sn btn* **17/2** | 48 |
| 0150 | **10** | *4* | **Danakim**[6] 2885 7-7-8 **50**........ DFentiman(7) 6<br>(JRWeymes) *chsd ldrs tl wknd fr 2f out* **25/1** | 28 |
| 600- | **11** | *18* | **Strawberry Patch (IRE)**[353] 2875 5-9-1 **64**........(p) JCarroll 2<br>(MissLAPerratt) *bhd on outside: wknd fr 1/2-way* **50/1** | — |

1m 13.03s (-0.69) **Going Correction** -0.025s/f (Good) **11** Ran **SP%** **113.6**
Speed ratings: **103,102,102,99,99 98,98,97,95,90 66**CSF £111.11 CT £726.07 TOTE £6.10: £2.30, £6.50, £2.50; EX 92.00.
**Owner** The Farmer Boys (Jock, Danny & Ally) **Bred** Sweetmans Bloodstock **Trained** Carluke, S Lanarks

**FOCUS**
A run of the mill event in which the field raced centre to stands side and the pace was sound. The form should stand up at a similar level.

**NOTEBOOK**
**Ulysees(IRE)** is a consistent sort who overcame trouble in running to win his second race of the season. He should not be going up too much for this success and can score again in exposed company.

**Legal Set(IRE)** confirmed the promise shown earlier this week and may be a bit better than the bare form as he had the worst draw. He is capable of winning races from this mark but his inconsistency has to be a concern.
**College Maid(IRE)**, back in trip and under a penalty for the previous evening's success, ran at least as well in defeat and this consistent sort, who is vulnerable to well handicapped or improving types, should continue to give a good account.
**Highland Warrior** for the fourth time in a row shaped as though better than the bare result, as he lost more ground at the start than he was beaten and made up his ground on the wide outside. He is capable of further success but he does need things to fall just right.
**Prince Of Blues(IRE)** looked in good condition and ran creditably, but he is not the most reliable of performers and his losing run means he is not one to place much faith in.
**Desert Arc(IRE)** was not disgraced under his penalty, but he may be better suited by a more strongly-run race on much quicker ground.
**Fair Spin** shaped as though retaining a fair amount of ability on this reappearance, and will be one to keep an eye on under more testing conditions.
**Friar Tuck** *Official explanation: jockey said gelding had a breathing problem*

## 3039 DAILY RECORD FIRST FOR SCOTTISH RACING CLASSIFIED STKS 1m
3:30 (3:31) (D) 3-Y-O+ £5,638 (£1,735; £867; £433) Stalls Low

Form RPR
2502 **1** **Tony Tie**[9] 2781 8-9-3 73 NMackay(3) 4 88
(JSGoldie) *trckd ldrs: led on bit over 1f out: pushed clr* 11/4[2]
1100 **2** 6 **Stoic Leader (IRE)**[30] 2226 4-9-7 79 DNolan(3) 7 78
(RFFisher) *midfield: effrt over 2f out: hung lft and styd on wl fnl f: nt rch wnr* 8/1
1223 **3** 2 **Samuel Charles**[7] 2838 6-9-6 72 SWKelly 2 70
(WMBrisbourne) *cl up: led 3f to over 1f out: outpcd ins last* 5/1[3]
-324 **4** shd **Lauro**[9] 2775 4-9-0 77 PMulrennan(5) 10 68
(MissJACamacho) *in tch: effrt over 2f out: no imp over 1f out* 5/2[1]
0061 **5** 3 **Western Roots**[17] 2545 3-8-13 78 ACulhane 3 65
(KAMorgan) *midfield: effrt and shkn up over 2f out: no imp over 1f out* 7/1
0004 **6** 3 **Telepathic (IRE)**[4] 2941 4-9-1 59 PBradley(5) 8 56
(ABerry) *hld up: hdwy over 2f out: btn over 1f out* 50/1
-024 **7** 1 3/4 **Francis Flute**[16] 2580 6-9-3 51 TEaves(3) 9 52
(BMactaggart) *trckd ldrs tl rdn and wknd wl over 1f out* 33/1
0000 **8** 5 **Percy Douglas**[22] 2423 4-9-6 45 AnnStokell 11 40
(MissAStokell) *bhd on outside: nvr on terms* 100/1
0200 **9** 1 1/4 **Anthemion (IRE)**[16] 2580 7-9-6 58 WDowling 1 37
(MrsJCMcgregor) *disp ld: led briefly 1/2-way: wknd 2f out* 50/1
-000 **10** 19 **Rosselli (USA)**[15] 2625 8-8-13 46 CEly(7) 5 —
(ABerry) *slt ld to 1/2-way: wknd over 2f out* 100/1
0500 **11** 9 **Blue Emperor (IRE)**[5] 2908 3-8-10 52 RFitzpatrick 12 —
(PTMidgley) *stdd s: nvr on terms* 100/1
30-0 **12** 2 **Unshaken**[9] 2779 10-8-13 57 JDO'Reilly(7) 6 —
(DANolan) *dwlt: a bhd* 50/1

1m 44.03s (0.91) **Going Correction** +0.35s/f (Good)
**WFA** 3 from 4yo+ 10lb 12 Ran SP% 107.3
Speed ratings: **109,103,101,100,97 94,93,88,86,67 58,56**CSF £21.26 TOTE £2.90: £1.30, £3.40, £1.80; EX 21.90.
**Owner** Frank Brady **Bred** Lord Crawshaw **Trained** Uplawmoor, E Renfrews
■ Stewards Enquiry : D Nolan caution: careless riding

**FOCUS**
The usual mixed bag but a sound pace and a decent time. Tony Tie improved on recent form but used to be capable of much better and is more reliable than mostof his opponents.

**NOTEBOOK**
**Tony Tie** is a tough and reliable sort who turned in his best effort of the year to win with plenty in hand. However he is likely to look vulnerable back in handicaps after reassessment.
**Stoic Leader(IRE)** put a poor run at Goodwood firmly behind him, but did not look the easiest of rides and he is likely to find life tough back in handicaps from his current mark.
**Samuel Charles** again looked ungainly under pressure (hangs and carries his head high), but he is a reliable type who again gave his running and who looks a good guide to the level of this form.
**Lauro** looked to have strong claims on recent evidence, despite the double figure draw, but was a shade disappointing. She is not one to write off just yet, though.
**Western Roots**, having his first run for new connections, was below his best and, although quicker ground may suit him ideally, is likely to look vulnerable from his current mark in handicaps.
**Telepathic(IRE)**, from an in-form stable, was not totally disgraced in the face of a stiff task but he is likely to be seen to much better effect in low-grade handicaps.

## 3040 UNBEATABLE OFFER (S) STKS 1m
4:05 (4:05) (F) 3-Y-O+ £2,975 (£850; £425) Stalls Low

Form RPR
0102 **1** **Ben Hur**[4] 2938 5-9-12 62 SWKelly 2 64
(WMBrisbourne) *in tch: hdwy to ld over 1f out: hung rt: kpt on wl: eased nr fin* 1/1[1]
-005 **2** 1 1/4 **Royal Windmill (IRE)**[50] 1718 5-9-0 45 (p) DFentiman(7) 8 56
(MDHammond) *plld hrd in midfield: hdwy to ld 1/2-way: sn kicked clr: hdd over 1f out: one pce fnl f* 25/1
0503 **3** 6 **Summer Special**[1] 3002 4-9-4 47 (p) LEnstone(3) 5 42
(DWBarker) *dwlt: hdwy 1/2-way: effrt and hung lft over 2f out: outpcd over 1f out* 8/1
5432 **4** 2 **Tinian**[16] 2594 6-9-7 53 DarrenWilliams 1 38
(KRBurke) *led 2f: cl up tl wknd fr 2f out* 4/1[2]
6000 **5** 5 **Andreyev (IRE)**[28] 2260 10-9-0 39 JCurrie(7) 11 26
(JSGoldie) *bhd tl sme late hdwy: nvr on terms* 50/1
030- **6** 3/4 **Ambushed (IRE)**[6] 4622 8-9-4 59 TEaves(3) 4 24
(PMonteith) *plld hrd: disp ld 2f: cl up tl wknd over 2f out* 7/1[3]
50 **7** 7 **Plattocrat**[14] 2664 4-9-7 SChin 10 8
(RPElliott) *in tch to 1/2-way: sn wknd* 50/1
500- **8** nk **Sherwood Forest**[249] 5534 4-9-4 44 (v) NMackay(3) 7 8
(MissLAPerratt) *midfield: rdn 1/2-way: sn btn* 16/1
600/ **9** 27 **Thwaab**[625] 5019 12-9-2 43 PMulrennan(5) 3 —
(FWatson) *a bhd* 40/1
0P00 **10** 5 **Lion's Domane**[45] 1868 7-9-7 52 JCarroll 9 —
(ABerry) *led after 2f: hdd 1/2-way: wknd 2f out* 25/1

1m 46.35s (3.23) **Going Correction** +0.35s/f (Good)
**WFA** 3 from 4yo+ 10lb 10 Ran SP% 113.5
Speed ratings: **97,95,89,87,82 82,75,74,47,42**CSF £36.61 TOTE £1.60: £1.10, £3.60, £2.40; EX 23.00.There was no bid for the winner.
**Owner** D C Rutter & H Clewlow **Bred** Blue Blood Investments **Trained** Great Ness, Shropshire

**FOCUS**
A modest event featuring mainly disappointing sorts. Ben Hur is a bit better than this grade, and there are unlikely to be too many winners coming from the minor placings downwards.

**NOTEBOOK**
**Ben Hur**, who had a good chance at the weights and on recent form, appreciated the decent gallop and won with a bit more in hand than the official margin suggests. He has reportedly had his problems but is a fair sort for this grade.
**Royal Windmill(IRE)** looks capable of winning a similar race in this grade, especially as he looks a bit better than the bare form. However, a career record of one win from 35 starts confirms he is not one to place too much faith in.
**Summer Special** turned out quickly, ran to a similar level and, although the return to further may help, the fact that he has yet to win in 30 starts inspires little confidence.
**Tinian** failed to confirm his recent Yarmouth run and remains one to place little faith in.
**Andreyev(IRE)** is a shadow of his former self and is not one to be interested in from a betting point of view.
**Ambushed(IRE)** , back on the Flat, did not give himself much chance of getting home given the early hold he took, and consistency has never been his strongest suit.

## 3041 KIDZPLAY H'CAP 1m 2f 192y
4:40 (4:41) (F) (0-55,55) 4-Y-O+ £3,178 (£908; £454) Stalls Low

Form RPR
-603 **1** **Scurra**[50] 1718 5-8-7 47 PMulrennan(5) 2 61
(ACWhillans) *trckd ldrs: led over 2f out: jnd ins fnl f: jst hld on* 14/1
0-62 **2** shd **Inchnadamph**[14] 2649 4-9-1 50 (t) ACulhane 14 64
(TJFitzgerald) *in tch: effrt over 2f out: edgd lft over 1f out: disp ld ins fnl f: jst failed* 5/1[2]
-000 **3** 10 **Border Terrier (IRE)**[14] 2649 6-8-7 45 (b[1]) NMackay(3) 13 42
(MDHammond) *keen: hld up: effrt over 2f out: no imp* 14/1
0405 **4** 5 **Escalade**[14] 2659 7-9-6 55 (p) SWKelly 12 44
(WMBrisbourne) *hld up: rdn and hdwy over 3f out: no imp fr 2f out* 15/2[3]
0300 **5** 2 **Mikasa (IRE)**[21] 2454 4-8-1 41 ow1 PBradley(5) 9 26
(RFFisher) *keen: led to over 2f out: sn btn* 33/1
-660 **6** shd **Grady**[10] 2753 5-7-10 38 DFentiman(7) 5 23
(WMBrisbourne) *hld up: rdn over 3f out: nt pce to chal* 25/1
-542 **7** 1 3/4 **Merlins Profit**[25] 2348 4-8-6 44 LEnstone(3) 4 26
(MDods) *cl up tl wknd over 2f out* 10/1
00-2 **8** 4 **Fairy Monarch (IRE)**[23] 2408 5-8-13 48 (p) RFitzpatrick 15 23
(PTMidgley) *racd wd towards rr: rdn 3f out: sn btn* 14/1
3045 **9** 2 1/2 **Optimum Night**[25] 2345 5-8-0 35 oh5 (p) PFessey 8 6
(PDNiven) *a bhd* 16/1
0-16 **10** 1 **Royal Melbourne (IRE)**[24] 2394 4-9-5 54 JCarroll 3 23
(MissJACamacho) *trckd ldrs tl wknd over 2f out* 10/1
2065 **11** 1 **Smarter Charter**[18] 2525 11-7-12 40 KristinStubbs(7) 1 8
(MrsLStubbs) *rrd s and rdr rode wout irons thrght: nvr on terms* 14/1
0-20 **12** 4 **Melograno (IRE)**[8] 2816 4-9-2 54 DNolan(3) 10 15
(MarkCampion) *dwlt: nvr on terms* 12/1
2000 **13** 12 **Good Timing**[18] 2346 6-8-5 40 DaleGibson 6 —
(JHetherton) *prom tl wknd over 2f out* 50/1
0305 **14** 6 **Repulse Bay (IRE)**[13] 2671 6-8-9 51 JCurrie(7) 11 —
(JSGoldie) *s.i.s: nvr on terms* 4/1[1]
0-00 **15** 12 **Burley Firebrand**[34] 2121 4-9-6 55 (b[1]) DarrenWilliams 7 —
(JGGiven) *midfield: rdn and wknd fr over 3f out* 14/1

2m 25.55s (2.23) **Going Correction** +0.35s/f (Good) 15 Ran SP% 122.3
Speed ratings: **105,104,97,94,92 92,91,88,86,85 85,82,73,69,60**CSF £81.99 CT £1027.91 TOTE £22.60: £5.00, £2.20, £5.00; EX 156.60.
**Owner** Mrs L M Whillans **Bred** Nawara Stud Co Ltd **Trained** Newmill-On-Slitrig, Borders
■ There was confusion after the judge initially called the result the other way round before changing his mind.

**FOCUS**
A low grade handicap on the rain-softened ground. The first two did well to pull clear of the remainder and record a fair time in the conditions, but the form doesn't look particularly solid.

**NOTEBOOK**
**Scurra** appreciated the return to this longer trip and got off the mark at the 29th attempt. Although he has taken a long time to get off the mark, he certainly showed the right attitude and may be able to win again in similar company.
**Inchnadamph**, whose latest Haydock form has been franked, ran at least as well and pulled clear of the remainder, but did not look an easy ride and may always be best under strong handling.
**Border Terrier(IRE)** ran a bit better in the first-time blinkers, despite taking a keen hold, but his inconsistency means he is not the best betting proposition around.
**Escalade** was again below his reappearance effort and, given his losing run stretches back to April 2002, he is another from this race to tread carefully with.
**Mikasa(IRE)**, back on turf and back up in trip, was again well beaten and this inconsistent maiden remains one to place little faith in.
**Grady** shaped as though a stiffer test of stamina would have been to his liking, but his record suggests he is an inconsistent maiden who remains one to place little faith in.
**Fairy Monarch(IRE)** *Official explanation: trainer said gelding was unsuited by the rain-softened ground*
**Royal Melbourne(IRE)** *Official explanation: jockey said gelding had lost its action on the bend*
**Smarter Charter** *Official explanation: jockey said saddle slipped*
**Good Timing** *Official explanation: jockey said gelding had hung right throughout*
**Repulse Bay(IRE)** *Official explanation: jockey said gelding had breathing problems*

## 3042 RACING HERE TOMORROW APPRENTICE MAIDEN H'CAP 1m 5f 13y
5:15 (5:16) (E) (0-70,67) 3-Y-O+ £3,474 (£1,069; £534; £267) Stalls Low

Form RPR
464P **1** **Merrymaker**[3] 2964 4-9-2 55 PPMathers 6 61
(WMBrisbourne) *hld up: hdwy 3f out: led over 1f out: kpt on wl* 11/4[1]
0-34 **2** hd **Dunlea Dancer**[16] 2567 3-7-6 53 AElliott(7) 7 59
(MJohnston) *keen: cl up: led over 2f to over 1f out: rallied: jst hld* 7/2[2]
456 **3** 5 **Caymans Gift**[20] 2487 4-9-2 60 AReilly(5) 1 59
(ACWhillans) *hld up in tch: effrt and ch over 2f out: no ex over 1f out* 16/1
-300 **4** 10 **Odabella (IRE)**[21] 2446 4-9-11 67 (t) JDO'Reilly(3) 5 52
(JohnBerry) *hld up in tch: hdwy to ld over 3f out: hdd over 2f out: sn btn* 7/2[2]
0-06 **5** 2 1/2 **Gaiety Girl (USA)**[11] 2732 3-8-5 64 AMullen(5) 8 46
(TDEasterby) *trckd ldrs tl hung lft and wknd fr 3f out* 7/1
-405 **6** 7 **Morvern (IRE)**[18] 2531 4-8-3 45 DTudhope(3) 4 17
(JGGiven) *led to over 3f out: sn rdn and wknd* 4/1[3]
6600 **7** 1 1/4 **Mr Moon**[10] 2760 3-7-9 52 oh17 DFentiman(3) 2 22
(MDHammond) *cl up: led briefly over 3f out: sn wknd* 50/1

3m 3.41s (7.56) **Going Correction** +0.35s/f (Good)
**WFA** 3 from 4yo+ 15lb 7 Ran SP% 111.5
Speed ratings: **90,89,86,80,79 74,74**CSF £11.92 CT £120.68 TOTE £3.40: £2.20, £2.60; EX 9.10 Place 6 £85.70, Place 5 £47.05.
**Owner** The Blacktoffee Partnership **Bred** Hascombe And Valiant Studs **Trained** Great Ness, Shropshire

**FOCUS**
An ordinary event, run at just a steady pace, and a modest winning time. However, the winner may be a bit better than the bare form.

**NOTEBOOK**
**Merrymaker**, whose saddle slipped last time, turned in an improved effort to win on only his fifth start for his current yard, and may be a bit better than the bare form as he was held up off a steady pace. He is in good hands and may be capable of better.

**Dunlea Dancer** did not really settle in a race run at just a steady gallop, but showed more than enough to suggest a similar race can be found in the near future.
**Caymans Gift** was not totally disgraced on this handicap debut, but is not going to be easy to place successfully from his current mark.
**Odabella(IRE)**, up to this trip for the first time, did not get home having travelled strongly for a long way. The return to shorter is likely to help but she has been a disappointing type.
**Gaiety Girl(USA)** did not improve for the step up to this longer trip and did not look the easiest of rides once put under pressure. She may not be the easiest to place successfully.
**Morvern(IRE)** had the run of the race but folded tamely, and this 16-race maiden remains one to tread carefully with.
T/Plt: £75.90 to a £1 stake. Pool £24,490.30, 235.45 winning tickets T/Qpdt: £18.10 to a £1 stake. Pool £2,167.55, 88.30 winning tickets RY

# 2837 GOODWOOD (R-H)

## Friday, June 18

**OFFICIAL GOING: Round course - good to firm; straight course - good**

## 3043 RACING UK APPRENTICE STKS (H'CAP) 6f

6:15 (6:15) (E) (0-70,70) 3-Y-0+ **£3,513** (£1,081; £540; £270) **Stalls** Low

Form RPR

2236 **1** **Aintnecessarilyso**[6] [2885] 6-8-0 **47** MHalford(5) 9 55
(NEBerry) *hld up towards rr: hdwy over 2f out: led 1f out: edgd lft ins fnl f: drvn out: jst hld on* **7/1**[3]

-000 **2** *shd* **Stokesies Wish**[23] [2399] 4-9-5 **61** HayleyTurner 8 69
(JLSpearing) *in tch: swtchd lft 1/2-way: rdn over 1f out: fin strly fnl f: jst failed* **20/1**

0-00 **3** *2* **Willheconquertoo**[12] [2703] 4-9-3 **64** (t) DerekNolan(5) 2 66
(AndrewReid) *b.hind: s.i.s: hdwy over 2f out: pressed ldrs appr fnl f: nt qckn ins last* **20/1**

0000 **4** *shd* **Beyond Calculation (USA)**[21] [2440] 10-9-0 **56** (p) NChalmers 6 57
(JMBradley) *hld up in mid-div: rdn and heaqdway over 1f out: kpt on fnl f* **11/1**

10-0 **5** *nk* **Polar Impact**[31] [2206] 5-10-0 **70** AQuinn 12 71
(GLMoore) *lw: a.p: led briefly olver 1f out: nt qckn ins fnl f* **7/2**[2]

4062 **6** *2 1/2* **Juwwi**[6] [2869] 10-8-13 **62** HazelBoyd(7) 5 55
(JMBradley) *slowly away and wl in rr: sme hdwy appr fnl f: nvr nr to chal* **14/1**

0110 **7** *3/4* **Somerset West (IRE)**[16] [2598] 4-9-10 **66** MSavage 10 57
(JRBest) *led tl hdd over 2f out: wknd over 1f out* **16/1**

-000 **8** *hd* **Toppling**[14] [2656] 6-8-13 **55** BSwarbrick 11 45
(JMBradley) *prom: led over 2f out: hdd over 1f out: wknd qckly* **10/1**

0/00 **9** *8* **Threezedzz**[15] [2614] 6-9-1 **60** SJDonohoe(3) 4 26
(PDEvans) *outpcd and nvr on terms* **7/1**[3]

3060 **10** *5* **Second Minister**[6] [2885] 5-8-1 **50** (b) JTucker(7) 1 1
(DFlood) *a bhd* **33/1**

04-1 **11** *19* **Millfields Dreams**[7] [2836] 5-8-12 **54** 7ex PMakin 7 —
(RBrotherton) *w ldrs: rdn over 2f out: wknd qckly: t.o* **15/8**[1]

1m 13.47s (0.63) **Going Correction** +0.225s/f (Good) **11 Ran SP% 124.4**
Speed ratings: **104,103,101,101,100 97,96,96,85,78 53**CSF £145.73 CT £2747.83 TOTE £8.70: £1.60, £5.30, £7.90; EX 101.90.
**Owner** Mrs Jan Adams **Bred** D R C And Mrs Elsworth **Trained** Earlswood, Monmouths

**FOCUS**
A sound pace, but just ordinary form.

**NOTEBOOK**
**Aintnecessarilyso** is a consistent individual but tricky to win with. Despite winning, he probably got to the front too soon, but the line came just in time as the runner-up produced a strong late challenge. He should continue to acquit himself well.
**Stokesies Wish**, who has been struggling for form this season, bounced back with a strong-finishing second. She ran well off 63 at Brighton last October, and perhaps she is not as badly handicapped as it seems.
**Willheconquertoo**, who is often slowly away, travelled well off the good pace and had his chance. He looks to be coming into form.
**Beyond Calculation(USA)**, who has not run off a mark as low as this since 1999, kept on well enough. This was his best performance of the season so far and hopefully he can build on it.
**Polar Impact** showed plenty of pace but was swamped by the closers late on.
**Juwwi** as usual got going all too late.
**Millfields Dreams**, who looked to have a strong chance of following up his runaway Chepstow win, ran way below form, but he had an excuse. *Official explanation: jockey said gelding lost its action*

## 3044 TAURUS WASTE RECYCLING MAIDEN STKS 1m 1f

6:45 (6:46) (D) 3-Y-0+ **£5,564** (£1,712; £856; £428) **Stalls** High

Form RPR

55- **1** **Goodwood Finesse (IRE)**[237] [5757] 3-8-7 GCarter 4 70
(JLDunlop) *mid-div: rdn and hdwy over 1f out: fin fast fnl f: led post* **7/1**

0 **2** *hd* **Woman In White (FR)**[63] [1441] 3-8-7 JFortune 6 70
(JHMGosden) *s.i.s: in rr tl hdwy over 2f out: strly rdn to ld wl ins fnl f: hdd post* **13/8**[1]

5-5 **3** *nk* **Gwen John (USA)**[14] [2647] 3-8-7 SDrowne 9 69
(HMorrison) *lw: trckd ldrs: led over 1f out: strly rdn and hdd wl ins fnl f: lost 2nd cl home* **7/4**[2]

00- **4** *5* **Spring Adieu**[224] [5938] 3-8-7 WSupple 1 59
(MrsAJPerrett) *scope: led: rdn and hdd over 1f out: fdd ins fnl f* **11/1**

0 **5** *shd* **Laugh 'n Cry**[15] [2632] 3-8-7 SWhitworth 3 59
(CACyzer) *w'like: t.k.h: a.p: rdn and wkng whn checked appr fnl f: no ex* **25/1**

6 **6** *11* **Nazzwah**[8] [2808] 3-8-7 CCatlin 8 37
(MRChannon) *w'like: trckd ldr: rdn over 2f out: wknd wl over 1f out* **6/1**[3]

0 **7** *3/4* **Royal Logic**[9] [2785] 3-8-7 ADaly 7 35
(MRChannon) *hld up: a rr: lost tch over 2f out* **20/1**

0-00 **8** *4* **Bee Dees Legacy**[6] [2882] 3-8-12 SCarson 2 32
(GLMoore) *towards rr: rdn over 4f out: sn wl bhd* **50/1**

1m 57.41s (0.55) **Going Correction** +0.225s/f (Good) **8 Ran SP% 120.1**
Speed ratings: **106,105,105,101,101 91,90,87**CSF £19.58 TOTE £6.10: £1.60, £1.30, £1.30; EX 19.00.
**Owner** Goodwood Racehorse Owners Group (Nine) **Bred** Yeomanstown Stud **Trained** Arundel, W Sussex
■ Stewards Enquiry : J Fortune one-day ban: failed to give filly time to respond to whip (Jun 29)

**FOCUS**
An ordinary looking maiden, but the first three pulled clear and the time was decent.

**NOTEBOOK**
**Goodwood Finesse(IRE)**, who is bred to stay middle distances, came with a strong late run to deny the favourite in the last moments. This did not look a great maiden, but she seems sure to get better as she steps up in trip.
**Woman In White(FR)**, whose dam won the Irish 1000 Guineas, had shown promise in a quality maiden at Newbury last time and stepped up on that effort, outbattling the eventual third only to be mugged close home. She also shapes as though she will be better when upped in trip.
**Gwen John(USA)** had the benefit of course experience having finished fifth in another maiden here a fortnight earlier. She picked up well under pressure but was eventually overhauled. She is now eligible for handicaps, but it is quite possible that she could yet find a weak maiden.
**Spring Adieu**, who made the running for her out-of-form stable, is out of a mare who won over ten furlongs and is a sister to the high-class filly Myself.
**Laugh 'n Cry**, whose dam was a triple sprint winner from a speedy family, is herself a half-sister to several multiple sprint winners. However, there is plenty of stamina on the sire's side of her pedigree.
**Nazzwah** was another representing a stable which is not quite at its very best at present.

## 3045 MIDSUMMER MAIDEN AUCTION FILLIES' STKS 6f

7:15 (7:16) (E) 2-Y-0 **£4,745** (£1,460; £730; £365) **Stalls** Low

Form RPR

52 **1** **Bentley's Bush (IRE)**[13] [2690] 2-8-10 JFortune 4 75
(RHannon) *lw: dwlt s: hdwy over 2f out: rdn to ld wl ins fnl f: r.o wl* **1/2**[1]

0 **2** *nk* **Shosolosa (IRE)**[9] [2786] 2-8-1 JFMcDonald(3) 3 68
(BJMeehan) *trckd ldrs: rdn to ld over 1f out: kpt on: hdd wl ins fnl f* **12/1**

**3** *1 1/4* **Sweet Coincidence** 2-8-2 GDuffield 2 62
(IAWood) *leggy: scope: s.i.s: in rr tl hdwy over 1f out: fine wl to take 3rd nr fin* **13/2**[2]

**4** *3/4* **Phlaunt** 2-8-2 SCarson 7 60
(RFJohnsonHoughton) *bkwd: hld up in tch: hdwy over 3f out: ev ch appr fnl f: one pce ins* **25/1**

00 **5** *1/2* **Elvina Hills (IRE)**[46] [1839] 2-8-3 ADaly 6 60
(WGMTurner) *led: rdn and hdd over 1f out: wknd ins fnl f* **20/1**

56 **6** *3/4* **Piddies Pride (IRE)**[29] [2234] 2-7-11 (v[1]) BSwarbrick(5) 1 56
(IAWood) *prom: rdn 2f out: wknd over 1f out* **20/1**

**7** *7* **Victory Hymn (IRE)** 2-8-3 CCatlin 8 36
(MRChannon) *w'like: bkwd: in tch: rdn 2f out: wknd over 1f out* **10/1**[3]

**8** *4* **Triple Zero (IRE)** 2-8-9 KMcEvoy 5 30
(APJarvis) *unf: in tch: rdn 2f out: sn wknd* **11/1**

1m 15.12s (2.28) **Going Correction** +0.225s/f (Good) **8 Ran SP% 118.5**
Speed ratings: **93,92,90,89,89 88,78,73**CSF £8.10 TOTE £1.60: £1.10, £2.40, £1.80; EX 6.60.
**Owner** Off Trak Partnership **Bred** Kilfrush Stud **Trained** East Everleigh, Wilts
■ Jimmy Fortune's first winner following ten months out with a back injury.
■ Stewards Enquiry : J Fortune caution: careless riding

**FOCUS**
Just an average maiden.

**NOTEBOOK**
**Bentley's Bush(IRE)**, who chased home Park Romance (fifth in the Albany Stakes at Royal Ascot earlier in the day) on her last outing, had less to do in this company but she did have to give weight all round, and it was anything but a walk in the park. She showed a good attitude though, and looks likely to be suited by farther than this in time.
**Shosolosa(IRE)** was slowly away on her debut but had clearly learnt plenty from that experience and was always near the pace on this occasion. She pushed the favourite close and is another expample of her trainer's juveniles improving a lot for their first runs.
**Sweet Coincidence**, a half-sister to juvenile sprint winner Sable 'n Silk, showed plenty of promise on her debut after missing the break and running green. Reluctant to challenge between horses, she stayed on well under a tender ride from her experienced jockey, and the chances are that she will improve a good deal for this experience.
**Phlaunt**, a sister to Pheisty, who won as a juvenile and later scored over middle distances, and half-sister to three other winners, shaped with a degree of promise, only being run out of the places inside the last.
**Elvina Hills(IRE)**, one of the more experienced fillies in the field, was tackling quicker ground than she had encountered on her previous two starts.

## 3046 RENAULT VAN STKS (H'CAP) 1m 4f

7:50 (7:51) (D) (0-85,85) 3-Y-0+ **£6,906** (£2,125; £1,062; £531) **Stalls** Low

Form RPR

-000 **1** **Wait For The Will (USA)**[29] [2240] 8-9-6 **82** (b) AQuinn(5) 8 94
(GLMoore) *hld up towards rr: tk clsr order over 5f out: led on bit ins fnl f: pushed out: comf* **8/1**

0035 **2** *1 3/4* **Northside Lodge (IRE)**[20] [2474] 6-9-5 **76** WSupple 2 85
(PWHarris) *lw: hld up in mid-div: rdn over 3f out: hdwy whn short of room and swtchd lft over 2f out: r.o fnl f to take 2nd cl home* **6/1**[3]

20-0 **3** *hd* **Sergeant Cecil**[58] [1539] 5-10-0 **85** SDrowne 1 94
(BRMillman) *mid-div: hdwy to 2nd over 3f out: led over 2f out: rdn and hdd ins fnl f: lost 2nd cl home* **33/1**

3-41 **4** *1/2* **Man At Arms (IRE)**[8] [2802] 3-8-3 **74** 5ex RLMoore 4 82
(RHannon) *s.i.s and in rr: rdn 3f out: styd on fnl f: nvr nrr* **5/2**[2]

-005 **5** *1 1/2* **Winners Delight**[17] [2557] 3-8-9 **80** KMcEvoy 7 86
(APJarvis) *lw: trckd ldr for 4f: sn mid-div: kpt on one pce ins fnl 2f* **16/1**

00-0 **6** *1/2* **Sunny Glenn**[14] [2639] 6-9-12 **83** RHavlin 9 88
(MrsPNDutfield) *lw: slowly away and in rr: styd on one pce fnl 2f* **40/1**

-611 **7** *1 1/4* **Tidal**[7] [2835] 5-8-3 **65** 5ex RThomas(5) 3 68
(AWCarroll) *trckd ldrs: led 6f out: hdd over 2f out: wknd appr fnl f* **7/4**[1]

4403 **8** *5* **Desert Island Disc**[5] [2914] 7-8-13 **73** JFMcDonald(3) 10 68
(JJBridger) *mid-div: rdn overe 2f out: sn btn* **16/1**

6301 **9** *10* **Private Benjamin**[10] [2767] 4-7-13 **55** 5ex oh1 ow1 CCatlin 5 35
(JamiePoulton) *mid-div: rdn over 3f out: wknd 2f out* **16/1**

3003 **10** *5* **Rainbow World (IRE)**[11] [2740] 4-8-8 **65** (p) JFEgan 6 36
(AndrewReid) *b.hind: prom: chsd ldr after 4f tl 6f out: rdn and wknd over 2f out* **33/1**

4004 **11** *23* **Richemaur (IRE)**[13] [2671] 4-9-2 **73** GDuffield 11 7
(MHTompkins) *plld hrd: led tl hdd 6f out: sn dropped rr and wl bhd fnl 3f* **14/1**

2m 38.36s (-0.57) **Going Correction** +0.225s/f (Good)
**WFA** 3 from 4yo+ 14lb **11 Ran SP% 123.0**
Speed ratings: **110,108,108,108,107 107,106,102,96,92 77**CSF £57.32 CT £1534.80 TOTE £9.40: £2.10, £2.40, £6.80; EX 70.50.
**Owner** Rdm Racing **Bred** Paul Mellon **Trained** Woodingdean, E Sussex

**FOCUS**
This looks reliable fom, despite a poor performance from the favourite. The winner won with any amount in hand and the time was good.

**NOTEBOOK**
**Wait For The Will(USA)** made it a hat-trick of wins in this race, having also been successful in 2002 and 2003. He had not shown anything on his previous three starts this term but had slipped to a mark 4lb lower than when successful in this race last year and clearly this had been the aim. He won so easily that he will surely go well if bidding to follow up under a penalty. *Official explanation: trainer said, regarding the improved form shown, gelding had taken time to come to itself this season following a lengthy break*
**Northside Lodge(IRE)** is currently on a fair mark and ran a solid race. It was just unfortunate for him that he ran into a well-handicapped animal ideally suited by the demands of this race.

**Sergeant Cecil** may have done his winning over a mile six but he has the ability to compete over this shorter distance too. Unfortunately, on this occasion he was merely a sitting duck for the winner.

**Man At Arms(IRE)** could have done with a stronger pace, as he got going all too late on this occasion.

**Winners Delight** was going into unknown territory on this step up in trip, but he seemed to see the trip out well enough.

**Tidal** looked to have plenty going for her on her hat-trick bid, but in the event she weakened tamely out of contention when the going got tougher in the straight. The race may have come too soon for her after her wide-margin Chepstow win, and she is due to be raised to a mark of 77 now, so things are not going to get any easier.

## 3047 PETERS PLC FILLIES' STKS (H'CAP) 7f

8:25 (8:25) (D) (0-85,82) 3-Y-O+ £5,382 (£1,656; £828; £414) Stalls High

| Form | | | | RPR |
|---|---|---|---|---|
| 1-00 | 1 | | **In The Pink (IRE)**[27] 2284 4-8-8 62 ... CCatlin 3<br>(MRChannon) *hld up in rr: swtchd lft and pushed along 3f out: rdn to ld ins fnl f: r.o wl* **9/1** | 71 |
| 0-30 | 2 | 1 1/4 | **Concubine (IRE)**[12] 2703 5-8-6 60 ... DSweeney 4<br>(JRBoyle) *trckd ldrs gng wl: short of room over 1f: r.o strly u.p whn got clr run ins fnl f* **4/1** | 66 |
| 3404 | 3 | 1 3/4 | **Bint Royal (IRE)**[6] 2875 6-8-6 60 ...(p) JFEgan 2<br>(MissVHaigh) *trckd ldr: led over 1f out: rdn and hdd ins fnl f and lost 2nd nr fin* **3/1**[1] | 61 |
| 2400 | 4 | 3/4 | **Annijaz**[6] 2886 7-8-1 55 ... RLMoore 6<br>(JMBradley) *stdd s: hld up: effrt over 1f out: styd on one pce fnl f* **11/2** | 54 |
| 0415 | 5 | 1 1/2 | **I Wish**[20] 2482 6-8-2 56 ... ADaly 1<br>(MMadgwick) *plld hrd thrght: hld up in rr: rdn over 1f out: no imp* **10/3**[2] | 51 |
| 0004 | 6 | 4 | **Riva Royale**[9] 2788 4-10-0 82 ... GDuffield 5<br>(IAWood) *stmbld s: sn led: hdd over 1f out: wknd qckly* **7/2**[3] | 67 |

1m 28.96s (0.93) **Going Correction** +0.225s/f (Good) 6 Ran SP% **115.7**

Speed ratings: **103,101,99,98,97 92**CSF £45.57 TOTE £6.00: £2.00, £2.80; EX 87.10.

**Owner** Mrs D J Buckley **Bred** Mount Coote Stud **Trained** West Ilsley, Berks

**FOCUS**

A modest race made up mostly of badly-handicapped fillies.

**NOTEBOOK**

**In The Pink(IRE)** had not hinted on her previous two starts this season that she was about to hit form, but she won this well, coming from last to first in the straight. She shapes as though a mile may be within her compass. *Official explanation: trainer's representative said, regarding the improved form shown, filly appeared better suited by being dropped in*

**Concubine(IRE)** did not get the best of runs next to the rail and the winner got first run on her. She finished well but the bird had flown, and she continues to be a hard horse to win with.

**Bint Royal(IRE)** is handicapped up to her best at present and in the circumstances this was a solid effort.

**Annijaz** is another who looks held by the Handicapper off her current mark, as she is still 3lb higher than when winning the last of the three handicaps she won last summer.

**I Wish** did not help her rider by failing to settle.

**Riva Royale** has generally struggled in handicap company off marks in the 80s, her only success coming when dropped to mark of 79 and beating a big field under top weight at Yarmouth last season. Once again heading the weights, she got her own way in front and really should have done better.

## 3048 RACING UK ON 425 STKS (H'CAP) 1m

8:55 (8:57) (D) (0-85,78) 3-Y-O+ £5,564 (£1,712; £856; £428) Stalls High

| Form | | | | RPR |
|---|---|---|---|---|
| -002 | 1 | | **Omaha City (IRE)**[23] 2406 10-9-1 69 ... MTebbutt 3<br>(BGubby) *stdd s: hld up in rr: rdn and hung rt 2f out: gd hdwy to ld over 1f out: pushed out* **13/2** | 80 |
| 6142 | 2 | 1 | **Ephesus**[6] 2891 4-9-10 78 ...(v) WSupple 9<br>(MissGayKelleway) *lw: trckd ldrs: led briefly over 1f out: rallied ins fnl f but no imp nr fin* **10/3**[2] | 87 |
| 2021 | 3 | 1/2 | **Best Before (IRE)**[4] 2945 4-8-12 73 6ex ... SJDonohoe[(7)] 1<br>(PDEvans) *hld up in mid-div: swtchd lft 2f out: hrd rdn over 1f out: styd on fnl f: nvr nrr* **4/1**[3] | 81 |
| 4055 | 4 | 4 | **Mad Carew (USA)**[7] 2845 5-9-8 76 ...(be) RLMoore 7<br>(GLMoore) *lw: hld up towards rr: rdn 3f out: one pce ins fnl 2f* **3/1**[1] | 75 |
| -006 | 5 | shd | **Recount (FR)**[11] 2727 4-9-7 75 ... NPollard 2<br>(JRBest) *a.p: trckd ldr 4f out to 2f out: sn one pce* **25/1** | 73 |
| 0451 | 6 | 3/4 | **Madamoiselle Jones**[18] 2521 4-9-0 68 ... DKinsella 6<br>(HSHowe) *led tl hdd over 1f out: wknd fnl f* **15/2** | 65 |
| 3350 | 7 | 4 | **Deeper In Debt**[37] 2030 6-9-0 68 ... GCarter 4<br>(JAkehurst) *trckd ldr to 4f out: rdn and wknd 2f out* **10/1** | 55 |
| 0100 | 8 | 1 1/4 | **Muyassir (IRE)**[8] 2806 9-8-9 63 ... SDrowne 8<br>(MissBSanders) *in tch: rdn 2f out: wknd appr fnl f* **12/1** | 48 |
| 10-2 | 9 | 18 | **Competitor**[160] 490 3-8-8 72 ... CCatlin 5<br>(JAkehurst) *in rr and outpcd: lost tch 3f out* **16/1** | 15 |

1m 41.41s (1.14) **Going Correction** +0.225s/f (Good)

**WFA** 3 from 4yo+ 10lb 9 Ran SP% **119.7**

Speed ratings: **103,102,101,97,97 96,92,91,73**CSF £29.59 CT £100.81 TOTE £7.80: £1.80, £1.60, £1.90; EX 22.50 Place 6 £410.64, Place 5 £67.65.

**Owner** Brian Gubby Ltd **Bred** Brownstown Stud Farm **Trained** Bagshot, Surrey

**FOCUS**

A race for course specialists, with no fewer than five (including the winner and runner-up) course and distance winners in the line-up. It was run at a good pace, the first three came clear, and the form should work out.

**NOTEBOOK**

**Omaha City(IRE)**, who had dropped to a career-low mark, is never one to underestimate at this track, and with the pace strong he had the race run to suit, too. He did it well but one would not be confident of him translating this form to another track.

**Ephesus** may not have achieved as much as the winner here yet, but he is certainly building up a decent record at the track, and this sound effort once again confirmed his liking for this unique course.

**Best Before(IRE)** did not run at all badly under his 6lb penalty considering this race came just four days after he won at Windsor. This should give connections hope that he can continue to run well off his revised mark.

**Mad Carew(USA)** had the headgear back on and the fast pace ought to have suited, as he finds this trip just on the short side. However, one cannot get away from the view that he is hardly well handicapped at present on a mark 15lb higher than when last successful on turf.

**Recount(FR)** is a middle-distance performer presumably being campaigned over this sort of distance in an attempt to get his handicap mark down. He is due to be dropped 3lb at the weekend.

**Madamoiselle Jones**, who has never won off a mark this high, went too quick for her own good and merely set it up for those coming from behind.

JS

# NEWMARKET (JULY) (R-H)

Friday, June 18

**OFFICIAL GOING: Good to firm**

There was a strong following wind, but no advantage to be gained by the draw.

Wind: Fresh behind Weather: Cloudy

## 3049 SIEMENS SMART HOME TECHNOLOGY APPRENTICE H'CAP 1m

6:30 (6:31) (E) (0-70,70) 3-Y-O+ £3,451 (£1,062; £531; £265) Stalls Low

| Form | | | | RPR |
|---|---|---|---|---|
| 2412 | 1 | | **Prime Offer**[8] 2803 8-9-2 61 ... CHaddon[(3)] 8<br>(JJay) *mde all: rdn out* **13/8**[1] | 71 |
| -200 | 2 | 1 3/4 | **Halcyon Magic**[16] 2597 6-8-1 48 ...(b) LauraPike[(5)] 9<br>(MissJFeilden) *chsd ldrs: rdn over 2f out: styd on* **10/1** | 54 |
| 00-0 | 3 | 1/2 | **Arran**[16] 2596 4-8-9 54 ... RoryMoore[(3)] 6<br>(VSmith) *hld up: hdwy to chse wnr over 2f out: rdn over 1f out: styd on* **8/1**[3] | 59 |
| 5006 | 4 | nk | **Single Track Mind**[6] 2886 6-7-11 44 ...(p) DeanWilliams[(5)] 7<br>(JRBoyle) *bhd: hdwy over 1f out: nt rch ldrs* **12/1** | 48 |
| 35-0 | 5 | 1/2 | **Welcome Signal**[6] 2881 4-9-6 67 ... SaleemGolam[(5)] 1<br>(JRFanshawe) *hld up: rdn over 3f out: hdwy over 1f out: styd on* **5/1**[2] | 70 |
| 450- | 6 | 4 | **Brooklands Lodge (USA)**[238] 5722 3-8-11 70 ... GEdwards[(7)] 3<br>(MJAttwater) *s.i.s: nvr trbld ldrs* **25/1** | 64 |
| -200 | 7 | 3/4 | **Queen Charlotte (IRE)**[23] 2410 5-9-5 66 ... WHogg[(5)] 5<br>(MrsKWalton) *prom: rdn over 2f out: wknd over 1f out* **5/1**[2] | 58 |
| 0000 | 8 | 4 | **Den'S-Joy**[16] 2594 8-8-2 47 ... StephanieHollinshead[(3)] 4<br>(VSmith) *s.i.s: hld up: effrt over 2f out: wknd over 1f out* **14/1** | 30 |
| 2125 | 9 | 10 | **Dalriath**[10] 2757 5-7-5 40 oh1 ... CharlotteKerton[(7)] 10<br>(MCChapman) *chsd wnr over 5f: sn wknd* **8/1**[3] | — |

1m 39.92s (-0.56) **Going Correction** +0.025s/f (Good)

**WFA** 3 from 4yo+ 10lb 9 Ran SP% **120.9**

Speed ratings: **103,101,100,100,99 95,95,91,81**CSF £20.83 CT £108.53 TOTE £2.30: £1.20, £3.20, £3.40; EX 22.40.

**Owner** Miss K A Bartlett **Bred** Cheveley Park Stud Ltd **Trained** Newmarket, Suffolk

**FOCUS**

An ordinary contest, but it looked to be run at a sound pace.

**NOTEBOOK**

**Prime Offer** soon tacked across to grab the far rail and, with Dalraith for company, had most of these in trouble some way out. Left with enough of an advantage when Dalraith cried enough, he saw his race out honestly.

**Halcyon Magic**, although yet to score beyond seven furlongs, stays this trip well enough and was back to form here.

**Arran**, tackling handicap company for the first time, attracted plenty of support in the market and although the money was left behind on this occasion, showed enough to suggest he can win a small race.

**Single Track Mind** stayed this trip well enough without ever threatening to reel in the leaders.

**Welcome Signal** appeared to find this trip, on the fast ground, an insufficient test.

## 3050 VIBE FM H'CAP 1m 4f

7:00 (7:01) (E) (0-75,70) 3-Y-O+ £3,445 (£1,060; £530; £265) Stalls Centre

| Form | | | | RPR |
|---|---|---|---|---|
| 04/2 | 1 | | **Swellmova**[27] 2302 5-8-13 59 ... KDarley 6<br>(JRBoyle) *hld up: hdwy over 3f out: rdn to ld ins fnl f: r.o* **5/1**[2] | 70 |
| -411 | 2 | 1 | **Prenup (IRE)**[9] 2774 3-8-7 67 5ex ... DHolland 8<br>(LMCumani) *chsd ldrs: led over 8f out: rdn over 1f out: hdd and unable qck ins fnl f* **1/2**[1] | 77 |
| 05-0 | 3 | 3 1/2 | **The Varlet**[15] 2631 4-9-7 70 ... DCorby[(3)] 10<br>(BICase) *s.i.s: hld up: outpcd over 2f out: swtchd lft and hdwy over 1f out: r.o* **50/1** | 74 |
| -100 | 4 | hd | **Jack Of Trumps (IRE)**[72] 1298 4-9-4 64 ... SSanders 2<br>(GWragg) *hld up in tch: plld hrd: rdn and ev ch over 1f out: no ex ins fnl f* **8/1**[3] | 68 |
| 3-02 | 5 | nk | **Summer Cherry (USA)**[11] 2728 7-7-12 44 oh3 ...(t) AMcCarthy 7<br>(JamiePoulton) *plld hrd and prom: rdn and ev ch over 1f out: no ex ins fnl f* **12/1** | 47 |
| 0-06 | 6 | 3 | **Saida Lenasera (FR)**[20] 2472 3-8-9 69 ... WRyan 3<br>(MrsPSly) *hld up: hdwy over 2f out: wknd over 1f out* **25/1** | 67 |
| -450 | 7 | 4 | **King Of Knight (IRE)**[35] 2097 3-8-4 67 ... BReilly[(3)] 1<br>(GProdromou) *hld up: hdwy over 3f out: wknd over 1f out* **50/1** | 59 |
| 326- | 8 | 10 | **Lahob**[291] 4624 4-9-4 64 ... KDalgleish 4<br>(PHowling) *sn led: hdd over 8f out: rdn 4f out: wknd over 1f out* **25/1** | 40 |
| 0010 | 9 | 3 1/2 | **Duc's Dream**[9] 2787 6-8-12 58 ... DMcGaffin 5<br>(DMorris) *prom over 9f* **12/1** | 28 |
| 0000 | 10 | 28 | **Lunar Leader (IRE)**[19] 1783 4-8-9 55 ... BDoyle 9<br>(MJGingell) *chsd ldrs: rdn over 4f out: wknd 3f out* **50/1** | — |

2m 32.75s (-0.21) **Going Correction** +0.025s/f (Good)

**WFA** 3 from 4yo+ 14lb 10 Ran SP% **123.4**

Speed ratings: **101,100,98,97,97 95,93,86,84,65**CSF £8.10 CT £119.47 TOTE £7.10: £1.60, £1.20, £12.80; EX 12.30.

**Owner** Robert Allen **Bred** Martyn Arbib **Trained** Epsom, Surrey

**FOCUS**

Not a strong contest, but the winner looks on the upgrade, while the runner-up was officially 9lbs well-in.

**NOTEBOOK**

**Swellmova** has had knee problems but managed to get away with the faster ground this time. He clearly has his fair share of ability and, granted an easier surface, should continue to progress.

**Prenup(IRE)**, 9lb well in here compared to her future mark, was something of a disappointment in this. She had the run of the race and the advantage of the rails to help her, and had no excuses.

**The Varlet** was doing his best work late on and ran his best race in a long while. However, he will need more help from the Handicapper if he is to get off the mark.

**Jack Of Trumps(IRE)**, stepping up in trip, was always doing too much and as a result did not quite get home. He is certainly worth another try over this distance.

**Summer Cherry(USA)** was not disgraced in this better race and is clearly on good terms with himself at present.

**Duc's Dream** *Official explanation: jockey said gelding finished lame*

## 3051 NGK SPARK PLUGS MAIDEN STKS 6f

7:30 (7:31) (D) 2-Y-O £3,108 (£3,108; £731; £365) Stalls Low

| Form | | | | RPR |
|---|---|---|---|---|
| | 1 | dht | **St Andrews Storm (USA)** 2-9-0 ... RHughes 3<br>(RHannon) *s.i.s: rcvrd to chse ldr 5f out: rdn to ld over 1f out: r.o: jnd post* **2/1**[2] | 84 |
| | 1 | | **Stagbury Hill (USA)** 2-9-0 ... MHills 4<br>(JWHills) *hld up: hdwy over 1f out: r.o wl ins fnl f to join wnr post* **16/1** | 84 |

3 1 1/4 **Northern Splendour (USA)** 2-9-0 LDettori 6 81
(SaeedBinSuroor) *chsd ldrs: rdn and ev ch over 1f out: unable qck ins fnl f* **5/4**[1]
4 1 1/4 **Coup D'Etat** 2-9-0 KDarley 1 77
(JLDunlop) *trckd ldrs: rdn over 1f out: styng on same pce whn n.m.r towards fin* **8/1**
0 5 1 1/4 **Monash Lad (IRE)**[18] 2522 2-9-0 PRobinson 5 73
(MHTompkins) *plld hrd and prom: outpcd and edgd lft over 1f out: styd on ins fnl f* **25/1**
0 6 1 1/4 **Lowestoft Playboy**[19] 2502 2-9-0 JPMurtagh 9 69
(MrsCADunnett) *led over 4f: wknd ins fnl f* **20/1**
7 3 **Wilford Maverick (IRE)** 2-9-0 SRighton 8 60
(MJAttwater) *mid-div: effrt over 2f out: wknd over 1f out* **66/1**
8 2 1/2 **Bellalou** 2-8-6 TPQueally(3) 7 48
(NACallaghan) *s.s: a in rr* **20/1**
6 9 1 1/4 **Hedingham Knight (IRE)**[19] 2502 2-9-0 DaneO'Neill 2 49
(NACallaghan) *hld up: wknd over 1f out* **7/1**[3]

1m 13.77s (0.45) **Going Correction** +0.025s/f (Good) **9** Ran SP% **122.1**
Speed ratings: **98,98,96,94,93 91,87,84,82**, £1.40 TRIFECTA Win SH 14.60, SAS 1.50; Pl SH 5.20, SAS 1.30; Ex SH-SAS 61.30, SAS-SH 40.70, CSF SH-SAS 24.75, SAS-SH 16.53.
**Owner** Nick Hubbard and Partners **Bred** H Heinlein **Trained** Upper Lambourn, Berks

**FOCUS**
Not a bad looking bunch and the race should produce its fair share of winners.

**NOTEBOOK**
**Stagbury Hill(USA)**, from the same family as the high-class Allied Forces, took a while to grasp what was required but, on meeting the rising ground, fairly took off. There should be plenty of improvement to come from him, especially as he steps up in trip.
**St Andrews Storm(USA)**, an early foal, showed a nice action to post. While he clearly knew his job, there should be more to come from him.
**Northern Splendour(USA)**, out of a mare that won as a juvenile, looked the likely winner going into the dip, but just flattened out in the closing stages. He will have learnt plenty from this.
**Coup D'Etat**, a half-brother to seven-furlong juvenile winner Peaceful Paradise, shaped with plenty of promise and can be found an opening in due course.
**Monash Lad(IRE)** had clearly learnt from his debut, and may have done better still had he not become unbalanced going into the dip.

## 3052 PORTLAND PLACE PROPERTIES RATED STKS (H'CAP) 7f
8:05 (8:06) (C) (0-95,95) 3-Y-0+ **£8,694** (£3,297; £1,648; £749) **Stalls** Low

Form RPR
3-51 1 **Ettrick Water**[16] 2575 5-9-7 **92** (v) DHolland 8 99
(LMCumani) *chsd ldr: rdn 1/2-way: led 2f out: hdd 1f out: rallied to ld nr fin* **11/4**[1]
2-60 2 shd **Colour Wheel**[27] 2295 3-8-8 **88** ow1 (t) RHughes 9 95
(RCharlton) *hld up: hdwy over 2f out: rdn to ld 1f out: edgd lft: hdd nr fin* **7/1**
31-5 3 hd **Leoballero**[28] 2279 4-8-7 **78** oh1 (t) DaneO'Neill 7 84
(DJDaly) *s.i.s: hld up: hdwy over 2f out: rdn and ev ch whn hung lft ins fnl f: nt run on* **25/1**
1534 4 2 **Molcon (IRE)**[5] 2907 3-8-3 **83** PRobinson 4 84
(NACallaghan) *prom: n.m.r and outpcd 2f out: styd on ins fnl f* **6/1**
0553 5 hd **Kool (IRE)**[16] 2575 5-9-5 **90** SSanders 11 90
(PFICole) *hld up: hdwy over 2f out: rdn and ev ch 1f out: no ex ins fnl f* **5/1**[3]
0-06 6 1 3/4 **Vindication**[19] 2503 4-9-6 **91** (t) JPMurtagh 10 87
(JRFanshawe) *hld up in tch: nt clr run over 1f out: sn rdn and no imp* **10/3**[2]
10-0 7 3 1/2 **Tahirah**[10] 2763 4-9-4 **89** CLowther 2 76
(RGuest) *sn pushed along in rr: hdwy over 1f out: wknd ins fnl f* **25/1**
512/ 8 1 1/2 **Ajeel (IRE)**[463] 5-8-9 **80** RHills 3 63
(JLDunlop) *chsd ldrs: n.m.r and wknd 2f out* **12/1**
0410 9 6 **Warden Warren**[13] 2673 6-8-4 **78** oh5 (p) BReilly(3) 1 45
(MrsCADunnett) *chsd ldrs: lost pl 5f out: wknd over 2f out* **25/1**
000- 10 3 1/2 **Funfair Wane**[272] 5060 5-9-10 **95** KDalgleish 6 53
(DNicholls) *led and sn clr: hdd 2f out: wknd 1f out* **20/1**
4-00 11 3 **Crafty Calling (USA)**[27] 2283 4-9-5 **90** (b[1]) KDarley 5 40
(PFICole) *hld up: wknd over 2f out* **20/1**

1m 24.77s (-2.00) **Going Correction** +0.025s/f (Good)
**WFA** 3 from 4yo+ 9lb **11** Ran SP% **122.0**
Speed ratings: **112,111,111,109,109 107,103,101,94,90 87**CSF £21.41 CT £392.43 TOTE £4.40: £1.70, £4.00, £3.70; EX 76.50.
**Owner** Mrs E H Vestey **Bred** Wickfield Farm Partnership **Trained** Newmarket, Suffolk

**FOCUS**
A decent handicap run at a fair pace, and the time was smart. There was no advantage in the draw.

**NOTEBOOK**
**Ettrick Water** has plenty of ability, but is not straightforward. However, he goes very well for Holland, who was partnering him to victory for the fourth time.
**Colour Wheel**, dropped in trip having given the impression he failed to stay a mile on his last couple of starts, albeit in better company than this, bounced back to form and was only just denied.
**Leoballero** let his rider down badly, having been produced with what looked a perfectly-timed challenge. He is certainly one to be wary of.
**Molcon(IRE)** is running well at present, and may have done better with a bit more luck in running.
**Kool(IRE)** had no excuses and is proving difficult to place.
**Vindication** travelled well on the heels of the leaders, but found disappointingly little off the bridle. He may be the sort who needs everything to go his way.

## 3053 SHARP MINDS BETFAIR E B F CLASSIFIED STKS 1m
8:40 (8:40) (C) 3-Y-0 **£9,841** (£3,028; £1,514; £757) **Stalls** Low

Form RPR
1204 1 **Appalachian Trail (IRE)**[27] 2295 3-9-0 89 RHughes 3 94
(ISemple) *trckd ldrs: rdn to ld over 1f out: edgd lft ins fnl f: r.o* **8/11**[1]
1400 2 2 1/2 **Bettalatethannever (IRE)**[14] 2642 3-9-0 87 DaneO'Neill 1 89
(SDow) *hld up: hdwy over 1f out: sn rdn: styng on same pce whn n.m.r ins fnl f* **6/1**[3]
10-5 3 2 **Bessemer (JPN)**[49] 1745 3-9-0 90 KDalgleish 4 84
(MJohnston) *led: hdd over 6f out: rdn to ld and hung lft over 1f out: sn hdd and no ex* **6/1**[3]
21-0 4 2 **Al Sifaat**[30] 2221 3-8-11 90 (t) LDettori 2 76
(SaeedBinSuroor) *trckd ldrs: plld hrd and led over 6f out: hdd nad hmpd over 1f out: sn btn* **3/1**[2]

1m 40.42s (-0.06) **Going Correction** +0.025s/f (Good) **4** Ran SP% **111.5**
Speed ratings: **101,98,96,94**CSF £5.72 TOTE £1.80; EX 6.70.
**Owner** G L S Partnership **Bred** Swettenham Stud **Trained** Carluke, S Lanarks

**FOCUS**
A messy contest, but considering the nature of the race the form looks fairly sound.

**NOTEBOOK**
**Appalachian Trail(IRE)** settled better than his rivals and confirmed the merit of his recent handicap form, although he probably did not have to run to his best.
**Bettalatethannever(IRE)** had nothing to do with the early pace, but came through to have a chance of sorts, before flattening out in the closing stages. A progressive performer on the Polytrack, this was the best of three attempts on turf.
**Bessemer(JPN)** is bred to be suited by much further than this, but will need to settle better if he is to progress.
**Al Sifaat** again gave herself no chance by refusing to settle.

## 3054 STUART GRANT BREAKFAST SHOW MAIDEN STKS 1m 2f
9:10 (9:11) (D) 3-Y-0 **£5,551** (£1,708; £854; £427) **Stalls** Centre

Form RPR
2 1 **Elmustanser**[17] 2562 3-9-0 (t) LDettori 8 84+
(SaeedBinSuroor) *mde all: shkn up over 1f out: r.o* **4/11**[1]
2 1 1/4 **Fortune's Princess** 3-8-9 KDarley 7 77
(MJWallace) *s.i.s: sn prom: chsd wnr over 2f out: rdn and edgd lft over 1f out: r.o* **25/1**
3 5 **Tashreefat (IRE)** 3-8-9 RHills 4 67
(ACStewart) *s.i.s: hld up: hdwy over 2f out: no imp fnl f* **11/2**[2]
6 4 7 **Zuri (IRE)**[13] 2693 3-8-9 DHolland 1 54
(LMCumani) *prom: eased whn btn over 1f out: edgd lft ins fnl f* **10/1**
5 2 1/2 **Conviction** 3-9-0 JPMurtagh 6 54
(JRFanshawe) *dwlt: sn prom: rdn 1/2-way: wknd 3f out* **8/1**[3]
6 shd **Chapelco** 3-9-0 SSanders 2 54
(JLDunlop) *s.i.s: hld up: wknd 3f out* **14/1**
0- 7 1 1/2 **Hold Up**[269] 5137 3-8-6 BReilly(3) 3 46
(MissJFeilden) *chsd wnr over 7f: sn wknd* **28/1**

2m 7.11s (0.65) **Going Correction** +0.025s/f (Good) **7** Ran SP% **122.9**
Speed ratings: **98,97,93,87,85 85,84**CSF £16.46 TOTE £1.40: £1.20, £3.60; EX 18.90 Place 6 £7.81, Place 5 £4.26.
**Owner** Godolphin **Bred** Shadwell Estate Company Limited **Trained** Newmarket, Suffolk

**FOCUS**
As it turned out this didn't take much winning.

**NOTEBOOK**
**Elmustanser** had the edge in experience and was always doing what was required. There should be plenty more to come from him.
**Fortune's Princess ◆**, out of a mare that won as a juvenile, is a half-sister to Fortunes Favourite, who stayed ten furlongs. She was a little green when coming off the bridle and is sure to be all the wiser next time.
**Tashreefat(IRE)**, a half-sister to three ten furlong winners, did not shape too badly, but never looked like being a threat.
**Zuri(IRE)** was not knocked around when her chance had gone and looks the sort to do better when she goes handicapping. *Official explanation: jockey said filly hung left*
**Conviction** looked clueless and needed plenty of driving throughout. His future lies in the hands of the Handicapper.
**Chapelco**, a half-brother to winning stayer Al's Alibi, was too green to do himself justice.
T/Plt: £6.20 to a £1 stake. T/Qpdt: £5.90 to a £1 stake. CR

# 2755 REDCAR (L-H)
Friday, June 18

**OFFICIAL GOING: Good (good to firm in places)**
A brisk almost head-on wind resulted in slow times.
Wind: Fresh 1/2 against Weather: Mainly fine after morning rain.

## 3055 INGS MAIDEN STKS 5f
2:10 (2:11) (D) 2-Y-0 **£3,406** (£1,048; £524; £262) **Stalls** Centre

Form RPR
04 1 **African Breeze**[16] 2568 2-8-9 DeanMcKeown 7 72
(RMWhitaker) *prom: drvn to ld over 1f out: r.o* **1/2**[1]
05 2 1 3/4 **Wonderful Mind**[13] 2686 2-9-0 RWinston 4 71
(TDEasterby) *mde most tl rdn and hdd over 1f out: no ex* **8/1**[3]
3 nk **Trim Image**[47] 1812 2-8-9 RLappin 6 65
(MsJoannaMorgan, Ire) *w ldr tl outpcd over 1f out: kpt on u.p ins last* **11/2**[2]
4 hd **Hillside Heather (IRE)** 2-8-9 FNorton 3 64
(ABerry) *dwlt: bhd: hdwy u.p over 1f out: kpt on same pce ins last* **20/1**
50 5 hd **Kilmovee**[17] 2550 2-8-9 SSanders 1 64
(NTinkler) *chsd ldrs: rdn and outpcd 2f out: kpt on fnl f* **12/1**
6 12 **For Nowt** 2-9-0 GFaulkner 2 27
(TDEasterby) *dwlt: bhd: rdn 1/2-way: lost tch over 1f out* **33/1**
0 7 7 **Tak's Girl**[9] 2773 2-8-9 DAllan 5 —
(PTMidgley) *dwlt: bhd and drvn along 1/2-way: lost tch over 1f out* **100/1**

62.30 secs (3.60) **Going Correction** +0.625s/f (Yiel) **7** Ran SP% **109.5**
Speed ratings: **96,93,92,92,92 72,61**CSF £4.51 TOTE £1.30: £1.10, £3.30; EX 3.50.
**Owner** G F Pemberton **Bred** The P B T Group And G F Pemberton **Trained** Scarcroft, W Yorks

**FOCUS**
A poor race apart from the winner who will appreciate a step up to six.

**NOTEBOOK**
**African Breeze** looked to have outstanding claims but made quite hard work of it and was well below her best in victory. She is ready for a step up to six.
**Wonderful Mind** is all speed but in the end was well outpointed by the winner. This qualifies him for nurseries.
**Trim Image**, placed in two maidens at Navan, is on the leg and wore a cross noseband. She stuck on under pressure and would have taken second place with a bit further to go.
**Hillside Heather(IRE)**, a March foal, is bred exclusively for speed. A moderate mover, she stuck on after a tardy start and this will have opened her eyes.
**Kilmovee**, having her third start, was not suited by the drop back to five. Putting in all her best work at the finish after being run off her feet at the halfway mark, this opens up the nursery route for her.

## 3056 NEWTON CLAIMING STKS 1m 2f
2:45 (2:45) (F) 3-Y-0+ **£2,968** (£848; £424) **Stalls** Low

Form RPR
-605 1 **Salut Saint Cloud**[7] 2854 3-8-3 46 FNorton 9 57
(MissVHaigh) *hld up in tch: smooth hdwy over 2f out: qcknd to ld over 1f out: rdn clr: eased ins last* **5/1**
-560 2 5 **Cezzaro (IRE)**[25] 2347 6-9-1 40 JBramhill 3 47
(SRBowring) *led: rdn 3f out: hdd over 1f out: kpt on: no ch w wnr* **9/1**
-066 3 nk **Erte**[8] 2801 3-8-4 58 ow1 SHitchcott(3) 1 50
(MRChannon) *trckd ldrs: rdn and outpcd over 2f out: styd on fnl f* **9/2**[3]
0000 4 1 **Turftanzer (GER)**[23] 2408 5-9-1 30 (t) KimTinkler 5 45?
(DonEnricoIncisa) *cl up: ev ch and rdn 2f out: no ex* **33/1**



The Form Book, Raceform Ltd, Compton, RG20 6NL

11-6 **5** 2 1/2 **Rojabaa**[16] 2594 5-9-7 53 LTreadwell(7) 7 53
(WGMTurner) *trckd ldrs: hdwy to chal over 2f out: ev ch and rdn over 1f out: wknd appr fnl f* **7/2**[2]

50-0 **6** *hd* **Face The Limelight (IRE)**[22] 1393 5-9-4 65 GFaulkner 2 42
(JeddO'Keeffe) *hld up: drvn along over 3f out: kpt on fnl 2f: n.d* **11/4**[1]

004- **7** 5 **Ultra Marine (IRE)**[198] 5917 4-9-4 54 (b) RWinston 8 33
(JSWainwright) *hld up: rdn 4f out: no hdwy* **7/1**

60 **8** 6 **Grey Samurai**[14] 2653 4-9-10 DAllan 6 28
(PTMidgley) *dwlt: a bhd* **33/1**

2m 9.97s (3.17) **Going Correction** +0.30s/f (Good)
**WFA** 3 from 4yo+ 12lb **8 Ran SP% 112.1**
Speed ratings: **99,95,94,93,91 91,87,83**CSF £46.62 TOTE £7.60: £2.10, £3.10, £2.00; EX 79.30.The winner was claimed by A Grinter for £5,500
**Owner** Miss V Haigh **Bred** Mill House Stud **Trained** Bawtry, S Yorks

**FOCUS**
A poor race even by claiming standards, but a facile winner, who changed hands afterwards.

**NOTEBOOK**
**Salut Saint Cloud**, with the visor left off and stepped up in trip, came there cantering and, but for being eased, would have scored by double the official margin. He changed hands afterwards.
**Cezzaro(IRE)**, three times successful in sellers, tried hard but in the end proved no match whatsoever.
**Erte**, well beaten in a seller last time, looks to have gone backwards from two to three.
**Turftanzer(GER)** had the least chance on official figures and boasts a rating of just 30.
**Rojabaa**, a flop over hurdles, had a fair bit to find.
**Face The Limelight(IRE)**, rated 16lb ahead of the winner, was settled in the rear but, driven along once in line for home, never looked a threat. His official rating belongs to the history books now.
**Ultra Marine(IRE)**, last seen in action over hurdles, seems to have lost what ability he showed at two.

## 3057 STAITHES MAIDEN STKS 1m 3f
3:20 (3:22) (D) 3-Y-0+ **£3,513** (£1,081; £540; £270) **Stalls** Low

Form RPR

**1** **Carte Diamond (USA)** 3-8-8 RFfrench 4 99
(MJohnston) *sn racing in 3rd: pushed along 1/2-way: hdwy over 3f out: led over 2f out: drvn out* **6/1**[2]

0-32 **2** 5 **Arrgatt (IRE)**[17] 2555 3-8-8 83 SSanders 2 91
(MAJarvis) *led 1f: trckd ldr after tl led over 3f out: rdn and hdd over 2f out: chsd wnr after: no imp* **1/5**[1]

**3** 26 **Hirayna**[251] 5-9-2 RWinston 3 44
(WMBrisbourne) *s.i.s: led after 1f tl hdd over 3f out: wknd qckly: t.o* **33/1**

**4** 17 **King Top** 3-8-8 DAllan 1 22
(TDEasterby) *s.i.s: bhd and sn pushed along: lost tch 1/2-way: t.o* **25/1**[3]

2m 22.14s (1.14) **Going Correction** +0.30s/f (Good)
**WFA** 3 from 5yo 13lb **4 Ran SP% 104.4**
Speed ratings: **107,103,84,72**CSF £7.52 TOTE £4.70; EX 14.30.
**Owner** Mr & Mrs Heywood & Mr & Mrs Bovingdon **Bred** The Thoroughbred Corporation **Trained** Middleham Moor, N Yorks

**FOCUS**
A decent time for the grade, despite there only being four runners. The favourite has been assessed as if running to form, but it is impossible to be sure.

**NOTEBOOK**
**Carte Diamond(USA)**, a good-bodied newcomer, was difficult to load. Pushed along once in line for home, he swept past the favourite and in the end scored in fine style. Exactly what the form is worth is open to doubt, but he is clearly a late-maturing type of some potential.
**Arrgatt(IRE)**, a headstrong type, went on travelling best but he carried his head high and looked quite happy to follow the winner home.
**Hirayna**, a bumper winner, was much too keen and, when headed by the runner-up, she stopped to nothing.
**King Top**, a rangy, unfurnished newcomer, missed the break slightly and was soon detached and being driven along.

## 3058 GO RACING IN YORKSHIRE H'CAP 1m
3:55 (3:55) (E) (0-70,66) 3-Y-0+ **£3,877** (£1,193; £596; £298) **Stalls** Centre

Form RPR

3411 **1** **Goodbye Mr Bond**[9] 2781 4-9-7 61 6ex FNorton 3 79+
(EJAlston) *trckd ldrs: rdn 2f out: led appr fnl f: edgd rt: drew clr ins last* **9/4**[1]

-622 **2** 3 1/2 **Alchemist Master**[3] 2965 5-9-0 54 (p) DeanMcKeown 8 61
(RMWhitaker) *trckd ldrs: chal and rdn 2f out: ev ch appr fnl f: no ex ins last* **5/2**[2]

-026 **3** 1 1/4 **Dara Mac**[3] 2965 5-8-6 53 SuzanneFrance(7) 2 57
(NBycroft) *hld up: hdwy and in tch 1/2-way: pushed along 2f out: no imp on first 2 ins fnl f* **20/1**

0000 **4** 1 1/2 **Mehmaas**[21] 2459 8-8-6 46 (v) RWinston 7 47
(REBarr) *led: rdn 2f out: hdd appr fnl f: sn btn* **20/1**

0054 **5** *hd* **Apache Point (IRE)**[17] 2551 7-9-2 56 KimTinkler 6 56
(NTinkler) *in tch: outpcd and rdn 3f out: styd on fnl 2f: n.d* **6/1**[3]

-030 **6** 5 **Mount Pekan (IRE)**[15] 2618 4-8-6 46 RFfrench 4 35
(JSGoldie) *hld up: keen early: drvn along 1/2-way: sn btn* **16/1**

4614 **7** 3 **Cashneem (IRE)**[13] 2673 6-9-10 64 DAllan 9 46
(WMBrisbourne) *trckd ldr: keen early: drvn along 1/2-way: wknd over 2f out* **13/2**

6003 **8** 18 **Night Wolf (IRE)**[20] 2492 4-9-9 66 SHitchcott(3) 5 6
(MRChannon) *hld up: drvn along 1/2-way: sn btn: lost tch over 1f out* **8/1**

1m 42.53s (4.83) **Going Correction** +0.625s/f (Yiel) **8 Ran SP% 113.5**
Speed ratings: **100,96,95,93,93 88,85,67**CSF £7.92 CT £82.00 TOTE £2.90: £1.60, £1.10, £6.60; EX 5.30.
**Owner** Peter J Davies **Bred** Michael Ng **Trained** Longton, Lancs

**FOCUS**
In effect a 0-66 handicap but in the end a quite impressive winner.

**NOTEBOOK**
**Goodbye Mr Bond**, who looked in peak condition, made light of the penalty, travelling strongly and quickening right away inside the last. In this sort of form connections will be looking to strike again before he is re-assessed.
**Alchemist Master**, fitted with cheekpieces this time, moved upsides two out but in the end proved no match. He is proving very frustrating.
**Dara Mac**, a maiden after 27 starts, ran a lot better than at Thirsk just three days earlier.
**Mehmaas**, bang out of form this year, ran a lot better and is now 13lb lower than his last success two years ago.
**Apache Point(IRE)**, who has slipped to a winning mark, found this trip on the sharp side. Staying on really well at the finish, he looks back to something like his best.
**Night Wolf(IRE)**, a negative on the exchanges, ran badly in trouble at halfway and eventually finishing tailed off. *Official explanation: trainer was unable to offer any explanation for poor form shown*

## 3059 GRIBDALE H'CAP 6f
4:30 (4:30) (D) (0-80,80) 3-Y-0 **£5,638** (£1,735; £867; £433) **Stalls** Centre

Form RPR

0405 **1** **Kingsmaite**[16] 2589 3-8-4 63 (b[1]) JBramhill 2 73
(SRBowring) *cl up: led 1/2-way: drvn out* **10/1**

-100 **2** 1 1/2 **Commando Scott (IRE)**[28] 2269 3-9-0 73 FLynch 5 78
(ABerry) *in tch: effrt over 2f out: wnt 2nd wl over 1f out: edgd lft u.p: no imp on wnr fnl f* **6/1**

0004 **3** 2 **Bright Sun (IRE)**[16] 2589 3-9-3 76 KimTinkler 4 75
(NTinkler) *dwlt: sn chsng ldrs: hung lft and rdn over 1f out: kpt on ins last* **3/1**[2]

6-06 **4** 1/2 **Tyne**[17] 2552 3-9-7 80 SSanders 3 78
(TDBarron) *dwlt: hld up: hdwy over 2f out: ch and rdn over 1f out: no ex ins last* **5/2**[1]

0023 **5** 5 **Fox Covert (IRE)**[21] 2457 3-8-0 59 (v) RFfrench 6 42
(DWBarker) *led tl hdd 1/2-way: wknd over 1f out* **7/2**[3]

30-2 **6** 1 1/2 **Wrenlane**[21] 2450 3-8-6 68 THamilton(3) 1 46
(RAFahey) *in tch: hung lft and rdn 1/2-way: wknd 2f out* **7/1**

1m 14.34s (2.64) **Going Correction** +0.625s/f (Yiel) **6 Ran SP% 111.7**
Speed ratings: **107,105,102,101,95 93**CSF £64.83 TOTE £14.90: £5.80, £3.50; EX 48.40.
**Owner** S R Bowring **Bred** S R Bowring **Trained** Edwinstowe, Notts
■ A welcome winner for John Bramhill after a run of 87 losers stretching back seven weeks.

**FOCUS**
All six in a line two furlongs out, but still a smart winning time.

**NOTEBOOK**
**Kingsmaite**, given a real chance by the Handicapper, responded to first-time blinkers and scored decisively.
**Commando Scott(IRE)**, dropped 5lb in two runs, seemed to benefit from a month on the sidelines and his stable is in much better form now.
**Bright Sun(IRE)**, who finished one place ahead of the winner at Nottingham, seems to be standing still.
**Tyne**, down 10lb since his handicap debut at two, was stepping up a furlong and came in for plenty of market support. This looks as good as he is now.
**Fox Covert(IRE)** has bags of toe but seems unable to break his duck.
**Wrenlane**, on his handicap bow, was a major negative on the exchanges and after hanging left dropped right out. He looks on a stiff mark.

## 3060 "HAND TO ROUF" LADY AMATEUR RIDERS' MAIDEN H'CAP 1m
5:05 (5:06) (G) (0-70,66) 3-Y-0+ **£2,639** (£754; £377) **Stalls** Centre

Form RPR

40-0 **1** **Zanjeer**[155] 541 4-9-7 50 MrsNWilson(5) 4 74
(NWilson) *mde virtually all: drew clr fr 1/2-way: easily* **16/1**

-400 **2** 8 **Regent's Secret (USA)**[27] 2292 4-10-11 63 MsCWilliams 12 69
(JSGoldie) *hld up: hdwy 1/2-way: wnt 2nd over 2f out: styd on u.p: no imp on wnr* **4/1**[1]

4004 **3** 2 1/2 **Shotley Dancer**[8] 2811 5-8-10 37 MissLEllison(3) 5 37
(NBycroft) *hld up: hdwy 1/2-way: disp 2nd and rdn over 2f out: kpt on same pce* **8/1**

0620 **4** 2 1/2 **Noble Penny**[13] 2673 5-9-8 49 MissKellyHarrison(3) 9 43
(MrsKWalton) *dwlt: hld up: hewday over 3f out: styd on u.p fnl 2f: nvr able to chal* **9/1**

2005 **5** *nk* **Boris The Spider**[6] 2880 3-9-7 55 MissEJJones 11 48
(MDHammond) *prom: outpcd by wnr over 3f out: rdn 2f out: no hdwy* **11/1**

6004 **6** 1 1/4 **Orion Express**[10] 2756 3-10-0 62 MissSBrotherton 1 53
(MWEasterby) *chsd ldrs tl outpcd 3f out: styd on fnl f* **4/1**[1]

0-03 **7** 3/4 **Orangino**[17] 2556 6-8-11 40 MissRDavidson(5) 8 29
(JSHaldane) *prom: outpcd by wnr whn rdn 2f out: no ex* **7/1**[3]

460- **8** 1 1/4 **Kama's Wheel**[239] 5717 5-9-0 38 MrsMMorris 6 24
(JohnAHarris) *s.i.s: sn midfield: outpcd and rdn 2f out: n.d* **33/1**

0-20 **9** 1 1/2 **Middleham Park (IRE)**[14] 2660 4-9-11 54 MissAArmitage(5) 3 36
(PCHaslam) *prom: rdn 3f out: wknd 2f out* **16/1**

2454 **10** 1 1/4 **Atholbrose (USA)**[16] 2571 3-9-5 53 MissAElsey 7 33
(TDEasterby) *chsd ldrs tl wknd over 3f out* **6/1**[2]

-004 **11** 6 **Banners Flying (IRE)**[7] 2851 4-10-7 66 MissRachelClark(7) 2 32
(DWChapman) *a bhd* **50/1**

-540 **12** *shd* **Campbells Lad**[13] 2688 3-8-5 46 oh2 MissDawnRankin(5) 13 10
(ABerry) *prom to 1/2-way: sn wknd* **28/1**

500- **13** 2 **Mandinka**[261] 5304 4-8-5 36 oh2 MissJoeyEllis(5) 10 —
(JFCoupland) *midfield to 1/2-way: sn bhd* **16/1**

1m 43.1s (5.40) **Going Correction** +0.625s/f (Yiel)
**WFA** 3 from 4yo+ 10lb **13 Ran SP% 122.2**
Speed ratings: **98,90,87,85,84 83,82,81,79,78 72,72,70**CSF £79.84 CT £590.67 TOTE £19.10: £5.00, £1.50, £2.30; EX 112.00 Place 6 £766.70, Place 5 £228.40.
**Owner** Malcom Wilson **Bred** D J Deer **Trained** Malton, N Yorks
■ Stewards Enquiry : Miss Rachel Clark one-day ban: used whip when out of contention (Jun 30)

**FOCUS**
A 0-66 handicap contested in the main by horses who are little better than platers. However, there appeared no fluke about the easy success of Zanjeer, who is unexposed and can hold his own in a much better grade.

**NOTEBOOK**
**Zanjeer** was having his first start for a new stable and was making his handicap debut on just his fifth career start. He did not go unbacked and had this won soon after halfway, coming clear in a manner which suggests he can hold his own in a much higher grade even from his revised mark.
**Regent's Secret(USA)**, who has slipped down the ratings, had a good pilot aboard. He went in pursuit of the winner but was no match whatsoever.
**Shotley Dancer**, a maiden now after 32 starts, seemed suited by the slight step up in trip and ten furlongs might bring out the best in her now.
**Noble Penny**, who is hardly a modeal of consistency, ran one of her better races.
**Boris The Spider** is happier on much easier ground.
**Orion Express** does not receive much mercy and here he had nothing on his outside.

T/Plt: £766.70 to a £1 stake. Pool: £20,429.60. 19.45 winning tickets. T/Qpdt: £228.40 to a £1 stake. Pool: £1,914.20. 6.20 winning tickets. JF

3061 - 3070a (Foreign Racing) - See Raceform Interactive

## 3031 ASCOT (R-H)

Saturday, June 19

**OFFICIAL GOING: Firm**

With no watering since yesterday, the rain that fell did not dampen the dust and there was again no bias between the two sides on the straight course.

Wind: nil Weather: unsettled, shower after race 2

### 3071 CHESHAM STKS (LISTED RACE) 7f
2:30 (2:32) (A) 2-Y-O **£23,200** (£8,800; £4,400; £2,000) **Stalls** Low

Form RPR

1 **1** **Whazzat**[10] 2786 2-8-7 ........ MHills 3 103
(BWHills) *hld up in tch: swtchd rt and squeezed through jst ins last 2f: qcknd to ld jst over 1f out: r.o wl* **7/1**[3]

11 **2** *3 ½* **Brecon Beacon**[27] 2321 2-9-0 ........ KFallon 4 101
(PFICole) *led early: trckd ldrs: rdn over 1f out: swtchd rt and squeezed through over 1f out: sn ev ch: one pce* **7/1**[3]

301 **3** *hd* **Wilko (USA)**[17] 2592 2-9-0 ........ EAhern 12 101
(JNoseda) *lw: plld hrd on outside: swtchd lft to stands' rail over 5f out: rdn over 3f out: swtchd rt and hdwy over 1f out: r.o* **16/1**

1 **4** *2* **Hearthstead Wings**[34] 2141 2-9-0 ........ JFanning 5 96
(MJohnston) *w'like: scope: sn led: rdn over 2f out: hdd jst over 1f out: one pce* **4/1**[1]

**5** *5* **In Excelsis (USA)**[58] 1574 2-9-0 ........ JPSpencer 2 83
(APO'Brien, Ire) *leggy: prom: rdn over 2f out: wknd over 1f out* **4/1**[1]

1 **6** *3* **Bolton Hall (IRE)**[17] 2570 2-9-4 ........ PHanagan 9 80
(RAFahey) *w'like: plld hrd: prom tl rdn and wknd over 2f out* **10/1**

1 **7** *hd* **Where With All (IRE)**[15] 2651 2-9-0 ........ LDettori 8 75
(SaeedBinSuroor) *lw: leggy: dwlt and bmpd s: sn rcvrd: ev ch 2f out: sn rdn and wknd* **5/1**[2]

01 **8** *2 ½* **Perfect Choice (IRE)**[9] 2804 2-9-0 ........ DHolland 10 76+
(BJMeehan) *sn w ldr: rdn wknd over 2f out: hmpd over 1f out: sn wknd* **10/1**

**9** *nk* **John Forbes** 2-8-12 ........ DaneO'Neill 1 66
(BEllison) *unf: bkwd: s.s: a bhd* **100/1**

4 **10** *1* **Darko Karim**[28] 2310 2-8-12 ........ TPQueally 6 64
(DRLoder) *trckd ldrs: rdn and wknd over 2f out* **12/1**

**11** *5* **Swell Lad** 2-8-12 ........ KDarley 7 51
(PFICole) *dwlt and wnt rt s: rn green: wl bhd fnl 5f* **40/1**

1m 29.55s (-0.12) **Going Correction** -0.075s/f (Good) **11** Ran SP% **116.9**
Speed ratings: **97,93,92,90,84 81,81,78,77,76 71**CSF £55.01 TOTE £9.10: £2.50, £1.70, £4.20; EX 68.30 Trifecta £1966.90 Pool £3,324.44 - 1.20 winning units..
**Owner** W J Gredley **Bred** Eurostrait Ltd **Trained** Lambourn, Berks

**FOCUS**
A weakish renewal and a modest winning time for the grade, continuing a recent trend which has seen the winning RPR slipping steadily. Nevertheless, the solitary filly Whazzat won in style from a field that featured five other unbeaten contenders.

**NOTEBOOK**
**Whazzat** confirmed the promise of her debut win and showed a nice turn of foot over this extra furlong. She won in the style of a smart filly and something like the May Hill at Doncaster's St Leger meeting could well be on the agenda.
**Brecon Beacon** had to wriggle his way through after being beaten to his first opening by the winner. His trainer feared that he had not returned sound and criticised the racecourse's watering policy. *Official explanation: vet said colt was lame*
**Wilko(USA)** ◆ saw too much daylight early on from his outside draw but still got the extra furlong well. There was no disgrace in this effort.
**Hearthstead Wings** ◆ was coltish in the preliminaries but gave a good account of himself despite looking uneasy on the quick ground. He is capable of further improvement.
**In Excelsis(USA)**, a $950,000 yearling, has a top-class American pedigree. A winner on heavy ground at Tipperary in April, he could not have had conditions more different.
**Bolton Hall(IRE)**, stepping up from the minimum trip, paid the penalty for running too freely.

### 3072 HARDWICKE STKS (GROUP 2) 1m 4f
3:05 (3:05) (A) 4-Y-O+ **£81,200** (£30,800; £15,400; £7,000) **Stalls** High

Form RPR

24-2 **1** **Doyen (IRE)**[15] 2639 4-8-9 121 ........ LDettori 7 129+
(SaeedBinSuroor) *b.hind: lw: hld up in 5th: smooth prog 3f out: led wl over 1f out: sn clr: pushed out: impressive* **6/5**[1]

12-4 **2** *6* **High Accolade**[15] 2639 4-8-9 116 ........ WSupple 2 115
(MPTregoning) *chsd ldng pair: rdn 5f out: outpcd 2f out: kpt on to take 2nd ins fnl f: no ch w wnr* **9/4**[2]

1-63 **3** *½* **Persian Majesty (IRE)**[31] 2220 4-8-9 113 ........ JPMurtagh 8 114
(PWHarris) *hld up in detached last: prog 3f out: rdn to dispute 2nd over 1f out: one pce fnl f* **6/1**[3]

2-52 **4** *2* **Songlark**[31] 2220 4-8-9 105 ........(vt) KMcEvoy 6 111
(SaeedBinSuroor) *lw: led at str pce: jnd over 4f out: hdd and btn wl over 1f out: fdd* **25/1**

3210 **5** *nk* **Systematic**[15] 2639 5-8-9 113 ........ KDarley 3 110
(MJohnston) *pressed ldr: chal and upsides over 4f out: outpcd wl over 1f out: fdd* **9/1**

/1-3 **6** *18* **Musanid (USA)**[49] 1767 4-8-9 107 ........ RHills 4 82
(SirMichaelStoute) *stmbld s: chsd ldrs tl wknd 3f out: t.o* **14/1**

2m 26.53s (-7.03) **Going Correction** -0.075s/f (Good) course record **6** Ran SP% **111.0**
Speed ratings: **120,116,115,114,114 102**CSF £3.96 TOTE £2.00: £1.50, £1.80; EX 3.00 Trifecta £11.80 Pool £2,347.80 - 140.65 winning units..
**Owner** Godolphin **Bred** Sheikh Mohammed Bin Rashid Al Maktoum **Trained** Newmarket, Suffolk
■ The sixth winner of the Royal Meeting for Godolphin, Saeed Bin Suroor and Frankie Dettori.

**FOCUS**
A highly impressive winner in Doyen, who recorded an outstanding winning time and broke a 21-year-old course record. The form is anchored to some extent by fourth-placed Songlark but still rates the best over middle distances so far this year.

**NOTEBOOK**
**Doyen(IRE)** ◆ produced a scintillating display. Ridden with a deal of confidence, he eased up to the leaders in the straight before quickening right away, breaking Stanerra's course record by 0.42 sec. He had never run on such fast ground before, but had no problems with the conditions and achieved the best middle-distance RPR of the year so far. He looks a worthy favourite for the King George over course and distance next month.
**High Accolade** got the best of a four-way scrap for second place but Doyen, who had finished just two short-heads in front of him at Epsom, was in a different league this time. Once again, he did very little wrong, but while he has plenty of fast-ground form connections believe this may have been a shade too firm for him.
**Persian Majesty(IRE)**, whose run at Goodwood against Papineau looks all the more impressive now, reverted to hold-up tactics and stayed on pretty well. He handles fast conditions but this ground was a little too firm for him.
**Songlark** did a good job as pacemaker for the favourite. He was joined by Systematic with over half a mile to run and the pair matched strides, but Doyen swamped the pair of them when unleashed.
**Systematic** disputed the lead with Songlark for more than three furlongs and it was rather disappointing that he could never actually get his head in front of that opponent.
**Musanid(USA)**, taking a step up in both class and trip, ought to have stayed on pedigree, but he failed to settle satisfactorily and was a spent force with three furlongs to run. *Official explanation: jockey said colt stumbled leaving the stalls*

### 3073 GOLDEN JUBILEE STKS (GROUP 1) 6f
3:45 (3:47) (A) 3-Y-O+ **£145,000** (£55,000; £27,500; £12,500) **Stalls** Low

Form RPR

0U-0 **1** **Fayr Jag (IRE)**[39] 2021 5-9-4 109 ........ WSupple 9 118
(TDEasterby) *hld up mid-div: hdwy to ld 2f out: edgd rt ins fnl f: drvn out* **12/1**

0-33 **2** *hd* **Crystal Castle (USA)**[23] 2438 6-9-4 ........(t) KFallon 2 117
(JEHammond, France) *hld up and bhd: hdwy and n.m.r on stands' rail over 1f out: swtchd rt ins fnl f: r.o* **8/1**

/3-2 **3** *hd* **Cape Of Good Hope**[4] 2955 6-9-4 ........(vt) MJKinane 1 116
(DOughton, Hong Kong) *lw: hld up: hdwy and n.m.r over 1f out: hrd rdn and r.o ins fnl f* **13/2**

5-04 **4** *¾* **Country Reel (USA)**[26] 2373 4-9-4 107 ........(vt) LDettori 12 114
(SaeedBinSuroor) *swtg: wnt rt s: sn prom: rdn over 2f out: nt qckn fnl f* **33/1**

3-21 **5** *¾* **Avonbridge**[13] 2719 4-9-4 113 ........ SDrowne 3 112
(RCharlton) *lw: a.p: rdn and ev ch over 1f out: no ex ins fnl f* **10/3**[1]

60-6 **6** *1 ½* **Airwave**[39] 2021 4-9-1 115 ........ DaneO'Neill 7 104
(HCandy) *s.i.s: hld up: hdwy over 2f out: sn rdn: one pce* **9/2**[2]

-302 **7** *nk* **Ashdown Express (IRE)**[26] 2373 5-9-4 111 ........ SSanders 14 107
(CFWall) *hld up and bhd: rdn and hdwy on outside over 1f out: wknd towards fin* **16/1**

2100 **8** *1* **Bahamian Pirate (USA)**[4] 2955 9-9-4 105 ........ GaryStevens 6 104
(DNicholls) *b.hind: hld up: swtchd rt 1f out: nvr nr to chal* **40/1**

-212 **9** *hd* **Steenberg (IRE)**[39] 2021 5-9-4 113 ........ RHills 13 103
(MHTompkins) *lw: s.i.s and hmpd s: hld up: hdwy over 2f out: wknd over 1f out* **16/1**

-430 **10** *nk* **Nights Cross (IRE)**[4] 2955 3-8-11 105 ........ TEDurcan 4 102
(MRChannon) *hld up: rdn over 2f out: nt clr run over wl over 1f out: n.d after* **40/1**

00-5 **11** *1* **Twilight Blues (IRE)**[26] 2373 5-9-4 114 ........ DHolland 11 99
(BJMeehan) *lw: led: rdn and hdd 2f out: sn wknd* **33/1**

-511 **12** *5* **Monsieur Bond (IRE)**[39] 2021 4-9-4 117 ........ FLynch 10 84
(BSmart) *prom: rdn over 2f out: nt clr run over 1f out: sn eased* **6/1**[3]

0-20 **13** *1 ½* **Lochridge**[4] 2955 5-9-1 106 ........ KDarley 8 77
(AMBalding) *prom: rdn over 2f out: wkng whn hmpd over 1f out* **20/1**

201- **14** *hd* **Polar Way**[238] 5737 5-9-4 111 ........ RHughes 5 79
(MrsAJPerrett) *lw: prom: ev ch jst over 2f out: sn rdn: wknd wl over 1f out* **16/1**

1m 13.35s (-2.64) **Going Correction** -0.075s/f (Good)
**WFA** 3 from 4yo+ 7lb **14** Ran SP% **120.9**
Speed ratings: **114,113,113,112,111 109,109,107,107,107 105,99,97,96**CSF £99.96 TOTE £13.50: £3.30, £2.80, £2.10; EX 108.60 Trifecta £1024.90 Pool £7,507.04 - 5.20 winning units..
**Owner** Jonathan Gill **Bred** Canice M Farrell Jnr **Trained** Great Habton, N Yorks
■ Stewards Enquiry : F Lynch one-day ban: careless riding (Jun 30)
L Dettori caution: careless riding

**FOCUS**
The lightning-fast ground contributed to some below-par efforts in what already looked a weak Group One. The time was a little slower than would be expected for a Group One.

**NOTEBOOK**
**Fayr Jag(IRE)** dead-heated in the Wokingham on similar conditions on the corresponding day last year, a race where the form has worked out remarkably well. Unsuited by the soft on his reappearance, he loves Ascot and his rider thought he probably hit the front too soon. The July Cup at Newmarket seems an obvious target.
**Crystal Castle(USA)** had a niggling injury last year but has been running well this term. He could not quite peg back the winner after not getting the best of runs. He is likely to renew rivalry with Fayr Jag in the July Cup at Newmarket.
**Cape Of Good Hope** did not have the edge taken off him by finishing second in the King's Stand on Tuesday. He had a slight altercation with the runner-up over a furlong out but did not finish quite as well as his rival. He is another who seems to be heading for the July Cup.
**Country Reel(USA)** improved on his two previous efforts this season and did seem to handle the lightning fast ground.
**Avonbridge** was not disgraced despite his rider reporting that he found the ground too firm.
**Airwave** was another whose jockey reported that the ground was too fast.
**Ashdown Express(IRE)**ran a bit better than his finishing position suggests and was not disgraced in this company.
**Monsieur Bond(IRE)** was unable to reproduce his York form on this much faster ground. *Official explanation: jockey said colt was unsuited by the firm ground*

### 3074 WOKINGHAM STKS (HERITAGE H'CAP) 6f
4:25 (4:25) (B) (0-110,102) 3-Y-O+ **£46,400** (£17,600; £8,800; £4,000) **Stalls** Low

Form RPR

0-03 **1** **Lafi (IRE)**[14] 2682 5-8-13 **91** ........ EAhern 30 106
(DNicholls) *trckd far side ldrs: effrt 2f out: rdn to ld 1f out: r.o wl and in command fnl f* **6/1**[1]

0-00 **2** *1 ½* **Coconut Penang (IRE)**[66] 1391 4-9-1 **93** ........ SWhitworth 7 103
(PWChapple-Hyam) *prom nr side: rdn and effrt 2f out: styd on wl to ld gp nr fin: nt on terms w wnr* **12/1**

4-36 **3** *nk* **High Reach**[49] 1765 4-8-11 **89** ........ KFallon 11 98
(TGMills) *prom nr side: led gp wl over 1f out: nt on terms w wnr ins fnl f: lost gp ld nr fin* **10/1**

6-01 **4** *½* **Royal Storm (IRE)**[48] 1789 5-9-6 **98** ........ MJKinane 16 106
(MrsAJPerrett) *mde most on far side to 1f out: kpt on wl u.p* **16/1**

-603 **5** *hd* **Dazzling Bay**[8] 2857 4-9-8 **100** ........ JFEgan 25 107
(TDEasterby) *cl up far side: drvn 2f out: ch 1f out: kpt on wl fnl f* **8/1**[3]

3163 **6** *shd* **Pic Up Sticks**[64] 1438 5-9-4 **96** ........ TEDurcan 26 103+
(MRChannon) *hld up in rr far side: plld to outer and effrt over 1f out: styd on fnl f: nt qckn nr fin* **12/1**

0602 **7** *½* **Simianna**[7] 2903 5-8-12 **90** ........ FNorton 4 95
(ABerry) *wl in tch nr side: chsd ldng pair over 1f out: styd on ins fnl f* **33/1**

0001 **8** *nk* **Cardinal Venture (IRE)**[16] 2626 6-8-12 **90** 5ex ........ GParkin 2 94+
(KARyan) *dwlt: racd in last trio nr side: rdn and effrt 2f out: styd on wl fnl f: nrst fin* **20/1**

3240 **9** *¾* **Boston Lodge**[14] 2679 4-9-2 **97** ........ TPQueally(3) 27 99
(GAButler) *lw: chsd far side ldrs: rdn and kpt on same pce fnl 2f* **40/1**

6030 **10** *½* **Dame De Noche**[11] 2750 4-8-10 **88** ........ MFenton 21 89
(JGGiven) *w far side ldrs: ev ch against rail 1f out: fdd ins fnl f* **50/1**

0446 **11** *nk* **Indian Spark**[16] 2625 10-9-0 **92** ........ GaryStevens 17 92
(JSGoldie) *hld up last of far side gp and wl bhd: swtchd to rail 2f out: nt clr run over 1f out: r.o wl last 100yds: hopeless task* **50/1**

0600 **12** *½* **Gaelic Princess**[11] 2763 4-8-4 **85** ........ LPKeniry(3) 15 83
(AGNewcombe) *racd far side: in rr: struggling 2f out: styd on ins fnl f: n.d* **66/1**

-442 **13** *shd* **Greenslades**[28] 2283 5-9-3 **95** ........ SSanders 22 93
(PJMakin) *racd in midfield far side: drvn and one pce fnl 2f* **13/2**[2]

0100 **14** *nk* **Whitbarrow (IRE)**[14] 2679 5-9-4 **96** ........ RLMoore 28 93
(JMBradley) *lw: w far side ldrs: rdn and ev ch 1f out: wknd* **33/1**

3-00 **15** *nk* **Fanny's Fancy**[38] 2041 4-8-12 **90** ........ JQuinn 18 86
(CFWall) *lw: s.s: racd far side: rchd midfield over 2f out: no prog and hanging u.p over 1f out* **11/1**

3401 **16** *½* **Circuit Dancer (IRE)**[8] 2857 4-9-8 **100** 8ex ........ FLynch 19 95
(ABerry) *dwlt: racd far side: wl in rr: effrt over 2f out: styng on whn nt clr run ins fnl f: eased* **50/1**

43-0 **17** *½* **Danehill Stroller (IRE)**[21] 2477 4-8-10 **88** ........(p) KMcEvoy 8 81
(RMBeckett) *chsd nr side ldrs: rdn and no prog 2f out: btn after* **33/1**

-401 **18** *hd* **Native Title**[14] 2682 6-8-13 **91** 8ex ........ PHanagan 24 83
(DNicholls) *chsd far side ldrs: cl up over 1f out: wknd fnl f* **33/1**

00/4 **19** *½* **Sheer Tenby (IRE)**[12] 2744 7-9-7 **99** ........(bt) JPMurtagh 20 90
(PaulARoche, Ire) *chsd far side ldrs: wknd u.p wl over 1f out* **33/1**

2466 **20** *nk* **Halmahera (IRE)**[8] 2857 9-9-8 **100** ........ KDarley 1 90
(KARyan) *prom nr side tl wknd wl over 1f out* **33/1**

0034 **21** *nk* **Fire Up The Band**[63] 1471 5-9-10 **102** ........ DHolland 6 91
(DNicholls) *mde most on nr side to wl over 1f out: sn wknd* **16/1**

4620 **22** *shd* **Johnston's Diamond (IRE)**[8] 2857 6-8-10 **88** ........ WSupple 29 77
(EJAlston) *racd far side: nvr beyond midfield: wknd over 1f out* **66/1**

-000 **23** *1 ¼* **Salviati (USA)**[21] 2488 7-8-9 **87** ........ DaneO'Neill 12 72
(JMBradley) *b.hind: s.s: racd in last trio nr side: effrt on outer 2f out: no prog fnl f* **66/1**

4426 **24** *¾* **Corridor Creeper (FR)**[14] 2679 7-8-11 **89** ........(p) RHills 3 72
(JMBradley) *w nr side ldr to over 2f out: sn wknd* **20/1**

21-0 **25** *4* **Cd Europe (IRE)**[35] 2132 6-9-0 **92** ........(p) NCallan 13 63
(KARyan) *racd nr side: nvr on terms w ldrs: struggling 2f out* **33/1**

3-24 **26** *2* **Texas Gold**[14] 2679 6-8-12 **90** ........ SDrowne 14 55
(WRMuir) *taken to post 15 minutes early: pressed ldrs to 1/2-way: sn wknd* **28/1**

0-53 **27** *1 ¼* **Tychy**[14] 2679 5-8-12 **90** ........ JPSpencer 10 51
(SCWilliams) *lw: b.hind: chsd nr side ldrs 4f: sn wknd* **12/1**

00-0 **28** *2 ½* **Boleyn Castle (USA)**[21] 2475 7-9-4 **96** ........ TGMcLaughlin 23 50
(PSMcentee) *lw: taken to post 15 minutes early: racd in midfield far side: wknd 1/2-way: bhd fnl 2f* **66/1**

0550 **29** *5* **Matty Tun**[28] 2293 5-9-0 **92** ........ LDettori 9 31
(JBalding) *b.hind: racd nr side: a in last trio: wl bhd over 1f out* **25/1**

1m 14.15s (-1.84) **Going Correction** -0.075s/f (Good) **29** Ran SP% **142.7**
Speed ratings: **109,107,106,105,105 105,104,104,103,102 102,101,101,101,100 100,99,99,98,98 97,97,95,94,89 86**CSF £69.11 CT £755.92 TOTE £7.70: £2.50, £4.40, £3.00, £3.20; EX 155.30 Trifecta £9019.80 Pool £16,515.30 - 1.30 winning units..
**Owner** Alfi and Partners **Bred** Biddestone Stud **Trained** Sessay, N Yorks
■ A first Royal Ascot winner for David Nicholls.

**FOCUS**
A competitive Wokingham, although not quite as classy as last year's, which worked out incredibly well. The field split into two, with eighteen going to the far side, but there seemed no appreciable draw bias. The winning time was spot on for a race of its type.

**NOTEBOOK**
**Lafi(IRE)** landed a reported £2.5 million gamble. Drawn against the far rail, but challenging four off the fence, he produced a decisive turn of foot to lead his group going to the furlong pole and was always in command thereafter. Like the majority of recent Wokingham winners, he stays farther, and this was his first win over six furlongs.
**Coconut Penang(IRE)**, previously trained by Rod Millman, had been given a chance by the handicapper having been high in the weights since a good juvenile season. Coming out on top of the twelve-strong group to race on the stands' side, but finding himself in front perhaps a little too early, he promises to stay seven and the Bunbury Cup at Newmarket could be his next target.
**High Reach** ◆ ran a cracking race and only just failed to emerge on top of his group. He is more effective held up for longer and there is a big sprint handicap in him this season.
**Royal Storm(IRE)**, whose yard is emerging from the doldrums, was no match for the favourite in the final furlong but this was still a fine effort. The stiff six furlongs suited him well.
**Dazzling Bay** showed plenty of dash and remains capable of winning another big sprint.
**Pic Up Sticks**, a versatile type, was staying on to good effort in the final furlong having been switched to the outside of his group.
**Simianna**, minus the cheekpieces this time, ran a solid race to finish third on the near side but looks likely to remain in the handicapper's pocket.
**Cardinal Venture(IRE)**, under his penalty, stays farther and was keeping on strongly having had plenty to do.
**Dame De Noche** disputed the lead with Royal Storm in the far-side bunch but had no chance with the favourite from the furlong pole. The handicapper has been slow to drop her.
**Indian Spark** ◆ was held up a long way off the pace and then found himself with nowhere to go when asked to improve his position against the rail. He finished full of running and there could be another race for him even at the age of ten.
**Whitbarrow(IRE)**, who had previously been confined to the minimum trip this season, showed plenty of pace to go with the leaders before the stiff finish found him out.
**Halmahera(IRE)** was beaten a short-head in this race in 1999 but has been found wanting in the five runnings since. He was without his usual headgear on this occasion.
**Fire Up The Band** led the stands'-side group for just over four furlongs before back-pedalling rapidly.
**Texas Gold** *Official explanation: jockey said gelding had stumbled and lost its action*
**Matty Tun** *Official explanation: jockey said gelding was unsuited by the firm ground*

## 3075 DUKE OF EDINBURGH STKS (HERITAGE H'CAP) 1m 4f
5:00 (5:02) (B) (0-105,104) 3-Y-0+ **£29,000** (£11,000; £5,500; £2,500) **Stalls** High

Form RPR

-001 **1** **Wunderwood (USA)**[14] 2691 5-9-1 **92** ........ SSanders 13 108
(LadyHerries) *hld up in tch: hdwy 2f out: rdn to ld over 1f out: rdn out* **15/2**

-342 **2** *3 ½* **Pagan Dance (IRE)**[49] 1768 5-9-1 **92** ........(p) MJKinane 8 102
(MrsAJPerrett) *hld up and bhd: rdn and hdwy over 1f out: r.o to take 2nd post* **8/1**

3412 **3** *shd* **Swift Tango (IRE)**[14] 2681 4-9-7 **98** ........ LDettori 6 108
(EALDunlop) *lw: hld up and bhd: hdwy 2f out: chsd wnr ins fnl f: no imp* **9/2**[1]

2-60 **4** *2* **Hambleden**[31] 2220 7-9-9 **100** ........ NCallan 12 107
(MAJarvis) *chsd ldr: led jst over 2f out tl over 1f out: one pce* **10/1**

2024 **5** *hd* **Highland Games (IRE)**[14] 2691 4-8-10 **87** ........ KDarley 17 93
(JGGiven) *hld up: hdwy on ins whn nt clr run and swtchd lft over 2f out: nt clr run and swtchd lft over 1f out: styd on ins fnl f* **20/1**

0203 **6** *1 ½* **Briareus**[16] 2624 4-8-1 **78** ........ JQuinn 14 82
(AMBalding) *hld up in tch: rdn over 2f out: wknd ins fnl f* **22/1**

0-04 **7** *hd* **Anticipating**[14] 2681 4-8-8 **85** ........ KFallon 10 89
(AMBalding) *hld up mid-div: hdwy on ins over 2f out: sn no imp* **11/2**[2]

31-1 **8** *1* **Ocean Avenue (IRE)**[28] 2305 5-8-7 **84** ........ DHolland 11 86
(CAHorgan) *led: rdn and hdd jst over 2f out: wknd 1f out* **8/1**

0-00 **9** *5* **Prince Nureyev (IRE)**[37] 2066 4-9-1 **92** ........ SDrowne 9 86
(BRMillman) *prom tl wknd over 1f out* **16/1**

-065 **10** *1 ¼* **Trust Rule**[14] 2681 4-9-4 **95** ........ MHills 3 87
(BWHills) *lw: hld up in tch: rdn and lost pl 5f out: sn struggling* **7/1**[3]

0-34 **11** *1* **Counsel's Opinion (IRE)**[15] 2638 7-9-13 **104** ........ JPMurtagh 4 94
(CFWall) *lw: a bhd* **9/1**

23/0 **12** *5* **Ocean Of Storms (IRE)**[15] 2637 9-7-11 **79** ow1 ........(t) RThomas(5) 16 61
(ChristianWroe, UAE) *rel to r: a in rr* **50/1**

0- **13** *dist* **Nopekan (IRE)**[36] 2103 4-9-3 **94** ........ VSlattery 1 —
(MissKMarks) *hld up in tch: lost pl over 6f out: t.o fnl 3f* **66/1**

2m 28.74s (-4.82) **Going Correction** -0.075s/f (Good) **13** Ran SP% **117.6**
Speed ratings: **113,110,110,109,109 108,108,107,104,103 102,99,—**CSF £62.83 CT £304.64 TOTE £10.30: £2.90, £3.20, £1.40; EX 92.70 Trifecta £238.10 Pool £4158.48 - 12.40 winning units..
**Owner** Tony Perkins **Bred** Darley Stud Management, L L C **Trained** Angmering, W Sussex

**FOCUS**
This handicap did not appear to be quite as competitive as usual, but the time was creditable and the form should work out.

**NOTEBOOK**
**Wunderwood(USA)** was raised only 3lb for his Newmarket win and ran out a clear-cut winner, looking very much at home on the firm ground and showing improved form again under a good ride.
**Pagan Dance(IRE)** came from well back on the wide outside, but the winner was home and dry. He could move up to two miles in the Northumberland Plate next time.
**Swift Tango(IRE)** was 8lb higher than when winning at Newbury last month. He travelled well, but the winner got first run on him and he was then pipped for second.
**Hambleden** likes fast ground and stepped up on his two previous starts this season. However, he continues on a career-high mark.
**Highland Games(IRE)** ◆ was 5lb better off than when just over four lengths behind Wunderwood at Newmarket. He got into all sorts of traffic problems in the home straight and can find a suitable opening while the ground remains fast.
**Briareus**, back on fast ground for the first time this season, ran his race again.
**Trust Rule** *Official explanation: jockey said colt was unsuited by the firm ground*
**Counsel's Opinion(IRE)** *Official explanation: jockey said gelding was unsuited by the firm ground*

## 3076 QUEEN ALEXANDRA STKS (CONDITIONS RACE) 2m 6f 34y
5:35 (5:35) (B) 4-Y-0+ **£20,300** (£7,700; £3,850; £1,750) **Stalls** High

Form RPR

**1** **Corrib Eclipse**[94] 5-9-0 ........ JFEgan 11 99
(JamiePoulton) *hld up in rr: drvn and effrt on inner 3f out: squeezed though over 2f out: qcknd to ld over 1f out: styd on wl* **25/1**

31/1 **2** *1 ½* **Dancing Bay**[14] 2684 7-9-0 100 ........ KFallon 5 98
(NJHenderson) *hld up in midfield: effrt whn nt clr run wl over 2f out and again over 1f out: chsd wnr fnl f: styd on: a hld* **11/2**[2]

30-3 **3** *1 ¾* **Romany Prince**[30] 2240 5-9-0 100 ........ DaneO'Neill 4 96
(DRCElsworth) *hld up wl in rr: effrt on outer 3f out: styd on to chse ldng pair wl ins fnl f: nvr able to chal* **6/1**[3]

60-4 **4** *3* **Holy Orders (IRE)**[24] 2416 7-9-0 ........(b) DJCondon 1 93
(WPMullins, Ire) *racd in midfield: prog over 3f out: rdn to ld briefly wl over 1f out: wknd fnl f* **9/1**

40-3 **5** *1 ¼* **Big Moment**[45] 1880 6-9-0 99 ........ MJKinane 10 92
(MrsAJPerrett) *chsd clr ldng pair: lost pl over 2f out: n.m.r wl over 1f out: nt qckn after* **5/1**[1]

-050 **6** *¾* **Don Fernando**[4] 2958 5-9-0 76 ........ GaryStevens 7 91
(MCPipe) *hld up in rr: effrt on outer over 2f out: nudged along and nvr nr ldrs* **25/1**

-040 **7** *shd* **Savannah Bay**[19] 2533 5-9-0 106 ........(b) LDettori 12 91
(BJMeehan) *hld up towards rr: effrt over 3f out: nt clr run 2f out: sn rdn and nt qckn* **7/1**

/30- **8** *1* **Double Honour (FR)**[31] 3198 6-9-0 102 ........ DHolland 6 90
(PJHobbs) *trckd ldr: led over 3f out: hdd & wknd wl over 1f out* **6/1**[3]

-550 **9** *1 ½* **Pugin (IRE)**[31] 2220 6-9-0 104 ........ JPSpencer 8 88
(DRLoder) *trckd clr ldrs: effrt and cl up 3f out: rdn and fnd nil 2f out: wknd* **9/1**

0-00 **10** *20* **Gallery God (FR)**[14] 2681 8-9-0 95 ........ RLMoore 2 68
(SDow) *hld up in last: rdn over 5f out: sn bhd* **66/1**

**11** *25* **Blackchurch Mist (IRE)**[20] 7-8-9 ........(t) ADaly 9 38
(BWDuke) *chsd ldrs tl wknd 5f out: t.o* **100/1**

52-1 **12** *6* **Windermere (IRE)**[24] 2416 5-9-5 ........ JPMurtagh 3 42
(TMWalsh, Ire) *led to over 3f out: wknd rapidly over 2f out: eased: t.o* **6/1**[3]

4m 57.41s (0.84) **Going Correction** -0.075s/f (Good) **12** Ran SP% **117.6**
Speed ratings: **95,94,93,92,92 92,91,91,91,83 74,72**CSF £153.70 TOTE £55.60: £10.30, £1.60, £2.50; EX 560.30 Trifecta £3457.60 Part won. Pool £4,869.96 - 0.10 winning units. Place 6 £369.92, Place 5 £76.62.
**Owner** M Ioannou **Bred** J Godfrey **Trained** Telscombe, E Sussex
■ Stewards Enquiry : J F Egan one-day ban: used whip with excessive frequency (Jun 30)

**FOCUS**
Mixed form, with some of the best horses clearly below their best, and though the early pace was reasonable the final time was modest. There were plenty in with a shout turning for home.

**NOTEBOOK**
**Corrib Eclipse** had not run since finishing tenth in the Champion Bumper at the Cheltenham Festival, and this was his first run on the Flat proper. Quickening up to lead in the straight, he stuck his neck out well and obviously has abundant stamina, a quality which will stand him in good stead when he goes over hurdles, although he is unlikely to be seen much on the Flat again. Easier ground may well suit him.
**Dancing Bay** was probably unfortunate not to win, as he was buffeted around turning into the straight and then had to wait for a gap to open, allowing the eventual winner to take first run. This was a fine effort especially as the firm ground was not ideal for him.
**Romany Prince**, stepping up a mile in trip, ran a solid race but his effort just petered out inside the last. He might remain hard to win with.
**Holy Orders(IRE)** briefly struck the front in the straight but was soon collared. It was a surprise that he appeared not to get home, having won over three miles over hurdles, but this was still a decent run.
**Big Moment** ran a creditable race, especially as he chased the pace, but could not produce a change of gear in the final quarter of a mile.
**Don Fernando**, having his second run of the week, was again given a fair bit to do but not to the extent he had been in the Ascot Stakes.
**Double Honour(FR)**, third in the last two runnings of this race, was a useful novice chaser in the latest season. Having tracked the leader, he struck for home early in the straight but was cut down below the distance.

**Pugin(IRE)** had his chance in the straight but appeared less than enthusiastic, although he probably failed to stay this marathon trip in any case.
**Windermere(IRE)**, under a penalty for his Listed-race defeat of Vinnie Roe, never really settled in front and failed to get home.
T/Plt: £217.40 to a £1 stake. Pool: £247,132.56. 829.65 winning tickets. T/Qpdt: £54.10 to a £1 stake. Pool: £14,088.25. 192.40 winning tickets. KH

## 3037 AYR (L-H)
### Saturday, June 19
**OFFICIAL GOING: Good (good to soft in places)**

## 3077 STANLEYBET.COM H'CAP — 5f
1:50 (1:53) (D) (0-85,85) 3-Y-O — **£6,799** (£2,092; £1,046; £523) **Stalls** High

Form — RPR
0036 **1** **Divine Spirit**[7] 2877 3-9-1 **79** ACulhane 2 — 88
(MDods) *swtchd to stands rail after 1f: hld up: nt clr run over 1f out: shkn up and hdwy to ld wl ins last: comf* **10/1**
4-60 **2** ½ **Sweet Cando (IRE)**[11] 2756 3-7-9 **62** oh3 (p) NMackay(3) 11 — 69
(MissLAPerratt) *prom: led appr fnl f to wl ins last: kpt on* **16/1**
2231 **3** 1¼ **Baron Rhodes**[7] 2889 3-8-11 **78** TEaves(3) 4 — 81
(JSWainwright) *sn pushed along bhd ldrs: effrt whn n.m.r wl over 1f out: ev ch ent last: one pce towards fin* **5/1**[1]
4230 **4** 2½ **Lualua**[7] 2877 3-8-8 **77** PMakin(5) 6 — 71
(TDBarron) *prom: effrt and ev ch over 1f out: edgd rt and one pce ins fnl f* **6/1**[2]
-031 **5** 2 **Champagne Cracker**[15] 2650 3-8-2 **66** DKinsella 10 — 52
(MissLAPerratt) *cl up: led briefly over 1f out: no ex whn hmpd ins fnl f* **7/1**[3]
-510 **6** 1½ **Four Amigos (USA)**[56] 1614 3-9-7 **85** SChin 7 — 66
(JGGiven) *chsd ldrs tl lost pl over 1f out* **5/1**[1]
0050 **7** hd **Peters Choice**[23] 2423 3-8-2 **66** JBramhill 8 — 46
(ISemple) *led to over 1f out: sn btn* **25/1**
3531 **8** shd **Blue Power (IRE)**[8] 2850 3-7-7 **62** oh4 BSwarbrick(5) 5 — 42
(KRBurke) *in tch: effrt 1/2-way: btn fnl f* **10/1**
4023 **9** shd **Only If I Laugh**[3] 2986 3-7-6 **63** StaceyRenwick(7) 9 — 42
(PABlockley) *prom: effrt whn n.m.r 2f out: sn rdn and outpcd* **16/1**
3040 **10** 1¼ **Baylaw Star**[7] 2889 3-8-7 **71** (p) JEdmunds 12 — 46
(JBalding) *cl up tl rdn and wknd over 1f out* **16/1**
0602 **11** 6 **Sir Ernest (IRE)**[15] 2650 3-8-12 **76** DarrenWilliams 1 — 29
(MJPolglase) *rrd s: nvr on terms* **16/1**
1203 **12** 18 **Sahara Silk (IRE)**[8] 2850 3-7-7 **62** (v) HayleyTurner(5) 3 — —
(DShaw) *sn outpcd: lost tch fr 1/2-way* **16/1**

61.62 secs (1.19) **Going Correction** +0.175s/f (Good) — **12 Ran SP% 111.6**
Speed ratings: **97,96,94,90,87 84,84,84,83,81 72,43**CSF £150.19 CT £892.25 TOTE £11.40: £2.30, £5.20, £1.60; EX 159.10.
**Owner** A Mallen **Bred** S R Hope And D Erwin Bloodstock **Trained** Piercebridge, Co Durham
■ Stewards Enquiry : T Eaves one-day ban: careless riding (Jun 30)

**FOCUS**
An ordinary handicap and not outstanding form, in which the winner and second raced against the stands side rail so the third, who made her ground on the outside, may be a bit better than the bare form.

**NOTEBOOK**
**Divine Spirit** confirmed recent promise but he did have plenty going for him, in that his rider switched him to the favoured stands' rail soon after the start and he got the gaps at the right time to win with a bit more in hand than the official margin suggests. Things went his way, but he should continue to give a good account.
**Sweet Cando(IRE)**, dropping in trip and tried in cheekpieces, had the run of the race, performed creditably and looks capable of winning a similar race on this evidence.
**Baron Rhodes** ◆, a most consistent sort, may be the one to take out of the race as she fared best of those that attempted to make ground away from the favoured stands' rail. She is admirably consistent and should continue to go well.
**Lualua** ran creditably but did not find as much off the bridle as seemed likely, and the minor inteference suffered late on made no difference to the result. Faster ground may suit him better.
**Champagne Cracker**, the winner of a messy flip-start race on her previous outing, showed plenty of dash for a long way but was beaten on merit and, although hampered late on, it made no difference to the placings.
**Four Amigos(USA)**, who beat Baron Rhodes in convincing fashion at Thirsk in April, looked sure to be suited by the drop to this trip and had conditions to suit, so was a shade disappointing.
**Sahara Silk(IRE)** *Official explanation: trainer said filly was never travelling*

## 3078 FREEPHONE STANLEYBET H'CAP — 1m 5f 13y
2:25 (2:25) (C) (0-95,89) 3-Y-O+ — **£9,646** (£2,968; £1,484; £742) **Stalls** Low

Form — RPR
-041 **1** **Trance (IRE)**[14] 2671 4-8-12 **82** PMakin(5) 3 — 91
(TDBarron) *prom: effrt over 2f out: hung lft and led 1f out: rdn out* **6/1**[3]
0401 **2** 1¼ **Sahem (IRE)**[5] 2935 7-9-0 **79** 6ex DKinsella 9 — 86
(DEddy) *led: rdn over 2f out: hdd 1f out: rallied: hld cl home* **9/2**[2]
361/ **3** 2½ **Monolith**[31] 5180 6-9-3 **82** WDowling 5 — 85
(LLungo) *chsd ldrs: effrt over 2f out: hung lft and no ex over 1f out* **9/1**
6/15 **4** 2½ **Colorado Falls (IRE)**[10] 2782 6-8-10 **78** LEnstone(3) 1 — 78
(PMonteith) *hld up: rdn 4f out: rallied over 1f out: no imp* **8/1**
1355 **5** ¾ **George Stubbs (USA)**[24] 2409 6-7-9 **63** NMackay(3) 4 — 61
(MJPolglase) *chsd ldrs tl rdn and no ex fr over 2f out* **7/1**
-512 **6** 3½ **Tawny Way**[37] 2062 4-9-7 **86** ACulhane 2 — 79
(WJarvis) *in tch: effrt over 2f out: btn over 1f out* **4/1**[1]
22-5 **7** 16 **Prince Holing**[55] 1286 4-9-7 **89** TEaves(3) 8 — 58
(MTodhunter) *hld up: effrt over 3f out: sn rdn and btn* **25/1**
-166 **8** 3½ **Graham Island**[32] 2203 3-8-5 **85** JCarroll 6 — 49
(GWragg) *trckd ldrs: effrt and rdn over 3f out: wknd 2f out* **9/2**[2]
31/ **9** 12 **Lord Dundee (IRE)**[743] 1962 6-9-6 **85** DarrenWilliams 7 — 31
(RCGuest) *hld up: rdn over 3f out: sn btn* **33/1**

2m 58.93s (3.08) **Going Correction** +0.45s/f (Yiel)
**WFA** 3 from 4yo+ 15lb — **9 Ran SP% 111.0**
Speed ratings: **108,107,105,104,103 101,91,89,82**CSF £31.21 CT £231.20 TOTE £8.70: £2.90, £2.70, £1.60; EX 49.50.
**Owner** Nigel Shields **Bred** Forenaghts Stud Co Ltd **Trained** Maunby, N Yorks

**FOCUS**
An ordinary handicap but one run at a steady pace and favoured those racing close to the pace. This bare form is fair but may not be entirely reliable.

**NOTEBOOK**
**Trance(IRE)** once again did not look an easy ride under pressure but turned in an improved effort over this longer trip. A more strongly-run race will suit, and he may be capable of defying a further rise in the weights kept away from progressive or well-handicapped types.
**Sahem(IRE)** once again was allowed the run of the race and performed right up to his recent best under his penalty. He is a versatile performer who is capable of winning again when allowed his own way in front, and he will be of even more interest when connections elect to send him back over hurdles.
**Monolith** ◆, an improved performer up to three miles on a sound surface over hurdles this year, would have been better suited by a stiffer test of stamina on quicker ground on this first Flat start since 2001. However, he showed more than enough to suggest he can win races in this sphere, granted more suitable conditions.
**Colorado Falls(IRE)** shaped as though a bit better than the bare result, as this race favoured those racing close to the steady pace. However, although a more strongly-run race would suit, he still looks high enough in the weights at present.
**George Stubbs(USA)** was not disgraced but, although a stiffer test of stamina may have seen him in a better light, he is not the most consistent around.
**Tawny Way** was below her best on her first attempt over this trip in the rain-softened ground, and may be suited by a more strongly-run race back over shorter distances. *Official explanation: vet said filly was found to be in season*
**Graham Island** looked to have fair claims back in this more suitable grade over a trip that should have been in his favour, but ran poorly and he may prefer a sound surface.

## 3079 STANLEYBET H'CAP — 7f 50y
2:55 (2:59) (C) (0-90,83) 3-Y-O+ — **£10,276** (£3,162; £1,581; £790) **Stalls** High

Form — RPR
222U **1** **Balakiref**[14] 2673 5-8-0 **64** HayleyTurner(5) 7 — 78
(MDods) *hld up and bhd: hdwy over 2f out: led ins fnl f: hld on wl* **16/1**
6005 **2** nk **Digital**[7] 2891 7-9-10 **83** ACulhane 10 — 96
(MRChannon) *hld up: gd hdwy 2f out: disp ld ins fnl f: kpt on: jst hld* **11/2**[2]
0533 **3** 3½ **Sarraaf (IRE)**[6] 2905 8-8-11 **70** VHalliday 13 — 74
(JSGoldie) *prom: rdn 3f out: kpt on ins fnl f* **12/1**
2233 **4** ½ **Samuel Charles**[1] 3039 6-8-8 **72** PMakin(5) 2 — 75
(WMBrisbourne) *w ldr: led 1/2-way: clr over 1f out: hdd and no ex ins fnl f* **7/1**[3]
-003 **5** 2 **Fair Shake (IRE)**[54] 1665 4-8-7 **66** (p) DKinsella 12 — 64
(DEddy) *hld up: effrt outside over 2f out: no imp fnl f* **10/1**
-064 **6** 1¾ **Ballyhurry (USA)**[21] 2492 7-8-9 **71** NMackay(3) 4 — 64
(JSGoldie) *midfield: effrt over 2f out: no imp fr over 1f out* **4/1**[1]
-060 **7** ¾ **Wessex (USA)**[10] 2781 4-9-3 **76** JCarroll 11 — 67
(JamesMoffatt) *midfield: rdn over 2f out: nt pce to chal* **33/1**
015U **8** 3½ **Tidy (IRE)**[56] 1608 4-9-7 **80** DarrenWilliams 5 — 62
(MDHammond) *in tch: rdn and outpcd whn n.m.r over 1f out: sn btn* **20/1**
3012 **9** 1¾ **El Palmar**[8] 2849 3-8-4 **72** JBramhill 9 — 49
(PABlockley) *chsd ldrs tl wknd fr 2f out* **33/1**
0024 **10** 3 **The Bonus King**[19] 2516 4-9-7 **80** SChin 6 — 50
(MJohnston) *prom: outpcd after 3f: sn n.d* **7/1**[3]
0216 **11** ½ **Desert Arc (IRE)**[1] 3038 6-8-1 **65** BSwarbrick(5) 3 — 33
(WMBrisbourne) *bhd: rdn 1/2-way: nvr on terms* **11/1**
00-1 **12** 4 **Flur Na H Alba**[28] 2291 5-9-7 **83** (p) TEaves(3) 1 — 41
(ISemple) *led to 1/2-way: wknd 2f out* **8/1**
20-3 **13** 7 **Bandos**[18] 2553 4-8-12 **74** (t) LEnstone(3) 8 — 14
(ISemple) *sn bhd: struggling fr 1/2-way* **20/1**

1m 34.61s (2.14) **Going Correction** +0.45s/f (Yiel)
**WFA** 3 from 4yo+ 9lb — **13 Ran SP% 117.9**
Speed ratings: **105,104,100,100,97 95,94,90,88,85 84,80,72**CSF £95.81 CT £1139.76 TOTE £23.30: £5.20, £2.20, £4.40; EX 133.30.
**Owner** Septimus Racing Group **Bred** S R Hope And D Erwin **Trained** Piercebridge, Co Durham

**FOCUS**
An open race but a strong pace teed things up for those coming from off the pace and so the bare form, which appears decent, may not be entirely reliable.

**NOTEBOOK**
**Balakiref**, appreciated the rain and the strongly-run race to turn in a career-best performance, but he may not have things fall as well for him next time and could be vulnerable back on faster ground from a higher mark.
**Digital** had the race run to suit and turned in his best effort of the year. However this bare form may flatter him to a certain extent, and he is likely to continue to look vulnerable from his current mark.
**Sarraaf(IRE)** is not the most predictable but ran well from his double figure draw. This underlined he is capable of winning races from his current mark, but his record suggests he is not one to place maximum faith in.
**Samuel Charles** is a model of consistency and ran well turned out quickly, especially as he was up with the strong pace throughout. He is a bit better than the bare form and should continue to give a good account.
**Fair Shake(IRE)**, who had conditions to suit, was not disgraced on this first run after a short break, but may prove more effective back over six furlongs when there is give in the ground.
**Ballyhurry(USA)**, from a stable that has been going well, had the race run to suit but did not pick up in the anticipated manner and, although he has run well on easy ground in the past, all his best form is on a quick surface. He is not one to write off yet back on top of the ground.
**Desert Arc(IRE)** *Official explanation: trainer said gelding was unsuited by the ground*
**Flur Na H Alba** was unable to get an easy lead and this inconsistent performer was a long way below his reappearance run.
**Bandos** *Official explanation: jockey said gelding would not face the cross noseband and became wound up at the start*

## 3080 STANLEYBET.COM MAIDEN AUCTION STKS — 6f
3:30 (3:33) (E) 2-Y-O — **£4,104** (£1,263; £631; £315) **Stalls** High

Form — RPR
**1** **Lamh Eile (IRE)** 2-7-13 NMackay(3) 12 — 80
(TDBarron) *mde all: clr whn edgd lft over 1f out: r.o strly* **12/1**
05 **2** 7 **Hymn Of Victory (IRE)**[17] 2579 2-8-4 TEaves(3) 10 — 64
(TJEtherington) *cl up: rdn over 2f out: kpt on fnl f: no ch w wnr* **12/1**
30 **3** 1¾ **Llamadas**[8] 2860 2-8-10 LEnstone(3) 5 — 65
(MDods) *in tch: rdn 1/2-way: rallied over 1f out: no imp* **8/1**[3]
**4** 1½ **Union Jack Jackson (IRE)** 2-8-13 JBramhill 11 — 60
(JGGiven) *chsd ldrs: outpcd over 2f out: rallied fnl f: no imp* **11/1**
3 **5** hd **Regal Lustre**[30] 2247 2-8-2 ow2 PMakin(5) 8 — 54
(JRWeymes) *midfield: drvn 1/2-way: nt pce to chal* **33/1**
0 **6** shd **Fly To Dubai (IRE)**[28] 2300 2-8-10 JCarroll 4 — 56
(EJO'Neill) *swtchd to stands rail sn after s: hld up: effrt over 2f out: no imp fnl f* **7/2**[1]
**7** 1¼ **I'm So Lucky** 2-8-10 SChin 7 — 53
(MJohnston) *sn pushed in rr: effrt and rn green over 2f out: btn fnl f* **9/2**[2]
03 **8** ½ **Whatatodo**[12] 2730 2-7-11 HayleyTurner(5) 1 — 43
(MLWBell) *prom on outside to 2f out: sn btn* **7/2**[1]
46 **9** shd **Zendaro**[28] 2300 2-8-5 BSwarbrick(5) 3 — 51
(WMBrisbourne) *sn bhd: nvr on terms* **16/1**
**10** 5 **Orphan (IRE)** 2-8-7 DarrenWilliams 9 — 33
(KRBurke) *chsd ldrs: rdn and edgd lft over 1f out: sn wknd* **20/1**

0 11 10 **Tillingborn Dancer (IRE)**[26] 2352 2-8-10 ACulhane 6 6
(MDHammond) *cl up to 1/2-way: sn lost pl* **25/1**

1m 15.13s (1.41) **Going Correction** +0.175s/f (Good) **11** Ran SP% **114.9**
Speed ratings: **97,87,85,83,83 82,81,80,80,73** **60**CSF £140.12 TOTE £24.30: £4.50, £5.90, £3.50; EX 191.00.
**Owner** Oghill House Stud **Bred** Oghill House Stud **Trained** Maunby, N Yorks

**FOCUS**
The proximity of the runner-up confirms this form is nothing special but a sound pace, the form looks reliable, and a most pleasing debut display from Lamh Eile, who is open to plenty of improvement and should stay further.

**NOTEBOOK**
**Lamh Eile(IRE)** ◆, a half-sister to a juvenile winner in Italy, had the advantageous stands rail pitch but created a favourable impression on this racecourse debut. She should prove equally effective over seven and looks the type to win more races.
**Hymn Of Victory(IRE)** has improved steadily and turned in his best effort over this longer trip. An even stiffer test of stamina should suit, and he is one to bear in mind in nursery company over seven furlongs or a mile.
**Llamadas** has still to reproduce debut form but was not disgraced over this trip for the first time and on this first start on easy ground. He too will be of more interest in modest nursery company in due course.
**Union Jack Jackson(IRE)**, a strong sort with plenty of scope, was nibbled at in the market and showed ability on this racecourse debut. He is likely to fare a good deal better in due course.
**Regal Lustre** probably ran to a simlar level of form as on her debut and she is likely to continue to look vulnerable in this grade. Low-grade handicaps over further may bring about improvement.
**Fly To Dubai(IRE)** again attracted market support but did not really improve on his debut form. He will need to do so if he is to win in similar company.
**I'm So Lucky**, a half-brother to five winners, looked as though the race would do him good beforehand and ran as though the experience was needed. He is not a bad sort and is the type to leave this form behind in due course.

## 3081 FREEPHONE STANLEYBET EUROPEAN BREEDERS FUND MAIDEN STKS 7f 50y
4:05 (4:10) (D) 2-Y-O £4,182 (£1,287; £643; £321) Stalls High

| Form | | | | | RPR |
|---|---|---|---|---|---|
| | 1 | | **Buddy Brown** 2-9-0 | DKinsella 4 | 70 |
| | | | (JHowardJohnson) *keen: hld up in tch: effrt on outside over 2f out: led ins last: kpt on wl* **4/1**[2] | | |
| 6 | 2 | hd | **Ballycroy Girl (IRE)**[29] 2256 2-8-6 | NMackay(3) 8 | 65 |
| | | | (ABailey) *cl up: led 2f out to ins fnl f: kpt on: jst hld* **16/1** | | |
| | 3 | 1 1/4 | **Dancer's Serenade (IRE)** 2-9-0 | DarrenWilliams 9 | 66 |
| | | | (TPTate) *s.i.s: hdwy and ev ch over 2f out: rdn and rn green: one pce fnl f* **25/1** | | |
| 0 | 4 | 1 3/4 | **Makepeace (IRE)**[12] 2736 2-9-0 | ACulhane 5 | 62 |
| | | | (MRChannon) *sn chsng ldrs: effrt over 2f out: one pce fnl f* **6/1**[3] | | |
| 0 | 5 | 1 1/2 | **Speagle (IRE)**[11] 2758 2-9-0 | JCarroll 6 | 58 |
| | | | (EJO'Neill) *keen: led after 2f to 2f out: sn one pce* **25/1** | | |
| | 6 | 6 | **Hawks Tor (IRE)** 2-9-0 | SChin 2 | 43 |
| | | | (MJohnston) *led 2f: prom tl outpcd over 2f out* **11/10**[1] | | |
| | 7 | 3 | **Spanish Law** 2-8-11 | LEnstone(3) 3 | 36 |
| | | | (MDods) *in tch: outpcd 1/2-way: n.d after* **25/1** | | |

1m 38.41s (5.94) **Going Correction** +0.45s/f (Yiel) **7** Ran SP% **99.3**
Speed ratings: **84,83,82,80,78 71,68**CSF £42.25 TOTE £5.90: £2.40, £4.40; EX 58.50.
**Owner** Andrea & Graham Wylie **Bred** Darley **Trained** Crook, Co Durham
■ Stewards Enquiry : N Mackay caution: used whip with excessive frequency

**FOCUS**
The proximity of those with previous form suggests this bare result is nothing special but a couple of the newcomers appeal as the types to improve with experience. The pace was only fair at best and the time was slow.

**NOTEBOOK**
**Buddy Brown** ◆, the second foal of a dam who is a sister to a multiple winner in Germany, failed to settle in the early stages but showed the right attitude to beat a more experienced rival. This bare form is nothing special, but he is the sort to progress again.
**Ballycroy Girl(IRE)** stepped up a good deal on her debut effort and, on this evidence, should be capable of winning a seven furlong event around this trip in due course.
**Dancer's Serenade(IRE)** ◆, a half-brother to Pirouettes, ran creditably despite his apparent greenness on this racecourse debut. He has plenty of scope and looks the type to improve, especially over further, and is capable of winning races.
**Makepeace(IRE)** improved on his debut form over this longer trip, and on easier ground and looks the type to do better in ordinary company at up to a mile.
**Speagle(IRE)** had the run of the race and fared better than on his debut but he will have to improve again to win in similar company.
**Hawks Tor(IRE)**, a Derby entry who cost 480,000gns and is a half-brother to seven furlong/mile winner Denver, was too green to do himself justice on this racecourse debut but he looks the type to improve a good deal for the experience.

## 3082 STANLEYBET.COM SUMMER H'CAP 1m 1f 20y
4:40 (4:42) (D) (0-80,75) 3-Y-0+ £5,486 (£1,688; £844; £422) Stalls Low

| Form | | | | | RPR |
|---|---|---|---|---|---|
| 4466 | 1 | | **Sting Like A Bee (IRE)**[23] 2424 5-7-11 **48** | NMackay(3) 10 | 59 |
| | | | (JSGoldie) *hld up: hdwy outside over 2f out: led 1f out: pushed out* **7/2**[1] | | |
| 0040 | 2 | 1 | **Lucky Largo (IRE)**[2] 3002 4-8-5 **53** | (b) DKinsella 6 | 62 |
| | | | (MissLAPerratt) *prom: led 3f to over 1f out: rallied: one pce towards fin* **16/1** | | |
| 1060 | 3 | 6 | **Harry Potter (GER)**[14] 2687 5-9-7 **69** | (b) DarrenWilliams 2 | 66 |
| | | | (KRBurke) *trckd ldrs: ev ch 3f out: sn rdn: wknd over 1f out* **7/1** | | |
| 1000 | 4 | 1 1/2 | **Pharoah's Gold (IRE)**[7] 2881 6-8-6 **54** ow1 | ACulhane 5 | 48 |
| | | | (DShaw) *hld up: effrt 2f out: no imp fnl f* **8/1** | | |
| 0000 | 5 | 5 | **Extinguisher**[10] 2776 5-8-11 **59** | (v[1]) SChin 8 | 43 |
| | | | (DNicholls) *trckd ldrs: tl rdn and wknd over 2f out* **14/1** | | |
| -044 | 6 | 1 | **Millagros (IRE)**[21] 2493 4-9-10 **75** | TEaves(3) 4 | 57 |
| | | | (ISemple) *in tch: rdn over 2f out: sn btn* **4/1**[2] | | |
| 0056 | 7 | 1 | **Nemo Fugat (IRE)**[10] 2781 5-8-11 **59** | JCarroll 1 | 39 |
| | | | (DNicholls) *hld up in tch: effrt over 2f out: btn over 1f out* **9/2**[3] | | |
| 00-0 | 8 | 9 | **Luxor**[29] 2272 7-7-7 **46** oh6 | BSwarbrick(5) 7 | 8 |
| | | | (WMBrisbourne) *led to 3f out: sn wknd* **20/1** | | |
| 0000 | 9 | 30 | **Buscador (USA)**[18] 2551 5-8-2 **50** | JBramhill 9 | — |
| | | | (WMBrisbourne) *cl up to 3f out: wknd qckly* **12/1** | | |
| 0000 | 10 | 4 | **Pharaoh Hatshepsut (IRE)**[24] 1992 6-7-7 **46** oh11 | HayleyTurner(5) 3 | — |
| | | | (JamesMoffatt) *s.v.s: t.o thrght* **100/1** | | |

2m 1.36s (4.82) **Going Correction** +0.45s/f (Yiel) **10** Ran SP% **110.0**
Speed ratings: **96,95,89,88,84 83,82,74,47,44**CSF £55.98 CT £344.13 TOTE £3.90: £1.40, £2.80, £2.20; EX 88.10 Place 6 £1617.53, Place 5 £499.63.
**Owner** Mrs C Brown **Bred** C H Wacker Iii **Trained** Uplawmoor, E Renfrews

**FOCUS**
A run of the mill handicap in which the pace was only fair and the winning time was modest. The form is ordinary and this does not look a race that will be throwing up too many winners.

**NOTEBOOK**
**Sting Like A Bee(IRE)** had been running a bit better than the bare form suggested on his last couple of starts and was seen to better effect this time. He will be up in the weights, but should continue to give a good account granted a suitable test of stamina.
**Lucky Largo(IRE)** ran his best race of the year under suitable conditions, but his record of no wins from 20 starts and his inconsistency means he is not one to be lumping on next time.
**Harry Potter(GER)** should have had no problems with the longer trip and had form in the ground but did not overly impress with his finishing effort and, although capable of winning from this mark, looks one to tread carefully with.
**Pharoah's Gold(IRE)** was not disgraced given he was dropped out, but his lack of consistency means he is one to tread warily with.
**Extinguisher**, tried in the first-time visor, did not get home over this longer trip trip and, although he has plummeted in the weights, remains a frustrating sort for his current stable.
**Millagros(IRE)** would probably have preferred a stronger pace on quicker ground, but she is not the most reliable betting proposition around.
T/Plt: £4,562.30 to a £1 stake. Pool: £36,873.65. 5.90 winning tickets. T/Qpdt: £200.50 to a £1 stake. Pool: £2,032.30. 7.50 winning tickets. RY

# 2881 LINGFIELD (L-H)
Saturday, June 19

**OFFICIAL GOING: Turf course - good to firm (good in places) ; all-weather course - standard**
Wind: light against Weather: unsettled

## 3083 LEN BURDFIELD'S BIRTHDAY MAIDEN AUCTION STKS 7f
6:30 (6:32) (E) 2-Y-0 £3,542 (£1,090; £545; £272) Stalls High

| Form | | | | | RPR |
|---|---|---|---|---|---|
| 05 | 1 | | **Lady Chef**[16] 2609 2-8-2 | AMcCarthy 10 | 67+ |
| | | | (BRMillman) *mde virtually all: rdn and qcknd over 2f out: pushed out and hld on cleverly fnl f* **10/1** | | |
| | 2 | hd | **Prize Fighter (IRE)** 2-8-10 | JQuinn 5 | 75 |
| | | | (PWChapple-Hyam) *str: scope: dwlt: hld up in midfield: hdwy over 2f out: hrd rdn and ev ch fnl f: r.o* **5/2**[1] | | |
| 0 | 3 | nk | **Bee Stinger**[11] 2761 2-8-5 | TPQueally(3) 3 | 72 |
| | | | (IAWood) *cl up: drvn to chse wnr 2f out: ev ch fnl f: r.o* **33/1** | | |
| 0 | 4 | 1 | **Time For You**[29] 2275 2-7-9 | KJackson(7) 9 | 64 |
| | | | (PJMcbride) *hld up in midfield: effrt over 2f out: styd on wl fnl f* **20/1** | | |
| 55 | 5 | 5 | **Silver Visage (IRE)**[36] 2095 2-8-7 | BReilly(3) 12 | 59 |
| | | | (MissJFeilden) *trckd wnr: hrd rdn over 2f out: wknd wl over 1f out* **25/1** | | |
| 0 | 6 | 1 1/2 | **Spaced (IRE)**[28] 2300 2-8-13 | PDobbs 17 | 58 |
| | | | (RHannon) *lw: sn pushed along towards rr: styd on fr over 1f out: nvr nrr* **4/1**[2] | | |
| | 7 | 1 | **Persian Carpet** 2-7-11 | RThomas(5) 1 | 45 |
| | | | (IAWood) *str: bkwd: mid-div: rdn over 2f out: no imp* **66/1** | | |
| 40 | 8 | nk | **Master Joseph**[9] 2804 2-8-12 | TEDurcan 4 | 54 |
| | | | (MRChannon) *mid-div: effrt over 2f out: no hdwy* **13/2**[3] | | |
| | 9 | 1 1/2 | **Daisy Bucket** 2-7-13 | FPFerris(3) 16 | 40 |
| | | | (DMSimcock) *compact: s.i.s: rn green and hung lft: bhd tl styd on fnl f* **16/1** | | |
| | 10 | 1 1/4 | **Play Up Pompey** 2-8-3 | NChalmers(5) 15 | 43 |
| | | | (JJBridger) *w'like: bkwd: s.i.s: outpcd and bhd: mod late hdwy* **50/1** | | |
| 000 | 11 | nk | **Fantasy Defender (IRE)**[14] 2674 2-8-8 | NPollard 6 | 42 |
| | | | (JJQuinn) *chsd ldrs over 4f* **20/1** | | |
| 06 | 12 | 1 3/4 | **Ahaz**[36] 2074 2-8-9 | SSanders 2 | 39 |
| | | | (IAWood) *prom over 4f* **50/1** | | |
| 00 | 13 | 1 1/4 | **Grand Welcome (IRE)**[36] 2087 2-8-8 | EAhern 11 | 35 |
| | | | (CTinkler) *in tch 4f* **9/1** | | |
| 0 | 14 | 1 3/4 | **Victimised (IRE)**[66] 1390 2-8-6 | LPKeniry(3) 14 | 32 |
| | | | (PBurgoyne) *chsd ldrs 4f* **33/1** | | |
| 0 | 15 | 3/4 | **Dara Girl (IRE)**[10] 2786 2-8-5 ow1 | RHavlin 8 | 26 |
| | | | (MrsPNDutfield) *dwlt: sn in mid-div: rdn 4f out: sn bhd* **16/1** | | |
| | 16 | hd | **Miss Cuisina** 2-8-4 | JoannaBadger 7 | 24 |
| | | | (PDEvans) *leggy: unf: dwlt: sn wl bhd* **100/1** | | |
| | 17 | 15 | **Chin Dancer** 2-8-2 | RSmith 13 | — |
| | | | (BRMillman) *neat: outpcd in rr: wl bhd fnl 3f* **50/1** | | |

1m 26.33s (2.12) **Going Correction** +0.225s/f (Good) **17** Ran SP% **120.4**
Speed ratings: **96,95,95,94,88 86,85,85,83,82 81,79,78,76,75 75,58**CSF £31.28 TOTE £13.40: £3.70, £1.50, £5.30; EX 50.90.
**Owner** Percys Country Hotel & Restaurant **Bred** Percys (north Harrow) Ltd **Trained** Kentisbeare, Devon

**FOCUS**
Just an average maiden and the first four were clear at the finish. The winner is little better than a plater on previous form, giving the race a modest look.

**NOTEBOOK**
**Lady Chef**, who had run distinctly green on both her previous outings, pinged out of the gates to make most of the running and score a shade cosily. This step up to an extra furlong helped work the oracle and she may have more to offer, but is more likely to fare better when the nurseries begin.
**Prize Fighter(IRE)**, an easy to back favourite, was not helped by a very sluggish start, but still recovered to hold every chance if good enough. This experience will not have been lost on him and he would have bright prospects of reversing form with the winner, granted the normal improvement.
**Bee Stinger** markedly stepped up on his debut form and went down fighting over this extra furlong. He again looked green under pressure late on and will come on again for this outing.
**Time For You**, who showed early pace before dropping out quickly on his debut, ran much better for being held up on this occasion and appreciated this longer trip.
**Spaced(IRE)**, the most expensive of these as a yearling, was hard at it from an early stage and proved slightly disappointing.
**Dara Girl(IRE)** *Official explanation: jockey said filly stumbled and lost her action two furlongs out*

## 3084 LADBROKES.COM H'CAP 5f
7:00 (7:01) (E) (0-70,63) 3-Y-0+ £3,601 (£1,108; £554; £277) Stalls High

| Form | | | | | RPR |
|---|---|---|---|---|---|
| 2420 | 1 | | **Enjoy The Buzz**[7] 2885 5-8-9 **43** | CCatlin 6 | 54 |
| | | | (JMBradley) *mid-div: rdn and hdwy over 1f out: r.o to ld fnl strides* **25/1** | | |
| 0260 | 2 | nk | **Inching**[9] 2800 4-8-12 **46** | EAhern 9 | 56 |
| | | | (RMHCowell) *lw: prom: led over 3f out: hrd rdn over 1f out: hdd fnl strides* **14/1** | | |
| 5321 | 3 | 1 1/4 | **Double M**[7] 2885 7-9-5 **58** | (v) RThomas(5) 14 | 63 |
| | | | (MrsLRichards) *lw: hld up in rr: hdwy and eased outside over 1f out: r.o wl fnl f: nrst fin* **11/4**[1] | | |
| 0601 | 4 | 1/2 | **Avit (IRE)**[9] 2800 4-8-5 **39** | JFEgan 10 | 42 |
| | | | (PLGilligan) *prom: hrd rdn over 2f out: kpt on* **16/1** | | |
| 050- | 5 | 1 1/2 | **Flapdoodle**[241] 5706 6-9-5 **56** | TPQueally(3) 3 | 53 |
| | | | (AWCarroll) *led over 1f: prom: one pce appr fnl f* **16/1** | | |

3043 **6** *hd* **Law Maker**[12] [2724] 4-8-12 **46**....(v) DHolland 2 42
(MABuckley) *racd alone far side: prom tl no ex 1f out* **10/1**
5624 **7** *1 ¼* **Boanerges (IRE)**[2] [3016] 7-9-10 **58**.... RLMoore 7 49
(JMBradley) *chsd ldrs: outpcd fnl 2f* **3/1**[2]
0-00 **8** *shd* **Tomthevic**[12] [2724] 6-9-9 **57**....(p) MFenton 4 48
(MrsPSly) *b.hind: s.i.s: sn chsng ldrs: wknd 2f out* **25/1**
5500 **9** *1* **Pompey Blue**[8] [2839] 3-9-8 **62**.... SSanders 5 49
(PJMcbride) *mid-div: rdn and no hdwy fnl 2f* **20/1**
5060 **10** *nk* **Forzenuff**[107] [959] 3-9-9 **63**.... VWenkaya 11 49
(JRBoyle) *sn pushed along towards rr: sme hdwy 2f out: wknd 1f out* **25/1**
-430 **11** *nk* **Catchthebatch**[95] [1027] 8-8-9 **50**.... LiamJones(7) 1 34
(EAWheeler) *mid-div towards centre: outpcd fnl 2f* **50/1**
-002 **12** *1 ¼* **Indian Bazaar (IRE)**[7] [2885] 8-8-12 **51**.... MSavage(5) 12 30
(NEBerry) *dwlt: outpcd: a in rr* **11/2**[3]
63-0 **13** *½* **Minimum Bid**[21] [2482] 3-9-2 **56**.... JQuinn 8 33
(MissBSanders) *rdn early and sn prom: wknd 2f out* **9/1**
06-0 **14** *½* **Ardkeel Lass (IRE)**[16] [2610] 3-9-1 **62**.... MHoward(7) 13 37
(DKIvory) *b.hind: hld up towards rr: effrt and nt clr run over 1f out: n.d after* **25/1**

59.55 secs (0.68) **Going Correction** +0.225s/f (Good)
**WFA** 3 from 4yo+ 6lb **14** Ran SP% **126.7**
Speed ratings: **103,102,100,99,97 97,95,94,93,92 92,90,89,88**CSF £332.02 CT £1327.11 TOTE £18.00: £4.10, £4.40, £1.70; EX 198.90.
**Owner** Miss F Fenley **Bred** Southern Seafoods **Trained** Sedbury, Gloucs

**FOCUS**
A moderate sprint run at a solid gallop, but the form is ordinary.

**NOTEBOOK**
**Enjoy The Buzz** produced a willing turn of foot to run on strongly and collar the leaders close home. This was a big improvement on his most recent efforts and he greatly appreciated this drop back to the minimum trip. Most known for his exploits on the sand, he still remains relatively unexposed on turf, and he confirmed the current well-being of his yard's runners.
**Inching**, heavily backed to score at Brighton last time when failing to handle the track, showed his true colours over this more suitable course and only just failed. He has a similar event within his grasp off this sort of mark.
**Double M** , who went into this at the top of his game, again came late and fast, but the line came too soon. The 5lb rise for winning last time has made its mark, but he can still pay his way at this level and is not one to write off just yet.
**Avit(IRE)** had every chance over one out and ran another sound race, but the recent rise in the ratings for winning her first-ever race at Brighton last time looks to have taken its toll.
**Boanerges(IRE)**, raised 3lb for finishing a close-up fourth latest, never really threatened and put up a below-par display. He may be better over six next time.
**Indian Bazaar(IRE)** blew his chance at the start and was never going the pace from that point onwards.

## 3085 VERITAS DGC SERVICES MAIDEN STKS 6f
**7:30** (7:31) (D) 3-Y-O+ **£3,799** (£1,169; £584; £292) **Stalls** High

Form RPR
-000 **1** **Piccleyes**[8] [2836] 3-8-12 59....(b) RLMoore 1 65
(RHannon) *sn pushed along towards rr: hdwy in centre 2f out: hung rt and led jst over 1f out: wnt 4l ahd: hrd rdn: jst hld on* **8/1**
0U4- **2** *shd* **Ragged Jack (IRE)**[192] [6159] 3-8-12 77.... SWKelly 8 65
(GAButler) *mid-div: effrt and nt clr run 2f out: hdwy over 1f out: str run fnl f: jst failed* **11/2**[3]
0-05 **3** *hd* **Ligne D'Eau**[8] [2836] 3-8-12 57.... RHavlin 9 64
(PDEvans) *chsd ldrs: drvn along over 2f out: styd on wl fnl f* **8/1**
**4** *¾* **Rachel's Verdict** 3-8-7.... OUrbina 5 57
(JRFanshawe) *w'like: bkwd: hld up in midfield: effrt and nt clr run 2f out: swtchd outside: r.o wl fnl f: improve* **5/1**[2]
0-5 **5** *2 ½* **Shibumi**[14] [2675] 3-8-7.... MFenton 4 49
(HMorrison) *prom: hrd rdn wl over 1f out: one pce* **7/1**
440- **6** *3* **Innstyle**[226] [5931] 3-8-4 67.... LisaJones(3) 7 40
(JLSpearing) *led at str pce: hdd & wknd jst over 1f out* **4/1**[1]
0 **7** *1 ¼* **Bunkhouse**[16] [2621] 4-9-5.... DHolland 2 42
(MissECLavelle) *chsd ldrs: 7th and btn whn hmpd over 1f out* **15/2**
0-00 **8** *1* **Themesofgreen**[10] [2785] 3-8-5.... TO'Brien(7) 10 39
(MRChannon) *rrd s: sn wl bhd: rdn over 2f out: styd on fnl f* **25/1**
0- **9** *¾* **Albertine**[437] [975] 4-8-11.... TPQueally(3) 12 31
(CADwyer) *bhd: rdn over 2f out: nvr trbld ldrs* **33/1**
40 **10** *¾* **Trifti**[67] [1382] 3-8-12.... SSanders 11 34
(CACyzer) *prom: hrd rdn over 2f out: wknd wl over 1f out* **14/1**
**11** *3* **Memory Man** 3-8-12.... JQuinn 3 25
(WRMuir) *str: bkwd: mid-div: btn whn hmpd over 2f out* **25/1**
**12** *2 ½* **Chem's Legacy (IRE)** 4-9-5.... EAhern 6 18
(WRMuir) *str: sn wl bhd* **20/1**

1m 12.84s (1.19) **Going Correction** +0.225s/f (Good)
**WFA** 3 from 4yo 7lb **12** Ran SP% **120.6**
Speed ratings: **101,100,100,99,96 92,90,89,88,87 83,79**CSF £50.07 TOTE £8.30: £2.00, £2.50, £4.00; EX 67.40.
**Owner** Paul J Dixon **Bred** Mrs M Gutkin **Trained** East Everleigh, Wilts
■ Stewards Enquiry : R L Moore caution: careless riding

**FOCUS**
A modest maiden run at a sound pace and the first four came clear, but formwise this contest does not look solid.

**NOTEBOOK**
**Piccleyes** , despite not looking to be going the early pace, really picked up under pressure to go join the pace and go clear approaching the final furlong, but soon hung in front and was all-out to hang on at the line. This was a first-ever victory for this tricky gelding, and he had dropped 4lb in the weights for this as a result of his recent poor form. That greatly helped and he clearly has ability, yet he is not an easy ride by any means and it is hard to know whether he will repeat this effort next time.
**Ragged Jack(IRE)**, who had not shown much as a juvenile last season, made a pleasing return to action and only lost by the narrowest of margins. He can also be counted a slightly unlucky loser, as he suffered a troubled passage when mounting a challenge two out. He has done well from two to three and can lose his maiden tag before long, possibly over an extra furlong.
**Ligne D'Eau** was not beaten at all far and again put up an improved showing. Granted his proximity at the finish drags down the form, but he looks to be slowly going the right way and is one to watch when reverting to handicaps.
**Rachel's Verdict ◆** , a half-sister to numerous winners in the US, made a pleasing debut and would have been closer but for meeting traffic problems two out. She looks the one to take out of the race and should go close next time.
**Shibumi** again ran a sound race and should do a lot better now she is eligible for handicaps.
**Innstyle** , making her three-year-old debut, paid for setting the strong pace late on and her lack of a recent run saw her quickly drop out.
**Trifti** *Official explanation: jockey said gelding was unsuited by the Good to Firm (Good in places) ground*

## 3086 LISTEN TO THE BAND AFTER RACING RATED STKS (H'CAP) 7f 140y
**8:05** (8:05) (D ) (0-80,79) 3-Y-O+ **£5,005** (£1,898; £949; £431) **Stalls** High

Form RPR
6111 **1** **A Woman In Love**[5] [2929] 5-9-1 **72** 3ex.... SSanders 13 84
(MissBSanders) *trckd ldrs: rdn to ld over 1f out: qcknd clr* **7/2**[1]
-000 **2** *2 ½* **Welcome Stranger**[19] [2537] 4-9-1 **75**.... LFletcher(3) 8 81
(JMPEustace) *mid-div: rdn and hdwy 2f out: styd on to take 2nd nr fin* **10/1**
-006 **3** *½* **Fleetwood Bay**[47] [1845] 4-8-12 **69**.... GBaker 14 74
(BRMillman) *w ldr: led after 2f tl over 1f out: nt pce of wnr* **12/1**
3166 **4** *¾* **Quantum Leap**[8] [2838] 7-9-0 **71**....(v) RLMoore 7 74
(SDow) *hld up towards rr: swtchd outside and effrt 2f out: styd on wl fnl f: nrst fin* **8/1**[3]
0433 **5** *nk* **Mistral Sky**[8] [2834] 5-8-9 **66**....(p) MFenton 5 68
(MrsStefLiddiard) *in tch: rdn to chse ldrs 2f out: one pce fnl f* **9/1**
4021 **6** *¾* **Climate (IRE)**[24] [2406] 5-9-6 **77**....(v) JPMurtagh 2 77
(JRBoyle) *hld up towards rr: rdn and hdwy 2f out: styd on fnl f* **7/2**[1]
4-05 **7** *7* **Roman Maze**[23] [2421] 4-8-8 **65**.... SWKelly 3 49
(WMBrisbourne) *dwlt: t.k.h towards rr: sn swtchd to stands' rail: rdn and sme hdwy 2f out: sn btn* **10/1**
0600 **8** *1* **Invader**[18] [2560] 8-9-7 **78**....(bt) EAhern 11 59
(CEBrittain) *prom: outpcd over 2f out: sn btn* **14/1**
0450 **9** *shd* **Mr Hullabalou (IRE)**[17] [2576] 3-8-6 **73**.... MHenry 12 54
(RIngram) *b.hind: led 2f: chsd ldr tl wknd wl over 1f out* **50/1**
2402 **10** *½* **And Toto Too**[10] [2788] 4-8-8 **68**....(b) FPFerris(3) 1 48
(PDEvans) *bhd: drvn along 1/2-way: nvr trbld ldrs* **15/2**[2]
0005 **11** *4* **Wood Fern (UAE)**[11] [2762] 4-8-8 **65** oh8.... CCatlin 6 35
(MRChannon) *a bhd* **25/1**
262 **12** *1 ½* **King Of Diamonds**[77] [1243] 3-8-10 **77**.... NPollard 10 44
(JRBest) *stdd s: plld hrd and sn in tch: wknd over 2f out* **16/1**
100- **13** *½* **Kindlelight Debut**[260] [5341] 4-9-8 **79**.... DHolland 4 44
(DKIvory) *a bhd* **16/1**

1m 32.12s (0.66) **Going Correction** +0.225s/f (Good)
**WFA** 3 from 4yo+ 10lb **13** Ran SP% **127.4**
Speed ratings: **105,102,102,101,100 100,93,92,92,91 87,86,85**CSF £43.16 CT £400.03 TOTE £4.20: £2.20, £4.50, £3.80; EX 63.40.
**Owner** High & Dry Racing **Bred** Stratford Place Stud **Trained** Epsom, Surrey

**FOCUS**
A fair handicap run at a decent clip and the form looks sound, with the winner producing a career-best effort.

**NOTEBOOK**
**A Woman In Love**, coming into this looking to land a four-timer having won three on the bounce at Brighton, produced a neat turn of foot to lead over one out and scored comfortably. This goes down as a personal best, she made mockery of a 3lb penalty on this occasion, and this former tricky mare is clearly in the form of her life at present.
**Welcome Stranger** improved for this drop back to a mile and stayed on best of all, without threatening the winner. This was his best display of the current campaign and he has dropped to a winning mark.
**Fleetwood Bay ◆** ran by far his race of the season and only found his stamina giving way late on. A drop back to seven furlongs should see him go closer and he appreciated the faster ground this time.
**Quantum Leap**, held up to get the trip, was doing all of his work too late in the day, but finished with purpose nonetheless. His current mark just looks to have his measure, but he can remain competitive and a more positive ride over this distance may see him get closer.
**Climate(IRE)** , off since winning on the Polytrack in May, was well-backed to follow-up on this switch back to turf, but could not get to the leaders at any stage and disappointed. A rise in the weights may mean the Handicapper has got his measure at present.
**Kindlelight Debut** *Official explanation: jockey said filly was unsuited by the Good to Firm (Good in Places) ground*

## 3087 COME RACING HERE AGAIN NEXT SATURDAY (S) STKS 1m 4f (P)
**8:35** (8:35) (G ) 3-Y-O+ **£2,618** (£748; £374) **Stalls** Low

Form RPR
0 **1** **Jelly Baby**[61] [1508] 3-8-3 ....(b[1]) JFEgan 10 51
(WJHaggas) *lw: b.hind: dwlt: pushed along in rr early: gd hdwy 4f out: led over 2f out: rdn clr over 1f out: styd on wl* **16/1**
050 **2** *3* **Tresor Secret (FR)**[19] [2516] 4-9-5 72.... TPQueally(3) 6 52
(NACallaghan) *lw: hld up towards rr: hdwy over 2f out: wnt 2nd over 1f out: styd on: nt pce of wnr* **9/2**[3]
0245 **3** *5* **Neptune**[40] [1989] 8-9-8 35.... MFenton 2 44
(JCFox) *sn wl bhd: gd hdwy 3f out: no ex appr fnl f* **12/1**
0020 **4** *¾* **Mandoob**[38] [2032] 7-9-10 65....(v[1]) J-PGuillambert(3) 7 48
(BRJohnson) *s.s: wl bhd tl gd hdwy 4f out: hrd rdn over 1f out: no ex* **3/1**[1]
-600 **5** *7* **Light Brigade**[25] [2381] 5-9-5 41....(v) FPFerris(3) 4 32
(JMPEustace) *cl up: chsd ldr 4f out tl wknd over 2f out* **6/1**
4 **6** *7* **Amusement**[15] [2662] 8-9-8.... SRighton 1 22
(DGBridgwater) *prom: rdn 4f out: sn wknd* **16/1**
0000 **7** *1* **Mister Completely (IRE)**[7] [2886] 3-8-8 47.... NPollard 11 20
(JRBest) *chsd ldrs: led over 4f out tl wknd over 2f out* **20/1**
5000 **8** *9* **Springalong (USA)**[13] [2705] 4-9-1 62.... SJDonohoe(7) 9 7
(PDEvans) *led 1f: w ldrs tl wknd over 3f out* **7/2**[2]
164- **9** *5* **Flyoff (IRE)**[120] [4285] 7-9-8 46....(v) PDoe 8 —
(KAMorgan) *prom over 6f* **6/1**
00-0 **10** *14* **Java Dawn (IRE)**[46] [1858] 4-9-3 45.... EAhern 3 —
(TEPowell) *led after 1f tl 5f out: 7th and wkng whn hmpd on rail over 3f out* **33/1**
**11** *dist* **Ydravlis**[27] 6-9-3.... SWhitworth 5 —
(DJSFfrenchDavis) *lengthy: str: plld hrd early and taken to outside: sn in midfield: rn wd and wknd bnd over 5f out: sn t.o* **50/1**

2m 36.19s (1.95) **Going Correction** +0.10s/f (Slow)
**WFA** 3 from 4yo+ 14lb **11** Ran SP% **123.1**
Speed ratings: **97,95,91,91,86 81,81,75,71,62** —CSF £89.35 TOTE £11.80: £3.20, £1.80, £4.00; EX 79.40.Jelly Baby was bought in for 9,800gns. Tresor Secret (no.7) was claimed by P. Butler for £6,000.
**Owner** B Haggas **Bred** J B Haggas **Trained** Newmarket, Suffolk

**FOCUS**
A fair event by selling standards and the field were strung out at the finish. Nevertheless the form has a dubious look.

**NOTEBOOK**
**Jelly Baby**, tailed off last on her only previous outing at Windsor in May, totally outclassed her rivals to score comfortably on this marked drop in grade. She was again slowly away, but it made little difference and she showed a neat turn of foot when asked to win her race entering two out. She should go onto better things and does stay well, but it would be wise not to get too carried away by this and she was racing in blinkers on this occasion, so is clearly not all that straightforward.

**Tresor Secret(FR)**, a former ten-furlong winner in France, ran his best race since switching to Britain. This drop in grade and step up in trip helped, and he stayed on to be a clear second without threatening the winner.
**Neptune**, well held in banded events recently, could not go the early pace, but stayed on late in the day for third. A step up in trip would suit.
**Mandoob**, in the first-time visor, lost all chance at the start.
**Springalong(USA)** looked to have a fair chance at the weights, but again showed very little and remains well out of form.

## 3088 PLAY GOLF & COME RACING H'CAP — 1m 2f (P)
**9:05** (9:05) (F ) (0-55,55) 4-Y-0+ — **£3,017** (£862; £431) **Stalls** Low

Form | | | | RPR
4411 **1** **Kingsdon (IRE)**[37] 2053 7-9-5 **52**......(vt) JFEgan 3 62
(TJFitzgerald) *lw: towards rr: rdn and outpcd 5f out: rallied 2f out: styd on to ld jst ins fnl f: drvn out* **11/2**[3]
3303 **2** *1 ½* **Fantasy Crusader**[13] 2705 5-9-1 **48**......(p) JQuinn 7 56
(JAGilbert) *chsd ldrs: led wl over 1f out tl jst ins fnl f: kpt on same pce* **12/1**
1136 **3** *2 ½* **Cumbrian Princess**[31] 2231 7-8-7 **45**...... RThomas(5) 4 48
(MBlanshard) *hld up in midfield: hdwy and nt clr run over 2f out: edgd lft and styd on fnl f* **25/1**
0-00 **4** *¾* **Nautical**[46] 1856 6-9-5 **52**...... MFenton 14 54
(AWCarroll) *hld up in rr: hdwy 4f out: ev ch over 1f out: one pce* **7/1**
4221 **5** *1* **Diamond Orchid (IRE)**[26] 2375 4-8-13 **46**......(v) JPMurtagh 10 46
(PDEvans) *dwlt: hld up towards rr: effrt on outside over 2f out: kpt on fnl f* **3/1**[1]
340 **6** *hd* **Fairland (IRE)**[5] 2939 5-8-9 **49**...... LSmith(7) 8 48
(SDow) *s.s and lost 12l: wl bhd tl hdwy on outside 3f out: styd on fnl f: nvr in chalng position* **25/1**
000- **7** *1 ¾* **Wavet**[173] 6249 4-9-0 **47**...... RPrice 1 43
(JPearce) *lw: prom: outpcd and drvn along 2f out: sn btn* **25/1**
0004 **8** *5* **Sammy's Shuffle**[17] 2594 9-8-13 **46**......(b) PDoe 6 33
(JamiePoulton) *towards rr: hdwy to ld over 3f out: hdd & wknd wl over 1f out* **10/1**
-346 **9** *½* **Magic Warrior**[126] 765 4-9-5 **52**...... PDobbs 13 38
(JCFox) *mid-div: rdn and wknd 2f out* **16/1**
220- **10** *6* **Blue Streak (IRE)**[68] 4874 7-9-1 **48**......(b) EAhern 11 24
(GLMoore) *in rr: rdn 1/2-way: nvr trbld ldrs* **12/1**
0363 **11** *½* **Icannshift (IRE)**[9] 2810 4-9-8 **55**...... RLMoore 9 30
(SDow) *lw: sn chsng ldr: led briefly 4f out: wknd 2f out* **8/1**
6530 **12** *7* **Happy Camper (IRE)**[32] 2209 4-8-10 **43**...... SWhitworth 2 5
(MRHoad) *chsd ldrs 4f: qckly lost pl* **33/1**
6005 **13** *10* **Horizontal (USA)**[17] 2598 4-9-6 **53**...... NDay 5 —
(RIngram) *led tl 4f out: sn wknd* **20/1**
4130 **14** *26* **My Lilli (IRE)**[17] 2597 4-9-7 **54**...... DHolland 12 —
(PMitchell) *prom over 7f* **4/1**[2]

2m 8.24s (0.39) **Going Correction** +0.10s/f (Slow) **14** Ran SP% **133.6**
Speed ratings: **102,100,98,98,97 97,95,91,91,86 86,80,72,51**CSF £73.00 CT £1594.52 TOTE £6.00: £2.80, £3.80, £6.40; EX 78.40 Place 6 £962.50, Place 5 £405.34.
**Owner** Mike Browne **Bred** Barronstown Stud **Trained** Norton, N Yorks
■ Stewards Enquiry : R Thomas one-day ban: careless riding (Jun 30)

**FOCUS**
A poor handicap that saw the field come home well strung out behind the front pair.

**NOTEBOOK**
**Kingsdon(IRE)**, coming into this on the back of successive victories in banded events, had to dig deep in the straight, but landed the hat-trick fairly comfortably in the end. This was his first handicap win and he is clearly in great heart.
**Fantasy Crusader** held every chance at the top of the straight, but could not go with the winner. This was a fair display however and, although he tends to find one too good, he is consistent enough.
**Cumbrian Princess**, held up to get the trip, would have been closer but for meeting trouble two out, but would not have got to the front pair.
**Nautical** found only the one pace when push came to shove in the straight. He has fallen in the weights and this was his best run for sometime.
**Diamond Orchid(IRE)**, a winner on the turf last time off a 3lb higher mark, did not show the same zest on this surface and disappointed.
**Fairland(IRE)** looked seriously up against it after blowing the start, but really flew late on. He has his quirks, but also a fair share of ability, and may be better than his current mark would suggest.
T/Plt: £804.40 to a £1 stake. Pool: £32,179.10. 29.20 winning tickets. T/Qpdt: £33.50 to a £1 stake. Pool: £2,320.60. 51.20 winning tickets. LM

# 3049 NEWMARKET (JULY) (R-H)
Saturday, June 19

**OFFICIAL GOING: Good to firm**
With the stalls placed on the stands' side it was beneficial to race on the rails.
Wind: Fresh behind Weather: Cloudy with the odd shower

## 3089 CAPITAL SPORTS EARLY PRICES AT 9.30 H'CAP — 7f
**1:35** (1:36) (D ) (0-80,80) 3-Y-O — **£6,955** (£2,140; £1,070; £535) **Stalls** High

Form | | | | RPR
6304 **1** **Dumnoni**[14] 2694 3-9-4 **77**...... NCallan 11 87
(JulianPoulton) *trckd ldrs: rdn to ld wl ins fnl f: edgd lft nr fin* **14/1**
2-15 **2** *nk* **Place Cowboy (IRE)**[22] 2444 3-9-1 **74**...... SWKelly 13 83
(JAOsborne) *w ldr: led over 2f out: rdn and hung lft over 1f out: hdd wl ins fnl f* **12/1**
4103 **3** *nk* **Pickle**[17] 2577 3-8-2 **61**...... AMcCarthy 12 69
(SCWilliams) *hld up: hdwy over 1f out: nt clr run ins fnl f: r.o* **7/1**[2]
-412 **4** *½* **Dr Thong**[31] 2224 3-9-6 **79**...... TQuinn 5 86
(PFICole) *plld hrd: w ldrs: rdn and ev ch fr over 1f out: no ex towards fin* **11/10**[1]
0000 **5** *2 ½* **Compton's Eleven**[18] 2557 3-9-7 **80**...... CCatlin 2 80
(MRChannon) *w ldrs: rdn over 1f out: no ex ins fnl f* **12/1**
2034 **6** *1 ¾* **Ask The Clerk (IRE)**[12] 2726 3-8-13 **72**...... MTebbutt 10 68
(VSmith) *trckd ldrs: nt clr run 2f out: sn rdn: no ex fnl f* **11/1**[3]
4-00 **7** *4* **Stevedore (IRE)**[18] 2557 3-9-1 **77**...... LPKeniry(3) 6 62
(BJMeehan) *led over 4f: wknd over 1f out* **14/1**
-006 **8** *1* **Who's Winning (IRE)**[12] 2726 3-8-4 **66**...... JFMcDonald(3) 3 49
(CADwyer) *hld up: plld hrd: wknd over 1f out* **25/1**
002- **9** *½* **Flame Queen**[236] 5785 3-9-1 **74**...... SCarson 7 55
(MissKBBoutflower) *hld up: nt clr run over 2f out: wknd over 1f out* **25/1**
13-0 **10** *nk* **Mountcharge (IRE)**[48] 1795 3-9-7 **80**...... IMongan 9 61
(CNAllen) *w ldrs to 1/2-way: wknd wl over 1f out* **25/1**
0-05 **11** *3 ½* **Patrixtoo (FR)**[56] 1612 3-8-1 **60**...... MHenry 1 31
(MHTompkins) *sn pushed along in rr: bmpd over 2f out: sn wknd* **16/1**
3-00 **12** *nk* **Epaminondas (USA)**[10] 2790 3-8-11 **70**...... PDobbs 4 41
(RHannon) *prom 5f* **25/1**
0004 **13** *shd* **Lord Of The Sea (IRE)**[8] 2842 3-8-5 **64**...... PDoe 8 34
(JamiePoulton) *hld up: hdwy over 2f out: wknd over 1f out* **14/1**

1m 23.93s (-2.84) **Going Correction** -0.25s/f (Firm) **13** Ran SP% **125.1**
Speed ratings: **106,105,105,104,101 99,95,94,93,93 89,88,88**CSF £171.60 CT £869.81 TOTE £17.00: £5.20, £3.00, £3.40; EX 313.30.
**Owner** Meddler Bloodstock **Bred** Southill Stud **Trained** Kentford, Suffolk

**FOCUS**
A competitive contest, but despite the steady early pace, the overall time was respectable.

**NOTEBOOK**
**Dumnoni** travelled really well through the race and took advantage of the leader just rolling off the rails in the latter stages to gain her first success on turf.
**Place Cowboy(IRE)**, who had the advantage of the rails to race against, stayed this longer trip well enough.
**Pickle** had no luck in the latter stages and would almost certainly had won had she enjoyed anything like a clear run.
**Dr Thong** would have been better suited to a stronger pace, for he was always doing a little too much early on.
**Compton's Eleven** turned in a sound effort from his wide draw, but left the impression this trip just stretched him.
**Ask The Clerk(IRE)** is well exposed and is probably better at trips short of this.

## 3090 CAPITAL SPORTS BET BY TELEPHONE 08000 288 233 CLASSIFIED STKS — 6f
**2:05** (2:05) (D ) 3-Y-O+ — **£6,773** (£2,084; £1,042; £521) **Stalls** High

Form | | | | RPR
5601 **1** **Willhewiz**[8] 2843 4-9-3 **78**......(v) SCarson 4 87
(RMStronge) *mde all: rdn out* **6/1**[2]
-062 **2** *¾* **Million Percent**[21] 2467 5-9-4 **81**...... KDalgleish 6 86
(KRBurke) *a.p: chsd wnr over 1f out: sn hrd rdn: unable qck nr fin* **2/1**[1]
0005 **3** *1 ¼* **Beauvrai**[12] 2724 4-9-3 **67**...... MTebbutt 7 81
(VSmith) *hld up in touch: nt clr run over 1f out: styd on* **16/1**
6460 **4** *1 ½* **Grey Pearl**[44] 1953 5-9-1 **81**...... IMongan 2 75
(MissGayKelleway) *dwlt: swtchd lft and hdwy over 2f out: one pce fnl f* **6/1**[2]
00-0 **5** *3* **Skyharbor**[44] 1900 3-9-1 **85**...... WRyan 5 73
(DNicholls) *chsd wnr over 4f: wknd ins fnl f* **12/1**[3]
0003 **6** *2 ½* **Najeebon (FR)**[11] 2763 5-9-5 **82**...... CCatlin 3 62
(MRChannon) *sn outpcd: rdn over 1f out: n.d* **2/1**[1]
0000 **7** *1* **Its Ecco Boy**[12] 2739 6-9-0 **60**...... LisaJones(3) 8 57
(PHowling) *hung rt thrght: chsd ldrs: rdn 1/2-way: wknd 2f out* **28/1**
U06/ **8** *9* **Garden Society (IRE)**[709] 2903 7-9-3 **75**...... BDoyle 1 30
(WAO'Gorman) *hld up: wknd over 2f out* **33/1**

1m 10.82s (-2.50) **Going Correction** -0.25s/f (Firm)
**WFA** 3 from 4yo+ 7lb **8** Ran SP% **115.2**
Speed ratings: **106,105,103,101,97 94,92,80**CSF £18.60 TOTE £6.90: £1.80, £1.20, £4.40; EX 19.90.
**Owner** Tim Bostwick **Bred** L T And M Foster **Trained** Beedon, Berks

**FOCUS**
A rare victory outside of claiming company for the winner, but one note of caution is that he did have the advantage of the stands' side rail. However, they did not hang about here and the time was good.

**NOTEBOOK**
**Willhewiz** was winning outside of claiming company for the first time since his juvenile days. However, he did have the advantage of the stands'-side rails to help.
**Million Percent** had his optimum conditions and had no excuses.
**Beauvrai** had plenty to find with his rivals on these terms and was far from disgraced.
**Grey Pearl**, who was done no favours by having to switch wide to launch her challenge, is probably better over an extra furlong.
**Skyharbor** has yet to convince in both of his outings this term.
**Najeebon(FR)** never went a yard and is better than he showed this time.

## 3091 BET ONLINE AT CAPITALSPORTS.COM FILLIES' H'CAP — 1m 2f
**2:40** (2:43) (C ) (0-90,88) 3-Y-O+ — **£9,412** (£2,896; £1,448; £724) **Stalls** High

Form | | | | RPR
4111 **1** **Polar Jem**[16] 2630 4-9-10 **86**...... AMcCarthy 8 98
(GGMargarson) *mde all: rdn out* **4/1**[3]
15 **2** *1 ½* **Fling**[24] 2403 3-8-6 **80**...... OUrbina 3 89
(JRFanshawe) *s.i.s: hld up: hdwy 2f out: edgd rt over 1f out: r.o* **7/2**[2]
2012 **3** *shd* **Grey Clouds**[10] 2775 4-9-2 **78**...... JFortune 10 87
(TDEasterby) *hld up in tch: rdn to chse wnr over 1f out: styd on* **10/3**[1]
31-0 **4** *1 ½* **Windy Britain**[21] 2474 5-9-12 **88**...... PRobinson 7 94
(LMCumani) *hld up: swtchd lft and hdwy over 1f out: sn rdn: no ex ins fnl f* **4/1**[3]
-510 **5** *1 ¾* **Astrocharm (IRE)**[21] 2471 5-9-0 **76**...... TQuinn 1 79
(MHTompkins) *hld up: hdwy over 4f out: n.m.r over 1f out: styd on same pce* **10/1**
23-0 **6** *nk* **Strategy**[28] 2284 4-9-4 **80**...... PDobbs 5 82
(PRWebber) *chsd wnr: rdn over 2f out: no ex fnl f* **12/1**
05-0 **7** *3* **Fragrant Star**[63] 1458 3-8-7 **81**...... BDoyle 9 77
(CEBrittain) *hld up: hdwy u.p over 1f out: wknd fnl f* **25/1**
0-03 **8** *¾* **Lady Peaches**[40] 2001 3-7-9 **72** oh5...... FPFerris(3) 6 67
(DMullarkey) *chsd ldrs: rdn and n.m.r over 2f out: wknd over 1f out* **20/1**
10-0 **9** *¾* **Rani Two**[11] 2752 5-8-7 **74**...... NChalmers(5) 2 67
(WMBrisbourne) *chsd ldrs: rdn over 2f out: wknd over 1f out* **25/1**
-004 **10** *6* **Island Rapture**[16] 2630 4-8-9 **74**...... LisaJones(3) 4 56
(JARToller) *hld up: plld hrd: hdwy 7f out: wknd over 1f out* **12/1**

2m 3.45s (-3.01) **Going Correction** -0.25s/f (Firm)
**WFA** 3 from 4yo+ 12lb **10** Ran SP% **122.2**
Speed ratings: **102,100,100,99,98 97,95,94,94,89**CSF £18.94 CT £52.12 TOTE £4.30: £1.40, £2.00, £1.60; EX 34.10.
**Owner** Norcroft Park Stud **Bred** Norcroft Park Stud **Trained** Newmarket, Suffolk

**FOCUS**
A fair handicap which did not appear to be that strongly run. The winner dictated the pace and found plenty when asked to extend her run.

**NOTEBOOK**
**Polar Jem**, a progressive filly, had something of a soft time up front, but she is game and kept finding more when tackled.
**Fling**, who was fitted with a rug for stalls entry put behind her a dismal effort last time. She clearly has her fair share of ability and should do better as she gets older.
**Grey Clouds** turned in a solid effort off this career-high mark and will find easier openings than she faced here.
**Windy Britain**, ridden with plenty of confidence ran a shade better than might first appear, for she made her challenge down the centre of the course, not the place to be.
**Astrocharm(IRE)** is well treated on the best of her form, but she never seems to run two races alike and was already beaten when short of room going to the furlong pole.

**Strategy** may have still needed this run to put an edge on her.

## 3092 CAPITAL SPORTS H'CAP 5f
3:15 (3:17) (B) (0-105,98) 3-Y-O £13,624 (£4,192; £2,096; £1,048) Stalls High

Form RPR
2103 1 **Green Manalishi**[7] 2877 3-8-12 89 TQuinn 3 96
(DWPArbuthnot) *trckd ldrs: rdn to ld ins fnl f: r.o: edgd lft nr fin* **7/1**
4-12 2 *nk* **Tony The Tap**[7] 2877 3-7-13 79 LisaJones(3) 2 85
(NACallaghan) *hld up in tch: rdn over 1f out: r.o* **7/2**[1]
1-12 3 *shd* **Autumn Pearl**[15] 2636 3-9-7 98 PRobinson 5 103
(MAJarvis) *led: rdn and hdd ins fnl f: r.o* **7/2**[1]
11-0 4 *shd* **Paradise Isle**[35] 2131 3-8-11 88 GBaker 10 93+
(CFWall) *dwlt: hld up: hdwy and nt clr run over 1f out: swtchd lft ins fnl f: running on whn hmpd nr fin* **7/1**
0-30 5 *1/2* **Wanchai Lad**[7] 2897 3-8-9 86 WRyan 8 89
(DNicholls) *chsd ldr: rdn and ev ch over 1f out: unable qck nr fin* **9/2**[2]
-040 6 *2 1/2* **Rydal (USA)**[7] 2897 3-8-3 83 (b) RMiles(3) 6 76
(GABulter) *hld up: rdn over 1f out: nvr trbld ldrs* **25/1**
-136 7 *1 1/2* **High Voltage**[7] 2897 3-9-7 98 (t) KDalgleish 7 85
(KRBurke) *chsd ldrs: rdn 2f out: wknd fnl f* **13/2**[3]
-063 8 *1 1/4* **Oro Verde**[7] 2892 3-8-10 87 PDobbs 1 69
(RHannon) *hld up: rdn over 1f out: n.d* **11/1**
1-50 9 *3/4* **Promenade**[18] 2552 3-8-6 83 JMackay 9 62
(MLWBell) *hld up: rdn 1/2-way: wknd wl over 1f out* **20/1**

58.38 secs (-1.27) **Going Correction** -0.25s/f (Firm) 9 Ran SP% **117.9**
Speed ratings: **100,99,99,99,98 94,92,90,88**CSF £32.45 CT £102.14 TOTE £9.10: £2.80, £1.50, £1.50; EX 32.00.
**Owner** Derrick C Broomfield **Bred** E Aldridge **Trained** Upper Lambourn, Berks

**FOCUS**
A competitive sprint run at a good pace and the form looks sound.

**NOTEBOOK**
**Green Manalishi** proved well suited to this strongly-run contest, and managed to reverse Leicester form with the runner-up on identical terms. Although he has had plenty of racing he still appears to be on the upgrade.
**Tony The Tap** was caught out wide from his low draw, but travelled much better than he had at Leicester. He is clearly learning all the time and looks to have a decent sprint in him.
**Autumn Pearl** soon bagged the favoured stands'-side rail and showed plenty of pace before finding the weight concession beyond her. She is a progressive filly who is equally at home over an extra furlong.
**Paradise Isle** is a quirky filly, but there is no doubt she has plenty of ability, and should find an opening before too long.
**Wanchai Lad** was far from disgraced and connections can be relied upon to find him plenty of opportunities through the summer.
**Rydal(USA)**, having his first run over the minimum trip, found things happening too quickly for him. However, he is beginning to slip down the weights and is one to keep an eye on over an extra furlong or two.

## 3093 FOOTBALL H'CAPS AT CAPITAL SPORTS MAIDEN 7f
3:50 (3:51) (D) 2-Y-O £4,754 (£1,463; £731; £365) Stalls High

Form RPR
2 1 **Fox**[15] 2644 2-9-0 BDoyle 1 90+
(CEBrittain) *chsd ldrs: rdn to ld ins fnl f: r.o* **5/6**[1]
2 *3/4* **In The Fan (USA)** 2-9-0 JFortune 5 88+
(JLDunlop) *led: rdn and hdd ins fnl f: styd on* **16/1**
3 *6* **Raza Cab (IRE)** 2-9-0 IMongan 6 73
(CNAllen) *chsd ldrs: rdn 1/2-way: wknd over 1f out* **40/1**
4 *1* **Sri Lipis** 2-9-0 TQuinn 9 71
(PFICole) *s.i.s: rcvrd to chse ldr 6f out: hung lft and wknd over 1f out* **7/1**[3]
5 *2* **Grand Marque (IRE)** 2-9-0 PDobbs 4 66
(RHannon) *prom: outpcd 1/2-way: styd on ins fnl f* **12/1**
6 *7* **Bobbie Love** 2-9-0 CCatlin 2 48
(MRChannon) *s.i.s: sn prom: wknd 2f out* **18/1**
4 7 *1 1/2* **Blue Kandora (IRE)**[39] 2024 2-9-0 PRobinson 3 44
(MAJarvis) *hld up: bhd fr 1/2-way* **7/2**[2]
8 *1* **Elizabeth's Choice** 2-8-9 MHenry 8 37
(MAJarvis) *s.i.s: sn prom: wknd 2f out* **33/1**
9 *2 1/2* **Robeson** 2-9-0 RMullen 7 36
(DMSimcock) *sn pushed along in rr: bhd fr 1/2-way* **33/1**
05 10 *15* **Parsley's Return**[9] 2817 2-9-0 WRyan 10 —
(NACallaghan) *sn outpcd* **50/1**

1m 25.11s (-1.66) **Going Correction** -0.25s/f (Firm) 10 Ran SP% **118.4**
Speed ratings: **99,98,91,90,87 79,78,77,74,57**CSF £17.39 TOTE £1.70: £1.10, £5.10, £7.80; EX 24.60.
**Owner** Sheikh Marwan Al Maktoum **Bred** Darley **Trained** Newmarket, Suffolk

**FOCUS**
Probably not that strong a maiden, but the front pair finished nicely clear and could be decent.

**NOTEBOOK**
**Fox**, who was colty in the paddock, had the benefit of a run and that made the difference. Well regarded by connections, he is capable of better.
**In The Fan(USA)**, out of a mare that won over five furlongs as a juvenile, was the only one to make a race of it with the winner and should be capable of winning a similar event.
**Raza Cab(IRE)**, a 31,000 gns yearling, was off the bridle some way out and should do better for the experience.
**Sri Lipis**, a 200,000 gns yearling is from the same family as the high-class Kahyasi. He was green during the race and can be expected to improve for the experience.
**Grand Marque(IRE)**, out of a mare that won over six furlongs as a juvenile, is from the same family as the top class pair Diamond Shoal and Glint Of Gold. He shaped very much as though he will appreciate middle distances next term.
**Bobbie Love**, a half-brother to seven-furlong winner Regimental Dance, should do better with this outing under his belt.

## 3094 CAPITAL SPORTS AT THE CENTRE OF RACING MAIDEN STKS 1m
4:20 (4:23) (D) 3-Y-O £5,525 (£1,700; £850; £425) Stalls High

Form RPR
1 **Namroc (IRE)** 3-9-0 PRobinson 2 80
(ACStewart) *hld up in tch: swtchd to stands' rail over 1f out: r.o to ld wl ins fnl f: sn clr* **10/1**[3]
35-4 2 *2* **Flamjica (USA)**[14] 2693 3-8-6 70 LisaJones(3) 1 71
(JARToller) *led: rdn over 1f out: hdd and unable qckn wl ins fnl f* **5/1**[2]
622 3 *2 1/2* **Grand But One (IRE)**[25] 2392 3-9-0 87 IMongan 8 70
(BWHills) *trckd ldr: rdn and ev ch over 2f out: hung lft over 1f out: one pce* **8/11**[1]
4 *nk* **Arrjook** 3-9-0 JMcAuley 13 69
(ACStewart) *s.s: hld up: hdwy and hung lft fnl f: nt rch ldrs* **33/1**
0 5 *1 1/4* **Dream Easy**[8] 2853 3-9-0 RPrice 10 66
(PLGilligan) *chsd ldrs: rdn over 2f out: styd on same pce appr fnl f* **50/1**
0 6 *3/4* **Nikiforos**[28] 2286 3-9-0 JFortune 9 64
(JWHills) *hld up in tch: racd keenly: rdn over 1f out: one pce* **33/1**
0-0 7 *hd* **North Sea (IRE)**[81] 1186 3-8-9 CCatlin 3 59
(MRChannon) *prom: rdn over 2f out: styd on same pce* **16/1**
0- 8 *7* **Silk Cravat (IRE)**[270] 5139 3-9-0 RHavlin 4 48
(GWragg) *chsd ldrs over 5f* **20/1**
0-00 9 *1* **Rawalpindi**[20] 2505 3-9-0 KDalgleish 12 46
(JARToller) *hld up: a in rr* **33/1**
10 *1 3/4* **Spes Bona (USA)** 3-9-0 SWKelly 5 42
(WJHaggas) *s.i.s: sn in tch: wknd 3f out* **14/1**
11 *5* **Capitole (IRE)** 3-9-0 PMcCabe 11 30
(ACStewart) *hld up: rdn 1/2-way: wknd 3f out* **40/1**
12 *4* **Artist Rifle (IRE)** 3-9-0 TQuinn 6 21
(JLDunlop) *s.i.s: a bhd* **12/1**
U **Aljafliyah** 3-8-2 AHamblett(7) 7 —
(LMCumani) *uns rdr s* **25/1**

1m 38.79s (-1.69) **Going Correction** -0.25s/f (Firm) 13 Ran SP% **125.7**
Speed ratings: **98,96,93,93,91 91,91,84,83,81 76,72,**—CSF £58.66 TOTE £12.30: £2.40, £1.30, £1.10; EX 75.40.
**Owner** Bruce Corman **Bred** Mount Coote Stud **Trained** Newmarket, Suffolk
■ Stewards Enquiry : Lisa Jones two-day ban: used whip with excessive frequency (Jun 30-Jul 1)

**FOCUS**
Probably not a great maiden with the runner-up rated 70, and the third is clearly flattered by his mark of 87.

**NOTEBOOK**
**Namroc(IRE)** took a while to hit top stride, but when the penny did finally drop he fairly took off. Out of a mare that stayed 11 furlongs, he can be expected to improve as he steps up in trip.
**Flamjica(USA)** had a soft time of things up front and had no excuses.
**Grand But One(IRE)** is proving expensive to follow and is clearly flattered by his current mark.
*Official explanation: vet said colt bled from the nose*
**Arrjook**, who is out of a mare that stayed ten furlongs took a while to get the hang of things, but there was plenty of promise in this effort.

## 3095 CAPITAL SPORTS £20 FREE BET H'CAP 1m 6f 175y
4:50 (4:55) (D) (0-85,85) 4-Y-0+ £5,460 (£1,680; £840; £420) Stalls High

Form RPR
11-0 1 **Dorothy's Friend**[14] 2684 4-9-7 78 JFortune 2 91
(RCharlton) *a.p: led 3f out: rdn out* **9/4**[1]
-0S2 2 *2* **Theatre (USA)**[21] 2480 5-9-10 81 PDoe 4 91
(JamiePoulton) *hld up: hdwy over 3f out: rdn and ev ch over 1f out: unable qck ins fnl f* **9/2**[2]
6502 3 *1 1/4* **Red Scorpion (USA)**[11] 2759 5-8-7 65 SWKelly 9 73
(WMBrisbourne) *chsd ldrs: nt clr run over 2f out: sn rdn: styd on same pce fnl f* **8/1**
-243 4 *nk* **Carrowdore (IRE)**[10] 2787 4-8-11 68 (p) IMongan 3 76
(CNAllen) *hld up: hdwy over 3f out: nt clr run and swtchd lft over 2f out: styd on same pce fnl f* **9/2**[2]
-106 5 *5* **Arresting**[14] 2691 4-10-0 85 OUrbina 7 86
(JRFanshawe) *hld up: hdwy over 2f out: wknd fnl f* **12/1**
30-6 6 *11* **Simon's Seat (USA)**[80] 1210 5-8-8 65 GCarter 6 52
(CDrew) *s.i.s: hld up: wknd 2f out* **16/1**
-060 7 *1 1/2* **Sovereign Dreamer (USA)**[14] 2671 4-9-5 76 (t) CCatlin 5 61
(PFICole) *led: rdn and hdd 3f out: wknd over 1f out* **20/1**
3-63 8 *14* **Hashid (IRE)**[16] 2611 4-8-13 70 (v[1]) KDalgleish 8 37
(PCRitchens) *chsd ldr: rdn over 3f out: wknd over 2f out* **10/1**
-300 P **Prairie Falcon (IRE)**[14] 2684 10-9-5 81 AMedeiros(5) 1 —
(BWHills) *racd alone for 2f: prom: racd keenly: broke leg and p.u over 9f out: dead* **15/2**[3]

3m 6.50s (-4.26) **Going Correction** -0.25s/f (Firm) 9 Ran SP% **117.4**
Speed ratings: **101,99,99,99,96 90,89,82,**—CSF £12.46 CT £69.22 TOTE £2.40: £1.50, £2.00, £2.30; EX 11.90 Place 6 £25.35, Place 5 £4.26.
**Owner** Mountgrange Stud **Bred** Floors Farming And Christopher J Heath **Trained** Beckhampton, Wilts

**FOCUS**
A modest handicap that was run at an even pace, but it was not that competitive.

**NOTEBOOK**
**Dorothy's Friend**, all the better for his run at Haydock, confirmed himself to be on the upgrade with a workmanlike success. His short-term target is the Northumberland Plate.
**Theatre(USA)** turned in a solid effort against an improving sort and deserves a change of luck.
**Red Scorpion(USA)** stepped up on his effort in a claimer last time, and may have done better still had he not had to switch to get a run.
**Carrowdore(IRE)** is proving very consistent and just about stayed this longer trip.
**Arresting** did not see his race out and may have found the ground faster than ideal.
**Hashid(IRE)** *Official explanation: jockey said gelding would not face the visor*
T/Plt: £16.60 to a £1 stake. Pool: £48,476.70. 2,122.00 winning tickets. T/Qpdt: £1.90 to a £1 stake. Pool: £3,248.80. 1,248.25 winning tickets. CR

# 3055 REDCAR (L-H)
Saturday, June 19

**OFFICIAL GOING: Good (good to firm in places)**
Wind: mod 1/2 against Weather: Heavy showers

## 3096 TEES COMPONENTS MAIDEN STKS 6f
1:45 (1:45) (D) 3-Y-O+ £3,474 (£1,069; £534; £267) Stalls Centre

Form RPR
-206 1 **Hartshead**[5] 2936 5-9-2 68 PMulrennan(5) 7 63
(GASwinbank) *cl up: led over 1f out: rdn ins last and kpt on* **7/2**[2]
0313 2 *1* **Compton Plume**[15] 2656 4-9-7 55 DaleGibson 3 60
(WHTinning) *hld up: swtchd rt and gd hdwy 2f out: rdn to chal ins last: kpt in* **4/1**[3]
03-3 3 *1/2* **Mistress Twister**[4] 2962 3-8-9 PFessey 4 54
(TDBarron) *hld up in tch: pushed along and sltly outpcd over 2f out: rdn and hdwy over 1f out: kpt on ins last* **11/4**[1]
0 4 *1 1/4* **Brain Washed**[16] 2621 3-8-9 DAllan 10 50
(TDEasterby) *hld up: hdwy 2f out: rdn and kpt on same pce appr last* **50/1**
0660 5 *nk* **Frimley's Mattery**[18] 2556 4-9-2 42 MLawson(5) 1 54?
(REBarr) *prom: rdn along 2f out: drvn and one pce appr last* **66/1**
040 6 *1* **Akiramenai (USA)**[26] 2367 4-9-2 58 RWinston 6 46
(MrsLStubbs) *led: rdn along and hdd wl over 1f out: sn wknd* **16/1**
0600 7 *6* **Man Crazy (IRE)**[17] 2577 3-8-9 60 GDuffield 9 28
(RMBeckett) *chsd ldrs: rdn along 2f out: sn wknd* **8/1**
-000 8 *3* **Designer City (IRE)**[6] 2908 3-8-4 50 PBradley(5) 8 19
(ABerry) *chsd ldrs: rdn along over 2f out: sn wknd* **33/1**



The Form Book, Raceform Ltd, Compton, RG20 6NL

422 **9** *1 1/4* **Urban Calm**[14] [2675] 3-8-6 **63**.................................... SHitchcott(3) 2 15
(RMHCowell) *cl up: rdn along 2f out and sn wknd* **7/2**[2]

00 **10** *15* **Casey's House**[38] [2040] 4-9-2.................................... RFfrench 5 —
(FWatson) *sn outpcd and wl bhd fr 1/2-way* **100/1**

1m 15.11s (3.41) **Going Correction** +0.40s/f (Good)
**WFA** 3 from 4yo+ 7lb **10** Ran SP% **115.5**
Speed ratings: **93,91,91,89,88 87,79,75,73,53**CSF £17.53 TOTE £5.30: £1.90, £1.90, £1.30; EX 30.90.
**Owner** Miss Sally R Haynes **Bred** Gainsborough Stud Management Ltd **Trained** Melsonby, N Yorks

**FOCUS**
A modest sprint maiden run at just a steady pace and a 42-rated horse finishing a creditable fifth, so form looks suspect.

**NOTEBOOK**
**Hartshead**, suited by this much flatter track, travelled strongly but in the end had to be kept right up to his work.
**Compton Plume**, well backed, had 13lb to find with the winner on official figures. In the end he pushed him hard and deserves to lose the maiden tag.
**Mistress Twister**, making a quick reappearance and dropping back in trip, was badly outpaced with over two furlongs left to run. Staying on in determined fashion at the line, she needs that seventh furlong.
**Brain Washed**, last of 16 on her only previous start two weeks earlier, shaped a lot better and can improve again.
**Frimley's Matterry**, on his 16th start, is rated just 42 putting a cap on the overall value of the form.
**Akiramenai(USA)**, suited by the easier ground, showed plenty of toe and five furlongs in handicap company may be as far as she wants to go.
**Urban Calm** travelled as well as the winner but when called on for an effort with over two furlongs left to run the response was negligible. *Official explanation: jockey said filly lost a front shoe*

## 3097 TOTEPOOL H'CAP 1m 2f
**2:20** (2:21) (C) (0-90,89) 3-Y-O+ **£13,585** (£4,180; £2,090; £1,045) **Stalls** Low

Form RPR

1330 **1** **Intricate Web (IRE)**[7] [2894] 8-9-3 **78**.................................... DAllan 9 88
(EJAlston) *hld up and bhd: hdwy over 4f out: snpushed along: swtchd outside and str run over 1f out: led ent last: kpt on* **11/1**

6600 **2** *3/4* **Cripsey Brook**[7] [2894] 6-9-9 **84**.................................... KimTinkler 5 92
(DonEnricoIncisa) *trckd ldrs: hdwy wl over 2f out: rdn to chse wnr ins last: kpt on* **11/2**[2]

0600 **3** *nk* **Stretton (IRE)**[7] [2894] 6-9-3 **78**.................................... RFfrench 11 86
(JDBethell) *hld up and bhd: hdwy on inner 3f out: n.m.r and hit in face w whip wl over 1f out: rdn and kpt on fnl f* **7/1**

2421 **4** *2* **Oldenway**[10] [2775] 5-8-12 **76**.................................... THamilton(3) 10 80
(RAFahey) *trckd ldesr: hdwy 4f out: led 21/2f out: rdn wl over 1f out: drvn and hdd ent last: wknd* **15/2**

0634 **5** *5* **Oscar Pepper (USA)**[3] [2982] 7-8-2 **63**....................(v) PFessey 1 58
(TDBarron) *in tch: hdwy 3f out: rdn over 2f out and sn one pce* **9/1**

0000 **6** *3/4* **Wahchi (IRE)**[17] [2583] 5-8-6 **67**.................................... DaleGibson 8 60
(GPKelly) *bhd tl styd on fnl 3f: nvr a factor* **100/1**

2003 **7** *1/2* **Arry Dash**[10] [2789] 4-9-5 **83**.................................... SHitchcott(3) 4 75
(MRChannon) *in tch: hdwy to chse ldrs over 3f out: rdn and btn over 2f out* **13/2**

6100 **8** *2 1/2* **Telemachus**[19] [2527] 4-10-0 **89**.................................... DeanMcKeown 12 76
(JGGiven) *chsd ldrs: rdn along over 3f out: sn wknd* **16/1**

5422 **9** *4* **Say What You See (IRE)**[8] [2845] 4-8-11 **72**....................(v) GDuffield 6 52
(JWHills) *led: rdn along 3f out: sn hdd and grad wknd* **6/1**[3]

0000 **10** *3/4* **Broadway Score (USA)**[10] [2775] 6-9-0 **80**.................. PMulrennan(5) 3 58
(MWEasterby) *a rr* **20/1**

4-12 **11** *5* **Trueno (IRE)**[16] [2612] 5-9-9 **84**.................................... RWinston 2 53
(LMCumani) *trckd ldrs: effrot over 3f out: sn rdn along and wknd over 2f out* **5/1**[1]

0000 **12** *11* **Gala Sunday (USA)**[10] [2775] 4-9-2 **77**.................................... TLucas 13 25
(MWEasterby) *midfield: hdwy on outer 4f out: rdn and wknd 3f out* **33/1**

0020 **13** *3* **Movie King (IRE)**[11] [2752] 5-8-4 **65**....................(p) GFaulkner 7 7
(SGollings) *cl up: rdn along 4f out: sn wknd* **33/1**

2m 6.45s (-0.35) **Going Correction** +0.225s/f (Good) **13** Ran SP% **119.8**
Speed ratings: **110,109,109,107,103 102,102,100,97,96 92,83,81**CSF £68.57 CT £464.73 TOTE £14.50: £4.20, £2.10, £2.00; EX 79.70.
**Owner** Morris, Oliver, Pierce **Bred** Moyglare Stud Farm Ltd **Trained** Longton, Lancs

**FOCUS**
A competitive 0-89 handicap run at a sound pace and the form looks solid.

**NOTEBOOK**
**Intricate Web(IRE)**, happier on this much easier ground, surged to the front and was always doing just enough. A fast run mile and a quarter brings out the best in him.
**Cripsey Brook**, down 2lb this year, was well backed to regain the winning thread, stayed on in most determined fashion but could never quite close the gap.
**Stretton(IRE)** had the strong pace to suit but, sticking to the inside, met traffic problems and looked to take a blow in the face from a rival rider's ship. Just found lacking inside the last, he is surely a winner waiting to happen.
**Oldenway**, raised 4lb, was running from a career high-mark and after showing ahead could not keep his head infront.
**Oscar Pepper(USA)**, who likes it here, was making a quick return to action and he found this Class C event too tough.
**Wahchi(IRE)**, who had started at 50/1 or longer on his four previous starts, has slipped over a stone in the ratings and this was his first worthwhile form this time.
**Trueno(IRE)**, a keen type, was in trouble early in the straight and this was well below his best for no apparent reason. *Official explanation: trainer was unable to offer any explanation for poor form shown*
**Movie King(IRE)** *Official explanation: jockey said gelding hung left handed in the straight*

## 3098 TETLEY'S SMOOTH H'CAP 6f
**2:50** (2:51) (C) (0-90,84) 3-Y-O+ **£13,942** (£4,290; £2,145; £1,072) **Stalls** Centre

Form RPR

2004 **1** **Cd Flyer (IRE)**[16] [2626] 7-9-8 **83**.................................... PMulrennan(5) 2 95
(BEllison) *dwlt and bhd: gd hdwy over 2f out: rdn ent last: styd on to ld nr fin* **14/1**

4062 **2** *hd* **Blackheath (IRE)**[7] [2899] 8-9-9 **79**.................................... AlexGreaves 6 90
(DNicholls) *trckd ldrs gng wl: hdwy wl over 1f out: rdn to ld ins last: hdd and no ex nr fin* **11/2**[1]

-040 **3** *3/4* **Midnight Parkes**[2] [3010] 5-8-8 **64**.................................... DAllan 1 73
(EJAlston) *cl up: led over 1f out: sn rdn and hdd ins last: no ex last 100 yds* **14/1**

5004 **4** *1 3/4* **Undeterred**[7] [2899] 8-9-2 **72**....................(v) PFessey 10 76
(TDBarron) *towards rr: effrt over 2f out: sn rdn and styd on fnl f: nrst fin* **8/1**[3]

3020 **5** *1 1/2* **Snow Bunting**[14] [2673] 6-8-3 **59**.................................... GDuffield 9 58
(JeddO'Keeffe) *towards rr: hdwy over 2f out: rdn wl over 1f out: hung lft and kpt in fnl f: nrst fin* **14/1**

5120 **6** *1 1/4* **Skip Of Colour**[92] [1057] 4-9-2 **75**.................................... DNolan(3) 4 71
(PABlockley) *led: rdn along 2f out: hdd over 1f out and sn wknd* **20/1**

0360 **7** *1 3/4* **Just One Smile (IRE)**[23] [2421] 4-8-4 **60**.................................... DaleGibson 5 50
(TDEasterby) *chsd ldrs: rdn 2f out: sn drvn and wknd over 1f out* **33/1**

4023 **8** *shd* **Obe One**[2] [3010] 4-8-6 **69**.................................... PPMathers(7) 11 59
(ABerry) *bhd tl styd on fnl 2f: nvr a factor* **13/2**[2]

5-50 **9** *hd* **Blythe Spirit**[7] [2899] 5-8-13 **72**.................................... THamilton(3) 7 62
(RAFahey) *chsd ldrs: rdn 2f out: sn wknd* **16/1**

2031 **10** *1* **Hiccups**[21] [2467] 4-9-12 **82**....................(p) RWinston 13 69
(MrsJRRamsden) *s.i.s and bhd: hdwy 1/2-way:s witched rt and rdn wl over 1f out: nvr nr ldrs* **11/2**[1]

-005 **11** *4* **Inter Vision (USA)**[35] [2132] 4-9-11 **84**.................................... ABeech(3) 17 59
(ADickman) *midfield: rdn along 1/2-way: nvr a factor* **8/1**[3]

0300 **12** *1/2* **Seafield Towers**[14] [2679] 4-9-5 **75**....................(p) DMcGaffin 3 48
(MissLAPerratt) *cl up: rdn along 2f out: sn wknd* **20/1**

0353 **13** *2 1/2* **Paddywack (IRE)**[2] [3016] 7-8-1 **64**....................(b) DFentiman(7) 14 30
(DWChapman) *s.i.s and bhd: hdwy over 2f out: sn rdn and btn* **8/1**[3]

0040 **14** *1 1/4* **Drury Lane (IRE)**[4] [2965] 4-8-0 **56**....................(b) PMQuinn 16 18
(DWChapman) *s.i.s: a rr* **16/1**

-440 **15** *shd* **Twice Upon A Time**[21] [2490] 5-8-12 **71**.................................... SHitchcott(3) 8 32
(BSmart) *chsd ldrs: rdn along 1/2-way: sn wknd* **25/1**

0000 **16** *3/4* **Safranine (IRE)**[6] [2909] 7-8-7 **63**....................(p) AnnStokell 15 22
(MissAStokell) *a bhd* **40/1**

0300 **17** *1/2* **Pride Of Kinloch**[7] [2899] 4-8-1 **57**.................................... RFfrench 12 15
(JHetherton) *in touc h: rdn along 1/2-way: sn wknd* **25/1**

1m 12.97s (1.27) **Going Correction** +0.40s/f (Good) **17** Ran SP% **131.8**
Speed ratings: **107,106,105,103,101 99,97,97,97,95 90,89,86,84,84 83,82**CSF £87.91 CT £775.43 TOTE £18.90: £4.30, £1.90, £3.60, £2.90; EX 114.70.
**Owner** Keith Middleton **Bred** Mrs J Reilly **Trained** Norton, N Yorks

**FOCUS**
A competitive 0-84 sprint handicap with the first ten stacked up at the line. The time was reasonable and the form is good.

**NOTEBOOK**
**Cd Flyer(IRE)**, greatly assisted by the ease in the ground, came from almost last to first to show ahead near the line. He needs cover and revels in big fields like this.
**Blackheath(IRE)** travelled strongly but, after being sent to the front, in the end just missed out. He is knocking on the door.
**Midnight Parkes**, making a quick return to action, was running from a career-low mark and was only edged out by the first two inside the last. His trainer could win with the stable hack at present.
**Undeterred**, meeting the runner-up on 3lb better terms, as usual put in all his best work late on. When he times it right he will end his losing run.
**Snow Bunting**, 4lb higher than when narrowly missing out at Newcastle two outings ago, may be better suited by seven now.
**Skip Of Colour**, who lost both his front shoes last time, was reappearing after a three-month break. He showed bags of toe to lead them a merry dance for over half a mile, and the minimum trip may prove to suit him better.
**Obe One**, having his second outing in three days, did not fire.
**Hiccups**, loaded last, ran into traffic problems soon after halfway and never threatened.
**Seafield Towers** *Official explanation: jockey said gelding was unsuited by the going*
**Safranine(IRE)** *Official explanation: jockey said mare was unsuited by the going*

## 3099 REDCAR GRANDSTAND "RUBY ANNIVERSARY" H'CAP 1m 6f 19y
**3:25** (3:25) (F) (0-55,55) 4-Y-O+ **£3,374** (£964; £482) **Stalls** Low

Form RPR

5003 **1** **Astromancer (USA)**[22] [2462] 4-8-9 **49**.................................... SaleemGolam(7) 2 56
(MHTompkins) *trckd ldrs: hdwy to ld over 3f out: rdn along and hdd over 2f out: ralied u.p ent last to ld last 100 yds* **10/3**[1]

5055 **2** *1* **Ipledgeallegiance (USA)**[3] [2978] 8-7-9 **35** oh5...........(b) DFentiman(7) 5 41
(DWChapman) *hld up: hdwy and in tch 1/2-way: effrt 3f out: led over 2f out: rdn: edgd lft and clr ent last: wknd and hdd last 100yds* **9/1**

0006 **3** *nk* **East Cape**[38] [2038] 7-8-10 **43**.................................... KimTinkler 9 48
(DonEnricoIncisa) *hld up in rr: hdwy 4f out: rdn 2f out: styd on wl fnl f: nrst fin* **13/2**[3]

20-0 **4** *5* **Circus Maximus (USA)**[28] [2299] 7-9-8 **55**....................(p) GFaulkner 3 53
(IanWilliams) *chsd ldrs: rdn 3f out: drvn and outpcd fnl 2f* **8/1**

0631 **5** *1/2* **Dash Of Magic**[9] [2816] 6-8-5 **41**.................................... THamilton(3) 8 38
(JHetherton) *hld up: hdwy over 4f out: rdn over 2f out: sn no imp* **4/1**[2]

4004 **6** *1/2* **Balalaika Tune (IRE)**[11] [2759] 5-8-2 **35**.................................... PMQuinn 7 32
(WStorey) *hld up in tch: smooth hdwy on inner 4f out: ev ch 3f out: rdn 2f out and sn wknd* **9/1**

000/ **7** *11* **Lady Stratagem**[13] [4863] 5-8-9 **47**.................................... PMulrennan(5) 11 28
(EWTuer) *a rr* **33/1**

042- **8** *1/2* **Oops (IRE)**[375] [2248] 5-8-12 **45**.................................... DAllan 1 26
(JFCoupland) *led: rdn along 4f out: sn hdd & wknd* **7/1**

5-06 **9** *12* **Copplestone (IRE)**[21] [1721] 8-7-9 **35** oh2....................(p) RoryMoore(7) 6 —
(WStorey) *mdfield: hdwy to chse ldrs 1/2-way: rdn along 4f out and sn wknd* **12/1**

00-0 **10** *1/2* **King's Mountain (USA)**[68] [1369] 4-9-3 **50**.................................... GDuffield 12 13
(MrsALMKing) *cl up: rdn along 5f out: sn wknd* **20/1**

3m 10.02s (5.02) **Going Correction** +0.225s/f (Good) **10** Ran SP% **115.4**
Speed ratings: **94,93,93,90,90 89,83,83,76,76**CSF £33.53 CT £185.38 TOTE £3.40: £2.40, £2.60, £1.80; EX 33.40.
**Owner** Mystic Meg Limited **Bred** Frank Cosgrove **Trained** Newmarket, Suffolk

**FOCUS**
A 0-55 handicap and a seller in all but name run at a very steady pace for the first mile confirming the form as modest.

**NOTEBOOK**
**Astromancer(USA)** made it 17th time lucky, rallying to collar the flagging runner-up well inside the last.
**Ipledgeallegiance(USA)**, 5lb out of the handicap, went on and took a decisive lead, but he lost concentration in front and, hanging badly left, was worried out of it in the closing stages.
**East Cape** came back after a spell in the doldrums and would have got there with a little further to go.
**Circus Maximus(USA)** ran a lot better than on his return to the Flat a month earlier, but he is hard to predict and really needs further.
**Dash Of Magic** could have done with a much stronger pace and on her return to turf found the leaders were not coming back to her.
**Balalaika Tune(IRE)**, unplaced in 15 previous starts, took a fierce grip but, after moving into the firing line, she was going up and down in the same place with two furlongs left to run.
**Magic Charm** *Official explanation: jockey said saddle slipped*

## 3100 BEST DRESSED ELVIS COMPETITION (S) STKS 7f
**4:00** (4:01) (G) 2-Y-O **£2,926** (£836; £418) **Stalls** Centre

Form RPR

041 **1** **Princely Vale (IRE)**[4] [2960] 2-8-10....................(p) CHaddon(7) 6 56
(WGMTurner) *cl up: led wl over 1f out: sn rdn and hung lft: drvn and hung bdly rt ins last: jst hld on* **9/4**[1]

64 **2** *shd* **Riverweld**$^{11}$ [2755] 2-8-4 ........ DFentiman$^{(7)}$ 5 50
(GMMoore) *trckd ldrs: hdwy to chal 2f out and ev ch: rdn and edgd rt ins last: jst failed* **14/1**

00 **3** *1 3/4* **Dishdasha (IRE)**$^{8}$ [2858] 2-8-11 ........ DAllan 7 45
(TDEasterby) *chsd ldrs: rdn along 2f out: kpt on ins last* **4/1**

456 **4** *shd* **Mount Ephram (IRE)**$^{30}$ [2248] 2-8-6 ........ PBradley$^{(5)}$ 2 45
(RFFisher) *hld up: hdwy 2f out: rdn and hung bdly lft ent last: kpt on* **7/2**$^{3}$

361 **5** *4* **Maureen's Lough (IRE)**$^{11}$ [2755] 2-8-12 ........ PFessey 4 36
(TDBarron) *led: rdn along over 2f out: hdd & wknd wl over 1f out* **11/4**$^{2}$

00 **6** *2* **Fransiscan**$^{30}$ [2248] 2-8-11 ........(v$^{1}$) GFaulkner 8 30
(PCHaslam) *chsd ldrs: rdn along 1/2-way: sn wknd* **25/1**

00 **7** *16* **Lady Indiana (IRE)**$^{6}$ [2904] 2-8-7 ow1........ RWinston 1 —
(JSWainwright) *s.i.s: a rr* **28/1**

**8** *22* **Kinfayre Boy** 2-8-4 ........ PPMathers$^{(7)}$ 3 —
(KWHogg) *a rr* **50/1**

1m 30.48s (5.58) **Going Correction** +0.40s/f (Good) **8** Ran SP% **115.6**
Speed ratings: **84,83,81,81,77 74,56,31**CSF £34.10 TOTE £3.50: £1.30, £3.40, £1.60; EX 46.20.There was no bid for the winner. Dishdasha (no.4) was claimed by C R Dore for £8,000
**Owner** Vale Racing **Bred** Brian Killeen **Trained** Sigwells, Somerset

**FOCUS**
A very slow pace for this seller and the form is moderate but appears solid enough for the grade.

**NOTEBOOK**
**Princely Vale(IRE)**, very coltish in the paddock, travelled strongly and looked to have it in the bag, but he hung badly inside the last and at the line had just a whisker to spare.
**Riverweld**, who looked very fit, seems to be improving with racing and in the end was only just denied.
**Dishdasha(IRE)**, down in grade and up in trip, was a 43/1 chance on the exchanges at one time but was heavily supported on course. After travelling strongly, he hit a flat spot before keeping on well in the closing stages. He was claimed.
**Mount Ephram(IRE)**, drawn one off the outside, gave his rider no help by persistently hanging badly left - just as he was reported to have done last time.
**Maureen's Lough(IRE)**, on her toes beforehand, led them a merry dance but could not see it out this time.
**Fransiscan**, in a visor this time, was down in grade but was struggling to keep up at halfway.

## 3101 ROMFORDS CATERERS CLASSIFIED STKS 7f
**4:35** (4:35) (E) 3-Y-0+ **£3,376** (£1,039; £519; £259) **Stalls** Centre

Form RPR

0-32 **1** **Mr Velocity (IRE)**$^{35}$ [2119] 4-9-3 70........ RFfrench 1 79
(ACStewart) *trckd ldrs: shkn up 2f out: rdn to ld over 1f out: drvna nd styd on ins last* **1/1**$^{1}$

0000 **2** *1 1/4* **Boundless Prospect (USA)**$^{9}$ [2806] 5-9-3 70........ GDuffield 2 76
(JWHills) *s.i.s and bhd: hdwy 1/2-way: swtchd rt and rdn 2f out: drvn over 1f out: styd on ins last: nrst fin* **4/1**$^{2}$

2315 **3** *shd* **Efidium**$^{14}$ [2673] 6-9-3 69........ GFaulkner 3 75
(NBycroft) *clsoe up: led 2f out: sn rdn and hdd: drvn and nt qckn ins last* **4/1**$^{2}$

-020 **4** *nk* **Reidies Choice**$^{22}$ [2448] 3-8-7 74........ PMulrennan$^{(5)}$ 4 79
(JGGiven) *trckd ldrs: hdwy 2f out: rdn over 1f out: kpt on ins last* **7/1**$^{3}$

-000 **5** *3 1/2* **Iberus (GER)**$^{32}$ [2215] 6-9-2 72........ SHitchcott$^{(3)}$ 8 68
(SGollings) *cl up: rdn along 2f out: wknd over 1f out* **14/1**

0605 **6** *8* **Linden's Lady**$^{4}$ [2963] 4-8-11 63........ THamilton$^{(3)}$ 5 42
(JRWeymes) *led: rdn along over 2f out: sn hdd & wknd* **20/1**

1m 27.46s (2.56) **Going Correction** +0.40s/f (Good)
**WFA** 3 from 4yo+ 9lb **6** Ran SP% **113.9**
Speed ratings: **101,99,99,99,95 85**CSF £5.50 TOTE £1.90: £1.80, £3.00; EX 9.10.
**Owner** A M Pickering **Bred** Mrs V Dubois **Trained** Newmarket, Suffolk

**FOCUS**
A tightly-matched classified stakes run at no pace to halfway but the decisive winner justified heavy support. The form is fair and rated through third and fourth.

**NOTEBOOK**
**Mr Velocity(IRE)**, whose Nottingham form has stood up well, found the drop back in trip no problem and stayed on with gusto to finally get off the mark
**Boundless Prospect(USA)**, dropping in trip, was switched off at the back. Making his effort on the stands' side, he was always tending to hang left and is not the most co-operative of individuals.
**Efidium** could have done with a much stronger gallop and, after showing ahead, was outspeeded by the winner inside the last, missing out for second spot on the line.
**Reidies Choice** travelled strongly but, forced to switch left when left short of room two furlongs out, was unable to raise his game sufficiently inside the last to threaten real danger.
**Iberus(GER)**, a one-time useful performer in Germany, is struggling to make any impact in this country.
**Linden's Lady**, very keen in front, stepped up the gallop at halfway but in the end dropped right away.

## 3102 BBC RADIO CLEVELAND H'CAP 1m 1f
**5:10** (5:11) (E) (0-75,71) 3-Y-0 **£3,532** (£1,087; £543; £271) **Stalls** Low

Form RPR

0304 **1** **Charlie Tango (IRE)**$^{6}$ [2915] 3-8-9 **62**........ SHitchcott$^{(3)}$ 6 72
(MRChannon) *hld up: hdwy over 4f out: str run on outer to ld over 1f out: sn rdn and hung lft ins last: drvn out* **5/1**$^{3}$

60-1 **2** *nk* **Richtee (IRE)**$^{11}$ [2760] 3-8-8 **61**........ THamilton$^{(3)}$ 7 70
(RAFahey) *tacked ldrs: hdwy 4f out: led 3f out: sn rdn: hdd over 1f out drvna nd rallied insdie last: jst hld* **2/1**$^{1}$

0000 **3** *hd* **Ghantoot**$^{25}$ [2392] 3-8-12 **62**........(v$^{1}$) RWinston 1 71
(LMCumani) *chsd ldrs: rdn along on inner 3f out: drvn and styd on whn n.m.r ins last* **9/1**

-000 **4** *5* **Gasparini (IRE)**$^{22}$ [2457] 3-8-9 **59**........ DAllan 3 58
(TDEasterby) *chsd ldrs: hdwy to chal 4f out and ev ch tl drvn and one pce fnl 2f* **20/1**

6-00 **5** *1/2* **Rigonza**$^{52}$ [1712] 3-9-6 **70**........ GFaulkner 2 68
(TDEasterby) *s.i.s and bhd: hdwy over 4f out: rdn to chse ldrs over 2f out: sn drvn and btn* **20/1**

345 **6** *5* **Foolish Groom**$^{15}$ [2654] 3-9-7 **71**........(p) GDuffield 9 59
(RHollinshead) *cl up: ev ch 3f out: sn rdn and gradyually wknd fnl 2f* **7/1**

6540 **7** *1 1/4* **Perfect Balance (IRE)**$^{15}$ [2665] 3-8-7 **57**........ KimTinkler 10 43
(NTinkler) *nvr nr ldrs* **10/1**

5266 **8** *1 3/4* **Always Flying (USA)**$^{25}$ [2390] 3-9-5 **69**........ RFfrench 5 51
(MJohnston) *led: rdn along and hdd 3f out: sn wknd* **3/1**$^{2}$

0000 **9** *1 1/2* **Royal Distant (USA)**$^{12}$ [2732] 3-9-6 **70**........ DaleGibson 11 49
(MWEasterby) *a rr* **18/1**

1406 **10** *nk* **Book Matched**$^{9}$ [2814] 3-9-1 **65**........ DMcGaffin 4 43
(BSmart) *midfield: hdwy to chse ldrs 4f out: sn rdn and wknd 3f out* **16/1**

030- **11** *7* **Venerdi Tredici (IRE)**$^{261}$ [5323] 3-7-12 **55**........ SYourston$^{(7)}$ 13 19
(PABlockley) *a rr* **33/1**

1m 55.62s (2.22) **Going Correction** +0.225s/f (Good) **11** Ran SP% **130.2**
Speed ratings: **99,98,98,94,93 89,88,86,85,84 78**CSF £16.80 CT £99.00 TOTE £6.60: £1.70, £1.80, £3.70; EX 15.20 Place 6 £43.21, Place 5 £28.64.
**Owner** P Trant **Bred** Newtown Stud And T J Pabst **Trained** West Ilsley, Berks

**FOCUS**
In effect a 0-71 handicap run at a sound pace, and with the first three clear the form looks sound.

**NOTEBOOK**
**Charlie Tango(IRE)** came there down the outer to show just ahead but, edging left, tightened up the two on his inside, getting off the mark at the 12th attempt.
**Richtee(IRE)**, 6lb higher, was heavily backed to follow up. After setting sail for home she fought back bravely when headed and in the end, crowded near the line, she just missed out.
**Ghantoot**, in a visor on his handicap debut, was left short of room but he was hanging violently left and it looked very much a case of giving away a race he was well capable of taking.
**Gasparini(IRE)**, stepping up in trip, travelled strongly but his stride shortened noticeably in the closing stages. A mile might be his trip.
**Rigonza**, absent for seven weeks, stayed on steadily late on and his trainer seems to be winning the mind battle with him.
**Foolish Groom**, in first-time cheekpieces, has started life in handicaps from a stiff mark.
**Always Flying(USA)** set a sound pace but seemed to drop out rather tamely.
T/Plt: £39.50 to a £1 stake. Pool: £35,027.75. 646.95 winning tickets. T/Qpdt: £6.30 to a £1 stake. Pool: £1,914.85. 222.50 winning tickets. JR

# 2939 WARWICK (L-H)
Saturday, June 19

**OFFICIAL GOING: Good to firm (firm in places)**

## 3103 PEUGEOT AMATEUR RIDERS' H'CAP 1m 22y
**6:45** (6:46) (F) (0-55,60) 3-Y-0+ **£3,188** (£911; £455) **Stalls** Low

Form RPR

00-0 **1** **Night Market**$^{23}$ [2128] 6-10-8 **47**........ MrsNWilson$^{(5)}$ 2 59
(NWilson) *hld up in tch on ins and gng wl: led 1f out: r.o wl* **12/1**

6643 **2** *1 1/2* **First Maite**$^{17}$ [2591] 11-11-2 **50**........ MrsMMorris 14 58
(SRBowring) *a.p on outside: c wd into st: r.o wl fnl f to take 2nd ins* **11/1**

0130 **3** *shd* **Bojangles (IRE)**$^{5}$ [2943] 5-10-11 **48**........ MrLNewnes$^{(3)}$ 5 56
(RBrotherton) *towards rr: hdwy over 2f out: r.o fnl f: nvr nrr* **13/2**$^{2}$

5-30 **4** *shd* **We'll Meet Again**$^{10}$ [2776] 4-11-5 **53**........ MissSBrotherton 13 61
(MWEasterby) *towards rr: hdwy 1/2-way: rdn 2f out on ins and tk 2nd briefly ins fnl f: no ex cl home* **10/1**

2210 **5** *2 1/2* **Londoner (USA)**$^{5}$ [2943] 6-11-7 **60**........ MrDHutchison$^{(5)}$ 1 62
(SDow) *a.p: led briefly appr fnl f: wknd ins* **9/2**$^{1}$

0-55 **6** *1* **Pension Fund**$^{15}$ [2649] 10-10-8 **49**........ MissJCoward$^{(7)}$ 12 49
(MWEasterby) *chsd ldrs tl lost pl 1/2-way: c wd into st and rallied over 1f out: r.o fnl f* **16/1**

4000 **7** *nk* **Mobo-Baco**$^{8}$ [2833] 7-11-1 **52**........ MrJJBest$^{(3)}$ 10 51
(RJHodges) *towards rr: rdn over 2f out: mde sme late hdwy* **9/1**$^{3}$

0232 **8** *nk* **Cargo**$^{25}$ [2379] 5-10-9 **48**........(tp) MrGGallagher$^{(5)}$ 7 47
(BAPearce) *led: edge3d rt 2f out: hdd appr fnl f: wknd* **12/1**

6312 **9** *1 1/2* **Shirley Oaks (IRE)**$^{7}$ [2886] 6-10-12 **51**........ MissGDGracey-Davison$^{(5)}$ 3 46
(MissZCDavison) *ptominent: rdn over 2f out: wknd appr fnl f* **9/1**$^{3}$

0160 **10** *2 1/2* **Shamwari Fire (IRE)**$^{5}$ [2943] 4-10-11 **50**........ MSeston$^{(5)}$ 9 39
(IWMcinnes) *chsd ldrs: 3rd ent st: wknd ent fnl f* **14/1**

00-0 **11** *1 1/4* **Lucky Archer**$^{18}$ [2547] 11-11-2 **50**........ MrsSBosley 6 36
(IanWilliams) *in tch tl wknd wl over 1f out* **16/1**

0103 **12** *2* **Our Imperial Bay (USA)**$^{37}$ [1547] 5-10-12 **51**........(p) MrDWeekes$^{(5)}$ 4 33
(MrsJCandlish) *vs lowly away: nvr on terms* **14/1**

0201 **13** *1 1/2* **Gran Clicquot**$^{15}$ [2643] 9-10-9 **48**........ MrJPemberton$^{(5)}$ 16 26
(GPEnright) *racd wd: bhd fr 1/2-way* **10/1**

-500 **14** *hd* **Dark Shah (IRE)**$^{23}$ [2426] 4-10-9 **50**........(tp) MrBEvans$^{(7)}$ 11 28
(DMSimcock) *a bhd* **25/1**

330- **15** *2* **Didoe**$^{249}$ [5564] 5-10-10 **49**........ MrsMarieKing$^{(5)}$ 15 22
(PWHiatt) *trckd ldrs: rdn over 2f out: sn wknd* **33/1**

0020 **16** *2 1/2* **The Gambler**$^{35}$ [2123] 4-10-12 **51**........(p) MrPEvans$^{(5)}$ 17 19
(PaulJohnson) *chsd ldrs for 5f: sn bhd* **16/1**

4-00 **P** **Grumpyintmorning**$^{42}$ [1969] 5-11-0 **53**........ MrsCThompson$^{(5)}$ 8 —
(MrsPTownsley) *mid-div: hdwy 1/2-way: wknd qckly over 2f out: sn p.u* **25/1**

1m 39.45s (0.15) **Going Correction** -0.175s/f (Firm) **17** Ran SP% **135.0**
Speed ratings: **92,90,90,90,87 86,86,86,84,82 80,78,77,77,75 72,—**CSF £148.76 CT £995.28 TOTE £12.90: £3.50, £2.90, £3.10, £2.50; EX 356.60.
**Owner** J Watson **Bred** Alan Gibson **Trained** Malton, N Yorks

**FOCUS**
Modest form typical of the type of race, which was run at a steady pace.

**NOTEBOOK**
**Night Market**, who is happier on turf than on the All-Weather, was not badly handicapped on his form last year and, under a hands and heels ride, came through to win nicely. He is a moderate performer but clearly goes well for an inexperienced rider.
**First Maite** has not won for an age but he remains a threat in this sort of grade.
**Bojangles(IRE)** usually makes the running, but he showed here he can run just as well from off the pace.
**We'll Meet Again** goes well on a fast surface but is probably at his best over seven furlongs.
**Londoner(USA)** has never won over this far and did not appear to get home after racing prominently for most of the way.
**Pension Fund** has not won for three years.
**Cargo** was another who failed to get home.
**Grumpyintmorning** *Official explanation: trainer said gelding lost its action but returned sound*

## 3104 LEE BEESLEY MAIDEN AUCTION STKS 5f
**7:15** (7:16) (E) 2-Y-0 **£3,656** (£1,125; £562; £281) **Stalls** Low

Form RPR

5232 **1** **The Crooked Ring**$^{36}$ [2087] 2-8-7 ........(v$^{1}$) KFallon 4 71
(PDEvans) *sn pushed along in tch: strly rdn ent fnl f: squeezed through to ld nr fin* **8/11**$^{1}$

34 **2** *nk* **Forzeen**$^{7}$ [2872] 2-8-10 ........ GGibbons 6 73
(JAOsborne) *trckd ldr: hrd rdn and led briefly ins fnl f: kpt on* **6/1**$^{2}$

03 **3** *nk* **Agilete**$^{29}$ [2263] 2-8-13 ........ SDrowne 7 75
(LGCottrell) *chsd ldrs: sltly outpcd 2f out: r.o wl fnl f* **8/1**$^{3}$

044 **4** *1* **Coleorton Dancer**$^{35}$ [2125] 2-8-7 ........ NCallan 5 65
(KARyan) *stmbld s sn led: strly rdn ent fnl f: hdd wl ins fnl f and fdd nr finsih* **6/1**$^{2}$

6 **5** *3 1/2* **Dove Cottage (IRE)**$^{32}$ [2208] 2-8-10 ........ IMongan 3 56
(WSKittow) *stdd s and t.k.h in rr: nvr nr to chal* **8/1**$^{3}$

**6** *2 1/2* **Pauline's Prince** 2-8-7 ........ DSweeney 8 44
(RHollinshead) *outpcd thrght* **33/1**

0 **7** *3* **Ivory Wolf**$^{13}$ [2702] 2-8-4 ........ RMiles$^{(3)}$ 2 34
(JLSpearing) *broke wl but sn in rr: lost tch wl over 1f out* **33/1**

59.32 secs (-0.88) **Going Correction** -0.35s/f (Firm) **7** Ran SP% **114.6**
Speed ratings: **93,92,92,90,84 80,76**CSF £5.72 TOTE £1.70: £1.20, £2.90; EX 4.00.

**Owner** J R Salter **Bred** W H R John And Partners **Trained** Pandy, Gwent

**FOCUS**

A modest maiden but one run at a fast early pace, although the overall time was ordinary.

**NOTEBOOK**

**The Crooked Ring**, visored for the first time on this drop back in distance, struggled to go the fast early pace but, receiving weight from the second and third, stayed on well to get up close home. On this evidence a stiffer track will suit over the minimum trip.

**Forzeen** had less trouble than the winner keeping tabs on the leader, but in the end he found the concession of 3lb to the favourite too much.

**Agilete** appears to be progressing along the right lines and this was a creditable effort giving weight all round.

**Coleorton Dancer** is a nippy type and showed plenty of speed around this sharp track, but he was overhauled inside the last.

**Dove Cottage(IRE)** finished sixth behind Royal Ascot winner Chateau Istana on his debut, and it was slightly disappointing to see him unable to go the pace and failing to land a blow with that experience behind him.

**Ivory Wolf** *Official explanation: jockey said gelding hung right-handed in the home straight*

## 3105 ETERNAL STKS (LISTED RACE) (FILLIES) — 7f 26y

**7:45** (7:47) (A) 3-Y-O — **£17,400** (£6,600; £3,300; £1,500) **Stalls** Low

Form — RPR

211 **1** — **Lucky Spin**[18] 2548 3-8-11 97 ........ KFallon 2 — 106
(RHannon) *sn prom: rdn to ld over 1f out: drvn clr fnl f* — **2/1**[1]

03-5 **2** 3 — **Lucky Pipit**[66] 1398 3-9-2 102 ........ MHills 9 — 104
(BWHills) *led: hung rt and hdd over 1f out: kpt on fnl f but no ch w wnr* — **8/1**

2-62 **3** 1 ¼ — **Kunda (IRE)**[15] 2641 3-8-11 96 ........ RHughes 1 — 95
(RHannon) *towards rr: hdwy on outside over 1f out: r.o strly fnl furlon: nvr nrr* — **7/1**

12-0 **4** ½ — **Snow Goose**[66] 1398 3-8-11 103 ........ TQuinn 8 — 94
(JLDunlop) *sn pushed along but in tch: nt pce to chal ins fnl 2f* — **5/1**[3]

2-15 **5** nk — **Catstar (USA)**[16] 2629 3-8-11 107 ........ (t) LDettori 3 — 93
(SaeedBinSuroor) *hld up in mid-div: hdwy on outside 2f out: sn ridden and fnd little fnl f* — **5/2**[2]

305- **6** ½ — **Dark Empress (IRE)**[246] 5613 3-8-11 90 ........ (b[1]) FLynch 5 — 92
(RMBeckett) *slowly away: sme hdwy 2f out but nvr nr to chal* — **66/1**

0000 **7** 1 — **Valjarv (IRE)**[28] 2309 3-8-11 93 ........ JFanning 10 — 89
(NPLittmoden) *a towards rr* — **16/1**

**8** 1 ¼ — **Maple Syrple (CAN)**[332] 3-8-11 ........ (t) KMcEvoy 7 — 86
(SaeedBinSuroor) *chsd ldr: rdn over 2f out: wknd appr fnl f* — **20/1**

-051 **9** 1 — **Sweet Reply**[13] 2704 3-8-11 75 ........ NCallan 6 — 84?
(IAWood) *racd mid-div: bhd fnl 2f* — **66/1**

-650 **10** 3 — **Withorwithoutyou (IRE)**[53] 1685 3-8-11 80 ........ GGibbons 11 — 76
(BAMcmahon) *trckd ldrs: rdn 2f out: sn wknd* — **66/1**

44 **11** 9 — **Laska (IRE)**[22] 2450 3-8-11 ........ DCorby 4 — 52
(MJWallace) *a in rr: rdn over 2f out and nvr on terms* — **100/1**

1m 21.26s (-3.64) **Going Correction** -0.175s/f (Firm) course record **11** Ran SP% **118.3**

Speed ratings: **113,109,108,107,107 106,105,104,102,99 89**CSF £18.70 TOTE £3.40: £1.60, £2.80, £2.00; EX 28.90.

**Owner** George C Scudder **Bred** Roland Hope **Trained** East Everleigh, Wilts

**FOCUS**

A strong Listed race, run at a proper gallop in a course record. The form is useful and should hold up.

**NOTEBOOK**

**Lucky Spin** picked up well off a fast pace to win going away in impressive style. She broke the track record here, is improving all the time and now fully deserves a crack at Group company.

**Lucky Pipit**, returning from a two-month absence following a slightly disappointing reappearance run in the Nell Gwyn, set a decent gallop and may have finished closer to the winner had she not hung badly right in the straight. This was still a good effort under her 5lb penalty, though, and she once again confirmed her liking for fast ground.

**Kunda(IRE)**, runner-up to Gonfilia over an extended mile at Epsom last time, came from way off the pace to grab third place close home. She clearly finds seven furlongs on the sharp side nowadays.

**Snow Goose**, like the runner-up, was having her first outing since running poorly in the Nell Gwyn two months earlier. This was far more encouraging and she too is well suited by a sound surface.

**Catstar(USA)**, whose stable is in such cracking form at present, appeared to have conditions to suit, but was rather disappointing. It would be unwise to write off this lightly-raced filly, though, as her second to Attraction in the Queen Mary and success in the UAE 1000 Guineas suggest that she is a lot better than she showed here.

**Dark Empress(IRE)**, who wore blinkers instead of cheekpieces this time, did not perform too badly against higher-class rivals. *Official explanation: jockey said filly sat down in the stalls and was outpaced early on*

**Valjarv(IRE)** has been disappointing this season.

**Maple Syrple(CAN)**, a sprint winner on dirt in America, was making her debut for Godolphin and racing on turf for the first time. This trip probably stretched her stamina to the limit.

## 3106 EVENING TELEGRAPH MAIDEN STKS — 7f 26y

**8:20** (8:21) (D) 3-Y-O+ — **£3,835** (£1,180; £590; £295) **Stalls** Low

Form — RPR

-332 **1** — **Kali**[17] 2577 3-8-9 76 ........ DSweeney 1 — 71
(RCharlton) *chsd ldrs: led and hung lft over 1f out: rdn out fnl f* — **8/11**[1]

52-3 **2** 1 ½ — **River Nurey (IRE)**[17] 2596 3-9-0 72 ........ MHills 6 — 72
(BWHills) *in tch tl outpcd 1/2-way: rdn and hdwy over 1f out: r.o to go 2nd ins fnl f: no ch w wnr* — **7/2**[2]

4 **3** 4 — **Kabeer**[17] 2596 6-9-9 ........ PMcCabe 5 — 62
(PSMcentee) *led: rdn and hdd over 1f out: fdd and lost 2nd ins fnl f* — **10/1**

0-25 **4** 1 — **Jarvo**[54] 1679 3-9-0 66 ........ (t) JFanning 8 — 59
(NPLittmoden) *in tch on outside: c wd into st: kpt on one pce but nvr on terms after* — **16/1**

0-0 **5** 7 — **Karma Chamelian (USA)**[21] 2479 3-8-9 ........ TQuinn 4 — 36
(JWHills) *t.k.h: in tch tl wknd over 1f out* — **33/1**

0550 **6** 5 — **Top Place**[46] 1859 3-8-6 35 ........ RMiles(3) 7 — 23
(BAPearce) *trckd ldr tl over 2f out: sn btn* — **100/1**

0 **7** 3 — **Eijaaz (IRE)**[20] 2505 3-9-0 ........ RHills 3 — 20
(ACStewart) *wnt lft leaving stalls and rel to r: a wl bhd* — **11/2**[3]

00 **8** 6 — **Heriot**[8] 2842 3-9-0 ........ (v[1]) DaneO'Neill 2 — 4
(HCandy) *v.s.a and bmpd s: a wl bhd* — **66/1**

1m 22.55s (-2.35) **Going Correction** -0.175s/f (Firm)

**WFA** 3 from 6yo 9lb — **8** Ran SP% **115.9**

Speed ratings: **106,104,99,98,90 84,81,74**CSF £3.57 TOTE £1.70: £1.10, £1.40, £2.30; EX 3.90.

**Owner** Mrs M D Low **Bred** Hollington Stud **Trained** Beckhampton, Wilts

**FOCUS**

Not a strong maiden despite a true gallop, and the runner-up provides the key to the race.

**NOTEBOOK**

**Kali** has been in good form and found a weak maiden. She did what was expected according to official ratings and should not go up for this.

**River Nurey(IRE)** ran as his rating suggested he should, chasing home the higher-rated filly without ever threatening for the win. He shapes as though he will stay farther.

**Kabeer** tried to make all, showing plenty of pace in the process, but the form horses had his measure in the closing stages. He is not without ability.

**Jarvo**, wearing a tongue strap for the first time, is an exposed performer who ran as well as could be expected.

**Eijaaz(IRE)** lost all chance at the start. *Official explanation: jockey said colt tried to whip round shortly after leaving the stalls*

## 3107 WEST MIDLANDS RACING CLUB H'CAP — 1m 2f 188y

**8:50** (8:50) (E) (0-70,70) 3-Y-O — **£4,290** (£1,320; £660; £330) **Stalls** Low

Form — RPR

5135 **1** — **Goblin**[5] 2949 3-9-7 70 ........ KFallon 1 — 77+
(DECantillon) *t.k.h: hld up: tk clsr order 7f out: rdn to ld over 1f out: kpt up to work* — **8/11**[1]

-002 **2** 1 ½ — **Regal Performer (IRE)**[24] 2402 3-8-8 57 ........ RHughes 6 — 59
(SKirk) *hld up: hdwy over 2f out: r.o fnl f to go 2nd nr fin* — **7/2**[2]

0246 **3** ½ — **Delightfully**[7] 2882 3-9-4 67 ........ MHills 4 — 68
(BWHills) *trckd ldr: led 4f out: hdd over 1f out: one pce and lost 2nd nr fin* — **15/2**[3]

-625 **4** 1 — **Scorchio (IRE)**[39] 2014 3-7-9 47 oh2 ........ JFMcDonald(3) 3 — 46
(MFHarris) *t.k.h: in tch: n.m.r and swtchd rt over 1f out: styd on fnl f* — **28/1**

05-6 **5** 5 — **African Star**[168] 415 3-8-8 57 ........ DaneO'Neill 7 — 48
(MrsAJPerrett) *in tch on outside: hung lft and wknd over 1f out* — **17/2**

045 **6** 1 — **Maidstone Midas (IRE)**[21] 2486 3-9-1 64 ........ IMongan 5 — 53
(WSKittow) *trckd ldrs tl hung lft and wknd 2f out* — **25/1**

0-40 **7** 2 ½ — **Verasi**[18] 2546 3-9-3 66 ........ (b[1]) SDrowne 2 — 51
(RCharlton) *led tl hdd 4f out: weakeneing whn hmpd over 1f out* — **12/1**

2m 17.98s (-1.42) **Going Correction** -0.175s/f (Firm) — **7** Ran SP% **117.4**

Speed ratings: **98,96,96,95,92 91,89**CSF £3.74 TOTE £1.70: £1.10, £2.30; EX 3.20.

**Owner** Mrs E M Clarke **Bred** G W Turner And Miss S J Turner **Trained** Carlton, Cambs

**FOCUS**

An uncompetitive handicap run at a moderate pace.

**NOTEBOOK**

**Goblin**, unlucky in running at Windsor, had a far clearer passage this time and won what was an uncompetitve handicap cosily. His trainer reportedly sees him as a hurdler in the making.

**Regal Performer(IRE)** stays farther than this and the modest pace over this shorter trip was not to his advantage. *Official explanation: jockey said gelding hung left*

**Delightfully** had her chance but the balance of her form suggests she is not particularly well handicapped at present.

**Scorchio(IRE)**, racing from 2lb out of the handicap, would hold stronger chances back in banded grade.

**Maidstone Midas(IRE)** *Official explanation: jockey said colt hung left throughout the race*

**Verasi**, blinkered for the first time, set just a modest gallop out in front and it was surprising to see him drop away so tamely. He is becoming disappointing, although easier ground may help.

## 3108 SYD MERCER MEMORIAL H'CAP — 2m 3f 13y

**9:20** (9:20) (E) (0-70,65) 3-Y-O+ — **£3,981** (£1,225; £612; £306) **Stalls** Low

Form — RPR

3060 **1** — **Darn Good**[8] 2840 3-7-10 60 ........ (b) JFMcDonald(3) 2 — 70
(RHannon) *mid-div: hdwy whn hmpd over 3f out: rdn over 2f out: fin strly fnl f to ld post* — **16/1**

0-50 **2** shd — **Accepting**[27] 1501 7-8-12 51 ........ (b) NCallan 12 — 61
(JMackie) *a in tch: chsd ldr 4f out: rdn to ld ins fnl f: hdd post* — **9/1**

0-00 **3** nk — **Caliban (IRE)**[17] 2590 6-8-6 45 ........ RFitzpatrick 3 — 55
(IanWilliams) *slowly away and t.k.h in rr: hdwy on outside 4f out: checked over 3f out: hrd rdn over 1f out and ev ch ins last* — **20/1**

6365 **4** 2 — **Moonshine Beach**[7] 2874 6-9-0 53 ........ DaneO'Neill 5 — 61
(PWHiatt) *trckd ldrs: lost pl over 5f out: hmpd over 3f out: swtchd lft and hdwy over 1f out: styd on wl fnl f* — **10/3**[2]

0-00 **5** 6 — **Dance Light (IRE)**[30] 2249 5-9-9 62 ........ TGMcLaughlin 9 — 64
(TTClement) *a in tch: led 4f out: drvn clr over 2f out: rdn and hdd ins fnl f: wknd* — **25/1**

0-06 **6** 6 — **Promote**[25] 2385 8-8-13 52 ow12 ........ PMcCabe 11 — 48
(MsAEEmbiricos) *hld up: hdwy 5f out: rdn over 2f out: wknd appr fnl f* — **40/1**

5-05 **7** ½ — **Dancing Pearl**[64] 1326 6-8-4 46 ow1 ........ DCorby(3) 7 — 41
(CJPrice) *trckd ldrs: rdn whn hmpd over 3f out: one pce ins fnl 2f* — **6/1**[3]

653/ **8** ½ — **Plain Chant**[14] 3156 7-7-8 38 oh2 ow1 ........ AMedeiros(5) 1 — 33
(CRoberts) *led for 2f: led 6f out: hdd 4f out: wknd 2f out* — **25/1**

2341 **9** ¾ — **Berkeley Heights**[31] 2230 4-8-5 45 ........ ADaly 10 — 39
(MrsJCandlish) *a struggling in rr* — **10/1**

00-0 **10** shd — **Ulshaw**[61] 1501 7-9-2 55 ........ DSweeney 4 — 49
(BJLlewellyn) *mid-div: bhd fr 1/2-way* — **25/1**

0200 **11** 1 ¼ — **Joely Green**[7] 2874 7-7-13 45 ........ (b) StevenHarrison(7) 6 — 38
(NPLittmoden) *a bhd* — **16/1**

0/0- **P** — **Quick**[31] 226 4-9-5 59 ........ (v) KFallon 13 — —
(MCPipe) *led after 2f: rdn and hdd 6f out: stl in tch on ins whn hmpd over 3f out: dropped out qckly and eased: p.u ins last* — **11/8**[1]

4m 12.59s

**WFA** 3 from 4yo 22lb 4 from 5yo+ 1lb — **12** Ran SP% **129.1**

Speed ratings: CSF £154.87 CT £2940.36 TOTE £16.60: £4.70, £4.40, £4.90; EX 123.20 Place 6 £91.08, Place 5 £20.53.

**Owner** J E Garrett **Bred** Mrs Patricia Conway **Trained** East Everleigh, Wilts

**FOCUS**

A weak race and there was no mad gallop on. The form is ordinary.

**NOTEBOOK**

**Darn Good** had the look of an exposed maiden but, off a 6lb lower mark and tackling a much longer trip for the first time, he saw this extreme distance out well, getting up in the final strides to break his duck.

**Accepting**, in contrast to some of the others, is a proven stayer over extreme distances. This quicker ground suited him and he was only narrowly denied.

**Caliban(IRE)** ran surprisngly well given that he failed to settle in the early stages.

**Moonshine Beach**, done no favours by the quickly weakening favourite, had to be snatched up and lost momentum. He picked up well in the straight to finish fourth, but had he got a clear run he would surely have been placed at least.

**Dance Light(IRE)**, who has been lightly raced in recent years, had her chance but remains below her best.

**Dancing Pearl** has run her best races with a bit of cut in the ground.

**Quick** stopped very quickly and presumably something was amiss.

T/Plt: £224.20 to a £1 stake. Pool: £34,906.70. 113.65 winning tickets. T/Qpdt: £37.10 to a £1 stake. Pool: £2,566.20. 51.10 winning tickets. JS

3109 - 3115a (Foreign Racing) - See Raceform Interactive



# 2730 PONTEFRACT (L-H)

Sunday, June 20

**OFFICIAL GOING: Good to firm**

## 3116 EBF BETFRED.COM MAIDEN FILLIES' STKS (DIV I) 6f

2:20 (2:20) (D) 2-Y-O £5,434 (£1,672; £836; £418) Stalls Low

Form RPR

53 1 **Missperon (IRE)**[19] 2550 2-8-11 ... NCallan 1 69
(KARyan) *qckly away: mde all: rdn and hung bdly rt ent last: drvn and kpt on* **13/8**[2]

2 1 ¼ **Consider This** 2-8-11 ... DAllan 9 65
(WMBrisbourne) *in tch: hdwy over 2f out: rdn and swtchd lft ent last: kpt on* **16/1**

0 3 2 ½ **Orpen Annie (IRE)**[34] 2177 2-8-8 ... BReilly(3) 4 58
(MissJFeilden) *cl up tl pushed along and outpcd 1/2-way: rdn and hdwy 2f out: styd on same pce ins last* **20/1**

0 4 ½ **Frantic**[18] 2585 2-8-11 ... TQuinn 7 56
(TDEasterby) *towards rr: hdwy over 2f out: sn rdn and kpt on appr last* **12/1**

5 5 **E Bride (USA)** 2-8-11 ... MFenton 11 41
(JGGiven) *a.p: hdwy to chse wnr 1/2-way: rdn wl over 1f out and grad wknd* **8/1**[3]

6 3 **Entertaining** 2-8-11 ... DaneO'Neill 3 32
(HCandy) *chsd wnr: pushed along 1/2-way rdn 2f out and sn wknd* **11/8**[1]

7 19 **Final Overture (IRE)** 2-8-8 ... TEaves(3) 10 —
(JSWainwright) *s.i.s: a bhd* **20/1**

8 20 **Agreat Dayoutwithu** 2-8-11 ... RFitzpatrick 6 —
(PTMidgley) *cl up to 1/2-way: sn rdn along and wknd* **50/1**

1m 18.73s (1.43) **Going Correction** -0.025s/f (Good) **8 Ran SP% 116.4**
Speed ratings: **89,87,84,83,76 72,47,20**CSF £26.81 TOTE £2.60: £1.30, £5.30, £2.60; EX 42.40.
**Owner** Mrs Angie Bailey **Bred** E O'Leary **Trained** Hambleton, N Yorks

**FOCUS**
An ordinary maiden run in a modest winning time and confidence in the form is not high.

**NOTEBOOK**
**Missperon(IRE)** put her experience to good use and was soon in the lead. Despite hanging markedly to the right she proved too strong for debutant Consider This, and it was the ground that may have been the cause of her hanging. She has plenty of speed and more to offer.
**Consider This** would have delighted connections with this staying on debut effort against a more experienced rival. If going the right way from this, she should land an ordinary maiden and will stay another furlong.
**Orpen Annie(IRE)** improved on her debut running and way staying on all the time.
**Frantic** was another to improve on her debut effort and is the type to do well in nurseries.
**E Bride(USA)** showed up well before tiring.
**Entertaining** was well supported throughout the course of the day and expected to go close. However, having been up there early, she weakened and dropped away. She is surely better than this.

## 3117 SKYBET FILLIES' H'CAP 1m 4y

2:50 (2:50) (E) (0-75,69) 3-Y-O+ £4,114 (£1,266; £633; £316) Stalls Low

Form RPR

65-5 1 **Sharp Secret (IRE)**[20] 2521 6-9-3 **55** ... LisaJones(3) 9 63
(JARToller) *dwlt: hld up: hdwy over 2f out: str run fr over 1f out: rdn ins last and styd on to ld last 100 yds* **9/2**[2]

-600 2 ¾ **Kindness**[18] 2597 4-8-13 **48** ... DaneO'Neill 1 54
(ADWPinder) *set stdy pce: qcknd over 2f out: rdn appr last: hdd and nt qckn last 100 yds* **16/1**

0006 3 hd **Uno Mente**[12] 2757 5-9-4 **53** ... KimTinkler 3 59
(DonEnricoIncisa) *chsd ldrs: hdwy 2f out: rdn and ent last and kpt on towards fin* **11/1**

-000 4 hd **Magical Mimi**[18] 2587 3-9-3 **69** ... LeanneKershaw(7) 5 74
(JeddO'Keeffe) *midfield: hdwy on outer 2f out: rdn to chal ins last: no ex last 100 yds* **33/1**

5005 5 1 ¼ **Hula Ballew**[3] 3006 4-9-5 **54** ... (p) DarrenWilliams 4 56
(MDods) *chsd ldrs: hdwy to chal 2f out: sn rdn and wknd ent last* **9/1**[3]

2-62 6 ¾ **Miss Eloise**[15] 2688 3-8-12 **57** ... DAllan 7 57
(TDEasterby) *hld up in tch: hdwy 1/2-way: rdn and wkng whn not much room over 1f out* **9/2**[2]

4501 7 3 **Classic Vision**[8] 2879 4-9-5 **54** ... (b) RHills 6 48
(WJHaggas) *hld up towards rr: hdwy and n.m.r wl over 1f out: sn rdn and no imp* **3/1**[1]

6004 8 4 **Transcendantale (FR)**[3] 3008 6-8-12 **47** ... KFallon 10 31
(MrsSLamyman) *chsd ldrs: rdn 2f out: sn wknd* **9/2**[2]

6-00 9 1 ¾ **Lark In The Park (IRE)**[57] 1606 4-8-9 **44** ... KDarley 2 24
(WMBrisbourne) *chsd ldr: rdn along 2f out: sn wknd* **11/1**

1m 47.24s (1.64) **Going Correction** -0.025s/f (Good)
**WFA** 3 from 4yo+ 10lb **9 Ran SP% 115.0**
Speed ratings: **90,89,89,88,87 86,83,79,78**CSF £72.21 CT £749.08 TOTE £6.00: £1.10, £4.50, £3.00; EX 111.80.
**Owner** John Drew **Bred** Canice M Farrell Jnr **Trained** Newmarket, Suffolk

**FOCUS**
A very slow time for the grade but a good performance from Sharp Secret who came from off the slow gallop.

**NOTEBOOK**
**Sharp Secret(IRE)** showed the benefit of her seasonal reappearance and came with a strong run from the rear of the field to win going away. Her stable are in decent form at the moment, and although a rise in the weights in likely, she will go close in a follow-up bid.
**Kindness** had the run of the race from the front and performed well in defeat, being unable to fend off the winners challenge.
**Uno Mente** was never far off the pace and ran on well to hold on for third.
**Magical Mimi** fared best of the three-year-olds and shaped much better than she had on previous runs this season.
**Miss Eloise** had her chance and faded late on. *Official explanation: trainer's representative had explanation for the poor form shown*
**Classic Vision** was a little short of room when trying to come with a challenge and did not pick up after. *Official explanation: trainer's representative had explanation for the poor form shown*
**Lark In The Park(IRE)** *Official explanation: jockey said filly had a breathing problem*

## 3118 STANLEYBET.COM CLASSIFIED STKS 1m 2f 6y

3:20 (3:23) (C) 3-Y-O+ £9,024 (£3,423; £1,711; £778) Stalls Low

Form RPR

1 1 **Mutasallil (USA)**[25] 2412 4-9-3 87 ... (t) LDettori 1 102
(SaeedBinSuroor) *mde all: qcknd 2f out: rdn over 1f out: styd on wl* **5/2**[1]

41-5 2 1 ¾ **Kingsword (USA)**[15] 2672 3-8-8 93 ... KFallon 2 102
(SirMichaelStoute) *trckd ldrs: pushed along 3f out: styd on to chse wnr over 1f out: drvn and kpt on ins last* **11/4**[2]

10-0 3 4 **Spuradich (IRE)**[33] 2196 4-9-6 93 ... JPMurtagh 6 94
(LMCumani) *hed up in toch: hdwy 3f out: rdn along wl over 1f out: no imp fnl f* **11/2**[3]

0054 4 2 ½ **Our Teddy (IRE)**[8] 2894 4-9-3 87 ... (b) KDarley 4 87
(AMBalding) *keen: chsd ldrs: hdwy over 2f out: rdn wl over 1f out: sn btn* **8/1**

-033 5 1 ½ **Crow Wood**[20] 2527 5-9-7 94 ... MFenton 7 88
(JGGiven) *cl up: rdn along 3f out: wknd 2f out* **11/4**[2]

0000 6 21 **Percy Douglas**[2] 3039 4-9-0 45 ... LFletcher(3) 8 44?
(MissAStokell) *a rr* **200/1**

0-00 7 2 **Eastern Dagger**[10] 2813 4-9-3 48 ... RFitzpatrick 3 40?
(PTMidgley) *s.i.s: plld hrd and sn chsng ldrs: rdn along and lost pl over 4f out: sn bhd* **200/1**

2m 11.5s (-2.41) **Going Correction** -0.025s/f (Good)
**WFA** 3 from 4yo+ 12lb **7 Ran SP% 109.4**
Speed ratings: **108,106,103,101,100 83,81**CSF £8.80 TOTE £3.50: £2.30, £2.30; EX 5.50.
**Owner** Godolphin **Bred** Shadwell Farm Llc **Trained** Newmarket, Suffolk
■ Stewards Enquiry : K Darley caution: careless riding

**FOCUS**
The two unexposed runners from the big yards dominated this and it was the Godolphin runner who came out on top.

**NOTEBOOK**
**Mutasallil(USA)** stepped up markedly on his maiden win and beat the useful Kingsword by a comfortable margin having made all the running. He is evidently progressive and gives the impression he will stay further, so remains one to keep on the right side of.
**Kingsword(USA)** shaped as though in need of the outing at Doncaster and just lacked the vital kick. A mile and a half will see him in a better light and he should improve again.
**Spuradich(IRE)** was four lengths adrift in third and no match for either of the front two.
**Our Teddy(IRE)** ran better than he had been last time and it was disappointing he could not run better.
**Crow Wood** held a good early position but folded disappointingly.

## 3119 WILLIAM HILL RATED STKS (H'CAP) 1m 4y

3:50 (3:50) (B) (0-105,101) 3-Y-O+ £12,093 (£4,587; £2,293; £1,042) Stalls Low

Form RPR

0211 1 **Ace Of Hearts**[7] 2905 5-8-10 **86** 3ex ... SSanders 5 98+
(CFWall) *trcke ldrs: pushed alng 3f out: ridden and nt clr run over 1f out: swtchd rt and drvn ins last: styd on wl to ld nr line* **11/8**[1]

0000 2 ½ **Calcutta**[4] 2969 8-9-5 **95** ... MHills 4 103
(BWHills) *hld up: hdwy over 2f out: effrt on outer over1f out: rdn to ld and edgd lft ins last: sn drvn and hdd nr fin* **11/2**[3]

4644 3 1 **King's Thought**[15] 2672 5-9-6 **96** ... JPMurtagh 10 102
(SGollings) *led: rdn wl over 1f out: drvn and hdd ins last: no ex* **16/1**

-200 4 ¾ **Always Esteemed (IRE)**[20] 2527 4-9-5 **95** ... JFEgan 9 99
(GWragg) *chsd ldrs: rdn along 2f out: drvn and edgd lft over 1f out: kpt on same pce inside last* **12/1**

4500 5 1 **Danelor (IRE)**[8] 2895 6-8-6 **85** ... THamilton(3) 1 87
(RAFahey) *hld up: hdwy and n.m.r wl over 1f out: swtchd ins and styd on fnl f* **9/1**

0-04 6 ½ **Narrative (IRE)**[18] 2588 6-9-10 **100** ... RHills 11 101
(DRLoder) *chsd ldr: rdn to chal wl over 1f out: sn drvn: edgd lft and wknd ent last* **14/1**

3010 7 3 ½ **Sea Storm (IRE)**[8] 2894 6-8-3 **84** oh2 ... (p) PMulrennan(5) 7 77
(DRMacleod) *cl up: rdn along over 3f out: wknd over 2f out* **12/1**

140- 8 30 **Russian Dance (USA)**[283] 4840 3-8-12 **98** ... KFallon 3 22
(SirMichaelStoute) *hld up in rr: pushed along 1/2-way: sn drvn and wknd: eased wl over 1f out* **7/2**[2]

1m 43.18s (-2.42) **Going Correction** -0.025s/f (Good)
**WFA** 3 from 4yo+ 10lb **8 Ran SP% 117.6**
Speed ratings: **111,110,109,108,107 107,103,73**CSF £9.72 CT £87.11 TOTE £2.40: £1.40, £1.70, £2.80; EX 12.50 Trifecta £263.60 Pool £10,770.79 - 29 winning units..
**Owner** Lady Stuttaford & W G Bovill **Bred** Whitsbury Manor Stud **Trained** Newmarket, Suffolk

**FOCUS**
A decent handicap despite the non runners, and a race that should work out. The good recent run of Ace Of Hearts continued and he won nicely in the end.

**NOTEBOOK**
**Ace Of Hearts** has been in great form and completed the hat-trick a shade cosily, just doing enough to get up in the final few yards. He should continue to thrive.
**Calcutta** looked to have come with his winning run, only to be collared by the winner close home. This was his best effort for a while and he may be nearing a win.
**King's Thought** ran a good race from the front but could not hold off the front pair. This was a good effort and he is evidently back to form.
**Always Esteemed(IRE)** had his chance and was not disgraced.
**Danelor(IRE)** was slightly unlucky not to finish closer and was keeping on at the line.
**Russian Dance(USA)**, making her three-year-old debut, was tailed off and something appeared to go amiss.

## 3120 TOTEEXACTA PONTEFRACT CUP (H'CAP) 2m 1f 216y

4:20 (4:20) (D) (0-80,77) 4-Y-O+ £6,776 (£2,085; £1,042; £521) Stalls Low

Form RPR

3403 1 **Thewhirlingdervish (IRE)**[9] 2855 6-9-13 **77** ... TQuinn 10 87
(TDEasterby) *hld up and bhd: stdy hdwy 5f out: rdn to ld wl over 1f out: sn clr* **7/2**[2]

0/25 2 2 **Magic Combination (IRE)**[6] 2935 11-9-7 **71** ... WDowling 3 79
(LLungo) *in tch:trckd ldrs 5f out: n.m.r and outpcd 3f out:swtchd rt and hdwy 2f out: chsd wnr and hung lft ins last: kpt on* **16/1**

3440 3 2 ½ **Ocean Tide**[17] 2613 7-9-8 **72** ... (b[1]) KDarley 4 77
(RFord) *led: rdn along 4f out: hdd over 2f out: rallied u.p appr last* **14/1**

-001 4 1 ½ **Stoop To Conquer**[13] 2731 4-9-8 **73** ... KFallon 8 76
(JLDunlop) *trckd ldrs: hdwy to ld over 2f out: sn rdn: hdd wl over 1f outa nd sn wknd* **5/4**[1]

3524 5 1 ½ **Toni Alcala**[6] 2935 5-9-4 **68** ... JFanning 2 70
(RFFisher) *trfacked ldrs: hdwy 4f out: rdn over 2f out and kpt on same pce* **15/2**

31-5 6 1 **Tilla**[17] 2631 4-8-13 **67** ... LFletcher(3) 11 67
(HMorrison) *held up: hdwy over 6f out: chal over 2f out and ev ch tl rdna nd wknd over 1f out* **11/2**[3]

60-0 7 14 **Peak Park (USA)**[22] 2480 4-7-9 **49** oh3 ... (v[1]) LisaJones(3) 9 34
(JARToller) *chsd ldng pair: rdn along over 3f out and sn wknd* **25/1**

1040 8 9 **Green 'N' Gold**[20] 2531 4-8-6 **57** ... DarrenWilliams 5 32
(MDHammond) *a rr* **20/1**

260 **9** *dist* **Indian Chase**[19] 2562 7-7-12 **55**....................(v) LucyRussell(7) 7 —
(DrJRJNaylor) *plld hrd: cl up tl rdn along and wknd qckly over 4f out*
**100/1**

3m 58.74s (-4.26) **Going Correction** -0.025s/f (Good)
**WFA** 4 from 5yo+ 1lb **9** Ran SP% **116.0**
Speed ratings: **108,107,106,105,104 104,98,94,**—CSF £55.26 CT £700.79 TOTE £4.40: £2.00, £2.20, £3.30; EX 61.50.
**Owner** Major I C Straker **Bred** Yeomanstown Stud **Trained** Great Habton, N Yorks

**FOCUS**
A fair gallop to this marathon.

**NOTEBOOK**
**Thewhirlingdervish(IRE)**, who showed signs of a revival at York last time, landed this contest two years ago off a 9lb lower mark. Given a patient ride, he was produced with his effort once in line for home and saw his race out really well.
**Magic Combination(IRE)** stayed on without ever looking likely to threaten the winner. He may be at the veteran stage now, but recently his efforts on the Flat have been much better than over hurdles.
**Ocean Tide** made the running at a fair pace and did well to hang on for third, considering he was taken on for the lead by the free-running Indian Chase for much of the way.
**Stoop To Conquer**, raised 7lb for his recent win at this track, had every chance and there seemed no obvious excuse except that this was a better race.
**Toni Alcala**, who is yet to win beyond 14 furlongs, was closely matched with Stoop To Conquer on recent running but, like that rival, he failed to land a blow in this better race.
**Tilla** ◆ was bang there turning in, but did not seem to see out this longer trip. She is still worth keeping in mind back over shorter.

## 3121 LADBROKES MAIDEN STKS 1m 4f 8y
**4:50** (4:51) (D) 3-Y-O **£5,538** (£1,704; £852; £426) **Stalls** Low

Form RPR
-034 **1** **Schapiro (USA)**[18] 2578 3-9-0 78....................(b) LDettori 4 79+
(JHMGosden) *trckd wnr: led 3f out: sn clr: easily* **15/8**[1]
45 **2** *6* **Race The Ace**[30] 2280 3-9-0 .................... SSanders 2 69
(JLDunlop) *hld up and bhd: hdwy 4f out: rdn 2f out: kpt on: no ch w wnr* **16/1**
3 **3** *6* **Sunday City (JPN)**[36] 2133 3-9-0 ....................(v1) KFallon 3 59
(DRLoder) *stmbld s: sn chsng ldrs: rdn along over 2f out: sn drvn and one pce fnl 2f* **9/4**[3]
43 **4** *2* **Zangeal**[17] 2632 3-9-0 .................... JQuinn 5 56
(CFWall) *dwlt: plld hrd and sn in tch: rdn along over 3f out and sn btn* **2/1**[2]
0 **5** *hd* **Molehill**[16] 2653 3-8-9 .................... MFenton 6 51
(JGGiven) *chsd ldrs: rdn along over 3f out: sn one pce* **25/1**
00-0 **6** *18* **Oniz Tiptoes (IRE)**[7] 2908 3-8-11 ....................(p) TEaves(3) 1 27
(JSWainwright) *led: rdn along and hdd 3f out: sn wknd* **100/1**
**7** *27* **Beseeka Runnin Fox** 3-8-6 .................... BReilly(3) 9 —
(MrsLWilliamson) *a rr: lost pl and bhd fnl 4f* **100/1**
**P** **Deangate (IRE)** 3-9-0 .................... RFitzpatrick 10 —
(PTMidgley) *a rr: lost tch qckly 5f out: t.o whn p.u andd dismntd 2f out* **50/1**

2m 39.3s (-0.75) **Going Correction** -0.025s/f (Good) **8** Ran SP% **112.6**
Speed ratings: **101,97,93,91,91 79,61,**—CSF £28.97 TOTE £2.90: £1.40, £2.30, £1.10; EX 30.00.
**Owner** Sangster Family **Bred** Midhurst Farm Inc Et Al **Trained** Manton, Wilts

**FOCUS**
Eight runners, but a three-horse race according to the market. The winner probably only needed to run to his handicap mark to score with ease, and using his mark of 78 as a guide, the rest look modest.

**NOTEBOOK**
**Schapiro(USA)** found this much easier than the handicap company he has been running in, and won with his head in his chest. This should have done his confidence a lot of good and, in beating this lot, his handicap mark should not suffer too much. He may prefer a greater test of stamina when returned to handicaps.
**Race The Ace** stayed on to win the separate race for second. He looks a real stayer and, using the winner as a guide, he should only get a modest handicap mark.
**Sunday City(JPN)**, visored for the first time, was made to look very one paced over the last couple of furlongs and did not really improve from his debut.
**Zangeal** was stepping up in trip and took a keen hold, but this was still disappointing. He now qualifies for handicaps, but will need to settle better if he is to make his mark in any type of contest.
**Molehill** was not completely disgraced and needs just one more run for a handicap mark.
**Deangate(IRE)** *Official explanation: jockey said gelding had a breathing problem*

## 3122 BET DIRECT H'CAP 6f
**5:20** (5:20) (D) (0-85,85) 3-Y-O **£5,499** (£1,692; £846; £423) **Stalls** Low

Form RPR
-244 **1** **Red Romeo**[9] 2839 3-8-11 **75**.................... KFallon 6 90
(GASwinbank) *a.p:led over 2f out: rdn clr ent last: styd on* **2/1**[1]
06-0 **2** *5* **Mind Alert**[30] 2269 3-8-6 **70**.................... DAllan 8 70
(TDEasterby) *in tch: hdwy over 2f out: rdn wl over 1f out: kpt on ins last* **28/1**
00-0 **3** *shd* **Bella Tutrice (IRE)**[8] 2877 3-8-8 **72**.................... JFanning 4 72
(IAWood) *led: rdn along over 2f out and sn hdd: drvn and kpt on same pce appr last* **25/1**
-504 **4** *hd* **Fiore Di Bosco (IRE)**[8] 2880 3-8-4 **73**.................... PMakin(5) 7 72
(TDBarron) *hld up: hdwy over 2f out: sn rdn and kpt on fnl f: nrst fin* **12/1**
041 **5** *1 ½* **Rene Barbier (IRE)**[15] 2675 3-8-5 **69**.................... DeanMcKeown 10 64
(JAGlover) *stdd s and bhd: hdwy over 2f out: sn rdn and kpt on fnl f* **16/1**
-630 **6** *shd* **Senor Bond (USA)**[67] 1392 3-8-7 **71** ow3.................... FLynch 2 65
(BSmart) *a rr* **16/1**
-012 **7** *shd* **Bo McGinty (IRE)**[4] 2981 3-9-4 **85**.................... THamilton(3) 5 79
(RAFahey) *cl up: rdn over 2f out: drvn and hung lft wl over 1f out: sn wknd* **2/1**[1]
0520 **8** *nk* **Lets Get It On (IRE)**[30] 2269 3-9-1 **79**.................... RWinston 3 72
(JJQuinn) *in tch:chsd along 1/2-way: nvr a factor* **7/1**[3]
-004 **9** *3 ½* **Imperial Echo (USA)**[4] 2981 3-9-2 **80**....................(v1) SSanders 1 63
(TDBarron) *cl up on inner: rdn along over 2f out: wkng whn bdly hmpd wl over 1f out and eased* **11/2**[2]

1m 16.53s (-0.77) **Going Correction** -0.025s/f (Good) **9** Ran SP% **121.3**
Speed ratings: **104,97,97,96,94 94,94,94,89**CSF £74.85 CT £1148.42 TOTE £3.10: £1.10, £6.30, £6.20; EX 72.80.
**Owner** J Yates **Bred** J O'Mulloy **Trained** Melsonby, N Yorks

**FOCUS**
A competitive handicap on paper and a decent pace, but ultimately a one-horse race.

**NOTEBOOK**
**Red Romeo** has won over seven furlongs, so this stiff six was ideal and he was never going to stop after hitting the front. The Handicapper is likely to punish him for this, so a quick reappearance under a penalty is the likely scenario.
**Mind Alert** is becoming well handicapped and even though he was eventually thrashed by the winner, this was still his best effort for a while.
**Bella Tutrice(IRE)** bowled along in front until soon after turning for home. This was a good deal better than on her reappearance and the minimum trip may be preferable when these tactics are employed.
**Fiore Di Bosco(IRE)** ◆ has dropped to a much more realistic mark and there was plenty of encouragement in this effort.
**Rene Barbier(IRE)**, making his handicap debut, came from off the pace to reach his final position and appeared to have no problem with the return to six. He still has some scope. *Official explanation: jockey said gelding had lost a shoe*
**Senor Bond(USA)** *Official explanation: jockey said gelding was denied a clear run in the closing stages*
**Bo McGinty(IRE)** was very disappointing and perhaps this came too soon after his Ripon effort.
**Imperial Echo(USA)** was not out of it when completely murdered against the inside rail soon after straightening up for home. This effort can be safely ignored.

## 3123 EBF BETFRED.COM MAIDEN FILLIES' STKS (DIV II) 6f
**5:50** (5:56) (D ) 2-Y-O **£5,434** (£1,672; £836; £418) **Stalls** Low

Form RPR
**1** **Krynica (USA)** 2-8-11 .................... KFallon 6 69
(SirMichaelStoute) *cl up: chal 2f out: rdn ent last: styd on to ld last 100 yds* **11/2**[3]
**2** *hd* **Secret History (USA)** 2-8-11 .................... JFanning 8 68
(MJohnston) *led: rdn along wl over 1f out: drvn ins last: hdd and nt qckn last 100 yds* **6/1**
**3** *1* **Balletto** 2-8-11 .................... DarrenWilliams 3 65
(KRBurke) *trckd ldrs: hdwy on inner 2f out: rdn and kpt on ins last* **16/1**
26 **4** *shd* **Taras Treasure (IRE)**[19] 2550 2-8-11 .................... RWinston 4 65
(JJQuinn) *keen: prom tl n.m.r and lost pl 1/2-way: effrt and nt clr run over 1f out:s witched rt and styd on wl fnl f* **5/2**[1]
**5** *¾* **Lottie Dundass** 2-8-11 .................... JPMurtagh 1 63
(PWHarris) *in rr: nt clr run and swtchd wd wl over 1f out: styd on wl ent last: nrst fin* **3/1**[2]
0 **6** *½* **Imperial Miss (IRE)**[22] 2481 2-8-11 .................... ADaly 5 61
(BWDuke) *cl up in inner: rdn along over 2f out: kpt on same pce appr last* **25/1**
**7** *1* **Princeable Lady (IRE)** 2-8-11 .................... DAllan 2 58
(TDEasterby) *bhd tl styd on fnl 2f* **18/1**
**8** *hd* **Rock Fever (IRE)** 2-8-11 .................... KDarley 10 58
(MJWallace) *s.i.s: hdwy to chse ldrs on outer 1/2-way: rdn wl over 1f out: one pce ent last* **6/1**
404 **9** *1* **Make Us Flush**[17] 2617 2-8-4 .................... PPMathers(7) 7 55
(ABerry) *chsd ldrs: rdn along 2f out: wknd appr last* **16/1**
**10** *1 ¼* **Scissors (IRE)** 2-8-8 .................... BReilly(3) 9 51
(MissJFeilden) *chsd ldrs: rdn along over 2f out: sn wknd* **66/1**

1m 18.61s (1.31) **Going Correction** -0.025s/f (Good) **10** Ran SP% **119.9**
Speed ratings: **90,89,88,88,87 86,85,85,83,82**CSF £39.71 TOTE £4.20: £1.90, £1.70, £6.80; EX 9.50 Place 6 £114.91, Place 5 £49.23..
**Owner** K Abdulla **Bred** Juddmonte Farms Inc **Trained** Newmarket, Suffolk

**FOCUS**
A marginally faster time than the first division, but still only a modest time for the grade. The form is only fair, but several of these looked capable of improvement though.

**NOTEBOOK**
**Krynica(USA)** ◆, whose dam was a winner over seven furlongs in her only start, responded bravely to hands and heels riding to score and, despite the narrow margin, it was noticeable that the champion never got truly serious with her. The form may be ordinary, but she is likely to have a great deal of improvement still in her.
**Secret History(USA)** ◆, a 25,000gns granddaughter of a very smart performer in the US, tried to make all the running but found the winner just too good. She should improve from this.
**Balletto** ◆, a 27,000gns yearling out of a winner in France, was rather intimidated by the winner up the home straight, but she was by no means knocked about and showed enough to suggest she has a race in her.
**Taras Treasure(IRE)** held a good position early, but got carried back against the inside rail before halfway and soon had a lot to do. She then had difficulty getting a run in the home straight and once in the clear had too much ground to make up. She may have been unlucky but, considering the three in front of her were making their debuts, she would be hard pressed to turn the form around with any of them in the future.
**Lottie Dundass** ◆, a 42,000gns half-sister to five winners including a dual Listed winner in France, raced in last place until staying on down the outside in the closing stages without being given at all a hard time. There should be a lot more to come.
**Rock Fever(IRE)**, a 25,000euros half-sister to five winners including Mac The Knife and Kettlesing, should be all the better for the experience.
T/Jkpt: £525.90 to a £1 stake. Pool: £10,000.00. 13.50 winning tickets. T/Plt: £129.30 to a £1 stake. Pool: £48,310.30. 272.65 winning tickets. T/Qpdt: £10.10 to a £1 stake. Pool: £3,513.40. 256.60 winning tickets. JR

# 3103 WARWICK (L-H)
Sunday, June 20

**OFFICIAL GOING: Firm (good to firm in places)**
Very quick ground descibed by one trainer as "hard"
Wind: Fresh half behind Weather: Cloudy with sunny spells

## 3124 EVENING TELEGRAPH CELEBRATION MAIDEN STKS 7f 26y
**2:30** (2:31) (D) 2-Y-O **£3,851** (£1,185; £592; £296) **Stalls** Low

Form RPR
0 **1** **Country Rambler (USA)**[22] 2470 2-9-0 .................... RHughes 6 83+
(BWHills) *mde all: clr over 2f out: eased ins fnl f* **5/2**[2]
05 **2** *5* **League Of Nations (IRE)**[23] 2453 2-9-0 .................... SDrowne 5 70
(PFICole) *chsd wnr: rdn over 2f out: sn outpcd* **9/2**[3]
45 **3** *¾* **Simplify**[18] 2592 2-8-11 .................... TPQueally(3) 3 68
(DRLoder) *hld up: hdwy 1/2-way: sn rdn: hung lft and no imp* **1/1**[1]
40 **4** *8* **Sharp N Frosty**[46] 1884 2-9-0 .................... SWKelly 2 48
(WMBrisbourne) *chsd ldrs: rdn 1/2-way: sn wknd* **12/1**
0 **5** *nk* **Dartanian**[38] 2057 2-9-0 .................... JoannaBadger 4 47
(PDEvans) *in tch: sn pushed along: wknd 1/2-way* **22/1**
**6** *14* **Robmantra** 2-9-0 .................... VSlattery 1 12
(BJLlewellyn) *s.s: outpcd* **66/1**

1m 22.9s (-2.00) **Going Correction** -0.175s/f (Firm) 2y crse rec **6** Ran SP% **110.3**
Speed ratings: **104,98,97,88,87 71**CSF £13.48 TOTE £3.80: £1.10, £3.40; EX 11.90.
**Owner** Ahmed Buhaleeba **Bred** M & B Delfiner Et Al **Trained** Lambourn, Berks

**FOCUS**
A very smart time for a race of its type and strong form from the winner, who could hold his own at a higher level.

**NOTEBOOK**
**Country Rambler(USA)**, who fell out of the stalls on his debut, had been re-schooled since and showed the benefit. He pinged the stalls on this occasion and showed good speed throughout to win pretty much as he liked. A fluent mover, he might always need quick ground to show his best. *Official explanation: trainer's representative said, regarding the improved form, colt missed the break completely at Doncaster last time out*
**League Of Nations(IRE)** is taking time to get the hang of things, but he is learning and should do better when going handicapping.
**Simplify** has become expensive to follow and looked a far from straightforward ride.

## 3125 EVENING TELEGRAPH PROPERTY GUIDE CLASSIFIED STKS 6f 21y
**3:00** (3:02) (E) 3-Y-0+ **£3,705** (£1,140; £570; £285) **Stalls** Low

Form RPR
1104 **1** **Parkside Pursuit**[12] 2763 6-9-2 70 RLMoore 5 77
(JMBradley) *hld up: hdwy over 1f out: hung lft and led wl ins fnl f* **7/2**[2]
1631 **2** ½ **Dizzy In The Head**[3] 3010 5-9-3 67 (b) NChalmers(5) 3 82
(PaulJohnson) *led 5f out: rdn over 1f out: hdd wl ins fnl f* **10/3**[1]
0011 **3** ½ **Hard To Catch (IRE)**[13] 2724 6-9-4 77 (b) MSavage(5) 2 81
(DKIvory) *chsd ldrs: rdn over 1f out: r.o* **7/2**[2]
10-2 **4** ¾ **Sweet Pickle**[23] 2444 3-8-3 70 TPQueally(3) 4 69
(DJCoakley) *s.i.s: sn chsng ldrs: rdn over 1f out: styd on same pce ins fnl f* **4/1**[3]
5-06 **5** 1½ **Compton Banker (IRE)**[9] 2834 7-9-2 70 (v) EAhern 1 67
(GAButler) *dwlt: hld up: hdwy and n.m.r over 1f out: styd on same pce* **6/1**
0106 **6** 2 **Byo (IRE)**[8] 2873 6-9-3 71 NPollard 6 62
(MQuinn) *led 1f: chsd ldr: rdn and edgd rt over 1f out: wknd ins fnl f* **12/1**
0060 **7** 8 **Speedfit Free (IRE)**[17] 2625 7-9-2 46 (p) AnnStokell 7 37
(MissAStokell) *chsd ldrs: sn drvn along: bhd fr 1/2-way* **100/1**

69.68 secs (-2.62) **Going Correction** -0.175s/f (Firm) course record
**WFA** 3 from 4yo+ 7lb **7** Ran **SP%** **110.5**
Speed ratings: **110,109,108,107,105 103,92**CSF £14.46 TOTE £4.70: £2.20, £2.20; EX 17.10.
**Owner** J M Bradley **Bred** J K Keegan **Trained** Sedbury, Gloucs

**FOCUS**
A smart time for the grade, even allowing for the conditions, and a course record.
**NOTEBOOK**
**Parkside Pursuit** took advantage of the drop in class, and proved well suited to this strongly-run contest. Despite having had plenty of racing, he looks as good as ever and should continue to give a good account for the time being
**Dizzy In The Head** took advantage of his low draw and soon got across to the rails, with the pair on his inside unable to go the early pace. He looked to run just as well as he ever he has.
**Hard To Catch(IRE)** looked to run his race despite not appearing to handle the bend as well as he might.
**Sweet Pickle** may be better when she is able to dominate.
**Compton Banker(IRE)** could not take advantage of the drop in class, but there were more encouraging signs here than of late.

## 3126 EVENING TELEGRAPH 1ST FOR JOBS H'CAP 5f
**3:30** (3:32) (E) (0-75,73) 3-Y-0+ **£4,273** (£1,315; £657; £328) **Stalls** Low

Form RPR
-011 **1** **Foley Millennium (IRE)**[8] 2869 6-8-12 **59** NPollard 13 67
(MQuinn) *chsd ldr: rdn to ld 1f out: all out* **7/1**[1]
0436 **2** *hd* **Law Maker**[1] 3084 4-7-13 **46** (v) JBramhill 15 53
(MABuckley) *a.p: rdn over 1f out: r.o* **16/1**
0000 **3** *shd* **Blessed Place**[6] 2943 4-7-9 **45** JFMcDonald(3) 2 52
(DJSFfrenchDavis) *chsd ldrs: rdn over 1f out: r.o* **66/1**
-000 **4** ¾ **Loch Inch**[13] 2724 7-8-4 **51** (b) EAhern 3 55
(JMBradley) *s.i.s: hdwy 1/2-way: rdn over 1f out: r.o* **25/1**
3664 **5** *hd* **Pulse**[13] 2724 6-9-0 **61** (p) RLMoore 17 64
(JMBradley) *hld up: hdwy over 1f out: r.o: nt rch ldrs* **15/2**[2]
1230 **6** *hd* **Justalord**[85] 1131 6-9-6 **67** (p) JEdmunds 4 69
(JBalding) *mde most 4f: no ex towards fin* **8/1**[3]
-000 **7** *hd* **Izmail (IRE)**[22] 2490 5-9-5 **66** SWhitworth 6 67
(DNicholls) *s.i.s: sn chsng ldrs: rdn over 1f out: styd on* **9/1**
0000 **8** *nk* **Safranine (IRE)**[1] 3098 7-9-2 **63** (p) AnnStokell 8 63
(MissAStokell) *hmpd s: outpcd: r.o ins fnl f: nvr nrr* **25/1**
-540 **9** 1 **Yorkies Boy**[8] 2885 9-8-6 **53** CCatlin 10 49
(JMBradley) *bhd: hdwy fnl f: nvr nrr* **14/1**
0136 **10** *hd* **Guns Blazing**[23] 2440 5-8-12 **66** (b) MHoward(7) 14 61
(DKIvory) *chsd ldrs: rdn over 1f out: no ex* **14/1**
00-0 **11** ¾ **Intellibet One**[16] 2656 4-8-10 **57** SDrowne 5 49
(PDEvans) *chsd ldrs: rdn over 1f out: styd on same pce* **50/1**
0020 **12** *nk* **Indian Bazaar (IRE)**[1] 3084 8-8-1 **53** ow2 NChalmers(5) 12 44
(NEBerry) *mid-div: sn pushed along: nvr trbld ldrs* **16/1**
5300 **13** 2 **Lady Pekan**[7] 2909 5-9-1 **62** (b) TGMcLaughlin 1 45
(PSMcentee) *chsd ldrs: rdn over 1f out: wknd towards fin* **12/1**
0002 **14** *nk* **One Last Time**[33] 2219 4-9-0 **61** RFfrench 9 43
(RBastiman) *outpcd: nvr nrr* **7/1**[1]
0-02 **15** *nk* **Sholto**[13] 2734 6-8-10 **64** (b) JDO'Reilly(7) 11 45
(JO'Reilly) *chsd ldrs: hrd rdn and wknd over 1f out* **9/1**
60-0 **16** 4 **College Hippie**[11] 2778 5-7-7 **47** ow2 (p) CHaddon(7) 16 12
(JFCoupland) *s.s: outpcd* **40/1**
0500 **17** 3½ **Chico Guapo (IRE)**[12] 2754 4-9-12 **73** (b[1]) RHughes 7 24
(JAGlover) *wnt rt s: sn prom: n.m.r and lost pl 4f out: wknd and eased fnl f* **8/1**[3]

58.72 secs (-1.48) **Going Correction** -0.20s/f (Firm) **17** Ran **SP%** **125.4**
Speed ratings: **103,102,102,101,101 100,100,99,98,97 96,96,93,92,92 85,80**CSF £114.61 CT £6976.44 TOTE £9.00: £2.60, £5.40, £13.10, £5.10; EX 251.80.
**Owner** Mrs S G Davies **Bred** Elperefa Bloodstock **Trained** Sparsholt, Oxon
■ Stewards Enquiry : J D O'Reilly two-day ban: careless riding (Jul 1,2)

**FOCUS**
This was quite a competitive low-grade sprint, run at a good pace. Although the winner and runner-up had high draws it would be wrong to assume that it was beneficial, as neither raced that wide.
**NOTEBOOK**
**Foley Millennium(IRE)**, 14lb higher than when starting his winning streak, is still well treated on his juvenile form.
**Law Maker** is well exposed, but this looked as good an effort as he has produced, and showed all is not lost with him yet.
**Blessed Place** is not the most consistent animal in training but, he does have a little ability and is certainly at the right end of the handicap to find an opening.
**Loch Inch** turned in a sound effort considering he missed a beat at the start, although it is worth noting that he has never won before August.
**Pulse** was done no favours by his wide draw and in the circumstances turned in a solid effort. He is one to keep an eye on in a similar contest, granted a decent box.
**Justalord** showed his customary early pace, but he could never shaken off his pursuers. While he is not as good on turf as he is on the All-Weather, his natural speed should ensure he continues to give a good account at this level.
**One Last Time**, having his first run over the minimum trip since his juvenile days, was soon taken off his legs. He had showed enough last time to suggest he retains some ability, and is one to keep an eye on back over an extra furlong.
**College Hippie** *Official explanation: trainer said mare missed the break*
**Chico Guapo(IRE)** *Official explanation: jockey said gelding slipped out of the stalls and cut himself*

## 3127 EVENING TELEGRAPH CUP H'CAP 1m 22y
**4:00** (4:02) (D ) (0-80,80) 3-Y-0+ **£5,876** (£1,808; £904; £452) **Stalls** Low

Form RPR
-020 **1** **Wind Chime (IRE)**[98] 1019 7-8-9 **64** LPKeniry(3) 1 72
(AGNewcombe) *a.p: rdn over 1f out: r.o to ld wl ins fnl f* **9/1**
-410 **2** ¾ **Tiber Tiger (IRE)**[21] 2504 4-9-11 **80** (b) J-PGuillambert(3) 7 86
(NPLittmoden) *hld up in tch: rdn over 1f out: edgd lft ins fnl f: r.o* **8/1**
0062 **3** *hd* **Answered Promise (FR)**[137] 672 5-8-3 **55** ow1 PDoe 2 61
(IAWood) *led 7f out: rdn clr over 1f out: hdd wl ins fnl f* **20/1**
-003 **4** *nk* **Adobe**[6] 2945 9-8-10 **67** MSavage(5) 12 72
(WMBrisbourne) *hld up: hung lft 2f out: hdwy over 1f out: r.o* **9/1**
6-23 **5** ¾ **Analyze (FR)**[10] 2304 6-9-7 **73** RLMoore 11 76
(BGPowell) *hld up: hdwy and nt clr run over 1f out: r.o* **15/2**[3]
0201 **6** 2½ **Pawan (IRE)**[6] 2941 4-9-3 **69** 6ex AnnStokell 8 67
(MissAStokell) *chsd ldr: rdn over 2f out: wknd ins fnl f* **11/1**
2304 **7** ¾ **Balerno**[8] 2886 5-7-13 **51** ow1 CCatlin 10 47
(RIngram) *hld up: styd on ins fnl f: nvr nrr* **9/1**
203 **8** 1 **Zafarshah (IRE)**[16] 2646 5-8-11 **63** SDrowne 4 57
(PDEvans) *chsd ldrs: rdn over 2f out: wknd over 1f out* **9/2**[2]
5406 **9** *nk* **Muqtadi (IRE)**[24] 2426 6-7-9 **50** oh6 JFMcDonald(3) 13 43
(MQuinn) *hld up: n.d* **18/1**
0601 **10** ¾ **Prince Of Gold**[11] 2776 4-9-1 **67** (p) RHughes 6 58
(RHollinshead) *led 1f: remained handy tl wknd over 1f out* **4/1**[1]
0050 **11** ¾ **Hoh's Back**[4] 2990 5-8-3 **60** (p) NChalmers(5) 9 49
(PaulJohnson) *hld up: rdn over 3f out: a in rr* **16/1**

1m 37.78s (-1.52) **Going Correction** -0.175s/f (Firm) **11** Ran **SP%** **115.3**
Speed ratings: **100,99,99,98,98 95,94,93,93,92 91**CSF £77.52 CT £1401.20 TOTE £10.80: £4.40, £2.80, £4.20; EX 69.40.
**Owner** M K F Seymour **Bred** Saeed Manana **Trained** Yarnscombe, Devon

**FOCUS**
They didn't go much of a gallop here, which resulted in a modest winning time.
**NOTEBOOK**
**Wind Chime(IRE)**, 1lb lower than when landing this last year, won a shade more cosily than the verdict suggeted.
**Tiber Tiger(IRE)** put behind him a poor effort at Doncaster last time and did not shirk the issue.
**Answered Promise(FR)** had something of an easy lead, but nonetheless turned in a sound effort on this return to action.
**Adobe** ◆ had his favoured ground, but lack of a decent pace was his undoing. He is well treated on the best of his form and, granted a strongly run race, can get back to winning ways.
**Analyze(FR)** ◆, who stays further than this, was not suited to the slow early pace, but still showed enough to suggest he will not be long in winning.
**Zafarshah(IRE)** *Official explanation: jockey said gelding was unsuited by the firm/good to firm ground*
**Prince Of Gold** was somewhat disappointing and may have found the ground faster than he likes.

## 3128 EVENING TELEGRAPH DRIVETIME H'CAP 1m 4f 134y
**4:30** (4:30) (E ) (0-75,72) 3-Y-0+ **£4,192** (£1,290; £645; £322) **Stalls** Low

Form RPR
3246 **1** **Compton Eclaire (IRE)**[20] 2514 4-8-7 **54** (v) EAhern 4 63
(GAButler) *hld up: hdwy over 2f out: edgd lft ins fnl f: r.o to ld nr fin* **10/1**
2405 **2** *hd* **Theatre Tinka (IRE)**[55] 1677 5-8-9 **56** (p) RHughes 2 65
(RHollinshead) *led: hdd over 5f out: rallied to ld 1f out: hdd nr fin* **20/1**
4122 **3** 1½ **Banningham Blaze**[23] 2443 4-7-12 **50** RThomas(5) 6 56
(AWCarroll) *hld up: hdwy over 1f out: r.o* **6/1**[3]
5232 **4** ½ **Bakiri (IRE)**[5] 2964 6-8-6 **60** RoryMoore(7) 3 66
(AndrewReid) *chsd ldrs: rdn to ld over 1f out: sn hdd: styd on same pce* **7/2**[1]
5034 **5** ½ **Most-Saucy**[12] 2767 8-8-9 **59** TPQueally(3) 11 64
(IAWood) *hld up: hdwy over 1f out: nt rch ldrs* **11/2**[2]
40-0 **6** 1½ **Tasneef (USA)**[23] 2449 5-8-10 **60** J-PGuillambert(3) 8 63
(TDMccarthy) *hld up: hdwy 1/2-way: led over 5f out: rdn and hdd over 1f out: wknd ins fnl f* **22/1**
4005 **7** ½ **Gallant Boy (IRE)**[12] 2752 5-9-4 **72** (vt) SJDonohoe(7) 1 74
(PDEvans) *prom: rdn over 2f out: styd on same pce appr fnl f* **7/1**
0-04 **8** ¾ **Red River Rebel**[23] 2449 6-8-8 **55** FNorton 7 56
(JRNorton) *chsd ldr: rdn over 2f out: wknd fnl f* **11/2**[2]
0-06 **9** 2 **Milk And Sultana**[9] 2835 4-8-7 **54** ow1 SDrowne 5 52
(GAHam) *hld up in tch: rdn over 2f out: wknd over 1f out* **25/1**
2114 **10** *nk* **Arms Acrossthesea**[19] 2547 5-9-0 **61** JEdmunds 9 58
(JBalding) *hld up: plld hrd: rdn over 2f out: a in rr* **9/1**
116- **11** 3 **Celtic Star (IRE)**[34] 4443 6-8-13 **63** (p) DNolan(3) 10 56
(MissKMGeorge) *hld up: rdn over 2f out: a in rr* **16/1**

2m 41.99s (-1.31) **Going Correction** -0.175s/f (Firm) **11** Ran **SP%** **117.7**
Speed ratings: **97,96,95,95,95 94,94,93,92,92 90**CSF £194.64 CT £1308.79 TOTE £10.60: £3.10, £5.80, £1.60; EX 90.40.
**Owner** Erik Penser **Bred** Declan And Catherine Macpartlin **Trained** Blewbury, Oxon

**FOCUS**
A poor contest and a moderate winning time.
**NOTEBOOK**
**Compton Eclaire(IRE)** is none too reliable, but she did not do anything wrong and looked to run somewhere near her best.
**Theatre Tinka(IRE)** had plenty of use made of him and it looked like paying off, until mugged in the shadow of the post. While he is not the most talented of animals, his heart is in the right place and should be capable of scoring at this level.
**Banningham Blaze** is running well at present and again ran to somewhere near her best.
**Bakiri(IRE)** had no excuses, he just was not good enough.
**Most-Saucy** had plenty to do turning for home and did well to finish as close as she did.
**Tasneef(USA)** looked to do too much, too soon, and did not get home as a consequence. However, he does look to be coming back to some sort of form.

## 3129 WATCH RACING UK LIVE ON 425 MAIDEN STKS 1m 2f 188y
**5:00** (5:00) (D) 3-Y-0+ **£3,818** (£1,175; £587; £293) **Stalls** Low

Form RPR
5-43 **1** **On Every Street**[16] 2645 3-8-13 72 (vt) WRyan 2 76
(HRACecil) *a.p: chsd ldr 4f out: rdn to ld wl ins fnl f* **5/1**[3]
3204 **2** ¾ **Beauchamp Star**[7] 2906 3-8-8 72 (b[1]) EAhern 5 70
(GAButler) *led: rdn over 1f out: hdd wl ins fnl f* **11/4**[2]

24 **3** *3* **Line Drawing**[8] 2888 3-8-13 ................................ RHughes 4 70
(BWHills) *hld up: hdwy 3f out: rdn and swished tail over 1f out: nt run on* **5/6**[1]

**4** *5* **Dafina (IRE)**[233] 5862 4-9-7 ................................ SDrowne 6 56
(HMorrison) *chsd ldr 7f: wknd 3 out* **9/1**

0046 **5** *16* **Celtic Vision (IRE)**[21] 2004 8-9-12 45 ................................(tp) SRighton 7 34
(MAppleby) *s.s: awlays bhd* **100/1**

2m 17.05s (-2.35) **Going Correction** -0.175s/f (Firm)
**WFA** 3 from 4yo+ 13lb **5** Ran SP% **108.9**
Speed ratings: **101,100,98,94,83**CSF £18.38 TOTE £7.20: £2.40, £1.50; EX 19.10 Place 6 £1,904.67, Place 5 £787.97..
**Owner** Colin Davey Racing **Bred** Genesis Green Stud Ltd **Trained** Newmarket, Suffolk

**FOCUS**
Not a strong maiden, but the pace looked fair.

**NOTEBOOK**
**On Every Street**, fitted with a tongue-strap for the first time, showed a nice turn of foot to wear down the long-time leader.
**Beauchamp Star**, fitted with a pair of blinkers after appearing not to go through with her effort last time, did nothing wrong and appeared well suited to the forcing tactics employed.
**Line Drawing** did not look that keen when push came to shove and one is to have reservations about. *Official explanation: jockey said mare hung right-handed in the early stages*
**Dafina(IRE)** had shown promise in a couple of maidens in Ireland, but did not exactly show a great deal. However, she may not have been entirely suited to this fast ground. *Official explanation: jockey said filly did not come round the last bend*
T/Plt: £2,485.00 to a £1 stake. Pool: £38,126.20. 11.20 winning tickets. T/Qpdt: £468.10 to a £1 stake. Pool: £2,720.40. 4.30 winning tickets. CR

3130 - 3133a (Foreign Racing) - See Raceform Interactive

# DORTMUND (R-H)
Sunday, June 20

**OFFICIAL GOING: Good**

## 3134a GROSSER PREIS DER WIRTSCHAFT (GROUP 3) 1m 165y
5:00 (5:20) 3-Y-0+ **£22,535** (£9,155; £4,577; £2,465)

RPR

**1** **Tahreeb (FR)**[22] 2476 3-8-2 ................................ WSupple 8 110
(MPTregoning) *chased leader til led just over 2f out, ran on well* 1

**2** *1 ¼* **Anolitas (GER)** 4-8-13 ................................(b) IFerguson 10 108
(UOstmann, Germany) *in touch, close 6th straight, ran on strongly to go 2nd 1f out, no chance with winner*

**3** *1 ¼* **Morbidezza (GER)**[36] 2138 4-8-11 ................................ LHammer-Hansen 3 103
(MTrinker, Germany) *mid-division, 7th straight, finished well to go 3rd final 50 yards*

**4** *¾* **Near Dock (GER)** 3-8-6 ow2................................ SChin 2 108
(PSchiergen, Germany) *raced in 3rd, went 2nd 2f out, one pace from 1f out* 2

**5** *1 ¼* **Roxagu (GER)**[260] 3-8-2 ................................ NRichter 7 101
(UStoltefuss, Germany) *prominent, 4th straight, kept on at one pace*

**6** *1 ¼* **Moon Over Miami (GER)** 3-8-2 ................................ AGoritz 1 99
(FrauEMader, Germany) *mid-division, 5th straight, no extra final stages*

**7** *½* **Rajpute (GER)**[50] 4-8-13 ................................ ABest 4 98
(DrABolte, Germany) *held up in rear, some late progress*

**8** *1 ¼* **Willingly (GER)**[273] 5109 5-8-13 ................................ FilipMinarik 9 96
(MTrybuhl) *held up, ran on from over 2f out but never dangerous*

**9** *5* **Blomquist (GER)**[355] 5-8-13 ................................ AStarke 11 86
(ASchutz, Germany) *in rear, never a factor* 3

**10** *10* **New Princess (GER)**[77] 5-8-11 ................................ SNemeth 5 65
(HHorwart, Germany) *always towards rear*

**11** *8* **Skythe (GER)**[294] 4608 4-8-13 ................................(b) THellier 6 52
(ASchutz, Germany) *led to straight, weakened quickly when headed just over 2f out*

1m 47.14s
**WFA** 3 from 4yo+ 11lb **11** Ran SP% **131.3**
Speed ratings: .
**Owner** Sheikh Ahmed Al Maktoum **Bred** S C E A Haras De Bois Carrouges **Trained** Lambourn, Berks

**NOTEBOOK**
**Tahreeb(FR)** broke his Group Race duck in convincing fashion and will probably bid to follow up in a similar continental contest.

# 2607 SAN SIRO (R-H)
Sunday, June 20

**OFFICIAL GOING: Good**

## 3135a PREMIO D'ESTATE (LISTED) 1m
3:50 (3:54) 3-Y-0 **£24,648** (£10,845; £5,915; £2,958)

RPR

**1** **Golden Wild**[323] 3820 3-8-11 ................................ DVargiu 1 —
(GFratini, Italy)

**2** *1 ¼* **Bipop (ITY)**[350] 3043 3-8-11 ................................ MTellini 3 —
(PPaciello, Italy)

**3** *1 ½* **Sogna Di Me** 3-8-8 ................................ SMulas 8 —
(BGrizzetti, Italy)

**4** *½* **Gioco Pericoloso (IRE)** 3-9-0 ................................ MEsposito 5 —
(MGasparini, Italy)

**5** *1 ¼* **Pippo Di Lucilla (IRE)**[50] 1777 3-8-11 ................................ CFiocchi 6 —
(MariaRitaSalvioni, Italy)

**6** *14* **Panshir (FR)**[11] 2790 3-8-11 ................................ PRobinson 7 —
(CFWall) *held up in rear, badly hampered by the fallers before half-way, no chance after SP 2.83-1* 1

**B** **Sfilzatore (ITY)** 3-8-11 ................................(b) IRossi 4 —
(A&GBotti, Italy)

**F** **Danzero Con Te** 3-8-11 ................................ MDemuro 2 —
(BGrizzetti, Italy)

1m 40.7s **8** Ran SP% **26.3**
Speed ratings: .
**Owner** Scuderia Golden Horse **Bred** Paul L Coe **Trained** Italy

**NOTEBOOK**
**Panshir(FR)** lost all chance when caught up in a melee and doing well to keep his feet after three furlongs.

## 3136a GRAN PREMIO DI MILANO (GROUP 1) 1m 4f
4:20 (4:31) 3-Y-0+ **£177,042** (£89,120; £51,901; £25,951)

RPR

**1** **Senex (GER)**[21] 2508 4-9-6 ................................ WMongil 1 117
(HBlume, Germany) *held up in rear, last straight, headway over 2f out, challenged 1 1/2f out, led 1f out, ridden out* **169/10**

**2** *2 ½* **Maktub (ITY)**[38] 2067 5-9-6 ................................ PRobinson 4 113
(MAJarvis) *set good pace, quickened over 4f out, headed 1f out, ran on same pace* **101/10**

**3** *1* **The Great Gatsby (IRE)**[357] 2832 4-9-6 ................................ JFortune 5 112
(JHMGosden) *tracked leader to straight, pushed along 4f out, hard ridden and every chance 1 1/2f out, no extra final furlong* **24/10**[2]

**4** *2* **Altieri**[35] 2155 6-9-6 ................................ MEsposito 3 109
(VCaruso, Italy) *held up, 5th straight, headway over 3f out, one pace final 2f* **16/10**[1]

**5** *1 ½* **Sa Fem Zifulum (IRE)**[21] 2510 3-8-6 ................................ DPorcu 2 107
(LCamici, Italy) *raced in 3rd, 6th straight, beaten 2f out* **44/1**

**6** *1* **Simonas (IRE)**[21] 2509 5-9-6 ................................ EPedroza 7 105
(AWohler, Germany) *raced in 4th, 3rd straight, ridden and no extra from 2f out* **46/10**

**7** *nk* **Groom Tesse**[21] 2510 3-8-6 ................................(b) DVargiu 6 105
(LCamici, Italy) *disputed 5th to 5f out, 4th straight, ridden 3f out, never a factor* **26/10**[3]

2m 28.7s
**WFA** 3 from 4yo+ 14lb **7** Ran SP% **130.3**
Speed ratings: .
**Owner** Stall Meerbusch **Bred** H Greis **Trained** Germany

**NOTEBOOK**
**Senex(GER)** had won nothing more than a maiden in 13 career starts, despite showing a decent level of form. Coming from last on the home turn, he quickened up well.
**Maktub(ITY)** ran much better than of late, back on a course where he has always run well. Setting an even pace, he repelled the challenge of The Great Gatsby at the furlong pole but had no answer to the winner's late thrust.
**The Great Gatsby(IRE)**, running for the first time since the 2003 Irish Derby and for a new yard, probably led for a few strides a furlong and a half out before his lack of fitness told. He should be all the better for the run.
**Altieri** is more at home over a mile and a quarter, but still found disappointingly little when asked for his effort two furlongs out. He hit the running rail and lost a shoe on the home bend so this run may be best forgotten.

## 3137a PREMIO MARIO INCISA (GROUP 3) (F&M) 1m 4f
4:50 (5:07) 3-Y-0+ **£37,254** (£17,025; £9,472; £4,736)

RPR

**1** **Vale Mantovani**[21] 2509 4-9-5 ................................ MEsposito 8 101
(VCaruso, Italy) *tracked leader, challenged 3f out, led 2f out, ran on well* 3

**2** *1 ½* **Deva (GER)**[36] 2138 5-9-5 ................................ KKerekes 5 99+
(DRonge, Germany) *held up in rear, last straight, tried to get through on rails 3f out, soon switched to outside, ran on well final 2f to tak* 1

**3** *hd* **Landinium (ITY)**[18] 2607 5-9-5 ................................ CColombi 7 99
(Waliani, Italy) *held up, 8th straight, headway on outside over 2f out, lost 2nd last strides* 2

**4** *nk* **Loriana (IRE)**[28] 2341 3-8-5 ................................ DVargiu 3 98
(RBrogi, Italy) *prominent, 5th straight, every chance on inside 2f out, stayed on but not quicken from over 1f out*

**5** *1 ½* **Holy Moon (IRE)**[36] 2138 4-9-5 ................................ EBotti 9 96
(A&GBotti, Italy) *mid-division, 3rd straight, switched out over 1f out, chased winner final furlong, no extra close home*

**6** *6* **Wigman (USA)**[36] 2138 4-9-5 ................................ MMonteriso 4 87
(Waliani, Italy) *4th straight, one pace final 2f*

**7** *1 ¾* **Musical Score**[18] 2607 5-9-5 ................................ EPedrota 1 84
(MGonnelli, Italy) *mid-division to straight, behind from over 2f out*

**8** *8* **Supereva (IRE)**[36] 2138 4-9-5 ................................ MTellini 2 72
(BGrizzetti, Italy) *led to 2f out*

**9** *3* **Dan Grey (IRE)**[36] 2138 4-9-5 ................................ MDemuro 6 68
(BGrizzetti, Italy) *held up, 7th straight, never a factor*

2m 35.5s
**WFA** 3 from 4yo+ 14lb **9** Ran SP% **133.7**
Speed ratings: .
**Owner** Scuderia Miragrigna **Bred** Scuderia Antonella Srl **Trained** Italy

# 2831 CHEPSTOW (L-H)
Monday, June 21

**OFFICIAL GOING: Good to firm**
Wind: nil Weather: showers and sunny spells

## 3138 VELINDRE HOSPITAL RACE NIGHT MAIDEN STKS 1m 4f 23y
6:50 (6:55) (D) 3-Y-0+ **£3,614** (£1,112; £556; £278) **Stalls** Low

Form RPR

5 **1** **Light Wind**[50] 1800 3-8-7 ................................ WSupple 2 81+
(MrsAJPerrett) *s.i.s: sn prom: led over 2f out: r.o wl* **15/8**[2]

**2** *2 ½* **Jayer Gilles** 4-9-12 ................................ DaneO'Neill 3 82
(HCandy) *s.i.s: hld up and bhd: rdn over 5f out: hdwy over 3f out: chsd wnr over 1f out: no imp* **16/1**

33 **3** *6* **At Your Request**[60] 1561 3-8-12 ................................ MHills 8 72
(EALDunlop) *prom: led over 7f out: rdn and hdd over 2f out: wknd over 1f out* **10/1**[3]

4 **4** *1 ¾* **Pope's Hill (IRE)**[31] 2273 3-8-12 ................................ LDettori 5 69
(LMCumani) *hld up: rdn over 5f out: hdwy over 4f out: wknd over 2f out* **4/5**[1]

4 **5** *19* **Uncle Batty**[21] 2520 4-9-9 ................................ SHitchcott(3) 7 39
(GJSmith) *hld up: hdwy over 7f out: rdn over 4f out: wknd over 3f out* **50/1**

04 **6** *10* **Delfinia**[10] 2832 3-8-4 ................................ TPQueally(3) 1 18
(HSHowe) *prom: rdn over 4f out: wknd over 3f out* **33/1**

000/ **7** *21* **Shannon's Dream**[564] 796 8-9-4 18................................ LisaJones(3) 6 —
(PWHiatt) *prom early: sn lost pl: dropped rr 7f out: t.o fnl 5f* **100/1**

0-5 **8** *13* **Fred's First**[24] 2454 3-8-12 ................................ CCatlin 4 —
(BPalling) *led: hdd over 7f out: wknd qckly: t.o fnl 5f* **100/1**

2m 38.48s (-0.02) **Going Correction** +0.025s/f (Good)
**WFA** 3 from 4yo+ 14lb **8** Ran SP% **112.2**
Speed ratings: **101,99,95,94,81 74,60,52**CSF £27.64 TOTE £2.70: £1.10, £3.60, £1.30; EX 30.30.

**Owner** Hesmonds Stud **Bred** Hesmonds Stud Ltd **Trained** Pulborough, W Sussex

**FOCUS**

A weak maiden, devalued by the poor showing of the odds-on favourite, but the first two were clear.

**NOTEBOOK**

**Light Wind** had no problem with this faster ground and ran out a fairly comfortable winner of what was admittedly a weak maiden. There should be more to come from her.

**Jayer Gilles**, whose dam was a winning staying hurdler, is a half-brother to Sergeant Cecil who was successful over a mile and six. He came from a good way off the pace to chase home the winner and, having showed signs of greenness, can be expected to improve when stepped up in trip.

**At Your Request**, having his third run, was tackling fast ground for the first time on this first start for two months.

**Pope's Hill(IRE)** was in trouble a good way out and never looked happy on this fast ground. The undulating track might not have suited him either.

**Uncle Batty**, who has left the Geoff Harker yard since his debut, failed to get home over this longer trip.

## 3139 EVERSHEDS SOLICITORS FILLIES' STKS (H'CAP) 1m 14y

**7:20** (7:21) (E) (0-75,75) 3-Y-O **£3,896** (£1,199; £599; £299) **Stalls** High

| Form | | | | RPR |
|---|---|---|---|---|
| 05-5 | **1** | | **Hot Lips Page (FR)**[12] 2788 3-9-1 **69** ........ DaneO'Neill 10<br>(RHannon) *hld up in tch: swtchd rt over 1f out: rdn to ld ins fnl f: r.o wl* **7/1** | 77+ |
| -552 | **2** | 1 3/4 | **Dami (USA)**[7] 2929 3-9-0 **68** ........ (p) BDoyle 8<br>(CEBrittain) *hld up and bhd: rdn and hdwy over 2f out: r.o wl ins fnl f: nt trble wnr* **10/3**[1] | 72+ |
| 51-4 | **3** | nk | **La Landonne**[75] 1303 3-9-0 **68** ........ SWKelly 2<br>(PMPhelan) *led: rdn over 2f out: edgd lft over 1f out: hdd ins fnl f: nt qckn* **16/1** | 71 |
| 0-06 | **4** | 1 3/4 | **Young Love**[26] 2401 3-8-1 **55** ........ CCatlin 4<br>(MissECLavelle) *a.p: rdn over 2f out: one pce* **16/1** | 54 |
| 0062 | **5** | hd | **Pella**[19] 2587 3-8-7 **61** ........ FNorton 1<br>(MBlanshard) *a.p: rdn over 3f out: one pce fnl 2f* **7/1** | 60 |
| 2610 | **6** | 2 | **Sunset Mirage (USA)**[10] 2847 3-9-2 **70** ........ WSupple 6<br>(EALDunlop) *hld up and bhd: plld out and hdwy over 2f out: sn rdn: one pce* **4/1**[2] | 64 |
| -442 | **7** | 5 | **Miss Adelaide (IRE)**[31] 2257 3-9-1 **69** ........ MHills 7<br>(BWHills) *hld up and bhd: hdwy on outside 3f out: sn rdn: wknd fnl f* **9/2**[3] | 52 |
| -063 | **8** | 3 1/2 | **Faraway Echo**[38] 2088 3-7-7 **52** oh2 ........ HayleyTurner(5) 9<br>(MLWBell) *hld up: rdn over 3f out: sn bhd* **12/1** | 27 |
| 060- | **9** | 5 | **Gone Loco**[290] 4705 3-7-9 **52** oh2 ........ LisaJones(3) 5<br>(HSHowe) *plld hrd: sn chsng ldr: rdn and wknd over 2f out* **25/1** | 15 |
| 6-02 | **10** | shd | **Vas Y Carla (USA)**[19] 2572 3-9-4 **75** ........ TPQueally(3) 3<br>(DRLoder) *s.i.s: hdwy over 4f out: rdn over 3f out: wknd over 2f out* **9/1** | 38 |

1m 34.67s (-1.23) **Going Correction** -0.075s/f (Good) **10 Ran SP% 119.6**

Speed ratings: **103,101,100,99,99 97,92,88,83,83**CSF £31.42 CT £378.19 TOTE £8.80: £2.90, £1.30, £5.70; EX 24.80.

**Owner** Bob Lalemant **Bred** Oostvlaamse Investering N V **Trained** East Everleigh, Wilts

**FOCUS**

A creditable time for the grade despite a modest early pace, but the form is ordinary.

**NOTEBOOK**

**Hot Lips Page(FR)** was drawn against the stands' rail, and just when O'Neill looked about to switch her off it a perfect gap opened up for her which she needed no second invitation to take. The extra furlong was ideal. *Official explanation: trainer's represenative had no explanation for the improved form shown*

**Dami(USA)** adopted different tactics on this occasion and, although she came home in good style, the winner had things under control by then.

**La Landonne** was on her toes in the paddock and went to post early. Dictating the pace, it looked at one stage as if she would make all but she came under pressure and edged away from the rail, allowing the eventual winner through. She has yet to run over seven furlongs but that could be her trip.

**Young Love** has begun life in handicaps on a lowly mark and this was a better effort.

**Pella**, raised 3lb for finishing second at Nottingham, lacked a change of gear and could need a step up to ten furlongs.

**Miss Adelaide(IRE)**, dropped in trip for her handicap debut, flattered only briefly with three to run.

**Vas Y Carla(USA)** *Official explanation: jockey said gelding was never travelling*

## 3140 TERRY JAYNE SCALLOPS (S) STKS 5f 16y

**7:50** (7:50) (G) 2-Y-O **£2,562** (£732; £366) **Stalls** High

| Form | | | | RPR |
|---|---|---|---|---|
| 5 | **1** | | **Royal Cozyfire (IRE)**[21] 2515 2-8-8 ........ SHitchcott(3) 2<br>(BPalling) *a.p: rdn over 2f out: led over 1f out: r.o wl* **9/2**[3] | 57 |
| 5634 | **2** | 3/4 | **Glasson Lodge**[7] 2946 2-8-6 ........ NCallan 10<br>(PDEvans) *wnt lft s: led 1f: prom: rdn over 3f out: kpt on ins fnl f* **2/1**[1] | 49 |
| | **3** | 1 | **Witty Girl** 2-8-1 ........ HayleyTurner(5) 3<br>(MDIUsher) *sn outpcd: hdwy whn swtchd lft ins fnl f: fin wl* **11/1** | 46 |
| 4630 | **4** | 1/2 | **Wizzskilad**[27] 2382 2-8-8 ........ LisaJones(3) 7<br>(MrsPNDutfield) *bmpd s: swtchd lft and hdwy over 2f out: sn rdn: r.o one pce fnl f* **9/4**[2] | 49 |
| 4 | **5** | hd | **Sapphire Princess**[14] 2725 2-8-3 ........ TPQueally(3) 6<br>(IAWood) *prom: rdn 3f out: outpcd over 1f out: kpt on towards fin* **9/1** | 43 |
| 5006 | **6** | 3/4 | **Zachy Boy**[7] 2946 2-8-4 ........ (p) DerekNolan(7) 9<br>(JSMoore) *carried lft s: led after 1f: rdn and hdd over 1f out: no ex ins fnl f* **12/1** | 45 |
| | **7** | 5 | **Fire At Will** 2-8-11 ........ WSupple 8<br>(AWCarroll) *s.i.s: outpcd* **12/1** | 28 |
| 050 | **8** | 1 | **Sabo Prince**[15] 2702 2-8-11 ........ DaneO'Neill 4<br>(JMBradley) *prom: rdn over 2f out: sn hung lft and wknd* **25/1** | 24 |
| 0 | **9** | 16 | **Angela's Girl**[15] 2702 2-8-6 ........ CCatlin 5<br>(JMBradley) *s.i.s: outpcd: t.o* **25/1** | — |

61.80 secs (2.30) **Going Correction** -0.075s/f (Good) **9 Ran SP% 123.7**

Speed ratings: **78,76,75,74,74 72,64,63,37**CSF £15.04 TOTE £7.00: £2.00, £1.20, £2.20; EX 19.20.There was no bid for the winner. Witty Girl was claimed by C. Dwyer for £6,000.

**Owner** Crosslee plc **Bred** Limestone And Tara Studs **Trained** Tredodridge, Vale Of Glamorgan

**FOCUS**

An average seller and a very slow winning time, even for a race like this.

**NOTEBOOK**

**Royal Cozyfire(IRE)** appreciated the drop in trip from his debut and duly improved past Glasson Lodge. Always in the front rank despite a low draw, he edged over to the stands' rail when in front.

**Glasson Lodge**, without the visor this time, was unable to cash in on the best draw. She has had plenty of chances.

**Witty Girl** ◆ could not go the early pace and was only sixth entering the final furlong but, after being switched around horses, she came home in taking style. Out of a mare who won a seven-furlong claimer as a juvenile, she is in need of a step up in trip and looks capable of winning in ordinary company for her new trainer Chris Dwyer.

**Wizzskilad**, an exposed perfomer, was found wanting on this drop into the bottom grade. *Official explanation: jockey said colt hung right-handed*

**Sapphire Princess**, who has more scope than most of these, looks in need of a sixth furlong.

**Zachy Boy**, in first-time cheekpieces, showed speed before fading.

## 3141 BETFRED SPRINT SERIES H'CAP (QUALIFIER) 6f 16y

**8:20** (8:20) (D) (0-80,76) 3-Y-O+ **£5,421** (£1,668; £834; £417) **Stalls** High

| Form | | | | RPR |
|---|---|---|---|---|
| 3203 | **1** | | **One Way Ticket**[9] 2873 4-8-10 **62** ........ (p) SWKelly 3<br>(JMBradley) *mde all: rdn over 1f out: r.o wl* **6/1** | 74 |
| 6463 | **2** | 2 1/2 | **Full Spate**[7] 2948 9-9-2 **68** ........ CCatlin 10<br>(JMBradley) *hld up: rdn over 2f out: hdwy over 1f out: r.o ins fnl f: nt trble wnr* **7/2**[2] | 73 |
| 2215 | **3** | nk | **Glencoe Solas (IRE)**[7] 2948 4-9-6 **72** ........ LDettori 7<br>(SKirk) *a.p: rdn over 2f out: kpt on same pce fnl f* **3/1**[1] | 76 |
| -406 | **4** | 1 3/4 | **Sewmuch Character**[16] 2673 5-8-13 **65** ........ NCallan 9<br>(MBlanshard) *hld up in tch: rdn over 1f out: one pce* **9/2**[3] | 64 |
| 0-00 | **5** | 4 | **Formalise**[13] 2763 4-8-10 **62** ........ FNorton 1<br>(GBBalding) *wnt lft s: hld up mid-div: rdn over 2f out: no hdwy* **9/1** | 49 |
| 00-0 | **6** | nk | **Golden Bounty**[56] 1673 5-9-9 **75** ........ PDobbs 5<br>(RHannon) *bhd: rdn over 2f out: n.d* **16/1** | 61 |
| -600 | **7** | 3/4 | **Among Friends (IRE)**[14] 2724 4-8-8 **63** ........ LisaJones(3) 2<br>(BPalling) *prom: rdn over 2f out: wknd 1f out* **25/1** | 47 |
| 2100 | **8** | 2 | **Boavista (IRE)**[9] 2875 4-8-7 **59** ........ JoannaBadger 8<br>(PDEvans) *w ldr: rdn over 2f out: wknd over 1f out* **16/1** | 37 |
| 0004 | **9** | 10 | **Currency**[12] 2784 7-9-10 **76** ........ DaneO'Neill 4<br>(JMBradley) *nvr gng wl: a in rr* **6/1** | 24 |

1m 10.8s (-1.40) **Going Correction** -0.075s/f (Good) **9 Ran SP% 119.6**

Speed ratings: **106,102,102,99,94 94,93,90,77**CSF £28.37 CT £77.54 TOTE £6.20: £2.40, £1.70, £1.60; EX 24.70.

**Owner** Saracen Racing **Bred** Woodsway Stud And Chao Racing And Bloodstock Ltd **Trained** Sedbury, Gloucs

**FOCUS**

An ordinary handicap but fair form, although the winner was allowed his own way out in front. The time was decent and the form looks sound.

**NOTEBOOK**

**One Way Ticket**, after crossing over from stall three to secure the stands'-rail berth, was allowed a soft lead and had the race in the bag before the furlong pole. He seemed to like being allowed his own way, but just how much he would have found had he needed to battle is questionable.

**Full Spate**, from the plum draw under the stands' fence, ran on in the latter stages but too late to trouble his stablemate.

**Glencoe Solas(IRE)**, 6lb higher than when winning at Doncaster earlier in the month, did not do anything wrong this time and there seemed no excuses.

**Sewmuch Character** was in second place passing the furlong pole but finished weakly. He might have done better going off in front from his favourable draw.

**Formalise** played up leaving the paddock and was reluctant to go to post. Certainly handicapped to win now, he could be worth a try over seven furlongs.

**Boavista(IRE)**, mounted on the course and taken early to post, showed up for over four furlongs before fading.

**Currency** *Official explanation: jockey said gelding lost its action*

## 3142 VELINDRE HOSPITAL CANCER RESEARCH MAIDEN FILLIES' STKS 1m 14y

**8:50** (8:50) (D) 3-Y-O **£3,731** (£1,148; £574; £287) **Stalls** High

| Form | | | | RPR |
|---|---|---|---|---|
| 33-4 | **1** | | **Game Dame**[11] 2805 3-8-11 78 ........ MHills 10<br>(BWHills) *hld up in tch: rdn 3f out: led 1f out: r.o* **3/1**[3] | 77 |
| 25-0 | **2** | 1 | **Powerful Parrish (USA)**[23] 2479 3-8-11 ........ SChin 11<br>(PFICole) *hld up mid-div: rdn and hdwy 2f out: swtchd lft ins fnl f: styd on: nt rch wnr* **20/1** | 74 |
| 5-2 | **3** | 1 | **Cantarna (IRE)**[17] 2654 3-8-11 76 ........ NCallan 1<br>(JMackie) *a.p: rdn over 2f out: ev ch over 1f out: nt qckn* **5/2**[2] | 72 |
| 2- | **4** | nk | **Strawberry Fair**[272] 5138 3-8-11 ........ LDettori 6<br>(SaeedBinSuroor) *led: rdn and hdd 1f out: one pce* **7/4**[1] | 71 |
| 32-5 | **5** | nk | **Cherubim (JPN)**[66] 1440 3-8-8 78 ........ TPQueally(3) 7<br>(DRLoder) *a.p: rdn over 3f out: one pce fnl 2f* **13/2** | 71 |
| 00 | **6** | 8 | **Cotton Easter**[21] 2517 3-8-11 ........ FNorton 2<br>(MrsAJBowlby) *s.i.s: bhd: sme hdwy over 2f out: sn no imp* **100/1** | 52 |
| 00 | **7** | 5 | **Palabelle (IRE)**[25] 2425 3-8-11 ........ BDoyle 9<br>(PWHarris) *bhd: short-lived effrt over 2f out* **25/1** | 41 |
| 50 | **8** | 2 1/2 | **Prelude**[17] 2647 3-8-11 ........ SWKelly 3<br>(WMBrisbourne) *a bhd* **50/1** | 35 |
| 0 | **9** | 3 1/2 | **Highlight Girl**[42] 2001 3-8-8 ........ SHitchcott(3) 8<br>(AWCarroll) *hld up mid-div: rdn over 3f out: bhd fnl 2f* **100/1** | 27 |
| 0-00 | **10** | 3 1/2 | **Ninah**[21] 2518 3-8-11 64 ........ CCatlin 4<br>(JMBradley) *plld hrd: chsd ldr: wknd 3f out* **50/1** | 19 |
| | **11** | 6 | **Way Out** 3-8-11 ........ MTebbutt 5<br>(BPJBaugh) *s.i.s: a wl bhd* **66/1** | 5 |

1m 35.2s (-0.70) **Going Correction** -0.075s/f (Good) **11 Ran SP% 119.3**

Speed ratings: **100,99,98,97,97 89,84,81,78,74 68**CSF £62.20 TOTE £3.30: £1.60, £3.00, £1.10; EX 24.60.

**Owner** Maktoum Al Maktoum **Bred** Gainsborough Stud Management Ltd **Trained** Lambourn, Berks

**FOCUS**

The first five came well clear in this routine fillies' maiden with several exposed performers close up. A high draw again proved an advantage.

**NOTEBOOK**

**Game Dame** was drawn near the rail but delivered her challenge some way off it. Resolute when it came down to a battle, she may struggle in handicaps off a mark in the 80s.

**Powerful Parrish(USA)**, well drawn, was the only one of the principals to come from off the pace and was only fifth passing the furlong pole. Likely to stay farther, she has a dirt pedigree and could be interesting on the All-Weather.

**Cantarna(IRE)** ran respectably but looks ready for a step up to ten furlongs.

**Strawberry Fair** had one run for David Loder as a juvenile. After tacking over to lead against the near rail, she stuck on when challenged but gave the impression that a drop to seven furlongs might suit.

**Cherubim(JPN)**, whose yard is going through a quiet spell, looks the sort to do better in handicaps over ten furlongs.

**Palabelle(IRE)** *Official explanation: jockey said filly was very unbalanced*

**Prelude** *Official explanation: jockey said filly had stumbled early on and had hung right-handed throughout*

## 3143 VELINDRE HOSPITAL H'CAP 1m 2f 36y

**9:20** (9:22) (E) (0-75,73) 3-Y-O+ **£3,750** (£1,154; £577; £288) **Stalls** Low

| Form | | | | RPR |
|---|---|---|---|---|
| 3612 | **1** | | **Realism (FR)**[10] 2835 4-9-1 **63** ........ LisaJones(3) 5<br>(PWHiatt) *chsd ldr: rdn to ld 2f out: drvn out* **11/4**[1] | 77 |

0-21 **2** 3/4 **Frontier**[13] [2752] 7-9-13 **72**..............(t) RHavlin 6 85
(BJLlewellyn) *a.p: ev ch over 1f out: sn rdn: nt qckn* **4/1**[3]

-003 **3** 5 **Billy Bathwick (IRE)**[10] [2835] 7-8-11 **56**..............DaneO'Neill 2 60
(JMBradley) *hld up in tch: rdn 2f out: wknd 1f out* **5/1**

0-41 **4** *shd* **Smart John**[31] [2272] 4-9-4 **63**..............SWKelly 9 66
(WMBrisbourne) *hld up: rdn 3f out: styd on same pce fnl f* **7/2**[2]

0000 **5** 1/2 **Sahaat**[37] [2116] 6-9-11 **73**..............TPQueally(3) 1 75
(JAOsborne) *hld up and bhd: hdwy 3f out: rdn and wknd over 1f out* **14/1**

0033 **6** *nk* **Rebate**[7] [2930] 4-9-3 **62**..............PDobbs 8 64
(RHannon) *led: rdn and hdd 2f out: wknd 1f out* **6/1**

-060 **7** 4 **Mr Dip**[49] [1845] 4-8-1 **53**..............CHaddon(7) 3 47
(AWCarroll) *plld hrd in rr: rdn over 2f out: no rspnse* **33/1**

044- **8** 12 **Zuleta**[233] [5877] 3-8-0 **57**..............FNorton 4 28
(MBlanshard) *bhd fnl 4f* **16/1**

2m 12.72s (3.12) **Going Correction** +0.025s/f (Good)
**WFA** 3 from 4yo+ 12lb **8** Ran SP% **115.3**
Speed ratings: **88,87,83,83,82 82,79,69**CSF £14.11 CT £51.49 TOTE £4.10: £1.50, £1.80, £1.30; EX 16.50 Place 6 £40.23, Place 5 £12.71.
**Owner** Miss Maria McKinney **Bred** Darley Stud Management Co Ltd **Trained** Hook Norton, Oxon

**FOCUS**
This was run at a steady pace until the winner went for home with two furlongs to run. The first two came clear but the form is ordinary. Wood Street (66/1) was withdrawn; refused to enter stalls.

**NOTEBOOK**
**Realism(FR)** ◆ paid a compliment to Tidal who slammed him over course and distance last time. After leading a quarter of a mile out he was immediately kicked for home, gaining valuable momentum running downhill into the dip and always holding the runner-up. He can score again over this trip.
**Frontier**, from a 3lb higher mark, travelled well, but the winner took first run and he was never quite going to peg him back. He finished clear of the rest and remains in good form.
**Billy Bathwick(IRE)** was weighted to reverse recent course placings with Realism, but was caught out when the tempo lifted with two to run and could never land a blow.
**Smart John**, who went up 3lb for his win at Haydock, tried to come from off the pace in a moderately-run race. He is worth another chance.
**Sahaat**, 11lb lower than at the start of the turf season, was going well enough when asked for his effort but could not quicken up. Connections appear unsure as to his optimum trip.
**Rebate**, who has been given a chance by the Handicapper, set only a moderate pace and had no answers when headed.
**Zuleta**, having her first run since November, became very warm in the preliminaries on what was a cool evening.
T/Plt: £41.50 to a £1 stake. Pool: £38,032.00. 667.40 winning tickets. T/Qpdt: £5.20 to a £1 stake. Pool: £2,648.70. 373.70 winning tickets. KH

## 2487 MUSSELBURGH (R-H)
Monday, June 21

**OFFICIAL GOING: Good to firm (firm in places)**

## 3144 RACING UK ON CHANNEL 425 (S) STKS 5f
**2:30** (2:31) (G) 2-Y-O **£2,877** (£822; £411) **Stalls** Low

Form RPR

6054 **1** **Our Louis**[5] [2980] 2-8-4 ow1..............TEaves(3) 7 51
(JSWainwright) *mde all: rdn wl over 1f out: kpt on fnl f* **16/1**

1254 **2** *nk* **Little Biscuit (IRE)**[10] [2858] 2-8-11..............DarrenWilliams 2 54
(KRBurke) *dwlt: sn chsng ldrs: n.m.r 1/2-way and wl over 1f out: rdn to chal ins last: sn drvn and kpt on* **6/5**[1]

300 **3** 1 1/2 **Almaty Express**[28] [2352] 2-8-11..............RWinston 4 52+
(MTodhunter) *hld up: hdwy whn n.m.r wl over 1f out: swtchd lft and hdwy ent last: rdn and kpt on: nrst fin* **9/4**[2]

5055 **4** 2 **Frisby Ridge (IRE)**[7] [2773] 2-8-6..............(b) DAllan 5 37
(TDEasterby) *cl up: rdn along 2f out: sn one pce* **16/1**

5050 **5** 1/2 **Voice Of An Angel (IRE)**[32] [2248] 2-7-13..............PPMathers(7) 6 35
(ABerry) *s.i.s: hdwy 1/2-way: sn rdn and kpt on same pce* **20/1**

P **6** 3/4 **Shatin Leader**[23] [2489] 2-8-6..............RFfrench 8 33
(MissLAPerratt) *wnt rt s: sn chsng ldrs: rdn 2f out and wknd over 1f out* **40/1**

23 **7** 5 **Songgaria**[7] [2946] 2-8-7 ow1..............GParkin 3 16
(JSWainwright) *sn outpcd and bhd* **11/2**[3]

000 **8** 3 **Boracay Beauty**[28] [2364] 2-8-3..............(b[1]) THamilton(3) 1 5
(JRWeymes) *c;lose up: rdn along 1/2-way: sn wknd* **66/1**

60.23 secs (-0.17) **Going Correction** -0.35s/f (Firm) **8** Ran SP% **112.1**
Speed ratings: **87,86,84,80,80 78,70,66**CSF £34.58 TOTE £18.40: £5.70, £1.02, £1.30; EX 45.10.There was no bid for the winner.
**Owner** Whitestonecliffe Racing Partnership **Bred** Mrs H Neshan **Trained** Kennythorpe, N Yorks

**FOCUS**
A modest time for this poor seller and it is unlikely to produce many future winners, although the second and third may be better than the bare result indicates.

**NOTEBOOK**
**Our Louis** found this rather easier than the novice event she ran in at Ripon the previous week, even though she has been beaten at this level before. Bouncing out of the gate from her wide draw, she showed good early speed and managed to keep enough in reserve to hold on. There was no interest in her at the auction.
**Little Biscuit(IRE)** did not see a great deal of daylight and only just failed to get up, but she does give the impression that an extra furlong and a slower surface suits her better now.
**Almaty Express** ◆, dropped into a seller for the first time, found the minimum trip on a fast surface much too sharp and can win in this grade under more suitable conditions.
**Frisby Ridge(IRE)**, with the blinkers back on, showed up for a while but looks exposed as very moderate.
**Songgaria**, who has now run three times for three different trainers, should have done much better based on her previous efforts, but she drifted alarmingly in the market and ran accordingly.

## 3145 WATCH RACING UK LIVE CHANNEL 425 NOVICE AUCTION STKS 7f 30y
**3:00** (3:00) (E) 2-Y-O **£3,987** (£1,227; £613; £306) **Stalls** Low

Form RPR

13 **1** **Society Music (IRE)**[24] [2447] 2-8-13..............FLynch 5 76
(MDods) *mde all: qcknd over 3f out: rdn wl over 1f out: edgd lft ins last: styd on wl* **3/1**[3]

262 **2** 1 **Forfeiter (USA)**[6] [2961] 2-8-12..............(b) RWinston 3 72
(TDBarron) *trcked ldr: hdwy to chal 3f out: rdn 2f out: drvn over 1f out and ev ch tl no ex wl ins last* **13/8**[1]

0 **3** 1/2 **Spinnakers Girl**[18] [2617] 2-8-0..............DFentiman(7) 4 66
(JRWeymes) *chsd ldrs: hdwy 3f out: riddedn 2f out: kpt on same pce appr last* **12/1**

514 **4** 14 **Indibraun (IRE)**[24] [2447] 2-9-4..............GFaulkner 1 42
(PCHaslam) *cl up: on outer: rdn along 3f out: drvn over 2f out and sn wknd* **7/4**[2]

000 **5** 25 **Countrywide Dream (IRE)**[4] [3009] 2-8-12..............(p) JCarroll 2 —
(ABerry) *outpcd and bhd fr 1/2-way* **66/1**

1m 28.45s (-1.08) **Going Correction** -0.35s/f (Firm) **5** Ran SP% **108.6**
Speed ratings: **92,90,90,74,45**CSF £8.08 TOTE £3.60: £2.40, £1.20; EX 5.30.
**Owner** M J K Dods **Bred** John Weld **Trained** Piercebridge, Co Durham

**FOCUS**
A fair pace, but an uncompetitive novice auction event and the order hardly changed throughout the contest. This is the winner's level.

**NOTEBOOK**
**Society Music(IRE)**, well beaten by a couple of fair sorts in a Pontefract conditions event last time, found this a much easier task. Given a positive ride over this longer trip, she always seemed to be holding the edge over the favourite and held on for a deserved victory. She did give the impression she was feeling the ground late on, and is probably better suited by an easier surface.
**Forfeiter(USA)** did not lead this time and every attempt to get past the filly was thwarted. He does not look to possess much in the way of a turn of foot and may always be best when able to dominate from the front.
**Spinnakers Girl** ◆ improved from her debut over this extra furlong and stayed right on the heels of the front pair all the way to the line. She was a cheap purchase, but there are winners on her dam's side and on this evidence she should be joining them.
**Indibraun(IRE)**, just behind Society Music at Pontefract last time, was meeting her on the same terms yet finished much further behind over this extra furlong and much of that was due to him hanging all over the track in the home straight. Despite winning on a sound surface, he may prefer easier ground.

## 3146 FORTH2 H'CAP 1m
**3:30** (3:31) (F) (0-55,53) 3-Y-O **£2,968** (£848; £424) **Stalls** Low

Form RPR

0-06 **1** **Cobalt Blue (IRE)**[16] [2688] 3-9-3 **50**..............(b) RWinston 1 55
(WJHaggas) *led: rdn along 3f out: hdd over 2f out: drvn: edgd rt and rallied to ld ins last: kpt on* **9/4**[1]

-616 **2** 3/4 **Son Of Thunder (IRE)**[4] [3007] 3-9-6 **53**..............DarrenWilliams 2 63+
(MDods) *i ntch: hdwy over 2f out: effrta nd nt clr run over 1f out: swtchd rt and hmpd ins last: swtchd lft and kpt on nr line* **11/4**[2]

1231 **3** *hd* **Roman The Park (IRE)**[28] [2349] 3-8-9 **42**..............DAllan 5 45
(TDEasterby) *trckd ldr: led over 2f out: sn rdn and edgd lft over 1f out: drvn and hdd ins last: no ex nr fin* **11/4**[2]

060- **4** 7 **A Monk Swimming (IRE)**[228] [5930] 3-8-2 **35**..............RFfrench 6 22
(JohnBerry) *trckd ldng pair: rdn along 3f out: wknd 2f out* **12/1**

00-0 **5** 3 **Polar Galaxy**[17] [2658] 3-9-3 **50**..............GFaulkner 4 30
(CWFairhurst) *hld up: hdwy 1/2-way: sn rdn along and nvr a factor* **25/1**

003 **6** 2 1/2 **Petrion**[11] [2815] 3-8-13 **46**..............CLowther 3 20
(RGuest) *a rr: bhd fr 1/2-way* **8/1**[3]

0-00 **7** 16 **Quintillion**[32] [2236] 3-8-8 **44**..............TEaves(3) 7 —
(TJEtherington) *a rr: bhd fr 1/2-way* **20/1**

1m 39.88s (-2.82) **Going Correction** -0.35s/f (Firm) **7** Ran SP% **111.5**
Speed ratings: **100,99,99,92,89 86,70**CSF £8.21 TOTE £2.80: £1.10, £2.30; EX 6.10.
**Owner** Peter S Jensen **Bred** Haras Du Gazon **Trained** Newmarket, Suffolk

**FOCUS**
A modest handicap, but a fair pace and a controversial outcome, with the runner-up unlucky.

**NOTEBOOK**
**Cobalt Blue(IRE)** seems to have improved in the blinkers and, even though he had never previously been placed, this was the weakest contest he had raced in. Making all the running, he faced a couple of serious challenges in the closing stages but, for one reason or another, managed to hold them off. This was an ordinary contest, but at least he should not go up too much. *Official explanation: trainer's representative had no explanation for the improved form shown other than that gelding may have benefited from the drop in class*
**Son Of Thunder(IRE)**, only 3lb higher than when winning over course and distance two outings ago, should have won this. He was travelling well behind the leaders over a furlong from home, but for some reason was switched to the inside and tried for an audacious gap between the winner and the rail which was always going to be tight. The gap closed and he was forced to snatch up, and then when switched left and finally seeing daylight, it was too late.
**Roman The Park(IRE)**, running in her first proper handicap, did little wrong but lacked a decisive turn of foot and probably found this sharp mile on quick ground an inadequate test.
**A Monk Swimming(IRE)**, making his handicap debut after three unplaced efforts at two and racing for the first time in seven months, showed up for a while until lack of a recent outing took its toll. He comes from a shrewd yard and this run should have brought him on, so it would be no surprise to see him improve a good deal on this.
**Polar Galaxy** was never in the race and looks exposed.
**Petrion**, making her handicap debut, improved when switched to Fibresand last time but did not maintain that progress back on turf. She may need a return to sand or easier ground, so should not be written off just yet.
**Quintillion** *Official explanation: trainer said gelding had a muscle problem, and was found to have been distressed after the race*

## 3147 RACING UK ON CHANNEL 425 FILLIES' H'CAP 5f
**4:00** (4:00) (E) (0-75,75) 3-Y-O+ **£4,026** (£1,239; £619; £309) **Stalls** Low

Form RPR

5040 **1** **Petana**[12] [2778] 4-7-5 **45** oh7..............(p) NataliaGemelova(7) 3 53
(MDods) *hld up: hdwy 1/2-way: rdn and qcknd to ld ins last: styd on* **20/1**

3100 **2** 1 1/4 **Scottish Exile (IRE)**[18] [2610] 3-9-1 **68**..............(v) DarrenWilliams 9 71
(KRBurke) *swtchd lft s: in tch: hdwy 2f out: sn rdn: styd on ins last: nrst fin* **14/1**

2632 **3** *nk* **Roxanne Mill**[8] [2912] 6-9-7 **75**..............CJDavies(7) 2 77
(JMBradley) *led: rdn and hung lft ent last: sn hdd and nt qckn* **1/1**[1]

0000 **4** *nk* **Mystery Pips**[12] [2778] 4-8-0 **47**..............(v) KimTinkler 1 48
(NTinkler) *cl up: ev ch 2f out: sn rdn and one pce appr last* **12/1**

-051 **5** 1/2 **Robwillcall**[5] [2975] 4-7-11 **51** 6ex..............(p) PPMathers(7) 7 50
(ABerry) *cl up: rdn along 2f out: drvn and one pce appr last* **9/1**

0-00 **6** 1/2 **Star Applause**[159] [530] 4-7-5 **45** oh11..............DFentiman(7) 4 42
(JSGoldie) *chsd ldrs: rdn along wl over 1f out: edgd lft and one pce appr last* **25/1**

5016 **7** *nk* **Pirlie Hill**[12] [2784] 4-8-8 **55**..............JCarroll 8 50
(MissLAPerratt) *sn outpcd and bhd: hdwy on outer 1/2-way: rdn and hung rt ins last* **8/1**[3]

6-00 **8** 5 **Gemini Girl (IRE)**[17] [2661] 3-7-12 **51** oh1..............PMQuinn 6 26
(MDHammond) *a outpcd and bhd* **33/1**

2602 **9** 3 **Inching**[2] [3084] 4-7-13 **46**..............DaleGibson 5 9
(RMHCowell) *cl up: rdn along 1/2-way: sn wknd* **5/1**[2]

59.04 secs (-1.36) **Going Correction** -0.35s/f (Firm)
**WFA** 3 from 4yo+ 6lb **9** Ran SP% **113.7**
Speed ratings: **96,94,93,93,92 91,90,82,78**CSF £258.37 CT £544.53 TOTE £23.50: £5.50, £4.30, £1.10; EX 485.80.
**Owner** The Four Aces **Bred** Red House Stud **Trained** Piercebridge, Co Durham

**FOCUS**
A modest fillies' handicap run at just a fair pace. The winner was getting off the mark at the 20th attempt which demonstrates the strength of the form.

**NOTEBOOK**
**Petana** finally got off the mark at the 20th attempt, but she had twice finished runner-up under today's rider, so she obviously gets on well with her and on this occasion everything went to plan. Given her previous history it is anyone's guess whether she will repeat this.
**Scottish Exile(IRE)** was doing all her best work late on and found this an inadequate test on the ground.
**Roxanne Mill** showed her usual speed out in front, but not for the first time ran about and threw it away. She has the ability, but has not won for nearly two years.
**Mystery Pips** ran her best race for a while, showing good speed under the stands' rail, and is now 2lb below her last winning mark.
**Robwillcall** put up a fair effort under a 6lb penalty for her Hamilton win, but is not the most consistent.
**Inching** showed her usual early speed, but looks a short runner and is still to win after 29 attempts.

## 3148 RECTANGLE GROUP H'CAP — 7f 30y
**4:30** (4:30) (F) (0-55,54) 3-Y-0+ — **£3,038** (£868; £434) **Stalls** Low

Form — RPR

3661 **1** **Sennen Cove**[28] 2345 5-9-1 **42**....(t) RFfrench 9 — 52
(RBastiman) *towards rr: hdwy over 2f out: nt clr run and swtchd rt over 1f out: rdn and styd on wl to ld on line* **20/1**

0-00 **2** *shd* **The Old Soldier**[62] 1526 6-9-6 **50**.... ABeech(3) 5 — 60
(ADickman) *towards rr: hdwy on outer over 2f out: rdn over 1f out: led ins last: edgd lft and hdd on line* **12/1**

3440 **3** *½* **Lord Chamberlain**[9] 2886 11-9-3 **51**....(b) CJDavies(7) 12 — 59
(JMBradley) *in tch: hdwy on wd outside 3f out: led wl over 1f out: rdn: edgd lft and hdd ins last: kpt on* **10/1**

2233 **4** *shd* **Tojoneski**[7] 2943 5-9-4 **45**....(p) DAllan 6 — 53
(IWMcinnes) *in tch: hdwy to chse ldrs over 2f out: rdn over 1f out: drvn and ev ch ins last: kpt on* **9/2**[2]

0006 **5** *2* **African Spur (IRE)**[11] 2823 4-9-3 **51**.... DTudhope(7) 10 — 54
(DCarroll) *cl up: rdn along over 2f out and ev ch tl drvn and wknd ent last* **10/1**

0540 **6** *hd* **Waltzing Wizard**[7] 2938 5-9-11 **52**.... FLynch 13 — 54
(ABerry) *chsd ldrs: hdwy 3f out: rdn to chal 2f out and ev ch tl drvn and wknd ent last* **4/1**[1]

0052 **7** *shd* **Royal Windmill (IRE)**[3] 3040 5-8-11 **45**....(p) DFentiman(7) 1 — 47
(MDHammond) *rrd s and s.i.s: beind tl hdwy over 2f out: rdn and styd on ins last: nrst fin* **10/1**

-003 **8** *½* **Mickledor (FR)**[12] 2778 4-8-11 **43**....(p) PMakin(5) 14 — 44
(MDods) *midfield: pushed along and sltly outpcd 3f out: hdwy and n.m.r 2f out: sn rdn and no imp fnl f* **8/1**[3]

0430 **9** *½* **Luke After Me (IRE)**[6] 2965 4-9-13 **54**.... RWinston 8 — 53
(GASwinbank) *midfield: hdwy 3f out: rdn 2f out and sn no imp* **12/1**

503 **10** *1 ¼* **Lieuday**[17] 2658 5-9-3 **49**....(p) PMulrennan(5) 2 — 45
(WMBrisbourne) *stdd s: bhd tl hdwy and n.m.r 2f out: sn rdn and no imp* **20/1**

40-0 **11** *3* **Hormuz (IRE)**[42] 1993 8-8-13 **45**.... MLawson(5) 11 — 33
(PaulJohnson) *led: rdn along 3f out: drvn 2f out: sn hdd & wknd* **33/1**

0200 **12** *3 ½* **The Gambler**[2] 3103 4-9-3 **51**....(p) NataliaGemelova(7) 4 — 30
(PaulJohnson) *hld up: a rr* **20/1**

-000 **13** *1 ¼* **Proud Western (USA)**[28] 2350 6-8-10 **40**.... TEaves(3) 3 — 16
(BEllison) *v.s.a: a bhd* **16/1**

0/0- **14** *1 ¾* **Always Daring**[275] 5070 5-8-10 **40**.... THamilton(3) 7 — 11
(CJTeague) *chsd ldrs: rdn over 3f out and sn wknd* **66/1**

1m 27.32s (-2.21) **Going Correction** -0.35s/f (Firm) **14** Ran SP% **116.6**
Speed ratings: **98,97,97,97,94 94,94,94,93,92 88,84,83,81**CSF £223.08 CT £2606.90 TOTE £18.20: £6.10, £3.50, £4.90; EX 987.50.
**Owner** Border Rail & Plant Limited **Bred** Fonthill Stud **Trained** Cowthorpe, N Yorks

**FOCUS**
A competitive if low-grade handicap run at an ordinary pace and a bunch finish. The form is modest.

**NOTEBOOK**
**Sennen Cove**, who got off the mark at the 29th attempt in a Beverley banded contest last time, has run well on this track before and was produced at the last possible moment to get up on the line. Once a long-standing maiden, now he cannot stop winning.
**The Old Soldier** did everything right and was unfortunate to be pipped. He is becoming reasonably handicapped and this was his best effort yet beyond six furlongs.
**Lord Chamberlain** usually likes to come late, but on this occasion he probably got there too soon and did nothing in front. The old engine has not quite conked out yet.
**Tojoneski** ran his race, but is without a win on turf in almost three years and keeps on finding one or two too good for him this year.
**African Spur(IRE)** ◆, rated 27lb lower than at this time last year, attracted market support in his most recent start and did not run at all badly on this occasion. He is worth keeping in mind.
**Waltzing Wizard** ran a little better on this drop back to seven, but does not look a winner waiting to happen.
**Royal Windmill(IRE)** deserves some extra credit for finishing where he did, as he was all over the place leaving the stalls and is probably better suited by a mile these days.
**Lieuday** *Official explanation: jockey said gelding was unsuited by the ground*

## 3149 WATCH RACING UK LIVE ON 425 H'CAP — 1m 4f
**5:00** (5:00) (F) (0-55,55) 4-Y-0+ — **£2,947** (£842; £421) **Stalls** High

Form — RPR

-314 **1** **Little Task**[4] 3018 6-8-1 **36**.... RFfrench 8 — 44
(JSWainwright) *hld up: hdwy 3f out: sn pushed along: rdn to chal wl over 1f out: drvn and styd on to ld ent last: r.o wl* **5/2**[1]

0210 **2** *nk* **Archirondel**[9] 2879 6-9-0 **54**.... PMulrennan(5) 7 — 61
(MDHammond) *trckd ldrs gng wl: smooth hdwy over 2f out: chal over 1f out and ev ch tl rdn and nt qckn wl ins last* **5/1**[3]

4240 **3** *1 ¼* **Platinum Charmer (IRE)**[19] 2584 4-9-6 **55**....(p) DarrenWilliams 5 — 60
(KRBurke) *trckd ldrs: hdwy 3f out: rdn 2f out: jnd and shkn up wl over 1f out: drvn and hdd ent last: one pce* **5/1**[3]

0650 **4** *2* **Smarter Charter**[3] 3041 11-7-12 **40**.... KristinStubbs(7) 2 — 42
(MrsLStubbs) *hld up in rr: hdwy 3f out: rdn to chse ldrs wl over 1f out: sn no imp* **11/1**

54-0 **5** *3 ½* **Minivet**[23] 461 9-9-6 **55**....(b) DAllan 1 — 51
(TDEasterby) *chsd ldrs: rdn along 3f out: sn one pce* **10/1**

5/-0 **6** *4* **Hibernate (IRE)**[28] 2347 10-8-2 **40**.... THamilton(3) 4 — 30
(CJTeague) *led: rdn along over 3f out: hdd wl over 2f out and sn wknd* **33/1**

4600 **7** *1* **Moyne Pleasure (IRE)**[5] 2990 6-7-10 **38**....(p) NataliaGemelova(7) 6 — 26
(PaulJohnson) *cl up: rdn along over 3f out: sn drvn and wknd* **10/1**

5-00 **8** *9* **Shalbeblue (IRE)**[13] 2753 7-8-7 **45**....(b) TEaves(3) 3 — 19
(BEllison) *stmbld s: hld up: hdwy over 4f out: sn rdn along and wknd* **7/2**[2]

2m 34.36s (-3.66) **Going Correction** -0.35s/f (Firm) **8** Ran SP% **113.6**
Speed ratings: **98,97,96,95,93 90,89,83**CSF £15.05 CT £56.74 TOTE £3.60: £1.10, £1.90, £1.50; EX 19.30 Place 6 £34.94, Place 5 £27.79.
**Owner** Keith Jackson **Bred** Stetchworth Park Stud Ltd **Trained** Kennythorpe, N Yorks
■ Stewards Enquiry : P Mulrennan three-day ban: used whip with excessive frequency and without allowing gelding time to respond (Jul 2-4)

**FOCUS**
A poor handicap, but the pace was fair and the form is modest.

**NOTEBOOK**
**Little Task** is a winner over hurdles and fences in recent seasons, but he has been running well and winning on the level this year. Patiently ridden, he was not going anything like as well as a few entering the last quarter-mile, but one thing he does is stay and in the end that was all that was required.
**Archirondel** travelled really well for a long way, but he is yet to win beyond ten furlongs and there was not enough left in the tank when he really needed it.
**Platinum Charmer(IRE)** was travelling every bit as well as the runner-up racing down the home straight, but he has often found little off the bridle in the past and that was the case again.
**Smarter Charter**, held up right out the back, stayed on to finish fourth but was never on terms with the front trio. He is an extremely hard ride and is without a win in over two years.
**Minivet**, better known as a hurdler, has not won on the Flat since September 1999 and never looked like improving that statistic.
**Shalbeblue(IRE)** ran poorly and is yet to recapture his best form this season.
T/Plt: £57.40 to a £1 stake. Pool: £35,302.10. 448.65 winning tickets. T/Qpdt: £20.10 to a £1 stake. Pool: £2,493.60. 91.80 winning tickets. JR

# 2585 NOTTINGHAM (L-H)
Monday, June 21

**OFFICIAL GOING: Good to firm**
There was quite a heavy rain/hail storm prior to racing and the ground appeared to be riding slower than the official description.
Wind: Moderate across. Weather: Cloudy with showers.

## 3150 EUROPEAN BREEDERS FUND MAIDEN STKS — 6f 15y
**2:15** (2:16) (D) 2-Y-0 — **£5,300** (£1,631; £815; £407) **Stalls** High

Form — RPR

6 **1** **Hornpipe**[10] 2846 2-9-0.... KFallon 1 — 79+
(SirMichaelStoute) *wnt lft s: sn w ldr: led over 4f out: clr over 2f out: canter* **13/8**[1]

504 **2** *5* **Gavioli (IRE)**[10] 2831 2-9-0....(t) RLMoore 7 — 58
(JMBradley) *prom: chsd wnr over 2f out: sn outpcd* **10/1**

**3** *2 ½* **Blakeshall Hope** 2-9-0.... DeanMcKeown 4 — 51
(PDEvans) *chsd ldrs over 3f* **66/1**

**4** *5* **Baddam** 2-9-0.... JPMurtagh 6 — 36
(JLDunlop) *s.i.s: outpcd* **8/1**

**5** *1 ½* **Rowan Warning** 2-9-0.... TQuinn 5 — 31
(WJHaggas) *s.i.s: sn pushed along in rr: wknd 1/2-way* **13/2**

5 **6** *7* **Town End Tom**[22] 2502 2-9-0.... MFenton 2 — 10
(DMSimcock) *hung lft thrght: led: hdd over 4f out: wknd over 2f out* **6/1**[3]

**7** *11* **Fact And Fiction (IRE)** 2-9-0.... KDalgleish 3 — —
(MJohnston) *sn pushed along and prom: wknd wl over 3f out* **4/1**[2]

1m 15.45s (0.65) **Going Correction** +0.05s/f (Good) **7** Ran SP% **107.4**
Speed ratings: **97,90,87,80,78 69,54**CSF £16.59 TOTE £2.40: £1.20, £7.20; EX 12.00.
**Owner** Cheveley Park Stud **Bred** Cheveley Park Stud Ltd **Trained** Newmarket, Suffolk

**FOCUS**
This did not look a strong race beforehand and Hornpipe won as he liked. The way these finished strung out suggested that the rain prior to racing had got into the ground, for some of them finished very tired.

**NOTEBOOK**
**Hornpipe**, as he had on his debut, went left as the gates opened, but none of his rivals could get him off the bridle and he soon made his way across to grab the favoured stands' side rail. Clear just past halfway, he won pretty much as he liked, but he would not have learnt a great deal in doing so.
**Gavioli(IRE)** filled the runner-up spot, but something had to.
**Blakeshall Hope**, out of a prolific winning seven-furlong mare, did not exactly shape like he was a winner waiting to happen, but he is entitled to come on for the experience.
**Baddam**, out of a mare that stayed two miles, is all legs at present and appeared clueless when the gates opened. He looks the sort who should do better in middle-distance handicaps next year.
**Rowan Warning**, a half-brother to juvenile winner Rowan Pursuit is a late foal, and should do better as the season goes on.
**Town End Tom** ruined his chance by hanging badly.

## 3151 PABLO PICASSO H'CAP — 6f 15y
**2:45** (2:49) (F) (0-55,55) 3-Y-0+ — **£3,584** (£1,024; £512) **Stalls** High

Form — RPR

-532 **1** **Miss Judgement (IRE)**[7] 2942 3-9-2 **53**.... FNorton 20 — 69
(WRMuir) *racd stands' side: chsd ldrs: rdn to ld over 1f out: r.o wl* **13/2**[1]

0100 **2** *5* **Redoubtable (USA)**[31] 2260 13-9-4 **48**.... ACulhane 4 — 49
(DWChapman) *racd far side: chsd ldrs: led that gp over 1f out: styd on same pce ins fnl f* **16/1**

0003 **3** *shd* **Blessed Place**[1] 3126 4-9-1 **45**....(t) PMcCabe 6 — 46
(DJSFfrenchDavis) *rcd far side: chsd ldrs: rdn over 1f out; styd on* **14/1**

0000 **4** *shd* **Toppling**[3] 3043 6-9-11 **55**.... RLMoore 19 — 55
(JMBradley) *racd stands' side: led over 4f: no ex* **13/2**[1]

00-0 **5** *1* **Cafe Americano**[29] 2322 4-9-1 **45**....(e[1]) JFortune 18 — 42
(DWPArbuthnot) *wnt lft s: racd stands' side: outpcd: hdwy u.p over 1f out: nt rch ldrs* **66/1**

-030 **6** *shd* **Beneking**[10] 2834 4-9-10 **54**.... NCallan 9 — 51
(RHollinshead) *s.i.s: racd far side: sn chsng ldrs: rdn over 1f styd on fnl f* **14/1**

0050 **7** *1 ¾* **Tender (IRE)**[9] 2885 4-9-9 **53**....(p) SDrowne 1 — 45
(MrsStefLiddiard) *racd far side: chsd ldrs: rdn over 2f out: no ex appr fnl f* **10/1**

5000 **8** *2* **Tamarella (IRE)**[9] 2875 4-9-5 **49**....(v) AMcCarthy 8 — 35
(GGMargarson) *led far side over 4f: no ex* **12/1**

-400 **9** *1* **Mannora**[9] 2885 4-9-7 **51**.... KFallon 11 — 34
(PHowling) *racd stands' side: chsd ldrs: rdn over 1f out: wknd fnl f* **17/2**[3]

5000 **10** *nk* **Komena**[11] 2823 6-9-1 **45**....(b[1]) JPMurtagh 14 — 27
(JWPayne) *racd stands' side: w ldr 4f: wknd over 1f out* **20/1**

00/0 **11** *1 ¾* **Dispol Verity**[17] 2663 4-9-1 **45**.... SWKelly 2 — 22
(WMBrisbourne) *racd far side: sn outpcd* **100/1**

0535 **12** *1* **Roan Raider (USA)**[8] 2908 4-9-2 **49**....(p) LFletcher(3) 10 — 23
(MJPolglase) *racd stands' side: chsd ldrs 4f* **33/1**

0406 **13** 1/2 **Tuscan Treaty**[9] 2875 4-9-3 **50** ........ JFMcDonald(3) 7 22
(TTClement) *racd far side: chsd ldrs: rdn over 2f out: wknd over 1f out* **16/1**

0150 **14** 1 1/4 **Sergeant Slipper**[15] 2707 7-9-0 **44** ........ (v) RFitzpatrick 3 12
(CSmith) *s.s: racd far side: outpcd* **28/1**

050- **15** *hd* **Vintage Style**[209] 6063 5-9-10 **54** ........ KDarley 16 22
(JRWeymes) *wnt rt s: racd stands' side: sn outpcd* **20/1**

3665 **16** 7 **Attorney**[9] 2885 6-9-4 **48** ........ (v) LVickers 17 —
(DShaw) *racd stands' side: hmpd s: outpcd* **12/1**

0-10 **17** 2 1/2 **Molotov**[17] 2663 4-9-2 **46** ........ KDalgleish 13 —
(IWMcinnes) *unruly to post: racd stands' side: w ldr 4f: sn wknd* **33/1**

0000 **18** 3 **Flying Faisal (USA)**[27] 2383 6-9-0 **44** ........ CCatlin 15 —
(JMBradley) *racd stands' side: outpcd* **33/1**

4200 **19** *nk* **Super Canyon**[23] 2473 6-9-10 **54** ........ (vt) TQuinn 5 —
(JPearce) *racd far side: dwlt: outpcd* **8/1**[2]

0600 **20** 5 **Speedfit Free (IRE)**[1] 3125 7-9-2 **46** ........ (p) AnnStokell 12 —
(MissAStokell) *racd stands' side: chsd ldrs: rdn and lost pl 4f out: sn bhd* **25/1**

1m 15.15s (0.35) **Going Correction** +0.05s/f (Good)
**WFA** 3 from 4yo+ 7lb **20** Ran SP% **126.0**
Speed ratings: **99,92,92,92,90 90,88,85,84,83 81,80,79,77,77 68,64,60,60,53**CSF £98.64 CT £1465.58 TOTE £5.40: £1.10, £7.50, £4.60, £1.80; EX 120.50.
**Owner** Double D Partnership **Bred** Yeomanstown Stud **Trained** Lambourn, Berks

**FOCUS**
A weak race overall but the winner is generally progressive. The field split into two with no real advantage to either side until the latter stages.

**NOTEBOOK**
**Miss Judgement(IRE)** took advantage of her good draw to confirm recent promise. Her trainer thought she had been a "slow learner", so there may well be more to come from her.
**Redoubtable(USA)** has been unlucky on his last two visit's here, having won his side on both occasions, only to find the winner on the opposite side.
**Blessed Place**, none the worse for run yesterday, confirmed himself in good form.
**Toppling** had the advantage of the rails to race against, but the rain prior to racing was not ideal for him.
**Cafe Americano** shaped with a bit more promise in the first-time eye-shield, over a trip which looked to be on the sharp side for him.
**Beneking** does have a little ability, but is proving difficult to place.
**Molotov** *Official explanation: jockey said gelding became very fractious prior to the race*
**Super Canyon** *Official explanation: trainer said gelding finished distressed*

## 3152 MIDSUMMERS DAY STKS (H'CAP) 1m 1f 213y
**3:15** (3:16) (D) (0-85,83) 3-Y-O **£5,954** (£1,832; £916; £458) **Stalls** Low

Form RPR

3-64 **1** **Penzance**[13] 2751 3-9-2 **78** ........ JPMurtagh 7 88+
(JRFanshawe) *a.p: rdn to ld over 1f out: r.o* **5/2**[2]

-000 **2** 1 1/4 **Swift Sailing (USA)**[12] 2790 3-8-7 **69** ........ ACulhane 2 73
(BWHills) *chsd ldrs: outpcd 5f out: rallied over 1f out: r.o* **33/1**

3-10 **3** *shd* **Incursion**[30] 2281 3-9-7 **83** ........ RHughes 4 87
(AKing) *s.i.s: hld up: hdwy over 2f out: rdn over 1f out: styd on same pce ins fnl f* **10/1**

31- **4** 1 1/4 **Kings Empire**[258] 5443 3-9-7 **83** ........ RFitzpatrick 8 84
(DCarroll) *hld up: hdwy over 4f out: rdn over 2f out: no ex ins fnl f* **16/1**

0-46 **5** 1 1/2 **Malibu (IRE)**[16] 2676 3-8-13 **75** ........ RLMoore 1 74
(SDow) *hld up: rdn over 3f out: styd on: nt pce to chal* **9/2**[3]

-203 **6** 1 **Fossgate**[19] 2571 3-8-9 **71** ........ TQuinn 3 68
(JDBethell) *sn led: hdd over 6f out: outpcd over 2f out: styd on ins fnl f* **14/1**

2-05 **7** 2 **Song Of Vala**[21] 2513 3-9-2 **78** ........ SDrowne 5 71
(RCharlton) *chsd ldr: rdn to ld over 2f out: hdd over 1f out: sn wknd* **10/1**

-041 **8** 2 **Nantucket Sound (USA)**[25] 2430 3-8-8 **70** ........ KFallon 9 59
(MCPipe) *hung rt and prom: led over 6f out: rdn and hdd over 2f out: wknd fnl f* **9/4**[1]

2m 12.48s (2.98) **Going Correction** +0.30s/f (Good) **8** Ran SP% **111.2**
Speed ratings: **100,99,98,97,96 95,94,92**CSF £70.22 CT £680.43 TOTE £3.30: £1.10, £15.30, £3.10; EX 64.70.
**Owner** Elite Racing Club **Bred** Elite Racing Club **Trained** Newmarket, Suffolk

**FOCUS**
Quite a competitive handicap, but the pace was only ordinary, and the form is sound.

**NOTEBOOK**
**Penzance** does not do anything quickly and looks sure to appreciate a step up in trip.
**Swift Sailing(USA)** stayed this longer trip well enough and may have done better with more of a gallop.
**Incursion** appeared to run his race with no excuses.
**Kings Empire**, whose maiden All-Weather win last year had been given a boost by the runner-up (three wins since), shaped well enough on this return to action. Although he will need placing with care off his current mark, he is open to improvement.
**Malibu(IRE)** takes a bit of winding up and may appreciate the return of the headgear.
**Fossgate** looked to run his race in snatches and may not be entirely straightforward.
**Nantucket Sound(USA)** hung quite badly over the far side and can be forgiven this lack-lustre effort. *Official explanation: jockey said colt had hung right*

## 3153 MIDLANDS RACING - 9 GREAT VENUES - CLASSIFIED STKS 2m 9y
**3:45** (3:47) (F) 4-Y-O+ **£3,178** (£908; £454) **Stalls** Low

Form RPR

0600 **1** **Sonoma (IRE)**[19] 2590 4-8-11 **60** ........ KDarley 6 68
(MLWBell) *chsd ldr: led over 3f out: styd on wl* **9/2**[3]

0341 **2** 2 **Spitting Image (IRE)**[13] 2759 4-8-11 **58** ........ ACulhane 2 66
(MrsMReveley) *a.p: chsd wnr over 2f out: sn rdn: styd on same pce ins fnl f* **10/3**[2]

-261 **3** 11 **Calamintha**[18] 2613 4-9-2 **65** ........ KFallon 1 58
(MCPipe) *led: rdn and hdd over 3f out: wknd 2f out* **5/4**[1]

0045 **4** *nk* **Squirtle Turtle**[11] 2798 4-8-9 **60** ........ NDeSouza(5) 3 55
(PFICole) *chsd ldrs: lost pl 5f out: wknd 3f out* **33/1**

-220 **5** 5 **Starry Mary**[52] 1754 6-8-11 **55** ........ GDuffield 4 46
(RMBeckett) *hld up: hdwy 11f out: wknd over 2f out* **12/1**

000 **6** 14 **Snow's Ride**[9] 2893 4-9-5 **65** ........ SDrowne 5 38
(WRMuir) *hld up: wknd over 3f out* **9/2**[3]

3m 37.21s (3.71) **Going Correction** +0.30s/f (Good) **6** Ran SP% **114.5**
Speed ratings: **102,101,95,95,92 85**CSF £20.27 TOTE £5.20: £3.00, £1.80; EX 48.50.
**Owner** Mrs P D Gray **Bred** Dr Michael Dargan **Trained** Newmarket, Suffolk

**FOCUS**
A moderate contest with the field finishing well strung out. The winner did not need to be at her best and the form is weak.

**NOTEBOOK**
**Sonoma(IRE)** appreciated the drop in class and never really looked in any danger after taking up the running.
**Spitting Image(IRE)** made a brave effort to follow up her Redcar victory and looked to run at least as well in defeat.
**Calamintha** had a soft time of things up front, so it was disappointing to see her drop away so tamely when headed.
**Squirtle Turtle** was on a none-going day.
**Snow's Ride**never looked like taking a hand and has plenty to prove now. *Official explanation: jockey said colt (as it was then) weakened very quickly*

## 3154 MONET MAIDEN STKS 1m 54y
**4:15** (4:17) (D) 3-Y-O+ **£4,046** (£1,245; £622; £311) **Stalls** Low

Form RPR

0000 **1** **Flashing Blade**[22] 2506 4-9-2 **70** ........ (t) GGibbons 12 73
(BAMcmahon) *trckd ldrs: racd keenly: led over 2f out: rdn and hung lft ins fnl f: all out* **10/1**

**2** 1/2 **Zathonia** 3-8-6 ........ SDrowne 10 72
(RCharlton) *s.i.s: hld up: hdwy over 1f out: r.o* **14/1**

05- **3** 1 3/4 **Pending (IRE)**[290] 4706 3-8-11 ........ JPMurtagh 11 72
(JRFanshawe) *w ldr: led over 6f out: hdd over 2f out: sn rdn: no ex ins fnl f* **3/1**[2]

000- **4** 1 3/4 **Jolizero**[209] 6069 3-8-11 ........ AMcCarthy 13 68?
(PWChapple-Hyam) *hld up: hdwy over 2f out: styd on* **40/1**

-500 **5** 1 1/2 **Little Englander**[20] 2547 4-9-7 **52** ........ SWhitworth 6 65?
(HCandy) *s.i.s: hld up: hdwy and hung lft 2f out: nt trble ldrs* **33/1**

2/0 **6** 1 1/4 **Successor**[17] 2654 4-9-7 ........ RHughes 7 62
(BWHills) *led: hdd over 6f out: remained handy: rdn over 2f out: wknd fnl f* **9/1**[3]

0-4 **7** 1 3/4 **Bluetoria**[27] 2392 3-8-6 ........ DeanMcKeown 1 53
(JAGlover) *hld up: rdn over 3f out: n.d* **12/1**

3 **8** 1 1/4 **Minority Report**[21] 2517 4-9-4 ........ NMackay(3) 5 55
(LMCumani) *s.i.s: sn prom: rdn over 2f out: wknd over 1f out* **15/8**[1]

6-0 **9** 3 **Rainbow Colours (IRE)**[34] 2198 3-8-6 ........ (t) GDuffield 8 43
(JRFanshawe) *prom 5f* **28/1**

/00- **10** *nk* **Pretty Kool**[394] 1837 4-9-2 ........ JBramhill 4 43
(SCWilliams) *s.i.s: hld up: nt clr run over 3f out: n.d* **100/1**

0-00 **11** 14 **Light The Dawn (IRE)**[18] 2621 4-9-2 ........ SWKelly 3 10
(WMBrisbourne) *hld up in tch: plld hrd: rdn and wknd over 2f out* **100/1**

**12** 1 1/2 **Super Boston**[132] 4-9-7 ........ RLappin 2 12
(RDEWoodhouse) *s.i.s: outpcd* **100/1**

5-0 **13** 2 1/2 **Torchlight (USA)**[35] 2182 4-9-2 ........ (bt[1]) JFortune 9 1
(JHMGosden) *hld up: plld hrd: hdwy over 5f out: wknd over 2f out* **14/1**

1m 48.34s (1.94) **Going Correction** +0.30s/f (Good)
**WFA** 3 from 4yo 10lb **13** Ran SP% **111.7**
Speed ratings: **102,101,99,98,96 95,93,92,89,88 74,73,70**CSF £126.22 TOTE £11.30: £4.10, £4.70, £1.60; EX 113.10.
**Owner** W D McClennon **Bred** Major C R And Mrs Philipson **Trained** Hopwas, Staffs

**FOCUS**
This didn't look a strong maiden with the exposed 70-rated Flashing Blade holding the call.

**NOTEBOOK**
**Flashing Blade** had looked exposed coming into this, but the step up in trip proved the ideal for her, although she did not have a lot to spare in the end. A half-sister to Group Three winner Needwood Blade, she will have boosted her paddock value no end.
**Zathonia**, a sister to smart ten-furlong filly Zante, still looked green and should improve for both the experience and a step up in trip.
**Pending(IRE)** looked fit enough to do herself justice and had quite a hard race in the process.
**Jolizero**, who is out of a mare that won over hurdles, shaped very much as though he needs a thorough test. He should find plenty of openings in handicaps.
**Little Englander** is exposed as moderate and did not improve any for the drop in trip.
**Bluetoria** *Official explanation: jockey said filly was unsuited by the loose ground*
**Minority Report** was one of the first off the bridle and dropped away tamely. He looks to have a touch of the slows.
**Light The Dawn(IRE)** *Official explanation: jockey said filly ran too keenly and did not handle the bend*
**Torchlight(USA)** *Official explanation: jockey said filly, wearing first-time blinkers, ran too keenly and stumbled in the straight*

## 3155 VAN GOGH H'CAP 1m 54y
**4:45** (4:46) (E) (0-75,72) 3-Y-O **£3,997** (£1,230; £615; £307) **Stalls** Low

Form RPR

50-4 **1** **Spring Jim**[14] 2727 3-9-5 **70** ........ JPMurtagh 8 85+
(JRFanshawe) *s.i.s: hld up: hdwy over 1f out: r.o to ld nr fin* **9/1**[3]

-202 **2** *nk* **Captain Marryat**[8] 2915 3-8-6 **57** ........ RLMoore 14 67+
(PWHarris) *hld up: hdwy over 2f out: led 1f out: rdn and hung lft ins fnl f: hdd nr fin* **4/1**[2]

0122 **3** 2 **Foley Prince**[10] 2847 3-9-7 **72** ........ KDarley 2 77
(MrsStefLiddiard) *led 5f: rdn over 1f out: no ex ins fnl f* **4/1**[2]

003 **4** 1 **Bertocelli**[14] 2727 3-9-4 **69** ........ AMcCarthy 5 72
(GGMargarson) *chsd ldr tl led 3f out: rdn and hdd 1f out: no ex* **14/1**

0-02 **5** 1 **Raysoot (IRE)**[17] 2667 3-8-9 **60** ........ RHughes 11 60
(ACStewart) *prom: rdn over 1f out: wknd ins fnl f* **3/1**[1]

04-0 **6** 1 1/2 **Violet Avenue**[31] 2259 3-8-8 **59** ........ MFenton 10 56
(JGGiven) *s.i.s: hld up: hdwy and nt clr run 2f out: nvr trbld ldrs* **66/1**

0005 **7** 3 1/2 **Go Green**[25] 2426 3-7-12 **49** ........ JoannaBadger 1 38
(PDEvans) *s.i.s: sn chsng ldrs: rdn over 3f out: wknd over 1f out* **25/1**

4546 **8** *hd* **Trojan Flight**[19] 2569 3-8-12 **63** ........ ACulhane 6 51
(MrsJRRamsden) *s.i.s: hld up: nt clr run 2f out: nvr trbld ldrs* **16/1**

0-00 **9** *hd* **My Hope (IRE)**[37] 2114 3-9-5 **70** ........ SDrowne 4 58
(RCharlton) *prom: rdn over 2f out: wknd over 1f out* **14/1**

3-00 **10** 2 1/2 **Solo Sole (ITY)**[42] 1997 3-8-11 **65** ........ NMackay(3) 9 47
(LMCumani) *prom: lost pl 6f out: hdwy 3f out: wknd over 1f out* **28/1**

-0P4 **11** 1 1/2 **Molinia**[12] 2790 3-8-9 **60** ........ GDuffield 13 39
(RMBeckett) *hld up: hdwy over 2f out: wknd over 1f out* **25/1**

45 **12** 6 **Breezit (USA)**[7] 2942 3-8-1 **52** ........ JBramhill 7 17
(SRBowring) *unruly stalls: s.i.s: hld up: hdwy 1/2-way: wknd 2f out* **25/1**

-236 **13** 8 **Joshua's Gold (IRE)**[32] 2251 3-8-5 **56** ........ RFitzpatrick 12 3
(DCarroll) *mid-div: rdn 1/2-way: wknd over 2f out* **40/1**

40-0 **14** 21 **Desert Diplomat (IRE)**[63] 1506 3-9-1 **66** ........ KFallon 3 —
(SirMichaelStoute) *sn pushed along in rr: bhd fr 1/2-way* **14/1**

1m 48.45s (2.05) **Going Correction** +0.30s/f (Good) **14** Ran SP% **119.8**
Speed ratings: **101,100,98,97,96 95,91,91,91,88 87,81,73,52**CSF £41.50 CT £175.60 TOTE £10.30: £6.70, £2.00, £1.10; EX 48.10 Place 6 £152.88, Place 5 £76.60.
**Owner** Andrew & Julia Turner **Bred** C I T Racing Ltd **Trained** Newmarket, Suffolk

**FOCUS**
An ordinary contest, but competitive nonetheless. The time was comparable with the earlier maiden and the form should work out.

**NOTEBOOK**
**Spring Jim** appreciated the step up in trip and now that he has proved he does stay, should find other openings.

**Captain Marryat**, a brother to Flashing Blade, who won the previous race, looked like making it a family double until hanging away from the whip and being caught in the dying strides.
**Foley Prince** more exposed than most, is holding his form well despite rising in the weights.
**Bertocelli**, having travelled well, did not quite get home. This trip just seems to stretch him.
**Raysoot(IRE)** had no excuses and is clearly of limited ability.
**Violet Avenue** looked as though she may appreciate a step up in trip.
T/Plt: £235.60 to a £1 stake. Pool: £36,059.70. 111.70 winning tickets. T/Qpdt: £30.20 to a £1 stake. Pool: £2,520.00. 61.70 winning tickets. CR

## 2945 WINDSOR (R-H)

Monday, June 21

**OFFICIAL GOING: Good to firm changing to good to soft after race 4 (8.10)**
The rain which fell before racing took the sting out of the ground, while the heavy rain during the evening softened the ground further.
Wind: nil Weather: hvy rain fr after race 2

### 3156 FORTUNE CENTRE OF RIDING THERAPY FILLIES' H'CAP 1m 2f 7y
6:40 (6:40) (E) (0-70,70) 3-Y-O £3,552 (£1,093; £546; £273) Stalls Low

Form RPR
-003 1 **Foxilla (IRE)**[7] 2949 3-7-12 **52** RThomas(5) 2 61
(DRCElsworth) *trckd ldrs: rdn over 2f out: led over 1f out: styd on wl* **9/2**[1]
264 2 1 **High School**[34] 2198 3-9-5 **68** EAhern 6 75
(DRLoder) *racd in midfield: swtchd to outer and effrt over 2f out: drvn to chal fnl f: unable qck* **8/1**
-404 3 1 1/4 **Bubbling Fun**[24] 2442 3-9-1 **64** TEDurcan 14 69
(EALDunlop) *trckd ldrs: nt clr run over 2f out to over 1f out: ch ent fnl f: nt qckn* **11/2**[2]
0055 4 1 3/4 **Blaeberry**[11] 2820 3-8-6 **55** GCarter 8 57
(PLGilligan) *dwlt: racd in rr tl prog 4f out: drvn 3f out: cl up on outer 1f out: fdd fnl f* **11/1**
444 5 3 1/2 **Queen Lucia (IRE)**[30] 2289 3-8-9 **58** TQuinn 11 53
(JGGiven) *trckd ldrs: unable qck wl over 1f out: one pce and btn over 1f out* **16/1**
0004 6 nk **Faith Healer (IRE)**[11] 2820 3-8-3 **52** (b) JQuinn 9 46
(VSmith) *trckd ldrs: rdn to ld 2f out: edgd rt and hdd over 1f out: wknd* **14/1**
4120 7 shd **Ivory Coast (IRE)**[7] 2949 3-8-11 **60** RMullen 7 54
(WRMuir) *wl in rr: rdn 1/2-way: kpt on u.p fnl 2f: nrst fin* **6/1**[3]
5-00 8 3/4 **Dream Of Dubai (IRE)**[27] 2377 3-8-11 **60** RLMoore 5 53
(PMitchell) *dwlt: hld up in last: prog 3f out: no imp on ldrs over 1f out* **33/1**
4-00 9 3 1/2 **Saharan Song (IRE)**[36] 2145 3-8-13 **62** IMongan 1 48
(BWHills) *mostly trckd ldr to over 2f out: grad wknd* **25/1**
0-00 10 nk **Elsinora**[29] 2325 3-8-1 **53** (v[1]) JFMcDonald(3) 13 39
(HMorrison) *a in rr: wandering u.p over 2f out: no prog* **33/1**
0-00 11 hd **Nabtat Saif**[102] 1005 3-9-0 **70** PGallagher(7) 12 55
(RHannon) *dwlt: hld up in rr: no prog over 2f out* **18/1**
0-50 12 1/2 **Daydream Dancer**[23] 2484 3-8-4 **53** PRobinson 10 37
(CGCox) *chsd ldrs: lost pl over 3f out: sn in rr: eased over 1f out* **10/1**
-345 13 15 **Nukhbah (USA)**[25] 2419 3-9-3 **66** SSanders 3 22
(LadyHerries) *led: rdn over 3f out: hdd & wknd rapidly 2f out: eased: t.o* **8/1**
-040 14 5 **Snow Joke (IRE)**[19] 2577 3-8-8 **57** RHavlin 4 3
(MrsPNDutfield) *a in rr: no prog 3f out: eased fnl 2f: t.o* **25/1**

2m 9.54s (1.24) **Going Correction** +0.10s/f (Good) **14** Ran SP% **118.9**
Speed ratings: **99,98,97,95,93 92,92,92,89,89 88,88,76,72**CSF £37.61 CT £202.61 TOTE £5.70: £1.90, £2.60, £2.10; EX 19.00.
**Owner** J Wotherspoon **Bred** Sugar Puss Corporation **Trained** Whitsbury, Hants

**FOCUS**
A modest handicap featuring only one previous winner.

**NOTEBOOK**
**Foxilla(IRE)** ran well from out of the handicap over course and distance last time, and won nicely off what was effectively a 3lb lower mark. No doubt the rain which had fallen was to her benefit.
**High School**, making her handicap debut, saw the trip out well and connections look to have every chance of realising the objective of getting a win out of this particularly well-bred filly, albeit in minor company. *Official explanation: jockey said filly was never travelling*
**Bubbling Fun** was travelling best of all turning into the straight and, although she had to wait for a gap, when it did appear her response was not all that had been expected.
**Blaeberry** finished clear of the fifth and shapes as though she will get even farther.
**Queen Lucia(IRE)** kept on well enough without ever threatening to challenge the principals, and she may need to be dropped a few pounds.
**Nabtat Saif**, for whom this longer trip was an unknown, should benefit from this first outing since March.
**Nukhbah(USA)** *Official explanation: jockey said filly was unsuited by the ground*

### 3157 MLL TELECOM MAIDEN AUCTION STKS 6f
7:10 (7:11) (E) 2-Y-O £3,630 (£1,117; £558; £279) Stalls High

Form RPR
02 1 **Don Pele (IRE)**[18] 2609 2-8-9 JFortune 6 86
(SKirk) *mde virtually all: rdn clr fr 2f out: styd on wl* **7/2**[2]
2 2 **Amazin** 2-8-9 RHughes 7 80
(RHannon) *dwlt: wl in rr: last after 2f: taken to wd outside 1/2-way: gd prog over 2f out: chsd wnr jst over 1f out: kpt on* **9/1**
3 1 1/4 **Ariodante** 2-8-7 SSanders 9 74
(JMPEustace) *dwlt: wl in rr: taken to outer and prog fr 1/2-way: styd on fnl 2f: nrst fin* **20/1**
5 4 1/2 **Transvestite (IRE)**[19] 2574 2-8-11 EAhern 11 77
(JWHills) *prom but sn pushed along: drvn and unable qck over 2f out: styd on same pce* **6/1**[3]
0 5 1 3/4 **Rosiella**[23] 2481 2-8-2 JQuinn 2 63
(MBlanshard) *sn chsd ldrs: rdn and disp 2nd pl over 1f out: one pce after* **80/1**
4 6 2 **Musico (IRE)**[18] 2609 2-9-0 SDrowne 15 69
(BRMillman) *prom: lost pl on inner 1/2-way: one pce fnl 2f* **3/1**[1]
04 7 1 **He's A Star**[7] 2927 2-8-2 PGallagher(7) 14 61
(RHannon) *wl in rr: pushed along on inner 2f out: kpt on steadily fnl f* **14/1**
5 8 1/2 **Dover Street**[8] 2904 2-8-11 PaulEddery 8 61
(PWD'Arcy) *sn rdn to chse ldrs: lost pl after 2f: wl in rr 1/2-way: kpt on u.p fnl f* **10/1**
9 nk **Ariane Star (IRE)** 2-8-4 PRobinson 10 53
(MAJarvis) *nvr beyond midfield: no prog fnl 2f* **12/1**
10 nk **Peppermint Tea (IRE)** 2-8-6 IMongan 4 54
(MLWBell) *dwlt: sn chsd ldrs: rdn and rn green over 2f out: fdd* **20/1**
11 1/2 **Picot De Say** 2-8-7 RMullen 18 54
(JohnBerry) *dwlt: nvr beyond midfield: rn green and btn wl over 1f out* **66/1**
12 1 1/2 **Grand Place** 2-8-9 RLMoore 1 51
(RHannon) *s.s: sn rcvrd and gd spd to press wnr: wknd over 1f out* **25/1**
13 3/4 **Marians Maid (IRE)** 2-8-2 DKinsella 16 42
(JSMoore) *racd in midfield: pushed along 1/2-way: wknd over 1f out* **66/1**
14 1 **Asteem** 2-8-7 SCarson 12 44
(RFJohnsonHoughton) *dwlt: a wl in rr* **40/1**
15 1 3/4 **Busaco** 2-8-9 TQuinn 17 41
(JLDunlop) *chsd ldrs: lost pl bef 1/2-way: in rr fnl 2f* **14/1**
46 16 1 **Blue Marble**[16] 2677 2-8-11 TEDurcan 5 40
(CEBrittain) *chsd ldrs: pushed along after 2f: wknd 2f out* **12/1**
17 1/2 **Emeraude Du Cap** 2-8-2 JMackay 3 29
(MLWBell) *a wl in rr* **66/1**
18 2 1/2 **Mister Elegant** 2-8-4 LPKeniry(3) 13 27
(JLSpearing) *racd in midfield to 1/2-way: sn wknd* **66/1**

1m 14.21s (0.34) **Going Correction** -0.025s/f (Good) **18** Ran SP% **132.3**
Speed ratings: **96,93,91,91,88 86,84,84,83,83 82,80,79,78,75 74,73,70**CSF £35.21 TOTE £4.40: £2.00, £3.30, £5.90; EX 20.30.
**Owner** Pedro Rosas **Bred** John J Cosgrave **Trained** Upper Lambourn, Berks

**FOCUS**
The draw did not play such a big part as usual in this fair maiden and the form is fairly strong.

**NOTEBOOK**
**Don Pele(IRE)**, second in a fast time at Chepstow, was quickly into his stride and stuck to the rail in the straight. He won fairly comfortably but his edge in racing experience was the difference on this occasion.
**Amazin** did well as he was last in the early stages but made up a huge amount of ground down the outside in the straight to finish a clear second. He should be able to build on this.
**Ariodante**, a half-brother to four winners, is bred to need a good deal farther than this in time and so this was a very encouraging effort on his debut.
**Transvestite(IRE)** ran a fair race and he looks more of a nursery type.
**Rosiella** improved a good deal on her debut when she was unruly before the start and never got into the race. She will need to progress again if she is to win a similar race, though.
**Musico(IRE)**, seven and a half lengths behind the winner on his debut, was 3lb worse off with that rival this time, but was surprisingly well supported. He finished exactly the same distance behind him on this occasion, though.
**He's A Star** looks another for whom handicaps will prove a more fruitful arena.
**Ariane Star(IRE)** *Official explanation: jockey said filly was hanging left*
**Grand Place**, a half-brother to juvenile winner Even Easier, showed plenty of speed and deserves a chance to prove his worth over five.

### 3158 KPMG LLP (UK) H'CAP 6f
7:40 (7:40) (D) (0-80,75) 3-Y-O £5,590 (£1,720; £860; £430) Stalls High

Form RPR
4641 1 **Bohola Flyer (IRE)**[14] 2741 3-9-7 **75** RHughes 9 80
(RHannon) *trckd ldrs: hrd rdn over 1f out: squeezed through to ld jst ins fnl f: rdr dropped whip: jst hld on* **13/8**[1]
4410 2 nk **Cherokee Nation**[14] 2726 3-8-3 **57** TQuinn 5 61
(PWD'Arcy) *t.k.h: hld up in tch: rdn and effrt over 1f out: pressed wnr wl ins fnl f: jst hld* **17/2**
0006 3 1/2 **Half A Handful**[34] 2211 3-8-11 **65** KFallon 10 68
(MJWallace) *settled in rr: effrt and eased to outer over 1f out: styd on wl last 100yds: nrst fin* **15/2**
-330 4 shd **General Feeling (IRE)**[10] 2836 3-8-11 **65** JFortune 8 67
(SKirk) *trckd ldrs: rdn to chal over 1f out: ev ch ent fnl f: one pce nr fin* **13/2**[3]
-303 5 nk **Whistful (IRE)**[14] 2741 3-9-1 **69** SSanders 4 70
(CFWall) *sn led: hdd and one pce jst ins fnl f* **7/2**[2]
0030 6 6 **Shielaligh**[19] 2589 3-9-4 **72** (tp) IMongan 3 64+
(MissGayKelleway) *dwlt: sn pressed ldr: starting to lose pl whn snatched up 1f out: eased* **12/1**
4-00 7 3 **Rockley Bay (IRE)**[12] 2790 3-8-8 **62** JQuinn 7 36
(PJMakin) *outpcd in last after 2f: nvr on terms* **20/1**
0-00 8 7 **Shebaan**[32] 2251 3-7-9 **52** oh2 FPFerris(3) 6 5
(PSMcentee) *a in rr: wknd 2f out* **66/1**
0-00 9 21 **Knight Onthe Tiles (IRE)**[136] 696 3-9-7 **75** (b) NPollard 2 —
(JRBest) *prom to 1/2-way: wknd over 2f out: t.o* **16/1**

1m 14.15s (0.28) **Going Correction** -0.025s/f (Good) **9** Ran SP% **115.8**
Speed ratings: **97,96,95,95,95 87,83,74,46**CSF £16.67 CT £82.74 TOTE £2.60: £1.40, £2.60, £1.50; EX 16.00 Trifecta £103.50 Pool of £1,531.70 - 10.50 winning units..
**Owner** William Durkan **Bred** Swordlestown Stud **Trained** East Everleigh, Wilts

**FOCUS**
A modest time for the grade, only fractionally faster than the preceding two-year-old maiden. The form is ordinary and somewhat messy.

**NOTEBOOK**
**Bohola Flyer(IRE)** took a while to pick up but she gains credit for having the courage to go through a narrow gap between horses. She was hardly impressive, but a stronger pace would have suited and the Handicapper cannot put her up much for this.
**Cherokee Nation** put a disappointing effort at Folkestone behind him and probably ran to form. He cannot expect any mercy from the Handicapper for this, though.
**Half A Handful** ◆ is a half-brother to three winners out of an unraced mare who herself is out of a half-sister to Irish Oaks winner Give Thanks. He really needs farther than this on breeding, and it is to his credit that he ran so well over this trip off a steady pace on his handicap debut. He is handicapped to win when stepped up in distance.
**General Feeling(IRE)** ran a fair race, just being edged out of the places close home. He should continue to give a good account off this sort of mark.
**Whistful(IRE)** was 3lb better off with the winner compared to a fortnight earlier, but the rain before racing would not have been to her advantage and she remains a maiden.
**Shielaligh** was beginning to beat a retreat when snatched up, and clearly she would have finished a lot closer had she not been hampered.

### 3159 FRASER MILLER CAN'T BELIEVE YOGI'S ONLY 50 CLASSIFIED STKS 1m 67y
8:10 (8:11) (D) 3-Y-O+ £5,687 (£1,750; £875; £437) Stalls High

Form RPR
412 1 **Diamond Lodge**[20] 2557 3-8-9 **80** EAhern 6 89+
(JNoseda) *hld up in tch: effrt over 2f out: drvn to ld over 1f out: hld on u.p* **4/5**[1]
1-0 2 nk **Ultimata**[31] 2278 4-9-5 **80** OUrbina 8 88+
(JRFanshawe) *hld up in rr: prog 3f out: shkn up to chal over 1f out: ev ch nr fin: nt qckn* **20/1**
0216 3 1 3/4 **Climate (IRE)**[2] 3086 5-9-5 **77** (v) JFortune 3 84
(JRBoyle) *trckd ldrs: hrd rdn and unable qck 2f out: styd on ins fnl f* **8/1**[3]
5300 4 3/4 **Jools**[21] 2537 6-9-6 **78** TQuinn 7 83
(DKIvory) *in tch: rdn to chal 2f out: ev ch 1f out: wknd ins fnl f* **14/1**

236- **5** *5* **Grandalea**[235] 5834 3-8-7 78 ........ KFallon 2 69
(SirMichaelStoute) *led to over 1f out: wknd fnl f* **4/1**[2]

6146 **6** *2 1/2* **Scottish River (USA)**[18] 2612 5-9-5 77 ........ WRyan 1 65
(MDIUsher) *rel to r: racd in last: effrt over 2f out: sn no prog* **25/1**

015 **7** *1 1/2* **Just Tim (IRE)**[11] 2806 3-8-12 80 ........ RHughes 5 65
(RHannon) *chsd ldr: hanging lft fr 3f out: sn wknd* **10/1**

0043 **8** *13* **Ile Michel**[10] 2856 7-9-6 78 ........ SSanders 4 33
(JGMO'Shea) *in tch: rdn and wknd over 2f out: eased* **25/1**

1m 48.98s (3.38) **Going Correction** +0.55s/f (Yiel)
**WFA** 3 from 4yo+ 10lb **8** Ran SP% **114.9**
Speed ratings: **105,104,102,102,97 94,93,80**CSF £22.84 TOTE £1.80: £1.10, £3.60, £3.10; EX 28.20.
**Owner** Mrs J Harris **Bred** Chippenham Lodge Stud Ltd **Trained** Newmarket, Suffolk

**FOCUS**
A fair classified event, but there was no mad gallop on as the surface was quite slippery with the rain falling, and the race turned into something of a sprint. The form is slightly mudding with the first two posting improved efforts.

**NOTEBOOK**
**Diamond Lodge** is improving with every run and, given the way the race was run, coped admirably well. Her narrow victory should ensure she does not go up too much and, given that she looks progressive, she may well go in again in the coming weeks.
**Ultimata** ran poorly on fast ground on her reappearance and the rain probably came just in time for her. The drop back in trip also looked in her favour.
**Climate(IRE)** ran well but he has a poor strike rate and is fairly high in the handicap at present, so he is not one to go overboard about.
**Jools** has a tremendous record at this track (6146114) but he is out of form at present and he ideally needs a stronger pace than he had here.
**Grandalea**, who became disappointing towards the end of last year, was making her reappearance and was treading water with a furlong to run.
**Just Tim(IRE)** has form on easy ground so this was a disappointing performance. *Official explanation: jockey said colt was unsuited by the Good to Soft ground*
**Ile Michel** *Official explanation: jockey said gelding was unsuited by the Good to Soft ground*

## 3160 SHARP MINDS BETFAIR H'CAP 1m 3f 135y
**8:40** (8:40) (E) (0-75,75) 3-Y-0 **£4,355** (£1,340; £670; £335) **Stalls** Low

Form RPR

1250 **1** **Bill Bennett (FR)**[20] 2561 3-9-7 75 ........ OUrbina 11 86
(JJay) *hld up in midfield: stdy prog over 3f out: led over 1f out: shkn up and edgd rt: sn clr* **6/1**[2]

0-34 **2** *4* **Blaze Of Colour**[21] 2513 3-9-2 70 ........ TQuinn 15 75
(SirMichaelStoute) *sn led: rdn and hdd over 1f out: one pce and no ch w wnr* **13/2**[3]

352- **3** *3/4* **Cellarmaster (IRE)**[275] 5087 3-9-4 72 ........ JFortune 5 76
(ACStewart) *trckd ldrs: effrt 3f out: kpt on same pce fnl 2f* **14/1**

5-00 **4** *1/2* **Bakhtyar**[42] 1998 3-8-4 58 ........ (b[1]) JQuinn 4 61
(RCharlton) *prom: cl up and rdn 2f out: one pce after* **20/1**

60-0 **5** *2* **Chanfron**[20] 2546 3-8-6 60 ........ AMcCarthy 13 60
(BRMillman) *racd in midfield: effrt to chse ldrs 4f out: fdd over 1f out* **20/1**

2-00 **6** *5* **In Deep**[16] 2676 3-9-2 70 ........ PaulEddery 6 62
(MrsPNDutfield) *trckd ldrs: effrt and rdn 3f out: wknd wl over 1f out* **14/1**

0-05 **7** *4* **Golden Drift**[16] 2693 3-8-6 60 ........ SDrowne 2 45
(GWragg) *towards rr: pushed along on outer 3f out: kpt on steadily: n.d* **16/1**

0433 **8** *2 1/2* **Gjovic**[11] 2809 3-9-4 75 ........ JFMcDonald[(3)] 14 56
(BJMeehan) *chsd ldrs: rdn and lost tch fr over 2f out* **8/1**

0001 **9** *2* **Planters Punch (IRE)**[20] 2547 3-9-1 69 ........ (v[1]) RHughes 16 47
(RHannon) *dwlt: sn trckd ldrs: rdn and btn whn n.m.r over 1f out: wknd* **5/1**[1]

6404 **10** *4* **Fiddlers Ford (IRE)**[9] 2881 3-9-4 72 ........ EAhern 3 44
(JNoseda) *hld up in rr: rdn over 3f out: nvr on terms* **9/1**

400- **11** *2* **Tungsten Strike (USA)**[282] 4883 3-9-0 68 ........ SCarson 10 37
(MrsAJPerrett) *prom tl wknd over 2f out* **40/1**

-003 **12** *shd* **Wild Pitch**[26] 2400 3-8-7 61 ........ RLMoore 7 29
(PMitchell) *pushed along in rr after 4f: nvr a factor* **10/1**

06-0 **13** *4* **Duke's View (IRE)**[49] 1843 3-8-12 66 ........ SSanders 1 28
(MrsAJPerrett) *s.s: a in rr: rdn and no prog over 3f out* **14/1**

2241 **14** *5* **Golden Empire (USA)**[56] 1662 3-9-5 73 ........ TEDurcan 12 27
(EALDunlop) *prom tl wknd 3f out* **10/1**

50-0 **15** *3* **Inchpast**[42] 1997 3-8-3 60 ........ FPFerris[(3)] 8 9
(MHTompkins) *a wl in rr* **20/1**

-000 **16** *dist* **Cashema (IRE)**[20] 2545 3-7-12 52 oh5 ........ DKinsella 9 —
(MrsPNDutfield) *prom 4f: wknd rapidly: last 5f out: t.o* **100/1**

2m 40.43s (10.33) **Going Correction** +0.65s/f (Yiel) **16** Ran SP% **127.2**
Speed ratings: **91,88,87,87,86 82,80,78,77,74 73,73,70,67,65** —CSF £43.85 CT £545.84 TOTE £10.30: £2.20, £1.50, £2.90, £5.70; EX 69.30.
**Owner** Mr & Mrs Jonathan Jay **Bred** J Jay **Trained** Newmarket, Suffolk

**FOCUS**
A fair handicap but a very slow time, even allowing for the deteriorating conditions. The race was run in a downpour.

**NOTEBOOK**
**Bill Bennett(FR)**, for whom the rain had come in time, won easily in the end, coping with conditions far better than anything else in the race. He will take a big hike in the weights for this though, and he would not make any appeal off a higher rating on quicker ground. He is one to remember for the autumn, however. *Official explanation: jockey said gelding hung right*
**Blaze Of Colour** ran a solid race considering the ground had probably gone against her. This was only her fourth run and handicap debut, and she is open to improvement.
**Cellarmaster(IRE)**, stepping up in trip on his seasonal reappearance and handicap debut, ran well given that he was squeezed up two furlongs out. He is entitled to improve for this outing.
**Bakhtyar**, blinkered for the first time, has done the majority of his racing on softish ground, and presumably conditions had come in his favour.
**Chanfron**, dropped 5lb for his reappearance effort, ran a bit better on the easiest ground he has so far encountered.
**Planters Punch(IRE)**, visored for the first time, appeared to be found out by the conditions. *Official explanation: jockey said colt was unsuited by the Good to Soft ground*
**Fiddlers Ford(IRE)** *Official explanation: jockey said gelding hung left*
**Cashema(IRE)** *Official explanation: jockey said filly was unsuited by the Good to Soft ground*

## 3161 YOGI BREISNER 50TH BIRTHDAY MAIDEN STKS 1m 67y
**9:10** (9:13) (D) 3-Y-0 **£4,459** (£1,372; £686; £343) **Stalls** High

Form RPR

02- **1** **Take A Bow**[271] 5153 3-9-0 ........ JQuinn 14 83+
(PRChamings) *t.k.h: trckd ldr: led 4f out: clr over 2f out: r.o wl* **8/1**

**2** *4* **Noble Mind** 3-9-0 ........ DKinsella 3 69
(PGMurphy) *wl in rr: plenty to do 4f out: gd prog on outer over 2f out: styd on wl to take 2nd wl ins fnl f* **50/1**

**3** *1 1/4* **Raakaan** 3-9-0 ........ JFortune 5 66+
(ACStewart) *dwlt: off the pce in midfield: shkn up 3f out: styd on steadily to take 3rd nr fin* **10/1**

3 **4** *hd* **Anatolian Queen (USA)**[49] 1830 3-8-9 ........ SSanders 10 61
(JMPEustace) *prom: chsd wnr over 2f out: no imp: lost 2nd wl ins fnl f* **3/1**[1]

44 **5** *3 1/2* **Different Planet**[21] 2519 3-9-0 ........ TQuinn 13 58
(JWHills) *chsd ldrs: rdn wl over 2f out: one pce after* **9/2**[3]

4 **6** *7* **Stage Right**[149] 597 3-8-11 ........ LPKeniry[(3)] 12 44
(DRCElsworth) *racd in midfield: drvn 4f out: btn over 2f out* **6/1**

**7** *1* **Homebred Star** 3-8-11 ........ DCorby[(3)] 11 41
(PBowen) *s.s: wl in rr: sme prog 3f out: wknd over 1f out* **33/1**

**8** *4* **Wedding Cake (IRE)** 3-8-9 ........ OUrbina 1 28
(SirMichaelStoute) *racd in midfield: pushed along and no prog over 3f out: btn after* **4/1**[2]

5 **9** *3 1/2* **Dan Di Canio (IRE)**[21] 2519 3-9-0 ........ TEDurcan 2 26
(PWHarris) *chsd ldrs tl wknd 3f out* **12/1**

00- **10** *1 3/4* **Argentum**[237] 5810 3-9-0 ........ RLMoore 4 22
(LadyHerries) *hld up in last: nvr nr ldrs* **33/1**

**11** *1* **Blaze The Trail** 3-8-9 ........ MHenry 9 15
(Jean-ReneAuvray) *s.v.s: a wl bhd* **50/1**

0 **12** *nk* **Benny Bathwick (IRE)**[13] 2765 3-9-0 ........ SDrowne 6 19
(BRMillman) *chsd ldrs tl wknd over 3f out* **25/1**

**13** *3 1/2* **Sayrianna** 3-8-6 ........ JFMcDonald[(3)] 7 7
(IAWood) *nvr on terms: rdn and struggling over 4f out: sn bhd* **50/1**

00- **14** *5* **Dont Let Go**[184] 6223 3-8-9 ........ SCarson 8 —
(MissBSanders) *racd freely: led to 4f out: chsd wnr to over 2f out: wknd rapidly* **50/1**

1m 50.42s (4.82) **Going Correction** +0.65s/f (Yiel) **14** Ran SP% **122.9**
Speed ratings: **101,97,95,95,92 85,84,80,76,74 73,73,70,65**CSF £371.80 TOTE £6.00: £1.80, £12.00, £2.50; EX 991.50 Place 6 £361.77, Place 5 £189.67 .
**Owner** Mrs J E L Wright **Bred** Heatherwold Stud **Trained** Baughurst, Hants

**FOCUS**
Probably not a strong maiden and the conditions played a huge part, resulting in a strung out field at the finish and the overall form is not strong.

**NOTEBOOK**
**Take A Bow**, runner-up to North Light in a Goodwood maiden on his final start last season, was surprisingly easy to back on his belated reappearance. He dotted up but probably did not beat a lot in the process.
**Noble Mind** is by a speedy sire but he showed surprising stamina on his debut, staying on well for second. He clearly does not take after his father.
**Raakaan**, who cost 72,000gns as a yearling, is a half-brother to two juvenile winners. He plugged on well on his debut and looks likely to appreciate farther in time.
**Anatolian Queen(USA)** had run well on bad ground on her debut and once again confirmed her liking for cut.
**Different Planet** finished nicely clear of the rest and is now eligible for a handicap mark.
**Wedding Cake(IRE)**, a half-sister to high-class middle-distance performers Multicoloured and Gamut, failed to run up to market expectations, although one can excuse her poor performance in these conditions.
T/Jkpt: £3,550 to a £1 stake. Pool of £10,000 - 2.00 winning units. T/Plt: £101.70 to a £1 stake. Pool: £50,034.95. 358.95 winning tickets. T/Qpdt: £36.80 to a £1 stake. Pool: £2,530.60. 50.80 winning tickets. JN

# 2923 CHANTILLY (R-H)
Monday, June 21

**OFFICIAL GOING: Good to soft**

## 3162a PRIX HAMPTON (LISTED) 5f
**1:50** (1:55) 3-Y-0+ **£15,845** (£6,338; £4,754; £3,169)

RPR

**1** **Chineur (FR)**[15] 2719 3-8-13 ........ ELegrix 3 108
(MDelzangles, France)

**2** *nk* **Rue La Fayette (SWE)**[20] 4-9-2 ........ ODoleuze 12 104
(FReuterskiold, Sweden)

**3** *1 1/2* **Bishops Court**[17] 2636 10-9-5 ........ TGillet 11 102
(MrsJRRamsden) *trckd ldrs, 3rd 1/2-wy, pushed along over 2f out, rdn & styd on fr over 1f out to take 3rd 100yds out, nrst at fin*

**4** *1/2* **Vasywait (FR)**[53] 1741 5-9-5 ........ DBoeuf 5 100
(J-LGay, France)

**5** *1/2* **Sister Moonshine (FR)**[26] 3-8-7 ........ CSoumillon 1 92
(RPritchard-Gordon, France)

**6** *shd* **Dobby Road (FR)**[15] 2719 5-9-2 ........ FSpanu 10 95
(MlleVDissaux, France)

**7** *nk* **Meliksah (IRE)**[36] 2162 10-9-5 ........ TJarnet 13 97
(WBaltromei, Germany)

**8** *hd* **Bali Royal**[8] 2913 6-9-2 ........ IMendizabal 2 93
(MSSaunders) *close up, 2nd half-way, soon pushed along, ridden and weakened from over 1f out*

**9** *nk* **Together (FR)**[285] 4831 4-8-13 ........ DSicaud 4 89
(MmeCBoqueho-Vergne, France)

**10** *1 1/2* **Melkior (FR)**[36] 2162 7-9-5 ........ C-PLemaire 6 90
(TLallie, France)

**0** **Grosgrain (USA)**[24] 3-8-7 ........ GaryStevens 8 —
(AFabre, France)

**0** **Davignon**[716] 2809 5-9-2 ........ TThulliez 9 —
(USuter, Germany)

**0** **Ela Merici (FR)**[56] 1682 4-8-13 ........ (b) OPeslier 7 —
(MmeCBarande-Barbe, France)

59.20 secs **Going Correction** +0.05s/f (Good)
**WFA** 3 from 4yo+ 6lb **13** Ran SP% **16.7**
Speed ratings: **110,109,107,106,105 105,104,104,104,101** —,—,—.
**Owner** Marquesa De Moratalla **Bred** Cyril Humphris **Trained** France

**NOTEBOOK**
**Bishops Court**, smartly into his stride, he was always well to the fore. He had every chance but could not quicken enough as the race came to an end, and his trainer felt his action was not as good as usual. He now goes for the City Wall Stakes at Chester.
**Bali Royal** broke well and was with the leaders early on. When things warmed up she could not go the pace and gradually dropped out of contention.

## 3163a PRIX DE LA JONCHERE (GROUP 3) (C&G) 1m

2:20 (2:23) 3-Y-O **£25,704** (£10,282; £7,711; £5,141)

RPR

1 **Art Master (USA)**[21] 2542 3-8-11 GaryStevens 2 104
(AFabre, France) *niggled along leaving stalls and led after 100 yards, made rest, pushed out, easily* 1

2 *3* **Joursanvault (FR)**[39] 2072 3-8-11 CSoumillon 1 98
(ADeRoyer-Dupre, France) *trckd ldr on ins, 3rd str, went 2nd and rdn over 1 1/2f out, kept on but no imp on wnr* 3

3 *1/2* **Charmo (FR)**[15] 2721 3-8-11 SPasquier 5 97
(PDemercastel, France) *held up, 4th straight, ridden over 1 1/2f out, headway on outside to go 3rd over 1f out, kept on*

4 *hd* **Sujimoto (USA)**[127] 3-8-11 IMendizabal 4 97
(J-CRouget, France) *held up, last straight, effort on inside well over 1f out, kept on* 2

5 *2 1/2* **Highland Dancer (FR)**[21] 2542 3-8-11 TGillet 3 92
(JEPease, France) *pulled hard in 2nd on outside, effort over 2f out, weakened over 1 1/2f out*

1m 38.0s **Going Correction** +0.05s/f (Good) **5** Ran SP% **123.9**
Speed ratings: **116,113,112,112,109.**
**Owner** K Abdulla **Bred** Juddmonte Farms Inc **Trained** France

**NOTEBOOK**
**Art Master(USA)**, a very promising colt, won this Group race in style. He went into the lead soon after the start and, quickening up two out, the race for first place was over shortly after. He drew clear and was eased in the final stages. Now unbeaten in three races, he has a big future and the Prix Eugene Adam is on the cards.
**Joursanvault(FR)** this very game and consistent colt was settled behind the leader early on. He picked up well from one and a half out and ran on gamely to take second place.
**Charmo(FR)**, towards the back of the field, he was brought with a challenge from the two-furlong marker. He quickened well and ran on gamely to hold third place. He is still a maiden and a drop in class will surely change that situation.
**Sujimoto(USA)**ran a little free early on and never really looked dangerous. Previously unbeaten in three races, he ran on in the final stages but in a rather one-paced manner.

# 3008 BEVERLEY (R-H)

## Tuesday, June 22

**OFFICIAL GOING: Good**

20mm of rain over the previous four days but the going was described as 'definitely on the fast side and rough against the running rail'.
Wind: Slight 1/2 behind Weather: Fine and sunny

## 3164 PADDOCK BAR MAIDEN AUCTION FILLIES' STKS 7f 100y

2:15 (2:16) (E) 2-Y-O **£3,822** (£1,176; £588; £294) **Stalls** High

Form RPR

0 1 **Three Pennies**[35] 2213 2-8-11 FLynch 9 69
(MDods) *tk ken hold: sn trcking ldrs: effrt over 2f out: edgd lft 1f out: styd on to ld last 50yds* **25/1**

06 2 *nk* **Chutney Mary (IRE)**[22] 2535 2-8-8 ACulhane 5 65
(JGPortman) *led: hdd and no ex wl ins last* **16/1**

550 3 *1 1/4* **Lady Misha**[21] 2550 2-8-2 PHanagan 11 56
(JeddO'Keeffe) *chsd ldrs: rdn over 2f out: styd on fnl f* **7/1**[2]

5 4 *3 1/2* **Louise Rayner**[12] 2819 2-8-5 KDarley 8 51
(MLWBell) *mid-div: hdwy over 3f out: kpt on fnl 2f: nvr nr to chal* **16/1**

0 5 *1 1/4* **Barnbrook Empire (IRE)**[19] 2609 2-8-2 GDuffield 4 45
(IAWood) *chsd ldrs: rdn over 2f out: wknd over 1f out* **50/1**

6 *1/2* **Golden Squaw** 2-8-2 DAllan 6 44
(TDEasterby) *s.i.s: bhd and drvn along 4f out: hdwy over 2f out: nvr nr ldrs* **14/1**[3]

40 7 *8* **Mrs Kepple**[35] 2208 2-8-11 JFanning 2 34
(MJohnston) *chsd ldrs: rdn over 2f out: sn wknd* **16/1**

05 8 *1 1/4* **Lanas Turn**[6] 2985 2-8-2 PRobinson 10 22
(TDEasterby) *dwlt: hdwy on wd outside over 2f out: wknd over 1f out* **20/1**

432 9 *2* **Lady Dan (IRE)**[11] 2860 2-8-5 TLucas 7 21
(MWEasterby) *plld v hrd: trckd ldrs: rdn 2f out: no rspnse and sn lost pl* **2/5**[1]

0 10 *dist* **Amanderica (IRE)**[38] 2129 2-8-2 JBramhill 1 —
(MCChapman) *dwlt: swtchd rt after s: t.o 4f out* **100/1**

1m 34.6s (0.30) **Going Correction** +0.025s/f (Good) **10** Ran SP% **119.8**
Speed ratings: **99,98,97,93,91 91,82,80,78,—**CSF £366.59 TOTE £31.40: £4.40, £4.60, £2.00; EX 235.60.
**Owner** W J P Jackson **Bred** Rockwell Bloodstock **Trained** Piercebridge, Co Durham

**FOCUS**
With the favourite refusing to settle it was a weak maiden but a decent time for the type of race.

**NOTEBOOK**
**Three Pennies**, a March foal, was a lot sharper this time. She took a fierce grip but stayed on up the hill to force her head in front near the line. With the favourite beating herself it took little winning, but she will improve again and will be suited by the full mile in nurseries.
**Chutney Mary(IRE)**, stepping up in trip, started on terms this time. She set a good gallop and kept straight this time only to find the winner fractionally too strong near the line.
**Lady Misha** ran better but she persisted in hanging left and did not look an easy ride. *Official explanation: jockey said filly hung left from four out*
**Louise Rayner**, beaten in selling company on her debut, stands over plenty of ground but she persisted in swishing her tail in the paddock. She should improve again and find a seller or claimer over a mile.
**Barnbrook Empire(IRE)** made little appeal in the paddock but improved on her debut effort.
**Golden Squaw**, a January foal, stands over a fair amount of ground but she needs to furnish to her frame. After a tardy start she stayed on in her own time and stamina looks her biggest asset.
**Lady Dan(IRE)** looked to have been found an easy opportunity but, stepping up over two furlongs in trip, she refused point blank to settle and was on the retreat with two furlongs left to run. *Official explanation: jockey said filly ran too free in early stages*

## 3165 WESTWOOD CLAIMING STKS 1m 4f 16y

2:45 (2:45) (F) 4-Y-O+ **£3,376** (£1,039; £519; £259) **Stalls** High

Form RPR

-615 1 **Life Is Beautiful (IRE)**[5] 3008 5-8-12 50 RWinston 2 61
(WHTinning) *trckd ldr: effrt over 3f out: led over 1f out: drvn rt out* **15/8**[2]

5602 2 *3* **Cezzaro (IRE)**[4] 3056 6-8-3 40 JBramhill 5 47
(SRBowring) *led: qcknd 1/2-way: hdd appr fnl f: no ex* **10/1**

53-6 3 *3 1/2* **Al Azhar**[5] 3022 10-8-5 68 SWKelly 1 44
(MDods) *trckd ldrs: effrt 3f out: hung rt and kpt on same pce* **7/2**[3]

0016 4 *2* **Piste Bleu (FR)**[22] 2525 4-8-4 54 PHanagan 4 39
(RFord) *hld up: hdwy over 3f out: sn rdn and one pce* **13/8**[1]

0004 5 *5* **Turftanzer (GER)**[4] 3056 5-8-9 30 (t) KimTinkler 6 36
(DonEnricoIncisa) *trckd ldrs: outpcd 5f out: wknd 2f out* **25/1**

0030 6 *9* **Jezadil (IRE)**[54] 1721 6-8-5 27 KristinStubbs[(7)] 3 25
(MrsLStubbs) *dwlt: hdwy on outside to chse ldr 9f out: edgd rt and lost pl over 2f out: sn bhd* **40/1**

2m 38.99s (-0.31) **Going Correction** +0.025s/f (Good) **6** Ran SP% **110.5**
Speed ratings: **102,100,97,96,93 87**CSF £19.32 TOTE £2.60: £2.00, £2.60; EX 14.40.
**Owner** W H & Mrs J A Tinning **Bred** Azienda Agricola Loreto Luciani **Trained** Thornton-le-Clay, N Yorks

**FOCUS**
A low-grade claimer run at just a steady pace to halfway.

**NOTEBOOK**
**Life Is Beautiful(IRE)**, a standing dish on this track, is very genuine and made it five wins from ten starts here. This is her trip.
**Cezzaro(IRE)** had his own way in front but in the end was very much second best.
**Al Azhar** had 25lb in hand of the winner on official ratings but, a pensioner now, he has had his fair share of problems and this is as good as he is.
**Piste Bleu(FR)**, held up in a race not run at a strong pace to halfway, could never land a blow.
**Turftanzer(GER)** had plenty to find and seems out of sorts at present.
**Jezadil(IRE)** had the least chance on official figures and so it proved.

## 3166 TOTEQUADPOT STKS (H'CAP) 1m 1f 207y

3:15 (3:15) (D) (0-80,76) 3-Y-O+ **£6,808** (£2,095; £1,047; £523) **Stalls** High

Form RPR

0316 1 **Rotuma (IRE)**[14] 2752 5-9-1 65 (b) SWKelly 3 78
(MDods) *chsd ldrs: drvn along 4f out: hung rt over 2f out: styd on wl to ld last 100yds* **7/2**[2]

0-00 2 *3* **Les Arcs (USA)**[50] 1821 4-9-6 70 (p) JFEgan 1 77
(RCGuest) *t.k.h: trckd ldrs: led over 1f out: hdd and no ex ins last* **10/3**[1]

1006 3 *1 3/4* **Tight Squeeze**[27] 2403 7-9-12 76 ACulhane 7 80
(PWHiatt) *hld up: hdwy 4f out: kpt on same pce fnl 2f* **10/3**[1]

00-0 4 *1/2* **Expected Bonus (USA)**[20] 2573 5-8-2 52 JBramhill 2 55
(SCWilliams) *led: qcknd over 6f out: hdd over 1f out: one pce* **7/1**

0230 5 *3* **Easibet Dot Net**[18] 2659 4-8-11 61 (p) RWinston 6 58
(ISemple) *bhd: pushed along over 4f out: hmpd 2f out: nvr on terms* **8/1**

0040 6 *2* **Vibe**[15] 2732 3-8-10 72 KDalgleish 5 66
(MJohnston) *in rr: effrt over 3f out: hung rt over 2f out: nvr a factor* **25/1**

-306 7 *hd* **Indian Solitaire (IRE)**[6] 2982 5-9-9 73 (v) PHanagan 4 66
(RAFahey) *trckd ldrs: diven along over 3f out: wkng whn bdly hmpd 2f out* **9/2**[3]

2m 6.44s (-0.76) **Going Correction** +0.025s/f (Good)
**WFA** 3 from 4yo+ 12lb **7** Ran SP% **114.0**
Speed ratings: **104,101,100,99,97 95,95**CSF £15.49 TOTE £4.60: £2.50, £2.30; EX 20.40.
**Owner** Denton Hall Racing Ltd **Bred** Sean Twomey **Trained** Piercebridge, Co Durham
■ Stewards Enquiry : S W Kelly two-day ban: careless riding (Jul 4-5)

**FOCUS**
A 0-76 handicap not run at a strong pace for the first half mile. The form is ordinary and the winner will need to improve to score off revised mark..

**NOTEBOOK**
**Rotuma(IRE)** came off a straight line and put his rider in hot water. In the end he saw it out much the better, maintaining his trainer's red-hot streak.
**Les Arcs(USA)**, down 15lb in two outings this year, had the cheekpieces on. A 9/1 shot on the morning line about £20,000 was invested on course. After taking a fierce grip, he looked home and dry when going a couple of lengths up, but in the end he was comprehensively outstayed. It was an expensive defeat.
**Tight Squeeze**, 4lb lower than her last success, would have preferred a much stronger pace in the early stages.
**Expected Bonus(USA)**, who has not won for over two years, has slipped to a very lenient mark but, after being given his own way in front, he was still not nearly good enough.
**Easibet Dot Net** has an awkward head carriage and was going nowhere when knocked out of his stride.
**Vibe**, 2lb lower than on his handicap debut, gave problems beforehand. He would not go forward in a straight line and may need blinkers.
**Indian Solitaire(IRE)**, who seems to have lost the winning habit, was on the retreat when put right out of the contest by the winner.

## 3167 MINSTER ENCLOSURE H'CAP 7f 100y

3:45 (3:47) (E) (0-75,68) 3-Y-O+ **£4,719** (£1,452; £726; £363) **Stalls** High

Form RPR

4000 1 **Libre**[6] 2990 4-9-1 55 (bt) JFEgan 4 65
(RCGuest) *hld up and bhd: hdwy on wd outside over 2f out: styd on to ld last 75yds* **25/1**

4-04 2 *3/4* **Tedsdale Mac**[8] 2936 5-8-10 50 KMcEvoy 6 58
(NBycroft) *bhd: swtchd outside over 2f out: styd on strly ins last: nt rch wnr* **11/1**

1004 3 *1/2* **Border Artist**[7] 2965 5-9-10 64 ANicholls 8 71
(DNicholls) *chsd ldrs: led jst ins last: hdd and no ex last 75yds* **6/1**[1]

0524 4 *3/4* **Shifty**[11] 2854 5-8-9 49 (v) JFanning 1 54
(DNicholls) *hld up in mid-div: hdwy and edgd rt 2f out: styd on ins last* **12/1**

0000 5 *nk* **Smith N Allan Oils**[7] 2965 5-9-1 55 (p) SWKelly 9 59
(MDods) *chsd ldrs: hung lft over 1f out: kpt on ins last* **12/1**

4500 6 *1/2* **Blunham**[83] 1197 4-8-8 48 GDuffield 3 51
(MCChapman) *chsd ldrs: led 2f out tl jst ins last: no ex* **66/1**

-004 7 *shd* **Jedeydd**[13] 2776 7-9-2 56 (t) PHanagan 7 59
(MDods) *hld up and bhd: hdwy on inner and n.m.r 2f out: swtchd rt ins last: styd on* **7/1**[2]

6240 8 *1 1/4* **Cryfield**[13] 2776 7-9-2 56 KimTinkler 11 56
(NTinkler) *in tch: outpcd fnl 2f* **8/1**[3]

000- 9 *1/2* **Maureen Ann**[209] 6075 4-8-10 55 PMulrennan[(5)] 13 54
(TJFitzgerald) *s.i.s: hdwy on ins and nt clr run 2f out: nvr nr ldrs* **50/1**

0-01 10 *1/2* **Senior Minister**[8] 2928 6-10-0 68 6ex ACulhane 15 65
(PWHiatt) *chsd ldrs: effrt over 2f out: wknd over 1f out* **12/1**

-040 11 *shd* **Jakeal (IRE)**[59] 1620 5-8-13 53 DeanMcKeown 16 50
(RMWhitaker) *led tl 2f out: wknd appr fnl f* **8/1**[3]

01-3 12 *4* **Mallard (IRE)**[20] 2580 6-9-10 64 MFenton 2 51
(JGGiven) *chsd ldrs: effrt over 2f out: lost pl over 1f out* **8/1**[3]

0500 13 *9* **Hoh's Back**[2] 3127 5-8-13 60 (p) JDO'Reilly[(7)] 14 25
(PaulJohnson) *chsd ldrs: wknd 2f out: eased ins last* **16/1**

0000 14 *3 1/2* **Bond Playboy**[35] 2215 4-9-8 62 FLynch 12 18
(BSmart) *s.i.s: a bhd: eased ins last* **16/1**

2005 15 *21* **Locombe Hill (IRE)**[13] 2779 8-9-6 60 JCarroll 5 —
(DNicholls) *mid-div: lost pl 3f out: sn bhd and eased* **25/1**

3051 **P** **Weet Watchers**[6] 2979 4-9-1 **55** KDarley 10 —
(PABlockley) *chsd ldrs: wknd and eased over 2f out: p.u and dismntd: b.b.v* **6/1**[1]

1m 33.94s (-0.36) **Going Correction** +0.025s/f (Good) **16** Ran SP% **128.7**
Speed ratings: **103,102,101,100,100 99,99,98,97,97 97,92,82,78,54** —CSF £287.93 CT £1899.65 TOTE £35.80: £9.20, £1.90, £1.90, £3.80; EX 546.40 TRIFECTA Not won..
**Owner** Willie McKay **Bred** J C S Wilson Bloodstock **Trained** Brancepeth, Co Durham
■ Trainer Richard Guest's first Flat winner.

**FOCUS**
In effect a 0-68 handicap run at a sound gallop with the first two coming from off the pace. The form is ordinary but solid enough.

**NOTEBOOK**
**Libre**, down 15lb this time, had the tongue tie back on. Settled right off the pace, he came steaming through down the wide outside to lead near the line. *Official explanation: trainer's representative had no explanation for the improved form shown*
**Tedsdale Mac**, who has not won for over two years, was stepping up in trip and had a poor draw. Pulled wide two furlongs out, he finished with quite a flourish but just too late to worry the winner out of it.
**Border Artist** was in the firing line throughout. After working hard to get his head in front, he was edged out near the line. He is clearly in very good form.
**Shifty**, with the visor back on, had the worst of the draw. He is running well at present but now has won just twice from 43 starts.
**Smith N Allan Oils**is not a straightforward ride and his last three wins have been on the Polytrack.
**Blunham**, last seen out in March, was drawn just two from the outside and so deserves credit for this bold effort.
**Jedeydd** has not won for over two years. He likes to come late and needs luck in running, which he certainly did not have here.
**Cryfield** was being tapped for toe when running short of racing room. *Official explanation: jockey said gelding suffered interference during the race*
**Maureen Ann**, having her first outing for her new stable and seeing a racecourse for the first time since November, did quite well after losing ground at the start then meeting traffic problems. *Official explanation: jockey said filly reared as stalls opened and missed break*
**Weet Watchers** stopped in two strides and was dismounted. He was found to have burst. *Official explanation: jockey said gelding bled from the nose*

## 3168 ST JOHN AMBULANCE MAIDEN STKS 1m 100y
4:15 (4:15) (D) 3-Y-O £5,687 (£1,750; £875; £437) Stalls High

Form RPR
44 **1** **Swainsworld (USA)**[7] 2962 3-9-0 DAllan 11 75
(TDEasterby) *chsd ldrs: led over 1f out and edgd rt: jst hld on* **11/2**[3]
-322 **2** *1/2* **Awesome Love (USA)**[13] 2777 3-9-0 79 KDalgleish 10 74
(MJohnston) *led tl over 1f out: rallied ins last: jst hld* **1/1**[1]
40 **3** *2 1/2* **Lillianna (IRE)**[36] 2182 3-8-9 WRyan 8 64
(HRACecil) *chsd ldrs: kpt on same pce fnl 2f* **16/1**
46 **4** *3* **Nistaki (USA)**[10] 2900 3-9-0 KDarley 6 63
(TDEasterby) *chsd ldrs: effrt over 2f out: kpt on one pce* **9/2**[2]
50-0 **5** *3 1/2* **Stephano**[88] 1111 3-9-0 75 ACulhane 1 55
(BWHills) *mid-div: drvn along and outpcd 5f out: kpt on fnl 2f* **15/2**
0 **6** *1 1/4* **Phone Tapping**[17] 2693 3-9-0 PRobinson 7 53
(MHTompkins) *dwlt: bhd tl kpt on fnl 2f* **50/1**
04 **7** *3* **Belshazzar (USA)**[27] 2412 3-9-0 DaleGibson 2 46
(TPTate) *bhd: sme hdwy 2f out: nvr on terms* **100/1**
0-00 **8** *3/4* **Gallas (IRE)**[10] 2900 3-9-0 61 GParkin 3 45
(JSWainwright) *chsd ldr: lost pl over 2f out* **100/1**
0 **9** *1 1/2* **Dalmarnock (IRE)**[37] 2144 3-9-0 FLynch 9 42
(BSmart) *dwlt: nvr nr ldrs* **100/1**
0 **10** *10* **Scott**[13] 2777 3-9-0 ANicholls 4 21
(JJay) *s.i.s: a bhd: t.o 3f out* **50/1**
0-0 **11** *7* **Fifth Column (USA)**[22] 2519 3-9-0 GDuffield 5 6
(JRFanshawe) *chsd ldrs: hung rt and wknd 2f out: sn bhd and eased* **14/1**

1m 47.95s (0.65) **Going Correction** +0.025s/f (Good) **11** Ran SP% **114.8**
Speed ratings: **97,96,94,91,87 86,83,82,81,71 64**CSF £11.05 TOTE £5.80: £1.70, £1.10, £2.90; EX 19.40.
**Owner** Bigwigs Bloodstock **Bred** Twelve Oaks Stud **Trained** Great Habton, N Yorks

**FOCUS**
Probably just a modest maiden but there should be better to come from both of the first two.

**NOTEBOOK**
**Swainsworld(USA)** is clearly going the right way. He took a decisive lead but in the end the line came just in time. With the runner-up rated 79 he cannot expect a lenient handicap mark, but should improve again.
**Awesome Love(USA)** made the running but looked definitely second best when the winner went by. Pulled off the fence, he rallied strongly and in the end was just held. He is still learning and deserves to open his account.
**Lillianna(IRE)**is only small and this is as good as she is.
**Nistaki(USA)** did not travel anywhere near as well as he had done at York. His new trainer is still learning about him and he can now compete in handicaps. He ought to be capable of a fair bit better.
**Stephano**, absent since March and already rated 75, struggled to keep up and only stayed on in his own time. A more galloping track and a longer distance may prove the answer.
**Phone Tapping**, a rangy, backward-type having just his second start, again lost ground at the start but looks capable of a bit better especially on less firm ground.
**Belshazzar(USA)** showed a glimmer of ability and is now qualified for handicaps.
**Fifth Column(USA)** did not impress at all going to post and never looked to be happy or striding out on the way back. *Official explanation: jockey said gelding moved badly throughout*

## 3169 RACING HERE AGAIN ON 2ND JULY APPRENTICE H'CAP 5f
4:45 (4:46) (F) (0-55,55) 3-Y-0+ £3,640 (£1,120; £560; £280) Stalls High

Form RPR
0000 **1** **Laurel Dawn**[15] 2734 6-9-4 **49** WHogg 17 73
(IWMcinnes) *mde all: clr over 1f out: unchal* **6/1**[2]
0003 **2** *5* **Flying Tackle**[15] 2735 6-9-3 **48** (p) DTudhope 4 54+
(MDods) *dwlt: swtchd rt after s: nt clr run 2f out: styd on wl to take 2nd ins last* **20/1**
0005 **3** *1* **Ballybunion (IRE)**[5] 3010 5-9-10 **55** MHalford 16 57
(DNicholls) *dwlt: sn outpcd: hdwy 2f out: edgd lft: styd on ins last* **5/2**[1]
5600 **4** *hd* **Travelling Times**[8] 2936 5-9-0 **45** (b) MHoward 12 47
(JSWainwright) *chsd ldr: hung rt over 2f out: kpt on same pce* **25/1**
3400 **5** *1* **Off Hire**[12] 2823 8-9-4 **49** (v) DerekNolan 13 47
(CSmith) *chsd wnr: one pce fnl 2f* **20/1**
5451 **6** *1/2* **Lydia's Look (IRE)**[13] 2778 7-9-6 **51** AMullen 11 47
(TJEtherington) *mid-div: styd on fnl 2f: nvr nr to chal* **8/1**[3]
-002 **7** *nk* **Fairgame Man**[29] 2350 6-9-0 **45** (p) DFentiman 6 40
(JSWainwright) *free to post: mid-div: kpt on fnl 2f: nvr nr ldrs* **14/1**
40-0 **8** *nk* **Blessingindisguise**[27] 2407 11-9-0 **45** (b) RKeogh 20 39
(MWEasterby) *dwlt: sn bhd: styd on appr fnl f* **12/1**
-000 **9** *hd* **Loughlorien (IRE)**[5] 3010 5-9-5 **50** JDO'Reilly 5 43
(RAFahey) *sn towards rr on outer: kpt on appr fnl f: nvr a factor* **20/1**
0004 **10** *3/4* **Efimac**[6] 2979 4-8-9 **40** (v[1]) SuzanneFrance 18 31
(NBycroft) *mid-div: edgd lft over 1f out: nvr a factor* **14/1**
5000 **11** *3/4* **Mr Spliffy (IRE)**[5] 3016 5-9-6 **51** AndrewWebb 19 39
(MCChapman) *chsd ldrs: edgd lft and fdd over 1f out* **12/1**
000- **12** *1 1/4* **Bowlegs Billy**[253] 5538 4-9-3 **52** KPierrepont[(4)] 14 36
(JBalding) *in tch: outpcd after 2f: n.d after* **33/1**
-000 **13** *nk* **Zietzig (IRE)**[5] 3024 7-9-6 **51** BO'Neill 3 33
(DNicholls) *racd wd: sn bhd* **100/1**
0503 **14** *hd* **Ace-Ma-Vahra**[10] 2875 6-8-9 **40** (b) SaleemGolam 10 22
(SRBowring) *hld up in rr: sme hdwy whn sltly hmpd over 1f out* **25/1**
0-00 **15** *1 3/4* **College Hippie**[2] 3126 5-9-0 **45** (p) DeanWilliams 15 20
(JFCoupland) *swvd rt s: a bhd* **16/1**
3040 **16** *hd* **Bond Shakira**[11] 2850 3-9-3 **54** MStainton 7 29
(BSmart) *chsd ldrs on outer. lost pl and edgd rt over 1f out* **50/1**
00-5 **17** *2* **Le Meridien (IRE)**[9] 2909 6-9-10 **55** AReilly 9 22
(JSWainwright) *racd wd: sn in rr* **14/1**
00-0 **18** *5* **Rum Destiny (IRE)**[18] 2656 5-9-5 **50** (v) KJackson 2 —
(JSWainwright) *sn bhd* **66/1**
5020 **19** *3 1/2* **Somethingabouther**[12] 2800 4-9-0 **45** StevenHarrison 8 —
(PWHiatt) *sn bhd* **40/1**

63.15 secs (-0.85) **Going Correction** -0.125s/f (Firm)
**WFA** 3 from 4yo+ 6lb **19** Ran SP% **127.0**
Speed ratings: **101,93,91,91,89 88,88,87,87,86 85,83,82,82,79 79,75,67,62**CSF £127.92 CT £395.67 TOTE £6.90: £2.30, £4.50, £1.80, £5.10; EX 197.10 Place 6 £237.52, Place 5 £31.04.
**Owner** Ivy House Racing **Bred** Mrs J M Berry **Trained** Catwick, E Yorks

**FOCUS**
With the top-weight rated just 55 this was a selling handicap in all but name. The winner showed a return to form but got the run of the race and could be flattered.

**NOTEBOOK**
**Laurel Dawn**, who has won from a 31lb higher mark in the past, had a favourable draw and took this from the front scoring by a decisive margin. His small stable is enjoying a fruitful campaign.
**Flying Tackle**, a winner just once from 38 starts now, had a poor draw and after missing a beat at the start made his way across to the favoured far side. Meeting traffic problems, he stuck on to take second spot near the line. Six seems to suit him better.
**Ballybunion(IRE)** had a favourable draw but missed the break slightly and lacks tactical speed. Making his way to the outer, he was again putting in his best work at the finish.
**Travelling Times** is now 33lb lower than his last success two years ago.
**Off Hire** has slipped to a mark 7lb lower than his last win, which was here two years ago.
**Lydia's Look(IRE)**, 6lb higher, was not as well drawn this time.
**Le Meridien(IRE)** *Official explanation: jockey said mare was never travelling*
T/Plt: £2,400.60 to a £1 stake. Pool: £40,942.85. 12.45 winning tickets. T/Qpdt: £28.40 to a £1 stake. Pool: £4,576.70. 119.10 winning tickets. WG

# 2927 BRIGHTON (L-H)
Tuesday, June 22

**OFFICIAL GOING: Firm**
There was a major bias towards those that were brought over to the nearside in the closing stages, so caution is advised when assessing each performance.
Wind: almost nil Weather: fine

## 3170 BET DIRECT ON ATTHERACES INTERACTIVE CLAIMING STKS 6f 209y
2:30 (2:31) (F) 2-Y-O £2,863 (£818; £409) Stalls Low

Form RPR
032 **1** **Lojo**[7] 2960 2-8-7 RThomas[(5)] 3 53
(CADwyer) *trckd ldng pair: brought to nr side st: effrt and led over 1f out: pushed clr* **10/3**[2]
00 **2** *2 1/2* **Jay (IRE)**[17] 2690 2-8-10 (b[1]) RLMoore 2 45
(NACallaghan) *s.s: reminder and sn jnd ldr: led 4f out: rdn over 2f out: hdd over 1f out: looked reluctant and btn after* **13/2**[3]
1111 **3** *2 1/2* **Goldhill Prince**[2] 2799 2-8-10 (p) CHaddon[(7)] 4 45
(WGMTurner) *t.k.h: led to 4f out: styd w ldr: shkn up and ev ch over 1f out: wknd ins fnl f* **4/7**[1]
0 **4** *5* **Lara's Girl**[15] 2730 2-7-11 FPFerris[(3)] 1 15
(IAWood) *dwlt: a in last: rdn 4f out: struggling after* **14/1**

1m 25.65s (3.05) **Going Correction** +0.10s/f (Good) **4** Ran SP% **106.7**
Speed ratings: **86,83,80,74**CSF £20.04 TOTE £4.40; EX 31.70.Lojo was claimed by Sheena West for £11,000.
**Owner** Miss Lilo Blum **Bred** D K Ivory **Trained** Newmarket, Suffolk

**FOCUS**
A poor race and a modest time even for a race of this nature, suggesting the form is weak.This contest gave the first signs that there was an advantage in coming stands' side.

**NOTEBOOK**
**Lojo**, making her debut for the yard, appreciated this extra furlong but it was almost certainly being brought over to the stands' side that enabled her to slam her three rivals. The track bias, the runner-up not looking keen, and the favourite possibly feeling his busy schedule means that the form probably does not add up to much.
**Jay(IRE)** missed the break, but in this contest it did not matter and she played an active role until the winner swooped down the outside late on. Her head carriage did not impress despite the first-time blinkers, but perhaps she was not liking the ground.
**Goldhill Prince** has been brilliantly placed of late, but was struggling to get on top of the runner-up even before the extra furlong became an issue. He may have had enough for the time being.
**Lara's Girl** again missed the break, but was never in the contest and looks very modest.

## 3171 LITTLEWOODS BET DIRECT MEDIAN AUCTION MAIDEN STKS 7f 214y
3:00 (3:00) (F) 3-4-Y-O £2,870 (£820; £410) Stalls Low

Form RPR
4-00 **1** **Aragon's Boy**[13] 2776 4-9-6 66 DaneO'Neill 1 74
(HCandy) *mde virtually all: shkn up and drew clr fr 2f out: hanging lft but in n.d 1f out: eased nr fin* **5/1**
2300 **2** *2 1/2* **Archerfield (IRE)**[20] 2577 3-8-5 63 (t) RLMoore 2 63
(JWHills) *t.k.h: hld up in tch: effrt 3f out: chsd wnr over 1f out: no imp* **7/2**[3]
3 **3** *5* **Chertsey (IRE)**[12] 2818 3-8-5 TEDurcan 5 52
(CEBrittain) *dwlt: t.k.h and hld up in last: effrt to press ldrs 3f out: wknd over 1f out* **2/1**[1]
4045 **4** *2 1/2* **Pregnant Pause (IRE)**[9] 2915 3-8-3 64 JDWalsh[(7)] 3 51
(SKirk) *t.k.h: cl up: pressed wnr 4f out: nt qckn and btn over 2f out: wknd over 1f out* **12/1**

622- **5** *17* **Suave Quartet (USA)**[209] 6074 3-8-10 78.........................(b[1]) EAhern 4 12
(GAButler) *t.k.h: w wnr to 4f out: rdn and wknd over 3f out: t.o* **11/4**[2]

1m 36.12s (1.12) **Going Correction** +0.10s/f (Good)
**WFA** 3 from 4yo 10lb **5** Ran SP% **106.6**
Speed ratings: **98,95,90,88,71**CSF £20.66 TOTE £5.60: £2.50, £2.50; EX 32.00.
**Owner** Paul & Linda Dixon **Bred** R S A Urquhart **Trained** Wantage, Oxon

**FOCUS**
A poor contest and only an ordinary pace. The whole field were brought to the centre of the track turning for home.

**NOTEBOOK**
**Aragon's Boy** found this easier after disappointing in handicap company this season and made all the running to win with ease despite looking at the crowd. He seems to like this ground, but will find things much more difficult back in handicap company.
**Archerfield(IRE)** made the frame for the fourth time, but was well beaten by the winner and probably achieved very little.
**Chertsey(IRE)**, given a patient ride, had every chance but ended up well beaten and certainly did not improve from her debut. The one ray of hope is that she is yet to encounter anything but fast ground.
**Pregnant Pause(IRE)** had his chance, but is totally exposed and made it 16 starts without a win.
**Suave Quartet(USA)**, runner-up a couple of times on Polytrack last autumn, was reappearing after a break of seven months but he put in a very mulish display in the first-time blinkers and looked very unhappy on the track. *Official explanation: jockey said gelding did not handle the track*

## 3172 NATIONAL TALKING NEWSPAPER MAIDEN H'CAP 1m 3f 196y
3:30 (3:32) (E) (0-75,75) 3-Y-O+ £3,396 (£1,045; £522; £261) Stalls High

Form RPR
2222 **1** **Sunny Lady (FR)**[11] 2840 3-10-0 **75**.............................. LDettori 2 82
(EALDunlop) *mde all: c to nr side rail in st: drvn 2f out: hrd pressed fnl f: hld on* **4/7**[1]
005 **2** *½* **Crocolat**[12] 2818 3-8-8 **55**.............................. RLMoore 3 61
(NACallaghan) *trckd ldrs: outpcd over 3f out: rdn and effrt to chse wnr 2f out: str chal fnl f: jst hld* **14/1**[3]
0022 **3** *8* **Regal Performer (IRE)**[3] 3107 3-8-10 **57**.............................. PDobbs 4 50
(SKirk) *pressed wnr: carried across to nr side rail st: rdn and btn 2f out: wknd* **11/4**[2]
-046 **4** *3 ½* **Ellina**[11] 2848 3-9-5 **66**.............................. SSanders 1 54
(JPearce) *hld up in tch: rdn and outpcd over 3f out: n.d after* **14/1**[3]
040 **5** *12* **Lucky Again (IRE)**[15] 2729 3-9-1 **62**.............................. GCarter 5 31
(JLDunlop) *in tch tl wknd over 3f out: sn bhd* **20/1**

2m 30.65s (-1.45) **Going Correction** +0.10s/f (Good) **5** Ran SP% **108.4**
Speed ratings: **108,107,102,100,92**CSF £9.47 TOTE £1.40: £1.10, £3.50; EX 7.70.
**Owner** Maktoum Al Maktoum **Bred** Gainsborough Stud Management Ltd **Trained** Newmarket, Suffolk

**FOCUS**
A modest contest and only a two-horse race according to the market, but a solid pace set by the winner and a smart winning time for a race of its type. All five runners brought wide in the straight, with the winner coming right over to the stands' rail.

**NOTEBOOK**
**Sunny Lady(FR)**, runner-up in all four of her previous starts this season, finally got off the mark under a well-judged front-running ride, but she had to fight hard to see off the runner-up. It would be unfair to downgrade this performance because of the proximity of the second, and the distance back to her only market rival is probably a better yardstick.
**Crocolat ◆**, making her handicap debut and stepping up in trip, was the revelation of the race. She never stopped trying, and along with the winner pulled right away from the rest of the field. It will be surprising if she does not go one better before too long.
**Regal Performer(IRE)** was carried over to the stands' rail by the winner, whether he liked it or not, before being made to look very one paced. He is completely exposed.
**Ellina** was well beaten, but is may be significant that her best effort to date came on soft ground.
**Lucky Again(IRE)** did not improve for the switch to handicap company or the step up in trip.

## 3173 WINDMILL CATERING CLAIMING STKS 1m 1f 209y
4:00 (4:01) (F) 3-Y-O+ £2,898 (£828; £414) Stalls High

Form RPR
-000 **1** **Zeis (IRE)**[38] 2120 4-9-8 68.............................. (t) LFletcher(3) 8 67
(HMorrison) *trckd ldrs: effrt to chse ldr 2f out: drvn to ld ins fnl f: styd on wl* **7/2**[2]
-000 **2** *2* **Cal Mac**[8] 2928 5-9-1 70.............................. MHenry 6 53
(RMHCowell) *led over 7f out: rdn over 2f out: hdd and one pce ins fnl f* **11/1**
5000 **3** *1 ½* **Private Seal**[8] 2939 9-9-1 41.............................. (t) NCallan 3 50
(JulianPoulton) *settled in rr: rdn over 3f out: styd on fr over 2f out: tk 3rd wl ins fnl f* **25/1**
4310 **4** *1 ½* **Our Destiny**[20] 2594 6-9-9 55.............................. IMongan 1 55
(AWCarroll) *hld up in rr: prog over 3f out: cl up 2f out: sn nt qckn: fdd ins fnl f* **9/4**[1]
1-65 **5** *8* **Rojabaa**[4] 3056 5-9-6 53.............................. (p) LTreadwell(7) 4 44
(WGMTurner) *t.k.h: prom: chsd ldr over 5f out to over 2f out: fnd nil and btn after* **13/2**
1000 **6** *7* **Coronado Forest (USA)**[32] 1522 5-9-7 49.............................. SWhitworth 7 25
(MRHoad) *t.k.h early: in tch: rdn over 3f out: sn wknd* **12/1**
5003 **7** *shd* **Bontadini**[12] 2801 5-9-3 42.............................. SSanders 2 21
(DMorris) *led to over 7f out: styd prom: cl up 2f out: wknd rapidly sn after: virtually p.u nr fin* **11/1**
000- **8** *9* **Skater Boy**[195] 6158 3-8-4.............................. NChalmers(5) 9 8
(MissSheenaWest) *in tch: rdn over 4f out: sn wknd: bhd fnl 3f* **25/1**
5516 **9** *26* **Regulated (IRE)**[15] 2740 3-8-9 67.............................. DaneO'Neill 5 —
(DBFeek) *hld up in rr: rdn and wknd over 3f out: t.o* **5/1**[3]

2m 1.93s (-0.61) **Going Correction** +0.10s/f (Good)
**WFA** 3 from 4yo+ 12lb **9** Ran SP% **115.0**
Speed ratings: **106,104,103,102,95 90,89,82,61**CSF £41.32 TOTE £4.90: £1.60, £5.80, £6.70; EX 56.40.
**Owner** D J Donner **Bred** David Jamison Bloodstock **Trained** East Ilsley, Berks

**FOCUS**
A fair pace and a decent winning time for a claimer, but the form is modest and is held down by the proximity of the third. The field stayed more towards the far side, but the winner still raced wider than most.

**NOTEBOOK**
**Zeis(IRE)**, well beaten in three starts this year, was taking a drop in grade and scored on his first attempt on fast ground. Racing wide of his nearest pursuers over the last couple of furlongs probably made all the difference.
**Cal Mac**, who had 9lb in hand of his rivals on adjusted official ratings, made much of the running but bucked the trend for the afternoon by sticking tight to the inside rail. Considering how long he held on to the lead and how far he was beaten, it would have been interesting had he made for the stands' rail instead.
**Private Seal** seemed to run well at the weights, but we have been here before and he is an habitual loser without a win in three and a half years.
**Our Destiny**, a winner over course and distance two starts ago, reverted to more patient tactics but, after threatening to get into it at halfway, found disappointingly little under pressure.
**Rojabaa** has not built on a promising effort following a break.
**Regulated(IRE)**, second best in on adjusted official ratings, ran a stinker. *Official explanation: jockey said gelding lost its action at the top of the hill*

## 3174 EDGAR'S COOL WATER H'CAP 6f 209y
4:30 (4:30) (E) (0-70,64) 3-Y-O+ £3,415 (£1,051; £525; £262) Stalls Low

Form RPR
22-0 **1** **Franksalot (IRE)**[24] 2483 4-10-0 **64**.............................. SSanders 11 76
(MissBSanders) *hld up in rr: prog on outer 1/2-way: rdn over 1f out: led ins fnl f: styd on wl* **10/1**
0200 **2** *1 ¼* **Ziet D'Alsace (FR)**[20] 2597 4-9-0 **50**.............................. IMongan 4 59
(AWCarroll) *prom: w ldrs fr 1/2-way: led wl over 1f out: hdd and one pce ins fnl f* **10/1**
2105 **3** *1 ¼* **Londoner (USA)**[3] 3103 6-9-10 **60**.............................. RLMoore 8 66
(SDow) *led for 2f: w ldrs tl lost pl over 2f out: hanging lft after: r.o again last 150yds* **4/1**[2]
063 **4** *½* **Mister Clinton (IRE)**[12] 2803 7-9-3 **53**.............................. DaneO'Neill 6 57
(DKIvory) *trckd ldrs: effrt over 2f out: drvn and cl up over 1f out: one pce fnl f* **9/2**[3]
1050 **5** *shd* **Warlingham (IRE)**[8] 2948 6-9-7 **57**.............................. CCatlin 1 61
(PHowling) *led after 2f: mde most tl wl over 1f out: one pce u.p* **9/1**
0-03 **6** *hd* **Jazzy Millennium**[16] 2707 7-9-3 **53**.............................. (b) NCallan 5 56
(BRMillman) *w ldrs: ev ch u.p 2f out: fdd ins fnl f* **3/1**[1]
0425 **7** *2 ½* **Tee Jay Kassidy**[12] 2803 4-8-1 **40**.............................. LisaJones(3) 9 37
(JulianPoulton) *in rr whn squeezed out over 5f: effrt over 2f out: one pce and nvr rchd ldrs* **12/1**
0000 **8** *3* **Goodwood Prince**[16] 2707 4-9-2 **52**.............................. SWhitworth 2 41
(SDow) *s.s: wl in rr: effrt on wd outside 3f out: wknd over 1f out* **20/1**
6556 **9** *½* **Zinging**[16] 2703 5-8-0 **36**.............................. DKinsella 3 24
(JJBridger) *stmbld s: hld up in rr: last and rdn 3f out: no imp on ldrs after* **20/1**
0-00 **10** *4* **Medusa**[13] 2788 4-9-10 **60**.............................. MTebbutt 7 37
(DMorris) *chsd ldrs: rdn over 3f out: wknd 2f out* **50/1**
5460 **11** *3 ½* **Kinsman (IRE)**[10] 2886 7-8-12 **51**.............................. (b) J-PGuillambert(3) 10 19
(TDMccarthy) *s.s: a in rr: brief effrt on wd outside 3f out: eased fnl 2f* **14/1**

1m 22.7s (0.10) **Going Correction** +0.10s/f (Good) **11** Ran SP% **117.2**
Speed ratings: **103,101,100,99,99 99,96,92,87 83**CSF £102.77 CT £480.22 TOTE £12.60: £2.80, £3.80, £2.40; EX 70.40.
**Owner** Peter Crate, Jane Byers, Roger Knight **Bred** J P Hardiman **Trained** Epsom, Surrey
■ Stewards Enquiry : Dane O'Neill one-day ban: careless riding (Jul 4)

**FOCUS**
A competitive handicap run at an even pace and the bias towards the stands' side was very much back in evidence. The form is sound.

**NOTEBOOK**
**Franksalot(IRE)**, beaten out of sight on his reappearance last month, had obviously benefited a huge amount from that and was brought widest of all to score and maintain his fine record on this track. Few jockeys ride Brighton better than Sanders. *Official explanation: trainer said, regarding the improved form shown, jockey was unable to cover gelding up at Lingfield last time out*
**Ziet D'Alsace(FR)**, dropping in the weights, put in a solid effort on a track where she has gone well before. Both her previous wins have been in selling company, but she has the ability to win a modest handicap over this trip.
**Londoner(USA)**, a winner over course and distance under similar conditions earlier this month, is a very difficult ride and tended to run in snatches on this occasion. Nothing was finishing quicker and the ability is there, but so are the quirks. *Official explanation: jockey said gelding never came down the hill*
**Mister Clinton(IRE)**, closely matched with Londoner on running here earlier in the month, was brought with his effort coming to the furlong pole, but he hung to the inside rail under pressure and that was no help given the way the track was riding.
**Warlingham(IRE)** has been around here a few times, but after being given a positive ride failed to get home on this occasion.
**Jazzy Millennium**, a multiple winner here including this race last year off a 1lb higher mark, was up there for a long way but faded rather disappointingly in the closing stages.
**Kinsman(IRE)** *Official explanation: jockey said saddle slipped*

## 3175 ALEXANDER CATERING H'CAP 5f 59y
5:00 (5:00) (F) (0-55,58) 3-Y-O+ £2,968 (£848; £424) Stalls Low

Form RPR
-063 **1** **Maluti**[8] 2932 3-8-12 **48**.............................. SSanders 8 61
(RGuest) *racd in midfield: effrt on outer over 1f out: drvn and r.o to ld wl ins fnl f* **10/3**[2]
0002 **2** *1* **Yorkie**[25] 2440 5-9-10 **54**.............................. IMongan 2 63
(PABlockley) *hld up in rr: prog 1/2-way: led wl over 1f out: hdd and no ex wl ins fnl f* **5/2**[1]
-400 **3** *¾* **Redwood Star**[10] 2875 4-9-10 **54**.............................. (e) RPrice 10 60
(PLGilligan) *hld up wl in rr: c wdst of all in st: rdn over 1f out: r.o wl fnl f: nrst fin* **10/1**
00-2 **4** *1 ¼* **Lucky Valentine**[12] 2800 4-9-3 **47**.............................. (b) RLMoore 9 48
(GLMoore) *w ldrs: ev ch over 1f out: fdd fnl f* **5/1**[3]
0-00 **5** *1 ¾* **Beenaboutabit**[88] 1121 6-8-1 **34** oh4.............................. JFMcDonald(3) 11 28
(MrsLCJewell) *w ldrs: led briefly 2f out: fdd fnl f* **66/1**
0050 **6** *hd* **Moonglade (USA)**[10] 2886 4-8-4 **34** oh1.............................. (b) JMcAuley 3 27
(MissJFeilden) *hld up in rr: drvn 2f out: one pce and nvr rchd ldrs* **25/1**
5204 **7** *hd* **Savernake Brave (IRE)**[8] 2932 3-8-10 **46**.............................. NCallan 6 38
(MrsHSweeting) *hld up: n.m.r after 1f and dropped to last: drvn on outer over 2f out: no imp over 1f out* **12/1**
5-00 **8** *1 ¼* **Ryan's Quest (IRE)**[24] 2482 5-8-9 **42**.............................. J-PGuillambert(3) 1 29
(TDMccarthy) *racd on inner: wl in tch: ch over 1f out: wknd fnl f* **20/1**
0000 **9** *1 ¾* **Bahamian Belle**[12] 2800 4-8-11 **48**.............................. LauraPike(7) 12 28
(PSMcentee) *chsd ldrs: effrt and in tch on outer 2f out: wknd over 1f out* **16/1**
0604 **10** *nk* **Must Be So**[12] 2800 3-7-13 **35**.............................. (t) DKinsella 5 14
(JJBridger) *racd in midfield: drvn over 2f out: wknd over 1f out* **16/1**
0601 **11** *shd* **Alizar (IRE)**[8] 2932 3-9-8 **58** 6ex.............................. CCatlin 7 37
(SDow) *w ldr: led over 3f out to 2f out: wknd* **7/1**
4000 **12** *2 ½* **Cedric Coverwell**[20] 2586 4-9-5 **49**.............................. DaneO'Neill 4 18
(DKIvory) *led to over 3f out: wknd 2f out* **25/1**

62.80 secs (0.53) **Going Correction** +0.10s/f (Good)
**WFA** 3 from 4yo+ 6lb **12** Ran SP% **123.3**
Speed ratings: **99,97,96,94,91 91,90,88,85,85 85,81**CSF £12.09 CT £79.93 TOTE £5.10: £2.00, £1.90, £2.50; EX 17.00 Place 6 £359.14, Place 5 £82.96.
**Owner** Mrs Jane Poulter **Bred** G S Shropshire **Trained** Newmarket, Suffolk

**FOCUS**
A low-level sprint handicap, but competitive enough and sound form. The field fanned right out across the track at halfway and the bias towards those on the stands' side probably proved crucial.

**NOTEBOOK**
**Maluti**, dropping back a furlong and again very well backed, was given another superb ride by Sanders who brought him with his effort right over against the stands' side, whilst at the same time his main rival was hanging his chance away.
**Yorkie** probably should have won this, for after being brought through the middle to hit the front at the ideal time, he then hung away towards the inside rail under a right-hand drive and the winner took full advantage.
**Redwood Star**, who is slowly dropping to a reasonable mark, followed the winner's path near the stands' rail and finished very strongly.
**Lucky Valentine** showed good speed with the blinkers back on and hung in there until well inside the last furlong.
**Beenaboutabit** has run well here before and put up her best performance for some time, but her official rating says it all about her overall record.
**Alizar(IRE)**, carrying a 6lb penalty for her win over an extra furlong here the previous week, showed good early speed but faded very tamely once headed.
T/Plt: £690.10 to a £1 stake. Pool: £34,933.35. 36.95 winning tickets. T/Qpdt: £43.10 to a £1 stake. Pool: £2,794.90. 47.90 winning tickets. JN

## 2804 NEWBURY (L-H)
Tuesday, June 22
**OFFICIAL GOING: Good to firm (firm in places)**

### 3176 STANJAMESUK.COM EBF MAIDEN STKS 5f 34y
6:30 (6:30) (D) 2-Y-O £5,538 (£1,704; £852; £426) Stalls High

Form RPR
1 **Southern Africa (USA)** 2-8-11 TPQueally(3) 4 85+
(GAButler) *rangy: scope: lw: in tch: pushed along 2f out: qcknd to chse ldrs over 1f out: edgd rt and led last half f: readily* **16/1**
6 2 hd **Lady Le Quesne (IRE)**[13] [2786] 2-8-9 SDrowne 7 80
(AMBalding) *lw: chsd ldr: led over 2f out: rdn 1f out: hdd last half f: kpt on but nt pce of wnr* **7/1**
3 2 **Bounty Quest** 2-9-0 RHughes 3 78
(RHannon) *str: bit bkwd: s.i.s: sn pushed along and trckd ldrs: rdn and effrt over 1f out: one pce ins last* **5/2**[2]
4 ¾ **Master Cobbler (IRE)** 2-9-0 EAhern 6 75
(GAButler) *lengthy: scope: s.i.s: bhd: shkn up 2f out: kpt on wl fnl f: gng on cl home* **14/1**
2450 5 nk **Alpaga Le Jomage (IRE)**[7] [2959] 2-9-0 LDettori 5 74
(BJMeehan) *led tl hdd over 2f out: styd pressing ldrs tl jst ins fnl f: wknd nr fin* **7/4**[1]
4 6 6 **Classic Guest**[11] [2837] 2-8-9 TEDurcan 8 48
(MRChannon) *chsd ldrs: rdn and wknd over 1f out* **11/2**[3]
0 7 5 **Follow My Lead**[8] [2947] 2-8-9 MHills 1 31
(BWHills) *chsd ldrs early: sn wknd* **20/1**
8 1 ¾ **Beauchamp Twist** 2-8-9 JFortune 2 24
(GAButler) *leggy: s.i.s: a bhd* **33/1**
60.87 secs (-1.78) **Going Correction** -0.40s/f (Firm) **8 Ran SP% 113.1**
Speed ratings: **98,97,94,93,92 83,75,72**CSF £119.15 TOTE £22.50: £2.80, £2.30, £1.50; EX 370.70.
**Owner** The International Carnival Partnership **Bred** H Ahamdi And Michael Anderson **Trained** Blewbury, Oxon
**FOCUS**
Probably not a bad maiden that should produce some winners.
**NOTEBOOK**
**Southern Africa(USA)**, a 52,000gns yearling out of a dual two-year-old winner, was quite easy to back on this racecourse debut. Despite that, he proved good enough to overcome his inexperience and make a winning debut. There should be plenty of improvement in him and he will be worthy of respect when stepped up in grade.
**Lady Le Quesne(IRE)** shaped well on her debut here over six furlongs and ran another good race on this drop in trip. She never looked like getting the better of the winner inside the final furlong, but there should be a similar event in her.
**Bounty Quest**, a 25,000gns sister to the top-class stayer Classic Cliche, out of a 12-furlong winner, was quite well supported and made a respectable debut. He should improve and it will be most disappointing if he does not find a maiden.
**Master Cobbler(IRE)**, a 50,000euros half-brother to Privy Seal, made a pleasing enough debut and is another who should improve. It is interesting he was allowed to go off a shorter price than his winning stablemate, and was arguably the first choice on the jockey bookings.
**Alpaga Le Jomage(IRE)** was a very short price even allowing for his respectable eighth of 15 in the Windsor Castle, given that he has had a few chances at this sort of level already. He had every chance, but does not appear to know how to win. He will find easier opportunities, but does not appeal as one to take a short price about.
**Classic Guest** failed to build on her debut running.

### 3177 STAN JAMES H'CAP 1m (S)
7:00 (7:03) (E) (0-75,75) 4-Y-O+ £4,420 (£1,360; £680; £340) Stalls High

Form RPR
0051 1 **Oh Boy (IRE)**[12] [2806] 4-9-3 64 RHughes 3 79
(RHannon) *lw: w ldrs: led jst ins fnl 2f: hung lft sn after: edgd rt to stands rail 1f out: pushed clr ins last: comf* **7/1**[2]
-006 2 3 **Sri Diamond**[21] [2560] 4-9-13 74 LDettori 11 82
(SKirk) *lw: narrow advantage tl hdd jst ins fnl 2f: styd chsng wnr: outpcd ins last but hld on wl for 2nd* **7/1**[2]
0213 3 shd **Best Before (IRE)**[4] [3048] 4-9-5 73 6ex SJDonohoe(7) 12 81
(PDEvans) *s.i.s: sn prom: rdn over 2f out: styd on u.p fnl f to press for 2nd but no ch w wnr* **5/1**[1]
0-30 4 1 **Crail**[21] [2560] 4-9-9 70 GBaker 7 75
(CFWall) *lw: hld up in rr: n.m.r over 2f out: rdn: carried hd awkwardly but r.o appr fnl f: kpt on ins last:nt rch ldrs* **5/1**[1]
3130 5 1 ½ **Parnassian**[18] [2643] 4-8-7 59 RThomas(5) 16 61
(GBBalding) *bhd: hdwy over 2f out: rdn and styd on fr over 1f out: nt pce to trble ldrs* **9/1**
0-25 6 ¾ **Labelled With Love**[12] [2801] 4-8-2 52 RMiles(3) 10 52
(JRBoyle) *lw: stdd s: hld up in rr: swtchd to outside and chsd ldrs 5f out: wknd fnl f* **33/1**
2000 7 1 ¼ **Te Quiero**[32] [2278] 6-10-0 75 (t) SDrowne 4 72
(MissGayKelleway) *hld up in rr: pushed along and sme hdwy over 2f out: kpt on fnl f but nvr gng pce to be dangerous* **12/1**
1205 8 nk **Wanna Shout**[26] [2430] 6-8-9 56 SRighton 6 53
(RDickin) *bhd: hdwy to chse ldrs 4f out: wknd ins fnl 2f* **16/1**
6542 9 3 **Phred**[8] [2945] 4-9-0 61 SCarson 2 51
(RFJohnsonHoughton) *pressed ldrs tl wknd ins fnl 2f* **8/1**[3]
2004 10 hd **Fortune Point (IRE)**[10] [2883] 6-8-13 60 JFortune 14 49
(AWCarroll) *nvr gng pce to rch ldrs* **12/1**
-040 11 6 **Duelling Banjos**[35] [2218] 5-9-2 63 EAhern 8 39
(JAkehurst) *lw: chsd ldrs: rdn 3f out: wknd 2f out* **10/1**
6-32 12 ½ **Have Some Fun**[150] [601] 4-8-12 59 JQuinn 15 33
(PRChamings) *chsd ldrs: rdn 3f out: wknd 2f out* **16/1**
0620 13 1 **Spy Gun (USA)**[25] [2459] 4-8-1 53 ow3 NChalmers(5) 1 25
(TWall) *chsd ldrs over 5f* **33/1**
1m 37.27s (-3.56) **Going Correction** -0.40s/f (Firm) **13 Ran SP% 121.6**
Speed ratings: **101,98,97,96,95 94,93,93,90,89 83,83,82**CSF £56.43 CT £279.38 TOTE £4.90: £1.90, £2.50, £2.70; EX 63.60.
**Owner** A F Merritt **Bred** Miss Brid Walsh **Trained** East Everleigh, Wilts
■ Stewards Enquiry : S J Donohoe two-day ban: careless riding (Jul 4, Sep 7)
**FOCUS**
Just a modest handicap but the form looks reliable, although the pace was ordinary and it proved hard to come from well off the speed.
**NOTEBOOK**
**Oh Boy(IRE)**, off the mark over course and distance on his previous start, followed up off a 4lb higher mark in good style. Clearly ahead of the Handicapper, he would be of interest if turned out under a penalty on similarly fast ground.
**Sri Diamond**, lightly-raced since gaining his only previous success on his debut in September 2002, appears to be running into a bit of form and should be placed to effect in similar company this summer.
**Best Before(IRE)**, 2lb well-in under his 6lb penalty for a success two starts back, ran his race and can have no real excuses. He has an All-Weather rating of just 56 and would be interesting if returned to that surface.
**Crail** represents a stable in fine form and did best of those from off the pace.
**Parnassian** lacked a change of pace and a stronger end-to-end gallop may have suited better.
**Duelling Banjos** *Official explanation: jockey said gelding was unsuited by the Good to Firm, Firm in places ground*
**Spy Gun(USA)** *Official explanation: trainer said gelding was scoped and found to have bled internally*

### 3178 OCTAGON TOYOTA FILLIES' H'CAP 6f 8y
7:30 (7:33) (D) (0-80,80) 3-Y-O+ £5,746 (£1,768; £884; £442) Stalls High

Form RPR
21 1 **Catherine Wheel**[24] [2468] 3-8-13 68 JPMurtagh 6 82+
(JRFanshawe) *led: rdn 2f out: edgd lft and hdd fnl 100yds: rallied to ld again last strides* **15/8**[1]
00-0 2 nk **Bee Minor**[17] [2694] 3-9-1 70 RHughes 5 75
(RHannon) *trckd wnr: rdn over 2f out: edgd lft ins last and led fnl 100yds: no ex and hdd last strides* **16/1**
4155 3 1 ¾ **I Wish**[4] [3047] 6-8-9 57 ow1 GBaker 7 57
(MMadgwick) *prom: rdn over 1f out: styd on u.p fnl f: nt rch ldrs* **14/1**
-302 4 2 **Concubine (IRE)**[4] [3047] 5-8-10 58 (p) JFortune 9 52
(JRBoyle) *lw: in tch: chsd ldrs 1/2-way: rdn over 1f out: wknd ins last* **13/2**
0132 5 1 **Amelia (IRE)**[10] [2875] 6-8-5 58 BSwarbrick(5) 2 49
(WMBrisbourne) *in tch: rdn 3f out: wknd appr fnl f* **11/2**[3]
0-20 6 nk **Go Between**[17] [2694] 3-9-11 80 SDrowne 4 70
(EALDunlop) *s.i.s: bhd: rdn over 2f out: nvr gng pce to be dangerous* **10/1**
2660 7 6 **Prima Stella**[95] [1051] 5-8-11 62 LisaJones(3) 12 34
(JARToller) *chsd ldrs tl wknd over 2f out* **9/1**
-402 8 6 **Cerulean Rose**[9] [2909] 5-9-5 67 LDettori 8 21
(AWCarroll) *lw: rdn 1/2-way: a bhd: lost tch fnl 2f* **11/4**[2]
1m 11.56s (-2.81) **Going Correction** -0.40s/f (Firm)
**WFA** 3 from 4yo+ 7lb **8 Ran SP% 121.8**
Speed ratings: **102,101,99,96,95 94,86,78**CSF £36.90 CT £348.46 TOTE £2.80: £1.30, £6.20, £3.00; EX 103.10.
**Owner** Cheveley Park Stud **Bred** Cheveley Park Stud Ltd **Trained** Newmarket, Suffolk
**FOCUS**
A modest handicap and, with four non-runners, it was not that competitive, although the winner is inexperienced and can rate higher. Once again it proved hard to come from off the pace.
**NOTEBOOK**
**Catherine Wheel** did not really impress when getting off the mark at Doncaster on her previous start, but she was well backed to follow up in this tougher heat over another furlong and did not disappoint. She did not have much in hand at the finish, but is clearly progressing and should not go up too much for this.
**Bee Minor**, still a maiden, improved on the form she showed on her reappearance and looks capable of picking up a similar contest.
**I Wish**, dropped back a furlong in trip, appeared to run her race. She has never won outside of Class E company and is on the sort of mark that allows her to race at a lower, more suitable level.
**Concubine(IRE)** had declared cheekpieces on for the first time, but they did not appear to bring around a great deal of improvement. She is hard to win with.
**Amelia(IRE)** did not run badly, but is not exactly well-handicapped at the moment.
**Go Between** did not help her chance with a slow start and could never get involved thereafter.
**Cerulean Rose** has never won beyond five furlongs, but was a long below form even allowing for the trip. *Official explanation: jockey said mare was never travelling*

### 3179 STAN JAMES 08000 383384 MAIDEN STKS 5f 34y
8:00 (8:02) (D) 3-Y-O £5,564 (£1,712; £856; £428) Stalls High

Form RPR
000- 1 **Tregarron**[225] [5966] 3-9-0 62 RLMoore 1 72
(RHannon) *lw: trckd ldr: rdn to ld wl over 1f out: hld on wl u.p fnl f* **10/1**
0- 2 hd **Royal Challenge**[227] [5947] 3-9-0 EAhern 7 71
(GAButler) *b.hind: lw: in tch: hdwy over 1f out: chsd wnr ins last: styd on wl: no ex last strides* **4/1**[2]
6 3 1 ¼ **Millinsky (USA)**[17] [2675] 3-8-9 SSanders 6 61
(RGuest) *lw: bhd: hdwy over 2f out: r.o wl to chsd ldrs fnl f: one pce nr fin* **6/1**
06-2 4 2 ½ **Green Ridge**[43] [1991] 3-8-9 68 PaulEddery 9 51
(PWD'Arcy) *lw: chsd ldrs: rdn and effrt over 1f out: wknd ins fnl f* **6/1**
-000 5 shd **Scarlett Breeze**[8] [2932] 3-8-9 48 MHills 8 51
(JWHills) *s.i.s: bhd: hdwy over 2f out: nvr gng pce to rch ldrs: wknd ins fnl f* **40/1**
0-04 6 shd **Eight Ellington (IRE)**[11] [2836] 3-9-0 58 IMongan 2 55
(MissGayKelleway) *in tch: pushed along 1/2-way: nvr gng pce to be dangerous but styd on ins last* **10/1**
0-40 7 ¾ **Indiana Blues**[19] [2621] 3-8-9 83 (b[1]) RHughes 5 47
(AMBalding) *sn led: hdd wl over 1f out: wkng whn sltly hmpd 1f out* **3/1**[1]
0 8 3 **Loveyoulongtime**[13] [2785] 3-8-9 LDettori 10 35
(AMBalding) *bit bkwd: sn in tch: rdn 1/2-way: wknd over 1f out* **16/1**
9 1 ¼ **Firenze** 3-8-9 JPMurtagh 3 30
(JRFanshawe) *w'like: bkwd: slowly away and bdly outpcd: kpt on fr over 1f out but nvr a danger* **9/2**[3]

000 **10** *1* **Batchworth Beau**[13] 2785 3-9-0 SCarson 4 31
(EAWheeler) *s.i.s: a outpcd* **50/1**
60.22 secs (-2.43) **Going Correction** -0.40s/f (Firm) **10** Ran SP% **120.2**
Speed ratings: **103,102,100,96,96 96,95,90,88,86**CSF £51.44 TOTE £16.40: £4.20, £2.10, £2.20; EX 98.20.
**Owner** J R Good **Bred** Mrs P Good **Trained** East Everleigh, Wilts
■ Stewards Enquiry : R L Moore caution: careless riding

**FOCUS**
A weak sprint maiden for the track.

**NOTEBOOK**
**Tregarron** had plenty of chances to win a race as a juvenile, but proved pretty disappointing. However, racing for the first time in 225 days, he finally showed what he is capable of with a game success. This was not a very good race and things are bound to be tougher in handicap company, but his confidence will be on a high and he should not be underestimated.
**Royal Challenge** was well held on his only start last season but, racing for the first time in 227 days, this represents improved form. There should be a similar race in him providing he goes the right way.
**Millinsky(USA)** did not shape badly in a weak race on her debut and again ran creditably. She is going the right way and should do even better when handicapped.
**Green Ridge** is proving quite frustrating and she was not at her best on this drop back from six furlongs.
**Scarlett Breeze**, rated just 48, gives a good guide to the strength of the form.
**Indiana Blues** is regressing and the first-time blinkers did not help matters.
**Firenze**, a sister to the high-class Frizzante, was easy to back on course and showed little after missing the break. However, she looked as though the run would bring her on and she should improve with this experience under her belt. *Official explanation: jockey said filly missed the break through inexperience*

## 3180 STAN JAMES TELEBETTING H'CAP 7f (S)
**8:30** (8:34) (E) (0-70,70) 3-Y-O **£4,446** (£1,368; £684; £342) **Stalls** High

Form RPR
4306 **1** **Evaluator (IRE)**[13] 2790 3-9-4 **70** RMiles(3) 19 79
(TGMills) *lw: bhd: hdwy on rails fr 2f out: str run ins fnl f to ld cl home* **9/1**
5344 **2** *½* **Here To Me**[10] 2871 3-9-5 **68** RHughes 11 76
(RHannon) *w ldrs tl led ins fnl 2f: hrd drvn ins last: hdd cl home* **14/1**
3351 **3** *1* **Kryssa**[20] 2577 3-9-1 **64** RLMoore 16 69
(GLMoore) *lw: hld up in rr: hdwy 2f out: str run to chse ldrs fnl f: nt qckn ins last* **5/1**[1]
0052 **4** *½* **Go Yellow**[11] 2836 3-8-12 **68** SJDonohoe(7) 3 72
(PDEvans) *chsd ldrs: chal 2f out: styd on same pce ins last* **33/1**
00-6 **5** *1 ¼* **Moscow Times**[40] 2063 3-9-7 **70** JPMurtagh 14 71+
(DRCElsworth) *hld up mid-div: hdwy and nt clr run 2f out: swtchd lft and kpt on fr over 1f out: styd on ins last but nt rch ldrs* **8/1**
-063 **6** *½* **Dr Synn**[40] 2063 3-9-2 **65** PDoe 7 64
(JAkehurst) *chsd ldrs: drvn to chal 2f out: wknd fnl f* **7/1**[3]
0-15 **7** *1 ¾* **Sforzando**[17] 2694 3-9-2 **68** LisaJones(3) 20 63
(JARToller) *lw: s.i.s: bhd and swtchd lft: hdwy 2f out: styd on fnl f but nvr gng pce to trble ldrs* **13/2**[2]
40-0 **8** *½* **Blue Java**[13] 2790 3-9-0 **63** SDrowne 12 56
(HMorrison) *chsd ldrs: rdn over 2f out: wknd ins fnl f* **33/1**
00-5 **9** *nk* **Trois Etoiles (IRE)**[19] 2621 3-8-12 **61** MHills 5 53
(JWHills) *bhd: hdwy 2f out: styd on fnl f but nvr gng pce to trble ldrs* **12/1**
246- **10** *2 ½* **Burlington Place**[193] 6165 3-8-7 **63** JDaly(7) 4 49
(SKirk) *chsd ldrs: pushed along and one pce 2f out: kpt on again ins last* **50/1**
6001 **11** *½* **Mister Trickster (IRE)**[19] 2614 3-8-13 **62** SRighton 17 46
(RDickin) *chsd ldrs: rdn over 2f out: wknd appr fnl f* **9/1**
0032 **12** *¾* **Adorata (GER)**[14] 2756 3-9-1 **64** OUrbina 10 46
(JJay) *sn slt ld tl narrowly hdd over 3f out: wknd over 1f out* **16/1**
6-00 **13** *2 ½* **Mutassem (FR)**[76] 1295 3-9-6 **69** RHills 13 44
(EALDunlop) *disp ld tl slt ld fr over 3f out: hdd ins fnl 2f: wknd qckly over 1f out* **16/1**
2-42 **14** *1 ¾* **Best Desert (IRE)**[28] 2377 3-9-3 **66** NPollard 8 37
(JRBest) *lw: chsd ldrs: rdn over 2f out: sn wknd* **16/1**
00-0 **15** *¾* **Nesnaas (USA)**[33] 2239 3-9-5 **68** WSupple 1 37
(BHanbury) *bhd: n.d* **33/1**
05-0 **16** *3 ½* **Total Force (IRE)**[22] 2517 3-8-13 **62** PDobbs 2 21
(RHannon) *a outpcd* **50/1**
3000 **17** *shd* **Off Beat (USA)**[13] 2790 3-9-2 **65** (b) SCarson 9 24
(RFJohnsonHoughton) *sn outpcd* **40/1**
0401 **18** *2 ½* **Whiplash (IRE)**[40] 2061 3-8-9 **58** CCatlin 6 10
(KOCunningham-Brown) *chsd ldrs 4f* **33/1**
-003 **19** *1 ¾* **Danish Monarch**[11] 2836 3-9-2 **65** DaneO'Neill 18 13
(ADWPinder) *chsd ldrs 4f* **33/1**
450- **20** *1 ½* **Scholarship (IRE)**[242] 5734 3-9-4 **67** SSanders 15 10
(CFWall) *a in rr* **12/1**
1m 24.37s (-2.85) **Going Correction** -0.40s/f (Firm) **20** Ran SP% **134.4**
Speed ratings: **100,99,98,97,96 95,93,93,92,89 89,88,85,83,82 78,78,75,73,72**CSF £130.73 CT £738.11 TOTE £12.10: £3.30, £2.20, £2.10, £8.50; EX 247.40.
**Owner** Mrs L M Askew **Bred** Airlie Stud **Trained** Headley, Surrey

**FOCUS**
A pretty ordinary handicap, but competitive enough and the form looks sound.

**NOTEBOOK**
**Evaluator(IRE)**, just as when racing over course and distance on his previous start, came right up the stands'-side rail, but this time ran on stronger than anything. There should be more to come.
**Here To Me** is still a maiden, but she is not doing anything wrong, the winner was simply too strong.
**Kryssa**, 6lb higher than when successful at Kempton on her previous start, again gave her running and can have no excuses.
**Go Yellow**, up a furlong in trip, posted a respectable effort, but remains a maiden. *Official explanation: jockey said gelding hung right handed*
**Moscow Times** would have finished closer with better luck in running. *Official explanation: jockey said gelding suffered interference in running*
**Adorata(GER)** *Official explanation: jockey said filly lost her action*
**Off Beat(USA)** *Official explanation: trainer said gelding was found to be lame on returning home*
**Scholarship(IRE)** *Official explanation: jockey said gelding was unsuited by the Good to Firm, Firm in places ground*

## 3181 STAN JAMES ONLINE H'CAP 1m 5f 61y
**9:00** (9:04) (E) (0-75,75) 3-Y-0+ **£4,387** (£1,350; £675; £337) **Stalls** Centre

Form RPR
1532 **1** **Anyhow (IRE)**[9] 2914 7-9-2 **63** JPMurtagh 8 73
(MissKMGeorge) *lw: mde all: shkn up over 1f out: qcknd and r.o wl fnl f: readily* **3/1**[1]
0000 **2** *¾* **Stolen Hours (USA)**[15] 2738 4-8-11 **58** JQuinn 2 67
(JAkehurst) *in tch: pushed along 3f out: styd on u.p to chse wnr fnl f: kpt on but readily hld nr fin* **8/1**
-000 **3** *1 ½* **Head To Kerry (IRE)**[10] 2893 4-8-11 **58** EAhern 14 65
(DJSFrenchDavis) *lw: t.k.h: bhd: hdwy to chse wnr 1m out: rdn over 3f out: no imp fr 2f out: lost 2nd and one pce fnl f* **10/1**
2250 **4** *1* **Classic Millennium**[13] 2787 6-8-7 **57** LisaJones(3) 7 62
(WJMusson) *s.i.s: hld up in rr: haedway 3f out: drvn to chse ldrs 2f out: one pce appr fnl f* **7/2**[2]
1-00 **5** *2 ½* **Beechy Bank (IRE)**[36] 2167 6-9-7 **68** VSlattery 13 70
(MrsMaryHambro) *chsd ldrs: rdn 3f out: wknd ins fnl 2f* **20/1**
0000 **6** *hd* **Persian King (IRE)**[19] 2631 7-9-4 **65** DaneO'Neill 4 66
(JABOld) *bhd: rdn over 3f out: kpt on fr over 1f out but nvr a danger* **20/1**
0345 **7** *¾* **Most-Saucy**[2] 3128 8-8-9 **59** TPQueally(3) 1 59
(IAWood) *bhd: hdwy 4f out: rdn to chse ldrs over 2f out: wknd over 1f out* **6/1**
4245 **8** *½* **Reminiscent (IRE)**[14] 2767 5-8-10 **57** (v) SCarson 11 56
(RFJohnsonHoughton) *s.i.s: rdn and sme hdwy 3f out: nt rch ldrs: wknd 2f out* **9/2**[3]
1230 **9** *11* **Dolzago**[23] 1832 4-9-4 **65** (b) RLMoore 3 48
(GLMoore) *lw: chsd ldr tl 1m out: rdn 4f out: wknd fr 3f out* **10/1**
**10** *2 ½* **Domart (POL)**[233] 4-9-12 **73** SDrowne 9 52
(MPitman) *bkwd: plld hrd: racd on outside: a bhd* **22/1**
0-00 **11** *½* **Royal Trigger**[39] 2084 4-9-9 **70** (t) CCatlin 10 48
(IanWilliams) *chsd ldrs 6f* **50/1**
2m 58.18s (7.19) **Going Correction** -0.40s/f (Firm)
**WFA** 3 from 4yo+ 15lb **11** Ran SP% **124.8**
Speed ratings: **61,60,59,59,57 57,56,56,49,48 47**CSF £28.20 CT £224.86 TOTE £3.40: £1.80, £3.20, £2.10; EX 43.10 Place 6 £209.62, Place 5 £61.47.
**Owner** Stableline **Bred** The Duke Of Marlborough **Trained** Higher Easington, Devon

**FOCUS**
With nobody willing to make the running, Johnny Murtagh used his initiative and sent Anyhow to the front. He was allowed an easy lead and was basically handed the race on a plate. Unsurprisingly, the winning time was incredibly slow time for a race of this grade and the form wants treating with caution.

**NOTEBOOK**
**Anyhow(IRE)** is usually held up but, with nobody wanting to make the running, Murtagh sent her to the front and the pair never really looked like being pegged back. Although the form of this success wants treating with some caution, she usually gives her running and should continue to go well.
**Stolen Hours(USA)**, still a maiden, attracted some support and ran a pleasing race.
**Head To Kerry(IRE)**, just 1lb higher than when last successful, showed real signs of a return to form.
**Classic Millennium**, back on a winning mark, did not run badly and is probably capable of even better in stronger-run race.
**Beechy Bank(IRE)** was a little bit below form and is one of many who would have preferred a stronger pace.
**Most-Saucy** was unsuited by the slow pace.
**Reminiscent(IRE)** is another who would have benefited from a stronger pace.
T/Jkpt: Not won. T/Plt: £343.80 to a £1 stake. Pool: £53,443.95. 113.45 winning tickets. T/Qpdt: £47.60 to a £1 stake. Pool: £3,793.40. 58.90 winning tickets. ST

3182 - 3189a (Foreign Racing) - See Raceform Interactive

# 2868 BATH (L-H)
### Wednesday, June 23

**OFFICIAL GOING: Firm (good to firm in places)**
Conditions were very windy indeed and caused some horses to be blown off course. Some caution is therefore advised when assessing the form.
Wind: v.str against Weather: overcast

## 3190 KLEENEZE EUROPEAN H'CAP 1m 2f 46y
**6:45** (6:46) (F) (0-55,56) 3-Y-O **£3,538** (£1,011; £505) **Stalls** Low

Form RPR
-600 **1** **Donastrela (IRE)**[28] 2402 3-8-10 **50** (v[1]) NChalmers(5) 4 62
(AMBalding) *in tch: hdwy over 2f out: chsd ldr 1f out: styd on u.p to ld fnl 50yds: edgd lft cl home* **33/1**
3426 **2** *1 ½* **Oktis Morilious (IRE)**[13] 2802 3-8-9 **44** DHolland 6 53
(AWCarroll) *chsd ldrs: led jst ins fnl 2f: sn rdn: hdd fnl 50yds: hld whn sltly hmpd cl home* **5/1**[2]
6605 **3** *5* **Saucy**[25] 2484 3-8-10 **48** (b) JFMcDonald(3) 13 48
(BJMeehan) *led 2f: styd trcking ldr: shkn up over 1f out and sn btn* **16/1**
0-01 **4** *1* **Fiddles Music**[72] 1375 3-8-3 **45** BO'Neill(7) 5 43
(MRChannon) *chsd ldrs: rdn and hung rt ins fnl 2f: one pce* **6/1**[3]
00-0 **5** *½* **Tell The Trees**[28] 2401 3-9-4 **53** MTebbutt 11 50
(RMBeckett) *chsd ldrs tl lost position and dropped rr over 4f out: rdn 3f out: styd on again fr over 1f out and fin wl: nt a danger* **33/1**
4003 **6** *1 ½* **Vrisaki (IRE)**[13] 2822 3-9-0 **49** AMcCarthy 1 43
(MissDMountain) *plld hrd: in tch: drvn to chse ldrs over 2f out: wknd over 1f out* **3/1**[1]
6106 **7** *½* **Larad (IRE)**[15] 2760 3-8-6 **48** (b) DerekNolan(7) 12 41
(JSMoore) *s.i.s: bhd: sme hdwy fnl 2f: n.m.r on rails over 1f out: nvr a danger* **8/1**
2000 **8** *shd* **Waltzing Beau**[12] 2840 3-9-3 **55** (v) TPQueally(3) 3 48
(BGPowell) *in tch: rdn 4f out: wknd over 2f out* **25/1**
0050 **9** *1 ¼* **The Footballresult**[15] 2762 3-8-10 **45** JoannaBadger 14 35
(MrsGHarvey) *bhd: sme hdwy on outside fr 3f out: nvr in contention* **25/1**
-400 **10** *½* **Nafferton Girl (IRE)**[25] 2484 3-8-12 **50** SHitchcott(3) 8 39
(JAOsborne) *in tch: rdn 3f out: wknd over 2f out* **14/1**
5050 **11** *5* **Hsi Wang Mu (IRE)**[27] 2425 3-8-11 **46** SWhitworth 10 26
(RBrotherton) *a in rr* **11/1**
0-00 **12** *17* **Joey Perhaps**[30] 2351 3-9-6 **55** NPollard 9 —
(JRBest) *led after 2f: hdd jst ins fnl 2f: wknd qckly and eased ins last* **28/1**
0-06 **13** *5* **Purr**[19] 2645 3-9-5 **54** (v[1]) DaneO'Neill 2 —
(JLDunlop) *chsd ldrs tl wknd qckly 1/2-way* **9/1**
5421 **14** *dist* **Jackie Kiely**[6] 3026 3-9-7 **56** 6ex TGMcLaughlin 7 —
(PSMcentee) *in tch tl wknd qckly over 2f out: virtually p.u fnl 50yds* **5/1**[2]
2m 13.2s (2.20) **Going Correction** +0.30s/f (Good) **14** Ran SP% **131.6**
Speed ratings: **103,101,97,97,96 95,95,94,93,93 89,75,71,—**CSF £199.99 CT £2830.48 TOTE £31.60: £10.60, £2.30, £5.20; EX 202.30.
**Owner** Guy Luck, Rosemary de Rougemont, Tom Cox **Bred** R H Thomas Cox And G William Robinson **Trained** Kingsclere, Hants
■ Stewards Enquiry : N Chalmers one-day ban: careless riding (Jul 4)

**FOCUS**
A modest race run in a fair time for the type of race given the very windy conditions, and the front pair finished clear.

**NOTEBOOK**

**Donastrela(IRE)** ◆, beaten out of sight in all four of her previous starts including in a handicap, looked a completely different animal and the first-time visor is one possible explanation. She did drift across the runner-up close home, but it made no difference to the result and she could be interesting under a penalty with the headgear kept on. *Official explanation: trainer's representative said filly had benefited from the fitting of a visor*

**Oktis Morilious(IRE)**, back over his best trip, seemed to be travelling better than anything for most of the home straight and he found plenty when asked for his effort, but was unfortunately mugged by an unexposed filly.

**Saucy** ran up to her best under a positive ride but she is beginning to look a very weak finisher, which is surprising considering her pedigree is packed with stamina.

**Fiddles Music**, making her handicap debut, ran a fair race but found this tougher than the Yarmouth seller she landed last time.

**Tell The Trees**, making her handicap debut, rather ran in snatches and might be worth stepping up again in trip.

**Vrisaki(IRE)** was dropping in trip, but still did not get home.

**Jackie Kiely** was carrying a 6lb penalty for his win on Fibresand the previous week, but he should have had no problem with these conditions and ran as though something was amiss.

## 3191 SKY BET PRESS RED TO BET NOW H'CAP — 1m 5y

**7:15** (7:18) (D ) (0-85,81) 3-Y-0+ — **£5,720** (£1,760; £880; £440) **Stalls** Low

Form — RPR

0020 **1** **St Pancras (IRE)**[19] 2638 4-9-11 **78** .... DHolland 8 — 86
(NACallaghan) *trckd ldrs: rn wd bnd 5f out: rdn over 3f out: styd on u.p to ld last half f: hld on all out* **5/2**[1]

1130 **2** *nk* **Voice Mail**[19] 2637 5-9-4 **78** .... TBlock(7) 2 — 86
(AMBalding) *hld up in rr: stl plenty to do ins fnl 2f: str run on outside fnl f: fin wl: nt quite get up* **8/1**

4011 **3** *nk* **Brazilian Terrace**[11] 2871 4-9-3 **75** .... HayleyTurner(5) 5 — 82
(MLWBell) *hld up in rr: hdwy over 2f out: str run fnl f to chal last half f: no ex nr fin* **5/1**[3]

0034 **4** *2* **Adobe**[3] 3127 9-8-9 **67** .... MSavage(5) 1 — 69
(WMBrisbourne) *chsd ldrs: rdn to ld appr fnl f: hdd last half f: wknd cl home* **7/1**

3022 **5** *nk* **Marnie**[11] 2871 7-7-13 **52** .... JQuinn 4 — 54
(JAkehurst) *in tch: rdn and one pce over 3f out: styd on u.p appr fnl f: one pce ins last* **13/2**

-110 **6** *shd* **Dance On The Top**[95] 1065 6-9-11 **81** .... (t) TPQueally(3) 7 — 82
(JRBoyle) *led: rdn 2f out: hdd appr fnl f: styd pressing ldrs tl wknd last half f* **4/1**[2]

2603 **7** *1 1/4* **Nuzzle**[11] 2871 4-7-9 **51** oh6 .... (v) JFMcDonald(3) 6 — 50
(MQuinn) *chsd ldrs: rdn and one pce fnl 2f* **33/1**

-004 **8** *1* **Bishopstone Man**[37] 2170 7-9-1 **68** .... DaneO'Neill 3 — 64
(HCandy) *bhd: rdn and effrt over 2f out: nvr gng pce to rch ldrs* **7/1**

1m 41.79s (0.79) **Going Correction** +0.30s/f (Good) — **8** Ran SP% **117.6**

Speed ratings: **108,107,107,105,105 105,103,102**CSF £24.23 CT £95.45 TOTE £3.90: £2.00, £2.00, £2.20; EX 48.00.

**Owner** Michael Hill **Bred** Thomas J Murphy **Trained** Newmarket, Suffolk

**FOCUS**

A competitive handicap run at a decent pace and the form should work out.

**NOTEBOOK**

**St Pancras(IRE)** ◆ has dropped 22lb since last summer, but has hinted at a return to form of late and was well backed on this occasion. He gamely forced his head in front where it mattered and win his first race since his racecourse debut two years ago but, given the fact that he was all over the place on the home bend and looked unhappy in general on the track, this effort was probably even better than it looked. He should be kept on the right side.

**Voice Mail** absolutely loves it here and ran a cracker under his inflated mark, especially as the recent rain would not have been in his favour. He even looked like scoring when flying down the outside well inside the last furlong, but the winner pulled out a little extra.

**Brazilian Terrace**, bidding for a hat-trick, was off just a 2lb higher mark than for her two recent wins. After being given a patient ride, she appeared to have timed her challenge just right but was worried out of it in the last 100 yards.

**Adobe** ran creditably, but he could have done without the rain and still looks capable of winning soon when conditions are favourable.

**Marnie**, closely matched with Brazilian Terrace on recent running here, was another that would have preferred the rain to have stayed away.

**Dance On The Top** has a great record fresh, so the layoff since March was not a problem. However, after making much of the running he was rather easily picked off.

## 3192 WITHY KING SOLICITORS MAIDEN STKS — 5f 161y

**7:45** (7:47) (D ) 2-Y-0 — **£3,614** (£1,112; £556; £278) **Stalls** Low

Form — RPR

2 **1** **Gee Bee Em**[12] 2837 2-8-9 .... TEDurcan 5 — 67
(MRChannon) *trckd ldrs: drvn to ld wl over 1f out: pushed out cl home: readily* **7/2**[2]

**2** *1/2* **Minnesota (USA)** 2-9-0 .... DaneO'Neill 8 — 70
(HCandy) *in tch: pushed along fr 1/2-way: hdwy over 1f out: str run ins last and fin wl to take 2nd last stride: nt rch wnr* **15/2**

0 **3** *shd* **Rusky Dusky (USA)**[39] 2111 2-9-0 .... PDobbs 4 — 70
(RHannon) *chsd ldrs: wnt 2nd and hrd drvn over 1f out: no imp on wnr ins last: ct for 2nd last stride* **10/1**

500 **4** *2* **Aberdeen Park**[11] 2884 2-8-9 .... GBaker 1 — 58
(MrsHSweeting) *led tl hdd over 3f out: styd chsng ldrs tl outpcd fnl f* **9/1**

4 **5** *1/2* **Ridder**[32] 2300 2-9-0 .... DHolland 9 — 62
(DJCoakley) *chsd ldr: led over 3f out: hdd wl over 1f out: n.m.r on rail and wknd last half f* **3/1**[1]

**6** *2 1/2* **Corker** 2-8-11 .... TPQueally(3) 2 — 54
(GAButler) *bhd: rdn and green over 3f out: styd on fr over 1f out but nvr gng pce to rch ldrs* **4/1**[3]

**7** *shd* **Good Wee Girl (IRE)** 2-8-9 .... JFEgan 3 — 48
(SKirk) *s.i.s: bhd: pushed along 3f out: styd on fnl f but nvr a danger* **12/1**

**8** *nk* **Voom** 2-8-2 .... BO'Neill(7) 6 — 47
(MRChannon) *bhd: shkn up 2f out: kpt on fnl f but nvr a danger* **14/1**

**9** *10* **Russian Servana (IRE)** 2-8-9 .... SRighton 7 — 14
(MJAttwater) *s.i.s: hung rt bnd over 3f out and green: a in rr* **40/1**

0 **10** *3 1/2* **Doughty**[15] 2749 2-9-0 .... VSlattery 10 — 8
(DJWintle) *rn green and a bhd* **50/1**

1m 14.89s (3.75) **Going Correction** +0.525s/f (Yiel) — **10** Ran SP% **116.8**

Speed ratings: **96,95,95,92,91 88,88,88,74,70**CSF £30.16 TOTE £4.50: £1.70, £3.50, £2.50; EX 36.70.

**Owner** Phil Jen Racing **Bred** Phil Jen Racing **Trained** West Ilsley, Berks

**FOCUS**

A modest contest, but these juveniles were running into a roaring headwind, so some flexibility can be applied when assessing the performances of the beaten horses.

**NOTEBOOK**

**Gee Bee Em** confirmed the promise of her debut, if only just, and given the conditions her previous experience was probably a major advantage.

**Minnesota(USA)** ◆, whose dam won over a mile and was placed in Listed company, showed a deal of promise on this debut in difficult conditions. He should not be hard to place.

**Rusky Dusky(USA)**, unplaced in a red-hot Newbury maiden on his debut, improved from that and reversed form with Aberdeen Park. He is going the right way and should be up to winning an ordinary contest.

**Aberdeen Park** was not beaten far, but she is more exposed than most in this contest and might need her sights lowered.

**Ridder** did not improve from his promising Kempton debut, but should be given another chance. *Official explanation: jockey said colt had hung left*

**Corker**, an 88,000gns yearling out of a half-sister to a French 1000 Guineas winner, was well backed to make a winning debut but never got into the race. He is obviously thought capable of much better.

## 3193 BATH CHRONICLE (S) H'CAP — 1m 5y

**8:15** (8:17) (G ) (0-55,52) 3-Y-0 — **£2,597** (£742; £371) **Stalls** Low

Form — RPR

0000 **1** **Mister Completely (IRE)**[4] 3087 3-8-8 **42** .... NPollard 3 — 49
(JRBest) *chsd ldrs: wnt 2nd over 1f out: hrd drvn to ld last half f* **8/1**

0030 **2** *3/4* **Delcienne**[15] 2760 3-8-8 **42** .... AMcCarthy 1 — 47
(GGMargarson) *s.i.s: bhd: stl plenty to do 2f out: rapid hdwy over 1f out: str run ins last: fin wl: nt rch wnr* **9/1**

4500 **3** *1* **Heartbeat**[13] 2822 3-8-7 **41** .... (bt) JQuinn 2 — 44
(PJMcbride) *bhd: stl plenty to do 2f out: swtchd to outside over 1f out and r.o ins fnl f: one pce cl home* **13/2**[2]

4033 **4** *1/2* **Roving Vixen (IRE)**[26] 2454 3-8-2 **41** .... (b) HayleyTurner(5) 6 — 43
(JLSpearing) *led: rdn and veered rt in str hdwind ins fnl 2f: hdd last half f and wknd cl home* **13/2**[2]

5206 **5** *1 3/4* **Avertaine**[25] 2484 3-9-2 **50** .... (b[1]) DHolland 10 — 48
(GLMoore) *chsd ldrs: rdn and effrt over 2f out: wknd ins fnl f* **9/2**[1]

6-06 **6** *2* **Buchanan Street (IRE)**[9] 2928 3-9-1 **49** .... OUrbina 13 — 42
(NACallaghan) *bhd: stl plenty to do over 2f out: r.o appr fnl f but nvr gng pce to trble ldrs* **12/1**

0600 **7** *1 1/2* **Livia (IRE)**[41] 2061 3-8-11 **45** .... (e[1]) TEDurcan 12 — 35
(JGPortman) *bhd: rdn 3f out: sme hdwy fr over 1f out: nvr a danger* **20/1**

0000 **8** *shd* **Johnny Alljays (IRE)**[9] 2932 3-8-5 **39** .... (b) SWhitworth 9 — 29
(JSMoore) *chsd ldrs tl wknd ins fnl 2f* **20/1**

4324 **9** *hd* **Soul Provider (IRE)**[72] 1366 3-9-1 **52** .... FPFerris(3) 11 — 41
(MJAttwater) *chsd ldrs: rdn over 2f out: wknd qckly fnl f* **7/1**[3]

0-40 **10** *4* **Charlieismydarling**[15] 2766 3-8-11 **48** .... TPQueally(3) 4 — 28
(JAOsborne) *chsd ldrs: rdn over 3f out: wknd over 2f out* **15/2**

6060 **11** *1 1/4* **Chase The Rainbow**[15] 2766 3-8-11 **52** .... DerekNolan(7) 7 — 29
(MissKMGeorge) *nvr bttr than mid-div: wknd over 2f out* **12/1**

0000 **12** *1* **Diverted**[64] 1519 3-8-6 **40** .... EStack 8 — 15
(MGQuinlan) *bhd: sme hdwy over 4f out: nvr nr ldrs and sn wknd* **25/1**

0105 **13** *16* **Lady Predominant**[44] 2005 3-8-13 **47** .... VSlattery 5 — —
(GFBridgwater) *sn bhd* **20/1**

1m 44.94s (3.94) **Going Correction** +0.30s/f (Good) — **13** Ran SP% **123.7**

Speed ratings: **92,91,90,89,88 86,84,84,84,80 78,77,61**CSF £76.28 CT £383.68 TOTE £10.60: £3.50, £4.50, £3.40; EX 98.00.There was no bid for the winner. Heartbeat (no.11) was claimed by I A Wood for £6,000

**Owner** Eastwell Manor Racing Ltd **Bred** Eamonn Griffin **Trained** Hucking, Kent

**FOCUS**

A poor seller, but the conditions took their toll and the last couple of furlongs were hard work for many.

**NOTEBOOK**

**Mister Completely(IRE)**, tried over 12 furlongs last time, was back to a more suitable trip. Racing more prominently than his two nearest pursuers probably gained him the day, as it enabled him to establish a decisive advantage when sent to the front a furlong from home. He was not going very quickly towards the end and would have been swallowed up with a little further to go, but just managed to hold on and get off the mark at the 14th attempt.

**Delcienne** is a very moderate maiden, but having been held up early she flew down the outside in the closing stages and would have prevailed with a little further to go.

**Heartbeat**, stepping back from middle distances, not for the first time finished well but too late. She is looking very hard to win with, but may have preferred even more rain.

**Roving Vixen(IRE)** was able to establish a soft lead and looked as though she might take some catching, but she had no cover from the wind and started to run all over the track passing the two-furlong pole. She grimly tried to hang on, but the winner had the impetus and she then lost two more places in the last 20 yards.

**Avertaine**, dropping into a seller and blinkered for the first time, was disappointing and the shorter trip did not bring about any improvement.

## 3194 M.J. CHURCH MAIDEN STKS — 1m 3f 144y

**8:45** (8:45) (D ) 3-Y-0+ — **£3,497** (£1,076; £538; £269) **Stalls** Low

Form — RPR

33 **1** **Leg Spinner (IRE)**[9] 2934 3-8-10 .... TEDurcan 4 — 76
(MRChannon) *led 1f: styd trcking ldrs: rdn over 2f out: led over 1f out: edgd led ins last: pushed out* **6/4**[2]

21- **2** *3 1/2* **Seeking A Way (USA)**[250] 5619 3-8-5 .... RHavlin 5 — 65
(JHMGosden) *t.k.h: trckd ldr after 2f: led over 2f out: rdn edgd lft and hdd over 1f out: sn btn* **5/4**[1]

0-50 **3** *4* **Opera Star (IRE)**[57] 1683 3-8-6 **63** ow1 .... DHolland 2 — 60
(BWHills) *led after 1f: hdd over 2f out: sn btn* **4/1**[3]

**4** *11* **Lord Nellsson**[18] 8-9-5 .... HayleyTurner(5) 6 — 46
(JSKing) *s.i.s: bhd and sn rdn: mod hdwy fnl 2f* **25/1**

**5** *6* **Chelsea's Diamond**[45] 4-9-5 .... (b[1]) VSlattery 1 — 32
(JAkehurst) *in tch tl wknd qckly 3f out* **33/1**

0 **6** *5* **Breaking The Rule (IRE)**[25] 2486 3-8-5 .... SWhitworth 3 — 24
(PRWebber) *bhd: hdwy to latch on to ldrs over 4f out: wknd ins fnl 3f* **16/1**

2m 33.45s (3.15) **Going Correction** +0.30s/f (Good)

**WFA** 3 from 4yo+ 14lb — **6** Ran SP% **117.1**

Speed ratings: **101,98,96,88,84 81**CSF £3.98 TOTE £2.70: £1.30, £1.70; EX 3.70.

**Owner** P D Savill **Bred** Steven Nolan **Trained** West Ilsley, Berks

**FOCUS**

A modest maiden run at an even pace dominated by the market principals.

**NOTEBOOK**

**Leg Spinner(IRE)** appreciated the longer trip and ground out a tidy victory. He still has a fair amount of scope and looks very much a staying handicapper in the making. Eventually the jumps trainers could be interested in him.

**Seeking A Way(USA)**, winner of the Newmarket Challenge Cup last October and therefore still qualifying as a maiden, saw out the longer trip on this first start since but looks rather one paced.

**Opera Star(IRE)** was allowed an uncontested lead, but was still nothing like good enough and connections will do very well to get a win out of her.

**Lord Nellsson**, making his Flat debut, is a poor performer over hurdles and fences and his stamina enabled him to pick up £269 for connections.

**Chelsea's Diamond**, unplaced in two bumpers, is very slow.

## 3195 OVAL OF BATH, PEUGEOT CLASSIFIED STKS 5f 161y
9:15 (9:17) (E) 3-Y-O+ £3,347 (£1,030; £515; £257) Stalls Low

Form RPR

0-00 **1** **Delegate**[11] 2869 11-9-0 63 ........ OUrbina 1 74
(NACallaghan) *hld up in rr: stdy hdwy fr 2f out to ld ins fnl f: nudged along and hld on wl* **16/1**

1-06 **2** 1/2 **Sparkling Jewel**[15] 2763 4-9-1 74 ........ (b[1]) DaneO'Neill 9 74
(RHannon) *sn in tch: hdwy whn carried lft over 2f out: styd on to press ldrs over 1f out tl nt qckn ins fnl f* **3/1**[2]

1041 **3** 2 **Parkside Pursuit**[3] 3125 6-9-6 70 ........ DHolland 2 73+
(JMBradley) *hld up in tch: hmpd on rail over 2f out: hdwy and nt clr run over 1f out: swtchd rt and kpt on ins last: nt rcvr* **5/4**[1]

0325 **4** 3/4 **Melody King**[15] 2754 3-8-7 68 ........ (b) TEDurcan 5 64
(PDEvans) *chsd ldrs: chal 2f out: sn led: hdd & wknd ins fnl f* **11/1**

0-00 **5** 6 **Landing Strip (IRE)**[65] 1504 4-9-1 74 ........ FPFerris(3) 3 50
(JMPEustace) *chsd ldrs: rdn 3f out: rallied to chse ldrs whn nt clr run appr fnl f: sn wknd* **10/1**

500- **6** nk **Bad Intentions (IRE)**[271] 5194 4-8-11 70 ........ AMcCarthy 7 42
(MissDMountain) *chsd ldrs: led 2f out: sn hdd: wknd appr fnl f* **20/1**

1066 **7** 1 1/2 **Byo (IRE)**[3] 3125 6-8-12 71 ........ TPQueally(3) 6 42
(MQuinn) *led tl hdd 2f out: sn wknd* **8/1**[3]

40-0 **8** 1 1/4 **Mimic**[46] 1974 4-8-4 70 ........ RMills(7) 8 34
(RGuest) *chsd ldrs: edgd lft over 2f out: sn wknd* **8/1**[3]

1m 14.1s (2.96) **Going Correction** +0.525s/f (Yiel) **8** Ran SP% **119.7**
**WFA** 3 from 4yo+ 7lb
Speed ratings: **101,100,97,96,88 88,86,84**CSF £66.85 TOTE £15.80: £3.30, £1.60, £1.40; EX 114.70 Place 6 £111.04, Place 5 £23.85.
**Owner** N A Callaghan **Bred** Juddmonte Farms **Trained** Newmarket, Suffolk

**FOCUS**
A messy classified event surprisingly run at a modest pace. The form should be treated with some caution, although the first two avoided trouble and appeared to run to form.

**NOTEBOOK**
**Delegate**, real character, was given a good ride by Urbina, who kept him interested by bringing him between horses even though he had every opportunity to come down the outside. His rider never once picked up his whip, which was another reason why the old boy probably agreed to put his best foot forward, but a repeat seems highly unlikely.
**Sparkling Jewel** had not shown much in two previous starts this season, but produced a little more in the first-time blinkers.
**Parkside Pursuit** was probably unlucky, as he was getting messed about behind a wall of horses at the same time as the front pair were establishing a significant advantage. When he was eventually switched, he had too much ground to make up.
**Melody King** ran a fair race against his elders despite not being able to dominate from the front.
**Landing Strip(IRE)** continues out of form this season.
T/Plt: £205.00 to a £1 stake. Pool: £40,060.10. 142.60 winning tickets. T/Qpdt: £29.40 to a £1 stake. Pool: £2,398.50. 60.30 winning tickets. ST

# 2933 CARLISLE (R-H)
Wednesday, June 23

**OFFICIAL GOING: Good (good to soft in places)**

## 3196 BORDER CONSTRUCTION MAIDEN AUCTION STKS 5f
2:20 (2:21) (E) 2-Y-O £5,772 (£1,776; £888; £444) Stalls High

Form RPR

0 **1** **Bond City (IRE)**[34] 2234 2-8-11 ........ FLynch 5 80
(BSmart) *sn rr and pushed along: hdwy 2f out: styd on wl u.p to ld ins fnl f: all out* **20/1**

0333 **2** shd **Gifted Gamble**[15] 2749 2-8-9 ........ (b) RWinston 3 78
(KARyan) *dwlt: sn pushed along in rr: gd hdwy u.p on outer 2f out: slt ld ins fnl f: sn hdd: styd on: jst hld* **9/2**[3]

30 **3** 4 **Holbeck Ghyll (IRE)**[6] 2996 2-8-11 ........ ACulhane 4 66+
(AMBalding) *cl up: ev ch ent fnl f: no ex ins last* **11/4**[1]

62 **4** 1/2 **Komac**[24] 2502 2-8-7 ........ GDuffield 8 60+
(BAMcmahon) *mde most tl rdn and hdd jst ins fnl f: no ex* **4/1**[2]

**5** hd **Big Hassle (IRE)** 2-8-9 ........ GFaulkner 1 62+
(TDEasterby) *dwlt: rr div: hdwy 1/2-way: ev ch appr fnl f: no ex ins last* **20/1**

33 **6** shd **Twice Nightly**[38] 2141 2-8-9 ........ JFanning 9 61+
(JDBethell) *midfield: rdn 2f out: kpt on fnl f: nvr able to chal* **6/1**

0 **7** 1/2 **Rancho Cucamonga (IRE)**[12] 2860 2-8-4 ........ KDarley 12 54
(TDBarron) *prom: rdn 2f out: fdd* **10/1**

36 **8** shd **Lorna Dune**[16] 2730 2-8-4 ........ LGoncalves 7 54
(MrsJRRamsden) *midfield: pushed along 2f out: no real hdwy* **16/1**

03 **9** 1 3/4 **Ryedane (IRE)**[23] 2526 2-8-9 ........ DAllan 6 53
(TDEasterby) *sn towards rr: n.d* **20/1**

6 **10** 2 1/2 **Borderlescott**[12] 2860 2-8-11 ........ RFfrench 10 46
(RBastiman) *midfield: rdn 2f out: sn btn* **16/1**

62 **11** 3/4 **Megell (IRE)**[40] 2096 2-8-2 ........ JMackay 2 35
(MGQuinlan) *a towards rr* **10/1**

0 **12** 13 **Outrageous Flirt (IRE)**[19] 2655 2-8-4 ........ PHanagan 11 —
(ADickman) *cl up to 1/2-way: sn wknd: t.o* **80/1**

6 **13** 1/2 **Alexia Rose (IRE)**[14] 2780 2-8-6 ........ FNorton 13 —
(ABerry) *s.i.s: bhd most of way: t.o* **25/1**

61.18 secs (-0.32) **Going Correction** -0.225s/f (Firm) **13** Ran SP% **128.4**
Speed ratings: **93,92,86,85,85 85,84,84,81,77 76,55,54**CSF £109.70 TOTE £22.00: £4.20, £2.90, £2.10; EX 237.50.
**Owner** R C Bond **Bred** David Ryan **Trained** Hambleton, N Yorks
■ Stewards Enquiry : L Goncalves four-day ban: failed to take all reasonable and permissible measures to obtain best possible placing (Jul 5-8)

**FOCUS**
This looked like quite a competitive maiden, but the first two in the betting disappointed and Bond City and Gifted Gamble were able to pull well clear, helped by racing on faster ground in the last furlong.

**NOTEBOOK**
**Bond City(IRE)**, who shaped with promise on his debut over six furlongs in a competitive Doncaster maiden, improved on that run to get off the mark. He struggled to go the early pace on this drop in trip and could improve again back over another furlong.
**Gifted Gamble** pulled well clear of all bar the winner and is holding his form well. He has had a few chances, but is not one to give up on and should soon be winning.
**Holbeck Ghyll(IRE)** offered some promise on his debut in a Chepstow maiden, but was outclassed in the Norfolk on his latest start. Dropped back to a more suitable grade, he was left behind by the front two and has to be considered disappointing. He has the ability to land a minor event, but this does not represent progressive form and he is not one to take a short price about.
**Komac**, a five-length second to the Norfolk third Skywards at Newmarket on his previous start, should have found this easier but was below form. An less-demanding track may suit better.
**Big Hassle(IRE)**, out of an unraced half-sister to high-class ten-furlong performer Batshoof, and champion miler in Hong Kong Regular Guest, offered plenty of encouragement. He should improve and may have a minor maiden in him.
**Twice Nightly** may not have been suited by this drop back from six furlongs.
**Lorna Dune** *Official explanation: jockey said filly hung right-handed*
**Alexia Rose(IRE)** *Official explanation: jockey said filly had hung right handed*

## 3197 SCOTTISH & NEWCASTLE PUB ENTERPRISES PENNINE REGION EBF MAIDEN STKS 5f 193y
2:50 (2:53) (D) 2-Y-O £5,772 (£1,776; £888; £444) Stalls High

Form RPR

**1** **King Of Love** 2-9-0 ........ JFanning 1 66
(MJohnston) *prom: faltered path after 1f: led 2f out: r.o u.p* **4/1**[2]

0 **2** 1 1/4 **Noodles**[19] 2651 2-9-0 ........ (v[1]) RWinston 3 62
(TDEasterby) *prom: drvn along 2f out: ev ch ent fnl f: no imp on wnr ins last* **10/1**

0 **3** 1 1/4 **Skiddaw Wolf**[12] 2860 2-8-9 ........ FLynch 6 53
(BSmart) *led: hdd 2f out: hung rt u.p: no ex fnl f* **9/2**[3]

4 **4** 1 3/4 **Banknote**[25] 2478 2-9-0 ........ KDarley 5 53
(AMBalding) *dwlt: in rr whn j. path after 1f: styd on u.p fnl 2f: nvr able to chal* **1/1**[1]

0 **5** 1 1/4 **Mr Maxim**[10] 2904 2-9-0 ........ VHalliday 2 49
(RMWhitaker) *in tch: rdn over 2f out: no imp on ldrs* **20/1**

0 **6** 1 1/2 **Frogs' Gift (IRE)**[38] 2141 2-8-6 ........ TEaves(3) 7 39
(GMMoore) *chsd ldrs: rdn over 2f out: sn btn* **40/1**

**7** 1/2 **Allstar Princess** 2-8-6 ........ THamilton(3) 4 38
(RAFahey) *sn in rr: n.d* **12/1**

**8** 3/4 **Wor Kid** 2-8-9 ........ KDalgleish 8 35
(RPElliott) *dwlt: sn in tch: rdn over 2f out: sn btn* **20/1**

0 **9** 4 **Toldo (IRE)**[18] 2686 2-9-0 ........ FNorton 9 28
(ABerry) *hld up in tch: hdwy to chse ldrs 1/2-way: wknd 2f out* **33/1**

1m 14.98s (0.78) **Going Correction** -0.225s/f (Firm) **9** Ran SP% **119.9**
Speed ratings: **85,83,81,79,77 75,75,74,68**CSF £41.78 TOTE £5.40: £2.30, £3.20, £2.60; EX 25.00.
**Owner** M Doyle **Bred** The Kingwood Partnership **Trained** Middleham Moor, N Yorks
■ A first winner as a sire for King's Best.

**FOCUS**
With the favourite below form, this was not a very good maiden and, with little pace on early, it proved hard to come from behind. The winning time was unsurprisingly modest for the grade.

**NOTEBOOK**
**King Of Love**, a 46,000gns yearling, half-brother to ten-furlong winner Premiership and seven-furlong scorer Sutton Common, out of a half-sister to the high-class pair Fruits Of Love and Mujadil, made a successful debut. Never too far off the pace, he travelled nicely for Fanning and found plenty when asked. With the favourite below form, this did not take a lot of winning and he will need to improve when raised in class, but a step up to seven furlongs should suit. Unfortunately, though, he struck into himself during the race.
**Noodles** stepped up on his debut running in the first-time visor and is going the right way.
**Skiddaw Wolf** was another to improve on his debut running and looks capable of progressing again, but he will need to in order to pick up a similar race.
**Banknote**, a 7/1 chance when a fair fourth a competitive conditions race at Kempton on his debut, failed to build on that, but had his excuses - he was slowly away and stumbled on a path soon after the start - and can be forgiven this.
**Mr Maxim** ran respectably, but may be more of a nursery type.
**Toldo(IRE)** *Official explanation: jockey said gelding hung left-handed*

## 3198 CARLISLE GLASS CARLISLE BELL (H'CAP) 7f 200y
3:20 (3:23) (D) (0-80,80) 3-Y-O+ £17,485 (£5,380; £2,690; £1,345) Stalls High

Form RPR

4111 **1** **Goodbye Mr Bond**[5] 3058 4-9-1 **67** 5ex ........ FNorton 7 79
(EJAlston) *midfield: hdwy over 1f out: edgd rt u.p and led wl ins fnl f* **5/1**[1]

0021 **2** nk **Countykat (IRE)**[7] 2989 4-9-3 **69** 5ex ........ (v) DarrenWilliams 1 80
(KRBurke) *cl up: led 1/2-way: hrd pressed and rdn fr over 1f out: styd on: hdd wl ins fnl f* **20/1**

0050 **3** 1/2 **Tedstale (USA)**[11] 2894 6-10-0 **80** ........ (b) JFanning 16 90
(TDEasterby) *hld up: hdwy to chse ldrs over 1f out: styd on wl u.p clsng stages* **20/1**

1002 **4** 3/4 **Stoic Leader (IRE)**[5] 3039 4-9-10 **79** ........ LFletcher(3) 6 87
(RFFisher) *cl up: chal 2f out: sn rdn: ev ch tl no ex wl ins fnl f* **33/1**

0225 **5** shd **Takes Tutu (USA)**[14] 2781 5-9-8 **74** ........ (p) KDarley 11 82
(KRBurke) *chsd ldrs: disp ld over 1f out: ev ch and rdn ins fnl f: no ex whn hmpd clsng stages* **20/1**

2016 **6** 1 **Pawan (IRE)**[3] 3127 4-9-2 **68** 5ex ........ AnnStokell 15 74
(MissAStokell) *midfield: rdn 2f out: styd on fnl f: nvr able to chal* **66/1**

4-44 **7** nk **Blonde Streak (USA)**[23] 2521 4-9-11 **77** ........ PHanagan 13 82
(TDBarron) *prom: rdn 2f out: fdd fnl f* **8/1**

2320 **8** shd **Top Dirham**[11] 2894 6-9-5 **71** ........ DaleGibson 9 76
(MWEasterby) *hld up: effrt over 2f out: kpt on fnl f: nvr able to chal* **15/2**[3]

1213 **9** hd **Kirkby's Treasure**[9] 2936 6-9-0 **66** ........ FLynch 17 71
(ABerry) *dwlt: hld up: effrt over 2f out: kpt on fnl f: n.d* **14/1**

0633 **10** nk **Cherished Number**[6] 3005 5-9-10 **76** ........ (v) RWinston 3 80
(ISemple) *chsd ldrs: rdn and ch over 1f out: wknd fnl f* **12/1**

4233 **11** hd **True Night**[5] 3036 7-9-11 **77** ........ EAhern 10 80
(DNicholls) *led tl hdd 1/2-way: remained prom tl wknd appr fnl f* **11/2**[2]

0300 **12** 1/2 **No Grouse**[16] 2735 4-9-3 **72** ........ (p) THamilton(3) 18 74
(RAFahey) *midfield: effrt 2f out: sn rdn and btn* **50/1**

4102 **13** shd **Tiber Tiger (IRE)**[3] 3127 4-9-11 **80** ........ (b) J-PGuillambert(3) 12 82
(NPLittmoden) *midfield rdn 2f out: sn btn* **14/1**

0000 **14** 1/2 **Everest (IRE)**[15] 2752 7-9-9 **78** ........ TEaves(3) 4 79
(BEllison) *dwlt: a bhd* **11/1**

1000 **15** nk **Caroubier (IRE)**[25] 2474 4-9-8 **74** ........ DeanMcKeown 14 74
(JGallagher) *hld up towards rr: sme hdwy over 2f out: wknd over 1f out* **50/1**

3-11 **16** 3 **Salinor**[32] 2304 4-10-0 **80** ........ ACulhane 5 73
(ACStewart) *midfield: rdn over 2f out: sn btn* **5/1**[1]

6-30 **17** 3 **Qualitair Wings**[33] 2271 5-9-7 **73** ........ DMcGaffin 8 59
(JHetherton) *dwlt: towards rr: hdwy into midfield 3f out: wknd 2f out* **33/1**

1m 40.53s (0.53) **Going Correction** +0.175s/f (Good) **17** Ran SP% **126.5**
Speed ratings: **104,103,103,102,102 101,101,100,100,100 100,99,99,99,98 95,92**CSF £111.56 CT £1951.86 TOTE £6.20: £2.00, £6.10, £4.10, £6.50; EX 142.10.
**Owner** Peter J Davies **Bred** Michael Ng **Trained** Longton, Lancs
■ Stewards Enquiry : Darren Williams caution: careless riding

**FOCUS**
Just a modest handicap, but very competitive nonetheless and strong form for the track.

**NOTEBOOK**

**Goodbye Mr Bond** defied a mark 15lb higher than when beginning his winning run to complete the four-timer. He was 3lb well-in under his penalty and things will be tougher when he is reassessed for this success, but he is the form of his life and there could yet be more to come.

**Countykat(IRE)**, 4lb well-in under his 5lb penalty for a success on Fibresand at Southwell on his previous start, has never won beyond seven furlongs, but this stiff mile was not a problem and he was just held.

**Tedstale(USA)** is on a winning mark and ran his best race of the season so far.

**Stoic Leader(IRE)**, 7lb higher than when last successful in handicap company, continues in the form of his life, but does look a little high in the weights. *Official explanation: jockey said gelding was struck across the nose approximately 2f out*

**Takes Tutu(USA)** is not running badly, but is proving very hard to win with. That said, he will face easier tasks than this one.

**True Night** was far too keen.

**Salinor** had looked to be progressing, but this was very disappointing.

## 3199 TOTEPLACEPOT CUMBERLAND PLATE (H'CAP) 1m 3f 206y

3:50 (3:52) (D) (0-80,80) 3-Y-O+ £17,257 (£5,310; £2,655; £1,327) Stalls Low

Form / RPR

23-2 **1** **Loves Travelling (IRE)**[18] 2671 4-9-11 **80**...................... NMackay(3) 11 88
(LMCumani) *midfield: hdwy 3f out: led 2f out: styd on u.p: all out* **15/2**[3]

0211 **2** *hd* **Bucks**[18] 2689 7-9-5 **78**........................................ MHoward(7) 17 86
(DKIvory) *hld up: hdwy u.p over 2f out: chsd wnr fnl f: styd on: jst hld* **11/1**

4/0 **3** *3/4* **Saltango (GER)**[11] 2881 5-9-1 **72**................................. PMakin(5) 13 79
(AMHales) *trckd ldrs: rdn to chal 2f out: ev ch ent fnl f: styd on* **33/1**

-054 **4** *1/2* **Sporting Gesture**[11] 2895 7-9-4 **75**.......................... PMulrennan(5) 2 81
(MWEasterby) *hld up: hdwy 3f out: rdn 2f out: edgd rt ins fnl f: styd on: nvr able to chal* **11/1**

1306 **5** *nk* **Rajam**[15] 2753 6-9-7 **73**..........................................(v) ANicholls 18 79
(DNicholls) *towards rr: hdwy u.p over 2f out: chsd ldrs ent fnl f: styd on: no ex* **33/1**

6341 **6** *2 1/2* **Mostarsil (USA)**[11] 2893 6-9-5 **71**...................................(p) EAhern 7 73
(GLMoore) *midfield: rdn 3f out: styd on fnl f: nvr able to chal* **7/1**[2]

0211 **7** *1/2* **Party Ploy**[8] 2964 6-8-13 **65** 5ex................................. DarrenWilliams 3 66
(KRBurke) *cl up: led over 3f out: rdn and hdd 2f out: btn whn hmpd ins fnl f* **14/1**

0-40 **8** *shd* **Vicious Prince (IRE)**[20] 2624 5-9-6 **72**....................... DeanMcKeown 20 73
(RMWhitaker) *midfield: drvn along 4f out: styd on fnl 2f: n.d* **20/1**

6115 **9** *1/2* **Red Forest (IRE)**[13] 2810 5-8-13 **65**................................(t) DaleGibson 5 65
(JMackie) *hld up: effrt 3f out: sn rdn: no hdwy* **20/1**

-212 **10** *shd* **Aleron (IRE)**[29] 2393 6-9-6 **72**........................................... RWinston 12 72
(JJQuinn) *in tch: tk clsr order over 2f out: rdn and ev ch over 1f out: wknd fnl f* **7/1**[2]

120/ **11** *2* **Valdesco (IRE)**[673] 4035 6-9-1 **70**.................................. LEnstone(3) 19 66
(MrsSJSmith) *hld up: effrt 3f out: sn rdn and btn* **40/1**

3311 **12** *3* **Millennium Hall**[7] 2978 5-8-7 **59**........................................ PFessey 14 51
(PMonteith) *hld up in rr: sme hdwy u.p over 2f out: no further prog fr over 1f out* **5/1**[1]

1523 **13** *6* **Field Spark**[8] 2964 4-8-7 **59**..........................................(p) GDuffield 15 41
(JAGlover) *hld up: keen: hung bdly lft after 4f out: effrt 3f out: sn rdn and btn* **16/1**

3003 **14** *3 1/2* **Greenwich Meantime**[9] 2935 4-9-11 **77**........................... ACulhane 16 53
(MrsJRRamsden) *prom: ev ch 3f out: wknd 2f out* **12/1**

23-0 **15** *1 3/4* **Montecristo**[53] 1768 11-9-8 **74**.......................................... CLowther 9 48
(RGuest) *bhd most of way* **20/1**

1-00 **16** *2 1/2* **Silvertown**[21] 2583 9-9-2 **68**........................................... PHanagan 6 38
(LLungo) *led tl hdd over 3f out: wknd over 2f out* **9/1**

1000 **17** *5* **Gran Dana (IRE)**[14] 2782 4-9-7 **73**.................................... JFanning 10 35
(MJohnston) *trckd ldrs: effrt over 3f out: wknd over 2f out* **33/1**

41-0 **18** *nk* **Mekuria (JPN)**[18] 2683 3-9-0 **80**.................................... KDalgleish 8 41
(MJohnston) *trckd ldrs: midfield tl wknd over 2f out* **25/1**

5200 **19** *18* **General**[39] 2110 7-9-1 **70**..........................................(b) J-PGuillambert(3) 4 2
(NPLittmoden) *dwlt: a bhd: t.o* **25/1**

2m 31.98s (-0.42) **Going Correction** +0.175s/f (Good)
**WFA** 3 from 4yo+ 14lb **19 Ran SP% 133.6**
Speed ratings: **108,107,107,107,106 105,104,104,104,104 103,101,97,94,93 91,88,88,76**CSF £82.27 CT £2647.42 TOTE £8.70: £2.40, £3.30, £10.90, £3.20; EX 62.40.
**Owner** G Robotti **Bred** J Hutchinson **Trained** Newmarket, Suffolk
■ Stewards Enquiry : P Mulrennan one-day ban: careless riding (Jul 5)

**FOCUS**

A fair and competitive handicap run at a sound gallop and the two top weights dominated the finish. The form looks reliable and the winner can rate higher.

**NOTEBOOK**

**Loves Travelling(IRE)**, who missed out narrowly on his seasonal reappearance last time, showed the benefit of that experience with a gritty display under top-weight. He put his proven stamina to good use when kicking for home two out, and showed a good attitude to repel the runner-up in the final strides. This progressive performer has come a long way since winning a claimer at Brighton in 2003, and there is no reason why he cannot build on this and score again.

**Bucks**, coming into this bidding for the hat-trick, went down with all guns blazing. This represented a personal best in defeat and he is clearly in rude health this season, the drop in trip was more against him than the 4lb rise in the weights for winning last time.

**Saltango(GER)** could not go with the front two in the final furlong, but improved markedly on his latest effort. This former winner in Germany can build on this and find a race at this level in which to get off the mark, but may need a slight drop in trip.

**Sporting Gesture** stayed on all too late in the day, but deserves credit for getting as close as he did from his wide draw.

**Rajam** ran a sound race in defeat, but continues to look vulnerable off his current mark in handicaps.

**Millennium Hall**, bidding for a hat-trick, never really got into this and looked unsuited by the drop in trip. Although this was slightly disappointing, he will find easier opportunities over farther.

**General** *Official explanation: trainer's representative said gelding was stopped in its run and lost interest thereafter*

## 3200 EUROPEAN BREEDERS FUND FILLIES' H'CAP 1m 1f 61y

4:20 (4:20) (D ) (0-80,80) 3-Y-O+ £7,052 (£2,170; £1,085; £542) Stalls High

Form / RPR

5-11 **1** **Heneseys Leg**[28] 2403 4-9-4 **70**........................................ ACulhane 4 83
(JohnBerry) *trckd ldrs: led over 3f out: drvn clr fnl f* **7/4**[2]

0-06 **2** *4* **Route Sixty Six (IRE)**[50] 1875 8-7-12 **50** oh7..................... DaleGibson 1 55
(JeddO'Keeffe) *hld up: rdn 3f out: wnt 2nd wl over 1f out: styd on: no ch w wnr* **14/1**

0000 **3** *1 1/2* **Penny Cross**[25] 2469 4-10-0 **80**.......................................... MFenton 3 82
(JGGiven) *cl up: chsd wnr fr 3f out tl wl over 1f out: no ex* **9/2**[3]

00-3 **4** *5* **Cyclonic Storm**[7] 2974 5-8-8 **60**...................................... PHanagan 2 52
(RAFahey) *s.i.s: hld up: rdn over 2f out: sn btn* **11/10**[1]

0005 **5** *1 3/4* **East Riding**[9] 2944 4-7-5 **50** oh13.................................... DFentiman(7) 5 39
(MissAStokell) *led tl hdd over 3f out: sn btn* **33/1**

1m 58.36s (0.33) **Going Correction** +0.175s/f (Good) **5 Ran SP% 111.8**
Speed ratings: **105,101,100,95,94**CSF £22.67 TOTE £2.60: £1.30, £4.60; EX 33.00.
**Owner** Peter J Skinner **Bred** J W Ford **Trained** Newmarket, Suffolk

**FOCUS**

A modest handicap run at a solid gallop despite the small field, but the overall form looks weak.

**NOTEBOOK**

**Heneseys Leg** landed the hat-trick in style. She only needed to be pushed out to score comfortably, having travelled sweetly off the decent early gallop. She had no trouble defying a 5lb rise for winning last time, and it is likely that her shrewd handler can place her to advantage once more, despite another inevitable rise in the weights for this.

**Route Sixty Six(IRE)**, although outclassed by the winner, ran by far her best race for some time from 7lb out of the handicap. She had the cheekpieces left off this time and it is hard to know what to make of this display, as she is inconsistent and has not won on the Flat since 2002.

**Penny Cross** had the run of the race, but again found very little at the business end and finished well held. She has looked a shadow of her former self since joining current connections and looks too high in the weights at present, so is likely continue to struggle in handicaps.

**Cyclonic Storm** ran a moody race and was never a threat. She failed to reproduce the form of her reappearance seven days previously and looks one to be wary of.

## 3201 SAFFIE JOSEPH & SONS H'CAP 5f

4:50 (4:50) (E ) (0-75,75) 3-Y-O £7,312 (£2,250; £1,125; £562) Stalls High

Form / RPR

5353 **1** **Treasure Cay**[11] 2889 3-9-7 **75**........................................(t[1]) KDarley 12 84
(PWD'Arcy) *prom: rdn to ld ins fnl f: r.o u.p: all out* **11/4**[1]

-562 **2** *nk* **True Magic**[22] 2552 3-8-12 **66**........................................ JFanning 6 74
(JDBethell) *chsd ldrs: hdwy to chal over 1f out: r.o u.p ins last: jst hld* **13/2**[3]

1-00 **3** *1 1/2* **Jadan (IRE)**[49] 1883 3-9-2 **70**............................................ EAhern 11 73
(EJAlston) *mde most tl rdn and hdd ins fnl f: no ex* **8/1**

0064 **4** *1 3/4* **Alchera**[20] 2610 3-8-12 **66**...........................................(b) GDuffield 7 62
(RFJohnsonHoughton) *in tch: rdn 2f out: kpt on fnl f: nvr able to chal* **9/1**

2001 **5** *1 1/4* **Obe Bold (IRE)**[7] 2986 3-8-7 **61** 7ex.................................. FNorton 5 53
(ABerry) *prom: rdn 2f out: wknd appr fnl f* **9/1**

0415 **6** *hd* **Rene Barbier (IRE)**[3] 3122 3-9-1 **69**............................... DeanMcKeown 4 60
(JAGlover) *cl up: rdn 2f out: wknd appr fnl f* **12/1**

-602 **7** *3 1/2* **Sweet Cando (IRE)**[4] 3077 3-8-2 **59**.................................(p) NMackay(3) 2 37
(MissLAPerratt) *hmpd and s.i.s: a bhd* **10/3**[2]

0202 **8** *1/2* **Leopard Creek**[14] 2778 3-8-3 **57**......................................(p) DAllan 3 34
(MrsJRRamsden) *s.i.s: hdwy to chse ldrs after 2f: hung bdly rt and drifted over to far rail 2f out: wknd fnl f* **9/1**

00-0 **9** *3* **Sujosise**[46] 1975 3-7-12 **52** oh3........................................ PHanagan 1 18
(JJQuinn) *s.i.s: a bhd* **33/1**

-000 **10** *1/2* **Multiple Choice (IRE)**[60] 1602 3-8-13 **70**.................. J-PGuillambert(3) 10 34
(NPLittmoden) *prom tl rdn and wknd 2f out* **20/1**

59.69 secs (-1.81) **Going Correction** -0.225s/f (Firm) **10 Ran SP% 119.6**
Speed ratings: **105,104,102,99,97 97,91,90,85,85**CSF £21.69 CT £130.83 TOTE £4.10: £1.40, £2.30, £2.20; EX 15.80 Place 6 £308.99, Place 5 £162.10.
**Owner** Bigwigs Bloodstock IV **Bred** D R Tucker **Trained** Newmarket, Suffolk

**FOCUS**

A modest sprint run at a decent early gallop and the front pair came clear. the form is ordinary but looks sound enough.

**NOTEBOOK**

**Treasure Cay**, who has blown his chances recently by missing the break, was this time smartly away and showed a great attitude to hold on all-out at the finish. He is lightly-raced and capable of better still, with this stiff five looking ideal, and the re-application of the eye-shield had a positive effect this time.

**True Magic** ◆ ran another solid race, but again found one too good. He only just failed on this occasion however, was clear of the rest, and should not be long in going one better over this trip.

**Jadan(IRE)** pinged out of the gates and made a bold bid from the front, but had nothing left in the tank when headed inside the final furlong. A recent 7lb drop in the weights helped bring about this improved effort and he looks to be coming back to himself, so a return to fast ground can see him in the winner's enclosure once again.

**Alchera** ran his race, but a recent slide in the weights has not brought about too much improvement and he looks a fairly tricky customer.

**Sweet Cando(IRE)** was done no favours at the start and faced a very stiff task from then on. This run is best forgiven. *Official explanation: jockey said filly missed the break*

**Leopard Creek** *Official explanation: jockey said filly hung right-handed throughout*

T/Jkpt: Part won. £7,100.00 to a £1 stake. Pool: £10,000.00. 0.50 winning tickets. T/Plt: £405.90 to a £1 stake. Pool: £41,479.65. 74.60 winning tickets. T/Qpdt: £49.50 to a £1 stake. Pool: £3,012.90. 45.00 winning tickets. JF

# 2573 KEMPTON (R-H)

### Wednesday, June 23

**OFFICIAL GOING: Good**

Wind: str across Weather: overcast & showery

## 3202 EUROPEAN BREEDERS FUND MAIDEN FILLIES' STKS 7f (J)

6:30 (6:34) (D ) 2-Y-O £5,310 (£1,634; £817; £408) Stalls High

Form / RPR

2 **1** **Maids Causeway (IRE)**[14] 2786 2-8-11 .................................. MHills 3 83+
(BWHills) *str: h.d.w: lw: dwlt: sn wl in tch: effrt 2f out: led 1f out: pushed clr* **2/5**[1]

**2** *2 1/2* **Park Law (IRE)** 2-8-11 .............................................. JFortune 1 77+
(JHMGosden) *rangy: scope: lw: dwlt: in rr tl prog 4f out: effrt to ld jst over 2f out: hdd 1f out: wknd nr fin* **7/1**[2]

**3** *1 1/2* **Little Miss Gracie** 2-8-8 ........................................... DCorby(3) 8 73
(PBurgoyne) *leggy: chsd ldrs: rdn over 2f out: kpt on fr over 1f out: nvr able to chal* **25/1**

**4** *3* **Danehill Dazzler (IRE)** 2-8-11 ....................................... KFallon 2 66
(APJarvis) *lengthy: str: bit bkwd: dwlt: rn green in last pair and bhd: styd on steadily fnl 2f: nvr nrr* **10/1**

**5** *1 1/4* **Gwyneth** 2-8-11 ........................................................ SSanders 6 62
(JLDunlop) *rangy: scope: dwlt: pushed along in last and wl off the pce: styd on fnl 2f: n.d* **14/1**

**6** *3* **Mulberry Wine** 2-8-11 ............................................... NCallan 7 55
(MBlanshard) *neat: bkwd: mostly chsd ldr to over 2f out: wknd* **33/1**

3 **7** *6* **Vondova**[9] 2940 2-8-11 ............................................... RHughes 4 40
(RHannon) *reluctant to enter stalls: led: rn green but clr 1/2-way: hdd jst over 2f out: wknd and eased* **8/1**[3]

0 **8** *16* **Just Beware**[25] 2481 2-8-11 ......................................... CCatlin 5 —
(MissZCDavison) *bit bkwd: chsd ldrs 3f: sn wknd: t.o* **100/1**

1m 31.92s (4.65) **Going Correction** +0.425s/f (Yiel) **8 Ran SP% 118.6**
Speed ratings: **90,87,85,82,80 77,70,52**CSF £4.13 TOTE £1.40: £1.02, £2.30, £4.50; EX 5.30.

**Owner** Lady Richard Wellesley **Bred** The Vallee Des Reves Syndicate **Trained** Lambourn, Berks
■ A first winner in Britain for the stallion Giant's Causeway.

**FOCUS**
A fair maiden full of inexperienced fillies. The time, not helped by the headwind, was 3.67sec slower than the later handicap, and as result confidence in the form cannot be high.

**NOTEBOOK**
**Maids Causeway(IRE)**, who had improved physically from her debut behind stable companion and subsequent Chesham winner Whazzat, made hard work of this, but may not have been entirely suited by the rain-softened ground. She can win again if not aimed too high.
**Park Law(IRE)** ◆, a half-sister to Lady High Havens and Middlemarch, made an encouraging debut, showing good acceleration to get to the front before being worn down by the favourite. She will come on for the run and should be able to win a maiden.
**Little Miss Gracie**, out of a two-year-old winner over this trip, ran quite well despite looking as if the experience was needed. If progressing she may be up to winning a small race.
**Danehill Dazzler(IRE)** was another to make an eyecatching debut, missing the break before keeping on steadily in the closing stages. She will be much better for the outing.
**Gwyneth**, a half-sister to five winners, was very green on this debut but was noted keeping on nicely at the death. She will do better in time.
**Mulberry Wine**, a half-sister to several winners at a modest level, showed ability on this debut.
**Vondova** found the conditions somewhat different to her debut over five furlongs on firm ground and, after being much too keen in front, emptied pretty quickly in the closing stages. *Official explanation: jockey said filly ran too free early on*

## 3203 WILLIAMHILLRADIO.COM CLASSIFIED STKS — 6f
7:00 (7:03) (D ) 3-Y-O — **£5,421** (£1,668; £834; £417) **Stalls** Centre

| Form | | | | | RPR |
|---|---|---|---|---|---|
| -311 | 1 | | **Kind (IRE)**[21] 2576 3-8-10 82 — RHughes 7 | *(RCharlton) b.hind: lw: trckd ldrs gng wl: squeezed through to ld 1f out: sn kicked on and in command: pushed out nr fin: cleverly* 11/4[1] | 84+ |
| 2050 | 2 | ½ | **Celtic Thunder**[11] 2877 3-8-13 82 — JFortune 4 | *(TJEtherington) lw: hld up in tch and gng wl: effrt and nt clr run jst over 1f out: effrt to chse wnr ins fnl f: r.o but readily hld* 12/1 | 85 |
| 3232 | 3 | hd | **Farewell Gift**[14] 2785 3-8-11 80 — KFallon 3 | *(RHannon) settled in tch: effrt over 1f out: pressed ldng pair ins fnl f: nt qckn* 11/4[1] | 82 |
| 021- | 4 | 3½ | **The Jobber (IRE)**[271] 5192 3-8-13 82 — NCallan 9 | *(MBlanshard) bkwd: t.k.h: led after 1f out: hdd 1f out: wknd last 100yds* 20/1 | 74 |
| 6460 | 5 | 1¾ | **Vienna's Boy (IRE)**[11] 2877 3-8-13 82 — RLMoore 2 | *(RHannon) lw: t.k.h: hld up in last: drvn and effrt on outer wl over 1f out: wknd ins fnl f* 11/2[2] | 69 |
| 50-2 | 6 | ½ | **Chance For Romance**[22] 2549 3-8-11 83 — SDrowne 6 | *(WRMuir) lw: led for 1f: prom tl wknd jst over 1f out* 8/1 | 65 |
| 00-3 | 7 | 1 | **Love Triangle (IRE)**[23] 2536 3-8-8 80 — LPKeniry(3) 8 | *(DRCElsworth) pressed ldr after 1f tl wknd over 1f out* 7/1[3] | 62 |
| 5450 | 8 | 3½ | **Dolce Piccata**[7] 2981 3-8-10 82 — TQuinn 1 | *(BJMeehan) in tch: drvn and wknd wl over 1f out* 20/1 | 51 |

1m 14.94s (1.87) **Going Correction** +0.425s/f (Yiel) — **8** Ran SP% **109.5**
Speed ratings: **104,103,103,98,96 95,94,89**CSF £34.72 TOTE £3.30: £1.60, £3.20, £1.30; EX 42.20.
**Owner** K Abdulla **Bred** Juddmonte Farms **Trained** Beckhampton, Wilts

**FOCUS**
A tight classified stakes with only 3lb between the field on official ratings. The form is sound enough, with the winner the most progressive in the race.

**NOTEBOOK**
**Kind(IRE)** ◆ completed a course hat-trick in cosy fashion, at the same time confirming form with Farewell Gift. She is clearly on the upgrade, but the narrow margin prevents the Handicapper from raising her too much, so the four-timer is on the cards.
**Celtic Thunder**, who has been gradually slipping in the handicap, handled this return to six furlongs and easier ground. He followed the winner through but never looked like overhauling her. He looks to be on the right mark now.
**Farewell Gift**, who has run into Kind in three of his last four races, ran to the ounce compared with their last meeting. Although still a maiden he is consistent and deserves to find a race before long.
**The Jobber(IRE)**, who won his maiden on soft ground but acts on fast, showed good speed on his first appearance for nine months. He only faded in the last furlong and the outing should be of benefit.
**Vienna's Boy(IRE)**, who failed to settle in the rear, did not really pick up, and despite some fair efforts has not won for a year.

## 3204 GIRLS' NIGHT OUT NEXT WEDNESDAY MAIDEN FILLIES' STKS — 1m 2f (J)
7:30 (7:35) (D ) 3-Y-O — **£5,642** (£1,736; £868; £434) **Stalls** High

| Form | | | | | RPR |
|---|---|---|---|---|---|
| | 1 | | **Tartouche** 3-8-11 — SSanders 1 | *(LadyHerries) lengthy: str: scope: bit bkwd: hld up in last trio: gd prog on wd outside fr over 3f out: led 2f out: sn clr: rdn out* 33/1 | 86+ |
| | 2 | 5 | **Apsara** 3-8-11 — (v[1]) WRyan 7 | *(HRACecil) leggy: lt-f: t.k.h: trckd ldrs: shkn up and unable qck 2f out: styd on fnl f to take 2nd on line* 16/1 | 76+ |
| 6 | 3 | shd | **Silver Sash (GER)**[13] 2805 3-8-11 — RHughes 12 | *(MLWBell) b.hind: led to 2f out: sn no ch w wnr: one pce and lost 2nd on line* 10/1 | 76+ |
| 0- | 4 | 2 | **Whole Grain**[254] 5541 3-8-11 — KFallon 8 | *(SirMichaelStoute) trckd ldrs: lost pl 4f out: nudged along and styd on steadily fnl 2f* 12/1 | 72+ |
| 4- | 5 | ¾ | **Daring Aim**[292] 4709 3-8-11 — JFortune 5 | *(SirMichaelStoute) settled in rr: shuffled along and styd on fr over 2f out: n.d* 7/2[2] | 71+ |
| 2-4 | 6 | 1¼ | **Maid To Treasure (IRE)**[22] 2562 3-8-11 — TQuinn 4 | *(JLDunlop) prom: effrt to chal over 2f out: sn ev ch: wknd over 1f out* 2/1[1] | 68+ |
| 26 | 7 | 3½ | **On Cloud Nine**[23] 2513 3-8-11 — RMullen 6 | *(MLWBell) racd towards rr: effrt 3f out: wandered and btn 2f out* 25/1 | 62 |
| 0- | 8 | ½ | **Persian Genie (IRE)**[243] 5733 3-8-11 — SDrowne 11 | *(GBBalding) chsd ldrs: lost pl 1/2-way: shkn up and no prog over 2f out* 100/1 | 61 |
| 0-0 | 9 | ½ | **Song Of The Sea**[22] 2562 3-8-11 — MHills 2 | *(JWHills) settled towards rr: effrt on outer over 3f out: no prog and btn 2f out* 25/1 | 60 |
| | 10 | 1 | **Arctic Silk** 3-8-11 — LDettori 3 | *(SaeedBinSuroor) scope: chsd ldr to over 2f out: sn wknd: eased fnl f* 4/1[3] | 58 |
| 0 | 11 | nk | **Paint The Lily (IRE)**[20] 2632 3-8-8 — LisaJones(3) 14 | *(JWHills) a in rr: pushed along and no prog over 2f out* 100/1 | 57 |
| | 12 | 8 | **Tanmeya** 3-8-11 — RLMoore 10 | *(ACStewart) rangy: bkwd: dwlt: rcvrd and prom after 2f: wknd over 2f out* 16/1 | 42 |
| 000 | 13 | hd | **Suspicious Minds**[32] 2311 3-8-11 — CCatlin 9 | *(GCBravery) a in last trio: wknd over 2f out* 66/1 | 42 |
| | 14 | 5 | **Disparity (USA)** 3-8-11 — JDSmith 13 | *(JRFanshawe) small: chsd ldrs: pushed along 1/2-way: wknd 3f out* 16/1 | 32 |

2m 11.47s (5.33) **Going Correction** +0.425s/f (Yiel) — **14** Ran SP% **124.1**
Speed ratings: **95,91,90,89,88 87,84,84,84,83 83,76,76,72**CSF £486.82 TOTE £49.50: £8.50, £4.90, £3.50; EX 750.90.
**Owner** Lady Herries **Bred** Angmering Park Stud **Trained** Angmering, W Sussex

**FOCUS**
A fair-looking maiden on paper, featuring a number of well-bred and unexposed sorts. The early pace was not especially strong, but they quickened up in the straight and the surprise winner scored in a style that suggests she could be decent.

**NOTEBOOK**
**Tartouche**, a half-sister to three winners, came right around her field and won going away. The form is difficult to evaluate, but she should benefit from the experience and could make up into a decent performer.
**Apsara**, who has plenty of speed on her dam's side, was visored for this debut. She was keen in the early stages, but rather than capitulate she was running on well at the finish and just snatched second.
**Silver Sash(GER)**, whose debut was in a maiden that has produced two subsequent winners already, took the field along and, although the winner brushed her aside, kept on and was only caught by the runner-up on the post. She will appreciate a longer trip and will be of interest once qualified for handicaps.
**Whole Grain**, a sister to Irish Oaks winner Pure Grain, was keeping on steadily without every looking a danger. She will appreciate a longer trip and should be better for this first outing in eight and a half months.
**Daring Aim**, a Daylami half-sister ot Oaks runner-up Flight Of Fancy, like her stable companion never got into contention but looks capable of better with this run under her belt.
**Maid To Treasure(IRE)**, both of whose previous runs have been with cut in the ground, looked to have every chance early in the straight but was soon in trouble and dropped away rather disappointingly. She now qualifies for handicaps.
**Arctic Silk**, the first foal of 1000 Guineas winner Cape Verdi, was close up until dropping away early in the straight and then was allowed to come home in her own time. She should do better in time.

## 3205 WILLIAM HILL ON 0800 44 40 40 H'CAP — 7f (J)
8:00 (8:05) (C ) (0-90,87) 3-Y-O+ — **£9,600** (£2,954; £1,477; £738) **Stalls** High

| Form | | | | | RPR |
|---|---|---|---|---|---|
| 3334 | 1 | | **Chateau Nicol**[21] 2575 5-9-4 78 — (v) TQuinn 2 | *(BGPowell) lw: hld up and sn in midfield: prog over 2f out: chsd ldr wl over 1f out: clsd fnl f: urged along and r.o to ld last 75yds* 10/1 | 89 |
| 0311 | 2 | hd | **Waterside (IRE)**[11] 2891 5-9-4 78 — RLMoore 11 | *(GLMoore) led: drvn 3l clr wl over 1f out: collared last 75yds* 7/1[3] | 88 |
| 6-02 | 3 | ¾ | **Gift Horse**[21] 2575 4-9-10 84 — LDettori 4 | *(JRFanshawe) lw: hld up in rr: nt clr run over 2f out and swtchd lft: hmpd sn after: r.o to take 3rd ins fnl f: nt rch ldng pair* 9/4[1] | 97+ |
| 0040 | 4 | 4 | **Marker**[25] 2477 4-9-1 80 — RThomas(5) 7 | *(GBBalding) hld up in rr: shuffled along 2f out: styd on steadily fr over 1f out : no ch* 10/1 | 78 |
| 0505 | 5 | hd | **Terraquin (IRE)**[12] 2838 4-8-10 70 — (p) DKinsella 6 | *(JJBridger) b: hld up in last pair: prog on outer over 2f out: unable qck wl over 1f out: one pce after* 25/1 | 68 |
| 0110 | 6 | 1½ | **Lifted Way**[23] 2534 5-9-6 80 — SDrowne 8 | *(PRChamings) lw: prom: chsd ldr 3f out to over 1f out: wknd fnl f* 14/1 | 74 |
| -000 | 7 | 2 | **Craiova (IRE)**[21] 2575 5-9-10 84 — MHills 12 | *(BWHills) lw: t.k.h: trckd ldrs: rdn and unable qck 2f out: wknd fnl f* 10/1 | 73 |
| 6045 | 8 | 2½ | **Fearby Cross (IRE)**[19] 2646 8-8-2 65 — LisaJones(3) 3 | *(WJMusson) hld up in last pair: swtchd rt and shkn up over 1f out: nvr nr ldrs* 14/1 | 47 |
| 005- | 9 | 1½ | **Great Scott**[258] 5459 3-9-4 87 — SChin 9 | *(MJohnston) lw: chsd ldrs: rdn and btn whn nt clr run 2f out: wknd* 20/1 | 65 |
| 5344 | 10 | 3 | **Molcon (IRE)**[5] 3052 3-9-0 83 — PRobinson 13 | *(NACallaghan) s.i.s: sn trckd ldrs: rdn on outer over 2f out: sn wknd and eased* 11/2[2] | 53 |
| 0304 | 11 | nk | **Jay Gee's Choice**[10] 2905 4-9-10 84 — CCatlin 10 | *(MRChannon) chsd ldr to 3f out: wknd 2f out* 12/1 | 54 |
| 5204 | 12 | shd | **Temper Tantrum**[31] 2325 6-7-9 60 — (p) BSwarbrick(5) 1 | *(AndrewReid) b: b.hind: hld up: effrt to chse ldrs over 3f out: wknd u.p over 2f out* 20/1 | 29 |

1m 28.25s (0.98) **Going Correction** +0.425s/f (Yiel)
**WFA** 3 from 4yo+ 9lb — **12** Ran SP% **120.3**
Speed ratings: **111,110,109,105,105 103,101,98,96,93 92,92**CSF £77.31 CT £219.12 TOTE £11.20: £3.90, £3.20, £1.80; EX 121.90.
**Owner** Basingstoke Commercials **Bred** Aston House Stud **Trained** Morestead, Hants

**FOCUS**
A decent time for the grade, 3.67 seconds faster than the juvenile fillies' maiden, and the first three home were clear. The form is fair and looks solid enough.

**NOTEBOOK**
**Chateau Nicol** came with a strong challenge entering the last furlong and really stuck his head out at the line to gain a much deserved success. He has not really had his ideal conditions since winning in April, yet has remained consistent and the easing in the ground went his way.
**Waterside(IRE)**, who has recently been rejuvenated by a change of stable, again took the field along at a fair clip and looked likely to bag the hat-trick approaching two out, but could not hold off the strong challenge of the winner at the finish. This was another bold front-running display nevertheless, and the recent 4lb rise in the weights may have been lenient on this evidence.
**Gift Horse** ◆ would have been closer but for meeting trouble two out and has to go down as a little unlucky. Better then the bare form, this lightly-raced performer is capable of making amends next time, yet would be more at home back over a mile on this evidence.
**Marker** made decent progress from off the pace to briefly threaten in the latter stages, but could not find a change of gear and just stayed on at the one npace. He clearly needs this easy going and has slipped in the ratings, so no doubt his shrewd connections will place him to advantage in due course.
**Terraquin(IRE)** looked booked for a place when challenging two out, but was made to look one paced under pressure and lost out for fourth close home. He may need things a bit quicker underfoot.
**Molcon(IRE)** never threatened and this must rate as a big disappointment. The form of his previous effort gave him every chance in this, but will have left connections scratching their heads.

## 3206 WILLIAMHILL.CO.UK FILLIES' H'CAP — 1m 1f (R)
8:30 (8:31) (D ) (0-80,80) 3-Y-O+ — **£5,473** (£1,684; £842; £421) **Stalls** High

| Form | | | | | RPR |
|---|---|---|---|---|---|
| 6411 | 1 | | **Unsuited**[21] 2573 5-8-9 61 — NataliaGemelova(7) 8 | *(JELong) settled in rr: smooth prog to ld wl over 1f out: shkn up and r.o wl* 11/4[1] | 72 |
| 2130 | 2 | 1½ | **Sunisa (IRE)**[11] 2887 3-9-8 78 — MHills 1 | *(BWHills) lw: trckd ldrs gng wl: effrt and w wnr wl over 1f out: r.o but readily hld fnl f* 11/4[1] | 86 |

34-0 **3** 2 ½ **Thirteen Tricks (USA)**[51] [1831] 3-9-5 **75** ................................ LDettori 5 78
(MrsAJPerrett) *trckd ldrs: effrt over 2f out: rdn and styd on one pce fr over 1f out* **10/1**

3616 **4** 1 **Springtime Romance (USA)**[12] [2841] 3-9-10 **80** .................... KFallon 2 81
(EALDunlop) *sn led: hdd and drvn wl over 1f out: one pce* **11/2**[3]

0504 **5** 1 ½ **Cuddles (FR)**[13] [2806] 5-9-0 **59** .................................. CCatlin 6 57
(KOCunningham-Brown) *s.s: hld up in last: prog and tried to get up on inner 2f out where no room: rdn and btn after* **10/1**

21-4 **6** ½ **Florida Heart**[32] [2284] 3-9-3 **76** ............................. LPKeniry(3) 10 73
(AMBalding) *hld up towards rr: effrt on outer over 2f out: no prog over 1f out* **9/2**[2]

0010 **7** 4 **Estimate**[26] [2446] 4-8-12 **57** ....................................(v) PaulEddery 3 46
(JohnAHarris) *b: chsd ldr to over 2f out: wknd over 1f out* **33/1**

-100 **8** 13 **Gretna**[32] [2281] 3-9-9 **79** .................................................. TQuinn 7 42
(JLDunlop) *sn prom: riddden and losing pl whn squeezed out over 2f out: eased and bhd after* **16/1**

1m 57.35s (3.02) **Going Correction** +0.425s/f (Yiel)
**WFA** 3 from 4yo+ 11lb **8** Ran SP% **113.9**
Speed ratings: **103,101,99,98,97 96,93,81**CSF £10.02 CT £63.32 TOTE £3.30: £1.10, £2.40, £3.20; EX 15.40.
**Owner** Amaroni Racing **Bred** Lawn Stud **Trained** Woldingham, Surrey

**FOCUS**
Ordinary form, but Unsuited achieved another personal best and had the rest well strung out behind her.

**NOTEBOOK**
**Unsuited** defied another hike in the weights and cosily landed the course hat-trick. She was given a fine ride by her capable apprentice, who has ridden her to all of her last three wins, and is clearly in the form of her life. A further rise in the weights is inevitable, but she obviously loves this track, and it would be folly to assume she has stopped improving yet.
**Sunisa(IRE)** put a poor run last time behind her with a sound effort in defeat, although no match for the in-form winner. This softer ground suited, and she was clear in second. An extra furlong should see her gain compensation soon in a similar event.
**Thirteen Tricks(USA)**, tailed off on her three-year-old debut in May when her stable was under a cloud, could only keep on at the one pace late in the day and was well held. She shaped as though this would again bring her on and was not disgraced.
**Springtime Romance(USA)** had the run of the race and took the field along at a modest clip, but found very little when challenged and could only muster the one pace late on. This ground looked easier than ideal and she is worth another chance when able to race on faster going.
**Florida Heart** could not quicken on this soft ground and is capable of better. *Official explanation: trainer said filly was scoped after the race and had bled internally*
**Gretna** *Official explanation: jockey said filly slipped coming out of the stalls*

## 3207 WILLIAMHILLCASINO.COM H'CAP 1m 4f
**9:00** (9:00) (D ) (0-85,85) 3-Y-O+ **£5,330** (£1,640; £820; £410) **Stalls** High

Form RPR

5231 **1** **Sangiovese**[13] [2810] 5-9-2 **73** ............................................. SDrowne 5 82
(HMorrison) *lw: trckd ldr for 4f: styd prom: drvn to ld over 1f out: kpt on wl* **7/2**[3]

2412 **2** 1 **Danakil**[18] [2689] 9-9-3 **74** .......................................... RLMoore 2 81
(SDow) *hld up in last: effrt 3f out: chsd wnr jst over 1f out: no imp ins fnl f* **3/1**[2]

11-0 **3** 1 ½ **Whispered Promises (USA)**[43] [2018] 3-8-11 **82** ........................ SChin 3 87
(MJohnston) *lw: in tch: drvn and outpcd over 2f out: kpt on again ins fnl f to take 3rd nr fin* **7/1**

3020 **4** hd **Mexican Pete**[18] [2671] 4-9-6 **77** ........................................ KFallon 1 81
(PWHiatt) *in tch: pushed along over 3f out: effrt u.p to chse ldng pair 1f out: one pce fnl f: lost 3rd nr fin* **11/4**[1]

/000 **5** 1 ¼ **Reviewer (IRE)**[14] [2787] 6-8-8 **65** ..................................(b) CCatlin 4 67
(MMeade) *chsd ldr after 4f to over 2f out: steadily fdd u.p* **10/1**

01-1 **6** 1 ¼ **Ski Jump (USA)**[20] [2612] 4-10-0 **85** ...............................(b) RHughes 6 85
(RCharlton) *rousted along to ld: hdd over 1f out: wknd fnl f* **5/1**

2m 37.39s (2.39) **Going Correction** +0.425s/f (Yiel)
**WFA** 3 from 4yo+ 14lb **6** Ran SP% **112.1**
Speed ratings: **109,108,107,107,106 105**CSF £14.33 TOTE £4.00: £2.40, £1.90; EX 22.90 Place 6 £84.67, Place 5 £68.07.
**Owner** Kentisbeare Quartet **Bred** Jeremy Green And Sons **Trained** East Ilsley, Berks

**FOCUS**
A reasonable handicap that produced a fair time for the grade. The form is ordinary but reliable.

**NOTEBOOK**
**Sangiovese** followed up his recent win at Newbury in good style, defying a 6lb rise in the process. He has improved of late for being upped in trip, and was his first attempt over the distance, so he could have more to offer. He is still well treated on turf in comparison to his All-Weather mark.
**Danakil** ran another sound race, but could not get to the winner, try as he might. He remains in good heart, yet the Handicapper looks to just about have his measure at present.
**Whispered Promises(USA)**, who flopped on his three-year-old debut last time, stayed on again having got outpaced at a crucial stage. He seemed to get the trip, but his best form as a juvenile was on a faster surface, and a return to quicker ground may see him get closer.
**Mexican Pete** had every chance if good enough on entering the straight, but was made to look very one paced when push came to shove and disappointed.
**Ski Jump(USA)** had the run of the race, but found disappointingly little off the bridle and dropped out tamely halfway up the straight. He is a moody sort, but may prefer a better surface.
T/Plt: £156.50 to a £1 stake. Pool: £46,497.00. 216.85 winning tickets. T/Qpdt: £103.50 to a £1 stake. Pool: £2,295.70. 16.40 winning tickets. JN

# 2910 SALISBURY (R-H)
## Wednesday, June 23

**OFFICIAL GOING: Good**
Rain eased the ground, which looked more testing than the official "good" might suggest. Many of the runners looked distinctly tired in the closing stages.
Wind: Fresh against Weather: Cool, dull and showery

## 3208 APPROACH VAUXHALL EBF MAIDEN FILLIES' STKS 5f
**2:10** (2:13) (D ) 2-Y-O **£5,057** (£1,556; £778; £389) **Stalls** High

Form RPR

4 **1** **Right Answer**[11] [2884] 2-8-11 ............................................ KFallon 2 83+
(APJarvis) *trckd stands' side ldr: led 2f out: rdn out* **13/2**

346 **2** 1 ¾ **Withering Lady (IRE)**[36] [2205] 2-8-11 ................................ RHavlin 4 77
(MrsPNDutfield) *hld up in tch stands' side: effrt over 2f out: ev ch 1f out: hrd rdn: nt qckn* **33/1**

**3** nk **Peeptoe (IRE)** 2-8-11 ........................................................ TQuinn 3 76
(JLDunlop) *w'like: bit bkwd: hld up in tch stands' side: rdn to chse ldrs 2f out: sltly outpcd 1f out: kpt on nr fin* **12/1**

**4** 2 **Clove (USA)** 2-8-11 ........................................................ RHughes 12 86+
(BWHills) *unf: lw: s.s: sn prom: led far side gp 1f out: no ch w stands' side* **9/4**[1]

2233 **5** hd **Bibury Flyer**[11] [2868] 2-8-11 .......................................... TEDurcan 1 68
(MRChannon) *led stands' side gp 3f: carried hd to one side and no ex over 1f out* **11/2**[3]

33 **6** hd **Angel Sprints**[27] [2427] 2-8-11 ............................................ ADaly 6 81+
(LGCottrell) *prom: j. path over 3f out: led far side gp over 2f out tl 1f out: no ch w stands' side* **8/1**

24 **7** 1 **Brag (IRE)**[27] [2427] 2-8-11 .......................................... SDrowne 11 78+
(RCharlton) *led far side gp over 2f: one pce appr fnl f* **7/2**[2]

263 **8** 5 **Azuree (IRE)**[11] [2876] 2-8-11 .......................................... PDobbs 5 60+
(RHannon) *in tch far side: outpcd fnl 2f* **14/1**

**9** 2 **Three Aces (IRE)** 2-8-11 .............................................. SSanders 10 53+
(RMBeckett) *leggy: s.s: racd far side: a bhd* **50/1**

**10** 3 ½ **Ruby Muja** 2-8-11 ........................................................ DaneO'Neill 9 41+
(RHannon) *unf: bit bkwd: s.s: towards rr far side: n.d fnl 2f* **25/1**

**11** 10 **Gold Majesty** 2-8-11 ........................................................ CCatlin 8 6+
(MRChannon) *w'like: bit bkwd: racd far side: sn outpcd and bhd* **20/1**

63.20 secs (1.63) **Going Correction** +0.30s/f (Good) **11** Ran SP% **120.7**
Speed ratings: **98,95,94,91,91 90,89,81,78,72 56**CSF £211.08 TOTE £6.90: £1.70, £12.80, £4.40; EX 279.70.
**Owner** Christopher Shankland **Bred** Bearstone Stud And T Herbert Jackson **Trained** Twyford, Bucks

**FOCUS**
The four who raced on the stands' side were clearly at an advantage, and Clove would have pushed the winner close had she been drawn lower. Nonetheless, a useful winning time for the type of race.

**NOTEBOOK**
**Right Answer** was helped by being one of the four to race on the stands' side, but won tidily. She still has plenty of strengthening to do around her middle and should progress on the track as she does so.
**Withering Lady(IRE)** was more exposed than many of her rivals but put in a fine performance, albeit from a favourable draw. She is well capable of finding a maiden on this evidence.
**Peeptoe(IRE)**, a Machiavellian filly, would be suited by six furlongs already. She is a nippy-looking sort who should learn plenty from this encouraging debut.
**Clove(USA)** ◆, the first home on the far side, would have gone close had she been in the other group and might even have won. She will improve as she strengthens and should have no problem finding races.
**Bibury Flyer** is beginning to look exposed and her finishing effort was rather tame.
**Angel Sprints** ran well on the unfavoured far side and is capable of winning a maiden or nursery.
**Brag(IRE)** did well from a poor draw. She is now qualified for nurseries and will be well at home in them.

## 3209 SMITH & WILLIAMSON MAIDEN FILLIES' STKS 6f 212y
**2:40** (2:40) (D ) 3-Y-O **£5,687** (£1,750; £875; £437) **Stalls** Centre

Form RPR

**1** **Alqwah (IRE)** 3-8-11 ...............................................(t) LDettori 3 87+
(SaeedBinSuroor) *unf: scope: mde all: set sedate pce: qcknd 3f out: rdn out* **5/1**[3]

2320 **2** 2 **Red Top (IRE)**[7] [2971] 3-8-11 **84** ........................................ RHughes 10 74
(RHannon) *lw: s.s: hld up and bhd: nt clr run on stands' rail over 2f out: gd hdwy to chse wnr ins fnl f: a hld* **1/1**[1]

-306 **3** nk **Ela Paparouna**[21] [2577] 3-8-11 **70** ...................................... SWhitworth 2 73
(HCandy) *mid-div: rdn over 2f out: hdwy over 1f out: styd on same pce fnl f* **9/2**[2]

60 **4** 1 **Scrunch**[35] [2223] 3-8-11 ................................................... KFallon 1 70
(BJMeehan) *prom: chsd wnr 2f out tl ins fnl f: one pce* **20/1**

**5** 2 ½ **Tetcott (IRE)** 3-8-11 ........................................................ DHolland 5 64
(MPTregoning) *neat: bit bkwd: hld up towards rr: shkn up and sme hdwy over 1f out: nvr nr to chal* **12/1**

3- **6** 2 ½ **Anna Panna**[175] [6266] 3-8-11 ............................................ DaneO'Neill 9 57
(HCandy) *in tch: rdn over 2f out: wknd over 1f out* **20/1**

30- **7** shd **Du Pre**[349] [3142] 3-8-11 ...................................................... SSanders 7 57
(MrsAJPerrett) *bit bkwd: towards rr: effrt over 2f out: no imp appr fnl f* **25/1**

**8** ¾ **Gay Romance** 3-8-11 ........................................................ MHills 6 55
(BWHills) *w'like: leggy: bhd: rdn 3f out: nvr rchd ldrs* **16/1**

20- **9** 2 ½ **Libera**[255] [5531] 3-8-11 ................................................... PMcCabe 8 49
(MGQuinlan) *hung rt thrght: chsd wnr 5f: sn lost pl* **25/1**

03 **10** 3 **Khafayif (USA)**[21] [2572] 3-8-11 ............................................ RHills 4 41
(BHanbury) *prom over 4f* **16/1**

1m 29.69s (0.69) **Going Correction** +0.30s/f (Good) **10** Ran SP% **121.5**
Speed ratings: **108,105,105,104,101 98,98,97,94,91**CSF £10.26 TOTE £6.10: £2.40, £1.10, £2.00; EX 7.00.
**Owner** Godolphin **Bred** Ballydoyle Stud **Trained** Newmarket, Suffolk

**FOCUS**
A routine maiden with a winner allowed the run of the race, but a very smart winning time indeed for the grade.

**NOTEBOOK**
**Alqwah(IRE)** arrived in the parade ring late and wearing a paddock sheet on an unseasonably cool day. Allowed to dictate terms by her rivals, she won with a bit to spare, but it will take another run to assess her more accurately.
**Red Top(IRE)**, very hot in the betting, did not get the run of the race, trying to come from behind off a pedestrian tempo and meeting trouble in running. She deserves another chance to show the support was justified.
**Ela Paparouna** looks the part, being strongly made and with plenty of scope, but this half-sister to top sprinter Kyllachy is not as speedy as he was. Indeed, an extra furlong might be in her favour.
**Scrunch** , who proved she stays this trip, seems to be improving and is now qualified for handicaps.
**Tetcott(IRE)** was not knocked about on this debut, but she lacks the scope of others and will need to step up soon.
**Anna Panna** needed the run after a long absence, so it was no surprise to see her fading away.
**Du Pre** was never competitive, but can do better in handicaps when the stable is in form.
**Khafayif(USA)** dropped back alarmingly, and may not have been suited by the slow ground.

## 3210 TOTETRIFECTA BIBURY CUP STKS (H'CAP) 1m 4f
**3:10** (3:10) (C ) (0-95,87) 3-Y-O **£15,587** (£5,912; £2,956; £1,343) **Stalls** High

Form RPR

-021 **1** **Albinus**[29] [2394] 3-9-1 **80** ...............................................(b) DHolland 10 96
(AMBalding) *w ldrs: led 3f out: rdn and styd on fnl 2f* **6/1**[3]

0111 **2** 1 ¾ **Selebela**[10] [2914] 3-9-8 **87** 5ex ........................................ LDettori 2 100
(LMCumani) *prom: chsd wnr over 2f out: kpt on* **3/1**[2]

-411 **3** 1 ¼ **Lochbuie (IRE)**[48] [1899] 3-9-7 **86** ........................................ JFEgan 7 97
(GWragg) *lw: t.k.h: rdn 5f out: hdwy to chse ldrs 3f out: kpt on* **9/4**[1]

1200 **4** *5* **Tiger Tiger (FR)**[18] 2676 3-9-5 **84** NCallan 6 87
(JamiePoulton) *lw: dwlt and hmpd s: in rr tl hdwy 4f out: one pce fnl 2f* **14/1**
0-30 **5** *3/4* **Pangloss (IRE)**[19] 2648 3-8-4 **69** (p) RLMoore 4 71
(GLMoore) *in rr: rdn and lost tch 4f out: hung rt and styd on fnl 2f* **25/1**
0012 **6** *1/2* **Watamu (IRE)**[28] 2397 3-9-7 **86** SSanders 3 87
(PJMakin) *chsd ldrs: rdn over 3f out: no ex fnl 2f* **6/1**[3]
-010 **7** *3/4* **Rarefied (IRE)**[48] 1899 3-9-3 **82** RHughes 9 82
(RCharlton) *t.k.h: chsd ldrs: lost pl 7f out: n.d fnl 3f* **20/1**
2451 **8** *nk* **Zaffeu**[11] 2870 3-8-3 **71** TPQueally[(3)] 1 71
(NPLittmoden) *b.off hind: s.s and early reminders: in rr tl rdn and hdwy 3f out: hung rt and btn 2f out* **25/1**
-140 **9** *3* **Bukit Fraser (IRE)**[21] 2578 3-9-4 **83** KFallon 8 78
(PFICole) *led tl 3f out: wknd 2f out* **7/1**
0421 **10** *23* **Horner (USA)**[9] 2944 3-9-6 **85** 5ex JQuinn 5 43
(PFICole) *lw: plld hrd: in tch: hrd rdn 4f out: wknd 3f out* **16/1**

2m 38.71s (2.36) **Going Correction** +0.30s/f (Good) **10** Ran SP% **121.8**
Speed ratings: **104,102,102,98,98 97,97,97,95,79**CSF £24.91 CT £53.35 TOTE £8.20: £2.20, £1.50, £1.60; EX 29.70 Trifecta £188.60 Pool £4,808.69 - 18.10 winning units.
**Owner** Miss K Rausing **Bred** Miss K Rausing **Trained** Kingsclere, Hants

**FOCUS**
A competitive race with a number of in-form horses and strong form overall. A number of decent prospects should emerge from this contest, with the winner capable of even better since he was idling a shade in front.

**NOTEBOOK**
**Albinus** ◆ was not doing much in front, though always finding enough. He looks progressive, with even more valuable handicaps than this within his range during the second half of the season.
**Selebela** had a tough task conceding weight to the colts, but ran a fine race. Whether she can cope with her scheduled 9lb rise in the weights is another matter.
**Lochbuie(IRE)** gets the trip well and appreciated the easing ground. He never stopped staying on, but the first two were always holding him.
**Tiger Tiger(FR)** goes well on ground with cut in it. He ran his race but was well held, and the incident at the start cannot be used as an excuse.
**Pangloss(IRE)** looked more exposed and less progressive than most of these, but he was still plodding on when others had given their all on the tiring ground.
**Watamu(IRE)** gets this trip on fast ground but these conditions just found him out at the finish.
**Rarefied(IRE)** is said to be better on fast ground, though he was coming back a bit at the finish after looking well out of it.
**Zaffeu** tends to hang on testing ground, and he had had enough a quarter of a mile from home.

## 3211 GOADSBY & HARDING FILLIES' H'CAP 6f
3:40 (3:40) (E) (0-75,75) 3-Y-O £4,338 (£1,335; £667; £333) **Stalls** High

Form RPR
0600 **1** **Rise**[16] 2741 3-8-1 **55** ow2 (b) JFEgan 1 65
(AndrewReid) *b: b.hind: w ldr: led wl over 1f out: rdn out* **14/1**
006- **2** *1 1/2* **Sabrina Brown**[189] 6210 3-7-10 **55** RThomas[(5)] 7 61
(GBBalding) *lw: mid-div: rdn to chse ldrs over 1f out: styd on to take 2nd ins fnl f* **14/1**
0504 **3** *1 1/2* **Wavertree Girl (IRE)**[32] 2290 3-8-13 **67** (b[1]) TGMcLaughlin 9 68
(NPLittmoden) *s.s: bhd: drvn and hdwy over 1f out: carried hd high: styd on* **14/1**
0412 **4** *1/2* **Estihlal**[12] 2839 3-8-10 **64** RHills 2 64
(EALDunlop) *dwlt: sn cl up: jnd ldrs and hung rt 2f out: one pce fnl f* **7/4**[1]
0504 **5** *shd* **Barabella (IRE)**[33] 2266 3-8-4 **58** RLMoore 8 57
(RJHodges) *outpcd towards rr: hdwy towards centre over 2f out: no imp fnl f* **14/1**
5250 **6** *3 1/2* **Missus Links (USA)**[11] 2875 3-9-3 **71** RHughes 11 60
(RHannon) *lw: racd alone early: jnd rest of field on stands' side after 2f: prom tl no ex fnl 2f* **11/2**[3]
3642 **7** *3/4* **Comeraincomeshine (IRE)**[16] 2741 3-8-6 **63** RMiles[(3)] 4 49
(TGMills) *led tl wknd wl over 1f out* **9/2**[2]
3005 **8** *1 1/4* **Black Oval**[13] 2800 3-7-9 **52** oh3 LisaJones[(3)] 10 35
(SDow) *dwlt: outpcd towards rr: nvr able to chal* **16/1**
-604 **9** *shd* **La Vie Est Belle**[23] 2518 3-9-2 **70** AMcCarthy 3 52
(BRMillman) *prom: n.m.r 2f out: sn wknd* **10/1**
-600 **10** *1 1/2* **Our Gamble (IRE)**[21] 2576 3-9-7 **75** DaneO'Neill 5 53
(RHannon) *mid-div tl wknd 2f out* **25/1**
0-05 **11** *12* **Even Hotter**[14] 2785 3-8-0 **54** JQuinn 6 —
(DWPArbuthnot) *dwlt: towards rr: rdn and n.d fr 1/2-way* **16/1**

1m 17.84s (2.90) **Going Correction** +0.30s/f (Good) **11** Ran SP% **121.3**
Speed ratings: **92,90,88,87,87 82,81,79,79,77 61**CSF £200.68 CT £2835.48 TOTE £15.00: £4.40, £3.40, £3.70; EX 213.10.
**Owner** A S Reid **Bred** Cheveley Park Stud Ltd **Trained** Mill Hill, London NW7

**FOCUS**
A run-of-the-mill contest with some well exposed types, many of them having an ordinary time of it this season. The form is moderate but sound.

**NOTEBOOK**
**Rise** had been well beaten in previous outings this season, but she ran a fair race on soft ground at Folkestone and obviously goes well with a bit of cut.
**Sabrina Brown**, from a family that enjoys soft ground, appreciated the easing conditions. She will stay farther and should find a race when things are in her favour.
**Wavertree Girl(IRE)** has become disappointing. She retains some ability and did fairly well after a stuttering start, but her finishing effort was not entirely convincing.
**Estihlal** began to wander as she tired on the rain-softened ground. Faster conditions suit her better.
**Barabella(IRE)** just plodded on but was never doing enough. She has done better on faster ground.
**Missus Links(USA)** cut the corner in the first two furlongs, a clever piece of riding, but one that did not make any difference in the end. The tiring ground eventually took its toll.
**Comeraincomeshine(IRE)** *Official explanation: jockey said filly was unsuited by the good ground*

## 3212 NOEL CANNON MEMORIAL TROPHY RATED STKS (H'CAP) 1m
4:10 (4:10) (C) (0-95,93) 3-Y-O+ £9,228 (£3,500; £1,750; £795) **Stalls** Centre

Form RPR
-014 **1** **Flowerdrum (USA)**[33] 2271 4-9-1 **83** RHills 12 94
(WJHaggas) *hld up in midfield: hdwy over 1f out: rdn to ld nr fin* **7/1**
1060 **2** *hd* **Consonant (IRE)**[11] 2894 7-9-7 **89** KFallon 3 100
(DGBridgwater) *lw: chsd ldrs: drvn to chal 1f out: ev ch whn n.m.r fnl 50 yds: kpt on* **8/1**
/3-5 **3** *1/2* **Presumptive (IRE)**[47] 1939 4-8-9 **77** SDrowne 2 87
(RCharlton) *lw: chsd ldrs: led over 1f out: hdd and nt qckn nr fin* **8/1**
-100 **4** *4* **Highland Reel**[7] 2969 7-9-5 **87** TQuinn 7 88
(DRCElsworth) *towards rr: rdn and hdwy over 2f out: nt pce to chal* **12/1**
0-00 **5** *nk* **Cornelius**[51] 1828 7-9-11 **93** SSanders 6 93
(PFICole) *s.s: rdn in rr early: styd on fnl 2f: nt rch ldrs* **20/1**
0512 **6** *nk* **Red Spell (IRE)**[18] 2692 3-8-3 **81** JFEgan 8 80
(RHannon) *prom: led over 2f out tl over 1f out: no ex* **5/1**[3]
0562 **7** *2 1/2* **Alrafid (IRE)**[19] 2637 5-9-6 **88** RLMoore 13 82
(GLMoore) *lw: in rr tl effrt into midfield 2f out: hrd rdn: no imp* **9/2**[2]
5040 **8** *1 1/2* **Norton (IRE)**[7] 2969 7-9-5 **90** (v[1]) RMiles[(3)] 4 80
(TGMills) *prom: ev ch 2f out: hrd rdn and wknd over 1f out* **7/2**[1]
6-05 **9** *nk* **Mezuzah**[18] 2687 4-8-12 **80** TEDurcan 11 69
(GWragg) *lw: outpcd in rr: effrt in centre 2f out: hrd rdn over 1f out: no imp* **16/1**
0040 **10** *1/2* **Irony (IRE)**[19] 2637 5-9-3 **85** LDettori 1 73
(AMBalding) *led tl over 2f out: sn wknd* **12/1**
5-00 **11** *7* **Captain Saif**[32] 2283 4-9-5 **87** RHughes 5 59
(RHannon) *mid-div tl outpcd over 2f out: n.d after* **33/1**
000- **12** *4* **Zucchero**[235] 5873 8-8-12 **80** DaneO'Neill 9 43
(DWPArbuthnot) *s.s: outpcd towards rr: rdn and n.d fnl 3f* **33/1**
-656 **13** *1 3/4* **Star Sensation (IRE)**[14] 2789 4-9-2 **84** DHolland 10 43
(PWHarris) *prom 5f* **16/1**

1m 44.58s (1.61) **Going Correction** +0.30s/f (Good) **13** Ran SP% **129.6**
**WFA** 3 from 4yo+ 10lb
Speed ratings: **103,102,102,98,98 97,95,93,93,92 85,81,80**CSF £66.37 CT £487.99 TOTE £8.70: £3.10, £2.80, £2.60; EX 99.00.
**Owner** J Caplan **Bred** Derry Meeting Farm & Christophe Clement **Trained** Newmarket, Suffolk

**FOCUS**
A race with some classy and seasoned handicappers, though many of them were largely out of form. However, the form should prove reliable.

**NOTEBOOK**
**Flowerdrum(USA)** has been doing well this season and deserved her success. She coped well with the easing ground.
**Consonant(IRE)**, a smart performer on sand, bounced back to form on turf with a spirited effort. His rider was unable to use his whip after becoming short of room near the finish and that did not help, though it probably did not cost him victory.
**Presumptive(IRE)**, having only his fourth race, ran remarkably well off a stiff-looking handicap mark. He has plenty of ability, and should win races if he can reproduce this and if the Handicapper does not lumber him with too much extra weight.
**Highland Reel** is inconsistent and ran only a fair race. He kept on from an unpromising position but was never going fast enough to make his presence felt.
**Cornelius** needs even softer ground to offset his lack of pace.
**Red Spell(IRE)** seemed not to get home up the hill on the rain-softened ground.
**Norton(IRE)** is a game old fellow in front, so the decision to put the visor on seemed strange. If anything, it had a negative effect. *Official explanation: trainer said race came too soon after his run seven days previously*
**Star Sensation(IRE)** *Official explanation: jockey said filly was unsuited by the good ground*

## 3213 JOHN S GLEDHILL & ASSOCIATES CHARTERED SURVEYORS CLASSIFIED STKS 1m 1f 198y
4:40 (4:40) (D) 3-Y-O £5,707 (£1,756; £878; £439) **Stalls** High

Form RPR
3-04 **1** **Red Birr (IRE)**[36] 2197 3-9-0 75 DHolland 9 82
(AMBalding) *lw: prom: led 3f out: rdn clr fnl f: readily* **4/1**[3]
0004 **2** *5* **Antigiotto (IRE)**[16] 2729 3-9-1 76 LDettori 8 74
(LMCumani) *b.off fore: hmpd in rr after 1f: mod 5th and drvn along over 4f out: styd on to take 2nd fnl 100 yds: no ch w wnr* **8/1**
1401 **3** *3/4* **Alfridini**[10] 2915 3-8-11 70 LPKeniry[(3)] 7 71
(DRCElsworth) *lw: hdwy to press ldrs over 3f out: hrd rdn 2f out: wnt mod 2nd 1f out tl fnl 100 yds* **10/3**[2]
2303 **4** *1 3/4* **Sailmaker (IRE)**[12] 2841 3-9-0 75 (t) SDrowne 4 68
(RCharlton) *mainly 2nd tl no ex 1f out* **5/2**[1]
5-55 **5** *1 3/4* **Mommkin**[15] 2751 3-8-8 74 SHitchcott[(3)] 5 61
(MRChannon) *led tl 3f out: sn outpcd* **6/1**
33-4 **6** *24* **Concert Hall (USA)**[85] 1186 3-8-11 75 RHughes 6 16
(MrsAJPerrett) *lw: hld up in rr: rdn 4f out: lost tch over 2f out: eased over 1f out* **8/1**

2m 11.67s (3.35) **Going Correction** +0.30s/f (Good) **6** Ran SP% **108.2**
Speed ratings: **98,94,93,92,90 71**CSF £31.35 TOTE £5.80: £3.10, £2.30; EX 68.10 Place 6 £1,552.04, Place 5 £195.58.
**Owner** John Nicholls (banbury) Ltd **Bred** Mrs Ellen Lyons **Trained** Kingsclere, Hants

**FOCUS**
A moderate contest and ordinary form, with a comfortable winner who clearly appreciated the ground.

**NOTEBOOK**
**Red Birr(IRE)** seemed to enjoy the easier conditions and should be noted on ground with cut in it.
**Antigiotto(IRE)**, caught up in scrimmaging early on, cannot use that as an excuse as second place was as good as he could have managed. However, he never stopped staying on and should get a bit farther.
**Alfridini** lacked a finishing spurt on this easier ground.
**Sailmaker(IRE)** is proving a disappointment and would only have a chance in handicaps if dropped a few pounds from his present mark.
**Mommkin** looks to be heading for mediocre handicaps, though this trip may be stretching her a bit.
**Concert Hall(USA)** has yet to prove she stays this trip and her stable is out of form.
T/Plt: £9,868.40 to a £1 stake. Pool: £37,175.75. 2.75 winning tickets. T/Qpdt: £354.60 to a £1 stake. Pool: £2,636.00. 5.50 winning tickets. LM

3214 - 3220a (Foreign Racing) - See Raceform Interactive

# 2972 HAMILTON (R-H)
Thursday, June 24
**OFFICIAL GOING: Good (good to soft in places)**

## 3221 DIET IRN-BRU LADY AMATEUR H'CAP 1m 5f 9y
7:05 (7:07) (E) (0-75,76) 3-Y-O+ £3,981 (£1,225; £612; £306) **Stalls** High

Form RPR
-622 **1** **Inchnadamph**[6] 3041 4-10-1 **50** (t) MissAElsey 9 63
(TJFitzgerald) *plld hrd: chsd ldr: led 3f out: r.o strly* **3/1**[2]
0403 **2** *3 1/2* **Sarn**[7] 3018 5-8-12 **40** MissMMullineaux[(7)] 7 48
(MMullineaux) *chsd ldrs: effrt over 2f out: chsd wnr over 1f out: kpt on: no imp* **7/1**
00-0 **3** *3* **Lady Netbetsports (IRE)**[7] 3008 5-10-9 **63** MissAArmitage[(5)] 10 67
(BSRothwell) *set slow pce: led to 3f out: one pce over 1f out* **25/1**
/0-1 **4** *1 3/4* **Latalomne (USA)**[7] 3018 10-11-10 **76** 6ex MrsNWilson[(3)] 8 77
(NWilson) *hld up in tch: outpcd over 2f out: r.o fnl f: no imp* **2/1**[1]
-103 **5** *hd* **Cosmic Case**[8] 2978 9-9-11 **46** MsCWilliams 3 47
(JSGoldie) *hld up last: outpcd 3f out: styd on fnl f: nrst fin* **8/1**
-550 **6** *shd* **Exalted (IRE)**[21] 2615 11-9-11 **51** MissHCuthbert[(5)] 6 52
(TAKCuthbert) *hld up in tch: hdwy and chsng ldrs over 2f out: outpcd over 1f out* **4/1**[3]


The Form Book, Raceform Ltd, Compton, RG20 6NL

-000 **7** *3* **Dark Cut (IRE)**[68] [1463] 4-9-5 **45**............................ MissDawnRankin(5) 2 42
(HAlexander) *chsd ldrs tl wknd fr 2f out* **33/1**

3m 3.76s (10.36) **Going Correction** +0.15s/f (Good) **7** Ran SP% **108.7**
Speed ratings: **74,71,70,68,68 68,66**CSF £21.45 CT £383.54 TOTE £3.90: £1.60, £2.80; EX 30.70.
**Owner** R N Cardwell **Bred** Bloomsbury Stud And R And A Craddock **Trained** Norton, N Yorks

**FOCUS**
An ordinary handicap and a ready winner, but the steady gallop and slow time means those held up were at a disadvantage and this bare form is modest and has a suspect look to it.

**NOTEBOOK**
**Inchnadamph**, already due to go up 5lb from Saturday, took a good hold over this longer trip but very much had the run of this slowly-run race. However, although again looking less than straightforward, he is just starting to get his act together and may well be capable of better.
**Sarn**, ran creditably in a race that placed the emphasis on speed rather than stamina. He is fairly versatile but his overall record suggests he is not one to place too much faith in.
**Lady Netbetsports(IRE)** ran her best race for some time but she did have the run of race and looks flattered by this bare form. He would not be one to rely on to reproduce this next time.
**Latalomne(USA)**, under a 6lb penalty, looks a bit better than the bare form as he was not suited by the way things unfolded and he will be much better suited by a more strongly-run event. He looks capable of winning again for new connections.
**Cosmic Case** was another not to be seen to best effect in a steadily-run race, and she is much better suited by a true gallop on a quicker surface.
**Exalted(IRE)**, who looked in tremendous condition, would have been suited by the rain but was not at his best in a race that would not have played to his strengths. He is worth another chance.

## 3222 ALONA HOTELS MAIDEN FILLIES' STKS 1m 1f 36y
**7:35** (7:35) (D ) 3-Y-O **£5,590** (£1,720; £860; £430) **Stalls** High

Form RPR
5-33 **1** **Secret Flame**[14] [2805] 3-8-11 78.............................. ACulhane 5 77
(WJHaggas) *trckd ldrs: led on bit over 2f out: shkn up and r.o strly: eased ins fnl f* **1/4**[1]

0- **2** *5* **Just Dance Me (FR)**[255] [5539] 3-8-8 ............................ NMackay(3) 3 67
(WJHaggas) *set stdy pce tl hdd 3f out: kpt on same pce fr 2f out* **10/1**[3]

0 **3** *3 1/2* **Burn**[14] [2805] 3-8-11 .................................................. FLynch 2 60
(MLWBell) *prom: effrt outside over 2f out: outpcd over 1f out* **7/1**[2]

0004 **4** *6* **Compassion (IRE)**[7] [3002] 3-8-11 53...................................... JCarroll 1 48
(MissLAPerratt) *cl up tl wknd over 2f out* **66/1**

2m 5.46s (5.86) **Going Correction** +0.15s/f (Good) **4** Ran SP% **103.1**
Speed ratings: **79,74,71,66**CSF £2.78 TOTE £1.30; EX 3.20.
**Owner** Cheveley Park Stud **Bred** Cheveley Park Stud Ltd **Trained** Newmarket, Suffolk

**FOCUS**
A most uncompetitive race in which the gallop was on the steady side and the time was pedestrian. The winner did not have to improve to win with more in hand than the winning margin suggests.

**NOTEBOOK**
**Secret Flame** did not have to improve to win an uncompetitive race with more in hand than the winning margin suggests. Life will be tougher from now on but she may be capable of further improvement.
**Just Dance Me(FR)**, up in trip for this reappearance, had the run of the race but was no match for the easy winner and looks flattered by her proximity. She is likely to fare better in modest handicaps in due course.
**Burn**, who is related to a couple of winners, also looks the type to do better in handicap company in due course.
**Compassion(IRE)** faced a stiff task at the weights and will continue to look vulnerable in this type of event.

## 3223 EUROPEAN BREEDERS FUND FILLIES' CONDITIONS STKS 1m 65y
**8:05** (8:05) (C ) 3-Y-O+ **£10,672** (£4,048; £2,024; £920) **Stalls** High

Form RPR
1- **1** **Antediluvian**[264] [5369] 3-7-13 .................................... NMackay(3) 6 103+
(SirMichaelStoute) *dwlt: sn chsng ldrs: nt clr run over 2f out: swtchd lft and hdwy to ld over 1f out: sn clr: kpt on wl* **5/1**[2]

2121 **2** *1 1/2* **Celtic Heroine (IRE)**[8] [2971] 3-8-2 89.............................. MHenry 2 100+
(MAJarvis) *prom: effrt whn nt clr run over 2f to over 1f out: swtchd lft: r.o strly fnl f: nt rch wnr* **1/2**[1]

230- **3** *9* **Sharplaw Venture**[335] [3548] 4-8-9 95.............................. ACulhane 1 76
(WJHaggas) *prom: ev ch over 2f out: outpcd over 1f out* **12/1**

3-05 **4** *1 1/4* **Play That Tune**[21] [2630] 4-8-9 93.......................................... JFanning 4 73
(MJohnston) *w ldr: led 3f to over 1f out: sn btn* **7/1**[3]

2402 **5** *2* **Rabitatit (IRE)**[8] [2974] 3-7-6 62.......................... NataliaGemelova(7) 5 69?
(JGMO'Shea) *set stdy pce to 3f out: btn over 1f out* **100/1**

0000 **6** *5* **Safranine (IRE)**[4] [3126] 7-8-9 63........................................ AnnStokell 3 57
(MissAStokell) *chsd ldrs tl wknd over 2f out* **200/1**

1m 48.48s (-0.82) **Going Correction** +0.15s/f (Good)
**WFA** 3 from 4yo+ 10lb **6** Ran SP% **105.0**
Speed ratings: **110,108,99,98,96 91**CSF £6.89 TOTE £5.30: £2.40, £1.10; EX 6.80.
**Owner** Lordship Stud **Bred** Mrs M L Parry And P M Steele-Mortimer **Trained** Newmarket, Suffolk

**FOCUS**
A fair time, but not the best turnout for the money on offer and a race that does not look a reliable form guide, as Celtic Heroine got into all the trouble going and would have gone very close with an uninterrupted passage.

**NOTEBOOK**
**Antediluvian** ◆, a good looker, overcame trouble on this reappearance to get first run on Celtic Heroine but, while it would have been close had the latter got a clear run, she looks the type to improve again and is capable of winning more races.
**Celtic Heroine(IRE)** ◆, turned out quickly after her Royal Ascot exertions, got into all the trouble going and did remarkably well to get as close as she did to the winner. She would have gone very close with a clear run and is well worth another chance to make amends.
**Sharplaw Venture** may have preferred a stronger gallop but seemed beaten on merit and is not going to be easy to place on this evidence from her current mark.
**Play That Tune** was again a fair way below the pick of last year's efforts and is another who is going to have to drop in the weights before returning to winning ways.
**Rabitatit(IRE)** faced a very stiff task at the weights and will be seen to much better effect in ordinary handicap company.
**Safranine(IRE)** was predictably outclassed.

## 3224 SCOTTISH DAILY MAIL NOVICE AUCTION STKS (QUALIFIER FOR THE HAMILTON PARK 2YO SERIES FINAL) 6f 5y
**8:35** (8:35) (D ) 2-Y-O **£4,823** (£1,484; £742; £371) **Stalls** Low

Form RPR
0 **1** **Tequila Sheila (IRE)**[17] [2730] 2-8-5 .................................. ANicholls 1 74
(KRBurke) *cl up: rdn and outpcd 2f out: rallied appr fnl f: styd on to ld cl home* **16/1**

5231 **2** *1/2* **Lincolneurocruiser**[16] [2758] 2-8-8 ................................ JDO'Reilly(7) 4 82
(JO'Reilly) *mde most tl hdd towards fin* **15/2**

321 **3** *2* **Katie Boo (IRE)**[10] [2933] 2-8-10 .............................................. FNorton 6 71
(ABerry) *cl up: hung rt thrght: effrt and ev ch over 1f out: no ex ins last* **6/1**

13 **4** *1* **Midnight Tycoon**[22] [2570] 2-9-1 ................................................ FLynch 3 73
(BSmart) *keen: chsd ldrs: rdn and one pce over 1f out* **13/8**[1]

12 **5** *6* **Selkirk Storm (IRE)**[20] [2655] 2-8-13 ............................ PMulrennan(5) 5 58
(MWEasterby) *prom tl rdn and wknd fr 2f out* **4/1**[2]

12 **6** *3* **Carte Royale**[12] [2868] 2-9-6 .................................................... SChin 2 51
(MJohnston) *w ldrs tl wknd fr 2f out* **9/2**[3]

1m 14.57s (1.47) **Going Correction** +0.05s/f (Good) **6** Ran SP% **108.2**
Speed ratings: **92,91,88,87,79 75**CSF £113.49 TOTE £14.30: £5.10, £4.90; EX 185.60.
**Owner** Lee Westwood **Bred** Martyn J McEnery **Trained** Middleham Moor, N Yorks

**FOCUS**
An interesting event but, with the three market leaders disappointing, this race did not take as much winning as had seemed likely and the placed horses provide the best line to the form. The early gallop was sound and the runners raced against the stands' side.

**NOTEBOOK**
**Tequila Sheila(IRE)** bettered her debut effort by some way and left the impression that the step up to seven furlongs will be in her favour. Life will be tougher from now on, but she may be capable of further improvement.
**Lincolneurocruiser** looks a good guide to the level of this form and again ran his race. He is a speedy sort who should continue to give a good account.
**Katie Boo(IRE)** up in grade, ran creditably, especially as she was inclined to hang to her right throughout. She is worth another try over this trip. *Official explanation: jockey said filly hung right-handed throughout*
**Midnight Tycoon**looked a useful prospect on his first two starts but pulled too hard and consequently did not improve for the step up to this trip. The return to five furlongs will suit and, with his stable in better form now, he is worth another chance back over the minimum trip.
**Selkirk Storm(IRE)** was disappointing back over this trip and on easier ground but, given he created a favourable impression on his first two starts, he may not be one to write off just yet.
**Carte Royale** had shaped as though the step up to this trip would have suited but was most disappointing and was beaten before stamina became an issue. He would be worth another chance back on a more conventional course, though.

## 3225 TOTEQUADPOT FILLIES' SPRINT H'CAP 5f 4y
**9:05** (9:05) (D ) (0-85,61) 3-Y-O+ **£6,753** (£2,078; £1,039; £519) **Stalls** Low

Form RPR
6532 **1** **Karminskey Park**[7] [3010] 5-9-10 **61**.......................................... JFanning 5 71
(TJEtherington) *cl up: led over 1f out: hld on wl fnl f* **11/8**[1]

-005 **2** *hd* **Aahgowangowan (IRE)**[15] [2784] 5-9-7 **58**............................(t) RFfrench 4 67+
(MDods) *stall opened fractionally late: sn prom: effrt and ev ch fnl f: edgd rt: kpt on: jst hld* **10/3**[2]

4403 **3** *1 3/4* **Tancred Times**[8] [2976] 9-9-4 **55**................................................ FLynch 7 58
(DWBarker) *led to over 1f out: rallied: no ex ins fnl f* **11/2**[3]

0160 **4** *3* **Pirlie Hill**[3] [3147] 4-9-4 **55**........................................................ JCarroll 8 47
(MissLAPerratt) *chsd ldrs outer: hung rt thrght: ev ch over 1f out: sn outpcd* **12/1**

2413 **5** *1/2* **College Maid (IRE)**[6] [3038] 7-9-2 **60** 6ex.............................. JCurrie(7) 6 50
(JSGoldie) *cl up tl rdn and outpcd fr over 1f out* **6/1**

0500 **6** *11* **Sugar Cube Treat**[17] [2734] 8-7-12 **35** oh4................................. SRighton 3 —
(MMullineaux) *s.v.s: t.o thrght* **20/1**

61.19 secs (-0.07) **Going Correction** +0.05s/f (Good) **6** Ran SP% **107.3**
Speed ratings: **102,101,98,94,93** **75**CSF £5.45 CT £14.03 TOTE £2.00: £1.40, £1.70; EX 6.10.
**Owner** Wold House Partnership **Bred** J T And Mrs Thomas **Trained** Norton, N Yorks

**FOCUS**
An ordinary event in which the field stayed on the stands' side but the result may have been different had Aahgowangowan's stall opened at the same time as the rest of the field. The form is sound enough otherwise.

**NOTEBOOK**
**Karminskey Park** extended her run of creditable efforts with another gutsy performance. She should not be going up too much for this win and should continue to give a good account.
**Aahgowangowan(IRE)**, from an in-form stable, confirmed the promise of her previous run over this course and distance and the result may well have been different had her stall opened at the same time as the rest of her field. Although her wins-to-runs ratio is only modest, she is capable of winning again from a similar mark.
**Tancred Times** had the run of the race and ran creditably and, although she has not won a handicap for over a year, she is mainly a consistent sort who should continue to give a good account. *Official explanation: jockey said mare hung right in the final 2f*
**Pirlie Hill** was not disgraced but again tended to go to her right and may be better suited by racing next to a right-handed rail. However, she does look vulnerable at present from her current rating.
**College Maid(IRE)** down further in trip, was comfortably held under her penalty and is going to continue to look vulnerable from this mark.
**Sugar Cube Treat** has not shown much for some time but lost all chance with a very tardy start. She remains one to place minimal confidence in.

## 3226 FLOWERSCENE H'CAP 6f 5y
**9:35** (9:35) (E ) (0-75,63) 4-Y-O+ **£3,932** (£1,210; £605; £302) **Stalls** Low

Form RPR
0042 **1** **Legal Set (IRE)**[6] [3038] 8-7-13 **45**.........................(t) NataliaGemelova(7) 2 58
(MissAStokell) *prom: shkn up to ld 1f out: r.o strly* **9/2**[3]

3001 **2** *1 3/4* **Silver Mascot**[10] [2936] 5-9-0 **56** 6ex.......................................... TEaves(3) 8 64
(ISemple) *keen: w ldr: shkn up 2f out: kpt on fnl f* **3/1**[2]

0022 **3** *3/4* **Bundy**[8] [2976] 8-9-10 **63** ............................................................. RWinston 9 69
(MDods) *dwlt: sn pushed along towards rr: hdwy over 1f out: kpt on fnl f* **7/4**[1]

5010 **4** *3/4* **My Bayard**[37] [2215] 5-8-11 **57**................................................ JDO'Reilly(7) 7 60
(JO'Reilly) *w ldrs: rdn and edgd rt fr 2f out: no ex fnl f* **7/1**

-000 **5** *shd* **Marshallspark (IRE)**[17] [2735] 5-9-8 **61**........................................ GParkin 6 64
(RAFahey) *prom: outpcd after 2f: hdwy appr fnl f: r.o: no imp* **8/1**

000- **6** *2 1/2* **Mutayam**[255] [5538] 4-8-0 **39**..........................................................(t) MHenry 4 34
(DANolan) *mde most tl hdd 1f out: sn btn* **66/1**

6400 **7** *4* **Friar Tuck**[6] [3038] 9-9-2 **55**......................................................... JCarroll 5 38
(MissLAPerratt) *sn outpcd: nvr rchd ldrs* **12/1**

00/0 **8** *3 1/2* **Saif Sareea**[15] [2779] 4-8-6 **52**.............................................. PPMathers(7) 3 25
(KWHogg) *towards rr: struggling fr 1/2-way* **100/1**

1m 13.3s (0.20) **Going Correction** +0.05s/f (Good) **8** Ran SP% **113.3**
Speed ratings: **100,97,96,95,95 92,86,82**CSF £18.07 CT £31.70 TOTE £4.60: £1.20, £1.20, £1.50; EX 22.80 Place 6 £98.99, Place 5 £27.72.
**Owner** Paul Byrne **Bred** John Kelsey-Fry **Trained** Brompton-on-Swale, N Yorks

**FOCUS**
An ordinary race but one run at a decent gallop and the field raced stands' side. This form should stand up at a similar level.

**NOTEBOOK**
**Legal Set(IRE)** confirmed Ayr promise and, although he has not always been reliable, is in good heart for his new stable. He is due to go up 5lb from Saturday but given the way he travelled, may well be capable of better.

**Silver Mascot**, under a 6lb penalty, ran right up to the level of his recent Carlisle win and, given he stays further, appeals as the type to win more races for his current stable.
**Bundy**, from an in-form stable, had conditions in his favour and the race run to suit and ran creditably. He is not the easiest to win with but should continue to give a good account.
**My Bayard** ran creditably but his record is one of inconsistency and he has yet to win on turf. He is not one to place too much faith in.
**Marshallspark(IRE)** looked in good shape and ran creditably but left the impression that the return to seven furlongs on faster ground would be to his liking. He is one to keep an eye on back over the longer trip.
**Mutayam** showed plenty of toe on this reappearance on only this second start over six furlongs but, given his record would be no certainty to reproduce this next time.
T/Plt: £76.70 to a £1 stake. Pool: £36,880.85. 350.70 winning tickets. T/Qpdt: £14.50 to a £1 stake. Pool: £2,150.90. 109.30 winning tickets. RY

## 2875 LEICESTER (R-H)
Thursday, June 24

**OFFICIAL GOING: Good**

Genuine good ground all round. The far side held the advantage throughout, even though the first winner was drawn low, he ended up drifting over there.
Wind: Fresh behind Weather: Cloudy with the odd shower

### 3227 MARK JARVIS G-RONN H'CAP (LADY AMATEUR RIDERS) 5f 2y
6:50 (6:51) (E) (0-70,66) 3-Y-O+ £3,581 (£1,102; £551; £275) Stalls Low

Form RPR
1100 **1** **Somerset West (IRE)**[6] 3043 4-10-9 **66** MissJFerguson(5) 3 78
(JRBest) *racd stands' side: outpcd: hdwy 1/2-way: led over 1f out: edgd rt: r.o* **20/1**
0001 **2** *1 1/2* **Torrent**[7] 3016 9-10-0 **52** 7ex (b) MissLynseyHanna 18 59
(DWChapman) *racd far side: chsd ldr: led overall over 1f out: hdd wl ins fnl f* **6/1**[1]
0232 **3** *nk* **Valazar (USA)**[30] 2383 5-9-4 **45** MissKellyHarrison(3) 5 51
(DWChapman) *racd stands' side: prom: rdn and ev ch over 1f out: edgd rt: styd on* **6/1**[1]
0030 **4** *3/4* **Tuscan Flyer**[12] 2899 6-10-5 **62** (b) MissRBastiman(5) 15 65
(RBastiman) *s.i.s: racd towards centre: hdwy 1/2-way: styd on* **9/1**
0230 **5** *nk* **Only If I Laugh**[5] 3077 3-10-0 **63** MissFayeBramley(5) 4 65
(PABlockley) *racd stands' side: outpcd: hdwy 1/2-way: styd on* **20/1**
060 **6** *1/2* **Travellers Joy**[13] 2836 4-8-5 **34** oh1 MissRD'Arcy(5) 14 34
(RJHodges) *racd centre: mid-div: hdwy 1/2-way: styd on same pce ins fnl f* **33/1**
-006 **7** *1 3/4* **Sir Sandrovitch (IRE)**[7] 3010 8-9-11 **54** (p) MissVTunnicliffe(5) 8 48
(RAFahey) *s.s: racd centre: outpcd: swtchd lft over 1f out: r.o ins fnl f: nvr nr to chal* **7/1**[2]
0000 **8** *2* **St Ivian**[9] 2965 4-10-8 **60** (p) MrsMMorris 10 47
(MrsNMacauley) *racd centre: chsd ldrs over 3f* **40/1**
0-02 **9** *shd* **Kallista's Pride**[13] 2843 4-9-13 **58** MissKManser(7) 16 44
(JRBest) *racd far side: s.i.s: hdwy 3f out: wknd over 1f out* **14/1**
4400 **10** *nk* **Repeat (IRE)**[108] 993 4-9-0 **45** MissMBritton(7) 11 30
(MissGayKelleway) *led centre to 1/2-way: wknd fnl f* **33/1**
0104 **11** *1* **Jinksonthehouse**[12] 2869 3-9-9 **58** MissAWallace(5) 19 40
(MDIUsher) *racd far side: chsd ldrs over 3f* **20/1**
0030 **12** *1/2* **Prime Recreation**[33] 2303 7-10-10 **62** MissSBrotherton 17 42
(PSFelgate) *led far side over 3f: wknd fnl f* **15/2**[3]
6-60 **13** *1/2* **Our Fred**[155] 578 7-10-0 (b) MissMSowerby(5) 13 35
(TGMills) *racd centre: outpcd fr 1/2-way* **14/1**
4300 **14** *1/2* **Port St Charles (IRE)**[11] 2912 7-10-10 **62** MissEJJones 1 38
(CRDore) *racd stands' side: s.s: outpcd* **7/1**[2]
-503 **15** *nk* **Diamond Ring**[12] 2869 5-8-11 **40** MissGwenMorris(5) 9 15
(MrsJCandlish) *racd centre: chsd ldrs: hmpd 1/2-way: wknd over 1f out* **12/1**
-005 **16** *1* **Beenaboutabit**[2] 3175 6-8-13 **44** oh4 ow10 MissLMcIntosh(7) 6 16
(MrsLCJewell) *s.s: outpcd: hdwy 1/2-way: wknd over 1f out* **66/1**
3000 **17** *shd* **Lady Pekan**[4] 3126 5-10-5 **62** (b) MissJCDuncan(5) 7 33
(PSMcentee) *w ldrs centre: led 1/2-way: hdd over 1f out: sn wknd* **20/1**
6600 **18** *3* **Cloudless (USA)**[27] 2451 4-9-6 **47** MissEFolkes(3) 2 8
(JWUnett) *racd stands' side: chsd ldrs to 1/2-way* **33/1**
6165 **19** *2* **Boisdale (IRE)**[20] 2663 6-9-6 **49** MissALTurner(5) 12 2
(SLKeightley) *racd centre: chsd ldrs 3f: eased* **16/1**

61.17 secs (0.24) **Going Correction** -0.025s/f (Good)
**WFA** 3 from 4yo+ 6lb **19** Ran SP% **134.0**
Speed ratings: **97,94,94,92,92 91,88,85,85,85 83,82,81,81,80 78,78,73,70**CSF £133.38 CT £865.53 TOTE £31.50: £4.50, £2.60, £1.80, £3.50; EX 243.40.
**Owner** J P Ferguson **Bred** Broguestown Stud **Trained** Hucking, Kent

**FOCUS**
An ordinary contest, but the winner did well to come from where he did, and the placed horses give the form a sound look.

**NOTEBOOK**
**Somerset West(IRE)** could not go with the fast early pace, but as his stamina came into play, was well on top in the end.
**Torrent** may have been a shade unlucky for he was left in front some way out.
**Valazar(USA)** turned in a sound effort from his draw and is clearly on good terms with himself at present, but he does find winning difficult.
**Tuscan Flyer**, with the blinkers back on, showed plenty of dash having missed a beat at the start.
**Only If I Laugh**, well treated on the best of his form, showed a bit more sparkle than of late and may be coming to hand.
**Sir Sandrovitch(IRE)** did all of his best work in the closing stages and, although he is not as good as he was, he is still one to keep an eye on at this level.
**Boisdale(IRE)** *Official explanation: trainer said jockey lost an iron immediately after the start*

### 3228 MARK JARVIS "SEE ANDY" MAIDEN AUCTION STKS 5f 218y
7:20 (7:22) (E) 2-Y-O £4,231 (£1,302; £651; £325) Stalls Low

Form RPR
**1** **Intoxicating** 2-8-9 GDuffield 3 83
(RFJohnsonHoughton) *s.s: hdwy 4f out: rdn to ld over 2f out: styd on* **14/1**
3 **2** *1 1/2* **Transaction (IRE)**[90] 1117 2-8-9 SSanders 5 79
(JMPEustace) *chsd ldrs: rdn and ev ch fr over 1f out: no ex towards fin* **5/1**
3332 **3** *1 1/2* **Edge Fund**[13] 2831 2-8-11 SDrowne 2 76
(BRMillman) *chsd ldrs: rdn and ev ch over 1f out: wknd ins fnl f* **4/1**[2]
**4** *1 1/2* **Scarlet Invader (IRE)** 2-8-11 KDarley 4 72
(JLDunlop) *dwlt: hdwy over 2f out: outpcd over 1f out: styd on ins fnl f* **7/1**
2 **5** *3/4* **Arthur Wardle (USA)**[15] 2780 2-8-11 DHolland 9 69
(MLWBell) *s.i.s: sn prom: rdn over 2f out: wknd over 1f out* **11/4**[1]
6 **6** *hd* **Nella Fantasia (IRE)**[22] 2585 2-8-9 MHills 10 67
(GCBravery) *chsd ldrs: rdn over 2f out: wknd over 1f out* **20/1**
**7** *3* **High Dyke** 2-8-7 PaulEddery 1 56
(DHaydnJones) *hld up: hdwy over 2f out: wknd over 1f out* **66/1**
66 **8** *5* **Taipan Tommy (IRE)**[31] 2360 2-8-11 WRyan 7 45
(SDow) *led over 3f: wknd wl over 1f out* **66/1**
**9** *nk* **Dahliyev (IRE)** 2-9-0 TQuinn 6 47
(PWHarris) *dwlt: hdwy 1/2-way: wknd over 2f out* **9/2**[3]
**10** *6* **Toby's Dream (IRE)** 2-8-11 KDalgleish 8 26
(MJohnston) *s.s: outpcd* **14/1**

1m 13.05s (-0.35) **Going Correction** -0.025s/f (Good) **10** Ran SP% **115.1**
Speed ratings: **101,99,97,95,94 93,89,83,82,74**CSF £80.54 TOTE £10.90: £3.00, £3.70, £1.30; EX 135.80.
**Owner** Anthony Pye-Jeary And Mel Smith **Bred** R P Williams **Trained** Blewbury, Oxon

**FOCUS**
A decent time for the grade. The third had shown a fair level of form in his four starts to date and is the guide to this race, giving the form a reasonably solid look.

**NOTEBOOK**
**Intoxicating**, who is out of a mare that won over seven furlongs, is a scopey sort who should do better as he gets stronger.
**Transaction(IRE)** turned in a sound enough effort on this return to action and should be capable of winning a similar contest.
**Edge Fund** had no excuses and continues to find one or two too good for him.
**Scarlet Invader(IRE)**, a half-brother to juvenile winner Scarlet Ribbons is from the same family as Oaks winner Circus Plume. Very green both at the start and through the race, she can only improve for the experience.
**Arthur Wardle(USA)** still looked a little green and was probably done no favours by having to race out wide.
**Nella Fantasia(IRE)** showed plenty of pace before dropping away, and her future looks to lie in nurseries.

### 3229 MARK JARVIS BUNCH O MOSS (S) STKS 7f 9y
7:50 (7:53) (G) 3-Y-O £3,045 (£870; £435) Stalls Low

Form RPR
-354 **1** **Willjojo**[13] 2849 3-8-9 **52** (v) MHills 14 57
(RAFahey) *racd far side: chsd ldr: led over 1f out: r.o* **11/2**[2]
0050 **2** *3* **Red Rocky**[10] 2942 3-8-4 **48** (p) StephanieHollinshead(5) 18 49
(RHollinshead) *led far side over 4f: no ex* **25/1**
0300 **3** *1/2* **Zonnebeke**[10] 2942 3-8-9 **50** (v[1]) KDalgleish 17 48
(KRBurke) *racd far side: prom: outpcd over 1f out: r.o ins fnl f* **11/1**
0-00 **4** *1 1/4* **Chubbes**[31] 2361 3-9-0 **69** (p) SDrowne 12 50
(MDHammond) *racd far side: outpcd: hdwy over 1f out: nt rch ldrs* **11/4**[1]
-566 **5** *1 1/2* **David's Girl**[16] 2766 3-8-9 **38** JMackay 6 41
(DMorris) *racd stands' side: chsd ldrs: hung rt and led that gp 1f out: no ch w far side* **8/1**
330- **6** *1 3/4* **Coco Reef**[296] 4640 3-8-9 **57** SSanders 16 36
(BPalling) *racd far side: chsd ldrs: rdn over 2f out: wknd fnl f* **11/1**
0000 **7** *1/2* **Jaolins**[16] 2766 3-9-0 **40** DKinsella 11 40
(PGMurphy) *s.s: hld up plld hrd: racd stands' side: hdwy over 2f out: edgd rt over 1f out: styd on same pce* **25/1**
00 **8** *nk* **Osla**[14] 2815 3-8-9 DHolland 8 34
(RBrotherton) *racd stands' side: chsd ldrs over 4f* **20/1**
6605 **9** *3/4* **Marksgold (IRE)**[26] 2485 3-9-0 **55** TQuinn 15 37
(PFICole) *racd far side: sn drvn along and prom: wknd 2f out* **6/1**[3]
0006 **10** *4* **Peace Treaty (IRE)**[20] 2661 3-8-9 **30** JBramhill 2 22
(SRBowring) *racd stands' side: chsd ldrs over 4f* **66/1**
3000 **11** *nk* **Emperor Cat (IRE)**[28] 2426 3-8-7 **50** (b) StaceyRenwick(7) 9 26
(PABlockley) *mde most stands' side over 4f: sn wknd* **40/1**
-502 **12** *5* **La Fonteyne**[8] 2986 3-8-9 **55** JMcAuley 13 8
(CBBBooth) *racd far side: prom 4f* **14/1**
0000 **13** *hd* **Dr Fox (IRE)**[12] 2886 3-8-9 **40** (p) AQuinn(5) 10 12
(KAMorgan) *racd far side: chsd ldrs to 1/2-way* **25/1**
0605 **14** *2 1/2* **Delta Lady**[20] 2657 3-8-9 **42** JFEgan 7 1
(RBastiman) *racd stands' side: chsd ldrs 4f* **14/1**
0-00 **15** *9* **Trinaree (IRE)**[11] 2908 3-9-0 NPollard 5 —
(SGollings) *racd stands' side: s.s: outpcd* **66/1**
0P- **16** *shd* **Back In Fashion**[240] 5816 3-8-9 MFenton 3 —
(JMackie) *racd stands' side: mid-div: wknd over 2f out* **66/1**
00 **17** *3/4* **Ragazzi (IRE)**[11] 2908 3-9-0 KDarley 1 —
(TDBarron) *racd stands' side: hld up: wknd 1/2-way* **10/1**

1m 26.5s (0.40) **Going Correction** -0.025s/f (Good) **17** Ran SP% **129.8**
Speed ratings: **96,92,92,90,88 86,86,85,85,80 80,74,74,71,61 60,60**CSF £150.12 TOTE £6.60: £3.20, £8.60, £4.00; EX 168.90.There was no bid for the winner.
**Owner** The Yorkshire Lancashire Alliance **Bred** Lostford Manor Stud **Trained** Musley Bank, N Yorks

**FOCUS**
A poor contest and an ordinary time. The high numbers held the call with the first two filling those places throughout.

**NOTEBOOK**
**Willjojo** proved well suited to this extra furlong and should have no trouble following up in similar company.
**Red Rocky**, tackling selling company for the first time showed plenty of pace on the favoured far side, and certainly looks capable of scoring at this level.
**Zonnebeke** finds this trip on the sharp side, but credit to her she kept plugging away without looking likely to take a hand in the finish.
**Chubbes**, even at this level was soon left toiling, but he did finish his race in a manner that suggested he is one to keep an eye on over an extra furlong.
**David's Girl** was the first of the stands'-side group home, although she drifted across the track and ended up nearly with the far-side group.
**Back In Fashion** *Official explanation: jockey said filly stumbled and lost a front shoe*
**Ragazzi(IRE)** *Official explanation: jockey said gelding had no more to give*

### 3230 MARK JARVIS "IT'S ONLY JUST CHANGED" H'CAP 1m 9y
8:20 (8:21) (D) (0-85,82) 3-Y-O £7,221 (£2,222; £1,111; £555) Stalls High

Form RPR
-121 **1** **Kamanda Laugh**[35] 2239 3-9-5 **80** MHills 1 86
(BWHills) *hld up in tch: rdn to ld over 1f out: r.o* **5/2**[1]
42-1 **2** *1* **Little Jimbob**[10] 2934 3-9-0 **75** 5ex SSanders 6 78
(RAFahey) *led: rdn and hdd over 1f out: unable qck nr fin* **10/1**
2000 **3** *hd* **Whitgift Rock**[13] 2847 3-8-12 **73** DHolland 8 76
(SDow) *prom: nt clr run and outpcd over 2f out: rallied over 1f out: r.o* **10/1**
31 **4** *shd* **Magic Merlin**[24] 2517 3-9-3 **78** BDoyle 3 81
(PWHarris) *hld up: hdwy over 2f out: rdn over 1f out: r.o* **7/2**[3]
-360 **5** *nk* **Rio De Jumeirah**[23] 2558 3-9-0 **75** TEDurcan 2 77
(CEBrittain) *a.p: rdn over 2f out: r.o* **20/1**
1200 **6** *5* **Inchloss (IRE)**[11] 2907 3-9-2 **77** GGibbons 9 68
(BAMcmahon) *hld up: hdwy over 2f out: wknd over 1f out* **20/1**
-004 **7** *shd* **Muhaymin (USA)**[13] 2841 3-9-7 **82** WSupple 7 72
(JLDunlop) *chsd ldrs: rdn over 1f out: wknd ins fnl f* **10/1**

-363 **8** *11* **Mr Jack Daniells (IRE)**[19] 2692 3-9-0 **75**.............................. SDrowne 5 40
(WRMuir) *trckd ldrs: slipped and lost pl 6f out: wknd over 2f out* **3/1**[2]

-645 **9** *2 1/2* **Carriacou**[47] 1969 3-8-9 **70**.................................................. PaulEddery 4 29
(PWD'Arcy) *sn drvn along to chse ldr: wknd over 2f out* **33/1**

1m 41.96s (-0.64) **Going Correction** -0.025s/f (Good) **9** Ran SP% **115.5**
Speed ratings: **102,101,100,100,100 95,95,84,81**CSF £27.57 CT £215.90 TOTE £3.10: £1.20, £3.00, £3.90; EX 23.30.
**Owner** John Sillett **Bred** Miss K Rausing **Trained** Lambourn, Berks

**FOCUS**
A competitive contest on paper, and the form looks reasonable even though the pace was only ordinary.

**NOTEBOOK**
**Kamanda Laugh** improved again for the step up in trip and looks one to keep on the right side of, for he only appears to do just enough.
**Little Jimbob** was far from disgraced in this better race, under his penalty.
**Whitgift Rock** has yet to strike on turf, but showed enough to suggest he can put that right before long.
**Magic Merlin** lacked the experience of his rivals, which probably cost him in the end. However, he still has some improvement in him, especially when tackling a little further.
**Rio De Jumeirah**, off the bridle some way out, stuck well enough to her task and shaped as though she really ought to stay further.
**Muhaymin(USA)**, as at Goodwood, stopped very quickly and may have a problem.
**Mr Jack Daniells(IRE)** can be forgiven this effort, for he did well to stand up having slipped leaving the back straight. *Official explanation: jockey said geldling slipped on the bend*

## 3231 JARVIS SIX FOOT INJURED JOCKEYS FUND H'CAP 1m 1f 218y
8:50 (8:52) (E) (0-70,69) 3-Y-O **£7,475** (£2,300; £1,150; £575) **Stalls** High

Form RPR

2232 **1** **Jakarmi**[20] 2665 3-9-0 **65**.............................................. RMiles[(3)] 2 75
(BPalling) *hld up: hdwy 1/2-way: rdn to ld over 1f out: r.o* **15/2**

5000 **2** *1 1/2* **Principessa**[13] 2848 3-9-3 **65**.............................................. TQuinn 11 72
(BPalling) *chsd ldr tl led over 7f out: hdd over 5f out: rdn over 1f out: r.o* **33/1**

0531 **3** *shd* **Habanero**[13] 2847 3-9-7 **69**.............................................. DHolland 8 76
(RHannon) *chsd ldrs: led over 5f out: rdn and hdd over 1f out: no ex ins fnl f* **6/1**[2]

0065 **4** *2 1/2* **Master Mahogany**[14] 2809 3-9-2 **64**.............................. SDrowne 7 66
(RJHodges) *hld up: hdwy 6f out: rdn over 1f out: styd on same pce* **40/1**

154 **5** *1* **Charmatic (IRE)**[17] 2732 3-9-3 **65**.............................. DeanMcKeown 4 65
(JAGlover) *trckd ldrs: rdn over 1f out: styd on same pce* **7/1**[3]

-304 **6** *3/4* **Inmom (IRE)**[14] 2814 3-8-10 **58**.............................................. JBramhill 1 57
(SRBowring) *hld up: hdwy over 4f out: rdn over 2f out: styd on same pce appr fnl f* **50/1**

4102 **7** *3/4* **Ile Facile (IRE)**[17] 2732 3-9-7 **69**..............................(t) TGMcLaughlin 14 67
(NPLittmoden) *hld up: hmpd wl over 2f out: styd on ins fnl f: nvr able to chal* **8/1**

0-30 **8** *nk* **Wyoming**[13] 2848 3-8-11 **59**.............................................. WRyan 12 56
(JARToller) *prom: rdn over 2f out: edgd rt over 1f out: wknd and eased ins fnl f* **14/1**

2220 **9** *3/4* **Late Opposition**[37] 2197 3-9-7 **69**.............................................. KDarley 19 65
(EALDunlop) *mid-div: hdwy 3f out: wknd fnl f* **9/1**

0-10 **10** *1/2* **Dagola (IRE)**[19] 2688 3-9-0 **62**.............................................. RSmith 18 57
(CGCox) *chsd ldrs: rdn over 2f out: wkng whn n.m.r over 1f out* **14/1**

66-0 **11** *1/2* **Music Mix (IRE)**[45] 1997 3-8-11 **59**..............................(e[1]) TEDurcan 15 53
(EALDunlop) *hld up: hdwy over 1f out: wknd fnl f* **33/1**

5611 **12** *1 1/4* **Magic Sting**[21] 2619 3-9-7 **69**.............................................. JMackay 17 60
(MLWBell) *led: hdd over 7f out: rdn over 2f out: wknd fnl f* **5/1**[1]

0000 **13** *1 1/4* **Munaawesh (USA)**[14] 2814 3-8-11 **59**.............................. GDuffield 5 48
(DWChapman) *hld up: a in rr* **66/1**

56-0 **14** *1 3/4* **Lawaaheb (IRE)**[22] 2578 3-9-7 **69**.............................................. WSupple 13 55
(JLDunlop) *chsd ldrs: lost pl over 7f out: hdwy over 2f out: wknd over 1f out* **14/1**

5-04 **15** *1 1/4* **Petite Colleen (IRE)**[10] 2949 3-9-3 **65**.............................. DKinsella 6 48
(DHaydnJones) *hld up: hdwy over 2f out: wknd over 1f out* **33/1**

-040 **16** *1/2* **Colloseum**[16] 2756 3-8-10 **58**.............................................. PaulEddery 9 40
(TJEtherington) *dwlt: a in rr* **50/1**

-605 **17** *1* **Badr (USA)**[24] 2529 3-9-0 **62**.............................................. KDalgleish 10 42
(MJohnston) *mid-div: hmpd 7f out: wknd over 2f out* **14/1**

4050 **18** *17* **Smokin Joe**[57] 1702 3-9-1 **63**.............................................. NPollard 3 11
(JRBest) *hld up: a in rr* **33/1**

2m 7.85s (-0.55) **Going Correction** -0.025s/f (Good) **18** Ran SP% **122.6**
Speed ratings: **101,99,99,97,96 96,95,95,94,94 94,93,92,90,89 89,88,74**CSF £249.06 CT £1597.50 TOTE £6.30: £1.70, £11.20, £2.30, £5.50; EX 164.80.
**Owner** Mrs M M Palling **Bred** Llety Stud **Trained** Tredodridge, Vale Of Glamorgan

**FOCUS**
An ordinary contest, but the pace was solid and the form looks reliable.

**NOTEBOOK**
**Jakarmi** gained reward for some consistent efforts of late, and he did well to overcome his wide draw.
**Principessa** had been somewhat disappointing since her debut and, although this was not a strong contest, there was at least some promise in this effort.
**Habanero**, keen to get on with things, stayed this longer trip well enough and had no excuses.
**Master Mahogany**, ridden with a little more restraint this time, is beginning to slip down the weights, but looks to need more help before he becomes competitive.
**Charmatic(IRE)** is a consistent filly, but she left the impression that this trip just stretches her.
**Ile Facile(IRE)** did not have the best of runs and is capable of better than he showed here.
**Music Mix(IRE)** *Official explanation: jockey said he was unable to ride the colt out in the closing stages as he did not have a clear run*

## 3232 MARK JARVIS "I KNOW MARK" CLASSIFIED STKS 1m 3f 183y
9:20 (9:21) (E) 3-Y-O+ **£4,202** (£1,293; £646; £323) **Stalls** High

Form RPR

14-5 **1** **Tender Falcon**[24] 2537 4-9-6 67.............................. JFMcDonald[(3)] 6 74
(RJHodges) *hld up: hdwy over 3f out: rdn over 1f out: styd on to ld post* **7/1**

5040 **2** *shd* **Rutters Rebel (IRE)**[15] 2782 3-8-12 70.............................. BDoyle 11 77
(GASwinbank) *led 1f: remained handy: chsd ldr over 2f out: rdn to ld over 1f out: hdd post* **10/1**

0-36 **3** *1* **Mungo Jerry (GER)**[33] 2298 3-8-12 70.............................. WSupple 1 75
(JGGiven) *hld up: hung rt over 2f out: hdwy u.p over 1f out: styd on* **20/1**

1024 **4** *3/4* **Isa'Af (IRE)**[15] 2782 5-9-2 65.............................. PMakin[(5)] 4 69
(PWHiatt) *prom: lost pl after 1f: hdwy over 2f out: rdn over 1f out: kpt on* **5/2**[2]

00-4 **5** *1/2* **Santa Caterina (IRE)**[42] 2059 3-8-8 69.............................. KDarley 8 69
(JLDunlop) *plld hrd: trckd ldr after 2f: led over 4f out: rdn and hdd over 1f out: styd on same pce* **9/4**[1]

0600 **6** *8* **Traveller's Tale**[16] 2767 5-9-7 64.............................. DKinsella 7 55
(PGMurphy) *hld up: hdwy 5f out: wknd over 1f out* **25/1**

0-20 **7** *1/2* **Perfect Punch**[22] 2591 5-9-9 67.............................. RMullen 3 57
(CFWall) *plld hrd and prom: rdn over 2f out: sn wknd* **5/1**[3]

0-30 **8** *nk* **Hoh Nelson**[38] 2179 3-8-12 70.............................. SDrowne 2 59
(HMorrison) *chsd ldrs: outpcd 4f out: n.d after* **33/1**

52-5 **9** *15* **Imperial Royale (IRE)**[20] 2653 3-8-7 65.............................. JBramhill 10 30
(PLClinton) *hld up: rdn and wknd over 2f out* **33/1**

1-00 **10** *2 1/2* **Red Skelton (IRE)**[13] 2841 3-8-12 70..............................(bt[1]) TQuinn 9 31
(WJHaggas) *led after 1f: hdd over 4f out: wknd over 2f out* **16/1**

2m 35.07s (0.39) **Going Correction** -0.025s/f (Good)
**WFA** 3 from 4yo+ 14lb **10** Ran SP% **118.0**
Speed ratings: **97,96,96,95,95 90,89,89,79,77**CSF £71.10 TOTE £8.80: £2.20, £2.20, £4.60; EX 49.50 Place 6 £1,624.10, Place 5 £578.08.
**Owner** P E Axon **Bred** P E Axon **Trained** Charlton Adam, Somerset

**FOCUS**
An ordinary contest run at a stop-start pace and a modest time, but the form looks solid enough.

**NOTEBOOK**
**Tender Falcon** proved well suited to this step up in trip and now connections have found he does stay, there will be other openings for him.
**Rutters Rebel(IRE)**, back at a more suitable level, did himself no favours by edging off a true line towards the finish, and may have been in front too soon.
**Mungo Jerry(GER)**, one of the few in this open to improvement, did not shape too badly and may have done better still with a stronger pace.
**Isa'Af(IRE)**, closely matched with the runner-up on their running at Hamilton, continues in good form and this consistent sort can be found another opening before too long.
**Santa Caterina(IRE)**, very free early on, would have been suited by a stronger pace. Off her current mark connections should have little difficulty placing her.
**Red Skelton(IRE)** *Official explanation: jockey said colt ran free when blinkered for the first time*
T/Plt: £341.90 to a £1 stake. Pool: £37,592.55. 80.25 winning tickets. T/Qpdt: £57.80 to a £1 stake. Pool: £2,385.90. 30.50 winning tickets. CR

# 2579 NEWCASTLE (L-H)
Thursday, June 24

**OFFICIAL GOING: Soft**
After over an inch and a half of rain the going was reckoned to be soft on the straight course and heavy on the round course.
Wind: Fresh 1/2 against. Weather: Persistent heavy rain.

## 3233 TSG SOPHOS MAIDEN AUCTION STKS 6f
2:20 (2:23) (F) 2-Y-O **£3,395** (£970; £485) **Stalls** High

Form RPR

335 **1** **Monsieur Mirasol**[31] 2352 2-9-0.............................................. NCallan 10 74
(KARyan) *racd far side: chsd ldrs led over 1f out: hdd jst ins last: styd on to ld last 75yds* **9/2**[1]

05 **2** *1 1/4* **Brace Of Doves**[14] 2812 2-8-9.............................................. JFEgan 9 65
(TDBarron) *racd far side: in tch: hdwy over 2f out: led jst ins fnl f: hdd & wknd last 75yds* **12/1**

**3** *2* **Propellor (IRE)** 2-8-11.............................................. ABeech[(3)] 14 64
(ADickman) *cmpt: unf: racd stands' side: chsd ldr: led that gp 3f out: kpt on wl fnl f* **25/1**

5 **4** *1 3/4* **Kaggamagic**[16] 2758 2-8-7.............................................. DarrenWilliams 19 52
(JRNorton) *racd stands' side: chsd ldrs: kpt on same pce fnl 2f* **7/1**[3]

**5** *1/2* **Artic Fox** 2-9-0.............................................. RWinston 18 58
(TDEasterby) *leggy: unf: scope: s.i.s: racd stands' side: bhd tl styd on fnl 2f* **16/1**

565 **6** *1 3/4* **Sound And Vision (IRE)**[7] 3009 2-9-0.............................. ACulhane 6 52
(MDods) *racd far side: chsd ldrs: rdn over 2f out: kpt on one pce* **6/1**[2]

0 **7** *3/4* **Gardasee (GER)**[14] 2812 2-8-9.............................................. JEdmunds 5 45
(TPTate) *racd far side: sn outpcd and bhd: styd on fnl 2f* **25/1**

**8** *3/4* **Heybrook Boy (USA)** 2-8-11.............................................. KDalgleish 4 45
(MJohnston) *rangy: unf: scope: dwlt: racd far side: bhd tl kpt on fnl 2f* **9/1**

5 **9** *1* **Classic Style (IRE)**[7] 3021 2-8-6.............................................. KDarley 20 37
(TDEasterby) *dwlt: racd stands' side: sn outpcd and bhd: hdwy fnl 2f: nvr a factor* **20/1**

**10** *2* **Morning Major (USA)** 2-8-9.............................................. PFessey 2 34
(TDBarron) *racd far side: in tch: rdn and outpcd over 2f out* **20/1**

0 **11** *nk* **Mister Buzz**[16] 2758 2-8-9.............................................. GDuffield 1 33
(MDHammond) *racd far side: chsd ldrs: outpcd over 2f out: sn lost pl* **25/1**

**12** *1 3/4* **Xaarist (IRE)** 2-8-11.............................................. DaleGibson 17 30
(TPTate) *w'like: leggy: unf: racd stands' side: sn outpcd and pushed along: nvr on terms* **10/1**

**13** *3* **Filey Buoy** 2-8-7.............................................. DeanMcKeown 15 17
(RMWhitaker) *leggy: unf: s.i.s: racd stands' side: sn bhd* **33/1**

**14** *1/2* **Flaxby** 2-8-6.............................................. TPQueally[(3)] 16 17
(JDBethell) *cmpt: unf: racd stands' side: chsd ldrs: rdn 3f out: sn btn* **20/1**

**15** *3/4* **Keyalzao (IRE)** 2-8-4 ow1.............................................. TEaves[(3)] 8 13
(ACrook) *neat: unf: s.i.s: racd far side: a bhd* **25/1**

0 **16** *1* **Davy Crockett**[22] 2579 2-8-7.............................................. LGoncalves 13 —
(MrsJRRamsden) *led stands' side gp tl 3f out: edgd lft and sn lost pl* **16/1**

062 **17** *1 1/2* **Brut**[7] 3003 2-8-6.............................................. LEnstone[(3)] 3 —
(DWBarker) *led far side tl hdeed and wknd over 1f out* **8/1**

**18** *2 1/2* **Norton Rose** 2-8-4.............................................. EAhern 11 —
(TJFitzgerald) *cmpt: unf: bkwd: dwlt: racd far side: a bhd* **25/1**

0 **19** *15* **Niteowl Lad (IRE)**[47] 1961 2-8-5 ow3.............................. JDO'Reilly[(7)] 12 —
(JO'Reilly) *racd far side: w ldr: edgd rt over 2f out: sn lost pl and bhd: eased* **20/1**

00 **20** *1/2* **The Terminator (IRE)**[20] 2651 2-8-9.............................................. JCarroll 7 —
(ABerry) *racd far side: sn bhd: eased* **50/1**

1m 20.36s (5.32) **Going Correction** +0.675s/f (Yiel) **20** Ran SP% **137.8**
Speed ratings: **91,89,86,84,83 81,80,79,78,75 74,72,68,67,66 65,63,60,40,39**CSF £54.33 TOTE £6.20: £2.20, £7.00, £16.80; EX 127.70.
**Owner** Mrs M Forsyth & Mrs E Jamieson **Bred** Lostford Manor Stud **Trained** Hambleton, N Yorks

**FOCUS**
Nothing more than an ordinary heat and the form is only modest. The field split into two groups, with those that raced far side coming out on top.

**NOTEBOOK**

**Monsieur Mirasol** had run well on his first two starts, but disappointed last time on very firm ground and enjoyed the cut in the ground. With the step up to six furlongs also helping, he improved on previous form and showed a good attitude in the process, picking up strongly once headed and ending up winning going away. Nurseries are sure to provide the best opportunity for him in future and as long as he gets a half decent mark, should be capable of winning again.

**Brace Of Doves** appreciated this return to turf, having run slightly below par on the Fibresand latest, and looked sure to win when going on inside the final furlong. However, he emptied out in the closing stages and was passed by the winner. He is now qualified for a handicap mark and will be best off in that sphere.

**Propellor(IRE)**, a newcomer by Pivotal, fared best of the stands' side bunch and showed good speed for most of the way without ever looking on terms with the front pair.

**Kaggamagic** has twice run well now and another who is sure to be winning winning when sent handicapping. *Official explanation: trainer said gelding was unsuited by the soft ground*

**Artic Fox** ◆ raced towards the back of the stands'-side pack after a tardy start, and was noted making good late headway. This was a pleasing effort and a maiden win should be a formality.

**Gardasee(GER)** shaped as though further would suit and improvement can be expected at seven.

**Heybrook Boy(USA)** comes from a stable whose juvenile can need their debut in terms of experience and this one looked a prime example.

**Classic Style(IRE)** improved on his initial outing and is slowly going the right way.

## 3234 TSG BRICE ASSOCIATES H'CAP 6f

2:50 (2:52) (F) (0-55,56) 3-Y-O £3,325 (£950; £475) Stalls High

| Form | | | | RPR |
|---|---|---|---|---|
| 0-05 | 1 | | **Shamrock Tea**[20] 2661 3-9-0 **52** ... THamilton(3) 2 | 62 |
| | | | (RAFahey) *racd far side: chsd ldr: led over 2f out: hld on towards fin* **6/1[2]** | |
| 0550 | 2 | ½ | **Musiotal**[27] 2457 3-8-8 **46** ... NMackay(3) 3 | 54 |
| | | | (JSGoldie) *racd far side: bhd: hdwy over 2f out: wnt 2nd that side over 1f out: n.m.r on inner and no ex last 50yds* **9/2[1]** | |
| -010 | 3 | 3½ | **Sam The Sorcerer**[36] 2232 3-8-10 **45** ... KDalgleish 12 | 43 |
| | | | (JRNorton) *led on stands' side: kpt on wl fnl f* **25/1** | |
| 0-50 | 4 | ½ | **Borodinsky**[9] 2962 3-8-7 **45** ... TEaves(3) 5 | 41 |
| | | | (REBarr) *racd wd on far side: in tch: rdn and outpcd over 2f out: kpt on fnl f* **50/1** | |
| -250 | 5 | 1¼ | **Westborough (IRE)**[14] 2815 3-9-4 **53** ... KimTinkler 8 | 45 |
| | | | (NTinkler) *swtchd elft s and racd far side: sn chsng ldrs: wknd fnl f* **14/1** | |
| 2066 | 6 | ¾ | **A Bid In Time (IRE)**[15] 2778 3-8-10 **45** ... DarrenWilliams 9 | 35 |
| | | | (DShaw) *s.s: racd stands' side: hdwy to chse ldr that side over 2f out: nt qckn* **8/1** | |
| 0500 | 7 | 1¾ | **Reversionary**[27] 2457 3-8-10 **45** ... (b) KDarley 6 | 30 |
| | | | (MWEasterby) *restless in stalls: dwlt: sn bhd: styd on appr fnl f* **12/1** | |
| 0550 | 8 | 6 | **Smart Danny**[31] 2350 3-8-8 **43** ... RWinston 4 | 10 |
| | | | (JJQuinn) *racd far side: chsd ldrs: hmpd by loose horse over 2f out: wknd over 1f out* **13/2[3]** | |
| 0-50 | 9 | 1¾ | **Caribbean Blue**[20] 2660 3-8-12 **47** ... DeanMcKeown 13 | 9 |
| | | | (RMWhitaker) *racd stands' side: chsd ldrs tl wknd 2f out* **25/1** | |
| -034 | 10 | 3½ | **Lord Wishingwell (IRE)**[23] 2556 3-8-2 **37** ... (v) PFessey 10 | — |
| | | | (JSWainwright) *racd stands' side: chsd ldrs tl lost pl 2f out* **12/1** | |
| 3001 | 11 | hd | **Garnock Venture (IRE)**[13] 2849 3-9-6 **55** ... (b) ACulhane 11 | 5 |
| | | | (ABerry) *racd stands' side: chsd ldrs: lost pl over 2f out* **7/1** | |
| P401 | 12 | 8 | **Wendy's Girl (IRE)**[10] 2942 3-9-0 **56** 6ex ... (b) DFentiman(7) 1 | — |
| | | | (RPElliott) *led on far side: clr that gp over 3f out: hdd over 2f out: sn lost pl and bhd* **7/1** | |
| 0605 | U | | **Killerby Nicko**[8] 2990 3-9-3 **52** ... (b[1]) DaleGibson 7 | — |
| | | | (TDEasterby) *restless in stalls and c out rdrless* **10/1** | |

1m 20.73s (5.69) **Going Correction** +0.675s/f (Yiel) **13** Ran SP% **122.7**

Speed ratings: **89,88,83,83,81 80,78,70,67,63 62,52,**—CSF £33.48 CT £667.82 TOTE £6.20: £2.50, £2.20, £5.50; EX 39.20.

**Owner** Keith Brown Properties (hull) Ltd **Bred** T J Cooper **Trained** Musley Bank, N Yorks

**FOCUS**

A slow time even in these conditions and an uninspiring event where those drawn low again prevailed. The form is modest.

**NOTEBOOK**

**Shamrock Tea**, who had a previous win to his name on the ground, was sent on at the two-furlong marker and that proved a decisive move, as he caught a couple out and then just found enough to hold on.

**Musiotal** finished well and looked sure to get to the winner until his challenge flattened out in the closing strides. He has run several good races in defeat and his turn will come.

**Sam The Sorcerer** ◆ ran his best race to date, making all on the stands' side and winning his 'race' by two and a half lengths. He may be worth looking out for in the coming weeks, as he is lowly rated and definitely on a winning mark.

**Borodinsky** left several miserable efforts behind in maidens with an improved showing on this handicap debut and clearly appreciates being able to get his toe in.

**Westborough(IRE)** has had more than enough chances and remains a maiden.

**A Bid In Time(IRE)** ran well without ever threatening.

**Reversionary** got a little upset in the stalls and ran well considering, staying on when it was all over.

**Smart Danny** *Official explanation: jockey said gelding was hampered by a loose horse*

**Caribbean Blue** *Official explanation: jockey said filly hung badly throughout*

## 3235 TSG SEATON DELAVAL TROPHY H'CAP 7f

3:20 (3:23) (C) (0-100,94) 3-Y-O+ £17,400 (£6,600; £3,300; £1,500) Stalls High

| Form | | | | RPR |
|---|---|---|---|---|
| 1-30 | 1 | | **Polar Bear**[8] 2969 4-9-10 **90** ... ACulhane 1 | 111+ |
| | | | (WJHaggas) *racd far side: hld up: gd hdwy 2f out: wnt 2nd over 1f out: qcknd to ld jst ins last: sn clr: easily* **9/4[1]** | |
| 0052 | 2 | 5 | **Digital**[5] 3079 7-9-0 **83** ... SHitchcott(3) 11 | 89 |
| | | | (MRChannon) *racd far side: chsd ldr: led 2f out tl jst ins last: no ch w wnr* **11/2[2]** | |
| 15U0 | 3 | 1½ | **Tidy (IRE)**[5] 3079 4-9-0 **80** ... DarrenWilliams 4 | 82 |
| | | | (MDHammond) *racd far side: hld up in rr: nt clr run and swtchd rt 2f out: styd on wl ins last* **25/1** | |
| 0130 | 4 | ¾ | **Mystic Man (FR)**[6] 3036 6-9-8 **88** ... NCallan 3 | 88 |
| | | | (KARyan) *racd far side: hld up: hdwy 2f out: sn chsng ldrs: one pce ins last* **8/1** | |
| 5333 | 5 | nk | **Sarraaf (IRE)**[5] 3079 8-8-1 **70** ... THamilton(3) 5 | 69 |
| | | | (JSGoldie) *racd far side: mid-div: effrt 2f out: kpt on same pce* **16/1** | |
| 5021 | 6 | 2 | **Tony Tie**[6] 3039 8-8-10 **79** 6ex ... NMackay(3) 15 | 73 |
| | | | (JSGoldie) *racd stands' side: chsd ldrs: styd on to ld that gp ins last* **12/1** | |
| 0-41 | 7 | 1½ | **Hills Of Gold**[61] 1620 5-8-5 **71** ... KDarley 6 | 62 |
| | | | (MWEasterby) *racd far side: one pce whn n.m.r over 1f out* **8/1** | |
| 1031 | 8 | shd | **Ulysees (IRE)**[6] 3038 5-8-7 **76** 6ex ... TEaves(3) 17 | 66 |
| | | | (ISemple) *s.i.s: racd stands' side: sn chsng ldrs: nt qckn fnl 2f* **16/1** | |
| 2315 | 9 | nk | **Soyuz (IRE)**[22] 2575 4-9-7 **87** ... PRobinson 14 | 77 |
| | | | (MAJarvis) *racd stands side: in rr: hdwy to ld that gp 2f out: hdd ins last: fdd* **10/1** | |
| 2214 | 10 | 3 | **Zilch**[53] 1789 6-9-9 **92** ... TPQueally(3) 16 | 74 |
| | | | (MLWBell) *racd stands' side: in rr: sme hdwy 2f out: nvr on terms* **7/1[3]** | |
| 000- | 11 | 1 | **Inchdura**[348] 3221 6-8-6 **72** ... KimTinkler 7 | 52 |
| | | | (NTinkler) *racd far side: chsd ldrs: n.m.r 2f out: sn wknd* **66/1** | |
| 2-00 | 12 | hd | **Pop Up Again**[14] 2806 4-8-7 **73** ... EAhern 13 | 52 |
| | | | (GASwinbank) *racd stands' side: chsd ldrs: hung lft 2f out: sn lost pl* **25/1** | |
| 1340 | 13 | 1 | **Sawwaah (IRE)**[6] 3036 7-9-4 **84** ... JCarroll 8 | 61 |
| | | | (DNicholls) *racd far side: hld up: hdwy 3f out: sn chsng ldrs: lost pl over 1f out* **33/1** | |
| -000 | 14 | 3½ | **Hit's Only Money (IRE)**[26] 2469 4-9-12 **92** ... DeanMcKeown 9 | 60 |
| | | | (PABlockley) *racd far side: chsd ldr: chal 2f out: sn wknd* **33/1** | |
| 0103 | 15 | 1¾ | **Raphael (IRE)**[9] 2963 5-8-13 **79** ... RWinston 19 | 43 |
| | | | (TDEasterby) *led stands' side gp tl 2f out: wknd* **25/1** | |
| 0000 | 16 | 9 | **Colemanstown**[15] 2779 4-7-12 **64** ... PFessey 18 | 5 |
| | | | (BEllison) *s.v.s: racd stands' side: a wl bhd* **33/1** | |
| 2515 | 17 | 12 | **Chappel Cresent (IRE)**[42] 2065 4-10-0 **94** ... ANicholls 10 | 5 |
| | | | (DNicholls) *led on far side tl 2f out: sn wknd and bhd: eased* **20/1** | |
| 0-30 | 18 | 27 | **Bandos**[5] 3079 4-8-8 **74** ... (t) GDuffield 12 | — |
| | | | (ISemple) *racd stands' side: chsd ldrs: lost pl over 2f out: sn bhd and eased* **66/1** | |

1m 31.3s (3.28) **Going Correction** +0.675s/f (Yiel) **18** Ran SP% **137.5**

Speed ratings: **108,102,100,99,99 97,95,95,94,91 90,90,88,84,82 72,58,28**CSF £13.72 CT £286.95 TOTE £3.30: £1.20, £1.70, £4.50, £2.70; EX 21.30 Trifecta £682.40 Pool of £1,441.88 - 1.50 winning tickets..

**Owner** B Haggas **Bred** Cheveley Park Stud Ltd **Trained** Newmarket, Suffolk

**FOCUS**

Polar Bear destroyed the opposition as he has been threatening to do for a while. The winner was impressive and the form is sound.

**NOTEBOOK**

**Polar Bear** simply bolted up on ground he loves. Sent off a 9/1 shot for the Royal Hunt Cup the previous week, he ran disappointingly on the firm ground, but back on this going he proved far too good for the opposition, pulling right away in the final furlong to win as he liked. However, soft ground form can be deceptive, and he is one to take on at short odds back on a faster surface.

**Digital** ran his usual solid race and was no match for the winner.

**Tidy(IRE)** was unlucky not to finish closer as he was held up in his run and stayed on well once switched to the outer of the far group. He is another who needs this ground to be seen at his best in the autumn.

**Mystic Man(FR)** had every chance and may need a short break to freshen him up.

**Sarraaf(IRE)** acts on the ground and ran well.

**Tony Tie** fared best of those on the near side and deserves some credit.

**Hills Of Gold** *Official explanation: jockey said gelding did not get a clear run*

**Soyuz(IRE)** should have fared better regardless of his draw.

**Colemanstown** *Official explanation: jockey said gelding missed the break*

**Chappel Cresent(IRE)** *Official explanation: jockey said colt lost its action*

**Bandos** *Official explanation: jockey said gelding had a breathing problem*

## 3236 TSG IBM H'CAP 2m 19y

3:50 (3:52) (E) (0-75,71) 3-Y-O+ £10,315 (£3,174; £1,587; £793) Stalls High

| Form | | | | RPR |
|---|---|---|---|---|
| 4015 | 1 | | **Lucky Judge**[8] 2987 7-9-3 **60** ... EAhern 6 | 73 |
| | | | (GASwinbank) *hld up in rr: hdwy 9f out: effrt over 3f out: led over 1f out: styd on wl* **14/1** | |
| 6-15 | 2 | 2½ | **Quedex**[21] 2613 8-9-2 **64** ... BSwarbrick(5) 9 | 74 |
| | | | (RJPrice) *chsd ldrs: drvn along 6f out: sn outpcd: hdwy over 2f out: styed on wl to take 2nd jst ins last* **5/1[2]** | |
| 1432 | 3 | 7 | **Next Flight (IRE)**[8] 2987 5-8-7 **50** ... PRobinson 12 | 53 |
| | | | (REBarr) *trckd ldrs: led over 3f out tl over 1f out: weakend ins last* **8/1** | |
| 050- | 4 | ½ | **Alrida (IRE)**[15] 4976 5-9-7 **67** ... THamilton(3) 8 | 70 |
| | | | (RAFahey) *hld up and bhd: hdwy over 3f out: kpt on fnl f* **8/1** | |
| 040- | 5 | 4 | **Simple Ideals (USA)**[198] 6156 10-7-12 **41** oh9 ... KimTinkler 13 | 40 |
| | | | (DonEnricoIncisa) *mid-div: effrt over 3f out: kpt on fnl f* **100/1** | |
| 0101 | 6 | 1¾ | **Best Port (IRE)**[24] 2531 8-9-2 **64** ... MLawson(5) 10 | 61 |
| | | | (JParkes) *hld up and bhd: effrt on inner 3f out: nvr trbld ldrs* **12/1** | |
| 200- | 7 | ¾ | **Hope Sound (IRE)**[21] 3471 4-9-2 **62** ... (p) TEaves(3) 2 | 58 |
| | | | (BEllison) *s.v.s: hdwy and in tch w main body of field 1/2-way: kpt on fnl 2f* **14/1** | |
| 0121 | 8 | 1¾ | **Considine (USA)**[14] 2821 3-8-8 **71** ... ACulhane 1 | 65 |
| | | | (JMPEustace) *led tl over 3f out: wknd over 1f out* **11/4[1]** | |
| 1054 | 9 | 1¼ | **Tandava (IRE)**[21] 2615 6-9-13 **70** ... (p) GDuffield 4 | 63 |
| | | | (ISemple) *chsd ldrs: rdn over 3f out: lost pl over 1f out* **25/1** | |
| -126 | 10 | 15 | **Red Sun**[17] 2731 7-9-3 **60** ... (t) NCallan 11 | 38 |
| | | | (JMackie) *chsd ldrs: effrt over 3f out: wknd over 1f out: eased ins last* **11/1** | |
| 5106 | 11 | dist | **Gargoyle Girl**[19] 2491 7-8-12 **58** ... NMackay(3) 3 | — |
| | | | (JSGoldie) *hld up towards rr: effrt over 3f out: sn wknd and bhd: t.o* **11/1** | |
| 22-2 | 12 | 10 | **Most Definitely (IRE)**[10] 2935 4-9-5 **62** ... (b) RWinston 7 | — |
| | | | (TDEasterby) *t.k.h in mid-div: effrt over 3f out: wknd 2f out: sn bhd: t.o* **12/1** | |
| -023 | 13 | 1¾ | **The Ring (IRE)**[47] 1958 4-10-0 **71** ... KDarley 5 | — |
| | | | (MrsMReveley) *trckd ldrs: pushed along 5f out: lost pl over 3f out: sn bhd: eased: t.o* **13/2[3]** | |

3m 47.28s (12.25) **Going Correction** +0.85s/f (Soft)

**WFA** 3 from 4yo+ 20lb **13** Ran SP% **129.1**

Speed ratings: **103,101,98,98,96 95,94,93,93,85** —,—,—CSF £89.25 CT £627.48 TOTE £23.90: £8.20, £2.00, £2.60; EX 187.60.

**Owner** Mrs I Gibson **Bred** K G Powter **Trained** Melsonby, N Yorks

**FOCUS**

This was a real test in the conditions and Lucky Judge stayed the best. The first two have been rated higher in the past and the race could prove better.

**NOTEBOOK**

**Lucky Judge** appreciated this soft surface and was always well placed to launch his challenge, off the pace on the outside. He had it won at the furlong marker and stayed on strongly. Connections may be tempted to put him by for a hurdle campaign if he does not get this ground again.

**Quedex** lost his position a little turning for home and was never getting to the winner in time. He has been running consistently well of late.

**Next Flight(IRE)** was seven lengths adrift in third and although running well, did not quite see out the trip.

**Alrida(IRE)**, a recent winner over obstacles, was never going quick enough despite the testing going.

**Considine(USA)**, who was well supported, may have done too much too early and did not get home.

**Red Sun** *Official explanation: jockey said gelding tired in the rain-softened ground*

**Gargoyle Girl** *Official explanation: jockey said mare was unsuited by the soft ground*

**The Ring(IRE)** *Official explanation: trainer had no explanation for the poor form shown*

**3237 TSG PEGASUS CLAIMING STKS** **1m 4f 93y**
4:20 (4:21) (F) 3-Y-0+ **£3,248** (£928; £464) **Stalls** Low

| Form | | | | RPR |
|---|---|---|---|---|
| 2215 | 1 | | **Hearthstead Dream**[8] 2973 3-8-3 63 (b) BSwarbrick(5) 3 | 60 |
| | | | (JGMO'Shea) *trckd ldrs: wnt 2nd over 2f out: rallied ins fnl f: led nr fin* **5/1** | |
| 3051 | 2 | nk | **Eton (GER)**[13] 2856 8-10-0 73 ANicholls 6 | 66 |
| | | | (DNicholls) *set mod pce: qcknd over 3f out: hdd nr fin* **6/1** | |
| 4345 | 3 | 2 ½ | **Paddy Mul**[87] 1173 7-8-11 40 (t) RoryMoore(7) 5 | 52? |
| | | | (WStorey) *hld up in last pl: hdwy on ins over 2f out: wnt 2nd over 1f out: one pce ins last* **8/1** | |
| 14-3 | 4 | 6 | **Lord Lamb**[16] 2759 12-9-4 65 ACulhane 1 | 44 |
| | | | (MrsMReveley) *rrd s: sn trcking ldrs: effrt over 3f out: sn rdn and outpcd* **9/2**[3] | |
| 4113 | 5 | 3 ½ | **Romil Star (GER)**[7] 3022 7-9-10 50 (v) DarrenWilliams 7 | 45 |
| | | | (KRBurke) *trckd ldr: t.k.h: effrt 3f out: lost pl over 1f out* **11/4**[1] | |
| 66-4 | 6 | 28 | **Tomasino**[13] 2856 6-10-0 83 KDarley 2 | 10 |
| | | | (MrsMReveley) *hld up: hdwy to trck ldrs 6f out: drvn along over 3f out: lost pl over 2f out: eased and sn bhd* **4/1**[2] | |

2m 58.2s (14.90) **Going Correction** +0.85s/f (Soft)
**WFA** 3 from 5yo+ 14lb **6 Ran SP% 106.9**
Speed ratings: **84,83,82,78,75 57**CSF £30.43 TOTE £7.00: £3.10, £4.00; EX 15.70.The winner was claimed by J. D. Bethell for £10,000.
**Owner** Gary Roberts **Bred** G And Mrs Middlebrook **Trained** Elton, Gloucs
■ Stewards Enquiry : Rory Moore one-day ban: careless riding (Jul 15)

**FOCUS**
Not much pace on here and the time was slow even in these conditions. It was the only three-year-old in the field who prevailed, just getting there in the dying strides to deny long-time leader Eton victory. The presence of the third diminshes confidence in the form.

**NOTEBOOK**
**Hearthstead Dream**, who was unsuited by the drop down to an extended mile at Hamilton on his previous outing, needed every yard of this distance and got there in the final strides to collar the long time leader.
**Eton(GER)** was originally not going to run if there was further rain, but he took his chance anyway and it nearly came off. He was conceding 25lb to the winner and deserves extra credit for his effort.
**Paddy Mul** looked a big danger at one stage but had nothing left to give in the final half furlong.
**Lord Lamb** ran slightly below par on ground he has won on, but at the age of 12 this has to be expected.
**Romil Star(GER)** raced a little too keenly for his own good and never really looked like it.
**Tomasino** is a talented individual who has had his problems, butr on ground he relishes was fully expected to take a lot of beating. However, he ran as if something was amiss.

**3238 TSG MICROSOFT CLASSIFIED STKS** **1m 2f 32y**
4:50 (4:51) (D) 3-Y-0+ **£5,876** (£1,808; £904; £452) **Stalls** High

| Form | | | | RPR |
|---|---|---|---|---|
| 50-5 | 1 | | **Burning Moon**[75] 1325 3-8-10 80 EAhern 7 | 87 |
| | | | (JNoseda) *trckd ldrs: shkn up over 3f out: smooth hdwy over 2f out: edgd lft over 1f out: r.o wl* **9/2**[2] | |
| 1103 | 2 | 5 | **Summer Bounty**[16] 2752 8-9-4 76 NCallan 6 | 74 |
| | | | (FJordan) *hld up: smooth hdwy over 2f out: n.m.r over 1f out: r.o: no imp* **5/1**[3] | |
| -402 | 3 | 5 | **Just A Fluke (IRE)**[10] 2934 3-8-7 77 SChin 2 | 67 |
| | | | (MJohnston) *led: qcknd over 3f out: hdd over 1f out: one pce* **9/2**[2] | |
| 6062 | 4 | 4 | **Go Tech**[8] 2982 4-9-4 76 RWinston 3 | 59 |
| | | | (TDEasterby) *sn trcking ldr: t.k.h: chal 3f out: wkng whn sltly hmpd over 1f out* **3/1**[1] | |
| 0200 | 5 | 2 ½ | **Internationalguest (IRE)**[80] 1272 5-9-3 75 (b) PRobinson 8 | 53 |
| | | | (GGMargarson) *sn bhd and pushed along: hdwy on ins 3f out: lost pl over 1f out* **3/1**[1] | |
| -000 | 6 | shd | **Eastern Dagger**[4] 3118 4-9-0 48 LEnstone(3) 5 | 53? |
| | | | (PTMidgley) *slwoly into stride: sn trcking ldrs: rdn and wknd 2f out* **100/1** | |
| -054 | 7 | 19 | **Leighton (IRE)**[28] 2424 4-9-5 80 (p) TPQueally(3) 1 | 26 |
| | | | (JDBethell) *trckd ldrs: rdn and lost pl 2f out* **14/1** | |
| 620- | 8 | dist | **John's Champ (IRE)**[392] 1943 4-9-0 50 TEaves(3) 4 | — |
| | | | (REBarr) *sn last: bhd and pushed along 6f out: t.o 3f out* **100/1** | |

2m 18.59s (6.99) **Going Correction** +0.85s/f (Soft)
**WFA** 3 from 4yo+ 12lb **8 Ran SP% 111.7**
Speed ratings: **106,102,98,94,92 92,77,**—CSF £25.85 TOTE £5.60: £1.50, £1.90, £1.40; EX 23.50 Place 6 £715.74, Place 5 £164.28.
**Owner** Hesmonds Stud **Bred** Hesmonds Stud Ltd **Trained** Newmarket, Suffolk
■ Stewards Enquiry : N Callan caution: careless riding

**FOCUS**
They went a decent pace considering the ground and they were strung out at the line. Even allowing for the proximity of the sixth, the form looks solid.

**NOTEBOOK**
**Burning Moon** improved on his previous form on this ground and jockey Eddie Ahern reported he felt a different colt on it. The decent pace that was set suited and he came through under a confident ride to win well. He is going the right way and can make his mark at handicap level. *Official explanation: trainer's representative said colt may have benefited from the step up in trip on this occasion*
**Summer Bounty** did best of the older bunch but was no match for the winner.
**Just A Fluke(IRE)** continues to disappoint - connections held him in the highest of regard as a two-year-old - and having set a decent gallop he was readily passed. He is running out of excuses.
**Go Tech** was disappointing as he had run his best race for a while on his previous outing.
**John's Champ(IRE)** *Official explanation: jockey said gelding had a breathing problem*
T/Jkpt: Not won. T/Plt: £508.20 to a £1 stake. Pool: £42,610.50. 61.20 winning tickets. T/Qpdt: £40.70 to a £1 stake. Pool: £3,460.15. 62.80 winning tickets. WG

## 3208 SALISBURY (R-H)
Thursday, June 24

**OFFICIAL GOING: Good (good to firm on loop)**

**3239 LEVY BOARD H'CAP** **1m 1f 198y**
1:40 (1:41) (D) (0-80,80) 3-Y-0+ **£5,648** (£1,738; £869; £434) **Stalls** High

| Form | | | | RPR |
|---|---|---|---|---|
| 12-1 | 1 | | **Hawridge Prince**[41] 2084 4-10-0 80 LDettori 4 | 95+ |
| | | | (LGCottrell) *hld up in rr: stdy hdwy on outside fr 3f out to ld 2f out: c clr over 1f out: easily* **8/11**[1] | |
| -032 | 2 | 6 | **Blue Mariner**[12] 2878 4-9-4 70 BDoyle 5 | 74 |
| | | | (PWHarris) *trckd ldr: drvn to chal appr fnl 2f: styd chsng wnr but sn no ch: edgd lft u.p ins last* **13/2**[3] | |
| 16-0 | 3 | ¾ | **My Galliano (IRE)**[27] 2000 8-9-2 68 TQuinn 3 | 71 |
| | | | (BGPowell) *sn led: rdn 3f out: hdd 2f out: sn outpcd but styd on again ins last to press for mod 2nd cl home* **25/1** | |
| -235 | 4 | 2 ½ | **Analyze (FR)**[4] 3127 6-9-7 73 RLMoore 1 | 71 |
| | | | (BGPowell) *hld up in tch: rdn and sme hdwy 3f out: n.d and no ch fnl 2f* **4/1**[2] | |
| -004 | 5 | 12 | **Yeoman Lad**[10] 2945 4-9-0 69 (v) LPKeniry(3) 2 | 44 |
| | | | (AMBalding) *chsd ldrs: rdn 5f out: wknd fr 3f out* **13/2**[3] | |

2m 9.43s (1.11) **Going Correction** +0.35s/f (Good) **5 Ran SP% 108.4**
Speed ratings: **109,104,103,101,92**CSF £5.76 TOTE £1.50: £1.10, £2.50; EX 3.50.
**Owner** Eric Gadsden **Bred** Downclose Stud **Trained** Dulford, Devon

**FOCUS**
A modest handicap run at a steady gallop, but the winner confirmed himself on the upgrade.

**NOTEBOOK**
**Hawridge Prince** won in a canter. The form of his win at Newbury last time gave him an obvious chance in this and, off a 4lb higher mark, he only had to be given an inch of rein before extending to victory. He is lightly raced and unexposed, so could be capable of even better than he has shown to date, and should get 12 furlongs.
**Blue Mariner** ran another fair race in defeat, but is greatly flattered by his proximity to the winner at the finish. This trip looks as far as he wants to go and a return to faster ground could see him nick a weak handicap.
**My Galliano(IRE)**, better known these days for his exploits over the sticks, was soon taking the field along at a modest clip, but got outpaced at a crucial stage and would have been better served by setting a quicker pace. He is another who found the recent ease in conditons against him.
**Analyze(FR)** would had ideally preferred a faster surface, but still showed little and looks to be going the wrong way.
**Yeoman Lad** never threatened and failed by a long way to reproduce the form of his latest effort at Windsor ten days previously.

**3240 HERBERT AND GWEN BLAGRAVE EBF MAIDEN STKS (DIV I)** **6f 212y**
2:10 (2:12) (D) 2-Y-O **£5,531** (£1,702; £851; £425) **Stalls** Centre

| Form | | | | RPR |
|---|---|---|---|---|
| | 1 | | **Perfectperformance (USA)** 2-8-11 LDettori 4 | 90+ |
| | | | (SaeedBinSuroor) *hld up in tch: stdy hdwy on outside fr 3f out: led over 1f out: shkn up and kpt on ins fnl f: readily* **4/1**[2] | |
| | 2 | nk | **Cape Greko** 2-8-11 JFortune 5 | 89+ |
| | | | (AMBalding) *hld up in rr: stdy hdwy 3f out: led ins fnl 2f: hdd over 1f out: styd on wl fnl f but nt pce of wnr nr fin* **25/1** | |
| | 3 | 5 | **Flag Point (IRE)** 2-8-11 TQuinn 7 | 76 |
| | | | (JLDunlop) *bhd: drvn and hdwy 3f out: edgd rt over 1f out: swtchd lft and r.o ins fnl f but no ch w ldrs* **25/1** | |
| 3 | 4 | hd | **Mushajer**[40] 2111 2-8-11 RHills 1 | 76 |
| | | | (MPTregoning) *trckd ldrs: led jst ins fnl 3f: rdn and hdd ins fnl 2f: wknd fnl f* **1/2**[1] | |
| 4 | 5 | 1 | **Royal Orissa**[14] 2804 2-8-11 PaulEddery 9 | 73 |
| | | | (DHaydnJones) *led tl hdd jst ins fnl 3f: styd pressing ldrs tl over 1f out: wknd ins fnl f* **25/1** | |
| | 6 | ¾ | **Hawridge Star (IRE)** 2-8-11 SSanders 6 | 71 |
| | | | (WSKittow) *s.i.s: bhd: rdn 2f out: kpt on fnl f but nvr gng pce to be dangerous* **50/1** | |
| | 7 | 3 | **Worth A Grand (IRE)** 2-8-6 RThomas(5) 8 | 63 |
| | | | (JWMullins) *chsd ldrs: wkng on rails whn nt clr run over 1f out: sn wknd* **66/1** | |
| | 8 | 7 | **Golden Dynasty** 2-8-11 RHughes 3 | 46 |
| | | | (RHannon) *sn chsng ldrs: wknd qckly 2f out* **7/1**[3] | |

1m 32.22s (3.22) **Going Correction** +0.35s/f (Good) **8 Ran SP% 114.2**
Speed ratings: **95,94,88,88,87 86,83,75**CSF £83.79 TOTE £5.00: £1.40, £4.00, £4.70; EX 64.00.
**Owner** Godolphin **Bred** Brushwood Stable **Trained** Newmarket, Suffolk

**FOCUS**
A decent-looking first division of the juvenile maiden, although the proximity of the sixth and seventh raises doubts. The pace was solid and the first two came clear.

**NOTEBOOK**
**Perfectperformance(USA)**, a $1,100,000 half-brother to top-class filly Russian Rhythm, made a winning debut in workmanlike fashion. He was appearing laboured at halfway and changed his legs on the turn for home, but the further he went the better he looked and he was always holding the runner-up close home. This experience will do him the world of good, he will be better on faster ground, and he looks a most exciting prospect.
**Cape Greko ◆**, a 35,000gns half-brother to the progressive three-year-old Royal Prince, made a very pleasing debut. He showed a neat turn of foot to lead two out until his lack of experience told, and he was always looking held by the winner late on. Well clear of the rest in second, the majority of his stable's juveniles improve for a run, so he should go very close next time out.
**Flag Point(IRE)**, a half-brother to smart juvenile Potaro, made a promising debut display and was doing all of his best work late in the day. He will come on a great deal for this experience and already looks in need of farther.
**Mushajer** disappointed. He seemed to have an obvious chance on the form of his debut at Newbury, which has really worked out well, but looked a different horse and something may have been amiss. It is unwise to write him off on just this below-par display, but he has an awful lot to prove now. *Official explanation: trainer had no explanation for the poor form shown*
**Royal Orissa**, who caught the eye when running on late over six furlongs at Newbury on his debut, tried late this time having shown plentry of early dash. He was far from disgraced however and looks the type to do well in nurseries.
**Golden Dynasty**, a grand-looking colt, dropped out quickly having shown early pace and was disappointing. He should be capable of much better in due course.

**3241 HERBERT AND GWEN BLAGRAVE EBF MAIDEN STKS (DIV II)** **6f 212y**
2:40 (2:41) (D) 2-Y-O **£5,512** (£1,696; £848; £424) **Stalls** Centre

| Form | | | | RPR |
|---|---|---|---|---|
| | 1 | | **Propinquity** 2-8-11 DHolland 8 | 75 |
| | | | (PWHarris) *trckd ldrs: rdn and styng on whn nt clr run and swtchd lft jst ins fnl f: qcknd wl to ld last strides* **4/1**[3] | |
| 2 | 2 | nk | **Chapter (IRE)**[12] 2890 2-8-11 RHughes 3 | 74 |
| | | | (RHannon) *w ldr: led ins fnl 3f: hung lft u.p over 1f out: kpt on wl u.p: ct last strides* **5/2**[1] | |
| | 3 | 1 ¼ | **Celestial Arc (USA)** 2-8-11 KFallon 4 | 71 |
| | | | (PFICole) *sn slt ld: hdd ins fnl 3f: styd pressing ldrs: edgd lft u.p jst ins last: kpt on same pce* **8/1** | |
| | 4 | 1 | **Tombola (FR)** 2-8-11 TQuinn 7 | 68 |
| | | | (JLDunlop) *chsd ldrs: pushed along 3f out: styd on fr over 1f out but nvr gng pce to trble ldrs* **14/1** | |
| 0 | 5 | 2 | **Merrymadcap (IRE)**[17] 2736 2-8-11 DaneO'Neill 2 | 63 |
| | | | (MBlanshard) *bhd: pushed along 2f out: styd on wl fnl f but nt rch ldrs* **40/1** | |
| | 6 | hd | **Benedict Bay** 2-8-11 SDrowne 9 | 63 |
| | | | (GBBalding) *bhd: pushed along 4f out: styd on fnl f: nt trble ldrs* **50/1** | |
| | 7 | ¾ | **Snow Tempest (USA)** 2-8-8 RMiles(3) 6 | 61 |
| | | | (TGMills) *s.i.s: bhd: shake up 2f out: r.o fnl f: nt a danger* **20/1** | |

8 ¾ **Rawaabet (IRE)** 2-8-11 .................... RHills 5 59
(MPTregoning) *stdd rr after 2f: hdwy 2f out: sn rdn: wknd over 1f out* **10/1**

9 5 **Mollzam (IRE)** 2-8-11 .................... LDettori 1 46
(MPTregoning) *sn chsng ldrs: rdn 3f out: wknd ins fnl 2f* **3/1**[2]

1m 34.24s (5.24) **Going Correction** +0.35s/f (Good) **9** Ran SP% **109.6**
Speed ratings: **84,83,82,81,78 78,77,76,71**CSF £13.08 TOTE £4.90: £1.90, £1.20, £2.50; EX 10.70.
**Owner** Mrs P W Harris **Bred** Pendley Farm **Trained** Ringshall, Bucks

**FOCUS**
A fair looking second division of the maiden, but it was run in a much slower time than the first, which governs the form.

**NOTEBOOK**
**Propinquity** ◆, a good-looking half-brother to the stable's progressive stayer Barolo, made a winning debut in taking style. He was always travelling best in behind the leaders, but had to be switched for a run after getting outpaced entering the final furlong, and deserves credit for picking up strongly when asked to win his race. He is better than the bare form, will stay further and looks worthy of a crack at a Listed event this year.
**Chapter(IRE)** confirmed the promise of his debut at Sandown last time and did everything right, but again found one too good. He pulled clear of the third horse, looks sure to lose his maiden tag before long and will have no problems staying a mile plus in time.
**Celestial Arc(USA)**, half-brother to the stable's Keplar who won his only outing as a juvenile, was smartly away and only lost out through greeness late on. This experience should see him hard to beat next time.
**Tombola(FR)** caught the eye staying on late and shaped with promise. Like most of his stable's two-year-old's to have run this term, he will be a lot sharper next time and would appreciate a stiffer test.
**Mollzam(IRE)**, a 115,000gns yearling and well-touted for this debut, found nil when push came to shove and dropped out alarmingly. Like his stable's runner in the first division of this maiden, he may well be capable of leaving this form behind in due course, but has an awful lot to prove now.

## 3242 PIPER HEIDSIECK CHAMPAGNE AUCTION STKS (CONDITIONS RACE) 6f
**3:10** (3:11) (B ) 2-Y-O **£12,600** (£4,779; £2,389; £1,086) **Stalls** High

Form RPR

1132 **1** **Polly Alexander (IRE)**[20] 2668 2-8-2 .................... RLMoore 2 88
(MJWallace) *trckd ldrs: led over 2f out: rdn and r.o gamely whn strly chal thrght fnl f* **13/2**[3]

2 **2** hd **Captain Hurricane**[14] 2817 2-8-7 .................... JFortune 6 92
(PWChapple-Hyam) *t.k.h: hld up in rr: hdwy 3f out: chsd wnr over 1f out: rdn and str chal thrght fnl f: no ex last strides* **2/1**[1]

225 **3** 4 **Asian Tiger (IRE)**[31] 2370 2-8-9 .................... DHolland 11 82
(RHannon) *chsd ldrs tl n.m.r on rails and lost position 3f out: rdn and styd on fr over 1f out: nt pce of ldrs ins last* **12/1**

15 **4** 2½ **Alvarinho Lady**[57] 1707 2-8-3 .................... PaulEddery 9 69
(DHaydnJones) *in tch: rdn and outpcd over 2f out: styd on again fnl f but nvr a danger* **33/1**

56 **5** ½ **Dusty Dane (IRE)**[7] 3009 2-8-4 .................... ADaly 1 68
(WGMTurner) *bhd: hrd rdn over 2f out: styd on u.p fnl f: nt trble ldrs* **66/1**

640 **6** 2 **Detonate**[37] 2205 2-8-3 .................... JFMcDonald 7 61
(IAWood) *chsd ldrs: rdn over 2f out: wknd ins fnl f* **33/1**

1 **7** 3 **Happy Event**[17] 2736 2-8-6 ow1 .................... SDrowne 10 55
(BRMillman) *sn led: hdd 3f out: wknd ins fnl 2f* **7/1**

2212 **8** 1 **Evanesce**[10] 2933 2-7-13 .................... CCatlin 8 45
(MRChannon) *chsd ldrs: led 3f out: hdd over 2f out: sn btn* **14/1**

2165 **9** nk **Im Spartacus**[26] 2478 2-8-6 .................... DKinsella 4 51
(IAWood) *a outpcd in rr* **66/1**

13 **10** 5 **Gortumblo**[19] 2677 2-8-7 .................... TQuinn 3 37
(DJSFfrenchDavis) *in tch: rdn 3f out: sn btn* **4/1**[2]

1m 16.35s (1.41) **Going Correction** +0.35s/f (Good) **10** Ran SP% **102.4**
Speed ratings: **104,103,98,95,94 91,87,86,86,79**CSF £14.96 TOTE £7.30: £2.00, £1.10, £3.60; EX 15.00.
**Owner** Mrs T A Foreman **Bred** Mrs T A Foreman **Trained** Newmarket, Suffolk

**FOCUS**
A fair line-up for this juvenile event that was run at a sound pace producing a decent time, and the front pair were clear at the death, the form suggesting they are progressive.

**NOTEBOOK**
**Polly Alexander(IRE)** showed a great attitude to fend off the runner-up close home and score all-out. She has shown decent form over five all season, but this was her first run over six furlongs and she got it well. Just touched off in Italy last time at Listed level, she is clearly a tough sort and could still have more to offer over further.
**Captain Hurricane** ◆, who only narrowly failed to score on his debut last time, ran a little keen early on and that proved costly late in the day, when trying to overhaul the eventual winner. He deserves a lot of credit for this, as he was conceding 5lb to a tough filly and it was only his second career outing. He looks set to land a maiden en-route to better things.
**Asian Tiger(IRE)** ran his best race since shaping with promise on his debut at York in May. He would have been closer but for meeting trouble on the rails before two out, without troubling the front pair. This extra furlong suited and he should find a small race this year.
**Alvarinho Lady** appreciated this better ground and shaped as though she may prefer a stiffer test.
**Detonate** may not have got this trip too well. He dropped out tamely having shown good early pace, but will most likely prosper back over the minimum trip when the nurseries begin.
**Im Spartacus** *Official explanation: jockey said colt lost its action*
**Gortumblo** was never a threat and proved most disappointing. It is possible that he may have been flattered by his third in Listed company at Epsom last time and he has it all to prove now. *Official explanation: jockey said colt was never travelling*

## 3243 ALDERHOLT SPRINT H'CAP 5f
**3:40** (3:41) (D ) (0-85,84) 3-Y-O+ **£6,942** (£2,136; £1,068; £534) **Stalls** High

Form RPR

0103 **1** **Whistler**[11] 2912 7-9-11 **81** .................... (p) RLMoore 3 90
(JMBradley) *hld up in rr: str run on outside fr over 1f led last half f: drvn out* **10/1**

4-04 **2** ½ **Domirati**[16] 2754 4-9-8 **78** .................... SDrowne 4 85
(RCharlton) *hld up in rr: hdwy 2f out: led appr fnl f: hdd and one pce last half f* **11/2**[2]

0042 **3** ½ **Further Outlook (USA)**[17] 2739 10-10-0 **84** .................... DaneO'Neill 9 89
(DKIvory) *son led: rdn 2f out: hdd appr fnl f: no ex ins last* **14/1**

4222 **4** hd **Romany Nights (IRE)**[16] 2754 4-9-8 **78** .................... (b) DHolland 5 82+
(JWUnett) *in tch: n.m.r ins fnl 2f: rdn and swtchd lft appr fnl f: r.o ins last: nt rch ledaders* **5/1**[1]

6015 **5** hd **Devise (IRE)**[12] 2873 5-9-10 **80** .................... SSanders 1 84+
(MSSaunders) *swtchd rt to far side s: hdwy on bit over 1f out: no room thrght fnl f: fin on bit* **10/1**

3213 **6** hd **Double M**[5] 3084 7-7-11 **58** .................... (v) RThomas(5) 12 61+
(MrsLRichards) *in tch: rdn to chse ldrs whn n.m.r over 1f out: styd on same pce ins last* **11/2**[2]

0-06 **7** 1¾ **Kathology (IRE)**[11] 2912 7-9-13 **83** .................... TQuinn 11 80
(DRCElsworth) *racd on rail: w ldr 3f: styd chsng ldrs tl wknd ins fnl f* **17/2**

3604 **8** ½ **Seven No Trumps**[11] 2912 7-9-5 **75** .................... (p) LDettori 7 70
(JMBradley) *chsd ldrs: rdn 2f out: wknd ins fnl f* **15/2**

0-00 **9** nk **Hey Presto**[16] 2763 4-8-13 **69** .................... KFallon 8 63+
(CGCox) *hld up in rr: hdwy on rails fr 2f out: trcking ldrs on bit whn nt clr run thrght fnl f: nt rcvr* **7/1**[3]

0/30 **10** ¾ **Sunley Sense**[7] 3016 8-9-2 **79** .................... TDean(7) 2 70
(MRChannon) *chsd ldrs over 3f* **25/1**

-500 **11** ¾ **Zargus**[60] 1642 5-8-3 **62** .................... LPKeniry(3) 10 50
(AMBalding) *chsd ldrs: rdn 1/2-way: wknd over 1f out* **16/1**

3006 **12** nk **Ok Pal**[48] 1937 4-9-7 **80** .................... (b[1]) RMiles(3) 6 67
(TGMills) *racd on outside w ldrs: hung bdly lft fr 2f out: wknd over 1f out* **14/1**

62.82 secs (1.25) **Going Correction** +0.35s/f (Good) **12** Ran SP% **123.5**
Speed ratings: **104,103,102,102,101 101,98,97,97,96 94,94**CSF £66.92 CT £804.88 TOTE £11.60: £3.70, £1.90, £4.00; EX 74.60.
**Owner** Raymond Tooth **Bred** Raymond Clive Tooth **Trained** Sedbury, Gloucs

**FOCUS**
A messy sprint which saw several hard luck stories and the form is unreliable. However, it was run at a solid gallop.

**NOTEBOOK**
**Whistler**, placed over course and distance last time off the same mark, looked to have it all to do three out, but really picked up under pressure on the outside of the pack and won a little cosily in the end. He enjoyed this decent early pace, was given a fine ride and is pretty useful when getting his ideal conditions.
**Domirati** ran his best race of the current campaign and went down fighting. He looks to be coming back to himself and will be one to look out for in a similar contest on faster ground.
**Further Outlook(USA)** did the best of those to force the pace and continues to run well, despite being a touch too high in the weights at present.
**Romany Nights(IRE)**, despite being a professional loser, would have gone closer with a clear run and can be considered a little unlucky. He remains in consistent form, but is fast running out of excuses.
**Devise(IRE)** ◆ was hardly off the bridle throughout, but had nowhere to go at a crucial stage and looked desperately unlucky. He is clearly in great heart at present and looks best over this trip. *Official explanation: jockey said gelding was unable to get a run*
**Double M** was another to be tightened for room on the rails and can be rated better than the bare form. That said, he is the type who needs everything to fall right in his races, and his supporters must take this into account.
**Hey Presto** was stopped in his run n the rail and is considerably better than this bare result suggests. He was flying at the death and looks like he may finally be about to capitalise on his slide in the ratings, most likely over an extra furlong. *Official explanation: jockey said gelding was unable to get a run*

## 3244 H. S. LESTER MEMORIAL H'CAP 1m 6f 15y
**4:10** (4:10) (D ) (0-80,78) 3-Y-O+ **£5,551** (£1,708; £854; £427) **Stalls** Far side

Form RPR

1162 **1** **Tudor Bell (IRE)**[11] 2910 3-8-9 **78** .................... KFallon 5 85
(JGMO'Shea) *mde all: shkn up 3f out: kpt on wl fnl f: readily* **3/1**[1]

62/0 **2** nk **Coalition**[19] 2671 5-9-9 **75** .................... DaneO'Neill 2 81
(HCandy) *chsd ldrs: pushed along 4f out: chsd wnr over 2f out: chal ins fnl f but a hld* **14/1**

410 **3** 3 **Glory Quest (USA)**[9] 2958 7-9-9 **75** .................... DHolland 4 77
(MissGayKelleway) *hld up: trckd ldrs: gng wl 2f out: rdn over 1f out: sn outpcd* **7/1**

3004 **4** ½ **Redspin (IRE)**[9] 2958 4-8-9 **68** .................... DerekNolan(7) 9 69
(JSMoore) *hld up in tch: switchued lft of rail over 2f out: kpt on u.p fr over 1f out: nt trble ldrs* **9/1**

03-3 **5** shd **Valance (IRE)**[34] 2277 4-9-10 **76** .................... SDrowne 6 77
(CREgerton) *hld up mid-div: rdn 3f out: styd on fr over 1f out: nt rch ldrs* **13/2**[3]

30 **6** 1¾ **Donald (POL)**[15] 2787 4-8-3 **55** .................... RLMoore 3 54
(MPitman) *bhd: rdn 3f out and one pce: kpt on again fr over 1f out: gng on nr fin* **20/1**

0555 **7** hd **Silver Prophet (IRE)**[15] 2787 5-9-3 **69** .................... GBaker 10 67
(MRBosley) *chsd ldr tl over 2f out: wknd appr fnl f* **10/1**

0-50 **8** nk **Sea Plume**[26] 2491 5-9-4 **70** .................... SSanders 8 68
(LadyHerries) *hld up in rr: hdwy on outside 3f out: flashed tail: hung rt and nt run on fnl 2f* **12/1**

4004 **9** 5 **San Hernando**[15] 2787 4-9-5 **71** .................... TQuinn 7 62
(DRCElsworth) *hld up in rr: swtchd lft to outside 3f out: sn rdn: edgd lft and btn 2f out* **7/2**[2]

0506 **10** 3½ **Fight The Feeling**[22] 2590 6-7-13 **51** oh5 ow1 .................... CCatlin 1 37
(JWUnett) *hld up in rr: hdwy 3f out: wknd fr 2f out* **40/1**

3m 9.63s (3.63) **Going Correction** +0.35s/f (Good)
**WFA** 3 from 4yo+ 17lb **10** Ran SP% **113.7**
Speed ratings: **103,102,101,100,100 99,99,99,96,94**CSF £45.00 CT £269.92 TOTE £3.30: £1.40, £3.20, £2.90; EX 46.30.
**Owner** K W Bell & Son Ltd **Bred** Michael Byrne **Trained** Elton, Gloucs

**FOCUS**
A modest handicap run at a fair clip.

**NOTEBOOK**
**Tudor Bell(IRE)** gamely made every yard of the running and was always just holding the runner-up close home. He was officially 4lb ahead of the Handicapper for this, so connections deserve credit, but he may struggle off a higher mark in the future despite the fact he is a tough cookie.
**Coalition**, a formerly progressive three-year-old in 2002, showed the benefit of his recent comeback outing and ran a sound race. He missed the whole of 2003, but clearly retains his ability and can find a race or two this summer, perhaps over farther.
**Glory Quest(USA)**, out of his depth in the Ascot Stakes recently, showed his true colours at this more realistic level and ran well. However, he looks too high in the weights at present.
**Redspin(IRE)**, a staying-on fourth in the Ascot Stakes last time, found this drop in trip totally against him.
**San Hernando** was again well supported to improve and end his losing run, but never really threatened from off the pace and again looked a tricky ride. He is one to avoid.

## 3245 CATISFIELD HINTON & STUD SUPPORTING THE R.N.L.I. MAIDEN STKS 1m 1f 198y
**4:40** (4:42) (D ) 3-Y-O+ **£5,804** (£1,786; £893; £446) **Stalls** High

Form RPR

4 **1** **Double Aspect (IRE)**[41] 2085 3-8-10 .................... KFallon 11 74
(SirMichaelStoute) *trckd ldrs: wnt 2nd 2f out: pushed along and led last half f: readily* **4/7**[1]

0-43 **2** ¾ **Michabo (IRE)**[10] 2950 3-8-10 .................... TQuinn 10 73
(DRCElsworth) *led: rdn 2f out: kpt on wl tl hdd last half f: nt pce of wnr* **14/1**

0- **3** 2½ **Dundry**[357] 2925 3-8-10 .................... RLMoore 14 68
(GLMoore) *in tch: chsd ldrs 4f out: pushed along fr 3f out: styd on fr over 1f out but no imp ins last* **25/1**

2 **4** *1 3/4* **Historic Place (USA)**[20] 2653 4-9-8 SDrowne 7 65
(GBBalding) *mid-div: pushed along over 2f out: r.o wl fnl f but nt rch ldrs* **11/1**

-030 **5** *shd* **Zuma (IRE)**[12] 2888 3-8-10 79 (v1) DHolland 5 65
(RHannon) *trckd ldrs: rdn to chal 3f out: styd front rnk tl sn btn fnl f* **8/1**[3]

4 **6** *1 1/4* **Warningcamp (GER)**[21] 2632 3-8-10 SSanders 4 62
(LadyHerries) *hld up mid-div: hdwy on outside to chal 3f out: wknd ins fnl f* **6/1**[2]

6-0 **7** *hd* **Masterman Ready**[21] 2632 3-8-10 BDoyle 1 62
(PWHarris) *bhd: pushed along and green 3f out: kpt on fr over 1f out: nt a danger* **50/1**

**8** *1 1/4* **Topkat (IRE)** 3-8-10 DaneO'Neill 8 60
(DRCElsworth) *slowly away: bhd: rn wd bnd after 3f: stl plenty to do over 2f out: kpt on fr over 1f out: nt a a danger* **16/1**

000- **9** *1/2* **Grey Admiral (USA)**[235] 5887 3-8-5 NChalmers(5) 12 59
(AMBalding) *sn chsng ldrs: rdn over 3f out: wknd 2f out* **25/1**

0- **10** *13* **Lasser Light (IRE)**[361] 2822 4-9-8 VSlattery 9 34
(DGBridgwater) *sn bhd* **100/1**

30 **11** *4* **Paddy Boy (IRE)**[96] 1064 3-8-7 RMiles(3) 3 26
(JRBoyle) *chsd ldrs: rn wd bnd over 6f out: wknd 3f out* **100/1**

**12** *dist* **Just Dashing** 5-9-8 CCatlin 13 —
(JELong) *sn bhd: t.o fnl 4f* **100/1**

00-0 **13** *dist* **Tartiruga (IRE)**[16] 2765 3-8-7 LPKeniry(3) 6 —
(LGCottrell) *rn v wd bnd after 3f: sddle slipped: t.o* **100/1**

2m 11.07s (2.75) **Going Correction** +0.35s/f (Good)
**WFA** 3 from 4yo+ 12lb **13** Ran SP% **123.5**
Speed ratings: **103,102,100,99,98 97,97,96,96,85 82,—,—**CSF £11.08 TOTE £1.60: £1.10, £4.00, £7.40; EX 10.00.

**Owner** The Celle Syndicate Incorporated **Bred** Lord Halifax **Trained** Newmarket, Suffolk

**FOCUS**
An ordinary maiden run at a fair pace, but the winner may be capable of better.

**NOTEBOOK**
**Double Aspect(IRE)** confirmed the promise of his debut at Newbury last time and scored with a bit up his sleeve. He is the type his yard do well with and will no doubt improve with more experience and over further, but he beat little on this occasion.

**Michabo(IRE)** tried to make all and went down all guns blazing, but could not hold off the winner when challenged. He settled better in the lead this time and looks to be at least going the right way.

**Dundry**, who showed little on his sole juvenile outing for Richard Hannon last year, stayed on to bag third having looked a little outpaced three out. He should come on a fair bit for this outing ,and is one to keep an eye on when eligible for handicaps, especially if upped in trip.

**Historic Place(USA)**, a former winner of an Ascot bumper, again ran on late as though he will be seen to a better effect over farther. He is another who is likely to fare better once handicapped and all of his decent bumper form was on easy ground.

**Zuma(IRE)**, tried in the first-time visor, had every chance but looked reluctant to go through with his effort. He is flattered by his current official rating.

**Warningcamp(GER)** made ground from off the pace three out, but failed to quicken and still looked green under pressure. He is capable of better.

**Tartiruga(IRE)** *Official explanation: jockey said saddle slipped*

## 3246 TELETEXT RACING "HANDS AND HEELS" APPRENTICE H'CAP 1m
**5:10** (5:10) (E) (0-70,66) 3-Y-O **£4,241** (£1,305; £652; £326) **Stalls** Centre

Form RPR

2203 **1** **Knickyknackienoo**[16] 2766 3-8-10 **55** MHalford 2 66
(AGNewcombe) *s.i.s: hld up rr: swtchd lft off rails ins fnl 2f: trckd ldrs and n.m.r 1f out: led jst ins last:kpt on wl* **11/2**

0603 **2** *1 3/4* **Gabana (IRE)**[14] 2820 3-9-3 **65** SO'Hara(3) 6 72
(CFWall) *trckd ldrs: hdwy on outside: carried hd high and changed action ins fnl f: no imp on wnr* **4/1**[2]

-243 **3** *1 3/4* **Ask The Driver**[26] 2484 3-8-9 **54** LiamJones 8 57
(DJSFfrenchDavis) *bhd: drvn and hdwy over 1f out: kpt on ins last: nt trble ldrs* **6/1**

2603 **4** *hd* **Chasing The Dream (IRE)**[17] 2737 3-9-3 **65** RJKilloran(3) 5 67
(AMBalding) *chsd ldrs: led over 2f out: hdd jst ins last: sn outpcd* **9/2**[3]

0644 **5** *nk* **Even Easier**[10] 2929 3-8-7 **55** (b) JemmaMarshall(3) 7 57
(GLMoore) *mid-div: hdwy to chse ldrs 3f out: sn pushed along: one pce fr over 1f out* **15/2**

006 **6** *1* **Miss Inkha**[13] 2842 3-8-10 **63** RMills(8) 1 63
(RGuest) *s.i.s: bhd: sme hdwy fr over 1f out* **16/1**

0-12 **7** *7* **Miss Porcia**[7] 3004 3-9-0 **59** BO'Neill 3 42
(PWChapple-Hyam) *led tl hdd over 2f out: wknd qckly ins fnl quarter m* **3/1**[1]

6-00 **8** *1/2* **First Dawn**[22] 2577 3-8-13 **66** LHarman(8) 4 48
(MRChannon) *chsd ldrs tl wknd 2f out* **16/1**

1m 45.98s (3.01) **Going Correction** +0.35s/f (Good) **8** Ran SP% **116.4**
Speed ratings: **98,96,94,94,94 93,86,85**CSF £28.29 CT £138.16 TOTE £5.50: £1.50, £1.70, £2.10; EX 23.90 Place 6 £116.79, Place 5 £82.55.

**Owner** A G Newcombe **Bred** Dunchurch Lodge Stud Co **Trained** Yarnscombe, Devon

**FOCUS**
A weak event run at a farcical early gallop. The form looks none too reliable.

**NOTEBOOK**
**Knickyknackienoo**, not for the first time, found all sorts of trouble in running, but still had too many guns close home for his rivals and lost his maiden tag at the 15th attempt. He is consistent enough but tricky, and would not be one for a follow-up bid.

**Gabana(IRE)** looked to duck the issue when holding every chance late on. She has ability, but also plenty of temperament as well.

**Ask The Driver** was not helped by the lack of early pace and was staying on all too late in the day. He can be rated slightly better than the bare form.

**Chasing The Dream(IRE)** held every chance if good enough, but found only the one pace under pressure. She again shaped as though she would prefer a stiffer test.

**Miss Porcia** had the run of the race out in front, but lacked the turn of pace to be competitive over this trip and disappointed.

T/Plt: £66.20 to a £1 stake. Pool: £33,454.40. 368.40 winning tickets. T/Qpdt: £10.20 to a £1 stake. Pool: £3,035.90. 218.45 winning tickets. ST

# 2960 THIRSK (L-H)
Thursday, June 24

**OFFICIAL GOING: Good to soft (soft in places) changing to soft after race 4 (4.00)**

## 3247 COLIN HAZELDEN BBC RADIO YORK (S) STKS 1m
**2:30** (2:30) (E) 4-Y-0+ **£3,721** (£1,145; £572; £286) **Stalls** Low

Form RPR

0263 **1** **Dara Mac**[6] 3058 5-8-4 53 SuzanneFrance(7) 12 60
(NBycroft) *hld up and bhd: gd hdwy on outer over 2f out: rdn to ld ent last: styd on wl* **13/2**[3]

5500 **2** *2 1/2* **Noble Pursuit**[9] 2965 7-8-11 53 RFfrench 10 55
(REBarr) *midfield: hdwy over 3f out: rdn to ld briefly over 1f out: hdd ent last: sn drvn and one pce* **20/1**

5-00 **3** *1 3/4* **Senor Eduardo**[73] 1373 7-8-11 51 NPollard 14 51
(SGollings) *a.p: rdn to chal over 2f out and ev ch tl drvn and one pce appr last* **50/1**

0143 **4** *hd* **Kelseas Kolby (IRE)**[10] 2928 4-9-2 55 (v) MFenton 6 56
(PABlockley) *hld up and bhd: hdwy over 2f out: rdn and ch over 1f out: sn one pce* **12/1**

5340 **5** *1 1/2* **Magic Mamma's Too**[55] 1748 4-8-6 50 (p) PMakin(5) 5 48
(TDBarron) *midfield: hdwy on inner wl over 2f out: riddcen and kpt on same pce appr last* **14/1**

0520 **6** *nk* **Royal Windmill (IRE)**[3] 3148 5-8-6 45 (p) PMulrennan(5) 3 47
(MDHammond) *trckd ldrs on inner: smooth hdwy 3f out: led on bit 2f out: sn shkn up: hdd and b eaten* **7/1**

0400 **7** *1 1/2* **Quicks The Word**[10] 2936 4-8-11 60 JFanning 9 44
(CWThornton) *chsd ldrs: rdn along over 2f out: drvn and one pce fr wl over 1f out* **20/1**

-320 **8** *3/4* **Rymer's Rascal**[10] 2938 12-8-11 51 WSupple 4 42
(EJAlston) *s.i.s and bhd: hdwy and n.m.r wl over 2f out: sn no imp* **6/1**[2]

-030 **9** *2* **Zarin (IRE)**[14] 2814 6-8-8 57 LisaJones(3) 8 38
(DWChapman) *s.i.s: a rr* **10/1**

65-0 **10** *3/4* **Zouche**[31] 2356 4-8-11 45 TEDurcan 15 36
(WMBrisbourne) *a midfield* **25/1**

4403 **11** *2* **Lord Chamberlain**[3] 3148 11-8-11 51 (b) FNorton 13 32
(JMBradley) *chsd ldrs: rdn along wl over 2f out: grad wknd* **11/2**[1]

6022 **12** *3* **Cezzaro (IRE)**[2] 3165 6-8-11 40 JBramhill 11 26
(SRBowring) *led: rdn along 1/2-way: sn hdd & wknd* **12/1**

0620 **13** *20* **Nicholas Nickelby**[12] 2895 4-8-11 60 GGibbons 1 —
(MJPolglase) *cl up: led 1/2-way: rdn and hdd over 2f out: sn wknd* **8/1**

0/00 **14** *3 1/2* **Stone Crest (IRE)**[8] 2990 6-7-13 30 SYourston(7) 16 —
(THCaldwell) *chsd ldrs to 1/2-way: sn lost pl and bhd* **100/1**

3606 **15** *26* **Inistrahull Island (IRE)**[8] 2979 4-8-11 56 OUrbina 17 —
(MHTompkins) *in tch outer: rdn along 1/2-way: sn lost pl and bhd* **20/1**

1m 43.21s (3.51) **Going Correction** +0.525s/f (Yiel) **15** Ran SP% **122.4**
Speed ratings: **103,100,98,98,97 96,95,94,92,91 89,86,66,63,37**CSF £139.18 TOTE £7.50: £3.60, £8.00, £23.30; EX 367.30.There was no bid for the winner.

**Owner** N Bycroft **Bred** N Bycroft And G Allison **Trained** Brandsby, N Yorks

**FOCUS**
A routine seller in which Dara Mac finally broke his duck and the form is poor.

**NOTEBOOK**
**Dara Mac** ran well in a handicap last time, the winner Goodbye Mr Bond having franked the form in the Carlisle Bell. Coming with a sweeping run down the outside to score comfortably, now that he has finally got his head in front he could win again.

**Noble Pursuit** put in a much better run on this second outing back on turf. He has shown his liking for soft ground in the past.

**Senor Eduardo** ran a better race on this drop in grade but remains a maiden.

**Kelseas Kolby(IRE)**, who was briefly short of room when about to come with his run, appeared to hang fire when the pressure was on.

**Magic Mamma's Too** wore cheekpieces rather than a visor on this first run after a break.

**Royal Windmill(IRE)** was again somewhat keen, but he travelled like the winner until finding nothing when asked to battle. This run underlines the fact that he is not one to trust. *Official explanation: jockey said gelding hung right-handed in the closing stages*

**Nicholas Nickelby** *Official explanation: jockey said gelding was unsuited by the ground*

## 3248 SANDIE DUNLEAVY BBC RADIO YORK MEDIAN AUCTION MAIDEN STKS 6f
**3:00** (3:01) (E) 2-Y-O **£3,701** (£1,139; £569; £284) **Stalls** High

Form RPR

**1** **Sir Anthony (IRE)** 2-9-0 FLynch 6 80
(BSmart) *hld up in tch: swtchd wd and hdwy wl over 1f out: str run to ld ins last: sn clr* **6/1**[2]

0 **2** *1 1/4* **Takhmin (IRE)**[16] 2758 2-9-0 WSupple 10 76
(MJohnston) *wnt bdly rt s: sn trcking ldrs: hdwy to ld wl over 1f out: sn ridde: hdd and nt qckn ins last* **5/2**[1]

0 **3** *1 1/4* **Rowan Lodge (IRE)**[17] 2736 2-9-0 JFanning 2 72
(MHTompkins) *promiennt: effrt to chal 2f out and evt ch tl rdn and one pce appr last* **14/1**

60 **4** *1* **Rich Albi**[13] 2860 2-9-0 (v1) DAllan 7 69
(TDEasterby) *cl up: rdn 2f out: one pce appr last* **7/1**

**5** *hd* **Commendable Coup (USA)** 2-9-0 GGibbons 11 68
(TDBarron) *bdly hmpd s and bhd: hdwy wl over 1f out: styd on ins last: nrst fin* **12/1**

**6** *hd* **Eukleia (USA)** 2-8-9 RFfrench 13 63
(TDBarron) *led: rdn along and hdd over 2f out: grad wknd appr last* **7/1**

**7** *1/2* **Ducal Diva** 2-8-9 JQuinn 3 61
(JRWeymes) *cl up: led 1/2-way: rdn and hdd wl over 1f out: sn wknd* **33/1**

**8** *1* **Regis Flight** 2-9-0 JBramhill 12 63
(RHollinshead) *hmpd s and b ehind tl styd on appr last* **25/1**

**9** *2* **Imperial Dynasty (USA)** 2-8-9 PMakin(5) 8 57
(TDBarron) *in tch: rdn along 2f out: sn wknd* **13/2**[3]

6 **10** *1 3/4* **Pee Jay's Dream**[40] 2125 2-8-9 PMulrennan(5) 9 52
(MWEasterby) *chsd ldrs: rdn along 1/2-way: sn wknd* **17/2**

**11** *3/4* **Herencia (IRE)** 2-9-0 MFenton 4 50
(PABlockley) *a rr* **20/1**

40 **12** *3* **Wedlock**[7] 3014 2-9-0 TEDurcan 1 41
(TDEasterby) *a bhd* **10/1**

0 **13** *2* **Fellbeck Fred**[19] [2686] 2-9-0 ........................................ GFaulkner 14 35
(CWThornton) *chsd ldrs to 1/2-way: sn wknd* **50/1**

1m 14.26s (1.76) **Going Correction** +0.025s/f (Good) **13** Ran SP% **128.7**
Speed ratings: **89,87,85,84,84 83,83,81,79,76 75,71,69**CSF £22.24 TOTE £7.80: £2.70, £1.80, £4.70; EX 31.50.
**Owner** Anthony D Gee **Bred** David Fitzgerald And Johnny Fitgerald **Trained** Hambleton, N Yorks

**FOCUS**
In all probability an ordinary maiden, but nothing solid on which to rate the form.

**NOTEBOOK**
**Sir Anthony(IRE)**, whose dam was a winner in Italy, came from off the pace once switched to the centre of the track to win going away in the end. He is still on the weak side and his trainer believes he will be better as a three-year-old.
**Takhmin(IRE)** stepped up on his debut effort, but he had to work hard to get to the lead and was cut down inside the last. He may need another furlong.
**Rowan Lodge(IRE)** had clearly learnt from his debut and was always in the front rank.
**Rich Albi** acquitted himself respectably in the first-time visor and is now eligible for nurseries.
**Commendable Coup(USA)**, a half-brother to seven-furlong juvenile winner Miss Ladybird and to winners in the United States, was the longest-priced of the Barron trio. Hampered by the eventual runner-up leaving the stalls, he was keeping on nicely at the death and ought to be capable of improvement.
**Eukleia(USA)**, a half-sister to a useful sprinter in the States, showed pace but may need better ground.
**Imperial Dynasty(USA)**, a half-brother to a winner in the United States, was well backed for this debut. A little slow to break, he was never within reach of the leaders.

## 3249 JACK CALVERT H'CAP 5f
**3:30** (3:30) (D ) (0-80,78) 3-Y-0+ **£5,590** (£1,720; £860; £430) **Stalls** High

Form RPR

3530 **1** **Paddywack (IRE)**[5] [3098] 7-8-10 **64**................................(b) LisaJones(3) 11 74
(DWChapman) *trckd ldrs: swtchd lft and hdwy over 2f out: rdn to ld ent last: styd on* **13/2**[3]

1200 **2** *¾* **Tally (IRE)**[7] [3010] 4-8-6 **57**........................................ GGibbons 7 64
(MJPolglase) *cl up: effrt over 1f out: sn rdn and edgd rt ent last: kpt on* **18/1**

0200 **3** *shd* **Strensall**[7] [3016] 7-9-7 **77**........................................ PMulrennan(5) 14 84
(REBarr) *cl up: led 1/2-way: rdn and hdd ent last: drvn and nt qckn* **12/1**

1440 **4** *hd* **Far Note (USA)**[7] [3010] 6-8-13 **64**................................(b) JBramhill 13 70
(SRBowring) *in tch: hdwy over 1f out: sn rdn and kpt on ins last: nrst fin* **5/1**[2]

4203 **5** *1* **Amanda's Lad (IRE)**[7] [3019] 4-8-2 **58**........................ DFox(5) 10 61
(MCChapman) *led: pushed along and hdd 1/2-way: rdn wl over 1f out: cl up whn hmpd ent last and wknd* **14/1**

6501 **6** *shd* **Awake**[16] [2754] 7-9-13 **78**........................................ TEDurcan 4 80
(DNicholls) *outpcd and bhd 1/2-way: hdwy wl over 1f out: styd on ins last: nrst fin* **9/2**[1]

-440 **7** *1 ¼* **Elliot's Choice (IRE)**[15] [2784] 3-8-4 **68**........................ DTudhope(7) 8 66
(DCarroll) *chsd ldrs: rdn along 2f out: grad wknd* **16/1**

463 **8** *shd* **Roman Mistress (IRE)**[19] [2670] 4-9-0 **65**........................(b) WSupple 9 62
(TDEasterby) *trckd ldrs: hdwy wl over 1f out: rdn and ev ch whn hmpd ent last: nt rcvr* **7/1**

0053 **9** *nk* **Ballybunion (IRE)**[2] [3169] 5-8-4 **55**........................ PMQuinn 6 51
(DNicholls) *chsd ldrs: rdn along 2f out: sn drvn and one pce* **9/2**[1]

0003 **10** *1* **Proud Native (IRE)**[13] [2843] 10-9-9 **74**........................ AlexGreaves 12 67
(DNicholls) *a rr* **14/1**

00-0 **11** *nk* **Miss Ceylon**[36] [2227] 4-7-7 **49** oh14........................ HayleyTurner(5) 3 41
(SPGriffiths) *cl up: rdn along 1/2-way: wknd wl over 1f out* **80/1**

6240 **12** *8* **Boanerges (IRE)**[5] [3084] 7-8-7 **58**........................................ FNorton 1 21
(JMBradley) *bhd fr 1/2-way* **8/1**

58.89 secs (-1.01) **Going Correction** +0.025s/f (Good)
**WFA** 3 from 4yo+ 6lb **12** Ran SP% **123.4**
Speed ratings: **109,107,107,107,105 105,103,103,102,101 100,88**CSF £122.29 CT £1409.43 TOTE £5.00: £1.40, £4.50, £4.50; EX 172.40.
**Owner** T S Redman **Bred** Colm McEvoy **Trained** Stillington, N Yorks

**FOCUS**
An ordinary sprint handicap though the time was fair for the grade and the form look solid.

**NOTEBOOK**
**Paddywack(IRE)** was 9lb lower than at the start of the year, but he has been held off this mark in recent runs. He came with his challenge down the centre where the better ground appeared to be, although he edged back across to the rail once in front.
**Tally(IRE)**, 7lb higher than when winning at Newcastle at the start of the month, was back to form after a couple of lacklustre efforts.
**Strensall**was 8lb higher than when going down by the minimum margin in this event last year. Racing against the stands' rail, this was a good effort on ground that was not ideal for him.
**Far Note(USA)** was arguably unlucky, as he was short of room on the rail before finishing strongly. He remains in good form.
**Amanda's Lad(IRE)** ran a fair race on this drop in trip but was held when buffeted in some scrimmaging entering the final furlong.
**Awake**, from an 8lb higher mark, stayed on too late to ever land a blow. The ground cannot be used as an excuse.
**Roman Mistress(IRE)** might have made the frame had she not been badly hampered when trying to go for a gap with a furlong to run.

## 3250 SKIPTON FILLIES' H'CAP 1m 4f
**4:00** (4:00) (E ) (0-70,68) 3-Y-0+ **£3,614** (£1,112; £556; £278) **Stalls** Low

Form RPR

-652 **1** **Charlotte Vale**[7] [3007] 3-9-7 **65**........................................ MFenton 7 71
(MDHammond) *hld up: hdwy 4f out: str run to chal wl over 1f out: sn rdn: drvn and styd on to ld last 50 yds* **11/2**[3]

0-35 **2** *hd* **Sand And Stars (IRE)**[13] [2848] 3-9-10 **68**........................ JFanning 2 74
(MHTompkins) *led: qcknd 4f out: rdn 2f out: drvn ins last: hdd and no ex last 50 yds* **5/1**[2]

1250 **3** *1 ½* **Dalriath**[6] [3049] 5-8-3 **38**........................................ DFox(5) 8 42
(MCChapman) *hld up in rr: hdwy 4f out: rdn to chse ldrs wl over 1f out: drvn and one pce ins last* **25/1**

-000 **4** *½* **Calomeria**[39] [2146] 3-9-2 **60**........................................ JQuinn 4 63
(RMBeckett) *cl up: rdn along 2f out and ev ch tl drvn and one pce appr last* **20/1**

-455 **5** *8* **Sea Cove**[14] [2816] 4-8-13 **43**........................................ RFfrench 3 34
(JMJefferson) *prom: rdn along 4f out and sn wknd* **6/1**

-000 **6** *5* **Theatre Belle**[7] [3026] 3-8-10 **54**........................................ DAllan 5 38
(TDEasterby) *in tch: rdn along over 5f out: wknd over 3f out* **33/1**

0-20 **7** *8* **Cantemerle (IRE)**[31] [2363] 4-9-10 **54**................................(b) TEDurcan 6 26
(WMBrisbourne) *hld up: hdwy to chse ldrs after 4f: rdn along over 3f out and sn wknd* **15/2**

3-31 **8** *2 ½* **Westcourt Dream**[7] [3008] 4-8-10 **45**........................ PMulrennan(5) 9 13
(MWEasterby) *trckd ldrs on inner: pushed along 5f out: rdn 3f out and sn wknd* **5/4**[1]

2m 43.42s (8.22) **Going Correction** +0.775s/f (Yiel)
**WFA** 3 from 4yo+ 14lb **8** Ran SP% **114.1**
Speed ratings: **103,102,101,101,96 92,87,85**CSF £31.93 CT £629.28 TOTE £7.20: £2.90, £2.10, £4.80; EX 37.30.
**Owner** Peter J Davies **Bred** Snailwell Stud Co Ltd **Trained** Middleham, N Yorks

**FOCUS**
A modest race with the favourite below par. The pace was only moderate early but picked up in the straight.

**NOTEBOOK**
**Charlotte Vale** was running beyond nine furlongs for the first time. She edged over to the far rail under pressure and had quite a hard race in getting off the mark.
**Sand And Stars(IRE)** settled better and stayed this longer trip as a consequence. With the benefit of the inside rail to race against, she went down fighting.
**Dalriath** was ridden with stamina in mind over this longer trip. She made steady progress from off the pace to have her chance but was unable to find any extra inside the last.
**Calomeria**, who flashed her tail when the pressure was on, is from a staying family and probably needs another couple of furlongs.
**Westcourt Dream** was able to race off a mark a pound lower than when winning a Beverley apprentice event. That was over ten furlongs on fast ground, and she never gave her supporters much hope under these different conditions. *Official explanation: trainer had no explanation for the poor form shown*

## 3251 JERRY SCOTT BBC RADIO YORK MAIDEN STKS 7f
**4:30** (4:32) (D ) 3-Y-0+ **£5,486** (£1,688; £844; £422) **Stalls** Low

Form RPR

**1** **Polar Magic** 3-9-0 ........................................ OUrbina 10 67
(JRFanshawe) *hld up: hdwy 3f out: effrt over 1f out: styd on to ld ins last: sn clr* **5/4**[1]

-642 **2** *1 ¾* **Flash Ram**[7] [3019] 3-9-0 66................................(b) WSupple 5 63
(TDEasterby) *cl up: led 3f out: rdn wl over 1f out: drvn and hdd ins last one pce* **11/2**[3]

6 **3** *1 ½* **Rosie Mac**[9] [2962] 3-8-2 ........................................ SuzanneFrance(7) 13 54
(NBycroft) *in tch: hdwy on outer 3f out: rdn to chal wl over 1f out: kpt on same pce ins last* **50/1**

00- **4** *3* **Edgehill (IRE)**[229] [5948] 3-9-0 ........................................ MFenton 9 52
(CREgerton) *hld up: hdwy 3f out: rdn wl over 1f out: kpt on same pce* **22/1**

**5** *1* **Dancer King (USA)** 3-9-0 ........................................ DaleGibson 11 49
(TPTate) *chsd ldrs: rdn along 3f out: drvn and wknd fnl 2f* **33/1**

**6** *nk* **Alpha Juliet (IRE)** 3-8-9 ........................................ NPollard 12 44
(GMMoore) *s.i.s and bhd: hdwy on outer over 2f out: styd on ins last: nrst fin* **40/1**

0- **7** *5* **Grele (USA)**[303] [4476] 3-8-9 ........................................ JFanning 3 31
(RHollinshead) *trckd ldrs: poushed along over 2f out: grad wknd* **50/1**

46 **8** *3 ½* **Harrington Bates**[8] [2984] 3-9-0 ........................................ VHalliday 7 27
(RMWhitaker) *keen: led: rdn along and hdd 3f out: sn wknd* **16/1**

24-3 **9** *1 ½* **Tropical Storm (IRE)**[33] [2301] 3-9-0 70........................................ JQuinn 2 24
(JNoseda) *in tch: rdn along 3f out: wknd 2f out* **7/4**[2]

6 **10** *nk* **Grand Rapide**[21] [2621] 3-8-4 ........................................ HayleyTurner(5) 8 18
(JLSpearing) *a towards rr* **16/1**

5 **11** *7* **Too Keen**[14] [2815] 3-8-9 ........................................ RFfrench 4 —
(JMJefferson) *keen: in tch:rdn along wl over 2f out and sn btn* **40/1**

**12** *1 ¾* **Blackburn Meadows** 7-8-11 ........................................ NataliaGemelova(7) 14 —
(PRWood) *a rr* **80/1**

06 **13** *3 ½* **Mary Carleton**[14] [2818] 3-8-6 ........................................ LisaJones(3) 6 —
(RMHCowell) *s.i.s: a rr* **100/1**

/00- **14** *3* **Fusillade (IRE)**[405] [1644] 4-9-9 ........................................ DMcGaffin 1 —
(AJLockwood) *dwlt: a rr* **100/1**

1m 32.21s (5.11) **Going Correction** +0.775s/f (Yiel)
**WFA** 3 from 4yo+ 9lb **14** Ran SP% **127.3**
Speed ratings: **101,99,97,93,92 92,86,82,80,80 72,70,66,63**CSF £9.11 TOTE £2.20: £1.40, £1.80, £14.40; EX 13.70.
**Owner** R C Thompson **Bred** Cheveley Park Stud Ltd **Trained** Newmarket, Suffolk

**FOCUS**
A moderate maiden won in decent style by newcomer Polar Magic, who is value for more thaan the winning margin and can rate higher.

**NOTEBOOK**
**Polar Magic**, whose dam was Listed-placed over this trip, came through from off the pace to score a shade comfortably. There should be a bit better to come from him.
**Flash Ram**, with blinkers replacing the visor, ran well enough but was no match for the favourite in the end. He is exposed and will remain vulnerable in maiden company.
**Rosie Mac** showed a hint of ability on her recent debut over course and distance, and she improved on that on this different ground.
**Edgehill(IRE)**, who was slowly away on both his starts as a juvenile, knew more here and was keeping on as if an extra furlong would not go amiss.
**Dancer King(USA)** is out of a multiple sprint winner in the States.
**Alpha Juliet(IRE)** found this too sharp and should be capable of better over a mile plus.
**Tropical Storm(IRE)** had run well on easy ground in the past, but he was a disappointment and looks one to be wary of.

## 3252 SKELTON H'CAP 7f
**5:00** (5:04) (E ) (0-75,73) 3-Y-0 **£3,653** (£1,124; £562; £281) **Stalls** Low

Form RPR

213 **1** **Snap**[22] [2569] 3-9-7 **73**........................................ JFanning 9 78
(MJohnston) *keen: cl up: led 3f out: hdd 2f out: sn ridden and rallied wl to ld ins last: kpt on* **7/4**[1]

1002 **2** *nk* **Commando Scott (IRE)**[6] [3059] 3-9-7 **73**........................ TEDurcan 8 77
(ABerry) *trckd ldrs: hdwy 3f out: led 2f out: sn rdna nd hdd ins last: kpt on* **3/1**[2]

2-00 **3** *1 ¼* **Acca Larentia (IRE)**[16] [2757] 3-7-7 **50** oh2.................. HayleyTurner(5) 6 51
(RMWhitaker) *chsd ldrs: rdn along and sltly outpcd over 2f out: styd on u.p fnl f* **25/1**

40-1 **4** *¾* **Cottingham (IRE)**[168] [473] 3-8-6 **65**........................ AndrewWebb(7) 4 64
(MCChapman) *hld up: hdwy on outer over 2f out: rdn and hung lft over 1f out: kpt on same pce ins last* **12/1**

0152 **5** *¾* **Tsarbuck**[13] [2854] 3-7-9 **50** oh1........................................ LisaJones(3) 3 47
(RMHCowell) *chsd ldrs: rdn along over 2f out: kpt on same pce* **3/1**[2]

060- **6** *5* **Plumpie Mac (IRE)**[394] [1893] 3-8-0 **59** oh1 ow9....... SuzanneFrance(7) 5 44
(NBycroft) *led: rdn along and hdd 3f out: sn wknd* **40/1**

360- **7** *4* **Chicago Bond (USA)**[248] [5671] 3-8-13 **65**........................ DMcGaffin 7 40
(BSmart) *in toch: rdn along 1/2-way: sn outpcd* **20/1**

0001 8 3/4 **Dark Day Blues (IRE)**[16] [2756] 3-9-1 **67**................................ MFenton 1 40
(MDHammond) *a rr: bhd fnl 3f* **7/1**[3]

1m 32.02s (4.92) **Going Correction** +0.775s/f (Yiel) **8** Ran SP% **117.6**
Speed ratings: **102,101,100,99,98 92,88,87**CSF £7.26 CT £94.46 TOTE £2.70: £1.10, £1.40, £5.50; EX 7.70 Place 6 £394.60, Place 5 £74.76.
**Owner** Duke Of Devonshire **Bred** Side Hill Stud **Trained** Middleham Moor, N Yorks

**FOCUS**
An ordinary handicap run at a fair pace and the form looks sound.

**NOTEBOOK**
**Snap** battled back well to gain his second win at this track. The soft ground was not a problem and he has the right attitude.
**Commando Scott(IRE)** got past the favourite with two to run but was worn down by that rival inside the last. The longer trip and easy ground were not a problem.
**Acca Larentia(IRE)**, who has been running over farther, ran her best race of the season on her first try on soft ground.
**Cottingham(IRE)**, off the track since winning on Fibresand in January, ran respectably back on turf although he did carry his head high.
**Tsarbuck** was 3lb out of the handicap, although that was negated by Jones's claim. This is his trip but he looks better on Fibresand.
T/Plt: £859.30 to a £1 stake. Pool: £29,487.35. 25.05 winning tickets. T/Qpdt: £40.10 to a £1 stake. Pool: £2,516.80. 46.40 winning tickets. JR

3253 - 3257a (Foreign Racing) - See Raceform Interactive

## 3162 CHANTILLY (R-H)
Thursday, June 24

**OFFICIAL GOING: Good to soft**

### 3258a PRIX CHLOE (GROUP 3) (FILLIES) 1m 1f
**2:50** (2:58) 3-Y-O £**25,704** (£10,282; £7,711; £5,141)

RPR

1 **Love And Bubbles (USA)**[11] [2925] 3-8-11 ................................ IMendizabal 4 106
(RobertCollet, France) *hld up, closing up on ins str, 4th whn swtchd out over 2f out, smooth hdwy to ld 1f out, pushed clr, easily* 3

2 3 **Cattiva Generosa**[39] [2160] 3-8-11 ................................ TJarnet 7 100
(RGibson, France) *led to 1f out, one pace* 2

3 1 1/2 **Cloon (USA)**[14] [2830] 3-8-11 ................................(b) C-PLemaire 6 97
(NClement, France) *hld up in rear to str, hdwy under pressure on outside fr wl over 1f out, took 3rd last strides*

4 snk **Bright Abundance (USA)**[18] [2720] 3-8-11 ....................... MBlancpain 1 97
(CLaffon-Parias, France) *always close up, 3rd straight, briefly 2nd 2f out, ridden & one pace approaching final f*

5 3 **Miss France (FR)**[44] [2028] 3-8-11 ................................ OPeslier 2 91
(ELellouche, France) *raced in 5th, 6th straight, never near to challenge*

6 2 1/2 **Step Danzer (IRE)**[32] [2341] 3-8-11 ................................ CSoumillon 5 86
(ABotti, Italy) *always close up, went 2nd 4f out, weakened quickly over 1f out* 1

7 2 **Iles Marquises (IRE)**[22] 3-8-11 ................................ GaryStevens 3 82
(AFabre, France) *dismounted & walked to start, trckd ldr, hung lft on turn over 4f out, squeezed back over 3f out, 4th straight, sn wknd*

1m 51.1s (-0.60) **7** Ran SP% **128.0**
Speed ratings: .
**Owner** B P Hayes **Bred** S D Plummer **Trained** France

**NOTEBOOK**
**Love And Bubbles(USA)**, supplemented into this race, she justified her generous confidence. After settling well early on she came with a smooth run in the straight and passed the runner-up a furlong out. The filly cruised into the lead and was never under the slightest of pressure. She may well go for races like the Beverly D and the E. P. Taylor Stakes in the future.
**Cattiva Generosa** set off to make all the running and she looked the likely winner until the furlong marker. She could not quicken in the final furlong but still stayed on bravely to the bitter end. Possible a longer trip may suit in the future.
**Cloon(USA)** was held up early on and did not appear on the scene until the furlong marker. She quickened well and pinched third place in the final few strides. This filly always runs up to expectations.
**Bright Abundance(USA)** fourth early on and raced on the rails, she was still well there two out but rather one-paced as the race drew to an end. She was caught for third place in the dying moments of the race.

## 2724 FOLKESTONE (R-H)
Friday, June 25

**OFFICIAL GOING: Good to firm**

### 3259 PILGRIMS HOSPICE MEDIAN AUCTION MAIDEN STKS 7f (S)
**2:30** (2:33) (F) 2-Y-O £**3,024** (£864; £432) **Stalls** Low

Form RPR

1 **Sky Crusader** 2-9-0 ................................ SDrowne 7 74+
(RIngram) *dwlt: trckd ldrs gng wl: effrt over 1f out: shkn up to ld last 150yds: sn drew clr* **6/1**[3]

23 2 2 1/2 **Laconicos (IRE)**[31] [2382] 2-8-11 ................................ TPQueally(3) 6 68
(DRLoder) *led: rdn and wandered over 2f out: hdd and outpcd last 150yds* **4/1**[2]

53 3 1/2 **Safendonseabiscuit**[27] [2470] 2-9-0 ................................ JFortune 9 67
(SKirk) *chsd ldr to over 1f out: swtchd rt ent fnl f: styd on same pce* **13/8**[1]

63 4 1/2 **Ride Safari**[11] [2927] 2-9-0 ................................ PDoe 1 65
(PWinkworth) *s.s: sn in tch on outer: rdn and unable qck over 2f out: styd on again ins fnl f* **25/1**

06 5 2 1/2 **Pacific Star (IRE)**[13] [2890] 2-9-0 ................................ TQuinn 10 59
(EALDunlop) *racd in midfield: prog on inner to chse ldrs over 2f out: wknd ins fnl f* **12/1**

0 6 shd **You Found Me**[16] [2786] 2-8-9 ................................ SSanders 3 54
(CTinkler) *chsd ldrs: rdn and outpcd over 2f out: one pce after* **6/1**[3]

0 7 2 1/2 **Bellalou**[7] [3051] 2-8-9 ................................ WRyan 5 48
(NACallaghan) *chsd ldrs: shkn up over 2f out: wknd over 1f out* **20/1**

0 8 3/4 **King Of Blues (IRE)**[12] [2904] 2-9-0 ................................ DaneO'Neill 11 51
(MAMagnusson) *racd in midfield: pushed along and outpcd 3f out: n.d after: kpt on* **25/1**

9 6 **Revivalist** 2-8-9 ................................ JMackay 14 31
(MLWBell) *prom tl wknd over 2f out* **16/1**

0 10 nk **Sarah Brown (IRE)**[35] [2263] 2-8-4 ................................(v[1]) BSwarbrick(5) 13 30
(IAWood) *sn outpcd and rdn: a wl in rr* **100/1**

11 3 **Fantasia's Forest (IRE)** 2-8-9 ................................ GCarter 4 22
(JLDunlop) *dwlt: outpcd and a wl bhd* **33/1**

12 nk **Ardasnails (IRE)** 2-8-11 ................................ DCorby(3) 12 27
(PBurgoyne) *dwlt: outpcd and a wl bhd* **100/1**

00 13 8 **Pie Corner**[43] [2058] 2-8-11 ................................ LPKeniry(3) 8 —
(MMadgwick) *s.s: racd in midfield: wknd 3f out* **100/1**

14 dist **Bregaglia** 2-8-9 ................................ BDoyle 2 —
(RMHCowell) *sn wl bhd: t.o* **100/1**

1m 26.47s (-1.33) **Going Correction** -0.45s/f (Firm) **14** Ran SP% **119.6**
Speed ratings: **89,86,85,85,82 82,79,78,71,71 67,67,58,—**CSF £28.26 TOTE £6.20: £2.50, £2.60, £1.10; EX 47.40.
**Owner** Pillar To Post Racing (IV) **Bred** M V S And Mrs Aram **Trained** Epsom, Surrey

**FOCUS**
An ordinary juvenile maiden run at a sound pace. The field came home well and truly strung out behind the winner, who is regarded the best prospect his small stable has had in a long while

**NOTEBOOK**
**Sky Crusader**, well-backed to oblige on this debut, showed a neat turn of foot to lead approaching the final furlong and win going away. He will come on a fair bit physically for this experience and looks promising, although the form is nothing special and it would be unwise to get too carried away.
**Laconicos(IRE)** held every chance if good enough on this step up in trip, but lacked the change of gear to go with the winner when challenged. It is likley that we will not see the best of him until the nurseries begin.
**Safendonseabiscuit** failed to build on the promise of his latest effort and still looked a little green when push came to shove over a furlong from home. This step up in trip looked to just stretch him and he will no doubt fare better once handicapped.
**Ride Safari**, again started slowly, but ran another promising race from his wide draw and deserves credit. He may not have handled this track all that well, but got the trip and can build on this. He should win a small race.
**Pacific Star(IRE)** held every chance two out on the rail, but was made to look very one-paced thereafter and finished tired. If he can finish one place better next time he will be eligible for nurseries.
**You Found Me** did not build on her debut display and may already need a stiffer test.
**Fantasia's Forest(IRE)** was not put in the race early on and this must go down as a very "educational" ride.

### 3260 MARK RAKE CLAIMING STKS 6f
**3:00** (3:08) (F) 3-Y-O+ £**2,926** (£836; £418) **Stalls** Low

Form RPR

0650 1 **Firework**[11] [2948] 6-9-2 60................................(p) TQuinn 2 69
(JAkehurst) *w ldr: led over 2f out: rdn over 1f out: styd on to draw clr ins fnl f* **9/4**[2]

0040 2 2 1/2 **Jasmine Pearl (IRE)**[31] [2380] 3-8-0 45................................ CCatlin 4 52
(TMJones) *w ldrs: rdn to chal over 1f out: ev ch ent fnl f: edgd lft and nt qckn* **50/1**

1000 3 2 1/2 **Pedro Jack (IRE)**[28] [2461] 7-9-6 62................................ SDrowne 7 58
(MABuckley) *racd in last pair: rdn 1/2-way: no prog tl kpt on fnl f to take 3rd nr fin* **9/1**[3]

-000 4 nk **Crafty Calling (USA)**[7] [3052] 4-9-8 90................................(t) KFallon 3 59
(PFICole) *chsd ldrs: pushed along after 2f: effrt 2f out: sn nt qckn and btn* **11/8**[1]

0000 5 1 **Power Bird (IRE)**[15] [2813] 4-8-5 52................................(b) NPollard 5 39
(BRJohnson) *s.i.s: racd in last pair: urged along and no rspnse 1/2-way : one pce after* **25/1**

0100 6 nk **Arogant Prince**[36] [2246] 7-9-4 59................................ JQuinn 1 51
(JPearce) *mde most to over 2f out: nt qckn and btn over 1f out* **14/1**

1m 11.39s (-2.21) **Going Correction** -0.45s/f (Firm)
**WFA** 3 from 4yo+ 7lb **6** Ran SP% **95.3**
Speed ratings: **96,92,89,88,87 87**CSF £52.41 TOTE £2.80: £1.30, £10.50; EX 60.30.
**Owner** The Grass Is Greener Partnership III **Bred** Cheveley Park Stud Ltd **Trained** Epsom, Surrey

**FOCUS**
The pace was nothing special and Crafty Calling has lost his way, but the form of the first two looks sound enough.

**NOTEBOOK**
**Firework** helped force the pace throughout and took advantage of a drop in grade. He had to pull out all the stops to shrug off the runner-up one out, but once he did so really found his stride and won going away. He is not the easiest horse to place in handicaps, but this will have done his confidence the world of good and he can continue to pay his way during the summer.
**Jasmine Pearl(IRE)** ran a much improved race and gave the winner plenty to think about, although ultimately well held. Her proximity at the finish holds the form down, but she may be able to finally get off the mark in this grade if able to maintain her current mood.
**Pedro Jack(IRE)** stayed on to grab third, but was never a threat to the principals at any stage. He would have been better served by a more positive ride.
**Crafty Calling(USA)**, by far the best of these on official figures, was never going the pace and found nil two out when still holding a chance. There is clearly something wrong and he is one to avoid at all costs until showing any sign of a revival.

### 3261 GUY PARKER MEDIAN AUCTION MAIDEN STKS 7f (S)
**3:30** (3:34) (F) 3-5-Y-O £**2,989** (£854; £427) **Stalls** Low

Form RPR

6420 1 **Midnight Ballard (USA)**[31] [2378] 3-8-12 80................................ SCarson 7 71
(RFJohnsonHoughton) *mde all: drew 4l clr wl over 1f out: rdn out fnl f* **6/4**[1]

-050 2 1 1/4 **Iphigenia (IRE)**[15] [2803] 3-8-4 50................................ RMiles(3) 8 63
(PWHiatt) *prom: rdn to chse wnr 2f out: hung lft over 1f out: styd on fnl f: nvr able to chal* **14/1**

04 3 6 **Set Alight**[15] [2818] 3-8-4 ................................ TPQueally(3) 6 47
(MissKBBoutflower) *racd in midfield: rdn 3f out: kpt on one pce to take 3rd fnl f* **25/1**

3-55 4 2 1/2 **Appetina**[18] [2729] 3-8-7 73................................ MFenton 3 40
(JGGiven) *chsd wnr to 2f out: sn btn* **11/2**[3]

5-03 5 1 1/2 **Truman**[16] [2785] 3-8-12 72................................ SSanders 1 41
(JARToller) *s.s: racd in last pair: prog on outer 3f out: wknd over 1f out* **9/4**[2]

5 6 shd **Tromp**[17] [2765] 3-8-12 ................................ DaneO'Neill 4 41
(DJCoakley) *racd in last pair: brief effrt 3f out: sn no prog and btn* **8/1**

0600 7 1 1/4 **Princess Bankes**[28] [2451] 3-8-7 45................................ SDrowne 9 32
(MissGayKelleway) *in tch on inner to 3f out: sn struggling* **33/1**

00-0 8 12 **Dont Let Go**[4] [3161] 3-8-7 ................................ JQuinn 2 —
(MissBSanders) *plld hrd: hld up bhd ldrs: wknd wl over 2f out* **50/1**

60-4 9 2 **Mrs Boz**[43] [2056] 4-8-11 29................................ BSwarbrick(5) 5 —
(AWCarroll) *chsd ldrs to 1/2-way: wknd* **150/1**

1m 25.04s (-2.76) **Going Correction** -0.45s/f (Firm)
**WFA** 3 from 4yo 9lb **9** Ran SP% **113.3**
Speed ratings: **97,95,88,85,84 84,82,68,66**CSF £23.17 TOTE £2.30: £1.50, £2.30, £5.00; EX 21.60.
**Owner** C W Sumner **Bred** Mark McEntee And John Bonziglia **Trained** Blewbury, Oxon

**FOCUS**
An average maiden run at a sound pace. Improved form from Iphigenia in finishing clear of the rest.

**NOTEBOOK**

**Midnight Ballard(USA)**, who flopped on fast ground last time, left that form behind with a tidy success. He was soon enjoying himself in the lead and always looked to be holding too many cards for the fast finishing runner-up. Although he was entitled to win as he did, it will have boosted his confidence no end.

**Iphigenia(IRE)**, well held in a handicap last time off a lowly mark, appeared to show much improved form over the extra furlong and finished a clear second. She ought to have a good chance back in handicap company off this mark.

**Set Alight** stayed on with no chance of getting to the front pair and now qualifies for handicaps.

**Appetina**, down in trip, again found little under pressure and is becoming very frustrating.

**Truman** found nothing off the bridle over the extra furlong and failed to build on his decent third at Newbury last time. This will have left connections scratching their heads.

**Tromp** never threatened over this slightly longer trip and was made to look very one-paced.

**Dont Let Go** *Official explanation: jockey said filly had run too free early on*

## 3262 JOHN ATKINS MAIDEN STKS — 5f

**4:00** (4:01) (D ) 3-Y-O+ — **£3,770** (£1,160; £580; £290) **Stalls** Low

Form — RPR

-002 **1** **Swinbrook (USA)**[23] 2576 3-9-0 80 ... SSanders 1 — 67
(JARToller) *trckd ldrs: nt clr run over 2f out tl got through to ld ins fnl f: drvn out* **2/9**[1]

5-42 **2** *nk* **Ex Mill Lady**[27] 2468 3-8-9 59 ... SDrowne 7 — 61
(JohnBerry) *pressed ldr: rdn over 1f out: w wnr ins fnl f: no ex nr fin* **9/2**[2]

0040 **3** *2* **Lakeside Guy (IRE)**[84] 1236 3-8-11 55 ... TPQueally(3) 4 — 58
(PSMcentee) *mde most tl hdd and one pce ins fnl f* **50/1**

30 **4** *1/2* **Otago (IRE)**[23] 2596 3-9-0 ... NPollard 3 — 56
(JRBest) *racd in last pair: pushed along 1/2-way: sn outpcd: kpt on ins fnl f* **20/1**[3]

0036 **5** *shd* **Ela Figura**[14] 2843 4-8-10 49 ... (p) BSwarbrick(5) 6 — 51
(AWCarroll) *racd on outer: trckd ldrs: effrt to chal over 1f out: sn rdn and fnd nil* **20/1**[3]

0000 **6** *8* **Firecat**[36] 2246 5-9-3 35 ... DCorby(3) 5 — 24
(APJones) *hld up in tch: rdn and wknd 2f out* **50/1**

59.02 secs (-1.68) **Going Correction** -0.45s/f (Firm)

**WFA** 3 from 4yo+ 6lb — **6** Ran SP% **113.5**

Speed ratings: **95,94,91,90,90 77**CSF £1.50 TOTE £1.20: £1.10, £1.30; EX 1.50.

**Owner** Lady Sophia Topley **Bred** B Bronstad **Trained** Newmarket, Suffolk

**FOCUS**

Very little strength in depth behind the favourite, who was well below form and won with nothing like the authority he should have done. The time was moderate for the grade.

**NOTEBOOK**

**Swinbrook(USA)** was going well behind the leaders, but had to wait for a gap, and when it came still only just scraped home. He needs producing just at the right time and only ever just does enough, but on official figures should have won with much more authority.

**Ex Mill Lady** cleverly tried to hold the eventual in a pocket two out and ran above herself in defeat, keeping on gamely. This confirmed her latest effort at Doncaster to be no fluke and she looks worth a switch into handicap company now off her modest mark.

**Lakeside Guy(IRE)**, making his turf debut, did his best from the front, but was a sitting duck for the faster finishers and had nothing left in the tank when challenged. This was however, his best run to date.

**Otago(IRE)** found this drop back to the minimum trip against him and will do better when handicapped over an extra furlong or two.

## 3263 MARTIN JORDAN H'CAP — 1m 4f

**4:30** (4:30) (F ) (0-55,55) 4-Y-O+ — **£3,052** (£872; £436) **Stalls** Low

Form — RPR

1/10 **1** **Cristoforo (IRE)**[62] 1611 7-9-3 55 ... TPQueally(3) 1 — 79+
(BJCurley) *hld up wl in rr: smooth prog fr 3f out: led on bit ins fnl f: sn clr* **5/2**[1]

00-0 **2** *3* **Absinther**[18] 2728 7-8-10 45 ... GBaker 5 — 51
(MRBosley) *dwlt: hld up in midfield: prog to chse ldrs 3f out: rdn and styd on fr over 1f out to take 2nd wl ins fnl f* **16/1**

4054 **3** *1/2* **Escalade**[7] 3041 7-9-1 55 ... (p) BSwarbrick(5) 13 — 60
(WMBrisbourne) *chsd ldrs: effrt on inner over 2f out: styd on u.p fr over 1f out* **16/1**

0-00 **4** *3/4* **Tintawn Gold (IRE)**[21] 2643 4-8-13 48 ... DSweeney 7 — 52
(SWoodman) *t.k.h: hld up in midfield: prog over 3f out: rdn to ld over 1f out: hdd and one pce ins fnl f* **33/1**

3612 **5** *3/4* **Make My Hay**[32] 2375 5-9-0 49 ... DaneO'Neill 9 — 52
(JGallagher) *hld up in last trio: wl off the pce over 2f out: rdn and r.o fr over 1f out: nvr nrr* **11/2**[3]

205 **6** *3/4* **Lazzaz**[8] 3018 6-8-9 47 ... RMiles(3) 12 — 48
(PWHiatt) *pushed up to join ldr: narrow ld 8f out tl hdd and nt qckn over 1f out* **6/1**

-025 **7** *1 1/2* **Summer Cherry (USA)**[7] 3050 7-8-10 45 ... (t) PDoe 15 — 44
(JamiePoulton) *dwlt: sn chsd ldrs: effrt to chal 2f out: wknd fnl f* **5/1**[2]

0-56 **8** *1 1/2* **Ripcord (IRE)**[12] 2055 6-7-11 35 oh5 ... JFMcDonald(3) 16 — 32
(BRJohnson) *settled towards rr: rdn and effrt over 2f out: one pce and no imp on ldrs* **16/1**

**9** *1 1/4* **Perida (IRE)**[10] 2025 4-8-13 48 ... SWhitworth 10 — 43
(BGPowell) *dwlt: hld up wl in rr: effrt on inner and nt clr run 3f out: sme prog 2f out: fdd fnl f* **50/1**

250- **10** *3/4* **Burnt Copper (IRE)**[193] 4874 4-9-3 52 ... NPollard 2 — 45
(JRBest) *dwlt: hld up in rr: rdn and effrt over 2f out: no prog over 1f out: wknd* **20/1**

0400 **11** *2* **River Of Fire**[13] 2874 6-7-7 35 oh5 ... (v) NataliaGemelova(7) 11 — 25
(CNKellett) *prom: pushed along fr 7f out: steadily wknd fr 3f out* **25/1**

5412 **12** *5* **Adjiram (IRE)**[43] 2055 8-8-4 39 ow2 ... (v) WRyan 4 — 21
(AWCarroll) *chsd ldrs: rn wd bnd over 9f out: wknd over 2f out* **14/1**

00-0 **13** *shd* **Wizard Of The West**[15] 2501 4-8-13 53 ... NChalmers(5) 6 — 35
(MissSheenaWest) *dwlt: hld up wl in rr: sme prog over 3f out: wknd 2f out* **33/1**

22-6 **14** *3* **African Dawn**[17] 2767 6-9-0 52 ... (t) LPKeniry(3) 14 — 29
(LGCottrell) *led to 8f out: w ldr to over 2f out: wknd* **10/1**

0130 **15** *8* **Ersaal (USA)**[46] 1989 4-8-7 42 ... (t) OUrbina 8 — 6
(JJay) *racd in midfield: rdn and wknd 3f out: eased over 1f out* **12/1**

0 **16** *5* **Watership Down (IRE)**[31] 2385 7-8-5 40 ... CCatlin 3 — —
(BGPowell) *a wl in rr: last and struggling 7f out: t.o 4f out* **50/1**

2m 37.71s (-2.69) **Going Correction** -0.10s/f (Good) — **16** Ran SP% **134.4**

Speed ratings: **104,102,101,101,100 100,99,98,97,96 95,92,92,90,84 81**CSF £50.11 CT £585.38 TOTE £3.80: £1.30, £5.10, £6.00, £2.10; EX 92.90.

**Owner** P Byrne **Bred** Bill Dwan And Tom Lynch **Trained** Newmarket, Suffolk

**FOCUS**

A tight-looking handicap, and solid form behind the winner, who won with any amount in hand.

**NOTEBOOK**

**Cristoforo(IRE)** was always travelling with ease off the pace and picked off his rivals effortlessly before extending away when shaken up inside the final furlong. He is useful on his day and was clearly primed for this after a charity win at Newbury. The Handicapper will make him pay - he already had an AW mark 10lb higher than this - but he could well defy a penalty.

**Absinther** ran his best race of the current campaign, but held no chance with the winner. He is not that consistent but appears to be running into form at his usual time again and could soon go one better.

**Escalade** ran a sound race under top-weight and only tired late on over this longer trip.

**Tintawn Gold(IRE)** was too keen in the early stages so did well to finish as close as she did, improving on recent efforts.

**Make My Hay** was running on well after looking to have a fair bit to do two out and is clearly in fair form at present. He looks capable of scoring again soon off this mark.

**Lazzaz** continues to run his race and find little at the business end.

## 3264 MIKE WHITE FILLIES' H'CAP — 1m 1f 149y

**5:00** (5:02) (E ) (0-70,68) 3-Y-O+ — **£3,523** (£1,084; £542; £271) **Stalls** Low

Form — RPR

2600 **1** **Lilli Marlane**[15] 2810 4-10-0 68 ... WRyan 12 — 78
(NACallaghan) *hld up towards rr: prog on inner over 2f out: rdn to ld jst ins fnl f: styd on wl* **5/1**[3]

6002 **2** *1 1/2* **Kindness**[5] 3117 4-8-8 48 ... DaneO'Neill 7 — 55
(ADWPinder) *t.k.h: sn led: drvn 2l clr 2f out: edgd lft over 1f out: hdd and one pce jst ins fnl f* **7/1**

0060 **3** *1 1/2* **Jessinca**[15] 2811 8-8-0 40 ... JMackay 9 — 44
(APJones) *t.k.h: hld up in last pair: prog on inner fr 2f out: styd on to take 3rd fnl f: no imp ldng pair* **33/1**

5426 **4** *nk* **Lara Falana**[13] 2881 6-10-0 68 ... SSanders 6 — 72
(MissBSanders) *trckd ldrs: effrt over 2f out: sn unable qckn: styd on same pce fr over 1f out* **4/1**[1]

552- **5** *3* **Scenic Lady (IRE)**[327] 3466 8-9-5 59 ... DSweeney 3 — 57
(LADace) *dwlt: hld up in rr: shkn up over 2f out: sn outpcd: prog over 1f out: one pce fnl f* **25/1**

0-06 **6** *2 1/2* **Sienna Sunset (IRE)**[56] 1752 5-9-3 57 ... SCarson 8 — 50
(WMBrisbourne) *prom: rdn to chse ldr 2f out to over 1f out: wknd fnl f* **9/1**

2132 **7** *3 1/2* **Princess Galadriel**[15] 2820 3-8-9 61 ... NPollard 1 — 47
(JRBest) *settled in last: rdn over 3f out: effrt on wd outside 2f out: sn btn* **9/2**[2]

-000 **8** *1* **Suerte**[28] 2456 4-8-9 49 ... BDoyle 11 — 34
(RMHCowell) *s.i.s: t.k.h and trckd ldr after 3f: rdn over 2f out: wknd over 1f out: eased* **10/1**

0-00 **9** *3/4* **Princess Magdalena**[18] 2740 4-8-9 52 ... LPKeniry(3) 5 — 35
(LGCottrell) *racd in midfield: rdn 3f out: wknd over 2f out* **16/1**

00/0 **10** *1/2* **Lady Jeannie**[18] 2737 7-8-5 48 ... RMiles(3) 2 — 30
(MJHaynes) *prom tl wknd over 2f out* **50/1**

1053 **11** *3* **Got To Be Cash**[8] 3008 5-8-7 52 ... BSwarbrick(5) 4 — 29
(WMBrisbourne) *chsd ldrs: drvn over 3f out: wknd 2f out* **5/1**[3]

2m 4.39s (-0.77) **Going Correction** -0.10s/f (Good)

**WFA** 3 from 4yo+ 12lb — **11** Ran SP% **117.7**

Speed ratings: **99,97,96,96,93 91,89,88,87,87 84**CSF £39.34 CT £1049.18 TOTE £6.20: £2.70, £3.20, £13.30; EX 55.40 Place 6 £61.82, Place 5 £47.82.

**Owner** Mrs T A Foreman **Bred** Mrs T A Foreman **Trained** Newmarket, Suffolk

**FOCUS**

A poor event run at a modest gallop, and unconvincing form. The first four were clear.

**NOTEBOOK**

**Lilli Marlane** took advantage of a gap on the inner two out and readily ran on to victory. This was her best effort since coming second at Ascot on her reappearance and the recent drop in the ratings has helped bring about her improvement. She could go in again.

**Kindness** again tried to nick the race from the front, only to find one too good late on. She is a tough sort who sould be winning soon, but her tactics often leave her vulnerable to anything with a turn of foot over this trip.

**Jessinca** did her rider no favours by running very free in the early stages, yet finished best of all. She improved for this switch back to turf.

**Lara Falana** could not quicken in the straight when holding a chance and looked very one-paced late on. She will be better served by a stronger gallop at this trip.

**Princess Galadriel** never looked like getting to the leaders from off the pace and slightly disappointed. A drop to seven furlongs may see her get closer once again.

T/Plt: £281.20 to a £1 stake. Pool: £35,171.30. 91.30 winning tickets. T/Qpdt: £36.00 to a £1 stake. Pool: £2,322.40. 47.70 winning tickets. JN

# 3233 NEWCASTLE (L-H)

Friday, June 25

**OFFICIAL GOING: Soft (heavy in places)**

## 3265 CANTORODDS.COM H'CAP (FOR GENTLEMAN AMATEUR RIDERS) — 1m 2f 32y

**6:55** (6:55) (F ) (0-75,69) 4-Y-O+ — **£3,425** (£1,054; £527; £263) **Stalls** High

Form — RPR

4111 **1** **Kingsdon (IRE)**[6] 3088 7-11-3 57 5ex ... (vt) MrNickyTinkler 10 — 69
(TJFitzgerald) *in tch: outpcd over 2f out: rallied to ld 1f out: kpt on wl* **6/1**[3]

6031 **2** *1 1/2* **Scurra**[7] 3041 5-10-5 52 5ex ... MrEWhillans(7) 7 — 61
(ACWhillans) *chsd ldrs: led 3f out: edgd lft: hdd 1f out and outpcd: r.o towards fin* **9/1**

1151 **3** *hd* **Pure Mischief (IRE)**[8] 3022 5-11-13 67 5ex ... MrSWalker 3 — 76
(CRDore) *hld up: hdwy over 3f out: disp ld appr fnl f: no ex wl ins last* **4/1**[2]

1-62 **4** *4* **Opening Ceremony (USA)**[8] 3005 5-11-9 68 ... (p) MrPCallaghan(5) 13 — 70
(RAFahey) *keen: hld up in tch: hdwy 3f out: hung lft: outpcd over 1f out* **7/2**[1]

3421 **5** *3/4* **Kid'Z'Play (IRE)**[8] 3005 8-11-8 69 5ex ... MrGGoldie(7) 12 — 70
(JSGoldie) *led to 3f out: wknd over 1f out* **7/1**

0006 **6** *2 1/2* **Every Note Counts**[11] 2945 4-11-3 62 ... MrMWalford(5) 11 — 58
(JJQuinn) *hld up: hdwy to chse ldrs over 2f out: wknd over 1f out* **9/1**

-503 **7** *3 1/2* **Untidy Daughter**[28] 2446 5-10-9 52 ... (p) MrEDehdashti(3) 8 — 42
(BEllison) *hld up in tch: hdwy to chse ldrs 4f out: wknd 2f out* **9/1**

4324 **8** *26* **Tinian**[7] 3040 6-10-10 53 ... MrSDobson(3) 2 — —
(KRBurke) *keen: prom to over 4f out: sn lost pl: sddle slipped* **16/1**

060- **9** *4* **Mafruz**[292] 4753 5-11-4 58 ... MrMJMcAlister 4 — —
(RAFahey) *chsd ldrs tl wknd over 3f out* **33/1**

33-0 **10** *15* **Able Mind**[16] 2779 4-11-4 65 ... MrSIrving(7) 1 — —
(ACWhillans) *keen: cl up to over 4f out: sn wknd* **33/1**



The Form Book, Raceform Ltd, Compton, RG20 6NL

6000 **L** **Moyne Pleasure (IRE)**[4] 3149 6-9-7 **38**........................(p) MrPEvans(5) 9 —
(PaulJohnson) *ref to r* **20/1**

2m 19.78s (8.18) **Going Correction** +0.40s/f (Good) **11** Ran SP% **115.5**
Speed ratings: **83,81,81,78,77 75,73,52,49,37** —CSF £56.52 CT £239.48 TOTE £7.10: £2.20, £4.30, £1.90; EX 78.70.
**Owner** Mike Browne **Bred** Barronstown Stud **Trained** Norton, N Yorks

**FOCUS**
Just an ordinary pace for this run-of-the-mill handicap, but a good test in the conditions and sound form. Kingsdon showed the right attitude to notch his fourth straight success.

**NOTEBOOK**
**Kingsdon(IRE)** is in tremendous form and, under a penalty for his latest success, notched his fourth straight win with a gutsy display to beat an in-form rival. He will be up in the weights again, but this was his best form in three years and he should continue to give a good account.
**Scurra**, whose Ayr win had been franked earlier in the week, ran to a similar level in these more testing conditions. He goes on any ground and has been much more consistent of late.
**Pure Mischief(IRE)**, who has been in good nick this year, had conditions to suit and once again gave it his best shot. However, he does look a shade vulnerable from his current mark.
**Opening Ceremony(USA)** was not totally disgraced in the first-time cheekpieces in the softest conditions she has encountered. A return to a sounder surface should suit, but she remains one to tread carefully with.
**Kid'Z'Play(IRE)**, under a 5lb penalty but back in a lower grade, had the run of the race but, unlike at Ayr last time, his response when tackled proved a shade disappointing.
**Every Note Counts** has slipped a fair way in the weights for his current and in-form stable and, although again below his best, left the impression that he may do better back on a sound surface. He is one to keep an eye on.
**Tinian** *Official explanation: jockey said saddle slipped*

## 3266 NORTHERN ROCK GOSFORTH PARK CUP (RATED STKS) (H'CAP) 5f
**7:25** (7:28) (B) (0-105,101) 3-Y-O+ **£17,400** (£6,600; £3,300; £1,500) **Stalls** High

Form RPR
-021 **1** **Caribbean Coral**[20] 2679 5-9-5 **96**........................ RWinston 7 106
(JJQuinn) *hld up: smooth hdwy 2f out: shkn up to ld ins fnl f: kpt on wl* **5/1**[1]
4260 **2** *3/4* **Corridor Creeper (FR)**[6] 3074 7-9-1 **92**..................(p) FNorton 11 99
(JMBradley) *cl up: ev ch over 1f out: kpt on fnl f: nt rch wnr* **12/1**
0125 **3** *3/4* **Steel Blue**[14] 2857 4-9-4 **95**........................ ACulhane 3 99
(RMWhitaker) *led to ins fnl f: kpt on same pce* **8/1**
114- **4** *1/2* **Philharmonic**[258] 5485 3-9-4 **101**........................ PHanagan 9 104
(RAFahey) *hld up: shkn up and hdwy over 1f out: kpt on wl fnl f* **20/1**
4660 **5** *hd* **Halmahera (IRE)**[6] 3074 9-9-7 **98**........................ NCallan 10 100
(KARyan) *hld up: hdwy over 1f out: kpt on fnl f: nrst fin* **16/1**
0100 **6** *nk* **Ptarmigan Ridge**[20] 2679 8-8-4 **84**........................ NMackay(3) 16 85
(MissLAPerratt) *trckd ldrs: rdn 2f out: one pce fnl f* **12/1**
00-0 **7** *1/2* **Funfair Wane**[7] 3052 5-9-4 **95**........................ ANicholls 8 94
(DNicholls) *w ldrs tl rdn and nt qckn fnl f* **33/1**
-004 **8** *shd* **Atlantic Viking (IRE)**[14] 2859 9-9-3 **94**........................ EAhern 1 93
(DNicholls) *trckd ldrs tl rdn and no ex over 1f out* **12/1**
1000 **9** *1 1/4* **Whitbarrow (IRE)**[6] 3074 5-9-6 **97**........................ RHills 6 92
(JMBradley) *hld up: hdwy and prom over 1f out: one pce fnl f* **11/2**[2]
5500 **10** *nk* **Matty Tun**[6] 3074 5-9-1 **92**........................ DaleGibson 5 86
(JBalding) *trckd ldrs tl rdn and outpcd over 1f out* **6/1**[3]
4460 **11** *1/2* **Indian Spark**[6] 3074 10-8-11 **91**........................ TEaves(3) 14 83
(JSGoldie) *in tch: outpcd 1/2-way: n.d after* **10/1**
0000 **12** *hd* **Salviati (USA)**[6] 3074 7-8-7 **84**........................ DeanMcKeown 4 75
(JMBradley) *dwlt: keen and sn prom: rdn and wknd appr fnl f* **16/1**
4300 **13** *nk* **Zarzu**[14] 2859 5-7-13 **81** oh9........................ RThomas(5) 2 71
(CRDore) *hld up: rdn over 2f out: btn fnl f* **25/1**
0100 **14** *4* **Proud Boast**[43] 2065 6-9-0 **91**........................ KDarley 13 68
(DNicholls) *sn pushed along in rr: nvr on terms* **20/1**
0001 **15** *13* **Piccled**[14] 2859 6-8-6 **83**........................ DAllan 15 16
(EJAlston) *bhd: rdn 1/2-way: sn btn* **16/1**

60.11 secs (-1.42) **Going Correction** +0.10s/f (Good)
**WFA** 3 from 4yo+ 6lb **15** Ran SP% **123.6**
Speed ratings: **115,113,112,111,111 111,110,110,108,107 106,106,105,99,78**CSF £62.54 CT £496.89 TOTE £5.70: £2.60, £6.10, £2.70; EX 63.30 Trifecta £682.40 Pool of £1,345.74 - 1.40 winning tickets.
**Owner** Dawson, Green, Quinn, Roberts **Bred** P And C Scott **Trained** Settrington, N Yorks

**FOCUS**
A competitive handicap run at a decent gallop in a smart time, in which the whole field raced in the centre of the track. The form should stand up and both the winner and the fourth look the types to do even better this term.

**NOTEBOOK**
**Caribbean Coral ◆**, who has improved with every outing for his current stable, turned in a career-best effort and, given the way he travelled through the race, he appeals as the type to win another decent handicap this term. He should prove equally effective over six furlongs and is one to keep on the right side.
**Corridor Creeper(FR)**, who found the competition too hot on very fast ground in the Wokingham last time, returned to something like his best. However he has paid the price for his consistency and, as he will be going up in the weights again for this run and will continue to look vulnerable to progressive or well handicapped rivals.
**Steel Blue**, who was a shade disappointing at York, was able to dominate this time and returned to his best. He goes on soft and fast ground but, while usually consistent, may continue to look vulnerable from his current mark.
**Philharmonic ◆** progressed with every outing last year but was making his handicap mark from a stiffish mark and encountering soft ground for the first time after an absence of more than eight months. He caught the eye in no uncertain terms and appeals strongly as the type to win a decent race this term, especially back over six furlongs.
**Halmahera(IRE)**, once again without his usual blinkers, goes on any ground and returned to something like his best. Although high enough in the weights, he looks as though he is being primed for a third consecutive win in Doncaster's Portland Handicap in September.
**Ptarmigan Ridge** had conditions to suit and ran creditably from his wide draw. However he is not the most consistent and is far from certain to put it all in next time.
**Funfair Wane**, back in trip, has slipped in the weights and showed very clear signs of retaining plenty of ability. He will be of interest returned to six furlongs back on a sound surface in the near future.
**Atlantic Viking(IRE)** was not disgraced and, although he handles easy ground, seems more effective on a sound surface and is well worth another chance to confirm the promise of his previous York start.
**Indian Spark** was disappointing in view of his eyecatching Royal Ascot performance but, given he has only won once since April 2002, he remains one to tread carefully with from a win-only perspective.
**Salviati(USA) ◆** won on easy ground last year but is almost certainly more effective on a sound surface and shaped as though better than the bare result. He travelled in his customary strong fashion for much of the way and, as he will be dropped a few pounds for this and usually comes to hand at this time of year, is one to keep an eye on granted more suitable conditions.
**Piccled** *Official explanation: jockey said gelding was unsuited by the soft ground*

## 3267 NITEX.CO.UK MAIDEN FILLIES' STKS 6f
**7:55** (7:56) (D) 3-Y-O **£3,750** (£1,154; £577; £288) **Stalls** High

Form RPR
**1** **Rampage** 3-8-11........................ RHills 3 73
(WJHaggas) *hld up in tch: smooth hdwy over 2f out: led and hung lft appr fnl f: r.o wl* **11/10**[1]
04 **2** *2 1/2* **Brain Washed**[6] 3096 3-8-11........................ DAllan 5 66
(TDEasterby) *cl up: effrt and ev ch over 1f out: kpt on fnl f: nt pce of wnr* **12/1**
3-35 **3** *2 1/2* **Island Spell**[32] 2367 3-8-11 **70**........................ PFessey 7 58
(CGrant) *cl up: led over 2f to appr fnl f: one pce* **13/2**[3]
044- **4** *shd* **Kamenka**[237] 5876 3-8-11 **73**........................ PHanagan 6 58
(RAFahey) *chsd ldrs tl rdn and nt qckn over 1f out* **7/2**[2]
05-0 **5** *1 1/4* **Speed Racer**[17] 2756 3-8-11 **57**........................ KimTinkler 2 54
(DonEnricoIncisa) *led to over 2f out: nt qckn over 1f out* **33/1**
60-5 **6** *1* **Scooby Dooby Do**[74] 1362 3-8-11 **60**........................ DeanMcKeown 1 51
(RMWhitaker) *chsd ldrs tl wknd fr 2f out* **8/1**
**7** *5* **Festive Chimes (IRE)** 3-8-11........................ RWinston 4 36
(JJQuinn) *missed break: sn rcvrd and hld up: effrt and prom 2f out: sn rdn and wknd* **14/1**

1m 15.8s (0.76) **Going Correction** +0.10s/f (Good) **7** Ran SP% **111.6**
Speed ratings: **98,94,91,91,89 88,81**CSF £15.24 TOTE £1.90: £1.50, £4.00; EX 17.30.
**Owner** Cheveley Park Stud **Bred** P Balding **Trained** Newmarket, Suffolk

**FOCUS**
An uncompetitive maiden in which the field raced in the centre. The pace was sound and the winner, who was green on this debut run, is likely to prove better than this bare form in due course.

**NOTEBOOK**
**Rampage ◆**, a 45,000gns half-sister to useful sprinter J M W Turner, created a favourable impression on this racecourse debut, despite running green. Although this bare form is only moderate, she looks the type to improve and is sure to win another race.
**Brain Washed** has improved with every outing to date and again left the impression that the step up to seven furlongs and switch to handicap company would help.
**Island Spell** was not disgraced back on an easy surface, but he did not find as much off the bridle as he might have done. He has had plenty of chances and will not be easy to place successfully.
**Kamenka** was not disgraced on this first start on soft ground on this reappearance run and left the impression that seven furlongs in handicap company back on a sound surface would suit.
**Speed Racer** is going to continue to look vulnerable in this grade.
**Festive Chimes(IRE)**, the fifth foal of a mile winner, shaped a bit better than the bare form suggests and looks the type to do better in ordinary handicaps in due course.

## 3268 CHAMPAGNE LANSON MEDIAN AUCTION MAIDEN STKS 1m (R)
**8:25** (8:25) (D) 3-5-Y-O **£6,708** (£2,064; £1,032; £516) **Stalls** Centre

Form RPR
2 **1** **Mr Mistral**[23] 2596 5-9-7........................ KDarley 1 81
(GWragg) *keen early: sn led: rdn over 1f out: hld on wl fnl f* **11/4**[2]
22 **2** *1* **Long Road (USA)**[34] 2311 3-8-11........................ EAhern 4 79
(JNoseda) *prom: smooth hdwy to press wnr over 1f out: rdn and kpt on fnl f* **4/7**[1]
-033 **3** *10* **Master Theo (USA)**[16] 2777 3-8-11 **77**........................ DeanMcKeown 2 59
(HJCollingridge) *trckd wnr: effrt and ev ch over 2f out: hung lft and wknd over 1f out* **7/1**[3]
0 **4** *9* **Rich Chic (IRE)**[21] 2654 3-8-3........................ NMackay(3) 3 36
(MDHammond) *chsd ldrs tl wknd over 2f out* **40/1**

1m 45.57s (2.09) **Going Correction** +0.40s/f (Good)
**WFA** 3 from 5yo 10lb **4** Ran SP% **105.3**
Speed ratings: **105,104,94,85**CSF £4.56 TOTE £3.20; EX 5.50.
**Owner** Howard Spooner And Partners (II) **Bred** J L C Pearce **Trained** Newmarket, Suffolk

**FOCUS**
A disappointing turnout for the money on offer and, although a couple of progressive types were on show, the steady gallop means this bare form has a shaky look to it.

**NOTEBOOK**
**Mr Mistral** fully confirmed his debut promise and, although he very much had the rub of this tactical race, is open to further improvement. He looks the type to win more races.
**Long Road(USA)** looked the one to beat if handling the conditions but, having travelled strongly, was outbattled in the closing stages by a rival that had been allowed an uncontested lead. He ought to win a similar race even though he has finished second on all his three starts.
**Master Theo(USA)** was below his best on this first start on testing ground. He did not look the easiest of rides and is not going to be easy to place.
**Rich Chic(IRE)** again achieved little.

## 3269 CANTOR ODDS CLAIMING STKS 6f
**8:55** (8:55) (F) 3-Y-O+ **£3,325** (£950; £475) **Stalls** High

Form RPR
6445 **1** **Miss Wizz**[16] 2778 4-7-13 **37**........................(p) RoryMoore(7) 7 52
(WStorey) *hld up in tch: effrt over 2f out: r.o wl to ld cl home* **20/1**
40-0 **2** *nk* **Haulage Man**[9] 2976 6-9-7........................ PHanagan 13 66
(DEddy) *prom: led over 1f out: kpt on wl: hdd cl home* **12/1**
4333 **3** *3* **Best Lead**[9] 2975 5-8-7 **52**........................(b) DTudhope(7) 5 50
(IanEmmerson) *led to over 1f out: nt qckn* **8/1**
0200 **4** *nk* **Type One (IRE)**[22] 2626 6-9-4 **67**........................ RWinston 8 53
(JJQuinn) *trckd ldrs: effrt and ev ch over 1f out: sn outpcd* **7/2**[1]
1030 **5** *2* **Pays D'Amour (IRE)**[8] 3025 7-9-0 **66**........................ AlexGreaves 15 43
(DNicholls) *hld up: effrt 2f out: sn no imp* **5/1**[2]
0626 **6** *1 3/4* **Juwwi**[7] 3043 10-8-12 **58**........................ DarrenWilliams 2 36
(JMBradley) *bhd tl styd on fr over 1f out: n.d* **7/1**[3]
0004 **7** *hd* **Beyond Calculation (USA)**[7] 3043 10-8-12 **56**..................(p) KDarley 12 35
(JMBradley) *in tch: outpcd 1/2-way: n.d after* **7/1**[3]
1025 **8** *1/2* **American Cousin**[9] 2975 9-9-0 **62**........................ ANicholls 10 36
(DNicholls) *hld up: effrt over 2f out: edgd lft and outpcd over 1f out* **15/2**
0-0 **9** *7* **Alpha Zeta**[22] 2621 3-8-9........................ DeanMcKeown 4 17
(CWThornton) *bhd: outpcd 1/2-way: nvr on terms* **66/1**
404L **10** *nk* **Queen Of Night**[9] 2979 4-8-6 **60**........................ ACulhane 1 6
(DWChapman) *rrd s: nvr on terms* **10/1**
0030 **11** *3/4* **Formeric**[46] 1986 8-8-12 **39**........................(v) PFessey 11 10
(MissLCSiddall) *a bhd* **25/1**
600- **12** *nk* **Nothing Daunted**[376] 2392 7-8-9 **55**........................ MLawson(5) 6 11
(TAKCuthbert) *chsd ldrs tl wknd over 2f out* **33/1**
0000 **13** *5* **Bettys Valentine**[9] 2975 4-8-6 **25**........................ EAhern 17 —
(DWBarker) *hld up: rdn 1/2-way: sn btn* **33/1**
00-0 **14** *12* **Cayman Mischief**[174] 424 4-8-5........................ TEaves(3) 3 —
(JamesMoffatt) *chsd ldrs to 1/2-way: sn wknd* **100/1**

1m 15.22s (0.18) **Going Correction** +0.10s/f (Good)
**WFA** 3 from 4yo+ 7lb **14** Ran SP% **120.5**
Speed ratings: **102,101,97,97,94 92,91,91,81,81 80,80,73,57**CSF £231.62 TOTE £24.10: £5.30, £3.50, £2.30; EX 503.70.
**Owner** Tony McCormick **Bred** S Hogg **Trained** Muggleswick, Co Durham

**FOCUS**
An ordinary race of its type in which the field again came down the centre. The gallop was sound, but those racing close to the pace held the edge. Only the first two have been rated as having run to form.
**NOTEBOOK**
**Miss Wizz** looked to have a bit to find at the weights but appreciated the return to this trip and turned in a career-best effort. She will face a stiffer task back in handicap company after reassessment, though.
**Haulage Man**, down in grade, ran creditably and looks well capable of winning a similar race. However the fact that he has not won since April 2002 means he is not one to be lumping on at short odds.
**Best Lead** is a consistent sort who again gave it his best shot. He should continue to give a good account and will not be inconvenienced by the return to five furlongs.
**Type One(IRE)**, dropped in grade and with the headgear left off, was not beaten far but could have been expected to fare better on these terms and he remains one to tread carefully with.
**Pays D'Amour(IRE)** fared the best of those that attempted to come from off the pace but was still below his best and is likely to struggle from his current mark back in competitive handicap company.
**Juwwi** was not totally disgraced considering the race favoured those racing prominently. His style of racing means he needs things to drop perfectly.
**Beyond Calculation(USA)** was below his best but is worth another chance in this grade back on a sound surface.

## 3270 WEATHERBYS BANK H'CAP — 5f
9:25 (9:25) (E) (0-75,70) 3-Y-O — £5,148 (£1,584; £792; £396) Stalls High

Form — RPR
-014 1 **Icenaslice (IRE)**[14] 2850 3-8-6 62 ........ DTudhope(7) 8 — 74
(JJQuinn) *trckd ldrs: effrt 2f out: kpt on fnl f to ld cl home* — **11/2**[3]
5310 2 hd **Blue Power (IRE)**[6] 3077 3-8-9 58 ........ DarrenWilliams 2 — 69
(KRBurke) *cl up: led 1f out: edgd lft: r.o fnl f: hdd cl home* — **13/2**
2025 3 nk **Hello Roberto**[109] 986 3-9-2 65 ........ RWinston 6 — 75
(MJPolglase) *hld up in tch: effrt 2f out: kpt on fnl f* — **6/1**
-204 4 1 **Volaticus (IRE)**[28] 2457 3-8-9 58 ........ (v[1]) ANicholls 5 — 65
(DNicholls) *keen: prom: rdn 2f out: kpt on same pce fnl f* — **10/1**
6020 5 hd **Sweet Cando (IRE)**[2] 3201 3-8-7 59 ........ (p) NMackay(3) 4 — 65
(MissLAPerratt) *prom: effrt 2f out: one pce fnl f* — **9/4**[1]
-003 6 1 **Jadan (IRE)**[2] 3201 3-9-7 70 ........ EAhern 7 — 73
(EJAlston) *led to 1f out: sn outpcd* — **4/1**[2]
00-0 7 2 ½ **Sir Loin**[21] 2650 3-8-11 60 ........ KimTinkler 3 — 55
(NTinkler) *trckd ldrs tl wknd over 1f out* — **25/1**
6030 8 2 ½ **Lord Baskerville**[32] 2351 3-8-1 57 ........ RoryMoore(7) 1 — 44
(WStorey) *in tch tl wknd fr 2f out* — **12/1**
62.21 secs (0.68) **Going Correction** +0.10s/f (Good) — **8 Ran SP% 114.4**
Speed ratings: **98,97,97,95,95 93,89,85**CSF £40.77 CT £223.20 TOTE £6.30: £2.20, £1.80, £1.70; EX 19.40 Place 6 £772.98, Place 5 £365.36.
**Owner** Miss D A Johnson **Bred** Mrs Roseanne And Paul McEnery **Trained** Settrington, N Yorks

**FOCUS**
A run-of-the-mill handicap comprising mainly exposed types. The runners again raced in the centre and the gallop was fair, so the form should prove reliable granted similar conditions.
**NOTEBOOK**
**Icenaslice(IRE)**, from an in-form stable, turned in a career-best effort back on turf. She should not be going up too much for this win and may be capable of better at a similar level.
**Blue Power(IRE)**, back on soft ground, ran his best race on turf and looks the type that will always be best suited to a test of speed. He is capable of winning a similar race if kept away from progressive types.
**Hello Roberto** is a consistent sort who ran up to his best on this first start for nearly four months. He has not won since last July but should continue to give a good account.
**Volaticus(IRE)** was not disgraced after taking a grip in the first-time visor and left the impression that the return to six furlongs would be in his favour. He is capable of winning a similar race.
**Sweet Cando(IRE)** jumped off on terms this time and ran creditably, but she will find life tougher in handicaps from now on as she is due to go up a further 6lb.
**Jadan(IRE)**, turned out quickly, was not disgraced but left the impression that the return to a sounder surface would be in his favour.
T/Jkpt: Not won. T/Plt: £270.40 to a £1 stake. Pool: £58,728.15. 158.50 winning tickets. T/Qpdt: £106.00 to a £1 stake. Pool: £2,766.80. 19.30 winning tickets. RY

# 3089 NEWMARKET (JULY) (R-H)
Friday, June 25

**OFFICIAL GOING: Good to firm**
As last week the stalls were placed on the far side, but there appeared no bias in the draw. A dry day saw the going change to good to firm.
Wind: Almost nil Weather: Sunny spells

## 3271 NEWMARKET NIGHTS CLAIMING STKS — 1m
6:40 (6:42) (E) 3-Y-O — £3,393 (£1,044; £522; £261) Stalls Low

Form — RPR
0-01 1 **The Fun Merchant**[8] 3002 3-8-1 63 ........ LisaJones(3) 6 — 64
(DCarroll) *chsd ldrs: rdn to ld ins fnl f: r.o* — **7/2**[2]
1-40 2 1 ¼ **Arkholme**[20] 2683 3-9-4 78 ........ (b[1]) DHolland 4 — 75
(WJHaggas) *hld up in tch: rdn over 1f out: r.o* — **13/2**
0-00 3 1 **Yashin (IRE)**[8] 3025 3-8-7 60 ........ JFanning 10 — 62
(MHTompkins) *plld hrd: led 7f out: rdn over 1f out: hdd and unable qck ins fnl f* — **50/1**
3101 4 nk **Lady Piste (IRE)**[31] 2379 3-8-0 61 ........ AMcCarthy 5 — 54
(GGMargarson) *led 1f: w ldr: rdn over 1f out: no ex ins fnl f* — **9/1**
0615 5 1 ½ **Western Roots**[7] 3039 3-8-10 78 ........ LDettori 8 — 61
(KAMorgan) *hld up: hdwy over 2f out: sn rdn: styd on* — **11/2**[3]
-600 6 ½ **Wizard Looking**[16] 2790 3-8-3 65 ........ (t) RLMoore 3 — 53
(RHannon) *hld up: hdwy over 1f out: nvr trbld ldrs* — **11/1**
1012 7 shd **Hawkit (USA)**[11] 2949 3-9-4 74 ........ KFallon 1 — 67
(PDEvans) *prom: lost pl 7f out: rdn over 2f out: styd on ins fnl f: nt trble ldrs: fin lame* — **2/1**[1]
0000 8 2 ½ **Eizawina Docklands**[8] 3002 3-8-3 ........ (t) JQuinn 2 — 47
(NPLittmoden) *hld up: sme hdwy over 1f out: n.d* — **50/1**
5033 9 1 ¼ **Four Kings**[9] 2973 3-8-2 63 ........ (t) FPFerris(3) 7 — 46
(JMPEustace) *dwlt: hld up: hdwy over 2f out: wknd over 1f out* — **14/1**
00- 10 9 **Saccharine**[276] 5142 3-7-12 ........ JBramhill 9 — 18
(NPLittmoden) *chsd ldrs over 5f* — **50/1**
1m 39.0s (-1.48) **Going Correction** +0.075s/f (Good) — **10 Ran SP% 115.2**
Speed ratings: **110,108,107,107,105 105,105,102,101,92**CSF £26.00 TOTE £5.20: £2.10, £2.70, £11.20; EX 38.90.The winner was claimed by Jeff Pearce for £11,000.
**Owner** Diamond Racing Ltd **Bred** Lostford Manor Stud **Trained** Warthill, N Yorks

**FOCUS**
A moderate contest run at a steady pace, which suited those racing handy. Despite that, the time was good for a claimer. The race has been rated through the third.
**NOTEBOOK**
**The Fun Merchant**, in the same ownership as the disappointing favourite, has certainly found his form since stepping up to this trip. Lightly raced, there should be more to come.
**Arkholme** was a bit keen early on in the first-time blinkers, on ground which would have been plenty quick enough for him. He should be capable of scoring in this grade.
**Yashin(IRE)**, stepping up in trip, was far too free early on and didn't quite get home. Still, this wasn't a bad effort on these terms.
**Lady Piste(IRE)** ran well enough over a trip which just seemed to stretch her.
**Western Roots** may have found this ground quicker than ideal.
**Hawkit(USA)** didn't move that well to post and was later found to be lame. *Official explanation: vet said gelding finished lame on the right foreleg*

## 3272 MOZART'S BISTRO EBF MAIDEN FILLIES' STKS — 6f
7:10 (7:11) (D) 2-Y-O — £4,745 (£1,460; £730; £365) Stalls Low

Form — RPR
1 **Borthwick Girl (IRE)** 2-8-11 ........ JFortune 6 — 76+
(BJMeehan) *chsd ldr tl led over 1f out: edgd lft ins fnl f: rdn clr* — **2/1**[1]
54 2 3 **Miss Cotswold Lady**[11] 2940 2-8-11 ........ JQuinn 5 — 67
(AWCarroll) *led over 4f: rdn and nt clr run ins fnl f: styd on same pce* **20/1**
3 1 ¼ **Keep Backckinhit (IRE)** 2-8-11 ........ RLMoore 8 — 63
(GLMoore) *s.i.s: hld up: hdwy over 2f out: one pce fnl f* — **9/1**
4 1 ¾ **Gennie Bond** 2-8-11 ........ RHughes 3 — 58
(RHannon) *dwlt: hdwy 1/2-way: sn rdn: wknd over 1f out* — **9/4**[2]
5 ¾ **Rosapenna (IRE)** 2-8-11 ........ RMullen 7 — 56
(CFWall) *chsd ldrs tl wknd ins fnl f* — **12/1**
6 3 ½ **Nordhock (USA)** 2-8-11 ........ AMackay 2 — 45
(NACallaghan) *sn outpcd* — **14/1**
7 2 ½ **Sabbiosa (IRE)** 2-8-11 ........ TQuinn 4 — 38
(JLDunlop) *chsd ldrs over 3f* — **5/1**[3]
1m 15.2s (1.88) **Going Correction** +0.075s/f (Good) — **7 Ran SP% 109.9**
Speed ratings: **90,86,84,82,81 76,73**CSF £37.26 TOTE £3.50: £2.40, £2.90; EX 36.60.
**Owner** Mrs Wendy English **Bred** Larry Ryan **Trained** Upper Lambourn, Berks
■ Stewards Enquiry : J Fortune caution: careless riding

**FOCUS**
This didn't look a good maiden by course standards and the pace was only steady.
**NOTEBOOK**
**Borthwick Girl(IRE)**, out of a mare that won over this trip as a juvenile, at least knew her job, unlike most of her rivals. While she is open to improvement, she will need to if she is to add to this.
**Miss Cotswold Lady** had the run of the race here and had no excuses.
**Keep Backckinhit(IRE)**, out of a mare that won as a juvenile, did not shape too badly and looks sure to benefit from the experience.
**Gennie Bond**, a half-sister to several sprint winners, was too green to do herself justice.
**Rosapenna(IRE)**, an early foal, ran as though she needed the outing. Better can be expected as she steps up in trip.
**Sabbiosa(IRE)**, out of a staying mare and from the same family as the high-class Snurge, should do better next year when tackling middle-distances.

## 3273 SIEMENS SMART HOME TECHNOLOGY H'CAP — 5f
7:40 (7:42) (D) (0-85,86) 3-Y-O — £5,434 (£1,672; £836; £418) Stalls Low

Form — RPR
4-00 1 **Jimmy Ryan (IRE)**[23] 2589 3-9-0 81 ........ J-PGuillambert(3) 7 — 92
(TDMcCarthy) *racd far side: chsd ldrs: led over 1f out: rdn and hung rt ins fnl f: r.o* — **20/1**
-122 2 1 ¼ **Tony The Tap**[6] 3092 3-9-1 79 ........ TQuinn 10 — 85
(NACallaghan) *swtchd to r stands' side over 4f out: led that duo: rdn over 1f out : r.o* — **5/4**[1]
-000 3 ½ **Silver Prelude**[13] 2877 3-9-2 80 ........ DHolland 4 — 84
(DKIvory) *racd far side: led: hdd over 3f out: rdn and ev ch over 1f out: no ex ins fnl f* — **20/1**
6004 4 1 ½ **Incise**[13] 2892 3-9-7 85 ........ (t) LDettori 2 — 83
(BJMeehan) *racd far side: chsd ldrs: rdn over 1f out: styd on same pce* — **13/2**[3]
-005 5 1 **Tribute (IRE)**[18] 2726 3-8-10 77 ........ (v[1]) TPQueally(3) 11 — 71
(DRLoder) *swtchd to chse ldr stands' side over 4f out: rdn over 1f out: styd on same pce* — **12/1**
5-02 6 nk **Signor Panettiere**[35] 2266 3-8-6 70 ........ PDobbs 1 — 63
(RHannon) *racd far side: chsd ldrs: rdn over 1f out: styd on same pce* — **10/1**
0361 7 hd **Divine Spirit**[6] 3077 3-9-5 86 7ex ........ LEnstone(3) 8 — 78
(MDods) *racd far side: chsd ldrs: rdn 1/2-way: hung rt and no ex over 1f out* — **11/2**[2]
1645 8 shd **Tizzy's Law**[21] 2650 3-8-3 67 ........ JBramhill 9 — 59
(MABuckley) *racd far side: led over 3f out: hung rt and hdd over 1f out: no ex* — **20/1**
2030 9 2 ½ **Sahara Silk (IRE)**[6] 3077 3-7-9 62 ........ (v) JFMcDonald(3) 5 — 44
(DShaw) *racd far side: sn outpcd* — **25/1**
0014 10 1 ¼ **Party Princess (IRE)**[18] 2741 3-8-0 64 ........ JQuinn 3 — 41
(JAGlover) *racd far side: chsd ldrs over 3f* — **10/1**
6-24 11 1 ¾ **Green Ridge**[3] 3179 3-8-4 68 ........ PaulEddery 6 — 38
(PWD'Arcy) *s.s: racd far side: outpcd* — **25/1**
58.41 secs (-1.24) **Going Correction** +0.075s/f (Good) — **11 Ran SP% 121.0**
Speed ratings: **112,110,109,106,105 104,104,104,100,98 95**CSF £43.90 CT £558.28 TOTE £21.80: £4.50, £1.20, £5.40; EX 90.80.
**Owner** James Ryan **Bred** Barronstown Stud And Orpendale **Trained** Godstone, Surrey

**FOCUS**
A messy race with the field splitting into two groups, but it was run at a fair clip and the time was good, so the form should stand up.
**NOTEBOOK**
**Jimmy Ryan(IRE)**, who took a fair grip to post, proved well suited by this strongly-run five and showed improved form. Fast ground suits him well. *Official explanation: trainer said, regarding the improved form shown, colt had settled better today having not been held up*
**Tony The Tap**, who went to post down the stands' side, was switched to race up the same side on the return, despite the stalls being placed on the far side. He is a genuine sort who deserves a change of luck.
**Silver Prelude** is beginning to drop in the weights and showed a bit more than of late. He looks to be returning to last year's nursery form.
**Incise** found this more her level, but she found little off the bridle having travelled well on the heels of leaders.
**Tribute(IRE)** followed the leader over to the stands' side, but never really looked like taking a hand in the first-time blinkers. A return to six-furlongs may help him.
**Signor Panettiere**, 3lbs higher than when beaten at Bath, had no excuses.
**Divine Spirit** *Official explanation: jockey said gelding hung right-handed*
**Green Ridge** *Official explanation: jockey said filly missed the break and jumped slowly from the stalls*

## 3274 NEWMARKETRACECOURSES.CO.UK RATED STKS (H'CAP) 1m 2f
8:10 (8:13) (D) (0-85,79) 3-Y-O+ £4,865 (£1,845; £666; £666) Stalls Centre

Form RPR
/034 1 **Ken's Dream**[18] 2738 5-9-10 **79**.............................. PMcCabe 6 87
(MsAEEmbiricos) *hld up: hdwy 2f out: nt clr run over 1f out: r.o to ld wl ins fnl f* **9/1**
0400 2 3/4 **Baileys Dancer**[23] 2587 3-8-7 **74**.............................. JFanning 7 81
(MJohnston) *led to 1/2-way: led 3f out: rdn over 1f out: hung lft and hdd wl ins fnl f* **9/1**
0065 3 nk **Kylkenny**[13] 2895 9-9-3 **72**..............................(t) JFortune 5 78
(HMorrison) *chsd ldrs: rdn over 2f out: ev ch over 1f out: unable qck nr fin* **7/2**[2]
1005 3 dht **Rasid (USA)**[13] 2881 6-9-4 **73**.............................. DHolland 9 79
(CADwyer) *sn pushed along and prom: nt clr run over 1f out: r.o: hmpd towards fin* **9/1**
3343 5 3/4 **Street Life (IRE)**[14] 2845 6-9-4 **73**.............................. KFallon 3 78
(WJMusson) *hld up in tch: pushed along over 3f out: nt clr run over 1f out: r.o: nvr able to chal* **11/4**[1]
3230 6 nk **Blazing The Trail (IRE)**[25] 2537 4-8-10 **65**.............................. MHills 1 69
(JWHills) *hld up: hdwy over 2f out: sn rdn: no ex towards fin* **5/1**[3]
0-60 7 1 3/4 **Glimmer Of Light (IRE)**[18] 2738 4-9-4 **73**.............................. IMongan 8 74
(PWHarris) *chsd ldr tl led 1/2-way: hdd 3f out: sn rdn: ev ch over 1f out: no ex ins fnl f* **14/1**
-623 8 1 3/4 **Piri Piri (IRE)**[16] 2782 4-8-13 **68**.............................. SWhitworth 2 65
(PJMcbride) *s.s: hld up: hdwy over 1f out: wknd ins fnl f* **11/2**

2m 5.13s (-1.33) **Going Correction** +0.075s/f (Good) **8 Ran SP% 117.6**
**WFA** 3 from 4yo+ 12lb
Speed ratings: **108,107,107,107,106 106,104,103**CSF £87.88 TOTE £12.00: £2.60, £2.20; EX 99.20 TRIFECTA Pl: Rasid 1.20, Kylkenny 1.00; Tri: Ken's Dream / Bailey's Dancer / Rasid £378.43, Ken's Dream / Bailey's Dancer / Kylkenny £170.64.
**Owner** Michael Underwood **Bred** Colin Bothway **Trained** Newmarket, Suffolk

**FOCUS**
The pace was sound, but there were plenty of traffic problems in the dip and they finished in a heap. The form is unconvincing.

**NOTEBOOK**
**Ken's Dream** had a dream run up the rails as others struggled for a run, and won without having to do too much.
**Baileys Dancer**, tackling older horses for the first time, turned in a solid effort and proved difficult to pass.
**Rasid(USA)**, for whom the ground would have been fast enough, turned in his best effort for a while, despite not having the best of runs.
**Kylkenny**, much better treated on turf than the All-Weather, had every chance on ground which was plenty quick enough for him.
**Street Life(IRE)** is a frustrating sort who needs everything to go his way.
**Blazing The Trail(IRE)**, forced to launch his challenge out wide, is yet to win on turf but again showed enough to suggest it is only a matter of time.
**Piri Piri(IRE)** *Official explanation: trainer's representative said filly was showing signs of possibly coming into season*

## 3275 VIBEFM.CO.UK FILLIES' CONDITIONS STKS 6f
8:40 (8:40) (C) 3-Y-O+ £8,294 (£3,146; £1,573; £715) Stalls Low

Form RPR
4604 1 **Grey Pearl**[6] 3090 5-8-5 81.............................. MFenton 1 90
(MissGayKelleway) *led: hdd over 4f out: led 2f out: hrd rdn fnl f: r.o* **20/1**
-260 2 1/2 **Cusco (IRE)**[9] 2971 3-8-1 89.............................. RSmith 2 91
(RHannon) *led over 4f out: hdd 2f out: sn rdn: r.o* **16/1**
5-23 3 1/2 **Topkamp**[13] 2903 4-8-6 104 ow1.............................. KFallon 4 88
(MLWBell) *trckd ldrs: plld hrd: rdn over 1f out: r.o* **1/2**[1]
0000 4 1/2 **Valjarv (IRE)**[6] 3105 3-8-1 93 ow3..............................(b[1]) TPQueally(3) 6 91
(NPLittmoden) *hld up: rdn over 2f out: hdwy and nt clr run over 1f out: r.o: nvr able to chal* **10/1**
614- 5 4 **Anthos (GER)**[295] 4692 3-7-12 93.............................. CCatlin 5 73
(JRFanshawe) *hld up: hdwy over 2f out: wknd over 1f out* **11/2**[2]
03-0 6 1/2 **Tentative (USA)**[59] 1685 3-8-1 90.............................. JQuinn 3 75
(RCharlton) *dwlt: hld up: hdwy over 2f out: wknd over 1f out* **9/1**[3]

1m 14.76s (1.44) **Going Correction** +0.075s/f (Good) **6 Ran SP% 111.8**
**WFA** 3 from 4yo+ 7lb
Speed ratings: **93,92,91,91,85 85**CSF £252.67 TOTE £10.80: £3.00, £4.50; EX 122.90.
**Owner** Andrea Wilkinson Gay Kelleway **Bred** Miss J Chaplin **Trained** Newmarket, Suffolk

**FOCUS**
A fair contest for the grade, but no pace and a slow time. The favourite failed to run her race, but the other principals have still been rated as having shown improved form.

**NOTEBOOK**
**Grey Pearl** had plenty to find on official figures, but she settled better than most of her rivals, and proved a willing partner at the business end. Her trainer will now try and get some "black type" for her, as she is destined for the paddocks next year.
**Cusco(IRE)**, who had been campaigned over further, had something of a soft lead, but battled on bravely when headed.
**Topkamp** found the lack of pace against her and did herself no favours by refusing to settle. She was a long way below form.
**Valjarv(IRE)**, sharpened up by the first-time blinkers, was another who would have been better suited by a stronger pace.
**Anthos(GER)**, although from a yard in fine form, dropped away tamely and may have needed this run.
**Tentative(USA)** dropped away tamely and looks to have something to prove now.

## 3276 LTM DIGITAL RATED STKS (H'CAP) 1m 4f
9:10 (9:11) (D) (0-85,85) 4-Y-O+ £4,848 (£1,839; £919; £418) Stalls Centre

Form RPR
0001 1 **Wait For The Will (USA)**[7] 3046 8-9-9 **85** 3ex..............................(b) RLMoore 7 91
(GLMoore) *trckd ldrs: nt clr run over 1f out: r.o to ld wl ins fnl f* **15/8**[1]
4/3- 2 3/4 **Genghis (IRE)**[426] 1221 5-9-4 **80**.............................. JFortune 4 85
(HMorrison) *led: rdn over 1f out: edgd lft: hdd and unable qck wl ins fnl f* **11/2**
5044 3 1 1/4 **Flotta**[14] 2855 5-9-3 **82**.............................. SHitchcott(3) 6 85
(MRChannon) *hld up: hdwy and nt clr run over 1f out: edgd lft 1f out: styd on* **3/1**[2]
323- 4 1 **Bendarshaan**[68] 4-9-7 **83**.............................. JFanning 2 84
(MJohnston) *chsd ldr: rdn over 2f out: ev ch over 1f out: no ex ins fnl f* **10/1**
40-0 5 1 3/4 **Team-Mate (IRE)**[139] 706 6-8-13 **78**.............................. BReilly(3) 3 76
(MissJFeilden) *hld up: hdwy over 1f out: no ex ins fnl f* **14/1**
0204 6 nk **Dovedon Hero**[13] 2893 4-9-0 **76**..............................(b) SSanders 1 74
(PJMcbride) *hld up: hdwy over 1f out: rdn whn bmpd 1f out: sn btn* **9/2**[3]
3606 7 5 **Sir Haydn**[35] 2277 4-8-2 **67**..............................(v[1]) LisaJones(3) 5 57
(JRJenkins) *dwlt: hld up: plld hrd: hdwy over 8f out: wknd over 1f out* **14/1**

2m 34.91s (1.95) **Going Correction** +0.075s/f (Good) **7 Ran SP% 115.8**
Speed ratings: **96,95,94,94,92 92,89**CSF £13.11 TOTE £3.00: £2.10, £2.20; EX 12.50 Place 6 £1,623.96, Place 5 £499.54.
**Owner** Rdm Racing **Bred** Paul Mellon **Trained** Woodingdean, E Sussex

**FOCUS**
Another slowly-run race which resulted in a moderate time and plenty of trouble in the dip. The form is nothing special.

**NOTEBOOK**
**Wait For The Will(USA)** had his optimum conditions and won a shade more cosily than the verdict suggested. Already due to go up another 6lb, before this success, he will not find things so easy in the future.
**Genghis(IRE)** had something of a soft lead on this return to action and didn't go down without a fight. Although he remains a maiden, he does have ability.
**Flotta** didn't have the best of runs and may have done better had more use been made of him.
**Bendarshaan** was not disgraced on this return to Britain. Due to go down 3lb in future events, he can be placed to advantage.
**Team-Mate(IRE)** isn't the most straightforward of rides and would not have been suited to the slow place. He can be expected to strip sharper for this outing.
**Dovedon Hero** is in danger of becoming well-treated, but he is a frustrating animal who needs things to go his way.
T/Plt: £1,730.20 to a £1 stake. Pool: £49,536.00. 20.90 winning tickets. T/Qpdt: £193.20 to a £1 stake. Pool: £4,021.80. 15.40 winning tickets. CR

# 3021 SOUTHWELL (L-H)
Friday, June 25

**OFFICIAL GOING: Standard**
Wind: Slight 1/2 behind. Weather: Fine and Sunny.

## 3277 FEAST OF THE OPTIONAL HOLIDAY H'CAP 6f (F)
2:20 (2:24) (F) (0-55,60) 3-Y-O+ £3,038 (£868; £434) Stalls Low

Form RPR
0341 1 **Never Without Me**[8] 3025 4-9-12 **60** 6ex.............................. MSavage(5) 1 75
(JFCoupland) *mde virtually all: hld on towards fin* **5/1**[1]
-000 2 nk **Jagged (IRE)**[39] 2166 4-9-8 **51**..............................(v[1]) NCallan 10 65
(JRJenkins) *chsd ldrs: chal and edgd rt over 1f out: styd on towards fin* **10/1**
-416 3 2 1/2 **Mallia**[8] 3024 11-8-10 **46**.............................. Laura-JayneCrawford(7) 15 53
(TDBarron) *bhd: styd on wl fnl 2f: nt rch ldrs* **14/1**
5365 4 3/4 **Mr Uppity**[15] 2823 5-8-3 **39**..............................(e) MHalford(7) 16 43
(JulianPoulton) *dwlt: racd wd: bhd tl styd on wl fnl 2f* **20/1**
3000 5 1/2 **New Options**[21] 2666 7-9-2 **48**..............................(b) LisaJones(3) 3 51
(WJMusson) *chsd ldrs: kpt on same pce fnl 2f* **25/1**
3324 6 3/4 **Indian Music**[8] 3024 7-9-1 **44**.............................. FLynch 13 45
(ABerry) *sn bhd: kpt on fnl 2f: nt rch ldrs* **12/1**
4002 7 shd **Kennington**[15] 2823 4-9-6 **54**..............................(v) HayleyTurner(5) 4 54
(MrsCADunnett) *w ldrs: wknd appr fnl f* **15/2**
5030 8 3 1/2 **Star Lad (IRE)**[13] 2885 4-9-2 **45**..............................(b) FNorton 8 35
(RBrotherton) *chsd ldrs: outpcd over 2f out: n.d after* **33/1**
1052 9 1/2 **Lucius Verrus (USA)**[21] 2663 4-9-9 **52**..............................(v) DarrenWilliams 12 40
(DShaw) *in tch: effrt over 2f out: nvr able chal* **9/1**
0065 10 1 3/4 **African Spur (IRE)**[4] 3148 4-9-1 **51**..............................(p) DTudhope(7) 9 34
(DCarroll) *chsd ldrs: wkng whn n.m.r over 1f out* **6/1**[2]
2331 11 1/2 **Levelled**[39] 2183 10-9-4 **47**.............................. GDuffield 11 28
(DWChapman) *dwlt: nvr on terms* **14/1**
2210 12 3/4 **Alastair Smellie**[41] 2123 8-9-4 **47**.............................. PMcCabe 2 26
(SLKeightley) *unruly s: a bhd* **20/1**
1350 13 hd **Rathmullan**[27] 2473 5-8-4 **40**..............................(b) LiamJones(7) 5 19
(EAWheeler) *sn wl bhd and drvn along: sme late hdwy* **20/1**
2151 14 1 1/2 **Turn Around**[8] 3024 4-10-0 **57** 6ex.............................. DeanMcKeown 7 31
(PABlockley) *dwlt: mid-div whn hung rt 3f out: sn lost pl* **7/1**[3]
3000 15 3/4 **Playful Spirit**[20] 2670 5-9-3 **46**..............................(v) JEdmunds 14 18
(JBalding) *chsd ldrs: edgd rt and lost pl over 1f out* **16/1**
6040 16 9 **Sounds Lucky**[57] 1738 8-9-10 **53**..............................(b) IMongan 6 —
(AndrewReid) *chsd ldrs: lost pl over 2f out: sn bhd and eased* **33/1**

1m 16.35s (-0.55) **Going Correction** -0.025s/f (Stan) **16 Ran SP% 125.2**
Speed ratings: **102,101,98,97,96 95,95,90,90,87 87,86,85,83,82 70**CSF £50.07 CT £699.96 TOTE £6.50: £1.80, £1.50, £6.50, £6.60; EX 58.80.
**Owner** J F Coupland **Bred** Miss Nathalie Lismonde **Trained** Grimsby, Lincs

**FOCUS**
An ordinary handicap, but the first two came clear and showed solid form.

**NOTEBOOK**
**Never Without Me**, hoisted 7lb after his win here last week, overcame a 6lb penalty, capitalising on the best of the draw and refusing to be denied.
**Jagged(IRE)**, down 9lb after three below-par efforts this time, had a visor on for the first time and very nearly made it 19th time lucky.
**Mallia**, drawn one from the outside, retains his enthusiasm in his 12th year.
**Mr Uppity**, worst drawn, missed the break slightly but put in some sterling late work. After 23 attempts now he has yet to taste victory.
**New Options** has slipped to a lenient mark but seems to have lost the winning habit.
**Indian Music** stayed on when it was all over and will be able to race from a lower mark in future.
**Star Lad(IRE)** *Official explanation: jockey said gelding had been struck into*
**Turn Around**, very weak in the market on his first outing for his new yard, became upset in the stalls, missed the break and then threw his head in the air turning in apparently resenting the kickback. *Official explanation: jockey said gelding became upset in the stalls, was slowly away and resented the kickback*

## 3278 CUSTER'S LAST STAND (S) STKS 7f (F)
2:50 (2:51) (G) 2-Y-O £2,548 (£728; £364) Stalls Low

Form RPR
05 1 **Diction (IRE)**[22] 2622 2-8-6.............................. DarrenWilliams 3 59+
(KRBurke) *trckd ldrs: led over 1f out: drvn clr: heavily eased nr fin* **7/2**[2]
000 2 4 **Diatonic**[14] 2858 2-8-8.............................. LisaJones(3) 6 47
(WJMusson) *chsd ldrs: outpcd over 3f out: styd on to take 2nd 1f out* **4/1**[3]
40 3 6 **Monashee Miss**[14] 2852 2-8-6.............................. DeanMcKeown 1 27
(JAPickering) *swvd rt s: sn chsng ldrs: led over 4f out: hdd over 1f out: sn wknd* **25/1**
34 4 3 **Petite Elle**[23] 2593 2-7-13.............................. KJackson(7) 7 20
(PJMcbride) *chsd ldrs on outer: effrt over 4f out: wknd over 1f out* **5/1**
036 5 1 3/4 **Concert Time**[32] 2364 2-8-1.............................. RThomas(5) 5 15
(CRDore) *led tl over 4f out: wknd over 1f out* **5/2**[1]

0 **6** *3* **Petite Noire**[78] 1307 2-8-6 ow3........(t) SHitchcott(3) 2 11
(JGPortman) *s.i.s: hdwy to chse ldrs over 3f out: lost pl over 1f out* **14/1**
4410 **7** *6* **Bowland Bride (IRE)**[22] 2622 2-8-5........ PPMathers(7) 4 —
(ABerry) *chsd ldrs: drvn along over 4f out: lost pl 3f out* **11/2**

1m 33.16s (2.36) **Going Correction** -0.025s/f (Stan) **7** Ran SP% **113.4**
Speed ratings: **85,80,73,70,68 64,57**CSF £17.53 TOTE £5.90: £1.60, £2.40; EX 15.60.There was no bid for the winner. Diatonic was claimed by Diamond Racing Ltd for £6,000.
**Owner** J C S Wilson **Bred** Heatherwold Stud **Trained** Middleham Moor, N Yorks

**FOCUS**
A rock bottom seller, but the winner was impressive and the runner-up improved a little for the step up in trip.

**NOTEBOOK**
**Diction(IRE)**, bred for stamina on her dam's side, was having her first taste of the All-Weather and proved different class. This was a very poor event though.
**Diatonic**, an excitable-type, proved suited by the step up in trip and is now expected to join Declan Carroll.
**Monashee Miss** had finished ahead of just two opponents in two previous starts, albeit in better class.
**Petite Elle** didn't seem to see out the extra furlong.
**Concert Time**, stepping up in trip on her All-Weather bow, didn't see the trip out by a fair way.

## 3279 ST EUROSIA'S DAY MAIDEN STKS 6f (F)
3:20 (3:21) (D) 3-Y-O+ £3,503 (£1,078; £539; £269) Stalls Low

Form RPR
0450 **1** **Point Calimere (IRE)**[43] 2064 3-9-0 70........(b1) NCallan 5 65
(CREgerton) *w ldr: led on bit over 2f out: shkn up and qcknd appr fnl f: rdn ins last: edgd rt: jst hld on* **11/4**[2]
00 **2** *nk* **Desert Leader (IRE)**[21] 2654 3-9-0........ GGibbons 11 64
(BAMcmahon) *hld up: hdwy on outer 2f out: styd on wl ins last: jst hld* **13/2**
5/ **3** *2 1/2* **Silent Storm**[672] 4108 4-9-7........ FLynch 10 56
(HJCyzer) *racd wd: chsd ldrs: outpcd 3f out: styd on ins last* **7/2**[3]
600 **4** *shd* **Irusan (IRE)**[22] 2621 4-9-0 57........ LeanneKershaw(7) 8 56
(JeddO'Keeffe) *chsd ldrs: outpcd over 3f out: hung lft: edgd lft 1f out: kpt on ins last* **12/1**
34 **5** *3 1/2* **Wunderbra (IRE)**[15] 2815 3-8-9........ IMongan 1 41
(MLWBell) *led tl over 2f out: weakend fnl f* **9/4**[1]
**6** *5* **Classic Expression** 3-8-9........ SRighton 6 26
(BAMcmahon) *s.i.s: bhd and drvn along: sme late hdwy* **14/1**
00-0 **7** *1/2* **Silver Island**[14] 2853 3-8-11........ LisaJones(3) 2 29
(RMHCowell) *chsd ldrs: n.m.r and lost pl over 3f out: n.d after* **33/1**
0 **8** *3/4* **Bank Games**[9] 2984 3-9-0........ DaleGibson 7 27
(MWEasterby) *chsd ldng pair: lost pl over 2f out* **40/1**
00 **9** *1 3/4* **Narciso (GER)**[16] 2777 4-9-7........ TLucas 3 22
(MWEasterby) *sn bhd and drvn along* **33/1**
0-00 **10** *2 1/2* **Savannah Sue**[15] 2815 3-8-9........ JBramhill 12 9
(JRNorton) *chsd ldrs: outpcd over 3f out: sn lost pl* **66/1**
00- **11** *shd* **Lord Arthur**[231] 5938 3-8-9........ PMulrennan(5) 4 14
(MWEasterby) *s.s: sn outpcd and bhd* **25/1**
**12** *10* **Peters Ploy** 4-9-4........ J-PGuillambert(3) 9 —
(TKeddy) *bhd and drvn along: t.o* **33/1**

1m 16.31s (-0.59) **Going Correction** -0.025s/f (Stan)
**WFA** 3 from 4yo 7lb **12** Ran SP% **124.0**
Speed ratings: **102,101,98,98,93 86,86,85,82,79 79,66**CSF £20.83 TOTE £5.50: £2.30, £3.70, £2.30; EX 33.20.
**Owner** Sangster Family & C R Egerton **Bred** Swettenham Stud **Trained** Chaddleworth, Berks

**FOCUS**
A very modest maiden. The winner didn't need to run up to his best, but the placed horses have a little potential.

**NOTEBOOK**
**Point Calimere(IRE)**looked very fit indeed and had first-time blinkers, but after taking it up running away only just lasted home.
**Desert Leader(IRE)** ◆, a rangy, well-made type, had run over a mile on his two previous outings. He was mowing the winner down at the line and should make his mark in handicap company.
**Silent Storm**, who showed ability in one start at two, changed hands cheaply at the autumn sales. He raced wide but after getting outpaced turning in he picked up in encouraging fashion late on. He will be suited by further but needs one more trip to the races before he qualifies for a handicap mark.
**Irusan(IRE)**, rated just 57, was making his All-Weather debut and the girl had difficulties keeping him on a straight line.
**Wunderbra(IRE)** had the plum draw but her stride shortened noticeably inside the last. Though dropping back in trip, she still didn't see it out and she may need the mud on turf.
**Classic Expression**, from a dam line that has served the stable well, looked on the backward side. A daughter of Classic Cliche, she will need more time and a stiffer test.

## 3280 TOTEEXACTA STKS (H'CAP) 7f (F)
3:50 (3:50) (D) (0-85,81) 3-Y-O £5,395 (£1,660; £830; £415) Stalls Low

Form RPR
4-00 **1** **Commander Bond**[36] 2239 3-8-7 **67**........ FLynch 4 74
(BSmart) *trcked ldr: hung lft and led wl over 1f out: hrd rdn: hld on gamely* **25/1**
-000 **2** *3/4* **Nine Red**[12] 2915 3-7-12 **58**........ RFfrench 5 63
(BWHills) *chsd ldrs: hrd drvn over 3f out: styd on ins last* **16/1**
0150 **3** *1/2* **Cotosol**[43] 2069 3-9-2 **76**........ GGibbons 2 80
(BAMcmahon) *s.i.s: outpcd over 4f out: hdwy 3f out: styd on ins fnl f* **4/1**[2]
-003 **4** *hd* **Ermine Grey**[20] 2688 3-9-7 **81**........(v) PaulEddery 1 84
(DHaydnJones) *s.i.s: sn drvn along to chse ldrs: ev ch on ins 1f out: nt qckn* **8/1**
6106 **5** *nk* **Generous Gesture (IRE)**[19] 2704 3-9-6 **80**........(v) IMongan 3 83
(MLWBell) *s.s: t.k.h: hdwy on ins over 2f out: ev ch 1f out: nt qckn* **6/1**[3]
2515 **6** *shd* **Fit To Fly (IRE)**[14] 2847 3-8-7 **67**........ FNorton 7 69
(SKirk) *trckd ldrs on outer: outpcd over 3f out: hrd rdn and styd on fnl 2f* **5/4**[1]
5630 **7** *3* **Wings Of Morning (IRE)**[28] 2448 3-8-6 **66**........(b1) GDuffield 8 61
(PABlockley) *led tl wl over 1f out: wknd fnl f* **20/1**
120- **8** *5* **Key Of Gold (IRE)**[256] 5535 3-9-5 **79**........ RFitzpatrick 6 61
(DCarroll) *trckd ldrs on outer: outpcd over 4f out: lost pl 3f out* **6/1**[3]

1m 30.07s (-0.73) **Going Correction** -0.025s/f (Stan) **8** Ran SP% **118.6**
Speed ratings: **103,102,101,101,101 100,97,91**CSF £366.20 CT £1945.99 TOTE £21.80: £2.50, £4.90, £2.50; EX 406.80.
**Owner** R C Bond **Bred** The Lavington Stud **Trained** Hambleton, N Yorks

**FOCUS**
There were seven in a line a furlong out and the time is nothing special, but the form overall looks okay.

**NOTEBOOK**
**Commander Bond**, dropped 5lb, made a winning All-Weather bow in the gamest possible fashion. He never flinched under a punishing ride.
**Nine Red**, down 6lb after three previous outings this time, made very hard work of it but was really finding his stride inside the last and only just held at bay. He is well worth another try over a mile.
**Cotosol**, suited by the trip and the surface here, is back on a winning mark, just one pound higher than his last success.
**Ermine Grey**, raised 11lb, stuck to the inner and as a result possibly saw more daylight than is ideal.
**Generous Gesture(IRE)**, on an all-time high mark, is basically too keen for her own good and had nothing more to give where it really matters.
**Fit To Fly(IRE)**, easily the paddock pick, found himself stuck on the outer and this trip looks on the sharp side for him now.
**Wings Of Morning(IRE)**, in first-time blinkers, set a sound gallop but dropped right away in the closing stages.

## 3281 ST MOLAUG'S DAY CLAIMING STKS 1m 4f (F)
4:20 (4:20) (F) 4-Y-O+ £2,961 (£846; £423) Stalls Low

Form RPR
1102 **1** **Maniatis**[8] 3022 7-9-8 73........(v) IMongan 9 76
(AndrewReid) *hld up: hdwy to chse ldrs 5f out: hung rt 1f out: styd on wl to ld post* **6/5**[1]
1135 **2** *shd* **Romil Star (GER)**[1] 3237 7-9-0 65........(v) DarrenWilliams 5 68
(KRBurke) *trckd ldr: led 8f out: hdd 2f out: led jst ins fnl f: jst ct* **5/1**[3]
1030 **3** *1 1/4* **Our Imperial Bay (USA)**[6] 3103 5-9-0 48........(p) ADaly 8 66?
(MrsJCandlish) *sn bhd and drvn along: hdwy on ins over 2f out: kpt on fnl f* **16/1**
2422 **4** *1/2* **Heathers Girl**[15] 2816 5-8-5 52........ PaulEddery 6 56
(DHaydnJones) *unruly in stalls: chsd ldrs: led 2f out tl jst ins fnl f: no ex* **7/2**[2]
0-04 **5** *1* **Big Smoke (IRE)**[8] 3022 4-8-5 69........(p) PMulrennan(5) 3 60
(JHowardJohnson) *chsd ldrs: drvn along 4f out: one pce appr fnl f* **12/1**
5052 **6** *20* **Western Command (GER)**[14] 2851 8-8-1 35........(p) HayleyTurner(5) 4 26
(MrsNMacauley) *in tch: drvn along 7f out: lost pl over 4f out: sn bhd* **20/1**
550- **7** *1 1/4* **Art Expert (FR)**[357] 1051 6-8-6........ RFitzpatrick 7 24
(MrsNMacauley) *chsd ldrs: drvn along 7f out: lost pl over 4f out: sn bhd* **66/1**
6003 **8** *shd* **Shatin Special**[15] 2816 4-8-1 40........(p) RFfrench 1 19
(GCHChung) *chsd ldrs: lost pl over 5f out: sn bhd* **14/1**
5000 **9** *14* **Bowing**[29] 2430 4-8-8 55........ DKinsella 2 5
(PGMurphy) *led tl 8f out: reminders 6f out: lost pl over 3f out: sn bhd* **28/1**

2m 40.27s (-1.83) **Going Correction** -0.025s/f (Stan) **9** Ran SP% **114.3**
Speed ratings: **105,104,104,103,103 89,88,88,79**CSF £7.14 TOTE £2.10: £1.10, £1.90, £4.90; EX 9.90.
**Owner** Nigel Shields **Bred** A Christodoulou **Trained** Mill Hill, London NW7

**FOCUS**
First impressions suggest that Our Imperial Bay holds the form down, but he used to be capable enough and so has been given the benefit of doubt.

**NOTEBOOK**
**Maniatis** looked held until hanging on to the stands' side rail a furlong out. A whirlwind finish put his head in front on the line.
**Romil Star(GER)**, better off with the winner, was having his second outing in two days. He regained the lead only to have it pinched from under his nose right on the line. He is clearly very tough.
**Our Imperial Bay(USA)** had 17lb to find with the first two but was backed at long odds on the exchanges and ran easily his best race for some time.
**Heathers Girl**, who had 4lb to find with the first two, played up badly in the stalls. After taking charge two furlongs out she was edged out inside the last. In the circumstances this was a commendable effort.
**Big Smoke(IRE)** had 8lb in hand of the first two on official rtaings but it did not work out that way. He looked to have no excuse and this may be as good as he is now.

## 3282 FESTIVAL OF RANTING AND VAPORING AMATEUR RIDERS' H'CAP 1m (F)
4:50 (4:50) (G ) (0-70,70) 4-Y-O+ £3,024 (£864; £432) Stalls Low

Form RPR
5140 **1** **Super Dominion**[21] 2666 7-9-1 **43**........(p) MissKTurbutt(7) 10 51
(RHollinshead) *chsd ldrs: led and hung lft over 1f out: jst hld on* **20/1**
2054 **2** *shd* **Paso Doble**[17] 2762 6-10-5 **61**........(p) MrJMillman(7) 9 69
(BRMillman) *led tl 4f out: kpt on wl ins fnl f: jst failed* **10/1**
6432 **3** *2 1/2* **First Maite**[6] 3103 11-11-2 **65**........ MrsMMorris 15 68
(SRBowring) *racd wd: chsd ldrs: styd on same pce fnl f* **8/1**
1303 **4** *1/2* **Bojangles (IRE)**[6] 3103 5-9-10 **48**........ MrLNewnes(3) 14 50
(RBrotherton) *racd wd: mid-div: hdwy whn nt clr run over 1f out: styd on ins last* **3/1**[1]
-405 **5** *hd* **Brandy Cove**[8] 3023 7-10-10 **62**........ JAJenkins(3) 12 63+
(BSmart) *s.s: bhd tl styd on fnl 2f* **7/1**[3]
0/0- **6** *1/2* **Chapter House (USA)**[81] 1806 5-11-0 **70**........(b) MrOGreenall(7) 8 70
(MWEasterby) *sn bhd and drvn along: kpt on fnl 2f* **25/1**
0015 **7** *3/4* **Littleton Zephir (USA)**[50] 1915 5-9-8 **48**........ MrsCThompson(5) 4 47
(MrsPTownsley) *trckd ldrs on inner: led 3f out tl over 1f out: sn wknd* **12/1**
-503 **8** *3/4* **Haunt The Zoo**[8] 3023 9-10-5 **57**........ MissKellyHarrison(3) 11 54
(JohnAHarris) *mid-div: rdn and outpcd over 2f out: kpt on ins last* **8/1**
2004 **9** *7* **Quiet Reading (USA)**[8] 3023 7-11-4 **67**........(v) MsCWilliams 13 50
(MRBosley) *mid-div on outer: effrt 3f out: sn btn* **4/1**[2]
0020 **10** *3/4* **Crusoe (IRE)**[8] 3023 7-10-2 **51**........(b) MissEJJones 7 33
(ASadik) *w ldrs: led 4f out: hdd 3f out: lost pl and edgd rt over 1f out* **14/1**
0-00 **11** *1 3/4* **Mutared (IRE)**[21] 2643 6-10-3 **55**........ MrsEmmaLittmoden(3) 2 33
(NPLittmoden) *prom: lost pl over 4f out* **16/1**
030- **12** *2 1/2* **Madaar (USA)**[53] 5696 5-8-12 **38** oh1........ MissJFoster(5) 1 11
(RBastiman) *chsd ldrs: wknd over 2f out* **20/1**
/0-5 **13** *6* **Kimoe Warrior**[15] 1514 6-8-10 **38** oh8........(p) MissMMullineaux(7) 5 —
(MMullineaux) *sn w ldrs: lost pl 3f out: sn bhd* **33/1**
000- **14** *8* **The Copt**[366] 2692 5-9-1 **43**........(t) MrSWarren(7) 3 —
(MrsSLamyman) *s.i.s: a in rr* **50/1**
00/0 **15** *dist* **Expectedtofli (IRE)**[67] 1510 6-10-0 **56** oh8 ow18......(t) MrLEdwards(7) 6 —
(TWall) *sn in rr: bhd fnl 3f: t.o* **50/1**

1m 45.05s (0.45) **Going Correction** -0.025s/f (Stan) **15** Ran SP% **129.3**
Speed ratings: **96,95,93,92,92 92,91,90,83,82 81,78,72,64,—**CSF £208.45 CT £1797.21 TOTE £21.00: £10.20, £3.00, £2.70; EX 556.70 Place 6 £372.12, Place 5 £129.89.
**Owner** Mrs Norman Hill **Bred** Norman Hill Plant Hire Ltd **Trained** Upper Longdon, Staffs
■ A first Flat winner for 22-year-old Kelly Turbutt.

**FOCUS**
A poor handicap which has been rated through the runner-up.

**NOTEBOOK**
**Super Dominion**, with his rider never picking up her whip, put his head in front right on the line.
**Paso Doble**, taken to post early, wore cheekpieces for the first time and very nearly doubled his career score on his 37th start.
**First Maite** was worst drawn and raced wide. Now a veteran, he is a stone higher on the All-weather than he is on turf.

**Bojangles(IRE)**, 15lb better off with First Maite, had shown little in two previous tries on this surface. He was out of luck here and looked third best on the day.
**Brandy Cove**, whose three wins have been here on this surface, was having his second outing after a break and looks back to something like his best.
**Chapter House(USA)**, out of form over hurdles, was on edge beforehand but stayed on late in the day, giving his young rider a memorable first experience. On breeding alone a lot more will be heard of this young man.
T/Plt: £433.40 to a £1 stake. Pool: £27,967.35. 47.10 winning tickets. T/Qpdt: £86.70 to a £1 stake. Pool: £1,900.00. 16.20 winning tickets. WG

3283 - 3285a (Foreign Racing) - See Raceform Interactive

## 2327 CURRAGH (R-H)
Friday, June 25

**OFFICIAL GOING: Good**

### 3286a THE GOFFS CHALLENGE — 6f 63y
7:30 (7:31) 2-Y-O — **£54,014** (£17,394; £8,239; £3,661)

RPR
1 **Kestrel Cross (IRE)**[7] 3064 2-9-0 ..... WSupple 3 88
(KevinPrendergast, Ire) *towards rr: impr into 6th and rdn 1 1/2f out: 3rd 1f out: r.o wl to ld on line* **14/1**
2 shd **Encanto (IRE)**[13] 2872 2-8-9 ..... JFEgan 8 83
(JSMoore) *hld up in tch: prog 2f out: 2nd 1f out: led cl home: hdd on line* **20/1**
3 1 **Nepro (IRE)**[29] 2431 2-9-0 ..... KJManning 13 85
(EJCreighton, Spain) *trckd ldrs on outer: 4th 2 1/2f out: led under 2f out: hdd cl home* **10/1**
4 1 **The Quiet Woman (IRE)**[47] 1976 2-8-9 ..... JAHeffernan 9 77
(FrancisEnnis, Ire) *chsd ldrs: 5th 1/2-way: sn rdn: kpt on ins fnl f* **14/1**
5 ½ **Lock And Key (IRE)**[27] 2494 2-8-9 ..... DPMcDonogh 11 75
(EdwardLynam, Ire) *prom: 2nd over 2f out: rdn and one pced* **12/1**
6 ¾ **Annatalia**[14] 2846 2-8-9 ..... FMBerry 14 73
(BJMeehan) *chsd ldrs on outer: kpt on one pced fr 2f out* **16/1**
7 hd **Miss Malone (IRE)**[16] 2786 2-8-9 ..... MJKinane 7 73
(RHannon) *cl up: led after 1/2-way: hdd 2f out: no ex over 1f out* **4/1**[2]
8 1 **Ektishaaf**[9] 2991 2-8-9 ..... PJSmullen 2 70
(DKWeld, Ire) *chsd ldrs: swtchd rt 2f out: no imp* **14/1**
9 2½ **Spirit Of Chester (IRE)**[7] 3031 2-8-9 ..... RHavlin 4 63
(MrsPNDutfield) *led: hdd after 1/2-way: sn wknd* **9/4**[1]
10 4 **Alsu (IRE)**[42] 2074 2-8-9 ..... JPSpencer 5 51
(AMBalding) *chsd ldrs early: towards rr and no imp fr 1/2-way* **8/1**[3]
11 ¾ **Benwilt Breeze (IRE)**[25] 2538 2-9-0 ..... PCosgrave 12 54
(GMLyons, Ire) *prom: 3rd 1/2-way: chal 2f out: sn wknd* **14/1**
12 14 **Kristikhab (IRE)**[14] 2852 2-9-0 ..... WMLordan 10 13
(ABerry) *a bhd: trailing fr 1/2-way: eased over 1f out: t.o* **20/1**
R **La Maitresse (IRE)**[19] 2708 2-8-9 ..... TPO'Shea 1 —
(MHalford, Ire) *cl up whn short of room and rn out through rail after 1f* **16/1**

1m 18.2s **Going Correction** -0.20s/f (Firm) **13** Ran SP% **126.6**
Speed ratings: **87,86,85,84,83 82,82,80,77,72 71,52,—**CSF £281.53 TOTE £18.60: £4.40, £6.50, £3.00; DF 519.20.
**Owner** Norman Ormiston **Bred** S J Macdonald **Trained** Friarstown, Co Kildare

**NOTEBOOK**
**Kestrel Cross(IRE)** won a 7f maiden week ago on his fourth attempt and got his head in front here virtually on the line. He needs the extra furlong already and this was a brave effort.
**Encanto(IRE)** showed improved form, flattering inside the last but being run out of it in the last stride.
**Nepro(IRE)** was bidding for a third success and flattered from two furlongs down despite an outside draw. Caught only in the closing stages he must have a bright future ahead when he goes to race in Spain, his imminent destination being Mijas.
**The Quiet Woman(IRE)** hardly boosted her Cork conqueror Damson's form here! She may be better suited by the minimum.
**Annatalia** ran moderately from a bad draw, just keeping on at the one pace.
**Miss Malone(IRE)** got her head in front after halfway but was done with over a furlong and a half out.
**Spirit Of Chester(IRE)** ran in front till after halfway but compounded quickly and was found to have a "nasal discharge" afterwards. *Official explanation: vet said filly was found to have a nasal discharge post race*
**Alsu(IRE)** was struggling from halfway.
**Kristikhab(IRE)** never went the pace and finished tailed-off.
**La Maitresse(IRE)** *Official explanation: jockey said filly lost her action, panicked and crashed through the rail after 1f*

3287 - 3289a (Foreign Racing) - See Raceform Interactive

## 2749 CHESTER (L-H)
Saturday, June 26

**OFFICIAL GOING: Good (good to soft in places)**

### 3290 WARWICK INTERNATIONAL EBF NOVICE STKS — 5f 16y
2:30 (2:32) (D) 2-Y-O — **£4,621** (£1,422; £711; £355) **Stalls** Low

Form RPR
3112 1 **Beckermet (IRE)**[10] 2980 2-9-9 ..... RFfrench 3 102
(RFFisher) *chsd ldrs: led over 1f out: sn clr: r.o wl* **5/1**[3]
2313 2 5 **Speed Dial Harry (IRE)**[24] 2592 2-8-12 .....(v) DarrenWilliams 8 74
(KRBurke) *midfield: hdwy over 2f out: sn rdn: wnt 2nd ins fnl f: no ch w wnr* **16/1**
412 3 nk **Doctor Hilary**[28] 2478 2-9-2 .....(v[1]) MHills 2 76+
(MLWBell) *outpcd: r.o fnl f: nvr nrr* **7/4**[1]
110 4 1 **Nova Tor (IRE)**[24] 2568 2-8-10 ..... J-PGuillambert[(3)] 11 70
(NPLittmoden) *towards rr: rdn and swtchd rt over 1f out: hung lft and styd on ins fnl f* **25/1**
160 5 nk **Handsome Lady**[24] 2568 2-8-4 ..... TEaves[(3)] 10 63
(ISemple) *sn in midfield: rdn over 2f out: nt pce to chal* **14/1**
05 6 hd **Tight Circle**[14] 2884 2-8-7 ..... SChin 5 62
(MrsGHarvey) *w ldrs tl over 3f out: one pce fnl f* **33/1**
5021 7 1¼ **Town House**[32] 2382 2-8-4 ..... RMiles[(3)] 1 58
(BPJBaugh) *led: rdn and hdd over 1f out: wknd ins fnl f* **7/2**[2]
03 8 1¼ **Moon Mischief (IRE)**[9] 3021 2-8-7 ..... JBramhill 6 53
(NPLittmoden) *towards rr: effrt whn nt clr run over 1f out: no imp after* **25/1**
661 9 3½ **Mytton's Dream**[39] 2194 2-8-9 ..... DAllan 9 43
(ABailey) *s.i.s: a outpcd* **33/1**
451 10 1¼ **Elisha (IRE)**[31] 2396 2-8-11 ..... GDuffield 4 41
(DMSimcock) *w ldr: rdn and wknd over 1f out* **7/1**

63.92 secs (1.94) **Going Correction** +0.50s/f (Yiel) **10** Ran SP% **113.9**
Speed ratings: **104,96,95,93,93 93,91,89,83,81**CSF £73.41 TOTE £7.30: £1.80, £3.90, £1.20; EX 132.20.
**Owner** Bishopthorpe Racing Two **Bred** Fritz Von Ball Moss **Trained** Ulverston, Cumbria

**FOCUS**
A competitive novices' event run at decent gallop on rain-sodden ground and a very smart time for the type of contest, although the track bias tempers confidence.

**NOTEBOOK**
**Beckermet(IRE)** quickened away from the field in the straight having raced prominently under two penalties. He showed he is quite versatile when it comes to ground conditions, and is now being aimed at Listed company after a short break, and it is possible he will stay six furlongs.
**Speed Dial Harry(IRE)** ran as though a return to six furlongs would not go amiss, staying on in hopeless pursuit of the winner.
**Doctor Hilary** could never go the pace in the first-time visor, but once in the short home straight flew home and would not be inconvenienced by a return to six furlongs. However, he has shown bags of pace in the past, suggesting that the minimum trip would not be a problem on a conventional track. *Official explanation: jockey said colt missed the break and lost all chance*
**Nova Tor(IRE)** made some good late progress from a high draw and another furlong may be needed. This was a decent effort.
**Handsome Lady** could never get into the contest from a bad draw.
**Tight Circle** lacked toe and will be better served in nursery company over six furlongs.
**Town House** was quick from the gate but faded late on. He was reportedly unsuited by the softish ground. *Official explanation: trainer said filly was unsuited by the easy ground*
**Elisha(IRE)** *Official explanation: trainer said filly was unsuited by the easy ground*

### 3291 EDWARDS HOMES "PREMIER" CLAIMING STKS — 1m 2f 75y
3:05 (3:05) (D) 3-Y-0+ — **£5,486** (£1,688; £844; £422) **Stalls** High

Form RPR
1021 1 **Ben Hur**[8] 3040 5-9-2 63 ..... CCatlin 3 82?
(WMBrisbourne) *prom: led over 7f out: drvn out* **10/3**[2]
0356 2 1 **Jabaar (USA)**[36] 2258 6-9-12 86 ..... AlexGreaves 6 91
(DNicholls) *hld up: hdwy over 3f out: chsd wnr over 2f out: styd on* **9/4**[1]
-310 3 7 **Giunchiglio**[24] 2573 5-9-2 64 ..... DarrenWilliams 2 68
(WMBrisbourne) *in tch: lost pl 4f out: rallied 2f out: chsd ldng pair over 1f out: one pce* **10/1**
-330 4 10 **Dick The Taxi**[9] 3018 10-8-13 67 ..... RMiles[(3)] 9 50
(RJSmith) *in tch: hdwy over 4f out: rdn over 3f out: wknd over 2f out* **6/1**[3]
0010 5 ½ **Hiawatha (IRE)**[19] 2738 5-9-2 75 ..... GFaulkner 5 49
(PABlockley) *trckd ldrs: wnt 2nd over 5f out: rdn over 3f out: lost 2nd over 2f out: sn wknd* **7/1**
0600 6 nk **Forest Tune (IRE)**[14] 2881 6-9-2 50 ..... GDuffield 1 49
(BHanbury) *trckd ldrs: rdn over 3f out: wknd over 2f out* **8/1**
-002 7 6 **Makulu (IRE)**[15] 2856 4-9-7 74 .....(p) SChin 8 43
(BJMeehan) *rdn over 6f out: a towards rr* **7/1**
000- 8 1½ **Blueberry Jim**[274] 5192 3-8-4 39 ..... DAllan 10 35
(THCaldwell) *dwlt: a bhd* **50/1**
0000 9 4 **Buthaina (IRE)**[21] 2687 4-8-8 55 ..... TEaves[(3)] 4 23
(THCaldwell) *led: hdd over 7f out: remained prom: pushed along 5f out: wknd over 3f out* **50/1**

2m 16.9s (4.35) **Going Correction** +0.50s/f (Yiel)
**WFA** 3 from 4yo+ 12lb **9** Ran SP% **117.3**
Speed ratings: **102,101,95,87,87 86,82,80,77**CSF £11.46 TOTE £3.40: £1.40, £1.60, £3.50; EX 9.10.
**Owner** D C Rutter & H Clewlow **Bred** Blue Blood Investments **Trained** Great Ness, Shropshire

**FOCUS**
Fair recent form had been achieved by a few of the runners in this claimer but in the end they were well strung out. The winner seems improved over the trip.

**NOTEBOOK**
**Ben Hur** has been fairly consistent of late and galloped relentlessly to the line to record his first win at this trip.
**Jabaar(USA)**, without headgear this time, was well in on the figures and settled better, running right to the line clear of the others.
**Giunchiglio** was no threat to the leading duo in the straight on this rain-softened ground.
**Dick The Taxi** was disappointing for the second consecutive occasion.
**Hiawatha(IRE)** was well beaten on this dead surface advertising the fact his Ayr win was in a soft race.
**Forest Tune(IRE)** was up against it on the figures and was duly well beaten.

### 3292 WARWICK INTERNATIONAL 25TH ANNIVERSARY H'CAP — 1m 4f 66y
3:40 (3:40) (D) (0-85,82) 3-Y-0 — **£5,486** (£1,688; £844; £422) **Stalls** Low

Form RPR
5351 1 **Peak Of Perfection (IRE)**[14] 2882 3-8-12 73 ..... MHenry 4 86
(MAJarvis) *led early: remained prom: led over 4f out: rdn over 2f out: r.o* **4/1**[2]
100 2 5 **Master Wells (IRE)**[21] 2683 3-9-4 79 ..... SChin 2 84
(JDBethell) *hld up: hdwy over 3f out: sn rdn and outpcd: styd on ins fnl f: snatched 2nd post: no ch w wnr* **8/1**
000 3 hd **Anousa (IRE)**[9] 2999 3-9-3 81 ..... RMiles[(3)] 3 86+
(PHowling) *in tch: hdwy over 4f out: rdn to chse wnr over 2f out: ev ch over 1f out: no ex and eased ins fnl f: lost 2nd post* **4/1**[2]
-435 4 2½ **Wou Oodd**[15] 2841 3-9-2 77 ..... CCatlin 5 78?
(MRChannon) *hld up: hdwy 4f out: rdn over 3f out: outpcd over 2f out* **14/1**
5 2 **Fire Dragon (IRE)**[46] 2026 3-9-7 82 .....(b) GDuffield 8 80
(JonjoO'Neill) *trckd ldrs: rdn and ev ch 3f out: wknd over 1f out* **5/1**[3]
-351 6 9 **Daytime Girl (IRE)**[18] 2751 3-9-3 78 ..... MHills 1 63
(BWHills) *trckd ldrs: rdn over 5f out: wknd 4f out* **5/2**[1]
-320 7 12 **Midshipman Easy (USA)**[25] 2562 3-8-7 75 ..... MCoumbe[(7)] 9 42
(PWHarris) *s.s: a struggling and bhd* **20/1**
5001 8 20 **Bold Blade**[29] 2452 3-8-4 65 .....(b) RFfrench 6 2
(MJPolglase) *sn led: hdd over 4f out: wknd over 3f out* **14/1**

2m 46.18s (5.66) **Going Correction** +0.50s/f (Yiel) **8** Ran SP% **114.4**
Speed ratings: **101,97,97,95,94 88,80,67**CSF £35.64 CT £135.15 TOTE £4.50: £1.60, £2.90, £1.90; EX 48.20.
**Owner** H R H Sultan Ahmad Shah **Bred** Hrh Sultan Ahmad Shah **Trained** Newmarket, Suffolk
■ Stewards Enquiry : R Miles 21-day ban: dropped hands and lost second place (Jul 7-17, 19-28)

**FOCUS**
Not the strongest race but the winner scored decisively and looked improved while the placed horses were below form.

**NOTEBOOK**
**Peak Of Perfection(IRE)** was always up with the slow pace to win well in the end. He showed his appreciation for going left-handed with cut in the ground, but this race did not take a great deal of winning.

**Master Wells(IRE)** was a fortuitous second as the eventual third's rider eased down towards the end. He has shown a liking for soft conditions in the past, but was well held having been tapped for toe, suggesting he may want further.
**Anousa(IRE)** tried to make a race of it with the winner in the straight before folding, only for his jockey to take things easy and lose second on the line. He showed with this effort that his big performance at Ascot was no flash in the pan.
**Wou Oodd** was found wanting before the straight on her step up in trip, though it is difficult to be adamant that she did not stay.
**Fire Dragon(IRE)** did not get home on his debut run for his current trainer. This close relative to leading hurdler Rigmarole looks to have been harshly treated in Britain after an easy recent success at Killarney.
**Daytime Girl(IRE)** was unable to dominate and disappointed on the dead ground which may have counted against her. For the second time this season she was beaten a fair way over this trip.
*Official explanation: trainer had no explanation for the poor form shown*

## 3293 WARWICK INTERNATIONAL H'CAP — 5f 16y
**4:15** (4:16) (C ) (0-95,89) 3-Y-O+ — **£9,737** (£2,996; £1,498; £749) **Stalls** Low

Form — RPR

2301 **1** **Frascati**[13] [2909] 4-8-4 **75** ........ PPMathers(7) 5 — 84
(ABerry) *led 1f: sn dropped in bhd ldrs: rdn and r.o to ld ins fnl f: hld on wl* — **9/1**

1060 **2** *nk* **Cape Royal**[21] [2679] 4-9-7 **85** ........ MHills 3 — 93
(MrsJRRamsden) *hld up: hdwy and swtchd lft over 1f out: r.o ins fnl f* **7/2**[1]

0630 **3** *hd* **Time N Time Again**[31] [2407] 6-8-4 **68** ........ DAllan 1 — 75
(EJAlston) *in tch: sn pushed along: hdwy 2f out: led 1f out: hdd ins fnl f: r.o u.p: hld towards fin* — **7/2**[1]

2002 **4** *1 3/4* **Tally (IRE)**[2] [3249] 4-7-12 **62** oh6 ........ RFfrench 9 — 63
(MJPolglase) *sn bhd and rdn along: hdwy and hung lft ins fnl f: styd on wl towards fin* — **20/1**

1206 **5** *nk* **Skip Of Colour**[7] [3098] 4-8-9 **73** ........ GFaulkner 2 — 73
(PABlockley) *led after 1f: rdn 2f out: hdd 1f out: no ex ins fnl f* — **13/2**

2224 **6** *hd* **Romany Nights (IRE)**[2] [3243] 4-9-0 **78** ........ (b) CCatlin 7 — 77
(JWUnett) *bhd: hdwy over 1f out: styd on ins fnl f* — **8/1**

0335 **7** *1 1/2* **Prince Of Blues (IRE)**[8] [3038] 6-7-5 **62** oh2 ........ (p) PVarley(7) 8 — 56
(MMullineaux) *midfield: effrt over 1f out: wknd ins fnl f* — **25/1**

1300 **8** *1* **Maktavish**[21] [2679] 5-9-2 **83** ........ (p) TEaves(3) 6 — 73
(ISemple) *chsd ldrs: wnt 2nd 2f out: sn rdn and lost 2nd: wknd ins fnl f* — **6/1**[3]

-305 **9** *5* **Wanchai Lad**[7] [3092] 3-9-2 **86** ........ AlexGreaves 4 — 58
(DNicholls) *w ldr: sn hung rt: rdn and wknd over 1f out* — **11/2**[2]

13-0 **10** *1/2* **Brave Burt (IRE)**[21] [2679] 7-9-5 **83** ........ SChin 10 — 53
(DNicholls) *chsd ldrs tl rdn and wknd over 1f out* — **16/1**

3040 **11** *19* **A Little Bit Yarie**[43] [2075] 3-8-7 **77** ........ (v) DarrenWilliams 12 — —
(KRBurke) *midfield: rdn and wknd over 2f out: eased over 1f out* — **25/1**

64.01 secs (2.03) **Going Correction** +0.50s/f (Yiel)
**WFA** 3 from 4yo+ 6lb — **11** Ran SP% **126.9**
Speed ratings: **103,102,102,99,98 98,96,94,86,85 55**CSF £42.91 CT £137.26 TOTE £9.60: £2.20, £2.20, £1.60; EX 41.20.
**Owner** Lord Crawshaw **Bred** Exors Of The Late Lord Crawshaw **Trained** Cockerham, Lancs
■ Stewards Enquiry : M Hills one-day ban: used whip with excessive frequency and without giving gelding time to respond (Jul 7)

**FOCUS**
Those who forced the early pace could not dominate and it was left to those coming from just off the gallop to take the honours. A career-best effort from the winner and the form look sound enough.

**NOTEBOOK**
**Frascati** came again having lost her decent early place to defy a rise in the weights. Although she has winning form on fast ground, connections feel she is better on a less lively surface.
**Cape Royal** finished strongly and his turn will come round again considering he hails from a late developing family.
**Time N Time Again** ran all the way to the line in his bid to win a third race at this venue.
**Tally(IRE)**, making a quick reappearance and running from 6lb out of the handicap, ran with credit from off the pace. All his winning has come over six furlongs.
**Skip Of Colour** showed plenty of pace and looks to have the ability to win over the minimum trip on turf.
**Romany Nights(IRE)** needs everything to drop his way and made late headway from off the pace.
**Wanchai Lad** struggled round the bends, hanging right. *Official explanation: jockey said colt hung right-handed throughout*

## 3294 WARWICK INTERNATIONAL CELEBRATION MAIDEN STKS — 1m 2f 75y
**4:50** (4:50) (D ) 3-Y-O — **£5,447** (£1,676; £838; £419) **Stalls** High

Form — RPR

0-32 **1** **Golden Island (IRE)**[23] [2632] 3-8-9 85 ........ MHills 3 — 86
(JWHills) *a.p: led 4f out: r.o wl to draw clr ins fnl f: comf* — **11/8**[1]

2023 **2** *5* **Rondelet (IRE)**[14] [2887] 3-9-0 76 ........ GDuffield 4 — 82
(RMBeckett) *trckd ldrs: wnt 2nd 3f out: rdn 2f out: hung lft 1f out: sn btn* — **9/4**[2]

0-63 **3** *11* **Turner**[18] [2751] 3-9-0 72 ........ DarrenWilliams 5 — 62
(WMBrisbourne) *hld up: hdwy over 3f out: rdn over 2f out: sn wknd* **6/1**[3]

00 **4** *6* **Paint The Lily (IRE)**[3] [3204] 3-8-9 ........ MHenry 2 — 46
(JWHills) *s.i.s: hld up: rdn over 3f out: sn wknd* — **16/1**

000 **5** *6* **Shaaban (IRE)**[15] [2842] 3-9-0 ........ CCatlin 3 — 41
(MRChannon) *led: hdd 4f out: rdn and wknd over 2f out* — **6/1**[3]

00- **6** *1 1/4* **Power Nap**[232] [5940] 3-8-9 ........ (t) KimTinkler 1 — 33
(NTinkler) *bhd: rdn over 3f out: nvr on terms* — **20/1**

2m 17.73s (5.18) **Going Correction** +0.50s/f (Yiel) — **6** Ran SP% **112.1**
Speed ratings: **99,95,86,81,76 75**CSF £4.65 TOTE £2.00: £1.40, £1.90; EX 3.10.
**Owner** D M Kerr And N Brunskill **Bred** Barouche Stud Ireland Ltd **Trained** Upper Lambourn, Berks

**FOCUS**
An uncompetitive maiden with only two serious contenders, but their form looks OK.

**NOTEBOOK**
**Golden Island(IRE)** trounced the field and may have more improvement in her, having been a backward sort, and is being touted as a candidate for the Group Three Golden Daffodil Stakes at Chepstow next month. She certainly seems quite versatile when it comes to ground requirements.
**Rondelet(IRE)** was the only plausible threat to the winner on paper but was put in his place in the straight, running to his best and finishing well clear of the others.
**Turner** ran below form with the give underfoot.

## 3295 BRYN THOMAS CRANE HIRE H'CAP — 7f 2y
**5:25** (5:25) (C ) (0-95,92) 3-Y-O — **£9,464** (£2,912; £1,456; £728) **Stalls** Low

Form — RPR

-005 **1** **Mrs Moh (IRE)**[13] [2907] 3-8-3 **74** ........ DAllan 4 — 82
(TDEasterby) *in tch: rdn 2f out: nt clr run over 1f out: r.o ins fnl f: led last strides* — **10/1**

2-00 **2** *shd* **Jazz Scene (IRE)**[9] [3001] 3-9-2 **87** ........ CCatlin 3 — 94
(MRChannon) *in rr: pushed along over 5f out: hdwy whn nt clr run over 1f out: r.o strly towards fin* — **3/1**[2]

13 **3** *shd* **Eisteddfod**[15] [2839] 3-8-1 **75** ........ RMiles(3) 8 — 82
(PFICole) *hld up: hdwy on wd outside over 2f out: led over 1f out: edgd lft ins fnl f: hdd last strides* — **3/1**[2]

44-6 **4** *4* **Baltic Wave**[13] [2907] 3-9-7 **92** ........ DarrenWilliams 1 — 89
(TDBarron) *led: rdn over 2f out: hdd over 1f out: wknd wl ins fnl f* — **11/2**[3]

-000 **5** *3/4* **Convince (USA)**[35] [2295] 3-8-13 **84** ........ RFfrench 2 — 79
(MABuckley) *trckd ldrs: rdn over 2f out: wknd over 1f out* — **11/1**

1-05 **6** *1 1/4* **Misaro (GER)**[24] [2569] 3-8-2 **73** ........ GDuffield 5 — 64
(PABlockley) *prom: rdn and ev ch 3f out: wknd fnl f* — **16/1**

-506 **7** *2 1/2* **Desert Dreamer (IRE)**[22] [2642] 3-9-5 **90** ........ MHills 7 — 75
(BWHills) *trckd ldrs: rdn 2f out: brief chal over 1f out: sn wknd* — **11/4**[1]

1m 30.71s (2.42) **Going Correction** +0.50s/f (Yiel) — **7** Ran SP% **115.4**
Speed ratings: **106,105,105,101,100 98,96**CSF £40.76 CT £114.18 TOTE £13.00: £3.70, £2.00; EX 71.10 Place 6 £34.37, Place 5 £21.13..
**Owner** Salifix **Bred** James Gleeson **Trained** Great Habton, N Yorks

**FOCUS**
A strong gallop was set with the principals coming from off the pace. The form has a decent, solid look about it.

**NOTEBOOK**
**Mrs Moh(IRE)** came with a strong run late on to prevail, having been denied a run early in the straight. Dropped in the weights since her last effort, she has shown she acts on any going.
**Jazz Scene(IRE)** was a shade unlucky, finishing well having been on the search for a passage early in the straight. Back in trip after his decent run in the Britannia at Ascot, he showed that effort to be no fluke.
**Eisteddfod** was the least experienced runner in the line-up and is definitely one to take out of this race. Having made ground round the outside of the field before hitting the front early in the straight, he then edged left through greenness at which point his jockey put his stick down and rode with hands and heels, only to be caught in the dying strides. There is probably more to come from this likeable individual.
**Baltic Wave** was on the front end and ran with credit before fading, offering plenty of encouragement for the remainder of the year.
**Convince(USA)** may need to return to sprinting.
**Misaro(GER)** came through to challenge at the top of the straight before disappointing. He seems to be struggling to find his feet at the moment.
T/Plt: £31.00 to a £1 stake. Pool: £52,576.20. 1,237.70 winning tickets. T/Qpdt: £17.60 to a £1 stake. Pool: £2,400.30. 100.50 winning tickets. DO

# 2904 DONCASTER (L-H)
### Saturday, June 26

**OFFICIAL GOING: Good**

## 3296 DONCASTER-RACECOURSE.COM EBF MAIDEN FILLIES' STKS — 6f
**6:50** (6:52) (D ) 2-Y-O — **£4,842** (£1,490; £745; £372) **Stalls** High

Form — RPR

**1** **Deeday Bay (IRE)** 2-8-11 ........ GBaker 7 — 69
(CFWall) *led 1f: cl up tl led again 2f out: rdn ins last: edgd lft and kpt on wl* — **16/1**

**2** *1/2* **Trylko (USA)** 2-8-11 ........ MFenton 1 — 67
(JGGiven) *led after 1f: pushed along and hdd 2f out: rdn and wandered ent last: kpt on* — **12/1**

**3** *hd* **Swan Nebula (USA)** 2-8-11 ........ (t) KMcEvoy 6 — 67
(SaeedBinSuroor) *in tch pshd along and sltly outpcd 1/2-way: hdwy 2f out: rdn and ev ch whn edgd hung lft wl ins last: kpt on* — **11/4**[2]

2 **4** *1 1/2* **Molly Marie (IRE)**[25] [2544] 2-8-11 ........ TQuinn 5 — 62
(TDEasterby) *trckd ldrs: hmpd and swtchd outside over 2f out: sn rdn and kpt on same pce fnl f* — **6/4**[1]

**5** *hd* **Generous Option** 2-8-11 ........ SChin 2 — 61
(MJohnston) *dwlt: sn cl up: effrt and ev ch 2f out: sn rdn and wknd ent last* — **10/1**

**6** *4* **Mitraillette (USA)** 2-8-11 ........ FLynch 4 — 49
(SirMichaelStoute) *trckd ldrs: hdwy 1/2-way: effrt and ev ch 2f out: sn rdn and wknd* — **7/2**[3]

0 **7** *1 1/2* **Tcherina (IRE)**[9] [3014] 2-8-11 ........ JCarroll 8 — 45
(TDEasterby) *t.k.h: a rr* — **33/1**

**8** *nk* **Nan Jan** 2-8-11 ........ NDay 3 — 44
(RIngram) *s.i.s: a rr* — **25/1**

1m 17.86s (3.58) **Going Correction** +0.275s/f (Good) — **8** Ran SP% **118.3**
Speed ratings: **87,86,86,84,83 78,76,76**CSF £193.06 TOTE £25.70: £4.20, £3.20, £1.60; EX 151.90.
**Owner** Peter Botham **Bred** Ocal Bloodstock **Trained** Newmarket, Suffolk

**FOCUS**
A modest time and probably just a fair race, but one that is likely to produce winners.

**NOTEBOOK**
**Deeday Bay(IRE)**, bred to be a speedy sort, was up on the pace throughout and showed plenty of early dash. She found plenty under pressure and ran on all the way to the line. This was a decent effort and there should be more to come from her.
**Trylko(USA)**, a half-sister to Bachelor Duke, ran a similar race to the winner but just ran around a little under pressure. This was a pleasing effort and she can win a similar race.
**Swan Nebula(USA)**, whose trainer's two-year-olds have been in good form, shaped with plenty of promise on this debut despite hanging a little to her left under pressure. Another furlong will suit and she should improve.
**Molly Marie(IRE)**, who shaped with plenty of promise on her debut when second to Queen Mary third Sharplaw Star, was disappointing and has evidently gone the wrong way.
**Generous Option** showed good early speed after an tardy start but did not know her job well enough to go on and win the race. She seemed to not fully let herself down, and better can be expected next time given how her trainer's juveniles usually improve dramatically from their first outing.
**Mitraillette(USA)** simply found this too sharp a test and like the Johnston filly better can be expected in future.
**Tcherina(IRE)** *Official explanation: jockey said filly hung right throughout*

## 3297 GO RACING IN YORKSHIRE MAIDEN STKS — 1m 2f 60y
**7:20** (7:24) (D ) 3-Y-O+ — **£5,777** (£1,777; £888; £444) **Stalls** Low

Form — RPR

**1** **Into The Dark** 3-8-11 ........ (vt[1]) KMcEvoy 15 — 89+
(SaeedBinSuroor) *sn led: qcknd over 3f out: rdn clr 2f out: eased ins last* — **15/2**[3]

03 **2** *5* **Forged (IRE)**[26] [2513] 3-8-8 ........ NMackay(3) 14 — 73
(LMCumani) *hld up in midfield: hdwy 3f out: rdn to chse ldrs over 2f out: styd on ins last: no ch w wnr* — **12/1**

-442 **3** *shd* **Little Bob**[30] [2419] 3-8-11 69 ........ TQuinn 7 — 73
(JDBethell) *trckd ldrs: hdwy to chse wnr over 2f out: sn rdn and kpt on same pce* — **14/1**

4 **2** *2* **Ouninpohja (IRE)** 3-8-11 ........ DeanMcKeown 8 69
(GASwinbank) *towards rr: hdwy 3f out: styd on fnl 2f: nrst fin* **50/1**

-234 **5** *8* **Templet (USA)**[23] [2619] 4-9-9 68........(v[1]) JCarroll 10 54
(ISemple) *chsd ldrs: effrt 3f out: rdn over 2f out and grad wknd* **16/1**

3- **6** *hd* **Maraakeb (FR)**[238] [5870] 3-8-11 ........ RHills 1 54
(JHMGosden) *in tch: swtchd rt and hdwy over 3f out: effrt on outer over 2f out: sn rdn and btn* **8/13**[1]

0- **7** *1 1/2* **Singlet**[238] [5870] 3-8-11 ........ MFenton 9 51
(DJDaly) *towards rr: hdwy on outer 3f out: rdn and edgd lft 2f out: kpt on: nvr rch ldrs* **50/1**

00 **8** *3 1/2* **Spot In Time**[44] [2060] 4-8-11 ........ NataliaGemelova(7) 12 39
(PRWood) *plld hrd: prom: hdwy to chse wnr 1/2-way: rdn along 3f out: sn wknd* **100/1**

0 **9** *7* **Hilltop Rhapsody**[73] [1395] 3-8-6 ........ ANicholls 4 26
(DJDaly) *s.i.s: a rr* **100/1**

0 **10** *1* **Bravely Does It (USA)**[22] [2653] 4-9-9 ........ GBaker 13 29
(WMBrisbourne) *a rr* **100/1**

0 **11** *1 1/4* **Dune Raider (USA)**[43] [2085] 3-8-11 ........ FLynch 6 27
(SirMichaelStoute) *midfield: hdwy over 4f out: rdn and btn 3f out* **5/1**[2]

00/0 **12** *1 1/2* **Home By Socks (IRE)**[28] [1533] 5-9-4 40........ LVickers 2 19
(MCChapman) *chsd wnr to 1/2-way: sn rdn along and wknd over 3f out* **100/1**

**13** *2 1/2* **Welkino's Boy** 3-8-11 ........ DaleGibson 11 19
(JMackie) *a bhd* **66/1**

5 **14** *2* **Conviction**[8] [3054] 3-8-11 ........ EAhern 16 15
(JRFanshawe) *a bhd* **25/1**

**15** *7* **West End Wonder (IRE)** 5-9-9 ........ TEDurcan 3 2
(MJWallace) *bhd fr 1/2-way* **50/1**

00-0 **16** *27* **Trofana Falcon**[22] [2653] 4-9-9 ........ JQuinn 5 —
(HJCollingridge) *b ehind fr 1/2-way* **66/1**

2m 12.72s (0.96) **Going Correction** +0.275s/f (Good)
**WFA** 3 from 4yo+ 12lb **16** Ran SP% **127.3**
Speed ratings: **107,103,102,101,94 94,93,90,85,84 83,82,80,78,72 51**CSF £95.40 TOTE £7.10: £2.30, £2.30, £2.10; EX 65.90.
**Owner** Godolphin **Bred** Gainsborough Stud Management Ltd **Trained** Newmarket, Suffolk
■ Stewards Enquiry : N Mackay caution: careless riding

**FOCUS**
No more than an average maiden, but a good performance from Into The Dark, who won tidily. The favourite was below par but the form is fair.

**NOTEBOOK**
**Into The Dark**, the first foal of quality sprinter Land Of Dreams, had the visor fitted for this debut and was soon taken into the lead. He quickened up smartly from the front and stayed on extremely well to win easily. This was a smart initial effort and there should be much more to come from him.
**Forged(IRE)** was a bad drifter on the exchanges throughout the course of the day, but that did not affect him running a big race. He stayed on well from the rear of the field to just get up for second, and he now qualifies for a handicap mark.
**Little Bob** will stay further than this and should improve for the switch to handicaps.
**Ouninpohja(IRE)** stayed on well for fourth - despite not really being bred to do so - and would have delighted connections with this debut. There can be more expected from him next time.
**Templet(USA)** was slightly disappointing and is another going to be better off in handicaps.
**Maraakeb(FR)** set the standard on form and, although this was his seasonal debut, was expected to win. Having sat in a good early position he tried to launch a challenge but there was nothing in reserve. Undoubtedly better than this, he may now be more the type for handicaps.
**Dune Raider(USA)** showed any amount of promise on his debut in what looked a decent Newbury maiden, but he failed to run up to anything like that form. Handicaps beckon. *Official explanation: jockey said colt was unsuited by the ground*
**Trofana Falcon** *Official explanation: jockey said gelding had a breathing problem*

## 3298 FINNINGLEY H'CAP 6f
7:50 (7:55) (D) (0-80,80) 3-Y-O+ **£5,839** (£1,796; £898; £449) **Stalls High**

Form RPR

2361 **1** **Aintnecessarilyso**[8] [3043] 6-7-6 **51**........ MHalford(7) 15 61
(NEBerry) *hld up stands side: gd hdwy 2f out: effrt whn rdr dropped stick over 1f out: styd on wl fnl f to ld last 50 yds* **10/1**

-653 **2** *nk* **Bollin Edward**[11] [2965] 5-8-8 **60**........(b) DAllan 12 69
(TDEasterby) *chsd ldrs: rdn 2f out: styd on to cge ent last: sn drvn and kpt on* **7/1**[3]

201 **3** *nk* **Lord Of The East**[11] [2965] 5-9-5 **71**........ AlexGreaves 9 79
(DNicholls) *cl up: led 11/2f out: sn rdn: hdd and no ex last 50 yds* **12/1**

0421 **4** *nk* **Legal Set (IRE)**[2] [3226] 8-7-12 57 7ex........(t) NataliaGemelova(7) 2 64
(MissAStokell) *a.p: rdn and edgd rt 2f out: kpt on u.p ins last* **12/1**

3256 **5** *3/4* **Soba Jones**[89] [1175] 7-9-4 **70**........ JEdmunds 14 75
(JBalding) *cl up: led over 3f out: rdn and hdd 11/2f out: drvn and no ex ins last* **14/1**

6600 **6** *1* **A Teen**[31] [2399] 6-8-6 **58**........ RHills 6 60
(PHowling) *bhd: hdwy 2f out: sn rdn and kpt on fnl f: nrst fin* **40/1**

4632 **7** *nk* **Full Spate**[5] [3141] 9-9-2 **68**........ KDalgleish 18 69
(JMBradley) *chsd ldrs: rdn and hung lft 2f out: drvn and btn whn edgd lft wl ins last* **6/1**[2]

4404 **8** *1* **Far Note (USA)**[2] [3249] 6-8-11 **63**........(b) JBramhill 11 61
(SRBowring) *dwlt: sn chsng ldrs: rdn along and n.m.r wl over 1f out: sn one pce* **9/1**

0000 **9** *nk* **Coranglais**[18] [2763] 4-8-9 **61**........(p) RWinston 8 58
(JMBradley) *chsd ldrs: rdn along and hmpd 2f out: swtchd rt and kpt on fnl f* **20/1**

0360 **10** *hd* **Armagnac**[32] [2391] 6-9-11 **77**........ JQuinn 10 74
(MABuckley) *in tch: hdwy whn hmpd and lost pl 2f out: kpt on ins last* **11/1**

-001 **11** *1 1/2* **Antonio Canova**[43] [2091] 8-9-12 **78**........ TWilliams 4 70
(BobJones) *chsd ldrs: rdn along 2f out: grad wknd* **10/1**

0002 **12** *1 1/2* **Stokesies Wish**[8] [3043] 4-8-7 **64**........ HayleyTurner(5) 17 52
(JLSpearing) *in tch stands side: rdn along 2f out: sn wknd* **14/1**

0600 **13** *1/2* **Oases**[39] [2215] 5-8-2 **57** ow2........ THamilton(3) 7 43
(DShaw) *dwlt and bhd: hdwy over 2f out: swtchd rt and rdn wl over 1f out: sn no imp* **33/1**

0060 **14** *3/4* **Time To Remember (IRE)**[22] [2656] 6-8-5 **57**........ JCarroll 5 41
(DNicholls) *led: hdd over 3f out: rdn and wknd 2f out* **25/1**

6000 **15** *5* **Quantica (IRE)**[14] [2899] 5-8-6 **58**........ KimTinkler 1 27
(NTinkler) *a rr: bhd fr 1/2-way* **16/1**

0001 **16** *1/2* **Sir Don (IRE)**[10] [2976] 5-9-0 **66**........(v) ANicholls 16 33
(DNicholls) *chsd ldrs: rdn along over 2f out: sn wknd* **14/1**

-041 **17** *1 1/4* **Pinchbeck**[43] [2094] 5-10-0 **80**........(p) PRobinson 13 44
(MAJarvis) *midfield: rdn along 1/2-way: sn wknd and eased* **5/1**[1]

0000 **18** *1 1/2* **Compton Arrow (IRE)**[21] [2673] 8-7-13 **51**........ SRighton 3 10
(AWCarroll) *s.i.s: a bhd* **50/1**

1m 14.34s (0.06) **Going Correction** +0.275s/f (Good) **18** Ran SP% **137.2**
Speed ratings: **110,109,109,108,107 106,106,104,104,104 102,100,99,98,91 91,89,87**CSF £83.07 CT £895.72 TOTE £12.10: £2.20, £3.00, £3.30, £3.80; EX 237.50.
**Owner** Mrs Jan Adams **Bred** D R C And Mrs Elsworth **Trained** Earlswood, Monmouths
■ Stewards Enquiry : K Dalgleish two-day ban: careless riding (Jul 7,9)

**FOCUS**
A tight finish to this competitive sprint handicap run in a decent time. Those with a high draw had a slight advantage as expected but the form looks sound enough.

**NOTEBOOK**
**Aintnecessarilyso**, who had a good draw in 15, was bidding to follow up his Goodwood win off a 4lb higher mark. He proved up to the task, coming through to lead well inside the final furlong and winning a shade cleverly considering his rider dropped his whip over a furlong out. He is finally getting his reward for many placed efforts, and a hat-trick cannot be ruled out.
**Bollin Edward** is without a win since 2002 but he came pretty close and is running into form.
**Lord Of The East**, who returned to winning ways at Thirsk recently over seven furlongs, ran his race but was not up to defying his 4lb higher mark.
**Legal Set(IRE)** has been running well of late and put up a good performance off a 12lb higher mark than when winning at Hamilton, especially considering the stall he came from.
**Soba Jones** was having his first start for 89 days and just got a little weary close home.
**A Teen** ran well at a price and returned to some sort of form.
**Full Spate** had the best of the draw but was unable to capitalise on it.
**Coranglais** ◆ was unlucky not to finish closer as he was squeezed out just when beginning to get going. He takes plenty of driving over this trip and may be worth trying back over seven. Either way he should be winning before long, as he is on a very good mark at present.
**Armagnac** lost his chance when hampered.
**Time To Remember(IRE)** *Official explanation: jockey said gelding lost its action*
**Sir Don(IRE)** *Official explanation: jockey said gelding was unsuited by the ground*
**Pinchbeck** ran a shocker and something was presumably amiss. *Official explanation: trainer had no explanation for the poor form shown*

## 3299 ASHGATE CROFT SCHOOL MEGAN POOL APPEAL CLASSIFIED STKS 1m (R)
8:20 (8:23) (D) 3-Y-O+ **£5,699** (£1,753; £876; £438) **Stalls High**

Form RPR

2510 **1** **Oddsmaker (IRE)**[9] [3001] 3-8-9 83........ DeanMcKeown 2 95
(PDEvans) *trckd ldrs:hdwy over 2f out: rdn to ld over 1f out: styd on* **9/1**

-040 **2** *1 1/2* **Devant (NZ)**[26] [2521] 4-8-13 79........ PRobinson 10 85+
(MAJarvis) *hld up: hdwy on outer 3f out: rdn wl over 1f out: kpt on ins last: nrst fin* **12/1**

5-60 **3** *1* **Winning Venture**[56] [1765] 7-9-5 83........ MFenton 13 89
(AWCarroll) *cl up: led 5f out and sn clr: rdn alobng over 2f out: hdd over 1f out: one pce* **20/1**

0-03 **4** *1/2* **Cat's Whiskers**[56] [1773] 5-9-3 81........ DaleGibson 4 86
(MWEasterby) *chsd ldrs: rdn along over 2f out: drvn and kpt on same pce fnl f* **12/1**

6002 **5** *1* **Cripsey Brook**[7] [3097] 6-9-9 87........ KimTinkler 7 90+
(DonEnricoIncisa) *keen: prom tl hampd and lost pl after 3f: rdn along 3f out: hdwy on inner 2f out: styng on whn n.m.r ins last* **14/1**

0004 **6** *nk* **Topton (IRE)**[27] [2504] 10-9-2 76........(b) RWinston 1 82+
(PHowling) *trckd ldrs: hdwy tl styd on fnl 2f: nrst fin* **16/1**

0600 **6** *dht* **African Sahara (USA)**[63] [1623] 5-9-2 80........(t) GCarter 6 82+
(MissDMountain) *hld up in rr: hdwy over 2f out: sn rdn and no imp appr last* **33/1**

30-4 **8** *1 1/4* **Dubrovsky**[63] [1623] 4-9-7 85........ EAhern 5 84
(JRFanshawe) *in tch: hdway 3f out: rdn 2f out and sn no imp* **13/8**[1]

0-00 **9** *1 1/2* **Machinist (IRE)**[8] [3036] 4-9-2 77........ AlexGreaves 9 76
(DNicholls) *trckd ldrs: smooth hdwy on outer 3f out: rdn 2f out and grad wknd* **16/1**

2-13 **10** *7* **Retirement**[50] [1927] 5-9-4 82........ NCallan 14 62
(MHTompkins) *chsd ldrs: rdn along over 2f out: sn wknd* **7/2**[2]

0006 **11** *7* **Percy Douglas**[6] [3118] 4-9-2 45........ AnnStokell 11 43
(MissAStokell) *led 3f: rdn along and wknd 3f out* **100/1**

5000 **12** *29* **Blue Emperor (IRE)**[8] [3039] 3-8-6 45........ RFitzpatrick 8 —
(PTMidgley) *a rr* **100/1**

1- **13** *dist* **Murashah (USA)**[281] [5046] 4-9-2 80........(t) RHills 3 —
(SaeedBinSuroor) *v.s.a and ref to r* **11/2**[3]

1m 40.96s (0.41) **Going Correction** +0.275s/f (Good)
**WFA** 3 from 4yo+ 10lb **13** Ran SP% **129.2**
Speed ratings: **108,106,105,105,104 103,103,102,100,93 86,57,—**CSF £118.97 TOTE £11.30: £2.70, £3.10, £6.00; EX 150.60.
**Owner** D Maloney **Bred** Margaret Conlon **Trained** Pandy, Gwent

**FOCUS**
A messy race with the principals disappointing, and it is hard to gauge how the form is going to work out.

**NOTEBOOK**
**Oddsmaker(IRE)** left a poor run on firm ground at Ascot behind and came right back to his best. He is a plucky character who always gives his all and should continue to pay his way.
**Devant(NZ)** has been shaping as though worth stepping back up to a mile two, and she was again staying on well close home.
**Winning Venture** showed his running last time to be all wrong and is on a winning mark.
**Cat's Whiskers** is currently only 1lb higher than when last scoring and his last two efforts both suggest he is nearing a win.
**Cripsey Brook** continues to run well in defeat but is still 7lb higher than when last winning.
**Dubrovsky** was made a short-priced favourite on the back of an unlucky fourth in a Sandown handicap when last seen back in April. However, he soon found himself struggling once coming under pressure and failed to pick up at all. This was too bad to be true and he is much better than this.
**Retirement** ran a rare bad race but deserves a chance to atone.
**Murashah(USA)** disgraced himself at the start.

## 3300 CASTLE WORKING MEN'S CLUB STAYERS' H'CAP 1m 6f 132y
8:50 (8:50) (D) (0-80,76) 4-Y-O+ **£5,512** (£1,696; £848; £424) **Stalls Low**

Form RPR

4103 **1** **Glory Quest (USA)**[2] [3244] 7-9-7 **73**........ MFenton 8 81
(MissGayKelleway) *prom:qcknd to ld 5f out: rdn 2f out: drvn ins last and hld on gamely* **7/2**[2]

4-01 **2** *shd* **Dr Sharp (IRE)**[49] [1958] 4-9-10 **76**........ DaleGibson 3 84
(TPTate) *trckd ldrs: effrt 3f out: rdn 2f out: drvn and styd on wl fnl f: jst failed* **5/2**[1]

-205 **3** *3 1/2* **Clarinch Claymore**[21] [2684] 8-9-5 **71**........ PHanagan 6 74
(JMJefferson) *hld up in rr: hdwy on outer 3f out: rdn wl over 1f out: drvn and one pce ins last* **7/2**[2]

-023 **4** *9* **Night Sight (USA)**[21] [2671] 7-9-4 **70**........ EAhern 5 62
(MrsSLamyman) *hld up: gd hdwy 5f out: rdn to chse wnr wl over 2f out: sn drvn and wknd wl over 1f out* **11/2**[3]

5060 **5** *3/4* **Fight The Feeling**[2] [3244] 6-7-7 **50** oh5 .......... DFox(5) 1 41
(JWUnett) *led: rdn along: edgd lft and hdd 5f out: wknd 3f out* **20/1**

40-0 **6** *3/4* **Bolshoi Ballet**[27] [1198] 6-8-3 **55** .......... (b) JFanning 4 45
(JMackie) *chsd ldrs: rdn along over 4f out: sn wknd* **9/1**

0-03 **7** *14* **Lady Netbetsports (IRE)**[2] [3221] 5-8-9 **61** .......... KDalgleish 7 33
(BSRothwell) *in tch: effrt 5f out: sn rdn and wknd over 3f out* **14/1**

0530 **8** *19* **Distant Cousin**[24] [2590] 7-8-8 **60** .......... (v) JQuinn 2 7
(MABuckley) *hld up in tch: hdwy over 6f out: rdn along over 4f out: sn wknd and bhd* **11/1**

3m 15.94s (6.20) **Going Correction** +0.275s/f (Good) **8** Ran SP% **118.2**
Speed ratings: **94,93,92,87,86 86,79,68**CSF £13.21 CT £32.81 TOTE £5.10: £1.70, £1.80, £1.60; EX 15.20.

**Owner** W R B Racing 40 (wrbracing.com) **Bred** Adelphian Ltd And Gainesway Farm **Trained** Newmarket, Suffolk

**FOCUS**
Only a moderate time for the grade, but an exciting finish between progressive Dr Sharp and winner Glory Quest who continues in good form and as such the race looks sound enough form-wise.

**NOTEBOOK**
**Glory Quest(USA)** was given a positive ride and quickened up smartly from the front to steal an advantage over Dr Sharp before repelling that rival's late challenge. This was a fine effort and he remains in decent form.

**Dr Sharp(IRE)** went close to following up his Beverley win and would have done so in another couple of strides. He is in good form and is a progressive three-year-old.

**Clarinch Claymore** stayed on from the rear to take a clear third but never troubled the front pair.

**Night Sight(USA)** was nine lengths adrift in fourth and slightly disappointing.

**Fight The Feeling** *Official explanation: jockey said gelding hung right throughout*

## 3301 BRANTON FILLIES' H'CAP 7f
**9:20** (9:25) (E) (0-70,69) 3-Y-O+ **£3,630** (£1,117; £558; £279) **Stalls** High

Form RPR

120- **1** **Gallery Breeze**[203] [6134] 5-9-11 **64** .......... VSlattery 15 78
(JLSpearing) *midfield: gd hdwy 2f out: rdn and qcknd to ld ent last: drvn nr fin and hld on wl* **25/1**

-001 **2** *nk* **In The Pink (IRE)**[8] [3047] 4-10-0 **67** .......... CCatlin 10 80
(MRChannon) *hld up: gd hdwy 2f out: nt clr run and swtchd lft over 1f out: rdn to chal ins last: drvn and nt qckn nr line* **3/1**[1]

000- **3** *4* **Pertemps Magus**[248] [5702] 4-9-4 **57** .......... PHanagan 11 60
(RAFahey) *trckd ldrs: hdwy wl over 1f out: rdn and kpt on ins last* **6/1**[3]

2405 **4** *1 1/4* **Jessie**[16] [2811] 5-8-4 **43** .......... (v) KimTinkler 18 43
(DonEnricoIncisa) *s.i.s and bhd: hdwy 2f out: n.m.r and swtchd lft over 1f out: styd on ins last: nrst fin* **16/1**

0000 **5** *1/2* **Zamyatina (IRE)**[12] [2943] 5-7-10 **42** .......... MHalford(7) 12 40
(PLClinton) *chsd ldrs: rdn along over 1f out: kpt on same pce fnl f* **16/1**

4004 **6** *2* **Annijaz**[8] [3047] 7-9-0 **53** .......... KDalgleish 14 46
(JMBradley) *hld up in midfield: hdwy 2f out: rdn to chal over 1f out: sn drvn and wknd ent last* **11/2**[2]

1060 **7** *nk* **Spark Up**[28] [2473] 4-9-7 **60** .......... (b) JFanning 8 52
(JWUnett) *cl up: led after 1f tl 2f out: sn rdn and wknd over 1f out* **16/1**

0-00 **8** *1* **Filliemou (IRE)**[22] [2648] 3-8-11 **59** .......... MFenton 19 49
(AWCarroll) *in tch: hdwy 2f out: sn rdn and no imp* **16/1**

0055 **9** *1* **Hula Ballew**[6] [3117] 4-8-9 **51** .......... (p) LEnstone(3) 16 38
(MDods) *cl up: rdn along 2f out: grad wknd* **9/1**

201 **10** *1* **Extremely Rare (IRE)**[47] [1991] 3-9-7 **69** .......... DAllan 9 53
(TDEasterby) *led 1f: cl up tl led 2f out: sn rdn: hdd & wknd ent last* **12/1**

0-00 **11** *2* **One Alone**[32] [2378] 3-7-7 **46** oh1 .......... DFox(5) 2 25
(Jean-ReneAuvray) *a towards rr* **50/1**

-002 **12** *shd* **True (IRE)**[22] [2657] 3-9-3 **65** .......... EAhern 4 44
(MrsSLamyman) *chsd ldrs: rdn over 2f out and sn wknd* **14/1**

5000 **13** *4* **Tapau (IRE)**[12] [2948] 6-9-9 **62** .......... (p) SChin 5 31
(JMBradley) *cl up: rdn along 1/2-way: sn wknd* **25/1**

3000 **14** *1 1/4* **Moonlight Song (IRE)**[16] [2811] 7-7-12 **44** .......... DFentiman(7) 6 9
(JohnAHarris) *a towards rr* **66/1**

-402 **15** *3* **Impulsive Bid (IRE)**[45] [2036] 3-9-1 **63** .......... TEDurcan 13 21
(JeddO'Keeffe) *bhd fr 1/2-way* **12/1**

-062 **16** *3 1/2* **Route Sixty Six (IRE)**[3] [3200] 8-8-4 **43** .......... DaleGibson 20 —
(JeddO'Keeffe) *a rr* **8/1**

0U44 **17** *2* **Park Star**[47] [1992] 4-9-2 **55** .......... RWinston 7 —
(DShaw) *a rr* **20/1**

40-0 **18** *nk* **Tokewanna**[22] [2666] 4-8-10 **54** .......... BSwarbrick(5) 1 —
(WMBrisbourne) *cl up on outer: rdn along 1/2-way and sn wknd* **33/1**

1m 28.99s (1.18) **Going Correction** +0.275s/f (Good)
**WFA** 3 from 4yo+ 9lb **18** Ran SP% **140.2**
Speed ratings: **104,103,99,97,97 94,94,93,92,91 88,88,84,82,79 75,72,72**CSF £106.15 CT £560.83 TOTE £43.30: £8.10, £1.70, £2.70, £4.00; EX 404.40 Place 6 £1,088.97, Place 5 £350.24 .

**Owner** Appleby Lodge Stud **Bred** G W Mills And Sons **Trained** Kinnersley, Worcs

**FOCUS**
Those drawn high again benefited - the first six home drawn in a double figure stall - and it was seasonal debutant Gallery Breeze who prevailed. The form looks fair.

**NOTEBOOK**
**Gallery Breeze**, making her seasonal debut off a 7lb higher mark than when last winning, had a good draw and showed she has progressed again from four to five. She showed a good attitude in the process and, if going on at all from this, will be capable of much better.

**In The Pink(IRE)** returned to winning ways at Goodwood on her most recent outing and went very near to following up. This confirmed she is right back to form and she came four lengths clear of the third.

**Pertemps Magus**, another seasonal debutant, showed improved form for the step up to seven furlongs and is entitled to progress again.

**Jessie** ran well on this return to turf and finished strongly. She can win a similar event if going the right way from this.

**Zamyatina(IRE)**, who was once rated in the high 70s, now competes off a lowly 42 and if building on it should soon be back winning.

**Route Sixty Six(IRE)** *Official explanation: jockey said mare lost her action*

T/Plt: £2,703.70 to a £1 stake. Pool: £45,185.65. 12.20 winning tickets. T/Qpdt: £235.80 to a £1 stake. Pool: £3,761.60. 11.80 winning tickets. JR

# 3083 LINGFIELD (L-H)
### Saturday, June 26

**OFFICIAL GOING: Turf course - good (good to firm in places); all-weather course - standard**

## 3302 EUROPEAN BREEDERS FUND MAIDEN STKS 5f
**6:35** (6:40) (D) 2-Y-O **£4,134** (£1,272; £636; £318) **Stalls** High

Form RPR

62 **1** **Tesary**[28] [2481] 2-8-9 .......... WSupple 4 74+
(EALDunlop) *trckd ldng pair: led over 1f out: shkn up and in command fnl f* **5/6**[1]

5 **2** *1 1/2* **African Storm (IRE)**[15] [2846] 2-9-0 .......... PDobbs 1 71
(SKirk) *w ldr: rdn and ev ch over 1f out: one pce* **14/1**

**3** *shd* **Louphole** 2-9-0 .......... RSmith 2 70
(PJMakin) *v s.i.s: off the pce in last trio: prog 1/2-way: rdn and styd on fr over 1f out* **33/1**

04 **4** *3/4* **First Rule**[12] [2947] 2-9-0 .......... RHavlin 3 68
(CFWall) *mde most to over 1f out: nt qckn u.p* **5/2**[2]

**5** *1 1/2* **Mulberry Lad (IRE)** 2-9-0 .......... DKinsella 7 63
(WRMuir) *dwlt: wl off the pce in last: pushed along 2f out: kpt on steadily: n.d* **33/1**

**6** *1 1/4* **Comtesse Lalande (USA)** 2-8-9 .......... IMongan 8 53
(MLWBell) *trckd ldrs: rdn 1/2-way: wknd over 1f out* **11/1**[3]

00 **7** *5* **Royal Accolade**[40] [2177] 2-8-9 .......... (b[1]) WRyan 5 36
(BHanbury) *a off the pce in last trio: struggling fnl 2f* **16/1**

59.68 secs (0.81) **Going Correction** -0.05s/f (Good) **7** Ran SP% **109.9**
Speed ratings: **91,88,88,87,84 82,74**CSF £13.48 TOTE £1.80: £1.20, £3.70; EX 10.30.
**Owner** Khalifa Sultan **Bred** Gainsborough Stud Management Ltd **Trained** Newmarket, Suffolk

**FOCUS**
A modest maiden run at a fair pace.

**NOTEBOOK**
**Tesary**, who had shown fair form in two previous outings, readily settled the issue entering the final furlong and won with a bit up her sleeve. She is the type to improve with age and this drop in trip was right up her street. Although her confidence will be high after this, her future probably lies in handicaps.
**African Storm(IRE)**, who ran distinctly green on her debut last time, put up a much-improved display and showed enough to suggest she will not be long in going one better.
**Louphole** would have been a lot closer but for blowing the start, but still put up an eye-catching debut display. This cheaply-bought gelding ran very much as though an extra furlong would be appreciated, and looks sure to improve for the experience.
**First Rule** lacked a change of gear late on, but still ran his best race to date and will be one to keep an eye on when the nurseries begin.

## 3303 DALLAS KIRKLAND (S) STKS 1m 4f (P)
**7:05** (7:05) (G) 3-Y-O+ **£2,597** (£742; £371) **Stalls** Low

Form RPR

2463 **1** **Delightfully**[7] [3107] 3-8-3 67 .......... (b[1]) RMullen 8 48
(BWHills) *led after 2f: rdn over 2f out: hdd ins fnl f: sn led again: hrd rdn and hld on* **15/8**[1]

0502 **2** *hd* **Tresor Secret (FR)**[7] [3087] 4-9-3 65 .......... RThomas(5) 4 53
(PButler) *trckd ldrs: wnt 2nd gng easily over 2f out: led ins fnl f: nt run on and sn hdd: would nt go past again nr fin* **9/2**[3]

0-00 **3** *3* **Java Dawn (IRE)**[7] [3087] 4-8-12 42 .......... AQuinn(5) 1 43
(TEPowell) *s.v.s: sn in tch in last: pushed along 3f out: nt clr run over 2f out: effrt over 1f out: styd on to take 3rd fnl f* **66/1**

0204 **4** *nk* **Mandoob**[7] [3087] 7-9-13 60 .......... (v) DaneO'Neill 3 53
(BRJohnson) *s.v.s: sn in tch: prog 1/2-way: rdn to dispute 2nd over 2f out: nt qckn and btn over 1f out* **5/2**[2]

2453 **5** *1* **Neptune**[7] [3087] 8-9-8 45 .......... PDobbs 7 46
(JCFox) *s.v.s: sn in tch in rr: effrt over 2f out: rdn and fnd nil wl over 1f out* **16/1**

2105 **6** *shd* **Blue Savanna**[19] [2740] 4-9-13 45 .......... (b) RLMoore 2 51
(JGPortman) *trckd ldrs: gng wl enough over 2f out: shkn up and fnd nil over 1f out* **10/1**

-000 **7** *9* **Kerristina**[13] [2911] 3-8-3 .......... (v[1]) SWhitworth 6 27
(DJSFfrenchDavis) *trckd wnr after 2f to over 2f out: wknd over 1f out* **40/1**

0063 **8** *5* **Coolfore Jade (IRE)**[15] [2851] 4-9-3 47 .......... MSavage(5) 5 25
(NEBerry) *led for 2f: styd prom tl wknd wl over 2f out* **8/1**

2m 39.36s (5.12) **Going Correction** +0.25s/f (Slow)
**WFA** 3 from 4yo+ 14lb **8** Ran SP% **111.6**
Speed ratings: **92,91,89,89,89 88,82,79**CSF £10.14 TOTE £2.20: £1.10, £1.80, £5.90; EX 8.20.The winner was sold to the Cartmel Syndicate for 8,000gns. Tresor Secret was claimed by J.Gallagher for £6,000.
**Owner** Stephen Crown **Bred** Lloyd Farm Stud **Trained** Lambourn, Berks

**FOCUS**
A poor seller and a weak race that saw the first two come clear.

**NOTEBOOK**
**Delightfully** gamely battled back, having been headed in the final furlong, to get up close home. This drop in grade was greatly appreciated, and the first-time blinkers had the desired effect. However, she was well favoured by the weights on this occasion and it looks about as good as she is.
**Tresor Secret(FR)** looked all over the winner approaching two out, but found less than expected off the bridle and looked most unwilling when the eventual winner rallied late on. She clearly has a race of this nature within her grasp, but looks a tricky ride and may need a drop in trip.
**Java Dawn(IRE)** would have been closer with a better run and can be rated superior to the bare form. She got a lot closer to the runner-up than when tailed off last time and significantly improved, but her finishing position greatly drags down the form.
**Mandoob** again blew his chances at the start and proved most disappointing.
**Neptune** *Official explanation: trainer's representative said jockey was unable to remove the blind and gelding was therefore slowly away*

## 3304 MERCEDES BENZ DIRECT MEDIAN AUCTION MAIDEN STKS 1m 2f (P)
**7:35** (7:36) (F) 3-Y-O **£2,982** (£852; £426) **Stalls** Low

Form RPR

00-6 **1** **Kentmere (IRE)**[26] [2519] 3-8-11 67 .......... (b[1]) TPQueally(3) 6 72
(WJHaggas) *trckd ldrs gng wl: effrt 2f out: drvn over 1f out: led ins fnl f: r.o wl* **7/1**[3]

5 **2** *1 1/4* **Hugs Destiny (IRE)**[14] [2900] 3-9-0 .......... IMongan 4 70
(JGGiven) *sn trckd ldr: rdn to ld wl over 1f out: hdd ins fnl f: r.o but hld after* **4/1**[2]

202 **3** *6* **Champagne Shadow (IRE)**[14] [2882] 3-9-0 69 .......... (b) RLMoore 7 59
(GLMoore) *trckd ldrs: cl up and rdn 3f out: nt qckn wl over 1f out: one pce after* **3/1**[1]

60-0 **4** 3/4 **Lady Blade (IRE)**[16] 2820 3-8-6 61 LisaJones(3) 5 53
(BHanbury) *hld up in midfield: effrt over 2f out: sn outpcd: rdn and hanging lft over 1f out: kpt on* **16/1**

0420 **5** nk **Principal Witness (IRE)**[9] 3001 3-9-0 82 SDrowne 2 57
(WRMuir) *led to wl over 1f out: wknd* **3/1**[1]

60 **6** hd **Shazana**[23] 2632 3-8-9 PDobbs 12 52
(BWHills) *walked to post: hld up in midfield: effrt to chse ldrs over 2f out: sn no prog and btn* **11/1**

6 **7** 5 **Sudden Impulse**[13] 2911 3-8-9 RSmith 3 43
(ACharlton) *t.k.h: hld up bhd ldrs: rdn and wknd wl over 1f out* **14/1**

0000 **8** shd **Steppenwolf**[40] 2168 3-8-7 37 CHaddon(7) 14 48?
(WDeBest-Turner) *settled wl in rr: struggling 3f out: modest late prog* **100/1**

5004 **9** 1 1/2 **Clare Galway**[28] 2484 3-8-4 49 RThomas(5) 1 40
(TDMccarthy) *prom tl wknd rapidly 2f out* **20/1**

0060 **10** 2 1/2 **Kitley**[13] 2915 3-9-0 60 SWhitworth 13 40
(BGPowell) *stdd s: hld up in last: sme prog into midfield 2f out: no ch: wknd fnl f* **20/1**

0 **11** 2 **Electras Dream (IRE)**[27] 2505 3-8-9 DSweeney 8 32
(MrsCADunnett) *racd in midfield: rdn 4f out: wl btn over 2f out* **66/1**

**12** 1 **Explicit (IRE)** 3-9-0 RMullen 11 35
(GCBravery) *s.i.s: a in rr: rdn 4f out: sn btn* **25/1**

**13** 1/2 **Little Gannet** 3-8-9 DaneO'Neill 10 29
(SDow) *s.v.s: a in rr: wknd 3f out* **50/1**

60 **14** 4 **Pine Bay**[22] 2647 3-8-9 WSupple 9 22
(PMitchell) *hld up: prog into midfield 4f out: wknd 3f out* **33/1**

2m 9.08s (1.23) **Going Correction** +0.25s/f (Slow) **14** Ran SP% **124.1**
Speed ratings: **105,104,99,98,98 98,94,94,92,90 89,88,88,84**CSF £34.03 TOTE £7.50: £2.90, £2.20, £1.50; EX 41.90.

**Owner** Mr & Mrs G Middlebrook **Bred** G And Mrs Middlebrook **Trained** Newmarket, Suffolk

**FOCUS**
An average maiden run at a sound pace and the first two came well clear. The winner is exposed and the form may not be that reliable.

**NOTEBOOK**
**Kentmere(IRE)**, who had not progressed as once looked likely prior to this, put up a much-improved performance and won readily. The blinkers really made a difference on this occasion and the step up in trip very much suited. There is no reason why he cannot progress further in handicaps over this distance.
**Hugs Destiny(IRE)** could not quicken after hitting the front one out and still looked green, but improved on his debut display as expected over this extra distance. He was clear in second, should come on again for the outing and another step up in trip would not go amiss.
**Champagne Shadow(IRE)**, whose previous effort looked to give him every chance in this, could not quicken late on over this shorter trip. It is unlikely that he will be in the winner's enclosure until he reverts to further.
**Lady Blade(IRE)** ran better than on her seasonal reappearance last time, but did little to suggest she is about to lose her maiden tag and looks tricky.
**Principal Witness(IRE)** was given a positive ride over this longer trip, but had nothing left in reserve when challenged late on. He needs to revert to shorter in order to score.

## 3305 MID-MARKET H'CAP 1m 4f (P)
8:05 (8:06) (F) (0-55,55) 3-Y-O £3,188 (£911; £455) Stalls Low

Form RPR

01 **1** **Jelly Baby**[7] 3087 3-9-3 55 (b) TPQueally(3) 12 63
(WJHaggas) *s.s: hld up wl in rr: plenty to do over 3f out: sustained prog after: rdn to ld ins fnl f: styd on wl* **3/1**[1]

0663 **2** 1 1/4 **Erte**[8] 3056 3-8-10 48 SHitchcott(3) 8 54
(MRChannon) *hld up towards rr: prog over 3f out: rdn over 2f out: effrt to chal ent fnl f: kpt on same pce* **12/1**

-004 **3** 3 1/2 **Rubaiyat (IRE)**[9] 3026 3-9-3 52 SDrowne 9 53
(GWragg) *prom: chsd ldr over 3f out: drvn to ld wl over 1f out: hdd & wknd ins fnl f* **11/2**[3]

5064 **4** 1 **Frambo (IRE)**[28] 2485 3-8-4 42 (t) LisaJones(3) 6 41
(JGPortman) *hld up in midfield: rdn and outpcd over 3f out: styd on fr over 1f out: no ch* **14/1**

-044 **5** nk **Ablaj (IRE)**[12] 2931 3-9-2 51 RMullen 4 50
(EALDunlop) *hld up in midfield: prog to chse ldrs over 2f out: no imp wl over 1f out: one pce* **9/1**

0-00 **6** 1 **Genuinely (IRE)**[68] 1507 3-8-5 40 SWhitworth 10 37
(WJMusson) *s.i.s: wl in rr: outpcd fr 4f out: kpt on one pce fnl 2f* **20/1**

0403 **7** nk **Shalati Princess**[44] 2054 3-8-8 43 PDobbs 11 39
(JCFox) *racd in midfield: outpcd over 3f out: n.d after: one pce* **12/1**

2256 **8** 3 1/2 **Danefonique (IRE)**[16] 2821 3-8-13 55 DTudhope(7) 3 46
(DCarroll) *s.s: hld up wl in rr: outpcd whn nt clr run over 3f out: plodded on* **7/1**

-330 **9** nk **Semelle De Vent (USA)**[47] 1998 3-9-6 55 (b[1]) RHavlin 15 45
(JHMGosden) *trckd ldr: led over 4f out: hdd & wknd rapidly wl over 1f out* **12/1**

0000 **10** nk **Forge Lane (IRE)**[42] 2114 3-9-6 55 RLMoore 16 45
(GLMoore) *prom: chsd ldr briefly 4f out: sn rdn: wknd 2f out* **4/1**[2]

0000 **11** 1 3/4 **Alianna (FR)**[25] 2562 3-8-5 40 RSmith 5 27
(SDow) *wl in rr: outpcd fr 4f out: plodded on fnl 2f* **33/1**

00-0 **12** 18 **Tshukudu**[61] 1678 3-8-7 42 DSweeney 14 —
(MBlanshard) *led to over 4f out: sn wknd: t.o* **33/1**

5-00 **13** 2 **Troubleinparadise (IRE)**[75] 1365 3-9-5 54 DaneO'Neill 1 9
(JGGiven) *chsd ldrs: wknd 4f out: t.o* **25/1**

00-0 **14** 1 1/2 **Absolutely Fab (IRE)**[24] 2596 3-8-0 35 JMcAuley 2 —
(MrsCADunnett) *chsd ldrs: wknd 4f out: t.o* **50/1**

0-00 **15** dist **Miss Hoofbeats**[58] 1740 3-8-4 42 BReilly(3) 7 —
(MissJFeilden) *prom: rel to r after 2f: sn bhd: t.o 4f out: sddle slipped* **50/1**

2m 38.02s (3.78) **Going Correction** +0.25s/f (Slow) **15** Ran SP% **131.0**
Speed ratings: **97,96,93,93,92 92,92,89,89,89 88,76,74,73,—**CSF £41.76 CT £203.34 TOTE £3.20: £1.40, £2.70, £2.00; EX 27.90.

**Owner** B Haggas **Bred** J B Haggas **Trained** Newmarket, Suffolk

**FOCUS**
A dire contest that saw the field well strung out at the finish. The winner appears to be improving and the form is fair for the grade.

**NOTEBOOK**
**Jelly Baby** followed up her win in selling company last time with a dour staying display, and was value for more than the official winning margin. She looked to have a fair bit to do turning for home, but really picked up under pressure and can be expected to improve again on this. Although she beat little this time, she looks progressive and will be hard to beat next time at this level.
**Erte**, who has been sliding down the weights this year on account of his poor form, ran by far his best race for some time over this longer trip. He can be placed to find a race of this rating.
**Rubaiyat(IRE)** again looked a non-stayer over this distance, having held every chance on turning for home. A slight drop in trip can see him get off the mark.
**Frambo(IRE)** was never a serious threat and only kept on at the one pace in the straight. She again did little to convince she gets the trip.
**Forge Lane(IRE)**, up in trip and making his handicap debut, was popular in the betting ring, but never looked like landing a blow to the leaders.
**Miss Hoofbeats** *Official explanation: jockey said filly hung badly right and saddle slipped*

## 3306 WEATHERBYS BANK FILLIES' H'CAP 7f
8:35 (8:35) (D) (0-85,83) 3-Y-O £5,622 (£1,730; £865; £432) Stalls High

Form RPR

661 **1** **Keyaki (IRE)**[16] 2818 3-8-13 75 RMullen 3 84
(CFWall) *dwlt: hld up in tch: prog 3f out: rdn 2f out: styd on wl fnl f to ld last strides* **7/2**[2]

6510 **2** 1/2 **Lorien Hill (IRE)**[17] 2788 3-8-7 69 WSupple 1 77
(BWHills) *pressed ldrs: led over 2f out: hrd rdn over 1f out: hdd last strides* **5/1**[3]

-610 **3** 2 **Verkhotina**[19] 2741 3-9-4 80 SDrowne 5 83
(RCharlton) *hld up in last pair: rdn and effrt 2f out: styd on to take 3rd wl ins fnl f* **7/2**[2]

621 **4** 1 3/4 **Capestar (IRE)**[28] 2479 3-9-3 79 DSweeney 8 77
(BGPowell) *cl up: rdn to press ldr 2f out: wknd ins fnl f* **10/3**[1]

4-40 **5** 1 1/2 **Zwadi (IRE)**[13] 2911 3-8-11 73 DaneO'Neill 2 67
(HCandy) *mde most to over 2f out: sn rdn and btn* **12/1**

0-55 **6** 3 **Glebe Garden**[43] 2089 3-9-7 83 IMongan 6 70
(MLWBell) *w ldrs: ev ch over 2f out: losing pl whn squeezed out sn after: hanging rt fr over 1f out* **5/1**[3]

-000 **7** 4 **Pink Supreme**[19] 2741 3-8-0 65 (t) FPFerris(3) 7 41
(IAWood) *wl in tch tl wknd 2f out* **22/1**

000- **8** nk **Zarneeta**[254] 5599 3-7-5 60 oh5 CHaddon(7) 4 35
(WDeBest-Turner) *w ldrs for 2f: sn lost pl: last and struggling 1/2-way: no ch after* **50/1**

1m 23.62s (-0.59) **Going Correction** -0.05s/f (Good) **8** Ran SP% **114.9**
Speed ratings: **101,100,98,96,94 91,86,86**CSF £21.48 CT £65.21 TOTE £6.10: £2.00, £1.60, £2.20; EX 19.00.

**Owner** Hintlesham SPD Partners **Bred** Rathbarry Stud **Trained** Newmarket, Suffolk

**FOCUS**
A fair fillies' handicap run at a solid pace. The form is ordinary with the runner-up being the key.

**NOTEBOOK**
**Keyaki(IRE)** really picked up under maximum pressure late on and really dug deep to get the better of the runner-up close home. She was following up on her maiden success last time, and has the look of a progressive filly who can improve further over another furlong.
**Lorien Hill(IRE)**, dropped 4lb from her last run, put up an improved show and did litle wrong in defeat.
**Verkhotina**, held up to get the trip, got going all too late in the day. This display suggested she could be better served by a more positive ride at this distance.
**Capestar(IRE)** held every chance if good enough, but could not find a change of gear and was made to look one paced late on. *Official explanation: trainer said filly was unsuited by the good, good to firm in places ground*
**Glebe Garden** *Official explanation: jockey said filly was slightly hampered 2f out*

## 3307 MERCEDES BENZ DIRECT H'CAP 5f
9:05 (9:05) (E) (0-75,76) 3-Y-O+ £3,779 (£1,163; £581; £290) Stalls High

Form RPR

1360 **1** **Guns Blazing**[6] 3126 5-8-12 66 (b) MHoward(7) 8 76
(DKIvory) *mde all: clr fnl 2f: rdn out: unchal* **11/1**

0200 **2** 2 **Indian Bazaar (IRE)**[6] 3126 8-8-2 52 ow1 TPQueally(3) 1 55
(NEBerry) *chsd wnr: rdn 2f out: kpt on: nvr able to chal* **14/1**

6645 **3** shd **Pulse**[6] 3126 6-9-0 61 (p) DaneO'Neill 12 64
(JMBradley) *racd nr side: prom: effrt 2f out: disp 2nd pl fnl f : no imp on wnr* **5/2**[1]

0-03 **4** 2 **Bella Tutrice (IRE)**[6] 3122 3-9-2 72 FPFerris(3) 2 67
(IAWood) *settled in midfield: effrt 2f out: styd on same pce fr over 1f out* **12/1**

6323 **5** 1 1/4 **Roxanne Mill**[5] 3147 6-10-1 76 (p) RLMoore 11 67
(JMBradley) *chsd wnr: rdn and no imp 2f out: fdd fnl f* **9/2**[2]

/00- **6** 3/4 **Another Victim**[366] 2713 10-8-3 50 DKinsella 3 38
(MRBosley) *hld up in rr: rdn 2f out: one pce and nvr rchd ldrs* **28/1**

0661 **7** 3/4 **Gone'N'Dunnett (IRE)**[16] 2823 5-8-7 57 (v) LisaJones(3) 4 43
(MrsCADunnett) *prom: rdn 1/2-way: wknd over 1f out* **9/2**[2]

6040 **8** 1 1/4 **Seven No Trumps**[2] 3243 7-9-8 76 (p) CJDavies(3) 10 57
(JMBradley) *chsd ldrs: bmpd along 1/2-way: struggling fnl 2f* **7/1**[3]

6020 **9** hd **Inching**[5] 3147 4-8-2 49 RMullen 5 29
(RMHCowell) *hld up in rr: rdn and no prog over 2f out* **14/1**

00-6 **10** 1/2 **Perfect Setting**[18] 2754 4-9-2 63 DSweeney 9 42
(PJMakin) *racd in midfield: rdn 1/2-way: wknd wl over 1f out* **10/1**

2530 **11** 1 1/4 **Empress Josephine**[28] 2482 4-8-6 53 (v) WSupple 6 27
(JRJenkins) *nvr on terms w ldrs: rdn and struggling 1/2-way* **20/1**

0600 **12** hd **Forzenuff**[7] 3084 3-8-6 59 VVenkaya 7 32
(JRBoyle) *a in rr: rdn and struggling 1/2-way* **20/1**

57.60 secs (-1.27) **Going Correction** -0.05s/f (Good)
**WFA** 3 from 4yo+ 6lb **12** Ran SP% **128.9**
Speed ratings: **108,104,104,101,99 98,97,95,94,93 91,91**CSF £164.04 CT £524.36 TOTE £7.50: £2.90, £4.00, £1.90; EX 153.20 Place 6 £25.13, Place 5 £15.89.

**Owner** R D Hartshorn **Bred** Mrs C A R Lockhart **Trained** Radlett, Herts

**FOCUS**
A modest sprint, but a decent time and the field were well strung out behind the decisive winner, who looks an inproved performer.

**NOTEBOOK**
**Guns Blazing** put up a bold display of front-running to win as he pleased. This was more like the form that made him a tough rival to pass earlier in the season.
**Indian Bazaar(IRE)** stayed on best of the remainder, but never looked like getting to the winner. This was his best run of the current campaign and he could be about to hit top form.
**Pulse** could not get to the winner under maximum pressure after two out, try as he might, and ultimately paid the price late in the day. He should not be written off on the back of this display.
**Bella Tutrice(IRE)** has started to find her form once more and is another to have slipped to a fair-looking mark. She can find an easier opportunity and get back in the winner's enclosure before long.
**Roxanne Mill** could only keep on at the one pace and ran slightly below par.
**Gone'N'Dunnett(IRE)**
T/Plt: £33.70 to a £1 stake. Pool: £33,805.40. 731.45 winning tickets. T/Qpdt: £12.10 to a £1 stake. Pool: £2,010.60. 122.20 winning tickets. JN

# 3265 NEWCASTLE (L-H)

Saturday, June 26

**OFFICIAL GOING: Soft (good to soft in places) changing to soft (heavy in places) after race 2 (2.25)**

A strip of fresh ground next to the far rail in the straight was uncovered, giving those racing up with the pace next to that rail the edge.

Wind: Moderate 1/2 behind. Weather: Persistent rain.

## 3308 FOSTER'S LAGER CHIPCHASE STKS (GROUP 3) 6f
**1:55** (1:56) (A) 3-Y-0+ **£29,000** (£11,000; £5,500; £2,500) **Stalls** High

Form RPR

425- **1** **Royal Millennium (IRE)**[223] 6009 6-9-2 110 TQuinn 4 115
(MRChannon) *prom far side: smooth hdwy over 1f out: shkn up to ld cl home* **8/1**

10-0 **2** *nk* **Somnus**[46] 2021 4-9-10 117 PRobinson 3 122
(TDEasterby) *chsd far side ldrs: led appr fnl f: kpt on: hdd cl home* **5/1**[2]

4-52 **3** *1/2* **Ruby Rocket (IRE)**[21] 2685 3-8-6 105 MFenton 8 110
(HMorrison) *hld up far side: n.m.r briefly 2f out and ins fnl f: rdn and r.o strly* **14/1**

-301 **4** *1* **The Kiddykid (IRE)**[35] 2316 4-9-6 111 RWinston 6 114
(PDEvans) *chsd ldrs: rdn over 2f out: one pce fnl f* **9/1**

6106 **5** *1/2* **Quito (IRE)**[23] 2623 7-9-2 110 (b) ACulhane 7 108
(DWChapman) *sn pushed along rr far side: hdwy over 1f out: kpt on: nrst fin* **13/2**

6-14 **6** *1/2* **Welsh Emperor (IRE)**[46] 2021 5-9-2 109 (b) DaleGibson 2 107
(TPTate) *led far side tl hdd appr fnl f: nt qckn* **6/1**[3]

6020 **7** *1 1/2* **Simianna**[7] 3074 5-8-13 96 (p) FNorton 5 99
(ABerry) *in tch far side: rdn over 2f out: no imp over 1f out* **33/1**

1-31 **8** *nk* **So Will I**[43] 2080 3-8-9 109 RHills 1 101
(MPTregoning) *prom far side: rdn over 2f out: btn over 1f out* **4/1**[1]

4011 **9** *9* **Celtic Mill**[33] 2373 6-9-2 107 LEnstone 9 74
(DWBarker) *led stands side: no ch w far side fr 1/2-way* **16/1**

1000 **10** *5* **Bahamian Pirate (USA)**[7] 3073 9-9-2 105 EAhern 11 59
(DNicholls) *chsd stands side ldrs: nvr on terms* **9/1**

0-15 **11** *11* **Goldeva**[46] 2021 5-8-13 102 NCallan 10 23
(RHollinshead) *chsd stands side ldr: rdn 1/2-way: sn no ch* **20/1**

1m 13.03s (-2.01) **Going Correction** +0.05s/f (Good)
**WFA** 3 from 4yo+ 7lb **11** Ran SP% **115.6**
Speed ratings: **115,114,113,112,111 111,109,108,96,90 75**CSF £46.92 TOTE £10.10: £4.10, £2.40, £3.40; EX 64.60.
**Owner** Jackie & George Smith **Bred** Mrs G Smith **Trained** West Ilsley, Berks

**FOCUS**
A decent quality event run at a sound pace and the form should stand up at a similar level. The three that raced on the stands side were readily left behind from halfway and their final placings are best ignored.

**NOTEBOOK**
**Royal Millennium(IRE)**, a tough sort who has been a model of consistency, confirmed himself at least as good as ever on this reappearance. He goes on any ground, stays seven furlongs and looks capable of winning again in minor Group company.
**Somnus**, carrying a Group One penalty, had the run of the race under ideal conditions and showed that he retains all his ability. The penalty means he may not be easy to place successfully on faster ground, but he will be a match for most over this trip with plenty of cut in the ground.
**Ruby Rocket(IRE)** ◆, a progressive performer, turned in a career-best effort on this first start on soft ground to fare the best of those that attempted to come from off the pace. She did not get the best of runs either, and looks well up to winning a race in Group company over sprint distances this term.
**The Kiddykid(IRE)**, an improved performer over this trip this term, had the run of the race and performed creditably under his penalty. He should continue to go well but is likely to continue to look vulnerable in this type of race under his penalty.
**Quito(IRE)** looked to have plenty in his favour, and ran almost as well as he has ever done under suitable conditions in a race where the leaders did not really come back. He is a smart performer who is equally effective over seven and should continue to give a good account.
**Welsh Emperor(IRE)** had conditions to suit and the run of the race next to the far rail and posted another creditable effort. He should continue to go well when he gets his favoured easy surface.
**Simianna** was not totally disgraced in the face of a stiff task, especially as she raced away from the favoured far side. However, she is high enough in the weights for handicaps and will continue to look vulnerable in this type of event.
**So Will I**, a progressive sort over six and seven furlongs, was a disappointment and he is worth another chance back on a sound surface. *Official explanation: jockey said gelding was unsuited by the soft ground*
**Celtic Mill**, a much-improved performer, showed his usual foot to lead the three that raced on the stands side, but that trio were readily left behind from halfway and this run is best overlooked.

## 3309 TOTESPORT NORTHERN SPRINT (H'CAP) 6f
**2:25** (2:28) (C) (0-95,91) 3-Y-0+ **£19,035** (£7,220; £3,610; £1,641) **Stalls** High

Form RPR

3005 **1** **Sierra Vista**[41] 2143 4-8-6 76 LEnstone(3) 10 89
(DWBarker) *keen early: trckd ldrs: led over 1f out: kpt on gamely* **33/1**

4244 **2** *nk* **Ellens Academy (IRE)**[28] 2467 9-8-12 79 FNorton 13 91
(EJAlston) *prom: effrt over 2f out: kpt on wl fnl f: jst hld* **50/1**

0100 **3** *1 1/4* **River Falcon**[15] 2857 4-9-3 84 GaryStevens 2 92
(JSGoldie) *led 2f: cl up: rdn 2f out: kpt on fnl f* **14/1**

0000 **4** *shd* **Fantasy Believer**[21] 2682 6-9-2 83 RWinston 6 91
(JJQuinn) *midfield: effrt 2f out: rdn and r.o fnl f: nrst fin* **8/1**

-134 **5** *3/4* **Bygone Days**[35] 2309 3-8-11 85 TQuinn 9 91
(WJHaggas) *hld up: rdn over 2f out: no imp tl kpt on fnl f: nrst fin* **13/2**[2]

6004 **6** *1/2* **Highland Warrior**[8] 3038 5-8-3 73 NMackay(3) 7 77
(JSGoldie) *dwlt: hld up: nt clr run fr over 2f out to ins fnl f: r.o wl* **16/1**

0000 **7** *nk* **Sharp Hat**[10] 2976 10-7-5 65 oh6 DFentiman(7) 16 68
(DWChapman) *cl up: effrt and ev ch over 1f out: nt qckn ins last* **66/1**

-042 **8** *shd* **Mutawaqed (IRE)**[21] 2682 6-9-5 86 (t) EAhern 14 89
(MAMagnusson) *hld up: hdwy and prom appr fnl f: no ex ins last* **15/2**[3]

0-04 **9** *1/2* **Pieter Brueghel (USA)**[15] 2857 5-9-1 82 JFanning 17 84
(DNicholls) *chsd ldrs tl rdn and outpcd fnl f* **28/1**

22U1 **10** *1/2* **Balakiref**[7] 3079 5-8-2 69 JQuinn 11 69
(MDods) *bhd tl swtchd rt and hdwy appr fnl f: nrst fin* **12/1**

0500 **11** *1* **Grey Cossack**[10] 2976 7-8-8 75 RFitzpatrick 1 72
(PTMidgley) *midfield: sn pushed along: no imp fr 2f out* **14/1**

003 **12** *nk* **Polar Kingdom**[56] 1765 6-8-8 75 RHills 5 71
(TDBarron) *in tch: n.m.r and lost pl after 2f: n.d after* **3/1**[1]

0041 **13** *hd* **Cd Flyer (IRE)**[7] 3098 7-9-1 87 PMulrennan(5) 18 83
(BEllison) *s.i.s: bhd tl sme late hdwy: nvr on terms* **16/1**

-064 **14** *1 1/2* **George The Best (IRE)**[43] 2075 3-7-13 73 DaleGibson 4 64
(MDHammond) *chsd ldrs tl wknd wl over 1f out* **25/1**

0035 **15** *1 3/4* **Fair Shake (IRE)**[7] 3079 4-7-13 66 (p) PHanagan 8 52
(DEddy) *sn outpcd: nvr on terms* **9/1**

4010 **16** *nk* **Native Title**[7] 3074 6-9-7 88 ANicholls 12 73
(DNicholls) *led after 2f to over 1f out: sn wknd* **25/1**

1-00 **17** *4* **Cd Europe (IRE)**[7] 3074 6-9-10 91 (p) NCallan 15 64
(KARyan) *hld up: rdn over 2f out: sn btn* **33/1**

4-30 **18** *1* **Sir Desmond**[152] 607 6-8-13 80 (p) PRobinson 3 50
(RGuest) *chsd ldrs to 2f out: sn btn* **20/1**

1m 14.4s (-0.64) **Going Correction** +0.05s/f (Good)
**WFA** 3 from 4yo+ 7lb **18** Ran SP% **129.2**
Speed ratings: **106,105,103,103,102 102,101,101,100,100 98,98,98,96,93 93,88,86**CSF £1170.68 CT £21946.41 TOTE £86.50: £12.40, £5.00, £4.20, £2.00; EX 2504.00 TRIFECTA Not won..
**Owner** David T J Metcalfe **Bred** Mrs M Beddis **Trained** Scorton, N Yorks
■ Stewards Enquiry : L Enstone caution: used whip with excessive frequency

**FOCUS**
A competitive sprint in which the pace was sound and in which the whole field tacked over to race towards the far rail. Once again those that raced up with the pace seemed to have the edge and the form looks a little below standard for the grade.

**NOTEBOOK**
**Sierra Vista** has gradually edged down the weights and turned in easily her best effort of the year to notch her first success since August 2002 for a stable that does well with speedy types. She had the run of the race to a larger degree than most, but should continue to give a good account.
**Ellens Academy(IRE)** is a most consistent sort who elected to put his best foot forward once again from his double-figure draw. He goes on any ground with the possible exception of heavy and should continue to give a good account.
**River Falcon** had the run of the race from his low draw and returned to something like his best. He goes on most ground, is effective over both sprint distances but is vulnerable to progressive or well handicapped types from his current mark.
**Fantasy Believer** ◆ had conditions to suit and ran his best race of the year. He has slipped back to a favourable mark and appeals as the type to win a similar handicap in the coming weeks, especially if there is any cut in the ground.
**Bygone Days** ◆ once again shaped as though a bit better than the bare form, as he fared the best of those to come from off the pace. He settled better than he has done in the past and looks well worth another try over seven furlongs. He is lightly raced enough to be open to further improvement, and looks sure to win another race.
**Highland Warrior**, not for the first time this season, fared a good deal better than the bare result suggests and would have achieved a minor placing at the very least had the gaps appeared at the right time. However he is the type that needs things to drop perfectly and, although capable of winning again from his current mark, is not one to be lumping on.
**Sharp Hat**, from a stable among the winners ran really well from 6lb out of the handicap and may be a bit better than the bare result suggests, as he was always racing a few lengths away from the favoured far rail. He will be of interest from his current mark when returned to a more suitable grade.
**Mutawaqed(IRE)** was another that was not seen to best advantage, as he had to make his ground away from the favoured far rail and was not knocked about when clearly held. He is worth another chance.
**Pieter Brueghel(USA)** was anything but disgraced from this widest draw and, as he will be down in the weights for this, will be of interest against exposed performers from this mark back on a sound surface in due course.
**Polar Kingdom**, who had conditions to suit, attracted plenty of support but could never get competitive after meeting early inteference and this run is best overlooked. *Official explanation: trainer said gelding had been struck into, adding that filly had run too freely*
**Cd Europe(IRE)** *Official explanation: jockey said gelding was unsuited by the soft ground*

## 3310 JOHN SMITH'S NORTHUMBERLAND PLATE (HERITAGE H'CAP) 2m 19y
**3:00** (3:02) (B) 3-Y-0+ **£104,400** (£39,600; £19,800; £9,000) **Stalls** High

Form RPR

04/3 **1** **Mirjan (IRE)**[37] 1316 8-8-3 86 (b) PHanagan 5 96
(LLungo) *midfield: effrt 3f out: led ins fnl f: styd on wl* **33/1**

-501 **2** *hd* **Swing Wing**[34] 2340 5-9-8 105 JFanning 7 115
(PFICole) *chsd ldrs: effrt and disp ld over 2f out: r.o fnl f: jst hld* **20/1**

2-11 **3** *3/4* **Anak Pekan**[52] 1880 4-9-4 101 PRobinson 10 110
(MAJarvis) *a cl up: led over 2f out to ins fnl f: kpt on: hld towards fin* **5/2**[1]

3-01 **4** *3* **Collier Hill**[43] 2076 6-9-4 101 RWinston 18 107
(GASwinbank) *hld up ins: n.m.r 4f out and over 2f out: rdn and r.o wl fnl f* **20/1**

5062 **5** *shd* **Kristensen**[28] 2491 5-7-12 81 (p) PFessey 3 87
(DEddy) *cl up: effrt over 2f out: outpcd appr fnl f* **25/1**

3422 **6** *1 1/4* **Pagan Dance (IRE)**[7] 3075 5-8-9 92 (p) ACulhane 19 97
(MrsAJPerrett) *hld up bhd: hdwy over 2f out: no imp fnl f* **25/1**

3-03 **7** *nk* **Defining**[21] 2691 5-8-12 95 OUrbina 8 100
(JRFanshawe) *hld up: hdwy over 2f out: nt qckn over 1f out* **14/1**

540/ **8** *1 1/2* **Self Defense**[72] 4024 7-9-0 100 JFMcDonald(3) 2 103
(PRChamings) *cl up tl rdn and wknd over 1f out* **40/1**

-002 **9** *2 1/2* **Promoter**[11] 2958 4-8-2 85 EAhern 9 86
(JNoseda) *keen in midfield: blkd 4f out: rdn and outpcd fr 2f out* **15/2**[3]

20-3 **10** *shd* **Zibeline (IRE)**[21] 2681 7-8-6 89 (b) FNorton 17 90
(BEllison) *keen: hld up: hdwy whn nt clr run over 2f out: n.d* **25/1**

1-02 **11** *3* **Escayola (IRE)**[15] 2855 4-8-4 87 (b) TQuinn 20 85
(WJHaggas) *keen: hld up: effrt over 2f out: hung lft and sn btn* **14/1**

3-42 **12** *2 1/2* **Distant Prospect (IRE)**[21] 2684 7-8-11 94 RHills 13 89
(AMBalding) *hld up: rdn 3f out: sn btn* **7/1**[2]

111- **13** *1/2* **Jagger**[272] 5253 4-9-0 97 GaryStevens 12 92
(GAButler) *hld up outer: effrt over 2f out: wknd over 1f out* **7/1**[2]

2136 **14** *1/2* **Red Lancer**[8] 3035 3-8-7 110 MFenton 14 104
(RJPrice) *hld up: effrt over 2f out: sn btn* **22/1**

02-0 **15** *1 1/2* **Mamcazma**[21] 2691 6-8-12 95 MTebbutt 11 88
(DMorris) *prom tl rdn and wknd over 2f out* **66/1**

6-00 **16** *3* **Rayshan (IRE)**[14] 2895 4-8-7 95 (b[1]) PMulrennan(5) 6 85
(JHowardJohnson) *hld up midfield: effrt over 2f out: wknd over 1f out* **66/1**

4-01 **17** *5* **Barolo**[37] 2240 5-9-10 107 JFortune 16 92
(PWHarris) *hld up: rdn 3f out: sn btn* **16/1**

6106 **18** *1 3/4* **Jorobaden (FR)**[21] 2684 4-8-6 89 JQuinn 15 72
(CFWall) *hld up: rdn 4f out: nvr on terms* **28/1**

30-0 **19** *20* **Spectrometer**[32] 1661 7-7-13 82 JMackay 1 45
(RCGuest) *led to over 2f out: sn wknd* **33/1**

3m 37.54s (2.51) **Going Correction** +0.40s/f (Good)
**WFA** 3 from 4yo+ 20lb **19** Ran SP% **124.7**
Speed ratings: **109,108,108,107,106 106,106,105,104,104 102,101,101,100,100 98,96,95,85**CSF £571.73 CT £2264.35 TOTE £42.50: £6.50, £4.40, £1.90, £2.60; EX 644.00 Trifecta £3952.10 Part won. Pool £5,566.40. 0.20 winning tickets..
**Owner** Mrs Barbara Lungo **Bred** His Highness The Aga Khan's Studs S C **Trained** Carrutherstown, D'fries & G'way



The Form Book, Raceform Ltd, Compton, RG20 6NL

**FOCUS**
A competitive renewal but the steady early gallop in the rain-softened conditions meant those held up were at a disadvantage. The form is not outstanding and for that reason this bare result is best treated with a degree of caution.

**NOTEBOOK**
**Mirjan(IRE)**, better known as a useful hurdler at up to three miles, has been very lightly raced on the Flat in recent years but showed he was capable of useful form with the blinkers back on (replacing a visor). He seems suited by a thorough test, did not mind the ground and will be interesting in a race like the Cesarewitch later in the year.
**Swing Wing ◆** turned in arguably a career-best effort and showed the right attitude in the closing stages. On this evidence he looks capable of picking up a minor Group race.
**Anak Pekan ◆**, a much-improved performer this year, had the run of the race but only narrowly failed to defy an 11lb rise in the weights. This represented a career-best effort and, as he is only relatively lightly raced, he may still be capable of better. He looks sure to win another decent race.
**Collier Hill** had conditions to suit and ran up to his best. Given that the race favoured those racing close to the pace, he could be a bit better than the bare form, as he was dropped in early on and met trouble on a couple of occasions. He has developed into a useful sort and should continue to give a good account on his favoured easy surface.
**Kristensen** is a consistent sort who had the run of the race and once again ran close to his best, but the fact his latest turf win was in April 2002 underlines his vulnerability from his current rating in this type of event.
**Pagan Dance(IRE)**, upped to this trip for the first time on the Flat, looks a bit better than the bare form as this race suited those racing prominently. However, he again looked less than straightforward under pressure and, as his effort flattened out in the closing stages, still has to prove conclusively his stamina in a truly-run race over this trip.
**Defining**, from an in-form stable, is at the top of his mark but was not disgraced on his first attempt over this trip. However he did leave the impression that the return to shorter distances and possibly a sounder surface would be in his favour.
**Promoter**, who turned in an improved effort at Royal Ascot last time, did not get home, having raced too keenly in the rain-softened conditions. Given his tendency to take a good hold, he may always be best on a sound surface.
**Escayola(IRE)** was drawn very wide and was not seen to best effect in this ground given the way the race unfolded. He is not one to write off just yet.
**Distant Prospect(IRE)** *Official explanation: trainer later said gelding was slowly away and could never find a position*

## 3311 EUROPEAN BREEDERS FUND HOPPINGS STKS (LISTED RACE) (F&M) 1m 2f 32y
**3:30** (3:34) (A ) 3-Y-0+ **£17,400** (£6,600; £3,300; £1,500) **Stalls High**

Form RPR
0-32 **1** **Ice Palace**[19] 2733 4-9-4 96 EAhern 5 95+
(JRFanshawe) *prom: rdn over 2f out: styng on whn nt clr run and swtchd ins fnl f: kpt on wl to ld cl home* **2/1**[1]
15 **2** *nk* **Blue Oasis (IRE)**[22] 2641 3-8-6 87 TQuinn 3 95
(RGuest) *s.i.s: hld up: effrt and rdn over 2f out: led ins fnl f: hdd cl home* **13/2**
0044 **3** *½* **Cote Quest (USA)**[19] 2733 4-9-4 92 ACulhane 6 94
(SCWilliams) *prom: effrt over 1f out: chal ins fnl f: kpt on: hld cl home* **14/1**
0-22 **4** *hd* **Shamara (IRE)**[23] 2630 4-9-4 85 PRobinson 8 94
(CFWall) *keen: cl up: rdn and led briefly ins fnl f: jst hld* **4/1**[3]
-330 **5** *1 ¾* **Crystal Curling (IRE)**[9] 2997 3-8-6 99 RHills 2 91+
(BWHills) *set stdy pce: rdn over 2f out: hdd and no ex ins fnl f* **3/1**[2]
0-00 **6** *dist* **Jubilee Treat (USA)**[31] 2403 4-9-4 74 FNorton 7 —
(GWragg) *keen: cl up tl wknd over 2f out: sn lost tch* **33/1**

2m 14.14s (2.54) **Going Correction** +0.40s/f (Good)
**WFA** 3 from 4yo 12lb **6** Ran **SP%** **101.3**
Speed ratings: **105,104,104,104,102** —CSF £12.14 TOTE £2.00: £1.30, £2.80; EX 16.60.
**Owner** Cheveley Park Stud **Bred** Cheveley Park Stud Ltd **Trained** Newmarket, Suffolk
■ Stewards Enquiry : T Quinn three-day ban: used whip with excessive frequency and without giving filly time to respond (Jul 7-9); caution: careless riding

**FOCUS**
A below-par renewal but a praiseworthy winner of a messy race. The gallop was steady and they raced wide for the first three furlongs until reaching the fresh strip of ground on the inside seven furlongs from home.

**NOTEBOOK**
**Ice Palace**, who looked at her very best, stuck to the inner on the best ground. With the doors slammed in her face, she eventually came six wide and showed a serious turn of foot to pull the prize out of the fire near the line. She deserves full marks for this.
**Blue Oasis(IRE)**, who won a Thirsk maiden two outings ago, is very much on the up. She never flinched under a punishing ride, but had the prize whipped from under her nose near the line.
**Cote Quest(USA)**, who likes the soft, had finished over five lengths behind the winner at Pontefract last time, and the way the race was run probably flatters her.
**Shamara(IRE)**, who had a bit to find, was keen to get on with it. After working her way into a narrow lead, she was outpointed in the final dash to the line.
**Crystal Curling(IRE)** had 3lb in hand of the winner on official figures. Having run over a mile and a half in the Group Two Ribblesdale at Royal Ascot just nine days earlier, she would surely have been better setting a much stronger pace. As it was she was found lacking in the final sprint.
**Jubilee Treat(USA)** had a lot to find but even so ran badly and eventually crossed the line in her own time. *Official explanation: jockey said filly ran too free*

## 3312 JOURNAL "GOOD MORNING" H'CAP 1m (R)
**4:05** (4:08) (D ) (0-80,82) 3-Y-0 **£11,971** (£4,540; £2,270; £1,032) **Stalls Centre**

Form RPR
3241 **1** **Majorca**[11] 2962 3-9-9 82 JFortune 10 93
(JHMGosden) *prom: smooth hdwy to ld over 1f out: rdn and edgd lft ins last: kpt on wl* **4/1**[1]
21-6 **2** *1* **Kibryaa (USA)**[21] 2692 3-9-3 76 PRobinson 2 85
(MAJarvis) *disp ld to over 1f out: kpt on ins fnl f* **10/1**
2622 **3** *¾* **Lets Roll**[14] 2887 3-8-8 72 PMulrennan(5) 11 79
(CWThornton) *hld up: hdwy outside 2f out: edgd lft: kpt on strly: nt rch first two* **11/2**[2]
-062 **4** *1 ½* **Double Vodka (IRE)**[24] 2571 3-8-4 63 FNorton 9 67
(MrsJRRamsden) *hld up: effrt whn nt clr run 2f out: kpt on fnl f: no imp* **14/1**
0-30 **5** *nk* **Third Empire**[47] 1995 3-8-1 60 PFessey 6 67+
(CGrant) *mde most to over 1f out: one pce whn hmpd and stmbld bdly ins fnl f: nt rcvr* **50/1**
2-23 **6** *¾* **Tytheknot**[59] 1712 3-9-2 75 PHanagan 12 77
(JeddO'Keeffe) *hld up: effrt outside 2f out: no imp fnl f* **16/1**
3-06 **7** *2 ½* **Chigorin**[15] 2847 3-8-11 70 EAhern 7 67
(JMPEustace) *prom tl rdn and outpcd fr 2f out* **9/1**
4-46 **8** *1* **Charnock Bates One (IRE)**[57] 1755 3-8-6 65 ow1 RWinston 3 60
(TDEasterby) *s.i.s: effrt over 2f out: no imp fnl 2f* **20/1**
-626 **9** *nk* **Miss Eloise**[6] 3117 3-7-13 58 ow1 JQuinn 4 52
(TDEasterby) *hld up: effrt over 2f out: nvr able to chal* **10/1**
5341 **10** *¾* **Lyca Ballerina**[17] 2777 3-9-2 75 RHills 5 68
(BWHills) *chsd ldrs tl outpcd fr 2f out* **7/1**[3]
0-13 **11** *2* **Ali Deo**[26] 2516 3-9-4 77 TQuinn 8 66
(WJHaggas) *hld up: effrt over 2f out: sn btn* **12/1**
3001 **12** *½* **Dispol Veleta**[10] 2988 3-8-9 68 JFanning 1 56
(TDBarron) *cl up tl wknd fr 2f out* **10/1**
3164 **13** *12* **Amankila (IRE)**[10] 2973 3-8-4 63 JMackay 13 27
(MLWBell) *prom tl wknd over 2f out* **11/1**

1m 45.14s (1.66) **Going Correction** +0.40s/f (Good) **13** Ran **SP%** **120.5**
Speed ratings: **107,106,105,103,103 102,100,99,98,98 96,95,83**CSF £44.53 CT £232.53 TOTE £4.80: £2.40, £3.90, £1.90; EX 73.80.
**Owner** Sheikh Mohammed **Bred** Shadwell Estate Company Limited **Trained** Manton, Wilts

**FOCUS**
A fair time for the grade and ordinary but reliable form. In effect a 0-82 handicap and a surprise when the Stewards deemed the interference accidental rather than careless.

**NOTEBOOK**
**Majorca**, in peak condition, found the totally different ground no problem. Making his final effort on the outer and, with his rider carrying his whip in his right hand, he came in, hampering the fifth and then the runner-up. He won going away and is clearly improving at a rate of knots.
**Kibryaa(USA)**, 2lb lower than his handicap debut three weeks earlier, clearly appreciated the ground and, making the most of his low draw, stuck on well, though held when his ankle was tapped by the winner near the line.
**Lets Roll** looked a shade unfortunate but he is not the easiest of rides. On and off the bit, he was still last with under three furlongs to go. Pulled wide, he persisted in edging back left before finishing with a flourish.
**Double Vodka(IRE)**, a maiden after seven starts, is invariably held up for a late surge and those tactics need luck, which he did not enjoy. That elusive first win is surely just around the corner.
**Third Empire** went head-to-head, but was clinging on to third spot when he nearly lost his rider inside the last as the winner edged in. This was a much-improved effort, but he seems incapable of running two races alike.
**Tytheknot** has form on easy ground and is well worth another try over a bit further.

## 3313 KRONENBOURG 1664 EBF MAIDEN STKS 6f
**4:40** (4:41) (D ) 2-Y-0 **£6,825** (£2,100; £1,050; £525) **Stalls High**

Form RPR
0 **1** **John Forbes**[7] 3071 2-8-9 PMulrennan(5) 3 76+
(BEllison) *chsd ldrs: rdn and outpcd 2f out: kpt on fnl f to ld cl home* **14/1**
3 **2** *½* **Turnaround (GER)**[21] 2686 2-9-0 ACulhane 7 74+
(MrsJRRamsden) *plld hrd: cl up: led 1/2-way: kpt on fnl f: hdd cl home* **5/2**[2]
**3** *¾* **Tsaroxy (IRE)** 2-9-0 PHanagan 4 72+
(JHowardJohnson) *sn prom: effrt over 1f out: edgd lft and ev ch ins fnl f: hld cl home* **2/1**[1]
**4** *6* **Lodgician (IRE)** 2-9-0 RWinston 5 54
(JJQuinn) *s.i.s: effrt over 2f out: no imp over 1f out* **8/1**
**5** *3 ½* **Middle Eastern** 2-9-0 NCallan 6 43
(PABlockley) *keen: cl up tl wknd fr 2f out* **25/1**
**6** *nk* **Hadrian (IRE)** 2-9-0 JFanning 2 42
(MJohnston) *led to 1/2-way: hung lft and wknd 2f out* **10/3**[3]
**7** *7* **Nowaday (GER)** 2-9-0 DaleGibson 1 21
(TPTate) *wnt lft s: sn in tch: wknd over 2f out* **33/1**

1m 17.7s (2.66) **Going Correction** +0.05s/f (Good) **7** Ran **SP%** **109.5**
Speed ratings: **84,83,82,74,69 69,59**CSF £45.09 TOTE £20.10: £4.80, £2.20; EX 63.20.
**Owner** Mrs Claire Ellison **Bred** Northmore Stud **Trained** Norton, N Yorks

**FOCUS**
Little strength in depth for the money on offer. The gallop was only fair and the time was slow. The bare form looks nothing out of the ordinary but a couple of these look capable of better.

**NOTEBOOK**
**John Forbes**, pitched in at the deep end on his racecourse debut at Royal Ascot, showed improved form back in this more realistic grade and shaped as though the step up to seven furlongs would be in his favour. He may well be capable of better.
**Turnaround(GER)**, up in trip, again showed more than enough to suggest he should have no problems winning a similar event. He may have to settle better than he did here if he is to fulfil his potential.
**Tsaroxy(IRE) ◆**, a 420,000 euro half-brother to six-furlong juvenile winner Lady's Mantle, attracted plenty of support and showed more than enough on this racecourse debut, despite his greenness, to suggest he can win a similar race at the very least.
**Lodgician(IRE)**, an 80,000gns to a seven-furlong winner in France, was relatively easy to back but showed ability on this racecourse debut and appeals as the type to do better in time.
**Middle Eastern**, a half-brother to five-furlong juvenile winner Schematic, failed to settle and was soundly beaten on this racecourse debut. He may be capable of better in due course.
**Hadrian(IRE)**, a 90,000gns half-brother to ten winners, most notably Classic Park, winner of the Irish 1000 Guineas. He attracted support but was too green to do himself justice, and looks the sort who will leave this bare form behind.

## 3314 MILLER UK H'CAP 5f
**5:10** (5:10) (E ) (0-70,69) 3-Y-0+ **£4,397** (£1,353; £676; £338) **Stalls High**

Form RPR
0412 **1** **Soaked**[10] 2975 11-9-2 57 (b) ACulhane 2 70
(DWChapman) *mde all far rail: rdn and r.o wl fnl f* **7/2**[1]
4004 **2** *1 ¾* **Blue Maeve**[9] 3016 4-8-9 50 SRighton 11 58
(JHetherton) *chsd ldrs: effrt over 2f out: kpt on same pce wl ins fnl f* **25/1**
0040 **3** *½* **Winthorpe (IRE)**[14] 2899 4-9-9 69 PMulrennan(5) 1 75+
(JJQuinn) *prom: outpcd over 2f out: rallied over 1f out: kpt on fnl f* **10/1**
1006 **4** *1 ¼* **Mynd**[19] 2734 4-9-9 64 VHalliday 3 67
(RMWhitaker) *trckd ldrs: effrt over 2f out: one pce fnl f* **7/1**[3]
0020 **5** *1* **Fairgame Man**[4] 3169 6-8-4 45 (p) RFitzpatrick 6 45+
(JSWainwright) *hld up: rdn 1/2-way: kpt on fnl f: n.d* **11/1**
3310 **6** *½* **Levelled**[1] 3277 10-7-13 47 DFentiman(7) 5 45
(DWChapman) *prom tl rdn and outpcd appr fnl f* **22/1**
0-50 **7** *½* **Le Meridien (IRE)**[4] 3169 6-8-9 53 (v) LEnstone(3) 4 50
(JSWainwright) *chsd ldrs tl rdn and outpcd over 1f out* **11/1**
0-00 **8** *1 ½* **Hilltime (IRE)**[22] 2656 4-9-3 58 JFanning 8 50
(JJQuinn) *bhd and outpcd: sme late hdwy: nvr rchd ldrs* **25/1**
-510 **9** *½* **Tatweer (IRE)**[19] 2734 4-9-3 58 (v) RWinston 7 49
(DShaw) *bhd and rdn 1/2-way: nvr rchd ldrs* **6/1**[2]
0L54 **10** *½* **Joyce's Choice**[10] 2975 5-8-9 50 DMcGaffin 10 39
(JSWainwright) *hld up: effrt over 2f out: wknd over 1f out* **20/1**
0015 **11** *1* **Obe Bold (IRE)**[3] 3201 3-8-13 60 NCallan 15 46
(ABerry) *prom: rdn and wkng whn n.m.r over 1f out* **16/1**
0000 **12** *1* **Viewforth**[14] 2899 6-10-0 69 JFortune 17 52
(JSGoldie) *a bhd* **15/2**
0300 **13** *2* **Lord Baskerville**[1] 3270 3-8-10 57 PFessey 16 34
(WStorey) *s.i.s: nvr on terms* **50/1**

0550 **14** 3/4 **Online Investor**[15] 2859 5-9-5 **67** ........ LTreadwell(7) 12 42
(DNicholls) *s.i.s: effrt over 2f out: wknd over 1f out* **10/1**
61.37 secs (-0.16) **Going Correction** +0.05s/f (Good)
**WFA** 3 from 4yo+ 6lb **14** Ran SP% **120.3**
Speed ratings: **103,100,99,97,95 95,94,91,91,90 88,87,83,82**CSF £105.80 CT £839.15 TOTE £2.90: £1.20, £7.80, £6.20; EX 132.60 Place 6 £422.08, Place 5 £136.76..
**Owner** David W Chapman **Bred** Stetchworth Park Stud Ltd **Trained** Stillington, N Yorks

**FOCUS**
An ordinary event but one in which the field raced towards the far side but one in which the winner very much had the run of the race against the favoured far rail and this bare form may not be entirely reliable.

**NOTEBOOK**
**Soaked**, back in handicap company and back on soft ground, turned in an improved effort, but it is worth remembering that he very much had the rub of things against the favoured far rail and may be one to field against from a higher mark next time if things are not stacked in his favour as much.
**Blue Maeve** has not always proved entirely reliable but ran creditably on only this fourth turf start and, although yet to win, showed enough to suggest he can get off the mark, especially as he deserves a bit more credit than the bare form indicates, as he raced a few widths off the far rail. He is one to keep an eye on.
**Winthorpe(IRE)**, from a stable among the winners, ran creditably and shaped as though the return to six furlongs would suit. However, he again left the impression he is not an easy ride and his inconsistency means he is not one to lump on next time.
**Mynd** had conditions to suit and was favourably drawn and returned to something like his best. He seemed beaten on merit though, and may continue to look vulnerable from his current mark.
**Fairgame Man** was not disgraced given this race favoured those racing close to the pace once again, but a losing run that stretches back nearly four years underlines the fact that he is not the best betting proposition around.
**Levelled** was not disgraced after racing away from the favoured far rail back on turf and, although he has not won on grass since 1999 (has won on sand this year), it will be no surprise to see him placed to best advantage by his excellent trainer.
**Le Meridien(IRE)** was favourably drawn and had the run of the race but will be of much more interest from a high draw on fast ground back at Beverley, the scene of all her three career wins.
**Tatweer(IRE)** *Official explanation: jockey said gelding missed the break*
**Joyce's Choice** *Official explanation: jockey said gelding missed the break*
**Obe Bold(IRE)** *Official explanation: trainer's representative said he was unable to fit declared tongue-strap and filly ran without it*
T/Plt: £478.20 to a £1 stake. Pool: £111,969.80. 170.90 winning tickets. T/Qpdt: £17.80 to a £1 stake. Pool: £6,292.70. 260.30 winning tickets. RY

# 3271 NEWMARKET (JULY) (R-H)
## Saturday, June 26

**OFFICIAL GOING: Good to firm**
Unlike the last meeting when the stalls were on the stands' side, there didn't appear to be that much bias in the draw.
Wind: Slight across Weather: Sunshine giving way to cloudy and an odd shower

## 3315 MCP FRED ARCHER STKS (LISTED RACE) 1m 4f
**1:35** (1:36) (A) 4-Y-0+ **£17,400** (£6,600; £3,300; £1,500) **Stalls** High

Form RPR
20-0 **1** **First Charter**[50] 1925 5-8-11 109 ........ KFallon 4 110
(SirMichaelStoute) *trckd ldrs: rdn to ld wl ins fnl f: edgd lft: r.o* **2/1**[1]
310- **2** 1/2 **Westmoreland Road (USA)**[287] 4880 4-8-11 112 ........ KDarley 1 109
(MrsAJPerrett) *hld up: racd keenly: hdwy over 4f out: led 2f out: rdn and hdd wl ins fnl f* **2/1**[1]
-305 **3** 2 **Island House (IRE)**[37] 2241 8-8-11 109 ........ SDrowne 3 106
(GWragg) *hld up in tch: rdn over 2f out: styd on same pce ins fnl f* **13/2**[3]
0250 **4** 3/4 **Tizzy May (FR)**[21] 2681 4-8-11 98 ........ DaneO'Neill 6 105
(RHannon) *hld up: outpcd over 2f out: nvr trbld ldrs* **12/1**
551- **5** 5 **Fruhlingssturm**[279] 5109 4-9-6 ........ TEDurcan 8 106
(MAJarvis) *chsd ldr: ev ch over 2f out: wknd over 1f out* **6/1**[2]
/52- **6** 1 1/2 **Calibre (USA)**[420] 1344 4-8-11 98 ........ RHughes 5 94
(JHMGosden) *led 10f: wknd over 1f out* **12/1**
0-06 **7** 5 **Sunny Glenn**[8] 3046 6-8-11 83 ........ PMcCabe 7 86?
(MrsPNDutfield) *hld up: racd keenly: hdwy over 4f out: wknd wl over 1f out* **50/1**
2m 32.59s (-0.37) **Going Correction** +0.125s/f (Good) 7 Ran SP% **111.6**
Speed ratings: **106,105,104,103,100 99,96**CSF £5.51 TOTE £2.80: £1.80, £1.70; EX 6.60.
**Owner** Saeed Suhail **Bred** W And R Barnett Ltd **Trained** Newmarket, Suffolk

**FOCUS**
This was up to its Listed status, although the pace did not appear that strong and the time was modest. The presence of the fourth holds the form down.

**NOTEBOOK**
**First Charter**, third in this contest last year, put matters right with a wormanlike display. He looks as good as ever and the March Stakes at Goodwood, which he has won for the past two years, would appear to be the the logical target.
**Westmoreland Road(USA)**, from a stable that has yet to click into top gear, looked in wonderful shape for this return to action. A progressive performer last year until disappointing in the St Leger, he looks to have done well from three to four and should have no trouble making his mark at Group level, with the Princess of Wales's Stakes a likely target at the July meeting here.
**Island House(IRE)**, stays this trip, even though he only has the one victory to his name over it. A solid performer in this grade, he is a good guide to the level of form.
**Tizzy May(FR)** appeared to stay this trip well enough, although the way the race was run hardly put the emphasis on stamina. He was not disgraced on these terms, but is going to continue to be difficult to place.
**Fruhlingssturm** looked pretty fit for this British debut and was not knocked around when his chance had gone. The winner of a Group Two in Germany, he had no easy task under his penalty, on ground which could well have been plenty quick enough for him.
**Calibre(USA)**, who wore a cross noseband, did not look to have come to himself just yet.

## 3316 CHEVELEY PARK STUD EMPRESS STKS (LISTED RACE) (FILLIES) 6f
**2:10** (2:14) (A) 2-Y-0 **£14,500** (£5,500; £2,750; £1,250) **Stalls** High

Form RPR
4 **1** **Slip Dance (IRE)**[19] 2745 2-8-11 ........ KMcEvoy 8 97
(EamonTyrrell, Ire) *chsd ldrs: led 1f out: rdn out* **16/1**
1 **2** 3/4 **Royal Alchemist**[43] 2087 2-8-8 ........ ADaly 9 92
(MDIUsher) *s.i.s: hld up: hdwy over 2f out: outpcd over 1f out: edgd lft ins fnl f: r.o* **7/1**
10 **3** 3/4 **Golden Anthem (USA)**[8] 3031 2-8-8 ........ TPQueally 2 90
(JPearce) *hld up: rdn over 2f out: r.o ins fnl f: nt rch ldrs* **50/1**
1 **4** nk **Baltic Dip (IRE)**[37] 2245 2-8-11 ........ RHughes 3 92
(RHannon) *led 5f: styd on same pce* **5/2**[1]
1334 **5** 3 **Umniya (IRE)**[8] 3031 2-8-8 ........ TEDurcan 7 80
(MRChannon) *chsd ldrs: rdn and ev ch 2f out: wknd ins fnl f* **9/2**[3]
51 **6** 1 1/2 **Kissing Lights (IRE)**[12] 2940 2-8-11 ........ KFallon 5 79
(MLWBell) *trckd ldr: ev ch over 1f out: wknd ins fnl f* **10/3**[2]
1 **7** 1/2 **Heres The Plan (IRE)**[36] 2275 2-8-11 ........ PMcCabe 1 77
(MGQuinlan) *plld hrd and prom: wknd over 1f out* **16/1**
110 **8** 1 3/4 **Polly Perkins (IRE)**[10] 2970 2-9-1 ........ KDarley 4 76
(NPLittmoden) *dwlt: hdwy to join ldrs over 4f out: ev ch 2f out: wknd over 1f out* **15/2**
1m 13.7s (0.38) **Going Correction** +0.125s/f (Good) **8** Ran SP% **107.8**
Speed ratings: **102,101,100,99,95 93,92,90**CSF £103.71 TOTE £21.40: £4.20, £2.20, £6.20; EX 120.80.
**Owner** M McLoughlin **Bred** Mary Rose Hayes **Trained** Ireland
■ A winner for Eamon Tyrell with his first runner in England.

**FOCUS**
With all eight runners having won this looked quite a hot little contest, but it was rather a messy affair and the form is probably nothing special by Listed standards.

**NOTEBOOK**
**Slip Dance(IRE)** looks to be going the right way and seemed to appreciate the more patient tactics employed here. She will stay further in time.
**Royal Alchemist** did not come down the hill at all well, but picked up in good style on meeting the rising ground. This was a big step up on her debut, and she should continue to progress, especially with an extra furlong likely to suit.
**Golden Anthem(USA)**, who suffered trouble in running at Ascot, belied her huge odds here with a solid effort. Off the bridle some way out, she picked up in good style in the latter stages and looks sure to appreciate an extra furlong.
**Baltic Dip(IRE)**, who missed Ascot to wait for this, had the run of the race and had no excuses. A step up in trip may prove beneficial.
**Umniya(IRE)** is a tough sort, having had seven outings in as many weeks. However, she did not see this out and may have had enough for the time being.
**Kissing Lights(IRE)** travelled well for much of the race, but left the impression that this trip was just too far for her. A return to the minimum should see her regain the winning thread.
**Heres The Plan(IRE)** gave herself no chance by refusing to settle.
**Polly Perkins(IRE)**

## 3317 LANCASTER RATED STKS (H'CAP) 6f
**2:40** (2:40) (D ) (0-85,82) 3-Y-0 **£5,509** (£1,695; £847; £423) **Stalls** High

Form RPR
0060 **1** **Mahmoom**[10] 2981 3-9-6 **81** ........(v) TEDurcan 1 93
(MRChannon) *hld up: hdwy over 1f out: rdn to ld ins fnl f: r.o* **14/1**
0-1 **2** 3/4 **Khalidia (USA)**[13] 2908 3-8-7 **71** ........ TPQueally(3) 5 81
(MAMagnusson) *led: rdn over 1f out: hdd ins fnl f: styd on* **8/1**
0-1 **3** 1 **Kschessinka (USA)**[17] 2785 3-9-3 **78** ........ KFallon 7 85
(WJHaggas) *hld up: plld hrd: nt clr run over 1f out: r.o ins fnl f: nt rch ldrs* **10/11**[1]
031 **4** 1 1/4 **Hawaajes**[23] 2621 3-9-0 **75** ........ WSupple 6 78
(BHanbury) *chsd ldrs: nt clr run over 1f out: styd on same pce ins fnl f* **9/2**[2]
0454 **5** 1 **Instant Recall (IRE)**[24] 2576 3-9-3 **78** ........(b1) KDarley 4 78
(BJMeehan) *prom: hmpd and n.m.r over 1f out: no ex* **12/1**
135- **6** nk **Rising Shadow (IRE)**[231] 5950 3-9-4 **82** ........ THamilton(3) 2 81
(RAFahey) *s.i.s: sn prom: rdn over 2f out: wknd ins fnl f* **12/1**
4214 **7** 1/2 **Mission Man**[32] 2378 3-9-6 **81** ........ RHughes 3 79
(RHannon) *w ldr: rdn over 2f out: wknd fnl f* **15/2**[3]
1m 13.19s (-0.13) **Going Correction** +0.125s/f (Good) 7 Ran SP% **115.5**
Speed ratings: **105,104,102,101,99 99,98**CSF £118.60 TOTE £13.60: £4.10, £5.00; EX 135.80.
**Owner** Sheikh Ahmed Al Maktoum **Bred** Barry Taylor **Trained** West Ilsley, Berks

**FOCUS**
Quite a competitive handicap run at a decent pace and the form looks reasonable.

**NOTEBOOK**
**Mahmoom**, racing off his lowest mark this term, finally got his act together and showed just what he is capable of when in the mood.
**Khalidia(USA)** stepped up on his maiden win, although he did have the run of the race. However, he is still open to improvement and can be found other openings off his curent mark
**Kschessinka(USA)** ◆ proved very difficult to settle early on and had no luck in searching for a gap when the race was on in earnest. Providing she settles better, she should have no trouble getting back to winning ways.
**Hawaajes** did not find much off the bridle and may not be entirely straightforward.
**Instant Recall(IRE)** travelled well enough in the first-time blinkers, but he looked held when given a nudge in the dip.
**Rising Shadow(IRE)** ran as though needing this first run of the season. However, he will need placing with care off his current mark.

## 3318 BANGO CRITERION STKS (GROUP 3) 7f
**3:15** (3:16) (A ) 3-Y-0+ **£29,000** (£11,000; £5,500; £1,875) **Stalls** High

Form RPR
1320 **1** **Arakan (USA)**[11] 2957 4-9-2 111 ........ KFallon 2 114
(SirMichaelStoute) *trckd ldrs: led ins fnl f: r.o* **7/4**[1]
54-0 **2** 3/4 **Desert Destiny**[23] 2623 4-9-2 105 ........(t) KMcEvoy 8 112
(SaeedBinSuroor) *prom: n.m.r and lost pl over 6f out: nt clr run over 1f out: r.o ins fnl f* **12/1**
15-0 **3** 2 **Trade Fair**[46] 2021 4-9-2 120 ........ RHughes 1 107
(RCharlton) *trckd ldr: rdn to ld 1f out: sn hdd and no ex* **7/2**[2]
1-35 **4** nk **Court Masterpiece**[23] 2623 4-9-2 106 ........ TEDurcan 6 106
(EALDunlop) *hld up: hdwy 2f out: swtchd lft over 1f out: no ex ins fnl f* **12/1**
0530 **4** dht **Kings Point (IRE)**[8] 3036 3-8-7 99 ........ DaneO'Neill 4 106
(RHannon) *chsd ldrs: pushed along 1/2-way: styd on same pce appr fnl f* **25/1**
/1-0 **6** 3 1/2 **Prince Tum Tum (USA)**[45] 2044 4-9-2 103 ........ KDarley 3 96
(JLDunlop) *chsd ldrs: rdn over 1f out: wknd fnl f* **12/1**
1-11 **7** 1 **Naahy**[17] 2793 4-9-7 106 ........ SHitchcott 7 99
(MRChannon) *led: rdn and hdd 1f out: edgd lft and sn wknd* **11/2**[3]
0-22 **8** 1 1/2 **Polar Ben**[56] 1758 5-9-7 112 ........ WSupple 5 95
(JRFanshawe) *hld up: rdn over 2f out: wknd over 1f out* **6/1**
1m 25.04s (-1.73) **Going Correction** +0.125s/f (Good)
**WFA** 3 from 4yo+ 9lb **8** Ran SP% **115.2**
Speed ratings: **114,113,110,110,110 106,105,103**CSF £25.04 TOTE £2.70: £1.20, £3.10, £1.80; EX 28.70.
**Owner** Niarchos Family **Bred** Flaxman Holdings Ltd **Trained** Newmarket, Suffolk

**FOCUS**
Worthy of its Group Three status and the pace was fair. The form is messy but useful.

**NOTEBOOK**
**Arakan(USA)** had faced some stiff tasks, one way or another, since making a winning reappearance, but he proved well up to this level and won a shade more cosily than the verdict suggests. Touched off last year in the Group Two Lennox Stakes at Glorious Goodwood last season, on ground which would have been soft enough for him, he will bid to gain compensation in this year's renewal.

**Desert Destiny**, wearing a tongue strap for the first time, came home in good style despite not having had the best of runs. He looks sure to make his mark at this level.
**Trade Fair**, the winner of this last year, had the ground in his favour and travelled well as usual. However, he found nothing off the bridle and does not look the horse he was.
**Kings Point(IRE)** got in here without having to carry a penalty for his Group Three win over course and distance last year. He had something to find on official ratings and was far from disgraced.
**Court Masterpiece** appeared to run his race and had no excuses, other than the ground may have been a shade faster than ideal.
**Prince Tum Tum(USA)** well supported to bounce back to form, ran as though the race was still needed.
**Naahy** had his ideal ground and the run of the race, but was anchored by his Group Three penalty.
**Polar Ben** never really threatened at any stage on this fast ground, and this effort is best forgotten.

## 3319 BRIDGEWELL SECURITIES MAIDEN STKS 7f
**3:50** (3:51) (D) 2-Y-0 **£4,774** (£1,469; £734; £367) **Stalls** High

Form RPR
1 **Solent (IRE)** 2-9-0 .......... DaneO'Neill 1 86+
(RHannon) *s.s: outpcd: hdwy over 1f out: r.o to ld wl ins fnl f* **25/1**
2 *1 ¼* **Daniel Thomas (IRE)** 2-9-0 .......... KDarley 11 83+
(MrsAJPerrett) *chsd ldrs: led over 1f out: hdd wl ins fnl f* **7/2**[2]
3 *¾* **Eqdaam (USA)** 2-9-0 .......... KFallon 9 81+
(JHMGosden) *always prom: rdn and ev ch over 1f out: styd on same pce ins fnl f* **8/1**[3]
3 4 *1 ¼* **Councellor (FR)**[16] 2804 2-9-0 .......... RHughes 10 78
(RHannon) *led over 5f: no ex ins fnl f* **7/4**[1]
5 *½* **Seyaadi** 2-9-0 .......... WSupple 6 77
(EALDunlop) *prom: rdn over 2f out: styd on same pce appr fnl f* **14/1**
6 *1 ¾* **Silverleaf** 2-9-0 .......... TEDurcan 4 72
(MRChannon) *s.i.s: hld up: hdwy over 1f out: nvr trbld ldrs* **16/1**
00 7 *hd* **Doctor's Cave**[16] 2804 2-8-11 .......... SHitchcott(3) 14 72
(CEBrittain) *w ldrs: rdn over 2f out: wkng whn hung lft ins fnl f* **33/1**
35 8 *hd* **Catch A Star**[21] 2690 2-8-9 .......... AMackay 2 66
(NACallaghan) *s.i.s: hld up: sme hdwy over 1f out: nvr nr to chal* **10/1**
9 *½* **Red Chairman** 2-8-11 .......... TPQueally(3) 3 70
(DRLoder) *hld up in tch: rdn 1/2-way: wknd over 1f out* **10/1**
10 *nk* **Velvet Heights (IRE)** 2-9-0 .......... GCarter 8 69
(JLDunlop) *s.s: outpcd: r.o ins fnl f: nvr nrr* **33/1**
6 11 *3* **Bibi Helen**[28] 2478 2-8-4 .......... DFox(5) 5 57
(NACallaghan) *s.s: outpcd* **40/1**
12 *½* **High Treason (USA)** 2-9-0 .......... DeanMcKeown 12 61
(JGGiven) *mid-div: rdn over 2f out: wknd over 1f out* **20/1**
13 *1 ½* **Rudaki** 2-8-7 .......... NicolPolli(7) 13 57
(MGQuinlan) *chsd ldrs over 5f* **8/1**[3]
06 14 *dist* **Oldstead Flyer (IRE)**[15] 2852 2-8-7 .......... DTudhope(7) 7 —
(DCarroll) *chsd ldrs over 4f* **100/1**

1m 28.61s (1.84) **Going Correction** +0.125s/f (Good) **14** Ran SP% **129.5**
Speed ratings: **94,92,91,90,89 87,87,87,86,86 82,82,80,—**CSF £113.92 TOTE £31.00: £5.90, £2.30, £2.90; EX 402.30.
**Owner** Mrs J Wood **Bred** Quay Bloodstock And Samac Ltd **Trained** East Everleigh, Wilts
■ Stewards Enquiry : A Mackay ten-day ban: failed to take all reasonable and permissible measures to obtain best possible placing (Jul 7-16)

**FOCUS**
This didn't look a strong maiden and although the stalls were on the stands' side, the field raced more towards the centre of the course.

**NOTEBOOK**
**Solent(IRE)**, a half-brother to seven-furlong juvenile winner Due Respect, did well to overcome a tardy start, although the pace did not appear to be that strong. However, he looked to be going nowhere until switched to the stands' rail going into the dip and, on meeting the rising ground, fairly flew up the hill. He will have no trouble staying further.
**Daniel Thomas(IRE)**, an early foal, is a half-brother to middle-distance winner Littlemissattitude. He shows plenty of knee action and should appreciate some give in the ground.
**Eqdaam(USA)**, an early foal, is out of a mare that won over this trip as a juvenile. He showed enough to suggest he can win his maiden.
**Councellor(FR)** showed promise on his debut in a race that has not worked out well, as yet. He travelled well in front until coming off the bridle, where there was no response.
**Seyaadi**, out of a mare that won over six furlongs as a juvenile, still looked a little green and will have learnt plenty from this.
**Silverleaf**, quite a late foal compared with some of these, is out of a Group Three-winning mare. He was given a nice introduction and looks sure to benefit from the experience.
**Catch A Star** caught the eye and should do better when stepping into nursery company.

## 3320 LANDCOM EBF FILLIES' H'CAP 1m
**4:25** (4:27) (C) (0-90,86) 3-Y-0+ **£9,529** (£2,932; £1,466; £733) **Stalls** High

Form RPR
-053 1 **Little Venice (IRE)**[17] 2788 4-9-1 **76** .......... LisaJones(3) 6 91
(CFWall) *raecd stands' side: chsd ldr: lft in clr ld over 3f out: rdn out* **6/1**[3]
411 2 *7* **Our Jaffa (IRE)**[24] 2587 3-9-1 **83** .......... KFallon 1 82
(DJDaly) *racd centre: prom: jnd stands' side gp 1/2-way: rdn to chse wnr fnl f: no imp* **3/1**[1]
5244 3 *1 ½* **Summer Shades**[11] 2963 6-8-7 **70** .......... BSwarbrick(5) 10 66
(WMBrisbourne) *racd stands' side: chsd ldrs: rdn over 2f out: styd on same pce* **20/1**
-065 4 *2* **Danclare (USA)**[10] 2971 3-9-3 **85** .......... RHughes 2 76
(JHMGosden) *led centre gp tl swtchd stands' side 1/2-way: rdn to chse wnr over 2f out: wknd fnl f* **9/2**[2]
4-10 5 *2 ½* **Pont Allaire (IRE)**[43] 2081 3-8-11 **79** .......... DaneO'Neill 5 64
(HCandy) *racd stands' side: chsd ldrs: rdn over 2f out: wknd wl over 1f out* **13/2**
-505 6 *2* **Mrs Pankhurst**[22] 2648 3-8-5 **73** .......... DeanMcKeown 9 54
(BWHills) *racd stands' side: hld up: hdwy 1/2-way: wknd over 2f out* **25/1**
0516 7 *9* **Enchanted Princess**[19] 2733 4-9-2 **74** .......... (b) WSupple 3 34
(WJHaggas) *swtchd to racd stands' side 7f out: hld up: wknd wl over 2f out* **7/1**
-024 8 *¾* **Hunter's Valley**[13] 2911 3-8-2 **70** .......... DKinsella 8 28
(RHannon) *racd stands' side: prom 5f* **25/1**
1-43 9 *5* **Salagama (IRE)**[23] 2630 4-9-8 **83** .......... TPQueally(3) 7 30
(PFICole) *led stands' side: rein broke and hung lft over 4f out: hdd & wknd over 3f out* **6/1**[3]
5-00 10 *7* **Fragrant Star**[7] 3091 3-8-10 **78** .......... TEDurcan 4 9
(CEBrittain) *racd centre: hld up: jnd stands' side 1/2-way: wknd over 2f out: eased* **25/1**

1m 40.67s (0.19) **Going Correction** +0.125s/f (Good)
**WFA** 3 from 4yo+ 10lb **10** Ran SP% **113.9**
Speed ratings: **104,97,95,93,91 89,80,79,74,67**CSF £22.44 CT £340.96 TOTE £6.70: £1.90, £1.40, £4.60; EX 17.00.
**Owner** Hintlesham SPD Partners **Bred** Limestone Stud **Trained** Newmarket, Suffolk

**FOCUS**
This did not look the strongest of fillies' contests and very few got into this. The form needs treating with caution.

**NOTEBOOK**
**Little Venice(IRE)**, left with a healthy advantage when the front-running Salagama's reins broke, never looked like being pegged back. This mile posed no problems for her, but she looks sure to pay for her wide-margin success.
**Our Jaffa(IRE)** was a shade disappointing, but she deserves another chance, for this turned out to be a strange race.
**Summer Shades** had her ground, but this company is a bit too hot for her. Back in her right grade, she will be one to keep an eye on.
**Danclare(USA)**, having her third run in as many weeks, seemed to run a little flat.
**Pont Allaire(IRE)** dropped away tamely and may need some give underfoot to show her best.
**Enchanted Princess** *Official explanation: jockey said filly was unable to get cover behind the other horses*
**Salagama(IRE)** was bowling along happily until her reins broke. Lightly raced, there is still plenty of time for her. *Official explanation: jockey said his rein broke*

## 3321 BANGO APPRENTICE H'CAP 7f
**5:00** (5:01) (E) (0-70,68) 3-Y-0+ **£3,484** (£1,072; £536; £268) **Stalls** High

Form RPR
0-60 1 **Mister Sweets**[14] 2899 5-9-9 **68** .......... DTudhope(5) 7 81
(DCarroll) *racd centre: chsd ldrs: led over 2f out: sn rdn: hung lft ins fnl f: r.o* **7/1**[3]
3040 2 *nk* **Balerno**[6] 3127 5-8-5 **50** .......... RoryMoore(5) 2 62
(RIngram) *hld up: racd centre: hdwy 1/2-way: rdn and ev ch fr over 2f out: hung lft ins fnl f: r.o* **8/1**
5000 3 *1 ¼* **Pagan Storm (USA)**[22] 2656 4-8-10 **55** .......... (t) KristinStubbs(5) 8 64
(MrsLStubbs) *hld up: racd centre: hdwy over 1f out: hung lft ins fnl f: r.o* **33/1**
2206 4 *¾* **Ranny**[43] 2098 4-8-8 **48** .......... DCorby 3 55
(DrJDScargill) *hld up: racd centre: nt clr run 2f out: hdwy over 1f out: r.o wl* **20/1**
3203 5 *nk* **Middleton Grey**[23] 2614 6-9-9 **63** .......... (b) LPKeniry 17 69
(AGNewcombe) *racd centre: hld up in tch: rdn over 1f out: styd on same pce* **6/1**[2]
0040 6 *shd* **Jedeydd**[4] 3167 7-9-2 **56** .......... (t) TPQueally 6 62
(MDods) *racd centre: trckd ldrs: rdn over 1f out: styd on u.p* **7/1**[3]
-100 7 *¾* **Iced Diamond (IRE)**[16] 2806 5-8-12 **55** .......... BSwarbrick(3) 5 58
(WMBrisbourne) *hld up: racd centre: hdwy 1/2-way: rdn over 1f out: no ex ins fnl f* **16/1**
0450 8 *shd* **Fearby Cross (IRE)**[3] 3205 8-9-11 **65** .......... LisaJones 12 68
(WJMusson) *hld up: racd centre: rdn over 2f out: r.o ins fnl f: nt rch ldrs* **7/1**[3]
0-00 9 *1 ¼* **Caerphilly Gal**[23] 2614 4-8-9 **52** .......... DFox(3) 1 52
(PLGilligan) *racd centre: hld up: plld hrd: rdn over 1f out: nvr trbld ldrs* **25/1**
0431 10 *nk* **Jubilee Street (IRE)**[28] 2473 5-8-13 **58** .......... SaleemGolam(5) 14 57
(MrsADuffield) *racd centre: hld up: rdn over 2f out: n.d* **9/2**[1]
-005 11 *1 ½* **Logistical**[15] 2834 4-9-0 **59** .......... PGallagher(5) 16 54
(ADWPinder) *s.i.s: hld up: racd centre: hdwy 2f out: wknd fnl f* **11/1**
0000 12 *1* **Dexileos (IRE)**[24] 2598 5-8-3 **43** .......... (t) FPFerris 10 35
(ADWPinder) *led: hdd over 5f out: wknd over 1f out* **40/1**
0000 13 *1 ½* **Its Ecco Boy**[7] 3090 6-9-3 **60** .......... HayleyTurner(3) 9 48
(PHowling) *racd centre: chsd ldrs over 5f* **33/1**
2002 14 *½* **Halcyon Magic**[8] 3049 6-8-1 **48** .......... (b) LauraPike(7) 4 35
(MissJFeilden) *racd alone far side: sn bhd* **20/1**
0065 15 *5* **Branston Tiger**[39] 2215 5-10-0 **68** .......... (b[1]) SHitchcott 15 41
(JGGiven) *racd centre: led over 5f out: hdd over 2f out: sn wknd* **14/1**
0004 16 *2* **Pharoah's Gold (IRE)**[7] 3082 6-8-12 **52** .......... (v) THamilton 18 20
(DShaw) *s.i.s: racd centre: hld up: hdwy 1/2-way: rdn and wknd over 2f out* **20/1**
0001 17 *8* **Albadi**[12] 2931 3-7-12 **52** .......... (b) DeanWilliams(5) 11 —
(CEBrittain) *racd centre: chsd ldrs 5f* **12/1**

1m 26.96s (0.19) **Going Correction** +0.125s/f (Good)
**WFA** 3 from 4yo+ 9lb **17** Ran SP% **136.1**
Speed ratings: **103,102,101,100,100 99,99,98,97,97 95,94,92,92,86 84,74**CSF £63.40 CT £1819.20 TOTE £10.40: £2.70, £5.90, £8.50, £6.00; EX 131.00 Place 6 £1,514.71, Place 5 £1,148.82..
**Owner** David Fravigar-Alan Mann **Bred** Juddmonte Farms **Trained** Warthill, N Yorks

**FOCUS**
Quite a competitive low-grade handicap and the pace appeared to be a fair one. The form looks sound enough.

**NOTEBOOK**
**Mister Sweets**, back over his optimum trip, appreciated the drop in class and saw his race out bravely.
**Balerno** proved a persistent challenger and only gave best near the finish. However, his overall profile is far from convincing.
**Pagan Storm(USA)** stuck to his task well enough, but he inconsistent and cannot be relied upon to reproduce this effort.
**Ranny** did not have the best of runs, but the way he stayed on up the suggested that a return to a mile will be in his favour.
**Middleton Grey** travelled as well as any through the race, but found less than anticipated off the bridle. Yet to win on turf, he is one to keep an eye on when returned to the Fibresand surface.
**Jedeydd** has become well-treated on his best form, and showed enough to suggest that all is not lost with him yet.
**Fearby Cross(IRE)** was doing his best work in the closing stages and may be returning to form.
**Jubilee Street(IRE)**, 6lb higher than when winning a similar contest at Doncaster, never really looked like taking a hand at any stage.
T/Plt: £4,704.50 to a £1 stake. Pool: £65,412.90. 10.15 winning tickets. T/Qpdt: £381.60 to a £1 stake. Pool: £3,868.30. 7.50 winning tickets. CR

# 3156 WINDSOR (R-H)
Saturday, June 26

**OFFICIAL GOING: Good to firm**
Several of the winners have form on easy ground, suggesting that the going was not as fast as it was described.

## 3322 "AT THE RACES:DEDICATED TO RACING" MAIDEN STKS 6f
**2:15** (2:16) (D) 3-Y-0 **£4,290** (£1,320; £660; £330) **Stalls** High

Form RPR
-034 1 **King's Caprice**[17] 2785 3-9-0 85 .......... SCarson 14 78+
(GBBalding) *trckd ldrs: led ins fnl 2f: drvn 1f out: styd on wl: comf* **3/1**[1]

02- **2** 2 1/2 **Stargem**[266] 5367 3-8-9 ............ RPrice 11 66
(JPearce) *w ldr tl slt advantage ins fnl 3f: hdd ins fnl 2f: rdn and kpt on wl to hold 2nd but no ch w wnr* **10/3**[2]

4 **3** shd **Corky (IRE)**[16] 2808 3-9-0 ............ RLMoore 15 71
(RHannon) *chsd ldrs: rdn over 2f out: styd on wl to press for 2nd ins fnl f but no ch w wnr* **4/1**[3]

**4** hd **Kostar** 3-9-0 ............ RSmith 9 70
(CGCox) *bhd: pushed along 1/2-way: hdwy over 1f out: styd on strly ins fnl f: nt rch ldrs* **25/1**

400 **5** 1 **Called Up**[18] 2765 3-9-0 64 ............ DSweeney 12 67
(HCandy) *slt advantage tl hdd ins fnl 3f: styd pressing ldrs tl over 1f out: wknd ins last* **11/1**

03- **6** 3 1/2 **Zazous**[358] 2956 3-9-0 ............ VSlattery 10 57
(AKing) *chsd ldrs: rdn 1/2-way: wknd fr 2f out* **14/1**

56 **7** 3 **Ridge Boy (IRE)**[26] 2517 3-9-0 ............ PDobbs 6 48
(RHannon) *mid-div: sn drvn along: styd on same pce fnl 2f* **12/1**

**8** nk **Highland Lass** 3-8-9 ............ GBaker 2 42
(MrsHSweeting) *wnt bdly lft s and bhd: swtchd rt to stands side fr 3f out: r.o ins fnl f but nvr a danger* **25/1**

000 **9** 2 **Radlett Lady**[37] 2236 3-8-9 ............ BDoyle 7 36
(DKIvory) *chsd ldrs over 3f* **33/1**

6220 **10** nk **Brown Dragon**[67] 1530 3-9-0 60 ............ PaulEddery 3 40
(DHaydnJones) *outpcd and nvr nr ldrs* **16/1**

0- **11** 2 1/2 **Paradise Breeze**[291] 4801 3-8-9 ............ NPollard 8 27
(CAHorgan) *s.i.s: stdd rr: a outpcd* **25/1**

0520 **12** 1/2 **Indian Edge**[32] 2377 3-8-7 63 ............ MHalford(7) 1 31
(BPalling) *hung lft to centre crse 1/2-way: sn bhd* **16/1**

05 **13** shd **Dane Rhapsody (IRE)**[24] 2586 3-8-9 ............ PDoe 5 25
(BPalling) *hung lft to centre crse: 1/2-way: a outpcd* **33/1**

1m 13.09s (-0.78) **Going Correction** -0.15s/f (Firm) **13** Ran SP% **120.0**
Speed ratings: **99,95,95,95,93 89,85,84,82,81 78,77,77**CSF £11.96 TOTE £3.90: £1.30, £1.60, £2.10; EX 14.10.
**Owner** Miss B Swire **Bred** Miss B Swire **Trained** Kimpton,Hants

**FOCUS**
A routine maiden, dominated by the form horses and a fair standard of form. The winner had something in hand.

**NOTEBOOK**
**King's Caprice** is not straightforward as he can pull, but after being saddled in the stables he settled well. He did it comfortably, easing over to the rail once in front, but as he is already rated 85 he may struggle in handicaps.
**Stargem**, runner-up in a race that has worked out well on her last start back in October, was always to the fore but the winner comfortably had her measure in the last quarter-mile.
**Corky(IRE)** was down a furlong in trip for this second run but was keeping on as if the return to seven would suit. However he was hanging away from the rail and his attitude may not be all that it should be.
**Kostar** made a promising debut and only just failed to snatch second after really finding his stride inside the last. He should know a lot more next time.
**Called Up**, down a furlong, showed pace to lead against the rail to past halfway.
**Zazous**, having his first run for nearly a year, shaped as if in need of farther. He is now eligible for handicaps.

## 3323 TOTEPOOL MIDSUMMER STKS (LISTED RACE) 1m 67y
2:50 (2:50) (A) 3-Y-O+ £17,400 (£6,600; £3,300; £1,500) Stalls High

Form RPR

1203 **1** **Gateman**[21] 2678 7-9-8 113 ............ KDalgleish 7 117
(MJohnston) *led tl hdd wl over 2f out: sn hrd rdn: styd on gamely u.p to ld again last strides* **5/2**[1]

5011 **2** hd **Shot To Fame (USA)**[24] 2588 5-9-3 101 ............ IMongan 5 112
(PWHarris) *trckd ldr: led wl over 2f out: styd on u.p fr over 1f out: ct last strides* **9/1**

-335 **3** 1 1/2 **Vanderlin**[21] 2678 5-9-3 107 ............ LPKeniry 6 108
(AMBalding) *trckd ldrs gng wl: rdn to chal 1f out: styd on same pce ins last* **14/1**

0-60 **4** nk **Beauchamp Pilot**[11] 2957 6-9-3 111 ............ NPollard 9 107
(GAButler) *chsd ldrs: outpcd and rdn 2f out: styd on again ins fnl f but nt pce to chal* **12/1**

-163 **5** 1/2 **Babodana**[56] 1758 4-9-6 111 ............ PDoe 3 109
(MHTompkins) *hld up in rr: hdwy on outside over 2f out: rdn to chal fr over 1f out: wknd nr fin* **8/1**[3]

1 **6** 3/4 **Binary Vision (USA)**[14] 2900 3-8-7 ............ RHavlin 2 105
(JHMGosden) *bhd: rdn and hdwy over 2f out: styd on fnl f but nvr gng pce to rch ldrs* **5/1**[2]

234- **7** 3 **Tarjman**[267] 5347 4-9-3 111 ............ RLMoore 8 98
(ACStewart) *chsd ldrs: rdn 3f out: wknd over 2f out* **5/1**[2]

1- **8** nk **Always First**[318] 4087 3-8-7 ............ BDoyle 1 97
(SirMichaelStoute) *bhd: rdn 3f out: nvr gng pce to rch ldrs and wknd fr 2f out* **9/1**

1-03 **9** 3 1/2 **Excelsius (IRE)**[47] 1999 4-9-6 103 ............ WRyan 4 92
(JLDunlop) *rdn 3f out: a bhd* **25/1**

1m 40.68s (-4.92) **Going Correction** -0.20s/f (Firm) course record
**WFA** 3 from 4yo+ 10lb **9** Ran SP% **111.2**
Speed ratings: **116,115,114,114,113 112,109,109,105**CSF £24.36 TOTE £3.00: £1.10, £2.50, £3.50; EX 22.10.
**Owner** Kennet Valley Thoroughbreds V **Bred** Miss K Rausing **Trained** Middleham Moor, N Yorks

**FOCUS**
A well-contested Listed event which saw the track record broken and the form is solid for the grade.

**NOTEBOOK**
**Gateman** carried a 5lb penalty for his Group Three win earlier in the season. Chased along from the stalls to secure an early lead, he was headed by the eventual runner-up early in the straight but rallied in great style to get back on top close home and break the course record by more than half a second. Tremendously game, he is worth a try over ten furlongs.
**Shot To Fame(USA)**, stepped up in grade, did nothing wrong at all and certainly battled, but was pipped close home. He remains in fine heart.
**Vanderlin** was unable to get closer to Gateman than he had at Epsom, despite being 2lb better off, but ran a solid race nevertheless. He has yet to win at this trip but certainly stays.
**Beauchamp Pilot**, down in this grade for the first time since November 2002, was keeping on again after losing his pitch.
**Babodana** had his chance but was inconvenienced by having to race down the centre. He has not quite lasted home in two runs at a mile since landing the Lincoln.
**Binary Vision(USA)**, stepped up in grade after an impressive maiden win on his debut, was found wanting. The way he was keeping on suggests he is ready for another furlong or two. *Official explanation: vet said colt finished lame*
**Tarjman** was a little disappointing on this seasonal reappearance. He has yet to prove that he stays a mile but was beaten too far out for the trip to have been solely to blame.
**Always First** was never in the hunt on this first start since August.

## 3324 ROYAL MARBELLA GROUP QUALITY HOMES ABROAD STKS (HERITAGE H'CAP) 6f
3:25 (3:28) (B) (0-105,102) 3-Y-O+ £29,000 (£11,000; £5,500; £2,500) Stalls High

Form RPR

2140 **1** **Zilch**[2] 3235 6-9-1 92 ............ RMullen 13 104
(MLWBell) *bhd: sn pushed along: str run u.p fr over 1f out: led wl ins last: r.o wl* **7/1**[2]

1111 **2** 3/4 **Caustic Wit (IRE)**[12] 2948 6-8-1 83 ............ (p) PMakin(5) 14 93
(MSSaunders) *trckd ldr: chal 2f out: led over 1f out: hdd and nt qckn wl ins last* **5/2**[1]

0000 **3** nk **Crimson Silk**[23] 2623 4-8-13 90 ............ (p) PaulEddery 17 99
(DHaydnJones) *bhd: rdn and hdwy fr 2f out: styd on wl u.p fnl f but no imp cl home* **25/1**

2000 **4** 1 1/2 **Smokin Beau**[11] 2955 7-9-6 97 ............ (b) TGMcLaughlin 18 101
(NPLittmoden) *led: rdn over 2f out: hdd over 1f out: one pce ins last* **20/1**

1031 **5** 1 **Green Manalishi**[7] 3092 3-8-7 91 ............ PDobbs 12 92
(DWPArbuthnot) *trckd ldrs: rdn and kpt on fr over 1f out: one pce ins last* **7/1**[2]

0622 **6** 3 **Million Percent**[7] 3090 5-8-3 80 ............ (v[1]) SWhitworth 15 72
(KRBurke) *chsd ldrs: rdn over 2f out: wknd appr fnl f* **10/1**[3]

0255 **7** shd **Watching**[15] 2859 7-8-8 85 ............ KDalgleish 9 77
(DNicholls) *chsd ldrs: rdn over 2f out: wknd over 1f out* **12/1**

0306 **8** 1 1/4 **Miss George**[33] 2373 6-8-7 84 ow2 ............ BDoyle 7 72
(DKIvory) *s.i.s: bhd: hdwy to chse ldrs 1/2-way: sn rdn: wknd ins fnl 2f* **12/1**

-600 **9** 3/4 **Bonus (IRE)**[33] 2373 4-9-11 102 ............ (t) RLMoore 10 88
(RHannon) *sn in tch: rdn 3f out: sn outpcd* **20/1**

52-0 **10** 3 1/2 **Pivotal Point**[44] 2065 4-8-13 90 ............ DSweeney 2 66
(PJMakin) *bhd: hdwy 1/2-way: sn rdn: wknd 2f out* **16/1**

0302 **11** 6 **Marsad (IRE)**[15] 2857 10-8-12 89 ............ PDoe 1 47
(JAkehurst) *rdn and hung bdly rt over 2f: a bhd* **12/1**

2200 **12** 3 1/2 **Mine Behind**[21] 2682 4-8-4 81 ............ NPollard 8 28
(JRBest) *a outpcd* **12/1**

6011 **13** 3/4 **Willhewiz**[7] 3090 4-8-4 81 ............ (v) SCarson 6 26
(RMStronge) *chsd ldrs 4f* **14/1**

-000 **14** 3/4 **Arctic Desert**[8] 3036 4-8-7 84 ............ (v[1]) SDrowne 11 27
(AMBalding) *chsd ldrs: wknd qckly: lost action and eased fnl f* **33/1**

0423 **15** shd **Further Outlook (USA)**[2] 3243 10-8-7 84 ............ IMongan 5 26
(DKIvory) *bhd: hdwy 1/2-way: wknd 2f out* **20/1**

-200 **16** 6 **Danzig River (IRE)**[14] 2897 3-8-11 95 ............ WRyan 4 19
(BWHills) *a outpcd* **25/1**

1m 11.61s (-2.26) **Going Correction** -0.15s/f (Firm)
**WFA** 3 from 4yo+ 7lb **16** Ran SP% **130.9**
Speed ratings: **109,108,107,105,104 100,100,98,97,92 84,80,79,78,78 70**CSF £23.90 CT £381.62 TOTE £8.30: £2.90, £1.60, £5.70, £4.40; EX 35.60.
**Owner** Mary Mayall, Linda Redmond, Julie Martin **Bred** Mrs Linda Corbett And Mrs Mary Mayall **Trained** Newmarket, Suffolk

**FOCUS**
A competitive field for this richly-endowed handicap resulting in solid, above-average form for the grade. With the stalls on the stands' side, a high draw proved a big advantage.

**NOTEBOOK**
**Zilch** came with a strong run once switched left over a furlong out and scored decisively. All his previous wins have come on easy ground, but the going here was nothing like as fast as it was described. *Official explanation: trainer said, regarding the improved form shown, gelding failed to get into the race from a high draw last time out*
**Caustic Wit(IRE)** was 11lb higher than when completing a four-timer over course and distance last time. He ran well, but had to work hard to get to the front and was cut down. He has been a nervy sort in the past, and the fact that he was in the stalls for quite some time did not help him.
**Crimson Silk** has gained both his career wins over this course and distance. Having only his second run in a handicap, after dropping to a more realistic mark, he finished well from off the pace over this shorter trip. There could be a race for him.
**Smokin Beau** showed his customary pace to bag the rail from the highest draw and stuck on once headed.
**Green Manalishi**, raised 2lb, ran a decent race on his first try over six furlongs but gave the impression he will be happier back over five.
**Million Percent** ran a decent race in the first-time visor, albeit from a favourable draw.
**Watching** fared best of those drawn in single figures.
**Pivotal Point** was poorly drawn and should be forgiven this.
**Arctic Desert** *Official explanation: jockey said saddle slipped*
**Further Outlook(USA)** *Official explanation: trainer's representative said gelding was struck into behind*

## 3325 LETHEBY & CHRISTOPHER H'CAP 1m 3f 135y
4:00 (4:04) (C) (0-95,93) 3-Y-O+ £17,225 (£5,300; £2,650; £1,325) Stalls Low

Form RPR

5-03 **1** **Vengeance**[66] 1539 4-9-11 90 ............ PDobbs 1 101
(MrsAJPerrett) *trckd ldrs: led jst ins fnl 2f: rdn over 1f out: r.o wl fnl f: readily* **13/2**[3]

6-42 **2** 1 1/4 **Nawamees (IRE)**[43] 844 6-9-5 84 ............ (p) KDalgleish 10 93
(GLMoore) *hld up rr:hdwy and nt clr run over 2f out:styng on whn n.m.r over 1f out: swtchd lft: str run ins last: nt pce of wnr* **20/1**

-212 **3** 1 3/4 **Frontier**[5] 3143 7-8-7 72 ............ (t) SWhitworth 9 78
(BJLlewellyn) *stdd rr: pushed along and hdwy over 3f out: chsd ldrs 2f out: kpt on same pce fnl f* **8/1**

1-02 **4** 1/2 **Desert Quest (IRE)**[22] 2638 4-9-13 92 ............ (b) SDrowne 4 97
(AMBalding) *hld up in rr: hdwy 3f out: chsd ldrs and rdn 2f out: sn one pce* **8/1**

-432 **5** 1/2 **Camrose**[18] 2764 3-8-8 87 ............ RLMoore 8 91
(JLDunlop) *chsd ldrs: rdn and outpcd 4f out: styd on again to chse ldrs 2f out: outpcd fnl f* **10/1**

01-1 **6** nk **Grooms Affection**[15] 2845 4-9-5 84 ............ IMongan 11 88
(PWHarris) *s.i.s:sn in tch: chsd ldrs over 3f out tl over 1f out: outpcd ins last* **9/4**[1]

0054 **7** 6 **Perfect Storm**[43] 2076 5-10-0 93 ............ DSweeney 2 87
(MBlanshard) *in tch: hdwy 3f out: drvn to chse ldrs over 2f out: sn wknd* **8/1**

-021 **8** nk **Shredded (USA)**[23] 2631 4-9-1 80 ............ RHavlin 12 74
(JHMGosden) *chsd ldrs: wnt 2nd 5f out: led ins fnl 3f: hdd & wknd jst ins fnl 2f* **11/2**[2]

024/ **9** 2 **Ranville**[652] 4584 6-9-13 92 ............ BDoyle 13 83
(MAJarvis) *bhd tl mod late hdwy* **33/1**

10-2 **10** 2 1/2 **Golano**[14] 2881 4-9-1 80 ............ RMullen 3 67
(CFWall) *in tch tl wknd over 3f out* **16/1**

0156 **11** 3 1/2 **Gig Harbor**[36] 1054 5-9-3 82 ............ SCarson 6 63
(MissECLavelle) *led tl hdd ins fnl 3f: wknd over 2f out* **25/1**

50-0 **12** *dist* **Herodotus**[21] 2681 6-9-3 **82** ........ NPollard 5 —
(KOCunningham-Brown) *drvn to chse ldr: wknd over 4f out: t.o* **100/1**

2m 25.83s (-4.27) **Going Correction** -0.20s/f (Firm)
**WFA** 3 from 4yo+ 14lb **12** Ran SP% **120.3**
Speed ratings: **106,105,104,103,103 103,99,98,97,95 93,**—CSF £134.61 CT £1065.70 TOTE £8.40: £2.30, £4.70, £3.80; EX 172.60.
**Owner** T Staplehurst **Bred** T Staplehurst **Trained** Pulborough, W Sussex

**FOCUS**
A valuable handicap run at a reasonable pace and the form looks up-to-standard and sound.

**NOTEBOOK**
**Vengeance** was returning from a two-month break, his yard having had a virus. After moving over to the rail once in front he won nicely, and there could be another decent handicap in him this season.
**Nawamees(IRE)** was having his first run on the Flat since February but has been running well over hurdles since then. In first-time cheekpieces, he was obliged to switch wide to deliver his run, but came home in good style.
**Frontier** ran another solid race from the same mark, but this longer trip just found him out.
**Desert Quest(IRE)**, raised 3lb for a good run in defeat at Epsom, was never nearer over this longer trip.
**Camrose** became outpaced with half a mile to run, but was sticking on again with the benefit of the rail to race against. He is edging up the handicap.
**Grooms Affection**, who went up 5lb after Sandown, took his time picking up but was keeping on at the end. He seemed to stay this longer trip.
**Perfect Storm** was inconvenienced by having to come down the centre of the track in the straight.
**Golano** *Official explanation: jockey said gelding was never travelling*

## 3326 SARACEN-PROMOTIONS.CO.UK CLASSIFIED STKS 6f
**4:35** (4:37) (E) 3-Y-O+ **£3,503** (£1,078; £539; £269) **Stalls** High

Form RPR
0-05 **1** **Polar Impact**[8] 3043 5-9-3 69 ........ RLMoore 10 81
(GLMoore) *hld up in tch: hdwy 2f out: drvn to ld 1f out: r.o wl* **7/2**[1]
0410 **2** *1* **The Fisio**[23] 2628 4-9-6 73 ........(v) SDrowne 5 81
(AMBalding) *led tl hdd over 3f out: led again over 2f out: sn rdn: hdd 1f out: styd on but nt pce of wnr ins last* **12/1**
-664 **3** *1 1/2* **Indian Steppes (FR)**[21] 2670 5-9-0 67 ........ IMongan 3 71
(JulianPoulton) *s.i.s: n.m.r sn after s but sn in tch:hdwy and rdn fr 3f out: styd on ins fnl f:nt pce of ldrs* **13/2**
00-0 **4** *2 1/2* **Indian Maiden (IRE)**[147] 646 4-8-11 72 ........ PMakin(5) 2 65
(MSSaunders) *bhd: hdwy and hung lft 2f out and over 1f out: nt keen but styd on ins last* **16/1**
2016 **5** *3 1/2* **Catch The Cat (IRE)**[15] 2859 5-9-5 72 ........(b) GParkin 8 58
(JSWainwright) *t.k.h: chsd ldrs tl led over 3f out: hdd over 2f out: wknd over 1f out* **6/1**
0415 **6** *1 1/2* **Silver Chime**[14] 2875 4-9-0 70 ........ RMullen 4 48
(DMSimcock) *chsd ldrs: riddeen in centre crse 3f out: wknd 2f out* **5/1**[3]
0050 **7** *5* **Cormorant Wharf (IRE)**[85] 1230 4-8-12 70 ........(p) AQuinn(5) 6 36
(TEPowell) *a outpcd* **14/1**
-555 **8** *9* **Isaz**[37] 2236 4-9-5 72 ........ DSweeney 7 11
(HCandy) *s.i.s: n.m.r sn after s: rdn and effrt 3f out: nt trble ldrs: eased whn btn fnl f* **12/1**
0232 **9** *6* **Another Glimpse**[29] 2455 6-9-3 69 ........(t) SCarson 1 —
(MissBSanders) *bhd: sme hdwy in centre crse 3f out: sn wknd: eased whn no ch over 1f out* **9/2**[2]

1m 12.44s (-1.43) **Going Correction** -0.15s/f (Firm) **9** Ran SP% **112.6**
Speed ratings: **103,101,99,96,91 89,83,71,63**CSF £45.01 TOTE £3.40: £1.60, £3.10, £2.50; EX 39.30.
**Owner** N J Jones **Bred** R And Mrs Heathcote **Trained** Woodingdean, E Sussex

**FOCUS**
A typically tight classified event, won by the favourite from the highest stall. The first two ran to form and overall the race looks fair handicap-wise.

**NOTEBOOK**
**Polar Impact**, who won three times on sand at Dos Hermanas in Spain over the winter, took advantage of the best draw to win his first race for this yard. Easy ground is reportedly ideal for him, another indication that the going was not as fast as it was described.
**The Fisio** showed plenty of pace against the stands' rail, but he has done his winning over five furlongs and the favourite had his measure inside the last.
**Indian Steppes(FR)** , who has a moderate strike rate, was keeping on well from a disadvantageous draw.
**Indian Maiden(IRE)**, having her first run since January, stayed on from the rear but did not look to be putting it all in.
**Catch The Cat(IRE)** seems a better horse over the minimum trip.
**Silver Chime** ran a respectable race given that his low draw meant he raced up the centre of the track.
**Isaz** *Official explanation: jockey said colt lost its action in the final furlong*
**Another Glimpse** *Official explanation: jockey said gelding was hanging and moving badly*

## 3327 ROYAL MARBELLA GROUP QUALITY HOMES ABROAD FILLIES' H'CAP 1m 2f 7y
**5:05** (5:16) (D) (0-85,85) 3-Y-O+ **£5,525** (£1,700; £850; £425) **Stalls** Low

Form RPR
4005 **1** **Miss Pebbles (IRE)**[35] 2284 4-8-8 **65** ........(v) NPollard 4 78
(BRJohnson) *bmpd s: hld up in rr: stdy hdwy over 2f out: chal 1f out: qcknd to ld last half f: easily* **7/1**
10-1 **2** *nk* **Mango Mischief (IRE)**[18] 2764 3-9-2 **85** ........ RLMoore 5 97
(JLDunlop) *t.k.h: hld up in rr: hdwy 3f out: chal 2f out: led appr fnl f: hdd and outpcd last half f* **3/1**[1]
5030 **3** *6* **Doris Souter (IRE)**[19] 2738 4-8-11 **68** ........ RSmith 8 69
(RHannon) *sn led: rdn and styd on fr over 2f out: hdd appr fnl f: sn btn but hld on for 3rd* **11/1**
1231 **4** *shd* **Olivia Rose (IRE)**[10] 2982 5-9-3 **79** ........ RThomas(5) 1 80
(JPearce) *chsd ldrs: rdn over 2f out: kpt on fnl f to press for mod 3rd* **4/1**[3]
31/ **5** *1 1/4* **Ballerina Suprema (IRE)**[645] 4771 4-10-0 **85** ........ SDrowne 10 83
(CREgerton) *in tch: pushed along on rails whn nt clr run 2f out: swtchd lft and r.o fnl f but nvr a danger* **14/1**
0-00 **6** *3/4* **Rani Two**[7] 3091 5-8-10 **72** ........ NChalmers(5) 2 69
(WMBrisbourne) *hld up in tch: hdwy on outside to chse ldrs over 2f out: wknd appr fnl f* **14/1**
0-10 **7** *hd* **Dreaming Of You (IRE)**[35] 2284 3-8-6 **73** ow2 ........ BDoyle 6 72
(SirMichaelStoute) *chsd ldrs: rdn 3f out: n.m.r whn wkng ins fnl 2f* **10/1**
3-06 **8** *nk* **Strategy**[7] 3091 4-9-7 **78** ........(v[1]) PDobbs 3 74
(PRWebber) *bmpd s: sn chsng ldrs: rdn 3f out: wknd qckly ins fnl 2f* **14/1**
5-00 **9** *1 1/2* **Lara Bay**[32] 2381 4-8-3 **60** ........(t) SWhitworth 9 53
(AMBalding) *hld up in rr: sme hdwy whn hmpd 2f out: n.d* **40/1**
40-2 **10** *1 3/4* **Czarina Waltz**[19] 2738 5-9-12 **83** ........ RMullen 7 73
(CFWall) *t.k.h: chsd ldrs: hung rt and wknd 2f out* **7/2**[2]

2m 6.56s (-1.74) **Going Correction** -0.20s/f (Firm)
**WFA** 3 from 4yo+ 12lb **10** Ran SP% **119.6**
Speed ratings: **98,97,92,92,91 91,91,90,89,88**CSF £29.06 CT £235.83 TOTE £10.10: £2.90, £1.50, £3.50; EX 41.80 Place 6 £92.63, Place 5 £70.81..
**Owner** A A Lyons **Bred** A Lyons Bloodstock **Trained** Epsom, Surrey

**FOCUS**
A steadily-run fillies' handicap in which the first two pulled well clear. The winner was back to her best and the runner-up produced another decent effort.

**NOTEBOOK**
**Miss Pebbles(IRE)** ◆, 5lb lower that at the start of the season, had no problem with ground that was riding slower than described. After travelling well, she only needed to be shaken up to put her head in front close home. She can win again while in this sort of mood.
**Mango Mischief(IRE)** was flattered in the end by the margin of defeat, but she finished well clear of the rest and is probably still on the upgrade.
**Doris Souter(IRE)** adopted her usual front-running tactics against the rail but had no answers when headed.
**Olivia Rose(IRE)** has enjoyed a good season, but a 6lb rise for her win at Ripon put her on a mark 19lb higher than at the beginning of the campaign.
**Ballerina Suprema(IRE)** won the second of her two runs as a juvenile when trained by Michael Bell but had not run since. She was keeping on after not getting the best of runs and promises to stay a mile and a half.
**Czarina Waltz** *Official explanation: trainer said filly was struck into and lost a hind shoe*
T/Plt: £173.30 to a £1 stake. Pool: £40,182.40. 169.25 winning tickets. T/Qpdt: £75.80 to a £1 stake. Pool: £2,070.20. 20.20 winning tickets. ST

# 3283 CURRAGH (R-H)
Saturday, June 26

**OFFICIAL GOING: Good (good to firm from 1m6f marker to 6f marker)**

## 3328a IRISH STALLION FARMS EUROPEAN BREEDERS FUND SUMMER FILLIES H'CAP (PREMIER HANDICAP) 7f
**2:10** (2:11) 3-Y-O+ **£36,676** (£10,760; £5,126; £1,746)

RPR
**1** **Sugarhoneybaby (IRE)**[24] 2604 3-7-5 79 ........ PBBeggy(7) 7 88
(NoelMeade, Ire) *hld up: hdwy over 1 1/2f out: rdn to ld ins fnl f: kpt on wl* **14/1**
**2** *1* **Alexander Duchess (IRE)**[52] 1879 3-8-13 97 ........ DJCondon(3) 10 103
(JGBurns, Ire) *hld up towards rr: hdwy 2f out: 2nd ins fnl f: kpt on wl* **16/1**
**3** *1 1/2* **Shoshana (IRE)**[13] 2920 3-7-5 79 ........ JEMoriarty(7) 4 81
(NoelMeade, Ire) *hld up: smooth hdwy to trckd ldrs 2f out: 3rd over 1f out: rdn and kpt on* **12/1**
**4** *1* **Little Whisper (IRE)**[41] 2150 3-8-5 89 ........ CatherineGannon(3) 6 88
(CCollins, Ire) *trckd ldrs: hdwy on stand side 2 1/2f out: led under 2f out tl hdd and no ex ins fnl f* **10/1**
**5** *hd* **Erreur (IRE)**[24] 2604 3-7-9 83 ........ RPCleary(7) 11 82
(EdwardLynam, Ire) *led: rdn and hdd under 2f out: kpt on same pce* **14/1**
**6** *shd* **Fairy Pass (IRE)**[13] 2921 3-7-13 80 ........ TPO'Shea 2 79
(GMLyons, Ire) *prom: 4th 1/2-way: rdn to chal 2f out: no imp fr over 1f out* **14/1**
**7** *1/2* **Hilites (IRE)**[14] 2877 3-7-13 80 ........ RMBurke 12 77
(JSMoore) *chsd ldrs: kpt on one pced fr 2f out* **14/1**
**8** *3/4* **Desert Gold (IRE)**[14] 2901 3-8-13 94 ........(t) JPSpencer 1 89
(DavidWachman, Ire) *in tch: 5th 1/2-way: rdn and no imp fr 2f out* **11/2**[3]
**9** *3/4* **Amourallis (IRE)**[251] 5657 3-7-10 82 ........ HelenKeohane(5) 5 75
(GMLyons, Ire) *bhd: sn trailing: kpt on ins fnl f* **20/1**
**10** *3/4* **Summer Sunset (IRE)**[10] 2971 3-9-0 95 ........ PJSmullen 9 86
(DKWeld, Ire) *trckd ldrs: effrt over 2f out: one pced* **12/1**
**11** *hd* **Aleida (IRE)**[20] 2709 3-8-2 83 ........ WMLordan 16 74
(JSBolger, Ire) *chsd ldrs on far side: 6th and effrt 2 1/2f out: sn no ex* **5/1**[2]
**12** *hd* **Dixie Evans**[63] 1634 4-9-10 96 ........(b) DMGrant 13 86
(HRogers, Ire) *cl up: 2nd and chal 3f out: wknd fr 2f out* **20/1**
**13** *1/2* **Dolce Voche (IRE)**[24] 2600 3-8-7 88 ........ MJKinane 15 77
(JohnMOxx, Ire) *hld up towards rr: no imp fr 2f out* **4/1**[1]
**14** *1/2* **Sudden Silence (IRE)**[48] 1980 3-8-13 94 ........ JAHeffernan 3 82
(DeclanGillespie, Ire) *chsd ldrs: 6th 1/2-way: no ex over 2f out* **14/1**
**15** *nk* **Triton Dance (IRE)**[34] 2328 4-9-2 88 ........(b) NGMcCullagh 8 75
(MJGrassick, Ire) *nvr a factor: bhd and trailing fr 2f out* **12/1**
**16** *7* **Doire-Chrinn (IRE)**[48] 1380 8-8-5 77 ........ JFEgan 14 46
(DPKelly, Ire) *cl up to 1/2-way: sn wknd: eased over 2f out: t.o* **14/1**

1m 24.1s **Going Correction** -0.40s/f (Firm)
**WFA** 3 from 4yo+ 9lb **16** Ran SP% **139.6**
Speed ratings: **100,98,97,96,95 95,95,94,93,92 92,92,91,90,90 82**CSF £251.89 CT £2811.86 TOTE £14.90: £2.40, £3.40, £5.60, £2.40; DF 276.60.
**Owner** Liam Queally **Bred** Mrs Bill O'Neill **Trained** Castletown, Co Meath

**NOTEBOOK**
**Hilites(IRE)** has shown her best form over six furlongs.
**Desert Gold(IRE)** *Official explanation: jockey said filly was checked in her run 1 1/2f out*

## 3331a AUDI PRETTY POLLY STKS (GROUP 1) (FILLIES) 1m 2f
**3:40** (3:40) 3-Y-O+ **£109,859** (£34,788; £16,478; £5,492)

RPR
**1** **Chorist**[19] 2733 5-9-7 ........ DHolland 1 119
(WJHaggas) *mde all: rdn and strly pressed fr under 2f out: styd on wl cl home* **7/4**[2]
**2** *1/2* **Alexander Goldrun (IRE)**[13] 2925 3-8-9 116 ........ KJManning 2 118
(JSBolger, Ire) *trckd ldrs in 4th: impr into 2nd and chal under 2f out: ev ch: no ex cl home* **6/4**[1]
**3** *6* **Ivowen (USA)**[28] 2498 4-9-7 101 ........ PJSmullen 3 107
(DKWeld, Ire) *chsd ldrs in 2nd: pushed along 3 1/2f out: 3rd and no ex under 2f out: kpt on same pce* **16/1**
**4** *3/4* **Soldera (USA)**[10] 2967 4-9-7 ........ JPMurtagh 5 105
(JRFanshawe) *settled 3rd: rdn over 3f out: 4th and no ex over 2f out* **11/2**[3]
**5** *nk* **Livadiya (IRE)**[24] 2603 8-9-7 107 ........ MJKinane 6 105
(HRogers, Ire) *hld up: 5th and effrt over 3f out* **12/1**
**6** *8* **Hanami**[35] 2318 4-9-7 ........ SSanders 4 89
(JARToller) *hld up: last fr over 4f out: sn wknd* **7/1**

2m 2.80s **Going Correction** -0.30s/f (Firm)
**WFA** 3 from 4yo+ 12lb **6** Ran SP% **117.8**
Speed ratings: **114,113,108,108,107 101**CSF £5.13 TOTE £2.90: £1.70, £1.10; DF 7.40.
**Owner** Cheveley Park Stud **Bred** Cheveley Park Stud Ltd **Trained** Newmarket, Suffolk

**FOCUS**
Doubled in prize money since last year and with new Group 1 status, this was still a weak contest.

**NOTEBOOK**
**Chorist**, a cosy winner on her seasonal reappearance in Listed company at Pontefract, was given a positive ride from the front and kept finding to hold the sole three-year-old in the field. She has evidently progressed well from four to five and was winning her first Group 1.
**Alexander Goldrun(IRE)** was already beginning to struggle when ridden to get upsides the winner with less than two furlongs to race. She was dominated physically by the winner and maybe just did not show the same zest for a struggle. A rest may do her good.
**Ivowen(USA)** was readily outpaced by the first pair.
**Soldera(USA)** struggled from early in the straight.
**Livadiya(IRE)** never looked entirely happy on the ground.
**Hanami** was not a factor in the straight. *Official explanation: trainer said filly finished lame*

## 3333a SHARP MINDS BETFAIR CURRAGH CUP (GROUP 3) 1m 6f
4:45 (4:45) 3-Y-O+ **£33,802** (£10,704; £5,070; £1,690)

RPR
1 **Mkuzi**[28] [2498] 5-9-10 109 ..... MJKinane 2 113
(JohnMOxx, Ire) *settled 3rd: hdwy 2f out: rdn to chal 1 1/2f out: led under 1f out: styd on wl* **7/1**[3]
2 ½ **Dubai Success**[22] [2639] 4-9-13 ..... JPMurtagh 5 115
(BWHills) *settled 2nd: rdn to chal 2f out: ev ch fr over 1f out: kpt on wl u.p* **10/3**[1]
3 1 **Cruzspiel**[266] [5386] 4-9-10 102 .....(b) FMBerry 4 111?
(JohnMOxx, Ire) *dwlt: sn led: rdn and strly pressed 2f out: hdd under 1f out: kpt on wl* **20/1**
4 2 **Mikado**[231] [5959] 3-8-7 102 ..... JPSpencer 6 108
(APO'Brien, Ire) *trckd ldrs in 5th: rdn 2f out: 4th and kpt on fnl f* **4/1**[2]
5 shd **The Whistling Teal**[42] [2108] 8-9-10 ..... JFEgan 1 108
(GWragg) *chsd ldrs: 4th 1/2-way: drvn along appr st: no imp fr 2f out: kpt on same pce* **10/3**[1]
6 4 ½ **Jade Quest (IRE)**[31] [2416] 4-9-10 100 ..... DHolland 7 102
(CharlesO'Brien, Ire) *hld up in rr: no imp st* **12/1**
7 20 **Maharib (IRE)**[55] [1814] 4-9-10 110 ..... PJSmullen 3 102
(DKWeld, Ire) *hld up: 6th and drvn along 5f out: wknd st: t.o* **4/1**[2]

2m 59.7s **Going Correction** -0.30s/f (Firm)
**WFA** 3 from 4yo+ 17lb 7 Ran SP% **111.1**
Speed ratings: **101,100,100,99,98 96,84**CSF £28.72 TOTE £11.10: £3.80, £2.00; DF 69.10.
**Owner** Sheikh Mohammed **Bred** Sheikh Mohammed Bin Rashid Al Maktoum **Trained** Currabeg, Co Kildare

**NOTEBOOK**
**Mkuzi** readily disposed of fears regarding stamina limitations. Always travelling strongly, he led a furlong out and galloped all the way to the line. He was holding the runner-up all the way in the closing stages.
**Dubai Success** delivered a sustained challenge over the last two furlongs but it was a one paced effort and he couldn't quicken under pressure.
**Cruzspiel**, a stable companion of the winner, set a fairly searching gallop and for a few strides a furlong and a half down, looked as though he may have stolen the race. But, having his first outing since last October, wilted inside the last.
**Mikado**, the only three year-old in the field and running here in preference to the Derby, travelled well until finding little from a furlong and a half down.
**The Whistling Teal** had every chance on the outside two furlongs out but could only stay on at the same pace under pressure.
**Maharib(IRE)** ran way below par, finishing tailed-off and never looked to be travelling. He is undoubtedly better than this.

3332 - 3334a (Foreign Racing) - See Raceform Interactive

# 2723 HAMBURG (R-H)
Saturday, June 26

**OFFICIAL GOING: Soft**

## 3335a DEUTSCHER HEROLD-PREIS (GROUP 3) 1m
4:05 (4:15) 3-Y-O+ **£22,535** (£9,155; £4,577; £2,465)

RPR
1 **Sambaprinz (GER)**[34] [2336] 5-9-2 ..... AStarke 7 111
(HHorwart, Germany) *raced in close 2nd, led entering straight, ridden over 1f out, held on well*
2 ½ **Pepperstorm (GER)**[41] [2158] 3-8-9 ..... ABoschert 11 113
(UOstmann, Germany) *midfield, disputing 4th straight, stayed on strongly down outside from over 1f out* 3
3 shd **Eagle Rise (IRE)**[24] [2608] 4-9-4 ..... ASuborics 6 112
(ASchutz, Germany) *held up, 6th straight, hard ridden and good headway from 1 1/2f out, went 2nd inside final f, no extra close home* 2
4 2 **Lazio (GER)**[41] [2158] 3-8-10 ow1 ..... ADeVries 8 110
(ATrybuhl, Germany) *in touch, disputing 4th straight, slightly outpaced over 1f out, rallied to take 4th close home* 1
5 nk **Peppercorn (GER)**[223] [6007] 7-9-2 ..... TMundry 2 105
(UOstmann, Germany) *always mid division*
6 hd **Askant (GER)**[244] [5779] 7-9-2 ..... JBojko 12 105
(HFanelsa, France) *in touch towards outside, ridden over 1 1/2f out, unable to challenge*
7 nse **Furioso Directa (GER)**[238] [5884] 4-9-4 .....(b) JPalik 1 107
(AndreasLowe, Germany) *midfield, 3rd on inside straight, hung badly right from 1 1/2f out, no extra final stages*
8 2 ½ **Forever Free (GER)**[37] 4-9-2 ..... ASchikora 4 100
(DKRichardson, Germany) *midfield, stayed on til one pace from over 1f out*
9 hd **Madresal (GER)**[34] [2336] 5-9-6 ..... THellier 10 103
(PSchiergen, Germany) *held up, disputing last straight, ridden over 1f out, never dangerous*
10 1 ¾ **Medici (GER)**[34] [2336] 4-9-2 ..... J-PCarvalho 9 96
(MarioHofer, Germany) *towards rear, disputing last entering straight, never a factor*
11 3 **Up And Away (GER)**[34] [2336] 10-9-2 ..... LHammer-Hansen 5 90
(FrauEMader, Germany) *led til headed entering straight, soon weakened*

1m 41.44s
**WFA** 3 from 4yo+ 10lb 11 Ran SP% **131.5**
Speed ratings: .
**Owner** A Von Mulert **Bred** A Von Mulert **Trained** Germany

# 3124 WARWICK (L-H)
Sunday, June 27

**OFFICIAL GOING: Good to firm (good in places)**
The 7mm of rain that fell overnight only eased the going marginally.
Wind: mod bhd Weather: showers last 2 races

## 3336 SOUTH WARWICKSHIRE BUSINESS CLUB MAIDEN AUCTION STKS 7f 26y
2:20 (2:21) (E) 2-Y-O **£3,851** (£1,185; £592; £296) Stalls Low

Form RPR
5 1 **Dry Ice (IRE)**[20] [2736] 2-8-9 ..... DaneO'Neill 7 79
(HCandy) *hld up in tch: lost pl sltly over 3f out: rdn over 2f out: rallied and edgd lft over 1f out: led and edgd lft ins fnl f: r.* **2/1**[2]
32 2 1 ½ **Mceldowney**[10] [3009] 2-8-11 ..... KDalgleish 5 77
(MJohnston) *led 1f: w ldr: rdn over 2f out: led and hung lft over 1f out: hdd ins fnl f: nt qckn* **7/2**[3]
6 3 1 ¾ **Coleorton Dane**[46] [2045] 2-8-7 ..... NCallan 6 72+
(KARyan) *trckd ldrs: rdn over 2f out: nt clr run jst over 1f out: swtchd rt ins fnl f: one pce* **15/8**[1]
0 4 ½ **Persian Carpet**[8] [3083] 2-8-2 ..... GDuffield 3 62
(IAWood) *led after 1f: rdn and hdd over 1f out: wknd ins fnl f* **20/1**
3 5 shd **Hawridge King**[34] [2360] 2-8-7 ..... MFenton 8 67
(WSKittow) *a.p: rdn and one pce fnl 2f* **16/1**
60 6 ¾ **Mirage Prince (IRE)**[38] [2234] 2-8-4 ..... BSwarbrick(5) 1 67
(WMBrisbourne) *hld up and bhd: rdn over 3f out: styd on fnl f: n.d* **66/1**
7 4 **Skidrow** 2-8-9 ..... IMongan 4 57
(MLWBell) *dwlt: sme hdwy over 3f out: rdn over 2f out: sn wknd* **14/1**
8 4 **Ansells Legacy (IRE)** 2-8-9 ..... GCarter 2 47
(ABerry) *dwlt: outpcd* **25/1**
9 10 **Sea Map** 2-8-9 ..... EAhern 9 22
(SKirk) *s.v.s: a wl bhd* **16/1**

1m 24.06s (-0.84) **Going Correction** -0.20s/f (Firm) 9 Ran SP% **118.9**
Speed ratings: **96,94,92,91,91 90,86,81,70**CSF £9.67 TOTE £2.90: £1.60, £1.30, £1.10; EX 10.50.
**Owner** Simon Broke And Partners **Bred** Corduff Stud And Partners **Trained** Wantage, Oxon

**FOCUS**
The form is solid and this could turn out to be an above-average event for its type.

**NOTEBOOK**
**Dry Ice(IRE)** built on the promise of his debut with the extra furlong to help. He is going the right way.
**Mceldowney** helped force the pace but was unable to cope with the winner on such an easy course.
**Coleorton Dane** made his debut in what turned out to be a hot race at York. Trying an extra furlong on faster ground, he did not get the run of the race but it is doubtful if he would have beaten the winner.
**Persian Carpet**, a half-sister to a couple of winners in Italy, showed significant improvement on her recent debut at Lingfield. She may be better suited to six at the moment.
**Hawridge King** was not inconvenienced by this longer trip.
**Mirage Prince(IRE)** is bred to appreciate this sort of trip.
**Sea Map** *Official explanation: jockey said colt missed the break*

## 3337 EUROPEAN BREEDERS FUND CLASSIFIED STKS 7f 26y
2:50 (2:51) (C) 3-Y-O+ **£9,999** (£3,792; £1,896; £862) Stalls Low

Form RPR
0201 1 **Material Witness (IRE)**[23] [2646] 7-9-4 89 ..... RMullen 1 95
(WRMuir) *mde all: rdn over 2f out: jst hld on* **13/2**[3]
-300 2 shd **Mysterinch**[23] [2637] 4-9-5 91 ..... PHanagan 10 96
(JeddO'Keeffe) *hld up and bhd: rdn and hdwy 2f out: r.o wl towards fin: jst failed* **14/1**
-336 3 nk **Look Here's Carol (IRE)**[22] [2685] 4-9-1 87 ..... GGibbons 6 91
(BAMcmahon) *hld up in tch: rdn 3f out: kpt on wl towards fin* **9/1**
5535 4 ¾ **Kool (IRE)**[9] [3052] 5-9-4 89 ..... TQuinn 11 92
(PFICole) *hld up: swtchd lft and hdwy 2f out: nt clr run on ins and swtchd rt over 1f out: hrd rdn and kpt on ins fnl f* **7/2**[1]
060 5 nk **Atavus**[9] [3036] 7-9-5 91 ..... JMackay 4 92
(GGMargarson) *chsd wnr: rdn over 2f out: ev ch 1f out: nt qckn* **6/1**[2]
0-06 6 shd **Binanti**[15] [2891] 4-9-4 88 ..... JQuinn 3 91
(PRChamings) *hld up in tch: rdn over 2f out: hung and swtchd lft ins fnl f: no ex* **7/1**
-066 7 4 **Vindication**[9] [3052] 4-9-4 89 .....(t) EAhern 12 80
(JRFanshawe) *hld up and bhd: short-lived effrt on outside over 1f out* **7/2**[1]
0000 8 5 **Rosselli (USA)**[9] [3039] 8-8-11 46 ..... CEly(7) 9 67?
(ABerry) *prom: rdn over 2f out: wknd over 1f out* **150/1**
0046 9 2 **Telepathic (IRE)**[9] [3039] 4-8-11 57 ..... PPMathers(7) 2 61
(ABerry) *s.i.s: sn prom: rdn over 2f out: wknd over 1f out* **150/1**
0602 10 3 **Jalouhar**[11] [2979] 4-9-4 46 ..... MTebbutt 5 53
(BPJBaugh) *s.i.s: a bhd* **100/1**
6000 11 1 ½ **Speedfit Free (IRE)**[6] [3151] 7-9-4 46 ..... AnnStokell 7 49
(MissAStokell) *a bhd* **200/1**

1m 21.59s (-3.31) **Going Correction** -0.20s/f (Firm)
**WFA** 3 from 4yo+ 9lb 11 Ran SP% **104.0**
Speed ratings: **110,109,109,108,108 108,103,97,95,92 90**CSF £70.01 TOTE £6.60: £2.30, £2.90, £2.00; EX 93.50.
**Owner** M J Caddy **Bred** M Henochsberg **Trained** Lambourn, Berks

**FOCUS**
The winner set a good pace which resulted in a fast time. The form is decent but this was a bit of a messy race.

**NOTEBOOK**
**Material Witness(IRE)** is a different animal when able to dominate. Like many front-runners, he is suited by a turning track.
**Mysterinch** ◆, dropping back to seven, found the post arriving a fraction too soon. A return to a mile can see him go one better.
**Look Here's Carol(IRE)** was suited by a return to seven especially on ground as quick as this. She is knocking on the door.
**Kool(IRE)** had his fair share of traffic problems in the home straight but did not finish as well as either the second or the third.
**Atavus** was always going to find it difficult to front-run with Material Witness in the field. A respectable effort in the circumstances.
**Binanti** was not helping his rider in the closing stages.
**Vindication** *Official explanation: jockey said gelding returned with a cut leg*

## 3338 MERCIA FM CLAIMING STKS 6f 21y
3:25 (3:25) (E) 3-Y-O £3,445 (£1,060; £530; £265) Stalls Low

Form RPR
-003 1 **Innclassic (IRE)**[16] 2849 3-8-1 67..........(b) JFMcDonald[(3)] 8 66
(BJMeehan) *a.p: hrd rdn to ld jst over 1f out: drvn out* **9/1**

0060 2 nk **Who's Winning (IRE)**[8] 3089 3-8-7 63..........(b[1]) EAhern 10 68
(CADwyer) *hld up: hdwy on outside bnd 3f out: rdn over 1f out: ev ch ins fnl f: nt qckn cl home* **5/1**[3]

0006 3 3/4 **One Upmanship**[16] 2833 3-8-7 61.......... NCallan 6 66
(JGPortman) *hld up in tch: lost pl 3f out: rdn and rallied over 1f out: kpt on wl towards fin* **16/1**

6020 4 1 1/4 **Sir Ernest (IRE)**[8] 3077 3-8-9 76.......... GDuffield 1 64
(MJPolglase) *led: rdn and hdd jst over 1f out: no ex towards fin* **7/2**[2]

0-00 5 1 3/4 **Dreaming Waters**[34] 2371 3-8-4 55.......... SCarson 4 54
(RFJohnsonHoughton) *stdd s: rdn and hdwy on outside over 1f out: one pce fnl f* **16/1**

1661 6 1 1/4 **Arfinnit (IRE)**[9] 3037 3-8-6 61.......... SHitchcott[(3)] 7 55
(MRChannon) *outpcd: hdwy whn nt clr run and swtchd rt jst over 1f out: nt rch ldrs* **6/4**[1]

0-05 7 2 1/2 **Karma Chamelian (USA)**[8] 3106 3-8-4 44.......... TQuinn 2 43
(JWHills) *s.i.s: hdwy on ins over 3f out: wknd over 1f out* **16/1**

00 8 2 **Parliament Act (IRE)**[25] 2586 3-8-7..........(t) GGibbons 3 40
(BAMcmahon) *prom: wnt 2nd 3f out: sn rdn: wknd wl over 1f out* **33/1**

10-5 9 1 1/2 **Mouseman**[35] 2326 3-8-7 59..........(b) MFenton 9 35
(CNKellett) *w ldr 3f: sn rdn and wknd* **14/1**

1m 10.15s (-2.15) **Going Correction** -0.20s/f (Firm) **9** Ran SP% **116.1**
Speed ratings: **106,105,104,102,100 98,95,92,90**CSF £53.82 TOTE £9.70: £2.70, £1.80, £3.60; EX 50.60.
**Owner** The Inn Partnership **Bred** Irish National Stud **Trained** Upper Lambourn, Berks

**FOCUS**
This was run in a fair time for the grade, but the form is not convincing.

**NOTEBOOK**
**Innclassic(IRE)**, again in the headgear, found a switch back to turf in similar company doing the trick.
**Who's Winning(IRE)** was blinkered for the first time for this drop in grade. He may have got his head in front in the last 200 yards but the winner would not be denied.
**One Upmanship** was without the headgear this time and needs a return to seven.
**Sir Ernest(IRE)**, down in class, was having only his second run at six and seems more effective at the minimum distance.
**Dreaming Waters**, dropped into claiming company, wants far more use made of her over this sort of trip.
**Arfinnit(IRE)** will do better with the visor back on on this evidence.
**Parliament Act(IRE)** *Official explanation: trainer said gelding bled from the nose*

## 3339 ST MARY'S LANDS RATED STKS (H'CAP) 5f 110y
4:00 (4:01) (D) (0-85,84) 3-Y-O+ £6,484 (£2,459; £1,229; £559) Stalls Low

Form RPR
6312 1 **Dizzy In The Head**[7] 3125 5-8-6 73..........(b) NChalmers[(5)] 7 86
(PaulJohnson) *mde all: rdn and edgd lft over 1f out: r.o* **6/1**

4-01 2 1 1/4 **Cape St Vincent**[30] 2455 4-8-10 72..........(v) MFenton 3 81
(HMorrison) *a.p: rdn over 2f out: chsd wnr fnl f: nt qckn* **11/2**

1512 3 1 **High Ridge**[13] 2948 5-8-4 69 oh1..........(p) SHitchcott[(3)] 1 74
(JMBradley) *a.p: rdn over 2f out: nt qckn fnl f* **9/4**[1]

0001 4 nk **Dancing Mystery**[14] 2912 10-9-7 83.......... SCarson 5 87
(EAWheeler) *hld up: rdn and hdwy over 1f out: nt qckn ins fnl f* **11/1**

0403 5 shd **Midnight Parkes**[8] 3098 5-8-7 69 oh4.......... DAllan 4 73
(EJAlston) *mid-div: rdn and outpcd over 3f out: hdwy jst over 1f out: kpt on ins fnl f* **7/2**[2]

5504 6 hd **Endless Summer**[16] 2843 7-8-12 74.......... TQuinn 8 77
(AWCarroll) *hld up and bhd: outpcd over 3f out: r.o ins fnl f* **25/1**

1031 7 1 1/2 **Whistler**[3] 3243 7-9-8 84 3ex..........(p) DaneO'Neill 10 82
(JMBradley) *hld up: rdn 3f out: no rspnse* **5/1**[3]

4400 8 hd **Twice Upon A Time**[8] 3098 5-8-7 69.......... EAhern 2 66
(BSmart) *rrd s: short-lived effrt on ins 2f out* **16/1**

0006 9 3/4 **Safranine (IRE)**[3] 3223 7-8-7 69 oh9..........(p) AnnStokell 6 63
(MissAStokell) *prom: rdn 2f out: wknd fnl f* **16/1**

63.60 secs (-0.71) **Going Correction** +0.025s/f (Good) course record**9** Ran SP% **123.3**
Speed ratings: **105,103,102,101,101 101,99,98,97**CSF £41.76 CT £99.69 TOTE £6.40: £1.50, £2.50, £1.80; EX 35.50.
**Owner** P And Mrs D M Johnson **Bred** Bearstone Stud And T Herbert Jackson **Trained** White-le-Head, Co Durham

**FOCUS**
Unlike many of his rivals, the winner was suited by a slightly shorter trip and he lowered the course record by .06 seconds. The form looks solid.

**NOTEBOOK**
**Dizzy In The Head** was narrowly beaten by a horse who broke the track record over six here last time. He went into the record books himself over this slightly shorter distance and continues in fine form.
**Cape St Vincent** showed his win at Wolverhampton in the first-time visor was no fluke over a trip that is on the short side for him.
**High Ridge** continues to run well but is another who probably wants the full six on a course as sharp as this.
**Dancing Mystery** could not quite sustain his effort off a 3lb higher mark.
**Midnight Parkes** is better suited to the full six furlongs.
**Endless Summer** is yet another who wants a shade further.
**Twice Upon A Time** *Official explanation: jockey said mare reared up in the stalls*

## 3340 ANDREW SYKES GROUP H'CAP 1m 2f 188y
4:35 (4:35) (D) (0-80,76) 3-Y-O £5,876 (£1,808; £904; £452) Stalls Low

Form RPR
4-10 1 **Cause Celebre (IRE)**[22] 2683 3-9-7 76.......... EAhern 2 83
(BWHills) *set slow pce: hdd after 2f: remained prom: rdn to ld jst over 1f out: r.o wl* **11/4**[3]

6335 2 1 3/4 **General Flumpa**[23] 2665 3-8-10 65.......... RMullen 4 69
(CFWall) *a.p: led over 2f out: rdn and hdd jst over 1f out: nt qckn* **5/1**

1351 3 shd **Goblin**[8] 3107 3-9-6 75.......... TQuinn 6 79
(DECantillon) *hld up: rdn over 2f out: hdwy over 1f out: ev ch ent fnl f: nt qckn* **5/2**[2]

0332 4 1 1/4 **Desert Image (IRE)**[15] 2870 3-9-1 73.......... DCorby[(3)] 1 75
(CTinkler) *a.p: rdn and one pce fnl 2f* **2/1**[1]

-002 5 5 **Spectested (IRE)**[30] 2452 3-7-5 53 oh3.......... CHaddon[(7)] 7 46
(AWCarroll) *plld hrd early: hld up: rdn 3f out: no rspnse* **20/1**

0-54 6 1 **Brough Supreme**[44] 2090 3-9-3 72.......... MFenton 5 64
(HMorrison) *plld hrd: hdwy to ld after 2f: qcknd over 5f out: hdd over 2f out: wknd over 1f out* **20/1**

2m 18.98s (-0.42) **Going Correction** -0.20s/f (Firm) **6** Ran SP% **114.8**
Speed ratings: **93,91,91,90,87 86**CSF £17.17 TOTE £3.70: £2.00, £2.10; EX 17.40.
**Owner** The Hon Mrs J M Corbett & C Wright **Bred** Epona Bloodstock Ltd **Trained** Lambourn, Berks

**FOCUS**
A slowly-run race led to a modest time for the grade, but the form looks sound enough.

**NOTEBOOK**
**Cause Celebre(IRE)** back down in both class and distance, ran out a decisive winner of a muddling sort of race.
**General Flumpa** may have preferred a stronger-run race given that he has tackled further on his last two outings.
**Goblin**, raised 5lb for his course and distance victory, was nearly a stone higher than when scoring at Beverley last month.
**Desert Image(IRE)** would have preferred more of an end to end gallop.

## 3341 WEATHERBYS INSURANCE MAIDEN STKS 2m 2f
5:05 (5:06) (D) 3-Y-O+ £4,251 (£1,308; £654; £327) Stalls Low

Form RPR
4040 1 **Fiddlers Ford (IRE)**[6] 3160 3-8-5 72.......... EAhern 9 64
(JNoseda) *hld up: rdn and hdwy 2f out: led jst over 1f out: styd on wl* **5/1**[3]

242 2 3 **Recognise (IRE)**[10] 3013 3-8-5 80.......... JFanning 4 61
(MJohnston) *w ldr: led after 3f: rdn over 2f out: hdd jst over 1f out: one pce* **11/8**[1]

-054 3 3 **Fu Fighter**[16] 2840 3-8-5 71.......... TQuinn 5 58
(JAOsborne) *plld hrd early: prom: wnt 2nd 10f out: rdn over 2f out: wknd fnl f* **3/1**[2]

2423 4 5 **Dora Corbino**[34] 2347 4-9-7 39.......... GDuffield 1 47?
(RHollinshead) *led 3f: prom: rdn over 3f out: wknd over 1f out* **20/1**

5 3/4 **My True Love (IRE)**[42] 5-9-13.......... VSlattery 2 51
(RJBaker) *dwlt: hld up: hdwy over 6f out: wknd over 3f out* **16/1**

-503 6 4 **Opera Star (IRE)**[4] 3194 3-8-0 63.......... PHanagan 3 42
(BWHills) *prom: rdn over 2f out: wknd over 1f out: eased fnl f* **10/1**

-065 7 2 1/2 **Victory Lap (GER)**[25] 2567 3-8-4 65 ow7.......... SHitchcott[(3)] 8 46
(MRChannon) *hld up: rdn over 3f out: sn struggling* **8/1**

0 P **Pridewood Dove**[24] 2611 5-9-8.......... MFenton 7 —
(RJPrice) *sn wl bhd: t.o 8f out: p.u over 4f out* **100/1**

3m 56.39s
**WFA** 3 from 4yo 22lb 4 from 5yo 1lb **8** Ran SP% **115.6**
Speed ratings: CSF £12.44 TOTE £6.80: £2.50, £1.30, £1.10; EX 19.20.
**Owner** Mrs Susan Roy **Bred** Gaines Centry Thoroughbreds Llc And Quay Bldst **Trained** Newmarket, Suffolk

**FOCUS**
This staying maiden did not probably take too much winning. The form is anchored by the fourth.

**NOTEBOOK**
**Fiddlers Ford(IRE)** relished the big step up in distance and it looks as if they have found the key to him.
**Recognise(IRE)** is bred to get this sort of trip but had no answer to the winner.
**Fu Fighter** eventually paid the penalty for running too freely early on over this extra half a mile.
**Opera Star(IRE)** *Official explanation: jockey said filly had a breathing problem*
**Pridewood Dove** *Official explanation: jockey said mare lost her action*

## 3342 HILL CLOSE GARDENS APPRENTICE H'CAP 1m 4f 134y
5:35 (5:36) (G) (0-70,66) 3-Y-O+ £3,122 (£892; £446) Stalls Low

Form RPR
5162 1 **Trusted Mole (IRE)**[13] 2939 6-9-4 56.......... DFentiman 4 65
(WMBrisbourne) *hld up in tch: chsd ldr over 3f out: r.o u.p to ld nr fin* **15/8**[1]

5220 2 1/2 **Ben Kenobi**[13] 2939 6-7-13 37.......... DeanWilliams 5 45
(MrsPFord) *hld up: sn in tch: led over 6f out: qckni clr 3f out: sn rdn: ct nr fin* **5/1**

0330 3 1 1/4 **Saxe-Coburg (IRE)**[19] 2767 7-9-8 60.......... WHogg 1 66
(GAHam) *a.p: outpcd over 3f out: rdn over 2f out: styd on fnl f* **3/1**[2]

0-00 4 1 3/4 **Bond May Day**[12] 2964 4-9-6 66.......... MStainton[(8)] 6 70
(BSmart) *set slow pce: hdd over 6f out: outpcd over 3f out: styd on ins fnl f* **7/1**

0000 5 3 1/2 **Silencio (IRE)**[24] 2611 3-8-2 60.......... BO'Neill[(5)] 8 59
(AKing) *prom: outpcd and rdn 3f out: rallied over 1f out: wknd fnl f* **9/2**[3]

/50- 6 1 1/2 **Pancake Role**[405] 1729 4-7-9 36 oh1.......... MHalford[(3)] 7 32
(AWCarroll) *rrd s: hld up: c wd st: rdn 2f out: no rspnse* **28/1**

0435 7 6 **Stylish Sunrise (IRE)**[18] 2783 3-8-1 64 ow8..........(t) JTucker[(10)] 2 51
(IAWood) *prom tl lost pl over 6f out: sn bhd* **12/1**

2m 50.65s (7.35) **Going Correction** -0.20s/f (Firm) **7** Ran SP% **118.3**
**WFA** 3 from 4yo+ 15lb
Speed ratings: **69,68,67,66,64 63,60**CSF £12.48 CT £27.52 TOTE £2.50: £1.40, £2.20; EX 9.30 Place 6 £145.34, Place 5 £129.30.
**Owner** P G Evans & David Manning Associates **Bred** Patrick Joseph O'Brien **Trained** Great Ness, Shropshire

**FOCUS**
This apprentices' event was run at a dawdle and the form is modest.

**NOTEBOOK**
**Trusted Mole(IRE)** was the first to react when the winner kicked for home off a slow pace at the three-furlong pole and eventually wore down his rival.
**Ben Kenobi** managed to slip his field on the home turn in this slowly-run race and the enterprising tactics very nearly paid off.
**Saxe-Coburg(IRE)** likes to come from behind off a good pace and was totally unsuited by the way things panned out.
**Bond May Day** might just as well have got on with things in the lead given the way things worked out.
**Silencio(IRE)** should have appreciated this trip but the race was falsely-run.
T/Plt: £212.60 to a £1 stake. Pool: £35,036.65 - 120.25 winning tickets. T/Qpdt: £25.10 to a £1 stake. Pool: £2,001.70 - 59.00 winning tickets. KH

# 3322 WINDSOR (R-H)
Sunday, June 27

**OFFICIAL GOING: Good to firm**

## 3343 READING EVENING POST NOVICE AUCTION STKS 6f
2:30 (2:30) (E) 2-Y-O £3,581 (£1,102; £551; £275) Stalls High

Form RPR
1 1 **Aastral Magic**[36] 2300 2-8-8.......... RLMoore 2 83
(RHannon) *mde virtually all: shkn up over 1f out: drew clr fnl f* **6/4**[1]

13 **2** *3* **Highland Cascade**[17] 2817 2-8-3 FPFerris(3) 1 72
(JMPEustace) *w wnr to wl over 1f out: rdn and nt qckn: hld after* **6/4**[1]
**3** *3 1/2* **Hidden Star** 2-8-12 JFortune 6 68+
(FJordan) *s.v.s and pushed along: prog to chse clr ldng pair over 2f out: kpt on but no imp* **13/2**[2]
0 **4** *6* **Hallucinate**[33] 2376 2-8-9 PDobbs 3 47
(RHannon) *chsd clr ldrs: hanging lft fr 3f out: sn btn* **11/1**[3]
6 **5** *5* **Robmantra**[7] 3124 2-8-7 SDrowne 5 30
(BJLlewellyn) *chsd clr ldng pair: hanging lft fr wl over 2f out: wknd* **33/1**
0 **6** *1* **Sirce (IRE)**[18] 2786 2-8-2 ow3 TPQueally(3) 4 25
(DJCoakley) *s.s: a struggling: wl bhd over 2f out* **25/1**

1m 12.1s (-1.77) **Going Correction** -0.225s/f (Firm) **6** Ran SP% **108.5**
Speed ratings: **102,98,93,85,78 77**CSF £3.47 TOTE £2.40: £1.30, £1.30; EX 4.20.
**Owner** Green Pastures Partnership **Bred** Green Pastures Farm **Trained** East Everleigh, Wilts

**FOCUS**
A decent time for the grade, but it was hand-timed. Only the first two ever counted.

**NOTEBOOK**
**Aastral Magic** made all the running and had seen off her only challenger inside the last. The form of her Kempton win has taken a knock, but she looks a progressive filly who will get a seventh furlong.
**Highland Cascade**, who drifted in the market beforehand, showed pace to go with the eventual winner but was held in the final furlong.
**Hidden Star** was very slow to go and trailed the field, so emerges with credit for eventually finishing third. A half-brother to four winners, he is bred to stay around ten furlongs in time and there are races to be won with him.
**Hallucinate** appeared unhappy on the ground and hung into the centre of the track.
**Robmantra** was another who hung and gave his rider problems. *Official explanation: jockey said colt had hung left*
**Sirce(IRE)** was left behind from halfway.

## 3344 RECTANGLE GROUP H'CAP 5f 10y
**3:05** (3:07) (E) (0-70,70) 3-Y-O **£3,552** (£1,093; £546; £273) **Stalls** High

Form RPR
1002 **1** **Scottish Exile (IRE)**[6] 3147 3-9-5 **68** (v) DarrenWilliams 14 74
(KRBurke) *pressed ldr: led 1/2-way: hrd rdn and hung lft fnl f: nt look keen but hld on* **5/1**[2]
6-00 **2** *nk* **Ardkeel Lass (IRE)**[8] 3084 3-8-8 **57** JFortune 6 62
(DKIvory) *s.i.s: hld up in rr and swtchd to nr side rail: prog 2f out: drvn and str chal ins fnl f:jst hld* **14/1**
6-30 **3** *nk* **Blue Moon Hitman (IRE)**[16] 2836 3-8-9 **58** FNorton 12 62
(RBrotherton) *chsd ldrs: rdn and effrt 2f out: chal and ev ch ins fnl f: nt qckn nr fin* **8/1**
4400 **4** *1* **Elliot's Choice (IRE)**[3] 3249 3-9-5 **68** SDrowne 10 68
(DCarroll) *racd towards rr: effrt 2f out: shkn up and styd on: nt rch ldrs* **7/1**[3]
5000 **5** *1* **Get To The Point**[13] 2931 3-8-13 **62** (b[1]) RLMoore 1 58
(PWD'Arcy) *dwlt: wl in rr and pushed along: styd on u.p fr over 1f out: nrst fin* **16/1**
6054 **6** *hd* **Cut And Dried**[37] 2265 3-9-4 **67** DHolland 2 62
(DMSimcock) *wl in rr: shkn up and styd on fnl 2f: nvr nrr* **9/1**
026 **7** *hd* **Signor Panettiere**[2] 3273 3-9-7 **70** PDobbs 16 64
(RHannon) *led: edgd lft and hdd 1/2-way: styd pressing ldrs tl hung lft and wknd ins fnl f* **7/2**[1]
2620 **8** *1 3/4* **Laconia (IRE)**[22] 2675 3-8-12 **68** DerekNolan(7) 13 55
(JSMoore) *prom: hung bdly lft fr 1/2-way: sn btn* **11/1**
-440 **9** *3/4* **Orchestration (IRE)**[44] 2097 3-9-1 **64** SWhitworth 8 48
(JWUnett) *chsd ldrs: rdn 1/2-way: fdd over 1f out* **33/1**
40-6 **10** *5* **Innstyle**[8] 3085 3-8-12 **64** LisaJones(3) 5 28
(JLSpearing) *racd on outer: chsd ldrs: hanging lft fr 1/2-way: sn wknd* **12/1**
0-60 **11** *2* **Maxi's Princess (IRE)**[46] 2033 3-8-3 **52** (p) KMcEvoy 4 8
(PJMakin) *v free to post: spd to 1/2-way: sn wknd* **20/1**
5000 **12** *2* **Pompey Blue**[8] 3084 3-8-6 **58** TPQueally(3) 3 6
(PJMcbride) *chsd ldrs to 1/2-way: wknd rapidly* **14/1**
6-00 **13** *10* **Tikitano (IRE)**[28] 2505 3-8-8 **57** ow2 FLynch 7 —
(DKIvory) *s.i.s: a struggling and wl bhd* **25/1**

59.77 secs (-1.43) **Going Correction** -0.225s/f (Firm) **13** Ran SP% **119.3**
Speed ratings: **102,101,101,99,97 97,97,94,93,85 82,78,62**CSF £71.27 CT £574.67 TOTE £5.00: £1.70, £5.40, £4.50; EX 130.90.
**Owner** Mrs Melba Bryce **Bred** D J And Mrs Deer **Trained** Middleham Moor, N Yorks

**FOCUS**
A modest handicap, with a high draw proving a big advantage.

**NOTEBOOK**
**Scottish Exile(IRE)**, back against her own age group, took advantage of the optimum draw, despite drifting away from the rail when in front. Her trainer is of the opinion that she is improving.
**Ardkeel Lass(IRE)** has dropped to a handy mark. After finding herself at the back following a tardy start, she got over to the stands' side and ran on strongly against the rail when an inviting gap appeared.
**Blue Moon Hitman(IRE)**, a fully exposed maiden, ran a decent race but was just held when carried across the track by the winner in the final furlong.
**Elliot's Choice(IRE)** was keeping on in good style and could be worth a try over six furlongs. He does not look particularly well treated at present, however.
**Get To The Point**, blinkered for the first time, although he has worn other forms of headgear in the past, gave himself plenty to do but was staying on quite nicely at the end.
**Cut And Dried** ran a respectable race from a poor draw and could be one to keep an eye on. *Official explanation: jockey said gelding had hung left*
**Signor Panettiere** showed his customary pace before hanging into the centre of the track when the pressure was on. *Official explanation: jockey said colt lost a front shoe*
**Innstyle** *Official explanation: jockey said filly had hung left*

## 3345 TOTESPORT.COM RATED STKS (H'CAP) 1m 2f 7y
**3:40** (3:41) (B) (0-95,92) 3-Y-O **£12,695** (£4,815; £2,407; £1,094) **Stalls** Low

Form RPR
-521 **1** **La Persiana**[14] 2906 3-8-9 **80** WRyan 10 91+
(WJarvis) *trckd ldrs: rdn over 2f out: led over 1f out: styd on wl* **10/1**
1342 **2** *1 1/4* **Royal Warrant**[22] 2676 3-9-0 **88** LPKeniry(3) 2 97+
(AMBalding) *hld up in rr: prog over 2f out: styng on whn bmpd jst ins fnl f: sn chsd wnr: clsd nr fin but a hld* **9/2**[2]
16-5 **3** *1 3/4* **Torinmoor (USA)**[56] 1799 3-9-6 **91** RLMoore 5 97
(MrsAJPerrett) *dwlt: pushed up to chse ldrs: rdn and nt qckn 3f out: effrt to chse wnr over 1f out: sn hung lft: one pce after* **10/1**
2511 **4** *2 1/2* **Gavroche (IRE)**[16] 2841 3-8-10 **84** J-PGuillambert(3) 4 85
(CADwyer) *settled in last trio: pushed along whn pce qcknd over 3f out: prog fr 2f out: nvr able to chal* **7/1**[3]
-536 **5** *nk* **Dumfries**[22] 2683 3-8-7 **78** (v[1]) JFortune 8 78
(JHMGosden) *prom: jnd ldr and rdn over 3f out: led 2f out to over 1f out: wknd* **10/1**
61 **5** *dht* **Lost Soldier Three (IRE)**[24] 2611 3-9-5 **90** DHolland 1 90+
(LMCumani) *trckd ldrs: rdn whn pce qcknd over 3f out: no imp on ldrs fnl 2f* **7/2**[1]
3-21 **7** *1 1/4* **Reservoir (IRE)**[23] 2645 3-8-11 **82** PRobinson 12 80
(WJHaggas) *mde most to 2f out: wknd over 1f out* **9/1**
4615 **8** *shd* **Sound Of Fleet (USA)**[15] 2896 3-8-11 **82** PDobbs 7 80
(PFICole) *hld up: hmpd on inner 6f out: rdn and no prog over 2f out: hanging bdly lft fnl f* **9/1**
41- **9** *nk* **Rinjani (USA)**[283] 5020 3-9-7 **92** (t) KMcEvoy 9 89
(SaeedBinSuroor) *t.k.h: trckd ldrs: n.m.r bnd 6f out: rdn and nt qckn 3f out: struggling after* **10/1**
0-43 **10** *3/4* **Irish Blade (IRE)**[56] 1800 3-8-8 **79** DSweeney 3 75
(HCandy) *a in last trio: rdn over 3f out: one pce and no prog* **20/1**

2m 5.32s (-2.98) **Going Correction** -0.225s/f (Firm) **10** Ran SP% **114.0**
Speed ratings: **102,101,99,97,97 97,96,96,96,95**CSF £53.39 CT £465.12 TOTE £11.30: £3.00, £1.60, £3.10; EX 65.00.
**Owner** Plantation Stud **Bred** Plantation Stud **Trained** Newmarket, Suffolk

**FOCUS**
A well contested handicap which should produce winners. The pace slowed rounding the loop and it developed into something of a sprint.

**NOTEBOOK**
**La Persiana**, returning to handicap company, stayed on strongly and will get twelve furlongs. She looks on the upgrade and, as a half-sister to Grand Lodge, will be worth a packet should she qualify for some black type.
**Royal Warrant**, 4lb higher than when second at Epsom, ran another solid race and was not helped by receiving a bump from the eventual third entering the final furlong, although the outcome was unaffected. He deserves to win a decent prize but is climbing the handicap.
**Torinmoor(USA)**, whose yard was out of form at the time he made his seasonal bow, ran much better but threw away what chance he had by hanging to his left.
**Gavroche(IRE)**, up another 6lb, was caught out when the tempo increased entering the pace and then had to make his ground down the centre of the track. He remains in good heart.
**Lost Soldier Three(IRE)** was another to be caught out when some pace was injected into the race and he then hung slightly. He was not knocked about when held and should not be written off, especialy if dropped a pound or two. *Official explanation: jockey said gelding had hung left in the latter stages*
**Dumfries**, in a visor for the first time, was ridden more prominently on this drop in trip but faded once headed.
**Reservoir(IRE)** *Official explanation: jockey said gelding had hung left*

## 3346 ROYAL MARBELLA GROUP QUALITY HOMES ABROAD EBF FILLIES' CONDITIONS STKS 5f 10y
**4:10** (4:12) (B) 2-Y-O **£12,087** (£4,584; £2,292; £1,042) **Stalls** High

Form RPR
313 **1** **Mary Read**[25] 2568 2-8-8 FLynch 5 93
(BSmart) *mde all: hung lft fr 1/2-way: drvn over 1f out: hld on gamely nr fin* **5/2**[1]
41 **2** *hd* **Right Answer**[4] 3208 2-8-11 DHolland 7 95
(APJarvis) *cl up: rdn to press wnr over 1f out: ev ch ins fnl f: nt qckn nr fin* **11/4**[2]
0105 **3** *4* **Celtic Spa (IRE)**[12] 2959 2-8-8 RLMoore 4 78
(MrsPNDutfield) *pressed wnr: carried lft fr 1/2-way: hld whn swtchd rt jst over 1f out: one pce after* **11/4**[2]
2 **4** *1* **Gold Quay (IRE)**[16] 2858 2-8-8 DSweeney 1 75
(NPLittmoden) *chsd ldrs: rdn 2f out: one pce and nvr able to chal* **16/1**
1 **5** *1 1/2* **Trempjane**[16] 2837 2-8-8 PDobbs 6 70
(RHannon) *s.s: a in last pair: rdn 1/2-way: no prog* **5/1**[3]
51 **6** *1 1/2* **Piper Lily**[22] 2686 2-8-11 FNorton 2 67
(MBlanshard) *a in last pair: rdn and struggling 1/2-way: no prog after* **9/1**

61.14 secs (-0.06) **Going Correction** -0.225s/f (Firm) **6** Ran SP% **114.5**
Speed ratings: **91,90,84,82,80 77**CSF £10.01 TOTE £3.10: £2.70, £2.60; EX 13.60.
**Owner** S J F racing **Bred** A S Denniff **Trained** Hambleton, N Yorks

**FOCUS**
A decent fillies' conditions event run but an unexceptional time.

**NOTEBOOK**
**Mary Read**, who hung left when trying to make all in the Hilary Needler Trophy last time, did so again but stuck to her task to hold off the runner-up. She is a tough filly and can win more races at the minimum trip on a sharp track.
**Right Answer** was stepping up in grade but looked to be running all over the winner when brought to challenge. However, she found that rival too tough in the closing stages and was unable to go past despite not shirking the issue. She was conceding 3lb and looks well capable of winning good races.
**Celtic Spa(IRE)**, whose win came on soft ground, had put up reasonable efforts in Listed company since. She was carried left by the winner in the straight which did not help her cause, but was unable to make pick up again once switched. She will not be easy to place but may find a decent nursery if not overburdened by the Handicapper.
**Gold Quay(IRE)**, claimed out of a York seller, was dropped in trip and up considerably in class on this first outing for new connections and found things happening too quickly. She will be better off in a lower-grade contest back over six.
**Trempjane**, who made a winning debut over six and looked as if seven would suit, was rather surprisingly dropped in trip. Not helped by missing the break, she never figured at any stage.
**Piper Lily**had her limitations exposed at this level.

## 3347 ROYAL MARBELLA GROUP QUALITY HOMES ABROAD H'CAP 1m 67y
**4:45** (4:47) (C) (0-90,90) 3-Y-O+ **£9,303** (£3,528; £1,764; £802) **Stalls** High

Form RPR
-431 **1** **A One (IRE)**[16] 2833 5-7-9 **60** oh4 FPFerris(3) 5 75
(HJManners) *mde all and sn clr: breather 1/2-way: kicked on again over 2f out: styd on wl: unchal* **25/1**
-315 **2** *2* **Bayhirr**[47] 2018 3-8-13 **85** PRobinson 2 95
(MAJarvis) *a chsng wnr: cl enough 3f out: rdn and unable qck over 2f out: kpt on same pce after* **5/2**[1]
0001 **3** *2 1/2* **Krugerrand (USA)**[15] 2894 5-9-8 **84** GCarter 6 89
(WJMusson) *s.s: hld up in last: effrt over 2f out but outpcd: shkn up and styd on fr over 1f out: nrst fin* **6/1**
3004 **4** *5* **Jools**[6] 3159 6-9-2 **78** DHolland 1 71
(DKIvory) *settled in midfield and off the pce: shkn up over 2f out: nt qckn and btn sn after* **7/1**
4200 **5** *3/4* **Star Pupil**[36] 2295 3-8-7 **82** LPKeniry(3) 7 73
(AMBalding) *dwlt: towards rr: outpcd over 2f out: struggling after* **14/1**
0050 **6** *7* **Desert Opal**[40] 2201 4-10-0 **90** JFortune 10 65
(JHMGosden) *chsd ldng pair: rdn 3f out: wknd 2f out* **4/1**[3]
0212 **7** *7* **Countykat (IRE)**[4] 3198 4-8-11 **73** (v) DarrenWilliams 9 32
(KRBurke) *racd in midfield: rdn 3f out: wknd over 2f out* **11/4**[2]

1m 40.95s (-4.65) **Going Correction** -0.225s/f (Firm)
**WFA** 3 from 4yo+ 10lb **7** Ran SP% **112.5**
Speed ratings: **114,112,109,104,103 96,89**CSF £84.35 CT £437.37 TOTE £28.50: £5.00, £2.20; EX 106.90.

**Owner** H J Manners **Bred** Humphrey Okeke **Trained** Highworth, Wilts

**FOCUS**
A fair handicap dominated by the first two throughout and producing a smart winning time.

**NOTEBOOK**
**A One(IRE)**, claimed after winning at Chepstow earlier in the month, gave his new connections an immediate return on their investment. Given a fine ride from the front - he was given a breather before the straight proper - he kicked on once in line for home and never looked likely to be caught. Racing from 4lb out of the handicap, he is likely to take a fair hike in the weights, but in this form may be able to defy it.
**Bayhirr**, dropped in trip and racing for the first time on ground faster than good to soft, had the winner in his sights throughout. However, he was unable to respond when that rival kicked and, although he never stopped trying, could make little impression. He will appreciate a return to further and a stiffer track.
**Krugerrand(USA)**, raised 7lb for winning a better race at York, dwelt in the stalls and, adopting his usual hold-up tactics, did not have the race run to suit him. He was doing his best work at the end and a longer trip will be in his favour.
**Jools**, a course and distance winner earlier in the season when he had Krugerrand behind, never landed a blow and seems more effective on easy ground on turf.
**Star Pupil**, who missed the break, has struggled in handicaps off his current mark, but a drop of a few pounds, which appears due, will enable him to compete at a slightly lower level.
**Countykat(IRE)** *Official explanation: trainer's representative said gelding ran flat today and may have been feeling the effects of having run four days ago; trainer later said gelding had sore feet*

## 3348 GAVIN & CLARE ENGAGEMENT CELEBRATION MEDIAN AUCTION MAIDEN STKS — 1m 3f 135y
**5:15** (5:18) (E) 3-4-Y-O — **£3,435** (£1,057; £528; £264) **Stalls** Low

Form — RPR
35-4 **1** **Bienvenue**[16] 2848 3-8-2 67 ... RLMoore 10 — 69
(MPTregoning) *trckd ldng gp: prog on outer wl over 3f out: led wl over 2f out and c to nr side: sn in command: rdn out fr over 1f out* **7/2**[1]
-004 **2** *1 1/4* **Pont Neuf (IRE)**[125] 863 4-9-2 55 ... (t) SWhitworth 17 — 67
(JWHills) *racd in midfield: prog over 3f out: chsd wnr fr 2f out: kpt on but a hld* **33/1**
43 **3** *3/4* **Shongweni (IRE)**[15] 2882 3-8-4 ... TPQueally(3) 14 — 71
(PJMcbride) *trckd ldrs: effrt 3f out: disp 2nd pl 2f out: hanging and nt qckn after: kpt on* **13/2**
**4** *5* **Garnett (IRE)** 3-8-8 ow1 ... DHolland 7 — 64
(AKing) *restless in stalls: dwlt: wl in rr: pushed along over 4f out: styd on fr 3f out: no ch w ldng trio* **12/1**
4 **5** *3/4* **Rossall Point**[24] 2611 3-8-7 ... SDrowne 8 — 62
(JLDunlop) *settled wl in rr: sme prog on wd outside fr 3f out: nudged along and nvr rchd ldrs* **9/1**
0-40 **6** *nk* **Maximinus**[15] 2882 4-9-4 56 ... LPKeniry(3) 16 — 61
(MMadgwick) *racd in midfield: rdn and effrt 3f out: one pce and no imp fnl 2f* **14/1**
0400 **7** *1/2* **Dance Party (IRE)**[15] 2881 4-9-2 60 ... (p) PRobinson 13 — 55
(AMBalding) *cl up: prog to press ldr over 3f out: ev ch wl over 2f out: wknd over 1f out* **11/1**
/0-6 **8** *2* **Secret Jewel (FR)**[26] 2562 4-9-2 72 ... KMcEvoy 2 — 52
(LadyHerries) *hld up wl in rr: shkn up and prog into midfield over 2f out: eased over 1f out but kpt on: nvr nr ldrs* **11/2**[3]
00 **9** *3* **Lookouthereicome**[122] 890 3-7-13 ... LisaJones(3) 18 — 47
(TTClement) *s.v.s and lost 10l: wl in rr: shkn up and kpt on fr 3f out: no ch* **66/1**
0-0 **10** *10* **Hold Up**[9] 3054 3-8-3 ow4 ... BReilly(3) 6 — 35
(MissJFeilden) *prom tl wknd 3f out* **25/1**
2224 **11** *shd* **Charleston**[15] 2882 3-8-7 73 ... (b[1]) JFortune 9 — 36
(JHMGosden) *mde most to wl over 2f out: sn wknd* **4/1**[2]
34-3 **12** *nk* **Frangipani (IRE)**[21] 2706 3-7-11 70 ... NDeSouza(5) 1 — 31
(PFICole) *chsd ldrs: rdn and effrt over 3f out: wknd over 2f out* **8/1**
**13** *5* **Samaria (GER)** 3-8-2 ... FNorton 5 — 23
(CFWall) *dwlt: racd in midfield: rdn and wknd 3f out* **16/1**
56-0 **14** *1* **Green Ocean**[66] 1560 4-9-2 50 ... DSweeney 3 — 21
(JWUnett) *a wl in rr* **50/1**
0 **15** *15* **Pitton Mill**[15] 2882 4-9-2 ... AQuinn(5) 11 — 2
(WGMTurner) *mostly chsd ldr to over 3f out: wknd rapidly* **100/1**
34 **16** *17* **Watchful Witness**[30] 2460 4-9-0 ... LucyRussell(7) 4 — —
(DrJRJNaylor) *a in rr: t.o fnl 3f* **33/1**
5000 **17** *dist* **Rumour Mill (IRE)**[23] 2667 3-8-7 45 ... PDoe 15 — —
(NEBerry) *prom tl wknd rapidly over 4f out: t.o* **66/1**

2m 30.78s (0.68) **Going Correction** -0.225s/f (Firm)
**WFA** 3 from 4yo 14lb — **17** Ran SP% **136.3**
Speed ratings: **88,87,86,83,82 82,82,80,78,72 72,72,68,68,58 46,—**CSF £141.31 TOTE £4.60: £2.20, £8.70, £2.50; EX 184.30 Place 6 £137.14, Place 5 £121.99.
**Owner** Stanley J Sharp **Bred** Stanley J Sharp **Trained** Lambourn, Berks

**FOCUS**
A moderate maiden run in a very modest winning time for the grade. A number of these will be jumping hurdles in the autumn.

**NOTEBOOK**
**Bienvenue**, a half-sister to a stayer, appreciated the step up in trip and, kicking for home early in the straight, was always holding her rivals from that point. This was only her second outing on turf and she appears likely to improve enough to win ordinary handicaps.
**Pont Neuf(IRE)** has had plenty of chances, but this was her first run on turf for nearly a year and her first outing for four months. Her earlier form suggests she appreciates cut, and handicaps in those conditions offer her best chance of getting off the mark.
**Shongweni(IRE)** is lightly raced and looks as though he has some maturing to do. He did not perform badly despite not looking happy on the ground, and now qualifies for a handicap mark.
**Garnett(IRE)** made an encouraging debut after playing up in the stalls and missing the break. He showed some promise, keeping on nicely at the finish, but with his connections this appears merely a prelude to a career over jumps.
**Rossall Point** never got involved but was staying on at the end. He will be of more interest once qualified for a handicap mark.
**Maximinus** has already run over hurdles, and has shown enough in three outings on the Flat this season to suggest that he is one to bear in mind when reverting to jumping, especially as he is qualified for handicaps in that sphere.
**Secret Jewel(FR)** has had little racing but was noted keeping on steadily under a sympathetic ride. She is one to keep in mind for a fillies' handicap.
**Charleston** was quite keen in the first-time blinkers, and dropped away badly in the straight. He appears to be going backwards, but he may be better suited by running in moderate handicaps with the headgear left off.
T/Plt: £138.20 to a £1 stake. Pool: £43,636.90. 230.40 winning tickets. T/Qpdt: £21.00 to a £1 stake. Pool: £2,682.90. 94.20 winning tickets. JN

3349 - (Foreign Racing) - See Raceform Interactive

# [3328]CURRAGH (R-H)
Sunday, June 27

**OFFICIAL GOING: Good to firm**

## 3350a KING OF BEERS STKS (REGISTERED AS RICHARD H FRAUGHT MEMORIAL) (LISTED RACE) — 5f
**2:05** (2:05) 3-Y-O+ — **£45,845** (£13,450; £6,408; £2,183)

RPR
**1** **Osterhase (IRE)**[20] 2744 5-9-7 104 ... (b) FMBerry 6 — 119
(JEMulhern, Ire) *mde all: rdn clr over 1f out: styd on strly: impressive* **3/1**[2]
**2** *4* **Moon Unit (IRE)**[53] 1893 3-8-12 102 ... DMGrant 1 — 100
(HRogers, Ire) *sn 2nd: rdn and no imp fr 2f out: kpt on u.p fnl f* **6/1**
**3** *1* **Orientor**[36] 2316 6-9-4 ... KFallon 5 — 96
(JSGoldie) *hld up: 5th and effrt on outer over 1f out: kpt on same pce* **5/1**
**4** *1/2* **Hanabad (IRE)**[36] 2316 4-9-7 107 ... MJKinane 2 — 97
(JohnMOxx, Ire) *chsd ldrs: 4th 1/2-way: sn rdn: no ex over 1f out* **2/1**[1]
**5** *shd* **Millbag (IRE)**[36] 2294 3-9-1 ... TEDurcan 4 — 97
(MRChannon) *chsd ldrs: 3rd 1/2-way: kpt on same pce fr 1 1/2f out* **9/2**[3]
**6** *4* **Tiger Royal (IRE)**[20] 2744 8-9-4 101 ... (b) PJSmullen 3 — 78
(DKWeld, Ire) *dwlt: hld up in rr: effrt 1/2-way: sn no ex: eased fnl f* **14/1**

57.30 secs **Going Correction** -0.425s/f (Firm)
**WFA** 3 from 4yo+ 6lb — **6** Ran SP% **114.1**
Speed ratings: **116,109,108,107,107 100**CSF £21.25 TOTE £3.50: £1.90, £3.10; DF 39.30.
**Owner** Michael Rosenfeld **Bred** E Kopica & M Rosenfeld **Trained** the Curragh, Co Kildare
■ Stewards Enquiry : F M Berry two-day ban: failed to keep straight stalls (Jul 6,7)

**NOTEBOOK**
**Osterhase(IRE)** set a new course record with a blinding display of speed. He came across quickly from an outside draw (two-day suspension for Berry) and was never headed.
**Moon Unit(IRE)** was slightly inconvenienced by the winner early but played second fiddle throughout on ground was generally assumed to be too fast for her.
**Orientor** was rather outpaced throughout and could never get in a challenge.
**Hanabad(IRE)** was struggling with the pace from halfway.
**Millbag(IRE)** could never get in any sort of a challenge from a furlong and a half down.
**Tiger Royal(IRE)** is out of form and the ground was much too fast.

## 3352a ANHEUSER BUSCH RAILWAY STKS (GROUP 2) — 6f
**3:10** (3:10) 2-Y-O — **£54,929** (£17,394; £8,239; £2,746)

RPR
**1** **Democratic Deficit (IRE)**[49] 1976 2-9-0 ... KJManning 6 — 104
(JSBolger, Ire) *chsd ldrs: 3rd and rdn after 1/2-way: chalng whn edgd lft over 1f out: led under 1f out: kpt on wl u.p* **7/1**[3]
**2** *3/4* **Russian Blue (IRE)**[36] 2314 2-9-0 ... JPSpencer 4 — 102
(APO'Brien, Ire) *dwlt and hld up in rr: impr into cl 5th and chal on outer over 1f out: kpt on wl u.p* **1/2**[1]
**3** *1* **L'Altro Mondo (IRE)**[36] 2314 2-9-0 ... TPO'Shea 3 — 99
(MHalford, Ire) *trckd ldr in 2nd: cl 3rd whn sltly hmpd over 1f out: sn 2nd and chalng: drifted lft wl ins fnl f: no ex* **12/1**
**4** *1 1/2* **Kay Two (IRE)**[36] 2314 2-9-0 ... FMBerry 1 — 94
(MsFMCrowley, Ire) *trckd ldrs on stands rail: 4th and chal over 1f out: 5th whn hmpd wl ins fnl f* **14/1**
**5** *1/2* **Joyce (IRE)**[18] 2792 2-9-0 ... JAHeffernan 2 — 93
(APO'Brien, Ire) *led: rdn and strly pressed under 2f out: hdd under 1f out: 4th and no ex whn hmpd wl ins fnl f* **14/1**
**6** *5* **Koolman (IRE)**[15] 2-9-0 ... ECreighton 7 — 78
(EJCreighton, Spain) *chsd ldrs on outer: wknd over 2f out* **33/1**
**7** *1/2* **Man O World (IRE)**[18] 2792 2-9-0 ... PJSmullen 5 — 76
(DKWeld, Ire) *towards rr: wknd over 2f out: eased fnl f* **5/1**[2]

1m 11.6s **Going Correction** -0.425s/f (Firm) — **7** Ran SP% **119.8**
Speed ratings: **103,102,100,98,98 91,90**CSF £11.68 TOTE £8.10: £2.50, £1.30; DF 12.20.
**Owner** D H W Dobson **Bred** J S Bolger **Trained** Coolcullen, Co Carlow
■ Stewards Enquiry : T P O'Shea two-day ban: careless riding (Jul 6-7)

**NOTEBOOK**
**Democratic Deficit(IRE)** showed improvement from his Leopardstown auction maiden and has done well himself in the intervening 7 weeks. He had the run of the race despite edging left before leading over a furlong out and was strong all the way to the line. It isn't easy to quantify this form though.
**Russian Blue(IRE)** missed the break and was in trouble from halfway. Switched, he got going on the outside from a furlong down but was never going to effectively get to the winner.
**L'Altro Mondo(IRE)** was inconvenienced by the winner well over a furlong down and then hung left causing damage to the fourth and fifth.
**Kay Two(IRE)** had finished his challenge when slightly hampered inside the last.
**Joyce(IRE)** made the running but was already beaten when hampered inside the last.
**Koolman(IRE)** was not a factor over the last quarter mile.
**Man O World(IRE)** was never in contention and there were no excuses offered.

## 3353a BUDWEISER IRISH DERBY (GROUP 1) (ENTIRE COLTS & FILLIES) — 1m 4f
**3:50** (3:50) 3-Y-O — **£518,732** (£176,830; £85,281; £30,352)

RPR
**1** **Grey Swallow (IRE)**[36] 2315 3-9-0 117 ... PJSmullen 6 — 126
(DKWeld, Ire) *trckd ldrs: 5th 1/2-way: smooth hdwy into 3rd 2f out: sn chal: led under 1f out: styd on wl* **10/1**
**2** *1/2* **North Light (IRE)**[22] 2680 3-9-0 ... KFallon 10 — 125
(SirMichaelStoute) *settled 3rd: drvn along 4f out: chal ent st: led under 2f out: hdd under 1f out: kpt on u.p* **8/11**[1]
**3** *1 1/2* **Tycoon**[266] 5405 3-9-0 103 ... CO'Donoghue 4 — 122
(APO'Brien, Ire) *hld up in rr: 9th into st: 6th 2f out: styd on wl to go 3rd cl home* **150/1**
**4** *nk* **Rule Of Law (USA)**[22] 2680 3-9-0 ... (t) LDettori 1 — 122
(SaeedBinSuroor) *cl up in 2nd: chal ent st: led over 2f out: hdd under 2f out: no ex ins fnl f* **13/2**[3]
**5** *2 1/2* **Let The Lion Roar**[22] 2680 3-9-0 ... (b[1]) MJKinane 11 — 118
(JLDunlop) *trckd ldrs in 4th: cl up ent st: no imp fr over 2f out: kpt on same pce* **11/2**[2]
**6** *1 1/2* **Book Of Kings (USA)**[84] 1257 3-9-0 ... PCosgrave 9 — 116
(APO'Brien, Ire) *trckd ldrs in 7th: 6th appr st: kpt on same pce* **66/1**
**7** *5* **Moscow Ballet (IRE)**[10] 3000 3-9-0 108 ... PJScallan 7 — 108
(APO'Brien, Ire) *led: rdn and hdd over 2f out: sn wknd* **50/1**
**8** *2 1/2* **Five Dynasties (USA)**[9] 3032 3-9-0 110 ... JAHeffernan 3 — 104
(APO'Brien, Ire) *hld up in 8th: wknd early st* **33/1**

9 *25* **Cobra (IRE)**[18] 2796 3-9-0 102 ........................................ JPSpencer 2 64
(APO'Brien, Ire) *5th early: 7th and rdn 4f out: wknd early st: t.o* **25/1**
10 *dist* **Percussionist (IRE)**[22] 2680 3-9-0 ........................................ KDarley 5 —
(JHMGosden) *nvr travelling: dropped to rr 1/2-way: sn wknd: completely t.o* **10/1**

2m 28.7s **Going Correction** -0.50s/f (Hard) **10** Ran SP% **115.7**
Speed ratings: **114,113,112,112,110 109,106,104,88,**—CSF £17.37 TOTE £7.10: £1.90, £1.10, £19.10; DF 27.90.
**Owner** Mrs Rochelle Quinn **Bred** Mrs C L Weld **Trained** The Curragh, Co Kildare

**NOTEBOOK**
**Grey Swallow(IRE)** showed an effective turn of foot to lead just inside the last furlong and outpace the Epsom winner. He appeared to get the trip well and his proven ability to quicken served him well. The Arc is the major Autumn target but the Irish Champion Stakes will suit ideally.
**North Light(IRE)** was being nudged along some way before the turn in. He led under two furlongs out but could not get away from the pack and was always going to prove vulnerable to the winner's bit of toe. It was later reported that he returned lame on his right hind and very sore in his quarters. He is an ideal St Leger type but that race seems to be unfashionable for Derby winners these days.
**Tycoon**, the rank outsider of Ballydoyle's five runners, had only one behind him turning for home but ran on well inside the last to snatch third place in the closing stages. He'll surely improve hugely on this delayed reappearance.
**Rule Of Law(USA)** was supplemented for 95,000 euros. He had his moment when leading over two furlongs out but he was headed in a matter of strides and found only the one pace under pressure. Stamina seems his sole asset.
**Let The Lion Roar** was right on terms turning for home but he just couldn't quicken when the pressure was turned on, just finding the one pace.
**Book Of Kings(USA)** stayed on without quickening and this was a fair effort for one with just a maiden success behind him.
**Moscow Ballet(IRE)** was used as pacemaker, a role which ended abruptly early in the straight.
**Five Dynasties(USA)** was never in serious contention.
**Cobra(IRE)**, the surprise choice of the stable jockey, was struggling well before the straight and trailed in.
**Percussionist(IRE)** appeared to hate the ground and was trailing five furlongs out. He was eased right down in the straight. *Official explanation: trainer said colt never travelled on the fast ground*

## 3355a BUDWEISER CELEBRATION STKS (LISTED RACE) 1m
**5:10** (5:10) 3-Y-O+ **£45,845** (£13,450; £6,408; £2,183)

RPR

1 **Grand Passion (IRE)**[18] 2796 4-9-7 106 ........................................ JFEgan 2 108
(GWragg) *in tch: 5th 1/2-way: hdwy on outer 2f out: led 1f out: r.o wl* **9/2**[3]
2 *1* **Solskjaer (IRE)**[20] 2748 4-9-7 ........................................ JPSpencer 6 106
(APO'Brien, Ire) *attempted to make all: strly pressed fr 2f out: hdd 1f out: edgd rt u.p: kpt on* **2/1**[1]
3 *1/2* **Latino Magic (IRE)**[18] 2793 4-9-10 104 ........................................ JPMurtagh 10 108
(RJOsborne, Ire) *settled 3rd: dropped to 5th on inner early st: short of room over 1f out: hmpd ins fnl f: swtchd and r.o wl* **4/1**[2]
4 *2* **Napper Tandy (IRE)**[18] 2796 4-9-10 107 ........................................ (bt) KJManning 1 103
(JSBolger, Ire) *hld up early: impr into 2nd early st: chal 2f out: no ex fnl f* **13/2**
5 *1/2* **Duck Row (USA)**[22] 2678 9-9-7 ........................................ SSanders 9 99
(JARToller) *trckd ldr in 2nd: 4th and pushed along ent st: kpt on same pce u.p* **6/1**
6 *3/4* **D'Anjou**[25] 2603 7-9-13 112 ........................................ MJKinane 5 103
(JohnMOxx, Ire) *hld up in rr: effrt on outer 2f out: kpt on same pce* **8/1**
7 *nk* **Favourite Nation (IRE)**[11] 2966 3-8-11 96 ........................................ PJSmullen 8 96
(DKWeld, Ire) *hld up in tch: sixth and rdn 2f out: no imp* **10/1**
8 *20* **Middlemarch (IRE)**[15] 2894 4-9-7 ........................................ (p) KFallon 4 50
(JSGoldie) *chsd ldrs early: rdn and wknd 4f out: virtually p.u st: t.o* **14/1**

1m 35.6s **Going Correction** -0.60s/f (Hard)
**WFA** 3 from 4yo+ 10lb **8** Ran SP% **126.0**
Speed ratings: **112,111,110,108,108 107,106,86**CSF £15.57 TOTE £5.80: £1.80, £1.50, £1.50; DF 15.40.
**Owner** Mr & Mrs H H Morriss **Bred** Mr & Mrs H H Morriss **Trained** Newmarket, Suffolk

**NOTEBOOK**
**Grand Passion(IRE)** appreciated this quick ground and paid tribute to his Leopardstown conqueror Medicinal, quickening to lead a furlong out and keeping on gamely.
**Solskjaer(IRE)** tried to make all as he had done at Naas on his reappearance. Once headed by the winner he edged right but kept up the gallop all the way to the line.
**Latino Magic(IRE)** earns decent place money in this company without winning and is difficult to place successfully.
**Napper Tandy(IRE)** got a couple of lengths closer to the winner than at Leopardstown but is becoming impossible to win with although he pays his way.
**Duck Row(USA)** was successful in this two years ago but is too long in the tooth now to be really competitive in this company.
**D'Anjou** did not carry through with his effort.
**Middlemarch(IRE)** dropped right out in the last half mile and was eased right down.

3354 - 3356a (Foreign Racing) - See Raceform Interactive

# 3335 HAMBURG (R-H)
Sunday, June 27

**OFFICIAL GOING: Soft**

## 3357a IDEE HANSA-PREIS (GROUP 2) 1m 3f
**4:15** (4:31) 3-Y-O+ **£45,775** (£17,606; £8,451; £4,930)

RPR

1 **Rotteck (GER)**[28] 2508 4-9-2 ........................................ J-PCarvalho 5 112
(HSteguweit, Germany) *trckd ldr, hdwy on ins to ld over 2f out, joined 1f out, ran on gamely under pressure final f to ld again post.* 2
2 *shd* **Storm Trooper (GER)**[56] 1802 4-9-2 ........................................ (b) ASuborics 1 112
(ASchutz, Germany) *set steady pace, headed over 2f out, rallied under pressure to join winner over 1f out, headed post.* 3
3 *1 3/4* **Aolus (GER)**[336] 3631 5-9-2 ........................................ AStarke 8 110
(ASchutz, Germany) *close up in 3rd or 4th, 4th straight, ridden over 1 1/2f out, stayed on at same pace.* 1
4 *1 1/4* **Well Made (GER)**[56] 1802 7-9-2 ........................................ WMongil 3 108
(HBlume, Germany) *hld up bhd steady pace, 7th str, slightly outpcd 2f out, stayed on well down outside to take 4th last 100yds*
5 *1/2* **Near Honor (GER)**[84] 1259 6-9-2 ........................................ JBojko 2 107
(TimGibson, Germany) *held up, 6th straight, stayed on under pressure towards outside final 1 1/2f.*
6 *1 3/4* **Fruhtau (GER)**[238] 5901 7-9-2 ........................................ THellier 6 104
(HHorwart, Germany) *held up in rear, headway on inside to go 5th straight, disputing 4th over 1f out, one pace final f.*

7 *2* **Mensatiger (GER)**[63] 1656 3-8-1 ........................................ NRichter 7 99
(THHansen, Germany) *prominent, 3rd straight, disputing 4th over 1f out, weakened.*
8 *2* **Russian Samba (IRE)**[84] 1259 5-8-12 ........................................ DSmith 9 94
(LordJFitzgerald, Germany) *held up in rear, last straight, never a factor.*
9 *dist* **Royal Fire (GER)**[378] 5-9-2 ........................................ TMundry 10 —
(THHansen, Germany) *close up on outside til weakened 3f out, tailed off final 2f.*

2m 24.63s
**WFA** 3 from 4yo+ 13lb **9** Ran SP% **130.9**
Speed ratings: .
**Owner** Stall Dagobert **Bred** A Birkmayer **Trained** Germany

# 3030 LONGCHAMP (R-H)
Sunday, June 27

**OFFICIAL GOING: Good to soft**

## 3359a PRIX DU LYS (GROUP 3) (C&G) 1m 4f
**2:15** (2:14) 3-Y-O **£25,704** (£10,282; £7,711; £5,141)

RPR

1 **Prospect Park**[21] 2722 3-8-11 ........................................ OPeslier 5 108+
(CLaffon-Parias, France) *hld up in 5th, disp 3rd fr over 5f out, 4th str, nt clr run whn stumbled over 2f out, pulled out, led ins fnl f, pushed out* 1
2 *1 1/2* **Lord Darnley (IRE)**[24] 3-8-11 ........................................ GaryStevens 6 106
(AFabre, France) *raced in 4th, 3rd straight, ridden to lead 1 1/2f out, headed inside final furlong, one pace.* 2
3 *1 1/2* **Lyonels Glory**[49] 3-8-11 ........................................ TJarnet 2 104
(USuter, Germany) *raced in 3rd to over 5f out, close 5th straight, stayed on at one pace to take 3rd close home.*
4 *nk* **Mister Farmer (FR)**[30] 3-8-11 ........................................ ODoleuze 1 104
(NBranchu, France) *held up in rear to straight, outpaced over 2f out, headway to go 3rd 1f out, lost 3rd close home.*
5 *3* **Malevitch (IRE)**[45] 2073 3-8-11 ........................................ TThulliez 4 99
(ELellouche, France) *led to over 5f out, 2nd straight, weakened approaching final f.*
6 *20* **Islero Noir (FR)**[26] 3-8-11 ........................................ CSoumillon 3 69
(YDeNicolay, France) *tracked leader, led and quickened over 5f out, headed 1 1/2f out, eased when beaten.* 3

2m 29.2s **Going Correction** -0.075s/f (Good) **6** Ran SP% **122.4**
Speed ratings: **114,113,112,111,109 96.**
**Owner** Wertheimer Et Frere **Bred** Wertheimer Et Frere **Trained** France

**NOTEBOOK**
**Prospect Park** looked extremely well in the paddock and was held up in a slowly run race. He was always travelling freely and a keenness caused him to stumble early in the straight. Once balanced he came with a sweeping run and totally outclassed his rivals. It was his first Group victory and a well deserved one for this colt who will now be rested and will take in either the Grosser Preis Von Baden or the Prix Niel before a tilt at the Arc de Triomphe.
**Lord Darnley(IRE)** raced on the outside and started a progressive run early in the straight before taking it up one and half out. He could not quicken in the final stages but it was a decent effort form an inexperienced colt.
**Lyonels Glory** was waited with and tried to go with the winner from one and a half out. He stayed on at the one pace and captured third position close home. This colt is still a maiden but should not be for much longer.
**Mister Farmer(FR)**, who sat out the back on his own for most of the way, did not really join the race until the straight. He made his run up the centre of the track and lost third place close home.

## 3360a JUDDMONTE GRAND PRIX DE PARIS (GROUP 1) (C&F) 1m 2f
**2:50** (2:49) 3-Y-O **£201,197** (£80,493; £40,246; £20,106)

RPR

1 **Bago (FR)**[21] 2721 3-9-2 ........................................ TGillet 2 113+
(JEPease, France) *last after 1f, 3rd straight and shaken up in centre 2f out, driven to challenge 1f out, led close home, pushed out.* **2/9**[1]
2 *1/2* **Cacique (IRE)**[21] 2721 3-9-2 ........................................ GaryStevens 4 112
(AFabre, France) *restrained in 2nd, led appr str, shaken up and ran on from 1 1/2f out til hdd and no extra close home.* **4/1**[2]
3 *5* **Alnitak (USA)**[21] 2721 3-9-2 ........................................ (b) C-PLemaire 1 103?
(JEPease, France) *led 2f, 3rd half-way, last on inside straight, never a danger but did take 3rd close home.* **100/1**
4 *nk* **Privy Seal (IRE)**[10] 3000 3-9-2 ........................................ (v) OPeslier 3 103
(JHMGosden) *last early stages but went on after 2f, hdd appr str, drvn and sn one pace fr over 2f out, lost 3rd cl hme.* **12/1**[3]

2m 5.60s **Going Correction** -0.075s/f (Good) **4** Ran SP% **110.5**
Speed ratings: **107,106,102,102.**
**Owner** Niarchos Family **Bred** Famille Niarchos **Trained** France

**NOTEBOOK**
**Bago(FR)** gave his connections a bit of a fright on this occasion and was forced to pull out all the stops for the first time in his life. Settled in last position, he was outpaced early in the straight and then gradually quickened to take control inside the final furlong. It was a muddling race and his pacemaker did not help his cause. Now unbeaten in six races, his main target will be the Breeders' Cup Classic and he may well take in the Arc de Triomphe beforehand.
**Cacique(IRE)** put up a magnificent display, racing in second position in a slowly run race and dashed into the lead early in the straight. One and a half out he looked the winner but he was run out of things in the final 100 metres. Still improving this beautifully bred colt is sure to be a Group winner in the not to distant future. He stays better than the other famous members of his family.
**Alnitak(USA)** took the lead soon after the start but was then checked. He then stayed in third place before running on well up the rail in the straight to take third place in the dying stages.
**Privy Seal(IRE)** went into the lead after the pacemaker slowed things up a furlong and a half after the start. He maintained his advantage until the straight and then stayed on at the one pace to the finish. He was robbed of third place close home.

## 3361a PRIX DE LA PORTE MAILLOT (GROUP 3) 7f
**4:35** (4:34) 3-Y-O+ **£25,704** (£10,282; £7,711; £5,141)

RPR

1 **Charming Groom (FR)**[14] 2923 5-9-2 ........................................ DBonilla 2 111
(FHead, France) *led, hdd 2f out and qckly pushed along, rdn and rallied fr over 1f out to chal, led again 150y out, ran on well, drvn out* 1
2 *shd* **Millennium Force**[24] 2623 6-9-2 ........................................ CCatlin 1 111
(MRChannon) *raced in close 2nd, jnd ldr 3f out, pushed along to ld 2f out, ran on but hdd 150y out, kpt on to press wnr to line*



The Form Book, Raceform Ltd, Compton, RG20 6NL

3 nse **Sunday Doubt (USA)**[10] 3-8-7 .......... OPeslier 6 111
(MmeCHead-Maarek, France) *raced in 5th, disputing 3rd str, short of room over 2 1/2f out, ev ch ins fnl f, kpt on* 1

4 1 1/2 **Suggestive**[24] [2623] 6-9-2 .......... (b) MHills 4 107
(WJHaggas) *raced in 4th, cl 5th str, pushed along 3f out & clsd up on ldrs, drvn to stay in tch 2f out, no ex fnl stages* 3

5 2 1/2 **Horeion Directa (GER)**[35] [2336] 5-9-2 .......... JPalik 3 101
(AndreasLowe, Germany) *raced in 3rd, disputing 3rd straight, pushed along 3f out, outpaced from over 2f out*

6 4 **Saratan (IRE)**[14] [2923] 7-9-2 .......... (b) ELegrix 5 91
(MDelzangles, France) *raced in last, effort over 2f out, never a factor* 2

1m 20.7s **Going Correction** -0.025s/f (Good)
**WFA** 3 from 5yo+ 9lb **6** Ran SP% **165.1**
Speed ratings: **111,110,110,109,106 101**.
**Owner** Wertheimer Et Frere **Bred** Wertheimer Et Frere **Trained** France

**NOTEBOOK**
**Charming Groom(FR)** quickly into his stride he led until halfway up the straight before rallying inside the final furlong to get up again on the line. He is a very brave and courageous individual who always runs his heart out. A campaign in the States at the end of the year is now envisaged for this five-year-old.
**Millennium Force** sweated up in the paddock but ran a blinder and was just pipped at the post. Second early on he took a neck advantage one and a half out and just failed to keep it in the final few yards. It was a very good effort and he lost nothing in defeat. This looks his perfect distance.
**Sunday Doubt(USA)** did not have the best of runs and waiting tactics were employed. He had to wait some time before having a clear run and then finished like a rocket going under by less than a head. This three-year-old is a real course and distance specialist and a Group race should go his way before the end of the season.
**Suggestive** was given every chance. After being well away he was settled in fourth place and looked dangerous halfway up the straight. He then just stayed on and his jockey reported he was unsuited by a lack of early pace.

## 3135 SAN SIRO (R-H)
### Sunday, June 27

**OFFICIAL GOING: Good to firm**

## 3362a PRIMI PASSI (GROUP 3) 6f
3:50 (3:57) 2-Y-O £33,891 (£15,631; £8,731; £4,365)

RPR

1 hd **Shifting Place** 2-8-8 .......... LManiezzi 2 87
(RMenichetti, Italy) *trckd ldrs gng well, effort but n.m.r appr fnl f, rallied closing stages & just failed, awarded race* 2

2 **Obe Gold**[22] [2677] 2-8-11 .......... ACulhane 7 90
(MRChannon) *a in tch, jnd ldrs 2f out, ev ch whn hung left jst ins fnl f, led 50y out, drvn out, disqualified, placed 2nd*

3 3/4 **Tenderlit (USA)**[23] [2668] 2-8-8 .......... MEsposito 4 84
(RMenichetti, Italy) *outpaced to half-way, finished well on inside to take 3rd on line* 2

4 nse **Golden Stravinsky (USA)**[23] [2669] 2-8-11 .......... DVargiu 1 87
(GFratini, Italy) *pressed ldr, quickened to lead 2f out, hung right approaching final furlong, caught 50 yards out, no extra* 1

5 1 1/4 **Gold Marie (IRE)** 2-8-8 .......... GBietolini 8 80
(BGrizzetti, Italy) *outpaced early, stayed on well on outside from over 1f out, nearest at finish*

6 nk **Fabios (IRE)** 2-8-11 .......... MTellini 3 82
(BGrizzetti, Italy) *always towards rear, stayed on final furlong*

7 1 3/4 **Patapan (USA)**[23] [2669] 2-8-11 .......... GTemperini 6 77
(RBrogi, Italy) *led 4f, weakened approaching final furlong* 3

8 10 **Nisri Di San Jore (IRE)** 2-8-11 .......... SLandi 9 47
(GianfrancoVerricelli, Italy) *always outpaced*

U **So Vain (ITY)**[23] [2669] 2-8-11 .......... PAragoni 5 —
(LRiccardi, Italy) *played up in stalls & unseated rider start*

1m 10.7s **9** Ran SP% **136.2**
Speed ratings: .
**Owner** Razza Dell'Olmo **Bred** Mrs C R Philipson **Trained** Italy

**NOTEBOOK**
**Shifting Place**, third in a Listed event last time out, she looks to be progressing with racing. However, she was certainly treated sympathetically by the stewards, and will probably struggle to top this effort.
**Obe Gold**, fourth in the Woodcote last time out, can be considered an unlucky loser, being blamed for causing the interference when to many eyes Golden Stravinsky was the main offender. He should win more races and could pick up a small listed event back here in Italy.
**Tenderlit(USA)**, a Listed winner in Rome previously, she found the pace too hot here in the early stages and a step up in trip seems sure to suit.

## 3144 MUSSELBURGH (R-H)
### Monday, June 28

**OFFICIAL GOING: Good (good to firm in places)**

## 3363 BOLLINGER CHAMPAGNE CHALLENGE SERIES H'CAP (FOR GENTLEMAN AMATEUR RIDERS) 2m
6:25 (6:25) (E) (0-70,68) 3-Y-0+ £4,017 (£1,236; £618; £309) Stalls Low

Form RPR

5245 1 **Toni Alcala**[8] [3120] 5-11-9 **68** .......... MSeston(5) 6 75
(RFFisher) *trckd ldr: hdwy over 3f out: led wl over 2f out: sn rdn and kpt on* 9/4[2]

/640 2 2 1/2 **Western Bluebird (IRE)**[31] [2462] 6-10-2 **42** .......... (b) MrMJMcAlister 2 46
(MissKateMilligan) *led: rdn along and edgd lft 3f out: sn hdd: drvn and one pce* 9/1

2556 3 8 **Muzio Scevola (IRE)**[56] [1823] 3-10-2 **65** .......... MrLNewnes(3) 1 59
(MRChannon) *hld up and bhd: hdwy 3f out: sn rdn and kpt on one pce* 12/1

-502 4 1 1/2 **Accepting**[9] [3108] 7-10-7 **54** .......... (b) MrStephenHarrison(7) 4 47
(JMackie) *in tch:effrt over 3f out: sn rdn and no imp* 2/1[1]

30-2 5 1/2 **Desert Quill (IRE)**[24] [2662] 4-10-12 **57** .......... MrCDavies(5) 5 49
(WMBrisbourne) *trckd ldrs: rdn along over 4f out: drvn wl over 2f out and plugged on one pce* 10/1

016/ 6 17 **Welsh Dream**[397] [4047] 7-10-9 **49** .......... MrCStorey 3 21
(MissSEForster) *chsd ldrs: rdn along 4f out: sn wknd* 6/1[3]

3m 37.93s (4.23) **Going Correction** -0.075s/f (Good)
**WFA** 3 from 4yo+ 20lb **6** Ran SP% **105.2**
Speed ratings: **86,84,80,80,79 71**CSF £18.82 TOTE £3.00: £1.50, £6.50; EX 26.60.
**Owner** Alan Willoughby **Bred** Mrs Agnes Steele Moore **Trained** Ulverston, Cumbria
■ Stewards Enquiry : Mr C Davies four-day ban: failed to ride out for fourth place (Jul 10,23,29, Aug 2)

**FOCUS**
A modest pace for this ordinary amateur riders' contest and a slow winning time, indicating the form is weak.

**NOTEBOOK**
**Toni Alcala** certainly knows his way around here and was always in the ideal position to strike once the leader hung away from the inside rail. His stamina was important even in a race run at such a modest pace.
**Western Bluebird(IRE)** was helped by being allowed to set a steady pace in an uncontested lead. An injection of pace starting up the home straight proved too much for the majority of his rivals, but the winner took full advantage when he hung away from the inside rail and basically outstayed him. In view of the way the race was run he might be slightly flattered.
**Muzio Scevola(IRE)** stayed on at very much the one pace down the home straight without ever getting anywhere near the winner. He is still relatively lightly raced and looks a real out-and-out stayer, so the modest gallop would not have suited him at all.
**Accepting** stays even longer trips than this, so the race was not run to suit and he could never land a blow.
**Desert Quill(IRE)** was comfortably held and this is as good as he is.
**Welsh Dream**, off since winning over hurdles 13 months ago, was entitled to need this and the majority of his best form has been on softer ground.

## 3364 WILKINSONCORR.COM (S) STKS 5f
6:55 (6:55) (F) 3-Y-0 £2,877 (£822; £411) Stalls Low

Form RPR

1040 1 **Jinksonthehouse**[4] [3227] 3-8-13 **58** .......... KDalgleish 4 53
(MDIUsher) *cl up: led 1/2-way: sn rdn: drvn and styd on wl fnl f* 5/2[2]

4002 2 3/4 **Beaver Diva**[10] [3037] 3-8-8 **40** .......... SWKelly 3 45
(WMBrisbourne) *bmpd and s.i.s: gd hdwy 2f out: rdn and ev ch ent last: sn hung bdly lft and reluctant to go past* 10/1

2305 3 1 1/2 **Only If I Laugh**[4] [3227] 3-8-13 **59** .......... DeanMcKeown 1 45
(PABlockley) *sn led: rdn along and hdd 1/2-way: drvn over 1f out and sn btn* 11/10[1]

0304 4 3/4 **Vaudevire**[10] [3037] 3-8-13 **23** .......... (b) SChin 2 42?
(RPElliott) *cl up: ev ch 2f out: sn rdn and wknd ent last* 40/1

3606 5 1/2 **Lavish Times**[35] [2353] 3-8-13 **48** .......... (b) FLynch 5 40
(ABerry) *sltly hmpd early and sn lost pl: rdn along and hdwy 2f out: drvn to chse ldrs 1f out: sn btn* 5/1[3]

-060 6 6 **Salonika Sky**[134] [780] 3-8-8 **40** .......... (b) JMcAuley 6 14
(CWThornton) *cl up on outer: rdn along 2f out: sn wknd* 25/1

60.99 secs (0.59) **Going Correction** -0.075s/f (Good) **6** Ran SP% **108.2**
Speed ratings: **92,90,88,87,86 76**CSF £24.02 TOTE £3.30: £1.70, £2.00; EX 26.00.There was no bid for the winner.
**Owner** Midweek Racing **Bred** Midweek Racing Club **Trained** Upper Lambourn, Berks
■ Stewards Enquiry : K Dalgleish one-day ban: used whip from above shoulder height (Jul 10)

**FOCUS**
A poor seller in which only two had a realistic chance on official ratings and not very much covering the front five home.

**NOTEBOOK**
**Jinksonthehouse**, back down to selling company, confirmed the form with Only If I Laugh having beaten him in a Bath claimer last month. However, she may have been the fortunate that the runner-up did not want to go past. Five furlongs and fast ground seems to bring out the best in her.
**Beaver Diva**, in a seller for the first time, though she has been well beaten in a banded stakes, was racing over the minimum trip for the first time since her racecourse debut last year. The drop in distance did not seem to be a problem even though she lost ground at the start, but her seeming reluctance to exert herself near the line when holding a winning chance certainly was.
**Only If I Laugh**, who has been mainly racing in better company since winning a couple of sellers last summer, was marginally best in on official ratings. He broke well enough, but the writing was on the wall some way out and he looks a very hard ride.
**Vaudevire** appeared to run well judged on official ratings, but at this level little should be read into that.
**Lavish Times** continues to perform moderately.

## 3365 GEORGE WIMPEY EAST SCOTLAND LTD H'CAP 7f 30y
7:25 (7:25) (D) (0-85,85) 3-Y-0+ £6,747 (£2,076; £1,038; £519) Stalls Low

Form RPR

2130 1 **Kirkby's Treasure**[5] [3198] 6-8-13 **67** .......... FLynch 2 79
(ABerry) *hld up in rr: hdwy whn n.m.r and swtchd rt 2f out: swtchd lft and rdn ent last: styd on wl to ld last 100 yds* 7/2[1]

0024 2 1 1/4 **Stoic Leader (IRE)**[5] [3198] 4-9-8 **79** .......... LFletcher(3) 3 88
(RFFisher) *trckd ldrs:hdwy to ld wl over 1f out: rdn ent last: hdd and no ex last 100 yds* 7/2[1]

0166 3 4 **Pawan (IRE)**[5] [3198] 4-8-12 **66** .......... AnnStokell 8 65
(MissAStokell) *chsd ldr: hdwy to ld over 3f out and sn clr: rdn over 2f out: hdd over 1f out and grad wknd* 7/1[3]

0351 4 hd **Low Cloud**[11] [3012] 4-9-8 **76** .......... (v) ANicholls 9 74
(DNicholls) *t.k.h: in tch: hdwy to chse ldrs 3f out: rdn 2f out and sn no imp* 7/1[3]

6-35 5 1 1/4 **Killala (IRE)**[30] [2492] 4-8-7 **64** .......... TEaves(3) 7 59
(ISemple) *hld up: hdwy 4f out: swtchd lft and rdn 2f out: sn drvn and btn* 8/1

0-53 6 3 **Bessemer (JPN)**[10] [3053] 3-9-8 **85** .......... JFanning 1 72
(MJohnston) *s.i.s and bhd: hdwy 3f out: rdn: hung and hung rt 2f out: sn btn* 8/1

0600 7 nk **Namroud (USA)**[10] [3036] 5-10-0 **82** .......... (b) PHanagan 4 68
(RAFahey) *chsd ldrs: rdn along 3f out: wkng whn n.m.r wl over 1f out* 5/1[2]

5002 8 5 **Silver Seeker (USA)**[28] [2528] 4-8-6 **60** .......... PFessey 10 33
(ARDicken) *keen: sn led: pushed along and hdd over 3f out: soo n wknd* 16/1

1m 27.5s (-2.03) **Going Correction** -0.075s/f (Good)
**WFA** 3 from 4yo+ 9lb **8** Ran SP% **114.2**
Speed ratings: **108,106,102,101,100 96,96,90**CSF £15.47 CT £80.26 TOTE £3.70: £2.10, £1.30, £2.20; EX 7.80.
**Owner** Kirkby Lonsdale Racing **Bred** Mrs J M Berry **Trained** Cockerham, Lancs
■ Stewards Enquiry : A Nicholls one-day ban: careless riding (Jul 9)

**FOCUS**
A decent handicap run at a strong pace and the form looks fair for the grade.

**NOTEBOOK**

**Kirkby's Treasure**, twice a winner over course and distance already this season, has crept up the handicap as a result but he has won off an even higher mark than this in the past. He was content to sit off the pace early, but when finally asked for his effort found a smart turn of foot to catch the wandering leader and in the end won going away.

**Stoic Leader(IRE)**, who finished in front of Kirkby's Treasure at Carlisle yet was 1lb better off, looked to have timed his challenge just right but he started to hang about once in front and was worried out of it. This was still a useful effort off this mark.

**Pawan(IRE)**, not the easiest horse to win with, was given a very positive ride and even though eventually well beaten by the front pair, arguably put up one of his best performances.

**Low Cloud** found this too sharp and lacked pace where it mattered.

**Killala(IRE)** ran another fair race, but his consistency means he is only very slowly dropping down the weights.

**Bessemer(JPN)** ◆ did not seem to take the home bend very well and looked unhappy racing down the home straight. He still has a little scope and a longer trip and possibly cut in the ground could well bring about improvement.

**Namroud(USA)** is now 5lb below his most recent winning mark, but the drop in the handicap is not bringing about any improvement.

## 3366 WILKINSONCORR.COM MAIDEN AUCTION STKS 7f 30y

**7:55** (7:58) (F) 2-Y-O **£3,360** (£1,034; £517; £258) **Stalls** Low

Form RPR

4564 **1** **Mount Ephram (IRE)**[9] 3100 2-8-13 ....................(p) PHanagan 5 63
(RFFisher) *unruly s: trckd ldrs: hdwy on inner 2f out: rdn to ld ent last: hung lft: kpt on* **8/1**

542 **2** *hd* **Lady Hopeful (IRE)**[12] 2985 2-8-4 .................... SChin 6 54
(RPElliott) *led: rdn along 2f out: edgd lft and hdd ent lft: drvn and kpt on nr fin* **9/4**[1]

0 **3** *3/4* **Cava Bien**[13] 2961 2-8-7 .................... MFenton 3 55
(JGGiven) *green and in rr: hdwy and edgd lft 3f out: rdn and hung bdly lft 2f out: kpt on wl fnl f* **11/2**[3]

0 **4** *1 3/4* **Young Thomas (IRE)**[37] 2300 2-8-11 .................... FLynch 4 55
(MLWBell) *chsd ldr: effrt and ev ch over 2f out: sn rdn and wknd over 1f out* **5/1**[2]

0 **5** *1* **Victory Hymn (IRE)**[10] 3045 2-8-6 .................... ACulhane 7 47
(MRChannon) *hld up: hdwy 4f out: rdn along wl ver 2f out and sn one pce* **5/1**[2]

0 **6** *2 1/2* **Bust (IRE)**[17] 2860 2-8-9 .................... KDalgleish 2 44
(TDEasterby) *chsd ldrs: rdn along 3f out: sn wknd* **5/1**[2]

00 **7** *dist* **Black Combe Lady (IRE)**[12] 2972 2-8-4 .................... JFanning 1 —
(ABerry) *a rr: outpcd and bhd fnl 3f* **66/1**

1m 30.5s (0.97) **Going Correction** -0.075s/f (Good) **7** Ran **SP% 108.8**

Speed ratings: **91,90,89,87,86 83,**—CSF £23.82 TOTE £10.20: £3.90, £1.90; EX 14.20.

**Owner** Great Head House Estates Limited **Bred** Twelve Oaks Stud Establishment **Trained** Ulverston, Cumbria

**FOCUS**

An ordinary maiden auction event run at an even pace in which a few took wayward courses. The form looks poor.

**NOTEBOOK**

**Mount Ephram(IRE)** has gradually got it together and ground out a dour victory. His tendency to hang left is beginning to look a trait, but it did not stop him from winning and he may be worth a try on a turning left-handed track.

**Lady Hopeful(IRE)**, given a positive ride, handed the winner the initiative by hanging away from the inside rail in the straight and letting him through. She did battle back once headed, but could never quite get up and is another that may be better going left handed.

**Cava Bien** still looks far from the finished article and threw his chance away by hanging right over to the stands' side in the home straight, possibly losing more ground than he was beaten by. Once the greenness is out of him, he is likely to turn out the best of these.

**Young Thomas(IRE)** ran better than on his debut, but this was a much less competitive contest and he is yet to prove he stays this far.

**Victory Hymn(IRE)** did not improve much from her debut and hardly looks one of the stable's better youngsters.

**Bust(IRE)** did not improve for the big step up in trip from his debut.

## 3367 GEORGE WIMPEY EAST SCOTLAND LTD CLAIMING STKS 1m 1f

**8:25** (8:25) (F) 3-Y-O+ **£2,947** (£842; £421) **Stalls** Low

Form RPR

0130 **1** **Bailieborough (IRE)**[11] 3023 5-9-11 67....................(v) AlexGreaves 7 75
(DNicholls) *in tch: smooth hdwy 3f out: led wl over 1f out: rdn clr ins last* **2/1**[2]

2660 **2** *3* **Always Flying (USA)**[9] 3102 3-8-8 67.................... JFanning 1 63
(MJohnston) *led: rdn along over 2f out: hdd wl over 1f out: sn drvn and one pce* **7/4**[1]

00-0 **3** *5* **Sherwood Forest**[10] 3040 4-8-10 44....................(v) LeanneKershaw(7) 5 51?
(MissLAPerratt) *towards rr: swtchd lft and hdwy over 2f out: rdn and styd on wl fnl f: nrst fin* **33/1**

30-6 **4** *1 3/4* **Ambushed (IRE)**[10] 3040 8-9-2 57.................... TEaves(3) 2 49
(PMonteith) *trckd ldrs: effrt on outer over 2f out: sn rdn and kpt on same pce* **14/1**

3000 **5** *1 1/2* **Kyle Of Lochalsh**[21] 2738 4-9-4 52....................(b[1]) AMcCarthy 8 45
(GGMargarson) *trckd ldrs on inner: hdwy 3f out: rdn 2f out and sn one pce* **13/2**[3]

0000 **6** *7* **Pharaoh Hatshepsut (IRE)**[9] 3082 6-8-12 32.................... FLynch 6 25
(JamesMoffatt) *cl up: rdn along 3f out: sn wknd* **100/1**

0055 **7** *1 1/4* **East Riding**[5] 3200 4-9-0 37.................... AnnStokell 10 25
(MissAStokell) *chsd ldrs: rdn along over 3f out: sn wknd* **33/1**

-000 **8** *7* **Environmentalist**[38] 2260 5-9-0 40....................(bt[1]) PFessey 3 11
(DANolan) *a rr* **66/1**

01-0 **9** *6* **Devine Light (IRE)**[38] 2258 4-9-6 60.................... PHanagan 4 5
(BMactaggart) *a rr* **10/1**

300- **10** *dist* **The Spook**[259] 5538 4-9-5 39.................... SWKelly 9 —
(WMBrisbourne) *s.i.s: a bhd* **20/1**

1m 52.49s (-0.71) **Going Correction** -0.075s/f (Good)

**WFA** 3 from 4yo+ 11lb **10** Ran **SP% 111.9**

Speed ratings: **100,97,92,91,90 83,82,76,71,**—CSF £5.27 TOTE £4.00: £1.20, £2.20, £6.90; EX 8.60.Always Flying was claimed by Mr Ian Glenton for £8,000.

**Owner** Middleham Park Racing Xviii **Bred** Churchtown Stud **Trained** Sessay, N Yorks

■ Stewards Enquiry : Alex Greaves caution: careless riding

**FOCUS**

A moderate claimer in which the pace was only fair and the finish was fought out by the pair best in on adjusted official ratings, though not in the right order. The form looks sound for the grade.

**NOTEBOOK**

**Bailieborough(IRE)**, back in the right grade, was one of those best in at the weights but was still meeting the runner-up on 6lb worse terms compared with a handicap. It certainly did not look that way when he arrived there on the bridle though, and he only needed a couple of cracks with the whip to leave his rival for dead. He will always be an effective tool at this level.

**Always Flying(USA)**, with upwards of 6lb in hand of his rivals on adjusted official ratings, had the run of the race out in front and proved to good for the bulk of the field, but was still made to look very pedestrian by the winner. He is always going to be vulnerable to a rival with a turn of foot.

**Sherwood Forest** might still have needed this and ran on into the placings without threatening the front pair. All is not lost though, as he had plenty on at the weights and this trip would have been sharp enough.

**Ambushed(IRE)** knows more about this game than most and ran just a fair race without looking like a winner waiting to happen.

**Kyle Of Lochalsh** ran marginally better in the first-time blinkers, but still has some way to go to regain his best form.

**Pharaoh Hatshepsut(IRE)** *Official explanation: jockey said mare suffered interference*

**Environmentalist** *Official explanation: jockey said horse had a breathing problem*

**Devine Light(IRE)** *Official explanation: jockey said filly hung left handed throughout*

**The Spook** *Official explanation: jockey said gelding was struck into and missed the break*

## 3368 WILKINSONCORR.COM H'CAP 7f 30y

**8:55** (8:55) (F) (0-55,55) 3-Y-O **£2,947** (£842; £421) **Stalls** Low

Form RPR

0005 **1** **Shinko Femme (IRE)**[11] 3002 3-8-10 48.................... PMulrennan(5) 1 59
(NTinkler) *hld up: hdwy whn n.m.r over 2f out: rdn and str run ent last: styd on to ld nr line* **10/1**

1160 **2** *shd* **Saros (IRE)**[17] 2854 3-9-6 53.................... FLynch 4 64
(BSmart) *led: pushed clr wl over 1f out: rdn and edgd lft ins last: hdd and no ex nr fin* **11/2**[1]

605U **3** *6* **Killerby Nicko**[4] 3234 3-9-3 50....................(b) KDalgleish 13 45
(TDEasterby) *chsd ldrs: hdwy on outer over 2f out: sn rdn and kpt on same pce appr last* **11/1**

0003 **4** *1/2* **Killoch Place (IRE)**[12] 2979 3-8-7 40....................(v) SWKelly 6 34
(JAGlover) *towards rr: pushed along 3f out: hdwy 2f out: nt clr run and swtchd lft over 1f out: styd on wl: nrst fin* **11/2**[1]

-000 **5** *3/4* **Themesofgreen**[9] 3085 3-9-7 54.................... ACulhane 2 46+
(MRChannon) *hld up and bhd: hdwy 2f out: rdn and styd on wl fnl f nrst fin* **8/1**[3]

60-0 **6** *nk* **Schinken Otto (IRE)**[23] 2688 3-9-1 48.................... PHanagan 8 39
(JMJefferson) *chsd ldrs: rdn along wl over 2f out: kpt on same pce* **10/1**

0010 **7** *nk* **Garnock Venture (IRE)**[4] 3234 3-9-5 55....................(b) LFletcher(3) 9 46
(ABerry) *chsd ldrs: ridden 2f out: wknd ent last* **11/2**[1]

00-0 **8** *3/4* **Luke Sharp**[25] 2621 3-8-2 35.................... PFessey 11 24
(KARyan) *chsd ldrs: hdwy over 2f out: rdn: edgd lft and wknd appr last* **25/1**

0-00 **9** *3/4* **St Tropez (IRE)**[49] 2001 3-9-3 50.................... JFanning 12 37
(BGPowell) *hld up: hdwy on inner over 2f out: rdn and no imp fr wl over 1f out* **6/1**[2]

0-00 **10** *3/4* **Aguilera**[15] 2908 3-8-12 45....................(p) DMcGaffin 7 30
(MDods) *prom: rdn along wl over 2f out: grad wknd* **12/1**

-050 **11** *1 3/4* **Be My Alibi (IRE)**[25] 2620 3-7-11 35.................... BSwarbrick(5) 10 15
(WMBrisbourne) *a rr* **12/1**

30-0 **12** *2 1/2* **Venerdi Tredici (IRE)**[9] 3102 3-9-5 52.................... DeanMcKeown 3 26
(PABlockley) *chsd ldrs: rdn along 3f out: sn wknd* **25/1**

-060 **13** *6* **Grey Orchid**[19] 2778 3-8-9 45.................... TEaves(3) 5 3
(TJEtherington) *bhd fr 1/2-way* **66/1**

1m 28.85s (-0.68) **Going Correction** -0.075s/f (Good) **13** Ran **SP% 122.6**

Speed ratings: **100,99,93,92,91 91,90,90,89,88 86,83,76**CSF £64.89 CT £654.45 TOTE £11.10: £2.50, £2.00, £4.50; EX 64.00.

**Owner** The Penniless Partnership **Bred** Rathbarry Stud **Trained** Langton, N Yorks

**FOCUS**

A competitive if low-grade handicap. The pace was solid and, although the form is modest, the front pair pulled a long way clear.

**NOTEBOOK**

**Shinko Femme(IRE)** has dropped 12lb since her last handicap outing and was also helped by dropping back a furlong, but still had plenty on from the worst draw. She did well to make up the ground on the clear leader, but keeping straight whilst her rival took a wayward course made all the difference to the result.

**Saros(IRE)** ◆ maintained the improvement he showed on sand in the spring on this return to turf. Hitting the gates running this time, he made a bold bid to run his opponents into the ground and it worked as far as most of his rivals were concerned. However, he hung persistently left in the closing stages and that enabled the winner to snatch the race from him. A return to a left-handed track can see him go one better.

**Killerby Nicko** was effectively in first-time blinkers as he came out of the stalls riderless with them last time and seemed to run a bit better as a result.

**Killoch Place(IRE)**, beaten in a seller last time, was doing his best work late and gives the impression he needs further, but he has already been tried over as far as ten furlongs and shown very little.

**Themesofgreen**, making his handicap debut, showed a little ability from a moderate draw and looks worth stepping up again in trip.

**Garnock Venture(IRE)** had every chance and there seemed no excuses, but he does look a better horse on Fibresand.

**Aguilera** *Official explanation: jockey said filly ran too free*

## 3369 EDINBURGH EVENING NEWS H'CAP 1m 4f

**9:25** (9:25) (F) (0-60,58) 3-Y-O+ **£2,975** (£850; £425) **Stalls** High

Form RPR

2102 **1** **Archirondel**[7] 3149 6-9-8 54.................... ACulhane 9 63+
(MDHammond) *hld up: hdwy 5f out: pushed along to trck ldrs 3f out: chal on bit 2f out: sn led: rdn and styd on wl fnl f* **5/2**[1]

20-2 **2** *2 1/2* **Ellway Heights**[12] 2978 7-9-7 53.................... SWKelly 10 61+
(WMBrisbourne) *hld up: stdy hdwy 5f out: effrt on inner and nt clr run wl over 1f out: swtchd lft and kpt on u.p fnl f* **5/2**[1]

-600 **3** *shd* **Saameq (IRE)**[11] 3007 3-7-12 44 oh2.................... PFessey 3 49
(ISemple) *bhd: hdwy on outer over 2f out: sn rdn and kpt on wl fnl f* **20/1**

/-06 **4** *hd* **Hibernate (IRE)**[7] 3149 10-8-5 40.................... TEaves(3) 1 45
(CJTeague) *led and sn clr: rdn along wl over 2f out: hdd wl over 1f out: kpt on u.p fnl f* **25/1**

450- **5** *1 3/4* **Chevin**[322] 4049 5-8-10 42.................... PHanagan 8 44
(RAFahey) *chsd clr ldr: hdwy 3f out: rdn and ev ch 2f out: drvn and wknd appr last* **7/1**[2]

0402 **6** *shd* **Lucky Largo (IRE)**[9] 3082 4-9-12 58....................(b) DMcGaffin 4 60
(MissLAPerratt) *bhd: rdn along over 3f out: kpt on u.p fnl 2f: nvr a factor* **12/1**

4060 **7** *2 1/2* **Howards Dream (IRE)**[12] 2978 6-7-12 30 oh2....................(t) JMcAuley 7 28
(DANolan) *chsd ldrs: rdn along over 3f out and sn wknd* **25/1**

4060 **8** *1 1/4* **Magic Charm**[11] 3018 6-7-10 35.................... LeanneKershaw(7) 6 31
(JeddO'Keeffe) *chsd ldrs: rdn 4f out: sn wknd* **14/1**

3050 **9** *9* **Repulse Bay (IRE)**[10] 3041 6-8-12 51.................... JCurrie(7) 2 32
(JSGoldie) *s.i.s: a bhd* **8/1**[3]

4563 **10** *1* **Caymans Gift**[10] 3042 4-9-7 **58** PMulrennan(5) 5 38
(ACWhillans) *in tch: rdn along over 3f out: sn wknd* **10/1**

2m 36.46s (-1.56) **Going Correction** -0.075s/f (Good) **10** Ran SP% **116.7**
**WFA** 3 from 4yo+ 14lb
Speed ratings: **102,100,100,100,98 98,97,96,90,89**CSF £7.67 CT £94.77 TOTE £3.40: £1.30, £1.80, £3.70; EX 7.40 Place 6 £93.44, Place 5 £31.15.
**Owner** The Archi Partnership **Bred** Jerry Sung **Trained** Middleham, N Yorks

**FOCUS**
A moderate handicap, but at least the early pace was solid with the leader going off at a rate at knots and the form is sound.

**NOTEBOOK**
**Archirondel** got the strong pace he needs and finally proved that he truly stays this trip in a race run at such a strong pace. Still on the bridle a couple of furlongs out, the only question was how much he had left in the tank and the answer was plenty. He has won off a higher mark in the past and might be capable of more over the trip, but may always need a sound surface to help him get it.
**Ellway Heights** was staying on when running into traffic approaching the furlong marker and had to be taken back and switched wide in order to see daylight. It is doubtful he would have won with a clear passage, but would have been a lot closer and still looks ready to strike.
**Saameq(IRE)** made the frame for the first time at the fifth attempt and the way he stayed on suggests he will get even further.
**Hibernate(IRE)**, a confirmed front-runner, went off at a cracking pace and showed great courage to hang on for fourth after losing the lead over a furlong from home. He is lasting longer in front each time since returning from his long layoff, and it may not be long before he does not come back to his rivals at all.
**Chevin** ◆ was far from disgraced on this first start in ten months, especially as she took a strong hold early. She is 1lb lower than for her two victories last summer and is one to watch for a similar contest.
T/Plt: £98.70 to a £1 stake. Pool: £37,695.60. 278.60 winning tickets. T/Qpdt: £13.50 to a £1 stake. Pool: £2,920.00. 159.50 winning tickets. JR

3116

## PONTEFRACT (L-H)
### Monday, June 28

**OFFICIAL GOING: Good to firm**

### 3370 GERRARD FINANCIAL PLANNING SERVICES MAIDEN AUCTION STKS 5f
**2:15** (2:15) (E) 2-Y-O **£4,784** (£1,472; £736; £368) **Stalls** Low

Form RPR
643 **1** **Mimi Mouse**[17] 2860 2-8-4 PRobinson 2 79
(TDEasterby) *mde virtually all: rdn over 1f out: hrd pressed: hung bdly rt and drifted over to stands side fnl f: hld on wl* **5/2**[2]
22 **2** *hd* **Tagula Sunrise (IRE)**[26] 2568 2-8-9 PHanagan 5 83
(RAFahey) *trckd wnr: effrt 2f out: sn rdn: disp ld ins fnl f: no ex clsng stages* **2/5**[1]
4 **3** *3* **Hillside Heather (IRE)**[10] 3055 2-8-2 FNorton 3 66
(ABerry) *prom: rdn and ev ch over 1f out: fdd fnl f* **16/1**[3]
**4** *2 ½* **Pro Tempore** 2-8-4 LGoncalves 4 59
(MrsJRRamsden) *hld up: plld v hrd 2f: effrt 2f out: sn rdn and btn* **40/1**
0 **5** *16* **Hamburg Springer (IRE)**[39] 2234 2-8-4 JFMcDonald(3) 6 —
(MJPolglase) *slowly away: a bhd: lost tch fr 1/2-way: t.o* **100/1**

63.95 secs (0.15) **Going Correction** -0.10s/f (Good) **5** Ran SP% **109.3**
Speed ratings: **94,93,88,84,59**CSF £3.79 TOTE £3.40: £1.60, £1.10; EX 5.30.
**Owner** Mrs Jean P Connew **Bred** Mrs P A Clark **Trained** Great Habton, N Yorks
■ Stewards Enquiry : P Robinson one-day ban: used whip with excessive frequency (Jul 9)
P Hanagan two-day ban: used whip with excessive frequency (Jul 20-21)

**FOCUS**
Hot favourite Tagula Sunrise was fully expected to win, although there was not much between the first two at the weights, but she ran a below-par race and it was Mimi Mouse who benefited.

**NOTEBOOK**
**Mimi Mouse** was having her fourth start on the course and put her previous experience to good use in the early stages, setting off in front testing her opposition, but she hung badly to her right in the final furlong and ended up just hanging on from the hot favourite. She should do well in nurseries.
**Tagula Sunrise(IRE)** was the one to beat on previous form with two second placings behind to useful opponents, the latter effort in a Listed race, so it was most disappointing she could not break her duck. This was a below-par effort and she deserves another chance to confirm that early promise.
**Hillside Heather(IRE)** ran a decent race and showed a progression in form from her debut. She has a similar race in her.
**Pro Tempore**, a Ramsden newcomer, pulled way too hard for her own good in the early stages and did well to finish as close as she did in the end. If settling better next time she can improve on this.

### 3371 SMEATON (S) H'CAP 1m 4f 8y
**2:45** (2:47) (F) (0-55,54) 3-Y-O **£3,458** (£1,064; £532; £266) **Stalls** Low

Form RPR
2505 **1** **Let It Be**[20] 2760 3-8-4 **40** PHanagan 2 47
(MrsMReveley) *in tch: effrt over 3f out: led over 2f out: rdn 4 l clr ent fnl f: styd on u.p: jst hld on* **7/2**[1]
0000 **2** *hd* **Bienheureux**[15] 2915 3-8-4 **40** RMullen 4 47
(WJMusson) *hld up: rdn 4f out: hdwy 2f out: styd on u.p to chse wnr ins fnl f: styd on wl towards fin: jst hld* **11/1**
53-5 **3** *5* **Defana**[174] 451 3-9-1 **54** LEnstone(3) 11 53
(MDods) *s.i.s: hld up: effrt 4f out: sn rdn: hdwy 2f out: styd on to go 3rd wl ins fnl f: nvr able to chal* **16/1**
2400 **4** *nk* **Valiant Air (IRE)**[27] 2554 3-8-4 **40** (b[1]) WSupple 5 38
(JRWeymes) *led after 1f: hdd over 2f out: no ex u.p* **5/1**[3]
0006 **5** *1 ¼* **Theatre Belle**[4] 3250 3-9-1 **51** (v[1]) DAllan 3 47
(TDEasterby) *midfield: rdn over 3f out: no hdwy* **14/1**
6254 **6** *shd* **Scorchio (IRE)**[9] 3107 3-8-9 **45** EAhern 6 41
(MFHarris) *led 1f: remained cl up: ev ch and rdn over 2f out: wknd over 1f out* **4/1**[2]
3265 **7** *24* **Royal Upstart**[18] 2822 3-7-8 **35** (b) BSwarbrick(5) 9 —
(WMBrisbourne) *midfield: rdn over 3f out: wknd over 2f out: t.o* **7/1**
0310 **8** *7* **Ciacole**[41] 2199 3-9-0 **50** DeanMcKeown 7 —
(RonaldThompson) *prom tl rdn and wknd wl over 2f out: t.o* **12/1**
-564 **9** *8* **Weaver Spell**[45] 2088 3-7-13 **35** FNorton 1 —
(JRNorton) *hld up: effrt 4f out: sn rdn and btn: t.o* **14/1**
0060 **10** *1 ¼* **Baroque**[27] 2554 3-7-6 **35** oh14 ow1 (b[1]) MHalford(7) 8 —
(CSmith) *cl up tl rdn and wknd over 3f out: t.o* **50/1**
2000 **11** *22* **Reedsman (IRE)**[27] 2556 3-8-4 **43** ow1 TEaves(3) 10 —
(RCGuest) *slowly away: hld up: effrt 4f out: sn rdn and btn: t.o and virtually p.u ins fnl f* **9/1**

2m 40.45s (0.40) **Going Correction** -0.10s/f (Good) **11** Ran SP% **118.6**
Speed ratings: **94,93,90,90,89 89,73,68,63,62 47**CSF £43.33 CT £552.52 TOTE £4.50: £1.70, £4.50, £6.20; EX 90.60.The winner was bought in for 6,600 guineas. Bienheureux was claimed by Gay Kelleway for £6,000.
**Owner** A Frame **Bred** Sir Eric Parker **Trained** Lingdale, N Yorks

**FOCUS**
A poor race with no strength in depth and only modest form, but a progressive winner who is up to following up if finding a similar event.

**NOTEBOOK**
**Let It Be** had run well in a better race on her latest outing and off a 2lb lower mark she was able to get get her head in front, just clinging on from the challenge of Bienheureux having gone clear at one stage. She is going the right way and is capable of winning again off such a lowly mark.
**Bienheureux** has always finished nearer last than first in his races and this represented a dramatic improvement in form. He had been running over shorter and this sort of trip is evidently what is required.
**Defana** ran on from the rear but was never in a winning position. He was stepping up from a mile and got the trip well.
**Valiant Air(IRE)** continues to struggle to find a race and the first-time blinkers failed to improve him.
**Theatre Belle** looks very one paced and is not one to make a habit of backing.
**Scorchio(IRE)** could offer no more, having raced prominently for most of the way.
**Ciacole** *Official explanation: jockey said filly had been unsuited by the ground*

### 3372 EBF GERRARD WEALTH MANAGEMENT FILLIES' H'CAP 6f
**3:15** (3:15) (D) (0-85,84) 3-Y-O+ **£10,452** (£3,216; £1,608; £804) **Stalls** Low

Form RPR
5-50 **1** **Sharoura**[16] 2875 8-8-3 **59** PHanagan 7 69
(RAFahey) *in tch: rdn 2f out: r.o u.p to ld wl ins fnl f: all out* **10/1**[3]
0624 **2** *nk* **Complication**[14] 2948 4-8-6 **65** (b) TPQueally(3) 3 74
(JARToller) *trckd ldrs: effrt 2f out: r.o u.p to dispute ld wl ins fnl f: no ex cl home* **9/2**[2]
0221 **3** *1 ¼* **Cloud Dancer**[16] 2899 5-9-6 **76** NCallan 9 81
(KARyan) *slowly away: hld up in rr: drvn along and hdwy into midfield 2f out: r.o u.p ins fnl f: nvr able to chal* **5/2**[1]
0-40 **4** *½* **Dani Ridge (IRE)**[15] 2909 6-9-7 **84** JDO'Reilly(7) 6 88
(EJAlston) *cl up: rdn to ld over 1f out: hdd wl ins fnl f: no ex* **11/1**
0654 **5** *½* **College Queen**[15] 2909 6-8-8 **64** (b) WSupple 10 66
(SGollings) *hld up: sme hdwy u.p over 1f out: kpt on fnl f: nvr able to chal* **16/1**
3-20 **6** *1* **Favour**[31] 2459 4-9-3 **73** JPMurtagh 4 72
(MrsJRRamsden) *hld up: pushed along 2f out: kpt on fnl f: n.d* **9/2**[2]
2313 **7** *nk* **Baron Rhodes**[9] 3077 3-8-12 **78** TEaves(3) 1 76
(JSWainwright) *mde most tl rdn and hdd over 1f out: wknd fnl f* **12/1**
4043 **8** *¾* **Bint Royal (IRE)**[10] 3047 6-7-9 **58** (p) MHalford(7) 11 54
(MissVHaigh) *in tch: rdn over 2f out: edgd lft u.p and wknd appr fnl f* **10/1**[3]
-500 **9** *1* **Bowling Along**[31] 2457 3-7-13 **62** oh8 ow1 RFfrench 5 55
(MESowersby) *hld up: effrt over 2f out: sn rdn and btn* **100/1**
3600 **10** *nk* **Just One Smile (IRE)**[9] 3098 4-8-1 **57** (b[1]) DAllan 8 49
(TDEasterby) *s.i.s: hld up in rr: drvn along and sme hdwy whn bdly hmpd jst ins fnl f: no ch after* **16/1**
2266 **11** *hd* **Marabar**[13] 2963 6-7-12 **59** (b) BSwarbrick(5) 2 51
(DWChapman) *chsd ldrs: rdn over 2f out: fdd* **20/1**

1m 16.1s (-1.20) **Going Correction** -0.10s/f (Good)
**WFA** 3 from 4yo+ 7lb **11** Ran SP% **116.7**
Speed ratings: **104,103,101,101,100 99,98,97,96,96 95**CSF £54.16 CT £151.68 TOTE £10.50: £2.80, £1.80, £1.70; EX 74.20 Trifecta £602.20 Pool of £1,781.20 - 2.10 winning units.
**Owner** Manor House Partnership **Bred** Mrs G M Peel **Trained** Musley Bank, N Yorks
■ Stewards Enquiry : M Halford two-day ban: careless riding (Jul 9,10)

**FOCUS**
A tight little affair and a good finish suggesting the form is sound and reliable.

**NOTEBOOK**
**Sharoura** was supported at Leicester as though a return to something like her best was expected, but she found trouble in running. Off a 1lb lower mark, she got the breaks on this occasion and stayed on too strongly for the second. Whether she can go on from this is open to question, but it was around this time last year she had a good spell.
**Complication** has run several good races in defeat this season and she is gradually getting nearer to winning.
**Cloud Dancer** blew the start and that may well have cost her the race. She was running off a 5lb lower mark than when winning at York and is up to winning off this rating.
**Dani Ridge(IRE)** is still 8lb higher than when last scoring over a year ago, and needs a further drop in the weights before she is winning.
**College Queen** is back on a winnable mark and can and will be winning when it all falls into place.
**Favour** needs to drop in the weights before she is winning again.
**Baron Rhodes** ran a rare bad race and will be better off back in her own age group.

### 3373 SPINDRIFTER CONDITIONS STKS 6f
**3:45** (3:45) (C) 2-Y-O **£7,238** (£2,745; £1,372; £624) **Stalls** Low

Form RPR
1 **1** **Leo's Lucky Star (USA)**[32] 2422 2-9-2 JFanning 2 101+
(MJohnston) *mde all: shkn up and qcknd over 2f out: clr over 1f out: eased clsng stages: unchal* **2/7**[1]
62 **2** *3 ½* **Tom Forest**[11] 3014 2-8-7 JFMcDonald(3) 9 78
(ACrook) *prom: wnt 2nd after 2f: rdn over 2f out: kpt on: no imp on wnr* **9/1**[2]
**3** *5* **Bunny Rabbit (USA)** 2-8-7 KMcEvoy 4 60
(BJMeehan) *dwlt: sn pushed along in rr: hdwy and in tch over 3f out: rdn over 2f out: sn btn* **10/1**[3]
3410 **4** *2* **Tiviski (IRE)**[26] 2568 2-8-11 WSupple 7 58
(EJAlston) *hld up in tch: rdn over 2f out: sn btn* **9/1**[2]
540 **5** *½* **Tantien**[26] 2568 2-8-2 TPQueally(3) 3 51
(JohnAHarris) *in tch: rdn over 2f out: sn btn* **40/1**
**6** *10* **The Plainsman** 2-8-7 EAhern 1 23
(PWHiatt) *dwlt: sn lost tch* **66/1**
60 **7** *3 ½* **Den Perry**[17] 2858 2-8-10 FLynch 6 15
(ABerry) *chsd wnr 2f: wknd and lost tch over 2f out* **100/1**

1m 16.94s (-0.36) **Going Correction** -0.10s/f (Good) **7** Ran SP% **111.8**
Speed ratings: **98,93,86,84,83 70,65**CSF £3.47 TOTE £1.30: £1.10, £3.00; EX 4.10.
**Owner** Mrs S J Brookhouse **Bred** Manganaro Llc **Trained** Middleham Moor, N Yorks

**FOCUS**
Another authoritative display from Leo's Lucky Star who outclassed the oppositon and the winner could be even better than the bare form.

**NOTEBOOK**

**Leo's Lucky Star(USA)**, an impressive winner on his racecourse debut at Ayr, was understandably upped in grade, but with his only realistic rivals both being non-runners he faced a simple task. Smartly into stride, he always had the race in his control and galloped on strongly for a smooth win. It was no mistake that connections chose this race for the colt - they won it last season with Lucky Story and are following a similar path - but his main aim will reportedly be the Champagne Stakes at Doncaster as connections feel Goodwood will not suit.

**Tom Forest** fared best of the remainder and, as he is still a maiden, is a ready-made winner for the forthcoming weeks.

**Bunny Rabbit(USA)**, a relative of winners in the States, gave plenty of encouragement for the future and will face easier tasks.

**Tiviski(IRE)** was a little disappointing, but her sole win came on soft ground and maybe this was too firm for her.

## 3374 WRAGBY MAIDEN FILLIES' STKS — 1m 2f 6y

**4:15** (4:15) (D) 3-Y-O — **£5,525** (£1,700; £850; £425) **Stalls** Low

| Form | | | Horse | RPR |
|---|---|---|---|---|
| 32 | **1** | | **Posteritas (USA)**[15] [2911] 3-8-11 .......... RHughes 6 (HRACecil) *hld up in tch: drvn along and hdwy 2f out: rdn to ld appr fnl f: styd on wl* **2/1**[2] | 81 |
| 2 | **2** | *3* | **Fortune's Princess**[10] [3054] 3-8-11 .......... EAhern 1 (MJWallace) *cl up: led 3f out: rdn and hdd approachinhg fnl f: no ex* **9/2**[3] | 75 |
| 0-3 | **3** | *1 ¾* | **Dalisay (IRE)**[16] [2888] 3-8-11 .......... FLynch 3 (SirMichaelStoute) *hld up in tch: drvn along over 2f out: kpt on fnl f: nvr able to chal* **9/2**[3] | 72 |
| 24 | **4** | *5* | **Chanteloup**[48] [2020] 3-8-11 .......... JPMurtagh 2 (JRFanshawe) *led: hdd 3f out: rdn over 1f out: sn btn: eased whn no ch wl ins last* **15/8**[1] | 62 |
| 0- | **5** | *1 ¼* | **Sierra**[279] [5138] 3-8-8 .......... TPQueally(3) 7 (CEBrittain) *s.i.s: hld up in rr: drvn along and outpcd over 2f out: n.d* **33/1** | 60 |
| 5 | **6** | *dist* | **Daring Games**[31] [2460] 3-8-11 .......... RFfrench 5 (BEllison) *rr: lost tch fr 4f out: t.o* **80/1** | — |

2m 12.17s (-1.74) **Going Correction** -0.10s/f (Good) — **6** Ran SP% **108.7**

Speed ratings: **102,99,98,94,93** —CSF £10.55 TOTE £2.80: £1.30, £2.00; EX 7.80.

**Owner** K Abdulla **Bred** Juddmonte Farms Inc **Trained** Newmarket, Suffolk

**FOCUS**

Not much strength in depth to this fillies' maiden and the form is only fair, but it was a nice performance from Posteritas.

**NOTEBOOK**

**Posteritas(USA)** appreciated this step up in trip and improved on her Salisbury running to win tidily. She is capable of making her mark in handicaps.

**Fortune's Princess** has run well on both starts to date and a run-of-the-mill maiden is hers for the taking.

**Dalisay(IRE)** is now qualified for a handicap mark, and the combination of an extra quarter mile on easier going should see her at her best.

**Chanteloup** was disappointing and could offer no more once challenged. *Official explanation: jockey said filly had hung right-handed throughout*

**Sierra** was not totally disgraced and is likely to do much better once handicapped. *Official explanation: jockey said filly had lost her action*

## 3375 BETFAIR.COM APPRENTICE SERIES (ROUND 3) H'CAP — 1m 2f 6y

**4:45** (4:46) (E) (0-70,70) 3-Y-O+ — **£4,173** (£1,284; £642; £321) **Stalls** Low

| Form | | | Horse | RPR |
|---|---|---|---|---|
| 6121 | **1** | | **Realism (FR)**[7] [3143] 4-9-10 **69** 6ex.......... StevenHarrison(3) 5 (PWHiatt) *in tch: hdwy over 2f out: rdn to ld ins fnl f: styd on wl* **11/2**[2] | 81 |
| -414 | **2** | *1* | **Smart John**[7] [3143] 4-9-7 **63**.......... DFentiman 9 (WMBrisbourne) *hld up: hdwy 1/2-way: led wl over 2f out: rdn and hdd ins fnl f: styd on* **15/2** | 74 |
| 002- | **3** | *6* | **Valeureux**[58] [5012] 6-8-10 **52**.......... MHalford 8 (JHetherton) *hld up: hdwy 4f out: chsng ldrs 2f out: rdn to go 3rd appr fnl f: no imp on first 2* **6/1**[3] | 51 |
| -000 | **4** | *shd* | **Derwent (USA)**[19] [2775] 5-9-7 **70**.......... (b) SShaw(7) 3 (JDBethell) *rr: hdwy 2f out: styd on u.p fnl f: nvr able to chal* **20/1** | 69 |
| -304 | **5** | *2 ½* | **We'll Meet Again**[9] [3103] 4-8-11 **53**.......... DTudhope 1 (MWEasterby) *hld up in tch: effrt 2f out: no real hdwy* **9/1** | 47 |
| 0220 | **6** | *8* | **Penwell Hill (USA)**[73] [1451] 5-8-12 **54**.......... Laura-JayneCrawford 2 (TDBarron) *mde most tl hdd wl over 2f out: rdn and wknd over 1f out* **14/1** | 33 |
| 06-6 | **7** | *4* | **Market Avenue**[41] [2216] 5-9-3 **62**.......... AMullen(3) 7 (RAFahey) *keen: sn prog: ev ch 2f out: sn rdn and btn* **7/4**[1] | 33 |
| 3426 | **8** | *6* | **Given A Chance**[26] [2571] 3-7-12 **52** oh6.......... DeanWilliams 4 (MrsSLamyman) *chsd ldrs tl rdn and wknd over 2f out* **50/1** | 12 |
| 0-01 | **9** | *dist* | **Night Market**[9] [3103] 6-8-10 **52**.......... JDO'Reilly 10 (NWilson) *keen: prom tl wknd rapidly 3f out: t.o and virtually p.u ins fnl f* **7/1** | — |
| 060/ | **10** | *1* | **Dragon Prince**[92] [5743] 4-9-9 **68**.......... AReilly(3) 6 (RCGuest) *plld v hrd early: bhd fr 1/2-way: t.o and virtually p.u ins fnl f: sddle slipped* **20/1** | — |

2m 12.66s (-1.25) **Going Correction** -0.10s/f (Good)

**WFA** 3 from 4yo+ 12lb — **10** Ran SP% **118.4**

Speed ratings: **101,100,95,95,93 86,83,78,—,—**CSF £45.89 CT £259.13 TOTE £5.90: £1.80, £1.90, £2.40; EX 34.00 Place 6 £24.66, Place 5 £23.05.

**Owner** Miss Maria McKinney **Bred** Darley Stud Management Co Ltd **Trained** Hook Norton, Oxon

**FOCUS**

Another good performance from Realism who confirmed Pontefract form with Smart John, but the form is not totally convincing.

**NOTEBOOK**

**Realism(FR)** continued his good recent spell of form and made it three wins from the last four. He is clearly thriving at the moment and not one to oppose in a hurry.

**Smart John** got closer to Realism on 6lb better terms than he had at Pontefract and remains progressive at this sort of level.

**Valeureux** was six lengths adrift in third and no match for the front pair.

**Derwent(USA)** ◆ kept on to run his best race for a while without posing a threat. He is back on a very good mark, 14lb lower than when last successful, and is one to keep an eye on in the coming weeks.

**Market Avenue** did a little too much too early and had nothing left when it mattered. This was disappointing. ( MB )

**Dragon Prince** *Official explanation: jockey said saddle slipped*

T/Jkpt: £4,405.20 to a £1 stake. Pool: £40,329.50. 6.50 winning tickets. T/Plt: £23.90 to a £1 stake. Pool: £44,137.50. 1,343.45 winning tickets. T/Qpdt: £5.40 to a £1 stake. Pool: £2,747.20. 370.40 winning tickets. JF

# 3277 SOUTHWELL (L-H)

### Monday, June 28

**OFFICIAL GOING: Standard**

Wind: Slight across Weather: Cloudy

## 3376 ST BASILIDES DAY APPRENTICE CLAIMING STKS — 7f (F)

**2:00** (2:00) (G) 4-Y-0+ — **£2,954** (£844; £422) **Stalls** Low

| Form | | | Horse | RPR |
|---|---|---|---|---|
| 52 | **1** | | **Ali Bruce**[11] [3002] 4-9-5 .......... HayleyTurner 6 (DECantillon) *s.i.s: rcvrd to join ld 6f out: led over 4f out: rdn clr over 2f out: jst hld on* **11/4**[2] | 67 |
| -000 | **2** | *½* | **Mac's Talisman (IRE)**[14] [2948] 4-9-0 55.......... RoryMoore(3) 3 (VSmith) *soon outpcd: hdwy 1/2-way: rdn over 2f out: chsd wnr over 1f out: r.o* **2/1**[1] | 64 |
| 3215 | **3** | *1* | **Countrywide Girl (IRE)**[40] [2229] 5-7-13 39.......... PPMathers(3) 8 (ABerry) *chsd ldrs: rdn over 2f out: hung lft ins fnl f: kpt on* **16/1** | 46 |
| 6200 | **4** | *2 ½* | **Nicholas Nickelby**[4] [3247] 4-9-1 62.......... (p) MSavage 1 (MJPolglase) *prom: rdn over 2f out: styd on same pce appr fnl f* **16/1** | 53 |
| 3031 | **5** | *1 ¼* | **Only One Legend (IRE)**[18] [2813] 6-8-4 60.......... (b) CWilliams(7) 7 (KARyan) *prom: lost pl over 4f out: rdn over 2f out: nt trble ldrs* **4/1**[3] | 46 |
| 3030 | **6** | *5* | **Headland (USA)**[11] [3024] 6-8-0 49.......... (b) DFentiman(5) 5 (DWChapman) *led: hdd over 4f out: wknd over 1f out* **10/1** | 27 |
| 0-05 | **7** | *6* | **Bandbox (IRE)**[11] [3024] 9-8-5 32.......... DFox 2 (MSalaman) *sn outpcd* **20/1** | 12 |
| 0-05 | **8** | *3* | **Matriarchal**[12] [2979] 4-7-13 30 ow4.......... JaniceWebster(7) 9 (DonEnricoIncisa) *dwlt: outpcd* **66/1** | 6 |
| 0300 | **9** | *1 ¾* | **Eager Angel (IRE)**[49] [1992] 6-8-3 56.......... (p) MNem(7) 4 (RFMarvin) *s.i.s: outpcd: sme hdwy 4f out: sn wknd* **12/1** | 5 |

1m 29.28s (-1.52) **Going Correction** -0.20s/f (Stan) — **9** Ran SP% **114.8**

Speed ratings: **100,99,98,95,94 88,81,78,76**CSF £8.58 TOTE £5.10: £1.70, £1.10, £4.70; EX 21.30.The winner was claimed by Nigel Shields for £12,000.

**Owner** Mrs Edward Cantillon **Bred** R J McCreery **Trained** Carlton, Cambs

**FOCUS**

A moderate claimer, with the third holding down the form, but the winner is unexposed and open to improvement.

**NOTEBOOK**

**Ali Bruce** started his career in bumpers and has been tried at up to ten furlongs on the Flat, but this sort of trip clearly suits best for he has plenty of pace. Given a good positive ride, he handled the surface well and always looked like holding on. He should be capable of holding his own in a higher grade and there is no reason why he should not confirm this promise back on turf.

**Mac's Talisman(IRE)** attracted significant market support on this return to claiming company despite having quite a bit to find at the weights, but he was unable to hold a position early on and, despite making plenty of ground up to get into a challenging position in the straight, he never really looked like getting there. He is on a fair mark and should be competitive if returned to handicaps.

**Countrywide Girl(IRE)**, who had done all of her racing in regional company this year, posted a respectable effort on this step up in grade.

**Nicholas Nickelby** looked to have lost his way on his last two starts, but he took well to the fitting of cheekpieces and posted an encouraging effort.

**Only One Legend(IRE)** is quite hard to win with and never once threatened under his inexperienced jockey, despite having a decent chance at the weights.

**Headland(USA)** dropped out very tamely.

## 3377 EUROPEAN BREEDERS FUND PUTNEY MAIDEN STKS — 7f (F)

**2:30** (2:32) (D) 2-Y-O — **£4,046** (£1,245; £622; £311) **Stalls** Low

| Form | | | Horse | RPR |
|---|---|---|---|---|
| 6 | **1** | | **Pauline's Prince**[9] [3104] 2-9-0 .......... DSweeney 5 (RHollinshead) *led early: remained handy: led over 1f out: rdn clr* **12/1** | 61 |
| 6 | **2** | *3* | **Ming Vase**[51] [1960] 2-8-7 .......... DTudhope(7) 3 (DCarroll) *s.i.s: hld up: outpcd 3f out: hdwy u.p over 1f out: no ch w wnr* **3/1**[2] | 54 |
| | **3** | *3* | **Keynes (JPN)** 2-9-0 .......... RHavlin 6 (JHMGosden) *w ldrs: rdn over 2f out: styd on same pce* **11/4**[1] | 46 |
| 00 | **4** | *1 ½* | **Ellis Cave**[23] [2674] 2-9-0 .......... (v[1]) RWinston 7 (JJQuinn) *s.s: sn prom: rdn over 2f out: wknd over 1f out* **7/1** | 42 |
| 0 | **5** | *1 ¼* | **Hiamovi (IRE)**[72] [1462] 2-9-0 .......... BDoyle 9 (RMHCowell) *dwlt: plld hrd and sn led: hdd & wknd over 1f out* **4/1**[3] | 39 |
| 06 | **6** | *2 ½* | **Hidden Jewel**[18] [2812] 2-9-0 .......... GGibbons 8 (BAMcmahon) *dwlt: sn prom: rdn and wknd over 1f out* **14/1** | 33 |
| 0 | **7** | *4* | **Ugly Sister (USA)**[45] [2096] 2-8-9 .......... SWhitworth 10 (GCBravery) *hld up in tch: plld hrd: wknd 2f out* **25/1** | 18 |
| 0 | **8** | *8* | **Miss Cuisina**[9] [3083] 2-8-9 .......... JoannaBadger 2 (PDEvans) *sn outpcd* **66/1** | — |
| 000 | **9** | *15* | **Lord Chalfont (IRE)**[17] [2852] 2-8-9 .......... MSavage(5) 1 (MJPolglase) *s.i.s: outpcd* **66/1** | — |
| | **10** | *5* | **Reaching Out (IRE)** 2-9-0 .......... SSanders 4 (GCBravery) *s.s: outpcd* **7/1** | — |

1m 31.23s (0.43) **Going Correction** -0.20s/f (Stan) — **10** Ran SP% **117.9**

Speed ratings: **89,85,82,80,79 76,71,62,45,39**CSF £48.25 TOTE £18.20: £3.50, £1.70, £1.20; EX 100.90.

**Owner** N Chapman **Bred** R Hollinshead **Trained** Upper Longdon, Staffs

**FOCUS**

Just a weak maiden and a seller in all but name, but Pauline's Prince created a good impression and should not be underestimated in slightly better company.

**NOTEBOOK**

**Pauline's Prince** ◆ showed nothing on his debut on fast ground at Warwick over five furlongs nine days previously, but had clearly learnt for that experience and was much better suited to these conditions. After travelling strongly, he pulled away in the straight and won in a manner that suggests he could well add to this in better company. He can also be given another chance back on turf.

**Ming Vase** confirmed the promise he showed on his debut 51 days previously on this step up from five furlongs and switch to Fibresand. He lost his position early, but kept on for pressure and is open to further improvement.

**Keynes(JPN)**, a half-brother to a couple of juvenile winners, including one who made a winning debut on Fibresand, was easy to back and was well held. He should improve and may do better on turf, but is clearly not one of his trainer's leading juveniles.

**Ellis Cave**, beaten a total of 33 lengths on his first two starts, improved for the fitting of a visor and switch to Fibresand. He should progress again providing the headgear continues to have a positive effect.

**Hiamovi(IRE)**, well beaten on his debut over five furlongs at Nottingham when last seen 72 days ago, was quite well backed on his return to action, but raced too keenly early on and failed to get home.

**Reaching Out(IRE)** showed nothing after starting very slowly, but he cost 52,000 euros and may just be capable of better in time.

## 3378 NATIONAL TAPIOCA DAY (S) STKS 5f (F)
3:00 (3:03) (G ) 3-Y-0+ £2,653 (£758; £379) Stalls High

Form RPR

04L0 **1** **Queen Of Night**[3] 3269 4-9-0 60........ DarrenWilliams 9 57
(DWChapman) *s.s: hdwy over 3f out: rdn to ld over 1f out: eased nr fin* **12/1**

0060 **2** *3* **Scary Night (IRE)**[24] 2663 4-9-10 51........(p) JEdmunds 2 56
(JBalding) *chsd ldrs: outpcd 1/2-way: r.o ins fnl f* **16/1**

0650 **3** *hd* **River Lark (USA)**[19] 2778 5-8-9 41........(b[1]) HayleyTurner[(5)] 10 45
(MABuckley) *chsd ldrs: rdn 1/2-way: styd on same pce appr fnl f* **16/1**

2323 **4** *nk* **Valazar (USA)**[4] 3227 5-9-5 45........ GDuffield 6 49
(DWChapman) *s.i.s: sn outpcd: hdwy over 1f out: nt trble ldrs* **9/2**[1]

0525 **5** *nk* **The Leather Wedge (IRE)**[60] 1738 5-8-12 45........(p) PPMathers[(7)] 4 48
(ABerry) *led over 3f: no ex ins fnl f* **11/2**[2]

0266 **6** *3/4* **Frenchmans Lodge**[16] 2869 4-9-2 39........(b) FPFerris[(3)] 5 46
(JMBradley) *chsd ldrs: rdn 1/2-way: styd on same pce appr fnl f* **25/1**

0310 **7** *hd* **Hagley Park**[24] 2663 5-9-0 48........ PMulrennan[(5)] 14 45
(MQuinn) *chsd ldrs: rdn 2f out: styd on same pce fnl f* **10/1**

6000 **8** *1/2* **Confuzed**[83] 1280 4-9-5 43........(e) SWhitworth 3 43
(DFlood) *mid-div: sn drvn along: nvr trbld ldrs* **20/1**

6650 **9** *1/2* **Attorney**[7] 3151 6-9-10 54........(v) LVickers 1 46
(DShaw) *chsd ldrs: rdn 1/2-way: wknd fnl f* **12/1**

3660 **10** *3* **Tickle**[42] 2178 6-9-0 45........(t) SSanders 7 26
(PJMakin) *chsd ldrs 3f* **10/1**

4300 **11** *1/2* **Catchthebatch**[9] 3084 8-9-5 47........ SCarson 11 29
(EAWheeler) *s.i.s: sn outpcd* **14/1**

-400 **12** *3/4* **Niteowl Dream**[16] 2879 4-9-0 48........ PMQuinn 8 22
(JO'Reilly) *sn outpcd* **33/1**

0060 **13** *nk* **Henry Tun**[16] 2869 6-9-5 52........(p) MSavage[(5)] 15 30
(NEBerry) *outpcd* **6/1**[3]

6266 **14** *nk* **Juwwi**[3] 3269 10-9-5 55........ CCatlin 12 24
(JMBradley) *s.i.s: outpcd* **7/1**

0056 **15** *12* **Brave Chief**[17] 2850 3-8-13 48........ NPollard 16 —
(JAPickering) *s.s: outpcd* **20/1**

59.47 secs (-0.93) **Going Correction** -0.20s/f (Stan)
**WFA** 3 from 4yo+ 6lb **15** Ran SP% **128.7**
Speed ratings: **99,94,93,93,92 91,91,90,89,85 84,83,82,82,62**CSF £192.85 TOTE £13.40: £5.40, £4.70, £6.70; EX 324.80.There was no bid for the winner.
**Owner** Michael Hill **Bred** Trevor Calver **Trained** Stillington, N Yorks

**FOCUS**
Quite a competitive seller despite several struggling for form. The 15 runners spread all over the track, but there did not appear to be a bias.

**NOTEBOOK**
**Queen Of Night** looked to have lost her way recently, not least when refusing to race two starts back, but her trainer is a master at rejuvenating 'characters' and she bounced back to form in emphatic style. She cannot be trusted to repeat this next time, but is most certainly in the right hands.
**Scary Night(IRE)** finished lame on his previous start, but is back in good form and ran a solid race.
**River Lark(USA)**, with blinkers replacing cheekpieces, showed up well throughout and can have no excuses.
**Valazar(USA)**, stablemate of the winner, stuck on well for pressure without ever really looking like winning.
**The Leather Wedge(IRE)** showed bags of pace and should benefit from a return to an easier track.
**Hagley Park** *Official explanation: jockey said mare had hung left*
**Attorney** had every chance against the far rail.
**Brave Chief** *Official explanation: jockey said colt jumped from the stalls with his head in the air, thereby losing many lengths*

## 3379 BATTLE OF VICKSBURG H'CAP 1m 4f (F)
3:30 (3:31) (E ) (0-70,67) 3-Y-0 £3,464 (£1,066; £533; £266) Stalls Low

Form RPR

1464 **1** **It's Blue Chip**[24] 2665 3-9-0 60........(e) PaulEddery 2 67
(PWD'Arcy) *hld up and bhd: hdwy 4f out: rdn over 1f out: r.o to ld post* **6/1**[3]

5543 **2** *hd* **Holly Walk**[11] 3026 3-7-11 46........(p) FPFerris[(3)] 6 53
(MDods) *chsd ldr: led over 7f out: hdd over 3f out: rdn to ld over 1f out: hdd post* **9/2**[2]

1100 **3** *1 1/2* **Fleetfoot Mac**[20] 2753 3-9-3 63........ RHavlin 4 68
(PDEvans) *chsd ldrs: led over 3f out: rdn and hdd over 1f out: styd on same pce ins fnl f* **12/1**

0052 **4** *nk* **Crocolat**[6] 3172 3-8-4 55........ DFox[(5)] 10 59
(NACallaghan) *chsd ldrs: outpcd over 6f out: hdwy over 3f out: rdn and edgd lft over 1f out: styd on* **9/2**[2]

1335 **5** *nk* **Siegfrieds Night (IRE)**[11] 3020 3-9-4 64........ LVickers 11 68
(MCChapman) *hld up: hdwy 6f out: rdn and ev ch fr over 2f out: styd on same pce ins fnl f* **7/1**

0563 **6** *12* **Rock Lobster**[24] 2665 3-9-7 67........ BDoyle 8 53
(JGGiven) *prom: rdn over 3f out: wknd wl over 1f out* **4/1**[1]

0000 **7** *5* **Munaawesh (USA)**[4] 3231 3-8-7 53........ GDuffield 3 31
(DWChapman) *hld up: effrt over 4f out: wknd over 3f out* **16/1**

0-06 **8** *30* **Commemoration Day (IRE)**[31] 2449 3-9-2 62........ SSanders 9 —
(JGGiven) *chsd ldrs: rdn 1/2-way: wknd over 3f out: eased* **7/1**

5610 **9** *17* **Peruvian Breeze (IRE)**[18] 2802 3-9-5 65........ TGMcLaughlin 1 —
(NPLittmoden) *led over 4f: wknd over 3f out* **12/1**

4-05 **10** *25* **Blue Viking (IRE)**[17] 2853 3-8-9 55........ RWinston 7 —
(JRWeymes) *hld up: rdn 1/2-way: wknd over 3f out: eased* **40/1**

60-5 **11** *dist* **Royal Approach**[58] 1761 3-9-3 63........ DSweeney 5 —
(MBlanshard) *prom to 1/2-way* **20/1**

2m 39.57s (-2.53) **Going Correction** -0.20s/f (Stan) **11** Ran SP% **124.1**
Speed ratings: **100,99,98,98,98 90,87,67,55,39** —CSF £35.18 CT £326.59 TOTE £8.40: £2.60, £2.20, £3.20; EX 36.30.
**Owner** Blue Chip Feed Ltd **Bred** G C Neate **Trained** Newmarket, Suffolk

**FOCUS**
A modest handicap and the early pace was just ordinary. The first five home finished close together, but were within 2lb of their previous marks.

**NOTEBOOK**
**It's Blue Chip** improved on his recent Wolverhampton fourth to reverse form with a below-par Rock Lobster. He did well to win this given that a stronger pace would surely have suited better, and he should progress again when stepped back up in trip.
**Holly Walk** is still a maiden, but is running well and was just denied. She should get her head in front sooner rather than later in similar company.
**Fleetfoot Mac** showed little on his only previous try on Fibresand, but the surface did not appear a problem this time and he posted a solid effort. He should stay further.
**Crocolat** made a respectable Fibresand debut. She is still a maiden, but is lightly raced and it will be disappointing if she does not improve enough to win a similar race.
**Siegfrieds Night(IRE)** lacked a change of pace in the closing stages.
**Rock Lobster** failed to run to the form he showed at Wolverhampton on his previous start and was most disappointing.
**Blue Viking(IRE)** *Official explanation: trainer's representative said gelding finished lame behind*

## 3380 SIGNING OF THE TREATY OF VERSAILLES H'CAP 1m (F)
4:00 (4:02) (F ) (0-55,55) 3-Y-0+ £3,003 (£858; £429) Stalls Low

Form RPR

2165 **1** **Downland (IRE)**[13] 2965 8-10-0 55........ KimTinkler 2 70
(NTinkler) *hld up in tch: plld hrd: rdn to ld ins fnl f: r.o* **10/1**

3002 **2** *1/2* **Midshipman**[11] 3023 6-10-0 55........(vt) SSanders 5 69
(AWCarroll) *sn outpcd: hdwy u.p over 1f out: ev ch ins fnl f: r.o* **9/4**[1]

4314 **3** *5* **Sudra**[132] 810 7-9-12 53........ CCatlin 4 57
(DJDaly) *prom: outpcd 5f out: hdwy u.p over 1f out: nt trble ldrs* **9/1**

004 **4** *1/2* **Magic Verse**[17] 2853 3-9-2 53........ CLowther 13 56
(RGuest) *chsd ldrs: rdn 1/2-way: outpcd 3f out: styd on fnl f* **16/1**

2503 **5** *3/4* **Dalriath**[4] 3250 5-8-7 39........ DFox[(5)] 11 41
(MCChapman) *chsd ldrs: led 2f out: hdd & wknd ins fnl f* **7/1**[2]

330P **6** *3/4* **Kenny The Truth (IRE)**[18] 2816 5-9-8 49........(t) ADaly 10 49
(MrsJCandlish) *sn outpcd: hdwy over 1f out: nvr nrr* **14/1**

2243 **7** *4* **Donegal Shore (IRE)**[63] 1681 5-9-2 48........(vt) NChalmers[(5)] 6 40
(MrsJCandlish) *s.i.s: outpcd: hdwy over 1f out: nvr nrr* **12/1**

0240 **8** *2* **Sea Ya Maite**[35] 2345 10-8-13 40........(t) SWhitworth 1 28
(SRBowring) *mid-div: nt clr run over 3f out: hdwy and n.m.r over 1f out: n.d* **20/1**

0321 **9** *1 1/2* **Mitzi Caspar**[18] 2815 3-9-3 54........ RPrice 9 39
(PLGilligan) *chsd ldrs: rdn and ev ch over 2f out: sn wknd* **14/1**

0050 **10** *3/4* **Tata Naka**[29] 2506 4-8-8 40........(tp) HayleyTurner[(5)] 3 24
(MrsCADunnett) *chsd ldr: led over 3f out: hdd & wknd 2f out* **33/1**

0-00 **11** *2 1/2* **Baby Barry**[14] 2936 7-10-0 55........(v) GDuffield 7 34
(MrsGSRees) *led over 4f: wknd wl over 1f out* **20/1**

4420 **12** *1/2* **Call Of The Wild**[14] 2938 4-9-7 51........(v) THamilton[(3)] 15 29
(RAFahey) *mid-div: rdn 1/2-way: n.d* **8/1**[3]

00/0 **13** *8* **Prince Of Aragon**[11] 3024 8-8-12 39........ DSweeney 16 —
(MissSuzySmith) *hdwy over 5f out: wknd wl over 2f out* **33/1**

0026 **14** *2 1/2* **Sonderborg**[24] 2660 3-9-1 52........ GCarter 12 9
(MissAMNewton-Smith) *chsd ldrs: rdn 1/2-way: wknd over 2f out* **14/1**

005- **15** *3 1/2* **Melford Red (IRE)**[385] 2225 4-9-2 43........ TGMcLaughlin 8 —
(RFMarvin) *s.i.s: a in rr* **50/1**

0-66 **16** *dist* **Muqarrar (IRE)**[158] 582 5-9-8 49........(bt) RWinston 14 —
(TJFitzgerald) *chsd ldrs 5f* **14/1**

1m 43.34s (-1.26) **Going Correction** -0.20s/f (Stan)
**WFA** 3 from 4yo+ 10lb **16** Ran SP% **131.1**
Speed ratings: **98,97,92,92,91 90,86,84,83,82 79,79,71,68,65** —CSF £33.09 CT £207.39 TOTE £12.30: £2.50, £1.10, £2.40, £5.80; EX 37.10.
**Owner** A Graham **Bred** Yeomanstown Stud **Trained** Langton, N Yorks

**FOCUS**
Just a moderate handicap, but the front two pulled well clear and would appear to be ahead of the Handicapper.

**NOTEBOOK**
**Downland(IRE)** has not had things go his way since scoring at Ayr three starts previously, but he made no mistake this time. Last on his only previous start on Fibresand, he handled the surface well and found just enough off the bridle after travelling strongly for Kim Tinkler. On this evidence, he looks capable of following up either on this surface or back on turf, but the fact he has never previously gained back-to-back wins cannot be ignored.
**Midshipman**, a winner on Fibresand off a mark of 85 at his best, he is dangerously well handicapped these days. After struggling to go the early pace, he kept on for pressure and found only the winner too strong. In this form he should soon end a losing run stretching back to December 2001, and would be particularly interesting at Wolverhampton where he has won three times.
**Sudra**, racing for the first time in 132 days and making his debut for new connections, was left behind by the front two, but kept on well to grab a place. He is entitled to improve on this.
**Magic Verse** showed just ordinary form in maidens, but this was a pleasing handicap debut and she would appear to be on a fair enough mark.
**Dalriath** has just a banded success to her name but, dropped half a mile in trip, this was a respectable effort.

## 3381 ST IRENAEUS' DAY H'CAP 6f (F)
4:30 (4:33) (F ) (0-55,59) 3-Y-0+ £3,087 (£882; £441) Stalls Low

Form RPR

1650 **1** **Boisdale (IRE)**[4] 3227 6-9-2 52........ LTreadwell[(7)] 4 63
(SLKeightley) *chsd ldrs: rdn over 1f out: r.o to ld post* **12/1**

3246 **2** *hd* **Indian Music**[3] 3277 7-8-6 42........ PPMathers[(7)] 1 52
(ABerry) *chsd ldrs: led over 3f out: hdd over 2f out: rallied to ld over 1f out: hdd post* **8/1**

0020 **3** *1 1/2* **Semper Paratus (USA)**[18] 2814 5-9-10 53........(b) MTebbutt 6 59
(VSmith) *sn outpcd: hdwy u.p over 1f out: ev ch ins fnl f: eased whn btn nr fin* **8/1**

0-00 **4** *3 1/2* **Shifty Night (IRE)**[23] 2675 3-8-1 42........ HayleyTurner[(5)] 9 37
(MrsCADunnett) *prom: outpcd over 4f out: rallied over 1f out: r.o* **33/1**

0520 **5** *1/2* **Lucius Verrus (USA)**[3] 3277 4-9-9 52........(v) DarrenWilliams 12 46
(DShaw) *s.s: swtchd lft sn after s: outpcd: hdwy u.p over 1f out: nt rch ldrs* **11/1**

5030 **6** *2* **Ace-Ma-Vahra**[6] 3169 6-9-3 46........(b) SWhitworth 10 34
(SRBowring) *chsd ldrs: led over 2f out: rdn and hdd over 1f out: wknd fnl f* **12/1**

-000 **7** *2* **Back In Spirit**[42] 2183 4-8-2 34 oh1........(t) FPFerris[(3)] 11 16
(BAMcmahon) *outpcd: hdwy over 3f out: nvr trbld ldrs* **33/1**

2031 **8** *1/2* **One Way Ticket**[7] 3141 4-9-9 59 7ex........(p) CJDavies[(7)] 16 39
(JMBradley) *prom tl rdn: hung lft and wknd over 1f out* **5/1**[1]

4201 **9** *nk* **Enjoy The Buzz**[9] 3084 5-9-2 45........ CCatlin 7 24
(JMBradley) *hld up: nt face kickbk over 3f out: n.d* **7/1**[3]

5065 **10** *hd* **Spy Master**[70] 1510 6-8-5 34 oh3........(tp) GDuffield 8 13
(JParkes) *w ldrs: rdn 1/2-way: wknd over 1f out* **16/1**

00-0 **11** *1/2* **Fizzy Lizzy**[27] 2556 4-8-7 36........ NPollard 5 13
(JeddO'Keeffe) *s.i.s: hld up: n.d* **25/1**

34-6 **12** *1* **Kiss The Rain**[168] 510 4-8-13 49........ StaceyRenwick[(7)] 3 23
(PABlockley) *prom over 4f* **14/1**

000 **13** *1* **Needwood Bucolic (IRE)**[12] 2975 6-8-12 41........ RWinston 15 12
(RAllan) *mid-div: rdn 1/2-way: sn wknd* **20/1**

10-0 **14** *2 1/2* **Haze Babybear**[11] 3025 4-9-8 54........ THamilton[(3)] 14 18
(RAFahey) *s.i.s: outpcd* **8/1**

00-1 **15** *3/4* **Strike Lucky**[175] 444 4-9-10 53........ SSanders 2 14
(PJMakin) *sn led: hdd over 3f out: hung lft and wknd over 1f out* **11/2**[2]

/040 **16** *14* **Bright Mist**[18] 2811 5-8-7 **36**............................................. DSweeney 13 —
(BPalling) *hld up: bhd fnl 2f* **20/1**

1m 15.89s (-1.01) **Going Correction** -0.20s/f (Stan)
**WFA** 3 from 4yo+ 7lb **16** Ran SP% **133.4**
Speed ratings: **98,97,95,91,90 87,85,84,84,83 83,81,80,77,76 57**CSF £107.62 CT £585.34 TOTE £13.00: £2.80, £1.60, £2.30, £9.40; EX 98.50 Place 6 £572.01, Place 5 £374.87.
**Owner** Ms S Gray & M F Galvin **Bred** G Ryan **Trained** Waltham-On-The-Wolds, Leics

**FOCUS**
A moderate sprint handicap but fairly sound with the principals up to their recent best.

**NOTEBOOK**
**Boisdale(IRE)** goes particularly well over this course and distance and was running over it for the first time since last successful. He will always be worthy of respect round here.
**Indian Music** has not won a handicap since April 2001, but he is running well enough in defeat and was just denied.
**Semper Paratus(USA)**, with the blinkers re-fitted on this drop back from a mile, struggled to go the early pace and may be better suited by seven furlongs - the trip he gained his last win over.
**Shifty Night(IRE)**, making her handicap debut, ran respectably over a trip that looked on the short side. She could improve for a step up in trip.
**Lucius Verrus(USA)** was dropped in from his high stall and could never really get on terms.
**One Way Ticket** could not make the most of an All-Weather mark that meant even with a 7lb penalty he was 3lb lower than when successful at Chepstow on his previous start. The surface probably did not suit and it is worth keeping in mind his trainer has a poor record round here.
**Strike Lucky** looked on a fair enough mark for his handicap debut, but disappointed. *Official explanation: jockey had no explanation for the poor form shown*

T/Plt: £312.60 to a £1 stake. Pool: £33,903.75. 79.15 winning tickets. T/Qpdt: £162.50 to a £1 stake. Pool: £2,427.70. 11.05 winning tickets. CR

# 3343 WINDSOR (R-H)

## Monday, June 28

**OFFICIAL GOING: Good (good to soft in places)**

Times suggested that the ground was riding on the quick side of good, rather than as the official going suggested.

Wind: lt bhd Weather: mostly sunny

## 3382 ROYAL MARBELLA GROUP QUALITY HOMES ABROAD FILLIES' MEDIAN AUCTION MAIDEN STKS 5f 10y

**6:40** (6:42) (E) 2-Y-O **£3,454** (£1,063; £531; £265) **Stalls** High

Form RPR

2 **1** **Roodeye**[32] 2427 2-8-11 ............................................ KFallon 4 85+
(RFJohnsonHoughton) *lw: mde all: pushed along and in command over 1f out: styd on wl* **9/4**[1]

320 **2** *1 ¾* **Castelletto**[12] 2970 2-8-11 ...................................... GGibbons 3 82+
(BAMcmahon) *pressed wnr: clr of remainder fr 2f out: rdn and no imp over 1f out: styd on* **4/1**[3]

**3** *3* **Noorain** 2-8-8 ............................................ SHitchcott(3) 8 69
(MRChannon) *w'like: chsd ldrs: rdn and outpcd 1/2-way: kpt on to take 3rd fnl f* **25/1**

**4** *½* **Magical Romance (IRE)** 2-8-11 ................................ JFortune 5 67
(BJMeehan) *neat: lw: dwlt: rcvrd to chse ldrs after 2f: disp 3rd but outpcd 2f out: one pce after* **7/1**

0 **5** *½* **Mabella (IRE)**[20] 2761 2-8-11 ................................ SDrowne 9 65
(BRMillman) *chsd ldrs: rdn 1/2-way: outpcd fr 2f out* **50/1**

0 **6** *3* **Saucepot**[16] 2884 2-8-11 ........................................ ADaly 7 55
(MDIUsher) *lw: chsd ldrs: outpcd and drvn 1/2-way: n.d after* **40/1**

3 **7** *10* **Liwa's Lake (USA)**[28] 2535 2-8-11 ........................(t) LDettori 2 20
(SaeedBinSuroor) *chsd ldng pair to 1/2-way: wknd rapidly* **11/4**[2]

23 **8** *3 ½* **Beautiful Mover (USA)**[20] 2758 2-8-11 ........................ RHills 1 7
(JWHills) *dwlt: effrt and in tch on outer after 2f: wknd rapidly 2f out* **7/1**

**9** *5* **Midnight Lace** 2-8-11 ............................................ RLMoore 6 —
(RHannon) *scope: bit bkwd: dwlt: outpcd and sn t.o* **16/1**

60.44 secs (-0.76) **Going Correction** -0.075s/f (Good) **9** Ran SP% **116.6**
Speed ratings: **103,100,95,94,93 89,73,67,59**CSF £11.53 TOTE £3.30: £1.40, £1.80, £4.80; EX 15.20.
**Owner** Mrs H Johnson Houghton **Bred** Mrs H Johnson Houghton And Mrs R F Johnson Houg **Trained** Blewbury, Oxon

■ Stewards Enquiry : G Gibbons one-day ban: failed to keep straight from stalls (Jul 9)
K Fallon one-day ban: failed to keep straight from stalls (Jul 9)

**FOCUS**
This looked a decent auction maiden on paper and it produced a very smart time indeed for a race of its type. The form looks strong.

**NOTEBOOK**
**Roodeye**, runner-up to the subsequent Queen Mary sixth on her debut, was quickly away and was never in any danger once she bagged the near-side rail in the straight. She won easily and should be capable of holding her own in better company, and the Lowther Stakes is now under consideration.
**Castelletto** finished second last in the Queen Mary last time out and found this company more suitable. She could not cope with the winner but pulled nicely clear of the third, and she will win her maiden.
**Noorain**, a half-sister to three winners in Makfool, Aldafra and Raheibb, shaped with promise. On breeding she is going to need farther than this in time, and her performance suggested as much.
**Magical Romance(IRE)**, a half-sister to two winners out of a mare who won over ten furlongs, came in for some market support on her debut. Her performance confirmed the impression given by her pedigree that she will do better when stepped up in trip.
**Mabella(IRE)**, undone by greenness on her debut, ran with more promise this time.
**Liwa's Lake(USA)**, third behind the Albany Stakes winner on her debut, had a tongue tie on for the first time and dropped out very quickly. She may have a problem. *Official explanation: jockey said filly was unsuited by today's ground - good, good to soft in places*

## 3383 COLLYER BRISTOW SOLICITORS FILLIES' H'CAP 1m 3f 135y

**7:10** (7:11) (E) (0-75,74) 3-Y-O+ **£4,121** (£1,268; £634; £317) **Stalls** Low

Form RPR

0-02 **1** **Feed The Meter (IRE)**[11] 3008 4-8-6 **52**.................... SaleemGolam(7) 8 58
(TTClement) *b. off hind: hld up: prog over 3f out: chsd ldr 2f out: chal fnl f: styd on to ld nr fin* **10/1**

-350 **2** *hd* **Kristal's Dream (IRE)**[20] 2751 3-9-7 **74**............................ LDettori 3 80
(JLDunlop) *lw: led: kicked on 3f out: hrd pressed fnl f: hdd nr fin* **5/1**[3]

-342 **3** *¾* **Blaze Of Colour**[7] 3160 3-9-3 **70**.......................................... KFallon 7 75
(SirMichaelStoute) *lw: sn chsd ldng pair: rdn over 3f out: effrt u.p over 1f out: ev ch ins fnl f: nt qckn nr fin* **9/4**[1]

0031 **4** *4* **Foxilla (IRE)**[7] 3156 3-8-3 **61** 6ex.................................... RThomas(5) 5 59
(DRCElsworth) *prom: rdn over 3f out: one pce and btn wl over 1f out* **11/4**[2]

5-00 **5** *½* **Chambray (IRE)**[28] 2517 3-8-0 **58**................................ NChalmers(5) 1 56
(AMBalding) *dwlt: in tch: rdn over 3f out: struggling over 2f out: kpt on one pce after* **12/1**

5243 **6** *5* **Vanilla Moon**[35] 2375 4-8-9 **48**.........................................(v) JFEgan 2 38
(JRJenkins) *lw: mostly chsd ldr to 2f out: wknd* **13/2**

030- **7** *dist* **Beauchamp Ribbon**[245] 5796 4-10-0 **67**.............................. VSlattery 6 —
(AJChamberlain) *v.s.i.s: in tch: rdn and wknd over 3f out: t.o* **25/1**

/00- **8** *¾* **Don't Matter**[388] 2176 4-9-6 **59**............................... JoannaBadger 4 —
(MrsSMJohnson) *dwlt: a in rr: rdn 5f out: wknd 4f out: t.o* **40/1**

2m 29.18s (-0.92) **Going Correction** -0.075s/f (Good)
**WFA** 3 from 4yo 14lb **8** Ran SP% **110.5**
Speed ratings: **100,99,99,96,96 93,—,—**CSF £55.11 CT £144.94 TOTE £11.20: £2.40, £1.60, £1.20; EX 64.10.
**Owner** P Harper **Bred** Lisieux Stud **Trained** Newmarket, Suffolk

**FOCUS**
Not a strong handicap and stamina won the day.

**NOTEBOOK**
**Feed The Meter(IRE)** stayed the trip best of all and came home well to grab the race close home. This was not a strong race but she is open to improvement.
**Kristal's Dream(IRE)**, who reportedly had a breathing problem last time, enjoyed the run of the race in front and Dettori appeared to have stolen a decisive advantage when quickening into a clear lead early in the straight, but in the end she was just outstayed over this longer trip and caught near the line. *Official explanation: jockey said filly had breathing problems*
**Blaze Of Colour** had the ground more in her favour this time and had every chance. It is early to write her off but she is becoming expensive to follow.
**Foxilla(IRE)** found the combination of a 9lb higher mark, including a 6lb penalty, and a longer trip finding her out on her return to the course where she was successful a week earlier.
**Chambray(IRE)**, as a half-sister to Hidden Meadow, Scorned, Kingsclere and Passing Glance, would be expected to be competing in better grade than this. Running off a mark of 58 on her handicap debut and stepping up from a mile for the first time, she found herself outpaced in the straight.

## 3384 WEATHERBYS BANK RATED STKS (H'CAP) 6f

**7:40** (7:40) (D) (0-85,85) 3-Y-O **£6,136** (£2,327; £1,163; £529) **Stalls** High

Form RPR

2441 **1** **Red Romeo**[8] 3122 3-9-0 **78** 3ex.......................................... KFallon 2 87
(GASwinbank) *lw: in tch: wnt to far side 1/2-way: effrt to ld gp 1f out: sn overall ldr: drvn out* **13/8**[1]

4605 **2** *1 ¼* **Vienna's Boy (IRE)**[5] 3203 3-9-4 **82**............................... DaneO'Neill 5 87
(RHannon) *lw: prom: wnt to far side 1/2-way and led gp: hdd 1f out: kpt on same pce* **12/1**

-062 **3** *nk* **Bathwick Bill (USA)**[38] 2264 3-9-3 **81**............................. GBaker 9 85
(BRMillman) *led: styd nr side: drvn 2f out: wknd and lost overall ld ins fnl f* **6/1**[3]

0346 **4** *hd* **Ask The Clerk (IRE)**[9] 3089 3-8-0 **71**.......................... RoryMoore(7) 8 74
(VSmith) *lw: in tch: styd nr side and chsd ldr of gp fr 1/2-way: drvn 2f out: kpt on ins fnl f* **8/1**

0636 **5** *nk* **Dr Synn**[6] 3180 3-8-4 **68** oh3............................................ JQuinn 6 71
(JAkehurst) *pushed along in rr: styd nr side and last of trio: hrd rdn over 2f out: styd on ins fnl f* **8/1**

32-1 **6** *2 ½* **Fictional**[16] 2877 3-9-7 **85**.............................................. GGibbons 1 80
(BAMcmahon) *lw: in tch: wnt far side 1/2-way: effrt 2f out: wknd fnl f* **4/1**[2]

2406 **7** *¾* **Trick Cyclist**[38] 2264 3-8-5 **76**.................................... TBlock(7) 4 69
(AMBalding) *chsd ldrs: wnt far side 1/2-way: rdn and no prog 2f out* **20/1**

4500 **8** *shd* **Mr Hullabalou (IRE)**[9] 3086 3-8-6 **70**............................... MHenry 3 62
(RIngram) *pushed along in rr: wnt far side 1/2-way: nvr on terms w ldrs* **50/1**

-165 **9** *1 ½* **River Treat (FR)**[12] 2981 3-9-4 **82**.................................... SDrowne 7 70
(GWragg) *pressed ldr: wnt far side 1/2-way: sn lost pl and struggling* **10/1**

1m 13.14s (-0.73) **Going Correction** -0.075s/f (Good) **9** Ran SP% **118.1**
Speed ratings: **101,99,98,98,98 94,93,93,91**CSF £24.36 CT £99.41 TOTE £2.50: £1.20, £3.00, £2.20; EX 22.10.
**Owner** J Yates **Bred** J O'Mulloy **Trained** Melsonby, N Yorks

**FOCUS**
There was a difference of opinion regarding where the best ground was in the straight and the field split into two, with the winner eventually coming from the far-side group. Events later in the evening suggest that the near side was favoured, so the first two perhaps deserve extra credit.

**NOTEBOOK**
**Red Romeo** had hacked up at Pontefract last time and only had to carry a 3lb penalty in his follow-up bid. He would have probably won whichever side he had come down in the straight, but things will be tougher in future as he is already due to go up another 7lb. *Official explanation: jockey said gelding hung left*
**Vienna's Boy(IRE)**, who has dropped 10lb in the handicap in the course of this year, appeared to see the trip out well enough on this sharp track.
**Bathwick Bill(USA)**, who won his two races at about this time last year, bounced back to form last time and narrowly won the race on the stands' side here. He looks on a fair mark.
**Ask The Clerk(IRE)**, narrowly beaten on the stands' side, is a consistent sort but evidence suggests he has nothing in hand of the Handicapper.
**Dr Synn** appeared not to see out seven furlongs last time but, back over six, once again found himself doing his best work at the finish. This was not a bad performance from 3lb out of the handicap, and he looks worth another try over seven.
**Fictional** had his chance but could not go with the leaders on the far side when it mattered. It is likely that the 6lb higher mark was his undoing.

## 3385 ROYAL MARBELLA GROUP QUALITY HOMES ABROAD PREMIER CLAIMING STKS 1m 2f 7y

**8:10** (8:10) (D) 3-Y-O+ **£6,948** (£2,138; £1,069; £534) **Stalls** Low

Form RPR

5-06 **1** **Kuster**[16] 2895 8-9-5 90.........................................(b) AHamblett(7) 4 95
(LMCumani) *lw: hld up in last: smooth prog 3f out: led 2f out: pushed clr* **5/1**[3]

-643 **2** *3* **Barking Mad (USA)**[21] 2738 6-9-10 82............................... KFallon 3 87
(MLWBell) *chsd ldr: led over 6f out: kicked on over 3f out: hrd rdn and hdd 2f out: nt qckn* **4/6**[1]

1021 **3** *3 ½* **Maniatis**[3] 3281 7-9-4 70..........................................(v) JFEgan 7 75
(AndrewReid) *b: b.hind: racd in 3rd: chsd ldr 4f out to over 2f out: one pce* **5/2**[2]

-066 **4** *12* **Cloudingswell**[21] 2737 3-7-10 57 ow2............................ NDeSouza(5) 1 47
(DLWilliams) *led to over 6f out: wknd wl over 2f out* **20/1**

2m 6.64s (-1.66) **Going Correction** -0.075s/f (Good)
**WFA** 3 from 4yo+ 12lb **4** Ran SP% **110.0**
Speed ratings: **103,100,97,88**CSF £9.18 TOTE £4.10; EX 5.40.
**Owner** Mrs Luca Cumani **Bred** London Thoroughbred Services Ltd **Trained** Newmarket, Suffolk

■ A first winner on only his second ride for Ashley Hamblett, son of former jockey Paul Hamblett.

**FOCUS**
A fair claimer. There was a reasonable pace on despite the small field.

**NOTEBOOK**
**Kuster** was best in at the weights, but he is ideally suited by a mile and a half these days and it was to his advantage that they went a decent gallop in this four-runner affair. Proven to go well for an inexperienced rider, he cruised through to lead and won well.
**Barking Mad(USA)** appeared to hold a strong chance in this grade, but he was taken on for the lead in the early stages and, although he kicked clear entering the straight, he could never shake off the attentions of the winner.
**Maniatis**, who is much happier over a mile and a half and prefers the All-Weather to grass, was taking on better opposition than when winning a claimer on turf in April.
**Cloudingswell**, whose rider put up 2lb overweight, had a bit to find at these weights. She dropped out once the tap was turned entering the straight.

## 3386 SLOUGH ESTATES H'CAP — 1m 67y
8:40 (8:42) (E) (0-70,69) 3-Y-0+ £5,447 (£1,676; £838; £419) Stalls High

Form | | | | RPR
000- **1** **Firewire**[273] 5279 6-9-3 **59** .......... SSanders 12 71
(MissBSanders) *lw: off the pce towards rr: rdn 1/2-way: prog 2f out: styd on wl to ld last 75yds* **8/1**
0600 **2** ¾ **El Chaparral (IRE)**[30] 2483 4-9-6 **62** .......... DaneO'Neill 11 73
(DKIvory) *stdd s: hld up in last and wl bhd: rapid prog over 2f out : styd on strly fnl f: too much to do* **25/1**
2022 **3** ¾ **Captain Marryat**[7] 3155 3-8-7 **59** .......... KFallon 10 68
(PWHarris) *lw: off the pce in midfield: rdn wl over 3f out: effrt u.p 2f out: nt qckn over 1f out: kpt on* **2/1**[1]
5045 **4** hd **Azreme**[11] 3025 4-9-6 **69** .......... MHoward(7) 8 78
(DKIvory) *lw: hld up in midfield and off the pce: prog over 3f out: led over 1f out : wknd and hdd last 75yds* **9/1**
0-00 **5** nk **Esperance (IRE)**[55] 1856 4-8-3 **45** .......... JQuinn 1 53
(JAkehurst) *chsd ldr and clr of rest: styd alone on nr side in st: wl on terms over 1f out: no ex ins fnl f* **40/1**
5010 **6** 1½ **Classic Vision**[8] 3117 4-8-12 **54** .......... (b) RHills 5 58
(WJHaggas) *hld up wl in rr: prog over 2f out: rdn and kpt on fr over 1f out: no ch* **15/2**[3]
3300 **7** 2 **Mythical Charm**[26] 2573 5-8-9 **51** .......... ADaly 7 51
(JJBridger) *chsd clr ldng pair over 5f out: clsd to ld over 2f out: hdd & wknd over 1f out* **20/1**
33-0 **8** 3½ **Florian**[16] 2883 6-9-4 **63** .......... (p) RMiles(3) 9 55
(TGMills) *led and spreadeagled field: hdd & wknd over 2f out* **10/1**
0206 **9** nk **Smoothly Does It**[14] 2949 3-9-0 **66** .......... EAhern 4 57
(MrsAJBowlby) *prom in chsng pack: rdn and wknd over 2f out* **13/2**[2]
-000 **10** 1¼ **One Alone**[2] 3301 3-7-7 **50** oh5 .......... DFox(5) 6 38
(Jean-ReneAuvray) *in tch in chsng gp: rdn over 4f out: steadily wknd* **66/1**
0016 **11** ½ **My Maite (IRE)**[22] 2705 5-8-5 **47** .......... (vt) NDay 3 34
(RIngram) *hld up in rr: a wl off the pce: bhd fnl 2f* **9/1**
0404 **12** 1½ **Coppington Flyer (IRE)**[96] 1102 4-8-3 **45** .......... CCatlin 14 29
(BWDuke) *racd in midfield: effrt and sme prog over 3f out: wknd over 2f out* **12/1**
0120 **13** 5 **Beltane**[77] 1373 6-8-4 **46** .......... JFEgan 13 18
(WDeBest-Turner) *bit bkwd: chsd clr ldng pair to over 5f out: sn u.p and btn* **25/1**
000- **14** 25 **Lady West**[99] 4005 4-7-6 **41** oh2 ow1 .......... LucyRussell(7) 2 —
(DrJRJNaylor) *s.s: a bhd: t.o* **66/1**

1m 43.91s (-1.69) **Going Correction** -0.075s/f (Good)
**WFA** 3 from 4yo+ 10lb **14 Ran SP% 124.2**
Speed ratings: **105,104,103,103,103 101,99,96,95,94 93,92,87,62**CSF £206.01 CT £495.25 TOTE £11.20: £3.00, £8.40, £1.80; EX 210.60.
**Owner** Miss Jennie Wisher **Bred** Miss Jennie Wisher **Trained** Epsom, Surrey

**FOCUS**
A competitive enough race and the form is sound. All but one headed towards the far side. The only one to stay stands' side, a 40-1 chance, finished fifth.

**NOTEBOOK**
**Firewire**, beaten narrowly at this track when sent off odds-on for a handicap off this mark last summer, shrugged off a 273-day absence to win on his seasonal reappearance. This was not a great heat but hopefully he can build on this.
**El Chaparral(IRE)** found the step up to a mile bringing about the improvement looked for. Held up to get the trip, in the event his rider probably had him too far out of his ground. At least this opens up new opportunities.
**Captain Marryat** had every chance but could only keep on at the one pace. He is becoming disappointing.
**Azreme**, best suited by some cut in the ground, has struggled to see this trip out in the past, and once again it looked beyond him.
**Esperance(IRE)**, who is still a maiden, came home on his own next to the stands'-side rail. It did not appear to be a disadvantage to him that he raced on the opposite side of the track to the rest of the field.
**Classic Vision** won in first-time blinkers but they do not appear to be having the same effect any longer.
**Florian** *Official explanation: jockey said gelding was unsuited by the slow ground*
**Beltane** *Official explanation: jockey said gelding was never travelling*

## 3387 AT THE RACES: DEDICATED TO RACING CLASSIFIED STKS — 1m 2f 7y
9:10 (9:11) (E) 3-Y-0+ £3,620 (£1,114; £557; £278) Stalls Low

Form | | | | RPR
-0U0 **1** **Hatch A Plan (IRE)**[21] 2732 3-8-6 62 .......... JQuinn 2 71
(RMBeckett) *hld up in last: styd alone nr side in st: on terms 3f out: overall ldr and clr fnl f: easily* **50/1**
0051 **2** 3 **Miss Pebbles (IRE)**[2] 3327 4-9-7 65 .......... (v) NPollard 4 68
(BRJohnson) *t.k.h: hld up in rr: gd prog 2f out: led gp ent fnl f: no ch w wnr* **9/4**[1]
10/2 **3** 1¼ **Cosi Fan Tutte**[21] 2740 6-9-1 65 .......... (vt) RMiles(3) 1 63
(MCPipe) *lw: prom: led main gp over 3f out tl ent fnl f: one pce* **10/1**
425- **4** nk **Malak Al Moulouk (USA)**[264] 5455 4-9-4 65 .......... SSanders 7 62
(JMPEustace) *lw: chsd ldrs: effrt over 2f out: chal over 1f out: nt qckn fnl f* **50/1**
6035 **5** 1½ **Mustang Ali (IRE)**[17] 2840 3-8-9 68 .......... JFEgan 11 63
(SKirk) *racd in midfield: effrt and prog 2f out: one pce fnl f* **12/1**
-032 **6** 1½ **Kirkham Abbey**[14] 2930 4-9-4 65 .......... (v) JFortune 12 57
(MAJarvis) *hld up: effrt over 2f out: nt qckn and no prog fnl f* **7/2**[2]
0010 **7** ¾ **Planters Punch (IRE)**[7] 3160 3-8-10 69 .......... (v) KFallon 5 59
(RHannon) *hld up in rr: rdn and effrt over 2f out: no imp on ldrs* **5/1**[3]
55-5 **8** 2 **Secluded**[21] 2738 4-9-8 69 .......... LDettori 6 55
(ACStewart) *lw: mde most to over 3f out: wknd 2f out* **5/1**[3]
361- **9** 2 **Almond Willow (IRE)**[224] 6012 3-8-6 68 .......... EAhern 10 48
(JNoseda) *lw: racd in midfield: flashing tail thrght r: rdn over 2f out: hanging lft and nt run on over 1f out* **12/1**
-000 **10** nk **Band**[11] 3023 4-9-4 62 .......... GGibbons 3 47
(BAMcmahon) *t.k.h: chsd ldrs tl wknd 2f out* **50/1**
000 **11** 1½ **Environment Audit**[58] 1768 5-9-4 65 .......... (v) VSlattery 8 44
(JRJenkins) *swtg: w ldr: ev ch 3f out: wknd over 2f out* **33/1**
0-20 **12** 8 **Competitor**[10] 3048 3-8-11 70 .......... CCatlin 9 34
(JAkehurst) *plld hrd: hld up in rr: rdn and wknd 4f out: sn bhd* **20/1**

2m 9.98s (1.68) **Going Correction** -0.075s/f (Good)
**WFA** 3 from 4yo+ 12lb **12 Ran SP% 124.4**
Speed ratings: **90,87,86,86,85 83,83,81,80,79 78,72**CSF £165.04 TOTE £87.90: £14.60, £2.10, £2.40; EX 622.10 Place 6 £116.08, Place 5 £62.09.
**Owner** T G S Sijpesteijn And Deal **Bred** Camogue Stud Ltd **Trained** Lambourn, Berks

**FOCUS**
A very slow winning time for the grade, 3.34 seconds slower than the claimer. There had looked little bias between either side throughout the evening and on this occasion the sole stands'-side runner came out well on top.

**NOTEBOOK**
**Hatch A Plan(IRE)** was the only one to stay next to the stands'-side rail in the straight. He won easily in the end and, while the evening's card as a whole suggested there was little between the two sides, the ease of his victory came as something as a surprise as he had shown little prior to this. We shall have to wait to see if there was an element of fluke about this victory. *Official explanation: trainer said, regarding the improved form shown, gelding had boiled over before the start last time out*
**Miss Pebbles(IRE)** was attempting to supplement her victory from two days previously. She won the race on her side well enough but found the stands'-side runner just too strong. She did confirm that she is holding her form well, though.
**Cosi Fan Tutte**, whose second here three weeks earlier came in a claimer, looked suited by the drop back in trip and ran a solid race.
**Malak Al Moulouk(USA)**, making his handicap debut, ran with promise and should be capable of stepping up on this form as this was his first outing for 264 days.
**Mustang Ali(IRE)** is becoming disappointing.
**Kirkham Abbey** has been performing consistently this term but this was a rare below-par effort.
T/Plt: £102.90 to a £1 stake. Pool: £57,373.65. 406.95 winning tickets. T/Qpdt: £38.00 to a £1 stake. Pool: £3,504.40. 68.10 winning tickets. JN

# 3258 CHANTILLY (R-H)
Monday, June 28

**OFFICIAL GOING: Good**

## 3388a PRIX DU BOIS (GROUP 3) — 5f
1:50 (1:50) 2-Y-O £25,704 (£10,282; £7,711; £5,141)

| | | | RPR
**1** **Divine Proportions (USA)**[33] 2-8-8 .......... C-PLemaire 2 111+
(PBary, France) *trckd ldrs, 3rd half-way, rdn 1 1/2f out, qcknd to ld appr fnl f, went clr ins last, easily* **3**
**2** 4 **Great Blood (FR)**[42] 2-8-8 .......... GaryStevens 1 97
(XThomas-Demeaulte, France) *led, jnd half-way, pushed along to tk clr ld appr 2f out, hdd appr fnl f, ran on but no ch with wnr* **1**
**3** 2½ **Salut Thomas (FR)**[18] 2828 2-8-11 .......... (b) CSoumillon 6 91
(RobertCollet, France) *close up in centre, joined leader half-way, pushed along 2f out, kept on at one pace, comfortably held 3rd* **2**
**4** nk **Lady Weasley (FR)**[18] 2828 2-8-8 .......... FSpanu 4 87
(MlleVDissaux, France) *in touch, 5th half-way, pushed along and stayed on from over 1f out to take 4th final strides*
**5** snk **Indiannie Star**[12] 2970 2-8-8 .......... TEDurcan 3 86
(MRChannon) *in touch, 4th half-way, pushed along 2f out, ran on at one pace til lost 4th final strides*
**6** 1½ **Ralpha (FR)** 2-8-8 .......... TJarnet 5 81
(JRossi, France) *in touch til outpaced before half-way*
**7** 1½ **Antioche (FR)**[59] 2-8-11 .......... OPeslier 7 79
(CLaffon-Parias, France) *outpaced throughout*

58.70 secs **7 Ran SP% 122.0**
Speed ratings: .
**Owner** Niarchos Family **Bred** Flaxman Holding Ltd **Trained** France

**NOTEBOOK**
**Divine Proportions(USA)** stamped herself the best juvenile filly seen out in France so far this season with an impressive fast-time clear-cut success in this Group Three. She is now unbeaten in two races and the Prix Robert Papin, followed by the Morny are next on the agenda.
**Great Blood(FR)** made the running and ran with credit but she could not hold a candle to the winner.
**Indiannie Star**, found out in graded company in England, was out of her depth here and in the circumstances fifth place was a good result.

# 3170 BRIGHTON (L-H)
Tuesday, June 29

**OFFICIAL GOING: Firm (good to firm in places)**
In view of the official going, race times were surprisingly slow. A combination of small fields and some slowly run races may have something to do with it.
Wind: Moderate across Weather: Fair

## 3390 JOHN CONNOR PRESS ASSOCIATES CLAIMING STKS — 5f 213y
2:30 (2:30) (F) 2-Y-O £2,905 (£830; £415) Stalls Low

Form | | | | RPR
0411 **1** **Princely Vale (IRE)**[10] 3100 2-8-5 .......... (p) CHaddon(7) 3 60
(WGMTurner) *chsd ldrs: drvn to ld wl over 1f out: sn clr* **7/4**[2]
5012 **2** 4 **Ronnies Lad**[19] 2799 2-8-8 .......... (p) J-PGuillambert(3) 1 47
(AndrewReid) *led 1f: outpcd and hung rt 2f out: kpt on fnl f: tk 2nd on line* **13/8**[1]
6454 **3** hd **General Nuisance (IRE)**[19] 2819 2-8-2 ow1 .......... (p) DerekNolan(7) 4 44
(JSMoore) *sn in rr: drvn along 1/2-way: hdwy 2f out: chsd wnr 1f out: styd on same pce: lost 2nd on line* **8/1**
3 **4** shd **Witty Girl**[8] 3140 2-8-6 .......... RThomas(5) 5 46
(CADwyer) *dwlt: in rr: c alone towards centre st: effrt over 2f out: styd on fnl f: nt pce to chal* **9/2**[3]
060 **5** 4 **Ahaz**[10] 3083 2-8-3 .......... (b[1]) TPQueally(3) 2 29
(IAWood) *chsd ldr: led after 1f and sn 4l clr: hdd wl over 1f out: sn wknd* **20/1**

1m 12.61s (2.51) **Going Correction** +0.275s/f (Good) **5 Ran SP% 108.5**
Speed ratings: **94,88,88,88,82** CSF £4.82 TOTE £2.90: £1.20, £1.70; EX 4.50.The winner was subject to a friendly bid. Witty Girl was claimed by Mark Polglase for £15,000.
**Owner** Vale Racing **Bred** Brian Killeen **Trained** Sigwells, Somerset

**FOCUS**
A poor claimer, but at least the pace was sound. Only one tried to come over to the stands' side.

**NOTEBOOK**
**Princely Vale(IRE)**, stepping back a furlong for his hat-trick bid, seemed to appreciate the strong gallop and once he hit the front the race was over. He is another example of some fine placing by his trainer, but he may not be in this country for very much longer.
**Ronnies Lad**, a close second behind the winner's stable companion Goldhill Prince over course and distance last time out, was disappointing as he held every chance but was made to look very pedestrian by the winner.
**General Nuisance(IRE)**, well beaten in a seller last time, may need easier ground but looks moderate in any case.
**Witty Girl** missed the break again and edged across to the stands' side turning for home. She could make no impression though, and the fact that she moved back to join the others in the latter stages suggests the earlier manoeuvre was not intentional.
**Ahaz** ran too freely in the first-time blinkers and paid the penalty.

## 3391 SALTWELL SIGNS (S) STKS — 7f 214y
**3:00** (3:00) (G ) 3-Y-O — **£2,562** (£732; £366) **Stalls** Low

Form — RPR
0302 **1** **Delcienne**[6] 3193 3-8-9 42 ... AMcCarthy 4 — 53
(GGMargarson) *hld up in rr: hdwy on outside over 2f out: led 1f out: pushed clr: readily* **4/1**[1]
-060 **2** 4 **Blaise Wood (USA)**[15] 2931 3-9-0 62 ... (p) RLMoore 7 — 49
(GLMoore) *hld up towards rr: hdwy over 2f out: led over 1f out: sn hdd and nt pce of wnr* **5/1**[2]
-000 **3** 1 1/2 **Magico**[12] 3024 3-8-7 48 ... (b[1]) DerekNolan(7) 9 — 46
(PBurgoyne) *stdd s: t.k.h: chsd ldrs: led over 2f out: hung lft and hdd over 1f out: no ex* **25/1**
0000 **4** 1 1/4 **Johnny Alljays (IRE)**[6] 3193 3-9-0 38 ... (p) JDSmith 1 — 43
(JSMoore) *sn led: hrd rdn and hdd over 2f out: no ex over 1f out* **33/1**
-014 **5** 1 1/2 **Fiddles Music**[6] 3190 3-9-0 45 ... TEDurcan 5 — 39
(MRChannon) *prom: rdn over 2f out: sn outpcd* **11/2**[3]
00- **6** 5 **Monash Girl (IRE)**[260] 5549 3-8-4 ... NChalmers(5) 6 — 23
(BRJohnson) *chsd ldrs 6f* **33/1**
0-60 **7** 2 1/2 **Roaming Vagabond (IRE)**[36] 2375 3-9-0 52 ... DHolland 2 — 22
(NACallaghan) *stmbld and bmpd s: sn bhd: rdn and lost tch 1/2-way* **15/2**
0000 **8** 2 **Mac The Knife (IRE)**[21] 2762 3-9-0 60 ... PDobbs 3 — 17
(RHannon) *in tch over 5f* **5/1**[2]
-500 **9** 2 1/2 **Sharplaw Destiny (IRE)**[21] 2766 3-8-6 47 ... TPQueally(3) 8 — 7
(WJHaggas) *plld hrd: prom over 5f* **4/1**[1]

1m 37.36s (2.36) **Going Correction** +0.275s/f (Good) **9** Ran SP% **110.2**
Speed ratings: **99,95,93,92,90 85,83,81,78**CSF £22.05 TOTE £5.00: £1.40, £1.70, £4.20; EX 26.30.The winner was bought in for 8,800 guineas. Fiddles Music was claimed by Sheena West for £6,000.
**Owner** The Del Boys **Bred** Castlemans Farms **Trained** Newmarket, Suffolk
■ Stewards Enquiry : Derek Nolan caution: careless riding

**FOCUS**
An poor seller but a fair winning time for the grade and solid enough form; the winner looks better than a plater.

**NOTEBOOK**
**Delcienne** had 13lb to find with the runner-up on adjusted official ratings, but she was possibly unlucky not to win when dropped into a seller at Bath last week and on this occasion her challenge was timed to perfection. Connections went to 8,800gns to keep her, so they must believe she is capable of more.
**Blaise Wood(USA)**, dropped into a seller for the first time and best in on official ratings, ran a good deal better than he did here last time but was still made to look very ordinary by the winner.
**Magico** appeared to run well, but he has already twice been well beaten at this level and his proximity does little for the form of the race outside the winner.
**Johnny Alljays(IRE)**, who finished well behind the winner at Bath last week, did so again and is still to prove he stays this trip.
**Fiddles Music** was done no favours by the drop in trip and failed to pick up.
**Sharplaw Destiny(IRE)**, dropped into a seller for the first time, did her chances little good by pulling too hard early but was still very disappointing. *Official explanation: reported that the filly had run too freely early on.*

## 3392 BRASSERIE ITALIAN RESTAURANT AT THE MARINA MAIDEN FILLIES' STKS — 1m 1f 209y
**3:30** (3:30) (D ) 3-Y-O — **£3,454** (£1,063; £531; £265) **Stalls** High

Form — RPR
2-55 **1** **Cherubim (JPN)**[8] 3142 3-8-8 78 ... TPQueally(3) 3 — 76
(DRLoder) *disp ld after 1f tl led 5f out: hdd over 2f out: led over 1f out: drvn out* **7/2**[2]
06 **2** 1 1/2 **Sea Of Gold**[43] 2182 3-8-11 ... RLMoore 5 — 73
(HJCyzer) *hdwy over 3f out: slt ld over 2f out tl over 1f out: kpt on same pce* **10/3**[1]
64 **3** 1 1/2 **Miss Monica (IRE)**[40] 2243 3-8-11 ... WRyan 6 — 70
(HRACecil) *hld up in rr: effrt over 2f out: edgd lft and styd on fr over 1f out: nt rch ldrs* **10/3**[1]
6-20 **4** 1 1/4 **Al Shuua**[22] 2732 3-8-11 79 ... TEDurcan 1 — 68
(CEBrittain) *led 1f: one pce fnl 2f* **7/2**[2]
06- **5** 14 **Kilminchy Lady (IRE)**[192] 6219 3-8-8 ... RMiles(3) 4 — 41
(WRMuir) *t.k.h: disp ld after 1f tl 5f out: wknd over 2f out* **20/1**
00 **6** 19 **Miss Shangri La**[15] 2950 3-8-11 ... DHolland 2 — 5
(GWragg) *chsd ldrs 7f: sn bhd* **7/1**[3]

2m 4.23s (1.69) **Going Correction** +0.275s/f (Good) **6** Ran SP% **107.9**
Speed ratings: **104,102,101,100,89 74**CSF £14.19 TOTE £5.00: £3.50, £2.00; EX 15.50.
**Owner** Sheikh Mohammed **Bred** Northern Farm **Trained** Newmarket, Suffolk

**FOCUS**
A fair maiden and a decent winning time for the grade when compared to other races on the day.

**NOTEBOOK**
**Cherubim(JPN)** appreciated the extra two furlongs and showed real gameness to rally after losing the lead. This is her ground and she should be able to hold her own in handicap company.
**Sea Of Gold** ran as though not staying judging by the way she did not get home after taking the lead, but she is bred to get the trip in which case the track and fast ground may be more valid excuses. She now qualifies for handicaps.
**Miss Monica(IRE)** made laboured late progress without being able to get on terms with the front pair, and may need an even greater stamina test.
**Al Shuua** disappointed for a second time after a promising return. Her handicap mark does not look generous so she may be difficult to place from now on.
**Miss Shangri La** *Official explanation: trainer said filly did not come down the hill well lost, her action and did not handle the firm ground*

## 3393 JOHN BLOOR MEMORIAL H'CAP FOR THE OPERATIC SOCIETY CHALLENGE CUP — 1m 3f 196y
**4:00** (4:01) (E ) (0-70,60) 3-Y-O+ — **£3,367** (£1,036; £518; £259) **Stalls** High

Form — RPR
0-02 **1** **Absinther**[4] 3263 7-9-1 45 ... GBaker 6 — 53
(MRBosley) *dwlt: hld up in rr: hdwy 1/2-way: rdn over 2f out: led 1f out: pushed out* **13/2**
2461 **2** 1 1/2 **Compton Eclaire (IRE)**[9] 3128 4-9-13 60 6ex ... (v) TPQueally(3) 7 — 66
(GAButler) *hld up in 5th: dropped to rr over 4f out: effrt over 2f out: styd on u.p to take 2nd nr fin* **7/2**[2]
6051 **3** 1 **Salut Saint Cloud**[11] 3056 3-8-8 52 ... SWhitworth 1 — 56
(GLMoore) *chsd ldrs: hrd rdn 2f out: kpt on same pce: sddle slipped* **3/1**[1]
6-00 **4** 2 1/2 **North Point (IRE)**[33] 2429 6-9-1 48 ... (b) RMiles(3) 5 — 48
(RCurtis) *led: sn 5l clr: hdd over 2f out: no ex fnl f* **14/1**
3010 **5** hd **Private Benjamin**[11] 3046 4-9-6 50 ... PDoe 4 — 50
(JamiePoulton) *chsd ldrs: sltly outpcd 4f out: styng on whn edgd lft over 1f out: no ex fnl f* **6/1**
1223 **6** 3/4 **Banningham Blaze**[9] 3128 4-9-6 50 ... DHolland 2 — 49
(AWCarroll) *chsd clr ldr: led over 2f out tl 1f out: wknd fnl f* **4/1**[3]
0250 **7** shd **Summer Cherry (USA)**[4] 3263 7-9-1 45 ... (t) IMongan 3 — 44
(JamiePoulton) *dwlt: t.k.h in rr: hdwy 7f out: rdn over 2f out: sn outpcd* **9/1**

2m 35.54s (3.44) **Going Correction** +0.275s/f (Good)
**WFA** 3 from 4yo+ 14lb **7** Ran SP% **111.5**
Speed ratings: **99,98,97,95,95 95,94**CSF £27.89 TOTE £8.10: £2.60, £2.30; EX 34.70.
**Owner** Mrs Jean M O'Connor **Bred** Ridgebarn Farm **Trained** Kingston Lisle, Oxon

**FOCUS**
A moderate pace for much of the way and all seven runners were within a couple of lengths at the furlong pole. The winning time was modest for the grade as a result and the form is ordinary.

**NOTEBOOK**
**Absinther**, who repeatedly shows his best form in the summer, confirmed the promise of his Folkestone effort in a race that ultimately became a two-furlong sprint. He should continue to go well, but one note of caution is that he has only managed to win one race every season since 2000.
**Compton Eclaire(IRE)**, under a 6lb penalty for her Warwick victory, stays further than this so she would not have been suited by the way the race was run and therefore performed with credit.
**Salut Saint Cloud**, claimed after winning at Redcar last time, was making his debut for the yard and attempting his longest trip to date. The slow pace should arguably have helped him in that respect, and he had every chance but was not good enough; although it is difficult to know how much effect a slipping saddle would have had. *Official explanation: jockey said saddle slipped*
**North Point(IRE)** did not get home despite setting only a modest pace and seems to have lost his way under both codes for the time being.
**Private Benjamin** would have preferred a proper end-to-end gallop.
**Banningham Blaze** has just looked held since winning a seller over course and distance last month.
**Summer Cherry(USA)** was probably the most inconvenienced by the moderate pace and he took too keen a hold as a result.

## 3394 UNIVERSITY OF SUSSEX NATALIE NAYLOR MEMORIAL STKS (H'CAP) — 1m 1f 209y
**4:30** (4:30) (E ) (0-75,70) 3-Y-O — **£3,396** (£1,045; £522; £261) **Stalls** High

Form — RPR
5522 **1** **Dami (USA)**[8] 3139 3-9-7 70 ... (p) DHolland 1 — 76
(CEBrittain) *pressed ldr: led over 1f out: rdn out* **6/4**[1]
0050 **2** 1 1/2 **Russalka**[57] 1843 3-7-10 52 ... MHalford(7) 2 — 55
(JulianPoulton) *hld up in rr: rdn over 2f out: hdwy on rail over 1f out: n.m.r: styd on to take 2nd ins fnl f* **14/1**
3041 **3** shd **Charlie Tango (IRE)**[10] 3102 3-9-1 67 ... SHitchcott(3) 4 — 70
(MRChannon) *t.k.h: trckd ldrs: rdn over 2f out: styd on fnl f* **11/4**[2]
0002 **4** 1/2 **Swift Sailing (USA)**[8] 3152 3-9-6 69 ... TEDurcan 6 — 71
(BWHills) *unruly in stalls: led: hrd rdn and hdd over 1f out: no ex ins fnl f* **7/2**[3]
6-00 **5** nk **Duke's View (IRE)**[8] 3160 3-9-3 66 ... (b[1]) DaneO'Neill 5 — 67?
(MrsAJPerrett) *chsd ldrs on outside: ev ch whn hung lft over 1f out: hrd rdn: no ex* **7/1**

2m 6.24s (3.70) **Going Correction** +0.275s/f (Good) **5** Ran SP% **108.1**
Speed ratings: **96,94,94,94,94**CSF £20.20 TOTE £2.30: £1.10, £4.10; EX 11.40.
**Owner** Saeed Manana **Bred** Newgate Stud Farm Inc **Trained** Newmarket, Suffolk

**FOCUS**
A moderate pace resulting in a modest winning time and a blanket could have covered the five runners a furlong from home. The form appears sound enough despite that.

**NOTEBOOK**
**Dami(USA)** ◆ needed all her rider's assistance to get her home in front, but she is a filly that has tended to run in snatches in the past so she may have won despite the way the race was run, not because of it. She may appreciate going back up in trip.
**Russalka**, slipping down the handicap, ran her best race so far on turf but, because of the way the race was run, the form may not be totally reliable.
**Charlie Tango(IRE)**, up 5lb for his Redcar win, took a keen hold in a slowly-run race and as a result was found wanting for pace where it mattered.
**Swift Sailing(USA)** was able to dictate at a modest pace, but he had managed to get himself awash with sweat and had little in reserve at the business end.
**Duke's View(IRE)**, blinkered for the first time, has not shown a great deal in five previous starts and did not look to fancy it when put under maximum pressure inside the last furlong.

## 3395 TOTESPORT.COM RATED STKS (H'CAP) — 5f 59y
**5:00** (5:00) (D ) (0-80,77) 3-Y-O+ — **£5,128** (£1,819; £909; £413) **Stalls** Low

Form — RPR
0413 **1** **Parkside Pursuit**[6] 3195 6-9-3 73 3ex ... RLMoore 2 — 83
(JMBradley) *cl up: led jst ins fnl f: drvn out* **7/4**[1]
-065 **2** 1 **Compton Banker (IRE)**[9] 3125 7-8-11 70 ... TPQueally(3) 3 — 76
(GAButler) *dwlt: hld up in tch: effrt ins fnl 2f: styd on to take 2nd ins fnl f: a hld* **5/1**[3]
0113 **3** 1/2 **Hard To Catch (IRE)**[9] 3125 6-9-2 77 ... (b) MSavage(5) 5 — 81
(DKIvory) *cl up: pressed ldr after 2f: slt ld over 1f out tl jst ins fnl f: nt qckn* **7/4**[1]
0000 **4** 1 1/4 **Coranglais**[3] 3298 4-8-5 61 ... (b) CCatlin 1 — 60
(JMBradley) *led tl over 1f out: no ex ins fnl f* **4/1**[2]

63.29 secs (1.02) **Going Correction** +0.275s/f (Good) **4** Ran SP% **109.4**
Speed ratings: **102,100,99,97**CSF £10.29 TOTE £2.90; EX 8.00 Place 6 £55.06, Place 5 £46.48.
**Owner** J M Bradley **Bred** J K Keegan **Trained** Sedbury, Gloucs

**FOCUS**
The winning time was ordinary though there were only four runners and not the strongest of form.

**NOTEBOOK**
**Parkside Pursuit** made up for his luckless run at Bath, though even on this occasion he did not have a great deal of room to play with. Fortunately enough of a gap appeared and he made full use of it. This was the highest mark he has ever won off but, as with many of his stablemates, it is hard to say how much more there is to come from him.
**Compton Banker(IRE)** ◆ did not have the race run to suit, so this was another encouraging effort, especially as he probably needs further than this now. He still looks favourably handicapped.
**Hard To Catch(IRE)** likes this track and did his best, but he looks to be on a very stiff mark now.
**Coranglais**, dropping down the handicap, set the pace with the blinkers back on but proved a sitting duck for his stable companion.
T/Plt: £95.10 to a £1 stake. Pool: £95.10 - 280.90 winning tickets. T/Qpdt: £38.50 to a £1 stake. Pool: £2,369.30 - 45.50 winning tickets. LM



The Form Book, Raceform Ltd, Compton, RG20 6NL

## [3221] HAMILTON (R-H)

Tuesday, June 29

**OFFICIAL GOING: Good to soft (good in places)**

### 3396 WEATHERBYS INSURANCE SERVICES H'CAP — 1m 4f 17y

2:20 (2:20) (E) (0-75,81) 3-Y-O — £3,883 (£1,195; £597; £298) Stalls High

| Form | | | | RPR |
|---|---|---|---|---|
| -342 | 1 | | **Dunlea Dancer**[11] 3042 3-8-3 **57** ... JFanning 3 <br> (MJohnston) *mde all: rdn clr 2f out: styd on wl* **11/4**[2] | 70 |
| 2255 | 2 | 6 | **Gold Card**[27] 2584 3-8-7 **61** ... (v[1]) RWinston 5 <br> (JRWeymes) *hld up: hdwy 4f out: rdn along to chse wnr over 2f out: sn drvn and kpt on: no ch w wnr* **6/1**[3] | 65 |
| -612 | 3 | 3 | **Habitual Dancer**[62] 1714 3-8-5 **59** ... GDuffield 4 <br> (JeddO'Keeffe) *trckd wnr: pushed along 5f out: rdn and outpcd 3f out: styd on u.p fnl f* **9/4**[1] | 59 |
| 2501 | 4 | ¾ | **Bill Bennett (FR)**[8] 3160 3-9-13 **81** 6ex ... OUrbina 2 <br> (JJay) *hld up: hdwy 4f out: rdn 2f out: sn btn* **9/4**[1] | 79 |
| 0044 | 5 | 6 | **Compassion (IRE)**[5] 3222 3-7-13 **53** oh5 ow1 ... RFfrench 6 <br> (MissLAPerratt) *chsd ldrs: rdn along over 3f out: sn btn* **20/1** | 42 |

2m 41.71s (2.51) **Going Correction** +0.175s/f (Good) **5** Ran SP% **107.3**
Speed ratings: **98,94,92,91,87**CSF £17.30 TOTE £3.20: £1.50, £5.20; EX 16.40.
**Owner** K Towey **Bred** Cheveley Park Stud Ltd **Trained** Middleham Moor, N Yorks

**FOCUS**
A moderate handicap run at a stop-start gallop, and the form looks modest but sound.

**NOTEBOOK**
**Dunlea Dancer** enjoyed being allowed to dictate the pace from the start and decisively made all under a fine ride. He has improved for being stepped up in trip recently and looks one to follow now he has hit form, as he is at the right end of the handicap.
**Gold Card**, in the first-time visor, tried in vain to get to the winner, but finished a clear second and this rates as his best effort yet in a handicap.
**Habitual Dancer** looked unsuited by the stop-start gallop and is capable of better, but he still proved slightly disappointing on this occasion.
**Bill Bennett(FR)** never looked a serious threat from off the pace and his penalty for winning last time proved his undoing. He could be hard to place now.

### 3397 HAMILTON PARK INVESTORS IN PEOPLE CLASSIFIED STKS — 1m 65y

2:50 (2:50) (E) 3-Y-O+ — £3,737 (£1,150; £575; £287) Stalls High

| Form | | | | RPR |
|---|---|---|---|---|
| -002 | 1 | | **Les Arcs (USA)**[7] 3166 4-9-3 70 ... KFallon 3 <br> (RCGuest) *hld up: pushed along 5f out: swtchd outside and gd hdwy 3f out: led wl over 1f out: pushed clr and styd on* **15/8**[1] | 82 |
| 1-31 | 2 | 1½ | **Munaawashat (IRE)**[13] 2973 3-8-5 71 ... WSupple 5 <br> (MJohnston) *led: rdn along 3f out: hdd wl over 1f out: kpt on same pce u.p* **11/4**[2] | 77 |
| 0004 | 3 | 4 | **Riska King**[12] 3012 4-9-0 66 ... THamilton(3) 2 <br> (RAFahey) *s.i.s and bhd: gd hdwy on outer 4f out: chsd ldr 3f out: sn rdn and kpt on same pce fnl 2f* **25/1** | 71 |
| 0140 | 4 | 3 | **Jordans Elect**[16] 2905 4-9-3 73 ... TEaves(3) 4 <br> (ISemple) *trckd ldng pair: rdn along over 3f out: sn one pce* **4/1**[3] | 67 |
| 046 | 5 | 1¼ | **J R Stevenson (USA)**[46] 2084 8-8-9 75 ... SWKelly 6 <br> (MWigham) *trckd ldrs: pushed along whn hmpd wl over 2f out and no ch after* **5/1** | 67 |
| -255 | 6 | 3 | **Catalini**[23] 2704 3-8-10 73 ... ACulhane 1 <br> (MRChannon) *cl up: rdn along 3f out: sn wknd* **10/1** | 58 |

1m 49.12s (-0.18) **Going Correction** +0.175s/f (Good)
**WFA** 3 from 4yo+ 10lb **6** Ran SP% **111.1**
Speed ratings: **107,105,101,98,97 94**CSF £7.08 TOTE £3.10: £1.70, £1.80; EX 7.10.
**Owner** Willie McKay **Bred** Elk Manor Farm **Trained** Brancepeth, Co Durham

**FOCUS**
Fair form, a creditable time for the grade and the first two came clear.

**NOTEBOOK**
**Les Arcs(USA)** ◆, a heavily gambled runner-up last time, again saw serious support in the ring and duly made amends in good style. He had the cheekpieces left off this time, and settled a lot better off the pace before readily going on to score with a bit up his sleeve. He can score again, this drop in trip looked ideal and a recent wind operation seems to have worked the oracle.
**Munaawashat(IRE)**, up 3lb for winning on much faster ground last time, again had the run of the race but had no answer to the winner's challenge approaching the final furlong. She kept on well however to finish a clear second and there was little disgrace in this defeat.
**Riska King** gave himself a stiff task by making a sluggish start and could not get to the leaders on this ground. He will appreciate a return to faster underfoot conditions and was not disgraced at the weights.
**Jordans Elect**, who disappointed last time when last at Doncaster, again ran a flat race and looks to be going the wrong way at present.
**J R Stevenson(USA)** was tightened for room two out and could not recover thereafter. He is better than the bare form, but has a habit of finding trouble in running and is does not look one to place any confidence in at present. *Official explanation: jockey said gelding suffered interference*

### 3398 EUROPEAN BREEDERS FUND MAIDEN STKS (A QUALIFIER FOR THE HAMILTON PARK 2-Y-O SERIES FINAL) — 6f 5y

3:20 (3:20) (D) 2-Y-O — £4,764 (£1,466; £733; £366) Stalls Low

| Form | | | | RPR |
|---|---|---|---|---|
| 3 | 1 | | **Shivaree**[40] 2245 2-8-9 ... ACulhane 2 <br> (MRChannon) *cl up: swtchd lft 1/2-way: rdn to ld ent last: styd on* **6/4**[1] | 75 |
| | 2 | 1¼ | **Value Plus (IRE)**[33] 2431 2-8-2 ... (p) AmyKathleenParsons(7) 1 <br> (MsJoannaMorgan, Ire) *rn free and sn led: hung rt 1/2-way: sn rdn: hdd ent last and kpt on same pce* **5/2**[3] | 71 |
| 2 | 3 | ¾ | **Secret History (USA)**[9] 3123 2-8-9 ... JFanning 4 <br> (MJohnston) *cl up: rdn along 2f out: kpt on ins last* **9/4**[2] | 69 |
| 5405 | 4 | nk | **No Commission (IRE)**[18] 2852 2-9-0 ... RWinston 5 <br> (RFFisher) *son outpcd in rr: hdwy 2f out: kpt on ins last: nrst fin* **33/1** | 73 |
| 0 | 5 | 3½ | **Scorpio Sally (IRE)**[22] 2730 2-8-9 ... GDuffield 3 <br> (MDHammond) *chsd ldrs: rdn along over 2f out: sn wknd* **33/1** | 58 |

1m 13.68s (0.58) **Going Correction** -0.025s/f (Good) **5** Ran SP% **105.2**
Speed ratings: **95,93,92,91,87**CSF £5.00 TOTE £2.20: £1.10, £1.10; EX 3.20.
**Owner** Sheikh Mohammed **Bred** Darley **Trained** West Ilsley, Berks

**FOCUS**
A modest juvenile maiden run at a fair pace.

**NOTEBOOK**
**Shivaree** confirmed the promise of her debut at Goodwood last time and duly got off the mark at the second attempt. She stuck to her task well under pressure, will improve again for this outing, and should have little trouble staying further in time.
**Value Plus(IRE)**, runner-up on all her three previous outings in Ireland previously, ran keen early on and lost her chance when hanging off the rail approaching two out. It may have been the first-time cheekpieces that had a negative effect, as she had shown no obvious signs of temperament previously. However, there may also be no coincidence in the fact she has found one too good on each of her starts to date
**Secret History(USA)** was never really going the pace of the leaders and looks sure to be seen in a better light when upped in trip. She will also no doubt fare better when handicapped.
**No Commission(IRE)**, who had shown little in five outings previously, was doing all of his best work late in the day. This was his best effort yet, but he does drag the form down somewhat.

### 3399 TOTEEXACTA STKS (H'CAP) — 5f 4y

3:50 (3:51) (D) (0-85,76) 3-Y-O+ — £8,209 (£2,526; £1,263; £631) Stalls Low

| Form | | | | RPR |
|---|---|---|---|---|
| 0052 | 1 | | **Aahgowangowan (IRE)**[5] 3225 5-8-6 **58** ... (t) RFfrench 3 <br> (MDods) *mde all:qcknd clr over 1f out: rdn and styd on wl* **9/4**[1] | 71 |
| -000 | 2 | 1¾ | **Beyond The Clouds (IRE)**[12] 3016 8-9-10 **76** ... RWinston 7 <br> (JSWainwright) *hld up: hdwy 2f out: sn rdn and kpt on fianl f* **8/1** | 83 |
| 0032 | 3 | hd | **Kings College Boy**[12] 3016 4-8-5 **60** ... (b) THamilton(3) 9 <br> (RAFahey) *bhd: hdwy on outer over 2f out: rdn and styed on fnl f: nrst fin* **9/2**[2] | 66 |
| 2003 | 4 | nk | **Strensall**[5] 3249 7-9-5 **76** ... PMulrennan(5) 1 <br> (REBarr) *chsd ldrs: rdn 2f out: hdwy to chae wnr ins last: kpt on same pce* **13/2** | 81 |
| -000 | 5 | 1¾ | **Northern Svengali (IRE)**[13] 2975 8-7-12 **50** oh14 ... (tp) JMcAuley 6 <br> (DANolan) *rrd s: bhd tl styd on fnl 2f* **66/1** | 49 |
| 0300 | 6 | hd | **Banjo Bay (IRE)**[11] 3036 6-9-10 **76** ... AlexGreaves 4 <br> (DNicholls) *trckd ldrs: rdn along 2f out: wknd over 1f out* **9/2**[2] | 74 |
| 5321 | 7 | shd | **Karminskey Park**[5] 3225 5-9-5 **71** 7ex ... JFanning 5 <br> (TJEtherington) *chsd ldrs: rdn 2f out: wknd over 1f out* **11/2**[3] | 69 |
| 00-6 | 8 | 3 | **Mutayam**[5] 3226 4-7-13 **51** oh11 ow1 ... (t) PFessey 8 <br> (DANolan) *cl up: rdn along 2f out: sn wknd* **40/1** | 38 |

60.14 secs (-1.12) **Going Correction** -0.025s/f (Good) **8** Ran SP% **110.9**
Speed ratings: **107,104,103,103,100 100,100,95**CSF £19.93 CT £70.63 TOTE £2.60: £1.20, £1.90, £1.90; EX 26.40.
**Owner** D Vic Roper **Bred** Seamus Phelan **Trained** Piercebridge, Co Durham
■ Stewards Enquiry : T Hamilton one-day ban: used whip down the shoulder in the forehand position (Jul 10)

**FOCUS**
A modest sprint which produced a fair time for the grade and the form looks reliable.

**NOTEBOOK**
**Aahgowangowan(IRE)**, an unlucky loser last time when her stall opened slightly late, pinged out this time to comfortably make all and score. She is in good heart at present and should prove hard to beat under penalty if found a similar event.
**Beyond The Clouds(IRE)** ran his best race for quite some time and appreciated this easier ground. He looks as though he may be about to capitalise on his slide in the weights.
**Kings College Boy** was staying on best at the end and this goes down as solid effort from his wide stall.
**Strensall** held every chance if good enough from his plum draw, but could not peg back the winner, try as he might.
**Northern Svengali(IRE)** did well from 14lb out of the handicap and may be worth another try back over seven furlongs.
**Banjo Bay(IRE)** failed to improve for this ease in grade and disappointed. He is well treated at present on his old form, but seems to be regressing.
**Karminskey Park** never looked like following up under her penalty for winning last time, and failed by some way to confirm form with Aahgowangowan.

### 3400 FRIENDS OF SCOTTISH RACING CLASSIFIED STKS — 6f 5y

4:20 (4:20) (E) 3-Y-O+ — £3,558 (£1,095; £547; £273) Stalls Low

| Form | | | | RPR |
|---|---|---|---|---|
| 12-6 | 1 | | **Fonthill Road (IRE)**[13] 2976 4-9-5 70 ... THamilton(3) 3 <br> (RAFahey) *trckd ldrs: hdwy on inner to ld ent last: sn rdn and kpt on* **15/8**[2] | 83+ |
| 0223 | 2 | ½ | **Bundy**[5] 3226 8-9-3 63 ... SWKelly 1 <br> (MDods) *led: rdn and hung rt over 1f out: hdd ent last: kptn on u.p* **13/8**[1] | 73 |
| 5610 | 3 | 5 | **Albashoosh**[15] 2936 6-9-8 70 ... AlexGreaves 4 <br> (DNicholls) *cl up: rdn 2f out: wknd over 1f out* **5/2**[3] | 63 |
| 4000 | 4 | 3½ | **Friar Tuck**[5] 3226 9-9-3 53 ... RFfrench 2 <br> (MissLAPerratt) *cl up: rdn along over 2f out: sn wknd* **14/1** | 48 |

1m 13.33s (0.23) **Going Correction** -0.025s/f (Good) **4** Ran SP% **108.1**
Speed ratings: **97,96,89,85**CSF £5.28 TOTE £2.60; EX 3.10.
**Owner** Mrs Una Towell **Bred** D N Wallace **Trained** Musley Bank, N Yorks

**FOCUS**
No early pace on for this tight classified event and that helped produce a slow winning time. Despite that the form is fair and the winner can rate higher.

**NOTEBOOK**
**Fonthill Road(IRE)** took advantage of a split on the rail over one out to lead and knuckled down well late on to score. He showed the benefit of his recent comeback run this time, is still relatively unexposed and can progress to a higher level this summer.
**Bundy** set a sedate gallop until he hung off the rail approaching the final furlong and let the eventual winner go past. He has finished in the frame over course and distance the last four times now, but is a very hard horse to win with.
**Albashoosh** was free in the early stages off the slow pace and could offer precious little under pressure when push came to shove. He can do better, but is another hard horse to predict. *Official explanation: jockey said gelding hung right throughout*

### 3401 SUPERCOUNTY H'CAP (A QUALIFIER FOR THE TOTEPOOL SERIES FINAL) — 1m 1f 36y

4:50 (4:50) (E) (0-75,70) 3-Y-O+ — £3,948 (£1,215; £607; £303) Stalls High

| Form | | | | RPR |
|---|---|---|---|---|
| -003 | 1 | | **Wahoo Sam (USA)**[15] 2938 4-8-12 **59** ... PMakin(5) 8 <br> (TDBarron) *cl up: led 4f out: rdn 2f out: edgd lft and drvn fnl f: hld on wl* **8/1**[3] | 71 |
| 4216 | 2 | ¾ | **Double Ransom**[45] 2120 5-9-2 **58** ... (b) GDuffield 1 <br> (MrsLStubbs) *hld up and bhd: hdwy on outer over 2f out: rdn to chal ins last: ev ch tl drvn and no ex last 100 yds* **9/2**[2] | 68 |
| -004 | 3 | ¾ | **No Chance To Dance (IRE)**[17] 2879 4-8-4 **46** ... (t) DeanMcKeown 6 <br> (HJCollingridge) *trckd ldrs gng wl: effrt 2f out and ev ch tl rdn and nt qckn ins last* **16/1** | 55 |
| 4002 | 4 | 5 | **Regent's Secret (USA)**[11] 3060 4-9-7 **63** ... WSupple 7 <br> (JSGoldie) *hld up and bhd: hdwy 2f out: swtchd rt and swtchd rt over 1f out: styd on wl fnl f: nrst fin* **10/1** | 62 |
| 555- | 5 | ½ | **Donna's Double**[237] 5928 9-8-9 **56** ... (p) PMulrennan(5) 3 <br> (DEddy) *towards rr: hdwy 3f out: rikdden wl over 1f out and kpt on same pce* **10/1** | 54 |
| 5-00 | 6 | hd | **Wood Dalling (USA)**[15] 2938 6-8-11 **53** ... RWinston 5 <br> (ISemple) *in tch: hdwy on outer 3f out: rdn and ev ch 2f out tl drvn and wknd ent last* **9/1** | 50 |

0400 **7** 1 1/4 **Newcorp Lad**[21] 2752 4-9-6 **62** ........ AClhane 12 57
(MrsGSRees) *in tch: hdwy 3f out: rdn 2f out and sn no imp* **8/1**[3]

006 **8** 8 **Chisel**[20] 2777 3-8-7 **60** ........ JFanning 2 39
(MJohnston) *chsd ldrs: rdn along 3f out: sn wknd* **20/1**

0001 **9** 2 **Libre**[7] 3167 4-9-3 **59** 6ex ........ (bt) KFallon 13 34
(RCGuest) *dwlt: in rr and sn poushed along: rdn and sme hdwy 3f out: nvr a factor* **11/4**[1]

2000 **10** 3 1/2 **Anthemion (IRE)**[11] 3039 7-8-13 **55** ........ DMcGaffin 10 23
(MrsJCMcgregor) *chsd ldrs: riden along over 3f out and sn wknd* **28/1**

2-05 **11** 3 **Peruvia (IRE)**[12] 3022 4-10-0 **70** ........ (vt) FLynch 11 32
(RMBeckett) *led: rdn along and hdd 4f out: sn wknd* **12/1**

0000 **12** 1 1/2 **Dark Cut (IRE)**[5] 3221 4-7-10 **45** ........ AmyKathleenParsons(7) 9 4
(HAlexander) *chsd ldrs: rdn along over 4f out: sn wknd* **50/1**

2m 0.46s (0.86) **Going Correction** +0.175s/f (Good)
**WFA** 3 from 4yo+ 11lb **12** Ran SP% **119.0**
Speed ratings: **103,102,101,97,96 96,95,88,86,83 80,79**CSF £43.20 CT £573.74 TOTE £10.00: £2.00, £2.10, £2.80; EX 64.80 Place 6 £85.30, Place 5 £26.57.
**Owner** C A Washbourn **Bred** Stonereath Farms Inc **Trained** Maunby, N Yorks
■ Stewards Enquiry : D McGaffin one-day ban: used whip from above shoulder height (Jul 21)

**FOCUS**
A weak handicap run at a modest gallop, and although the form is ordinary it looks reliable.

**NOTEBOOK**
**Wahoo Sam(USA)**, who hinted at a return to form last time at Carlisle, appreciated this extra distance and did the job nicely. He settled well on the pace and, as he still looks well-treated on his juvenile form, could be one to side with next time.
**Double Ransom** came there with every chance inside the last furlong, but could not quicken past the winner. He deserves extra credit as he had the worst of the draw this time and can win a similar event off this mark.
**No Chance To Dance(IRE)** found less than expected off the bridle and looked very one paced in the final stages. This was his best effort to date however, and the way in which he travelled through the race would suggest he is slowly going the right way.
**Regent's Secret(USA)**, restrained early on, was staying on all too late in the day and had no chance with the front three.
**Libre** was well-backed to follow up his suprise win at Beverley a week earlier, but was always up against it after a sluggish start and never threatened. *Official explanation: jockey said gelding was unsuited by the soft ground*
T/Plt: £67.40 to a £1 stake. Pool: £37,662.80. 407.60 winning tickets. T/Qpdt: £14.40 to a £1 stake. Pool: £2,253.60. 115.80 winning tickets. JR

3402 - 3405a (Foreign Racing) - See Raceform Interactive

## 1196 CATTERICK (L-H)
### Wednesday, June 30

**OFFICIAL GOING: Good to firm (good in places)**
After a three month break while the racecourse stables were re-developed the ground was described as 'near perfect with a lush covering'.
Wind: Fresh 1/2 behind. Weather: Heavy shower race 1, fine but fresh after.

## 3406 EUROPEAN BREEDERS FUND ZETLAND MEDIAN AUCTION MAIDEN STKS 7f
2:30 (2:31) (E) 2-Y-O £4,251 (£1,308; £654; £327) Stalls Low

Form RPR

50 **1** **Al Garhoud Bridge**[27] 2609 2-9-0 ........ TEDurcan 3 86
(MRChannon) *trckd ldrs: nt clr run briefly 2f out: sn rdn to chse ldr: led fnl 7yds: styd on* **11/4**[1]

352 **2** nk **Jane Jubilee (IRE)**[14] 2972 2-8-9 ........ KDalgleish 10 80
(MJohnston) *cl up: led over 2f out: rdn and hdd fnl 75yds: styd on* **7/2**[2]

264 **3** 5 **Taras Treasure (IRE)**[10] 3123 2-8-9 ........ RWinston 6 68
(JJQuinn) *trckd ldrs: ev ch 2f out: sn rdn: outpcd by first 2 fnl f* **7/2**[2]

**4** 1 3/4 **Little Dalham** 2-9-0 ........ AMcCarthy 7 68
(PWChapple-Hyam) *small: cmpt: towards rr whn j. path over 5f out: styd on fnl 2f: n.d* **4/1**[3]

006 **5** 3 **Kashmar Flight**[15] 2961 2-8-9 ........ DAllan 8 56
(TDEasterby) *dwlt: sn midfield: sme hdwy 3f out: rdn 2f out: no further prog* **66/1**

4 **6** 2 1/2 **King Henrik (USA)**[15] 2961 2-9-0 ........ KDarley 1 55
(ACrook) *led tl hdd over 2f out: sn btn* **14/1**

02 **7** 1/2 **Dan's Heir**[22] 2755 2-9-0 ........ GFaulkner 5 53
(PCHaslam) *midfield: drvn along 3f out: no hdwy* **33/1**

3 **8** 1 1/4 **Drax**[15] 2961 2-8-11 ........ TPQueally(3) 11 50
(DRLoder) *s.i.s: a bhd* **7/1**

00 **9** 1 3/4 **Tillingborn Dancer (IRE)**[11] 3080 2-9-0 ........ ACulhane 4 46
(MDHammond) *bhd fr 1/2-way* **100/1**

**10** 3 1/2 **Harry's Simmie (IRE)** 2-8-9 ........ DaleGibson 2 32
(RHollinshead) *leggy: unf: s.i.s: a bhd* **50/1**

1m 25.51s (-1.99) **Going Correction** -0.275s/f (Firm) **10** Ran SP% **117.7**
Speed ratings: **100,99,93,91,88 85,85,83,81,77**CSF £12.55 TOTE £4.10: £1.60, £1.20, £1.50; EX 13.60.
**Owner** Jaber Abdullah **Bred** S R Hope And D Erwin **Trained** West Ilsley, Berks

**FOCUS**
Just an ordinary maiden, but the first two pulled well clear and the time was decent for the grade.

**NOTEBOOK**
**Al Garhoud Bridge**, who looked very fit indeed, overcame a glitch to show ahead near the line. The step up to seven seemed to suit him and he is a likely nursery type.
**Jane Jubilee(IRE)**, drawn one from the outside, proved suited by the step up in trip and was just edged out. She is going the right away and deserves to go one better.
**Taras Treasure(IRE)**, a keen type, did not improve for the step up to seven.
**Little Dalham**, a February foal, is well named. A posistive on the exchanges, he never really threatened and a more galloping track might see him in a better light.
**Kashmar Flight**, having her fourth outing, would have a better chance of paying her way in nursery company.
**King Henrik(USA)** didn't improve on his debut effort.
**Drax** hung violently left and does not look by any means straightforward.

## 3407 PROJECT MANAGEMENT SCOTLAND CATTERICK H'CAP 5f
3:00 (3:00) (E) (0-75,73) 3-Y-O+ £3,542 (£1,090; £545; £272) Stalls Low

Form RPR

0-00 **1** **Wicked Uncle**[22] 2754 5-10-0 **73** ........ (v) KDarley 3 87
(SGollings) *racd far side: mde all: clr appr fnl f: r.o wl u.p* **11/1**

0600 **2** 4 **Brigadier Monty (IRE)**[13] 3010 6-7-12 **50** ........ DFentiman(7) 1 48
(MrsSLamyman) *midfield far side: hdwy over 1f out: wnt 2nd ins fnl f: r.o: no ch w wnr* **16/1**

0000 **3** 1 **Sharp Hat**[4] 3309 10-9-0 **59** ........ ACulhane 13 53
(DWChapman) *dwlt: towards rr far side: hdwy appr fnl f: r.o ins last: nrst fin* **10/1**

2035 **4** nk **Amanda's Lad (IRE)**[6] 3249 4-8-6 **56** ........ DFox(5) 7 49
(MCChapman) *chsd ldrs far side: drvn along 1/2-way: kpt on wl fnl f* **25/1**

0001 **5** 3/4 **Laurel Dawn**[8] 3169 6-7-11 **49** ........ NataliaGemelova(7) 14 39
(IWMcinnes) *towards rr far side: hdwy over 1f out: kpt on ins last: nvr able to chal* **4/1**[1]

-300 **6** shd **Count Cougar (USA)**[13] 3010 4-8-11 **56** ........ DaleGibson 6 45
(SPGriffiths) *prom far side: rdn over 1f out: no ex ins last* **100/1**

0022 **7** nk **Yorkie**[8] 3175 5-8-9 **54** ........ DeanMcKeown 9 42
(PABlockley) *midfield far side: kpt on fnl f: n.d* **11/1**

2025 **8** nk **Chairman Bobby**[14] 2976 6-9-13 **72** ........ TEDurcan 2 59
(DWBarker) *midfield far side: kpt on fnl f: n.d* **13/2**[2]

5541 **9** 1/2 **Malahide Express (IRE)**[21] 2784 4-8-6 **58** ........ JDO'Reilly(7) 5 43
(EJAlston) *dwlt: sn in tch far side: rdn 2f out: no hdwy* **15/2**[3]

0000 **10** shd **Mr Spliffy (IRE)**[8] 3169 5-8-5 **50** ........ GDuffield 4 35
(MCChapman) *prom far side: rdn over 1f out: wknd ins last* **16/1**

5224 **11** 1 1/2 **Valiant Romeo**[13] 3010 4-8-10 **55** ........ (v) RFfrench 10 34
(RBastiman) *chsd ldrs far side: rdn 1/2-way: wknd over 1f out* **10/1**

5000 **12** shd **Chico Guapo (IRE)**[10] 3126 4-10-0 **73** ........ (b) RWinston 12 51
(JAGlover) *led stands side gp thrght: no ch w far side gp* **20/1**

3000 **13** nk **Lord Baskerville**[4] 3314 3-7-13 **57** ........ RoryMoore(7) 8 34
(WStorey) *dwlt: racd far side: a bhd* **66/1**

0200 **14** hd **Kangarilla Road**[13] 3010 5-9-2 **66** ........ PMulrennan(5) 17 42
(MrsJRRamsden) *chsd stands side ldr: rdn over 1f out: no imp: no ch w far side gp* **15/2**[3]

0000 **15** 3/4 **Zuhair**[33] 2461 11-9-8 **67** ........ AlexGreaves 16 40
(DNicholls) *racd stands side: a bhd* **33/1**

-050 **16** nk **Vigorous (IRE)**[37] 2369 4-9-9 **68** ........ JCarroll 15 40
(DNicholls) *racd stands side: bhd fnl 2f* **25/1**

0060 **17** 1 3/4 **Safranine (IRE)**[3] 3339 7-9-1 **60** ........ (p) AnnStokell 11 25
(MissAStokell) *racd centre 2f: jnd stands side gp: sn bhd* **28/1**

58.59 secs (-2.01) **Going Correction** -0.275s/f (Firm)
**WFA** 3 from 4yo+ 6lb **17** Ran SP% **124.8**
Speed ratings: **105,98,97,96,95 95,94,94,93,93 90,90,90,89,88 88,85**CSF £167.07 CT £1892.93 TOTE £13.10: £4.00, £2.80, £4.60, £4.00; EX 177.90.
**Owner** Northern Bloodstock Racing **Bred** Lady Jennifer Green **Trained** Scamblesby, Lincs

**FOCUS**
A competitive 0-73 handicap but the wide-margin winner was the only one to run to form. They split into two separate groups but at the finish those on the stands' side were out with the washing.

**NOTEBOOK**
**Wicked Uncle**, whose last success over two years ago came from a 5lb higher mark, showed them a clean pair of heels on the far side and had this won before the final furlong. *Official explanation: trainer said, regarding the improved form shown, gelding was suited by the drop in class and the reapplication of a visor*
**Brigadier Monty(IRE)**, who is tumbling down the weights, had pole position here and will be better suited by six furlongs.
**Sharp Hat**, seeking his 23rd win on his 160th run, had an unfavourable draw and made a sluggish start. He stuck on with gusto inside the last and is as enthusiastic as ever.
**Amanda's Lad(IRE)**, seeking to break his duck at the 50th attempt, keeps running well, but like Tim Henman at Wimbledon seems doomed to fail.
**Laurel Dawn**, banged up 10lb after Beverley, ran here without a penalty, but didn't have the best of draws and none of his seven career wins has been on a downhill track.
**Count Cougar(USA)**, having his second outing in two weeks after a five-month break, shaped a lot better. His one success so far was achieved on the All-Weather.
**Yorkie** *Official explanation: jockey said gelding was never travelling*
**Kangarilla Road**, one of the quintet to stick to the stands' side, was found to have bled. *Official explanation: jockey said gelding bled from the nose*

## 3408 EUROPEAN BREEDERS FUND MAIDEN FILLIES' STKS 5f
3:30 (3:31) (D) 2-Y-O £4,160 (£1,280; £640; £320) Stalls Low

Form RPR

**1** **Oh Dara (USA)** 2-8-11 ........ DeanMcKeown 3 81
(PABlockley) *mde all: clr over 1f out: readily* **10/3**[2]

2335 **2** 3 1/2 **Bibury Flyer**[7] 3208 2-8-11 ........ TEDurcan 7 69
(MRChannon) *chsd ldrs: wnt clr 2nd over 2f out: no ch w wnr* **6/4**[1]

34 **3** 1 1/4 **Angelofthenorth**[16] 2933 2-8-11 ........ SChin 10 65
(JDBethell) *swvd rt s: sn chsng ldrs: kpt on fnl f* **16/1**

6 **4** hd **Epitomise**[18] 2884 2-8-11 ........ GDuffield 9 64
(RMBeckett) *chsd ldrs: sn drvn along: outpcd after 2f: kpt on appr fnl f* **11/2**[3]

505 **5** nk **Kilmovee**[12] 3055 2-8-11 ........ KDarley 2 63
(NTinkler) *restless in stalls: chsd ldrs: outpcd after 2f: styd on fnl 2f* **8/1**

006 **6** 5 **Serene Pearl (IRE)**[16] 2933 2-8-11 ........ (t) RWinston 6 45
(GMMoore) *sn outpcd: bhd fnl 2f* **66/1**

263 **7** 3 1/2 **Nee Lemon Left**[14] 2980 2-8-4 ........ PPMathers(7) 5 33
(ABerry) *dwlt: sn chsng ldrs: wknd 2f out: sn bhd* **11/2**[3]

000 **8** 11 **Hunipot**[21] 2773 2-8-11 ........ RFfrench 1 —
(MESowersby) *chsd ldrs over 2f: sn lost pl and wl bhd* **100/1**

60.19 secs (-0.41) **Going Correction** -0.275s/f (Firm) **8** Ran SP% **113.3**
Speed ratings: **92,86,84,84,83 75,70,52**CSF £8.54 TOTE £6.10: £1.90, £1.10, £4.10; EX 20.20.
**Owner** Mrs Joanna Hughes **Bred** Bricklow Ltd And Hyperion Stud Ltd **Trained** Southwell, Notts

**FOCUS**
The favourite may not have been seen at her best but the winner was still impressive.

**NOTEBOOK**
**Oh Dara(USA)**, a January foal, cost 26,000gns at the breeze-up sales. A positive on the exchanges, she is a good walker and was easily the pick of the paddock. She knew her job and had this won some way out, and is clearly useful.
**Bibury Flyer** is finding it hard to break her duck. It was disconcerting to see the next three home on her coat tail.
**Angelofthenorth**, who has a pronounced knee action, seemed to run easily her best race on this her third start, appreciating the much better ground.
**Epitomise**, who lacks substance, is bred exclusively for speed but on this showing will appreciate six.
**Kilmovee**, who became upset in the stalls, looks to be crying out for a step up to six furlongs.
**Nee Lemon Left**, a slip of a thing, was a major negative on the exchanges and the crystal ball was proved right.

## 3409 DERBY HOUSE STABLING H'CAP 7f
4:00 (4:01) (D) (0-80,80) 4-Y-O+ £5,752 (£1,770; £885; £442) Stalls Low

Form RPR

6222 **1** **Alchemist Master**[12] 3058 5-8-5 **57** ........ (p) DeanMcKeown 9 78
(RMWhitaker) *trckd ldr: led wl over 1f out: rdn and drew clr appr fnl f: styd on wl* **5/1**[2]

0005 **2** 5 **Smith N Allan Oils**[8] 3167 5-8-2 **54** ........ (p) PFessey 7 62
(MDods) *hld up midfield: sltly hmpd over 2f out: styd on wl u.p fnl f to go 2nd clsng stages* **14/1**

5406 **3** hd **Waltzing Wizard**[9] 3148 5-7-13 **51** ........ FNorton 13 58
(ABerry) *a chsng ldrs: styd on wl u.p fnl f* **25/1**

1030 **4** 1 **Raphael (IRE)**[6] 3235 5-9-6 **79** AMullen(7) 17 83
(TDEasterby) *hld up midfield: hdwy 2f out: rdn over 1f out: styd on ins fnl f: nvr able to chal* **20/1**
0055 **5** nk **Ronnie From Donny (IRE)**[21] 2776 4-8-13 **65** ACulhane 5 69
(BEllison) *a chsng ldrs: rdn 2f out: kpt on same pce* **11/1**
0200 **6** hd **King Harson**[12] 3036 5-10-0 **80** (v) GDuffield 6 83
(JDBethell) *led tl hdd wl over 1f out: kpt on same pce* **9/1**
3000 **7** nk **No Grouse**[7] 3198 4-9-3 **72** (p) THamilton(3) 11 74
(RAFahey) *hld up midfield: hdwy 2f out: rdn over 1f out: styd on ins fnl f: nvr able to chal* **12/1**
-300 **8** 1 1/4 **Qualitair Wings**[7] 3198 5-9-7 **73** DMcGaffin 1 72
(JHetherton) *dwlt: hld up in rr: hdwy over 2f out: rdn over 1f out: kpt on fnl f: nvr able to chal* **14/1**
4044 **9** hd **What-A-Dancer (IRE)**[19] 2838 7-9-4 **75** PMulrennan(5) 3 74
(GASwinbank) *in tch: hmpd over 2f out: rdn over 1f out: sn btn* **9/2**[1]
0040 **10** nk **Mr Bountiful (IRE)**[15] 2965 6-7-13 **51** (p) RFfrench 10 49
(MDods) *hld up: sme hdwy over 2f out: rdn over 1f out: no further prog* **14/1**
1663 **11** 1 **Pawan (IRE)**[2] 3365 4-9-0 **66** AnnStokell 2 61
(MissAStokell) *hld up: hdwy u.p over 1f out: hmpd and nt clr run fnl f: nt rcvr* **12/1**
04-0 **12** nk **Skylark**[20] 2813 7-8-5 **57** KimTinkler 16 51
(DonEnricoIncisa) *dwlt: a towards rr: n.d* **66/1**
0305 **13** hd **Pays D'Amour (IRE)**[5] 3269 7-9-0 **66** AlexGreaves 12 60
(DNicholls) *trckd ldrs tl rdn and wknd over 1f out* **33/1**
0005 **14** shd **Extinguisher**[11] 3082 5-8-5 **57** (v) JCarroll 8 51
(DNicholls) *sn in rr: n.d* **33/1**
0001 **15** 1 **Smart Minister**[13] 3019 4-8-12 **64** KDalgleish 4 55
(JJQuinn) *a towards rr* **25/1**
5065 **16** 1 1/2 **Flying Edge (IRE)**[16] 2936 4-8-5 **57** DAllan 18 44
(EJAlston) *sn towards rr* **16/1**
2255 **17** 1 1/4 **Takes Tutu (USA)**[7] 3198 5-9-8 **74** (b) KDarley 15 58
(KRBurke) *in tch: rdn wl over 1f out: hung bdly rt and lost pl fnl f* **6/1**[3]
000- **18** 6 **Martin House (IRE)**[42] 5458 5-8-8 **60** RWinston 14 28
(MrsKWalton) *a rr div* **66/1**

1m 24.53s (-2.97) **Going Correction** -0.275s/f (Firm) **18 Ran SP% 130.1**
Speed ratings: **105,99,99,97,97 97,97,95,95,95 93,93,93,93,92 90,88,82**CSF £72.46 CT £1653.04 TOTE £7.10: £2.20, £3.70, £7.20, £12.10; EX 127.20 Trifecta £589.30 Part won. Pool of £830.10 - 0.10 winning units..
**Owner** T L Adams **Bred** Mrs John Van Geest **Trained** Scarcroft, W Yorks

**FOCUS**
Another wide-margin winner and this is fair form.

**NOTEBOOK**
**Alchemist Master** travelled strongly and had this won in a matter of strides. He never had time to change his mind and is still potentially well treated on his All-Weather form.
**Smith N Allan Oils** is finding his form and snatched second spot near the line.
**Waltzing Wizard**, whose last success over two years ago was from a 10lb higher mark, ran one of his better races but these days he is hard to predict.
**Raphael(IRE)**, drawn wide, receives no mercy.
**Ronnie From Donny(IRE)** has three career wins to his credit, all on the All-Weather.
**King Harson** made all to win here over this trip in November but it was from a 3lb lower mark.
**No Grouse** ran with credit but would have preferred quicker ground.
**What-A-Dancer(IRE)** was playing catch-up after being left short of room on the inner turning in.
**Pawan(IRE)** ran out of racing room completely otherwise he would have finished a fair bit closer. *Official explanation: jockey said gelding was denied a run in the closing stages*
**Takes Tutu(USA)**, with the blinkers back on, was forced to race wide, and in the end he hung violently right and proved almost unsteerable. *Official explanation: jockey said gelding hung right in the closing stages*

## 3410 WE RACE AGAIN NEXT WEDNESDAY MEDIAN AUCTION MAIDEN STKS 5f 212y
4:30 (4:31) (F) 3-4-Y-O £3,017 (£862; £431) Stalls Low

Form RPR
3132 **1** **Compton Plume**[11] 3096 4-9-6 55 DaleGibson 2 70
(WHTinning) *chsd ldrs: led over 2f out: hld on wl* **9/2**[3]
24-0 **2** 3/4 **Cyfrwys (IRE)**[46] 2112 3-8-8 75 ACulhane 12 63
(BPalling) *chsd ldrs: styd on ins fnl f: no real imp* **5/1**
0063 **3** 3/4 **Half A Handful**[9] 3158 3-8-13 65 KDarley 5 66
(MJWallace) *trckd ldrs: effrt and hung bdly lft over 1f out: kpt on ins last* **4/1**[2]
-222 **4** 1/2 **Flying Bantam (IRE)**[17] 2908 3-8-10 70 (p) THamilton(3) 1 64
(RAFahey) *led after 1f: hung rt bnd over 3f out: hdd over 2f out: kpt on same pce* **11/4**[1]
3004 **5** 1 1/2 **Dark Champion**[13] 3019 4-9-6 59 RWinston 13 60
(REBarr) *led 1f: chsd ldrs: kpt on same pce fnl 2f* **25/1**
6422 **6** 1/2 **Flash Ram**[6] 3251 3-8-13 64 (b) DAllan 9 58
(TDEasterby) *chsd ldrs: one pce fnl 2f* **9/2**[3]
4- **7** 2 **Harrison's Flyer (IRE)**[413] 1594 3-8-13 GParkin 14 52
(RAFahey) *sn bhd: hdwy over 2f out: kpt on fnl f* **20/1**
0235 **8** 1/2 **Fox Covert (IRE)**[12] 3059 3-8-8 58 PMulrennan(5) 7 51
(DWBarker) *chsd ldrs: one pce fnl 2f* **10/1**
00 **9** 2 **Prince Renesis**[15] 2962 3-8-13 RFfrench 3 45
(IWMcinnes) *s.i.s: bhd tl sme hdwy fnl 2f* **100/1**
0550 **10** 1/2 **East Riding**[2] 3367 4-9-1 37 (p) AnnStokell 10 38
(MissAStokell) *s.i.s: sme hdwy on outside over 2f out: nvr on terms* **100/1**
0000 **11** 24 **Designer City (IRE)**[11] 3096 3-8-8 45 JCarroll 6 —
(ABerry) *s.i.s: bhd and eased over 1f out* **100/1**
**12** 1 1/4 **Miss Chancelot** 3-8-8 RLappin 8 —
(SPGriffiths) *s.i.s: sn bhd: t.o 3f out* **66/1**

1m 12.62s (-1.38) **Going Correction** -0.275s/f (Firm)
**WFA** 3 from 4yo 7lb **12 Ran SP% 121.9**
Speed ratings: **98,97,96,95,93 92,90,89,86,86 54,52**CSF £27.10 TOTE £4.50: £1.80, £2.40, £2.30; EX 52.50.
**Owner** W H Tinning **Bred** Mrs D A La Trobe **Trained** Thornton-le-Clay, N Yorks

**FOCUS**
A modest sprint maiden with the first 10 stacked up at the line and the winner finally lost the maiden tag at the 25th attempt, making up for his luckless defeat at Redcar three outings ago. The form looks sound.

**NOTEBOOK**
**Compton Plume**, with a plum draw, made no mistake and always looked like coming out on top. He had plenty to find on official figures and faces a stiff rise in the ratings.
**Cyfrwys(IRE)**, officially rated 20lb ahead of the winner, never really looked like overhauling him.
**Half A Handful**, officially rated 10lb in advance of the winner, looked in peak condition but he proved very difficult to keep straight. He stayed on well inside the last and will appreciate a much more galloping track.
**Flying Bantam(IRE)**, officially rated 15lb ahead of the winner, was a negative on the exchanges. In first-time cheekpieces, he had the plum draw but he hung badly away from the running rail on the home turn. *Official explanation: jockey said gelding hung right throughout*
**Dark Champion**, drawn wide, had plenty to find and would appreciate a much more galloping track.
**Flash Ram**, a maiden after seven previous starts, will appreciate a return to seven furlongs.
**Designer City(IRE)** *Official explanation: jockey said filly bled from the nose*

## 3411 STOCKTON H'CAP 1m 3f 214y
5:00 (5:01) (F ) (0-55,55) 4-Y-O+ £3,073 (£878; £439) Stalls Low

Form RPR
000/ **1** **Sovereign State (IRE)**[17] 4926 7-8-8 **41** (p) FNorton 14 51
(DWThompson) *trckd ldrs: rdn to ld appr fnl f: hld on wl clsng stages* **20/1**
0-20 **2** 1/2 **Fairy Monarch (IRE)**[12] 3041 5-8-13 **46** (p) RFitzpatrick 12 55
(PTMidgley) *midfield: drvn along and hdwy over 3f out: styd on u.p to go 2nd ins fnl f: no ex clsng stages* **25/1**
3453 **3** 1 1/2 **Paddy Mul**[6] 3237 7-8-0 **40** (t) RoryMoore(7) 18 47
(WStorey) *hld up: hdwy u.p 2f out: styd on wl fnl f: nvr able to chal* **8/1**
056 **4** 1 **Lazzaz**[5] 3263 6-8-8 **46** (p) PMakin(5) 9 51
(PWHiatt) *mde most tl rdn and hdd appr fnl f: no ex* **5/1**[1]
0000 **5** 1 1/2 **Cryptogam**[22] 2757 4-8-8 **41** ow1 DMcGaffin 15 44
(MESowersby) *hld up in rr: hdwy u.p 2f out: styd on fnl f: nvr able to chal* **66/1**
410- **6** 1/2 **Prize Ring**[34] 5624 5-9-5 **52** RWinston 16 54
(GMMoore) *in tch: rdn over 2f out: no hdwy* **12/1**
-133 **7** 3/4 **Righty Ho**[37] 2348 10-8-12 **45** VHalliday 10 46
(WHTinning) *proninent: rdn 3f out: fdd fnl 2f* **12/1**
501- **8** 1/2 **Millkom Elegance**[10] 4948 5-8-12 **45** (b) GParkin 4 45
(KARyan) *w ldr: ev ch and rdn over 1f out: wknd ins last* **10/1**
0-50 **9** 1 **Stepastray**[29] 2551 7-8-11 **44** DAllan 11 42
(REBarr) *in tch: rdn over 2f out: sn btn* **28/1**
0 **10** shd **Regal Fantasy (IRE)**[16] 2939 4-8-3 **36** PFessey 13 34
(PABlockley) *sn towards rr: styd on fnl 2f: n.d* **66/1**
0552 **11** 3/4 **Ipledgeallegiance (USA)**[11] 3099 8-8-2 **35** (b) GDuffield 2 32
(DWChapman) *towards rr: hdwy into midfield 1/2-way: no further prog* **6/1**[2]
0003 **12** shd **Border Terrier (IRE)**[12] 3041 6-8-7 **40** (b) KDarley 20 37
(MDHammond) *in tch: hung bdly rt paddock bnd after 3f: wknd over 2f out* **12/1**
0004 **13** 1 1/2 **Blue Venture (IRE)**[35] 2408 4-9-4 **51** GFaulkner 19 45
(PCHaslam) *sn towards rr: sme hdwy u.p over 2f out: n.d* **16/1**
3141 **14** 1 1/4 **Little Task**[9] 3149 6-8-11 **44** 6ex RFfrench 5 36
(JSWainwright) *midfield: outpcd 4f out: n.d* **7/1**[3]
4-00 **15** 10 **Sea Of Happiness**[22] 2759 4-8-4 **40** THamilton(3) 3 16
(CGrant) *midfield to 1/2-way: sn bhd* **100/1**
046/ **16** 1 1/2 **Free Will**[18] 3231 7-9-8 **55** DeanMcKeown 6 29
(RCGuest) *hld up: hdwy into midfield 5f out: nt clr run 4f out: wknd 2f out* **14/1**
04-0 **17** 3 **Ultra Marine (IRE)**[12] 3056 4-8-12 **50** (b) MLawson(5) 17 19
(JSWainwright) *hld up: keen early: drvn along 4f out: sn btn* **50/1**
-003 **18** 3 **Margold (IRE)**[35] 2408 4-9-1 **48** ACulhane 7 12
(RHollinshead) *midfield whn hmpd and lost pl 4f out: n.d after* **12/1**
000- **19** 7 **Natmsky (IRE)**[510] 477 5-7-9 **35** DFentiman(7) 1 —
(GAHarker) *bhd most of way* **66/1**
0/06 **20** 5 **Norma Speakman (IRE)**[13] 3008 4-8-5 **43** PMulrennan(5) 8 —
(EWTuer) *in tch: rdn 4f out: sn wknd* **50/1**

2m 37.55s (-1.45) **Going Correction** -0.275s/f (Firm) **20 Ran SP% 128.4**
Speed ratings: **93,92,91,91,90 89,89,88,88,88 87,87,86,85,79 78,76,74,69,66**CSF £444.50 CT £4311.17 TOTE £32.30: £7.10, £11.80, £2.90, £1.90; EX 770.40 Place 6 £200.25, Place 5 £151.46.
**Owner** J Greenbank **Bred** Lord Harrington **Trained** Bolam, Co Durham
■ A first Flat winner for David Thompson.

**FOCUS**
A 0-55 handicap run at just a steady pace in a moderate time. This is ordinary form but fairly sound.

**NOTEBOOK**
**Sovereign State(IRE)**, a winner of five hurdles races, was returning to the level after an absence of over two years. Always handy, in the end he did just enough.
**Fairy Monarch(IRE)**, who hasn't won for over two years, put a poor effort at Ayr less than two weeks ago behind him.
**Paddy Mul** is running out of his skin at present and is much better given a stiffer test. He deserves credit for coming off the pace in a race not run at a true gallop.
**Lazzaz** has won from an 8lb higher mark on the All-Weather. A positive on the betting front, he was in the right position throughout but was still not good enough.
**Cryptogam**, a maiden after 14 previous outings, has slipped to a very lenient mark after being bang out of form so far this time. This was a much better effort.
**Prize Ring**, who has won twice over hurdles since he was last seen in action on the level last year, looks to need a stiffer test of stamina now.
T/Jkpt: Not won. T/Plt: £614.60 to a £1 stake. Pool: £43,023.60. 51.10 winning tickets. T/Qpdt: £72.70 to a £1 stake. Pool: £3,385.70. 34.45 winning tickets. JF

# 3202 KEMPTON (R-H)
Wednesday, June 30

**OFFICIAL GOING: Good to firm**

## 3412 MORE O'FERRALL AMATEUR RIDERS' H'CAP (FOR LADY AND GENTLEMAN AMATEUR RIDERS) 1m 1f (R)
6:40 (6:41) (E) (0-75,71) 3-Y-O+ £3,581 (£826; £826; £275) Stalls High

Form RPR
6200 **1** **Graft**[13] 3018 5-10-5 **60** (b) MrsCThompson(5) 7 69
(MrsPTownsley) *lw: mid div: stdy hdwy 2f out: swtchd lft over 1f out: str run inide last to ld cl home: readily* **25/1**
2010 **2** 1 1/4 **Gran Clicquot**[11] 3103 9-9-7 **48** MrJPemberton(5) 12 54
(GPEnright) *in tch: hdwy 2f out: chal 1f out: styd pressing ldr ins lasst tl no ex cl home* **16/1**
4436 **2** dht **Todlea (IRE)**[23] 2738 4-11-4 **71** JAJenkins(3) 9 77
(JAOsborne) *lw: mid-div: hdwy on outside fr 3f out: drvn to ld 1f out: kpt on tl press: hdd and no ex cl home* **11/2**[1]
4005 **4** 2 1/2 **Pas De Surprise**[28] 2573 6-10-0 **53** MissEFolkes(3) 11 54
(PDEvans) *b: b.hind: chsd ldrs: rdn over 2f out: pressed ldrs 1f out: one pce ins last* **10/1**

3034 **5** $^{1}/_{2}$ **Bojangles (IRE)**$^{5}$ [3282] 5-9-9 **48** MrLNewnes(3) 1 48
(RBrotherton) *bhd: stl plenty to do over 2f out: str run fr over 1f out: fin wl: nt rch ldrs* **12/1**

0020 **6** *nk* **Madame Marie (IRE)**$^{16}$ [2943] 4-9-9 **50** MrDHutchison(5) 2 49
(SDow) *bhd: hdwy fr 2f out: r.o wl fnl f: nt rch ldrs* **25/1**

6560 **7** *hd* **Rainstorm**$^{22}$ [2753] 9-9-4 **43** oh1 MrsSOwen(3) 19 42
(WMBrisbourne) *s.i.s: bhd: hdwy on outside over 2f out: kpt on fr over 1f out: nt trble ldrs* **12/1**

6063 **8** $1^{1}/_{4}$ **Liberty Royal**$^{26}$ [2643] 5-11-0 **64** (p) MrSWalker 18 61
(PJMakin) *chsd ldrs: led 2f out: hdd 1f out: wknd ins last* **13/2**$^{2}$

-050 **9** *shd* **Jacaranda (IRE)**$^{19}$ [2834] 4-11-3 **67** MsCWilliams 13 63
(MrsALMKing) *lw: bhd: gd hdwy fr 2f out: r.o wl fnl f: nt rch ldrs* **25/1**

5420 **10** $3^{1}/_{2}$ **Phred**$^{8}$ [3177] 4-10-10 **60** MissEJohnsonHoughton 6 49
(RFJohnsonHoughton) *chsd ldrs: rdn over 2f out: wknd over 1f out* **14/1**

0325 **11** *nk* **Oh So Rosie (IRE)**$^{18}$ [2871] 4-10-4 **57** MrsSMoore(3) 10 46
(JSMoore) *chsd ldrs: rdn over 2f out: wknd over 1f out* **14/1**

000- **12** *nk* **Ark Admiral**$^{23}$ [3645] 5-11-0 **67** MissCTizzard(3) 15 55
(CLTizzard) *w ldr: led 5f out: hdd 4f out: wknd ins fnl 2f* **25/1**

00-0 **13** $1^{1}/_{4}$ **Honeystreet (IRE)**$^{22}$ [2753] 4-10-2 **52** MissSBrotherton 3 38
(JDFrost) *b: mid-div: rdn and no hdwy fr over 2f out* **20/1**

0542 **14** $^{3}/_{4}$ **Paso Doble**$^{5}$ [3282] 6-10-0 **57** (p) MrJMillman(7) 16 41
(BRMillman) *lw: led tl hdd 5f out: styd pressing ldrs: rdn over 2f out: wknd ins fnl quarter m* **7/1**$^{3}$

0-00 **15** *hd* **Somayda (IRE)**$^{20}$ [2810] 9-9-0 **43** oh3 JDoyle(7) 4 27
(MissJacquelineSDoyle) *b: bhd most of way* **50/1**

-002 **16** $^{1}/_{2}$ **Chevronne**$^{19}$ [2833] 4-10-9 **59** MrLJefford 17 42
(LGCottrell) *bhd most of way* **7/1**$^{3}$

12U0 **17** *1* **The Gaikwar (IRE)**$^{44}$ [2170] 5-10-8 **65** (b) MrJoshuaHarris(7) 20 46
(NEBerry) *w ldrs: led 4f out: hdd 2f out: snw wknd* **20/1**

3500 **18** *4* **Deeper In Debt**$^{12}$ [3048] 6-10-8 **65** MrSGascoyne(7) 14 38
(JAkehurst) *nvr bttr than mid-div* **25/1**

640- **19** $1^{1}/_{4}$ **Titian Flame (IRE)**$^{31}$ [2857] 4-10-3 **58** MissAWallace(5) 8 28
(MrsPNDutfield) *in tch 6f* **33/1**

0124 **20** *28* **Leyaaly**$^{14}$ [2990] 5-9-4 **43** oh5 (p) MissLJHarwood(3) 5 —
(BAPearce) *lw: a in rr* **33/1**

1m 55.28s (0.95) **Going Correction** +0.125s/f (Good) **20** Ran SP% **134.0**
Speed ratings: **100,98,98,96,96 95,95,94,94,91 91,90,89,89,88 88,87,84,82,58** TOTE £35.80: £11.00 TRIFECTA PL: T £2.30, GC £4.40, PDS £2.40; EX: G/T £179.70, G/GC £87.50; CSF: G/T £76.30, G/GC £185.71; TRICAST: G/T/GC £1,179.69, G/GC/T £1.
**Owner** Paul Townsley **Bred** Raffin Stud **Trained** Dunsfold, Surrey

**FOCUS**
The pace was strong but this is ordinary form. The winner is well treated if building on this.

**NOTEBOOK**
**Graft**, who has left Mick Easterby's yard since his latest start, was taking a drop in trip. He came with a well timed run between horses to win cosily, his rider not having to do anything on him.
**Gran Clicquot**, who had every chance, was 3lb higher than when winning at Goodwood two runs back for the same rider.
**Todlea(IRE)**, who is proving consistent this season, came with a sweeping run down the outside but could not sustain the effort close home.
**Pas De Surprise** was successful in this event a year ago from a pound higher mark. He looks to be running into form.
**Bojangles(IRE)** finished in good style from his poor draw.
**Madame Marie(IRE)**, who was poorly drawn, ran her usual race, finishing strongly from the back of the field but too late. She is still a maiden but is capable of winning a race when things drop right.
**Rainstorm** has dropped to a mark a pound lower than when last visiting the winner's enclosure in August and he could be about to strike form.
**Liberty Royal** *Official explanation: trainer said gelding finished distressed*

## 3413 GIRLS NIGHT OUT MAIDEN STKS 5f
7:10 (7:11) (D) 2-Y-O **£4,797** (£1,476; £738; £369) **Stalls** Low

Form RPR

**1** **Notjustaprettyface (USA)** 2-8-9 SDrowne 3 84+
(HMorrison) *cmpt: str: bit bkwd: s.i.s: bhd: stdy hdwy fr 2f out: qcknd to ld last half f: easily* **9/1**

52 **2** *2* **African Storm (IRE)**$^{4}$ [3302] 2-9-0 LDettori 5 82
(SKirk) *lw: led: rdn 2f out: hdd and nt pce of wnr last half f* **5/1**$^{2}$

0 **3** $1^{1}/_{2}$ **Lady Ann Summers (USA)**$^{14}$ [2970] 2-8-9 JFortune 8 72
(BJMeehan) *chsd ldrs: rdn 2f out: nt pce of ldrs 1f out: wknd last half f* **11/10**$^{1}$

0 **4** $^{1}/_{2}$ **Grand Place**$^{9}$ [3157] 2-9-0 RLMoore 7 75
(RHannon) *lw: s.i.s: bhd: hdwy 1/2-way: pressed ldrs and rdn 2f out: wknd ins fnl f* **11/2**$^{3}$

06 **5** *2* **Lowestoft Playboy**$^{12}$ [3051] 2-9-0 JPMurtagh 2 68
(MrsCADunnett) *chsd ldrs: rdn and outpcd over 2f out: n.d after* **10/1**

660 **6** $2^{1}/_{2}$ **Taipan Tommy (IRE)**$^{6}$ [3228] 2-9-0 DaneO'Neill 9 59
(SDow) *swtg: rrd stalls: bhd: sme hdwy fr over 1f out* **66/1**

**7** *hd* **Looking Great (USA)** 2-9-0 SCarson 6 59
(RFJohnsonHoughton) *leggy: unf: sn pushed along to stay in tch: wknd fr 2f out* **14/1**

44 **8** *nk* **Ninah's Intuition**$^{57}$ [1871] 2-8-11 SHitchcott(3) 4 58
(JMBradley) *chsd ldrs tl wknd 1/2-way* **20/1**

59.63 secs (-1.58) **Going Correction** -0.20s/f (Firm) **8** Ran SP% **111.7**
Speed ratings: **104,100,98,97,94 90,90,89**CSF £50.79 TOTE £11.10: £3.40, £1.70, £1.10; EX 61.40.
**Owner** Loddington Bloodstock **Bred** Hargus Sexton And Sandra Sexton **Trained** East Ilsley, Berks

**FOCUS**
A very smart time indeed for a race of its type and an impressive start for Notjustaprettyface. She looks one to follow.

**NOTEBOOK**
**Notjustaprettyface(USA)**, a close relative of high-class juvenile and successful sire Sri Pekan, cost 45,000gns at the breeze-ups. Shaken up to improve at halfway, she ran up the backs of her rivals and her rider temporarily had to take a pull, before she quickened up nicely to take command inside the last and score in the style of a useful filly. She did not appear fully wound up for this debut and it will be disappointing if she cannot step up on this.
**African Storm(IRE)**, making a quick reappearance, ran his race but was ultimately no match for the filly. His turn should not be delayed for long.
**Lady Ann Summers(USA)**, who made her debut in the Queen Mary at Ascot, was below that form on this second run. Caught a bit flat-footed going to the final furlong, she promises to stay six.
**Grand Place** looked a danger when pulled to the outside for his effort but faded inside the last. He has ability but may need a bit more time to strengthen.
**Lowestoft Playboy** showed pace against the rail to dispute the lead to halfway before being left behind by the principals.
**Looking Great(USA)** is out of a half-sister to Princess Royal Stakes winner Delilah. Green for this debut, he was quickly outpaced and is going to need farther.

## 3414 WILLIAMHILLPOKER.COM EBF NOVICE STKS 6f
7:40 (7:40) (D) 2-Y-O **£5,343** (£1,644; £822; £411) **Stalls** Low

Form RPR

2 **1** **Amazin**$^{9}$ [3157] 2-8-12 RHughes 2 84
(RHannon) *lw: t.k.h early: trckd ldrs:qcknd to ld wl over 1f out:shkn up ins last: readily* **8/13**$^{1}$

**2** $1^{1}/_{4}$ **Goodwood Spirit** 2-8-8 TQuinn 1 76+
(JLDunlop) *leggy: scope: lw: trckd ldrs: hdwy on rails and nt clr run appr fnl f: swtchd rt and r.o to take 2nd but no ch w wnr* **8/1**

2321 **3** $^{1}/_{2}$ **The Crooked Ring**$^{11}$ [3104] 2-9-2 KFallon 3 83
(PDEvans) *led tl narrowly hdd over 3f out: styd chalng: led 2f out: hdd wl over 1f out: no imp and lost 2nd nr fin* **10/3**$^{2}$

21 **4** *5* **Gee Bee Em**$^{7}$ [3192] 2-8-11 SHitchcott(3) 4 66
(MRChannon) *w ldr: led over 3f out: hdd 2f out: sn wknd* **15/2**$^{3}$

1m 12.78s (-0.29) **Going Correction** -0.20s/f (Firm) **4** Ran SP% **107.9**
Speed ratings: **93,91,90,84**CSF £5.88 TOTE £1.70; EX 6.10.
**Owner** K Panos **Bred** Theobalds Stud **Trained** East Everleigh, Wilts

**FOCUS**
The two previous winners in this small field help set the standard for the form. Amazin ran close to his debut form, while Goodwood Spirit made an eye-catching debut.

**NOTEBOOK**
**Amazin**, who has done well since his debut, gave Hannon his third consecutive victory in this event. He scored comfortably, despite idling a little in front, and should continue to progress.
**Goodwood Spirit** is a half-brother to four winners at between six and eight furlongs. Encountering trouble when beginning his run, he finished well once switched off the rail, although the winner scored with a bit up his sleeve. His stable's juveniles have not been firing but he should soon go one better.
**The Crooked Ring**, without the visor he wore when off the mark at Warwick, was also back up in trip. He was not disgraced conceding weight all round.
**Gee Bee Em**, who faced a stiff task under her penalty, was the first beaten and this was disappointing.

## 3415 CLEAR CHANNEL H'CAP 1m 1f (R)
8:10 (8:11) (C) (0-90,90) 3-Y-0+ **£9,555** (£2,940; £1,470; £735) **Stalls** High

Form RPR

-005 **1** **Spanish Don**$^{21}$ [2789] 6-9-7 **83** TQuinn 3 92
(DRCElsworth) *lw: hld up in rr: hdwy on outside over 1f out: str run and edgd rt ins last: led last strides* **8/1**

-622 **2** *nk* **James Caird (IRE)**$^{18}$ [2894] 4-9-8 **84** JPMurtagh 8 92
(MHTompkins) *lw: chsd ldrs: edgd rt 2f out: led over 1f out: hrd drvn ins last: hdd last strides* **3/1**$^{1}$

-010 **3** $1^{1}/_{2}$ **Guilded Flyer**$^{26}$ [2638] 5-9-11 **87** WSupple 2 92
(WSKittow) *chsd ldr after 3f: led ins fnl 3f: hdd over 1f out: outpcd ins last* **14/1**

-000 **4** *1* **Chinkara**$^{14}$ [2969] 4-9-11 **90** JFMcDonald(3) 5 94+
(BJMeehan) *bhd: hdwy on outside 3f out: chal over 1f out: one pce whn n.m.r ins last* **20/1**

1-00 **5** $1^{1}/_{4}$ **Best Be Going (IRE)**$^{30}$ [2537] 4-9-0 **76** EAhern 4 77
(PWHarris) *led 1f: styd chsng ldrs: rdn over 2f out: one pce whn n.m.r ins fnl f and eased cl home* **9/1**

4030 **6** *1* **Desert Island Disc**$^{12}$ [3046] 7-8-4 **71** NChalmers(5) 10 70
(JJBridger) *lw: chsd ldrs: rdn over 2f out: wknd appr fnl f* **20/1**

1302 **7** *hd* **Voice Mail**$^{7}$ [3191] 5-8-13 **78** LPKeniry(3) 7 76
(AMBalding) *hld up in rr: rdn over 2f out: nvr gng pce to rch ldrs* **9/1**

0-01 **8** *5* **Portmanteau**$^{43}$ [2198] 3-8-12 **85** KFallon 6 73
(SirMichaelStoute) *lw: stdd rr after 1f: pushed along over 2f out: a in rr* **11/2**$^{2}$

60-6 **9** $^{1}/_{2}$ **Giocoso (USA)**$^{26}$ [2646] 4-9-3 **82** SHitchcott(3) 9 69
(BPalling) *bhd: sme hdwy on rails whn bdly hmpd 2f out* **25/1**

-315 **10** *1* **Tannoor (USA)**$^{23}$ [2732] 3-8-5 **78** PRobinson 12 63
(MAJarvis) *s.i.s: a in rr* **10/1**

1-13 **11** $1^{1}/_{2}$ **Penrith (FR)**$^{22}$ [2764] 3-9-2 **89** JFanning 11 71
(MJohnston) *chsd ldrs: wknd whn hmpd on rails jst ins fnl 2f* **6/1**$^{3}$

0-60 **12** *8* **Shamrock City (IRE)**$^{14}$ [2969] 7-9-12 **88** SDrowne 1 54
(PHowling) *swtg: b: led after 1f: hdd ins fnl 3f: wkng on rails whn bdly hmpd 2f out* **66/1**

1m 53.11s (-1.22) **Going Correction** +0.125s/f (Good)
**WFA** 3 from 4yo+ 11lb **12** Ran SP% **116.4**
Speed ratings: **110,109,108,107,106 105,105,100,100,99 98,91**CSF £30.10 CT £342.08 TOTE £10.50: £3.50, £1.40, £4.90; EX 33.10.
**Owner** Richard J Cohen **Bred** Juddmonte Farms **Trained** Whitsbury, Hants

**FOCUS**
There was a fair pace on here for what was on paper a competitive affair. The form looks reliable without being outstanding.

**NOTEBOOK**
**Spanish Don**, who appeared to be coming into form when running well at Newbury last time out, confirmed that impression with success off a 1lb higher mark than for his last win. The decent gallop suited him as he likes to be held up off the pace and come late.
**James Caird(IRE)** was finishing runner-up for the fourth time in his last five races. He took up the running approaching the furlong marker and looked the most likely winner, but he does not do a lot in front and the winner came with a rare rattle. He probably needs producing later.
**Guilded Flyer** did not run at all badly given that he did not get the outright lead, which he craves, and had anything but an easy time of it once he did get to the front.
**Chinkara** was taking a drop in grade and ran a far more promising race. He suffered incidental interference late on but it made no real difference. He probably needs to drop a few more pounds but will be interesting back at Goodwood, where he won last year.
**Best Be Going(IRE)** did not help himself by doing so much early in the race, but he too probably still needs dropping a pound or two.
**Desert Island Disc** did not run too badly over a trip short of her best.
**Voice Mail** saves his best for Bath.
**Penrith(FR)** got squeezed up two furlongs out and soon dropped out of contention. He ran better than his finishing position suggests but he would not have threatened for the places.

## 3416 WILLIAMHILLCASINO.COM H'CAP 6f
8:40 (8:42) (D) (0-80,77) 3-Y-0+ **£5,499** (£1,692; £846; £423) **Stalls** Low

Form RPR

00-0 **1** **Prince Dayjur (USA)**$^{46}$ [2132] 5-9-10 **74** (v1) KFallon 3 85
(MJWallace) *lw: mde all: rdn and qcknd fr 2f out: styd on wl nr fin* **14/1**

-212 **2** $^{3}/_{4}$ **Devon Flame**$^{18}$ [2873] 5-9-8 **75** JFMcDonald(3) 8 84
(RJHodges) *lw: chsd wnr thrght: styd on u.p fr over 1f out but no imp nr fin* **11/4**$^{2}$

0463 **3** *hd* **Mr Malarkey (IRE)**$^{18}$ [2899] 4-9-13 **77** JPMurtagh 1 85
(MrsCADunnett) *pressed ldrs: rdn 2f out: kpt on fnl f but nt qckn nr fin* **5/2**$^{1}$



The Form Book, Raceform Ltd, Compton, RG20 6NL

5002 **4** *nk* **Astrac (IRE)**[19] 2834 13-7-13 **49**............................. PMQuinn 11 56
(MrsALMKing) *hld up in rr: rapid hdwy over 2f out: chsd ldrs ins fnl f: nt qckn cl home* **16/1**

-000 **5** *hd* **Hey Presto**[6] 3243 4-9-5 **69**............................. PRobinson 2 75
(CGCox) *lw: hld up in rr: rdn 2f out: swtchd rt and styd on fr over 1f out: r.o ins last: kpt on but nt rch ldrs* **7/2**[3]

0040 **6** *1 ¼* **Currency**[9] 3141 7-9-12 **76**............................. RLMoore 9 79
(JMBradley) *b: pushed along in rr: swtchd rt: rdn and rapid hdwy appr fnl f: kpt on but nt pce to trble ldrs ins last* **20/1**

6-00 **7** *½* **Canterloupe (IRE)**[32] 2477 6-9-12 **76**.............................(t) DSweeney 7 77
(PJMakin) *chsd ldrs: rdn 1/2-way: styd prom tl wknd wl ins last* **14/1**

-062 **8** *1 ½* **Sparkling Jewel**[7] 3195 4-9-10 **74**............................. DaneO'Neill 4 71
(RHannon) *sn rdn along in rr: styd on fnl f but n.d* **12/1**

-005 **9** *4* **Formalise**[9] 3141 4-8-12 **62**............................. SCarson 10 47
(GBBalding) *swtg: bhd: sme hdwy on outside 1/2-way: wknd ins fnl 2f* **20/1**

0-06 **10** *nk* **Golden Bounty**[9] 3141 5-9-11 **75**............................. RHughes 5 59
(RHannon) *lw: chsd ldrs: rdn 2f out: wknd qckly over 1f out* **20/1**

1m 11.92s (-1.15) **Going Correction** -0.20s/f (Firm) **10** Ran SP% **118.7**
Speed ratings: **99,98,97,97,97 95,94,92,87,87**CSF £51.97 CT £132.32 TOTE £19.00: £3.20, £1.50, £1.60; EX 68.50.

**Owner** Lucayan Stud **Bred** Golden Gate Stud **Trained** Newmarket, Suffolk

**FOCUS**
A modest winning time for what looks just a fair handicap. The winner has slipped a long way down the ratings, but the form is best viewed through the ageing fourth Astrac.

**NOTEBOOK**
**Prince Dayjur(USA)** was a smart two-year-old but his form since had given little cause for optimism. However, he had dropped a full 33lb since his peak, and with the visor on for the first time and Fallon booked to ride on his second start for his new stable, he made every yard. He looks ahead of the Handicapper, but his trainer warns he will fold quickly if headed. *Official explanation: trainer said, regarding the improved form shown, gelding had benefited from wearing a visor for the first time today*

**Devon Flame** ran a sound race, but he was running off a 4lb higher mark than when beaten at Bath last time and the Handicapper looks to be getting his measure now.

**Mr Malarkey(IRE)** has never won without blinkers and for some reason they were left off on this occasion.

**Astrac(IRE)** came home well and this performance in addition to his Chepstow effort shows him to be in fine form at present.

**Hey Presto** ran well enough. He is the type who needs everything to drop just right, as his record of one win from 19 starts suggests.

**Currency** continues to struggle for his best form.

## 3417 BOOK NOW FOR GALA NIGHT MAIDEN STKS 1m 4f
**9:10** (9:10) (D) 3-Y-O **£5,564** (£1,712; £856; £428) **Stalls** High

Form RPR

46 **1** **Stage Right**[9] 3161 3-9-0 ............................. DaneO'Neill 2 82+
(DRCElsworth) *lw: chsd ldrs: rdn to ld over 1f out: styd on wl fnl f: readily* **25/1**

60-2 **2** *1 ½* **Meissen**[18] 2888 3-8-9 75............................. TQuinn 7 75
(ACStewart) *chsd ldrs: t.k.h early: rdn to chal over 1f out: chsd wnr ins last: one pce* **5/1**[3]

0 **3** *3* **Gift Voucher (IRE)**[47] 2085 3-9-0 ............................. KFallon 4 75+
(SirMichaelStoute) *bit bkwd: hld up in rr: styd on fr over 1f out: fin wl to take 3rd cl home: nt a danger: should improve* **9/1**

**4** *nk* **Dahjee (USA)** 3-9-0.............................(t) LDettori 9 74
(SaeedBinSuroor) *w'like: s.i.s: sn in tch: rdn and outpcd 3f out:styd on again fr 2f out: chsd ldrs over 1f out: wknd and lost 3rd nr fin* **13/8**[1]

6 **5** *3* **Roman Forum**[35] 2412 3-9-0 ............................. RHughes 6 70
(HRACecil) *bit bkwd: led: hdd 2f out: wknd qckly over 1f out* **14/1**

44 **6** *nk* **Pope's Hill (IRE)**[9] 3138 3-9-0 ............................. JPMurtagh 5 69
(LMCumani) *bhd: hdwy on outside 3f out: nvr gng pce to rch ldrs and wknd over 1f out* **7/1**

05 **7** *½* **Vicat Cole**[18] 2882 3-9-0 ............................. JFortune 3 68
(HJCyzer) *chsd ldr: led and carried hdd high 2f out: hdd & wknd qckly over 1f out* **33/1**

5 **8** *1* **Qudraat (IRE)**[27] 2632 3-9-0 ............................. WSupple 8 67
(ACStewart) *lw: bhd: effrt 3f out: n.d: bhd fnl 2f* **4/1**[2]

0-0 **9** *dist* **Tout Les Sous**[37] 2357 3-9-0 ............................. SWKelly 10 —
(Jean-ReneAuvray) *a in rr: t.o* **100/1**

2m 36.01s (1.01) **Going Correction** +0.125s/f (Good) **9** Ran SP% **111.7**
Speed ratings: **101,100,98,97,95 95,95,94,**—CSF £139.25 TOTE £24.90: £4.70, £1.30, £2.80; EX 151.50 Place 6 £57.20, Place 5 £19.09.

**Owner** J C Smith **Bred** Littleton Stud **Trained** Whitsbury, Hants

**FOCUS**
The performance of the 75-rated runner-up suggests this was just a fair maiden.

**NOTEBOOK**
**Stage Right**, whose dam was fourth in the Oaks, is a half-brother to four winners, including Gold Medallist, who stays well. He looked sure to appreciate the step up in trip from a mile but it still came as something of a surprise that he was good enough to take this race. He should stay farther in time.

**Meissen**, another stepping up in trip, was one of the most experienced in the line-up and ran well in defeat, although her performance probably says a lot about the overall quality of the race.

**Gift Voucher(IRE)** ◆ looks the one to take out of the race. A half-brother to Golan and to two other middle-distance winners, he was not given a hard ride on his second start but stayed on takingly for third place. He looks sure to come into his own once handicapped and is one to look out for in that sphere.

**Dahjee(USA)**, the only previously unraced runner in the field, is a full-brother to Dubai Millennium and half-brother to several other winners. He has a fantastic pedigree, but on this evidence he is going to struggle to live up to it.

**Roman Forum** made more of an impression this time, but he was treading water inside the final two furlongs and this step up in trip may not have been what he wanted.

**Pope's Hill(IRE)** will surely be of more interest when he ventures into handicap company.

T/Plt: £79.30 to a £1 stake. Pool: £53,602.85. 493.20 winning tickets. T/Qpdt: £16.10 to a £1 stake. Pool: £3,037.80. 139.20 winning tickets. ST

# 3302 LINGFIELD (L-H)
## Wednesday, June 30

**OFFICIAL GOING: Turf course - good to firm (firm in places); all-weather course - standard**
Wind: fresh bhd Weather: fine but cloudy

## 3418 WHIPS AND TEES MAIDEN AUCTION STKS 5f (P)
**2:10** (2:10) (E) 2-Y-O **£3,406** (£1,048; £524; £262) **Stalls** High

Form RPR

052 **1** **Russian Rocket (IRE)**[24] 2702 2-8-2 ............................. HayleyTurner(5) 8 77
(MrsCADunnett) *chsd ldrs: rdn over 2f out: c wd bnd wl over 1f out: r.o to ld wl ins fnl f: edgd lft: kpt on* **7/2**[2]

2 **2** *½* **Connotation**[16] 2927 2-8-4 ............................. EAhern 1 73
(PWD'Arcy) *chsd ldrs: rdn over 2f out: effrt to chal ins fnl f: jst outpcd* **9/2**[3]

342 **3** *¾* **Forzeen**[11] 3104 2-8-9 ............................. LDettori 7 75
(JAOsborne) *led: rdn 2f out: edgd rt over 1f out: hdd and nt qckn wl ins fnl f* **11/8**[1]

06 **4** *½* **Kempsey**[16] 2947 2-8-7 ............................. ADaly 5 71
(JJBridger) *chsd ldr: rdn and hanging rt fr 2f out: ev ch ins fnl f: hld whn squeezed out last 50yds* **20/1**

0 **5** *4* **Kingsgate Bay (IRE)**[22] 2761 2-8-9 ............................. NPollard 3 59
(JRBest) *s.s: detached in last pair: nudged along over 1f out: nvr nr ldrs* **16/1**

5 **6** *½* **Peopleton Brook**[18] 2872 2-8-7 ............................. TQuinn 4 56
(DWPArbuthnot) *chsd ldrs: snatched up over 4f out: wknd over 1f out* **7/1**

3530 **7** *11* **Dustini (IRE)**[47] 2095 2-8-2 .............................(b) MHalford(7) 2 19
(WGMTurner) *outpcd and a wl bhd: t.o* **20/1**

60.51 secs (0.73) **Going Correction** +0.10s/f (Slow) **7** Ran SP% **110.4**
Speed ratings: **98,97,96,95,88 88,70**CSF £18.11 TOTE £4.10: £2.40, £2.60; EX 12.10.

**Owner** Mrs Christine Dunnett **Bred** Tally-Ho Stud **Trained** Hingham, Norfolk
■ Stewards Enquiry : Hayley Turner two-day ban: careless riding (Jul 11-12)

**FOCUS**
An ordinary maiden run at a fair pace and the first four were well clear. The form looks solid enough.

**NOTEBOOK**
**Russian Rocket(IRE)**, who had shown fair form in three previous outings, got off the mark in game fashion. He was carried wide off the home turn and lost ground in the process, but really stuck to his task well under pressure and ran out a deserved winner. He should be placed to advantage when the nurseries begin.
**Connotation** travelled well into the straight and looked the most likely winner, but found less than expected under serious pressure. This was, however, another promising effort and she clearly has what it takes to win a maiden.
**Forzeen** held every chance in the straight, but could not find a change of gear when it mattered. He looks in need of another furlong, as he looks exposed over this trip, and will no doubt fare better once handicapped.
**Kempsey** was looking just held when he met trouble close home. This represented his best effort to date and he looks to be slowly going the right way.
**Kingsgate Bay(IRE)**, as on his debut, fell out of the gates and was up against it from then on. However, he found his stride as the race went on and shaped with promise.

## 3419 FORMOST FABRICATIONS SUMMER CLASSIFIED STKS 1m (P)
**2:40** (2:40) (E) 3-Y-O+ **£3,393** (£1,044; £522; £261) **Stalls** High

Form RPR

6000 **1** **Invader**[11] 3086 8-9-7 74.............................(bt) DHolland 2 82
(CEBrittain) *racd in midfield: lost pl 1/2-way: last 2f out: drvn and prog over 1f out: styd on strly to ld last stride* **14/1**

1-30 **2** *shd* **Mallard (IRE)**[8] 3167 6-9-7 74............................. MFenton 6 82
(JGGiven) *trckd ldrs: effrt 2f out: rdn to ld 1f out: edgd rt fnl f: hdd last stride* **11/1**

0040 **3** *1* **Island Rapture**[11] 3091 4-9-1 71............................. LDettori 8 74
(JARToller) *dwlt: hld up in rr: prog on wd outside over 2f out: rdn to chal ins fnl f: nt qckn* **7/1**[3]

0151 **4** *2* **Tre Colline**[13] 3023 5-9-8 75............................. GBaker 11 76
(NTinkler) *lw: hld up in rr: prog on wd outside 3f out: hrd rdn and chsd ldrs over 1f out: one pce* **7/1**[3]

0600 **5** *nk* **Flying Treaty (USA)**[80] 1345 7-9-6 73............................. SDrowne 9 73
(JLSpearing) *chsd ldrs: rdn over 3f out: cl up u.p over 1f out: wknd ins fnl f* **25/1**

43-0 **6** *nk* **Morning After**[41] 2237 4-9-4 74............................. JPMurtagh 1 71
(JRFanshawe) *hld up in rr: effrt and swtchd lft over 1f out: one pce and nvr rchd ldrs* **7/1**[3]

3-10 **7** *2* **Slalom (IRE)**[74] 1460 4-9-8 75.............................(e) WSupple 10 70
(MissGayKelleway) *b. hind: dwlt: racd wd early: wnt prom over 5f out: rdn to ld over 1f out: hdd and fnd nil 1f out* **10/1**

0110 **8** *hd* **Athboy**[118] 959 3-8-7 70.............................(v) KFallon 3 65
(MJWallace) *lw: settled in rr: effrt 2f out: swtchd lft and drvn over 1f out: fnd nil* **13/2**[2]

0113 **9** *½* **Brazilian Terrace**[7] 3191 4-9-0 75............................. HayleyTurner(5) 5 66
(MLWBell) *trckd ldrs: pushed along over 3f out: steadily lost pl fr over 2f out* **5/1**[1]

065 **10** *1 ½* **Certain Justice (USA)**[30] 2516 6-9-8 75.............................(p) TQuinn 7 65
(PFICole) *taken down early and mounted on crse: prom: w ldr over 5f out: ev ch over 1f out: nt run on* **11/1**

505 **11** *3* **Certifiable**[17] 2906 3-8-11 74............................. SCarson 4 57
(AndrewReid) *b: b.hind: led for 2f: rdn and lost pl over 3f out: sn struggling* **8/1**

0065 **12** *1 ½* **Recount (FR)**[12] 3048 4-9-5 72............................. NPollard 12 52
(JRBest) *led after 2f to over 1f out: wknd rapidly* **33/1**

1m 40.82s (1.27) **Going Correction** +0.10s/f (Slow)
**WFA** 3 from 4yo+ 10lb **12** Ran SP% **117.8**
Speed ratings: **97,96,95,93,93 93,91,91,90,89 86,84**CSF £158.50 TOTE £11.70: £4.70, £3.80, £2.80; EX 119.50.

**Owner** R J Swinbourne **Bred** Sheikh Mohammed Obaid Al Maktoum **Trained** Newmarket, Suffolk

**FOCUS**
A fair and competitive handicap run at a solid pace.

**NOTEBOOK**
**Invader** really picked up under heavy pressure in the straight and collared the runner-up on the line. He appreciated this drop in class and was given a great ride on this occasion, but may find life tougher off a higher mark and back in handicaps.
**Mallard(IRE)** looked all over the winner when hitting the front over one out, but could not hold on come the line. He showed his poor effort from a bad draw at Beverley last time to be all wrong, and a reproduction of this form back on turf would see him in the winner's enclosure once again.

**Island Rapture** settled much better and ran with great credit. She would have been closer but for blowing the start and, as she looks well treated on her best form, a step back up to ten furlongs could see her end the losing run.
**Tre Colline** was taken off his feet early on this sharper circuit, but was staying on well in the straight. He did enough to suggest that he can go close off this mark when reverting to the Fibresand once again.
**Flying Treaty(USA)** did well to sustain his gallop under pressure and ran his best race for quite some time. The recent change of stable looks to have rekindled some enthusiasm, but his next run will tell us more.
**Morning After** looked like getting involved in the straight, having made ground from off the pace turning for home, but could not quicken and finished well held. She will come on again for this and is not one to write off.
**Brazilian Terrace** quickly came under pressure when holding a good position approaching the home turn and dropped out tamely. This was a well below-par effort.

## 3420 ENERGY & POWER CONSULTANTS H'CAP 6f (P)
**3:10** (3:11) (D ) (0-85,83) 3-Y-O **£5,609** (£1,726; £863; £431) **Stalls** Low

Form RPR
4545 **1** **Instant Recall (IRE)**[4] [3317] 3-9-4 **80**....(b) JFortune 5 88
(BJMeehan) *trckd ldrs: effrt over 1f out: led ins fnl f: drvn out* **6/1**[3]
0513 **2** ½ **Tag Team (IRE)**[23] [2726] 3-8-12 **77**.... LPKeniry(3) 1 83
(AMBalding) *trckd ldrs: effrt on inner over 1f out: led jst ins fnl f: edgd rt and sn hdd: nt qckn* **9/2**[2]
3000 **3** 1 **Torquemada (IRE)**[21] [2790] 3-7-9 **60** oh3.... FPFerris(3) 7 63
(WJarvis) *dwlt: wl in rr: prog 2f out: swtchd rt and drvn 1f out: styd on to take 3rd nr fin* **20/1**
4110 **4** ¾ **Eccentric**[81] [1333] 3-9-0 **76**.... SSanders 9 77
(AndrewReid) *w ldrs: led over 2f out: hdd and one pce jst ins fnl f* **14/1**
0-05 **5** 1 **Catch The Wind**[40] [2264] 3-9-0 **76**.... DHolland 2 74
(IAWood) *led for 1f: styd prom: ev ch fr 2f out tl fdd ent fnl f* **25/1**
54-0 **6** ½ **Sweetest Revenge (IRE)**[23] [2741] 3-8-10 **77**.... HayleyTurner(5) 4 73
(MDIUsher) *racd in midfield: rdn and no prog wl over 1f out: kpt on nr fin* **14/1**
1-50 **7** ½ **Ace Club**[40] [2269] 3-8-8 **70**.... MHills 10 65
(WJHaggas) *b.hind: chsd ldrs: rdn and unable qck over 1f out: wknd fnl f* **10/1**
400 **8** ½ **Trifti**[11] [3085] 3-8-3 **65**.... EAhern 8 58
(CACyzer) *a towards rr: rdn and no prog 2f out* **33/1**
2310 **9** 4 **Emtilaak**[23] [2726] 3-9-2 **78**.... WSupple 6 59
(BHanbury) *b: led after 1f to over 2f out: wknd over 1f out* **9/1**
-034 **10** 2½ **Bella Tutrice (IRE)**[4] [3307] 3-8-10 **72**.... KFallon 11 46
(IAWood) *racd wd: hld up in rr: shuffled along and no prog over 1f out: eased fnl f* **14/1**
3120 **11** 19 **Morse (IRE)**[39] [2309] 3-9-7 **83**.... LDettori 3 —
(JAOsborne) *a in rr: last and losing tch 1/2-way: t.o* **6/4**[1]

1m 13.27s (0.35) **Going Correction** +0.10s/f (Slow) **11** Ran **SP%** **123.1**
Speed ratings: **101,100,99,98,96 96,95,94,89,86 60**CSF £34.07 CT £533.32 TOTE £9.30: £2.80, £2.20, £4.60; EX 48.00.
**Owner** Mrs Susan Roy **Bred** Frank Dunne **Trained** Upper Lambourn, Berks

### FOCUS
A fair sprint run at a solid gallop and the form looks reliable.

### NOTEBOOK
**Instant Recall(IRE)**, far from disgraced in the first-time blinkers just four days previously at Newmarket, won well under a positive ride. He clearly likes this surface, having posted his only previous win at the track in March, and should continue to pay his way over this trip, but a higher mark will make life tougher back on turf.
**Tag Team(IRE)**, a dual winner on this surface in February, again edged right when hitting the front and could not fend off the winner's late challenge. This was another sound effort, and although he is probably weighted to his best, he may improve for a drop back to five furlongs and should continue to pay his way at this level.
**Torquemada(IRE)** was yet again sluggish at the start and gave himself plenty to do, but was really staying on with purpose in the final stages and posted a decent effort from 3lb out of the handicap. He likes this surface and is at the right end of the handicap, but is frustrating and must learn to break from the gates.
**Eccentric** was not allowed to dominate as he would prefer, but still ran with credit and will find easier opportunities. A step back up to seven furlongs around this circuit will be of benefit.
**Catch The Wind** showed plenty of early dash and was not beaten far. A drop to five furlongs could see this sharp filly get closer.
**Sweetest Revenge(IRE)** stayed on well enough, but lacked the early toe to adopt her favoured handy position and should improve again for this outing.
**Bella Tutrice(IRE)** *Official explanation: jockey said filly was never travelling*
**Morse(IRE)**, 8lb lower than if racing on turf, was really well backed for this, but never once looked like landing the odds. He was soon detatched and ran too badly to be true. His connections reported that he hated the kickback, but he was placed on this surface as a juvenile and there is hardly any kickback compared to the Fibresand, so something was clearly amiss. *Official explanation: trainer said colt missed the break and resented the kickback*

## 3421 LADBROKES.COM FILLIES' H'CAP 1m 3f 106y
**3:40** (3:41) (E ) (0-70,67) 3-Y-O **£3,445** (£1,060; £530; £265) **Stalls** High

Form RPR
406- **1** **Mazuna (IRE)**[271] [5337] 3-8-13 **59**.... EAhern 5 69
(CEBrittain) *trckd ldrs: led over 2f out: rdn and pressed fnl f: styd on wl nr fin* **20/1**
6042 **2** 1¼ **La Petite Chinoise**[14] [2977] 3-9-6 **66**.... SSanders 1 74
(RGuest) *lw: in tch: effrt over 3f out: chsd wnr 2f out: rdn to chal fnl f: no imp last 100yds* **5/1**[3]
4043 **3** 2½ **Bubbling Fun**[9] [3156] 3-9-4 **64**.... KFallon 10 68
(EALDunlop) *lw: hld up in rr: prog over 2f out: rdn to chse ldng pair jst over 1f out: kpt on but no imp* **4/1**[2]
-030 **4** 2½ **Lady Peaches**[11] [3091] 3-9-4 **67**.... J-PGuillambert(3) 9 67
(DMullarkey) *dwlt: t.k.h and hld up in last pair: effrt on outer 3f out: hrd rdn and kpt on fr over 1f out: no ch* **14/1**
02-0 **5** 3 **Macchiato**[77] [1394] 3-8-10 **56**.... SCarson 4 51
(RFJohnsonHoughton) *led to over 2f out: steadily wknd u.p* **16/1**
1320 **6** ¾ **Princess Galadriel**[5] [3264] 3-9-1 **61**.... NPollard 3 55
(JRBest) *t.k.h: hld up in midfield: rdn over 2f out: no prog over 1f out: wknd* **9/1**
0464 **7** ¾ **Ellina**[8] [3172] 3-9-6 **66**.... LDettori 11 59
(JPearce) *t.k.h: hld up in last pair: effrt on outer 3f out: no prog and btn 2f out* **14/1**
5-66 **8** nk **Alaloof (USA)**[45] [2146] 3-9-6 **66**.... WSupple 6 58
(JLDunlop) *in tch: rdn over 3f out: sn struggling and btn* **4/1**[2]
001 **9** 1 **Illeana (GER)**[28] [2584] 3-8-12 **58**.... DHolland 8 49
(WRMuir) *hld up in midfield: prog and prom 5f out: wknd over 2f out* **7/2**[1]
-500 **10** nk **Daydream Dancer**[9] [3156] 3-8-7 **53**.... PRobinson 7 43
(CGCox) *mostly chsd ldr to over 3f out: sn lost pl and btn* **16/1**
0004 **11** 18 **Out Of My Way**[62] [1726] 3-7-9 **44** oh17.... FPFerris(3) 2 —
(TMJones) *lw: prom tl wknd rapidly 3f out: t.o* **66/1**

2m 32.0s (2.48) **Going Correction** +0.225s/f (Good) **11** Ran **SP%** **120.2**
Speed ratings: **99,98,96,94,92 91,91,90,90,90 76**CSF £119.88 CT £496.25 TOTE £26.10: £4.50, £1.40, £2.20; EX 219.40.
**Owner** Saeed Manana **Bred** B Freiha **Trained** Newmarket, Suffolk

### FOCUS
A moderate affair run at a fair gallop.

### NOTEBOOK
**Mazuna(IRE)** ◆, last seen in a Polytrack maiden over six furlongs 271 days ago, defied her absence in good style and had absolutely no problems with this much longer trip. She is almost certainly capable of better and looks one to follow while she is at this lowly end of the handicap.
**La Petite Chinoise** again found one too good, but confirmed she has improved a touch since stepping up to this trip and was a clear second.
**Bubbling Fun** ran slightly below form and continues to frustrate. The potential to get off the mark is there and she may be worth a try over farther on this evidence.
**Lady Peaches** was very keen early on and obviously has her quirks, but looks the type to do better with more racing.
**Macchiato** had the run of the race and dictated the pace until finding little under pressure in the final two furlongs. She is entitled to improve a touch for this outing and a drop in trip would be of benefit.
**Alaloof(USA)** again frustrated and looks one to lay rather than play.
**Illeana(GER)**, well-backed to follow-up her win in a dire race last time, never looked a serious threat off this same mark. *Official explanation: jockey said filly was unsuited by the track and the firm ground*

## 3422 HENRY STREETER MAIDEN STKS 1m 2f
**4:10** (4:11) (D ) 3-Y-O+ **£3,877** (£1,193; £596; £298) **Stalls** Low

Form RPR
0- **1** **Alphecca (USA)**[313] [4348] 3-8-12.... KFallon 2 93+
(SirMichaelStoute) *rousted along to ld after 1f: mde rest: shkn up over 1f out: clr fnl f: comf* **2/1**[2]
2322 **2** 3 **Ganymede**[26] [2645] 3-8-12 81....(v[1]) DHolland 7 73
(MLWBell) *trckd wnr after 1f: pushed along 3f out: rdn to chal wl over 1f out: hung lft and nt run on* **8/11**[1]
**3** 5 **Safirah** 3-8-7.... PRobinson 4 58
(MAJarvis) *unf: led for 1f: restrained bhd ldrs: outpcd 3f out: shkn up and one pce after* **10/1**[3]
**4** nk **St Barchan (IRE)** 3-8-12.... TQuinn 3 63
(WJarvis) *w'like: bit bkwd: lw: s.s: hld up in last pair: outpcd 3f out: pushed along and kpt on fnl 2f* **33/1**
4 **5** 2½ **Port 'n Starboard**[26] [2645] 3-8-12.... LDettori 5 58
(CACyzer) *trckd ldrs: shkn up and outpcd over 2f out: disputing 3rd pl whn hung bdly rt over 1f out* **16/1**
00 **6** ½ **Scott**[8] [3168] 3-8-12.... GBaker 6 57
(JJay) *a in last pair: drvn and no prog 3f out* **66/1**

2m 10.48s (0.88) **Going Correction** +0.225s/f (Good)
**WFA** 3 from 5yo 12lb **6** Ran **SP%** **110.6**
Speed ratings: **105,102,98,98,96 95**CSF £3.63 TOTE £3.00: £1.90, £1.10; EX 4.00.
**Owner** Niarchos Family **Bred** Flaxman Holdings Ltd **Trained** Newmarket, Suffolk

### FOCUS
A modest maiden, but the winner won impressively and should have plenty more to offer. The time compares well with the later handicap.

### NOTEBOOK
**Alphecca(USA)** ◆, unplaced in a warm maiden on his sole juvenile outing, showed he has wintered well with a smooth display to get off the mark. He was rushed up to lead early on and ran distinctly green throughout, but the further he went, the better he shaped and there was an awful lot to like about the way he settled the argument late on. Considerably better than the bare result, he should stay further, be better for the run, and looks a most promising colt.
**Ganymede**, in the first-time visor, again found one too good and again looked to be slightly reluctant to fully go through with his effort under pressure. He is flattered by his current rating, but is the benchmark for the form, and time will no doubt tell there was little disgrace in this defeat. *Official explanation: jockey said colt hung left handed down the straight*
**Safirah**, a physically backward debutante who looked fit enough, shaped with promise and will come on a bundle for this experience. However, she did look a little one paced and may need further.
**Port 'n Starboard** looked like getting involved in the finish when challenging in the straight, but hung markedly right under pressure and obviously has his quirks. That said, he is entitled to improve again and looks one to do better when handicapped. *Official explanation: jockey said gelding hung right handed down the straight*

## 3423 DON'T FORGET LADIES EVENING 17TH JULY APPRENTICE H'CAP 1m 2f
**4:40** (4:40) (F ) (0-55,55) 4-Y-O+ **£3,031** (£866; £433) **Stalls** Low

Form RPR
3104 **1** **Our Destiny**[8] [3173] 6-9-6 **55**.... LTreadwell 2 63
(AWCarroll) *hld up in rr: stdy prog fr 3f out: pushed into ld jst ins fnl f: hanging lft but sn in command* **10/1**
0603 **2** 1½ **Jessinca**[5] [3264] 8-8-0 **40**.... LiamJones(5) 11 45
(APJones) *prom: effrt to ld 2f out: hdd and one pce jst ins fnl f* **10/1**
1000 **3** nk **Molly's Secret**[118] [966] 6-8-3 **45**....(p) AshleighHorton(7) 4 50
(CGCox) *led at stdy pce: pushed along and hdd 2f out: kpt on fnl f: a hld* **16/1**
2404 **4** 1 **Holly Rose**[16] [2939] 5-8-12 **52**....(p) LauraPike(5) 10 55
(DECantillon) *dwlt: hld up in tch: effrt on outer over 2f out: pressed ldrs over 1f out: hanging and nt qckn fnl f* **7/1**
5343 **5** nk **Vandenberghe**[16] [2939] 5-8-9 **49**.... RKeogh(5) 13 51
(JAOsborne) *trckd ldrs: effrt to chal over 2f out: one pce fr over 1f out* **13/2**[3]
-004 **6** 4 **Nautical**[11] [3088] 6-9-0 **52**.... WHogg(3) 5 47
(AWCarroll) *dwlt: hld up in last pair: prog on outer over 2f out: rdn and no imp fr over 1f out* **6/1**[2]
0064 **7** ½ **Single Track Mind**[12] [3049] 6-8-7 **42**.... StephanieHollinshead 8 36
(JRBoyle) *settled in rr: pushed along over 2f out: one pce and no imp on ldrs* **14/1**
0634 **8** 1½ **Mister Clinton (IRE)**[8] [3174] 7-9-1 **53**.... MHoward(3) 3 44
(DKIvory) *t.k.h: prom: lost pl over 2f out: n.d after* **7/1**
3032 **9** ½ **Fantasy Crusader**[11] [3088] 5-8-12 **50**....(p) MHalford(3) 9 40
(JAGilbert) *rrd bdly in stalls bef s: hld up in tch: rdn and struggling over 2f out* **4/1**[1]
5465 **10** ¾ **Miss Peaches**[28] [2597] 6-8-11 **46**.... KristinStubbs 1 34
(GGMargarson) *hld up in last pair: pushed along and no prog over 2f out* **10/1**
-000 **11** shd **Night Driver (IRE)**[29] [2560] 5-8-8 **48**....(e[1]) JemmaMarshall(5) 7 36
(GLMoore) *racd in midfield: rdn 3f out: sn btn* **10/1**



The Form Book, Raceform Ltd, Compton, RG20 6NL

0150 **12** *2* **Antony Ebeneezer**[34] 1281 5-7-11 **35**........................ DeanWilliams(3) 12 19
(CRDore) *pressed ldr to 3f out: wknd* **20/1**

2m 11.75s (2.15) **Going Correction** +0.225s/f (Good) **12** Ran SP% **126.3**
Speed ratings: **100,98,98,97,97 94,93,92,92,91 91,90**CSF £113.21 CT £1620.58 TOTE £12.90: £3.10, £3.00, £3.20; EX 143.40 Place 6 £584.27, Place 5 £238.55.
**Owner** Dennis Deacon **Bred** D A And Mrs Hicks **Trained** Wixford, Warwicks

**FOCUS**
A poor contest run at just a sedate galllop.

**NOTEBOOK**
**Our Destiny** won comfortably under a well-judged ride. He needs everything to fall right, but has been a rejuvenated character for current connections this year and he had no trouble defying top-weight, but the fact he was well held in a claimer latest sums up the form.
**Jessinca** ran another sound race, but had no answer to the winner when challenged. She is running into form.
**Molly's Secret** set the sedate pace until being outpaced two out, but stuck on once headed and ran one of her better races.
**Holly Rose** could only find the one pace and was hanging under pressure late in the day. Well treated on her old form, she looks to be going the wrong way at present.
**Vandenberghe** had every chance if good enough in the straight, but found little and just kept on at the same pace.
**Fantasy Crusader** played up at the start and showed little in the race. This was a poor show considering her latest efforts looked to give her an obvious chance in this. *Official explanation: jockey said gelding was injured after rearing in the stalls*
T/Plt: £377.80 to a £1 stake. Pool: £31,082.35. 60.05 winning tickets. T/Qpdt: £20.60 to a £1 stake. Pool: £2,386.40. 85.70 winning tickets. JN

## 2817 YARMOUTH (L-H)
### Wednesday, June 30

**OFFICIAL GOING: Firm (good to firm in places)**
A strong wind across the course ensured the ground was very firm.
Wind: Strong across. Weather: Cloudy.

### 3424 EUROPEAN BREEDERS FUND ADIOS MAIDEN STKS — 6f 3y
6:25 (6:26) (D) 2-Y-O — £4,735 (£1,457; £728; £364) Stalls High

Form RPR
**1** **Personify** 2-9-0 ........................ KMcEvoy 2 80
(SaeedBinSuroor) *sn w ldr: led 2f out: hdd over 1f out: rallied to ld wl ins fnl f* **9/4**[2]
**2** *nk* **Sovereignty (JPN)** 2-8-11 ........................ TPQueally(3) 3 79
(DRLoder) *plld hrd and prom: led over 1f out: rdn and hdd wl ins fnl f* **11/1**
**3** *2* **Motarassed** 2-9-0 ........................ RHills 5 73
(JLDunlop) *chsd ldrs: pushed along over 2f out: wandered over 1f out: styd on* **11/8**[1]
**4** *3* **Tanzani (USA)** 2-9-0 ........................ DHolland 4 64
(CEBrittain) *chsd ldrs: n.m.r and dropped rr 4f out: n.d after* **6/1**[3]
**5** *1 1/4* **Dralion** 2-9-0 ........................ SSanders 6 60
(JMPEustace) *edgd rt s: sn led: hdd 2f out: wknd fnl f* **7/1**
**6** *20* **African Emperor (FR)** 2-9-0 ........................ MTebbutt 7 —
(WJarvis) *chsd ldrs over 3f* **28/1**

1m 14.38s (0.78) **Going Correction** -0.025s/f (Good) **6** Ran SP% **111.4**
Speed ratings: **93,92,89,85,84 57**CSF £25.02 TOTE £3.40: £2.50, £4.20; EX 15.40.
**Owner** Godolphin **Bred** Darley **Trained** Newmarket, Suffolk

**FOCUS**
These were quite a nice bunch to look at with some well-related newcomers on show. However, with little to go on and a modest time the form is rated as just average for the time being, but may prove better.

**NOTEBOOK**
**Personify**, out of a Group Three-winning juvenile, knew his job and showed the right attitude to see off the runner-up, who looked to have his measure when going on. He looked as though he will stay an extra furlong in time.
**Sovereignty(JPN)** ◆, like the winner, is out of a mare that won a Group Three as a juvenile. He was always doing a little too much due to the steady pace and, with improvement to come as he steps up in trip, should not have too much trouble winning his maiden.
**Motarassed**, from the same family as Derby winner Erhaab, lacked the knowledge of the front pair. A lengthy colt, he looks certain to benefit from the experience.
**Tanzani(USA)**, a half-brother to Group One winner Pearl Of Love, looked in need of both the outing and the experience, and should do better in time.
**Dralion**, a half-brother to Rapscallion, is all legs at present, but he showed enough to suggest he can make his mark in due course.

### 3425 HAPPINOSE (S) STKS — 7f 3y
6:55 (6:55) (G) 3-Y-O — £2,583 (£738; £369) Stalls High

Form RPR
2-55 **1** **Mugeba**[130] 843 3-8-9 **59**........................ GCarter 2 52
(WJMusson) *racd centre: hld up: hdwy 3f out: rdn to ld and edgd rt wl ins fnl f: r.o* **11/4**[1]
4350 **2** *3/4* **City General (IRE)**[22] 2762 3-8-7 **49**........................(p) DerekNolan(7) 10 55
(JSMoore) *led stands' side over 4f: rdn over 1f out: edgd lft ins fnl f: r.o* **11/1**
0343 **3** *3/4* **Wares Home (IRE)**[12] 3037 3-9-0 **60**........................ DarrenWilliams 12 53
(KRBurke) *racd stands' side: chsd ldrs: rdn over 2f out: hung lft over 1f out: r.o ins fnl f* **5/1**[3]
3003 **4** *hd* **Zonnebeke**[6] 3229 3-8-9 **45**........................(v) IMongan 5 48
(KRBurke) *racd centre: chsd ldr: led that gp over 3f out: overall ldr over 2f out: clr over 1f out: hdd wl ins fnl f* **4/1**[2]
3240 **5** *6* **Soul Provider (IRE)**[7] 3193 3-8-9 **52**........................ SRighton 9 32
(MJAttwater) *chsd ldr stands' side: rdn and hung lft over 2f out: wknd over 1f out* **15/2**
6055 **6** *3* **Bookiesindexdotcom**[19] 2849 3-8-6 **39**........................(p) TPQueally(3) 3 24
(JRJenkins) *racd centre: chsd ldrs: rdn over 3f out: nt run on* **20/1**
0200 **7** *1 1/2* **Maybe Someday**[20] 2813 3-9-0 **55**........................(b) DHolland 6 25
(JBalding) *led centre to 1/2-way: wknd 2f out* **12/1**
5665 **8** *3/4* **David's Girl**[6] 3229 3-8-9 **38**........................ RMullen 1 18
(DMorris) *racd centre: bhd fr 1/2-way* **15/2**
**9** *1 1/2* **Trivial Pursuit** 3-9-0 ........................ MTebbutt 7 19
(WJarvis) *racd centre: bhd fr 1/2-way* **10/1**
0000 **10** *6* **Justice Jones**[24] 2705 3-9-0 **47**........................ DKinsella 11 4
(JLSpearing) *s.i.s: sn prom in centre: wknd 1/2-way* **40/1**
-000 **11** *16* **St George's Girl**[19] 2849 3-8-9 **25**........................ SWhitworth 4 —
(JRJenkins) *s.s: racd centre: outpcd* **100/1**

1m 26.63s (0.13) **Going Correction** -0.025s/f (Good) **11** Ran SP% **120.2**
Speed ratings: **98,97,96,96,89 85,84,83,81,74 56**CSF £35.21 TOTE £3.20: £1.60, £3.00, £2.00; EX 57.40.Mugeba was sold to Gay Kelleway for 9,000gns.
**Owner** Billings & Broughton Thermal Insulation **Bred** Broughton Bloodstock And M Billings **Trained** Newmarket, Suffolk

**FOCUS**
A moderate seller in which the field split into two, but there was no advantage to be gained by either side and the form appears sound for the level.

**NOTEBOOK**
**Mugeba**, tackling turf for the first time, was less exposed than the majority of her rivals and took advantage of the drop in class, landing something of a touch for connections. She was sold at the auction to Gay Kelleway.
**City General(IRE)** has plenty of form at this level and seemed to run his race, but was probably a bit unlucky to come up against an unexposed type.
**Wares Home(IRE)** again gave the impression he was far from straightforward.
**Zonnebeke** is proving difficult to place, but in her defence she may have been left in front plenty soon enough.
**Soul Provider(IRE)** looked to be hating the fast ground.
**Maybe Someday** *Official explanation: jockey said gelding was never travelling*
**David's Girl** *Official explanation: jockey said filly finished lame*

### 3426 AEROPAK H'CAP — 1m 3y
7:25 (7:25) (D) (0-80,80) 3-Y-O+ — £5,395 (£1,660; £830; £415) Stalls High

Form RPR
0002 **1** **Welcome Stranger**[11] 3086 4-9-7 **76**........................ LFletcher(3) 6 86
(JMPEustace) *s.i.s: hdwy 1/2-way: led over 1f out: rdn out* **10/3**[2]
0046 **2** *1 1/2* **Topton (IRE)**[4] 3299 10-9-10 **76**........................(b) SSanders 4 83
(PHowling) *hld up: hdwy over 2f out: rdn to chse wnr fnl f: styd on* **9/2**[3]
0623 **3** *5* **Answered Promise (FR)**[10] 3127 5-7-9 **54**........................ CHaddon(7) 7 49
(IAWood) *w ldrs: led over 3f out: rdn and hdd over 1f out: wknd ins fnl f* **7/1**
0000 **4** *1* **Hurricane Floyd (IRE)**[12] 3036 6-9-11 **80**........................ TPQueally(3) 2 73
(DRLoder) *trckd ldrs: rdn and ev ch over 1f out: wknd ins fnl f* **6/1**
3-00 **5** *1 1/2* **Mountcharge (IRE)**[11] 3089 3-9-1 **77**........................ IMongan 3 66
(CNAllen) *w ldrs to 1/2-way: sn rdn: wknd over 1f out* **16/1**
2-20 **6** *hd* **Borrego (IRE)**[18] 2891 4-9-12 **78**........................ DHolland 5 67
(CEBrittain) *chsd ldrs: rdn over 3f out: wknd over 1f out* **9/4**[1]
0-26 **7** *1/2* **Magic Amour**[20] 2806 6-8-8 **60**........................ CCatlin 1 48
(IanWilliams) *w ldrs over 4f: rdn and ev ch over 1f out: wknd ins fnl f* **12/1**

1m 39.15s (-0.55) **Going Correction** -0.025s/f (Good)
**WFA** 3 from 4yo+ 10lb **7** Ran SP% **112.4**
Speed ratings: **101,99,94,93,92 91,91**CSF £17.96 CT £95.87 TOTE £4.00: £3.40, £2.20; EX 18.50.
**Owner** H R Moszkowicz **Bred** Henry And Mrs Rosemary Moszkowicz **Trained** Newmarket, Suffolk

**FOCUS**
A fair handicap that was run at a steady early pace and the form is nothing out of the ordinary.

**NOTEBOOK**
**Welcome Stranger**, just 1lb higher than when last successful, had his optimum conditions and, getting first run on Topton, never looked likely to be reeled in.
**Topton(IRE)** did not have the strong pace he needs, so in the circumstances this was a fine effort.
**Answered Promise(FR)** seemed to run a bit flat and may have found this coming too soon after Warwick.
**Hurricane Floyd(IRE)** would have picked this lot up and carried them at his best, but sadly those days look long gone.
**Mountcharge(IRE)** *Official explanation: jockey said gelding hung left in the final furlong and a half*

### 3427 DIOMED DEVELOPMENTS CLAIMING STKS — 1m 3y
7:55 (7:55) (F) 3-Y-O+ — £2,947 (£842; £421) Stalls High

Form RPR
031- **1** **The Prince**[277] 4940 10-9-5 **85**........................ CCatlin 5 65
(IanWilliams) *hld up: hdwy over 2f out: rdn to ld ins fnl f: r.o* **15/8**[2]
0004 **2** *hd* **Heversham (IRE)**[24] 2704 3-9-0 **73**........................ DHolland 8 69
(WJHaggas) *led: rdn and hdd ins fnl f: r.o* **13/8**[1]
505 **3** *6* **Soviet Spirit**[21] 2777 3-8-8 **63**........................ OUrbina 2 50
(JRFanshawe) *chsd ldrs: rdn over 1f out: sn wknd* **10/3**[3]
**4** *3* **The Nibbler** 3-9-0 ........................ BDoyle 4 49
(GCHChung) *s.s: hld up: n.m.r and dropped rr over 2f out: kpt on ins fnl f* **80/1**
0000 **5** *nk* **Naughty Girl (IRE)**[18] 2869 4-8-10 **55**........................(t) NCallan 6 34
(PDEvans) *hld up: rdn over 2f out: wknd over 1f out* **20/1**
00 **6** *3 1/2* **Love Of Life**[84] 1295 3-8-3 ........................ PDoe 10 29
(JulianPoulton) *dwlt: sn chsng ldr: rdn and wknd over 1f out* **100/1**
0334 **7** *4* **Roving Vixen (IRE)**[7] 3193 3-8-0 **41**........................(b) JMackay 1 17
(JLSpearing) *plld hrd and prom: rdn over 2f out: sn wknd* **12/1**
0-0 **8** *18* **Albertine**[11] 3085 4-8-13 ........................ TPQueally(3) 7 —
(CADwyer) *s.i.s: sn prom: rdn and wknd over 3f out* **66/1**

1m 39.19s (-0.51) **Going Correction** -0.025s/f (Good)
**WFA** 3 from 4yo+ 10lb **8** Ran SP% **112.1**
Speed ratings: **101,100,94,91,91 88,84,66**CSF £5.03 TOTE £2.80: £1.10, £1.30, £1.10; EX 4.60.Heversham was claimed by J. Hetherton for £15,000.
**Owner** Patrick Kelly **Bred** Bottisham Heath Stud **Trained** Portway, Warwicks

**FOCUS**
Not much strength in depth here and the front three finished in the correct order on official ratings. The first two were clear but the winner was below his best.

**NOTEBOOK**
**The Prince** was entitled to win on official figures, but was made to work hard in the end. He clearly goes well fresh and is limited to the amount of racing he has, for he does not like soft ground and has arthritic joints.
**Heversham(IRE)**, much happier over this trip, had something of a soft lead and battled back bravely when headed. Although he has yet to strike on turf, it can only be a matter of time. *Official explanation: jockey said his whip was knocked out of his hand approaching the winning line*
**Soviet Spirit** showed plenty of knee action to post and would not have been ideally suited to the fast surface.

### 3428 BAZUKA H'CAP — 6f 3y
8:25 (8:28) (E) (0-70,70) 3-Y-O+ — £3,896 (£1,199; £599; £299) Stalls High

Form RPR
4102 **1** **Cherokee Nation**[9] 3158 3-8-8 **57**........................ DHolland 9 68
(PWD'Arcy) *hld up: hdwy over 1f out: r.o to ld nr fin* **9/2**[1]
0056 **2** *1/2* **Yomalo (IRE)**[16] 2948 4-9-6 **62**........................ SSanders 1 71
(RGuest) *a.p: rdn to ld over 1f out: hdd nr fin* **5/1**[2]
6610 **3** *shd* **Gone'N'Dunnett (IRE)**[4] 3307 5-9-1 **57**........................(v) TGMcLaughlin 6 66
(MrsCADunnett) *led over 4f: rdn and hung rt ins fnl f: r.o* **9/1**[3]
6200 **4** *1/2* **Illusive (IRE)**[13] 3010 7-9-2 **58**........................(b) MTebbutt 2 66
(MWigham) *chsd ldrs: rdn over 1f out: edgd rt ins fnl f: styd on* **14/1**
10-0 **5** *1* **Bob's Buzz**[67] 1608 4-9-13 **69**........................ OUrbina 11 74
(SCWilliams) *chsd ldrs: outpcd wl over 1f out: r.o ins fnl f* **12/1**
00-0 **6** *nk* **Stagnite**[19] 2836 4-8-13 **55**........................ DarrenWilliams 4 59
(MrsHSweeting) *w ldr: rdn and ev ch over 1f out: no ex towards fin* **50/1**

1-04 **7** *nk* **Cold Climate**[91] 1204 9-9-0 **56** ........ BDoyle 12 59
(BobJones) *hld up in tch: rdn over 1f out: styd on* **5/1**[2]
0505 **8** *hd* **Warlingham (IRE)**[8] 3174 6-9-0 **56** ........ CCatlin 13 58
(PHowling) *hld up in tch: lost pl over 3f out: r.o ins fnl f: nt trble ldrs* **9/1**[3]
3-04 **9** *hd* **Charlottebutterfly**[30] 2524 4-9-0 **56** ........ JMackay 5 58
(TTClement) *hld up: hdwy over 1f out: styd on same pce ins fnl f* **14/1**
2400 **10** *¾* **Multahab**[25] 2675 5-8-11 **53** ........ (t) CLowther 8 52
(MissGayKelleway) *hld up: hdwy over 2f out: rdn and ev ch over 1f out: no ex ins fnl f* **16/1**
00-0 **11** *1 ¼* **Angel Isa (IRE)**[16] 2936 4-8-7 **49** ow1 ........ NCallan 14 45
(RAFahey) *chsd ldrs over 3f* **20/1**
004 **12** *4* **Chatshow (USA)**[17] 2908 3-8-11 **60** ........ PDoe 10 44
(LADace) *s.i.s: n.d* **16/1**
5005 **13** *1 ½* **Haydn (USA)**[19] 2839 3-9-7 **70** ........ JQuinn 2 49
(PWChapple-Hyam) *prom over 3f* **14/1**
00-6 **14** *2 ½* **Bad Intentions (IRE)**[7] 3195 4-10-0 **70** ........ AMcCarthy 15 42
(MissDMountain) *chsd ldrs over 3f* **33/1**

1m 12.93s (-0.67) **Going Correction** -0.025s/f (Good)
**WFA** 3 from 4yo+ 7lb **14** Ran SP% **120.6**
Speed ratings: **103,102,102,101,100 99,99,99,98,97 96,90,88,85**CSF £25.69 CT £204.44 TOTE £4.40: £2.00, £2.20, £3.80; EX 30.50.
**Owner** Walt Sylvester **Bred** Miss Paula Sylvester And W Sylvester **Trained** Newmarket, Suffolk

**FOCUS**
An ordinary contest, but it was run at a fair pace and the form is sound.

**NOTEBOOK**
**Cherokee Nation** was ridden with plenty of confidence and is value for more than the winning margin.
**Yomalo(IRE)** was probably done no favours by having to launch her challenge out wide. However, she is clearly on good terms with herself at present, and as she has dropped to her last winning mark is one to keep an eye on for a similar contest.
**Gone'N'Dunnett(IRE)** turned in a solid effort off this 7lb higher mark than when successful here last month, but consistency is not his middle name.
**Illusive(IRE)** is a funny customer who needs everything to go right for him.
**Bob's Buzz** shaped with a bit more promise but, one note of caution, he does seem to carry his head at a strange angle.
**Stagnite** showed plenty of pace, but is essentially a disappointing sort.
**Warlingham(IRE)** ran a strange race, losing his pitch before staying on when it was all but over.

## 3429 4HEAD FOR HEADACHES H'CAP — 1m 6f 17y

**8:55** (8:55) (F) (0-55,53) 4-Y-0+ **£3,290** (£940; £470) **Stalls** Low

Form RPR
2215 **1** **Diamond Orchid (IRE)**[11] 3088 4-8-13 **53** ........ (v) SJDonohoe(7) 4 64
(PDEvans) *hld up: hdwy 5f out: led 3f out: rdn out* **9/2**[2]
0-00 **2** *1 ¾* **Peak Park (USA)**[10] 3120 4-8-13 **46** ........ (v) SSanders 8 55
(JARToller) *chsd ldrs: rdn over 2f out: styd on same pce ins fnl f* **7/1**
643 **3** *nk* **Ambersong**[23] 2728 6-8-8 **41** ........ IMongan 3 49
(AWCarroll) *a.p: chsd wnr over 2f out: styd on same pce ins fnl f* **7/2**[1]
-000 **4** *2 ½* **Annakita**[36] 2385 4-8-7 **40** ........ GCarter 7 45
(WJMusson) *hld up in tch: outpcd 3f out: styd on u.p fr over 1f out* **20/1**
6504 **5** *1 ¼* **Smarter Charter**[9] 3149 11-8-0 **40** ........ KristinStubbs(7) 1 43
(MrsLStubbs) *sn pushed along in rr: hdwy 3f out: styd on same pce appr fnl f* **10/1**
2066 **6** *3* **Lissahanelodge**[21] 2787 5-8-9 **42** ........ (p) SWhitworth 6 41
(PRHedger) *hld up: hdwy and stmbld over 2f out: n.d* **5/1**[3]
0031 **7** *¾* **Astromancer (USA)**[11] 3099 4-8-10 **50** ........ SaleemGolam(7) 9 48
(MHTompkins) *hld up in tch: rdn over 4f out: wknd over 1f out* **7/2**[1]
2045 **8** *6* **Free Style (GER)**[23] 2728 4-9-1 **48** ........ DarrenWilliams 2 37
(MrsHSweeting) *chsd ldr over 10f: wknd 2f out: eased* **12/1**
0-00 **9** *5* **Little Sky**[31] 2501 7-8-6 **42** ow2 ........ (e[1]) J-PGuillambert(3) 5 24
(DMullarkey) *led 11f: wknd 2f out* **50/1**

3m 3.77s (-1.43) **Going Correction** -0.025s/f (Good) **9** Ran SP% **115.3**
Speed ratings: **103,102,101,100,99 97,97,94,91**CSF £35.88 CT £122.35 TOTE £5.40: £1.40, £1.80, £2.50; EX 42.60 Place 6 £37.27, Place 5 £9.50.
**Owner** Diamond Racing Ltd **Bred** Eamon O'Mahony **Trained** Pandy, Gwent

**FOCUS**
A poor staying contest, but it was run at a nice even pace and the form is sound enough for the grade.

**NOTEBOOK**
**Diamond Orchid(IRE)** looked to find improvement for the step up in trip and, with her ability to handle most types of ground, should have other opportunities.
**Peak Park(USA)**, dropping down in trip, may have found the ground faster than ideal.
**Ambersong** stayed this trip well enough, he just lacks a change of pace.
**Annakita** is only moderate, but she did keep battling away on ground which looked fast enough for her.
**Smarter Charter** is of little account nowadays.
**Lissahanelodge** was about to get into the action when stumbling badly going to the two-furlong pole. *Official explanation: jockey said gelding lost action*
**Astromancer(USA)** is an in-and-out performer, who was on a non-going day.
**Free Style(GER)** *Official explanation: jockey said filly was unsuited by tonight's firm, good to firm in places*
T/Plt: £37.60 to a £1 stake. Pool: £38,020.75. 736.35 winning tickets. T/Qpdt: £14.20 to a £1 stake. Pool: £2,909.10. 151.10 winning tickets. CR

3430 - 3433a (Foreign Racing) - See Raceform Interactive

# 3357 HAMBURG (R-H)

Wednesday, June 30

**OFFICIAL GOING: Good**

## 3434a FAHRHOFER STUTENPREIS (GROUP 3) (F&M) — 1m

**7:00** (7:07) 3-Y-0+ **£22,535** (£9,155; £4,577; £2,465)

RPR
**1** **Eyeq (IRE)** 4-9-6 ........ NCordrey 11 —
(GJensen, Denmark) *in tch on outside, disp cl 5th str, rdn to chal 1 1/2f out, disp ld over 1f out, tk clr ld cl hme, ran on well* 3
**2** *shd* **Nightdance Forest (IRE)** 3-8-9 ........ FilipMinarik 1 —
(PSchiergen, Germany) *held up, driven and headway entering straight, ridden and every chance final furlong, kept on*
**3** *nk* **Arlecchina (GER)**[38] 2336 4-9-4 ........ TMundry 10 —
(UStoltefuss, Germany) *towards rr, prog app str, disp cl 5th str, rdn to chal 1 1/2f out, disp ld over 1f out, ev ch ins last, ran on*
**4** *2* **Ripley (GER)**[234] 5963 4-9-4 ........ (b) NRichter 5 —
(MarioHofer, Germany) *hld up in last, pushed along and only 3l off ldr ent str, kpt on steadily at one pace to tk 4th cl home*
**5** *hd* **Nicolaia (GER)**[214] 6101 4-9-4 ........ WMongil 2 —
(HSteinmetz, Germany) *towards rear, some late headway under pressure but never a threat*
**6** *nk* **Arlekinada (IRE)**[647] 4852 5-9-4 ........ J-PCarvalho 3 —
(HBlume, Germany) *in touch, driven towards inside entering straight, stayed on steadily at one pace*
**7** *shd* **Lysuna (GER)**[277] 5241 4-9-4 ........ THellier 12 —
(ATrybuhl, Germany) *led, ridden and ran on from 2f out til headed over 1f out, no extra*
**8** *shd* **Mysterix (IRE)**[297] 4-9-4 ........ AStarke 7 —
(ASchutz, Germany) *close up, 2nd straight, ridden and ran on til no extra from well over 1f out* 2
**9** *1* **Attilia (GER)**[52] 1983 3-8-9 ........ ASuborics 6 —
(PSchiergen, Germany) *pulled early in mid-division, shaken up over 1 1/2f out, unable to quicken* 1
**10** *½* **Kolina (FR)** 3-8-9 ........ EPedroza 9 —
(PVovcenko, Germany) *in touch, 3rd and pushed along straight, outpaced from over 1 1/2f out*
**11** *1 ¾* **Avenir Rubra (GER)**[248] 5779 4-9-6 ........ JBojko 4 —
(FrauEMader, Germany) *sweating, raced in touch, 4th and effort straight, weakened from 1 1/2f out*
**12** *1 ¼* **Prunelle (GER)**[52] 1983 3-8-9 ........ AHelfenbein 8 —
(PRau, Germany) *mid-division, outpaced and behind from over 2f out*

1m 39.93s
**WFA** 3 from 4yo+ 10lb **12** Ran SP% **131.4**
Speed ratings: .
**Owner** Stal Kentaur As **Bred** Skymarc Farm Inc & Castlemartin Stud **Trained** Denmark

# 3362 SAN SIRO (R-H)

Wednesday, June 30

**OFFICIAL GOING: Good to firm**

## 3435a PREMIO DONGO (MAIDEN) (C&G) — 6f

**3:20** (3:22) 2-Y-0 **£10,000** (£4,400; £2,400; £1,200)

RPR
**1** **Ally Boy (IRE)** 2-9-0 ........ MTellini 5 —
(GianfrancoVerricelli, Italy)
**2** *¾* **Garmud** 2-9-0 ........ MMonteriso 6 —
(EBorromeo, Italy) *finished 3rd, placed 2nd*
**3** *1* **Mac Millennium** 2-8-11 ........ APolli 3 —
(MGQuinlan) *led tl hung rt and hit rails ins fnl f, jinked lft and bumped Garmud close home, fin 2nd, placed 3rd 1.95-1*
**4** *6* **Bluvet (IRE)** 2-9-0 ........ LPanici 1 —
(MCiciarelli, Italy)
**5** *14* **Trull's Trump (ITY)** 2-9-0 ........ MDemuro 4 —
(BGrizzetti, Italy)
**6** *dist* **Dovizioso (IRE)** 2-8-11 ........ ACarboni 2 —
(PCaravati, Italy)

1m 11.1s **6** Ran
Speed ratings: .
**Owner** Scuderia Fert **Bred** Eugenia Farms **Trained** Italy

**NOTEBOOK**
**Mac Millennium**made a promising debut, and the colt should progress from this. Although he wandered around and hit the rails in the final stages, he should leave those signs of greeness behind next time.

## 3436a PREMIO VARENNA (MAIDEN) (FILLIES) — 6f

**4:20** (4:31) 2-Y-0 **£10,000** (£4,400; £2,400; £1,200)

RPR
**1** **Miss Kiss** 2-9-0 ........ LManiezzi 5 —
(RMenichetti, Italy)
**2** *1* **Pagnottella (IRE)** 2-9-0 ........ MDemuro 7 —
(BGrizzetti, Italy)
**3** *1 ¼* **Mac Rhapsody** 2-8-11 ........ APolli 6 —
(MGQuinlan) *mid-div, prog bef half-way and led over 2f out, drvn and ran on til hdd and no ex from appr fnl f SP 3.83-1*
**4** *shd* **Natikhab** 2-9-0 ........ DPorcu 2 —
(MGuarnieri, Italy)
**5** *1 ½* **Alien (ITY)** 2-9-0 ........ EBotti 11 —
(FrankSheridan, Italy)
**6** *4* **Kawaha (IRE)** 2-9-0 ........ SUrru 8 —
(BGrizzetti, Italy)
**7** *snk* **Bakira (GER)** 2-8-11 ........ MTellini 9 —
(FrauEMader, Germany)
**8** *2 ½* **Calderini (FR)** 2-9-0 ........ MMonteriso 1 —
(VValiani, Italy)
**9** *3 ½* **Pridaisy (IRE)** 2-9-0 ........ GBietolini 4 —
(JHeloury, Italy)
**10** *nk* **Piccola Giada (IRE)** 2-9-0 ........ LPanici 10 —
(MCiciarelli, Italy)
**11** *2 ½* **Dlinnoukiy (IRE)** 2-9-0 ........ PConvertino 3 —
(MInnocenti, Italy)

1m 11.1s **11** Ran
Speed ratings: .
**Owner** Razza Dell'Olmo **Bred** B Minty **Trained** Italy

**NOTEBOOK**
**Mac Rhapsody**like her stablemate ran a really encouraging race. She clearly has ability and should not be long in winning races.

# [2676]EPSOM (L-H)

Thursday, July 1

**OFFICIAL GOING: Good to firm (good in places)**

Wind: It across Weather: fine but cloudy

## 3437 TOTEQUADPOT H'CAP 1m 4f 10y

6:25 (6:28) (E) (0-70,70) 3-Y-O+ **£4,810** (£1,480; £740; £370) **Stalls** Centre

Form RPR

/101 **1** **Cristoforo (IRE)**[6] 3263 7-9-1 **60** 5ex TPQueally[(3)] 9 78+
(BJCurley) *hld up: 7th and plenty to do st: prog 3f out: chsd clr ldr over 1f out: urged along and r.o to ld last stride* **8/11**[1]

0002 **2** *shd* **Stolen Hours (USA)**[9] 3181 4-9-2 **58** JQuinn 8 72
(JAkehurst) *prom: trckd ldr 7f out: cl 2nd st and clr of rest: led 3f out: clr wl over 1f out: kpt on fnl f: hdd last stride* **7/2**[2]

0006 **3** *6* **Persian King (IRE)**[9] 3181 7-9-9 **65** VSlattery 6 69
(JABOld) *trckd ldrs: lost pl 1/2-way: 6th and pushed along st: n.d to ldrs after: kpt on fnl 2f to take 3rd nr fin* **20/1**

0000 **4** *1 1/2* **Lunar Lord**[20] 2835 8-8-8 **50** JDSmith 7 52
(DBurchell) *led: set stdy pce tl kicked on 5f out: clr w one rival st: rdn and hdd 3f out: grad fdd* **16/1**

3035 **5** *3* **Rome (IRE)**[19] 2893 5-9-6 **65** (p) SHitchcott[(3)] 4 62
(GPEnright) *chsd ldrs: pushed along 1/2-way: hanging downhill over 4f out: 4th and rdn st: n.d after: plodded on* **10/1**[3]

5-03 **6** *8* **The Varlet**[13] 3050 4-9-11 **70** DCorby[(3)] 1 54
(BICase) *s.s: hld up in last: outpcd over 4f out: no ch after: wknd 2f out* **14/1**

52-5 **7** *1 3/4* **Scenic Lady (IRE)**[6] 3264 8-9-3 **59** DSweeney 2 41
(LADace) *s.s: hld up: 5th st: sn shkn up and struggling: wknd over 2f out* **16/1**

2300 **8** *12* **Dolzago**[9] 3181 4-9-4 **65** (b) AQuinn[(5)] 3 27
(GLMoore) *chsd ldr to 7f out: 3rd and rdn st: wknd 3f out: t.o* **16/1**

2m 41.06s (2.34) **Going Correction** +0.125s/f (Good) **8** Ran SP% **118.3**

Speed ratings: **97,96,92,91,89 84,83,75**CSF £3.61 CT £26.89 TOTE £1.60: £1.10, £1.20, £3.70; EX 2.70.

**Owner** P Byrne **Bred** Bill Dwan And Tom Lynch **Trained** Newmarket, Suffolk

**FOCUS**

As the market suggested, this was not a competitive race, and the finish was dominated by two in-form horses who were both ahead of the Handicapper. The time was modest for the grade.

**NOTEBOOK**

**Cristoforo(IRE)**, turned out quickly under a penalty, was 11lb well in here. He got up only in the final stride and on this evidence looks likely to struggle off his new mark. His rider said the ground was faster than ideal.

**Stolen Hours(USA)**, who was 2lb well in, may still be a maiden but he has a race in him judged on this effort. He pulled nicely clear of the remainder under a good ride and was unlucky to run into a very well-handicapped horse in top form.

**Persian King(IRE)** kept on past beaten horses to take third. He shapes as though he needs farther these days.

**Lunar Lord** was successful on his last visit here two years ago off this mark, and he had the race run to suit. He is not in the same form, however.

**Rome(IRE)**, fitted with cheekpieces for the first time, failed to handle Tattenham Corner. *Official explanation: jockey said gelding hung right throughout*

## 3438 MCKEEVER ST LAWRENCE EBF MEDIAN AUCTION MAIDEN STKS 7f

6:55 (6:56) (E) 2-Y-O **£4,254** (£1,309; £654; £327) **Stalls** Low

Form RPR

54 **1** **Emerald Penang (IRE)**[29] 2592 2-9-0 SWhitworth 1 76
(PWChapple-Hyam) *prom: led ent st: mde rest: rdn over 1f out: styd on wl* **9/2**[1]

030 **2** *1 1/4* **Flying Pass**[24] 2736 2-9-0 TQuinn 4 73
(DJSFfrenchDavis) *prom: cl 3rd st: rdn to chse wnr over 1f out: kpt on but no imp* **13/2**[2]

0 **3** *1/2* **Dreemon**[24] 2736 2-9-0 GBaker 3 72
(BRMillman) *chsd ldrs: 4th st: rdn and hanging over 2f out: styd on fnl f: unable to chal* **8/1**

503 **4** *1* **Madam Caversfield**[19] 2890 2-8-9 PDobbs 8 64
(RHannon) *racd in midfield: 7th st: rdn and effrt 2f out: styd on u.p fnl f: nrst fin* **8/1**

0 **5** *nk* **Tuvalu (GER)**[19] 2890 2-8-11 LPKeniry[(3)] 11 69
(AMBalding) *s.s: wl in rr: 11th st: prog over 2f out: nt clr run sn after: styd on fnl f: nrst fin* **16/1**

005 **6** *1 1/4* **Elvina Hills (IRE)**[13] 3045 2-8-6 ABeech[(3)] 2 60
(WGMTurner) *led tl hung rt and hdd ent st: pressed wnr tl over 1f out: hung rt and wknd fnl f* **20/1**

3 **7** *2 1/2* **Bint Il Sultan (IRE)**[20] 2837 2-8-9 EAhern 6 54
(EALDunlop) *chsd ldrs: prog and 5th st: rdn and cl up 2f out: wknd 1f out* **9/2**[1]

6 **8** *nk* **Bobbie Love**[12] 3093 2-8-11 SHitchcott[(3)] 10 58
(MRChannon) *racd wd in midfield: 8th st: rdn and effrt on outer over 2f out: no prog over 1f out: wknd fnl f* **16/1**

0 **9** *1 1/4* **Chek Oi**[36] 2396 2-9-0 JQuinn 12 55
(WRMuir) *chsd ldrs: 6th st: rdn over 2f out: wknd over 1f out* **33/1**

0 **10** *3 1/2* **Wise Dennis**[43] 2225 2-9-0 SSanders 9 47
(APJarvis) *a in rr: 10th st: lost tch w ldng gp over 2f out* **15/2**[3]

0 **11** *11* **Liquid Lover (IRE)**[21] 2804 2-9-0 RSmith 7 19
(RHannon) *a towards rr: 9th st: wknd 3f out: wl bhd fnl 2f: t.o* **33/1**

**12** *3/4* **Cool Cristal** 2-8-9 BDoyle 13 12
(RMHCowell) *s.s: immediately hopelessly t.o in last: styd there tl r.o ins fnl f* **33/1**

**13** *nk* **Dizzy Lizzy** 2-8-6 BReilly[(3)] 5 11
(NickWilliams) *squeezed out sn after s and sn bhd: 12th and detached st: sn t.o* **25/1**

1m 25.32s (1.37) **Going Correction** +0.125s/f (Good) **13** Ran SP% **112.9**

Speed ratings: **97,95,95,93,93 92,89,88,87,83 70,70,69**CSF £28.52 TOTE £5.40: £1.90, £1.90, £2.70; EX 48.30.

**Owner** Mrs A K H Ooi **Bred** Pat Fullam **Trained** Newmarket, Suffolk

**FOCUS**

Just an average maiden, made up mostly of horses who will be contesting nurseries in time. Most of the principals ran close to their pre-race marks.

**NOTEBOOK**

**Emerald Penang(IRE)** stepped up considerably on his debut when making his debut for his new stable last time, and he built on that promise here, having been handy throughout from his inside draw. This was not a great race and he should not be overburdened when it comes to nurseries. He should get farther.

**Flying Pass**, one of the most experienced runners in the field, had his chance but could only find the one pace when it mattered. He looks another who will soon be plying his trade in handicaps.

**Dreemon** had shaped with promise on his debut and this was another step in the right direction. He is a half-brother to six winners and there is stamina on the dam's side, so he should get a mile.

**Madam Caversfield** was staying on well at the finish for a yard who had sent out three winners of this race in the previous five years.

**Tuvalu(GER)**, who was slowly away, shaped encouragingly and looks capable of better, as he did not get the clearest of runs. He will probably not come into his own until he starts running in handicaps.

**Elvina Hills(IRE)** had difficulty coping with the track and did not appear to get home over this longer trip. *Official explanation: jockey said filly hung right*

**Bint Il Sultan(IRE)** was disappointing and perhaps the track was to blame.

## 3439 TOTEEXACTA H'CAP 6f

7:25 (7:29) (C) (0-90,79) 3-Y-O+ **£9,600** (£2,954; £1,477; £738) **Stalls** High

Form RPR

2500 **1** **Loyal Tycoon (IRE)**[13] 3036 6-9-3 **79** LTreadwell[(7)] 4 97
(DNicholls) *trckd ldrs gng wl: cl 5th st: rdn to ld jst over 1f out: sn wl clr* **5/1**

013 **2** *5* **Lord Of The East**[5] 3298 5-9-2 **71** AlexGreaves 1 74
(DNicholls) *mde most: drvn over 2f out: hdd jst over 1f out: no ch w wnr after* **9/2**[3]

0434 **3** *2* **Jayanjay**[26] 2682 5-9-8 **77** SSanders 8 74
(MissBSanders) *chsd ldrs: 6th st: rdn 3f out: hanging lft fr 2f out: sn outpcd: kpt on to take 3rd ins fnl f* **5/1**

3112 **4** *1 3/4* **Waterside (IRE)**[8] 3205 5-9-9 **78** EAhern 2 70
(GLMoore) *stmbld bdly s: sn chsd ldrs: cl 4th st: wknd over 1f out* **4/1**[2]

-003 **5** *1/2* **Willheconquertoo**[13] 3043 4-8-8 **63** (t) JFEgan 9 53
(AndrewReid) *dwlt: sn pressed ldng pair: chsd ldr 2f out to over 1f out: wknd* **12/1**

4156 **6** *1/2* **Silver Chime**[5] 3326 4-8-12 **70** LPKeniry[(3)] 6 59
(DMSimcock) *pressed ldr to 2f out: wknd over 1f out* **25/1**

-012 **7** *2* **Cape St Vincent**[4] 3339 4-9-0 **72** (v) TPQueally[(3)] 5 55
(HMorrison) *dwlt: outpcd and wl bhd in last: nvr any ch: r.o ins fnl f* **3/1**[1]

5050 **8** *2 1/2* **Madrasee**[17] 2948 6-9-4 **73** TQuinn 7 48
(LMontagueHall) *stmbld bdly s: nvr on terms w ldrs: 7th st: no prog: eased ins fnl f* **20/1**

35-0 **9** *2 1/2* **Esatto**[17] 2948 5-9-3 **72** (t) SRighton 3 40
(MJAttwater) *outpcd and a struggling: 8th and wl bhd st: eased ins fnl f* **33/1**

68.91 secs (-1.72) **Going Correction** +0.125s/f (Good) **9** Ran SP% **115.8**

Speed ratings: **116,109,106,104,103 103,100,97,93**CSF £27.10 CT £119.22 TOTE £6.60: £2.50, £2.50, £1.10; EX 28.90.

**Owner** Michael A J Hall & Mrs Mandy Hall **Bred** Paul Starr **Trained** Sessay, N Yorks

**FOCUS**

An outstanding winning time for a race of this class.

**NOTEBOOK**

**Loyal Tycoon(IRE)**, who won his last race over this course and distance last year off a 5lb higher mark, had run well at Royal Ascot last time and found this competition less demanding. He won easily in a fast time, is clearly in top form, and the Stewards' Cup consolation race looks the ideal target, although there is an outside chance that he could get into the big race itself.

**Lord Of The East**, four times a course winner, albeit in claimers on three of those occasions, set a decent pace, which suited his stablemate perfectly. He still ran a good race himself, though, finishing clear of the third.

**Jayanjay**, last year's winner off a 2lb lower mark, briefly threatened to take a hand but his challenge never materialised. His overall strike-rate is poor.

**Waterside(IRE)**, best when making the running over seven furlongs, was dropping back in distance and could never get to the front on this occasion after stumbling leaving the stalls. *Official explanation: jockey said gelding stumbled leaving the stalls*

**Willheconquertoo** had his chance but his challenge flattened out approaching the furlong marker. *Official explanation: jockey said gelding lost its action*

**Cape St Vincent**, who is still chasing his first win on turf, was competing in the highest grade he has ever run in, but even allowing for that fact, this performance was too bad to be true. Up until this race he appeared to have lost last season's habit of starting slowly, but he showed here that it should remain a concern. *Official explanation: jockey said colt was unsuited by the track*

**Madrasee** *Official explanation: jockey said mare slipped coming out of the stalls*

**Esatto** *Official explanation: jockey said gelding had choked*

## 3440 SCOTTISH EQUITABLE/JOCKEYS ASSOCIATION H'CAP 7f

7:55 (7:56) (D) (0-85,82) 3-Y-O+ **£6,938** (£2,135; £1,067; £533) **Stalls** Low

Form RPR

0-22 **1** **Pango**[24] 2737 5-9-2 **72** PDobbs 4 83
(HMorrison) *trckd ldrs: 5th st: effrt 2f out: rdn to ld ins fnl f: r.o wl* **5/1**[2]

1664 **2** *1 1/4* **Quantum Leap**[12] 3086 7-9-1 **71** (v) TQuinn 3 79
(SDow) *led: hrd pressed fr 2f out: kpt on wl tl hdd and unable qck ins fnl f* **15/2**

4100 **3** *nk* **H Harrison (IRE)**[13] 3036 4-9-11 **81** LVickers 8 88
(IWMcinnes) *trckd ldr: chal 2f out: nt look keen and nt go past: kpt on ins fnl f* **15/2**

2-01 **4** *shd* **Franksalot (IRE)**[9] 3174 4-8-13 **69** 5ex SSanders 1 76
(MissBSanders) *trckd ldrs: 4th st: rdn and nt qckn 2f out: styd on ins fnl f* **9/2**[1]

2040 **5** *1* **Temper Tantrum**[8] 3205 6-8-1 **60** (p) JFMcDonald[(3)] 5 64
(AndrewReid) *dwlt: settled in rr: 7th st: effrt on ins 2f out: one pce and no imp on ldrs* **14/1**

0063 **6** *1 1/4* **Fleetwood Bay**[12] 3086 4-8-13 **69** GBaker 2 70
(BRMillman) *chsd ldng pair to over 1f out: sn lost pl u.p* **6/1**[3]

3024 **7** *1 1/4* **Concubine (IRE)**[9] 3178 5-8-6 **62** (p) DSweeney 6 59
(JRBoyle) *hld up in rr: 8th st: nt clr run over 2f out to over 1f out: keeping on but no ch whn squeezed out 1f out* **15/2**

3400 **8** *nk* **Sawwaah (IRE)**[7] 3235 7-9-12 **82** AlexGreaves 7 79
(DNicholls) *hld up in last: rdn over 2f out: nt qckn and no real prog* **10/1**

0060 **9** *8* **Margalita (IRE)**[17] 2948 4-8-9 **65** (t) JFEgan 9 40
(PMitchell) *chsd ldrs: 6th and rdn st: sn btn: bhd fnl 2f* **20/1**

0000 **10** *11* **Colemanstown**[7] 3235 4-8-8 **64** EAhern 10 9
(BEllison) *racd on outer: in rr: 9th and rdn st: wknd 3f out: t.o* **8/1**

1m 23.29s (-0.66) **Going Correction** +0.125s/f (Good) **10** Ran SP% **116.1**

Speed ratings: **108,106,106,106,104 103,102,101,92,80**CSF £42.11 CT £285.90 TOTE £5.50: £1.90, £2.00, £3.20; EX 32.40.

**Owner** Pangfield Partners **Bred** T J Billington **Trained** East Ilsley, Berks

■ Stewards Enquiry : J F McDonald one-day ban: careless riding (Jul 12)

**FOCUS**

A competitive race, but ordinary form.

**NOTEBOOK**

**Pango** has not been the easiest to win with in the past but enjoyed an untroubled passage on this occasion and finished well down the outside, winning comfortably in the end. He had no problem with the shorter trip.

**Quantum Leap** runs well on undulating tracks and had the run of the race, so there were no excuses.
**H Harrison(IRE)** usually likes a sharp track but he did not look particularly happy on this course, carrying his head high and hanging under pressure.
**Franksalot(IRE)**, carrying a 5lb penalty for his recent Brighton win, is another who goes well on undulating tracks. He stayed on but was never going to trouble the winner.
**Temper Tantrum** has yet to find his best form this season but this was a respectable effort.
**Concubine(IRE)** could not find a way through from over two furlongs out and met all the trouble going. She has a poor strike-rate but this run can be forgotten.

## 3441 DRIVERS JONAS CLAIMING STKS 1m 114y
8:25 (8:28) (E) 3-Y-O+ £4,153 (£1,278; £639; £319) Stalls Low

Form RPR
0036 **1** **Burgundy**[21] [2810] 7-8-13 57 (b) TPQueally(3) 3 59
(PMitchell) *dwlt and pushed along early: wl bhd: last st: hrd rdn over 2f out: styd on strly over 1f out: edgd lft but led nr fin* **11/2**[3]
2334 **2** *nk* **Tojoneski**[10] [3148] 5-9-0 47 (p) JFMcDonald(3) 7 59
(IWMcinnes) *pressed ldr and sn clr of rest: rdn over 2f out: led over 1f out: tired fnl f: hdd nr fin* **10/1**
3002 **3** *shd* **Archerfield (IRE)**[9] [3171] 3-8-4 63 (t) EAhern 8 56
(JWHills) *wl off the pce in midfield: rdn 1/2-way: 5th st: styd on strly on outer fr over 1f out: jst hld* **15/2**
-000 **4** *1 1/2* **Captain Saif**[8] [3212] 4-9-3 87 PDobbs 2 56
(RHannon) *chsd clr ldng pair: rdn 3f out: wandering after: tried to cl over 1f out: kpt on but nvr able to chal* **5/2**[2]
0211 **5** *1* **Ben Hur**[5] [3291] 5-9-5 63 SWKelly 6 56
(WMBrisbourne) *taken down early: led at str pce: clr w one rival st: drvn over 2f out: hdd over 1f out: wandering and v tired fnl f* **7/4**[1]
065- **6** *8* **Gameset'N'Match**[311] [4436] 3-8-0 70 CHaddon(7) 1 37
(WGMTurner) *sn wl off the pce: poor 6th st: no prog* **16/1**
0640 **7** *8* **Single Track Mind**[1] [3423] 6-8-8 42 (p) AQuinn(5) 5 16
(JRBoyle) *s.i.s: sn wl off the pce: poor 7th st: wl bhd after* **33/1**
5000 **8** *2 1/2* **Figura**[17] [2929] 6-8-8 41 (t) NDay 4 —
(RIngram) *racd in 4th but nt on terms: rdn over 3f out: hanging and wknd over 2f out* **33/1**

1m 46.12s (0.38) **Going Correction** +0.125s/f (Good)
**WFA** 3 from 4yo+ 10lb **8** Ran SP% **112.9**
Speed ratings: **103,102,102,101,100 93,86,83**CSF £56.59 TOTE £7.30: £1.80, £2.10, £1.90; EX 44.70.
**Owner** Nigel Shields **Bred** Cheveley Park Stud Ltd **Trained** Epsom, Surrey

**FOCUS**
A modest heat, but one run at a good clip. With such a disparity of ratings among the first five home, the form is hard to assess.

**NOTEBOOK**
**Burgundy** had not won on turf for two years and did not look particularly favoured by the weights. He looked to be going nowhere turning into the straight, but the leaders stopped in front and he stayed on well to pick them up close home. The chances are he was flattered by the way the race was run.
**Tojoneski** is a consistent type but keeps meeting one or two too good. For one who had been beaten on numerous occasions in banded grade earlier this year, this was a great effort, especially at these weights and given the pace he helped set with the eventual fifth.
**Archerfield(IRE)** is still a maiden but this was the fifth time she has made the frame in 11 starts. She finished her race strongly but, like the winner, may be flattered, as the leaders were stopping in front.
**Captain Saif**, who had plenty in hand of his rivals on official figures, was most disappointing. He appears to be on a steep downward curve at present.
**Ben Hur**, chasing the hat-trick, was not given much peace in front despite setting a strong gallop, and in the end that was his undoing.

## 3442 LEWIS SILKIN CLASSIFIED STKS 1m 2f 18y
8:55 (8:55) (D) 3-Y-O+ £5,330 (£1,640; £820; £410) Stalls Low

Form RPR
2166 **1** **Woody Valentine (USA)**[19] [2887] 3-8-6 80 SChin 1 84
(MJohnston) *chsd ldr: rdn over 1f out: led ent fnl f: drvn and hld on* **2/1**[1]
610- **2** *nk* **Silver City**[262] [5550] 4-9-3 80 PDobbs 2 83
(MrsAJPerrett) *led: clr w wnr over 2f out: rdn and hdd ent fnl f: rallied nr fin: jst hld* **10/1**
6001 **3** *1/2* **Mr Tambourine Man (IRE)**[17] [2949] 3-8-7 81 TQuinn 7 83
(PFICole) *racd in 4th: rdn 3f out: sn outpcd: styd on fnl 2f: clsd ins fnl f: a hld* **2/1**[1]
3/00 **4** *5* **Ocean Of Storms (IRE)**[12] [3075] 9-8-12 78 (t) RThomas(5) 4 73
(ChristianWroe, UAE) *s.v.s: t.k.h and sn chsd ldng pair: pushed along over 2f out: wknd wl over 1f out* **20/1**
1456 **5** *3* **Dissident (GER)**[26] [2681] 6-9-0 84 JTucker(7) 6 72
(DFlood) *hld up in last: hmpd 4f out: sn rdn: no prog and btn after* **8/1**[3]
0030 **6** *4* **Arry Dash**[12] [3097] 4-9-0 80 SHitchcott(3) 5 61
(MRChannon) *racd in 5th: drvn over 3f out: no prog and sn btn* **10/3**[2]

2m 10.97s (2.27) **Going Correction** +0.125s/f (Good)
**WFA** 3 from 4yo+ 11lb **6** Ran SP% **114.7**
Speed ratings: **95,94,94,90,87 84**CSF £23.39 TOTE £3.20: £2.00, £3.20; EX 47.90 Place £101.19, Place 5 £79.24.
**Owner** Favourites Racing **Bred** J I Amos And Barbara F Amos **Trained** Middleham Moor, N Yorks
■ Stewards Enquiry : S Hitchcott four-day ban: careless riding (Jul 12-15)

**FOCUS**
A very modest winning time for a race of this grade and the form might not be as good as it looks.

**NOTEBOOK**
**Woody Valentine(USA)** had had excuses for his last two defeats and the step back up to a mile and a quarter looked likely to suit. He took his time to pick up but always looked like getting there, although he had to withstand a rally from the runner-up close home. He looks sure to continue to progress and should not go up much for this.
**Silver City**, whose only win to date came in an uncompetitive Beverley maiden, made a brave attempt to make every yard on his seasonal debut. He rallied when headed and, following this promising reappearance, looks sure to win again when returned to a mile and a half.
**Mr Tambourine Man(IRE)** had his chance but his challenge flattened out inside the last. He was put up 6lb by the Handicapper for his narrow Windsor success, but he is still relatively lightly raced and, on fast ground, is open to further improvement back on a more conventional track.
**Ocean Of Storms(IRE)** had less to do in this company but he did not settle in the early stages and never really threatened the principals.
**Dissident(GER)** was without the visor and tongue strap which he wore when running well here from out of the handicap on Derby Day. A stronger pace would have probably suited him, too.
**Arry Dash**, whose previous record in this type of contest looked decent, ran a disappointing race.
T/Plt: £130.70 to a £1 stake. Pool: £41,238.05. 230.25 winning tickets. T/Qpdt: £42.10 to a £1 stake. Pool: £2,759.40. 48.50 winning tickets. JN

# [2683] HAYDOCK (L-H)
Thursday, July 1

**OFFICIAL GOING: Good (good to soft in places)**
Wind: It against Weather: fine

## 3443 FAUCETS FOR MIRA SHOWERS FILLIES' H'CAP 1m 3f 200y
2:20 (2:21) (D) (0-80,76) 3-Y-O+ £5,632 (£1,733; £866; £433) Stalls High

Form RPR
5105 **1** **Astrocharm (IRE)**[12] [3091] 5-9-12 74 LDettori 4 83
(MHTompkins) *trckd ldrs: led 2f out: comf* **3/1**[1]
5-41 **2** *2 1/2* **Act Of The Pace (IRE)**[15] [2983] 4-10-0 76 KDalgleish 7 81
(MJohnston) *a.p: led over 4f out: rdn and hdd 2f out: one pce fnl f* **5/1**
-254 **3** *1 1/2* **Swynford Pleasure**[27] [2659] 8-8-3 51 DaleGibson 2 54
(JHetherton) *hld up: rdn and hdwy over 2f out: kpt on one pce* **9/2**[3]
0040 **4** *4* **Transcendantale (FR)**[11] [3117] 6-7-13 47 FNorton 3 43
(MrsSLamyman) *in tch: rdn whn nt clr run over 2f out: no imp on ldrs* **9/1**
6063 **5** *1 1/2* **Infidelity (IRE)**[14] [3007] 3-7-7 59 oh2 (v[1]) HayleyTurner(5) 5 53
(ABailey) *s.s: hld up: effrt whn swtchd rt 3f out: hung lft over 1f out: no imp* **4/1**[2]
-200 **6** *1/2* **Cantemerle (IRE)**[7] [3250] 4-8-6 54 (b) KDarley 1 47
(WMBrisbourne) *s.s: hld up: hdwy 7f out: rdn over 3f out: wknd over 2f out* **15/2**
0-25 **7** *13* **Desert Quill (IRE)**[3] [3363] 4-8-9 57 WSupple 6 29
(WMBrisbourne) *led: hdd over 4f out: sn rdn: wknd over 2f out* **16/1**
PU0 **8** *6* **Harambee (IRE)**[15] [2982] 4-9-11 73 RWinston 8 36
(BSRothwell) *cl up: rdn over 3f out: wknd over 2f out* **40/1**

2m 33.71s (-1.45) **Going Correction** -0.10s/f (Good)
**WFA** 3 from 4yo+ 13lb **8** Ran SP% **109.9**
Speed ratings: **100,98,97,94,93 93,84,80**CSF £16.66 CT £59.88 TOTE £3.00: £1.10, £1.70, £1.90; EX 8.70.
**Owner** Mystic Meg Limited **Bred** Miss D J Merson **Trained** Newmarket, Suffolk

**FOCUS**
No strength in depth to this handicap and the field were well strung out as a result of the tactical pace. Astrocharm was back to her best, while Act Of The Pace continues to improve.

**NOTEBOOK**
**Astrocharm(IRE)** pressed the button two out, having travelled well to that point, and quickly settled the issue. This represented her easiest assignment for a while and she had her ideal conditions, but while still well treated on her best form, she can be a bit in-and-out.
**Act Of The Pace(IRE)** got outpaced over this distance but still showed improved form in finishing a clear second, as she had been set a stiff task. She will be suited by further and has more improvement inher.
**Swynford Pleasure** ran with credit, considering she would have preferred faster ground and a much stronger early gallop. She is coming right, looks well-weighted at present and is certainly one to bear in mind when getting her ideal conditions.
**Transcendantale(FR)** may have finished a little closer with a better run entering the final two furlongs, but was made to look very one paced late on. She is very hard to win with.
**Infidelity(IRE)** disappointed in the first time visor and remains a frustrating performer.

## 3444 DALKIA & LAND SECURITIES TRILLIUM PARTNERSHIP MAIDEN CLAIMING STKS 6f
2:50 (2:51) (F) 2-Y-O £3,206 (£916; £458) Stalls Centre

Form RPR
4040 **1** **Make Us Flush**[11] [3123] 2-8-6 FNorton 8 66
(ABerry) *trckd ldrs: rdn 2f out: led 1f out: r.o* **5/1**[1]
**2** *2 1/2* **As Handsome Does** 2-9-0 (t) ACulhane 13 66
(NTinkler) *s.i.s: bhd: hdwy over 1f out: r.o ins fnl f: nrst fin* **33/1**
0 **3** *shd* **Alzarma**[28] [2609] 2-8-7 TEaves(3) 6 62
(MrsLWilliamson) *led: rdn over 2f out: hdd 1f out: no ex towards fin* **33/1**
566 **4** *nk* **Piddies Pride (IRE)**[13] [3045] 2-8-2 (v) JFanning 3 53
(IAWood) *midfield: hdwy 3f out: rdn and ev ch over 1f out: r.o same pce ins fnl f* **10/1**[3]
0 **5** *3* **Kerry's Blade (IRE)**[48] [2096] 2-9-0 GFaulkner 10 56
(PCHaslam) *trckd ldrs: rdn 3f out: hung rt over 1f out: one pce* **20/1**
060 **6** *2* **Miss Good Time**[48] [2087] 2-7-9 HayleyTurner(5) 20 36
(JGGiven) *prom: rdn 3f out: wknd fnl f* **12/1**
0 **7** *1/2* **Ladruca**[41] [2275] 2-8-8 RLMoore 4 43
(RHannon) *in tch: pushed along 3f out: no ex ins fnl f* **8/1**[2]
5 **8** *shd* **Magic Genie (IRE)**[20] [2858] 2-8-7 DaleGibson 1 41
(MWEasterby) *midfield: rdn 3f out: hdwy over 2f out: kpt on one pce fnl f* **16/1**
3664 **9** *hd* **Turtle Magic (IRE)**[42] [2248] 2-7-12 CHaddon(7) 16 39
(WGMTurner) *towards rr: rdn 3f out: hdwy over 2f out: edgd rt 1f out: sn wknd* **5/1**[1]
**10** *2 1/2* **Hopelessly Devoted** 2-8-3 RoryMoore(7) 5 36
(PCHaslam) *dwlt: midfield: rdn and hdwy over 1f out: wknd ins fnl f* **14/1**
00 **11** *1 3/4* **Roko**[20] [2858] 2-8-10 PMulrennan(5) 17 36
(MWEasterby) *trckd ldrs: rdn 3f out: wknd over 1f out* **33/1**
6 **12** *1/2* **For Nowt**[13] [3055] 2-9-1 WSupple 18 34
(TDEasterby) *wnt lft s: towards rr: rdn 3f out: sme hdwy 2f out: eased whn no ex ins fnl f* **25/1**
0 **13** *1/2* **Xeight Express (IRE)**[16] [2960] 2-8-3 RFfrench 2 21
(MABuckley) *trckd ldrs tl rdn and wknd wl over 1f out* **50/1**
6 **14** *1* **Cash Time**[28] [2622] 2-8-3 PMQuinn 11 18
(JO'Reilly) *dwlt: midfield: rdn and outpcd 3f out* **50/1**
0 **15** *1 1/4* **Elliebow**[30] [2550] 2-8-7 DAllan 19 18
(TDEasterby) *in tch: rdn 3f out: sn wknd* **14/1**
**16** *1* **Carmania (IRE)** 2-8-9 THamilton(3) 12 20
(RPElliott) *prom: rdn over 2f out: sn wknd* **25/1**
**17** *3* **Winter Mist** 2-8-10 KDarley 7 9
(NPLittmoden) *a bhd* **12/1**
**18** *3/4* **Miss Trendsetter (IRE)** 2-8-10 NCallan 14 7
(KARyan) *in tch: rdn and wknd over 2f out* **14/1**
00 **19** *5* **Tak's Girl**[13] [3055] 2-8-4 RFitzpatrick 9 —
(PTMidgley) *a bhd* **66/1**
20 **20** *3/4* **Mas O Menos (IRE)**[34] [2453] 2-8-8 IMongan 15 —
(MsDeborahJEvans) *prom tl rdn and wknd 3f out* **25/1**

1m 17.24s (2.35) **Going Correction** +0.125s/f (Good) **20** Ran SP% **125.3**
Speed ratings: **89,85,85,85,81 78,77,77,77,74 71,71,70,69,67 66,62,61,54,53**CSF £187.59 TOTE £5.70: £1.60, £9.90, £22.60; EX 293.30.Alzarma was claimed by Diamond Racing Ltd. for £10,000.
**Owner** The Bath Tub Boys **Bred** Bearstone Stud **Trained** Cockerham, Lancs

**FOCUS**
A dire event and they were strung out at the finish.

**NOTEBOOK**
**Make Us Flush**, down in grade, responded well to pressure and really found her stride late on to run out a ready winner. She had shown bits of ability prior to a poor effort last time (when reportedly struck into) but is likely to find life a lot tougher back up at a higher level.
**As Handsome Does** blew his chance with a slow start and still looked to have plenty to do two out, but the penny dropped and he flew home to finish best of all. This was a nice debut and he should improve plenty, with a step up in trip likley to suit.
**Alzarma** improved on his debut in this lower grade and showed fair speed until tiring late in the day. He is only moderate, but may nick a similar event on a sharper track.
**Piddies Pride(IRE)** ran her race, but never really looked like troubling the winner. This looks to be her level and she can find a similar race this summer, as she looks the type to improve with more experience.
**Turtle Magic(IRE)** was never really in it and proved most disappointing.
**Cash Time** *Official explanation: jockey said filly ran very greenly*
**Mas O Menos(IRE)** *Official explanation: trainer said gelding had a sore throat*

## 3445 EUROPEAN BREEDERS FUND NOVICE FILLIES' STKS 6f
3:20 (3:22) (D) 2-Y-0 £4,998 (£1,538; £769; £384) Stalls Centre

| Form | | | | RPR |
|---|---|---|---|---|
| 1225 | 1 | | **Bright Moll**[15] 2970 2-8-11 ... IMongan 2 | 86 |
| | | | (MLWBell) *a.p: led over 1f out: edgd rt ins fnl f: r.o* **5/4**[1] | |
| 5 | 2 | 3 ½ | **All Night Dancer (IRE)**[24] 2745 2-9-2 ... LDettori 5 | 81 |
| | | | (DavidWachman, Ire) *trckd ldrs: rdn over 2f out: wnt 2nd ins fnl f: nt pce of wnr* **9/4**[2] | |
| 521 | 3 | ¾ | **Rockburst**[28] 2617 2-8-13 ... DarrenWilliams 4 | 75 |
| | | | (KRBurke) *led: rdn over 2f out: hdd over 1f out: no ex towards fin* **7/1**[3] | |
| 041 | 4 | nk | **African Breeze**[13] 3055 2-9-2 ... DeanMcKeown 3 | 77 |
| | | | (RMWhitaker) *hld up: hdwy 3f out: one pce ins fnl f* **15/2** | |
| | 5 | 1 | **Howards Princess** 2-8-5 ... WSupple 7 | 63 |
| | | | (JSGoldie) *s.s: in rr: rn green: rdn and hdwy over 2f out: wknd ins fnl f* **33/1** | |
| 4106 | 6 | hd | **Mitchelland**[27] 2655 2-8-13 ... TEaves(3) 1 | 74 |
| | | | (JamesMoffatt) *hld up in rr: rdn over 2f out: kpt on ins fnl f: nvr able to chal* **25/1** | |
| 5 | 7 | 3 ½ | **Menna**[23] 2749 2-8-9 ... ACulhane 6 | 56 |
| | | | (RHollinshead) *racd keenly: prom tl wknd over 2f out* **33/1** | |

1m 16.14s (1.25) **Going Correction** +0.125s/f (Good) 7 Ran SP% **109.2**
Speed ratings: **96,91,90,89,88 88,83**CSF £3.71 TOTE £2.20: £1.10, £1.70; EX 4.50.
**Owner** A Buxton P Fenwick & Lostford Manor Stud **Bred** Lostford Manor Stud **Trained** Newmarket, Suffolk

**FOCUS**
A decent race run at a generous pace and the form should work out.
**NOTEBOOK**
**Bright Moll** confirmed her fifth in the Queen Mary was no fluke and won with authority over this extra furlong. This slightly easier ground was right up her street and she looks worthy of a crack at a higher level once again, with the Princess Margaret Stakes back at Ascot a likely target.
**All Night Dancer(IRE)**, not disgraced when unplaced in Listed company last time, ran her race with no obvious excuses. Conceding 5lb, she did well to get as close as she did to the winner, and this sharp Irish filly should continue to progress over this trip.
**Rockburst** made a bold bid from the front and again showed good early speed, but could not keep up the gallop and was readily passed by the winner entering the final furlong. There was no disgrace in this defeat and she can win again when getting faster ground.
**African Breeze**, held up to get the trip, ran on at the one pace late in the day. She fared well enough under her penalty, but may need to revert to the minimum trip in order to get closer again.

## 3446 SILVER CROSS PRAMS H'CAP 6f
3:50 (3:51) (D) (0-80,78) 3-Y-0+ £6,223 (£1,915; £957; £478) Stalls Centre

| Form | | | | RPR |
|---|---|---|---|---|
| 3120 | 1 | | **Savile's Delight (IRE)**[33] 2477 5-9-1 **70** ... DNolan(3) 8 | 78 |
| | | | (RBrotherton) *mde v all: rdn and hung lft over 1f out: edgd rt and lft ins fnl f: r.o* **11/2**[3] | |
| 6303 | 2 | hd | **Time N Time Again**[5] 3293 6-9-2 **68** ... (p) DAllan 5 | 76 |
| | | | (EJAlston) *w ldr thrght: rdn over 2f out: r.o* **8/1** | |
| 0432 | 3 | 1 | **Brantwood (IRE)**[14] 3025 4-8-7 **59** ... (t) GGibbons 10 | 64 |
| | | | (BAMcmahon) *trckd ldrs: rdn over 2f out: styd on ins fnl f* **8/1** | |
| 0050 | 4 | shd | **Locombe Hill (IRE)**[9] 3167 8-8-8 **60** ... (v¹) JCarroll 4 | 64 |
| | | | (DNicholls) *bhd: swtchd rt over 2f out: r.o ins fnl f: nrst fin* **25/1** | |
| -000 | 5 | ¾ | **William's Well**[29] 2581 10-8-3 **60** ow2 ... (b) PMulrennan(5) 7 | 62 |
| | | | (MWEasterby) *prom: rdn over 2f out: hmpd whn n.m.r ins fnl f: no ex cl home* **25/1** | |
| 0046 | 6 | 1 | **Highland Warrior**[5] 3309 5-9-7 **73** ... WSupple 1 | 72+ |
| | | | (JSGoldie) *s.i.s: towards rr: rdn and hdwy over 1f out: n.m.r and bdly hmpd ins fnl f: nt rcvr* **5/1**[2] | |
| 4214 | 7 | ½ | **Legal Set (IRE)**[5] 3298 8-7-11 **56** 6ex ... (t) NataliaGemelova(7) 12 | 54 |
| | | | (MissAStokell) *midfield: rdn 3f out: kpt on same pce fnl f* **8/1** | |
| 6-00 | 8 | 1 | **Smirfys Party**[24] 2735 6-7-13 **51** ... (v) PMQuinn 9 | 46 |
| | | | (DNicholls) *s.i.s: midfield: rdn and hdwy over 2f out: one pce ins fnl f* **33/1** | |
| 4035 | 9 | 1 ¼ | **Midnight Parkes**[4] 3339 5-8-13 **65** ... RHughes 11 | 56 |
| | | | (EJAlston) *dwlt: hld up: rdn 3f out: nvr able to chal* **9/2**[1] | |
| 0530 | 10 | ¾ | **Ballybunion (IRE)**[7] 3249 5-8-3 **55** ... JFanning 2 | 44 |
| | | | (DNicholls) *in tch: hdwy over 2f out: ev ch over 1f out: wknd ins fnl f* **10/1** | |
| 20-0 | 11 | 5 | **Key Of Gold (IRE)**[6] 3280 3-9-3 **75** ... LDettori 6 | 49 |
| | | | (DCarroll) *a bhd* **16/1** | |
| -000 | 12 | 2 ½ | **Bollin Janet**[14] 3016 4-9-3 **69** ... RWinston 13 | 35 |
| | | | (TDEasterby) *a outpcd* **20/1** | |
| 1166 | 13 | 1 ¾ | **Mr Wolf**[15] 2981 3-9-6 **78** ... KDarley 14 | 39 |
| | | | (DWBarker) *w ldrs tl wknd over 2f out* **10/1** | |

1m 14.76s (-0.13) **Going Correction** +0.125s/f (Good)
**WFA** 3 from 4yo+ 6lb 13 Ran SP% **123.0**
Speed ratings: **105,104,103,103,102 100,100,98,97,96 89,86,83**CSF £48.26 CT £360.89 TOTE £8.00: £2.80, £2.70, £2.90; EX 107.10 Trifecta £1476.90 Part won. Pool of £2080.26 - 0.90 winning units..
**Owner** Roy Brotherton **Bred** Romany Investements Ltd **Trained** Elmley Castle, Worcs

**FOCUS**
A modest sprint that saw plenty of hard luck stories. Ordinary form.
**NOTEBOOK**
**Savile's Delight(IRE)** hit the front late on, having been handy throughout, but idled and wandered under pressure, so deserves credit for sticking his head out at the line. He is value for a bit more than the official winning margin and is a consistent sort at this level.
**Time N Time Again** ran another sound race, but just got worried out of it late on. He is hard to win with, but is always capable of paying his way in this grade.
**Brantwood(IRE)** was staying on all too late in the day, but improved a little on his latest effort at Southwell. He is running well and deserves to win before long.
**Locombe Hill(IRE)**, in the first-time visor, put up a much improved effort and has to be rated better than the bare form. If the headgear has the same effect next time, he should get closer.
**William's Well** was full of running when he got stopped late on, and would have been placed at least, with a clear run. *Official explanation: jockey said gelding suffered interference in running*
**Highland Warrior** was another to suffer a troubled passage and would have been a lot closer but for that. This did rate a slight improvement on recent efforts. *Official explanation: jockey said horse suffered interference in running*

## 3447 PERFORMANCE CAR HIRE MAIDEN STKS (DIV I) 1m 30y
4:20 (4:22) (D) 3-Y-0 £5,629 (£1,732; £866; £433) Stalls Low

| Form | | | | RPR |
|---|---|---|---|---|
| | 1 | | **Balavista (USA)** 3-9-0 ... RHughes 8 | 83+ |
| | | | (RCharlton) *a.p: led over 2f out: qcknd clr over 1f out: comf* **4/1**[2] | |
| 0 | 2 | 3 | **News Sky (USA)**[75] 1461 3-9-0 ... WSupple 5 | 70 |
| | | | (BWHills) *midfield: rdn and hdwy over 2f out: chsd wnr over 1f out: no imp* **4/1**[2] | |
| | 3 | 3 | **Go Garuda** 3-9-0 ... RLMoore 10 | 63+ |
| | | | (DWPArbuthnot) *hld up: rdn and hdwy over 2f out: styd on and hung lft ins fnl f: nt trble ldng pair* **33/1** | |
| 0 | 4 | 1 ¼ | **Mesayan (IRE)**[26] 2693 3-9-0 ... (t) JMcAuley 2 | 60 |
| | | | (ACStewart) *s.i.s: in tch: rdn over 2f out: one pce* **16/1** | |
| 50 | 5 | 2 ½ | **Dan Di Canio (IRE)**[10] 3161 3-9-0 ... IMongan 4 | 54 |
| | | | (PWHarris) *in tch: pushed along over 2f out: nvr trbld ldrs* **10/1**[3] | |
| 06- | 6 | 1 ¼ | **Kinkozan**[243] 5867 3-8-11 ... J-PGuillambert(3) 6 | 51 |
| | | | (NPLittmoden) *prom: rdn 4f out: wknd wl over 1f out* **33/1** | |
| | 7 | nk | **Java Dancer** 3-9-0 ... DAllan 7 | 50 |
| | | | (TDEasterby) *hld up: struggling over 2f out: nvr on terms* **25/1** | |
| -0 | 8 | hd | **Howards Rocket**[48] 2077 3-9-0 ... KDalgleish 9 | 50 |
| | | | (JSGoldie) *bhd: rdn over 2f out: nvr on terms* **50/1** | |
| | 9 | 2 | **Eltihaab (USA)** 3-8-9 ... LDettori 3 | 40 |
| | | | (SaeedBinSuroor) *led: rdn and hdd over 2f out: wknd 1f out* **5/4**[1] | |
| | 10 | 1 | **Classic Lease** 3-9-0 ... NCallan 1 | 43 |
| | | | (RHollinshead) *trckd ldrs: rdn over 2f out: wknd over 1f out* **33/1** | |
| 40- | 11 | dist | **Treason Trial**[246] 5830 3-9-0 ... ACulhane 11 | — |
| | | | (NTinkler) *a bhd: t.o* **12/1** | |

1m 44.21s (-1.34) **Going Correction** -0.10s/f (Good) 11 Ran SP% **121.7**
Speed ratings: **102,99,96,94,92 90,90,90,88,87** —CSF £20.22 TOTE £5.20: £1.50, £1.80, £7.70; EX 32.50.
**Owner** K Abdulla **Bred** Juddmonte Farms Inc **Trained** Beckhampton, Wilts

**FOCUS**
This was run at a modest gallop, yet they all came home strung out behind the easy winner. The time was slower than that recorded in division two, and the form is not outstanding, but there were some promising performances.
**NOTEBOOK**
**Balavista(USA)** was always travelling best in behind the leaders, and there was a lot to like about the way he quickened twice in the straight to settle the issue and post a comfortable debut success. He should stay further and improve plenty for this experience, and though he may now have to step up into a classified event or Listed company, looks promising.
**News Sky(USA)** was flattered by his promitity to the winner, but was himself a clear second and ran a much improved race. He will far better with more experience and when handicapped.
**Go Garuda** was doing all of his best work late in the day and came home with effect to bag third. This was a fair debut effort and he is entitled to improve on this.
**Mesayan(IRE)**, as on his debut last time, was slow to go and looked one-paced when making his effort two out. He is a late maturing sort who will do better in time.
**Dan Di Canio(IRE)** *Official explanation: jockey said gelding got his tongue over the bit*
**Eltihaab(USA)**, a choicely-bred debutante, led the field along and looked sure to be in the finish coming into the straight, but quickly came under heavy pressure and dropped out tamely. She was well backed for this and is presumably thought capable of better, so may need a drop in trip.
**Treason Trial** *Official explanation: jockey said gelding ran too freely to post*

## 3448 PERFORMANCE CAR HIRE MAIDEN STKS (DIV II) 1m 30y
4:50 (4:52) (D) 3-Y-0 £5,629 (£1,732; £866; £433) Stalls Low

| Form | | | | RPR |
|---|---|---|---|---|
| 3 | 1 | | **New Order**[50] 2046 3-8-9 ... RHughes 5 | 75 |
| | | | (BWHills) *led 1f: remained prom: regained ld 3f out: r.o* **5/4**[1] | |
| 0 | 2 | 1 | **Revenir (IRE)**[21] 2808 3-9-0 ... LDettori 2 | 78 |
| | | | (ACStewart) *hld up hdwy over 2f out: rdn over 1f out: ev ch ins fnl f: nt qckn cl home* **13/2** | |
| | 3 | 2 ½ | **Clipperdown (IRE)** 3-9-0 ... RLMoore 6 | 72 |
| | | | (PWHarris) *s.i.s: hld up: hdwy whn swtchd rt over 1f out: styd on and edgd lft ins fnl f: nt rch ldrs* **11/2**[3] | |
| 4 | 4 | 1 ¾ | **Premier Rouge**[22] 2777 3-9-0 ... KDarley 7 | 68 |
| | | | (ACStewart) *trckd ldrs: rdn over 2f out: ch over 1f out: wknd ins fnl f* **9/2**[2] | |
| 000 | 5 | ¾ | **Palabelle (IRE)**[10] 3142 3-8-9 ... IMongan 4 | 61 |
| | | | (PWHarris) *midfield: rdn over 2f out: kpt on one pce* **20/1** | |
| 60 | 6 | 2 ½ | **Cronkyvoddy**[20] 2853 3-9-0 ... (t) NCallan 10 | 61 |
| | | | (MissGayKelleway) *in tch: hdwy over 3f out: wknd 1f out* **25/1** | |
| 0 | 7 | 3 | **Warbreck**[61] 1771 3-9-0 ... JFortune 8 | 54 |
| | | | (CREgerton) *towards rr: effrt over 2f out: nvr able to chal* **25/1** | |
| 06 | 8 | 5 | **Nikiforos**[12] 3094 3-9-0 ... (p) KDalgleish 9 | 42 |
| | | | (JWHills) *trckd ldrs: rdn and ev ch over 2f out: wkng whn n.m.r and hmpd over 1f out* **16/1** | |
| 000 | 9 | 3 ½ | **Gustavo**[50] 2046 3-9-0 ... WSupple 1 | 34 |
| | | | (BWHills) *hld up: rdn over 2f out: nvr on terms* **25/1** | |
| 0 | 10 | 18 | **Way Out**[10] 3142 3-8-9 ... DarrenWilliams 11 | — |
| | | | (BPJBaugh) *midfield: rdn over 3f out: wknd over 2f out* **100/1** | |
| 00-0 | 11 | 6 | **Blueberry Jim**[5] 3291 3-9-0 39 ... RWinston 3 | — |
| | | | (THCaldwell) *led after 1f: pushed along over 4f out: hdd 3f out: sn wknd* **100/1** | |

1m 42.96s (-2.59) **Going Correction** -0.10s/f (Good) 11 Ran SP% **115.5**
Speed ratings: **108,107,104,102,102 99,96,91,88,70 64**CSF £8.64 TOTE £2.30: £1.10, £2.80, £2.20; EX 13.00.
**Owner** K Abdulla **Bred** Juddmonte Farms **Trained** Lambourn, Berks

**FOCUS**
Although the form looks nothing special, it was a smart winning time for the class, 1.25 seconds faster than the first division. The winner stepped up on his debut effort and the fifth and sixth both improved too.
**NOTEBOOK**
**New Order** got off the mark at the second attempt in workmanlike fashion. However, she showed the benefit of her debut in May, appreciated this extra furlong and looks the type to improve again.
**Revenir(IRE)** held every chance, but could not quicken past the winner late on and shaped as though he will again come on for this run. The trip suited and he has a race in him.
**Clipperdown(IRE)** ◆ looks the one to take from the race for the future. He was very slowly away and had to be switched markedly wide to throw down a challenge entering the final furlong. He ran green under pressure, but was still staying on with effect and should be a lot sharper next time.
**Premier Rouge** failed to quicken when having a chance late in the day and shaped as though he needs further.
**Palabelle(IRE)** ran her best race to date and would appreciate a switch to handicaps now.
**Cronkyvoddy** ran his best race so far and is now qualified for handicaps.

## 3449 GOOSE GREEN H'CAP 1m 6f
5:20 (5:20) (D) (0-80,80) 3-Y-O+ £5,648 (£1,738; £869; £434) Stalls Low

Form RPR

-012 **1** **Dr Sharp (IRE)**[5] 3300 4-9-10 **76** ........ JEdmunds 2 85
(TPTate) *trckd ldrs: rdn over 3f out: led over 1f out: kpt on* **4/1**[2]

2111 **2** ½ **My Legal Eagle (IRE)**[22] 2787 10-8-1 **58** ........ HayleyTurner(5) 3 66
(RJPrice) *hld up in tch: rdn and hdwy 3f out: ev ch ins fnl f: styd on* **4/1**[2]

3004 **3** 1¼ **Sudden Flight (IRE)**[33] 2480 7-9-1 **67** ........ RHavlin 5 73
(PDEvans) *a.p: rdn over 3f out: edgd lft ins fnl f: nt qckn* **7/2**[1]

5623 **4** nk **Northern Nymph**[27] 2652 5-8-9 **66** ........ StephanieHollinshead(5) 8 72
(RHollinshead) *trckd ldrs: rdn over 4f out: one pce towards fin* **14/1**

/3-2 **5** 3 **Genghis (IRE)**[6] 3276 5-10-0 **80** ........ JFortune 4 82
(HMorrison) *racd keenly: hld up: rdn and hdwy whn nt clr run wl over 2f out: sn swtchd lft: wknd ins fnl f* **11/2**[3]

2212 **6** nk **Nakwa (IRE)**[27] 2652 6-9-6 **72** ........ DAllan 7 73
(EJAlston) *led: rdn over 3f out: hdd over 1f out: wknd ins fnl f* **7/1**

4032 **7** 6 **Sarn**[7] 3221 5-7-13 **51** oh6 ow1 ........ RFfrench 1 44
(MMullineaux) *in tch: lost pl after 6f: bhd after* **25/1**

5023 **8** 1 **Red Scorpion (USA)**[12] 3095 5-8-13 **65** ........ KDarley 6 57
(WMBrisbourne) *hld up: pushed along over 4f out: nvr on terms* **8/1**

3m 2.98s (-3.17) **Going Correction** -0.10s/f (Good) **8** Ran SP% **111.7**
Speed ratings: **105,104,104,103,102 101,98,97**CSF £19.39 CT £58.86 TOTE £5.40: £2.10, £1.70, £1.70; EX 12.40 Place 6 £78.41, Place 5 £48.75.
**Owner** The Ivy Syndicate **Bred** Mrs Ann Fortune **Trained** Tadcaster, N Yorks

**FOCUS**
A modest race, but the gallop was true and the form looks sound.

**NOTEBOOK**
**Dr Sharp(IRE)** appreciated this decent gallop, and responded gamely to pressure in the straight, to get back to winning ways. He looks fairly progressive, will be better over farther and should find more races this season on route to a possible tilt at the Cesarewitch.
**My Legal Eagle(IRE)** ran a blinder off his new mark. On this evidence the Handicapper still might not have a proper hold of him.
**Sudden Flight(IRE)** was well backed for this and ran with credit in defeat. He can make amends, but often runs his best races at this venue.
**Northern Nymph** again looked very one paced under pressure, but ran his race nevertheless and deserves to end his long losing run.
**Genghis(IRE)** paid for running too keen early, when finding little under pressure from two out. He may not have stayed this longer trip, but would have brighter prospects if settling next time.
T/Jkpt: £9,445.40 to a £1 stake. Pool: £13,303.50. 1.00 winning ticket. T/Plt: £113.50 to a £1 stake. Pool: £37,954.95. 244.10 winning tickets. T/Qpdt: £11.90 to a £1 stake. Pool: £2,263.30. 139.60 winning tickets. DO

# 3176 NEWBURY (L-H)
Thursday, July 1

**OFFICIAL GOING: Good to firm**

## 3450 KERRIDGE COMPUTERS APPRENTICE H'CAP 1m 3f 5y
6:40 (6:42) (E) (0-75,70) 4-Y-O+ £3,640 (£1,120; £560; £280) Stalls Centre

Form RPR

0-01 **1** **Lucky Leo**[33] 2471 4-9-4 **68** ........ DeanWilliams(5) 7 81+
(IanWilliams) *bhd: hdwy 5f out: trckd ldrs 3f out: led over 2f out: rdn and edgd lft u.p ins last: all out* **13/2**

5036 **2** ½ **Man The Gate**[32] 2501 5-8-10 **55** ........ NChalmers 5 64
(PDCundell) *hld up in rr: stdy hdwy fr 4f out: chsd wnr ins fnl 2f: chal ins last: no ex u.p last half f* **9/2**[1]

4662 **3** 1¾ **Eastborough (IRE)**[21] 2810 5-9-1 **60** ........ MSavage 3 66
(BGPowell) *s.i.s: hld up in rr: hdwy on ins fr 3f out: pressed ldrs 2f out: kpt on same pce ins last* **11/2**[3]

0543 **4** 2½ **Escalade**[6] 3263 7-8-7 **52** ........(p) BSwarbrick 4 54
(WMBrisbourne) *bhd: rdn along 5f out: styd on u.p fr 2f out: r.o ins last: nt rch ldrs* **5/1**[2]

3504 **5** 3 **Galey River (USA)**[21] 2810 5-7-7 **43** oh3 ........ MHalford(5) 10 40
(JJSheehan) *chsd ldrs: rdn to chal fr 3f out: stl wl there 2f out: sn wknd* **14/1**

0-06 **6** 1½ **Tasneef (USA)**[11] 3128 5-9-1 **60** ........ PMakin 8 55
(TDMcCarthy) *chsd ldrs: slt ld 3f out: hdd over 2f out: sn wknd* **7/1**

2324 **7** 1¼ **Bakiri (IRE)**[11] 3128 6-9-0 **64** ........ DerekNolan(5) 1 57
(AndrewReid) *b: b.hind: hld up in tch: trckd ldrs gng wl 3f out: sn rdn: wknd qckly 2f out* **13/2**

-300 **8** ¾ **Bluegrass Boy**[21] 2810 4-9-2 **61** ........ RThomas 9 53
(GBBalding) *chsd ldrs: rdn to chal over 3f out: wknd over 2f out* **16/1**

0040 **9** ½ **Richemaur (IRE)**[13] 3046 4-9-6 **70** ........ SaleemGolam(5) 2 61
(MHTompkins) *led after 3f: hdd 3f out: sn wknd* **11/1**

0520 **U** **Royal Axminster**[14] 3018 9-7-8 **46** oh3 ow3 ........ AmyBaker(7) 6 —
(MrsPNDutfield) *sn led: hdd after 3f: wkng whn hmpd an uns rdr ins fnl 3f* **16/1**

2m 22.3s (-0.51) **Going Correction** -0.05s/f (Good) **10** Ran SP% **116.2**
Speed ratings: **99,98,97,95,93 92,91,90,90,**—CSF £35.72 CT £172.85 TOTE £5.10: £1.90, £2.10, £2.50; EX 23.20.
**Owner** B and S Vaughan **Bred** J K And Mrs Keegan **Trained** Portway, Warwicks
■ Stewards Enquiry : N Chalmers two-day ban: careless riding (Jul 12,13)

**FOCUS**
A messy race and a modest winning time for the grade.

**NOTEBOOK**
**Lucky Leo**, whose confidence appears to have been boosted by his Doncaster victory, was racing off a 4lb higher mark. Kept wide of the field racing down the straight, he missed the trouble on his inside and stayed on in resolute style to hold off the challenge of the runner-up. These conditions are ideal.
**Man The Gate** made his effort between horses and caused problems for Royal Axminster as he did so. He had every chance throughout the final furlong but, not for the first time, lacked that killer punch. He is hard to win with.
**Eastborough(IRE)**, up 2lb for getting beaten in an amateur riders' handicap last time, had every chance but is another that lacks a decisive turn of foot these days. His last win in a handicap came two years ago off a 6lb higher mark, which suggests he is on the downgrade.
**Escalade**, reverting to more patient tactics, stayed on without being able to offer a threat. Despite several placings, he is on a very long losing run and is not getting much help from the Handicapper.
**Galey River(USA)** was attempting his longest trip on the Flat and did not quite see it out.
**Royal Axminster** was already on the retreat when clipping heels and getting rid of his rider three furlongs out.

## 3451 CHOISIR EBF MAIDEN STKS 7f (S)
7:10 (7:13) (D) 2-Y-O £5,824 (£1,792; £896; £448) Stalls Centre

Form RPR

5 **1** **Grand Marque (IRE)**[12] 3093 2-9-0 ........ KFallon 3 85
(RHannon) *lw: trckd ldrs: led over 4f out: pushed along fr 2f out: styd on wl fnl f: readily* **9/2**[1]

**2** 2 **Mastman (IRE)** 2-9-0 ........ JFortune 13 80
(BJMeehan) *w'like: scope: lw: chsd ldrs: rdn to chal wl over 2f out:wnt 2nd ins fnl 2f: kpt on but nt pce of wnr fnl f* **12/1**

**3** 1¼ **Transgress (IRE)** 2-9-0 ........ MartinDwyer 11 77
(RHannon) *str: bit bkwd: w ldrs: chall and rdn 3f out: styd on wl u.p fnl 2f but nt pce of ldrs ins last* **28/1**

**4** 1½ **Jonquil (IRE)** 2-9-0 ........ RHavlin 5 73
(JHMGosden) *cmpt: bit bkwd: chsd ldrs: rdn to chal ins fnl 3f: wknd fnl f* **13/2**

**5** 1¾ **Wansdyke Lass** 2-8-9 ........ CCatlin 1 64
(MRChannon) *leggy: bhd: rdn and hdwy 3f out: styd on same pce u.p fr 1f out* **33/1**

**6** hd **North Shore (IRE)** 2-9-0 ........ DHolland 10 68
(RHannon) *str: bit bkwd: s.i.s: bhd: hdwy 3f out: rdn and styd on fr over 1f out: nvr gng pce to trble ldrs* **5/1**[2]

**7** ½ **Ball Boy** 2-8-7 ........ TO'Brien(7) 9 67
(MRChannon) *lengthy: athletic: bit bkwd: s.i.s: bhd: pushed along 2f out: styd on ins fnl f but nvr a danger* **33/1**

**8** nk **Worth Abbey** 2-9-0 ........ RLMoore 8 66
(RHannon) *w'like: scope: bit bkwd: led tl hdd over 4f out: rdn over 2f out: wknd appr fnl f* **33/1**

**9** hd **Scale The Heights (IRE)** 2-9-0 ........ MHills 15 66
(BWHills) *leggy: unf: bit bkwd: sn bhd: rdn over 2f out: styd on fnl f but nvr a danger* **8/1**

**10** hd **Dunmaglass (USA)** 2-9-0 ........ SDrowne 2 65
(PFICole) *w'like: scope: bit bkwd: in tch: pushed along after 3f: rdn 3f out: wknd fnl f* **20/1**

**11** nk **Garance** 2-8-9 ........ DaneO'Neill 4 60
(RHannon) *unf: bit bkwd: s.i.s: hdwy 4f out: rdn 3f out: wknd over 1f out* **16/1**

**12** ½ **Discomania** 2-9-0 ........ RHughes 12 63
(RCharlton) *w'like: scope: sn in rr: pushed along 3f out: nvr gng pce to get beyond mid-div* **6/1**[3]

**13** 1½ **Voir Dire** 2-9-0 ........ MFenton 7 60
(MrsPNDutfield) *bhd: sn pushed along: sme hdwy fnl f* **33/1**

0 **14** 1¼ **Bakke**[47] 2111 2-9-0 ........ ADaly 14 56
(MPTregoning) *stdd s: plld hrd and sn prom: wknd 2f out* **8/1**

**15** 1¼ **Guyana (IRE)** 2-9-0 ........ JPMurtagh 6 53
(SKirk) *w'like: chsd ldrs tl wknd ins fnl 3f* **20/1**

1m 28.49s (1.27) **Going Correction** -0.05s/f (Good) **15** Ran SP% **123.0**
Speed ratings: **90,87,86,84,82 82,81,81,81,80 80,80,78,76,75**CSF £54.43 TOTE £4.80: £1.90, £3.20, £5.50; EX 89.70.
**Owner** Noodles Racing **Bred** S N C Ecurie J L Bouchard **Trained** East Everleigh, Wilts

**FOCUS**
An ordinary winning time for the class and experience told, but there were still some eyecatching performances behind the winner.

**NOTEBOOK**
**Grand Marque(IRE)** made his experience tell under a positive ride. He was well on top at the line and on the evidence will have no problem getting a mile.
**Mastman(IRE)** ◆, a 35,000gns yearling from the family of Bireme and Yawl, is a good type and ran a cracker on this debut. He should improve and will get much further than this.
**Transgress(IRE)** ◆, a 35,000gns half-brother to Simply The Guest, is a good-bodied colt and responded well to pressure to grab a place in the frame. His pedigree suggests that this sort of trip will suit him best and he should be all the better for the experience.
**Jonquil(IRE)** ◆, a 130,000gns half-brother to Desert Quest, showed distinct ability for a long way and will be a different proposition next time.
**Wansdyke Lass**, who cost just 4,200gns as a two-year-old, is a half-sister to a couple of winners and ran with credit on this racecourse debut. Her dam won at up to 13 furlongs and the way she looked suggests she will improve with time. *Official explanation: trainer said filly was lame*
**North Shore(IRE)** ◆, a 37,000gns half-brother to three winners including Sergeyev, could never get on terms with the leaders but is probably capable of a good deal better.
**Ball Boy**, an 80,000euros half-brother to four winners including Tanzilla, looked more likely to finish right out the back for a long way but did hint at ability in the latter stages. There is plenty of stamina on the dam's side so there should be better to come from him over further in time.
**Scale The Heights(IRE)**, a 30,000gns half-brother to Softly and Spitting Image, has plenty of stamina in his pedigree so it was no great surprise to see him lack the pace to get competitive. It is likely to be a different story when he is faced with a stiffer test.
**Discomania**, a brother to Clog Dance and half-brother to other winners including the Ebor winner Tuning, is entitled to come on from this debut and will need further, but it still would have been nice to have seen a more prominent showing.

## 3452 JURYS DOYLE HOTELS H'CAP 1m (S)
7:40 (7:43) (D) (0-85,85) 3-Y-O £6,136 (£1,888; £944; £472) Stalls Centre

Form RPR

3-01 **1** **Another Bottle (IRE)**[35] 2419 3-9-0 **78** ........ DaleGibson 7 90+
(TPTate) *lw: plld hrd: stdd rr: hdwy 3f out: led ins fnl f: drvn out* **11/2**[2]

62-2 **2** ¾ **Taaqaah**[16] 2962 3-9-0 **78** ........ MartinDwyer 8 88+
(MPTregoning) *stdd s: t.k.h in rr: hdwy over 2f out: drvn to chse wnr ins fnl f: no imp last half f* **10/3**[1]

5126 **3** 1½ **Red Spell (IRE)**[8] 3212 3-9-3 **81** ........ RHughes 2 88+
(RHannon) *trckd ldrs: led jst ins fnl 2f: hung bdly lft appr fnl f: hdd ins last: one pce* **11/2**[2]

3630 **4** 2½ **Mr Jack Daniells (IRE)**[7] 3230 3-8-11 **75** ........ SDrowne 10 76
(WRMuir) *hld up in rr: hdwy over 2f out: rdn: edgd lft and kpt on fnl f: nvr gng pce of ldrs* **8/1**

-012 **5** 1 **Doctorate**[29] 2569 3-9-6 **84** ........ DHolland 4 83
(EALDunlop) *chsd ldrs: rdn 3f out: wknd over 1f out* **7/1**

10-3 **6** 2½ **Have Faith (IRE)**[14] 3017 3-9-7 **85** ........ MHills 5 78
(BWHills) *chsd ldr 5f: rdn over 2f out: sn btn* **12/1**

4130 **7** ½ **Barathea Dreams (IRE)**[14] 3000 3-9-7 **85** ........ KFallon 1 77
(JSMoore) *led tl hdd ins fnl 2f: sn wknd* **6/1**[3]

4-54 **8** 3 **Geller**[23] 2764 3-8-8 **72** ........ RLMoore 11 57
(RHannon) *wnt rt s: sn rcvrd to chse ldrs: rdn 3f out: wknd 2f out* **25/1**

-003 **9** 2 **Scientist**[22] 2790 3-8-10 **74** ........ JFortune 6 55
(JHMGosden) *hld up in tch: wknd 3f out* **9/1**

0-42 **10** 19 **Barons Spy (IRE)**[17] 2941 3-8-1 **65** ........ CCatlin 3 —
(AWCarroll) *in tch: rdn 1/2-way: sn wknd* **20/1**

1m 39.8s (-1.03) **Going Correction** -0.05s/f (Good) **10** Ran SP% **118.0**
Speed ratings: **103,102,100,98,97 94,94,91,89,70**CSF £24.50 CT £109.47 TOTE £5.40: £1.90, £1.80, £2.90; EX 26.50.


The Form Book, Raceform Ltd, Compton, RG20 6NL

**Owner** J Hanson **Bred** Killeen Castle Stud **Trained** Tadcaster, N Yorks

**FOCUS**
A tight little handicap, run at a sound pace. This looks decent form and the first three are all progressive, particularly the first and second.

**NOTEBOOK**
**Another Bottle(IRE)** ◆, 6lb higher than for his last appearance in a handicap, won this in game fashion despite the shorter trip and again taking a good grip early. He looks progressive and is capable of better, especially in a strongly run race.
**Taaqaah** ◆, making his handicap debut, like the winner took a good hold early but had every chance and was just unable to peg him back. He should be able to win a similar contest.
**Red Spell(IRE)**, who looked very fit, had the ground in his favour and looked to have timed his effort just right, but after hitting the front then hung his chance away. It would be no surprise to see him sporting blinkers in the future.
**Mr Jack Daniells(IRE)** stayed on in the closing stages and again gave the impression he is worth a try over a bit further.
**Doctorate**, raised 4lb for finishing second at Beverley, should not have had a problem with the trip but did not get home. It is worth remembering that his only previous win came on soft ground.
**Have Faith(IRE)** again gave the impression she did not stay.
**Barathea Dreams(IRE)**, set the early pace, but was rather easily picked off. He is 12lb higher than for his last win and is yet to show he can handle this sort of ground on turf.

## 3453 INVESCO PERPETUAL RATED STKS (H'CAP) 6f 8y
**8:10** (8:11) (C ) (0-95,91) 3-Y-O+ **£9,247** (£3,507; £1,753; £797) **Stalls** Centre

Form RPR
0004 **1** **Fantasy Believer**[5] 3309 6-8-13 **83** ........ DHolland 5 100
(JJQuinn) *hld up mid-div: stdy hdwy over 1f out: led jst ins last: qcknd clr: easily* **5/1**[3]
1112 **2** *2 ½* **Caustic Wit (IRE)**[5] 3324 6-8-10 **83** ........ (p) RMiles(3) 8 93
(MSSaunders) *trckd ldr 1/2-way: led ins fnl 2f: rdn and hdd jst ins last: kpt on but no ch w wnr* **7/2**[2]
0036 **3** *hd* **Najeebon (FR)**[12] 3090 5-8-10 **80** ........ CCatlin 10 89
(MRChannon) *in tch: drvn along 1/2-way: styd on fr 2f out: kpt on u.p ins last* **10/1**
312- **4** *nk* **Khabfair**[260] 5575 3-9-1 **91** ........ DaneO'Neill 7 99
(MrsAJPerrett) *hld up in rr: gd hdwy fr 2f out: chsd ldrs: appr fnl f: kpt on ins last* **16/1**
3341 **5** *¾* **Chateau Nicol**[8] 3205 5-8-11 **81** 3ex........ (v) JPMurtagh 9 87
(BGPowell) *hld up in rr: rdn and hdwy appr fnl f: nvr gng pce to rch ldrs* **15/2**
0000 **6** *½* **Nivernais**[18] 2912 5-8-0 **75** ........ NChalmers(5) 3 79
(HCandy) *bhd: hdwy and n.m.r ins fnl 2f: rdn: hung lft and fnd no ex ins fnl f* **16/1**
-363 **7** *shd* **High Reach**[12] 3074 4-9-7 **91** ........ KFallon 1 95
(TGMills) *hld up: hdwy to trck ldrs 1/2-way: rdn and effrt over 1f out: wknd ins fnl f* **7/4**[1]
0110 **8** *5* **Willhewiz**[5] 3324 4-8-11 **81** ........ (v) SCarson 11 70
(RMStronge) *led tl hdd ins fnl 2f: wknd over 1f out* **25/1**
3-00 **9** *hd* **Danehill Stroller (IRE)**[12] 3074 4-9-2 **86** ........ (p) JFortune 6 74
(RMBeckett) *bhd: sn drvn along: a outpcd* **25/1**
000- **10** *1 ½* **Golden Dixie (USA)**[258] 5616 5-8-12 **82** ........ MartinDwyer 2 66
(AMBalding) *chsd ldr to 1/2-way: wknd over 1f out* **25/1**
0300 **11** *6* **Dame De Noche**[12] 3074 4-9-1 **85** ........ MFenton 4 51
(JGGiven) *in tch: rdn 1/2-way: sn bhd* **20/1**

1m 11.8s (-2.57) **Going Correction** -0.05s/f (Good)
**WFA** 3 from 4yo+ 6lb **11** Ran SP% **124.2**
Speed ratings: **115,111,111,111,110 109,109,102,102,100 92**CSF £23.07 CT £171.88 TOTE £5.70: £1.90, £1.50, £2.80; EX 20.30.
**Owner** The Fantasy Fellowship B **Bred** John Khan **Trained** Settrington, N Yorks

**FOCUS**
A most competitive handicap, and the winning time was very smart indeed for the grade. A very solid race that looks sure to work out.

**NOTEBOOK**
**Fantasy Believer**, whose yard have been going great guns in valuable sprint handicaps in recent weeks, was given a chance by the Handicapper and won this in grand style. What was even more impressive was that his best recent form has been on easier ground than this. The time was excellent, but the Handicapper is likely to punish him.
**Caustic Wit(IRE)** seems to have lost none of his dash despite being 27lb higher than for the start of his winning sequence back in May. Despite doing nothing wrong, he was again beaten by a rival with a superior turn of foot and a further 3lb rise in the handicap will not make things any easier.
**Najeebon(FR)** needs fast ground and ran much better back in handicap company. He is now 5lb lower than for his last win in October and is running well enough to take advantage.
**Khabfair** ◆, making his handicap debut and running for the first time in nine months, was racing for only the second time on turf and ran a blinder against a field of battled-hardened sprinters off what had looked a stiff mark. His stable's runners have returned to action in fine form and he looks sure to pay his way. An extra furlong should be well within his compass.
**Chateau Nicol** ran with a great deal of credit off a career-high mark over an inadequate trip.
**Nivernais** is dropping back to a realistic mark and, despite not seeing much daylight, ran his best race since returning from his break.
**High Reach**, who started short enough following his cracking effort in the Wokingham, was racing off just a 2lb higher mark but faded rather disappointingly in the closing stages. He may have still been feeling the effects of Royal Ascot and he remains a serious contender for the Stewards' Cup.
**Willhewiz** *Official explanation: jockey said colt lost a front shoe*

## 3454 HUGHIE CAMERON-ROSE MEMORIAL MAIDEN STKS 1m 4f 5y
**8:40** (8:41) (D ) 3-Y-O **£5,850** (£1,800; £900; £450) **Stalls** Centre

Form RPR
020 **1** **Massif Centrale**[26] 2680 3-9-0 100........ DaneO'Neill 1 82+
(DRCElsworth) *lw: led after 2f: shkn up whn chal over 2f out: c clr appr fnl f: v easily* **2/7**[1]
40-4 **2** *7* **Four Pence (IRE)**[17] 2944 3-9-0 65........ MHills 6 71
(BWHills) *hld up in tch: hdwy 4f out: chsd wnr 3f out: drvn to chal 2f out: sn outpcd by wnr but styd on for clr 2nd* **20/1**
0 **3** *10* **Shastye (IRE)**[38] 2374 3-8-9 ........ JFortune 7 50
(JHMGosden) *chsd ldrs: chsd wnr 4f out: no imp and lost 2nd 3f out: sn wknd u.p* **6/1**[2]
0-00 **4** *6* **Song Of The Sea**[8] 3204 3-8-9 ........ (t) RHughes 4 40
(JWHills) *a in rr* **25/1**
0-2 **5** *5* **Devito (FR)**[38] 2357 3-9-0 ........ VSlattery 2 37
(AKing) *chsd ldrs: rdn 5f out: sn btn* **16/1**[3]
0 **6** *7* **Blaze The Trail**[10] 3161 3-8-9 ........ MartinDwyer 3 21
(Jean-ReneAuvray) *led 2f: styd chsng ldr tl wknd 4f out* **100/1**
6 **7** *5* **Chapelco**[13] 3054 3-9-0 ........ RLMoore 5 18
(JLDunlop) *a bhd: lost tch fnl 5f* **33/1**

2m 34.33s (-1.96) **Going Correction** -0.05s/f (Good) **7** Ran SP% **110.5**
Speed ratings: **104,99,92,88,85 80,77**CSF £10.01 TOTE £1.40: £1.10, £4.80; EX 5.20.
**Owner** Raymond Tooth **Bred** Cliveden Stud Ltd **Trained** Whitsbury, Hants

**FOCUS**
An uncompetitive maiden, and Massif Centrale did not need to be anywhere near his best, but at least he made it a true gallop. This was the first subsequent victory for a horse that ran in the Epsom Derby, but given the nature of this contest that probably has little relevance.

**NOTEBOOK**
**Massif Centrale**, an imposing sort who looked really well, needed this confidence booster after finishing 11th in the Derby. He had to be shaken up briefly passing the two-furlong pole, but besides that it was plain sailing and this victory told us little new about him.
**Four Pence(IRE)** came from off the pace to offer a brief threat to the favourite two furlongs from home, but he was then firmly put in his place. He looks flattered, as he is relatively exposed and this type of race can be notoriously misleading. His official mark remains a reasonable measure of his ability.
**Shastye(IRE)** did not build on her promising Windsor debut and ran as if not staying.
**Song Of The Sea**, unplaced in three maidens before this, achieved little in finishing a remote fourth.

## 3455 MOTOR NEURONE DISEASE ASSOCIATION H'CAP 7f (S)
**9:10** (9:12) (D ) (0-85,83) 3-Y-O+ **£5,902** (£1,816; £908; £454) **Stalls** Centre

Form RPR
1221 **1** **Goodenough Mover**[20] 2834 8-9-7 **77**........ KFallon 4 89
(JSKing) *mde all: pushed along over 2f out: styd on gamely whn chal fr over 1f out: kpt on wl fnl f: asserted fnl 100yds: readily* **3/1**[1]
0005 **2** *½* **Compton's Eleven**[12] 3089 3-9-0 **78**........ CCatlin 6 89
(MRChannon) *chsd ldrs: rdn over 2f out: styd on wl to chse wnr fnl f but no imp fnl 100yds* **14/1**
0002 **3** *nk* **Boundless Prospect (USA)**[12] 3101 5-9-0 **70**........ RHughes 10 80
(JWHills) *stdd s: hld up in rr: hdwy 2f out: rdn and r.o to chse ldrs ins fnl f: no ex fnl 100yds* **12/1**
-000 **4** *½* **Craic Sa Ceili (IRE)**[31] 2521 4-8-4 **63**........ RMiles(3) 12 72
(MSSaunders) *chsd ldrs: chal ins fnl 2f: styd chsng wnr tl appr fnl f: nt qckn ins last* **25/1**
302- **5** *hd* **Point Of Dispute**[260] 5574 9-9-10 **80**........ (v) JFortune 11 88
(PJMakin) *bhd: rdn and hdwy over 1f out: edgd lft u.p and r.o ins last: nt rch ldrs* **25/1**
0020 **6** *1* **Blue Patrick**[17] 2948 4-9-2 **75**........ (p) LFletcher(3) 5 81
(JMPEustace) *hld up in rr: hdwy fr 2f out: styd on u.p ins last: nt rch ldrs* **14/1**
5055 **7** *½* **Terraquin (IRE)**[8] 3205 4-9-0 **70**........ (p) ADaly 7 74
(JJBridger) *in tch: rdn and effrt over 2f out: nt pce to trble ldrs: wknd ins last* **10/1**
0-02 **8** *2* **Bee Minor**[9] 3178 3-8-6 **70**........ RLMoore 13 69
(RHannon) *sn in tch: drvn along 3f out: kpt on same pce fnl 2f* **13/2**
100- **9** *¾* **Indian Trail**[306] 4586 4-9-13 **83**........ DaneO'Neill 2 80
(DRCElsworth) *t.k.h: hld up mid-div: rdn and hdwy over 2f out: wknd appr fnl f* **16/1**
0404 **10** *1* **Marker**[8] 3205 4-9-10 **80**........ RHavlin 14 74
(GBBalding) *stdd s: bhd: hdwy fr 3f out: chsd ldrs and rdn over 2f out: wknd over 1f out* **6/1**[3]
1363 **11** *1 ½* **Primo Way**[18] 2907 3-9-4 **82**........ MHills 9 72
(BWHills) *bhd: pushed along 1/2-way: n.d* **11/2**[2]
-556 **12** *9* **Handsome Cross (IRE)**[29] 2576 3-9-3 **81**........ SDrowne 1 47
(HMorrison) *bhd: sme hdwy 3f out: wknd 2f out* **11/1**
0030 **13** *15* **Night Wolf (IRE)**[13] 3058 4-8-3 **66**........ TDean(7) 8 —
(MRChannon) *prom early: wknd qckly 1/2-way* **33/1**

1m 25.85s (-1.37) **Going Correction** -0.05s/f (Good)
**WFA** 3 from 4yo+ 8lb **13** Ran SP% **123.0**
Speed ratings: **105,104,104,103,103 102,101,99,98,97 95,85,68**CSF £48.96 CT £474.64 TOTE £4.20: £2.10, £3.10, £4.70; EX 62.80 Place 6 £39.95, Place 5 £21.47.
**Owner** D Goodenough Removals & Transport **Bred** G Foster **Trained** Broad Hinton, Wilts

**FOCUS**
A competitive handicap run at a sound pace. Solid form.

**NOTEBOOK**
**Goodenough Mover**, put up 7lb after his Chepstow win, was running in his 50th race and had the champion jockey on board for the very first time. The tactics were the same though, and he showed wonderful determination to hold off his rivals and record his tenth career victory. The handicapper will no doubt have another go at him, but he will still be fairly treated on his 2002 form.
**Compton's Eleven** is becoming well handicapped and ran his best race for a while. He saw the trip out much better this time, but just found the winner far too determined.
**Boundless Prospect(USA)**, now 8lb below his last winning mark which was more than two years ago, had every chance but could not force his head in front. He should be capable of winning off this sort of mark.
**Craic Sa Ceili(IRE)** ◆ has plummeted 12lb since the start of the season and this was certainly much better. She handles this ground, but her only previous win came in the soft and she would be very interesting under similar conditions off this sort of mark.
**Point Of Dispute**, who looked fit despite his nine-month absence, made up a lot of late ground, but he is a notoriously hard ride who has thrown away winning chances in the past.
**Blue Patrick** ran with credit back up a furlong, but he is very much an in-and-out performer and there is no guarantee he will build on this.
**Indian Trail** looked fit after his absence, but ran as though needing it. This is his ground.
**Primo Way** should have been suited by the conditions, but he has disappointed when appearing to have a good chance in the past and this was certainly another very poor effort.
**Handsome Cross(IRE)** *Official explanation: jockey said colt was hanging badly left handed*
T/Plt: £38.10 to a £1 stake. Pool: £47,703.40. 911.65 winning tickets. T/Qpdt: £7.20 to a £1 stake. Pool: £3,332.10. 340.30 winning tickets. ST

# 3424 YARMOUTH (L-H)
## Thursday, July 1

**OFFICIAL GOING: Firm (good to firm in places)**
Another dry night with a strong breeze meant that conditions remained on the fast side.
Wind: Strong across Weather: Sunshine giving way to cloud.

## 3456 EUROPEAN BREEDERS FUND MAIDEN FILLIES' STKS 7f 3y
**2:30** (2:31) (D ) 2-Y-O **£4,793** (£1,475; £737; £368) **Stalls** High

Form RPR
**1** **Queen Of Poland** 2-8-11 ........ NPollard 9 80
(DRLoder) *chsd ldrs: rdn to ld and edgd lft ins fnl f: r.o* **16/1**
0 **2** *nk* **Great Opinions (USA)**[29] 2585 2-8-11 ........ RHills 4 79
(JHMGosden) *s.i.s: sn chsng ldrs: led over 1f out: hdd ins fnl f: r.o* **16/1**
**3** *nk* **Glorious Step (USA)** 2-8-11 ........ SSanders 7 78
(JHMGosden) *s.i.s: sn prom: rdn over 1f out: r.o* **16/1**
4 **4** *1 ¾* **Night Of Joy (IRE)**[19] 2876 2-8-11 ........ PRobinson 12 74
(MAJarvis) *led over 5f: no ex ins fnl f* **3/1**[2]

5 1 1/4 **Theas Dance** 2-8-8 ........ TPQueally(3) 2 71
(DRLoder) *hld up: hdwy 1/2-way: rdn and wknd ins fnl f* **13/2**
6 1 3/4 **Eccentricity (USA)** 2-8-11 ........ WRyan 1 67
(HRACecil) *s.i.s: outpcd: nvr nrr* **9/2**[3]
7 shd **Lunar Sky (USA)** 2-8-11 ........ DHolland 11 66
(CEBrittain) *prom over 4f* **12/1**
8 1/2 **Georgina** 2-8-11 ........ MHenry 10 65
(MAJarvis) *prom: lost pl 5f out: n.d after* **28/1**
9 11 **Meditation** 2-8-11 ........ GDuffield 8 38
(IAWood) *chsd ldr: wkng whn stmbld 2f out* **66/1**
10 8 **Riyma (IRE)** 2-8-11 ........ KFallon 6 —
(SirMichaelStoute) *dwlt: outpcd* **5/2**[1]

1m 26.18s (-0.32) **Going Correction** -0.10s/f (Good) **10** Ran SP% **115.4**
Speed ratings: **97,96,96,94,92 90,90,90,77,68**CSF £242.52 TOTE £18.60: £5.40, £5.80, £4.40; EX 807.30.
**Owner** Sheikh Mohammed **Bred** Darley **Trained** Newmarket, Suffolk

**FOCUS**
Some well-bred newcomers on show but, the majority of these refused to let themselves down on the fast ground. A fair amount of guesswork is involved in assessing the form.

**NOTEBOOK**
**Queen Of Poland**, a half-sister to winning juvenile Grizel, is quite a nice filly who looked as though the race would do her good. She handled conditions better than most, and is clearly open to improvement.
**Great Opinions(USA)** stepped up considerably on her debut effort but continually changed legs and looked to be hating the ground.
**Glorious Step(USA)**, a $35,000 yearling, comes from a useful American family. She took a while to grasp what was required, but was staying on to good effect in the latter stages and should appreciate a little further in time.
**Night Of Joy(IRE)** had something of a soft lead, but when coming off the bridle left the impression she wasn't enjoying the fast ground. *Official explanation: jockey said filly hung left*
**Theas Dance**, out of a Group 1 winning mare, looked the likely winner going into the final furlong, but found little off the bridle. She looks sure to benefit from the experience.
**Eccentricity(USA)**, from a top-class, middle-distance family, was the first of her stables juveniles to run this term. She looked very green during the race and should do better in time.
**Meditation** *Official explanation: jockey said filly was unsuited by the ground - firm, good to firm in places*
**Riyma(IRE)**, out of a dual winning, middle-distance mare, looked clueless and is surely better than she showed here.

## 3457 CUSTOM KITCHENS FILLIES' H'CAP 7f 3y
**3:00** (3:00) (D ) (0-80,79) 3-Y-0+ **£5,577** (£1,716; £858; £429) **Stalls** High

Form RPR
5-4 1 **Pintle**[19] [2873] 4-9-4 **65** ........ KMcEvoy 2 75
(JLSpearing) *mde virtually all: edgd rt wl over 1f out: r.o* **16/1**
512- 2 1 1/4 **Search Mission (USA)**[304] [4613] 3-9-10 **79** ........ PRobinson 4 86
(MrsAJPerrett) *trckd ldrs: plld hrd: shkn up over 1f out: styd on* **16/1**
06-0 3 hd **Moon Legend (USA)**[32] [2505] 3-8-10 **65** ........ SSanders 1 71
(WJarvis) *hld up: plld hrd: hdwy over 1f out: r.o wl* **66/1**
4020 4 nk **And Toto Too**[12] [3086] 4-9-6 **67** ........(b) KFallon 12 72
(PDEvans) *hld up: hdwy 1/2-way: rdn and edgd lft over 1f out: styd on same pce* **11/1**
6121 5 1/2 **Lady Georgina**[20] [2838] 3-9-9 **78** ........ OUrbina 6 82
(JRFanshawe) *hld up in tch: racd keenly: n.m.r wl over 1f out: styd on same pce ins fnl f* **15/8**[1]
-053 6 nk **Cara Bella**[26] [2694] 3-9-2 **74** ........ TPQueally(3) 5 77
(DRLoder) *chsd ldrs: outpcd over 1f out: r.o ins fnl f* **8/1**[3]
0046 7 3/4 **Annijaz**[5] [3301] 7-8-3 **53** ........ FPFerris(3) 11 54
(JMBradley) *s.i.s: hld up: rdn and n.m.r over 2f out: nvr trbld ldrs* **22/1**
0000 8 3/4 **Tapau (IRE)**[5] [3301] 6-9-1 **62** ........(p) DHolland 3 61
(JMBradley) *hld up: nt clr run 2f out: nvr trbld ldrs* **33/1**
0430 9 3/4 **Bint Royal (IRE)**[3] [3372] 6-8-11 **58** ........(p) RMullen 9 55
(MissVHaigh) *chsd ldrs: rdn over 2f out: no ex fnl f* **14/1**
0012 10 shd **In The Pink (IRE)**[5] [3301] 4-9-6 **67** ........ TEDurcan 8 64
(MRChannon) *hld up: n.m.r 2f out: n.d* **5/2**[2]
5003 11 2 **Wodhill Be**[44] [2209] 4-7-12 **45** oh1 ........ JMackay 7 36
(DMorris) *s.i.s: hld up: plld hrd: a in rr* **66/1**
0-00 12 3/4 **Angel Isa (IRE)**[1] [3428] 4-8-1 **48** ........ GDuffield 10 37
(RAFahey) *w ldr over 4f: wknd over 1f out* **33/1**

1m 26.26s (-0.24) **Going Correction** -0.10s/f (Good)
**WFA** 3 from 4yo+ 8lb **12** Ran SP% **114.4**
Speed ratings: **97,95,95,95,94 94,93,92,91,91 89,88**CSF £225.98 CT £8519.85 TOTE £19.50: £3.90, £3.60, £12.80; EX 168.50.
**Owner** Robert Heathcote **Bred** R And Mrs Heathcote **Trained** Kinnersley, Worcs

**FOCUS**
Not a strong race for the grade and the time was only moderate.

**NOTEBOOK**
**Pintle**, tackling this trip for the first time, had a soft lead and never looked likely to be pegged back. She is clearly at home on a fast surface.
**Search Mission(USA)**, from a stable that has had a quite time so far this season, was a little keen in the early stages, more so than at the business end.
**Moon Legend(USA)**, tackling handicap company for the first time, did her best to extended her jockeys arms for much of the race, and deserves plenty of credit for seeing her race out in the manner she did.
**And Toto Too** turned in a sound enough effort, but may have done better still had there been more pace on .
**Lady Georgina** was a little disappointing for she always looked to be in the right place. It could be that this ground was plenty quick enough for her.
**Cara Bella** stayed on again having lost her pitch and may be worth another try over a mile.
**Tapau(IRE)** *Official explanation: jockey said he suffered interference approaching final furlong*

## 3458 STREET CONSTRUCTION IN PARTNERSHIP WITH NORTHERN RACING (S) STKS 6f 3y
**3:30** (3:35) (G ) 2-Y-0 **£2,541** (£726; £363) **Stalls** High

Form RPR
6 1 **Nordhock (USA)**[6] [3272] 2-8-3 ........ TPQueally(3) 4 59
(NACallaghan) *s.i.s: sn prom: rdn over 1f out: led ins fnl f: r.o* **3/1**[2]
1342 2 1 **Zimbali**[29] [2593] 2-8-11 ........ DHolland 6 61
(JMBradley) *led: rdn and hdd ins fnl f: unable qck* **11/4**[1]
344 3 1 3/4 **Petite Elle**[6] [3278] 2-8-6 ........ RMullen 3 51
(PJMcbride) *chsd ldrs: rdn over 1f out: styd on same pce* **14/1**
0 4 1 3/4 **Voom**[8] [3192] 2-8-6 ........ TEDurcan 2 46
(MRChannon) *chsd ldrs: rdn over 1f out: no ex ins fnl f* **11/2**[3]
0066 5 3/4 **Zachy Boy**[10] [3140] 2-8-8 ........(p) FPFerris(3) 1 48
(JSMoore) *unruly stalls: w ldr: rdn and ev ch over 1f out: wknd ins fnl f* **33/1**
05 6 2 1/2 **Dartanian**[11] [3124] 2-8-11 ........ GDuffield 5 41
(PDEvans) *chsd ldrs: rdn 1/2-way: wknd over 1f out* **7/1**
2064 7 23 **Urabande**[16] [2960] 2-8-6 ........ GCarter 7 —
(JulianPoulton) *s.i.s: sn outpcd* **15/2**
8 2 1/2 **Tiger Hunter** 2-8-11 ........ KFallon 8 —
(PHowling) *sn outpcd* **8/1**

1m 14.5s (0.90) **Going Correction** -0.10s/f (Good) **8** Ran SP% **112.0**
Speed ratings: **90,88,86,84,83 79,49,45**CSF £11.18 TOTE £4.50: £2.10, £1.30, £3.90; EX 11.90.The winner was bought in for 10,400gns. Zimbali was claimed by J. Billson for £6,000.
**Owner** Mrs J Doyle & Mrs P Shanahan **Bred** P J B Bloodstock **Trained** Newmarket, Suffolk

**FOCUS**
Probably a fair seller, with the runner-up having shown useful enough form at this level previously.

**NOTEBOOK**
**Nordhock(USA)** showed a fluent action to post and appreciated this drop in class, having shown nothing in better company on her debut. There is no reason why she can't go on from here.
**Zimbali** is a tough and consistent sort, and lost nothing in defeat giving plenty of weight away.
**Petite Elle** looked to run nearly to the form she showed behind the runner-up on their meeting here last month.
**Voom** showed a bit more on this drop in class. Her dam was a winner over a mile, and there is every reason to believe she will be suited by further.
**Zachy Boy**, who got upset in the stalls, had already looked exposed at this level.

## 3459 STREET CONSTRUCTION H'CAP 1m 2f 21y
**4:00** (4:03) (E ) (0-70,68) 3-Y-0+ **£3,935** (£1,211; £605; £302) **Stalls** Low

Form RPR
0033 1 **Billy Bathwick (IRE)**[10] [3143] 7-8-12 **56** ........ FPFerris(3) 1 63
(JMBradley) *a.p: rdn to ld ins fnl f: r.o* **7/1**
2434 2 hd **Carrowdore (IRE)**[12] [3095] 4-9-13 **68** ........ RMullen 8 74
(CNAllen) *hld up: hdwy over 1f out: edgd lft ins fnl f: r.o wl* **7/2**[2]
0302 3 1 1/4 **Ember Days**[29] [2573] 5-9-4 **59** ........(p) KMcEvoy 2 63
(JLSpearing) *chsd ldrs: led over 1f out: hdd and unable qck ins fnl f* **7/1**
6000 4 1 1/4 **Adalar (IRE)**[23] [2753] 4-9-5 **60** ........ KFallon 6 62
(PDEvans) *hld up: hdwy over 2f out: rdn over 1f out: no ex ins fnl f* **13/2**[3]
0040 5 2 1/2 **Sammy's Shuffle**[12] [3088] 9-8-4 **45** ........(b) PDoe 7 42
(JamiePoulton) *s.i.s: hld up: hdwy over 2f out: rdn over 1f out: styd on same pce fnl f* **16/1**
06-0 6 nk **Niagara (IRE)**[43] [1282] 7-9-11 **66** ........ PRobinson 3 62
(MHTompkins) *trckd ldrs: racd keenly: rdn over 1f out: styd on same pce* **16/1**
0211 7 hd **Kernel Dowery (IRE)**[17] [2930] 4-9-9 **64** ........(e) DHolland 5 60
(PWHarris) *chsd ldr: led over 2f out: rdn and hdd over 1f out: wknd ins fnl f* **13/8**[1]
36-0 8 10 **Cazisa Star (USA)**[20] [2848] 3-8-8 **60** ........ NPollard 9 37
(PWHarris) *led over 7f: wknd over 1f out* **33/1**
000 9 11 **Daimajin (IRE)**[45] [2170] 5-8-11 **52** ........ WRyan 4 8
(MrsLucindaFeatherstone) *s.i.s: hld up: hdwy over 3f out: wknd over 2f out* **33/1**

2m 7.76s (-0.21) **Going Correction** +0.125s/f (Good)
**WFA** 3 from 4yo+ 11lb **9** Ran SP% **116.3**
Speed ratings: **105,104,103,102,100 100,100,92,83**CSF £31.98 CT £177.65 TOTE £7.50: £2.00, £1.90, £2.80; EX 30.10.
**Owner** Ms A M Williams **Bred** Burgage Stud **Trained** Sedbury, Gloucs

**FOCUS**
An ordinary handicap, but it was run at a fair pace.

**NOTEBOOK**
**Billy Bathwick(IRE)** managed to get first run on Carrowdore, which made all the difference. However, he wasn't winning out of turn.
**Carrowdore(IRE)**, who has been campaigned over further this year, proved just as well suited by this shorter trip and continues to run well, without getting his head in front. *Official explanation: jockey said colt hung left in latter stages*
**Ember Days**, without a win for a couple of years, is more realistically treated now and turned in a sound effort, on ground which could well have been plenty quick enough for her.
**Adalar(IRE)** has found life difficult since coming over from Ireland and as a consequence has seen his mark plummet. He showed that he still retains some abiltity and was reported by his jockey not to have stayed. *Official explanation: jockey said gelding didn't stay*
**Sammy's Shuffle** has won more than his fair share in the past, but lacks consistency nowadays.
**Kernel Dowery(IRE)**, had no excuses and could well be in the grip of the Handicapper for the time being.

## 3460 GROSVENOR CASINO GREAT YARMOUTH MAIDEN STKS 1m 3f 101y
**4:30** (4:30) (D ) 3-Y-0+ **£3,682** (£1,052; £526) **Stalls** Low

Form RPR
32-2 1 **Asaleeb**[21] [2805] 3-8-7 80 ........ RHills 2 64+
(ACStewart) *trckd ldr: led 3f out: pushed clr fnl f: eased nr fin* **1/16**[1]
00-0 2 3 1/2 **Boogie Magic**[29] [2596] 4-9-5 62 ........ RMullen 1 58
(CNAllen) *sn led: rdn and hdd 3f out: no ch w wnr* **22/1**[3]
4 3 5 **Wodhill Hope**[48] [2090] 4-9-5 ........ DMcGaffin 4 50
(DMorris) *dwlt: sn chsng ldr: rdn over 3f out: wknd over 1f out* **20/1**[2]

2m 32.05s (4.65) **Going Correction** +0.125s/f (Good)
**WFA** 3 from 4yo 12lb **3** Ran SP% **103.2**
Speed ratings: **88,85,81**CSF £2.00 TOTE £1.10; EX 1.90.
**Owner** Hamdan Al Maktoum **Bred** Shadwell Estate Company Limited **Trained** Newmarket, Suffolk

**FOCUS**
A non-event with the winner outclassing her rivals. A slow time for the grade.

**NOTEBOOK**
**Asaleeb** told us nothing new and was entitled to beat her rivals with ease.
**Boogie Magic** was flaterred by the winning margin, but she never stopped trying.
**Wodhill Hope** at least picked up some prize money, but achieved little in doing so.

## 3461 ROY & JOAN TANNER AMATEUR RIDERS' H'CAP 1m 3f 101y
**5:00** (5:00) (F ) (0-55,55) 3-Y-0+ **£3,017** (£862; £431) **Stalls** Low

Form RPR
42-0 1 **Golden Chance (IRE)**[14] [3018] 7-11-0 **48** ........ MissSBrotherton 13 55
(MWEasterby) *a.p: led over 1f out: rdn out* **5/1**[1]
2403 2 1/2 **Platinum Charmer (IRE)**[10] [3149] 4-11-4 **55** ........(p) MrSDobson(3) 4 61
(KRBurke) *hld up: swtchd rt and hdwy over 1f out: hung lft and r.o u.p ins fnl f* **13/2**[3]
0036 3 2 1/2 **Vrisaki (IRE)**[8] [3190] 3-10-3 **49** ........ MrsSBosley 1 51
(MissDMountain) *hld up: hdwy over 2f out: styd on* **8/1**
0264 4 2 **Jade Star (USA)**[70] [1560] 4-11-3 **51** ........ MissEJJones 3 50
(MissGayKelleway) *chsd ldrs: rdn and hung lft over 1f out: no ex ins fnl f* **5/1**[1]
43-0 5 nk **Final Dividend (IRE)**[14] [3018] 8-10-8 **45** ........ MissJoannaRees(3) 8 43
(JMPEustace) *s.i.s: sn prom: rdn and ev ch 2f out: no ex ins fnl f* **8/1**
5-65 6 1/2 **African Star**[12] [3107] 3-10-6 **55** ........ MissLJHarwood(3) 10 53
(MrsAJPerrett) *led: hdd over 9f out: chsd ldr: led over 2f out: rdn and hdd over 1f out: wknd ins fnl f* **14/1**



The Form Book, Raceform Ltd, Compton, RG20 6NL

5305 **7** 1 1/2 **Roppongi Dancer**[6] 699 5-10-1 **35** oh5.....................(b) MrsMMorris 7 30
(MrsNMacauley) *chsd ldrs: led over 8f out: hdd over 2f out: wknd fnl f*
**40/1**

45-4 **8** 1 1/2 **Ellovamul**[15] 2974 4-10-13 **52**.................................... MrCDavies(5) 9 45
(WMBrisbourne) *hld up: pushed along 7f out: hdwy over 2f out: wknd over 1f out*
**11/2**[2]

000- **9** 6 **Arctic Blue**[341] 2906 4-10-13 **52**.................................... SWalsh(5) 6 35
(MJGingell) *hld up: plld hrd: hdwy u.p over 3f out: wknd over 1f out* **14/1**

/5-3 **10** 3 **Tommy Carson**[88] 684 9-10-3 **40**............................. MrEDehdashti(3) 2 18
(JamiePoulton) *hmpd after 1f: a bhd*
**12/1**

3566 **11** 4 **Theatre Lady (IRE)**[17] 2939 6-10-7 **44**.....................(v) MissEFolkes(3) 12 16
(PDEvans) *trckd ldrs: racd keenly: wknd over 2f out*
**10/1**

6606 **12** 1 **Grady**[13] 3041 5-9-12 **35**.................................... MrsSOwen(3) 5 5
(WMBrisbourne) *dwlt: outpcd*
**16/1**

0-40 **13** 8 **Bid Spotter (IRE)**[6] 1238 5-10-3 **42** ow7........................ MrNPearce(5) 11 —
(MrsLucindaFeatherstone) *chsd ldrs: led over 9f out: hdd over 8f out: wknd 5f out*
**25/1**

2m 28.26s (0.86) **Going Correction** +0.125s/f (Good) **13** Ran SP% **126.6**
**WFA** 3 from 4yo+ 12lb
Speed ratings: **101,100,98,97,97 96,95,94,90,88 85,84,78**CSF £39.36 CT £268.00 TOTE £7.50: £2.10, £3.00, £3.80; EX 28.70 Place 6 £2,974.75, Place 5 £175.81.
**Owner** Miss S Brotherton **Bred** Gainsborough Stud Management Ltd **Trained** Sheriff Hutton, N Yorks

**FOCUS**
A low-grade handicap and ordinary form, but the pace looked fair for the grade.

**NOTEBOOK**
**Golden Chance(IRE)** had his favoured fast surface and goes well for his amateur rider, who was seen to good effect.
**Platinum Charmer(IRE)** looked to have been given plenty to do, but he stuck willingly to his task and was closing the winner down all the way to the line, despite drifting to his left.
**Vrisaki(IRE)** again showed a little promise, but doesn't look the easiest of rides.
**Jade Star(USA)** had no excuses and has yet to convince she truly stays this far.
**Final Dividend(IRE)** isn't the most consistent animal in training but, he is well-treated on the best of his form and it would come as no surprise to see him pop up in similar company.
**African Star** had plenty of use made of him and had no excuses. However, unlike most of his rivals, he is at least open to a little improvement.
T/Plt: £2,941.40 to a £1 stake. Pool: £31,630.80. 7.85 winning tickets. T/Qpdt: £6.00 to a £1 stake. Pool: £3,111.90. 381.00 winning tickets. CR

3465 - 3467a (Foreign Racing) - See Raceform Interactive

## 3164 BEVERLEY (R-H)

Friday, July 2

**OFFICIAL GOING: Good to firm**
Times suggested the ground was riding softer than the official going suggested.

### 3468 EUROPEAN BREEDERS FUND WELLBEING NOVICE STKS (GUARANTEED SWEEPSTAKES) 5f
**6:45** (6:45) (D) 2-Y-O **£4,387** (£1,350; £675; £337) **Stalls** High

Form RPR
122 **1** **Melalchrist**[15] 3011 2-9-2 .................................... RWinston 4 91
(JJQuinn) *trckd ldrs: swtchd lft and hdwy wl over 1f out: rdn to ld ent last: drvn out*
**7/2**[2]

1 **2** 1 1/4 **Imperial Sound**[15] 3011 2-9-5 .................................... SSanders 5 90+
(TDBarron) *hmpd early and sn towards rr: hdwy 1/2-way: rdn to chal over 1f out: drvn and one pce ins last*
**2/5**[1]

01 **3** 3 **Bond City (IRE)**[9] 3196 2-9-2 .................................... FLynch 1 76
(BSmart) *chsd ldr: hdwy to ld 2f out: sn rdn: hdd ent last: sn wknd* **7/1**[3]

**4** 9 **Zanderido** 2-8-8 .................................... DarrenWilliams 3 36
(BSRothwell) *dwlt: sn outpcd and b ehind*
**50/1**

0541 **5** 2 1/2 **Our Louis**[11] 3144 2-8-4 .................................... TEaves(3) 2 26
(JSWainwright) *led: rdn along and hdd 2f out: sn wknd*
**33/1**

66.49 secs (2.49) **Going Correction** +0.425s/f (Yiel) **5** Ran SP% **111.1**
Speed ratings: **97,95,90,75,71**CSF £5.39 TOTE £4.80: £1.70, £1.10; EX 7.30.
**Owner** T G S Wood **Bred** A C M Spalding **Trained** Settrington, N Yorks
■ Stewards Enquiry : R Winston caution: careless riding

**FOCUS**
Only three mattered here. The form is decent.

**NOTEBOOK**
**Melalchrist** turned around course and distance form with the runner-up on 11lb better terms. Both his wins have come with give in the ground - the surface here looked softer than the official going suggested - although he appears equally at ease on a faster surface.
**Imperial Sound** had easier ground to contend with this time and was 11lb worse off with the winner compared with when he beat him here on his debut. This was still a decent effort giving weight all round, though, especially as things did not really go his way. There will be other days for him.
**Bond City(IRE)** took up the running with a quarter of a mile to run but could not hold off the principals when challenged. He should appreciate a return to six.
**Our Louis** was out of his depth in this grade but he showed plenty of early dash.

### 3469 HULL MITSUBISHI GRANDIS MAIDEN STKS 5f
**7:15** (7:16) (D) 2-Y-O **£4,686** (£1,442; £721; £360) **Stalls** High

Form RPR
052 **1** **Wonderful Mind**[14] 3055 2-9-0 .................................... RWinston 13 71
(TDEasterby) *chsd ldr: hdwy to ld wl over 1f out: rdn out* **11/10**[1]

0 **2** 1 3/4 **Rasa Sayang (USA)**[76] 1462 2-9-0 .................................... SSanders 4 64+
(TDBarron) *in tch: hdwy 2f out: sn rdn and kpt on wl fnl f* **9/1**

**3** shd **Claret And Amber** 2-9-0 .................................... RFfrench 3 64+
(RAFahey) *swtchd rt and bhd: hdwy 2f out: styd on wl fnl f: nrst fin* **14/1**

06 **4** 1 **Sowerby**[21] 2858 2-8-9 .................................... MLawson(5) 6 60
(MBrittain) *prom: rdn 2f out: chsd wnr ent last: sn drvn and one pce* **40/1**

**5** 3/4 **Wayward Shot (IRE)** 2-9-0 .................................... DaleGibson 2 57
(MWEasterby) *s.i.s and swvd rt start: in rr tl hdwy wl over 1f out: styd on wl fnl f: nrst fin*
**40/1**

0 **6** 1 **Zarova (IRE)**[43] 2234 2-9-0 .................................... TLucas 14 53
(MWEasterby) *in tch: lost pl and bhd 1/2-way: swtchd lft wl over 1f out: styd on wl fnl f: nrst fin*
**12/1**

**7** shd **Choreographic (IRE)** 2-8-11 .................................... THamilton(3) 7 52
(RAFahey) *s.i.s and bhd tl styd on wl appr last: nrst fin* **8/1**[3]

6 **8** nk **Paula Jo**[15] 3011 2-8-6 .................................... TEaves(3) 11 46
(JSWainwright) *in tch: rdn along 2f out: grad wknd* **20/1**

5033 **9** 2 **Chilali (IRE)**[15] 3003 2-8-9 .................................... FLynch 8 38
(ABerry) *led: rdn along 2f out: sn hdd & wknd* **7/2**[2]

0 **10** 1/2 **Star Of Kildare (IRE)**[21] 2860 2-8-9 .................................... KimTinkler 10 36
(NTinkler) *in tch: rdn along 2f out: sn wknd* **25/1**

0 **11** 6 **Samalan**[43] 2248 2-9-0 .................................... GDuffield 5 17
(JParkes) *bhd fr 1/2-way* **66/1**

**12** 2 **Cadogen Square** 2-8-9 .................................... DarrenWilliams 12 4
(DWChapman) *bhd fr 1/2-way* **20/1**

**13** 1 1/2 **Exponential (IRE)** 2-9-0 ....................................(be[1]) VHalliday 9 3
(SCWilliams) *midfield: rdn along 1/2-way: sn wknd* **25/1**

66.69 secs (2.69) **Going Correction** +0.425s/f (Yiel) **13** Ran SP% **128.9**
Speed ratings: **95,92,92,90,89 87,87,87,83,83 73,70,67**CSF £12.42 TOTE £1.90: £1.40, £3.00, £2.80; EX 19.50.
**Owner** T G & Mrs M E Holdcroft **Bred** Bearstone Stud **Trained** Great Habton, N Yorks

**FOCUS**
An ordinary maiden.

**NOTEBOOK**
**Wonderful Mind** had shown enough in three starts to suggest he could win an average maiden and, from a good draw, showed his usual early pace to maintain a good position before picking off the leader in the straight. He should pay his way in handicap company.
**Rasa Sayang(USA)**, a half-brother to two winners in the US, was not well drawn but improved a good deal on his debut effort. He shapes as though he will be suited by a step up to six.
**Claret And Amber**, a brother to dual winner Riska King and half-brother to three other winners, came home well from his low draw. He achieved more than his better-fancied stablemate and hopefully he can build on this.
**Sowerby**, beaten in a seller last time out, is improving with every run.
**Wayward Shot(IRE)** took a while to get the hang of things and to understand what was required. He should derive plenty from this debut experience and is going to be suited by farther in time.
**Zarova(IRE)**, whose dam was a middle-distance winner in France, did not really have the pace to take advantage of his draw.
**Chilali(IRE)** came in for plenty of support in the ring. Although she showed plenty of dash, she was easily brushed aside and her place is in selling grade.
**Samalan** *Official explanation: jockey said gelding hung left handed throughout*

### 3470 AUNT BESSIE'S YORKSHIRE PUDDING H'CAP 1m 100y
**7:45** (7:45) (D) (0-85,80) 4-Y-O+ **£6,922** (£2,130; £1,065; £532) **Stalls** High

Form RPR
2400 **1** **Cryfield**[10] 3167 7-8-3 **56**.................................... KimTinkler 4 68
(NTinkler) *wnt bdly lft s: hld up: hdwy on outer wl over 1f out: str run to ld ent last: styd on wl*
**12/1**

5-01 **2** 1 **Torrid Kentavr (USA)**[37] 1502 7-8-12 **65**........................ RWinston 11 75
(BEllison) *hld up: gd hdwy over 2f out: rdn to chal over 1f out and ev ch tl nt qckn ins last*
**13/2**[3]

0021 **3** 2 1/2 **Les Arcs (USA)**[3] 3397 4-9-9 **76** 6ex.................................... JFEgan 8 81
(RCGuest) *hld up: gd hdwy 3f out: rdn to ld briefly over 1f out: drvn and hdd ent last: sn one pce*
**2/1**[1]

0005 **4** nk **Iberus (GER)**[13] 3101 6-8-13 **69**.................................... TEaves(3) 10 73
(SGollings) *trckd ldrs: hdwy to chal and ev ch whn n.m.r 2f out: sn rdn and outpcd over 1f out: styd on ins last*
**20/1**

-042 **5** 1 1/4 **Tedsdale Mac**[10] 3167 5-7-12 **51** oh1.................................... RFfrench 7 52
(NBycroft) *in tch: hdwy on outer to ld and edgd rt 2f out: sn rdn and hdd over 1f out: sn one pce*
**9/1**

0503 **6** nk **Tedstale (USA)**[9] 3198 6-9-13 **80**....................................(b) SSanders 12 81
(TDEasterby) *trckd ldrs on inner: effrt and nt clr run 2f out: swtchd lft and sn rdn: no imp appr last*
**9/2**[2]

4310 **7** 2 **Jubilee Street (IRE)**[6] 3321 5-8-5 **58**.................................... GDuffield 9 55
(MrsADuffield) *t.k.h: trckd ldrs on inner: pushed along over 3f out: sn btn*
**7/1**

0006 **8** 4 **Atlantic Ace**[34] 2493 7-9-6 **73**.................................... FLynch 3 61
(BSmart) *hmpd s: puled hrd: a rr*
**14/1**

0-06 **9** 1 1/4 **Wuxi Venture**[44] 2078 9-8-9 **65**.................................... THamilton(3) 2 51
(RAFahey) *hmpd s: a rr*
**25/1**

0000 **10** 1 1/2 **Arawan (IRE)**[16] 2982 4-8-9 **62**.................................... DaleGibson 5 44
(MWEasterby) *led: rdn along 1/2-way: hdd & wknd 3f out*
**16/1**

0000 **11** 2 **Broadway Score (USA)**[13] 3097 6-9-8 **75**.................................... TLucas 6 53
(MWEasterby) *cl up: led 3f out tl 2f out: sn wknd*
**25/1**

0-53 **12** 5 **Aswan (IRE)**[15] 3012 6-8-13 **66**....................................(t) JBramhill 1 34
(SRBowring) *hmpd s and behyind: hdwy on outer 3f out: rdn and btn 2f out*
**20/1**

1m 48.25s (0.95) **Going Correction** +0.225s/f (Good) **12** Ran SP% **124.8**
Speed ratings: **104,103,100,100,98 98,96,92,91,89 87,82**CSF £87.92 CT £229.47 TOTE £16.80: £3.40, £2.00, £1.80; EX 228.80.
**Owner** Mrs Andrea O'Grady **Bred** G And Mrs Middlebrook **Trained** Langton, N Yorks

**FOCUS**
There was a decent pace on here and the principals came from off the gallop. The form is ordinary.

**NOTEBOOK**
**Cryfield**, a previous course and distance winner, had the race run to suit and stayed on well from off the pace. He should remain fairly handicapped even after being reassessed.
**Torrid Kentavr(USA)**, last seen running over fences, is another who likes to challenge from off the pace, so the good gallop suited him, too.
**Les Arcs(USA)**, making a quick reappearance under a 6lb penalty, ran well but perhaps this third run in 11 days proved too much.
**Iberus(GER)** got outpaced early in the straight but was staying on again at the finish, suggesting a step back up in trip will suit.
**Tedsdale Mac** is a model of consistency but has a poor strike-rate.
**Tedstale(USA)** remains stubbornly high in the handicap.
**Aswan(IRE)** *Official explanation: jockey said gelding was unsuited by the rain softened ground*

### 3471 WESTWOOD BARRATT HOMES (S) H'CAP 7f 100y
**8:15** (8:15) (F) (0-55,55) 3-Y-O+ **£3,339** (£954; £477) **Stalls** High

Form RPR
1002 **1** **Redoubtable (USA)**[11] 3151 13-9-5 **48**.................................... ACulhane 8 57
(DWChapman) *hld up towards rr: gd hdwy 2f out: str run to ld wl ins last: sn clr*
**7/1**[3]

0400 **2** 2 1/2 **Jakeal (IRE)**[10] 3167 5-9-10 **53**....................................(p) VHalliday 9 56
(RMWhitaker) *led: pushed clr 2f out: rdn over 1f out: hdd and no ex wl ins last*
**12/1**

1600 **3** 2 1/2 **Shamwari Fire (IRE)**[13] 3103 4-9-7 **50**.................................... RFfrench 15 47
(IWMcinnes) *chsd ldrs: rdn along 2f out: kpt on u.p fnl f*
**15/2**

5002 **4** shd **Noble Pursuit**[8] 3247 7-9-6 **49**.................................... FLynch 13 51+
(REBarr) *hld up and bhd: gd hdwy 3f out: rdn wl over 1f out: kpt on ins last*
**11/2**[2]

0105 **5** nk **Open Handed (IRE)**[34] 2473 4-9-9 **55**....................................(t) TEaves(3) 16 51
(BEllison) *towards rr: hdwy 3f out: rdn along 2f out: kpt on appr last: nrst fin*
**5/1**[1]

40-0 **6** 1/2 **Alpine Hideaway (IRE)**[7] 2473 11-9-1 **47**.................................(p) THamilton(3) 14 42
(JSWainwright) *chsd ldr: rdn along 2f out: drvn and wknd over 1f out* **14/1**

0506 **7** 1/2 **Celtic Romance**[15] 3006 5-9-3 **46**.................................... JCarroll 4 39
(MrsMReveley) *wnt lft s and bhd: hdwy on outer 2 out: kpt on ins last: nrst fin*
**14/1**

0-60 **8** *nk* **Delightful Gift**[22] [2814] 4-8-11 **45**........ MLawson(5) 5 38
(MBrittain) *midfield: hdwy on outer 2f out: sn rdn and one pce fnl f* **50/1**
05U3 **9** *3/4* **Killerby Nicko**[4] [3368] 3-8-13 **50**........(b) SSanders 2 41
(TDEasterby) *chsd ldrs: rdn 2f out: drvn and wknd over 1f out* **12/1**
00-0 **10** *hd* **Maureen Ann**[10] [3167] 4-9-12 **55**........ JBramhill 11 45
(TJFitzgerald) *chsd ldrs: rdn over 2f out: sn wknd* **12/1**
0606 **11** *3* **Clann A Cougar**[24] [2762] 4-9-12 **55**........(b) GDuffield 12 38
(IAWood) *slowly in to stride: a rr* **9/1**
0-02 **12** *2* **Canlis**[20] [2879] 5-9-4 **47**........ RWinston 1 25
(DWThompson) *midfield: hdwy to chse ldrs 3f out: rdn and btn 2f out* **12/1**
0000 **13** *1 1/2* **Moonlight Song (IRE)**[6] [3301] 7-8-13 **45** ow1........(b1) LFletcher(3) 10 19
(JohnAHarris) *chsd ldrs: rdn over 2f out: sn wknd* **33/1**
306- **14** *1 3/4* **Splodger Mac (IRE)**[297] [4792] 5-8-7 **43**........ SuzanneFrance(7) 7 13
(NBycroft) *a rr* **25/1**
0230 **15** *3/4* **Dasar**[21] [2854] 4-9-5 **48**........(v) DarrenWilliams 3 16
(MBrittain) *prom: rdn along over 3f out: sn wknd* **25/1**
0006 **16** *14* **Eastern Dagger**[8] [3238] 4-9-5 **48**........ RFitzpatrick 6 —
(PTMidgley) *s.i.s and bhd: effrt and sme hdwy on outer 3f out: sn rdn and wknd* **28/1**

1m 35.41s (1.11) **Going Correction** +0.225s/f (Good)
**WFA** 3 from 4yo+ 8lb **16** Ran SP% **126.5**
Speed ratings: **102,99,96,96,95 95,94,94,93,93 89,87,85,83,82 66**CSF £86.89 CT £691.84 TOTE £6.00: £1.80, £4.60, £2.00, £1.90; EX 255.50.There was no bid for the winner
**Owner** David W Chapman **Bred** Wooden Horse Inv Inc And Post Syndicate **Trained** Stillington, N Yorks

**FOCUS**
A moderate handicap and the form, which has been rated through the second, is modest.

**NOTEBOOK**
**Redoubtable(USA)** appreciated the decent pace and came from well back to take the race. This was his fourth win of the year and he clearly retains plenty of enthusiasm.
**Jakeal(IRE)** set a decent gallop in front and it is to his credit that he kept on for second. This was a welcome return to form in the first-time cheekpieces and he is not badly handicapped now.
**Shamwari Fire(IRE)** won his only race over this course and distance and once again showed his liking for the track.
**Noble Pursuit** ran a respectable race but is on a long losing run. *Official explanation: jockey said gelding failed to act down hill in early stages*
**Open Handed(IRE)**, for whom the ground appeared to have come in his favour, was putting in his best work at the finish.
**Alpine Hideaway(IRE)**, runner-up over hurdles last time, has done all his most recent winning over farther.

## 3472 FERGUSON FAWSITT ARMS H'CAP — 1m 4f 16y
**8:45** (8:45) (E) (0-70,62) 3-Y-0+ **£4,550** (£1,400; £700; £350) **Stalls** High

Form RPR
0-52 **1** **Sualda (IRE)**[15] [3018] 5-9-7 **62**........ THamilton(3) 8 73
(RAFahey) *trckd ldrs: hdwy 3f out: rdn to chal wl over 1f out: drvn to ld ent last: kpt on wl* **7/2**[1]
-040 **2** *nk* **Red River Rebel**[12] [3128] 6-9-3 **55**........ DarrenWilliams 4 66
(JRNorton) *led: rdn along 2f out: drvn and hdd ent last: kpt on gamely u.p* **7/2**[1]
5434 **3** *5* **Escalade**[1] [3450] 7-9-0 **52**........(p) ACulhane 10 55
(WMBrisbourne) *hld up in tch: hdwy to chse ldrs wl over 1f out: swtchd rt and drvn ent last: one pce* **11/2**[2]
1410 **4** *2* **Little Task**[2] [3411] 6-8-6 **44** 6ex........ RFfrench 6 43
(JSWainwright) *hld up in rr: hdwy on inner 3f out: rdn along 2f out: drvn and one pce appr last* **10/1**
0063 **5** *1/2* **East Cape**[13] [3099] 7-8-5 **43**........ KimTinkler 9 42
(DonEnricoIncisa) *bhd: hdwy over 2f out: sn rdn and kpt on same pce* **9/1**[3]
6151 **6** *3* **Life Is Beautiful (IRE)**[10] [3165] 5-9-4 **56** 6ex........ RWinston 2 50
(WHTinning) *chsd ldrs: ridden along over 2f out: sn drvn and wknd over 1f out* **7/2**[1]
4250 **7** *1 1/4* **Dubai Dreams**[150] [671] 4-9-1 **53**........ JBramhill 7 45
(SRBowring) *in tch: rdn along 4f out: wknd 3f out* **16/1**
30/6 **8** *6* **Cyber Santa**[27] [2689] 6-8-7 **45**........ DaleGibson 1 27
(JHetherton) *hld up: hdwy to chse ldrs over 5f out: rdn 3f out and sn wknd* **16/1**
-160 **9** *23* **Royal Melbourne (IRE)**[14] [3041] 4-9-2 **54**........ JCarroll 3 —
(MissJACamacho) *s.i.s: hdwy to join ldrs 1/2-way: cl up tl rdn along over 3f out and sn wknd* **20/1**

2m 40.5s (1.20) **Going Correction** +0.225s/f (Good) **9** Ran SP% **117.7**
Speed ratings: **105,104,101,100,99 97,96,92,77**CSF £15.70 CT £66.43 TOTE £4.40: £1.90, £1.70, £2.00; EX 20.90.
**Owner** J H Tattersall **Bred** St Simon Foundation **Trained** Musley Bank, N Yorks

**FOCUS**
Ordinary form, with the first two only running to their best in pulling wel clear.

**NOTEBOOK**
**Sualda(IRE)** has been in good form this season and a 3lb rise in the handicap was not enough to stop him recording his first win of the year. He should continue to run with credit.
**Red River Rebel** has a remarkable record at this track (form figures of 1211262) and once again acquitted himself with credit, only going down narrowly.
**Escalade** is running fairly consistently at present but has now gone 40 races without success.
**Little Task** looks likely to struggle off this higher mark.
**East Cape** appreciates a mile six these days.
**Life Is Beautiful(IRE)** had more to do in this company under a 6lb penalty having won a claimer last time.
**Cyber Santa** *Official explanation: jockey said gelding lost its action*

## 3473 WILLIAM JACKSON BAKERY FILLIES' STKS (H'CAP) — 1m 1f 207y
**9:15** (9:15) (E) (0-70,68) 3-Y-O **£3,770** (£1,160; £580; £290) **Stalls** High

Form RPR
6260 **1** **Miss Eloise**[6] [3312] 3-8-3 **57**........ AMullen(7) 12 65
(TDEasterby) *in tch on inner: swtchd lft and hdwy 2f out: rdn to ld ins last: kpt on* **11/2**[3]
0002 **2** *nk* **Principessa**[8] [3231] 3-9-4 **65**........ ACulhane 9 72
(BPalling) *cl up: rdn to ld wl over 1f out: drvn and hdd inside last: kpt on wl u.p* **5/2**[1]
0530 **3** *4* **Aesculus (USA)**[23] [2790] 3-9-6 **67**........ DaleGibson 7 67
(LMCumani) *trckd ldrs: effrt over 2f out: rdn and one pce over 1f out* **11/2**[3]
4445 **4** *2* **Queen Lucia (IRE)**[11] [3156] 3-8-11 **58**........ DarrenWilliams 10 55
(JGGiven) *led: rdn along 3f out: hdd wl over 1f out: grad wknd* **10/1**
4-00 **5** *2 1/2* **Adees Dancer**[45] [2198] 3-8-11 **58**........ DMcGaffin 6 50
(BSmart) *towards rr: hdwy 1/2-way: chsd ldrs over 2f out: sn rdn and one pce* **33/1**
3046 **6** *1/2* **Inmom (IRE)**[8] [3231] 3-8-11 **58**........ JBramhill 2 49
(SRBowring) *in tch on outer: rdn along over 2f out: sn one pce* **25/1**
5000 **7** *1 3/4* **Nod's Star**[15] [3026] 3-7-12 **45**........ RFfrench 8 33
(MissJACamacho) *towards rr: hdwy 4f out: rdn wl over 2f out and no imp* **22/1**
0000 **8** *1 3/4* **Royal Distant (USA)**[13] [3102] 3-9-7 **68**........ TLucas 5 53
(MWEasterby) *a rr* **20/1**
00-4 **9** *shd* **Spring Adieu**[14] [3044] 3-9-5 **66**........ SSanders 11 51
(MrsAJPerrett) *trckd ldrs on inner: effrt 2f out: sn rdn and wknd over 1f out* **7/2**[2]
5100 **10** *3* **Prairie Sun (GER)**[15] [3026] 3-8-10 **57**........(v1) GDuffield 13 36
(MrsADuffield) *a rr* **8/1**
60-0 **11** *16* **Chicago Bond (USA)**[8] [3252] 3-9-4 **65**........ FLynch 3 16
(BSmart) *plld hrd: chsd ldrs on outer to 1/2-way: sn wknd* **25/1**
006 **12** *3 1/2* **Wedowannagiveuthat (IRE)**[30] [2572] 3-8-8 **55**........ RWinston 4 —
(TDEasterby) *chsd ldrs: rdn along 3f out: wknd over 2f out* **20/1**

2m 9.82s (2.62) **Going Correction** +0.225s/f (Good) **12** Ran SP% **126.3**
Speed ratings: **98,97,94,92,90 90,89,87,87,85 72,69**CSF £18.96 CT £84.63 TOTE £6.60: £1.80, £1.80, £2.30; EX 22.80 Place 6 £11.82, Place 5 £11.08.
**Owner** Slatch Farm Stud **Bred** Slatch Farm Stud **Trained** Great Habton, N Yorks
■ Stewards Enquiry : A Culhane one-day ban: used whip with excessive frequency (Jul 13)

**FOCUS**
A modest event run at a steady early gallop. Fair form for the grade.

**NOTEBOOK**
**Miss Eloise** appreciated the step up in trip and picked up well off the steady pace to score narrowly. This was a modest contest but she and the runner-up pulled nicely clear and she could be capable of improvement.
**Principessa** raced closer to the pace than the winner and was better suited by the steady pace as a result. She was only beaten narrowly and while in this form a similar contest is surely within her ability.
**Aesculus(USA)** was taking a big step up in trip and ran a much better race as a result. She is open to further improvement at the distance.
**Queen Lucia(IRE)** enjoyed the run of the race in front as there was no great gallop on. She may be flattered by her performance.
**Adees Dancer**, who was held up at the rear, did not really have the race run to suit.
T/Plt: £11.60 to a £1 stake. Pool: £38,055.70. 2,386.25 winning tickets. T/Qpdt: £11.20 to a £1 stake. Pool: £2,308.40. 152.10 winning tickets. JR

# 3443 HAYDOCK (L-H)
### Friday, July 2

**OFFICIAL GOING: Good (good to soft in places)**
Wind: lt against Weather: lt showers

## 3474 DAVE AND DEBBIE WATKINS WEDDING ANNIVERSARY APPRENTICE H'CAP — 1m 3f 200y
**7:00** (7:01) (E) (0-85,85) 3-Y-0+ **£3,471** (£1,068; £534; £267) **Stalls** High

Form RPR
4142 **1** **Smart John**[4] [3375] 4-8-7 **63**........ BSwarbrick 8 78+
(WMBrisbourne) *hld up: hdwy gng wl 3f out: led over 1f out: r.o* **5/2**[1]
64P1 **2** *3* **Merrymaker**[14] [3042] 4-8-1 **60**........ PPMathers(3) 4 68
(WMBrisbourne) *hld up in tch: rdn and outpcd over 3f out: rallied to chse wnr 1f out: no imp* **6/1**[2]
1212 **3** *4* **Yankeedoodledandy (IRE)**[93] [1201] 3-8-3 **75**........ RoryMoore(3) 9 77
(PCHaslam) *prom: rdn and outpcd over 3f out: kpt on one pce fnl f* **5/2**[1]
0/60 **4** *1 1/4* **Spree Vision**[12] [1661] 8-7-9 **54** oh1........(v) DFentiman(3) 3 54
(PMonteith) *led after 1f tl after 2f: led again 7f out: hdd over 3f out: stl ev ch whn rdn over 2f out: wknd over 1f out* **16/1**
331 **5** *nk* **Always Waining (IRE)**[32] [2513] 3-8-11 **85**........ WHogg(5) 7 84+
(MJohnston) *sddle sn slipped: led after 2f: hdd 7f out whn racing wd: led again over 3f out: hdd over 1f out: wknd and eased ins fnl fu* **13/2**[3]
3110 **6** *nk* **Millennium Hall**[9] [3199] 5-8-9 **68**........ DTudhope(3) 2 68+
(PMonteith) *s.s: hld up: hdwy 5f out: rdn and ev ch over 2f out: wkng and hanging lft whn n.m.r and hmpd ins finl* **9/1**
6-04 **7** *7* **Colophony (USA)**[20] [2878] 4-9-4 **74**........(t) PMakin 5 61
(KAMorgan) *trckd ldrs: rdn and lost pl over 3f out: n.d after* **16/1**
2-50 **8** *1 1/2* **Prince Holing**[13] [3078] 4-10-0 **84**........(t) RThomas 1 69
(MTodhunter) *led 1f: remained prom: lost pl 6f out: renewed effrt over 3f out: wknd wl over 1f out* **20/1**
31/0 **9** *21* **Lord Dundee (IRE)**[13] [3078] 6-9-3 **78**........(t) AReilly(5) 6 29
(RCGuest) *hld up: lft bhd 3f out* **40/1**

2m 35.75s (0.59) **Going Correction** +0.075s/f (Good)
**WFA** 3 from 4yo+ 13lb **9** Ran SP% **113.7**
Speed ratings: **101,99,96,95,95 95,90,89,75**CSF £17.68 CT £40.01 TOTE £3.40: £1.60, £2.30, £1.20; EX 19.40.
**Owner** Mr & Mrs D J Smart **Bred** D J And Mrs K D Smart **Trained** Great Ness, Shropshire
■ Stewards Enquiry : Rory Moore two-day ban: careless riding (Jul 13-14)

**FOCUS**
An apprentice race of reasonable quality, featuring a winner in fine form with more to come. There were excuses for several of those down the field.

**NOTEBOOK**
**Smart John** was attempting this trip for the first time but saw it out tidily. He is holding his form well and can improve a bit more at this distance.
**Merrymaker** stays farther than this. He ran well, but the winner had too much finishing speed.
**Yankeedoodledandy(IRE)** ran respectably after a three-month absence but has plenty of weight at present on turf. His all-weather mark is significantly lower. *Official explanation: jockey said gelding lost a front shoe*
**Spree Vision** ran one of his better races on the Flat, though comfortably beaten in the end. There is plenty of life in him yet.
**Always Waining(IRE)** was troubled by a slipping saddle. He is lightly raced and there is room for improvement in better circumstances. *Official explanation: jockey said saddle slipped*
**Millennium Hall** has been heading up the weights and did not look well handicapped. He also looks more effective on fast ground.

## 3475 MERCHANT RENTALS PLC CLAIMING STKS — 1m 2f 120y
**7:30** (7:32) (D) 3-4-Y-0 **£7,832** (£2,410; £1,205; £602) **Stalls** High

Form RPR
1056 **1** **Jimmy Byrne (IRE)**[15] [3018] 4-9-6 67........ SDrowne 9 63
(BEllison) *a.p: rdn to ld over 1f out: sn edgd lft: pushed out* **5/1**[3]
-100 **2** *1 1/4* **Allied Victory (USA)**[150] [671] 4-10-0 69........ JPMurtagh 5 69
(EJAlston) *racd keenly: prom: rdn over 2f out: styd on fnl f* **10/1**
-U0L **3** *nk* **Tagula Blue (IRE)**[37] [2410] 4-9-7 78........(bt1) DeanMcKeown 1 61
(JAGlover) *rel to r and s.v.s: plld hrd: hld up: hdwy whn bmpd over 2f out: hung lft over 1f out: kpt on u.p* **16/1**

1020 **4** nk **Ile Facile (IRE)**[8] 3231 3-8-7 69 ........ TPQueally(3) 8 62
(NPLittmoden) *prom: led over 3f out: rdn over 2f out: hdd over 1f out: sn n.m.r: no ex ins fnl f* **5/2**[1]

-033 **5** 5 **Go Solo**[21] 2847 3-8-12 77 ........ MHills 2 55+
(BWHills) *hld up in tch: lost pl over 3f out: rdn whn n.m.r and hmpd over 2f out: n.d after* **5/2**[1]

0 **6** nk **Charlie George**[15] 3002 3-8-1 ........ DFentiman(7) 7 51?
(PMonteith) *s.s: bhd: rdn and hdwy to chse ldrs over 2f out: wknd ent fnl f* **80/1**

0-0 **7** shd **Nopekan (IRE)**[13] 3075 4-9-7 89 ........ PMakin(5) 4 57
(MissKMarks) *midfield: rdn 3f out: no imp* **9/2**[2]

0 **8** nk **Hollywood Critic (USA)**[15] 3002 3-8-8 ........ GFaulkner 10 50?
(PMonteith) *hld up: hdwy 3f out: wknd over 1f out* **50/1**

0- **9** 14 **Red Mountain**[296] 4818 3-8-13 ........ LEnstone(3) 6 34
(DWBarker) *led: rdn and hdd over 3f out: sn wknd* **50/1**

2m 18.12s (0.39) **Going Correction** +0.075s/f (Good) **9** Ran SP% **112.1**
**WFA** 3 from 4yo 12lb
Speed ratings: **101,100,99,99,96 95,95,95,85**CSF £50.88 TOTE £6.80: £1.70, £2.30, £3.70; EX 71.00.
**Owner** Keith Middleton **Bred** Austin Well Stud **Trained** Norton, N Yorks

**FOCUS**
A fair claimer in which the best-weighted runner, Nopekan, ran poorly, leaving the form with a hollow look.

**NOTEBOOK**
**Jimmy Byrne(IRE)**, who has been running with credit in handicap company, found these rivals eminently beatable and he did so convincingly.
**Allied Victory(USA)** had a tough task at the weights but ran well after a five-month absence. He is effective on sand and turf and should find another race with this sharpener behind him .
**Tagula Blue(IRE)** has become what is politely known as a "character" and was blinkered for the first time. It did not improve his behaviour, but he ended up running a good race on paper.
**Ile Facile(IRE)** was not favourably weighted but showed he retains a fair level of ability by finishing so close.
**Go Solo** was a shade disappointing and is probably best on slightly faster ground. *Official explanation: jockey said colt suffered interference*
**Charlie George** showed little on his debut but this improved effort showed he does have some ability.
**Nopekan(IRE)**was best-in on official figures but did not perform. The easier ground should not have been a problem.
**Hollywood Critic(USA)** , who left Jeremy Noseda cheaply before his racecourse debut, is still learning the job but this was a step up on his first effort.

## 3476 MTB GROUP MAIDEN AUCTION STKS — 6f
**8:00** (8:01) (E) 2-Y-O — **£3,809** (£1,172; £586; £293) **Stalls** Centre

Form — RPR

22 **1** **Harvest Warrior**[24] 2749 2-8-9 ........ DAllan 12 90
(TDEasterby) *a.p: led 2f out: rdn clr fnl f: r.o wl* **10/3**[1]

62 **2** 5 **Malinsa Blue (IRE)**[27] 2674 2-8-2 ........ JQuinn 13 68
(JAGlover) *in tch: hdwy 2f out: chsd wnr over 1f out: no imp fnl f* **4/1**[2]

**3** 2 **Sambarina (IRE)** 2-8-6 ........ RSmith 6 66
(CGCox) *chsd ldrs: rdn over 2f out: kpt on same pce* **33/1**

3 **4** 1 **Bounty Quest**[10] 3176 2-8-9 ........ DaneO'Neill 3 66
(RHannon) *chsd ldrs: rdn 3f out: one pce fnl f* **10/3**[1]

**5** 1 1/4 **Seamless** 2-8-11 ........ MHills 9 64
(WJHaggas) *hld up: rdn over 2f out: hdwy over 1f out: kpt on: nvr trbld ldrs* **11/2**[3]

5 **6** nk **Shujune Al Hawaa (IRE)**[45] 2205 2-8-3 ........ SHitchcott(3) 10 58
(MRChannon) *midfield: rdn and outpcd over 2f out: kpt on fnl f: nvr able to chal* **9/1**

4 **7** 1 **Union Jack Jackson (IRE)**[13] 3080 2-8-9 ........ MFenton 2 58
(JGGiven) *led: rdn and hdd 2f out: wknd fnl f* **18/1**

**8** 1 1/2 **Blaise Hollow (USA)** 2-8-9 ........ SDrowne 5 54
(RCharlton) *s.s: bhd: nvr trbld ldrs* **20/1**

**9** nk **Peters Delite** 2-8-11 ........ GParkin 4 55
(RAFahey) *a outpcd* **33/1**

50 **10** 3/4 **Tiffin Deano (IRE)**[63] 1743 2-8-0 ........ RoryMoore(7) 7 49
(PCHaslam) *midfield: rdn over 2f out: wknd 1f out* **33/1**

0 **11** 7 **Peppermint Tea (IRE)**[11] 3157 2-8-4 ........ JMackay 1 25
(MLWBell) *in tch: rdn 3f out: wknd over 1f out* **14/1**

**12** 14 **Gallego** 2-8-9 ........ FNorton 11 —
(SLKeightley) *s.s: a outpcd* **66/1**

1m 15.4s (0.51) **Going Correction** +0.075s/f (Good) **12** Ran SP% **118.5**
Speed ratings: **99,92,89,88,86 86,84,82,82,81 72,53**CSF £15.64 TOTE £4.30: £1.70, £2.10, £7.70; EX 15.10.
**Owner** Mr & Mrs W J Williams **Bred** Campbell Stud **Trained** Great Habton, N Yorks

**FOCUS**
A mixed bunch, but a creditable time for the type of race. The winner is a likeable sort who should continue to run well, and there will be winners at various levels among those behind.

**NOTEBOOK**
**Harvest Warrior** got the extra furlong really well and acts on fast, good and heavy ground. He is versatile and looks a reliable sort.
**Malinsa Blue(IRE)** was comfortably beaten by the useful winner but should be placed to win her maiden. If not, nurseries are now an option.
**Sambarina(IRE)** has plenty of speed in her pedigree and made a promising debut. Runners from her stable usually improve for their first outings.
**Bounty Quest** has now run creditably at both five and six furlongs but it is not yet clear which trip suits him better at present.
**Seamless** made a satisfactory debut and should improve with time. He ought to get at least a mile in due course, and maybe significantly farther.
**Shujune Al Hawaa(IRE)**, not inconvenienced by the extra furlong, was well beaten in the end but is worth another try. Nurseries are beginning to look a likelihood in the longer term.
**Union Jack Jackson(IRE)** did the donkey work this time but merely set the race up for the others. Connections are still trying to find his best trip and how to ride him.

## 3477 JOHN SUFFIELD MEMORIAL RATED STKS (H'CAP) — 1m 30y
**8:30** (8:31) (C) (0-95,95) 3-Y-O+ — **£8,856** (£3,359; £1,679; £763) **Stalls** Low

Form — RPR

312- **1** **Primus Inter Pares (IRE)**[265] 5483 3-8-13 95 ........ JPMurtagh 10 104+
(JRFanshawe) *midfield: hdwy over 2f out: led ins fnl f: r.o* **11/1**

1-20 **2** 1 1/2 **Hello It's Me**[52] 2018 3-8-3 85 ........ JQuinn 5 91+
(HJCollingridge) *a.p: rdn 2f out: bmpd over 1f out: ev ch wl ins fnl f: nt qckn cl home* **16/1**

0602 **3** 1/2 **Consonant (IRE)**[9] 3212 7-8-13 89 ........ DNolan(3) 7 93
(DGBridgwater) *trckd ldrs: rdn over 2f out: led over 1f out: hdd ins fnl f: styd on same pce cl home* **6/1**[1]

-403 **4** 1 1/2 **Sew'N'So Character (IRE)**[20] 2896 3-8-13 95 ........ FNorton 4 96
(MBlanshard) *trckd ldrs: rdn whn bmpd over 1f out: styd on* **6/1**[1]

5101 **5** hd **Oddsmaker (IRE)**[6] 3299 3-8-4 86 3ex ........ DeanMcKeown 13 87
(PDEvans) *racd keenly: led: rdn and hdd over 1f out: no ex wl ins fnl f* **8/1**[2]

0610 **6** 1 **Flighty Fellow (IRE)**[16] 2969 4-9-7 94 ........ (b) JFortune 9 92
(TDEasterby) *hld up: rdn 3f out: nt clr run over 1f out: styd on towards fin* **16/1**

3002 **7** 3/4 **Mysterinch**[5] 3337 4-9-4 91 ........ JFanning 3 91+
(JeddO'Keeffe) *hld up: rdn over 1f out: keeping on whn nt much wl ins fnl f: sn eased* **8/1**[2]

-230 **8** 1/2 **Alekhine (IRE)**[27] 2676 3-8-4 86 ........ RLMoore 8 81
(PWHarris) *midfield: rdn over 2f out: one pce fnl f* **9/1**[3]

0000 **9** 1/2 **Craiova (IRE)**[9] 3205 5-8-11 84 ........ MHills 2 78
(BWHills) *in tch: rdn to chse ldrs over 2f out: one pce whn n.m.r wl ins fnl f: sn eased* **16/1**

3301 **10** 1 **Intricate Web (IRE)**[13] 3097 8-8-10 83 ........ DAllan 1 75
(EJAlston) *towards rr: rdn over 2f out: nt clr run over 1f out: nvr trbld ldrs* **12/1**

-206 **11** 1 3/4 **Borrego (IRE)**[2] 3426 4-8-4 80 oh2 ........ TPQueally(3) 12 68
(CEBrittain) *in tch: rdn over 2f out: wknd 1f out* **14/1**

540 **12** 3 **Starbeck (IRE)**[16] 2967 6-8-13 86 ........ NCallan 11 67
(PHowling) *a bhd* **25/1**

24-0 **13** 3/4 **Travelling Band (IRE)**[163] 577 6-8-4 80 ........ LPKeniry(3) 6 59
(AMBalding) *a bhd* **33/1**

1-01 **14** nk **Bishopric**[27] 2687 4-9-7 94 ........ (v[1]) DaneO'Neill 14 73
(HCandy) *prom: rdn and ev ch 2f out: wknd over 1f out* **8/1**[2]

1m 43.87s (-1.68) **Going Correction** +0.075s/f (Good) **14** Ran SP% **119.0**
**WFA** 3 from 4yo+ 9lb
Speed ratings: **111,109,109,107,107 106,105,105,104,103 101,98,98,97**CSF £173.86 CT £1163.27 TOTE £8.40: £2.60, £3.60, £3.00; EX 230.70.
**Owner** Colin Davey Racing **Bred** Pacelco S A And Gaines-Centry Thoroughbreds Llc **Trained** Newmarket, Suffolk

**FOCUS**
A competitive mid-grade handicap run in a fair time, in which the first two home in particular should continue to progress. The form looks solid and others down the field will also find suitable opportunities in due course.

**NOTEBOOK**
**Primus Inter Pares(IRE)**, was running in his first handicap and looks as if he will be very much at home in similar contests, even allowing for the inevitable rise in the weights. Lightly raced, he should have a lively future. He will reportedly move to David Nicholls now, having been sold on the morining of the race.
**Hello It's Me** did not find the drop from an extended ten furlongs to be a problem. Only beaten by a relatively unexposed rival, he emerged with great credit and there is more to come.
**Consonant(IRE)** is a tough sort and he is particularly effective on slowish ground. He has now run two fine races in the space of just over a week.
**Sew'N'So Character(IRE)** has been running well from his present mark and would only need to be dropped a couple of pounds to have a major chance of success.
**Oddsmaker(IRE)** was not well drawn and had to use himself early to get to the front. In the circumstances, a respectable effort.
**Flighty Fellow(IRE)**, with the blinkers back on, ran a satisfactory race without ever quite threatening.
**Mysterinch**, without actually being unlucky, did not find things going for him late on. He has shown enough this season to give cause for optimism.
**Alekhine(IRE)** has not really fired in his last two outings but is capable of better when in top form.
**Craiova(IRE)** showed signs of a return to form.

## 3478 OCS FILLIES' H'CAP — 1m 30y
**9:00** (9:02) (D) (0-80,76) 3-Y-O — **£5,950** (£1,831; £915; £457) **Stalls** Low

Form — RPR

-400 **1** **Keeper's Lodge (IRE)**[19] 2905 3-8-11 66 ........ GGibbons 4 73
(BAMcmahon) *trckd ldrs: rdn over 2f out: r.o to ld wl ins fnl f* **20/1**

0-00 **2** 1/2 **Eboracum (IRE)**[16] 2989 3-8-5 60 ........ DAllan 5 66
(TDEasterby) *trckd ldrs: rdn to ld over 2f out: hdd wl ins fnl f* **22/1**

0625 **3** 2 1/2 **Pella**[11] 3139 3-8-6 61 ........ FNorton 3 61
(MBlanshard) *towards rr: rdn over 2f out: hdwy over 1f out: styd on: nt rch ldrs* **5/1**[2]

4-06 **4** nk **Violet Avenue**[11] 3155 3-8-5 60 ow1 ........ MFenton 6 59
(JGGiven) *racd keenly: midfield: rdn over 2f out: hdwy over 1f out: kpt on u.p* **20/1**

-005 **5** 2 1/2 **Blue Daze**[20] 2887 3-8-13 68 ........ RSmith 1 62
(RHannon) *midfield: rdn and hdwy over 2f out: one pce ins fnl f* **8/1**

-130 **6** 2 1/2 **Night Frolic**[21] 2848 3-8-10 65 ........ MHills 10 53
(JWHills) *led: rdn and hdd over 2f out: wknd ins fnl f* **7/1**[3]

6-15 **7** 2 1/2 **Baffle**[60] 1831 3-9-7 76 ........ JPMurtagh 12 58
(JLDunlop) *prom: rdn and ev ch over 2f out: wknd over 1f out* **10/3**[1]

-065 **8** 1 **Gaiety Girl (USA)**[14] 3042 3-8-5 60 ........ RMullen 11 40
(TDEasterby) *trckd ldrs: rdn over 2f out: wknd over 1f out* **14/1**

150- **9** 1 **Beauty Of Dreams**[293] 4882 3-9-2 74 ........ SHitchcott(3) 9 52
(MRChannon) *midfield: rdn over 2f out: wknd over 1f out* **20/1**

641- **10** 3 **Hi Darl**[401] 1925 3-7-10 56 ........ BSwarbrick(5) 2 27
(WMBrisbourne) *midfield: rdn and wknd over 2f out* **33/1**

02-0 **11** shd **Flame Queen**[13] 3089 3-9-2 71 ........ SDrowne 8 41
(MissKBBoutflower) *s.s: a bhd* **20/1**

5340 **P** **Poppys Footprint (IRE)**[19] 2907 3-9-6 75 ........ NCallan 7 —
(KARyan) *upset in stalls: s.s: a bhd: eased 2f out: sn p.u* **5/1**[2]

1m 46.6s (1.05) **Going Correction** +0.075s/f (Good) **12** Ran SP% **113.0**
Speed ratings: **97,96,94,93,91 88,86,85,84,81 81,—**CSF £353.84 CT £2524.06 TOTE £28.80: £4.60, £6.80, £2.60; EX 450.10.
**Owner** W D McClennon **Bred** Darpat S L **Trained** Hopwas, Staffs

**FOCUS**
A moderate contest, in which most of the runners had been underperforming in recent races.

**NOTEBOOK**
**Keeper's Lodge(IRE)**, who seemed to be suited by the easier ground, proved she gets this trip well and got off the mark at the ninth attempt. *Official explanation: trainer said, regarding the improved form shown, gelding was better suited by the softer ground*
**Eboracum(IRE)** bounced back to form with a spirited bid that nearly came off. She stays well and acts on ground with cut in it.
**Pella** did not seem to stay ten furlongs earlier in the season but she looked here as if a slightly longer trip or stiffer track would be in her favour.
**Violet Avenue** lacks a serious turn of foot but she clearly stays a mile and is worth campaigning at this trip or a little farther.
**Blue Daze** retains ability but has yet to strike peak form this season. She looks a few pounds too high in the weights at present.
**Night Frolic**, left in front for the second race running, ran moderately, and is probably more effective when arriving from behind.
**Flame Queen** *Official explanation: jockey said filly became upset in starting stalls and was slowly away*
**Poppys Footprint(IRE)** *Official explanation: vet said filly injured her head in starting stalls*

## 3479 STEVE VINCENT 30TH BIRTHDAY H'CAP — 1m 6f
9:30 (9:32) (E) (0-70,64) 3-Y-0 — £3,757 (£1,156; £578; £289) Stalls Low

Form / RPR

6-05 **1** **Euippe**[22] [2821] 3-9-3 **60**........ MFenton 6 74+
(JGGiven) *trckd ldrs: rdn to ld over 2f out: clr 1f out: eased towards fin* **33/1**

0461 **2** 3 1/2 **Winslow Boy (USA)**[22] [2822] 3-9-1 **58**........ JQuinn 5 65
(CFWall) *hld up in midfield: hdwy over 3f out: chsd winner over 1f out: no imp* **10/1**[3]

0-52 **3** 2 1/2 **Princess Kiotto**[64] [1740] 3-8-12 **55**........ DAllan 18 58+
(TDEasterby) *dwlt: bhd: rdn over 3f out: hdwy over 1f out: styd on: nt rch ldrs* **50/1**

44-0 **4** 1 **Penny Stall**[39] [2361] 3-9-5 **62**........ RLMoore 11 64+
(JLDunlop) *midfield: rdn over 2f out: hdwy over 1f out: kpt on: nt rch ldrs* **11/1**

6-16 **5** 1/2 **Zalda**[15] [3020] 3-9-7 **64**........ SDrowne 14 65
(RCharlton) *prom: rdn over 3f out: wknd over 1f out* **16/1**

3421 **6** 1/2 **Dunlea Dancer**[3] [3396] 3-9-6 **63** 6ex........ JFanning 3 63
(MJohnston) *led 2f: remained prom: regained ld over 3f out: sn rdn: hdd over 2f out: wknd fnl f* **5/2**[1]

2222 **7** hd **Ilwadod**[15] [3020] 3-9-2 **62**........(v) SHitchcott[(3)] 13 62
(MRChannon) *s.i.s: bhd: hdwy over 2f out: one pce over 1f out* **3/1**[2]

30-0 **8** 7 **Restart (IRE)**[43] [2251] 3-8-10 **60**........ RoryMoore[(7)] 9 50
(PCHaslam) *towards rr: rdn 4f out: hdwy over 2f out: no imp on ldrs* **50/1**

2504 **9** 3/4 **Bollin Annabel**[31] [2554] 3-8-10 **53**........ GGibbons 1 42
(TDEasterby) *led after 2f: rdn and hdd over 3f out: wknd over 2f out* **20/1**

6562 **10** 4 **Cunning Pursuit**[22] [2822] 3-8-4 **47**........ RMullen 7 31
(MLWBell) *trckd ldrs: rdn over 3f out: wkng whn n.m.r over 2f out* **20/1**

6123 **11** 2 **Habitual Dancer**[3] [3396] 3-9-2 **59**........ DaneO'Neill 17 40
(JeddO'Keeffe) *in tch: tk clsr order after 6f: rdn and wknd over 2f out* **12/1**

0020 **12** 2 **Timbuktu**[59] [1862] 3-8-1 **44**........ FNorton 4 22
(CWThornton) *dwlt: bhd: sme hdwy over 2f out: wknd over 1f out* **33/1**

030 **13** 3/4 **Muslin**[20] [2882] 3-8-12 **55**........ JPMurtagh 2 32
(JRFanshawe) *midfield: rdn over 3f out: wknd 2f out* **12/1**

-000 **14** 1 1/4 **Quay Walloper**[15] [3026] 3-7-7 **41** oh1........(v[1]) BSwarbrick[(5)] 12 16
(JRNorton) *midfield: pushed along 6f out: wknd over 1f out* **100/1**

030 **15** 3 1/2 **Great Gidding**[25] [2729] 3-9-2 **59**........ JFortune 8 29
(HMorrison) *tarcked ldrs: rdn over 2f out: wknd over 1f out* **40/1**

3031 **16** 9 **Crackleando**[56] [1947] 3-9-2 **62**........ TPQueally[(3)] 10 20
(NPLittmoden) *midfield: rdn over 3f out: wknd over 2f out* **14/1**

5400 **17** 7 **Perfect Balance (IRE)**[13] [3102] 3-9-0 **57**........ GBaker 16 5
(NTinkler) *a bhd* **20/1**

0-30 **18** 2 1/2 **Dawn Air (USA)**[48] [2133] 3-9-0 **57**........(p) NCallan 15 1
(KARyan) *midfield: rdn over 4f out: wknd 3f out* **33/1**

3m 6.64s (0.49) **Going Correction** +0.075s/f (Good) **18** Ran SP% **129.4**
Speed ratings: **101,99,97,97,96 96,96,92,91,89 88,87,86,86,84 79,75,73**CSF £326.95 CT £15404.33 TOTE £64.50: £10.40, £2.10, £4.60, £2.70; EX 441.60 Place 6 £1,068.69, Place 5 £834.03.

**Owner** C G Rowles Nicholson **Bred** Limestone Stud **Trained** Willoughton, Lincs

**FOCUS**

A decent enough race of its type and the form should prove reliable. The winner is coming on race by race and has plenty of stamina. Many of her rivals were honest enough but a bit on the slow side.

**NOTEBOOK**

**Euippe** appreciated the easier ground and won well. She stays this trip well and will be one to consider in similar events.

**Winslow Boy(USA)** stayed the trip alright, but was simply beaten by an improving and well-weighted rival.

**Princess Kiotto** is short on pace, so trips of this magnitude, and maybe even around two miles, represent her best chance of getting off the mark.

**Penny Stall** was stepping up in trip and stayed it okay, though she was never quite getting there. Staying is her game, with easy ground more in her favour than fast.

**Zalda**, facing a stiff task from the top of the handicap, did not quite get home. The combination of weight and distance conspired against her.

**Dunlea Dancer** was carrying a penalty but his position in the market suggested that should not have been a problem. However, while he nearly stays this trip, he has yet to prove he gets the last 200 yards or so.

**Ilwadod** could not be accused of arriving too late this time.He is effective at a mile and a half and beyond and stamina is his main asset.

T/Plt: £1,908.10 to a £1 stake. Pool: £55,153.85. 21.10 winning tickets. T/Qpdt: £84.20 to a £1 stake. Pool: £3,812.40. 33.50 winning tickets. DO

# [2887] SANDOWN (R-H)
Friday, July 2

**OFFICIAL GOING: Good to soft**

Rain had turned the ground testing and race times suggest it was softer on the straight course than the round.

## 3480 FRIENDS OF JONATHAN COOPER RATED STKS (H'CAP) — 5f 6y
2:05 (2:07) (C) (0-95,95) 3-Y-0+ — £9,651 (£2,969; £1,484; £742) Stalls High

Form / RPR

0310 **1** **Whistler**[5] [3339] 7-8-10 **84** 3ex........(p) RHills 9 97
(JMBradley) *hld up in last: prog on wd outside fr over 1f out: led last 150yds: pushed clr* **13/2**[2]

0550 **2** 1 1/4 **Talbot Avenue**[27] [2679] 6-8-7 **81** oh1........ PDobbs 3 90
(MMullineaux) *hld up in rr: prog on outer 2f out: drvn to chal and ev ch jst ins fnl f: outpcd by wnr* **10/1**

2602 **3** 1 3/4 **Corridor Creeper (FR)**[7] [3266] 7-9-3 **91**........(p) DHolland 2 93
(JMBradley) *lw: trckd ldrs on outer: rdn 2f out: led briefly ent fnl f: sn hdd and one pce* **5/1**[1]

-240 **4** 2 **Connect**[21] [2859] 7-8-12 **86**........(b) PRobinson 10 81
(MHTompkins) *chsd ldrs: rdn and unable qck over 1f out: one pce after* **5/1**[1]

5000 **5** 1 **Matty Tun**[7] [3266] 5-9-2 **90**........ RHughes 5 81
(JBalding) *b: trckd ldrs: smooth prog to ld 2f out: hung rt over 1f out: hdd & wknd jst ins fnl f* **8/1**

-060 **6** 1 1/2 **Absent Friends**[34] [2488] 7-9-4 **92**........ JEdmunds 11 78
(JBalding) *b: prom: led 1/2-way to 2f out: wknd fnl f* **20/1**

-600 **7** 1 1/4 **Malapropism**[27] [2682] 4-8-10 **84**........ TEDurcan 6 66
(MRChannon) *s.i.s: a in rr: rdn and no hdwy 2f out* **12/1**

-060 **8** 5 **Kathology (IRE)**[8] [3243] 7-8-8 **82**........ KFallon 7 46
(DRCElsworth) *w ldrs to 2f out: sn wknd* **7/1**[3]

0006 **9** nk **Repertory**[19] [2913] 11-9-7 **95**........ TGMcLaughlin 8 57
(MSSaunders) *led to 1/2-way: sn wknd and bhd* **16/1**

0303 **10** 5 **Henry Hall (IRE)**[21] [2859] 8-9-6 **94**........ KimTinkler 12 38
(NTinkler) *in tch to 1/2-way: sn wknd and bhd* **8/1**

5005 **11** 8 **Little Edward**[19] [2913] 6-9-4 **92**........ TQuinn 1 8
(BGPowell) *racd alone nr side: nvr on terms: wl bhd fnl 2f* **12/1**

63.96 secs (1.77) **Going Correction** +0.575s/f (Yiel) **11** Ran SP% **116.5**
Speed ratings: **108,106,103,100,98 96,94,86,85,77 64**CSF £69.23 CT £359.20 TOTE £7.50: £2.40, £3.70, £1.50; EX 110.70.

**Owner** Raymond Tooth **Bred** Raymond Clive Tooth **Trained** Sedbury, Gloucs

**FOCUS**

A race run in a downpour. The winning time was slow, but that was due to the deteriorating ground and when allowing for the overall conditions it was not bad at all.

**NOTEBOOK**

**Whistler** was not at all inconvenienced by the softening ground and with Repertory in the field it meant he got the strong pace he needs. He did not look well treated, but once switched left for his effort he picked up really well. He has never been in better nick.

**Talbot Avenue ◆**, 1lb out of the handicap, made his effort at just the right time and did nothing wrong, but the winner had the greater impetus in the run to the line. This was a decent effort considering all his best form has been on fast ground, and it will surely not be long before he hits the target.

**Corridor Creeper(FR)** is high enough in the weights, but with his ability to handle softening ground proven he again gave it his very best shot. Unfortunately his consistency is not getting him much help from the Handicapper.

**Connect** ran with great credit, but could definitely have done without the rain.

**Matty Tun** scored under similar conditions over course and distance two years ago, but that was off a 26lb lower mark. After moving to the front just after halfway he hung right, something he has done a few times before, and found the final climb to the line too much for him in the conditions.

**Absent Friends** showed good speed for a fair way before fading. He is still 8lb above his highest winning, having paid for running well in conditions events and Listed company last season.

**Malapropism** has run well on an easy surface in the past, but all his wins have been on faster ground and he could never land a blow.

**Kathology(IRE)** showed his usual good early speed, but he has not been in top form this season and he was on the retreat shortly after halfway.

**Repertory**, who would not have been bothered by the rain, set the field a merry dance early but he stopped very quickly once headed. One of the very fastest horses on the scene in his prime and a winner 13 times, including in the Group 3 Prix du Petit Couvert three times, he can no longer dominate in the manner he used to and he has reportedly been retired.

**Henry Hall(IRE)** could have done without the rain, but still showed little sparkle.

**Little Edward** was brought across to the stands' side from his low draw to race alone, but the tactic did not help. *Official explanation: jockey said gelding was unsuited by the good to soft ground*

## 3481 DRAGON STKS (LISTED RACE) — 5f 6y
2:40 (2:41) (A) 2-Y-0 — £14,875 (£5,500; £2,750; £1,250) Stalls High

Form / RPR

1100 **1** **Polly Perkins (IRE)**[6] [3316] 2-9-0........ J-PGuillambert 1 101
(NPLittmoden) *lw: a gng wl: hld up in last: eased to outer 2f out: led jst over 1f out: drew rt away fnl f: rdn out* **8/1**

1 **2** 8 **Southern Africa (USA)**[10] [3176] 2-8-12........ RHughes 3 72
(GAButler) *lw: chsd ldng pair: effrt 2f out: kpt on to take 2nd ins fnl f: no ch w wnr* **9/4**[2]

2315 **3** 1 3/4 **Empire's Ghodha**[15] [2996] 2-8-12........(b) JFortune 2 66
(BJMeehan) *swtg: chsd ldr: led wl over 1f out: hdd & wknd jst over 1f out* **10/1**

134 **4** 2 **Bunditten (IRE)**[16] [2970] 2-8-10........ JFEgan 4 57
(AndrewReid) *b: b.hind: led at str pce to wl over 1f out: wknd* **3/1**[3]

1110 **5** 7 **Lady Filly**[16] [2970] 2-8-10........ ADaly 5 33
(WGMTurner) *chsd ldrs: rdn 1/2-way: wknd over 1f out* **15/8**[1]

65.00 secs (2.81) **Going Correction** +0.575s/f (Yiel) **5** Ran SP% **110.8**
Speed ratings: **100,87,84,81,70**CSF £26.29 TOTE £8.50: £2.30, £1.80; EX 20.40.

**Owner** Miss Vanessa Church **Bred** David John Brown **Trained** Newmarket, Suffolk

**FOCUS**

Only a fair time even allowing for the conditions. The ground was very different to what most of these juveniles have been encountering and there was a complete turnaround in the Queen Mary form. In view of that, the beaten horses should be forgiven to a degree.

**NOTEBOOK**

**Polly Perkins(IRE)**, back a furlong and on soft ground for the first time, was given a patient ride before taking off and pulling right away to reverse Queen Mary form with Bunditten and Lady Filly in no uncertain terms. She probably handled the ground that much better than the three that followed her home and her other rival finished lame, which raises questions over the value of the form, but she should still be able to add to this in similar conditions.

**Southern Africa(USA)**, on different ground compared to his successful Newbury debut, was the least experienced in the field and even though ultimately beaten pointless by the winner, still emerges with some credit.

**Empire's Ghodha**, fifth in the Norfolk Stakes, was encountering soft ground for the first time, and after taking over in front soon after passing the two-furlong pole he quickly emptied. He was more experienced that his four rivals and therefore may not have much in the way of scope.

**Bunditten(IRE)**, who finished in front of both the winner and Lady Filly in the Queen Mary, established her usual position out in front, but she barely gets the trip and the softening ground on such a stiff track eventually proved too much for her.

**Lady Filly**, whose three wins before her Queen Mary defeat had all been on soft ground, should have relished these conditions but she never looked happy. It transpired that she was lame behind. *Official explanation: vet said filly was lame behind*

## 3482 ACTION ONLINE CASINO SUMMER STKS (H'CAP) — 1m 2f 7y
3:15 (3:16) (B) (0-105,98) 3-Y-0+ — £17,400 (£6,600; £3,300; £1,500) Stalls High

Form / RPR

0601 **1** **Silvaline**[20] [2881] 5-7-7 **74**........ CHaddon[(7)] 1 87
(TKeddy) *hld up in midfield: prog and brought to wd outside over 3f out: led over 2f out: rdn over 1f out: clr fnl f: pushed out* **7/1**

-000 **2** 2 1/2 **Prince Nureyev (IRE)**[13] [3075] 4-8-13 **87**........ KFallon 3 96
(BRMillman) *hld up in last pair: prog and brought to outer over 3f out: chsd wnr 2f out: drvn and no imp over 1f out* **7/1**

-323 **3** 3/4 **Shahzan House (IRE)**[28] [2638] 5-9-8 **96**........(p) PRobinson 8 103
(MAJarvis) *lw: led: hdd and shkn up over 2f out: styd on same pce fr over 1f out* **9/4**[1]

6003 **4** 1/2 **Stretton (IRE)**[13] [3097] 6-8-6 **80**........ TQuinn 11 86
(JDBethell) *settled in last: brought to outer 3f out: rdn and prog 2f out: kpt on one pce fr over 1f out* **5/1**[2]

-115 **5** 1 1/2 **Fine Palette**[27] [2691] 4-8-13 **87**........ WRyan 10 91
(HRACecil) *lw: hld up in midfield: effrt 3f out: hanging rt and nt qckn 2f out: one pce after* **11/2**[3]

0-06 **6** 1/2 **Foodbroker Founder**[14] [3034] 4-9-10 **98**........ KDarley 7 101
(DRCElsworth) *pressed ldr: rdn over 3f out: ev ch over 2f out: fdd jst over 1f out* **16/1**

6060 **7** *shd* **Nero's Return (IRE)**[20] [2897] 3-8-10 **95** KDalgleish 4 97
(MJohnston) *swtg: chsd ldrs: rdn over 2f out: one pce and btn over 1f out* **25/1**

0-60 **8** *1 3/4* **Millafonic**[14] [3034] 4-9-7 **95** (v[1]) DHolland 9 94
(LMCumani) *lw: sn trckd ldng pair: rdn over 3f out: lost pl fr 2f out: wknd ins fnl f* **6/1**

5-30 **9** *1 3/4* **Definite Guest (IRE)**[20] [2894] 6-8-8 **82** MartinDwyer 6 78
(RAFahey) *racd in midfield: rdn over 2f out: wknd over 1f out* **16/1**

2m 12.9s (2.72) **Going Correction** +0.425s/f (Yiel)
**WFA** 3 from 4yo+ 11lb **9** Ran SP% **117.7**
Speed ratings: **106,104,103,103,101 101,101,99,98**CSF £56.18 CT £146.36 TOTE £9.20: £2.40, £1.70, £1.50; EX 72.00 Trifecta £365.80 Pool £1,648.79, 3.20 winning units.
**Owner** Andrew Duffield **Bred** P D And Mrs Player **Trained** Newmarket, Suffolk

**FOCUS**
A decent-class handicap run at just a fair pace. The whole field were brought over to the nearside half of the track turning for home and the first two were the ones that were brought widest. Fair form.

**NOTEBOOK**
**Silvaline**, just 3lb higher than when winning in similar conditions over course and distance last August, had shown his well-being with a recent victory on Polytrack and his apprentice jockey gave him a fine ride. Brought right over to the stands' side after turning for home, he answered his rider's every call and was well on top at the line. At least this decent prize will help ease the effect of the stiff rise he is likely to suffer at the hands of the Handicapper.
**Prince Nureyev(IRE)**, a winner in similar conditions here as a juvenile, has been finding life tough in handicap company but has dropped to a mark 10lb lower than he started the season. This was by far his best effort for about a year and being brought right over to the stands' side in the home straight probably helped him.
**Shahzan House(IRE)**, who looks high enough in the weights considering he is yet to win a proper handicap, was able to dictate at his own pace but he stayed more towards the centre of the track turning in, whereas the front pair came widest, and that may have had an effect. He seems to handle cut in the ground well enough.
**Stretton(IRE)** has bits and pieces of soft ground form, but all his best efforts have been on fast ground. Held up out the back early, he followed the front pair right up the stands' side after turning for home and did make some progress, but it was laboured and he could never land a serious blow.
**Fine Palette** should have relished the conditions, but an 8lb higher mark than for his Leicester handicap success seems to have nailed him and he was simply not good enough.
**Foodbroker Founder** is sliding down the handicap, but is still a stone higher than for his last win after the Handicapper had panned him for finishing runner-up in Listed company last year.
**Millafonic** did not improve for the application of a visor and it may be that despite his victory on easy ground at Ayr last spring, he may prefer it faster.

## 3483 EUROPEAN BREEDERS FUND MAIDEN STKS 7f 16y
**3:45** (3:50) (D) 2-Y-O **£6,357** (£1,956; £978; £489) **Stalls** High

Form RPR

5 **1** **Melrose Avenue (USA)**[20] [2890] 2-9-0 KDalgleish 1 96
(MJohnston) *lw: mde all: rdn clr over 3f out: in n.d fnl 2f: drvn out* **11/4**[1]

**2** *6* **Ground Rules (USA)** 2-9-0 RHughes 5 81
(BWHills) *unf: angular: dwlt: hld up in last: plenty to do over 3f out: smooth prog to chse wnr over 2f out: shkn up and no imp* **3/1**[2]

**3** *8* **Road To Heaven (USA)** 2-9-0 TQuinn 4 61
(EALDunlop) *w'like: bit bkwd: in tch: pushed along and outpcd 3f out: plugged on to take 3rd over 1f out: no imp ldng pair* **12/1**

**4** *2* **Off Colour** 2-9-0 KDarley 3 56
(MrsAJPerrett) *w'like: bit bkwd: chsd wnr: rdn and outpcd over 3f out: lost 2nd over 2f out: fin tired* **4/1**

**5** *3/4* **Almanshood (USA)** 2-9-0 RHills 7 54
(JHMGosden) *w'like: scope: s.i.s: hld up in last pair: pushed along and outpcd 3f out: effrt 2f out: fdd over 1f out* **7/2**[3]

**6** *2* **Spill A Little** 2-9-0 TEDurcan 6 49
(MRChannon) *leggy: scope: tall: chsd ldrs: rdn and outpcd 3f out: no ch after* **16/1**

**7** *1 1/4* **Tumbleweed Galore (IRE)** 2-9-0 JFortune 2 46
(BJMeehan) *w'like: bit bkwd: prom: rdn over 3f out: sn lost pl and struggling* **20/1**

1m 34.31s (3.22) **Going Correction** +0.425s/f (Yiel) **7** Ran SP% **112.2**
Speed ratings: **98,91,82,79,78 76,75**CSF £10.84 TOTE £3.90: £2.10, £2.30; EX 9.20.
**Owner** Sheikh Mohammed **Bred** Lantern Hill Farm Llc Et Al **Trained** Middleham Moor, N Yorks

**FOCUS**
Little to go on, but a creditable time and probably a fair maiden. Again the field came over to the stands' side in the straight and experience counted for plenty, as the winner was the only one with previous racecourse experience and conditions were testing enough for the debutants.

**NOTEBOOK**
**Melrose Avenue(USA)**, the only one with previous experience, having finished fifth on different ground here last month, bounced out of the stalls in front and gradually wound things up as the race progressed. He forged right away in the closing stages to win with ease and looks a nice prospect, though the true merit of the form is hard to establish.
**Ground Rules(USA)** ◆, out of a half-sister to Danehill, Eagle Eyed, Shibboleth and Harpia, was given a very patient ride and was brought right over to the stands' side turning in. He made good progress to move into second place halfway up the straight, but was never in the same parish as the winner. The fact that he beat the others easily enough suggests he should be able to go one better before too long and he may also improve for better ground.
**Road To Heaven(USA)**, a $110,000 yearling out of a half-sister to a high-class performer in the US and a multiple winner in Germany, ran as though stamina is going to be his forte.
**Off Colour** ◆, a full brother to Him Of Distinction and half-brother to Man Of Distinction out of the Group-Three winner Air Of Distinction, got weary in the conditions late on, but should improve for the experience.
**Almanshood(USA)** ◆, first foal of the 1,000 Guineas winner Lahan, did not offer any immediate encouragement but the stable's juveniles often improve for a run and better ground may also suit him.
**Spill A Little**, a half-brother to Claradotnet and Generous Diana, is bred to need middle distances so is probably more of a long-term prospect.
**Tumbleweed Galore(IRE)**, a 30,000gns half-brother to Compton Banker, has a pedigree that is all speed so it was not surprising that he struggled with these conditions on his debut.

## 3484 CHAMPAGNE J LASSALLE IMPORTED BY O. W. LOEB GALA STKS (LISTED RACE) 1m 2f 7y
**4:20** (4:21) (A) 3-Y-0+ **£17,400** (£6,600; £3,300; £1,500) **Stalls** High

Form RPR

6322 **1** **Crocodile Dundee (IRE)**[15] [3000] 3-8-8 105 JFEgan 3 113
(JamiePoulton) *lw: t.k.h: hld up in tch: chsd ldr 3f out: drvn to ld jst over 1f out: edgd lft ins fnl f: battled on wl* **7/1**

-120 **2** *nk* **Silence Is Golden**[32] [2543] 5-9-0 100 JFortune 2 107
(BJMeehan) *racd wd in bk st: hld up: effrt over 2f out: drvn to chal and ev ch over 1f out: kpt on wl: jst hld* **7/1**

-343 **3** *3* **Sunstrach (IRE)**[31] [2559] 6-9-5 112 JPMurtagh 5 107
(LMCumani) *lw: led after 2f: 3l clr 3f out: hrd rdn 2f out: hdd jst over 1f out: fdd ins fnl f* **85/40**[1]

5410 **4** *3* **Alkaadhem**[17] [2957] 4-9-8 108 RHills 8 104
(MPTregoning) *lw: trckd ldrs: shkn up and nt qckn over 2f out: one pce and n.d after* **10/3**[2]

0052 **5** *1 1/2* **Dutch Gold (USA)**[27] [2678] 4-9-5 110 (b) DHolland 7 99
(CEBrittain) *chsd ldr after 3f to 3f out: rdn and nt qckn over 2f out: no ch after: wknd ins fnl f* **9/2**[3]

3250 **6** *3 1/2* **Compton Bolter (IRE)**[14] [3034] 7-9-8 109 RHughes 4 95
(GAButler) *racd wd in bk st: led for 2f: shkn up 3f out: no rspnse and btn after* **7/1**

154- **7** *25* **Weecandoo (IRE)**[260] [5589] 6-9-0 90 GCarter 6 42
(CNAllen) *a in last: bhd over 3f out: t.o* **33/1**

2m 10.99s (0.81) **Going Correction** +0.425s/f (Yiel)
**WFA** 3 from 4yo+ 11lb **7** Ran SP% **113.7**
Speed ratings: **113,112,110,107,106 103,83**CSF £53.10 TOTE £7.10: £2.20, £2.90; EX 42.90.
**Owner** R W Huggins **Bred** T J Pabst **Trained** Telscombe, E Sussex

**FOCUS**
A couple of important withdrawals weakened the contest, but the winning time suggests the race was up to standard. Silence Is Golden and Compton Bolter raced wide of the others down the back straight and the whole field came right over to the stands' side in the home straight. The result was a triumph for the classic generation, the winner being the only three-year-old in the line up.

**NOTEBOOK**
**Crocodile Dundee(IRE)**, the only three-year-old in the field, has done nothing but improve this season and did so again on this first encounter with soft ground. What was especially impressive was the way he stuck his neck right out in a driving finish, despite having taken a good hold racing down the back straight, and it will be a surprise if he does not enjoy further success in Pattern company under suitable conditions.
**Silence Is Golden** handles this sort of ground and ran another fine race, only just going down in a driving finish. She has not enjoyed much luck at this level in the past and now that she is in foal, she is not going to get many more chances to gain that illusive victory in Listed company.
**Sunstrach(IRE)** loves this ground and was stepping down in class, but despite getting the run of the race out in front he was unable to hang on. It later transpired he had fractured a cannon bone and he is unlikely to race again. *Official explanation: jockey said horse was lame*
**Alkaadhem**, back at a more realistic level, could have done without the rain and failed to pick up in the conditions.
**Dutch Gold(USA)** failed to build on his cracking effort in the Diomed over yet another different trip, though to be fair he has never shown much on this sort of ground. *Official explanation: jockey said colt was unsuited by good to soft ground*
**Compton Bolter(IRE)** was not on one of his going days.
**Weecandoo(IRE)** *Official explanation: jockey said mare was unsuited by good to soft ground*

## 3485 SUNDOWN AT SANDOWN H'CAP 1m 6f
**4:50** (4:50) (C) (0-90,86) 3-Y-0+ **£9,750** (£3,000; £1,500; £750) **Stalls** Centre

Form RPR

-152 **1** **Quedex**[8] [3236] 8-8-0 **64** JFMcDonald[(3)] 7 80
(RJPrice) *trckd ldrs: c to outer in st: shkn up to ld 2f out: drew clr fnl f* **4/1**[2]

00-2 **2** *7* **Mr Ed (IRE)**[9] [2893] 6-8-11 **75** (p) DCorby[(3)] 5 85+
(PBowen) *lw: dwlt: hld up in last pair: plenty to do over 3f out: prog over 2f out to chse wnr over 1f out: no imp: eased last 75yds* **7/2**[1]

0S22 **3** *shd* **Theatre (USA)**[13] [3095] 5-9-8 **83** PDoe 3 89
(JamiePoulton) *dwlt: hld up in last pair: rdn 4f out: prog u.p 2f out: nt clr run and swtchd rt over 1f out: kpt on* **9/1**

0044 **4** *5* **Redspin (IRE)**[8] [3244] 4-8-7 **68** MartinDwyer 10 67
(JSMoore) *trckd ldr: led 3f out to 2f out: wknd fnl f* **14/1**

0-03 **5** *5* **Sergeant Cecil**[14] [3046] 5-9-11 **86** KFallon 6 78
(BRMillman) *t.k.h: trckd ldng pair: rdn over 2f out: wknd over 1f out* **4/1**[2]

221 **6** *nk* **Twofan (USA)**[49] [2090] 3-8-6 **82** SChin 9 74
(MJohnston) *led: wandered and hdd 3f out: wknd over 1f out* **5/1**[3]

0443 **7** *10* **Flotta**[7] [3276] 5-9-7 **82** TEDurcan 2 60
(MRChannon) *racd in 5th pl: rdn and wknd over 2f out: sn bhd* **6/1**

3m 10.31s (5.94) **Going Correction** +0.425s/f (Yiel)
**WFA** 3 from 4yo+ 15lb **7** Ran SP% **109.8**
Speed ratings: **100,96,95,93,90 90,84**CSF £16.84 CT £106.83 TOTE £5.70: £3.20, £2.20; EX 25.70 Place 6 £178.78, Place 5 £74.90.
**Owner** Fox And Cub Partnership **Bred** Leo Van Hijkoop **Trained** Ullingswick, H'fords

**FOCUS**
A moderately run staying handicap which would not have suited a few of these and the race became virtually a three-furlong sprint. The winning time was therefore very modest for the grade. The field came wide once into the home straight, though not right over, and again the winner was the one that came widest.

**NOTEBOOK**
**Quedex** handles this sort of ground and found by far the best turn of foot in what became a sprint up the home straight. Even though his winning distance was exacerbated by the runner-up being heavily eased, he was still a clear winner and is still very well handicapped on his best form.
**Mr Ed(IRE)**, runner-up to Sergeant Cecil in this last year, is an out-and-out stayer so the modest pace was no help to him. Under the circumstances he did well to finish second again, especially as he raced closest to the far side of the track, and he would have been a more comfortable runner-up had his rider not prematurely eased him and very nearly got caught.
**Theatre(USA)** ran with credit considering that the ground was softer than ideal and he would not have been helped by the modest pace.
**Redspin(IRE)** did not have the race run to suit over an inadequate trip and probably did too much too soon.
**Sergeant Cecil**, winner of this race last year off a 4lb lower mark, pulled far too hard due to the lack of pace and there was little left in the tank when asked for his final effort.
**Twofan(USA)**, making his handicap debut, was able to dictate at his own pace for most of the way but was done for foot in the sprint up the home straight. He may have been put on a stiff mark based on what he has actually achieved, but may still be capable of better when setting a more searching gallop.

T/Jkpt: Not won. T/Plt: £661.90 to a £1 stake. Pool: £59,579.45. 65.70 winning tickets. T/Qpdt: £91.70 to a £1 stake. Pool: £3,955.80. 31.90 winning tickets. JN

# 3336 WARWICK (L-H)

Friday, July 2

**OFFICIAL GOING: Good to firm**

The course missed all the heavy rain that had been around and riders described the ground as quick.

Wind: mod bhd Weather: mainly fine

## 3486 YORKSHIRE BANK MAIDEN STKS — 6f 21y

2:15 (2:17) (D) 3-Y-O+ — £4,465 (£1,374; £687; £343) Stalls Low

Form — RPR

3442 **1** **Here To Me**[10] 3180 3-8-10 68 ........ RLMoore 3 — 73
(RHannon) *mde all: rdn over 1f out: hld on wl* — **11/8**[1]

3-6 **2** *hd* **Anna Panna**[9] 3209 3-8-10 ........ DaneO'Neill 1 — 73
(HCandy) *w wnr: rdn over 1f out: ev ch fnl f: r.o* — **5/1**[3]

U4-2 **3** *2* **Ragged Jack (IRE)**[13] 3085 3-9-1 72 ........ SWKelly 9 — 72
(GAButler) *hld up: rdn and hdwy over 2f out: one pce fnl f* — **2/1**[2]

64-4 **4** *3 ½* **Troodos Jet**[16] 2984 3-9-1 65 ........ FNorton 4 — 61
(ABerry) *prom: rdn over 1f out: wknd ins fnl f* — **20/1**

33 **5** *¾* **Chertsey (IRE)**[10] 3171 3-8-10 ........ BDoyle 5 — 54
(CEBrittain) *s.i.s: t.k.h: no real prog fnl 2f* — **20/1**

0-00 **6** *shd* **Pick A Berry**[87] 1288 3-8-10 ........ SDrowne 2 — 53
(GWragg) *s.i.s: hld up: hdwy on ins over 2f out: sn rdn: wknd over 1f out* — **66/1**

-046 **7** *1* **Eight Ellington (IRE)**[10] 3179 3-9-1 58 ........ IMongan 7 — 55
(MissGayKelleway) *hld up and bhd: rdn over 2f out: no rspnse* — **12/1**

5-00 **8** *hd* **Perfect Hindsight (IRE)**[45] 2207 3-9-1 55 ........ RSmith 8 — 55
(CGCox) *a bhd* — **50/1**

50- **9** *3 ½* **Fleet Anchor**[252] 5733 3-9-1 ........ CCatlin 6 — 44
(JMBradley) *prom tl wknd wl over 1f out* — **40/1**

1m 10.24s (-2.06) **Going Correction** -0.35s/f (Firm) — **9** Ran SP% **115.2**

Speed ratings: **99,98,96,91,90 90,88,88,84**CSF £8.21 TOTE £2.20: £1.10, £1.30, £1.40; EX 11.90.

**Owner** Mrs D Joly **Bred** Mrs D O Joly **Trained** East Everleigh, Wilts

**FOCUS**

An ordinary maiden with plenty of exposed runners, but the form looks more sound than most races of its type. The handicapper will have a good line to it.

**NOTEBOOK**

**Here To Me**finally earned winning brackets at the 14th attempt. Tackling this trip for the first time this year, she was pushed along to secure an early lead and dug deep to repel several challengers in the straight. She is unlikely to go up too much for this and a return to seven furlongs will not inconvenience her judged on the way she was sticking to her task.

**Anna Panna**, stepping down a furlong, stuck to the inside in the straight and had every chance, but she flashed her tail under pressure and the smaller filly was always just about holding her. She is eligible for a mark now.

**Ragged Jack(IRE)** was worst drawn in nine. He was close enough in the straight but lacked a change of gear and this sharp six was not ideal for him.

**Troodos Jet** briefly looked a threat with two to run but did not find much. He could well want easier ground.

**Chertsey(IRE)** failed to settle properly in the early stages and was not knocked about when held. She did not shape as if the drop to six furlongs was what she needed and is now eligible for handicaps.

**Eight Ellington(IRE)** was well backed on this step back up in trip but was never near enough to land a blow.

## 3487 MCDONALDS SERVICE CELEBRATION MAIDEN STKS — 7f 26y

2:50 (2:53) (D) 3-Y-O+ — £4,719 (£1,452; £726; £363) Stalls Low

Form — RPR

20-0 **1** **Three Secrets (IRE)**[78] 1413 3-8-8 85 ........ AMcCarthy 7 — 76
(PWChapple-Hyam) *a.p: wnt 2nd over 3f out: led over 2f out: rdn over 1f out: r.o wl* — **9/4**[2]

0-2 **2** *2* **Admiral Compton**[21] 2842 3-8-13 ........ SDrowne 4 — 76
(ACStewart) *chsd ldrs: rdn over 2f out: wnt 2nd jst over 1f out: nt qckn* — **2/1**[1]

**3** *3* **Majors Cast (IRE)** 3-8-13 ........ SWKelly 2 — 68
(JNoseda) *s.s: hld up: hdwy on ins over 1f out: r.o: bttr for r* — **16/1**

0 **4** *1 ¼* **Memory Man**[13] 3085 3-8-13 ........ FNorton 1 — 65
(WRMuir) *chsd ldr over 3f: rdn over 2f out: wknd ins fnl f* — **66/1**

0-36 **5** *½* **Moors Myth**[62] 1771 3-8-13 80 ........ RMullen 10 — 63
(BWHills) *chsd ldrs: rdn and one pce fnl 2f* — **7/1**

00 **6** *2* **Cayman Calypso (IRE)**[22] 2808 3-8-13 ........ NCallan 12 — 58
(MAJarvis) *hld up mid-div: rdn over 3f out: no hdwy fnl 2f* — **20/1**

2 **7** *nk* **Noble Mind**[11] 3161 3-8-13 ........ DKinsella 5 — 57
(PGMurphy) *hld up: rdn and sme hdwy 2f out: no imp fnl f* — **6/1**[3]

3 **8** *1 ½* **Hirayna**[14] 3057 5-9-2 ........ GBaker 8 — 48
(WMBrisbourne) *s.s: nvr nr ldrs* — **66/1**

000- **9** *2 ½* **Scarpia**[295] 4835 4-9-7 39 ........ RSmith 3 — 46?
(JCFox) *hld up: hdwy on ins 4f out: wknd 2f out* — **100/1**

00 **10** *1 ¾* **Black Sabbeth**[22] 2808 3-8-13 ........ DSweeney 9 — 41
(PJMakin) *hld up mid-div: rdn and wkng over 1f out* — **66/1**

43 **11** *1 ¼* **Kabeer**[13] 3106 6-9-7 ........ NPollard 13 — 38
(PSMcentee) *led: hdd over 2f out: wknd over 1f out* — **10/1**

63 **12** *1 ½* **Pure Imagination (IRE)**[24] 2765 3-8-13 ........ RLMoore 14 — 34
(JMBradley) *s.i.s: a bhd* — **25/1**

00 **13** *13* **Bunkhouse**[13] 3085 4-9-7 ........ MFenton 11 — —
(MissECLavelle) *sn rdn along: a bhd* — **50/1**

**14** *nk* **Jimmy Hay** 3-8-10 ........ LPKeniry(3) 6 — —
(JCFox) *s.s: sn wl bhd* — **100/1**

1m 22.3s (-2.60) **Going Correction** -0.35s/f (Firm)

**WFA** 3 from 4yo+ 8lb — **14** Ran SP% **122.9**

Speed ratings: **100,97,94,92,92 90,89,87,85,83 81,79,65,64**CSF £6.95 TOTE £3.20: £2.00, £1.30, £3.00; EX 8.70.

**Owner** Norcroft Park Stud **Bred** Swettenham Stud **Trained** Newmarket, Suffolk

**FOCUS**

There was no great pace on in this ordinary maiden.

**NOTEBOOK**

**Three Secrets(IRE)**, thought good enough to contest the Lowther Stakes as a two-year-old, had not run since a lacklustre debut for this yard at the Craven meeting. Always well placed, she went for home as the leader dropped away and had soon opened up a decisive advantage. She liked this ground but may struggle in handicaps from a likely mark in the high 80s.

**Admiral Compton** chased the winner hard through the final furlong but lacked a gear change. A return to a mile should pay dividends.

**Majors Cast(IRE)**, who fetched the not inconsiderable sum of 190,000gns as a yearling, drifted in the market prior to this debut. Well drawn on the inner, he made steady late progress but the first two were beyond recall. He ought to step up on this next time.

**Memory Man** showed a good deal more than he had on his debut but might have been flattered from the best draw of all.

**Moors Myth**, returning from a two-month break, was a little keen early on and then appeared reluctant to let himself down on the fast ground in the straight. He is proving disappointing. *Official explanation: , returning from a two-month break, was a little keen early on and then appeared reluctant to let himself down on the fast ground in the straight. He is proving disappointing.*

**Noble Mind**was unsuited by the drop in trip and faster ground, and was never within striking distance.

**Kabeer**made the running but stopped pretty quickly. He now qualifies for handicaps but may need more time.

## 3488 PYMENTS TROPHY H'CAP — 1m 6f 213y

3:25 (3:26) (E) (0-70,64) 3-Y-O+ — £4,621 (£1,422; £711; £355) Stalls Low

Form — RPR

0601 **1** **Darn Good**[13] 3108 3-8-10 64 ........ (b) RLMoore 11 — 74
(RHannon) *a.p: rdn over 3f out: led ins fnl f: drvn out* — **6/1**[2]

0303 **2** *½* **Noble Calling (FR)**[20] 2874 7-9-1 52 ........ FNorton 2 — 61
(RJHodges) *hld up: nt clr run on ins over 3f out: swtchd rt and hdwy 2f out: led 1f out: sn hdd: styd on* — **6/1**[2]

0065 **3** *3* **Persian Dagger (IRE)**[22] 2802 3-8-10 64 ........ SDrowne 1 — 69+
(JLDunlop) *hld up: lost pl over 3f out: hrd rdn and hdwy over 1f out: one pce fnl f* — **8/1**

0350 **4** *1 ¾* **Makarim (IRE)**[101] 1081 8-8-1 43 ........ (p) HayleyTurner(5) 13 — 46
(MRBosley) *hld up and bhd: hdwy on outside over 3f out: one pce fnl 2f* — **20/1**

0003 **5** *2* **Head To Kerry (IRE)**[10] 3181 4-9-7 58 ........ SWhitworth 9 — 58
(DJSFfrenchDavis) *hld up and bhd: hdwy 6f out: rdn to ld over 2f out: hdd 1f out: wknd ins fnl f* — **5/1**[1]

0/40 **6** *2* **Hernandita**[17] 2958 6-9-10 61 ........ MFenton 3 — 59
(MissECLavelle) *led early: chsd ldr: rdn over 3f out: wknd fnl f* — **8/1**

00/0 **7** *1 ¼* **Real Estate**[25] 2740 10-8-8 48 ........ LisaJones(3) 8 — 44
(JSKing) *hld up in tch: lost pl 9f out: n.d after* — **66/1**

4052 **8** *¾* **Theatre Tinka (IRE)**[12] 3128 5-9-0 56 ........ (p) StephanieHollinshead(5) 5 — 51
(RHollinshead) *sn led: clr 10f out: rdn and hdd over 2f out: wknd fnl f* — **8/1**

/0-P **9** *1* **Quick**[13] 3108 4-9-3 59 ........ (v) PMakin(5) 7 — 53
(MCPipe) *bhd: hdwy 6f out: wknd 4f out* — **7/1**[3]

0-00 **10** *1 ¼* **Heart Springs**[18] 2950 4-8-8 45 ........ SCarson 4 — 37
(DrJRJNaylor) *prom: rdn over 3f out: wknd wl over 1f out* — **40/1**

00-0 **P** **Western Ridge (FR)**[46] 1858 7-8-13 50 ........ DSweeney 10 — —
(BJLlewellyn) *hld up: hdwy 8f out: wknd 2f out: p.u lame 1f out* — **16/1**

3654 **P** **Moonshine Beach**[13] 3108 6-9-3 54 ........ DaneO'Neill 12 — —
(PWHiatt) *hld up in tch: lost pl 9f out: p.u over 6f out: sddle slipped* — **6/1**[2]

3m 13.8s (-1.40) **Going Correction** -0.05s/f (Good)

**WFA** 3 from 4yo+ 17lb — **12** Ran SP% **119.9**

Speed ratings: **101,100,99,98,97 96,95,95,94,93** —,—CSF £41.79 CT £295.57 TOTE £6.80: £2.10, £1.70, £3.10; EX 49.00.

**Owner** J E Garrett **Bred** Mrs Patricia Conway **Trained** East Everleigh, Wilts

**FOCUS**

Modest fare, with the topweight running off only 61 in this 0-70 handicap. It was run at a decent clip thanks to front-running Theatre Tinka.

**NOTEBOOK**

**Darn Good**won here last month over half a mile further. Raised 4lb for that success, he was fifth and hard at work turning into the short straight, but responded well to pressure to get on top. A step back up in trip will obviously suit him and he is clearly in fine heart at present.

**Noble Calling(FR)**, whose last win a year ago came from this mark, put his head narrowly in front but edged to his left under pressure and could not hold on. There was not much wrong with this effort especially as he did not enjoy a trouble-free run.

**Persian Dagger(IRE)**, stepped up in trip, was staying on after being caught flat-footed on the approach to the home turn. His trainer traditionally does well in long-distance handicaps and this one can get off the mark over a couple of furlongs farther.

**Makarim(IRE)**, who proved very reluctant to go down to the start, kept on past toiling rivals in the latter stages. He is very well handicapped these days but despite this more encouraging effort would not be one to get too interested in.

**Head To Kerry(IRE)** looked set to score when striking the front but was soon treading water. He has taken time to find his form this year and is handicapped to win again.

**Hernandita**, who has dropped to a handy mark, stuck on reasonably well considering she had chased the pace.

**Quick**, who was pulled up here last time, looked a little reluctant right from the start and could never get near the front.

**Western Ridge(FR)** *Official explanation: jockey said gelding was lame*

**Moonshine Beach** *Official explanation: jockey said saddle slipped*

## 3489 CALTHORPE ESTATES (S) H'CAP — 1m 22y

3:55 (3:58) (F) (0-55,52) 3-Y-O+ — £3,241 (£926; £463) Stalls Low

Form — RPR

0000 **1** **Mobo-Baco**[13] 3103 7-9-13 52 ........ RLMoore 3 — 63
(RJHodges) *hld up: hdwy on ins 2f out: rdn to ld ins fnl f: r.o wl* — **6/1**[1]

4030 **2** *1 ¼* **Lord Chamberlain**[8] 3247 11-9-5 51 ........ (b) CJDavies(7) 15 — 59
(JMBradley) *hld up: hdwy on outside over 2f out: rdn to ld over 1f out: hdd ins fnl f: nt qckn* — **8/1**

4000 **3** *¾* **Over To You Bert**[10] 2833 5-9-1 40 ........ RHavlin 2 — 46
(RJHodges) *a.p: rdn and ev ch over 1f out: nt qckn* — **33/1**

0353 **4** *nk* **Ivy Moon**[21] 2833 4-8-13 45 ........ SJDonohoe(7) 5 — 50
(BJLlewellyn) *dwlt: hld up: swtchd rt and hdwy over 1f out: kpt on ins fnl f* — **7/1**[3]

-003 **5** *1* **Senor Eduardo**[8] 3247 7-9-12 51 ........ IMongan 4 — 54
(SGollings) *hld up mid-div: rdn and hdwy over 2f out: one pce fnl f* — **8/1**

4000 **6** *nk* **Repeat (IRE)**[8] 3227 4-9-1 45 ........ MSavage(5) 17 — 47
(MissGayKelleway) *a.p: ev ch over 1f out: one pce* — **20/1**

30-0 **7** *3 ½* **Didoe**[13] 3103 5-9-5 47 ........ LisaJones(3) 6 — 41
(PWHiatt) *hld up in rr: rdn 2f out: hdwy fnl f: nvr nr ldrs* — **16/1**

460 **8** *shd* **Enna (POL)**[22] 2811 5-9-12 51 ........ SDrowne 13 — 45
(MrsStefLiddiard) *prom: led 3f out: rdn and hdd over 1f out: wknd ins fnl f* — **20/1**

4415 **9** *¾* **Espada (IRE)**[18] 2945 8-9-13 52 ........ (b) SWKelly 7 — 44
(JAOsborne) *hld up mid-div: rdn wl over 1f out: no hdwy* — **13/2**[2]

4060 **10** *2 ½* **Muqtadi (IRE)**[12] 3127 6-9-5 44 ........ FNorton 1 — 31
(MQuinn) *s.s: hld up: hdwy over 1f out: no imp fnl f* — **8/1**

0-00 **11** *hd* **Lucky Archer**[13] 3103 11-9-2 48 ........ LTreadwell(7) 10 — 34
(IanWilliams) *hld up towards rr: rdn 3f out: no rspnse* — **25/1**

0005 **12** *1 ½* **Power Bird (IRE)**[7] 3260 4-9-13 52 ........ (b) NPollard 9 — 35
(BRJohnson) *prom: rdn 2f out: wknd over 1f out* — **20/1**

0600 **13** *½* **Fife And Drum (USA)**[24] 2594 7-9-3 45 ........ (p) BReilly(3) 12 — 27
(MissJFeilden) *prom: rdn over 2f out: wknd over 1f out* — **25/1**



The Form Book, Raceform Ltd, Compton, RG20 6NL

2250 **14** *2 ½* **Benjamin (IRE)**[38] 2387 6-9-3 **42**..............................(bt) RMullen 11 18
(JaneSouthcombe) *hld up and bhd: short-lived effrt on outside 3f out* **14/1**

5100 **15** *½* **Flying Spud**[28] 2667 3-9-2 **50**.............................. DeanMcKeown 16 25
(JLSpearing) *prom tl wknd over 2f out* **14/1**

6005 **16** *5* **Light Brigade**[13] 3087 5-9-1 **40**.............................. SCarson 8 3
(JMPEustace) *led: hdd 3f out: sn rdn: wknd wl over 1f out* **14/1**

0000 **17** *dist* **Lunar Leader (IRE)**[14] 3050 4-9-6 **45**..............................(v[1]) MFenton 14 —
(MJGingell) *s.i.s: bhd: rdn over 3f out: t.o fnl 2f* **25/1**

1m 38.68s (-0.62) **Going Correction** -0.05s/f (Good) **17** Ran SP% **128.1**
**WFA** 3 from 4yo+ 9lb
Speed ratings: **101,99,99,98,97 97,93,93,93,90 90,88,88,85,85 80,**—CSF £49.30 CT £1561.11 TOTE £6.60: £2.00, £1.80, £6.50, £2.70; EX 59.60.There was no bid for the winner.
**Owner** Frome Racing **Bred** C J Hill **Trained** Charlton Adam, Somerset

**FOCUS**
Plenty of old adversaries in opposition for a seller in which the whole field was rated between 40 and 52.

**NOTEBOOK**
**Mobo-Baco** had a bit on his plate turning in, but his low draw meant he could stick to the inside rail and he finished strongly to get his head in front. He was very well treated on last season's form and has done all his winning on fast ground. Unfortunately he finished sore.
**Lord Chamberlain** raced wide apart from the winner in the straight and went down fighting. The draw beat him, but this infrequent winner could yet score again if things go his way.
**Over To You Bert**, a stablemate of the winner, ran his best race since successful on the Lingfield Polytrack in March but was aided by a favourable draw.
**Ivy Moon** was well drawn, but she was slowly away and found herself behind a stack of horses turning into the straight. Switched right, she ended up near the stands' rail and finished as well as any bar the winner, seeing out the mile on this sharp track.
**Senor Eduardo** is running creditably at present and promises to stay a little farther.
**Repeat(IRE)** did well to challenge for the lead from his draw but finished weakly. Due to be dropped 3lb, he will appreciate the return to seven furlongs.
**Espada(IRE)** needs to dominate but could never get to the front.
**Flying Spud** *Official explanation: jockey said gelding was unsuited by the good to firm going*
**Lunar Leader(IRE)** *Official explanation: jockey said filly had a breathing problem*

## 3490 SHOOSMITHS MAIDEN H'CAP 1m 2f 188y
**4:30** (4:32) (F ) (0-55,53) 4-Y-0+ **£3,458** (£988; £494) **Stalls** Low

Form RPR

006- **1** **Toccata Aria**[276] 5289 6-8-12 **45**.............................. RLMoore 4 55
(JMBradley) *hld up: rdn and hdwy over 1f out: r.o wl to ld nr fin* **25/1**

-004 **2** *¾* **Tintawn Gold (IRE)**[7] 3263 4-9-1 **48**.............................. DSweeney 11 57
(SWoodman) *hld up: hdwy 4f out: rdn to ld over 1f out: hdd nr fin* **4/1**[1]

3604 **3** *nk* **Pacific Ocean (ARG)**[18] 2943 5-9-6 **53**..............................(t) SDrowne 2 61
(MrsStefLiddiard) *a.p: rdn over 2f out: nt qckn ins fnl f* **4/1**[1]

0060 **4** *2 ½* **Castaigne (FR)**[36] 2430 5-9-5 **52**.............................. RHavlin 10 56
(BWDuke) *s.i.s: hld up: hdwy over 4f out: rdn over 2f out: one pce fnl f* **10/1**

0600 **5** *1* **Mr Dip**[11] 3143 4-8-13 **53**.............................. LTreadwell[(7)] 3 55
(AWCarroll) *s.i.s: hld up: hdwy over 3f out: rdn over 1f out: swtchd rt ins fnl f: one pce* **33/1**

346- **6** *shd* **Eboracum Lady (USA)**[254] 5703 4-9-3 **50**.............................. CCatlin 16 52
(JDBethell) *chsd ldr: led over 3f out tl over 1f out: wknd fnl f* **16/1**

-000 **7** *¾* **Dash For Glory**[66] 1693 5-7-9 **33** oh3.............................. HayleyTurner[(5)] 5 34
(JSKing) *prom tl wknd over 2f out* **10/1**

5 **8** *5* **Latin Queen (IRE)**[19] 2914 4-9-3 **50**.............................. SWhitworth 13 42
(JDFrost) *hld up and bhd: hdwy 2f out: n.d* **20/1**

5320 **9** *1 ¾* **Ryan's Bliss (IRE)**[18] 2939 4-8-8 **44**.............................. RMiles[(3)] 14 33
(TDMccarthy) *prom: ev ch 2f out: wknd over 1f out* **6/1**[2]

0005 **10** *7* **Zalkani (IRE)**[30] 2594 4-9-2 **49**.............................. VSlattery 7 26
(BGPowell) *prom: rdn over 3f out: wknd over 2f out* **7/1**[3]

-00P **11** *5* **Grumpyintmorning**[13] 3103 5-9-1 **53**..............................(b[1]) MSavage[(5)] 9 22
(MrsPTownsley) *s.i.s: hdwy over 6f out: rdn over 3f out: wknd over 2f out* **40/1**

600 **12** *hd* **Grey Samurai**[14] 3056 4-8-2 **35**..............................(p) FNorton 8 3
(PTMidgley) *a bhd* **50/1**

5-00 **13** *6* **Zouche**[8] 3247 4-8-12 **45**.............................. SWKelly 15 3
(WMBrisbourne) *hld up: rdn 6f out: sn struggling* **20/1**

0300 **P** **Dances With Angels (IRE)**[38] 2385 4-8-2 **35**.............................. PMQuinn 12 —
(MrsALMKing) *s.v.s: a wl bhd: t.o* **14/1**

-400 **P** **Puri**[28] 2666 5-9-3 **50**..............................(b[1]) MFenton 1 —
(JGGiven) *plld hrd: led: clr 8f out: hdd over 3f out: sn wknd: p.u 2f out* **16/1**

2m 17.57s (-1.83) **Going Correction** -0.05s/f (Good) **15** Ran SP% **124.1**
Speed ratings: **104,103,103,101,100 100,100,96,95,90 86,86,81,**—,—CSF £118.39 CT £507.80 TOTE £27.20: £6.20, £2.60, £2.00; EX 167.10.
**Owner** Terry Warner **Bred** Southill Stud **Trained** Sedbury, Gloucs
■ A 3,025/1 four-timer for Ryan Moore.

**FOCUS**
A typically weak maiden handicap, run at a good pace. The runners were spread across the track in the straight.

**NOTEBOOK**
**Toccata Aria**, who put up what on paper was an improving showing on her final run of last season, stayed on past tiring rivals to score, overcoming an absence of nine months in the process.
**Tintawn Gold(IRE)** had run well behind the previous day's winner Cristoforo last time, form that gave her a sound chance in this. She was travelling well on the home turn and looked the winner when kicking for home, but was run out of it despite appearing to do nothing wrong.
**Pacific Ocean(ARG)**, who has had plenty of chances but looked as if this longer trip would suit last time, ran his race, but the inability to change gear is his problem. *Official explanation: jockey said horse hung left*
**Castaigne(FR)**, another long-standing maiden, raised connections' hopes early in the straight before fading.
**Mr Dip** was noted staying on well in the closing stages and, being lightly raced, at least offers the possibility that he can win a race at this level. *Official explanation: jockey said gelding hung right*
**Eboracum Lady(USA)** did not fare too badly on her first outing since October, keeping on having been close to the pace throughout.
**Ryan's Bliss(IRE)**, who was well backed, looked sure to figure in the finish turning in but dropped away disappointingly in the closing stages.
**Dances With Angels(IRE)** *Official explanation: jockey said filly hit front gates as the stalls opened*
**Puri** ran too free in the first-time blinkers and set a good pace before weakening quickly and eventually being pulled up. *Official explanation: jockey said gelding lost its action, but returned sound*

## 3491 BIRMINGHAM GARRICK CLUB MEDIAN AUCTION MAIDEN STKS 5f
**5:00** (5:05) (E ) 2-Y-O **£3,786** (£1,165; £582; £291) **Stalls** Low

Form RPR

2 **1** **Godsend**[46] 2177 2-8-9.............................. DaneO'Neill 7 76
(RHannon) *chsd ldrs: rdn 2f out: led wl ins fnl f: r.o wl* **4/6**[1]

03 **2** *1* **Bold Minstrel (IRE)**[20] 2872 2-9-0.............................. FNorton 1 77
(MQuinn) *w ldr: rdn over 2f out: ev ch ins fnl f: nt qckn* **5/1**[2]

6 **3** *1 ½* **Anfield Dream**[30] 2574 2-9-0.............................. JMackay 4 71
(JRJenkins) *a.p: rdn over 2f out: edgd rt and led over 1f out: hdd and no ex wl ins fnl f* **16/1**

4500 **4** *1 ¾* **Next Time (IRE)**[27] 2677 2-8-9.............................. GGibbons 2 59
(MJPolglase) *led: rdn and hdd over 1f out: wknd wl ins fnl f* **16/1**

0 **5** *1 ½* **High Dyke**[8] 3228 2-9-0.............................. PaulEddery 5 58
(DHaydnJones) *s.i.s: hdwy fnl f: nvr nrr* **50/1**

56 **6** *½* **Town End Tom**[11] 3150 2-9-0.............................. CCatlin 11 56
(DMSimcock) *chsd ldrs tl wknd over 1f out* **50/1**

**7** *2 ½* **Fadael (IRE)** 2-8-9.............................. RLMoore 3 41
(PWD'Arcy) *s.i.s: sme hdwy on ins 2f out: n.d* **8/1**[3]

4 **8** *shd* **Our Fugitive (IRE)**[63] 1751 2-9-0.............................. IMongan 10 46
(AWCarroll) *s.i.s: short-lived effrt on outside over 2f out* **25/1**

4 **9** *shd* **Phlaunt**[14] 3045 2-8-9.............................. SCarson 9 40
(RFJohnsonHoughton) *outpcd* **12/1**

0 **10** *3 ½* **Beauchamp Twist**[10] 3176 2-8-9.............................. SWKelly 8 26
(GAButler) *mid-div: rdn over 2f out: wknd wl over 1f out* **66/1**

**11** *11* **Absolut Edge** 2-9-0.............................. DSweeney 6 —
(JAPickering) *s.v.s: a wl bhd* **50/1**

58.90 secs (-1.30) **Going Correction** -0.40s/f (Firm) **11** Ran SP% **118.4**
Speed ratings: **94,92,90,87,84 84,80,79,79,74 56**CSF £4.00 TOTE £1.60: £1.10, £1.40, £3.90; EX 6.50.
**Owner** The Queen **Bred** The Queen **Trained** East Everleigh, Wilts

**FOCUS**
Not a bad auction maiden. The pace was sound and the time decent. The main action took place down the centre in the straight.

**NOTEBOOK**
**Godsend** had looked a sure future winner on her debut when runner-up to a decent filly. She briefly looked in trouble when ridden along, but ran on well to score a shade readily in the end. She would not mind a step up to six furlongs.
**Bold Minstrel(IRE)**, who had run well in a warm little race at Bath last time, had his chance but was unable to capitalise on his good draw. There was no disgrace in this and he should make his mark in nurseries.
**Anfield Dream** threw away his chance when edging over to the right in the straight, but this was a step up on his debut running and he obviously possesses ability.
**Next Time(IRE)**, tackling a more suitable grade, showed plenty of speed and stuck to the inner once in line for home, but was soon put in her place when headed.
**High Dyke**, who took his chance despite the lack of overnight rain, was unsuited by the drop back in trip and was finishing quite well. *Official explanation: jockey said colt was unsuited by the good to firm ground*
**Fadael(IRE)** was well backed, but that could have been due to fact that her rider was in such sparkling form. She never got into the hunt and will need stepping up in trip.
**Absolut Edge** *Official explanation: jockey said gelding missed break and hung left.*

## 3492 BOLLINGER CHAMPAGNE CHALLENGE SERIES H'CAP (GENTLEMAN AMATEUR RIDERS) 1m 4f 134y
**5:30** (5:31) (F ) (0-70,70) 4-Y-0+ **£3,542** (£1,090; £545; £272) **Stalls** Low

Form RPR

0044 **1** **Skylarker (USA)**[21] 2835 6-11-13 **69**.............................. MrLJefford 3 78
(WSKittow) *a.p: led over 5f out: rdn over 1f out: edgd lft ins fnl f: r.o* **5/1**

1240 **2** *nk* **Great View (IRE)**[33] 2501 5-11-6 **62**..............................(v) MrSWalker 6 71
(MrsALMKing) *hld up: hdwy over 2f out: sn rdn: edgd lft and ev ch fnl f: r.o* **7/2**[2]

6062 **3** *7* **Giko**[24] 2767 10-9-12 **40**.............................. MrAdamJones 2 39
(JaneSouthcombe) *hld up in tch: rdn 3f out: wknd fnl f* **9/2**[3]

0/0- **4** *2* **Karakum**[232] 3551 5-9-9 **44**.............................. MrGTumelty[(7)] 5 40
(AJChamberlain) *prom tl wknd over 1f out* **66/1**

3303 **5** *2* **Saxe-Coburg (IRE)**[5] 3342 7-10-11 **60**.............................. MrGDenvir[(7)] 7 53
(GAHam) *hld up: lost pl 3f out: n.d after* **9/1**

045- **6** *½* **Javelin**[189] 4469 8-10-2 **51**.............................. MrBGallagher[(7)] 4 43
(IanWilliams) *hld up: rdn over 4f out: hdwy on ins over 3f out: rdn over 2f out: wknd over 1f out* **8/1**

/0-6 **7** *nk* **Chapter House (USA)**[7] 3282 5-11-7 **70**..............................(b) MrOGreenall[(7)] 8 61
(MWEasterby) *hld up: dropped rr 5f out: n.d after* **25/1**

1621 **8** *1* **Trusted Mole (IRE)**[5] 3342 6-10-9 **56**.............................. MrCDavies[(5)] 9 46
(WMBrisbourne) *hld up: sn in tch: wknd over 3f out* **5/2**[1]

-004 **9** *8* **Jack Durrance (IRE)**[25] 2740 4-10-0 **45**.............................. MrEDehdashti[(3)] 1 23
(GAHam) *prom: ev ch over 2f out: sn rdn: wknd wl over 1f out* **14/1**

0035 **10** *7* **Morris Dancing (USA)**[21] 2851 5-9-5 **38** oh8......(v) MrJPemberton[(5)] 10 5
(BPJBaugh) *led: hdd over 5f out: rdn 4f out: wknd 3f out* **100/1**

2m 42.56s (-0.74) **Going Correction** -0.05s/f (Good) **10** Ran SP% **119.7**
Speed ratings: **100,99,95,94,93 92,92,91,87,82**CSF £23.40 CT £86.29 TOTE £6.50: £2.60, £2.10, £2.10; EX 30.00 Place 6 £ 18.38, Place 5 £16.69.
**Owner** Midd Shire Racing **Bred** P Pritchard **Trained** Blackborough, Devon

**FOCUS**
A moderate event, and the pace was not as strong as in a lot of amateurs' races. The first two pulled clear.

**NOTEBOOK**
**Skylarker(USA)**was winning only his second race from 29 starts. Suited by the return to this trip, he travelled well in front and his rider only really needed to get busy with him inside the final furlong for him to hold on.
**Great View(IRE)**, who has a good record in these events, was back to form after a couple of below-par runs. He came with a strong challenge towards the stands' side, but edged across the track under pressure and could not get his head in front.
**Giko** was unable to repeat last year's victory in this event, when 2lb lower, and there appeared no excuses.
**Karakum** ran respectably on this return from a break but has always been a weak finisher.
**Javelin**, runner-up in this race two years ago when 5lb higher, was having his first run since Boxing Day over hurdles. He was already feling the pinch when stumbling slightly on the home turn.
**Trusted Mole(IRE)**, unpenalised for his win in an apprentice race here at the weekend, failed to pick up and this might have come too soon.
T/Plt: £12.80 to a £1 stake. Pool: £29,570.75. 1,685.85 winning tickets. T/Qpdt: £8.90 to a £1 stake. Pool: £1,641.10. 135.50 winning tickets. KH

3497 - 3503a (Foreign Racing) - See Raceform Interactive

## 3434 HAMBURG (R-H)

Friday, July 2

**OFFICIAL GOING: Very soft**

### 3504a PREIS DER JUNGHEINRICH GABELSTAPLER (GROUP 3) 1m 3f

6:40 (6:54) 3-Y-O+ **£24,648** (£9,859; £4,930; £2,817)

RPR

1 **Vallera (GER)**[26] 2723 3-8-7 TMundry 9 102
(UOstmann, Germany) *held up towards rear, headway & moved to stands rail 2f out, strong run from over 1f out to lead 100y out, driven out* 2

2 1 3/4 **Next Gina (GER)**[271] 5403 4-9-4 AStarke 3 99
(ASchutz, Germany) *always in touch, headway 3f out, 2nd straight, driven to lead 1 1/2f out, headed 100y out, no extra* 1

3 2 1/2 **Give Me Five (GER)**[26] 2723 3-8-7 FilipMinarik 10 96
(FrauEMader, Germany) *led til headed 1 1/2f out, weakened final f, just held 3rd*

4 hd **Mity Dancer (GER)**[48] 2138 4-9-4 LHammer-Hansen 11 95
(DKRichardson, Germany) *held up, headway & 6th straight, cut corner & soon went 3rd in middle, one pace from over 1f out*

5 2 1/2 **Iduna (GER)**[26] 2723 3-8-7 ASuborics 13 92
(WHickst, Germany) *tracked leaders, 3rd straight, soon ridden & one pace* 3

6 6 **Seraphine (GER)**[56] 1952 4-9-4 THellier 1 82
(WHimmel, Germany) *held up in rear, headway over 3f out, 7th straight, ridden well over 1f out, never near to challenge*

7 nk **Kastoria (GER)**[292] 5-9-4 EPedroza 4 82
(AWohler, Germany) *in touch, 5th straight, soon beaten*

8 1 1/2 **Fleurie Domaine**[56] 1952 5-9-4 (b) J-PCarvalho 8 79
(MarioHofer, Germany) *prominent, tracked leader half-way, 4th straight, soon beaten*

9 2 1/2 **Delightful Sofie (GER)**[314] 4-9-4 JPalik 14 76
(AndreasLowe, Germany) *in touch on outside to over 3f out*

10 6 **Daytona (GER)**[26] 2723 3-8-7 ABoschert 6 68
(FrauABertram, Germany) *mid-division, 8th straight, soon beaten*

11 hd **Dalicia (GER)**[26] 2723 3-8-7 AHelfenbein 5 67
(PRau, Germany) *always towards rear*

12 11 **Corrine (IRE)** 5-9-4 FJohansson 7 50
(S-ELilja, Norway) *prominent til weakening quickly over 3f out, last straight*

13 11 **Anna Victoria (GER)**[35] 4-9-6 CCzachary 2 35
(GSybrecht, Germany) *always towards rear, beaten 3f out*

2m 27.89s
**WFA** 3 from 4yo+ 12lb **13** Ran SP% **132.3**
Speed ratings: .
**Owner** Gestut Auenquelle **Bred** Gestut Auenquelle **Trained** Germany

## 3468 BEVERLEY (R-H)

Saturday, July 3

**OFFICIAL GOING: Good to soft**

Race times suggested conditions were even more testing than the official going description would suggest.

### 3505 COACHMAN CARAVANS NOVICE STKS 7f 100y

1:45 (1:45) (D) 2-Y-O **£4,621** (£1,422; £711; £355) **Stalls** High

Form RPR

1 **Gypsy Johnny** 2-8-8 IMongan 3 74+
(MLWBell) *trckd ldng pair: hdwy 2f out: qcknd to ld appr last: sn rdn and styd on wl* **9/4**[2]

2 4 **Love Palace (IRE)** 2-8-8 KDalgleish 2 65+
(MJohnston) *cl up: green and pushed along 1/2-way: rdn along 2f out: hdwy to chal over 1f out: one pce ins last* **9/4**[2]

01 3 3/4 **Three Pennies**[11] 3164 2-8-11 FLynch 4 66
(MDods) *set slow pce: shkn up over 1f out: sn hdd and btn* **2/1**[1]

4 5 **Eborarry (IRE)** 2-8-8 DAllan 1 52
(TDEasterby) *s.i.s: a rr* **7/1**[3]

1m 41.77s (7.47) **Going Correction** +0.825s/f (Soft) **4** Ran SP% **107.4**
Speed ratings: **90,85,84,78**CSF £7.46 TOTE £3.50; EX 7.20.
**Owner** H E Sheikh Rashid Bin Mohammed **Bred** A C Birkle **Trained** Newmarket, Suffolk

**FOCUS**
A small field and only one of the quartet had previous experience. This was a stiff test for juveniles in the conditions and the winning time was modest for the grade.

**NOTEBOOK**
**Gypsy Johnny**, who fetched 34,000gns as a two-year-old, is a half-brother to several winners including Coconut Johnny, out of a winning half-sister to Cape Town. Given a patient ride, he had no problem with the trip or the ground and was well on top of his three rivals at the line. Despite having beaten a previous winner on this debut, the form is difficult to assess, though he shapes as though he will get further.
**Love Palace(IRE)**, a 110,000euros half-brother to Hunting Lodge out of a multiple winner in the US and France, was well and truly put in his place by the winner, but suggested he needed the experience and should be all the better for it.
**Three Pennies**, penalised for winning a fillies' maiden over course and distance last time, put the form of that contest into perspective as, despite being able to dictate from the front at her own pace, she was still nothing like good enough.
**Eborarry(IRE)**, a 13,5000euros half-brother to Montone and Pride Of May, did not show much on this debut but is likely capable of better in time.

### 3506 HAPPY BIRTHDAY ROBERT (S) STKS 7f 100y

2:15 (2:17) (F) 2-Y-O **£3,160** (£903; £451) **Stalls** High

Form RPR

1 **Pon My Soul (IRE)** 2-8-11 RFitzpatrick 2 58
(MGQuinlan) *bhd: hdwy on outer 1/2-way: led 2f out: sn rdn: drvn and hung bdly lft ins last: kpt on* **8/1**

230 2 1/2 **Songgaria**[12] 3144 2-8-3 TEaves(3) 4 52
(JSWainwright) *towards rr: hdwy on outer over 2f out: rdn and hung rt wl over 1f out: drvn to chal and edgd rt ins last: kpt on* **15/2**

30 3 shd **Cois Na Tine Eile**[17] 2985 2-8-6 GParkin 8 52
(KARyan) *in rr and sn pushed along: rdn along and hdwy 2f out: drvn and r.o strly ins last* **9/1**

3615 4 nk **Maureen's Lough (IRE)**[14] 3100 2-8-13 DarrenWilliams 7 58
(TDBarron) *trckd ldrs: effrt 2f out: sn rdn and kpt on u.p fnl f* **5/1**[2]

642 5 nk **Riverweld**[14] 3100 2-8-4 DFentiman(7) 5 55
(GMMoore) *chsd ldrs: rdn 2f out: drvn and styng on whn hmpd and swtchd rt ins last: kpt on* **9/2**[1]

06 6 3/4 **Forpetesake**[18] 2960 2-8-11 IMongan 10 54
(MrsJRRamsden) *bhd and sn pushed along: hdwy wl over 1f out: rdn and kpt on fnl f: nrst fin* **10/1**

6500 7 4 **Lane Marshal**[31] 2570 2-8-11 (b[1]) GGibbons 16 44
(MESowersby) *cl up: led after 1f: rdn along and hdd 2f out: grad wknd* **20/1**

6 8 1 1/4 **Faithful Flash**[23] 2819 2-8-3 THamilton(3) 6 37
(CADwyer) *in tch: hdwy on inner 3f out: rdn 2f out and sn no imp* **33/1**

0554 9 1 1/2 **Frisby Ridge (IRE)**[12] 3144 2-8-6 DAllan 12 33
(TDEasterby) *led 1f: cl up tl rdn along over 2f out and grad wknd* **13/2**[3]

000 10 1/2 **Hollingwood Soul**[24] 2773 2-8-6 DeanMcKeown 9 32
(RonaldThompson) *a rr* **20/1**

000 11 4 **Timmy**[24] 2773 2-8-11 DMcGaffin 14 28
(MESowersby) *chsd ldrs: rdn over 2f out: drvn and wknd over 1f out* **33/1**

30 12 8 **Shuchbaa**[22] 2858 2-8-6 RFfrench 15 4
(KARyan) *a bhd* **8/1**

13 3 **Tewitfield Lass** 2-8-6 ow3 LEnstone(3) 3 —
(JRWeymes) *s.i.s: a bhd* **33/1**

00 14 3/4 **Amanderica (IRE)**[11] 3164 2-8-1 DFox(5) 11 —
(MCChapman) *s.i.s: a bhd* **100/1**

1m 42.46s (8.16) **Going Correction** +0.825s/f (Soft) **14** Ran SP% **120.6**
Speed ratings: **86,85,85,84,84 83,79,77,76,75 70,61,58,57** CT £16.30 TOTE £4.50: £2.10, £3.80, £; EX126.50 1.The winner was bought in for 6,800gns. Cois Na Tine Eile was claimed by Ms D. J. Evans for £6000; Forpetesake was claimed by Ms D. J.
**Owner** Archangels **Bred** Miss M Archdeacon **Trained** Newmarket, Suffolk

**FOCUS**
A poor seller in which less than two lengths covered the first six home and the way the race was run null and voided the effect of the draw. The leaders went a good pace early, but eventually paid for it due to the conditions and they were walking near the line. The winning time was slow, even for a race like this.

**NOTEBOOK**
**Pon My Soul(IRE)**, out of a full sister to a winner in Germany, has already been gelded. Held up off the strong pace early, he was suddenly produced to lead approaching the last two furlongs in what turned out to be a race-winning move, as despite him getting tired and wandering all over the track, none of his rivals were quite good enough to take advantage. This was a tough introduction and he is not going to be easy to place from now on.
**Songgaria**, stepping up in trip, seemed to appreciate the greater test of stamina, though despite staying on she could never quite reel the winner in. There may be a similar race in her under similar conditions.
**Cois Na Tine Eile**, much happier back on turf, made up a lot of late ground but the post was always going to arrive too soon. She could be interesting in modest company in the autumn when faced with a mile and similar ground to this.
**Maureen's Lough(IRE)** deserves credit for finishing so close as she had a penalty to carry and was close to the fierce pace from the off. She goes on any ground and there should be another small race in her, especially if she is allowed to dominate on her own.
**Riverweld** is another that deserves credit for hanging in there after being prominent from the start.
**Forpetesake** came from a long way back, but seemed to find even this an insufficient test. His 37,000gns price tag suggests he should be better than a mere plater. *Official explanation: jockey said gelding missed break*
**Lane Marshal**, stepping up in trip and tried in blinkers, was partly responsible for the strong early pace and ultimately paid for it.
**Frisby Ridge(IRE)**, taking a significant step up in trip on her seventh start, did far too much too soon and eventually fell in a heap.

### 3507 BP SALTEND H'CAP 1m 100y

2:50 (2:50) (D) (0-85,78) 3-Y-O **£5,557** (£1,710; £855; £427) **Stalls** High

Form RPR

-460 1 **Charnock Bates One (IRE)**[7] 3312 3-8-6 63 GGibbons 5 74
(TDEasterby) *pushed along and edgd rt after 2f: sn trcking ldrs: hdwy and rdn along whn hung rt 2f out: drvn to ld inside last: kpt on* **7/1**[3]

2122 2 hd **Riley Boys (IRE)**[16] 3012 3-9-3 74 IMongan 6 85
(JGGiven) *led 1f: cl up tl led again over 3f out: rdn over 2f out: drvn and hdd ins last: kpt on* **9/2**[1]

2125 3 8 **Man Of Letters (UAE)**[32] 2558 3-9-7 78 KDalgleish 2 72+
(MJohnston) *prom: pushed along and outpcd 3f out: hdwy on inner whn hmpd 2f out: swtchd lft and kpt on u.p fianl f* **9/2**[1]

2-12 4 5 **Little Jimbob**[9] 3230 3-9-3 77 THamilton(3) 4 60
(RAFahey) *chsd ldrs: hdwy 3f out: rdn 2f out and sn wknd* **11/2**[2]

-002 5 5 **Annie Harvey**[17] 2988 3-8-13 70 FLynch 1 43
(BSmart) *wnt lft s: hdwy to ld after 1f: rdn along and hdd over 3f: sn wknd* **12/1**

0-14 6 hd **Cottingham (IRE)**[9] 3252 3-8-3 65 DFox(5) 3 37
(MCChapman) *a rr* **12/1**

6-50 7 1 **Fairlie**[17] 2973 3-8-5 62 RFfrench 9 32
(MrsJRRamsden) *hld up: hdwy onm outer over 3f out: sn rdn and wknd* **12/1**

441 8 shd **Swainsworld (USA)**[11] 3168 3-9-7 78 DAllan 8 48
(TDEasterby) *hld up: hdwy on inner 1/2-way: effrt and ch whn n.m.r 2f out: sn rdn and grad wknd* **9/2**[1]

0000 9 3 **Mount Vettore**[26] 2732 3-9-4 75 DeanMcKeown 7 39
(MrsJRRamsden) *in tch whn hmpd and lost pl after 2f: hdwy 3f out: sn rdn and wknd* **9/1**

1m 52.1s (4.80) **Going Correction** +0.825s/f (Soft) **9** Ran SP% **115.5**
Speed ratings: **109,108,100,95,90 90,89,89,86**CSF £38.52 CT £159.49 TOTE £12.50: £1.90, £1.30, £2.20; EX 46.40.
**Owner** Charnock Bates **Bred** Gerry Flannery **Trained** Great Habton, N Yorks
■ Stewards Enquiry : T Hamilton caution: careless riding

**FOCUS**
A good pace and a decent time for the grade. The front two finished well clear, although the margin is a bit flattering, and the form looks solid.

**NOTEBOOK**
**Charnock Bates One(IRE)** ◆, getting off the mark at the tenth attempt, appeared to relish the testing conditions and just came out best after a prolonged duel with the runner-up. She looks as though she would get further and, now that she has broken her duck, may well be able to add to this in the near future.
**Riley Boys(IRE)** ◆, as tough and consistent as they come and proven in testing conditions, was given his usual positive ride, but never had it easy at the front and the fact that he still only went down narrowly and pulled miles clear of the third marks this as yet another a cracking effort. It will be very surprising if he does not regain the winning thread soon.
**Man Of Letters(UAE)**, never far away, met trouble against the inside rail inside the last two furlongs when still in with a shout, but given how far the front pair forged clear it is highly unlikely he would have done any better than third in any case.

**Little Jimbob** ran his race, but looks plenty high enough in the weights now and all his best form is on fast ground.
**Annie Harvey** managed to get to the front early despite swerving left from her outside stall, but probably did too much too soon and did not get home.
**Swainsworld(USA)**, making his handicap debut, did not get the best of runs, but was still beaten a long way and perhaps the ground was not suitable.

## 3508 ELTHERINGTON STKS (H'CAP) 2m 35y
**3:25** (3:25) (E) (0-70,70) 3-Y-O+ **£3,900** (£1,200; £600; £300) **Stalls** High

Form RPR
42-0 **1** **Oops (IRE)**[14] 3099 5-7-7 **42** ow1 DeanWilliams(7) 3 47
(JFCoupland) *led tl rn wd bnd after 6f: cl up: rdn 2f out: drvn and styd on ins last to ld last 100 yds* **6/1**[3]
-030 **2** ½ **Lady Netbetsports (IRE)**[7] 3300 5-9-0 **61** MLawson(5) 6 66
(BSRothwell) *cl up: led after 6f: rdn along 3f out: drvn and edgd lft ins last: hdd and no0 ex last 100 yds* **11/1**
-005 **3** ½ **Dance Light (IRE)**[14] 3108 5-9-4 **60** TGMcLaughlin 7 64
(TTClement) *hld up: hdwy on inner 5f out: rdn to chal over 1f out and ev chance tl drvn and no ex last 100 yds* **3/1**[2]
/06- **4** 5 **Galleon Beach**[278] 5266 7-10-0 **70** LVickers 4 68
(BDLeavy) *hld up: hdwy 4f out: swtchd lft and rdn over 2f out: sn one pce* **16/1**
0-60 **5** 11 **Ashtaroute (USA)**[24] 2133 4-8-2 **49** DFox(5) 2 34
(MCChapman) *hld up: hdwy on outer 1/2-way: rdn along 4f out and sn btn* **16/1**
000/ **6** ½ **Only Words (USA)**[13] 4153 7-7-13 **41** oh6 ow1 RFfrench 5 25
(AJLockwood) *trckd ldrs: pushed along 1/2-way: lost pl over 5f out and sn bhd* **9/1**
3030 **7** 8 **Riyadh**[18] 2958 6-9-9 **65** (v) KDalgleish 1 40
(MJohnston) *trckd ldrs: pushed along and lost pl briefly 5f out: rdn to chse ldrs 3f out: drvn 2f out: edgd rt and sn wknd* **11/10**[1]

3m 56.18s (16.78) **Going Correction** +0.825s/f (Soft) **7** Ran SP% **117.0**
Speed ratings: **91,90,90,88,82 82,78**CSF £68.70 TOTE £5.40: £2.50, £5.50; EX 105.60.
**Owner** J F Coupland **Bred** Mrs Clodagh McStay **Trained** Grimsby, Lincs
■ Stewards Enquiry : M Lawson two-day ban: used whip with excessive frequency (Jul 14,15)

**FOCUS**
A race run in a downpour at a modest gallop and a moderate winning time for the grade. Despite the lack of pace, very few got into it and first two home were at the front throughout. The form is modest.

**NOTEBOOK**
**Oops(IRE)**, an uncooperative individual last season, seems to have turned the corner after a change of stables and was getting off the mark at the 13th attempt. Always up with the pace on just his second start for his new yard, he needed to battle hard to get the best of a three-way fight to the line and on this occasion his resolution could not be faulted.
**Lady Netbetsports(IRE)**, without a win on the Flat after 19 attempts, was given a positive ride and looked the one to catch racing up the home straight, but she started to wander approaching the furlong pole and was eventually worried out of it.
**Dance Light(IRE)** has dropped to a decent mark and had every chance in the final couple of furlongs, but could not produce a telling blow. She could have done without the rain.
**Galleon Beach** has gained all his wins on faster ground, but does have form on soft ground in his younger days so that may not have been a problem. However, he is a dour stayer so the lack of a proper pace probably was.
**Riyadh**, seventh in the Ascot Staks at the Royal Meeting, has had a questionable attitude in the past and on this occasion he ran a thoroughly moody race. *Official explanation: trainer was unable to offer any explanation for poor form shown*

## 3509 MONDI HYPAC STKS (H'CAP) 5f
**3:55** (3:55) (C) (0-90,90) 3-Y-O+ **£13,884** (£4,272; £2,136; £1,068) **Stalls** High

Form RPR
5301 **1** **Paddywack (IRE)**[9] 3249 7-7-13 **68** (b) RoryMoore(7) 18 79+
(DWChapman) *towards rr: swtchd lft and hdwy 2f out: str run to ld ins last: styd on* **11/2**[2]
0403 **2** ½ **Winthorpe (IRE)**[7] 3314 4-8-7 **69** KDalgleish 14 78+
(JJQuinn) *squeezed out after 100 yds and bhd: nt clr run on inner 1/2-way and over 1f out: swtchd lft and nt clr run over 1f out:fin* **6/1**[3]
4060 **3** nk **Bond Boy**[62] 1789 7-10-0 **90** FLynch 13 98
(BSmart) *towards rr: hdwy 2f out: rdn and styd on to chse wnr ins last: drvn and one pce nr fin* **12/1**
0024 **4** 1½ **Tally (IRE)**[7] 3293 4-7-7 **60** oh1 DFox(5) 16 63
(MJPolglase) *chsd ldrs: effrt on inner and nt clr run over 1f out: squeezed through ent last: sn rdn and kpt on* **7/1**
6002 **5** 2 **Brigadier Monty (IRE)**[3] 3407 6-7-5 **60** oh10 DFentiman(7) 9 56+
(MrsSLamyman) *hld up in rr: hdwy whn nt clr run over 1f out: styd on wl fnl f: nrst fin* **33/1**
0622 **6** ¾ **Blackheath (IRE)**[14] 3098 8-9-6 **82** AlexGreaves 15 75
(DNicholls) *trckd ldrs: c lose up 2f out and ev ch tl rdn and wknd ent last* **4/1**[1]
0165 **7** shd **Catch The Cat (IRE)**[7] 3326 5-8-10 **72** (b) GParkin 17 65
(JSWainwright) *led: rdn along 2f out: hdd & wknd ins last* **6/1**[3]
0323 **8** nk **Kings College Boy**[4] 3399 4-7-12 **60** (v[1]) JMcAuley 8 52
(RAFahey) *midfield: hdwy whn n.m.r over 1f out: kpt on fnl f* **20/1**
0002 **9** 2½ **Beyond The Clouds (IRE)**[4] 3399 8-9-0 **76** DAllan 6 59
(JSWainwright) *cl up: rdn wl over 1f out: grad wknd* **18/1**
2550 **10** ½ **Watching**[7] 3324 7-9-8 **84** ANicholls 12 65
(DNicholls) *chsd ldrs: rdn 2f out: grad wknd* **10/1**
0304 **11** 1¼ **Tuscan Flyer**[9] 3227 6-7-13 **61** (b) RFfrench 10 37
(RBastiman) *midfield: rdn 2f out: no imp* **16/1**
0350 **12** 5 **Vita Spericolata (IRE)**[28] 2682 7-9-4 **83** (b) TEaves(3) 3 41
(JSWainwright) *cl up: rdn 2f out: grad wknd* **40/1**
-000 **13** 1½ **Rectangle (IRE)**[22] 2859 4-8-10 **72** IMongan 5 25
(DNicholls) *a rr* **66/1**
3121 **14** hd **Dizzy In The Head**[6] 3339 5-9-5 **86** 6ex (b) NChalmers(5) 7 38
(PaulJohnson) *chsd ldrs to 1/2-way: sn wknd* **12/1**
0210 **15** 1¼ **Artie**[52] 2041 5-9-7 **83** JCarroll 1 31
(TDEasterby) *dwlt: a bhd* **25/1**

67.19 secs (3.19) **Going Correction** +0.825s/f (Soft) **15** Ran SP% **127.6**
Speed ratings: **107,106,105,103,100 98,98,98,94,93 91,83,81,80,78**CSF £38.66 CT £398.45 TOTE £6.50: £2.40, £2.90, £4.10; EX 54.40.
**Owner** T S Redman **Bred** Colm McEvoy **Trained** Stillington, N Yorks
■ Stewards Enquiry : Rory Moore three-day ban: careless riding (Jul 15-17)

**FOCUS**
A competive sprint handicap run at a decent pace. The form looks sound enough and the first three are all potentially well treated. The draw played its usual part with the six highest stalls finishing in the first seven. Those drawn low had no chance. The winning time was still acceptable for the grade, despite being 0.6 seconds slower than the first division of the maiden.

**NOTEBOOK**
**Paddywack(IRE)**, raised 4lb for his Thirsk victory, had the best of the draw but had to sit and wait for the gaps to appear. Fortunately he was able to angle out at just the right time and deliver a race-winning turn of foot that was to prove decisive.
**Winthorpe(IRE)** ◆, nicely handicapped at present, endured a rough passage at various stages of the contest and had to be pulled wide to deliver his final challenge. He fairly flew when in the clear, but it was always going to be a couple of strides too late. With anything like a clear run he would have won easily and he deserves to make amends.
**Bond Boy**, for whom the rain was very welcome, was at the back early but came home in great style. He is back on a winning mark and looks capable of winning another big handicap when underfoot conditions are suitable.
**Tally(IRE)**, 1lb out of the handicap, found this stiff five furlongs in the conditions offsetting the inadequate trip and this was a very solid effort.
**Brigadier Monty(IRE)** ◆, who showed his best form in Ireland on this sort of ground, ran an absolute cracker from 10lb out of the handicap and was the only one from a single-figure draw to get anywhere near. If he can reproduce this on his favoured surface off his proper mark it will not be long before he breaks his duck in this country.
**Blackheath(IRE)**, raised another 3lb despite not winning, was close enough if good enough for much of the way and there seemed no excuses this time. *Official explanation: jockey said gelding was never travelling*
**Catch The Cat(IRE)**, a natural front-runner, had no choice but to try and force the issue from his good draw, but in these conditions he did not get home.
**Kings College Boy** was snatched up after taking a bump when the winner was pulled out over a furlong from home. It probably cost him a length or two.

## 3510 COACHMAN CARAVANS H'CAP 1m 1f 207y
**4:30** (4:30) (E ) (0-75,75) 3-Y-O+ **£3,770** (£1,160; £580; £290) **Stalls** High

Form RPR
-321 **1** **Santiburi Lad (IRE)**[29] 2649 7-8-7 **57** THamilton(3) 1 73
(NWilson) *mde all: rdn clr wl over 1f out: comf* **9/4**[1]
5225 **2** 8 **Compton Dragon (USA)**[18] 2964 5-10-0 **75** (v) ANicholls 6 77
(DNicholls) *t.k.h: trckd ldrs: pushed along and hdwy whn hmpd wl over 1f out: sn rdn and styd on: no ch w wnr* **7/2**[3]
1111 **3** 2 **Kingsdon (IRE)**[8] 3265 7-9-2 **63** (vt) KDalgleish 3 61
(TJFitzgerald) *in tch: pushed along after 2: rdn along and outpcd 4f out: drvn and styd on fnl 2f* **5/2**[2]
-004 **4** hd **Bond May Day**[6] 3342 4-9-5 **66** FLynch 5 64
(BSmart) *cl up: pushed along 3f out: rdn and hung rt wl over 1f out: sn drvn and wknd* **11/2**
4-65 **5** 3 **Lucayan Dancer**[75] 1502 4-8-13 **60** AlexGreaves 4 53
(DNicholls) *chsd ldrs: rdn along over 3f out and sn wknd* **9/2**

2m 12.2s (5.00) **Going Correction** +0.825s/f (Soft) **5** Ran SP% **115.1**
Speed ratings: **113,106,105,104,102**CSF £10.93 TOTE £3.50: £2.10, £3.00; EX 14.40.
**Owner** Mrs Karan Ridley **Bred** Rathbarry Stud **Trained** Malton, N Yorks

**FOCUS**
A small field, but a powerful piece of front-running by the winner who looked different class. The time was very decent indeed for the grade given the conditions.

**NOTEBOOK**
**Santiburi Lad(IRE)**, 3lb higher than for his Haydock victory in a race that looks better than it did at the time, produced another powerful front-running display and had pounded his rivals into the turf before reaching the furlong pole. He obviously relishes these conditions, but his future prospects depend on what the Handicapper does and whether he can get his own way out in front.
**Compton Dragon(USA)** took a keen grip early and also met some traffic problems when trying to make an effort over a furlong from home, but given the winner's superiority it would be pushing things to say it made any difference and he is still looking for his first win on turf.
**Kingsdon(IRE)** found his winning run coming to an end off this 6lb higher mark and did not appear to handle the home bend too well. This was a better race than he has been contesting.
**Bond May Day** had every chance before fading under pressure over the last couple of furlongs, but all his best form has come on fast ground.
**Lucayan Dancer** ended up well beaten, but may have just needed it after a short break.

## 3511 GEORGE KILBURN MEMORIAL STKS (MAIDEN) (DIV I) 5f
**5:00** (5:04) (D ) 3-Y-O+ **£3,435** (£1,057; £528; £264) **Stalls** High

Form RPR
0-2 **1** **Royal Challenge**[11] 3179 3-9-0 IMongan 4 82
(GAButler) *trckd ldrs: hdwy on inner 1/2-way: led wl over 1f out: kpt on* **4/6**[1]
4-0 **2** 3 **Harrison's Flyer (IRE)**[3] 3410 3-9-0 GParkin 11 71?
(RAFahey) *led: rdn along 2f out: sn hdd and kpt on same pce* **6/1**[3]
0 **3** 8 **Red Hot Ruby**[30] 2621 3-8-6 THamilton(3) 1 37
(RAFahey) *outpcd in rr: hdwy 2f out: styd on ins last* **25/1**
0042 **4** 1¾ **Blue Maeve**[7] 3314 4-9-5 51 SRighton 8 36
(JHetherton) *cl up: rdn along 2f out: sn wknd* **4/1**[2]
0- **5** ½ **Mecca's Mate**[334] 3833 3-8-6 LEnstone(3) 6 29
(DWBarker) *outpcd and bhd: stmbld after 2f: headway 2f out: sn rdn and one pce* **50/1**
000 **6** 1½ **Cottam Karminski**[20] 2908 3-8-2 RoryMoore(7) 7 24
(JSWainwright) *sn outpcd: a rr* **50/1**
00-5 **7** 1¾ **Hamaasy**[17] 2984 3-9-0 61 AlexGreaves 5 22
(DNicholls) *in tch: rdn along 1/2-way: sn wknd* **12/1**
00-0 **8** 1½ **Bowlegs Billy**[11] 3169 4-8-12 48 (p) KPierrepont(7) 9 17
(JBalding) *a rr* **16/1**
020- **9** 5 **Bond Romeo (IRE)**[225] 6037 3-9-0 70 DMcGaffin 3 —
(BSmart) *cl up on outer: rdn along over 2f out: sn wknd* **11/1**
0-00 **10** hd **Alpha Zeta**[8] 3269 3-9-0 DeanMcKeown 10 —
(CWThornton) *sn outpcd and bhd fr 1/2-way* **66/1**

66.59 secs (2.59) **Going Correction** +0.825s/f (Soft)
**WFA** 3 from 4yo 5lb **10** Ran SP% **125.4**
Speed ratings: **112,107,94,91,90 88,85,83,75,74**CSF £5.88 TOTE £1.60: £1.10, £1.50, £4.40; EX 5.50.
**Owner** Cheveley Park Stud **Bred** Capt A L Smith-Maxwell **Trained** Blewbury, Oxon

**FOCUS**
An uncompetitive maiden in which the field finished well strung out, but still an outstanding winning time for the grade, 1.65 seconds faster than the second division and 0.6 seconds faster than the earlier 0 to 90 handicap.

**NOTEBOOK**
**Royal Challenge** ◆ was taking on much easier company than at Newbury, albeit on different ground, but could not be faulted in the way he hugged the inside rail and came right away from his rivals to score with ease. The winning time gives encouragement that he may be capable of finding something quite a bit better than this.
**Harrison's Flyer(IRE)** ◆ showed good early speed from the best draw and even though he hung away from the inside rail as the race progressed, letting the winner through in the process, he still finished clear second best by some margin. This was encouraging on his second run back following a long layoff and he can now be handicapped.
**Red Hot Ruby** made some late progress without ever getting anywhere near the front two, but this was still an improvement from her debut. *Official explanation: jockey said filly hung left throughout*

**Blue Maeve**, proven on the ground, showed speed until past halfway. He is completely exposed though, having had more runs than the front three put together, and would be better off back in handicaps.
**Mecca's Mate**, racing for the first time since her debut 11 months ago, was fortunate not to come down when squeezed out passing the three-furlong pole.
**Hamaasy** was again disappointing and the change of yards has yet to work the oracle.
**Bond Romeo(IRE)**, racing for the first time in eight months, showed little and his handicap mark looks far from generous when compared to some that finished ahead of him. *Official explanation: jockey said gelding hung left in final two furlongs*

## 3512 GEORGE KILBURN MEMORIAL STKS (MAIDEN) (DIV II) 5f

**5:30** (5:32) (D ) 3-Y-O+ **£3,425** (£1,054; £527; £263) **Stalls** High

Form RPR

4- **1** **Chimali (IRE)**[332] 3887 3-9-0 .......... ANicholls 6 61+
(JNoseda) *mde virtually all: shkn up and qcknd over 1f out: rdn ins last and kpt on* **7/4**[1]

5350 **2** *nk* **Roan Raider (USA)**[12] 3151 4-9-5 53 .......... (v) GGibbons 9 54
(MJPolglase) *a.p: effrt 2 f out: sn rdn and styd on to chal ins last: drvn and no ex nr fin* **14/1**

4004 **3** *1 1/2* **Elliot's Choice (IRE)**[6] 3344 3-8-11 66 .......... DNolan(3) 7 49
(DCarroll) *broke wl: hld up and sn in rr: hdwy 2f out: rdn over 1f out: styd on wl fnl f: too much to do* **2/1**[2]

66 **4** *4* **Intavac Boy**[31] 2586 3-9-0 .......... JCarroll 8 34
(CWThornton) *sn outpcd in rr: hdwy over 2f out: pushed along and styng on whn n.m.r over 1f out: kpt on ins last: nrst fin* **10/1**

0354 **5** *hd* **Amanda's Lad (IRE)**[3] 3407 4-9-0 56 .......... DFox(5) 1 33
(MCChapman) *cl up on outer: rdn along 2f out: sn drvn and wknd over 1f out* **7/1**[3]

60 **6** *10* **Grey Gurkha**[30] 2621 3-9-0 .......... RFitzpatrick 2 —
(PTMidgley) *dwlt: sn in tch: rdn along on outer 2f out and soo wknd* **33/1**

0406 **7** *nk* **Akiramenai (USA)**[14] 3096 4-9-0 55 .......... IMongan 5 —
(MrsLStubbs) *chsd ldrs: rdn along 1/2-way: sn wknd* **25/1**

00 **8** *1* **Estoille**[28] 2675 3-8-2 .......... (t) DFentiman(7) 10 —
(MrsSLamyman) *a rr* **50/1**

60- **9** *25* **Io Callisto**[352] 3339 3-8-9 .......... GParkin 4 —
(RAFahey) *cl up: rdn along after 2f: sn outpcd and bhd* **25/1**

68.24 secs (4.24) **Going Correction** +0.825s/f (Soft)
**WFA** 3 from 4yo 5lb **9** Ran SP% **110.5**
Speed ratings: **99,98,96,89,89 73,72,71,31**CSF £23.30 TOTE £2.80: £1.40, £3.80, £1.10; EX 33.00 Place 6 £1,037.96, Place 5 £295.53.
**Owner** Mrs Susan Roy **Bred** Redpender Stud Ltd **Trained** Newmarket, Suffolk
■ Stewards Enquiry : G Gibbons four-day ban: used whip with excessive frequency and without giving gelding time to respond (Jul 14-17)

**FOCUS**
Not much to get excited about in this weak maiden and a modest winning time for the class, 1.65 seconds slower than the first division.

**NOTEBOOK**
**Chimali(IRE)**, off for 11 months since his debut, soon bagged pole position in front against the far rail and showed real determination to hold off the highly experienced if exposed runner-up in the closing stages. He can probably still improve a bit and connections will be hoping the Handicapper establishes his mark through the second rather than the third horse.
**Roan Raider(USA)** appeared to run above his handicap mark and was closing down the winner at the line, but as this was his 30th start it was probably his experience and a good draw that enabled him to get so close.
**Elliot's Choice(IRE)** stayed on from the back to finish a clear third, but he is becoming exposed and using the runner-up as a guide he did not even run up to his handicap mark.
**Intavac Boy** ◆, not for the first time, ran as though he needs much further than this and the tact that he is a half-brother to 12-furlong winner Alessandro Severo certainly backs that up. He could be very interesting if stepped up in trip now that he qualifies for handicaps, especially if the market speaks in his favour.
**Amanda's Lad(IRE)** is one of the longest-standing maidens in training in terms of starts and it is hard to imagine that changing.
**Akiramenai(USA)** *Official explanation: jockey said filly was in season*
**Io Callisto** *Official explanation: jockey said filly had lost her action*
T/Plt: £1,684.40 to a £1 stake. Pool: £30,458.25. 13.20 winning tickets. T/Qpdt: £118.30 to a £1 stake. Pool: £2,303.20. 14.40 winning tickets. JR

# 3196 CARLISLE (R-H)

Saturday, July 3

**OFFICIAL GOING: Good (good to soft in places)**
The ground was described as 'just on the slow side of good'.
Wind: Fresh 1/2 against. Weather: Dry and breezy.

## 3513 AZURE (S) STKS 7f 200y

**7:05** (7:05) (F ) 3-Y-O **£3,094** (£884; £442) **Stalls** High

Form RPR

5000 **1** **Reversionary**[9] 3234 3-8-12 43 .......... (b) RWinston 7 49
(MWEasterby) *sn chsng ldrs: led over 1f out: hdd ins last: bmpd and regained ld nr line* **8/1**

-000 **2** *nk* **Elsinora**[12] 3156 3-8-7 50 .......... (p) MFenton 5 43
(HMorrison) *dwlt: sn trcking ldrs: nt clr run and swtchd lft over 1f out: hung bdly rt and led ins last: hdd nr fin* **5/1**[3]

0200 **3** *2* **Bargain Hunt (IRE)**[25] 2760 3-8-12 46 .......... JBramhill 1 44
(WStorey) *bhd: drvn along and hdwy over 3f out: ev ch 1f out: nt qckn* **9/2**[2]

-004 **4** *1* **Chubbes**[9] 3229 3-8-12 60 .......... (v) ACulhane 8 41
(MDHammond) *led tl over 1f out: wknd ins last* **1/1**[1]

5400 **5** *shd* **Campbells Lad**[15] 3060 3-8-12 40 .......... PBradley 4 41
(ABerry) *trckd ldrs: rdn and outpcd over 1f out: styd on ins last* **16/1**

00-0 **6** *10* **Cute Cait**[16] 3024 3-8-7 49 .......... WSupple 2 13
(MrsGSRees) *trckd ldrs: effrt over 2f out: sn btn* **12/1**

0505 **7** *8* **Knight To Remember (IRE)**[17] 2986 3-8-9 40 .......... TEaves(3) 3 —
(REBarr) *hld up in rr: drvn along over 3f out: sn bhd* **20/1**

0 **8** *3 1/2* **Raybers Magic**[16] 3015 3-8-7 .......... JFanning 6 —
(JRWeymes) *trckd ldrs: lost pl over 2f out: sn bhd* **33/1**

1m 42.71s (2.71) **Going Correction** +0.35s/f (Good) **8** Ran SP% **117.2**
Speed ratings: **100,99,97,96,96 86,78,75**CSF £48.76 TOTE £13.10: £4.10, £1.80, £1.40; EX 80.90.No bid for winner.
**Owner** A G Black & A M Hedley **Bred** P And Mrs Venner **Trained** Sheriff Hutton, N Yorks

**FOCUS**
A rock-bottom seller.

**NOTEBOOK**
**Reversionary**, who had a bit to find, appreciated the step up in trip but was basically handed it on a plate.
**Elsinora**, who had 12lb in hand of the winner on official ratings, wore first-time cheekpieces. Switched to get a run, she went a neck up inside the last but then threw it away, giving the winner a hefty bump. If there was ever a case of a winning opportunity thrown out of the window this was it.
**Bargain Hunt(IRE)**, a maiden after 17 previous starts, had 3lb in hand of the winner but raced nearest the slowest ground on the far side.
**Chubbes**, who had 5lb and upwards in hand on official figures, is only small and prefers much quicker ground.
**Campbells Lad**, unplaced in eight previous starts, ran in snatches, suddenly taking a fierce grip at halfway. Brought widest of all, in the end he finished best but he clearly has a mind of his own.

## 3514 VILLAGE NIGHTCLUB MAIDEN AUCTION STKS 5f

**7:35** (7:37) (E ) 2-Y-O **£3,542** (£1,090; £545; £272) **Stalls** High

Form RPR

**1** **Strawberry Dale (IRE)** 2-8-6 .......... JFanning 8 77
(JDBethell) *leggy: unf: scope: chsd ldrs: led 1f out: hld on wl* **18/1**

5 **2** *1/2* **Big Hassle (IRE)**[10] 3196 2-8-9 .......... WSupple 11 78
(TDEasterby) *sn trcking ldrs: chal 1f out: nt qckn towards fin* **6/4**[1]

**3** *2* **On The Bright Side** 2-8-4 .......... PMQuinn 9 66+
(DNicholls) *s.s: bhd: hdwy 2f out: r.o wl ins last: improve* **20/1**

4 **4** *2 1/2* **Dispol Isle (IRE)**[22] 2860 2-8-2 .......... PFessey 1 55
(TDBarron) *w ldrs: fdd appr fnl f* **5/2**[2]

060 **5** *hd* **Desert Buzz (IRE)**[25] 2758 2-8-7 .......... MFenton 3 59
(JHetherton) *sn outpcd and towards rr: hdwy 2f out: kpt on* **20/1**

03 **6** *nk* **Skiddaw Wolf**[10] 3197 2-8-2 .......... RFfrench 6 53
(BSmart) *led tl hdd & wknd 1f out* **6/1**[3]

05 **7** *1 1/4* **Ochil Hills Dancer (IRE)**[30] 2617 2-8-6 .......... VHalliday 2 53
(ACrook) *chsd ldrs: sn drvn along: outpcd fnl 2f* **14/1**

4054 **8** *1* **No Commission (IRE)**[4] 3398 2-8-11 .......... ACulhane 4 54
(RFFisher) *chsd ldrs: wknd fnl 2f* **8/1**

00 **9** *6* **Toldo (IRE)**[10] 3197 2-8-9 .......... FLynch 7 31
(ABerry) *outpcd and bhd fr 1/2-way* **50/1**

**10** *3* **Danceinthevalley (IRE)** 2-8-9 .......... RWinston 5 20
(GASwinbank) *lengthy: s.s: a bhd* **16/1**

00 **11** *1 1/2* **Robury**[35] 2470 2-8-7 .......... DeanMcKeown 10 —
(EJAlston) *chsd ldrs: lost pl over 2f out: sn bhd* **100/1**

**12** *3* **Titus Rock (IRE)** 2-8-2 .......... JBramhill 12 —
(DMccain) *lengthy: unf: s.i.s: sn bhd* **100/1**

62.61 secs (1.11) **Going Correction** +0.025s/f (Good) **12** Ran SP% **125.2**
Speed ratings: **92,91,88,84,83 83,81,79,70,65 62,58**CSF £46.63 TOTE £19.60: £4.80, £1.20, £2.80; EX 85.50.
**Owner** M J Dawson **Bred** Bryan Ryan **Trained** Middleham Moor, N Yorks

**FOCUS**
Just an ordinary event but the first three should progress.

**NOTEBOOK**
**Strawberry Dale(IRE)**, a March foal, went on travelling best but in the end had to dig deep. Six, or even seven furlongs will suit her better in due course.
**Big Hassle(IRE)**, drawn one from the inside, travelled strongly but he was racing on the slightly slower ground near the far side. He made the winner pull out all the stops and deserves to go one better.
**On The Bright Side**, a March foal, is on the leg and looks some way short of the finished article. Only eighth a furlong out, she finished with quite a flourish and looks capable of a fair bit better in due course.
**Dispol Isle(IRE)** looked very fit and did not improve on her initial effort.
**Desert Buzz(IRE)**, unplaced in three previous outings, will be much happier back over six or even seven furlongs.
**Skiddaw Wolf** showed bags of toe but even over this furlong shorter trip did not get home.
**Toldo(IRE)** *Official explanation: jockey said gelding hung left and right*

## 3515 CRANEMAKERS CLASSIFIED STKS 5f 193y

**8:05** (8:06) (E ) 3-Y-O+ **£3,623** (£1,115; £557; £278) **Stalls** High

Form RPR

2061 **1** **Hartshead**[14] 3096 5-9-3 68 .......... DeanMcKeown 4 81
(GASwinbank) *trckd ldrs: shkn up to ld last 150yds: comf* **10/1**

3032 **2** *1 1/2* **Time N Time Again**[2] 3446 6-9-3 70 .......... (p) WSupple 3 75
(EJAlston) *led: qcknd 3f out: sn hdd: nt qckn ins last* **7/4**[1]

0104 **3** *1 1/2* **My Bayard**[9] 3226 5-8-10 56 .......... (b[1]) JDO'Reilly(7) 2 70?
(JO'Reilly) *trckd ldrs: led over 2f out: hrd rdn and hung rt over 1f out: hdd ins last: unable qckn* **20/1**

2565 **4** *2 1/2* **Soba Jones**[7] 3298 7-9-3 70 .......... JEdmunds 6 61
(JBalding) *chsd ldrs: effrt over 2f out: wknd appr fnl f* **3/1**[3]

0310 **5** *1 3/4* **Ulysees (IRE)**[9] 3235 5-9-4 74 .......... TEaves(3) 7 59
(ISemple) *hld up: effrt 3f out: wknd over 1f out* **11/4**[2]

5044 **6** *1/2* **Fiore Di Bosco (IRE)**[13] 3122 3-8-6 73 .......... PMakin(5) 9 53
(TDBarron) *hld up: effrt over 2f out: nvr a threat* **8/1**

1m 13.61s (-0.59) **Going Correction** +0.025s/f (Good)
**WFA** 3 from 4yo+ 6lb **6** Ran SP% **113.0**
Speed ratings: **104,102,100,96,94 93**CSF £28.44 TOTE £9.90: £2.80, £1.30; EX 23.10.
**Owner** B Valentine **Bred** Gainsborough Stud Management Ltd **Trained** Melsonby, N Yorks
■ Stewards Enquiry : J D O'Reilly six-day ban: used whip with excessive force, above shoulder height and in the incorrect place (Jul 14-17,19,20)

**FOCUS**
A depleted field and no real gallop. The winner and third showed improved form.

**NOTEBOOK**
**Hartshead** is clearly going the right away and, racing hard against the stands'-side rail, took this with the minimum of fuss.
**Time N Time Again**, having his second outing in three days, setepped up the gallop at halfway but the winner always looked likely to take him.
**My Bayard**, in first-time blinkers, went on near the stands'-side rail but, under extreme pressure, went right, leaving the door open for the winner. His young rider will have to learn to restrict his use of the stick otherwise the six-day ban handed out here will be the first of many.
**Soba Jones** continues to run well but he is finding it hard to hit the target at present.
**Ulysees(IRE)**, warm on a cool night, was below his best.
**Fiore Di Bosco(IRE)** was best in on official figures but it did not work out that way. Unless his rating of 73 is chopped he will continue to struggle to make his mark in handicap company.

## 3516 CARLING H'CAP 6f 192y

**8:35** (8:36) (D ) (0-80,80) 3-Y-O+ **£6,032** (£1,856; £928; £464) **Stalls** High

Form RPR

3425 **1** **Young Mr Grace (IRE)**[35] 2493 4-9-1 **74** .......... AMullen(7) 1 83
(TDEasterby) *led: kpt on wl fnl f: jst hld on* **12/1**

1301 **2** *1/2* **Kirkby's Treasure**[5] 3365 6-9-7 **73** 6ex .......... FLynch 5 81
(ABerry) *chsd ldrs: effrt on outside over 2f out: hung rt: styd on ins last: nt qckn fnl strides* **9/2**[2]

0043 **3** *hd* **Riska King**[4] 3397 4-9-0 **66** .......... RWinston 6 73
(RAFahey) *in tch: pushed lft over 2f out: kpt on wl fnl f* **11/1**

4063 **4** ½ **Waltzing Wizard**[3] 3409 5-7-13 **51** PFessey 10 57
(ABerry) *t.k.h: trckd ldrs: styd on fnl f* **9/1**

3153 **5** 1 **Efidium**[14] 3101 6-9-3 **69** DeanMcKeown 8 72
(NBycroft) *hld up: effrt on outer over 2f out: styd on same pce fnl f* **9/1**

0242 **6** 1½ **Stoic Leader (IRE)**[5] 3365 4-9-10 **79** LFletcher(3) 7 78
(RFFisher) *trckd ldrs: ev ch tl fdd jst ins last* **15/8**[1]

5U03 **7** 1½ **Tidy (IRE)**[9] 3235 4-10-0 **80** ACulhane 9 75
(MDHammond) *trckd ldrs: hmpd over 2f out: no ch after* **8/1**[3]

-003 **8** nk **Tantric**[33] 2528 5-8-6 **65** ow7 JDO'Reilly(7) 2 60
(JO'Reilly) *s.i.s: effrt on outer whn nt clr run 2f out: n.d after* **8/1**[3]

5244 **9** 1¼ **Shifty**[11] 3167 5-7-12 **50** oh1 (v) PMQuinn 3 41
(DNicholls) *s.i.s: sn drvn along: hdwy over 2f out: edgd rt: nvr on terms* **12/1**

0650 **10** ½ **Flying Edge (IRE)**[3] 3409 4-8-5 **57** WSupple 4 47
(EJAlston) *t.k.h in mid-div: nt clr run over 2f out: n.d after* **14/1**

1m 28.55s (1.45) **Going Correction** +0.35s/f (Good) **10** Ran SP% **125.6**
Speed ratings: **105,104,104,103,102 100,99,98,97,96**CSF £70.45 CT £650.73 TOTE £16.00: £3.40, £1.90, £3.00; EX 154.00.
**Owner** Norman Jackson **Bred** Michael Greany **Trained** Great Habton, N Yorks
■ Stewards Enquiry : A Mullen caution: careless riding

**FOCUS**
Quite a rough race, but fair form and it should prove reliable.

**NOTEBOOK**
**Young Mr Grace(IRE)** looked at his best after an absence of seven weeks. Considered possibly short of work after rapping himself on his previous start, he came wide in search of the quicker ground, causing a concertina effect, and in the end just held on to record his first win for over two years. His rider looks to have a future.
**Kirkby's Treasure**, under a 6lb penalty, raced hard against the stands'-side rail. Despite a tendency to hang, he stuck on really well and in the end just missed out.
**Riska King**, back in handicap company, had to dig deep to hold his place when left short of room. He stuck on well inside the last despite the going not being as quick as he likes, and he looks back to his best.
**Waltzing Wizard**, who hasn't won for over two years, took a keen grip and kept on stoutly despite racing close to the slower ground on the far side.
**Efidium**, warm beforehand, never looked a real threat despite his proximity at the finish. He really prefers quicker ground than he encountered here.
**Stoic Leader(IRE)**, weighted to turn the tables on Kirkby's Treasure, saw a lot of daylight and didn't truly see it out.
**Tidy(IRE)** looked to be just starting to struggle when running out of racing room completely against the stands'-side rail with two furlongs left to run.
**Tantric**, fitted with a net muzzle, found himself behind a wall and that was that.

## 3517 CARLISLE BRASS H'CAP — 6f 192y
**9:05** (9:07) (E) (0-70,71) 3-Y-O **£3,672** (£1,130; £565; £282) **Stalls High**

Form RPR

0635 **1** **Menai Straights**[25] 2756 3-8-10 **59** RFfrench 6 63
(RFFisher) *chsd ldrs: led appr fnl f: hld on towards fin* **12/1**

0320 **2** nk **Adorata (GER)**[11] 3180 3-9-1 **64** ACulhane 10 68
(JJay) *mid-div: effrt over 2f out: ev ch fnl f: nt qckn towards fin* **8/1**

0004 **3** 1 **Gasparini (IRE)**[14] 3102 3-8-8 **57** RWinston 4 58
(TDEasterby) *led after 1f tl appr fnl f: kpt on wl* **7/1**[3]

43-4 **4** 1½ **Micklegate**[19] 2937 3-8-12 **61** JFanning 5 58
(JDBethell) *chsd ldrs: styd on same pce appr fnl f* **14/1**

4020 **5** 1 **Impulsive Bid (IRE)**[7] 3301 3-9-0 **63** DarrenWilliams 3 58
(JeddO'Keeffe) *led 1f: chsd ldrs: one pce appr fnl f* **12/1**

-503 **6** 1½ **Firebird Rising (USA)**[19] 2937 3-8-10 **64** PMakin(5) 2 55
(TDBarron) *rrd s: bhd: hdwy over 2f out: kpt on fnl f* **12/1**

-504 **7** 1¼ **Borodinsky**[9] 3234 3-7-12 **47** oh3 PFessey 7 34
(REBarr) *mid-div: effrt over 2f out: kpt on: nvr rchd ldrs* **14/1**

50-0 **8** hd **Yorke's Folly (USA)**[17] 2984 3-8-7 **56** DeanMcKeown 11 43
(CWFairhurst) *bhd: effrt and nt clr run over 2f out: kpt on fnl f* **16/1**

-001 **9** 1¼ **Commander Bond**[8] 3280 3-9-8 **71** FLynch 1 55
(BSmart) *chsd ldrs: one pce whn nt clr run over 1f out* **9/2**[2]

1000 **10** 2½ **Capetown Girl**[16] 3006 3-9-4 **67** (p) VHalliday 8 44
(KRBurke) *mid-div: effrt 3f out: wknd appr fnl f* **12/1**

0-51 **11** 3 **Neqaawi**[19] 2937 3-9-3 **66** (t) WSupple 9 35
(BHanbury) *trckd ldrs: effrt on ins over 3f out: hung rt: lost pl over 1f out* **15/8**[1]

1m 29.64s (2.54) **Going Correction** +0.35s/f (Good) **11** Ran SP% **126.6**
Speed ratings: **99,98,97,95,94 92,91,91,89,87 83**CSF £112.57 CT £755.26 TOTE £17.30: £2.60, £3.20, £3.30; EX 280.30.
**Owner** M Maclennan **Bred** Theakston Stud **Trained** Ulverston, Cumbria
■ Stewards Enquiry : P Makin caution: careless riding

**FOCUS**
Another low-grade handicap with traffic problems. The form is sound but moderate.

**NOTEBOOK**
**Menai Straights**, with the cheekpieces left off, made it tenth time lucky.
**Adorata(GER)**continually swished her tail in the paddock. She seemed suited by the bit of give underfoot and, racing towards the inside, was in the end just held.
**Gasparini(IRE)** went on and soon stepped up the gallop. He fought back well and there may be even better to come.
**Micklegate**, who gave a problem or two at the start, showed a lot more than on her return here two weeks ago and clearly appreciates getting her toe in.
**Impulsive Bid(IRE)** ran a lot better and is clearly not at her best on fast ground.
**Firebird Rising(USA)**, slipping down the ratings, gave away ground standing on her back legs in the stalls. This was only her fifth ever start and she ought to be capable of better.
**Commander Bond**, 4lb higher on his return to turf, was going nowhere when left short of room towards the stands'-side rail.
**Neqaawi**, 7lb higher, looked to have run up very light. Sticking to the slower ground near the far side, she continually hung and dropped right away.

## 3518 RICHMOND HOTEL MAIDEN H'CAP — 2m 1f 52y
**9:35** (9:36) (F) (0-55,51) 4-Y-O+ **£3,066** (£876; £438) **Stalls High**

Form RPR

**1** **The Kelt (IRE)**[11] 3189 7-8-4 **35** (t) WSupple 14 48
(EoinDoyle, Ire) *s.i.s: hld up in rr: hdwy 8f out: led over 3f out: styd on strly ins last* **11/4**[1]

2044 **2** 4 **Tom Bell (IRE)**[17] 2978 4-8-11 **47** BSwarbrick(5) 9 56
(JGMO'Shea) *hld up in rr: hdwy on far side over 3f out: wnt 2nd 2f out: edgd lft: nt qckn fnl f* **11/2**[2]

-050 **3** 6 **Dancing Pearl**[14] 3108 6-8-12 **43** DarrenWilliams 5 45
(CJPrice) *s.i.s: hdwy 7f out: sn chsng ldrs: led 4f out: sn hdd: one pce fnl 2f* **6/1**[3]

00/5 **4** 1 **Percy-Verance (IRE)**[21] 2214 6-8-9 **40** RWinston 11 41
(JJQuinn) *in tch: effrt over 3f out: one pce* **16/1**

-054 **5** ¾ **Purdey**[21] 2874 4-8-12 **43** MFenton 6 43
(HMorrison) *hld up and bhd: effrt over 3f out: kpt on: nvr rchd ldrs* **11/4**[1]

3-60 **6** 13 **Ton-Chee**[35] 2186 5-8-0 **31** oh11 PMQuinn 2 17
(KWHogg) *trckd ldrs: t.k.h: effrt over 3f out: wknd over 1f out* **33/1**

064- **7** ¾ **Fly Kicker**[35] 3868 7-8-0 **31** oh1 (p) JBramhill 13 16
(WStorey) *mid-div: rn wd bnd over 4f out: lost pl over 1f out* **14/1**

-000 **8** nk **Bulgaria Moon**[25] 2759 4-8-8 **39** ACulhane 8 24
(CGrant) *chsd ldrs: drvn along 4f out: lost pl over 1f out* **25/1**

/506 **9** 2½ **Kristineau**[17] 2978 6-8-5 **43** (tp) PPMathers(7) 4 25
(MrsDianneSayer) *hld up and bhd: hdwy on wd outside whn hmpd bnd over 4f out: lost pl over 1f out* **14/1**

3005 **10** 1¼ **Mikasa (IRE)**[15] 3041 4-8-5 **36** RFfrench 1 17
(RFFisher) *trckd ldrs: rdn and lost pl over 3f out* **16/1**

0000 **11** shd **Diva Dancer**[25] 2759 4-7-9 **33** (b) DFentiman(7) 12 13
(JHetherton) *led 5f: chsd ldrs tl lost pl over 3f out* **25/1**

002/ **12** nk **Westernmost**[35] 3813 6-8-6 **40** TEaves(3) 10 20
(MTodhunter) *mid-div: drvn along 7f out: lost pl over 3f out* **8/1**

0046 **13** 15 **Balalaika Tune (IRE)**[14] 3099 5-7-8 **32** RoryMoore(7) 3 —
(WStorey) *led after 5f: hdd 4f out: lost pl and eased over 2f out* **16/1**

0040 **14** ½ **Blue Venture (IRE)**[3] 3411 4-8-13 **51** GBartley(7) 7 14
(PCHaslam) *hld up in last pl: a bhd* **14/1**

3m 59.18s (9.28) **Going Correction** +0.35s/f (Good) **14** Ran SP% **142.4**
Speed ratings: **92,90,87,86,86 80,80,79,78,78 78,77,70,70**CSF £20.96 CT £97.68 TOTE £3.80: £2.40, £2.00, £2.90; EX 23.30 Place 6 £288.79, Place 5 £123.48.
**Owner** J J P Murphy **Bred** Miss C Benson **Trained** Ireland
■ Eoin Doyle's first Flat winner in Britain.

**FOCUS**
A seller in all but name, and a modest pace in the early stages resulting in a slow winning time.

**NOTEBOOK**
**The Kelt(IRE)**, a winner over hurdles at Huntingdon in April, is a real stayer who seems suited by give in the ground. In the end he took this rock-bottom maiden handicap going right away.
**Tom Bell(IRE)**, stepping up in trip, made his effort on the inner turning in. He edged right across the track, joining the winner near the stands' side, and in the end proved very much second best.
**Dancing Pearl**, a winner three times over hurdles, is finding it hard to make an impact on the level.
**Percy-Verance(IRE)**, last seen in action over hurdles, looks devoid of any speed and all he does is stay.
**Purdey**, unplaced in eight starts now, tried to come from off what was not a strong early pace and she never looked like summoning up the speed to do so.
**Ton-Chee** took a keen hold on the heels of the leaders and was a contributor to trouble beginning the home turn.
**Westernmost** *Official explanation: jockey said gelding had finished lame; trainer confirmed this*
T/Plt: £589.80 to a £1 stake. Pool: £41,490.90. 51.35 winning tickets. T/Qpdt: £175.50 to a £1 stake. Pool: £3,416.50. 14.40 winning tickets. WG

# 3474 HAYDOCK (L-H)
Saturday, July 3

**OFFICIAL GOING: Good (good to soft in places)**
Wind: mod against Weather: fine

## 3519 BET365 LANCASHIRE OAKS (GROUP 2) (F&M) — 1m 3f 200y
**1:50** (1:51) (A) 3-Y-O+ **£58,000** (£22,000; £11,000; £5,000) **Stalls High**

Form RPR

0-31 **1** **Pongee**[42] 2297 4-9-3 96 JFortune 6 109
(LMCumani) *in tch: rdn over 4f out: hdwy u.p over 1f out: r.o to ld towards fin* **9/2**[2]

-222 **2** 1 **Sahool**[16] 2997 3-8-4 107 WSupple 4 107
(MPTregoning) *a.p: rdn over 2f out: struck on nose by rival's whip over 1f out: led 1f out: hdd towards fin* **11/8**[1]

5441 **3** nk **Danelissima (IRE)**[6] 3356 3-8-4 (b) TPQueally 8 107
(JSBolger, Ire) *hld up: rdn over over 2f out: wandered u.p over 1f out: r.o ins fnl f: nrst fin* **10/1**

-215 **4** ¾ **Hidden Hope**[16] 2997 3-8-5 106 ow1 SDrowne 1 106
(GWragg) *hld up in tch: hdwy over 2f out: kpt on u.p ins fnl f* **13/2**[3]

-214 **5** ½ **New Morning (IRE)**[16] 2997 3-8-5 104 ow1 NCallan 5 106
(MAJarvis) *led: rdn over 2f out: hdd 1f out: no ex towards fin* **13/2**[3]

2-32 **6** nk **Summitville**[17] 2993 4-9-3 107 MFenton 3 104
(JGGiven) *hld up: rdn and hdwy over 2f out: kpt on same pce towards fin* **7/1**

3-03 **7** 12 **Chantress**[42] 2297 4-9-3 92 JFanning 7 85
(MrsJRRamsden) *trckd ldrs tl rdn and wknd over 2f out* **66/1**

-445 **8** 3 **Si Si Amiga (IRE)**[23] 2807 3-8-4 94 MHills 2 80
(BWHills) *prom: rdn 4f out: wknd over 2f out* **50/1**

2m 32.9s (-2.26) **Going Correction** +0.10s/f (Good)
**WFA** 3 from 4yo 13lb **8** Ran SP% **112.0**
Speed ratings: **111,110,110,109,109 109,101,99**CSF £10.59 TOTE £5.30: £1.40, £1.10, £2.10; EX 11.70.
**Owner** Fittocks Stud **Bred** Fittocks Stud **Trained** Newmarket, Suffolk

**FOCUS**
Not a great Group Two, with Ribblesdale Stakes form (race 2997) more or less reproduced. It was run at a good gallop into a headwind in the home straight, making stamina a crucial factor in the closing stages. An acceptable winning time for the type of race.

**NOTEBOOK**
**Pongee**, a winner over course and distance six weeks ago, was being raised in class. However, she acted well on the easy ground and her undoubted stamina proved decisive.
**Sahool** finished second for the fourth race running but, that apart, does not appear to be doing anything wrong. She is clearly capable of winning a Group Two contest.
**Danelissima(IRE)**, with the blinkers back on, gets every yard of this trip and showed she is Group Two quality by going close. The Group One Yorkshire Oaks is now on the agenda.
**Hidden Hope** lacked a little tactical speed early in the straight, again falling only just short of what was required at this level.
**New Morning(IRE)**, whose stable has a good record in this race, is capable of winning a Group Three at least.
**Summitville** is close to top class at her best but fell below that level here. She was more exposed than some of her rivals, but faster ground would have helped.
**Si Si Amiga(IRE)** *Official explanation: jockey said filly emptied in the home straight*

## 3520 BIRCHLEY H'CAP — 1m 30y
**2:25** (2:26) (E) (0-70,70) 3-Y-O+ **£4,069** (£1,252; £626; £313) **Stalls Low**

Form RPR

1305 **1** **Parnassian**[11] 3177 4-9-2 **58** SDrowne 4 67
(GBBalding) *towards rr: pushed along over 4f out: hdwy whn swtchd rt over 1f out: edgd lft ins fnl f: sn led: r.o* **6/1**[3]

3200 **2** 1¼ **Rymer's Rascal**[9] 3247 12-8-7 **49** WSupple 11 55
(EJAlston) *midfield: hdwy over 2f out: led briefly ins fnl f: styd on* **25/1**

00-0 **3** ½ **Fair Spin**[15] 3038 4-9-7 **63** ACulhane 9 68
(MDHammond) *midfield: pushed along over 4f out: hdwy over 1f out: nt clr run ins fnl f: r.o* **16/1**

-660 **4** *nk* **Didnt Tell My Wife**[21] 2883 5-9-7 **63**........................ RMullen 17 67
(CFWall) *midfield: rdn over 2f out: hdwy over 1f out: n.m.r and struck by rival's whip ins fnl f: styd on* **16/1**

0545 **5** *1/2* **Apache Point (IRE)**[15] 3058 7-8-12 **54**........................ KimTinkler 1 57
(NTinkler) *midfield: hdwy over 2f out: chal ins fnl f: nt qckn towards fin* **8/1**

-302 **6** *nk* **Mallard (IRE)**[3] 3419 6-9-7 **63**........................ MFenton 2 65
(JGGiven) *prom: rdn and ev ch 1f out: no ex towards fin* **4/1**[1]

3342 **7** *hd* **Tojoneski**[2] 3441 5-8-1 **46**........................(p) JFMcDonald(3) 8 48
(IWMcinnes) *in tch: rdn over 2f out: hmpd ins fnl f: one pce towards fin* **11/2**[2]

6546 **8** *1 1/2* **Bought Direct**[30] 2614 5-8-13 **55**........................ KMcEvoy 3 53
(RJSmith) *towards rr: rdn and hdwy over 1f out: nvr trbld ldrs* **10/1**

3000 **9** *3* **Creskeld (IRE)**[50] 2078 5-10-0 **70**........................ RWinston 13 62
(BSmart) *prom: led over 4f out: hdd ins fnl f: sn btn and eased* **20/1**

6010 **10** *3/4* **Prince Of Gold**[13] 3127 4-9-11 **67**........................(p) NCallan 7 57
(RHollinshead) *trckd ldrs: rdn over 2f out: ev ch 1f out: no ex ins fnl f* **12/1**

0000 **11** *1 3/4* **Buthaina (IRE)**[7] 3291 4-8-3 **50**........................ PMakin(5) 6 36
(THCaldwell) *bhd: hdwy u.p over 1f out: no imp on ldrs* **33/1**

0000 **12** *1/2* **The Loose Screw (IRE)**[36] 2462 6-7-7 **40**........................(p) BSwarbrick(5) 18 25
(GMMoore) *prom: rdn over 2f out: sn wknd* **50/1**

-020 **13** *8* **Gemini Lady**[21] 2879 4-8-4 **46**........................ GDuffield 15 12
(MrsGSRees) *midfield: rdn over 2f out: wknd over 1f out* **33/1**

23-6 **14** *7* **How's Things**[131] 862 4-9-7 **63**........................ PaulEddery 16 13
(DHaydnJones) *trckd ldrs tl rdn and wknd over 3f out* **20/1**

6301 **15** *2 1/2* **Zawrak (IRE)**[40] 2356 5-8-11 **60**........................ NataliaGemelova(7) 10 4
(IWMcinnes) *a bhd* **12/1**

24-0 **16** *3/4* **Iftikhar (USA)**[43] 2272 5-9-4 **60**........................ NPollard 5 3
(WMBrisbourne) *s.i.s: a bhd* **25/1**

0306 **17** *5* **Mount Pekan (IRE)**[15] 3058 4-8-2 **44**........................ JMackay 12 —
(JSGoldie) *led: hdd over 4f out: wknd over 2f out* **33/1**

1m 45.56s (0.01) **Going Correction** +0.10s/f (Good) **17** Ran SP% **125.0**
Speed ratings: **103,101,101,100,100 100,99,98,95,94 92,92,84,77,74 74,69**CSF £157.67 CT £2391.26 TOTE £7.10: £2.00, £5.10, £3.90, £3.30; EX 151.80.
**Owner** Miss B Swire **Bred** Miss B Swire **Trained** Kimpton,Hants

**FOCUS**
The first three ran to form in what was only an average event.

**NOTEBOOK**
**Parnassian** often finds trouble in running but made his effort on the outside this time. He was winning for only the second time in 26 outings but the easy ground was in his favour.
**Rymer's Rascal**, well beaten in selling company last time, has otherwise run some fine races this season. He is still capable of winning at the age of 12.
**Fair Spin** has run over a variety of trips in recent races but a mile looks to suit him well nowadays.
**Didnt Tell My Wife**, well at home on turf over a mile on softish ground, bounced back to form after a below-par effort on sand.
**Apache Point(IRE)**, fourth and second in the two previous runnings of this race, is on a winning mark at present and looks to be gradually running back to peak form.
**Mallard(IRE)** is better on sand and had run well on Polytrack three days earlier. He put in a respectable effort but the Handicapper just has his measure on turf.
**Tojoneski** continues to run well and must surely win from his current mark one day if staying fresh.
**Gemini Lady** *Official explanation: jockey said filly hung right in home straight*

## 3521 BET365 OLD NEWTON CUP (HERITAGE H'CAP) 1m 3f 200y
2:55 (2:55) (B) (0-110,103) 3-Y-0+ **£40,600** (£15,400; £7,700; £3,500) **Stalls** High

Form RPR

22-2 **1** **Alkaased (USA)**[28] 2691 4-9-1 **94**........................ JFortune 11 111+
(LMCumani) *trckd ldrs: led 2f out: edgd lft over 1f out: sn clr: r.o wl* **7/1**[2]

0335 **2** *4* **Crow Wood**[13] 3118 5-9-1 **94**........................ KMcEvoy 5 103+
(JGGiven) *midfield: hdwy 2f out: nt clr run over 1f out: wnt 2nd wl ins fnl f: no ch w wnr* **33/1**

/262 **3** *nk* **Grampian**[28] 2672 5-9-9 **102**........................ MFenton 17 109
(JGGiven) *bhd: hdwy over 1f out: sn hung lft: styd on* **33/1**

-604 **4** *1 1/4* **Hambleden**[14] 3075 7-9-6 **99**........................ NCallan 7 104
(MAJarvis) *led: rdn and hdd 2f out: styd on same pce* **16/1**

-014 **5** *shd* **Royal Cavalier**[57] 1925 7-9-5 **98**........................ ACulhane 14 103
(RHollinshead) *midfield: rdn over 2f out: hdwy over 1f out: kpt on* **16/1**

4123 **6** *nk* **Swift Tango (IRE)**[14] 3075 4-9-7 **100**........................ KDarley 6 105
(EALDunlop) *hld up: rdn and hdwy over 2f out: styd on same pce fnl f* **10/1**

4214 **7** *1* **Oldenway**[14] 3097 5-7-12 **77** oh1........................ PFessey 16 80
(RAFahey) *midfield: rdn over 2f out: hdwy over 1f out: kpt on one pce* **40/1**

-116 **8** *1/2* **Swagger Stick (USA)**[16] 2999 3-7-12 **90**........................ JMackay 1 92
(JLDunlop) *prom: ev ch 2f out: wknd ins fnl f* **9/2**[1]

-340 **9** *shd* **Counsel's Opinion (IRE)**[14] 3075 7-9-10 **103**........................ RMullen 3 105
(CFWall) *s.i.s: t.k.h: midfield after 2f: effrt whn n.m.r 1f out: one pce* **14/1**

-231 **10** *nk* **Bourgeois**[40] 2365 7-9-5 **98**........................ RWinston 12 100
(TDEasterby) *midfield: rdn and hdwy over 3f out: wknd ins fnl f* **14/1**

0650 **11** *1 1/4* **Trust Rule**[14] 3075 4-9-1 **94**........................ MHills 8 97+
(BWHills) *prom: rdn 2f out: wknd over 1f out* **9/1**

1-61 **12** *6* **Balkan Knight**[53] 2022 4-8-5 **84**........................(v) TPQueally 15 74
(DRLoder) *towards rr: effrt over 2f out: no imp* **7/1**[2]

-004 **13** *5* **Turbo (IRE)**[49] 2110 5-9-0 **93**........................(p) SDrowne 2 75
(GBBalding) *a bhd* **8/1**[3]

5305 **14** *4* **Santando**[133] 849 4-9-4 **97**........................(v) GDuffield 9 73
(CEBrittain) *trckd ldrs: rdn over 4f out: wknd over 2f out* **20/1**

314 **15** *20* **Haadef**[15] 3032 3-8-7 **99**........................ WSupple 4 43
(JHMGosden) *hmpd after 2f: a bhd* **8/1**[3]

2m 32.3s (-2.86) **Going Correction** +0.10s/f (Good)
**WFA** 3 from 4yo+ 13lb **15** Ran SP% **122.7**
Speed ratings: **113,110,110,109,109 109,108,108,107,107 106,102,99,96,83**CSF £232.96 CT £6995.40 TOTE £7.70: £2.70, £6.60, £11.80; EX 180.80 Trifecta £1193.20 Part won. Pool: £1,680.70. 0.10 winning tickets..
**Owner** M R Charlton **Bred** Clovelly Farms **Trained** Newmarket, Suffolk

**FOCUS**
An apparently competitive renewal of this valuable handicap, but taken with incredible ease by the improving winner. With hindsight, the placed horses probably had an impossible task at the weights. The form looks solid and the winning time was very creditable for the grade, 0.6 seconds faster than the Lancashire Oaks.

**NOTEBOOK**
**Alkaased(USA)** had never previously raced on ground softer than good but proved a revelation. He looks highly progressive and connections could be eyeing up Pattern company soon.
**Crow Wood** had no chance with the impressive winner but looked well suited by the longer trip and now has options from ten furlongs upwards.
**Grampian** ran well from a tough handicap mark and a tricky draw. Unfortunately, the Handicapper is unlikely to relent if he continues to produce performances like this.
**Hambleden**, again adopting the role of front-runner, ran his race but time will show it was impossible to concede weight to the winner.
**Royal Cavalier** did well again but, like so many of those who chased the winner home, he was up against it at the weights.
**Swift Tango(IRE)** is an admirable performer in every respect, and again acquitted himself well from a tough handicap mark. Connections believe he is better on faster ground, but there was little wrong with this effort.
**Oldenway** was in better company here but ran with credit, albeit off joint bottom weight.
**Swagger Stick(USA)** ran respectably but is 10lb higher than for his last win, and he was not able to make the necessary improvement off the same mark as when beaten last time.
**Counsel's Opinion(IRE)** had an unenviable task off topweight in a race as competitive as this. Nonetheless, he was not disgraced.
**Bourgeois** was not far off the placed horses but found a 3lb rise too much in this company.
**Turbo(IRE)** *Official explanation: jockey said gelding was never travelling*
**Haadef** *Official explanation: vet said colt injured its near fore*

## 3522 THWAITES SMOOTH BEER CONDITIONS STKS 6f
3:35 (3:36) (C) 3-Y-0+ **£8,932** (£3,388; £1,694; £770) **Stalls** Centre

Form RPR

1065 **1** **Quito (IRE)**[7] 3308 7-8-10 **110**........................(b) ACulhane 7 104
(DWChapman) *hld up: hdwy over 1f out: led wl ins fnl f: r.o* **7/4**[1]

6035 **2** *1* **Dazzling Bay**[14] 3074 4-8-10 **102**........................(b) WSupple 6 101
(TDEasterby) *racd keenly: hld up in tch: rdn and hdwy over 1f out: led ins fnl f: sn wandered and hdd: nt pce of wnr cl home* **10/3**[2]

600- **3** *1 3/4* **Continent**[301] 4714 7-8-10 **112**........................ JFortune 4 96
(DNicholls) *s.s: in rr: hdwy 2f out: led 1f out: sn hdd: nt qckn towards fin* **8/1**

020 **4** *1* **Tom Tun**[30] 2625 9-9-1 **93**........................(b) MFenton 9 98
(JBalding) *in tch: effrt 2f out: one pce ins fnl f* **12/1**

4010 **5** *nk* **Circuit Dancer (IRE)**[14] 3074 4-8-10 **96**........................ KDarley 2 92
(ABerry) *led: rdn and hdd 2f out: no ex ins fnl f* **11/2**[3]

1-54 **6** *4* **Dowager**[21] 2903 3-8-4 **97**........................ RLMoore 1 80
(RHannon) *in tch: led 2f out: rdn and hdd 1f out: wknd ins fnl f* **7/1**

6020 **7** *10* **Jalouhar**[6] 3337 4-8-10 **46**........................ TWoodley 8 50
(BPJBaugh) *prom tl rdn and wknd over 2f out* **125/1**

0000 **8** *12* **Rosselli (USA)**[6] 3337 8-8-3 **46**........................ CEly(7) 5 14
(ABerry) *prominent tl rdn and wknd over 2f out* **125/1**

1m 16.48s (1.59) **Going Correction** +0.30s/f (Good)
**WFA** 3 from 4yo+ 6lb **8** Ran SP% **107.7**
Speed ratings: **101,99,97,96,95 90,76,60**CSF £6.58 TOTE £2.40: £1.20, £1.50, £2.50; EX 6.60.
**Owner** Michael Hill **Bred** Sheikh Mohammed Bin Rashid Al Maktoum **Trained** Stillington, N Yorks

**FOCUS**
The form looks mixed, with the seventh not far enough behind despite having been beaten 20l to have the winner running to form. Some smart sprinters, with Continent and Quito, in that order, most favoured by the conditions. The winning time was moderate for the grade, 0.45 seconds slower than the following 0 to 95 handicap for three-year-olds.

**NOTEBOOK**
**Quito(IRE)**, second best to Continent at the weights, has developed into a smart sprinter and takes his racing well. This race did not play to his strengths, and it would be no surprise to see him win in Group company before the end of the season.
**Dazzling Bay** made a bold bid but again showed a tendency to come off a straight line. Nonetheless, a good effort at the weights.
**Continent** was best-in at the weights but was out of form last year. However, there are better days in store this time round, particularly on easy ground, if he can reproduce the promise of this seasonal debut.
**Tom Tun**, a useful handicapper, was up against it here, so his finishing position represented a decent effort.
**Circuit Dancer(IRE)** often misses the break but quickly found himself in front here. Despite the change in tactics, he still ran close to the level that might have been expected.
**Dowager** had a bit to do at the weights. *Official explanation: jockey said filly stopped very quickly in final furlong*

## 3523 DUKE OF LANCASTER'S OWN YEOMANRY H'CAP 6f
4:05 (4:05) (C) (0-95,94) 3-Y-0 **£10,270** (£3,160; £1,580; £790) **Stalls** Centre

Form RPR

-422 **1** **Flipando (IRE)**[20] 2907 3-8-6 **79**........................ KDarley 5 93
(TDBarron) *trckd ldrs: rdn over 1f out: r.o to ld last strides* **3/1**[1]

1 **2** *hd* **Doitnow (IRE)**[17] 2984 3-8-8 **81**........................ RWinston 9 94
(RAFahey) *towards rr: hdwy 3f out: led over 1f out: sn hung rt: hdd last strides* **8/1**[3]

5106 **3** *3* **Four Amigos (USA)**[14] 3077 3-8-10 **83**........................ KMcEvoy 11 87
(JGGiven) *bhd: hdwy over 1f out: styd on ins fnl f: nt rch ldrs* **11/1**

6411 **4** *3/4* **Bohola Flyer (IRE)**[12] 3158 3-8-5 **78**........................ RLMoore 1 80
(RHannon) *in rr: hdwy 2f out: kpt on ins fnl f* **7/1**[2]

5200 **5** *shd* **Lets Get It On (IRE)**[13] 3122 3-8-4 **77**........................ PFessey 2 79
(JJQuinn) *bhd: rdn and hdwy whn swtchd lft over 1f out: kpt on ins fnl f* **20/1**

0640 **6** *3 1/2* **George The Best (IRE)**[7] 3309 3-7-7 **71** oh1........................ BSwarbrick(5) 10 62
(MDHammond) *prom: rdn to ld briefly wl over 1f out: wknd ins fnl f* **25/1**

0502 **7** *1* **Celtic Thunder**[10] 3203 3-8-11 **84**........................ JFortune 14 72
(TJEtherington) *hld up: rdn and hdwy over 1f out: kpt on: nvr trbld ldrs* **7/1**[2]

2510 **8** *1 3/4* **Times Review (USA)**[21] 2897 3-8-11 **84**........................ WSupple 7 67
(TDEasterby) *midfield: rdn 2f out: sn outpcd* **20/1**

6000 **9** *1* **Iskander**[17] 2981 3-8-8 **81**........................(b) NCallan 6 61
(KARyan) *midfield: rdn 2f out: no imp* **16/1**

2251 **10** *3/4* **Under My Spell**[21] 2875 3-8-3 **76**........................ RMullen 16 54
(PDEvans) *trckd ldrs: rdn over 1f out: wknd fnl f* **14/1**

0-05 **11** *1/2* **Skyharbor**[14] 3090 3-8-7 **80**........................ MHills 12 56
(DNicholls) *chsd ldrs tl rdn and wknd over 2f out* **16/1**

1504 **12** *1/2* **Foursquare (IRE)**[21] 2877 3-9-2 **89**........................ ACulhane 15 64
(JMackie) *led after 1f: rdn and hdd wl over 1f out: sn wknd* **10/1**

2-10 **13** *4* **Bonne De Fleur**[21] 2897 3-9-7 **94**........................ TPQueally 13 57
(BSmart) *led 1f: remained cl up: rdn 2f out: wknd over 1f out* **16/1**

2020 **14** *3* **Piccolo Prince**[17] 2981 3-7-12 **71** oh3........................ JBramhill 4 25
(EJAlston) *in tch: rdn 2f out: wknd over 1f out* **33/1**

6-02 **15** *1* **Mind Alert**[13] 3122 3-7-12 **71** oh1........................ JMackay 3 22
(TDEasterby) *in tch: rdn 2f out: wknd over 1f out* **16/1**

1m 16.03s (1.14) **Going Correction** +0.30s/f (Good) **15** Ran SP% **125.0**
Speed ratings: **104,103,99,98,98 93,92,90,88,87 87,86,81,77,75**CSF £25.11 CT £245.57 TOTE £3.70: £1.80, £2.50, £2.40; EX 28.90.
**Owner** Mrs J Hazell **Bred** Denis McDonnell **Trained** Maunby, N Yorks

**FOCUS**
A well-contested race, and decent form, particularly from the first two, who dominated the finish. The winner looks progressive and the runner-up did particularly well from the middle of the weights on only his second outing.

**NOTEBOOK**
**Flipando(IRE)** had been raised 2lb for finishing second last time, but just made it. He is versatile, being effective at both six and seven furlongs and on fast and soft ground, and can probably progress a bit more.
**Doitnow(IRE)** is probably still a bit green and seemed to get lonely in the closing stages, hence his tendency to wander. Nonetheless, this was a fine run from a challenging handicap mark considering his lack of experience.
**Four Amigos(USA)**, comfortable on the easy ground, showed he gets this trip, though unable to trouble the leading pair.
**Bohola Flyer(IRE)** continues to rise in the weights, but she has been in fine form and this was another decent effort.
**Lets Get It On(IRE)** has never won in handicap company but she has been running well at this trip and any concession from the Handicapper should be noted.

## 3524 ELLESMERE H'CAP 5f
**4:40** (4:41) (E ) (0-70,68) 3-Y-0+ **£3,913** (£1,204; £602; £301) **Stalls Centre**

Form RPR
0111 **1** **Foley Millennium (IRE)**[13] 3126 6-9-7 **62**.......... NPollard 9 74
(MQuinn) *mde all: rdn over 1f out: jst hld on* **9/2[1]**
0015 **2** *shd* **Laurel Dawn**[3] 3407 6-9-1 **59**.......... JFMcDonald(3) 8 71
(IWMcInnes) *bmpd s: bhd: hdwy over 1f out: r.o strly ins fnl f: jst failed* **10/1**
0-00 **3** *nk* **Intellibet One**[13] 3126 4-8-13 **54**.......... NCallan 13 65
(PDEvans) *in tch: rdn over 1f out: r.o ins fnl f* **25/1**
0000 **4** *3/4* **Viewforth**[7] 3314 6-9-12 **67**..........(b) WSupple 7 75
(JSGoldie) *stmbld s: hld up: rdn over 2f out: hdwy over 1f out: styd on same pce towards fin* **7/1[2]**
0033 **5** *nk* **Blessed Place**[12] 3151 4-8-6 **47**..........(p) TPQueally 12 54
(DJSFfrenchDavis) *chsd ldrs: rdn over 1f out: nt qckn ins fnl f* **14/1**
2050 **6** *1/2* **Dunn Deal (IRE)**[37] 2423 4-9-4 **64**.......... BSwarbrick(5) 6 69
(WMBrisbourne) *chsd ldrs: rdn over 1f out: kpt on same pce* **16/1**
0003 **7** *1* **Sharp Hat**[3] 3407 10-9-7 **62**.......... ACulhane 17 64
(DWChapman) *midfield: rdn over 1f out: one pce ins fnl f* **7/1[2]**
6100 **8** *1/2* **Full Pitch**[36] 2455 8-9-6 **68**.......... KirbyHarris(7) 10 68
(WJenks) *dwlt: bhd: styd on fnl f: nvr nrr* **33/1**
5410 **9** *1* **Malahide Express (IRE)**[3] 3407 4-8-10 **58**.......... JDO'Reilly(7) 2 54
(EJAlston) *prom: rdn over 1f out: wknd ins fnl f* **10/1**
0050 **10** *1/2* **Certa Cito**[28] 2670 4-9-0 **55**.......... JFortune 4 50
(TDEasterby) *in tch: rdn over 1f out: wknd wl ins fnl f* **25/1**
-240 **11** *1/2* **Green Ridge**[8] 3273 3-9-5 **65**.......... PaulEddery 11 58
(PWD'Arcy) *dwlt: in tch: lost pl 3f out: sn nt clr run: no imp after* **20/1**
0-00 **12** *1 1/4* **Blues Princess**[24] 2778 4-8-8 **49** ow1..........(b) RWinston 5 37
(RAFahey) *dwlt: towards rr: effrt 2f out: no imp* **25/1**
5000 **13** *1/2* **Zargus**[9] 3243 5-8-13 **57**.......... LPKeniry(3) 15 43
(AMBalding) *prom tl rdn and wknd over 1f out* **15/2[3]**
0064 **14** *hd* **Mynd**[7] 3314 4-9-1 **63**.......... DTudhope(7) 16 49
(RMWhitaker) *in tch: rdn and wknd over 1f out* **16/1**
0004 **15** *shd* **Mystery Pips**[12] 3147 4-8-5 **46**..........(v) KimTinkler 19 31
(NTinkler) *racd alone stands' side: in tch: rdn over 1f out: sn wknd* **20/1**
-006 **16** *1 1/2* **Star Applause**[12] 3147 4-8-1 **42**.......... JMackay 18 22
(JSGoldie) *a bhd* **40/1**
0-00 **17** *1 1/2* **Blessingindisguise**[11] 3169 11-8-2 **43**..........(b) PFessey 20 18
(MWEasterby) *towards rr: rdn over 2f out: no imp* **16/1**
0060 **18** *1 1/2* **Percy Douglas**[7] 3299 4-8-4 **45**..........(v) AnnStokell 1 14
(MissAStokell) *in tch: rdn over 2f out: sn wknd* **40/1**

62.92 secs (0.85) **Going Correction** +0.30s/f (Good)
**WFA** 3 from 4yo+ 5lb **18 Ran SP% 132.9**
Speed ratings: **105,104,104,103,102 101,100,99,97,97 96,94,93,93,93 90,88,85**CSF £47.52 CT £1065.25 TOTE £4.10: £1.60, £2.70, £7.20, £2.40; EX 44.90 Place 6 £226.66, Place 5 £118.22.
**Owner** Mrs S G Davies **Bred** Elperefa Bloodstock **Trained** Sparsholt, Oxon

**FOCUS**
Plenty of runners, though no great depth. The winner continues in fine form and many of the others will win in their turn.

**NOTEBOOK**
**Foley Millennium(IRE)** putting his natural speed to good use, was winning for the fourth time in succession. He only just held on but is in such good form there could be more to come.
**Laurel Dawn** has risen 10 lbs in the weights but is still favourably handicapped on his form of past seasons. On his day, he is still capable of winning, as he nearly demonstrated here.
**Intellibet One**, on a winning mark and returning to form, could be dangerous in the coming weeks.
**Viewforth** is handicapped to win at present and seems to coming back to his best, so he should be kept in mind from now on.
**Blessed Place** stays six furlongs but is at least as effective over this trip. He has been back in form in his last three races and can win off his current mark.
**Dunn Deal(IRE)** is 5lb above his winning mark, so this was not a bad effort. He appreciated the easier ground.
**Sharp Hat** continues to show plenty of life and a 23rd success is quite possible.
T/Plt: £98.10 to a £1 stake. Pool: £76,651.25. 570.25 winning tickets. T/Qpdt: £12.70 to a £1 stake. Pool: £3,276.50. 190.00 winning tickets. DO

# 3227 LEICESTER (R-H)
## Saturday, July 3

**OFFICIAL GOING: Good (good to firm in places)**
After recent rain the course looked in magnificent condition. There was quite a fresh wind helping the horses in the straight.
Wind: Fresh behind Weather: Cloudy

## 3525 VISTA CLASSIFIED STKS 7f 9y
**2:00** (2:00) (E ) 3-Y-0+ **£5,512** (£1,696; £848; £424) **Stalls Low**

Form RPR
01- **1** **Alinda (IRE)**[256] 5687 3-8-5 70.......... SCarson 9 83+
(PWHarris) *racd stands' side: s.i.s: hld up: hdwy 2f out: rdn to ld ins fnl f: edgd rt: r.o* **12/1**
2334 **2** *3 1/2* **Samuel Charles**[14] 3079 6-9-3 71.......... SWKelly 11 78
(WMBrisbourne) *racd alone far side: w ldrs: rdn over 2f out: styd on same pce fnl f* **9/2[2]**
3410 **3** *3/4* **Lyca Ballerina**[7] 3312 3-8-8 73.......... WRyan 10 75
(BWHills) *racd stands' side: mid-div: rdn 1/2-way: styd on same pce fnl f* **5/1[3]**
4335 **4** *1* **Mistral Sky**[14] 3086 5-9-2 66..........(b) BDoyle 6 72
(MrsStefLiddiard) *racd stands' side: chsd ldrs: led over 2f out: sn rdn: hdd & wknd ins fnl f* **7/1**
60-1 **5** *3* **Override (IRE)**[129] 886 4-9-4 75.......... LFletcher(3) 5 70
(JMPEustace) *racd stands' side: hld up: hdwy over 2f out: wknd fnl f* **8/1**
0524 **6** *1 3/4* **Go Yellow**[11] 3180 3-8-2 69 ow1.......... DerekNolan(7) 4 61
(PDEvans) *racd stands' side: chsd ldrs: rdn and ev chnace over 2f out: wknd over 1f out* **12/1**
2641 **7** *1 1/2* **Baker Of Oz**[26] 2737 3-8-10 72.......... PDobbs 8 58
(RHannon) *racd stands' side: chsd ldr: rdn over 2f out: wknd over 1f out* **7/2[1]**
0034 **8** *6* **Bertocelli**[12] 3155 3-8-8 68.......... AMcCarthy 2 41
(GGMargarson) *led stands' side: hdd over 5f out: wknd over 2f out* **11/1**
-040 **9** *1 3/4* **Juste Pour L'Amour**[22] 2845 4-9-6 74..........(b[1]) RPrice 3 40
(PLGilligan) *racd stands' side: led over 5f out: rdn and hdd over 2f out: sn wknd* **10/1**
00-0 **10** *5* **Cross Ash (IRE)**[70] 1603 4-9-4 72.......... DSweeney 7 25
(RHollinshead) *unruly stalls: racd stands' side: hld up: rdn and wknd over 2f out* **40/1**

1m 23.66s (-2.44) **Going Correction** -0.275s/f (Firm)
**WFA** 3 from 4yo+ 8lb **10 Ran SP% 115.9**
Speed ratings: **102,98,97,96,92 90,88,82,80,74**CSF £64.96 TOTE £11.90: £3.50, £2.00, £2.60; EX 71.60.
**Owner** Mrs P W Harris & E Jehu **Bred** Yeomanstown Stud **Trained** Ringshall, Bucks

**FOCUS**
An ordinary contest, but it was run at a sound pace. The form is sound and the unexposed winner posted a decent effort for the grade.

**NOTEBOOK**
**Alinda(IRE)**, the least exposed in the field, won with something in hand and looks capable of scoring again.
**Samuel Charles**, switched to race alone on the far side, was always up with the pace and was beaten only by a progressive animal. He is proving wonderfully consistent and deserves a change of luck.
**Lyca Ballerina** kept plugging away, but this trip looked to be on the sharp side for her.
**Mistral Sky** had quite a stiff task on these terms, but was far from disgraced.
**Override(IRE)** ran as though he needed this outing, his first since February.
**Baker Of Oz**, off the bridle soon after halfway, looked to find this trip too sharp.

## 3526 VISTA (S) STKS 5f 2y
**2:30** (2:31) (G ) 2-Y-0 **£2,912** (£832; £416) **Stalls Low**

Form RPR
5000 **1** **Tipsy Lillie**[23] 2812 2-7-13.......... MHalford(7) 9 48
(JulianPoulton) *trckd ldrs: led over 1f out: r.o* **7/2[2]**
0 **2** *hd* **Russian Servana (IRE)**[10] 3192 2-8-3.......... FPFerris(3) 7 47
(MJAttwater) *s.i.s: hld up: hdwy over 1f out: swtchd rt ins fnl f: r.o u.p* **20/1**
0365 **3** *2 1/2* **Concert Time**[8] 3278 2-8-1.......... RThomas(5) 5 38
(CRDore) *led over 3f: edgd lft and no ex ins fnl f* **6/1**
606 **4** *1 1/2* **Justenjoy Yourself**[16] 3021 2-8-3.......... BReilly(3) 3 33
(CADwyer) *chsd ldrs: rdn and ev ch over 1f out: styd on same pce* **11/2[3]**
0135 **5** *1* **Story Of One (IRE)**[23] 2799 2-9-2.......... BDoyle 2 39
(NPLittmoden) *chsd ldrs: rdn 1/2-way: wknd ins fnl f* **11/4[1]**
60 **6** *nk* **Jonny Fox'S (IRE)**[24] 2773 2-8-11..........(b[1]) DSweeney 6 33
(JGallagher) *s.i.s and bmpd s: sn prom: rdn over 1f out: wknd fnl f* **8/1**
00 **7** *1 3/4* **Fellbeck Fred**[9] 3248 2-8-11.......... SWKelly 8 27
(CWThornton) *hld up: outpcd over 3f out: n.d after* **20/1**
00 **8** *1/2* **Eternal Sunshine (IRE)**[18] 2960 2-8-3.......... RMiles(3) 4 20
(RPElliott) *w ldr 3f: wknd over 1f out* **50/1**
200 **9** *3* **Mermaid's Cry**[23] 2812 2-8-6.......... RHavlin 1 —
(RBrotherton) *s.i.s: hdwy 1/2-way: wknd over 1f out* **8/1**

61.98 secs (1.05) **Going Correction** -0.275s/f (Firm) **9 Ran SP% 112.3**
Speed ratings: **80,79,75,73,71 71,68,67,62**CSF £69.79 TOTE £5.20: £1.50, £4.30, £3.20; EX 83.50.There was no bid for the winner. Russian Servana was claimed by Jeff Pearce for £6,000.
**Owner** Mrs A C Guinle **Bred** Southill Stud **Trained** Kentford, Suffolk

**FOCUS**
A poor race and a very slow time, even for a two-year-old seller.

**NOTEBOOK**
**Tipsy Lillie** took advantage of the drop in class, although she had little to spare in the end.
**Russian Servana(IRE)** still looked a little green, but showed enough to suggest she can win one of these events, especially as it looks as though another furlong may well bring about a bit of improvement.
**Concert Time**, who gave the impression she didn't stay last time, had no excuses here.
**Justenjoy Yourself** didn't find any improvement for the drop in class.
**Story Of One(IRE)** probably didn't run too badly considering he was giving plenty of weight away all round. However, he does look below the form he showed earlier on in the season.
**Mermaid's Cry** *Official explanation: trainer said filly lost its action*

## 3527 VISTA CHARITY H'CAP 1m 9y
**3:05** (3:05) (D ) (0-80,79) 3-Y-0 **£7,299** (£2,246; £1,123; £561) **Stalls High**

Form RPR
4124 **1** **Dr Thong**[14] 3089 3-9-2 **79**.......... NDeSouza(5) 3 87
(PFICole) *plld hrd and prom: trckd ldr 6f out: led over 2f out: rdn clr over 1f out: jst hld on* **5/1[2]**
3061 **2** *hd* **Evaluator (IRE)**[11] 3180 3-9-0 **75**.......... RMiles(3) 9 91+
(TGMills) *hld up: hdwy over 3f out: nt clr run and lost pl over 2f out: swtchd lft and rapid hdwy ins fnl f: fin wl: unlucky* **9/2[1]**
3310 **3** *1 1/4* **Burley Flame**[16] 3001 3-9-5 **77**.......... BDoyle 5 82
(JGGiven) *chsd ldrs: shkn up over 3f out: outpcd over 1f out: r.o ins fnl f* **13/2[3]**
0403 **4** *3/4* **Spin King (IRE)**[21] 2880 3-8-13 **76**.......... HayleyTurner(5) 8 79
(MLWBell) *a.p: chsd wnr over 2f out: rdn and edgd rt over 1f out: no ex ins fnl f* **8/1**
0-50 **5** *1/2* **Trois Etoiles (IRE)**[11] 3180 3-8-2 **60**.......... DKinsella 10 62
(JWHills) *hld up: hdwy over 2f out: rdn and edgd rt over 1f out: styd on same pce ins fnl f* **14/1**
1223 **6** *2 1/2* **Foley Prince**[12] 3155 3-9-0 **72**.......... RHavlin 11 68
(MrsStefLiddiard) *hld up: hdwy u.p 3f out: styd on same pce appr fnl f* **8/1**
50-4 **7** *nk* **Iffy**[150] 675 3-8-2 **60**.......... CCatlin 1 55
(PDCundell) *s.i.s: hld up: hdwy over 2f out: styd on same pce appr fnl f* **16/1**
1204 **8** *3/4* **Phluke**[38] 2400 3-9-0 **72**.......... SCarson 2 66
(RFJohnsonHoughton) *mid-div: sn pushed along: hdwy over 3f out: wknd fnl f* **9/1**
-424 **9** *4* **Leaping Brave (IRE)**[22] 2834 3-9-4 **76**.......... AMcCarthy 4 60
(BRMillman) *led over 5f: wknd over 1f out* **14/1**
40-3 **10** *3* **Flying Adored**[74] 1519 3-9-0 **72**.......... SWKelly 7 50
(JLDunlop) *s.i.s: hld up: rdn over 3f out: n.d* **9/1**
00-0 **11** *1* **Binnion Bay (IRE)**[31] 2576 3-9-6 **78**.......... PDobbs 12 53
(RHannon) *s.i.s: hld up: a in rr* **33/1**

-254 **12** *nk* **Jarvo**[14] 3106 3-8-8 **66** DSweeney 6 41
(NPLittmoden) *prom over 5f* **16/1**

1m 40.89s (-1.71) **Going Correction** -0.075s/f (Good) **12** Ran SP% **118.4**
Speed ratings: **105,104,103,102,102 99,99,98,94,91 90,90**CSF £27.72 CT £152.08 TOTE £4.00: £2.20, £2.60, £2.30; EX 19.90.
**Owner** Frank Stella **Bred** Mascalls Stud **Trained** Whatcombe, Oxon
■ Nelson De Souza's first British winner, to go with 30 in his native Brazil.

**FOCUS**
A competitive-enough contest and the pace was sound. The form should prove reliable, with the second unlucky and rated as the clear winner.

**NOTEBOOK**
**Dr Thong** was again very keen early on, just as he had been at Newmarket. He was a lucky winner as the race turned out, but he still looks to be on the upgrade and should be capable of adding to this.
**Evaluator(IRE)** ◆ was a most unlucky loser, for having just moved onto the heels of the leaders he was carried back by the weakening Leaping Brave, losing him at least five lengths in the process. He ran on to such good effect when eventually switched outside inside the final furlong that he would have been a clear winner in another few strides.
**Burley Flame** found this more his level, but may have appreciated more use being made of him.
**Spin King(IRE)** is gradually dropping in the weights, but this trip just seems to stretch him.
**Trois Etoiles(IRE)** seemed to stay this longer trip well enough and will certainly find easier opportunities than she faced here.

## 3528 EUROPEAN BREEDERS FUND FILLIES' H'CAP — 1m 3f 183y
**3:40** (3:40) (D) (0-85,82) 3-Y-0+ **£8,092** (£2,490; £1,245; £622) **Stalls** High

Form RPR
3131 **1** **Portrait Of A Lady (IRE)**[23] 2809 3-9-8 **81** WRyan 1 89
(HRACecil) *trckd ldr: led over 3f out: rdn out* **1/1**[1]
1-50 **2** *1 1/4* **Keep On Movin' (IRE)**[80] 1394 3-8-10 **72** RMiles(3) 2 78
(TGMills) *a.p: rdn and ev ch fr over 2f out: edgd rt over 1f out: styd on* **9/1**
650- **3** *5* **Gaelic Roulette (IRE)**[266] 5490 4-9-10 **70** BDoyle 3 68
(PWHarris) *sn led: hdd over 3f out: outpcd fnl 2f* **9/1**
4612 **4** *2 1/2* **Compton Eclaire (IRE)**[4] 3393 4-8-12 **58** CCatlin 4 52
(GAButler) *s.i.s: hld up: outpcd over 3f out: n.d* **10/3**[2]
3-31 **5** *11* **Karamea (SWI)**[63] 1770 3-9-9 **82** SWKelly 5 58
(JLDunlop) *chsd ldrs over 8f* **5/1**[3]

2m 33.42s (-1.26) **Going Correction** -0.075s/f (Good)
**WFA** 3 from 4yo 13lb **5** Ran SP% **109.7**
Speed ratings: **101,100,96,95,87**CSF £10.52 TOTE £1.70: £1.10, £3.30; EX 8.60.
**Owner** J Shack **Bred** Pat Garvey **Trained** Newmarket, Suffolk

**FOCUS**
An ordinary gallop which didn't suit the winner, who looks capable of better. This was not all that competitive but the first two showed improved form.

**NOTEBOOK**
**Portrait Of A Lady(IRE)** doesn't do anything quickly and wouldn't have been suited by the steady pace. With more to come as she steps up in trip, she looks one to keep on the right side of.
**Keep On Movin'(IRE)** proved a persistent challenger, but you always felt that the winner could have found more had she needed to.
**Gaelic Roulette(IRE)** had something of a soft lead, but was easily brushed aside once the race began in earnest. However, she should strip sharper for the outing.
**Compton Eclaire(IRE)**, held up in a slowly-run race, didn't have things fall right for her.
**Karamea(SWI)** dropped away tamely when the pace lifted and was most disappointing.

## 3529 VISTA CLAIMING STKS — 1m 1f 218y
**4:15** (4:15) (E) 3-Y-0 **£4,114** (£1,266; £633; £316) **Stalls** High

Form RPR
5045 **1** **Canadian Storm**[19] 2930 3-8-10 58 FPFerris(3) 2 64
(MHTompkins) *sn led: clr 8f out: jnd over 2f out: rdn clr again over 1f out: eased nr fin* **11/2**[3]
-000 **2** *2 1/2* **Epaminondas (USA)**[14] 3089 3-9-3 66 PDobbs 4 63
(RHannon) *chsd ldrs: rdn over 2f out: wnt 2nd ins fnl f: no ch w wnr* **9/2**[2]
5-00 **3** *6* **Simonovski (USA)**[67] 1688 3-9-3 67 VSlattery 6 52
(JAOsborne) *chsd clr ldrs: rdn over 4f out: r.o ins fnl f: n.d* **7/1**
06 **4** *1/2* **Laurens Girl (IRE)**[26] 2729 3-8-8 RHavlin 8 42
(MGQuinlan) *chsd wnr: rdn and ev ch over 2f out: hung lft and wknd fnl f* **12/1**
0-00 **5** *3/4* **House Of Blues**[29] 2665 3-8-9 57 SWKelly 1 41
(JAOsborne) *hld up: r.o ins fnl f: nvr nrr* **16/1**
0001 **6** *nk* **Bosco (IRE)**[23] 2801 3-8-7 52 (t) WRyan 3 39
(PSMcentee) *hld up: r.o ins fnl f: nvr nrr* **7/1**
0000 **7** *1 3/4* **Eizawina Docklands**[8] 3271 3-8-5 50 (t) CCatlin 7 34
(NPLittmoden) *in rr: rdn over 4f out: n.d* **16/1**
4-00 **8** *3 1/2* **Tardis**[23] 2820 3-7-13 61 HayleyTurner(5) 11 26
(MLWBell) *chsd clr ldrs: rdn over 3f out: wknd over 1f out* **3/1**[1]
6064 **9** *2 1/2* **Anisette**[23] 2822 3-7-11 46 MHalford(7) 5 21
(JulianPoulton) *s.s: a bhd* **9/1**
000 **10** *3* **Osla**[9] 3229 3-8-3 RThomas(5) 9 19
(RBrotherton) *hld up: wknd 4f out* **50/1**
000 **11** *26* **Fly So High**[98] 1127 3-8-4 ow2 SWhitworth 10 —
(DShaw) *sn outpcd and bhd* **50/1**

2m 7.60s (-0.80) **Going Correction** -0.075s/f (Good) **11** Ran SP% **116.9**
Speed ratings: **100,98,93,92,92 91,90,87,85,83 62**CSF £30.28 TOTE £6.10: £2.10, £2.90, £2.40; EX 31.40.Canadian Storm was claimed by Miss Venetia Williams for £10,000.
**Owner** P A & D G Sakal **Bred** P V And J P Jackson **Trained** Newmarket, Suffolk

**FOCUS**
A fair claimer and the pace was sound. The race is difficult to rate with several of these on the downgrade and has been rated through the winner's handicap form.

**NOTEBOOK**
**Canadian Storm** finally got his act together, but owes much to the splendid ride given by his jockey.
**Epaminondas(USA)** found this more his level, and stayed on gamely having been off the bridle some way out. This trip was well within his compass.
**Simonovski(USA)**, although filling third spot, hardly gave encouraging signs.
**Laurens Girl(IRE)** paid late on for trying to keep tabs on the winner. However, as this was only her third outing, she should be capable of a bit more.
**Tardis** didn't improve for the step back up in trip.
**Anisette** *Official explanation: jockey said filly hit her head on starting stalls and missed break*

## 3530 VISTA FILLIES' H'CAP — 5f 218y
**4:45** (4:48) (E) (0-70,68) 3-Y-0 **£5,837** (£1,796; £898; £449) **Stalls** Low

Form RPR
4124 **1** **Estihlal**[10] 3211 3-9-3 **64** WRyan 8 79+
(EALDunlop) *s.i.s: hld up: hdwy to ld over 1f out: sn clr* **4/1**[2]
6001 **2** *2 1/2* **Rise**[10] 3211 3-9-3 **64** (b) JFEgan 12 72
(AndrewReid) *hld up in tch: rdn over 1f out: kpt on: no ch w wnr* **9/1**
5321 **3** *2 1/2* **Miss Judgement (IRE)**[12] 3151 3-9-4 **65** FNorton 10 65+
(WRMuir) *prom: nt clr run over 2f out and over 1f out: hung rt ins fnl f: nt trble ldrs* **5/2**[1]
-465 **4** *3/4* **Fair Compton**[30] 2610 3-9-1 **62** PDobbs 11 60
(RHannon) *chsd ldrs: rdn and ev ch over 1f out: no ex* **20/1**
4020 **5** *hd* **Indrani**[47] 2187 3-7-11 **49** oh2 ow4 RThomas(5) 1 46
(JohnAHarris) *hld up: hdwy over 2f out: rdn and ev ch over 1f out: no ex* **40/1**
1-43 **6** *nk* **La Landonne**[12] 3139 3-9-7 **68** SWKelly 5 64
(PMPhelan) *outpcd: hdwy over 2f out: hung rt and outpcd over 1f out: styd on ins fnl f* **12/1**
5060 **7** *1* **Indian Lily**[19] 2942 3-8-6 **53** SWhitworth 13 46
(CFWall) *hld up: hdwy over 2f out: rdn and ev ch over 1f out: wknd ins fnl f* **12/1**
-560 **8** *2* **Turkish Delight**[26] 2741 3-8-12 **59** CCatlin 3 46
(JBalding) *hld up: hdwy over 2f out: wknd fnl f* **28/1**
305- **9** *hd* **Annie Miller (IRE)**[285] 5127 3-9-1 **65** DCorby(3) 18 52
(MJWallace) *s.i.s: outpcd: nt clr run ins fnl f: nt rch ldrs* **20/1**
0004 **10** *nk* **Danifah (IRE)**[19] 2942 3-7-12 **45** JoannaBadger 6 31
(PDEvans) *chsd ldrs: outpcd over 3f out: n.d after* **12/1**
0000 **11** *1 1/4* **Pink Supreme**[7] 3306 3-8-6 **60** (t) DerekNolan(7) 16 42
(IAWood) *hld up: sme hdwy over 1f out: n.d* **33/1**
0-04 **12** *1 1/2* **Bahama Belle**[25] 2765 3-8-10 **57** DKinsella 4 35
(HSHowe) *chsd ldrs: rdn 1/2-way: wknd over 1f out* **33/1**
0140 **13** *1/2* **Party Princess (IRE)**[8] 3273 3-9-2 **63** BDoyle 14 39
(JAGlover) *chsd ldrs: rdn over 1f out: sn hdd: wknd ins fnl f* **8/1**[3]
0460 **14** *1/2* **Lizhar (IRE)**[86] 1312 3-8-3 **50** MHenry 20 25
(JJQuinn) *chsd ldrs: rdn and ev ch over 1f out: wknd ins fnl f* **20/1**
1105 **15** *3/4* **Melaina**[33] 2518 3-9-1 **65** (p) RMiles(3) 19 37
(MSSaunders) *chsd ldrs: rdn and ev ch over 1f out: wknd and eased ins fnl f* **20/1**
0502 **16** *hd* **Red Rocky**[9] 3229 3-7-12 **50** ow4 (p) StephanieHollinshead(5) 2 22
(RHollinshead) *w ldrs: rdn 1/2-way: wknd wl over 1f out* **20/1**
1235 **17** *1* **Smart Starprincess (IRE)**[130] 868 3-8-11 **61** FPFerris(3) 9 30
(MJAttwater) *led over 3f: sn wknd* **20/1**
1040 **18** *nk* **Pardon Moi**[19] 2932 3-7-10 **48** HayleyTurner(5) 17 16
(MrsCADunnett) *s.i.s: outpcd* **25/1**
00-0 **19** *3 1/2* **Carla Moon**[50] 2097 3-8-13 **60** GBaker 15 17
(CFWall) *s.i.s: outpcd* **20/1**

1m 11.86s (-1.54) **Going Correction** -0.275s/f (Firm) **19** Ran SP% **141.7**
Speed ratings: **99,95,92,91,91 90,89,86,86,86 84,82,81,81,80 79,78,78,73**CSF £37.16 CT £118.42 TOTE £5.20: £1.70, £2.70, £1.70, £5.60; EX 49.80 Place 6 £55.48, Place 5 £25.89.
**Owner** Hamdan Al Maktoum **Bred** Shadwell Estate Company **Trained** Newmarket, Suffolk

**FOCUS**
A moderate contest run at a steady pace, but a runaway winner.

**NOTEBOOK**
**Estihlal** had her ground this time and won with plenty in hand. She is on the upgrade.
**Rise** was 9lb worse off with the winner for three and a half lengths and was put firmly in her place, although this was her best run yet on turf.
**Miss Judgement(IRE)**, 12lb higher than when bolting up at Nottingham, moved poorly to post, and didn't have the best of runs this time.
**Fair Compton** had his chance, but just wasn't good enough.
**Indrani** picked up ground stylishly before her effort petered out in the latter stages. While she remains a maiden, she does have a little ability and is one to keep an eye on if dropped into selling company.
**La Landonne** found this trip on the sharp side for her, but even so didn't look an easy ride.
**Lizhar(IRE)** *Official explanation: jockey said filly lost her action*
**Melaina** *Official explanation: jockey said filly was unsuited by the fast ground*
**Carla Moon** *Official explanation: jockey said filly had a breathing problem*
T/Plt: £104.70 to a £1 stake. Pool: £31,488.45. 219.50 winning tickets. T/Qpdt: £8.20 to a £1 stake. Pool: £2,267.00. 203.90 winning tickets. CR

# 3150 NOTTINGHAM (L-H)
### Saturday, July 3

**OFFICIAL GOING: Good changing to good (good to soft in places) after race 2 (7.20) and good to soft (soft in places) after race 3 (7.50)**
The going was much softer than expected after total of 9mm of rain fell before and during racing.
Wind: almost nil Weather: showers

## 3531 BET WITH THE BOOKIES MEDIAN AUCTION MAIDEN STKS — 5f 13y
**6:50** (6:50) (F) 2-Y-0 **£3,360** (£960; £480) **Stalls** High

Form RPR
460 **1** **Blue Marble**[12] 3157 2-8-11 J-PGuillambert(3) 8 73
(CEBrittain) *w ldrs: rdn 2f out: led ins fnl f: r.o wl* **8/1**[3]
**2** *1 1/2* **Lucky Emerald (IRE)** 2-8-9 KDarley 10 62
(BPalling) *s.i.s: sn chsng ldrs: rdn 2f out: hung lft fnl f: kpt on* **12/1**
54 **3** *shd* **Transvestite (IRE)**[12] 3157 2-9-0 RLMoore 9 67
(JWHills) *w ldrs: led over 1f out: rdn and hdd ins fnl f: nt qckn* **2/1**[2]
04 **4** *1 1/4* **Frantic**[13] 3116 2-8-9 GDuffield 2 58
(TDEasterby) *chsd ldrs: rdn over 3f out: no ex fnl f* **9/1**
0 **5** *nk* **Three Aces (IRE)**[10] 3208 2-8-9 MTebbutt 5 56
(RMBeckett) *s.i.s: rdn over 2f out: kpt on ins fnl f: nt rch ldrs* **25/1**
624 **6** *3* **Komac**[10] 3196 2-9-0 SSanders 1 51
(BAMcmahon) *led: rdn and hdd over 1f out: wknd ins fnl f* **13/8**[1]
**7** *9* **Katie Killane** 2-8-9 ADaly 6 13
(MWellings) *s.s: a bhd* **33/1**
**8** *3 1/2* **Starlight River (IRE)** 2-8-9 SDrowne 7 1
(WRMuir) *prom tl rdn and wknd 2f out* **16/1**
**9** *3* **Independent Spirit** 2-8-11 RMiles(3) 3 —
(RPElliott) *s.s: sn hung lft and racd alone in centre: a bhd* **33/1**

64.51 secs (2.71) **Going Correction** +0.50s/f (Yiel) **9** Ran SP% **115.8**
Speed ratings: **98,95,95,93,92 88,73,68,63**CSF £95.32 TOTE £13.80: £2.60, £2.60, £1.10; EX 108.20.
**Owner** H E Sheikh Rashid Bin Mohammed **Bred** Exors Of The Late Lord Crawshaw **Trained** Newmarket, Suffolk

**FOCUS**
A decent winning time for an ordinary maiden. The form is probably fair.

**NOTEBOOK**
**Blue Marble**, a half-brother to five-furlong winners Frascati and Birikina, found a return to the minimum trip on softer ground doing the trick. He has improved past the third on their Windsor running.
**Lucky Emerald(IRE)**, a half-sister to a couple of five-furlong winners, snatched second place on the line despite showing signs of inexperience. She should have learnt a lot from this.



The Form Book, Raceform Ltd, Compton, RG20 6NL

**Transvestite(IRE)**, reverting back to the minimum trip on a slower surface, ran a sound enough race.
**Frantic** was another back down in distance on the softest surface she has encountered so far.
**Three Aces(IRE)** ◆, a half-sister to six-furlong juvenile scorer Bad Intentions, stepped up considerably on her debut. Further improvement can be expected over a longer trip.
**Komac** has shown his best form on faster ground.

## 3532 SATURDAY NIGHT RACING MAIDEN AUCTION FILLIES' STKS 6f 15y

**7:20** (7:21) (E) 2-Y-0 **£4,062** (£1,250; £625; £312) **Stalls** High

| Form | Pos | Dist | Horse | Jockey/Draw | RPR |
|---|---|---|---|---|---|
| 00 | 1 | | **Rancho Cucamonga (IRE)**[10] 3196 2-8-4 ow2 ... KDarley 15 | | 71 |
| | | | (TDBarron) *chsd ldrs: swtchd lft over 2f out: sn rdn: led 1f out: drvn out* **14/1** | | |
| 02 | 2 | 2 | **Shosolosa (IRE)**[15] 3045 2-8-7 ow1 ... JFortune 13 | | 68 |
| | | | (BJMeehan) *a.p: rdn and n.m.r 1f out: kpt on same pce* **5/1**[3] | | |
| 225 | 3 | shd | **Agent Kensington**[24] 2786 2-8-2 ... RLMoore 1 | | 63 |
| | | | (RHannon) *prom: led far side over 2f out: r.o* **4/1**[2] | | |
| 340 | 4 | nk | **Gaudalpin (IRE)**[21] 2884 2-8-2 ... SRighton 11 | | 62 |
| | | | (MJAttwater) *led: rdn 2f out: hdd 1f out: nt qckn* **25/1** | | |
| 2 | 5 | 3 | **Consider This**[13] 3116 2-8-2 ... CCatlin 6 | | 53 |
| | | | (WMBrisbourne) *prom far side: rdn over 2f out: wknd fnl f* **9/1** | | |
| 544 | 6 | nk | **Sweet Marguerite**[16] 3003 2-8-6 ... DAllan 5 | | 56 |
| | | | (TDEasterby) *led far side over 2f: sn rdn: wknd fnl f* **16/1** | | |
| | 7 | ¾ | **Before The Dawn** 2-7-13 ... FPFerris(3) 16 | | 50 |
| | | | (AGNewcombe) *rdn and hdwy over 2f out: sn hung lft: wknd fnl f* **33/1** | | |
| 3 | 8 | ½ | **Sweet Coincidence**[15] 3045 2-8-2 ... GDuffield 14 | | 48 |
| | | | (IAWood) *dwlt: hdwy over 2f out: wknd fnl f* **10/3**[1] | | |
| 022 | 9 | 1¾ | **Lakesdale (IRE)**[23] 2819 2-7-11 ... HayleyTurner(5) 17 | | 43 |
| | | | (MrsCADunnett) *no hdwy fnl 2f* **33/1** | | |
| 0 | 10 | ½ | **Emeraude Du Cap**[12] 3157 2-8-2 ... ADaly 2 | | 41 |
| | | | (MLWBell) *dwlt: outpcd far side* **100/1** | | |
| 0 | 11 | shd | **Ariane Star (IRE)**[12] 3157 2-8-6 ... PRobinson 3 | | 45 |
| | | | (MAJarvis) *spd far side over 2f: eased over 1f out* **6/1** | | |
| 0 | 12 | 3 | **Oceanico Dot Com (IRE)**[25] 2749 2-8-2 ... FNorton 9 | | 32 |
| | | | (ABerry) *chsd ldrs tl wknd 2f out* **33/1** | | |
| 052 | 13 | shd | **Clinet (IRE)**[38] 2396 2-8-3 ow1 ... JFEgan 7 | | 33 |
| | | | (PMPhelan) *s.i.s: sn prom: wknd over 1f out* **8/1** | | |
| 0 | 14 | 1 | **Good Wee Girl (IRE)**[10] 3192 2-8-2 ow3 ... RMiles(3) 8 | | 32 |
| | | | (SKirk) *prom tl wknd over 1f out* **33/1** | | |
| | 15 | shd | **Royal Abigail (IRE)** 2-8-6 ... SDrowne 4 | | 33 |
| | | | (EALDunlop) *s.s: outpcd far side* **40/1** | | |
| 050 | 16 | 1½ | **Lanas Turn**[11] 3164 2-8-2 ow7 ... SaleemGolam(7) 12 | | 31 |
| | | | (TDEasterby) *dwlt: outpcd* **66/1** | | |
| | 17 | 3½ | **Pride Of London (IRE)** 2-8-2 ... TPQueally 10 | | 14 |
| | | | (IAWood) *outpcd* **66/1** | | |

1m 19.35s (4.55) **Going Correction** +0.50s/f (Yiel) **17 Ran SP% 129.7**
Speed ratings: **89,86,86,85,81 81,80,79,77,76 76,72,72,71,71 69,64**CSF £82.22 TOTE £27.20: £9.30, £2.10, £3.20; EX 167.70.
**Owner** P D Savill **Bred** P D Savill **Trained** Maunby, N Yorks

**FOCUS**
There was probably no material advantage in the draw. A fair maiden on paper but the form is probably not as strong as it could have been.

**NOTEBOOK**
**Rancho Cucamonga(IRE)** may be bred for speed but this extra furlong did not prove to be against her.
**Shosolosa(IRE)**, a half-sister to a seven-furlong selling winner at two, gave the impression she will stay further.
**Agent Kensington** had already shown she can handle soft ground and was the first home on the far side.
**Gaudalpin(IRE)** is bred to stay at least this trip and got the extra furlong well enough despite the easier ground.
**Consider This** may have found this softer surface against her.
**Sweet Marguerite**, reverting back to six, did not appear to get home on this softer surface.

## 3533 LETHEBY & CHRISTOPHER (S) H'CAP 6f 15y

**7:50** (7:54) (G) (0-55,55) 3-Y-0+ **£2,800** (£800; £400) **Stalls** High

| Form | Pos | Dist | Horse | RPR |
|---|---|---|---|---|
| 0030 | 1 | | **Mickledor (FR)**[12] 3148 4-8-5 **43** ... (p) DTudhope(7) 19 | 57 |
| | | | (MDods) *hld up: hdwy over 1f out: led ins fnl f: r.o wl* **10/1** | |
| 0306 | 2 | 1¾ | **Headland (USA)**[5] 3376 6-9-4 **49** ... (be) SSanders 20 | 58 |
| | | | (DWChapman) *a.p: led jst over 1f out tl ins fnl f: nt qckn* **12/1** | |
| 0300 | 3 | ¾ | **Shady Deal**[39] 2383 8-8-11 **45** ... FPFerris(3) 4 | 52 |
| | | | (JMBradley) *s.i.s: racd far side: bhd tl hdwy 2f out: kpt on ins fnl f* **16/1** | |
| 0040 | 4 | nk | **Beyond Calculation (USA)**[8] 3269 10-9-10 **55** ... (b[1]) RLMoore 6 | 61 |
| | | | (JMBradley) *chsd ldrs: led far side 3f out: no ex ins fnl f* **12/1** | |
| 0000 | 5 | nk | **Komena**[12] 3151 6-8-12 **43** ... GDuffield 1 | 48 |
| | | | (JWPayne) *chsd ldrs far side: kpt on ins fnl f* **12/1** | |
| 2420 | 6 | 1 | **My Girl Pearl (IRE)**[22] 2836 4-9-2 **47** ... VSlattery 18 | 49 |
| | | | (MSSaunders) *mid-div: rdn and hdwy over 1f out: nt rch ldrs* **7/1**[2] | |
| 2320 | 7 | hd | **Cargo**[14] 3103 5-9-0 **48** ... (tp) RMiles(3) 12 | 49 |
| | | | (BAPearce) *led: hdd jst over 1f out: no ex* **12/1** | |
| 0000 | 8 | 1¼ | **Zietzig (IRE)**[11] 3169 7-9-0 **45** ... PDobbs 13 | 43 |
| | | | (DNicholls) *bhd tl hdwy over 1f out: nvr able to chal* **33/1** | |
| 0000 | 9 | ¾ | **Loughlorien (IRE)**[11] 3169 5-8-12 **46** ... (v) THamilton(3) 16 | 41 |
| | | | (RAFahey) *prom tl wknd over 1f out* **10/3**[1] | |
| 4415 | 10 | 5 | **Bells Beach (IRE)**[22] 2843 6-9-0 **45** ... SDrowne 5 | 25 |
| | | | (PHowling) *sn outpcd far side* **7/1**[2] | |
| 650- | 11 | 1¼ | **Octennial**[422] 1461 5-9-5 **50** ... RFitzpatrick 17 | 27 |
| | | | (CSmith) *outpcd* **33/1** | |
| 0010 | 12 | hd | **Rileys Dream**[22] 2833 5-8-12 **43** ... DSweeney 9 | 19 |
| | | | (BJLlewellyn) *s.i.s: swtchd to stands' side gp: a bhd* **16/1** | |
| 1500 | 13 | ½ | **Danakim**[15] 3038 7-9-0 **45** ... CCatlin 10 | 20 |
| | | | (JRWeymes) *racd alone centre: spd 4f* **9/1**[3] | |
| 6000 | 14 | 1½ | **Sabana (IRE)**[47] 2178 6-8-12 **43** ... FNorton 8 | 13 |
| | | | (JMBradley) *led far side after 1f to 3f out: sn wknd* **28/1** | |
| 0400 | 15 | nk | **Sounds Lucky**[8] 3277 8-9-0 **45** ... (b) JFEgan 14 | 14 |
| | | | (AndrewReid) *prom 4f* **25/1** | |
| 0000 | 16 | ¾ | **Cedric Coverwell**[11] 3175 4-9-0 **45** ... RHughes 3 | 12 |
| | | | (DKIvory) *racd far side: sn bhd* **33/1** | |
| 0000 | 17 | 1¾ | **Ridicule**[22] 2843 5-9-2 **47** ... (vt) NCallan 11 | 9 |
| | | | (JGPortman) *mid-div: wknd 2f out* **10/1** | |
| 5300 | 18 | 2 | **Blade's Edge**[16] 3004 3-9-4 **55** ... (b[1]) JFortune 15 | 11 |
| | | | (ABailey) *bhd fnl 2f* **14/1** | |
| 50-0 | 19 | 3½ | **Vintage Style**[12] 3151 5-9-9 **54** ... (v[1]) KDarley 2 | — |
| | | | (JRWeymes) *racd far side: sn bhd* **40/1** | |
| 1500 | 20 | 7 | **Foolish Thought (IRE)**[88] 1279 4-8-13 **47** ... (p) LEnstone(3) 7 | — |
| | | | (IAWood) *led far side 1f: rdn 3f out: sn wknd* **33/1** | |

1m 17.87s (3.07) **Going Correction** +0.50s/f (Yiel)
**WFA** 3 from 4yo+ 6lb **20 Ran SP% 147.0**
Speed ratings: **99,96,95,95,94 93,93,91,90,83 82,82,81,79,78 77,75,72,68,58**CSF £138.95 CT £2027.39 TOTE £13.10: £3.00, £4.10, £5.20, £4.00; EX 77.80.No bid for winner.
**Owner** D B Stanley **Bred** Gillian C Stanley **Trained** Piercebridge, Co Durham

**FOCUS**
There again appeared to be no bias between the two sides. Ordinary form for the grade.

**NOTEBOOK**
**Mickledor(FR)** does seem to have benefited from a switch to cheekpieces and six furlongs on soft ground suited her well.
**Headland(USA)** has tumbled down the ratings and liked the soft ground.
**Shady Deal**, with ground conditions in his favour, came through to win the race on the far side.
**Beyond Calculation(USA)**, blinkered for the first time, found top weight anchoring him in the closing stages.
**Komena**, again in blinkers, ran better back in this lower grade.
**My Girl Pearl(IRE)** was in a seller for the first time but needs a return to seven.
**Bells Beach(IRE)** *Official explanation: jockey said mare was unsuited by Good to Soft, Soft in places going*
**Sounds Lucky** *Official explanation: jockey said gelding had breathing problems*
**Cedric Coverwell** *Official explanation: jockey said gelding hung right*
**Ridicule** *Official explanation: jockey said gelding's cross noseband became dislodged and restricted his breathing*

## 3534 SEARCH CONSULTANCY'S GRAHAME & DEBBIE WEDDING H'CAP 1m 1f 213y

**8:20** (8:21) (D) (0-80,76) 3-Y-0+ **£5,882** (£1,810; £905; £452) **Stalls** Low

| Form | Pos | Dist | Horse | RPR |
|---|---|---|---|---|
| 0053 | 1 | | **Rasid (USA)**[8] 3274 6-9-7 **73** ... DHolland 5 | 83 |
| | | | (CADwyer) *led after 2f: rdn over 2f out: r.o wl* **4/1**[3] | |
| 3161 | 2 | 2 | **Rotuma (IRE)**[11] 3166 5-9-3 **72** ... (b) LEnstone(3) 3 | 78 |
| | | | (MDods) *hld up in tch: hmpd and lost pl after 3f: hdwy on ins over 3f out: rdn over 2f out: nt qckn ins fnl f* **4/1**[3] | |
| 2566 | 3 | ½ | **Active Account (USA)**[19] 2938 7-8-9 **61** ... SDrowne 8 | 66 |
| | | | (MrsHDalton) *led 2f: chsd wnr: rdn and ev ch 2f out: nt qckn fnl f* **11/1** | |
| 1-00 | 4 | 1¼ | **Mekuria (JPN)**[10] 3199 3-8-12 **75** ... SChin 2 | 78 |
| | | | (MJohnston) *s.i.s: sn rcvrd: rdn over 2f out: one pce* **9/1** | |
| 6060 | 5 | ½ | **Sir Haydn**[8] 3276 4-8-13 **65** ... (v) TPQueally 4 | 67 |
| | | | (JRJenkins) *s.i.s: hld up: hdwy over 2f out: sn rdn: one pce fnl f* **16/1** | |
| 0624 | 6 | 3½ | **Go Tech**[9] 3238 4-9-10 **76** ... DAllan 6 | 72 |
| | | | (TDEasterby) *t.k.h: prom: rdn over 3f out: wknd fnl f* **8/1** | |
| 6001 | 7 | 7 | **Lilli Marlane**[8] 3264 4-9-6 **72** ... WRyan 1 | 55 |
| | | | (NACallaghan) *hld up and bhd: plld out over 2f out: sn rdn: no rspnse* **10/3**[1] | |
| 4220 | 8 | 12 | **Karaoke (IRE)**[22] 2845 4-9-1 **67** ... RLMoore 7 | 28 |
| | | | (SKirk) *a in rr* **7/2**[2] | |

2m 17.12s (7.62) **Going Correction** +0.825s/f (Soft)
**WFA** 3 from 4yo+ 11lb **8 Ran SP% 120.6**
Speed ratings: **102,100,100,99,98 95,90,80**CSF £21.69 CT £167.17 TOTE £4.80: £1.60, £2.50, £3.00; EX 15.20.
**Owner** David L Bowkett **Bred** Shadwell Farm Inc **Trained** Newmarket, Suffolk

**FOCUS**
A slowly-run race in what had basically become soft ground. The form is ordinary.

**NOTEBOOK**
**Rasid(USA)** loves soft ground and would not have been in the line-up had the surface not been deemed suitable.
**Rotuma(IRE)** had no real excuses apart from the fact he had been raised 7lb.
**Active Account(USA)** ran his race on this return to a longer trip.
**Mekuria(JPN)** had apparently failed to stay on her two attempts at a mile and a half last month.
**Sir Haydn** settled much better than when first fitted with a visor over further last time.
**Go Tech** struggles to get this distance on soft ground.
**Karaoke(IRE)** *Official explanation: jockey said gelding was unsuited by Good to Soft, Soft in places going*

## 3535 BDN CONSTRUCTION CLASSIFIED STKS 1m 1f 213y

**8:50** (8:50) (E) 3-Y-0 **£3,948** (£1,215; £607; £303) **Stalls** Low

| Form | Pos | Dist | Horse | RPR |
|---|---|---|---|---|
| 2321 | 1 | | **Jakarmi**[9] 3231 3-8-13 72 ... RMiles(3) 11 | 76 |
| | | | (BPalling) *hld up: hdwy 5f out: led over 1f out: r.o wl* **6/5**[1] | |
| 0003 | 2 | 2 | **Whitgift Rock**[9] 3230 3-9-3 73 ... DHolland 10 | 73 |
| | | | (SDow) *led early: prom: led over 3f out: rdn and hdd over 1f out: nt qckn* **13/2**[3] | |
| -606 | 3 | 1½ | **Bailaora (IRE)**[39] 2378 3-9-3 73 ... (b) RLMoore 7 | 71 |
| | | | (BWDuke) *trckd ldrs: rdn over 3f out: one pce fnl f* **20/1** | |
| -236 | 4 | ½ | **Tytheknot**[7] 3312 3-9-4 74 ... RHughes 1 | 71 |
| | | | (JeddO'Keeffe) *sn led: rdn and hdd over 3f out: one pce fnl 2f* **10/1** | |
| 65-3 | 5 | ½ | **Trullitti (IRE)**[70] 1619 3-9-2 75 ... KDarley 6 | 68 |
| | | | (JLDunlop) *sn bhd: rdn 4f out: hdwy over 1f out: nt rch ldrs* **7/2**[2] | |
| 2-50 | 6 | 2½ | **Imperial Royale (IRE)**[9] 3232 3-8-7 62 ... MHalford(7) 9 | 61 |
| | | | (PLClinton) *hld up: hdwy 5f out: rdn over 3f out: wknd over 1f out* **50/1** | |
| -000 | 7 | ½ | **The Violin Player (USA)**[28] 2692 3-9-4 74 ... TPQueally 2 | 65 |
| | | | (WJarvis) *s.i.s: sn in tch: rdn over 3f out: wknd over 2f out* **12/1** | |
| 043 | 8 | nk | **Honeymooning**[16] 3013 3-8-11 68 ... WRyan 3 | 57 |
| | | | (HRACecil) *s.i.s: a bhd* **12/1** | |
| 5156 | 9 | 1 | **Fit To Fly (IRE)**[8] 3280 3-8-12 75 ... JDWalsh(7) 8 | 63 |
| | | | (SKirk) *hld up: hdwy 5f out: rdn over 3f out: wknd over 2f out* **14/1** | |
| -163 | 10 | 3½ | **Vengerov**[21] 2870 3-8-7 70 ... SaleemGolam(7) 5 | 52 |
| | | | (MLWBell) *prom: rdn over 4f out: wknd over 2f out* **14/1** | |

2m 17.66s (8.16) **Going Correction** +0.825s/f (Soft) **10 Ran SP% 125.5**
Speed ratings: **100,98,97,96,96 94,94,93,92,90**CSF £10.68 TOTE £2.20: £1.20, £2.50, £3.40; EX 12.60.
**Owner** Mrs M M Palling **Bred** Llety Stud **Trained** Tredodridge, Vale Of Glamorgan

**FOCUS**
They again went no pace in the soft ground. The form has a sound look although the winner was the only one proven in the conditions.

**NOTEBOOK**
**Jakarmi** is as tough as they come and still appears to be improving.
**Whitgift Rock** got the extra quarter-mile well enough despite the testing surface and simply met one too good.
**Bailaora(IRE)** was another up in distance who did not seem to be beaten for a lack of stamina.
**Tytheknot** was back up in distance having failed to stay this trip on desperate ground at Pontefract in April.
**Trullitti(IRE)** ◆ still appears likely to do better over a mile and a half.

## 3536 MIDLANDS RACING - 9 GREAT VENUES - H'CAP 1m 54y

9:20 (9:20) (E) (0-75,72) 3-Y-O+ £4,095 (£1,260; £630; £315) Stalls Low

Form RPR

5005 **1** **Little Englander**[12] 3154 4-8-8 **55**........................ DSweeney 1 65
(HCandy) *hld up: hdwy over 3f out: led ins fnl f: drvn out* **12/1**

0350 **2** 1 ¼ **Johannian**[17] 2982 6-9-10 **71**........................ RLMoore 11 78
(JMBradley) *hld up and bhd: hdwy 3f out: ev ch ins fnl f: nt qckn* **12/1**

01 **3** nk **Trousers**[91] 1247 5-9-1 **62**........................ JFEgan 12 69
(AndrewReid) *led early: w ldr: led 3f out tl ins fnl f: nt qckn* **2/1**[1]

3445 **4** ½ **Disabuse**[31] 2583 4-8-3 **50**........................(b[1]) GDuffield 6 56
(MWEasterby) *s.i.s: sn prom: rdn over 2f out: nt qckn ins fnl f* **9/2**[2]

-043 **5** ¾ **Habshan (USA)**[23] 2806 4-9-7 **68**........................ RHughes 9 72
(NAGraham) *hld up: hdwy over 2f out: sn rdn and swtchd rt: one pce fnl f* **9/2**[2]

6620 **6** 1 ¾ **Vermilion Creek**[21] 2879 5-8-1 **53**........................ StephanieHollinshead(5) 14 53
(RHollinshead) *hld up: hdwy over 2f out: sn rdn: no further prog* **16/1**

0001 **7** 5 **Flashing Blade**[12] 3154 4-9-9 **70**........................(t) GGibbons 5 60
(BAMcmahon) *hld up in mid-div: rdn over 3f out: eased whn btn ins fnl f* **7/1**

42-0 **8** 6 **Sheriff's Deputy**[43] 2271 4-9-9 **70**........................ DHolland 13 47
(JWUnett) *hld up: rdn over 3f out: sn struggling* **6/1**[3]

50-6 **9** 2 **Brooklands Lodge (USA)**[15] 3049 3-8-11 **67**........................ SRighton 7 40
(MJAttwater) *chsd ldrs: rdn over 4f out: sn lost pl* **40/1**

0005 **10** 3 ½ **Sahaat**[12] 3143 6-9-11 **72**........................(b[1]) TPQueally 4 38
(JAOsborne) *hld up in tch: rdn 3f out: wknd 2f out* **10/1**

6000 **11** 3 **Among Friends (IRE)**[12] 3141 4-8-8 **58**........................ LisaJones(3) 2 17
(BPalling) *plld hrd: sn led: hdd 3f out: sn wknd* **20/1**

6000 **12** 2 **Aimee's Delight**[25] 2757 4-9-6 **67**........................(b[1]) SSanders 15 22
(JGGiven) *a bhd* **16/1**

1m 50.44s (4.04) **Going Correction** +0.825s/f (Soft)
**WFA** 3 from 4yo+ 9lb **12 Ran SP% 139.9**
Speed ratings: **112,110,110,109,109 107,102,96,94,90 87,85**CSF £174.05 CT £430.38 TOTE £16.80: £4.50, £5.30, £1.80; EX 504.40 Place 6 £143.39, Place 5 £72.64.
**Owner** The Earl Cadogan **Bred** The Earl Cadogan **Trained** Wantage, Oxon

**FOCUS**
An outstanding time for the grade in what were now quite testing conditions, and sound form.

**NOTEBOOK**
**Little Englander** seemed to appreciate the soft ground and travelled well for most of the trip.
**Johannian** could not quite take advantage of being 13lb lower than at the start of the season.
**Trousers**, raised 7lb and back up in trip, is still well handicapped compared with his All-Weather rating.
**Disabuse** was tried in blinkers for this drop back to a mile.
**Habshan(USA)** had already shown he could handle these conditions.
T/Plt: £229.70 to a £1 stake. Pool: £40,831.50. 129.75 winning tickets. T/Qpdt: £55.30 to a £1 stake. Pool: £3,095.00. 41.40 winning tickets. KH

# 3480 SANDOWN (R-H)

Saturday, July 3

**OFFICIAL GOING: Good to soft**

## 3537 CHAMPAGNE LAURENT-PERRIER SPRINT STKS (GROUP 3) 5f 6y

1:35 (1:40) (A) 3-Y-O+ £29,000 (£11,000; £5,500; £2,500) Stalls High

Form RPR

5053 **1** **Orientor**[6] 3350 6-9-3 105........................ KFallon 3 118
(JSGoldie) *hld up towards rr: prog 1/2-way: led wl over 1f out: edgd rt but in command fnl f* **5/1**[3]

6134 **2** 2 ½ **Ringmoor Down**[18] 2955 5-9-0 106........................ TQuinn 1 107
(DWPArbuthnot) *stdd s: hld up in last trio: prog 2f out: chsd wnr jst over 1f out: r.o but unable to chal* **7/1**

6550 **3** 4 **Colonel Cotton (IRE)**[18] 2955 5-9-3 100........................ PRobinson 9 96
(NACallaghan) *hld up towards rr: prog 1/2-way: hanging and nt qckn over 1f out: plugged on fnl f to take 3rd last stride* **14/1**

3216 **4** shd **Boogie Street**[18] 2955 3-8-12 111........................ RHughes 12 96
(RHannon) *lw: led: hdd and shkn up wl over 1f out: nt qckn and sn btn: lost 3rd last stride* **7/2**[1]

0-50 **5** nk **Twilight Blues (IRE)**[14] 3073 5-9-3 105........................(p) EAhern 6 95
(BJMeehan) *pushed along to chse ldrs: outpcd over 1f out: no imp on ldrs after* **25/1**

3014 **6** ¾ **The Kiddykid (IRE)**[7] 3308 4-9-7 111........................ JPSpencer 11 96
(PDEvans) *chsd ldrs: rdn and outpcd over 1f out: n.d after* **7/1**

4000 **7** ½ **Stormont (IRE)**[18] 2955 4-9-9 104........................(v[1]) JQuinn 7 96
(HJCollingridge) *dwlt: racd in last trio and sn pushed along: nvr on terms* **25/1**

4440 **8** hd **Fromsong (IRE)**[20] 2913 6-9-3 97........................ TEDurcan 2 90
(BRMillman) *hld up in rr: rdn on outer 2f out: sn outpcd and btn* **33/1**

2341 **9** 1 ¼ **The Tatling (IRE)**[18] 2955 7-9-9 115........................ DHolland 10 91
(JMBradley) *lw: stdd s: racd on inner and hld up towards rr: effrt whn nt clr run 2f out: no prog after* **4/1**[2]

0-01 **10** 6 **Night Prospector**[29] 2636 4-9-9 105........................ JPMurtagh 8 71
(JWPayne) *lw: pressed ldrs: rdn whn n.m.r over 1f out: wknd and eased fnl f* **25/1**

2-00 **11** ¾ **Mornin Reserves**[18] 2955 5-9-3 105........................ LDettori 5 62
(ISemple) *w ldr to 1/2-way: wknd rapidly 2f out* **10/1**

-640 **12** 1 ½ **Bali Royal**[12] 3162 6-9-0 102........................ DaneO'Neill 4 54
(MSSaunders) *fractious coming on to crse: w ldrs to 1/2-way: sn wknd (rn wout one front shoe)* **20/1**

62.38 secs (0.19) **Going Correction** +0.375s/f (Good)
**WFA** 3 from 4yo+ 5lb **12 Ran SP% 118.9**
Speed ratings: **113,109,102,102,101 100,99,99,97,88 86,84**CSF £36.87 TOTE £6.80: £1.80, £3.20, £5.20; EX 50.10.
**Owner** S Bruce **Bred** R T And Mrs Watson **Trained** Uplawmoor, E Renfrews
■ This was elevated from Listed status to Group 3 for the first time.

**FOCUS**
Many of these wanted faster ground and/or six furlongs. Orientor was back to his very best, and Ringmoor Down ran to form, but the rest were well below their best.

**NOTEBOOK**
**Orientor** had never previously won over the minimum trip, but he did finish sixth in the Abbaye in 2002. He travelled well on this rain-softened surface and went on to win decisively. The Nunthorpe could now be on the cards, but the ground will be the key to his chance.
**Ringmoor Down** did not get the best of runs at Ascot and enjoyed a much happier time of it here. She finished well clear of the rest, once again showing that she has the ability to win a Group race.
**Colonel Cotton(IRE)**, who goes on any ground, had the blinkers left off this time. He ran well from off the pace but is notoriously difficult to win with.
**Boogie Street** ◆ showed his usual good early pace, but on this rain-softened ground he burnt himself out. He did well to finish fourth and will be a different propsition back on a fast surface. The King George Stakes at Goodwood and Nunthorpe at York still look realistic targets.
**Twilight Blues(IRE)** was racing over five furlongs for the first time since winning on his debut three years ago and unsurprsingly ran as though finding this trip on the short side.
**The Kiddykid(IRE)** was another running over five furlongs for the first time in a long while. He too looked to find the pace too hot over this shorter trip.
**The Tatling(IRE)** did not get the run of the race but even so it is unlikely he would have played a part in the finish. The ground had gone against him. *Official explanation: jockey said gelding suffered interference in running*
**Bali Royal** *Official explanation: trainer said mare lost a front plate*

## 3538 ADDLESHAW GODDARD STKS (REGISTERED AS THE ESHER STAKES) (LISTED RACE) 2m 78y

2:05 (2:09) (A) 4-Y-O+ £17,400 (£6,600; £3,300; £1,500) Stalls High

Form RPR

4-33 **1** shd **Silver Gilt**[28] 2672 4-8-12 100........................ LDettori 3 110
(JHMGosden) *trckd ldr for 4f: styd prom: effrt to chse wnr over 2f out: sltly checked wl over 1f out: clsd fnl f: jst failed: subs. awr* **7/2**[1]

0-33 **2** **Romany Prince**[14] 3076 5-8-12 100........................ DaneO'Neill 9 110
(DRCElsworth) *lw: hld up in last: prog on outer to ld 3f out: edgd rt 2f out: drvn and jst hld on: fin 1st, shd: subs. disq* **6/1**[3]

0260 **3** 5 **Misternando**[16] 2998 4-9-1 109........................(v[1]) SHitchcott 4 107
(MRChannon) *rn in snatches: lost pl 10f out: last and rdn 4f out: prog to chse ldng pair over 1f out: no imp: wknd last 100yds* **5/1**[2]

/504 **4** 3 ½ **Royal Rebel**[16] 2998 8-8-12 110........................ JPMurtagh 7 100
(MJohnston) *drvn and prog to press ldr after 4f: styd in 2nd pl u.p to 3f out: sn outpcd* **5/1**[2]

6-03 **5** 3 **Gulf (IRE)**[49] 2108 5-8-12 105........................ KFallon 6 96
(DRCElsworth) *t.k.h: hld up in rr: n.m.r 5f out: effrt to chse ldrs 3f out: wknd wl over 1f out* **13/2**

1 **6** 6 **Corrib Eclipse**[14] 3076 5-8-12 105........................ JFEgan 8 92+
(JamiePoulton) *pushed along and prog to chse ldng trio over 10f out: rdn over 3f out: sn wknd* **6/1**[3]

03-6 **7** 13 **Gold Medallist**[49] 2108 4-8-12 102........................ TQuinn 2 73
(DRCElsworth) *lw: led to 3f out: sn wknd* **10/1**

2504 **8** dist **Tizzy May (FR)**[7] 3315 4-8-12 98........................ RHughes 1 —
(RHannon) *trckd ldrs tl lost pl over 3f out: eased over 2f out: t.o* **16/1**

3m 41.17s (2.94) **Going Correction** +0.225s/f (Good) **8 Ran SP% 112.4**
Speed ratings: **100,101,98,96,95 92,85,**—CSF £26.33 TOTE £6.90: £2.00, £1.50, £2.00; EX 30.30.
**Owner** The Dukes of Roxburghe & Devonshire **Bred** Side Hill Stud And Floors Farming **Trained** Manton, Wilts
■ Stewards Enquiry : Dane O'Neill caution: careless riding
L Dettori caution: careless riding

**FOCUS**
A very modest winning time by Listed standards, and only fair form for the grade. The Stewards looked into an incident involving the first two and took over 20 minutes to announce that the result stood, but the result was amended in favour of Silver Gilt after an appeal.

**NOTEBOOK**
**Silver Gilt**, who needs some cut in the ground, came in for market support on this step up in trip and very nearly justified it, staying on strongly after being slightly checked momentarily when the winner went across him and only just failing. Only lightly raced and open to improvement, he should be capable of winning a similar race.
**Romany Prince**, whose only previous victory came in soft ground, benefited from the decent pace set by his stablemate and came through to lead a fair way out. He has looked a difficult horse to win with in the past, and he probably hit the front too soon on this occasion, as he was hard pressed again close home. He is not short on ability, though, and the Melbourne Cup is reportedly the long-term target.
**Misternando** had a visor on for the first time and, despite running in snatches, performed with credit to finish third on ground which would have been much softer than he likes.
**Royal Rebel**, who is lazy and needs plenty of encouragement from his rider, tends to reserve his best for the Ascot Gold Cup.
**Gulf(IRE)** was keen early on in ground that would have been softer than ideal. To date he must be classed as something of an underachiever.
**Corrib Eclipse** was running over a shorter trip and racing on softer ground than when springing a shock at Royal Ascot.
**Gold Medallist** effectively ran as a pacemaker for the winner.
**Tizzy May(FR)** had his stamina limitations exposed. *Official explanation: jockey said colt failed to stay*

## 3539 TOTESCOOP6 STKS (HERITAGE H'CAP) 1m 14y

2:40 (2:46) (B) 3-Y-O+ £58,000 (£22,000; £11,000; £5,000) Stalls High

Form RPR

-060 **1** **Pentecost**[17] 2969 5-8-10 **94**........................ LDettori 1 105
(AMBalding) *stdd s: hld up in last pair: rapid prog over 1f out: swtchd rt ent fnl f: r.o to ld last 75yds: hld on* **20/1**

4/26 **2** hd **St Andrews (IRE)**[15] 3036 4-8-8 **92**........................ PRobinson 8 103
(MAJarvis) *lw: hld up in midfield: prog to trck ldrs 2f out: plld out over 1f out: drvn to ld last 75yds: sn hdd: jst hld* **6/1**[2]

-001 **3** 1 ½ **Unshakable (IRE)**[70] 1623 5-8-10 **94**........................ FNorton 2 101
(BobJones) *prom: rdn to chal over 1f out: ev ch wl ins fnl f: no ex nr fin* **11/2**[1]

4211 **4** nk **Tahreeb (FR)**[13] 3134 3-9-1 **108**........................ MartinDwyer 6 115
(MPTregoning) *lw: trckd ldr: led main gp to nr side in st: overall ldr wl over 1f out: hrd pressed 1f out: hdd & wknd last 75yds* **6/1**[2]

2311 **5** shd **Mine (IRE)**[17] 2969 6-9-10 **108**........................(v) TQuinn 3 115
(JDBethell) *hld up in rr: effrt 2f out: drvn and styd on fnl f: unable to chal* **9/1**

10-3 **6** nk **Colisay**[40] 2358 5-9-3 **101**........................ KFallon 14 107
(ACStewart) *racd in midfield: rdn and prog over 2f out: drvn and cl up 1f out: one pce ins fnl f* **9/1**

-045 **7** shd **Camp Commander (IRE)**[17] 2969 5-8-12 **96**........................(t) DHolland 5 102
(CEBrittain) *hld up in rr: prog over 1f out: styd on ins fnl f: nt pce to chal* **14/1**

2400 **8** 1 **Boston Lodge**[14] 3074 4-8-12 **96**........................(b) RHughes 11 100
(GAButler) *hld up towards rr: rdn 2f out: styd on fnl f: nvr able to chal* **33/1**

2111 **9** ½ **Ace Of Hearts**[13] 3119 5-8-7 **91**........................ SSanders 13 94
(CFWall) *lw: racd in midfield: pushed along 1/2-way: rdn and prog to chal over 1f out: wknd ins fnl f* **8/1**[3]

0530 **10** ¾ **Finished Article (IRE)**[17] 2969 7-8-6 **90** ow1........................ DaneO'Neill 4 91
(DRCElsworth) *dwlt: hld up in last pair: prog over 1f out: kpt on ins fnl f: n.d* **14/1**

-203 **11** 14 **Thyolo (IRE)**[16] 3001 3-8-6 **99**........................ JPSpencer 18 71
(CGCox) *led: styd far side in st: lost overall ld wl over 1f out: wknd and eased fnl f* **9/1**

0002 **12** *3 1/2* **Calcutta**[13] 3119 8-8-13 **97** RHills 16 61
(BWHills) *racd in midfield: eventually c w main gp to nr side in st: wknd 2f out* **20/1**

0100 **13** *shd* **Pablo**[52] 2044 5-9-2 **100** JPMurtagh 17 64
(BWHills) *prom: rdn and cl up 2f out: wknd rapidly over 1f out* **12/1**

0544 **14** *5* **Our Teddy (IRE)**[13] 3118 4-8-3 **87** (b) EAhern 12 41
(AMBalding) *a wl in rr: losing tch over 2f out: t.o* **25/1**

0000 **15** *19* **Tuning Fork**[15] 3034 4-8-8 **92** (t) JQuinn 7 6
(JAkehurst) *t.k.h: prom: styd far side in st: hrd rdn and no ch w ldr over 2f out: wknd: t.o* **33/1**

1m 43.25s (-0.67) **Going Correction** +0.225s/f (Good)
**WFA** 3 from 4yo+ 9lb **15** Ran SP% **125.3**
Speed ratings: **112,111,110,110,109 109,109,108,108,107 93,89,89,84,65**CSF £132.99 CT £787.97 TOTE £23.10: £5.20, £3.50, £2.80; EX 204.30 Trifecta £2174.40 Part won. Pool: £3,062.66. 0.80 winning tickets..
**Owner** J C, J R And S R Hitchins **Bred** Miss S N Ralphs **Trained** Kingsclere, Hants

**FOCUS**
There was a strong pace on here and the majority came stands' side in the straight. The time was solid for the class and the form is strong.

**NOTEBOOK**
**Pentecost**, whose last two victories came off marks of 91 and 92, has been struggling of late, but the Handicapper had dropped him 6lb since the start of the season and, with the race run to suit, he came to win the race well inside the last. All his previous wins had been on fast ground, but he handles a little cut. *Official explanation: trainer has no explanation for the improved form shown*
**St Andrews(IRE)** ◆ ran really well at Royal Ascot on his previous start and improved again, tackling the softest ground he has ever encountered here. He lost nothing in defeat and it would be no surprise to see him pick up a decent handicap. Indeed, the William Hill Mile at Goodwood is next on the agenda.
**Unshakable(IRE)**, 6lb higher than for his course and distance success in April, was up with the pace throughout and ran a solid race. He should remain competitive off this sort of mark.
**Tahreeb(FR)** ◆ chased a decent gallop before taking up the running himself, with his rider keen to head for the stands' side. He only dropped out of the places close home and this was a big run by a three-year-old giving weight away to most of his rivals. Already a Group 3 winner abroad, he can pay his way again back in minor Pattern company.
**Mine(IRE)**, a model of consistency in big-field handicaps, ran another brave race under top weight. He is worth another try in Listed grade, although the possible lack of pace is the worry there.
**Colisay** left a disappointing reappearance run behind and can hopefully build on this. He may need some help from the Handicapper, though.
**Camp Commander(IRE)** is a consistent type in this sort of event but the Handicapper knows all about him. *Official explanation: jockey said horse hung right*
**Boston Lodge** had the blinkers back on and the return to a mile suited him, having been running over sprint distances of late.
**Ace Of Hearts** has been in cracking form lately, but his run of success came on fast ground.
**Finished Article(IRE)** will have his chances back at his favourite track Goodwood, where his record reads 61242175052125.
**Thyolo(IRE)** was probably at a disadvantage staying towards the inside in the straight, but the ground had also gone against him. He should be a different proposition back on a fast surface.

## 3540 CORAL-ECLIPSE STKS (GROUP 1) 1m 2f 7y
3:15 (3:23) (A) 3-Y-O+ £237,220 (£89,980; £44,990; £20,450) Stalls High

Form RPR

-001 **1** **Refuse To Bend (IRE)**[18] 2957 4-9-7 (t) LDettori 9 126
(SaeedBinSuroor) *lw: t.k.h early: cl up: effrt over 2f out: led wl over 1f out: drvn out: jst hld on* **15/2**[3]

-531 **2** *hd* **Warrsan (IRE)**[29] 2639 6-9-7 **118** DHolland 6 126
(CEBrittain) *chsd ldrs: effrt over 2f out: drvn to press wnr over 1f out: styd on wl nr fin: jst failed* **12/1**

2-21 **3** *4* **Kalaman (IRE)**[38] 2398 4-9-7 **116** KFallon 3 123+
(SirMichaelStoute) *lw: hld up in last pair: hmpd 3f out: nt clr run 2f out: rdn and prog over 1f out: hung lft ins fnl f: tk 3rd nr fin* **12/1**

-430 **4** *1/2* **Norse Dancer (IRE)**[18] 2957 4-9-7 **117** (b[1]) TQuinn 11 118
(DRCElsworth) *lw: hld up in last: nt clr run briefly 2f out: prog wl over 1f out: styd on ins fnl f: n.d* **20/1**

3-12 **5** *hd* **Powerscourt**[17] 2968 4-9-7 JPSpencer 10 118
(APO'Brien, Ire) *lw: prom: led 4f out to 3f out: styd w ldr: ev ch over 1f out: fdd ins fnl f* **11/2**[2]

3623 **6** *1 3/4* **Ikhtyar (IRE)**[17] 2968 4-9-7 **116** RHills 7 115
(JHMGosden) *settled towards rr: shkn up and prog over 2f out: no imp on ldrs jst over 1f out: fdd* **8/1**

-360 **7** *2* **Imperial Dancer**[29] 2639 6-9-7 **117** TEDurcan 4 111
(MRChannon) *settled in rr: rdn 3f out: no prog over 2f out: one pce after* **25/1**

12-1 **8** *nk* **Rakti**[17] 2968 5-9-7 **121** PRobinson 12 111+
(MAJarvis) *dwlt: plld hrd and rapid prog to go prom after 1f: led 3f out to wl over 1f out: wknd* **13/8**[1]

-165 **9** *nk* **Salford City (IRE)**[28] 2680 3-8-10 **115** JPMurtagh 2 110
(DRCElsworth) *hld up towards rr: hrd rdn and no prog 2f out: no ch after* **8/1**

1111 **10** *2 1/2* **African Dream**[57] 1924 3-8-10 **113** JQuinn 5 106
(PWChapple-Hyam) *racd in midfield: styd on inner bnd over 4f out: drvn wl over 2f out: wknd over 1f out* **16/1**

-062 **11** *2 1/2* **Maktub (ITY)**[13] 3136 5-9-7 **110** GCarter 1 102
(MAJarvis) *led to 4f out: wknd over 2f out* **100/1**

0100 **12** *30* **Chancellor (IRE)**[32] 2559 6-9-7 **110** SSanders 13 51
(JLDunlop) *trckd ldrs: styd on inner bnd over 4f out and prom 3f out: sn rdn and wknd: t.o* **66/1**

2m 8.31s (-1.87) **Going Correction** +0.225s/f (Good)
**WFA** 3 from 4yo+ 11lb **12** Ran SP% **119.8**
Speed ratings: **116,115,112,112,112 110,109,108,108,106 104,80**CSF £91.89 TOTE £7.30: £2.40, £2.10, £4.00; EX 63.00 Trifecta £550.60 Pool: £5,118.78. 6.60 winning tickets.
**Owner** Godolphin **Bred** Moyglare Stud Farm Ltd **Trained** Newmarket, Suffolk
■ Stewards Enquiry : D Holland one-day ban: careless riding (Jul 14)

**FOCUS**
An acceptable, if not outstanding, winning time for a Group One whose field featured 5 individual winners at that level but lacked a strong contender from the Classic generation. The winner has initially been awarded an identical RPR to that recorded by Falbrav and Hawk Wing after their wins in the corresponding race.

**NOTEBOOK**
**Refuse To Bend(IRE)** had easier ground to cope with and his stamina for this longer trip was unproven. Neither factor proved any problem, though, and he saw the race out strongly. He is clearly now back to his very best and should continue a force to be reckoned with in top races from a mile to ten furlongs throughout the rest of the season.
**Warrsan(IRE)**, a dual Coronation Cup winner, twice won over a mile six earlier in his career so this drop back to ten furlongs was a worry. The rain-softened ground made it a test, though, and he ran a cracker to finish a narrow runner-up. The King George is next on the agenda and the return to a mile and a half will suit at Ascot.
**Kalaman(IRE)**, who looked outstanding beforehand, has been something of an underachiever, having started favourite for seven of his previous eight career starts but won only three of them. He would have finished closer but for being hampered twice, and he can hopefully now start fulfilling some of his potential.
**Norse Dancer(IRE)** ran poorly at Ascot but put up a more typical display in the first-time blinkers. He is not the heartiest of battlers but is fairly consistent at the top level.
**Powerscourt** is by Sadler's Wells, has form on soft ground and over farther, and so was expected by some to reverse Ascot form with Rakti. He did that, but having looked likely to be at least placed early in the straight, he weakened disappointingly out of contention. Perhaps faster ground suits him better after all.
**Ikhtyar(IRE)** had no excuses on the ground front this time and is becoming slightly disappointing. He deserves a chance to pick up a confidence-boosting win at a lower level.
**Imperial Dancer** once again found the competition at this level too tough.
**Rakti**, although a winner on soft ground in the past, is clearly much happier on a fast surface, as he showed at Ascot. Having missed the break, he was rushed up to make up the lost ground and was soon pulling strongly in behind the leader. He got away with racing keenly at Ascot but in this ground he gave himself little chance of getting home. He could be his own worst enemy. *Official explanation: jockey said horse was unsuited by good to soft ground*
**Salford City(IRE)**, running on the softest surface he has encountered to date, did not do a lot for the Derby form, but his run can be excused on account of the ground.
**African Dream** appeared to have conditions to suit but he too failed to advertise the Classic generation's form.

## 3541 PACEMAKER DISTAFF STKS (LISTED RACE) (FILLIES) 1m 14y
3:50 (3:59) (A) 3-Y-O £17,400 (£6,600; £3,300; £1,500) Stalls High

Form RPR

1-1 **1** **Antediluvian**[9] 3223 3-8-11 KFallon 7 104
(SirMichaelStoute) *lw: settled in midfield: prog 3f out: rdn to chal 2f out: disp ld after tl drvn to assert last 100yds* **9/4**[1]

2-04 **2** *3/4* **Snow Goose**[14] 3105 3-8-11 **100** TQuinn 4 102
(JLDunlop) *led: 4l clr 1/2-way: jnd 2f out: kpt on wl tl hdd and no ex last 100yds* **8/1**

-365 **3** *1 1/2* **Ithaca (USA)**[50] 2081 3-8-11 **94** RHughes 3 99
(HRACecil) *trckd ldr: chal 2f out: disp ld after tl nt qckn last 100yds* **25/1**

3414 **4** *4* **Brindisi**[17] 2971 3-8-11 **95** MartinDwyer 1 91
(BWHills) *t.k.h: trckd ldrs: rdn 2f out: nt qckn and btn over 1f out* **14/1**

14 **5** *3/4* **Moon Dazzle (USA)**[15] 3033 3-8-11 **106** RHills 2 89
(WJHaggas) *lw: t.k.h: hld up in tch: rdn and nt qckn 2f out: one pce and btn after* **3/1**[2]

5056 **6** *3/4* **Kelucia (IRE)**[15] 3033 3-8-11 **98** JPMurtagh 8 88
(JSGoldie) *hld up in last pair: rdn and sme prog over 2f out: no imp over 1f out* **16/1**

-623 **7** *1 1/2* **Kunda (IRE)**[14] 3105 3-8-11 **96** LDettori 6 85
(RHannon) *hld up in last pair: effrt over 2f out: no prog and btn over 1f out* **7/1**

10-4 **8** *7* **Donna Vita**[56] 1963 3-8-11 **90** DHolland 5 70
(PWChapple-Hyam) *t.k.h: chsd ldrs tl wknd over 2f out* **33/1**

3-30 **9** *2 1/2* **Nataliya**[62] 1791 3-8-11 **110** SSanders 9 65
(JLDunlop) *hld up: last and rdn over 3f out: wl btn after: wknd fnl f* **11/2**[3]

1m 44.59s (0.67) **Going Correction** +0.225s/f (Good) **9** Ran SP% **114.1**
Speed ratings: **105,104,102,98,98 97,95,88,86**CSF £20.81 TOTE £2.60: £1.50, £2.10, £3.90; EX 29.00.
**Owner** Lordship Stud **Bred** Mrs M L Parry And P M Steele-Mortimer **Trained** Newmarket, Suffolk

**FOCUS**
A decent Listed contest won by a progressive type. Moon Dazzle and Kelucia failed to advertise the Coronation Stakes form, although the ground was very different.

**NOTEBOOK**
**Antediluvian**, a well-made filly, is progressing well and took another step up the class ladder. She was nicely on top at the finish and a mile and a quarter looks sure to suit her even better.
**Snow Goose** was given a positive ride over this longer trip and a lack of stamina certainly was not her undoing. She handled the easier conditions well and a race of similar quality looks within her ability.
**Ithaca(USA)** ran a much better race back in trip and clearly lack of stamina has been the problem earlier this year. She finished clear of the fourth and hopefully this performance will begin to get her career back on track.
**Brindisi**, tackling the slowest ground she has ever encountered, raced keenly in the early stages and could not go with the front three when they upped the tempo.
**Moon Dazzle(USA)**, an excellent fourth in the Coronation Stakes on only her second start, had her chance but just could not pick up in this ground. She deserves a chance to prove this form all wrong back on a fast surface.
**Kelucia(IRE)** looks as though she is going to be difficult to place this season.
**Kunda(IRE)** is another who looks difficult to place.
**Nataliya** *Official explanation: jockey said filly lost her action*

## 3542 WOODHURST CONSTRUCTION H'CAP 7f 16y
4:20 (4:33) (C) (0-100,92) 3-Y-O £12,528 (£4,752; £2,376; £1,080) Stalls High

Form RPR

211- **1** **Silk Fan (IRE)**[288] 5040 3-9-7 **92** MartinDwyer 6 101
(PWHarris) *hld up in rr: stdy prog over 2f out: led over 1f out: drvn and kpt on wl fnl f* **9/2**[2]

-002 **2** *3/4* **Jazz Scene (IRE)**[7] 3295 3-9-4 **92** SHitchcott[(3)] 11 99
(MRChannon) *hld up in last pair: rdn wl over 2f out: prog over 1f out: styd on wl to snatch 2nd on post* **9/1**

4230 **3** *shd* **Zonus**[16] 3001 3-9-5 **90** RHills 13 97
(BWHills) *trckd ldrs: effrt to chal over 2f out: hanging and nt qckn over 1f out: styd on ins fnl f* **3/1**[1]

-152 **4** *shd* **Place Cowboy (IRE)**[14] 3089 3-8-5 **76** EAhern 15 83
(JAOsborne) *settled towards rr: prog over 2f out: rdn to chal over 1f out : styd on same pce fnl f* **11/1**

6121 **5** *1* **Distant Connection (IRE)**[16] 3017 3-8-10 **81** SSanders 9 85
(APJarvis) *trckd ldr 5f out: led gng easily over 2f out: hdd and rdn over 1f out: edgd lft and nt qckn fnl f* **8/1**

2041 **6** *1/2* **Appalachian Trail (IRE)**[15] 3053 3-9-5 **90** RHughes 3 93+
(ISemple) *t.k.h: hld up in last pair: gng wl whn nt clr run over 2f out to ins fnl f: no ch* **11/2**[3]

0341 **7** *nk* **King's Caprice**[7] 3322 3-9-0 **85** DHolland 7 87
(GBBalding) *t.k.h: hld up in tch: effrt to press ldrs 2f out: one pce and hld whn nt clr run wl ins fnl f* **12/1**

2-60 **8** *2 1/2* **Bentley's Ball (USA)**[16] 3001 3-9-5 **90** DaneO'Neill 2 86
(RHannon) *hld up towards rr: rdn over 2f out: one pce and no imp on ldrs* **20/1**

41-3 **9** *2* **King Of Cashel (IRE)**[22] 2844 3-9-1 **86** KFallon 8 76
(RHannon) *racd in midfield: drvn and no rspnse wl over 2f out: sn btn* **8/1**

05-0 **10** *3* **Great Scott**[10] 3205 3-9-2 **87** SChin 12 70
(MJohnston) *led for 1f: lost pl 4f out: renewed effrt u.p to chal 3f out: wknd over 1f out* **25/1**

0-30 **11** *nk* **Love Triangle (IRE)**[10] 3203 3-8-9 **80**...................................... JQuinn 10 62
(DRCElsworth) *led after 1f to over 2f out: sn lost pl and eased* **20/1**

1m 31.66s (0.57) **Going Correction** +0.225s/f (Good) **11** Ran SP% **120.2**
Speed ratings: **105,104,104,103,102 102,101,99,96,93 92**CSF £44.39 CT £145.08 TOTE £6.30: £2.30, £2.40, £2.20; EX 39.40.
**Owner** Harris, Clark, Swinburn & Harris **Bred** Abbeville And Meadow Court Partners **Trained** Ringshall, Bucks

**FOCUS**
A decent pace and it paid to be held up off the gallop.

**NOTEBOOK**
**Silk Fan(IRE)**, who looked fit, was well supported on her belated reappearance. She has clearly had one or two problems but looks sure to make up for lost time on this evidence, and black type must surely be the immediate objective.
**Jazz Scene(IRE)**, up 5lb for his Chester effort, like the winner came from off the pace. This was a good effort under top weight but as a result the Handicapper will probably end up keeping hold of him for the time being.
**Zonus** has now started favourite for his last four starts and has been beaten every time. He is proving expensive to follow but there was not much wrong with this run.
**Place Cowboy(IRE)**, who was only having his fifth ever start, was in second a few yards from the line but just lost out on a place close home. He is going the right way and is open to further improvement.
**Distant Connection(IRE)** arrived here in top form and did best of the prominent racers, but he was racing off a 7lb higher mark and on softer ground.
**Appalachian Trail(IRE)**, ideally suited by another furlong, did not get the best of runs and by the time he saw daylight the race was over. He has the ability to win a race off this mark, but a return to a mile will suit.
**King's Caprice** did not appear to fail through lack of stamina.

## 3543 DEBORAH SHAILER H'CAP — 1m 2f 7y
4:55 (5:03) (D ) (0-85,84) 3-Y-O — **£14,202** (£4,370; £2,185; £1,092) **Stalls** High

Form — RPR

-050 **1** **Hezaam (USA)**[29] 2648 3-8-11 **74**.............................................. RHills 14 84
(JLDunlop) *hld up wl in rr: prog on outer over 2f out: chsd ldr 1f out: r.o wl to ld last strides* **12/1**

-414 **2** *½* **Boule D'Or (IRE)**[23] 2809 3-9-4 **81**............................................... NDay 5 90
(RIngram) *hld up in midfield: prog over 2f out: led over 1f out and drvn 3l clr: wknd and hdd last strides* **9/1**

0055 **3** *1 ¼* **Winners Delight**[15] 3046 3-9-2 **79**............................................ KFallon 9 86
(APJarvis) *hld up in last trio: nt clr run 3f out: prog 2f out: drvn to chse ldng pair ins fnl f: no imp nr fin* **4/1**[1]

5510 **4** *2 ½* **Whitsbury Cross**[16] 3000 3-9-3 **80**........................................... TQuinn 3 83
(DRCElsworth) *lw: trckd ldrs: lost pl and pushed along 3f out: no prog u.p 2f out: r.o again fnl f* **14/1**

0244 **5** *¾* **Cartronageeraghlad (IRE)**[21] 2887 3-9-0 **77**.................. DaneO'Neill 8 78
(JAOsborne) *hld up towards rr: nt clr run 3f out: rdn and prog 2f out: styd on fnl f: n.d* **12/1**

2240 **6** *shd* **Baawrah**[100] 1108 3-8-2 **65**.............................................................. PDoe 1 66
(MRChannon) *hld up in rr: rdn over 2f out: no prog tl styd on fr over 1f out: n.d* **25/1**

-041 **7** *2 ½* **Red Birr (IRE)**[10] 3213 3-9-5 **82**........................................ MartinDwyer 4 78
(AMBalding) *settled in rr: effrt over 2f out: nt clr run briefly over 1f out: kpt on fnl f: nrst fin* **15/2**[3]

00-0 **8** *shd* **American Duke (USA)**[24] 2790 3-8-3 **66**................................. SChin 12 62
(BJMeehan) *t.k.h: pressed ldrs: rdn over 2f out: fdd over 1f out* **50/1**

1-00 **9** *1 ¼* **Breathing Sun (IRE)**[51] 2069 3-8-13 **76**.............................(t) GCarter 7 70
(WJMusson) *dwlt: hld up in last trio: nt clr run 3f out and wl over 1f out: kpt on after: no ch* **20/1**

-100 **10** *¾* **Over The Rainbow (IRE)**[16] 2999 3-9-5 **82**.................(b[1]) JPMurtagh 11 75
(BWHills) *racd freely: led to over 2f out: wknd and eased over 1f out* **12/1**

-465 **11** *½* **Malibu (IRE)**[12] 3152 3-8-12 **75**................................................ JQuinn 13 67
(SDow) *prom: led over 2f out: hdd over 1f out: wknd rapidly* **25/1**

-005 **12** *3* **Top Spec (IRE)**[30] 2612 3-9-3 **80**.......................................... RHughes 16 66
(RHannon) *dwlt: rushed up to chse ldrs: rdn and cl up over 2f out: wknd rapidly over 1f out* **25/1**

-301 **13** *2 ½* **Pagan Magic (USA)**[31] 2578 3-8-10 **76**.............................. LisaJones(3) 2 58
(JARToller) *lw: racd in midfield: rdn 3f out: wknd 2f out* **5/1**[2]

6010 **14** *¾* **Balearic Star (IRE)**[21] 2887 3-8-4 **70** ow1...................... SHitchcott(3) 18 51
(BRMillman) *prom tl wknd over 2f out* **14/1**

6-06 **15** *shd* **Hoh Bleu Dee**[32] 2557 3-9-5 **82**............................................. LDettori 15 62
(SKirk) *settled towards rr: shuffled along and nt clr run over 2f out: sn wknd* **16/1**

3412 **16** *3* **Swainson (USA)**[22] 2841 3-9-7 **84**.......................................... DHolland 6 59
(PMitchell) *t.k.h: racd wd: trckd ldrs tl wknd 3f out* **8/1**

2m 11.45s (1.27) **Going Correction** +0.225s/f (Good) **16** Ran SP% **130.1**
Speed ratings: **103,102,101,99,99 98,96,96,95,95 94,92,90,89,89 87**CSF £116.35 CT £527.11 TOTE £16.60: £3.90, £2.90, £1.30, £4.80; EX 211.70 Place 6 £203.69, Place 5 £48.51.
**Owner** Hamdan Al Maktoum **Bred** Shadwell Farm Llc **Trained** Arundel, W Sussex

**FOCUS**
Once again most of the principals came from off the pace. This looks fair form.

**NOTEBOOK**
**Hezaam(USA)** had not run on ground as soft as this since winning his maiden last autumn and clearly the ground is the key to him. He got up in the last strides and his rider looked particularly pleased, waving his stick in the air as though he had won a Group One.
**Boule D'Or(IRE)** ◆ failed to stay a mile and a half last time out and appreciated the drop back in trip. He accelerated away from his field in good style and looked to have the race won until collared close home. It might be that his rider went too soon on him, and he definitely looks capable of winning again, even off a higher mark, as he has a smart turn of foot.
**Winners Delight**, an eye-catcher at Kempton in the spring, was heavily backed but did not enjoy the best of luck. He was doing all his best work at the finish and is probably worth another try over a mile and a half.
**Whitsbury Cross**, outclassed in Listed grade last time, found his second wind inside the final furlong and finished well.
**Cartronageeraghlad(IRE)**, who has dropped 5lb since the start of the season, always looks vulnerable to less exposed rivals.
**Baawrah** was another to stay on late in the day. He is entitled to come on for this first run since March.
**Red Birr(IRE)** had the ground to suit but was ridden less prominently on this occasion. He shapes as though he will get farther.
**Breathing Sun(IRE)** did not enjoy much luck in running and ran a fair bit better than his finishing position implies. This was a step up on his previous form this season. *Official explanation: jockey said colt suffered interference in running*
**Pagan Magic(USA)** *Official explanation: jockey said colt had been struck into*
**Swainson(USA)** *Official explanation: jockey said colt was unsuited by good to soft ground*
T/Plt: £782.80 to a £1 stake. Pool: £123,380.65. 115.05 winning tickets. T/Qpdt: £73.10 to a £1 stake. Pool: £7,228.40. 73.10 winning tickets. JN

3544 - 3546a (Foreign Racing) - See Raceform Interactive

# [3214]LEOPARDSTOWN (L-H)
Saturday, July 3

**OFFICIAL GOING: Good to yielding**

## 3547a IRISH STALLION FARMS EUROPEAN BREEDERS FUND BROWNSTOWN STKS (GROUP 3) (F&M) — 7f
7:15 (7:15) 3-Y-O+ — **£41,197** (£12,042; £5,704; £1,901)

RPR

**1** **Tropical Lady (IRE)**[6] 3349 4-9-5 112.................................. KJManning 5 108+
(JSBolger, Ire) *chsd ldrs: rdn in 4th fr early st: 3rd 1f out: r.o strly fnl f to ld cl home* **11/4**[2]

**2** *nk* **Majestic Desert**[15] 3033 3-9-0 ............................................. TEDurcan 1 110+
(MRChannon) *trckd ldrs: chal in 2nd fr under 2f out: led 1f out: kpt on wl fnl f: hdd cl home* **11/10**[1]

**3** *2* **Red Feather (IRE)**[15] 3065 3-8-11 103...........................(t) NGMcCullagh 8 102
(EdwardLynam, Ire) *led: rdn and strly pressed fr under 2f out: hdd 1f out: sn dropped to 3rd: kpt on one pce* **10/1**

**4** *3* **Dangle (IRE)**[31] 2601 3-8-11 88............................................ MJKinane 2 94
(EdwardLynam, Ire) *towards rr and t.k.h early: impr into 5th and rdn fr 2f out: no imp fr 1 1/2f out: kpt on same pce* **12/1**

**5** *2* **Royal Tigress (USA)**[15] 3033 3-8-11 105.............................. JPSpencer 6 89
(APO'Brien, Ire) *trckd ldrs: rdn in 4th fr 2f out: no imp fr 1 1/2f out: kpt on one pce* **9/2**[3]

**6** *3 ½* **Follow (USA)**[41] 2330 3-8-11 92.................................... CO'Donoghue 7 80
(APO'Brien, Ire) *rr: rdn and kpt on wout threatening fr 2f out* **25/1**

**7** *nk* **Summer Sunset (IRE)**[7] 3328 3-8-11 94.........................(b) PJSmullen 4 79
(DKWeld, Ire) *chsd ldrs and t.k.h early: rdn and no imp fr early st* **20/1**

**8** *3 ¼* **Dixie Evans**[7] 3328 4-9-5 94...............................................(b) DMGrant 3 70
(HRogers, Ire) *s.i.s: sn trckd ldrs: rdn and wknd fr 2f out* **25/1**

1m 29.2s **Going Correction** -0.05s/f (Good)
**WFA** 3 from 4yo 8lb **8** Ran SP% **121.7**
Speed ratings: **115,114,112,108,106 102,102,98**CSF £6.45 TOTE £3.50: £1.40, £1.10, £1.90; DF 5.30.
**Owner** George J Kent **Bred** John Boden & Willie Kane **Trained** Coolcullen, Co Carlow

**FOCUS**
Another weak link in the Irish Pattern with an improving handicapper emerging on top.

**NOTEBOOK**
**Tropical Lady(IRE)**'s three handicap wins this season have seen her climb 28 lb from her starter mark of 84. This was a step up in class on paper and she showed more stamina than speed when wearing down the runner-up close home. She stays a mile comfortably and will get ten furlongs.
**Majestic Desert** was weak in the market. She got her head in front a furlong down but had nothing more to give in the closing stages.
**Red Feather(IRE)** ran in front until headed a furlong out.
**Dangle(IRE)** is an ordinary maiden winner with no pretensions in this company.
**Royal Tigress(USA)** was supported to turn Ascot form around with Majestic Desert but held out no hope in the straight.

3548 - 3551a (Foreign Racing) - See Raceform Interactive

# [3504]HAMBURG (R-H)
Saturday, July 3

**OFFICIAL GOING: Heavy**

## 3552a HOLSTEN-TROPHY (GROUP 3) — 6f
4:20 (4:37) 3-Y-O+ — **£42,254** (£14,789; £7,746; £3,873)

RPR

**1** **Lucky Strike**[36] 2466 6-9-3 ..................................................... ADeVries 7 110
(ATrybuhl, Germany) *prom early, mid-div & came widest to stands rail str, hdwy wl over 1f out, led 1f out, hung rt (into whip), driven out* 1

**2** *1 ¼* **Fiepes Shuffle (GER)**[36] 2466 4-9-3 ................................ J-PCarvalho 3 107
(MarioHofer, Germany) *always close up, led over 2f out to 1f out, ran on one pace*

**3** *1* **Areias (GER)**[36] 2466 6-9-1 ........................................................ AStarke 5 102
(ASchutz, Germany) *outpcd early, last at half-way, styd towards far side & mde hdwy to 5th ent str, 2nd over 1f out, one pace fnl f*

**4** *¾* **Gold Type (IRE)**[36] 2466 5-8-12 ............................................ WMongil 10 98
(KWoodburn) *outpaced, last straight, ran on final 2f to take 4th close home*

**5** *½* **Welsh Emperor (IRE)**[7] 3308 5-9-1 ..............................(b) DaleGibson 14 99
(TPTate) *s.i.s, mid-div str, switched lft over 1f out, disp 3rd appr fnl f, kpt on one pace & lost 4th cl hme* 2

**6** *2 ½* **Bodyguard Of Spain (GER)**[400] 1983 5-9-1 ...................... TMundry 13 93
(CZschache, Germany) *prominent on outside, 4th straight, disputed 2nd well over 1f out, weakened final f*

**7** *3* **Raffelberger (GER)**[64] 1756 3-8-7 ...................................... ASuborics 1 84
(MarioHofer, Germany) *always outpaced* 3

**8** *9* **Sacho (GER)**[36] 2466 6-9-1 .............................................. AHelfenbein 11 63
(WKujath, Germany) *prominent, 3rd straight, weakened well over 1f out*

**9** *¾* **Aristaios (GER)**[41] 2335 3-8-7 ...........................................(b) IFerguson 4 59
(BruceHellier, Germany) *in rear to straight, never a factor*

**10** *1 ¼* **Rue La Fayette (SWE)**[12] 3162 4-8-10 ................. LHammer-Hansen 2 53
(FReuterskiold, Sweden) *set strong pace to over 2f out, soon weakened*

**11** *½* **Musadif (USA)**[20] 6-9-1 ........................................................ FJohansson 6 57
(RoyArneKvisla, Sweden) *always outpaced*

**12** *½* **Lores Joy (ARG)** 5-9-5 ................................................................ GSolis 9 60
(DiegoLowther, Sweden) *speed over 3f*

**13** *¾* **Media Hora (CHI)** 4-9-1 ...................................................(b) MSantos 8 54
(FCastro, Sweden) *speed over 3f*

1m 15.07s
**WFA** 3 from 4yo+ 6lb **13** Ran SP% **131.5**
Speed ratings: .
**Owner** Stall Lucky Stables International **Bred** Red House Stud **Trained** Germany

**NOTEBOOK**
**Lucky Strike**, the best sprinter in Germany at present, won well despite hanging again. He now heads to Deauville for the Prix Maurice de Gheest in August.
**Fiepes Shuffle(GER)**, a regular in these events, posted his best effort of the season. He is a fair performer, though one any decent British sprinter should have little trouble in accounting for.
**Welsh Emperor(IRE)** had ground conditions come in his favour, but was landed with the worst of the draw. After being slowly away, his jockey reported he could never get him into the position he wanted.

# [3390] BRIGHTON (L-H)

Sunday, July 4

**OFFICIAL GOING: Good to firm (firm in places) changing to good after race 2 (3.00)**

In all six races the runners raced towards the near-side rail in the straight. The exception was Taboor in the last race, who stayed far side, but was well held.

## 3553 STAN JAMES IN-RUNNING MAIDEN AUCTION STKS — 6f 209y

2:30 (2:31) (E) 2-Y-O — £3,701 (£1,139; £569; £284) Stalls Low

Form — RPR

5 **1** **He's A Diamond**[26] 2761 2-8-8 ........ RMiles(3) 2 71
(TGMills) *a in tch: rdn to ld appr fnl f: jst hld on: all out* 5/2[2]

0505 **2** *shd* **Campeon (IRE)**[20] 2947 2-8-9 ........ RLMoore 7 69
(MJWallace) *a front rnk: led after 3f: hdd appr fnl f: rallied ins last u.p to press wnr to line* 7/1[3]

565 **3** *1* **Dusty Dane (IRE)**[10] 3242 2-8-8 ........ ADaly 1 65
(WGMTurner) *hld up in tch: rdn 2f out: styd on ins fnl f: nvr nrr* 7/1[3]

533 **4** *1 3/4* **Safendonseabiscuit**[9] 3259 2-8-9 ........ JFortune 4 62
(SKirk) *led for 3f: styd prom: rdn over 1f out: fdd ins last* 15/8[1]

063 **5** *1 1/4* **Be Bop Aloha**[18] 2985 2-8-2 ........ TPQueally 8 51
(IAWood) *t.k.h: in tch on outside: rdn 2f out: no hdwy after* 33/1

065 **6** *shd* **Pacific Star (IRE)**[9] 3259 2-8-10 ........ TEDurcan 5 59
(EALDunlop) *s.i.s: sn prom: wknd over 1f out* 7/1[3]

**7** *3* **Top Pursuit** 2-8-7 ........ SDrowne 9 48
(JLSpearing) *in tch early: sn outpcd* 33/1

0 **8** *nk* **Lord Normacote**[51] 2096 2-8-9 ........ SSanders 6 49
(CADwyer) *s.i.s: a bhd* 20/1

1m 25.67s (3.07) **Going Correction** +0.25s/f (Good) **8** Ran SP% **111.5**

Speed ratings: **92,91,90,88,87 87,83,83**CSF £18.91 TOTE £2.70: £1.20, £2.70, £2.10; EX 12.40.

**Owner** Ms Tracey Barker **Bred** Tattersalls Ltd **Trained** Headley, Surrey

**FOCUS**

Just a modest maiden run at an ordinary pace.

**NOTEBOOK**

**He's A Diamond** offered promise on his debut in a modest contest over six furlongs at Salisbury and, with the benefit of that experience, improved enough to get off the mark. His long-term future lies in the hands of the Handicapper.

**Campeon(IRE)** appreciated this step up from five furlongs and was just denied. There is a similar race in him, but he is not one to take a short price about.

**Dusty Dane(IRE)** looked to run above himself in a conditions event at Salisbury on his previous start, but this was another solid run.

**Safendonseabiscuit** was well held and does not appear to be progressing. That said, it could be worth keeping an eye on him in nurseries.

**Be Bop Aloha** ran respectably, but just lacked a change of pace.

## 3554 STAN JAMES ONLINE MAIDEN STKS — 7f 214y

3:00 (3:00) (D) 3-Y-O — £5,473 (£1,684; £842; £421) Stalls Low

Form — RPR

5-36 **1** **Carry On Doc**[44] 2267 3-9-0 73 ........ SWhitworth 8 79
(JWHills) *hld up: hdwy on stands' rail whn short of room over 1f out: swtchd ledt: rdn and r.o to ld fnl 100yds* 11/2[2]

30-0 **2** *hd* **Du Pre**[11] 3209 3-8-9 74 ........ SSanders 4 74
(MrsAJPerrett) *w.w: hdwy over 2f out: rdn to ld wl over 1f out: hdd fnl 100yds: kpt on* 6/1[3]

-400 **3** *3* **Indiana Blues**[12] 3179 3-8-6 75 ........ LPKeniry(3) 6 67
(AMBalding) *t.k.h: a.p: ev ch over 1f out: fdd ins fnl f* 9/1

00 **4** *1* **Eijaaz (IRE)**[15] 3106 3-9-0 ........ RHills 9 69
(ACStewart) *hld up in rr: hdwy over 1f out: styd on fnl f: nvr nr to chal* 12/1

2-32 **5** *1 1/2* **River Nurey (IRE)**[15] 3106 3-9-0 72 ........ DHolland 2 66
(BWHills) *led: hdd wl over 1f out: sn wknd* 10/11[1]

5-60 **6** *6* **Regal Flight (IRE)**[20] 2949 3-9-0 50 ........ RLMoore 7 52
(JMBradley) *tok t.k.h: prom tl wknd 2f out* 33/1

**7** *8* **Ceylon Round (FR)** 3-8-6 ........ DCorby(3) 1 29
(MJWallace) *trckd ldrs tl rdn and wknd wl over 1f out* 33/1

0052 **8** *3/4* **Bahama Reef (IRE)**[20] 2931 3-9-0 57 ........(p) SCarson 5 32
(BGubby) *mid-div: rdn 3f out: sn wknd* 25/1

66 **9** *3/4* **Nazzwah**[16] 3044 3-8-9 ........ TEDurcan 3 25
(MRChannon) *a struggling in rr* 16/1

1m 36.99s (1.99) **Going Correction** +0.25s/f (Good) **9** Ran SP% **115.4**

Speed ratings: **100,99,96,95,94 88,80,79,78**CSF £37.46 TOTE £7.50: £2.50, £2.60, £2.30; EX 42.00.

**Owner** Stuart Whitehouse & Abbott Racing Partne **Bred** Bearstone Stud **Trained** Upper Lambourn, Berks

**FOCUS**

With four horses officially rated in the 70s, this looked reasonablly competitive, but it was contested by mainly disappointing sorts and is not a race to follow.

**NOTEBOOK**

**Carry On Doc** had not looked to be progressing, but this was more like it. He justified good market support with a narrow victory and this will have boosted his confidence.

**Du Pre** ran a solid race, pulling clear of all bar the winner. There is a similar race in her.

**Indiana Blues** did not improve for the removal of blinkers or the step back up in trip. She is becoming disappointing and is not one to follow.

**Eijaaz(IRE)** never really threatened, but is now qualified for a handicap mark and may do better in that sphere.

**River Nurey(IRE)** was given every chance from the front, but dropped out disappointingly. He has had a few chances.

## 3555 STAN JAMES TELEBETTING H'CAP — 7f 214y

3:30 (3:30) (E) (0-75,72) 3-Y-O+ — £3,721 (£1,145; £572; £286) Stalls Low

Form — RPR

6340 **1** **Mister Clinton (IRE)**[4] 3423 7-8-9 53 ........ DHolland 2 65
(DKIvory) *hld up: hdwy whn short of room 2f out tl gap eappeared on stands' rail appr fnl f: led jst ins last: drvn clr* 13/2[3]

-005 **2** *2 1/2* **Tuscarora (IRE)**[20] 2943 5-8-8 52 ........ IMongan 8 58
(AWCarroll) *slowly away: t.k.h and hld up in rr: rdn and hdwy over 2f out: ev ch appr fnl f but nt pce of wnr* 5/1[2]

0U36 **3** *1* **Poppyline**[22] 2879 4-8-9 53 ........ SDrowne 4 57
(WRMuir) *in tch: rdn and ev ch appr fnl f: nt qckn ins last* 12/1

0043 **4** *hd* **Border Artist**[12] 3167 5-9-7 65 ........ ANicholls 9 68
(DNicholls) *a.p: edgd lft appr fnl f: and hdd jst ins last: stl wnt lft and no ex after* 5/1[2]

-014 **5** *6* **Franksalot (IRE)**[3] 3440 4-9-12 70 ........ SSanders 7 60
(MissBSanders) *in rr: t.k.h: effrt 2f out: eased whn btn ins fnl f* 11/4[1]

6005 **6** *2* **Flying Treaty (USA)**[4] 3419 7-9-2 60 ........(b[1]) JMackay 5 45
(JLSpearing) *trckd ldrs: rdn 4f out: wknd over 2f out* 12/1

-001 **7** *1/2* **Aragon's Boy**[12] 3171 4-10-0 72 ........ DSweeney 10 56
(HCandy) *led for 3f: wknd over 1f out* 8/1

-010 **8** *1 1/2* **Senior Minister**[12] 3167 6-9-1 62 ........ RMiles(3) 1 42
(PWHiatt) *trckd ldr: led 4f out: hdd over 2f out: sn wknd* 12/1

0050 **9** *7* **Wood Fern (UAE)**[15] 3086 4-8-10 57 ........ SHitchcott(3) 3 21
(MRChannon) *outpcd and a bhd* 10/1

3060 **10** *nk* **Estrella Levante**[97] 1165 4-8-9 53 ........ TPQueally 11 17
(RMFlower) *slowly away: a bhd* 33/1

1m 36.34s (1.34) **Going Correction** +0.25s/f (Good) **10** Ran SP% **119.6**

Speed ratings: **103,100,99,99,93 91,90,89,82,82**CSF £40.09 CT £398.53 TOTE £8.50: £1.80, £2.40, £3.20; EX 40.20.

**Owner** J B Waterfall **Bred** C N Hart **Trained** Radlett, Herts

**FOCUS**

Just a moderate handicap.

**NOTEBOOK**

**Mister Clinton(IRE)**, 2lb higher than when last successful, goes well round here and gained his third course win in decisive fashion.

**Tuscarora(IRE)** has tumbled in the weights recently and this was an encouraging effort.

**Poppyline** ran respectably, but is still a maiden and simply very hard to win with.

**Border Artist** is 6lb higher than when last successful and may just be in the grip of the Handicapper.

**Franksalot(IRE)** has run well over a mile in the past, but he does most of his racing over seven furlongs and, back up in trip, he was not at his best.

**Senior Minister** *Official explanation: jockey said gelding was unsuited by loose ground*

**Wood Fern(UAE)** *Official explanation: jockey said gelding was unsuited by loose ground*

## 3556 STANJAMESUK.COM H'CAP — 1m 1f 209y

4:00 (4:00) (E) (0-70,70) 3-Y-O — £3,770 (£1,160; £580; £290) Stalls High

Form — RPR

0003 **1** **Ghantoot**[15] 3102 3-9-3 66 ........(v) DHolland 1 78
(LMCumani) *rdn fr s in mid-div: hdwy 2f out: kpt on u.str.p to ld fnl 50yds* 5/2[1]

0000 **2** *nk* **Littlestar (FR)**[39] 2402 3-7-13 48 ........ JMackay 10 59
(JLDunlop) *hld up: hdwy over 2f out: led appr fnl f: rdn and hdd fnl 50yds* 25/1

5323 **3** *4* **Resplendent King (USA)**[24] 2802 3-9-7 70 ........(p) IMongan 8 73
(TGMills) *led: hdd over 3f out: styd prom and ev ch 1f out: no ex* 5/1[3]

5-00 **4** *3/4* **Uncle John**[23] 2841 3-8-11 60 ........ JFortune 7 62
(SKirk) *trckd ldrs: rdn and wknd fnl f* 9/1

-005 **5** *3* **Duke's View (IRE)**[5] 3394 3-9-0 63 ........(b) SSanders 6 59
(MrsAJPerrett) *hld up in mid-div: gd hdwy to ld over 3f out: rdn and hdd appr fnl f: wknd qckly* 12/1

0030 **6** *5* **Wild Pitch**[13] 3160 3-8-11 60 ........ RLMoore 11 47
(PMitchell) *a towards rr* 7/1

2433 **7** *1 1/4* **Ask The Driver**[10] 3246 3-8-4 53 ........ SWhitworth 9 37
(DJSFfrenchDavis) *hld up: a bhd* 4/1[2]

1300 **8** *17* **Three Welshmen**[21] 2915 3-8-3 55 ........(b) RMiles(3) 4 7
(BRMillman) *plld hrd and trckd ldr: wknd over 2f out* 14/1

0005 **9** *2* **Glendale**[18] 2988 3-8-0 52 ........(v[1]) LisaJones(3) 5 —
(CADwyer) *plld hrd: prom tl wknd over 3f out* 10/1

2m 4.01s (1.47) **Going Correction** +0.25s/f (Good) **9** Ran SP% **115.0**

Speed ratings: **104,103,100,99,97 93,92,78,77**CSF £69.26 CT £294.45 TOTE £3.10: £2.00, £5.80, £1.90; EX 114.80.

**Owner** Sheikh Mohammed Obaid Al Maktoum **Bred** Mrs R F Johnson Houghton **Trained** Newmarket, Suffolk

**FOCUS**

Fair form for the grade. The front two pulled clear of the third.

**NOTEBOOK**

**Ghantoot** had his mind made up for him under a fantastically determined ride from Holland. He could well follow up, but is not exactly an easy ride.

**Littlestar(FR)** ◆ had shown nothing this year but, dropped in trip with the blinkers removed, he ran a fine race, pulling clear of all bar the winner. On a very attractive mark, he should be able to pick up a similar race.

**Resplendent King(USA)**, with cheekpieces on for the first time, was readily held by the front two and is proving hard to win with.

**Uncle John** ran respectably and looks to be running into form.

**Duke's View(IRE)** found disappointingly little under pressure.

**Wild Pitch** *Official explanation: jockey said gelding hung right*

**Ask The Driver** was not at his best and may not have been suited by the track. *Official explanation: jockey said gelding did not handle the track*

**Three Welshmen** *Official explanation: jockey said gelding ran too freely early on*

## 3557 STANJAMESUK.COM CLASSIFIED STKS — 1m 3f 196y

4:30 (4:31) (E) 3-Y-O+ — £3,692 (£1,136; £568; £284) Stalls High

Form — RPR

0306 **1** **Desert Island Disc**[4] 3415 7-9-1 71 ........ TPQueally 2 77
(JJBridger) *led tl hdd over 3f out: rdn to ld 1f out: kpt up to work* 6/1

5-43 **2** *1* **Kythia (IRE)**[23] 2848 3-8-4 73 ........ RLMoore 4 77
(HMorrison) *hld up in rr: pushed along 5f out: hdwy to trck ldrs 2f out: swtchd rt to stands'rail 1f out: r.o to chse wnr fnl f* 15/8[1]

0512 **3** *1 1/4* **Eton (GER)**[10] 3237 8-9-6 73 ........ ANicholls 3 78
(DNicholls) *trckd ldr: led over 3f out: hung lft fr 2f out and hdd 1f out: lost 2nd ins fnl f* 8/1

2221 **4** *4* **Sunny Lady (FR)**[12] 3172 3-8-11 80 ........ TEDurcan 1 76
(EALDunlop) *disp 3rd: rdn 2f out: wknd over 1f out* 7/2[3]

1-40 **5** *1/2* **Stealing Beauty (IRE)**[34] 2514 4-9-5 75 ........ DHolland 5 70
(LMCumani) *hld up: hdwy 4f out: wknd over 1f out* 9/4[2]

2m 33.75s (1.65) **Going Correction** +0.25s/f (Good)

**WFA** 3 from 4yo+ 13lb **5** Ran SP% **113.2**

Speed ratings: **104,103,102,99,99**CSF £18.20 TOTE £7.70: £1.50, £1.80; EX 25.30.

**Owner** W Wood **Bred** Southill Stud **Trained** Liphook, Hants

**FOCUS**

Quite a tight race on the figures. They went a decent enough pace considering the size of the field, but they remained quite well bunched and all five could be given a chance two out. The winner did not need to run to her very best to score, and the second and third ran to form.

**NOTEBOOK**

**Desert Island Disc** confirmed the promise she showed over an inadequate trip on her previous start under a good front-running ride from Tom Queally. She has followed up in the past, but is not that far ahead of the Handicapper and could be one to take on next time.

**Kythia(IRE)**, in contrast to the winner, was given a waiting ride, but it suited her well and she ran her race. She had to be switched to the near-side rail for her run, but it did not affect the result.

**Eton(GER)**, in good form in claiming company recently, ran respectably but is high enough in the weights.

**Sunny Lady(FR)**, off the mark in a weak race over course and distance on her previous start, failed to build on that and was disappointing.
**Stealing Beauty(IRE)**, disappointing at Chepstow on her previous start (sent off favourite), again ran below expectations.

## 3558 STAN JAMES H'CAP — 5f 59y

**5:00** (5:00) (E) (0-75,73) 3-Y-O+ — **£3,721** (£1,145; £572; £286) **Stalls** Low

Form — RPR

6103 **1** **Gone'N'Dunnett (IRE)**[4] [3428] 5-8-7 **57**....................(v) HayleyTurner(5) 9 — 66
(MrsCADunnett) *a.p: led 1f out: hld on wl* — **13/2**[2]

3130 **2** ½ **Harbour House**[28] [2707] 5-8-0 **45**.................................................. ADaly 4 — 52
(JJBridger) *hld up: gd hdwy over 1f out: r.o to chse wnr fnl f* — **16/1**

-036 **3** *shd* **Jazzy Millennium**[12] [3174] 7-8-8 **53**...........................................(b) SDrowne 6 — 60
(BRMillman) *in rr and plenty to do 2f out: tk hold of bit appr fnl f and fin strly to go past btn horses* — **7/1**[3]

6616 **4** ¾ **Arfinnit (IRE)**[7] [3338] 3-8-8 **61**..........................................(v) SHitchcott(3) 7 — 65
(MRChannon) *bmpd leaving stalls and in rr: rdn after 2f: hdwy appr f: fin wl* — **14/1**

2400 **5** *1* **Boanerges (IRE)**[10] [3249] 7-8-10 **55**.........................................(p) TEDurcan 10 — 56
(JMBradley) *led tl hdd 1f out: fdd fnl f* — **12/1**

5020 **6** *shd* **Taboor (IRE)**[21] [2912] 6-8-11 **56**...............................................(b) DHolland 1 — 56
(JWPayne) *in tch: styd alone on far side ent st: no real ch ins fnl 2f* — **9/1**

6453 **7** *hd* **Pulse**[8] [3307] 6-9-3 **62**.......................................................................(p) RLMoore 3 — 61
(JMBradley) *prom tl wknd ent fnl f* — **10/3**[1]

3601 **8** *5* **Guns Blazing**[8] [3307] 5-9-7 **73**..........................................(b) MHoward(7) 5 — 54
(DKIvory) *plld hrd: prom tl wknd wl over 1f out* — **7/1**[3]

0004 **9** *1 ¼* **Loch Inch**[14] [3126] 7-8-6 **51**................................................(b) CCatlin 8 — 28
(JMBradley) *t.k.h: prom tl wknd 2f out* — **9/1**

0000 **10** *shd* **Izmail (IRE)**[14] [3126] 5-9-7 **66**.............................................. SWhitworth 11 — 43
(DNicholls) *racd wd: btn 1/2-way* — **7/1**[3]

-005 **11** *11* **Landing Strip (IRE)**[11] [3195] 4-9-10 **72**............................... LFletcher(3) 2 — 9
(JMPEustace) *a towards rr: eased whn no ch fnl f* — **20/1**

63.44 secs (1.17) **Going Correction** +0.25s/f (Good)
**WFA** 3 from 4yo+ 5lb — **11** Ran **SP%** **118.9**
Speed ratings: **100,99,99,97,96 96,95,87,85,85 68**CSF £106.42 CT £769.55 TOTE £8.80: £1.70, £5.50, £2.40; EX 230.20 Place 6 £161.80, Place 5 £84.44..
**Owner** College Farm Thoroughbreds **Bred** Ocal Bloodstock **Trained** Hingham, Norfolk

**FOCUS**
A moderate sprint handicap and ordinary form.

**NOTEBOOK**
**Gone'N'Dunnett(IRE)**, 7lb higher than when successful three starts previously, was not inconvenienced by this drop back in trip and ran out a narrow winner. He is holding his form better than has often been the case in the past.
**Harbour House** does not win very often and was last successful in banded company, but this was a fine effort.
**Jazzy Millennium**, five times a course winner, is a pound lower than when last successful and showed himself ready to strike with a good effort over a trip short of his best.
**Arfinnit(IRE)** acquitted himself well on this return to handicap company and shaped as though he will be capable of even better over six furlongs.
**Boanerges(IRE)** fared best of three Milton Bradley runners, but remains on a long losing run.
**Taboor(IRE)** ran respectably on his own against the far rail.
**Pulse** was a little keen and below form.
T/Plt: £471.10 to a £1 stake. Pool: £44,181.20. 68.45 winning tickets. T/Qpdt: £91.30 to a £1 stake. Pool: £3,319.50. 26.90 winning tickets. JS

# 3096 REDCAR (L-H)

Sunday, July 4

**OFFICIAL GOING: Soft (good to soft in places) changing to soft after race 5 (4.20)**
After 18mm of rain before racing and further rain during the afternoon the going was soon described as 'genuine soft'.
Wind: Moderate 1/2 against. Weather: Persistent rain.

## 3559 YANKEE DOODLE DAY APPRENTICE H'CAP — 1m

**2:20** (2:21) (E) (0-75,66) 3-Y-O+ — **£3,620** (£1,114; £557; £278) **Stalls** Centre

Form — RPR

0000 **1** **Parisian Playboy**[40] [2387] 4-7-9 **42**........................ LeanneKershaw(5) 6 — 52
(JeddO'Keeffe) *hld up: hdwy and swtchd lft 3f out: hrd rdn over 1f out: kpt on to ld last 50yds* — **66/1**

6345 **2** *nk* **Oscar Pepper (USA)**[15] [3097] 7-9-4 **63**..............................(v) PMakin(3) 8 — 72
(TDBarron) *mid-div: hdwy over 2f out: led over 1f out: wnt lft: hdd wl ins last* — **6/1**[2]

0300 **3** *1* **Eastern Hope (IRE)**[25] [2776] 5-8-13 **60**.................... KristinStubbs(5) 4 — 67
(MrsLStubbs) *dwlt: sn bhd: gd hdwy 3f out: keeping on same pce whn n.m.r last 50yds* — **16/1**

-000 **4** *1* **Basinet**[14] [2551] 6-8-7 **54**..................................................... DTudhope(5) 7 — 59
(JJQuinn) *dwlt: hld up in rr: hdwy over 2f out: styd on same pce fnl f* — **12/1**

4121 **5** *shd* **Prime Offer**[16] [3049] 8-9-4 **65**.................................................... CHaddon(5) 3 — 70
(JJay) *led tl over 2f out: kpt on same pce appr fnl f* — **7/1**

0-01 **6** *hd* **Zanjeer**[16] [3060] 4-9-5 **66**..................................................... LTreadwell(5) 10 — 70
(NWilson) *w ldrs: led over 2f out tl over 1f out: unable qckn* — **13/2**[3]

2631 **7** ¾ **Dara Mac**[10] [3247] 5-8-8 **55**.............................................. SuzanneFrance(5) 1 — 58
(NBycroft) *sn bhd: hdwy stands' side over 2f out: styd on same pce appr fnl f* — **10/1**

3560 **8** *1* **Encounter**[22] [2879] 8-7-13 **46**............................................. DFentiman(5) 16 — 47
(JHetherton) *hld up in rr: kpt on fnl 2f: nvr nr ldrs* — **14/1**

6140 **9** *1 ½* **Cashneem (IRE)**[16] [3058] 6-9-8 **64**................................................ DAllan 5 — 62
(WMBrisbourne) *mid-div: drvn along over 2f out: nvr on terms* — **14/1**

-000 **10** *1 ¾* **Hilltime (IRE)**[8] [3314] 4-8-11 **53**................................................ DNolan 11 — 47
(JJQuinn) *chsd ldrs: wknd over 1f out* — **16/1**

0-02 **11** *1 ¼* **Haulage Man**[9] [3269] 6-9-3 **59**................................................... TEaves 9 — 51
(DEddy) *s.s: sme hdwy whn nt clr run 3f out: nvr on terms* — **14/1**

1 **12** *7* **Sedge (USA)**[34] [2528] 4-9-4 **60**................................................ LEnstone 13 — 38
(PTMidgley) *sn trcking ldrs: effrt over 2f out: wknd over 1f out* — **20/1**

0004 **13** *1 ¾* **Mehmaas**[16] [3058] 8-7-13 **44**.......................................(v) BSwarbrick(3) 14 — 18
(REBarr) *w ldrs: lost pl 2f out* — **14/1**

0/00 **14** *12* **Saif Sareea**[10] [3226] 4-8-1 **48**......................................... PPMathers(5) 2 — —
(KWHogg) *w ldrs: lost pl over 3f out: sn bhd: eased* — **100/1**

500- **15** *2 ½* **Loner**[299] [4796] 6-8-10 **52**................................................... THamilton 12 — —
(RAFahey) *chsd ldrs: rdn and lost pl 3f out: sn bhd: eased* — **5/1**[1]

6605 **16** *2* **Frimley's Matterry**[15] [3096] 4-8-3 **50**.................... NataliaGemelova(5) 15 — —
(REBarr) *a bhd: eased* — **66/1**

1m 41.3s (3.60) **Going Correction** +0.50s/f (Yiel) — **16** Ran **SP%** **120.7**
Speed ratings: **102,101,100,99,99 99,98,97,96,94 93,86,84,72,69 67**CSF £425.97 CT £6620.87 TOTE £40.40: £6.60, £1.50, £11.90, £3.90; EX 1063.20.
**Owner** Playboy Partnership **Bred** Paul Scholes **Trained** Middleham Moor, N Yorks
■ Stewards Enquiry : P Makin caution: careless riding

**FOCUS**
Only modest form, and not particularly strong. The first three finished up racing on the far side.

**NOTEBOOK**
**Parisian Playboy**, placed once in eight previous starts, was suited by the rain-softened ground and in the end did just enough.
**Oscar Pepper(USA)**, whose three turf wins have been here, dived left when hitting the front, ending up on the far side and getting in the way of the third.
**Eastern Hope(IRE)**, with the blinkers left off, as usual missed the break. Detached at halfway, he was only keeping on in his own time when left short of room near the line. This trip stretches him to the very limit.
**Basinet**, last seen in action over hurdles, came out best of those who raced towards the stands' side.
**Prime Offer**, 4lb higher, did not enjoy an uncontested lead and the rain was not in his favour.
**Zanjeer**, 16lb higher, may not have been at his very best on the rain-soaked ground.
**Sedge(USA)** *Official explanation: jockey said gelding was unsuited by the soft ground*
**Loner**, a major positive on every betting front, had the cheekpieces left off on his first outing for 10 months and his first for his new yard. He was in trouble at halfway and eventually completed in his own time.

## 3560 EUROPEAN BREEDERS FUND MAIDEN STKS — 7f

**2:50** (2:54) (D) 2-Y-O — **£4,498** (£1,384; £692; £346) **Stalls** Centre

Form — RPR

3 **1** **Northern Splendour (USA)**[16] [3051] 2-9-0 ......................... KMcEvoy 10 — 85+
(SaeedBinSuroor) *trckd ldrs: effrt 2f out: hung lft and led jst ins fnl f: styd on wl* — **8/11**[1]

0 **2** *1 ¾* **Gone Fishing (IRE)**[36] [2481] 2-8-9 ......................................... PRobinson 2 — 76
(MAJarvis) *sn trcking ldrs: led over 2f out tl jst ins last: wknd nr fin* — **7/2**[2]

3 **3** ½ **Little Miss Gracie**[11] [3202] 2-8-2 ................................... DerekNolan(7) 5 — 74
(PBurgoyne) *trckd ldrs: effrt and swtchd rt 2f out: hung lft and kpt on same pce fnl f* — **14/1**

04 **4** *5* **Aire De Mougins (IRE)**[29] [2674] 2-9-0 ........................................ KDarley 6 — 67
(PCHaslam) *led tl over 5f out: outpcd whn sltly hmpd 2f out: kpt on fnl f* — **14/1**

3 **5** *1* **Dancer's Serenade (IRE)**[15] [3081] 2-9-0 ......................... DaleGibson 11 — 64
(TPTate) *swvd rt s: w ldrs: outpcd over 2f out: n.d after* — **16/1**

0 **6** *1 ¼* **Paris Heights**[19] [2961] 2-9-0 ........................................... DeanMcKeown 4 — 61
(RMWhitaker) *chsd ldrs: outpcd and hung lft over 2f out* — **100/1**

**7** *hd* **Wolf Hammer (USA)** 2-9-0 ....................................................... RWinston 1 — 61
(JHowardJohnson) *dwlt: sn chsng ldrs: led over 5f out tl over 2f out: grad wknd* — **10/1**[3]

05 **8** *6* **Mr Maxim**[11] [3197] 2-9-0 .......................................................... VHalliday 9 — 46
(RMWhitaker) *outpcd and bhd fr 1/2-way* — **100/1**

0 **9** *12* **Wor Kid**[11] [3197] 2-8-6 ........................................................ THamilton(3) 7 — 11
(RPElliott) *bhd whn swvd bdly lft over 4f out: wnt rt and sn lost tch* — **100/1**

06 **10** *6* **Loyalty Lodge (IRE)**[17] [3014] 2-9-0 ............................................. JPMurtagh 3 — —
(JDBethell) *outpcd and bhd fr 1/2-way: sn lost tch* — **40/1**

1m 28.56s (3.66) **Going Correction** +0.50s/f (Yiel) — **10** Ran **SP%** **113.8**
Speed ratings: **99,97,96,90,89 88,87,81,67,60**CSF £3.17 TOTE £1.60: £1.10, £1.40, £2.90; EX 4.50.
**Owner** Godolphin **Bred** Darley **Trained** Newmarket, Suffolk

**FOCUS**
Probably an above-average two-year-old maiden for the track with the first three clear. The form could prove better than rated.

**NOTEBOOK**
**Northern Splendour(USA)** looked in peak condition and in the end, despite a tendency to hang, ran out a most convincing winner.
**Gone Fishing(IRE)**, a quality filly, looked to be travelling better than the winner at one stage but in the end did not see out the seven furlongs anywhere near as well as him in the conditions. She looks sure to find a race.
**Little Miss Gracie** again showed ability, but in the longer term this will not have done her nursery mark any good at all.
**Aire De Mougins(IRE)** stayed on when it was all over and this third outing tees him up for a nursery campaign.
**Dancer's Serenade(IRE)** didn't look totally at home in the soft ground and is the type who will need more time yet.
**Loyalty Lodge(IRE)** *Official explanation: jockey said colt was unsuited by the soft ground*

## 3561 FORMICA SURFACING YOUR WORLD H'CAP — 1m 3f

**3:20** (3:22) (D) (0-80,80) 3-Y-O — **£14,365** (£4,420; £2,210; £1,105) **Stalls** Low

Form — RPR

6223 **1** **Lets Roll**[8] [3312] 3-9-0 **73**................................................ DeanMcKeown 6 — 80
(CWThornton) *hld up and bhd: hdwy on outside 3f out: hung lft: styd on to ld last 150yds: hld on nr fin* — **11/2**[3]

4112 **2** ½ **Prenup (IRE)**[16] [3050] 3-9-0 **73**................................................ JPMurtagh 11 — 79
(LMCumani) *trckd ldrs: led over 3f out: rdn and hung rt over 1f out: hdd jst ins last: r.o* — **10/3**[1]

6521 **3** ¾ **Charlotte Vale**[10] [3250] 3-8-9 **68**............................................. ACulhane 13 — 73
(MDHammond) *in tch: effrt over 3f out: styd on fnl f* — **10/1**

0000 **4** *shd* **Munaawesh (USA)**[6] [3379] 3-7-5 **57** oh2..................(b[1]) DFentiman(7) 9 — 62?
(DWChapman) *bhd: effrt over 4f out: hdwy over 2f out: styd on fnl f* — **50/1**

0-12 **5** *shd* **Richtee (IRE)**[15] [3102] 3-8-3 **65**.......................................... THamilton(3) 2 — 69
(RAFahey) *chsd ldrs: rdn and outpcd over 3f out: styd on fnl f* — **9/1**

-123 **6** *1 ½* **Meadaaf (IRE)**[27] [2732] 3-9-7 **80**.................................................. KDarley 5 — 82
(ACStewart) *chsd ldrs: effrt over 2f out: kpt on same pce* — **5/1**[2]

0624 **7** *hd* **Double Vodka (IRE)**[8] [3312] 3-8-4 **63**........................................ KMcEvoy 3 — 65
(MrsJRRamsden) *trckd ldrs: effrt over 2f out: kpt on same pce* — **10/1**

0332 **8** *3 ½* **Wing Collar**[25] [2774] 3-8-9 **68**................................................ WSupple 12 — 64
(TDEasterby) *mid-div: hdwy on outside over 5f out: swtchd lft over 1f out: btn whn n.m.r and eased ins last* — **12/1**

052 **9** *2* **Manhattan Jack**[25] [2783] 3-8-10 **69**........................................... RWinston 7 — 62
(GASwinbank) *bhd: effrt on outer 4f out: sn pushed along: nvr nr ldrs* — **12/1**

0 **10** *2* **Sharadi (IRE)**[30] [2645] 3-8-11 **70**............................................ MTebbutt 4 — 60
(VSmith) *in tch: drvn along over 4f out: hung lft and n.d* — **33/1**

5324 **11** *1 ½* **Havetoavit (USA)**[17] [3020] 3-8-4 **63**.......................................... SChin 10 — 50
(JDBethell) *led tl over 3f out: lost pl over 1f out* — **16/1**

-500 **12** *3 ½* **Hernando's Boy**[55] [1995] 3-8-0 **59**........................................... PFessey 1 — 41
(MrsMReveley) *s.i.s: hdwy on ins 4f out: lost pl over 2f out* — **20/1**



The Form Book, Raceform Ltd, Compton, RG20 6NL

-005 **13** *1 ¼* **Rigonza**[15] 3102 3-8-9 **68**........................................(v[1]) DAllan 8 48
(TDEasterby) *unruly s: s.s: bhd and drvn along 4f out* **33/1**

2m 24.93s (3.93) **Going Correction** +0.50s/f (Yiel) **13** Ran SP% **117.2**
Speed ratings: **105,104,104,104,103 102,102,100,98,97 96,93,92**CSF £22.68 CT £180.70 TOTE £5.50: £1.90, £1.50, £3.10; EX 17.20 Trifecta £287.10 Pool £7,561.84 - 18.70 winning units..
**Owner** A Crute and Partners **Bred** G G A Gregson **Trained** Middleham Moor, N Yorks

**FOCUS**
Quite a competitive 0-80 handicap but no great pace and they tended to get in each other's way. The form is therefore not as strong as it might have been.

**NOTEBOOK**
**Lets Roll**, as usual settled at the rear, came down the outside, missing any trouble. He again hung left but did enough to nail the runner-up, who looked to be waiting for something to go past.
**Prenup(IRE)**, 6lb higher, again travelled strongly, but in front she hung away from the running rail and seemed to hang fire. This looked a good opportunity thrown out of the window.
**Charlotte Vale**, 3lb higher, could have done with a much stronger pace. She stuck on in sterling fashion and will be suited by a return to a mile and a half.
**Munaawesh(USA)**, in first-time blinkers, was putting in all his best work at the finish and will appreciate a stiffer test.
**Richtee(IRE)**, 10lb higher than when successful here two outings ago, was trapped on the inner and never had that much room to work in. On this eveidence she will get further.
**Meadaaf(IRE)** didn't have the run of the race but it would be over-egging the pudding to put him down as an unlucky loser. *Official explanation: jockey said colt was denied a clear run*
**Double Vodka(IRE)**, stepping up in trip, again met traffic problems. *Official explanation: jockey said gelding was denied a clear run*

## 3562 "WIN A HOLIDAY TO ORLANDO" - RACECARD COMPETITION H'CAP 5f

**3:50** (3:52) (E ) (0-70,70) 3-Y-O **£3,935** (£1,211; £605; £302) **Stalls** Centre

Form RPR

2162 **1** **Nanna (IRE)**[23] 2850 3-8-9 **58**........................................ FLynch 18 65
(RHollinshead) *mde all on stands' side: gained upper hand overall wl ins last* **8/1**

0401 **2** *¾* **Short Chorus**[58] 1934 3-8-1 **50**..............................(p) DaleGibson 3 54
(JBalding) *racd far side: w ldr: led that gp over 1f out: no ex wl ins last* **7/1**[3]

02-0 **3** *½* **Fitzwarren**[37] 2457 3-9-4 **67**..............................(v) DeanMcKeown 4 69
(NBycroft) *led far side tl over 1f out: no ex ins last* **16/1**

0631 **4** *¾* **Maluti**[12] 3175 3-8-4 **53**........................................ KDarley 1 53
(RGuest) *racd far side: chsd ldrs: hung rt over 1f out: wknd towards fin* **5/1**[1]

0-00 **5** *shd* **Sir Loin**[9] 3270 3-8-6 **55**........................................ KimTinkler 14 54
(NTinkler) *racd stands' side: chsd ldrs: hrd rdn over 1f out: kpt on wl* **25/1**

0036 **6** *nk* **Jadan (IRE)**[9] 3270 3-9-7 **70**........................................ WSupple 10 68
(EJAlston) *racd stands' side: hld up: stdy hdwy over 2f out: hit in face by rival's whip over 1f out: styd on same pce* **7/1**[3]

2010 **7** *shd* **Extremely Rare (IRE)**[8] 3301 3-9-5 **68**........................................ DAllan 13 66
(TDEasterby) *racd stands' side: sn outpcd: styd on wl appr fnl f* **10/1**

5500 **8** *½* **Smart Danny**[10] 3234 3-7-12 **47** oh6........................................ RFfrench 8 43
(JJQuinn) *bdly hmpd s: racd far side: bhd: gd hdwy over 1f out: fin wl* **14/1**

0253 **9** *hd* **Hello Roberto**[9] 3270 3-9-3 **66**........................................ RWinston 12 62
(MJPolglase) *racd stands' side: prom: outpcd over 2f out: kpt on appr fnl f* **6/1**[2]

1360 **10** *1 ½* **He's A Rocket (IRE)**[30] 2650 3-8-13 **62**..............................(b) DarrenWilliams 6 53
(KRBurke) *swvd rt s: racd far side: sn chsng ldrs: outpcd fnl 2f* **8/1**

30-0 **11** *1 ½* **Royal Awakening (IRE)**[144] 744 3-8-5 **57** ow2.................... TEaves(3) 9 42
(REBarr) *hmpd s: racd stands' side: bhd: sme hdwy 2f out: nvr a factor* **66/1**

-000 **12** *shd* **Gemini Girl (IRE)**[13] 3147 3-7-12 **47** oh1........................................ PMQuinn 2 32
(MDHammond) *racd far side: chsd ldrs: wknd over 1f out* **25/1**

0-05 **13** *1 ¼* **From The North (IRE)**[36] 2468 3-8-2 **56** ow2..............(v) PMakin(5) 11 37
(ADickman) *racd stands' side: sn outpcd and in rr* **16/1**

-000 **14** *2 ½* **Savannah Sue**[9] 3279 3-7-5 **47** oh17........................................ DFentiman(7) 7 19
(JRNorton) *swvd rt s: racd far side: sn bhd* **66/1**

-353 **15** *2 ½* **Island Spell**[9] 3267 3-9-5 **68**........................................ PFessey 16 32
(CGrant) *racd stands' side: chsd ldrs: lost pl over 2f out: sn bhd* **25/1**

60.60 secs (1.90) **Going Correction** +0.50s/f (Yiel) **15** Ran SP% **120.2**
Speed ratings: **104,102,102,100,100 100,100,99,98,96 94,93,91,87,83**CSF £59.54 CT £901.91 TOTE £9.20: £2.40, £2.90, £5.80; EX 99.40.
**Owner** Mrs G A Weetman **Bred** Mark Clarke **Trained** Upper Longdon, Staffs

**FOCUS**
They split into two groups and the winner did easily best of those towards the stands' side. This is ordinary form but it should work out at a lowish level.

**NOTEBOOK**
**Nanna(IRE)**, taken to post early, was 7lb higher on her return to turf. She knuckled down well and was firmly in command at the line.
**Short Chorus**, absent for two months, worked hard to gain the upper hand on the far side but at the line had to settle for second best.
**Fitzwarren**, awkward to load, showed a lot more than on his return to action seven weeks earlier.
**Maluti**, 5lb higher, was drawn right against the far-side running rail but gave problems, persisting in hanging away from it. The rain did not help his cause.
**Sir Loin**, down 5lb, ran better but is still a maiden now after eight starts.
**Jadan(IRE)** was trying hard to close when struck over the head by a rival's whip. He basically needs some respite.
**Extremely Rare(IRE)**, who has started life in handicaps from a tough mark, fins the minimum trip much too sharp.
**Smart Danny**, 6lb out of the handicap, did really well after being knocked sideways at the start.

## 3563 REDCARRACING.CO.UK CLASSIFIED STKS 1m 1f

**4:20** (4:21) (E ) 3-Y-O+ **£3,503** (£1,078; £539; £269) **Stalls** Low

Form RPR

6630 **1** **Pawan (IRE)**[4] 3409 4-9-3 66........................................ AnnStokell 6 74
(MissAStokell) *trckd ldrs: outpcd over 5f out: hdwy on outside over 2f out: styd on to ld towards fin* **16/1**

-624 **2** *½* **Opening Ceremony (USA)**[9] 3265 5-8-11 70........................................ THamilton(3) 4 70
(RAFahey) *hld up: stdy hdwy 3f out: ev ch and hung lft over 1f out: no ex wl ins last* **7/2**[2]

432 **3** *nk* **Pinching (IRE)**[48] 2182 3-8-9 75..............................(v) WRyan 5 74
(HRACecil) *led early: trckd ldr: led over 2f out: hdd and no ex wl ins last* **7/2**[2]

2120 **4** *2 ½* **Aleron (IRE)**[11] 3199 6-9-5 72........................................ RWinston 7 69
(JJQuinn) *trckd ldrs on outer: t.k.h: drvn along 3f out: hung lft: keeping on same pce whn n.m.r jst ins last: eased nr fin* **6/4**[1]

2443 **5** *2* **Summer Shades**[8] 3320 6-8-9 69........................................ BSwarbrick(5) 3 60
(WMBrisbourne) *hld up: effrt on outer over 2f out: nvr rchd ldrs* **9/1**[3]

0000 **6** *13* **Gala Sunday (USA)**[15] 3097 4-9-5 72........................................ DaleGibson 1 39
(MWEasterby) *sn led: hdd over 2f out: wkng whn hung lft and hit rail over 1f out: lost pl and eased* **14/1**

-000 **7** *5* **Rifleman (IRE)**[31] 2618 4-9-5 72..............................(p) GDuffield 2 29
(MrsADuffield) *trckd ldrs: shkn up over 3f out: lost pl over 2f out: sn bhd* **14/1**

1m 58.39s (4.99) **Going Correction** +0.50s/f (Yiel)
**WFA** 3 from 4yo+ 10lb **7** Ran SP% **113.7**
Speed ratings: **97,96,96,94,92 80,76**CSF £70.07 TOTE £21.40: £4.10, £1.90; EX 211.40.
**Owner** Ms Caron Stokell **Bred** Hadi Al Tajir **Trained** Brompton-on-Swale, N Yorks

**FOCUS**
No gallop and a very messy race, with the winner, through whom the race has been rated, at least showing a good attitude.

**NOTEBOOK**
**Pawan(IRE)**, who had the least chance on official figures, had stamina to prove. Helped by the modest gallop, he came down the outside and looked the only genuine horse.
**Opening Ceremony(USA)** persisted in hanging left and in the end seemed quite happy to follow the winner over the line.
**Pinching(IRE)**, with the visor fitted once again, carried her head high in front and never seemed to be putting her best foot forward.
**Aleron(IRE)** wouldn't drop his bit as a result of the steady gallop. Making his effort on the outer, he persisted in hanging left and ended up on the running rail. He was going nowhere when running out of room inside the last and if he is to be seen in a more favourable light he needs further and a stronger gallop. *Official explanation: jockey said gelding hung left in the straight*
**Summer Shades** tried to come from off the pace in a race not run at a strong pace. She never threatened to take a hand.
**Gala Sunday(USA)**looks to have lost his way completely.

## 3564 CAR BOOT FAIRS EVERY SATURDAY AND SUNDAY H'CAP 2m 4y

**4:50** (4:51) (E ) (0-75,75) 3-Y-O+ **£3,779** (£1,163; £581; £290) **Stalls** Low

Form RPR

0151 **1** **Lucky Judge**[10] 3236 7-9-7 **68**........................................ DaleGibson 4 78+
(GASwinbank) *trckd ldrs: nt clr run over 3f out: styd on to go 2nd over 1f out: kpt on wl to ld last 50yds* **2/1**[1]

/252 **2** *¾* **Magic Combination (IRE)**[14] 3120 11-9-11 **72**........................................ WDowling 11 79
(LLungo) *hld up: shkn up over 5f out: hdwy to ld 3f out: hdd and no ex towards fin* **5/1**[2]

3412 **3** *2* **Spitting Image (IRE)**[13] 3153 4-8-11 **58**........................................ ACulhane 8 63
(MrsMReveley) *trckd ldrs: led over 3f out: sn hdd: edgd rt and and pce fnl 2f* **8/1**

40-5 **4** *1 ¼* **Simple Ideals (USA)**[10] 3236 10-7-12 **45** oh13........................................ KimTinkler 3 48?
(DonEnricoIncisa) *hld up in rr: hdwy 7f out: styd on appr fnl f* **16/1**

-400 **5** *3* **Vicious Prince (IRE)**[11] 3199 5-9-5 **70**........................................ DeanMcKeown 1 70
(RMWhitaker) *hld up in rr: outpcd 5f out: swtchd outside over 3f out: kpt on fnl f* **6/1**[3]

2-20 **6** *1* **Most Definitely (IRE)**[10] 3236 4-9-1 **62**........................................ DAllan 6 60
(TDEasterby) *sn chsng ldrs: pushed along 9f out: one pce fnl 3f* **12/1**

50/0 **7** *2* **Ebinzayd (IRE)**[20] 2935 8-10-0 **75**........................................ RWinston 7 71
(LLungo) *hld up in rr: effrt 4f out: nvr nr ldrs* **20/1**

4-34 **8** *hd* **Lord Lamb**[10] 3237 12-8-13 **60**........................................ KDarley 5 56
(MrsMReveley) *sn trcking ldrs: hung rt: n.m.r and lost pl 4f out* **12/1**

1405 **9** *14* **Prince Of The Wood (IRE)**[27] 2731 4-8-2 **49**..............................(p) JFanning 2 28
(ABailey) *led at mod pce: qcknd 9f out: hdd over 3f out: sn lost pl: eased over 1f out: sn bhd* **6/1**[3]

3m 40.6s (9.10) **Going Correction** +0.50s/f (Yiel) **9** Ran SP% **115.7**
Speed ratings: **97,96,95,95,93 93,92,91,84**CSF £11.81 CT £65.48 TOTE £2.90: £1.40, £2.70, £1.80; EX 12.30 Place 6 £190.80, Place 5 £47.15..
**Owner** Mrs I Gibson **Bred** K G Powter **Trained** Melsonby, N Yorks

**FOCUS**
No gallop until once in line for home. This is ordinary form.

**NOTEBOOK**
**Lucky Judge**, 8lb higher, gave the runner-up first run and had to dig deep to get the better of him close home. The way the race was run did not play to his strengths.
**Magic Combination(IRE)** struck for home and it looked as though he had poached a winning lead, but in the end the winning combination proved just too strong.
**Spitting Image(IRE)** took it up and stepped up the pace, but when headed all she wanted to do was go right. A return to claiming company looks on the cards.
**Simple Ideals(USA)**, a winner here three times in the past, was racing from 13lb out of the handicap. He stayed on when it was all over.
**Vicious Prince(IRE)**, slipping down the ratings, was stepping up in trip but had no chance ridden this way in a slowly-run race.
**Most Definitely(IRE)**, struggling to keep up at halfway, prefers much quicker ground but the fact remains he has yet to get his head in front.
**Ebinzayd(IRE)** was by no means knocked about and may yet slip to a winning mark.
T/Jkpt: Not won. T/Plt: £235.00 to a £1 stake. Pool: £47,100.70. 146.30 winning tickets. T/Qpdt: £29.80 to a £1 stake. Pool: £2,754.90. 68.40 winning tickets. WG

# 3552 HAMBURG (R-H)

Sunday, July 4

**OFFICIAL GOING: Heavy**

## 3565a BMW DEUTSCHES DERBY (GROUP 1) (C&F) 1m 4f

**4:15** (4:19) 3-Y-O **£223,944** (£74,648; £44,789; £22,394)

RPR

**1** **Shirocco (GER)**[21] 2926 3-9-2........................................ ASuborics 7 120
(ASchutz, Germany) *always close up, 2nd straight, led over 2f out, driven clear, ran on well* **6/1**[3]

**2** *4* **Malinas (GER)**[21] 2926 3-9-2........................................ WMongil 8 115
(PSchiergen, Germany) *mid-division, 7th straight, switched to rails over 2f out, ran on under pressure to go 2nd over 1f out, one pace final f* **4/1**[2]

**3** *6* **Omikron (IRE)**[21] 2926 3-9-2........................................ ADeVries 13 108
(MarioHofer, Germany) *always in touch, 5th straight, switched outside 2f out, ran on under pressure to go 3rd 1f out, one pace* **20/1**

**4** *1 ½* **Saldentigerin (GER)**[28] 2723 3-9-2........................................ TQuinn 10 106
(PSchiergen, Germany) *8th straight, stayed on to take 4th close home* **10/1**

**5** *¾* **Gentle Tiger (GER)**[34] 2541 3-9-2........................................ THellier 4 105
(PSchiergen, Germany) *always in touch, 4th straight, ridden & beaten over 1f out* **16/1**

**6** *hd* **El Tiger (GER)**[259] 5660 3-9-2........................................ FilipMinarik 16 105
(PSchiergen, Germany) *mid-division to straight, never near to challenge* **20/1**

**7** *nk* **Salonhonor (GER)**[77] 3-9-2........................................ JPalik 1 104
(AndreasLowe, Germany) *led to over 2f out, weakened over 1f out* **20/1**

8 1 **Farouge (FR)** 3-9-2 ............ FJohansson 2 103
(WidoNeuroth, Norway) *towards rear to straight, stayed on but never a factor* **50/1**

9 1 ¼ **Apeiron (GER)**[35] 2510 3-9-2 ............ JCarvalho 11 102
(MarioHofer, Germany) *towards rear to straight, some progress under pressure on outside 2f out, beaten over 1f out* **20/1**

10 ½ **Fight Club (GER)**[34] 2541 3-9-2 ............ AStarke 12 101
(ASchutz, Germany) *prominent, 4th straight, weakened well over 1f out* **7/2**[1]

11 nse **Dayano (GER)**[35] 2510 3-9-2 ............ EPedroza 6 101
(AWohler, Germany) *mid-div, brought to stands side str, no prog* **16/1**

12 2 **Egerton (GER)**[34] 2541 3-9-2 ............ AHelfenbein 3 98
(PRau, Germany) *6th straight, soon ridden & beaten* **20/1**

13 2 ½ **Delsun (IRE)**[34] 2541 3-9-2 ............(b) ODoleuze 17 95
(MarioHofer, Germany) *rear early, progress to mid-division half-way, beaten 3f out* **33/1**

14 12 **Classic Croco (GER)**[35] 3-9-2 ............ MJKinane 19 80
(CVonDerRecke, Germany) *in touch to 4f out* **33/1**

15 ¾ **Oakboy (GER)** 3-9-2 ............(b) JBojko 5 79
(HSteinmetz, Germany) *behind final 4f* **100/1**

16 8 **Intendant (GER)**[21] 2926 3-9-2 ............ ABoschert 15 69
(FrauABertram, Germany) *always behind* **33/1**

17 7 **Sweet Wake (GER)**[99] 3-9-2 ............ LDettori 9 61
(MarioHofer, Germany) *tracked leader, 3rd straight, weakened quickly* **7/1**

18 11 **Golden Millenium (GER)** 3-9-2 ............ LHammer-Hansen 18 47
(THHansen, Germany) *behind final 4f* **50/1**

2m 39.64s **18** Ran SP% **127.4**
Speed ratings: .
**Owner** Baron G Von Ullmann **Bred** Baron G Von Ullmann **Trained** Germany

# 2542 SAINT-CLOUD (L-H)
Sunday, July 4

**OFFICIAL GOING: Good to soft**

## 3566a PRIX DE MALLERET (GROUP 2) (FILLIES) 1m 4f
**2:50** (2:50) 3-Y-O **£42,148** (£16,268; £7,764; £5,176)

RPR

1 **Lune D'Or (FR)**[21] 3-8-9 ............ TJarnet 4 98
(RGibson, France) *held up, 6th straight, edged out & headway from well over 1f out, driven to lead last strides*

2 nk **Buoyant (IRE)**[12] 3-8-9 ............ DBonilla 7 97
(FHead, France) *set steady pace, quickened well over 2f out, hard ridden over 1f out, caught last strides*

3 1 ½ **Dream Play (IRE)**[33] 3-8-9 ............ GaryStevens 1 95
(AFabre, France) *tracked leader, 2nd straight, ridden over 2f out, stayed on one pace from over 1f out* 2

4 shd **Reverie Solitaire (IRE)**[29] 2700 3-8-9 ............ MBlancpain 3 95
(CLaffon-Parias, France) *racd in 3rd to str, disp 2nd on rails fr over 2f out, shut in wl over 1f out, swtchd out 1f out, kpt on one pace*

5 3 **Kalatuna (FR)**[29] 2700 3-8-9 ............ TThulliez 6 91
(JVanHandenhove, France) *disputed 3rd, 4th straight, effort well over 1f out, weakened inside final furlong*

6 1 ½ **Super Lina (FR)**[29] 2700 3-8-9 ............ DBoeuf 5 88
(YDeNicolay, France) *held up in rear, last straight, never a factor* 3

7 3 **Silverskaya (USA)**[29] 2700 3-8-9 ............ IMendizabal 2 84
(J-CRouget, France) *held up in last til headway 4f out, 5th straight, ridden & beaten well over 1f out* 1

2m 42.6s **Going Correction** +0.225s/f (Good) **7** Ran SP% **116.3**
Speed ratings: **97,96,95,95,93 92,90.**
**Owner** Mme P De Moussac **Bred** Haras De Mezeray S A **Trained** France

### NOTEBOOK
**Lune D'Or(FR)** raced in mid-division early on in a very slowly run race. She still had plenty to do at the furlong marker, but put under pressure she ran on to get up in the final few strides. She is a very promising filly who not only stays but accelerates and will probably be more impressive with a stronger pace. The Prix Vermeille is now her long-term target.
**Buoyant(IRE)** was asked to make all the running and did so at a moderate pace until entering the final turn. She quickened well and looked the winner at the furlong marker, but was finally run out it in the dying strides. She looks sure to be a Group winner in the future.
**Dream Play(IRE)**, always handy, settled behind the leader and challenged persistently during the straight. She could only stay on at one pace and was certainly unsuited to the way the race was run.
**Reverie Solitaire(IRE)** was always well up there, but was not too lucky on the rail at the furlong marker. She stayed on, but lost third place close home.

## 3567a GRAND PRIX DE SAINT-CLOUD (GROUP 1) 1m 4f
**3:25** (3:30) 3-Y-O+ **£140,838** (£56,345; £28,173; £14,074)

RPR

1 **Gamut (IRE)**[63] 1792 5-9-9 ............ KFallon 6 121
(SirMichaelStoute) *always close up, went 2nd after 3f, led well over 2f out (entering straight), ridden clear approaching final f, ran on well* **7/2**[1]

2 3 **Policy Maker (IRE)**[21] 2924 4-9-9 ............ TThulliez 3 117
(ELellouche, France) *raced in 4th to straight, chased winner from 1 1/2f out, one pace final f* **7/2**[1]

3 ½ **Visorama (IRE)**[34] 2543 4-9-6 ............ ELegrix 2 113
(AFabre, France) *mid-division, close 6th straight, stayed on one pace from over 1f out, never reached first two* **14/1**

4 nk **Short Pause**[21] 2924 5-9-9 ............ TGillet 5 116
(AFabre, France) *held up, 8th straight, headway on rails final f to take 4th on line* **10/1**

5 shd **Pride (FR)**[34] 2543 4-9-6 ............ DBonilla 4 112
(ADeRoyer-Dupre, France) *mid-division, 7th straight, stayed on same pace from over 1f out, lost 4th on line* **14/1**

6 ¾ **Phoenix Reach (IRE)**[18] 2968 4-9-9 ............ MartinDwyer 1 114
(AMBalding) *raced in 3rd to straight, disputed 2nd to 1 1/2f out, gradually weakened* **8/1**[3]

7 1 ½ **Polish Summer**[63] 1804 7-9-9 ............ GaryStevens 9 112
(AFabre, France) *held up, headway & 5th straight, beaten over 1f out (reported to have lost his right fore plate)* **7/2**[1]

8 ½ **Touch Of Land (FR)**[35] 2508 4-9-9 ............ C-PLemaire 8 111
(H-APantall, France) *held up in rear, 9th straight, never a factor* **10/1**

9 ¾ **Westerner**[17] 2998 5-9-9 ............ OPeslier 7 110
(ELellouche, France) *held up in rear, last straight, hard ridden 1 1/2f out, no headway* **6/1**[2]

10 20 **Poussin (IRE)**[120] 980 6-9-9 ............ SCoffigny 10 80
(ELellouche, France) *led to entering straight (well over 2f out)* **100/1**

2m 36.1s **Going Correction** +0.225s/f (Good) **10** Ran SP% **124.6**
Speed ratings: **119,117,116,116,116 115,114,114,114,100.**
**Owner** Mrs G Smith **Bred** Ballymacoll Stud Farm Ltd **Trained** Newmarket, Suffolk

### NOTEBOOK
**Gamut(IRE)**, who looked superb in the paddock, settled behind the pacemaker and was always travelling well. He took control of the race on entering the straight and began to draw the sting from his rivals. The race was in the bag at the two-furlong marker and he passed the post on his own. This was an outstanding performance and the King George VI and Queen Elizabeth Diamond Stakes and the Arc are both possibilities.
**Policy Maker(IRE)** followed the winner throughout and was given every possible chance, but could not quicken with that rival and just stayed on during the final two furlongs. He will now be aimed at either the Grand Prix de Deauville or the Grosser Preis at Baden-Baden.
**Visorama(IRE)**, settled in mid-division, was brought with a late run up the centre of the track. She really began to motor from a furlong out and this was a decent effort.
**Short Pause** had plenty to do on entering the straight, but really began to motor on the far rail from a furlong out and finished best of all. He looks capable of making the grade at Group level in the future.
**Phoenix Reach(IRE)**, always up there, was still going well rounding the final turn. When asked to quicken early in the straight, he was found wanting but still stayed on bravely to the line. He has not been easy to train and this race will have done him the power of good. He will be allowed to take his chance in the King George.

# 3435 SAN SIRO (R-H)
Sunday, July 4

**OFFICIAL GOING: Good**

## 3568a PREMIO OGGEBBIO (MAIDEN) (C&G) 6f
**2:50** (2:55) 2-Y-O **£7,042** (£3,099; £1,690; £845)

RPR

1 **Golden Pyramid (IRE)**[30] 2669 2-9-2 ............ MEsposito 1 —
(GFratini, Italy)

2 2 ½ **Sacranun** 2-8-8 ............ MMonteriso 2 —
(LMCumani) *always prominent, every chance over 1f out, stayed on same pace final f (178/100)*

3 15 **Deusexmachina** 2-9-2 ............ MDemuro 3 —
(MMarcialis, Italy)

4 7 **Dorange (ITY)** 2-8-8 ............ LPanici 5 —
(VPanici, Italy)

1m 12.0s **4** Ran
Speed ratings: .
**Owner** Scuderia Golden Horse **Bred** A M F Persse **Trained** Italy

### NOTEBOOK
**Sacranun** showed a little promise on his debut and can improve. However, he was receiving a generous weight allowance from the more experienced winner.

## 3569a PREMIO BESANA (FILLIES) 1m 2f
**4:25** (4:25) 3-Y-O **£10,563** (£4,648; £2,535; £1,268)

RPR

1 **Salse Bravo**[63] 1805 3-8-9 ............ MPasquale 5 —
(LBrogi, Italy)

2 3 ½ **Entusiasmo (ITY)**[32] 2607 3-8-9 ............ GBietolini 2 —
(JHeloury, Italy)

3 nse **Sogna Di Me**[14] 3135 3-8-9 ............ MDemuro 3 —
(BGrizzetti, Italy)

4 2 ½ **Love Of The Game (IRE)** 3-8-9 ............ SLandi 7 —
(EBorromeo, Italy)

4 dht **Rock Of Angels (IRE)** 3-8-9 ............ MEsposito 8 —
(GiorgioVerricelli, Italy)

6 5 **Indian Filly**[42] 2341 3-8-9 ............ LPanici 4 —
(MCicarelli, Italy)

7 5 **Tapioka City (USA)** 3-8-9 ............ MMonteriso 1 —
(LMCumani) *last throughout (633/100 coupled with Salse Bravo)* 1

2m 4.80s **7** Ran SP% **13.7**
Speed ratings: .
**Owner** Allevamento La Nuova Sbarra **Bred** Azienda Agricola Velino **Trained** Italy

### NOTEBOOK
**Tapioka City(USA)** was always struggling in rear. However, anyone who backed her was still rewarded as she was coupled to win with Salse Bravo.

# 3190 BATH (L-H)
Monday, July 5

**OFFICIAL GOING: Firm**

## 3570 E.B.F./SPONSORSHIP RACEDAY EVENT MAIDEN STKS 5f 11y
**2:00** (2:12) (D) 2-Y-O **£4,449** (£1,369; £684; £342) **Stalls** Low

Form RPR

46 1 **Annatalia**[10] 3286 2-8-9 ............ LDettori 6 85+
(BJMeehan) *mde all: pushed clr over 1f out: easily* **8/11**[1]

5 2 6 **Mulberry Lad (IRE)**[9] 3302 2-9-0 ............ RMullen 8 69
(WRMuir) *sn chsng wnr: no imp whn rdn 2f out but styd on for clr 2nd* **9/1**[3]

65 3 3 ½ **Dove Cottage (IRE)**[16] 3104 2-9-0 ............ WSupple 5 57
(WSKittow) *bhd: rdn 3f out: styd on fr over 1f out to take modest 3rd last strides* **16/1**

4 shd **Danzili Bay** 2-9-0 ............ TQuinn 9 56
(RMBeckett) *wnt rt s: bhd and rdn hdwy 3f out: chsd ldrs over 2f out: no imp: ct and lost mod 3rd last strides* **9/1**[3]

5 1 ¼ **Averting** 2-9-0 ............ SCarson 3 52
(RFJohnsonHoughton) *sn pushed along in rr: modest prog fr over 1f out* **5/1**[2]

66 6 5 **Dominer (IRE)**[45] 2263 2-9-0 ............ RLMoore 4 35
(JMBradley) *chsd ldrs to 1/2-way* **66/1**

0 **7** *nk* **Our Nigel (IRE)**[32] [2627] 2-9-0 ................................................ RHavlin 1 33
(MrsPNDutfield) *chsd ldrs to 1/2-way* **50/1**
61.27 secs (-1.23) **Going Correction** -0.075s/f (Good) **7** Ran SP% **103.9**
Speed ratings: **106,96,90,90,88 80,80**CSF £6.27 TOTE £1.60: £1.30, £3.00; EX 5.90.
**Owner** Mrs Sheila Tucker **Bred** Compton Down Stud **Trained** Upper Lambourn, Berks

**FOCUS**
An uncompetitive maiden, but Annatalia did what was required and in a fair time.

**NOTEBOOK**
**Annatalia ◆**, a fair sixth in a valuable Sales race at The Curragh on her previous start, was far too good for this lot and the result was never in doubt. Things are bound to be tougher in future, but she deserves to take her chance in a higher grade and could go well in something like the Super Sprint at Newbury.
**Mulberry Lad(IRE)** offered some promise on his debut, but failed to show significant improvement.
**Dove Cottage(IRE)** does not appear to be progressing and may do better in nurseries.
**Danzili Bay**, a 38,000gns purchase, half-brother to six- to eight-furlong scorer Moten Swing, out of a winner over ten furlongs, showed signs of inexperience and should improve, but he will need to in order to find a similar race.
**Averting**, a 24,000gns purchase, out of a seven-furlong two-year-old winner, showed little and may benefit from a step up in trip. *Official explanation: jockey said colt missed the break*

## 3571 OVAL OF BATH, PEUGEOT (S) STKS — 5f 11y
**2:30** (2:41) (G) 2-Y-O — **£2,527** (£722; £361) **Stalls** Low

Form RPR
3254 **1** **Straffan (IRE)**[25] [2799] 2-8-7 ........................................ SSanders 2 49
(EJO'Neill) *chsd ldrs: rdn to chse ldr appr fnl 2f: rdn to ld ins fnl f: drvn out* **7/2**[2]
6342 **2** *3/4* **Glasson Lodge**[14] [3140] 2-8-8 ow1 ........................................ NCallan 4 47
(PDEvans) *chsd ldrs: rdn fr 3f out: styd on u.p fnl f: tk 2nd last strides: nt rch wnr* **11/4**[1]
04 **3** *nk* **Voom**[4] [3458] 2-8-6 ow2 ........................................ SHitchcott(3) 1 47
(MRChannon) *in tch: rdn over 2f out: hdwy on rails over 1f out: chsd ldrs ins last: kpt on same pce* **4/1**[3]
0665 **4** *hd* **Zachy Boy**[4] [3458] 2-8-5 ........................................(b[1]) DerekNolan(7) 3 50
(JSMoore) *rrd and taken out of stalls: sn led: edgd rt over 1f out: hdd ins last: styd on same pce* **14/1**
45 **5** *1* **Sapphire Princess**[14] [3140] 2-8-7 ........................................ TPQueally 5 41
(IAWood) *racd wout tongue strap: in tch and rdn 3f out: hdwy over 1f out: styng on whn nt clr run and eased cl home* **7/1**
0 **6** *1 1/2* **Tip Toes (IRE)**[48] [2208] 2-8-0 ........................................ TDean(7) 7 36
(MRChannon) *s.i.s: bhd: shkn up and sme hdwy fr over 1f out: kpt on cl home* **16/1**
0 **7** *nk* **Fire At Will**[14] [3140] 2-8-12 ........................................ WSupple 6 40
(AWCarroll) *s.i.s: sn rdn and outpcd: styd on fr over 1f out: n.d* **20/1**
3300 **8** *1* **Nutty Times**[51] [2124] 2-8-0 ........................................ CHaddon(7) 8 31
(WGMTurner) *chsd ldr tl over 2f out: wknd ins fnl f* **5/1**
64.87 secs (2.37) **Going Correction** -0.075s/f (Good) **8** Ran SP% **115.4**
Speed ratings: **78,76,76,76,74 72,71,69**CSF £13.73 TOTE £4.30: £1.30, £1.10, £1.50; EX 12.90.The winner was sold to W. Clifford for 8,500gns.
**Owner** Mrs Melissa O'Neill **Bred** Mountarmstrong Stud **Trained** Newmarket, Suffolk
■ Stewards Enquiry : C Haddon one-day ban: careless riding (Jul 16); further one-day ban: failed to keep straight from stalls (Jul 17)

**FOCUS**
Little strength in depth to this seller and the winner did not have to be at her best to score.

**NOTEBOOK**
**Straffan(IRE)** had been running respectably in claimers and this drop into selling company proved just what was required. A penalty will make things tougher in this grade and her overall record suggests she could struggle if stepped back up in class.
**Glasson Lodge** ran her race, but again found one too good. She is not one to follow, but will surely find a similar race.
**Voom** ran respectably over a trip probably shorter than ideal.
**Zachy Boy** was lit up by the first-time blinkers and did not appear to quite get home.
**Sapphire Princess** did not have things go her way - she got bumped soon after the start and was denied a clear run inside the final furlong - but she looks to need another furlong in any case.

## 3572 LANSDOWN MAIDEN H'CAP — 1m 3f 144y
**3:00** (3:08) (E) (0-75,68) 3-Y-O — **£3,692** (£1,136; £568; £284) **Stalls** Low

Form RPR
-364 **1** **Velvet Waters**[25] [2821] 3-8-10 **57** ........................................ SCarson 7 59
(RFJohnsonHoughton) *led: rdn over 2f out: narrowly hdd ins fnl f: rallied gamely to ld again cl home* **7/2**[2]
0503 **2** *hd* **Lucky Arthur (IRE)**[19] [2977] 3-8-12 **59** ........................................ DSweeney 5 61
(JGMO'Shea) *bhd: hdwy on outside over 2f out: styd on wl to press ldrs ins last: kpt on to take 2nd cl home: nt rch wnr* **7/1**
0355 **3** *hd* **Mustang Ali (IRE)**[7] [3387] 3-9-7 **68** ........................................ LDettori 9 70
(SKirk) *hld up in tch:rdn and hdwy 3f out:chsd wnr over 1f out:slt advantage ins last: sn drvn: hdd and fnd no ex cl home* **3/1**[1]
5402 **4** *1 3/4* **The King Of Rock**[18] [3026] 3-8-9 **56** ........................................ SWhitworth 2 55
(AGNewcombe) *hld up rr but in tch: hdwy over 2f out: styd on u.p fnl f: nt rch ldrs* **6/1**[3]
0-03 **5** *1/2* **Dhehdaah**[26] [2774] 3-9-0 **61** ........................................(b[1]) WSupple 8 59
(NAGraham) *chsd ldrs: rdn to chse wnr over 2f out tl over 1f out: wknd ins fnl f* **13/2**
0-05 **6** *3/4* **Science Academy (USA)**[42] [2363] 3-8-7 **54** ........................................ TQuinn 10 51
(PFICole) *chsd wnr tl rdn and edgd lft over 2f out: kpt on tl no ex and wknd ins fnl f* **10/1**
0005 **7** *5* **Silencio (IRE)**[8] [3342] 3-8-13 **60** ........................................ VSlattery 4 49
(AKing) *t.k.h: chsd ldrs: rdn 3f out: wknd over 2f out* **16/1**
00-0 **8** *1 1/4* **Royal Starlet**[24] [2842] 3-8-6 **53** ........................................ PDobbs 1 40
(MrsAJPerrett) *chsd ldrs: rdn 3f out: wknd over 2f out* **10/1**
6060 **9** *3* **Signora Panettiera (FR)**[25] [2822] 3-8-3 **50** ........................................ CCatlin 6 32
(MRChannon) *a bhd: rdn over 2f out: no rspnse* **50/1**
0350 **10** *hd* **Almost Welcome**[84] [1356] 3-8-8 **55** ........................................ RLMoore 3 37
(SDow) *a in rr* **20/1**
2m 30.42s (0.12) **Going Correction** -0.075s/f (Good) **10** Ran SP% **118.1**
Speed ratings: **96,95,95,94,94 93,90,89,87,87**CSF £28.82 CT £82.53 TOTE £4.70: £1.70, £3.00, £1.20; EX 39.00.
**Owner** R Crutchley **Bred** R E Crutchley **Trained** Blewbury, Oxon

**FOCUS**
A moderate if competitive maiden handicap and the form looks good for the grade.

**NOTEBOOK**
**Velvet Waters** appeared to find a mile six stretching her stamina on her previous start and this drop back in trip suited well. She ran out a particularly game winner and, now she has got her head in front, could go on from this.
**Lucky Arthur(IRE)** finished well from off the pace and was just denied. There is a similar race in her, although maiden handicaps are not that common.
**Mustang Ali(IRE)** can have no excuses, as he ranged upsides the eventual winner but could not go past.
**The King Of Rock** is better handicapped on the All-Weather and may do better on that surface.
**Dhehdaah** did not improve for the fitting of blinkers.

## 3573 GROSVENOR CASINOS STKS (H'CAP) — 1m 2f 46y
**3:30** (3:33) (E) (0-75,71) 3-Y-O+ — **£4,459** (£1,372; £686; £343) **Stalls** Low

Form RPR
3023 **1** **Ember Days**[4] [3459] 5-8-13 **59** ........................................(p) EAhern 4 69
(JLSpearing) *hld up in tch: hdwy 3f out: chsd ldr ins fnl 2f: drvn to chal ins last: styd on to ld last strides* **4/1**[2]
4362 **2** *shd* **Todlea (IRE)**[5] [3412] 4-9-11 **71** ........................................ LDettori 3 81
(JAOsborne) *led after 1f: rdn and styd on fr 2f out: no ex u.p whn chal last half f: ct last strides* **5/4**[1]
0336 **3** *1 1/4* **Rebate**[14] [3143] 4-9-0 **60** ........................................ PDobbs 5 67
(RHannon) *hld up in rr: hdwy 2f out: chsd ldrs ins last: no ex u.p* **5/1**[3]
3-40 **4** *3/4* **Maria Bonita (IRE)**[49] [2169] 3-8-8 **65** ........................................(b[1]) RLMoore 1 71?
(RMBeckett) *t.k.h: disp 2nd tl ins fnl 2f: one pce u.p fnl f* **16/1**
4262 **5** *hd* **Oktis Morilious (IRE)**[12] [3190] 3-7-5 **55** oh7 ........................................ CHaddon(7) 2 61
(AWCarroll) *stdd rr but in tch: pushed along and hdwy ins fnl 2f: kpt on ins last but nvr gng pce to rch ldrs* **8/1**
16-0 **6** *3* **Celtic Star (IRE)**[15] [3128] 6-8-11 **60** ........................................ DNolan(3) 6 60
(MissKMGeorge) *led 1f: styd disputing 2nd tl over 2f out: wknd wl over 1f out* **25/1**
6006 **7** *2* **Traveller's Tale**[11] [3232] 5-9-1 **61** ........................................ SDrowne 7 57
(PGMurphy) *held up in rr: hdwy 4f out: drvn to chse ldrs and edgd lft 2f out: sn wknd* **8/1**
2m 8.37s (-2.63) **Going Correction** -0.075s/f (Good)
**WFA** 3 from 4yo+ 11lb **7** Ran SP% **113.1**
Speed ratings: **107,106,105,105,105 102,101**CSF £9.19 TOTE £5.00: £1.80, £1.60; EX 11.10.
**Owner** Mrs Carol J Welch **Bred** Mrs Carol Jacqueline Welch **Trained** Kinnersley, Worcs

**FOCUS**
Just the seven runners, but this modest handicap was pretty competitive. The form looks sound without being all that strong.

**NOTEBOOK**
**Ember Days** ended a losing run stretching back to July 2002 off a mark 12lb lower than when gaining her last success. There was next to nothing in it at the line, but she should not go up much for this and a follow up could not be ruled out.
**Todlea(IRE)** continues in good heart without winning - he was last successful in May 2003. He had no obvious excuse and does not appeal as one to take a short price about in similar company.
**Rebate**, with waiting tactics employed this time, kept on well for a respectable third. With just one win to his name in 26 career starts, he does not appeal as one to follow, but is 13lb lower than when gaining his sole success and becoming dangerously well handicapped.
**Maria Bonita(IRE)** has been given a chance by the Handicapper, but was quite keen in the first-time blinkers.
**Oktis Morilious(IRE)** had it all to do from 7lb out of the handicap and never really looked like winning. His proximity at the line does not help the form.

## 3574 WEATHERBYS BANK MAIDEN STKS — 1m 2f 46y
**4:00** (4:01) (D) 3-Y-O — **£3,536** (£1,088; £544; £272) **Stalls** Low

Form RPR
023 **1** **Vamp**[28] [2729] 3-8-9 **73** ........................................ SSanders 5 73
(RMBeckett) *trckd ldrs: rdn to ld ins fnl 2f: hld on wl fnl f* **11/4**[2]
-545 **2** *1* **Mouftari (USA)**[44] [2298] 3-9-0 **84** ........................................ LDettori 3 76
(BWHills) *led: hdd ins fnl 2f: styd chsng wnr but nt qckn ins f* **5/1**
0 **3** *1* **Wedding Cake (IRE)**[14] [3161] 3-8-9 ........................................ EAhern 2 69
(SirMichaelStoute) *hld up rr but in tch: swtchd to outside and hdwy fr 2f out: changed legs but kpt on fnl f: nt rch ldrs* **7/1**
5-02 **4** *3 1/2* **Powerful Parrish (USA)**[14] [3142] 3-8-9 **78** ........................................ TQuinn 6 62
(PFICole) *chsd lesder after 2f: rdn over 2f out: wknd appr fnl f* **15/8**[1]
33 **5** *3 1/2* **Sunday City (JPN)**[15] [3121] 3-9-0 ........................................(v) TPQueally 1 61
(DRLoder) *chsd ldrs: rdn over 2f out: sn btn* **4/1**[3]
**6** *4* **Whenwillitwin** 3-8-7 ........................................ DerekNolan(7) 4 53
(JSMoore) *s.i.s: bhd: sme hdwy 4f out: nvr a danger and sn rr* **100/1**
2m 9.37s (-1.63) **Going Correction** -0.075s/f (Good) **6** Ran SP% **111.6**
Speed ratings: **103,102,101,98,95 92**CSF £16.40 TOTE £3.80: £2.10, £3.30; EX 17.30.
**Owner** A D G Oldrey **Bred** A D G Oldrey **Trained** Lambourn, Berks

**FOCUS**
Just a fair maiden, with a couple of these looking flattered by their current ratings.

**NOTEBOOK**
**Vamp** confirmed the promise she showed in similar events despite having a little bit to find at the weights with her two main market rivals. As a result, she will probably be raised for this and will find things tougher next time.
**Mouftari(USA)** again failed to justify his rating of 84. There is a maiden in him, but it will be a pretty ordinary one.
**Wedding Cake(IRE)**, one of the less exposed runners, kept on nicely for pressure and would appear to be going the right way.
**Powerful Parrish(USA)** shaped as though this sort of trip would suit when runner-up at Chepstow on his previous start, but failed to confirm that promise. At least this run should see her drop a few pounds.
**Sunday City(JPN)**, dropped back from a mile and a half, was a long way below form.

## 3575 TELETEXT RACING "HANDS AND HEELS" APPRENTICE H'CAP — 5f 11y
**4:30** (4:31) (G) (0-55,58) 3-Y-O+ — **£2,653** (£758; £379) **Stalls** Low

Form RPR
0032 **1** **Flying Tackle**[13] [3169] 6-9-2 **48** ........................................(p) WHogg 14 58
(MDods) *in tch: hdwy over 2f out: chal and hung lft 1f out: sn led: hld on all out* **4/1**[1]
2010 **2** *hd* **Enjoy The Buzz**[7] [3381] 5-9-1 **47** ........................................ MHalford 13 56
(JMBradley) *bhd: hdwy over 2f out: str run fnl f: fin wl: nt quite get up* **5/1**[2]
0-24 **3** *shd* **Lucky Valentine**[13] [3175] 4-8-8 **46** ........................................(b) JemmaMarshall(6) 2 55
(GLMoore) *chsd ldrs: drvn and slt led 1f out: sn hdd: kpt on: no ex cl home* **9/1**
0335 **4** *1 1/2* **Blessed Place**[2] [3524] 4-9-1 **47** ........................................(p) DerekNolan 9 50
(DJSFfrenchDavis) *w ld tl def advantage over 3f out: drvn 2f out: hdd 1f out: outpcd ins last* **5/1**[2]
0000 **5** *nk* **Tamarella (IRE)**[14] [3151] 4-9-1 **47** ........................................(b[1]) MHoward 8 49
(GGMargarson) *s.i.s: bhd: hdwy 2f out:kpt on wl fnl f but nt rch ldrs* **12/1**
4000 **6** *hd* **Fiamma Royale (IRE)**[62] [1855] 6-8-13 **45** ........................................ StevenHarrison 4 46
(MSSaunders) *chsd ldrs: drvn over 2f out: styd on fnl f: nvr gng pce to chal* **16/1**
-000 **7** *1 1/2* **Tomthevic**[16] [3084] 6-9-7 **53** ........................................ SaleemGolam 16 48
(MrsPSly) *sn led: hdd over 3f out: styd chsng ldr tl over 1f out: wknd ins last* **20/1**
0000 **8** *hd* **Bennanabaa**[24] [2834] 5-8-8 **43** ........................................(t) BO'Neill(3) 3 37
(SCBurrough) *bhd: pushed along over 2f out: kpt on fnl f: nt trble ldrs* **50/1**

3100 **9** *hd* **Hagley Park**$^{7}$ [3378] 5-9-2 **48**........(v) KMay 12 41
(MQuinn) *chsd ldrs: stl wl there whn hmpd and wknd 1f out* **25/1**

0603 **10** *1 1/4* **Xsynna**$^{73}$ [1591] 8-8-2 **37**........KJackson$^{(3)}$ 6 25
(MissMERowland) *bhd: pushed along 2f out: r.o fnl f: n.d* **33/1**

4005 **11** *shd* **Boanerges (IRE)**$^{1}$ [3558] 7-9-6 **58** ow3........(p) CJDavies$^{(6)}$ 5 46
(JMBradley) *in tch: drvn to chse ldrs whn n.m.r and wknd 1f out* **7/1**$^{3}$

50-5 **12** *1* **Flapdoodle**$^{16}$ [3084] 6-9-8 **54**........RLucey-Butler 11 38
(AWCarroll) *chsd ldrs: rdn over 2f out: wknd over 1f out* **12/1**

0040 **13** *hd* **Danifah (IRE)**$^{2}$ [3530] 3-8-5 **45**........(b) RJKilloran$^{(3)}$ 15 28
(PDEvans) *s.i.s: outpcd: sme late prog* **20/1**

0200 **14** *1/2* **Somethingabouther**$^{13}$ [3169] 4-8-6 **43**........FrancesPickard$^{(5)}$ 7 24
(PWHiatt) *sn outpcd* **50/1**

3003 **15** *nk* **Shady Deal**$^{2}$ [3533] 8-8-13 **45**........DeanWilliams 17 25
(JMBradley) *racd on outside: sn outpcd* **10/1**

0305 **16** *nk* **Tappit (IRE)**$^{23}$ [2869] 5-8-12 **52**........HazelBoyd$^{(8)}$ 1 31
(JMBradley) *sn outpcd* **20/1**

-000 **17** *2* **Diaphanous**$^{118}$ [1000] 6-7-13 **37**........(b) LiamJones$^{(6)}$ 10 8
(EAWheeler) *chsd ldrs over 3f* **33/1**

62.34 secs (-0.16) **Going Correction** -0.075s/f (Good)
**WFA** 3 from 4yo+ 5lb **17 Ran SP% 134.1**
Speed ratings: **98,97,97,95,94 94,91,91,91,89 89,87,87,86,85 85,82**CSF £22.89 CT £189.34 TOTE £5.30: £1.80, £2.00, £2.20, £1.40; EX 28.70 Place 6 £10.11, Place 5 £7.46.
**Owner** Neil Harrison **Bred** Raffin Stud **Trained** Piercebridge, Co Durham

**FOCUS**
A very moderate handicap but it looks sound form for the level.

**NOTEBOOK**
**Flying Tackle** had been running into form lately and was able to confirm the promise of his recent efforts to gain his first win since October 2001. This should have boosted his confidence and he could well add to this for his in-form yard.
**Enjoy The Buzz** did not appear to face the kickback on the Fibresand last time but, returned to turf, this was much better and he was just denied.
**Lucky Valentine** has just a maiden win to her name, but she is running well and has a similar race in her.
**Blessed Place** is in fine form at the moment but, with just one win to his name from 27 starts, he is clearly hard to win with.
**Tamarella(IRE)** ran a little better with blinkers replacing the visor.
T/Plt: £10.30 to a £1 stake. Pool: £36,953.25. 2,606.80 winning tickets. T/Qpdt: £6.50 to a £1 stake. Pool: £2,004.00. 226.50 winning tickets. ST

## 3363 MUSSELBURGH (R-H)
### Monday, July 5
**OFFICIAL GOING: Round course - good; straight course - good to soft**

### 3576 PETER WALKER GROUP STAYERS H'CAP — 2m
**2:15** (2:15) (F) (0-55,55) 4-Y-0+ **£2,954** (£844; £422) **Stalls** Low

Form RPR

4533 **1** **Paddy Mul**$^{5}$ [3411] 7-9-0 **49**........(t) JBramhill 4 55
(WStorey) *hld up towards rr: stdy hdwy over 6f out: led 3f out: rdn and styd on wl fnl 2f* **10/1**

0-22 **2** *1/2* **Ellway Heights**$^{7}$ [3369] 7-8-11 **51**........BSwarbrick$^{(5)}$ 3 56
(WMBrisbourne) *hedl up towards rr: hdwy 1/2-way: effrt to chse wnr over 2f out and sn rdn: drvn and hung rt over 1f out: kpt on* **4/1**$^{2}$

5520 **3** *nk* **Ipledgeallegiance (USA)**$^{5}$ [3411] 8-7-7 **35**........(b) DFentiman$^{(7)}$ 9 40
(DWChapman) *slowly to stride and bhd: hdwy over 5f out: str run on outer to chse ldng pair wl over 1f out: sn rdn and kpt on* **14/1**

4323 **4** *5* **Next Flight (IRE)**$^{11}$ [3236] 5-9-1 **50**........DHolland 8 49
(REBarr) *trckd ldrs: hdwy 4f out: rdn wl over 2f out and sn one pce* **10/3**$^{1}$

500/ **5** *12* **Billy Two Rivers (IRE)**$^{5}$ [4631] 5-8-0 **35** oh2........(p) RFfrench 12 19
(DRMacleod) *chsd ldrs: rdn along 5f out and sn wknd* **16/1**

-050 **6** *1/2* **Mr Fortywinks (IRE)**$^{38}$ [2462] 10-8-9 **47**........TEaves$^{(3)}$ 10 31
(BEllison) *led 3f: chsd ldr tl rdn along 5f out and sn wknd* **11/2**$^{3}$

6402 **7** *15* **Western Bluebird (IRE)**$^{7}$ [3363] 6-8-7 **42**........(b) PFessey 11 8
(MissKateMilligan) *chsd ldrs: rdn along over 5f out: sn wknd* **16/1**

0400 **8** *1* **Green 'N' Gold**$^{15}$ [3120] 4-9-6 **55**........ACulhane 2 19
(MDHammond) *in tch: rdn along over 5f out: sn wknd* **12/1**

000/ **9** *1 1/2* **End Of An Error**$^{29}$ [4859] 5-7-7 **35** oh4........NataliaGemelova$^{(7)}$ 1 —
(MrsDianneSayer) *bhd fr 1/2-way* **20/1**

-606 **10** *21* **Ton-Chee**$^{2}$ [3518] 5-8-0 **35** oh15........PMQuinn 6 —
(KWHogg) *cl up: led after 3f and sn clr: rdn along over 4f out: hdd 3f out and sn wknd* **33/1**

0400 **11** *24* **Washington Pink (IRE)**$^{26}$ [2462] 5-8-2 **40** ow2........(p) THamilton$^{(3)}$ 7 —
(CGrant) *in tch: rdn along and bhd fr 1/2-way* **33/1**

3410 **12** *dist* **Berkeley Heights**$^{16}$ [3108] 4-8-7 **42**........RWinston 5 —
(MrsJCandlish) *dwlt: a rr* **16/1**

3m 30.05s (-3.65) **Going Correction** -0.025s/f (Good) **12 Ran SP% 110.2**
Speed ratings: **108,107,107,105,99 98,91,90,90,79 67,—**CSF £45.05 CT £529.67 TOTE £8.60: £2.50, £1.40, £5.30; EX 29.70.
**Owner** Gremlin Racing **Bred** G Piper **Trained** Muggleswick, Co Durham
■ Stewards Enquiry : J Bramhill two-day ban: excessive use of the whip (Jul 16-17)

**FOCUS**
A very weak event that suited those held up off the pace, and it saw the front three pull clear. Ordinary form with the winner defying a career-high mark.

**NOTEBOOK**
**Paddy Mul**, back up in trip, made a decisive move for home that caught his main rivals napping and kept to his task well late in the day to score a deserved success. He has been in consistent form of late and had been raised 9lb, but he does look best suited by this trip and should continue to pay his way at this level.
**Ellway Heights** again found one too good and looked a little reluctant under maximum pressure late on. He will find a race in due course off this mark, but is not one to trust.
**Ipledgeallegiance(USA)** improved a touch for this step up in trip and ran to the line. He is a very tricky ride nowadays, but is threatening to win a race off his current mark and it may well come over a slightly shorter trip.
**Next Flight(IRE)** ran a little below par and may have been better served by a slightly more patient ride.
**Mr Fortywinks(IRE)** paid for setting the generous early pace and is capable of better, but this veteran has a bit to prove now.
**Berkeley Heights** *Official explanation: jockey said filly was never travelling*

### 3577 EUROPEAN BREEDERS FUND MEDIAN AUCTION MAIDEN STKS — 5f
**2:45** (2:45) (E) 2-Y-0 **£4,361** (£1,342; £671; £335) **Stalls** Low

Form RPR

4505 **1** **Alpaga Le Jomage (IRE)**$^{13}$ [3176] 2-9-0........DHolland 6 80
(BJMeehan) *mde all: rdn over 1f out: drvn out* **1/1**$^{1}$

0 **2** *1 1/2* **Madame Topflight**$^{27}$ [2749] 2-8-6........NMackay$^{(3)}$ 3 70
(MrsGSRees) *cl up: rdn along 2f out: kpt on u.p ins last* **25/1**

3 **3** *1 1/4* **Trim Image**$^{17}$ [3055] 2-8-9........RLappin 4 65
(WJarvis) *chsd ldrs: swtchd rt and hdwy 2f out: rdn over 1 out and sn one pce* **11/4**$^{2}$

3003 **4** *3 1/2* **Almaty Express**$^{14}$ [3144] 2-9-0........RWinston 5 58
(MTodhunter) *chsd ldrs: rdn along 2f out: wknd over 1f out* **12/1**

**5** *1 3/4* **Premier Times** 2-9-0........ACulhane 1 52
(MDHammond) *s.i.s and bhd tl sme late hdwy* **50/1**

2630 **6** *1 1/4* **Nee Lemon Left**$^{5}$ [3408] 2-8-2........(p) PPMathers$^{(7)}$ 2 43
(ABerry) *prom:rdn along 1/2-way: sn wknd* **16/1**

**7** *14* **Bond Puccini** 2-9-0........FLynch 7 —
(BSmart) *s.i.s: rn green and sn outpcd: a wl bhd* **11/2**$^{3}$

61.23 secs (0.83) **Going Correction** +0.125s/f (Good) **7 Ran SP% 111.4**
Speed ratings: **98,95,93,88,85 83,60**CSF £28.64 TOTE £1.70: £1.40, £6.60; EX 23.80.
**Owner** The Top Banana Partnership **Bred** Patrick M Ryan **Trained** Upper Lambourn, Berks

**FOCUS**
An ordinary juvenile affair that saw the field come home well strung out. The form looks sound enough for its level.

**NOTEBOOK**
**Alpaga Le Jomage(IRE)** pinged out of the gates, and although never really looking in danger, this goes down as a workmanlike performance. He is consistent enough, but could be hard to place in the future, as he looks totally exposed.
**Madame Topflight** improved plenty on her debut effort and looks the type to improve again for another furlong. She is by a proper Fibresand sire and will be very interesting if turning up at Southwell or Wolverhampton.
**Trim Image** seemd to run her race with no obvious excuses. This does look about as good as she is, but at least she was clear of the rest and she may be worth a try over an extra furlong.
**Bond Puccini** was taken off his feet on this debut and can only improve.

### 3578 PETER WALKER GROUP FILLIES' H'CAP — 1m 4f
**3:15** (3:15) (F) (0-55,55) 4-Y-0+ **£3,354** (£1,032; £516; £258) **Stalls** High

Form RPR

020/ **1** **Woodwind Down**$^{29}$ [2787] 7-8-12 **45**........RWinston 2 52
(MTodhunter) *mde all: rdn over 2f out: wandered ent last: drvn and styd on wl* **10/1**

1035 **2** *1 3/4* **Cosmic Case**$^{11}$ [3221] 9-8-9 **45**........NMackay$^{(3)}$ 7 49
(JSGoldie) *trckd ldrs: hdwy 3f out: rdn wl over 1f out: kpt on u.p ins last* **9/4**$^{2}$

0460 **3** *1/2* **Balalaika Tune (IRE)**$^{2}$ [3518] 5-8-2 **35** oh3........JBramhill 6 38
(WStorey) *hld up: hdwy on inner 3f out: swtchd lft and hdwy 2f out: rdn and ch whn n.m.r and swtchd rt ins last: kpt on* **12/1**

5-40 **4** *1/2* **Ellovamul**$^{4}$ [3461] 4-9-0 **52**........PMakin$^{(5)}$ 1 54
(WMBrisbourne) *trckd ldrs: hdwy 3f out: rdn and ch wl over 1f out: drvn and no ex ins last* **11/2**$^{3}$

0042 **5** *3/4* **Pont Neuf (IRE)**$^{8}$ [3348] 4-9-8 **55**........(t) KDarley 3 56
(JWHills) *hld up: rdn along 4f out: drvn over 2f out: kpt on same pce appr last* **2/1**$^{1}$

0002 **6** *3* **Miss Fleurie**$^{60}$ [1917] 4-8-2 **35** oh3........PFessey 4 31
(RCraggs) *chsd wnr to 1/2-way: rdn along 4f out: wknd 3f out* **11/1**

0200 **7** *12* **Miss Ocean Monarch**$^{18}$ [3008] 4-8-6 **39**........(be$^{1}$) ACulhane 5 16
(DWChapman) *keen: prom: hdwy to chse wnr 1/2-way: rdn along over 3f out: wknd 2f out* **20/1**

2m 39.71s (1.69) **Going Correction** -0.025s/f (Good) **7 Ran SP% 109.4**
Speed ratings: **93,91,91,91,90 88,80**CSF £30.03 TOTE £9.40: £4.20, £1.90; EX 48.20.
**Owner** Domino Racing **Bred** Fares Stables Ltd **Trained** Orton, Cumbria

**FOCUS**
A very poor contest run at a tactical pace and the form is suspect.

**NOTEBOOK**
**Woodwind Down**, last seen when placed over hurdles a month ago, scored a first ever win on the Flat under a canny ride from Winston. She dictated the stop-start gallop from the off and used her proven stamina to good effect late on when asked to win her race. This versatile mare does stay well and is genuine, but very much had the run of the race this time.
**Cosmic Case** went in vain pursuit of the winner, but would have preffered a stronger gallop and faster underfoot conditions.
**Balalaika Tune(IRE)** can be rated slightly better than the bare form, and bettered her effort just two days previously, but is a hard mare to catch right and is not one to trust.
**Ellovamul** shaped like a non-stayer over this trip and the recent ease in the ground had gone against her.
**Pont Neuf(IRE)** could not reproduce the form of her previous outing, which looked to give her an obvious chance in this, and this run confirmed her as a most in-and-out individual.

### 3579 YSC SCOTLAND (S) STKS — 1m
**3:45** (3:47) (F) 3-Y-0+ **£2,982** (£852; £426) **Stalls** Low

Form RPR

0600 **1** **Artistic Style**$^{48}$ [2218] 4-8-11 63........TEaves$^{(3)}$ 11 61
(BEllison) *chsd ldrs: pushed along and hdxway 3f out: rdn 2f out: drvn ent last and styd on to ld nr fin* **7/2**$^{1}$

4000 **2** *hd* **Quicks The Word**$^{11}$ [3247] 4-9-0 54........KDarley 6 61
(CWThornton) *trckd ldrs: hdwy on outer oevr 2f out: rdn to ld over 1f out: drvn ins last: hdd and no ex nr fin* **8/1**

0002 **3** *2 1/2* **Mac's Talisman (IRE)**$^{7}$ [3376] 4-9-0 55........MTebbutt 3 55
(VSmith) *hld up: hdwy over 2f out: rdn and n.m.r over 1f out: kpt on ins last* **11/2**$^{3}$

0406 **4** *1 1/2* **Jedeydd**$^{9}$ [3321] 7-9-0 55........(tp) RWinston 1 52
(MDods) *stdd s and bhd: hdwy 3f out: rdn and n.m.r wl over 1f out: kpt on u.p ins last* **9/2**$^{2}$

0100 **5** *nk* **Forest Air (IRE)**$^{19}$ [2974] 4-9-0 46........RFfrench 10 51
(MissLAPerratt) *midfield: hdwy on outer over 2f out: rdn wl over 1f out: kpt on fnl f* **33/1**

5206 **6** *3/4* **Royal Windmill (IRE)**$^{11}$ [3247] 5-9-0 46........(p) ACulhane 8 49
(MDHammond) *hld up in tch: smooth hdwy 3f out: chal on bit 2f out: rdn and one pce fnl f* **7/1**

5033 **7** *3 1/2* **Summer Special**$^{17}$ [3040] 4-8-11 44........LEnstone$^{(3)}$ 9 41
(DWBarker) *cl up: led over 2f out: sn rdn: hdd over 1f out and sn wknd* **12/1**

P000 **8** *hd* **Lion's Domane**$^{17}$ [3040] 7-9-0 47........FLynch 2 41
(ABerry) *led: rdn along and hdd over 2f out: grad wknd* **33/1**

-503 **9** *shd* **Erupt**$^{19}$ [2990] 11-9-0 40........DHolland 4 41
(REBarr) *bhd tl sme late hdwy* **16/1**

0650 **10** *1* **African Spur (IRE)**$^{10}$ [3277] 4-8-7 49........DTudhope$^{(7)}$ 12 38
(DCarroll) *chsd ldng pair: rdn along 3f out: drvn and wknd over 1f out* **14/1**

60-0 **11** *18* **Mafruz**$^{10}$ [3265] 5-8-11 55........THamilton$^{(3)}$ 13 —
(RAFahey) *sn rdn alonga nd a bhd* **14/1**

000 **12** *1/2* **Welcome Archie**$^{42}$ [2346] 4-9-0........PMQuinn 14 —
(JSHaldane) *s.i.s: a b ehind* **100/1**

13 *dist* **Crazy Like A Fool (IRE)**[53] 5-8-11 .................................. NMackay(3) 5 —
(BMactaggart) *s.i.s: a bhd* **100/1**
1m 41.18s (-1.52) **Going Correction** -0.025s/f (Good)
**WFA** 3 from 4yo+ 9lb **13** Ran SP% **114.2**
Speed ratings: **106,105,103,101,101 100,97,97,96,95 77,77,**—CSF £29.52 TOTE £4.60: £1.20, £3.00, £3.60; EX 68.40.The winner was bought in for 5,200gns.
**Owner** Mr & Mrs D A Gamble **Bred** Juddmonte Farms **Trained** Norton, N Yorks

**FOCUS**
A fair seller but little strength in depth and the first two pulled clear at the finish.

**NOTEBOOK**
**Artistic Style**, clear best in at the weights, relished this drop into selling company, but had to pull out all the stops to register a first ever success. This looks about as good as he is.
**Quicks The Word** only just went down and ran a much improved race, confirming that he gets this trip.
**Mac's Talisman(IRE)** was finishing best of all, having been held up to get this trip, and will be better served by a more positive ride next time. However, he is fiendishly hard to win with.
**Jedeydd**, with the cheekpieces back on, did not get the best of runs entering the final furlong, but it made little difference to the result. He looks better over shorter.
**Royal Windmill(IRE)**, winner of this last year, ran too freely early on and never looked like getting there.

## 3580 PETER WALKER GROUP LE GARCON D'OR STKS (H'CAP) 5f
**4:15** (4:17) (D) (0-80,78) 3-Y-O+ **£6,786** (£2,088; £1,044; £522) **Stalls** Low

Form RPR
3000 **1** **Zarzu**[10] [3266] 5-9-1 **72**.......................................... RThomas(5) 4 88+
(CRDore) *trckd ldrs: hdwy 2f out: rdn and qcknd to ld ent last: sn clr* **9/2**[2]
3011 **2** *2 1/2* **Frascati**[9] [3293] 4-9-5 **78**.......................................... PPMathers(7) 6 80
(ABerry) *cl up: led wl over 1f out: sn rdn: hdd ent fnl f and nt qckn* **7/1**[3]
0004 **3** *nk* **Viewforth**[2] [3524] 6-8-12 **67**..........................................(b) NMackay(3) 3 68
(JSGoldie) *chsd ldrs: rdn 2f out: kpt on ins last* **9/4**[1]
1604 **4** *1 1/2* **Pirlie Hill**[11] [3225] 4-8-1 **53**.......................................... RFfrench 7 49
(MissLAPerratt) *n.m.r and lost pl after 1f: hdwy 1/2-way: effrt and nt clr run over 1f out and ent last: kpt on* **16/1**
0005 **5** *1* **Northern Svengali (IRE)**[6] [3399] 8-7-12 **50** oh14..........(tp) JMcAuley 5 42
(DANolan) *hld up: hdwy 2f out: styd on fnl f: nrst fin* **50/1**
0-60 **6** *shd* **Mutayam**[6] [3399] 4-7-7 **50** oh11..........................................(t) BSwarbrick(5) 10 42
(DANolan) *cl up: ev ch 2f out: sn rdna nd wknd ent last* **100/1**
0034 **7** *1 1/4* **Strensall**[6] [3399] 7-9-12 **78**.......................................... RFitzpatrick 8 65
(REBarr) *cl up on outer: rdn 2f out: wknd appr last* **10/1**
460 **8** *1* **Finger Of Fate**[42] [2350] 4-7-12 **50** oh8..........................................(b) PMQuinn 2 34
(MJPolglase) *led: rdn along 1/2-way: hdd wl over 1f out and sn wknd* **40/1**
-064 **9** *1 3/4* **Tyne**[17] [3059] 3-9-6 **77**.......................................... KDarley 9 55
(TDBarron) *hmpd s: sn cl up on outer: rdn 2f out and sn wknd* **7/1**[3]
00-0 **10** *1/2* **Strawberry Patch (IRE)**[17] [3038] 5-8-8 **60**..........................................(p) JCarroll 1 36
(MissLAPerratt) *a rr* **33/1**
60.85 secs (0.45) **Going Correction** +0.125s/f (Good)
**WFA** 3 from 4yo+ 5lb **10** Ran SP% **97.3**
Speed ratings: **101,97,96,94,92 92,90,88,85,85**CSF £24.89 CT £52.54 TOTE £5.70: £2.10, £1.90, £1.10; EX 32.90.
**Owner** Page, Pickering, Taylor, Ward, Marsh **Bred** Compton Down Stud **Trained** West Pinchbeck, Lincs
■ Soaked (7/1) was withdrawn on vet's advice. R4 applies, deduct 10p in the £.

**FOCUS**
A modest sprint that saw those drawn low at an advantage. The form is held down a little by the fifth and sixth horses from out of the handicap.

**NOTEBOOK**
**Zarzu** ran out a most ready winner and really stepped up on his most recent efforts. He had been dropped to a fair mark after running a dire race at Newcastle last time and had a decent low draw, but granted a fast pace he is more than capable of adding to this.
**Frascati**, coming into this bidding for the hat-trick, looked to be travelling best of all with two to run, but failed to quicken with the winner late on. She was far from disgraced off this new mark.
**Viewforth**, who hinted at a return to form last time, shaped very much as though he needs a stiffer test over this trip. He is worth another chance.
**Pirlie Hill** was running on well after meeting interference at a crucial point and is slightly better than the bare form would suggest.
**Tyne**, a costly faliure at Recar last time over an extra furlong, was again well supported to make amends, but never looked like going in on this drop back to five.

## 3581 MATTHEW MCLEOD H'CAP 1m 1f
**4:45** (4:46) (F) (0-55,55) 3-Y-O **£3,380** (£1,040; £520; £260) **Stalls** Low

Form RPR
0025 **1** **Pearl Of York (DEN)**[18] [3026] 3-9-6 **55**.......................................... KDarley 8 66
(RGuest) *hld up and bhd: stdy hdwy on outer over 2f out: str run to ld over 1f out: styd on wl* **9/2**[2]
0004 **2** *4* **Munaawesh (USA)**[1] [3561] 3-9-6 **55**..........................................(b[1]) ACulhane 3 58
(DWChapman) *s.i.s and bhd: hdwy 2f out: swtchd rt over 1f out: rid and kpt on fnl f* **5/1**[3]
0445 **3** *1* **Compassion (IRE)**[6] [3396] 3-8-12 **47**..........................................(p) RWinston 2 48
(MissLAPerratt) *cl up: led 1/2-way: rdn clrover 2f out: drvn and hdd over 1f out: one pce* **25/1**
2313 **4** *2 1/2* **Roman The Park (IRE)**[14] [3146] 3-8-2 **44**.......................................... AMullen(7) 10 40
(TDEasterby) *chsd ldrs: rdn 2f out: sn one pce* **7/2**[1]
6053 **5** *3* **Saucy**[12] [3190] 3-8-12 **47**.......................................... DHolland 6 37
(BJMeehan) *chsd ldng pair: hdwy3f out: rdn 2f out: kpt on same pce* **9/2**[2]
2003 **6** *3* **Bargain Hunt (IRE)**[2] [3513] 3-8-6 **46**..........................................(v) BSwarbrick(5) 4 30
(WStorey) *chsd ldng apir: hdwy 3f out: rdn 2f out and sn wknd* **15/2**
00-4 **7** *shd* **River Line (USA)**[34] [2555] 3-9-1 **50**.......................................... KDalgleish 9 34
(CWFairhurst) *a towards rr* **25/1**
-060 **8** *7* **Koodoo**[27] [2760] 3-9-0 **52**..........................................(p) LEnstone(3) 1 22
(ACrook) *s.i.s: a rr* **12/1**
0-60 **9** *6* **Saratoga Splendour (USA)**[40] [2411] 3-8-10 **45**.......... DarrenWilliams 5 3
(JeddO'Keeffe) *chsd ldrs: rdn along 3f out: sn wknd* **50/1**
0-64 **10** *16* **Kintore**[18] [3007] 3-8-9 **47**.......................................... NMackay(3) 7 —
(JSGoldie) *bhd fr 1/2-way* **14/1**
-400 **11** *4* **Stiletto Lady (IRE)**[30] [2688] 3-9-6 **55**..........................................(b[1]) MFenton 11 —
(JGGiven) *dwlt: rdn along and sn led: hdd 1/2-way: sn drvn and wknd over 3f out* **25/1**
1m 54.62s (1.42) **Going Correction** -0.025s/f (Good) **11** Ran SP% **114.9**
Speed ratings: **92,88,87,85,82 80,79,73,68,54 50**CSF £25.40 CT £510.53 TOTE £7.20: £2.30, £2.50, £6.10; EX 33.80 Place 6 £65.30, Place 5 £23.69.
**Owner** N Elsass **Bred** York Stutteri **Trained** Newmarket, Suffolk

**FOCUS**
A modest handicap that was run at a fair clip. The winner looks improved.

**NOTEBOOK**
**Pearl Of York(DEN)** produced a fair turn of foot to lead entering the final furlong and won going away in the end. She had disappointed on the Fibresand latest, but this was much more her true form and the shorter trip proved ideal. However, she beat mainly out-of-form rivals and it would be wise not to get too carried away by this.
**Munaawesh(USA)** missed the kick and was staying on all too late in the day. He had finished fourth over further at Redcar 24 hours previously, and may have found this coming too quick, but is a most frustrating sort who has run out of excuses now.
**Compassion(IRE)**, dropped in the weights for this, had the cheeekpieces back on and improved on recent efforts as a result. However, she had the run of the race and it does look about as good as she is.
**Roman The Park(IRE)** held every chance over this slightly longer trip, but could not quicken late on.
**Saucy**, with the blinkers left off, ran too keen early and disappointed. She is regressive and cannot run two races alike. *Official explanation: jockey said filly was unsuited by the loose ground*
**Kintore** *Official explanation: jockey said colt was not suited by the good to soft ground*
T/Plt: £84.20 to a £1 stake. Pool: £34,846.65. 301.90 winning tickets. T/Qpdt: £19.70 to a £1 stake. Pool: £2,694.70. 100.80 winning tickets. JR

# 3014 RIPON (R-H)
## Monday, July 5

**OFFICIAL GOING: Good**
The going was described as 'near perfect'.
Wind: Almost nil. Weather: Fine and sunny.

## 3582 MARY DODDS 90TH BIRTHDAY CELEBRATION (S) STKS 1m 2f
**6:50** (6:50) (F) 3-Y-O **£3,255** (£930; £465) **Stalls** High

Form RPR
2220 **1** **Biscar Two (IRE)**[41] [2390] 3-8-12 48..........................................(b[1]) VHalliday 5 58
(RMWhitaker) *s.i.s and early reminders: towards rr: hdwy u.p over 3f out: led 2f out: drew clr appr fnl f* **7/4**[1]
-066 **2** *5* **Buchanan Street (IRE)**[12] [3193] 3-8-12 44.......................................... PRobinson 6 48
(NACallaghan) *trckd ldrs: drvn along and outpcd 3f out: styd on u.p to go 2nd wl ins fnl f: no ch w wnr* **3/1**[2]
0030 **3** *1 3/4* **Bonjour Bond (IRE)**[48] [2199] 3-8-12 51..........................................(b) DMcGaffin 2 45
(BSmart) *trckd ldrs: led 4f out: rdn and hdd 2f out: no ex* **6/1**[3]
0-06 **4** *3 1/2* **Oniz Tiptoes (IRE)**[15] [3121] 3-8-12 35..........................................(b[1]) GParkin 3 38
(JSWainwright) *hld up: effrt 4f out: sn rdn: kpt on fnl 2f: n.d* **20/1**
3100 **5** *8* **Ciacole**[7] [3371] 3-8-12 50.......................................... DeanMcKeown 7 23
(RonaldThompson) *dwlt: w ldr after 3f: disp ld 4f out: sn rdn: wknd over 2f out* **6/1**[3]
0000 **6** *nk* **Lupine Howl**[27] [2756] 3-8-12 44..........................................(p) GGibbons 8 22
(BAMcmahon) *hld up: hmpd over 4f out: sn rdn and btn* **7/1**
00-0 **7** *6* **Ballin Rouge**[48] [2195] 3-8-7..........................................(t) DAllan 4 6
(TJFitzgerald) *led tl hdd 4f out: sn wknd* **12/1**
2m 10.29s (2.29) **Going Correction** +0.10s/f (Good) **7** Ran SP% **114.9**
Speed ratings: **94,90,88,85,79 79,74**CSF £7.20 TOTE £2.40: £1.40, £2.30; EX 9.10.There was no bid for the winner. Buchanan Street was claimed by Gary Roberts for £6,000.
**Owner** M J O'Dwyer **Bred** Michael O'Dwyer **Trained** Scarcroft, W Yorks

**FOCUS**
A rock-bottom seller in which the first two ran to form.

**NOTEBOOK**
**Biscar Two(IRE)**, with blinkers on this time, seemed to appreciate this trip and hit the target on his tenth start. He will be lucky to come across an equally bad race.
**Buchanan Street(IRE)**, a decent type for a plater, stayed on after getting outpaced to secure a remote second spot. He was claimed and juvenile hurdles beckon.
**Bonjour Bond(IRE)**, who had the best chance on official figures, was having his first outing for seven weeks. He took it up on the bridle but found little when challenged by the winner.
**Oniz Tiptoes(IRE)** was dropping in trip in first-time blinkers.
**Ciacole**, who had two handlers in the paddock, seems to have lost the plot since her success in this grade at Beverley in May.
**Lupine Howl** had only run at up to seven furlongs previously. He seems to be going from bad to worse.

## 3583 SKY BET JUST PRESS RED TO BET MAIDEN AUCTION FILLIES' STKS 5f
**7:20** (7:22) (F) 2-Y-O **£4,143** (£1,275; £637; £318) **Stalls** Low

Form RPR
3202 **1** **Castelletto**[7] [3382] 2-8-11 .......................................... GGibbons 3 82
(BAMcmahon) *w ldr: rdn to ld over 1f out: r.o wl ins fnl f* **8/15**[1]
43 **2** *1 3/4* **Hillside Heather (IRE)**[7] [3370] 2-8-2 .......................................... FNorton 9 67
(ABerry) *in tch: hdwy 1/2-way: hung lft and rdn over 1f out: sn ev ch: no imp on wnr ins fnl f* **16/1**
23 **3** *1/2* **Wise Wager (IRE)**[21] [2933] 2-8-2 .......................................... PFessey 6 65
(RAFahey) *slowly away: bhd: hdwy and in tch 2f out: r.o wl to go 3rd wl ins fnl f: nvr able to chal* **8/1**[3]
432 **4** *1* **Colonial Girl (IRE)**[18] [3021] 2-8-8 .......................................... DAllan 5 68
(TDEasterby) *led tl rdn and hdd over 1f out: no ex ins fnl f* **9/2**[2]
**5** *6* **Baymist** 2-8-5 .......................................... DaleGibson 12 44
(MWEasterby) *dwlt: towards rr: kpt on fnl 2f: n.d* **100/1**
**6** *1/2* **Desert Phoenix (IRE)** 2-8-1 .......................................... NataliaGemelova(7) 10 45
(RAFahey) *slowly away: bhd: r.o fnl f: n.d* **50/1**
00 **7** *1/2* **Outrageous Flirt (IRE)**[12] [3196] 2-7-12 .......................................... DFentiman(7) 1 40
(ADickman) *chsd ldrs to 1/2-way: sn wknd* **33/1**
542 **8** *1/2* **Miss Cotswold Lady**[10] [3272] 2-8-5 .......................................... JQuinn 7 39
(AWCarroll) *chsd ldrs tl wknd 2f out* **16/1**
**9** *11* **Misty Bay** 2-8-2 .......................................... JBramhill 8 —
(JBalding) *s.i.s: a bhd* **100/1**
**10** *nk* **Aleshanee** 2-8-8 .......................................... JFanning 4 —
(JRBest) *chsd ldrs tl wknd 2f out* **16/1**
60.23 secs (0.03) **Going Correction** +0.10s/f (Good) **10** Ran SP% **119.1**
Speed ratings: **103,100,99,97,88 87,86,85,68,67**CSF £12.27 TOTE £1.50: £1.10, £2.50, £1.70; EX 13.10.
**Owner** J C Fretwell **Bred** Capt J H Wilson **Trained** Hopwas, Staffs

**FOCUS**
A very ordinary race and the winner had 15lb in hand on RPR.

**NOTEBOOK**
**Castelletto** looked to have been found a good opening, and after hanging right in front she was firmly in command at the line.
**Hillside Heather(IRE)** hung left on to the stands'-side rail and in the end she was very definitely second best. *Official explanation: jockey said filly hung left in the closing stages*
**Wise Wager(IRE)** again started slowly and never seemed to be racing on an even keel. The penny must surely drop eventually and she looks likely nursery material. *Official explanation: jockey said filly dwelt and hung throughout the race*

**Colonial Girl(IRE)**, having her fourth outing, looked very fit. She had plenty to find with the winner on Nottingham running.
**Baymist**, a January foal, is a moderate walker and was very green to post. Worst drawn, she picked up in her own time very late on.
**Miss Cotswold Lady** *Official explanation: jockey said bit slipped*
**Misty Bay** *Official explanation: jockey said filly was slow away and became unbalanced*
**Aleshanee** *Official explanation: jockey said filly lost her action in the closing stages*

## 3584 RIPON LAND ROVER H'CAP — 1m 4f 60y
7:50 (7:53) (D) (0-80,80) 3-Y-O — £6,825 (£2,100; £1,050; £525) Stalls High

Form — RPR
-352 **1** **Sand And Stars (IRE)**[11] 3250 3-8-11 **70**........................ PRobinson 10 — 83
(MHTompkins) *mde all: rdn 2f out: styd on wl* **9/2**[2]
-330 **2** *5* **Dr Cerullo**[69] 1688 3-8-13 **72**........................ JQuinn 7 — 77
(CTinkler) *prom: rdn 3f out: styd on u.p fnl f: no ch w wnr* **33/1**
3355 **3** *3/4* **Siegfrieds Night (IRE)**[7] 3379 3-8-0 **64**........................ DFox(5) 2 — 68
(MCChapman) *cl up: ev ch and rdn 2f out: no ex* **11/1**
0402 **4** *1 1/2* **Rutters Rebel (IRE)**[11] 3232 3-8-13 **72**........................ KDarley 5 — 73
(GASwinbank) *s.i.s: sn in tch: hdwy over 3f out: chsng ldrs and rdn 2f out: no further prog* **13/2**
0041 **5** *nk* **Masked (IRE)**[19] 2977 3-8-12 **71**........................ DaleGibson 1 — 72
(JWHills) *hld up: keen early: hdwy 4f out: sn drvn along: in tch and rdn 2f out: no further prog* **5/1**[3]
1360 **6** *3 1/2* **Jomacomi**[30] 2683 3-9-5 **78**........................ JFanning 6 — 73
(MJohnston) *trckd ldrs: drvn along 4f out: fdd fnl 2f* **8/1**
1002 **7** *hd* **Master Wells (IRE)**[9] 3292 3-9-2 **80**........................ NChalmers(5) 3 — 75
(JDBethell) *hld up: sme hdwy 4f out: sn drvn along and btn* **10/1**
-414 **8** *11* **Man At Arms (IRE)**[17] 3046 3-9-5 **78**........................(v[1]) DHolland 4 — 55
(RHannon) *in tch: drvn along over 3f out: sn btn: bhd and eased fnl f: t.o* **7/2**[1]
011 **9** *18* **Jelly Baby**[9] 3305 3-8-6 **65**........................(b) ACulhane 8 — 14
(WJHaggas) *midfield: pushed along whn short of room 4f out: sn lost tch: wl bhd and eased fnl f: t.o* **7/1**

2m 38.68s (-1.22) **Going Correction** +0.10s/f (Good) — **9** Ran SP% **114.4**
Speed ratings: **108,104,104,103,102 100,100,93,81**CSF £131.12 CT £1528.77 TOTE £6.70: £1.90, £4.90, £2.80; EX 124.40.
**Owner** Pollards Stables **Bred** Pollards Stables **Trained** Newmarket, Suffolk

**FOCUS**
Just a steady gallop until once in line for home and full marks to master tactician Philip Robinson. The winner improved to the tune of 8lb and three of the next four home ran to a pound of their pre-race marks.

**NOTEBOOK**
**Sand And Stars(IRE)**, 2lb higher, dictated things from the front. Winding up the gallop once in line for home, she never looked like being challenged and broke her duck at the seventh attempt.
**Dr Cerullo**, down 3lb, was having his first run for ten weeks. He stuck on to claim second spot but the winner was gone beyond recall.
**Siegfrieds Night(IRE)**, 6lb higher than his last win, did not impress at all going to post, but he is all heart and did not go down without a fight.
**Rutters Rebel(IRE)**, 2lb higher, moved short going to post and never looked like picking up sufficiently to get in a blow at the winner.
**Masked(IRE)**, fitted with a cross noseband, was very keen to post and the lack of early pace was against him.
**Jomacomi**, who started life in handicap company from a stiff mark, has only been dropped 2lb after three runs. He moved moderately to post and was in trouble the minute the winner stepped up the pace.
**Man At Arms(IRE)**, who hung both left and right under pressure, was never a threat and in the end his rider gave up. *Official explanation: jockey said colt had hung both ways in the home straight*

## 3585 SKYBET.COM H'CAP — 6f
8:20 (8:21) (D) (0-80,76) 3-Y-O — £10,393 (£3,198; £1,599; £799) Stalls Low

Form — RPR
1021 **1** **Cherokee Nation**[5] 3428 3-8-9 **64** 6ex........................ DHolland 8 — 74+
(PWD'Arcy) *dwlt: hld up in tch: keen early: hdwy over 1f out: drvn to ld ins fnl f: r.o wl* **3/1**[1]
0022 **2** *1 1/4* **Commando Scott (IRE)**[11] 3252 3-9-7 **76**........................ FLynch 10 — 82+
(ABerry) *cl up: slt ld and rdn ent fnl f: hdd ins last: kpt on* **7/1**[2]
5103 **3** *1* **Neon Blue**[19] 2981 3-8-13 **68**........................ ACulhane 3 — 71
(RMWhitaker) *cl up: led over 2f out: rdn and hdd ent fnl f: no ex* **3/1**[1]
-051 **4** *nk* **Shamrock Tea**[11] 3234 3-8-2 **60** ow1........................ THamilton(3) 6 — 62
(RAFahey) *s.i.s: hld up in rr: hdwy 1/2-way: chsng ldrs and rdn ent fnl f: no ex ins last* **8/1**[3]
304 **5** *3/4* **Otago (IRE)**[10] 3262 3-8-2 **57**........................ DaleGibson 4 — 57
(JRBest) *dwlt: midfield and drvn along 1/2-way: kpt on u.p fnl f: n.d* **11/1**
0043 **6** *nk* **Elliot's Choice (IRE)**[2] 3512 3-8-11 **66**........................ JFanning 5 — 65
(DCarroll) *trckd ldrs: effrt 2f out: sn drvn along: no hdwy* **12/1**
0043 **7** *2 1/2* **Bright Sun (IRE)**[17] 3059 3-9-5 **74**........................ KimTinkler 12 — 65
(NTinkler) *in tch: rdn 1/2-way: no hdwy* **10/1**
4156 **8** *3/4* **Rene Barbier (IRE)**[12] 3201 3-8-10 **65**........................(v[1]) DeanMcKeown 1 — 54
(JAGlover) *mde most tl hdd over 2f out: wknd over 1f out* **25/1**
0100 **9** *nk* **Extremely Rare (IRE)**[1] 3562 3-8-13 **68**........................ DAllan 7 — 56
(TDEasterby) *cl up tl wknd over 1f out* **22/1**
-030 **10** *1/2* **Louisiade (IRE)**[33] 2589 3-8-10 **65**........................ KDarley 9 — 52
(TDEasterby) *bhd most of way* **14/1**
0403 **11** *shd* **Xpres Digital**[38] 2455 3-9-3 **72**........................(t) JBramhill 11 — 59
(SRBowring) *s.i.s: rr div: sme hdwy over 2f out: sn rdn and btn* **14/1**

1m 13.14s (0.24) **Going Correction** +0.10s/f (Good) — **11** Ran SP% **120.3**
Speed ratings: **102,100,99,98,97 97,93,92,92,91 91**CSF £24.78 CT £71.06 TOTE £4.10: £1.90, £2.10; EX 24.90 Trifecta £100.00 Pool: £1,704.85. 12.10 winning tickets.
**Owner** Walt Sylvester **Bred** Miss Paula Sylvester And W Sylvester **Trained** Newmarket, Suffolk

**FOCUS**
In effect a 0-76 handicap, with the first two home both favourably drawn. An ordinary race but competitive enough.

**NOTEBOOK**
**Cherokee Nation**, who looked in tip-top shape, missed a beat at the start which helped him settle. When set alight he was soon in command, and his action suggest that Fibresand will be no problem. He will not be resting on his laurels.
**Commando Scott(IRE)**, raised 3lb, went down fighting but in the end was definitely second best.
**Neon Blue**, better drawn this time, ran right up to his best but this is as good as he is.
**Shamrock Tea**, 7lb higher, ran into traffic problems and did well to finish so close. He would not want the ground any faster. *Official explanation: jockey said gelding missed the break*
**Otago(IRE)**, who has started life in handicap company from a sensible mark, stayed on after missing a beat at the start and he is still learning what the game is all about.
**Elliot's Choice(IRE)** keeps running well but is still a maiden now after 12 starts.

## 3586 DUFELL ROOFING H'CAP — 1m
8:50 (8:50) (E) (0-70,70) 3-Y-O+ — £4,231 (£1,302; £651; £325) Stalls High

Form — RPR
2221 **1** **Alchemist Master**[5] 3409 5-9-10 **63** 6ex........................(p) DeanMcKeown 7 — 79+
(RMWhitaker) *trckd ldr: nt clr run over 2f out: led over 1f out: pushed clr fnl f: eased cl home* **1/1**[1]
5006 **2** *5* **Blunham**[13] 3167 4-8-8 **47**........................ DHolland 4 — 51
(MCChapman) *led tl rdn and hdd over 1f out: no ex* **10/1**
4054 **3** *1/2* **Jessie**[9] 3301 5-8-4 **43**........................(v) KimTinkler 3 — 46
(DonEnricoIncisa) *s.i.s: bhd: rdn and outpcd 1/2-way: hdwy over 1f out: styd on wl fnl f: nvr able to chal* **14/1**
6310 **4** *1 1/4* **Premier Dream (USA)**[46] 2251 3-9-8 **70**........................ JFanning 1 — 70
(MJohnston) *in tch: rdn over 2f out: kpt on same pce* **16/1**
00-2 **5** *shd* **Eddies Jewel**[41] 2386 4-7-13 **38** oh2 ow1........................ RFfrench 5 — 38
(JSWainwright) *prom: rdn and ev ch over 2f out: kpt on same pce* **25/1**
6204 **6** *shd* **Noble Penny**[17] 3060 5-8-7 **49**........................(p) TEaves(3) 10 — 49
(MrsKWalton) *s.i.s: hld up: hdwy over 3f out: in tch and rdn over 2f out: no further prog* **16/1**
-004 **7** *hd* **Gifted Flame**[21] 2938 5-9-10 **63**........................ KDarley 6 — 62
(TDBarron) *dwlt: hld up: hdwy to trck ldrs 1/2-way: ev ch and rdn over 2f out: kpt on same pce* **6/1**[2]
0106 **8** *3/4* **Classic Vision**[7] 3386 4-9-1 **54**........................(b) ACulhane 2 — 51
(WJHaggas) *hld up towards rr: short of room over 4f out: sn pushed along: styd on fnl 2f: short of room ins last: nvr able to chal* **7/1**[3]
2440 **9** *1 1/4* **Shifty**[2] 3516 5-8-10 **49**........................ ANicholls 9 — 43
(DNicholls) *towards rr: hdwy over 3f out: no further prog fnl 2f: short of room ins last* **10/1**
06-0 **10** *3/4* **Splodger Mac (IRE)**[3] 3471 5-8-4 **43**........................ JQuinn 8 — 36
(NBycroft) *trckd ldrs to 1/2-way: sn wknd* **50/1**
0-04 **11** *8* **Esteban**[31] 2658 4-8-13 **52**........................ RWinston 11 — 26
(JJQuinn) *midfieold whn hmpd over 4f out: sn bhd* **20/1**

1m 41.87s (0.77) **Going Correction** +0.10s/f (Good)
**WFA** 3 from 4yo+ 9lb — **11** Ran SP% **124.0**
Speed ratings: **100,95,94,93,93 93,92,92,90,90 82**CSF £12.90 CT £103.01 TOTE £2.10: £1.20, £2.70, £3.10; EX 10.10.
**Owner** T L Adams **Bred** Mrs John Van Geest **Trained** Scarcroft, W Yorks
■ Stewards Enquiry : J Quinn one-day ban: careless riding (Jul 16)

**FOCUS**
In effect a 0-63 handicap, run at just a steady pace. The form is not all that solid but the winner was well treated under his penalty and could rate a bit higher yet.

**NOTEBOOK**
**Alchemist Master**, his confidence sky-high, made light of his 6lb penalty. The leader rolled off the fence at just the right moment and he went through the gap without hesitation.
**Blunham**, given a soft lead, wound it up once in line for home. He rolled off the fence, leaving the door ajar for the winner, and that was that. A true-run seven furlongs suits him better.
**Jessie**, who hasn't tasted success for the best part of three years, was bang last with two furlongs left to run. She snatched third place on the line but is not sure to reproduce this effort next time.
**Premier Dream(USA)**, last of 14 when he last ran six weeks ago, wore a cross noseband and seemed to appreciate the less-firm ground. He looks weighted to the hilt.
**Eddies Jewel**, 2lb out of the handicap, had two handlers in the paddock and is still a maiden now after 11 outings.
**Classic Vision**, who is only small, had no luck at all and this is best ignored.

## 3587 KIRKGATE MAIDEN STKS — 1m
9:20 (9:22) (D) 3-Y-O+ — £4,832 (£1,487; £743; £371) Stalls High

Form — RPR
6223 **1** **Grand But One (IRE)**[16] 3094 3-8-12 87........................ DHolland 13 — 82+
(BWHills) *mde all: styd on wl: comf* **10/11**[1]
4- **2** *1* **Triple Jump**[270] 5460 3-8-12........................ KDalgleish 7 — 80
(TDEasterby) *trckd ldrs: wnt 2nd over 2f out: rdn and ch over 1f out: styd on: no imp on wnr fnl f* **16/1**
4 **3** *2 1/2* **Ouninpohja (IRE)**[9] 3297 3-8-12........................ DeanMcKeown 10 — 74+
(GASwinbank) *hld up: hdwy 1/2-way: chsd first 2 fr over 1f out: styd on: no imp* **6/1**[3]
0 **4** *10* **Spes Bona (USA)**[16] 3094 3-8-12........................ ACulhane 14 — 51+
(WJHaggas) *bhd: hdwy 1/2-way: short of room briefly over 2f out: styd on fnl f: nvr able to chal* **14/1**
0 **5** *shd* **Glencalvie (IRE)**[64] 1794 3-8-12........................ KDarley 6 — 51+
(JNoseda) *midfield: hdwy 1/2-way: chsng ldrs and rdn 2f out: no further prog* **9/1**
06 **6** *3/4* **Phone Tapping**[13] 3168 3-8-12........................ PRobinson 8 — 49
(MHTompkins) *midfield: drvn along over 2f out: no hdwy* **5/1**[2]
43 **7** *1 1/2* **Farne Isle**[19] 2983 5-9-2........................ RWinston 9 — 41
(GAHarker) *slowly away: bhd: styd on fnl 3f: n.d* **20/1**
04 **8** *1/2* **Rich Chic (IRE)**[10] 3268 3-8-7........................ DarrenWilliams 11 — 39
(MDHammond) *in tch tl wknd over 2f out* **100/1**
5 **9** *nk* **Dancer King (USA)**[11] 3251 3-8-12........................ DaleGibson 1 — 44
(TPTate) *keen early: prom tl wknd 2f out* **20/1**
0 **10** *2 1/2* **Dee En Ay (IRE)**[54] 2046 3-8-12........................ DAllan 15 — 38
(TDEasterby) *in tch tl wknd over 2f out* **50/1**
0- **11** *shd* **Alethea Gee**[347] 3534 6-9-2........................ GParkin 2 — 33
(MrsMReveley) *sn bhd: n.d* **66/1**
**12** *5* **High Class Pet**[138] 4-8-13........................ THamilton(3) 12 — 21
(FPMurtagh) *sn bhd* **100/1**
**13** *3/4* **Transkei** 3-8-7........................ RFfrench 16 — 20
(MrsLStubbs) *a bhd* **66/1**
**14** *1/2* **Rouge Et Noir**[10] 6-9-7........................ JFanning 3 — 23
(MrsMReveley) *slowly away: a bhd* **20/1**
56 **15** *2* **Daring Games**[7] 3374 3-8-5 ow1........................ TEaves(3) 4 — 15
(BEllison) *midfield to 1/2-way: sn bhd* **100/1**
**16** *10* **Wild Tide**[29] 5-9-2........................ PBradley 5 — —
(DWThompson) *cl up tl wknd qckly over 2f out: t.o* **100/1**

1m 41.39s (0.29) **Going Correction** +0.10s/f (Good)
**WFA** 3 from 4yo+ 9lb — **16** Ran SP% **129.1**
Speed ratings: **102,101,98,88,88 87,86,85,85,82 82,77,77,76,74 64**CSF £19.32 TOTE £2.00: £1.30, £4.10, £1.90; EX 20.70 Place 6 £13.29, Place 5 £9.28.
**Owner** Enton Thoroughbred Racing 2 **Bred** Musaid Abo Salim **Trained** Lambourn, Berks

**FOCUS**
A weakish maiden dominated from the front by the winner who had 18lb and upwards in hand on RPR. The form is not easy to pin down but has been rated through the third.

**NOTEBOOK**
**Grand But One(IRE)**, who bled from the nose when third in much stronger company at Newmarket just 16 days earlier, had a favourable draw and was always in command from the front. He will struggle in handicaps from a mark of 87.

**Triple Jump**, a disapointment in one backend outing at two, went in pursuit of the winner but in truth he was always going to come off second best. He clearly has some ability and is capable of a bit better.
**Ouninpohja(IRE)** travelled very strongly and was by no means knocked about, finishing a long way clear of dead wood. He needs another outing before he can ply his trade in handicap company.
**Spes Bona(USA)**, fitted with a cross noseband, was on edge and behaving like a headstrong schoolboy in the paddock. He picked up from the rear in his own time and plan A will be to teach him to settle and behave better.
**Glencalvie(IRE)**, well beaten on his debut two months earlier, is a good-bodied type. Fitted with a cross noseband, he shaped a fraction better and connections will be hoping for something better in due course.
**Phone Tapping**, having his third start, came in for market support, but never threatened. A rangy type, he can can surely do better in handicap company.
**Farne Isle**, a heavy-ground bumper winner, was having her third run and came from a long way back to finish on the heels of the second group. She is worth bearing in mind for a handicap over a fair bit further.
**Alethea Gee**, who had just one previous outing at five, is not without some ability but needs one more away day before she qualifies for a handicap mark.
T/Plt: £15.10 to a £1 stake. Pool: £47,688.60. 2,303.95 winning tickets. T/Qpdt: £12.90 to a £1 stake. Pool: £2,955.30. 169.30 winning tickets. JF

## 3382 WINDSOR (R-H)

Monday, July 5

**OFFICIAL GOING: Good to firm**

Wind: almost nil Weather: sunny

### 3588 GREAT ORMOND STREET HOSPITAL EBF MAIDEN STKS (SPONSORED BY MRS JOHN MAGNIER) 6f

**6:35** (6:38) (D) 2-Y-O **£5,421** (£1,668; £834; £417) **Stalls** High

Form RPR

1 **Street Cred** 2-9-0 MartinDwyer 7 79
(AMBalding) *pressed ldrs: rdn to ld 1f out: kpt on wl* **25/1**

03 2 ½ **Rusky Dusky (USA)**[12] 3192 2-9-0 PDobbs 20 77
(RHannon) *mde most to 1f out: styd on but hld by wnr last 100yds* **6/1**[3]

3 1 ¼ **Dane's Castle (IRE)** 2-8-11 LPKeniry(3) 11 73
(BJMeehan) *s.i.s: racd in midfield: prog over 2f out: chsd ldng pair ins fnl f: hanging lft but styd on* **33/1**

46 4 1 ¾ **Musico (IRE)**[14] 3157 2-9-0 SDrowne 8 68
(BRMillman) *a.p: shkn up over 1f out: one pce fnl f* **16/1**

5 *shd* **Blazing View (USA)** 2-8-9 WSupple 6 63
(EALDunlop) *racd towards rr: shkn up and sme prog 2f out: styd on fnl f: nrst fin* **50/1**

03 6 *nk* **Pitch Up (IRE)**[24] 2846 2-9-0 KFallon 3 67
(TGMills) *sn w ldrs: drvn and ch jst over 1f out: fdd ins fnl f* **4/1**[2]

7 *hd* **Je Suis Belle** 2-8-4 AMedeiros(5) 1 61
(BWHills) *s.s: racd on wd outside: prog and prom 1/2-way: ch over 1f out: wknd ins fnl f* **50/1**

8 1 **Jack The Giant (IRE)** 2-9-0 MHills 2 63
(BWHills) *s.s: wl in rr: pushed along over 2f out: prog over 1f out: styng on wl nr fin* **12/1**

9 ¾ **Naval Force** 2-9-0 RHughes 12 61
(HMorrison) *trckd ldrs: nudged along 2f out: losing pl whn nt clr run briefly 1f out: bttr for r* **12/1**

0 10 3 **Worth Abbey**[4] 3451 2-9-0 RLMoore 19 52
(RHannon) *racd in midfield: shkn up over 2f out: no imp on ldrs* **20/1**

11 ½ **Gypsy Royal (IRE)** 2-8-9 NDay 13 45
(RIngram) *towards rr: pushed along and no prog over 2f out: no ch after* **33/1**

12 ½ **Maggie Tulliver (IRE)** 2-8-9 TQuinn 15 44
(PWHarris) *outpcd: detached in last pair and rdn after 2f: r.o fr over 1f out* **16/1**

25 13 ½ **Arthur Wardle (USA)**[11] 3228 2-9-0 IMongan 5 47
(MLWBell) *dwlt: wl in rr: pushed along and no real prog fr 2f out* **20/1**

14 ¾ **Lama Albarq (USA)** 2-9-0 LDettori 14 45
(SaeedBinSuroor) *w ldr over 3f: wknd rapidly* **9/4**[1]

0 15 3 **In Dream'S (IRE)**[48] 2205 2-9-0 JFEgan 18 36
(BGubby) *reluctant to enter stalls: rrd s: a towards rr* **33/1**

16 ½ **Mickey Pearce (IRE)** 2-9-0 DSweeney 16 35
(JGMO'Shea) *outpcd: detached in last pair 4f out: kpt on fnl f* **33/1**

17 1 **Global Banker (IRE)** 2-9-0 OUrbina 10 32
(GCHChung) *s.i.s: a towards rr: wknd over 1f out* **50/1**

0 18 ¾ **Pips Pearl (IRE)**[44] 2300 2-8-9 RHavlin 9 24
(MrsPNDutfield) *in rr by 1/2-way: wknd over 1f out* **100/1**

00 19 *nk* **Doughty**[12] 3192 2-9-0 VSlattery 4 29
(DJWintle) *hld up wl in rr: pushed along and no prog 2f out* **100/1**

P **Cavaradossi** 2-9-0 JFortune 17 —
(BJMeehan) *s.s: p.u after 100yds: dismntd* **20/1**

1m 13.77s (-0.10) **Going Correction** -0.20s/f (Firm) **20** Ran SP% **130.0**
Speed ratings: **92,91,89,87,87 86,86,85,84,80 79,78,78,77,73 72,71,70,69,—**CSF £159.80 TOTE £37.30: £10.10, £1.90, £19.10; EX 375.70.
**Owner** Young Guns Syndicate **Bred** C R Withers **Trained** Kingsclere, Hants

**FOCUS**
A fair maiden in which the fourth helps confirm the standard.

**NOTEBOOK**
**Street Cred**, whose dam was a winner over six furlongs, is reportedly lazy at home and connections were not expecting too much on his debut, but he showed good speed throughout and did it well. He could be open to improvement.
**Rusky Dusky(USA)** had the best draw and made the most of it, making the running to the last furlong. He could be one for nurseries.
**Dane's Castle(IRE)**, a half-brother to a coulpe of juvenile winners, overcame a slow start to post a good debut effort, despite running green.
**Musico(IRE)** ran a better race than on his previous visit, but he once again found a few too good. He will have more opportunities now that nurseries are open to him.
**Blazing View(USA)**, whose dam is from the top-class family of Zafonic, Zamindar and Reams Of Verse, was putting in her best work late on, and on breeding she will come into her own over farther.
**Pitch Up(IRE)** has started at 4-1 or shorter on each of his three starts but has disappointed his supporters on each occasion. The extra furlong did not appear to help this time.
**Je Suis Belle** showed pace and can build on this.
**Jack The Giant(IRE)**, a half-brother to middle-distance performers Crystal Curling, True Crystal and Time Crystal, was slowly away and struggled to go the early pace, but he came home in good style and there is plenty more to come when he steps up in trip.
**Arthur Wardle(USA)** *Official explanation: jockey said colt missed the break*
**Lama Albarq(USA)**, whose dam is a half-sister to top-class US middle-distance performer Pleasantly Perfect, was not particularly strong in the market and dropped away tamely in the race itself.
**Cavaradossi** *Official explanation: jockey said colt lost his action*

### 3589 TRINITY HOSPICE H'CAP (SPONSORED BY MRS URS SCHWARZENBACH) 1m 67y

**7:05** (7:06) (E ) (0-70,67) 3-Y-O **£3,640** (£1,120; £560; £280) **Stalls** High

Form RPR

560 1 **Ridge Boy (IRE)**[9] 3322 3-9-7 **67** PDobbs 1 72
(RHannon) *led at modest pce: jnd and kicked on over 3f out: hdd 2f out: hrd rdn and rallied fnl f: edgd lft but led last stride* **40/1**

04-2 2 *shd* **Rosacara**[18] 3006 3-9-6 **66** (t) JPMurtagh 9 71
(DJDaly) *trckd wnr to 5f out: styd prom: rdn to ld 2f out: hrd rdn fnl f: hdd last stride* **8/1**

-100 3 *shd* **Dagola (IRE)**[11] 3231 3-9-2 **62** JFortune 4 67
(CGCox) *t.k.h: trckd wnr 5f out: chal 3f out: hrd rdn over 1f out: ev ch nr fin: jst hld* **14/1**

0306 4 1 ¾ **Little Eye (IRE)**[23] 2883 3-9-2 **62** (v[1]) NPollard 12 63
(JRBest) *t.k.h: trckd ldrs: hrd rdn and effrt 2f out: nt qckn 1f out: kpt on* **33/1**

50-6 5 ¾ **Kinbrace**[35] 2536 3-9-0 **60** MartinDwyer 14 59
(MPTregoning) *t.k.h: hld up in midfield: rdn over 2f out: kpt on ins fnl f: n.d* **7/1**

1033 6 *shd* **Pickle**[16] 3089 3-9-3 **63** SSanders 7 62
(SCWilliams) *hld up in rr: rdn 2f out: styd on fnl f: nvr able to chal* **7/2**[2]

2031 7 1 **Knickyknackienoo**[11] 3246 3-8-13 **59** SWhitworth 5 55
(AGNewcombe) *dwlt: hld up in rr: rdn over 2f out: sme prog u.p over 1f out: nvr rchd ldrs* **9/1**

0033 8 1 ½ **Fuel Cell (IRE)**[22] 2915 3-9-5 **65** RHughes 13 58
(RHannon) *s.i.s: hld up in rr: rdn over 3f out: btn whn nt clr run briefly 2f out* **10/3**[1]

3500 9 *hd* **Keepers Knight (IRE)**[84] 1365 3-9-0 **65** NDeSouza(5) 6 58
(PFICole) *dwlt: hld up in midfield: rdn 3f out: no prog* **40/1**

1200 10 2 **Jomus**[24] 2847 3-9-1 **61** TQuinn 8 49
(LMontagueHall) *taken down early: dwlt: hld up in last pair: taken to outer and drvn over 2f out: no ch* **12/1**

-510 11 ¾ **Carte Noire**[19] 2989 3-8-13 **59** EAhern 11 45
(JGPortman) *hld up towards rr: pushed along and sme prog 2f out: wknd fnl f* **33/1**

006 12 1 ¼ **Cotton Easter**[14] 3142 3-8-13 **59** TEDurcan 2 42
(MrsAJBowlby) *dwlt: hld up wl in rr: taken to wd outside and effrt over 2f out: wknd over 1f out* **50/1**

0-06 13 6 **Nebraska City**[45] 2266 3-8-13 **59** DaneO'Neill 3 29
(PMitchell) *t.k.h: hld up in midfield: wknd 2f out* **40/1**

-012 14 5 **Cornwallis**[53] 2063 3-9-4 **64** KFallon 10 22
(JSKing) *t.k.h: trckd ldrs tl wknd over 2f out: eased* **5/1**[3]

1m 43.59s (-2.01) **Going Correction** -0.30s/f (Firm) **14** Ran SP% **125.1**
Speed ratings: **98,97,97,96,95 95,94,92,92,90 89,88,82,77**CSF £336.85 CT £4843.89 TOTE £62.80: £11.50, £2.60, £6.80; EX 174.40.
**Owner** Mrs Chris Harrington **Bred** Mrs Chris Harrington **Trained** East Everleigh, Wilts

**FOCUS**
There was a slow pace to this modest contest and those held up were at a disadvantage.

**NOTEBOOK**
**Ridge Boy(IRE)** did not look particularly well handicapped beforehand but the step back up to a mile on his handicap debut suited and he did get the run of the race in front. He battled when headed, though, showing the right attitude, and he should get farther. *Official explanation: trainer's representative said, regarding the improved form shown, colt had taken time to come to hand*
**Rosacara** was also suited by the way the race was run as she was up there tracking the leader for most of the contest. She just lost out in the battle to the line and as a result will likely go up again for this effort.
**Dagola(IRE)** appreciated the drop back to his winning distance of a mile and was another to benefit from racing prominently in a slowly-run race.
**Little Eye(IRE)** ran a creditable race in the first-time visor, but he is still a maiden.
**Kinbrace** did not really have the race to suit and raced too keenly for her own good. She is not to be written off as this trip had previously looked likely to suit.
**Pickle** was another whose chance was seriously compromised by the slow pace.
**Fuel Cell(IRE)** missed the break and was held up at the back of the field. That was not the place to be in the circumstances as the slow pace played into the hands of the leaders.
**Cornwallis** *Official explanation: jockey said gelding lost his action*

### 3590 JOBS @ PERTEMPS EBF CLASSIFIED STKS 1m 3f 135y

**7:35** (7:36) (D ) 3-Y-O+ **£6,890** (£2,120; £1,060; £530) **Stalls** Low

Form RPR

51 1 **Light Wind**[14] 3138 3-8-1 79 RLMoore 1 87+
(MrsAJPerrett) *disp ld tl led 3f out: jnd and rdn over 2f out: styd on wl to draw clr ins fnl f* **9/4**[2]

-040 2 3 **Anticipating**[16] 3075 4-9-7 84 MartinDwyer 6 89
(AMBalding) *hld up in rr: prog over 3f out: jnd wnr over 2f out: ev ch tl wknd ins fnl f* **2/1**[1]

4142 3 5 **Obay**[25] 2809 3-8-8 84 (b[1]) KFallon 5 81
(EALDunlop) *disp ld to 3f out: sn hrd rdn and fnd nil: wl btn fr over 1f out* **4/1**

-200 4 1 ¼ **Asiatic**[18] 2999 3-8-9 85 SChin 2 80
(MJohnston) *prom: rdn and outpcd wl over 2f out: no ch after: plugged on* **7/2**[3]

/4-0 5 14 **Don't Sioux Me (IRE)**[22] 706 6-9-6 83 IMongan 3 56?
(CRDore) *wl in tch: rdn 4f out: sn wknd and bhd* **20/1**

500/ 6 9 **Little Fox (IRE)**[676] 4277 9-9-0 45 ADaly 4 35
(JJBridger) *in tch to 4f out: sn wknd and bhd* **100/1**

2m 24.4s (-5.70) **Going Correction** -0.30s/f (Firm)
**WFA** 3 from 4yo+ 13lb **6** Ran SP% **112.1**
Speed ratings: **107,105,101,100,91 85**CSF £7.15 TOTE £3.80: £2.00, £1.90; EX 10.30.
**Owner** Hesmonds Stud **Bred** Hesmonds Stud Ltd **Trained** Pulborough, W Sussex

**FOCUS**
A tight race on the ratings, run at a sound pace. This looks decent form.

**NOTEBOOK**
**Light Wind** is a half-sister to seven winners and is keeping up the family tradition of success well. She is not the type who has a turn of foot, but she does gallop well and had her field strung out at the end of this race. She can progress again.
**Anticipating** appeared to have less to do in this company than on his previous starts this term, but he found the concession of 20lb to a progressive three-year-old too much on this occasion.
**Obay**, who made all for his only previous win, would probably have appreciated an easy lead in the first-time blinkers.
**Asiatic** has disappointed since a promising run at Chester in May and perhaps easier ground is the key to him.

**Don't Sioux Me(IRE)**, having only his third run on the Flat since October 2002, was soon beaten off.

## 3591 TOTE SUPPORTS THE G.O.S.H.C.C. AND TRINITY HOSPICE H'CAP 1m 2f 7y
8:05 (8:05) (D) (0-85,78) 3-Y-O+ £5,525 (£1,700; £850; £425) Stalls Low

Form RPR

4311 **1** **A One (IRE)**[8] 3347 5-8-8 **62** 6ex........ FPFerris(3) 8 77
(HJManners) *mde all: racd freely and nvr less than 3l clr: in n.d fnl 2f: pushed out* **2/1**[1]

0303 **2** *5* **Doris Souter (IRE)**[9] 3327 4-9-3 **68**........ RHughes 6 74
(RHannon) *racd in 3rd: shkn up wl over 2f out: chsd wnr wl over 1f out: no imp* **4/1**[2]

0030 **3** *1 1/2* **Rainbow World (IRE)**[17] 3046 4-8-8 **59**........(p) JFEgan 1 62
(AndrewReid) *chsd wnr: rdn over 3f out: no imp: lost 2nd wl over 1f out* **14/1**

1-00 **4** *1 3/4* **Best Flight**[52] 2084 4-9-5 **70**........ MHills 7 69
(BWHills) *s.i.s: hld up in midfield: rdn 3f out: one pce and no prog* **10/1**

2005 **5** *1 1/2* **Internationalguest (IRE)**[11] 3238 5-9-8 **73**........(v) SSanders 3 69
(GGMargarson) *trckd ldng trio: pushed along 4f out: hrd rdn and btn over 2f out* **8/1**

0050 **6** *1/2* **Gallant Boy (IRE)**[15] 3128 5-8-11 **69**........(vt) SJDonohoe(7) 4 65
(PDEvans) *last of main gp: rdn and struggling wl over 3f out: one pce after* **5/1**[3]

1 **7** *10* **Littleton Telchar (USA)**[21] 2950 4-9-6 **78**........ MHalford(7) 5 55
(MJRyan) *hld up: prog 3f out: wknd rapidly over 1f out* **7/1**

0-06 **8** *14* **Rolex Free (ARG)**[75] 899 6-9-2 **67**........ RSmith 9 17
(DFlood) *a last: wl bhd 6f out: continued t.o* **33/1**

2m 3.38s (-4.92) **Going Correction** -0.30s/f (Firm) **8** Ran SP% **112.3**
Speed ratings: **107,103,101,100,99 98,90,79**CSF £9.53 CT £83.07 TOTE £2.90: £1.40, £1.60, £3.20; EX 10.80.
**Owner** H J Manners **Bred** Humphrey Okeke **Trained** Highworth, Wilts

**FOCUS**
A fair handicap and the form looks solid. The time recorded was less than half a second outside the course record.

**NOTEBOOK**
**A One(IRE)**, chasing the hat-trick, never gave his supporters much to worry about as he was quickly into his stride and bounded clear for an authoritative win in a time just outside the course record. The change of stables has clearly done him the world of good and he is likely to go to Chepstow on Friday in an attempt to record the four-timer.
**Doris Souter(IRE)** usually runs well here and put up a creditable performance to bring home the rest of the field. She likes to make the running so the fact that she could never get to the front probably counted against her.
**Rainbow World(IRE)** never seems to be able to follow up a decent effort like this one with a similarly good run next time.
**Best Flight** has failed to build on the promise of his maiden win last autumn.
**Internationalguest(IRE)** needs soft ground to be seen at his best.
**Gallant Boy(IRE)** never got into contention.

## 3592 SUNLEY MAIDEN FILLIES' STKS 1m 67y
8:35 (8:36) (D) 3-Y-O £4,342 (£1,336; £668; £334) Stalls High

Form RPR

00 **1** **Hilltop Rhapsody**[9] 3297 3-8-11........ JPMurtagh 13 73
(DJDaly) *trckd ldr: led wl over 2f out: rdn wl over 1f out: kpt on wl* **50/1**

**2** *1/2* **Liberty Flag (USA)** 3-8-11........ JFortune 7 72
(JHMGosden) *s.i.s: hld up wl in rr: outpcd 1/2-way: plenty to do after: gd prog 2f out: r.o strly to take 2nd nr fin* **14/1**

2 **3** *3/4* **Zathonia**[14] 3154 3-8-11........ RHughes 14 70
(RCharlton) *s.i.s: sn trckd ldng pair: chsd wnr wl over 1f out: shuffled along and nt qckn fnl f: lost 2nd nr fin* **9/4**[1]

34 **4** *1/2* **Supamach (IRE)**[23] 2900 3-8-11........ TQuinn 4 69
(PFICole) *t.k.h: chsd ldng trio: outpcd and rdn over 3f out: effrt again u.p 2f out: kpt on* **6/1**[2]

64 **5** *1 1/4* **Double Dagger Lady (USA)**[21] 2950 3-8-11........ EAhern 3 66
(JNoseda) *chsd ldrs: outpcd and rdn over 3f out: effrt on outer 2f out: kpt on same pce* **9/1**[3]

0 **6** *nk* **Alenushka**[25] 2805 3-8-11........ DaneO'Neill 12 65
(HCandy) *racd in midfield: outpcd 4f out: n.d after: rdn 2f out: styd on fnl f* **16/1**

2-4 **7** *nk* **Strawberry Fair**[14] 3142 3-8-11........(t) LDettori 2 65
(SaeedBinSuroor) *led: qcknd 1/2-way: hdd wl over 2f out: fdd* **9/4**[1]

0 **8** *2 1/2* **Medica Boba**[22] 2911 3-8-11........ SDrowne 8 59
(HMorrison) *chsd ldrs: outpcd 1/2-way: struggling 3f out: one pce after* **66/1**

64 **9** *3/4* **Zuri (IRE)**[17] 3054 3-8-11........ TEDurcan 5 57
(LMCumani) *hld up wl in rr: outpcd 1/2-way: no ch after: nudged along and one pce fnl 2f* **25/1**

0 **10** *1 1/2* **Gay Romance**[12] 3209 3-8-11........ MHills 10 54
(BWHills) *hld up: outpcd 1/2-way: stuck firmly in the rr after* **25/1**

03 **11** *3/4* **Burn**[11] 3222 3-8-11........ IMongan 6 52
(MLWBell) *hld up: sme prog into midfield 1/2-way: sn outpcd: no ch after* **25/1**

**12** *1/2* **Gold Relic (USA)** 3-8-11........ MartinDwyer 9 51
(AMBalding) *hld up in rr: outpcd 1/2-way: nvr a factor* **14/1**

**13** *1/2* **Primeshade Promise** 3-8-11........ RPrice 1 50
(DBurchell) *a in last pair: outpcd 1/2-way: bhd after* **66/1**

**14** *1/2* **Rosings** 3-8-11........ RLMoore 11 48
(PWHarris) *hld up in last pair: outpcd 1/2-way: bhd after* **25/1**

1m 43.57s (-2.03) **Going Correction** -0.30s/f (Firm) **14** Ran SP% **125.4**
Speed ratings: **98,97,96,96,95 94,94,91,91,89 88,88,87,87**CSF £636.23 TOTE £59.80: £9.00, £3.60, £1.50; EX 596.70.
**Owner** G Noble **Bred** G Noble **Trained** Newmarket, Suffolk

**FOCUS**
This looked a fair maiden on paper but it was run in a poor time and the form looks dubious, although the runner-up certainly looks capable of better.

**NOTEBOOK**
**Hilltop Rhapsody** had shown little on her previous two starts but her trainer had thought enough of her to run her in the Wood Ditton first time out, and she came good at the third time of asking. Her dam is a half-sister to a winning stayer/hurdler and she should get farther than this in time.
**Liberty Flag(USA)** ◆, a half-sister to A P Five Hundred, placed in Grade Two company in the US, and to Gold Streamer, a Stakes winner Stateside, shaped with plenty of promise for the future. Despite running green, she would probably have won had she not been given so much to do, and with this experience behind her a similar maiden should be easy pickings.
**Zathonia** was slightly disappointing, as she had every chance but failed to pick up as well as some might have expected. Perhaps she needs a step up to ten furlongs.
**Supamach(IRE)** was running on fast ground again and previous observations suggest she will be seen to better effect when she gets some cut underfoot. This effort does make her eligible for a handicap mark, however, and she looks one to keep an eye on in that sphere.
**Double Dagger Lady(USA)** has now had her three runs for a mark and perhaps she will be capable of better now that she moves into handicap company.
**Alenushka** needs one more run for a mark.
**Strawberry Fair** was fitted with a tongue tie this time, indicating that she may have breathing problems.

## 3593 CLAUDIA SWINBURN PETER PAN CENTENARY H'CAP 6f
9:05 (9:05) (E) (0-70,70) 3-Y-O+ £3,601 (£1,108; £554; £277) Stalls High

Form RPR

0035 **1** **Willheconquertoo**[4] 3439 4-9-7 **63**........(t) JFEgan 20 78
(AndrewReid) *mde all: 5l clr after 2f: unchal* **10/1**

4064 **2** *3 1/2* **Sewmuch Character**[14] 3141 5-9-7 **63**........ DSweeney 19 67
(MBlanshard) *prom in chsng gp: rdn to chse wnr jst over 1f out: r.o but no ch* **8/1**[3]

3000 **3** *3 1/2* **Mythical Charm**[7] 3386 5-8-9 **51**........(t) ADaly 14 45
(JJBridger) *dwlt: hld up in last pair: effrt on inner and nt clr run over 1f out: r.o wl fnl f to take 3rd nr fin* **16/1**

-003 **4** *3/4* **Intellibet One**[2] 3524 4-8-12 **54**........ NCallan 5 45+
(PDEvans) *prom in chsng gp: rdn 1/2-way: effrt to dispute 2nd pl 2f out: kpt on same pce* **8/1**[3]

0020 **5** *shd* **Stokesies Wish**[9] 3298 4-9-8 **64**........ LDettori 16 55
(JLSpearing) *chsd wnr: no imp fr 1/2-way: one pce and lost 2nd pl jst over 1f out* **6/1**[1]

4-45 **6** *1 1/2* **Royal Advocate**[23] 2883 4-9-4 **60**........ SWhitworth 17 46
(JWHills) *hld up in rr: effrt 2f out: styd on fnl f: nrst fin* **14/1**

0020 **7** *1/2* **Kennington**[10] 3277 4-8-6 **53**........(v) HayleyTurner(5) 10 38
(MrsCADunnett) *prom in chsng gp: rdn over 2f out: fdd over 1f out* **11/1**

6600 **8** *nk* **Prima Stella**[13] 3178 5-8-13 **58**........ LisaJones(3) 18 42
(JARToller) *racd in midfield: rdn 1/2-way: one pce and no prog fnl 2f* **12/1**

6000 **9** *1/2* **Night Worker**[26] 2790 3-8-5 **53**........ RSmith 9 36
(RHannon) *dwlt: racd on outer: towards rr: effrt over 2f out: no imp* **25/1**

6006 **10** *3/4* **A Teen**[9] 3298 6-9-1 **57**........ KFallon 4 37
(PHowling) *settled in last pair of main gp: rdn and effrt over 2f out: hanging lft and no ch over 1f out: eased* **10/1**

0001 **11** *1* **Piccleyes**[16] 3085 3-9-1 **63**........(b) RLMoore 15 40
(RHannon) *wl in tch in chsng gp: rdn and struggling over 2f out: fdd* **10/1**

5550 **12** *1* **Isaz**[9] 3326 4-10-0 **70**........ DaneO'Neill 1 44
(HCandy) *racd wd: rr: rdn 1/2-way: no prog 2f out: fdd* **33/1**

0000 **13** *3 1/2* **Super Song**[21] 2948 4-9-2 **58**........(t) JoannaBadger 13 22
(PDEvans) *in tch in chsng gp tl wknd over 2f out* **25/1**

1601 **14** *1 1/4* **Doctor Dennis (IRE)**[29] 2707 7-8-10 **52**........(v) SSanders 12 12
(JPearce) *a outpcd and wl in rr* **7/1**[2]

0500 **15** *1* **Tender (IRE)**[14] 3151 4-8-9 **51**........(v[1]) SDrowne 11 8
(MrsStefLiddiard) *prom to 1/2-way: wknd rapidly* **18/1**

2002 **16** *3* **Indian Bazaar (IRE)**[9] 3307 8-8-4 ........ MHalford(7) 3 1
(NEBerry) *a in rr: struggling over 2f out* **12/1**

3063 **17** *18* **Onefortheboys (IRE)**[67] 1724 5-7-13 **41** oh1 ow1........ CCatlin 6 —
(DFlood) *restless stalls: rrd stalls: a t.o* **33/1**

1m 11.69s (-2.18) **Going Correction** -0.20s/f (Firm)
**WFA** 3 from 4yo+ 6lb **17** Ran SP% **131.4**
Speed ratings: **106,101,96,95,95 93,92,92,91,90 89,88,83,81,80 76,52**CSF £90.62 CT £1309.08 TOTE £12.80: £2.90, £2.40, £4.30, £3.00; EX 62.80 Place 6 £949.95, Place 5 £137.51.
**Owner** A S Reid **Bred** A S Reid **Trained** Mill Hill, London NW7

**FOCUS**
An ordinary handicap rated through the second. The high draws had it.

**NOTEBOOK**
**Willheconquertoo**, whose speed has been masked by slow starts recently, was well drawn here, got away from the gate in great style and never saw another rival. He came home a clear winner and, while his handicap mark will suffer as a result, he will surely be turned out quickly under a penalty in the interim.
**Sewmuch Character**, also well berthed, could never get in a blow at the winner but kept on well for a clear second place. He is beginning to look favourably handicapped.
**Mythical Charm** has done her winning over much farther so this was a cracking performance to finish third over six. The strong pace set by the winner no doubt helped, and she will appreciate a step back up in trip.
**Intellibet One** can take credit for being the only one drawn in single figures to make it into the first eight. She is finally back down to her last winning mark and looks primed to take advantage of it.
**Stokesies Wish**, whose jockey booking was probably responsible for the market making her favourite, did too much too soon in attempting to keep up with the pace set by the winner. She has a poor strike-rate.
**Royal Advocate**, dropping back down to sprinting, looks capable of a bit better than he has shown so far. He did not get the best of runs here and his rider was not hard on him.
**A Teen** *Official explanation: jockey said horse was never travelling*
**Onefortheboys(IRE)** *Official explanation: jockey said gelding reared up in stalls and missed break*
T/Jkpt: Not won. T/Plt: £1,012.60 to a £1 stake. Pool: £60,688.55. 43.75 winning tickets. T/Qpdt: £13.00 to a £1 stake. Pool: £4,794.80. 271.80 winning tickets. JN

3594 - 3596a (Foreign Racing) - See Raceform Interactive

# 3315 NEWMARKET (JULY) (R-H)
Tuesday, July 6

**OFFICIAL GOING: Good changing to good to firm after race 2 (1.50)**
There did not appear any draw bias but front runners had a hard time of it.
Wind: Slight across. Weather: Bright and sunny.

## 3597 H & K COMMISSIONS BOOKMAKERS H'CAP 1m
1:20 (1:23) (C) (0-90,90) 3-Y-O+ £14,014 (£4,312; £2,156; £1,078) Stalls Low

Form RPR

0000 **1** **Everest (IRE)**[13] 3198 7-9-0 **76**........ DaneO'Neill 8 87
(BEllison) *racd far side: hld up: pushed along 1/2-way: str run ins fnl f to ld nr post* **6/1**[2]

0000 **2** *shd* **Audience**[20] 2969 4-10-0 **90**........(p) JQuinn 15 101
(JAkehurst) *lw: racd stands' side: chsd ldrs: led that gp over 2f out: rdn over 1f out: r.o* **16/1**

2330 **3** *shd* **True Night**[13] 3198 7-9-2 **78**........ EAhern 19 89
(DNicholls) *racd stands' side: hld up in tch: ev ch that gp fnl f: r.o* **16/1**

1400 **4** *shd* **Blue Trojan (IRE)**[18] 3036 4-9-7 **83**........ JFEgan 3 94
(SKirk) *racd far side: chsd ldrs: rdn to ld that gp ins fnl f: hdd post* **33/1**

0201 **5** *1 1/4* **St Pancras (IRE)**[13] 3191 4-9-4 **80**........ DHolland 9 88
(NACallaghan) *lw: racd far side: led that gp over 2f out: hdd and unable qck ins fnl f* **15/2**[3]

0462 **6** *3/4* **Topton (IRE)**[6] 3426 10-9-0 **76**........(b) MHills 20 82
(PHowling) *racd stands' side: dwlt: hld up: hdwy over 1f out: sn ev ch: styd on* **20/1**

000- **7** *hd* **Rafferty (IRE)**263 5616 5-9-6 **82**........................................(b) TEDurcan 7 87
(CEBrittain) *racd far side: hld up: nt clr run over 2f out: hdwy over 1f out: r.o* **40/1**

-023 **8** *hd* **Gift Horse**13 3205 4-9-11 **87**........................................ JPMurtagh 4 92
(JRFanshawe) *b: racd far side: hld up: hdwy over 1f out: r.o* **4/1**1

6006 **9** *½* **African Sahara (USA)**10 3299 5-9-3 **79**..............................(t) GCarter 17 83
(MissDMountain) *lw: chsd ldrs stands' side: rdn over 1f out: styd on same pce* **33/1**

1122 **10** *½* **Harrison Point (USA)**32 2646 4-9-8 **84**.............................. JFortune 16 87
(PWChapple-Hyam) *racd stands' side: hld up: hdwy fnl f: nt rch ldrs* **20/1**

0531 **11** *hd* **Little Venice (IRE)**10 3320 4-9-10 **86**.............................. SSanders 6 88
(CFWall) *racd far side: chsd ldrs: rdn over 2f out: styd on same pce fnl f* **20/1**

0021 **12** *½* **Omaha City (IRE)**18 3048 10-8-12 **74**.............................. MTebbutt 11 75
(BGubby) *racd far side: hld up: nt clr run over 2f out: n.d* **50/1**

3-53 **13** *½* **Presumptive (IRE)**13 3212 4-9-2 **78**.............................. SDrowne 14 78
(RCharlton) *lw: racd far side: hld up: hdwy 1/2-way: rdn over 2f out: no ex fnl f* **12/1**

0402 **14** *1* **Devant (NZ)**10 3299 4-9-3 **79**........................................ PRobinson 18 77
(MAJarvis) *racd stands' side: chsd ldrs: rdn over 2f out: styd on same pce appr fnl f* **14/1**

-210 **15** *½* **Langford**20 2969 4-9-9 **85**........................................ LDettori 2 82
(MHTompkins) *lw: led far side over 5f: wknd fnl f* **10/1**

0015 **16** *2* **Atlantic Quest (USA)**23 2905 5-9-1 **82**....................(v) PMulrennan(5) 12 74
(GAHarker) *racd far side: chsd ldrs: rdn over 2f out: wknd fnl f* **40/1**

0511 **17** *1* **Oh Boy (IRE)**14 3177 4-8-10 **72**........................................ RHughes 5 62
(RHannon) *racd far side: chsd ldrs: rdn over 2f out: wkng whn n.m.r ins fnl f* **10/1**

1422 **18** *½* **Ephesus**18 3048 4-9-5 **81**........................................(v) WSupple 10 69
(MissGayKelleway) *swtg: racd far side: mid-div: rdn over 2f out: wknd over 1f out* **33/1**

1020 **19** *12* **Tiber Tiger (IRE)**13 3198 4-9-1 **80**....................(b) J-PGuillambert(3) 1 41
(NPLittmoden) *racd far side: chsd ldrs over 6f* **33/1**

-430 **20** *14* **Salagama (IRE)**10 3320 4-9-7 **83**..............................(b1) KFallon 13 12
(PFICole) *b.hind: racd stands' side: dwlt: sn rcvrd to ld: rdn and hdd over 2f out: sn wknd* **20/1**

1m 38.13s (-2.35) **Going Correction** -0.15s/f (Firm) **20** Ran SP% **128.0**
Speed ratings: **105,104,104,104,103 102,102,102,101,101 101,100,100,99,98 96,95,95,83,69**CSF £86.00 CT £1530.52 TOTE £8.10: £3.30, £4.80, £3.50, £11.20; EX 167.20 Trifecta £964.30 Part won..
**Owner** I S Sandhu And Partners **Bred** Sir Eric Parker **Trained** Norton, N Yorks

**FOCUS**
A really competitive handicap run at a decent pace. The form looks solid with only four and a half lengths covering the first twelve. The field split into two groups, but there was no bias.

**NOTEBOOK**
**Everest(IRE)**, beaten a short head in this race last year off a 7lb higher mark, ended a losing run stretching back over a year off the rating he gained his last success from. He is always worthy of respect in big-field handicaps when the money is down.
**Audience ◆**, not beaten very far at all in the Royal Hunt Cup at Ascot on his previous start, confirmed that promise to 'win' the race on the stands' side. He started the season off a mark of 101, so does not look badly treated off his current mark and could be one to keep in mind for something like the William Hill Mile at Goodwood.
**True Night**, just 2lb higher than when last successful, returned to form with a fine effort. On this form, he clearly has a similar event in him, but his wins-to-runs record does not inspire that much confidence.
**Blue Trojan(IRE)** posted a career-best effort on the RPRs. Held in competitive handicaps at Epsom and Royal Ascot on his two most recent starts, he improved significantly on those runs and came home second best on the far side.
**St Pancras(IRE)**, raised just 2lb for a recent success at Bath, ran respectably in this better contest.
**Topton(IRE)** had conditions to suit and ran well.
**Rafferty(IRE) ◆** hails from a yard in good form and made a pleasing, albeit belated, reappearance (first run in 263 days). He just got a little tired in the closing stages, but was entitled to and should be capable of improvement.
**Gift Horse** shaped as though the step up to a mile would suit when a slightly unlucky third over seven furlongs at Kempton on his previous start, but he was raised 3lb for that effort and proved unable to confirm the promise.
**Salagama(IRE)** was quite free in the first-time blinkers and did not get home.

## 3598 TOTESPORT RATED STKS (H'CAP) 6f
**1:50** (1:55) (B) (0-105,105) 3-Y-O **£34,800** (£13,200; £6,600; £3,000) **Stalls** Low

Form RPR

5214 **1** **Alderney Race (USA)**24 2897 3-8-7 **91**.............................. SDrowne 17 101
(RCharlton) *lw: racd stands' side: prom: rdn to ld ins fnl f: r.o* **13/2**2

0601 **2** *¾* **Mahmoom**10 3317 3-8-5 **89**........................................ TEDurcan 13 97
(MRChannon) *lw: racd stands' side: hld up: hdwy over 1f out: r.o* **14/1**

-641 **3** *nk* **Two Step Kid (USA)**24 2897 3-8-11 **95**.............................. EAhern 5 102
(JNoseda) *lw: racd far side: chsd ldr: rdn to ld that gp 1f out: r.o* **5/1**1

0004 **4** *nk* **Valjarv (IRE)**11 3275 3-8-6 **90**..............................(b) TPQueally 15 96
(NPLittmoden) *racd stands' side: dwlt: sn pushed along in rr: hdwy over 1f out: r.o* **40/1**

0000 **5** *½* **Spanish Ace**32 2642 3-8-4 **88**..............................(v) MartinDwyer 10 93
(AMBalding) *b: sn led far side: rdn and hdd 1f out: styd on same pce* **40/1**

5422 **6** *¾* **Mac Love**23 2913 3-9-7 **105**........................................ GCarter 1 107
(JAkehurst) *racd far side: hld up: hdwy over 2f out: kpt on* **14/1**

13-5 **7** *shd* **Doohulla (USA)**24 2897 3-8-6 **90** ow1.............................. RHughes 11 91
(GAButler) *racd stands' side: chsd ldrs: rdn over 1f out: styd on* **9/1**

5013 **8** *hd* **Traytonic**24 2897 3-9-3 **101**........................................ JPMurtagh 3 102
(JRFanshawe) *lw: racd far side: hld up: nt clr run wl over 1f out: r.o: nt rch ldrs* **7/1**3

1003 **9** *1* **Fancy Foxtrot**32 2642 3-8-5 **89**........................................ KMcEvoy 12 87
(BJMeehan) *racd stands' side: prom: rdn over 2f out: styd on same pce fnl f* **14/1**

14-4 **10** *¾* **Philharmonic**11 3266 3-9-0 **101**.............................. THamilton(3) 14 97
(RAFahey) *racd stands' side: chsd ldrs: rdn over 1f out: no ex* **9/1**

4-64 **11** *¾* **Baltic Wave**10 3295 3-8-6 **90**........................................ KDarley 7 84
(TDBarron) *racd far side: mid-div: lost pl over 3f out: n.d after* **33/1**

1-10 **12** *shd* **Spliff**45 2309 3-8-10 **94**........................................ DaneO'Neill 16 88
(HCandy) *racd stands' side: s.i.s: hld up: nvr trbld ldrs* **14/1**

5000 **13** *hd* **Barbajuan (IRE)**38 2476 3-9-2 **100**..............................(b1) DHolland 9 93
(NACallaghan) *racd far side: mid-div: rdn over 2f out: wknd over 1f out* **20/1**

-120 **14** *nk* **Fun To Ride**24 2897 3-8-9 **93**........................................ MHills 4 85
(BWHills) *racd far side: chsd ldrs: rdn over 1f out: wknd ins fnl f* **12/1**

-220 **15** *shd* **Moonlight Man**45 2308 3-9-5 **103**.............................. RLMoore 19 95
(RHannon) *racd stands' side: chsd ldrs: rdn over 2f out: wknd fnl f* **40/1**

0-20 **16** *¾* **Big Bradford**24 2897 3-8-6 **90**..............................(v) DKinsella 8 80
(PGMurphy) *racd far side: chsd ldrs: rdn over 2f out: wknd fnl f* **33/1**

1360 **17** *½* **High Voltage**17 3092 3-8-12 **96**..............................(t) DarrenWilliams 18 84
(KRBurke) *led stands' side tl wknd and hdd ins fnl f* **25/1**

5050 **18** *shd* **Local Poet**24 2897 3-8-5 **89**..............................(t) GGibbons 2 77
(BAMcmahon) *raqced far side: chsd ldrs over 4f* **50/1**

1-01 **19** *5* **Corps De Ballet (IRE)**34 2589 3-8-4 **88**.............................. JQuinn 6 61
(JLDunlop) *lw: racd far side: chsd ldrs over 4f* **16/1**

1m 11.02s (-2.30) **Going Correction** -0.15s/f (Firm) **19** Ran SP% **126.5**
Speed ratings: **109,108,107,107,106 105,105,105,103,102 101,101,101,101,100 99,99,99,92**CSF £88.20 CT £517.93 TOTE £7.20: £2.10, £2.90, £1.90, £11.40; EX 326.30 Trifecta £1073.10 Pool of £1,662.56 - 1.10 winning units.
**Owner** Britton House Stud Ltd **Bred** Britton House Stud Inc **Trained** Beckhampton, Wilts

**FOCUS**
A competitive sprint handicap in which the William Hill Trophy form worked out well. The fourth horse sets the standard.

**NOTEBOOK**
**Alderney Race(USA)** did not have things go his way when a creditable fourth to Two Step Kid in the William Hill Trophy and, granted a smoother passage this time, he was good enough to reverse the placings. Connections have ruled out the Stewards' Cup, but he should be capable of further progression and is likely to stay seven furlongs.
**Mahmoom**, without the visor and 8lb higher than when successful over course and distance on his previous start, found only the winner too strong. However, he will go up again for this and does not look to have that much in hand of the assessor.
**Two Step Kid(USA)**, up 7lb for his success in the William Hill Trophy, won the race on the far side but, with there being no apparent course bias, he cannot be considered unlucky. This was just the fifth run of his life and there should be more to come. The Stewards' Cup could be his next target.
**Valjarv(IRE)** did not help her chance with a slow start, but still managed to post her best effort of the season so far according to RPRs. She has taken well to the fitting of blinkers.
**Spanish Ace** has proved quite hard to place since getting off the mark in April 2003, but he has tumbled in the weights this season and, dropped back in trip, ran respectably.
**Mac Love** ran a blinder when a close second to Moss Vale in Listed company on his previous start and acquitted himself with credit on this return to handicap company under his big weight.
**Doohulla(USA)** was just a neck behind today's winner at York on his previous start and again ran respectably, although the winner has clearly progressed.
**Traytonic** had today's winner behind when third in the William Hill Trophy on his previous start, but he did not get the clearest of runs this time and can be forgiven this run. *Official explanation: jockey said he suffered interference at start*
**Corps De Ballet(IRE)** *Official explanation: jockey said filly ran too free early on*

## 3599 CHIPPENHAM LODGE STUD CHERRY HINTON STKS (GROUP 2) (FILLIES) 6f
**2:20** (2:21) (A ) 2-Y-O **£40,600** (£15,400; £7,700; £3,500) **Stalls** Low

Form RPR

11 **1** **Jewel In The Sand (IRE)**18 3031 2-8-9 .............................. RHughes 8 105+
(RHannon) *lw: trckd ldrs: nt clr run 2f out: swtchd lft and led over 1f out: qcknd clr: rdn out* **2/1**1

13 **2** *hd* **Salsa Brava (IRE)**18 3031 2-8-9 .............................. J-PGuillambert 9 104+
(NPLittmoden) *h.d.w: s.i.s: hld up: hung rt over 1f out: r.o wl ins fnl f: edgd lft: jst failed* **11/2**3

610 **3** *5* **Extreme Beauty (USA)**18 3031 2-8-9 .............................. DHolland 3 89
(CEBrittain) *hld up: hdwy over 1f out: r.o: nt trble ldrs* **25/1**

31 **4** *½* **Shivaree**7 3398 2-8-9 ........................................ TEDurcan 1 88
(MRChannon) *outpcd: hdwy over 1f out: r.o* **33/1**

26 **5** *1 ½* **Arabian Dancer**18 3031 2-8-9 ........................................ KFallon 2 83
(MRChannon) *mid-div: sn pushed along: hdwy to ld wl over 1f out: sn hdd & wknd* **16/1**

10 **6** *2 ½* **Masa (USA)**18 3031 2-8-9 ........................................ LDettori 7 76
(SaeedBinSuroor) *w ldrs: led 1/2-way: rdn and hdd over 1f out: wknd fnl f* **7/2**2

110 **6** *dht* **Miss Meggy**20 2970 2-8-9 ........................................ DAllan 4 76
(TDEasterby) *sn pushed along in rr: hdwy over 2f out: wknd fnl f* **33/1**

310 **8** *1* **Nufoos**18 3031 2-8-9 ........................................ RHills 6 73
(MJohnston) *lw: w ldrs: rdn and ev ch over 1f out: wknd fnl f* **11/2**3

1321 **9** *1* **Polly Alexander (IRE)**12 3242 2-8-9 .............................. KDarley 10 70
(MJWallace) *lw: chsd ldrs: rdn over 2f out: wknd over 1f out* **11/1**

1 **10** *1* **Satin Kiss (USA)**24 2876 2-8-9 ........................................ KMcEvoy 5 67
(SaeedBinSuroor) *led to 1/2-way: ev ch over 1f out: wkng whn n.m.r fnl f* **16/1**

1m 11.55s (-1.77) **Going Correction** -0.15s/f (Firm) **10** Ran SP% **116.2**
Speed ratings: **105,104,98,97,95 92,92,90,89,88**CSF £12.89 TOTE £3.00: £1.30, £2.20, £5.10; EX 18.70 Trifecta £233.10 Pool of £1,628.77 - 4.96 winning units.
**Owner** Sand Associates **Bred** Gerrardstown House Stud **Trained** East Everleigh, Wilts

**FOCUS**
This looked like a pretty decent renewal of the Cherry Hinton, but the leaders - who included Masa, Nufoos and Satin Kiss - went off too fast and the first two home, who finished clear, are surely flattered by the bare form. Having said that, this was a good boost for the Albany form.

**NOTEBOOK**
**Jewel In The Sand(IRE)** proved good enough to follow up her Albany Stakes success, although Salsa Brava - two and a half lengths third at Ascot - was able to get a lot closer this time. Connections feel she has a chance of getting the Guineas mile, but that is a long way off and she has still to prove just how good she is, given that this run only confirmed her Royal Ascot form.
**Salsa Brava(IRE)** did not have things go her way when two and a half lengths third behind Jewel In The Sand in the Albany at Royal Ascot on her previous start and managed to close the gap despite once again things not panning out ideally. After a slow start, she had to make her challenge wider than anything and just got going too late.
**Extreme Beauty(USA)** had something of a disaster in the Albany - her saddle was slipping and she did not get a clear run - but things went better this time and she did not look to have any major excuses. A good effort, but she may just need dropping in grade.
**Shivaree**, off the mark in a Hamilton maiden on her previous outing, could not go the furious early pace and was doing her best work late on. A good effort considering and she looks sure to stay another furlong.
**Arabian Dancer ◆**, a creditable sixth in the Albany at Royal Ascot on her previous start, looked to get to the front a little too soon. That said, this was still a good effort and, clearly held in very high regard, she should win her maiden before stepping back up in grade.
**Masa(USA)**, unlucky when a beaten favourite in Listed company at Royal Ascot, looked to go too fast and did not last home. She can be given another chance.
**Nufoos** was another who looked to do too much early.
**Polly Alexander(IRE)**, whose recent Salisbury success was given a boost when Captain Hurricane won the July Stakes, was below form and may not have been suited by the fast ground, or racing close to the fast pace.
**Satin Kiss(USA)** looked to go too fast. Being a full-sister to Lujian, she is surely not one to give up on just yet.

## 3600 UAE EQUESTRIAN AND RACING FEDERATION FALMOUTH STKS (GROUP 1) (F&M) 1m

**2:55** (2:57) (A ) 3-Y-0+ **£116,000** (£44,000; £22,000; £10,000) **Stalls** Low

| Form | | | | RPR |
|---|---|---|---|---|
| 2312 | 1 | | **Soviet Song (IRE)**[21] 2957 4-9-1 114 JPMurtagh 3 (JRFanshawe) *lw: swtg: hld up: hdwy over 2f out: rdn to ld over 1f out: r.o* **11/4**[2] | 122 |
| -111 | 2 | 2 ½ | **Attraction**[18] 3033 3-8-6 119 KDarley 4 (MJohnston) *lw: led: rdn and hdd over 1f out: unable qck ins fnl f* **4/5**[1] | 116 |
| 11 | 3 | 2 ½ | **Baqah (IRE)**[30] 2720 3-8-6 (t) DBonilla 6 (FHead, France) *gd sort: neat: chsd ldrs: rdn over 1f out: sn outpcd* **33/1** | 111 |
| -362 | 4 | ¾ | **Monturani (IRE)**[20] 2967 5-9-1 104 DHolland 5 (GWragg) *chsd ldr over 6f: no ex* **50/1** | 109 |
| 113 | 5 | 7 | **Illustrious Miss (USA)**[44] 2330 3-8-6 112 TPQueally 1 (DRLoder) *plld hrd and prom: rdn and wknd over 1f out* **14/1** | 93 |
| 15-1 | 6 | 1 ½ | **Favourable Terms**[20] 2967 4-9-1 108 KFallon 7 (SirMichaelStoute) *lw: hld up: pushed laong over 4f out: hdwy 3f out: rdn and wknd over 1f out* **6/1**[3] | 89 |
| 6 | 7 | 3 ½ | **Tizdubai (USA)**[32] 2641 3-8-6 (t) KMcEvoy 2 (SaeedBinSuroor) *b.hind: chsd ldrs over 5f* **100/1** | 81 |

1m 36.11s (-4.37) **Going Correction** -0.15s/f (Firm)
**WFA** 3 from 4yo+ 9lb **7** Ran SP% **109.1**
Speed ratings: **115,112,110,109,102 100,97**CSF £4.77 TOTE £3.50: £1.80, £1.20; EX 6.40.
**Owner** Elite Racing Club **Bred** Elite Racing Club **Trained** Newmarket, Suffolk

**FOCUS**
The first running of the Falmouth Stakes as a Group One and this line-up fully justified the decision to upgrade it - the only top-class British-based filly missing was Russian Rhythm. All eyes were on the record-breaking Attraction, but she was not good enough on the day. Interestingly, no horse managed the make all on the seven-race card and this was one of the fastest races ever run over a mile on the July course.

**NOTEBOOK**
**Soviet Song(IRE)** never really fulfilled her immense potential during a frustrating campaign last season, but she is running better than ever this term and confirmed the promise of her Queen Anne second behind subsequent Eclipse winner Refuse To Bend. Ridden confidently by Murtagh, she showed an impressive turn of foot to sweep past Attraction a furlong out and the result never looked in doubt. Her trainer's immediate reaction was to skip the Sussex Stakes and bring her back in the autumn - wherever she goes next, she will take a lot of beating.
**Attraction**, who has recovered from injury to become the leading filly of her generation, came up short on her first run against her elders, running probably a few pounds below her best. If one was looking for excuses, maybe she could have gone faster in a bid to get her rivals off the bridle earlier than they would have liked, although the fact that this was one of the fastest races ever run over a mile on the July course puts that theory in doubt. It could also be argued that this race came a bit too soon for her after Ascot. Whatever the case, surprisingly for such an exceptional filly, she has something to prove, although the subsequent discovery that she was in season looks a valid enough reason for this below-par effort.
**Baqah(IRE)** has been progressing well in France, winning a Listed race and a Group Two on her last two outings, and posted a fine effort on this step up to the highest level. There ought to be more to come, but she has a little way to go yet to make a winning mark in a Group One.
**Monturani(IRE)** has never won outside of Listed company, or since May 2002, but she is capable on her day and ran a cracker. Even if she has run a little way above herself, she is surely the best guide as to the strength of the form.
**Illustrious Miss(USA)**, three lengths third to Attraction in the Irish Guineas, was far too keen and ran below form. It would be unwise to write her off already.
**Favourable Terms** looked as though she would be capable of fulfilling her potential this season when winning the Windsor Forest Stakes (Monturani two lengths second) at Royal Ascot on her previous start, but this represented a step back. She is better than this, but is capable of throwing in the odd poor performance.
**Tizdubai(USA)** is clearly not up to this class on turf and, as a full sister to dual Breeders' Cup Classic winner Tiznow, why is she not running on dirt?

## 3601 STRUTT & PARKER MAIDEN STKS 7f

**3:30** (3:31) (D ) 2-Y-0 **£8,443** (£2,598; £1,299; £649) **Stalls** Low

| Form | | | | RPR |
|---|---|---|---|---|
| | 1 | | **Belenus (IRE)** 2-9-0 LDettori 5 (SaeedBinSuroor) *nice colt: a.p: led over 1f out: r.o wl* **13/8**[1] | 86+ |
| | 2 | 1 ½ | **Frith (IRE)** 2-9-0 MHills 7 (BWHills) *w'like: scope: lw: chsd ldr: rdn over 1f out: r.o* **9/1** | 82+ |
| | 3 | 2 ½ | **L'Escapade (IRE)** 2-9-0 MartinDwyer 1 (AMBalding) *w'like: scope: s.i.s: sn prom: rdn over 1f out: nt clr run ins fnl f: styd on same pce* **25/1** | 76+ |
| 4 | 4 | nk | **Sri Lipis**[17] 3093 2-9-0 KFallon 10 (PFICole) *hld up: hdwy and hung lft fr over 2f out: styd on same pce fnl f* **7/2**[2] | 75 |
| 0 | 5 | 1 | **Red Chairman**[10] 3319 2-9-0 TPQueally 11 (DRLoder) *chsd ldrs: led 5f out: rdn and hdd over 1f out: hung lft and wknd ins fnl f* **18/1** | 73 |
| | 6 | ¾ | **King Forever** 2-9-0 EAhern 12 (JNoseda) *gd sort: wl grwn: s.i.s: hld up: hdwy and nt clr run over 2f out: and over 1f out: nvr able to chal* **8/1**[3] | 71 |
| | 7 | 2 ½ | **Northern Secret** 2-8-9 RMullen 15 (AMBalding) *w'like: leggy: hld up: rdn over 2f out: nvr trbld ldrs* **33/1** | 59 |
| | 8 | hd | **River Biscuit (USA)** 2-9-0 RLMoore 8 (RHannon) *str: bit bkwd: prom: rdn and hmpd over 2f out: wknd over 1f out* **14/1** | 64 |
| | 9 | nk | **Following Flow (USA)** 2-9-0 KDarley 6 (WJarvis) *neat: sn outpcd: nvr nrr* **40/1** | 63 |
| | 10 | hd | **Cape Quest** 2-9-0 RHughes 13 (RHannon) *leggy: scope: hld up: hdwy over 1f out: wknd ins fnl f* **16/1** | 63 |
| 4 | 11 | hd | **Love Beauty (USA)**[27] 2780 2-9-0 JFanning 3 (MJohnston) *lw: led 2f: rdn and ev ch over 1f out: wknd fnl f* **16/1** | 62 |
| 30 | 12 | 1 | **Drax**[6] 3406 2-8-11 ABeech(3) 2 (DRLoder) *lw: a in rr* **33/1** | 60 |
| | 13 | ½ | **Young Mick** 2-9-0 AMcCarthy 9 (GGMargarson) *w'like: prom: sn pushed along: lost pl over 4f out: wknd over 2f out* **40/1** | 58 |
| | 14 | 1 ½ | **Gurrun** 2-9-0 AMackay 14 (NACallaghan) *gd sort: bit bkwd: s.i.s: outpcd* **66/1** | 55 |
| | 15 | 2 ½ | **Kandidate** 2-9-0 DHolland 4 (CEBrittain) *w'like: bkwd: s.i.s: plld hrd and sn prom: lost pl 1/2-way: sn bhd* **20/1** | 48 |

1m 26.3s (-0.47) **Going Correction** -0.15s/f (Firm) **15** Ran SP% **126.0**
Speed ratings: **96,94,91,91,89 89,86,86,85,85 85,84,83,81,78**CSF £16.63 TOTE £2.70: £1.60, £2.90, £7.30; EX 18.90.
**Owner** Godolphin **Bred** Gainsborough Stud Management Ltd **Trained** Newmarket, Suffolk

**FOCUS**
This maiden can produce a classy performer or two, the likes of Alhaarth, Colonel Collins, Mark Of Esteem and Dubai Destination, and this year's renewal looked pretty decent. It has been rated through the fourth and fifth who both ran to the pound of their respective debuts.

**NOTEBOOK**
**Belenus(IRE)** ◆, by the great Dubai Millennium (his second winner from as many runners), out of a useful eight- to ten-furlong winner, really took the eye in the paddock and clearly has ability to match his looks. Always going nicely for Dettori, he quickened up smartly and soon settled the issue. He is held in quite high regard by connections and was made a general 25/1 shot for the 2000 Guineas, although he will not be rushed this season.
**Frith(IRE)** ◆, a half-brother to an eight-furlong two-year-old winner, made a very encouraging debut, finishing clear of all bar the winner. He should win a maiden soon rather than later.
**L'Escapade(IRE)** ◆, out of an eight-furlong three-year-old winner, sister to a Listed scorer, hails from a stable that had a first-time-out winner at the same price the previous day. He showed signs of inexperience before finishing to good effect and will surely pick up a maiden.
**Sri Lipis**, fourth to the promising Fox (who was second behind the only other Dubai Millennium offspring to have run, Dubawi) on his debut, stepped up on that effort and fared the best of those with previous experience. An ordinary race should come his way.
**Red Chairman**, well held on his debut over course and distance, showed improved form and is going the right way.
**King Forever** ◆, a 65,000gns purchase, half-brother to eight-furlong three-year-old winner Baffle, out of an unraced half-sister to Prince Of Wales's Stakes winner Perpendicular, was noted travelling well in the middle part of the contest, but he could never really land a telling blow. He should improve enough to win a maiden.
**Northern Secret**, a 20,000gns yearling, half-sister to a juvenile winner in France, offered some promise and should progress.

## 3602 RACINGPOST.CO.UK FILLIES' RATED STKS (H'CAP) 7f

**4:05** (4:06) (B ) (0-100,96) 3-Y-0 **£12,081** (£4,582; £2,291; £1,041) **Stalls** Low

| Form | | | | RPR |
|---|---|---|---|---|
| 3-11 | 1 | | **Peeress**[21] 2963 3-8-6 88 KFallon 8 (SirMichaelStoute) *lw: hld up in tch: led 1f out: edgd lft: drvn out* **2/1**[1] | 103+ |
| 1151 | 2 | 1 ¼ | **Oasis Star (IRE)**[25] 2844 3-8-5 87 MartinDwyer 9 (PWHarris) *lw: hld up: hdwy over 1f out: r.o* **7/2**[3] | 95+ |
| -400 | 3 | 1 | **Malvern Light**[31] 2685 3-9-0 96 RHills 10 (WJHaggas) *lw: hld up: swtchd rt over 1f out: r.o ins fnl f: nt rch ldrs* **25/1** | 101+ |
| -244 | 4 | ¾ | **Solar Power (IRE)**[45] 2306 3-8-2 84 EAhern 1 (JRFanshawe) *trckd ldrs: rdn and ev ch 1f out: styd on same pce ins fnl f* **9/2** | 87 |
| 3-21 | 5 | shd | **Dawn Surprise (USA)**[23] 2911 3-8-8 90 (t) LDettori 4 (SaeedBinSuroor) *led: rdn and hdd 1f out: no ex* **11/4**[2] | 93 |
| 0300 | 6 | 2 | **Hilites (IRE)**[10] 3328 3-7-11 82 oh2 NMackay(3) 6 (JSMoore) *s.i.s: hld up: rdn over 2f out: nvr trbld ldrs* **50/1** | 80 |
| 1-00 | 7 | ¾ | **First Candlelight**[32] 2642 3-8-0 82 JQuinn 7 (JGGiven) *chsd ldr: rdn and ev ch over 1f out: wknd ins fnl f* **50/1** | 78 |
| 6500 | 8 | 2 ½ | **Withorwithoutyou (IRE)**[17] 3105 3-8-0 82 oh2 JMackay 2 (BAMcmahon) *hld up: rdn over 2f out: wknd over 1f out* **40/1** | 72 |
| 2602 | 9 | nk | **Cusco (IRE)**[11] 3275 3-8-6 88 RLMoore 5 (RHannon) *chsd ldrs: pushed along 3f out: wknd over 1f out* **20/1** | 77 |

1m 23.95s (-2.82) **Going Correction** -0.15s/f (Firm) **9** Ran SP% **115.4**
Speed ratings: **110,108,107,106,106 104,103,100,100**CSF £8.78 CT £125.72 TOTE £2.80: £1.40, £1.50, £5.20; EX 7.10.
**Owner** Cheveley Park Stud **Bred** Cheveley Park Stud Ltd **Trained** Newmarket, Suffolk

**FOCUS**
A decent handicap run in a creditable time. The first three could be up to Listed class but a couple of others look high enough in the weights.

**NOTEBOOK**
**Peeress**, up 6lb for her recent Thirsk win, completed the hat-trick in good style on this drop back from a mile. Always going well for Fallon, she picked up nicely and did what was required when in front. Her style of racing means she could just remain ahead of the assessor if kept to handicaps, and a 5lb penalty increases her chances of making the cut in Goodwood's William Hill Mile, but connections could now aim for some black type.
**Oasis Star(IRE)** is probably a little flattered to get this close to the winner as that one may have been idling in front, but she is clearly still progressing and remains one to keep on the right side of.
**Malvern Light** had quite a task off a mark of 96 for her handicap debut, but she ran respectably.
**Solar Power(IRE)**, dropped back to seven furlongs for the first time since making a winning debut, looked set to pose a threat when making a move against the rail a furlong out, but she could not quicken.
**Dawn Surprise(USA)** won well enough in a Salisbury maiden on her previous start, but the Handicapper had not taken any chances putting her on a mark of 90. She had every chance from the front but just lacked a change of pace and may be better suited a mile.

## 3603 ROBIN PARKE MEMORIAL MAIDEN STKS 1m 2f

**4:40** (4:41) (D ) 3-Y-0 **£8,346** (£2,568; £1,284; £642) **Stalls** High

| Form | | | | RPR |
|---|---|---|---|---|
| 222 | 1 | | **Long Road (USA)**[11] 3268 3-9-0 85 EAhern 3 (JNoseda) *lw: s.i.s: hld up: hdwy over 3f out: led ins fnl f: rdn clr* **11/4**[1] | 79+ |
| 53 | 2 | 3 ½ | **Mikao (IRE)**[24] 2900 3-9-0 PRobinson 8 (MHTompkins) *led over 8f out: rdn and hdd over 1f out: outpcd ins fnl f* **10/1** | 72+ |
| 2-3 | 3 | ¾ | **Flamboyant Lad**[102] 1116 3-9-0 MHills 4 (BWHills) *lw: hld up: hdwy over 2f out: rdn and ev ch over 1f out: styd on same pce* **9/2** | 71+ |
| | 4 | ½ | **Articulation** 3-9-0 RHughes 5 (HRACecil) *gd sort: bkwd: trckd ldrs: rdn to ld over 1f out: hdd and no ex ins fnl f* **13/2** | 70+ |
| | 5 | 1 ¾ | **Stream Of Gold (IRE)** 3-9-0 KFallon 9 (SirMichaelStoute) *gd sort: scope: plld hrd and prom: shkn up over 1f out: no ex* **7/2**[3] | 66+ |
| 00 | 6 | ¾ | **Bold Phoenix (IRE)**[24] 2888 3-9-0 MartinDwyer 6 (ACStewart) *sn led: hdd over 8f out: remained w ldr: rdn and ev ch over 1f out: wknd ins fnl f* **66/1** | 65 |
| 0-00 | 7 | 2 | **Hold Up**[9] 3348 3-8-6 BReilly(3) 7 (MissJFeilden) *plld hrd and prom: rdn over 3f out: wknd wl over 1f out* **100/1** | 56? |
| 0 | 8 | 2 | **Ogilvy (USA)**[80] 1461 3-9-0 JFortune 1 (JHMGosden) *lw: hld up: hdwy over 4f out: sn rdn: wknd wl over 1f out* **10/3**[2] | 57 |

2m 6.64s (0.18) **Going Correction** -0.15s/f (Firm) **8** Ran SP% **115.1**
Speed ratings: **93,90,89,89,87 87,85,84**CSF £31.55 TOTE £4.50: £1.20, £2.20, £1.60; EX 35.20 Place 6 £51.37, Place 5 £9.10.
**Owner** Syd Belzberg **Bred** Syd Belzberg & Budget Stable **Trained** Newmarket, Suffolk

**FOCUS**
A fair maiden but the time was slow and the form was not what it might have been. Having said that, some of these are probably capable of better than they showed.

**NOTEBOOK**

**Long Road(USA)** had been a beaten favourite on his last two starts, but this step up from a mile suited well and he ran out a most decisive winner, picking up nicely when a gap against the rail appeared. His rating of 85 means he will face no easy task in handicaps, but he will be worthy of respect on the back of this performance.

**Mikao(IRE)** showed real signs of inexperience when readily held over a mile at York on his previous start, but he did not look to have any excuses this time. He is now eligible for a handicap mark.

**Flamboyant Lad** failed to build on the promise he showed when last seen 102 days ago and may have preferred a stronger pace. He is at least now qualified for handicaps.

**Articulation**, out of a full-sister to Derby winner Commander In Chief, looked in need of the run in the paddock and should improve on this encouraging effort.

**Stream Of Gold(IRE)**, a full brother to the top-class Spectrum, proved easy to back and was well held after racing keenly. He took the eye in the paddock, however, and given his breeding is not one to write off just yet.

**Ogilvy(USA)** was supported in the market, but showed nothing.

T/Jkpt: £6,758.60 to a £1 stake. Pool: £28,557.50. 3.00 winning tickets. T/Plt: £49.00 to a £1 stake. Pool: £102,704.15. 1,528.70 winning tickets. T/Qpdt: £4.00 to a £1 stake. Pool: £6,271.80. 1,157.30 winning tickets. CR

## 3370 PONTEFRACT (L-H)

Tuesday, July 6

**OFFICIAL GOING: Good to firm**

### 3604 PONTEFRACT LADIES H'CAP (FOR LADY AMATEUR RIDERS) 1m 2f 6y

2:05 (2:06) (F) (0-55,54) 3-Y-0+ £5,057 (£1,556; £778; £389) Stalls Low

Form RPR

50-0 **1** **Burnt Copper (IRE)**[11] 3263 4-10-10 50 .................. MissKManser(7) 16 62
*(JRBest) dwlt: hld up and wl bhd: hmpd over 3f out: gd hdwy 2f out: styd on strly u.p to ld post* 20/1

02-3 **2** *shd* **Valeureux**[8] 3375 6-11-5 52 .................. MrsSBosley 3 64
*(JHetherton) midfield: hdwy to trck ldrs over 2f out: rdn to ld wl ins fnl f: ct post* 10/3[1]

0564 **3** *3/4* **Lazzaz**[6] 3411 6-10-7 45 .................. MrsMarieKing(5) 7 56
*(PWHiatt) led: qcknd clr over 1f out: hdd wl ins fnl f: no ex* 9/2[2]

-556 **4** *3 1/2* **Pension Fund**[17] 3103 10-10-9 49 .................. MissJCoward(7) 12 53
*(MWEasterby) midfield: sme hdwy 2f out: nt clr run over 1f out: styd on ins last: nvr able to chal* 11/1

4323 **5** *5* **First Maite**[11] 3282 11-11-3 50 .................. MrsMMorris 15 44
*(SRBowring) bhd: hdwy on outer into midfield over 3f out: kpt on fnl 2f: nvr able to chal* 10/1

3-05 **6** *hd* **Final Dividend (IRE)**[5] 3461 8-10-9 45 .................. MissJoannaRees(3) 6 39
*(JMPEustace) prom: ch over 2f out: kpt on same pce* 17/2

-500 **7** *hd* **Stepastray**[6] 3411 7-10-11 44 .................. MissSBrotherton 1 38
*(REBarr) in tch: effrt over 2f out: no hdwy* 25/1

032- **8** *1* **Healey (IRE)**[372] 2851 6-10-12 48 .................. MissKellyHarrison(3) 9 40
*(PRWood) in tch: effrt over 2f out: no hdwy* 16/1

0000 **9** *nk* **Dark Cut (IRE)**[7] 3401 4-10-4 42 .................. MissDawnRankin(5) 13 33
*(HAlexander) s.i.s: towards rr: hdwy into midfield 1/2-way: no further prog* 50/1

00/0 **10** *3/4* **Lady Stratagem**[17] 3099 5-10-7 45 .................. MissMSowerby(5) 19 35
*(EWTuer) bhd: styd on fnl 2f: n.d* 50/1

5600 **11** *1 1/2* **Rainstorm**[6] 3412 9-10-6 42 .................. MrsSOwen(3) 11 29
*(WMBrisbourne) midfield: hdwy and prom 4f out: ev ch 2f out: wknd qckly over 1f out* 7/1[3]

-200 **12** *shd* **Melograno (IRE)**[18] 3041 4-11-3 50 .................. MissAGoschen 10 37
*(MarkCampion) midfield: rdn wl over 1f out: no hdwy* 33/1

0024 **13** *2* **Noble Pursuit**[4] 3471 7-10-10 50 .................. MissVBarr(7) 14 33
*(REBarr) towards rr: sme hdwy on outer 1/2-way: no further prog* 25/1

2206 **14** *nk* **Penwell Hill (USA)**[8] 3375 5-11-7 54 .................. MsCWilliams 8 36
*(TDBarron) trckd ldrs: ch over 2f out: wknd qckly over 1f out* 14/1

-000 **15** *1* **Outward (USA)**[19] 3018 4-10-12 50 .................. MissRBastiman(5) 5 30
*(RBastiman) bhd most of way* 50/1

-000 **16** *5* **Mutared (IRE)**[11] 3282 6-10-10 46 ..................(p) MrsEmmaLittmoden(3) 2 17
*(NPLittmoden) cl up: ev ch over 2f out: wknd qckly over 1f out* 33/1

0-04 **17** *15* **Expected Bonus (USA)**[14] 3166 5-11-1 51 .................. MissEFolkes(3) 18 —
*(SCWilliams) chsd ldrs tl rdn and wknd 3f out: t.o* 14/1

5060 **18** *13* **Kristineau**[3] 3518 6-10-5 43 ..................(t) MissBeverleyKendall(5) 4 —
*(MrsDianneSayer) dwlt: a bhd: lost tch over 2f out: t.o* 25/1

2m 15.24s (1.33) **Going Correction** +0.075s/f (Good) 18 Ran SP% 129.0

Speed ratings: **97,96,96,93,89 89,89,88,88,87 86,86,84,84,83 79,67,57**CSF £82.92 CT £373.73 TOTE £35.20: £7.20, £1.50, £1.40, £2.50; EX 137.90.

**Owner** R Blake **Bred** Premier Enterprises **Trained** Hucking, Kent

■ Kylie Manser's first winner.

**FOCUS**

A typical event for the division run at a fair pace, and the first three came clear.

**NOTEBOOK**

**Burnt Copper(IRE)**, despite dwelling at the start and meeting with interference, really flew home and collared the runner-up on the line. He had been sharpened up by a recent comeback effort, but this was a much improved run and a first win in 24 attempts.

**Valeureux** did everything right, but was just found wanting towards the line as the eventual winner came with his late challenge. He certainly can score off this mark, but is not one to take a short price about.

**Lazzaz** again took the field along for most of the way, but was a sitting duck for the first two late on and finished very tired. He is a most consistent performer in this division, and a banker for each-way punters, but is a desperately hard horse to win with.

**Pension Fund**, ridden by today's rider on his last four outings, improved a touch and was staying on well enough late in the day. He is dropping in the weights, but is clearly in decline and has not won since 2001.

**First Maite** again found less than expected off the bridle and ran below par.

### 3605 DIANNE NURSERY 6f

2:35 (2:37) (D) 2-Y-0 £7,241 (£2,228; £1,114; £557) Stalls Low

Form RPR

030 **1** **Prospect Court**[21] 2959 2-8-8 75 .................. TQuinn 2 75
*(JDBethell) trckd ldrs: wnt 2nd over 1f out: styd on wl u.p to ld post* 8/1[3]

221 **2** *shd* **Spirit Of France (IRE)**[19] 3014 2-9-7 88 .................. KDalgleish 9 88
*(MJohnston) disp ld: led over 2f out: rdn over 1f out: styd on wl: ct post* 5/4[1]

052 **3** *2 1/2* **Brace Of Doves**[12] 3233 2-8-0 67 .................. PFessey 8 60
*(TDBarron) hld up: drvn along over 2f out: hdwy to chse first 2 appr fnl f: no imp ins last* 9/1

6610 **4** *3* **Mytton's Dream**[10] 3290 2-7-7 65 oh3 .................. DFox(5) 7 49
*(ABailey) towards rr: drvn along over 2f out: styd on u.p fr over 1f out: n.d* 25/1

030 **5** *1 1/2* **Ryedane (IRE)**[13] 3196 2-8-2 69 .................. ANicholls 1 48
*(TDEasterby) disp ld tl over 2f out: rdn and btn over 1f out* 25/1

052 **6** *1 3/4* **Hymn Of Victory (IRE)**[17] 3080 2-8-6 73 .................. RHavlin 3 47
*(TJEtherington) chsd ldrs: rdn over 2f out: sn btn* 16/1

51 **7** *3/4* **Snookered Again**[26] 2812 2-8-4 71 .................. DaleGibson 6 43
*(MWEasterby) sn bhd and drvn along: kpt on fnl f: n.d* 10/1

3351 **8** *nk* **Monsieur Mirasol**[12] 3233 2-8-9 76 .................. NCallan 4 47
*(KARyan) sn towards rr: drvn along 1/2-way: no hdwy* 4/1[2]

030 **9** *12* **Moon Mischief (IRE)**[10] 3290 2-8-1 68 .................. JBramhill 5 —
*(NPLittmoden) chsd ldrs: rdn over 2f out: sn btn: bhd whn eased and lost tch fnl f* 12/1

1m 18.16s (0.86) **Going Correction** +0.075s/f (Good) 9 Ran SP% 115.9

Speed ratings: **97,96,93,89,87 85,84,83,67**CSF £18.46 CT £92.48 TOTE £11.50: £3.80, £1.10, £2.10; EX 35.50.

**Owner** John E Lund **Bred** Mrs G Slater **Trained** Middleham Moor, N Yorks

**FOCUS**

The first nursery of the season and the time was fair. The figures shown as 'official ratings' are estimates for guidance only.

**NOTEBOOK**

**Prospect Court**, last seen when tailed off in the Windsor Castle Stakes at the Royal Meeting, showed a willing attitude to peg back the runner-up close home. He was getting off the mark at the fourth attempt, appreciated the extra furlong and was obviously fairly well in for this, so may be capable of better still.

**Spirit Of France(IRE)**, who had shown fair form in three outings previously, made a bold bid under top-weight, but had no more to offer when challenged in the final strides. This was a decent effort and he looks sure to find compensation soon.

**Brace Of Doves** could not find the change of gear to trouble the principals late on and may have preferred softer ground. He was clear of the rest and will find easier opportunities than this.

**Mytton's Dream**, a winner over five furlongs in May, stayed on late to finish a never-dangerous fourth from out of the handicap.

**Hymn Of Victory(IRE)** *Official explanation: jockey said colt hung right throughout*

**Monsieur Mirasol** was never in it and proved most disappointing.

### 3606 ST. GILES H'CAP 6f

3:10 (3:11) (D) (0-85,83) 3-Y-0+ £14,235 (£4,380; £2,190; £1,095) Stalls Low

Form RPR

6242 **1** **Complication**[8] 3372 4-8-6 65 ..................(b) LisaJones(3) 12 78
*(JARToller) midfield: hdwy over 1f out: r.o wl u.p to ld wl ins fnl f* 8/1[3]

2140 **2** *1 3/4* **Legal Set (IRE)**[5] 3446 8-7-12 59 ..................(t) DFox(5) 15 67
*(MissAStokell) prom: rdn over 2f out: ev ch ent fnl f: r.o* 28/1

0350 **3** *shd* **Midnight Parkes**[5] 3446 5-8-9 65 ..................(p) MHenry 16 72
*(EJAlston) led: rdn over 1f out: hdd wl ins fnl f: no ex* 14/1

0044 **4** *3/4* **Undeterred**[17] 3098 8-9-1 71 ..................(v) SSanders 10 76
*(TDBarron) towards rr: hdwy 2f out: kpt on u.p fnl f: nvr able to chal* 13/2[1]

3611 **5** *hd* **Aintnecessarilyso**[10] 3298 6-7-7 56 .................. MHalford(7) 4 61
*(NEBerry) rr div: hdwy 2f out: kpt on u.p fnl f: nvr able to chal* 12/1

0310 **6** *1 3/4* **Hiccups**[17] 3098 4-9-11 81 ..................(p) TQuinn 14 80
*(MrsJRRamsden) midfield: hdwy to trck ldrs 2f out: sn rdn: no further prog* 9/1

6532 **7** *3/4* **Bollin Edward**[10] 3298 5-8-8 64 ..................(v) JCarroll 8 61
*(TDEasterby) bhd: styd on fr over 1f out: n.d* 7/1[2]

2232 **8** *1* **Bundy**[7] 3400 8-8-7 63 .................. SWKelly 6 57
*(MDods) s.i.s: bhd: styd on fr over 1f out: n.d* 12/1

6010 **9** *nk* **Pax**[31] 2682 7-9-13 83 .................. AlexGreaves 2 76
*(DNicholls) midfield: rdn appr fnl f: no hdwy* 14/1

-040 **10** *nk* **Pieter Brueghel (USA)**[10] 3309 5-9-10 80 .................. RWinston 11 72
*(DNicholls) chsd ldrs tl rdn and wknd over 1f out* 7/1[2]

0250 **11** *shd* **Chairman Bobby**[6] 3407 6-8-13 72 .................. LEnstone(3) 13 64
*(DWBarker) cl up: rdn over 2f out: wknd over 1f out* 33/1

-500 **12** *1 1/2* **Blythe Spirit**[17] 3098 5-8-6 69 .................. NataliaGemelova(7) 1 57
*(RAFahey) midfield: effrt 2f out: no hdwy* 16/1

-501 **13** *shd* **Sharoura**[8] 3372 8-8-10 66 7ex .................. GParkin 17 53
*(RAFahey) in tch: rdn over 2f out: wknd over 1f out* 25/1

2004 **14** *1/2* **Illusive (IRE)**[6] 3428 7-8-2 58 ..................(b) FNorton 5 44
*(MWigham) prom tl rdn and wknd 2f out* 20/1

-000 **15** *2 1/2* **Pop Up Again**[12] 3235 4-9-1 71 .................. DeanMcKeown 3 49
*(GASwinbank) in tch: rdn over 2f out: wknd over 1f out* 33/1

2246 **16** *hd* **Romany Nights (IRE)**[10] 3293 4-9-5 78 ..................(b) SHitchcott(3) 9 56
*(JWUnett) chsd ldrs to 1/2-way: sn drvn along and wknd* 9/1

0555 **17** *27* **Ronnie From Donny (IRE)**[6] 3409 4-8-6 65 .................. TEaves(3) 7 —
*(BEllison) bhd: lost tch and eased fnl f: t.o* 16/1

1m 16.7s (-0.60) **Going Correction** +0.075s/f (Good) 17 Ran SP% 127.9

Speed ratings: **107,104,104,103,103 100,99,98,98,97 97,95,95,94,91 91,55**CSF £232.35 CT £1850.19 TOTE £7.10: £1.40, £8.00, £6.20, £2.50; EX 475.60.

**Owner** Miss Julia Staughton **Bred** Limestone Stud **Trained** Newmarket, Suffolk

**FOCUS**

A decent contest for the grade, although the time was not good. A high draw proved an advantage.

**NOTEBOOK**

**Complication**, a narrow loser over course and distance last time, quickened up in good style late on to run out a ready winner. She enjoyed this fast pace, has been in good heart of late and would be of definite interest if turned out under a penalty.

**Legal Set(IRE)** stepped up on his latest effort and ran a solid race off this new mark. He is in good form, appreciated this faster ground and should continue to pay his way this summer.

**Midnight Parkes** showed good early speed to get to the lead from his high draw and only gave way late on. He is hard to win with, but looks on a fair mark now and could end his long losing run soon if he can maintain this form.

**Undeterred** did well to finish as he did, as he looked to have it all to do turning for home. He was forced to race wide this time and can be rated better than the bare form.

**Aintnecessarilyso** ran another sound race and fared the best of those drawn low.

**Bollin Edward** got shuffled back at an early stage and could not recover. He is capable of better.

**Ronnie From Donny(IRE)** *Official explanation: jockey said gelding had a breathing problem*

### 3607 WILFRED UNDERWOOD MEMORIAL MAIDEN STKS 1m 2f 6y

3:45 (3:46) (D) 3-Y-0+ £5,811 (£1,788; £894; £447) Stalls Low

Form RPR

2 **1** **Apsara**[13] 3204 3-8-5 ..................(v) WRyan 1 85
*(HRACecil) mde all: rdn over 1f out: styd on wl* 4/1[2]

6 **2** *3* **Mijdaaf (FR)**[24] 2888 3-8-10 .................. SSanders 10 84
*(ACStewart) trckd ldrs: wnt 2nd 4f out: rdn over 1f out: styd on: no imp on wnr* 4/1[2]

24- **3** *1 1/4* **Hills Spitfire (IRE)**[248] 5871 3-8-10 .................. TQuinn 5 82
*(PWHarris) s.i.s: sn midfield: drvn along 1/2-way: rdn into 3rd over 2f out: styd on: no imp on first 2 fnl f* 10/11[1]

0 **4** *10* **Capitole (IRE)**[17] 3094 3-8-10 RWinston 7 63
(ACStewart) *slowly away: bhd: hdwy 1/2-way: in tch 3f out: no further prog* **50/1**
5-23 **5** *6* **Cantarna (IRE)**[15] 3142 3-8-5 76 DaleGibson 9 46
(JMackie) *chsd wnr to 4f out: wknd over 2f out* **15/2**[3]
00 **6** *2 1/2* **Bravely Does It (USA)**[10] 3297 4-9-7 SWKelly 3 46
(WMBrisbourne) *in tch tl outpcd 4f out: n.d after* **100/1**
5 **7** *1/2* **Sharabad (FR)**[17] 3115 6-9-7 LVickers 2 46
(MrsLBNormile) *dwlt: towards rr: outpcd 4f out: n.d* **100/1**
30-0 **8** *8* **Madaar (USA)**[11] 3282 5-9-7 46 RFfrench 4 30
(RBastiman) *towards rr: outpcd 4f out* **100/1**
4206 **9** *3 1/2* **Giust In Temp (IRE)**[155] 652 5-9-4 36 LisaJones(3) 6 24
(PWHiatt) *keen: trckd ldrs to 1/2-way: outpcd 4f out* **100/1**
**10** *1 1/2* **Shyshiyra (IRE)** 3-8-5 GParkin 11 16
(KARyan) *slowly away: a bhd* **50/1**
0-00 **11** *dist* **Svenson**[174] 529 3-8-10 PMQuinn 8 —
(JSWainwright) *dwlt: towards rr: outpcd 4f out: t.o and eased fnl f* **150/1**

2m 11.13s (-2.78) **Going Correction** +0.075s/f (Good)
**WFA** 3 from 4yo+ 11lb **11** Ran **SP% 112.7**
Speed ratings: **114,111,110,102,97 95,95,89,86,85** —CSF £19.39 TOTE £5.20: £1.10, £1.40, £1.10; EX 16.80.
**Owner** Dr Catherine Wills **Bred** St Clare Hall Stud **Trained** Newmarket, Suffolk

**FOCUS**
A very fast time indeed for the grade, 2.5 seconds faster than the classified stakes and 4.11 seconds faster than the amateur riders' event over the same trip. The first three were clear.

**NOTEBOOK**
**Apsara**, who shaped with promise when staying on last time, showed the benefit of that debut success and won cosily. She settled a lot better in front here and will improve again for this experience. It will be interesting to see where her connections aim her next and she should get further.
**Mijdaaf(FR)** looked a threat turning for home, but failed to quicken and could only keep on at the one pace thereafter. This was, however, an improvement on his debut and he will fare better once handicapped.
**Hills Spitfire(IRE)**, who showed definite promise in two backend events last year, was hard ridden from an early stage and ran as though this outing was badly needed. He has a bit to prove now, but is entitled to improve on this three-year-old debut. *Official explanation: jockey said colt was slow away and never travelling*
**Capitole(IRE)** significantly improved on his debut effort over this longer trip and will no doubt be seen to a better effect once eligible for handicaps.

## 3608 BRADLEY MAIDEN STKS 1m 4f 8y
**4:20** (4:23) (D ) 3-Y-O+ **£5,577** (£1,716; £858; £429) **Stalls** Low

Form RPR
23-4 **1** **Bendarshaan**[11] 3276 4-9-7 81 KDalgleish 3 84
(MJohnston) *hld up: pushed along and hdwy over 3f out: rdn to ld over 1f out: styd on wl* **6/4**[1]
2 **2** *2 1/2* **Jayer Gilles**[15] 3138 4-9-7 DSweeney 9 80
(HCandy) *prom: led 3f out: rdn and hdd over 1f out: styd on* **7/4**[2]
0 **3** *5* **Encompass (FR)**[33] 2632 3-8-4 ow1 WRyan 1 68
(HRACecil) *prom: rdn 4f out: outpcd by ldrs 3f out: styd on fnl 2f* **11/2**[3]
05 **4** *2 1/2* **Molehill**[16] 3121 3-8-3 JBramhill 4 63
(JGGiven) *prom: ch and rdn 3f out: wknd over 1f out* **16/1**
0 **5** *1 1/4* **Welkino's Boy**[10] 3297 3-8-8 DaleGibson 2 66?
(JMackie) *bhd: drvn along 4f out: kpt on: n.d* **100/1**
00/ **6** *11* **All Bleevable**[44] 649 7-9-7 LVickers 10 48
(MrsSLamyman) *led tl rdn and hdd 3f out: wknd 2f out* **25/1**
05 **7** *23* **Stylish Dancer**[32] 2645 3-8-3 FNorton 6 7
(MBlanshard) *towards rr: outpcd 4f out: lost tch and eased fnl f: t.o* **16/1**
00/0 **8** *dist* **Joey The Schnoze**[153] 676 6-9-0 DerekNolan(7) 11 —
(MissDAMchale) *sn prom: rdn 5f out: wknd qckly: t.o and eased fnl 2f* **100/1**
00 **9** *dist* **Charnwood Pride (IRE)**[33] 2632 3-8-8 (t) NCallan 8 —
(PWHarris) *towards rr: outpcd 5f out: t.o fnl 2f: virtually p.u* **25/1**

2m 39.82s (-0.23) **Going Correction** +0.075s/f (Good)
**WFA** 3 from 4yo+ 13lb **9** Ran **SP% 113.2**
Speed ratings: **103,101,98,96,95 88,72,—,—**CSF £4.07 TOTE £2.40: £1.10, £1.30, £2.00; EX 4.40.
**Owner** Malih L Al Basti **Bred** The Duke Of Roxburghe's Stud, Beckhampton Stables **Trained** Middleham Moor, N Yorks

**FOCUS**
A weak maiden and the field came home well strung out. The time was poor.

**NOTEBOOK**
**Bendarshaan** responded well to pressure three out and in the end ran out a ready winner. He had become frustrating last year, when with Ed Dunlop, and although his confidence will be high after this, he beat little and may struggle back in handicaps.
**Jayer Gilles** failed to improve on his debut effort, but should again come on for this run and can do better when handicapped.
**Encompass(FR)** was easy to back and ran very much to the form of her debut effort last time out. By Sadler's Wells, she may improve on easier going.
**Molehill** quickly faded in the straight, but now qualifies for handicaps and could stay further, as there is plenty of stamina in her pedigree.
**Charnwood Pride(IRE)** *Official explanation: jockey said gelding hung right again*

## 3609 KING RICHARD III STKS (FILLIES' H'CAP) 1m 4y
**4:55** (4:55) (E ) (0-70,67) 3-Y-O+ **£4,914** (£1,512; £756; £378) **Stalls** Low

Form RPR
0550 **1** **Hula Ballew**[10] 3301 4-8-12 51 (p) SWKelly 4 67
(MDods) *midfield gng wl: hdwy over 1f out: qcknd to ld ent fnl f: sn rdn clr* **8/1**[2]
0100 **2** *6* **Estimate**[13] 3206 4-8-13 52 (v) DeanMcKeown 5 54
(JohnAHarris) *prom: hmpd over 6f out: drvn along over 2f out: styd on fnl f to go 2nd clsg stages* **25/1**
6030 **3** *1/2* **Nuzzle**[13] 3191 4-8-6 45 (v) FNorton 8 46
(MQuinn) *led tl rdn and hdd ent fnl f: no ex* **9/1**
2405 **4** *3/4* **Graceful Air (IRE)**[19] 3004 3-8-11 59 (p) RWinston 13 58
(JRWeymes) *towards rr: hdwy 3f out: in tch and rdn 2f out: kpt on u.p fnl f* **22/1**
-000 **5** *1 1/4* **Lark In The Park (IRE)**[16] 3117 4-7-12 42 (t) BSwarbrick(5) 11 38
(WMBrisbourne) *hld up: hdwy u.p 2f out: kpt on fnl f: n.d* **33/1**
0600 **6** *3/4* **Spark Up**[10] 3301 4-9-3 59 SHitchcott(3) 10 54
(JWUnett) *dwlt: towards rr: reminder over 3f out: kpt on u.p fnl 2f: n.d* **16/1**
0063 **7** *2* **Uno Mente**[16] 3117 5-9-0 53 KimTinkler 12 43
(DonEnricoIncisa) *rr: sme hdwy whn nt clr run over 1f out: n.d* **17/2**[3]
5-51 **8** *1/2* **Sharp Secret (IRE)**[16] 3117 6-9-1 57 LisaJones(3) 1 46
(JARToller) *hld up in rr: effrt 2f out: kpt on fnl f: n.d* **2/1**[1]
0000 **9** *2* **Aimee's Delight**[3] 3536 4-10-0 67 MFenton 14 51
(JGGiven) *cl up: ev ch and rdn 2f out: wknd appr fnl f* **14/1**
0-34 **10** *1 1/4* **Cyclonic Storm**[13] 3200 5-9-7 60 (b[1]) GParkin 7 42
(RAFahey) *slowly away: hld up: hdwy over 3f out: chsng ldrs and rdn 2f out: sn btn* **9/1**
-000 **11** *1* **Cut Ridge (IRE)**[27] 2778 5-8-2 41 ow1 PBradley 2 20
(JSWainwright) *keen: cl up: hung rt bnd over 6f out: ev ch over 2f out: wknd over 1f out* **33/1**
-006 **12** *3 1/2* **Balmacara**[22] 2943 5-8-6 45 SCarson 6 16
(MissKBBoutflower) *prom: rdn 3f out: sn wknd* **9/1**
3250 **13** *3 1/2* **Oh So Rosie (IRE)**[6] 3412 4-8-11 57 DerekNolan(7) 3 20
(JSMoore) *dwlt: hld up: effrt 3f out: sn rdn and btn* **8/1**[2]
600- **14** *1* **Hum (IRE)**[255] 5745 3-8-8 56 NCallan 9 17
(MissDAMchale) *dwlt: hld up: effrt 3f out: sn rdn and btn* **25/1**

1m 46.01s (0.41) **Going Correction** +0.075s/f (Good)
**WFA** 3 from 4yo+ 9lb **14** Ran **SP% 126.6**
Speed ratings: **100,94,93,92,91 90,88,88,86,85 84,80,77,76**CSF £207.49 CT £1854.84 TOTE £12.30: £3.20, £7.70, £2.80; EX 330.20.
**Owner** Mrs J W Hutchinson & Mrs P A Knox **Bred** T K & Mrs P A Knox **Trained** Piercebridge, Co Durham

**FOCUS**
A very ordinary fillies' contest that saw the field strung out behind the easy winner.

**NOTEBOOK**
**Hula Ballew**, who has dropped in the weights this year on account of her loss of form, relished the change of tactics and quickened up nicely off the strong pace to win comfortably. A rise in the weights is inevitable, but she would go very close under a penalty and holding her up could be the making of her. *Official explanation: trainer said, regarding the improved form shown, filly has shown a tendency to run free in her races but settled better today*
**Estimate ◆**, dropping back a furlong, was no match for the winner, but would have been closer but for meeting interference early on. This was an improved effort and she can score off this mark when upped in trip once more.
**Nuzzle** had no more to give when headed in the final furlong. She ran her race but is a very hard horse to win with.
**Graceful Air(IRE)**, who found seven furlongs too sharp last time, ran her race back over this extra furlong and with cheekpieces reapplied, but remains a maiden after 16 outings.
**Sharp Secret(IRE)**, who bounced back to form last time, never looked like following up off this 2lb higher mark and ran well below par. *Official explanation: trainer said mare failed to get the run of the race*

## 3610 MONKHILL CLASSIFIED STKS 1m 2f 6y
**5:25** (5:26) (D ) 3-Y-O **£5,408** (£1,664; £832; £416) **Stalls** Low

Form RPR
001 **1** **Trew Class**[24] 2888 3-8-12 76 TQuinn 7 80
(MHTompkins) *cl up: led over 2f out: rdn and hdd over 1f out: styd on wl u.p to ld again ins fnl f* **11/2**[3]
2252 **2** *1/2* **My Paris**[23] 2906 3-9-3 78 NCallan 5 84
(KARyan) *trckd ldrs: led over 1f out: rdn and hdd ins fnl f: no ex* **9/1**
15-6 **3** *2 1/2* **Night Spot**[56] 2018 3-9-5 80 RWinston 4 81
(RCharlton) *hld up: hdwy 3f out: chsd first 2 fnl 2f: kpt on: no imp* **3/1**[1]
2445 **4** *1 1/4* **Cartronageeraghlad (IRE)**[3] 3543 3-9-2 77 SWKelly 2 76
(JAOsborne) *hld up: effrt whn nt clr run briefly 2f out: sn rdn: kpt on fnl f: nvr able to chal* **3/1**[1]
0042 **5** *4* **Heversham (IRE)**[6] 3427 3-9-0 73 MTebbutt 3 66
(JHetherton) *led: hung rt over 3f out: hdd over 2f out: sn btn* **16/1**
3222 **6** *5* **Awesome Love (USA)**[14] 3168 3-9-2 77 KDalgleish 1 59
(MJohnston) *trckd ldrs: effrt over 2f out: sn rdn and btn* **4/1**[2]
310 **7** *1 1/4* **Yaahomm**[28] 2751 3-8-13 77 (v[1]) DNolan(3) 6 56
(DRLoder) *towards rr: rdn 3f out: sn btn* **12/1**

2m 13.63s (-0.28) **Going Correction** +0.075s/f (Good) **7** Ran **SP% 113.2**
Speed ratings: **104,103,101,100,97 93,92**CSF £36.96 TOTE £6.90: £3.40, £2.90; EX 67.40 Place 6 £34.21, Place 5 £17.69.
**Owner** Russell Trew Roofing Ltd **Bred** Aylesfield Farms Stud **Trained** Newmarket, Suffolk

**FOCUS**
A tight-knit affair run at just a steady gallop.

**NOTEBOOK**
**Trew Class** followed up her recent Sandown maiden win in game fashion. She was handy throughout, kicked for home before two out and did well to battle back having been headed entering the final furlong. She loves this ground and looks progressive, but the race was run to suit this time.
**My Paris** looked to get worried out of it close home, having gone past the eventual winner approaching the final furlong. Although he has a habit of finding one too good, he is consistent and may be slightly better when reverting to shorter.
**Night Spot** stayed on the best of those to be held up off the steady gallop and is capable of better, granted a true pace. He remains fairly unexposed.
**Cartronageeraghlad(IRE)** was another who found the early pace against him. However, he does seem weighted to his best at present.
**Heversham(IRE)**, making his debut for new connections, set the modest pace, but did not look to stay this trip. *Official explanation: jockey said colt hung right*
**Awesome Love(USA)** again disappointed and looks regressive.
T/Plt: £51.90 to a £1 stake. Pool: £35,826.00. 503.40 winning tickets. T/Qpdt: £18.40 to a £1 stake. Pool: £2,526.50. 101.20 winning tickets. JF

# 3376 SOUTHWELL (L-H)
Tuesday, July 6

**OFFICIAL GOING: Standard**
Wind: nil Weather: fine

## 3611 ST MARIA GORETTI'S DAY MAIDEN AUCTION STKS 7f (F)
**6:30** (6:31) (E ) 2-Y-O **£3,454** (£1,063; £531; £265) **Stalls** Low

Form RPR
2 **1** **Prize Fighter (IRE)**[17] 3083 2-8-9 AMcCarthy 7 79+
(PWChapple-Hyam) *hld up in tch: wnt 2nd over 2f out: rdn to ld wl over 1f out: r.o wl* **4/5**[1]
062 **2** *3* **Chutney Mary (IRE)**[14] 3164 2-8-5 TPQueally 11 68
(JGPortman) *w ldr: led over 3f out: rdn over 2f out: hdd wl over 1f out: one pce* **11/1**
**3** *8* **Uncle Bulgaria (IRE)** 2-8-8 SSanders 10 51
(GCBravery) *rdn over 4f out: hdwy over 3f out: one pce fnl 2f* **11/2**[2]
303 **4** *1 1/2* **Llamadas**[17] 3080 2-8-7 (p) LEnstone(3) 2 49
(MDods) *sn pushed along: rdn over 4f out: hdwy 2f out: sn no imp* **12/1**
62 **5** *1 3/4* **Ming Vase**[6] 3377 2-8-1 DTudhope(7) 1 42
(DCarroll) *bhd: rdn and hdwy over 2f out: no further prog* **6/1**[3]
00 **6** *1* **Gardasee (GER)**[12] 3233 2-8-8 DaleGibson 8 40
(TPTate) *sn outpcd: nvr nr ldrs* **66/1**

50 **7** *1 ¼* **Classic Style (IRE)**[12] 3233 2-8-6 ............ DAllan 5 35
(TDEasterby) *chsd ldrs: rdn over 4f out: wknd 3f out* **40/1**

0 **8** *½* **Mister Aziz (IRE)**[45] 2300 2-8-9 ............ DHolland 12 37
(JMPEustace) *prom tl rdn and wknd 2f out* **20/1**

060 **9** *20* **Oldstead Flyer (IRE)**[10] 3319 2-8-7 ............ FLynch 6 —
(DCarroll) *led over 3f: sn wknd: t.o* **80/1**

403 **10** *19* **Monashee Miss**[11] 3278 2-8-2 ............ DKinsella 3 —
(JAPickering) *prom: rdn over 3f out: sn wknd: t.o* **100/1**

0 **11** *hd* **Welcome Dream**[83] 1390 2-8-2 ............ JQuinn 9 —
(MrsADuffield) *a bhd: t.o* **25/1**

1m 30.71s (-0.09) **Going Correction** -0.20s/f (Stan) **11** Ran SP% **116.0**
Speed ratings: **92,88,79,77,75 74,73,72,49,28 27**CSF £9.97 TOTE £1.50: £1.02, £3.20, £2.10; EX 10.20.
**Owner** Diamond Racing Ltd **Bred** G Dunne **Trained** Newmarket, Suffolk

**FOCUS**
This looks a decent race for the track and class.

**NOTEBOOK**
**Prize Fighter(IRE)** had less to do than when narrowly beaten on his turf debut at Lingfield last month.
**Chutney Mary(IRE)** again showed how well she stays on this switch to sand and came clear of the others. She can take a similar event.
**Uncle Bulgaria(IRE)** shaped as if he is going to need further which his breeding would suggest.
**Llamadas**, again up in distance, was fitted with cheekpieces for this switch to sand.
**Ming Vase** was rather disappointing, having come in for some market support based on his second over course and distance last week.
**Oldstead Flyer(IRE)** *Official explanation: jockey said colt was very weak and tired rapidly*
**Monashee Miss** *Official explanation: jockey said filly lost her action*
**Welcome Dream** *Official explanation: jockey said filly was moving awkwardly and never travelling*

## 3612 NATIONAL PICKLE FESTIVAL (S) H'CAP 1m (F)
**7:00** (7:04) (G) (0-55,50) 3-Y-0+ **£2,597** (£742; £371) **Stalls** Low

Form RPR

0642 **1** **Bulawayo**[19] 3024 7-9-8 **47** ............(b) BSwarbrick(5) 5 57
(AndrewReid) *t.k.h: trckd ldr: led 3f out: rdn 2f out: hung lft 1f out: r.o* **10/3**[1]

0000 **2** *3* **Late Arrival**[22] 2938 7-9-2 **36** ............(v) DarrenWilliams 3 40
(MDHammond) *s.i.s: hld up: hdwy over 3f out: rdn over 2f out: kpt on to take 2nd nr fin: nt trble wnr* **8/1**

0-10 **3** *½* **Tancred Miss**[19] 3006 5-9-3 **40** ............ TEaves(3) 6 43
(DWBarker) *a.p: rdr over 2f out: chsd wnr fnl f: no imp* **12/1**

2153 **4** *6* **Countrywide Girl (IRE)**[8] 3376 5-9-5 **39** ............ FLynch 7 30
(ABerry) *led 5f: sn rdn: wknd fnl f* **11/2**[2]

0043 **5** *3* **Shotley Dancer**[18] 3060 5-8-9 **36** ............ SuzanneFrance(7) 8 21
(NBycroft) *s.i.s: hld up: no real prog fnl 2f* **13/2**

0001 **6** *2 ½* **Mister Completely (IRE)**[13] 3193 3-9-7 **50** ............ NPollard 4 30
(JRBest) *prom: rdn over 3f out: wknd over 2f out* **6/1**[3]

2400 **7** *2 ½* **Sea Ya Maite**[8] 3380 10-9-6 **40** ............(t) JBramhill 10 15
(SRBowring) *in tch: rdn 4f out: wknd over 2f out* **16/1**

0040 **8** *10* **Mehmaas**[2] 3559 8-9-9 **43** ............(v) RFfrench 2 —
(REBarr) *w ldr 4f: rdn and wknd 3f out* **15/2**

-000 **9** *25* **Forest Queen**[33] 2620 7-8-0 **27** oh7............ PPMathers(7) 1 —
(KWHogg) *s.i.s: a bhd: t.o fnl 3f* **66/1**

1m 43.17s (-1.43) **Going Correction** -0.20s/f (Stan)
**WFA** 3 from 5yo+ 9lb **9** Ran SP% **104.0**
Speed ratings: **99,96,95,89,86 84,81,71,46**CSF £23.60 CT £176.25 TOTE £3.70: £1.30, £3.30, £2.30; EX 32.00.The winner was bought in for 3,200gns.
**Owner** A S Reid **Bred** D J Allen **Trained** Mill Hill, London NW7

**FOCUS**
A typically modest selling handicap which went to form.

**NOTEBOOK**
**Bulawayo**, who caught a tartar in a similar event over seven here last month, was scoring for the first time both at this track and over a mile.
**Late Arrival** was in selling company for the first time on this return to the All-Weather.
**Tancred Miss** has yet to prove she can be effective at this distance.
**Countrywide Girl(IRE)** had her stamina limitations exposed.

## 3613 MUSIC FOR LIFE MEDIAN AUCTION MAIDEN STKS 1m (F)
**7:30** (7:35) (F) 3-4-Y-0 **£2,919** (£834; £417) **Stalls** Low

Form RPR

3- **1** **Rumour**[340] 3763 4-9-2 ............ OUrbina 2 75+
(JRFanshawe) *a gng wl: sn trcking ldr: carried hd awkwardly and led over 1f out: pushed clr: comf* **13/8**[1]

2-40 **2** *5* **Telefonica (USA)**[31] 2694 3-8-7 74............ FLynch 3 65
(SirMichaelStoute) *mde most: rdn and hdd over 1f out: sn btn* **11/2**[3]

4 **3** *4* **Dafina (IRE)**[16] 3129 4-9-2 ............ DHolland 9 57
(HMorrison) *prom: rdn and outpcd 3f out: styd on again fnl f* **5/2**[2]

00 **4** *2* **Petrolina (IRE)**[24] 2882 3-8-7 ............ JQuinn 7 53
(HMorrison) *w ldr: rdn 4f out: wknd over 1f out* **50/1**

00-2 **5** *2 ½* **Go Free**[26] 2815 3-8-12 56............ ANicholls 4 53
(AMHales) *prom: rdn 4f out: wknd wl over 1f out* **12/1**

-055 **6** *2* **Viola Da Braccio (IRE)**[20] 2977 3-8-7 63............ RFfrench 6 44
(DJDaly) *reluctant and led to post: s.i.s: bhd tl sme hdwy over 1f out: nvr nr ldrs* **14/1**

2-00 **7** *¾* **Super King**[24] 2900 3-8-5 65............ SuzanneFrance(7) 5 48
(NBycroft) *s.i.s: bhd fnl 3f* **33/1**

50 **8** *12* **Too Keen**[12] 3251 3-8-4 ............ TEaves(3) 8 19
(JMJefferson) *bhd fnl 4f* **40/1**

0346 **9** *15* **Big Bad Burt**[20] 2973 3-8-5 66............(tp) DeanWilliams(7) 1 —
(GCHChung) *s.i.s: a bhd: t.o* **8/1**

00 **10** *26* **Hello Tiger**[85] 1371 3-8-5 ............ RoryMoore(7) 10 —
(JASupple) *in tch: rdn 5f out: wknd qckly: t.o fnl 2f* **100/1**

1m 42.39s (-2.21) **Going Correction** -0.20s/f (Stan)
**WFA** 3 from 4yo 9lb **10** Ran SP% **115.9**
Speed ratings: **103,98,94,92,89 87,86,74,59,33**CSF £10.83 TOTE £2.60: £1.10, £1.60, £1.50; EX 14.80.
**Owner** T & J Vestey **Bred** T R G Vestey **Trained** Newmarket, Suffolk

**FOCUS**
This was not very competitive and the value of the form remains to be seen.

**NOTEBOOK**
**Rumour** has obviously been difficult to train but proved much too good for this lot despite her demeanour. Connections will have to hope the Handicapper does not take this defeat of a 74-rated filly literally.
**Telefonica(USA)**, trying her luck on sand, was swiftly brushed aside by the winner after travelling well in the lead. She has yet to really prove she stays a mile.
**Dafina(IRE)** ◆ needs a return to a longer trip and is better than this bare form suggests.

## 3614 CROWNING OF RICHARD THE LIONHEART H'CAP 1m 4f (F)
**8:00** (8:00) (E) (0-75,75) 3-Y-0+ **£3,334** (£1,026; £513; £256) **Stalls** Low

Form RPR

000- **1** **Elusive Dream**[220] 6091 3-8-1 **61**............ JMackay 9 75+
(SirMarkPrescott) *dwlt: sn rcvrd: hdwy over 7f out: rdn 3f out: hung rt 2f out: sn hdd: led and hung rt ins fnl f: r.o* **4/1**[3]

0022 **2** *5* **Midshipman**[8] 3380 6-8-8 **55**............(vt) IMongan 2 66+
(AWCarroll) *s.i.s: hdwy over 7f out: rdn and w wnr whn carried rt 2f out: sn led: hdd and hmpd ins fnl f: n* **13/8**[1]

1150 **3** *2 ½* **Red Forest (IRE)**[13] 3199 5-9-2 **63**............(t) DaleGibson 7 65
(JMackie) *hld up: hdwy over 8f out: rdn over 3f out: one pce fnl 2f* **3/1**[2]

0-60 **4** *1 ½* **Alpine Special (IRE)**[29] 2732 3-8-9 **69**............ GFaulkner 4 69
(PCHaslam) *t.k.h: prom: rdn over 3f out: wknd fnl f* **14/1**

-003 **5** *8* **Mexican (USA)**[48] 2231 5-7-9 **45** oh8............(p) LisaJones(3) 10 33
(MDHammond) *hld up: hdwy over 3f out: wknd over 2f out* **25/1**

0000 **6** *½* **Caroubier (IRE)**[13] 3198 4-9-7 **75**............ SaleemGolam(7) 6 62
(JGallagher) *hld up: hdwy over 3f out: wknd 2f out* **16/1**

1030 **7** *8* **Dance World**[33] 2612 4-9-11 **75**............ BReilly(3) 8 50
(MissJFeilden) *hld up: lost pl over 7f out: hdwy over 4f out: wknd wl over 1f out* **9/1**

1023 **8** *4* **Magic Amigo**[23] 2906 3-9-0 **74**............ DHolland 1 43
(JRJenkins) *prom: led 7f out tl over 4f out: wknd over 3f out* **9/1**

6006 **9** *11* **Mcqueen (IRE)**[19] 3023 4-9-7 **68**............ DSweeney 5 21
(MrsHDalton) *dwlt: rdn 5f out: a bhd* **16/1**

000- **10** *dist* **Midmaar (IRE)**[199] 6222 3-8-3 **63**............ FNorton 3 —
(MWigham) *led 5f: wknd over 5f out: t.o fnl 3f* **40/1**

2m 37.53s (-4.57) **Going Correction** -0.20s/f (Stan)
**WFA** 3 from 4yo+ 13lb **10** Ran SP% **127.8**
Speed ratings: **107,103,102,101,95 95,90,87,80,—**CSF £12.07 CT £24.15 TOTE £3.60: £3.50, £1.10, £2.40; EX 22.20.
**Owner** Cheveley Park Stud **Bred** Cheveley Park Stud Ltd **Trained** Newmarket, Suffolk
■ Stewards Enquiry : J Mackay two-day ban: careless riding (Jul 17,19); further caution: careless riding

**FOCUS**
An eventful race with the stewards rightly allowing the result to stand. The time was creditable for the grade and the form looks sound. The runner-up has been rated as having been beaten two lengths.

**NOTEBOOK**
**Elusive Dream**, stepping up in distance on his handicap debut, proved a difficult ride and twice took the runner-up's ground. However, there seems little doubt that he was best on merit. This was a big improvement on his previous form and he can do better still. *Official explanation: trainer's representative said, regarding the improved form shown, colt had benefited from the step up in trip*
**Midshipman** was twice done no favours by the winner but it is difficult to argue it affected the final outcome given the margin of his defeat.
**Red Forest(IRE)** could not take advantage of the antics ahead of him and is probably flattered by his proximity to the runner-up.
**Alpine Special(IRE)** will need to settle better if he is going to get this sort of trip.
**Magic Amigo** *Official explanation: jockey said gelding would not face the kickback*

## 3615 BEATRIX POTTER CLASSIFIED STKS 7f (F)
**8:30** (8:34) (F) 3-Y-0+ **£2,961** (£846; £423) **Stalls** Low

Form RPR

0003 **1** **Chorus Beauty**[24] 2883 3-8-13 63............ FNorton 8 72
(GWragg) *hld up: hdwy 4f out: hrd rdn wl over 1f out: led wl ins fnl f: r.o* **7/1**

-000 **2** *½* **Merdiff**[19] 3023 5-9-9 62............ SWKelly 14 73
(WMBrisbourne) *racd wd: a.p: rdn over 2f out: ev ch ins fnl f: r.o* **16/1**

6002 **3** *½* **Teehee (IRE)**[20] 2989 6-9-4 60............(b) RMiles(3) 3 70
(BPalling) *a.p: led on bit over 2f out: rdn over 1f out: hdd and nt qckn wl ins fnl f* **4/1**[2]

3600 **4** *2* **Spindor (USA)**[41] 2406 5-9-7 60............(b) DHolland 11 65
(JAOsborne) *racd wd: hld up: hdwy over 2f out: rdn over 1f out: one pce* **20/1**

2441 **5** *2 ½* **Danger Bird (IRE)**[80] 1479 4-9-4 57............ DSweeney 10 56
(RHollinshead) *hld up: rdn over 3f out: hdwy 1f out: nt trble ldrs* **12/1**

6004 **6** *3* **Irusan (IRE)**[11] 3279 4-9-3 63............ LeanneKershaw(7) 4 54
(JeddO'Keeffe) *prom: rdn and hung lft over 2f out: wknd over 1f out* **33/1**

0300 **7** *shd* **Zarin (IRE)**[12] 3247 6-9-7 63............(b[1]) LisaJones(3) 12 54
(DWChapman) *s.i.s: nvr nrr* **25/1**

2020 **8** *½* **Zagala**[20] 2989 4-9-1 64............(t) LTreadwell(7) 9 51
(SLKeightley) *hld up and bhd: rdn over 3f out: n.d* **10/1**

0100 **9** *1 ½* **Old Bailey (USA)**[20] 2989 4-9-7 59............(v) RWinston 7 46
(TDBarron) *chsd ldrs: rdn 3f out: sn wknd* **14/1**

6306 **10** *½* **Senor Bond (USA)**[16] 3122 3-9-4 65............ FLynch 13 50
(BSmart) *led over 2f: rdn over 3f out: wknd over 1f out* **16/1**

00-0 **11** *1 ¼* **White Ledger (IRE)**[19] 3025 5-9-4 60............ THamilton(3) 5 41
(RAFahey) *rdn 4f out: a bhd* **33/1**

0012 **12** *¾* **Silver Mascot**[12] 3226 5-9-4 60............ TEaves(3) 15 40
(ISemple) *racd wd: plld hrd: hung rt over 4f out: sn bhd* **11/2**[3]

0315 **13** *hd* **Only One Legend (IRE)**[8] 3376 6-9-7 60............(b) RFfrench 6 39
(KARyan) *a bhd* **12/1**

0512 **14** *3* **Diamond Shannon (IRE)**[20] 2990 3-8-3 59............ DTudhope(7) 2 29
(DCarroll) *prom: led over 3f out: rdn and hdd over 2f out: wknd wl over 1f out* **10/3**[1]

3064 **15** *3 ½* **Feast Of Romance**[26] 2823 7-9-7 56............ IMongan 1 23
(CNAllen) *prom: led over 4f out: rdn and hdd over 3f out: wknd 2f out* **16/1**

1m 29.09s (-1.71) **Going Correction** -0.20s/f (Stan)
**WFA** 3 from 4yo+ 8lb **15** Ran SP% **134.2**
Speed ratings: **101,100,99,97,94 91,91,90,88,88 86,86,85,82,78**CSF £121.83 TOTE £8.60: £3.30, £2.60, £3.50; EX 289.10.
**Owner** Mrs Claude Lilley **Bred** B W Hills Southbank Ltd And R A N Bonnycastle **Trained** Newmarket, Suffolk

**FOCUS**
A modest event but the form looks sound. The race has been rated through the runner-up.

**NOTEBOOK**
**Chorus Beauty** had to work hard to land the spoils on this first run on Fibresand. She needs a mile now on surfaces less demanding than this.
**Merdiff** showed definite signs of a return to form and it is interesting that the only time he has been fitted with a tongue strap he won.
**Teehee(IRE)** appeared set to score when taking it up but in hindsight he was probably in front too soon.
**Spindor(USA)** travelled well for a long way before getting chopped for speed.
**Danger Bird(IRE)** found this distance on the short side.
**Senor Bond(USA)** *Official explanation: jockey said gelding would not face the kickback*

**Silver Mascot** *Official explanation: jockey said gelding had hung throughout the race*

## 3616 FESTIVAL OF BUDDHA'S EYE TOOTH H'CAP 6f (F)
**9:00** (9:05) (F) (0-55,58) 3-Y-0+ **£3,024** (£864; £432) **Stalls** Low

Form RPR

103 **1** **Jonny Ebeneezer**[19] 3024 5-9-7 **51**....(b[1]) RSmith 14 64
(DFlood) *a.p: led 3f out: rdn over 1f out: drvn out* **11/2**[3]

4163 **2** *2* **Mallia**[11] 3277 11-8-8 **45**.... Laura-JayneCrawford[(7)] 16 52
(TDBarron) *mid-div: rdn over 3f out: hdwy on outside over 1f out: r.o ins fnl f: nt rch wnr* **13/2**

0306 **3** *3/4* **Ace-Ma-Vahra**[8] 3381 6-9-2 **46**....(b) JBramhill 11 51
(SRBowring) *chsd ldrs: rdn over 2f out: kpt on ins fnl f* **20/1**

6000 **4** *3/4* **Aguila Loco (IRE)**[26] 2803 5-9-8 **52**....(p) FNorton 10 55
(MrsStefLiddiard) *led 3f: sn rdn: no ex ins fnl f* **12/1**

3106 **5** *shd* **Levelled**[10] 3314 10-8-12 **45**.... LisaJones[(3)] 8 47
(DWChapman) *chsd ldrs: rdn over 2f out: one pce fnl f* **18/1**

5205 **6** *1/2* **Lucius Verrus (USA)**[8] 3381 4-9-6 **50**....(v) DarrenWilliams 9 51
(DShaw) *dwlt: bhd tl hdwy over 1f out: fin wl* **7/1**

2462 **7** *1* **Indian Music**[8] 3381 7-8-10 **40**.... FLynch 1 38
(ABerry) *bhd tl hdwy over 1f out: nrst fin* **7/2**[1]

6500 **8** *nk* **Attorney**[8] 3378 6-9-10 **54**....(e) DHolland 12 51
(DShaw) *chsd ldrs: outpcd 3f out: kpt on ins fnl f* **12/1**

6501 **9** *1/2* **Boisdale (IRE)**[8] 3381 6-9-7 **58** 6ex.... LTreadwell[(7)] 6 53
(SLKeightley) *chsd ldrs: rdn over 2f out: wknd fnl f* **4/1**[2]

2100 **10** *3 1/2* **Alastair Smellie**[11] 3277 8-9-0 **47**....(v) LPKeniry[(3)] 4 32
(SLKeightley) *s.i.s: sn mid-div: rdn over 3f out: sn bhd* **33/1**

3451 **11** *1 3/4* **Sotonian (HOL)**[42] 2384 11-8-3 **38**.... StephanieHollinshead[(5)] 5 18
(PSFelgate) *prom: rdn over 3f out: wknd 2f out* **33/1**

30-6 **12** *1/2* **Coco Reef**[12] 3229 3-9-5 **55**.... DSweeney 13 33
(BPalling) *w ldrs tl rdn and wknd 2f out* **20/1**

0/00 **13** *1 3/4* **Nifty Roy**[43] 2356 4-8-5 **35**.... ADaly 7 8
(KWHogg) *sn outpcd* **50/1**

0000 **14** *3 1/2* **Speedfit Free (IRE)**[9] 3337 7-8-13 **43**....(v) AnnStokell 2 5
(MissAStokell) *a bhd* **25/1**

00-0 **15** *3 1/2* **The Copt**[11] 3282 5-8-8 **38**....(t) VHalliday 3 —
(MrsSLamyman) *dwlt: rdn 4f out: a bhd* **66/1**

1m 16.85s (-0.05) **Going Correction** -0.20s/f (Stan)
**WFA** 3 from 4yo+ 6lb **15** Ran SP% **126.8**
Speed ratings: **92,89,88,87,87 86,85,84,84,79 77,76,74,69,64**CSF £40.05 CT £509.61 TOTE £5.80: £1.90, £3.40, £6.00; EX 52.00 Place 6 £41.30, Place 5 £14.60.
**Owner** Mrs Ruth M Serrell **Bred** John Purcell **Trained** Upper Lambourn, Berks

**FOCUS**
This was no better than a seller and the time was slow for the class. The form looks sound for the level.

**NOTEBOOK**
**Jonny Ebeneezer** , thrown in on last year's form, was blinkered for the first time on this drop back to six.
**Mallia** continues to run well but found the winner had gone beyond recall.
**Ace-Ma-Vahra** seems worth a try back over further.
**Aguila Loco(IRE)**, not inconvenienced by a return to Fibresand, only gave best in the closing stages.
**Levelled** is more effective at the minimum distance on this surface.
**Lucius Verrus(USA)** again found himself with too much to do after a poor start.
T/Plt: £41.30 to a £1 stake. Pool: £40,116.90. 707.45 winning tickets. T/Qpdt: £14.60 to a £1 stake. Pool: £2,680.70. 135.80 winning tickets. KH

3617 - 3619a (Foreign Racing) - See Raceform Interactive

# [3406]CATTERICK (L-H)
Wednesday, July 7

**OFFICIAL GOING: Good to firm**
It was very difficult for horses to come from off the pace at this meeting and those that managed to do so deserve extra credit.

## 3620 JOHN CHURCH (S) STKS 5f
**2:30** (2:30) (G) 2-Y-0 **£2,891** (£826; £413) **Stalls** Low

Form RPR

0034 **1** **Almaty Express**[2] 3577 2-8-11.... RWinston 4 52
(MTodhunter) *trckd ldrs: short of room 3f out: drvn along and swtchd rt over 1f out: r.o wl u.p fnl f: led post* **4/5**[1]

**2** *hd* **Dispol In Mind** 2-8-6.... RFitzpatrick 7 46
(PTMidgley) *chsd ldrs: rdn to ld appr fnl f: r.o: ct post* **14/1**

0633 **3** *2 1/2* **Danehill Fairy (IRE)**[22] 2960 2-8-6....(v) JCarroll 3 38
(MrsADuffield) *led tl rdn and hdd appr fnl f: no ex* **2/1**[2]

60 **4** *1* **Cash Time**[6] 3444 2-8-6.... PMQuinn 6 34
(JO'Reilly) *dwlt: bhd: rdn 1/2-way: kpt on fnl 2f: n.d* **25/1**

4100 **5** *3 1/2* **Bowland Bride (IRE)**[12] 3278 2-7-13....(b[1]) PPMathers[(7)] 2 22
(ABerry) *s.i.s: in tch tl outpcd 1/2-way* **12/1**[3]

0000 **6** *3 1/2* **Hunipot**[7] 3408 2-8-6....(b[1]) RFfrench 5 10
(MESowersby) *cl up: ev ch 2f out: rdn and wknd qckly over 1f out* **40/1**

61.79 secs (1.19) **Going Correction** 0.0s/f (Good) **6** Ran SP% **109.5**
Speed ratings: **90,89,85,84,78 72**CSF £13.05 TOTE £1.80: £1.10, £6.70; EX 13.80.Dispol In Mind was claimed by Ian Wood for £6,000.
**Owner** Abbadis Racing Club **Bred** P G Airey **Trained** Orton, Cumbria

**FOCUS**
A moderate juvenile seller and only the front pair showed any real encouragement for the future.

**NOTEBOOK**
**Almaty Express**, back in selling company, appeared to have quite a bit to do at halfway but he picked up well and nailed the runner-up right on the line. He may be capable of more given an extra furlong or a slower surface.
**Dispol In Mind**, a 5,500gns half-sister to Bonny Ruan, has very much a speed-oriented pedigree and despite drifting badly in the market showed good pace on this debut, only having the race snatched from her on the line. She dumped her rider soon afterwards, but that did not stop Ian Wood from claiming her for £6,000.
**Danehill Fairy(IRE)** made the running as usual, but once again did not get home. She probably prefers easier ground, but looks totally exposed.
**Cash Time** was not suited by the drop back to five. *Official explanation: jockey said filly ran very greenly*
**Bowland Bride(IRE)** was not suited by the drop back in trip or the first-time blinkers.

## 3621 DRAGON TROOP TURMERIC H'CAP 1m 7f 177y
**3:05** (3:06) (D) (0-85,83) 3-Y-0+ **£5,443** (£1,675; £837; £418) **Stalls** Low

Form RPR

1-31 **1** **Yoshka**[20] 3020 3-8-5 **81**.... RFfrench 3 97+
(MJohnston) *trckd ldrs: wnt 2nd over 3f out: led 2f out: drifted rt fr over 1f out: styd on u.p* **1/1**[1]

2610 **2** *3/4* **Tiyoun (IRE)**[26] 2855 6-9-10 **81**.... DarrenWilliams 5 88
(JeddO'Keeffe) *hld up: effrt over 3f out: wnt 2nd ent fnl f: styd on wl u.p: no imp on wnr clsng stages* **14/1**

1621 **3** *5* **Tudor Bell (IRE)**[13] 3244 3-8-7 **83**.... DSweeney 6 84
(JGMO'Shea) *led tl rdn and hdd 2f out: no ex* **2/1**[2]

00-0 **4** *3 1/2* **Hope Sound (IRE)**[13] 3236 4-8-1 **61** ow1....(p) THamilton[(3)] 2 58
(BEllison) *hld up: sme hdwy u.p over 2f out: no further prog fr over 1f out* **16/1**

4403 **5** *2 1/2* **Ocean Tide**[17] 3120 7-8-8 **70**....(b) BSwarbrick[(5)] 4 64
(RFord) *cl up: rdn 4f out: wknd 3f out* **6/1**[3]

2000 **6** *hd* **Vicars Destiny**[30] 2731 6-8-8 **65**.... RWinston 1 59
(MrsSLamyman) *hld up: effrt 4f out: no hdwy* **20/1**

3m 25.89s (-5.51) **Going Correction** -0.20s/f (Firm)
**WFA** 3 from 4yo+ 19lb **6** Ran SP% **114.9**
Speed ratings: **105,104,102,100,99 99**CSF £17.27 TOTE £1.80: £1.30, £3.70; EX 10.00.
**Owner** Saeed Buhaleeba **Bred** Bloomsbury Stud **Trained** Middleham Moor, N Yorks

**FOCUS**
A fair little staying handicap run at a decent pace and it is likely we will be hearing a lot more of the winner.

**NOTEBOOK**
**Yoshka ◆**, raised 5lb for his Ripon victory, relished the longer trip as befits a half-brother to Royal Rebel. Taking over soon after turning for home, he ran on right to the line despite drifting out into the centre of the track to record his third win from just four outings. He is probably still learning and looks a smart staying handicapper in the making.
**Tiyoun(IRE)** showed his York running to be all wrong and gave valiant chase to the winner down the home straight. He could never quite take advantage of the winner hanging, but still pulled right away from the others and will not always run into such a progressive type.
**Tudor Bell(IRE)**, raised another 5lb following his Salisbury win, set the pace but was rather easily picked off after turning for home. The Handicapper may have caught up with him, but equally this was his first attempt beyond 14 furlongs and he may not have seen it out.
**Hope Sound(IRE)**, having only his fifth outing on the Flat, could never get into the thick of the action and may prefer easier ground.
**Ocean Tide** ended up well beaten and there seemed no obvious excuse.

## 3622 5TH REGIMENT ROYAL ARTILLERY H'CAP 7f
**3:40** (3:40) (E) (0-75,73) 3-Y-0 **£3,532** (£1,087; £543; £271) **Stalls** Low

Form RPR

3541 **1** **Willjojo**[13] 3229 3-8-1 **53**....(v) RFfrench 1 62
(RAFahey) *trckd ldrs: chal 2f out: sn rdn: led ent fnl f: styd on* **5/1**[3]

0204 **2** *1 1/4* **Reidies Choice**[18] 3101 3-9-7 **73**.... MFenton 3 81+
(JGGiven) *s.i.s: hld up: hdwy whn hmpd over 1f out: styd on fnl f: nt trble wnr* **7/2**[1]

0020 **3** *1/2* **True (IRE)**[11] 3301 3-8-11 **63**.... RWinston 7 67
(MrsSLamyman) *dwlt: hld up: hdwy 2f out: hung lft and nt clr run appr fnl f and ins fnl f: styd on towards fin* **25/1**

5000 **4** *nk* **Bowling Along**[9] 3372 3-8-1 **56** ow3.... THamilton[(3)] 5 59
(MESowersby) *sn led: hrd pressed and rdn 2f out: hdd 1f out: no ex* **16/1**

334- **5** *1 1/2* **Christina's Dream**[275] 5422 3-9-7 **73**.... DeanMcKeown 4 72
(PWHarris) *in tch: short of room and checked over 2f out: nt clr run and swtchd rt over 1f out: no hdwy fnl f* **9/2**[2]

006- **6** *1* **Midnight Prince**[263] 5632 3-8-1 **53**.... DaleGibson 2 49
(MWEasterby) *prom early: bhd 1/2-way: styd on fnl 2f: n.d* **66/1**

1602 **7** *nk* **Saros (IRE)**[9] 3368 3-7-8 **53**.... MStainton[(7)] 9 48
(BSmart) *prom: rdn over 2f out: wknd over 1f out* **5/1**[3]

3-33 **8** *hd* **Mistress Twister**[18] 3096 3-8-13 **70**.... PMakin[(5)] 10 65
(TDBarron) *in tch: effrt over 2f out: sn rdn and btn* **8/1**

0051 **9** *1* **Shinko Femme (IRE)**[9] 3368 3-8-2 **54** 6ex.... KimTinkler 6 46
(NTinkler) *s.i.s: towards rr: rdn 2f out: no hdwy* **12/1**

300 **10** *6* **Mister Regent**[44] 2367 3-8-12 **64**....(b[1]) NCallan 8 40
(KARyan) *chsd ldrs: hung lft over 2f out: rdn and btn whn hmpd over 1f out* **10/1**

1m 25.39s (-2.11) **Going Correction** -0.20s/f (Firm) **10** Ran SP% **112.9**
Speed ratings: **104,102,102,101,99 98,98,98,97,90**CSF £22.03 CT £399.63 TOTE £6.70: £2.00, £1.30, £5.90; EX 20.90.
**Owner** The Yorkshire Lancashire Alliance **Bred** Lostford Manor Stud **Trained** Musley Bank, N Yorks

**FOCUS**
A modest handicap run at a fair pace and a creditable time for the grade. The draw played its part with the first six home coming from the bottom seven stalls.

**NOTEBOOK**
**Willjojo**, stepping up from selling company, was able to take a good position from her inside draw and showed a superior turn of foot to settle it. She is now unbeaten in two starts since being stepped up to this strip.
**Reidies Choice** ran with credit considering he met trouble in running and this was a meeting where it was very difficult to make up significant ground. He looks capable of winning a similar event off this sort of mark.
**True(IRE)**, still a maiden, is becoming well handicapped and did not enjoy the clearest of passages, but that was mainly due to her hanging towards the inside rail in the home straight. She does not look an easy ride.
**Bowling Along**, who boasts a record of one win and three placings from five previous visits here, tried to make all the running but did not get home. Her style of running is suited to this track and she does not look so effective elsewhere.
**Christina's Dream**, making her handicap debut and stepping up a furlong in trip, did not enjoy a clear passage in the home straight and is worth another chance. *Official explanation: jockey said filly suffered interference in running*
**Saros(IRE)**, who should have been suited by going this way round after hanging badly left last time, still did not look happy and it may be that he needs an easier surface than this.

## 3623 LOUISBURG CLASSIFIED STKS 7f
**4:15** (4:16) (E) 3-Y-0+ **£3,445** (£1,060; £530; £265) **Stalls** Low

Form RPR

1520 **1** **Effective**[23] 2948 4-9-3 63.... NCallan 7 73
(APJarvis) *cl up: led 2f out: styd on u.p* **11/2**[3]

0052 **2** *1 3/4* **Smith N Allan Oils**[7] 3409 5-9-0 54....(p) LEnstone[(3)] 3 68
(MDods) *midfield: hmpd after 1f: rdn 3f out: hdwy 2f out: chsd wnr fnl f: no imp* **4/1**[1]

0010 **3** *1 3/4* **Sir Don (IRE)**[11] 3298 5-9-4 66....(v) AlexGreaves 11 64
(DNicholls) *chsd ldrs: rdn over 2f out: kpt on same pce* **9/1**

0350 **4** *nk* **Scotland The Brave**[22] 2963 4-9-1 66.... DSweeney 1 60
(JDBethell) *chsd ldrs: rdn over 1f out: no ex* **9/2**[2]



The Form Book, Raceform Ltd, Compton, RG20 6NL

0-11 **5** *1 3/4* **Tap**[60] 1971 7-8-10 58.....(p) DFentiman(7) 4 58
(IanEmmerson) *cl up early: sn midfield: rdn 2f out: kpt on fnl f* **13/2**

4135 **6** *1* **College Maid (IRE)**[13] 3225 7-8-7 62..... JCurrie(7) 10 52
(JSGoldie) *hld up in rr: rdn 2f out: styd on fnl f: n.d* **7/1**

0000 **7** *1* **No Grouse**[7] 3409 4-9-5 70.....(p) THamilton(3) 9 57
(RAFahey) *midfield: drvn along over 2f out: no hdwy* **7/1**

0-50 **8** *hd* **Give Him Credit (USA)**[50] 2218 4-9-3 60.....(p) JCarroll 2 52
(MrsADuffield) *led tl hdd 2f out: fdd fnl f* **40/1**

0030 **9** *2* **Tantric**[4] 3516 5-8-10 58..... JDO'Reilly(7) 12 46
(JO'Reilly) *hld up: rdn 2f out: no hdwy* **12/1**

-005 **10** *3 1/2* **Alice Blackthorn**[23] 2937 3-7-13 64..... MStainton(7) 6 34
(BSmart) *slowly away: wl bhd whn stmbld 3f out: sme hdwy u.p appr fnl f: n.d* **20/1**

0000 **11** *5* **Arctic Burst (USA)**[20] 3010 4-9-3 63.....(v) DarrenWilliams 5 23
(DShaw) *s.i.s: hld up in rr: rdn 2f out: no hdwy* **40/1**

60/0 **12** *3* **Dragon Prince**[9] 3375 4-9-3 68..... TEaves(3) 8 18
(RCGuest) *keen: trckd ldrs to 1/2-way: sn wknd* **33/1**

1m 26.06s (-1.44) **Going Correction** -0.20s/f (Firm)
**WFA** 3 from 4yo+ 8lb **12** Ran SP% **122.2**
Speed ratings: **100,98,96,95,93 92,91,91,88,84 79,75**CSF £27.71 TOTE £8.70: £3.90, £1.70, £3.40; EX 25.30.
**Owner** Eurostrait Ltd **Bred** Peter Balding **Trained** Twyford, Bucks

**FOCUS**
A modest contest run at just a fair pace. Ordinary form.

**NOTEBOOK**
**Effective**, a dual winner on sand, had not previously won on turf and his best form has been over six furlongs, but this trip on fast ground on such a sharp track proved ideal and he was in a good position throughout. He may be able to win again under similar conditions.
**Smith N Allan Oils** was worst in on adjusted official figures, but he came into this in some sort of form and was well suited by the conditions. He could never quite get on terms with the winner, but still emerges with credit.
**Sir Don(IRE)** ran with credit under conditions that suit, especially from such a high draw, but he is a very hard horse to predict.
**Scotland The Brave**, best in on adjusted official ratings, was taking a big step down in class but it failed to bring about much improvement. She is beginning to look very disappointing.
**Tap**, bidding for a hat-trick following a short absence, broke well enough but did not try and maintain his position and was soon playing catch-up. He did stay on late, but only very slowly and would almost certainly have preferred easier ground.
**College Maid(IRE)** could never get into the race from her high draw.

## 3624 SPHINX & WORKSHOPS H'CAP 5f 212y
**4:50** (4:53) (E) (0-70,66) 3-Y-O **£3,552** (£1,093; £546; £273) **Stalls** Low

Form RPR

4010 **1** **Wendy's Girl (IRE)**[13] 3234 3-8-8 **56**.....(b) THamilton(3) 6 64
(RPElliott) *w ldr: led after 2f: rdn clr over 1f out: in command fnl f* **12/1**

0000 **2** *1 1/2* **Lord Baskerville**[7] 3407 3-8-8 **53**..... JBramhill 2 56
(WStorey) *midfield: hdwy u.p over 1f out: wnt 2nd ins fnl f: nt trble wnr* **40/1**

0500 **3** *3/4* **Uhuru Peak**[29] 2756 3-8-9 **54**..... DaleGibson 10 55
(MWEasterby) *sn bhd and pushed along: hdwy over 1f out: r.o wl fnl f: nrst fin* **25/1**

00-4 **4** *nk* **Thornaby Green**[44] 2353 3-8-11 **61**..... PMakin(5) 5 61
(TDBarron) *chsd ldrs: rdn and outpcd 1/2-way: r.o u.p fnl 2f: nvr able to chal* **10/1**[3]

-140 **5** *2* **Game Flora**[42] 2411 3-8-8 **56**..... TEaves(3) 14 50
(MESowersby) *chsd ldrs: rdn 2f out: no hdwy* **25/1**

00-0 **6** *hd* **Calculaite**[47] 2270 3-8-5 **50**..... MFenton 13 43
(MrsGSRees) *midfield: outpcd 1/2-way: kpt on u.p fnl 2f: n.d* **50/1**

0300 **7** *hd* **Sahara Silk (IRE)**[12] 3273 3-8-13 **58**.....(v) DarrenWilliams 4 51
(DShaw) *midfield: hdwy u.p 2f out: wnt 2nd appr fnl f: wknd ins last* **25/1**

0666 **8** *hd* **A Bid In Time (IRE)**[13] 3234 3-7-9 **45**..... BSwarbrick(5) 12 37
(DShaw) *slowly away: bhd: sme hdwy u.p over 1f out: no further prog fnl f* **20/1**

0315 **9** *3/4* **Champagne Cracker**[18] 3077 3-9-7 **66**..... RFfrench 1 56
(MissLAPerratt) *in tch: drvn along over 2f out: sn btn* **12/1**

0211 **10** *hd* **Cherokee Nation**[2] 3585 3-9-5 **64** 6ex..... RWinston 9 53+
(PWD'Arcy) *slowly away: towards rr: drvn along over 2f out: no hdwy* **5/6**[1]

0-00 **11** *1 1/4* **Sujosise**[14] 3201 3-8-2 **47**.....(v[1]) PFessey 3 32
(JJQuinn) *hld up: sme hdwy over 2f out: sn rdn and btn* **25/1**

2044 **12** *2* **Volaticus (IRE)**[12] 3270 3-8-13 **58**.....(v) AlexGreaves 7 37+
(DNicholls) *s.i.s: towards rr: effrt and wandered 2f out: no hdwy* **4/1**[2]

5-04 **13** *1 3/4* **Maunby Raver**[43] 2389 3-9-4 **63**.....(v[1]) GFaulkner 8 37
(PCHaslam) *led 2f: chsd wnr after: rdn over 2f out: wknd over 1f out* **14/1**

5-05 **14** *3* **Speed Racer**[12] 3267 3-8-12 **57**..... KimTinkler 11 22
(DonEnricoIncisa) *sn wl bhd* **66/1**

1m 13.26s (-0.74) **Going Correction** -0.20s/f (Firm) **14** Ran SP% **131.7**
Speed ratings: **96,94,93,92,89 89,89,89,88,87 86,83,81,77**CSF £442.49 CT £11641.27 TOTE £15.40: £3.70, £7.90, £7.20; EX 571.80.
**Owner** E Grayson **Bred** Lars Pearson **Trained** Formby, Lancs

**FOCUS**
A competitive handicap on paper, but very few got into it and the winning time was modest for the grade.

**NOTEBOOK**
**Wendy's Girl(IRE)** loves to hear her feet rattle so this return to fast ground was perfect. Soon finding herself dictating from the front, she was kicked into a clear lead off the final bend and the advantage she established was to prove decisive. She had the run of the race here, but that will not always be the case. *Official explanation: trainer said, regarding the improved form shown, filly was taken on by a loose horse and ran too freely last time, adding that she was possibly suited by today's faster ground*
**Lord Baskerville**, who is still a maiden, was awkward going down to the start but did little wrong in the race itself and came home in good style. This was a big improvement on his previous outings and much of that may have been down to a good draw.
**Uhuru Peak** ◆ put up a fair effort from his wide draw and finished to good effect. He still has a little scope and a return to further and easier ground may eventually see him off the mark.
**Thornaby Green** did not really improve much from his reappearance and considering his best previous form has been over the minimum trip, it was surprising that he ran as though finding this too sharp.
**Game Flora** did not run at all badly considering she came from the widest draw and her best previous form has been on soft ground.
**Calculaite** ran with some credit from his high draw and could be interesting back on Fibresand now that he is handicapped. *Official explanation: jockey said gelding slipped on the bend turning into the straight*
**Cherokee Nation**, bidding for a hat-trick and even with the penalty off the same mark as when winning at Ripon 48 hours earlier, ran a shocker even allowing for a modest draw. It may be that so many races close together have finally found him out. *Official explanation: jockey said colt suffered interference in running*

**Volaticus(IRE)**, backed off the boards, soon had a lot to do and get never got himself into a challenging position. He does not look an easy ride.

## 3625 SANNA'S POST MEDIAN AUCTION MAIDEN STKS 1m 5f 175y
**5:20** (5:23) (F) 3-4-Y-0 **£2,891** (£826; £413) **Stalls** Low

Form RPR

63 **1** **Silver Sash (GER)**[14] 3204 3-8-6..... MFenton 2 77+
(MLWBell) *in tch: tk clsr order over 4f out: led on bit over 3f out: drew clr over 2f out: unextended* **1/5**[1]

6-00 **2** *15* **Duncanbil (IRE)**[26] 2854 3-8-6 45..... RFfrench 3 45
(RFFisher) *keen early: trckd ldrs: drvn along and outpcd over 3f out: styd on u.p to go 2nd ins fnl f: no ch w wnr* **25/1**

0- **3** *1 1/2* **Bien Good**[247] 5905 3-8-3..... TEaves(3) 5 43
(MrsMReveley) *hld up: rdn over 5f out: styd on u.p to chse wnr 2f out: no imp: lost 2nd ins fnl f* **50/1**

00 **4** *2 1/2* **Twilight Years**[20] 3013 3-8-11..... GGibbons 6 44
(TDEasterby) *hld up: sme hdwy over 3f out: outpcd over 2f out: n.d* **33/1**

**5** *5* **Kyber** 3-8-11..... RWinston 4 37
(RFFisher) *hld up in rr: hdwy over 3f out: disp poor 2nd 2f out: wknd appr fnl f* **10/1**[2]

46 **6** *21* **Aston Lad**[20] 3015 3-8-11..... DarrenWilliams 1 8
(MDHammond) *cl up: hung rt bnd after 5f: led over 5f out: rdn and hdd over 3f out: lost tch fnl 2f: t.o* **25/1**

05 **7** *16* **I'm A Dark Horse**[23] 2934 3-8-11..... NCallan 7 —
(KARyan) *led: hung rt bnd after 5f: hdd over 5f out: wknd qckly 2f out: t.o and eased fnl f* **20/1**[3]

3m 2.14s (-2.36) **Going Correction** -0.20s/f (Firm) **7** Ran SP% **109.8**
Speed ratings: **98,89,88,87,84 72,63**CSF £9.32 TOTE £1.20: £1.10, £12.80; EX 7.70 Place 6 £144.63, Place 5 £88.15.
**Owner** Baron F C Oppenheim **Bred** Baron Fr C Von Oppenheim **Trained** Newmarket, Suffolk

**FOCUS**
Am ordinary pace, but a meaningless maiden in which the beaten horses will have to improve out of all recognition to win a race.

**NOTEBOOK**
**Silver Sash(GER)**, stepping up a long way in trip, only had to show a glimpse of her previous form to beat this field with ease and duly did so. She would have burned up more energy on the gallops and this told us little new about her, though she did appear to see the trip out well.
**Duncanbil(IRE)**, unplaced in all nine of her previous starts, was still able to put one foot in front of the other in the closing stages and that was all it took to earn her a remote second place and earn a little prize money for connections. Her official rating puts the ability of those behind her in perspective.
**Bien Good** looks very slow and hopefully she will be able to show a bit more over hurdles.
**Twilight Years** again looked very slow.
**Kyber**, a half-brother to the winning hurdler Hamadeena, made a very brief move mid-race but it came to nothing. He is another who will hopefully show a little bit more over obstacles. *Official explanation: jockey said gelding hung left handed throughout final circuit*
T/Plt: £327.90 to a £1 stake. Pool: £24,818.55. 55.25 winning tickets. T/Qpdt: £65.10 to a £1 stake. Pool: £1,760.10. 20.00 winning tickets. JF

# 3412 KEMPTON (R-H)
## Wednesday, July 7

**OFFICIAL GOING: Good to firm**
Wind: str across Weather: overcast, rain after race 4

## 3626 BETFRED "THE BONUS KING" GIRL APPRENTICE H'CAP 7f (J)
**6:30** (6:30) (E) (0-75,73) 3-Y-0+ **£4,182** (£1,287; £643; £321) **Stalls** High

Form RPR

1245 **1** **Fen Gypsy**[14] 2833 6-9-0 **59**..... DonnaBashton 5 68
(PDEvans) *lw: trckd ldrs: drvn to ld jst ins fnl f: rdn out* **6/1**[3]

-002 **2** *1/2* **Bi Polar**[30] 2727 4-10-0 **73**..... NataliaGemelova 3 81
(DRCElsworth) *lw: trckd ldrs: chal over 3f out tl slt ld 2f out: hdd jst ins fnl f: styd on but no ex cl home* **5/1**[2]

0201 **3** *1/2* **Wind Chime (IRE)**[17] 3127 7-9-7 **66**..... LisaJones 6 72+
(AGNewcombe) *bhd: hdwy over 2f out: str run ins fnl f: fin wl: nt rch ldrs* **4/1**[1]

4150 **4** *nk* **Espada (IRE)**[5] 3489 8-8-2 **52**.....(b) DanielleDeverson(5) 9 58
(JAOsborne) *swtg: slt advantage: rdn whn chal fr 4f out: narrowly hdd 2f out: kpt on same pce ins fnl f* **14/1**

0003 **5** *1/2* **Mythical Charm**[2] 3593 5-8-6 **51**.....(t) LucyRussell 7 55
(JJBridger) *lw: chsd ldrs: drvn over 2f out: styd on same pce fnl f* **10/1**

0020 **6** *nk* **Halcyon Magic**[11] 3321 6-8-3 **48**.....(b) LauraPike 1 52+
(MissJFeilden) *mid-div: outpcd over 3f out: hdwy over 1f out: styng on but nt pce to trble ldrs whn n.m.r cl home* **16/1**

3502 **7** *nk* **City General (IRE)**[7] 3425 3-7-7 **51** oh2.....(p) LauraReynolds(5) 12 54
(JSMoore) *chased ldrs: chal 4f out tl 2f out: styd on same pce appr fnl f* **20/1**

0003 **8** *hd* **Pagan Storm (USA)**[11] 3321 4-8-11 **56**.....(t) KristinStubbs 4 58
(MrsLStubbs) *bhd: pushed along 3f out: hdwy over 1f out: kpt on ins last but nvr gng pce to rch ldrs* **8/1**

0-03 **9** *3/4* **Arran**[19] 3049 4-8-8 **53**..... StephanieHollinshead 10 53
(VSmith) *b: s.i.s: bhd: sme hdwy 2f out: nvr gng pce to rch ldrs* **8/1**

2002 **10** *1/2* **Ziet D'Alsace (FR)**[15] 3174 4-8-8 **53**..... LeanneKershaw 13 52
(AWCarroll) *s.i.s: bhd: hdwy over 2f out: sn rdn: one pce fr over 1f out* **12/1**

3045 **11** *5* **Otago (IRE)**[2] 3585 3-8-4 **57**..... HayleyTurner 2 43
(JRBest) *lw: broke wl: sn bhd and n.d* **8/1**

2110 **12** *9* **Frank's Quest (IRE)**[20] 3023 4-8-5 **55**..... VictoriaHill(5) 14 18
(PBurgoyne) *in tch: chsd ldrs over 3f out: wknd qckly ins fnl 2f* **14/1**

00-0 **13** *9* **Fulvio (USA)**[25] 2883 4-9-1 **60**..... JemmaMarshall 11 —
(JamiePoulton) *lw: chsd ldrs tl wknd qckly 2f out* **16/1**

1m 27.02s (-0.25) **Going Correction** +0.125s/f (Good)
**WFA** 3 from 4yo+ 8lb **13** Ran SP% **130.9**
Speed ratings: **106,105,104,104,103 103,103,103,102,101 95,85,75**CSF £39.81 CT £142.78 TOTE £8.00: £2.60, £3.20, £1.60; EX 51.60.
**Owner** P D Evans **Bred** Juddmonte Farms **Trained** Pandy, Gwent

**FOCUS**
An ordinary apprentices' handicap, and straightforward form to assess. Most of the principals ran close to form, and while third-placed Wind Chime was a bit below, he was the only one who was not ridden prominently.

**NOTEBOOK**
**Fen Gypsy**, last seen unplaced over hurdles in June, showed a good attitude to score and posted a welcome return to form. He is best at this trip and had the race run to suit this time.
**Bi Polar** again found one too good, but ran his race and looks to be coming right again. He has slipped to a fair mark and can make amends soon.

**Wind Chime(IRE)**, a winner over an extra furlong last time, failed to hold a handy position early on and was staying on all too late in the day over this shorter trip. He will be well suited by a return to a mile and remains in good form.
**Espada(IRE)**was not beaten far, but could only muster the one pace under pressure and was unsuited by being taken on for the early lead.
**Mythical Charm** did not improve as expected for this extra furlong and may have found this coming too quick.

## 3627 EUROPEAN BREEDERS FUND MAIDEN FILLIES' STKS 7f (J)
**7:00** (7:04) (D ) 2-Y-O **£4,940** (£1,520; £760; £380) **Stalls** High

Form RPR
2 **1** **Park Law (IRE)**[14] 3202 2-8-11 ........ JFortune 7 77+
(JHMGosden) *lw: b.hind: mde all: drvn along over 1f out: styd on wl fnl f: readily* **1/1**[1]
**2** *1 1/4* **Arbella** 2-8-8 ........ NMackay(3) 1 74
(PWHarris) *gd sort: rangy: str: bit bkwd: bhd: pushed along 3f out: hdwy 2f out: str run ins fnl f to chse wnr cl home but no imp* **12/1**
**3** *3/4* **Sharaby (IRE)** 2-8-11 ........ WSupple 9 72
(EALDunlop) *neat: scope: in tch: hdwy over 2f out: chsd wnr over 1f out: no imp and lost 2nd cl home* **25/1**
**4** *nk* **Heat Of The Night** 2-8-11 ........ SSanders 8 73+
(JLDunlop) *scope: trckd ldrs: hdwy on rails whn n.m.r ins fnl 2f: kpt on fnl f but nt pce to chal* **25/1**
**5** *1/2* **Autumn Melody (FR)** 2-8-11 ........(t) LDettori 12 70
(SaeedBinSuroor) *lengthy: scope: bit bkwd: chsd ldrs: wnt 2nd over 2f out tl over 1f out: wknd last half f* **7/2**[2]
0 **6** *3* **Spinning Coin**[28] 2786 2-8-8 ........ LisaJones(3) 16 63
(JGPortman) *in tch: early: sn outpcd: drvn over 2f out: r.o wl fnl f: nt rch ldrs* **33/1**
**7** *1/2* **Hidden Chance** 2-8-11 ........ DaneO'Neill 2 61
(RHannon) *unf: bhd: rdn over 2f out: r.o fnl f: nt rch ldrs* **20/1**
06 **8** *hd* **Imperial Miss (IRE)**[17] 3123 2-8-11 ........ ADaly 15 61
(BWDuke) *trckd wnr over 4f: rdn over 2f out: wknd qckly over 1f out* **33/1**
**9** *1/2* **Take It There** 2-8-11 ........ PDobbs 3 60
(RHannon) *w'like: bhd: hdwy whn nt clr run over 2f out: r.o fr over 1f out: nt a danger* **20/1**
**10** *shd* **Par Jeu** 2-8-11 ........ BDoyle 6 59
(DJDaly) *neat: lw: hld up in tch: pushed along to chse ldrs over 2f out: wknd over 1f out* **11/2**[3]
**11** *1/2* **She's My Outsider** 2-8-11 ........ TPQueally 13 58
(IAWood) *small: bhd: veered lft over 2f out: sme hdwy fr over 1f out but nvr a danger* **33/1**
**12** *nk* **Entertain** 2-8-11 ........ JMackay 11 67+
(MLWBell) *str: cmpt: bhd: stdy hdwy fr 2f out: n.m.r over 1f out and ins last: styd on but n.d* **25/1**
**13** *3/4* **Magic Tree (UAE)** 2-8-11 ........ TEDurcan 4 55
(MRChannon) *w'like: chsd ldrs: pushed along over 2f out: wknd wl over 1f out* **20/1**
0 **14** *1 1/2* **Triple Zero (IRE)**[19] 3045 2-8-11 ........ EStack 10 52
(APJarvis) *swtg: hrd drvn over 2f out: a bhd* **50/1**
6 **15** *1 1/2* **Liameliss**[25] 2876 2-8-11 ........ CCatlin 5 48
(MAAllen) *chsd ldrs until wknd ins fnl 2f* **50/1**
**16** *8* **Big Hoo Hah** 2-8-8 ........ JFMcDonald(3) 14 28
(CACyzer) *w'like: a in rr* **33/1**

1m 28.82s (1.55) **Going Correction** +0.125s/f (Good) **16** Ran SP% **136.8**
Speed ratings: **96,94,93,93,92 89,88,88,88,87 87,86,86,84,82 73**CSF £14.72 TOTE £2.00: £1.10, £2.80, £10.40; EX 16.60.
**Owner** Sangster Family **Bred** Swettenham Stud And Hugo Lascelles **Trained** Manton, Wilts

**FOCUS**
Potentially an above average fillies' maiden which looks sure to throw up it's fair share of winners.

**NOTEBOOK**
**Park Law(IRE)**, second over course and distance last time, showed the benefit of that debut display, by readily making all. She has a lot of scope, and should take higher order in due course, most likely over a mile next year.
**Arbella** stayed on most promisingly, having run green in the early parts, and would have given the winner plenty more to think about over another 100 yards. This was a taking debut and she should have no trouble in losing her maiden tag.
**Sharaby(IRE)** ◆, a half-sister to the smart stayer Shanty Star, tired in the closing stages, but ran a race full of promise and will go a lot closer next time out.
**Heat Of The Night** was done no favours when hampered on the rail in the straight, but had travelled well up to that point and is another to have made a most promising debut. Like the majority of her yard's juveniles this season, she will improve a bundle for this experience.
**Autumn Melody(FR)** kept on at the one pace, having run distinctly green at a crucial stage. This choicely-bred filly can be expected to leave this form behind in due course.
**Par Jeu** was fairly well-supported for this debut, but faded tamely in the straight and looked to find this too hot.

## 3628 BETFRED "WE PAY DOUBLE RESULT" H'CAP 5f
**7:30** (7:34) (E ) (0-75,73) 3-Y-O **£4,114** (£1,266; £633; £316) **Stalls** Centre

Form RPR
6-00 **1** **Red Sovereign**[55] 2063 3-9-2 **68** ........ SSanders 11 77
(IAWood) *b.hind: racd far side and trckd ldr: led that side over 1f out and overall advantage 1f out: drvn out* **14/1**
3-00 **2** *2* **Minimum Bid**[18] 3084 3-8-2 **54** ........ JQuinn 1 56+
(MissBSanders) *lw: bhd: hdwy appr fnl f: str run to chse wnr ins last but no imp* **10/1**
3254 **3** *1* **Melody King**[14] 3195 3-9-1 **67** ........(b) JFortune 12 65
(PDEvans) *led far side: rdn and hdd by wnr over 1f out: one pce ins last* **6/1**[2]
0546 **4** *1/2* **Cut And Dried**[10] 3344 3-9-1 **67** ........ MartinDwyer 2 64
(DMSimcock) *chsd ldrs: rdn 1/2-way: styd on same pce fnl f* **7/1**[3]
0403 **5** *hd* **Lakeside Guy (IRE)**[12] 3262 3-8-6 **58** ........ TPQueally 7 54
(PSMcentee) *lw: led overall in centre crse: rdn 1/2-way: hdd 1f out: sn wknd* **10/1**
0046 **6** *hd* **Mirasol Princess**[25] 2889 3-9-7 **73** ........ DHolland 9 68
(DKIvory) *chsd ldrs: rdn 1/2-way: one pce fnl f* **6/1**[2]
1130 **7** *3/4* **Imperium**[25] 2877 3-9-7 **73** ........ SDrowne 6 65
(MrsStefLiddiard) *lw: chsd ldrs: rdn over 2f out: wknd fnl f* **8/1**
0005 **8** *nk* **Scarlett Breeze**[15] 3179 3-7-9 **50** oh3 ........ JFMcDonald(3) 4 41
(JWHills) *in tch: rdn to chse ldrs 2f out: outpcd fnl f* **12/1**
4-06 **9** *1/2* **Sweetest Revenge (IRE)**[7] 3420 3-9-6 **72** ........ ADaly 8 62
(MDIUsher) *stdd s: bhd: rdn 1/2-way: nvr gng pce to rch ldrs* **14/1**
0644 **10** *1 1/4* **Alchera**[14] 3201 3-8-12 **64** ........(b) SCarson 5 49
(RFJohnsonHoughton) *lw: chsd ldrs: rdn 1/2-way: wknd over 1f out* **11/2**[1]
0006 **11** *1/2* **Sworn To Secrecy**[30] 2741 3-8-7 **59** ........ RLMoore 3 42
(SKirk) *a outpcd* **14/1**
-030 **12** *11* **The Butterfly Boy**[26] 2836 3-7-12 **55** ........ NDeSouza(5) 10 —
(PFICole) *n tch: rdn 1/2-way: wknd qckly* **14/1**

59.52 secs (-1.69) **Going Correction** -0.325s/f (Firm) **12** Ran SP% **120.1**
Speed ratings: **100,96,95,94,94 93,92,92,91,89 88,70**CSF £148.91 TOTE £14.90: £4.60, £3.00, £2.30; EX 181.50.
**Owner** Miss Jacqueline Goodearl **Bred** Miss Jacqueline Goodearl **Trained** Upper Lambourn, Berks

**FOCUS**
A modest afair in which racing against the far side rail looked to be an advantage. The winner looked back to his best, and the runner-up reproduced last year's Kempton maiden form.

**NOTEBOOK**
**Red Sovereign**, a useful juvenile last year, bounced back to that form and won nicely under a fine ride. She had excuses for her two below par efforts this term and could be the type to follow up on this while at this end of the handicap. *Official explanation: trainer had no explanation for the improved form shown*
**Minimum Bid** stayed on best of all and ran her best race to date. She can be placed to advantage off this mark and she confirmed the recent good form of her stable.
**Melody King** held every chance and had the run of the race from the front, but could not quicken with the eventual winner late on.
**Cut And Dried** improved a touch on recent displays, but he does looks weighted to his best at present.
**Alchera** ran below par and looks tricky.

## 3629 HH ASSOCIATES H'CAP 1m 6f 92y
**8:00** (8:02) (D ) (0-80,80) 3-Y-O+ **£8,092** (£2,490; £1,245; £622) **Stalls** High

Form RPR
00-0 **1** **Tungsten Strike (USA)**[16] 3160 3-8-0 **66** ow1 ........ MartinDwyer 7 81+
(MrsAJPerrett) *lw: hld up rr but in tch: pushed along and hdwy 3f out: led jst ins fnl 2f: shkn up and clr fnl f: comf* **20/1**
0-02 **2** *5* **Levitator**[23] 2944 3-8-0 **70** ........ NMackay(3) 4 73+
(SirMichaelStoute) *lw: t.k.h early: disp 2nd 4f: styd chsng ldrs: pushed along and kpt on wl for 2nd ins fnl f: no ch w wnr* **7/2**[3]
3035 **3** *3/4* **Saxe-Coburg (IRE)**[5] 3492 7-8-5 **60** ........ JFMcDonald(3) 8 62
(GAHam) *hld up in rr: hdwy and rdn over 2f out: styd on fr over 1f out to press for 2nd ins last: no ch w wnr* **8/1**
0506 **4** *shd* **Gallant Boy (IRE)**[2] 3591 5-9-0 **69** ........(t) FPFerris(3) 6 71
(PDEvans) *bhd: rdn and hdwy over 2f out: styd on to press for 3rd ins fnl f but nvr gng pce to trble wnr* **14/1**
2112 **5** *shd* **Bucks**[14] 3199 7-10-0 **80** ........ DHolland 1 82
(DKIvory) *lw: disp 2nd tl chsd ldr after 4f: led 4f out: hdd jst ins fnl 2f: styd on one pce u.p* **13/8**[1]
0/00 **6** *23* **Ursa Major**[35] 2594 10-7-9 **50** oh2 ........ LisaJones(3) 3 20
(TKeddy) *bit bkwd: b: in tch: rdn to chse ldrs over 3f out: wknd qckly over 2f out* **25/1**
3416 **7** *15* **Mostarsil (USA)**[14] 3199 6-9-4 **70** ........(p) RLMoore 2 19
(GLMoore) *led tl hdd 4f out: wknd qckly over 2f out: eased whn no ch* **3/1**[2]

3m 10.96s (0.30) **Going Correction** +0.125s/f (Good)
**WFA** 3 from 4yo+ 15lb **7** Ran SP% **111.7**
Speed ratings: **104,101,100,100,100 87,78**CSF £84.33 CT £611.27 TOTE £8.40: £3.60, £2.00; EX 82.30.
**Owner** John Connolly **Bred** Minster Stud **Trained** Pulborough, W Sussex

**FOCUS**
An ordinary affair run at a reasonable gallop.

**NOTEBOOK**
**Tungsten Strike(USA)** put in a massively improved display to win as he pleased over this longer trip. He looks well suited to a test of stamina and can surely strike again off this pretty lowly mark. *Official explanation: trainer said, regarding the improved form shown, stable had been out of form when gelding ran poorly last time, adding that gelding was better suited by today's step up in trip and the good, good to firm in places ground*
**Levitator** ran keen early on, but soon settled and looked a threat to all turning for home, only to find the one pace when coming under pressure in the straight. He is improving and can find a weak heat off this current mark, but is certainly one of his stable's lesser lights.
**Saxe-Coburg(IRE)** stayed on well enough to finish a never dangerous third.
**Gallant Boy(IRE)** reamins badly out of form and still shows no sign of capitalising on his fall in the ratings.
**Bucks** disappointingly found nil off the bridle after holding every chance turning for home. This was a well below-par display.
**Mostarsil(USA)** set the pace for most of the way on this step back up in trip, but dropped out alarmingly late on and something may have been amiss.

## 3630 PLATINUM SECURITY MAIDEN FILLIES' STKS 1m 2f (J)
**8:30** (8:34) (D ) 3-Y-O **£5,590** (£1,720; £860; £430) **Stalls** High

Form RPR
0223 **1** **Anna Pallida**[33] 2653 3-8-11 80 ........ DHolland 6 82+
(PWHarris) *lw: trckd ldrs: hmpd and slipped ins fnl 3f:drvn and qcknd to ld wl over 1f out: comf* **7/2**[2]
**2** *2* **Autumn Wealth (IRE)** 3-8-11 ........ KDarley 15 78
(MrsAJPerrett) *str: scope: bit bkwd: b: hld up in tch: pushed along 3f out: styd on to chse wnr wl ins last but no imp* **5/1**[3]
2 **3** *1/2* **Summer Serenade**[23] 2950 3-8-11 ........ LDettori 5 77
(LMCumani) *trckd ldr: drvn to ld and wnt lft to stands rail ins fnl 3f: hdd wl over 1f out: styd on same pce ins last* **6/4**[1]
0- **4** *1 1/2* **Castagna (USA)**[284] 5218 3-8-11 ........ WRyan 1 75
(HRACecil) *stdd rr after 3f: hdwy whn nt clr run ins fnl 3f: n.m.r over 1f out: kpt on wl cl home* **16/1**
**5** *1 1/4* **Wait For Spring (USA)** 3-8-11 ........ RHavlin 9 73
(JHMGosden) *lengthy: scope: chsd ldrs: hmpd ins fnl 3f: sn rdn: wknd fnl f* **25/1**
02 **6** *2 1/2* **Woman In White (FR)**[19] 3044 3-8-11 ........ JFortune 13 68
(JHMGosden) *chsd ldrs: rdn 3f out: wknd fnl f* **13/2**
**7** *3/4* **Niobe's Way** 3-8-11 ........ SDrowne 10 67
(PRChamings) *leggy: bit bkwd: in tch: hdwy 4f out: rdn 3f out: wknd over 1f out* **33/1**
0-0 **8** *2 1/2* **Persian Genie (IRE)**[14] 3204 3-8-11 ........ SCarson 8 62
(GBBalding) *in tch: rdn over 3f out: wknd 2f out* **50/1**
00- **9** *2 1/2* **Gliding By**[224] 6072 3-8-11 ........ JQuinn 12 58
(PRChamings) *bhd: styd on fnl 2f: nt trble ldrs* **50/1**
0 **10** *1 3/4* **Lady Taverner**[51] 2182 3-8-11 ........ DaneO'Neill 3 55
(HJCyzer) *bhd most of way* **50/1**
0 **11** *1 3/4* **Sayrianna**[16] 3161 3-8-11 ........ TPQueally 11 51
(IAWood) *in tch: rdn over 3f out: wknd over 2f out* **50/1**
**12** *2 1/2* **Under My Skin (IRE)** 3-8-11 ........(t) JPMurtagh 4 47
(TGMills) *str: bit bkwd: a in rr* **14/1**

0 **13** *1 ¼* **Trinity Fair**[25] 2900 3-8-11 .................................... IMongan 2 45
(JGGiven) *led tl hdd & wknd ins fnl 3f* **33/1**

2m 7.49s (1.35) **Going Correction** +0.125s/f (Good) **13** Ran SP% **122.3**
Speed ratings: **99,97,97,95,94 92,92,90,88,86 85,83,82**CSF £20.89 TOTE £4.90: £2.10, £2.00, £1.30; EX 22.40.
**Owner** Aboobaker, Harris & Taylor **Bred** Gateway Bloodstock **Trained** Ringshall, Bucks

**FOCUS**
A fair fillies' maiden, but run at a modest pace. The winner showed improved form and there were some promising efforts behind her.

**NOTEBOOK**
**Anna Pallida** got off the mark at the fifth attempt in good style and greatly appreciated this drop in trip. She quickened up nicely this time and may be able to progress further, with connections hoping to pick up some black type in due course.
**Autumn Wealth(IRE)**, an expensive purchase, made a most promising, if somewhat belated debut. She stayed on best of all, having run green early on, should have no problem winning her maiden and taking higher order over this trip in the future.
**Summer Serenade**, as on her debut, ran well enough without suggesting she is anything special. She should find a maiden and looks the type to do better with further experience.
**Castagna(USA)** improved on her sole juvenile outing and ran as though another step up in trip would suit. Her future looks to lie within handicaps.
**Wait For Spring(USA)** made a pleasing debut and would have been closer but for interference three out. She will improve plenty for this and clearly has abitlity.
**Woman In White(FR)** failed to find the expected improvement over this longer trip, but now qualifies for handicaps and is one to keep an eye on.

## 3631 "BOOK NOW FOR GALA NIGHT" H'CAP — 1m 1f (R)
**9:00** (9:02) (D) (0-80,80) 3-Y-0+ **£6,955** (£2,140; £1,070; £535) **Stalls** High

Form RPR
3044 **1** **Momtic (IRE)**[20] 3017 3-9-4 **80** .................................... KDarley 11 90
(WJarvis) *trckd ldrs: rdn over 2f out: led 1f out: hld on all out* **8/1**
0-41 **2** *hd* **Spring Jim**[16] 3155 3-8-13 **75** .................................... JPMurtagh 2 85+
(JRFanshawe) *lw: hld up in rr: hdwy and edgd lft 2f out: swtchd rt and hdwy over 1f out: str run ins last: nt ex last strides* **7/2**[1]
2133 **3** *2 ½* **Best Before (IRE)**[15] 3177 4-9-1 **74** .................................... SJDonohoe(7) 3 79+
(PDEvans) *lw: bhd: hdwy whn badly hmpd jst ins fnl 2f: swtchd rt and rapid hdwy fnl f: nt rch ldrs* **9/1**
005 **4** *nk* **Desert Hawk**[26] 2842 3-8-7 **69** .................................... RLMoore 10 73
(RHannon) *lw: chsd ldrs: drvn to chal over 1f out: styd on same pce ins last* **12/1**
1560 **4** *dht* **Gig Harbor**[11] 3325 5-10-0 **80** .................................... TPQueally 1 84
(MissECLavelle) *lw: chsd ldrs: chal 4f out and stl chalng over 1f out: outpcd ins last* **33/1**
0044 **6** *1* **Jools**[10] 3347 6-9-11 **77** .................................... DHolland 9 79
(DKIvory) *b: sn led: rdn and kpt on wl fr over 2f out: hdd 1f out: wknd ins last* **14/1**
0550 **7** *½* **Terraquin (IRE)**[6] 3455 4-9-3 **69** .................................... (p) ADaly 8 70
(JJBridger) *b: chsd ldrs: rdn 2f out: one pce ins fnl f* **20/1**
-043 **8** *hd* **Freeloader (IRE)**[25] 2878 4-9-6 **72** .................................... EAhern 7 72+
(JWHills) *lw: hld up mid-div: hdwy on rails whn bdly hmpd ins fnl 2f: nt clr run 1f out: nt rcvr but styd on* **7/1**[3]
2200 **9** *½* **Karaoke (IRE)**[4] 3534 4-9-1 **67** .................................... LDettori 5 66
(SKirk) *hld up in rr: gd hdwy over 2f out: chsd ldrs over 1f out: wknd ins last* **10/1**
06-4 **10** *½* **Resonate (IRE)**[55] 2064 6-9-6 **72** .................................... DaneO'Neill 4 70+
(AGNewcombe) *hld up in rr: hdwy on rails whn hmpd ins fnl 2f: stl n.m.r 1f out: nt rcvr but kpt on* **9/1**
4-53 **11** *1* **Stateroom (USA)**[43] 2393 6-9-3 **72** .................................... (b) LisaJones(3) 15 68
(JARToller) *bhd: sme hdwy whn nt clr run ins fnl 2f: nt rcvrd and n.d after* **12/1**
2004 **12** *2* **Catch The Fox**[35] 2573 4-7-5 **50** oh8 .................................... LucyRussell(7) 14 42
(JJBridger) *chsd ldrs tl wknd ins fnl 2f* **25/1**
5000 **13** *4* **Must Be Magic**[35] 2573 7-8-6 **58** .................................... (v) WSupple 6 42
(HJCollingridge) *chsd ldrs: rdn 3f out: wknd fr 2f out* **12/1**
0322 **14** *½* **Blue Mariner**[13] 3239 4-9-4 **70** .................................... BDoyle 12 53
(PWHarris) *chsd ldrs 6f* **14/1**
0000 **15** *4* **Learned Lad (FR)**[33] 2643 6-8-3 **55** ow2 .................................... PDoe 13 30
(JamiePoulton) *lw: a in rr* **25/1**
00-1 **16** *2 ½* **Firewire**[9] 3386 6-8-13 **65** 6ex .................................... SSanders 16 35
(MissBSanders) *lw: bhd most of way* **6/1**[2]

1m 54.48s (0.15) **Going Correction** +0.125s/f (Good)
**WFA** 3 from 4yo+ 10lb **16** Ran SP% **141.0**
Speed ratings: **104,103,101,101,101 100,100,99,99,98 98,96,92,92,88 86**CSF £40.17 CT £294.22 TOTE £10.30: £2.60, £3.00, £2.10; EX 102.20 TRIFECTA PL: GH £4.10, DH £1.50. Place 6 £188.00, Place 5 £106.34.
**Owner** Heath, Keenan & Verrier **Bred** Janic Thoroughbreds **Trained** Newmarket, Suffolk

**FOCUS**
A muddling race that saw plenty of hard luck stories and the form looks unreliable. Owing to poor visibility there was no photo finish, and the distances after the dead-heat for fourth have been estimated from a video recording.

**NOTEBOOK**
**Momtic(IRE)** dug deep under pressure and won in gritty fashion. He had slightly lost his form, having promised to win earlier in the season, but although it was an improved effort this does looks about as good as he is.
**Spring Jim** stayed on from a difficult position all too late in the day. He looks a fairly progressive type and should make amends for this narrow failure, but his need to be held up means he will always need things to fall right.
**Best Before(IRE)** has to go down as an unlucky loser, as he was stopped in his tracks at a crucial point and could not recover. He is value for more than the bare form and could be winning again soon on this evidence.
**Gig Harbor** ran a very respectable race under top-weight and looks to be coming right.
**Desert Hawk** had every chance and ran a much improved race, as expected, on this handicap debut. He will find easier opportunites against his own age group.
**Freeloader(IRE)** was full of running when hampered and would have been a lot closer with a clear run. He looks to be finding his form once again.
**Resonate(IRE)** would have been closer but for meeting a wall of horses when full of running. He was not given a hard time when beaten and looks worth keeping an eye out for next time. *Official explanation: jockey said horse suffered interference in running*
**Firewire** *Official explanation: jockey said gelding was never travelling*
T/Plt: £50.80 to a £1 stake. Pool: £45,235.80. 649.10 winning tickets. T/Qpdt: £67.00 to a £1 stake. Pool: £3,193.70. 35.25 winning tickets. ST

# 3418 LINGFIELD (L-H)
Wednesday, July 7

**OFFICIAL GOING: Turf course - good to firm (firm in places) all-weather - standard**
Wind: str hlf against Weather: overcast; heavy rain race three onwards

## 3632 COME EVENING RACING ON 17TH JULY MAIDEN AUCTION STKS (DIV I) — 6f
**1:40** (1:41) (E) 2-Y-O **£3,435** (£1,057; £528; £264) **Stalls** High

Form RPR
04 **1** **Time For You**[18] 3083 2-8-2 .................................... RMullen 8 60
(PJMcbride) *trckd ldrs: rdn over 2f out: led jst over 1f out: kpt on fnl f* **10/3**[2]
**2** *¾* **Tybalt** 2-8-7 .................................... IMongan 7 63
(PWHarris) *s.s: detached in last pair: prog 1/2-way: chsd ldrs 2f out: shkn up and rn green 1f out: styd on to take 2nd nr fin* **10/1**
**3** *nk* **Trackattack** 2-8-13 .................................... SWKelly 2 68
(JAOsborne) *dwlt: detached in last pair: prog 1/2-way: chsd ldrs 2f out: shkn up over 1f out: v green and hanging: kpt on to take 3rd o* **14/1**
**4** *shd* **Bamzooki** 2-8-5 .................................... OUrbina 5 60
(JRFanshawe) *dwlt: trckd ldrs: nt clr run 1/2-way and swtchd to wd outside over 2f out: plenty to do after: styd on fr over 1f out: nrst* **4/5**[1]
**5** *½* **Avertigo** 2-8-8 ow1 .................................... SSanders 9 61
(WRMuir) *mde most to over 1f out: one pce fnl f: lost 3 pls nr fin* **25/1**
0 **6** *3* **Marians Maid (IRE)**[16] 3157 2-8-3 ow1 .................................... JFEgan 3 47
(JSMoore) *pressed ldrs: rdn over 2f out: one pce and btn whn squeezed out last 100yds* **8/1**[3]
**7** *5* **Coombe Centenary** 2-8-2 .................................... CCatlin 1 31
(SDow) *racd on outer: chsd ldrs tl wknd 2f out* **50/1**
04 **8** *1 ¾* **Lara's Girl**[15] 3170 2-7-13 .................................... JFMcDonald(3) 6 26
(IAWood) *pressed ldr: rdn 1/2-way: sn wknd* **33/1**
60 **9** *5* **Dancing Moonlight (IRE)**[21] 2985 2-8-8 .................................... JoannaBadger 4 17
(MrsNMacauley) *prom to 1/2-way: sn wknd and bhd* **100/1**

1m 13.4s (1.75) **Going Correction** +0.025s/f (Good) **9** Ran SP% **115.2**
Speed ratings: **89,88,87,87,86 82,76,73,67**CSF £34.48 TOTE £4.70: £1.10, £2.50, £3.90; EX 31.50.
**Owner** Saracen Racing **Bred** Mrs J M Langmead **Trained** Newmarket, Suffolk

**FOCUS**
Only an ordinary maiden, but one that is likely to produce the occasional winner.

**NOTEBOOK**
**Time For You**, a staying-on fourth over seven furlongs at the course last month, handled this drop back in trip well and was always holding the second. She is definitely the type to make her mark in nurseries and is versatile with regards to trip.
**Tybalt** made a pleasing debut, staying on well from the rear of the field despite showing distinct signs of inexperience. He has a similar race in him and will stay further.
**Trackattack**, a late foal who is bred for speed, ran a similar race to the second, staying on for pressure despite running green. He would have learned from this and is up to winning his maiden.
**Bamzooki** was a strongly supported favourite and can count herself unlucky not to reach at least a place. She was denied a clear run at one stage and had to deliver her challenge out wide. She too should win her maiden. *Official explanation: jockey said filly was unsuited by the Good to Firm, Firm in places ground*
**Avertigo** should come into his own later in the season and can be expected to improve on this.
**Marians Maid(IRE)** is more of a nursery type.

## 3633 COME EVENING RACING ON 17TH JULY MAIDEN AUCTION STKS (DIV II) — 6f
**2:10** (2:10) (E) 2-Y-O **£3,425** (£1,054; £527; £263) **Stalls** High

Form RPR
3 **1** **Ariodante**[16] 3157 2-8-10 .................................... SSanders 4 77
(JMPEustace) *racd on outer: w ldrs: rdn 2f out: drvn ahd jst ins fnl f: styd on wl* **11/8**[1]
03 **2** *1* **Bee Stinger**[18] 3083 2-8-7 .................................... IMongan 7 71
(IAWood) *mde most tl jst ins fnl f: unable qck* **9/1**
05 **3** *½* **Monash Lad (IRE)**[19] 3051 2-8-7 .................................... FPFerris(3) 6 73
(MHTompkins) *t.k.h: w ldrs: rdn 2f out: ev ch ent fnl f: no ex last 100yds* **5/1**
3 **4** *¾* **Louphole**[11] 3302 2-8-7 .................................... RSmith 5 67
(PJMakin) *w ldrs: led briefly 2f out: ev ch 1f out: wknd last 100yds* **9/2**[3]
**5** *1 ¼* **Sunny Times (IRE)** 2-7-13 .................................... LisaJones(3) 8 59
(JWPayne) *chsd ldrs: rdn 2f out: nvr pce to chal: kpt on* **25/1**
50 **6** *hd* **Zolash (IRE)**[29] 2761 2-8-3 .................................... DerekNolan(7) 2 66
(JSMoore) *dwlt: in tch: rdn 1/2-way: nt on terms after: kpt on fnl f* **50/1**
**7** *1 ½* **The Keep** 2-8-5 .................................... JFEgan 3 56
(RHannon) *dwlt: in tch: shkn up over 2f out: no prog over 1f out: one pce after* **4/1**[2]
0 **8** *½* **Play Up Pompey**[18] 3083 2-8-2 .................................... NChalmers(5) 9 57
(JJBridger) *s.i.s: mostly last but wl in tch: rdn over 2f out: no imp fnl 2f* **50/1**

1m 12.04s (0.39) **Going Correction** +0.025s/f (Good) **8** Ran SP% **114.7**
Speed ratings: **98,96,96,95,93 93,91,90**CSF £15.12 TOTE £2.00: £1.20, £1.90, £2.00; EX 15.70.
**Owner** The Macdougall Partnership **Bred** Bishop's Down Farm **Trained** Newmarket, Suffolk

**FOCUS**
A creditable time for the grade and the stronger of the two divisions on a line through Bee Stinger, who had previously finished ahead of the winner of division one.

**NOTEBOOK**
**Ariodante** was the form pick coming into the race and, despite racing out wide, proved too good for the opposition. He will stay another furlong and can win a nursery.
**Bee Stinger** had finished ahead of Time For You - winner of the first division - here last month and the fact he could only manage second suggests this was the stronger division. He had his chance and was trying to get back at the winner close home, suggesting a return to seven will see him winning.
**Monash Lad(IRE)** travelled nicely before being unable to up his game under pressure. He is now qualified for a handicap mark and will be more at home in nurseries.
**Louphole** is a gelding of modest ability and one who will do better once handicapped.
**Sunny Times(IRE)** made a pleasing debut, keeping on steadily, and will improve for the outing.
**The Keep** did not really know her job as well as some of the others and, although this was a disappointing effort, she will be capable of better next time.

## 3634 RYDON GROUP NURSERY — 6f

2:40 (2:40) (E) 2-Y-O — £4,134 (£1,272; £636; £318) Stalls High

Form — RPR

2234 **1** **Lateral Thinker (IRE)**[58] [2002] 2-8-8 **66** ........ SWKelly 6 — 66
(JAOsborne) *mde virtually all: set stdy pce to 2f out: hrd pressed fnl f: hld on* **7/1**

453 **2** *hd* **Simplify**[17] [3124] 2-9-2 **74** ........ (b[1]) NPollard 3 — 73
(DRLoder) *t.k.h: cl up: trckd wnr over 1f out: rdn to chal fnl f: hung lft and fnd nil* **7/1**

51 **3** *1* **Aberdovey**[36] [2550] 2-9-5 **77** ........ IMongan 7 — 73
(MLWBell) *s.i.s: hld up in last: swtchd to outer over 2f out: drvn and r.o fr over 1f out: nt rch ldng pair* **3/1**[2]

621 **4** *¾* **Tesary**[11] [3302] 2-9-0 **72** ........ WSupple 8 — 66
(EALDunlop) *t.k.h: hld up bhd ldrs: nt clr run over 1f out: nt qckn fnl f* **9/4**[1]

6265 **5** *½* **Queen's Glory (IRE)**[23] [2927] 2-8-13 **71** ........ RMullen 5 — 63
(WRMuir) *s.i.s: t.k.h: hld up bhd ldrs: shkn up 2f out: nt qckn* **20/1**

31 **6** *2½* **Earl Of Links (IRE)**[64] [1871] 2-9-7 **79** ........ PDobbs 4 — 64
(RHannon) *t.k.h: w wnr to wl over 1f out: wknd* **4/1**[3]

1m 13.65s (2.00) **Going Correction** +0.15s/f (Good) — **6** Ran SP% **105.5**
Speed ratings: **92,91,90,89,88 85**CSF £46.13 CT £144.00 TOTE £7.60: £2.10, £3.00; EX 75.50.
**Owner** Mrs Patricia Hughes **Bred** Joe Rogers **Trained** Upper Lambourn, Berks

**FOCUS**
Just modest form. There was not much pace on here and Lateral Thinker had the run of things from the front. The figures shown as 'official ratings' are estimates for guidance only.

**NOTEBOOK**
**Lateral Thinker(IRE)** improved on previous form on this nursery debut, leading at a steady pace throughout and battling under pressure to hold the runner-up. She clearly appreciated the step up to six furlongs but did have the rub of the green.
**Simplify** had his chance but did not look to keen to go by in the first-time blinkers. He is one to leave alone for the time being.
**Aberdovey** was slightly unlucky as she had to come wide after being tardy at the gate and was held up off the slow pace. This run should not be taken at face value and she is worth another chance in a similar race.
**Tesary** was another not suited by being held up off the slow pace and failed to get the gaps when she was trying to make a forward move. She, like the third, is better than this and deserves another chance to shine.
**Queen's Glory(IRE)** had her chance and may need a drop in to lesser company to get off the mark.
**Earl Of Links(IRE)** was disappointing, dropping away tamely having raced up with the pace.

## 3635 SILKS SUITE MEDIAN AUCTION MAIDEN STKS — 5f

3:15 (3:15) (F) 3-4-Y-O — £2,884 (£824; £412) Stalls High

Form — RPR

-422 **1** **Ex Mill Lady**[12] [3262] 3-8-9 59 ........ BDoyle 1 — 65
(JohnBerry) *cl up: rdn 2f out: led 1f out: drvn out* **1/2**[1]

**2** *½* **Sokoke** 3-9-0 ........ JMackay 3 — 68
(RMBeckett) *rn green and jst in tch: prog on outer 2f out: r.o to press wnr ins fnl f: no imp nr fin* **16/1**

-303 **3** *1½* **Blue Moon Hitman (IRE)**[10] [3344] 3-8-11 58 ........ DNolan[(3)] 7 — 62
(RBrotherton) *w ldr: led 3f out to 1f out: nt qckn u.p* **11/4**[2]

00 **4** *5* **Loveyoulongtime**[15] [3179] 3-8-4 ........ NChalmers[(5)] 5 — 37
(AMBalding) *prom: chsd ldr 3f out to wl over 1f out: wknd rapidly fnl f* **14/1**[3]

0000 **5** *nk* **Cedric Coverwell**[4] [3533] 4-9-5 45 ........ JFEgan 6 — 41
(DKIvory) *led to 3f out: sn lost pl and btn: eased over 1f out: shkn up nr fin* **33/1**

**6** *6* **Panfield Belle (IRE)** 3-8-9 ........ WSupple 2 — 12
(HJCollingridge) *s.i.s: outpcd and a bhd* **33/1**

59.28 secs (0.41) **Going Correction** +0.15s/f (Good)
**WFA** 3 from 4yo 5lb — **6** Ran SP% **111.8**
Speed ratings: **102,101,98,90,90 80**CSF £10.75 TOTE £1.40: £1.10, £3.70; EX 8.60.
**Owner** Mrs Rosemary Moszkowicz **Bred** Henry And Mrs Rosemary Moszkowicz **Trained** Newmarket, Suffolk

**FOCUS**
A poor event that did not take much winning, although the form looks sound enough.

**NOTEBOOK**
**Ex Mill Lady** faced a relatively simple task and was the obvious form choice. She did it in workmanlike fashion, but still got the result and off such a lowly rating can make her mark in handicaps.
**Sokoke** is bred to be speedy and made a pleasing debut, running on well to make the winner work despite showing signs of inexperience. He is evidently no star but three-year-olds-plus sprint maidens are usually very weak affairs and he should not have too much trouble finding a suitable opening.
**Blue Moon Hitman(IRE)** had his chance and remains well exposed.
**Loveyoulongtime** showed up well before fading tamely - not the first time she has done this - and maybe she has a problem.
**Cedric Coverwell** *Official explanation: jockey said gelding hung left throughout*

## 3636 FURLONGS AND FAIRWAYS AT LINGFIELD PARK H'CAP — 7f

3:50 (3:51) (F) (0-55,55) 3-Y-O — £3,017 (£862; £431) Stalls High

Form — RPR

0554 **1** **Blaeberry**[16] [3156] 3-9-8 **55** ........ (b[1]) JFEgan 8 — 65
(PLGilligan) *mde most: clr bef 1/2-way: rdn over 2f out: kpt on fr over 1f out: unchal* **11/2**[1]

60-6 **2** *2* **Choristar**[25] [2880] 3-9-8 **55** ........ RMullen 14 — 60
(WRMuir) *hld up in last trio: drvn and hanging rt over 2f out: plld out over 1f out: styd on strly to snatch 2nd last stride* **25/1**

4-06 **3** *shd* **United Spirit (IRE)**[20] [3004] 3-9-5 **55** ........ (p) SHitchcott[(3)] 11 — 60
(MAMagnusson) *prom in chsng gp: rdn to chse wnr wl over 1f out: no imp: lost 2nd last stride* **16/1**

0-55 **4** *½* **Shibumi**[18] [3085] 3-9-3 **53** ........ LFletcher[(3)] 1 — 57
(HMorrison) *racd towards far side for 1f: jnd main gp in rr: drvn 3f out: styd on fr over 1f out: nrst fin* **10/1**

-065 **5** *1½* **Beautiful Noise**[28] [2790] 3-9-7 **54** ........ WSupple 2 — 54
(DMorris) *in tch in chsng gp: effrt over 2f out: one pce and no hdwy over 1f out* **9/1**[3]

0000 **6** *¾* **Night Worker**[2] [3593] 3-9-6 **53** ........ PDobbs 6 — 51
(RHannon) *in tch in chsng gp: rdn over 2f out: one pce and no prog* **20/1**

0501 **7** *1* **Accendere**[29] [2766] 3-9-8 **55** ........ SSanders 4 — 50
(RMBeckett) *s.i.s: hld up towards rr: prog over 2f out: rdn and no hdwy over 1f out* **6/1**[2]

0040 **8** *½* **Dellagio (IRE)**[25] [2889] 3-9-3 **53** ........ BReilly[(3)] 3 — 47
(CADwyer) *hld up towards rr: gng wl enough over 2f out: sme prog wl over 1f out: rdn and nt qckn sn after* **20/1**

2360 **9** *3½* **Joshua's Gold (IRE)**[16] [3155] 3-9-0 **54** ........ DTudhope[(7)] 10 — 39
(DCarroll) *prom in chsng gp: rdn over 2f out: wknd wl over 1f out* **9/1**[3]

3111 **10** *¾* **Dial Square**[69] [1726] 3-9-7 **54** ........ CCatlin 16 — 37
(PHowling) *hld up in last trio: rdn and no real prog over 2f out* **9/1**[3]

3540 **11** *nk* **Barras (IRE)**[26] [2850] 3-9-3 **55** ........ (v) MSavage[(5)] 7 — 37
(MissGayKelleway) *mostly chsd wnr to wl over 1f out: wknd rapidly* **25/1**

6000 **12** *¾* **Forzenuff**[11] [3307] 3-9-8 **55** ........ (t) VVenkaya 5 — 35
(JRBoyle) *racd towards far side for 1f: prom whn joining main gp: disp 2nd pl over 2f out: wkng rapidly and unbalanced over 1f out* **33/1**

-050 **13** *½* **Averami**[99] [1184] 3-9-1 **55** ........ (v) RJKilloran[(7)] 15 — 34
(AMBalding) *wl plcd in chsng gp: effrt over 2f out: sn rdn and wknd rapidly* **40/1**

-064 **14** *3½* **Young Love**[16] [3139] 3-9-4 **54** ........ LPKeniry[(3)] 13 — 24
(MissECLavelle) *prom in chsng gp but sn pushed along: wknd 3f out: eased over 1f out* **9/1**[3]

**15** *3* **Newtown Chief**[336] [3906] 3-9-0 **54** ........ StevenHarrison[(7)] 9 — 16
(NPLittmoden) *a wl bhd* **40/1**

4305 **16** *dist* **Wonky Donkey**[26] [2850] 3-9-7 **54** ........ OUrbina 12 — —
(SCWilliams) *a bhd: t.o fnl 2f* **12/1**

1m 27.6s (3.39) **Going Correction** +0.45s/f (Yiel) — **16** Ran SP% **117.4**
Speed ratings: **98,95,95,95,93 92,91,90,86,85 85,84,84,80,76** —CSF £143.78 CT £2052.95 TOTE £8.00: £1.60, £8.60, £3.20, £2.40; EX 182.20.
**Owner** Lady Bland **Bred** Lady Bland **Trained** Newmarket, Suffolk

**FOCUS**
Modest form. Blaeberry led for most of the way and had built up such a lead that she was never going to be caught.

**NOTEBOOK**
**Blaeberry**, who has been running over further, was droped back in trip for this and had the aid of blinkers for the first time. She was a clear leader at the half-mile pole and had gone beyond recall at the furlong marker. Whether the headgear will have the same effect next time is open to question, and she could be one to take on if made a short price to follow up.
**Choristar** came from a long way back to grab second on the line and ran his best race to date. If going on from this he should be up to winning in this sort of company.
**United Spirit(IRE)** ran a good race in defeat, just getting nabbed for second in the dying strides.
**Shibumi** showed improved form on this handicap debut and was closing with every stride at the line from her modest draw. She will be of interest when upped to a mile.
**Beautiful Noise** has a small race in her and also did well from a low stall.
**Accendere** *Official explanation: trainer said gelding was unsuited by the ground which had eased from good to firm due to heavy rain for an hour before the race*
**Young Love** was reported to have been unsuited by the ground and deserves a chance to show she is better than this. *Official explanation: trainer said filly was unsuited by the Good to Firm, firm in places ground*
**Wonky Donkey** *Official explanation: jockey said gelding bled from the nose*

## 3637 SEAHOLME MARQUEES (S) STKS — 1m 2f (P)

4:25 (4:26) (G) 3-Y-O+ — £2,576 (£736; £368) Stalls Low

Form — RPR

0361 **1** **Burgundy**[6] [3441] 7-9-12 58 ........ (b) IMongan 6 — 66+
(PMitchell) *rousted along in rr early: sn in tch: prog over 5f out: led wl over 2f out: rdn clr fr over 1f out* **3/1**[1]

4430 **2** *5* **Bretton**[49] [2231] 3-8-6 35 ........ BReilly[(3)] 12 — 51
(BAPearce) *hld up wl in rr: stdy prog on outer over 3f out: chsd ldng pair over 2f out: kpt on to take 2nd last strides* **33/1**

0006 **3** *hd* **Piquet**[40] [2443] 6-9-7 47 ........ GBaker 13 — 51
(JJBridger) *hld up in rr: smooth prog over 3f out: chsd wnr over 2f out: sn rdn and no imp: lost 2nd last strides* **12/1**

0000 **4** *5* **One Alone**[9] [3386] 3-8-4 45 ........ (v[1]) WSupple 11 — 36
(Jean-ReneAuvray) *hld up wl in rr: prog on wd outside 3f out: drvn to chse clr ldng trio wl over 1f out: no imp* **33/1**

5160 **5** *5* **Regulated (IRE)**[15] [3173] 3-8-12 65 ........ J-PGuillambert[(3)] 5 — 37
(DBFeek) *settled in rr: rdn over 4f out: sn struggling and no ch: plodded on* **4/1**[2]

0P0- **6** *1¾* **Frixos (IRE)**[60] [4837] 4-9-6 70 ........ (b) VSlattery 8 — 28
(MScudamore) *racd in midfield: rdn 7f out: lost pl u.p 5f out: plugged on* **14/1**

-000 **7** *1* **Buckenham Stone**[21] [2990] 5-9-1 30 ........ RPrice 4 — 21
(JPearce) *trckd ldrs: rdn and lost pl 5f out: n.d after* **66/1**

0045 **8** *8* **Yeoman Lad**[13] [3239] 4-9-3 69 ........ (v) LPKeniry[(3)] 9 — 11
(AMBalding) *racd in midfield: pushed along 6f out: struggling over 4f out: no ch after: wl bhd fnl 2f* **3/1**[1]

-656 **9** *7* **Lilian**[141] [811] 4-8-11 37 ow1 ........ MSavage[(5)] 1 — —
(MissGayKelleway) *chsd ldrs: rdn and wknd 5f out: t.o fnl 2f* **12/1**

0006 **10** *¾* **Coronado Forest (USA)**[15] [3173] 5-9-12 59 ........ (b[1]) SSanders 10 — 2
(MRHoad) *prom: led over 4f out to wl over 2f out: wknd rapidly: t.o* **9/1**[3]

6500 **11** *1¼* **African Spur (IRE)**[2] [3579] 4-8-13 49 ........ DTudhope[(7)] 14 — —
(DCarroll) *led after 1f to over 4f out: wknd rapidly: t.o* **16/1**

46 **12** *1¾* **Amusement**[18] [3087] 8-9-6 ........ SRighton 2 — —
(DGBridgwater) *led for 1f: rdn 7f out: sn btn: t.o 3f out* **25/1**

0-00 **13** *¾* **Boom Or Bust (IRE)**[28] [857] 5-9-3 35 ........ (p) DNolan[(3)] 3 — —
(MissKMGeorge) *racd in midfield: rdn over 4f out: nt run on: t.o over 2f out* **16/1**

2m 9.73s (1.88) **Going Correction** +0.275s/f (Slow)
**WFA** 3 from 4yo+ 11lb — **13** Ran SP% **125.0**
Speed ratings: **103,99,98,94,90 89,88,82,76,76 75,73,73**CSF £123.10 TOTE £3.50: £2.30, £14.70, £3.10; EX 83.70.No bid for the winner.
**Owner** Nigel Shields **Bred** Cheveley Park Stud Ltd **Trained** Epsom, Surrey

**FOCUS**
A creditable time for a seller. With Yeoman Lad running badly the winner had nothing to beat.

**NOTEBOOK**
**Burgundy**, successful in claiming company last week, had to be ridden along early to take an interest, but once back racing keenly he came through to take it two out and came right away in the final furlong.
**Bretton** remains a maiden after 17 starts, but this was his best effort for some time.
**Piquet** left a couple of uninspiring runs behind with a decent third.
**One Alone** ran well for one of her price. She had shown nothing prior to this and although well held, at least beat nine rivals.
**Yeoman Lad** ran a shocker on this first crack at selling company and is best left alone until showing more. *Official explanation: jockey said gelding was never travelling*

## 3638 LADBROKES.COM FILLIES' H'CAP — 1m 4f (P)

5:00 (5:00) (E) (0-70,68) 3-Y-O+ — £3,454 (£1,063; £531; £265) Stalls Low

Form — RPR

112- **1** **Nadeszhda**[348] [3582] 4-9-12 **66** ........ SSanders 4 — 80+
(SirMarkPrescott) *sn trckd ldr: led over 3f out: gng easily 2f out: rdn out whn pressed last 100yds: improve* **4/7**[1]

1134 **2** *¾* **Regal Gallery (IRE)**[125] [964] 6-9-11 **65** ........ PaulEddery 3 — 78
(CAHorgan) *dwlt: hld up in tch: prog over 3f out: chsd wnr 2f out: tried to chal fnl f: r.o but readily hld* **10/1**

0010 **3** 5 **Illeana (GER)**[7] 3421 3-8-5 **58**.......... RMullen 5 63
(WRMuir) *hld up in last: prog wl over 2f out: drvn wl over 1f out: kpt on to take 3rd ins fnl f* **33/1**

2132 **4** 1 3/4 **Fleeting Moon**[51] 2167 4-9-6 **63**.......... LPKeniry(3) 2 65
(AMBalding) *hld up: lost pl and last wl over 2f out: sn rdn: kpt on same pce after* **9/1**[3]

0414 **5** 1 **Royale Pearl**[43] 2385 4-8-2 **42**.......... CCatlin 1 43
(RIngram) *prom: rdn 3f out: outpcd and btn over 2f out* **16/1**

2050 **6** 3 1/2 **Wanna Shout**[15] 3177 6-9-4 **58**.......... JoannaBadger 8 53
(RDickin) *cl up: chsd wnr 3f out to 2f out: wknd u.p* **33/1**

-042 **7** 3 1/2 **Dispol Evita**[125] 962 5-8-13 **53**.......... IMongan 7 42
(JamiePoulton) *dwlt: hld up in rr: effrt u.p 3f out: wknd 2f out* **16/1**

5321 **8** 5 **Anyhow (IRE)**[15] 3181 7-9-11 **68**.......... DNolan(3) 6 49
(MissKMGeorge) *led: hdd and pushed along over 3f out: sn lost pl: last over 2f out : eased sn after* **4/1**[2]

2m 37.88s (3.64) **Going Correction** +0.275s/f (Slow) **8** Ran SP% **120.4**
**WFA** 3 from 4yo+ 13lb
Speed ratings: **98,97,94,93,92 90,87,84**CSF £8.54 CT £102.47 TOTE £1.70: £1.10, £1.60, £5.80; EX 9.30 Place 6 £408.12, Place 5 £95.03.
**Owner** Miss K Rausing **Bred** Miss K Rausing **Trained** Newmarket, Suffolk

**FOCUS**
An uncompetitive event. A nice reappearance win for the well handicapped Nadeszhda who did it a shade cosily. For handicapping purposes the runner-up has been rated a 5lb winner from the rest.

**NOTEBOOK**
**Nadeszhda**, who holds an entry in the Group One Yorkshire Oaks, was last seen in July of last year when turned over at odds of 2/11 in a poor four-runner event at Wolverhampton. Her yard have been quiet - laid low by a bug for most of the year - and this run was expected to do her good despite her being made such a short price. They went no gallop early on but she had taken it up before turning in and just had to be kept up to her work to score, appearing to get tired. Almost certain to score again in this sort of race, her Yorkshire Oaks entry is flying too high but she is undoubtedly a promising filly.
**Regal Gallery(IRE)** was the only one to come after the winner and she did not let her have it easy. This was her first run since March and improvement should be forthcoming.
**Illeana(GER)** made some late headway from the rear but never threatened.
**Fleeting Moon** is only one-paced and kept plodding on.
**Anyhow(IRE)** dropped out tamely having made the early running and ran a rare bad race. *Official explanation: jockey said mare ran flat*
T/Plt: £118.20 to a £1 stake. Pool: £22,817.35. 140.85 winning tickets. T/Qpdt: £27.60 to a £1 stake. Pool: £1,780.80. 47.60 winning tickets. JN

# 3597 NEWMARKET (JULY) (R-H)
## Wednesday, July 7

**OFFICIAL GOING: Good to firm**
A strong headwind made things difficult for the front-runners. There appeared to be no bias in the draw.
Wind: Strong against. Weather: Cloudy with rain for the last race.

## 3639 BAHRAIN TROPHY (LISTED RACE) 1m 6f 175y
**1:20** (1:22) (A) 3-Y-O **£18,600** (£6,600; £3,300; £1,500) **Stalls** High

Form RPR

003 **1** **Anousa (IRE)**[11] 3292 3-8-11 82.......... KFallon 3 97
(PHowling) *lw: chsd ldrs: shkn up to ld over 1f out: styd on wl* **13/2**[3]

2403 **2** 3 1/2 **Top Seed (IRE)**[19] 3035 3-8-11 108.......... TEDurcan 2 92
(MRChannon) *lw: chsd ldr tl led over 2f out: edgd rt and hdd over 1f out: styd on same pce* **10/11**[1]

3144 **3** 3/4 **Bumptious**[19] 3035 3-8-11 90..........(b) PRobinson 1 91
(MHTompkins) *hld up in tch: rdn and ev ch over 1f out: no ex ins fnl f* **4/1**[2]

-444 **4** 16 **Isidore Bonheur (IRE)**[62] 1901 3-8-11 98.......... DHolland 4 69
(BWHills) *set stdy pce: hdd over 2f out: sn rdn: hmpd and wknd over 1f out* **4/1**[2]

3m 17.83s (7.07) **Going Correction** +0.30s/f (Good) **4** Ran SP% **105.7**
Speed ratings: **93,91,90,82**CSF £12.66 TOTE £6.30; EX 11.20.
**Owner** Arkland International (uk) Ltd **Bred** Michael Dalton **Trained** Newmarket, Suffolk

**FOCUS**
This was not a strong Listed race and it was run at a steady pace due to the wind. The time was pedestrian for a race of its class, and the form is highly suspect.

**NOTEBOOK**
**Anousa(IRE)** had plenty of cover from the wind even in this small field, and handled the fast ground better than his rivals. This step up in trip clearly suited, and there is no reason why he can't continue to progress, although he will find life more difficult now with a revised mark and a Listed penalty.
**Top Seed(IRE)** had plenty in hand on these terms, but the combination of a steady pace and fast ground found him out.
**Bumptious** ran pretty close to his Ascot form with the runner-up but, like Top Seed, wouldn't have been suited to the steady pace.
**Isidore Bonheur(IRE)** had the worst of the conditions cutting out the running, and dropped away tamely going into the dip.

## 3640 TNT JULY STKS (GROUP 2) (C&G) 6f
**1:50** (1:52) (A) 2-Y-O **£40,600** (£15,400; £7,700; £3,500) **Stalls** Low

Form RPR

22 **1** **Captain Hurricane**[13] 3242 2-8-10.......... JFortune 6 107
(PWChapple-Hyam) *lw: hld up: hdwy over 1f out: edgd lft ins fnl f: r.o to ld nr fin* **10/1**

12 **2** shd **Council Member (USA)**[22] 2954 2-8-10.......... LDettori 5 107
(SaeedBinSuroor) *lw: led: rdn over 1f out: edgd rt and hdd nr fin* **7/4**[1]

212 **3** 1 1/4 **Mystical Land (IRE)**[20] 2996 2-8-10.......... KFallon 4 105+
(JHMGosden) *lw: chsd ldrs: rdn over 1f out: looked hld whn n.m.r towards fin* **15/8**[2]

1 **4** 1 1/2 **St Andrews Storm (USA)**[19] 3051 2-8-10.......... RHughes 2 99
(RHannon) *s.i.s: hld up: outpcd over 2f out: styd on ins fnl f: nvr able to chal* **14/1**

14 **5** shd **Tony James (IRE)**[22] 2954 2-8-10.......... DHolland 7 98
(CEBrittain) *h.d.w: prom: chsd ldr 1/2-way: rdn over 1f out: wknd ins fnl f* **10/1**

212 **6** 4 **Moscow Music**[37] 2532 2-8-10.......... RLMoore 1 86
(MGQuinlan) *hld up: effrt over 1f out: wknd fnl f* **33/1**

611 **7** 5 **Chateau Istana**[22] 2959 2-8-10.......... TPQueally 3 71
(NPLittmoden) *chsd ldr to 1/2-way: wknd over 1f out* **7/1**[3]

1m 13.61s (0.29) **Going Correction** +0.30s/f (Good) **7** Ran SP% **111.4**
Speed ratings: **110,109,108,106,106 100,94**CSF £26.59 TOTE £12.00: £3.90, £1.70; EX 39.40.
**Owner** The Comic Strip Heroes **Bred** Highclere Stud Ltd **Trained** Newmarket, Suffolk

**FOCUS**
This looked well up to standard and produced a creditable time for the grade. The first three ran close to their Ascot form.

**NOTEBOOK**
**Captain Hurricane** settled much better here in a cross noseband, which enabled him to show a nice turn of foot at the business end, confirming the promise he had shown in his two previous starts. He still looks open to improvement and looks sure to play a major role in his next intended target, the Gimcrack.
**Council Member(USA)**, although beaten, comes out of this with plenty of credit, for he was exposed to the elements up front. A likeable type, he looks the sort to benefit from an extra furlong in time.
**Mystical Land(IRE)** looked to improve a little for the step up in trip, and would certainly have finished closer had he not been short of room towards the finish. With his ability to handle most types of ground, he is sure to find other opportunities.
**St Andrews Storm(USA)**, although never threatening to get competitive, had clearly improved from his debut and looks capable of making his mark at this level as he steps up in trip.
**Tony James(IRE)** had no excuses and will need to lower his sights to get back on the winning trail.
**Moscow Music** didn't improve for the step up in trip, but there is stamina on the dam's side and he shouldn't be written off just yet.
**Chateau Istana** was very disappointing and dropped away tamely. He is better than he showed here.

## 3641 JOSS COLLINS STKS (HERITAGE H'CAP) 1m 2f
**2:20** (2:24) (B) (0-105,97) 3-Y-O **£29,000** (£11,000; £5,500; £2,500) **Stalls** High

Form RPR

-120 **1** **Woodcracker**[20] 2999 3-9-0 **90**.......... DHolland 9 104
(MLWBell) *trckd ldrs: nt clr run 2f out: swtchd lft and led over 1f out: edgd lft ins fnl f: rdn out* **10/1**

3422 **2** shd **Royal Warrant**[10] 3345 3-8-12 **88**.......... MartinDwyer 7 102
(AMBalding) *chsd ldrs: ev ch whn hmpd over 1f out: r.o* **5/1**[3]

6-53 **3** 4 **Torinmoor (USA)**[10] 3345 3-9-1 **91**.......... JPMurtagh 8 98
(MrsAJPerrett) *dwelt, hld up: rdn over 2f out: hdwy over 1f out: styd on same pce ins fnl f* **12/1**

-410 **4** 3 1/2 **Silent Hawk (IRE)**[32] 2676 3-8-13 **89**..........(vt) LDettori 13 89
(SaeedBinSuroor) *lw: hld up: hdwy over 2f out: rdn and ev ch over 1f out: wknd ins fnl f* **12/1**

1212 **5** 3/4 **Celtic Heroine (IRE)**[13] 3223 3-9-7 **97**.......... KDarley 5 96
(MAJarvis) *lw: hld up: hdwy over 3f out: rdn and ev ch whn hmpd over 1f out: sn wknd* **7/2**[2]

2130 **6** 3 **Mystical Girl (USA)**[21] 2971 3-9-4 **94**.......... SChin 2 87
(MJohnston) *led and sn clr: hdd & wknd over 1f out* **16/1**

0-61 **7** 2 1/2 **Galvanise (USA)**[20] 3015 3-8-11 **87**.......... RHughes 14 75
(BWHills) *lw: chsd ldr over 6f: hung rt wl over 1f out: hung lft and hmpd over 1f out: sn wknd* **17/2**

512 **8** 3 1/2 **Motive (FR)**[25] 2896 3-9-0 **90**.......... KFallon 6 71
(SirMichaelStoute) *lw: hld up in tch: chsd ldr over 3f out: rdn whn hmpd over 1f out: sn wknd* **9/4**[1]

-210 **9** 16 **Tarandot (IRE)**[19] 3035 3-8-11 **87**.......... AMcCarthy 3 38
(GGMargarson) *chsd ldrs over 6f* **28/1**

521- **10** 2 1/2 **Quartino**[292] 5045 3-8-13 **89**.......... JFortune 11 35
(JHMGosden) *h.d.w: hld up: wknd 3f out* **22/1**

15-6 **11** 11 **Lunar Exit (IRE)**[25] 2896 3-9-4 **94**.......... KMcEvoy 1 19
(LadyHerries) *hld up: bhd fnl 6f* **40/1**

2m 8.51s (2.05) **Going Correction** +0.30s/f (Good) **11** Ran SP% **120.8**
Speed ratings: **103,102,99,96,96 93,91,89,76,74 65**CSF £59.95 CT £622.51 TOTE £11.40: £3.20, £1.80, £3.60; EX 70.80 Trifecta £507.60 Pool of £3,288.99 - 4.60 winning units..
**Owner** Sir Thomas Pilkington **Bred** Sir Thomas Pilkington **Trained** Newmarket, Suffolk

**FOCUS**
Not as strong as this race usually is, with the topweight rated 8lb below the ceiling.

**NOTEBOOK**
**Woodcracker** proved much better suited by this trip having failed to stay last time. Just as effective on an easier surface, he should find other openings.
**Royal Warrant**, more exposed than his rivals, still looks to be on the upgrade and the way he kept on here suggested there may be more to come when stepped up a little in trip.
**Torinmoor(USA)** closely matched with Royal Warrant on Windsor form, didn't quite see his race out, but he may have not have been done any favours by launching his challenge on the outside of the field *Official explanation: jockey said colt missed the break*
**Silent Hawk(IRE)** had no excuses, and even though he won a weak maiden over this trip on the Rowley Mile, he left the impression that the trip at this level is beyond him.
**Celtic Heroine(IRE)** was done no favours when messed around in the dip, but she was already under pressure and looked held at the time.
**Mystical Girl(USA)** , at her best when allowed to bowl along, faced a difficult task running into the strong headwind.
**Galvanise(USA)** looked to face a stiff task on this first venture into handicap company, and probably didn't run too badly considering he was later found to have mucus in his throat. *Official explanation: trainer's representative said colt had mucus in his throat*
**Motive(FR)** had to work quite hard to go in pusuit of the clear leader, and that didn't look to do him any favours for he was already struggling when squeezed out going into the dip. He deserves another chance.
**Quartino** *Official explanation: jockey said colt was unsuited by the Good to Firm ground*
**Lunar Exit(IRE)** *Official explanation: jockey said gelding was unsuited by the Good to Firm ground*

## 3642 PRINCESS OF WALES'S CANTORODDS.COM STKS (GROUP 2) 1m 4f
**2:55** (2:59) (A) 3-Y-O+ **£58,000** (£22,000; £11,000; £5,000) **Stalls** High

Form RPR

1110 **1** **Bandari (IRE)**[21] 2968 5-9-2 117.......... RHills 8 123
(MJohnston) *lw: hld up: swtchd rt and hdwy over 1f out: sn led: rdn out* **12/1**

15-4 **2** 1/2 **Sulamani (IRE)**[21] 2968 5-9-7 125..........(t) LDettori 7 127
(SaeedBinSuroor) *lw: b: hld up: hdwy and swtchd lft over 2f out: hung rt and ev ch fr over 1f out: r.o* **11/8**[1]

2-42 **3** 2 1/2 **High Accolade**[18] 3072 4-9-2 116.......... MartinDwyer 2 118
(MPTregoning) *chsd ldrs: led over 2f out: rdn and hdd over 1f out: styd on same pce ins fnl f* **6/1**[3]

22-6 **4** 3 1/2 **Magistretti (USA)**[33] 2639 4-9-2 121.......... DHolland 5 113
(NACallaghan) *lw: hld up: hdwy 3f out: sn ev ch: rdn and wknd over 1f out* **10/3**[2]

-633 **5** hd **Persian Majesty (IRE)**[18] 3072 4-9-2 113.......... JPMurtagh 6 112
(PWHarris) *chsd ldrs: rdn and ev ch over 2f out: hung lft and wknd over 1f out* **8/1**

2105 **6** 3 **Systematic**[18] 3072 5-9-2 113.......... KDarley 1 107
(MJohnston) *lw: hld up: hdwy over 3f out: wknd wl over 1f out* **20/1**

25-3 **7** 12 **The Great Gatsby (IRE)**[17] 3136 4-9-2 119.......... JFortune 4 88
(JHMGosden) *chsd ldr 9f: wknd wl over 1f out* **10/1**

5-35 **8** *dist* **Naheef (IRE)**[45] [2329] 5-9-2 111..........................................(vt) KMcEvoy 3 —
(SaeedBinSuroor) *lw: led and sn clr: hdd & wknd over 2f out* **66/1**

2m 32.9s (-0.06) **Going Correction** +0.30s/f (Good) **8** Ran SP% **113.6**
Speed ratings: **112,111,110,107,107 105,97,**—CSF £28.68 TOTE £10.90: £2.80, £1.40, £2.30; EX 31.50 Trifecta £83.20 Pool of £2,531.83 - 21.60 winning units..
**Owner** Hamdan Al Maktoum **Bred** Rathasker Stud **Trained** Middleham Moor, N Yorks

**FOCUS**
This looked a strong Group Two, but it was a fairly modest time. A line through High Accolade suggests there is very little between Sulamani and Doyen, although the latter is better than the bare form he showed at Ascot.

**NOTEBOOK**
**Bandari(IRE)** was fitted with earplugs in the preliminaries in an effort to keep him calm. The way the race was run suited him well, and he showed plenty of resolution to hold on from the persistent Sulamani. His earlier wins this year were back at ten furlongs, but he has always stayed further and, on RPRs, this was a career best.
**Sulamani(IRE)** wasn't disgraced under his Group One penalty, but his attitude left something to be desired. However, connections are certain he will benefit from easier ground.
**High Accolade** was left in front sooner than ideal and was readily picked off. He seems to be racing with a bit more enthusiasm this season but, while he is effective over this trip, he may need to step back up in distance to win.
**Magistretti(USA)** had no excuses and has yet to fully convince over this trip.
**Persian Majesty(IRE)** was far from disgraced, but this company was just too hot for him.
**Systematic**, ridden with more patience than usual, dropped away tamely and doesn't look up to this level.

## 3643 CAPANNELLE RACECOURSE EBF NOVICE STKS 6f
**3:30** (3:32) (D ) 2-Y-O **£8,859** (£2,726; £1,363; £681) **Stalls** Low

Form RPR
**1** **Stetchworth Prince** 2-8-8 .................................................. TPQueally 6 89
(DRLoder) *gd sort: trckd ldrs: led over 1f out: rdn out* **9/2**[3]
**2** 1 3/4 **Army Of Angels (IRE)** 2-8-8 ..........................................(t) LDettori 7 83
(SaeedBinSuroor) *nice colt: bit bkwd: hld up: nt clr run over 1f out: hdwy to chse wnr ins fnl f: no imp towards fin* **7/2**[2]
**3** *nk* **Paper Talk (USA)** 2-8-8 ............................................... DHolland 1 83
(BWHills) *gd sort: trckd ldrs: nt clr run over 1f out: r.o* **11/8**[1]
**4** *1* **Love Angel (USA)** 2-8-8 ............................................... JFanning 4 80
(MJohnston) *cmpt: scope: bit bkwd: w ldr: rdn over 1f out: styd on same pce ins fnl f* **16/1**
15 **5** 2 1/2 **Trempjane**[10] [3346] 2-8-11 ............................................... RHughes 3 75
(RHannon) *lw: led: rdn and hdd over 1f out: wknd ins fnl f* **8/1**
**6** 1/2 **Sign Writer (USA)** 2-8-8 .............................................. EAhern 8 71
(JNoseda) *wl grwn: bkwd: swvd rt s: hld up: plld hrd: rdn over 1f out: wknd ins fnl f* **9/1**

1m 14.35s (1.03) **Going Correction** +0.30s/f (Good) **6** Ran SP% **109.5**
Speed ratings: **105,102,102,100,97 96**CSF £19.35 TOTE £4.90: £2.80, £2.00; EX 24.80.
**Owner** Lucayan Stud **Bred** Highclere Stud Ltd **Trained** Newmarket, Suffolk

**FOCUS**
Some guesswork involved in assessing the form, but a smart time for a race of its type, just 0.74 seconds slower than the July Stakes.

**NOTEBOOK**
**Stetchworth Prince**, a half-brother to the useful Smirk, showed a nice turn of foot to score. While it is difficult to know what to make of this novice, the time was comparable with the July Stakes, and with some well-regarded newcomers filling the frame, there is every reason to believe it was a fair race.
**Army Of Angels(IRE)**, a half-brother to several sprint winners, shaped well enough and can be found an opening before long.
**Paper Talk(USA)** ◆, out of a mare that was successful as a juvenile, is from the same family as the smart sprinter Sheer Viking. He was handled with kid gloves, and should have no trouble repaying the kindness shown here
**Love Angel(USA)**, a half-brother to winners in the States, shaped with plenty of promise and will certainly stay further.
**Trempjane** had the benefit of experience and the rails to race against. Although well beaten in the end, time may tell she wasn't disgraced under her penalty.
**Sign Writer(USA)** was green and pulled far too hard to give himself a chance.

## 3644 ROLLS ROYCE H'CAP 2m 24y
**4:05** (4:08) (C ) (0-95,91) 4-Y-O+ **£10,166** (£3,128; £1,564; £782) **Stalls** High

Form RPR
3-35 **1** **Valance (IRE)**[13] [3244] 4-8-12 **75**........................................ JPMurtagh 10 88
(CREgerton) *lw: trckd ldr over 6f: remained handy: rdn to ld and hung rt over 1f out: drvn out* **9/2**[1]
0506 **2** 1 3/4 **Don Fernando**[18] [3076] 5-9-3 **80**............................................ KFallon 9 91
(MCPipe) *hld up: hdwy and nt clr run over 1f out: styd on* **9/1**
110- **3** 1 1/4 **Ten Carat**[263] [5639] 4-10-0 **91**.......................................... RHughes 11 100
(MrsAJPerrett) *prom: lost pl over 4f out: hdwy and nt clr run over 1f out: swtchd lft: r.o* **9/2**[1]
-015 **4** 1/2 **Land 'n Stars**[22] [2958] 4-9-2 **79**........................................... PDoe 2 88
(JamiePoulton) *hld up: hdwy 1/2-way: rdn over 1f out: styd on same pce ins fnl f* **5/1**[2]
0230 **5** *shd* **The Ring (IRE)**[13] [3236] 4-8-7 **70**........................................ KDarley 3 79
(MrsMReveley) *hld up: hdwy over 2f out: sn rdn: one pce fnl f* **20/1**
2333 **6** 2 1/2 **High Point (IRE)**[39] [2480] 6-9-3 **80**................................. DaneO'Neill 13 86
(GPEnright) *hld up: racd keenly: hdwy u.p over 1f out: wknd wl ins fnl f* **7/1**[3]
-266 **7** *1* **Teresa**[22] [2958] 4-9-0 **77**................................................ JQuinn 12 81
(JLDunlop) *chsd ldrs: rdn over 2f out: wknd fnl f* **15/2**
2200 **8** *3* **Madiba**[35] [2590] 5-7-12 **61** oh2.......................................... AMcCarthy 6 62
(PHowling) *prom: chsd ldr over 9f out: rdn to ld and edgd rt over 2f out: hdd over 1f out: sn wknd* **66/1**
3020 **9** 3/4 **King Flyer (IRE)**[22] [2958] 8-9-3 **80**................................... SWhitworth 7 80
(MissJFeilden) *hld up: rdn over 3f out: nvr trbld ldrs* **9/1**
2126 **10** *3* **Nakwa (IRE)**[6] [3449] 6-8-9 **72**............................................ DAllan 5 68
(EJAlston) *lw: prom: rdn 6f out: wknd over 1f out* **20/1**
3555 **11** *9* **George Stubbs (USA)**[18] [3078] 6-7-13 **67** ow5................ RThomas(5) 1 53
(MJPolglase) *sn led: rdn and hdd over 2f out: wknd over 1f out* **20/1**
0444 **12** *3* **Redspin (IRE)**[5] [3485] 4-8-4 **67**.................................... MartinDwyer 4 49
(JSMoore) *hld up: hdwy 6f out: wknd over 1f out* **12/1**

3m 31.74s (4.75) **Going Correction** +0.30s/f (Good) **12** Ran SP% **120.8**
Speed ratings: **100,99,98,98,98 96,96,94,94,93 88,87**CSF £43.72 CT £196.85 TOTE £5.50: £1.80, £2.90, £2.50; EX 62.70.
**Owner** M Haynes, A & J Allison, J Weatherby **Bred** B H Bloodstock **Trained** Chaddleworth, Berks

**FOCUS**
A very modest time for a race of its class, but the form looks sound enough.

**NOTEBOOK**
**Valance(IRE)** got first run on his rivals and took advantage of traffic problems in behind. This trip suited well and there may be more to come from him.
**Don Fernando** didn't have the best of runs, but confirmed himself in good order. While he only has a maiden victory to his name, there is no doubt he is more than capable when things fall right for him.
**Ten Carat** ◆ covered most of the track in the latter stages and would certainly have given the winner a fight with anything like a clear run.
**Land 'n Stars** had no excuses other than he may have preferred a stronger pace.
**The Ring(IRE)** may have found the ground faster than ideal.

## 3645 NGK SPARK PLUGS RATED STKS (H'CAP) 5f
**4:40** (4:40) (D ) (0-85,83) 3-Y-O+ **£10,249** (£3,153; £1,576; £788) **Stalls** Low

Form RPR
0003 **1** **Silver Prelude**[12] [3273] 3-8-13 **80**...................................... PRobinson 11 91
(DKIvory) *b: racd far side: led that gp 1f: led again 1f out: hung lft: rdn out* **25/1**
5016 **2** *nk* **Awake**[13] [3249] 7-9-2 **78**.............................................. ANicholls 12 88
(DNicholls) *racd far side: hld up: hdwy over 1f out: r.o wl* **14/1**
0406 **3** *nk* **Currency**[7] [3416] 7-9-0 **76**..........................................(p) RLMoore 19 85
(JMBradley) *lw: b: racd stands' side: chsd ldrs: nt clr run over 1f out: r.o wl* **20/1**
0155 **4** 1/2 **Devise (IRE)**[13] [3243] 5-9-4 **80**........................................ KMcEvoy 7 87
(MSSaunders) *racd far side: a.p: rdn over 1f out: r.o* **6/1**[2]
0010 **5** 1/2 **Piccled**[12] [3266] 6-9-7 **83**................................................ DAllan 18 88
(EJAlston) *raecd stands' side: s.i.s: hld up: hdwy over 1f out: r.o* **16/1**
00-3 **6** *nk* **Semenovskii**[158] [646] 4-8-10 **72**........................................ RHills 9 76
(PWD'Arcy) *lw: racd far side: chsd ldrs: rdn over 1f out: styd on* **12/1**
-042 **7** *nk* **Domirati**[13] [3243] 4-9-3 **79**............................................ SDrowne 1 81
(RCharlton) *racd far side: prom: rdn over 1f out: styd on* **8/1**
4633 **8** 1/2 **Mr Malarkey (IRE)**[7] [3416] 4-9-1 **77**.................................(b) PDoe 4 77
(MrsCADunnett) *w ldr far side: rdn and ev ch 1f out: no ex* **7/1**[3]
1300 **9** *nk* **Turibius**[39] [2477] 5-9-2 **78**............................................ RHughes 3 77
(TEPowell) *racd far side: hld up: r.o ins fnl f: nt rch ldrs* **33/1**
21-4 **10** 1/2 **The Jobber (IRE)**[14] [3203] 3-9-1 **82**................................... FNorton 16 79
(MBlanshard) *racd stands' side: chsd ldrs: rdn over 1f out: no ex* **25/1**
0-01 **11** 3/4 **Prince Dayjur (USA)**[7] [3416] 5-9-1 **77** 3ex.............................(v) KFallon 14 71
(MJWallace) *lw: led stands' side tl hdd and no ex ins fnl f* **9/1**
3060 **12** 1/2 **Miss George**[11] [3324] 6-9-6 **82**........................................ SChin 15 74
(DKIvory) *b: racd stands' side: chsd ldrs: rdn and hung lft over 1f out: sn btn* **14/1**
0053 **13** *hd* **Beauvrai**[18] [3090] 4-8-11 **73**......................................... MTebbutt 17 64
(VSmith) *chsd ldrs stands' side: rdn over 1f out: no ex* **18/1**
3-00 **14** 1/2 **Brave Burt (IRE)**[11] [3293] 7-9-6 **82**...................................... EAhern 10 71
(DNicholls) *lw: b: racd far side: led 4f out: rdn and hdd over 1f out: sn wknd* **10/1**
0000 **15** *1* **Salviati (USA)**[12] [3266] 7-8-13 **80**.................................. RThomas(5) 5 65
(JMBradley) *racd far side: dwlt: hld up: wknd over 1f out* **14/1**
4032 **16** 1 3/4 **Winthorpe (IRE)**[4] [3509] 4-8-7 **69**..................................... DHolland 6 47
(JJQuinn) *racd fars ide: chsd ldrs over 3f* **10/3**[1]

59.20 secs (-0.45) **Going Correction** +0.30s/f (Good)
**WFA** 3 from 4yo+ 5lb **16** Ran SP% **134.3**
Speed ratings: **115,114,114,113,112 111,111,110,110,109 108,107,107,106,104 101**CSF £360.36 CT £7270.49 TOTE £42.50: £7.10, £3.80, £5.00, £2.60; EX 310.30 Place 6 £481.50, Place 5 £49.60.
**Owner** Mrs A Shone **Bred** Bearstone Stud **Trained** Radlett, Herts

**FOCUS**
The wind died down a little for this race, but it was still a cracking winning time for the grade. The field split into two with no bias. Solid sprint form.

**NOTEBOOK**
**Silver Prelude** bounced back to form with a vengeance and, although a narrow winner, he had gone for home quite a way out.
**Awake** confirmed himself in good form and, although 8lb higher than when successful last month, is still well treated on the best of his form.
**Currency** ◆ showed more sparkle in the first-time cheekpieces and was unlucky not to have collected, having been forced wide.
**Devise(IRE)** ran his race and had no excuses this time. There will be other days for him.
**Piccled** did himself no favours by missing the break, but confirmed he is on good terms with himself at present.
**Semenovskii** ◆ turned in a solid effort on this return to action, and is 4lb lower now than when last successful.
**Prince Dayjur(USA)** *Official explanation: jockey said gelding lost his action in latter stages*
**Winthorpe(IRE)** *Official explanation: trainer said gelding may have felt the effects of being raced twice within four days*
T/Jkpt: Not won. T/Plt: £1,026.30 to a £1 stake. Pool: £87,031.65. 61.90 winning tickets. T/Qpdt: £46.60 to a £1 stake. Pool: £7,190.05. 113.95 winning tickets. CR

3646 - 3651a (Foreign Racing) - See Raceform Interactive

# 3296 DONCASTER (L-H)
Thursday, July 8

**3652 Meeting Abandoned** - Waterlogged

# 3437 EPSOM (L-H)
Thursday, July 8

**OFFICIAL GOING: Good to soft**
Three-quarters-of-an-inch of rain resulted in a going change - good to soft from the good to firm - and runners came stands' side all evening.

## 3658 EPROCUREMENT APPRENTICE H'CAP 1m 4f 10y
**6:25** (6:29) (E ) (0-70,70) 3-Y-O+ **£4,026** (£1,239; £619; £309) **Stalls** Centre

Form RPR
0362 **1** **Man The Gate**[7] [3450] 5-8-10 **55**................................ NChalmers(3) 8 65
(PDCundell) *lw: hld up in rear: stdy hdwy fr 4f out: ch ldr inside final 2f: drvn to ld 1f out; hung bdly left to far rail: drvn out* **7/2**[3]
-312 **2** *2* **Garston Star**[28] [2802] 3-7-9 **55**................................... RoryMoore(5) 6 62
(JSMoore) *led: styd on wl whn strly chal appr fnl 2f: hdd 1f out: carried lft and nt qckn ins fnl f* **10/1**
0022 **3** *7* **Stolen Hours (USA)**[7] [3437] 4-9-4 **60**.......................... J-PGuillambert 1 57
(JAkehurst) *lw: s.i.s: sn rcvrd and chsd ldrs: rdn to chal over 2f out tl over 1f out: wknd ins fnl f* **11/4**[2]
2-32 **4** *2* **Valeureux**[2] [3604] 6-8-5 **52**.................................. NataliaGemelova(5) 5 46
(JHetherton) *b: chased ldr until rdn and wknd inside final 3f* **2/1**[1]



The Form Book, Raceform Ltd, Compton, RG20 6NL

2000 **5** ½ **General**[15] 3199 7-9-7 **70** StevenHarrison(7) 4 63
(NPLittmoden) *lw: sn in tch: chsd ldrs 5f out: sn pushed along: wknd ins fnl 3f* **8/1**

5045 **6** 1 ¾ **Smarter Charter**[8] 3429 11-7-11 **44** oh2 ow4 KristinStubbs(5) 3 34
(MrsLStubbs) *b: rdn 5f out: a in rr* **20/1**

-040 **7** 2 **Half Inch**[25] 1560 4-9-2 **58** (p) DCorby 2 45
(BICase) *in tch: rdn 5f out: sn wknd* **16/1**

2m 44.13s (5.41) **Going Correction** +0.55s/f (Yiel)
**WFA** 3 from 4yo+ 13lb **7** Ran SP% **113.1**
Speed ratings: **103,101,97,95,95 94,92**CSF £36.07 CT £107.81 TOTE £4.00: £2.20, £2.90; EX 26.10.
**Owner** John G Morley **Bred** J G Morley **Trained** Compton, Berks
■ Stewards Enquiry : N Chalmers one-day ban: careless riding (Jul 19)

**FOCUS**
Runners came stands' side and the field finished strung out. Ordinary form.

**NOTEBOOK**
**Man The Gate** has been in good enough form of late and deserved to get his head in front again. He did so despite hanging badly left and ending up far side and is value for a bit more than the two official lengths he won by. However, he was still a little below last year's best.
**Garston Star**, the sole three-year-old in the field, led for most of the journey and saw off all rivals bar the winner, pulling seven lengths clear of the third.
**Stolen Hours(USA)** momentarily looked as though he was going to get involved but had nothing left to offer from over a furlong out. The ground had probably gone against him.
**Valeureux** has won on this ground in the past and was disappointing as his second earlier in the week entitled him to be bang there.

## 3659 EHRM MAIDEN AUCTION STKS 6f
6:55 (6:57) (E) 2-Y-0 £4,065 (£1,251; £625; £312) Stalls High

Form RPR

62 **1** **Lady Le Quesne (IRE)**[16] 3176 2-8-6 SDrowne 6 81
(AMBalding) *lw: mde all: c to stands rails: drvn fr 2f out: styd on wl fnl f: readily* **9/4**[2]

0622 **2** 1 ¾ **Encanto (IRE)**[13] 3286 2-8-4 JFEgan 2 74
(JSMoore) *disp 2nd:chsd wnr over 3f out:drvn to chal on rail whn nt clr run over 2f out: swtchd lft: r.o ins last: no imp* **7/4**[1]

0 **3** 5 **Guinea A Minute (IRE)**[29] 2786 2-8-9 KFallon 4 64
(MLWBell) *in toich: drvn to chse ldrs over 3f out: sn rdn and one pce: edgd lft fr 2f out: styd on again ins last but n.d* **4/1**[3]

0 **4** 1 ¼ **Sastre (IRE)**[38] 2522 2-8-5 ow1 NChalmers(5) 3 61
(PMPhelan) *s.i.s: sn rcvrd to dispute 2nd tl over 3f out: wknd over 2f out* **40/1**

0 **5** 2 ½ **Asteem**[17] 3157 2-8-9 ANicholls 1 53
(RFJohnsonHoughton) *t.k.h: bhd: rdn an effrt on outside 3f out: nvr gng pce to rch ldrs and wknd over 2f out* **25/1**

424 **6** 4 **Mauro (IRE)**[52] 2177 2-8-4 JQuinn 5 36
(PMPhelan) *swtg: a outpcd: lost tch fr over 2f out* **7/1**

1m 12.39s (1.76) **Going Correction** +0.20s/f (Good) **6** Ran SP% **105.9**
Speed ratings: **96,93,87,85,82 76**CSF £5.76 TOTE £3.00: £1.60, £1.60; EX 5.20.
**Owner** Coriolan Partnership V **Bred** Rozelle Bloodstock **Trained** Kingsclere, Hants
■ Stewards Enquiry : S Drowne caution: careless riding

**FOCUS**
A good performance from Lady Le Quesne who is only small but a useful juvenile.

**NOTEBOOK**
**Lady Le Quesne(IRE)**, who is only a small filly, had shown more than enough to suggest she was capable of winning a race of this nature and having bounced out in front, found plenty when asked in the straight to win well. This is a decent standard of form and she will no doubt be given a busy time of it as she does not look the type to train on.
**Encanto(IRE)** finished second in a sales race in Ireland on her latest start and set the standard. She had every chance but could never get to the winner. Her winning turn will come.
**Guinea A Minute(IRE)** improved on her Newbury debut running and kept on for third. Better can be expected of her once handicapping.
**Mauro(IRE)** ran below par but is worth another chance in nurseries.

## 3660 EXTENDED FINANCE H'CAP 1m 114y
7:25 (7:26) (D) (0-85,84) 3-Y-0+ £8,112 (£2,496; £1,248; £624) Stalls Low

Form RPR

010 **1** **Nimello (USA)**[71] 1708 8-9-9 **75** LDettori 7 86
(AGNewcombe) *mde all: qcknd 6l clr 5f out: stdd over 3f out: hrd drvn over 1f out: kpt on wl* **9/2**[3]

3000 **2** 1 ¼ **Qualitair Wings**[8] 3409 5-9-5 **71** KFallon 2 79
(JHetherton) *bhd: hdwy 5f out: drvn to chse wnr over 1f out: kpt on u.p but no imp ins last* **7/2**[2]

15-3 **3** 1 **Mbosi (USA)**[42] 2420 3-9-8 **84** SChin 6 90
(MJohnston) *swtg: sn chsng wnr: lost position 5f out: rdn and hdwy 3f out: styd on to chse ldrs fnl f but no imp cl home* **13/2**

4516 **4** 1 ¼ **Madamoiselle Jones**[20] 3048 4-9-1 **67** SDrowne 4 70
(HSHowe) *chsd wnr 5f out: pushed along over 2f out: lost 2nd over 1f out: one pce ins last* **8/1**

3514 **5** 15 **Low Cloud**[10] 3365 4-9-10 **76** (v) ANicholls 9 48
(DNicholls) *lw: slowly away and lost 6l: plld hrd in rr: sme hdwy to chse ldrs 3f out: sn rdn: wknd 2f out: eased whn btn ins last* **5/1**

00-1 **6** 2 **Hollywood Henry (IRE)**[24] 2943 4-8-4 **56** (p) JQuinn 1 24
(JAkehurst) *lw: chsd ldrs tl qckly wknd over 2f out* **5/2**[1]

1m 50.53s (4.79) **Going Correction** +0.55s/f (Yiel)
**WFA** 3 from 4yo+ 10lb **6** Ran SP% **110.1**
Speed ratings: **100,98,98,96,83 81**CSF £19.57 CT £93.12 TOTE £5.60: £2.60, £2.20; EX 11.90.
**Owner** Ms Gerardine P O'Reilly **Bred** Glencrest Farm **Trained** Yarnscombe, Devon

**FOCUS**
A modest winning time for the grade and the form might not be all it seems. The result has provisionally been taken at face value, but there were doubts over several of the principals.

**NOTEBOOK**
**Nimello(USA)** was given an astute ride by Dettori in conditions in which he acts well and had stolen a decisive advantage before being given a breather. He picked up well again and held the second comfortably.
**Qualitair Wings** ran well over seven furlongs last time and appreciated this stiffer test. He is well worth trying at ten furlongs but remains 8lb higher than when last winning.
**Mbosi(USA)** lost his position turning into the straight and dropped back to last. He made up plenty of ground in the final couple of furlongs and deserves credit for his effort.
**Madamoiselle Jones** has done all her winning on fast ground and would not have been helped by the rain.
**Low Cloud** should have this run forgotten as he lost ground at the start and pulled once getting back on terms. He unsurprisingly dropped out.
**Hollywood Henry(IRE)** came right back to form to win for the first time at Warwick last month so it was disappointing he could not run better in his follow up bid, the only possible excuse being the ground.

## 3661 COLLABORATIVE PLANNING CONDITIONS STKS 1m 2f 18y
7:55 (7:55) (C ) 4-Y-0+ £8,932 (£3,388; £1,694; £770) Stalls Low

Form RPR

51-5 **1** **Fruhlingssturm**[12] 3315 4-9-4 **111** PRobinson 3 114
(MAJarvis) *lw: racd in 2nd: hdwy to cl hom clr ldr over 2f out: drvn to ld ins fnl f: hld on all out* **9/2**[3]

31-2 **2** shd **Imtiyaz (USA)**[43] 2398 5-8-12 **109** (t) LDettori 2 108
(SaeedBinSuroor) *led: wnt 5l clr after 6f out: rdn whn chal over 1f out: hdd ins last: kpt on wl but no ex last strides* **5/6**[1]

35 **3** 6 **Shambar (IRE)**[24] 2950 5-8-12 RLMoore 6 98?
(PRChamings) *s.i.s: sn rcvrd: chsd ldrs and wnt 3rd over 2f out but nvr a danger: no ch fnl 2f but kpt on for clr 3rd* **66/1**

-320 **4** 3 **Bustan (IRE)**[75] 1622 5-8-12 **107** RHills 5 93
(MPTregoning) *lw: racd in 3rd but nvr gng pce of ldrs: shkn up ins fnl 3f: no rspnse and wknd over 2f out* **6/1**

5205 **5** 9 **Bonecrusher**[20] 3034 5-8-12 **105** KFallon 1 77
(DRLoder) *bhd: rdn over 4f out: no rspnse* **4/1**[2]

0 **6** dist **Mantel Mini**[128] 948 5-8-7 (p) JFEgan 4 —
(BAPearce) *b: slowly into a bhd: t.o* **200/1**

2m 10.84s (2.14) **Going Correction** +0.55s/f (Yiel) **6** Ran SP% **109.0**
Speed ratings: **113,112,108,105,98** —CSF £8.18 TOTE £5.80: £3.30, £1.10; EX 9.60.
**Owner** Gary A Tanaka **Bred** J H A Baggen **Trained** Newmarket, Suffolk

**FOCUS**
A very smart time and a fine effort from from the winner, giving 6lb to the second. However, the proximity of Shambar, seemingly improving around 20lb on his maiden form, is worrying.

**NOTEBOOK**
**Fruhlingssturm**, a German import who shaped with plenty of promise on his British debut behind First Charter at Newmarket - bang there until two out when the combination of first run since September over a mile four found him out - had clearly progressed for the run and put up a smart performance in beating Imtiyaz a short head, especially as he was giving him 6lb.
**Imtiyaz(USA)** was given a similar ride by Dettori to Nimello in the previous race. He did not quite pull it off this time, although he was trying to get back at the winner close home. His best form has come on fast ground.
**Shambar(IRE)** has shown promise in maidens since arriving from France but this looks vastly improved form if it can be believed. He will have done his future handicap mark no good but should win his maiden.
**Bustan(IRE)** was most disappointing and clearly has problems. He is a shadow of the horse we knew of two seasons ago.
**Bonecrusher** was another to run no sort of race on ground he has won on. *Official explanation: jockey said gelding was never travelling*

## 3662 PORTALS H'CAP 1m 2f 18y
8:25 (8:28) (E ) (0-75,75) 3-Y-0+ £4,784 (£1,472; £736; £368) Stalls Low

Form RPR

1466 **1** **Scottish River (USA)**[17] 3159 5-9-9 **75** HayleyTurner(5) 8 88
(MDIUsher) *lw: s.i.s : hld up in rear: improved 4f out: hdwy on rails to ld app final 2f: drvn and held on well final f* **9/2**[3]

0500 **2** 2 ½ **Jacaranda (IRE)**[8] 3412 4-9-6 **67** SDrowne 7 76
(MrsALMKing) *lw: bhd: hdwy 4f out: chsd wnr wl over 1f out: no imp ins last* **8/1**

3630 **3** 3 ½ **Icannshift (IRE)**[19] 3088 4-8-8 **55** RLMoore 6 58
(SDow) *led tl hdd appr fnl 2f: wknd fnl f* **5/2**[1]

0-60 **4** 3 ½ **Mount Benger**[27] 2835 4-9-1 **62** (p) SSanders 2 59
(RMBeckett) *lw: bhd: impr over 2f out: styng on whn hmpd on rails ins fnl 2f: no rcvr and sn btn* **12/1**

-005 **5** 2 ½ **Esperance (IRE)**[10] 3386 4-7-13 **46** ow1 JQuinn 1 39
(JAkehurst) *swtg: bhd: sme hdwy and rdn over 2f out: nvr nr ldrs but styd on u.p fnl f* **6/1**

6-03 **6** shd **My Galliano (IRE)**[14] 3239 8-9-7 **68** KFallon 4 61
(BGPowell) *ch ldrs: rdn to go 2nd over 3f out: wknd quickly 2f out* **7/2**[2]

0002 **7** 4 **Cal Mac**[16] 3173 5-8-12 **59** MHenry 10 45
(RMHCowell) *chsd ldr tl over 3f out: sn wknd* **12/1**

0000 **U** **Lunar Leader (IRE)**[6] 3489 4-7-6 **46** ow1 NataliaGemelova(7) 3 —
(MJGingell) *chsd ldrs tl wknd rapidly over 4f out: t.o* **25/1**

2m 13.37s (4.67) **Going Correction** +0.55s/f (Yiel)
**WFA** 3 from 4yo+ 11lb **8** Ran SP% **113.6**
Speed ratings: **103,101,98,95,93 93,90,**—CSF £39.28 CT £107.97 TOTE £5.80: £1.70, £1.80, £1.60; EX 48.10.
**Owner** M D I Usher **Bred** The Thoroughbred Corporation **Trained** Upper Lambourn, Berks

**FOCUS**
This was not a great race, but a good effort from Scottish River to defy top-weight nonetheless.

**NOTEBOOK**
**Scottish River(USA)** left a couple of slightly disappointing efforts in classified events behind and stayed on well to win a shade comfortably.
**Jacaranda(IRE)** stayed on for second without ever looking likely to get to the winner and appreciate this trip.
**Icannshift(IRE)** ran his race from the head of affairs without quite lasting out.
**Mount Benger** would have finished closer but for being hampered by the loose horse and has a small race in him.
**Cal Mac** *Official explanation: jockey said gelding hung left*

## 3663 CEDAR OPEN ACCOUNTS H'CAP 6f
8:55 (8:59) (D ) (0-80,78) 3-Y-0+ £5,421 (£1,668; £834; £417) Stalls High

Form RPR

4343 **1** **Jayanjay**[7] 3439 5-9-12 **77** SSanders 3 86
(MissBSanders) *lw: bhd: hdwy 3f out: str run fr over 1f out: hrd drvn ins last to ld last stride* **4/1**[3]

2153 **2** shd **Glencoe Solas (IRE)**[17] 3141 4-9-7 **72** JFEgan 9 81
(SKirk) *led: rdn 2f out: styd on wl fnl f: ct last stride* **8/1**

0132 **3** ½ **Lord Of The East**[7] 3439 5-9-9 **74** AlexGreaves 4 81
(DNicholls) *chsd ldr: rdn and effrt 1f out: lost 2nd and styd on wl ins last* **7/2**[2]

6642 **4** nk **Quantum Leap**[7] 3440 7-9-6 **71** (v) RLMoore 5 77
(SDow) *chsd ldrs: rdn over 2f out: one pce ins fnl f* **8/1**

4210 **5** 5 **Kingscross**[40] 2477 6-9-13 **78** DSweeney 8 69
(MBlanshard) *bhd: rdn and hdwy fr 2f out: kpt on fnl f but nvr gng pce to rch ldrs* **5/2**[1]

5000 **6** nk **Attorney**[2] 3616 6-7-7 **49** oh3 (v) HayleyTurner(5) 1 39
(DShaw) *bhd: rdn and styd on fr 2f out: kpt on ins last but nvr a danger* **20/1**

0652 **7** ¾ **Compton Banker (IRE)**[9] 3395 7-9-0 **68** DNolan(3) 7 56
(GAButler) *s.i.s: bhd: rdn 3f out and sme hdwy: styd on same pce fnl 2f* **11/1**

2000 **8** 2 **Social Contract**[101] 1176 7-7-9 **49** oh1 LisaJones(3) 10 31
(SDow) *chsd ldrs tl wknd 2f out* **25/1**

6501 **9** 3 **Firework**[13] 3260 6-8-13 **64**......(p) JQuinn 2 37
(JAkehurst) *lw: chsd ldrs: styd far side and racd alone: no ch w stands side ins fnl 2f* **14/1**

5100 **10** 1 **Tatweer (IRE)**[12] 3314 4-8-5 **56**......(v) SWhitworth 6 26
(DShaw) *s.i.s: a outpcd* **16/1**

1m 11.38s (0.75) **Going Correction** +0.20s/f (Good) **10** Ran SP% **122.5**
Speed ratings: **103,102,102,101,95 94,93,91,87,85**CSF £38.20 CT £128.68 TOTE £5.40: £1.60, £2.80, £1.80; EX 53.10 Place 6 £60.17, Place 5 £10.11.
**Owner** Peter Crate **Bred** P D Crate **Trained** Epsom, Surrey

**FOCUS**
A good finish and sound form, with the second running her best race yet, and the other principals pretty much to form.

**NOTEBOOK**
**Jayanjay**, whose last win came around a year ago over course and distance, finished strongly under a full-on ride from Seb Sanders and caught the long-time leader in the dying strides. He has an indifferent strike-rate however, and is not one to rely on for a follow up.
**Glencoe Solas(IRE)** was a hard done by loser as she had led for most of the way and looked to have done enough until getting nailed on the line. Career best form neverthless, as she did not look well treated.
**Lord Of The East** has done all his winning on fast ground and ran well considering. He is versatile with regards to trip and is worth watching out for when the ground firms up again.
**Quantum Leap** had his chance and was not quite good enough.
**Kingscross** should really have shown more on his favoured easy going and could only keep on at the one pace having been held up.
T/Plt: £92.10 to a £1 stake. Pool: £59,931.50. 474.85 winning tickets. T/Qpdt: £23.40 to a £1 stake. Pool: £5,314.00. 167.80 winning tickets. ST

# 3259 FOLKESTONE (R-H)

Thursday, July 8

**OFFICIAL GOING: Good to soft**
Wind: lt against Weather: rain much of afternoon

## 3664 EUROPEAN BREEDERS FUND MEDIAN AUCTION MAIDEN STKS (DIV I) 7f (S)

**2:10** (2:12) (F) 2-Y-O **£3,101** (£886; £443) **Stalls** Low

Form RPR

**1** **Montgomery's Arch (USA)** 2-9-0 ...... JQuinn 1 89+
(PWChapple-Hyam) *t.k.h: hld up: gd prog on outer over 2f out: led wl over 1f out: rn green but sn in command: shkn up fnl f: promising* **6/4**[1]

5 **2** 2 ½ **Lottie Dundass**[18] 3123 2-8-9 ...... BDoyle 6 73
(PWHarris) *sn pressed ldr: led 3f out to wl over 1f out: styd on but no ch w wnr* **2/1**[2]

**3** 1 ¾ **Jamaaron** 2-9-0 ...... RLMoore 7 74
(RHannon) *cl up: shkn up and unable qck over 1f out: one pce after* **10/1**

0 **4** 1 ½ **Bazelle**[29] 2786 2-8-9 ...... PaulEddery 9 65
(PWD'Arcy) *trckd ldrs: pushed along 2f out: rn green after: one pce* **33/1**

**5** 1 ½ **Merchant (IRE)** 2-9-0 ...... IMongan 8 66
(MLWBell) *dwlt: sn trckd ldrs: pushed along and outpcd wl over 1f out: n.d after* **8/1**

05 **6** 1 ¼ **Merrymadcap (IRE)**[14] 3241 2-9-0 ...... DSweeney 3 63
(MBlanshard) *in tch in rr: outpcd and shkn up over 2f out: one pce and no ch after* **16/1**

**7** ½ **Chairman Rick (IRE)** 2-9-0 ...... NPollard 2 62
(DRLoder) *settled in tch: outpcd and pushed along over 2f out: no ch after* **7/1**[3]

0 **8** ½ **Scissors (IRE)**[18] 3123 2-8-6 ...... BReilly(3) 10 56
(MissJFeilden) *mde most to 3f out: wknd over 1f out* **40/1**

**9** 7 **Rhapsody In Silver (FR)** 2-9-0 ...... MTebbutt 4 43
(JJay) *outpcd and bhd after 3f: nvr on terms* **66/1**

00 **10** 25 **Ivory Wolf**[19] 3104 2-9-0 ......(p) SCarson 5 —
(JLSpearing) *prom tl wknd rapidly over 2f out: t.o* **66/1**

1m 30.09s (2.29) **Going Correction** +0.175s/f (Good) **10** Ran SP% **120.3**
Speed ratings: **93,90,88,86,84 83,82,82,74,45**CSF £4.72 TOTE £2.30: £1.70, £1.10, £2.90; EX 6.50.
**Owner** Franconson Partners **Bred** Sycamore Hall Farm Llc **Trained** Newmarket, Suffolk

**FOCUS**
Just an average juvenile event, but the winner was impressive and looks sure to go on to better things.

**NOTEBOOK**
**Montgomery's Arch(USA)** ran distinctly green through the early parts, but showed an eye-catching turn of foot to win going away. This was an impressive display and he should improve a great deal again for the experience. He looks sure to take a higher order over farther in due course.
**Lottie Dundass** improved on her debut display over this extra furlong and softer ground, but had no chance with the winner. There was little disgrace in this defeat.
**Jamaaron** showed good early speed and was only caught out late on by lack of experience. This was a pleasing debut, and with her yard's juveniles continuing in fine form she should make the necessary improvement to find a race.
**Bazelle** stepped up markedly on the form of her debut and appreciated the extra furlong. She still looked green late on and will fare better once handicapped.
**Rhapsody In Silver(FR)** *Official explanation: jockey said colt was hanging left throughout*

## 3665 EUROPEAN BREEDERS FUND MEDIAN AUCTION MAIDEN STKS (DIV II) 7f (S)

**2:40** (2:42) (F) 2-Y-O **£3,101** (£886; £443) **Stalls** Low

Form RPR

06 **1** **Spaced (IRE)**[19] 3083 2-9-0 ...... RLMoore 3 79
(RHannon) *w ldr: led wl over 2f out: rdn and kpt on wl fr over 1f out* **11/1**

2 **2** 1 ½ **Sunset Strip**[42] 2422 2-9-0 ...... CCatlin 4 75
(MRChannon) *led to wl over 2f out: pressed wnr after: nt qckn u.p 1f out* **4/5**[1]

**3** ¾ **Fairmile** 2-9-0 ...... IMongan 2 73
(PWHarris) *dwlt: racd on outer and sn trckd ldrs: rn green and unable qck 2f out: styd on again fnl f* **3/1**[2]

6 **4** 2 **Mulberry Wine**[15] 3202 2-8-9 ...... DSweeney 1 63
(MBlanshard) *cl up: rdn to chal and ev ch 2f out: sn nt qckn and edgd rt: one pce after* **50/1**

40 **5** 3 ½ **Marianis**[29] 2786 2-8-9 ...... SCarson 7 55
(JGPortman) *rn green in last pair: rdn 1/2-way: kpt on one pce fr over 1f out* **16/1**

03 **6** ½ **Orpen Annie (IRE)**[18] 3116 2-8-9 ...... JMcAuley 8 53
(MissJFeilden) *cl up: rdn wl over 2f out: wknd wl over 1f out* **14/1**

00 **7** 4 **Countrywide Sun**[55] 2087 2-8-11 ......(b[1]) J-PGuillambert(3) 9 48
(NPLittmoden) *in tch: rdn whn jinked rt over 2f out: wknd* **33/1**

**8** 2 ½ **Precious Sammi** 2-9-0 ...... JFEgan 5 42
(JulianPoulton) *chsd ldrs: rdn 3f out: sn wknd* **7/1**[3]

**9** ¾ **Olivia Twist** 2-8-6 ...... ABeech(3) 6 35
(WGMTurner) *a in last pair: rdn 1/2-way: struggling after* **33/1**

1m 29.7s (1.90) **Going Correction** +0.175s/f (Good) **9** Ran SP% **121.8**
Speed ratings: **96,94,93,91,87 86,82,79,78**CSF £21.29 TOTE £18.20: £2.20, £1.02, £2.10; EX 21.50.
**Owner** de La Warr Racing **Bred** Tally-Ho Stud **Trained** East Everleigh, Wilts

**FOCUS**
Just an ordinary maiden, run at a fair gallop, but improved form from the first two.

**NOTEBOOK**
**Spaced(IRE)** stuck to his task well late in the day to shrug off his challenger and get off the mark at the third attempt. He has improved with every outing so far and is the type to improve through the nursery ranks.
**Sunset Strip**, who shaped with promise behind a smart juvenile on his debut last time, was well backed to go one better, but could not quicken with the winner and finished well held. He may be worth another chance back on faster ground.
**Fairmile** , a half-brother to his stable's useful ten furlong performer Poppy Carew, ran green early on and was not helped by a slow start. He stayed on well however, and should know a lot more next time.
**Mulberry Wine** had every chance, but could not quicken on this ground when it mattered. She will not be seen to best effect until eligible for nurseries.

## 3666 COME EVENING RACING ON 22ND JULY MAIDEN STKS 7f (S)

**3:15** (3:16) (D ) 3-Y-O **£3,493** (£1,075; £537; £268) **Stalls** Low

Form RPR

43 **1** **Corky (IRE)**[12] 3322 3-9-0 ...... RLMoore 3 80
(RHannon) *prom: trckd ldr 1/2-way: led wl over 1f out: sn rdn clr* **3/1**[2]

**2** 5 **Violet Park** 3-8-9 ...... CCatlin 9 62
(BJMeehan) *dwlt: racd in last pair: wl bhd 1/2-way: gd prog over 2f out: styd on wl to take 2nd last 75yds: no ch w wnr* **12/1**[3]

3 **3** 2 ½ **Deuxieme (IRE)**[28] 2808 3-8-9 ...... DSweeney 1 56
(RCharlton) *led: gng easily tl hdd and fnd nil wl over 1f out: lost 2nd last 75yds* **4/7**[1]

0 **4** 6 **Cazenove**[92] 1306 3-9-0 ...... JFEgan 6 45
(MGQuinlan) *chsd ldrs: pushed along 3f out: cl up 2f out: wknd* **12/1**[3]

00-0 **5** 5 **Argentum**[17] 3161 3-9-0 ...... JQuinn 2 32
(LadyHerries) *nudged along in last trio: wl bhd 1/2-way: kpt on steadily fnl 2f: do bttr* **33/1**

00 **6** 5 **Preston Hall**[110] 1064 3-9-0 ...... SCarson 7 19
(MrsLCJewell) *chsd ldrs: rdn and lost tch 3f out: wl bhd whn nt clr run 1f out* **66/1**

0 **7** 3 **Homebred Star**[17] 3161 3-8-11 ...... DCorby(3) 4 11
(PBowen) *s.i.s: sn chsd ldrs: rdn and wknd 3f out* **25/1**

000- **8** 2 **Sixtilsix (IRE)**[254] 5812 3-9-0 ...... RLappin 11 6
(WJarvis) *cl up tl wknd rapidly wl over 2f out* **25/1**

0-0 **9** 3 **Paradise Breeze**[12] 3322 3-8-9 ...... PaulEddery 5 —
(CAHorgan) *in tch to 1/2-way: nudged along and sn bhd: eased over 1f out* **50/1**

0 **10** 5 **Till There Was You**[173] 553 3-8-6 ...... ABeech(3) 10 —
(WGMTurner) *w ldr for 3f: sn wknd and bhd* **66/1**

0-0 **11** dist **Native Turk (USA)**[87] 1371 3-9-0 ......(b[1]) WRyan 8 —
(JARToller) *sn rdn and wl bhd in last: t.o* **25/1**

1m 28.88s (1.08) **Going Correction** +0.175s/f (Good) **11** Ran SP% **123.5**
Speed ratings: **100,94,91,84,78 73,69,67,64,58** —CSF £37.08 TOTE £4.20: £1.30, £3.20, £1.02; EX 25.70.
**Owner** Robert Whitworth & Jane Whitworth **Bred** A Stroud And J Hanly **Trained** East Everleigh, Wilts

**FOCUS**
A maiden lacking any strength in depth and the field came home well strung out.

**NOTEBOOK**
**Corky(IRE)** ran out a comfortable winner on this softer ground and got off the mark at the third attempt. He looks fairly progressive and this return to seven furlongs was clearly to his liking.
**Violet Park** ran green in the early stages and looked to have a fair bit to do at half-way, but really picked up under pressure late on and finished best of all. She would not have troubled the winner, but rates better than the bare form and should improve on this.
**Deuxieme(IRE)** looked the most likely winner inside the final two furlongs, but she found nothing could not even hold on for second. She may well have hated this easier surface, but has it all to prove now. *Official explanation: trainer representative said filly did not act on the Good to Soft ground*
**Cazenove** , popular at big prices in the betting ring, could not quicken on this drop in trip and finished well beaten. He still looked inexperienced and may be worth another chance when handicapped.
**Argentum** caught the eye under a tender ride, staying on all too late. He is one to keep on the right side of if the market speaks in his favour.

## 3667 LADIES EVENING ON THE 5TH AUGUST H'CAP 2m 93y

**3:50** (3:51) (F) (0-55,52) 4-Y-O+ **£2,996** (£856; £428) **Stalls** Low

Form RPR

4000 **1** **River Of Fire**[13] 3263 6-7-7 **32** oh2......(v) NataliaGemelova(7) 2 46
(CNKellett) *led after 3f: mde rest: kicked on 2f out: clr and in n.d fnl f* **14/1**

20-1 **2** 5 **High Drama**[11] 2874 7-8-5 **40** ow2...... DCorby(3) 11 48
(PBowen) *led for 3f: chsd wnr after: rdn over 2f out: no imp over 1f out* **4/1**[2]

0120 **3** 1 ½ **Galandora**[26] 2893 4-8-13 **52**...... LucyRussell(7) 4 58
(DrJRJNaylor) *hld up in rr: prog to chse ldrs over 3f out: unable qck 2f out: kpt on same pce after* **12/1**

0442 **4** 3 ½ **Tom Bell (IRE)**[5] 3518 4-8-8 **47**...... PPMathers(7) 13 49
(JGMO'Shea) *trckd ldrs: gng wl 4f out: v one-pced and btn fr 2f out* **3/1**[1]

3220 **5** nk **Mr Whizz**[23] 2430 7-8-4 **36**...... DKinsella 1 38
(APJones) *hld up in last pair: prog 5f out: kpt on fr over 2f out: nvr on terms* **25/1**

-003 **6** 4 **Java Dawn (IRE)**[12] 3303 4-8-10 **42**...... JFEgan 10 39
(TEPowell) *t.k.h: hld up in last pair: prog to chse ldrs over 3f out : no imp 2f out: wknd over 1f out* **20/1**

6-62 **7** nk **Harik**[13] 2874 10-8-11 **43**......(bt) RLMoore 12 39
(GLMoore) *hld up in midfield: prog and cl up 3f out: sn rdn: wknd over 1f out* **6/1**[3]

0/00 **8** 4 **Real Estate**[6] 3488 10-8-11 **48**...... HayleyTurner(5) 16 40
(JSKing) *wl in tch: rdn and effrt over 3f out: wknd 2f out* **33/1**

0-00 **9** 6 **Wizard Of The West**[13] 3263 4-8-12 **49**...... NChalmers(5) 8 33
(MissSheenaWest) *w ldrs to 4f out: rdnn and steadily wknd fnl 3f* **40/1**

-002 **10** 3 ½ **Peak Park (USA)**[8] 3429 4-8-10 **45**......(v) LisaJones(3) 5 25
(JARToller) *trckd ldrs: lost pl 5f out: rdn and no prog 3f out: sn wknd* **8/1**

06 **11** hd **Dalon (POL)**[28] 2816 5-9-0 **46**......(b) MTebbutt 3 26
(DBFeek) *t.k.h: hld up in midfield: rdn and wknd 3f out* **16/1**

0-04 **12** 2 ½ **Circus Maximus (USA)**[19] 3099 7-9-4 **50**......(b) CCatlin 9 27
(IanWilliams) *towards rr: reminder 9f out: rdn and struggling 6f out: bhd fnl 3f* **8/1**



The Form Book, Raceform Ltd, Compton, RG20 6NL

005 **13** *19* **Stopwatch (IRE)**[122] [889] 9-8-0 **32** oh7..............................(p) MHenry 15 —
(MrsLCJewell) *dwlt: a in rr: wknd over 4f out: wl bhd fnl 3f* **50/1**
0-50 **14** *10* **El Hamra (IRE)**[100] [1187] 6-8-4 **36**.............................................. ADaly 7 —
(MJHaynes) *sn in rr: last and losing tch over 5f out: t.o* **33/1**
2000 **15** *10* **Joely Green**[19] [3108] 7-8-8 **40**..............................................(b) IMongan 6 —
(NPLittmoden) *dwlt: rdn to go prom after 3f: wknd 4f out: virtually p.u fnl f* **14/1**

3m 49.51s (8.91) **Going Correction** +0.50s/f (Yiel) **15** Ran SP% **127.3**
Speed ratings: **97,94,93,92,91 89,89,87,84,82 82,81,72,67,62**CSF £68.31 CT £727.93 TOTE £23.10: £5.00, £2.40, £3.60; EX 213.20.
**Owner** J E Titley **Bred** Littleton Stud **Trained** Swadlincote, Derbys

**FOCUS**
A seller in disguise and it produced a modest time, even for such a low grade.

**NOTEBOOK**
**River Of Fire** repeated last year's win, having taken the race by the scruff of the neck early on, and was value for even more than the official winning margin. This was a much improved effort on this softer ground, and although he is only plating-class, his manner of victory suggests he could follow up.
**High Drama**, disappointing over fences the last twice, ran a fair race off this higher mark and on this softer ground. He will improve on faster ground and seems in good heart on the Flat at this lowly level.
**Galandora** improved for this step back up in distance, but failed to quicken on this softer ground. She can do better over this trip, back on a quicker surface.
**Tom Bell(IRE)** fell in a hole in the straight, having travelled well to that point, and looked all at sea on this slower ground.
**Java Dawn(IRE)** *Official explanation: jockey said filly was too keen throughout*
**Harik** looked to be in with a shout over three out, but found little and looked to be hating the ground late on. He is worth another chance back on his favoured fast ground.

## 3668 FAVERSHAM H'CAP 5f
**4:25** (4:26) (E ) (0-70,64) 3-Y-O+ **£3,445** (£1,060; £530; £265) **Stalls** Low

Form RPR
0102 **1** **Enjoy The Buzz**[3] [3575] 5-8-9 **47**............................................ RLMoore 2 58
(JMBradley) *hld up in last: pushed along 1/2-way: struggling 2f out: swtchd rt over 1f out: styd on strly to ld last 100yds: sn clr* **1/1**[1]
6545 **2** *1 ½* **College Queen**[10] [3372] 6-9-12 **64**..........................................(b) IMongan 1 70
(SGollings) *led: 3l clr 2f out: rdn over 1f out: tired and hdd last 100yds* **7/2**[3]
6-04 **3** *¾* **Lake Verdi (IRE)**[43] [2404] 5-9-2 **54**...........................................(t) WRyan 5 57
(BHanbury) *hld up in tch: effrt 2f out: chsd ldr over 1f out tl ins fnl f: kpt on one pce* **3/1**[2]
4220 **4** *7* **Urban Calm**[19] [3096] 3-9-6 **63**................................................ MHenry 3 41
(RMHCowell) *chsd ldr to over 1f out: wknd and eased* **8/1**
0000 **5** *4* **Bahamian Belle**[16] [3175] 4-8-7 **45**............................................... JQuinn 4 9
(PSMcentee) *t.k.h: trckd ldrs tl wknd wl over 1f out* **20/1**

61.68 secs (0.98) **Going Correction** +0.175s/f (Good)
**WFA** 3 from 4yo+ 5lb **5** Ran SP% **113.1**
Speed ratings: **99,96,95,84,77**CSF £5.06 TOTE £2.00: £1.90, £1.40; EX 6.40.
**Owner** Miss F Fenley **Bred** Southern Seafoods **Trained** Sedbury, Gloucs

**FOCUS**
A modest winning time for the grade, but the winner improved again.

**NOTEBOOK**
**Enjoy The Buzz**, a narrow loser on firm ground last time, was heavily backed to go one better and ultimately landed the odds in tidy fashion, although his prospects did not look good at halfway. Value for more than the official winning margin, he has been in good heart since resuming this summer and can improve yet again on faster ground.
**College Queen** had every chance form the front, but was no match for the eventual winner's turn of foot late on under her big weight. She is slowly dropping back to a fair mark and ideally needs softer ground. She has a race in her at this level.
**Lake Verdi(IRE)** lacked a change of gear when it mattered on this drop back to the minimum trip.
**Urban Calm** did not improve for this handicap debut and drop back to five furlongs. She is going the wrong way.

## 3669 HYTHE FESTIVAL H'CAP 1m 4f
**5:00** (5:00) (E ) (0-70,67) 3-Y-O **£4,316** (£1,328; £664; £332) **Stalls** Low

Form RPR
00-1 **1** **Elusive Dream**[2] [3614] 3-9-13 **67** 6ex.................................... SSanders 9 87+
(SirMarkPrescott) *prom: led 3f out: shkn up 2f out: clr fnl f: won w plenty in hand* **4/6**[1]
5133 **2** *5* **Vicario**[21] [3020] 3-9-7 **61**....................................................... IMongan 7 65
(MLWBell) *in tch: pushed along 4f out: prog 3f out: chsd wnr 2f out: sn brushed aside* **6/1**[2]
-005 **3** *4* **Rinneen (IRE)**[43] [2402] 3-8-9 **49**...........................................(v) RLMoore 1 47
(RHannon) *cl up: trckd ldr 6f out: ev ch over 2f out: sn outpcd and btn* **8/1**[3]
0223 **4** *1* **Regal Performer (IRE)**[16] [3172] 3-9-4 **58**.............................. JFEgan 8 55
(SKirk) *hld up in tch: prog to trck ldrs 3f out: rdn and no rspnse 2f out: wknd fnl f* **14/1**
0200 **5** *1 ½* **Varuni (IRE)**[27] [2848] 3-9-3 **60**......................................... LisaJones(3) 11 54
(JGPortman) *wl in tch: rdn and effrt 3f out: outpcd and btn over 2f out* **9/1**
0145 **6** *16* **Fiddles Music**[9] [3391] 3-8-5 **45**............................................... CCatlin 10 15
(MissSheenaWest) *led for 2f: prom tl lost pl over 4f out: wl bhd fnl 2f* **33/1**
-300 **7** *½* **Wyoming**[14] [3231] 3-9-5 **59**..................................................... WRyan 5 29
(JARToller) *hld up in tch: effrt over 3f out: wknd over 2f out: sn bhd* **12/1**
-060 **8** *3 ½* **Frankies Wings (IRE)**[28] [2821] 3-9-6 **60**.............................(b1) BDoyle 2 24
(TGMills) *dwlt: reminders and rushed up to ld after 2f: hdd & wknd rapidly 3f out* **14/1**
-000 **9** *11* **Bee Dees Legacy**[20] [3044] 3-9-5 **59**..................................(b1) RBrisland 3 7
(GLMoore) *racd in rr: rn wd bnd over 9f out: wknd 5f out: t.o* **50/1**
0000 **10** *dist* **High View (USA)**[34] [2654] 3-9-4 **58**............................................ JQuinn 4 —
(FJordan) *t.k.h early: hld up: rdn 8f out: lost tch 6f out: t.o* **14/1**

2m 46.23s (5.83) **Going Correction** +0.50s/f (Yiel) **10** Ran SP% **128.0**
Speed ratings: **100,96,94,93,92 81,81,79,71,—**CSF £6.06 CT £23.40 TOTE £1.60: £1.10, £1.70, £2.80; EX 6.70.
**Owner** Cheveley Park Stud **Bred** Cheveley Park Stud Ltd **Trained** Newmarket, Suffolk

**FOCUS**
A modest heat and the field came home well strung out. The winner was different class, but there could well be future winners in behind him.

**NOTEBOOK**
**Elusive Dream** ◆ followed up his controversial Fibresand success readily under his 6lb penalty. He looked different class and could well run up a sequence en-route to a crack at something bigger.
**Vicario** had no chance with the winner, but was clear second best and again ran a solid race. He can clearly find a race off this mark.
**Rinneen(IRE)** has improved a touch the last twice for the application of a visor, and although he looked very one-paced late on, may be able to find a weak heat off his declining mark.
**Regal Performer(IRE)**, although still a maiden, has become consistent and would have preferred faster ground.

## 3670 FOLKESTONE FILLIES' H'CAP 1m 1f 149y
**5:30** (5:32) (E ) (0-70,69) 3-Y-O+ **£3,503** (£1,078; £539; £269) **Stalls** Low

Form RPR
06-1 **1** **Toccata Aria**[6] [3490] 6-8-10 **51** 6ex......................................... RLMoore 14 59
(JMBradley) *well placed: chsd ldr over 2f out: led over 1f out: hard rdn and hld on nr finish* **7/1**[2]
4044 **2** *½* **Holly Rose**[8] [3423] 5-8-6 **52**..........................................(p) HayleyTurner(5) 2 59
(DECantillon) *s.i.s: hld up: prog on outer fr 4f out: chsd wnr over 1f out: upsides fnl f: reminder and jinked lft nr fin* **9/1**
0231 **3** *¾* **Ember Days**[3] [3573] 5-9-10 **65** 6ex..........................................(p) SCarson 5 71
(JLSpearing) *settled towards rr: rdn and effort 3f out: progress over 1f out: staying on but held when checked nr fin* **9/2**[1]
0604 **4** *1* **Castaigne (FR)**[6] [3490] 5-8-11 **52**............................................... RHavlin 9 56
(BWDuke) *hld up in midfield: effort 2f out: not clear run over 1f out: styd on fnl f: nrst fin* **16/1**
4025 **5** *1* **Rabitatit (IRE)**[14] [3223] 3-8-4 **63**........................................ PPMathers(7) 12 65
(JGMO'Shea) *pressed ldr: led over 5f out to over 1f out: wknd fnl f* **14/1**
-405 **6** *¾* **Maxilla (IRE)**[29] [2775] 4-9-7 **69**........................................... AHamblett(7) 10 70
(LMCumani) *hld up wl in rr: last over 2f out: nudged along and styd on steadily after: nvr nr ldrs* **10/1**
0206 **7** *hd* **Madame Marie (IRE)**[8] [3412] 4-8-6 **50**.................................. LisaJones(3) 1 50
(SDow) *s.i.s: hld up in last trio: prog on outer over 3f out: nt rch ldrs fr 2f out: one pce* **8/1**[3]
0150 **8** *1 ½* **Littleton Zephir (USA)**[13] [3282] 5-8-7 **48**...................... JoannaBadger 11 46
(MrsPTownsley) *wl in rr: in last trio whn nt clr run over 3f out: rdn and kpt on same pce fnl 2f: no ch* **25/1**
6032 **9** *1* **Jessinca**[8] [3423] 8-7-12 **39**........................................................ DKinsella 6 35
(APJones) *racd in midfield: prog 5f out: chsd ldrs over 2f out: wknd over 1f out* **9/2**[1]
6106 **10** *1 ½* **Sunset Mirage (USA)**[17] [3139] 3-9-3 **69**................................ SSanders 8 62
(EALDunlop) *racd in midfield: rdn and effrt 3f out: chsd ldrs over 1f out: sn wknd* **11/1**
0/00 **11** *hd* **Lady Jeannie**[13] [3264] 7-8-2 **43**................................................. CCatlin 4 36
(MJHaynes) *mounted on crse: reluctant to enter stalls: prom: chsd ldr 3f out to over 2f out: sn wknd* **50/1**
260 **12** *7* **On Cloud Nine**[15] [3204] 3-9-0 **66**.............................................. IMongan 3 46
(MLWBell) *hld up in rr: shkn up 3f out: no prog over 2f out: wknd* **16/1**
0-00 **13** *13* **Havantadoubt (IRE)**[47] [2302] 4-9-0 **55**................................(p) DSweeney 7 12
(MRBosley) *prom tl wknd rapidly wl over 2f out* **16/1**
2644 **14** *1* **Jade Star (USA)**[7] [3461] 4-8-3 **51**.........................(p) RachelCostello(7) 13 6
(MissGayKelleway) *led to over 5f out: wknd rapidly 3f out* **7/1**[2]

2m 9.27s (4.11) **Going Correction** +0.50s/f (Yiel)
**WFA** 3 from 4yo+ 11lb **14** Ran SP% **130.0**
Speed ratings: **103,102,102,101,100 99,99,98,97,96 96,90,80,79**CSF £74.59 CT £328.39 TOTE £8.20: £2.60, £2.30, £2.30; EX 80.10 Place 6 £5.76, Place 5 £4.53.
**Owner** Terry Warner **Bred** Southill Stud **Trained** Sedbury, Gloucs

**FOCUS**
A sound pace, but a moderate handicap and weak form.

**NOTEBOOK**
**Toccata Aria** was always well placed and had no problem defying a 6lb penalty. She showed a good attitude to shrug off the runner-up close home and did well to maintain her form on this slower surface. Although she has clearly improved this year, she will need to do so again in order to defy another rise in the weights.
**Holly Rose** again had her chance, but looked reluctant to pass the eventual winner in the last furlong. She is on a fair mark and is often one to fill the frame, but remains very hard to win with.
**Ember Days** ran her race under a 6lb penalty and gives the form a solid enough look for the grade.
**Castaigne(FR)** was staying on best of all, having been set a fair bit to do, and ran a fair race in the circumstances.
**Rabitatit(IRE)** appreciated the return to handicap company, but was unsuited by the softened ground.
**Jessinca**, in the frame in weaker events the last twice, ran no sort of race on this easier surface and in this better company.
T/Plt: £9.10 to a £1 stake. Pool: £24,410.65. 1,957.15 winning tickets. T/Qpdt: £6.20 to a £1 stake. Pool: £1,268.00. 150.70 winning tickets. JN

# 3639 NEWMARKET (JULY) (R-H)
### Thursday, July 8

**OFFICIAL GOING: Good to soft**
Just under an inch of rain fell through the night. The far side appeared to be favoured.
Wind: Slight across. Weather: Cloudy with an occasional shower.

## 3671 VENTURE LIFESTYLE PHOTOGRAPHY H'CAP 1m
**1:20** (1:22) (C ) (0-100,100) 3-Y-O **£13,884** (£4,272; £2,136; £1,068) **Stalls** Low

Form RPR
1 **1** **Kehaar**[28] [2808] 3-8-9 **86**............................................................ EAhern 1 99
(MAMagnusson) *midfield far side: rdn over 2f out: wnt 2nd 1f out: determined chal to ld cl home* **10/1**
31- **2** *shd* **Mister Monet (IRE)**[370] [2963] 3-9-1 **92**................................. KDalgleish 8 105
(MJohnston) *overall ldr on far side: rdn over 2f out: 3 l clr ins fnl f: jst ct* **12/1**
04 **3** *1 ¾* **Aperitif**[27] [2847] 3-7-9 **75** oh2........................................... NMackay(3) 4 84
(WJHaggas) *taken to post 20 minutes bef r: rrd s: bhd far side tl prog over 2f out: no imp ins fnl f* **14/1**
1-60 **4** *1 ¼* **Resplendent One (IRE)**[21] [3001] 3-9-7 **98**.......................... JPMurtagh 9 104
(TGMills) *b.hind: lw: t.k.h and chsd ldr far side: demoted 1f out: nt qckn after* **50/1**
-310 **5** *3* **Alshawameq (IRE)**[21] [3001] 3-8-9 **86**........................................ RHills 7 86
(JLDunlop) *bhd far side: sme hdwy over 2f out: styd on but nvr rchd ldrs* **11/1**
215 **6** *1 ¼* **Rehearsal**[47] [2307] 3-9-5 **96**.................................................. JFortune 10 93
(CGCox) *lw: racd freely and prom far side: rdn and wknd over 1f out* **13/2**[2]
3310 **7** *1* **Credit (IRE)**[21] [3001] 3-8-10 **87**................................................. KFallon 6 82
(RHannon) *chsd ldrs far side: rdn 2f out: sn no imp* **14/1**
-510 **8** *1 ½* **State Dilemma (IRE)**[21] [3001] 3-9-3 **94**...................................... MHills 2 85
(BWHills) *bhd far side: no ch fnl 2f* **14/1**
0205 **9** *nk* **Secretary General (IRE)**[33] [2692] 3-8-11 **88**.......................... KDarley 11 79
(PFICole) *cl up on stands' side: rdn and no ch w far side fnl 2f* **16/1**
13-0 **10** *½* **Sweet Indulgence (IRE)**[47] [2306] 3-8-7 **84**......................... KMcEvoy 12 74
(DrJDScargill) *t.k.h on stands' side: no ch w far gp fnl 2f* **10/1**

0536 **11** ½ **Qasirah (IRE)**[22] [2971] 3-9-4 **95**........................................(b) PRobinson 13 84
(MAJarvis) *lw: racd stands' side: rdn and btn over 2f out* **16/1**
3130 **12** *shd* **Taruskin (IRE)**[34] [2642] 3-8-8 **85**........................................ DHolland 5 73
(NACallaghan) *lw: last on far side: nvr on terms* **25/1**
4205 **13** *shd* **Principal Witness (IRE)**[12] [3304] 3-8-3 **80**........................ MartinDwyer 3 68
(WRMuir) *prom far side: drvn 2f out: wknd wl over 1f out* **66/1**
110- **14** 3 ½ **Hunting Lodge (IRE)**[300] [4870] 3-9-5 **96**........................ TPQueally 14 76
(DRLoder) *bhd on stands' side: rdn 3f out: sn btn* **25/1**
2411 **15** ¾ **Majorca**[12] [3312] 3-8-10 **87**........................................ LDettori 16 66
(JHMGosden) *lw: led 5 disadvantaged rivals on stands side most of way tl wknd 2f out* **4/1**[1]
12-1 **16** *nk* **Primus Inter Pares (IRE)**[6] [3477] 3-9-9 **100** 5ex........... AlexGreaves 17 78
(DNicholls) *trckd ldrs gng wl on stands' side but no ch w far gp fnl 2f: eased* **7/1**[3]

1m 38.65s (-1.83) **Going Correction** +0.10s/f (Good) **16** Ran SP% **123.0**
Speed ratings: **113,112,111,109,106 105,104,103,102,102 101,101,101,98,97 97**CSF £122.22 CT £1766.73 TOTE £10.40: £2.30, £3.10, £4.00, £15.50; EX 152.20 Trifecta £914.80 Part won. Pool: £1,288.48. 0.50 winning tickets..
**Owner** East Wind Racing Ltd **Bred** Watership Down Stud **Trained** Upper Lambourn, Berks

**FOCUS**
A fair handicap run at a good clip and a very decent winning time for the grade. Low numbers certainly had an advantage, with the first three home racing tight to the far rail for much of the trip.

**NOTEBOOK**
**Kehaar** lacked the expeience of his rivals, but it didn't show and he made good use of having the plum draw next to the rails.His trainer still thinks he is "immature" and he will prove to be a better horse next year.
**Mister Monet(IRE)** ◆ has reportedly had problems, and ran here as though just needing the outing. However, there is no doubt he retains plenty of ability and he must be difficult to beat in similar company next time.
**Aperitif** taken to post early, clearly has his problems, but he also has his fair share of ability. Providing he can keep his head right, he should be able to take advantage of his current mark.
**Resplendent One(IRE)**, keen to post and during the race, didn't quite get home as well as he might have. He will need to learn to settle if he is to progress.
**Alshawameq(IRE)** may need a faster surface to bring out the best in him.
**Rehearsal**, who missed a race here on Wednesday to wait for the rain, dropped out tamely and looks to have something to prove now.
**Majorca**, although taking the field along on the stands' side, always looked to be playing second fiddle to the far side.

## 3672 WEATHERBYS SUPERLATIVE STKS (GROUP 3) 7f
**1:50** (1:52) (A) 2-Y-O **£23,200** (£8,800; £4,400; £2,000) **Stalls** Low

Form RPR
1 **1** **Dubawi (IRE)**[34] [2644] 2-8-11 ........................................ LDettori 12 104+
(SaeedBinSuroor) *lw: hld up: hdwy over 1f out: r.o to ld towards fin* **15/8**[1]
1 **2** ½ **Henrik**[50] [2225] 2-8-11 ........................................ TEDurcan 9 103
(MRChannon) *trckd ldrs: led over 1f out: sn rdn: hdd towards fin* **14/1**
3013 **3** *nk* **Wilko (USA)**[19] [3071] 2-8-11 ........................................ EAhern 1 102
(JNoseda) *hld up: hdwy over 1f out: r.o* **11/1**
21 **4** 1 ¼ **Fox**[19] [3093] 2-8-11 ........................................ DHolland 11 99
(CEBrittain) *lw: s.i.s: hld up: hdwy over 1f out: r.o* **10/1**
1 **5** 1 ¼ **Pivotal Flame**[57] [2045] 2-8-11 ........................................ SSanders 3 96
(BAMcmahon) *hld up: hdwy over 1f out: nt rch ldrs* **11/2**[2]
14 **6** ¾ **Hearthstead Wings**[19] [3071] 2-8-11 ........................................ JFanning 6 94
(MJohnston) *chsd ldrs: led 2f out: hdd over 1f out: no ex* **14/1**
01 **7** ½ **Country Rambler (USA)**[18] [3124] 2-8-11 ........................................ RHughes 5 93
(BWHills) *trckd ldrs: plld hrd: hmpd 2f out: styd on same pce fnl f* **10/1**
**8** *nk* **Rowan Tree**[12] [3329] 2-8-11 ........................................ JPSpencer 7 92
(APO'Brien, Ire) *gd sort: leggy: mid-div: pushed along 1/2-way: nvr trbld ldrs* **7/1**[3]
01 **9** *shd* **Destinate (IRE)**[47] [2310] 2-8-11 ........................................ PDobbs 2 92
(RHannon) *hld up: effrt and swtchd lft over 1f out: n.d* **20/1**
01 **10** 2 **John Forbes**[12] [3313] 2-8-11 ........................................ RWinston 4 87
(BEllison) *hld up in tch: hmpd and lost pl 2f out: hmpd again over 1f out: n.d* **50/1**
1 **11** 3 ½ **Jalamid (IRE)**[26] [2890] 2-8-11 ........................................(t) RHills 10 78
(JHMGosden) *w ldr tl led wl over 2f out: hdd 2f out: wknd fnl f* **16/1**
51 **12** 11 **Al Qudra (IRE)**[27] [2852] 2-8-11 ........................................ JFortune 8 51
(BJMeehan) *led: plld hrd: hdd wl over 2f out: wkng whn hmpd over 1f out* **50/1**

1m 26.48s (-0.29) **Going Correction** +0.10s/f (Good) **12** Ran SP% **117.1**
Speed ratings: **105,104,104,102,101 100,99,99,99,97 93,80**CSF £30.06 TOTE £2.90: £1.50, £4.10, £3.10; EX 33.60 Trifecta £350.00 Pool: £1,133.86. 2.30 winning tickets..
**Owner** Godolphin **Bred** Darley **Trained** Newmarket, Suffolk
■ Stewards Enquiry : P Dobbs two-day ban: careless riding (Jul 19-20)

**FOCUS**
With 12 individual winners taking part this looked well up to Group 3 standard and it was an acceptable winning time for the grade. Wilko and Hearthstead Wings ran close to their Chesham form in defeat, and the race has a solid look about it. Indeed it could be rated higher.

**NOTEBOOK**
**Dubawi(IRE)** ◆ was only a narrow winner but always looked like getting there. A likeable colt, he still has plenty of improvement in him and will certainly stay further in time.
**Henrik** took this step up in class in his stride and comes out of this with plenty of credit. He has his fair share of pace and will equally at home over a furlong less.
**Wilko(USA)** turned in another solid effort despite the ground being easier than connections believe he cares for. Granted his favoured fast surface he should have no trouble scoring at this level.
**Fox** confirmed himself to be progressive, even though he was beaten further by the winner here than when they met on their debuts.
**Pivotal Flame** ◆, whose maiden win had worked out well, had a fair bit to do and deserves plenty of credit for finishing as close as he did. Out of a mare that won over two miles, another furlong will not come amiss.
**Hearthstead Wings** looked to run close to his Ascot form with Wilko, and didn't appear to have any excuses.
**Country Rambler(USA)**, allowed to bowl along and use his stride at Warwick, was ridden with more restraint here, but he was always doing too much. A likeable sort, he is still open to improvement.
**Rowan Tree** was never really travelling and is surely better than he showed here.
**John Forbes** ran much better than his final position suggested, for he was almost knocked over twice. There will be other days for him.
**Jalamid(IRE)** raced prominently but failed to confirm the promise of his succesful debut at Sandown. That form is not working out especially well, but he is surely capable of better than this.

## 3673 LADBROKES BUNBURY CUP (HERITAGE H'CAP) 7f
**2:20** (2:23) (B) (0-105,105) 3-Y-O+ **£45,500** (£14,000; £7,000; £3,500) **Stalls** Low

Form RPR
2011 **1** **Material Witness (IRE)**[11] [3337] 7-9-3 **94** 5ex................. MartinDwyer 6 105
(WRMuir) *overall ldr far side: drvn fnl f and kpt on gamely: jst hld on* **25/1**
-354 **2** *shd* **Court Masterpiece**[12] [3318] 4-10-0 **105**........................................ KFallon 5 116+
(EALDunlop) *dwlt: hdwy 2f out: rdn and nt clr passage through fnl f: kpt on stoutly: jst failed* **10/1**
4420 **3** 1 ¼ **Greenslades**[19] [3074] 5-9-4 **95**........................................ SSanders 10 103
(PJMakin) *stdd s: sn midfield: effrt over 1f out: rdn and nt qckn last 100 yds* **8/1**[1]
5000 **4** *nk* **El Coto**[22] [2969] 4-9-9 **100**........................................(b[1]) LDettori 17 107+
(BAMcmahon) *rr of disadvantaged stands quintet: gd hdwy over 1f out: fin strly: btn by draw* **14/1**
020- **5** ¾ **Grizedale (IRE)**[250] [5873] 5-9-3 **94**........................................(t) RHughes 16 99
(JAkehurst) *swtchd to r on outside of far gp: t.k.h in rr: hdwy 2f out: one pce fnl f* **25/1**
-014 **6** *shd* **Royal Storm (IRE)**[19] [3074] 5-9-8 **99**........................................ MJKinane 9 104
(MrsAJPerrett) *lw: chsd far side ldr tl drvn 1f out: nt qckn ins* **9/1**[3]
0024 **7** *hd* **Amandus (USA)**[22] [2969] 4-9-4 **95**........................................ TPQueally 12 99
(DRLoder) *chsd far side ldrs: rdn over 1f out: sn no imp* **14/1**
0210 **8** 2 ½ **Makfool (FR)**[21] [3001] 3-8-13 **98**........................................ TEDurcan 1 96
(MRChannon) *lw: cl up far side tl drvn 1f out: wknd fnl 100 yds* **14/1**
0160 **9** ½ **Master Robbie**[20] [3036] 5-8-11 **91**........................................ SHitchcott[(3)] 11 87
(MRChannon) *lw: s.s: bhd far side: styd on over 1f out: nt rch ldrs ins fnl f* **33/1**
532 **10** *hd* **Maghanim**[20] [3036] 4-9-7 **98**........................................ RHills 14 94+
(JLDunlop) *led stands quintet over 6f: sn btn* **12/1**
1401 **11** *hd* **Zilch**[12] [3324] 6-9-7 **98**........................................ RMullen 2 93
(MLWBell) *s.s: rchd midfield but drvn 1/2-way: n.d after* **17/2**[2]
5-00 **12** ½ **Vicious Knight**[22] [2969] 6-9-7 **98**........................................ AlexGreaves 3 92
(DNicholls) *pressed far side ldrs tl wknd 1f out* **33/1**
5304 **13** 1 ½ **Kings Point (IRE)**[12] [3318] 3-9-1 **100**........................................ DaneO'Neill 15 90+
(RHannon) *swtg: stand quintet: rdn and btn 2f out* **25/1**
0-45 **14** 1 ¼ **Chookie Heiton (IRE)**[67] [1789] 6-9-11 **102**........................ RWinston 13 89
(ISemple) *b.hind: lw: effrt far side 3f out: rdn and fdd over 1f out* **50/1**
0605 **15** *hd* **Atavus**[11] [3337] 7-9-0 **91**........................................ JMackay 7 77
(GGMargarson) *cl up far side: drvn 1f out: tired bdly ins fnl f* **33/1**
0010 **16** 1 ¾ **Cardinal Venture (IRE)**[19] [3074] 6-9-4 **95**........................ NCallan 4 77
(KARyan) *prom far side 5f: sn lost pl: eased ins fnl f* **8/1**[1]
0010 **17** *nk* **Golden Chalice (IRE)**[47] [2283] 5-9-0 **91**........................ JPMurtagh 8 72
(AMBalding) *midfield far side: chsd along 2f out: btn whn n.m.r ins fnl f: eased* **10/1**
-002 **18** 2 ½ **Coconut Penang (IRE)**[19] [3074] 4-9-5 **96**........................ SWhitworth 19 71+
(PWChapple-Hyam) *cl up in stands quintet tl rdn and btn over 2f out: eased* **11/1**
0-14 **19** 11 **Heretic**[71] [1705] 6-10-0 **105**........................................ OUrbina 20 51+
(JRFanshawe) *last of stands quintet and a struggling* **16/1**

1m 26.2s (-0.57) **Going Correction** +0.10s/f (Good)
**WFA** 3 from 4yo+ 8lb **19** Ran SP% **125.2**
Speed ratings: **107,106,105,105,104 104,103,101,100,100 100,99,97,96,96 94,93,90,78**CSF £247.10 CT £2212.00 TOTE £33.20: £6.50, £3.40, £2.90, £3.60; EX 225.00 TRIFECTA Not won..
**Owner** M J Caddy **Bred** M Henochsberg **Trained** Lambourn, Berks
■ Stewards Enquiry : Martin Dwyer two-day ban: used whip with whip arm above shoulder height (Jul 19-20)

**FOCUS**
A decent handicap, run in a good time. The field split into two, with the low numbers again holding the advantage.

**NOTEBOOK**
**Material Witness(IRE)**, at his best when allowed to bowl along, confirmed himself a much improved performer with a typically gutsy display. Just as effective over six, he holds an entry in the Stewards Cup, where he can race off the same mark as he did in the dip, looked a most unlucky loser.
**Court Masterpiece** ◆, all dressed up and nowhere to go in the dip, looked a most unlucky loser. He is clearly on good terms with himself at present and connections have said they intend to take in the Totesport International at Ascot towards the end of the month. He deserves compensation.
**Greenslades** is a consistent colt, but difficult to place. These big field handicaps are ideal for him, but while he seems to handle most types of ground, his trainer feels he doesn't want it too firm.
**El Coto** ◆ ran a cracker from his high draw, and the first-time blinkers clearly had the desired effect. More at home over an extra furlong, he can be found a winning opportunity in the coming weeks.
**Grizedale(IRE)**, runner-up in this in 2002, was switched to race towards the far side. This was a soild effort on this return to action, on ground which may well have been on the easy side for him. If he can build on this, he should have no trouble adding to his tally, although he does take a fair grip and is always going to need a bit of luck in running.
**Royal Storm(IRE)** probably turned in his best effort to date, on ground which would have been slow enough for him.
**Amandus(USA)** didn't have the best of runs, and although he has yet to win on turf, it is surely only a matter of time.
**Makfool(FR)** proved his Ascot run all wrong and was much better suited by this easier surface.
**Master Robbie**, for whom the ground would have been easier than ideal, never really got competitive after missing the break.
**Zilch** never really recovered from a tardy start.
**Cardinal Venture(IRE)** had no excuses and looks to be in the grip of the Handicapper for the time being.
**Heretic** even allowing for being on the "wrong side", turned in another dismal effort and looks to have plenty to prove now.

## 3674 DARLEY JULY CUP (GROUP 1) 6f
**2:55** (2:58) (A) 3-Y-O+ **£145,000** (£55,000; £27,500; £12,500) **Stalls** Low

Form RPR
-213 **1** **Frizzante**[23] [2955] 5-9-2 111........................................ JPMurtagh 18 119
(JRFanshawe) *s.i.s: hld up: hung lft over 1f out: r.o to ld wl ins fnl f* **14/1**
3020 **2** *nk* **Ashdown Express (IRE)**[19] [3073] 5-9-5 111........................ SSanders 11 121
(CFWall) *swtg: hld up: gd hdwy to chal ins fnl f: r.o* **100/1**
120- **3** 2 **Balmont (USA)**[264] [5640] 3-8-13 115........................................ EAhern 16 115
(JNoseda) *swtg: racd centre: chsd ldrs: jnd main gp over 3f out: rdn to ld ins fnl f: sn hdd and unable qck* **25/1**
3-23 **4** *nk* **Cape Of Good Hope**[19] [3073] 6-9-5 ........................................(vt) MJKinane 20 114
(DOughton, Hong Kong) *racd centre: hld up: jnd main gp 4f out: hdwy u.p over 1f out: r.o* **20/1**
0-02 **5** *hd* **Somnus**[12] [3308] 4-9-5 117........................................ TEDurcan 17 114
(TDEasterby) *racd centre: jnd main gp over 4f out: mid-div: hdwy 1/2-way: sn rdn: styng on whn edgd lft ins fnl f* **12/1**
5110 **6** *nk* **Monsieur Bond (IRE)**[19] [3073] 4-9-5 117........................ FLynch 14 113
(BSmart) *chsd ldrs: rdn over 2f out: styd on* **14/1**
-253 **7** *nk* **Antonius Pius (USA)**[23] [2956] 3-8-13 ........................................(t) JPSpencer 5 112
(APO'Brien, Ire) *gd sort: neat: chsd ldrs: pushed along 1/2-way: kpt on* **5/1**[2]
15-2 **8** *hd* **Porlezza (FR)**[32] [2719] 5-9-2 ........................................ OPeslier 13 108
(YDeNicolay, France) *gd-sort: hld up: nt clr run over 1f out: r.o ins fnl f: nvr nrr* **33/1**

0-66 **9** *nk* **Airwave**[19] 3073 4-9-2 115 DaneO'Neill 15 107+
(HCandy) *lw: hld up: nt clr run over 1f out: r.o ins fnl f: nvr able to chal* **20/1**

11-3 **10** *shd* **Patavellian (IRE)**[53] 2162 6-9-5 115 (b) SDrowne 12 110
(RCharlton) *b: w ldr: rdn to ld over 1f out: hdd and no ex ins fnl f* **7/1**[3]

-044 **11** *1 1/4* **Country Reel (USA)**[19] 3073 4-9-5 104 (vt) RHills 4 106
(SaeedBinSuroor) *lw: chsd ldrs: rdn over 1f out: styd on same pce* **25/1**

**12** *hd* **Seeking The Dia (USA)**[60] 3-8-13 YTake 1 106
(HideyukiMori, Japan) *gd-sort: b: b.hind: chsd ldrs: rdn and ev ch over 1f out: no ex ins fnl f* **50/1**

U-01 **13** *shd* **Fayr Jag (IRE)**[19] 3073 5-9-5 109 WSupple 10 105
(TDEasterby) *lw: hld up: nt clr run over 1f out: nvr trbld ldrs* **25/1**

10-1 **14** *shd* **Kheleyf (USA)**[22] 2966 3-8-13 108 LDettori 8 105+
(SaeedBinSuroor) *lw: hld up: nt clr run over 1f out: r.o ins fnl f: nvr trbld ldrs* **8/1**

00-3 **15** *nk* **Continent**[5] 3522 7-9-5 112 JFortune 19 104
(DNicholls) *lw: s.s: bhd: hdwy fnl f: n.d* **50/1**

02-3 **16** *nk* **Nayyir**[103] 1146 6-9-5 RHughes 7 103+
(GAButler) *s.i.s: hld up: hdwy over 2f out: rdn whn hmpd over 1f out: sn wknd* **12/1**

0000 **17** *1* **Bahamian Pirate (USA)**[12] 3308 9-9-5 105 KDarley 9 100
(DNicholls) *b. off hind: s.i.s: hld up: n.d* **66/1**

2120 **18** *3/4* **Steenberg (IRE)**[19] 3073 5-9-5 113 PRobinson 6 98
(MHTompkins) *chsd ldrs: lost pl over 2f out: wknd fnl f* **22/1**

**19** *1* **Exceed And Excel (AUS)**[124] 4-9-5 (t) KMcEvoy 3 95
(TMartin, Australia) *nice colt: str: led: rdn and hdd over 1f out: wknd ins fnl f* **4/1**[1]

4111 **20** *1* **Moss Vale (IRE)**[25] 2913 3-8-13 112 MHills 2 92
(BWHills) *chsd ldrs: rdn over 2f out: wknd fnl f* **14/1**

1m 11.51s (-1.81) **Going Correction** +0.10s/f (Good)
**WFA** 3 from 4yo+ 6lb **20 Ran SP% 130.4**
Speed ratings: **116,115,112,112,112 111,111,111,110,110 109,108,108,108,108 107,106,105,104,102**CSF £1046.56 TOTE £20.20: £4.30, £26.30, £8.90; EX 914.20 Trifecta £3430.20 Pool: £5,314.46. 1.10 winning tickets..
**Owner** Mrs Jan Hopper & Mrs Elizabeth Grundy **Bred** Mrs J P Hopper And Mrs E M Grundy **Trained** Newmarket, Suffolk

**FOCUS**
A truly international field for this prestigeous contest and the sort of winning time you would expect for a Group One in the conditions. Most of the top sprinters were present, but there was no stand-out and while the winner is progressive, Ashdown Express is relatively exposed. The form, taken at face value for now, might need to come down a few pounds.

**NOTEBOOK**
**Frizzante** has come on no end this season and had her optimum conditions for the first time. A confirmed hold-up mare, she was well suited to the strong pace and swooped late to land her first Group 1. While she may not be as easy to place now in lesser company under her penalty, she should still continue to give a good account at this level and has the Stanley Leisure Sprint a likely target.
**Ashdown Express(IRE)** enjoyed a lovely run through the pack after beingheld up in rear, and looked the winner for a moment when bursting through. He appeared to improve between 5lb and 7lb on his previous best, which on his 31st start, seems a little unlikely, but his provisional RPR gives him the benefit of doubt.
**Balmont(USA)** ◆ turned in a cracking effort on this return to action, especially as it was reported after the race that he was cast in his box overnight. A top-class juvenile, he has clearly trained on and is going to be a major player in all of the top sprints. The Nunthorpe is first on the agenda, and he will be a major player there.
**Cape Of Good Hope**, drawn worst of all gradually made his way across to join the main group. This was another solid effort at this level, although this may well have been his last race over here.
**Somnus** ran his usual honest race, but may have done even better had there been more give underfoot.
**Monsieur Bond(IRE)**, one of the first off the bridle, stuck to his task well on ground which would have been plenty quick enough for him. Given his favoured soft ground, he will be a match for them all.
**Antonius Pius(USA)** lacked the tactical speed on this return to sprinting, but he saw his race out honestly enough this time and should be suited by an extra furlong.
**Porlezza(FR)** didn't look to be given the best of rides, and is certainly capable of better than she showed here.
**Airwave** ◆ hasn't had much luck of late, one way or the other, and it was the same story here. She had to wait for a run and by the time she got one, the race was all over. She appeared to have plenty left in the tank at the finish and is still capable of landing another major prize when she gets the breaks. *Official explanation: jockey said filly was unlucky in running throughout*
**Patavellian(IRE)** had the run of the race and had no excuses.
**Country Reel(USA)** was always in the right place but lacked a change of gear.
**Seeking The Dia(USA)**, a winner at up to 1m in Japan, enjoyed the benefit of having the rails to race against but folded tamely up the hill after holding every chance in the dip..
**Fayr Jag(IRE)** was done no favours by the overnight rain and is better than he showed here, for he had little luck in running.
**Kheleyf(USA)** did not enjoy the best of runs but essentially found things happening too quickly for him over this trip, and needs to return to seven furlongs.
**Continent**, the winner of this two years ago, never recovered from a slow start. *Official explanation: jockey said gelding missed the break*
**Nayyir** was just beginning to feel the pinch when squeezed out going into the dip. A return to an extra furlong will be in his favour.
**Bahamian Pirate(USA)**, runner-up to his stablemate in this two years ago, is clearly on the downgrade now.
**Steenberg(IRE)**, off the bridle some way out, looked well below his best.
**Exceed And Excel(AUS)** was an outstanding sprinter in his native Australia but had missed his itended debut over here at Royal Ascot following an interrupted preparation and probably still was not himself here, for despite showing plenty of pace he could never get away from his field and he folded tamely when headed. It was decided afterwards to retire him, and he will return to stud in Australia. *Official explanation: trainer was unable to offer any explanation for poor form shown*
**Moss Vale(IRE)** had a progressive profile coming here, but this was a step too far. *Official explanation: jockey said colt was kicked at Start*

## 3675 MICHAEL POWLES BENTLEY MAIDEN FILLIES' STKS (DIV I) 6f
3:30 (3:30) (D) 2-Y-O **£8,092** (£2,490; £1,245; £622) **Stalls** Low

Form RPR

**1** **Winds Of Time (IRE)** 2-8-11 MJKinane 11 81
(MrsAJPerrett) *cmpt: scope: s.i.s: towards rr tl progres over 1f out: styd on wl to ld fnl 20 yds* **9/1**

6 **2** *nk* **Unreal**[55] 2083 2-8-11 RHughes 3 80
(BWHills) *led: rdn over 1f out: hdd and wnt rt fnl 20 yds* **9/2**[2]

350 **3** *3/4* **Catch A Star**[12] 3319 2-8-11 JPMurtagh 4 78
(NACallaghan) *gd sort: stdd s: t.k.h in rr: hdwy over 1f out: kpt on wl to chal between horses but jst hld whn snatched up nr fin* **5/1**[3]

**4** *nk* **Satin Finish (IRE)** 2-8-11 TEDurcan 7 77
(MRChannon) *neat: pressed ldrs: rdn and effrt 1f out: hld after but kpt on gamely towards fin* **7/1**

**5** *2 1/2* **Papality** 2-8-11 MartinDwyer 10 70
(WJarvis) *leggy: scope: cl up and keen: wnt 2nd 1/2-way: rdn over 1f out: tired ins fnl f* **4/1**[1]

**6** *1/2* **Della Salute** 2-8-8 LPKeniry(3) 8 68
(AMBalding) *cmpt: stdd s: effrt 1/2-way: rdn and btn over 1f out* **33/1**

**7** *1/2* **Madhavi** 2-8-11 PDobbs 1 67
(RHannon) *cmpt: scope: midfield: rdn over 1f out: sn tired and btn* **16/1**

**8** *1 3/4* **Lady Hen** 2-8-11 KFallon 6 61
(MJWallace) *w'like: scope: bit bkwd: chsd ldrs: niggled 1/2-way: outpcd over 1f out* **8/1**

**9** *shd* **Velveteen Rabbit** 2-8-11 LDettori 2 61
(SaeedBinSuroor) *neat: scope: dwlt: getting outpcd whn hmpd over 2f out: bhd after* **6/1**

**10** *dist* **Captain Margaret** 2-8-11 KDarley 5 —
(JPearce) *w'like: leggy: chsd ldr tl 1/2-way: stopped to nil: t.o and eased over 1f out* **50/1**

1m 15.58s (2.26) **Going Correction** +0.10s/f (Good) **10 Ran SP% 113.5**
Speed ratings: **88,87,86,86,82 82,81,79,79,**—CSF £47.92 TOTE £10.50: £3.40; EX 43.40.
**Owner** Mr & Mrs R Scott **Bred** C C And Mrs D J Buckley **Trained** Pulborough, W Sussex
■ Stewards Enquiry : R Hughes two-day ban: careless riding (Jul 19-20)

**FOCUS**
Little to go on, but this didn't look a strong maiden and it produced a modest winning time for the grade.

**NOTEBOOK**
**Winds Of Time(IRE)**, out of a mare that stayed 14f, would hardly have been suited by the steady pace, but may be capable of better as she steps up in trip.
**Unreal** had the benefit of a run and looked to have improved a little from her debut. Her future looks to lie in nurseries.
**Catch A Star** still looked a little green, despite having had three visit's to the racecourse. She will have learnt plenty from this.
**Satin Finish(IRE)**, an early foal, is from the same family as the high-class Belmez and should do better as she steps up in trip.
**Papality** is a 100,000 gns yearling from the same family as the high-class Grand Lodge. She will certainly be better for the outing.
**Della Salute**, out of a mare that won over a mile at three, should do better as she faces a stiffer test.
**Captain Margaret** *Official explanation: jockey said filly was holding her breath during the race*

## 3676 MICHAEL POWLES BENTLEY MAIDEN FILLIES' STKS (DIV II) 6f
4:05 (4:06) (D) 2-Y-O **£8,092** (£2,490; £1,245; £622) **Stalls** Low

Form RPR

30 **1** **Vondova**[15] 3202 2-8-11 DaneO'Neill 6 82
(RHannon) *racd keenly: led 5f out: rdn and hung lft over 1f out: r.o gamely* **20/1**

**2** *shd* **Almansoora (USA)** 2-8-11 LDettori 5 82
(SaeedBinSuroor) *gd sort: leggy: scope: hld up in tch: chsd wnr over 1f out: sn ev ch: r.o* **5/2**[2]

**3** *1 1/4* **Ahdaaf (USA)** 2-8-11 RHills 2 78
(JLDunlop) *gd sort: scope: b. off fore: tacked ldrs: rdn over 1f out: unable qck ins fnl f* **2/1**[1]

**4** *3* **Indiena** 2-8-11 JFortune 4 69
(BJMeehan) *w'like: scope: led 1f: chsd wnr tl outpcd fnl f* **8/1**

**5** *1* **Ringarooma** 2-8-11 PRobinson 1 66
(MHTompkins) *neat: s.i.s: hld up: rdn over 1f out: nvr trbld ldrs* **20/1**

**6** *shd* **Cerebus** 2-8-11 EAhern 9 66
(NPLittmoden) *wl grwn: bkwd: hld up: rdn over 2f out: n.d* **28/1**

**7** *1 1/2* **Yeldham Lady** 2-8-11 RPrice 7 61
(JPearce) *w'like: bit bkwd: hld up: pushed along 1/2-way: n.d* **50/1**

**8** *nk* **Silent Spring (USA)** 2-8-11 MHills 8 60
(BWHills) *leggy: scope: hld up: effrt over 1f out: sn wknd* **9/2**[3]

**9** *1/2* **Never Away** 2-8-11 JPMurtagh 10 59
(NACallaghan) *w'like: leggy: lw: rrd over bef s: s.i.s: hld up: wknd over 1f out* **16/1**

0 **10** *nk* **Saffa Garden (IRE)**[44] 2388 2-8-11 DHolland 3 58
(CEBrittain) *lw: chsd ldrs over 4f* **14/1**

1m 15.0s (1.68) **Going Correction** +0.10s/f (Good) **10 Ran SP% 118.7**
Speed ratings: **92,91,90,86,84 84,82,82,81,81**CSF £68.82 TOTE £22.70: £3.80, £1.80, £1.40; EX 85.10.
**Owner** W J Gredley **Bred** Middle Park Stud Ltd **Trained** East Everleigh, Wilts

**FOCUS**
Despite being 0.58 seconds faster than the first division, the winning time was still only average for the grade. The form has provisionally been rated marginally higher than the earlier race but still does not look strong by the meeting's normal standards.

**NOTEBOOK**
**Vondova** was one of only two in the race with previous experience and saw her race out properly this time, showing admirable battling qualities and recording much her best form. She had not got home over 7f on her previous start, having been too free, and this trip looked to suit her much better.
**Almansoora(USA)** ◆ is a half-sister to several winners, most of whom stay well. She kept battling away over a trip which will prove to be on the sharp side for her, and she can pay her way when facing a stiffer test.
**Ahdaaf(USA)** ◆ comes from the same family as champion sprinter Elnadim as well as 1000 Guineas winner Mehtaaf. Although clearly well fancied, she still looked a little green and is sure to benefit from the experience.
**Indiena**, a 75,000 guineas yearling, showed plenty of pace and looks sure to benefit from the outing.
**Ringarooma**, a half-sister to juvenile winner Trimming, was not knocked around and should do better in time.
**Cerebus**, from a speedy family, looked as though the outing would do her good.

## 3677 NEWMARKETRACECOURSES.CO.UK NURSERY 7f
4:40 (4:41) (C) 2-Y-O **£10,237** (£3,150; £1,575; £787) **Stalls** Low

Form RPR

21 **1** **Satchem (IRE)**[28] 2817 2-9-6 86 TPQueally 13 94+
(DRLoder) *lw: hmprd st: held up: hdwy 2f out: ld insde fnl f: rn on wl* **7/2**[1]

014 **2** *3/4* **Sea Hunter**[52] 2180 2-8-11 78 SHitchcott(3) 2 86
(MRChannon) *lw: led: drvn and hdd jst ins fnl f: kpt on wl but a hld fnl 100 yds* **14/1**

4211 **3** *1/2* **Silver Wraith (IRE)**[26] 2868 2-9-7 87 JPMurtagh 10 92
(NACallaghan) *trckd ldrs: effrt 2f out: hung lft fr over 1f out: flattered briefly ins: no ex cl home* **10/1**

532 **4** *nk* **Marching Song**[24] 2947 2-9-2 80 RHughes 9 86
(RHannon) *lw: pressed ldrs: edgd lft over 1f out: ev ch briefly 100 yds out: nt qckn cl home* **13/2**[3]

2253 **5** *3 1/2* **Asian Tiger (IRE)**[14] 3242 2-9-5 83 DHolland 5 80
(RHannon) *pressed ldr tl over 1f out: rdn and sn outpcd by first four* **8/1**

1650 **6** *hd* **Im Spartacus**[14] 3242 2-7-10 **67** ........................................ CHaddon(7) 8 64
(IAWood) *chsd ldrs: rdn over 1f out: edgd lft and sn btn* **40/1**

023 **7** *hd* **Mac Cois Na Tine**[21] 3009 2-8-6 **70** ow1 ........................................ NCallan 6 66
(KARyan) *cl up: rdn over 2f out: btn over 1f out* **33/1**

4630 **8** *nk* **Gryskirk**[26] 2890 2-8-1 **65** ........................................ MartinDwyer 11 61
(PWD'Arcy) *swtg: bhd: drvn and slt prog 2f out: nvr nr ldrs and sn one pced* **10/1**

423 **9** *2* **Langston Boy**[61] 1960 2-8-6 **70** ........................................ RMullen 3 61
(MLWBell) *dwlt: towards rr: driven and struggling over 2f out* **25/1**

141 **10** *½* **Lisa Mona Lisa (IRE)**[28] 2819 2-8-6 **70** ow1 ........................................ KFallon 12 59
(VSmith) *wnt rt s: w ldrs: rdn 2f out: sn wknd* **9/1**

503 **11** *shd* **Amphitheatre (IRE)**[27] 2858 2-7-6 **63** ........................................ MHalford(7) 4 52
(RFJohnsonHoughton) *midfield: rdn 1/2-way: btn 2f out* **33/1**

325 **12** *½* **Adoration**[33] 2677 2-8-13 **77** ........................................ KDarley 7 65
(MJohnston) *last early: wl btn fnl 2f* **5/1**[2]

014 **13** *12* **Apologies**[66] 1819 2-8-11 **75** ........................................ GGibbons 1 33
(BAMcmahon) *pressed ldrs: rdn over 2f out: sn fdd: t.o and eased fnl f* **12/1**

1m 26.37s (-0.40) **Going Correction** +0.10s/f (Good) **13** Ran SP% **118.0**
Speed ratings: **106,105,104,104,100 100,99,99,97,96 96,95,82**CSF £52.15 CT £468.27 TOTE £4.30: £1.90, £4.40, £3.10; EX 78.10.
**Owner** Lucayan Stud & D D Clee **Bred** K Molloy **Trained** Newmarket, Suffolk

**FOCUS**
A competitive nursery - easily the best so far this season - and a very smart time. In a race in which they tended towards the centre of the course, the first four pulled clear and all look ahead of the handicapper. The figures shown as 'official ratings' are estimates for guidance only.

**NOTEBOOK**
**Satchem(IRE)**, whose Yarmouth form was given an almighty boost when the runner-up won the July Stakes earlier in the week, looked thrown in on that form. He didn't let his supporters down and won with more in hand than the bare verdict suggested. He looks well capable of holding his own at a higher level.
**Sea Hunter** found plenty of improvement for the step up in trip. He is sure to go up a bit for this effort, but will continue to give a good account.
**Silver Wraith(IRE)**, tackling his easiest surface to date, was another to improve significantly for the step up in trip. He aquitted himself really well under his big weight, and he should continue to perform with credit.
**Marching Song**, stepping up in trip and running in his first nursery, left his maiden form behind with an excellent effort. However, while he stayed this longer trip well enough, he may be better suited by six furlongs at this stage of his career.
**Asian Tiger(IRE)** has proved wonderfully consistent, without quite hitting the bullseye.
**Im Spartacus** has found life difficult since winning his maiden and was easily shaken off here once the dash to the line began.

## 3678 DULLINGHAM H'CAP 1m 4f
**5:10** (5:13) (C) (0-90,88) 3-Y-0+ **£13,858** (£4,264; £2,132; £1,066) **Stalls** High

Form RPR

-051 **1** **Mephisto (IRE)**[26] 2895 5-10-0 **88** ........................................ DHolland 11 108+
(LMCumani) *a.p: jnd ldrs 5f out: rdn over 1f out: led ins fnl f: styd on gamely* **8/1**

1051 **2** *½* **Astrocharm (IRE)**[7] 3443 5-9-6 **80** 6ex ........................................ NCallan 2 94+
(MHTompkins) *lw: hld up: hdwy over 2f out: sn rdn: r.o* **16/1**

3315 **3** *1½* **Always Waining (IRE)**[6] 3474 3-8-12 **85** ........................................ JFanning 15 97+
(MJohnston) *sn led: rdn and hdd ins fnl f: unable qck* **16/1**

3435 **4** *1¼* **Street Life (IRE)**[13] 3274 6-8-13 **73** ........................................ KFallon 7 83
(WJMusson) *hld up: hdwy over 1f out: nt rch ldrs* **6/1**[2]

0-05 **5** *6* **Team-Mate (IRE)**[13] 3276 6-8-13 **76** ........................................ BReilly(3) 14 76
(MissJFeilden) *hld up in tch: rdn over 2f out: wknd over 1f out* **50/1**

4/21 **6** *nk* **Swellmova**[20] 3050 5-8-7 **67** ow1 ........................................ JFortune 10 67
(JRBoyle) *chsd ldr: rdn over 3f out: wknd over 1f out* **7/1**[3]

2311 **7** *nk* **Sangiovese**[15] 3207 5-9-4 **78** ........................................ SDrowne 8 77
(HMorrison) *prom: rdn over 2f out: wknd over 1f out* **9/1**

1-03 **8** *2½* **Whispered Promises (USA)**[15] 3207 3-8-9 **82** ........................................ KDalgleish 12 77
(MJohnston) *lw: chsd ldrs tl wknd over 2f out* **14/1**

-011 **9** *1¾* **Lucky Leo**[7] 3450 4-8-8 **68** ........................................ RHughes 4 60
(IanWilliams) *b: hld up: rdn over 4f out: n.d* **7/1**[3]

3110 **10** *hd* **Another Choice (IRE)**[54] 2107 3-8-5 **78** ........................................(t) RMullen 6 70
(NPLittmoden) *hld up: rdn over 2f out: n.d* **33/1**

0352 **11** *7* **Northside Lodge (IRE)**[20] 3046 6-9-4 **78** ........................................ MartinDwyer 5 59
(PWHarris) *hld up in tch: racd keenly: rdn and wknd over 2f out* **14/1**

2046 **12** *3* **Dovedon Hero**[13] 3276 4-9-1 **75** ........................................(b) MHills 3 51
(PJMcbride) *hld up: a in rr* **33/1**

-434 **13** *1¾* **Crathorne (IRE)**[23] 2964 4-9-5 **79** ........................................(p) JPMurtagh 13 52
(JDBethell) *b: hld up: rdn over 4f out: wknd over 2f out* **9/1**

00-0 **14** *5* **Back In Action**[24] 2945 4-8-10 **70** ........................................(t) DaneO'Neill 1 35
(MAMagnusson) *lw: s.s: hld up: rdn over 4f out: sn wknd* **50/1**

0-51 **15** *1¼* **Burning Moon**[14] 3238 3-8-13 **86** ........................................ EAhern 9 49
(JNoseda) *hld up: rdn and wknd over 2f out* **9/2**[1]

2m 32.91s (-0.05) **Going Correction** +0.10s/f (Good)
**WFA** 3 from 4yo+ 13lb **15** Ran SP% **123.5**
Speed ratings: **104,103,102,101,97 97,97,95,94,94 89,87,86,83,82**CSF £129.09 CT £2012.53 TOTE £10.40: £4.30, £4.10, £5.40; EX 122.60 Place 6 £1,358.97, Place 5 £255.19.
**Owner** Mrs Angie Silver **Bred** Shadwell Estate Company Limited **Trained** Newmarket, Suffolk

**FOCUS**
They went a fair pace and came down the centre of the track once in line for home. The first four came right away, and the winner continues to progress.

**NOTEBOOK**
**Mephisto(IRE)** ◆ has a powerful action and really appreciated this easier ground. He is a progressive performer, and with more improvement likely over a bit further, he could prove an ideal type for the Ebor.
**Astrocharm(IRE)** has now put a couple of decent efforts together, and proved beyond doubt that she truly stays this far. While she handles fast ground, she may prefer an easier surface now that she is a bit older.
**Always Waining(IRE)**, like so many from his yard, is as tough as teak. Relatively unexposed, this easier surface seemed to bring about some improvement from him and he should continue to run well at this level.
**Street Life(IRE)** continues to frustrate, although there was nothing wrong with this effort.
**Team-Mate(IRE)** flattered briefly before being left behind. He may have found the ground softer than ideal.
**Swellmova**, 8lbs higher than when winning here last month, wasn't disgraced in this much better race.
**Northside Lodge(IRE)** could never get any cover on the outside of the field and as a consequence raced too freely.
**Burning Moon** was most disappointing, never threatening to get competitive at any stage and beaten well before stamina became an issue. *Official explanation: jockey said colt did not stay the distance*

T/Jkpt: Not won. T/Plt: £2,131.90 to a £1 stake. Pool: £105,719.60. 36.20 winning tickets. T/Qpdt: £155.10 to a £1 stake. Pool: £7,654.60. 36.50 winning tickets. CR

# 3486 WARWICK (L-H)
Thursday, July 8

**OFFICIAL GOING: Good**
Rain-softened ground, and on the easy side of Good. A bias existed towards the stands' side in the straight, though in only two races did the jockeys try it.
Wind: slt against Weather: cloudy

## 3679 DLA NOVICE AUCTION STKS 7f 26y
**2:30** (2:39) (E) 2-Y-O **£3,867** (£1,190; £595; £297) **Stalls** Low

Form RPR

0 **1** **I'm So Lucky**[19] 3080 2-8-6 ........................................ RFfrench 3 80
(MJohnston) *a.p: rdn over 2f out: led ins fnl f: drvn out* **8/1**[3]

54 **2** *shd* **Group Captain**[26] 2890 2-8-6 ........................................ JDSmith 7 80
(SKirk) *s.s: sn prom: led jst over 1f out: sn rdn: edgd lft and hdd ins fnl f: r.o* **9/4**[1]

0110 **3** *3½* **Justaquestion**[20] 3031 2-8-13 ........................................ FNorton 2 78
(IAWood) *a.p: rdn over 2f out: n.m.r and swtchd rt over 1f out: one pce fnl f* **9/4**[1]

04 **4** *1¼* **Young Thomas (IRE)**[10] 3366 2-8-6 ........................................ MFenton 9 68
(MLWBell) *w ldr: rdn to ld wl over 1f out: sn hdd: hld whn n.m.r ins fnl f* **16/1**

**5** *¾* **Blackcomb Mountain (USA)** 2-7-12 ........................................ FPFerris(3) 11 61
(MFHarris) *hld up: rdn over 3f out: rn green: styd on fnl f* **40/1**

1 **6** *hd* **Treat Me Wild (IRE)**[91] 1307 2-8-5 ........................................ RSmith 6 65
(RHannon) *hld up and bhd: hdwy over 1f out: n.d* **11/2**[2]

54 **7** *1½* **Kaggamagic**[14] 3233 2-8-6 ........................................ DarrenWilliams 5 62
(JRNorton) *hld up in mid-div: rdn and effrt 2f out: wknd jst over 1f out* **16/1**

0 **8** *7* **Scale The Heights (IRE)**[7] 3451 2-8-12 ........................................ DeanMcKeown 4 50
(BWHills) *s.i.s: a bhd* **12/1**

50 **9** *½* **Dixie Queen (IRE)**[35] 2617 2-8-4 ........................................ DaleGibson 8 41
(MDods) *led: rdn and hdd wl over 1f out: sn wknd* **14/1**

0 **10** *6* **Chin Dancer**[19] 3083 2-8-1 ........................................ AMcCarthy 10 23
(BRMillman) *prom over 3f* **66/1**

00 **11** *2* **Amalgam (IRE)**[47] 2300 2-7-12 ........................................ JFMcDonald(3) 1 18
(MrsPNDutfield) *s.i.s: a bhd* **50/1**

1m 26.82s (1.92) **Going Correction** +0.175s/f (Good) **11** Ran SP% **120.1**
Speed ratings: **96,95,91,90,89 89,87,79,79,72 69**CSF £26.73 TOTE £10.00: £2.50, £1.40, £1.20; EX 41.80.
**Owner** Mrs S J Brookhouse **Bred** Leydens Farm Stud **Trained** Middleham Moor, N Yorks
■ Stewards Enquiry : F Norton two-day ban: careless riding (Jul 19,20)

**FOCUS**
A routine event of its type, though the time was fair.

**NOTEBOOK**
**I'm So Lucky**, all the better for his debut, was off the bridle some way out but showed plenty of guts to outbattle the runner-up. Nurseries seem the likely option and on this evidence he would have no problem getting a mile.
**Group Captain** looked to be travelling best passing the two-furlong pole, but although he did very little wrong he does appear to lack a change of gear and was just worried out of it. He might be better ridden more positively and now qualifies for nurseries.
**Justaquestion** would have welcomed the rain and could possibly have done with even more. She was still battling away when having to be switched after losing out in trying for the same gap as the winner. However, given the distance she was beaten it made little difference to her finishing position.
**Young Thomas(IRE)**, given a positive ride, looked to be getting the worst of it when squeezed out by the front pair and still looks to find this trip too far. *Official explanation: jockey said gelding became unbalanced in the final furlong*
**Blackcomb Mountain(USA)** ◆, who cost only 4,000gns as a two-year-old, was inclined to hang about in the home straight but still showed distinct signs of ability. She should come on plenty for the experience and her pedigree suggests she will stay much further than this.
**Treat Me Wild(IRE)**, not seen since winning a Bath claimer on her debut in April, was stepping up two furlongs in trip but it was not lack of stamina that beat her.
**Scale The Heights(IRE)**, as on his debut, was always struggling after missing the break but it is still quite possible we will eventually see a different horse when he steps right up in trip.
**Dixie Queen(IRE)** *Official explanation: jockey said filly lost her action*

## 3680 BARRATT MERCIA FILLIES' H'CAP 5f 110y
**3:05** (3:06) (E) (0-70,70) 3-Y-O+ **£4,095** (£1,260; £630; £315) **Stalls** Low

Form RPR

12-2 **1** **Come Away With Me (IRE)**[55] 2098 4-8-13 **55** ........................................ VSlattery 15 62
(MABuckley) *a.p: rdn to ld over 1f out: r.o* **4/1**[1]

1000 **2** *hd* **Boavista (IRE)**[17] 3141 4-8-13 **62** ow4 ........................................ SJDonohoe(7) 12 68
(PDEvans) *s.i.s: hdwy over 2f out: sn rdn: ev ch ins fnl f: r.o* **11/1**

1325 **3** *1½* **Amelia (IRE)**[16] 3178 6-8-10 **57** ........................................ BSwarbrick(5) 14 58
(WMBrisbourne) *t.k.h: hdwy over 2f out: rdn and ev ch over 1f out: nt qckn* **5/1**[2]

5000 **4** *1¾* **Tender (IRE)**[3] 3593 4-8-9 **51** ........................................(p) SWKelly 8 46
(MrsStefLiddiard) *w ldr: rdn over 3f out: ev ch over 1f out: no ex ins fnl f* **10/1**

5160 **5** *nk* **Red Leicester**[21] 3010 4-8-9 **51** ........................................(v) DeanMcKeown 9 45
(JAGlover) *led: rdn and hdd over 1f out: wknd wl ins fnl f* **12/1**

0406 **6** *¾* **Bettys Pride**[25] 2909 5-8-11 **53** ........................................ DarrenWilliams 13 45
(MDods) *hld up: sn in tch: rdn over 2f out: no imp fnl f* **5/1**[2]

-500 **7** *¾* **Le Meridien (IRE)**[12] 3314 6-8-9 **51** ........................................(v) RFfrench 3 40
(JSWainwright) *in tch: n.m.r and bmpd after 1f: effrt 2f out: wknd 1f out* **14/1**

0606 **8** *¾* **Travellers Joy**[14] 3227 4-7-9 **40** oh8 ........................................ JFMcDonald(3) 7 27
(RJHodges) *s.i.s: rdn and short-lived effrt 2f out* **14/1**

3003 **9** *1¼* **Blonde En Blonde (IRE)**[21] 3006 4-8-11 **53** ........................................(b) JBramhill 4 36
(NPLittmoden) *bmpd after 1f: sn bhd* **10/1**

0-60 **10** *nk* **Bad Intentions (IRE)**[8] 3428 4-9-7 **70** ........................................ SaleemGolam(7) 2 52
(MissDMountain) *bmpd on ins after 1f: sn bhd* **25/1**

3035 **11** *7* **Whistful (IRE)**[17] 3158 3-9-7 **69** ........................................ MFenton 19 28
(CFWall) *in tch on outside: rdn over 2f out: sn wknd* **8/1**[3]

67.24 secs (2.93) **Going Correction** +0.50s/f (Yiel)
**WFA** 3 from 4yo+ 5lb **11** Ran SP% **115.8**
Speed ratings: **100,99,97,95,95 94,93,92,90,89 80**CSF £47.91 CT £224.81 TOTE £4.20: £2.10, £3.40, £1.70; EX 52.60.
**Owner** C C Buckley **Bred** Gestut Sohrenhof **Trained** Castle Bytham, Lincs

**FOCUS**
A modest contest weakened by eight non-runners, and the pace was only ordinary. There was a big advantage to those that came stands' side in the home straight and the front three, all drawn high, were very much favoured as a result.

**NOTEBOOK**

**Come Away With Me(IRE)** had no problem lying up with the pace despite the shorter trip and battled on well to score after being brought wide into the home straight. The track bias flatters her to a degree, but she is relatively lightly raced and still open to improvement.

**Boavista(IRE)**, a hard filly to win with, managed yet another placing but it would be hard to criticise her as she carried significant overweight and did very little wrong. However, as things turned out being brought over to the stands' side in the straight probably enhanced her performance.

**Amelia(IRE)** was not at all inconvenienced by the easing of the ground and ran her race off what still looks a stiff enough mark. She may be slightly flattered though, as she was brought right over to the stands' side in the home straight and that looked to be a major advantage.

**Tender(IRE)**, with the cheekpieces refitted after flopping in a visor, was always up with the pace and deserves credit for emerging best of those that stayed towards the far side in the home straight.

**Red Leicester** showed her usual early pace, but she only just gets the minimum trip. This extended five may have found her out, and she could probably have done without the rain as well.

**Bettys Pride**, rated 83 at the start of last season, is on the decline, as her current mark will testify.

## 3681 CHURCHILL OFFICE SOLUTIONS (S) STKS — 1m 2f 188y

**3:40** (3:40) (G ) 3-Y-O — **£3,136** (£896; £448) **Stalls** Low

Form — RPR

2625 **1** — **Oktis Morilious (IRE)**[3] 3573 3-8-11 48 ... LTreadwell(7) 2 — 61
(AWCarroll) *a.p: rdn to ld over 1f out: r.o wl* **5/2**[1]

0000 **2** 1½ **Waltzing Beau**[15] 3190 3-8-13 53 ... GBaker 3 — 53
(BGPowell) *sn chsng ldr: rdn and ev ch over 1f out: nt qckn* **5/1**[2]

3-53 **3** 3½ **Defana**[10] 3371 3-8-10 54 ... LEnstone(3) 1 — 47
(MDods) *a.p: rdn 3f out: one pce fnl 2f* **5/2**[1]

0664 **4** ¾ **Cloudingswell**[10] 3385 3-8-3 57 ... (v[1]) NDeSouza(5) 4 — 41
(DLWilliams) *led: rdn and hdd over 1f out: wknd ins fnl f* **13/2**[3]

6603 **5** 17 **Come What July (IRE)**[40] 2485 3-9-4 60 ... (b) CLowther 10 — 22
(RGuest) *hld up: rdn over 4f out: hdwy over 3f out: edgd lft and wknd wl over 1f out* **5/1**[2]

0000 **6** 5 **Osla**[5] 3529 3-8-3 ... RThomas(5) 9 — 3
(RBrotherton) *hld up: rdn over 7f out: eased whn no ch fnl 2f* **40/1**

00 **7** 8 **Saint Zita (IRE)**[131] 916 3-8-5 ... (b[1]) JFMcDonald(3) 5 — —
(BJMeehan) *s.s: plld hrd in rr: rdn and struggling over 3f out* **20/1**

00 **8** 14 **Barholm Charlie**[36] 2586 3-8-13 ... VSlattery 6 — —
(MABuckley) *t.k.h early: rdn over 5f out: t.o fnl 4f* **40/1**

2m 21.03s (1.63) **Going Correction** +0.175s/f (Good) **8** Ran SP% **113.4**
Speed ratings: **101,99,97,96,84 80,75,64**CSF £15.05 TOTE £5.00: £1.30, £2.60, £1.70; EX 23.30.Oktis Morilious was bought in for 3,600gns.

**Owner** Dennis Deacon **Bred** Lord Vestey **Trained** Wixford, Warwicks

■ Stewards Enquiry : L Enstone four-day ban: used whip with excessive frequency (Jul 19-22)

**FOCUS**

A good pace and a fair time for a race of its type.

**NOTEBOOK**

**Oktis Morilious(IRE)**, taking a drop in class, still had a bit to do on adjusted official ratings but won this with a degree of comfort, the easing in the ground not bothering him at all. He should have another modest race in him.

**Waltzing Beau**, another dropped in grade, was 16lb better off with Oktis Morilious for a beating of around nine lengths at Bath and managed to narrow the gap, though still comfortably held.

**Defana** was well backed and had every chance, but lacked pace in the closing stages. His best trip is still to be established.

**Cloudingswell** ran freely enough out in front in the first-time visor and did not get home. She still has to convince she stays this far, especially given her style of running.

**Come What July(IRE)**, held up out the back, tried to make a move mid-race but it came to nothing and he was heavily eased once beaten. He seems to reserve his best for the sand these days.

**Saint Zita(IRE)** *Official explanation: jockey said filly ran too freely in early stages*

## 3682 BRYANT HOMES H'CAP — 1m 4f 134y

**4:15** (4:15) (F ) (0-55,55) 4-Y-O+ — **£3,430** (£980; £490) **Stalls** Low

Form — RPR

0-05 **1** — **Danebank (IRE)**[37] 2547 4-9-0 47 ... DaleGibson 9 — 56
(JMackie) *chsd ldr: rdn to ld wl over 1f out: drvn out* **8/1**[3]

0402 **2** ½ **Red River Rebel**[6] 3472 6-9-4 51 ... DarrenWilliams 2 — 59
(JRNorton) *set modest pce: qcknd 3f out: sn rdn: hdd wl over 1f out: ev ch ins fnl f: r.o* **9/4**[1]

0345 **3** ¾ **Bojangles (IRE)**[8] 3412 5-8-12 48 ... DNolan(3) 7 — 55
(RBrotherton) *hld up and bhd: hdwy over 1f out: r.o ins fnl f* **11/2**[2]

00/1 **4** ½ **Sovereign State (IRE)**[8] 3411 7-9-0 47 6ex ... (p) FNorton 4 — 53
(DWThompson) *a.p: rdn and outpcd over 2f out: rallied ins fnl f* **9/1**

6125 **5** nk **Make My Hay**[13] 3263 5-8-11 49 ... BSwarbrick(5) 8 — 55
(JGallagher) *hld up in tch: rdn and outpcd 3f out: rallied ins fnl f* **11/2**[2]

01-0 **6** 6 **Boing Boing (IRE)**[40] 2473 4-9-4 54 ... JFMcDonald(3) 12 — 51
(MissSJWilton) *prom: rdn over 2f out: wknd over 1f out* **20/1**

1041 **7** 1¼ **Our Destiny**[8] 3423 6-9-1 55 ... LTreadwell(7) 6 — 50
(AWCarroll) *hld up: rdn and no hdwy fnl 3f* **8/1**[3]

-060 **8** ½ **Milk And Sultana**[18] 3128 4-9-4 51 ... RSmith 5 — 45
(GAHam) *hld up in tch: rdn and lost pl on ins over 3f out* **25/1**

2-60 **9** ½ **African Dawn**[13] 3263 6-9-0 50 ... (t) FPFerris(3) 11 — 44
(LGCottrell) *hld up in mid-div: rdn over 2f out: wknd over 1f out* **14/1**

4-00 **10** 5 **Migration**[54] 2126 8-9-3 50 ... LVickers 10 — 36
(MrsSLamyman) *hld up in mid-div: c wd ent st: sn rdn and btn* **25/1**

501- **11** 10 **Denise Best (IRE)**[262] 5672 6-9-4 51 ... VSlattery 1 — 22
(MissKMGeorge) *s.i.s: a bhd* **16/1**

0450 **12** 12 **Free Style (GER)**[8] 3429 4-9-1 48 ... GBaker 3 — 1
(MrsHSweeting) *a bhd* **25/1**

4-00 **13** 3½ **Ultra Marine (IRE)**[8] 3411 4-9-0 50 ... LFletcher(3) 13 — —
(JSWainwright) *hld up: rdn over 5f out: sn struggling* **40/1**

2m 46.03s (2.73) **Going Correction** +0.175s/f (Good) **13** Ran SP% **125.0**
Speed ratings: **98,97,97,96,96 93,92,91,91,88 82,75,72**CSF £25.79 CT £115.17 TOTE £8.70: £2.40, £1.50, £2.70; EX 37.30.

**Owner** Ms L A Machin **Bred** Sweetmans Bloodstock **Trained** Church Broughton, Derbys

**FOCUS**

An ordinary handicap and only a modest pace for the first mile. Despite his uninspiring form figures, the winner showed enough last year to have a serious chance. The second failed to reproduce his recent good effort, but the next three were roughly to form.

**NOTEBOOK**

**Danebank(IRE)**, unplaced in all 15 of his previous starts, including one over hurdles, was nonetheless backed off the boards. Always in the front two, he kept responding to pressure in order to outbattle the favourite and land the gamble. In fairness, he had shown glimpses of form from higher marks and was having only his third run on the Flat for his new trainer, who was sure he would appreciate the rain. Whether he will reproduce this is anyone's guess, but those who were in the know here are unlikely to be too bothered .

**Red River Rebel** was able to set a moderate gallop before trying to quicken things up half a mile from home. He never stopped trying and battled back really well when the gambled-on winner challenged him, but he just lost out in the very closing stages. This easy track may not have been ideal, and he would be interesting if sent back to his beloved Beverley. However, he was already going up 9lb.

**Bojangles(IRE)** has shown his best form over shorter, but the modest gallop helped him get the longer trip and he was never closer than at the line.

**Sovereign State(IRE)**, carrying a 6lb penalty for his Catterick victory, ran creditably but would have preferred a stronger gallop and for the rain to have stayed away.

**Make My Hay** was another totally unsuited by the way the race was run.

**Our Destiny**, unpenalised for his Lingfield win, is yet another that failed to pick up off a modest pace.

**Free Style(GER)** *Official explanation: jockey said filly lost her action*

## 3683 THREE A'S PERTEMPS H'CAP — 2m 39y

**4:50** (4:50) (E ) (0-75,70) 3-Y-O+ — **£4,348** (£1,338; £669; £334) **Stalls** Low

Form — RPR

654P **1** — **Moonshine Beach**[6] 3488 6-8-9 54 ... DarrenWilliams 8 — 69+
(PWHiatt) *chsd ldr: led over 8f out: qcknd clr over 3f out: sn rdn: eased ins fnl f* **11/4**[2]

6011 **2** 1 **Darn Good**[6] 3488 3-8-3 70 6ex ... (b) JFMcDonald(3) 5 — 76
(RHannon) *hld up: stdy hdwy over 6f out: wnt 2nd over 1f out: styd on: nt rch eased wnr* **5/2**[1]

-005 **3** 10 **Beechy Bank (IRE)**[16] 3181 6-9-6 65 ... VSlattery 2 — 59
(MrsMaryHambro) *hld up: stdy hdwy over 6f out: wknd over 1f out* **12/1**

3-50 **4** 6 **Henry Island (IRE)**[42] 2429 11-9-6 65 ... FNorton 7 — 52
(MrsAJBowlby) *a.p: chsd wnr over 7f out: rdn over 4f out: wknd over 1f out* **7/2**[3]

0-05 **5** 7 **Chanfron**[17] 3160 3-7-12 62 oh4 ... AMcCarthy 3 — 40
(BRMillman) *prom tl wknd 2f out* **8/1**

006/ **6** nk **Three Eagles (USA)**[15] 2211 7-7-7 43 oh12 ... (b) BSwarbrick(5) 4 — 21
(MScudamore) *led: reminders over 9f out: hdd over 8f out: rdn over 7f out: sn lost pl* **11/1**

00-0 **7** 1½ **Lillebror (GER)**[89] 1326 6-9-3 62 ... SWKelly 6 — 38
(BJCurley) *hld up in rr: rdn over 4f out: no rspnse* **12/1**

3m 37.48s (5.67) **Going Correction** +0.175s/f (Good)
**WFA** 3 from 6yo+ 19lb **7** Ran SP% **112.3**
Speed ratings: **92,91,86,83,80 79,79**CSF £9.68 CT £66.09 TOTE £5.00: £2.60, £1.60; EX 12.10.

**Owner** Ken Read **Bred** Lawrence Shepherd **Trained** Hook Norton, Oxon

**FOCUS**

A moderate pace until well past halfway and a very slow winning time for the grade. The winner was value for a wide margin, but he did rather steal the race.

**NOTEBOOK**

**Moonshine Beach** whose last two starts were both in races won by Darn Good here, had excuses on both occasions. A sudden injection of pace from the front over half a mile from home proved a race-winning move, as it caught his rivals flat-footed, and having held an unassailable lead turning in he was eased right down, despite being very tired. He was value for considerably more and his rider will not have fooled the Handicapper.

**Darn Good**, carrying a 6lb penalty in his hat-trick bid, was patiently ridden but was rather caught on heels when the winner quickened from the front half a mile out. Even though he kept on and cut right into the advantage, that was more down to the winning jockey's antics than anything else. He could probably have done without the rain.

**Beechy Bank(IRE)** was trying this trip for the first time, but despite the lack of early pace she still seemed to find it too far in the ground.

**Henry Island(IRE)** is dropping back to a reasonable mark, but was nonetheless well beaten and looks well past his best.

**Chanfron**, a maiden stepping up more than half a mile in trip, did not stay.

## 3684 HALL BROS H'CAP — 1m 22y

**5:20** (5:22) (E ) (0-70,69) 3-Y-O — **£3,981** (£1,225; £612; £306) **Stalls** Low

Form — RPR

0025 **1** — **Hazewind**[27] 2835 3-8-6 57 ... (t) FPFerris(3) 15 — 61
(PDEvans) *w ldr: rdn over 3f out: led 1f out: r.o* **9/2**[2]

3000 **2** hd **Three Welshmen**[4] 3556 3-8-7 55 ... (p) SWKelly 13 — 59
(BRMillman) *led: rdn over 2f out: hdd 1f out: r.o* **12/1**

6032 **3** nk **Gabana (IRE)**[14] 3246 3-9-3 65 ... GBaker 11 — 68
(CFWall) *hld up: hdwy over 1f out: r.o ins fnl f* **9/2**[2]

0502 **4** 4 **Iphigenia (IRE)**[13] 3261 3-8-12 65 ... PMakin(5) 16 — 59
(PWHiatt) *hld up and bhd: rdn over 2f out: hdwy over 1f out: nvr nr to chal* **9/1**

0055 **5** 4 **Blue Daze**[6] 3478 3-9-6 68 ... (b[1]) RSmith 7 — 53
(RHannon) *prom: rdn over 2f out: wknd over 1f out* **8/1**[3]

4260 **6** hd **Given A Chance**[10] 3375 3-7-12 46 ... SRighton 2 — 30
(MrsSLamyman) *prom: rdn over 2f out: wknd wl over 1f out* **12/1**

320- **7** 5 **Text**[315] 4526 3-9-1 63 ... FNorton 12 — 36
(MrsStefLiddiard) *hld up: rdn over 2f out: no rspnse* **20/1**

6162 **8** shd **Son Of Thunder (IRE)**[17] 3146 3-8-6 57 ... LEnstone(3) 4 — 30
(MDods) *hld up: rdn and wknd wl over 1f out* **3/1**[1]

-000 **9** 10 **Rockley Bay (IRE)**[17] 3158 3-8-10 58 ... (b[1]) MFenton 10 — 8
(PJMakin) *hld up: rdn over 3f out: sn struggling* **25/1**

0063 **10** 3½ **Kings Rock**[37] 2545 3-8-3 58 ... DonnaCaldwell(7) 3 — —
(KARyan) *a towards rr* **10/1**

0400 **11** dist **Snow Joke (IRE)**[17] 3156 3-8-0 53 ... BSwarbrick(5) 8 — —
(MrsPNDutfield) *bhd: hmpd wl over 3f out: sn t.o* **16/1**

-000 **U** **Don Argento**[35] 2614 3-7-7 46 oh6 ... DFox(5) 5 — —
(MrsAJBowlby) *s.s: in rr tl hmpd and uns rdr wl over 3f out* **33/1**

3060 **F** **Tonto (FR)**[116] 1017 3-8-13 68 ... (p) SaleemGolam(7) 6 — —
(MissDMountain) *bhd tl broke leg and fell wl over 3f out: dead* **22/1**

1m 40.55s (1.25) **Going Correction** +0.175s/f (Good) **13** Ran SP% **128.7**
Speed ratings: **100,99,99,95,91 91,86,86,76,72** —,—,—CSF £59.55 CT £228.27 TOTE £9.20: £3.20, £3.20, £1.80; EX 71.30 Place 6 £10.54, Place 5 £7.91.

**Owner** Waterline Racing Club **Bred** Gainsborough Stud Management Ltd **Trained** Pandy, Gwent

**FOCUS**

A modest event, but a dramatic contest. The pace was only fair, but despite that very few got into it and the first two home were the front pair throughout. As with the second race, there was an advantage in coming stands' side in the home straight and the front pair, who were drawn high, both took that route.

**NOTEBOOK**

**Hazewind** helped force the pace along with the runner-up and, after being brought over to the stands' side in the straight, battled on really well to score narrowly. This is probably his best trip and he is likely to win a few more races like this in his career, even though he obviously has his quirks as he dumped his rider on returning to the winner's enclosure.

**Three Welshmen**, who would probably have preferred even more rain, ran very well under a positive ride but being brought over to the stands' side after turning for home almost certainly helped him get so close.

**Gabana(IRE)** came from off the pace to finish very close. She may have been a bit unlucky as she stayed more towards the far side than the front pair and also wandered about in the closing stages, possibly losing more ground than she was beaten by. On the other hand, she has shown wayward tendencies in the past so it may be wise not to make too many excuses.
**Iphigenia(IRE)** appeared to run way above herself in a Folkestone maiden last time and as a result found herself racing off a 13lb higher mark than for her last start in a handicap. Not surprisingly she found that far too much, despite doing her very best, and hopefully she will now be shown some mercy.
**Blue Daze** may need to drop back a furlong, but still needs some help from the Handicapper.
**Son Of Thunder(IRE)**, raised 4lb for getting beaten at Musselburgh, could have done without the rain but was still disappointing.
**Snow Joke(IRE)** *Official explanation: jockey said he was hampered by a fallen horse*
T/Plt: £20.00 to a £1 stake. Pool: £28,583.35. 1,039.80 winning tickets. T/Qpdt: £10.10 to a £1 stake. Pool: £1,553.10. 113.50 winning tickets. KH

3685 - 3688a (Foreign Racing) - See Raceform Interactive

3071
# ASCOT (R-H)
Friday, July 9

**OFFICIAL GOING: Good (good to soft in places on round course)**
Rain resulted in a change in the going with the official description being 'Good, good to soft in places on the round course' and it rode loose on top.
Wind: lt against Weather: fine but cloudy

## 3689 SONY CLAIMING STKS — 1m (R)
2:15 (2:18) (D) 3-Y-O — £10,237 (£3,150; £1,575; £787) Stalls High

| Form | | | | RPR |
|---|---|---|---|---|
| -402 | 1 | | **Arkholme**[14] 3271 3-9-0 76 (b) DHolland 7 | 83 |
| | | | (WJHaggas) *racd in rr: plld wd and prog over 2f out: led over 1f out: edgd rt but rdn clr* **7/2**[2] | |
| -060 | 2 | 3 | **Hoh Bleu Dee**[6] 3543 3-9-0 82 JFEgan 4 | 76 |
| | | | (SKirk) *pushed along in midfield: reminder 4f out: prog on inner over 2f out: ev ch over 1f out: one pce* **12/1** | |
| -010 | 3 | 1 3/4 | **Toparudi**[34] 2692 3-9-0 73 FPFerris(3) 2 | 75 |
| | | | (MHTompkins) *trckd ldrs: rdn and nt qckn 2f out: kpt on one pce after* **12/1** | |
| 0520 | 4 | 1/2 | **Tranquil Sky**[34] 2692 3-9-2 85 LDettori 10 | 73 |
| | | | (NACallaghan) *prom: effrt over 2f out: ev ch over 1f out: wknd fnl f* **11/4**[1] | |
| 1560 | 5 | 2 | **Fit To Fly (IRE)**[6] 3535 3-8-12 75 SWhitworth 9 | 64 |
| | | | (SKirk) *lw: snatched up after 1f: nvr gng wl after: rdn in rr over 2f out: no prog* **14/1** | |
| 1230 | 6 | hd | **Lady Mo**[37] 2577 3-8-8 60 AMcCarthy 1 | 60 |
| | | | (GGMargarson) *chsd ldr: led over 2f out to over 1f out: wknd* **33/1** | |
| 0-65 | 7 | 3/4 | **Moscow Times**[17] 3180 3-9-7 70 JPMurtagh 5 | 71 |
| | | | (DRCElsworth) *lw: dwlt: hld up in last: rdn over 2f out: fnd nil* **7/1** | |
| 0002 | 8 | 1 1/4 | **Epaminondas (USA)**[6] 3529 3-8-12 66 RLMoore 3 | 59 |
| | | | (RHannon) *racd in midfield: rdn 3f out: sn btn* **12/1** | |
| 0-00 | 9 | nk | **Binnion Bay (IRE)**[6] 3527 3-9-0 78 DaneO'Neill 6 | 61 |
| | | | (RHannon) *dwlt: racd on outer: prog fr rr 1/2-way: wknd over 2f out* **33/1** | |
| 122- | 10 | 13 | **Queenstown (IRE)**[205] 6203 3-9-1 88 (b) JFortune 8 | 32 |
| | | | (BJMeehan) *led to over 2f out: wknd rapidly over 1f out: t.o* **6/1**[3] | |

1m 43.31s (0.27) **Going Correction** +0.325s/f (Good) **10 Ran SP% 111.3**
Speed ratings: **111,108,106,105,103 103,102,101,101,88**CSF £42.66 TOTE £4.50: £1.60, £4.00, £6.40; EX 76.40.The winner was claimed by P.Winkworth for £22,000. Fit To Fly (IRE) was claimed by Mrs J. Candlish for £14,000.
**Owner** Mr & Mrs G Middlebrook **Bred** G And Mrs Middlebrook **Trained** Newmarket, Suffolk

**FOCUS**
A good claimer and a decent time for the grade, giving the form a sound look. A fine performance from Arkholme, who appreciated this easy going.

**NOTEBOOK**
**Arkholme** ran a solid second when dropped into this grade a week ago and, on this easier ground, found the necessary improvement. He picked up strongly once switched to come with his run and ran out a cosy winner. He is capable of winning back in handicap company.
**Hoh Bleu Dee** appreciated this less demanding company and ran a better race than of late. He is not easy to place as he is on a stiff mark and will struggle to win any time soon.
**Toparudi** appreciated this easy surface and could ideally do with a stiffer test. He won a handicap on his penultimate start and can win again back in that company.
**Tranquil Sky** had a clear chance at the weights and was made favourite despite being unproven on an easy surface. She was well positioned throughout and had her chance but was not up to the task.
**Fit To Fly(IRE)** was cut up early in the race and never really going that well thereafter. He can be given another chance.
**Moscow Times**, although not favoured by the weights, had to be respected on connections alone, and had promised better to come when a running-on fifth at Newbury last time. He was held up last for most of the way and found nothing when asked to improve his position. He is one to avoid on the evidence of this.
**Epaminondas(USA)** *Official explanation: jockey said colt hung left round the bend*
**Queenstown(IRE)** raced too keenly for his own good on this three-year-old debut and stopped very quickly. He has something to prove now. *Official explanation: jockey said gelding pulled hard and did not get home*

## 3690 WOODCOTE STUD H'CAP — 7f
2:45 (2:47) (C) (0-90,90) 3-Y-O+ — £14,144 (£4,352; £2,176; £1,088) Stalls Low

| Form | | | | RPR |
|---|---|---|---|---|
| 3303 | 1 | | **True Night**[3] 3597 7-9-3 78 DHolland 9 | 89 |
| | | | (DNicholls) *lw: pressed ldr after 2f: led 3f out and kicked on: hrd pressed fnl f: drvn and hld on wl* **7/2**[1] | |
| -050 | 2 | nk | **Manaar (IRE)**[21] 3036 4-9-6 81 LDettori 7 | 91 |
| | | | (JNoseda) *hld up in rr: prog on outer 2f out: drvn and str chal fnl f: jst hld* **7/1**[3] | |
| 0454 | 3 | 1/2 | **Azreme**[11] 3386 4-8-6 69 IMongan 3 | 78 |
| | | | (DKIvory) *b: b.hind: hld up in midfield: rdn and squeezed through 2f out: chal jst over 1f out: ev ch: no ex last 75yds* **11/1** | |
| 1111 | 4 | 1 1/2 | **A Woman In Love**[20] 3086 5-9-4 79 SSanders 13 | 84 |
| | | | (MissBSanders) *hld up towards rr: pushed along and effrt whn nt clr run over 1f out: styd on same pce* **10/1** | |
| 0446 | 5 | shd | **Jools**[2] 3631 6-9-2 77 DaneO'Neill 14 | 82 |
| | | | (DKIvory) *b: hld up in last: swtchd to wd outside and prog 2f out: cl up 1f out: one pce after* **33/1** | |
| 3415 | 6 | 1 1/2 | **Chateau Nicol**[8] 3453 5-9-9 84 (v) JFortune 6 | 85 |
| | | | (BGPowell) *lw: hld up towards rr: gng wl enough whn nt clr run over 1f out: fnd nil after* **12/1** | |
| 3211 | 7 | 3/4 | **Warden Complex**[26] 2907 3-9-3 86 JPMurtagh 8 | 85 |
| | | | (JRFanshawe) *settled wl in rr: nt clr run briefly 2f out: rdn and styd on fnl f: no ch* **4/1**[2] | |
| 4015 | 8 | 1 1/4 | **Taranaki**[40] 2503 6-9-10 88 LisaJones(3) 4 | 84 |
| | | | (PDCundell) *prom: pressed wnr over 2f out to over 1f out: wknd* **16/1** | |
| 0000 | 9 | 3/4 | **Craiova (IRE)**[7] 3477 5-9-5 80 CCatlin 12 | 74 |
| | | | (BWHills) *racd towards outer: in tch: rdn 2f out: wknd jst over 1f out* **12/1** | |
| 5-01 | 10 | 3 1/2 | **Music Maid (IRE)**[30] 2788 6-8-4 65 TPQueally 2 | 50 |
| | | | (HSHowe) *dwlt: sn trckd ldrs: rdn over 2f out: wknd wl over 1f out* **20/1** | |
| -602 | 11 | 5 | **Colour Wheel**[21] 3052 3-9-7 90 (t) RHughes 10 | 62 |
| | | | (RCharlton) *racd towards outer: trckd ldrs: rdn over 2f out: sn lost pl and btn* **11/1** | |
| 0000 | 12 | nk | **Te Quiero**[17] 3177 6-8-8 72 (t) SHitchcott(3) 1 | 43 |
| | | | (MissGayKelleway) *led at stdy pce to 3f out: sn u.p and struggling* **33/1** | |
| 010 | 13 | 7 | **Secret Place**[35] 2642 3-9-7 90 WRyan 5 | 43 |
| | | | (EALDunlop) *trckd ldr: rdn over 2f out: wknd rapidly over 1f out* **14/1** | |

1m 30.8s (1.13) **Going Correction** +0.325s/f (Good)
**WFA** 3 from 4yo+ 8lb **13 Ran SP% 119.1**
Speed ratings: **106,105,105,103,103 101,100,99,98,94 88,88,80**CSF £27.05 CT £253.36 TOTE £4.50: £1.80, £2.70, £3.50; EX 40.60 Trifecta £702.00 Pool of £11,964.74 - 12.10 winning tickets.
**Owner** Benton And Partners **Bred** Crichel Farms Ltd **Trained** Sessay, N Yorks

**FOCUS**
A competitive handicap, but run at only a modest pace, that went to True Night who has a real liking for this place. The form is fair and looks solid enough.

**NOTEBOOK**
**True Night** has been threatening to get his head in front again and was given a full-on ride from Holland to repel all challengers once taking it up three out. He goes well at this course but, with his strike rate, would not be one to bank on for a follow up, even if returning here.
**Manaar(IRE)**, 3lb better off with the winner for just under four lengths on Royal Ascot form, bridged the cap and went very close to reversing the placings. He is still relatively unexposed and is progressing.
**Azreme** came to win his race but, as at Windsor last time, did not quite see it out. He is undoubtedly running into form and likes this sort of ground, but could do with an easier course.
**A Woman In Love** has been in the form of her life, winning her last four, and produced another good effort. She is currently 21lb higher than when last winning and may struggle now the Handicapper appears to have caught up with her.
**Jools** ran a better race under hold-up tactics than he had done from the front at Kempton earlier in the week, staying on at the one pace around the outside of his field.
**Chateau Nicol** travelled nicely before meeting a dead-end and failed to pick up thereafter. He is currently 6lb higher than when last scoring and needs a drop in the weights before he is winning again.
**Warden Complex** never really got involved, running on all too late having been denied a clear passage. He is better than this and deserves another chance back on his favoured fast ground.
**Craiova(IRE)** travelled nicely on the outer before finding little. He has become most disappointing.
**Colour Wheel** *Official explanation: trainer was unable to offer any explanation for the poor form shown*
**Secret Place** *Official explanation: jockey said gelding lost its action*

## 3691 RENDEZVOUS CASINO RATED STKS (H'CAP) — 6f 110y
3:15 (3:17) (C) (0-90,90) 3-Y-O+ — £8,733 (£3,312; £1,656; £752) Stalls Low

| Form | | | | RPR |
|---|---|---|---|---|
| 1315 | 1 | | **Prince Aaron (IRE)**[34] 2682 4-9-2 81 GCarter 5 | 92+ |
| | | | (CNAllen) *lw: wl plcd: prog and cruising 2f out: led ent fnl f: shkn up and sn clr* **11/2**[3] | |
| 3600 | 2 | 1 1/2 | **Armagnac**[13] 3298 6-8-10 75 DaneO'Neill 9 | 82+ |
| | | | (MABuckley) *dwlt: hld up in last pair: snatched up over 2f out: swtchd to wd outside over 1f out and gd prog: r.o to take 2nd last stri* **12/1** | |
| 1102 | 3 | hd | **Idle Power (IRE)**[28] 2838 6-8-12 77 (p) JPMurtagh 10 | 83 |
| | | | (JRBoyle) *hld up in midfield: rdn and effrt wl over 1f out: r.o to chse wnr wl ins fnl f: lost 2nd last strides* **12/1** | |
| 2122 | 4 | 1 | **Devon Flame**[9] 3416 5-8-7 75 JFMcDonald(3) 4 | 78 |
| | | | (RJHodges) *lw: racd freely: led tl ent fnl f: one pce* **12/1** | |
| 400 | 5 | 3/4 | **Starbeck (IRE)**[7] 3477 6-9-7 86 TGMcLaughlin 7 | 87 |
| | | | (PHowling) *b: b.hind: restless stalls: dwlt: hld up in last pair: effrt 2f out: kpt on fr over 1f out: nt pce to rch ldrs* **33/1** | |
| 1200 | 6 | shd | **Morse (IRE)**[9] 3420 3-9-3 90 LDettori 1 | 90 |
| | | | (JAOsborne) *chsd ldrs: rdn 2f out: kpt on same pce u.p* **14/1** | |
| 0363 | 7 | 1 1/4 | **Najeebon (FR)**[8] 3453 5-8-12 80 SHitchcott(3) 6 | 77 |
| | | | (MRChannon) *lw: trckd ldrs: rdn over 2f out: styd clos up u.p tl wknd ins fnl f* **8/1** | |
| 5001 | 8 | 2 1/2 | **Loyal Tycoon (IRE)**[8] 3439 6-9-3 82 3ex JFortune 2 | 71 |
| | | | (DNicholls) *hld up towards rr: nt clr run twice over 1f out: shkn up ent fnl f: nt clr run sn after and eased* **5/1**[2] | |
| -342 | 9 | 5 | **Bandit Queen**[31] 2750 4-9-4 86 LisaJones(3) 3 | 60 |
| | | | (WJarvis) *mostly chsd ldr tl wknd over 1f out* **12/1** | |
| 0041 | 10 | 2 | **Fantasy Believer**[8] 3453 6-9-8 87 3ex DHolland 11 | 55 |
| | | | (JJQuinn) *v restless in stalls: hld up: rdn and effrt on outer 2f out: no prog over 1f out: wknd fnl f* **11/4**[1] | |
| 5042 | 11 | 5 | **Mister Saif (USA)**[28] 2844 3-9-0 87 RHughes 8 | 40 |
| | | | (RHannon) *prom tl wknd over 2f out* **20/1** | |

1m 23.54s
**WFA** 3 from 4yo+ 6lb **11 Ran SP% 115.0**
Speed ratings: CSF £68.10 CT £771.18 TOTE £5.90: £1.90, £4.70, £3.80; EX 125.60 Trifecta £2089.50 Pool of £2,943.07 - 0.40 winning tickets.
**Owner** Black Star Racing **Bred** Peter Charles And J R Bamforth **Trained** Newmarket, Suffolk
■ Stewards Enquiry : R Hughes one-day ban: failed to keep straight from stalls (Jul 21)

**FOCUS**
A decent handicap and a smart performance from Prince Aaron, who was chopped from both the Wokingham and Bunbury Cup, but got his just desserts here. There are no speed figures for this race as the distance is used very rarely, but the form looks sound.

**NOTEBOOK**
**Prince Aaron(IRE)**, who ran well in defeat despite reportedly not handling the track on Derby Day, missed the cut in both the Wokingham and Bunbury Cup - races he would have ran well in if this performance is anything to go by. Always holding a good position, he was never going to be caught once hitting the front just inside the furlong. A horse who does not want soft ground, he looks sure to play a big part in the outcome of races such as the Stewards Cup - if getting in - and the Ayr Gold Cup if getting his favoured fast surface.
**Armagnac** ◆ was unlucky not to finish closer, but whether he would have won is open to debate. He was reported to have momentarily lost his action when crossing the path and that cost him momentum. He flew home once getting going and, as he is currently racing off a 3lb lower mark than when last winning, should be ready to strike in the coming weeks. *Official explanation: jockey said gelding lost its action on the crossings*
**Idle Power(IRE)**, who has been in great form this season, winning twice and finishing second when last seen, ran his race but was not good enough on the day.
**Devon Flame** has done all his winning on good to firm ground and coped well enough with this easier surface in what was the best race he has ever run in. He could offer no more having run a bit free, and although currently 7lb higher than when last winning, he seems to be progressing well enough to defy it and win again.
**Starbeck(IRE)** stayed on at the one pace through tiring rivals and remains hard to place off her mark.
**Morse(IRE)** fared best of the two three-year-olds but never threatened.


The Form Book, Raceform Ltd, Compton, RG20 6NL

**Loyal Tycoon(IRE)** *Official explanation: jockey said gelding suffered interference in running*
**Fantasy Believer** played up in the stalls and that may have had something to do with his dire effort. He is better than this and deserves another chance. *Official explanation: vet said gelding suffered lacerations to its head probably sustained when reared in the starting stalls*

## 3692 SONY WEGA H'CAP — 1m 4f
**3:50** (3:53) (C) (0-90,90) 3-Y-O+ — **£9,782** (£3,010; £1,505; £752) **Stalls** High

Form — RPR

-035 **1** **Sergeant Cecil**[7] 3485 5-9-13 **86** ........ JFortune 8 95
(BRMillman) *hld up in last: rapid prog on outer over 2f out: led over 1f out: idled fnl f and drvn: jst hld on* **16/1**

-316 **2** *shd* **Cutting Crew (USA)**[50] 2244 3-9-4 **90** ........ DHolland 10 99
(PWHarris) *trckd ldng pair: rdn and unable qck wl over 1f out: drvn and r.o to chse wnr ins fnl f: clsd fin: jst failed* **4/1**[2]

3-30 **3** *1 ¼* **Fort**[34] 2676 3-9-1 **87** ........ SChin 2 94
(MJohnston) *led after 1f: rdn and hdd over 1f out: kpt on wl fnl f: a hld* **11/1**

0204 **4** *shd* **Mexican Pete**[16] 3207 4-9-4 **77** ........ JFEgan 9 84
(PWHiatt) *swtg: racd in midfield: lost pl 4f out: in last pair over 3f out: prog again on inner 2f out: styd on: nvr quite able to ch* **25/1**

-412 **5** *hd* **Zeitgeist (IRE)**[30] 2782 3-9-1 **87** ........ LDettori 3 93
(LMCumani) *racd in midfield: lost pl over 3f out and in rr: drvn over 2f out: styd on wl fr over 1f out: nrst fin* **9/4**[1]

0030 **6** *4* **Barry Island**[39] 2537 5-9-3 **76** ........ SSanders 6 76
(DRCElsworth) *t.k.h: hld up in midfield: trckd ldrs gng wl whn nt clr run briefly wl over 1f out: fnd nil after* **20/1**

2036 **7** *1 ¾* **Briareus**[20] 3075 4-9-4 **77** ........ RLMoore 7 74
(AMBalding) *lw: t.k.h: led for 1f: trckd ldr to wl over 1f out: wknd* **7/1**[3]

6011 **8** *¾* **Silvaline**[7] 3482 5-8-13 **79** 5ex ........ CHaddon(7) 12 75
(TKeddy) *t.k.h: hld up in last pair: prog on outer 5f out: c v wd ent st: edgd rt 2f out: bmpd along and wknd* **10/1**

4-51 **9** *shd* **Tender Falcon**[15] 3232 4-8-7 **69** ........ JFMcDonald(3) 4 65
(RJHodges) *trckd ldrs: rdn and wknd over 2f out* **14/1**

-641 **10** *shd* **Penzance**[18] 3152 3-8-10 **82** ........ JPMurtagh 5 78
(JRFanshawe) *lw: racd in midfield: losing pl whn squeezed out wl over 1f out: wknd* **7/1**[3]

-021 **11** *3* **Feed The Meter (IRE)**[11] 3383 4-7-9 **57** 5ex ........ FPFerris(3) 1 48
(TTClement) *t.k.h: racd on outer: hld up: effrt 1/2-way: rdn and wknd 3f out* **20/1**

2m 34.86s (1.30) **Going Correction** +0.325s/f (Good)
**WFA** 3 from 4yo+ 13lb — **11** Ran SP% **119.1**
Speed ratings: **108,107,107,107,106 104,103,102,102,102 100**CSF £77.99 CT £756.50 TOTE £19.80: £4.10, £1.90, £2.70; EX 137.20.
**Owner** Terry Cooper **Bred** D E Hazzard **Trained** Kentisbeare, Devon

**FOCUS**
A decent handicap and close finish between Sergeant Cecil and three-year-old Cutting Crew, but the form is just fair for the grade.

**NOTEBOOK**
**Sergeant Cecil**, who raced too freely when disappointing last week, settled well in rear and came with a sweeping run around the outside of the field to take it up approaching the final furlong. However, he found little in front but just did enough to hold on. This was the highest mark he has ever won off, and he will need to progress further if he is to defy another rise. *Official explanation: trainer said, regarding the improved form shown, gelding pulled too hard in a slowly-run race at Sandown last time*
**Cutting Crew(USA)** stays this trip well and only really hit top gear in the final furlong. He flew home under Holland and would have got there in another stride. Although on a high-enough mark, he is evidently progressive and will stay further.
**Fort**, who caught the eye of many when meeting with interference in a competitive handicap on Derby Day, adopted different tactics and tried to make most of the running. He was passed over a furlong out but, as with most of his trainer's runners, kept battling away and held on for third. He has a similar race in him.
**Mexican Pete** ran a good race in defeat and was closing with every stride at the line, but remains 11lb higher than when last successful and needs a drop in the weights before he is winning again.
**Zeitgeist(IRE)** is progressing but not well enough to defy his 10lb higher mark for winning at Redcar off 77. He will stay farther and that may be the source of the improvement he needs to find.
**Penzance** was disappointing and beaten by the time he was squeezed out.

## 3693 WOODCOTE STUD MAIDEN FILLIES' STKS — 6f
**4:25** (4:25) (D) 2-Y-O — **£5,538** (£1,704; £852; £426) **Stalls** Low

Form — RPR

**1** **Valentin (IRE)** 2-8-11 ........ DaneO'Neill 1 85+
(RHannon) *rangy: scope: dwlt: rn green and last to 1/2-way: prog to chse ldrs over 1f out : burst through to ld jst ins fnl f: sn clr* **10/1**

**2** *3 ½* **Dance Flower (IRE)** 2-8-11 ........ CCatlin 6 75
(MRChannon) *leggy: scope: pressed ldr: led over 2f out: hdd and outpcd jst ins fnl f* **10/1**

4 **3** *¾* **Gennie Bond**[14] 3272 2-8-11 ........ RHughes 4 73
(RHannon) *dwlt: sn trckd ldrs on outer: rdn and unable qck over 1f out: styd on ins fnl f* **4/1**[1]

03 **4** *hd* **Lady Ann Summers (USA)**[9] 3413 2-8-11 ........ JFortune 2 72
(BJMeehan) *trckd ldrs: nt clr run over 2f out: effrt to chal over 1f out : ev ch ent fnl f: nt qckn and sn btn* **9/2**[2]

**5** *¾* **Subyan Dreams** 2-8-11 ........ AMcCarthy 3 70
(PWChapple-Hyam) *str: scope: bit bkwd: trckd ldrs: shkn up and ev ch over 1f out: fdd fnl f* **7/1**

**6** *4* **Tamora** 2-8-11 ........ DHolland 7 58
(APJarvis) *cmpt: bit bkwd: rn green: in tch tl shied at path over 3f out and dropped to last: no ch after: kpt on* **10/1**

3 **7** *nk* **African Gift**[35] 2651 2-8-11 ........ SSanders 5 57
(JGGiven) *b.hind: wnt lft s: led to over 2f out: wknd over 1f out* **13/2**[3]

5 **8** *15* **Theas Dance**[8] 3456 2-8-11 ........ TPQueally 8 12
(DRLoder) *lw: wnt rt s: racd on outer: wl in tch tl wknd rapidly 2f out: t.o* **4/1**[1]

1m 18.47s (2.48) **Going Correction** +0.325s/f (Good) — **8** Ran SP% **111.3**
Speed ratings: **96,91,90,90,89 83,83,63**CSF £97.71 TOTE £17.50: £3.40, £2.70, £1.90; EX 158.80.
**Owner** Mrs Valerie Hubbard & A J Ilsley **Bred** Rockhart Trading Ltd **Trained** East Everleigh, Wilts

**FOCUS**
Hard to know what to make of the form of the race with a couple of the fancied runners not giving their running, and suggesting it may be unreliable; but an impressive winner nonetheless and nothing should be taken away from her.

**NOTEBOOK**
**Valentin(IRE)** is bred for speed and showed plenty, sprinting throught the pack to make her field look pedestrian and winning impressively. This was a smart performance considering she was tardy at the start and ran green, so there is definitely more to come and a step up in grade is warranted.
**Dance Flower(IRE)** made a pleasing debut and seemed to know her job, racing up with the pace before being mown down by the winner. She had two fillies with previous experience directly behind and she looks a ready-made winner.
**Gennie Bond** showed a little improvement on her debut and kept on well. Her turn will come.
**Lady Ann Summers(USA)** seemed better suited to this trip of six furlongs but is not really progressing as well as she could have done.
**Subyan Dreams** ◆ is sure to appreciate further than this, so it was encouraging she could show some early pace. Her stable have done well with their two-year-olds so far and she will be winning in the not too distant future, possibly over further.
**Tamora**, representing last year's winning stable, looked very inexperienced on this debut and it is to her credit that she stayed on after dropping to last.
**African Gift** never looked at ease and failed to give her running. On her debut form she should have little trouble landing a maiden.
**Theas Dance** ran as though something was wrong and reportedly got upset in the stalls. She is better than this. *Official explanation: trainer's representative said filly became upset in the starting stalls*

## 3694 SODEXHO FILLIES' H'CAP — 1m 2f
**5:00** (5:00) (C ) (0-90,87) 3-Y-O+ — **£9,392** (£2,890; £1,445; £722) **Stalls** High

Form — RPR

1 **1** **Tartouche**[16] 3204 3-9-0 **87** ........ SSanders 6 93
(LadyHerries) *lw: trckd ldng pair: rdn and rn green 2f out: ev ch ent fnl f: rallied to ld last strides* **5/2**[1]

1-04 **2** *shd* **Windy Britain**[20] 3091 5-9-11 **87** ........ DHolland 5 93
(LMCumani) *lw: hld up in last pair: nt clr run over 1f out: got through and rdn to ld last 100yds: wandered and idled: hdd last stride* **11/2**

-304 **3** *½* **Spring Goddess (IRE)**[27] 2896 3-8-8 **81** ........ AMcCarthy 3 86
(APJarvis) *hld up in last pair: prog on outer 2f out: led jst over 1f out: hdd and nt qckn last 100yds* **8/1**

1 **4** *1 ½* **Hasaiyda (IRE)**[44] 2401 3-7-13 **75** ........ LisaJones(3) 4 77
(SirMichaelStoute) *lw: trckd ldng pair: shkn up and rn green 2f out: sn outpcd: kpt on again ins fnl f* **11/4**[2]

-321 **5** *1 ¼* **Golden Island (IRE)**[13] 3294 3-8-12 **85** ........ RLMoore 1 85
(JWHills) *lw: t.k.h: pressed ldr: rdn to ld wl over 1f out to jst over 1f out: wknd ins fnl f* **5/1**[3]

-024 **6** *¾* **Pink Sapphire (IRE)**[39] 2536 3-8-0 **73** ........ CCatlin 2 71
(DRCElsworth) *led: hrd rdn and hdd wl over 1f out: fdd* **8/1**

2m 10.6s (1.87) **Going Correction** +0.325s/f (Good)
**WFA** 3 from 5yo 11lb — **6** Ran SP% **109.5**
Speed ratings: **105,104,104,103,102 101**CSF £15.52 TOTE £3.40: £2.30, £2.20; EX 13.60 Place 6 £410.61, Place 5 £145.79.
**Owner** Lady Herries **Bred** Angmering Park Stud **Trained** Angmering, W Sussex

**FOCUS**
Fair form but somewhat messy, with a modest gallop resulting in this turning into a bit of a sprint, which did not suit Tartouche, but the filly proved good enough to win despite this.

**NOTEBOOK**
**Tartouche** ◆, having only her second start having made a smart winning debut at Kempton - both second and third won since - raced a tad keenly and ran green under pressure. However she really picked up once Windy Britain went by and got up close close home. There is more to come from her and this will have taught her a lot.
**Windy Britain** may have looked unlucky in not being able to get through, but judging by the way she idled once hitting the front, it was a good job she did not get there sooner. A good effort nonetheless, she remains in good form.
**Spring Goddess(IRE)** looked the likely winner a furlong out, but had no answer when the front two went by. She continues to run well in defeat.
**Hasaiyda(IRE)** ◆ coming into this on the back of a maiden win like the winner, still looked green and undoubtedly wants further. She will be winning when upped to a mile and a half.
**Golden Island(IRE)** raced keenly and was ultimately disappointing.
**Pink Sapphire(IRE)** did not stay the trip despite leading at only a moderate pace.
T/Jkpt: Not won. T/Plt: £803.20 to a £1 stake. Pool: £81,319.60. 73.90 winning tickets. T/Qpdt: £56.80 to a £1 stake. Pool: £4,799.70. 62.50 winning tickets. JN

# 3138 CHEPSTOW (L-H)
### Friday, July 9

**OFFICIAL GOING: Good**
Wind: nil Weather: fine and becoming sunny

## 3695 MEDINET APPRENTICE H'CAP — 1m 4f 23y
**6:35** (6:36) (E) (0-70,68) 3-Y-O+ — **£3,373** (£1,038; £519; £259) **Stalls** Low

Form — RPR

5223 **1** **Dickie Deadeye**[56] 2084 7-9-5 **57** ........ DerekNolan(3) 7 76
(GBBalding) *mde all: clr over 5f out: rdn over 1f out: unchal* **9/2**[1]

6005 **2** *11* **Mr Dip**[7] 3490 4-8-12 **50** ........ WHogg(3) 12 52
(AWCarroll) *dwlt: hld up in rr: hdwy on ins over 2f out: sn rdn: wnt 2nd ins fnl f: no ch w wnr* **8/1**

5032 **3** *5* **Lucky Arthur (IRE)**[4] 3572 3-8-11 **59** ........ MLawson 5 54
(JGMO'Shea) *hld up: hdwy over 5f out: rdn to chse wnr 4f out: no imp: lost 2nd ins fnl f* **5/1**[2]

0000 **4** *1 ¾* **Sholay (IRE)**[58] 2034 5-8-5 **47** ow2 ........ CrystalCaetano(7) 9 39
(PMitchell) *hld up: hdwy on outside over 3f out: rdn and sddle slipped over 2f out: one pce* **66/1**

4343 **5** *nk* **Escalade**[7] 3472 7-9-6 **55** ........(p) PPMathers 10 46
(WMBrisbourne) *plld hrd: prom: chsd wnr over 5f out to 4f out: sn rdn: wknd fnl f* **6/1**[3]

/20- **6** *nk* **Diamonds Will Do (IRE)**[187] 5817 7-9-7 **56** ........ LTreadwell 4 47
(MissVenetiaWilliams) *prom: rdn over 3f out: wknd over 2f out* **12/1**

6060 **7** *1 ¼* **Grady**[8] 3461 5-8-0 **35** ........ DFentiman 2 24
(WMBrisbourne) *s.i.s: rdn over 4f out: hdwy over 3f out: wknd fnl f* **25/1**

2202 **8** *¾* **Ben Kenobi**[12] 3342 6-7-13 **37** ........ DeanWilliams(3) 3 25
(MrsPFord) *dwlt: sn rcvrd: hdwy over 4f out: rdn over 2f out: wknd fnl f* **6/1**[3]

035/ **9** *6* **Barcelona**[10] 1789 7-9-11 **63** ........(b) HPoulton(3) 8 42
(GLMoore) *hld up in mid-div: rdn and hdwy 4f out: wknd over 2f out* **6/1**[3]

00-0 **10** *11* **Grey Admiral (USA)**[15] 3245 3-9-1 **68** ........ TBlock(5) 1 30
(AMBalding) *a bhd* **16/1**

0-00 **11** *nk* **Tartiruga (IRE)**[15] 3245 3-7-13 **47** ........ StephanieHollinshead 6 9
(LGCottrell) *plld hrd: chsd ldr over 6f: rdn over 4f out: wknd over 3f out* **40/1**

4/0- **12** *4* **Stage Direction (USA)**[444] 1180 7-8-8 **43** ........ PGallagher 11 —
(JDFrost) *dwlt: hld up: rdn 5f out: bhd fnl 4f* **14/1**

2m 40.27s (1.77) **Going Correction** +0.225s/f (Good)
**WFA** 3 from 4yo+ 13lb — **12** Ran SP% **116.8**
Speed ratings: **103,95,92,91,90 90,89,89,85,78 77,75**CSF £39.31 CT £187.78 TOTE £5.80: £2.30, £2.90, £1.70; EX 49.90.
**Owner** Miss B Swire **Bred** Miss B Swire **Trained** Kimpton,Hants

**FOCUS**
A modest handicap and a slowly-run race until the winner effectively stole it on the long home turn.
**NOTEBOOK**
**Dickie Deadeye** was ridden as if this longer trip would not be a problem and connections were proven to be spot on.
**Mr Dip**, ridden to get the longer distance, found himself with a lot to do and the winner was certainly not stopping. He looks well handicapped at the moment.
**Lucky Arthur(IRE)** eventually paid the penalty for going in vain pursuit of the winner.
**Sholay(IRE)**, disappointing since his two-year-old days, is down to the mark of a plater and would have finished closer had his saddle not slipped. *Official explanation: jockey said saddle slipped*
**Escalade** was set to drop 3lb tomorrow.

## 3696 EUROPEAN BREEDERS FUND NOVICE STKS — 5f 16y
7:05 (7:06) (D) 2-Y-O — **£5,651** (£1,739; £869; £434) **Stalls** High

Form — RPR
1605 **1** **Indiannie Star**[11] [3388] 2-8-6 ........ SHitchcott(3) 5 — 73
(MRChannon) *w ldr: led jst over 2f out: rdn over 1f out: r.o* **11/4**[2]
21 **2** *nk* **Kwame**[27] [2884] 2-8-9 ........ SWKelly 1 — 72
(MissECLavelle) *a.p: carried sltly lft 2f out: ev ch ins fnl f: rdn and r.o* **6/1**[3]
65 **3** *1 3/4* **Robmantra**[12] [3343] 2-8-12 ........ SWhitworth 4 — 69?
(BJLlewellyn) *hld up: n.m.r over 1f out: kpt on ins fnl f* **66/1**
13 **4** *1 1/4* **Safari Sunset (IRE)**[24] [2959] 2-9-2 ........ PDoe 2 — 68
(PWinkworth) *led: hdd jst over 2f out: sn rdn and edgd lft: edgd rt over 1f out: wknd ins fnl f* **8/13**[1]
0 **5** *18* **Dizzy Lizzy**[8] [3438] 2-8-7 ........ MHenry 3 — —
(NickWilliams) *prom: rdn 3f out: sn wknd* **50/1**
61.59 secs (2.09) **Going Correction** +0.225s/f (Good) **5** Ran SP% **106.3**
Speed ratings: **92,91,88,86,57**CSF £16.98 TOTE £3.40: £1.40, £2.20; EX 10.90.
**Owner** Timberhill Racing Partnership **Bred** Timber Hill Racing Partnership **Trained** West Ilsley, Berks
**FOCUS**
A fair event but the form affected by the sub-standard effort of the favourite and the proximity of the third. However, the first two ran almost exactly to their form at Lingfield in May.
**NOTEBOOK**
**Indiannie Star**, highly tried since winning at Lingfield, found this company more to her liking with the stands' rail to help in the closing stages.
**Kwame** had been beaten a length and a quarter by Indiannie Star at Lingfield. She looked likely to reverse the form when challenging but the winner would not be denied.
**Robmantra** ◆ showed tremendous improvement on this first start over the minimum trip. It could be that he previously found the ground too lively and he may be an interesting proposition back at six.
**Safari Sunset(IRE)** got worked up in the preliminaries and unseated his rider in the paddock. Inclined to drift away from the whip, he was rather disappointing on this slightly slower ground.

## 3697 BET365 08000 322365 (S) H'CAP — 1m 14y
7:35 (7:35) (G) (0-55,58) 3-Y-O+ — **£2,653** (£758; £379) **Stalls** High

Form — RPR
0320 **1** **Chandelier**[43] [2426] 4-9-0 **42** ........ DaneO'Neill 17 — 58
(MSSaunders) *a.p: led over 3f out: rdn clr wl over 1f out: readily* **10/1**
0050 **2** *5* **Go Green**[18] [3155] 3-8-6 **46** ........ (t) FPFerris(3) 8 — 51
(PDEvans) *s.i.s: rdn over 3f out: hdwy over 2f out: wnt 2nd jst ins fnl f: no ch w wnr* **16/1**
0003 **3** *2 1/2* **Over To You Bert**[7] [3489] 5-8-12 **40** ........ RHavlin 14 — 39
(RJHodges) *a.p: rdn and ev ch over 2f out: one pce* **13/2**[2]
4600 **4** *nk* **Enna (POL)**[7] [3489] 5-9-9 **51** ........ SDrowne 13 — 49
(MrsStefLiddiard) *hld up and bhd: rdn and swtchd rt to stands' rail over 2f out: hdwy over 1f out: nvr nrr* **20/1**
0001 **5** *1* **Mobo-Baco**[7] [3489] 7-10-2 **58** 6ex ........ JFortune 12 — 54
(RJHodges) *led to post: mid-div: rdn and hdwy over 2f out: one pce fnl f* **7/1**[3]
-004 **6** *1 1/2* **Leitrim Rock (IRE)**[29] [2801] 4-9-2 **44** ........ SWhitworth 4 — 36
(AGNewcombe) *s.i.s and swtchd rt to stands' side: rdn over 3f out: hdwy 2f out: no imp fnl f* **16/1**
0302 **7** *1/2* **Lord Chamberlain**[7] [3489] 11-9-2 **51** ........ (b) CJDavies(7) 16 — 42
(JMBradley) *hld up in tch: rdn and hdwy 2f out: wknd fnl f* **9/2**[1]
2065 **8** *3* **Avertaine**[16] [3193] 3-8-12 **49** ........ (b) RLMoore 2 — 33
(GLMoore) *led far side: clr of that gp over 2f out: eased whn btn ins fnl f* **9/1**
3364 **9** *3/4* **Zahunda (IRE)**[76] [1606] 5-8-10 **38** ........ SWKelly 20 — 21
(WMBrisbourne) *hld up: hdwy over 3f out: rdn over 2f out: wknd wl over 1f out* **15/2**
0000 **10** *1 1/2* **In Tune**[28] [2833] 4-8-12 **40** ........ (t) GBaker 18 — 19
(SCBurrough) *led over 4f: wknd over 2f out* **25/1**
0050 **11** *2* **Zalkani (IRE)**[7] [3490] 4-9-0 **49** ........ AHindley(7) 11 — 23
(BGPowell) *s.i.s: sn chsng ldrs: rdn and wknd over 2f out* **20/1**
000- **12** *6* **Southampton Joe (USA)**[30] [5376] 4-9-2 **51** ........ PPMathers(7) 7 — 12
(JGMO'Shea) *prom far side: rdn over 3f out: wknd over 2f out* **16/1**
0600 **13** *2 1/2* **Muqtadi (IRE)**[7] [3489] 6-9-2 **44** ........ NPollard 19 — —
(MQuinn) *s.i.s: sn chsng ldrs: rdn over 3f out: wknd over 2f out* **12/1**
00-0 **14** *2 1/2* **Variety Club**[28] [2833] 3-8-11 **55** ........ (v[1]) TBlock(7) 6 — 4
(AMBalding) *prom far side: rdn over 3f out: sn wknd* **33/1**
1000 **15** *shd* **Margarets Wish**[28] [2835] 4-9-0 **42** ........ SSanders 5 — —
(TWall) *prom far side 4f* **20/1**
00-0 **16** *2 1/2* **Brevity**[23] [2975] 9-9-13 **55** ........ VSlattery 15 — —
(JGMO'Shea) *a bhd* **33/1**
5050 **17** *1 1/2* **Young Dynasty**[35] [2643] 4-8-5 **40** ........ (b) LiamJones(7) 3 — —
(EAWheeler) *prom far side over 3f* **50/1**
1m 37.53s (1.63) **Going Correction** +0.225s/f (Good)
**WFA** 3 from 4yo+ 9lb **17** Ran SP% **126.2**
Speed ratings: **100,95,92,92,91 89,89,86,85,83 81,75,73,70,70 68,66**CSF £150.54 CT £1177.78 TOTE £14.80: £2.60, £4.60, £1.80, £6.10; EX 761.10.The winner was bought in for 7,000gns.
**Owner** Chris Scott & Peter Hall **Bred** W H Joyce **Trained** Haydon, Somerset
**FOCUS**
Poor form with little solid to go on, and the five that raced on the far side were all well beaten in the end.
**NOTEBOOK**
**Chandelier** made short work of this big field of platers and his rider was swinging off him in the closing stages.
**Go Green**, down 3lb for this drop into a seller, found that the winner had gone way beyond recall.
**Over To You Bert** ran another sound race but could not cope with the runner-up let alone the winner.
**Enna(POL)** had finished just over five lengths behind Over To You Bert on identical terms in a similar event at Warwick a week ago. Adopting totally different tactics, she got going too late.
**Mobo-Baco** could not confirm the Warwick form with the two who finished directly in front of him here under his penalty.
**Leitrim Rock(IRE)** was 11lb lower than when last in a handicap.
**Avertaine**, the first horse home on the far side, ran a lot better than her finishing position suggests. *Official explanation: jockey said filly hung right handed*

## 3698 S.E.T. OFFICE SUPPLIES H'CAP — 7f 16y
8:05 (8:07) (D) (0-85,85) 3-Y-O+ — **£16,796** (£5,168; £2,584; £1,292) **Stalls** High

Form — RPR
-221 **1** **Pango**[8] [3440] 5-9-3 **77** 5ex ........ LFletcher(3) 17 — 90
(HMorrison) *hld up in tch: rdn and swtchd lft 2f out: hrd rdn to ld post* **9/2**[2]
4004 **2** *shd* **Blue Trojan (IRE)**[3] [3597] 4-9-12 **83** ........ JFEgan 9 — 96
(SKirk) *chsd ldrs: rdn over 3f out: led ins fnl f: hdd post* **11/1**
3041 **3** *2* **Dumnoni**[20] [3089] 3-9-1 **80** ........ NCallan 20 — 88
(JulianPoulton) *a.p: rdn over 2f out: kpt on towards fin* **9/1**
0166 **4** *hd* **Hurricane Coast**[67] [1828] 5-9-2 **73** ........ (b) RSmith 10 — 80
(DFlood) *a.p: ev ch 2f out: rdn over 1f out: one pce* **20/1**
2211 **5** *3/4* **Goodenough Mover**[8] [3455] 8-9-6 **82** 5ex ........ HayleyTurner(5) 2 — 87
(JSKing) *swtchd to stands' side gp after 1f: sn prom: led over 2f out: rdn over 1f out: hdd ins fnl f: no ex* **8/1**[3]
0052 **6** *hd* **Tuscarora (IRE)**[5] [3555] 5-7-5 **55** oh3 ........ DFentiman(7) 7 — 60+
(AWCarroll) *swtchd rt s: hld up: hdwy fnl f: nrst fin* **16/1**
0460 **7** *shd* **Annijaz**[8] [3457] 7-7-12 **55** oh3 ........ DKinsella 18 — 60
(JMBradley) *s.i.s: hld up: rdn over 1f out: hdwy fnl f: nvr nrr* **25/1**
3111 **8** *1/2* **A One (IRE)**[4] [3591] 5-8-1 **61** 5ex ........ FPFerris(3) 8 — 64
(HJManners) *led: rdn and hdd over 2f out: wknd over 1f out* **4/1**[1]
0636 **9** *1* **Fleetwood Bay**[8] [3440] 4-8-12 **69** ........ GBaker 19 — 70
(BRMillman) *prom: rdn over 2f out: wknd wl over 1f out* **20/1**
4040 **10** *3/4* **Marker**[8] [3455] 4-9-8 **79** ........ (v) SDrowne 5 — 78
(GBBalding) *swtchd to stands' side gp after 1f: mid-div: rdn over 3f out: no hdwy fnl 2f* **20/1**
2030 **11** *1/2* **Zafarshah (IRE)**[19] [3127] 5-8-5 **62** ........ NPollard 16 — 59
(PDEvans) *n.d* **16/1**
4-10 **12** *hd* **Millfields Dreams**[21] [3043] 5-7-12 **60** ........ RThomas(5) 6 — 57
(RBrotherton) *led far side: rdn over 1f out: wknd ins fnl f* **20/1**
2030 **13** *1 1/4* **Just Fly**[37] [2575] 4-9-7 **78** ........ JFortune 12 — 72
(SKirk) *a bhd* **20/1**
1400 **14** *shd* **Cashneem (IRE)**[5] [3559] 6-8-7 **64** ........ SWKelly 3 — 57
(WMBrisbourne) *chsd ldr far side: wknd ins fnl f* **50/1**
0200 **15** *3 1/2* **Cheese 'n Biscuits**[37] [2575] 4-9-2 **73** ........ (p) RLMoore 14 — 57
(GLMoore) *a bhd* **33/1**
0020 **16** *hd* **Chevronne**[9] [3412] 4-7-13 **59** ........ JFMcDonald(3) 13 — 43
(LGCottrell) *mid-div: rdn over 3f out: bhd fnl 2f* **50/1**
2U00 **17** *1/2* **The Gaikwar (IRE)**[9] [3412] 5-8-8 **65** ........ (b) DaneO'Neill 11 — 47
(NEBerry) *s.i.s: a bhd* **50/1**
0000 **18** *1 3/4* **Arctic Desert**[13] [3324] 4-9-11 **82** ........ (v) KDarley 1 — 60
(AMBalding) *dwlt: racd far side: sn chsng ldrs: wknd over 1f out* **25/1**
3150 **19** *3* **Soyuz (IRE)**[15] [3235] 4-10-0 **85** ........ MHenry 15 — 55
(MAJarvis) *a bhd* **12/1**
0000 **20** *4* **Tapau (IRE)**[8] [3457] 6-8-2 **59** ........ (p) CCatlin 4 — 19
(JMBradley) *racd far side: bhd fnl 2f* **50/1**
1m 23.73s (0.53) **Going Correction** +0.225s/f (Good)
**WFA** 3 from 4yo+ 8lb **20** Ran SP% **129.4**
Speed ratings: **105,104,102,102,101 101,101,100,99,98 98,97,96,96,92 92,91,89,86,81**CSF £45.31 CT £449.41 TOTE £5.60: £1.90, £2.90, £2.50, £8.80; EX 93.00.
**Owner** Pangfield Partners **Bred** T J Billington **Trained** East Ilsley, Berks
**FOCUS**
A fair handicap and this looked good sound form for the track, although those who raced on the far side were again disadvantaged.
**NOTEBOOK**
**Pango** would have had a pound less to carry had his new mark been in force. He had to give his all to snatch the verdict.
**Blue Trojan(IRE)**, making a quick reappearance, just got touched off and is obviously in fine fettle at the moment.
**Dumnoni**, raised 3lb, found a second wind after looking held and a return to a mile would not bother her.
**Hurricane Coast** travelled well for much of the trip and had no excuses.
**Goodenough Mover** was unable to dominate from the outset because of his draw. He was also trying to complete a hat-trick off a mark 12lb higher than the first of his back-to-back victories.
**Tuscarora(IRE)**, set to drop 3lb in future handicaps, is beginning to look well treated.
**A One(IRE)** would have had another 6lb to carry had his new mark been in force. Unless this came too soon, it does not augur well for the future.
**Soyuz(IRE)** *Official explanation: jockey said gelding did not handle the track*

## 3699 OAKGROVE STUD GOLDEN DAFFODIL STKS (GROUP 3) (F&M) — 1m 2f 36y
8:35 (8:35) (A) 3-Y-O+ — **£29,000** (£11,000; £5,500; £2,500) **Stalls** Low

Form — RPR
-034 **1** **Felicity (IRE)**[48] [2297] 4-9-2 94 ........ JFortune 6 — 102
(JHMGosden) *chsd ldr: led over 2f out: hrd rdn and hdd 1f out: led wl ins fnl f: all out* **12/1**
1-45 **2** *nk* **Kinnaird (IRE)**[21] [3033] 3-8-5 110 ........ KDarley 10 — 101
(PCHaslam) *hld up: rdn and hdwy 3f out: led 1f out tl wl ins fnl f: nt qckn* **7/4**[1]
6110 **3** *7* **Tidal**[21] [3046] 5-9-2 74 ........ TPQueally 1 — 88
(AWCarroll) *led: rdn and hdd over 2f out: wknd over 1f out* **20/1**
2031 **4** *2* **Incheni (IRE)**[29] [2807] 3-8-5 102 ........ SDrowne 11 — 84
(GWragg) *hld up and bhd: rdn over 3f out: hdwy 2f out: nvr nrr ldrs* **3/1**[2]
6-40 **5** *1* **Doctrine**[23] [2971] 3-8-5 96 ........ RHavlin 4 — 82
(JHMGosden) *hld up towards rr: rdn 3f out: sme hdwy over 1f out: n.d* **20/1**
0443 **6** *3 1/2* **Cote Quest (USA)**[13] [3311] 4-9-2 92 ........ RLMoore 2 — 76
(SCWilliams) *chsd ldrs: rdn 3f out: wknd 2f out* **25/1**
-224 **7** *1* **Shamara (IRE)**[13] [3311] 4-9-2 90 ........ SSanders 3 — 74
(CFWall) *hld up: rdn over 3f out: sme hdwy over 2f out: wknd wl over 1f out* **14/1**
-123 **8** *1 1/2* **Classical Dancer**[29] [2807] 3-8-5 99 ........ DaneO'Neill 8 — 71
(HCandy) *hld up in rr: rdn 3f out: no rspnse* **7/2**[3]
2003 **9** *1* **Castaway Queen (IRE)**[25] [2929] 5-9-2 59 ........ JFEgan 7 — 69
(WRMuir) *hld up and bhd: rdn over 3f out: no rspnse* **100/1**
1650 **10** *12* **Tamarillo**[21] [3035] 3-8-5 99 ........ TEDurcan 9 — 46
(MLWBell) *bmpd s: hld up and bhd: rdn over 3f out: sn struggling* **16/1**
2m 9.40s (-0.20) **Going Correction** +0.225s/f (Good)
**WFA** 3 from 4yo+ 11lb **10** Ran SP% **118.2**
Speed ratings: **109,108,103,101,100 97,97,95,95,85**CSF £32.66 TOTE £14.00: £3.20, £1.10, £3.00; EX 47.40.
**Owner** George Strawbridge **Bred** George Strawbridge **Trained** Manton, Wilts
**FOCUS**
This Group Three event was run at a good pace and few got into it. The form is fair for the grade with the first two clear.



The Form Book, Raceform Ltd, Compton, RG20 6NL

**NOTEBOOK**
**Felicity(IRE)**, back down in distance, rather outbattled the runner-up for a hard-fought victory.
**Kinnaird(IRE)**, stepping up from a mile, appeared to be getting on top in the final furlong but it would be hard to say that she did not stay.
**Tidal** set a good pace on this big step up in class but she had run her race once collared. There was no disgrace in this.
**Incheni(IRE)** took a while to pick up and could never get competitive.
**Doctrine** was ridden to get this longer trip and could never land a blow.
**Tamarillo** *Official explanation: jockey said filly ran flat*

## 3700 MEDINET FILLIES' H'CAP — 1m 14y
**9:05** (9:06) (E) (0-70,67) 3-Y-O — **£6,851** (£2,108; £1,054; £527) **Stalls** High

Form — RPR
3513 **1** **Kryssa**[17] [3180] 3-9-6 **66** ... RLMoore 4 — 80
(GLMoore) *hld up in tch: hdwy 3f out: rdn 2f out: led 1f out: r.o wl* **9/4**[1]
06-2 **2** *¾* **Sabrina Brown**[16] [3211] 3-8-9 **60** ... RThomas(5) 1 — 72
(GBBalding) *prom: led over 5f out: rdn and hdd 1f out: nt qckn* **11/2**[3]
5000 **3** *3* **Daydream Dancer**[9] [3421] 3-8-4 **50** ... (b[1]) RSmith 10 — 55
(CGCox) *led over 3f: rdn over 2f out: r.o one pce* **33/1**
-342 **4** *½* **Keshya**[60] [2005] 3-9-3 **63** ... DaneO'Neill 7 — 67
(DJCoakley) *a.p: rdn over 2f out: one pce* **5/1**[2]
-000 **5** *2* **Filliemou (IRE)**[13] [3301] 3-8-11 **57** ... NCallan 9 — 56
(AWCarroll) *bmpd s: hld up in mid-div: rdn 3f out: no hdwy fnl 2f* **22/1**
0000 **6** *nk* **Just One Look**[23] [2988] 3-9-1 **61** ... DSweeney 13 — 60
(MBlanshard) *hld up and bhd: hdwy over 1f out: n.d* **16/1**
5000 **7** *1 ¼* **Venetian Romance (IRE)**[26] [2915] 3-7-7 **44** oh4 ... HayleyTurner(5) 3 — 40
(APJones) *s.i.s: in rr: rdn 2f out: nvr nrr* **33/1**
-000 **8** *2 ½* **My Hope (IRE)**[18] [3155] 3-9-7 **67** ... SSanders 2 — 57
(RCharlton) *hld up in mid-div: rdn and effrt on outside over 2f out: wknd over 1f out* **16/1**
0000 **9** *2 ½* **The Stick**[31] [2760] 3-8-6 **52** ... CCatlin 5 — 36
(MRChannon) *hld up and bhd: rdn 3f out: sme hdwy on outside over 2f out: no further prog* **20/1**
0051 **10** *1 ½* **Deign To Dance (IRE)**[27] [2883] 3-9-5 **65** ... TPQueally 12 — 46
(JGPortman) *hld up in mid-div: rdn over 2f out: wknd over 1f out* **15/2**
4410 **11** *hd* **Fizzy Lady**[32] [2727] 3-8-13 **64** ... (t) MSavage(5) 8 — 44
(NEBerry) *chsd ldrs: rdn and wknd over 2f out* **25/1**
-000 **12** *nk* **Dream Of Dubai (IRE)**[18] [3156] 3-9-0 **60** ... JFortune 14 — 40
(PMitchell) *hld up in mid-div: rdn 3f out: wknd 2f out* **20/1**
050 **13** *2 ½* **Gentle Raindrop (IRE)**[29] [2808] 3-9-5 **65** ... JFEgan 11 — 39
(SKirk) *hld up towards rr: swtchd lft wl over 2f out: sn nt clr run: eased whn btn fnl f* **20/1**
3450 **14** *15* **Nukhbah (USA)**[18] [3156] 3-9-5 **65** ... SWhitworth 6 — —
(AGNewcombe) *prom 5f: t.o* **12/1**

1m 37.4s (1.50) **Going Correction** +0.225s/f (Good) — **14** Ran SP% **122.4**
Speed ratings: **101,100,97,96,94 94,93,90,88,86 86,86,83,68**CSF £12.32 CT £334.88 TOTE £2.90: £2.00, £2.50, £7.40; EX 18.40 Place 6 £199.71, Place 5 £87.99.
**Owner** D J Deer **Bred** D J And Mrs Deer **Trained** Woodingdean, E Sussex

**FOCUS**
A modest fillies' handicap and not particularly solid form in which they all raced on the stands' side because of the slightly smaller field.

**NOTEBOOK**
**Kryssa**, raised another 2lb, found the step up to a mile on slower ground to her liking and scored with something in hand.
**Sabrina Brown ◆**, 5lb higher for this first attempt at a mile, is certainly knocking on the door.
**Daydream Dancer**, blinkered for the first time, has been struggling to find the right trip and probably wants a bit further.
**Keshya** is another who will probably have preferred a longer distance on a course as easy as this.
**Filliemou(IRE)** has not been firing this year and has dropped 8lb as a consequence.
**Gentle Raindrop(IRE)** *Official explanation: jockey said filly did not handle the track*
T/Plt: £313.30 to a £1 stake. Pool: £46,708.00. 108.80 winning tickets. T/Qpdt: £72.70 to a £1 stake. Pool: £3,726.10. 37.90 winning tickets. KH

# [3290] CHESTER (L-H)
### Friday, July 9

**OFFICIAL GOING: Good**
Wind: almost nil Weather: fine

## 3701 CLAIMS UK MAIDEN FILLIES' STKS — 7f 122y
**6:50** (6:51) (D) 3-Y-O+ — **£5,382** (£1,656; £828; £414) **Stalls** Low

Form — RPR
3202 **1** **Red Top (IRE)**[16] [3209] 3-8-12 82 ... FNorton 1 — 69+
(RHannon) *trckd ldr: led 2f out: clr over 1f out: v easily* **4/9**[1]
52-6 **2** *3 ½* **Heart's Desire (IRE)**[35] [2647] 3-8-12 77 ... MHills 7 — 60+
(BWHills) *led: rdn and hdd 2f out: no ch w wnr fnl f* **5/2**[2]
0-00 **3** *3 ½* **Tokewanna**[13] [3301] 4-9-7 50 ... (t) RWinston 4 — 51
(WMBrisbourne) *in tch: hdwy 4f out: rdn 2f out: flashed tail u.p and wknd fnl f* **40/1**
30 **4** *1 ¼* **Hirayna**[7] [3487] 5-9-7 ... DAllan 2 — 48
(WMBrisbourne) *t.k.h: trckd ldrs: rdn over 3f out: wknd 2f out* **12/1**[3]
0-0 **5** *1* **Grele (USA)**[15] [3251] 3-8-12 ... JCarroll 3 — 46
(RHollinshead) *towards rr: niggled along over 4f out: kpt on fnl f: nvr able to chal* **50/1**
**6** *2 ½* **Reem Two** 3-8-9 ... LEnstone(3) 6 — 39
(DMccain) *bhd: rdn and hdwy over 3f out: wknd 2f out* **50/1**
0-00 **7** *20* **Let's Party (IRE)**[72] [1710] 4-9-4 45 ... (t) J-PGuillambert(3) 5 — —
(PLClinton) *a bhd* **50/1**

1m 33.41s (-1.34) **Going Correction** -0.075s/f (Good)
**WFA** 3 from 4yo+ 9lb — **7** Ran SP% **113.8**
Speed ratings: **103,99,96,94,93 91,71**CSF £1.76 TOTE £1.40: £1.20, £1.30; EX 1.70.
**Owner** William Durkan **Bred** K Molloy **Trained** East Everleigh, Wilts

**FOCUS**
An uncompetitive maiden that worked out just as one would have expected, and the winner did not have to be at her best to score.

**NOTEBOOK**
**Red Top(IRE)** did not get the run of the race when unable to justify favouritism at Salisbury on her previous start, but things were much more straightforward this time and she ran out a comfortable winner. She is high enough in the weights and could go up even more for this, so it would not surprise if she were to turn up back in Listed company.
**Heart's Desire(IRE)** had every chance from the front, but was simply not good enough.
**Tokewanna** had beaten just one horse home on her previous two starts this term but, fitted with a tongue-tie for the first time, this was better.
**Hirayna** was well held, but is now qualified for handicaps.
**Grele(USA)** is another now qualified for a handicap mark.

## 3702 KATHLEEN B. CORBETT MEMORIAL H'CAP — 5f 16y
**7:20** (7:21) (C) (0-95,92) 3-Y-O — **£9,509** (£2,926; £1,463; £731) **Stalls** Low

Form — RPR
2530 **1** **Hello Roberto**[5] [3562] 3-7-12 **69** oh3 ... JMackay 3 — 75
(MJPolglase) *midfield: hdwy whn nt clr run over 1f out: r.o ins fnl f to ld towards fin* **8/1**
0204 **2** *¾* **Sir Ernest (IRE)**[12] [3338] 3-8-5 **76** ... RFfrench 1 — 79
(MJPolglase) *led: rdn over 1f out: hdd towards fin* **7/1**
3610 **3** *nk* **Divine Spirit**[14] [3273] 3-9-0 **85** ... RWinston 4 — 87
(MDods) *chsd ldrs: rdn over 1f out: chalng ins fnl f: styd on* **9/2**[2]
2112 **4** *hd* **Enchantment**[27] [2892] 3-9-7 **92** ... MHills 5 — 93
(JMBradley) *prom: rdn over 1f out: ev ch ins fnl f: nt qckn towards fin* **7/2**[1]
0315 **5** *shd* **Green Manalishi**[13] [3324] 3-9-6 **91** ... PDobbs 9 — 92+
(DWPArbuthnot) *midfield: hdwy whn nt clr run and hmpd over 1f out: edgd lft ins fnl f: r.o* **6/1**[3]
2543 **6** *¾* **Melody King**[2] [3628] 3-7-12 **69** oh2 ... (b) PMQuinn 2 — 67
(PDEvans) *chsd ldrs: rdn over 2f out: styd on same pce fnl f* **7/1**
1063 **7** *4* **Four Amigos (USA)**[6] [3523] 3-8-12 **83** ... JFanning 8 — 67
(JGGiven) *bhd: rdn over 1f out: nvr trbld ldrs* **8/1**
64-0 **8** *nk* **Molly Moon (IRE)**[55] [2131] 3-9-1 **86** ... FNorton 7 — 69
(MBlanshard) *bhd: rdn over 1f out: nvr trbld ldrs* **25/1**
1660 **9** *2* **Mr Wolf**[8] [3446] 3-8-4 **78** ... LEnstone(3) 10 — 53
(DWBarker) *prom: rdn over 2f out: wknd over 1f out* **25/1**
61- **10** *hd* **Dvinsky (USA)**[301] [4868] 3-9-5 **90** ... (t) RHughes 11 — 65
(GAButler) *sn pushed along and outpcd* **10/1**

60.73 secs (-1.25) **Going Correction** -0.075s/f (Good) — **10** Ran SP% **118.7**
Speed ratings: **107,105,105,105,104 103,97,96,93,93**CSF £64.12 CT £237.34 TOTE £12.50: £2.40, £2.30, £2.30; EX 23.00.
**Owner** G A Lucas and I Buckley **Bred** I B Barker **Trained** Southwell, Notts
■ Stewards Enquiry : J Mackay two-day ban: careless riding (Jul 20-21)

**FOCUS**
A fair, competitive sprint, predictably dominated by the low stalls. The form is not particularly strong, with the runner-up having been beaten in a claimer previously.

**NOTEBOOK**
**Hello Roberto** had just a claiming win to her name going into this and was 3lb out of the handicap, but she had just a feather weight on her back and showed herself as good as ever with a narrow win, overcoming a slow start to collar her stablemate. Given she should have been racing off a mark of 66, she is likely to take a significant rise in the weights and would therefore be interesting under a penalty.
**Sir Ernest(IRE)**, beaten in a claimer over six furlongs on his previous start, made full use of stall one on this drop in trip and was only just pegged back.
**Divine Spirit**, 6lb higher than when last successful two starts back, ran his race for his in-form yard and can have no excuses. *Official explanation: jocke said gelding hung right-handed throughout*
**Enchantment** is arguably at her best when gaining an uncontested lead, but she was unable to get to the front and just lacked a decisive change of pace in the straight under her big weight. Having said that, she remains in good form and is still one to have on your side.
**Green Manalishi ◆** could not really get into the thick of things from his high stall and is much better than he showed.

## 3703 NEXUS GSA CONDITIONS STKS — 5f 16y
**7:50** (7:50) (B) 2-Y-O — **£10,300** (£3,907; £1,953; £888) **Stalls** Low

Form — RPR
1121 **1** **Beckermet (IRE)**[13] [3290] 2-9-3 ... RFfrench 2 — 101
(RFFisher) *prom: led over 1f out: r.o* **5/4**[1]
21 **2** *2 ½* **Amazin**[9] [3414] 2-9-0 ... RHughes 1 — 89
(RHannon) *pushed along to sn chse ldrs: swtchd rt 3f out: styd on to take 2nd wl ins fnl f: nt trble wnr* **5/2**[2]
1 **3** *1* **Oh Dara (USA)**[9] [3408] 2-8-9 ... DeanMcKeown 7 — 81
(PABlockley) *led: rdn and hdd over 1f out: lost 2nd and no ex wl ins fnl f* **15/2**[3]
3213 **4** *5* **The Crooked Ring**[9] [3414] 2-8-11 ... EAhern 4 — 65
(PDEvans) *outpcd: sme hdwy over 1f out: nvr trbld ldrs* **12/1**
4104 **5** *nk* **Tiviski (IRE)**[11] [3373] 2-8-9 ... WSupple 3 — 62
(EJAlston) *chsd ldrs: n.m.r 3f out: sn lost pl and rdn: n.d after* **9/1**
24 **6** *1 ¼* **Gold Quay (IRE)**[12] [3346] 2-8-6 ... JFanning 5 — 55
(NPLittmoden) *towards rr: effrt wl over 1f out: sn wknd* **25/1**
600 **7** *7* **Den Perry**[11] [3373] 2-8-11 ... CEly 6 — 35
(ABerry) *a outpcd* **100/1**
124 **8** *3* **Bigalos Bandit**[37] [2570] 2-9-0 ... RWinston 9 — 28
(JJQuinn) *chsd ldrs tl rdn and wknd over 2f out* **10/1**

60.85 secs (-1.13) **Going Correction** -0.075s/f (Good) — **8** Ran SP% **116.4**
Speed ratings: **106,102,100,92,91 89,78,73**CSF £4.55 TOTE £2.20: £1.40, £1.60, £1.90; EX 3.50.
**Owner** Bishopthorpe Racing Two **Bred** Fritz Von Ball Moss **Trained** Ulverston, Cumbria

**FOCUS**
A reasonable conditions event won in style by Beckermet, and the winning time was excellent for the type of race.

**NOTEBOOK**
**Beckermet(IRE)** made it four wins from six starts with a most decisive success, picking up well in the straight having got a nice lead off Oh Dara. He could now head for the Molecomb Stakes at Goodwood and that looks an ideal target. He has boosted the form no end of a Roger Charlton-trained colt called Pike Bishop, who is the only horse to have beaten him in his last five starts, and did so easily.
**Amazin**, off the mark at Kempton on his previous start, gave up his good draw with a slow start and lacked the pace to threaten the winner. This was his first run over five furlongs and a return to six should be in his favour.
**Oh Dara(USA)**, off the mark on her debut at Catterick, did well to get to the front from stall seven, but was left behind by the winner in the straight and may have done just a little too much.
**The Crooked Ring** does not have a progressive profile and was out of his depth.
**Tiviski(IRE)** has not really gone on from her course and distance maiden win and may need her sights lowered.

## 3704 NEW VAUXHALL TIGRA NURSERY — 5f 16y
**8:20** (8:21) (D) 2-Y-O — **£4,745** (£1,460; £730; £365) **Stalls** Low

Form — RPR
1104 **1** **Nova Tor (IRE)**[13] [3290] 2-8-12 **75** ... IMongan 2 — 76+
(NPLittmoden) *mde all: rdn over 1f out: r.o* **7/2**[1]
3040 **2** *1 ¾* **I'm Aimee**[45] [2376] 2-8-9 **72** ... EAhern 8 — 67
(PDEvans) *w wnr: rdn and ev ch over 1f out: no ex wl ins fnl f* **11/1**
6406 **3** *shd* **Detonate**[15] [3242] 2-8-11 **74** ... RHughes 1 — 69+
(IAWood) *t.k.h: trckd ldrs: rdn over 1f out: styd on same pce towards fin* **9/2**[2]
41 **4** *nk* **Talcen Gwyn (IRE)**[25] [2927] 2-9-2 **79** ... WSupple 3 — 72
(MFHarris) *midfield: nt clr run over 1f out: sn rdn and hdwy: styd on* **9/2**[2]

3213 **5** ½ **Katie Boo (IRE)**[15] 3224 2-9-0 **77**.................................. JCarroll 5 69
(ABerry) *trckd ldrs: lost pl 3f out: rallied 1f out: styd on* **9/2**[2]

2542 **6** *nk* **Little Biscuit (IRE)**[18] 3144 2-7-7 **61** oh2.................. BSwarbrick(5) 9 52
(KRBurke) *hld up: rdn over 1f out: styd on towards fin* **10/1**[3]

0444 **7** ¾ **Coleorton Dancer**[20] 3104 2-8-3 **66**.................................. PFessey 7 54
(KARyan) *hld up: rdn over 1f out: nvr able to chal* **11/1**

516 **8** *3* **Piper Lily**[12] 3346 2-9-7 **84**.................................. FNorton 6 62
(MBlanshard) *trckd ldrs: rdn over 1f out: sn wknd* **10/1**[3]

62.15 secs (0.17) **Going Correction** -0.075s/f (Good) **8** Ran SP% **111.6**
Speed ratings: **95,92,92,91,90 90,89,84**CSF £40.31 CT £172.20 TOTE £4.20: £1.90, £3.00, £1.60; EX 41.10.
**Owner** Nigel Shields **Bred** Newlands House Stud **Trained** Newmarket, Suffolk

**FOCUS**
Quite a tight nursery, although the pace was just steady and first two home were in the first two throughout, giving the form a messy and somewhat unreliable look. The figures shown as 'official ratings' are estimates for guidance only.

**NOTEBOOK**
**Nova Tor(IRE)** ran well from a high stall over course and distance on her previous start and, better drawn this time, was good enough to confirm that promise. There should be more to come in similar company.
**I'm Aimee**, returning from a short break, had every chance and ran her race.
**Detonate** forfeited his good draw with a sluggish start before racing keenly. A stronger pace would have suited better in the circumstances.
**Talcen Gwyn(IRE)**, off the mark in a weak Brighton maiden on his previous start, came from an unpromising position to post a respectable effort.
**Katie Boo(IRE)** was not at her best on this handicap debut.

## 3705 ETHEL AUSTIN PROPERTY GROUP CLASSIFIED STKS 1m 2f 75y
**8:50** (8:53) (D) 4-Y-0+ **£5,382** (£1,656; £828; £414) **Stalls** High

Form RPR

6432 **1** **Barking Mad (USA)**[11] 3385 6-9-0 82.................................. IMongan 5 71
(MLWBell) *mde all: rdn over 1f out: r.o gamely* **10/3**[2]

0123 **2** *shd* **Grey Clouds**[20] 3091 4-8-9 79.................................. WSupple 4 66+
(TDEasterby) *hld up: swtchd rt and hdwy over 1f out: rdn: edgd lft and ev ch ins fnl f: hld cl home* **5/4**[1]

3020 **3** 2 ½ **Voice Mail**[9] 3415 5-8-9 79.................................. LPKeniry(3) 3 64
(AMBalding) *a.p: rdn over 1f out: styd on same pce fnl f* **13/2**

2115 **4** ½ **Ben Hur**[8] 3441 5-8-12 73.................................. EAhern 9 63
(WMBrisbourne) *prom: rdn and ev ch 2f out: no ex ins fnl f* **5/1**[3]

2426 **5** *6* **Stoic Leader (IRE)**[6] 3516 4-8-12 79.................................. RWinston 6 53
(RFFisher) *in tch: rdn 2f out: wknd 1f out* **8/1**

0500 **6** *shd* **Phoenix Nights (IRE)**[131] 937 4-8-5 52.................................. CEly(7) 2 52?
(ABerry) *s.i.s: in rr: rdn over 2f out: nvr on terms* **40/1**

3350 **7** *3* **Prince Of Blues (IRE)**[13] 3293 6-8-12 59.................................. PDobbs 8 47
(MMullineaux) *rdn over 2f out: a bhd* **33/1**

0000 **8** *19* **Buscador (USA)**[20] 3082 5-8-7 47.................................. BSwarbrick(5) 7 13
(WMBrisbourne) *racd keenly: in tch: rdn and wknd over 4f out* **50/1**

2m 11.11s (-1.44) **Going Correction** -0.075s/f (Good) **8** Ran SP% **116.0**
Speed ratings: **102,101,99,99,94 94,92,77**CSF £7.95 TOTE £4.40: £1.50, £1.20, £1.90; EX 7.70.
**Owner** Christopher Wright **Bred** Andrade Farm **Trained** Newmarket, Suffolk
■ Stewards Enquiry : I Mongan two-day ban: used whip with excessive frequency (Jul 20-21)
W Supple caution: used whip in an incorrect place

**FOCUS**
Not that strong a classified event, although there was just 4lb separating the first three home at the weights, few appeared to perform to their best.

**NOTEBOOK**
**Barking Mad(USA)** is not exactly easy to win with, but he got the uncontested lead that suits him so well and made the most of it under a fantastically determined ride from Mongan. He has never previously followed up and could be one to take on next time.
**Grey Clouds** always looked to be travelling best of all but, despite responding to pressure in the straight, the winner proved just too strong.
**Voice Mail** may just be better covered up in slightly bigger fields for, after moving well early, he found little off the bridle.
**Ben Hur** had quite a task at the weights (7lb to find with the eventual winner) and was well held. *Official explanation: jockey said gelding hung right-handed throughout*
**Stoic Leader(IRE)** was best in at the weights, but he had never previously raced beyond a mile and did not look to get the trip. He should drop in the handicap for this.

## 3706 ASPECTS BEAUTY COMPANY CHESHIRE YEOMANRY H'CAP 1m 2f 75y
**9:20** (9:20) (D) (0-85,84) 3-Y-0 **£5,421** (£1,668; £834; £417) **Stalls** High

Form RPR

5114 **1** **Gavroche (IRE)**[12] 3345 3-9-4 **84**.................................. J-PGuillambert(3) 4 95
(CADwyer) *hld up and bhd: hdwy over 3f out: rdn to ld over 1f out: r.o* **10/3**[2]

0U01 **2** *1* **Hatch A Plan (IRE)**[11] 3387 3-8-5 **68** 6ex.................................. JQuinn 1 77
(RMBeckett) *hld up: hdwy over 3f out: rdn 2f out: chsd wnr ins fnl f: nt qckn cl home* **3/1**[1]

6110 **3** 2 ½ **Magic Sting**[15] 3231 3-8-5 **68**.................................. JMackay 3 73
(MLWBell) *chsd ldrs: clsd over 4f out: led over 3f out: rdn and hdd over 1f out: no ex ins fnl f* **3/1**[1]

31-4 **4** *4* **Kings Empire**[18] 3152 3-8-13 **83**.................................. DTudhope(7) 2 81
(DCarroll) *led early: chsd ldr: rdn and ev ch 2f out: sn wknd* **5/1**[3]

0305 **5** 1 ¼ **Zuma (IRE)**[15] 3245 3-8-13 **76**..................................(b[1]) RHughes 5 71
(RHannon) *rdn to sn ld: hdd over 3f out: wknd 2f out* **11/2**

500 **6** *hd* **Prelude**[18] 3142 3-7-9 **63**.................................. BSwarbrick(5) 6 58
(WMBrisbourne) *hld up: rdn over 3f out: sn btn* **22/1**

2m 11.83s (-0.72) **Going Correction** -0.075s/f (Good) **6** Ran SP% **109.5**
Speed ratings: **99,98,96,93,92 91**CSF £12.97 TOTE £4.00: £1.60, £1.90; EX 5.90 Place 6 £9.91, Place 5 £9.54.
**Owner** J L Guillambert **Bred** John O'Connor **Trained** Newmarket, Suffolk

**FOCUS**
A fair handicap but an ordinary pace, although the winner continues his improvement.

**NOTEBOOK**
**Gavroche(IRE)** did not have things go his way at Windsor on his previous start, but he made no mistake this time and gained his third win from his last four outings. A rise in the weights for this will force him up in grade, but he must be respected whilst in this heart.
**Hatch A Plan(IRE)** showed his recent Windsor success was no fluke with a solid effort under his 6lb penalty.
**Magic Sting**, a disappointing favourite at Leicester on his previous start, did not look to have any excuses, but better cannot be ruled out when he returns to a more conventional track.
**Kings Empire** had quite a bit of use made of him and was ultimately well held. He looks high enough in the weights.
**Zuma(IRE)**, with blinkers replacing a visor, looked to do too much early on. *Official explanation: jockey said colt hung to the left*
T/Plt: £9.60 to a £1 stake. Pool: £55,724.95. 4,202.40 winning tickets. T/Qpdt: £3.20 to a £1 stake. Pool: £3,335.00. 754.10 winning tickets. DO

# 3611 SOUTHWELL (L-H)
Friday, July 9

**OFFICIAL GOING: Standard**
The track looked to be riding quite deep and as the fields were rather small, there appeared no advantage as to were they raced.
Wind: Slight behind. Weather: Overcast.

## 3707 1ST WIMBLEDON FINAL CLAIMING STKS 1m (F)
**2:25** (2:29) (F) 3-Y-0 **£2,912** (£832; £416) **Stalls** Low

Form RPR

6035 **1** **Come What July (IRE)**[1] 3681 3-8-10 70..................................(b) CLowther 9 61
(RGuest) *sn outpcd: hung lft and hdwy over 2f out: nt clr run ins fnl f: r.o to ld nr fin* **3/1**[2]

0000 **2** *shd* **Multiple Choice (IRE)**[16] 3201 3-9-0 65..................................(t[1]) J-PGuillambert(3) 7 68
(NPLittmoden) *w ldrs: rdn to ld 1f out: hung rt ins fnl f: hdd nr fin* **10/1**

00 **3** 1 ¼ **Hinode (IRE)**[68] 1794 3-9-5.................................. MTebbutt 10 67
(JARToller) *chsd ldrs: outpcd over 4f out: hdwy u.p over 2f out: styd on* **4/1**[3]

-000 **4** *2* **Stevedore (IRE)**[20] 3089 3-8-10 74..................................(b[1]) LPKeniry(3) 1 57
(BJMeehan) *sn led: rdn and hdd over 4f out: styd on same pce fnl f* **9/4**[1]

0040 **5** *3* **Chatshow (USA)**[9] 3428 3-9-2 60.................................. PMakin(5) 5 59
(LADace) *w ldr: led over 4f out: hdd & wknd 1f out* **20/1**

0000 **6** 2 ½ **Jaolins**[15] 3229 3-8-0 52.................................. DKinsella 4 33
(PGMurphy) *s.s: outpcd: effrt over 2f out: n.d* **14/1**

6660 **7** *3* **Brother Cadfael**[56] 2088 3-8-7 47..................................(p) PaulEddery 6 34
(JohnAHarris) *chsd ldrs: outpcd over 4f out: n.d after* **16/1**

40-0 **8** *2* **Snow Chance (IRE)**[31] 2760 3-7-9 34.................................. BSwarbrick(5) 11 23
(WMBrisbourne) *chsd ldrs: outpcd over 4f out: n.d after* **40/1**

3200 **9** *9* **Zuloago (USA)**[76] 1627 3-8-10 55.................................. OUrbina 3 15
(SLKeightley) *sn outpcd* **12/1**

0-00 **10** *4* **Absolutely Fab (IRE)**[13] 3305 3-8-7 31.................................. HayleyTurner(5) 2 9
(MrsCADunnett) *sn outpcd* **66/1**

0040 **11** 3 ½ **Maria Maria (IRE)**[29] 2822 3-8-6 45.................................. RFitzpatrick 8 —
(MrsNMacauley) *s.i.s: outpcd* **66/1**

1m 46.76s (2.16) **Going Correction** +0.025s/f (Slow) **11** Ran SP% **115.3**
Speed ratings: **90,89,88,86,83 81,78,76,67,68 59**CSF £34.36 TOTE £5.00: £1.20, £4.00, £1.20; EX 18 [overprinted: The winner was claimed by ... Stevedore was claimed by S. Keightley for]
£8,000\n\x\x Stevedore (IRE)\n\x\x s. keightley £8000
**Owner** The Storm Again Syndicate **Bred** Pat Beirne **Trained** Newmarket, Suffolk

**FOCUS**
An ordinary claimer with little strength in depth, and the time was slow which makes the overall form modest.

**NOTEBOOK**
**Come What July(IRE)**, who had finished third on his only other run here, found thiings happening too quickly for him over this trip. However, once in line for home, his stamina came into play and he always looked like getting there. Ten furlongs could prove to be his optimum trip.
**Multiple Choice(IRE)** with an eyeshield and tongue-tie to help, bounced back to form on this first attempt beyond six-furlongs. Rated 84 last year, he is a long way below that nowadays, but showed he still retains ability and, if the aids have the same effect next time, he will be hard to beat in minor company.
**Hinode(IRE)**, who proved difficult to load into the stalls, stayed on well enough having got outpaced leaving the back staright. This drop in class suited well and he looks capable of finding a similar contest.
**Stevedore(IRE)** had no excuses in the first-time blinkers, and looks to have something to prove now.
**Chatshow(USA)**, paying his first visit here, showed a bit more than of late, although this trip just seemed to stretch him.

## 3708 ST VERONICA GUILIANI H'CAP 6f (F)
**2:55** (2:57) (E) (0-70,66) 3-Y-0 **£3,458** (£1,064; £532; £266) **Stalls** Low

Form RPR

-004 **1** **Shifty Night (IRE)**[11] 3381 3-7-7 **43** oh1.................................. HayleyTurner(5) 6 54
(MrsCADunnett) *chsd ldrs: led 2f out: rdn out* **14/1**

1525 **2** 1 ¾ **Tsarbuck**[15] 3252 3-8-13 **58**.................................. GFaulkner 4 64
(RMHCowell) *mde most 4f: rdn and edgd lft over 1f out: styd on same pce* **5/2**[1]

3202 **3** 1 ½ **Adorata (GER)**[6] 3517 3-9-5 **64**.................................. OUrbina 3 66
(JJay) *prom: rdn over 2f out: styd on same pce fnl f* **7/2**[2]

0-50 **4** *1* **Megabond**[23] 2989 3-9-0 **59**.................................. FLynch 2 58
(BSmart) *sn outpcd: hdwy u.p over 1f out: nt trble ldrs* **8/1**

0100 **5** 1 ¼ **Garnock Venture (IRE)**[11] 3368 3-9-3 **62**..................................(b) DaleGibson 1 57
(ABerry) *sn pushed along and prom: rdn over 2f out: wknd fnl f* **11/2**[3]

2200 **6** *4* **Brown Dragon**[13] 3322 3-9-4 **63**.................................. PaulEddery 7 46
(DHaydnJones) *s.i.s: hld up: outpcd 4f out: n.d* **8/1**

5003 **7** *3* **Noble Mount**[36] 2620 3-9-0 **59**.................................. JQuinn 8 33
(RGuest) *chsd ldrs over 3f* **12/1**

0436 **8** 1 ½ **Elliot's Choice (IRE)**[4] 3585 3-9-4 **66**.................................. DNolan(3) 5 35
(DCarroll) *chsd ldrs: rdn 1/2-way: wknd over 1f out* **7/1**

1m 16.25s (-0.65) **Going Correction** +0.025s/f (Slow) **8** Ran SP% **115.3**
Speed ratings: **105,102,100,99,97 92,88,86**CSF £49.66 CT £154.47 TOTE £17.60: £2.80, £1.40, £1.30; EX 71.80.
**Owner** G R Price **Bred** Epona Bloodstock Ltd **Trained** Hingham, Norfolk

**FOCUS**
This moderate handicap was not that competitive and the winner probably did not have to improve much to get off the mark. The form is modest but the time was fair for the grade though.

**NOTEBOOK**
**Shifty Night(IRE)** all the better for her first experience of the track last time, won with a little more in hand than the verdict suggested.
**Tsarbuck** turned in a solid enough effort, over a trip which could well be on the sharp side for him. He has yet to finish out of the frame here.
**Adorata(GER)** looked to find this trip on the sharp side.
**Megabond** found things happening far too quickly for him over this trip.
**Garnock Venture(IRE)** has never won in handicap company and is probably better off in claimers.

## 3709 TOM HANKS BIRTHDAY (S) STKS 5f (F)
**3:30** (3:33) (G) 2-Y-0 **£2,520** (£720; £360) **Stalls** High

Form RPR

0353 **1** **Eternally**[29] 2799 2-8-11..................................(p) BDoyle 2 45+
(RMHCowell) *chsd ldr tl led 1/2-way: hung lft fnl f: r.o* **2/5**[1]

06 **2** *3* **Itsa Monkey (IRE)**[29] 2799 2-8-4.................................. KGhunowa(7) 3 35
(MJPolglase) *s.i.s: sn chsng ldrs: outpcd over 3f out: styd on to go 2nd ins fnl f: no ch w wnr* **10/1**[3]



The Form Book, Raceform Ltd, Compton, RG20 6NL

000 **3** 1 3/4 **Eternal Sunshine (IRE)**[6] 3526 2-8-6 ..........................(v[1]) RFitzpatrick 4 23
(RPElliott) *led to 1/2-way: sn rdn: wknd fnl f* **20/1**
000 **4** 1 3/4 **Fellbeck Fred**[6] 3526 2-8-8 .......................................... TEaves(3) 1 22
(CWThornton) *dwlt: sn chsng ldrs: rdn 1/2-way: sn outpcd* **10/1**[3]
500 **5** 8 **Northern Revoque (IRE)**[26] 2904 2-8-6 .............................. PBradley 6 —
(ABerry) *chsd ldrs to 1/2-way* **6/1**[2]
0 **6** 3 **Absolut Edge**[7] 3491 2-8-11 .................................................. DSweeney 5 —
(JAPickering) *dwlt: outpcd: hung lft for over 3f: swvd rt ins fnl f* **20/1**

63.10 secs (2.70) **Going Correction** +0.30s/f (Slow) **6** Ran SP% **113.4**
Speed ratings: **90,85,82,79,66 62**CSF £5.67 TOTE £1.10: £1.10, £5.90; EX 5.10.There was no bid for the winner.
**Owner** Bottisham Heath Stud **Bred** Mrs E M Gauvain **Trained** Six Mile Bottom, Cambs

**FOCUS**
A very weak seller in which both the first and second dropped their riders on the way to post. It was a slow time even for this grade and the winner did not have to run up to previous form to score.

**NOTEBOOK**
**Eternally**, like the runner-up, dropped his rider on the way to post. However, he did little wrong in the race itself and was not hard pressed to score.
**Itsa Monkey(IRE)** is well named for he does look something of a character, having deposited his rider on the way to the start, and although he filled the runner-up spot, achieved little in doing so.
**Eternal Sunshine(IRE)** showed a bit of speed in the first-time visor but, when push came to shove, there was little response.
**Absolut Edge** *Official explanation: jockey said gelding hung left-handed*

## 3710 LOBSTER CARNIVAL MAIDEN FILLIES' H'CAP 1m (F)
**4:00** (4:02) (F) (0-55,55) 3-Y-0+ **£3,038** (£868; £434) **Stalls** Low

Form RPR
0046 **1** **Faith Healer (IRE)**[18] 3156 3-9-4 **50**.......................................(b) JQuinn 10 61
(VSmith) *mde all: clr over 1f out: rdn out* **9/2**[1]
00-0 **2** 3 **Wavet**[20] 3088 4-9-9 **46**.................................................................. RPrice 1 51
(JPearce) *prom: n.m.r and lost pl 5f out: rallied over 1f out: nt rch ldr* **14/1**
0-03 **3** 2 **Essex Star (IRE)**[29] 2811 3-9-3 **49**.............................................. JMcAuley 6 50
(MissJFeilden) *chsd ldrs: rdn over 3f out: styd on same pce fnl 2f* **5/1**[2]
0044 **4** shd **Magic Verse**[11] 3380 3-9-7 **53**.................................................... CLowther 12 54
(RGuest) *chsd ldrs: rdn over 3f out: styd on same pce fnl 2f* **5/1**[2]
46-6 **5** 2 1/2 **Eboracum Lady (USA)**[7] 3490 4-9-13 **50**..................................... OUrbina 5 46
(JDBethell) *sn pushed along in rr: hdwy over 5f out: outpcd over 3f out: n.d after* **7/1**[3]
-545 **6** 3 1/2 **Hilarious (IRE)**[27] 2879 4-9-1 **45**............................................ LucyRussell(7) 2 34
(DrJRJNaylor) *sn outpcd: styd on ins fnl f: nvr nrr* **15/2**
6-20 **7** 1 1/2 **Candy Anchor (FR)**[79] 1545 5-9-4 **41**....................................(b) VSlattery 8 27
(REPeacock) *s.i.s: outpcd: nvr nrr* **14/1**
00-0 **8** 1 **Lola Lola (IRE)**[28] 2842 3-8-13 **45**............................................... DKinsella 15 29
(JLDunlop) *chsd ldrs 6f* **22/1**
0000 **9** 2 **Chiqitita (IRE)**[64] 1907 3-8-12 **49**............................................ PMakin(5) 7 29
(MissMERowland) *prom over 4f* **20/1**
3220 **10** 1 1/4 **Divina**[46] 2345 3-8-6 **38**.........................................................................(v) ADaly 14 15
(SLKeightley) *prom to 1/2-way* **11/1**
0/00 **11** 4 **Dispol Verity**[18] 3151 4-9-0 **42**............................................. BSwarbrick(5) 11 11
(WMBrisbourne) *hld up: wknd 5f out* **20/1**
0060 **12** 7 **Wedowannagiveuthat (IRE)**[7] 3473 3-9-9 **55**................................ FLynch 3 10
(TDEasterby) *s.i.s: outpcd: rdn over 3f out: a in rr* **20/1**
0000 **13** 7 **Suerte**[14] 3264 4-9-6 **43**................................................................... BDoyle 9 —
(RMHCowell) *s.i.s: outpcd: sme hdwy over 3f out: sn wknd* **14/1**

1m 45.68s (1.08) **Going Correction** +0.025s/f (Slow)
**WFA** 3 from 4yo+ 9lb **13** Ran SP% **122.7**
Speed ratings: **95,92,90,89,87 83,82,81,79,78 74,67,60**CSF £62.80 CT £302.45 TOTE £6.10: £3.00, £14.30, £4.50; EX 55.30.
**Owner** V Smith **Bred** Ruairi O'Coileain **Trained** Exning, Suffolk

**FOCUS**
A moderate maiden handicap, and despite the large field this was not that competitive with the runners having had 116 runs between them without scoring. The form looks solid enough for the grade.

**NOTEBOOK**
**Faith Healer(IRE)**, who had been held up over longer trips, appreciated the forcing tactics employed over this mile. This was the first time she has encountered this surface, so may be capable of further improvement.
**Wavet**, one of the less exposed in the field, was doing her best work in the closing stages and gave the impression she should stay further, even though she has been well beaten when tried over longer distances.
**Essex Star(IRE)** was treading water all the way up the straight and may have found this trip beyond her.
**Magic Verse** was not disgraced, but she will need to come down in the weights if she is to score at this level.
**Eboracum Lady(USA)** tended to run her race in snatches and may not have been entirely happy on this surface.
**Hilarious(IRE)** took a while to get the hang of this surface and was never nearer than at the line.
**Suerte** *Official explanation: jockey said filly had a breathing problem*

## 3711 EVERY BREATH YOU TAKE AT NUMBER 1 MAIDEN STKS 6f (F)
**4:35** (4:35) (D) 3-Y-0 **£3,341** (£1,028; £514; £257) **Stalls** Low

Form RPR
2223 **1** **Extra Cover (IRE)**[28] 2853 3-9-0 69.........................................(b) DSweeney 4 75+
(RCharlton) *hld up in tch: led on bit ins fnl f: shkn up and r.o* **2/1**[2]
4-02 **2** 4 **Cyfrwys (IRE)**[9] 3410 3-8-9 75....................................................... JQuinn 1 58
(BPalling) *w ldr tl led over 4f out: rdn over 1f out: hdd and unable qck ins fnl f* **15/8**[1]
604 **3** 2 **Scrunch**[16] 3209 3-8-6 68............................................................ LPKeniry(3) 2 52
(BJMeehan) *w ldrs: hung rt over 1f out: styd on same pce* **2/1**[2]
00-0 **4** 2 1/2 **Lord Arthur**[14] 3279 3-9-0 ................................................................. DaleGibson 6 50
(MWEasterby) *sn outpcd: styd on ins fnl f: nvr nr to chal* **50/1**
5020 **5** 1 1/2 **La Fonteyne**[15] 3229 3-8-6 50................................................... TEaves(3) 5 40
(CBBBooth) *chsd ldrs: rdn 1/2-way: sn outpcd* **25/1**
6-53 **6** 3 1/2 **Palvic Moon**[60] 1991 3-8-9 60....................................................... RFitzpatrick 3 30
(CSmith) *led: hdd over 4f out: n.m.r and rdn over 3f out: wknd over 1f out* **14/1**[3]

1m 16.69s (-0.21) **Going Correction** +0.025s/f (Slow) **6** Ran SP% **113.9**
Speed ratings: **102,96,94,90,88 84**CSF £6.34 TOTE £3.40: £2.60, £1.10; EX 8.00.
**Owner** John Livock Bloodstock Limited **Bred** Robert Phelan **Trained** Beckhampton, Wilts

**FOCUS**
A fair maiden for the course, but the placed horses were below form and the winner only needed to run to previous best.

**NOTEBOOK**
**Extra Cover(IRE)**, whose effort here last time left something to be desired, proved better suited by this trip and, although he won with plenty in hand, it was noticeable that his rider wanted to delay his effort as long as possible.
**Cyfrwys(IRE)** handled this surface well enough and should have no trouble winning her maiden on this surface.
**Scrunch** had no excuses and again did herself no favours by hanging.
**Lord Arthur** found things happening too quickly over this trip and, as he is out of a mare that won over 12 furlongs, better can be expected when he goes handicapping over a more suitable trip.
**Palvic Moon** *Official explanation: jockey said filly did not handle bend into the straight*

## 3712 RUN A MILE FOR SPORT RELIEF TOMORROW H'CAP 1m 6f (F)
**5:10** (5:13) (F) (0-55,55) 4-Y-0+ **£2,975** (£850; £425) **Stalls** Low

Form RPR
000- **1** **Magic Red**[62] 4297 4-8-5 **40**.................................................................. RPrice 9 53
(MJRyan) *w ldr: led over 7f out: rdn over 2f out: styd on wl* **33/1**
4154 **2** 3 **Mercurious (IRE)**[53] 2186 4-8-7 **42**........................................... DaleGibson 10 51
(JMackie) *a.p: rdn and ev ch fr over 2f out tl no ex ins fnl f* **9/2**[2]
-060 **3** 13 **Kalanisha (IRE)**[29] 2816 4-8-3 **38** ow2..........................(b[1]) PaulEddery 4 30
(NAGraham) *prom: rdn over 3f out: sn wknd* **33/1**
4555 **4** 6 **Sea Cove**[15] 3250 4-8-4 **42** ow1................................................. TEaves(3) 1 26
(JMJefferson) *chsd ldrs: rdn over 5f out: wknd over 3f out* **7/1**
0/00 **5** nk **Lake Of Dreams**[25] 2950 5-7-12 **40**........................................ LucyRussell(7) 7 24
(DrJRJNaylor) *hld up: hdwy over 5f out: wknd over 3f out* **40/1**
0303 **6** 7 **Our Imperial Bay (USA)**[14] 3281 5-9-6 **55**.................................(p) ADaly 6 30
(MrsJCandlish) *hld up: pushed along and bhd over 9f out: a bhd* **5/1**[3]
0526 **7** 6 **Western Command (GER)**[14] 3281 8-8-0 **35**.............. JoannaBadger 2 2
(MrsNMacauley) *hld up: rdn 7f out: wknd over 4f out* **14/1**
/00- **8** 30 **Heartbreaker (IRE)**[336] 3461 4-8-4 **39**...................................... SCarson 3 —
(MWEasterby) *led over 6f: wknd over 4f out* **33/1**
1 **P** **The Kelt (IRE)**[6] 3518 7-8-6 **41** 6ex...........................................(t) JQuinn 8 —
(EoinDoyle, Ire) *s.i.s: hld up: p.u 5f out: lame* **13/8**[1]

3m 7.39s (-2.31) **Going Correction** +0.025s/f (Slow) **9** Ran SP% **103.4**
Speed ratings: **107,105,97,94,94 90,86,69,—**CSF £138.60 CT £3613.93 TOTE £44.20: £6.40, £1.80, £7.50; EX 283.00 Place 6 £51.79, Place 5 £19.33.
**Owner** M J Ryan **Bred** Cheveley Park Stud Ltd **Trained** Newmarket, Suffolk

**FOCUS**
A very moderate handicap that was little better than a seller, but there appeared to be plenty of pace on and the time was very good for the grade with the first two were clear.

**NOTEBOOK**
**Magic Red**, tackling his furthest trip to date on the Flat, trounced his rivals. There was plenty to like about this performance and he should have no trouble scoring again at this level.
**Mercurious(IRE)**, who stays further than this, looked the likely winner when looming large at the two-furlong pole but, off the bridle, the response was disappointing.
**Kalanisha(IRE)** did not improve any for the step up in trip.
**Sea Cove** was easily left behind turning for home.
**Our Imperial Bay(USA)** has his own ideas about the game.
**The Kelt(IRE)** sadly went lame before leaving the back straight. *Official explanation: jockey said gelding was lame*
CR

# [2894]YORK (L-H)
## Friday, July 9

**OFFICIAL GOING: Good to soft**
The ground was described as 'good to soft'.
Wind: Moderate 1/2 against. Weather: Overcast but mainly fine and dry.

## 3713 GRAMPIAN COUNTRY FOOD GROUP STKS (H'CAP) 5f
**2:00** (2:01) (C) (0-95,92) 3-Y-0+ **£10,601** (£3,262; £1,631; £815) **Stalls** Centre

Form RPR
2100 **1** **Artie**[6] 3509 5-9-2 **83**........................................................................ RWinston 10 93
(TDEasterby) *led early: chsd ldrs: styd on to ld last 75yds* **12/1**
0400 **2** 1/2 **Seven No Trumps**[13] 3307 7-8-8 **75**......................................(p) KDarley 5 83
(JMBradley) *w ldrs: led over 1f out: hdd and no ex wl ins last* **12/1**
0244 **3** nk **Tally (IRE)**[6] 3509 4-7-12 **65** oh6............................................ PMQuinn 11 72
(MJPolglase) *sn outpcd and bhd: hdwy over 1f out: styd on wl towards fin* **14/1**
6226 **4** 1/2 **Blackheath (IRE)**[6] 3509 8-9-1 **82**....................................... AlexGreaves 6 87
(DNicholls) *in tch: hdwy over 1f out: styd on wl ins last* **9/1**
1006 **5** 1 **Ptarmigan Ridge**[14] 3266 8-8-13 **83**........................................ NMackay(3) 2 85
(MissLAPerratt) *chsd ldrs: ev ch 1f out: wknd last 150yds* **5/1**[1]
230 **6** hd **Obe One**[20] 3098 4-8-1 **68**................................................................. FNorton 3 69
(ABerry) *sn drvn along: hdwy over 1f out: swtchd lft ins last: kpt on* **11/2**[2]
1650 **7** 2 **Catch The Cat (IRE)**[6] 3509 5-7-12 **72**.......................(v) RoryMoore(7) 8 66
(JSWainwright) *sn led: hdd over 1f out: wknd ins last* **10/1**
0602 **8** 1 **Cape Royal**[13] 3293 4-9-6 **87**................................................................ MHills 1 77
(MrsJRRamsden) *sn chsng ldrs: effrt over 2f out: wknd fnl f* **6/1**[3]
0020 **9** 3/4 **Beyond The Clouds (IRE)**[6] 3509 8-8-9 **76**................................ DAllan 9 63
(JSWainwright) *outpcd and bhd 1/2-way: kpt on appr fnl f: nvr on terms* **8/1**
0606 **10** 2 1/2 **Absent Friends**[7] 3480 7-9-11 **92**........................................... JEdmunds 4 70
(JBalding) *trckd ldrs: wknd over 1f out* **25/1**
5500 **11** hd **Watching**[6] 3509 7-9-3 **84**.................................................... WSupple 12 62
(DNicholls) *mid-div: lost pl over 2f out* **9/1**
/300 **12** 2 1/2 **Sunley Sense**[15] 3243 8-8-10 **77**............................................ TEDurcan 7 46
(MRChannon) *lost pl over 2f out: sn bhd* **25/1**

61.32 secs (2.04) **Going Correction** +0.525s/f (Yiel) **12** Ran SP% **116.3**
Speed ratings: **104,103,102,101,100 100,96,95,94,90 89,85**CSF £145.33 CT £2045.04 TOTE £15.10: £3.30, £4.00, £4.60; EX 158.10.
**Owner** A Arton **Bred** Mrs D Ellis **Trained** Great Habton, N Yorks

**FOCUS**
In effect a 0-92 handicap and as usual they stayed away from both rails. The form is fair and reasonably solid with the first two running close to best and the third posting another good effort.

**NOTEBOOK**
**Artie**, who had the coffin box draw at Beverley, looked at his very best and appreciated the ease in the ground. He seems equally at home over both five and six furlongs.
**Seven No Trumps** last tasted success over two years ago but from a 21lb higher mark. He ran his best race for some time and career win number seven is surely just around the corner.
**Tally(IRE)** did really well considering he was 6lb out of the handicap and he has done all his winning over six furlongs.
**Blackheath(IRE)**, 6lb higher than his last winning mark, is not at his very best on ground as easy as he encountered here.
**Ptarmigan Ridge** raced a lot more prominently than usual and his rider seemed to get in a tangle with his reins late on.
**Obe One** keeps running well but needs everything to fall just right to get his head in front where it matters most.
**Catch The Cat(IRE)**, with a visor instead of blinkers, is all speed but he is still 3lb higher than his last winning mark.
**Cape Royal**, 2lb higher, was simply not up to the task.

**Absent Friends** dropped out in a matter of strides and was found to have bled from the nose. *Official explanation: jockey said gelding bled from nose*

## 3714 HEARTHSTEAD HOMES STKS (H'CAP) 7f 205y
**2:35** (2:36) (D) (0-85,83) 3-Y-O+ **£5,980** (£1,840; £920; £460) **Stalls** Low

Form RPR

-440 **1** **Blonde Streak (USA)**[16] [3198] 4-9-6 **75** ... KDarley 9 86
(TDBarron) *led: qcknd over 4f out: hld on towards fin* **8/1**[3]

0425 **2** *nk* **Tedsdale Mac**[7] [3470] 5-8-0 **55** ow2 ... FNorton 8 65
(NBycroft) *in rr: hdwy over 2f out: edgd lft over 1f out: kpt on wl: no ex towards fin* **25/1**

-410 **3** *1* **Hills Of Gold**[15] [3235] 5-8-11 **71** ... PMulrennan(5) 10 79
(MWEasterby) *trckd ldrs: effrt over 3f out: nt qcknd ins last* **9/1**

2211 **4** *1 1/2* **Alchemist Master**[4] [3586] 5-8-8 **63** 6ex ... (p) DeanMcKeown 7 68
(RMWhitaker) *trckd ldrs: effrt and ev ch over 1f out: wknd ins last* **2/1**[1]

1440 **5** *1* **Honest Injun**[55] [2134] 3-8-12 **76** ... MHills 2 79
(BWHills) *trckd ldrs: one pce appr fnl f* **8/1**[3]

4001 **6** *1 1/2* **Cryfield**[7] [3470] 7-8-6 **61** 6ex ... KimTinkler 5 61
(NTinkler) *bhd: sn pushed along: hdwy whn nt clr over 2f out and over 1f out: nvr rchd ldrs* **14/1**

6246 **7** *3 1/2* **Go Tech**[6] [3534] 4-9-7 **76** ... WSupple 6 69
(TDEasterby) *swtchd wd sn after s: t.k.h towards rr: hdwy over 3f out: wknd over 1f out* **11/1**

5005 **8** *1 1/2* **Danelor (IRE)**[19] [3119] 6-9-11 **83** ... THamilton(3) 3 72
(RAFahey) *hld up in mid-div: drvn along over 3f out: nvr a threat* **8/1**[3]

6301 **9** *1 1/2* **Pawan (IRE)**[5] [3563] 4-9-3 **72** 6ex ... AnnStokell 1 58
(MissAStokell) *sn chsng wnr: wknd over 1f out* **25/1**

-130 **10** *10* **Retirement**[13] [3299] 5-9-13 **82** ... JFanning 4 47
(MHTompkins) *trckd ldrs: effrt over 3f out: lost pl over 1f out: eased* **11/2**[2]

1m 40.24s (2.50) **Going Correction** +0.525s/f (Yiel)
**WFA** 3 from 4yo+ 9lb **10** Ran **SP% 114.7**
Speed ratings: **108,107,106,105,104 102,99,97,96,86**CSF £182.12 CT £1240.49 TOTE £6.10: £1.90, £6.70, £2.90; EX 169.20.
**Owner** Mrs Liz Jones **Bred** Shadwell Farm Inc **Trained** Maunby, N Yorks

**FOCUS**
A 0-83 handicap run at a sound pace but lacking real strength in depth. The form is ordinary but reliable enough.

**NOTEBOOK**
**Blonde Streak(USA)**, only 1lb higher than for her last win, appreciated the ease in the ground and proved very game in a tight finish.
**Tedsdale Mac**, without a win for over two years, was in the end only just denied carrying 2lb overweight.
**Hills Of Gold**, 5lb higher than for his last win, probably ran right up to his best.
**Alchemist Master**, attempting a quick follow up, looked a bit tucked up. He moved upsides seemingly travelling the better but on this rain-softened ground did not really see it out. He will have a lot more to do when his revised rating clicks in. *Official explanation: jockey said gelding failed to stay on good to soft ground*
**Honest Injun**, having his first outing for two months, gave a good account of himself but looks in need of a little more leniency.
**Cryfield**, under his penalty, met trouble in running and was never on terms.
**Retirement** dropped right out in a matter of strides and looked to struggle to cross the finishing line. He clearly has a problem. *Official explanation: jockey said gelding was never travelling and finished exhausted*

## 3715 CUISINE DE FRANCE SUMMER STKS (GROUP 3) (F&M) 6f
**3:05** (3:05) (A) 3-Y-O+ **£29,000** (£11,000; £5,500; £2,500) **Stalls** Centre

Form RPR

40-1 **1** **Tante Rose (IRE)**[34] [2685] 4-9-0 107 ... MHills 1 116
(RCharlton) *stdd and swtchd rt s:hld up: nt clr run over 2f out: smooth hdwy over 1f out: qcknd to ld 150yds out: impressive* **11/4**[1]

-523 **2** *2 1/2* **Ruby Rocket (IRE)**[13] [3308] 3-8-8 105 ... MFenton 7 109
(HMorrison) *trckd ldr: hung lft and led over 1f out: hdd jst ins last: no ch w wnr* **3/1**[2]

-200 **3** *1 1/2* **Lochridge**[20] [3073] 5-9-0 103 ... DeanMcKeown 5 104
(AMBalding) *led tl over 1f out: nt qckn* **13/2**

1342 **4** *nk* **Ringmoor Down**[6] [3537] 5-9-0 106 ... KDarley 9 103
(DWPArbuthnot) *trckd ldrs: effrt over 2f out: styd on same pce appr fnl f* **4/1**[3]

-150 **5** *1 1/4* **Goldeva**[13] [3308] 5-9-0 101 ... (t) NCallan 2 99
(RHollinshead) *trckd ldrs: kpt on same pce fnl 2f* **25/1**

-233 **6** *shd* **Topkamp**[14] [3275] 4-9-0 102 ... RMullen 10 99
(MLWBell) *trckd ldrs: effrt over 2f out: one pce* **25/1**

3131 **7** *shd* **Golden Nun**[27] [2903] 4-9-4 101 ... (b) RWinston 3 103+
(TDEasterby) *rrd s: bhd tl hdwy over 2f out: nvr rchd ldrs* **8/1**

3500 **8** *nk* **Vita Spericolata (IRE)**[6] [3509] 7-9-0 83 ... GParkin 6 98?
(JSWainwright) *t.k.h in mid-div: effrt over 2f out: swtchd lft over 1f out: wknd ins last* **100/1**

1050 **9** *1 1/4* **Silca's Gift**[23] [2966] 3-8-12 107 ... TEDurcan 11 98
(MRChannon) *hld up: effrt on ins over 2f out: wknd 1f out* **14/1**

1m 13.26s (0.69) **Going Correction** +0.525s/f (Yiel)
**WFA** 3 from 4yo+ 6lb **9** Ran **SP% 111.5**
Speed ratings: **116,112,110,110,108 108,108,107,106**CSF £10.49 TOTE £3.90: £1.70, £1.40, £2.40; EX 13.70.
**Owner** B E Nielsen **Bred** Addison Racing Ltd Inc **Trained** Beckhampton, Wilts

**FOCUS**
A line-up fully justifying the Group Three status and an impressive winner. The time was very good for the class and the form is sound for a race of its type.

**NOTEBOOK**
**Tante Rose(IRE)** ◆, who narrowly accounted for the runner-up at Haydock, looked in tip-top trim after a month off. She travelled supremely well and made light of traffic problems, producing a serious turn of foot, and was back on the bridle at the line. In this frame of mind she can take a Group Two and would not be out of place at the top level.
**Ruby Rocket(IRE)**, 2lb better off with the winner compared to Haydock, again gave a good account of herself but this time was very much second best.
**Lochridge** put two poor runs behind her and is even more effective on genuinely quick ground. She seems at her best in the second half of the season.
**Ringmoor Down** is in good form but this may be as good as she is.
**Goldeva** ran right up to her best, suited by the ease in the ground.
**Topkamp**, fourth last year, ran out of her skin.
**Golden Nun**, runner-up a year ago, was up against it under her 4lb penalty and she blew what chance she had by rearing when the gates opened. *Official explanation: jockey said filly reared as stalls opened*
**Silca's Gift** seems to have lost her way since her Nell Gwyn success.

## 3716 JOHN WEST TUNA STKS (RATED STAKES) (H'CAP) 1m 3f 198y
**3:40** (3:40) (B) (0-100,99) 3-Y-O+ **£12,910** (£4,897; £2,448; £1,113) **Stalls** Low

Form RPR

1 **1** **Carte Diamond (USA)**[21] [3057] 3-8-3 **90** ... JFanning 10 104+
(MJohnston) *trckd ldrs: led over 2f out: hung lft and hdd 1f out: wnt lft bt styd on wl to ld last 50yds* **8/1**

3-21 **2** *nk* **Loves Travelling (IRE)**[16] [3199] 4-8-8 **85** oh2 ... NMackay(3) 1 99+
(LMCumani) *hld up in rr: stdy hdwy over 2f out: edgd rt and led 1f out: rdn and wnt bdly lft ins last: hdd and no ex* **9/2**[2]

2365 **3** *1 3/4* **Gold Ring**[28] [2855] 4-8-11 **85** ... SDrowne 4 96
(GBBalding) *chsd ldrs: ev ch over 3f out: nt qckn fnl f* **4/1**[1]

2124 **4** *2 1/2* **Desert Royalty (IRE)**[23] [2993] 4-9-4 **92** ... WSupple 3 99
(EALDunlop) *trckd ldrs: ev ch over 3f out: fdd ins last* **12/1**

-031 **5** *hd* **Vengeance**[13] [3325] 4-9-10 **98** ... PDobbs 7 105
(MrsAJPerrett) *hld up towards rr: effrt 3f out: styd on wl fnl f* **5/1**[3]

0005 **6** *1* **Dunaskin (IRE)**[23] [2982] 4-8-6 **85** oh4 ... PMulrennan(5) 9 90
(DEddy) *trckd ldrs: chal over 4f out: outpcd over 2f out: n.d after* **40/1**

-130 **7** *nk* **Destination Dubai (USA)**[22] [2999] 3-8-5 **92** ... (t) KMcEvoy 2 97
(SaeedBinSuroor) *led: hung rt thrght: hdd over 2f out: lost pl over 1f out* **13/2**

1000 **8** *2 1/2* **Telemachus**[20] [3097] 4-8-13 **87** ... MFenton 6 88
(JGGiven) *rr-div: sn pushed along: sme hdwy 3f out: nvr on terms* **20/1**

41-0 **9** *1 1/2* **Urowells (IRE)**[34] [2691] 4-9-4 **92** ... TEDurcan 8 90
(EALDunlop) *bhd: sme hdwy 3f out: nvr a factor* **40/1**

000- **10** *shd* **Fourth Dimension (IRE)**[265] [5639] 5-8-12 **86** ... AlexGreaves 11 84
(DNicholls) *mid-div: effrt on wd outside 3f out: nvr a factor* **50/1**

110- **11** *11* **Conquering Love (IRE)**[325] [4267] 6-8-8 **85** oh2 ... THamilton(3) 5 65
(BEllison) *s.i.s: sn t.o: sme hdwy 4f out: lost pl 3f out: eased* **33/1**

214- **12** *5* **Lodger (FR)**[323] [4325] 4-9-4 **92** ... KDarley 12 64
(JNoseda) *sn trcking ldrs on outer: lost pl over 2f out: sn bhd and eased* **17/2**

3- **13** *6* **Astronomic**[264] [5663] 4-9-11 **99** ... RWinston 13 62
(JHowardJohnson) *trckd ldrs: drvn along 4f out: lost pl over 2f out: sn bhd and eased* **16/1**

2m 34.15s (5.29) **Going Correction** +0.525s/f (Yiel)
**WFA** 3 from 4yo+ 13lb **13** Ran **SP% 117.9**
Speed ratings: **103,102,101,99,99 99,98,97,96,96 88,85,81**CSF £41.25 CT £168.40 TOTE £7.10: £2.20, £2.20, £1.80; EX 23.40.
**Owner** Mr & Mrs Heywood & Mr & Mrs Bovingdon **Bred** The Thoroughbred Corporation **Trained** Middleham Moor, N Yorks

**FOCUS**
A good contest and strong handicap form, but just a steady pace until in line for home and a modest final time. The unexposed winner can go on to better things.

**NOTEBOOK**
**Carte Diamond(USA)**, who has a long stride, made it two from two despite showing signs of inexperience. He has a willing attitude and will go on from here, especially over further.
**Loves Travelling(IRE)**, 5lb higher, proved hard to keep on an even keel and in the end just missed out. He would not want the ground any softer than he encountered here.
**Gold Ring**, who has won just once from 21 starts now, usually gives a good account of himself but he looks weighted to the limit.
**Desert Royalty(IRE)**, 10lb higher than her last win, found this more her level but this is as good as she is.
**Vengeance**, 8lb higher, found himself in a hopeless position and his sterling late work was to no avail.
**Dunaskin(IRE)**, due to race from a 4lb lower mark in future, is better over shorter when able to dominate. *Official explanation: jockey said gelding hung right*
**Destination Dubai(USA)**, very edge beforehand, made the running but, with the visor left off, he persisted in hanging away from the running rail. He is clearly not straightforward. *Official explanation: jockey said colt hung right*
**Urowells(IRE)** *Official explanation: jockey said gelding hung left*

## 3717 TULIP BACON RATED STKS (H'CAP) 7f 205y
**4:15** (4:16) (B) (0-100,100) 3-Y-O+ **£12,852** (£4,875; £2,437; £1,108) **Stalls** Low

Form RPR

2102 **1** **St Petersburg**[67] [1828] 4-9-0 **93** ... KDarley 7 103
(MHTompkins) *trckd ldrs: led 2f out: drvn along and hld on wl* **7/2**[2]

6106 **2** *1 1/2* **Flighty Fellow (IRE)**[7] [3477] 4-9-1 **94** ... WSupple 1 101
(TDEasterby) *hld up: nt clr run over 2f out: swtchd ins: styd on to go 2nd ins last: no real imp* **11/2**[3]

-054 **3** *1/2* **Play That Tune**[15] [3223] 4-8-10 **89** ... JFanning 2 95
(MJohnston) *hld up: effrt over 2f out: sn chsng wnr: nt qckn fnl f* **9/1**

5603 **4** *1 1/4* **Blue Sky Thinking (IRE)**[49] [2258] 5-9-0 **93** ... DarrenWilliams 5 96
(KRBurke) *sn trckings ldrs: effrt on outside over 2f out: edgd lft and no ex fnl f* **6/1**

-260 **5** *3/4* **Wizard Of Noz**[23] [2969] 4-9-7 **100** ... MHills 6 102
(JNoseda) *hld up: effrt on outer over 2f out: kpt on: no imp* **10/1**

6310 **6** *5* **Putra Kuantan**[23] [2969] 4-9-7 **100** ... NCallan 4 91
(MAJarvis) *led: qcknd over 3f out: hdd 2f out: wknd 1f out* **11/4**[1]

0020 **7** *2 1/2* **Mysterinch**[7] [3477] 4-8-12 **91** ... TEDurcan 3 77
(JeddO'Keeffe) *sn chsng ldrs: reminders after s: effrt over 3f out: lost pl over 1f out: eased* **7/1**

1m 40.0s (2.26) **Going Correction** +0.525s/f (Yiel) **7** Ran **SP% 110.2**
Speed ratings: **109,107,107,105,105 100,97**CSF £21.08 TOTE £3.60: £2.30, £2.30; EX 16.50.
**Owner** P Heath **Bred** Kirtlington Stud Ltd **Trained** Newmarket, Suffolk

**FOCUS**
A tactical affair with the pace only lifting in the final half mile, but the form is fair for the level.

**NOTEBOOK**
**St Petersburg**, helped by the ease in the ground, went to the front two furlongs out and his rider was in his most determined mood.
**Flighty Fellow(IRE)**, with the blinkers left off, could have done with a much stronger pace. He met traffic problems but in the end was definitely second best.
**Play That Tune**, down 7lb in three outings this time, showed a return to form and should continue to give a good account of herself.
**Blue Sky Thinking(IRE)**, given seven weeks on the sidelines, could have done with a much stronger pace and this trip is his bare minimum.
**Wizard Of Noz**, 4lb lower, tried to come from off the pace in a tactical race and never looked like picking up sufficiently. He will be seen to much better effect in a truly-run race.
**Putra Kuantan**, 6lb higher than Sandown, was given a fine tactical ride but was still not good enough and in the end dropped out in disappointing fashion. *Official explanation: jockey said colt was unsuited by the ground*

## 3718 RAMESYS MAIDEN STKS — 6f 217y

4:50 (4:51) (D) 2-Y-O — £5,255 (£1,617; £808; £404) Stalls Low

| Form | | | | | RPR |
|---|---|---|---|---|---|
| | 1 | | **Elliots World (IRE)** 2-9-0 | JFanning 2 | 93+ |
| | | | (MJohnston) *rangy: tall: scope: trckd ldrs: led over 2f out: sn drew clr: pushed out* | **7/2**[3] | |
| 5 | 2 | 6 | **Seyaadi**[13] [3319] 2-9-0 | RHills 3 | 77 |
| | | | (EALDunlop) *trckd ldrs: led over 3f out: hdd over 2f out: kpt on: no ch w wnr* | **2/1**[1] | |
| 4 | 3 | 5 | **Lodgician (IRE)**[13] [3313] 2-9-0 | DarrenWilliams 4 | 64 |
| | | | (JJQuinn) *trckd ldrs: one pce fnl 2f* | **14/1** | |
| | 4 | 2 ½ | **Jackadandy (USA)** 2-8-9 | PMulrennan(5) 9 | 58+ |
| | | | (JHowardJohnson) *w'like: sltly hmpd s: s.i.s: outpcd and bhd over 3f out: kpt on fnl f* | **11/1** | |
| 62 | 5 | 1 ¼ | **Ballycroy Girl (IRE)**[20] [3081] 2-8-6 | NMackay(3) 5 | 49 |
| | | | (ABailey) *chsd ldrs: outpcd and lost pl over 3f out: n.d after* | **11/1** | |
| | 6 | 2 | **Zoripp (IRE)** 2-9-0 | MFenton 8 | 49 |
| | | | (JGGiven) *w'like: cmpt: sltly hmpd s: in rr and outpcd after 2f: nver a threat after* | **22/1** | |
| | 7 | nk | **Masquerader (USA)** 2-9-0 | KMcEvoy 1 | 48 |
| | | | (SaeedBinSuroor) *w'like: lengthy: sn trcking ldrs: effrt over 3f out: hung lft 2f out: sn lost pl* | **11/4**[2] | |
| | 8 | 24 | **Bahamian Bay** 2-8-9 | GParkin 6 | — |
| | | | (MBrittain) *cmpt: unf: swvd rt s: led tl over 3f out: lost pl over 2f: sn bhd and eased* | **50/1** | |

1m 27.63s (4.32) **Going Correction** +0.525s/f (Yiel) **8** Ran SP% **111.9**
Speed ratings: **96,89,83,80,79 76,76,49**CSF £10.40 TOTE £4.50: £1.60, £1.40, £3.40; EX 12.80 Place 6 £482.91, Place 5 £44.58.
**Owner** Atlantic Racing Limited **Bred** K And Mrs Cullen **Trained** Middleham Moor, N Yorks

**FOCUS**
Just a steady pace to halfway but in the end an impressive wide-margin winner who may well be up to Pattern company.

**NOTEBOOK**
**Elliots World(IRE)** ◆, a May foal, is a half-brother to Bachir, winner of the Irish and French Guineas. Very much up in the air and inclined to be warm and coltish beforehand, he came right away and looks a smart prospect.
**Seyaadi**, who has a round action, went on and stepped up the pace but in the end was left toiling in the winner's wake. He should be well up to taking a run-of-the-mill maiden.
**Lodgician(IRE)**, taking quietly to post, again showed ability but in the end the first two were much too good.
**Jackadandy(USA)**, a May foal, picked up in his own time late on and this will have taught him something.
**Ballycroy Girl(IRE)** was left behind the moment the pace increased.
**Masquerader(USA)**, a March foal, is long in the back and he hung when asked a question and soon dropped right away. The artificial surface at Lingfield might be the next step.
T/Plt: £410.00 to a £1 stake. Pool: £65,606.05. 116.80 winning tickets. T/Qpdt: £8.40 to a £1 stake. Pool: £6,790.55. 595.50 winning tickets. WG

3719 - 3722a (Foreign Racing) - See Raceform Interactive

# 3689 ASCOT (R-H)

Saturday, July 10

**OFFICIAL GOING: Good (good to soft in places)**
Wind: lt against Weather: mostly fine

## 3723 MILLENNIUM & COPTHORNE HOTELS H'CAP — 5f

1:30 (1:31) (C) (0-100,97) 3-Y-0+ — £10,645 (£4,038; £2,019; £917) Stalls Low

| Form | | | | | RPR |
|---|---|---|---|---|---|
| 2-00 | 1 | | **Pivotal Point**[14] [3324] 4-9-5 **88** | LDettori 6 | 104 |
| | | | (PJMakin) *lw: mde virtually all: shkn up 1f out: styd on wl* | **5/1**[1] | |
| -001 | 2 | 1 | **Jimmy Ryan (IRE)**[15] [3273] 3-8-12 **86** | TQuinn 8 | 98 |
| | | | (TDMccarthy) *swtg: taken down early: pressed wnr: rdn and ev ch over 1f out: nt qckn fnl f* | **11/2**[2] | |
| -300 | 3 | 1 | **Sir Desmond**[14] [3309] 6-8-8 **77** | (p) EAhern 1 | 86 |
| | | | (RGuest) *lw: racd in last pair: pushed along 1/2-way: eased towards outer fr 1f out: nt clr run tl ins fnl f: r.o wl last 100yds* | **14/1** | |
| 3101 | 4 | 1 ¼ | **Whistler**[8] [3480] 7-9-8 **91** | (p) DaneO'Neill 2 | 95 |
| | | | (JMBradley) *pushed along in last after 1f: prog on outer wl over 1f out: chsd ldng pair ins fnl f: no imp: lost 3rd nr fin* | **6/1**[3] | |
| 0014 | 5 | ¾ | **Dancing Mystery**[13] [3339] 10-8-13 **82** | SCarson 4 | 84 |
| | | | (EAWheeler) *settled in last trio: effrt over 1f out: no imp on ldrs* | **5/1**[1] | |
| -240 | 6 | ½ | **Texas Gold**[21] [3074] 6-9-6 **89** | MartinDwyer 7 | 89 |
| | | | (WRMuir) *lw: taken down early: t.k.h: cl up: pushed along over 1f out: wknd fnl f* | **5/1**[1] | |
| 4400 | 6 | dht | **Fromsong (IRE)**[7] [3537] 6-10-0 **97** | JPMurtagh 9 | 97 |
| | | | (BRMillman) *lw: cl up: rdn and nt qckn over 1f out: fdd* | **10/1** | |
| 0000 | 8 | 9 | **Whitbarrow (IRE)**[15] [3266] 5-9-13 **96** | RLMoore 3 | 63 |
| | | | (JMBradley) *pressed ldrs to 1/2-way: wknd wl over 1f out: bhd fnl f* | **13/2** | |

62.66 secs (0.73) **Going Correction** +0.275s/f (Good)
**WFA** 3 from 4yo+ 5lb **8** Ran SP% **108.8**
Speed ratings: **105,103,101,99,98 97,97,83**CSF £29.06 CT £322.63 TOTE £5.90: £1.70, £2.10, £3.60; EX 44.90.
**Owner** R A Bernard **Bred** T R Lock **Trained** Ogbourne Maisey, Wilts

**FOCUS**
Numerically not as competitive as it might have been, and the pace through the first furlong was pretty steady, with nobody that keen to lead. As a result, it proved hard to come from off the pace, and while the winner has been rated as back to his best and the second improving again, the result may want treating with a little caution.

**NOTEBOOK**
**Pivotal Point** had excuses on his first two starts, but there were no problems this time around and he made no mistake. He had the run of the race in front and may be slightly flattered by the bare form, but he is lightly raced this season and open to some improvement. He picks up just a 3lb penalty for the Stewards Cup, but connections indicated he is more likely to return here under an 8lb penalty for the Hong Kong Jockey Club Sprint. *Official explanation: trainer said, regarding the improved form shown, gelding had been unsuited by the low draw over 6f last time out at Windsor*
**Jimmy Ryan(IRE)**, up 5lb for his recent Newmarket success, ran well considering he got quite warm and jumped the path soon after the start. However, he was well placed considering how the race was run. *Official explanation: jockey said colt jumped the road crossing and was unsuited by good ground*
**Sir Desmond** ◆ did best of those from off the pace. He did not enjoy the best of runs and posted a fine effort considering a stronger pace would have suited better. He gained his last success in this month last year and, back on a winning mark, is one to keep an eye on for a similar event.
**Whistler** did not have the race run to suit and is better than this.
**Dancing Mystery** would have preferred a stronger gallop. *Official explanation: jockey said gelding stumbled a furlong out*
**Texas Gold** would have been seen to better effect in a stronger-run race. *Official explanation: trainer said gelding was unsuited by the good ground*
**Fromsong(IRE)** *Official explanation: jockey said gelding had a breathing problem and lost its action*

## 3724 MICHAEL PAGE INTERNATIONAL SILVER TROPHY STKS (GROUP 3) — 1m (R)

2:00 (2:01) (A) 4-Y-0+ — £31,900 (£12,100; £6,050; £2,750) Stalls High

| Form | | | | | RPR |
|---|---|---|---|---|---|
| 0112 | 1 | | **Shot To Fame (USA)**[14] [3323] 5-8-13 107 | LDettori 10 | 114 |
| | | | (PWHarris) *trckd ldr to over 5f out: styd prom: rdn and effrt over 1f out: narrow ld ins fnl f: jst hld on* | **6/1**[2] | |
| 2031 | 2 | hd | **Gateman**[14] [3323] 7-9-2 113 | JFanning 4 | 117 |
| | | | (MJohnston) *b.hind: led: rdn and jnd over 2f out: battled on wl: narrowly hdd ins fnl f: rallied: jst hld* | **13/2**[3] | |
| 3150 | 3 | ¾ | **Hurricane Alan (IRE)**[25] [2957] 4-9-4 114 | PDobbs 5 | 117 |
| | | | (RHannon) *lw: hld up in last trio: prog over 2f out: styd on wl to take 3rd nr fin* | **16/1** | |
| 0601 | 4 | shd | **Pentecost**[7] [3539] 5-8-13 94 | MartinDwyer 7 | 112 |
| | | | (AMBalding) *hld up in last: rdn 2f out: prog over 1f out: r.o wl last 150yds: gaining fast at fin* | **20/1** | |
| 1635 | 5 | ½ | **Babodana**[14] [3323] 4-8-13 110 | TQuinn 8 | 110 |
| | | | (MHTompkins) *trckd ldrs: effrt on inner 2f out: chsd ldng pair ins fnl f: no imp and lost 2 pls nr fin* | **16/1** | |
| -430 | 6 | 1 | **Bowman's Crossing (IRE)**[25] [2957] 5-8-13 | MJKinane 6 | 108 |
| | | | (DOughton, Hong Kong) *racd in midfield: rdn over 2f out: one pce and no prog* | **6/1**[2] | |
| -023 | 7 | 1 ¼ | **Salselon**[25] [2957] 5-9-2 118 | (b) JPMurtagh 2 | 108 |
| | | | (LMCumani) *lw: trckd ldrs: shkn up wl over 1f out: fnd nil and btn after* | **7/4**[1] | |
| 1-24 | 8 | nk | **New Seeker**[22] [3036] 4-8-13 103 | JQuinn 3 | 105 |
| | | | (CGCox) *lw: prom: trckd ldr over 5f out: chal and upsides over 2f out to jst over 1f out: wknd* | **7/1** | |
| 0525 | 9 | 5 | **Dutch Gold (USA)**[8] [3484] 4-8-13 110 | (b) EAhern 9 | 93 |
| | | | (CEBrittain) *a in last trio: rdn and no prog over 2f out: sn wknd* | **33/1** | |
| 5214 | 10 | 2 ½ | **Suggestive**[13] [3361] 6-8-13 109 | (b) MHills 1 | 87 |
| | | | (WJHaggas) *racd freely in midfield: rdn over 2f out: fnd nil: wknd wl over 1f out* | **25/1** | |

1m 42.49s (-0.55) **Going Correction** +0.275s/f (Good) **10** Ran SP% **114.1**
Speed ratings: **113,112,112,111,111 110,109,108,103,101**CSF £42.50 TOTE £6.50: £2.00, £2.20, £4.40; EX 28.10.
**Owner** The Conquistadors **Bred** Eric Puerari **Trained** Ringshall, Bucks

**FOCUS**
This had the look of a really competitive Group Three, but the early pace was surprisingly moderate and several horses failed to give their true running. The form is anchored by fourth-placed Pentecost and may want treating with a little caution.

**NOTEBOOK**
**Shot To Fame(USA)**, just outbattled by Gateman in Listed company at Windsor on his previous start, managed to get the better of that rival this time around, but it was hard work. He is in the form of his life and would command respect wherever he goes next.
**Gateman** is as tough as they come and ran another blinder, only just failing to confirm recent Windsor placings with the eventual winner. Connections are itching to step him up to ten furlongs and are eyeing the Royal Whip at The Curragh.
**Hurricane Alan(IRE)** did well to finish so close considering he was held up well off the ordinary early pace. This was a good effort under his penalty, and he will be given his chance in the Sussex Stakes, which his stable won last year with a similar sort.
**Pentecost** deserved to take his chance in this company off the back of his recent Sandown success, despite having it all to do at the weights. He justified the decision with what was a fine run considering a stronger pace would have suited better. He is now set to take his chance in the William Hill Mile at Goodwood off a mark of 98.
**Babodana** ran respectably, but he is just not quite seeing his races out for whatever reason.
**Bowman's Crossing(IRE)** failed to build on his Queen Anne effort.
**Salselon**, a good third despite not having things go his way in the Queen Anne on his previous start, ran a long way below that form on this drop in grade. A stronger pace would surely have seen him in better light and he may be worth another chance, although he appears quite hard to win with.
**New Seeker**, stepping up to Group company for the first time, looked the most likely winner two out, but dropped out disappointingly.
**Suggestive** would have been unsuited by the moderate early pace.

## 3725 TOTESPORT STKS (HERITAGE H'CAP) — 2m 45y

2:30 (2:31) (B) (0-105,100) 3-Y-0+ — £37,700 (£14,300; £7,150; £3,250) Stalls High

| Form | | | | | RPR |
|---|---|---|---|---|---|
| 1-01 | 1 | | **Dorothy's Friend**[21] [3095] 4-8-13 **85** | SDrowne 6 | 96 |
| | | | (RCharlton) *lw: racd in midfield: rdn and prog fr 2f out: styd on wl to ld last 50yds: hld on* | **5/1**[1] | |
| -000 | 2 | nk | **Random Quest**[35] [2684] 6-8-12 **84** | RLMoore 4 | 95 |
| | | | (BJLlewellyn) *lw: racd towards rr: plenty to do wl over 2f out: gd prog on outer over 1f out: r.o to chal last 100yds: jst hld* | **22/1** | |
| 4031 | 3 | nk | **Thewhirlingdervish (IRE)**[20] [3120] 6-8-10 **82** | TQuinn 2 | 92 |
| | | | (TDEasterby) *lw: led after 2f to after 3f: sttd bhd ldrs: effrt over 2f out: chsd ldr wl over 1f out: led last 100yds to last 50yds: kpt* | **14/1** | |
| 0020 | 4 | nk | **Promoter**[14] [3310] 4-9-2 **88** | EAhern 13 | 98 |
| | | | (JNoseda) *t.k.h: hld up towards rr: rdn and prog fr 2f out: carried hd high but styd on to chal fnl f: nt qckn* | **12/1** | |
| 0001 | 5 | ¾ | **Double Obsession**[25] [2958] 4-9-9 **95** | (v) JFEgan 8 | 104 |
| | | | (MJohnston) *mde most: drew 4l clr over 3f out: hdd & wknd last 100yds* | **8/1**[3] | |
| 40/0 | 6 | 2 | **Self Defense**[14] [3310] 7-10-0 **100** | JPMurtagh 9 | 107 |
| | | | (PRChamings) *lw: prom: n.m.r and steadily lost pl fr 7f out: wl in rr 3f out: gd prog on wd outside over 1f out: wknd last 100yds* | **25/1** | |
| 4330 | 7 | 1 ½ | **Sentry (IRE)**[25] [2958] 4-8-13 **85** | DaneO'Neill 11 | 90 |
| | | | (JHMGosden) *trckd ldrs: steadily lost pl fr 6f out: wl in rr 3f out: nt clr run over 2f out: styd on again fr over 1f out* | **20/1** | |
| 6-00 | 8 | ½ | **High Action (USA)**[41] [1821] 4-8-13 **85** | (t) PDobbs 1 | 89 |
| | | | (IanWilliams) *lw: trckd ldrs: rdn over 2f out: no imp: fdd over 1f out* | **50/1** | |
| 0121 | 9 | 1 ¼ | **Dr Sharp (IRE)**[9] [3449] 4-8-8 **80** | DaleGibson 16 | 83 |
| | | | (TPTate) *lw: t.k.h: prom: chsd ldr wl over 2f out to wl over 1f out: wknd* | **9/1** | |
| 0625 | 10 | 5 | **Kristensen**[14] [3310] 5-8-10 **82** | MJKinane 7 | 79 |
| | | | (DEddy) *prom: chsd ldr 11f out to 9f out: hrd rdn to dispute 2nd pl over 2f out: wknd over 1f out* | **14/1** | |
| 0500 | 11 | ½ | **Mana D'Argent (IRE)**[25] [2958] 7-9-0 **86** | JFanning 3 | 82 |
| | | | (MJohnston) *settled wl in rr: sme prog on inner over 3f out: nt clr run sn after: no hdwy fnl 2f* | **8/1**[3] | |

-420 **12** *1 1/4* **Distant Prospect (IRE)**[14] 3310 7-9-7 **93**.................... MartinDwyer 14 88
(AMBalding) *hld up in rr: lost pl and last whn hmpd 4f out: no ch after: modest late prog* **14/1**

4226 **13** *6* **Pagan Dance (IRE)**[14] 3310 5-9-8 **94**................................(p) LDettori 10 82
(MrsAJPerrett) *settled towards rr: plenty to do whn nt clr run 3f out: no prog after: wknd over 1f out* **11/2**[2]

**14** *3/4* **Almah (SAF)**[343] 6-9-6 **95**.................................... LisaJones(3) 15 82
(MissVenetiaWilliams) *a towards rr: rdn and struggling 3f out* **100/1**

S223 **15** *2 1/2* **Theatre (USA)**[8] 3485 5-8-10 **82**........................................ PDoe 5 66
(JamiePoulton) *dwlt and rdn early: wl in rr: effrt on outer whn squeezed out wl over 1f out: wknd* **22/1**

-020 **16** *hd* **Escayola (IRE)**[14] 3310 4-9-1 **87**..........................................(b) MHills 17 70
(WJHaggas) *t.k.h: racd on inner in midfield: nt clr run over 3f out and over 2f out: hanging rt and wknd rapidly over 1f out* **10/1**

4012 **17** *3* **Sahem (IRE)**[21] 3078 7-8-10 **82**........................................ RHughes 12 62
(DEddy) *hld up in last trio: rapid prog to chse ldr 9f out: rdn 5f out: wknd wl over 2f out* **33/1**

3m 35.97s (1.13) **Going Correction** +0.275s/f (Good) **17** Ran SP% **124.3**
Speed ratings: **108,107,107,107,107 106,105,105,104,102 101,101,98,97,96 96,94**CSF £121.07 CT £1478.57 TOTE £4.90: £1.40, £7.70, £2.40, £5.30; EX 220.20 TRIFECTA Not won..
**Owner** Mountgrange Stud **Bred** Floors Farming And Christopher J Heath **Trained** Beckhampton, Wilts

**FOCUS**
A really competitive staying handicap and strong form. They went just an ordinary gallop for most of the race, but things really quickened over three out when Double Obsession kicked for home, and it was no surprise to see them finish so close together.

**NOTEBOOK**
**Dorothy's Friend** would have been completing a five-timer but for a below-par reappearance. Raised 7lb for his recent Newmarket success, he was 23lb higher than when gaining his first win and showed himself still highly progressive with a narrow victory, responding well to pressure to get on top close home. There could yet be more to come and the Cesarewitch is his main aim.
**Random Quest** bounced right back to form off a mark 7lb lower than when last successful, finishing as well as anything from a long way off the speed. He now heads for the Goodwood Stakes.
**Thewhirlingdervish(IRE)**, 5lb higher than when successful at Pontefract on his previous outing, was only just held. He remains one to keep on the right side of.
**Promoter** was given plenty to do and did not look overly keen to make up ground in the straight. He has just a maiden win to his name.
**Double Obsession**, 9lb higher than when successful at the Royal meeting on his previous outing, benefited from a positive ride and only just failed to nick this. A fine effort considering faster ground would have suited better.
**Self Defense** followed up his good Northumberland Plate run with another sound effort. The Handicapper has taken no chances putting him on a mark of 100, but he should remain competitive in similar events.
**Mana D'Argent(IRE)** ◆ loves this place, but was not at his best. He only needs to drop 2lb to be back on his last winning mark and is one to keep an eye on, especially considering this is his time of year.
**Pagan Dance(IRE)** *Official explanation: jockey said gelding stumbled coming out of the stalls and lost its action in home straight*

## 3726 ALFRED FRANKS & BARTLETT SUNGLASSES NOVICE STKS 7f
**3:05** (3:10) (D) 2-Y-O **£5,564** (£1,712; £856; £428) **Stalls** Low

Form RPR

2 **1** **Cape Greko**[16] 3240 2-8-12 ........................................ MartinDwyer 3 93+
(AMBalding) *lw: t.k.h: hld up bhd ldrs: prog to chse ldr over 1f out: shkn up to ld ins fnl f: styd on wl* **7/2**[2]

16 **2** *3/4* **Berkhamsted (IRE)**[25] 2954 2-9-0 ...................................... LDettori 4 93
(JAOsborne) *lw: trckd ldr: led wl over 1f out: rdn and hdd ins fnl f: styd on but a hld* **11/4**[1]

1 **3** *1 3/4* **Propinquity**[16] 3241 2-9-5 ........................................ JPMurtagh 9 94
(PWHarris) *led to wl over 1f out: sn outpcd: kpt on ins fnl f* **4/1**[3]

**4** *1 1/4* **Kharish (IRE)** 2-8-8 ........................................ EAhern 8 80
(JNoseda) *lengthy: scope: s.s: hld up in rr: prog on outer 2f out: one pce fr over 1f out* **7/1**

23 **5** *2 1/2* **Chalison (IRE)**[52] 2225 2-8-12 ........................................ RHughes 1 77
(RHannon) *racd in midfield: rdn over 2f out: outpcd and btn over 1f out* **5/1**

1 **6** *1/2* **Sky Crusader**[15] 3259 2-9-0 ........................................ SDrowne 2 78
(RIngram) *lw: prom: rdn and ev ch wl over 1f out: wknd* **8/1**

**7** *nk* **Zabeel Palace** 2-8-8 ........................................ NPollard 7 71
(DRLoder) *unf: scope: bit bkwd: trckd ldrs: pushed along and lost pl over 2f out: n.d after* **16/1**

**8** *1 1/4* **Clasp** 2-8-8 ........................................ IMongan 6 68
(MLWBell) *neat: dwlt: rn green: in tch to 2f out: wknd* **66/1**

**9** *11* **Patronofconfucius (IRE)** 2-8-8 ........................................ TQuinn 5 41
(JRBoyle) *tall: narrow: bit bkwd: s.s: a last: wknd over 2f out* **50/1**

1m 32.99s (3.32) **Going Correction** +0.275s/f (Good) **9** Ran SP% **118.5**
Speed ratings: **92,91,89,87,84 84,83,82,69**CSF £13.99 TOTE £4.70: £1.80, £1.50, £1.70; EX 17.30.
**Owner** Holistic Racing Ltd **Bred** Snailwell Stud Co Ltd **Trained** Kingsclere, Hants
■ Stewards Enquiry : L Dettori one-day ban: hit colt in an incorrect place (Jul 21st)

**FOCUS**
A competitive looking novice, featuring a mix of winners, promising maidens and well-bred newcomers. Strong form, and the winner improved around three lengths on his promising debut.

**NOTEBOOK**
**Cape Greko**, runner-up to a half-brother to Russian Rhythm on his debut (five lengths clear of third) at Salisbury, confirmed that promise to get off the mark. His stable have some nice juveniles in their care this season and this Derby entry should progress again. He could head for the Champagne Stakes at Doncaster.
**Berkhamsted(IRE)**, sixth in arguably just an ordinary Coventry Stakes off the back of a break, ran his race on this step up in trip and cannot have any excuses.
**Propinquity** created a good impression when making a winning debut at Salisbury and improved on that run with a good effort under his big penalty.
**Kharish(IRE)** ◆, a 300,000euros yearling, half-brother to a useful five-furlong two-year-old winner, and a mile three-year-old scorer, made a very pleasing debut. He should improve and it will be most disappointing if he does not find a maiden before stepping back up in class.
**Chalison(IRE)** was a little bit disappointing on this step up to seven furlongs, although this was his first run in 52 days. He will find things much easier in maiden company.
**Sky Crusader** landed a bit of a touch when winning on his debut at Folkestone, but was well held in this better company. Given the way he travelled, he may just prove better over six furlongs.

## 3727 MICHAEL PAGE INTERNATIONAL NURSERY 6f
**3:40** (3:40) (D) 2-Y-O **£5,369** (£1,652; £826; £413) **Stalls** Low

Form RPR

51 **1** **Sacred Nuts (IRE)**[24] 2972 2-9-1 **82**.................................... LDettori 6 90+
(MLWBell) *lw: hld up in midfield: squeezed through to chse ldr over 1f out: r.o wl to ld last 50yds* **3/1**[1]

541 **2** *nk* **Fiefdom (IRE)**[27] 2904 2-9-7 **88**.................................... JFanning 3 95
(MJohnston) *lw: fast away: led: 2l clr ent fnl f: collared last 50yds* **10/3**[2]

521 **3** *2 1/2* **Bentley's Bush (IRE)**[22] 3045 2-9-1 **82**.................................... RHughes 1 82
(RHannon) *lw: wl in tch: chsd ldr 2f out to over 1f out: edgd lft and one pce fnl f* **11/2**[3]

614 **4** *1/2* **Canton (IRE)**[66] 1878 2-9-5 **86**.................................... RLMoore 5 84
(RHannon) *hld up in midfield: effrt 2f out: styng on same pce whn n.m.r ins fnl f* **13/2**

0520 **5** *1 1/4* **Clinet (IRE)**[7] 3532 2-7-12 **65** oh1.................................... JQuinn 4 59
(PMPhelan) *s.s: last and sn detached: rdn and prog over 2f out: one pce fnl f* **33/1**

310 **6** *3/4* **Alsu (IRE)**[15] 3286 2-8-6 **73**.................................... MartinDwyer 9 65
(AMBalding) *prom on outer: rdn over 2f out: wknd jst over 1f out* **12/1**

13 **7** *2* **Observer (IRE)**[29] 2831 2-9-4 **85**.................................... NPollard 8 71
(DRLoder) *hld up in rr: nt clr run briefly wl over 1f out: rdn and no prog after* **8/1**

2160 **8** *3/4* **Norcroft**[57] 2086 2-9-3 **84**.................................... JPMurtagh 2 68
(NACallaghan) *lw: racd in last pair: rdn over 2f out: sn no prog and btn* **14/1**

043 **9** *1 1/4* **Lily Lenat**[28] 2884 2-8-5 **72**.................................... EAhern 7 52
(JRBoyle) *lw: chsd ldr to 2f out: losing pl whn bmpd over 1f out* **12/1**

1m 18.12s (2.13) **Going Correction** +0.275s/f (Good) **9** Ran SP% **112.9**
Speed ratings: **96,95,92,91,89 88,86,85,83**CSF £12.69 CT £50.69 TOTE £3.00: £1.10, £1.70, £1.50; EX 13.40.
**Owner** Fitzroy Thoroughbreds **Bred** John Foley **Trained** Newmarket, Suffolk

**FOCUS**
A reasonable nursery and the winner is clearly progressing. The figures shown as 'official ratings' are estimates for guidance only.

**NOTEBOOK**
**Sacred Nuts(IRE)** followed up his Hamilton maiden success with a really game effort. He had to be brave to take the gaps and really picked up when in the clear. There should be even more to come.
**Fiefdom(IRE)** got a very easy lead and nearly made every yard with a really tough effort. He had everything go his way and this would as good as he is, although improvement cannot be ruled out.
**Bentley's Bush(IRE)**, off the mark at Goodwood on her previous start, could not go by the Johnston runner when making her effort and was well held.
**Canton(IRE)**, racing for the first time in 66 days, appreciated this return to a galloping track and ran respectably.
**Clinet(IRE)** was given plenty to do and never really threatened.
**Lily Lenat** *Official explanation: jockey said filly hung right throughout and lost its action from half way*

## 3728 MITSUBISHI ELECTRIC CLASSIFIED STKS 1m (R)
**4:15** (4:16) (D) 3-Y-O **£5,499** (£1,692; £846; £423) **Stalls** High

Form RPR

5-10 **1** **Dubois**[39] 2558 3-8-13 82..........................................(vt) LDettori 7 96
(SaeedBinSuroor) *lw: mde all: racd against far rail to 1/2-way: 6l clr whn crossed to inner over 3f out: coaxed along fnl 2f: unchal* **9/2**[1]

-404 **2** *3* **Saffron Fox**[39] 2557 3-8-9 81.......................................... EAhern 3 85
(JGPortman) *prom in chsng gp: rdn over 2f out: styd on to take 2nd wl ins fnl f: no ch w wnr* **9/1**

5-26 **3** *3/4* **Desert Cristal (IRE)**[73] 1704 3-8-8 80.............................. MartinDwyer 6 82
(JRBoyle) *racd in 2nd: 6l bhd wnr over 3f out but clr of rest: no imp 2f out: lost 2nd wl ins fnl f* **14/1**

2140 **4** *nk* **Mission Man**[14] 3317 3-8-11 80.......................................... RLMoore 10 85
(RHannon) *lw: hld up towards rr: prog over 2f out: kpt on fr over 1f out: n.d* **20/1**

321 **5** *2* **Marbush (IRE)**[42] 2487 3-9-2 85.......................................... MJKinane 9 85
(MAJarvis) *hld up in rr: prog over 2f out: disp 3rd pl 1f out: wknd* **9/2**[1]

51 **6** *3* **Pass The Port**[29] 2853 3-8-11 80.......................................... JPMurtagh 5 73
(JRFanshawe) *hld up in rr: kpt on fnl 2f: no ch* **7/1**[3]

0-40 **7** *1/2* **Lord Links (IRE)**[23] 3001 3-9-1 84.......................................... RHughes 8 76
(RHannon) *lw: racd towards rr: effrt but no ch whn hmpd on inner wl over 1f out: no prog after* **10/1**

6103 **8** *2* **Verkhotina**[14] 3306 3-8-8 80.......................................... SDrowne 11 64
(RCharlton) *b. off hind: hld up in last pair: no prog 2f out* **6/1**[2]

4142 **9** *1/2* **Boule D'Or (IRE)**[7] 3543 3-9-2 85.......................................... NDay 1 71
(RIngram) *lw: prom in chsng gp: wknd over 1f out* **9/2**[1]

-000 **10** *1 3/4* **Fragrant Star**[14] 3320 3-8-8 74.......................................... JQuinn 2 59
(CEBrittain) *prom in chsng gp: wknd and edgd rt 2f out* **50/1**

-556 **11** *1/2* **Glebe Garden**[14] 3306 3-8-9 81.......................................... IMongan 4 59
(MLWBell) *b.hind: dwlt: a in last trio: no prog 2f out* **25/1**

1m 43.44s (0.40) **Going Correction** +0.275s/f (Good) **11** Ran SP% **117.7**
Speed ratings: **109,106,105,104,102 99,99,97,96,95 94**CSF £44.71 TOTE £3.70: £1.80, £2.40, £4.70; EX 62.50 Place 6 £95.06, Place 5 £39.05.
**Owner** Godolphin **Bred** Cheveley Park Stud Ltd **Trained** Newmarket, Suffolk

**FOCUS**
The form could be suspect even though the winning time was very good for the grade. Dettori gave his weighing room colleagues a lesson in riding, taking Dubois over to the far rail soon after the start so he could race alone and possibly enjoy better ground. When he re-joined the main group, he was well clear and nothing could land a blow.

**NOTEBOOK**
**Dubois**, dropped back from ten furlongs, appeared to show much improved form but benefited from a very shrewd ride from Dettori and may well have been flattered. He was taken over to the far rail soon after the start whilst every other jockeys elected to stay where they were and, well clear when re-joining the main group, he had no trouble maintaining the advantage.
**Saffron Fox**, well favoured by the weights, was unable to peg back the winner in the straight, but fnished best of the rest and emerged with credit.
**Desert Cristal(IRE)** found this easier than the Listed race she contested last time, but could simply not land a telling blow.
**Mission Man**, back up to a mile, did not have the race run to suit.
**Marbush(IRE)** is another who did not have things go his way and he should be capable of much better.
**Verkhotina**, stepping up from seven furlongs, could not get into it.
**Boule D'Or(IRE)** was below form, even allowing for the way the race was run, and has to be considered disappointing.
**Fragrant Star** *Official explanation: jockey said filly had a breathing problem*
T/Plt: £316.30 to a £1 stake. Pool: £89,121.80. 205.65 winning tickets. T/Qpdt: £30.10 to a £1 stake. Pool: £5,258.00. 129.10 winning tickets. JN

# 3701 CHESTER (L-H)

## Saturday, July 10

**OFFICIAL GOING: Good**

Wind: almost nil Weather: lt showers

## 3729 MERCEDES-BENZ OF NORTH WALES MAIDEN AUCTION STKS — 5f 16y

**2:25** (2:29) (E) 2-Y-O — **£3,376** (£1,039; £519; £259) **Stalls** Low

Form — RPR

032 **1** **Bold Minstrel (IRE)**[8] [3491] 2-8-7 .......... FNorton 7 70
(MQuinn) *prom: rdn to ld 1f out: hld on wl* **15/8**[1]

**2** *shd* **Sound That Alarm** 2-8-11 .......... SWKelly 4 74
(GAButler) *chsd ldrs: rdn over 1f out: ev ch ins fnl f: r.o* **10/3**[2]

0330 **3** *2* **Chilali (IRE)**[8] [3469] 2-8-2 .......... SRighton 1 58
(ABerry) *led: rdn and hdd 1f out: no ex ins fnl f* **10/1**

0 **4** *2 ½* **Open Verdict (IRE)**[29] [2860] 2-8-9 .......... EStack 5 56
(APJarvis) *pushed along and outpcd after 1f: styd on fnl f* **12/1**

0 **5** *nk* **Carmania (IRE)**[9] [3444] 2-8-7 .......... WSupple 8 53
(RPElliott) *in tch: rdn over 2f out: wknd fnl f* **50/1**

053 **6** *¾* **Leonalto (IRE)**[76] [1638] 2-8-7 .......... (b) JFortune 3 50
(BJMeehan) *chsd ldrs: rdn over 2f out: wknd 1f out* **9/2**[3]

5422 **7** *½* **Lady Hopeful (IRE)**[12] [3366] 2-7-9 .......... DFentiman(7) 9 43
(RPElliott) *outpcd: effrt whn hung rt over 1f out: no imp* **13/2**

**8** *5* **Swallow Falls (IRE)** 2-8-2 .......... ANicholls 2 26
(DMccain) *s.i.s: a outpcd* **20/1**

00 **9** *6* **Xeight Express (IRE)**[9] [3444] 2-8-2 .......... CCatlin 6 5
(MABuckley) *a outpcd* **66/1**

61.61 secs (-0.37) **Going Correction** -0.125s/f (Firm) **9** Ran SP% **114.4**

Speed ratings: **97,96,93,89,89 87,87,79,69**CSF £7.86 TOTE £2.80: £1.20, £1.80, £2.60; EX 10.60.

**Owner** The Boys From The Shed Partnership **Bred** John & Denis Dunne **Trained** Sparsholt, Oxon

**FOCUS**

A modest maiden auction in which the winner did not need to be at his best.

**NOTEBOOK**

**Bold Minstrel(IRE)** overcame an unfavourable draw to break his duck, holding on well in the end. Although possessing plenty of pace, he may not be inconvenienced by another furlong.

**Sound That Alarm**, a 29,000gns purchase and half-brother to juvenile winners in Italy and Spain, ran a race full of promise on his debut at a track not considered an ideal venue for racecourse debutants. He made the winner fight in the short straight and looks the type to step up on this effort, possibly over further, even though there is plenty of speed on the dam's side.

**Chilali(IRE)**, the most experienced runner in the line-up, made good use of pole position, showing plenty of pace before being mastered by the front pair. This was a better effort than when last seen. *Official explanation: jockey said filly hung right-handed, especially in closing stages*

**Open Verdict(IRE)** struggled to go the early pace around the tight turns, but this was an improved run from his debut effort and a more conventional track will help.

**Carmania(IRE)** showed a bit more this time before fading.

**Leonalto(IRE)** may have a needed this run after a lay off, but that said, his previous form was nothing to write home about and this is about as good as he is.

**Lady Hopeful(IRE)** was inconvenienced by the track and drop in trip.

## 3730 MERCEDES-BENZ OF LIVERPOOL CONDITIONS STKS — 7f 2y

**3:00** (3:00) (B) 3-Y-O+ — **£12,383** (£4,697; £2,348; £1,067) **Stalls** Low

Form — RPR

3353 **1** **Vanderlin**[14] [3323] 5-9-2 107 .......... LPKeniry 6 112
(AMBalding) *hld up: hdwy over 2f out: led ins fnl f: r.o* **10/3**[3]

5542 **2** *1 ¾* **Makhlab (USA)**[37] [2623] 4-9-2 108 .......... (b¹) WSupple 5 107
(BWHills) *rdn along to chse ldrs: r.o ins fnl f* **2/1**[2]

0042 **3** *½* **Millennium Force**[13] [3361] 6-8-13 107 .......... CCatlin 4 103
(MRChannon) *w ldr: led over 1f out: hdd ins fnl f: no ex* **7/4**[1]

0300 **4** *1 ½* **Glaramara**[24] [2966] 3-8-7 97 ow2 .......... JFortune 3 101
(ABailey) *hld up: rdn over 1f out: styd on* **6/1**

0460 **5** *3 ½* **Telepathic (IRE)**[13] [3337] 4-8-13 57 .......... PPMathers 2 90?
(ABerry) *trckd ldrs: rdn over 1f out: sn wknd* **50/1**

0200 **6** *6* **Jalouhar**[7] [3522] 4-8-13 46 .......... TWoodley 1 75?
(BPJBaugh) *led: rdn and hdd over 1f out: sn wknd* **66/1**

1m 25.36s (-2.93) **Going Correction** -0.125s/f (Firm)

**WFA** 3 from 4yo+ 8lb **6** Ran SP% **110.5**

Speed ratings: **111,109,108,106,102 95**CSF £10.09 TOTE £4.70: £2.30, £1.70; EX 15.00.

**Owner** J C, J R And S R Hitchins **Bred** Ellway Breeding **Trained** Kingsclere, Hants

**FOCUS**

The pace was strong but the result was messy, with no-hopers too close for comfort from a handicapping point of view.

**NOTEBOOK**

**Vanderlin** was suited by the turning nature of this course and the strong gallop. He is reportedly being aimed at Goodwood's Group Three Lennox Stakes, where he will need to show improvement.

**Makhlab(USA)** was ridden along early to get a decent position and, in first-time blinkers, ran respectably considering he lost a shoe. *Official explanation: trainer's representative said colt lost a front shoe*

**Millennium Force** was favoured on the official figures but for the third time this year finished behind the runner-up. This was disappointing.

**Glaramara** ran as well as could have been expected on ground to suit. *Official explanation: jockey said colt hung badly left-handed*

**Telepathic(IRE)** had a mountain to climb but was not beaten out of sight as the figures seem to suggest he would be.

## 3731 MERCEDES-BENZ OF SOUTHPORT H'CAP — 1m 2f 75y

**3:35** (3:36) (D) (0-80,80) 4-Y-O+ — **£5,512** (£1,696; £848; £424) **Stalls** High

Form — RPR

6242 **1** **Opening Ceremony (USA)**[6] [3563] 5-9-4 **70** .......... LVickers 8 80
(RAFahey) *hld up: hdwy 2f out: nt clr run fr over 1f out tl ins fnl f: qcknd to ld towards fin* **9/1**

5112 **2** *½* **Yenaled**[32] [2753] 7-8-9 **68** .......... DonnaCaldwell(7) 12 77
(KARyan) *s.i.s: bhd: hdwy whn swtchd rt over 1f out: r.o ins fnl f* **8/1**[3]

1204 **3** *½* **Aleron (IRE)**[6] [3563] 6-9-3 **72** .......... (p) LPKeniry(3) 7 80
(JJQuinn) *chsd ldrs: rdn to ld 1f out: hdd and nt qckn towards fin* **8/1**[3]

5145 **4** *¾* **Low Cloud**[2] [3660] 4-9-10 **76** .......... FNorton 6 83
(DNicholls) *midfield: hdwy 2f out: r.o ins fnl f* **14/1**

-006 **5** *hd* **Rani Two**[14] [3327] 5-9-5 **71** .......... CCatlin 1 77
(WMBrisbourne) *in tch: hdwy over 3f out: nt clr run over 1f out: sn rdn: r.o ins fnl f* **6/1**[1]

3103 **6** *shd* **Giunchiglio**[14] [3291] 5-8-12 **64** .......... SWKelly 5 70
(WMBrisbourne) *midfield: hdwy over 2f out: rdn and ev ch over 1f out: nt qckn towards finsih* **16/1**

0-00 **7** *hd* **Luxor**[21] [3082] 7-7-5 **50** oh13 .......... DFentiman(7) 14 56?
(WMBrisbourne) *led: rdn 3f out: hdd 1f out: no ex towards fin* **33/1**

5064 **8** *1 ¼* **Gallant Boy (IRE)**[3] [3629] 5-9-0 **69** .......... (vt) FPFerris(3) 3 73+
(PDEvans) *hld up: hdwy over 1f out: nt clr run ins fnl f: nt rcvr* **8/1**[3]

3501 **9** *shd* **War Owl (USA)**[33] [2738] 7-9-4 **73** .......... ABeech(3) 15 77
(IanWilliams) *in tch: hdwy 4f out: rdn over 1f out: no ex towards fin* **10/1**

1032 **10** *hd* **Summer Bounty**[16] [3238] 8-9-10 **76** .......... JFortune 10 79
(FJordan) *midfield: hdwy whn nt clr run 2f out: swtchd rt over 1f out: styd on ins fnl f* **7/1**[2]

0303 **11** *1 ½* **Nuzzle**[4] [3609] 4-7-12 **50** oh5 .......... RBrisland 4 50
(MQuinn) *chsd ldr: rdn and ev ch over 1f out: wknd ins fnl f* **20/1**

2252 **12** *1 ¼* **Compton Dragon (USA)**[7] [3510] 5-9-8 **74** .......... (v) ANicholls 16 72
(DNicholls) *held up: rdn 2f out: n.d* **12/1**

4004 **13** *3 ½* **Lennel**[27] [2753] 6-8-12 **64** .......... (b) JoannaBadger 2 56
(ABailey) *s.s: a bhd* **12/1**

0100 **14** *2* **Prince Of Gold**[7] [3520] 4-9-0 **66** .......... (p) WSupple 9 54
(RHollinshead) *a bhd* **25/1**

-034 **15** *19* **Cat's Whiskers**[14] [3299] 5-9-11 **80** .......... LFletcher(3) 13 34
(MWEasterby) *chsd ldrs: rdn and wkng whn hmpd 2f out: sn eased* **11/1**

2m 11.65s (-0.90) **Going Correction** -0.125s/f (Firm) **15** Ran SP% **127.0**

Speed ratings: **98,97,97,96,96 96,96,95,95,94 93,92,89,88,73**CSF £81.30 CT £620.38 TOTE £17.30: £5.20, £2.40, £3.20; EX 128.10.

**Owner** H Hurst **Bred** Juddmonte Farms Inc **Trained** Musley Bank, N Yorks

**FOCUS**

A decent early pace was set but in the end there were a few denied a run and there was little more than 6 lengths covering the first 12 home, among them a horse 13lb 'wrong' at the weights. The final time was moderate for the class.

**NOTEBOOK**

**Opening Ceremony(USA)** can be a tricky customer but, having waited for daylight down the straight, the gaps eventually appeared for her to pounce at just the right time. Whether she can repeat this is another matter.

**Yenaled** benefited from coming off the strong pace to record a solid effort.

**Aleron(IRE)** chased the leaders before hitting the front for a time in the straight and ran well considering he is probably better over further.

**Low Cloud** performed with credit at a trip he has yet to win over, his two wins having been over a mile.

**Rani Two** ◆ met with trouble in running but showed she could be coming back to form and is one to note, as she is almost down to her last winning mark again.

**Giunchiglio** held every chance but may want the ground a shade faster.

**Luxor** set a good pace and performed admirably considering he was well out of the handicap.

**Gallant Boy(IRE)**, having his third run of the week, was totally denied a run in the straight.

**War Owl(USA)** was not beaten far coming from a wide draw.

**Summer Bounty** did not enjoy the run of the race from a high draw.

**Cat's Whiskers** *Official explanation: jockey said gelding suffered interference in running*

## 3732 MERCEDES-BENZ OF CHESTER CITY WALL STKS (LISTED RACE) — 5f 16y

**4:10** (4:11) (A) 3-Y-O+ — **£17,400** (£6,600; £3,300; £1,500) **Stalls** Low

Form — RPR

0340 **1** **Fire Up The Band**[21] [3074] 5-9-0 99 .......... ANicholls 2 98+
(DNicholls) *sn led: rdn over 1f out: all out* **7/2**[2]

5502 **2** *shd* **Talbot Avenue**[8] [3480] 6-9-0 80 .......... SRighton 5 98
(MMullineaux) *plld hard: in tch: hdwy over 1f out: rdn and r.o ins fnl f* **16/1**

0000 **3** *1 ¼* **Dragon Flyer (IRE)**[25] [2955] 5-8-9 98 .......... FNorton 3 89
(MQuinn) *prom: rdn 2f out: ev ch ins fnl f: no ex cl home* **4/1**[3]

**4** *1 ¼* **Dorubako (IRE)**[48] 3-8-9 .......... SWKelly 1 103+
(HideyukiMori, Japan) *s.i.s: sn outpcd: hdwy over 1f out: nt clr run ins fnl f: nt rcvr* **6/1**

05-4 **5** *1 ¾* **Curfew**[74] [1685] 5-8-9 94 .......... PMakin 6 78
(JRFanshawe) *hld up: nt clr run 3f out: sn rdn and outpcd: styd on ins fnl f: nt trble ldrs* **10/1**

-404 **6** *3* **Dani Ridge (IRE)**[12] [3372] 6-8-9 84 .......... WSupple 4 67
(EJAlston) *prom: rdn over 1f out: sn wknd* **20/1**

2033 **7** *shd* **Bishops Court**[19] [3162] 10-9-0 107 .......... JFortune 9 72
(MrsJRRamsden) *hld up: rdn over 1f out: no imp: b.b.v* **5/2**[1]

0 **8** *½* **Steve's Champ (CHI)**[9] 4-9-4 .......... (t) FDiaz 8 74
(RuneHaugen, Norway) *prom tl pushed along and lost pl 3f out: n.d after* **16/1**

1210 **9** *14* **Dizzy In The Head**[7] [3509] 5-9-0 80 .......... (b) FPFerris 7 19
(PaulJohnson) *led early: remained prom tl rdn: rn wd and wknd over 2f out* **20/1**

59.74 secs (-2.24) **Going Correction** -0.125s/f (Firm)

**WFA** 3 from 4yo+ 5lb **9** Ran SP% **115.5**

Speed ratings: **112,111,109,107,105 100,100,99,76**CSF £57.25 TOTE £4.70: £1.80, £4.00, £1.70; EX 55.80.

**Owner** P Crane, A Barker & S Short **Bred** Miss A J Rawding And P M Crane **Trained** Sessay, N Yorks

**FOCUS**

A good time but the form may not be totally reliable, with the fourth appearing to be unlucky and the favourite breaking a blood vessel.

**NOTEBOOK**

**Fire Up The Band** returned to form with a pacy performance from his low draw to gain compensation for being balloted out of the July Cup. He has entries in some of the top sprint handicaps and the Nunthorpe Stakes this summer.

**Talbot Avenue** ran out of his skin, making the winner run right to the line. It is doubtful if he ran quite as well as the figures suggest, but if he made the cut he would obviously be interesting off his old mark in the Hong Kong Jockey Club Sprint.

**Dragon Flyer(IRE)** was placed yet again in this race. Although without a win for nearly two years, she is certainly game.

**Dorubako(IRE)** ◆ was the hard luck story if the race, as he was slow to get going and denied a run when keeping on inside the final furlong. The Japanese runner was brought over to this country with a stablemate for the July Cup, but was balloted out of that Group One contest. It is difficult to know the strength of his Japanese form, though he has won two races over six furlongs in his homeland this year, but the Prix Maurice de Gheest at Deauville is an objective now. *Official explanation: jockey said colt suffered interference shortly after start*

**Curfew** returned from a short break but struggled to live with the pace and needs further.

**Dani Ridge(IRE)** ran well considering she faced a stiff task at the weights.

**Bishops Court** was disappointing in search of his third win in this race, though it transpired he had bled from the nose. *Official explanation: vet said gelding bled from the nose*

## 3733 MERCEDES-BENZ OF WIRRAL H'CAP — 1m 7f 195y

**4:45** (4:45) (D) (0-80,75) 3-Y-O+ — **£5,447** (£1,676; £838; £419) **Stalls** Low

Form — RPR

0043 **1** **Sudden Flight (IRE)**[9] [3449] 7-8-13 **67** .......... FPFerris(3) 4 74
(PDEvans) *led after 1f: mde rest: rdn over 1f out: styd on wl* **5/4**[1]

3/00 **2** *4* **Weet For Me**[45] [2409] 8-9-10 **75** .......... WSupple 2 77
(RHollinshead) *led 1f: trckd ldr tl jst bef 1/2-way: regained 2nd over 2f out: one pce ins fnl f* **12/1**

P/00 **3** 2 1/2 **Grand Fromage (IRE)**[37] 2613 6-8-9 **60** ... FNorton 1 59
(AKing) *trckd ldrs: rdn and lost pl over 3f out: kpt on ins fnl f* **3/1**[2]
0320 **4** shd **Sarn**[9] 3449 5-7-12 **49** oh6 ... SRighton 6 48
(MMullineaux) *hld up: hdwy over 3f out: outpcd over 2f out: kpt on ins fnl f* **12/1**
0-10 **5** 5 **Herne Bay (IRE)**[13] 2590 4-8-6 **60** ... (p) ABeech(3) 3 53
(ABailey) *trckd ldrs: chsd wnr jst bef 1/2-way: ev ch 3f out: sn rdn and lost 2nd: wknd over 1f out* **7/2**[3]
00/0 **6** 5 **King Halling**[41] 2501 5-8-11 **62** ... (p) JoannaBadger 5 49
(RFord) *hld up: niggled along over 5f out: hdwy 4f out: wknd over 2f out* **14/1**

3m 27.11s (-6.67) **Going Correction** -0.125s/f (Firm) **6** Ran SP% **113.7**
Speed ratings: **111,109,107,107,105 102**CSF £18.06 TOTE £1.90: £1.50, £3.40; EX 18.00.
**Owner** Norbury Ten **Bred** Gainsborough Stud Management Ltd **Trained** Pandy, Gwent

**FOCUS**
This was an uncompetitive event, won well by the favourite, but the time was good.

**NOTEBOOK**
**Sudden Flight(IRE)** was given a fine ride from the front to land his first win over the trip with authority. He is in good heart at the moment, and should not go up in the weights too much for this success.
**Weet For Me** recorded by far and away his best performance of the season when plugging on at one pace in vain pursuit of the winner.
**Grand Fromage(IRE)**, winner of this race two years ago and off the track last year, showed he retains ability by keeping on in the straight. *Official explanation: jockey said gelding finished lame*
**Sarn** ran a fair race from out of the handicap, though the jury is still out on whether he truly stays this trip.
**Herne Bay(IRE)** was bang in contention before the straight before weakening, ultimately running below form.

## 3734 MERCEDES-BENZ OF WARRINGTON APPRENTICE H'CAP 7f 122y
**5:15** (5:16) (E) (0-70,65) 3-Y-O+ **£3,571** (£1,099; £549; £274) **Stalls** Low

Form RPR
0002 **1** **Merdiff**[4] 3615 5-9-0 **55** ... PPMathers(3) 13 67
(WMBrisbourne) *trckd ldrs: rdn over 1f out: led ins fnl f: edgd lft: r.o* **11/1**
2451 **2** 1 3/4 **Fen Gypsy**[3] 3626 6-9-6 **65** 6ex ... DonnaBashton(7) 11 73
(PDEvans) *in tch: rdn to chal over 1f out: styd on* **13/2**[3]
-000 **3** shd **Baby Barry**[12] 3380 7-8-9 **47** ... ABeech 14 55
(MrsGSRees) *chsd ldr: rdn to ld over 1f out: hdd ins fnl f: nt qckn* **25/1**
0054 **4** hd **Pas De Surprise**[10] 3412 6-9-1 **53** ... FPFerris 1 60
(PDEvans) *midfield: rdn over 2f out: hdwy whn swtchd rt over 1f out: styd on and edgd lft ins fnl f* **4/1**[2]
0000 **5** 1 3/4 **Proud Western (USA)**[19] 3148 6-7-13 **40** ... (t) NataliaGemelova(3) 3 43
(BEllison) *hld up: hdwy whn nt clr run over 1f out: styd on ins fnl f: nvr nrr* **16/1**
0021 **6** 1/2 **Redoubtable (USA)**[8] 3471 13-8-11 **54** ... DFentiman(5) 4 56
(DWChapman) *hld up: rdn and hdwy over 1f out: kpt on ins fnl f* **7/1**
1000 **7** hd **Iced Diamond (IRE)**[14] 3321 5-8-11 **54** ... PGallagher(5) 2 56
(WMBrisbourne) *midfield: rdn over 2f out: kpt on same pce fnl f* **7/1**
3026 **8** 1 3/4 **Mallard (IRE)**[7] 3520 6-9-10 **62** ... AQuinn 5 60
(JGGiven) *hld up: hdwy over 3f out: rdn over 1f out: sn one pce* **7/2**[1]
0005 **9** 1/2 **Zamyatina (IRE)**[14] 3301 5-8-0 **41** ... CHaddon(3) 10 38
(PLClinton) *midfield: rdn over 2f out: wknd ins fnl f* **16/1**
535- **10** 1 **Risk Free**[308] 4734 7-9-2 **59** ... (b) SJDonohoe(5) 7 53
(PDEvans) *led: rdn 2f out: hdd over 1f out: wknd ins fnl f* **10/1**
0-00 **11** 2 **Hormuz (IRE)**[19] 3148 8-8-1 **42** ... StephanieHollinshead(3) 12 32
(PaulJohnson) *in tch: rdn over 3f out: wknd over 1f out* **20/1**
3000 **12** 3 **Blade's Edge**[7] 3533 3-7-13 **53** ... (b) DawnWatson(7) 9 36
(ABailey) *t.k.h: chsd ldrs: rdn 2f out: wknd over 1f out* **25/1**
0306 **13** shd **Beneking**[19] 3151 4-8-8 **53** ... (p) HFellows(7) 8 35
(RHollinshead) *a towards rr* **12/1**
5000 **14** 5 **Hoh's Back**[18] 3167 5-9-0 **57** ... (p) LeanneKershaw(5) 6 28
(PaulJohnson) *bmpd sn after s: a bhd* **20/1**
000/ **15** 3 **Midnight Arrow**[42] 6-8-5 **50** ... CEly(7) 15 14
(ABerry) *midfield: rdn 3f out: sn wknd* **33/1**

1m 34.17s (-0.58) **Going Correction** -0.125s/f (Firm)
**WFA** 3 from 4yo+ 9lb **15** Ran SP% **137.6**
Speed ratings: **97,95,95,94,93 92,92,90,90,89 87,84,84,79,76**CSF £86.20 CT £1200.91 TOTE £19.00: £4.30, £3.20, £5.50; EX 123.20 Place 6 £131.98, Place 5 £88.76.
**Owner** Team Racing **Bred** Sheikh Ahmed Bin Rashid Al Maktoum **Trained** Great Ness, Shropshire

**FOCUS**
A modest race, with only a few in form beforehand, and one which saw horses drawn high occupying the first three positions.

**NOTEBOOK**
**Merdiff** is in good heart and, having always been on the pace from his high draw, hit the front inside the final furlong to land a first victory on turf.
**Fen Gypsy**, from a high draw, mounted a big effort at the top of the straight under his penalty for winning three days earlier.
**Baby Barry** put in his best effort for some time but it remains to be seen whether he can build on this.
**Pas De Surprise** ◆ was drawn in pole position but found he had to switch around the field in the straight before staying on, confirming he is coming back to form.
**Proud Western(USA)** showed his best form for some time when coming from off the pace in the straight.
**Redoubtable(USA)** ran with credit, coming wide turning in to keep on from a 6lb higher mark than when winning recently.
**Mallard(IRE)** raced on the outside and looked to struggle with the turning track, finishing a bit flat in the end.
**Risk Free** was out in front for a long way before folding. This was his seasonal debut, and he should come on for it.
T/Plt: £245.00 to a £1 stake. Pool: £59,767.25. 178.05 winning tickets. T/Qpdt: £112.90 to a £1 stake. Pool: £2,609.80. 17.10 winning tickets. DO

# 3396 HAMILTON (R-H)
Saturday, July 10

**OFFICIAL GOING: Good**
Wind: almost nil Weather: cloudy

## 3735 SATURDAY NIGHTS ARE BACK APPRENTICE RIDERS STKS (ROUND 2) (H'CAP) 6f 5y
**6:50** (6:50) (E) (0-70,64) 3-Y-O+ **£4,030** (£1,240; £620; £310) **Stalls** Low

Form RPR
0301 **1** **Mickledor (FR)**[7] 3533 4-8-13 **50** ... (p) MHoward 3 60
(MDods) *hld up stands side: hdwy and swtchd lft over 1f out: led ins fnl f: r.o wl* **8/1**[3]
-030 **2** hd **Orangino**[22] 3060 6-7-10 **40** ... RKennemore(7) 14 50
(JSHaldane) *swtchd to stands side gp after 2f: cl up: led over 1f out to ins last: kpt on* **10/1**
5010 **3** 1 1/4 **Sharoura**[4] 3606 8-9-13 **64** ... DeanWilliams 13 70
(RAFahey) *racd far side: a cl up: ev ch fr over 1f out: no ex wl ins last* **4/1**[1]
2320 **4** 1/2 **Bundy**[4] 3606 8-9-13 **64** ... WHogg 1 69
(MDods) *hld up stands side: hdwy over 1f out: kpt on fnl f* **4/1**[1]
1000 **5** 1 1/2 **Old Bailey (USA)**[4] 3615 4-8-8 **45** ... (p) JDO'Reilly 10 45
(TDBarron) *swtchd to stands side after 2f: prom on outer: rdn over 2f out: one pce fnl f* **8/1**[3]
0055 **6** hd **Northern Svengali (IRE)**[5] 3580 8-8-2 **44** ... (tp) BO'Neill(5) 12 43
(DANolan) *cl up far side tl rdn and no ex ins last* **16/1**
-101 **7** 1/2 **Massey**[158] 669 8-9-6 **57** ... Laura-JayneCrawford 6 55
(TDBarron) *led stands side to over 1f out: btn ins last* **7/1**[2]
3333 **8** 1/2 **Best Lead**[15] 3269 5-8-12 **54** ... (b) KJackson(5) 9 50
(IanEmmerson) *chsd stands side ldrs tl outpcd over 1f out* **12/1**
0000 **9** 1/2 **Needwood Bucolic (IRE)**[12] 3381 6-7-12 **40** ... MStainton(5) 2 35
(RAllan) *in tch: outpcd 1/2-way: n.d after* **33/1**
20 **10** 1 1/2 **Xanadu**[23] 3010 8-8-11 **53** ... (p) JemmaMarshall(5) 5 43
(MissLAPerratt) *chsd stands side ldrs tl wknd over 1f out* **10/1**
/000 **11** 2 1/2 **Nifty Roy**[4] 3616 4-7-9 **37** ow2 ... SYourston(5) 7 20
(KWHogg) *s.i.s: n.d* **66/1**
6004 **12** 1/2 **Travelling Times**[18] 3169 5-8-1 **41** ... (v) AReilly(3) 4 22
(JSWainwright) *chsd stands side ldrs to 1/2-way: sn btn* **12/1**
0000 **13** 3 **Speedfit Free (IRE)**[4] 3616 7-8-2 **44** ow1 ... (v) RKeogh(5) 8 16
(MissAStokell) *towards rr on outside of stands side gp: outpcd fr 1/2-way* **33/1**
2006 **14** 5 **Vijay (IRE)**[24] 2975 5-8-8 **52** ... (p) GBartley(7) 11 9
(ISemple) *swtchd to outer of stands side gp after 2f: prom tl wknd fr 2f out* **20/1**

1m 13.35s (0.25) **Going Correction** -0.025s/f (Good) **14** Ran SP% **126.3**
Speed ratings: **97,96,95,94,92 92,91,90,90,88 84,84,80,73**CSF £87.26 CT £386.92 TOTE £11.30: £3.60, £6.50, £2.20; EX 417.60.
**Owner** D B Stanley **Bred** Gillian C Stanley **Trained** Piercebridge, Co Durham
■ Stewards Enquiry : R Kennemore two-day ban: careless riding (Jul 21,22)

**FOCUS**
A run-of-the-mill sprint in which the pace was sound and the form should stand up at a similar level. The bulk of the field raced stands' side, but the proximity of the two that raced on the far side showed there was little advantage in the draw.

**NOTEBOOK**
**Mickledor(FR)**, up in the weights and up in grade, turned in an improved effort to follow up her recent Nottingham win. She should not be going up too much for this and can continue to give a good account. She should prove equally effective back over seven.
**Orangino**, over a more suitable trip, ran well, especially as he tacked over to join the stands'-side group before halfway. He is capable of winning a race of this nature, but his record of no wins from 25 starts means he is not one to be lumping on.
**Sharoura**, one of the two to race on the far-side group, returned to something like her best and is capable of winning again from this sort of mark when things go her way.
**Bundy**, a stable companion of the winner, extended his run of creditable efforts but he is the type that does need things to fall just right and, as a result, is not really one to take a short price about.
**Old Bailey(USA)** ran creditably returned to turf and left the impression that the return to seven furlongs would be in his favour. However his lack of consistency is a bit of a concern.
**Northern Svengali(IRE)** was far from disgraced having raced on the far side, but the fact that he has not won a race for over three years has to be a big worry.
**Massey**, easy to back, looked and shaped as though the race was just needed and he is not one to write off just yet over sprint distances on turf.
**Travelling Times** *Official explanation: jockey said gelding hung right handed throughout*

## 3736 JOE PUNTER NOVICE AUCTION STKS (A QUALIFIER FOR HAMILTON PARK 2-Y-O SERIES FINAL) 5f 4y
**7:20** (7:21) (F) 2-Y-O **£2,940** (£840; £420) **Stalls** Low

Form RPR
3132 **1** **Speed Dial Harry (IRE)**[14] 3290 2-8-10 ... (v) DarrenWilliams 5 75
(KRBurke) *sn crossed to stands rail: mde all: pushed clr fr over 1f out* **7/4**[2]
35 **2** 7 **Regal Lustre**[21] 3080 2-8-1 ... BSwarbrick(5) 4 47
(JRWeymes) *in tch: rdn 1/2-way: kpt on fnl f: no ch w wnr* **25/1**
6 **3** hd **Underthemistletoe (IRE)**[53] 2213 2-8-6 ... DMcGaffin 2 46
(BSmart) *chsd wnr: rdn over 2f out: flashed tail and no ex fnl f* **8/1**[3]
000 **4** 4 **Toldo (IRE)**[7] 3514 2-8-11 ... (b[1]) PBradley 3 37
(ABerry) *prom tl wknd fr 2f out* **50/1**
21 **5** 9 **Sweet Royale**[23] 3003 2-8-13 ... RWinston 1 —
(MissLAPerratt) *hung rt thrght: lost pl over 3f out: sn struggling* **8/11**[1]

61.61 secs (0.35) **Going Correction** -0.025s/f (Good) **5** Ran SP% **111.2**
Speed ratings: **96,84,84,78,63**CSF £32.67 TOTE £2.40: £1.10, £5.50; EX 47.20.
**Owner** Nigel Shields **Bred** Brendan Lavery **Trained** Middleham Moor, N Yorks

**FOCUS**
With Sweet Royale running no sort of race this was a straightforward task for Speed Dial Harry, who nevertheless imrpoved on his previous turf best.

**NOTEBOOK**
**Speed Dial Harry(IRE)** faced a straightforward task when his main market rival dropped out at an early stage and won as he was entitled to. He will be of interest in nursery company when the emphasis is on speed.
**Regal Lustre** had little chance with the easy winner but again hinted at ability and looks the type to do better in nursery company over further in due course.
**Underthemistletoe(IRE)** attracted support on only this second outing but, although she ran creditably for a long way, the way she flashed her tail in the closing stages means she is one to tread carefully with.
**Toldo(IRE)** faced a very stiff task at the weights and again offered little immediate promise in the first-time blinkers.
**Sweet Royale** looked to have solid claims on her recent Ayr win, but looked ill-at-ease on this downhill track and was struggling from an early stage. She is worth another chance back on a more conventional course. *Official explanation: jockey said gelding hung right handed throughout*

## 3737 MAILSPORT WEEKLY CLASSIFIED STKS 6f 5y
**7:50** (7:50) (D) 3-Y-O **£6,162** (£1,896; £948; £474) **Stalls** Low

Form RPR
0052 **1** **Compton's Eleven**[9] 3455 3-9-5 **80** ... CCatlin 5 93
(MRChannon) *trckd ldr: rdn over 2f out: led ins fnl f: r.o strly* **9/4**[2]
0040 **2** 3 **Imperial Echo (USA)**[20] 3122 3-8-12 **78** ... PMakin(5) 1 82
(TDBarron) *led: hung rt 1/2-way: hdd ins fnl f: one pce* **13/2**
2005 **3** 4 **Lets Get It On (IRE)**[7] 3523 3-8-12 **76** ... RWinston 3 65
(JJQuinn) *hld up: effrt 2f out: sn no imp* **11/4**[3]
0150 **4** 1 1/2 **Obe Bold (IRE)**[14] 3314 3-8-11 **57** ... PBradley 4 60
(ABerry) *chsd ldrs tl outpcd fr 2f out* **33/1**

1121 **5** *4* **Bridgewater Boys**[24] 2981 3-9-5 80....................................(b) RFfrench 2 56
(KARyan) *chsd ldrs tl rdn and wknd over 2f out* **7/4**[1]

1m 11.86s (-1.24) **Going Correction** -0.025s/f (Good) **5** Ran SP% **110.1**
Speed ratings: **107,103,97,95,90**CSF £16.10 TOTE £3.10: £2.00, £2.60; EX 20.80.
**Owner** PCM Racing **Bred** Lady Cobham **Trained** West Ilsley, Berks

**FOCUS**
With two market leaders failing to run up to their best this race did not take as much winning as seemed likely. The pace was fair and the time was good for the grade, but this bare form does not look entirely reliable with only the first two showing their best.

**NOTEBOOK**
**Compton's Eleven**, back in trip, confirmed recent promise to win his first race since last September but, with his main market rivals below their best, this race did not take as much winning as seemed likely. He may be vulnerable after reassessment back in handicaps.
**Imperial Echo(USA)** ran creditably in terms of form but, given he was sweating in the preliminaries and hanging to his right for much of the way, he looks one to tread carefully with.
**Lets Get It On(IRE)** had run well on both previous outings at this track, but was below her best in a race that suited those racing up with the pace. She is better than this but she has not proved the most reliable.
**Obe Bold(IRE)** faced a stiff task on these terms and ran accordingly.
**Bridgewater Boys**, who had a good chance at the weights and a progressive profile, ran poorly and this undulating track may have been to blame. Given his improvement coming into this race, he may not be one to write off just yet.

## 3738 SPORTS RELIEF H'CAP (A QUALIFIER FOR THE TOTEPOOL SERIES FINAL) 1m 1f 36y
**8:20** (8:22) (E) (0-75,67) 3-Y-0+ **£4,176** (£1,285; £642; £321) **Stalls** High

Form RPR
0031 **1** **Wahoo Sam (USA)**[11] 3401 4-9-4 **64**.................................. PMakin(5) 8 72
(TDBarron) *set stdy pce: mde all: rdn over 2f out: hld on wl fnl f* **2/1**[1]

5455 **2** *3/4* **Apache Point (IRE)**[7] 3520 7-8-12 **53**................................ KimTinkler 1 60
(NTinkler) *in tch: rdn over 3f out: rallied 2f out: r.o fnl f* **11/4**[2]

0043 **3** *nk* **Coustou (IRE)**[20] 2292 4-9-4 **59**.................................. SWKelly 4 65
(ARDicken) *trckd ldrs: rdn over 2f out: kpt on fnl f* **16/1**

4000 **4** *1 3/4* **Newcorp Lad**[11] 3401 4-9-0 **60**.............................. BSwarbrick(5) 5 63
(MrsGSRees) *prom: rdn over 3f out: one pce over 1f out* **12/1**

6-60 **5** *1* **Market Avenue**[12] 3375 5-9-7 **62**................................ ANicholls 2 63
(RAFahey) *hld up: hdwy centre 2f out: no imp fnl f* **4/1**[3]

55-5 **6** *1 1/2* **Donna's Double**[11] 3401 9-8-10 **56**..........................(p) PMulrennan(5) 9 54
(DEddy) *hld up in tch: effrt over 2f out: no imp over 1f out* **7/1**

6050 **7** *5* **Badr (USA)**[16] 3231 3-8-8 **59**.................................... RFfrench 6 47
(MJohnston) *chsd ldrs tl wknd fr 3f out* **12/1**

505- **8** *8* **Kristiansand**[278] 5418 4-9-7 **65**.............................. LEnstone(3) 7 37
(PMonteith) *keen: cl up tl wknd fr over 2f out* **20/1**

4440 **9** *22* **Rare Coincidence**[30] 2814 3-9-2 **67**...............................(p) RWinston 3 —
(RFFisher) *chsd ldrs to 1/2-way: qckly lost pl* **14/1**

1m 58.1s (-1.50) **Going Correction** -0.025s/f (Good)
**WFA** 3 from 4yo+ 10lb **9** Ran SP% **125.2**
Speed ratings: **105,104,104,102,101 100,95,88,69**CSF £8.39 CT £73.06 TOTE £3.60: £1.50, £1.30, £3.30; EX 11.10.
**Owner** C A Washbourn **Bred** Stonereath Farms Inc **Trained** Maunby, N Yorks

**FOCUS**
An ordinary event and, although the first three appeared to run to form, the steady pace favoured those racing close to the pace which raises slight doubts.

**NOTEBOOK**
**Wahoo Sam(USA)**, up 5lb in the weights for his recent course victory had the run of the race but showed the right attitude once pressed. Although things went his way again, he looks the type to progress further for his shrewd stable.
**Apache Point(IRE)** ◆ looked in good shape and confirmed his recent return to form. A stronger overall gallop would have been in his favour, and he looks capable of winning a similar event in the near future from his current mark.
**Coustou(IRE)** has not won since 2002 but had the run of the race and performed creditably. He left the impression that a stiffer test of stamina over this trip would have been in his favour.
**Newcorp Lad** had the run of the race and turned in his best effort of the year back at his favourite course. He currently figures on a handy mark and may well be capable of further success at a modest level.
**Market Avenue** is capable of winning a similar race from this sort of mark and she shaped as though a bit better than the bare result, as she was held up off a steady gallop and made her ground in the centre. She has disappointed on occasions but remains one to keep an eye on.
**Donna's Double** again left the impression that he retains ability and he figures on a handy mark at present. A strongly-run race over a mile and a quarter are his requirements, and he is one to keep an eye on.
**Badr(USA)** was again soundly beaten and remains one to tread carefully with.
**Kristiansand** *Official explanation: jockey said gelding had no more to give*
**Rare Coincidence** *Official explanation: jockey said gelding hung left handed up home straight*

## 3739 SUNDAY MAIL MEDIAN AUCTION MAIDEN STKS 5f 4y
**8:50** (8:50) (E) 3-Y-0 **£3,786** (£1,165; £582; £291) **Stalls** Low

Form RPR
4-23 **1** **Ragged Jack (IRE)**[8] 3486 3-9-0 72....................................(b1) SWKelly 4 60+
(GAButler) *chsd ldr: led 2f out: drvn out* **2/7**[1]

2505 **2** *1 1/2* **Westborough (IRE)**[16] 3234 3-9-0 51................................. KimTinkler 1 55
(NTinkler) *keen: trckd ldrs: effrt 2f out: kpt on fnl f: hld towards fin* **9/2**[2]

03 **3** *5* **Red Hot Ruby**[7] 3511 3-8-9 ........................................ GParkin 2 32
(RAFahey) *stdd s: hld up: shkn up 1/2-way: nvr rchd ldrs* **8/1**[3]

-000 **4** *7* **Aguilera**[12] 3368 3-8-6 43...................................(p) LEnstone(3) 3 7
(MDods) *led: hung rt and hdd 2f out: sn wknd* **20/1**

61.70 secs (0.44) **Going Correction** -0.025s/f (Good) **4** Ran SP% **111.8**
Speed ratings: **95,92,84,73**CSF £2.16 TOTE £1.40; EX 2.20.
**Owner** Mrs W W Fleming **Bred** Norelands Bloodstock **Trained** Blewbury, Oxon

**FOCUS**
A weak maiden and a most uncompetititve event in which Ragged Jack failed to impress when beating a rival he would have been conceding lumps of weight to in a handicap.

**NOTEBOOK**
**Ragged Jack(IRE)**, in the first-time blinkers, had to work hard to beat a rival he would have been conceding plenty of weight to in a handicap. Although the return to further should suit, he will look vulnerable from his current mark back in handicap company.
**Westborough(IRE)** is exposed as modest and, although running creditably, is going to continue to look vulnerable in this grade or from higher marks back in handicap company.
**Red Hot Ruby** ◆'s bare form amounts to little, but she was not knocked about and appeals as the type to leave this form a long way behind in modest handicap company over further in due course. *Official explanation: jockey said filly did not come down hill and hung left from half way*
**Aguilera** is a poor performer who looks to need a drop in grade.

## 3740 SUPPORT VELVET FAIR FRIDAY H'CAP 1m 5f 9y
**9:20** (9:21) (E) (0-75,68) 3-Y-0+ **£4,143** (£1,275; £637; £318) **Stalls** High

Form RPR
6221 **1** **Inchnadamph**[16] 3221 4-9-0 **58**.........................................(t) RWinston 4 70+
(TJFitzgerald) *in tch: smooth hdwy over 2f: rdn to ld over 1f out: kpt on wl* **11/4**[1]

-521 **2** *1* **Sualda (IRE)**[8] 3472 5-9-10 **68**.................................. GParkin 5 75
(RAFahey) *trckd ldrs: nt clr run over 2f out: rdn wl over 1f out: kpt on fnl f: nt rch wnr* **5/1**

0352 **3** *1 1/2* **Cosmic Case**[5] 3578 9-8-1 **45**.................................. ANicholls 2 50
(JSGoldie) *led to over 1f out: kpt on same pce* **6/1**

0312 **4** *1* **Scurra**[15] 3265 5-8-6 **55**...................................... PMulrennan(5) 7 58
(ACWhillans) *hld up in tch: effrt over 2f out: no imp fnl f* **8/1**

-222 **5** *shd* **Ellway Heights**[5] 3576 7-8-4 **53**................................ BSwarbrick(5) 3 56
(WMBrisbourne) *keen: trckd ldrs: n.m.r over 2f out: rdn and no ex over 1f out* **3/1**[2]

1106 **6** *6* **Millennium Hall**[8] 3474 5-9-1 **62**.............................. LEnstone(3) 6 56
(PMonteith) *hld up: hdwy over 3f out: sn rdn: btn over 1f out* **7/2**[3]

0600 **7** *5* **Howards Dream (IRE)**[12] 3369 6-7-12 **42** oh17..............(t) KimTinkler 1 29
(DANolan) *keen: cl up tl wknd over 1f out* **50/1**

2m 52.26s (-1.14) **Going Correction** -0.025s/f (Good) **7** Ran SP% **117.9**
Speed ratings: **102,101,100,99,99 96,93**CSF £17.80 TOTE £3.30: £2.30, £3.10; EX 13.70 Place 6 £71.74, Place 5 £30.50.
**Owner** R N Cardwell **Bred** Bloomsbury Stud And R And A Craddock **Trained** Norton, N Yorks

**FOCUS**
An ordinary handicap in which the pace was on the steady side and, as a result, the bare form does not look entirely reliable. However the winner is a progressive sort who should continue to go well.

**NOTEBOOK**
**Inchnadamph** ◆ is an improved performer in recent times and turned in his best effort from this 8lb higher mark. He shapes as though he will be better suited by a more strongly-run race, and appeals as the type to progress again.
**Sualda(IRE)**, up 6lb in the weights, did not get the best of runs but performed creditably against the far-side rail and he should continue to give a good account for his in-form stable.
**Cosmic Case**, who is usually held up, had the run of the race and ran creditably under very different tactics. She is capable of winning again from her current mark, but will be more of interest when it looks as though a decent gallop is likely.
**Scurra** did not really get his suspect stamina tested to the full over this longer trip, but failed to confirm recent Ayr placings with Inchnadamph. The return to shorter will not be an inconvenience.
**Ellway Heights**pulled too hard in a race that was not really run to suit and did not get the gaps at the right time. This run is best ignored and he looks worth another chance.
**Millennium Hall** was disappointing even allowing for the fact that he was dropped out in a steadily-run race, and he seems to have gone off the boil for the time being.
T/Plt: £124.00 to a £1 stake. Pool: £36,869.55. 216.95 winning tickets. T/Qpdt: £11.90 to a £1 stake. Pool: £3,121.30. 192.50 winning tickets. RY

# 3531 NOTTINGHAM (L-H)
Saturday, July 10

**OFFICIAL GOING: Good (good to soft in places)**
A shower prior to racing ensured the ground remained on the easy side. It was a big advantage to be drawn low on the straight course.
Wind: Slight across. Weather: Cloud giving way to sunny spells.

## 3741 EUROPEAN BREEDERS FUND MAIDEN FILLIES' STKS 6f 15y
**2:15** (2:15) (D) 2-Y-0 **£6,041** (£1,859; £929; £464) **Stalls** Low

Form RPR
5 **1** **Generous Option**[14] 3296 2-8-11 ........................................ RFfrench 2 81
(MJohnston) *racd far side: chsd ldrs: led that gp over 1f out: rdn clr* **7/2**[2]

3 **2** *3* **Peeptoe (IRE)**[17] 3208 2-8-11 ........................................ GCarter 15 81+
(JLDunlop) *rrd s: racd stands' side: sn chsng ldrs: led her gp and hung lft fr over 1f out: no ch w far side* **6/4**[1]

04 **3** *1 1/4* **Burton Ash**[39] 2550 2-8-11 ........................................ MFenton 4 68
(JGGiven) *led far side over 4f: styd on same pce* **12/1**

**4** *1* **Authenticate** 2-8-11 ........................................ GGibbons 3 65
(BAMcmahon) *s.s: racd far side: hdwy and nt clr run over 2f out: styd on same pce fnl f* **20/1**

**5** *2* **Rapid Romance (USA)** 2-8-11 ........................................ OUrbina 6 59
(EALDunlop) *racd far side: chsd ldrs tl hung rt and wknd fnl f* **28/1**

**6** *3* **Icing** 2-8-11 ........................................ BDoyle 16 59+
(WJHaggas) *racd stands' side: chsd ldrs over 4f* **8/1**[3]

**7** *1 1/4* **Resistance Heroine** 2-8-11 ........................................ WRyan 8 55+
(EALDunlop) *s.s: racd stands' side: outpcd: nvr nrr* **14/1**

0 **8** *nk* **Royal Pardon**[32] 2758 2-8-11 ........................................ JMackay 9 54+
(MLWBell) *racd stands' side: mid-div: sme hdwy 2f out: edgd lft and sn wknd* **14/1**

0 **9** *1 3/4* **Midnight Lace**[12] 3382 2-8-11 ........................................ ADaly 5 40
(RHannon) *racd far side: prom over 4f* **50/1**

0 **10** *nk* **Princeable Lady (IRE)**[20] 3123 2-8-11 ........................................ DAllan 1 39
(TDEasterby) *racd far side: w ldr over 3f: wknd over 1f out* **20/1**

**11** *shd* **Montjeu Baby (IRE)** 2-8-11 ........................................ JCarroll 12 48+
(RHannon) *racd stands' side: sn outpcd: hdwy over 2f out: wknd over 1f out* **25/1**

0 **12** *3* **Mercari**[23] 3014 2-8-11 ........................................ RFitzpatrick 13 39+
(GMMoore) *racd stands' side: prom tl hung lft and wknd over 1f out* **80/1**

5600 **13** *3* **Misty Princess**[29] 2852 2-8-11 ........................................ MTebbutt 14 30+
(MJPolglase) *led stands' side: hung lft: hdd & wknd over 1f out* **50/1**

5 **14** *shd* **Rosapenna (IRE)**[15] 3272 2-8-11 ........................................ RMullen 10 30+
(CFWall) *racd stands' side: prom over 4f* **12/1**

**15** *9* **Mina Alsalaam** 2-8-11 ........................................ RLappin 7 —
(MRChannon) *racd far side: dwlt: sn prom: wknd over 2f out* **28/1**

00 **16** *15* **Mrs Willy Nilly**[68] 1839 2-8-11 ...................................(p) SWhitworth 11 —
(JMBradley) *racd stands' side: hung lft thrght: chsd ldrs to 1/2-way* **100/1**

1m 17.4s (2.60) **Going Correction** +0.15s/f (Good) **16** Ran SP% **128.5**
Speed ratings: **88,84,82,81,78 74,72,72,69,69 69,65,61,61,49 29**CSF £8.64 TOTE £4.30: £2.40, £1.10, £3.60; EX 16.60.
**Owner** Maktoum Al Maktoum **Bred** Gainsborough Stud Management Ltd **Trained** Middleham Moor, N Yorks

**FOCUS**
A fair maiden in which the field finished well strung out, despite the steady pace. It was an advantage to be drawn low.

**NOTEBOOK**
**Generous Option** had clearly learnt from her debut, and this daughter of Cadeaux Genereux clearly relished this easier surface. She is open to plenty of improvement as she steps up in trip.

**Peeptoe(IRE)**, drawn on the wrong side, hung most of the way across the course in the latter stages. She clearly has ability and should have no trouble scoring at this level.
**Burton Ash**, one of the nicer ones in the paddock, is gradually getting the hang of things, and will certainly have more options open to her now in nurseries.
**Authenticate**, a 24,000gns yearling, was green as the gates opened, but showed enough to suggest she should find a race in due course. *Official explanation: jockey said filly was slowly away and got left*
**Rapid Romance(USA)**, a half-sister to the high-class juvenile Raphane, is a late foal who has plenty of catching up to do. She did not shape too badly, but better will be seen of her later on in the season.
**Icing**, a half-sister to a Listed winner in Italy, had little chance from her draw.

## 3742 NOTTINGHAMSHIRE LIFEBOATS (S) STKS 6f 15y
**2:50** (2:51) (G ) 3-Y-0+ **£2,901** (£829; £414) **Stalls** Low

Form RPR
0000 **1** **Sabana (IRE)**[7] 3533 6-9-10 41..............(p) RMullen 6 58
(JMBradley) *racd far side: chsd ldrs: rdn to ld wl ins fnl f* **33/1**
0000 **2** *1 1/4* **Back In Spirit**[12] 3381 4-9-4 30..............(t) GCarter 3 48
(BAMcmahon) *racd far side: w ldr tl led over 2f out: rdn and hdd wl ins fnl f* **50/1**
2004 **3** *2* **Nicholas Nickelby**[12] 3376 4-9-4 58..............(p) MFenton 4 42
(MJPolglase) *led far side over 3f: rdn and ev ch over 1f out: styd on same pce* **15/2**
0404 **4** *hd* **Beyond Calculation (USA)**[7] 3533 10-9-4 54..............(b) SWhitworth 5 42
(JMBradley) *racd far side: chsd ldrs: rdn over 1f out: styd on* **4/1**[1]
0000 **5** *1/2* **Zietzig (IRE)**[7] 3533 7-9-4 42.............. JCarroll 18 40
(DNicholls) *led stands' side tl rdn over 1f out: r.o: no ch w far side* **16/1**
2430 **6** *1 1/4* **Donegal Shore (IRE)**[12] 3380 5-9-4 46..............(vt) ADaly 9 36
(MrsJCandlish) *racd far side: dwlt: outpcd: styd on ins fnl f: nvr nrr* **25/1**
031 **7** *1 3/4* **Jonny Ebeneezer**[4] 3616 5-9-10 56..............(b) TJMurphy 11 37
(DFlood) *w ldr stands' side tl wknd fnl f* **9/2**[2]
0030 **8** *2 1/2* **Shady Deal**[5] 3575 8-9-1 45.............. DCorby(3) 17 24
(JMBradley) *racd stands' side: sn chsng ldrs: rdn and wknd over 1f out* **9/1**
1041 **9** *1/2* **King Nicholas (USA)**[64] 1941 5-9-5 53..............(b[1]) MLawson(5) 14 28
(JParkes) *racd stands' side: prom 4f* **6/1**[3]
0654 **10** *nk* **Niteowl Express (IRE)**[54] 2187 3-8-7 36.............. VHalliday 16 16
(JO'Reilly) *racd stands' side: s.i.s: sme hdwy 2f out: wknd fnl f* **20/1**
0650 **11** *nk* **Spy Master**[12] 3381 6-9-4 31..............(bt) DAllan 15 20
(JParkes) *racd stands' side: hld up: effrt over 2f out: nvr trbld ldrs* **33/1**
0000 **12** *2* **Gruff**[29] 2854 5-9-4 32.............. JBramhill 19 14
(PTMidgley) *racd stands' side: in tch: rdn over 2f out: wknd over 1f out* **50/1**
50-0 **13** *1 1/2* **Octennial**[7] 3533 5-9-4 50.............. RFitzpatrick 10 10
(CSmith) *racd far side: dwlt: outpcd* **33/1**
0006 **14** *hd* **Repeat (IRE)**[8] 3489 4-9-5 42.............. MSavage(5) 12 15
(MissGayKelleway) *racd stands' side: chsd ldrs 4f* **14/1**
0630 **15** *1/2* **Onefortheboys (IRE)**[5] 3593 5-8-12 39 ow1.............. LTreadwell(7) 7 9
(DFlood) *racd far side: rrd and swvd lft s: outpcd* **16/1**
0000 **16** *2* **Justice Jones**[10] 3425 3-8-12 43..............(b[1]) DKinsella 2 2
(JLSpearing) *racd far side: sn outpcd* **40/1**
6503 **17** *3 1/2* **River Lark (USA)**[12] 3378 5-8-8 41..............(b) HayleyTurner(5) 8 —
(MABuckley) *racd far side: chsd ldrs 4f* **12/1**
660 **18** *4* **My Country Club**[43] 2454 7-9-4 47..............(b[1]) VSlattery 13 —
(AGJuckes) *racd stands' side: dwlt: outpcd* **33/1**
1000 **19** *5* **Grand View**[28] 2886 8-9-10 36..............(p) MTebbutt 1 —
(JRWeymes) *racd far side: chsd ldrs over 3f* **25/1**

1m 16.43s (1.63) **Going Correction** +0.15s/f (Good)
**WFA** 3 from 4yo+ 6lb **19** Ran SP% **130.9**
Speed ratings: **95,93,90,90,89 88,85,82,81,81 80,78,76,76,75 72,68,62,56**CSF £1179.62 TOTE £37.00: £9.90, £8.60, £2.60; EX 765.70.There was no bid for the winner.
**Owner** E A Hayward **Bred** Churchtown House Stud **Trained** Sedbury, Gloucs

**FOCUS**
A poor seller and once again the field split into two, with the far-side group holding the call. The first four home on the far side were always up with the pace.

**NOTEBOOK**
**Sabana(IRE)** was woken up by the first-time cheekpieces. He stays much further than this and, with his stamina coming into play, saw his race out well. *Official explanation: trainer said, regarding the improved form shown, gelding may have benefited from the application of sheepskin cheek pieces for the first time*
**Back In Spirit** made a mockery of the ratings but, while he is lightly-raced on turf and may be open to a little improvement on this surface, this run still needs to be treated with caution.
**Nicholas Nickelby** does stay further, but really ought to have beaten those in front of him on these terms.
**Beyond Calculation(USA)** is a long way below his best and may have found the ground slower than ideal.
**Zietzig(IRE)** turned in a solid effort on these terms from the "wrong" side, and looks to be running into form.
**Donegal Shore(IRE)** never really recovered from a tardy start.
**Octennial** *Official explanation: jockey said gelding was never travelling*
**Grand View** *Official explanation: jockey said gelding lost his action*

## 3743 LES STONE MEMORIAL H'CAP 1m 6f 15y
**3:25** (3:25) (E ) (0-75,73) 3-Y-0+ **£3,965** (£1,220; £610; £305) **Stalls** Low

Form RPR
0244 **1** **Isa'Af (IRE)**[16] 3232 5-9-0 **64**.............. HayleyTurner(5) 13 75
(PWHiatt) *hld up in tch: led over 3f out: edgd lft fr over 1f out: all out* **10/3**[2]
0004 **2** *hd* **Lunar Lord**[9] 3437 8-7-13 **44**.............. JBramhill 3 55
(DBurchell) *hld up: plld hrd: hdwy 5f out: rdn to chse wnr and hung lft wl over 1f out: nt clr run ins fnl f: styd on* **7/1**
452 **3** *2* **Race The Ace**[20] 3121 3-8-8 **68**.............. GCarter 9 76
(JLDunlop) *trckd ldr: racd keenly: ev ch over 2f out: hmpd wl over 1f out: styd on* **3/1**[1]
6001 **4** *1 1/4* **Sonoma (IRE)**[19] 3153 4-9-3 **62**.............. MFenton 1 68
(MLWBell) *chsd ldrs: rdn 5f out: styd on same pce fnl f* **9/2**[3]
4454 **5** *hd* **Disabuse**[7] 3536 4-8-4 **49**.............. RMullen 8 55
(MWEasterby) *hld up: hdwy 2f out: styd on same pce fnl f* **13/2**
34-0 **6** *1 1/4* **Majestic Vision**[82] 1508 3-8-4 **67**.............. DCorby(3) 12 71
(PWHarris) *led over 10f: wknd fnl f* **12/1**
0230 **7** *1* **Stocking Island**[30] 2805 3-8-13 **73**.............. JCarroll 6 76
(BHanbury) *hld up: styd on appr fnl f: nvr trbld ldrs* **9/1**
-546 **8** *3/4* **Brough Supreme**[13] 3340 3-8-7 **67**.............. JMackay 5 69
(HMorrison) *hld up: hdwy 4f out: rdn and wknd over 1f out* **14/1**
060/ **9** *4* **Welsh Main**[49] 4483 7-9-11 **70**.............. GBaker 7 66
(FJordan) *hld up: a in rr* **25/1**
0004 **10** *13* **Calomeria**[16] 3250 3-7-10 **61** ow2.............. RThomas(5) 2 39
(RMBeckett) *hld up: a wknd 2f out* **11/1**
4160 **11** *2* **Stolen Song**[58] 1457 4-9-0 **59**.............. BDoyle 4 34
(MJRyan) *chsd ldrs: rdn 5f out: wknd and eased wl over 1f out* **12/1**
165/ **12** *dist* **King Spinner (IRE)**[936] 5950 7-8-10 **55**.............. VSlattery 11 —
(MrsAJBowlby) *prom over 9f* **33/1**

3m 7.77s (0.57) **Going Correction** +0.15s/f (Good)
**WFA** 3 from 4yo+ 15lb **12** Ran SP% **139.3**
Speed ratings: **104,103,102,102,101 101,100,100,97,90 89,**—CSF £32.81 CT £86.11 TOTE £5.60: £1.60, £3.60, £1.40; EX 58.70.
**Owner** Miss Maria McKinney **Bred** T Monaghan **Trained** Hook Norton, Oxon

**FOCUS**
A low-grade contest, but quite competitive and run at an even pace. The form looks reasonably sound.

**NOTEBOOK**
**Isa'Af(IRE)**, who had reportedly suffered a setback since his last run, confirmed himself an improved performer in winning off his highest mark. His trainer thought he may have 'blown up' here, in which case there may be more to come.
**Lunar Lord**, without a win for two years, did not have the best of runs and has now slipped to a competitive mark.
**Race The Ace** ◆ proved well suited to this step up in trip and will have no trouble staying further still. There are races to be won with him.
**Sonoma(IRE)** did not turn in a bad effort considering the ground would have been on the easy side for her.
**Disabuse**, who has yet to win on turf, appeared to stay this longer trip well enough.

## 3744 RECTANGLE GROUP FILLIES' H'CAP 5f 13y
**4:00** (4:00) (C ) (0-90,89) 3-Y-0+ **£10,569** (£3,252; £1,626; £813) **Stalls** Low

Form RPR
3042 **1** **Fruit Of Glory**[47] 2372 5-10-0 **89**.............. WRyan 2 99
(JRJenkins) *w ldr tl led 1/2-way: rdn out* **5/1**[3]
1-04 **2** *1/2* **Paradise Isle**[21] 3092 3-9-8 **88**.............. GBaker 8 96+
(CFWall) *hld up: hdwy and hung rt 2f out: hung lft and chsd wnr over 1f out: r.o* **9/4**[1]
2-06 **3** *1 1/4* **Dispol Katie**[55] 2143 3-9-1 **81**.............. MFenton 4 85
(TDBarron) *chsd ldrs: outpcd 2f out: r.o ins fnl f* **12/1**
4000 **4** *1/2* **Twice Upon A Time**[13] 3339 5-8-6 **67**.............. RMullen 7 69
(BSmart) *s.s: hld up: hdwy over 1f out: styd on same pce ins fnl f* **20/1**
630 **5** *nk* **Roman Mistress (IRE)**[16] 3249 4-8-4 **65**..............(b) DAllan 6 66
(TDEasterby) *hld up: rdn 1/2-way: hung lft and r.o ins fnl f: nt rch ldrs* **8/1**
3235 **6** *1/2* **Roxanne Mill**[14] 3307 6-8-9 **75**..............(p) RThomas(5) 3 74
(JMBradley) *s.i.s: hld up: nt clr run fr over 1f out: nvr able to chal* **9/1**
3210 **7** *1* **Karminskey Park**[11] 3399 5-8-4 **65**.............. DKinsella 5 60+
(TJEtherington) *trckd ldrs: hmpd over 1f out: btn whn hmpd ins fnl f* **9/1**
0112 **8** *1 1/2* **Frascati**[5] 3580 4-9-3 **78**.............. JCarroll 9 68
(ABerry) *chsd ldrs: wkng whn hmpd ins fnl f* **4/1**[2]
0000 **9** *3 1/2* **Bollin Janet**[9] 3446 4-8-4 **65**..............(b) JMackay 1 42
(TDEasterby) *sn led: hdd 1/2-way: wknd fnl f* **33/1**

61.04 secs (-0.76) **Going Correction** +0.15s/f (Good)
**WFA** 3 from 4yo+ 5lb **9** Ran SP% **118.3**
Speed ratings: **112,111,109,108,107 107,105,103,97**CSF £17.10 CT £130.92 TOTE £6.70: £2.70, £1.40, £2.70; EX 16.90.
**Owner** R B Hill **Bred** The Buy And Sell Partnership **Trained** Royston, Herts

**FOCUS**
A decent sprint run at a good pace and a useful final time, giving the form a solid look.

**NOTEBOOK**
**Fruit Of Glory** appreciated this easier task and took advantage of a favourable draw to gain due reward for some consistent efforts.
**Paradise Isle** stuck out wide from her draw, did a fair bit of running around and, although she does not look the easiest of rides, certainly has her fair share of ability.
**Dispol Katie** acquitted herself well but this track appeared sharp enough for her.
**Twice Upon A Time** is beginning to get some respite from the Handicapper now, and shaped as though she is about to return to form.
**Roman Mistress(IRE)** ◆ tackling better company than she is used to, turned in a sound effort despite hanging quite badly in the closing stages. She can return to winning ways when back in her right grade.
**Roxanne Mill**, another tackling better company than she is used to, could never get competitive.

## 3745 LETHEBY & CHRISTOPHER CLASSIFIED STKS 1m 54y
**4:35** (4:35) (E ) 3-Y-0+ **£3,818** (£1,175; £587; £293) **Stalls** Centre

Form RPR
2006 **1** **Inchloss (IRE)**[16] 3230 3-8-12 74.............. WRyan 3 81
(BAMcmahon) *prom: nt clr run and lost pl over 2f out: hdwy over 1f out: rdn to ld wl ins fnl f* **12/1**
1222 **2** *nk* **Riley Boys (IRE)**[7] 3507 3-9-3 79..............(p) MFenton 1 85
(JGGiven) *chsd ldrs: rdn and edgd rt over 2f out: led ins fnl f: sn hdd: styd on* **11/4**[1]
00-0 **3** *1 1/2* **Zucchero**[17] 3212 8-9-8 75..............(p) ADaly 5 78
(DWPArbuthnot) *trckd ldrs: rdn and hmpd over 2f out: styd on* **16/1**
6330 **4** *3/4* **Cherished Number**[17] 3198 5-9-8 75..............(v) JCarroll 9 76
(ISemple) *hld up in tch: led over 1f out: hdd and no ex ins fnl f* **11/2**[2]
-100 **5** *1/2* **Slalom (IRE)**[10] 3419 4-9-2 74..............(p) MSavage(5) 2 74
(MissGayKelleway) *s.i.s: hld up: hdwy over 1f out: nt rch ldrs* **14/1**
1514 **6** *1 1/2* **Tre Colline**[10] 3419 5-9-6 73.............. GBaker 6 70
(NTinkler) *hld up: rdn over 1f out: nvr trbld ldrs* **7/1**[3]
0000 **7** *2* **Motu (IRE)**[31] 2790 3-8-8 70.............. GCarter 4 62
(JLDunlop) *hld up: effrt and hung lft over 1f out: n.d* **11/2**[2]
05-3 **8** *nk* **Pending (IRE)**[19] 3154 3-8-13 75.............. OUrbina 10 66
(JRFanshawe) *hld up: plld hrd: hdwy over 2f out: sn rdn: wknd over 1f out* **11/4**[1]
0/ **9** *5* **Lizarazu (GER)**[244] 5-9-8 75.............. BDoyle 7 55
(FJordan) *chsd ldr 6f out: led over 2f out: hdd & wknd over 1f out* **16/1**
0000 **10** *6* **Daimajin (IRE)**[9] 3459 5-9-3 47.............. JMcAuley 8 36
(MrsLucindaFeatherstone) *led over 5f: sn wknd* **100/1**

1m 46.42s (0.02) **Going Correction** +0.15s/f (Good)
**WFA** 3 from 4yo+ 9lb **10** Ran SP% **123.7**
Speed ratings: **105,104,103,102,101 100,98,98,93,87**CSF £47.95 TOTE £15.20: £2.90, £1.20, £4.70; EX 56.30.
**Owner** R Thornhill **Bred** John McEnery **Trained** Hopwas, Staffs
■ Stewards Enquiry : M Fenton one-day ban: careless riding (Jul 21)
W Ryan caution: used whip without allowing gelding time to respond between strokes

**FOCUS**
Quite a tight classified stakes on adjusted figures. The pace was reasonable and the form looks fairly sound for the grade.

**NOTEBOOK**
**Inchloss(IRE)**, well suited by the easy surface, was value for a little more than the winning margin.
**Riley Boys(IRE)** is proving wonderfully consistent, despite plenty of wool about the head.


The Form Book, Raceform Ltd, Compton, RG20 6NL

**Zucchero** is a long way below his best nowadays, but he did show a little more zest in the first-time cheekpieces.
**Cherished Number**, facing his easiest task for a while, was disappointing, for he had gone to the front easily enough, but found nothing off the bridle.
**Slalom(IRE)** was doing his best work in the closing stages and looks to need a stiffer test.
**Pending(IRE)** was far too free early on and did not get home.

## 3746 NOTTINGHAM EVENING POST FAMILY DAY H'CAP 1m 1f 213y
**5:10** (5:10) (E) (0-75,76) 3-Y-O **£4,192** (£1,290; £645; £322) **Stalls** Low

Form RPR
52-3 **1** **Cellarmaster (IRE)**[19] 3160 3-9-4 **72**........ BDoyle 3 85
(ACStewart) *trckd ldrs: led over 3f out: rdn clr over 1f out* **8/1**
0-45 **2** 3 ½ **Santa Caterina (IRE)**[16] 3232 3-9-2 **70**........ GCarter 2 76
(JLDunlop) *s.i.s: hdwy 8f out: rdn over 2f out: styd on* **12/1**
2200 **3** ½ **Late Opposition**[16] 3231 3-9-0 **68**........(v[1]) OUrbina 14 73
(EALDunlop) *hld up: hdwy to chse wnr over 2f out: hung lft: styd on same pce fnl f* **16/1**
-600 **4** 3 **Canni Thinkaar (IRE)**[30] 2821 3-8-9 **63**........ JCarroll 8 62
(PWHarris) *chsd ldr: rdn over 3f out: wknd over 1f out* **33/1**
-061 **5** 1 ½ **Cobalt Blue (IRE)**[19] 3146 3-8-0 **54**........(b) JBramhill 9 50
(WJHaggas) *prom: rdn over 3f out: wknd over 1f out* **16/1**
3352 **6** 1 ¼ **General Flumpa**[13] 3340 3-8-11 **65**........ RMullen 13 59
(CFWall) *chsd ldrs 8f* **7/1**[3]
4050 **7** ½ **Auroville**[26] 2949 3-8-3 **62**........(v[1]) HayleyTurner(5) 7 55
(MLWBell) *hld up: hdwy over 1f out: nvr nrr* **16/1**
2601 **8** nk **Miss Eloise**[8] 3473 3-8-2 **63**........ AMullen(7) 16 56
(TDEasterby) *mid-div: rdn over 3f out: wknd wl over 1f out* **11/1**
00-4 **9** nk **Jolizero**[19] 3154 3-8-4 **58**........ MHenry 5 50
(PWChapple-Hyam) *hld up in tch: lost pl over 5f out: rdn whn stmbld wl over 1f out: n.d* **5/1**[2]
006- **10** 3 ½ **Abbeygate**[224] 6091 3-8-10 **64**........ MTebbutt 10 49
(TKeddy) *s.i.s: hld up: a in rr* **20/1**
06-0 **11** 1 **Trilemma**[59] 2039 3-8-9 **63**........ JMackay 1 46
(SirMarkPrescott) *sn led: rdn and hdd over 3f out: wknd over 2f out* **10/1**
-555 **12** ¾ **Snowed Under**[31] 2774 3-8-6 **60**........ DAllan 6 42
(JDBethell) *s.i.s: hld up: hmpd over 5f out: a in rr* **25/1**
4354 **13** 8 **Wou Oodd**[14] 3292 3-9-7 **75**........ RLappin 12 42
(MRChannon) *hld up: a in rr* **16/1**
3211 **14** 7 **Jakarmi**[7] 3535 3-9-3 **76**........ MSavage(5) 11 30
(BPalling) *hld up: hdwy over 4f out: rdn and wknd 2f out* **2/1**[1]
-060 **15** 5 **Commemoration Day (IRE)**[12] 3379 3-8-6 **60**........ MFenton 15 4
(JGGiven) *prom: lost pl 4f out: sn bhd* **25/1**

2m 10.67s (1.17) **Going Correction** +0.15s/f (Good) **15 Ran SP% 137.7**
Speed ratings: **101,98,97,95,94 93,92,92,92,89 88,88,81,76,72**CSF £109.99 CT £1564.73 TOTE £11.10: £3.10, £4.00, £5.10; EX 111.00 Place 6 £600.20, Place 5 £449.52.
**Owner** Hill-Smith, Fine, Goddard, Sangster **Bred** Peter Gibbons And Dermot Forde **Trained** Newmarket, Suffolk

**FOCUS**
An ordinary handicap and not the strongest of races, but the winner pulled well clear and looks a progressive sort.

**NOTEBOOK**
**Cellarmaster(IRE)** ◆ all the better for his Windsor outing, fairly ran away from his rivals. Lightly-raced, there is almost certainly more to come.
**Santa Caterina(IRE)** ◆, who was not suited to the steady pace at Leicester, found things happening a bit too quickly for her over this trip. A return to 12 furlongs will be in her favour.
**Late Opposition**, fitted with a visor for the first-time, again left the impression he was saving a bit for himself.
**Canni Thinkaar(IRE)** is beginning to look tripless.
**Jakarmi**, who has been on the go since making his debut last November, was reported to have run flat. *Official explanation: jockey said gelding ran flat possibly as a result of being over the top*
T/Plt: £411.70 to a £1 stake. Pool: £30,316.70. 53.75 winning tickets. T/Qpdt: £47.40 to a £1 stake. Pool: £2,158.70. 33.70 winning tickets. CR

# 3239 SALISBURY (R-H)
Saturday, July 10

**OFFICIAL GOING: Good (good to firm in places) changing to good to soft after race 2 (7:05)**
Wind: lt against Weather: showers

## 3747 CARNARVON AMATEUR RIDERS' H'CAP 6f
**6:35** (6:35) (E) (0-75,72) 3-Y-0+ **£3,575** (£1,100; £550; £275) **Stalls** Centre

Form RPR
-020 **1** **Kallista's Pride**[16] 3227 4-9-9 **58**........ MissKManser(5) 12 64
(JRBest) *trckd ldrs: rdn over 1f out: r.o to ld cl home* **14/1**
5-50 **2** nk **Calusa Lady (IRE)**[31] 2788 4-9-1 **52**........ MissJHannaford(7) 11 57
(GBBalding) *s.i.s: sn mid-div: led briefly ins fnl f: hdd cl home* **11/1**
-000 **3** ½ **Somayda (IRE)**[10] 3412 9-8-3 **40**........(p) JDoyle(7) 1 44
(MissJacquelineSDoyle) *trckd ldr: ev ch ent fnl f: nt qckn wl ins fnl f* **66/1**
6000 **4** shd **Man Crazy (IRE)**[21] 3096 3-8-12 **55**........(b) MrRVMoore(7) 7 58
(RMBeckett) *hampered s: plld hrd and towards rr tl hdwy 3f out: led over 1f out: hdd wl ins fnl f and no ex nr fin* **25/1**
0050 **5** ½ **Formalise**[10] 3416 4-9-7 **58**........ MissKCuthbertson(7) 3 60
(GBBalding) *led tl hdd over 1f out: one pce fnl f* **14/1**
0500 **6** ½ **Cormorant Wharf (IRE)**[14] 3326 4-10-3 **68**........(v[1]) MissJPowell(7) 2 68
(TEPowell) *in rr: hdwy over 1f out: hmpd ins fnl f but nvr nr to chal* **14/1**
1001 **7** hd **Somerset West (IRE)**[16] 3227 4-10-7 **72**........ MissLBaldwin(7) 9 72
(JRBest) *t.k.h: hld up in rr: hdwy on ins wl over 1f out but nvr nr to chal* **13/2**[3]
2445 **8** hd **Lily Of The Guild (IRE)**[28] 2886 5-9-8 **52**........ MrsSBosley 8 51
(WSKittow) *slowly away: gd hdwy over 1f out: nt clr run ins fnl f and could nt chal* **5/1**[1]
03 **9** nk **Secam (POL)**[99] 1233 5-8-11 **46** ow1........ MrsCThompson(5) 10 44
(MrsPTownsley) *in tch: rdn over 2f out: one pce after* **14/1**
00-0 **10** ½ **Ark Admiral**[10] 3412 5-10-2 **63**........(t) MissCTizzard(3) 6 60
(CLTizzard) *t.k.h: hld up: rdn 3f out: wknd wl over 1f out* **14/1**
5-60 **11** 3 ½ **Emerald Fire**[168] 599 5-10-3 **66**........ MissMSowerby(5) 4 52
(AMBalding) *hld up: effrt over 2f out: sn one pce* **11/2**[2]
060- **12** 4 **Saintly Place**[351] 3564 3-9-10 **63**........ MrLNewnes(3) 13 37
(MRChannon) *slowly away: sn in tch: rdn and wknd over 2f out* **14/1**
2160 **13** 8 **Desert Arc (IRE)**[21] 3079 6-10-7 **65**........ MrSWalker 5 15
(WMBrisbourne) *t.k.h: in tch tl wknd 1/2-way: eased* **11/2**[2]

1m 17.58s (2.64) **Going Correction** +0.325s/f (Good)
**WFA** 3 from 4yo+ 6lb **13 Ran SP% 114.4**
Speed ratings: **95,94,93,93,93 92,92,91,91,90 86,80,70**CSF £153.19 CT £9725.72 TOTE £25.10: £7.80, £4.00, £21.20; EX 161.00.
**Owner** G G Racing **Bred** Miss K S Buckley And J S Middleton **Trained** Hucking, Kent

**FOCUS**
A tight event and runners were packed together at the line, the first ten being split by no more than three lengths. Plenty of them were struggling for form previously, so this might not be that reliable.

**NOTEBOOK**
**Kallista's Pride**, claimed after her second at Sandown, was well suited by the extra furlong. She looked beaten when dropping back around two furlongs out, but came with a renewed challenge to get up in the final yards. On this showing she is worth another try over 7f.
**Calusa Lady(IRE)** ran one of her better races and was only run out of it in the final strides.
**Somayda(IRE)** raced towards the centre of the track for most of the way and produced an improved effort in the cheekpieces. He is currently 43lb lower than when last winning nearly six years ago and looks capable of scoring if holding this level of form.
**Man Crazy(IRE)** did not quite see her race out, having pulled in rear, but still ran well.
**Formalise** is a frustrating sort and remains one to leave alone.
**Cormorant Wharf(IRE)** was a little unlucky not to finish closer, being hampered as he was trying to get involved.
**Somerset West(IRE)**, a stablemate of the winner, could not defy a 6lb higher mark for his win at Leicester.
**Lily Of The Guild(IRE)** was luckless in the final furlong, getting no run and having to sit and suffer.

## 3748 PETER & SARAH GRUBB WEDDING ANNIVERSARY NOVICE AUCTION STKS 6f
**7:05** (7:07) (F) 2-Y-O **£3,523** (£1,084; £542; £271) **Stalls** Centre

Form RPR
1 **1** **Johnny Jumpup (IRE)**[67] 1853 2-9-3........ SSanders 7 90
(RMBeckett) *hld up: rdn over 2f out: short of room sn after and swtchd lft to ld ins fnl f: r.o wl* **13/8**[1]
4 **2** ¾ **Little Dalham**[10] 3406 2-8-9........ JFortune 6 80
(PWChapple-Hyam) *led over 2f out: rdn and hdd wl ins fnl f: nt pce of wnr* **9/1**
1 **3** 1 ½ **Intoxicating**[16] 3228 2-9-4........ SCarson 8 84
(RFJohnsonHoughton) *a.p: ev ch ent fnl f: nt qckn ins last* **5/2**[2]
1 **4** 1 ¼ **Deeday Bay (IRE)**[14] 3296 2-9-1........ JQuinn 5 78
(CFWall) *in tch: rdn whn hmpd over 2f out: got clr run and styd on ins fnl f* **8/1**[3]
0 **5** 1 ¼ **Worth A Grand (IRE)**[16] 3240 2-8-7........ PDoe 9 66
(JWMullins) *prom: strly rdn and wknd ent fnl f* **33/1**
06 **6** 5 **Pennestamp (IRE)**[32] 2761 2-8-9........ RHavlin 3 53
(MrsPNDutfield) *led: started to hang rt and hdd over 2f out: continued to drift rt and weakened over 1f out* **66/1**
45 **7** ½ **Ridder**[17] 3192 2-8-12........ MartinDwyer 11 54
(DJCoakley) *chsd ldrs tl rdn and wknd over 1f out* **16/1**
00 **8** 2 ½ **Pips Pearl (IRE)**[5] 3588 2-8-4 ow2........ NPollard 2 37
(MrsPNDutfield) *a bhd: no ch fnl 2f* **80/1**
00 **9** 3 **Dara Girl (IRE)**[21] 3083 2-8-4........(t) JFEgan 1 30
(MrsPNDutfield) *a outpcd in rr* **66/1**
5042 **10** 1 ¼ **Gavioli (IRE)**[19] 3150 2-8-9........(t) RLMoore 4 31
(JMBradley) *prom tl hung rt and wknd over 1f out* **16/1**
**11** 7 **David's Symphony (IRE)** 2-8-12........ DaneO'Neill 10 13
(RHannon) *swvd rt leaving stalls and always hopelessly in rr* **10/1**

1m 16.7s (1.76) **Going Correction** +0.325s/f (Good) **11 Ran SP% 115.8**
Speed ratings: **101,100,98,96,94 88,87,84,80,78 69**CSF £17.02 TOTE £2.70: £1.60, £2.10, £1.60; EX 17.30.
**Owner** Mr & Mrs A Briars **Bred** Mill House Stud **Trained** Lambourn, Berks

**FOCUS**
A decent event, much better than its class F status and a smart winning time for the grade. Johnny Jumpup missed Ascot but confirmed himself a useful prospect, despite making hard work of winning.

**NOTEBOOK**
**Johnny Jumpup(IRE)**, who claimed the scalp of subsequent Coventry winner Iceman back in May, was having his first start since and appreciated the rain. He was being ridden some way from the finish and struggled for a good position, but sneaked up the rail in the final 100 yards to eventually score a shade cosily. This extra furlong suited well and he is clearly a useful prospect.
**Little Dalham** showed promise over seven furlongs on his debut and was not inconvenienced by the drop back in trip. He looked the likely winner over a furlong out but wandered off the rail late on, allowing the winner to slip through. He should win his maiden.
**Intoxicating** was a good winner on his debut at Leicester and ran well in defeat, just being unable to go with the front pair late on, after racing off the advantageous stands' rail.
**Deeday Bay(IRE)** created a good impression when winning on her debut at Doncaster, the fifth-placed horse there having won earlier in the day, and was unlucky not to finish closer, being hampered and having to wait for a run. She is capable of better.
**Worth A Grand(IRE)** improved on course debut form and is one to watch out for once handicapped.
**Pennestamp(IRE)**, although hanging and looking an awkward ride, undoubtedly has ability and is another nursery type. *Official explanation: jockey said colt was hanging badly right*
**Gavioli(IRE)** *Official explanation: jockey said colt was hanging right*
**David's Symphony(IRE)** lost any chance he had by swerving right at the stalls and was never going thereafter. He is no doubt better than this.

## 3749 GEORGE SMITH HORSEBOXES E B F MAIDEN STKS 6f 212y
**7:35** (7:36) (D) 2-Y-O **£6,077** (£1,870; £935; £467) **Stalls** Low

Form RPR
**1** **Liakoura (GER)** 2-9-0........ SSanders 15 85
(MrsAJPerrett) *a in tch: rdn to ld appr fnl f: styd on wl* **4/1**[2]
**2** ¾ **Woodsley House (IRE)** 2-9-0........ NPollard 1 83
(MrsPNDutfield) *led tl hdd appr fnl f: kpt on gamely but nt peg bk wnr* **66/1**
**3** 3 ½ **Bay Hawk** 2-9-0........ MartinDwyer 7 74
(AMBalding) *mid-div: rdn over 2f out: styd on wl fnl f: nvr nrr* **25/1**
**4** 1 ½ **Desert Commander (IRE)** 2-9-0........ LDettori 8 71
(SaeedBinSuroor) *a in tch: shkn up over 1f out and one pce after* **4/1**[2]
**5** ½ **Mister Genepi** 2-9-0........ JQuinn 4 69
(WRMuir) *wl in rr tl hdwy over 1f out: styd on fnl f: nvr nrr* **25/1**
**6** nk **Chinese Puzzle** 2-9-0........(t) RHughes 5 69
(HRACecil) *prom: rdn over 2f out: fdd appr fnl f* **11/1**
**7** 1 **Kamakiri (IRE)** 2-9-0........ PDobbs 11 66
(RHannon) *wl in rr tl styd on past btn horses ins fnl 2f* **50/1**
3 **8** 5 **Transgress (IRE)**[9] 3451 2-9-0........ DaneO'Neill 2 54
(RHannon) *prom: rdn over 2f out: sn btn* **10/3**[1]
0 **9** 1 ¾ **Snow Tempest (USA)**[16] 3241 2-9-0........ RLMoore 13 49
(TGMills) *a towards rr* **16/1**
6 **10** ½ **Benedict Bay**[16] 3241 2-9-0........ SCarson 10 48
(GBBalding) *nvr on terms* **33/1**
3 **11** ¾ **Celestial Arc (USA)**[16] 3241 2-9-0........ SDrowne 14 46
(PFICole) *prom tl rdn and wknd qckly wl over 1f out* **8/1**[3]
0 **12** hd **Mollzam (IRE)**[16] 3241 2-9-0........ SWhitworth 6 46
(MPTregoning) *wnt rt s: plld hrd: sn in tch: wknd over 1f out* **20/1**

13 *1* **Storm Fury (USA)** 2-9-0 ........ RHavlin 12 43
(PWChapple-Hyam) *in tch: rdn over 2f out: sn wknd* **20/1**

14 *6* **Happy Banker (IRE)** 2-8-7 ........ TO'Brien(7) 9 28
(MRChannon) *mid-div: rdn sn after 1/2-way: sn bhd* **20/1**

15 *nk* **Rum Creek** 2-9-0 ........ JFEgan 3 27
(SKirk) *prom tl rdn and wknd 2f out* **66/1**

16 *1* **Northanger Abbey (IRE)** 2-9-0 ........ JFortune 16 25
(JHMGosden) *racd on outside fr wd draw: sn bhd* **10/1**

1m 31.51s (2.51) **Going Correction** +0.325s/f (Good) **16** Ran SP% **127.4**
Speed ratings: **98,97,93,91,90 90,89,83,81,81 80,80,78,72,71 70**CSF £274.22 TOTE £6.00: £2.40, £16.50, £5.60; EX 2162.20.
**Owner** Mark Tracey **Bred** Dr Chr Berglar **Trained** Pulborough, W Sussex

**FOCUS**
In all probability this was a useful maiden, and one that is sure to produce future winners.

**NOTEBOOK**
**Liakoura(GER)**, whose stable got off the mark with their juveniles in the week - also at the first time of asking - was supported on the exchanges throughout the day and was clearly 'expected'. He did not let supporters down and ran on well to hold one of the rank outsiders. Clearly a useful prospect, he can be placed to advantage in a conditions event and has the scope to stay a mile.
**Woodsley House(IRE)** ◆ comes from a stable that can get a good two-year-old and although he had the advantage of the favoured stands' rail throughout, pulled far enough clear of the third to suggest it was no fluke. He should have little bother winning his maiden and may be a fair price to do so, due to relatively discreet connections.
**Bay Hawk** ◆ comes from a stable that has had a great start to the season with their two-year-olds - roughly a 22% strike rate - and although this one was a cheap purchase, he shaped with any amount of promise, staying on well in the closing stages to take third. Out of a dam who won at up to 18 furlongs, he is going to relish a mile in time and looks another likely maiden winner. He holds a Derby entry.
**Desert Commander(IRE)**, a Gimcrack entrant, is a half-brother to Lucky Pipit - a useful two-year-old herself who won at Listed level - and he showed enough to suggest he is going to be a winning juvenile himself, if not one of the stable's 'top dogs'.
**Mister Genepi** comes from a stable whose juveniles usually need a run or two to put them straight, so it was encouraging he finished where he did. If going the right way from this he can get his head in front. *Official explanation: jockey said colt lost its action*
**Chinese Puzzle**, although shaping with promise, was not among those going on at the finish and is nothing to get excited about. He was wearing a tongue tie.
**Kamakiri(IRE)** ◆ would have appreciated the ease in the ground and ran better than his price suggested he would, being given a sympathetic ride and staying on nicely through the final couple of furlongs. A mile will suit and improvement can be expected.
**Transgress(IRE)** shaped with any amount of promise on his debut when a staying on third at Newbury and was bitterly disappointing. He is better than this and needs one more run to qualify for nurseries.
**Celestial Arc(USA)** was another who failed to progress from his promising debut, stopping sharply as though there may be a problem.
**Northanger Abbey(IRE)**, who has a blend of speed and stamina in his pedigree, was forced to race on the outside of the field. Although a disappointing effort, he boasts excellent connections and is sure to show this running to be all wrong in time.

## 3750 JACKSONS GROUP MERCEDES-BENZ RATED STKS (H'CAP) 1m
8:05 (8:06) (D) (0-85,85) 3-Y-O **£7,269** (£2,236; £1,118; £559) **Stalls** Centre

Form RPR

02-1 **1** **Take A Bow**[19] 3161 3-9-6 **84** ........ JQuinn 2 95
(PRChamings) *a.p: swtchd rt to ld 1f out: rdn out* **5/1**[3]

0612 **2** *½* **Evaluator (IRE)**[7] 3527 3-9-0 **78** ........ RLMoore 6 88
(TGMills) *in tch: rdn over 2f out: styd on to chse wnr fnl f* **6/4**[1]

-150 **3** *3* **Apex**[35] 2692 3-9-0 **78** ........ LDettori 7 82
(EALDunlop) *led: carried hd high: rdn and hdd 1f out: nt qckn* **8/1**

1 **4** *1* **Namroc (IRE)**[21] 3094 3-9-7 **85** ........ MartinDwyer 3 87
(ACStewart) *hld up in rr: hdwy and swtchd rt over 2f out: sn rdn and outpcd* **4/1**[2]

4013 **5** *1 ¾* **Alfridini**[17] 3213 3-8-6 **73** ........ LPKeniry(3) 9 71
(DRCElsworth) *trckd ldr: rdn and u.p whn bmpd appr fnl f: sn wknd* **12/1**

0010 **6** *1 ¾* **Flip Flop And Fly (IRE)**[36] 2642 3-9-7 **85** ........ JFEgan 4 80
(SKirk) *a towards rr: no hdwy fnl 2f* **10/1**

2-00 **7** *3* **I Won't Dance (IRE)**[34] 2704 3-9-0 **78** ........ PDobbs 8 66
(RHannon) *s.i.s: sn in tch: wknd 2f out* **20/1**

-420 **8** *1* **Best Desert (IRE)**[18] 3180 3-8-4 **68** oh2 ........ NPollard 11 54
(JRBest) *a struggling in rr* **33/1**

-300 **9** *shd* **Love Triangle (IRE)**[7] 3542 3-9-1 **79** ........ DaneO'Neill 1 65
(DRCElsworth) *prom tl rdn and wknd 2f out* **20/1**

1m 45.7s (2.73) **Going Correction** +0.325s/f (Good) **9** Ran SP% **117.0**
Speed ratings: **99,98,95,94,92 91,88,87,86**CSF £12.75 CT £60.22 TOTE £6.60: £1.60, £1.30, £2.70; EX 15.70.
**Owner** Mrs J E L Wright **Bred** Heatherwold Stud **Trained** Baughurst, Hants

**FOCUS**
This featured several horses who are high enough in the weights but still looks a reasonable three-year-old handicap.

**NOTEBOOK**
**Take A Bow** was an easy winner from a good draw at Windsor most recently and, although introduced into handicaps on a stiff enough mark - mainly as a result of finishing second to North Light at two - put up a smart performance in beating Evaluator. Likely to take a further rise in the weights, he will need to progress again to defy it.
**Evaluator(IRE)**, unlucky in running when trying to supplement his Newbury win last time, pulled clear of the third but could not get to the winner. He will go up again despite not winning.
**Apex** had the favoured rail to run against but was not good enough. He carried his head slightly high but did at least return to form.
**Namroc(IRE)**, a Newmarket winner on his only previous start, ran well for one so inexperienced and improved around 7lb, but he was not up to defying his stiff-looking mark of 85. He may need to drop a few pounds before he is winning in handicap company. *Official explanation: jockey said colt lost its action*

## 3751 EBF LADIES EVENING CLASSIFIED STKS 6f 212y
8:35 (8:35) (B) 3-Y-O **£14,935** (£5,665; £2,832; £1,287) **Stalls** Low

Form RPR

4312 **1** **Delphie Queen (IRE)**[28] 2897 3-8-11 95 ........ JFEgan 2 107
(SKirk) *hld up in tch: swtchd rt over 2f out: led appr fnl n f: qcknd clr: easily* **15/8**[1]

-033 **2** *5* **Jedburgh**[52] 2224 3-9-2 97 ........ TQuinn 6 99
(JLDunlop) *trckd ldrs: gng 2nd whn hmpd by wnr appr fnl f: readily outpcd* **3/1**[2]

22-0 **3** *1 ¾* **Golden Sahara (IRE)**[70] 1764 3-9-1 96 ........(vt) LDettori 3 93
(SaeedBinSuroor) *hld up: hdwy over 1f out but nvr nr to chal* **4/1**[3]

0-00 **4** *1 ½* **Sgt Pepper (IRE)**[24] 2966 3-9-0 95 ........ PDobbs 5 89
(RHannon) *led tl hdd & wknd appr fnl f* **12/1**

1 **5** *½* **Camberwell**[32] 2765 3-9-0 90 ........ JFortune 7 87
(TGMills) *wnt rt s: lost tch ins fnl 2f* **8/1**

131- **6** *3 ½* **Polonius**[262] 5707 3-9-0 91 ........ DaneO'Neill 1 78
(HCandy) *t.k.h: trckd ldr tl wknd over 1f out* **13/2**

1m 30.04s (1.04) **Going Correction** +0.325s/f (Good) **6** Ran SP% **111.9**
Speed ratings: **107,101,99,97,97 93**CSF £7.64 TOTE £3.10: £2.00, £2.80; EX 8.10.
**Owner** Nicholas Hartery **Bred** Mrs C Hartery **Trained** Upper Lambourn, Berks
■ Stewards Enquiry : J F Egan caution: careless riding

**FOCUS**
A decent classified event and a smart performance from Delphie Queen who showed a good change of pace to settle the issue and looks progressive.

**NOTEBOOK**
**Delphie Queen(IRE)** was racing off a 5lb higher mark than when second to Two Step Kid in the William Hill Trophy at York, blitzed her rivals and has evidently improved again. On this evidence and according to her rating, she has to have a go at Listed level as she is in blinding form, acts on any ground and is fully effective over six and seven furlongs. *Official explanation: jockey said filly hung left handed*
**Jedburgh** is on a stiff mark and although slightly hampered by the winner, it made no difference to the outcome. This type of race is his best hope for winning again.
**Golden Sahara(IRE)**, used as a pacemaker when last of 14 in the 2000 Guineas, ran just a fair race and is on a much stiffer mark than he can handle. He is likely to continue to struggle.
**Sgt Pepper(IRE)** has yet to run a race this season and folded disappointingly.
**Camberwell** simply seemed to come up short of what was required, finding this much tougher than his easy course debut win over modest opposition.
**Polonius** was a useful juvenile and should come on appreciably for this.

## 3752 FTX LOGISTICS H'CAP 1m 4f
9:05 (9:06) (E) (0-75,75) 3-Y-O+ **£3,523** (£1,084; £542; £271) **Stalls** High

Form RPR

1004 **1** **Jack Of Trumps (IRE)**[22] 3050 4-9-3 **64** ........ DHolland 6 75
(GWragg) *a in tch: hdwy to ld over 1f out: edgd lft: styd on u.p* **5/1**[2]

5060 **2** *½* **Aoninch**[32] 2767 4-8-9 **56** ........ NPollard 4 67
(MrsPNDutfield) *wl in rr tl hdwy 2f out: swtchd rt jst ins fnl f: styd on strly to cl on wnr* **14/1**

-420 **3** *3* **Turnstile**[39] 2561 3-8-12 **72** ........ RHughes 1 78
(RHannon) *a.p: rdn and one pce appr fnl f* **15/2**

0653 **4** *hd* **Kylkenny**[15] 3274 9-9-8 **72** ........(t) LFletcher(3) 14 78
(HMorrison) *trckd ldrs: lft in ld 7f out: rdn and hdd over 1f out: kpt on one pce* **4/1**[1]

0005 **5** *1 ¼* **Reviewer (IRE)**[17] 3207 6-9-2 **63** ........ RHavlin 3 67
(MMeade) *a.p: rdn over 2f out: fdd appr fnl f* **12/1**

6-00 **6** *2 ½* **Masterman Ready**[16] 3245 3-8-10 **70** ........ RLMoore 8 70
(PWHarris) *in tch: rdn and wknd over 1f out* **9/1**

500- **7** *3* **Flamenco Bride**[245] 5949 4-9-8 **69** ........ SSanders 2 65
(DRCElsworth) *towards rr: sme hdwy ins fnl 2f: nvr nr to chal* **20/1**

2600 **8** *1 ½* **Indian Chase**[20] 3120 7-7-5 **45** ........ LucyRussell(7) 5 39
(DrJRJNaylor) *hld up:: rdn and hdwy over 3f out: wknd 2f out* **33/1**

**9** *¾* **Onward To Glory (USA)**[397] 4-9-12 **73** ........ LDettori 9 65
(JLDunlop) *mid-div: rdn and wknd over 2f out* **6/1**[3]

0105 **10** *3* **Private Benjamin**[11] 3393 4-8-3 **50** ow1 ........ PDoe 7 38
(JamiePoulton) *a towards rr* **15/2**

-200 **11** *15* **Western (IRE)**[112] 899 4-9-13 **74** ........ TQuinn 12 39
(JAkehurst) *towards rr: effrt over 2f out: sn btn* **20/1**

-630 **12** *2 ½* **Hashid (IRE)**[21] 3095 4-9-9 **70** ........ MartinDwyer 11 32
(PCRitchens) *led for 1f: wknd 6f out* **25/1**

0-00 **13** *20* **Herodotus**[14] 3325 6-10-0 **75** ........(t) JFEgan 10 7
(KOCunningham-Brown) *hld up: lost tch 3f out and eased whn btn* **40/1**

-060 **U** **Nick The Silver**[31] 2787 3-7-10 **61** ow1 ........ RThomas(5) 13 —
(GBBalding) *led after 1f: rn out on bnd 7f out and uns rdr* **25/1**

2m 40.1s (3.75) **Going Correction** +0.325s/f (Good)
**WFA** 3 from 4yo+ 13lb **14** Ran SP% **121.4**
Speed ratings: **100,99,97,97,96 95,93,92,91,89 79,77,64,—**CSF £66.00 CT £531.97 TOTE £5.80: £2.60, £3.70, £2.70; EX 164.00 Place 6 £292.00, Place 5 £35.80.
**Owner** Mollers Racing **Bred** Miss Susan Bates **Trained** Newmarket, Suffolk

**FOCUS**
An ordinary race in which there was little to pin the form on. The front two pulled three lengths clear.

**NOTEBOOK**
**Jack Of Trumps(IRE)** did not quite get home after pulling on his first attempt at this trip at Newmarket last month, but he settled better and saw his race out well, running on to hold the slightly unlucky late challenge of Aoninch. He is only moderate but is at least going the right way.
**Aoninch** was arguably unlucky not to win as she was running on strongly when blocked by the winner in her bid to come up the rail and had to check in her run. Back on a reasonable mark, she could land a similar race in the not too distant future.
**Turnstile** travelled strongly and looked the most likely winner until coming under pressure and finding less than looked likely. Although weakening over a mile six last time, he is not the quickest and looks worth another go under more restrained tactics.
**Kylkenny** was bang there throughout until being unable to quicken late on.
**Masterman Ready** was slightly disappointing as he had shaped as though this trip would suit. He may be worth another chance back on faster ground to prove he stays.
**Flamenco Bride** did not really go on after her win at the course last year, but this was an encouraging reappearance.
**Onward To Glory(USA)** was having his first start in this country having previously been with Andre Fabre in France. He did not do enough to suggest he will be winning next time, but is no doubt better than this.
**Western(IRE)** *Official explanation: jockey said gelding got tired*
T/Plt: £408.60 to a £1 stake. Pool: £41,763.55. 74.60 winning tickets. T/Qpdt: £71.50 to a £1 stake. Pool: £3,579.30. 37.00 winning tickets. JS

# 3713 YORK (L-H)
Saturday, July 10

**OFFICIAL GOING: Good (good to soft in places)**
The ground was described as 'tacky' after a dry night.
Wind: Slight 1/2 against. Weather: Overcast but mainly fine and dry.

## 3753 JOHN SMITH'S "AVE IT" STKS (NURSERY) 5f
2:05 (2:06) (C) 2-Y-O **£8,697** (£2,676; £1,338; £669) **Stalls** Centre

Form RPR

11 **1** **Key Secret**[40] 2523 2-7-13 **72** ........ AMcCarthy 6 77
(MLWBell) *trckd ldrs: hdwy 2f out: rdn over 1f out: led ent last and styd on wl* **7/1**

412 **2** *1 ¼* **Right Answer**[13] 3346 2-9-7 **94** ........ KFallon 2 95
(APJarvis) *led: rdn wl over 1f out: drvn and hdd ent last: kpt on* **5/1**[2]

531 **3** *1* **Missperon (IRE)**[20] 3116 2-8-3 **76** ........ PFessey 8 74
(KARyan) *chsd ldrs: rdn 2f out: styd on u.p fnl f* **11/1**

6 **19** 3/4 **Polygonal (FR)**[28] 2894 4-8-10 **89** TEDurcan 22 63
(MrsJRRamsden) *s.i.s: a rr* **25/1**
1333 **20** 1 3/4 **Mutafanen**[23] 3000 3-8-9 **99** RHills 15 69
(EALDunlop) *stdd s: a rr* **12/1**
-400 **21** 15 **Lundy's Lane (IRE)**[84] 1456 4-9-4 **100** J-PGuillambert(3) 19 42
(CEBrittain) *aways rr* **66/1**

2m 10.01s (0.57) **Going Correction** +0.35s/f (Good)
**WFA** 3 from 4yo+ 11lb **21** Ran SP% **129.6**
Speed ratings: **111,110,108,108,107 107,107,105,103,101 100,98,97,96,95 95,94,94,93,92 80**CSF £82.45 CT £646.80 TOTE £36.10: £6.30, £1.60, £1.90, £3.20; EX 182.50 Trifecta £1897.30 Pool £, w/u.
**Owner** Andrea & Graham Wylie **Bred** P E Clinton **Trained** Crook, Co Durham

**FOCUS**
A high draw was not the disadvantage it was predicted to be, and four of the first six were in double figures. The pace was sound and the form looks typically strong.

**NOTEBOOK**
**Arcalis** was up 7lb and had a wide drawn to overcome. On top of that, his rider dropped his whip inside the last, but he still did enough to edge out the favourite near the line and improve around 10lb on his previous best. Bought as a potential hurdler, connections are reluctant to continue with him on the Flat and regard these two wins as a bonus.
**Promotion** tends to live on his nerves. He surged to the front looking all over a winner but he looked to hang fire well inside the last and was just edged out. He certainly has the ability to find a major handicap from this sort of mark but will need everything to fall just right.
**Starry Lodge(IRE)**, 3lb higher, was attempting to make it seven wins from his last 11 starts. Dropping back in trip, he could not match the first two where it matters and did not aid his cause by tending to hang left. *Official explanation: jockey said colt hung left*
**Red Fort(IRE)**had been hoisted 16lb after his runaway Royal Ascot success but had just an 8lb penalty. He did not impress at all going to post and, like the winner, had a supposedly unfavourable draw, but he ran really well, again putting up a performance plenty good enough to win in Listed or minor Group company.
**Jabaar(USA)**, beaten in a claimer last time, had the visor back on and seemed to run out of his skin. Will he reproduce it next time though ?
**Polar Jem**, under an 8lb penalty, had a good draw for a front-runner and she confirmed that she is a highly-progressive filly. She must be worth a chance in Listed company now.
**Vicious Warrior**, a late call up as first reserve, hasn't won for two years, but he had the ground in his favour and was far from disgraced.
**Wing Commander**, whose sole win was in a maiden at two, usually gives a good account of himself in these competitive handicaps and so it was again here.
**Ionian Spring(IRE)**, 5lb higher and from a career-high mark, was last in the parade and virtually walked to post. After a tardy start he was merely staying on in his own time at the finish, but at nine he is a credit to his yard.
**Blue Spinnaker(IRE)** looked at his best but never really got competitive. He prefers much quicker ground and there will be other days.
**Coat Of Honour(USA)**, whose trainer had enjoyed two big high profile wins in this race in the past, was awash with sweat at the start and his supporters knew their fate early in the home straight.

## 3757 JOHN SMITH'S EXTRA SMOOTH SILVER CUP RATED STKS (H'CAP) (LISTED RACE) 1m 5f 197y

4:25 (4:26) (A) (0-110,105) 4-Y-0+ £17,400 (£6,600; £3,300; £1,500) Stalls Low

Form RPR
5-05 **1** **Distinction (IRE)**[56] 2108 5-9-7 **105** KFallon 1 119
(SirMichaelStoute) *lw: hld up: hdwy on ins over 3f out: led 1f out: hld on wl* **11/2**[1]
5141 **2** 1/2 **Star Member (IRE)**[29] 2855 5-8-8 **92** KMcEvoy 12 105
(APJarvis) *hld up: hdwy over 3f out: led over 1f out: sn hdd: nt qckn toards fin* **6/1**[2]
-014 **3** 5 **Collier Hill**[14] 3310 6-9-6 **104** DeanMcKeown 6 110
(GASwinbank) *hld up: hdwy to ld over 2f out: hdd over 1f out: styd on same pce* **6/1**[2]
2-00 **4** 1 1/2 **Mamcazma**[14] 3310 6-8-8 **92** TEDurcan 14 96
(DMorris) *chsd ldrs: effrt over 3f out: one pce fnl 2f* **16/1**
-234 **5** 3/4 **Prins Willem (IRE)**[35] 2684 5-8-7 **91** oh1 TPQueally 5 94
(JRFanshawe) *lw: hld up and bhd: hdwy on outer over 3f out: kpt on: nvr nr ldrs* **8/1**[3]
-061 **6** shd **Kuster**[12] 3385 8-8-7 **91** oh1 (b) NMackay 3 94
(LMCumani) *s.i.s: bhd: hdwy on ins 3f out: nvr nrr* **12/1**
1-00 **7** 4 **Morson Boy (USA)**[35] 2684 4-8-13 **97** SChin 4 94
(MJohnston) *chsd ldr: chal over 3f out: hung lft: lost pl 2f out* **25/1**
3050 **8** 1/2 **Santando**[7] 3521 4-8-10 **94** (v) DHolland 8 90
(CEBrittain) *mid-div: effrt on outer over 3f out: no imp* **20/1**
0145 **9** 3/4 **Royal Cavalier**[7] 3521 7-9-0 **98** NCallan 7 93
(RHollinshead) *chsd ldrs: effrt 3f out: wknd 2f out* **12/1**
24/0 **10** 3 **Ranville**[14] 3325 6-8-7 **91** oh1 PRobinson 10 82
(MAJarvis) *chsd ldrs: lost pl over 3f out* **14/1**
**11** 3/4 **Theme Song (IRE)**[13] 3356 5-8-11 **95** (p) CatherineGannon 11 85
(AnthonyMullins, Ire) *trckd ldr: led over 6f out tl over 2f out: sn lost pl* **11/2**[1]
2310 **12** 5 **Bourgeois**[7] 3521 7-9-0 **98** RWinston 13 81
(TDEasterby) *chsd ldrs on outer: effrt over 3f out: lost pl over 2f out* **11/1**
110- **13** dist **Montmartre (IRE)**[281] 5349 4-8-8 **92** PMulrennan 2 —
(JHowardJohnson) *trckd ldrs: hmpd over 4f out: bhd and eased over 2f out: t.o* **33/1**
52-6 **14** dist **Calibre (USA)**[14] 3315 4-9-0 **98** KDarley 9 —
(JHMGosden) *led tl over 6f out: lost pl over 4f out: bhd and eased over 3f out: wl t.o* **20/1**

2m 58.44s (2.04) **Going Correction** +0.35s/f (Good) **14** Ran SP% **123.0**
Speed ratings: **108,107,104,104,103 103,101,100,100,98 98,95,—,—**CSF £36.44 CT £211.29 TOTE £4.80: £2.30, £2.40, £3.00; EX 42.90.
**Owner** Highclere Thoroughbred Racing Ltd **Bred** Orpendale And Minch Bloodstock **Trained** Newmarket, Suffolk

**FOCUS**
In effect a 0-105 handicap, not run at a strong pace in the middle third of the race. The form reads well, however, Distinction putting up one of the handicap performances of the season and Star Member confirming himself a progressive sort.

**NOTEBOOK**
**Distinction(IRE)**, who looked in magnificent condition, was a positive on the betting front and digging deep, in the end did just enough. This was a top-class handicap performance and a return for the Ebor is on the cards. In the longer term he looks ideal material for the Melbourne Cup.
**Star Member(IRE)**, 7lb higher, went a neck up but could not quite contain the winner. He is still on the upgrade and is another who looks likely to return for a crack at the Ebor next month.
**Collier Hill**, 3lb higher, did not impress at all going to post and was a negative on the exchanges. He is starting to look in the grip of the handicapper, but this was still a decent effort, especially as he prefers more give underfoot.
**Mamcazma**, runner-up in this a year ago from a 3lb higher mark, ran a lot better than on his two previous outings this time and would have preferred much quicker ground.
**Prins Willem(IRE)**, running from a career-high mark, was held up to get the trip. He stayed on up the wide outside but was never on terms. Now his stamina is proven more posititive tactics can be adopted.
**Kuster** ambled out of the stalls and was in arrears until picking up late in the day. Stamina did not seem to be a problem.
**Morson Boy(USA)**, who looked to have lost his way in two previous starts this time, ran a lot better and is hopefully on the way back.
**Theme Song(IRE)**, 10lb higher than for his Curragh success, was a major mover on the betting front but after showing ahead and setting sail for home he dropped right out with two furlongs left to run.
**Bourgeois** *Official explanation: jockey said gelding ran very flat*
**Montmartre(IRE)** *Official explanation: jockey said filly ran too keen early on and got very tired*
**Calibre(USA)** *Official explanation: jockey said colt lost its action*

## 3758 JOHN SMITH'S HERON & BREARLEY MEDIAN AUCTION MAIDEN STKS (DIV I) 6f

5:00 (5:01) (E) 2-Y-O £6,906 (£2,125; £1,062; £531) Stalls Centre

Form RPR
**1** **Visionist (IRE)** 2-9-0 DHolland 2 89+
(JAOsborne) *w'like: lengthy: scope: trckd ldrs: led jst ins fnl f: r.o wl* **7/1**
**2** 1 **Yajbill (IRE)** 2-9-0 TEDurcan 8 86
(MRChannon) *w'like: cmpt: hmpd s: sn trcking ldrs: led over 1f out: hdd jst ins fnl f: nt qckn* **8/1**
0 **3** 3 **Wavertree Warrior (IRE)**[30] 2804 2-8-11 J-PGuillambert(3) 5 77
(NPLittmoden) *trckd ldrs: ev ch 2f out: wknd ins last* **20/1**
**4** hd **Bahamian Magic** 2-9-0 TPQueally 12 76
(DRLoder) *lengthy: unf: sn trcking ldrs: effrt over 2f out: styd on same pce* **9/2**[2]
3 **5** 3 **Claret And Amber**[8] 3469 2-9-0 KFallon 9 67
(RAFahey) *hdwy over 2f out: styd on wl fnl f: improve* **3/1**[1]
0 **6** hd **Regis Flight**[16] 3248 2-9-0 DeanMcKeown 6 67
(RHollinshead) *trckd ldrs: effrt over 2f out: kpt on same pce* **50/1**
5 **7** hd **Commendable Coup (USA)**[16] 3248 2-9-0 GGibbons 3 66
(TDBarron) *t.k.h: trckd ldrs: stmbld path after 150yds: one pce fnl 2f* **12/1**
**8** 1 3/4 **Jeune Loup** 2-9-0 GFaulkner 1 61
(PCHaslam) *leggy: unf: scope: bhd: sme hdwy over 2f out: nvr nr ldrs* **66/1**
**9** 3/4 **Spence Appeal (IRE)** 2-9-0 NCallan 10 59
(KARyan) *w'like: bit bkwd: s.i.s: bhd tl sme hdwy fnl 2f* **25/1**
**10** 4 **Mostanad** 2-9-0 RHills 4 47
(EALDunlop) *w ldrs: wkng whn hmpd over 1f out* **12/1**
60 **11** 1 **Paula Jo**[8] 3469 2-8-6 TEaves(3) 7 39
(JSWainwright) *led tl 2f out: sn wknd* **66/1**
5 **12** 3/4 **Artic Fox**[16] 3233 2-9-0 PRobinson 11 41
(TDEasterby) *rr div: outpcd over 2f out: nvr a danger* **6/1**[3]
2 **13** 3 1/2 **As Handsome Does**[9] 3444 2-9-0 (t) KDarley 13 31
(NTinkler) *s.i.s: a bhd* **15/2**

1m 14.01s (1.44) **Going Correction** +0.125s/f (Good) **13** Ran SP% **121.8**
Speed ratings: **95,93,89,89,85 85,84,82,81,76 74,73,69**CSF £60.61 TOTE £8.30: £2.70, £2.20, £8.20; EX 65.70.
**Owner** Pat Eddery Racing (Alvaro) **Bred** Frank Barry **Trained** Upper Lambourn, Berks
■ A first success for Pat Eddery's syndicates.

**FOCUS**
Just a steady gallop for the first four furlongs, but strong maiden form and a winner who has the potential to go on to much better things.

**NOTEBOOK**
**Visionist(IRE)** ◆, an April foal, was easily the paddock pick but he was very green to post. Firmly in command at the line, he looks sure to improve and make his mark in much stronger company.
**Yajbill(IRE)**, a February foal, already looks mature. After taking a bump at the start he took it up travelling nicely but in the end simply met one too good. He looks a ready-made winner.
**Wavertree Warrior(IRE)**, a May foal, showed a lot more than on his debut a month earlier and should improve again.
**Bahamian Magic**, a March foal, is bred for speed. He made a satisfactory bow and will know more next time.
**Claret And Amber** is still learning and will be of serious interest in nursery company with another away day under his belt.
**Regis Flight** improved on his initial outing and there may be even better to come.
**Commendable Coup(USA)** was again out of luck, losing ground at the path early on. He is definitely better than he has shown in two outings so far.

## 3759 JOHN SMITH'S "NO NONSENSE RACING" MAIDEN FILLIES' STKS 6f 217y

5:30 (5:31) (D) 3-Y-O £5,616 (£1,728; £864; £432) Stalls Low

Form RPR
34 **1** **Anatolian Queen (USA)**[19] 3161 3-8-11 KDarley 4 77
(JMPEustace) *trckd ldrs: effrt 2f out: styd on to ld last 75yds* **11/2**[3]
0-20 **2** 1 **Noora (IRE)**[52] 2223 3-8-11 80 RHills 6 74
(MPTregoning) *lw: led: qckn 4f out: kpt on wl: hdd wl ins last* **11/4**[2]
**3** 1 **Lake Charlotte (USA)** 3-8-11 TPQueally 2 71
(DRLoder) *w'like: lengthy: trckd ldrs: effrt 2f out: ev ch 1f out: n.m.r and fdd nr fin* **1/1**[1]
63 **4** 5 **Rosie Mac**[16] 3251 3-8-4 SuzanneFrance(7) 7 58
(NBycroft) *chsd ldrs: fdd over 1f out* **25/1**
65- **5** 1/2 **Miss Procurer (IRE)**[324] 4308 3-8-11 SChin 9 57
(PFICole) *swtchd lft after s: hld up: effrt and swtchd rt over 2f out: put hd in air: wknd over 1f out* **20/1**
0-5 **6** 2 1/2 **Mecca's Mate**[7] 3511 3-8-11 FLynch 8 51
(DWBarker) *in tch: outpcd over 3f out: kpt on fnl 2f* **100/1**
**7** 5 **Lottie** 3-8-11 AMcCarthy 3 38
(MissVHaigh) *cmpt: bit bkwd: chsd ldrs: outpcd over 2f out: sn wknd* **50/1**
U **8** 1 1/2 **Aljafliyah**[21] 3094 3-8-8 NMackay(3) 5 34
(LMCumani) *s.v.s: a bhd* **20/1**
00-6 **9** 1 **Power Nap**[14] 3294 3-8-8 48 (t) TEaves(3) 1 31
(NTinkler) *chsd ldrs: outpcd and pushed along 4f out: lost pl 3f out* **66/1**

1m 27.24s (3.93) **Going Correction** +0.575s/f (Yiel) **9** Ran SP% **109.9**
Speed ratings: **100,98,97,92,91 88,82,81,80**CSF £18.40 TOTE £7.20: £1.90, £1.60, £1.30; EX 21.20.
**Owner** Y Gelgin **Bred** Flaxman Holdings Ltd **Trained** Newmarket, Suffolk

**FOCUS**
A maiden lacking strength in depth and run at a very steady pace to almost halfway. The form of the principals is okay, but some big-priced horses behind may be flattered.

**NOTEBOOK**
**Anatolian Queen(USA)**, dropping back in trip, had the leader covered and in the end did just enough. This was improved form, but with the runner-up rated 80 she cannot expect a lenient mark in handicaps.
**Noora(IRE)**, absent for over seven weeks, looked fresh and well and on good terms with herself. Allowed to set her own pace, in the end she was still not good enough.

3153 **4** *shd* **Empire's Ghodha**[8] 3481 2-9-0 **87**....(b) TEDurcan 10 84
(BJMeehan) *towards rr: hdwy halfway: rdn and hung lft over 1f out: kpt on ins last: nrst fin* **10/1**

0521 **5** *nk* **Wonderful Mind**[8] 3469 2-7-13 **72**.... PMQuinn 7 68
(TDEasterby) *cl up: rdn and ev ch over 1f out: wknd ins last* **13/2**[3]

4320 **6** *1* **Lady Dan (IRE)**[18] 3164 2-7-10 **72**.... JFMcDonald(3) 1 65
(MWEasterby) *in tch: hdwy to chse ldrs 2f out: sn rdn and one pce* **4/1**[1]

4601 **7** *1 ¾* **Blue Marble**[7] 3531 2-8-1 **77**.... NMackay(3) 3 63
(CEBrittain) *bhd tl styd in fnl 2f* **15/2**

015 **8** *½* **Dorn Dancer (IRE)**[23] 3011 2-8-7 **83**.... LEnstone(3) 4 68
(DWBarker) *sn rdn along and a rr* **16/1**

213 **9** *nk* **World At My Feet**[56] 2129 2-8-6 **86**.... SuzanneFrance(7) 5 70
(NBycroft) *cl up: rdn along 1/2-way and sn wknd* **13/2**[3]

064 **10** *¾* **Sowerby**[8] 3469 2-7-7 **71** oh8.... BSwarbrick(5) 9 52
(MBrittain) *a towards rr* **33/1**

60.12 secs (0.84) **Going Correction** +0.125s/f (Good) **10** Ran SP% **113.8**
Speed ratings: **98,96,94,94,93 92,89,88,88,86**CSF £40.87 CT £390.09 TOTE £9.20: £3.30, £1.90, £4.10; EX 31.20.
**Owner** Joy And Valentine Feerick **Bred** Barry Minty **Trained** Newmarket, Suffolk
■ Stewards Enquiry : P Fessey two-day ban: used whip without giving filly time to respond (Jul 21)

**FOCUS**
The time was decent and the fourth is a particularly good yardstick, so this looks rock-solid nursery form. The figures shown as 'official ratings' are estimates for guidance only.

**NOTEBOOK**
**Key Secret**, who is not very big, was having her first outing for her new connections. Awkward to load, she edged left inside the last but was firmly in command at the line, making it three from three. The ease in the ground was no problem.
**Right Answer**, conceding weight all round, showed a very scratchy action. She went down fighting and deserves credit for this.
**Missperon(IRE)**, dropping back in trip and racing on easy ground for the first time, was very keen to post, at a cost to her rider. She stayed on despite being carried left and is better suited by six.
**Empire's Ghodha**, very warm beforehand, was taken very gingerly to post. She showed a marked tenedency to hang and does not look straightfoward, but this was another decent effort at the weights.
**Wonderful Mind**, a positive on the exchanges, showed plenty of toe but did not truly see it out on the easy ground.
**Lady Dan(IRE)**, quite keen to post, was taking a big drop in trip on a track at which she has run well in the past. Six looks the happy medium.

## 3754 JOHN SMITH'S EXTRA COLD H'CAP 6f
**2:40** (2:40) (C) (0-90,92) 3-Y-0+ **£10,738** (£3,304; £1,652; £826) **Stalls** Centre

Form RPR

0400 **1** **Pieter Brueghel (USA)**[4] 3606 5-9-4 **80**.... RWinston 1 94
(DNicholls) *mde all: rdn over 1f out: kpt on* **13/2**[3]

2442 **2** *½* **Ellens Academy (IRE)**[14] 3309 9-9-7 **83**.... SSanders 6 95
(EJAlston) *hmpd s and bhd: hdwy 1/2-way: swtchd lft and rdn wl over 1f out: styd on strly ins last* **13/2**[3]

0100 **3** *1 ¾* **Native Title**[14] 3309 6-9-11 **87**.... AlexGreaves 7 94
(DNicholls) *trckd ldrs gng wl: smooth hdwy 2f out: rdn over 1f out: nt qckn ins last* **11/1**

1402 **4** *¾* **Legal Set (IRE)**[4] 3606 8-7-9 **60** oh2....(t) CatherineGannon(3) 3 65
(MissAStokell) *cl up: rdn along and sltly outpcd 2f out: kpt on wl u.p ins last* **14/1**

2213 **5** *shd* **Cloud Dancer**[12] 3372 5-9-1 **77**.... NCallan 5 81
(KARyan) *lw: hmpd s: towards rr: hdwy over 2f out: sn rdn and kpt same pce appr last* **5/1**[1]

0051 **6** *1 ¼* **Sierra Vista**[14] 3309 4-9-2 **81**.... LEnstone(3) 10 81
(DWBarker) *chsd ldrs: rdn 2f out kpt on same pce appr last* **8/1**

3011 **7** *3 ½* **Paddywack (IRE)**[7] 3509 7-8-4 **73**....(b) RoryMoore(7) 11 63
(DWChapman) *trckd ldrs: rdn wl over 2f out: wknd wl over 1f out* **6/1**[2]

0603 **8** *5* **Bond Boy**[7] 3509 7-10-2 **92**.... FLynch 4 67
(BSmart) *wnt rt s: a rr* **13/2**[3]

400- **9** *2* **Mitsuki**[264] 5673 5-8-4 **66**.... PRobinson 12 35
(JDBethell) *a rr* **33/1**

4600 **10** *7* **Indian Spark**[15] 3266 10-10-0 **90**.... KFallon 2 38
(JSGoldie) *in tch: rdn along 1/2-way: sn lost pl and bhd* **6/1**[2]

1m 12.3s (-0.27) **Going Correction** +0.125s/f (Good) **10** Ran SP% **114.3**
Speed ratings: **106,105,103,102,101 100,95,88,86,76**CSF £47.34 CT £467.97 TOTE £11.80: £3.30, £2.00, £6.20; EX 74.10.
**Owner** David Faulkner **Bred** Huckleberry Farm Llc **Trained** Sessay, N Yorks

**FOCUS**
A hat-trick in this race for sprint-king David Nicholls. The form is solid, with the winner approaching his best form again and the runner-up putting up his best effort in ages.

**NOTEBOOK**
**Pieter Brueghel(USA)**, 15lb lower than his last win two years ago, was the best-backed horse in the race and justified the confidence. *Official explanation: jockey said, regarding the improved form shown, gelding had been unsuited by crowding from other runners at Pontefract last time*
**Ellens Academy(IRE)**, on the back foot after being hampered at the start, had a luckless run otherwise he would have given the winner even more to do.
**Native Title**, who looked in tip-top trim, put two poor efforts behind him, moving up on the bridle but not really finding much as expected when asked a question.
**Legal Set(IRE)**, 2lb out of the handicap, is in really good form at present.
**Cloud Dancer**, who looked in peak condition, took a bump at the start but on this easy ground never really looked like picking up.
**Sierra Vista**, 5lb higher, found this too tough. Her trainer must despair of ever saddling a winner here.
**Paddywack(IRE)** seems best suited by the minimum trip these days.

## 3755 JOHN SMITH'S CASK H'CAP 6f 217y
**3:15** (3:15) (C) (0-90,89) 3-Y-0+ **£10,692** (£3,290; £1,645; £822) **Stalls** Low

Form RPR

3363 **1** **Look Here's Carol (IRE)**[13] 3337 4-9-12 **87**.... DHolland 14 96
(BAMcmahon) *sn cl up: effrt 2f out: rdn to ld over 1f out: drvn ins last and hld on wl* **13/2**[3]

0522 **2** *hd* **Digital**[16] 3235 7-9-9 **87**.... SHitchcott(3) 13 95
(MRChannon) *midfield and pushed along 1/2-way: hdwy over 2f out: rdn to chal over 1f out: drvn and ev ch ins last: jst hld* **6/1**[2]

1215 **3** *¾* **Distant Connection (IRE)**[7] 3542 3-8-12 **81**.... KFallon 9 88
(APJarvis) *sn led: qcknd 4f out: rdn along over 2f out: hdd over 1f out: drvn and rallied ins last: no ex nr fin* **6/1**[2]

0410 **4** *¾* **Cd Flyer (IRE)**[14] 3309 7-9-7 **87**.... PMulrennan(5) 6 92
(BEllison) *hld up towards rr: hdwy wl over 2f out: rdn over 1f out and kpt on same pce* **16/1**

-601 **5** *nk* **Mister Sweets**[14] 3321 5-8-5 **73**.... DTudhope(7) 7 77
(DCarroll) *trckd ldrs: effrt 2f out:sn rdn and kpt on same pce* **9/1**

0040 **6** *1 ½* **Kareeb (FR)**[22] 3036 7-8-7 **75**.... ARutter(7) 10 75
(WJMusson) *hld up in tch: effrt 2f out: wandered over 1f out: sn rdn and kep# on same pce* **14/1**

-050 **7** *½* **Roman Maze**[21] 3086 4-7-11 **63**.... BSwarbrick(5) 1 62
(WMBrisbourne) *plld hrd: effrt and nt clr run on inner 3f out: rdn and kpt on appr last: nrst fin* **20/1**

0304 **8** *shd* **Raphael (IRE)**[10] 3409 5-9-2 **77**.... RWinston 2 75
(TDEasterby) *in tch on inner: rdn along over 2f out and kpt on same pce* **11/1**

2U10 **9** *hd* **Balakiref**[14] 3309 5-8-8 **69**.... FLynch 8 67
(MDods) *hmpd s and bhd: hdwy 3f out: rdn: edgd lft and hmpd wl over 1f out: no ch after* **10/1**

-000 **10** *1 ¼* **Cd Europe (IRE)**[14] 3309 6-10-0 **89**....(b[1]) NCallan 15 84
(KARyan) *keen: in tch: effrt over 2f out: sn rdn and wknd wl over 1f out* **25/1**

-321 **11** *shd* **Mr Velocity (IRE)**[21] 3101 4-8-11 **72**.... KDarley 3 66
(ACStewart) *chsd ldrs: rdn along over 2f out: sn wknd* **11/2**[1]

**12** *1 ¾* **Mobane Flyer**[273] 5491 4-8-9 **70**.... GParkin 5 60
(RAFahey) *keen and hmpd after 1f: a towards rr* **66/1**

0000 **13** *½* **Will He Wish**[22] 3036 8-9-12 **87**....(b) TPQueally 11 75
(SGollings) *chsd ldrs: rdn over 2f out: sn hung lft and wknd* **16/1**

00-0 **14** *¾* **Inchdura**[16] 3235 6-8-11 **72**.... KimTinkler 16 59
(NTinkler) *hld up in rr: hdwy 1/2-way: rdn along 3f out a sn wknd* **50/1**

U030 **15** *2 ½* **Tidy (IRE)**[7] 3516 4-9-5 **80**.... DarrenWilliams 4 60
(MDHammond) *a rr* **16/1**

1m 25.82s (2.51) **Going Correction** +0.575s/f (Yiel)
**WFA** 3 from 4yo+ 8lb **15** Ran SP% **121.1**
Speed ratings: **108,107,106,106,105 104,103,103,103,101 101,99,98,98,95**CSF £43.64 CT £252.19 TOTE £6.20: £2.10, £2.30, £2.60; EX 30.50.
**Owner** S L Edwards **Bred** S L Edwards **Trained** Hopwas, Staffs

**FOCUS**
Just a steady gallop until once in line for home, enabling the winner to take a good position from her outside draw. Sound form, but far from outstanding.

**NOTEBOOK**
**Look Here's Carol(IRE)** is not that big but is all heart. With the ease in the ground in her favour she overcame an unfavourable draw to make it two career wins on her 20th start.
**Digital**, who took this three years ago, was another with a less than favourable draw. He drew upsides coming to the final furlong but the suspicion was that the filly had the more will to win.
**Distant Connection(IRE)**, despite his high draw soon showed in front. Stepping up the pace once in line for home, he proved extra game but in the end was just held. This was a fine effort on ground much easier than he truly prefers.
**Cd Flyer(IRE)**, stepping up in trip, likes to come from the back and could have done with a much stronger early pace.
**Mister Sweets**, 5lb higher, ran well but prefers much quicker ground.
**Kareeb(FR)** took this a year ago from a 3lb lower mark on much quicker ground. As usual he travelled strongly but he didn't have the best of luck in running. By no means knocked about he is surely a winner waiting to happen.
**Roman Maze**, a positive on the exchanges, is a poor mover. Drawn one, he had no luck in running but his action suggest the artificial surfaces suit him better.
**Balakiref** had no luck at all.
**Cd Europe(IRE)**, stepping up in trip in first- time blinkers, was not helped by the lack of early pace and pulled much too hard.
**Mr Velocity(IRE)** looked at his best but was a major negative on the exchanges and those who opposed him were proved right.
**Tidy(IRE)** *Official explanation: jockey said colt would be better suited by softer ground*

## 3756 45TH JOHN SMITH'S CUP (HERITAGE H'CAP) 1m 2f 88y
**3:50** (3:50) (B) (0-110,105) 3-Y-0+ **£91,000** (£28,000; £14,000; £7,000) **Stalls** Low

Form RPR

12-1 **1** **Arcalis**[50] 2258 4-9-2 **95**.... RWinston 18 110
(JHowardJohnson) *midfield: hdwy over 3f out: rdn to chal over 1f out: rdr dropped whip ins last: styd on wl to ld nr line* **20/1**

2-12 **2** *hd* **Promotion**[22] 3034 4-9-2 **95**.... KFallon 9 110
(SirMichaelStoute) *midfield: swtchd rt and hdwy over 3f out: str run to ld over over 1f: sn rdn and hung lft ins last: drvn and hdd nr line* **7/2**[1]

21-1 **3** *2 ½* **Starry Lodge (IRE)**[35] 2681 4-9-2 **95**.... DHolland 1 105+
(LMCumani) *hld up in tch: hdwy over 2f out: rdn over 1f out: kpt on same pce fnl f* **8/1**

-131 **4** *shd* **Red Fort (IRE)**[22] 3034 4-9-12 **105** 8ex.... PRobinson 16 115
(MAJarvis) *trckd ldrs: hdwy 3f out: rdn to chal 2f out and ev ch tl drvn and one pce ent last* **15/2**[3]

3562 **5** *1* **Jabaar (USA)**[14] 3291 6-8-4 **86**....(v) TEaves(3) 12 94
(DNicholls) *chsd ldrs: rdn along over 3f out: drvn and outpcd over 2f out: swtchd rt and styd on u.p fnl f* **50/1**

1111 **6** *¾* **Polar Jem**[21] 3091 4-9-1 **94** 8ex.... AMcCarthy 3 101
(GGMargarson) *led: rdn along 3f out: hdd wl over 1f out: kpt on same pce u.p fnl f* **14/1**

2053 **7** *nk* **Vicious Warrior**[28] 2894 5-8-7 **86**.... DeanMcKeown 21 92
(RMWhitaker) *prom: rdn along 3f out: drvn and one pce fnl 2f* **50/1**

4300 **8** *2 ½* **Wing Commander**[24] 2969 5-8-13 **92**.... GParkin 4 93
(RAFahey) *towards rr: pushed along on inner over 3f out: styd on fnl 2f: nrst fin* **25/1**

-101 **9** *1 ¾* **Ionian Spring (IRE)**[37] 2624 9-9-2 **95**.... RSmith 6 93
(CGCox) *s.i.s and bhd: hdwy over 3f out: kpt on fnl 2f: nrst fin* **25/1**

0141 **10** *3* **Blue Spinnaker (IRE)**[40] 2527 5-9-4 **102**.... PMulrennan(5) 8 94
(MWEasterby) *lw: midfield: pushed along and outpcd over 4f out: drvn and no imp fnl 2f* **13/2**[2]

-024 **11** *1 ¼* **Desert Quest (IRE)**[14] 3325 4-8-13 **92**....(b) FLynch 5 82
(AMBalding) *s.i.s and bhd: hdwy over 3f out: sn rdn along and no imp fnl 2f* **12/1**

-140 **12** *2 ½* **Zero Tolerance (IRE)**[24] 2969 4-8-13 **92**.... KDarley 20 77
(TDBarron) *cl up: rdn along 3f out: drvn and wknd over 2f out* **20/1**

1205 **13** *1* **Eastern Breeze (IRE)**[87] 1397 6-9-9 **102**....(e) PaulEddery 14 85
(PWD'Arcy) *swtg: towards rr: hdwy on outer over 3f out: sn rdn along and no further prog* **50/1**

6023 **14** *1* **Consonant (IRE)**[8] 3477 7-8-7 **89**.... DNolan(3) 2 70
(DGBridgwater) *chsd ldrs on inner: rdn along over 3f out: wknd over 2f out* **25/1**

1463 **15** *1 ½* **Blythe Knight (IRE)**[22] 3034 4-9-10 **103**.... KMcEvoy 17 81
(EALDunlop) *hld up: a rr* **33/1**

132- **16** *hd* **Coat Of Honour (USA)**[288] 5193 4-8-13 **92**....(b) SSanders 13 70
(SirMarkPrescott) *swtg: chsd ldrs: rdn along over 3f out: sn wknd* **9/1**

5500 **17** *¾* **Bourgainville**[40] 2527 6-9-1 **99**.... NChalmers(5) 10 76
(AMBalding) *a rr* **50/1**

-046 **18** *¾* **Narrative (IRE)**[20] 3119 6-9-7 **100**.... TPQueally 11 75
(DRLoder) *towards rr: sme hdwy 4f out: sn rdn and wknd* **50/1**

**Lake Charlotte(USA)**, a long-backed newcomer, looked very fit. She sat in behind the first two but when the gap came she was simply not good enough and she was held in third when crowded near the line. She finished clear of the remainder and should have little difficulty finding an opportunity to get off the mark.
**Rosie Mac** again showed ability and her chances are enhanced now she is qualified to run in handicaps. The lack of early pace almost certainly flattered her.
**Miss Procurer(IRE)**, absent since her second and final outing at two at Folkestone in August, carried her head high and looks one to have reservations about.

## 3760 JOHN SMITH'S HERON & BREARLEY MEDIAN AUCTION MAIDEN STKS (DIV II) 6f
**6:00** (6:01) (E) 2-Y-O **£6,890** (£2,120; £1,060; £530) **Stalls** Centre

Form RPR
32 **1** **Transaction (IRE)**[16] 3228 2-9-0 .......... TEDurcan 9 86
(JMPEustace) *chsd ldrs: effrt over 2f out: styd on to ld nr fin* **11/2**[3]
4 **2** ½ **Coup D'Etat**[22] 3051 2-9-0 .......... KDarley 3 85
(JLDunlop) *w ldrs: slt ld over 1f out: hdd nr fin* **9/4**[1]
**3** *hd* **For Life (IRE)** 2-9-0 .......... KFallon 8 84
(APJarvis) *w'like: trckd ldrs: outpcd over 2f out: styd on wl fnl f* **11/2**[3]
**4** ¾ **Querido (USA)** 2-9-0 .......... KMcEvoy 2 82
(SaeedBinSuroor) *neat: w ldrs: ev ch over 1f out: nt qckn ins last* **11/2**[3]
**5** ¾ **Lubeck** 2-9-0 .......... TPQueally 4 79
(DRLoder) *lengthy: unf: trckd ldrs: t.k.h: effrt over 2f out: styd on same pce fnl f* **9/1**
**6** *shd* **Reqqa** 2-9-0 .......... RHills 6 79
(MJohnston) *tall: unf: led: qcknd over 2f out: hdd over 1f out: nt qckn* **9/2**[2]
**7** 6 **Superstitious (IRE)** 2-9-0 .......... GGibbons 12 61
(BAMcmahon) *wl grwn: bit bkwd: s.i.s: outpcd and drvn along over 2f out: nvr on terms* **25/1**
00 **8** *shd* **Mister Buzz**[16] 3233 2-9-0 .......... FLynch 11 61
(MDHammond) *in tch: outpcd over 2f out: sn lost pl* **100/1**
**9** 1½ **Last Pioneer (IRE)** 2-9-0 .......... JEdmunds 10 56
(TPTate) *rangy: angular: swvd bdly lft s: hdwy 3f out: hung lft and sn lost pl* **100/1**
**10** 1½ **Tiffin Brown** 2-9-0 .......... GFaulkner 1 52
(PCHaslam) *w'like: leggy: Scope: bit bkwd: s.i.s: a bhd* **66/1**
0 **11** 1¾ **Allstar Princess**[17] 3197 2-8-9 .......... PMQuinn 5 42
(RAFahey) *trckd ldrs: rdn and lost pl over 2f out* **66/1**
4 **12** 12 **Zanderido**[8] 3468 2-8-11 .......... TEaves(3) 7 11
(BSRothwell) *sn outpcd and pushed along: lost tch 2f out* **100/1**

1m 14.12s (1.55) **Going Correction** +0.125s/f (Good) **12 Ran SP% 114.9**
**Speed ratings: 94,93,93,92,91 90,82,82,80,78 76,60**CSF £17.40 TOTE £6.70: £2.00, £1.60, £2.00; EX 19.50 Place 6 £460.37, Place 5 £150.12.
**Owner** George Darling **Bred** George Darling **Trained** Newmarket, Suffolk

**FOCUS**
Five in line a furlong out after a steady pace to past halfway, and fractionally the slower of the two divisions. But a bit more strength in depth and a reasonably solid race, with the two form horses first and second.

**NOTEBOOK**
**Transaction(IRE)** made his experience tell, sticking on in game fashion to show ahead near the line.
**Coup D'Etat** had been in the stalls quite some time and became rather upset late on. He took a narrow lead coming to the final furlong but could not quite last out. A true-run race over seven will see him go one better.
**For Life(IRE)** ◆, a February foal, is a good-bodied, most likeable type. Tapped for toe when the pace increased, he came with a sustained run towards the stands' side in the final furlong and will improve a good deal for the outing.
**Querido(USA)**, a March foal is bred for stamina not speed. Not very big, he travelled strongly down the outside and was only found wanting inside the last. Seven furlongs or even a mile will surely play to his strengths a lot better.
**Lubeck**, a January foal, has a mixture of speed and stamina in his pedigree. He took some settling as a result of the moderate pace but to his credit stuck on all the way to the line. He will know a lote more next time.
**Reqqa** ◆, a February foal, is bred for pure speed and is a half-brother to four winners, including Airwave. Very much in the air and full of himself beforehand, he showed plenty of toe but couldn't last out. A drop back to five will not be a problem and this will have taught him what life is all about.
T/Plt: £226.30 to a £1 stake. Pool: £127,310.60. 410.65 winning tickets. T/Qpdt: £24.00 to a £1 stake. Pool: £9,593.70. 295.05 winning tickets. WG

3761 - 3768a (Foreign Racing) - See Raceform Interactive

# 3688 DEAUVILLE (R-H)
## Saturday, July 10
**OFFICIAL GOING: Turf course - soft; all-weather course - standard**

## 3769a PRIX DE RIS-ORANGIS (GROUP 3) 6f
**3:20** (3:23) 3-Y-0+ **£25,704** (£10,282; £7,711; £5,141)

RPR
**1** **The Trader (IRE)**[25] 2955 6-9-4 ..........(b) DSweeney 2 118
(MBlanshard) *held up towards rear, headway on outside from over 1f out, led 150 yards out, ran on strongly* 1
**2** 2 **Swedish Shave (FR)**[55] 2162 6-9-0 .......... TJarnet 11 108
(RGibson, France) *led after 1f, 2 lengths clear over 1f out, headed 150 yards out, no extra*
**3** 2 **Vasywait (FR)**[19] 3162 5-9-0 .......... DBoeuf 7 102
(J-LGay, France) *raced in 2nd, ridden and hung left 1 1/2f out, kept on at same pace* 2
**4** ½ **The Wise Lady (FR)**[35] 4-8-10 .......... GaryStevens 5 97
(MNigge, France) *led 1f, raced in 3rd, effort on inside when forced to switch 1 1/2f out, kept on final f to take 4th close home*
**5** ½ **Blanche (FR)**[44] 2438 5-9-1 .......... DBonilla 6 100
(JRossi, France) *raced in 5th, ridden and one pace from over 1f out*
**6** 1½ **Miss Emma (IRE)**[75] 1682 4-8-10 .......... TGillet 4 91
(JEHammond, France) *held up, effort when denied run on inside 1 1/2f out, one pace* 3
**7** ¾ **Malaica (FR)**[127] 3-8-5 .......... C-PLemaire 8 89
(RPritchard-Gordon, France) *held up in last, never a factor*
**8** 1½ **Art Moderne (USA)**[27] 2923 4-9-0 ..........(b) OPeslier 9 88
(ELellouche, France) *raced in 4th til weakened over 1f out*
**9** ¾ **Glad To Be Fast (IRE)**[41] 2511 4-9-4 .......... J-PCarvalho 3 90
(MarioHofer, Germany) *held up in 8th on inside, always in rear*

1m 10.7s **Going Correction** -0.05s/f (Good)
**WFA** 3 from 4yo+ 6lb **9 Ran SP% 122.1**
Speed ratings: **113,110,107,107,106 104,103,101,100.**
**Owner** Mrs C J Ward **Bred** Lady Bland **Trained** Upper Lambourn, Berks

**NOTEBOOK**
**The Trader(IRE)** proved conclusively that he now stays six furlongs with a convincing victory under his 4lb penalty. Enjoying the cut in the ground, he came with a strong run to sweep past Swedish Shave inside the final furlong. The Nunthorpe and the Prix de l'Abbaye are now top of his agenda, although the style of this success suggests that the Haydock Sprint Cup is another sensible target.
**Swedish Shave(FR)** is a solid performer in this grade but found the winner much too strong.

# 3570 BATH (L-H)
## Sunday, July 11
**OFFICIAL GOING: Good (good to firm in places) changing to good after race 7 (4:50)**
Wind: lt bhd Weather: cloudy, occasional showers

## 3770 HAVEN HOLIDAYS AT DEVONCLIFFS MEDIAN AUCTION MAIDEN FILLIES' STKS 5f 161y
**2:20** (2:22) (F) 2-Y-0 **£3,353** (£958; £479) **Stalls** Low

Form RPR
**1** **Bridge T'The Stars** 2-8-11 .......... SCarson 11 71
(RFJohnsonHoughton) *towards rr whn sltly hmpd after 1f: rdn and hdwy over 2f out: drvn to ld 1f out: hld on u.p* **50/1**
**2** ½ **Scrooby Baby** 2-8-11 .......... SWKelly 1 69
(JAOsborne) *s.i.s: hld up in tch: led briefly over 1f out: one pce after* **12/1**
6 **3** ¾ **Geisha Lady (IRE)**[38] 2627 2-8-11 .......... MartinDwyer 6 67
(RMBeckett) *s.i.s: hrd rdn and in rr tl hdwy 1/2-way: styd on: nvr nrr* **16/1**
3 **4** ¾ **Noorain**[13] 3382 2-8-8 .......... SHitchcott(3) 3 65
(MRChannon) *trckd ldrs: led over 2f out: rdn and hdd over 1f out: sn n btn* **11/4**[1]
2343 **5** 1½ **Ruby's Dream**[35] 2702 2-8-11 .......... CCatlin 2 60
(JMBradley) *trckd ldrs: ev ch over 1f out: sn wknd* **10/1**
20 **6** 2½ **Dreamer's Lass**[47] 2382 2-8-11 .......... SDrowne 10 52
(JMBradley) *on outside whn taken further wd after 1f: nvr on terms* **50/1**
**7** ½ **Miss Patricia** 2-8-11 .......... NCallan 13 50
(JGPortman) *s.i.s: hampered after 1f: nvr on terms after* **33/1**
06 **8** 20 **Sirce (IRE)**[14] 3343 2-8-11 .......... DaneO'Neill 12 —
(DJCoakley) *bhd whn hmpd after 1f: sn t.o* **80/1**
006 **9** 1¾ **Gloria Nimbus**[33] 2749 2-8-11 .......... SRighton 9 —
(MMullineaux) *led tl hdd over 2f out: wknd rapidly: t.o* **80/1**
3 **10** *dist* **Keep Bacckinhit (IRE)**[16] 3272 2-8-11 .......... RLMoore 8 —
(GLMoore) *v bdly hmpd after 1f and virtually p.u after* **13/2**[3]
2 **B** **Value Plus (IRE)**[12] 3398 2-8-11 .......... DHolland 5 —
(JosephQuinn, Ire) *b.d after 1f* **11/4**[1]
32 **S** **Miss Cassia**[29] 2884 2-8-11 .......... PDobbs 7 —
(RHannon) *prom whn slipped up on bnd and fell after 1f* **4/1**[2]

1m 15.22s (4.08) **Going Correction** +0.325s/f (Good) **12 Ran SP% 118.7**
**Speed ratings: 85,84,83,82,80 77,76,49,47,— —,—**CSF £558.88 TOTE £62.80: £11.70, £4.60, £4.10; EX 489.10.
**Owner** Mrs Zara Campbell-Harris **Bred** Mrs Zara Campbell-Harris And Adam Barker **Trained** Blewbury, Oxon

**FOCUS**
An ordinary time for the grade. There was a nasty incident after nearly a furlong when Miss Cassia slipped up, bringing down Value Plus and causing problems for several others behind. As the two stricken horses were amongst the top three in the market, the race's competitiveness must have been affected and the standard is just fair.

**NOTEBOOK**
**Bridge T'The Stars**, a cheap foal whose siblings managed to make the frame without winning, was hampered in the melee after a furlong, though not as badly as a few others, but that did not stop her from grinding out a debut victory. This was a poor maiden made weaker by the fallers, and with the winning time also moderate the form probably does not add up to much.
**Scrooby Baby**, a 100,000gns half-sister to Milk It Mick, showed some ability but this was such a poor race that she will have to improve significantly in order to uphold the family tradition.
**Geisha Lady(IRE)** came from well off the pace and, despite hanging out into the centre of the track, finished best of all. She had the edge in experience on the front pair, but should appreciate an extra furlong.
**Noorain** was disappointing in that she did not build on the promise of her Windsor debut even with her two main market rivals out of the way.
**Ruby's Dream** had experience on her side, but could not make it count and would probably be better off dropped in grade or in modest nurseries.
**Dreamer's Lass** was forced to take evasive action after a furlong, but then whether by accident or design hung right out to the centre of the track and made no further impression.
**Miss Patricia**, whose dam was a winner over the minimum trip, did well to finish as close as she did having met serious interference after a furlong. She is probably quite a bit better than this.
**Keep Bacckinhit(IRE)**, well backed, lost all chance in the melee after a furlong and was very fortunate not to come down. *Official explanation: jockey said filly was badly hampered*
**Miss Cassia** was up with the pace when appearing to lose her footing on the bend after almost a furlong.
**Value Plus(IRE)** had no chance of staying on her feet when Miss Cassia came down right alongside her after a furlong.

## 3771 BE HOPEFUL H'CAP 1m 5y
**2:50** (3:13) (E) (0-75,68) 3-Y-0+ **£4,478** (£1,378; £689; £344) **Stalls** Low

Form RPR
0033 **1** **Over To You Bert**[2] 3697 5-7-9 **42** oh3.......... JFMcDonald(3) 8 51
(RJHodges) *trckd ldrs: rdn over 1f out: r.o to ld wl ins fnl f* **7/1**[3]
0344 **2** ½ **Adobe**[18] 3191 9-9-3 **66**.......... MSavage(5) 7 74
(WMBrisbourne) *hld up in tch: rdn and hdwy to ld 1f out: kpt on but hdd wl ins fnl f* **11/2**[1]
2-00 **3** 1¾ **Sheriff's Deputy**[8] 3536 4-9-7 **68**.......... SHitchcott(3) 2 72
(JWUnett) *hld up: hdwy 3f out on outside: styd on fnl f but no ch w first 2* **14/1**
0046 **4** 1 **Nautical**[11] 3423 6-8-6 **50**.......... RLMoore 5 52
(AWCarroll) *slowly away: in rr tl hdwy 3f out: rdn over 1f out and one pce after* **7/1**[3]
0225 **5** *hd* **Marnie**[18] 3191 7-8-7 **51**.......... JMackay 1 52
(JAkehurst) *a in tch: rdn and one pce ins fnl 2f* **6/1**[2]
0040 **6** *nk* **Bishopstone Man**[18] 3191 7-9-8 **66**.......... DaneO'Neill 9 67
(HCandy) *sn led: rdn and hdd 1f out: fdd ins fnl f* **11/2**[1]
0004 **7** ¾ **Adalar (IRE)**[10] 3459 4-9-2 **60**.......... NCallan 3 59
(PDEvans) *in tch tl rdn and wknd over 1f out* **11/2**[1]
6233 **8** 5 **Answered Promise (FR)**[11] 3426 5-8-10 **54**.......... SSanders 11 41
(IAWood) *trckd ldr: rdn over 2f out: wknd over 1f out* **8/1**
0000 **9** 4 **Steppenwolf**[15] 3304 3-7-5 **51** oh14.......... CHaddon(7) 4 29
(WDeBest-Turner) *towards rr: rdn over 3f out and sn lost tch* **100/1**

1000 **10** ¾ **Muyassir (IRE)**[23] 3048 9-9-2 **60** SDrowne 6 36
(MissBSanders) *bhd after 2f and styd there* **16/1**

-320 **11** 3½ **Have Some Fun**[19] 3177 4-8-11 **55** JQuinn 10 23
(PRChamings) *s.i.s: plld hrd: sn prom: wknd over 2f out* **14/1**

1m 43.01s (2.01) **Going Correction** +0.15s/f (Good)
**WFA** 3 from 4yo+ 9lb **11** Ran SP% **116.8**
Speed ratings: **95,94,92,91,91 91,90,85,81,80 77**CSF £44.97 CT £538.45 TOTE £10.50: £2.30, £2.40, £5.20; EX 64.20.
**Owner** R J Hodges **Bred** J K S Cresswell **Trained** Charlton Adam, Somerset

**FOCUS**
Following an incident in the first race the track was inspected before being given the all-clear. A very steady pace until past halfway resulted in a slow winning time for the grade and several were pulling for their heads as a result. The form looks ordinary.

**NOTEBOOK**
**Over To You Bert**, beaten in a seller last time, was 3lb out of the handicap but he was always in the ideal position in a slowly-run race and that enabled him to deliver his race-winning move at just the right time. The way the race was run suggests the form may not be that reliable though.
**Adobe** would have preferred the ground rattling fast and a strong pace, but potentially an even bigger handicap was seeing so much daylight on the outside down the home straight. In the circumstances he did not perform at all badly.
**Sheriff's Deputy** stays further than this, so the slow pace was no help and he probably did well to finish as close as he did.
**Nautical** was another who stays further than this, so would not have been at all suited by the way the race was run.
**Marnie**, a regular here, needs the ground lightning fast so the goodish ground was no use to her at all.
**Bishopstone Man** is dropping to a decent mark, but after setting his own modest pace he found himself done for foot in the closing stages.
**Adalar(IRE)** dropping back in trip, was in a good position to strike in a slowly-run race, but found nothing off the bridle.
**Have Some Fun** *Official explanation: jockey said gelding lost its action*

## 3772 DEVONCLIFFS BUY A CARAVAN HERE! CLASSIFIED STKS 5f 11y
**3:20** (3:41) (F) 3-Y-0+ **£3,318** (£948; £474) **Stalls** Low

Form RPR

0004 **1** **Coranglais**[12] 3395 4-9-3 58 (p) RLMoore 6 74
(JMBradley) *mid-div: rdn and hdwy over 1f out: drvn out to ld wl ins fnl f* **15/2**

0002 **2** ¾ **Boavista (IRE)**[3] 3680 4-9-0 58 NCallan 7 68
(PDEvans) *a in tch: led 2f out: hrd rdn and led wl ins fnl f* **3/1**[1]

5030 **3** 5 **Diamond Ring**[17] 3227 5-9-0 40 ADaly 11 50
(MrsJCandlish) *hld up in rr: hdwy and r.o wl fnl f to go 3rd nr fin: no ch w first 2* **33/1**

-002 **4** ½ **Ardkeel Lass (IRE)**[14] 3344 3-8-9 59 PaulEddery 13 48
(DHaydnJones) *stdd in rr s: t.k.h: hdwy 2f out: sn rdn and one pce* **12/1**

0000 **5** ¾ **Run On**[29] 2885 6-9-3 46 SRighton 9 49
(DGBridgwater) *outpce: swtchd lft 2f out: kpt on one pce* **40/1**

0020 **6** *nk* **Indian Bazaar (IRE)**[6] 3593 8-8-10 53 MHalford[(7)] 10 47
(NEBerry) *prom whn hmpd after 1f: rdn over 2f out: kpt on but nvr on terms after* **16/1**

1600 **7** *nk* **Erracht**[43] 2482 6-8-12 63 NChalmers[(5)] 3 46
(MrsHSweeting) *prom tl lost pl 1/2-way: nvr on terms after* **8/1**

6164 **8** *nk* **Arfinnit (IRE)**[7] 3558 3-8-9 60 (v) SHitchcott[(3)] 2 45
(MRChannon) *in tch: rdn 1/2-way: wknd over 1f out* **6/1**[3]

0-60 **9** 2 **Perfect Setting**[15] 3307 4-9-3 60 SSanders 12 38
(PJMakin) *mid-div: rdn 2f out: wknd over 1f out* **16/1**

30-0 **10** 4 **Giverand**[64] 1969 5-9-0 42 JFEgan 5 21
(MissJacquelineSDoyle) *sn bhd and styd there* **25/1**

2660 **11** ¾ **Juwwi**[13] 3378 10-9-3 50 CCatlin 14 21
(JMBradley) *a bhd* **16/1**

1111 **12** *shd* **Foley Millennium (IRE)**[8] 3524 6-9-9 66 NPollard 15 27
(MQuinn) *led on outside tl rdn and hdd 2f out: wknd qckly* **4/1**[2]

5045 **13** 2 **Barabella (IRE)**[18] 3211 3-8-9 58 SDrowne 1 10
(RJHodges) *prom tl rdn after 2f: sn bhd* **20/1**

63.36 secs (0.86) **Going Correction** +0.325s/f (Good)
**WFA** 3 from 4yo+ 5lb **13** Ran SP% **121.5**
Speed ratings: **106,104,96,96,94 94,93,93,90,83 82,82,79**CSF £29.46 TOTE £11.20: £2.70, £1.90, £4.60; EX 40.10.
**Owner** John Brookman **Bred** Slatch Farm Stud **Trained** Sedbury, Gloucs

**FOCUS**
A modest contest, but the pace was sound and the form looks solid. The front pair pulled well clear and the time was very good for the grade. It was noticeable that the jockeys were keen to give the inside rail a wide berth.

**NOTEBOOK**
**Coranglais**, with cheekpieces back on instead of blinkers, was ridden more patiently this time and showed a good turn of foot to pick off the runner-up. He was rated 80 at this time last year, which shows how much he has declined, but now that the Bradley magic has worked again he could be very well handicapped.
**Boavista(IRE)** could have done with the ground remaining genuinely fast, but nonetheless ran another fine race in defeat and, along with the winner, pulled right away from the rest of the field. She deserves to find a race in the near future.
**Diamond Ring** had plenty on at the weights, but stayed on to finish third at a respectable distance. Her previous record suggests it may be wise not to get carried away with this performance though.
**Ardkeel Lass(IRE)**, making her debut for the yard, could never land a blow and perhaps she needs genuinely fast ground.
**Run On**, no closer than 12th in four previous starts this term, appeared to run well at the weights but it would be dangerous to take this form at face value.
**Indian Bazaar(IRE)** never figured after early trouble, but is proving extremely inconsistent this term.
**Juwwi** *Official explanation: vet said gelding bled from nose*
**Foley Millennium(IRE)**, bidding for a five-timer, was off a 21lb higher mark than when the sequence started in banded company. He showed his usual early pace, but dropped away very quickly and there was surely more than his high draw to blame for this modest effort. *Official explanation: jockey said gelding was unsuited by ground (Good, Good to Firm in places)*

## 3773 FAVOURITES RACING CLASSIFIED STKS 1m 2f 46y
**3:50** (4:06) (F) 3-Y-0+ **£3,626** (£1,036; £518) **Stalls** Low

Form RPR

1101 **1** **Doctored**[45] 2426 3-8-6 60 (b) NCallan 6 71
(PDEvans) *in tch: led 3f out: hdd 2f out: hung rt ent fnl f: rallied to ld ins* **10/1**

6623 **2** 1¼ **Eastborough (IRE)**[10] 3450 5-8-12 60 MSavage[(5)] 5 69
(BGPowell) *hld up in tch: smooth hdwy to ld on bit 2f out: hdd over 1f out: squeezed out appr fnl f: one pce after* **4/1**[1]

5045 **3** *hd* **Cuddles (FR)**[18] 3206 5-9-0 59 DaneO'Neill 8 66
(KOCunningham-Brown) *hld up: hdwy over 2f out: hung lft and led over 1f out: kpt gng lft and hdd ins fnl f* **7/1**[3]

6001 **4** 1½ **Donastrela (IRE)**[18] 3190 3-8-0 57 ow2 (v) NChalmers[(5)] 4 65
(AMBalding) *hld up: hdwy 3f out: rdn 2f out: one pce after* **9/1**

3010 **5** 6 **Zawrak (IRE)**[8] 3520 5-8-10 60 NataliaGemelova[(7)] 13 54
(IWMcinnes) *prom early: sn mid-div: hdwy 3f out: wknd over 1f out* **16/1**

0654 **6** 5 **Master Mahogany**[17] 3231 3-8-10 64 SDrowne 1 49
(RJHodges) *disputing ld tl def advantage 5f out: hdd 3f out: sn wknd* **11/1**

0331 **7** 3 **Billy Bathwick (IRE)**[10] 3459 7-9-3 59 RLMoore 10 39
(JMBradley) *trckd ldrs tl rdn and wknd over 2f out* **11/2**[2]

0-00 **8** 1½ **Sweet Az**[30] 2836 4-9-0 37 (p) SRighton 11 33
(SCBurrough) *mid-div: bhd fnl 4f* **100/1**

1-46 **9** 3 **So Sure (IRE)**[12] 914 4-9-3 60 (b) DSweeney 2 31
(JGMO'Shea) *chsd ldrs: rdn overe 3f out: sn bhd* **25/1**

400- **10** 5 **Optimal (IRE)**[298] 4986 3-8-5 62 SSanders 12 20
(SirMarkPrescott) *hld up in tch: rdn over 3f out: sn btn* **4/1**[1]

1200 **11** 5 **Ivory Coast (IRE)**[20] 3156 3-8-3 59 MartinDwyer 3 9
(WRMuir) *plld hrd: w ldrs: wnt wd on bnd over 4f out: sn bhd* **8/1**

00-0 **12** ½ **Zarneeta**[15] 3306 3-7-10 55 CHaddon[(7)] 7 8
(WDeBest-Turner) *bhd fr 1/2-way* **100/1**

2-05 **13** 1½ **Macchiato**[11] 3421 3-8-3 54 SCarson 14 5
(RFJohnsonHoughton) *t.k.h: disp ld tl taken wd on bnd over 4f out: sn bhd* **25/1**

2m 11.43s (0.43) **Going Correction** +0.15s/f (Good)
**WFA** 3 from 4yo+ 11lb **13** Ran SP% **122.0**
Speed ratings: **104,103,102,101,96 92,90,89,86,82 78,78,77**CSF £49.85 TOTE £8.60: £2.60, £2.40, £1.60; EX 83.30.
**Owner** Treble Chance Partnership **Bred** Wickfield Farm Partnership **Trained** Pandy, Gwent

**FOCUS**
A modest contest, but the pace was sound and the form looks solid enough for the grade. The field fanned right out across the track turning for home.

**NOTEBOOK**
**Doctored**, making his debut for the yard, saw his race out in good style and was a deserved winner even though he hung right and gave the runner-up a bump well inside the last furlong. This victory made it four wins from his last five starts and winning over this longer trip gives his new trainer a few more options with him.
**Eastborough(IRE)** was going better than anything approaching the two-furlong pole, but did not find as much off the bridle as seemed likely. He was done no favours by the pair either side of him in the closing stages, but it made little difference to the result and he does have a tendency to find one or two too good for him these days.
**Cuddles(FR)** came from off the pace down the outside to hold every chance entering the last furlong, but once there she tended to roll about and appeared to be saving a bit for herself. She is developing a rather lengthy losing run.
**Donastrela(IRE)**, carrying 2lb overweight, could never get on terms with the front trio and this was probably a better race than she won in the first-time visor here last month.
**Zawrak(IRE)** did not get home and may be best over a stiff mile these days.
**Optimal(IRE)**, a half-sister to the very smart One Off out of the equally prolific On Call, was making her handicap debut on her first run in ten months after the obligatory three outings at two. She never got into the race though, and this was a rare reverse for the yard since their recent return to the track.
**Macchiato** *Official explanation: trainer's representative said filly was unsuited by the ground (Good, Good to Firm in places)*

## 3774 BATHWICK TYRES LADY RIDERS' H'CAP 1m 3f 144y
**4:20** (4:34) (F) (0-55,55) 4-Y-0+ **£3,419** (£1,052; £526; £263) **Stalls** Low

Form RPR

5660 **1** **Theatre Lady (IRE)**[10] 3461 6-9-11 **41** MissEFolkes[(3)] 17 53
(PDEvans) *mid-div: hdwy over 3f out: led over 1f out: styd on wl* **16/1**

0600 **2** 1½ **Milk And Sultana**[3] 3682 4-10-7 **51** MrsSOwen[(3)] 13 61
(GAHam) *hld up: hdwy 3f out: rdn 2f out: kpt on to chse wnr fnl f* **20/1**

4535 **3** 2 **Neptune**[15] 3303 8-9-3 **35** MissSarah-JaneDurman[(5)] 9 41
(JCFox) *towards rr: rdn over 2f out: styd on: nvr nrr* **20/1**

5643 **4** 1¾ **Lazzaz**[5] 3604 6-9-13 **45** MrsCThompson[(5)] 12 49
(PWHiatt) *prom: led 8f out: hdd over 2f out: one pce after* **5/1**[1]

-104 **5** ¾ **Heathyards Pride**[48] 2356 4-10-4 **50** MissSSharratt[(5)] 14 52
(RHollinshead) *trckd ldrs: led briefly appr 2f out: wknd ins fnl f* **20/1**

3435 **6** *shd* **Vandenberghe**[11] 3423 5-10-7 **48** MissSBeddoes 11 50
(JAOsborne) *mid-div: rdn over 2f out: kpt on one pce* **9/1**[3]

6060 **7** *nk* **Clann A Cougar**[9] 3471 4-10-7 **53** (p) MissMSowerby[(5)] 16 55
(IAWood) *mid-div: rdn over 2f out: styd on one pce* **25/1**

0-01 **8** 2 **Burnt Copper (IRE)**[5] 3604 4-10-9 **55** 5ex MissKManser[(5)] 7 54
(JRBest) *v.s.a and wl in rr tl sme late hdwy* **7/1**[2]

-605 **9** 3 **Compton Aviator**[47] 2381 8-10-7 **51** (t) MissJoannaRees[(3)] 5 45
(AWCarroll) *hld up in mid-div: rdn over 3f out: nvr on terms* **12/1**

/0-4 **10** 1½ **Karakum**[9] 3492 5-9-8 **42** MissEJTuck[(7)] 3 33
(AJChamberlain) *trckd ldrs tl lost pl over 4f out: nvr on terms after* **33/1**

433 **11** *hd* **Ambersong**[11] 3429 6-10-0 **41** MrsSBosley 10 32
(AWCarroll) *in rr: hdwy after 3f: wknd over 2f out* **5/1**[1]

5/00 **12** 1¾ **Deferlant (FR)**[32] 2787 7-10-4 **50** (p) MissJoeyEllis[(5)] 4 38
(KBell) *t.k.h: bhd fnl 3f* **20/1**

0164 **13** 4 **Piste Bleu (FR)**[19] 3165 4-10-11 **52** MissEJJones 6 34
(RFord) *mid-div: rdn and sme hdwy over 3f out: wknd over 2f out* **10/1**

2450 **14** 10 **Reminiscent (IRE)**[19] 3181 5-11-0 **55** (v) MsCWilliams 15 21
(RFJohnsonHoughton) *s.i.s: a bhd* **7/1**[2]

2500 **15** 9 **Benjamin (IRE)**[9] 3489 6-9-9 **39** (t) MissKellyHarrison[(3)] 1 —
(JaneSouthcombe) *led tl hdd 8f out: wknd wl over 2f out* **33/1**

000- **16** 7 **Waterline Spirit**[230] 6057 4-9-11 **43** MissAWallace[(5)] 8 —
(PDEvans) *trckd ldrs tl rdn and wknd over 2f out* **50/1**

00-0 **17** 15 **I See No Ships**[24] 3019 4-9-4 **38** MissMMullineaux[(7)] 2 —
(MMullineaux) *prom tl wknd 4f out* **50/1**

2m 34.73s (4.43) **Going Correction** +0.15s/f (Good) **17** Ran SP% **123.7**
Speed ratings: **91,90,88,87,87 86,86,85,83,82 82,81,78,71,65 61,51**CSF £309.02 CT £6293.06 TOTE £14.90: £2.80, £5.20, £6.20, £1.70; EX 374.80.
**Owner** Waterline Racing Club **Bred** Terry Keaney **Trained** Pandy, Gwent

**FOCUS**
A very moderate ladies' handicap run at only a steady gallop and the form may not work out.

**NOTEBOOK**
**Theatre Lady(IRE)** is only banded class, but was given a good ride and, gaining a decisive advantage before the elbow, stayed on well to gain her first success over this trip. She is tough and consistent and should not go up much for this. *Official explanation: trainer said, regarding the improved form shown, mare was better suited by not wearing a visor today*
**Milk And Sultana**, a Fibresand winner who has struggled on turf, ran her best race of the season. She may be of interest if reverting to Fibresand, although she is rated higher.
**Neptune**, another better known for his exploits on sand, is more at home in sellers and confirms the level of the form.
**Lazzaz** ran his race, but did not get home and the ease in the ground may have been against him.
**Heathyards Pride**, suited by the easier ground, was taking a big step up in trip and ran well having been in contention from the start.

**Vandenberghe** has been generally running well this year, and may be capable of picking up a minor contest on turf.
**Clann A Cougar**, taking a big step up in trip and with the cheekpieces re-applied, did not perform too badly without ever getting in a blow.
**Burnt Copper(IRE)** lost his chance at the start by walking out of the stalls.
**Ambersong**, dropping back in trip, never reached a challenging position and it may be that a fast surface on turf suits him best. *Official explanation: jockey said gelding was unsuited by ground (Good, Good to Firm in places)*
**Reminiscent(IRE)** *Official explanation: jockey said gelding was unsuited by ground (Good, Good to Firm in places)*

## 3775 TOTESPORT.COM H'CAP — 5f 161y
4:50 (4:59) (D) (0-85,80) 3-Y-0+ — £6,864 (£2,112; £1,056; £528) Stalls Low

Form / RPR
2000 **1** **Mine Behind**[15] 3324 4-9-8 **79** MSavage(5) 3 — 89
(JRBest) *a in tch: led 2f out: hrd rdn: all out* **8/1**[3]
2460 **2** *shd* **Romany Nights (IRE)**[5] 3606 4-9-9 **78** (b) SHitchcott(3) 10 — 88
(JWUnett) *hld up: gd hdwy 1/2-way: hrd rdn to press wnr clly fnl f: jst failed* **14/1**
6115 **3** *1 ¾* **Aintnecessarilyso**[5] 3606 6-7-10 **55** MHalford(7) 5 — 59
(NEBerry) *mid-div: str run on outside over 1f out: no ex u.p ins fnl f* **8/1**[3]
5123 **4** *1 ¾* **High Ridge**[14] 3339 5-9-3 **69** (p) CCatlin 4 — 67
(JMBradley) *towards rr: hdwy over 1f out: r.o fnl f: nvr nr to chal* **11/2**[2]
0152 **5** *nk* **Laurel Dawn**[8] 3524 6-8-6 **61** JFMcDonald(3) 1 — 58
(IWMcinnes) *s.i.s: hdwy 1/2-way: kpt on one pce fnl f* **8/1**[3]
1532 **6** *3* **Glencoe Solas (IRE)**[3] 3663 4-9-6 **72** JFEgan 6 — 60
(SKirk) *trckd ldrs: rdn over 1f out: sn btn* **5/1**[1]
0310 **7** *½* **One Way Ticket**[13] 3381 4-9-3 **69** (p) RLMoore 11 — 55
(JMBradley) *trckd ldr: rdn over 1f out: wknd ins fnl f* **10/1**
0000 **8** *2* **Salviati (USA)**[4] 3645 7-9-7 **80** (p) CJDavies(7) 8 — 59
(JMBradley) *in tch tl rdn and wknd over 1f out* **16/1**
0010 **9** *½* **Somerset West (IRE)**[1] 3747 4-9-6 **72** NPollard 7 — 50
(JRBest) *in tch: rdn and wknd over 1f out* **10/1**
6-01 **10** *¾* **Wyatt Earp (IRE)**[58] 2082 3-9-4 **76** SSanders 12 — 51
(JARToller) *slowly away: nvr on terms* **11/2**[2]
0-04 **11** *5* **Indian Maiden (IRE)**[15] 3326 4-9-4 **70** SCarson 9 — 29
(MSSaunders) *led tl hdd 2f out: wknd qckly* **20/1**
0660 **12** *10* **Byo (IRE)**[18] 3195 6-9-4 **70** SDrowne 2 — —
(MQuinn) *in tch early: wknd 2f out: sn eased* **20/1**

1m 12.45s (1.31) **Going Correction** +0.325s/f (Good)
**WFA** 3 from 4yo+ 6lb — **12** Ran SP% **121.0**
Speed ratings: **104,103,101,99,98 94,94,91,90,89 83,69**CSF £117.19 CT £939.80 TOTE £13.30: £3.90, £5.30, £2.90; EX 160.50 Trifecta £1619.50 Pool: £5,930.65. 2.60 winning units..
**Owner** M Folan R Lees R Crampton **Bred** Hesmonds Stud Ltd **Trained** Hucking, Kent

**FOCUS**
A fair but tight handicap in which the well-backed winner scored with a decisive move halfway up the straight.

**NOTEBOOK**
**Mine Behind**, the subject of good market support, picked up nicely when a gap appeared halfway up the straight, and had just enough in reserve to hold off the runner-up. He has been successful on both occasions Savage has ridden, and he should not go up a great deal for this effort. *Official explanation: trainer said, regarding the improved form shown, gelding was better suited by today's drop in class, adding that the yard had been out of form when gelding ran poorly previously*
**Romany Nights(IRE)** extended his losing sequence to 23, but did little wrong in defeat and kept responding to his rider's urgings. He is clearly a frustrating sort, but is basically consistent, which prevents the Handicapper from dropping him.
**Aintnecessarilyso** is in good heart and put up another decent effort before his run came to an end.
**High Ridge**, a dual course and distance winner this season, ran well enough but looks in the Handicapper's grip now.
**Laurel Dawn** touched off last time, was 2lb higher but effectively lost his race leaving the stalls and did well to finish where he did.
**Glencoe Solas(IRE)**, just caught last time, appeared to have every chance from her low draw but was comfortably brushed aside. *Official explanation: jockey said filly hung left handed*
**Wyatt Earp(IRE)** was another to lose his chance at the gate.
**Byo(IRE)** *Official explanation: jockey said gelding was unsuited by ground (Good, Good to Firm in places)*

## 3776 BUY HERE! IMPROVE YOUR LIFESTYLE WITH DEVONCLIFFS H'CAP — 2m 1f 34y
5:20 (5:26) (F) (0-55,59) 4-Y-0+ — £3,601 (£1,108; £554; £277) Stalls Low

Form / RPR
54P1 **1** **Moonshine Beach**[3] 3683 6-9-10 **59** 5ex DaneO'Neill 13 — 68
(PWHiatt) *a.p: led 2f out: styd on wl fnl f* **2/1**[1]
-040 **2** *nk* **Circus Maximus (USA)**[3] 3667 7-9-1 **50** (p) SSanders 10 — 59
(IanWilliams) *towards rr: hdwy 1/2-way: rdn 3f out: chal appr fnl f: no imp fnl 100yds* **20/1**
1203 **3** *2 ½* **Galandora**[3] 3667 4-8-10 **52** LucyRussell(7) 5 — 58
(DrJRJNaylor) *a.p: rdn 3f out: kpt on one pce fnl 2f* **10/1**
0000 **4** *nk* **Cool Bathwick (IRE)**[39] 2590 5-8-9 **44** SWKelly 4 — 50
(BRMillman) *hld up: hdwy 1/2-way: pressed ldrs 2f out: nt qckn after* **20/1**
06-0 **5** *1 ¾* **Pertemps Sia**[29] 2874 4-7-9 **37** CHaddon(7) 8 — 41
(ADSmith) *bhd tl hdwy 6f out: rdn and styd on fnl 2f* **50/1**
10-0 **6** *hd* **Top Trees**[33] 2767 6-8-10 **45** NCallan 20 — 48
(WSKittow) *mid-div: rdn and hdwy 3f out: ev ch 2f out: wknd appr fnl f* **22/1**
0004 **7** *2* **Sninfia (IRE)**[39] 2590 4-9-4 **53** ADaly 14 — 54
(GAHam) *slowly away: hdwy over 4f out: chsd ldrs over 2f out: wknd appr fnl f* **20/1**
000/ **8** *1* **Knight Of Silver**[34] 618 7-8-3 **45** MHalford(7) 18 — 45
(JDFrost) *in rr: mde sme late hdwy* **33/1**
0-P0 **9** *hd* **Polanski Mill**[32] 2787 5-9-6 **55** PaulEddery 7 — 55
(CAHorgan) *bhd: passed sme btn horses fnl 2f* **25/1**
0040 **10** *2 ½* **Jack Durrance (IRE)**[9] 3492 4-8-4 **42** JFMcDonald(3) 16 — 39
(GAHam) *slowly away: hld up in rr: effrt 3f out: wknd wl over 1f out* **25/1**
0623 **11** *9* **Giko**[9] 3492 10-8-0 **38** LisaJones(3) 11 — 25
(JaneSouthcombe) *trckd ldr tl rdn over 3f out: sn wknd* **8/1**[3]
/000 **12** *2* **Real Estate**[3] 3667 10-8-8 **43** RLMoore 3 — 28
(JSKing) *trckd ldrs tl rdn and wknd wl over 1f out* **16/1**
306 **13** *shd* **Donald (POL)**[17] 3244 4-9-3 **52** SDrowne 19 — 37
(MPitman) *in tch: rdn over 3f out: sn wknd* **13/2**[2]
3504 **14** *nk* **Makarim (IRE)**[9] 3488 8-8-9 **44** ow1 (p) GBaker 12 — 29
(MRBosley) *in tch: hdwy: gng wl 1/2-way: wknd over 2f out* **12/1**
-000 **15** *nk* **Royal Trigger**[19] 3181 4-9-6 **55** (bt[1]) CCatlin 17 — 39
(IanWilliams) *prom: led over 4f out: rdn and hdd 2f out: wknd qckly* **25/1**
0-00 **16** *½* **Ulshaw**[22] 3108 7-8-10 **45** DSweeney 1 — 29
(BJLlewellyn) *led tl hdd over 4f out: sn wknd* **20/1**
**17** *½* **Deo Gratias (POL)**[42] 4-9-0 **49** JFEgan 6 — 32
(MPitman) *a bhd* **22/1**
0-50 **18** *1 ¼* **Port Moreno (IRE)**[25] 812 4-8-5 **40** (v) RHavlin 9 — 22
(JGMO'Shea) *in tch tl wknd 3f out* **20/1**
0 **19** *9* **Perida (IRE)**[16] 3263 4-8-10 **45** SWhitworth 2 — 17
(BGPowell) *mid-div tl lost pl 6f out: sn wl bhd* **10/1**

3m 55.99s (6.39) **Going Correction** +0.15s/f (Good) — **19** Ran SP% **138.5**
Speed ratings: **90,89,88,88,87 87,86,86,86,84 80,79,79,79,79 79,78,78,74**CSF £53.39 CT £380.77 TOTE £3.80: £1.20, £4.60, £2.50, £7.30; EX 82.20 Place 6 £6,777.19, Place 5 £172.68.
**Owner** Ken Read **Bred** Lawrence Shepherd **Trained** Hook Norton, Oxon

**FOCUS**
A modest event and a moderate winning time for the grade, so the form may not be totally reliable. The runners came centre to stands' side in the straight.

**NOTEBOOK**
**Moonshine Beach**, a winner of arguably a better race at Warwick, was always in contention and established a clear advantage halfway up the straight which he never looked like relinquishing. He may be up to completing the hat-trick.
**Circus Maximus(USA)**, better known as a chaser/hurdler, was making a quick reappearance and put up a decent effort on this sounder surface. He is on a fair mark at present.
**Galandora**, who finished ahead of the runner-up last time, kept on quite well considering she was quite keen and up with the pace from the start.
**Cool Bathwick(IRE)**, with the headgear left off, seemed suited by the longer trip and ran better than of late.
**Pertemps Sia**, having only his second run in over a year, put up a fair effort without ever looking likely to trouble the principals. Off his current mark a long-distance seller may be the best option.
**Top Trees**, arrived on the scene looking sure to figure, but faded in the straight as if the trip was beyond him. Presumably connections will be considering a return to hurdles before long.
**Sninfia(IRE)**, who ran well over a mile and six last time, was another who did not appear to get home over this extended trip.
**Giko** *Official explanation: trainer said gelding was unsuited by the ground (Good)*
**Royal Trigger**pulled too hard in the first-time blinkers and, after going to the front early in the straight, ran out of steam. *Official explanation: trainer's representative said gelding was unsuited by the trip*
**Deo Gratias(POL)** *Official explanation: jockey said colt got tired*
**Port Moreno(IRE)** *Official explanation: jockey said gelding hung right handed*
T/Plt: £9,914.80 to a £1 stake. Pool: £46,858.00. 3.45 winning tickets. T/Qpdt: £55.60 to a £1 stake. Pool: £4,188.70. 55.70 winning tickets. JS

# 3519 HAYDOCK (L-H)
### Sunday, July 11

**OFFICIAL GOING: Good to soft (soft in places)**
The card was billed as 'Football Furlong'; the jockeys wore the colours of Premiership clubs and took part in a points competition.
Wind: lt against Weather: overcast

## 3777 PADDY POWER NSPCC H'CAP — 5f
2:10 (2:12) (D) (0-80,86) 3-Y-0 — £6,971 (£2,145; £1,072; £536) Stalls Centre

Form / RPR
0366 **1** **Jadan (IRE)**[7] 3562 3-8-11 **70** WSupple 1 — 79
(EJAlston) *restless in stalls: in rr: rdn and hdwy over 1f out: edgd lft ins fnl f: sn swtchd rt: r.o to ld cl home* **7/1**
0406 **2** *nk* **Rydal (USA)**[22] 3092 3-9-7 **80** (b) TPQueally 2 — 88
(GAButler) *cl up: led wl over 1f out: rdn whn edgd rt ins fnl f: hdd cl home* **14/1**
2304 **3** *3 ½* **Lualua**[22] 3077 3-9-3 **76** KFallon 10 — 72
(TDBarron) *hld up: rdn and hdwy over 1f out: styd on and edgd lft ins fnl f: nt trble ldrs* **5/1**[2]
4-1 **4** *1 ¼* **Chimali (IRE)**[8] 3512 3-8-8 **67** EAhern — 58
(JNoseda) *prom: rdn 2f out: no ex ins fnl f* **13/2**[3]
3130 **5** *2 ½* **Baron Rhodes**[13] 3372 3-9-1 **77** TEaves(3) 8 — 60
(JSWainwright) *prom: rdn 2f out: wknd ins fnl f* **8/1**
-055 **6** *hd* **Catch The Wind**[11] 3420 3-8-11 **73** LEnstone(3) 5 — 55
(IAWood) *led: rdn 2f out: sn hdd: wknd fnl f* **16/1**
1050 **7** *1 ¼* **Peruvian Style (IRE)**[58] 2082 3-9-0 **73** JFanning 3 — 51
(NPLittmoden) *in tch: pushed along 3f out: nt pce to chal* **12/1**
0031 **8** *hd* **Silver Prelude**[4] 3645 3-9-13 **86** 6ex PRobinson 7 — 63
(DKIvory) *prom: rdn over 1f out: wknd ins fnl f* **5/1**[2]
3531 **9** *nk* **Treasure Cay**[18] 3201 3-9-6 **79** (t) KDarley 9 — 55
(PWD'Arcy) *restless in stalls: in tch: rdn over 1f out: wknd fnl f* **9/2**[1]
2-03 **10** *1* **Fitzwarren**[7] 3562 3-8-8 **67** (v) DeanMcKeown — 39
(NBycroft) *chsd ldrs: rdn 2f out: wknd over 1f out* **20/1**

63.12 secs (1.05) **Going Correction** +0.40s/f (Good) — **10** Ran SP% **113.5**
Speed ratings: **107,106,100,98,94 94,92,92,91,90**CSF £97.02 CT £542.13 TOTE £10.90: £2.50, £3.90, £2.00; EX 209.70.
**Owner** Derrick Mossop **Bred** Michael Rourke **Trained** Longton, Lancs

**FOCUS**
A fair sprint that produced a decent winning time for the grade, with the first two improving but will need to find more off higher marks.

**NOTEBOOK**
**Jadan(IRE)**was keen early on, but the decent early pace played to his strengths, and he came through late on to collar the runner-up and score. This performance allayed any fears about soft ground and he is in good heart, but is not the easiest ride.
**Rydal(USA)**, who has failed to build on his juvenile form so far this year over a variety of trips, ran his best race of the season on this softer surface and was only just denied. He did everything right until wandering about late on under pressure, and that cost him, but he clearly has a race in him over this trip.
**Lualua**was doing all of his best work late on and shaped as though a return to six furlongs is required. He is capable of better.
**Chimali(IRE)**, who made all to get off the mark last time, was unable to dominate on this handicap debut and although he remains open to improvement, he is clearly no great shakes.
**Catch The Wind** could not sustain her good early pace on this slow ground and is a different propostion on a quick surface.
**Silver Prelude** had every chance to follow-up his recent Newmarket win under this penalty, but failed to quicken on the soft ground.
**Treasure Cay** played up in the stalls and never looked a threat when coming out of them. He looks firmly in the Handicapper's grip and has his quirks, so may be one to avoid. *Official explanation: jockey said colt was unsuited by the good to soft ground*

## 3778 PADDY POWER BET IN-RUNNING H'CAP — 6f
2:40 (2:41) (D) (0-85,82) 4-Y-0+ — £7,182 (£2,210; £1,105; £552) Stalls Centre

Form / RPR
0410 **1** **Pinchbeck**[15] 3298 5-9-12 **80** (p) PRobinson 7 — 97
(MAJarvis) *racd keenly: bhd: hdwy over 1f out: led ins fnl f: pushed out* **9/2**[1]

00-0 **2** *1 1/4* **Golden Dixie (USA)**[10] [3453] 5-9-12 **80** KFallon 4 93
(AMBalding) *prom: led 1/2-way: rdn over 1f out: hdd ins fnl f: nt qckn* **5/1**[2]

0322 **3** *2* **Time N Time Again**[8] [3515] 6-9-2 **70** (p) DAllan 6 77
(EJAlston) *a.p: rdn 2f out: styd on same pce fnl f* **9/2**[1]

0504 **4** *nk* **Locombe Hill (IRE)**[10] [3446] 8-8-6 **60** JCarroll 10 66
(DNicholls) *in tch: rdn and outpcd over 2f out: styd on u.p ins fnl f* **8/1**[3]

5000 **5** *1 3/4* **Grey Cossack**[15] [3309] 7-9-5 **73** RFitzpatrick 2 74
(PTMidgley) *s.s: sn in midfield: rdn and hdwy over 2f out: no ex ins fnl f* **12/1**

6226 **6** *2 1/2* **Million Percent**[15] [3324] 5-9-11 **79** DarrenWilliams 9 72
(KRBurke) *midfield: rdn and hdwy over 2f out: wknd ins fnl f: sn eased* **9/2**[1]

0050 **7** *nk* **Inter Vision (USA)**[22] [3098] 4-9-11 **82** ABeech(3) 1 74
(ADickman) *in tch: rdn over 1f out: wknd ins ins fnl f* **16/1**

-005 **8** *1 1/4* **Smirfys Systems**[43] [2467] 5-9-8 **76** TGMcLaughlin 5 65
(WMBrisbourne) *s.s: towards rr: rdn and hdwy over 2f out: wknd 1f out* **12/1**

0000 **9** *2* **Zuhair**[11] [3407] 11-8-12 **66** AlexGreaves 8 49
(DNicholls) *a bhd* **25/1**

1133 **10** *10* **Hard To Catch (IRE)**[12] [3395] 6-9-4 **79** (b) MHoward(7) 3 32
(DKIvory) *led: hdd 1/2-way: sn rdn: wknd over 1f out* **11/1**

1m 17.43s (2.54) **Going Correction** +0.40s/f (Good) **10 Ran SP% 115.8**
Speed ratings: **99,97,94,94,91 88,88,86,83,70**CSF £26.62 CT £106.91 TOTE £5.40: £2.90, £1.90, £1.70; EX 23.70.
**Owner** T G Warner **Bred** Red House Stud **Trained** Newmarket, Suffolk

**FOCUS**
A fair contest that only produced a modest winning time for the grade, but the form appears solid enough.

**NOTEBOOK**
**Pinchbeck** looked to have a fair bit to do at half-way, but showed his resilience and picked up well under pressure to out-stay his rivals in the final furlong. He put a poor run last time behind him, likes this venue and should continue to pay his way this summer.
**Golden Dixie(USA)** ◆ bounced back to form and only tired out of it late on. He handled this ground, but is better on a quick surface, and should go close next time if getting his favoured underfoot conditions. *Official explanation: jockey said gelding hung right handed*
**Time N Time Again** again held every chance and ran to form, but continues to frustrate at the business end of his races. Although he has been placed on a soft surface, he has never won on ground easier than good.
**Locombe Hill(IRE)** again shaped as though he is about to hit form, so is one to respect when racing over another furlong, and especially if the market speaks in his favour.
**Grey Cossack** ran his best race since winning in April and has slipped back to a favourable mark. He can build on this and loves a testing surface.
**Million Percent**, whose recent efforts gave him an obvious chance in this, failed to pick up on the soft ground and is worth another chance when reverting to a quick surface.
**Zuhair**, who has slipped in the ratings, was never put in the race. Connections will be aiming to have him spot on for his beloved Goodwood at the end of July, and he looks on the sort of mark to do himself justice there.

## 3779 PADDY POWER H'CAP 7f 30y
**3:10** (3:11) (E) (0-70,74) 4-Y-0+ **£5,720** (£1,760; £880; £440) **Stalls** Low

Form RPR

1201 **1** **Savile's Delight (IRE)**[10] [3446] 5-10-1 **74** DNolan(3) 4 86
(RBrotherton) *prom: led over 5f out: rdn and wandered fr over 1f out: kpt on wl* **11/2**[2]

2035 **2** *1/2* **Middleton Grey**[15] [3321] 6-9-4 **63** (b) LPKeniry(3) 3 74
(AGNewcombe) *midfield: hdwy 2f out: styd on ins fnl f* **11/2**[2]

2-61 **3** *nk* **Fonthill Road (IRE)**[12] [3400] 4-9-11 **70** THamilton(3) 2 80
(RAFahey) *s.i.s: midfield: hdwy 3f out: rdn 2f out: ev ch fr over 1f out: hld towards fin* **9/4**[1]

1535 **4** *2 1/2* **Efidium**[8] [3516] 6-9-13 **69** DeanMcKeown 7 73
(NBycroft) *hld up: hdwy over 2f out: kpt on u.p ins fnl f* **10/1**

4300 **5** *3/4* **Bint Royal (IRE)**[10] [3457] 6-8-13 **55** (p) PRobinson 57
(MissVHaigh) *led: hdd over 5f out: remained handy: rdn over 2f out: no ex ins fnl f* **16/1**

3-00 **6** *5* **Able Mind**[16] [3265] 4-9-3 **62** TEaves(3) 5 51
(ACWhillans) *hld up in rr: pushed along over 2f out: kpt on ins fnl f: nvr trbld ldrs* **40/1**

0650 **7** *3/4* **Branston Tiger**[15] [3321] 5-9-9 **65** MFenton 9 52
(JGGiven) *in rr: rdn and hdwy over 3f out: wknd over 1f out* **9/1**

0000 **8** *1 1/2* **Creskeld (IRE)**[8] [3520] 5-9-11 **67** FLynch 8 50
(BSmart) *prom: rdn over 3f out: wknd over 1f out* **11/1**

530 **9** *5* **Aswan (IRE)**[9] [3470] 6-9-9 **65** (t) KFallon 6 35
(SRBowring) *midfield: rdn over 2f out: wknd over 1f out: eased ins fnl f* **8/1**[3]

4040 **10** *18* **Far Note (USA)**[15] [3298] 6-9-9 **65** (b) KDarley 10 —
(SRBowring) *prom: rdn over 3f out: wknd 2f out: eased ins fnl f* **10/1**

1m 33.64s (1.48) **Going Correction** +0.275s/f (Good) **10 Ran SP% 117.5**
Speed ratings: **102,101,101,98,97 91,90,89,83,62**CSF £36.15 CT £88.06 TOTE £9.30: £2.60, £2.10, £1.70; EX 54.20.
**Owner** Roy Brotherton **Bred** Romany Investements Ltd **Trained** Elmley Castle, Worcs

**FOCUS**
A modest event run at a sound gallopand the form looks fair for the grade.

**NOTEBOOK**
**Savile's Delight(IRE)** bravely followed-up his previous win at the track over this extra furlong and off his 4lb higher mark. He does idle in front, but is the type Handicapper's find hard to assess, so he could well have more to offer and does look best with a bit of give in the ground.
**Middleton Grey** again ran on late in the day, but although he is dangerously well-treated on his All-Weather form, he remains winless on turf and is clearly a tricky ride.
**Fonthill Road(IRE)** missed the kick, but still recovered to hold every chance and ultimately proved disappointing. He is dangerous to write off however, as he has a habit of bouncing back, and may have found this trip stretching him.
**Efidium** was not disgraced on ground less than ideal and over a distance that just looks to find him out.
**Far Note(USA)** *Official explanation: jockey said gelding had a breathing problem*

## 3780 PADDYPOWER.COM H'CAP 1m 30y
**3:40** (3:41) (E) (0-70,69) 3-Y-0 **£5,655** (£1,740; £870; £435) **Stalls** Low

Form RPR

-424 **1** **Silverhay**[25] [2977] 3-9-4 **66** KFallon 5 71
(TDBarron) *mde virtually all: rdn out* **13/8**[1]

61-0 **2** *3/4* **Almond Willow (IRE)**[13] [3387] 3-9-4 **66** EAhern 2 70
(JNoseda) *hld up: pushed along 3f out: hdwy on ins over 1f out: flashed tail u.p: swtchd rt ins fnl f: r.o cl home* **12/1**

3456 **3** *1/2* **Foolish Groom**[22] [3102] 3-9-7 **69** (tp) WSupple 10 72
(RHollinshead) *midfield: rdn and hdwy over 2f out: edgd lft wl over 1f out: ev ch ins fnl f: no ex cl home* **12/1**

0046 **4** *3/4* **Orion Express**[23] [3060] 3-8-9 **62** PMulrennan(5) 7 63
(MWEasterby) *midfield: rdn over 2f out: styd on ins fnl f: nrst fin* **9/1**

040 **5** *nk* **Belshazzar (USA)**[19] [3168] 3-9-7 **69** JEdmunds 8 69
(TPTate) *in rr: rdn and swtchd rt over 2f out: styd on ins fnl f: nvr nrr* **33/1**

4000 **6** *shd* **Morag**[35] [2703] 3-9-2 **64** TPQueally 3 64
(IAWood) *trckd ldrs: rdn 2f out: styd on same pce fnl f* **20/1**

002 **7** *2* **Desert Leader (IRE)**[16] [3279] 3-9-7 **69** GGibbons 4 65
(BAMcmahon) *trckd ldrs: rdn and nt clr run 2f out: sn lost pl: kpt on one pce ins fnl f: eased whn btn cl home* **4/1**[2]

6604 **8** *3/4* **Acuzio**[24] [3004] 3-9-1 **63** KDarley 6 57
(WMBrisbourne) *prom: rdn and ev ch 2f out: wknd fnl f* **25/1**

0010 **9** *hd* **Dispol Veleta**[15] [3312] 3-9-2 **67** NMackay(3) 9 61
(TDBarron) *trckd ldrs: rdn whn n.m.r wl over 1f out wknd fnl f* **7/1**[3]

5104 **10** *nk* **Mission Affirmed (USA)**[25] [2988] 3-9-4 **66** DaleGibson 1 59
(TPTate) *hld up: pushed along over 2f out: nvr trbld ldrs* **14/1**

1m 48.99s (3.44) **Going Correction** +0.275s/f (Good) **10 Ran SP% 114.2**
Speed ratings: **93,92,91,91,90 90,88,87,87,87**CSF £21.87 CT £182.24 TOTE £2.10: £1.50, £2.30, £3.00; EX 19.20.
**Owner** D C Rutter P J Huntbach **Bred** Major W R Hern And W H Carson **Trained** Maunby, N Yorks

**FOCUS**
A moderate affair that saw just an ordinary winning time for the grade and a close finish, suggesting this was not a strong heat.

**NOTEBOOK**
**Silverhay** bounced back from a disappointing effort last time to score and really enjoyed being able to dictate affairs over this shorter trip. He was much more settled in the lead this time, and now connections have seemingly found his optimum distance, he is entitled to improve again.
**Almond Willow(IRE)** improved on her comeback effort and was finishing best of all, yet again flashed her tail under pressure and does look quirky. It would however, be a surprise if she were not placed to advantage of this mark.
**Foolish Groom**, in the tongue tie for the first time, improved a touch for this softer ground. He does little to suggest he is well handicapped and needs some respite in the weights.
**Orion Express**, held up to get the trip, stayed on well enough to suggest he is worth another try at this trip with a more positive ride.
**Desert Leader(IRE)**, making his handicap debut after the mandatory three previous starts, was tight for room two out, but it made little difference to the result. He is capable of better and, being a son of Green Desert, should relish the chance to race on faster ground.

## 3781 PADDY POWER DIAL-A-BET H'CAP 1m 2f 120y
**4:10** (4:10) (E) (0-70,76) 3-Y-0+ **£5,785** (£1,780; £890; £445) **Stalls** High

Form RPR

0561 **1** **Jimmy Byrne (IRE)**[9] [3475] 4-9-11 **70** TEaves(3) 1 80
(BEllison) *a.p gng wl: led ins fnl f: sn edgd lft: drvn out* **6/1**[3]

3211 **2** *1 3/4* **Santiburi Lad (IRE)**[8] [3510] 7-9-10 **66** KFallon 10 75+
(NWilson) *led 2f: remained prom: regaine ld over 2f out: rdn over 1f out: hdd ins fnl f: hld whn sn checked* **6/4**[1]

2305 **3** *3/4* **Easibet Dot Net**[19] [3166] 4-9-4 **60** (p) PFessey 9 66
(ISemple) *prom: rdn over 2f out: nt qckn over 1f out: kpt on u.p cl home* **12/1**

0000 **4** *2* **Band**[13] [3387] 4-9-2 **58** GGibbons 60
(BAMcmahon) *hld up: hdwy 4f out: sn rdn: one pce ins fnl f* **33/1**

2421 **5** *1 1/4* **Opening Ceremony (USA)**[1] [3731] 5-10-3 **76** 6ex THamilton(3) 4 76
(RAFahey) *hld up: rdn and hdwy over 1f out: nvr able to chal* **9/2**[2]

0040 **6** *1 1/4* **Lennel**[1] [3731] 6-9-8 **64** (b) TPQueally 8 62
(ABailey) *towards rr: hdwy 3f out: one pce over 1f out* **12/1**

20/0 **7** *1* **Valdesco (IRE)**[18] [3199] 6-9-8 **67** (p) LEnstone(3) 3 63
(MrsSJSmith) *led after 2f: rdn and hdd over 2f out: wknd over 1f out* **16/1**

1002 **8** *8* **Allied Victory (USA)**[9] [3475] 4-10-5 **75** WSupple 7 58
(EJAlston) *t.k.h: in tch: hdwy 4f out: wknd over 2f out* **16/1**

5663 **9** *6* **Active Account (USA)**[8] [3534] 7-9-5 **61** KDarley 5 34
(MrsHDalton) *trckd ldrs: rdn 4f out: sn lost pl: n.d after* **12/1**

5000 **10** *26* **Mi Odds**[51] [2272] 8-9-11 **67** JFanning 6 —
(MrsNMacauley) *hld up: rdn over 2f out: nvr on terms* **25/1**

2m 19.49s (1.76) **Going Correction** +0.275s/f (Good) **10 Ran SP% 114.1**
Speed ratings: **104,102,102,100,99 98,98,92,88,69**CSF £14.96 CT £104.30 TOTE £5.70: £2.00, £1.50, £3.70; EX 12.50.
**Owner** Keith Middleton **Bred** Austin Well Stud **Trained** Norton, N Yorks
■ Stewards Enquiry : L Enstone two-day ban: used whip when gelding showing no response (Jul 23,25)
T Eaves caution: careless riding

**FOCUS**
A moderate event lacking any strength in depth and the field came home well strung out.

**NOTEBOOK**
**Jimmy Byrne(IRE)** readily followed-up his claiming win over course-and-distance to land his first handicap success. He appreciated this softer surface and is clearly in great nick at present.
**Santiburi Lad(IRE)**, who came into this bidding for the hat-trick, ran another brave race. However, he had the run of the race and the 12lb rise in the weights for winning the last twice looks to have found him out.
**Easibet Dot Net** put in a better effort on this easier ground, but is a very hard horse to catch right and could do with a drop in the weights.
**Band**, who has lost his form this year, showed his best form for a long while and has clearly appreciated a recent slide in the ratings.
**Opening Ceremony(USA)**, who got back to winning ways at Chester just 24-hours previously, was never a threat under her penalty and found this coming way too soon.

## 3782 PADDY POWER FOOTBALL FURLONG H'CAP 1m 6f
**4:40** (4:40) (E) (0-75,72) 3-Y-0+ **£5,590** (£1,720; £860; £430) **Stalls** Low

Form RPR

2522 **1** **Magic Combination (IRE)**[7] [3564] 11-9-6 **72** PMulrennan(5) 7 86+
(LLungo) *hld up: hdwy gng wl over 2f out: rdn to ld ins fnl f: sn edgd lft: styd on wl* **9/4**[1]

10-6 **2** *3* **Prize Ring**[11] [3411] 5-8-3 **50** RFfrench 3 57
(GMMoore) *trckd ldrs: rdn over 3f out: led over 2f out: hdd ins fnl f: no ex* **9/1**

1421 **3** *6* **Smart John**[9] [3474] 4-9-4 **70** BSwarbrick(5) 6 69+
(WMBrisbourne) *hld up: hdwy 3f out: rdn 2f out: edgd lft 1f out: no ex whn jinked rt wl ins fnl f* **11/4**[2]

0040 **4** *1 1/2* **Perestroika (IRE)**[43] [2491] 6-8-5 **55** TEaves(3) 8 52
(BEllison) *hld up: rdn over 3f out: nvr able to chal* **14/1**

0250 **5** *3/4* **Bramantino (IRE)**[44] [2449] 4-8-6 **56** (b) THamilton(3) 2 52
(RAFahey) *in tch: hdwy over 3f out: rdn and led briefly over 2f out: wknd ins fnl f* **12/1**

**6** *nk* **Bushido (IRE)**[45] [1867] 5-8-9 **59** LEnstone(3) 1 55
(MrsSJSmith) *prom: rdn to ld wl over 3f out: hdd over 2f out: wkng whn n.m.r 1f out and again wl ins fnl f* **9/1**

6234 **7** *6* **Northern Nymph**[10] [3449] 5-9-0 **66** StephanieHollinshead(5) 4 54
(RHollinshead) *in tch: rdn 5f out: wknd 1f out* **13/2**[3]

0302 **8** *20* **Lady Netbetsports (IRE)**[8] 3508 5-8-10 **62**.................... MLawson(5) 5 24
(BSRothwell) *sn led: rdn and hdd wl over 3f out: sn wknd* **16/1**

3m 7.84s (1.69) **Going Correction** +0.275s/f (Good) 8 Ran SP% **111.0**
Speed ratings: **106,104,100,100,99 99,95,84**CSF £21.74 CT £54.27 TOTE £3.40: £1.60, £2.60, £1.70; EX 22.70 Place 6 £16.40, Place 5 £4.06.
**Owner** Sw Transport (swindon) Ltd & R J Gilbert **Bred** William J O'Regan **Trained** Carrutherstown, D'fries & G'way

**FOCUS**
A weak heat run at a furious early gallop. The field trailed in well strung out as a result and the form does not look all that solid.

**NOTEBOOK**
**Magic Combination(IRE)**, a decent hurdler in his pomp, relished this strong gallop and shorter trip and won readily. He has returned to the Flat in admirably consistent form, and his yard do well with their few raiders on the level, but whether this one can follow-up off a higher mark is another matter entirely.
**Prize Ring**, in fair form this summer over hurdles, ran a much improved race and was a clear second best. He looks well suited by a test of stamina and proved he can go on this easy ground.
**Smart John**, 7lb higher than when winning over shorter last time, looked all at sea on this softer ground and is well worth another chance back on faster ground.
**Perestroika(IRE)** was made to look very one-paced late in the day, but was not disgraced at the weights and would have preferred faster going.
T/Jkpt: Not won. T/Plt: £30.60 to a £1 stake. Pool: £58,729.35. 1,400.05 winning tickets. T/Qpdt: £2.60 to a £1 stake. Pool: £3,978.10. 1,105.70 winning tickets. DO

3783 - 3789a (Foreign Racing) - See Raceform Interactive

## 3768 DEAUVILLE (R-H)
Sunday, July 11

**OFFICIAL GOING: Turf course - good to soft; all-weather course - standard**

### 3790a PRIX ROLAND DE CHAMBURE (LISTED) (STRAIGHT COURSE) 7f (S)
**1:30** (1:31) 2-Y-O **£15,845** (£6,338; £4,754; £3,169)

RPR

**1** **Inhabitant**[18] 2-9-0 .................... ODoleuze 6 96
(MmeCHead-Maarek, France)

**2** *1 ½* **Kappelmann (FR)**[20] 2-9-0 .................... TJarnet 7 92
(RobertCollet, France)

**3** *½* **Royal Mistress**[40] 2-8-11 .................... OPeslier 5 88
(RGibson, France)

**4** *1 ½* **Medigating (FR)**[34] 2-9-0 .................... TGillet 9 87
(MRoussel, France)

**5** *hd* **Ascot Dream (IRE)**[91] 2-8-11 ....................(b) YBarberot 1 84
(SWattel, France)

**6** *nk* **Dahteer (IRE)**[30] 2831 2-9-0 .................... TEDurcan 3 86
(MRChannon) *disputed lead on inside after 1f, headed and weakened 1 1/2f out*

**7** *1 ½* **Faussaire (IRE)** 2-9-0 .................... IMendizabal 2 82
(J-CRouget, France)

**8** *2* **Riverbride (USA)** 2-8-11 .................... C-PLemaire 4 74
(NClement, France)

1m 28.2s **Going Correction** -0.125s/f (Firm) **8 Ran**
Speed ratings: **89,87,86,85,84 84,82,80.**
**Owner** K Abdulla **Bred** Juddmonte Farms **Trained** France

**NOTEBOOK**
**Inhabitant** is still green but won smoothly here and can make his mark in a higher grade.
**Dahteer(IRE)** was up with the pace from the off, but found little when popped the question a furlong and a half out. Durcan was convinced that this was not his true form.

### 3791a PRIX MESSIDOR (GROUP 3) (STRAIGHT COURSE) 1m
**2:30** (2:29) 3-Y-O+ **£25,704** (£10,282; £7,711; £5,141)

RPR

**1** **Ryono (USA)**[233] 6044 5-9-2 .................... TCastanheira 6 118?
(PLautner, Germany) *held up in last, headway on inside to lead over 1f out, quickened clear*

**2** *2 ½* **Diamond Green (FR)**[26] 2956 3-8-7 .................... GaryStevens 7 113?
(AFabre, France) *pressed leader on outside til led narrowly just under 2f out, headed over 1f out, no extra* 1

**3** *½* **Special Kaldoun (IRE)**[71] 1780 5-9-2 .................... DBoeuf 4 112?
(DSmaga, France) *disputed 3rd, switched outside and ridden over 1f out, stayed on at same pace* 3

**4** *¾* **Joursanvault (FR)**[20] 3163 3-8-7 .................... OPeslier 2 110?
(ADeRoyer-Dupre, France) *tracked leader towards inside, ridden and slightly outpaced 1 1/2f out, stayed on final f to take 4th close home*

**5** *snk* **Maxwell (FR)**[71] 1780 4-9-2 .................... C-PLemaire 1 110?
(MmeCHead-Maarek, France) *led til headed just under 2f out, one pace* 2

**6** *nk* **Almond Mousse (FR)**[28] 2923 5-8-13 .................... IMendizabal 5 106?
(RobertCollet, France) *always in rear*

1m 39.6s **Going Correction** -0.125s/f (Firm)
**WFA** 3 from 4yo+ 9lb **6 Ran SP% 124.5**
Speed ratings: **113,110,110,109,109 108.**
**Owner** Frau H Focke **Bred** Hildegard Focke **Trained** Germany

**NOTEBOOK**
**Ryono(USA)**, who had somehow been allowed to start at over 50-1 when landing a Milan Listed race on his previous start, was again outsider of the field. Held up in last, he came up the inside rail as the others preferred to race a few yards off it. Exhibiting a fine turn of foot, he won in taking style. Connections are keen to keep things low-key, with further Group Three events at Cologne and Deauville being considered, but he would not need to improve much to make his mark in better company.
**Diamond Green(FR)** was primed for a morale-boosting victory prior to a return to Group Onecompany in the Jacques Le Marois. Instead, he suffered a clear-cut and dispiriting defeat and, although Stevens was inclined to blame the ground, he won a Group Three on soft as a two-year-old and this result gave further credence to those who believe the classic crop of 2004 are sub-standard.
**Special Kaldoun(IRE)** ran better than of late as he tried to repeat last year's victory but may need softer ground to return to his best.

## HOPPEGARTEN (R-H)
Sunday, July 11

**OFFICIAL GOING: Good**

### 3792a BERLIN BRANDENBURG TROPHY (GROUP 2) 1m
**3:40** (3:50) 3-Y-O+ **£44,366** (£15,493; £7,746; £4,225)

RPR

**1** **Martillo (GER)**[26] 2957 4-9-6 .................... WMongil 2 111+
(RSuerland, Germany) *raced in 3rd on inside, no room 1 1/2f out, switched outside, strong run to lead post* 1

**2** *shd* **Assiun (GER)**[56] 2158 3-8-9 .................... ASuborics 1 109
(PSchiergen, Germany) *raced in 4th, headway to dispute lead from 1 1/2f out, headed post* 2

**3** *hd* **Checkit (IRE)**[26] 2957 4-9-6 .................... ACulhane 6 111
(MRChannon) *raced in 2nd, disputed lead 1 1/2f out, headed and no extra close home* 3

**4** *3 ½* **Arlecchina (GER)**[11] 3434 4-9-2 .................... ADeVries 3 100
(UStoltefuss, Germany) *slowly into stride, last straight, stayed on to take 4th 1f out but never near leaders*

**5** *2* **Sambaprinz (GER)**[15] 3335 5-9-6 .................... AStarke 5 100
(HHorwart, Germany) *set slow pace til headed 1 1/2f out, weakened*

**6** *2 ½* **Bear King (GER)**[49] 2336 7-9-6 .................... NRichter 4 95
(CSprengel, Germany) *raced in 5th, ridden and unable to quicken 2f out*

1m 39.4s
**WFA** 3 from 4yo+ 9lb **6 Ran SP% 128.0**
Speed ratings: .
**Owner** Gestut Hony-Hof **Bred** Gestut Katharinenhof **Trained** Germany

**NOTEBOOK**
**Martillo(GER)** was more at home back on a round mile, but so nearly got beaten in a race he should have won comfortably. Ill-suited by the slow pace, he then got boxed in against the running rail in the straight and only just got out in time. He needs a gap between his races an is unlikely to run again before the end of next month, when the Celebration Mile at Goodwood and the Oettingen-Rennen at Baden-Baden are possible targets.
**Assiun(GER)** turned in a solid effort and should not be long in breaking his Group race duck.
**Checkit(IRE)**, outclassed in the Queen Anne last time, found this level more suitable and ran a decent race in defeat. He continues to run with credit but now has six Pattern race placings since his Group Two win as a juvenile. If he keeps knocking at the door it should finally re-open.

## 3077 AYR (L-H)
Monday, July 12

**OFFICIAL GOING: Good (good to firm in places)**
Wind: fresh, hlf across Weather: bright but cloudy

### 3793 EUROPEAN BREEDERS FUND MAIDEN STKS 6f
**2:15** (2:17) (D) 2-Y-O **£5,447** (£1,676; £838; £419) **Stalls High**

Form RPR

**1** **Shamardal (USA)** 2-9-0 .................... JFanning 5 97+
(MJohnston) *mde all: shkn up and qcknd clr fr over 1f out: readily* **11/10**[1]

0540 **2** *8* **No Commission (IRE)**[9] 3514 2-9-0 .................... FNorton 6 73
(RFFisher) *chsd ldrs: rdn over 2f out: kpt on fnl f: no ch w wnr* **50/1**

3 **3** *1 ½* **Tsaroxy (IRE)**[16] 3313 2-9-0 .................... RWinston 2 69
(JHowardJohnson) *cl up: effrt and chsd wnr over 1f out: no imp ins fnl f* **9/4**[2]

**4** *3* **Tartan Special** 2-9-0 .................... DarrenWilliams 4 60
(KRBurke) *dwlt: hld up in tch: rdn over 2f out: sn no imp* **66/1**

6 **5** *3 ½* **Corker**[19] 3192 2-9-0 .................... KDarley 1 49
(GAButler) *cl up: rdn over 2f out: sn btn* **20/1**

**6** *6* **Geojimali** 2-8-11 .................... TEaves(3) 3 31
(JSGoldie) *hld up: outpcd after 2f: n.d after* **150/1**

**F** **Stretford End (IRE)** 2-9-0 .................... FLynch 7 —
(BSmart) *keen: in tch on ins: edgd rt: hit rail: faltered bdly and fell over 4f out* **7/2**[3]

1m 11.63s (-2.09) **Going Correction** -0.275s/f (Firm) 7 Ran SP% **109.5**
Speed ratings: **102,91,89,85,72 80,**—CSF £57.10 TOTE £1.90: £1.60, £10.20; EX 74.20.
**Owner** Abdulla Buhaleeba **Bred** Brilliant Stable **Trained** Middleham Moor, N Yorks

**FOCUS**
Little strength in depth, but a very smart winning time for the grade and the winner appeals as the sort to go on to better things.

**NOTEBOOK**
**Shamardal(USA)** ◆, who cost 50,000gns and is a half brother to seven-furlong winner Lushs Lad, took the eye in the paddock and created a lasting impression on this racecourse debut. He has plenty of physical scope and appeals strongly as the type to hold his own in stronger company.
**No Commission(IRE)** ran creditably back over this longer trip, but is a fully exposed performer who is likely to remain vulnerable in this type of event. However, he again shaped as though worth a try over seven furlongs.
**Tsaroxy(IRE)** failed to come on for his debut effort on this quicker ground, but was not disgraced and may be capable of better over seven furlongs in nursery company in due course.
**Tartan Special**, who cost 27,000gns and is the third foal of a winner in France, was not disgraced on this racecourse debut and left the impression that he could improve granted a stiffer test in due course.
**Corker**, easy to back, failed by some way to confirm the bit of promise shown on his debut. He is not one to write off yet, though, and is another that may be seen to better effect in nursery company.
**Geojimali** looked in need of the race but was well beaten on this racecourse debut. He has physical scope and is likely to do better in time.
**Stretford End(IRE)**, a half-brother to seven furlong winner Weavers Pride, is not a bad sort on looks but, after attracting support on this racecourse debut, suffered a nasty fall soon after the start. It is to be hoped he is none the worse for this experience.

### 3794 GARRY OWEN H'CAP 1m 2f 192y
**2:45** (2:45) (E) (0-70,65) 3-Y-O+ **£3,623** (£1,115; £557; £278) **Stalls Low**

Form RPR

2110 **1** **Party Ploy**[19] 3199 6-9-8 **63**.................... DarrenWilliams 5 70
(KRBurke) *set stdy pce: mde all: rdn 2f out: hld on wl* **7/4**[1]

/604 **2** *1* **Spree Vision**[10] 3474 8-8-7 **51** ow1....................(v) LEnstone(3) 3 56
(PMonteith) *cl up: disp ld over 2f out: sn rdn: r.o fnl f* **10/1**

2345 **3** *hd* **Templet (USA)**[16] 3297 4-9-10 **65**....................(b[1]) JCarroll 2 70
(ISemple) *chsd ldrs: rdn over 2f out: kpt on fnl f* **10/1**

0030 **4** *1 ¾* **Border Terrier (IRE)**[12] 3411 6-7-12 **39** oh2....................(b) RFfrench 6 41
(MDHammond) *in tch: rdn over 2f out: kpt on fnl f: no imp* **8/1**

4661 **5** 2 ½ **Sting Like A Bee (IRE)**[23] 3082 5-8-11 **55** NMackay[(3)] 1 53
(JSGoldie) *keen in tch: effrt over 2f out: btn fnl f* **4/1**[2]

0-03 **6** 1 ¾ **Sherwood Forest**[14] 3367 4-7-10 **44** (v) LeanneKershaw[(7)] 4 39
(MissLAPerratt) *prom on outside: rdn over 2f out: btn over 1f out* **7/1**[3]

4026 **7** 1 ¾ **Lucky Largo (IRE)**[14] 3369 4-8-11 **57** (b) PMulrennan[(5)] 7 49
(MissLAPerratt) *hld up: pushed along 3f out: sn struggling* **11/1**

2m 24.59s (1.27) **Going Correction** -0.05s/f (Good) 7 Ran SP% **106.5**
Speed ratings: **93,92,92,90,89 87,86**CSF £17.16 TOTE £2.50: £1.10, £7.20; EX 14.30.
**Owner** Ian A McInnes **Bred** I McInnes **Trained** Middleham Moor, N Yorks
■ Stewards Enquiry : L Enstone caution: used whip with excessive frequency

**FOCUS**
A field of inconsistent performers and a sedate pace not surprisingly resulted in a very moderate winning time. This race favoured those racing close to the pace and bare form looks less than reliable.

**NOTEBOOK**
**Party Ploy**, a consistent sort, was allowed to do his own thing in front and he comfortably outbattled a few unreliable rivals. A rise in the weights will leave him vulnerable in stronger company, but he will always be of interest in this grade when it looks like he can dominate.
**Spree Vision**, always well placed in a steadily-run race, elected to put his best foot forward and ran creditably with his rider putting up overweight. However, given his record and his losing run on the Flat, he would not be certain to put it all in next time.
**Templet(USA)**, with the visor replaced by first-time blinkers, ran creditably but he does look high enough in the weights. While a stronger gallop may have suited, it is no certainty that aid will have the same effect next time.
**Border Terrier(IRE)** is on a fair mark and was not disgraced from out of the handicap, given this race favoured those racing right up with the pace, but is too unreliable to be a betting proposition next time.
**Sting Like A Bee(IRE)** was not totally disgraced given he did not settle in this messy race over this longer trip and left the impression that a more strongly run race over shorter would have suited. He is better than this bare form.
**Sherwood Forest** had his limitations exposed back in handicap company and remains one to tread carefully with.

## 3795 TOTEEXACTA STKS H'CAP 5f
**3:15** (3:15) (C ) (0-95,89) 3-Y-0+ **£10,927** (£4,144; £2,072; £942) **Stalls** High

Form RPR

0065 **1** **Ptarmigan Ridge**[3] 3713 8-9-5 **83** MFenton 7 92
(MissLAPerratt) *bhd stands rail: nt clr run 1/2-way: swtchd lft and hdwy over 1f out: led and edgd rt ins fnl f: r.o wl* **12/1**

1000 **2** 1 **Proud Boast**[17] 3266 6-9-11 **89** KDarley 5 98+
(DNicholls) *sn niggled in rr: effrt whn no clr run fr 1/2-way to last half f: r.o wl: no ch w wnr* **16/1**

5040 **3** shd **Foursquare (IRE)**[9] 3523 3-9-5 **88** DaleGibson 2 93
(JMackie) *cl up: effrt over 2f out: one pce ins fnl f* **12/1**

3000 **4** nk **Maktavish**[16] 3293 5-9-0 **81** (p) TEaves[(3)] 9 85
(ISemple) *disp ld stands side to over 1f out: one pce ins last* **7/1**[3]

0521 **5** hd **Aahgowangowan (IRE)**[13] 3399 5-7-13 **63** (t) RFfrench 3 66
(MDods) *disp ld: led over 1f out to ins last: no ex* **5/1**[2]

6000 **6** shd **Malapropism**[10] 3480 4-9-4 **82** CCatlin 6 85
(MRChannon) *sn niggled towards rr: hdwy 2f out: no imp wl ins fnl f* **9/1**

306 **7** ½ **Obe One**[3] 3713 4-8-4 **68** FNorton 10 69
(ABerry) *in tch: no room fr 1/2-way: nt rcvr* **9/2**[1]

0043 **8** ½ **Viewforth**[7] 3580 6-8-0 **67** (b) NMackay[(3)] 8 66+
(JSGoldie) *in tch: rdn 1/2-way: no room fr 2f out: nt rcvr* **9/2**[1]

3000 **9** 6 **Seafield Towers**[23] 3098 4-8-9 **73** (p) JFanning 4 51+
(MissLAPerratt) *chsd ldrs: wkng whn hmpd over 1f out* **18/1**

156 **10** 9 **Musical Fair**[25] 3016 4-8-13 **77** (v[1]) RWinston 1 22
(JAGlover) *racd wd: hung lft thrght: wknd fr 1/2-way* **12/1**

59.01 secs (-1.42) **Going Correction** -0.275s/f (Firm)
**WFA** 3 from 4yo+ 5lb 10 Ran SP% **109.8**
Speed ratings: **100,98,98,97,97 97,96,95,86,71**CSF £173.44 CT £2230.07 TOTE £12.90: £5.20, £4.90, £6.10; EX 85.40 Trifecta £888.10 Pool of £1,375.95. 1.10 winning units..
**Owner** The Hon Miss Heather Galbraith **Bred** Miss Heather Galbraith **Trained** Ayr, Strathclyde

**FOCUS**
An ordinary handicap and a modest winning time for the type of race. The first eight home finished in a heap and, given there were several hard luck stories, this bare form may prove misleading.

**NOTEBOOK**
**Ptarmigan Ridge**, back on the same mark as when last successful, got the breaks at the right time and got first run on a rival who met plenty of trouble. He is a fair sort on his day but he would be by no means sure to put it all in next time.
**Proud Boast**, back on a sound surface, returned to something like her recent best and would have gone very close with a clear run. She is not the most consistent but is capable of winning races from her current mark.
**Foursquare(IRE)**, back over a more suitable trip, had the run of the race and gave it his best shot with no excuses. He looks high enough in the weights at present though, and is likely to remain vulnerable to progressive or well handicapped types.
**Maktavish** had the run of the race next to the stands' rail and returned to form. However, a couple of these would almost certainly have finished ahead of him granted a clear run, and he remains a bit below his early season form.
**Aahgowangowan(IRE)** had the run of the race, despite the low draw and ran creditably in this tougher grade. She has been in good heart and, although she does not win very often, should continue to give a good account.
**Malapropism** has slipped to a decent-looking mark and ran his best race of the year. As he made ground on the wide outside he may be a shade better than the bare form, and he is one to keep an eye on in similar company from now on.
**Obe One** ◆ looks considerably better than the bare form as he got no run at any stage and, while his modest strike rate prevents him from being a serious betting proposition, he is more than capable of winning more races when things go his way.
**Viewforth** was another that looks a good deal better than the bare form, as he got no run at all in the last quarter mile. He is another that is not 100% reliable but is capable of winning again from his current mark.
**Seafield Towers** *Official explanation: jockey said gelding hung right handed final two furlongs*
**Musical Fair** looked a less than easy ride from this wide draw in the first-time visor, and this run is best overlooked. *Official explanation: jockey said filly hung left handed*

## 3796 KIDZPLAY CLAIMING STKS 1m 2f
**3:45** (3:45) (E ) 3-Y-0+ **£3,506** (£1,079; £539; £269) **Stalls** Low

Form RPR

2552 **1** **Gold Card**[13] 3396 3-8-9 60 (v) RWinston 4 63
(JRWeymes) *prom: rdn to ld appr fnl f: edgd lft: r.o wl* **8/1**

1005 **2** ½ **Forest Air (IRE)**[7] 3579 4-8-10 46 (p) RFfrench 2 52
(MissLAPerratt) *hld up in tch: hdwy over 1f out: kpt on fnl f: nt rch wnr* **25/1**

4215 **3** 1 **Kid'Z'Play (IRE)**[17] 3265 8-9-5 69 TEaves[(3)] 6 62
(JSGoldie) *led to over 2f out: rallied: kpt on same pce ins fnl f* **5/2**[2]

0413 **4** nk **Charlie Tango (IRE)**[13] 3394 3-8-9 68 CCatlin 8 60
(MRChannon) *hld up last: smooth hdwy outside over 2f out: rdn over 1f out: nt qckn* **9/4**[1]

10/4 **5** 1 **Minstrel Hall**[69] 1867 5-9-3 50 LEnstone[(3)] 3 58
(PMonteith) *pressed ldr: led over 2f out to appr fnl f: no ex* **50/1**

1301 **6** ¾ **Bailieborough (IRE)**[14] 3367 5-9-11 70 (v) AlexGreaves 5 61
(DNicholls) *hld up: stdy hdwy 3f out: rdn and no ex over 1f out* **3/1**[3]

6-46 **7** 3 **Tomasino**[18] 3237 6-9-11 76 (t) KDarley 7 56
(MrsMReveley) *prom: n.m.r and lost pl over 2f out: sn btn* **16/1**

0-64 **8** 1 ¼ **Ambushed (IRE)**[14] 3367 8-8-13 52 PMulrennan[(5)] 1 46
(PMonteith) *trckd ldrs tl wknd fr 2f out* **25/1**

2m 9.36s (-2.83) **Going Correction** -0.05s/f (Good)
**WFA** 3 from 4yo+ 11lb 8 Ran SP% **111.0**
Speed ratings: **109,108,107,107,106 106,103,102** CT £7.20 TOTE £3.00: £4.00, £1.10, £; EX67.60 1.The winner was claimed by J. Best for £10,000. Charlie Tango was claimed by Killoran Civil Engineering Ltd. for £10,000. Kid'Z'Play
**Owner** Mrs R L Heaton **Bred** Roseland Thoroughbreds Ltd **Trained** Middleham Moor, N Yorks

**FOCUS**
With two of the market leaders failing to give their running this race did not take as much winning as seemed likely and the form is modest, but a decent gallop resulted in a fair time for the grade.

**NOTEBOOK**
**Gold Card**, a consistent sort, proved suited by the drop in grade and the good gallop over this shorter trip to get off the mark. However, given the proximity of the runner-up and the fact that two market leaders disappointed, he will find life tougher from his current mark in competitive handicap company
**Forest Air(IRE)**, who seems to go well at this course, ran well in the face of a stiff task over this longer trip in the first-time cheekpieces. However, she is not guaranteed to reproduce this next time and will face a tough task after reassessment.
**Kid'Z'Play(IRE)** looked to have a good chance at the weights and ran creditably, despite being pushed for the lead throughout. He has mainly been in good heart up to middle distances this year and should continue to give a good account.
**Charlie Tango(IRE)**, dropped in grade, travelled strongly for a long way but found less than anticipated off the bridle. The return to shorter may suit, but he may be one to tread carefully with.
**Minstrel Hall** was not disgraced in the face of a stiff task after a short break, but her record suggests she would not be one to place maximum faith in.
**Bailieborough(IRE)**, who had a good chance at the weights and came here in good form, was below his best and left the impression that the return to shorter distances would be in his favour.
**Tomasino** continues to disappoint and has still to prove he can run anywhere near his current rating.

## 3797 DAWN GROUP CLASSIFIED STKS 1m
**4:15** (4:15) (D ) 3-Y-0+ **£5,376** (£1,654; £827; £413) **Stalls** Low

Form RPR

0216 **1** **Tony Tie**[18] 3235 8-9-3 83 NMackay[(3)] 5 88
(JSGoldie) *prom: hdwy to ld appr fnl f: hld on wl* **5/2**[2]

4265 **2** shd **Stoic Leader (IRE)**[3] 3705 4-9-6 83 RWinston 6 88
(RFFisher) *in tch: nt clr run over 2f out: swtchd and effrt over 1f out: sn chsng wnr: edgd lft ins fnl f: r.o* **12/1**

-011 **3** 2 **Another Bottle (IRE)**[11] 3452 3-8-11 83 DaleGibson 1 83+
(TPTate) *t.k.h: chsd ldrs: rdn 2f out: kpt on same pce fnl f* **1/1**[1]

1401 **4** 3 ½ **Brief Goodbye**[33] 2789 4-9-4 81 MFenton 3 73
(JohnBerry) *led: rdn and hdd over 1f out: sn btn* **9/2**[3]

0000 **5** nk **Anthemion (IRE)**[13] 3401 7-9-3 50 RFfrench 4 71?
(MrsJCMcgregor) *pressed ldr tl wknd over 1f out* **150/1**

4605 **6** 8 **Telepathic (IRE)**[2] 3730 4-9-3 57 PBradley 2 53
(ABerry) *hld up: rdn over 2f out: sn btn* **100/1**

1m 41.71s (-1.41) **Going Correction** -0.05s/f (Good)
**WFA** 3 from 4yo+ 9lb 6 Ran SP% **106.1**
Speed ratings: **105,104,102,99,99 91**CSF £26.52 TOTE £3.20: £1.80, £4.90; EX 15.60.
**Owner** Frank Brady **Bred** Lord Crawshaw **Trained** Uplawmoor, E Renfrews

**FOCUS**
A few in with a chance but a race run at less than a true gallop early, and the bare form may not be totally reliable.

**NOTEBOOK**
**Tony Tie** has been in good heart and notched his second course and distance win of the season. He is likely to look vulnerable back in handicaps from his current mark, but he is a consistent sort who should continue to give a good account.
**Stoic Leader(IRE)** is another tough and reliable sort and he gave it his best shot back over this more suitable trip, despite once again edging off a true line. He too is likely to look vulnerable from his current mark back in handicap company.
**Another Bottle(IRE)** left the impression that he was a bit better than the bare form suggests and this hitherto progressive type looks worth another chance, especially granted a stiffer test over this trip or when upped to a mile and a quarter.
**Brief Goodbye**'s run has to go down as disappointing, especially as he was proven in the conditions and very much had the run of the race. He has plenty of ability but may not be one to place too much faith in.
**Anthemion(IRE)** was not disgraced in the face of a very stiff task, but the fact that he lasted so long was due to the steady pace and it would be unwise to mark this down as an improved effort.
**Telepathic(IRE)** faced a very stiff task at the weights and ran accordingly.

## 3798 SCOTTISH RACING H'CAP 7f 50y
**4:45** (4:45) (E ) (0-70,65) 3-Y-0 **£3,643** (£1,121; £560; £280) **Stalls** Low

Form RPR

5502 **1** **Musiotal**[18] 3234 3-8-5 **52** NMackay[(3)] 6 56
(JSGoldie) *in tch: effrt over 2f out: rallied fnl f to ld towards fin* **11/2**[3]

0633 **2** ½ **Half A Handful**[12] 3410 3-9-7 **65** KDarley 2 68
(MJWallace) *chsd ldrs: shkn up and hung lft fr over 2f out: led over 1f out: hdd towards fin* **11/4**[1]

6351 **3** ¾ **Menai Straights**[9] 3517 3-9-1 **64** PMulrennan[(5)] 1 65
(RFFisher) *chsd ldrs: effrt and swtchd rt over 1f out: kpt on fnl f* **4/1**[2]

0600 **4** 1 ¾ **Hana Dee**[34] 2756 3-9-1 **59** CCatlin 7 56
(MRChannon) *hld up: rdn over 2f out: kpt on fnl f: nrst fin* **14/1**

5411 **5** nk **Willjojo**[5] 3622 3-8-12 **59** 6ex (v) THamilton[(3)] 3 55
(RAFahey) *cl up: led over 2f to over 1f out: one pce: fin lame* **11/4**[1]

4453 **6** 1 ½ **Compassion (IRE)**[7] 3581 3-8-3 **47** (p) RFfrench 5 39
(MissLAPerratt) *led to over 2f out: wknd ins fnl f* **8/1**

0000 **7** 6 **Gemini Girl (IRE)**[8] 3562 3-8-2 **46** PMQuinn 4 22
(MDHammond) *hld up: rdn over 2f out: btn over 1f out* **33/1**

1m 34.21s (1.74) **Going Correction** -0.05s/f (Good) 7 Ran SP% **109.4**
Speed ratings: **88,87,86,84,84 82,75**CSF £19.15 TOTE £6.00: £3.30, £2.50; EX 26.00 Place 6 £504.74, Place 5 £263.82.
**Owner** Frank Brady **Bred** Cheveley Park Stud Ltd **Trained** Uplawmoor, E Renfrews

**FOCUS**
An ordinary handicap and, although the gallop was fair, it resulted in a very slow time for the grade and the form is distinctly modest.

**NOTEBOOK**
**Musiotal** is not very big but finally got off the mark with his best effort yet on only his second start over seven furlongs. A more strongly-run race would have suited and he may be capable of further success in this grade.
**Half A Handful** proved suited by the step up to this grade and ran his best race yet, but once again looked anything but an easy ride. Although capable of winning a similar event, he looks one to tread carefully with.
**Menai Straights**, 5lb higher than his Carlisle success, ran right up to that level and left the impression that a stiffer test of stamina would have suited. He should continue to give a good account.
**Hana Dee** ◆ ran her best race of the year and looks a bit better than the bare form, as she fared the best of those coming off the the ordinary gallop. She looks well worth another chance over a mile and is one to keep an eye on.
**Willjojo**, who had the best of the draw and the run of the race last time, ran creditably under her penalty, especially as it transpired that she finished lame. She should continue to give a good account. *Official explanation: jockey said filly finished lame*
**Compassion(IRE)** was not disgraced in this stronger grade, but did not really leave the impression that she would be getting off the mark over this trip in handicap company in the near future.
T/Plt: £601.90 to a £1 stake. Pool: £42,673.25. 51.75 winning tickets. T/Qpdt: £105.00 to a £1 stake. Pool: £3,620.20. 25.50 winning tickets. RY

# 3707 SOUTHWELL (L-H)
Monday, July 12

**OFFICIAL GOING: Standard**
Wind: Slight across. Weather: Cloudy.

## 3799 ST JOHN GUALBERT'S DAY CLASSIFIED CLAIMING STKS 1m 4f (F)
**6:10** (6:11) (F) 3-Y-0+ **£2,940** (£840; £420) **Stalls** Low

Form RPR
0524 **1** **Crocolat**[14] 3379 3-8-12 57 NCallan 6 69+
(NACallaghan) *chsd ldrs: led on bit over 3f out: sn clr: eased fnl f* **8/15**[1]
3006 **2** 2 ½ **Think Quick (IRE)**[104] 1194 4-8-11 20 HFellows(7) 9 43
(RHollinshead) *chsd ldrs: rdn over 3f out: sn outpcd: wnt mod 2nd over 1f out: no ch w wnr* **100/1**
3240 **3** 15 **Tinian**[17] 3265 6-9-9 45 GFaulkner 10 26
(KRBurke) *hld up in tch: rdn over 4f out: wknd over 2f out: no ch whn hung lft over 1f out* **17/2**[3]
0040 **4** hd **Banners Flying (IRE)**[24] 3060 4-9-10 55 ACulhane 2 26
(DWChapman) *led 1f: remained handy tl wknd over 3f out* **20/1**
6360 **5** ¾ **Kentucky Bullet (USA)**[32] 2816 8-9-6 42 LPKeniry(3) 5 24
(AGNewcombe) *hld up: hdwy over 5f out: chsd wnr over 3f out: wknd over 2f out* **13/2**[2]
**6** 3 **Invogue (FR)**[56] 2191 4-9-6 40 GParkin 4 17
(RAFahey) *led after 1f: sn hdd: led over 5f out: hdd & wknd over 3f out* **28/1**
300 **7** 3 **Spanish Star**[88] 1426 7-9-2 47 SarahSayer(7) 8 15
(MrsNMacauley) *s.i.s: in rr: rdn and wknd over 4f out* **20/1**
5260 **8** 12 **Western Command (GER)**[3] 3712 8-9-10 35 (p) JoannaBadger 3 —
(MrsNMacauley) *led over 10f out: hdd over 5f out: wknd 4f out* **22/1**
005/ **9** 10 **Cosmic Ranger**[22] 347 6-9-0 32 (bt) RKeogh(7) 7 —
(HAlexander) *s.s: outpcd* **100/1**
0-50 **10** 2 **Fred's First**[21] 3138 3-8-10 35 SSanders 1 —
(BPalling) *prom: lost pl 8f out: sn bhd* **66/1**
**11** 14 **Dante's Battle (IRE)**[37] 2836 12-9-8 60 DeanMcKeown 11 —
(MissKMarks) *s.i.s: bhd fnl 8f* **16/1**
2m 40.78s (-1.32) **Going Correction** -0.175s/f (Stan)
**WFA** 3 from 4yo+ 13lb **11** Ran SP% **115.8**
Speed ratings: **97,95,85,85,84 82,80,72,66,64 55**CSF £116.12 TOTE £1.30: £1.02, £46.70, £2.60; EX 38.30.The winner was claimed by Mrs Stef Liddiard for £10,000
**Owner** Lord Clinton **Bred** Addison Racing Ltd Inc **Trained** Newmarket, Suffolk
**FOCUS**
A weak contest and a one-horse race on recent form, and that is the way it worked out.
**NOTEBOOK**
**Crocolat** ◆, fourth in a course and distance handicap on her previous start, found this much easier and won with any amount in hand. She was claimed for £10,000 by Stef Liddiard and should do well back in handicaps for her new trainer.
**Think Quick(IRE)**, second last in a regional seller when last seen 104 days previously, showed improved form, but is greatly flattered to get so close to the winner. All she did was stay and will get two miles.
**Tinian** showed very little on this step back up to a mile and a half.
**Banners Flying(IRE)** again failed to prove her effectiveness over this trip.
**Kentucky Bullet(USA)** continues out of sorts.
**Dante's Battle(IRE)** was best off the weights, but beaten a mile.

## 3800 DOCTOR IN THE HOUSE H'CAP 7f (F)
**6:40** (6:44) (E) (0-70,66) 3-Y-0+ **£3,386** (£1,042; £521; £260) **Stalls** Low

Form RPR
1651 **1** **Downland (IRE)**[14] 3380 8-9-5 **61** KimTinkler 4 81
(NTinkler) *hld up: hdwy 1/2-way: chsd ldr over 1f out: hung lft and led ins fnl f: rdn clr* **9/2**[2]
0021 **2** 3 ½ **Merdiff**[2] 3734 5-9-6 **62** SWKelly 11 73
(WMBrisbourne) *chsd ldrs: led over 4f out: rdn over 1f out: hdd and unable qck ins fnl f* **5/2**[1]
5252 **3** 2 **Tsarbuck**[3] 3708 3-8-8 **58** GFaulkner 5 64
(RMHCowell) *a.p: chsd ldrs 1/2-way: rdn over 1f out: styd on same pce* **5/1**[3]
0023 **4** hd **Teehee (IRE)**[6] 3615 6-9-4 **60** (b) SSanders 9 66
(BPalling) *prom: rdn over 2f out: styd on same pce appr fnl f* **13/2**
4133 **5** 2 ½ **Roman Empire**[25] 3025 4-9-2 **58** (b) NCallan 12 57
(KARyan) *dwlt: bhd: c wd st: r.o ins fnl f: nvr nrr* **6/1**
0000 **6** 2 ½ **Emperor Cat (IRE)**[18] 3229 3-7-7 **50** ow2 SYourston(7) 7 43
(PABlockley) *hld up: hdwy 1/2-way: edgd lft and wknd over 1f out* **80/1**
0000 **7** 1 ¼ **St Ivian**[18] 3227 4-9-10 **66** (p) RFitzpatrick 1 56
(MrsNMacauley) *sn drvn along in rr: sme hdwy u.p 2f out: sn wknd* **33/1**
0160 **8** 1 **Sandorra**[32] 2811 6-8-5 **47** DeanMcKeown 13 34
(MBrittain) *prom over 4f* **25/1**
2000 **9** nk **Super Canyon**[21] 3151 6-9-9 **65** (t) ACulhane 3 52
(JPearce) *s.i.s: sn outpcd* **25/1**
6000 **10** nk **Caribe (FR)**[25] 3025 5-8-1 **50** PPMathers(7) 10 36
(ABerry) *broke wl: sn lost pl: n.d after* **100/1**
/0-0 **11** 11 **Always Daring**[21] 3148 5-7-6 **41** oh5 ow1 NataliaGemelova(7) 8 —
(CJTeague) *led 1f: wknd 1/2-way* **100/1**
006 **12** 6 **Arogant Prince**[17] 3260 7-9-1 **57** (b) JBramhill 6 —
(JPearce) *led 6f out: hdd over 4f out: wknd over 2f out: bhd whn edgd lft over 1f out* **18/1**
0000 **13** 4 **Moonlight Song (IRE)**[10] 3471 7-7-5 **40** oh10 DFentiman(7) 2 —
(JohnAHarris) *chsd ldrs 4f: bhd whn hmpd over 1f out* **100/1**
1m 28.85s (-1.95) **Going Correction** -0.175s/f (Stan)
**WFA** 3 from 4yo+ 8lb **13** Ran SP% **111.1**
Speed ratings: **104,100,97,97,94 91,90,89,88,88 75,69,64**CSF £14.21 CT £56.23 TOTE £5.00: £1.90, £1.60, £1.60; EX 17.10.
**Owner** A Graham **Bred** Yeomanstown Stud **Trained** Langton, N Yorks
**FOCUS**
Just a modest handicap, but the pace was reasonable and the form is fair for the grade and sound.
**NOTEBOOK**
**Downland(IRE)**, 6lb higher than when successful over a mile round here on his previous start, took a little while to hit full stride and did not help his chance by hanging under pressure, but he eventually pulled clear. There should be more to come and he will be hard to beat when he goes for the hat-trick.
**Merdiff**, racing off a mark 7lb higher than when successful at Chester two days previously, ran his race on this switch to Fibresand (a surface he has won on) but just found the winner too strong.
**Tsarbuck** ran respectably, but just lacked a change of pace. He has yet to finish out of the first three at Southwell.
**Teehee(IRE)** is 4lb lower than when last successful but, after travelling quite well, he did not find much.
**Roman Empire** should have been suited by this step up to seven furlongs, but he never got into it.

## 3801 RAIN OF FROGS (S) STKS 5f (F)
**7:10** (7:13) (G) 3-4-Y-0 **£2,534** (£724; £362) **Stalls** High

Form RPR
4L01 **1** **Queen Of Night**[14] 3378 4-9-5 55 ACulhane 4 66
(DWChapman) *w ldr: hrd rdn ins fnl f: r.o to ld post* **7/4**[1]
0031 **2** hd **Innclassic (IRE)**[15] 3338 3-8-11 65 (b) LPKeniry(3) 1 65
(BJMeehan) *led: rdn and edgd rt ins fnl f: hdd post* **2/1**[2]
600 **3** 5 **Finger Of Fate**[7] 3580 4-9-2 38 (b) LFletcher(3) 6 48
(MJPolglase) *hld up: hmpd over 3f out: swtchd rt and hdwy 1/2-way: nvr trbld ldrs* **10/1**
0400 **4** 3 **Bond Shakira**[20] 3169 3-8-9 52 DMcGaffin 9 32
(BSmart) *s.i.s: sn chsng ldrs: rdn and wknd over 1f out* **9/1**[3]
0560 **5** nk **Brave Chief**[14] 3378 3-8-7 46 DFentiman(7) 2 36
(JAPickering) *chsd ldrs: rdn 3f out: wknd 2f out* **33/1**
0-00 **6** 2 ½ **Haze Babybear**[14] 3381 4-9-0 52 (b[1]) GParkin 7 23
(RAFahey) *lsowly into stride: outpcd* **9/1**[3]
6065 **7** 7 **Lavish Times**[14] 3364 3-8-7 45 (p) PPMathers(7) 10 3
(ABerry) *chsd ldrs: rdn and lost pl 3f out: sn bhd* **22/1**
**8** 1 ¼ **Mistblack** 4-9-0 DeanMcKeown 3 —
(ASenior) *s.s: outpcd* **66/1**
5000 **9** 4 **Shanghai Surprise**[38] 2661 3-9-0 40 (b) SSanders 8 —
(JBalding) *chsd ldrs to 1/2-way* **22/1**
0-00 **10** 3 ½ **Miss Noteriety**[26] 2979 4-8-7 23 (bt[1]) NataliaGemelova(7) 5 —
(CJTeague) *s.s: outpcd* **100/1**
59.26 secs (-1.14) **Going Correction** -0.25s/f (Stan)
**WFA** 3 from 4yo 5lb **10** Ran SP% **112.9**
Speed ratings: **99,98,90,85,85 81,70,68,61,56**CSF £4.86 TOTE £3.00: £1.10, £1.10, £3.40; EX 4.80.Innclassic was claimed by M. J. Polglase for £6000
**Owner** Michael Hill **Bred** Trevor Calver **Trained** Stillington, N Yorks
**FOCUS**
A moderate contest, but the front two had a good tussle and pulled well clear, giving it a sound look.
**NOTEBOOK**
**Queen Of Night** is a real credit to David Chapman. She appeared to have lost the plot when refusing to race a month previously, but is back in fine form and followed up her recent course and distance success in this grade with a gritty display.
**Innclassic(IRE)**, well clear on adjusted official figures, did not appear to be inconvenienced by this drop in trip or switch back to Fibresand and was just denied.
**Finger Of Fate** had it all to do at the weights and was never a danger.
**Bond Shakira** was better in at the weights than the winner, but she was well beaten.
**Brave Chief** may find things easier in handicaps.

## 3802 JULIUS CAESAR MAIDEN AUCTION STKS 6f (F)
**7:40** (7:42) (E) 2-Y-0 **£3,415** (£1,051; £525; £262) **Stalls** Low

Form RPR
**1** **Comic Strip** 2-8-13 SSanders 2 84+
(SirMarkPrescott) *s.s: sn chsng ldrs: rdn to ld 1f out: r.o wl* **11/4**[2]
3 **2** 4 **Dane's Castle (IRE)**[7] 3588 2-8-6 LPKeniry(3) 3 68
(BJMeehan) *chsd ldr: rdn to ld over 1f out: sn edgd rt and hdd: styd on same pce* **5/2**[1]
4 **3** 2 ½ **Sister Gee (IRE)**[26] 2985 2-8-2 JBramhill 1 54
(RHollinshead) *led over 4f: wknd ins fnl f* **25/1**
62 **4** ½ **Caitlin (IRE)**[32] 2812 2-8-7 ow1 DMcGaffin 9 57
(BSmart) *dwlt: outpcd: hdwy u.p over 1f out: nt rch ldrs* **10/1**
3 **5** ¾ **Trackattack**[5] 3632 2-8-9 SWKelly 8 57
(JAOsborne) *s.i.s: sn prom: rdn 1/2-way: sn outpcd* **4/1**[3]
00 **6** 5 **Namking**[56] 2173 2-8-7 DeanMcKeown 6 40
(CWThornton) *prom over 3f* **33/1**
004 **7** shd **Ellis Cave**[14] 3377 2-8-4 DTudhope(7) 10 43
(JJQuinn) *dwlt: outpcd* **16/1**
3 **8** 1 **Blakeshall Hope**[21] 3150 2-8-9 ow2 ACulhane 4 38
(PDEvans) *chsd ldrs: lost pl over 4f out: sn bhd* **11/1**
0 **9** 1 ½ **Wilford Maverick (IRE)**[24] 3051 2-8-7 NCallan 7 32
(MJAttwater) *chsd ldrs over 4f* **15/2**
1m 16.88s (-0.02) **Going Correction** -0.175s/f (Stan) **9** Ran SP% **117.1**
Speed ratings: **93,87,84,83,82 76,75,74,72**CSF £10.24 TOTE £3.40: £1.80, £1.20, £6.00; EX 12.20.
**Owner** Neil Greig - Osborne House **Bred** Floors Farming And Side Hill Stud **Trained** Newmarket, Suffolk
**FOCUS**
Just modest form, but a nice performance from Comic Strip, who showed signs of inexperience, but was still able to pull upwards of four lengths clear and may prove capable of better.
**NOTEBOOK**
**Comic Strip**, a 26,000gns purchase out of a ten and 11-furlong winner, has already been gelded. Despite showing signs of inexperience, most notably a slow start, he responded well to Sanders' urgings to eventually pull clear of his rivals. There should be plenty of improvement to come.
**Dane's Castle(IRE)**, third of 20 on his debut in a fair Windsor maiden, failed to build on that on this switch to Fibresand and has to be considered disappointing. Having said that, he may well be worth giving another chance to back on turf.
**Sister Gee(IRE)** showed plenty of pace on this drop in trip, but was ultimately well held and may do better when handicapped.
**Caitlin(IRE)** did not build on the promise she showed when runner-up in a course and distance maiden on her previous start, but is now qualified for a handicap mark.
**Trackattack**, third in just a modest maiden on his debut, was never a danger on this switch to Fibresand.

**Ellis Cave** went well in a first-time visor on his previous start but, dropped a furlong in trip, the headgear was left off this time and he was well beaten. He could be one to keep in mind for a nursery, especially if the headgear is re-fitted.

## 3803 HOLDING BACK THE YEARS H'CAP — 1m 6f (F)

**8:10** (8:12) (F) (0-55,55) 4-Y-O+ — **£2,933** (£838; £419) **Stalls** Low

Form — RPR

00-1 **1** **Magic Red**[3] 3712 4-8-12 **47** 7ex.................................. RPrice 2 64+
(MJRyan) *mde virtually all: rdn clr and edgd lft over 1f out: eased ins fnl f* **4/1**[2]

5203 **2** *6* **Ipledgeallegiance (USA)**[7] 3576 8-7-7 **35** oh5.........(b) DFentiman(7) 11 41
(DWChapman) *hld up: hdwy 6f out: chsd wnr over 3f out: outpcd fnl 2f* **13/2**

3036 **3** *8* **Our Imperial Bay (USA)**[3] 3712 5-9-6 **55**..........................(p) NCallan 1 50
(MrsJCandlish) *chsd ldrs: drvn along over 8f out: wknd 3f out* **11/1**

5331 **4** *1* **Paddy Mul**[7] 3576 7-9-0 **49** 7ex..........................................(t) JBramhill 5 42
(WStorey) *hld up: hdwy over 4f out: rdn over 3f out: sn wknd* **11/2**[3]

3044 **5** *1* **Broughton Melody**[26] 2987 5-8-5 **40**........................... DeanMcKeown 8 32
(WJMusson) *hld up: rdn 7f out: n.d* **9/1**

3234 **6** *5* **Next Flight (IRE)**[7] 3576 5-9-1 **50**........................................ RFitzpatrick 9 35
(REBarr) *dwlt: sn pushed along in rr: n.d* **3/1**[1]

4234 **7** *3 1/2* **Dora Corbino**[15] 3341 4-8-0 **40**........................ StephanieHollinshead(5) 6 20
(RHollinshead) *s.i.s: sn chsng wnr: wknd over 3f out* **16/1**

0-54 **8** *9* **Simple Ideals (USA)**[8] 3564 10-8-0 **35** oh8......................... KimTinkler 3 3
(DonEnricoIncisa) *prom 10f* **9/1**

03-5 **9** *10* **Karyon (IRE)**[47] 2408 4-8-3 **38**.............................................. ANicholls 7 —
(MissKateMilligan) *chsd ldrs tl wknd over 3f out* **66/1**

406- **10** *dist* **Eastwell Violet**[238] 3136 4-8-9 **44**........................................ SSanders 10 —
(RTPhillips) *hld up: racd keenly: wknd over 6f out: eased* **16/1**

3m 6.06s (-3.64) **Going Correction** -0.175s/f (Stan) **10** Ran SP% **115.3**
Speed ratings: **103,99,95,94,93 91,89,83,78,**—CSF £29.90 CT £264.17 TOTE £3.50: £1.50, £1.60, £6.10; EX 39.50.
**Owner** M J Ryan **Bred** Cheveley Park Stud Ltd **Trained** Newmarket, Suffolk

**FOCUS**
A moderate race in which it proved hard to come from off the pace. The winner aside the form is weak.

**NOTEBOOK**
**Magic Red** showed his recent 33/1 course and distance success was no fluke by readily defying a 7lb penalty. He may be slightly flattered by the ease of this success, given that nothing could get into the race, but there should be more to come and he is at the right end of the handicap.
**Ipledgeallegiance(USA)** found the winner far too strong, but did at least finish clear of the remainder.
**Our Imperial Bay(USA)** continues to frustrate.
**Paddy Mul** was racing off the same mark he won off at Musselburgh on his previous start, but was unable to repeat the trick on this drop back from two miles and return to Fibresand (he has won on the surface).
**Broughton Melody** did not offer a great deal of promise.
**Next Flight(IRE)** was never going and ran a shocker. It would be hard to blame the surface given that he has gone well on it in the past. *Official explanation: jockey said gelding was never travelling*
**Eastwell Violet** *Official explanation: jockey said filly was never travelling*

## 3804 JOSIAH WEDGEWOOD H'CAP — 1m (F)

**8:40** (8:42) (F) (0-55,55) 3-Y-O+ — **£3,017** (£862; £431) **Stalls** Low

Form — RPR

00-2 **1** **Masafi (IRE)**[120] 1019 3-9-2 **53**........................................ SSanders 13 77+
(SirMarkPrescott) *a.p: chsd ldr 2f out: rdn to ld and edgd lft over 1f out: styd on wl: eased nr fin* **11/8**[1]

0035 **2** *4* **Mexican (USA)**[6] 3614 5-8-9 **37**...............................(v) SWKelly 6 44
(MDHammond) *led 7f out: rdn 3f out: hdd over 1f out: no ex* **16/1**

3063 **3** *3/4* **Ace-Ma-Vahra**[6] 3616 6-9-3 **45**.............................................. JBramhill 15 50
(SRBowring) *hld up: hdwy over 2f out: nt rch ldrs* **20/1**

0003 **4** *2* **Rocky Reppin**[31] 2854 4-8-11 **46**.................................. KPierrepont(7) 8 47
(JBalding) *chsd ldrs: outpcd over 3f out: hdwy over 1f out: styd on* **20/1**

30P6 **5** *1* **Kenny The Truth (IRE)**[14] 3380 5-9-6 **48**..............................(t) ADaly 9 47
(MrsJCandlish) *hld up: sn outpcd: hdwy over 1f out: nt rch ldrs* **14/1**

0002 **6** *hd* **Late Arrival**[6] 3612 7-8-9 **37** ow1.....................................(b) ACulhane 3 36
(MDHammond) *s.s: hdwy over 3f out: n.d* **11/1**[3]

4306 **7** *2* **Donegal Shore (IRE)**[2] 3742 5-9-4 **46**..................................(vt) NCallan 10 41
(MrsJCandlish) *s.i.s: sn prom: rdn and wknd over 1f out* **16/1**

6421 **8** *3* **Bulawayo**[6] 3612 7-9-7 **54** 7ex....................................(b) BSwarbrick(5) 7 43
(AndrewReid) *prom: lost pl over 6f out: n.d after* **3/1**[2]

0245 **9** *1 1/2* **Air Of Esteem**[32] 2813 8-8-13 **41**.......................................(p) ANicholls 5 27
(IanEmmerson) *s.s: outpcd* **14/1**

1401 **10** *hd* **Super Dominion**[17] 3282 7-9-0 **47**..............(p) StephanieHollinshead(5) 4 32
(RHollinshead) *chsd ldrs: rdn over 3f out: sn wknd* **14/1**

550 **11** *3/4* **Knight Of Hearts (IRE)**[42] 2519 3-8-8 **45**.................... DeanMcKeown 2 29
(PABlockley) *sn bhd* **66/1**

5030 **12** *2* **Haunt The Zoo**[17] 3282 9-9-10 **55**......................................... LFletcher(3) 1 35
(JohnAHarris) *chsd ldrs to 1/2-way* **20/1**

-000 **13** *nk* **Ash Laddie (IRE)**[28] 2943 4-9-7 **49**.....................................(p) DAllan 16 28
(EJAlston) *chsd ldrs over 5f* **66/1**

4-00 **14** *7* **Skylark**[12] 3409 7-9-10 **52**................................................ KimTinkler 11 17
(DonEnricoIncisa) *a in rr* **33/1**

030/ **15** *1* **Magic Box**[17] 4450 6-9-6 **48**..........................................(p) GFaulkner 14 11
(MissKateMilligan) *s.i.s: hld up: racd wd: bhd fr 1/2-way* **50/1**

002- **16** *19* **Icecap**[195] 6257 4-9-4 **51**............................................ PMakin(5) 12 —
(MissECLavelle) *led 1f: wknd over 3f out* **20/1**

1m 43.68s (-0.92) **Going Correction** -0.175s/f (Stan)
**WFA** 3 from 4yo+ 9lb **16** Ran SP% **134.1**
Speed ratings: **97,93,92,90,89 89,87,84,82,82 81,79,79,72,71 52**CSF £27.83 CT £383.11 TOTE £2.90: £1.20, £5.70, £4.70, £7.90; EX 49.80 Place 6 £12.92, Place 5 £10.02.
**Owner** G D Waters **Bred** G D Waters **Trained** Newmarket, Suffolk

**FOCUS**
Just a moderate handicap, but the winner, having raced over inadequate trips at two, showed himself well ahead of the assessor. The time was ordinary time for the grade.

**NOTEBOOK**
**Masafi(IRE)** offered plenty of promise on his handicap debut when last seen 120 days ago, and he was unsurprisingly good enough to confirm that given that he gained his initial rating off the back of three runs over six furlongs, despite clearly needing this sort of trip. He will be incredibly hard to beat if turned out under a penalty.
**Mexican(USA)** ran a fine race and was unlucky to have bumped into such a well-handicapped horse.
**Ace-Ma-Vahra** appreciated the step back up in trip, but he was running for second and was just denied that position.
**Rocky Reppin**, back up in trip, ran respectably, but was not good enough on the day.
**Bulawayo**, successful in a seller on his previous start, was below form switched back to handicap company.

T/Plt: £12.20 to a £1 stake. Pool: £35,541.20. 2,112.40 winning tickets. T/Qpdt: £12.20 to a £1 stake. Pool: £2,413.60. 146.00 winning tickets. CR

# 3588 WINDSOR (R-H)

### Monday, July 12

**OFFICIAL GOING: Good**
Wind: Moderate half behind Weather: Cloudy

## 3805 C.I. TRADERS LTD E B F MEDIAN AUCTION MAIDEN STKS — 5f 10y

**6:30** (6:32) (E) 2-Y-O — **£3,464** (£1,066; £533; £266) **Stalls** High

Form — RPR

**1** **Sundance (IRE)** 2-9-0 .................................................. JQuinn 6 85+
(HJCollingridge) *w ldr: led over 2f out: rdn clr over 1f out: comf* **14/1**

**2** *4* **Dancing Rose (IRE)** 2-8-9 ........................................ PRobinson 1 66
(CGCox) *chsd ldrs: rdn and ev ch 2f out: nt pce of wnr* **7/1**

**3** *2* **Great Belief (IRE)** 2-8-11 ...................................... J-PGuillambert(3) 7 64
(TDMccarthy) *s.s and lost 8l: bhd tl rdn and hdwy in centre over 1f out: nt rch ldrs* **20/1**

**4** *1* **Ninja Storm (IRE)** 2-9-0 ........................................... RLMoore 9 60
(GLMoore) *dwlt: plld hrd: sn chsng ldrs: one pce fnl 2f* **11/4**[1]

033 **5** *shd* **Agilete**[23] 3104 2-9-0 ..................................................... SDrowne 5 60
(LGCottrell) *chsd ldrs: one pce fnl 2f* **4/1**[3]

0 **6** *shd* **Il Pranzo**[97] 1276 2-9-0 ................................................... JFEgan 8 59
(SKirk) *mid-div: rdn and hdwy 2f out: no ex over 1f out* **20/1**

2 **7** *1 1/4* **Lucky Emerald (IRE)**[9] 3531 2-8-9 ...................................... TQuinn 11 50
(BPalling) *chsd ldrs 2f: sn rdn and outpcd* **3/1**[2]

0 **8** *hd* **Ruby Muja**[19] 3208 2-8-9 ............................................. DaneO'Neill 2 49
(RHannon) *led tl over 2f out: sn wknd* **12/1**

**9** *5* **Champagne Rossini (IRE)** 2-9-0 ..................................... TPQueally 4 37
(MCChapman) *dwlt: outpcd and hung lft: a bhd* **20/1**

**10** *4* **A Qui Le Tour** 2-9-0 ............................................. SWhitworth 3 23
(MRHoad) *rdn along: sn wl bhd* **66/1**

**11** *1* **Little Indy** 2-8-11 ............................................ DNolan(3) 10 19
(RBrotherton) *dwlt: rdn along towards rr: no ch fnl 2f* **20/1**

61.27 secs (0.07) **Going Correction** -0.05s/f (Good) **11** Ran SP% **119.1**
Speed ratings: **97,90,87,85,85 85,83,83,75,68 67**CSF £100.85 TOTE £21.30: £5.50, £2.10, £5.30; EX 167.20.
**Owner** Richard Farquhar **Bred** Mrs Noelle Walsh **Trained** Exning, Suffolk

**FOCUS**
A good race for the sire Namid, but there is little to go on in assessing the race, and it may be best to apply caution in the short term.

**NOTEBOOK**
**Sundance(IRE)**, a half-brother to two juvenile winners, one in Italy, ran out a clear-cut winner on his debut. He comes from a yard not known for its winning juvenile debutants but there was no fluke about this.
**Dancing Rose(IRE)**, a half-sister to Oh So Rosie and quite useful juvenile Vienna's Boy, could not live with the winner in the closing stages, but she finished clear of the rest. She will need to improve on this to win a similar race.
**Great Belief(IRE)**, a half-brother to a multiple winner in Italy, including in Listed company, is sired by Namid, like the winner and fourth. Given how much ground he lost with his slow start, he ran really well to finish third. He will have chances of going two better if breaking on terms next time.
**Ninja Storm(IRE)**, yet another sired by Namid, was popular in the ring and did not run too badly given that he failed to settle. *Official explanation: jockey said colt ran too keen early on*
**Agilete** had as much racing experience as the rest of the field put together and continues to find a few too good at this level.
**Il Pranzo** *Official explanation: jockey said colt hung left*
**Lucky Emerald(IRE)** was weak in the market and failed to build on the promise of her debut. Maybe nurseries will be her thing. *Official explanation: jockey said filly went too keen to post*
**Champagne Rossini(IRE)** *Official explanation: jockey said gelding hung left*

## 3806 BDO STOY HAYWARD H'CAP — 1m 3f 135y

**7:00** (7:04) (D) (0-85,85) 3-Y-O — **£5,687** (£1,750; £875; £437) **Stalls** Low

Form — RPR

1430 **1** **Settlement Craic (IRE)**[25] 2999 3-9-7 **85**.................................. JFortune 4 95+
(TGMills) *hld up in midfield to rr: hdwy in centre 3f out: drvn to ld ins fnl f* **4/1**[2]

5-41 **2** *1/2* **Bienvenue**[15] 3348 3-8-5 **69**............................................... MartinDwyer 2 78
(MPTregoning) *chsd ldrs: led 2f out tl ins fnl f: kpt on* **7/1**[3]

-430 **3** *3/4* **Gironde**[25] 2999 3-9-7 **85**................................................... KFallon 7 93+
(SirMichaelStoute) *dwlt: sn in tch: hrd rdn over 2f out: styd on fnl f* **2/1**[1]

1003 **4** *1 3/4* **Fleetfoot Mac**[14] 3379 3-7-12 **65**......................................... FPFerris(3) 8 70
(PDEvans) *std s: hld up in tch: ev ch whn led: hdd 2f out: styd on same pce* **12/1**

2264 **5** *1 1/4* **Absolutelythebest (IRE)**[29] 2910 3-9-2 **80**.............................. TEDurcan 6 83
(EALDunlop) *stdd s: hld up in midfield: effrt over 2f out: styd on fnl f* **16/1**

-040 **6** *nk* **Petite Colleen (IRE)**[18] 3231 3-7-12 **62**...............................(p) DKinsella 9 65
(DHaydnJones) *prom: drvn along and swtchd lft over 2f out: 6th and hld whn nt clr run over 1f out* **50/1**

-103 **7** *nk* **Incursion**[21] 3152 3-9-6 **84**............................................... RHughes 1 87
(AKing) *prom: rdn and ev ch 2f out: no ex over 1f out* **7/1**[3]

0410 **8** *6* **Nantucket Sound (USA)**[21] 3152 3-8-6 **70**............................. RLMoore 10 64
(MCPipe) *dwlt: chsd ldrs tl lost pl after 4f: rallied in centre 3f out: wknd over 1f out* **12/1**

0025 **9** *1/2* **Spectested (IRE)**[15] 3340 3-7-6 **63** oh16 ow1..............(p) MHalford(7) 12 56
(AWCarroll) *in tch: rdn 3f out: sn outpcd* **66/1**

4641 **10** *4* **It's Blue Chip**[14] 3379 3-8-2 **66** ow1.......................................(e) PaulEddery 5 53
(PWD'Arcy) *dwlt: a bhd* **16/1**

004 **11** *8* **Starmix**[55] 2204 3-8-5 **69**........................................................ TQuinn 3 44
(PFICole) *in rr: hdwy into midfield 1/2-way: wknd over 2f out* **14/1**

4140 **12** *1 1/2* **Man At Arms (IRE)**[7] 3584 3-9-0 **78**........................................ JQuinn 11 51
(RHannon) *sn bhd* **20/1**

2m 29.32s (-0.78) **Going Correction** -0.05s/f (Good) **12** Ran SP% **120.4**
Speed ratings: **100,99,99,98,97 96,96,92,92,89 84,83**CSF £32.36 CT £73.03 TOTE £5.10: £2.00, £2.40, £1.70; EX 46.10.
**Owner** Buxted Partnership **Bred** Pollards Stables **Trained** Headley, Surrey

**FOCUS**
A decent handicap, providing one or two with an easier task following outings at Royal Ascot, and solid form.

**NOTEBOOK**
**Settlement Craic(IRE)** found the competition less taxing than at Ascot and Sandown and responded well to pressure. Lightly raced, he remains open to further improvement, but he will take a hike in the handicap for this.
**Bienvenue** won what was a modest maiden over course and distance last time out. She ran well in this better race and is clearly going the right way.
**Gironde** never got into the race at Ascot after a slow start, and this was more like his true form. He shapes as though he will handle a step up in trip.

**Fleetfoot Mac** is not open to as much improvement as some of his more lightly-raced rivals, but ran a solid race from the front.
**Absolutelythebest(IRE)** ran poorly on fast ground on his last two starts and the easier conditions here brought about a better show.
**Petite Colleen(IRE)** ran a better race in the first-time cheekpieces, but faster ground would have suited her.
**Starmix** *Official explanation: jockey said colt got tired*
**Man At Arms(IRE)** *Official explanation: jockey said colt hung both ways in the home straight*

## 3807 BARCLAYS CAPITAL FILLIES' H'CAP 1m 67y
**7:30** (7:31) (D) (0-85,80) 3-Y-O+ **£5,508** (£1,695; £847; £423) **Stalls** High

Form RPR
0526 **1** **Tuscarora (IRE)**[3] 3698 5-8-5 **52** TPQueally 1 64
(AWCarroll) *in rr tl hdwy over 2f out: drvn to ld over 1f out: hld on wl* **7/2**[1]
-166 **2** *hd* **Red Sahara (IRE)**[37] 2694 3-9-7 **77** PRobinson 8 89
(WJHaggas) *stdd in rr s: bhd tl hdwy in centre 3f out: str chal fnl f: jst hld* **9/2**[3]
36-5 **3** *4* **Grandalea**[21] 3159 3-9-5 **75** KFallon 4 78
(SirMichaelStoute) *led and set str pce: hrd rdn and hdd over 1f out: no ex* **4/1**[2]
0005 **4** *3/4* **Naughty Girl (IRE)**[12] 3427 4-8-0 **50** (vt) FPFerris(3) 6 52
(PDEvans) *chsd ldrs: hrd rdn and styd on same pce fnl 2f* **16/1**
0404 **5** *3* **Transcendantale (FR)**[11] 3443 6-7-6 **46** oh3 ow1 MHalford(7) 2 41
(MrsSLamyman) *towards rr: effrt in centre 2f out: no imp* **12/1**
60-0 **6** *1 3/4* **Dry Wit (IRE)**[37] 2694 3-8-6 **62** JQuinn 7 54
(RMBeckett) *chsd ldrs over 4f: n.d fnl 3f* **16/1**
-150 **7** *1* **Sforzando**[20] 3180 3-8-8 **67** LisaJones(3) 3 57
(JARToller) *in tch: effrt 3f out: wknd 2f out* **7/2**[1]
6164 **8** *22* **Springtime Romance (USA)**[19] 3206 3-9-10 **80** (v[1]) TEDurcan 5 23
(EALDunlop) *chsd ldr: hrd rdn 3f out: sn wknd: eased whn no ch over 1f out* **7/1**

1m 44.38s (-1.22) **Going Correction** -0.05s/f (Good)
**WFA** 3 from 4yo+ 9lb **8** Ran SP% **114.6**
Speed ratings: **104,103,99,99,96 94,93,71**CSF £19.50 CT £65.09 TOTE £5.10: £1.80, £1.90, £1.70; EX 27.10.
**Owner** Pursuit Media **Bred** Yeomanstown Stud **Trained** Wixford, Warwicks

**FOCUS**
This was run at a strong pace and the first two came from off the gallop. The form is not easy to rate but appears reasonable.

**NOTEBOOK**
**Tuscarora(IRE)**, who probably appreciated the fact that the ground was drying out, saw out the trip well. However, she is pretty exposed and a hike in the handicap for this is likely to make things a good deal more difficult.
**Red Sahara(IRE)**, held up at the rear, appeared to be ridden with the intention of getting to the front as late as possible. She never quite got there though, and is likely to go up in the handicap again for this.
**Grandalea**set a gallop which she could not sustain. She is currently burning herself out over a mile and might be worth dropping in distance.
**Naughty Girl(IRE)**, whose stamina over a mile is still in question, at least made a better fist of it this time.
**Transcendantale(FR)** has only won one race from 40 starts, and that was two years ago.
**Sforzando** had looked sure to appreciate the step up to a mile, but in the event she looked a non-stayer.

## 3808 CHOISIR MAIDEN STKS 6f
**8:00** (8:02) (D) 2-Y-O **£5,382** (£1,656; £828; £414) **Stalls** High

Form RPR
4 **1** **Galeota (IRE)**[60] 2057 2-9-0 RLMoore 6 87
(RHannon) *pressed ldr: led ins fnl f: rdn out* **7/2**[1]
4 **2** *1 1/4* **Loaderfun (IRE)**[42] 2522 2-9-0 DaneO'Neill 10 83
(HCandy) *led tl ins fnl f: nt qckn* **7/2**[1]
45 **3** *1 1/2* **Royal Orissa**[18] 3240 2-9-0 PaulEddery 5 79
(DHaydnJones) *chsd ldrs: rdn 2f out: styd on same pce* **25/1**
2 **4** *1/2* **Sovereignty (JPN)**[12] 3424 2-9-0 TPQueally 9 77
(DRLoder) *t.k.h: chsd ldrs: one pce fnl 2f* **9/2**[2]
**5** *1/2* **Disguise** 2-9-0 RHughes 1 76
(BWHills) *chsd ldrs: effrt 2f out: no ex fnl f* **8/1**
**6** *2 1/2* **Embossed (IRE)** 2-9-0 PDobbs 15 68+
(RHannon) *s.s: bhd: swtchd to centre 1/2-way: shkn up and r.o fnl 2f: improve* **14/1**
5 **7** *1 3/4* **Arc Of Light (IRE)**[51] 2310 2-9-0 MHills 14 63
(BWHills) *hld up in midfield: rdn 1/2-way: nvr able to chal* **20/1**
**8** *shd* **Viking Spirit** 2-9-0 TQuinn 12 62
(PWHarris) *mid-div: drvn along and no imp fr 1/2-way* **7/1**[3]
**9** *1 3/4* **Look At The Stars (IRE)** 2-9-0 PRobinson 8 57
(CGCox) *s.s: outpcd in rr: nvr rchd ldrs* **33/1**
**10** *1 1/4* **Grandma's Girl** 2-8-9 CLowther 13 48
(RGuest) *sn outpcd in midfield: n.d fr 1/2-way* **66/1**
**11** *3/4* **Valios (IRE)** 2-9-0 TEDurcan 3 51
(LMCumani) *dwlt: a outpcd in rr gp* **33/1**
**12** *1* **Danger Zone** 2-9-0 EAhern 4 48
(MrsAJPerrett) *dwlt: a outpcd in rr gp* **12/1**
**13** *6* **Young Boldric** 2-8-11 DCorby(3) 7 30
(KBell) *reluctant to load: dwlt: a bhd* **100/1**
0 **14** *nk* **Looking Great (USA)**[12] 3413 2-9-0 SCarson 2 29
(RFJohnsonHoughton) *mid-div tl 1/2-way: bhd fnl 2f* **33/1**
0 **15** *2 1/2* **Kenwyn**[60] 2058 2-9-0 DSweeney 11 22
(MBlanshard) *mid-div tl wknd over 2f out* **66/1**

1m 13.85s (-0.02) **Going Correction** -0.05s/f (Good) **15** Ran SP% **122.0**
Speed ratings: **98,96,94,93,93 89,87,87,84,83 82,80,72,72,69**CSF £14.06 TOTE £5.30: £2.20, £1.80, £5.80; EX 34.70.
**Owner** J A Lazzari **Bred** W Maxwell Ervine **Trained** East Everleigh, Wilts

**FOCUS**
This looked a fairly decent maiden and previous experience proved critical. The form looks strong and reliable.

**NOTEBOOK**
**Galeota(IRE)**, sent off at odds-on on his debut, was too green to do himself justice that day, but he had clearly learnt plenty from that and made amends in what looked a fairly decent maiden. He is entered in the Gimcrack and, while that might be aiming a bit high, he could be up to taking a conditions race.
**Loaderfun(IRE)**, the form of whose debut outing at Salisbury is working out well, made most of the running and was only overhauled inside the last. He looks capable of winning his maiden.
**Royal Orissa** ran another solid race in defeat. He is now eligible to run in nurseries and may have greater opportunities in that sphere.
**Sovereignty(JPN)** once more showed that he has plenty of ability, but he did not help his rider by again failing to settle.
**Disguise**, another Gimcrack entry, is a half-brother to three-time winner Desert Opal. He shaped with a degree of promise, coming out best of the newcomers, and should come on for this debut effort.
**Embossed(IRE)**, who came in for some market support, is a half-brother to a juvenile winner First Village. Slowly away, he was held up at the rear of the field before making steady progress in the straight under a kind ride. He looks sure to have derived plenty from this experience. *Official explanation: jockey said colt ran green*
**Viking Spirit** *Official explanation: jockey said colt hung right*
**Look At The Stars(IRE)** *Official explanation: jockey said colt ran very green and hung left early on*

## 3809 ROYAL WINDSOR WELCOMES BACK TALKSPORT RADIO (S) STKS 1m 3f 135y
**8:30** (8:31) (E) 3-4-Y-O **£3,435** (£1,057; £528; £264) **Stalls** Low

Form RPR
0425 **1** **Pont Neuf (IRE)**[7] 3578 4-9-3 65 (t) SWhitworth 3 50
(JWHills) *stdd s: hld up in rr: hdwy over 2f out: led over 1f out: drvn clr* **5/2**[1]
30-5 **2** *3 1/2* **White Park Bay (IRE)**[107] 431 4-8-10 48 MHalford(7) 9 44
(MissSuzySmith) *towards rr whn hmpd on bnd 6f out: hdwy over 2f out: ev ch over 1f out: nt pce of wnr* **14/1**
0-02 **3** *2 1/2* **Boogie Magic**[11] 3460 4-9-3 62 RMullen 7 40
(CNAllen) *sn led: hdd over 1f out: one pce* **7/2**[2]
1056 **4** *2 1/2* **Blue Savanna**[16] 3303 4-9-13 40 (b) RLMoore 5 46
(JGPortman) *hld up in tch: drvn to chal 2f out: no ex over 1f out* **10/1**
3055 **5** *1/2* **Sir Frank Gibson**[45] 2452 3-8-9 50 DSweeney 1 40
(MrsJaneGalpin) *chsd ldr: hrd rdn 4f out: wknd 2f out* **25/1**
6 **6** *nk* **Whenwillitwin**[7] 3574 3-8-2 DerekNolan(7) 6 40
(JSMoore) *t.k.h: chsd ldrs: effrt and hung lft to centre 3f out: hrd rdn and wknd 2f out* **16/1**
-000 **7** *6* **Princess Magdalena**[17] 3264 4-9-3 50 SCarson 8 25
(LGCottrell) *prom 9f* **8/1**[3]
0016 **8** *4* **Bosco (IRE)**[9] 3529 3-9-0 52 (t) KFallon 4 29
(PSMcentee) *hld up in midfield to rr: n.m.r bnd after 2f: mod effrt 3f out: sn btn* **7/2**[2]
0000 **9** *17* **Altares**[47] 2395 3-8-9 35 MHills 2 —
(PHowling) *dropped to rr after 3f: no ch fnl 3f* **33/1**

2m 32.96s (2.86) **Going Correction** -0.05s/f (Good)
**WFA** 3 from 4yo 13lb **9** Ran SP% **112.6**
Speed ratings: **88,85,84,82,82 81,77,75,63**CSF £38.39 TOTE £3.40: £1.40, £3.20, £1.50; EX 54.50.The winner was sold to M.W. Lawrence for 7,000gns
**Owner** J W Hills **Bred** Mull Enterprises Ltd **Trained** Upper Lambourn, Berks

**FOCUS**
A poor race, run in a very slow winning time, even for a seller.

**NOTEBOOK**
**Pont Neuf(IRE)**, best in at the weights, was given a confident ride and won with authority on her first start in selling grade. She was subsequently sold for 7,000gns and will now join David Evans.
**White Park Bay(IRE)**, having her first run on the turf for almost a year, has changed stables. This was more encouraging as she would have been receiving 17lb from the winner had this been a handicap.
**Boogie Magic**, who was flattered in a maiden last time, was the only other runner who could be given a chance on the ratings. The fact that she was eventually sandwiched by two lowly-rated rivals though, suggests she is undeserving of her current mark.
**Blue Savanna** was joint worst in at the weights and in the circumstances put up a creditable effort.
**Sir Frank Gibson**, a regressive type, remains a maiden.

## 3810 LADBROKES.COM H'CAP 5f 10y
**9:00** (9:01) (E) (0-70,68) 3-Y-O+ **£3,493** (£1,075; £537; £268) **Stalls** High

Form RPR
3354 **1** **Blessed Place**[7] 3575 4-8-6 **47** (t) TQuinn 13 59
(DJSFrenchDavis) *prom: led 1f out: rdn out* **13/2**[2]
0310 **2** *1/2* **Jonny Ebeneezer**[2] 3742 5-9-7 **62** 6ex (b) RSmith 15 73
(DFlood) *stmbld s and missed break: sn in tch: effrt and nt clr run over 1f out: r.o wl to take 2nd nr fin* **13/2**[2]
0605 **3** *1/2* **Playtime Blue**[29] 2912 4-9-4 **59** GBaker 2 68
(MrsHSweeting) *prom: hrd rdn over 1f out: kpt on* **16/1**
0040 **4** *shd* **Loch Inch**[8] 3558 7-8-10 **51** (b) DaneO'Neill 12 60
(JMBradley) *dwlt: hdwy in centre 2f out: nt qckn fnl f* **14/1**
0025 **5** *1/2* **Brigadier Monty (IRE)**[9] 3509 6-8-12 **53** KFallon 3 60
(MrsSLamyman) *mid-div: rdn to chse ldrs 2f out: one pce fnl f* **5/1**[1]
0506 **6** *3/4* **Dunn Deal (IRE)**[9] 3524 4-9-8 **63** TEDurcan 10 67
(WMBrisbourne) *mid-div: squeezed and lost pl after 1f: rallied and r.o wl fnl f* **12/1**
0034 **7** *1* **Intellibet One**[7] 3593 4-8-12 **56** FPFerris(3) 7 57
(PDEvans) *rrd s: sn in midfield: rdn 1/2-way: nvr able to chal* **13/2**[2]
0365 **8** *1* **Ela Figura**[17] 3262 4-8-8 **49** (p) TPQueally 5 46
(AWCarroll) *towards rr: hdwy over 2f out: no ex over 1f out* **33/1**
0351 **9** *3/4* **Willheconquertoo**[7] 3593 4-9-13 **68** 6ex (t) JFEgan 1 63
(AndrewReid) *pressed ldr: led 2f out tl wknd 1f out* **7/1**[3]
000- **10** *hd* **Montana**[226] 6088 4-9-10 **65** KMcEvoy 4 59
(JLSpearing) *chsd ldrs 2f: same pl fr 1/2-way* **25/1**
4530 **11** *nk* **Pulse**[8] 3558 6-9-7 **62** (p) RLMoore 9 55
(JMBradley) *a mid-div* **9/1**
3502 **12** *1 1/4* **Roan Raider (USA)**[9] 3512 4-8-5 **53** (v) KGhunowa(7) 11 42
(MJPolglase) *sn outpcd* **25/1**
0-00 **13** *nk* **Giverand**[1] 3772 5-8-1 **42** JQuinn 8 29
(MissJacquelineSDoyle) *dwlt: a outpcd in rr* **50/1**
0000 **14** *5* **Diaphanous**[7] 3575 6-7-7 **41** oh2 ow2 (b) LiamJones(7) 14 11
(EAWheeler) *led tl wknd qckly 2f out* **40/1**
00-6 **15** *1 1/4* **Another Victim**[16] 3307 10-8-5 **46** DSweeney 6 12
(MRBosley) *in tch: hrd rdn 2f out: sn wknd* **14/1**

60.59 secs (-0.61) **Going Correction** -0.05s/f (Good) **15** Ran SP% **121.1**
Speed ratings: **102,101,100,100,99 98,96,95,93,93 93,91,90,82,80**CSF £45.87 CT £675.29 TOTE £8.90: £3.20, £2.90, £5.80; EX 71.60 Place 6 £123.79, Place 5 £12.17.
**Owner** S J Edwards **Bred** Mrs W H Gibson Fleming **Trained** Lambourn, Berks

**FOCUS**
Those drawn high held the call in this typically competitive finale, although the form is only ordinary.

**NOTEBOOK**
**Blessed Place** only had one previous win to his name - on the Polytrack - but he has been running well in big-field sprints over the last four weeks and deserved to pick up a race of this nature. He had a good draw, was well positioned throughout, and did everything that was required.
**Jonny Ebeneezer** did not break well from his plum draw and as a result he ended up behind horses, albeit having kept his stands'-side rail position. He had nowhere to go approaching the final furlong, and in the end could do no more than follow the winner through. He may have been slightly unlucky.
**Playtime Blue**, whose last win on turf came off this mark over this course and distance, showed plenty of pace and was still battling away at the finish. This was a good effort from his poor draw.

**Loch Inch** is an inconsistent sort, but he is currently running off his last winning mark and put up a fair effort from what was admittedly a favourable draw.
**Brigadier Monty(IRE)** ran a cracker at Beverley last time but found the drying ground against him on this occasion, and the fact that the runners all came stands' side meant that his low stall position was no help either. He is capable of better than this given some luck.
**Willheconquertoo**, in contrast to last time when he had the plum draw, found himself in the worst stalls position of all on this occasion. He once again showed plenty of speed to lead the field early in the straight, but his early efforts cost him dear in the closing stages.
**Another Victim** *Official explanation: jockey said gelding pulled up lame*
T/Jkpt: Not won. T/Plt: £993.00 to a £1 stake. Pool: £65,499.80. 48.15 winning tickets. T/Qpdt: £18.20 to a £1 stake. Pool: £5,063.60. 204.80 winning tickets. LM

3811 - 3815a (Foreign Racing) - See Raceform Interactive

# NAPLES (R-H)
## Sunday, July 11

**OFFICIAL GOING: Good to firm**

### 3816a GRAN PREMIO CITTA' DI NAPOLI SIS (GROUP 3) 5f
**10:00** (10:15) 3-Y-0+ **£34,194** (£15,821; £8,857; £4,429)

RPR
1 **T E Lawrence (USA)**[238] [6007] 4-8-12 ........ OFancera 10 —
(ARenzoni, Italy) *tracked leaders, led 150 yards out, just held on*
2 *hd* **Regina Saura**[42] [2511] 6-8-8 ........ (b) LManiezzi 13 —
(MCiciarelli, Italy) *held up in rear, headway 2f out, finished well, just failed* 3
3 *hd* **Benbaun (IRE)**[29] [2892] 3-8-7 ........ (v) DCorby 5 —
(MJWallace) *missed break and soon pushed along to chase leaders, stayed on under pressure final f* 1
4 *1 1/2* **Dasami**[42] [2511] 5-8-12 ........ GUda 12 —
(GPucciatti, Italy) *led to 150 yards out, one pace*
5 *1/2* **Cottage Flower (ITY)**[42] [2511] 5-8-8 ........ (b) CFiocchi 1 —
(LBrogi, Italy) *always prominent, one pace final f*
6 *1/2* **Breid (IRE)** 5-8-12 ........ (b) APolli 6 —
(GrazianoVerricelli, Italy) *in touch behind leaders, unable to quicken over 1f out*
7 *1* **St Paul House**[42] [2511] 6-9-2 ........ PAragoni 15 —
(OCamuffo, Italy) *close up on outside, oner pace final 1 1/2f* 2
8 *1/2* **Krisman (IRE)**[42] [2511] 5-9-0 ........ WGambarota 7 —
(MCiciarelli, Italy) *held up, headway 2f out, one pace final f* 3
9 *2* **San Dany (IRE)**[42] [2511] 4-8-12 ........ SDiana 9 —
(LAntonacci, Italy) *never a factor*
10 *1* **Golden Danetime (IRE)**[84] 4-8-12 ........ PBorrelli 14 —
(RSantini, Italy) *prominent to halfway*
11 *2* **Kathy Pekan (IRE)**[42] [2511] 5-8-10 ow2........ (b) MPasquale 11 —
(APeraino, Italy) *chased leaders to over 2f out*
12 *3* **Colledoro** 4-8-12 ........ MBelli 8 —
(ARenzoni, Italy) *always towards rear, eased closing stages*
13 *nse* **Minerwa (GER)**[147] 4-8-8 ........ DVargiu 3 —
(MGonnelli, Italy) *prominent til weakened 3f out*
14 *4* **San Rachele (USA)** 3-8-5 ........ GTemperini 2 —
(LAntonacci, Italy) *always behind*
15 *6* **Nietta** 4-8-10 ow2........ MCangiano 4 —
(GMatrullo, Italy) *always behind*

56.57 secs
**WFA** 3 from 4yo+ 5lb **15** Ran SP% **161.6**
Speed ratings: .
**Owner** Scuderia Jerome **Bred** C E S Racing Ltd **Trained** Italy

**NOTEBOOK**
**Benbaun(IRE)** crucially missed the break. Soon off the bridle, he kept on gamely and was never nearer than at the line. This is a very sharp furlongs, which did not suit, but a quick start would have made all the difference.

# 3505 BEVERLEY (R-H)
## Tuesday, July 13

**OFFICIAL GOING: Good to soft (good in places)**
The high draw did not appear consistently advantageous throughout the meeting.

### 3817 DAVE DREW IS OUR PLUMBER CLAIMING STKS 7f 100y
**2:15** (2:16) (E) 3-Y-0 **£3,523** (£1,084; £542; £271) **Stalls** High

Form RPR
-500 1 **Fairlie**[10] [3507] 3-8-3 59........ LGoncalves 4 55
(MrsJRRamsden) *stdd s and bhd: gd hdwy on inner 2f out: rdn to ld appr last: drvn out* **10/1**
-000 2 *3 1/2* **Gallas (IRE)**[21] [3168] 3-8-4 57........ (v) RFfrench 11 47
(JSWainwright) *hld up in midfield: hdwy 1/2-way: effrt and n.m.r wl over 1f out: swtchd rt and rdn to chse wnr ins last: kpt on* **25/1**
5560 3 *2 1/2* **Heathyards Joy**[50] [2346] 3-7-13 32........ JBramhill 2 36
(RHollinshead) *midfield: hdwy on outer 3f out: rdn to chal 2f out: sn drvn and one pce appr last* **40/1**
4530 4 *1 3/4* **Turf Princess**[39] [2657] 3-7-11 56........ DFentiman(7) 1 37
(IanEmmerson) *led: rdn over 2f out: drvn over 1f out: sn hdd and btn* **12/1**
000 5 *3/4* **Trysting Grove (IRE)**[28] [2962] 3-8-4 ........ PFessey 14 35
(KARyan) *stmbld s and bhd: hdwy 3f out: swtchd lft and rdn 2f out: swtchd rt and kpt on ins last: nrst fin* **12/1**
0000 6 *2 1/2* **Pink Supreme**[10] [3530] 3-8-2 58........ TPQueally 5 27
(IAWood) *chsd ldrs: hdwy over 2f out: rdn and ch wl over 1f out: sn drvn and wknd* **10/1**
6602 7 *1 1/2* **Always Flying (USA)**[15] [3367] 3-9-0 64........ PMulrennan(5) 9 40
(NWilson) *chsd ldrs: rdn over 2f out: sn drvn and one pce* **5/1**[2]
2405 8 *2 1/2* **Soul Provider (IRE)**[13] [3425] 3-8-0 50........ SRighton 6 15
(MJAttwater) *midfield: effrt over 2f out: sn rdn and no imp* **16/1**
000- 9 *1 1/4* **Skelthwaite**[231] [6066] 3-8-8 ........ MNem(7) 8 26
(MissDAMchale) *chsd ldrs: rdn along 3f out and sn wknd* **100/1**
-003 10 *1/2* **Acca Larentia (IRE)**[19] [3252] 3-7-13 50........ HayleyTurner(5) 3 14
(RMWhitaker) *nvr a factor* **7/1**[3]
60-6 11 *nk* **Plumpie Mac (IRE)**[19] [3252] 3-8-2 49........ SuzanneFrance(7) 12 18
(NBycroft) *cl up: rdn along over 3f out: sn wknd* **66/1**
3-44 12 *3* **Micklegate**[10] [3517] 3-8-5 60........ TQuinn 13 7
(JDBethell) *trckd ldrs: effrt over 2f out and sn cl up: rdn and edgd rt wl over 1f out: wkng whn n.m.r ent last* **5/2**[1]
00 13 *12* **Raybers Magic**[10] [3513] 3-7-12 ........ JQuinn 7 —
(JRWeymes) *s.i.s: a bhd* **100/1**
-000 14 *14* **Knight Onthe Tiles (IRE)**[22] [3158] 3-8-7 72........ (b) NPollard 10 —
(JRBest) *stmbld s: a bhd* **10/1**

1m 35.09s (0.79) **Going Correction** +0.20s/f (Good) **14** Ran SP% **116.0**
Speed ratings: **103,99,96,94,93 90,88,85,84,83 83,80,66,50**CSF £242.14 TOTE £12.60: £3.00, £5.30, £9.70; EX 898.80.The winner was claimed by A. Crook for £9,000
**Owner** L C Sigsworth **Bred** L C And Mrs A E Sigsworth **Trained** Sandhutton, N Yorks
■ The first British winner for Brazilian rider Leandro Goncalves.

**FOCUS**
A moderate claimer and the proximity of 32-rated Heathyards Joy in third holds down the form. They went a strong pace, giving those drawn low half a chance to get into the race.

**NOTEBOOK**
**Fairlie** appreciated the drop in both trip and class and ran out a clear-cut winner under a good ride from Goncalves who, despite being slowly away, managed to get a good run against the far rail in the straight. Things will be tougher back in handicaps, but she deserves another chance at that level.
**Gallas(IRE)** had shown little this year but, with the visor re-fitted and dropped in grade, he posted an encouraging effort, despite proving no match for the winner.
**Heathyards Joy**, rated just 32 and beaten in a regional maiden claimer over course and distance when last seen 50 days ago, ran much better than she was entitled to at the weights and clearly showed improved form, but she still holds the form down.
**Turf Princess** may have gone off just a touch too fast, but still fared best of those to race on the pace.
**Trysting Grove(IRE)** ◆ attracted support on this drop in grade, but was very slowly away from her good draw and found a lot of troubling when trying to make up lost ground in the straight. She is now qualified for a handicap mark and could be capable of better in that grade.
**Always Flying(USA)** was not at his best on this drop in trip.
**Micklegate**, dropped into a very realistic grade, looked to have every chance, but found nothing for pressure. *Official explanation: jockey said filly was never travelling*
**Knight Onthe Tiles(IRE)** was very well in at the weights, but remains out of sorts.

### 3818 BAMBOO BISTRO MAIDEN AUCTION STKS 5f
**2:45** (2:47) (E) 2-Y-0 **£4,153** (£1,278; £639; £319) **Stalls** High

Form RPR
52 1 **Big Hassle (IRE)**[10] [3514] 2-8-7 ........ TQuinn 14 87+
(TDEasterby) *mde all: shkn up over 2f out and sn clr* **4/7**[1]
2 *3 1/2* **Breaking Shadow (IRE)** 2-8-7 ........ KDarley 11 72+
(RAFahey) *in tch: hdwy 2f out: rdn to chse wnr ins last: no imp* **10/1**[3]
60 3 *5* **Borderlescott**[20] [3196] 2-8-10 ........ RFfrench 12 57
(RBastiman) *trckd ldrs: effrt whn noy much room over 1f out: sn rdn and kpt on fnl f* **33/1**
000 4 *nk* **Roko**[12] [3444] 2-8-3 ow1........ PMulrennan(5) 15 54
(MWEasterby) *chsd ldrs on inner: rdn along 2f out: sn one pce* **40/1**
0 5 *2 1/2* **Detroit Dancer**[30] [2904] 2-8-7 ........ DeanMcKeown 16 44
(RonaldThompson) *chsd ldrs: rdn along 1/2-way: sn btn* **25/1**
5 6 *1/2* **Baymist**[8] [3583] 2-8-2 ........ DaleGibson 7 37
(MWEasterby) *hmpd after 1f out and bhd tl sme late hdwy* **50/1**
03 7 *3/4* **Alzarma**[12] [3444] 2-8-7 ........ RWinston 10 40
(ABailey) *dwlt: towards rr: hdwy and n.m.r over wl over 1f out: kpt on: nrst fin* **10/1**[3]
8 *3/4* **Summer Silks** 2-8-2 ........ PFessey 4 32
(RAFahey) *s.i.s and bhd tl sme late hdwy* **50/1**
5 9 *shd* **Waggledance (IRE)**[41] [2570] 2-8-7 ........ GParkin 3 37
(JSWainwright) *sn cl up: chsed wnr 1/2-way: sn rdn and wknd wl over 1f out* **33/1**
10 *1* **Tiger Bond** 2-8-7 ........ DMcGaffin 8 40+
(BSmart) *bhd: hdwy on outer 2f out: nvr a factor* **20/1**
11 *1/2* **Breeder's Folly** 2-7-12 ........ AReilly(7) 6 30
(TJFitzgerald) *s.i.s: a rr* **66/1**
12 *3 1/2* **Diamond Heritage** 2-8-10 ........ MFenton 13 22
(JAGlover) *slowly into strdie: a rr* **16/1**
13 *2 1/2* **Peaceful Frontier** 2-8-2 ow3........ RFitzpatrick 5 6
(CSmith) *bhd fr 1/2-way* **66/1**
0 14 *5* **Mighty Empire (IRE)**[45] [2470] 2-8-7 ........ PRobinson 2 —
(MHTompkins) *hdwy to chse ldrs after 1f: rdn and hung rt 2f out: sn wknd* **8/1**[2]
15 *1 1/4* **Marlenes Girl (IRE)** 2-8-5 ........ FNorton 9 —
(ABerry) *chsd ldrs to 1/2-way: sn wknd* **33/1**

65.08 secs (1.08) **Going Correction** +0.20s/f (Good) **15** Ran SP% **125.6**
Speed ratings: **99,93,85,84,80 80,78,77,77,75 75,69,65,57,55**CSF £6.43 TOTE £1.60: £1.10, £3.20, £7.80; EX 9.50.
**Owner** Lee Connolly and Jason Jones **Bred** Mount Coote Stud **Trained** Great Habton, N Yorks

**FOCUS**
A weak maiden in which the front two look the horses to concentrate on. It is also worth noting that double figure stalls filled the first five places despite the easy ground. The time was decent time for the grade, slightly faster than the later handicap for older horses.

**NOTEBOOK**
**Big Hassle(IRE)** bumped into a potentially useful sort when second to Strawberry Dale at Carlisle on his previous start, but there was nothing of the same quality in this field and he ran out a very comfortable winner. He is progressing and looks worth keeping on the right side of.
**Breaking Shadow(IRE)**, a 12,000gns purchase, half-brother to six winners, including three as juveniles, made a pleasing debut from his good draw. Given normal improvement, he should find a maiden.
**Borderlescott** failed to confirm his debut promise when well beaten at Carlisle on his previous start but, well drawn, this was better.
**Roko**, beaten in a seller and claimer on his last two starts, had the best draw of all and ran his race. A good guide to the strength of the form.
**Detroit Dancer** could find things easier in nurseries or claimers.
**Baymist** *Official explanation: jockey said filly suffered interference at the start*
**Alzarma** *Official explanation: jockey said, regarding the running and riding, in trying to settle gelding in he may have given it too much to do, owing to gelding being so light-mouthed and overreacting to restraint, adding that he did not get the clearest of runs; vet said gelding had a sore mouth.*
**Mighty Empire(IRE)** ran poorly from his low stall, failing to show any improvement on his debut running.

### 3819 TOTEJACKPOT STKS (H'CAP) 7f 100y
**3:15** (3:17) (D) (0-85,83) 3-Y-0 **£6,776** (£2,085; £1,042; £521) **Stalls** High

Form RPR
3103 1 **Burley Flame**[10] [3527] 3-9-1 77........ MFenton 13 82
(JGGiven) *trckd ldrs: hdwy 3f out: swtchd left and ridden to ld over 1f out: drvn out* **9/2**[2]
1-62 2 *1/2* **Kibryaa (USA)**[17] [3312] 3-9-2 78........ PRobinson 11 82
(MAJarvis) *in tch: hdwy to trck ldrs 1/2-way: swtchd lft and hdwy whn bmpd over 1f out: sn rdn and kpt on u.p fnl f* **2/1**[1]

3100 **3** *nk* **St Savarin (FR)**[49] 2378 3-8-10 **72** ........ NPollard 6 75
(JRBest) *sn led: stdd and jnd 1/2-way: rdn 2f out: drvn and hdd over 1f out: kpt in wl u.p fnl f* **16/1**

0203 **4** *nk* **True (IRE)**[6] 3622 3-8-1 **63** ........ JQuinn 12 65
(MrsSLamyman) *in tch: hdwy on outer over 2f out: rdn to chal over 1f out and ev ch tl drvn and no ex wl ins last* **12/1**

0-26 **5** *shd* **Wrenlane**[25] 3059 3-8-2 **64** ........ PFessey 4 66+
(RAFahey) *hmpd s and bhd: hdwy 3f out: swtchd rt and rdn ent last: styd on wl: nrst fin* **33/1**

0222 **6** *2* **Commando Scott (IRE)**[8] 3585 3-8-7 **76** ........ PPMathers(7) 1 73
(ABerry) *chsd ldrs on outer: rdn along 2f out: kpt on same pce appr last* **16/1**

6513 **7** *1* **Futoo (IRE)**[26] 3004 3-7-13 **61** ........ RFrench 8 56
(GMMoore) *bhd tl styd on fnl 2f: nrst fin* **11/1**[3]

-000 **8** *½* **Super King**[7] 3613 3-8-3 **65** ........ DeanMcKeown 2 58
(NBycroft) *hmpd s: bhd tl sme late hedaway* **100/1**

0043 **9** *2½* **Gasparini (IRE)**[10] 3517 3-7-12 **60** oh1 ........ JMackay 9 47
(TDEasterby) *bhd fr 1/2-way* **25/1**

0510 **10** *¾* **Sweet Reply**[24] 3105 3-8-13 **75** ........ TPQueally 10 60
(IAWood) *chsd ldrs: rdn over 2f out: wknd wl over 1f out* **14/1**

1241 **11** *1½* **Dr Thong**[10] 3527 3-9-7 **83** ........ KDarley 5 64
(PFICole) *plld hrd: wnt lft s and sn chsng ldrs: hdwy to dispute ld 1/2-way: rdn along whn bmpd over 1f out and sn wknd* **9/2**[2]

4-02 **12** *7* **Harrison's Flyer (IRE)**[10] 3511 3-8-2 **67** ........ THamilton(3) 7 31
(RAFahey) *chsd ldrs: rdn along wl over 2f out and sn wknd* **14/1**

6406 **13** *3* **George The Best (IRE)**[10] 3523 3-8-6 **68** ........ DarrenWilliams 3 24
(MDHammond) *bmpd s: a bhd* **28/1**

1m 35.2s (0.90) **Going Correction** +0.20s/f (Good) **13** Ran SP% **122.0**
Speed ratings: **102,101,101,100,100 98,97,96,93,92 91,83,79**CSF £13.72 CT £141.90 TOTE £6.40: £2.10, £1.30, £4.10; EX 14.20 Trifecta £329.30 Pool £1,345.04, 2.90 w/u.
**Owner** Burley Appliances Ltd **Bred** Miss D Fleming **Trained** Willoughton, Lincs
■ Stewards Enquiry : M Fenton one-day ban: careless riding (Jul 25)

**FOCUS**
Quite a competitive handicap. There appeared quite a good pace on in the early stages, but Neil Pollard on St Savarin appeared to slow things up over four furlongs out and the field became slightly bunched before the pace increased again. As a result, there may be a couple of these better than the bare form suggests but the form is difficult to weigh up.

**NOTEBOOK**
**Burley Flame**, returned to the course and distance he gained his only previous win over, had to be pushed along to hold his position despite having the best draw, and the slowing of the pace four out helped his cause. He eventually ran out a game winner, but did not have much in hand and will find a follow up even tougher.
**Kibryaa(USA)**, dropping back from a mile, finished to good effect, finding only the winner too strong. In this sort of form, he should soon be winning a similar race.
**St Savarin(FR)** returned to form and has clearly benefited from a short break. Despite being drawn low, he got a good trip and can have no excuses.
**True(IRE)** did not appear to find as much as had looked likely at one stage and may have benefited from a stronger end-to-end gallop. This was, however, still a good effort and she has dropped to an attractive mark.
**Wrenlane** was well beaten on his handicap debut, but he has been dropped 4lb and this was much better. He got no luck at the start from an already bad draw and got going all too late in the closing stages. There should be more to come.
**Dr Thong** dropped out disappointingly after racing keenly. A better draw and stronger pace would have suited better.

## 3820 HALL GOLDEN ANNIVERSARY H'CAP STKS 5f
**3:45** (3:47) (F ) (0-55,55) 3-Y-0+ **£3,250** (£1,000; £500; £250) **Stalls High**

Form RPR

0205 **1** **Fairgame Man**[17] 3314 6-8-11 **43** ........(p) GParkin 4 54+
(JSWainwright) *midfield: hdwy on outer wl over 1f out: rdn ent last and styd on wl to ld nr line* **33/1**

2216 **2** *nk* **Larky's Lob**[26] 3025 5-8-6 **45** ........ JDO'Reilly(7) 16 55
(JO'Reilly) *led: rdn along wl over 1f out: drvn ins last: edgd lft: hdd and no ex nr line* **8/1**

2134 **3** *nk* **On The Trail**[33] 2813 7-8-13 **45** ........ JMackay 8 54+
(DWChapman) *towards rr: hdwy on outer over 1f out: rdn and styd on wl fnl f: nrst fin* **33/1**

0204 **4** *¾* **Bella Beguine**[26] 3006 5-9-2 **48** ........ RWinston 7 54+
(ABailey) *in rr: hdwy over 1f out: nt clr run and swtchd rt ins last: styd on wl: nrst fin* **33/1**

2240 **5** *½* **Valiant Romeo**[13] 3407 4-9-8 **54** ........(v) RFfrench 14 59
(RBastiman) *chsd ldrs: rdn wl over 1f out: kpt on u.p ins last* **9/1**

5000 **6** *hd* **Le Meridien (IRE)**[5] 3680 6-9-2 **51** ........(v) LFletcher(3) 19 55
(JSWainwright) *a.p: rdn wl over 1f out: drvn and one pce ins last* **13/2**[3]

0012 **7** *¾* **Torrent**[19] 3227 9-9-5 **54** ........(b) LisaJones(3) 18 55
(DWChapman) *cl up: rdn wl over 1f out: drvna nd wknd ent last* **6/1**[2]

0040 **8** *hd* **Mystery Pips**[10] 3524 4-8-13 **45** ........(v) KimTinkler 9 46
(NTinkler) *cl up: rdn along wl over 1f out: grad wknd* **50/1**

5300 **9** *½* **Ballybunion (IRE)**[12] 3446 5-9-6 **52** ........ ANicholls 1 51
(DNicholls) *s.i.s and swtchd rt s: bhd tl sme late hdwy* **40/1**

0-00 **10** *½* **Rosie's Result**[34] 2784 4-8-8 **45** ........ PMulrennan(5) 10 42
(MTodhunter) *in tch: hdwy to chase ldrs 2f out: sn rdn and wknd over 1f out* **33/1**

4005 **11** *1* **Off Hire**[21] 3169 8-9-0 **46** ........(v) RFitzpatrick 2 40
(CSmith) *chsd ldrs on outer: rdn along 2f out: grad wknd* **66/1**

L540 **12** *nk* **Joyce's Choice**[17] 3314 5-8-9 **48** ........ PPMathers(7) 20 41
(JSWainwright) *prom: rdn along 2f out: grad wknd* **12/1**

4516 **13** *¾* **Lydia's Look (IRE)**[21] 3169 7-9-1 **50** ........ TEaves(3) 6 40
(TJEtherington) *a midfield* **50/1**

1065 **14** *hd* **Levelled**[7] 3616 10-8-13 **45** ........ JQuinn 5 34
(DWChapman) *a towards rr* **50/1**

0321 **15** *1½* **Flying Tackle**[6] 3575 6-8-9 **48** ........(p) DTudhope(7) 15 32
(MDods) *dwlt: in tch on inner: effrt and n.m.r wl over 1f out: no hdwy* **5/2**[1]

2020 **16** *1¼* **Leopard Creek**[20] 3201 3-9-4 **55** ........(p) DAllan 13 35
(MrsJRRamsden) *swtchd rt s: in tch: rdn along wl over 1f out and grad wknd* **20/1**

0002 **17** *shd* **Burkees Graw (IRE)**[39] 2661 3-8-3 **47** ........ DFentiman(7) 12 26
(MrsSLamyman) *a bhd* **66/1**

0000 **18** *1½* **John O'Groats (IRE)**[26] 3010 6-9-9 **55** ........(p) SWKelly 17 29
(MDods) *midfield: rdn along 1/2-way: sn wknd* **9/1**

5/00 **19** *6* **Smirfys Night**[36] 2734 5-9-9 **55** ........ JFanning 11 8
(DNicholls) *a rr* **50/1**

0-00 **20** *4* **Rum Destiny (IRE)**[21] 3169 5-8-12 **47** ........(v) LEnstone(3) 3 —
(JSWainwright) *a rr* **80/1**

65.25 secs (1.25) **Going Correction** +0.20s/f (Good)
**WFA** 3 from 4yo+ 5lb **20** Ran SP% **126.0**
Speed ratings: **98,97,97,95,95 94,93,93,92,91 90,89,88,88,85 83,83,81,71,65**CSF £265.22 CT £8747.96 TOTE £52.20: £6.90, £1.90, £5.20, £5.90; EX 1139.00.
**Owner** Mrs P Wake **Bred** Mrs E McKee **Trained** Kennythorpe, N Yorks
■ Stewards Enquiry : J D O'Reilly caution: careless riding

**FOCUS**
A modest handicap and moderate form, but a strange race in that the high stalls did not dominate like they so often do.

**NOTEBOOK**
**Fairgame Man** ended a losing run stretching back to August 2000, despite having an unfavourably low draw. He cannot be backed with much confidence to follow up given his recent wins-to-run record, but he has gained back-to-back wins in the past and this is likely to have boosted his confidence.
**Larky's Lob ◆**, 18lb lower than on the All-Weather, appreciated this drop back from six furlongs and was only just denied under a good, positive ride. On this evidence, he should be able to exploit his current mark in a similar event.
**On The Trail** has never won on the turf and is more used to Fibresand, but he is rated accordingly and ran well off an 11lb lower mark, especially considering his best recent form has been over six furlongs. *Official explanation: jockey said gelding was struck into behind*
**Bella Beguine**, dropped two furlongs in trip and with the visor left off, probably would have won with a clearer run. However, she is no sure thing to repeat this next time.
**Valiant Romeo** ran his race, but remains without a win since 2002.
**Rosie's Result** *Official explanation: jockey said gelding suffered interference at start*
**Flying Tackle** got no luck and this run is best forgotten.
**Leopard Creek** *Official explanation: jockey said saddle slipped*
**John O'Groats(IRE)** *Official explanation: jockey said gelding was never travelling*
**Smirfys Night** *Official explanation: jockey said gelding suffered interference at the start*

## 3821 119TH YEAR OF THE WATT MEMORIAL H'CAP 2m 35y
**4:15** (4:16) (D ) (0-85,85) 3-Y-0+ **£5,586** (£1,719; £859; £429) **Stalls High**

Form RPR

2053 **1** **Clarinch Claymore**[17] 3300 8-8-11 **71** ........ TEaves(3) 6 78
(JMJefferson) *hld up in tch gng wl: smooth hdwy on inner over 4f out: swtchd lft and hdwy 2f out: rdn to ld ent last: kpt on wl* **7/2**[1]

4035 **2** *¾* **Ocean Tide**[6] 3621 7-8-13 **70** ........(v) KDarley 4 76
(RFord) *cl up: led after 2f: rdn along 3f out: drvn over 1f out: hdd ent last: edgd lft and kpt on wl u.p* **11/2**[3]

060- **3** *hd* **Celtic Blaze (IRE)**[54] 4405 5-7-13 **56** ........(tp) JQuinn 9 62
(BSRothwell) *hld up and bhd: hdwy on inner over 2f out: nt clr run ent last: swtchd rt and styd on nr fin* **25/1**

0006 **4** *½* **Vicars Destiny**[6] 3621 6-8-8 **65** ........ RWinston 2 70
(MrsSLamyman) *s.i.s: hdwy to chse ldrs 1/2-way: rdn along on outer and ev ch 2f out: drvn and no ex ent last* **11/1**

41-0 **5** *shd* **Astyanax (IRE)**[59] 2116 4-9-2 **73** ........ JMackay 8 78
(SirMarkPrescott) *trckd ldrs: effrt 3f out: rdn along and ch over 1f out: drvn and no ex ins last* **8/1**

/56- **6** *3½* **Contact Dancer (IRE)**[234] 6053 5-10-0 **85** ........ JFanning 3 86
(MJohnston) *a rpominent: hdwy to chal ofer 2f out and evry ch tl rdn and wknd over 1f out* **5/1**[2]

0030 **7** *nk* **Greenwich Meantime**[20] 3199 4-9-4 **75** ........ LGoncalves 5 76
(MrsJRRamsden) *outpcd and bhd: hdwy 3f out: rdn to chse ldrs over 1f out: sn drvn and wknd* **11/1**

06-4 **8** *7* **Galleon Beach**[10] 3508 7-8-9 **66** ........ RFfrench 1 58
(BDLeavy) *prom: rdn along over 3 out: wknd 2f out* **50/1**

1330 **9** *1¼* **Nessen Dorma (IRE)**[25] 3035 3-8-7 **83** ........ MFenton 7 74
(JGGiven) *led 2f: cl up tl rdn along and lost pl after 6f: bhd fnl 5f* **7/2**[1]

3m 42.46s (3.06) **Going Correction** +0.20s/f (Good)
**WFA** 3 from 4yo+ 19lb **9** Ran SP% **110.1**
Speed ratings: **100,99,99,99,99 97,97,93,93**CSF £20.99 CT £378.92 TOTE £4.80: £1.40, £1.70, £5.60; EX 17.90.
**Owner** John Donald **Bred** Arthur Symons Key **Trained** Norton, N Yorks

**FOCUS**
A fair staying handicap and competitive enough, although the time was modest for the grade and the form is rated through the in-form winner.

**NOTEBOOK**
**Clarinch Claymore** had not won since taking this race last year, but he was just 1lb higher than when gaining that success and ended the year-long losing run in game fashion. Given that he did not follow up his success in this race last year, he would obviously not be one to take too short a price about next time.
**Ocean Tide**, with a visor replacing blinkers, is 6lb lower than when last winning and was just held.
**Celtic Blaze(IRE)**, just 1lb higher than when gaining her only previous win, is fit from hurdling and ran well on this return to the Flat, especially considering she did not get the clearest of runs.
**Vicars Destiny** has never won on the Flat (all of her wins have come over hurdles), but this ground would have suited and she ran well.
**Astyanax(IRE)**, last of 18 on his only previous start this term, ran better on his first start in 59 days and one could not rule of further improvement.
**Contact Dancer(IRE)**, having his first run since leaving John Dunlop, looked set to be in the shake up turning in, but dropped out and may have needed this first run in 234 days.
**Greenwich Meantime ◆** looked like posing a big threat inside the final two furlongs, but was unable to sustain his effort and eventually finished well beaten. This was a better effort than his finishing position suggests.
**Nessen Dorma(IRE)** had the ground in his favour, but ran a shocker. He has yet to convince this trip suits, but was below form in any case and losing a front shoe cannot have helped. *Official explanation: jockey said gelding lost a hind shoe*

## 3822 19 JULY IS MEDIEVAL NIGHT APPRENTICE H'CAP 1m 100y
**4:45** (4:46) (F ) (0-55,53) 3-Y-0 **£3,353** (£958; £479) **Stalls High**

Form RPR

000- **1** **Boppys Princess**[263] 5725 3-8-6 **38** ........ THamilton 1 46
(RAFahey) *bhd: hdwy on inner over 2f out: n.m.r wl over 1f out: swtchd rt and styd on wl fnl f: led last 50 yds* **40/1**

1000 **2** *1* **Flying Spud**[11] 3489 3-9-2 **48** ........ DNolan 13 54
(JLSpearing) *prom: hdwy to chse clr ldr 3f out: rdn to ld over 1f out drvn ins last: wknd and hdd last 50 yds* **8/1**

2606 **3** *2½* **Given A Chance**[5] 3684 3-8-9 **46** ........ DFentiman(5) 12 47
(MrsSLamyman) *led: clr 1/2-way: rdn along over 2f out: hdd and drvn over 1f out: kpt on u.p ins last* **8/1**

0055 **4** *2½* **Boris The Spider**[25] 3060 3-9-6 **52** ........ LisaJones 14 48
(MDHammond) *midfield: hdwy 3f out: rdn along 2f out: kpt on same pce* **13/2**[3]

3021 **5** *½* **Delcienne**[14] 3391 3-9-2 **48** ........ ABeech 11 42
(GGMargarson) *bhd: hdwy on outer over 2f out: sn rdn and kpt on fnl f nrst fin* **6/1**[2]

-000 **6** ½ **Joey Perhaps**[20] 3190 3-9-1 **50**........ MSavage(3) 2 43
(JRBest) *rrd and hmpd s: bhd tl hdwy on inner over 2f out: sn rdn along and kpt on u.p fnl f: nrst fin* **16/1**

0-06 **7** ¾ **Schinken Otto (IRE)**[15] 3368 3-9-0 **46**........ TEaves 4 38
(JMJefferson) *chsd ldr: rdn along 3f out: drvn and wknd wl over 1f out* **25/1**

0034 **8** 1 **Killoch Place (IRE)**[15] 3368 3-8-8 **40**........(v) DAllan 5 30
(JAGlover) *nvr nr ldrs* **12/1**

0001 **9** 4 **Reversionary**[10] 3513 3-9-2 **51**........(b) PMulrennan(3) 15 32
(MWEasterby) *chsd ldrs: rdn along 3f out: drvn 2f out and sn wknd* **5/1**[1]

0303 **10** 1¾ **Bonjour Bond (IRE)**[8] 3582 3-9-0 **51**........(b) MStainton(5) 7 29
(BSmart) *in to0uch: rdn along 3f out: sn wknd* **14/1**

2010 **11** 5 **A Bit Of Fun**[50] 2349 3-8-3 **40**........ DTudhope(5) 16 7
(JJQuinn) *a rr* **5/1**[1]

4540 **12** 4 **Athollbrose (USA)**[25] 3060 3-9-1 **52**........(b[1]) AMullen(5) 3 11
(TDEasterby) *wnt lft s: sn in tch: rdn along over 3f out and sn wknd* **10/1**

-645 **13** 1¼ **Airedale Lad (IRE)**[68] 1916 3-7-10 **33** oh1........ DeanWilliams(5) 9 —
(JRNorton) *a bhd* **66/1**

0006 **14** 1¾ **Cottam Karminski**[10] 3511 3-8-8 **40**........ LEnstone 8 —
(JSWainwright) *chsd ldrs: rdn along 1/2-way: wknd wl over 2f out* **50/1**

0030 **15** ½ **Lenwade**[61] 2054 3-8-3 **38**........ PMakin(3) 6 —
(GGMargarson) *bhd fr 1/2-way* **20/1**

1m 49.2s (1.90) **Going Correction** +0.20s/f (Good) **15** Ran SP% **127.0**
Speed ratings: **98,97,94,92,91 91,90,89,85,83 78,74,73,71,71**CSF £340.42 CT £2917.97 TOTE £76.10: £23.40, £3.50, £4.00; EX 915.40 Place 6 £3,439.95, Place 5 £233.73.
**Owner** Mrs S Bond **Bred** Mrs Sylvia Bond **Trained** Musley Bank, N Yorks

**FOCUS**
A very moderate race run at a furious early pace, but the form is little better than selling grade.

**NOTEBOOK**
**Boppys Princess** showed little as a juvenile at up to this trip, including in a visor. However, with the headgear left off on this first run in 263 days, she was found a very moderate race by connections and overcame being drawn in the lowest stall of all, and trouble in running, to get off the mark. She will avoid a penalty if turned out before she is reassessed and would be worthy of respect in a similarly weak event. *Official explanation: trainer's representative said, regarding the improved form shown, this was filly's first run from the yard*
**Flying Spud** had every chance but, after picking off the long-time leader, he had no answer to the winner's late bust.
**Given A Chance** nearly stole this under a really positive ride from Fentiman, but was just found out by the stiff finish and remains a maiden.
**Boris The Spider** would have appreciated the ground, but he just lacked a change of pace.
**Delcienne**, off the mark in a seller on very fast ground on her previous start, was unable to land a blow on this very different ground.
**Reversionary** was unable to build on his recent Carlisle selling win and has to be considered disappointing.
**A Bit Of Fun** had a good draw, but never posed a threat.
**Cottam Karminski** *Official explanation: jockey said filly lost her action*
T/Jkpt: Not won. T/Plt: £5,475.90 to a £1 stake. Pool: £63,385.50. 8.45 winning tickets. T/Qpdt: £174.80 to a £1 stake. Pool: £5,433.50. 23.00 winning tickets. JR

# 3553 BRIGHTON (L-H)
## Tuesday, July 13

**OFFICIAL GOING: Good to firm**
Wind: mod hlf against Weather: sunny intervals

## 3823 ANDREX PUPPY DASH/E.B.F. MEDIAN AUCTION MAIDEN STKS 5f 213y
2:30 (2:31) (E) 2-Y-O £3,359 (£1,033; £516; £258) Stalls Low

Form RPR

03 **1** **Rowan Lodge (IRE)**[19] 3248 2-9-0........ LDettori 1 81
(MHTompkins) *w ldr: led over 2f out: edgd lft: rdn out* **9/4**[2]

00 **2** 1½ **Good Wee Girl (IRE)**[10] 3532 2-8-9........ JFEgan 2 71
(SKirk) *chsd ldrs: swtchd to rail and ev ch 2f out: n.m.r wl over 1f out: hrd rdn: kpt on same pce* **66/1**

5 **3** ½ **Avertigo**[6] 3632 2-9-0........ RMullen 5 75
(WRMuir) *rdn along in rr: edgd lft & r.o fnl 2f: nrst fin* **8/1**

5052 **4** 1¾ **Campeon (IRE)**[9] 3553 2-9-0........ JFortune 6 70
(MJWallace) *led tl over 2f out: no ex over 1f out* **11/8**[1]

0 **5** 2½ **Top Form (IRE)**[38] 2690 2-8-9........ WSupple 3 57
(EALDunlop) *in tch: rdn to chse ldrs over 2f out: wknd over 1f out* **9/2**[3]

6606 **6** 5 **Taipan Tommy (IRE)**[13] 3413 2-9-0........ RLMoore 4 47
(SDow) *in tch: wd st: wknd over 2f out* **20/1**

1m 11.69s (1.59) **Going Correction** +0.125s/f (Good) **6** Ran SP% **108.4**
Speed ratings: **94,92,91,89,85 79**CSF £78.76 TOTE £3.40: £2.10, £7.10; EX 43.80.
**Owner** The Rowan Stud and Clique Partnership **Bred** M P B Bloodstock Ltd **Trained** Newmarket, Suffolk

**FOCUS**
A weak juvenile heat but run at a fair pace, and the form looks sound enough for the grade.

**NOTEBOOK**
**Rowan Lodge(IRE)** appreciated the drop to five furlongs and racing on this faster ground to get off the mark at the third attempt. He beat little this time and did not have to improve on his previous outing to score, but did the job well and should be able to land a nursery. *Official explanation: jockey said colt hung left in the last two furlongs*
**Good Wee Girl(IRE)**, half-sister to the useful sprinter Morse, ran her best race to date and now qualifies for nurseries where she should do better.
**Avertigo** failed to fully act on the track and was unable to go the early pace on this drop back to five furlongs. He will be capable of improving with more racing. *Official explanation: trainer's representative said colt was unsuited by the track*
**Campeon(IRE)** showed good early pace on this drop back to the minimum trip, but was unable to sustain his gallop and finished well beaten. He is the benchmark for the form and he may be capable of better back over another furlong, most likely in nurseries. *Official explanation: jockey said gelding ran too free*
**Top Form(IRE)** was very easy to back for this second outing and showed little, but could well leave this form behind when handicapped.

## 3824 RENDEZVOUS CASINO AT THE MARINA (S) STKS 5f 213y
3:00 (3:00) (G) 2-Y-O £2,550 (£728; £364) Stalls Low

Form RPR

5664 **1** **Piddies Pride (IRE)**[12] 3444 2-8-6........ SSanders 7 59+
(IAWood) *trckd ldrs: led 2f out: rdn clr over 1f out: readily* **5/2**[2]

4543 **2** 3½ **General Nuisance (IRE)**[14] 3390 2-8-4........(p) DerekNolan(7) 6 53
(JSMoore) *sn in tch: rdn over 2f out: kpt on to take 2nd ins fnl f* **9/1**

00 **3** *shd* **Bellalou**[18] 3259 2-8-6........ RLMoore 8 48
(NACallaghan) *in tch on outside: pushed along after 2f: outpcd over 2f out: kpt on fnl f* **7/4**[1]

60 **4** 1¾ **Faithful Flash**[10] 3506 2-8-6........ EAhern 5 43
(CADwyer) *sn rdn in rr of main gp: struggling and hung lft fr 1/2-way: kpt on fnl f* **25/1**

00 **5** 1 **Victimised (IRE)**[24] 3083 2-8-8........ LPKeniry(3) 2 45
(PBurgoyne) *led tl 2f out: wknd fnl f* **50/1**

3422 **6** *nk* **Glasson Lodge**[8] 3571 2-8-3........ FPFerris(3) 3 39
(PDEvans) *pressed ldr: rdn and ev ch 2f out: sn outpcd: lost pl fnl f* **7/2**[3]

06 **7** 7 **Tip Toes (IRE)**[8] 3571 2-8-6........ CCatlin 4 17
(MRChannon) *sn outpcd and bhd* **14/1**

06 **8** 3 **Kentucky Bankes**[43] 2515 2-8-11........(b[1]) ADaly 1 13
(WGMTurner) *dwlt: sn rdn to chse ldrs on rail: wknd over 2f out* **33/1**

1m 12.45s (2.35) **Going Correction** +0.125s/f (Good) **8** Ran SP% **112.6**
Speed ratings: **89,84,84,81,80 80,70,66**CSF £23.80 TOTE £3.40: £1.10, £2.80, £1.40; EX 22.10.The winner was sold to Phil McEntee for 9,200gns. Bellalou was the subject of a friendly claim
**Owner** Mrs Sue Pidcock **Bred** B Kennedy **Trained** Upper Lambourn, Berks

**FOCUS**
A very weak juvenile event, but reliable form and the winner may be capable of better.

**NOTEBOOK**
**Piddies Pride(IRE)** put up a much improved display on this drop into selling company and ran out a comfortable victor. She had lost ground last time at Haydock, but without the visor this time, pinged the gates and showed her true clours. She can build on this and could be placed to advantage in a higher grade. She was claimed afterwards for 9,200gns.
**General Nuisance(IRE)** stayed on best of all and again ran his race with no excuses. He is exposed, but reliable enough and is the benchmark for this lowly form.
**Bellalou**, from a yard that landed a gamble with a similar type at Yarmouth earlier this month, improved a touch for this drop in grade. However, he was well-backed for this and should have done better, so looks one to avoid.
**Glasson Lodge** again proved disappointing and has now run out of excuses. Her trainer does well with this type, but even he will have trouble getting this one to break it's duck.

## 3825 KIMBERLY-CLARK PROFESSIONAL CLASSIFIED STKS 1m 3f 196y
3:30 (3:32) (F) 3-Y-O+ £2,947 (£842; £421) Stalls High

Form RPR

0-11 **1** **Elusive Dream**[5] 3669 3-8-12 **61**........ SSanders 2 79+
(SirMarkPrescott) *led 4f: led 6f out: rdn over 3f out: drew clr 1f out: styd on wl* **1/3**[1]

-004 **2** 5 **Uncle John**[9] 3556 3-8-5 **60**........ JFEgan 5 64
(SKirk) *chsd ldrs: jnd wnr 3f out: hrd rdn: one pce appr fnl f* **25/1**

2402 **3** ¾ **Great View (IRE)**[11] 3492 5-9-9 **65**........(v) SDrowne 6 68
(MrsALMKing) *hdwy on outside 4f out: ev ch over 2f out: one pce* **7/1**[2]

0002 **4** 2½ **Treetops Hotel (IRE)**[29] 2943 5-9-4 **55**........ DaneO'Neill 1 59
(BRJohnson) *stdd in rr s: hdwy in centre 3f out: hung bdly lft fnl 2f: one pce* **33/1**

0304 **5** 13 **Lady Peaches**[13] 3421 3-8-7 **65**........ RLMoore 4 40
(DMullarkey) *prom 9f* **25/1**

0000 **6** 6 **Kirov King (IRE)**[43] 2537 4-9-9 **65**........ LDettori 7 33
(BGPowell) *stdd in rr s: mod effrt over 3f out: sn btn* **20/1**

0/23 **7** 22 **Cosi Fan Tutte**[15] 3387 6-9-9 **65**........(vt) WSupple 3 —
(MCPipe) *pressed wnr: led after 4f tl 6f out: wknd qckly over 3f out* **12/1**[3]

2m 31.28s (-0.82) **Going Correction** +0.125s/f (Good)
**WFA** 3 from 4yo+ 13lb **7** Ran SP% **110.6**
Speed ratings: **107,103,103,101,92 88,74**CSF £14.15 TOTE £1.40: £1.20, £5.20; EX 10.90.
**Owner** Cheveley Park Stud **Bred** Cheveley Park Stud Ltd **Trained** Newmarket, Suffolk

**FOCUS**
A race lacking strength in depth, but the winner recorded a smart winning time and the form appears sound enough.

**NOTEBOOK**
**Elusive Dream** won his third outing in seven days, but although he was clear at the line, it was a workmanlike performance. He was forced to make the running early on, as the pace was just modest, and the ground may have been fast enough on this occasion. He ought to improve again for this experence, can again score under another penalty and still looks certain to take higher order in the handicap ranks.
**Uncle John**, stepping up in trip, did well to make the winner work over this longer distance and posted his best effort to date. He looks to be coming right and could get closer with a slight drop in trip.
**Great View(IRE)** again ran his race with no excuses, but although he is in good heart and should remain consistent at this level, he looks weighted to the hilt now.
**Treetops Hotel(IRE)** had a stiff task at these weights and ran accordingly. He will be better served by a return to handicaps.
**Lady Peaches** *Official explanation: jockey said filly was unsuited by Good to Firm ground*
**Kirov King(IRE)** *Official explanation: jockey said colt pulled hard to post*

## 3826 TOTESPORT.COM H'CAP 7f 214y
4:00 (4:01) (D) (0-80,79) 3-Y-O+ £5,352 (£1,646; £823; £411) Stalls Low

Form RPR

4650 **1** **Malibu (IRE)**[10] 3543 3-8-12 **73**........ RLMoore 6 83
(SDow) *mde all: drvn clr over 1f out: styd on* **7/2**[2]

0403 **2** 2½ **Island Rapture**[13] 3419 4-9-5 **71**........ LDettori 3 75
(JARToller) *chsd ldrs: disp 2nd over 2f out: hung lft over 1f out: styd on same pce* **7/2**[2]

0464 **3** ½ **Nautical**[2] 3771 6-7-6 **51** ow1........ MHalford(7) 8 54
(AWCarroll) *stdd s: plld hrd in rr: hdwy to dispute 2nd over 2f out: one pce appr fnl f* **7/2**[2]

0405 **4** *nk* **Temper Tantrum**[12] 3440 6-8-6 **58**........(p) JFEgan 7 60
(AndrewReid) *in tch: drvn to dispute 2nd over 2f out: no ex fnl f* **9/4**[1]

-055 **5** 8 **Nephetriti Way (IRE)**[32] 2844 3-9-3 **78**........ SDrowne 5 62
(PRChamings) *hld up towards rr: rdn 4f out: btn over 2f out* **10/1**[3]

0-00 **6** 1½ **Sky Galaxy (USA)**[41] 2587 3-9-0 **75**........(v[1]) JFortune 4 55
(EALDunlop) *t.k.h: chsd wnr tl wknd over 2f out* **16/1**

0-00 **7** 4 **Fulvio (USA)**[6] 3626 4-8-8 **60**........(v) PDoe 1 31
(JamiePoulton) *t.k.h: chsd ldrs 5f* **25/1**

1m 35.83s (0.83) **Going Correction** +0.125s/f (Good)
**WFA** 3 from 4yo+ 9lb **7** Ran SP% **116.3**
Speed ratings: **100,97,97,96,88 87,83**CSF £16.70 CT £45.52 TOTE £5.10: £2.80, £2.60; EX 20.00.
**Owner** John Robinson and Derek Stubbs **Bred** Liscannor Stud Ltd **Trained** Epsom, Surrey

**FOCUS**
A moderate handicap and not a race to dwell on, as it produced a modest winning time for the class.

**NOTEBOOK**
**Malibu(IRE)**, taking a drop in trip, put his stamina to great effect by gamely making all of the running. He dug deep under maximum pressure in the straight and was given a fine ride on this occasion, so although he may still have a bit more to offer at this trip, he could be vulnerable off a higher mark in the furture.
**Island Rapture** spoilt his chance by hanging late on under pressure, but still turned in another fair display and she has clearly dropped to a handy mark.

**Nautical**, well-backed in the ring, ran too keen in through the early stages and had nothing left to give when asked for maximum effort in the straight.
**Temper Tantrum**, a triple course-and-distance winner, found very little under pressure and was soon beaten.

## 3827 ANDREX WITH ALOE VERA H'CAP — 1m 1f 209y
4:30 (4:33) (F) (0-55,55) 3-Y-0+ — £3,045 (£870; £435) Stalls High

Form — RPR
4210 1 **Jackie Kiely**[20] 3190 3-9-3 55 ........ (t) LDettori 15 — 65
(PSMcentee) *hld up in midfield: rdn and hdwy 3f out: led 2f out: drvn clr ins fnl f* — **9/1**
30-0 2 2 1/2 **Bhutan (IRE)**[38] 2689 9-9-0 46 ........ RThomas(5) 8 — 51
(GBBalding) *hld up in tch: hdwy on bit 2f out: wnt 2nd over 1f out: rdn: nt qckn* — **20/1**
000U 3 hd **Don Argento**[5] 3684 3-8-2 40 ........ DKinsella 12 — 45
(MrsAJBowlby) *stdd s: hld up in rr: hdwy on outside 3f out: edgd lft fnl 2f: styd on* — **66/1**
0000 4 shd **Forge Lane (IRE)**[17] 3305 3-9-3 55 ........ SSanders 13 — 59
(GLMoore) *towards rr: effrt and nt clr run over 2f out tl over 1f out: styd on strly fnl f* — **16/1**
6601 5 shd **Theatre Lady (IRE)**[2] 3774 6-9-3 47 6ex ........ FPFerris(3) 6 — 51
(PDEvans) *in tch: rdn and ev ch 2f out: one pce* — **6/1[2]**
0502 6 1 **Russalka**[14] 3394 3-8-8 53 ........ MHalford(7) 11 — 55
(JulianPoulton) *hld up in rr: rdn and hdwy over 2f out: swtchd rt 1f out: 6th and styng on whn nt clr run fnl 50 yds* — **10/1**
6445 7 nk **Even Easier**[19] 3246 3-9-1 53 ........ (b) RLMoore 7 — 55
(GLMoore) *dwlt: hld up in midfield: hdwy over 2f out: one pce appr fnl f* — **8/1**
0022 8 2 **Kindness**[18] 3264 4-9-7 48 ........ DaneO'Neill 14 — 46
(ADWPinder) *hld up in midfield: hdwy on outside 4f out: hrd rdn 2f out: one pce* — **15/2[3]**
0-00 9 2 **Didoe**[11] 3489 5-9-4 45 ........ EAhern 16 — 39
(PWHiatt) *chsd ldrs: led 3f out tl 2f out: sn btn* — **20/1**
6303 10 2 **Icannshift (IRE)**[5] 3662 4-10-0 55 ........ JFortune 1 — 45+
(SDow) *led tl 3f out: 4th and hld whn n.m.r on rail over 1f out: eased whn wl btn ins fnl f* — **4/1[1]**
6044 11 2 **Castaigne (FR)**[5] 3670 5-9-9 50 ........ RHavlin 3 — 37
(BWDuke) *chsd ldrs: drvn along over 2f out: sn outpcd* — **12/1**
300P 12 3/4 **Dances With Angels (IRE)**[11] 3490 4-8-8 35 ........ SDrowne 9 — 20
(MrsALMKing) *mid-div: n.m.r on rail 5f out: sn rdn and outpcd* — **25/1**
2500 13 3 1/2 **Summer Cherry (USA)**[14] 3393 7-8-13 40 ........ (t) PDoe 10 — 18
(JamiePoulton) *prom over 7f* — **8/1**
50-6 14 7 **Pancake Role**[16] 3342 4-8-1 35 oh3 ........ CHaddon(7) 2 — —
(AWCarroll) *prom 5f* — **50/1**
0-06 15 16 **Briery Mec**[47] 539 9-8-8 35 oh4 ........ JFEgan 5 — —
(HJCollingridge) *a bhd* — **50/1**
0260 16 24 **Sonderborg**[15] 3380 3-9-3 55 ........ GCarter 4 — —
(MissAMNewton-Smith) *a bhd: no ch whn virtually p.u over 2f out* — **33/1**

2m 3.92s (1.38) **Going Correction** +0.125s/f (Good)
**WFA** 3 from 4yo+ 11lb — **16** Ran SP% **122.7**
Speed ratings: **99,97,96,96,96 95,95,94,92,90 89,88,85,80,67 48**CSF £183.62 CT £10719.42 TOTE £10.80: £2.20, £5.20, £13.00, £5.90; EX 124.30.
**Owner** P S J Croft **Bred** Mrs M Chaworth Musters **Trained** Newmarket, Suffolk
■ Stewards Enquiry : F P Ferris one-day ban: careless riding (Jul 24)

**FOCUS**
A poor handicap run at a generous early gallop, but not really form to be interested in away from here.

**NOTEBOOK**
**Jackie Kiely**, who had definite excuses over course-and-distance three runs back, put a dismal run last time well behind her with a tidy success. The tongue tie had a very positive effect and he clearly enjoyed this undulating test. *Official explanation: trainer had no explanation for the improved form shown*
**Bhutan(IRE)**, who last ran over a trip this short in 2000, showed the benefit of his recent spin at Newmarket and turned in an improved effort. He did enough to suggest he could go one better off this mark when upped in trip once again.
**Don Argento** was staying on well at the death and ran by far his best-ever race. He was well out of the handicap proper, and his finishing position drags the form down, but he has obviously improved for stepping up in distance. *Official explanation: jockey said gelding hung left*
**Forge Lane(IRE)**, well-backed when disappointing on his handicap bow last time over further, was denied a clear run approaching two out and can be rated better than the bare result, as he was flying a the death. He is slowly getting the hang of things and may be able to exploit his current mark this summer.
**Theatre Lady(IRE)** ran her race, but it is most likely that this shorter trip was her undoing, rather than the penalty she got for winning a ladies' race two days previously.
**Icannshift(IRE)** was not suited by being taken on for the early lead and dropped out tamely when headed in the straight. He prefers to dominate and can do better, but this laboured effort may take it's toll.
**Briery Mec** *Official explanation: jockey said gelding was unsuited by the good to firm ground*
**Sonderborg** *Official explanation: jockey said filly lost its action due to the good to firm ground*

## 3828 WHARTON SLANEY LTD RAILS BOOKMAKERS H'CAP — 6f 209y
5:00 (5:01) (F) (0-55,58) 3-Y-0+ — £3,038 (£868; £434) Stalls Low

Form — RPR
0020 1 **Ziet D'Alsace (FR)**[6] 3626 4-9-12 53 ........ RLMoore 2 — 64
(AWCarroll) *trckd ldrs: swtchd rt 2f out: drvn to ld ins fnl f: sn clr* — **8/1**
3401 2 3 **Mister Clinton (IRE)**[9] 3555 7-10-3 58 6ex ........ JFortune 11 — 61+
(DKIvory) *hld up in rr: rdn and hdwy fnl 2f: styd on wl to take 2nd nr fin* — **7/1[3]**
0363 3 1/2 **Jazzy Millennium**[9] 3558 7-9-12 53 ........ (b) SDrowne 5 — 55
(BRMillman) *chsd ldr: hrd rdn and ev ch over 1f out: nt qckn* — **3/1[1]**
4206 4 shd **My Girl Pearl (IRE)**[10] 3533 4-9-4 45 ........ DaneO'Neill 1 — 44
(MSSaunders) *led: hrd rdn over 1f out: hdd and no ex ins fnl f* — **16/1**
0500 5 1 **Loch Laird**[31] 2886 9-9-8 49 ........ GBaker 3 — 48
(MMadgwick) *in tch: hrd rdn over 2f out: kpt on fnl f* — **25/1**
6010 6 3/4 **Doctor Dennis (IRE)**[8] 3593 7-9-11 52 ........ (v) SSanders 6 — 49
(JPearce) *in rr: hdwy on ins 3f out: one pce ent fnl f* — **11/1**
4634 7 3/4 **Due To Me**[33] 2803 4-9-4 45 ........ (p) SWhitworth 12 — 40
(GLMoore) *towards rr: rdn and hdwy over 1f out: nt rch ldrs* — **10/1**
0000 8 1 1/4 **Social Contract**[5] 3663 7-9-7 48 ........ CCatlin 4 — 39
(SDow) *chsd ldrs 3f: rdn and lost pl: sme hdwy over 1f out: no imp* — **40/1**
0-05 9 3/4 **Cafe Americano**[22] 3151 4-9-3 44 ........ (e) ADaly 17 — 33
(DWPArbuthnot) *s.s: bhd tl hdwy 2f out: styng on whn n.m.r on rail over 1f out: no further prog* — **33/1**
U363 10 hd **Poppyline**[9] 3555 4-9-12 53 ........ RMullen 10 — 42
(WRMuir) *in tch: rdn and no hdwy fnl 2f* — **12/1**
3120 11 2 1/2 **Shirley Oaks (IRE)**[24] 3103 6-9-10 51 ........ LDettori 8 — 33
(MissZCDavison) *towards rr: rdn 3f out: nvr rchd ldrs* — **6/1[2]**
6004 12 1/2 **Enna (POL)**[4] 3697 5-9-7 48 ........ EAhern 14 — 28
(MrsStefLiddiard) *towards rr: rdn 3f out: n.d* — **14/1**
0066 13 1/2 **Susiedil (IRE)**[29] 2929 3-9-3 52 ........ (v[1]) IMongan 18 — 31
(PWHarris) *wd: chsd ldrs over 4f* — **20/1**
-000 14 1 1/4 **Silistra**[36] 2728 5-9-2 46 ........ (p) JFMcDonald(3) 13 — 22
(MrsLCJewell) *mid-div tl wknd over 2f out* — **100/1**
-530 15 6 **Peregian (IRE)**[74] 1748 6-9-7 48 ........ JFEgan 9 — 8
(AndrewReid) *prom 5f* — **20/1**
0005 16 1 **Komena**[10] 3533 6-9-1 42 ........ GCarter 16 — —
(JWPayne) *wd: a bhd* — **20/1**
4040 17 7 **Coppington Flyer (IRE)**[15] 3386 4-9-1 42 ........ RHavlin 7 — —
(BWDuke) *prom over 4f* — **25/1**

1m 23.03s (0.43) **Going Correction** +0.125s/f (Good)
**WFA** 3 from 4yo+ 8lb — **17** Ran SP% **128.9**
Speed ratings: **102,98,98,96,97 95,95,93,92,92 89,89,88,87,80 79,71**CSF £59.55 CT £221.75 TOTE £10.10: £1.80, £2.60, £1.50, £3.90; EX 89.50 Place 6 £103.01, Place 5 £37.71.
**Owner** Dennis Deacon **Bred** J L Oberle **Trained** Wixford, Warwicks

**FOCUS**
A moderate contest run at a sound pace and the field came home strung out behind the cosy winner, who was running up to her best.

**NOTEBOOK**
**Ziet D'Alsace(FR)** returned to the form that has seen her twice finish second previously over course and distance, with a cosy success. She is obviously a quirky type, but goes well on this type of track and got a fine ride this time from the fast-improving Ryan Moore.
**Mister Clinton(IRE)**, a good winner over a mile at this venue nine days previously, again ran on all too late over this shorter trip, but still posted a sound effort off his welter weight. He is a hard horse to predict and will no doubt find life a lot tougher off a higher mark.
**Jazzy Millennium**, who often saves his best for this track, had every chance over this more suitable trip but could not quicken when it mattered and was beaten fair and square.
**My Girl Pearl(IRE)** enjoyed being allowed to lead and ran a much-improved race, only tiring out of it late on. She remains winless after 27 outings, but she looks worth a try at five furlongs and clearly liked the track.
**Loch Laird** turned in an improved display, having been dropped a few pounds for this, but was again made to look very one-paced under pressure.
**Poppyline**, closely matched with the runner-up on her latest effort at this venue over a mile, was tight for room on several occasions and can be rated better than the bare form. She is worth another chance at this trip.
**Shirley Oaks(IRE)** could never get into the argument over this slightly shorter trip and looks to be high enough in the weights at present.
**Susiedil(IRE)** *Official explanation: jockey said filly hung left in the latter stages*
T/Plt: £498.80 to a £1 stake. Pool: £53,707.80. 78.60 winning tickets. T/Qpdt: £81.50 to a £1 stake. Pool: £4,564.75. 41.40 winning tickets. LM

3829 - 3833a (Foreign Racing) - See Raceform Interactive

# [3620]CATTERICK (L-H)
### Wednesday, July 14

**OFFICIAL GOING: Good to firm**
Wind: fresh, hlf against Weather: fine, sunny

## 3834 MIDDLEHAM SUITE NOVICE AUCTION STKS — 7f
2:30 (2:30) (F) 2-Y-0 — £3,454 (£1,063; £531; £265) Stalls Low

Form — RPR
1 1 **Lamh Eile (IRE)**[25] 3080 2-8-4 ........ NMackay(3) 7 — 82+
(TDBarron) *trckd ldrs: shkn up and qcknd to ld appr fnl f: pushed out: comf* — **1/1[1]**
63 2 5 **Coleorton Dane**[17] 3336 2-8-6 ........ NCallan 2 — 63+
(KARyan) *mde most tl rdn and hdd appr fnl f: styd on: no ch w wnr* — **9/4[2]**
131 3 2 **Society Music (IRE)**[23] 3145 2-8-12 ........ LEnstone(3) 6 — 67
(MDods) *w ldr: rdn and ev ch over 1f out: hung rt and faltered jst ins last: no ex* — **4/1[3]**
5641 4 shd **Mount Ephram (IRE)**[16] 3366 2-8-12 ........ (b[1]) RWinston 9 — 64
(RFFisher) *s.i.s: sn in tch: rdn 2f out: no imp on ldrs whn hung lft appr fnl f* — **16/1**
506 5 3 1/2 **Uredale (IRE)**[44] 2526 2-8-8 ........ MTebbutt 1 — 51
(MrsADuffield) *towards rr: outpcd 1/2-way: n.d* — **66/1**
0 6 7 **Harbour Legend**[37] 2730 2-8-1 ........ JBramhill 5 — 27
(JGGiven) *sn bhd* — **66/1**
0 7 1 1/2 **Filey Buoy**[20] 3233 2-8-6 ........ DeanMcKeown 3 — 28
(RMWhitaker) *sn bhd* — **66/1**

1m 25.98s (-1.52) **Going Correction** -0.225s/f (Firm) — **7** Ran SP% **111.1**
Speed ratings: **99,93,91,90,86 78,77**CSF £3.22 TOTE £1.70: £1.20, £1.70; EX 4.00.
**Owner** Oghill House Stud **Bred** Oghill House Stud **Trained** Maunby, N Yorks

**FOCUS**
A modest event, lacking any real strength in depth, and the field were strung out at the finish.

**NOTEBOOK**
**Lamh Eile(IRE)** confirmed the promise of his impressive debut success by following up with a similarly taking display. Always travelling with ease just in behind the leaders, she only needed to be pushed out to score under her penalty and had no problems with this extra furlong. Although she will enter nurseries on a high-enough mark, she will be a tough nut to crack when going for the hat-trick.
**Coleorton Dane** ◆ was made to look pedestrian when the winner went past late on, but turned in another creditable effort nonetheless, and was clear of the remainder. He will find a similar race.
**Society Music(IRE)** looked to have a fairly stiff task in giving the weight away and so it proved. She did not look comfortably on this track and is capable of better, but basically looks vulnerable in this division under her penalty. *Official explanation: jockey said filly hung right handed throughout*
**Mount Ephram(IRE)** was not disgraced at the weights, but ran way too freely in the first-time blinkers, and hung badly late on under pressure. He is obviously temperamental and now looks well exposed.

## 3835 MALTON SUITE CLAIMING STKS — 1m 3f 214y
3:00 (3:00) (F) 3-Y-0+ — £3,484 (£1,072; £536; £268) Stalls Low

Form — RPR
000- 1 **Peter's Imp (IRE)**[263] 3997 9-9-7 25 ........ PPMathers(7) 12 — 52
(ABerry) *hld up: gd hdwy over 2f out: rdn to ld ent fnl f: styd on* — **33/1**
4603 2 1 1/4 **Balalaika Tune (IRE)**[9] 3578 5-8-13 28 ........ (t) JBramhill 10 — 35
(WStorey) *midfield: hdwy over 3f out: led 2f out: rdn and hdd ent fnl f: no ex* — **9/1**
3-63 3 3/4 **Al Azhar**[22] 3165 10-9-8 60 ........ SWKelly 2 — 43
(MDods) *hld up: pushed along over 3f out: hdwy 2f out: styd on fnl f: nrst fin* — **7/1**
5060 4 2 1/2 **Celtic Romance**[12] 3471 5-9-1 44 ........ JCarroll 8 — 32
(MrsMReveley) *hld up: hdwy 5f out: chsng ldrs and rdn over 1f out: no further prog* — **6/1[3]**
-340 5 7 **Lord Lamb**[10] 3564 12-9-3 60 ........ NeilBrown(7) 5 — 30
(MrsMReveley) *slowly away: hdwy and prom chsng gp after 3f: racd on outer: lost pl 4f out: n.d after* — **7/1**

1330 **6** *nk* **Righty Ho**[14] 3411 10-9-8 44 RWinston 11 27
(WHTinning) *led chsng gp: ch and rdn over 2f out: fdd* **4/1**[1]

0-06 **7** *3/4* **Face The Limelight (IRE)**[26] 3056 5-9-8 62 GFaulkner 9 26
(JeddO'Keeffe) *midfield: outpcd over 3f out: n.d* **9/2**[2]

/40- **8** *nk* **Marton Mere**[336] 4066 8-8-13 36 AMullen(7) 1 23
(AJLockwood) *prom chsng gp to 1/2-way: wknd over 3f out* **33/1**

00-0 **9** *5* **Natmsky (IRE)**[14] 3411 5-8-13 30 PMulrennan(5) 3 13
(GAHarker) *hld up in rr: effrt 4f out: sn btn* **66/1**

-064 **10** *3/4* **Hibernate (IRE)**[16] 3369 10-9-7 39 TEaves(3) 4 18
(CJTeague) *w ldr and clr of remainder: rdn to ld over 2f out: sn hdd: wknd qckly* **6/1**[3]

0050 **11** *4* **Mikasa (IRE)**[11] 3518 4-9-3 30 DNolan(3) 6 8
(RFFisher) *slt ld: drvn along over 4f out: hdd over 2f out: wknd qckly* **50/1**

2m 39.16s (0.16) **Going Correction** -0.225s/f (Firm)
**WFA** 3 from 4yo+ 13lb **11** Ran SP% **111.1**
Speed ratings: **90,89,88,87,82 82,81,81,78,77 74**CSF £285.65 TOTE £27.60: £8.30, £2.10, £2.00; EX 395.90.
**Owner** Ian & Arthur Bolland **Bred** Don Kelly **Trained** Cockerham, Lancs

**FOCUS**
A poor race that is difficult to assess and a modest time, even for a claimer, being 2.27 seconds slower than the later handicap over the same trip.

**NOTEBOOK**
**Peter's Imp(IRE)** came with a well-timed run halfway up the straight to win going away. He looked to have an impossible task at these weights plus he was returning after a 263-day absence, and this was his first win on the Flat since scoring at Ascot in 2000 off a mark of 67. He is inconsistent and was greatly aided by the strong early pace this time, but has clearly come back in good heart.
**Balalaika Tune(IRE)** improved for this drop in grade and application of the tongue tie. Although she has yet to score in 19 outings, she has found some form since dropping back in trip and should remain competitive at this lowly level.
**Al Azhar** stayed on too late in the day and remains a very hard horse to predict. This was a poor effort at the weights, even by his declining standards.
**Celtic Romance** , restrained early to get the trip, found this a bit too far. She did improve on her recent efforts and looks well worth a try over ten furlongs.
**Lord Lamb** ran as though he needs to step back up to around two miles, and is not one to write off just yet in this grade.
**Righty Ho** held every chance if good enough, but found nil off the bridle and ran below his best. He did not have the easiest task on the ratings, however. *Official explanation: jockey said gelding finished very tired*
**Face The Limelight(IRE)** again ran a moody race and looks to have completely lost the plot.
**Hibernate(IRE)** paid for setting a suicidal gallop and would have been seen to better effect with an uncontested early lead. If this has not taken its toll, he should leave this form behind in due course.

## 3836 LUNCHEON SUITE (S) STKS 5f 212y
**3:30** (3:31) (G) 3-Y-0+ **£2,996** (£856; £428) **Stalls** Low

Form RPR

4033 **1** **Tancred Times**[20] 3225 9-8-6 55 LEnstone(3) 4 55
(DWBarker) *mde virtually all: hrd pressed over 1f out: edgd rt ins fnl f: r.o wl u.p: all out* **11/4**[1]

3433 **2** *shd* **Wares Home (IRE)**[14] 3425 3-8-8 55 DarrenWilliams 3 60
(KRBurke) *cl up: rdn to chal over 1f out: ev ch fnl f: r.o u.p: jst hld* **6/1**[2]

0000 **3** *3/4* **Loughlorien (IRE)**[11] 3533 5-8-11 44 THamilton(3) 2 57
(RAFahey) *in tch: hdwy over 2f out: n.m.r and swtchd rt ent fnl f: r.o u.p: no imp on first 2* **7/1**[3]

3000 **4** *2* **Port St Charles (IRE)**[20] 3227 7-8-9 60 RThomas(5) 13 51
(CRDore) *in tch: effrt 2f out: sn rdn: kpt on same pce* **6/1**[2]

0005 **5** *1 3/4* **Old Bailey (USA)**[4] 3735 4-9-1 45 (b) PMakin(5) 6 52
(TDBarron) *in tch: drvn along 2f out: kpt on same pce* **12/1**

0005 **6** *nk* **Zietzig (IRE)**[4] 3742 7-9-0 42 AlexGreaves 14 45
(DNicholls) *midfield: sme hdwy under presssure and in tch 2f out: no further prog* **8/1**

0610 **7** *2 1/2* **Mister Mal (IRE)**[40] 2656 8-9-3 54 (be) TEaves(3) 1 44
(BEllison) *s.i.s: sn midfield: rdn 2f out: no hdwy* **9/1**

3150 **8** *nk* **Only One Legend (IRE)**[8] 3615 6-9-6 52 (b) NCallan 8 43
(KARyan) *hld up: effrt 2f out: sn rdn: no hdwy* **12/1**

5000 **9** *hd* **Danakim**[11] 3533 7-8-13 42 (be) DFentiman(7) 11 42
(JRWeymes) *hld up: keen early: rdn 2f out: no hdwy* **33/1**

0036 **10** *1 1/4* **Bargain Hunt (IRE)**[9] 3581 3-8-8 46 (v) JBramhill 12 32
(WStorey) *rr div: sme hdwy whn nt clr run ins fnl f: n.d* **50/1**

-500 **11** *1 1/2* **Give Him Credit (USA)**[7] 3623 4-9-0 60 (p) MTebbutt 5 28
(MrsADuffield) *sn drvn along in midfield: wknd 2f out* **14/1**

4620 **12** *2* **Indian Music**[8] 3616 7-8-13 46 PPMathers(7) 7 28
(ABerry) *towards rr most of way* **25/1**

0004 **13** *1 1/4* **Aguilera**[4] 3739 3-8-5 43 ow2 SWKelly 10 15
(MDods) *cl up tl wknd over 2f out* **40/1**

0606 **14** *nk* **Salonika Sky**[16] 3364 3-8-3 35 JMcAuley 9 12
(CWThornton) *sn bhd* **100/1**

1m 12.19s (-1.81) **Going Correction** -0.225s/f (Firm)
**WFA** 3 from 4yo+ 6lb **14** Ran SP% **123.1**
Speed ratings: **103,102,101,99,96 96,93,92,92,90 88,86,84,84**CSF £18.17 TOTE £4.20: £1.50, £2.00, £3.10; EX 18.40.There was no bid for the winner.
**Owner** D W Barker **Bred** W L Barker **Trained** Scorton, N Yorks
■ Stewards Enquiry : D Fentiman caution: careless riding

**FOCUS**
A fair time for a seller and a low draw proved most advantageous, but difficult to pin down the form so some caution advised.

**NOTEBOOK**
**Tancred Times** was rightly quick to take advantage of her favourable draw and showed a good attitude in fending off the runner-up in the closing stages to score. This was a deserved success, but she needed this drop in grade and had plenty in her favour this time.
**Wares Home(IRE)** again filled the frame and is never far away at this level, but again looked reluctant to got through with his effort under pressure inside the final furlong, having travelled well to that point. He looks well worth a try in blinkers.
**Loughlorien(IRE)** ran one of his best races for some time from his low draw, and did not get the best of runs late on so can be rated slightly unlucky. He looks to be coming right, but his next run will reveal more.
**Port St Charles(IRE)** did the best of those drawn high, but found less than expected under pressure. He always needs luck in running and has not won on the turf since 2002, but could be placed to advantage at this lowly level.
**Give Him Credit(USA)** *Official explanation: jockey said gelding lost a right front shoe*
**Indian Music** *Official explanation: jockey said gelding was reluctant to travel in the early part of race*

## 3837 BOOK YOUR RACEDAY HOSPITALITY ON 01777 247103 H'CAP 1m 3f 214y
**4:00** (4:00) (E) (0-70,70) 3-Y-0 **£4,192** (£1,290; £645; £322) **Stalls** Low

Form RPR

0204 **1** **Ile Facile (IRE)**[12] 3475 3-9-5 68 (t) JFanning 4 73
(NPLittmoden) *mde virtually all: hld on wl u.p fnl f* **7/1**[3]

066- **2** *3/4* **Our Emmy Lou**[288] 5288 3-8-10 59 JMackay 1 63
(SirMarkPrescott) *prom: wnt 2nd 4f out: ev ch and drvn along 3f out: outpcd by wnr over 1f out: styd on u.p ins last* **6/1**[2]

3254 **3** *2* **Savannah River (IRE)**[35] 2774 3-7-12 47 oh5 (t) JMcAuley 5 48
(CWThornton) *in tch: chsng ldrs and rdn over 2f out: styd on: no imp* **33/1**

0-00 **4** *nk* **Inchpast**[23] 3160 3-8-6 55 (b[1]) NCallan 10 56
(MHTompkins) *midfield: plld hrd early: hdwy over 3f out: in tch and rdn over 2f out: kpt on same pce* **25/1**

0422 **5** *1 1/2* **La Petite Chinoise**[14] 3421 3-9-7 70 JCarroll 3 68
(RGuest) *in tch: drvn along and sme hdwy 3f out: no further prog fnl 2f* **6/1**[2]

1332 **6** *2 1/2* **Vicario**[6] 3669 3-8-7 61 HayleyTurner(5) 9 55
(MLWBell) *hld up: sme hdwy u.p 2f out: hung bdly lft over 1f out: no further prog fnl f* **11/4**[1]

3553 **7** *3 1/2* **Siegfrieds Night (IRE)**[9] 3584 3-8-9 65 CHaddon(7) 14 54
(MCChapman) *midfield: rdn 3f out: no hdwy* **8/1**

00-6 **8** *5* **Bay Solitaire**[43] 2555 3-7-13 48 PMQuinn 7 29
(TDEasterby) *slowly away: bhd most of way* **50/1**

-013 **9** *12* **Ego Trip**[36] 2760 3-8-5 54 DaleGibson 12 15
(MWEasterby) *slowly away and sn pushed along: a bhd* **9/1**

-506 **10** *2* **Imperial Royale (IRE)**[11] 3535 3-8-6 62 MHalford(7) 13 20
(PLClinton) *chsd ldrs: rdn 3f out: wknd qckly 2f out* **33/1**

-000 **11** *3* **Barton Flower**[27] 3008 3-7-12 47 PFessey 11 —
(MWEasterby) *sn bhd* **66/1**

053 **12** *3 1/2* **Jalousie Dream**[27] 3015 3-7-13 48 ow1 RFfrench 6 —
(GMMoore) *prom to 1/2-way: sn lost pl: bhd fnl 3f* **40/1**

5432 **13** *nk* **Holly Walk**[16] 3379 3-8-1 50 (p) ANicholls 8 —
(MDods) *cl up: rdn over 4f out: fdd: bhd and eased fnl f* **9/1**

6606 **14** *7* **Fire Finch**[34] 2809 3-9-6 69 ACulhane 2 5
(MRChannon) *midfield tl wknd over 3f out* **20/1**

2m 36.89s (-2.11) **Going Correction** -0.225s/f (Firm) **14** Ran SP% **119.2**
Speed ratings: **98,97,96,95,94 93,90,87,79,78 76,73,73,69**CSF £45.02 CT £1313.73 TOTE £8.50: £2.70, £1.70, £10.20; EX 67.70.
**Owner** Paul J Dixon **Bred** John Foley **Trained** Newmarket, Suffolk

**FOCUS**
A moderate handicap and a race lacking any strength in depth and the pace was modest.

**NOTEBOOK**
**Ile Facile(IRE)**, a winner over six furlongs back in February, won well under a surprisingly positive ride. A beaten favourite in a claimer last time, this was the longest trip he had tackled to date and he got it well, but very much had the run of the race.
**Our Emmy Lou** , a handicap debutante and stepping up in trip, got outpaced at a crucial stage, but was staying on well and showed more than enough to suggest she is capable of breaking her duck off this mark.
**Savannah River(IRE)** was well-placed throughout, and although she lacked a change of gear late on, did very well from 5lb out of the handicap.
**Inchpast** ran keen early in the first-time blinkers, but as he settled he looked a different animal, and this was his first worthwhile form to date.
**La Petite Chinoise** is paying for her recent consistency with the Handicapper and this looks as good as she is.
**Vicario**, seriously supported in the betting ring, had an excellent chance on the form of his previous efforts, but proved a bitter disappointment. She has attitude questions to answer now.
**Ego Trip** *Official explanation: jockey said colt anticipated the start causing him to become unbalanced leaving stalls*
**Fire Finch** *Official explanation: jockey said filly was never travelling*

## 3838 RICHMOND SUITE H'CAP 5f
**4:30** (4:31) (E ) (0-75,71) 3-Y-O **£4,182** (£1,287; £643; £321) **Stalls** Low

Form RPR

1621 **1** **Nanna (IRE)**[10] 3562 3-9-0 64 6ex ACulhane 2 74
(RHollinshead) *mde all: hld on wl u.p fnl f* **4/1**[1]

-005 **2** *3/4* **Sir Loin**[10] 3562 3-8-5 55 KimTinkler 3 62
(NTinkler) *cl up: rdn 2f out: ch ent fnl f: edgd rt and no ex ins last* **12/1**

1504 **3** *nk* **Obe Bold (IRE)**[4] 3737 3-8-0 57 PPMathers(7) 6 63
(ABerry) *slowly away: sn in tch: rdn 2f out: kpt on u.p fnl f: nvr able to chal* **9/1**

4012 **4** *1/2* **Short Chorus**[10] 3562 3-8-0 50 (p) DaleGibson 8 54
(JBalding) *chsd ldrs: rdn 2f out: kpt on same pce* **5/1**[3]

460 **5** *1/2* **Harrington Bates**[20] 3251 3-9-0 64 DeanMcKeown 1 66
(RMWhitaker) *chsd ldrs: rdn 2f out: kpt on same pce* **9/2**[2]

0101 **6** *shd* **Wendy's Girl (IRE)**[7] 3624 3-8-9 62 6ex (b) THamilton(3) 7 64
(RPElliott) *dwlt: towards rr: kpt on u.p fr over 1f out: nvr able to chal* **12/1**

0-50 **7** *3 1/2* **Sea Fern**[48] 2423 3-8-0 50 PFessey 9 38
(DEddy) *dwlt: rr div: kpt on u.p fnl 2f: n.d* **40/1**

0141 **8** *1/2* **Icenaslice (IRE)**[19] 3270 3-8-11 66 PMulrennan(5) 11 52
(JJQuinn) *in tch: drvn along 2f out: sn btn* **13/2**

600- **9** *nk* **First Eclipse (IRE)**[251] 5931 3-8-3 53 JEdmunds 10 37
(JBalding) *nvr bttr than mid-div* **50/1**

3530 **10** *3/4* **Island Spell**[10] 3562 3-8-11 68 AMullen(7) 5 49
(CGrant) *rr div: rdn over 2f out: no hdwy* **20/1**

0021 **11** *1 1/2* **Scottish Exile (IRE)**[17] 3344 3-9-7 71 (v) DarrenWilliams 12 46
(KRBurke) *s.i.s: sn midfield: wknd over 1f out* **8/1**

0-50 **12** *14* **Mouseman**[17] 3338 3-8-5 55 SWKelly 4 —
(CNKellett) *sn bhd: lost tch and eased appr fnl f: t.o* **40/1**

60.00 secs (-0.60) **Going Correction** -0.10s/f (Good) **12** Ran SP% **117.7**
Speed ratings: **100,98,98,97,96 96,90,90,89,88 86,63**CSF £50.54 CT £411.88 TOTE £5.40: £2.00, £3.50, £2.40; EX 77.60.
**Owner** Mrs G A Weetman **Bred** Mark Clarke **Trained** Upper Longdon, Staffs

**FOCUS**
A modest sprint which again saw those drawn low at an advantage, butr the form looks sound enough.

**NOTEBOOK**
**Nanna(IRE)** controlled the tempo from the off, and proved game late on to hold off her challengers and defy a 6lb penalty in the process. She is clearly progressing along the right lines and this faster ground was no problem, but she was greatly aided by her draw this time.
**Sir Loin** ran to his recent form with the winner on these better terms, and was helped by his low draw. He has improved the last twice and could be nearing that first career success.
**Obe Bold(IRE)** would have been closer but for blowing the start and ran much better for this return to handicap company.
**Short Chorus**, 6lb better off with the winner for a three-quarter length defeat last time, could not quicken late in the day, having used up plenty of energy early on from unfavourable draw.
**Harrington Bates**, making his handicap debut, could not muster the early speed to take advantage of his low draw and never really looked like scoring. Another furlong can see him get closer.
**Wendy's Girl(IRE)** , who made all over six furlongs at this venue seven days previously, was unable to dominate on this drop in trip and looked anchored by her penalty late on.
**Icenaslice(IRE)**, who had won her last two turf starts prior to this, was never in it from her high stall. Although she may be capable of better, she looks high enough in the weights now. *Official explanation: jockey said filly hung right handed in final three furlongs*


The Form Book, Raceform Ltd, Compton, RG20 6NL

**Scottish Exile(IRE)** *Official explanation: jockey said filly ran very flat; trainer said filly was in season*
**Mouseman** *Official explanation: jockey said gelding became upset in the stalls*

## 3839 PADDOCK SUITE MEDIAN AUCTION MAIDEN STKS 7f
**5:00** (5:02) (F) 3-Y-O **£3,454** (£1,063; £531; £265) **Stalls** Low

Form RPR

50- **1** **Listen To Reason (IRE)**[333] 4193 3-9-0 ACulhane 5 67
(JGGiven) *led tl hdd ent fnl f: r.o wl u.p to regain ld ins last* **9/2**[3]

0063 **2** *nk* **One Upmanship**[17] 3338 3-9-0 64 NCallan 7 66
(JGPortman) *cl up: slt ld ent fnl f: rdn and hdd ins last: no ex* **15/8**[2]

0 **3** *1 3/4* **Festive Chimes (IRE)**[19] 3267 3-8-9 RWinston 6 56
(JJQuinn) *hld up in tch: hdwy to chse first 2 over 2f out: rdn over 1f out: styd on: no imp* **14/1**

0-00 **4** *5* **Royal Awakening (IRE)**[10] 3562 3-8-11 55 TEaves(3) 3 48
(REBarr) *rr: drvn along over 2f out: styd on fnl f: n.d* **20/1**

042 **5** *1* **Brain Washed**[19] 3267 3-8-9 72 DAllan 9 40
(TDEasterby) *in tch: drvn along bnd wl over 2f out: disputing 3rd and rdn 2f out: sn btn* **7/4**[1]

0-6 **6** *nk* **Comic Tales**[31] 2908 3-9-0 SRighton 2 44
(MMullineaux) *rr: rdn over 2f out: no hdwy* **14/1**

60- **7** *6* **Rusty Boy**[275] 5533 3-9-0 JFanning 1 28
(ACrook) *trckd ldrs tl wknd over 2f out* **40/1**

1m 26.78s (-0.72) **Going Correction** -0.225s/f (Firm) **7** Ran SP% **109.9**
Speed ratings: **95,94,92,86,85 85,78**CSF £12.29 TOTE £5.70: £1.40, £1.50; EX 15.00 Place 6 £249.05, Place 5 £216.34.
**Owner** Mike Beadle and John Furness **Bred** Jerry Russell **Trained** Willoughton, Lincs

**FOCUS**
A moderate maiden, and only limited lines of form to go on, but the pace was fair and the winner may be capable of better.

**NOTEBOOK**
**Listen To Reason(IRE)**, who injured himself on his final outing as a juvenile last year, rallied gamely inside the closing stages to bravely get off the mark. He is entitled to improve on this return from a 333-day layoff, and he should not be too harshly treated by the Handicapper for this success.
**One Upmanship** held every chance back over this extra furlong, but was worried out of it late on by the winner. He is an honest sort and is the benchmark for the form, but will not find many better opportunities to lose his maiden tag.
**Festive Chimes(IRE)** improved a good deal on his recent debut effort and will no doubt fare better once handicapped.
**Royal Awakening(IRE)** could only plug on at the one pace over this longer trip. He has failed to build on his debut as a two-year-old, but is worth another chance back in handicaps when dropped a furlong.
**Brain Washed** looked all at sea on this track and was unsuited by the faster ground. That said, this still rates a disappointing effort and he could be flattered by his official rating, so may struggle in handicaps. *Official explanation: jockey said filly was unsuited by the ground*
T/Plt: £185.80 to a £1 stake. Pool: £36,711.60. 144.20 winning tickets. T/Qpdt: £31.90 to a £1 stake. Pool: £2,320.20. 53.80 winning tickets. JF

# 3626 KEMPTON (R-H)
Wednesday, July 14
**OFFICIAL GOING: Good to firm (good in places)**

## 3840 CITY & SUBURBAN E B F MEDIAN AUCTION MAIDEN FILLIES' STKS 6f
**6:25** (6:26) (E) 2-Y-O **£4,280** (£1,317; £658; £329) **Stalls** Centre

Form RPR

4 **1** **Magical Romance (IRE)**[16] 3382 2-8-11 JFortune 1 84+
(BJMeehan) *lw: racd stands side: sn chsng ldrs and led that gp after 2f: drvn to take overall ld appr fnl f: rdn out* **3/1**[1]

00 **2** *2 1/2* **Miss Malone (IRE)**[19] 3286 2-8-11 RLMoore 12 76
(RHannon) *racd far side: chsd ldr that gp tl led ins fnl 2f and w wnr stands side 1f out: nt qckn ins last: kpt on wl* **11/2**[3]

**3** *1 3/4* **Wedding Party** 2-8-11 KFallon 4 71+
(MrsAJPerrett) *str: scope: bit bkwd: bmpd s: racd stands side: sn in tch: rdn to chse ldrs 1/2-way: styd on same pce ins last* **4/1**[2]

2630 **4** *shd* **Azuree (IRE)**[21] 3208 2-8-11 (b[1]) RHughes 13 70
(RHannon) *racd far side: led that gp tl hdd ins fnl 2f: wknd ins last* **14/1**

**5** *shd* **Crocodile Kiss (IRE)** 2-8-11 LDettori 5 70
(JAOsborne) *w'like: neat: bmpd s: sn in tch and racd stands side: chsd ldrs and rdn 2f out: kpt on ins last but nt a danger* **8/1**

**6** *2* **Toffee Vodka (IRE)** 2-8-11 MHills 10 64
(JWHills) *unf: bit bkwd: s.i.s: racd stands side: rdn over 2f out: kpt on but nvr gng pce to rch ldrs* **20/1**

05 **7** *5* **Mabella (IRE)**[16] 3382 2-8-11 SDrowne 2 49
(BRMillman) *pressed ldrs stands side 2f: styd chsng ldrs tl wknd ins fnl 2f* **20/1**

0 **8** *2* **Gold Majesty**[21] 3208 2-8-11 CCatlin 14 43
(MRChannon) *racd far side: outpcd and n.d* **50/1**

**9** *shd* **Molly Dancer** 2-8-11 TEDurcan 3 43
(MRChannon) *w'like: scope: bit bkwd: wnt rt s: racd stands side: sn led: hdd after 2f: wknd 2f out* **13/2**

0 **10** *1* **Elizabeth's Choice**[25] 3093 2-8-11 PRobinson 7 40
(MAJarvis) *racd stands side: chsd ldrs 4f* **20/1**

**11** *1 1/2* **Rockys Girl** 2-8-11 BDoyle 9 35
(MJRyan) *w'like: bit bkwd: led briefly stands side: sn bhd* **50/1**

30 **12** *1* **Bint Il Sultan (IRE)**[13] 3438 2-8-11 EAhern 6 32
(EALDunlop) *racd stands side: outpcd* **20/1**

060 **13** *7* **Mystery Maid (IRE)**[35] 2786 2-8-11 DKinsella 11 11
(HSHowe) *hmpd s: sn in tch: stands side: wknd 1/2-way* **66/1**

1m 13.59s (0.52) **Going Correction** +0.10s/f (Good) **13** Ran SP% **116.0**
Speed ratings: **100,96,94,94,94 91,84,82,81,80 78,77,67**CSF £16.73 TOTE £3.40: £2.00, £2.80, £2.00; EX 15.10.
**Owner** F C T Wilson **Bred** Quay Bloodstock And Samac Ltd **Trained** Upper Lambourn, Berks

**FOCUS**
A decent looking maiden, the two most recent runnings of which were won by won by Soviet Song and Ruby Rocket. The time was excellent for a race of its type, just 0.22 seconds slower than the later 0 to 80 classified stakes for three-year-olds.

**NOTEBOOK**
**Magical Romance(IRE)** confirmed the promise of her Windsor debut and improved to run out a ready winner. This extra furlong suited, she recorded a decent time and can be expected to improve again on this. A step up to Listed company looks in order now for this well-regarded filly.
**Miss Malone(IRE)**, who went off second favourite for a valuable sales race in Ireland last time, ran her race on the far side and again showed promise. She can win a maiden over this trip, but now also qualifies for nurseries.
**Wedding Party**, a good-bodied filly, made an eye-catching debut and should come on plenty for this experience. Another furlong will be well within her compass.
**Azuree(IRE)** improved for the application of blinkers, and showed good pace to lead the far side group, until tiring late on. He could go in over five furlongs on this evidence, providing the headgear has the same effect next time, but may have to switch to nurseries in order to find the best opportunity.
**Crocodile Kiss(IRE)**, who looked quite straight for this debut, was staying on nicely at the death. She was bumped at the start and took time to recover, but should be a lot sharper mentally next time and looks to have a future.
**Toffee Vodka(IRE)** did not shape too badly late on, having run green early, and will do better with further experience.
**Molly Dancer** was backed for this and is clearly thought capable of better, so should come on a fair bit for this debut effort.

## 3841 NEWTON INVESTMENT MANAGEMENT H'CAP 7f (J)
**6:55** (6:56) (E) (0-70,70) 3-Y-O+ **£4,280** (£1,317; £658; £329) **Stalls** High

Form RPR

0402 **1** **Balerno**[18] 3321 5-8-12 54 NDay 13 68
(RIngram) *mid-div: hdwy 3f out: led appr fnl f: drvn and styd on wl* **12/1**

3102 **2** *1 1/4* **Jonny Ebeneezer**[2] 3810 5-9-6 62 6ex (b) RSmith 8 73
(DFlood) *lw: mid-div: hdwy over 2f out: str run appr fnl f to chse wnr ins last: no ex cl home* **9/2**[1]

6000 **3** *3/4* **Oases**[18] 3298 5-8-12 54 (v) SWhitworth 4 63
(DShaw) *slowly away: hld up in rr: hdwy 2f out: swtchd lft and rapid hdwy appr fnl f: fin wl* **40/1**

4512 **4** *1* **Fen Gypsy**[4] 3734 6-9-0 59 FPFerris(3) 10 65
(PDEvans) *bhd: hdwy 3f out: rdn to chse ldrs fr 2f out: kpt on same pce fnl f* **9/2**[1]

-040 **5** *1/2* **Cold Climate**[14] 3428 9-8-13 55 OUrbina 16 60
(BobJones) *chsd ldrs: led ins fnl 2f: hdd appr fnl: wknd ins last* **11/1**[3]

0000 **6** *1* **Super Song**[9] 3593 4-9-2 58 (t) RMullen 17 60
(PDEvans) *in tch: chsd ldrs 3f out: rdn 2f out: wknd ins fnl f* **50/1**

3354 **7** *hd* **Mistral Sky**[11] 3525 5-9-10 66 (v) SDrowne 1 67
(MrsStefLiddiard) *chsd ldrs: rdn over 2f out: wknd ins fnl f* **14/1**

-040 **8** *1 3/4* **Charlottebutterfly**[14] 3428 4-8-10 55 JFMcDonald(3) 2 52
(TTClement) *bhd: hdwy ins fnl 2f: kpt on fnl f but n.d* **25/1**

0000 **9** *1/2* **Iced Diamond (IRE)**[4] 3734 5-8-12 54 TEDurcan 11 49
(WMBrisbourne) *in tch: hdwy 2f out: trcking ldrs whn n.m.r on rails over 1f out: nt rcvr and n.d after* **16/1**

-150 **10** *nk* **Artistry**[85] 1531 4-9-4 60 JFortune 6 54
(BJMeehan) *lw: in tch: chsd ldrs over 3f out: rdn over 2f out: wknd fnl f* **14/1**

6002 **11** *1/2* **El Chaparral (IRE)**[16] 3386 4-9-7 63 DaneO'Neill 9 56
(DKIvory) *mid-div: racd on outside: n.d* **10/1**[2]

0030 **12** *4* **Swift Alchemist**[32] 2883 4-9-3 59 GBaker 12 41
(MrsHSweeting) *b.hind: chsd ldrs: rdn over 2f out: wknd over 1f out* **14/1**

3-00 **13** *1/2* **Florian**[16] 3386 6-9-5 61 (p) KFallon 15 42
(TGMills) *led tl hdd ins fnl 2f: eased whn no ch ins last* **9/2**[1]

60-0 **14** *5* **Sister Sophia (USA)**[93] 1372 4-9-9 65 GCarter 14 32
(WJMusson) *s.i.s: n.d* **33/1**

0050 **15** *5* **Logistical**[18] 3321 4-9-0 56 (t) DSweeney 7 10
(ADWPinder) *in tch over 4f* **20/1**

0300 **16** *7* **Night Wolf (IRE)**[13] 3455 4-9-2 65 LHarman(7) 5 —
(MRChannon) *racd on outside: n.d* **33/1**

1m 27.52s (0.25) **Going Correction** +0.10s/f (Good) **16** Ran SP% **124.4**
Speed ratings: **102,100,99,98,98 96,96,94,94,93 93,88,88,82,76 68**CSF £62.09 CT £2249.94 TOTE £16.20: £2.70, £1.90, £10.10, £1.50; EX 81.80.
**Owner** The Three Amigos **Bred** Juddmonte Farms **Trained** Epsom, Surrey

**FOCUS**
A moderate affair, but run at a solid gallop. The form looks fair for the grade.

**NOTEBOOK**
**Balerno**, raised 4lb for a decent second at Newmarket last time, responded well to pressure to lead late on and score tidily. This was only his second win in 35 starts and he is far from certain to follow up off an inevitably higher mark, but this is his trip and he should remain competitive at this level.
**Jonny Ebeneezer**, having his third outing since winning at Southwell only nine days previously, came from out of the clouds to bag second and posted another sound effort over this longer trip.
**Oases** ran on well in the home straight, having made a sluggish start, and posted his most worthwhile form for sometime. The visor had the desired effect, he has slipped to a winning mark and is capable of scoring when able to get his toe into the ground.
**Fen Gypsy**, officially 6lb well-in for this, ran his race and can have no excuses. He may struggle off his new mark now, but remains in fair heart.
**Cold Climate** tired out of it late on having helped set the pace for a long way and shaped as though he may get closer again for a drop back to six furlongs. *Official explanation: jockey said gelding was unsuited by the ground*
**El Chaparral(IRE)** *Official explanation: jockey said gelding ran too free*
**Florian** had his favoured lead, but once again dropped out tamely under pressure and seems to have totally lost the plot at present.
**Logistical** *Official explanation: jockey said colt resented tongue strap*

## 3842 TOTEEXACTA STKS (H'CAP) 1m 2f (J)
**7:25** (7:25) (C) (0-90,90) 3-Y-O+ **£9,737** (£2,996; £1,498; £749) **Stalls** High

Form RPR

0051 **1** **Spanish Don**[14] 3415 6-9-9 88 LPKeniry(3) 8 106
(DRCElsworth) *lw: hld up in rr:hdwy ins fnl 2f: styng on whn hmpd gng to fnl f: swtchd lft and str run to ld cl home: readily* **6/1**[2]

2-11 **2** *nk* **Hawridge Prince**[20] 3239 4-10-0 90 LDettori 10 107
(LGCottrell) *lw: hld up in rr: hdwy 4f out: chsd ldrs 3f out: chal 1f out: sn led and rdn: ct cl home* **9/4**[1]

2000 **3** *5* **Karaoke (IRE)**[7] 3631 4-8-5 67 RLMoore 12 75
(SKirk) *bhd: hdwy 4f out: chsng ldrs whn n.m.r and lost position 2f out: rdn and kpt on again fnl f: tk 3rd cl home* **20/1**

4220 **4** *nk* **Say What You See (IRE)**[25] 3097 4-8-10 72 (v) MHills 6 79
(JWHills) *trckd ldr: chal 4f out tl led over 2f out: sn rdn: hdd jst ins fnl f: sn wknd: ct for 3rd cl home* **14/1**

1642 **5** *3/4* **Ofaraby**[41] 2624 4-10-0 90 PRobinson 7 96
(MAJarvis) *t.k.h: chsd ldrs: rdn 2f out: hung rt and wknd appr fnl f* **8/1**[3]

0013 **6** *4* **Krugerrand (USA)**[17] 3347 5-9-8 84 GCarter 4 82
(WJMusson) *chsd ldrs: racd on outside: wknd ins fnl 2f* **12/1**

3-00 **7** *1* **Liquid Form (IRE)**[41] 2624 4-9-7 83 RHughes 5 79
(BHanbury) *s.i.s: hld up: hdwy 3f out: n.m.r and rdn over 2f out: sn btn* **10/1**

0103 **8** 1 ¾ **Guilded Flyer**[14] 3415 5-9-11 **87** ........ WSupple 11 80
(WSKittow) *chsd ldrs: chal 4f out: slt ld 3f out tl over 2f out: wkng whn hmpd over 1f out* **9/1**

0-60 **9** 1 ¼ **Giocoso (USA)**[14] 3415 4-9-4 **80** ........ KDarley 2 71
(BPalling) *led tl narrowly hdd 3f out: wknd 2f out* **25/1**

0001 **10** 3 **Invader**[14] 3419 8-9-2 **78** ........ (bt) SSanders 1 63
(CEBrittain) *bhd: rdn 3f out: nvr a danger and sn rr* **20/1**

0306 **11** 1 ¾ **Arry Dash**[13] 3442 4-9-3 **79** ........ TEDurcan 3 61
(MRChannon) *bhd fr 1/2-way* **16/1**

4050 **12** *dist* **Dream Magic**[44] 2537 6-8-13 **75** ........ BDoyle 9 —
(MJRyan) *in tch: rdn 4f out: sn bhd: t.o* **8/1**[3]

2m 6.90s (0.76) **Going Correction** +0.10s/f (Good) **12** Ran SP% **120.0**

Speed ratings: **100,99,95,95,94 91,90,89,88,86 84**,—CSF £19.44 CT £262.58 TOTE £6.80: £2.40, £1.80, £6.70; EX 18.50 Trifecta £209.60 Pool: £1,033.48. 3.50 winning tickets.

**Owner** Richard J Cohen **Bred** Juddmonte Farms **Trained** Whitsbury, Hants

**FOCUS**

No-one wanted to go on, resulting in a slow pace and several pulling for their heads early. The winning time was modest for the grade but the form looks solid, with the winner back to his very best, the runner-up still progressing, and the next three close to their marks.

**NOTEBOOK**

**Spanish Don**, raised 5lb for his win over a furlong shorter here two weeks ago, did not get the strong pace he normally needs but that did not stop him and, despite having to change positions a few times in the home straight in order to get a run, was produced with precision timing to get up ten yards from the line. This is the highest mark he has ever won off and he has never been better.

**Hawridge Prince**, bidding for a hat-trick off a 10lb higher mark, seemed to have done everything right and hit the front at the right time, but was mugged by the winner. He remains competitive, even off this mark.

**Karaoke(IRE)** showed a bit more than of late, but even though he ran into traffic problems in the home straight it would be pushing things to say he was an unlucky loser.

**Say What You See(IRE)** was never far away and ran his race, but looks a better horse when dominating.

**Ofaraby** did not have circumstances to suit having taken a good hold early, being 11lb higher than his last winning mark, and racing on ground faster than ideal. *Official explanation: jockey said gelding was keen early on and hung right*

**Krugerrand(USA)** tends to run more moderate races than good ones and this was ordinary.

**Liquid Form(IRE)** *Official explanation: jockey said gelding was never travelling*

**Guilded Flyer** does not look so effective when restrained like this.

**Dream Magic** *Official explanation: jockey said he had no explanation for his run*

## 3843 ROYAL BRITISH LEGION MAIDEN STKS 1m 2f (J)

**7:55** (7:57) (D) 3-Y-O **£5,707** (£1,756; £878; £439) **Stalls** High

Form RPR

**1** **Deep Purple** 3-9-0 ........ MartinDwyer 10 88
(MPTregoning) *leggy: scope: slowly away: bhd: hdwy over 4f out: chsd ldrs over 2f out: wnt 2nd 1f out: led last half f: pushed out and ed* **12/1**

4 **2** *hd* **Plummet (USA)**[51] 2374 3-8-9 ........ RHughes 9 82
(JHMGosden) *lw: chsd ldr: led over 2f out: rdn over 1f out: hdd last half f: hld whn bmpd last strides* **3/1**[2]

0-3 **3** 3 ½ **Dundry**[20] 3245 3-9-0 ........ RLMoore 3 81
(GLMoore) *uns rdr bef s: in tch: hdwy to chse ldrs ins fnl 2f: kpt on same pce fnl f* **14/1**

3 **4** 3 ½ **Tashreefat (IRE)**[26] 3054 3-8-9 ........ RHills 15 69
(ACStewart) *chsd ldrs: rdn over 2f out: wknd over 1f out* **7/1**[3]

3 **5** 1 ¾ **Safirah**[14] 3422 3-8-9 ........ PRobinson 13 66
(MAJarvis) *bhd: pushed along 4f out: styd on fr 2f out: nt trble ldrs* **14/1**

-432 **6** 2 **Michabo (IRE)**[20] 3245 3-9-0 80 ........ TQuinn 2 67
(DRCElsworth) *led: sn clr: stdd 4f out: hdd over 2f out: wknd over 1f out* **11/4**[1]

0-00 **7** ½ **Persian Genie (IRE)**[7] 3630 3-8-9 ........ SDrowne 14 61
(GBBalding) *bhd: hdwy on rails 4f out: chsd ldrs 3f out: sn rdn: wknd ins fnl 2f* **25/1**

0-0 **8** *nk* **Singlet**[18] 3297 3-9-0 ........ MFenton 11 65
(DJDaly) *chsd ldrs: rdn 3f out: wknd over 2f out* **14/1**

0 **9** *nk* **Safa Park**[49] 2401 3-9-0 ........ (t) LDettori 4 65
(SaeedBinSuroor) *lw: chsd ldrs: rdn over 2f out: sn wknd* **8/1**

**10** 2 ½ **Cugina Nicola** 3-8-9 ........ RHavlin 7 55
(GBBalding) *w'like: bit bkwd: bhd: j. path over 5f out: shkn up over 3f out and wnt mid-div: sn bhd* **66/1**

**11** ¾ **Charmed By Fire (USA)** 3-9-0 ........ KDarley 6 59
(MrsAJPerrett) *w'like: scope: bit bkwd: in tch: chsd ldrs 4f out: wknd over 2f out* **12/1**

**12** 12 **Anna Gayle** 3-8-9 ........ DaneO'Neill 5 31
(MrsAJPerrett) *leggy: slowly away and veered lft s: effrt into mid-div 1/2-way: sn bhd* **33/1**

**13** *dist* **Oration** 3-9-0 ........ KFallon 8 —
(SirMichaelStoute) *w'like: bit bkwd: a bhd: t.o fnl 2f* **12/1**

2m 7.32s (1.18) **Going Correction** +0.10s/f (Good) **13** Ran SP% **126.6**

Speed ratings: **99,98,96,93,91 90,89,89,89,87 86,77**,—CSF £50.21 TOTE £14.00: £2.80, £2.00, £4.30; EX 81.00.

**Owner** Byculla Thoroughbreds **Bred** Bricklow Ltd **Trained** Lambourn, Berks

■ Stewards Enquiry : Martin Dwyer caution: careless riding

**FOCUS**

The early pace was decent. This is probably a fair maiden for the time of year, but little to go on and only time will tell

**NOTEBOOK**

**Deep Purple**, a tall and leggy debutant who has some filling out to do, came from way off the pace to win on his debut. A 40,000gns yearling, he is a half-brother to several winners out of a mare who was a fairly useful middle-distance performer, and he was not knocked about at all to score. His future is in the hands of the Handicapper.

**Plummet(USA)**, who was prominent in the chasing pack, grabbed a clear lead around the two-furlong pole but was eventually overhauled by the winner. She finished clear of the rest, though, and her form to date suggests she can find a maiden.

**Dundry** unseated his rider before the start but the incident clearly had no affect on his performance. He finished his race well and will appreciate another two furlongs in handicap company.

**Tashreefat(IRE)** is a half-sister to high-class middle-distance filly Mezzogiorno, but she is not in that class. Her best chance of success will be in handicap company after one more run.

**Safirah** stayed on steadily from the rear and this half-sister to 11-furlong winner Zeyaarah and very useful hurdler Salhood looks sure to do better when granted a stiffer test.

**Michabo(IRE)** had the benefit of a good deal more racing experience than most of his rivals, and put that to good use in making the running. He went too quick, though, and burnt himself out.

**Persian Genie(IRE)** may do better when she gets some cut underfoot.

## 3844 LEONARD CURTIS "FLOATING CHARGE" H'CAP 1m 1f (R)

**8:25** (8:27) (E) (0-75,73) 3-Y-O+ **£4,260** (£1,311; £655; £327) **Stalls** Low

Form RPR

0430 **1** **Freeloader (IRE)**[7] 3631 4-9-12 **72** ........ RHills 2 83
(JWHills) *bhd: hdwy on outside fr 3f out: led appr fnl f: edgd rt: drvn out* **7/2**[2]

6253 **2** 1 **Pella**[12] 3478 3-8-4 **60** ........ FNorton 7 69
(MBlanshard) *hmpd after 1f: bhd: hdwy to chse ldrs and n.m.r 3f out: styd on fr over 1f out: fin wl: nt rch wnr* **9/1**

3622 **3** *hd* **Todlea (IRE)**[9] 3573 4-9-11 **71** ........ LDettori 13 80
(JAOsborne) *sn led: drvn over 2f out: hdd appr fnl f: no ex ins last: ct for 2nd cl home* **11/4**[1]

0160 **4** 1 ¼ **My Maite (IRE)**[16] 3386 5-8-0 **46** ........ (tp) CCatlin 12 52
(RIngram) *s.i.s: bhd: rdn 3f out:hdwy fr 2f out: str run fnl f: nt rch ldrs* **33/1**

0544 **5** *nk* **Pas De Surprise**[4] 3734 6-8-4 **53** ........ FPFerris(3) 15 59
(PDEvans) *chsd ldrs: rdn over 2f out: one pce fr over 1f out* **7/1**[3]

0360 **6** *hd* **Indian Blaze**[105] 1207 10-8-4 **50** ........ TPQueally 6 55
(AndrewReid) *b: b.hind: bhd: rdn and hdwy over 2f out: kpt on fnl f but nt trble ldrs* **33/1**

0303 **7** 1 ¼ **Rainbow World (IRE)**[9] 3591 4-8-13 **59** ........ (p) JFEgan 3 62
(AndrewReid) *b: b.hind: chsd ldrs: rdn 3f out: wknd fnl f* **20/1**

004/ **8** *nk* **Lawrence Of Arabia (IRE)**[620] 5601 4-8-12 **58** ........ SSanders 9 60
(SirMarkPrescott) *s.i.s: bhd: pushed along 4f out: swtchd to outside and styd on fr over 1f out: nt rch ldrs* **10/1**

3502 **9** ½ **Johannian**[11] 3536 6-9-12 **72** ........ RLMoore 8 73
(JMBradley) *bhd: rdn and sme hdwy over 3f out: nt rch ldrs and one pce appr fnl f* **10/1**

1036 **10** *nk* **Giunchiglio**[4] 3731 5-9-4 **64** ........ KFallon 14 64
(WMBrisbourne) *mid-div: hdwy 3f out: chsng ldrs whn n.m.r over 2f out: styd on same pce* **9/1**

0650 **11** 2 ½ **Recount (FR)**[14] 3419 4-9-10 **70** ........ NPollard 16 65
(JRBest) *chsd ldrs: rdn 3f out: wknd over 1f out* **33/1**

5601 **12** 1 ½ **Ridge Boy (IRE)**[9] 3589 3-9-3 **73** 6ex ........ RHughes 11 65
(RHannon) *chsd ldrs: hmpd 1/2-way: styd chsng ldrs: nt clr run and lost position 2f out: styd on again fnl f* **14/1**

5000 **13** 1 ¼ **Deeper In Debt**[14] 3412 6-9-2 **62** ........ GCarter 17 52
(JAkehurst) *bhd: mod late hdwy* **25/1**

5/5- **14** 5 **Polish Spirit**[470] 894 9-9-5 **65** ........ TQuinn 4 45
(BRMillman) *chsd ldrs tl wknd qckly fr 2f out* **33/1**

0000 **15** *nk* **Learned Lad (FR)**[7] 3631 6-8-7 **53** ........ PDoe 1 32
(JamiePoulton) *chsd ldrs: rdn over 3f out: wknd qckly 2f out* **50/1**

0040 **16** 23 **Costa Del Sol (IRE)**[52] 2322 3-7-9 **54** oh14 ........ JFMcDonald(3) 10 —
(JJBridger) *a in rr* **66/1**

1m 54.11s (-0.22) **Going Correction** +0.10s/f (Good)

**WFA** 3 from 4yo+ 10lb **16** Ran SP% **130.1**

Speed ratings: **104,103,102,101,101 101,100,100,99,99 97,95,94,90,89 69**CSF £34.74 CT £108.96 TOTE £4.20: £1.70, £2.00, £1.60, £5.10; EX 48.60.

**Owner** Scott Hardy Partnership **Bred** David Commins **Trained** Upper Lambourn, Berks

**FOCUS**

The early pace was only steady and the race was won by the horse with the best turn of foot. Fair form nevertheless.

**NOTEBOOK**

**Freeloader(IRE)**, unlucky in running over this course and distance last week, enjoyed a clear run on the outside this time. He found a useful change of gear inside the final two and a half furlongs to come and claim the race, and is clearly at the top of his game at present.

**Pella** stayed on well to grab the runner-up spot. While she did not appear to get ten furlongs plus on easier ground in the spring, she certainly shapes as though she needs that distance now, and she should stay the trip well on fast ground.

**Todlea(IRE)** is ultra consistent but continues to find one or two too good. His only victory came when hitting the front with 50 yards to run, and perhaps he needs to be brought with as late a run as possible.

**My Maite(IRE)**, who finished well from off the pace, is a difficult horse to catch right.

**Pas De Surprise** is currently racing off a mark 1lb lower than for his last win and has put up four creditable performances this summer without hitting the scoresheet. His overall strike-rate is modest.

**Indian Blaze** last won on turf three years ago.

**Lawrence Of Arabia(IRE)** was making his handicap debut and was weak in the market on his return from a 620-day layoff. Slowly away and held up, he struggled to go the early pace but put in some good late work. He is going to need farther, and softer ground would not go amiss, either.

**Polish Spirit** *Official explanation: jockey said gelding hung right*

## 3845 FIREWORK FINALE CLASSIFIED STKS 6f

**8:55** (8:57) (D) 3-Y-O **£5,421** (£1,668; £834; £417) **Stalls** Centre

Form RPR

4411 **1** **Red Romeo**[16] 3384 3-9-4 84 ........ KFallon 1 92+
(GASwinbank) *lw: hld up in rr: hdwy over 2f out: str run to ld appr fnl f: drvn out* **11/4**[1]

5451 **2** 1 ¼ **Instant Recall (IRE)**[14] 3420 3-9-0 78 ........ (b) JFortune 10 84
(BJMeehan) *in tch: rdn and hdwy 2f out: chsd wnr ins last but no imp* **10/1**

3104 **3** 1 ¾ **Borzoi Maestro**[32] 2889 3-8-11 76 ........ (p) LisaJones(3) 3 79
(JLSpearing) *led: rdn 2f out: hdd appr fnl f: no ex ins last* **33/1**

5020 **4** 1 ½ **Celtic Thunder**[11] 3523 3-9-4 84 ........ EAhern 7 79
(TJEtherington) *racd wd: hdwy over 2f out: chsd ldrs and rdn over 1f out: wknd ins last* **16/1**

6052 **5** 1 **Vienna's Boy (IRE)**[16] 3384 3-9-3 83 ........ DaneO'Neill 4 75
(RHannon) *chsd ldrs: rdn and outpcd over 2f out: styd on again fnl f but nt a danger* **14/1**

1-40 **6** ½ **The Jobber (IRE)**[7] 3645 3-9-2 82 ........ FNorton 9 72
(MBlanshard) *chsd ldrs: rdn over 2f out: wknd fnl f* **11/2**

211 **7** ½ **Buy On The Red**[53] 2309 3-9-4 84 ........ RMullen 5 73
(WRMuir) *s.i.s: bhd: rdn 2f out: a outpcd* **5/1**[3]

0623 **8** 3 ½ **Bathwick Bill (USA)**[16] 3384 3-9-1 81 ........ GBaker 2 59
(BRMillman) *in tch: chsd ldrs 1/2-way: wknd fr 2f out* **12/1**

0120 **9** 2 ½ **Snow Wolf**[28] 2981 3-9-1 81 ........ RLMoore 6 52
(JMBradley) *fly j. s: outpcd fr 1/2-way* **25/1**

2-22 **10** 7 **Taaqaah**[13] 3452 3-9-1 81 ........ MartinDwyer 8 31
(MPTregoning) *lw: chsd ldrs tl wknd qckly 2f out* **7/2**[2]

1m 13.37s (0.30) **Going Correction** +0.10s/f (Good) **10** Ran SP% **117.1**

Speed ratings: **102,100,98,96,94 94,93,88,85,76**CSF £31.63 TOTE £3.30: £1.70, £2.80, £6.00; EX 38.70 Place 6 £41.70, Place 5 £31.55.

**Owner** J Yates **Bred** J O'Mulloy **Trained** Melsonby, N Yorks

**FOCUS**

A tight little classified stakes in which the pace was sound, without being breakneck.



The Form Book, Raceform Ltd, Compton, RG20 6NL

**NOTEBOOK**
**Red Romeo**, who had Vienna's Boy and Bathwick Bill close behind him when winning a rated stakes at Windsor last time, extended his advantage over that pair despite meeting them on disadvantageous terms and completed the hat-trick, all under Fallon, in good style. He looks vastly improved this summer and has already shown he stays further than this.
**Instant Recall(IRE)**, whose two wins to date have come on Polytrack, pressed the winner right to the line. He has won over this trip on sand, but might prefer an extra furlong on a sound surface like this.
**Borzoi Maestro** was able to dictate from the front at his own pace and ran right up to his best as a result.
**Celtic Thunder** was gradually taken to race alone closer to the far rail and it hard to know whether that helped him or not.
**Vienna's Boy(IRE)** should have given the winner more to think about based on their running at Windsor, but rather ran in snatches and did not fail through lack of stamina.
**The Jobber(IRE)** attracted market support, but faded rather disappointingly late on.
**Buy On The Red** is suited by forcing tactics and never looked happy after missing the break.
*Official explanation: trainer said colt was restless in the stalls and missed the break*
**Bathwick Bill(USA)** *Official explanation: jockey said gelding ran flat*
**Taaqaah**, racing over his shortest trip to date, ran too badly to be true. *Official explanation: trainer was unable to offer any explanation for poor form shown*
T/Jkpt: Not won. T/Plt: £71.00 to a £1 stake. Pool: £76,683.35. 788.15 winning tickets. T/Qpdt: £40.10 to a £1 stake. Pool: £4,717.20. 87.00 winning tickets. ST

## 3632 LINGFIELD (L-H)
### Wednesday, July 14

**OFFICIAL GOING: Turf course - good (good to firm in places); all-weather - standard**

## 3846 DORMANSLAND MEDIAN AUCTION MAIDEN STKS (DIV I) 1m (P)
**1:50** (1:51) (F) 3-4-Y-O **£2,919** (£834; £417) **Stalls** High

Form RPR
34 **1** **Nordwind (IRE)**[40] [2654] 3-8-12 .......... TQuinn 6 78
(PWHarris) *chsd ldrs: rdn to go 2nd wl over 2f out: drvn to ld over 1f out: styd on wl* **11/8**[2]
02 **2** 3 1/2 **Revenir (IRE)**[13] [3448] 3-8-12 .......... LDettori 1 70
(ACStewart) *led: shkn up 2f out: hanging and hdd over 1f out: fnd nil* **10/11**[1]
50-0 **3** 1/2 **Scholarship (IRE)**[22] [3180] 3-8-12 67.......... SSanders 4 69
(CFWall) *racd in midfield: rdn to chse clr ldng pair over 2f out: kpt on fnl f* **16/1**[3]
000- **4** 7 **French Gigolo**[389] [2569] 4-9-7 59.......... GCarter 5 53
(CNAllen) *b: t.k.h: hld up towards rr: outpcd 3f out: nudged along to chse clr ldng trio wl over 1f out: nvr on terms* **50/1**
0- **5** 7 **Fisby**[398] [2302] 3-8-12 .......... JFEgan 7 37
(SKirk) *bit bkwd: s.s: rcvrd and prom after 2f: nudged along and steadily lost pl fr 3f out* **40/1**
4 **6** nk **The Nibbler**[14] [3427] 3-8-12 .......... BDoyle 9 36
(GCHChung) *a towards rr: shkn up and outpcd 3f out: wl off the pce after* **40/1**
**7** 1 **Coco Point Breeze** 3-8-7 .......... MFenton 3 29
(JGGiven) *w'like: bit bkwd: chsd ldr to wl over 2f out: rn green and wknd* **25/1**
0-00 **8** 6 **Albertine**[14] [3427] 4-8-13 ..........(t) J-PGuillambert(3) 8 15
(CADwyer) *a in rr: drvn and wknd 3f out* **66/1**
**9** 1 3/4 **The Palletman**[279] 4-9-7 .......... SDrowne 2 16
(MFHarris) *w'like: tall: angular: dwlt: last and drvn over 5f out: struggling after* **100/1**

1m 39.3s (-0.25) **Going Correction** +0.075s/f (Slow)
**WFA** 3 from 4yo 9lb 9 Ran SP% **113.5**
Speed ratings: **104,100,100,93,86 85,84,78,76**CSF £2.73 TOTE £2.80: £1.10, £1.10, £4.10; EX 3.70.
**Owner** Mrs P W Harris **Bred** Christoph Berglar **Trained** Ringshall, Bucks

**FOCUS**
A modest-looking maiden beforehand, but the front three pulled a long way clear and the winning time was creditable for the type of race, being 1.67 seconds faster than the second division. The third provides the level of the form.

**NOTEBOOK**
**Nordwind(IRE)** appreciated the return to a sounder surface despite this being his sand debut, but his cause did not look hopeful approaching the home bend as he was off the bridle and the favourite was going much better. However, he kept responding to pressure and after taking the lead gradually forged clear. He should carry on improving and looks a nice prospect for handicaps at around this trip.
**Revenir(IRE)** very much had the run of the race out in front and looked to be running all over his rivals approaching the turn for home, but the winner gave him no peace and ultimately saw his race out much the better. He should be able to find a race as maidens like this get progressively weaker, but he also now qualifies for handicaps and using the third as a benchmark he should get a fairly modest rating.
**Scholarship(IRE)** is much more exposed than the front pair and his proximity does not appear to do much for the form, but this was still a much better performance than on his belated reappearance and he should be able to find an ordinary race somewhere.
**French Gigolo** had managed just one placing from seven attempts prior to this and achieved very little in finishing a remote fourth.
**Fisby** ended up well beaten, but he can be forgiven to some extent as he walked out of the stalls and this was his first outing since his racecourse debut 13 months ago.
**Coco Point Breeze** *Official explanation: jockey said filly had a breathing problem*

## 3847 EUROPEAN BREEDERS FUND MAIDEN STKS 6f (P)
**2:20** (2:20) (D) 2-Y-O **£4,303** (£1,324; £662; £331) **Stalls** Low

Form RPR
**1** **Afrashad (USA)** 2-9-0 .......... LDettori 6 98+
(SaeedBinSuroor) *w'like: str: scope: mde all and sn 10l clr: shkn up over 1f out: unchal* **1/2**[1]
**2** 5 **Wazir (USA)** 2-9-0 .......... KFallon 5 86+
(JHMGosden) *unf: dwlt: rcvrd to chse clr wnr over 4f out: tried to cl 2f out: no imp after* **3/1**[2]
**3** 4 **Sant Jordi** 2-9-0 .......... JFortune 1 71
(BJMeehan) *w'like: bit bkwd: chsd wnr to over 4f out: outpcd in 3rd after* **20/1**
**4** 3/4 **Hypnotic** 2-9-0 .......... SSanders 3 69
(SirMarkPrescott) *w'like: tall: bit bkwd: outpcd in midfield: shuffled along 2f out: nvr on terms: kpt on* **14/1**[3]
**5** 5 **Vale De Lobo** 2-8-2 .......... SArcher(7) 2 49
(SirMarkPrescott) *unf: bit bkwd: outpcd in midfield: rdn and no prog over 2f out: wknd fnl f* **40/1**
0 **6** 1 **Chairman Rick (IRE)**[6] [3664] 2-9-0 .......... TPQueally 4 51
(DRLoder) *s.s: bdly outpcd in last and nt look keen: a bhd* **14/1**[3]
00 **7** 1/2 **Chek Oi**[13] [3438] 2-9-0 .......... SDrowne 7 49
(WRMuir) *outpcd and bhd: wknd fnl f* **40/1**

1m 12.1s (-0.82) **Going Correction** +0.075s/f (Slow) 7 Ran SP% **114.6**
Speed ratings: **108,101,96,95,88 87,86**CSF £2.21 TOTE £1.60: £1.10, £2.20; EX 2.50.
**Owner** Godolphin **Bred** F Mehew **Trained** Newmarket, Suffolk

**FOCUS**
A hugely impressive winner and a truly outstanding winning time for the type of race, 1.2 seconds faster than the later three-year-old handicap over the same trip.

**NOTEBOOK**
**Afrashad(USA)** ◆, a good type in the paddock who was resold for $500,000 as a two-year-old after fetching just $15,500 as a yearling, comes from a successful American family and it showed on this surface as he pinged the gate and the race was effectively over after a furlong. He just needed a couple of love taps in the closing stages to see him home and record a most impressive debut victory in a tremendous time. He looks to be all speed and is a very exciting prospect indeed.
**Wazir(USA)** ◆, out of a winning half-sister to Mozart, did his very best to cut into the winner's huge advantage during the contest and did get a bit closer on the home bend, but that was as near as he got. He was unfortunate to run into something a bit special in a race like this and, as his stable's youngsters often come on for a run, he should not be long in going one better.
**Sant Jordi**, a 25,000gns yearling out of a half-sister to eight winners, could not match the speed of the front pair and was struggling from halfway. He still showed enough to suggest he has some ability though and might appreciate further.
**Hypnotic**, first foal of the Listed winner Hypnotize, has speed in his pedigree but ran as though an extra furlong would not come amiss. He is sure to come on for this.
**Vale De Lobo**, a half-sister to a couple of winners for the same yard including the stayer Froglet, is very likely to improve a lot when eventually stepped right up in trip.
**Chairman Rick(IRE)** had the benefit of previous experience, so it was surprising he fluffed the start but he still showed little once under way and just might not be very good.

## 3848 DORMANSLAND MEDIAN AUCTION MAIDEN STKS (DIV II) 1m (P)
**2:50** (2:51) (F) 3-4-Y-O **£2,919** (£834; £417) **Stalls** High

Form RPR
**1** **Komoto** 3-8-12 .......... TPQueally 2 70+
(GAButler) *w'like: leggy: bit bkwd: dwlt: in tch in rr: pushed along over 3f out: rdn and prog over 2f out: styd on strly fnl f to ld* **6/1**
**2** shd **Cashbar** 3-8-7 .......... OUrbina 4 64+
(JRFanshawe) *unf: lengthy: hld up in tch gng wl: prog 3f out: swtchd to inner and led jst ins fnl f: pushed along and hdd last stride* **11/2**[3]
04 **3** 1 1/2 **Memory Man**[12] [3487] 3-8-12 .......... FNorton 5 66
(WRMuir) *lw: led 1f: restrained bhd ldng pair: led again 2f out: drvn and hdd jst ins fnl f: one pce* **8/1**
4000 **4** 1 3/4 **Trifti**[14] [3420] 3-8-12 62.......... LDettori 6 62
(CACyzer) *trckd ldrs: prog to chal 2f out: ev ch u.p 1f out: fdd* **6/1**
-054 **5** 4 **Stanley Crane (USA)**[30] [2934] 3-8-12 66..........(t) DaneO'Neill 9 53
(BHanbury) *b: s.i.s: sn rcvrd and led after 2f: hdd 2f out: sn wknd* **11/4**[1]
**6** 2 **Port Sodrick** 3-8-12 .......... ADaly 1 48
(MDIUsher) *w'like: bit bkwd: s.s: detached in last and rdn: no prog tl styd on fr over 1f out: nrst fin* **33/1**
**7** 2 1/2 **In Every Street (USA)** 3-8-7 .......... EAhern 7 37+
(MAMagnusson) *w'like: bit bkwd: b: b.hind: towards rr: rdn 1/2-way: brief effrt u.p over 2f out: sn btn* **5/1**[2]
000 **8** 8 **Bunkhouse**[12] [3487] 4-9-7 .......... SDrowne 3 24
(MissECLavelle) *chsd ldrs to 1/2-way: wknd 3f out* **33/1**
-256 **9** 11 **Labelled With Love**[22] [3177] 4-9-2 50.......... AQuinn(5) 8 —
(JRBoyle) *s.i.s: rcvrd to ld after 1f: hdd after 2f: w ldr to 3f out: wknd rapidly: t.o* **12/1**

1m 40.97s (1.42) **Going Correction** +0.075s/f (Slow)
**WFA** 3 from 4yo 9lb 9 Ran SP% **112.0**
Speed ratings: **95,94,93,91,87 85,83,75,64**CSF £37.30 TOTE £6.70: £2.00, £2.50, £2.10; EX 29.30.
**Owner** Mr & Mrs Michael C Kwee **Bred** The Kwee Family **Trained** Blewbury, Oxon

**FOCUS**
Very much the weaker of the two divisions and a modest winning time for the grade, 1.67 seconds slower than the first division. The front two were debutants though, so are entitled to improve.

**NOTEBOOK**
**Komoto**, a half-brother to Gryngolette, did well to make a winning debut as he only had one behind him and was off the bridle at halfway, but he got stronger as the race progressed and got up to win the race on the nod. He should improve, but had a much harder race than the runner-up and would not be fancied to confirm the form with her.
**Cashbar**, a lean first foal of the winning hurdler Barford Sovereign, came from off the pace and was produce with a well-timed challenge a furlong out, but her rider did very little on her and she had the race snatched from her grasp. She probably should have won this, but the kindness will probably be repaid in the longer term.
**Memory Man** showed up for a long way and appeared to see the longer trip out well enough. He now qualifies for handicaps and that may be his best option.
**Trifti**, one of three in a line turning in, did not get home. He is looking exposed and connections seem to be having trouble identifying his best trip.
**Stanley Crane(USA)**, backed to get off the mark despite looking exposed, was probably not helped by being taken on for the early lead and finished weakly, but he is running out of excuses.
**In Every Street(USA)**, who has an American pedigree, was weak in the market and always struggling.

## 3849 BELLWAY STKS (H'CAP) 6f (P)
**3:20** (3:21) (E) (0-75,75) 3-Y-O **£4,277** (£1,316; £658; £329) **Stalls** Low

Form RPR
211 **1** **Catherine Wheel**[22] [3178] 3-9-5 73.......... LDettori 1 82+
(JRFanshawe) *hld up: lost pl over 3f out and in rr: prog on inner 2f out: led ins fnl f: drvn out* **11/8**[1]
1104 **2** 1/2 **Eccentric**[14] [3420] 3-9-7 75.......... JFEgan 4 82
(AndrewReid) *b: b.hind: led: drvn and edgd rt over 1f out: hdd ins fnl f: kpt on nr fin: a hld* **9/2**[2]
0340 **3** 3/4 **Bella Tutrice (IRE)**[14] [3420] 3-9-1 69.......... KFallon 7 74
(IAWood) *lw: pressed ldr: rdn and ev ch 2f out: edgd rt over 1f out: unable qck ins fnl f* **14/1**
4-34 **4** nk **Pure Folly (IRE)**[151] [764] 3-8-3 57.......... TPQueally 3 61+
(SirMarkPrescott) *trckd ldrs on inner: effrt 2f out: hrd rdn over 1f out: kpt on same pce* **10/1**
5464 **5** nk **Cut And Dried**[7] [3628] 3-8-12 66.......... MartinDwyer 6 69
(DMSimcock) *t.k.h early: trckd ldrs: rdn and cl up fr 2f out: one pce fr over 1f out* **6/1**[3]
0466 **6** 3/4 **Mirasol Princess**[7] [3628] 3-9-5 73.......... IMongan 9 74
(DKIvory) *chsd ldrs on outer: rdn 2f out: cl up over 1f out: no ex fnl f* **25/1**
46-0 **7** 2 1/2 **Burlington Place**[22] [3180] 3-8-11 65.......... EAhern 2 58
(SKirk) *dwlt: hld up in rr: pushed along over 2f out: no imp on ldrs* **20/1**
3213 **8** 1 **Miss Judgement (IRE)**[11] [3530] 3-8-11 65.......... FNorton 10 55
(WRMuir) *pressed ldrs: rdn and lost pl over 2f out: no prog after* **6/1**[3]

6010 **9** ½ **Alizar (IRE)**[22] 3175 3-8-5 **59** ........ RLMoore 11 48
(SDow) *racd in last pair: rdn and struggling 1/2-way: kpt on fnl f* **16/1**
1300 **10** ¾ **Imperium**[7] 3628 3-9-4 **72** ........ SDrowne 8 59
(MrsStefLiddiard) *lw; s.i.s: a in rr: rdn and no prog 2f out* **33/1**
-000 **11** 5 **Ticero**[32] 2880 3-9-1 **72** ........ (b[1]) J-PGuillambert(3) 12 44
(CEBrittain) *dwlt: t.k.h and hld up in rr: effrt over 2f out: sn wknd* **50/1**

1m 13.3s (0.38) **Going Correction** +0.075s/f (Slow) **11** Ran SP% **124.0**
Speed ratings: **100,99,98,97,97 96,93,91,91,90 83**CSF £7.64 CT £67.48 TOTE £2.50: £1.10, £2.30, £3.60; EX 10.10.
**Owner** Cheveley Park Stud **Bred** Cheveley Park Stud Ltd **Trained** Newmarket, Suffolk

**FOCUS**
A fairly competitive handicap run at a sound pace and the time was average for the grade despite being 1.2 seconds slower than the earlier two-year-old maiden. The form looks solid enough for the class.

**NOTEBOOK**
**Catherine Wheel**, raised 5lb following her Newbury victory, was always travelling well and was helped by the leaders edging out into the centre of the track turning for home, leaving a nice big gap for her to come through and complete the hat-trick. She may not have stopped improving yet.
**Eccentric** set the pace, but never had a soft lead and kept battling right to the line. This was a decent effort over a trip probably short of his best.
**Bella Tutrice(IRE)**, who continues to slip down the handicap, was always up with the pace and appeared to be going particularly well approaching the home turn, but she again lacked a change of gear when it was needed.
**Pure Folly(IRE)**, making her handicap debut and running for the first time in five months, had every chance and was not beaten far. She still has some scope and has a similar race in her.
**Cut And Dried**, a winner twice over the minimum trip here at the start of the year, saw the extra furlong out better than he had in his only previous attempt and is now back on a winning mark.
**Mirasol Princess** has become disappointing and, even though this was not a bad effort, she still has to convince over this trip.

## 3850 E B F PAUL KELLEWAY MEMORIAL CLASSIFIED STKS 1m (P)
**3:50** (3:50) (C) 3-Y-O+ **£8,572** (£3,251; £1,625; £739) **Stalls** High

Form RPR
2004 **1** **Always Esteemed (IRE)**[24] 3119 4-9-7 94 ........ MartinDwyer 4 104
(GWragg) *chsd ldrs: rdn over 3f out: prog over 2f out: led jst over 1f out: edgd lft and drvn out* **6/1**[2]
2005 **2** 1½ **Fiveoclock Express (IRE)**[45] 2504 4-9-3 90 ........ (p) IMongan 1 97
(MissGayKelleway) *prom: chsd ldr 2f out: sn rdn and nt qckn: kpt on to chse wnr ins fnl f: a hld* **10/1**
1-4 **3** ½ **Warrad (USA)**[82] 1587 3-8-8 88 ........ SSanders 10 96+
(GAButler) *lw: hld up in last trio: prog on wd outside over 2f out: styd on to take 3rd wl ins fnl f: nt rch ldng pair* **9/1**
-400 **4** 1¼ **Selective**[26] 3036 5-9-7 94 ........ KFallon 7 97
(ACStewart) *b: hld up in midfield: effrt over 2f out: rdn wl over 1f out: styd on but nt pce to chal* **7/1**[3]
1106 **5** ½ **Dance On The Top**[21] 3191 6-9-7 94 ........ (t) DSweeney 2 96
(JRBoyle) *led for 2f: led again 3f out: kicked 2l clr 2f out: hdd and fdd jst over 1f out* **6/1**[2]
4002 **6** nk **Bettalatethannever (IRE)**[26] 3053 3-8-13 95 ........ DaneO'Neill 12 96
(SDow) *lw: s.i.s: hld up in rr: rdn and effrt over 2f out: kpt on fr over 1f out: nvr able to chal* **6/1**[2]
0030 **7** 1¼ **Fancy Foxtrot**[8] 3598 3-8-8 90 ........ JFortune 3 88
(BJMeehan) *t.k.h early: hld up in midfield: effrt over 2f out: rdn and nt qckn over 1f out* **4/1**[1]
30-3 **8** 4 **Sharplaw Venture**[20] 3223 4-9-0 90 ........ RHills 6 76
(WJHaggas) *chsd ldrs: rdn whn bdly hmpd on inner over 2f out: nt rcvr* **12/1**
-066 **9** 3 **Binanti**[17] 3337 4-9-3 88 ........ JQuinn 11 72
(PRChamings) *settled in rr: outpcd 2f out: rdn over 1f out: no ch* **20/1**
4220 **10** 1 **Ephesus**[8] 3597 4-9-3 81 ........ (v) WSupple 5 70
(MissGayKelleway) *settled in rr: rdn and struggling over 2f out: wknd* **20/1**
1304 **11** hd **Hatch**[33] 2844 3-8-8 88 ........ LDettori 9 69
(RMHCowell) *racd v wd early: led after 2f to 3f out: wknd 2f out* **10/1**
0- **12** 19 **Outside Investor (IRE)**[173] 5603 4-9-3 75 ........ EAhern 8 26
(TPMcgovern) *a in rr: t.o fnl 3f* **66/1**

1m 39.22s (-0.33) **Going Correction** +0.075s/f (Slow)
**WFA** 3 from 4yo+ 9lb **12** Ran SP% **122.2**
Speed ratings: **104,102,102,100,100 99,98,94,91,90 90,71**CSF £65.43 TOTE £7.20: £2.50, £3.90, £3.80; EX 117.90.
**Owner** Mollers Racing **Bred** Haras De La Perelle **Trained** Newmarket, Suffolk

**FOCUS**
A decent-quality contest and the form looks sound enough, although the pace was by no means strong and the time was ordinary for the grade.

**NOTEBOOK**
**Always Esteemed(IRE)**, who has been finding life tough in regular handicaps on turf, at last found a race he could win and took to this surface at the first time of asking to record his first victory since his racecourse debut 15 months ago. This seems to be his best trip, and he looks worth persevering with on this surface if a suitable opportunity can be found.
**Fiveoclock Express(IRE)**, rated 9lb higher on the All-Weather than he is on turf, ran a pleasing race and even though his best performance on sand came on the now-defunct Wolverhampton Fibresand, he looks more than capable of winning on this surface.
**Warrad(USA)**, whose three outings to date have been well spaced out, came from well off the pace and was staying on nicely at the end. He still has scope and should be suited by a bit further.
**Selective**, making his sand debut, would probably have preferred a much stronger pace as, even though he was staying on, he never looked like getting there.
**Dance On The Top** helped force the pace until swamped racing down the home straight. He looks to be on a stiff mark on sand now, forcing him to race against rivals like these, and his best options may be off a lower mark back on grass, even though he is not so effective on it.
**Bettalatethannever(IRE)** did not perform badly, but he is now 13lb higher than the mark he won off here in January and has paid dearly for finishing fourth on disadvantageous terms in a Listed contest here in the spring.
**Fancy Foxtrot**, ridden very differently compared with when he made all here in April, has only shown glimpses of form on turf since then and this return to Polytrack did not produce an upturn in his fortunes.
**Sharplaw Venture** already looked to be on the retreat when getting pinched against the inside rail turning for home.
**Outside Investor(IRE)** *Official explanation: jockey said gelding would not face the kickback*

## 3851 LADIES NIGHT THIS SATURDAY H'CAP 2m
**4:20** (4:21) (E) (0-75,74) 3-Y-O+ **£4,251** (£1,308; £654; £327) **Stalls** Low

Form RPR
0-01 **1** **Tungsten Strike (USA)**[7] 3629 3-8-6 71 5ex ........ MartinDwyer 7 91+
(MrsAJPerrett) *mostly trckd ldr: rdn to ld over 2f out: drew clr fr over 1f out: readily* **15/8**[1]
221 **2** 4 **Belle Rouge**[98] 1297 6-8-13 **59** ........ LDettori 4 67
(CAHorgan) *b: trckd ldrs: smooth prog to chal over 2f out: sn rdn: fdd and btn over 1f out* **6/1**[3]
510/ **3** 1 **Bow Strada**[21] 5693 7-9-10 **70** ........ EAhern 5 77
(PJHobbs) *lw: prom: drvn 3f out: unable qck: kpt on again fr over 1f out* **8/1**
0040 **4** shd **San Hernando**[20] 3244 4-9-10 **70** ........ DaneO'Neill 9 77
(DRCElsworth) *hld up in rr: effrt 3f out: outpcd over 2f out: kpt on to dispute 3rd over 1f out: no imp after* **10/1**
333- **5** 1¾ **Marrel**[15] 485 6-7-13 **45** oh5 ow1 ........ (v) JQuinn 6 50
(DBurchell) *settled in midfield: rdn and nt qckn over 2f out: hanging but kpt on one pce after* **5/1**[2]
0431 **6** 3½ **Sudden Flight (IRE)**[4] 3733 7-9-5 **72** 5ex ........ SJDonohoe(7) 12 73
(PDEvans) *led: rdn and hdd over 2f out: grad wknd* **8/1**
50-0 **7** ¾ **Cedar Master (IRE)**[17] 2893 7-9-0 **65** ........ (bt) AQuinn(5) 1 65
(JRBoyle) *settled in midfield: rdn 3f out: no prog 2f out: wknd over 1f out* **100/1**
0466 **8** 4 **Moon Emperor**[32] 2893 7-10-0 **74** ........ JFortune 11 69
(JRJenkins) *hld up in rr: rdn over 3f out: sn outpcd and struggling* **11/1**
026- **9** 13 **Dear Sir (IRE)**[227] 4765 4-8-3 **49** ........ CCatlin 10 28
(MrsPNDutfield) *hld up in last pair: lost tch 5f out: wl bhd after* **50/1**
-066 **10** 9 **Promote**[25] 3108 8-7-12 **44** oh4 ........ AMcCarthy 2 13
(MsAEEmbiricos) *trckd ldrs: rdn and effrt 3f out: wknd rapidly over 2f out* **33/1**
2000 **P** **Madiba**[7] 3644 5-8-13 **59** ........ KFallon 3 —
(PHowling) *nvr gng wl: t.o after 5f: p.u 1/2-way* **12/1**

3m 35.92s (2.73) **Going Correction** +0.15s/f (Good)
**WFA** 3 from 4yo+ 19lb **11** Ran SP% **119.0**
Speed ratings: **99,97,96,96,95 93,93,91,84,80** —CSF £13.19 CT £75.29 TOTE £3.10: £1.70, £1.70, £2.60; EX 9.50.
**Owner** John Connolly **Bred** Minster Stud **Trained** Pulborough, W Sussex

**FOCUS**
A routine staying handicap run at an ordinary pace and a modest winning time for the grade. The winner looks progressive though.

**NOTEBOOK**
**Tungsten Strike(USA)** ◆, the only three-year-old in the field, had a 5lb penalty to carry for his Kempton victory but he was always going well just behind the leader and found plenty when asked for his effort. The form is nothing to write home about, but he could do little more than win as he did and should be able to add to this.
**Belle Rouge**, off since winning in April, was 5lb higher this time but ran with credit, especially as she could have done with more rain.
**Bow Strada**, who has been successful over hurdles and fences since his last outing on the Flat in November 2001, ran with credit but would probably have preferred a stronger gallop as he lacked pace at the business end.
**San Hernando** came from well off the pace and made up a lot of late ground. This looked promising, but we have been here before and he did appear to be carrying his head rather high down the home straight.
**Marrel**, a winner over hurdles last time, was taking part in a Flat turf race for the first time in almost two years. He could never land a blow and is another that would have been better suited by a proper test.
**Sudden Flight(IRE)**, carrying a 5lb penalty for his Chester win, was again able to set his own pace out in front. He looked to be travelling well turning in, and his rider must have liked what he saw when he looked over his left shoulder passing the three-furlong pole, but then when he looked over his right there were several dangers stacking up on his outside and he quickly went from one extreme to the other.
**Promote** *Official explanation: jockey said gelding had a breathing problem*
**Madiba** *Official explanation: jockey said gelding was uncomfortable on the good, good to firm places ground*

## 3852 COME RACING HERE ON SATURDAY NIGHT CLASSIFIED STKS 1m 2f
**4:50** (4:56) (F) 3-Y-O **£3,038** (£868; £434) **Stalls** Low

Form RPR
1011 **1** **Doctored**[3] 3773 3-9-0 60 ow1 ........ (b) SJDonohoe(7) 1 77
(PDEvans) *racd in midfield: plld out and effrt 3f out: prog over 2f out: rdn to ld ins fnl f: styd on wl* **7/2**[2]
-050 **2** ½ **Golden Drift**[23] 3160 3-8-11 58 ........ SDrowne 2 66
(GWragg) *trckd ldrs: effrt 3f out: prog on inner to ld over 1f out: drvn and hdd ins fnl f: styd on but a hld* **14/1**
63-0 **3** 5 **Polar Dancer**[65] 1998 3-8-11 59 ........ DaneO'Neill 9 57
(MrsAJPerrett) *s.i.s: hld up in last trio: wl off the pce and rdn over 3f out: prog 2f out: styd on to take 3rd wl ins fnl f* **8/1**
0-00 **4** ¾ **Rajayoga**[51] 2371 3-8-11 60 ........ FPFerris(3) 8 58
(MHTompkins) *racd on outer: trckd ldrs: effrt 3f out: rdn and ev ch 2f out: fdd fnl f* **16/1**
-505 **5** 1¼ **Trois Etoiles (IRE)**[11] 3527 3-8-11 58 ........ RHills 6 53+
(JWHills) *trckd ldrs: nt clr run wl over 2f out to wl over 1f out: rdn and no prog after* **3/1**[1]
**6** 1¼ **Kalimenta (USA)**[68] 3-9-2 65 ........ JFEgan 13 55+
(SKirk) *bolted on way to post and led to s: hld up in last pair: wl off the pce and brought wd 3f out: shuffled along and kpt on st* **33/1**
006 **7** 3 **Cayman Calypso (IRE)**[12] 3487 3-9-5 65 ........ MHenry 12 53
(MAJarvis) *prom: chsd wnr 4f out: rdn and ev ch 2f out: sn wknd* **16/1**
0-00 **8** shd **Autumn Flyer (IRE)**[30] 2949 3-9-2 62 ........ RSmith 5 49
(CGCox) *led: hanging rt and hdd over 1f out: nt run on* **50/1**
0005 **9** nk **Palabelle (IRE)**[13] 3448 3-8-11 60 ........ MartinDwyer 3 44
(PWHarris) *t.k.h: trckd ldr to 4f out: losing pl whn n.m.r 2f out: wknd* **5/1**[3]
403 **10** 2½ **Lillianna (IRE)**[22] 3168 3-9-2 65 ........ WRyan 7 44
(HRACecil) *racd in midfield: rdn and struggling 3f out: no ch after* **6/1**
0600 **11** nk **Frankies Wings (IRE)**[6] 3669 3-9-0 60 ........ (b) BDoyle 10 42
(TGMills) *hld up in last: wl bhd over 3f out: n.d after* **20/1**

2m 10.54s (0.94) **Going Correction** +0.15s/f (Good) **11** Ran SP% **117.4**
Speed ratings: **102,101,97,97,96 95,92,92,92,90 90**CSF £50.51 TOTE £3.90: £1.60, £4.30, £2.30; EX 59.30 Place 6 £25.41, Place 5 £24.27.
**Owner** Treble Chance Partnership **Bred** Wickfield Farm Partnership **Trained** Pandy, Gwent

**FOCUS**
A modest classified event, but at least the pace was sound.

**NOTEBOOK**
**Doctored** continued in cracking form and bagged his fifth win from his last six starts. He was always travelling well and even though in the end he had to be kept up to his work, he always had the situation under control.
**Golden Drift**, unplaced in all four of her previous starts, kept on to the line and made sure the winner could not take things easy. This was a much-improved effort from her and it appears to devalue the form, but given the distance back to the third it may be wise to give her the benefit of the doubt.
**Polar Dancer** made up a lot of late ground without ever looking like getting on terms with the front pair and looks worth stepping back up in trip.
**Rajayoga** was stepping up a quarter of a mile in trip and did not appear to see it out.
**Trois Etoiles(IRE)**, stepping up another two furlongs in trip and well backed to get off the mark, managed to find all sorts of traffic problems in the home straight, but given how far the front pair pulled clear it probably cost her a place in the frame at best.

**Kalimenta(USA)** ◆, making her handicap and British debuts after three runs in the French Provinces, caused all sorts of trouble before the start, but in the race she was noted making some late headway having been right out the back early. She should improve from this and may not be a lost cause if her temperament can be sorted out.
**Palabelle(IRE)**, up in trip, did her chances no good by pulling hard early.
T/Plt: £18.80 to a £1 stake. Pool: £30,732.70. 1,190.05 winning tickets. T/Qpdt: £15.90 to a £1 stake. Pool: £1,695.20. 78.55 winning tickets. JN

3853 - 3858a (Foreign Racing) - See Raceform Interactive

## [3544]LEOPARDSTOWN (L-H)

Wednesday, July 14

**OFFICIAL GOING: Good to yielding**

### 3859a SILVER FLASH STKS (LISTED RACE) (FILLIES) 6f

7:30 (7:30) 2-Y-O £22,922 (£6,725; £3,204; £1,091)

RPR

1 **Silk And Scarlet**[35] 2791 2-8-11 .......... JPSpencer 10 102
(APO'Brien, Ire) *settled in rr: impr eighth ent st: chal on outer ins fnl f: led last 100yds* **7/2[1]**

2 *1 ½* **Alexander Icequeen (IRE)**[46] 2494 2-8-11 .......... PJSmullen 8 98
(DKWeld, Ire) *mid-div: 8th half-way: impr 6th ent st: led ins fnl f: hdd last 100yds: kpt on* **6/1[3]**

3 *4 ½* **La Maitresse (IRE)**[9] 3594 2-8-11 .......... TPO'Shea 6 84
(MHalford, Ire) *bhd: 9th half-way: r.o wl fr over 1f out* **10/1**

4 *2* **Desert Tigress (USA)**[6] 3685 2-8-11 .......... CO'Donoghue 2 78
(APO'Brien, Ire) *led: hdd ins fnl f: no ex* **10/1**

5 *1* **National Swagger (IRE)**[18] 3329 2-8-11 .......... KJManning 11 75
(JSBolger, Ire) *settled sixth: impr 4th ent st: no ex fnl f* **6/1[3]**

6 *1* **Belle Artiste (IRE)**[12] 3497 2-8-11 .......... MCHussey 3 72
(JosephCrowley, Ire) *chsd ldr 2nd: rdn over 1f out: sn wknd* **12/1**

7 *3* **Luas Line (IRE)** 2-8-11 .......... JAHeffernan 1 63
(DavidWachman, Ire) *chsd ldrs 4th: rdn 2f out: sn wknd* **5/1[2]**

8 *1* **Glinting Desert (IRE)** 2-8-11 .......... DJCondon 5 60
(JGBurns, Ire) *bhd: nvr able to chal* **10/1**

9 *¾* **Abbeylara (USA)**[20] 3253 2-8-11 .......... PCosgrave 7 58
(DavidWachman, Ire) *chsd ldrs 5th early: seventh half-way: rdn bef st: sn btn* **11/1**

10 *½* **All Night Dancer (IRE)**[13] 3445 2-8-11 .......... NGMcCullagh 9 56
(DavidWachman, Ire) *chsd ldrs 3rd: rdn 2f out: sn wknd* **10/1**

11 *2* **Dipterous (IRE)**[31] 2917 2-8-11 .......... DMGrant 13 50
(JosephCrowley, Ire) *a bhd* **14/1**

12 *1 ½* **Midnight Grace (IRE)**[25] 3110 2-8-11 ..........(t) FMBerry 4 46
(MsFMCrowley, Ire) *chsd ldrs 5th: impr 3rd ent st: sn rdn and wknd qckly* **12/1**

1m 15.7s **Going Correction** +0.15s/f (Good) **12** Ran SP% **134.2**
Speed ratings: **98,96,90,87,86 84,80,79,78,77 75,73**CSF £27.81 TOTE £4.20: £1.60, £2.10, £2.70; DF 16.90.
**Owner** Mrs John Magnier **Bred** Juddmonte Farms **Trained** Ballydoyle, Co Tipperary

**NOTEBOOK**
**Silk And Scarlet** was dropping back a furlong in trip after a promising debut run and had only three behind her turning for home. Fourth over a furlong out, she was soon second and ran on sweetly to lead inside the last 100 yards. Well-regarded, she will improve further.
**Alexander Icequeen(IRE)** was not hustled early but came through strongly to go third over a furlong out, in front early inside the last, she was then outpaced by the winner.
**La Maitresse(IRE)** stayed on well inside the last without actually quickening to be nearest at the finish.
**Desert Tigress(USA)** led until tackled and outpaced by the first pair.
**National Swagger(IRE)** made a bit of headway turning for home but was never an effective challenger.
**Belle Artiste(IRE)** ran second till weakening inside the last.
**Luas Line(IRE)** chased the leaders until weakening from two furlongs out.
**Glinting Desert(IRE)** was very green and needs further but showed some ability when keeping on late.

### 3862a CHALLENGE STKS (LISTED RACE) 1m 6f

9:00 (9:01) 3-Y-O+ £22,922 (£6,725; £3,204; £1,091)

RPR

1 **Barolo**[18] 3310 5-9-9 .......... JPMurtagh 3 99
(PWHarris) *led: rdn two fs out: styd on wl* **4/1[2]**

2 *1 ½* **Two Miles West (IRE)**[26] 3035 3-8-8 .......... JPSpencer 4 97
(APO'Brien, Ire) *chsd ldrs in 4th: impr to 3rd bef st: 2nd 2f out: no ex fnl f* **5/4[1]**

3 *1* **Valentina Guest (IRE)**[21] 3219 3-8-5 91 .......... CatherineGannon 7 93
(PeterCasey, Ire) *settled rr: impr to go 6th ent st: hmpd over 1f out: styd on wl fnl f* **9/1**

4 *½* **Ivowen (USA)**[18] 3331 4-9-6 103 .......... PJSmullen 5 92
(DKWeld, Ire) *settled 7th: impr 5th 2f out: styd on fnl f* **11/2**

5 *3* **Liss Ard (IRE)**[19] 3284 3-8-8 88 .......... DMGrant 9 91
(JohnJosephMurphy, Ire) *chsd ldrs in 5th: rdn 2f out: kpt on one pce* **16/1**

6 *9* **Jade Quest (IRE)**[18] 3333 4-9-12 100 .......... FMBerry 2 81
(CharlesO'Brien, Ire) *settled 6th: impr 4th bef st: rdn 2f out and wknd* **12/1**

7 *7* **Cruzspiel**[18] 3333 4-9-12 108 ..........(b) MJKinane 1 71
(JohnMOxx, Ire) *chsd ldr 2nd: 3rd half-way: rdn ent st: sn wknd* **9/2[3]**

8 *20* **Chimes At Midnight (USA)**[17] 3356 7-9-7 87 ..........(b) JAHeffernan 8 40
(LukeComer, Ire) *slowly away: impr rapidly to 3rd after 2f: chsd ldr in 2nd half-way: rdn 4f out and wknd* **33/1**

9 *15* **Sunday Joy (AUS)**[270] 5652 5-9-6 .......... KJManning 6 16
(DKWeld, Ire) *a bhd* **16/1**

3m 3.70s **Going Correction** +0.15s/f (Good)
**WFA** 3 from 4yo+ 15lb **9** Ran SP% **130.4**
Speed ratings: **112,111,110,110,108 103,99,88,79**CSF £10.77 TOTE £4.90: £1.90, £1.30, £2.50; DF 7.30.
**Owner** Mrs P W Harris **Bred** Pendley Farm **Trained** Ringshall, Bucks

**NOTEBOOK**
**Barolo** put his disappointing Northumberland Plate run behind him here with a display of front running that saw him dominate throughout under a canny ride and stay on too strongly for the favourite. He remains progressive.
**Two Miles West(IRE)** was made look very one-paced over the last furlong.
**Valentina Guest(IRE)**, successful here in handicaps this season off 76 and 84 is still improving. She managed to find what trouble was going in the straight and looked a shade unlucky not to finish closer.
**Ivowen(USA)** stayed on well inside the last but was never on terms to launch an effective challenge.
**Liss Ard(IRE)** was not disgraced and needs further.
**Cruzspiel** ran into difficulties over a furlong out and was eased.
**Sunday Joy(AUS)** was always behind and showed approaching the form that made her a successful Group performer in Australia.
T/Jkpt: @424.20. Pool of @15,840.50. 28 winning units. T/Plt: @181.30. Pool of @967.00. 4 winning units. II

3860 - 3862a (Foreign Racing) - See Raceform Interactive

## [3833]MAISONS-LAFFITTE (R-H)

Wednesday, July 14

**OFFICIAL GOING: Soft**

### 3863a PRIX EUGENE ADAM (GROUP 2) 1m 2f (S)

2:20 (2:24) 3-Y-O £42,148 (£16,268; £7,764; £5,176)

RPR

1 **Valixir (IRE)**[38] 2722 3-8-11 .......... ELegrix 3 117
(AFabre, France) *made all, set steady pace, pushed clear over 1 1/2f out, easily* **1**

2 *3* **Delfos (IRE)**[38] 2722 3-8-11 .......... MBlancpain 4 112
(CLaffon-Parias, France) *raced in 2nd or 3rd, 3rd straight, went 2nd again just under 2f out, stayd on but not pace of winner* **2**

3 *½* **Hazyview**[39] 2680 3-8-11 .......... IMendizabal 2 111
(NACallaghan) *prom, pushed along to press ldr 3f out, dropped back to 4th 2f out, styd on und str pressure to regain 2nd ins fnl f*

4 *2 ½* **African Dream**[11] 3540 3-8-11 .......... ODoleuze 5 107
(PWChapple-Hyam) *held up in 4th, headway on outside to dispute 2nd pressing winner 2f out, soon ridden and outpaced* **3**

5 *2* **Mohandas (FR)**[52] 3-8-11 .......... J-MBreux 7 103
(WHefter, Germany) *held up in last, ridden 2f out, took 5th close home, never a factor*

6 *snk* **Tiganello (GER)**[16] 3389 3-8-11 .......... OPeslier 6 103
(FHead, France) *raced in 5th, ridden and outpaced from over 2f out*

2m 7.90s **Going Correction** +0.025s/f (Good) **6** Ran SP% **123.5**
Speed ratings: **112,109,109,107,105 105**.
**Owner** Lagardere Family **Bred** S N C Lagardere Elevage **Trained** France

**NOTEBOOK**
**Valixir(IRE)** won readily without needing to be hit with the whip and is progressing well. Legrix used his initiative when Valixir's front-running stablemate Ecolde d'Art refused to enter the stalls and changed tactics to set a steady pace. Three different challengers had a crack at him early in the straight, but Valixir was still travelling easily and moved away smoothly when asked. He is likely to be rested until the autumn, when the Prix Niel is a possible target.
**Delfos(IRE)** ran much better than in the Jockey-Club, giving credence to his trainer's belief that he does not stay a mile and a half.
**Hazyview** was meant to make the running, but instead was dropped in behind the leader much to Callaghan's fury. Shoved along to challenge up the inside early in the straight, he then got outpaced before staying on again in the closing stages. A more enterprising ride might have seen him finish second.
**African Dream** was ill-suited by the modest gallop. Using up his energy to draw alongside the winner with two furlongs to run, he was a spent force in the closing stages. Chapple-Hyam is considering dropping him back to a mile in the hope of finding a race with a decent pace.

## [3296]DONCASTER (L-H)

Thursday, July 15

**OFFICIAL GOING: Good to soft**

### 3864 ST JOHNS AMBULANCE APPRENTICE H'CAP 5f

6:40 (6:41) (F) (0-55,55) 3-Y-O+ £3,708 (£1,141; £570; £285) Stalls High

Form RPR

-000 1 **Rosie's Result**[2] 3820 4-8-12 **45** .......... JemmaMarshall[(3)] 19 54
(MTodhunter) *in tch centre: hdwy over 2f out: effrt to chal ins last: sn rdn and styd on to ld nr line* **12/1**

5020 2 *hd* **Roan Raider (USA)**[3] 3810 4-9-6 **53** ..........(v) KGhunowa[(3)] 10 61
(MJPolglase) *a.p centre: hdwy to ld wl over 1f out: rdn ent last: hdd nr line* **16/1**

2162 3 *1 ¾* **Larky's Lob**[2] 3820 5-8-10 **45** .......... HFellows[(5)] 13 47
(JO'Reilly) *cl up c entre: ev ch 2f out tl rdn and one pce ent last* **7/2[1]**

0200 4 *½* **Kennington**[10] 3593 4-9-6 **53** ..........(b[1]) LauraPike[(3)] 9 53
(MrsCADunnett) *overall ldr centre: rdn along over 2f out: hdd wl over 1f out: kpt on same pce ins last* **20/1**

0006 5 *1 ½* **Le Meridien (IRE)**[2] 3820 6-9-4 **51** ..........(p) DonnaCaldwell[(3)] 20 46
(JSWainwright) *cl up stands rail: evc hance 2f out: sn rdna nd kpt on same pce* **6/1[2]**

0650 6 *¾* **Levelled**[2] 3820 10-8-12 **45** .......... RKeogh[(3)] 18 38
(DWChapman) *in tch: rdn along 2f out: drvn and one pce appr last* **16/1**

0600 7 *shd* **Percy Douglas**[12] 3524 4-8-10 **43** ..........(t) MStainton[(3)] 17 35
(MissAStokell) *sn rdn along towards rr: hdwy 2f out: styd on strly ins last: nrst fin* **25/1**

0000 8 *½* **Pompey Blue**[18] 3344 3-8-13 **54** .......... KJackson[(6)] 3 44
(PJMcbride) *cl up far side: hdwy to ld that gp 2f out: sn rdn and one pce appr last* **33/1**

3000 9 *hd* **Ballybunion (IRE)**[2] 3820 5-9-3 **52** .......... PJBenson[(5)] 1 42
(DNicholls) *dwlt and towards rr far side: hdwy after 2f: cl up 2f out: sn rdn and one pce appr last* **9/1**

5400 10 *nk* **Joyce's Choice**[2] 3820 5-9-1 **48** ..........(b[1]) BO'Neill[(3)] 15 37
(JSWainwright) *s.i.s and bhd tl sme late hdwy* **20/1**

0006 11 *hd* **Attorney**[7] 3663 6-8-13 **46** ..........(v) LucyRussell[(3)] 2 34
(DShaw) *chsd ldrs far side: rdn along 2f out: sn one pce* **12/1**

0430 12 *½* **So Sober (IRE)**[52] 2350 6-8-7 **40** .......... StaceyRenwick[(3)] 6 26
(DShaw) *chsd ldrs centre: rdn along 2f out: sn wknd* **25/1**

-000 13 *½* **Rum Destiny (IRE)**[2] 3820 5-8-12 **47** ..........(v) CEly[(5)] 11 32
(JSWainwright) *in tch centre: rdn along over 2f out: sn n o imp* **40/1**

-000 14 *1 ¾* **College Hippie**[23] 3169 5-8-12 **45** ..........(b[1]) SYourston[(3)] 5 23
(JFCoupland) *chsd ldrs centre: rdn along 2f out: sn wknd* **40/1**

0050 15 *nk* **Boanerges (IRE)**[10] 3575 7-9-5 **55** ..........(p) CJDavies[(6)] 7 32
(JMBradley) *a towards rr* **16/1**

1605 16 *1* **Red Leicester**[7] 3680 4-8-13 **51** ..........(v) JRoberts[(8)] 4 25
(JAGlover) *led far side gp: rdn along and hdd 2f out: sn wknd* **15/2[3]**

6600 17 *¾* **Juwwi**[4] 3772 10-8-12 **50** .......... HazelBoyd[(8)] 14 21
(JMBradley) *sn outpcd and bhd* **16/1**

0602 18 *nk* **Scary Night (IRE)**[17] 3378 4-8-13 **51** ..........(p) KPierrepont[(8)] 8 21
(JBalding) *in tch: rdn along 1/2-way: sn btn* **16/1**

0-00 **19** *11* **Miss Ceylon**[21] 3249 4-8-8 **41**............ ARutter(3) 16 —
(SPGriffiths) *bhd fr 1/2-way* **25/1**

62.65 secs (1.23) **Going Correction** +0.30s/f (Good)
**WFA** 3 from 4yo+ 5lb **19** Ran SP% **132.9**
Speed ratings: **102,101,98,98,95 94,94,93,93,92 92,91,90,88,87 85,84,84,66**CSF £183.41 CT £853.93 TOTE £16.50: £3.30, £4.60, £1.60, £6.00; EX 454.50.
**Owner** Mrs J Mandle **Bred** P G Airey And R R Whitton **Trained** Orton, Cumbria

**FOCUS**
Those drawn high held the call.

**NOTEBOOK**
**Rosie's Result** has been struggling for form of late but ran a bit better at Beverley last time, although it was difficult to see how he could reverse the form with Larky's Lob. He stayed on well to get up near the line, but this was a modest heat and a repeat performance next time is far from guaranteed.
**Roan Raider(USA)** remains a maiden after 32 starts, but he did little wrong here, coming down the centre of the track and only being headed in the final yards.
**Larky's Lob** never quite got to the lead, which seems crucial to his performance, and he could not confirm Beverley form with Rosie's Result.
**Kennington**, wearing blinkers instead of a visor, showed plenty of speed for a horse who has won over seven furlongs.
**Le Meridien(IRE)**, wearing cheekpieces instead of a visor, ran well enough from her good draw, but she appears to reserve his best for Beverley.
**Levelled**, another Beverley also-ran, shaped better from a good draw here.

## 3865 RECTANGLE GROUP NOVICE STKS 6f
**7:10** (7:11) (D) 2-Y-O **£4,945** (£1,521; £760; £380) **Stalls** High

Form RPR
1 **1** **Abraxas Antelope (IRE)**[36] 2780 2-9-4 ............ RWinston 5 101+
(JHowardJohnson) *cl up tl pushed along and sltly outpcd 1/2-way: swtchd wd and hdwy over 1f out: rdn to ld ins last: styd on gamely* **7/2**[3]
1220 **2** *1 1/4* **Dario Gee Gee (IRE)**[30] 2954 2-9-1 ............ NCallan 2 94
(KARyan) *cl up: effrt to ld over 1f out: sn rdn: drvn and hdd ins last: kpt on* **3/1**[2]
1 **3** *5* **Sir Anthony (IRE)**[21] 3248 2-9-1 ............ FLynch 7 79
(BSmart) *s.i.s and bhd: hdwy 1/2-way: rdn wl over 1f out kpt on same pce* **14/1**
1 **4** *nk* **Krynica (USA)**[25] 3123 2-8-13 ............ KFallon 3 76
(SirMichaelStoute) *cl up: effrt to chal 2f out: rdn and edgd rt over 1f out: sn btn* **6/1**
221 **5** *4* **Harvest Warrior**[13] 3476 2-9-1 ............ DaleGibson 1 66
(TDEasterby) *sn led: rdn along wl over 2f out: hdd and wkng whn bdly hmpd over 1f out* **9/4**[1]
1 **6** *22* **Elgin Marbles**[79] 1686 2-8-13 ............ JFanning 4 —
(RHannon) *trckd ldrs: effrt 1/2-way: sn rdn and wknd 2f out: eased* **8/1**
0 **7** *2 1/2* **Cadogen Square**[13] 3469 2-8-6 ............ DarrenWilliams 6 —
(DWChapman) *trckd ldrs: rdn along 1/2-way: sn outpcd and bhd: eased* **200/1**

1m 15.93s (1.65) **Going Correction** +0.30s/f (Good) **7** Ran SP% **110.6**
Speed ratings: **101,99,92,92,86 57,54**CSF £13.41 TOTE £4.50: £2.70, £2.50; EX 14.00.
**Owner** Andrea & Graham Wylie **Bred** Gerry Flannery **Trained** Crook, Co Durham

**FOCUS**
This looked a decent event, with six previous winners lining up. The pace was good for the grade and the form looks strong.

**NOTEBOOK**
**Abraxas Antelope(IRE)**, the only Gimcrack entry in the line-up, had made a good impression on his debut and the easing of the ground looked sure to suit him. It was still a good performance to give weight and a beating to his six rivals, though, and he certainly looks worth trying in Group company.
**Dario Gee Gee(IRE)**, the most experienced of these, finished eighth at Royal Ascot and found this level more suitable. He was receiving 3lb from the winner, though, so it is difficult to see him reversing the form if they were to meet again.
**Sir Anthony(IRE)** struggled to go the early pace but stayed on well to be third. He was beaten a fair wayy by the first two, but will be suited by another furlong.
**Krynica(USA)**, whose Pontefract form did not look that strong, was found out in this better grade, although the easier ground may have been against her.
**Harvest Warrior** showed plenty of speed early on but he was already beating a retreat when badly hampered and almost brought down a furlong out.
**Elgin Marbles** ran as though something was amiss.

## 3866 RASCAL.UK.COM VIP HOSPITALITY H'CAP 1m 4f
**7:40** (7:40) (D) (0-80,75) 3-Y-0+ **£5,652** (£1,739; £869; £434) **Stalls** Low

Form RPR
2231 **1** **Dickie Deadeye**[6] 3695 7-8-1 **57**............ RThomas(5) 1 72+
(GBBalding) *mde all: clr over 4f out: rdn wl over 1f out: kpt on wl fnl f* **4/6**[1]
5230 **2** *2 1/2* **Field Spark**[22] 3199 4-8-6 **57**............(p) FNorton 4 63
(JAGlover) *towards rr: hdwy over 4f out: rdn along 3f out: drvn and styd on fnl 2f: nt rch wnr* **10/1**[3]
0106 **3** *1/2* **Maritime Blues**[30] 2964 4-8-13 **64**............ BDoyle 8 69
(JGGiven) *midfield: hdwy to chse ldng pair over 4f out: drvn to chse wnr over 2f out: kpt on same pce* **16/1**
0234 **4** *20* **Night Sight (USA)**[19] 3300 7-9-4 **69**............ KFallon 2 44
(MrsSLamyman) *in tch: hdwy to chse wnr 5f out: rdn over 3f out: wknd over 2f out* **7/2**[2]
0-60 **5** *7* **Secret Jewel (FR)**[18] 3348 4-9-6 **71**............ KMcEvoy 3 36
(LadyHerries) *a bhd* **12/1**
3200 **6** *7* **Midshipman Easy (USA)**[19] 3292 3-8-10 **74**............ MFenton 6 28
(PWHarris) *a towards rr* **20/1**
0060 **7** *26* **Zan Lo (IRE)**[41] 2659 4-8-4 **55**............ JQuinn 7 —
(BSRothwell) *chsd ldng pair to 1/2-way: sn wknd* **66/1**
-500 **8** *dist* **Prince Holing**[13] 3474 4-9-10 **75**............ RWinston 5 —
(MTodhunter) *cl up: rdn along 1/2-way and sn wknd* **22/1**

2m 42.67s (6.97) **Going Correction** +0.375s/f (Good)
**WFA** 3 from 4yo+ 13lb **8** Ran SP% **115.5**
Speed ratings: **91,89,89,75,71 66,49,—**CSF £8.54 CT £60.16 TOTE £1.80: £1.10, £2.90, £3.00; EX 9.00.
**Owner** Miss B Swire **Bred** Miss B Swire **Trained** Kimpton,Hants

**FOCUS**
An ordinary handicap in which the pace was slow.

**NOTEBOOK**
**Dickie Deadeye**, who got away with not having to carry a penalty as his win six days earlier was in an apprentices' event, made every yard again and was never really under any threat. His mark goes up 13lb from Saturday so things will be tougher in future, however.
**Field Spark** stayed on from the back of the field but never threatened the winner. His best form is on faster ground.
**Maritime Blues** went in pursuit of the winner but it was a lost cause. His effort cost him second place but he finished well clear of the rest. *Official explanation: jockey said gelding had no more to give in closing stages*
**Night Sight(USA)**, who has not won for over two years, prefers quicker ground, but this was still a disappointing effort.

## 3867 REAL RADIO "WINNERS" FILLIES' H'CAP 7f
**8:10** (8:12) (C) (0-95,93) 3-Y-0+ **£9,646** (£2,968; £1,484; £742) **Stalls** High

Form RPR
3504 **1** **Scotland The Brave**[6] 3623 4-8-5 **66**............(p) KMcEvoy 5 76
(JDBethell) *led: rdn along over 2f out: hdd wl over 1f out: rallied gamely u.p to ld ins last: edgd rt and styd on wl* **12/1**
3040 **2** *3/4* **Raphael (IRE)**[5] 3755 5-9-2 **77**............ RWinston 4 85
(TDEasterby) *trckd ldrs: hdwy 2f out: rdn to challenge over 1f out: drvn and styng on wehn n.m.r wl ins last* **5/1**[2]
0543 **3** *nk* **Play That Tune**[6] 3717 4-10-0 **89**............ JFanning 9 96
(MJohnston) *cl up: led wl over 1f out: sn rdn and hdd ins last: hld whn n.m.r and swtchd lft nr fin* **5/2**[1]
005 **4** *3* **Starbeck (IRE)**[6] 3691 6-9-7 **82**............ PMcCabe 7 87+
(PHowling) *dwlt and towards rr: hdwy whn hmpd over 2f out: swtchd rt and styd on wl under pessre aproaching last: nrst fin* **9/1**
-040 **5** *1/2* **Totally Yours (IRE)**[29] 2971 3-9-6 **89**............ RMullen 2 88
(WRMuir) *hld up in tch: hdwy 2f out: sn rdn and kpt on same pce ent last* **20/1**
0010 **6** *shd* **Flashing Blade**[12] 3536 4-8-7 **68**............(t) WSupple 11 66
(BAMcmahon) *keen: in tch: effrt over 2f out: sn rdn and one pce appr last* **9/1**
-206 **7** *1 1/2* **Favour**[17] 3372 4-8-10 **71**............ KFallon 3 66
(MrsJRRamsden) *hld up: hdwy and n.m.r 2f out: sn rdn and no imp* **13/2**
3005 **8** *1 1/2* **Bint Royal (IRE)**[4] 3779 6-7-13 **60** oh4 ow1............(p) JQuinn 6 51
(MissVHaigh) *chsd ldrs: rdn along 3f out: drvn 2f out and grad wknd* **20/1**
0-63 **9** *shd* **Strong Hand**[100] 1284 4-8-12 **78**............ PMulrennan(5) 1 69
(MWEasterby) *chsd ldrs on outer: rdn along over 2f out: sn wknd* **6/1**[3]
6-30 **10** *3 1/2* **Surf The Net**[29] 2971 3-9-6 **92**............ DaneO'Neill 10 74
(RHannon) *cl up: rdn along 3f out: sn wknd* **11/1**
0 **11** *17* **Live Wire Lucy (USA)**[32] 2913 3-9-10 **93**............ JFEgan 8 32
(CTinkler) *a rr* **50/1**

1m 29.98s (2.17) **Going Correction** +0.30s/f (Good)
**WFA** 3 from 4yo+ 8lb **11** Ran SP% **120.4**
Speed ratings: **99,98,97,94,93 93,91,90,90,86 66**CSF £71.15 CT £206.63 TOTE £16.70: £3.90, £2.10, £1.80; EX 116.10.
**Owner** Robert Gibbons **Bred** R F Gibbons **Trained** Middleham Moor, N Yorks
■ Stewards Enquiry : P McCabe two-day ban: used whip with excessive frequency and down the mare's shoulder in the forehand position (Jul 26-27)

**FOCUS**
No great pace on, and that favoured those who raced prominently.

**NOTEBOOK**
**Scotland The Brave** has been largely disappointing since her debut, but the first-time cheekpieces worked the oracle and she rallied well once headed to get back up and win. She had the run of the race in front, though, and one wonders if she will repeat this effort.
**Raphael(IRE)** handles cut well and ran a solid race havnig been up there throughout. She remains on a high enough mark, though.
**Play That Tune** had less to do in this grade and was perfectly placed to go and win her race, but she continues to frustrate.
**Starbeck(IRE)** ran a fair race given that she did not get the best of runs, but she simply does not win.
**Totally Yours(IRE)** has had some tough tasks this season and on the balance of her form she looks too high in the handicap.
**Flashing Blade** did not help her chances by racing keenly in this steadily-run affair.
**Favour** *Official explanation: jockey said saddle slipped*
**Strong Hand** needs a longer trip than this.
**Surf The Net** *Official explanation: jockey said filly hung left handed*
**Live Wire Lucy(USA)** *Official explanation: jockey said filly hung right handed throughout; trainer said filly wasn't suited by the good to soft going*

## 3868 SASHA LYONS MEMORIAL TROPHY EBF NOVICE FILLIES' STKS 5f
**8:40** (8:40) (D) 2-Y-O **£4,732** (£1,456; £728; £364) **Stalls** High

Form RPR
31 **1** **Word Perfect**[91] 1415 2-9-2 ............ DaleGibson 1 91
(MWEasterby) *quic kly away and sn clr: rdn along 2f out: drvn ent last and styd on wl* **5/6**[1]
3352 **2** *1 1/2* **Bibury Flyer**[15] 3408 2-8-9 ............ TEDurcan 3 79
(MRChannon) *trckd wnr: hdwy to chal 2f out and ev ch tl drvn and nt qckn ins last* **10/3**[3]
**3** *4* **Pivotal's Princess (IRE)** 2-8-5 ............ WSupple 2 61
(BAMcmahon) *s.i.s: rn green and bhd: hdwy 1/2-way: rdn to chse ldng pair 2f out: sn wknd* **9/4**[2]
050 **4** *9* **Ochil Hills Dancer (IRE)**[12] 3514 2-8-9 ............ VHalliday 4 34
(ACrook) *chsd ldng pair: rdn along 1/2-way: sn outpcd* **16/1**

63.64 secs (2.22) **Going Correction** +0.30s/f (Good) **4** Ran SP% **114.3**
Speed ratings: **94,91,85,70**CSF £4.34 TOTE £1.90; EX 3.10.
**Owner** Mrs Jean Turpin **Bred** Mrs Jean Turpin **Trained** Sheriff Hutton, N Yorks

**NOTEBOOK**
**Word Perfect**, quickly into her stride, gave weight and a beating to her rivals. A likeable filly, she responded well to pressure and, judged on this effort, is going to appreciate a step up to six furlongs.
**Bibury Flyer** once again had to settle for the runner-up position. She has plenty of ability but might be keeping a bit back.
**Pivotal's Princess(IRE)** was slowly away and ran green. Her inexperience found her out against her rivals on this occasion but she should have derived plenty from this.
**Ochil Hills Dancer(IRE)** was out of her depth in this grade.

## 3869 "DONCASTER CHAMBER SPONSORSHIP PREVIEW" H'CAP 1m (R)
**9:10** (9:11) (D) (0-85,84) 3-Y-0+ **£5,652** (£1,739; £869; £434) **Stalls** High

Form RPR
3051 **1** **Parnassian**[12] 3520 4-8-4 **61**............ RThomas(5) 6 81+
(GBBalding) *hld up: smooth hdwy 3f out: led wl over 1f out: rdn and hung rt ent last: sn clr* **5/1**[3]
4103 **2** *5* **Hills Of Gold**[6] 3714 5-9-0 **71**............ PMulrennan(5) 9 77
(MWEasterby) *trckd ldrs: pushed along 3f out: rdn 2f out: styd on u.p ins last* **4/1**[2]
0060 **3** *3/4* **African Sahara (USA)**[9] 3597 5-9-13 **79**............(t) GCarter 2 83
(MissDMountain) *chsd ldrs: rdn along 2f out: kpt on same pce appr last* **9/1**
13 **4** *1 1/4* **Trousers**[12] 3536 5-8-10 **62**............ JFEgan 1 64
(AndrewReid) *led: rdn along over 2f out: hdd wl over 1f out: sn drvn and one pce* **3/1**[1]
4626 **5** *nk* **Topton (IRE)**[9] 3597 10-9-13 **79**............(b) KFallon 3 80
(PHowling) *hld up in rr: hdwy over 2f out: sn rdn and no imp appr last* **6/1**


The Form Book, Raceform Ltd, Compton, RG20 6NL

4251 **6** ¾ **Young Mr Grace (IRE)**[12] 3516 4-9-3 **76** .......................... AMullen(7) 5 76
(TDEasterby) *chsd ldr: rdn along 2f out: sn drvn and wknd* **11/1**
1055 **7** 8 **Open Handed (IRE)**[13] 3471 4-8-1 **53** .......................... (t) JQuinn 4 36
(BEllison) *a rr* **22/1**
5-33 **8** 10 **Mbosi (USA)**[7] 3660 3-9-9 **84** .......................... JFanning 8 46
(MJohnston) *chsd ldrs: rdn along 3f out: sn wknd* **6/1**
0060 **9** 8 **Atlantic Ace**[13] 3470 7-9-4 **70** .......................... FLynch 7 15
(BSmart) *dwlt: a rr* **18/1**

1m 42.64s (2.09) **Going Correction** +0.375s/f (Good)
**WFA** 3 from 4yo+ 9lb **9** Ran SP% **118.2**
Speed ratings: **104,99,98,97,96 95,87,77,69**CSF £26.00 CT £178.38 TOTE £6.30: £1.80, £1.70, £3.20; EX 25.80 Place 6 £54.96, Place 5 £19.25..
**Owner** Miss B Swire **Bred** Miss B Swire **Trained** Kimpton,Hants

**FOCUS**
A 0-85 handicap but the top-weight was rated just 79. A runaway winner in a fair time, and the form should work out.

**NOTEBOOK**
**Parnassian**, whose stable is in good form, had the ground in his favour and, off just a 3lb higher mark, ran away with the race. He looks progressive but the Handicapper may put the brakes on that when he gets a chance to reassess him.
**Hills Of Gold** ran a solid race but never threatened the well-handicapped winner. He did appreciate the return to a mile, though.
**African Sahara(USA)** goes well enough on this sort of ground, but still looks slightly high in the weights.
**Trousers** is another who handles cut in the ground well, and he had the run of the race in front, but he was easily brushed aside in the closing stages.
**Topton(IRE)** is happier on a quicker surface although he has won on this sort of ground before. He won this race last year off a 1lb higher mark, but never came close to repeating that feat this time around.
**Young Mr Grace(IRE)** did not look harshly treated for his Carlisle success, but he made all for that win and was unable to get to the front on this occasion.
T/Plt: £77.70 to a £1 stake. Pool: £43,208.50. 405.90 winning tickets. T/Qpdt: £17.60 to a £1 stake. Pool: £2,827.50. 118.40 winning tickets. JR

## 3658 EPSOM (L-H)
### Thursday, July 15

**OFFICIAL GOING: Good**

## 3870 FTS EBF MEDIAN AUCTION MAIDEN STKS 7f
**6:25** (6:26) (E) 2-Y-O **£4,849** (£1,492; £746; £373) **Stalls** Low

Form RPR
2 **1** **In The Fan (USA)**[26] 3093 2-9-0 .......................... TQuinn 1 83+
(JLDunlop) *mde all: j. path ent st: pushed along and rn green over 2f out: styd on stoutly* **8/11**[1]
**2** 1¼ **Kiswahili** 2-8-9 .......................... SSanders 6 72+
(SirMarkPrescott) *unf: lengthy: lw: trckd ldrs: 4th st: shkn up over 2f out: chsd wnr over 1f out: styd on but no imp ins fnl f* **8/1**[3]
42 **3** 3 **Secret Pact (IRE)**[64] 2035 2-9-0 .......................... RFfrench 7 69
(MJohnston) *chsd wnr: rdn and no imp over 2f out: lost 2nd over 1f out: wl btn after* **5/2**[2]
0 **4** hd **Discomania**[14] 3451 2-9-0 .......................... RHughes 3 69
(RCharlton) *wl in tch: 5th st: effrt over 2f out: shuffled along and outpcd wl over 1f out: kpt on* **20/1**
0 **5** hd **Ball Boy**[14] 3451 2-9-0 .......................... CCatlin 5 68
(MRChannon) *s.i.s: in tch in rr: 6th st: outpcd over 2f out: styd on again ins fnl f* **20/1**
05 **6** 4 **Speagle (IRE)**[26] 3081 2-9-0 .......................... JFortune 4 58
(EJO'Neill) *prom: 3rd st: cl up over 2f out: fdd wl over 1f out* **40/1**
**7** 9 **Yardstick** 2-9-0 .......................... RLMoore 2 36
(SKirk) *w'like: dwlt: a in last pair: 7th and out of tch st: wl bhd fnl 2f* **20/1**
**8** ½ **Mickehaha** 2-9-0 .......................... PDoe 8 34
(IAWood) *w'like: leggy: bkwd: wnt rt s: a in fnl pair: last and wl adrift st: no prog* **50/1**

1m 25.31s (1.36) **Going Correction** +0.175s/f (Good) **8** Ran SP% **116.3**
Speed ratings: **99,97,94,93,93 89,78,78**CSF £6.92 TOTE £1.80: £1.02, £3.00, £1.10; EX 8.80.
**Owner** Oliver Murphy (Dublin) **Bred** C Grosso **Trained** Arundel, W Sussex

**FOCUS**
No more than a fair maiden, but reliable form. The front two were nicely clear and are likely to rate quite a bit higher in time..

**NOTEBOOK**
**In The Fan(USA)**, runner-up in a reasonable Newmarket maiden on his debut, built on that promise to get off the mark. He still showed signs of inexperience, jumping the path on turning in and continually changing his legs, so there should be plenty of improvement to come.
**Kiswahili**, a half-sister to a couple of three-year-old middle-distance winners, out of a 12-furlong scorer, made a pleasing debut and is very much the type to progress with time and distance.
**Secret Pact(IRE)** offered promise on his first two starts, but had not been seen for 64 days and was well held on his return. He is better than this.
**Discomania** did not show a great deal on his debut at Newbury, but this was a little better and he appears to be going the right way.
**Ball Boy** was unable to confirm his debut placings with Discomania and may be more of a nursery type.

## 3871 PINNACLE INSURANCE CLAIMING STKS 7f
**6:55** (6:55) (E) 3-Y-O+ **£4,065** (£1,251; £625; £312) **Stalls** Low

Form RPR
2306 **1** **Lady Mo**[6] 3689 3-8-7 60 .......................... SSanders 7 69
(GGMargarson) *trckd ldrs: 4th st: effrt to chal 2f out: rdn to ld jst over 1f out: styd on wl* **12/1**
1323 **2** 2 **Lord Of The East**[7] 3663 5-9-10 73 .......................... AlexGreaves 4 72
(DNicholls) *walked to post: t.k.h: led for 1f: trckd ldr tl led again 3f out: rdn over 2f out: hdd jst over 1f out: nt qckn* **5/4**[1]
0004 **3** nk **Captain Saif**[14] 3441 4-9-0 75 .......................... (t) RLMoore 10 62
(RHannon) *lw: prom: 3rd st: rdn to chse ldr over 2f out: ev ch jst over 1f out: nt qckn* **7/2**[2]
0000 **4** hd **Arabie**[9] 1328 6-9-2 86 .......................... MartinDwyer 1 63
(IanWilliams) *in tch: 7th st: prog to trck ldrs 2f out: sn rdn and nt qckn: kpt on ins fnl f* **8/1**[3]
650 **5** 2½ **Certain Justice (USA)**[15] 3419 6-9-12 70 .......................... TQuinn 5 67
(PFICole) *hld up: nt handle downhill and 8th st: sn rdn and struggling: no prog tl r.o fnl f* **8/1**[3]
1504 **6** 2 **Espada (IRE)**[8] 3626 8-8-12 52 .......................... (b) SWKelly 6 47
(JAOsborne) *led after 1f to 3f out: wknd over 2f out* **11/1**
0000 **7** ½ **Dexileos (IRE)**[19] 3321 5-8-9 40 .......................... (t) NChalmers(5) 3 48
(ADWPinder) *prom: n.m.r on inner 5f out: 6th and losing pl st: edgd rt and wknd over 2f out* **66/1**
0000 **8** 2 **Social Contract**[2] 3828 7-8-12 48 .......................... CCatlin 9 41
(SDow) *a in rr: last st: sn rdn: no prog* **40/1**
0010 **9** ¾ **Piccleyes**[10] 3593 3-8-8 63 .......................... (b) RHughes 8 43
(RHannon) *racd on outer: hld up: prog and 5th st: no imp on ldrs 2f out: sn wknd* **16/1**

1m 24.01s (0.06) **Going Correction** +0.175s/f (Good)
**WFA** 3 from 4yo+ 8lb **9** Ran SP% **114.7**
Speed ratings: **106,103,103,103,100 98,97,95,94**CSF £27.27 TOTE £11.50: £2.10, £1.20, £1.40; EX 24.90.Captain Saif (no.5) was claimed by N Wilson for £8,000.
**Owner** The Gunnicks Partnership **Bred** Mrs M S Teversham **Trained** Newmarket, Suffolk

**FOCUS**
A claimer contested mainly by disappointing sorts who are on the downgrade now putting questions over the form. The time was decent and the winner, who had quite a task on at the weights, was gaining her first win outside of selling company and running her best race so far on turf.

**NOTEBOOK**
**Lady Mo** had plenty to find with some of these at the weights, but she got a near-perfect run under Seb Sanders and recorded her first win for her current connections in decisive fashion. This was her first success outside of selling company and she is as good as ever.
**Lord Of The East** had 6lb in hand of the eventual winner at the weights, but had no answer to that one's challenge after racing too freely.
**Captain Saif** had 16lb in hand of the winner at the weights, but has been below form all season and did not improve much for the fitting of a tongue tie. He has not won since his two-year-old days, but the £8,000 it cost to claim him here would look pretty cheap if his new connections could get him back in form.
**Arabie** showed nothing on his debut for his current connections on his first run over hurdles on his previous start and was disappointing on this switch back to the Flat, especially considering he was the best in at the weights.
**Certain Justice(USA)** did not go down the hill very well and was unable to get on terms.

## 3872 PINNACLE DIRECT & AFFINITY MARKETING CLASSIFIED STKS 1m 2f 18y
**7:25** (7:28) (D) 3-Y-O+ **£6,906** (£2,125; £1,062; £531) **Stalls** Low

Form RPR
0232 **1** **Rondelet (IRE)**[19] 3294 3-8-7 76 .......................... SSanders 7 85
(RMBeckett) *lw: hld up towards rr: prog and 7th st: stdy hdwy on outer over 2f out: led over 1f out: hanging lft but in command fnl f* **5/1**[2]
4661 **2** 1¼ **Scottish River (USA)**[7] 3662 5-9-4 75 .......................... HayleyTurner(5) 4 88
(MDIUsher) *hld up in last trio: prog 6f out: 9th st: hdwy on outer 2f out: hanging lft and nt qckn over 1f out: kpt on to take 2nd fin* **10/1**
000 **3** hd **Kentucky King (USA)**[56] 2237 4-9-7 79 .......................... JFortune 16 86
(PWHiatt) *racd in midfield: prog and 6th st: hdwy on outer over 2f out: rdn and ev ch over 1f out: one pce fnl f* **40/1**
1103 **4** nk **Tidal**[6] 3699 5-9-0 74 .......................... RHughes 15 78
(AWCarroll) *led after 1f: rdn and hdd over 1f out: one pce* **4/1**[1]
5123 **5** 5 **Eton (GER)**[11] 3557 8-9-3 73 .......................... AlexGreaves 14 72
(DNicholls) *t.k.h: prom: 3rd st: bmpd along to chse ldr briefly 2f out: wknd jst over 1f out* **20/1**
4-00 **6** 1½ **Travelling Band (IRE)**[13] 3477 6-8-12 77 .......................... TBlock(7) 3 71
(AMBalding) *hld up towards rr: 11th st: effrt over 2f out: one pce and no imp on ldrs* **33/1**
64-1 **7** nk **Waziri (IRE)**[41] 2648 3-8-8 77 .......................... SDrowne 10 71
(HMorrison) *racd in midfield: 10th and rdn st: sn struggling: no prog fnl 2f* **5/1**[2]
0110 **8** 2½ **Acomb**[36] 2781 4-9-5 77 .......................... JPMurtagh 11 66
(MWEasterby) *prom: cl 4th st: wknd 2f out* **9/1**[3]
5-50 **9** nk **Ryan's Future (IRE)**[166] 649 4-9-7 79 .......................... CCatlin 1 68
(JAkehurst) *hld up wl in rr: 14th st: pushed along over 2f out: no prog tl styd on wl fnl f: nvr nr ldrs* **25/1**
0032 **10** 1¾ **Whitgift Rock**[12] 3535 3-8-6 73 .......................... MartinDwyer 6 61
(SDow) *led for 1f: pressed ldr tl wknd rapidly 2f out* **12/1**
2354 **11** 2 **Analyze (FR)**[21] 3239 6-9-3 72 .......................... RLMoore 5 57
(BGPowell) *a towards rr: 12th and rdn st: no prog and sn btn* **25/1**
2014 **12** 1 **Katiypour (IRE)**[38] 2737 7-9-0 75 .......................... LisaJones(3) 9 55
(MissBSanders) *trckd ldrs: 5th st: wknd 2f out: eased* **9/1**[3]
4023 **13** 3½ **Just A Fluke (IRE)**[21] 3238 3-8-8 77 .......................... RFfrench 2 51
(MJohnston) *lw: hld up in rr: last and struggling st: sn wl bhd: plodded on fnl f* **12/1**
0010 **14** 1¾ **Lilli Marlane**[12] 3534 4-9-0 72 .......................... WRyan 13 43
(NACallaghan) *hld up in last trio: 13th st: sn no prog: wknd over 1f out* **16/1**
3253 **15** 10 **Perfidious (USA)**[152] 768 6-9-3 73 .......................... DSweeney 12 28
(JRBoyle) *chsd ldrs: 8th and losing pl st: sn no ch: eased* **20/1**

2m 9.77s (1.07) **Going Correction** +0.175s/f (Good)
**WFA** 3 from 4yo+ 11lb **15** Ran SP% **126.3**
Speed ratings: **102,101,100,100,96 95,95,93,92,91 89,89,86,84,76**CSF £51.44 TOTE £8.00: £2.80, £3.60, £15.20; EX 112.10.
**Owner** Richard A Pegum & Mrs Richard Aykroyd **Bred** Mount Coote Stud,Richard Pegum And M Bell Racing **Trained** Lambourn, Berks

**FOCUS**
Tidal was clear at the weights following her recent third in a Group Three, but she was unable to reproduce the form. The rest of the field were separated by just 3lb, so it looked pretty tight on the figures, though not many showed their form.

**NOTEBOOK**
**Rondelet(IRE)** had been in good from this season without managing to win a race, but he attracted good market support and gained a deserved victory in convincing fashion. There should be more to come now he has finally got his head in front.
**Scottish River(USA)**, successful in a modest handicap over course and distance on his previous start, continues in good form, but was readily held by the winner.
**Kentucky King(USA)** has never won beyond a mile, but this trip did not appear to pose a problem and he returned to form with a good effort.
**Tidal** was theoretically very well in at the weights, as she is due to go up to a mark of 87 following her recent third in a Chepstow Group Three, but she was unable to take advantage despite appearing to have every chance. Her new rating will make things tough, but the Handicapper will surely have a rethink now.
**Eton(GER)** may find things easier back in claiming company.
**Waziri(IRE)** failed to build on his successful reappearance and was disappointing.

## 3873 PINNACLE WARRANTY SERVICES H'CAP 1m 4f 10y
**7:55** (8:00) (E) (0-75,75) 3-Y-O+ **£5,460** (£1,680; £840; £420) **Stalls** Centre

Form RPR
2-11 **1** **Flying Spirit (IRE)**[20] 2798 5-9-8 **69** .......................... RLMoore 3 82+
(GLMoore) *trckd ldr: pushed along over 5f out: led ent st and kicked on: styd on strly fnl 2f* **10/3**[2]

3065 **2** 2 ½ **Rajam**[22] 3199 6-9-12 **73** (v) AlexGreaves 7 82
(DNicholls) *hld up in tch: 6th st: prog to chse wnr over 2f out: drvn and hanging lft after: no imp over 1f out* **10/1**

0203 **3** 2 **Pay The Silver**[35] 2798 6-9-4 **65** (p) TPQueally 5 71
(IAWood) *lw: settled in last pair: 7th st: rdn 3f out: kpt on one pce to take 3rd ins fnl f* **7/1**

3450 **4** ¾ **Most-Saucy**[23] 3181 8-8-5 **57** HayleyTurner(5) 8 62
(IAWood) *in rr: rdn 1/2-way: last st: effrt on outer 3f out: kpt on one pce fnl 2f* **4/1**[3]

3621 **5** ¾ **Man The Gate**[7] 3658 5-8-10 **57** SSanders 6 60+
(PDCundell) *lw: w.w: nt clr run on inner 4f out: 5th st: hmpd on inner over 2f out: chsd ldng pair 1f out: no imp: wknd last 100yds* **3/1**[1]

2441 **6** 3 ½ **Isa'Af (IRE)**[5] 3743 5-9-6 **70** 6ex LPKeniry(3) 1 68
(PWHiatt) *mde most tl ent st: losing pl whn n.m.r over 2f out: wknd over 1f out* **8/1**

-502 **7** 3 **Keep On Movin' (IRE)**[12] 3528 3-9-1 **75** JFortune 9 68
(TGMills) *uns rdr on way to post: trckd ldrs: 3rd st: rdn wl over 2f out: wknd wl over 1f out: eased* **10/1**

630- **8** dist **Sir Alfred**[314] 4710 5-8-11 **58** EAhern 2 —
(AKing) *swtg: chsd ldng pair: 4th and wkng st: sn bhd: virtually p.u fnl f* **25/1**

2m 41.76s (3.04) **Going Correction** +0.175s/f (Good)
**WFA** 3 from 5yo+ 13lb **8** Ran SP% **113.7**
Speed ratings: **96,94,93,92,92 89,87,**—CSF £35.64 CT £217.80 TOTE £3.00: £1.70, £3.50, £2.10; EX 41.00.
**Owner** Richard Green (fine Paintings) **Bred** Sean Madigan **Trained** Woodingdean, E Sussex

**FOCUS**
Just a modest handicap, but another career-best from Flying Spirit.

**NOTEBOOK**
**Flying Spirit(IRE)** is as well as ever and completed the hat-trick in good style. He will be hard to beat when he attempts the four-timer, either under a penalty or when reassessed, but could be given another spin over hurdles in the meantime. A lower All-Weather mark also gives connections more options.
**Rajam** came from off the pace, but was no match for the bang in-form winner.
**Pay The Silver**, 4lb lower than when last successful, runs most of hsi bets races in bigger fields and took an age to pick up. He has an All-Weather mark of 59 and could be worth another try on the dirt.
**Most-Saucy**, successful in this race last year off a 7lb lower mark, was never really going that well and was unable to pose a threat. She looks worth try over further.
**Man The Gate**, 6lb lower than in future off the back of a convincing win in a course and distance apprentice race the previous week, would have been at least second with a clear run. *Official explanation: jockey said gelding hung left in final furlong*
**Isa'Af(IRE)**, dropped two furlongs in trip, was easy to back and below form.
**Sir Alfred** *Official explanation: jockey said gelding lost its action*

## 3874 PINNACLE CREDITOR H'CAP 7f
8:25 (8:26) (D ) (0-80,80) 3-Y-O **£8,326** (£2,562; £1,281; £640) **Stalls** Low

Form RPR

0336 **1** **Pickle**[10] 3589 3-8-4 **63** MartinDwyer 7 73
(SCWilliams) *b.off hind: trckd ldrs: cl 4th st: plld out and effrt 2f out: rdn to ld jst over 1f out: styd on wl* **5/1**[3]

-003 **2** 1 ¾ **Yashin (IRE)**[20] 3271 3-7-11 **59** FPFerris(3) 4 64
(MHTompkins) *mde most: rdn and hrd pressed over 2f out: hdd jst over 1f out: one pce fnl f* **16/1**

4421 **3** ½ **Here To Me**[13] 3486 3-8-13 **72** RLMoore 6 76
(RHannon) *w ldr: rdn over 2f out: ev ch jst over 1f out: nt qckn and btn ins fnl f* **8/1**

0565 **4** ¾ **Head Boy**[70] 1908 3-7-9 **57** oh4 LisaJones(3) 8 59
(SDow) *n.m.r s: in rr: 8th and out of tch st: effrt u.p and nt clr run briefly 2f out: r.o over 1f out: nvr nrr* **33/1**

1222 **5** ¾ **Tony The Tap**[20] 3273 3-9-7 **80** TQuinn 5 80
(NACallaghan) *hld up: 6th st: sn pushed along: effrt on wd outside 2f out: one pce and nvr rchd ldrs* **10/3**[2]

1524 **6** 1 ¾ **Place Cowboy (IRE)**[12] 3542 3-9-4 **77** EAhern 3 72
(JAOsborne) *lw: hld up: nt handle downhill: rdn in 7th st: one pce fr over 2f out and nvr on terms w ldrs* **9/4**[1]

5000 **7** ½ **Mr Hullabalou (IRE)**[17] 3384 3-8-6 **65** MHenry 9 59
(RIngram) *trckd ldrs: 3rd st: rdn over 2f out: wknd wl over 1f out* **33/1**

306- **8** 3 ½ **Darla (IRE)**[259] 5835 3-8-11 **70** JPMurtagh 1 55
(JWPayne) *trckd ldrs: cl 5th st: unable qck over 2f out: wknd wl over 1f out* **16/1**

-025 **9** 5 **Raysoot (IRE)**[24] 3155 3-7-13 **58** JMcAuley 2 30
(ACStewart) *sn in last: bdly outpcd downhill and wl adrift st: no prog after* **11/2**

1m 24.32s (0.37) **Going Correction** +0.175s/f (Good) **9** Ran SP% **114.7**
Speed ratings: **104,102,101,100,99 97,97,93,87**CSF £79.49 CT £622.55 TOTE £6.10: £2.00, £3.60, £1.90; EX 99.70.
**Owner** S P Tindall **Bred** Simon Tindall **Trained** Newmarket, Suffolk

**FOCUS**
Ordinary form, but even though the two market leaders both disappointed the pace was decent and the form looks reasonably sound.

**NOTEBOOK**
**Pickle** had her excuses on her last couple of runs, but there no problems this time around and she gained her second career success off an 8lb higher mark than when first winning. She is clearly progressing and could now head to Leicester for a valuable fillies' handicap.
**Yashin(IRE)** ran her best race to date on this step up from claiming company and drop in trip. She is going the right way and should be able to find a similar race.
**Here To Me**, off the mark over six furlongs at Warwick on her previous start, was back on her highest-ever rating. Stepped back up a furlong in trip, she posted a fair effort.
**Head Boy**, racing from 4lb out of the handicap, came from a very unpromising position to grab fourth despite not getting the clearest of runs. A promising effort.
**Tony The Tap**, a beaten favourite or joint favourite on his last three starts, failed to convince on this step up from five furlongs.
**Place Cowboy(IRE)** did not handle the hill very well on the home bend and this run is best forgotten. *Official explanation: jockey said colt was unsuited by good ground*
**Raysoot(IRE)**, a beaten favourite on his last two starts, ran a shocker and may not have been suited by the track.

## 3875 PINNACLE INVESTMENTS MAIDEN H'CAP 1m 114y
8:55 (8:56) (E ) (0-70,70) 3-Y-O **£4,290** (£1,320; £660; £330) **Stalls** Low

Form RPR

00-5 **1** **Desert Reign**[118] 1052 3-9-2 **65** TPQueally 13 71+
(APJarvis) *lw: trckd ldrs: 6th and gng easily st: chsd ldr 2f out: sn rdn and wandering: led jst ins fnl f: drvn and hld on* **6/1**[2]

00-0 **2** nk **Quarrymount**[64] 2029 3-8-6 **55** SSanders 15 61+
(SirMarkPrescott) *settled in midfield: 10th and wl in tch st: prog on outer 2f out: drvn and styd on wl fnl f: gaining at fin* **7/1**[3]

0023 **3** nk **Archerfield (IRE)**[14] 3441 3-8-10 **59** (t) EAhern 12 64
(JWHills) *racd in midfield: 9th st: prog on wd outside over 2f out: pressed wnr ins fnl f: hld and lost 2nd nr fin* **14/1**

0-40 **4** ¾ **Iffy**[12] 3527 3-8-9 **58** SCarson 9 61
(PDCundell) *towards rr: 11th and pushed along st: effrt u.p over 2f out: styd on wl fnl f: nrst fin* **9/1**

5024 **5** 3 ½ **Iphigenia (IRE)**[7] 3684 3-9-2 **65** RLMoore 16 61+
(PWHiatt) *prom: 3rd st: led over 2f out and kicked 2l clr: hdd & wknd jst ins fnl f* **16/1**

40-0 **6** 1 ½ **Treason Trial**[14] 3447 3-8-13 **62** GBaker 10 55
(NTinkler) *n.m.r s: hld up in rr: 14th and plenty to do st: prog over 2f out: hanging lft after: nt rch ldrs* **33/1**

3064 **7** nk **Little Eye (IRE)**[10] 3589 3-8-13 **62** (v) NPollard 11 54
(JRBest) *chsd ldrs: 7th and pushed along st: no prog over 2f out: kpt on same pce fr over 1f out* **16/1**

-540 **8** 1 ¼ **Geller**[14] 3452 3-9-5 **68** RHughes 2 58
(RHannon) *led for 1f: trckd ldr tl led again over 3f out to over 2f out: wknd over 1f out* **20/1**

2023 **9** ½ **Adorata (GER)**[6] 3708 3-9-5 **68** OUrbina 5 57
(JJay) *wl in rr: 13th st: rdn and effrt 3f out: hung lft fr 2f out: no prog after* **12/1**

2540 **10** 3 ½ **Jarvo**[12] 3527 3-8-6 **62** (t) StevenHarrison(7) 6 43
(NPLittmoden) *prom: 4th st: rdn and wknd 2f out: no ch whn bdly hmpd on inner 1f out* **33/1**

0-03 **11** 6 **Growler**[31] 2931 3-8-8 **57** TQuinn 1 26
(JLDunlop) *prom: 5th and rdn st: struggling 3f out: wknd* **12/1**

0-00 **12** nk **Blue Java**[23] 3180 3-8-12 **61** SDrowne 4 29
(HMorrison) *b.hind: dwlt: wl in rr: 12th and rdn st: no prog* **11/1**

3233 **13** 7 **Resplendent King (USA)**[11] 3556 3-9-7 **70** (b) JFortune 14 23
(TGMills) *led after 1f to over 3f out: sn wknd* **7/1**[3]

00-0 **14** 8 **Hum (IRE)**[9] 3609 3-8-2 **56** (p) HayleyTurner(5) 7 —
(MissDAMchale) *a wl in rr: 15th and wl bhd st* **66/1**

4-22 **15** 4 **Rosacara**[10] 3589 3-9-3 **66** (t) JPMurtagh 3 —
(DJDaly) *racd in midfield: 8th and pushed along st: jockey looking down 3f out: sn wknd and eased* **11/4**[1]

60-0 **16** dist **Turtle Patriarch (IRE)**[99] 1293 3-8-13 **62** MartinDwyer 8 —
(MrsAJPerrett) *squeezed out and stmbld sn after s: t.o and allowed to coast arnd* **14/1**

1m 47.63s (1.89) **Going Correction** +0.175s/f (Good) **16** Ran SP% **136.9**
Speed ratings: **98,97,97,96,93 92,92,90,90,87 82,81,75,68,64** —CSF £52.40 CT £439.91 TOTE £7.30: £2.00, £3.30, £2.70, £2.80; EX 72.50 Place 6 £136.36, Place 5 £125.31..
**Owner** Allen B Pope **Bred** Miss L C Siddall **Trained** Twyford, Bucks
■ Stewards Enquiry : O Urbina five-day ban: careless riding (Jul 26-30)

**FOCUS**
A modest maiden handicap, but it was run at a fair pace. The first two home were unexposed and look capable of improving further.

**NOTEBOOK**
**Desert Reign**, the subject of serious support in the betting ring, was all-out to land the odds having wandered about under pressure close home. He was well-regarded as a juvenile, but has been plagued with problems since and his recent gelding looks to have done the trick. Clearly open to further improvement, he could be one to follow and should stay further on breeding. *Official explanation: trainer said, regarding the improved form shown, gelding had progressed and was entitled to win a contest of this nature*
**Quarrymount ◆**, a typical improver form the Prescott yard, stayed on strongly in the straight and may well have won in a few more strides. He is at right end of the handicap and, on this evidence, should be hard to beat next time.
**Archerfield(IRE)** , placed in a claimer over course and distance latest, ran well and held every chance. This was an improved effort, but she is fiendishly difficult to win with.
**Iffy** was doing all of his best work too late in the day and shaped as though he could get closer with a step up in distance. This was an encouraging effort.
**Iphigenia(IRE)** had every chance under a positive ride but she is high in the handicap now and might not have stayed.
**Rosacara** was never happy and ran too badly to be true. Something was presumably amiss, as her previous efforts looked to give her every chance in this. *Official explanation: jockey said filly suffered interference in running*
**Turtle Patriarch(IRE)** *Official explanation: jockey said colt suffered interference shortly after the start and lost his action.*
T/Jkpt: £322,364.09 to a £1 stake. Pool: £454,034.00. 1.00 winning ticket. T/Plt: £231.40 to a £1 stake. Pool: £68,371.10. 215.60 winning tickets. T/Qpdt: £184.00 to a £1 stake. Pool: £4,005.20. 16.10 winning tickets. JN

# 3735 HAMILTON (R-H)
Thursday, July 15
**OFFICIAL GOING: Good to firm (good in places)**

## 3876 SHOPMOBILITY MAIDEN AUCTION STKS (A QUALIFIER FOR THE HAMILTON PARK 2-Y-O SERIES FINAL) 6f 5y
2:20 (2:21) (D ) 2-Y-O **£4,842** (£1,490; £745; £372) **Stalls** Low

Form RPR

3 **1** **Propellor (IRE)**[21] 3233 2-8-7 ABeech(3) 5 83
(ADickman) *mde all: rdn and kpt on strly fr 2f out* **7/2**[2]

**2** 2 ½ **Spy King (USA)** 2-8-11 KDarley 4 77
(MJohnston) *chsd ldrs: rdn and outpcd over 2f out: kpt on fnl f: no ch w wnr* **6/1**[3]

053 **3** ¾ **Monash Lad (IRE)**[8] 3633 2-8-8 KFallon 3 71
(MHTompkins) *n.m.r and blkd sn after s: prom: effrt on outside 2f out: hung lft fr 1f out: r.o* **8/13**[1]

**4** 3 **Invertiel (USA)** 2-8-10 RWinston 6 64
(ISemple) *cl up: outpcd whn n.m.r 1f out* **20/1**

0 **5** ½ **Patxaran (IRE)**[38] 2730 2-7-10 DFentiman(7) 1 56
(PCHaslam) *blkd sn after s: sn drvn bhd ldrs: hung rt over 3f out: no imp fr 2f out* **50/1**

**6** 1 ¼ **Arabian Ana (IRE)** 2-8-10 FLynch 2 59
(BSmart) *missed break: a outpcd* **14/1**

1m 11.96s (-1.14) **Going Correction** -0.275s/f (Firm) **6** Ran SP% **111.8**
Speed ratings: **96,92,91,87,87 85**CSF £23.74 TOTE £5.10: £2.00, £4.10; EX 19.00.
**Owner** The Marooned Crew **Bred** T Hirschfeld **Trained** Sandhutton, N Yorks

**FOCUS**
An ordinary maiden in which the winner, who had the favoured rail, fully confirmed debut promise.

**NOTEBOOK**
**Propellor(IRE)** fully confirmed debut promise on this much quicker ground to win with a bit more in hand than the official margin suggests. He is not very big and had the rail to assist, but may well be capable of better.

**Spy King(USA)** ◆, who cost $35,000 and is related to a couple of winners in the United States, looked in need of the run but showed enough to suggest a similar race can be found, especially granted a stiffer test of stamina.
**Monash Lad(IRE)** did not really have the chance the betting suggested nor did he have the run of the race but he was not disgraced and may be capable of picking up a nursery on a more conventional course. He should stay seven furlongs.
**Invertiel(USA)**, who has a bit of physical scope, is related to a couple of winners in the States and showed enough on this racecourse debut before tiring to suggest he has ability and he looks the type to improve in due course.
**Patxaran(IRE)** did not look entirely happy at this course or over this trip, and should do better over further in modest handicap company in due course. *Official explanation: jockey said filly hung right until half way*
**Arabian Ana(IRE)**, who cost 17,000gns and is related to a couple of winners abroad, was easy to back and showed precious little on this racecourse debut. However, he is not a bad type physically and is likely to do better in time.

## 3877 ARTHUR BALDING STKS (H'CAP) 6f 5y
**2:50** (2:52) (E) (0-70,70) 3-Y-0 **£4,436** (£1,365; £682; £341) **Stalls** Low

Form RPR
0-44 **1** **Thornaby Green**[8] 3624 3-8-7 **61** PMakin(5) 9 67
(TDBarron) *trckd far side ldrs: effrt and swtchd lft over 1f out: led ins fnl f: r.o wl* **6/1**[3]
0002 **2** ½ **Lord Baskerville**[8] 3624 3-8-3 **52** JBramhill 7 56
(WStorey) *hld up far side: effrt whn checked over 1f out: kpt on fnl f* **11/2**[2]
5600 **3** *hd* **Turkish Delight**[12] 3530 3-8-8 **57** JEdmunds 1 60
(JBalding) *hld up stands side: effrt to ld that gp appr fnl f: r.o wl fnl f: nt rch far side* **10/1**
2350 **4** 1 ¼ **Fox Covert (IRE)**[15] 3410 3-8-8 **57** (v) RWinston 10 57
(DWBarker) *led far side to ins fnl f: one pce* **11/2**[2]
5000 **5** 2 **Smart Danny**[11] 3562 3-7-7 **47** oh6 BSwarbrick(5) 6 41
(JJQuinn) *in tch far side: sn pushed along: effrt 1/2-way: no imp over 1f out* **5/1**[1]
0-06 **6** *shd* **Calculaite**[8] 3624 3-8-1 **50** PFessey 5 43
(MrsGSRees) *led stands side to appr fnl f: no ex* **14/1**
2224 **7** 3 ½ **Flying Bantam (IRE)**[15] 3410 3-9-4 **70** THamilton(3) 3 53
(RAFahey) *chsd stands side ldrs tl wknd over 1f out* **8/1**
0205 **8** 3 ½ **Sweet Cando (IRE)**[20] 3270 3-9-1 **64** (p) KDarley 8 36
(MissLAPerratt) *chsd far side ldrs tl wknd over 1f out* **6/1**[3]
0205 **9** ¾ **Indrani**[12] 3530 3-7-5 **47** oh4 DFentiman(7) 4 17
(JohnAHarris) *cl up stands side tl wknd over 1f out* **14/1**
0-00 **10** 1 ¼ **Yorke's Folly (USA)**[12] 3517 3-8-5 **54** GFaulkner 2 20
(CWFairhurst) *in tch stands side: brief effrt centre over 1f out: sn wknd* **33/1**

1m 11.53s (-1.57) **Going Correction** -0.275s/f (Firm) **10** Ran SP% **112.5**
Speed ratings: **99,98,98,96,93 93,88,84,83,81**CSF £37.50 CT £328.98 TOTE £7.20: £1.90, £2.90, £2.00; EX 52.90.
**Owner** Thornaby Racing Club **Bred** Mrs S Broadhurst **Trained** Maunby, N Yorks
■ Stewards Enquiry : P Makin caution: careless riding

**FOCUS**
A run of the mill handicap in which the field split into two even groups and there was little advantage in the draw.

**NOTEBOOK**
**Thornaby Green** had conditions to suit and turned in his best effort of the year. He should not be going up too much for this win and looks the sort to improve again for his astute trainer.
**Lord Baskerville** has not been entirely consistent but once again ran creditably, and would have finished even closer had he not met a bit of trouble. He is capable of winning a similar event, but the fact he has yet to score is a bit of a worry.
**Turkish Delight** ◆ turned in easily her best effort of the year to finish clear of those that raced on the stands'-side group and, given she is in very capable hands, appeals as the type to win a similar race in the near future.
**Fox Covert(IRE)** has slipped a fair way in the weights but, although performing creditably, did have the run of the race. Also, the fact he is still winless after 19 starts is a concern.
**Smart Danny**, back up in trip and back on a sound surface, was not disgraced but left the impression that a stiffer test of stamina would be in his favour. He is from a late-maturing family and would not be one to write off yet.
**Calculaite** showed a fair bit of foot to finish second home on the stands'-side group, and this full-brother to the speedy Playtime Blue looks worth a try over five furlongs on either turf or All-Weather surfaces.
**Indrani** *Official explanation: trainer said filly sustained a cut to her off fore knee*

## 3878 DAILY RECORD CONDITIONS STKS 1m 1f 36y
**3:20** (3:23) (C) 3-Y-0 **£9,582** (£3,400; £1,700; £772) **Stalls** High

Form RPR
31-2 **1** **Mister Monet (IRE)**[7] 3671 3-8-12 92 KDalgleish 1 98+
(MJohnston) *mde all: qcknd over 2f out: kpt on strly* **4/7**[1]
1-0 **2** 4 **Always First**[19] 3323 3-9-3 95 KFallon 3 95+
(SirMichaelStoute) *chsd wnr: rdn over 2f out: one pce fnl f* **11/8**[2]
**3** 10 **Banana Grove (IRE)** 3-8-2 PPMathers(7) 2 67?
(ABerry) *hld up in tch: rdn over 3f out: sn outpcd* **100/1**[3]
4054 **4** 1 ¼ **Graceful Air (IRE)**[9] 3609 3-8-7 59 RWinston 4 63?
(JRWeymes) *chsd ldrs tl rdn and outpcd fr over 2f out* **100/1**[3]

1m 55.94s (-3.66) **Going Correction** -0.35s/f (Firm) **4** Ran SP% **107.7**
Speed ratings: **102,98,89,88**CSF £1.59 TOTE £1.50; EX 1.70.
**Owner** Syndicate 2002 **Bred** Barronstown Stud, Orpendale And Mrs T Stack **Trained** Middleham Moor, N Yorks

**FOCUS**
Only two serious contenders who can possibly be rated higher. Although the pace was nothing special and Mister Monet had the run of the race, he appeals as the type to hold his own in more competitive company.

**NOTEBOOK**
**Mister Monet(IRE)** ◆, one of only two serious contenders, had the run of this steadily-run race and showed the right attitude in the closing stages. Although this told us little new about him, he appeals as the type to win more races, even when upped in grade.
**Always First** took the eye in the paddock and ran creditably under his penalty. He shaped as though he will stay further and, given he is open to more improvement, looks sure to win another race
**Banana Grove(IRE)**, a cheap purchase, faced an impossible task at the weights on this racecourse debut and is flattered by his proximity to the first two.
**Graceful Air(IRE)**, exposed as modest, was predictably outclassed.

## 3879 RECTANGLE GROUP CLASSIFIED STKS 1m 65y
**3:55** (4:03) (D) 3-Y-0+ **£5,817** (£1,790; £895; £447) **Stalls** High

Form RPR
2100 **1** **Langford**[9] 3597 4-9-8 85 KFallon 4 79
(MHTompkins) *prom: shkn up to ld 1f out: kpt on wl: eased cl home* **6/4**[1]
1661 **2** *nk* **Woody Valentine (USA)**[14] 3442 3-8-10 82 SChin 6 75
(MJohnston) *chsd ldrs: outpcd over 3f out: rallied over 1f out: kpt on wl* **6/4**[1]
0005 **3** 1 **Anthemion (IRE)**[3] 3797 7-9-3 50 DMcGaffin 2 71?
(MrsJCMcgregor) *led: clr after 2f: hdd 1f out: nt qckn* **100/1**
5036 **4** *nk* **Tedstale (USA)**[13] 3470 6-9-4 81 (b) KDarley 5 71
(TDEasterby) *in tch: effrt 3f out: hung rt over 1f out: no imp towards fin* **3/1**[2]
6056 **5** 11 **Telepathic (IRE)**[3] 3797 4-8-10 57 PPMathers(7) 3 45
(ABerry) *chsd ldr tl wknd over 2f out* **100/1**
1/ **6** 24 **Elsundus (USA)**[1050] 4380 6-9-8 85 RWinston 1 —
(KAMorgan) *s.i.s: lost tch fr 1/2-way* **16/1**[3]

1m 44.84s (-4.46) **Going Correction** -0.35s/f (Firm)
**WFA** 3 from 4yo+ 9lb **6** Ran SP% **112.9**
Speed ratings: **108,107,106,106,95 71**CSF £4.00 TOTE £2.50: £1.80, £1.10; EX 4.50.
**Owner** Marlborough Electronics **Bred** Summertree Stud **Trained** Newmarket, Suffolk
■ Stewards Enquiry : S Chin two-day ban: careless riding (Jul 26,27)

**FOCUS**
A mixed bag and a race in which the third home was allowed to dominate. Although the pace was sound, this bare form does not look entirely reliable.

**NOTEBOOK**
**Langford**, ridden with more restraint than is usually the case, returned to winning ways in this much easier grade and was value for a bit more in hand than the official margin. He will find things much tougher back in handicaps.
**Woody Valentine(USA)**, back in trip, did not look entirely happy over the trip or at this course but ran creditably, especially as a stiffer test of stamina would have suited. He is likely to win more races back over a mile and a quarter.
**Anthemion(IRE)** looked to have a bit to find at the weights but was allowed to do his own thing in front and seemed to excel himself. However, he is almost certainly flattered by his proximity and, as he has not won for over four years, will be one to take on back in handicaps.
**Tedstale(USA)** looked to have a fair chance at the weights and was not disgraced in terms of form but looked a less than easy ride and appears to be saving something for himself. He remains one to tread carefully with.
**Telepathic(IRE)** faced a stiff task on these terms and ran accordingly.
**Elsundus(USA)**, off the course since his debut success nearly three years ago, looked in need of the run on this first start for his current stable but ran poorly.

## 3880 FAMOUS GROUSE PREMIER CLAIMING STKS 1m 1f 36y
**4:30** (4:30) (D) 3-Y-0+ **£5,590** (£1,720; £860; £430) **Stalls** High

Form RPR
2140 **1** **Oldenway**[12] 3521 5-9-9 76 THamilton(3) 6 83
(RAFahey) *mde all: edgd lft u.p over 1f out: r.o wl fnl f* **4/6**[1]
0540 **2** ½ **Leighton (IRE)**[21] 3238 4-9-10 78 SChin 5 80
(JDBethell) *chsd ldrs: outpcd over 3f out: rallied over 1f out: kpt on: hld nr fin* **9/2**[3]
0446 **3** 4 **Millagros (IRE)**[26] 3082 4-9-4 74 TEaves(3) 3 69
(ISemple) *pressed ldr: ev ch tl wknd over 1f out* **3/1**[2]
0040 **4** 9 **Jamestown**[31] 2943 7-9-4 45 ACulhane 4 48
(MJPolglase) *in tch tl wknd over 3f out* **20/1**
5000 **5** *shd* **Stepastray**[9] 3604 7-9-4 41 PFessey 1 48
(REBarr) *hld up in tch: rdn and wknd over 3f out* **66/1**

1m 56.1s (-3.50) **Going Correction** -0.35s/f (Firm) **5** Ran SP% **109.4**
Speed ratings: **101,100,97,89,88**CSF £4.08 TOTE £1.50: £1.10, £1.70; EX 4.00.The winner was bought by M. Stavrou for £30,000. Leighton (IRE) was claimed by Robert Stronge for £25,000.
**Owner** J J Staunton **Bred** Snailwell Stud Co Ltd **Trained** Musley Bank, N Yorks

**FOCUS**
An uncompetitive race in which the winner had the rub of things. Given the gallop was on the steady side this bare form does not look entirely reliable.

**NOTEBOOK**
**Oldenway** is a fairly reliable sort who had a good chance at the weights and the run of the race and got first run on Leighton. He was subsequently claimed for £30,000 but should continue to go well back in handicaps.
**Leighton(IRE)**, well beaten on unsuitably soft ground last time, ran creditably in terms of form but once again did not look an easy ride and will be one to field against from his current mark back in handicap company.
**Millagros(IRE)** looked to have a decent chance at the weights, but was below her best after enjoying the run of the race. She is not the most reliable of performers.
**Jamestown** had plenty to find on these terms and was well beaten. He is not one to place any faith in.
**Stepastray** faced a very stiff task on these terms and was not surprisingly well beaten.

## 3881 SAFFIE JOSEPH & SONS H'CAP 1m 3f 16y
**5:00** (5:00) (E) (0-70,68) 3-Y-0+ **£4,225** (£1,300; £650; £325) **Stalls** High

Form RPR
020/ **1** **Tiger Frog (USA)**[35] 4774 5-8-11 **55** (b) TEaves(3) 4 66+
(JMackie) *prom: reminders over 3f out: rallied to ld over 1f out: kpt on strly* **7/1**[3]
2151 **2** 5 **Hearthstead Dream**[21] 3237 3-8-10 **68** (b) BSwarbrick(5) 6 71
(JDBethell) *in tch: rdn over 3f out: rallied over 1f out: no ch w wnr* **10/1**
5212 **3** *nk* **Sualda (IRE)**[5] 3740 5-9-10 **68** THamilton(3) 5 71
(RAFahey) *led to over 1f out: nt qckn* **6/4**[1]
6003 **4** 1 **Saameq (IRE)**[17] 3369 3-7-12 **51** oh8 PFessey 8 52
(ISemple) *dwlt: effrt centre 2f out: no imp fnl f* **20/1**
1021 **5** 2 ½ **Archirondel**[17] 3369 6-9-5 **60** ACulhane 1 57
(MDHammond) *trckd ldrs: effrt over 2f out: outpcd over 1f out* **7/2**[2]
4104 **6** *shd* **Little Task**[13] 3472 6-7-5 **39** DFentiman(7) 7 36
(JSWainwright) *hld up: rdn over 3f out: btn over 1f out* **7/1**[3]
-221 **7** 1 ½ **Turks And Caicos (IRE)**[149] 804 3-8-5 **58** GFaulkner 2 52
(PCHaslam) *cl up: ev ch over 3f out: wknd over 1f out* **16/1**
-036 **8** ½ **Sherwood Forest**[3] 3794 4-7-10 **44** (v) LeanneKershaw(7) 3 38
(MissLAPerratt) *hld up: rdn over 2f out: hung rt and sn btn* **25/1**

2m 22.27s (-4.23) **Going Correction** -0.35s/f (Firm)
**WFA** 3 from 4yo+ 12lb **8** Ran SP% **110.8**
Speed ratings: **101,97,97,96,94 94,93,93**CSF £68.66 CT £152.11 TOTE £7.10: £1.90, £2.00, £1.10; EX 66.90 Place 6 £33.88, Place 5 £7.29.
**Owner** Fools Who Dream **Bred** Camberwell Investments **Trained** Church Broughton, Derbys

**FOCUS**
An ordinary event in which the gallop was only fair at best and those racing close to the pace were at an advantage.

**NOTEBOOK**
**Tiger Frog(USA)**, a consistent sort over hurdles for current connections, turned in an improved effort back on the Flat and, given that he would have preferred a stiffer test over this trip, may be capable of better, even after reassessment.
**Hearthstead Dream**, having his first run for his new stable, was not disgraced and is not the easiest of rides, but is another that would have preferred a more end-to-end gallop. He should continue to give a good account.

**Sualda(IRE)** had conditions to suit and had the run of the race against the favoured inside rail, but was beaten on merit and looks vulnerable to progressive or well handicapped types from his current mark.
**Saameq(IRE)** was not disgraced from 8lb out of the handicap given that this race favoured those racing prominently, and he looks a bit better than the bare form. He is in good hands and it will be no surprise to see him pick up a small race in due course.
**Archirondel**, 6lb higher than his Musselburgh success, is best held up off a strong pace so, although below his best racing close up in a much more tactical race, would not be one to write off completely just yet.
**Little Task** was not seen to best effect in a race that suited those racing close to the pace, but he is likely to continue to look vulnerable in this grade.
RY

# 3525 LEICESTER (R-H)

Thursday, July 15

**OFFICIAL GOING: Good to firm (good in places)**
Wind: Slight behind Weather: Cloudy

## 3882 RACECOURSE SPONSORSHIP AND ADVERTISING MEDIAN AUCTION MAIDEN STKS — 1m 1f 218y

**2:10** (2:15) (F) 3-4-Y-O — **£3,552** (£1,093; £546; £273) **Stalls** High

Form — RPR

3 **1** **Raakaan**[24] 3161 3-8-9 .................... SDrowne 6 76+
(ACStewart) *chsd ldrs: led over 1f out: edgd rt ins fnl f: r.o wl* **6/4**[1]

0042 **2** *2* **Antigiotto (IRE)**[22] 3213 3-8-9 76 .................... DHolland 1 72+
(LMCumani) *led 3f: chsd ldr tl led over 2f out: rdn and hdd over 1f out: no ex ins fnl f* **5/2**[2]

46 **3** *1* **Warningcamp (GER)**[21] 3245 3-8-9 .................... SSanders 9 71+
(LadyHerries) *dwlt: hld up: hdwy over 2f out: rdn over 1f out: styd on same pce* **7/2**[3]

0 **4** *5* **Disparity (USA)**[22] 3204 3-8-5 ow1 .................... (t) OUrbina 7 57
(JRFanshawe) *hld up in tch: shkn up over 2f out: wknd fnl f* **14/1**

00 **5** *1 3/4* **Bayou Princess**[45] 2513 3-8-4 .................... AMcCarthy 10 53
(BDeHaan) *chsd ldr tl led 7f out: rdn and hdd over 2f out: wknd over 1f out* **100/1**

05 **6** *3* **Welkino's Boy**[9] 3608 3-8-9 .................... DaleGibson 13 52
(JMackie) *prom: rdn over 3f out: wknd over 1f out* **25/1**

**7** *4* **Through The Slips (USA)** 3-8-4 .................... JMackay 2 39
(JGGiven) *s.i.s: sn prom: wknd over 1f out* **25/1**

**8** *5* **Blue Track (IRE)** 3-8-9 .................... SRighton 11 35
(MJAttwater) *s.s: hld up: rdn 1/2-way: a bhd* **66/1**

00 **9** *shd* **Electras Dream (IRE)**[19] 3304 3-7-13 .................... HayleyTurner(5) 5 30
(MrsCADunnett) *plld hrd and prom: wknd over 3f out* **100/1**

0 **10** *17* **Peters Ploy**[20] 3279 4-9-3 .................... J-PGuillambert(3) 8 2
(TKeddy) *chsd ldrs over 6f* **66/1**

**11** *19* **Cromarty Bay** 3-8-4 .................... JQuinn 3 —
(APJames) *s.s and swvd lft: a bhd* **66/1**

2m 8.23s (-0.17) **Going Correction** 0.0s/f (Good)
**WFA** 3 from 4yo 11lb — **11** Ran SP% **111.6**
Speed ratings: **91,89,88,84,83 80,77,73,73,59 44**CSF £4.72 TOTE £2.10: £1.10, £1.10, £1.50; EX 3.50.
**Owner** Sheikh Ahmed Al Maktoum **Bred** Wickfield Farm Partnership **Trained** Newmarket, Suffolk

**FOCUS**
A fair maiden, but one with very little strength in depth.

**NOTEBOOK**
**Raakaan**, whose debut third last time gave him an obvious chance in this, got off the mark tidily and was value for more than the official winning margin. He should enter handicaps on a fair enough mark and is entitled to improve again for this experience.
**Antigiotto(IRE)** turned in another solid effort. Although he is clearly limited, he has improved with every outing and can be placed to win a similar event.
**Warningcamp(GER)** took his time to find his full stride and, when he finally got going, looked a bit unbalanced and could not close on the leaders. He is now eligible for handicaps, got an educational ride this time and should fare much better in that sphere.
**Disparity(USA)** improved on her debut and the tongue tie had a positive effect. She is another who can step up on this form in due course and will stay further.

## 3883 RACEDAY HOSPITALITY (S) STKS — 5f 2y

**2:40** (2:40) (G) 2-Y-O — **£2,898** (£828; £414) **Stalls** Low

Form — RPR

0 **1** **Marcela Zabala**[101] 1264 2-8-6 .................... MFenton 6 51
(JGGiven) *swvd rt s: sn chsng ldr: rdn to ld over 1f out: r.o* **10/1**[3]

2541 **2** *nk* **Straffan (IRE)**[10] 3571 2-8-11 .................... SSanders 5 55
(EJO'Neill) *led: rdn and hdd over 1f out: r.o* **9/4**[1]

6640 **3** *shd* **Turtle Magic (IRE)**[14] 3444 2-7-13 .................... (b[1]) CHaddon(7) 1 50
(WGMTurner) *sn pushed along in rr: hdwy fnl f: nt run on nr fin* **9/4**[1]

0001 **4** *2* **Tipsy Lillie**[12] 3526 2-8-4 .................... MHalford(7) 2 48
(JulianPoulton) *chsd ldrs: rdn 1/2-way: styd on same pce fnl f* **5/2**[2]

000 **5** *1 1/2* **Amalgam (IRE)**[7] 3679 2-8-6 .................... RHavlin 4 37
(MrsPNDutfield) *chsd ldr: rdn 1/2-way: styd on same pce appr fnl f* **40/1**

5000 **6** *3 1/2* **Lane Marshal**[12] 3506 2-8-11 .................... (b) RFfrench 3 30
(MESowersby) *in tch: sn pushed along: wknd wl over 1f out* **11/1**

61.04 secs (0.11) **Going Correction** -0.225s/f (Firm) — **6** Ran SP% **110.0**
Speed ratings: **90,89,89,86,83** 78CSF £31.49 TOTE £11.50: £2.20, £1.90; EX 37.00.There was no bid for the winner. Straffan was bought by Dandy Nicholls for £6,000.
**Owner** Zaha Racing Syndicate **Bred** A Smith **Trained** Willoughton, Lincs
■ Stewards Enquiry : M Fenton one-day ban: excessive use of the whip (Jul 26)
S Sanders caution: used whip with excessive frequency

**FOCUS**
A very poor contest that saw the first three finish in a heap.

**NOTEBOOK**
**Marcela Zabala** stayed on well under pressure to win all-out. She has done well physically since her debut in April, and as she was still distinctly green early this time could improve again, but this looks to be her level.
**Straffan(IRE)**, off the mark in a Bath seller last time, was only narrowly denied. She ran up to her best and is the benchmark for the form. He was claimed afterwards by David Nicholls.
**Turtle Magic(IRE)**, tried in the first-time blinkers, held every chance if good enough, but again looked reluctant to go through with her effort close home. She was only just denied however, and has the ability to land a similarly poor event, but is not one to trust by any means.
**Tipsy Lillie**, winner of a seller over course and distance last time out, was well held and now looks throughly exposed.

## 3884 TOTEPOOL H'CAP — 7f 9y

**3:10** (3:12) (D ) (0-80,80) 3-Y-O+ — **£7,065** (£2,174; £1,087; £543) **Stalls** Low

Form — RPR

-41 **1** **Pintle**[14] 3457 4-9-3 69 .................... KMcEvoy 1 80
(JLSpearing) *racd alone towards stands' side: w ldrs: hung rt and led over 1f out: rdn out* **8/1**

2550 **2** *3/4* **Takes Tutu (USA)**[15] 3409 5-9-8 74 .................... (b) SSanders 3 83
(KRBurke) *racd centre: hld up: hdwy over 1f out: r.o* **8/1**

2015 **3** *3/4* **St Pancras (IRE)**[9] 3597 4-10-0 80 .................... DHolland 7 87
(NACallaghan) *racd centre: sn pushed along and prom: rdn and ev ch over 1f out: styd on* **5/2**[1]

-260 **4** *2* **Magic Amour**[15] 3426 6-8-6 58 .................... PRobinson 4 60
(IanWilliams) *stmbld s: sn led centre: rdn and hdd over 1f out: no ex ins fnl f* **25/1**

1-53 **5** *1/2* **Leoballero**[27] 3052 4-10-0 80 .................... (t) DaneO'Neill 6 80
(DJDaly) *racd centre: hld up: hdwy over 1f out: sn rdn: styd on same pce ins fnl f* **11/2**[3]

2114 **6** *1 3/4* **Alchemist Master**[6] 3714 5-9-8 74 6ex .................... (p) DeanMcKeown 11 70
(RMWhitaker) *racd centre: hld up: hdwy 1/2-way: rdn over 1f out: wknd ins fnl f* **5/1**[2]

0500 **7** *nk* **Roman Maze**[5] 3755 4-8-11 63 .................... SWKelly 10 58
(WMBrisbourne) *s.i.s: racd centre: hld up: rdn over 2f out: nvr trbld ldrs* **9/1**

4201 **8** *1 1/4* **Midnight Ballard (USA)**[20] 3261 3-9-6 80 .................... SCarson 9 71
(RFJohnsonHoughton) *racd centre: w ldrs: rdn and ev ch over 1f out: sn wknd and eased* **14/1**

0024 **9** *1 1/2* **Astrac (IRE)**[15] 3416 13-7-12 50 oh1 .................... PMQuinn 2 37
(MrsALMKing) *racd centre: hld up: rdn over 2f out: n.d* **25/1**

4323 **10** *1 1/4* **Brantwood (IRE)**[14] 3446 4-8-7 59 .................... (t) WSupple 5 43
(BAMcmahon) *chsd ldrs centre over 5f* **11/1**

0240 **11** *2* **The Bonus King**[26] 3079 4-9-12 78 .................... OUrbina 8 56
(JJay) *racd centre: bhd fr 1/2-way* **25/1**

1m 23.6s (-2.50) **Going Correction** -0.225s/f (Firm)
**WFA** 3 from 4yo+ 8lb — **11** Ran SP% **119.4**
Speed ratings: **105,104,103,101,100 98,98,96,94,93 91**CSF £69.87 CT £208.99 TOTE £10.80: £3.80, £3.60, £1.20; EX 61.00 Trifecta £145.30 Pool of £1,043.88 - 5.10 winning tickets.
**Owner** Robert Heathcote **Bred** R And Mrs Heathcote **Trained** Kinnersley, Worcs

**FOCUS**
A fair event run at a reasonable gallop. The form is ordinary but looks sound enough.

**NOTEBOOK**
**Pintle** followed up her recent Yarmouth success in good style off this 4lb higher mark. Having raced alone up the stands'-side rail, she found a fair turn of foot to go clear inside the last furlong, and always looked like holding off the fast-finishing runner-up. She is lightly raced and remains open to further improvement this summer.
**Takes Tutu(USA)** was finishing fast and best of all, but again left the impression that he has his own ideas about the game. He is very well-treated on his old form, yet cannot be backed with any confidence at present.
**St Pancras(IRE)** was not disgraced off his big weight, but ran as though this drop back a furlong was slightly against him. He has found his form again of late and has another prize within his compass.
**Magic Amour** walked out of the gates and had to be rushed up to lead early on, which took its toll late on, as he had nothing more to offer when headed. This was not a bad effort in the circumstances however, and he will find easier opportunites off this mark.
**Leoballero** failed to run up to the form of his latest third at Newmarket and is starting to frustrate.
**Alchemist Master** held every chance, but ran very much as though the Handicapper now has his measure off this much higher mark.
**The Bonus King** *Official explanation: trainer said gelding bled internally*

## 3885 BARNSDALE HALL HOTEL COUNTY AIR AMBULANCE CLAIMING STKS — 1m 3f 183y

**3:45** (3:45) (F) 4-Y-O+ — **£4,075** (£1,254; £627; £313) **Stalls** High

Form — RPR

0001 **1** **Zeis (IRE)**[23] 3173 4-9-4 68 .................... (t) LFletcher(3) 7 67
(HMorrison) *mid-div: hdwy 1/2-way: rdn to ld over 1f out: styd on* **10/3**[2]

0-00 **2** *2 1/2* **Relative Hero (IRE)**[45] 2520 4-8-6 57 .................... (p) JFMcDonald(3) 6 51
(MissSJWilton) *chsd ldrs: rdn over 4f out: ev ch over 1f out: no ex ins fnl f* **80/1**

610- **3** *nk* **Forbearing (IRE)**[18] 5458 7-9-3 73 .................... DHolland 4 59
(MCPipe) *chsd ldrs: rdn over 4f out: nt run on* **10/11**[1]

0/20 **4** *1 1/4* **Cracow (IRE)**[35] 2816 7-8-7 46 .................... AMcCarthy 5 47
(AMHales) *chsd clr ldr tl led 3f out: rdn and hdd over 1f out: no ex* **16/1**

2236 **5** *3 1/2* **Banningham Blaze**[16] 3393 4-8-8 50 .................... TPQueally 9 42
(AWCarroll) *hld up: nt clr run over 3f out: sn rdn: nt trble ldrs* **11/2**[3]

**6** *1 1/2* **Ben's Revenge**[22] 4-8-9 .................... VSlattery 8 41
(MWellings) *s.i.s: hld up: hdwy u.p 4f out: wknd fnl f* **80/1**

4 **7** *2* **Lord Nellsson**[22] 3194 8-9-2 .................... HayleyTurner(5) 2 49
(JSKing) *s.s: outpcd: nvr nrr* **33/1**

6560 **8** *shd* **Lilian**[8] 3637 4-8-0 46 .................... (v) JQuinn 3 28
(MissGayKelleway) *a in rr* **40/1**

0/60 **9** *1/2* **Jazil**[40] 2689 9-8-5 50 .................... (t) DeanMcKeown 10 32
(KAMorgan) *chsd ldrs 8f* **50/1**

64-0 **10** *1 1/2* **Flyoff (IRE)**[26] 3087 7-8-0 45 .................... (v) RThomas(5) 1 30
(KAMorgan) *sn led and clr: hdd 3f out: wknd 2f out* **14/1**

2m 33.87s (-0.81) **Going Correction** 0.0s/f (Good) — **10** Ran SP% **113.2**
Speed ratings: **93,91,91,90,87 86,85,85,85,84**CSF £242.57 TOTE £5.30: £1.60, £9.20, £1.10; EX 310.90.The winner was claimed by P. M. Phelan for £12,000
**Owner** D J Donner **Bred** David Jamison Bloodstock **Trained** East Ilsley, Berks

**FOCUS**
Moderate stuff.

**NOTEBOOK**
**Zeis(IRE)** followed up his Brighton win in relatively decisive fashion, staying on strongly once getting to the lead. With the favourite looking awkward and an 80/1 shot finishing second he probably failed to achieve much, but is at least in good form.
**Relative Hero(IRE)** has run some shockers of late and this signalled a welcome return to form. He is capable of winning if holding this level of form.
**Forbearing(IRE)** had the highest official rating of these but did not look overly keen under pressure. He is one to be wary of at short odds in future.
**Cracow(IRE)** ran in the Derby many years ago and, although obviously not up to that now, he is capable in this grade.

## 3886 INTRODUCTION TO SPONSORSHIP NURSERY — 5f 218y

**4:20** (4:22) (E) 2-Y-O — **£5,629** (£1,732; £866; £433) **Stalls** Low

Form — RPR

206 **1** **Colonel Bilko (IRE)**[48] 2439 2-7-13 65 ow1 .................... FNorton 1 67
(BRMillman) *w ldrs: rdn over 1f out: r.o to ld wl in side fnl f* **16/1**

5334 **2** 1 ½ **Safendonseabiscuit**[11] 3553 2-8-10 **76**................................ KMcEvoy 12 73
(SKirk) *chsd ldrs: rdn to ld 1f out: hdd wl ins fnl f* **8/1**[3]

4111 **3** ½ **Princely Vale (IRE)**[16] 3390 2-8-0 **73**.............................(p) CHaddon(7) 15 68
(WGMTurner) *s.i.s: sn chsng ldrs: led 1/2-way: hung lft and hdd 1f out: styd on* **14/1**

040 **4** nk **Lord John**[59] 2173 2-7-12 **64** oh3........................................ DaleGibson 8 59
(MWEasterby) *chsd ldrs: rdn over 1f out: styd on* **25/1**

4532 **5** nk **Simplify**[8] 3634 2-8-8 **74**...................................................(b) TPQueally 13 68+
(DRLoder) *s.i.s: hld up: hdwy 2f out: sn rdn: nt clr run ins fnl f: styd on* **5/1**[1]

042 **6** 1 ½ **Haroldini (IRE)**[45] 2523 2-8-3 **69**...................................... SCarson 14 58
(MrsPNDutfield) *chsd ldrs: lost pl over 4f out: outpcd 1/2-way: hdwy over 1f out: styd on same pce ins fnl f* **16/1**

2655 **7** ½ **Queen's Glory (IRE)**[8] 3634 2-8-5 **71**..................................... RMullen 7 59
(WRMuir) *prom: rdn whn hmpd ins fnl f: styd on same pce* **25/1**

504 **8** ½ **Ivana Illyich (IRE)**[47] 2481 2-8-5 **71**...................................... JFEgan 2 57
(SKirk) *chsd ldrs: rdn over 2f out: no ex fnl f* **13/2**[2]

0420 **9** 2 **Gavioli (IRE)**[5] 3748 2-8-0 **69**..................................(t) JFMcDonald(3) 11 49
(JMBradley) *hld up: hdwy 1/2-way: wknd fnl f* **20/1**

261 **10** 2 ½ **Chilly Cracker**[28] 3021 2-8-5 **71**.................................. DeanMcKeown 9 43
(RHollinshead) *led to 1/2-way: wknd fnl f* **14/1**

061 **11** ½ **Don't Tell Trigger (IRE)**[45] 2515 2-7-13 **65**............................ JQuinn 6 36
(JSMoore) *chsd ldrs over 4f* **16/1**

2312 **12** 2 **Lincolneurocruiser**[21] 3224 2-9-7 **87**...................................... DAllan 10 52
(JO'Reilly) *prom over 3f* **5/1**[1]

3404 **13** 2 ½ **Gaudalpin (IRE)**[12] 3532 2-8-0 **66**......................................... SRighton 5 23
(MJAttwater) *prom: racd keenly: wknd wl over 1f out* **20/1**

344 **14** 8 **English Fellow**[37] 2758 2-8-12 **78**........................................... WSupple 3 11
(BAMcmahon) *s.i.s: sn outpcd* **5/1**[1]

1m 12.11s (-1.29) **Going Correction** -0.225s/f (Firm) **14** Ran SP% **122.6**
Speed ratings: **99,97,96,95,95 93,92,92,89,86 85,82,79,68**CSF £134.01 CT £1897.57 TOTE £24.80: £7.60, £2.80, £3.70; EX 174.50.
**Owner** Ray Gudge, Colin Lewis, Malcolm Calvert **Bred** Redpender Stud Ltd **Trained** Kentisbeare, Devon
■ Stewards Enquiry : C Haddon two-day ban: careless riding (Jul 26,27)

**FOCUS**
A weak nursery but it is still likely to produce winners at a lowly level. The figures shown as 'official ratings' are estimates for guidance only.

**NOTEBOOK**
**Colonel Bilko(IRE)** went backward in maidens, being well beaten in blinkers on his latest outing, but came back to his best on this nursery debut and ran on strongly off his feather weight to win well from stall 1.
**Safendonseabiscuit** ran another solid race in defeat on this handicap debut but continues to find at least one too good. His turn will come eventually.
**Princely Vale(IRE)** has been on a roll in claiming and selling company - winning his last three - and produced an improved effort on his nursery debut from the outside stall. He can win back down in grade.
**Lord John** showed an improvement in form and can win a small race when stepping up to seven furlongs.
**Simplify** was unlucky not to finish closer, being tardy at the start and not getting the clearest of runs.
**Haroldini(IRE)** appears to have benefited from a break and should pick up a small race when running over seven furlongs.
**Queen's Glory(IRE)** was hampered in the last furlong but had had her chance.
**Lincolneurocruiser** *Official explanation: trainer said colt was struck into behind*
**English Fellow** *Official explanation: jockey said colt changed his leading leg on a number of occasions*

## 3887 LEICESTER RACECOURSE CONFERENCE CENTRE H'CAP 5f 218y
**4:50** (4:52) (E) (0-75,75) 3-Y-0+ **£5,850** (£1,800; £900; £450) **Stalls** Low

Form RPR

0005 **1** **Marshallspark (IRE)**[21] 3226 5-8-13 **60**.................................. GParkin 4 71
(RAFahey) *chsd ldrs: rdn to ld 1f out: jst hld on* **7/1**

3411 **2** shd **Never Without Me**[20] 3277 4-8-9 **56**...................................... SWhitworth 1 67
(JFCoupland) *chsd ldrs: nt clr run over 1f out: swtchd lft r.o wl* **13/2**[3]

0004 **3** 2 **Bowling Along**[8] 3622 3-7-11 **53**.................................... NMackay(3) 13 58
(MESowersby) *chsd ldrs: rdn and ev ch 1f out: unable qck* **14/1**

0205 **4** hd **Stokesies Wish**[10] 3593 4-9-3 **64**........................................ KMcEvoy 8 68
(JLSpearing) *w ldrs: led over 1f out: sn hdd: styd on same pce* **10/1**

/00- **5** hd **Asbo**[423] 1723 4-8-13 **60**..................................................... CLowther 10 64
(DrJDScargill) *w ldrs: rdn and ev ch 1f out: no ex* **40/1**

0005 **6** ¾ **Hey Presto**[15] 3416 4-9-8 **69**.............................................. PRobinson 11 70
(CGCox) *mid-div: pushed along 1/2-way: hdwy over 1f out: nt clr run ins fnl f: nt trble ldrs* **3/1**[1]

3-36 **7** 1 ½ **Chickado (IRE)**[101] 1266 3-8-9 **62**...................................... PaulEddery 15 59
(DHaydnJones) *hld up: hdwy over 1f out: styd on same pce ins fnl f* **22/1**

3100 **8** nk **One Way Ticket**[4] 3775 4-9-8 **69**........................................(p) RMullen 3 65
(JMBradley) *prom: led over 2f out: rdn and hdd over 1f out: wknd ins fnl f* **6/1**[2]

6320 **9** nk **Full Spate**[19] 3298 9-9-7 **68**............................................... DaneO'Neill 9 63
(JMBradley) *s.i.s: nvr trbld ldrs* **7/1**

0060 **10** ½ **A Teen**[10] 3593 6-8-10 **57**.................................................... DKinsella 6 50
(PHowling) *sn outpcd* **14/1**

6000 **11** ½ **Just One Smile (IRE)**[17] 3372 4-8-8 **55**............................(b) WSupple 12 47
(TDEasterby) *sn outpcd* **16/1**

2350 **12** 3 ½ **Smart Starprincess (IRE)**[12] 3530 3-8-7 **60**............................ SRighton 7 41
(MJAttwater) *led over 3f: wknd over 1f out* **40/1**

-110 **13** hd **Bronx Bomber**[34] 2854 6-8-4 **51**............................................. JQuinn 2 32
(DrJDScargill) *mid-div: sn pushed along: wknd over 2f out* **12/1**

0000 **14** 8 **Its Ecco Boy**[19] 3321 6-8-11 **58**........................................... JMackay 14 15
(PHowling) *mid-div: wknd over 2f out* **25/1**

1m 10.71s (-2.69) **Going Correction** -0.225s/f (Firm)
**WFA** 3 from 4yo+ 6lb **14** Ran SP% **126.7**
Speed ratings: **108,107,105,104,104 103,101,101,100,100 99,94,94,83**CSF £53.02 CT £653.49 TOTE £7.90: £2.00, £2.60, £5.00; EX 81.90 Place 6 £108.91, Place 5 £102.78.
**Owner** J J Staunton **Bred** Mrs Teresa Bergin **Trained** Musley Bank, N Yorks

**FOCUS**
A good finish to a weak race that was run at a good gallop. The form is ordinary but solid.

**NOTEBOOK**
**Marshallspark(IRE)** showed signs he was nearing a win when a staying on fifth at Hamilton last month, and confirmed the impression, just clinging on the lead in the dying strides. He may improve again on this.
**Never Without Me** was an unlucky loser, being denied a clear passage through when picking up and failing to get there by the narrowest of margins. He has been in great form on the All-Weather and should continue to run well.
**Bowling Along** fared best of the fillies but remains with just a selling win to her name.
**Stokesies Wish** had her chance and will be better back on a sharper track.
**Asbo** having her first run for 423 days, showed plenty of reason for optimism, coming there with every hope before tiring late on. She can win if going on from this.
**Hey Presto** was again unlucky and just seems one of those horses that always finds trouble.
T/Plt: £51.10 to a £1 stake. Pool: £33,306.20. 475.65 winning tickets. T/Qpdt: £55.20 to a £1 stake. Pool: £2,226.60. 29.80 winning tickets. CR

3888 - 3891a (Foreign Racing) - See Raceform Interactive

# [3513] CARLISLE (R-H)
Friday, July 16

**OFFICIAL GOING: Good to firm (firm in places)**
After just 1mm over the last 10 days the going was described as 'very firm' in the home straight but slightly easier in the back straight.
Wind: Moderate 1/2 against. Weather: Fine and sunny.

## 3892 CUBBY CONSTRUCTION LIMITED CLAIMING STKS 1m 3f 206y
**2:10** (2:10) (F ) 3-Y-0+ **£3,052** (£872; £436) **Stalls** Low

Form RPR

-460 **1** **Tomasino**[4] 3796 6-9-12 76.........................................(t) KDarley 3 72+
(MrsMReveley) *led after 1f: set mod pce: qckdn 4f out: styd on strly fnl f: eased nr fin* **12/1**

6042 **2** 5 **Spree Vision**[4] 3794 8-9-7 50...............................................(v) GBaker 2 59?
(PMonteith) *hld up: hdwy over 3f out: wnt 2nd 2f out: hung rt: no ch w wnr* **5/2**[2]

-045 **3** 5 **Big Smoke (IRE)**[21] 3281 4-8-12 60.............................(p) PMulrennan(5) 7 47
(JHowardJohnson) *dwlt: sn led: hdd after 1f: chsd ldrs: wknd fnl f* **5/1**[3]

1/00 **4** nk **Lord Dundee (IRE)**[14] 3474 6-9-2 65.......................(t) DeanMcKeown 1 46
(RCGuest) *hld up: lost pl 1/2-way: hdwy 2f out: styd on towards fin* **20/1**

4032 **5** 2 **Platinum Charmer (IRE)**[15] 3461 4-9-9 57..............(p) DarrenWilliams 6 49
(KRBurke) *led eraly: t.k.h: trckd ldrs: effrt over 2f out: wknd over 1f out* **1/1**[1]

1-00 **6** 14 **Devine Light (IRE)**[18] 3367 4-9-1 60.................................(p) RWinston 4 19
(BMactaggart) *t.k.h: trckd ldrs: rdn and edgd lft over 2f out: sn lost pl* **16/1**

60-0 **7** 30 **Rusty Boy**[2] 3839 3-8-5 ..................................................... VHalliday 5 —
(ACrook) *trckd ldrs: t.k.h: lost pl over 3f out: sn bhd* **100/1**

2m 35.21s (2.81) **Going Correction** -0.15s/f (Firm)
**WFA** 3 from 4yo+ 12lb **7** Ran SP% **114.6**
Speed ratings: **84,80,77,77,75 66,46**CSF £42.38 TOTE £8.50: £4.50, £1.70; EX 75.90.
**Owner** P D Savill **Bred** P D Savill **Trained** Lingdale, N Yorks

**FOCUS**
A tactical race and a very slow pace, with Kevin Darley dictating things from the front, suggesting the form may not be all that sound.

**NOTEBOOK**
**Tomasino**, who would have eaten these in his prime, was given his own way in front and in the end was able to ease right down. If nothing else this will have done his confidence a power of good.
**Spree Vision**, who had plenty to find, went in pursuit of the winner but he was inclined to hang and was never doing anything like enough.
**Big Smoke(IRE)** tried to keep tabs on the winner but he became very leg weary in the final furlong.
**Lord Dundee(IRE)**, last in two handicaps this time, was detached at halfway. He stayed on in his own time and this was more encouraging.
**Platinum Charmer(IRE)**, heavily supported, would not settle as a result of the strong pace and found himself rather stuck out in the middle. This is safely ignored. *Official explanation: jockey said gelding was unsuited by slow pace*
**Devine Light(IRE)**, who took a maiden at 100/1 last backend, again showed a tendency to go left-handed. Her win is starting to look more and more like a flash in the pan. *Official explanation: jockey said filly hung left handed*

## 3893 BORDER CONSTRUCTION LTD MAIDEN AUCTION STKS 5f
**2:45** (2:46) (E ) 2-Y-0 **£3,607** (£1,110; £555; £277) **Stalls** High

Form RPR

4 **1** **Pro Tempore**[18] 3370 2-8-6 ow1...................................... ACulhane 10 66
(MrsJRRamsden) *led tl over 2f out: styd on to ld ins last: hld on* **9/2**[2]

00 **2** nk **Niteowl Lad (IRE)**[22] 3233 2-8-7 ........................................ DAllan 6 66
(JO'Reilly) *w ldr: led over 2f out: hung rt and hdd ins last: no ex* **14/1**

P6 **3** nk **Shatin Leader**[25] 3144 2-8-2 ........................................... RFfrench 8 60
(MissLAPerratt) *chsd ldrs: outpcd over 2f out: hung rt 1f out: styd on ins last: fin wl* **25/1**

**4** 2 ½ **Hansomelle (IRE)** 2-8-4 ow7......................................... PMulrennan(5) 9 58
(BMactaggart) *unf: scope: s.s: bhd tl styd on fnl 2f* **20/1**

**5** shd **Tahlal (IRE)** 2-8-10 ........................................................ SSanders 3 59
(MrsADuffield) *rangy: chsd ldrs: outpcd over 3f out: kpt on fnl 2f* **7/1**[3]

360 **6** 1 ¼ **Lorna Dune**[23] 3196 2-8-2 ............................................... PFessey 7 46
(MrsJRRamsden) *sn drvn along: outpcd over 3f out: sme hdwy 2f out: nvr a danger* **10/3**[1]

4200 **7** 1 ½ **Kristikhab (IRE)**[21] 3286 2-8-10 .......................................... FLynch 5 49
(ABerry) *s.i.s: hung rt and hdwy over 2f out: nvr nr ldrs* **9/2**[2]

00 **8** 1 **Slate Grey**[33] 2904 2-8-7 ........................................ DarrenWilliams 2 43
(KRBurke) *s.i.s: sme hdwy on outer whn hmpd over 1f out: eased* **12/1**

0 **9** 1 **Danceinthevalley (IRE)**[13] 3514 2-8-7 ............................ DeanMcKeown 1 39
(GASwinbank) *chsd ldrs: outpcd over 3f out: swvd lft over 1f out: sn wknd* **11/1**

0 **10** 1 ¾ **Negas (IRE)**[35] 2860 2-8-10 .............................................. RWinston 4 36
(JHowardJohnson) *rrd s: bhd and edgd lft 2f out: nvr a factor* **9/1**

61.06 secs (-0.44) **Going Correction** -0.175s/f (Firm) **10** Ran SP% **113.2**
Speed ratings: **96,95,95,91,90 88,86,84,83,80**CSF £63.44 TOTE £4.90: £1.60, £4.50, £5.80; EX 72.30.
**Owner** P R C Morrison **Bred** P Onslow **Trained** Sandhutton, N Yorks

**FOCUS**
A very ordinary maiden with the first two one-two throughout.

**NOTEBOOK**
**Pro Tempore**, a rangy type, had clearly learnt plenty first time. With the rail to help she battled back under a forceful ride to force her head in front again near the line. She should improve again.
**Niteowl Lad(IRE)**, whose two previous outings were on soft ground, looked very fit indeed. He went a neck up but did not give his rider a real of help and in the end just missed out.
**Shatin Leader**, well beaten in a seller last time, tended to edge in behind the first two. Pulled wide, she would have made it with a little further to go.
**Hansomelle(IRE)**, a March foal, lost ground at the start but was picking up in good style late on. This will have taught her plenty.
**Tahlal(IRE)**, a March foal, has size and scope and looks capable of better in due course.
**Lorna Dune**, the shorter priced of Lynda Ramsden's pair, never went a yard and looks to need at least six furlongs.
**Kristikhab(IRE)**, a handful at the start, lost ground when the stalls opened and wanted to do nothing but hang right-handed. *Official explanation: jockey said gelding was fractious at start and slow away*

**Danceinthevalley(IRE)** *Official explanation: trainer said colt was unsuited by the ground and was struck into*
**Negas(IRE)** *Official explanation: jockey said gelding missed break and was unsuited by the ground*

## 3894 KINGMOOR PARK H'CAP — 5f
3:15 (3:20) (E) (0-70,72) 3-Y-O+ — £7,897 (£2,430; £1,215; £607) Stalls High

| Form | Pos | Dist | Horse | Jockey | RPR |
|---|---|---|---|---|---|
| 0000 | 1 | | **Izmail (IRE)**[12] 3558 5-9-4 **66** (DNicholls) *w ldr: kpt on wl to ld nr fin* **25/1** | LTreadwell(7) 11 | 79 |
| 0500 | 2 | nk | **Peters Choice**[27] 3077 3-9-1 **63** (ISemple) *led: hrd rdn and edgd lft over 1f out: wnt rt ins last: hdd nr fin* **33/1** | (b[1]) TEaves(3) 13 | 75 |
| 6053 | 3 | ¾ | **Playtime Blue**[4] 3810 4-9-4 **59** (MrsHSweeting) *chsd ldrs: styd on ins last* **10/1** | GBaker 9 | 68 |
| 3040 | 4 | shd | **Tuscan Flyer**[13] 3509 6-9-5 **60** (RBastiman) *chsd ldrs: kpt on fnl f: hmpd nr fin* **12/1** | (b) RFfrench 16 | 69 |
| 4121 | 5 | hd | **Soaked**[20] 3314 11-9-8 **63** (DWChapman) *hld up: hdwy 2f out: edgd rt ins fnl f: nt clr run nr fin* **10/1** | (b) ACulhane 2 | 71 |
| 00 | 6 | 1 | **Xanadu**[6] 3735 8-8-12 **53** (MissLAPerratt) *mid-div: kpt on wl fnl f* **25/1** | (p) JCarroll 7 | 57 |
| 1043 | 7 | shd | **My Bayard**[13] 3515 5-9-5 **60** (JO'Reilly) *w ldrs: chalng whn sltly hmpd over 1f out: nt qckn* **16/1** | (b) DAllan 10 | 63 |
| 2051 | 8 | nk | **Fairgame Man**[3] 3820 6-8-8 **49** 6ex (JSWainwright) *bhd: hdwy on inner 2f out: styng on whn nt clr run wl ins last* **7/1**[3] | (p) GParkin 19 | 51 |
| 3210 | 9 | hd | **Flying Tackle**[3] 3820 6-8-7 **48** (MDods) *mid-div: hdwy on inner 2f out: keeping on same pce whn nt clr run nr fin* **15/2** | (p) DarrenWilliams 18 | 49 |
| 5301 | 10 | ½ | **Hello Roberto**[7] 3702 3-9-6 **72** 6ex (MJPolglase) *swtchd rt after s: bhd tl kpt on wl appr fnl f* **16/1** | KGhunowa(7) 1 | 71 |
| 6044 | 11 | hd | **Pirlie Hill**[11] 3580 4-8-12 **53** (MissLAPerratt) *sn bhd on outer: styd on fnl 2f: nvr rchd ldrs* **25/1** | KDarley 4 | 52 |
| 0045 | 12 | nk | **Dark Champion**[16] 3410 4-9-4 **59** (REBarr) *rr-div: sme hdwy over 1f out: nvr on terms* **50/1** | (p) RWinston 3 | 56 |
| 4066 | 13 | shd | **Bettys Pride**[8] 3680 5-8-9 **53** (MDods) *in tch: outpcd fnl 2f* **20/1** | (p) LEnstone(3) 6 | 50 |
| 0250 | 14 | ¾ | **American Cousin**[21] 3269 9-9-3 **58** (DNicholls) *hld up and bhd: sme hdwy and n.m.r 2f out: nvr a factor* **25/1** | ANicholls 8 | 52 |
| 0430 | 15 | ½ | **Viewforth**[4] 3795 6-9-12 **67** (JSGoldie) *trckd ldrs: effrt over 1f out: no imp: eased ins last* **5/1**[2] | (b) SSanders 15 | 59 |
| 2443 | 16 | shd | **Tally (IRE)**[7] 3713 4-9-1 **59** (MJPolglase) *s.i.s: sme hdwy whn nt clr run over 1f out: nvr a factor* **9/2**[1] | LFletcher(3) 17 | 51 |
| 5500 | 17 | 1 | **Online Investor**[20] 3314 5-9-9 **64** (DNicholls) *s.v.s: a bhd* **16/1** | (v[1]) AlexGreaves 5 | 52 |
| 6100 | 18 | 3½ | **Feu Duty (IRE)**[37] 2784 3-9-8 **67** (TJEtherington) *v unruly leaving paddock: a in rr* **20/1** | (be[1]) DMcGaffin 20 | 41 |

60.31 secs (-1.19) **Going Correction** -0.175s/f (Firm)
**WFA** 3 from 4yo+ 4lb — **18** Ran SP% **132.4**
Speed ratings: **102,101,100,100,99 98,98,97,97,96 96,95,95,94,93 93,91,86**CSF £685.08 CT £8513.30 TOTE £36.70: £9.00, £6.30, £3.10, £3.00; EX 1019.50.
**Owner** G M McGuinness **Bred** Kildaragh Stud **Trained** Sessay, N Yorks
■ Stewards Enquiry : T Eaves three-day ban: careless riding (Jul 27-29); one-day ban: hit winner over head with whip (Jul 30)

**FOCUS**
A rough race and those drawn low at a disadvantage.

**NOTEBOOK**
**Izmail(IRE)**, who has slipped to a lenient mark, is a real firm-ground specialist and, despite taking a crack over the head from the rider of the runner-up's whip, he showed ahead near the line.
**Peters Choice**, in first-time blinkers, showed bags of toe but, under a punishing ride, came off a straight line and was pipped near the finish. His two career wins were on the All-Weather.
**Playtime Blue**, making a quick reappearance, appreciated the quick ground and looks right back to his best.
**Tuscan Flyer**, who hardly seems to run two races alike, was held when left short of room by the runner-up near the line.
**Soaked**, drawn one off the outside, was ridden much more patiently than usual. Making headway towards the far side, he found himself short of racing room near the line. This hardy veteran is clearly in very good form.
**Fairgame Man**, racing on different ground under a penalty, was keeping on when running out of racing room inside the last.
**Viewforth** had no excuse this time and his rider eventually drew stumps.
**Tally(IRE)**, raised 7lb after York, gave away ground at the start and was making no real impression and with plenty to do when left short of room.

## 3895 KEN HOPE LTD H'CAP — 6f 192y
3:45 (3:47) (E) (0-70,68) 3-Y-O+ — £3,851 (£1,185; £592; £296) Stalls High

| Form | Pos | Dist | Horse | Jockey | RPR |
|---|---|---|---|---|---|
| -006 | 1 | | **Wood Dalling (USA)**[17] 3401 6-8-11 **52** (ISemple) *mid-div: hdwy 2f out: styd on to ld nr fin* **10/1** | RWinston 15 | 63 |
| -001 | 2 | nk | **Pepper Road**[32] 2938 5-8-10 **51** (RBastiman) *chsd ldrs: led 1f out: hdd and no ex nr fin* **4/1**[1] | RFfrench 13 | 61 |
| -016 | 3 | hd | **Zanjeer**[12] 3559 4-9-6 **66** (NWilson) *chsd ldrs: led over 1f out: sn hdd: nt qckn wl ins last* **8/1** | PMulrennan(5) 3 | 75 |
| 0522 | 4 | 2½ | **Smith N Allan Oils**[9] 3623 5-8-10 **54** (MDods) *rr-div: hdwy 2f out: kpt on: nvr rchd ldrs* **9/2**[2] | (p) LEnstone(3) 10 | 57 |
| 0434 | 5 | hd | **Border Artist**[12] 3555 5-9-10 **65** (DNicholls) *rr-div: hdwy on outer 2f out: nvr nr to chal* **13/2**[3] | ANicholls 8 | 67 |
| 0020 | 6 | 2½ | **Silver Seeker (USA)**[18] 3365 4-9-1 **56** (ARDicken) *chsd ldrs: drvn along over 3f out: one pce* **50/1** | PFessey 6 | 52 |
| 0600 | 7 | 1½ | **Time To Remember (IRE)**[20] 3298 6-9-2 **57** (DNicholls) *s.s: hdwy on outer over 4f out: wknd 1f out* **25/1** | SSanders 1 | 49 |
| 0216 | 8 | nk | **Redoubtable (USA)**[6] 3734 13-8-13 **54** (DWChapman) *sn chsng ldrs: lost pl over 1f out* **14/1** | ACulhane 11 | 45 |
| 3513 | 9 | 2 | **Menai Straights**[4] 3798 3-9-2 **64** (RFFisher) *chsd ldrs: wknd over 1f out* **8/1** | JFanning 4 | 50 |
| 4064 | 10 | 1¼ | **Jedeydd**[11] 3579 7-9-0 **55** (MDods) *hld up and bhd: sme hdwy on ins 2f out: nvr a factor* **12/1** | (t) SWKelly 14 | 38 |
| 5044 | 11 | ¾ | **Locombe Hill (IRE)**[5] 3778 8-9-5 **60** (DNicholls) *led: hung rt and hdd over 1f out: sn lost pl* **14/1** | (v) JCarroll 2 | 41 |
| 0010 | 12 | ½ | **Libre**[17] 3401 4-9-5 **60** (RCGuest) *s.i.s: hld up and bhd: sme hdwy over 2f out: nvr a factor* **12/1** | (bt) DeanMcKeown 12 | 40 |
| 0634 | 13 | 1¾ | **Waltzing Wizard**[13] 3516 5-8-10 **51** (ABerry) *a in rr* **12/1** | FLynch 9 | 26 |
| 0/00 | 14 | 7 | **Dragon Prince**[9] 3623 4-9-10 **68** (RCGuest) *t.k.h: a in rr* **100/1** | PAspell(3) 7 | 25 |

1m 25.28s (-1.82) **Going Correction** -0.175s/f (Firm)
**WFA** 3 from 4yo+ 7lb — **14** Ran SP% **124.2**
Speed ratings: **103,102,102,99,99 96,94,94,92,90 89,89,87,79**CSF £50.87 CT £359.88 TOTE £9.00: £2.50, £2.10, £3.20; EX 44.40.
**Owner** William Laird **Bred** Orpendale And Kilboy Estates **Trained** Carluke, S Lanarks

**FOCUS**
A low-grade handicap run at a strong pace.

**NOTEBOOK**
**Wood Dalling(USA)**, whose one previous win was over three years ago, was backed at long odds on the exchanges. Down 6lb in three previous outings this time, he was put in front almost on the line before he could have a change of mind.
**Pepper Road**, 3lb higher, worked hard to take a narrow lead only to be edged out near the line. A mile suits him marginally better.
**Zanjeer**, much happier on this far quicker ground, just missed out in a tight three-way finish.
**Smith N Allan Oils**, fifth in this a year ago, continues in good form but that sixth career win is proving elusive.
**Border Artist** had the trip and the ground in his favour, but he was handicapped by ending up racing wide.

## 3896 BAINES WILSON MAIDEN STKS — 6f 192y
4:20 (4:21) (D) 3-Y-O+ — £5,824 (£1,792; £896; £448) Stalls High

| Form | Pos | Dist | Horse | Jockey | RPR |
|---|---|---|---|---|---|
| 4226 | 1 | | **Flash Ram**[16] 3410 3-9-0 64 (TDEasterby) *led early: w ldr: led over 1f out: edgd rt ins last: jst hld on* **8/1**[3] | (b) SSanders 3 | 67 |
| 43 | 2 | shd | **Ouninpohja (IRE)**[11] 3587 3-9-0 (GASwinbank) *trckd ldrs: wnt 2nd 1f out: styd on wl and jst failed* **4/1**[2] | DeanMcKeown 7 | 67 |
| 043 | 3 | 5 | **Aperitif**[8] 3671 3-9-0 73 (WJHaggas) *taken to post early and walked down; mid-div: effrt over 2f out: sn rdn and hung rt: kpt on ins last* **1/3**[1] | SWKelly 1 | 54 |
| 30 | 4 | 2½ | **Good Time Bobby**[42] 2662 7-9-4 (JO'Reilly) *sn led: hdd over 1f out: fdd jst ins last* **25/1** | DNolan(3) 4 | 47 |
| | 5 | 7 | **Minstrel's Double** 3-9-0 (FPMurtagh) *rangy: s.i.s: sme hdwy 3f out: fdd over 1f out* **50/1** | PBradley 10 | 29 |
| 0 | 6 | 5 | **Sonearsofar (IRE)**[37] 2777 4-9-2 (JParkes) *bhd: sme hdwy 2f out: nvr a factor* **66/1** | MLawson(5) 9 | 16 |
| 000 | 7 | 4 | **Spot In Time**[20] 3297 4-8-13 (PRWood) *chsd ldrs: rdn 3f out: sn lost pl* **50/1** | LFletcher(3) 2 | — |
| 0-0 | 8 | 1 | **Alethea Gee**[11] 3587 6-8-13 (MrsMReveley) *hld up in rr: effrt over 2f out: nvr a factor* **50/1** | TEaves(3) 8 | — |
| | 9 | ½ | **Lumback (IRE)**[34] 5-9-4 (NWilson) *s.i.s: t.k.h in rr: nvr a factor* **50/1** | (t) PAspell(3) 5 | 2 |
| 000 | 10 | 2½ | **Narciso (GER)**[21] 3279 4-9-2 (MWEasterby) *chsd ldrs: lost pl over 3f out: sn bhd* **50/1** | PMulrennan(5) 6 | — |

1m 26.06s (-1.04) **Going Correction** -0.175s/f (Firm)
**WFA** 3 from 4yo+ 7lb — **10** Ran SP% **121.3**
Speed ratings: **98,97,92,89,81 75,71,69,69,66**CSF £39.92 TOTE £8.00: £1.30, £1.10, £1.10; EX 42.80.
**Owner** Lee Connolly **Bred** Bearstone Stud **Trained** Great Habton, N Yorks

**FOCUS**
With the favourite well below form this was barely better than a seller but the runner-up should do better now he is qualified for handicaps.

**NOTEBOOK**
**Flash Ram**, placed five times, made it ninth time lucky but in the end it was a close-run thing.
**Ouninpohja(IRE)** went in pursuit of the winner and would have made it in one more stride. There is better to come and he should make his mark in handicap company over a mile plus.
**Aperitif**, taken to post early and lead all the way to the start, was never happy and hung, probably feeling the very firm ground. He is by no means straightforward but is a lot better than he showed here. *Official explanation: trainer said gelding was unsuited by the ground*
**Good Time Bobby**, third in a claimer on his first outing on the Flat and tailed off on the All-Weather last time, was on his toes beforehand and led them a merry dance but did not get home.
**Minstrel's Double** looks as though he needs more time and is a prospective juvenile hurdler.

## 3897 LORNE STEWART PLC H'CAP — 1m 1f 61y
4:50 (4:50) (E) (0-70,69) 3-Y-O — £3,753 (£1,155; £577; £288) Stalls High

| Form | Pos | Dist | Horse | Jockey | RPR |
|---|---|---|---|---|---|
| 0-21 | 1 | | **Masafi (IRE)**[4] 3804 3-8-11 **59** 6ex (SirMarkPrescott) *trckd ldrs: effrt over 2f out: hung rt: styed on strly fnl f to ld last 75yds* **8/15**[1] | SSanders 2 | 69+ |
| -305 | 2 | 1 | **Third Empire**[20] 3312 3-8-12 **60** (CGrant) *led: qcknd 4f out: hdd and no ex wl ins last* **14/1**[3] | RWinston 5 | 68 |
| 0251 | 3 | 6 | **Pearl Of York (DEN)**[11] 3581 3-8-13 **61** 6ex (RGuest) *trckd ldrs: effrt over 2f out: one pce whn eased ins last* **5/2**[2] | KDarley 3 | 57 |
| -610 | 4 | 1 | **Dance To My Tune**[57] 2251 3-8-7 **60** (MWEasterby) *stdd s: hld up: hdwy on ins over 2f out: nvr able chal* **16/1** | PMulrennan(5) 6 | 54 |
| 0004 | 5 | shd | **Magical Mimi**[26] 3117 3-9-0 **69** (JeddO'Keeffe) *trckd ldr: lost pl over 1f out* **16/1** | LeanneKershaw(7) 4 | 63 |
| 5460 | 6 | 9 | **Trojan Flight**[25] 3155 3-8-12 **60** (MrsJRRamsden) *hld up: effrt 3f out: hung rt: lost pl and eased over 1f out* **16/1** | JFanning 1 | 36 |

1m 55.36s (-2.67) **Going Correction** -0.15s/f (Firm) — **6** Ran SP% **118.1**
Speed ratings: **105,104,98,97,97 89**CSF £11.31 TOTE £1.70: £1.10, £6.80; EX 18.70 Place 6 £226.34, Place 5 £78.19.
**Owner** G D Waters **Bred** G D Waters **Trained** Newmarket, Suffolk

**FOCUS**
A tactical race with no gallop to past halfway and the form is somewhat mixed, but the winner was right on top at the finish.

**NOTEBOOK**
**Masafi(IRE)**, on his first try on turf, made hard work of it, not helped by the modest gallop. After hanging fire, in the end he was firmly in command and no doubt will not be resting on his laurels.
**Third Empire**, placed once in seven previous starts, was given a fine tactical but in the end was still not good enough.
**Pearl Of York(DEN)**, hoisted 8lb, had a 6lb penalty to overcome but in the end she was no match whatsoever for the first two.
**Dance To My Tune**, absent for eight weeks, was dropped in at the start. She never really looked like picking up and may not appreciate the ground as quick as this.
**Magical Mimi** did not see it out even though the pace to past halfway was steady to say the least.
**Trojan Flight** would not go forward in a straight line and in the end his stamina seemed to give out completely. He looks one to avoid. *Official explanation: jockey said gelding hung right*
T/Plt: £632.60 to a £1 stake. Pool: £27,514.05. 31.75 winning tickets. T/Qpdt: £30.30 to a £1 stake. Pool: £2,599.00. 63.30 winning tickets. WG

# [3876]HAMILTON (R-H)

Friday, July 16

**OFFICIAL GOING: Good to firm**

## 3898 JOHN BANKS NURSERY 6f 5y
6:50 (6:51) (D) 2-Y-O £6,831 (£2,102; £1,051; £525) Stalls Low

Form RPR
5402 1 **No Commission (IRE)**[4] [3793] 2-8-11 **69** .... RWinston 2 73+
(RFFisher) *hld up: swtchd rt over 2f out: led and edgd lft over 1f out: rdn out* **7/2**[3]
322 2 ½ **Mceldowney**[19] [3336] 2-9-6 **78** .... JFanning 3 81+
(MJohnston) *chsd ldrs: nt clr run over 2f out: squeezed through and bmpd over 1f out: sn chsng wnr: kpt on fnl f* **5/2**[1]
343 3 5 **Angelofthenorth**[16] [3408] 2-8-11 **69** .... SChin 1 57
(JDBethell) *w ldrs: ev ch over 1f out: outpcd fnl f* **14/1**
403 4 2½ **Melvino**[30] [2972] 2-9-0 **77** ....(v[1]) PMakin(5) 5 57
(TDBarron) *disp ld tl wknd over 1f out* **7/2**[3]
4220 5 1¾ **Lady Hopeful (IRE)**[6] [3729] 2-8-4 **65** ....(v[1]) TEaves(3) 4 40
(RPElliott) *dwlt: sn chsng ldrs: effrt whn bmpd over 1f out: sn btn* **20/1**
01 6 3½ **Tequila Sheila (IRE)**[22] [3224] 2-9-7 **79** .... DarrenWilliams 6 43+
(KRBurke) *led: jst hdd whn bdly hmpd and lost pl over 1f out: nt rcvr* **3/1**[2]

1m 12.17s (-0.93) **Going Correction** -0.40s/f (Firm) **6** Ran SP% **109.4**
Speed ratings: **90,89,82,79,77 72**CSF £11.99 TOTE £4.90: £2.30, £1.60; EX 18.00.
**Owner** Great Head House Estates Limited **Bred** N D Cronin **Trained** Ulverston, Cumbria

**FOCUS**
A fair nursery run at a frenetic early gallop and it suited those held up off the pace. The figures shown as 'official ratings' are estimates for guidance only.

**NOTEBOOK**
**No Commission(IRE)** came from last to first and got off the mark at the ninth attempt. He had looked exposed in maidens prior to this, but relished this switch to a nursery and was well suited by being held up off the strong gallop. However, he still looks a tricky customer and will most likely struggle off a higher mark.
**Mceldowney ◆** , who had shown fair form in three maidens previously, was unlucky on this handicap debut. He failed to go the early pace on this drop in trip, then was tightened for room twice late on, before running on all too late. A clear second, he was well-backed for this and should recoup losses before long, especially granted a stiffer test.
**Angelofthenorth** had every chance, but could not quicken when it mattered over this extra furlong. On this evidence, she has been given a stiff mark and looks to need some respite in the weights.
**Melvino** , who has shown fair form previously and was fitted with a visor for this nursery bow, dropped out of contention late on, having helped set the pace for most of the way. This was a disappointing effort, but he could be capable of better with a more patient ride.
**Tequila Sheila(IRE)** went off too fast and was beating a retreat when hampered approaching the final furlong. She can do better, but does look vulnerable off this mark.

## 3899 VELVET FAIR FRIDAY MAIDEN STKS 1m 65y
7:20 (7:22) (D) 3-Y-O+ £7,007 (£2,156; £1,078; £539) Stalls High

Form RPR
-322 1 **Arrgatt (IRE)**[28] [3057] 3-8-13 83 .... NCallan 8 64+
(MAJarvis) *keen: w ldr: led after 3f: r.o strly fr 3f out* **1/9**[1]
0-00 2 3½ **Islands Farewell**[67] [1993] 4-9-7 45 .... ANicholls 6 56?
(DNicholls) *chsd ldrs: effrt over 2f out: kpt on fnl f: nt rch wnr* **50/1**
2/0 3 7 **Awwal Marra (USA)**[62] [2133] 4-9-2 .... PFessey 1 35
(EWTuer) *in tch: rdn over 3f out: sn no imp* **33/1**
4 1¼ **Bijou Dan** 3-8-13 .... RWinston 7 37
(ISemple) *dwlt: wl bhd tl styd on fr 2f out: n.d* **16/1**[2]
00 5 ¾ **Hollywood Critic (USA)**[14] [3475] 3-8-10 .... LEnstone(3) 4 35
(PMonteith) *led 3f: cl up tl wknd fr 2f out* **25/1**
-00 6 ¾ **Howards Rocket**[15] [3447] 3-8-8 .... PMulrennan(5) 2 34
(JSGoldie) *hld up and a bhd* **66/1**
0 7 1 **Rouge Et Noir**[11] [3587] 6-9-4 .... TEaves(3) 5 31
(MrsMReveley) *hld up: rdn 1/2-way: n.d* **20/1**[3]
8 8 **Dalkeys Lass** 3-8-8 .... SChin 3 8
(MrsLBNormile) *chsd ldrs tl wknd fr 1/2-way* **80/1**

1m 45.11s (-4.19) **Going Correction** -0.40s/f (Firm)
**WFA** 3 from 4yo+ 8lb **8** Ran SP% **112.1**
Speed ratings: **104,100,93,92,91 90,89,81**CSF £15.81 TOTE £1.20: £1.02, £8.70, £2.90; EX 17.50.
**Owner** Sheikh Ahmed Al Maktoum **Bred** Mrs Max Morris **Trained** Newmarket, Suffolk

**FOCUS**
A poor maiden totally lacking strength in depth, and although the winner is clear it is difficult to be confident about the form.

**NOTEBOOK**
**Arrgatt(IRE)**, whose previous efforts stood way above that of his rivals, duly won as he was entitled to. He was keen over this shorter trip, and should do better when upped once again in distance, but will need to improve again to justify his current mark back in handicaps.
**Islands Farewell** ran on to be a clear second, but held no chance with the winner. This was still his best effort to date, and he greatly appreciated this return to a faster surface, so may be able to exploit his current handicap mark.
**Awwal Marra(USA)** turned in a more credible effort than her reappearance last time, and will surely fare better now she qualifies for handicaps.
**Bijou Dan** ran green on this belated debut and looks only modest.
**Rouge Et Noir** was never a threat over this inadequate trip, but he will could be one to keep an eye on once handicapped and when racing over much further.

## 3900 CHARD CONSTRUCTION E B F MAIDEN STKS (A QUALIFIER FOR THE HAMILTON PARK 2-Y-O SERIES FINAL 5f 4y
7:50 (7:50) (D) 2-Y-O £5,894 (£1,684; £842) Stalls Low

Form RPR
1 **Andronikos** 2-9-0 .... KDarley 4 79+
(PFICole) *pressed ldr: shkn up to ld over 1f out: kpt on wl fnl f* **13/8**[2]
3332 2 2 **Gifted Gamble**[23] [3196] 2-9-0 ....(b) NCallan 1 72
(KARyan) *led to over 1f out: kpt on same pce ins fnl f* **5/2**[3]
3 ½ **Countdown** 2-9-0 .... SSanders 6 70+
(SirMarkPrescott) *chsd ldrs: sn rn green and outpcd: kpt on fnl f: bttr for r* **11/8**[1]

60.01 secs (-1.25) **Going Correction** -0.40s/f (Firm) **3** Ran SP% **108.8**
Speed ratings: **94,90,90**CSF £5.48 TOTE £2.60; EX 4.70.
**Owner** C Shiacolas **Bred** Mrs R D Peacock **Trained** Whatcombe, Oxon

**FOCUS**
A maiden weakened by the three non-runners, but the winner won well and could take higher order this year.

**NOTEBOOK**
**Andronikos** made a winning debut in pleasing fashion. He readily took the lead approaching the final furlong, but still looked distinctly green under pressure, and will improve significantly for another furlong. It will be interesting to see where connections aim him next time and he clearly has a future.
**Gifted Gamble** had every chance if good enough, but lacked the pace to go with the winner when it mattered. He is looking exposed, but has some fair form to his name, and should find easier opportunities to get off the mark.
**Countdown ◆**, an expensive debutant, ran very green, and was unbalanced coming down the hill before running on again when meeting the rising ground. This experience will do him the world of good and he can be expected to leave this form behind in due course, most probably over another furlong.

## 3901 TENNENTS SCOTTISH STEWARDS CUP H'CAP 6f 5y
8:20 (8:26) (B) (0-105,102) 3-Y-O+ £18,478 (£7,009; £3,504; £1,593) Stalls Low

Form RPR
2264 1 **Blackheath (IRE)**[7] [3713] 8-8-3 **82** .... PMakin(5) 11 96
(DNicholls) *mde all far side: clr fnl f: kpt on wl* **8/1**
204 2 2½ **Tom Tun**[13] [3522] 9-9-8 **96** ....(b) JFanning 1 103
(JBalding) *prom stands side: effrt over 1f out: carried rt ins last: kpt on: no ch w wnr* **10/1**
4001 3 ½ **Pieter Brueghel (USA)**[6] [3754] 5-8-12 **86** 6ex .... RWinston 2 91
(DNicholls) *led stands side gp: rdn over 2f out: hung rt ins last: no ex last 75yds* **4/1**[1]
0200 4 ½ **Simianna**[20] [3308] 5-8-12 **93** ....(p) PPMathers(7) 13 97
(ABerry) *cl up far side: effrt over 2f out: one pce fnl f* **10/1**
0010 5 ½ **Loyal Tycoon (IRE)**[7] [3691] 6-9-2 **90** .... ANicholls 4 92
(DNicholls) *chsd stands side ldrs: rdn over 2f out: kpt on same pce fnl f* **9/2**[2]
0000 6 ½ **Cd Europe (IRE)**[6] [3755] 6-9-1 **89** ....(b) NCallan 8 90
(KARyan) *swtchd to far side sn after s: chsd ldrs tl rdn and no ex over 1f out* **16/1**
0000 7 1¾ **Seafield Towers**[4] [3795] 4-7-6 **73** ....(p) LeanneKershaw(7) 6 68
(MissLAPerratt) *bhd stands side: hung rt and outpcd 1/2-way: sme late hdwy: n.d* **20/1**
0100 8 nk **Pax**[10] [3606] 7-8-9 **83** .... KDarley 12 77
(DNicholls) *chsd far side ldrs tl wknd over 1f out* **16/1**
6200 9 3 **Johnston's Diamond (IRE)**[27] [3074] 6-9-1 **89** .... DAllan 3 74
(EJAlston) *cl up stands side: rdn 1/2-way: wknd over 1f out* **16/1**
4024 10 3 **Legal Set (IRE)**[6] [3754] 8-7-9 **72** oh14 ....(t) CatherineGannon(3) 5 48
(MissAStokell) *chsd stands side ldrs tl wknd fr over 2f out* **33/1**
450 11 ¾ **Chookie Heiton (IRE)**[8] [3673] 6-9-11 **102** .... TEaves(3) 7 76
(ISemple) *prom on outside of stands side gp: rdn over 2f out: sn btn* **6/1**[3]

69.92 secs (-3.18) **Going Correction** -0.40s/f (Firm) **11** Ran SP% **107.1**
Speed ratings: **105,101,100,100,99 99,96,96,92,88 87**CSF £66.74 CT £239.99 TOTE £9.60: £2.90, £3.20, £2.00; EX 100.00.
**Owner** Middleham Park Racing Xx & Streamhill **Bred** John McKay **Trained** Sessay, N Yorks
■ Stewards Enquiry : P Makin one-day ban: failed to keep straight from stalls (Jul 27)

**FOCUS**
A decent sprint, which again saw the field split into two groups, and this time the winner came form the far side. The form looks solid enough.

**NOTEBOOK**
**Blackheath(IRE)** showed decent early speed to bag the far-side rail and put up a solid front-running display to win in great style. This was by far his best effort for some time, but will find things much tougher off a higher future mark.
**Tom Tun** lost ground when he was carried right when challenging late on and can be considered better than the bare form. He rarely runs a bad race at the track and would have been better suited by an easier surface. *Official explanation: jockey said gelding hung right*
**Pieter Brueghel(USA)**, penalised for a gutsy win at York last time, pinged out to lead on the stands' side and held every chance until hanging under pressure well inside the final furlong. He is in good heart, but needs all to fall right and may struggle off his future mark. *Official explanation: jockey said gelding hung right*
**Simianna** ran a sound race, but may not have been totally happy on the ground and looks anchored by her current rating at present.
**Loyal Tycoon(IRE)** never looked a serious threat, and has looked held by the Handicapper since his impressive success at Epsom.
**Chookie Heiton(IRE)** again disappointed and has shown little since returning this season. *Official explanation: trainer said gelding was found to have a low-grade throat infection*

## 3902 VELVET H'CAP STKS (FOR THE TENNENT TROPHY) 1m 5f 9y
8:50 (8:52) (D) (0-80,80) 3-Y-O+ £11,059 (£3,403; £1,701; £850) Stalls High

Form RPR
-111 1 **Elusive Dream**[3] [3825] 3-8-4 **67** 6ex .... SSanders 2 79+
(SirMarkPrescott) *cl up: rdn to ld 2f out: edgd rt: styd on wl* **4/9**[1]
6150 2 1¼ **Sound Of Fleet (USA)**[19] [3345] 3-9-3 **80** .... JFanning 6 91
(PFICole) *hld up midfield: effrt over 2f out: hung lft fr over 1f out: kpt on wl fnl f* **25/1**
1503 3 5 **Red Forest (IRE)**[10] [3614] 5-8-13 **63** ....(t) RWinston 10 66
(JMackie) *prom: effrt 3f out: one pce over 1f out* **12/1**[3]
3314 4 1¾ **Paddy Mul**[4] [3803] 7-7-12 **48** 6ex ....(t) PMQuinn 3 48
(WStorey) *bhd tl styd on fr 2f out: nrst fin* **25/1**
0540 5 nk **Tandava (IRE)**[22] [3236] 6-9-6 **70** ....(p) NCallan 7 70
(ISemple) *led to 2f out: sn btn* **50/1**
-412 6 1¾ **Act Of The Pace (IRE)**[15] [3443] 4-9-7 **78** .... WHogg(7) 5 75
(MJohnston) *keen: cl up tl wknd over 2f out* **7/1**[2]
3523 7 ½ **Cosmic Case**[6] [3740] 9-8-0 **48** oh3 ow2 .... ANicholls 8 47
(JSGoldie) *hld up: rdn over 3f out: n.d* **25/1**
/154 8 1½ **Colorado Falls (IRE)**[15] [3078] 6-9-11 **78** .... LEnstone(3) 4 72
(PMonteith) *hld up: effrt centre over 3f out: btn over 2f out* **25/1**
2305 9 2 **The Ring (IRE)**[9] [3644] 4-9-6 **70** .... KDarley 1 61
(MrsMReveley) *hld up: effrt over 3f out: sn btn* **14/1**
1260 10 ½ **Nakwa (IRE)**[9] [3644] 6-9-6 **70** .... DAllan 11 61
(EJAlston) *chsd ldrs tl wknd over 3f out* **33/1**

2m 46.04s (-7.36) **Going Correction** -0.40s/f (Firm)
**WFA** 3 from 4yo+ 13lb **10** Ran SP% **116.4**
Speed ratings: **106,105,102,101,100 99,99,98,97,97**CSF £21.65 CT £73.58 TOTE £1.60: £1.60, £3.30, £2.60; EX 15.90.
**Owner** Cheveley Park Stud **Bred** Cheveley Park Stud Ltd **Trained** Newmarket, Suffolk

**FOCUS**
A modest handicap that saw the two three-year-old's dominate the finish, but the pace was sound and the first two were clear, giving the form a reasonably reliable look.

**NOTEBOOK**
**Elusive Dream** completed the four-timer with another improved display. He was officially 19lb 'well-in' for this and will have to race off his new mark in the future, so will again need to step-up on what he has previously achieved. However, his confidence will be sky high and he could stay further on this evidence.

**Sound Of Fleet(USA)** ◆, up in trip, ran a game race in defeat and was clear of the rest. He greatly appreciated this drop on class, and although he hung badly late on this time, can be placed to win a similar event. *Official explanation: jockey said colt hung badly left handed*
**Red Forest(IRE)** produced another sound effort, but could not quicken late on, and now looks weighted to the hilt.
**Paddy Mul** was doing all of his best work all too late, but still improved on his latest outing, and looks worth stepping up in distance once again.

## 3903 SCOTTISH RACING YOUR BEST BET H'CAP — 1m 1f 36y
**9:20** (9:20) (E) (0-70,70) 3-Y-O+ — **£4,322** (£1,330; £665; £332) **Stalls** High

Form — RPR
0053 **1** **Anthemion (IRE)**[1] 3879 7-8-13 **50** ........ DMcGaffin 5 69+
(MrsJCMcgregor) *mde all: shkn up and drew clr fr over 2f out: eased wl ins fnl f* **8/1**
5600 **2** *6* **Encounter**[12] 3559 8-8-9 **46** ........ DAllan 6 51
(JHetherton) *keen in tch: effrt over 2f out: kpt on fnl f: no ch w wnr* **12/1**
5-56 **3** *½* **Donna's Double**[6] 3738 9-9-0 **56** ........ (p) PMulrennan(5) 8 60
(DEddy) *keen: prom: rdn over 2f out: one pce fnl f* **6/1**
3452 **4** *¾* **Oscar Pepper (USA)**[12] 3559 7-9-7 **63** ........ (v) PMakin(5) 7 66
(TDBarron) *chsd ldrs: rdn over 2f out: no ex over 1f out* **10/3**[2]
0326 **5** *shd* **Kirkham Abbey**[18] 3387 4-10-0 **65** ........ (v) KDarley 1 67
(MAJarvis) *cl up tl rdn and outpcd fr 2f out* **3/1**[1]
05-0 **6** *¾* **Kristiansand**[6] 3738 4-9-11 **65** ........ LEnstone(3) 9 66
(PMonteith) *dwlt: keen in tch: rdn 3f out: nvr rchd ldrs* **20/1**
0433 **7** *¾* **Coustou (IRE)**[6] 3738 4-9-5 **59** ........ (p) TEaves(3) 4 58
(ARDicken) *cl up tl rdn and wknd fr over 2f out* **5/1**[3]
3110 **8** *21* **Ace Coming**[63] 2078 3-9-10 **70** ........ PFessey 3 27
(DEddy) *hld up in tch: struggling 1/2-way: sn btn* **10/1**

1m 55.95s (-3.65) **Going Correction** -0.40s/f (Firm)
**WFA** 3 from 4yo+ 9lb — **8 Ran SP% 111.7**
Speed ratings: **100,94,94,93,93 92,92,73**CSF £92.15 CT £606.75 TOTE £13.60: £3.20, £3.20, £2.20; EX 96.40 Place 6 £67.05, Place 5 £35.58.
**Owner** On The Level **Bred** C And R O'Brien **Trained** Milnathort, Perth & Kinross

**FOCUS**
A modest handicap full of exposed performers and run at a steady gallop. The form may be suspect.

**NOTEBOOK**
**Anthemion(IRE)**, who tried to make all from out of the handicap at the track just 24-hours earlier, showed the benefit of this drop in grade to comfortably make all the running. He finished runner-up at this track off a much higher mark in May and could well folllow-up on this, granted he can grab an early lead.
**Encounter** stayed on well to finish a never-dangerous second and ran his best race for a while. He needs all to fall right and is not the force of old, but could go one better with a stronger pace at this level.
**Donna's Double** paid late on for running keenly through the early stages, but would have been seen to a better effect with a stronger gallop, and was not disgraced in the circumstances.
**Oscar Pepper(USA)** ran below form on this faster ground and has become a very hard horse to win with.
**Kirkham Abbey** would have been much better suited by a faster gallop and got badly outpaced when the tempo quickend from two out. He is high in the weights at present and may be best left alone until he drops in the ratings.
**Coustou(IRE)** *Official explanation: trainer said gelding ran flat and race may have come too soon after previous run*
**Ace Coming** *Official explanation: jockey said gelding was never travelling*
T/Plt: £99.20 to a £1 stake. Pool £32,950.65. 242.30 winning units T/Qpdt: £52.30 to a £1 stake. Pool £2,129.80, 30.10 winning units RY

# 3450 NEWBURY (L-H)
## Friday, July 16
**OFFICIAL GOING: Good (good to firm in places)**

## 3904 EBF STARLIGHT MAIDEN FILLIES' STKS — 6f 8y
**2:00** (2:06) (D) 2-Y-O — **£7,605** (£2,340; £1,170; £585) **Stalls** Centre

Form — RPR
**1** **Free Lift** 2-8-11 ........ SDrowne 8 81+
(RCharlton) *rangy: lw: hld up rr but in tch: hdwy fr 2f out: pushed along and qckND fnl f to ld fnl 100yds: readily* **33/1**
**2** *¾* **Quickfire** 2-8-11 ........ KFallon 6 79+
(SirMichaelStoute) *tall: str: lw: trckd ldrs:ld appr fnl f: rdn ins last: hdd and no ex fnl 100yds* **4/9**[1]
0 **3** *1* **Madhavi**[8] 3675 2-8-11 ........ RHughes 4 76
(RHannon) *pressed ldrs: rdn over 1f out: nt qckn ins last* **33/1**
**4** *nk* **Miss L'Augeval** 2-8-11 ........ TEDurcan 10 75
(GWragg) *str: scope: s.i.s: bhd: pushed along and hdwy appr fnl f: fin wl and gng on cl home* **25/1**
4 **5** *1* **Indiena**[8] 3676 2-8-11 ........ JFortune 5 72
(BJMeehan) *mde most tl rdn and hdd appr fnl f: wknd last half f* **10/1**[3]
25 **6** *1 ½* **Alexander Capetown (IRE)**[64] 2071 2-8-11 ........ MartinDwyer 3 68
(BWHills) *lw: w ldr: rdn 2f out: wknd fnl f* **25/1**
**7** *1 ¾* **Bountiful** 2-8-11 ........ DSweeney 1 62
(MBlanshard) *w'like: in tch: rdn over 2f out: sn outpcd: wknd fnl f* **40/1**
**8** *1 ¼* **Cabin Fever** 2-8-11 ........ RSmith 11 59
(JCFox) *neat: slowly away: bhd: styd on fnl 2f: nvr nr ldrs* **100/1**
**9** *½* **Modraj** 2-8-11 ........ RHills 2 57
(JLDunlop) *leggy: unf: sn chsng ldrs: rdn 2f out: sn wknd* **14/1**
**10** *nk* **Evasive Quality (FR)** 2-8-11 ........ TPQueally 12 56
(DRLoder) *tall: bit bkwd: in tch: rdn over 2f out: sn wknd* **7/1**[2]
**11** *nk* **Divine Diva** 2-8-11 ........ DaneO'Neill 9 55
(RHannon) *lengthy: rdn 3f out: a bhd* **33/1**
**12** *4* **Midcap (IRE)** 2-8-11 ........ MHills 7 43
(BWHills) *slowly away: a in rr* **25/1**

1m 14.56s (0.19) **Going Correction** -0.15s/f (Firm) — **12 Ran SP% 121.3**
Speed ratings: **92,91,89,89,87 85,83,81,81,80 80,75**CSF £47.61 TOTE £23.80: £4.50, £1.10, £4.20; EX 72.30.
**Owner** The Queen **Bred** The Queen **Trained** Beckhampton, Wilts

**FOCUS**
Only three of the 12 runners had previous experience, making this a hard race to weigh up. While the form might not be that special, there were several very nice prospects, notably the first two and the fourth.

**NOTEBOOK**
**Free Lift** ◆, by the sprinter Cadeaux Generaux out of a Shirley Heights mare, showed a fine turn of foot to make a winning debut. The style of her victory suggests she will be a force in better grade, and she was quoted at 25-1 for next year's 1,000 Guineas after the race.
**Quickfire** ◆, the first daughter of Dubai Millennium to reach the racecourse, came into the race with a smart reputation and there was plenty to like about this first effort despite her failure to land the odds. She will stay farther and can be expected to win good races.
**Madhavi** showed the benefit of her debut, chasing home two fillies of some potential. There are races to be won with her.
**Miss L'Augeval** ◆, an Entrepreneur filly, made a promising debut and will be suited by seven furlongs before long. The stable's juveniles often come on for their first outings, so her future looks bright.
**Indiena** did the donkey work again and those who beat her will win their share of races, so this was a good performance.
**Alexander Capetown(IRE)** had more experience than any in the field, having run twice previously. She is up to winning a routine maiden, or a nursery now she is eligible.
**Cabin Fever** caught the eye down the field and should be monitored for signs of improvement.
**Modraj** should be more effective over a slightly longer trip in due course.

## 3905 MOUNTGRANGE STUD MAIDEN FILLIES' STKS — 7f (S)
**2:35** (2:38) (D) 2-Y-O — **£7,572** (£2,330; £1,165; £582) **Stalls** Centre

Form — RPR
**1** **Windscreamer** 2-8-11 ........ MHills 10 89
(JWHills) *rangy: str: scope: hld up in rr: stdy hdwy over 2f out: led appr fnl f: pushed along and r.o strly ins last: comf* **12/1**[3]
**2** *2 ½* **Proud Scholar (USA)** 2-8-11 ........ RHughes 11 82
(MrsAJPerrett) *well grown: lw: s.i.s: sn rcvrd and in tch: chsd ldr ins fnl 2f: chsd wnr fnl f but no imp* **7/1**[2]
**3** *2 ½* **Dubai Surprise (IRE)** 2-8-11 ........ TPQueally 7 76
(DRLoder) *leggy: prom: rdn over 2f out: styd on fnl f but nvr gng pce of ldrs* **7/1**[2]
**4** *hd* **Something Exciting** 2-8-11 ........ NPollard 12 76
(DRCElsworth) *unf: chsd ldrs: rdn over 2f out: styd on fnl f but nvr a danger* **40/1**
3 **5** *1* **Swan Nebula (USA)**[20] 3296 2-8-11 ........ (t) LDettori 6 73
(SaeedBinSuroor) *led: hdd appr fnl f: wknd qckly ins last* **5/4**[1]
**6** *1 ¼* **Cassydora** 2-8-11 ........ TQuinn 1 70
(JLDunlop) *rangy: scope: s.i.s: bhd and sn pushed along: styd on fnl 2f but nvr gng pce to rch ldrs* **16/1**
**7** *hd* **Kalmini (USA)** 2-8-11 ........ CCatlin 9 69
(MRChannon) *w'like: in tch: rdn to chse ldrs over 2f out: outpcd fnl f* **40/1**
**8** *¾* **Sadie Thompson (IRE)** 2-8-11 ........ TEDurcan 4 68
(MRChannon) *leggy: mid-div: rdn over 2f out: kpt on fnl f but nvr nr ldrs* **16/1**
**9** *1 ½* **Silver Highlight (CAN)** 2-8-11 ........ MartinDwyer 8 64
(AMBalding) *tall: str: bkwd: bhd: pushed along 3f out: sme hdwy fnl f* **20/1**
0 **10** *nk* **Take It There**[9] 3627 2-8-11 ........ DaneO'Neill 5 63
(RHannon) *chsd ldrs: rdn over 2f out: wknd over 1f out* **12/1**[3]
**11** *1* **Musical Day** 2-8-11 ........ JFortune 2 61
(BJMeehan) *lenghty: bhd: pushed along 1/2-way and n.d* **40/1**
**12** *13* **Corniche Dancer** 2-8-8 ........ SHitchcott(3) 13 28
(MRChannon) *lenghty: str: plld hrd: pressed ldr 4f out tl wknd qckly appr fnl 2f* **66/1**
**13** *3* **Ushindi (IRE)** 2-8-11 ........ KFallon 3 21
(MLWBell) *neat: chsd ldrs tl wknd qckly 2f out* **12/1**[3]

1m 26.8s (-14.54) **Going Correction** -0.15s/f (Firm) — **13 Ran SP% 117.9**
Speed ratings: **96,93,90,90,88 87,87,86,84,84 83,68,64**CSF £88.54 TOTE £23.10: £4.60, £2.30, £2.40; EX 189.20.
**Owner** Mrs Stevie Richards **Bred** T R Lock **Trained** Upper Lambourn, Berks

**FOCUS**
Little previous form to go on, but the winner looks useful and the runner-up should also make her mark. Some of those farther down the field need to improve to have hopes of success outside routine company.

**NOTEBOOK**
**Windscreamer** ◆, just a 10,000 guineas purchase but well regarded at home, is from a winning family and produced an impressive debut performance. If her trainer is correct, she will be capable of holding her own in Pattern company as she gains experience.
**Proud Scholar(USA)** was no match for the winner but is capable of winning a similar contest.
**Dubai Surprise(IRE)**, a 220,000 guineas King's Best filly out of an unraced mare, was the most expensive of these. She can be expected to win her maiden before long.
**Something Exciting**, a 20,000 guineas Halling filly, looks the sort to improve with time, so this was a satisfactory debut.
**Swan Nebula(USA)** had the benefit of previous run, so this was rather disappointing. She has ability but does not look to be a stable star.
**Cassydora**, whose dam won over a mile as a juvenile, should come into her own over ten furlongs and more next year, and anything this season will be a bonus. In the circumstances, a satisfactory debut.
**Kalmini(USA)**, whose dam won over a mile and a half, is not bred to be precocious but made a fair debut. She should be watched for signs of improvement.
**Sadie Thompson(IRE)** cost 130,000 guineas as a yearling but her position in the market did not suggest anything special, and so it proved. She is nicely bred, but her next run will show if she is going in the right direction.

## 3906 TATTERSALLS CONDITIONS STKS — 7f (S)
**3:05** (3:08) (B) 3-Y-O+ — **£13,050** (£4,950; £2,475; £1,125) **Stalls** Centre

Form — RPR
**1** **Fong's Thong (USA)**[349] 3-8-7 ........ JFortune 3 114
(BJMeehan) *well grown: lw: trckd ldr: led jst ins fnl 2f: drvn clr ins last* **25/1**
2200 **2** *3 ½* **Moonlight Man**[10] 3598 3-8-7 103 ........ DaneO'Neill 6 105
(RHannon) *lw: trckd ldrs: chsd wnr over 1f out: kpt on to hold narrow 2nd thrght fnl f but no ch w wnr* **50/1**
01-0 **3** *shd* **Polar Way**[27] 3073 5-9-0 110 ........ RHughes 7 105
(MrsAJPerrett) *s.i.s: hld up in rr and t.k.h: hdwy over 2f out: kpt on to dispute 2nd thrght fnl f but no ch w wnr* **9/2**[2]
1-06 **4** *2 ½* **Prince Tum Tum (USA)**[20] 3318 4-8-11 101 ........ TQuinn 5 95
(JLDunlop) *in tch: rdn to chse ldrs over 2f out: sn one pce: wknd ins last* **20/1**
4-02 **5** *nk* **Desert Destiny**[20] 3318 4-8-11 110 ........ (t) LDettori 8 94
(SaeedBinSuroor) *lw: hld up in rr: shkn up and effrt over 2f out: little rspnse and wknd fnl f* **10/11**[1]
3240 **6** *3 ½* **Psychiatrist**[30] 2966 3-8-7 100 ........ KFallon 2 88
(RHannon) *chsd ldrs: rdn 3f out: wknd 2f out* **12/1**[3]
20-3 **7** *½* **Orcadian**[48] 2476 3-8-4 103 ........ RHills 1 84
(JMPEustace) *led tl hdd ins fnl 2f: wknd over 1f out* **9/2**[2]

0000 **8** *nk* **Stormont (IRE)**[13] 3537 4-9-7 104........ TEDurcan 4 93
(HJCollingridge) *s.i.s: hld up rr: sme hdwy over 2f: nt pce to trble ldrs and sn btn* **22/1**

1m 23.88s (-3.34) **Going Correction** -0.15s/f (Firm)
**WFA** 3 from 4yo+ 7lb **8** Ran SP% **111.4**
Speed ratings: **113,109,108,106,105 101,101,100**CSF £811.22 TOTE £14.30: £2.10, £5.20, £1.60; EX 256.40.
**Owner** Joe L Allbritton **Bred** W A Hamilton **Trained** Upper Lambourn, Berks

**FOCUS**
Some very smart performers, though many of them are underachieving this season. However, the surprise winner was impressive and posted a very good time for the grade, and his next outing will be keenly awaited.

**NOTEBOOK**
**Fong's Thong(USA)** was formerly a smart American dirt track performer, successful once at 1m and placed twice from three outings. This was a remarkably good first effort on turf and his attitude looks sound, so there should be plenty more to come.
**Moonlight Man** had been out of sorts in recent outings and this represented a return to form. He had no chance with the winner, but there were some smart performers behind.
**Polar Way**was running more in his grade this time but was comfortably held. He stays seven furlongs but the balance of his form is better over six.
**Prince Tum Tum(USA)** retains some ability; the problem will be finding the right race for him.
**Desert Destiny** should have gone close if past form was anything to go by, but he has become an expensive horse to follow despite being gelded.
**Psychiatrist** is probably more effective over a mile or so on slightly easier ground.
**Orcadian** had the chance to control things from the front but ultimately proved a disappointment.
**Stormont(IRE)** had a tough task at the weights.

## 3907 NAYEF ROSE BOWL STKS (LISTED RACE) 6f 8y
3:35 (3:36) (A) 2-Y-O £14,500 (£5,500; £2,750; £1,250) **Stalls** Centre

Form RPR
021 **1** **Don Pele (IRE)**[25] 3157 2-8-11 ........ JFortune 3 106
(SKirk) *h.d.w: lw: mde virtually all: rdn and edgd rt to stands side fnl f: r.o wl* **5/1**[3]
1 **2** *2* **Black Velvet**[64] 2058 2-8-11 ........ MartinDwyer 7 100
(MPTregoning) *trckd ldrs: chsd wnr fr 4f out: rdn over 2f out: kpt on u.p fnl f: no imp on wnr* **13/8**[1]
6051 **3** *3 ½* **Indiannie Star**[7] 3696 2-8-6 ........ TEDurcan 6 85
(MRChannon) *hld up in rr: t.k.h: hdwy 2f out: styd on fr over 1f out but nvr gng pce to rch ldrs* **25/1**
14 **4** *nk* **St Andrews Storm (USA)**[9] 3640 2-8-11 ........ RHughes 8 89
(RHannon) *lw: stdd s: hld up in rr: hdwy over 2f out: hrd rdn over 1f out styd on same pce ins fnl* **11/4**[2]
510 **5** *shd* **Al Qudra (IRE)**[8] 3672 2-8-11 ........ RLMoore 5 88
(BJMeehan) *chsd ldrs: rdn over 2f out: sn btn* **40/1**
3210 **6** *1 ¼* **Beaver Patrol (IRE)**[31] 2954 2-9-0 ........ SCarson 4 88
(RFJohnsonHoughton) *in tch: rdn over 2f out: nvr gng pce to rch ldrs and sn bhd* **14/1**
4 **7** *1 ¼* **Tanzani (USA)**[16] 3424 2-8-11 ........ MHills 1 81
(CEBrittain) *chsd ldrs: shkn up over 2f out and sn btn* **33/1**
1 **8** *2 ½* **Street Cred**[11] 3588 2-8-11 ........ KFallon 2 73
(AMBalding) *chaed wnr 2f: rdn over 2f out: sn wknd* **6/1**

1m 13.15s (-1.22) **Going Correction** -0.15s/f (Firm) **8** Ran SP% **111.6**
Speed ratings: **102,99,94,94,94 92,90,87**CSF £12.85 TOTE £6.40: £2.10, £1.40, £3.50; EX 21.00.
**Owner** Pedro Rosas **Bred** John J Cosgrave **Trained** Upper Lambourn, Berks

**FOCUS**
Not the strongest renewal of this Listed race, but the form is reasonable, the time was up to scratch and Don Pele is progressing really well.

**NOTEBOOK**
**Don Pele(IRE)** is improving with racing and paid another compliment to Chepstow winner CaesarBeware. A tough sort with natural speed, he looked happier once he found the rail and beat some potentially useful rivals.
**Black Velvet**, considered a Pattern standard performer by his stable, was readily held but finished clear of the rest. He could go to Goodwood for his next race.
**Indiannie Star** was more exposed than most in the race but had previously run only at five furlongs. This longer trip did not appear to be a problem, but the first two were much too good for her.
**St Andrews Storm(USA)** had run well in the July Stakes the previous week and may not have fully recovered, because he failed to build on that effort.
**Al Qudra(IRE)** has taken on some smart rivals in his last two races and is showing a creditable level of form despite failing to make a major impact.
**Beaver Patrol(IRE)** had a hard job conceding weight all round in this company.

## 3908 BAILEYS HORSE FEEDS FILLIES' H'CAP 1m 2f 6y
4:10 (4:11) (D) (0-80,80) 3-Y-O £6,032 (£1,856; £928; £464) **Stalls** Low

Form RPR
0522 **1** **Wee Dinns (IRE)**[35] 2848 3-9-2 **75** ........ JFEgan 10 89+
(SKirk) *lw: hld up rr but in tch: stdy hdwy on outside fr 3f out: sn pressing ldrs: led 2f out: drvn clr fnl f* **9/2**[2]
06-1 **2** *3* **Mazuna (IRE)**[16] 3421 3-8-8 **67** ........ RLMoore 7 73
(CEBrittain) *in tch: rdn over 2f out: chsd ldrs over 1f out: styd on to take 2nd cl home but no ch w wnr* **7/1**
523 **3** *1* **Tree Tops**[59] 2198 3-8-13 **72** ........ JFortune 11 76
(JHMGosden) *chsd ldrs: chal over 3f out tl slt ld over 2f out: sn hdd: no ch w wnr fnl f: lost 2nd cl home* **13/2**[3]
4-03 **4** *2* **Thirteen Tricks (USA)**[23] 3206 3-9-2 **75** ........ JPMurtagh 2 75
(MrsAJPerrett) *chsd ldrs: rdn 3f out: styd on same pce fnl 2f* **8/1**
55-1 **5** *5* **Goodwood Finesse (IRE)**[28] 3044 3-9-2 **75** ........ GCarter 12 66
(JLDunlop) *bhd: rdn over 4f out: kpt on u.p fnl 2f but nvr nr ldrs* **4/1**[1]
-101 **6** *1* **Cause Celebre (IRE)**[19] 3340 3-9-7 **80** ........ MHills 9 69
(BWHills) *chsd ldr tl led 4f out: rdn 3f out: hdd over 2f out: sn btn* **9/1**
00-4 **7** *1* **Land Of Nod (IRE)**[100] 1304 3-8-4 **63** ........ EAhern 6 50
(GAButler) *bit bkwd: chsd ldrs: rdn and one pce whn hmpd over 2f out: swtchd rt and sn wknd* **14/1**
-006 **8** *1 ½* **In Deep**[25] 3160 3-8-6 **65** ........ MartinDwyer 1 49
(MrsPNDutfield) *bhd: rdn 3f out: n.d* **22/1**
0022 **9** *nk* **Principessa**[14] 3473 3-8-11 **70** ........ TEDurcan 3 53
(BPalling) *led tl hdd 4f out: wknd ins fnl 3f* **11/1**
2551 **10** *nk* **Dark Raider (IRE)**[29] 3007 3-8-8 **70** ........ DCorby(3) 5 53
(APJones) *chsd ldrs: rdn and wkng whn n.m.r and wknd over 2f out* **14/1**
5-53 **11** *hd* **Gwen John (USA)**[28] 3044 3-9-1 **74** ........ SDrowne 4 57
(HMorrison) *rdn 3f out: a in rr* **10/1**
-024 **12** *2 ½* **Powerful Parrish (USA)**[11] 3574 3-9-5 **78** ........ KFallon 8 56
(PFICole) *lw: in tch: rdn and wknd 3f out* **16/1**

2m 6.86s (-1.85) **Going Correction** -0.15s/f (Firm) **12** Ran SP% **126.1**
Speed ratings: **101,98,97,96,92 91,90,89,89,88 88,86**CSF £38.78 CT £213.53 TOTE £6.60: £2.10, £3.60, £2.30; EX 61.00.
**Owner** F B O T Racing **Bred** Swordlestown Stud **Trained** Upper Lambourn, Berks

**FOCUS**
A fair 0-80 fillies' handicap won by a horse at the top of her form. In contrast, many of the others failed to produce their best, and several could do with dropping a few pounds..

**NOTEBOOK**
**Wee Dinns(IRE)** has been threatening to win a race and was able to overcome a 5 lb rise in the weights. The Handicapper is the main threat to further success, for she is is a filly in flying form at present.
**Mazuna(IRE)** performed with credit over the shorter trip, only to run into an in-form rival.
**Tree Tops**'s handicap mark is not far wrong, and she should continue to be thereabouts in similar contests.
**Thirteen Tricks(USA)** did not progress from her previous run, but a little sympathy from the Handicapper should see her drop to a winning mark.
**Goodwood Finesse(IRE)**, racing off a stiff mark, was drawn wide and soon struggling. *Official explanation: trainer said filly was outpaced early*
**Cause Celebre(IRE)** is becoming inconsistent, but she had plenty of weight here.
**Powerful Parrish(USA)** *Official explanation: jockey said filly lost its action*

## 3909 WINDSOR PLC H'CAP 1m 3f 5y
4:40 (4:42) (D) (0-85,85) 3-Y-O+ £5,850 (£1,800; £900; £450) **Stalls** Low

Form RPR
3653 **1** **Gold Ring**[7] 3716 4-10-0 **85** ........ SCarson 7 97
(GBBalding) *trckd ldrs: kpt on ins rail and rdn to pressed ldrs fr 3f out: led ins fnl 2f: drvn and styd on wl fnl f* **3/1**[1]
3-25 **2** *2 ½* **Genghis (IRE)**[15] 3449 5-9-9 **80** ........ JFortune 10 88
(HMorrison) *lw: slt ld after 1f: styd in centre crse and rdn fr 3f out: hdd ins fnl 2f: edgd lft u.p and nt qckn ins last* **6/1**
4111 **3** *1 ¼* **Unsuited**[23] 3206 5-8-5 **69** ........ NataliaGemelova(7) 6 75
(JELong) *in tch: hdwy 3f out: pushed along to chal 2f out: one pce ins last* **8/1**
0341 **4** *½* **Ken's Dream**[21] 3274 5-9-11 **82** ........ PMcCabe 8 87
(MsAEEmbiricos) *t.k.h: hld up in rr: stdy hdwy over 2f out: chsd ldrs and rdn over 1f out: nt qckn ins last* **5/1**[3]
/004 **5** *3 ½* **Ocean Of Storms (IRE)**[15] 3442 9-9-2 **78** ........(t) RThomas(5) 4 78
(ChristianWroe, UAE) *slowly away: bhd: hdwy on outside fr 3f out: nvr gng pce to rch ldrs* **25/1**
0360 **6** *5* **Briareus**[7] 3692 4-9-6 **77** ........ MartinDwyer 9 69
(AMBalding) *chsd ldrs: rdn over 3f out: wknd over 2f out* **9/2**[2]
10-2 **7** *1* **Silver City**[15] 3442 4-9-10 **81** ........ RHughes 11 71
(MrsAJPerrett) *sn chsng ldr: rdn over 3f out: wknd qckly over 2f out* **8/1**
-000 **8** *½* **Financial Future**[41] 2681 4-10-0 **85** ........ BrigitteRenk 5 74
(MJohnston) *chsd ldrs tl wknd over 3f out* **33/1**
30-0 **9** *11* **Victory Venture (IRE)**[39] 2738 4-9-3 **74** ........ TEDurcan 1 46
(IanWilliams) *lw: rdn 4f out: a bhd* **50/1**
**10** *½* **Dawton (POL)**[15] 6-9-7 **78** ........ RLMoore 3 49
(TRGeorge) *chsd ldrs: rdn over 3f out: sn wknd* **7/1**
16-0 **11** *4* **Vin Du Pays**[100] 1302 4-7-12 **55** ........ AMcCarthy 2 19
(MBlanshard) *lw: a in rr* **40/1**

2m 19.67s (-3.14) **Going Correction** -0.15s/f (Firm) **11** Ran SP% **120.0**
Speed ratings: **105,103,102,101,99 95,95,94,86,86 83**CSF £21.07 CT £134.16 TOTE £4.20: £1.90, £2.20, £2.00; EX 25.50.
**Owner** Miss B Swire **Bred** Miss B Swire **Trained** Kimpton,Hants

**FOCUS**
Solid handicap form. The winner is better than ever, and the placed horses were right up to their best too.

**NOTEBOOK**
**Gold Ring** had previously won only once in 21 starts, but this sterling effort showed how cruel statistics can be. He stays farther than this and may go hurdling next winter.
**Genghis(IRE)** seemed at home over the shorter trip. He is still relatively unexposed and should find a race soon. *Official explanation: jockey said gelding hung right on bend*
**Unsuited** ran well considering she has been racing up the handicap. Her winning run may have been ended, but this looks improved form yet again.
**Ken's Dream** needs a strong pace to stop him pulling, so this was not a bad effort off a 3 lb higher mark.
**Ocean Of Storms(IRE)** is on a lenient mark if he can recapture his old form. Learning to break properly would be a good place to start. *Official explanation: jockey said horse missed break*
**Briareus** is handicapped to go close at present, but has not run convincingly in recent races.
**Silver City** did not reproduce the form of his good seasonal debut, and may have "bounced".

## 3910 LADBROKES.COM H'CAP 7f (S)
5:10 (5:13) (D) (0-80,80) 3-Y-O+ £6,032 (£1,856; £928; £464) **Stalls** Centre

Form RPR
0023 **1** **Boundless Prospect (USA)**[15] 3455 5-9-5 **71** ........ MHills 6 82
(JWHills) *bhd: reminders over 4f out: hdwy over 2f out: led appr fnl f: drvn kpt on strly ins last* **12/1**
02-5 **2** *1 ½* **Point Of Dispute**[15] 3455 9-10-0 **80** ........(v) MartinDwyer 4 87
(PJMakin) *hld up in rr: hdwy 2f out: drvn to chal over 1f out: kpt on ins last but nt pce on wnr* **14/1**
621- **3** *¾* **Star Of Light**[241] 6021 3-9-3 **76** ........ JFortune 8 81
(BJMeehan) *led 2f: styd pressing ldrs and ev ch u.p fnl 2f: no ex ins last* **50/1**
0204 **4** *nk* **And Toto Too**[15] 3457 4-9-1 **67** ........(b) RLMoore 2 71
(PDEvans) *slowl;y into stride: bhd: hdwy fr 3f out: styd on to chse ldrs fnl f but nt pce to chal* **16/1**
0110 **5** *1 ¾* **Yorkshire Blue**[31] 2965 5-8-6 **58** ........ TEDurcan 16 58
(JSGoldie) *chsd ldrs tl n.m.r and outpcd 2f out: rdn and kpt on fr over 1f out: fin wl: nt rch ldrs* **11/1**
3201 **6** *1* **Chandelier**[7] 3697 4-7-12 **48** 6ex oh2........ AMcCarthy 7 47
(MSSaunders) *chsd ldrs: led ins fnl 2f: hdd appr fnl f: wknd ins last* **20/1**
0006 **7** *2 ½* **Nivernais**[15] 3453 5-9-2 **73** ........(t) NChalmers(5) 3 64
(HCandy) *chsd ldrs: rdn and ev ch 2f out: wknd fnl f* **12/1**
0300 **8** *hd* **Just Fly**[7] 3698 4-9-5 **78** ........ JDaly(7) 15 68
(SKirk) *in tch: pushed along and chse ldrs 2f out: outpcd fnl f* **25/1**
5261 **9** *1 ½* **Tuscarora (IRE)**[4] 3807 5-8-6 **58** 6ex........ TPQueally 17 44
(AWCarroll) *bhd: rdn and some hdwy over 2f out: nt rch ldrs and n.d after* **8/1**[3]
-000 **10** *nk* **Nabtat Saif**[25] 3156 3-8-8 **67** ........(t) RSmith 10 53
(RHannon) *bhd: sme hdwy whn n.m.r over 2f out: n.d after* **50/1**
20-1 **11** *hd* **Gallery Breeze**[20] 3301 5-9-4 **70** ........ VSlattery 9 55
(JLSpearing) *fly j. s: sn in tch: outpcd over 2f out: kpt on again ins fnl f* **12/1**
4543 **12** *¾* **Azreme**[7] 3690 4-9-3 **69** ........ IMongan 14 52
(DKIvory) *b.hind: chsd ldrs: ev ch 2f out: wknd fnl f* **6/1**[1]
0022 **13** *1 ½* **Bi Polar**[9] 3626 4-9-4 **73** ........ LPKeniry(3) 11 52
(DRCElsworth) *chsd ldrs: led after 2f: hdd 3f out: wknd over 1f out* **7/1**[2]
6-22 **14** *½* **Sabrina Brown**[7] 3700 3-7-10 **60** ........ RThomas(5) 12 38
(GBBalding) *pressed ldrs: led over 2f out: hdd ins fnl 2f: sn wknd* **6/1**[1]

0500 **15** *3 ½* **Wood Fern (UAE)**[12] 3555 4-8-5 **60** ow3.....................(v[1]) SHitchcott[(3)] 5 29
(MRChannon) *in tch: chsd ldrs 3f out to 2f out: sn wknd* **33/1**
5110 **16** *1 ¾* **Oh Boy (IRE)**[10] 3597 4-9-6 **72**.......................................... RHughes 13 36
(RHannon) *lw: w ldrs: led 3f out tl over 2f out: wknd over 1f out* **7/1**[2]
00-0 **17** *4* **Kindlelight Debut**[27] 3086 4-9-4 **77**................................. MHoward[(7)] 1 31
(DKIvory) *lw: chsd ldrs in centre crse tl wknd qckly 2f out* **40/1**

1m 25.58s (-1.64) **Going Correction** -0.15s/f (Firm)
**WFA** 3 from 4yo+ 7lb **17** Ran SP% **126.6**
Speed ratings: **103,101,100,100,98 96,94,93,92,91 91,90,89,88,84 82,77**CSF £164.55 CT £7902.43 TOTE £14.10: £2.90, £4.80, £7.20, £2.40; EX 169.20 Place 6 £155.90, Place 5 £111.55.
**Owner** M Wauchope,Sir Simon Dunning,R Cottam **Bred** Mrs Edgar Scott Jr & Mrs Lawrence Macelree **Trained** Upper Lambourn, Berks

**FOCUS**
A routine 0-80 handicap, with the field initially racing in two groups before converging in the middle. The first four home were all in the bottom half of the draw and raced in the centre.

**NOTEBOOK**
**Boundless Prospect(USA)** has been coming back into form in recent races. He was on a winning mark, and this is his trip.
**Point Of Dispute** is unpredictable but runs enough good races to keep him high in the weights, though he has dropped a little in recent outings. He could win off this mark if only he were to finish off his races properly.
**Star Of Light** ◆ had run mainly on the all-weather until now. However, this fine effort, following an eight-month absence, suggests he can win a similar race on turf, with races over longer trips an option.
**And Toto Too** continues to go close off her current mark, which does not encourage the Handicapper to drop her a couple of pounds. This was another solid effort.
**Yorkshire Blue** ran better than last time and did not get the run of the race. He is still well capable of figuring in similar races, despite having gone up the weights for his two earlier successes.
**Chandelier** found it tough under a 6lb penalty for his selling win.
**Oh Boy(IRE)** *Official explanation: trainer said he had no explanation for colt's poor performance*
T/Jkpt: Not won. T/Plt: £211.40 to a £1 stake. Pool: £46,265.30. 159.75 winning tickets. T/Qpdt: £51.10 to a £1 stake. Pool: £3,288.10. 47.60 winning tickets. ST

## 3671 NEWMARKET (JULY) (R-H)
### Friday, July 16

**OFFICIAL GOING: Good**
Plenty of rain throughout the morning ensured the ground, at least on the straight course, looked to be riding slower than the official Good.
Wind: Slight across Weather: Cloudy

### 3911 VIBE FM SALES BABES H'CAP — 1m
6:00 (6:01) (E) (0-75,74) 4-Y-0+ **£4,251** (£1,308; £654; £327) **Stalls** Low

Form RPR
1333 **1** **Best Before (IRE)**[9] 3631 4-9-11 **74**.................................... FPFerris[(3)] 2 87
(PDEvans) *racd far side: chsd ldrs: rdn to ld 1f out: r.o wl* **7/1**[3]
0002 **2** *2* **Quicks The Word**[11] 3579 4-8-8 **54**.......................................... OUrbina 20 62
(CWThornton) *led stands' side: rdn over 1f out: styd on* **14/1**
6604 **3** *nk* **Didnt Tell My Wife**[13] 3520 5-9-0 **63**.............................. LisaJones[(3)] 15 70
(CFWall) *racd stands' side: hld up: hdwy over 1f out: r.o* **11/2**[2]
0000 **4** *hd* **Huxley (IRE)**[63] 2084 5-9-10 **70**............................................ JPMurtagh 13 77
(MGQuinlan) *lw: racd stands' side: chsd ldrs: rdn over 1f out: styd on* **5/1**[1]
-000 **5** *2 ½* **Mamore Gap (IRE)**[107] 1213 6-9-3 **70**................................ PGallagher[(7)] 18 71
(RHannon) *lw: racd stands' side: hld up: hdwy and nt clr run over 1f out: nt rch ldrs* **25/1**
0043 **6** *1* **No Chance To Dance (IRE)**[17] 3401 4-8-3 **49** ow1........(t) KMcEvoy 14 48
(HJCollingridge) *lw: racd stands' side: hld up in tch: rdn over 1f out: styd on same pce* **12/1**
0040 **7** *nk* **Gifted Flame**[11] 3586 5-9-3 **63**..............................................(p) KFallon 9 61
(TDBarron) *racd far side: hld up: swtchd rt and hdwy over 3f out: led 2f out : rdn and hdd 1f out: sn wknd* **10/1**
1005 **8** *hd* **Slalom (IRE)**[6] 3745 4-10-0 **74**..........................................(p) MFenton 17 72
(MissGayKelleway) *racd stands' side: dwlt: hld up: hdwy over 1f out: nvr trbld ldrs* **20/1**
1360 **9** *½* **Royal Racer (FR)**[34] 2886 6-8-4 **50** ow1...............................(v[1]) EAhern 1 47
(JRBest) *racd far side: chsd ldrs: rdn over 2f out: wknd over 1f out* **50/1**
0400 **10** *½* **Juste Pour L'Amour**[13] 3525 4-9-12 **72**.................................. JFEgan 4 67
(PLGilligan) *led far side 6f: wknd over 1f out* **20/1**
1060 **11** *½* **Classic Vision**[11] 3586 4-8-7 **53**..............................................(b) RHills 19 47
(WJHaggas) *racd stands' side: chsd ldrs: rdn over 2f out: wknd fnl f* **12/1**
0206 **12** *1* **Halcyon Magic**[9] 3626 6-7-11 **48**...........................(b) HayleyTurner[(5)] 11 40
(MissJFeilden) *racd far side: mid-div: effrt 1/2-way: nvr trbld ldrs* **25/1**
4060 **13** *3 ½* **Tuscan Treaty**[25] 3151 4-8-1 **47**...........................................(v) JMackay 3 31
(TTClement) *racd far side: n.d* **50/1**
5-50 **14** *4* **Secluded**[18] 3387 4-9-7 **67**......................................................... SDrowne 6 42
(ACStewart) *racd far side: chsd ldrs 6f* **9/1**
0023 **15** *2* **Mac's Talisman (IRE)**[11] 3579 4-8-10 **56**.............................. MTebbutt 10 26
(VSmith) *racd far side: hld up in tch: rdn and wknd over 2f out* **20/1**
3003 **16** *nk* **Eastern Hope (IRE)**[12] 3559 5-8-7 **60**......................... KristinStubbs[(7)] 7 29
(MrsLStubbs) *racd stands' side: dwlt: bhd: pushed along 1/2-way: a in rr* **20/1**
0320 **17** *nk* **Fantasy Crusader**[16] 3423 5-8-4 **50**......................................(p) WRyan 16 19
(JAGilbert) *racd stands' side: disp ld 6f: wknd over 1f out* **16/1**
620/ **18** *3 ½* **Night Dance**[250] 12-7-5 **44** oh19.................................. FrancesPickard[(7)] 5 5
(MWigham) *swtg: racd far side: bhd fr 1/2-way* **50/1**
000/ **19** *hd* **We'Re Stonybroke (IRE)**[45] 2563 5-8-11 **57**....................... CLowther 8 17
(ThomasCooper, Ire) *unruly stalls: racd far side: plld hrd: w ldrs: rdn over 2f out: wknd over 1f out* **25/1**
40-0 **20** *2* **Pirouettes (IRE)**[191] 469 4-8-7 **53**........................................ PaulEddery 12 9
(EROertel) *racd far side: chsd ldrs over 5f* **50/1**

1m 40.13s (-0.35) **Going Correction** +0.075s/f (Good) **20** Ran SP% **130.0**
Speed ratings: **104,102,101,101,99 98,97,97,97,96 96,95,91,87,85 85,84,81,81,79**CSF £90.11 CT £602.77 TOTE £8.50: £1.70, £3.90, £1.70, £1.80; EX 136.70.
**Owner** Waterline Racing Club **Bred** Joe Rogers **Trained** Pandy, Gwent

**FOCUS**
The field split into two and there appeared to be no advantage to either side.

**NOTEBOOK**
**Best Before(IRE)**, who has been tackling better company of late, took advantage of this easier task and won with something in hand.
**Quicks The Word** had the advantage of the rails to help and won the race on his side. This trip suits him well and he should be able to find compensation off his current mark.
**Didnt Tell My Wife** turned in another solid effort and looks to be running into form.
**Huxley(IRE)**, well handicapped on his best Irish form, attracted plenty of support throughout the day and, although landing the place money, never really looked like scoring.
**Mamore Gap(IRE)** showed a bit more sparkle on this return to action, and as this is his time of year is one to keep an eye on in the coming weeks.

### 3912 VIBE FM NEWS TEAM CONDITIONS STKS — 1m 4f
6:30 (6:32) (C ) 3-Y-0+ **£8,502** (£3,225; £1,612; £733) **Stalls** Centre

Form RPR
2050 **1** **Eastern Breeze (IRE)**[6] 3756 6-9-1 102..........................(e) PaulEddery 5 110
(PWD'Arcy) *swtg: chsd ldrs: led over 4f out: rdn over 1f out: edgd lft ins fnl f: styd on* **16/1**
10-2 **2** *¾* **Westmoreland Road (USA)**[20] 3315 4-9-4 112................. JPMurtagh 7 112
(MrsAJPerrett) *lw: hld up in tch: jnd wnr over 2f out: rdn over 1f out: unable qck ins fnl f* **6/5**[1]
3053 **3** *1* **Island House (IRE)**[20] 3315 8-9-1 106.................................. DHolland 3 107
(GWragg) *lw: hld up: rdn over 3f out: hdwy over 1f out: styd on* **8/1**[3]
21-0 **4** *½* **Supremacy**[79] 1703 5-9-4 104............................................... KFallon 2 109
(SirMichaelStoute) *hld up: hdwy over 4f out: outpcd over 1f out: styd on towards fin* **9/1**
4-02 **5** *hd* **Delsarte (USA)**[62] 2108 4-9-1 111.........................................(t) KMcEvoy 1 106
(SaeedBinSuroor) *sn chsng ldr: rdn over 1f out: styd on same pce* **5/2**[2]
11-3 **6** *4* **Carini**[58] 2221 3-7-12 94........................................................ CCatlin 4 95
(HCandy) *mid-div: hdwy over 4f out: sn rdn: wknd over 1f out* **14/1**
-100 **7** *1* **Putra Sandhurst (IRE)**[41] 2681 6-9-9 102........................... PRobinson 9 106
(MAJarvis) *b.hind: led 1f: remained handy tl wknd over 1f out* **20/1**
24 **8** *5* **Historic Place (USA)**[22] 3245 4-9-1 ..................................... SDrowne 6 90?
(GBBalding) *hld up: rdn over 3f out: a in rr* **100/1**
5 **9** *20* **My True Love (IRE)**[19] 3341 5-9-1 ........................................ EAhern 8 58?
(RJBaker) *s.s: rcvrd to ld after 1f: hdd over 4f out: wknd over 3f out* **200/1**

2m 30.01s (-2.95) **Going Correction** -0.075s/f (Good)
**WFA** 3 from 4yo+ 12lb **9** Ran SP% **113.9**
Speed ratings: **106,105,104,104,104 101,101,97,84**CSF £35.21 TOTE £19.20: £4.20, £1.10, £2.30; EX 88.30.
**Owner** Colin Cage and Peter Lupson **Bred** Limestone Stud **Trained** Newmarket, Suffolk

**FOCUS**
A decent contest worthy of Listed status at least. The pace was good and with the 2nd and 3rd running close to their form here last month, the form looks solid enough.

**NOTEBOOK**
**Eastern Breeze(IRE)** appeared to have something to find on these terms with the principals, but looked to turn in an improved performance.There was certainly no fluke about the result and it will be interesting to see where he goes from here. *Official explanation: trainer said, regarding the improved form shown, gelding had benefited from its previous run at York, which came after a lengthy break, and also appreciated the step up in distance to 1m4f*
**Westmoreland Road(USA)** looked the part beforehand and had had no excuses, other than he may have found the ground easier than he cares for.
**Island House(IRE)**, closely matched with the runner-up on their running here last month, is a reliable yardstick and again gave it his best shot.
**Supremacy** ◆, over a trip short of his best, was far from disgraced. Back over a more suitable trip can see him return to winning ways.
**Delsarte(USA)** had no excuses and although he stays this far, is probably better at shorter.

### 3913 VIBE FM PRODUCTION KINGS MAIDEN STKS — 7f
7:00 (7:02) (D ) 2-Y-0 **£5,031** (£1,548; £774; £387) **Stalls** Low

Form RPR
**1** **Librettist (USA)** 2-9-0 .................................................................. LDettori 1 93+
(SaeedBinSuroor) *gd sort: s.s: hld up: hdwy over 2f out: led ins fnl f: r.o wl* **7/2**[2]
**2** *2 ½* **Baradore (IRE)** 2-8-9 ............................................................ RLMoore 11 79
(MGQuinlan) *w'like: b.off hind: a.p: chsd ldr 3f out: led over 1f out: hdd and unable qck ins fnl f* **6/1**[3]
**3** *1 ½* **Road Rage (IRE)** 2-8-9 ........................................................... EAhern 5 75
(EALDunlop) *neat: chsd ldrs: rdn over 1f out: styd on same pce* **10/1**
**4** *hd* **Etaar** 2-9-0 ................................................................................ DHolland 2 80
(NAGraham) *w'like: leggy: chsd ldrs: shkn up over 1f out: styd on same pce* **10/1**
**5** *½* **Home Affairs** 2-9-0 ..................................................................... KFallon 7 78
(SirMichaelStoute) *gd sort: lw: hld up: hdwy over 2f out: rdn over 1f out: styd on same pce ins fnl f* **5/2**[1]
5 **6** *2 ½* **Trainos (USA)**[36] 2804 2-9-0 ..................................................... TQuinn 3 72
(PFICole) *lw: led over 5f: wknd ins fnl f* **9/1**
**7** *1 ½* **Wujood** 2-9-0 .............................................................................. RHills 8 68
(JLDunlop) *compact: bkwd: hld up: nvr trbld ldrs* **9/1**
**8** *2 ½* **The Coires (IRE)** 2-9-0 ........................................................ DaneO'Neill 9 62
(RHannon) *w;like: scope: s.i.s: hld up: pushed along 1/2-way: n.d* **20/1**
0 **9** *2 ½* **Gurrun**[10] 3601 2-9-0 .................................................................. WRyan 6 56
(NACallaghan) *lw: chsd ldr 4f: sn wknd* **50/1**
**10** *1* **Rhoslan (IRE)** 2-9-0 ........................................................... JPMurtagh 4 53
(CADwyer) *w'like: b.: hld up: wknd over 2f out* **14/1**
**11** *6* **Penalty Kick (IRE)** 2-9-0 ...................................................... OUrbina 10 38
(NACallaghan) *gd sort: hld up: wknd over 2f out* **33/1**

1m 27.98s (1.21) **Going Correction** +0.075s/f (Good) **11** Ran SP% **119.6**
Speed ratings: **96,93,91,91,90 87,86,83,80,79 72**CSF £24.92 TOTE £4.10: £1.90, £2.10, £2.50; EX 36.20.
**Owner** Godolphin **Bred** Calumet Farm **Trained** Newmarket, Suffolk

**FOCUS**
A smart performance from the winner, despite the slow time.

**NOTEBOOK**
**Librettist(USA)**, a half-brother to the top-class Dubai Destination, showed a smart turn of foot to score with plenty in hand. While it is hard to know quite what he beat here, he showed a nice attitude and looks certain to hold his own in better company.
**Baradore(IRE)**, out of a mare that stayed 12 furlongs, would not have been suited by the steady early pace, but showed enough to suggest she can pay her way when facing a stiffer test.
**Road Rage(IRE)**, out of a mare that won over two miles, was another who would have been better suited to a stronger pace.
**Etaar**, a 36,000 gns yearling is related to several winners between five and 12 furlongs. He did not shape at all badly, and being by Zafonic may prefer a sounder surface than he faced here.
**Home Affairs** ◆, out of a Group Three-winning mare, looks sure to improve for the experience and can be found an opening before too long.
**Trainos(USA)** had the run of the race and had no excuses. His future looks to lie in nurseries.
**The Coires(IRE)**, who is from the same family as the high-class Height Of Fashion, looked very green and should do better next term over middle-distances.

### 3914 VIBE FM FILLIES' RATED STKS (H'CAP) — 6f
7:30 (7:30) (C) (0-95,92) 3-Y-0+ **£8,477** (£3,215; £1,607; £730) **Stalls** Low

Form RPR
3111 **1** **Kind (IRE)**[23] 3203 3-8-13 **86**.................................................. RHughes 8 92+
(RCharlton) *b.hind: trckd ldrs: rdn to ld ins fnl f: jst hld on* **3/1**[1]

0044 **2** *shd* **Valjarv (IRE)**[10] [3598] 3-9-3 **90**....(b) TPQueally 4 96+
(NPLittmoden) *hld up: nt clr run over 1f out: rdr dropped reins and r.o wl ins fnl fnl f: jst failed* **7/1**[2]

-000 **3** *¾* **Fanny's Fancy**[27] [3074] 4-9-6 **88**....(t) JFortune 6 92
(CFWall) *hld up: hdwy over 1f out: sn rdn: r.o* **3/1**[1]

0421 **4** *hd* **Fruit Of Glory**[6] [3744] 5-9-10 **92** 3ex.... DHolland 1 95
(JRJenkins) *lw: led: rdn and hdd ins fnl f: unable qck* **3/1**[1]

4114 **5** *1* **Bohola Flyer (IRE)**[13] [3523] 3-8-5 **78**.... RLMoore 5 78
(RHannon) *swtg: sddle slipped after leaving stalls: w ldr: rdn and ev ch ins fnl f: eased nr fin* **12/1**[3]

441- **6** *shd* **Chanterelle (IRE)**[294] [5190] 3-9-0 **87**.... TQuinn 2 87
(JLDunlop) *chsd ldrs: rdn over 1f out: styd on same pce ins fnl f* **20/1**

6643 **7** *hd* **Indian Steppes (FR)**[20] [3326] 5-7-11 **72** oh6.... MHalford[(7)] 3 71+
(JulianPoulton) *lw: trckd ldrs: racd keenly: n.m.r ins fnl f: styd on same pce* **25/1**

14-5 **8** *3½* **Anthos (GER)**[21] [3275] 3-9-3 **90**.... JPMurtagh 7 79
(JRFanshawe) *lw: hld up: wknd over 1f out* **20/1**

1m 13.41s (0.09) **Going Correction** +0.075s/f (Good)
**WFA** 3 from 4yo+ 5lb **8** Ran SP% **108.6**
Speed ratings: **102,101,100,100,99 99,98,94**CSF £22.17 CT £59.12 TOTE £3.60: £1.20, £2.10, £1.80; EX 18.70.
**Owner** K Abdulla **Bred** Juddmonte Farms **Trained** Beckhampton, Wilts

**FOCUS**
A decent contest, but the pace didn't appear that strong. A narrow, but progressive winner.

**NOTEBOOK**
**Kind(IRE)**, tackling handicappers for the first time, again did just what was required. Well placed this term, she is clearly gaining in confidence all the time and there may well be more to come.
**Valjarv(IRE)** would have preferred a stronger pace, and did not have the best of luck in running. She lost vital momentum when her rider dropped his reins for a couple of strides on meeting the rising ground, which may well have cost her the race, and while her win-to-run ratio is hardly inspiring, there is no doubt she does have plenty of ability.
**Fanny's Fancy** has yet to win on turf and is a filly who needs everthing to drop just right for her.
**Fruit Of Glory** had the run of the race and was just undone by her penalty.
**Bohola Flyer(IRE)** ◆ produced a remarkable performance, for her saddle was almost back on her quarters from an early stage. She is certainly on the upgrade and is one to keep in mind for a similar event. *Official explanation: jockey said saddle slipped*
**Chanterelle(IRE)** made a pleasing return to action and is sure to be sharper for the outing.

## 3915 VIBE FM VIBE TRIBE RATED STKS (H'CAP) 1m 2f
**8:00** (8:02) (C ) (0-95,90) 3-Y-O **£8,565** (£3,248; £1,624; £738) **Stalls** Centre

Form RPR

1 **1** **Into The Dark**[20] [3297] 3-9-7 **90**....(vt) LDettori 4 109+
(SaeedBinSuroor) *mde virtually all: r.o wl* **10/3**[1]

14- **2** *1½* **Art Trader (USA)**[252] [5944] 3-9-5 **88**.... JPMurtagh 2 104+
(MrsAJPerrett) *lw: hld up in tch: swtchd rt over 1f out: rdn and ev ch ins fnl f: unable qck* **6/1**[3]

22-5 **3** *1¼* **Notable Guest (USA)**[88] [1508] 3-9-1 **84**.... KFallon 3 98+
(SirMichaelStoute) *hld up: hdwy over 1f out: sn edgd rt: styd on* **7/1**

615 **4** *2* **Lost Soldier Three (IRE)**[19] [3345] 3-9-5 **88**.... DHolland 7 98+
(LMCumani) *a.p: chsd wnr 3f out: rdn and hung lft ins fnl f: no ex* **11/2**[2]

321 **5** *1¼* **Posteritas (USA)**[18] [3374] 3-9-1 **84**.... RHughes 1 92
(HRACecil) *hld up: hdwy and hung rt over 1f out: nt trble ldrs* **12/1**

2300 **6** *hd* **Alekhine (IRE)**[14] [3477] 3-9-1 **84**.... RLMoore 6 91?
(PWHarris) *hld up: hdwy over 1f out: n.m.r and no ex 1f out* **14/1**

0553 **7** *1¾* **Winners Delight**[13] [3543] 3-8-12 **81**.... KMcEvoy 5 85
(APJarvis) *hld up: hdwy u.p over 1f out: nvr trbld ldrs* **10/1**

3222 **8** *4* **Ganymede**[16] [3422] 3-8-11 **80**.... MFenton 9 76
(MLWBell) *lw: plld hrd and prom: hmpd over 8f out: rdn 4f out: wknd wl over 1f out* **16/1**

1253 **9** *3* **Man Of Letters (UAE)**[13] [3507] 3-8-9 **78**.... AMcCarthy 8 69
(GGMargarson) *chsd ldrs 8f* **25/1**

1160 **10** *2* **Swagger Stick (USA)**[13] [3521] 3-9-7 **90**.... TQuinn 11 77
(JLDunlop) *chsd wnr 7f: wkng whn n.m.r wl over 1f out* **11/2**[2]

1100 **11** *1¾* **Another Choice (IRE)**[8] [3678] 3-8-9 **78**....(t) TPQueally 10 61
(NPLittmoden) *swtg: prom: rdn over 3f out: wknd 2f out* **33/1**

2m 3.59s (-2.87) **Going Correction** -0.075s/f (Good) **11** Ran SP% **116.8**
Speed ratings: **108,106,105,104,103 103,101,98,96,94 93**CSF £22.63 CT £132.33 TOTE £2.90: £1.80, £2.20, £1.90; EX 26.10.
**Owner** Godolphin **Bred** Gainsborough Stud Management Ltd **Trained** Newmarket, Suffolk

**FOCUS**
This looked a competitive contest and the pace was solid. With several progressive sorts close up the form is expected to work out.

**NOTEBOOK**
**Into The Dark** confirmed himself a progressive performer and was well on top in the end, having looked to be in trouble on the final climb. He has a willing attitude and should be capable of better still.
**Art Trader(USA)** ◆ looked a huge threat as he loomed large inside the final furlong until lack of a recent outing found him out. He can be expected to be sharper next time.
**Notable Guest(USA)**, tackling handicappers for the first time, was doing his best work in the closing stages. Out of a mare that won over 12 furlongs, there is every reason to believe he will prove at least as effective over that trip.
**Lost Soldier Three(IRE)** had every chance and had no excuses, although he was not disgraced. *Official explanation: jockey said gelding hung left*
**Posteritas(USA)**, tackling handicappers for the first time, found things happening too quickly for her. Out of a mare that won over seven furlongs, she shapes as though she will stay further still.
**Alekhine(IRE)**, short of room in the dip, did not get up the hill and may be better suited by a mile.
**Swagger Stick(USA)** *Official explanation: jockey said colt stumbled a furlong out when beaten*

## 3916 HUGO AND THE HUGUENOTES MAIDEN STKS 1m
**8:30** (8:35) (D ) 3-Y-O **£5,590** (£1,720; £860; £430) **Stalls** Low

Form RPR

**1** **Hermitage Court (USA)** 3-9-0.... KMcEvoy 12 86
(BJMeehan) *w'like: scope: racd stands' side: chsd ldr: rdn to ld ins fnl f: r.o* **25/1**

3 **2** *hd* **Kauri Forest (USA)**[95] [1352] 3-9-0.... JPMurtagh 18 85
(JRFanshawe) *lw: racd stands' side: trckd ldrs: rdn and ev ch ins fnl f: r.o* **11/4**[1]

0 **3** *½* **Arctic Silk**[23] [3204] 3-8-9....(t) LDettori 15 79
(SaeedBinSuroor) *racd stands' side: led: rdn and hdd ins fnl f: styd on* **8/1**

**4** *3½* **Gentleman's Deal (IRE)** 3-9-0.... RHughes 2 76+
(EALDunlop) *well grown: racd far side: trckd ldrs: swtchd rt and continued to hang rt fr over 2f out: no ex ins fnl f* **16/1**

**5** *nk* **Sea Nymph (IRE)** 3-8-9.... KFallon 20 70
(SirMichaelStoute) *gd sort: lw: racd stands' side: hld up: hdwy over 1f out: nt trble ldrs* **12/1**

**6** *hd* **Countrywide Luck** 3-9-0.... TPQueally 19 75+
(NPLittmoden) *w'like: racd stands' side: hld up: hdwy whn stmbld 1f out: nt trble ldrs* **66/1**

3 **7** *1¾* **Clipperdown (IRE)**[15] [3448] 3-9-0.... RLMoore 4 71+
(PWHarris) *racd far side: chsd ldr tl led that gp over 3f out: wknd ins fnl f* **7/2**[2]

**8** *½* **Danze Romance** 3-8-9.... TQuinn 11 65
(JLDunlop) *neat: racd stands' side: hld up: n.d* **33/1**

**9** *shd* **One So Marvellous** 3-8-9.... DHolland 13 65+
(LMCumani) *gd sort: racd stands' side: hld up: n.d* **12/1**

**10** *hd* **Tadawul (USA)** 3-8-9.... RHills 10 64+
(ACStewart) *w'like: racd far side: hld up: r.o ins fnl f: nvr nrr* **25/1**

**11** *nk* **Royal Lustre** 3-9-0.... JFortune 14 68+
(JHMGosden) *leggy: scope: racd stands' side: hld up: n.d* **6/1**[3]

0- **12** *¾* **Radish (IRE)**[258] [5869] 3-8-9.... PRobinson 1 62+
(ACStewart) *racd far side: mid-div: rdn over 2f out: wknd over 1f out* **25/1**

4323 **13** *nk* **Pinching (IRE)**[12] [3563] 3-8-9 75....(v) WRyan 6 61
(HRACecil) *racd far side: chsd ldrs: rdn and ev ch that gp over 1f out: wknd fnl f* **9/1**

**14** *hd* **Inviting (USA)** 3-8-9.... SDrowne 16 61
(RCharlton) *gd sort: leggy: racd stands' side: chsd ldrs over 6f* **20/1**

05 **15** *¾* **Glencalvie (IRE)**[11] [3587] 3-9-0.... EAhern 17 64
(JNoseda) *racd stands' side: chsd ldrs over 6f* **40/1**

00 **16** *5* **Hoops And Blades**[41] [2693] 3-9-0....(t) TGMcLaughlin 5 52
(NPLittmoden) *racd far side: dwlt: a in rr* **100/1**

0 **17** *½* **Bonnetts (IRE)**[58] [2223] 3-8-9.... DaneO'Neill 3 46
(HCandy) *led far side over 4f: wknd over 1f out* **80/1**

**18** *1¾* **Alfhala (IRE)** 3-8-2.... LauraWells[(7)] 7 42
(ACStewart) *bit bkwd: racd far side: s.i.s: a in rr* **100/1**

**19** *1* **Zak Attack** 3-9-0.... CCatlin 8 45
(DJDaly) *unruly stalls: dwlt: racd far side: hld up: plld hrd: wknd over 3f out* **40/1**

**20** *16* **Southburgh (IRE)** 3-8-9.... HayleyTurner[(5)] 9 8
(MrsCADunnett) *unf: racd far side: slowly in to stride: hdwy over 3f out: sn wknd* **100/1**

1m 40.63s (0.15) **Going Correction** +0.075s/f (Good) **20** Ran SP% **135.4**
Speed ratings: **102,101,101,97,97 97,95,95,94,94 94,93,93,93,92 87,86,85,84,68**CSF £94.49 TOTE £57.40: £8.90, £2.20, £3.00; EX 246.50.
**Owner** Gallagher Equine Ltd **Bred** Curtis C Green **Trained** Upper Lambourn, Berks

**FOCUS**
The field split into two groups with the stands' side having the best of it filling five of the first six places, and the fourth home ending up on the stands' side having hung all the way across the track.

**NOTEBOOK**
**Hermitage Court(USA)**, a $100,000 first foal is a scopey sort, who should do even better with this outing under his belt.
**Kauri Forest(USA)** had the advantage of a run, but was just beaten by a better animal on the day.
**Arctic Silk** had clearly learnt from her debut, but does not look like being a patch on her mum at this stage.
**Gentleman's Deal(IRE)**, like the third, is out of a 1000 Guineas winner. A fine, rangy type, he was very green and should certainly be capable of plenty of improvement.
**Sea Nymph(IRE)** comes from a well-related family and will benefit from a step up in trip in the furture.
**Countrywide Luck**, a half-brother to winning stayer Furness, as well as German Listed winner Orfisio, showed enough to suggest he can make his mark when facing a stiffer test.
**Clipperdown(IRE)** although well beaten in the end, looked to be racing on the slower side and can be forgiven this effort.

## 3917 VIBE FM ADMIN HUNNIES H'CAP 1m 2f
**9:00** (9:04) (E ) (0-70,72) 3-Y-O+ **£4,260** (£1,311; £655; £327) **Stalls** Centre

Form RPR

2101 **1** **Jackie Kiely**[3] [3827] 3-8-10 **61** 6ex....(t) LDettori 2 73+
(PSMcentee) *hld up: hdwy over 1f out: n.m.r 1f out: styd on to ld wl ins fnl f* **9/2**[1]

2313 **2** *¾* **Ember Days**[8] [3670] 5-9-10 **65** 6ex....(p) EAhern 16 73
(JLSpearing) *chsd ldrs: rdn to ld ins fnl f: sn hdd: kpt on* **15/2**

0031 **3** *1* **Ghantoot**[12] [3556] 3-9-7 **72** 6ex....(v) DHolland 1 81+
(LMCumani) *hld up: pushed along 1/2-way: hdwy over 1f out: r.o* **6/1**[2]

6006 **4** *nk* **Forest Tune (IRE)**[20] [3291] 6-8-9 **50**.... TEDurcan 17 56
(BHanbury) *a.p: chsd ldr 3f out: led over 1f out: edgd lft and hdd ins fnl f: no ex* **12/1**

5-05 **5** *nk* **Welcome Signal**[28] [3049] 4-9-10 **65**....(p) JPMurtagh 12 70
(JRFanshawe) *lw: hld up: hdwy over 3f out: rdn over 1f out: styd on same pce* **8/1**

**6** *1¾* **Prairie Law (GER)**[160] 4-7-12 **42**.... LisaJones[(3)] 15 44
(IanWilliams) *hld up in tch: hung rt over 1f out: wknd ins fnl f* **16/1**

03-3 **7** *nk* **Kalou (GER)**[68] [966] 6-8-7 **48**.... TPQueally 7 49
(BJCurley) *b.off hind: hld up in tch: rdn over 1f out: wknd ins fnl f* **13/2**[3]

/006 **8** *1¼* **Ursa Major**[9] [3629] 10-8-7 **48**.... KMcEvoy 14 47
(TKeddy) *led over 8f: wknd ins fnl f* **25/1**

0100 **9** *3½* **Planters Punch (IRE)**[18] [3387] 3-9-3 **68**....(v) KFallon 4 60
(RHannon) *hld up: rdn 1/2-way: hdwat over 1f out: eased whn btn ins fnl f* **8/1**

0210 **10** *3½* **Feed The Meter (IRE)**[7] [3692] 4-9-0 **55**.... GCarter 11 40
(TTClement) *hld up: plld hrd: n.d* **16/1**

5045 **11** *5* **Galey River (USA)**[15] [3450] 5-7-13 **40**.... AMcCarthy 10 16
(JJSheehan) *chsd ldrs: rdn over 3f out: wknd over 1f out* **12/1**

5106 **12** *3½* **Sinjaree**[88] [1503] 6-8-1 **42**.... SRighton 6 11
(MrsSLamyman) *chsd ldr 6f: wknd 2f out* **33/1**

0160 **13** *2* **Bosco (IRE)**[4] [3809] 3-7-12 **52**....(t) FPFerris[(3)] 9 17
(PSMcentee) *s.i.s: rdn 1/2-way: a in rr* **25/1**

**14** *2½* **Birchall (IRE)**[75] [1818] 5-8-13 **54**.... CCatlin 13 15
(IanWilliams) *hld up: rdn 6f out: a in rr* **25/1**

4-30 **15** *3½* **Mr Fleming**[64] [2053] 5-7-6 **40**....(b) MHalford[(7)] 3 —
(DrJDScargill) *swtg: chsd ldrs: rdn over 3f out: wknd over 2f out* **66/1**

6-06 **16** *9* **Niagara (IRE)**[15] [3459] 7-9-9 **64**.... PRobinson 8 1
(MHTompkins) *chsd ldrs over 6f* **16/1**

-000 **17** *dist* **Migration**[8] [3682] 8-8-9 **50**.... MTebbutt 5 —
(MrsSLamyman) *s.i.s: wknd over 4f out* **50/1**

2m 5.39s (-1.07) **Going Correction** -0.075s/f (Good)
**WFA** 3 from 4yo+ 10lb **17** Ran SP% **130.8**
Speed ratings: **101,100,99,99,99 97,97,96,93,90 86,84,82,80,77 70,—**CSF £37.34 CT £217.01 TOTE £4.00: £1.40, £2.20, £1.90, £3.30; EX 52.50 Place 6 £32.60, Place 5 £15.61.
**Owner** P S J Croft **Bred** Mrs M Chaworth Musters **Trained** Newmarket, Suffolk

**FOCUS**
Just an ordinary handicap, but it was run at a good pace.

**NOTEBOOK**
**Jackie Kiely**, for whom the tongue-tie certainly appears to have worked, proved most resolute under his penalty.
**Ember Days** has proved wonderfully consistent of late and turned in another solid peformance.
**Ghantoot** tended to run his race in snatches and looks one to treat with caution.
**Forest Tune(IRE)**, well treated on the best of his form, turned in a solid effort and it would be a surprise if connections cannot place him to win off his current mark.
**Welcome Signal**, wearing cheekpieces for the first time has become a frustrating type and is clearly far from straightforward.
**Prairie Law(GER)**, the winner of an All-Weather maiden in Germany, did not shape too badly on this first effort over here. He has worn blinkers in the past, and is one to keep an eye on at this level if they are re-fitted.
T/Plt: £62.20 to a £1 stake. Pool: £41,772.05. 490.10 winning tickets. T/Qpdt: £34.50 to a £1 stake. Pool: £2,338.60. 50.10 winning tickets. CR

## 3604 PONTEFRACT (L-H)

Friday, July 16

**OFFICIAL GOING: Good to firm (good in places)**

## 3918 BETFRED.COM MAIDEN AUCTION STKS — 6f

**6:40** (6:40) (E) 2-Y-O — **£4,241** (£1,305; £652; £326) **Stalls** Low

Form — RPR

1 **El Rey Royale** 2-8-4 — NMackay[(3)] 4 — 73
(MDHammond) *midfield: hdwy over 2f out: str run ent last: led last 50 yds* **33/1**

04 2 ¾ **Persian Carpet**[19] 3336 2-8-2 — FNorton 8 — 66+
(IAWood) *led: rdn and hdd briefly over 1f out: sn rallied to ld again ent last: hdd and no ex last 50 yds* **9/2**[2]

3 ½ **Good Investment** 2-8-7 — GFaulkner 1 — 69
(PCHaslam) *towards rr: hdwy 1/2-way: swtchd ins and rdn over 1f out: styd on wl towards fin* **22/1**

0 4 shd **Heybrook Boy (USA)**[22] 3233 2-8-9 — RFfrench 10 — 71
(MJohnston) *chsd ldrs: rdn wl over 1f out: kpt on* **11/2**

00 5 2 **Davy Crockett**[22] 3233 2-8-7 — SWhitworth 5 — 63
(MrsJRRamsden) *midfield: hdwy and n.m.r wl over 1f out: swtchd rt and styd on fnl f: nrst fin* **22/1**

3 6 ¾ **Hidden Star**[19] 3343 2-8-11 ow2 — KDalgleish 11 — 65+
(FJordan) *cl up: effrt to ld over 1f out: sn rdn and hdd ent last: wknd* **2/1**[1]

7 nk **Along The Nile** 2-9-0 — LGoncalves 9 — 67
(MrsJRRamsden) *s.i.s and bhd: hdwy on outer over 1f out: styd on wl fnl f: nrst fin* **16/1**

02 8 ¾ **Noodles**[23] 3197 2-8-11 — (v) WSupple 12 — 62
(TDEasterby) *chsd ldrs: rdn wl over 1f out: grad wknd* **5/1**[3]

9 ½ **Lightening Fire (IRE)** 2-8-7 — DKinsella 2 — 56
(TJEtherington) *s.i.s and bhd tl styd on fnl f* **33/1**

64 10 nk **Royal Flynn**[29] 3009 2-8-11 — VHalliday 14 — 59
(MDods) *in tch: rdn along 2f out: sn wknd* **12/1**

11 1¼ **Comical Errors (USA)** 2-8-2 — GBartley[(7)] 13 — 53
(PCHaslam) *s.i.s and bhd tl sme late hdwy* **40/1**

12 ¾ **Tidal Fury (IRE)** 2-8-11 — GBaker 3 — 53
(JJay) *racd wd: a rr* **12/1**

13 ½ **Hows That** 2-8-2 — RMullen 7 — 43
(PJMcbride) *s.i.s: hdwy and in tch 1/2-way: rdn 2f out and s wknd* **40/1**

00 14 8 **Live In Hope**[39] 2730 2-8-2 — DaleGibson 6 — 19
(JeddO'Keeffe) *chsd ldrs to 1/2-way: sn wknd* **66/1**

06 15 2½ **Zarova (IRE)**[14] 3469 2-9-0 — TLucas 15 — 23
(MWEasterby) *cl up: rdn along 1/2-way: sn wknd and eased* **18/1**

1m 19.61s (2.31) **Going Correction** +0.225s/f (Good) — **15** Ran SP% **131.0**
Speed ratings: **93,92,91,91,88 87,87,86,85,85 83,82,81,71,67**CSF £182.07 TOTE £94.20: £13.60, £2.40, £4.00; EX 485.10.
**Owner** A Walker **Bred** A G Greenwood **Trained** Middleham, N Yorks

**FOCUS**
An ordinary-looking maiden auction run 1.26sec slower than the concluding classified event.

**NOTEBOOK**
**El Rey Royale**, by a sire who is having a good season out of a mare who won as a juvenile, was held up off the pace and then picked up nicely to catch the long-time leader close home. He looks capable of going on from this.
**Persian Carpet** is progressing with her racing and was made plenty of use of on this drop in trip. She had no sooner fought off the challenge of the favourite than the winner arrived on the scene and she was cut down near the finish. She looks capable of winning a small race and now qualifies for a handicap mark.
**Good Investment ◆**, a half-brother to six winners, including a couple of sprinters, looked in need of the experience but took advantage of a gap up the rail to finish as well as anything. He should be considerably better for the outing.
**Heybrook Boy(USA)**, as is often the case with runners from his yard, improved for his debut and was keeping on steadily having been on the heels of the leaders throughout. He looks as if another furlong will not go amiss.
**Davy Crockett** caught the eye staying on late, He had finished much further behind the fourth at Newcastle and may have appreciated the faster surface. He is one to keep in mind for nurseries later in the season.
**Hidden Star**, a well-backed favourite following his promising debut, got in a battle with the runner-up which eventually cost both of them. He was the first to crack and was a little disappointing, but can be given the chance to put this effort behind him.
**Along The Nile** showed some promise on this debut and is likely to do better in time.
**Noodles** was easy in the market and was somewhat disappointing on this third outing, although he may have found the ground too fast. However, the form of his Carlisle second is not working out as yet.
**Tidal Fury(IRE)** missed the break on this debut and ran better than his finishing position suggests, as he had to go around the outside.

## 3919 TOTEQUADPOT FILLIES' H'CAP — 1m 4f 8y

**7:10** (7:14) (E) (0-70,76) 3-Y-O+ — **£5,538** (£1,704; £852; £426) **Stalls** Low

Form — RPR

5213 1 **Charlotte Vale**[12] 3561 3-9-3 **68** — ACulhane 3 — 79
(MDHammond) *trckd ldrs: hdwy to chse ldr wl over 1f out: rdn to chal ent last: drvn and kpt on to ld nr line* **9/2**[2]

3521 2 shd **Sand And Stars (IRE)**[11] 3584 3-9-11 **76** 6ex — MHenry 6 — 87
(MHTompkins) *trckd ldr: hdwy to ld 3f out: rdn over 1f out: drvn ins last: hdd and no ex nr line* **7/2**[1]

0435 3 7 **Shotley Dancer**[10] 3612 5-8-0 **39** oh1 ow2 — FNorton 13 — 39
(NBycroft) *bhd: hdwy 3f out: sn rdn and kpt on appr last* **33/1**

5006 4 3 **Olympias (IRE)**[35] 2840 3-8-7 **58** — JCarroll 2 — 53
(HMorrison) *midfield: hdwy over 4f out: rdn along wl over 2f out: no imp* **18/1**

0040 5 2 **Staff Nurse (IRE)**[30] 2987 4-7-12 **37** oh2 — KimTinkler 10 — 29
(DonEnricoIncisa) *bhd tl sme late hdwy* **25/1**

-666 6 ½ **Lebenstanz**[32] 2950 4-9-11 **67** — NMackay[(3)] 14 — 58
(LMCumani) *hld up in rr: hdwy over 4f out: sn pshd along and nvr a factor* **10/1**

0026 7 4 **Miss Fleurie**[11] 3578 4-7-12 **37** oh5 — DKinsella 8 — 22
(RCraggs) *led: rdn along 4f out: hdd 3f out and sn wknd* **50/1**

0-04 8 ½ **Lady Blade (IRE)**[20] 3304 3-8-9 **60** — WSupple 1 — 44
(BHanbury) *chsd ldrs: rdn along over 2f out: sn wknd* **20/1**

6-11 9 3 **Toccata Aria**[8] 3670 6-8-9 **53** 6ex — RThomas[(5)] 7 — 32
(JMBradley) *trckd ldrs: effrt over 3f out: sn rdn along and wknd* **8/1**[3]

004 10 1¾ **Paint The Lily (IRE)**[20] 3294 3-8-7 **58** — SWhitworth 9 — 34
(JWHills) *a rr* **25/1**

0005 11 7 **Cryptogam**[16] 3411 4-8-0 **39** — RFfrench 4 — 4
(MESowersby) *in tch: rdn along 4f out: sn wknd* **33/1**

660 12 9 **Nassiria**[36] 2805 3-9-1 **69** — J-PGuillambert[(3)] 12 — 20
(CEBrittain) *a rr* **16/1**

0604 13 12 **Ribbons And Bows (IRE)**[33] 2914 4-9-9 **62** — FLynch 11 — —
(CACyzer) *in tch: rdn along 4f out: sn wknd* **12/1**

2m 40.98s (0.93) **Going Correction** +0.225s/f (Good)
**WFA** 3 from 4yo+ 12lb — **13** Ran SP% **99.7**
Speed ratings: **105,104,100,98,96 96,93,93,91,90 85,79,71**CSF £12.54 CT £236.66 TOTE £4.10: £1.60, £1.60, £6.20; EX 7.30.
**Owner** Peter J Davies **Bred** Snailwell Stud Co Ltd **Trained** Middleham, N Yorks

**FOCUS**
A modest fillies' handicap but run at a decent gallop with the first two coming clear. Swynford Pleasure (7/2) was withdrawn after refusing to go into the stalls; deduction 20p in the pound.

**NOTEBOOK**
**Charlotte Vale** stays well and appreciated this stiff track, but it took all of Culhane's strength to get her up to confirm Thirsk form with the runner-up despite being 5lb better off. She is consistent but will not find things easy off her revised mark.
**Sand And Stars(IRE)**, who deservedly got off the mark when making all last time, had a stiff task with the winner under her penalty. However, again given a positive ride, she was only just collared and is clearly improving. She may gain compensation on a less-testing track.
**Shotley Dancer**, who was already 1lb out of the handicap before her rider put up 2lb overweight, is still a maiden but ran quite well over the longest trip she has tried to date. She likes fast ground and some of her best efforts have been at this time of year.
**Olympias(IRE)**, dropping back in trip, was being niggled at just after halfway but stayed on steadily without offering immediate promise that she can find a race.
**Staff Nurse(IRE)** was another to run on late in the day from the rear.
**Lebenstanz**, easy in the market for this handicap debut, was always behind and never got into contention. She has now finished sixth on all four outings, and looks high enough in the handicap based on this performance.
**Toccata Aria**, attempting a hat-trick under a 6lb penalty, appeared to find the task and the longer trip beyond her, but should not be written off yet.

## 3920 ANTONIA DEUTERS RATED STKS (H'CAP) — 5f

**7:40** (7:41) (D) (0-80,80) 3-Y-O+ — **£9,303** (£3,528; £1,764; £802) **Stalls** Low

Form — RPR

3503 1 **Midnight Parkes**[10] 3606 5-8-8 **67** — (p) MHenry 4 — 78
(EJAlston) *cl up: led over 1f out: rdn ent last: styd on wl* **10/1**

5654 2 nk **Soba Jones**[13] 3515 7-8-10 **69** — JEdmunds 2 — 79
(JBalding) *trckd ldrs: hdwy to chse wnr ent last: sn rdn to chal and ev ch tl drvn and nt qckn nr fin* **33/1**

0110 3 1¼ **Paddywack (IRE)**[6] 3754 7-9-0 **73** — (b) ACulhane 7 — 78+
(DWChapman) *in tch: effrt and n.m.r wl over 1f out: hdwy on inner ins last: sn rdn and kpt on* **12/1**

060 4 ¾ **Obe One**[4] 3795 4-8-9 **68** — FNorton 8 — 70
(ABerry) *in tch: hdwy wl over 1f out: sn rdn and kpt on ins last: nrst fin* **6/1**[1]

0320 5 ½ **Winthorpe (IRE)**[9] 3645 4-8-10 **72** — THamilton[(3)] 13 — 72+
(JJQuinn) *towards rr: hdwy 2f out: swtchd rt and rdn over 1f out: kpt on ins last: nrst fin* **14/1**

0001 6 ¾ **Zarzu**[11] 3580 5-8-11 **75** 3ex — RThomas[(5)] 11 — 72
(CRDore) *towards rr: hdwy 2f out: rdn over 1f out: kpt on ins last: nrst fin* **7/1**[3]

2100 7 1½ **Karminskey Park**[6] 3744 5-8-7 **66** oh1 — DKinsella 9 — 57
(TJEtherington) *chsd ldrs: rdn 2f out: drvn and one pce appr last* **22/1**

1525 8 shd **Laurel Dawn**[5] 3775 6-8-4 **66** oh5 — JFMcDonald[(3)] 14 — 56
(IWMcinnes) *bhd: hdwy wl over 1f out: swtchd lft ent last and kpt on* **16/1**

0162 9 hd **Awake**[9] 3645 7-9-5 **78** — WSupple 17 — 68+
(DNicholls) *hld up in rr: hdwy 2f out: kpt on ins last* **9/1**

6500 10 nk **Catch The Cat (IRE)**[7] 3713 5-8-12 **71** — (p) GParkin 16 — 59
(JSWainwright) *midfield: rdn along 2f out: no hdwy* **33/1**

0510 11 ½ **Merlin's Dancer**[29] 3016 4-9-7 **80** — AlexGreaves 6 — 66
(DNicholls) *sn led: rdn along over 2f out: hdd wl over 1f out and sn wknd* **13/2**[2]

0000 12 ½ **Salviati (USA)**[5] 3775 7-9-4 **80** — (p) LFletcher[(3)] 5 — 64+
(JMBradley) *s.i.s and bhd tl sme late hdwy* **16/1**

202- 13 1¾ **Sion Hill (IRE)**[277] 5548 3-9-1 **78** — FLynch 12 — 55
(SirMichaelStoute) *stdd and swtchd lft s: a rr* **10/1**

0004 14 2 **Twice Upon A Time**[6] 3744 5-8-8 **67** — RMullen 10 — 36+
(BSmart) *s.i.s: a rr* **14/1**

4131 15 5 **Parkside Pursuit**[17] 3395 6-9-3 **76** — RFfrench 18 — 25
(JMBradley) *bhd fr 1/2-way* **12/1**

0010 16 3½ **Tommy Smith**[35] 2859 6-8-13 **72** — (b) KDalgleish 15 — 7
(JSWainwright) *in tch: rdn along 2f out: sn wknd* **25/1**

2042 17 2½ **Sir Ernest (IRE)**[7] 3702 3-8-2 **72** — KGhunowa[(7)] 3 — —
(MJPolglase) *cl up: rdn along over 2f out: sn wknd* **20/1**

63.75 secs (-0.05) **Going Correction** +0.225s/f (Good)
**WFA** 3 from 4yo+ 4lb — **17** Ran SP% **127.6**
Speed ratings: **109,108,106,105,104 103,100,100,100,99 99,98,95,92,84 78,74**CSF £326.82 CT £2317.15 TOTE £14.10: £2.80, £4.00, £2.30, £2.10; EX 134.40.
**Owner** Joseph Heler **Bred** Joseph Heler **Trained** Longton, Lancs

**FOCUS**
A competitive rated handicap run at a good pace, in which those drawn low appeared to have an advantage. However, the form looks solid and reliable.

**NOTEBOOK**
**Midnight Parkes**, who signalled a return to form over six furlongs here earlier in the month, was helped by the drop in trip and battled on well to resist the persistent challenge of the runner-up. He is not on a bad mark, having won off 73 two years ago, and could possibly follow up whilst in such good heart.
**Soba Jones** has been holding his form well and, given a good ride, again ran his race. However, he has yet to win on any surface other than Fibresand during the last two years.
**Paddywack(IRE) ◆**, back to his best trip, got through on the inside but then had nowhere to go. Had he found an opening he would have finished closer, and he may not have finished winning yet.

**Obe One**, who was made favourite following some consistent efforts, appeared to have a good position from the start but failed to pick up until staying on late in the day. He has a moderate strike rate, and it may be that some form of headgear could produce the improvement needed.
**Winthorpe(IRE)**, who has failed to win since completing a hat-trick at this time last year, again finished really well after being some way off the pace. He has climbed the handicap following a couple of decent recent efforts, but looks capable of scoring if things fall right for him.
**Zarzu**, under a penalty for his win on easy ground last time, stayed on but gave the impression that he may requre a bit of cut these days.
**Karminskey Park** has been running consistently well, but looks in the Handicapper's grip at present.
**Tommy Smith** *Official explanation: jockey said gelding hung right throughout*

## 3921 WEATHERBYS INJURED JOCKEYS FUND H'CAP — 1m 4y
**8:10** (8:10) (E) (0-70,70) 3-Y-0+ — **£4,377** (£1,347; £673; £336) **Stalls** Low

Form — RPR

6240 **1** **Time To Regret**32 2938 4-8-5 **50** ........ THamilton(3) 6 — 57
(JSWainwright) *mde all: rdn clr over 1f out: drvn ins last: jst hld on* **25/1**

0105 **2** *hd* **Zawrak (IRE)**5 3773 5-9-1 **60** ........ (v1) JFMcDonald(3) 1 — 69+
(IWMcInnes) *midfield: pushed along on inner 1/2-way: hdwy and n.m.r 2f out: swtchd rt and nt clr run 1f out: str run ins last: jst fail* **20/1**

6003 **3** *1 1/4* **Shamwari Fire (IRE)**14 3471 4-8-8 **50** ........ RFfrench 5 — 54
(IWMcInnes) *chsd ldrs: hdwy 2f out: sn rdn and hung rt over 1f out: drvn and kpt on fnl f* **16/1**

0004 **4** *hd* **Newcorp Lad**6 3738 4-9-4 **60** ........ WSupple 14 — 63
(MrsGSRees) *trckd ldrs: hdwy to chse wnr 2f out: rdn and ch 1f out: sn drvn and one pce* **10/1**3

5501 **5** *hd* **Hula Ballew**10 3609 4-9-1 **57** 6ex ........ (p) SWKelly 4 — 60+
(MDods) *hld up towards rr: hdwy 3f out: swtchd rt and rdn wl over 1f out: drvn and styd on ins last: nrst fin* **11/4**1

U0L3 **6** *hd* **Tagula Blue (IRE)**14 3475 4-10-0 **70** ........ DeanMcKeown 10 — 72+
(JAGlover) *dwlt and bhd: hdwy on outer 2f out: sn rdn and kpt on fnl f: nrst fin* **12/1**

0-03 **7** *hd* **Fair Spin**13 3520 4-9-7 **63** ........ ACulhane 8 — 65
(MDHammond) *in tch: hdwy to chse ldrs 2f out: sn rdn and one pce appr last* **5/1**2

0004 **8** *hd* **Basinet**12 3559 6-8-12 **54** ........ KDalgleish 9 — 55
(JJQuinn) *dwlt and bhd: hdwy on inner over 2f out:s witched rt over 1f out: sn rdn and kpt on ins last: nrst fin* **10/1**3

0630 **9** *1 3/4* **Uno Mente**10 3609 5-8-11 **53** ........ KimTinkler 11 — 50
(DonEnricoIncisa) *bhd tl styd on fnl 2f* **20/1**

2500 **10** *3 1/2* **Dubai Dreams**14 3472 4-8-3 **50** ........ BSwarbrick(5) 13 — 39
(SRBowring) *chsd ldrs: rdn along 3f out: wkng whn n.m.r over 1f out* **25/1**

2060 **11** *1 1/2* **Penwell Hill (USA)**10 3604 5-8-9 **54** ........ NMackay(3) 18 — 40
(TDBarron) *cl up: rdn along 2f out: wkng whn hmpd over 1f out* **12/1**

32-0 **12** *3/4* **Healey (IRE)**10 3604 6-8-6 **48** ........ VHalliday 15 — 32
(PRWood) *bhd fr 1/2-way* **40/1**

6310 **13** *1 1/4* **Dara Mac**12 3559 5-8-6 **55** ........ SuzanneFrance(7) 19 — 36
(NBycroft) *a rr* **25/1**

0-65 **14** *3/4* **Kalishka (IRE)**56 2259 3-8-13 **63** ........ JCarroll 2 — 43
(AndrewTurnell) *alwasy rr* **14/1**

-350 **15** *2* **Golden Spectrum (IRE)**32 2936 5-9-1 **57** ........ AlexGreaves 17 — 32
(DNicholls) *bhd fr 1/2-way* **25/1**

10 **16** *3/4* **Sedge (USA)**12 3559 4-9-4 **60** ........ GParkin 20 — 33
(PTMidgley) *chsd ldrs: rdn along 3f out: wknd 2f out* **33/1**

0000 **17** *5* **Daimajin (IRE)**6 3745 5-9-0 **59** ow12 ........ DNolan(3) 7 — 21
(MrsLucindaFeatherstone) *dwlt: a rr* **50/1**

300 **18** *2 1/2* **Aswan (IRE)**5 3779 6-9-9 **65** ........ (t) SWhitworth 12 — 21
(SRBowring) *in tch: rdn along over 3f out: sn wknd* **25/1**

1m 46.99s (1.39) **Going Correction** +0.225s/f (Good)
**WFA** 3 from 4yo+ 8lb — **18** Ran SP% **125.5**
Speed ratings: **102,101,100,100,100 100,100,99,98,94 93,92,91,90,88 87,82,80**CSF £438.10 CT £4144.95 TOTE £23.10: £4.40, £5.80, £2.80, £2.80; EX 280.80.
**Owner** Denison Arms **Bred** Speedlith Group **Trained** Kennythorpe, N Yorks

**FOCUS**
A moderate handicap in which few came from off the pace and a low draw was an advantage.

**NOTEBOOK**
**Time To Regret**, a maiden going into this, was having his first run for his current trainer and was racing off his lowest mark to date. Dictating the pace from the front, he eventually did just enough to hold on after looking likely to win by further entering the final furlong. He should not go up a great deal for this.
**Zawrak(IRE)**, who has struggled since winning an apprentice handicap in May, responded to the first-time visor and, finishing strongly, was unlucky not to get up. If the headgear works again next time he may be able to gain compensation at a similar level.
**Shamwari Fire(IRE)** ran to Beverley form with the winner, if the latter's apprentice allowance is taken into consideration. However, that race was a maiden claimer, which re-inforces the moderate standard of this contest.
**Newcorp Lad**, who usually saves his best efforts for Hamilton, posted a decent performance from his wide draw and was only run out of the placings close home. In this form, he may be capable of scoring again back on his favourite track.
**Hula Ballew**was made favourite to defy a 6lb penalty for her win in a fillies' handicap over course and distance last time. However, she could not pick up until the race was over.
**Tagula Blue(IRE)**, with the tongue tie and blinkers left off this time, again missed the break but was less reluctant than of late and ran quite well in the circumstances. He has been given a chance by the Handicapper and, if he can be kept sweet, is back on a winning mark.
**Fair Spin**, who was well backed to complete a treble for the yard, had a chance early in the straight and was done no favours by the runner-up inside the last. He is another who looks reasonably handicapped at present, but may prefer an easier surface.

## 3922 TENERIFE HOLIDAY MAIDEN STKS — 1m 2f 6y
**8:40** (8:42) (D) 3-Y-0 — **£7,280** (£2,240; £1,120; £560) **Stalls** Low

Form — RPR

22 **1** **Fortune's Princess**18 3374 3-8-9 ........ SWKelly 4 — 72
(MJWallace) *trckd ldrs: hmpd bnd after 3f: hdwy 3f out: rdn over 1f out styd on to ld ins last* **3/1**2

2 **2** *3/4* **Mandatum**30 2983 3-8-11 ........ NMackay(3) 7 — 76+
(LMCumani) *stmbld s: hld up in rr: hdwy over 2f out: rdn wl over 1f out: kpt on ins last* **6/1**3

53-0 **3** *1/2* **Turn 'n Burn**94 1387 3-9-0 73 ........ DeanMcKeown 5 — 75
(CACyzer) *bhd: pushed along over 3f out: hdwy 2f out: sn rdn and kpt on u.p ins last* **14/1**

03 **4** *nk* **Shastye (IRE)**15 3454 3-8-9 ........ RHavlin 2 — 69
(JHMGosden) *chsd ldr: led 2 1/2f out: rdn clr over 1f out: drvn and hdd ins last: one pce* **12/1**

**5** *2* **Barathea Blue** 3-9-0 ........ DaleGibson 6 — 71+
(PWHarris) *rn green and sn outpcd in rr: hdwy 2f out: kpt on ins last: nrst fin* **16/1**

0-5 **6** *15* **Sierra**18 3374 3-8-6 ........ J-PGuillambert(3) 3 — 37
(CEBrittain) *chsd ldrs on outer: rdn along 3f out: chsd ldr 2f out: sn wknd* **33/1**

0 **7** *2* **Baranook (IRE)**32 2950 3-9-0 ........ RMullen 10 — 38+
(PWHarris) *a rr* **33/1**

03 **8** *2* **Gift Voucher (IRE)**16 3417 3-9-0 ........ FLynch 1 — 35+
(SirMichaelStoute) *trckd ldrs on inner: hmpd and hung out bnd over 6f out: pushed along and put hd in air 3f out: sn lost pl and eased* **13/8**1

6052 **9** *12* **Sharaab (USA)**34 2900 3-9-0 73 ........ (t) WSupple 8 — 12
(BHanbury) *chsd ldrs: hmpd bnd over 6f out: rdn along over 3f out: sn wknd and eased* **7/1**

0 **10** *30* **Explicit (IRE)**20 3304 3-9-0 ........ SWhitworth 9 — —
(GCBravery) *led: rdn along over 3f out: hdd 21/2f out and wknd quic kly* **50/1**

2m 16.19s (2.28) **Going Correction** +0.225s/f (Good) — **10** Ran SP% **118.0**
Speed ratings: **99,98,98,97,96 84,82,80,71,47**CSF £21.48 TOTE £4.30: £1.70, £2.10, £3.10; EX 20.40.
**Owner** Lucayan Stud **Bred** Lucayan Stud Ltd And Whatton Manor Stud **Trained** Newmarket, Suffolk

**FOCUS**
A fair maiden featuring backward sorts from top stables, but run at a moderate pace and the form may have been slightly devalued by the below-par effort of the favourite.

**NOTEBOOK**
**Fortune's Princess**, who had run well in both starts over this trip, overcame being hampered by the favourite on the first bend. She gives the impression another two furlongs would not be beyond her and should be competitive in handicaps off a mark in the low 70s.
**Mandatum**, a half-brother to the stayer Boreas, was rather surprisingly dropped in trip on this second outing, having been placed over a mile and a half on his debut. He ran as if the return to a longer trip was needed, and an ordinary maiden is within his compass.
**Turn 'n Burn**, returning from a three-month absence and encountering fast ground for the first time, ran well enough but is likely to find his best opportunities in handicaps in due course.
**Shastye(IRE)**, a half-sister to Arc winner Sagamix among others, travelled well for a long way, but again gave the impression she did not get home. It could be that she is still a little weak at present.
**Barathea Blue ◆**, a brother to the useful stayer Barathea Blazer, caught the eye on this debut, finishing on the heels of the placed horses under a considerate ride. He should come on a good deal for this and is sure to be placed to win a maiden before long.
**Gift Voucher(IRE)** failed to build on his recent Kempton effort over this shorter trip. However, he may have had excuses as he failed to handle the first bend and may have done himself some damage in the process. *Official explanation: trainer's representative said colt had sustained a leg injury*

## 3923 INJURED JOCKEYS CLASSIFIED STKS — 6f
**9:10** (9:10) (E) 3-Y-0+ — **£4,927** (£1,516; £758; £379) **Stalls** Low

Form — RPR

1234 **1** **High Ridge**5 3775 5-9-4 69 ........ (p) DeanMcKeown 9 — 78
(JMBradley) *stdd s: hld up in rr: hdwy on outer 2f out: rdn to chal ent last: styd on to ld last 100 yds* **11/4**1

0000 **2** *1/2* **Rectangle (IRE)**13 3509 4-9-3 68 ........ AlexGreaves 5 — 75
(DNicholls) *chsd ldr: rdn and hdwy to ld over 1f out: drvn ins last: hdd and no ex last 100 yds* **12/1**

0300 **3** *2* **Tantric**9 3623 5-9-0 58 ........ ACulhane 3 — 66
(JO'Reilly) *hld up: hdwy 2f out: rdn to chse ldrs over 1f out: kpt on u.p ins last* **8/1**3

3204 **4** *3* **Bundy**6 3735 8-9-0 64 ........ SWKelly 2 — 57
(MDods) *chsd ldrs: rdn 2f out: sn drvn and no imp* **3/1**2

6056 **5** *nk* **Linden's Lady**27 3101 4-8-4 60 ........ (be1) DFentiman(7) 1 — 53
(JRWeymes) *led: rdn 2f out: hdd over 1f out and sn wknd* **12/1**

0010 **6** *2 1/2* **Smart Minister**16 3409 4-9-0 64 ........ KDalgleish 4 — 49
(JJQuinn) *prom: rdn along 2f out and sn wknd* **12/1**

0642 **7** *2* **Sewmuch Character**11 3593 5-9-0 63 ........ DSweeney 6 — 43
(MBlanshard) *hld up in tch: hdwy to chse ldng pair 2f out: sn rdn and wknd over 1f out* **11/4**1

1m 18.35s (1.05) **Going Correction** +0.225s/f (Good)
**WFA** 3 from 4yo+ 5lb — **7** Ran SP% **112.5**
Speed ratings: **102,101,98,94,94 90,88**CSF £33.99 TOTE £3.80: £2.00, £3.60; EX 28.50 Place 6 £750.97, Place 5 £152.75.
**Owner** James Leisure Ltd **Bred** Buckram Thoroughbred Enterprises Inc **Trained** Sedbury, Gloucs

**FOCUS**
A tight classified contest judged on official ratings, but the winner defied the outside draw.

**NOTEBOOK**
**High Ridge** has been running consistently this season and was not unduly inconvenienced by the outside stall and he is usually dropped in. He picked up well to take the advantage and did enough to resist the renewed effort of the runner-up. He should not go up a great deal for this effort, as he looks handicapped up to the limit.
**Rectangle(IRE)** seems well suited by a positive ride and, back on a fast surface, did best of those that raced up with the pace. He did not give up once beaten and is now on his lowest-ever mark.
**Tantric**, who has raced mainly over seven furlongs and a mile of late, had a stiff task on official ratings and ran on quite well from the rear without ever appearing likely to score. He is on a fair mark now, and will be interesting if returning to Carlisle for the classified stakes he won in early August last year.
**Bundy** continues to run well without really sparkling. He may need to drop a few pounds before he is able to regain the winning thread.
**Linden's Lady**, with blinkers and eyeshield for the first time, set off at a rate of knots but did not last home. The same tactics may well work on an easier course.
**Sewmuch Character**, returning to the course where he gained his last win, travelled well but faded disappointingly in the final furlong. Despite dropping in the handicap he does not seem to be getting any nearer winning again.
T/Plt: £657.60 to a £1 stake. Pool: £36,531.65. 40.55 winning tickets. T/Qpdt: £179.80 to a £1 stake. Pool: £2,819.50. 11.60 winning tickets. JR

# 3777 HAYDOCK (L-H)
Saturday, July 17

**OFFICIAL GOING: Soft**
11 m of rain overnight and a further 5mm through the day led to testing conditions being prevalent.
Wind: almost nil Weather: fine

## 3924 HAYDOCK PARK PONY CLUB NURSERY — 5f
**6:40** (6:42) (E) 2-Y-0 — **£3,588** (£1,104; £552; £276) **Stalls** Centre

Form — RPR

0401 **1** **Make Us Flush**16 3444 2-8-3 **69** ........ FNorton 5 — 72
(ABerry) *racd far-side: chsd leaders: rdn 1/2-way: r.o to ld overall wl ins fnl f: jst hld on* **12/1**

0402 **2** *shd* **I'm Aimee**[8] 3704 2-8-6 **72** KFallon 6 75
(PDEvans) *racd far-side and overall ld: rdn over 1f out: hdd wl ins fnl f: rallied last strides* **4/1**[1]
1066 **3** *1 ½* **Mitchelland**[16] 3445 2-8-7 **73** RWinston 2 72
(JamesMoffatt) *racd far-side: towards rr: pushed along 1/2-way: hdwy over 1f out: r.o towards fin: nt rch ldrs* **9/1**[3]
5426 **4** *5* **Little Biscuit (IRE)**[8] 3704 2-7-7 **64** oh5 BSwarbrick(5) 8 48
(KRBurke) *racd stands' side: prom: led gp over 1f out: edgd lft ins fnl f: no ch w far-side* **9/1**[3]
0620 **5** *1 ½* **Brut**[23] 3233 2-8-1 **67** RFfrench 1 46
(DWBarker) *racd far-side: prom: rdn and ev ch over 1f out: wknd ins fnl f* **25/1**
0140 **6** *2* **Apologies**[9] 3677 2-8-11 **77** RLMoore 4 50
(BAMcmahon) *racd far-side: sn outpcd* **11/2**[2]
0210 **7** *nk* **Town House**[21] 3290 2-8-6 **72** JFEgan 7 44
(BPJBaugh) *led stands' side tl hdd over 1f out: wkng whn edgd lft ins fnl f* **14/1**
120 **8** *14* **Dance Anthem**[32] 2954 2-9-7 **87** PMcCabe 3 17
(MGQuinlan) *racd far-side: t.k.h: in rr: outpcd 2f out* **4/1**[1]
134 **9** *9* **Midnight Tycoon**[23] 3224 2-9-7 **87** FLynch 9 —
(BSmart) *chsd ldr stands'side 2f: sn wknd* **4/1**[1]

64.40 secs (2.33) **Going Correction** +0.45s/f (Yiel) **9 Ran SP% 113.6**
Speed ratings: **99,98,96,88,86 82,82,59,45**CSF £58.58 CT £460.52 TOTE £11.30: £2.70, £1.50, £4.00; EX 36.90.
**Owner** The Bath Tub Boys **Bred** Bearstone Stud **Trained** Cockerham, Lancs

**FOCUS**
A decent pace with the draw playing a major part. The figures shown as 'official ratings' are estimates for guidance only.

**NOTEBOOK**
**Make Us Flush**, a winner of a claimer at the track last time did not need to step up on that to win a nursery that lacked strength in depth. Racing on the favoured far side, she responded well to pressure to win on the nod.
**I'm Aimee** set a good even pace on the far side but remains a maiden after eight starts and lacks a change of gear.
**Mitchelland** had been disappointing since winning a four-runner Newcastle maiden on her second start, and was under pressure early on in the race before staying on past beaten horses.
**Little Biscuit(IRE)** would be interesting back in selling company.
**Brut** weakened quickly over a furlong out having tried to go with the pacesetter, and looks harshly treated at the present time.
**Apologies**, supported in the market, ran poorly for the second race in succession and is best watched for the time being.
**Town House** *Official explanation: jockey said filly was unsuited by the soft going*
**Dance Anthem** failed to run any sort of race, apparently hating the ground. *Official explanation: jockey said colt was unsuited by soft going*
**Midnight Tycoon** ran as if something was amiss with the jockey constantly looking down. *Official explanation: trainer was unable to offer any explanation for poor form shown*

## 3925 MERCEDES-BENZ DIRECT BIRTHDAY EBF MAIDEN STKS 6f
**7:10** (7:13) (D ) 2-Y-O **£5,310** (£1,634; £817; £408) **Stalls** Centre

Form RPR
**1** **Josh** 2-9-0 PRobinson 2 88
(MAJarvis) *racd keenly: trckd ldrs: rdn over 1f out: led ins fnl f: r.o* **11/2**[3]
**2** *2 ½* **Throw The Dice** 2-9-0 NCallan 11 81
(KARyan) *dwlt: towards rr: hdwy over 3f out: led 2f out: sn hung lft: hdd ins fnl f: kpt on same pce* **11/1**
2 **3** *hd* **Sacranun**[13] 3568 2-9-0 DHolland 14 80
(LMCumani) *a.p: rdn and ev ch fr over 1f out: nt qckn ins fnl f* **5/1**[2]
62 **4** *5* **Mozafin**[34] 2904 2-9-0 ACulhane 1 80+
(MRChannon) *w ldr: rdn whn n.m.r and hmpd over 1f out: sn lost pl: kpt on ins fnl f* **9/4**[1]
0 **5** *¾* **Orphan (IRE)**[28] 3080 2-9-0 DarrenWilliams 10 63
(KRBurke) *midfield: rdn and hdwy over 1f out: wknd ins fnl f* **50/1**
**6** *1 ¼* **Love And Laughter (IRE)** 2-8-9 JFEgan 8 69+
(TDEasterby) *s.s: in rr: rn green: hdwy whn nt clr run ins fnl f: n.d* **16/1**
**7** *1* **Chief Scout** 2-9-0 KFallon 4 56
(BJMeehan) *midfield: rn green: pushed along 1/2-way: nvr trbld ldrs* **11/2**[3]
**8** *2 ½* **Wizardmicktee (IRE)** 2-9-0 RWinston 5 48
(ABailey) *dwlt: midfield: nt pce to chal* **40/1**
**9** *¾* **Sydneyroughdiamond** 2-9-0 SRighton 13 46
(MMullineaux) *dwlt: a in rr div* **66/1**
23 **10** *hd* **Mytton's Bell (IRE)**[50] 2453 2-8-9 VSlattery 12 41
(ABailey) *led: rdn and hdd 2f out: n.m.r and hmpd over 1f out: sn wknd* **10/1**
**11** *3* **Mickledo** 2-9-0 RLMoore 7 37
(ABailey) *trckd ldrs tl rdn and wknd over 2f out* **33/1**
**12** *shd* **Allizam** 2-9-0 WSupple 9 36
(BAMcmahon) *midfield: lost palce 1/2-way: bhd after* **25/1**

1m 18.88s (3.99) **Going Correction** +0.45s/f (Yiel) **12 Ran SP% 114.2**
Speed ratings: **91,87,87,80,79 78,76,73,72,72 68,68**CSF £58.92 TOTE £7.00: £2.30, £3.80, £2.10; EX 65.40.
**Owner** T G & Mrs M E Holdcroft **Bred** Bearstone Stud **Trained** Newmarket, Suffolk
■ Stewards Enquiry : D Holland one-day ban: careless riding (Jul 29)

**FOCUS**
A fair maiden with an even split of precocious and backward types on show.

**NOTEBOOK**
**Josh** ◆, a home-bred colt by Josr Algarhoud, he raced very keenly through the first furlong and a half but was always well positioned. He saved enough for the latter stages of the race, and quickened away readily from his rivals in the soft ground in the style of a useful colt. This was his stable's first juvenile winner of the season and a step up in grade is warranted.
**Throw The Dice** was slowly away and, after hitting the front two furlongs out, he was hanging left throughout the final furlong. Being a half-brother to the useful Hazyview, he should improve for experience and a step up in trip.
**Sacranun**, beaten in Milan on his debut, ran well enough, however he is not over big and has less scope for improvement than the front two.
**Mozafin** would have finished much closer had he not been badly hampered over a furlong out by the weakening Mytton's Bell. His future will depend on the Handicapper's assessment.
**Orphan(IRE)** showed huge improvement from his debut and this cheap purchase may be capable of better still.
**Love And Laughter(IRE)**, supported in the market, was a big eyecatcher on her debut. The daughter of Theatrical was very slowly away and was last during the early stages, and she only started to get the hang of things after Egan livened her up with one slap of the whip. She then started to eat up the ground and would have surely taken close order had she not been brought to a standstill by Mytton's Bell, who was a menace throughout the race. She is capable of far better than this and will be very interesting on her next start.
**Chief Scout**, by Tomba, who was very successful for connections and loved this sort of ground, did not know his job and can be expected to improve on this.
**Mickledo** weakened noticeably after holding a prominent position, and the hope must be that he will improve on a sounder surface.

## 3926 KNIGHTS PHARMACY RATED STKS (H'CAP) 6f
**7:40** (7:43) (D ) (0-85,82) 3-Y-O **£5,165** (£1,959; £979; £445) **Stalls** Centre

Form RPR
2226 **1** **Commando Scott (IRE)**[4] 3819 3-9-3 **78** FLynch 4 91
(ABerry) *chsd ldr: led 2f out: r.o wl* **6/1**[3]
35-6 **2** *3* **Rising Shadow (IRE)**[21] 3317 3-9-7 **82** DHolland 9 86
(RAFahey) *wnt rt s: in tch: rdn and hdwy over 2f out: chsd wnr and hung lft over 1f out: no imp fnl f* **14/1**
1033 **3** *2 ½* **Neon Blue**[12] 3585 3-8-7 **68** KFallon 2 65
(RMWhitaker) *in tch: rdn and outpcd over 2f out: styd on ins fnl f* **4/1**[1]
4062 **4** *½* **Rydal (USA)**[6] 3777 3-9-5 **80** (b) SWKelly 14 75
(GAButler) *s.s: in rr: hdwy over 2f out: sn rdn and swtchd lft: no ex ins fnl f* **9/2**[2]
1300 **5** *2* **Distant Times**[31] 2981 3-9-1 **76** (v) DAllan 5 65
(TDEasterby) *trckd ldrs: rdn and edgd rt over 2f out: wknd ins fnl f* **12/1**
0000 **6** *nk* **Iskander**[14] 3523 3-9-2 **77** (b) JCarroll 7 65
(KARyan) *led: rdn 1/2-way: hdd 2f out: wknd 1f out* **33/1**
0012 **7** *nk* **Rise**[14] 3530 3-8-4 **65** (b) JFEgan 6 52
(AndrewReid) *midfield: rdn whn nt clr run over 2f out: sn swtchd rt: nt clr run again over 1f out: kpt on ins fnl f* **7/1**
4001 **8** *shd* **Keeper's Lodge (IRE)**[15] 3478 3-8-9 **70** RLMoore 10 57
(BAMcmahon) *towards rr: rdn over 2f out: nvr able to chal* **14/1**
0630 **9** *1 ¼* **Four Amigos (USA)**[8] 3702 3-9-7 **82** JFanning 8 65
(JGGiven) *trckd ldrs: rdn over 2f out: wknd over 1f out* **11/1**
50-0 **10** *½* **Beauty Of Dreams**[15] 3478 3-8-10 **71** ACulhane 1 53
(MRChannon) *midfield: rdn over 2f out: wknd over 1f out* **25/1**
4060 **11** *7* **George The Best (IRE)**[4] 3819 3-8-7 **68** DarrenWilliams 11 29
(MDHammond) *hld up: rdn and hdwy 1/2-way: sn wknd* **14/1**
0314 **12** *11* **Hawaajes**[21] 3317 3-9-0 **75** WSupple 13 3
(BHanbury) *hld up: brief effrt 1/2-way: sn wknd* **9/1**

1m 17.16s (2.27) **Going Correction** +0.45s/f (Yiel) **12 Ran SP% 117.8**
Speed ratings: **102,98,94,94,91 90,90,90,88,88 78,64**CSF £86.55 CT £383.32 TOTE £7.70: £2.50, £4.60, £2.10; EX 194.60.
**Owner** Mrs Ann Morris **Bred** Noel Finegan **Trained** Cockerham, Lancs

**FOCUS**
A run-of-the-mill handicap in which the pace was reasonable, although not many showed their form in the conditions.

**NOTEBOOK**
**Commando Scott(IRE)**, winner of a soft-ground maiden in April and poorly drawn on his previous outing, produced a career-best effort, gradually drawing away from his field after taking up the running fully two furlongs from home. On this evidence he has further improvement in him.
**Rising Shadow(IRE)** is still lightly raced and showed that his turn is not far away. Running down the centre of the track until edging over to the far side, he kept on well for second but had no chance with the winner.
**Neon Blue** stayed on and may be suited to a return to seven furlongs.
**Rydal(USA)** found plenty of trouble in running and is far better than his placing suggests.
**Rise** *Official explanation: jockey said filly missed break*
**George The Best(IRE)**, representing a trainer in form, appeared to run below par. *Official explanation: jockey said gelding lost his action*
**Hawaajes** hated the soft ground and this run should be ignored. *Official explanation: jockey said gelding was unsuited by soft ground*

## 3927 H2O STKS (REGISTERED AS THE JULY TROPHY) (LISTED RACE) (C&G) 1m 3f 200y
**8:10** (8:11) (A ) 3-Y-O **£17,400** (£6,600; £3,300; £1,500) **Stalls** High

Form RPR
6131 **1** **Frank Sonata**[42] 2683 3-8-10 **101** RLMoore 6 108
(MGQuinlan) *hld up in tch: hdwy over 3f out: rdn 2f out: led 1f out: hld on wl* **10/3**[2]
1-10 **2** *nk* **Pukka (IRE)**[42] 2680 3-8-10 **105** DHolland 4 108
(LMCumani) *a.p: rdn and nt qckn over 2f out: r.o cl home* **9/4**[1]
0211 **3** *shd* **Albinus**[24] 3210 3-8-10 **90** (b) MartinDwyer 7 107
(AMBalding) *led: rdn 2f out: hdd 1f out: stl ev ch ins fnl f: no ex cl* **5/1**[3]
401 **4** *10* **Protective**[43] 2653 3-8-10 **88** WSupple 2 92
(JGGiven) *hld up in rr: effrt over 2f out: no imp* **50/1**
-315 **5** *shd* **Lord Mayor**[30] 3000 3-8-10 **103** KFallon 3 92
(SirMichaelStoute) *racd keenly: prom: rdn 2f out: wknd over 1f out* **9/4**[1]
1360 **6** *8* **Red Lancer**[21] 3310 3-9-3 **108** MFenton 1 87
(RJPrice) *hld up in tch: hdwy over 3f out: rdn and wknd over 2f out* **12/1**
0031 **7** *1 ½* **Anousa (IRE)**[10] 3639 3-9-0 **82** RWinston 5 82
(PHowling) *hld up in tch: rdn and wknd over 2f out* **25/1**

2m 39.53s (4.37) **Going Correction** +0.55s/f (Yiel) **7 Ran SP% 114.8**
Speed ratings: **107,106,106,100,100 94,93**CSF £11.38 TOTE £4.00: £1.90, £2.00; EX 10.40.
**Owner** Adams, Flynn, Arnold **Bred** Bishop Wilton Stud **Trained** Newmarket, Suffolk

**FOCUS**
A decent little Listed race, although there were no real stars on show. The time was ordinary for the grade.

**NOTEBOOK**
**Frank Sonata** was well in at the weights and continued his progress with a hard-fought success, holding the winner gamely on the run to the line. Always travelling strongly behind the pacesetter, his jockey had to get serious two furlongs out and in the end he dug deep to score. The easy ground suited him, unlike some of his rivals, and he would not be sure to confirm the form next time. The St Leger is said to be on the agenda.
**Pukka(IRE)**, ninth in the Derby on his previous start, ran well here despite not liking the ground according to his trainer. He ran all the way to the line and the St Leger is still under consideration.
**Albinus** set a steady pace on this step up into Listed Company for the first time. This was much improved form and he is remains highly progressive.
**Protective** was held up last for much of the race and made little impact, although in fairness he faced a very tough task and was not disgraced.
**Lord Mayor** was bang in contention two furlongs from home but patently didn't stay here and this effort should be ignored. He will be a different proposition back to ten furlongs on drier ground.
**Red Lancer** had a difficult task at the weights but still ran poorly. The trainer blamed the going, but he had won a Group Three at Chester in similar conditions and may have had enough for now.
**Anousa(IRE)** was struggling a long way out and needs further.

## 3928 MICK SHERWOOD 50TH BIRTHDAY H'CAP 2m 45y
**8:40** (8:40) (E ) (0-75,70) 3-Y-O+ **£3,575** (£1,100; £550; £275) **Stalls** Low

Form RPR
1521 **1** **Quedex**[15] 3485 8-9-4 **70** LTreadwell(7) 8 76
(RJPrice) *hld up: hdwy 5f out: rdn to ld 2f out: edgd rt over 1f out: styd on* **9/4**[1]
4-04 **2** *1* **Penny Stall**[15] 3479 3-8-0 **62** DKinsella 5 67
(JLDunlop) *in tch: led over 4f out: rdn and hdd 2f out: styd on same pce* **11/2**

0040 **3** *1* **Calomeria**[7] 3743 3-7-13 **61** oh3 ow1 ....................(b[1]) FNorton 4 65
(RMBeckett) *led for 7f: remained prom: rdn and flashed tail fr 3f out: kpt on* **33/1**

-051 **4** *3 1/2* **Euippe**[15] 3479 3-8-8 **70** .................... MFenton 1 71
(JGGiven) *hld up: hdwy over 4f out: rdn and ev ch over 2f out: no ex ins fnl f* **4/1**[2]

0352 **5** *19* **Ocean Tide**[4] 3821 7-9-9 **68** .................... MartinDwyer 6 50
(RFord) *prom: pushed along 1/2-way: wknd over 4f out* **9/2**[3]

2-01 **6** *6* **Oops (IRE)**[14] 3508 5-7-7 **45** .................... DeanWilliams(7) 7 21
(JFCoupland) *racd wd thrght: prom: led bef 1/2-way: hdd over 5f out: wknd over 3f out* **11/2**

2006 **7** *3 1/2* **Cantemerle (IRE)**[16] 3443 4-8-0 **50** ....................(b) BSwarbrick(5) 3 22
(WMBrisbourne) *a bhd* **33/1**

51/0 **8** *4* **Congo Man**[31] 2978 11-8-0 **45** .................... RFfrench 10 13
(DWWhillans) *a bhd* **66/1**

0-00 **9** *5* **Allez Mousson**[102] 1287 6-8-7 **52** ....................(b) WSupple 9 15
(ABailey) *sn prom: led after 7f: hdd bef 1/2-way: rdn and wknd 4f out* **33/1**

3020 **10** *23* **Lady Netbetsports (IRE)**[6] 3782 5-9-3 **62** .................... RWinston 2 2
(BSRothwell) *trckd ldrs: led over 5f out: hdd over 4f out: sn wknd: eased: t.o* **25/1**

3m 44.46s (6.56) **Going Correction** +0.55s/f (Yiel)
**WFA** 3 from 4yo+ 17lb **10** Ran SP% **113.9**
Speed ratings: **105,104,104,102,92 89,88,86,83,72**CSF £13.80 CT £311.43 TOTE £3.60: £1.70, £1.60, £9.30; EX 13.00.
**Owner** Fox And Cub Partnership **Bred** Leo Van Hijkoop **Trained** Ullingswick, H'fords

**FOCUS**
A slowly run staying race. The leading quartet drew a long way clear of the others, but the form doesn't look that solid.

**NOTEBOOK**
**Quedex** followed up his Sandown win with a battling success here. Held up off the pace, he joined issue under a confident ride and showed the right attitude in a good tussle to the line. He should not go up to much for this and could win again.
**Penny Stall** stepped up to two miles for the first time here and this lightly raced maiden travelled strongly for much of the race. She looks to possess enough ability to win a similar race.
**Calomeria** was out of the handicap and had the blinkers on for the first time. She is not one to trust, flashing her tail under pressure and refusing to go through with her effort despite having the far side rail to run against.
**Euippe**, who was stepping up in trip, didn't quite get home having held every chance.
**Oops(IRE)** may have been closer if he had not raced down the centre of the track
**Allez Mousson** seemed reluctant to race and had to be vigorously ridden leaving the stalls. On a long losing run, he looks out of love with the game.

## 3929 RECTANGLE GROUP H'CAP 1m 2f 120y
9:10 (9:11) (E) (0-70,76) 3-Y-O+ £3,692 (£1,136; £568; £284) Stalls High

Form RPR

-604 **1** **Mount Benger**[9] 3662 4-9-4 **60** ....................(p) FLynch 7 69
(RMBeckett) *bhd: rdn and hdwy whn edgd rt over 1f out: str run ins fnl f to ld post* **8/1**

1513 **2** *shd* **Pure Mischief (IRE)**[22] 3265 5-9-9 **70** .................... RThomas(5) 9 79
(CRDore) *hld up: hdwy 3f out: rdn 2f out: hung lft and r.o to ld wl ins fnl f: ct post* **5/1**[2]

5611 **3** *hd* **Jimmy Byrne (IRE)**[6] 3781 4-10-1 **76** 6ex .................... PMulrennan(5) 11 84
(BEllison) *trckd ldrs gng wl: rdn to ld 1f out: sn hung lft: hdd wl ins fnl f* **9/4**[1]

0406 **4** *1 1/4* **Lennel**[6] 3781 6-9-8 **64** ....................(b) VSlattery 10 70
(ABailey) *s.i.s: towards rr: rdn 4f out: hdwy over 3f out: styd on ins fnl f* **16/1**

000/ **5** *3/4* **Mr Midaz**[27] 5170 5-8-3 **45** .................... RFfrench 12 50
(DWWhillans) *in tch: rdn 4f out: ev ch over 1f out: nt qckn ins fnl f* **14/1**

0052 **6** *1 1/2* **Mr Dip**[8] 3695 4-8-3 **50** .................... PMakin(5) 15 53
(AWCarroll) *midfield: hdwy over 3f out: led over 1f out: sn hdd: kpt on same pce* **11/2**[3]

0530 **7** *3/4* **Got To Be Cash**[22] 3264 5-8-5 **52** .................... BSwarbrick(5) 2 53
(WMBrisbourne) *midfield: hdwy over 3f out: rdn over 1f out: one pce ins fnl f* **12/1**

0004 **8** *1 1/2* **Band**[6] 3781 4-9-2 **58** .................... WSupple 5 57
(BAMcmahon) *s.i.s: midfield: rdn over 2f out: hdwy over 1f out: one pce whn nt clr run wl ins fnl f* **9/1**

00-0 **9** *8* **Martin House (IRE)**[17] 3409 5-8-13 **55** .................... JFanning 6 40
(MrsKWalton) *hdwy after 2f: in tch: rdn and wknd over 1f out* **33/1**

3530 **10** *3* **Arjay**[37] 2816 6-8-5 **47** .................... JCarroll 13 27
(AndrewTurnell) *hld up: effrt over 2f out: no imp* **25/1**

040/ **11** *3* **The Roundsills**[569] 4562 10-7-12 **40** .................... SRighton 8 15
(MMullineaux) *led: rdn 2f out: hdd over 1f out: sn wknd* **100/1**

0P65 **12** *1/2* **Kenny The Truth (IRE)**[5] 3804 5-8-0 **42** ....................(t) PMQuinn 4 16
(MrsJCandlish) *midfield: rdn and wknd over 3f out* **25/1**

650- **13** *7* **Saddler's Quest**[77] 3649 7-9-7 **63** .................... DarrenWilliams 3 25
(BPJBaugh) *prom tl rdn and wknd over 2f out* **25/1**

4-00 **14** *6* **Iftikhar (USA)**[14] 3520 5-9-1 **57** .................... SWKelly 14 9
(WMBrisbourne) *hld up: nt clr run over 3f out: rdn and btn over 2f out* **33/1**

-003 **15** *12* **Sheriff's Deputy**[6] 3771 4-9-12 **68** .................... RWinston 16 —
(JWUnett) *racd keenly: midfield: in tch: rdn and wknd over 3f out* **16/1**

000/ **16** *dist* **Gablesea**[428] 4025 10-7-8 **43** oh16 ow3 .................... DeanWilliams(7) 17 —
(BPJBaugh) *prom: rdn over 4f out: wknd over 3f out: t.o* **100/1**

2m 22.89s (5.16) **Going Correction** +0.55s/f (Yiel) **16** Ran SP% **129.5**
Speed ratings: **103,102,102,101,101 100,99,98,92,90 88,88,82,78,69** —CSF £48.09 CT £125.60 TOTE £10.60: £3.00, £1.40, £1.40, £5.00; EX 45.40 Place 6 £56.20, Place 5 £19.27.
**Owner** Young Guns Syndicate **Bred** London Thoroughbred Services Ltd And John Gaines **Trained** Lambourn, Berks

**FOCUS**
A tight little handicap but only a fair pace. While the overall level of form is ordinary, it looks solid, with the first two running their best races since they were juveniles and the third confirming recent improvement.

**NOTEBOOK**
**Mount Benger**, who had shown improved form last time in first-time cheek pieces, showed that was no fluke winning the first race of his career here at the ninth time of asking. Given a patient ride and sitting last at half way he gradually worked his way through the field and finished well to lead on the post.
**Pure Mischief(IRE)** was supported in the betting market and did nothing wrong. However his current handicap mark will always leave him exposed to improving types.
**Jimmy Byrne(IRE)** was looking for a hat-trick, having won his previous 2 races over course and distance. He travelled extremely well with his apprentice but found disappointingly little under a big weight. He has been called a few names in the past and although not beaten far will struggle once reassessed.
**Lennel** ran his usual race, slowly away before staying on. For the time being he appears to be fighting a losing battle with the handicapper.
**Mr Midaz**, a winner over hurdles, showed enough on his first Flat run in 20 months to suggest he could win on the level, but he does not have a change of gear and may need to be stepped up.
**Mr Dip** ran a fair race back over this shorter trip and continues to threaten to break his duck.
**Got To Be Cash** could muster only one pace inside the final furlong on ground which he appreciates.
**Band** got within striking distance but could not quicken, but at least the signs are a little encouraging.
**Martin House(IRE)** had the run of the race but again ran poorly. He is running out of excuses and although falling in the handicap he is unlikely to trouble the judge at present.
**Gablesea** *Official explanation: jockey said gelding slipped and lost his action turning into home straight*
T/Plt: £136.10 to a £1 stake - Pool: £51,074.90. 273.85 winning tickets. T/Qpdt: £13.50 to a £1 stake - Pool: £3,641.10. 199.10 winning tickets. DO

# 3846 LINGFIELD (L-H)
Saturday, July 17

**OFFICIAL GOING: Turf course - good; all-weather - standard**

## 3930 INDEPENDENT CATERING NURSERY 5f
6:25 (6:25) (E) 2-Y-O £3,484 (£1,072; £536; £268) Stalls High

Form RPR

3423 **1** **Forzeen**[17] 3418 2-8-13 **73** .................... EAhern 2 83+
(JAOsborne) *racd on outer in midfield: prog 2f out: rdn to ld 1f out: r.o wl: readily* **6/1**[3]

0521 **2** *1 3/4* **Russian Rocket (IRE)**[17] 3418 2-8-11 **76** .................... HayleyTurner(5) 3 80
(MrsCADunnett) *racd towards outer in midfield: prog 2f out: rdn to chal jst over 1f out: styd on but no ch w wnr ins fnl f* **9/1**

6214 **3** *2* **Tesary**[10] 3634 2-9-0 **74** .................... LDettori 12 71
(EALDunlop) *hld up in midfield: nt clr run briefly 2f out: rdn and hanging over 1f out: kpt on fnl f to take 3rd nr fin* **2/1**[1]

064 **4** *3/4* **Kempsey**[17] 3418 2-8-10 **70** .................... ADaly 11 64
(JJBridger) *racd on inner: chsd ldrs: outpcd and rdn 2f out: kpt on again ins fnl f* **20/1**

2414 **5** *shd* **Smiddy Hill**[43] 2655 2-9-7 **81** .................... JQuinn 6 75
(RBastiman) *racd freely: led to 1f out: wknd* **4/1**[2]

4510 **6** *1/2* **Elisha (IRE)**[21] 3290 2-8-12 **72** .................... CCatlin 7 64
(DMSimcock) *chsd ldr to over 1f out: wknd fnl f* **20/1**

414 **7** *1 3/4* **Talcen Gwyn (IRE)**[8] 3704 2-9-5 **79** .................... IMongan 9 65
(MFHarris) *s.i.s: wl in rr: pushed along 1/2-way: kpt on fnl f: no ch* **12/1**

044 **8** *1/2* **First Rule**[21] 3302 2-8-11 **71** .................... SSanders 5 55
(CFWall) *chsd ldrs tl wknd wl over 1f out* **8/1**

0021 **9** *1/2* **Keresforth**[40] 2725 2-8-4 **64** .................... PDoe 1 47
(IAWood) *racd on outer: outpcd and pushed along 3f out: nvr a factor* **20/1**

340 **10** *hd* **Majestical (IRE)**[53] 2376 2-8-1 **61** .................... AMcCarthy 4 43
(WRMuir) *a towards rr: rdn and hanging 2f out: fnd nil* **20/1**

406 **11** *3 1/2* **Ms Polly Garter**[51] 2427 2-7-5 **58** oh5 .................... MHalford(7) 10 28
(JMBradley) *s.s: outpcd and wl bhd in last: no prog* **33/1**

536 **12** *3 1/2* **Baileys Applause**[57] 2275 2-8-6 **66** ....................(b[1]) RHavlin 8 23
(CADwyer) *chsd ldrs: wkng whn hmpd over 1f out: eased* **16/1**

58.73 secs (-0.14) **Going Correction** +0.025s/f (Good) **12** Ran SP% **124.3**
Speed ratings: **102,99,96,94,94 93,91,90,89,89 83,77**CSF £56.44 CT £151.42 TOTE £9.50: £2.50, £2.60, £1.60; EX 63.30.
**Owner** Cavendish Racing **Bred** James Clark **Trained** Upper Lambourn, Berks
■ Stewards Enquiry : L Dettori caution: careless riding

**FOCUS**
A nursery of reasonable quality run in a decent time, with the first two home still on the upgrade. The figures shown as 'official ratings' are estimates for guidance only.

**NOTEBOOK**
**Forzeen** gained his reward for some solid efforts in maiden auction company and looks a useful nursery performer. He was 5lb better off with the runner-up compared with their race on Polytrack last time.
**Russian Rocket(IRE)** had beaten the winner on sand here last time but was now 5lb worse off. Nonetheless, he ran his race and can be expected to go well again in turf nurseries off a similar mark.
**Tesary** ran a fair race but the first two home beat her fair and square in the end. This was a shade disappointing considering the promise of earlier performances.
**Kempsey** seems to be steadily improving and is capable of winning a routine maiden or nursery.
**Smiddy Hill** has bags of early speed and is very effective when bowling along, but on this occasion she was a bit too fresh in front under her big weight.
**Elisha(IRE)** is happier on faster ground than last time, coming back to her earlier form here, but the main contenders were too strong at the weights.
**Talcen Gwyn(IRE)** had previously run three good races but was carting plenty of weight against these rivals. He then handicapped himself unnecessarily by missing the break.

## 3931 EUROPEAN BREEDERS FUND MAIDEN STKS 7f
6:55 (7:00) (D) 2-Y-O £4,459 (£1,372; £686; £343) Stalls High

Form RPR

2 **1** **Minnesota (USA)**[24] 3192 2-9-0 .................... DaneO'Neill 6 76
(HCandy) *racd against nr side rail: mde all: rdn whn pressed over 1f out: r.o wl fnl f* **3/1**[2]

46 **2** *1 3/4* **Ragged Glory (IRE)**[52] 2396 2-9-0 .................... RSmith 4 72
(RHannon) *trckd ldrs: rdn and unable qck 2f out: styd on wl fnl f to take 2nd last stride* **14/1**

0 **3** *shd* **Dahliyev (IRE)**[23] 3228 2-9-0 .................... EAhern 1 72
(PWHarris) *wl in tch: chsd wnr over 2f out: rdn to chal over 1f out: no imp fnl f: lost 2nd last stride* **12/1**

**4** *1/2* **Creative Character (USA)** 2-8-11 ow2 .................... NDeSouza(5) 9 73
(PFICole) *prom: u.p 2f out: styd on ins fnl f: nvr able to chal* **28/1**

0 **5** *1 1/4* **Blaise Hollow (USA)**[15] 3476 2-9-0 .................... SDrowne 11 67
(RCharlton) *uns rdr on way to post: hld up in midfield: shkn up over 2f out: kpt on ins fnl f: n.d* **16/1**

**6** *hd* **Zalaal (USA)** 2-9-0 .................... LDettori 14 67
(SaeedBinSuroor) *hld up towards rr: effrt 3f out: rdn and no prog 2f out: one pce after* **9/4**[1]

0 **7** *shd* **Dunmaglass (USA)**[16] 3451 2-9-0 .................... SSanders 8 67
(PFICole) *sn chsd ldrs: rdn over 2f out: one pce and no imp* **25/1**

03 **8** *nk* **Dreemon**[16] 3438 2-9-0 .................... GBaker 3 66
(BRMillman) *uns rdr bef s: mostly chsd wnr to over 2f out: wknd over 1f out* **9/1**

9 shd **Karlu (GER)** 2-9-0 ........ RHughes 5 69+
(JLDunlop) *dwlt: rdn in last pair 4f out: prog over 2f out: styng on whn nt clr run ins fnl f: nvr nrr* **14/1**

10 ¾ **Asaateel (IRE)** 2-9-0 ........ RHills 13 64
(JLDunlop) *hld up towards rr: prog 3f out: chsd ldrs 2f out: rdn and m green sn after: fdd* **4/1[3]**

11 1 ¾ **Lady Luisa (IRE)** 2-8-9 ........ SWhitworth 12 54
(JSMoore) *s.i.s: a in rr: rdn and no prog 3f out* **66/1**

12 6 **Blue Spectrum (IRE)** 2-9-0 ........ JDSmith 16 44
(JSMoore) *dwlt: a in rr: rdn and struggling 1/2-way: wknd 2f out* **50/1**

00 13 ¾ **Liquid Lover (IRE)**[16] 3438 2-8-7 ........ PGallagher(7) 2 43
(RHannon) *dwlt: racd on outer: chsd ldrs: rdn 4f out: wknd 3f out* **50/1**

00 14 shd **Snow Tempest (USA)**[7] 3749 2-9-0 ........ IMongan 10 42
(TGMills) *dwlt: a in rr: struggling 1/2-way: wknd 2f out* **25/1**

15 30 **Pralin Star (IRE)** 2-8-9 ........ NChalmers(5) 7 —
(MrsHSweeting) *dwlt: chsd ldrs 2f: sn wknd u.p: t.o 3f out* **66/1**

1m 25.71s (1.50) **Going Correction** +0.025s/f (Good) **15** Ran SP% **130.7**
Speed ratings: **92,90,89,89,87 87,87,87,87,86 84,77,76,76,42**CSF £46.65 TOTE £4.00: £1.90, £4.10, £4.00; EX 57.80.

**Owner** Philip Newton **Bred** P Newton **Trained** Wantage, Oxon

**FOCUS**
A fair maiden, with the winner looking particularly useful. Others behind, though not looking anything special at this stage, should win their maidens or in nursery company when they are qualified.

**NOTEBOOK**
**Minnesota(USA)** was well at home over the longer trip, not only being able to lay up better, but to lead from start to finish. He looks a smart sort in the making
**Ragged Glory(IRE)** looks to need this trip already, and should be capable of finding a seven-furlong event with so few juveniles seeing out the trip at this stage of the season.
**Dahliyev(IRE)** looked happier over the extra furlong, though clearly no match for the winner.
**Creative Character(USA)** is from a family with winners at a variety of trips. Unraced at shorter trips, he got the seven furlongs well, suggesting that middle distances will be his game in the long run.
**Blaise Hollow(USA)** showed more ability than on his debut and ought to be capable of winning a seven-furlong nursery in due course *Official explanation: jockey said colt suffered interference in running*
**Zalaal(USA)**, a son of the American dirt champion AP Indy, failed to live up to market expectations. There will be some improvement to come, but there needs to be plenty for him to take high rank.
**Dunmaglass(USA)**, though not setting the world on fire, is showing enough to give connections hope in nurseries after one more run.
**Dreemon** should be placed to effect around the minor tracks, and is now qualified for nurseries.
**Karlu(GER)**, a 32,000 guineas purchase from a good winning family, was done for early speed but looks a potential improver as he matures. *Official explanation: jockey said colt was slowly away and suffered interference in running*
**Asaateel(IRE)** is a middle-distance horse in the making, and should improve with racing.

## 3932 ANEELA ROSE BOUTIQUE, THE LANES, BRIGHTON CLAIMING STKS — 1m (P)
7:25 (7:26) (F) 3-5-Y-0 — £3,003 (£858; £429) Stalls High

Form — RPR

5146 1 **Tre Colline**[7] 3745 5-9-13 75 ........ LDettori 6 82
(NTinkler) *settled in rr: prog over 3f out: chsd ldr over 1f out: urged along to ld last 10yds: fnd jst enough to hold on* **7/4[1]**

160- 2 nk **Zariano**[309] 4866 4-9-8 90 ........ RHavlin 3 76
(SLKeightley) *led: clr 1/2-way: stl gng wl enough 2f out: rdn and hdd last 100yds: kpt on but hld nr fin* **12/1**

22-0 3 3 ½ **Queenstown (IRE)**[8] 3689 3-9-0 84 ........ (b) JFMcDonald(3) 10 71
(BJMeehan) *chsd ldr: rdn over 2f out: lost 2nd over 1f out: fdd* **5/2[2]**

0-50 4 1 ¼ **Dixie Dancing**[30] 3023 5-9-0 56 ........ SSanders 1 57
(CACyzer) *trckd ldrs: rdn over 2f out: one pce fr over 1f out* **12/1**

-000 5 2 ½ **Fulvio (USA)**[4] 3826 4-9-3 58 ........ (v) PDoe 7 55
(JamiePoulton) *hld up: prog to chse ldng pair briefly over 2f out: u.p and wknd over 1f out* **16/1**

4010 6 1 **Whiplash (IRE)**[25] 3180 3-8-7 55 ........ CCatlin 12 50
(KOCunningham-Brown) *settled in last trio: lost tch and wl bhd 1/2-way: rdn over 3f out: styd on fnl 2f: no ch* **14/1**

6006 7 3 ½ **Wizard Looking**[22] 3271 3-8-6 60 ........ (bt[1]) DaneO'Neill 4 41
(RHannon) *wl in tch: rdn to chse ldng pair over 3f out to over 2f out: wknd* **9/2[3]**

0640 8 1 **Anisette**[14] 3529 3-7-8 45 ........ MHalford(7) 2 34
(JulianPoulton) *dwlt: sn rcvrd to chse ldng pair: wknd over 3f out* **16/1**

0-00 9 1 **Tshukudu**[21] 3305 3-8-2 38 ........ JQuinn 9 33
(MBlanshard) *t.k.h: hld up: wl bhd in last trio 1/2-way: struggling after* **66/1**

5560 10 2 ½ **Zinging**[25] 3174 5-9-0 45 ........ TPQueally 11 31
(JJBridger) *racd in midfield: rdn 1/2-way: struggling after: wknd over 2f out* **14/1**

5-00 11 1 ¼ **Singularity**[15] 1723 4-8-12 37 ........ (p) AMcCarthy 8 26
(KFClutterbuck) *s.s: sn in tch in rr: wknd 3f out* **66/1**

06 12 nk **Mantel Mini**[9] 3661 5-8-12 ........ (p) GBaker 5 25
(BAPearce) *s.i.s: hld up in last trio: wl bhd 1/2-way: rdn and no prog 2f out* **100/1**

1m 40.71s (1.16) **Going Correction** +0.175s/f (Slow)
**WFA** 3 from 4yo+ 8lb **12** Ran SP% **127.6**
Speed ratings: **101,100,97,95,93 92,88,87,86,84 83,82**CSF £27.94 TOTE £2.80: £1.80, £3.60, £1.80; EX 26.40.

**Owner** Peter Alderson Mike Gosse Adrian Mornin **Bred** Hesmonds Stud Ltd **Trained** Langton, N Yorks

**FOCUS**
A modest claimer, though the winner is a fair sort and the runner-up needs to run at this level because he is on too high a mark in handicaps at present.

**NOTEBOOK**
**Tre Colline** took advantage of the drop to claiming company, though he only just made it.
**Zariano** is not well handicapped at present and his best chance of success must be in claimers. Given a good ride from the front, he nearly pulled it off.
**Queenstown(IRE)** is effective on the All-Weather as well as turf, and this would appear to be his kind of race.
**Dixie Dancing** performed respectably considering her stable is out of form. She has run some of her best races on this track.
**Fulvio(USA)** has never won beyond seven furlongs, and that was as far as wanted to go here.
**Whiplash(IRE)** ran an odd race for a horse that had won over seven furlongs two outings earlier. Nonetheless, claimers are his scene.
**Mantel Mini** *Official explanation: jockey said mare hung right throughout*

## 3933 RECTANGLE GROUP FILLIES' H'CAP — 1m 2f (P)
7:55 (8:05) (D) (0-85,85) 3-Y-0+ — £5,443 (£1,675; £837; £418) Stalls Low

Form — RPR

4264 1 **Lara Falana**[22] 3264 6-8-4 61 ........ JQuinn 6 67
(MissBSanders) *racd in 4th tl rdn to chse ldng pair over 2f out: drvn to ld ins fnl f: styd on wl* **9/4[2]**

-551 2 1 ¼ **Cherubim (JPN)**[18] 3392 3-8-8 75 ........ TPQueally 1 79
(DRLoder) *led: set stdy pce to 3f out: hrd rdn 2f out: hung rt and hdd ins fnl f: nt qckn* **6/1**

0506 3 2 **Wanna Shout**[10] 3638 6-7-12 55 ........ JoannaBadger 5 55
(RDickin) *dwlt: sn trckd ldr: rdn to chal and upsides fr over 2f out to 1f out: edgd rt and nt qckn* **14/1**

0420 4 2 ½ **Dispol Evita**[10] 3638 5-7-12 55 oh3 ........ AMcCarthy 4 50
(JamiePoulton) *hld up in last: outpcd over 2f out: kpt on over 1f out: no ch* **14/1**

-111 5 ½ **Heneseys Leg**[24] 3200 4-8-13 73 ........ LisaJones(3) 3 68
(JohnBerry) *sweating profusely: hld up in 5th: outpcd over 2f out: effrt wl over 1f out: no ch: wknd ins fnl f* **10/3[3]**

0-20 6 2 **Czarina Waltz**[21] 3327 5-10-0 85 ........ RMullen 2 76
(CFWall) *trckd ldng pair to over 2f out: sn wknd* **7/4[1]**

2m 8.12s (0.27) **Going Correction** +0.175s/f (Slow)
**WFA** 3 from 4yo+ 10lb **6** Ran SP% **117.8**
Speed ratings: **105,104,102,100,100 98**CSF £16.93 TOTE £3.60: £1.80, £3.30; EX 26.50.

**Owner** Exors of the late R Lamb **Bred** Mrs I A Balding **Trained** Epsom, Surrey

**FOCUS**
An ordinary race devalued by the below-par efforts of Heneseys Leg and Czarina Waltz. The form is modest.

**NOTEBOOK**
**Lara Falana** finally got off the mark on sand after nine previous efforts. She had been running with credit for some time, so this win was well deserved.
**Cherubim(JPN)** had her fair share of weight on this handicap debut but her mark was just about right. Dictating things, she was eventually beaten by a more experienced performer but undoubtedly proved her effectiveness on the surface.
**Wanna Shout** had a stiff task, and ran at least as well as could be expected over a trip which is at her upper limit.
**Dispol Evita**, 3lb out of the weights, will find easier opportunities over this track, where she is a standing dish.
**Heneseys Leg** boiled over before the start and did not appear to be at her best. *Official explanation: jockey said filly was upset by the delayed start*
**Czarina Waltz** disappointed for the second race in succession. She had a big weight, but at her best she would have gone close to carrying it. *Official explanation: trainer was unable to offer any explanation for poor form shown*

## 3934 NUTFIELD PRIORY, SPONSORS OF THE BEST HAT, (S) STKS — 1m 2f (P)
8:25 (8:35) (G) 3-Y-0+ — £2,632 (£752; £376) Stalls Low

Form — RPR

3611 1 **Burgundy**[10] 3637 7-9-11 58 ........ (b) IMongan 2 70+
(PMitchell) *dwlt and str reminders sn after s: prog to trck ldrs 1/2-way: drvn to ld over 2f out: sn wl clr* **5/6[1]**

0003 2 7 **Private Seal**[25] 3173 9-8-12 45 ........ (t) MHalford(7) 1 49
(JulianPoulton) *settled wl in rr: outpcd 4f out: rdn 3f out: kpt on fr over 2f out to take 2nd last stride* **16/1**

4350 3 shd **Stylish Sunrise (IRE)**[20] 3342 3-8-9 56 ........ (t) SSanders 9 49
(IAWood) *racd wd in midfield: effrt but outpcd 3f out: kpt on to chse wnr ins fnl f: no imp: lost 2nd last stride* **12/1**

0040 4 nk **Enna (POL)**[4] 3828 5-9-0 45 ........ SDrowne 6 43
(MrsStefLiddiard) *settled in rr: outpcd 4f out: effrt over 2f out: kpt on one pce u.p* **12/1**

0000 5 1 ¾ **Figura**[16] 3441 6-9-0 54 ........ NDay 4 40
(RIngram) *settled towards rr: prog over 4f out: outpcd over 3f out: hrd rdn and one pce fnl 2f* **4/1[2]**

000/ 6 1 ½ **Zeloso**[464] 1643 6-9-5 ........ (v) ADaly 8 42
(MFHarris) *trckd ldrs: outpcd over 3f out: lost pl over 2f out: no ch whn nt clr run 1f out* **14/1**

0/0- 7 ½ **Ragasah**[530] 458 6-8-11 ........ LisaJones(3) 14 36
(EROertel) *mostly pressed ldr: led over 4f out to over 2f out: no ch w wnr after: wknd fnl f* **66/1**

-060 8 9 **Rolex Free (ARG)**[12] 3591 6-9-5 60 ........ (bt) RSmith 13 24
(DFlood) *pushed up to join ldrs 7f out: wknd 3f out* **20/1**

0555 9 5 **Sir Frank Gibson**[5] 3809 3-8-9 40 ........ (p) DSweeney 3 15
(MrsJaneGalpin) *chsd ldrs: pushed along 6f out: sn struggling: wl bhd fnl 2f* **28/1**

0020 10 10 **Cal Mac**[9] 3662 5-9-5 57 ........ MHenry 5 —
(RMHCowell) *mde most to over 4f out: sn wknd: wl bhd fnl 2f* **9/1[3]**

0000 11 11 **In Tune**[8] 3697 4-9-5 42 ........ (t) GBaker 10 —
(SCBurrough) *s.s: a wl in rr: t.o fnl 3f* **50/1**

00- 12 12 **Russian Icon**[260] 5847 3-8-4 ........ CCatlin 12 —
(LADace) *a bhd: t.o 1/2-way* **100/1**

000/ 13 3 ½ **Father Seamus**[14] 1126 6-8-13 20 ow1 ........ (p) RLucey-Butler(7) 7 —
(PButler) *chsd ldrs for 3f: sn u.p and lost pl: t.o fnl 4f* **66/1**

2m 8.59s (0.74) **Going Correction** +0.175s/f (Slow)
**WFA** 3 from 4yo+ 10lb **13** Ran SP% **126.6**
Speed ratings: **104,98,98,98,96 95,95,87,83,75 67,57,54**CSF £18.54 TOTE £1.90: £1.40, £5.20, £2.00; EX 21.60.The winner was bought in for 10,000gns.

**Owner** Nigel Shields **Bred** Cheveley Park Stud Ltd **Trained** Epsom, Surrey

**FOCUS**
A weak seller with the exception of the winner, who bolted up and completed a hat-trick.

**NOTEBOOK**
**Burgundy** has made the most of the drop to claiming and selling level. He can be a bit moody, but he could have picked this lot up and carried them.
**Private Seal** is capable of winning a seller, but the presence of an in-form Burgundy in the line-up gave him no chance.
**Stylish Sunrise(IRE)** had been tailed off on his only previous run on Polytrack, so this was an improved effort. Sellers are the right place for him, and he is not without hope.
**Enna(POL)** is very moderate, but she is at home in sellers.
**Figura** was beaten for the 22nd time in succession, but she is on a fair mark if returning to her best.
**Zeloso** last ran over hurdles 15 months earlier. This was a satisfactory return to action, but he looks a plater nowadays.
**In Tune** *Official explanation: trainer said gelding had a breathing problem*

## 3935 DP CARUANA WONGA H'CAP 6f

8:55 (9:00) (F) (0-55,58) 3-Y-O+ £3,136 (£896; £448) Stalls High

Form RPR

3363 **1** **Adantino**37 2823 5-9-9 **54**....(b) GBaker 12 64
(BRMillman) *wl off the pce in rr: nt clr run over 2f out: prog u.p wl over 1f out: styd on strly to ld last strides* **6/1**3

0-06 **2** *nk* **Stagnite**17 3428 4-9-4 **54**....(p) NChalmers(5) 2 63
(MrsHSweeting) *disp ld clr of rest: hrd rdn 2f out: hdd last strides* **25/1**

0002 **3** *nk* **Jagged (IRE)**22 3277 4-9-10 **55**....(b1) TPQueally 15 63
(JRJenkins) *disp ld and sn clr of rest: hrd rdn 2f out: hdd nr fin* **11/2**2

0400 **4** *3/4* **Drury Lane (IRE)**28 3098 4-9-8 **53**....(b) EAhern 14 59+
(DWChapman) *dwlt: settled in last and wl off the pce: swtchd to outer 1/2-way: plenty to do 2f out: styd on strly fnl f: nrst fin* **7/1**

0-62 **5** *nk* **Choristar**10 3636 3-9-5 **55**.... RMullen 6 60
(WRMuir) *towards rr and wl off the pce: rdn whn nt clr run 2f out: gd prog fnl f: nrst fin* **12/1**

0001 **6** *1 1/4* **Sabana (IRE)**7 3742 6-9-0 **48**....(p) LisaJones(3) 11 49
(JMBradley) *off the pce in midfield: rdn and no prog over 2f out: kpt on fnl f* **8/1**

1021 **7** *3/4* **Enjoy The Buzz**9 3668 5-9-6 **51**.... CCatlin 10 50
(JMBradley) *chsd clr ldrs: v hrd rdn 2f out: no imp: fdd ins fnl f* **4/1**1

0-10 **8** *shd* **Strike Lucky**19 3381 4-9-6 **51**....(p) DSweeney 4 50
(PJMakin) *racd on outer: chsd clr ldng pair: rdn over 2f out: no imp: wknd fnl f* **20/1**

-002 **9** *nk* **Minimum Bid**10 3628 3-9-5 **55**.... JQuinn 8 53
(MissBSanders) *hld up in rr and wl off the pce: nt clr run 2f out: rdn and kpt on fr over 1f out: no ch* **7/1**

0004 **10** *1 1/4* **Man Crazy (IRE)**7 3747 3-9-5 **55**....(b) SSanders 16 49
(RMBeckett) *chsd clr ldrs: rdn and no imp over 2f out: wknd over 1f out* **7/1**

4000 **11** *1 1/4* **Mannora**26 3151 4-9-5 **50**.... SDrowne 7 40
(PHowling) *racd on outer: wl off the pce in rr: brief effrt over 2f out: sn btn* **33/1**

5400 **12** *1/2* **Yorkies Boy**27 3126 9-9-1 **51**.... MSavage(5) 1 40
(NEBerry) *racd in midfield and off the pce: rdn wl over 2f out: sn struggling* **14/1**

0004 **13** *1/2* **Toppling**26 3151 6-9-3 **55**.... CJDavies(7) 5 42
(JMBradley) *chsd clr ldrs tl wknd wl over 1f out* **12/1**

4060 **14** *3* **Akiramenai (USA)**14 3512 4-9-8 **53**.... SWhitworth 9 31
(MrsLStubbs) *off the pce in midfield: rdn 1/2-way: wknd wl over 1f out* **66/1**

1m 11.62s (-0.03) **Going Correction** +0.025s/f (Good)
**WFA** 3 from 4yo+ 5lb **14** Ran SP% **133.4**
Speed ratings: **101,100,100,99,98 97,96,96,95,93 92,91,90,86**CSF £165.08 CT £929.51 TOTE £7.40: £2.60, £9.00, £2.60; EX 219.60 Place 6 £70.08, Place 5 £48.32.
**Owner** Tarka Two Racing **Bred** S D Bevan **Trained** Kentisbeare, Devon

**FOCUS**
A low-grade sprint but a number of the field had been in reasonable form. The second and third dominated the race most of the way and, though both still maidens, should not be dismissed as hopeless causes.

**NOTEBOOK**
**Adantino** was patiently ridden, as if his jockey was intent on not getting there too soon. Still going easily but with plenty to do two furlongs from home, he was produced with a perfectly-timed run.
**Stagnite** dominated the race with Jagged, only for both of them to be done by the late run of the winner. He is still a maiden but runs like this give him every chance of getting off the mark at long last.
**Jagged(IRE)** is, like the runner-up, still a maiden, but they dominated the race for all but the last 50 yards and there is still hope of finding an opening for him.
**Drury Lane(IRE)** is very well handicapped on his best form and looks to be on the way back. Fast ground races over this trip are his speciality.
**Choristar**, dropped in distance, got going just too late. He should find a race soon and a return to an extra furlong would suit him, though success over this trip cannot be ruled out.
**Sabana(IRE)** pops up in the winner's enclosure from time to time, but was never quite going the pace this time.
**Enjoy The Buzz** has been in good form on turf but he has had a busy time of late.
**Strike Lucky** had only run on sand this season, and this was a respectable if unspectacular first run on turf in 2004.
**Akiramenai(USA)** *Official explanation: trainer said filly was in season*
T/Plt: £62.50 to a £1 stake. Pool: £36,104.00. 421.30 winning tickets. T/Qpdt: £20.20 to a £1 stake. Pool: £2,502.60. 91.50 winning tickets. JN

# 3904 NEWBURY (L-H)

Saturday, July 17

**OFFICIAL GOING: Good to firm (good in places in back straight)**

## 3936 CANTORODDS.COM STEVENTON STKS (LISTED RACE) 1m 2f 6y

1:50 (1:52) (A) 3-Y-O+ £17,400 (£6,600; £3,300; £1,500) Stalls High

Form RPR

4-01 **1** **Muqbil (USA)**42 2672 4-9-3 113.... RHills 4 120
(JLDunlop) *lw: hld up in rr: stdy hdwy on outside over 3f out: trckd ldr 2f out: rdn to ld jst ins fnl f: drvn out* **11/4**2

2220 **2** *3/4* **Vespone (IRE)**42 2678 4-9-3 118....(vt) LDettori 3 119
(SaeedBinSuroor) *lw: led: 5l clr 6f out: shkn up 2f out: rdn over 1f out: hdd jst ins last: rdr dropped whip and no ex fnl 100yds* **6/1**3

1-36 **3** *6* **Musanid (USA)**28 3072 4-9-3 107.... KFallon 1 108
(SirMichaelStoute) *bhd: pushed along over 4f out: styd on fr 2f out: kpt on u.p fnl f but nt trble ldrs* **11/1**

2-64 **4** *1 1/2* **Magistretti (USA)**10 3642 4-9-3 121.... DHolland 2 105
(NACallaghan) *lw: chsd ldrs: rdn to chse ldr ins fnl 3f but sn no imp: wknd fr 2f out* **15/8**1

0-60 **5** *3* **Kaieteur (USA)**31 2968 5-9-3 114....(b1) JFortune 6 99
(BJMeehan) *prom: rdn to press for 2nd ins fnl 3f but no imp on ldr: wknd fr 2f out* **10/1**

4-02 **6** *2* **Elshadi (IRE)**29 3032 3-8-7 104....(b) MartinDwyer 5 95
(MPTregoning) *chsd ldr tl rdn ins fnl 3f: sn wknd* **11/1**

1- **7** *dist* **Tree Chopper (USA)**279 5499 3-8-2.... RLMoore 7 —
(MPTregoning) *s.i.s: rdn over 5f out: sn lost tch: t.o* **12/1**

2m 4.12s (-4.59) **Going Correction** -0.075s/f (Good)
**WFA** 3 from 4yo+ 10lb **7** Ran SP% **109.2**
Speed ratings: **115,114,109,108,106 104,**—CSF £17.59 TOTE £4.30: £2.70, £2.70; EX 24.40.
**Owner** Hamdan Al Maktoum **Bred** Shadwell Farm Llc **Trained** Arundel, W Sussex

**FOCUS**
A decent Listed contest that featured several Group One performers. The first two came clear in a good time.

**NOTEBOOK**
**Muqbil(USA)**, whose profile suggests he is at his best on a flat track and a sound surface, got those conditions and did everything right. This was a strong contest for the grade and he looks capable of winning another Group race; the Winter Hill Stakes or the Strensall Stakes at the end of next month may provide suitable conditions.
**Vespone(IRE)**, given a canny waiting-in-front ride by Dettori, was given a breather early in the straight and when picking up again had all bar the winner in trouble. He responded well when headed and, although his rider losing his whip did not affect the result, he would have finished closer. He has not won since taking the Grand Prix de Paris last year but, on this evidence, another Group-race win is not far away.
**Musanid(USA)**, who ran no sort of race in the Hardwicke on fast ground, settled better on this drop in trip and grade. Although he never got into contention, he was keeping on steadily and can be placed to win a Pattern race, possibly abroad.
**Magistretti(USA)**, a proven Group performer, looked to have been found a good opportunity prior to another tilt at the Juddmonte International. However, he was disappointing, finding little when asked after having every chance, and now has something to prove.
**Kaieteur(USA)** appeared to run too free in the first-time blinkers, and did not get home. Possibly cheekpieces may work better for him, and he has options such as another crack at the Arlington Million, or the Dallmyr Preis, which he won in 2002, as alternatives to the Juddmonte International.
**Elshadi(IRE)**, found this tougher than the substandard King Edward VII in which he finished runner-up last time.

## 3937 LADBROKES.COM H'CAP 1m (S)

2:25 (2:26) (B) (0-105,103) 3-Y-O+ £23,200 (£8,800; £4,400; £2,000) Stalls Centre

Form RPR

0001 **1** **Everest (IRE)**11 3597 7-8-6 **80**.... KFallon 15 93
(BEllison) *hld up in rr: pushed along and hdwy 3f out: str run to ld appr fnl f: drvn out ins last: jst hld on* **11/2**2

0130 **2** *shd* **Vortex**31 2969 5-9-10 **98**....(t) LDettori 8 111+
(MissGayKelleway) *b.hind: hld up in rr: stdy hdwy whn n.m.r ins fnl 2f: rapid hdwy over 1f out: fin fast: nt quite get up* **14/1**

030- **3** *1 1/2* **Battle Chant (USA)**254 5936 4-10-0 **102**.... RLMoore 14 111
(MrsAJPerrett) *lw: hld up in rr: hdwy 3f out: drvn to chal over 1f out: nt qckn ins last* **14/1**

0002 **4** *1* **Audience**11 3597 4-9-5 **93**....(p) JQuinn 4 100
(JAkehurst) *lw: hld up in rr: hdwy over 2f out: styd on to chse ldrs ins fnl f: kpt on same pce* **12/1**

0260 **5** *1* **Impeller (IRE)**31 2969 5-8-13 **87**.... SDrowne 18 92
(WRMuir) *hld up in rr: hdwy whn n.m.r 2f out: styd on fr over 1f out but no imp on ldrs ins last* **20/1**

4006 **6** *1* **Lago D'Orta (IRE)**31 2969 4-9-12 **100**.... JFortune 5 102
(CGCox) *b.front: s.i.s: bhd: hdwy whn n.m.r over 1f out: kpt on wl fnl f but nt pce to rch ldrs* **10/1**3

6222 **7** *1* **James Caird (IRE)**17 3415 4-8-13 **87**.... RHills 7 87
(MHTompkins) *lw: chsd ldrs: rdn to chal ins fnl 2f: wknd ins fnl f* **10/1**3

0-42 **8** *1 1/2* **Able Baker Charlie (IRE)**31 2969 5-9-5 **93**.... OUrbina 16 90
(JRFanshawe) *lw: hld up in rr: stdy hdwy over 3f out to trck ldrs 2f out: pushed along over 1f out: wknd ins last* **7/2**1

1004 **9** *3/4* **Highland Reel**24 3212 7-8-9 **86**.... LPKeniry(3) 13 81
(DRCElsworth) *mid-div: pushed along halway: kpt on fr over 1f out: nt pce to rch ldrs* **33/1**

0-03 **10** *1 1/4* **Zucchero**7 3745 8-8-1 **75**....(p) ADaly 12 67
(DWPArbuthnot) *trckd ldrs: rdn to take slt ld ins fnl 2f: hdd appr fnl f and sn wknd* **20/1**

0042 **11** *1/2* **Blue Trojan (IRE)**8 3698 4-8-12 **86**.... JFEgan 17 77
(SKirk) *bhd: hdwy 4f out: trckd ldrs 3f out: sn rdn: wknd over 1f out* **10/1**3

0/ **12** *1* **Rebel Leader**530 7-9-2 **90**.... MartinDwyer 9 79
(WRMuir) *chsd ldrs: styng on whn nt clr run 2f out: sn wknd* **50/1**

5604 **13** *1 1/2* **Gig Harbor**10 3631 5-8-6 **80**.... SWhitworth 11 65
(MissECLavelle) *led tl hdd ins fnl 2f: sn wknd* **40/1**

3030 **14** *1 3/4* **King's County (IRE)**31 2969 6-9-7 **95**.... DHolland 6 76
(LMCumani) *chsd ldrs: rdn over 3f out: wknd qckly ins fnl 2f* **12/1**

-300 **15** *3* **Definite Guest (IRE)**15 3482 6-8-3 **80**.... THamilton(3) 10 54
(RAFahey) *chsd ldrs: rdn 1/2-way: wknd over 2f out* **20/1**

2135 **16** *1* **Gold History (USA)**29 3032 3-9-7 **103**.... KDalgleish 1 75
(MJohnston) *chsd ldrs: chall 3f out: wknd qckly 2f out* **25/1**

0450 **17** *5* **Camp Commander (IRE)**14 3539 5-9-7 **95**....(t) TEDurcan 3 55
(CEBrittain) *s.i.s: bhd: effrt 3f out: sn bhd* **14/1**

0002 **18** *9* **Serieux**91 1456 5-9-2 **90**.... RHughes 2 30
(MrsAJPerrett) *chsd ldrs: rdn 3f out: n.m.r and wknd appr fnl 2f* **16/1**

1m 38.1s (-2.73) **Going Correction** -0.075s/f (Good)
**WFA** 3 from 4yo+ 8lb **18** Ran SP% **131.6**
Speed ratings: **110,109,108,107,106 105,104,102,102,100 100,99,97,96,93 92,87,78**CSF £78.73 CT £1094.65 TOTE £7.20: £2.10, £2.90, £3.60, £4.50; EX 98.70 TRIFECTA Not won..
**Owner** I S Sandhu And Partners **Bred** Sir Eric Parker **Trained** Norton, N Yorks

**FOCUS**
A decent, competitive handicap run at a good pace and dominated by those that were held up in the early stages. Solid form.

**NOTEBOOK**
**Everest(IRE)**, who narrowly won a decent handicap at the Newmarket July meeting, repeated the feat in this more valuable contest. Held up in the rear he burst through when the opening presented itself and gained enough of an advantage to just resist then strong late thrust of the runner-up. The Handicapper cannot put him up that much for this, and one of the mile handicaps at either York or Doncaster may offer his best chance of a hat-trick.
**Vortex** ◆ held up like the winner, followed that rival through but unfortunately could not quite reduce the leeway. It was a very close thing and he fully deserves to gain compensation, possibly in the Tote International at Ascot, providing he gets a more favourable draw than in the Victoria Cup there.
**Battle Chant(USA)**was the subject of a gamble, despite carrying top weight and this being his seasonal reappearance. He looked likely to score when making his move, but ultimately the first too quickened past him. He is verging on Pattern class, and has moved to a stable that has done well with similar types in the past.
**Audience**, 1lb better off with the winner for a narrow defeat at Newmarket, ran his race again without quite repeating that effort. He has the William Hill Mile at Goodwood as his likely target.
**Impeller(IRE)** is a pretty consistent performer at this level but does not win very often. He ran his race and may be better suited by Goodwood's William Hill Mile, on a track where he scored his last victory, although his style of racing means he does tend to find trouble in running and will need things to fall just right there.
**Lago D'Orta(IRE)** had finished ahead of the fourth and fifth in the Royal Hunt Cup, but was given a fair amount to do and never looked like reaching the front rank. He may need a confidence booster in a conditions race after struggling in Pattern company earlier in the season.
**James Caird(IRE)**, who has put up a series of creditable efforts at around nine and ten furlongs without scoring, again ran his race but was done for pace in the closing stages. He is now 20lb above his last winning mark and will not find it easy to regain the winning thread.

**Able Baker Charlie(IRE)** was a well-backed favourite, having finished ahead of a number of these in the Royal Hunt Cup. He appeared to have every chance but could not pick up. He may take on several of these gain in the William Hill Mile.
**Blue Trojan(IRE)**, who had been touched off at Chepstow since being narrowly beaten by Everest at Newmarket, had a chance at one stage but eight races in as many weeks may have taken their toll.
**King's County(IRE)** *Official explanation: jockey said gelding had carried its head high and hung left-handed*
**Serieux** *Official explanation: jockey said horse had got tired*

## 3938 WEATHERBYS SUPER SPRINT 5f 34y
**3:00** (3:02) (B) 2-Y-O **£78,300** (£29,700; £14,850; £6,750) **Stalls** Centre

| Form | | | | RPR |
|---|---|---|---|---|
| 110 | **1** | | **Siena Gold**[31] [2970] 2-8-1 JFMcDonald 9<br>(BJMeehan) *mde virtually all: def advantage 1/2-way: hrd drvn and edgd lft ins last: all out* **11/2**[3] | 93 |
| 16 | **2** | ¾ | **Don't Tell Mum (IRE)**[31] [2970] 2-8-2 RLMoore 5<br>(RHannon) *w wnr to 1/2-way: styd chalng: kpt on u.p and carried lft ins last: no ex cl home* **9/2**[1] | 91 |
| 013 | **3** | ¾ | **Bond City (IRE)**[15] [3468] 2-8-8 FLynch 1<br>(BSmart) *chsd ldrs: rdn and styd on wl: fr over 1f out: no imp on ldrs last half f* **33/1** | 95 |
| 5051 | **4** | 1 | **Alpaga Le Jomage (IRE)**[12] [3577] 2-8-5 JFEgan 3<br>(BJMeehan) *lw: chsd ldrs: rdn over 2f out: kpt on same pce ins fnl f* **33/1** | 88 |
| 6144 | **5** | hd | **Canton (IRE)**[7] [3727] 2-8-13 DaneO'Neill 19<br>(RHannon) *chsd ldrs: rdn over 2f out: kpt on same pce u.p ins fnl f* **25/1** | 96 |
| 3522 | **6** | 1 ¼ | **Bibury Flyer**[2] [3868] 2-8-10 SHitchcott 4<br>(MRChannon) *mid-div: hrd drvn 1/2-way: fin wl fnl f: gng on cl home* **33/1** | 88 |
| 3462 | **7** | hd | **Withering Lady (IRE)**[24] [3208] 2-8-0 DKinsella 18<br>(MrsPNDutfield) *lw: mid-div: hdwy 2f out: styd on fnl f but nvr gng pce to rch ldrs* **66/1** | 77 |
| 122 | **8** | hd | **Tournedos (IRE)**[32] [2959] 2-8-10 TEDurcan 2<br>(MRChannon) *chsd ldrs: rdn 1/2-way: styd on same pce fnl f* **5/1**[2] | 87 |
| 422 | **9** | nk | **Chiselled (IRE)**[60] [2208] 2-8-9 DarrenWilliams 16<br>(KRBurke) *swtg: pressed ldrs: chal over 1f out: wknd fnl f* **33/1** | 85 |
| 12 | **10** | ½ | **Imperial Sound**[15] [3468] 2-9-2 DHolland 14<br>(TDBarron) *lw: chsd ldrs: rdn over 2f out: wkng and no ch whn n.m.r wl ins last* **14/1** | 90 |
| 2120 | **11** | ¾ | **Evanesce**[23] [3242] 2-7-13 CCatlin 11<br>(MRChannon) *chsd ldrs: hrd rdn over 2f out: wknd fnl f* **33/1** | 70 |
| 410 | **12** | nk | **Alta Petens**[29] [3031] 2-7-12 AMcCarthy 20<br>(MLWBell) *pressed ldrs: rdn 1/2-way: wknd fnl f* **12/1** | 68 |
| 1053 | **13** | ¾ | **Celtic Spa (IRE)**[20] [3346] 2-7-13 JQuinn 8<br>(MrsPNDutfield) *bhd: sme hdwy fnl f but n.d* **25/1** | 67 |
| 4 | **14** | 1 ¼ | **The Quiet Woman (IRE)**[22] [3286] 2-8-1 MartinDwyer 21<br>(FrancisEnnis, Ire) *compact: sn outpcd: rdn 1/2-way: styd on ins fnl 2f but nvr gng pce of ldrs* **14/1** | 64 |
| 222 | **15** | 1 ¾ | **Tagula Sunrise (IRE)**[19] [3370] 2-8-10 THamilton 22<br>(RAFahey) *chsd ldrs tl wknd fnl f* **33/1** | 67 |
| 2341 | **16** | hd | **Lateral Thinker (IRE)**[10] [3634] 2-7-12 RThomas 7<br>(JAOsborne) *pressed ldrs early: sn rdn and outpcd* **50/1** | 54 |
| 23 | **17** | nk | **Exit Smiling**[64] [2074] 2-8-11 KDalgleish 10<br>(MJohnston) *s.i.s: n.m.r whn rdn 2f out: nvr nr ldrs* **40/1** | 66 |
| 56 | **18** | 1 ½ | **Peopleton Brook**[17] [3418] 2-8-5 LPKeniry 17<br>(DWPArbuthnot) *outpcd tl sme hdwy fr over 1f out* **100/1** | 55 |
| 10 | **19** | nk | **Happy Event**[23] [3242] 2-8-7 SDrowne 6<br>(BRMillman) *s.i.s: outpcd* **50/1** | 56 |
| 2325 | **20** | ½ | **Grand Option**[52] [2396] 2-8-5 (b[1]) ADaly 13<br>(BWDuke) *spd to 1/2-way* **100/1** | 52 |
| 461 | **21** | shd | **Annatalia**[12] [3570] 2-8-10 LDettori 23<br>(BJMeehan) *chsd ldrs over 3f* **13/2** | 57 |
| 3323 | **22** | 1 | **Edge Fund**[23] [3228] 2-9-0 (p) JFortune 24<br>(BRMillman) *sn drvn along: outpcd most of way* **50/1** | 58 |
| 04 | **23** | 1 | **Grand Place**[17] [3413] 2-8-7 KFallon 15<br>(RHannon) *s.i.s: effrt 1/2-way: sn wknd* **20/1** | 47 |
| 316 | **24** | 3 ½ | **Earl Of Links (IRE)**[10] [3634] 2-8-10 RHughes 12<br>(RHannon) *chsd ldrs tl wknd 2f out* **25/1** | 38 |

61.89 secs (-0.76) **Going Correction** -0.075s/f (Good) **24** Ran SP% **130.3**
Speed ratings: **103,101,100,99,98 96,96,96,95,94 93,93,91,89,87 86,86,83,83,82 82,80,79,73**CSF £25.70 TOTE £6.90: £2.70, £2.80, £18.10; EX 34.60 Trifecta £1368.30 Pool of £1,927.20 - 0.30 winning tickets..
**Owner** N Attenborough & Mrs L Mann **Bred** Limestone Stud **Trained** Upper Lambourn, Berks

**FOCUS**
Not quite as strong as usual, but pretty competitive nevertheless and a decent time. Two fillies who had contested the Queen Mary at Royal Ascot dominated a finish in which six of the first eight home were drawn in single figures.

**NOTEBOOK**
**Siena Gold ◆**, who finished eighth in the Queen Mary, was able to get to the front this time and was well suited by this flatter track. She stuck to her task in resolute fashion and connections are now targeting a similar race at the Doncaster St Leger meeting.
**Don't Tell Mum(IRE)**, who finished a length ahead of the winner in the Queen Mary, had evidently become jarred up in that contest, but she appeared to run her race, although her rider reported she may have been feeling the ground late on, when she was carried left by the winner. She is likely to look for a Listed or Group race next, in order to gain some black type.
**Bond City(IRE)**, stepping up in grade, ran well from his low draw and connections felt he would have been closer had he been able to find cover in the middle of the main group. He once again gave the impression that a return to six furlongs would be in his favour, and there are several similar races at around that trip, but connections are thinking in terms of the Flying Childers at Doncaster.
**Alpaga Le Jomage(IRE)** is a consistent performer and put up another creditable effort. He seems well suited to a little cut in the ground, and may well pick up another race at a slightly lower level.
**Canton(IRE)**, who was beaten in a nursery on his return from a break last time, may find his rating going up following this good effort from his high draw, for he was conceding weight to all those that finished ahead of him and emerged the best horse at the weights
**Bibury Flyer**, who is still a maiden despite having finished runner-up four times, ran much her best race. She was doing her best work at the finish and looks worth a try at six furlongs.
**Withering Lady(IRE)** continues to show ability, and looks capable of finding a race at a lower level.
**Tournedos(IRE)**, who finished four lengths ahead of today's fourth in the Windsor Castle, never got to grips with the leaders and the form of that Royal Ascot race is working out disappointingly.
**Chiselled(IRE)**, returning from a two-month break, again showed plenty of speed and ought to get off the mark before long.
**Celtic Spa(IRE)** *Official explanation: jockey said filly had hung right*

## 3939 CANTORODDS.COM CONDITIONS STKS 7f (S)
**3:30** (3:35) (C) 2-Y-O **£7,482** (£2,838; £1,419; £645) **Stalls** Centre

| Form | | | | RPR |
|---|---|---|---|---|
| 51 | **1** | | **Grand Marque (IRE)**[16] [3451] 2-8-13 KFallon 3<br>(RHannon) *lw: slt ld tl narrowly hdd appr fnl f: styd chalng and r.o gamely to ld again last half f* **7/2**[2] | 97 |
| 1 | **2** | nk | **Blues And Royals (USA)**[35] [2898] 2-8-13 LDettori 4<br>(SaeedBinSuroor) *h.d.w: lw: hld up in tch: hdwy 2f out: slt ld and gng wl appr fnl f: rdn: no ex and hdd last half f* **5/4**[1] | 96 |
| 0 | **3** | 1 | **Kandidate**[11] [3601] 2-8-10 RLMoore 1<br>(CEBrittain) *chsd ldrs: rdn 2f out: styd on wl to chal appr fnl f: kpt on same u.p ins last* **40/1** | 91 |
| 3141 | **4** | 6 | **Obe Gold**[20] [3362] 2-8-13 TEDurcan 6<br>(MRChannon) *chsd ldrs: rdn over 3f out: outpcd over 2f out: wknd over 1f out* **4/1**[3] | 79 |
| 2 | **5** | ¾ | **Mastman (IRE)**[16] [3451] 2-8-10 JFortune 8<br>(BJMeehan) *w wnr over 3f: styd chsng ldrs: wknd over 1f out* **13/2** | 74 |
| | **6** | 3 | **William Tell (IRE)** 2-8-4 SHitchcott[(3)] 7<br>(MRChannon) *neat: scope: bhd: rdn 3f out: rn green: hung bdly lft and wknd 2f out* **25/1** | 63 |
| 0 | **7** | 1 ½ | **Voir Dire**[16] [3451] 2-8-10 RHavlin 2<br>(MrsPNDutfield) *bkwd: chsd ldrs: rdn over 3f out: wknd and hung lft 2f out* **66/1** | 63 |
| | **8** | 13 | **Just A Try (USA)** 2-8-7 RHughes 5<br>(RHannon) *s.i.s: bhd: lost tch fnl 2f* **20/1** | 27 |

1m 26.92s (-0.30) **Going Correction** -0.075s/f (Good) **8** Ran SP% **112.5**
Speed ratings: **98,97,96,89,88 85,83,68**CSF £7.87 TOTE £5.20: £1.70, £1.10, £8.40; EX 10.90.
**Owner** Noodles Racing **Bred** S N C Ecurie J L Bouchard **Trained** East Everleigh, Wilts

**FOCUS**
A decent conditions event in which the first three came clear. The time is well up to standard for the grade and the form looks sound enough on a line through the fourth.

**NOTEBOOK**
**Grand Marque(IRE)**, who won his maiden over course and distance, produced a really tough display to reagain the lead from the favourite in the closing stages. He is from a family that improve with age, and his attitude will enable him to win more than his share of races.
**Blues And Royals(USA)**, stepping up in trip, ran his race and looked sure to win when taking the advantage entering the final furlong. However, he came up against a really tough cookie on this occasion and was run out of it. He will not always come up against such a battler and has more races in him.
**Kandidate**, who missed the break then pulled too hard when last on his debut, showed what he is capable of with a fine effort. Always close to the pace, he joined battle with the first two and lost little in defeat. He should have no trouble picking up a maiden and should go on from this if not aimed too high.
**Obe Gold**, already in the frame in Group company in Italy, was beaten fair and square and gives the form solid look.
**Mastman(IRE)**, who finished two lengths behind the winner here on his debut, was 3lb better off but never landed a blow. This was a little disappointing.
**Just A Try(USA)** *Official explanation: jockey said colt went lame*

## 3940 RACING UK STKS (REGISTERED AS THE HACKWOOD STAKES) (LISTED RACE) 6f 8y
**4:05** (4:11) (A) 3-Y-O+ **£17,400** (£6,600; £3,300; £1,500) **Stalls** Centre

| Form | | | | RPR |
|---|---|---|---|---|
| 11-2 | **1** | | **Pastoral Pursuits**[44] [2629] 3-8-12 110 SDrowne 1<br>(HMorrison) *s.i.s: pushed along and hdwy over 2f out: chsd ldr appr fnl f: drvn to ld ins last: r.o wl* **15/8**[1] | 112 |
| 0-33 | **2** | hd | **Cartography (IRE)**[31] [2966] 3-8-12 106 (t) LDettori 6<br>(SaeedBinSuroor) *lw: trckd ldr: led ins fnl 2f: rdn and hdd ins fnl f: kpt on but nt pce of wnr* **11/4**[2] | 111 |
| -546 | **3** | nk | **Dowager**[14] [3522] 3-8-7 96 DaneO'Neill 7<br>(RHannon) *lw: hld up in rr: hdwy 2f out: styng on whn nt clr run appr fnl f: rdn and str run ins last: fin wl* **50/1** | 105? |
| -310 | **4** | 1 ¼ | **So Will I**[21] [3308] 3-9-2 109 RHills 9<br>(MPTregoning) *lw: chsd ldrs: rdn over 2f out and kpt on tl outpcd ins fnl f* **15/2** | 110 |
| 01-6 | **5** | ¾ | **Phantom Wind (USA)**[91] [1458] 3-8-7 98 RHughes 5<br>(JHMGosden) *trckd ldrs: rdn and effrt over 1f out: outpcd ins fnl f* **7/1**[3] | 99 |
| 4226 | **6** | 1 ¼ | **Mac Love**[11] [3598] 3-8-12 105 GCarter 3<br>(JAkehurst) *hld up in tch: hdwy 2f out: rdn to chse ldrs over 1f out: wknd ins last* **16/1** | 100 |
| 4300 | **7** | hd | **Nights Cross (IRE)**[28] [3073] 3-8-12 107 TEDurcan 12<br>(MRChannon) *in tch: chsd ldrs 1/2-way: wknd ins fnl f* **11/1** | 100 |
| 0146 | **8** | shd | **The Kiddykid (IRE)**[14] [3537] 4-9-10 110 DHolland 11<br>(PDEvans) *led tl hdd ins fnl 2f: wknd fnl f* **16/1** | 106 |
| 2-16 | **9** | nk | **Iqte Saab (USA)**[56] [2308] 3-8-12 104 MartinDwyer 13<br>(JLDunlop) *bhd: rdn 2f out: kpt on fnl f but nvr gng pce to rch ldrs* **14/1** | 99 |
| 5503 | **10** | shd | **Colonel Cotton (IRE)**[14] [3537] 5-9-7 100 RLMoore 4<br>(NACallaghan) *hld up rr but in tch: rdn over 2f out: sn one pce* **25/1** | 102 |
| 0003 | **11** | 5 | **Crimson Silk**[21] [3324] 4-9-3 92 (p) PaulEddery 8<br>(DHaydnJones) *rdn over 3f out: a outpcd* **33/1** | 83 |

1m 12.91s (-1.46) **Going Correction** -0.075s/f (Good)
**WFA** 3 from 4yo+ 5lb **11** Ran SP% **121.2**
Speed ratings: **106,105,105,103,102 101,100,100,100,100 93**CSF £6.99 TOTE £2.70: £1.80, £1.70, £12.60; EX 7.40.
**Owner** The Pursuits Partnership **Bred** Red House Stud **Trained** East Ilsley, Berks

**FOCUS**
A decent Listed contest run fractionally faster than the following handicap over the same trip. Twilight Blues (25/1) was withdrawn after rearing over in the stalls.

**NOTEBOOK**
**Pastoral Pursuits**, who was a very useful juvenile and was only narrowly beaten on his return over seven last month, appreciated the drop back to this trip and, although made to fight quite hard, stuck to his task well. He had apparently banged his head in the saddling boxes and been kicked when Twilight Blues played up in the stalls, so this effort was all the more creditable. He is capable of winning another Group race, and if returning to seven the Hungerford Stakes back here would be an option.
**Cartography(IRE)**, who has been third in two decent three-year-old races this season, including the Jersey Stakes, ran his race on this drop in trip, battling back when headed, and he should pick up a similar contest sooner rather than later.
**Dowager ◆**, who had a stiff task judged on official ratings, was the unlucky horse of the race. Held up at the back, she was checked just as she was beginning her run and then finished strongly to nearly overhaul the first two. This was a step up on what she had previously achieved this season, and can pick up a similar race soon, especially against her own sex.
**So Will I**, both of whose wins have been over course and distance, seemed to run his race and improved on his previous form with the sixth and seventh, but just did not appear good enough. He may be worth a try over an extra furlong.

**Phantom Wind(USA)**, having her first outing since April, showed plenty of dash before failing to pick up. She will appreciate a return to seven furlongs and may even get a mile.

**Mac Love** ran about 7lb below previous course form with So Will I. He is struggling at this level and may need to go abroad to gain another victory.

**Nights Cross(IRE)** was also below previous course form with So Will I, and has a similar profile to Mac Love.

## 3941 DORIC SIGNS RATED STKS (H'CAP) 6f 8y

**4:40** (4:41) (C ) (0-90,89) 3-Y-0+ **£8,755** (£3,321; £1,660; £754) **Stalls** Centre

Form RPR

00-0 **1** **Indian Trail**[16] 3455 4-9-4 **83**........ DaneO'Neill 9 96
(DRCElsworth) *hld in rr: hdwy and swtchd rt to stands side over 1f out: str run u.p to ld fnl 100yds* **14/1**

12 **2** *¾* **Doitnow (IRE)**[14] 3523 3-9-0 **87**........ THamilton(3) 6 97
(RAFahey) *bhd: rdn and gd hdwy over 1f out: str run to chal ins last: flashed tail u.p but kpt on to chse wnr cl home* **6/1**[1]

6002 **3** *shd* **Armagnac**[8] 3691 6-8-12 **77**........ SDrowne 12 87
(MABuckley) *bhd: gd hdwy over 1f out: drvn to ld ins fnl f: hdd fnl 100yds* **13/2**[2]

-000 **4** *1 ¼* **Danehill Stroller (IRE)**[16] 3453 4-9-4 **83**........(p) FLynch 10 89
(RMBeckett) *lw: hld up in rr: hdwy and swtchd rt over 1f out: styd ins last but nt pce to rch ldrs* **16/1**

0005 **5** *1 ¼* **Spanish Ace**[11] 3598 3-9-4 **88**........(v) MartinDwyer 15 91
(AMBalding) *swtg: led: rdn 2f out: hdd ins last: wknd last half f* **8/1**

4156 **6** *shd* **Chateau Nicol**[8] 3690 5-9-4 **83**........(v) KFallon 14 85
(BGPowell) *chsd ldrs: drvn to chal jst ins fnl f: wknd last half f* **10/1**

-000 **7** *1* **Canterloupe (IRE)**[17] 3416 6-8-8 **73**........ RSmith 2 72
(PJMakin) *in tch: rdn over 2f out: chsd ldrs 1f out: wknd ins last* **25/1**

1023 **8** *nk* **Idle Power (IRE)**[8] 3691 6-9-0 **79**........(p) JFortune 11 77
(JRBoyle) *chsd ldrs: rdn over over 1f out: wknd ins last* **12/1**

1122 **9** *½* **Caustic Wit (IRE)**[16] 3453 6-9-2 **86**........(p) PMakin(5) 13 83
(MSSaunders) *chsd ldrs: rdn 2f out: wknd 1f out* **6/1**[1]

1224 **10** *1* **Devon Flame**[8] 3691 5-8-8 **76**........ JFMcDonald(3) 16 70
(RJHodges) *lw: in tch: rdn over 2f out: wknd appr fnl f* **15/2**[3]

-100 **11** *1* **Millfields Dreams**[8] 3698 5-8-4 **69** oh10........ JFEgan 4 60
(RBrotherton) *pressed ldr 4f: wknd appr fnl f* **50/1**

3630 **12** *nk* **Najeebon (FR)**[8] 3691 5-8-12 **80**........ SHitchcott(3) 5 70
(MRChannon) *behind: rdn and hdwy 3f out: chsd ldrs ins fnl 2f: wknd fnl f* **10/1**

00-0 **13** *3 ½* **Sir Edwin Landseer (USA)**[29] 3036 4-8-9 **79**........ RThomas(5) 8 58
(ChristianWroe, UAE) *chsd ldrs: rdn over 2f out: wknd over 1f out* **33/1**

2006 **14** *2* **Morse (IRE)**[8] 3691 3-9-2 **89**........ LFletcher(3) 1 62
(JAOsborne) *pressed ldrs: rdn 1/2-way: wknd over 1f out* **25/1**

4046 **15** *1 ¼* **Dani Ridge (IRE)**[7] 3732 6-9-5 **84**........ TEDurcan 7 54
(EJAlston) *lw: chsd ldrs 4f* **25/1**

-020 **16** *1 ¼* **Bee Minor**[16] 3455 3-8-4 **74**........ RLMoore 3 40
(RHannon) *bhd: sme hdwy 2f out: sn wknd* **25/1**

1m 12.96s (-1.41) **Going Correction** -0.075s/f (Good)
**WFA** 3 from 4yo+ 5lb **16** Ran SP% **123.5**
Speed ratings: **106,105,104,103,101 101,100,99,99,97 96,95,91,88,86 85**CSF £89.72 CT £616.88 TOTE £20.80: £3.80, £2.00, £2.10, £4.70; EX 104.80.
**Owner** The Trail Blazers **Bred** Whitsbury Manor Stud **Trained** Whitsbury, Hants

**FOCUS**
A decent sprint handicap run only fractionally slower than the earlier Listed race and dominated by those that came from off the pace.

**NOTEBOOK**
**Indian Trail**, who only returned to action at the beginning of the month, showed the benefit of that with a narrow win. He travelled well at the rear of the field before having to switch to the stands' side to get a run. Once in the clear he picked up well to deny the pair racing towards the centre of the track. He looks capable of going on from this providing he is not raised too much in the weights.

**Doitnow(IRE)**, narrowly beaten against his own age group on his handicap debut, had a stiff task from a 6lb higher mark against older rivals. He was produced at the right time, and came back to head the third despite swishing his tail under pressure. This was another fine effort, as the eventual winner was on the near side, and he should pick up a decent handicap if maintaining this level of form.

**Armagnac** has been running into form of late and posted another good effort. He was produced to win his race but was outbattled by the second, with the winner coming wide of the pair. He is still 1lb lower than his last winning mark, and should find a winning opportunity before long.

**Danehill Stroller(IRE)** ran into form about this time last year, and looks to be doing the same again. Like the winner, he had to switch to the nearside to get a run and, although no match for that rival, looks capable of winning off his current mark. He is worth bearing in mind.

**Spanish Ace** has been helped to re-discover some form by the drop in the weights, return to sprinting and the fitting of a visor. He may be able to lead all the way if dropped back to five furlongs.

**Chateau Nicol** continues to run with credit but is now 15lb higher than at the start of the season and looks to be in the Handicappers grasp.

**Caustic Wit(IRE)**, whose good recent run has seen him rise 30lb in the ratings, ran as if the assessor has finally got his measure.

**Devon Flame**, who ran so well at Ascot last time and is yet another who has been in fine form, is 34lb higher than the mark from which he began the season and never landed a blow on this occasion.

## 3942 CISTM RACING CLUB APPRENTICE H'CAP 1m 4f 5y

**5:10** (5:10) (E ) (0-75,74) 3-Y-0+ **£4,192** (£1,290; £645; £322) **Stalls** High

Form RPR

4P12 **1** **Merrymaker**[15] 3474 4-9-1 **62**........ PPMathers 8 76
(WMBrisbourne) *s.i.s: hld up in rr: stdy hdwy 3f out: trckd ldr ins fnl 2f: drvn to ld last half f: hld on wl* **11/2**[3]

0415 **2** *nk* **Masked (IRE)**[12] 3584 3-8-9 **71**........ DerekNolan(3) 5 85
(JWHills) *lw: trckd ldr: led ins fnl 2f: sn hrd drvn: hdd last half f: kpt on wl but no ex nr fin* **4/1**[2]

0035 **3** *5* **Head To Kerry (IRE)**[15] 3488 4-8-10 **57**........(t) PGallagher 2 63
(DJSFrenchDavis) *led: rdn 3f out: hdd ins fnl 2f: wknd fnl f* **4/1**[2]

0353 **4** *3* **Saxe-Coburg (IRE)**[10] 3629 7-8-8 **58**........ WHogg(3) 6 59
(GAHam) *bhd: hdwy 5f out: rdn 3f out: no ch w ldrs fnl 2f* **11/2**[3]

1255 **5** *5* **Make My Hay**[9] 3682 5-8-2 **49**........ NataliaGemelova 1 42
(JGallagher) *chsd ldrs: rdn over 4f out: wknd 3f out* **13/2**

0/50 **6** *6* **Greyfield (IRE)**[36] 2835 8-8-3 **53**........ MHoward(3) 3 36
(KBishop) *s.i.s: bhd: sme hdwy 5f out: wknd over 3f out* **16/1**

1211 **7** *2* **Realism (FR)**[19] 3375 4-9-8 **74**........ StevenHarrison(5) 7 54
(PWHiatt) *swtg: t.k.h: chsd ldrs tl wknd ins fnl 3f* **7/2**[1]

0/00 **8** *12* **Enchanted Ocean (USA)**[39] 2767 5-8-3 **55**........ TBlock(5) 4 16
(GBBalding) *bhd: sme hdwy 6f out: wknd 4f out* **14/1**

2m 35.12s (-1.17) **Going Correction** -0.075s/f (Good)
**WFA** 3 from 4yo+ 12lb **8** Ran SP% **118.9**
Speed ratings: **100,99,96,94,91 87,85,77**CSF £28.96 CT £99.33 TOTE £6.40: £1.70, £1.80, £1.90; EX 23.20 Place 6 £58.98, Place 5 £19.86.
**Owner** The Blacktoffee Partnership **Bred** Hascombe And Valiant Studs **Trained** Great Ness, Shropshire

**FOCUS**
A modest handicap for the track and an ordinary time, but the first two had the last furlong to themselves.

**NOTEBOOK**
**Merrymaker** had run well in similar races for the same apprentice and was given a nice waiting ride. After creeping on to the heels of the leaders, he picked up well when asked and resisted the renewed effort of the runner-up. He is sure to go up again, but is in good hands and might not have finished progressing yet..

**Masked(IRE)** was always close to the pace but, when he made his move, had to work harder than expected to get the better of Head To Kerry. This left him with little in reserve when the winner arrived on the scene, but he rallied in fine fashion and showed improved form in going down only narrowly. He is progressing with experience and should be able to win another ordinary handicap.

**Head To Kerry(IRE)** has been threatening a return to form and took a fair amount of passing before eventually weakening. His two wins last year came in August and September, and he is back on the same mark as when winning the second of them.

**Saxe-Coburg(IRE)** has done most of his recent racing on fast ground, but interestingly his only win this year was on soft going.

**Realism(FR)**, who came into this on a hat-trick, failed to settle in the early stages and was in trouble early in the straight. He is a stone higher than when scoring in June, but can be given an opportunity to atone for this.

T/Plt: £84.50 to a £1 stake. Pool: £85,253.90. 736.35 winning tickets. T/Qpdt: £9.30 to a £1 stake. Pool: £4,561.15. 361.30 winning tickets. ST

# 3911 NEWMARKET (JULY) (R-H)

Saturday, July 17

**OFFICIAL GOING: Good**

After a dry night the ground was unchanged from the previous evening. However, it certainly looked to be riding faster.

Wind: Slight across Weather: Cloudy with sunny spells

## 3943 NEWMARKET TROPHY (A RATED STKS) (H'CAP) 1m

**2:10** (2:11) (B ) (0-100,97) 3-Y-O **£17,400** (£6,600; £3,300; £1,500) **Stalls** High

Form RPR

4121 **1** **Diamond Lodge**[26] 3159 3-8-7 **83** oh2........ EAhern 3 91+
(JNoseda) *hld up in tch: rdn to ld ins fnl f: r.o* **12/1**

4014 **2** *¾* **Fine Silver (IRE)**[30] 3001 3-9-1 **91**........ TQuinn 6 98+
(PFICole) *lw: chsd ldrs: rdn to ld over 1f out: hdd ins fnl f: kpt on* **6/1**[2]

1015 **3** *¾* **Oddsmaker (IRE)**[15] 3477 3-8-11 **87**........ IMongan 10 92
(PDEvans) *hld up: hdwy over 2f out: rdn over 1f out: r.o* **20/1**

4034 **4** *1 ¼* **Sew'N'So Character (IRE)**[15] 3477 3-9-5 **95**........ DSweeney 13 97
(MBlanshard) *s.s: hdwy over 6f out: rdn over 1f out: kpt on* **12/1**

3-00 **5** *2* **Sweet Indulgence (IRE)**[9] 3671 3-8-8 **84**........ TPQueally 7 82
(DrJDScargill) *hld up: outpcd over 3f out: styd on ins fnl f: nvr trbld ldrs* **16/1**

0416 **6** *½* **Appalachian Trail (IRE)**[14] 3542 3-9-0 **90**........ KDarley 2 86+
(ISemple) *hld up: hdwy over 1f out: wknd ins fnl f* **11/2**[1]

2303 **7** *nk* **Zonus**[14] 3542 3-9-1 **91**........ MHills 11 87
(BWHills) *hld up: pushed along 1/2-way: n.d* **6/1**[2]

0-12 **8** *1* **Invasian (IRE)**[30] 3017 3-8-12 **88**........ WRyan 8 81
(HRACecil) *prom: chsd ldr over 3f out: led over 2f out: rdn and hdd over 1f out: wknd ins fnl f* **8/1**

00-4 **9** *1 ¾* **Enford Princess**[76] 1797 3-8-12 **88**........ SSanders 9 77
(RHannon) *hld up: rdn over 2f out: n.d* **50/1**

0000 **10** *7* **Barbajuan (IRE)**[11] 3598 3-9-7 **97**........(b) JPMurtagh 5 70
(NACallaghan) *led over 5f: wknd over 1f out* **33/1**

3152 **11** *nk* **Bayhirr**[20] 3347 3-8-10 **86**........ PRobinson 4 59
(MAJarvis) *chsd ldrs: rdn over 2f out: sn wknd* **7/1**[3]

-101 **12** *hd* **Dubois**[7] 3728 3-9-0 **90**........(vt) KMcEvoy 1 62
(SaeedBinSuroor) *lw: chsd ldrs 6f* **15/2**

0456 **13** *5* **Forthright**[30] 3001 3-8-11 **90**........(p) J-PGuillambert(3) 12 51
(CEBrittain) *chsd ldrs over 5f* **14/1**

1m 40.2s (-0.28) **Going Correction** +0.125s/f (Good) **13** Ran SP% **116.9**
Speed ratings: **106,105,104,103,101 100,100,99,97,90 90,90,85**CSF £79.15 CT £1488.71 TOTE £10.00: £3.20, £2.40, £7.90; EX 79.60.
**Owner** Mrs J Harris **Bred** Chippenham Lodge Stud Ltd **Trained** Newmarket, Suffolk

**FOCUS**
Quite a competitive affair and decent form. The first two are among several still open to some improvement.

**NOTEBOOK**
**Diamond Lodge** confirmed herself a progressive performer and showed fine battling qualities to hold off the persistent Fine Silver. She appears to handle most types of ground.

**Fine Silver(IRE)**, raised 3lb for his effort in the Britannia, is a consistent colt and continues in fine form. The way he kept battling on here suggested he may well stay a little further.

**Oddsmaker(IRE)** has had plenty of racing but this run confirmed he is as good as ever.

**Sew'N'So Character(IRE)** ran as though this trip was on the sharp side for him now.

**Sweet Indulgence(IRE)** tended to run his race in snatches and may benefit from some form of headgear.

**Appalachian Trail(IRE)** came there to have every chance up the centre of the course, before dropping away in the closing stages.

**Zonus** is a frustrating character who needs things to go his way.

**Invasian(IRE)** does not do anything quickly and might have appreciated more use being made of him.

**Bayhirr** *Official explanation: jockey said colt became extremely tired in the latter stages*

## 3944 APHRODITE STKS (LISTED RACE) 1m 4f

**2:45** (2:45) (A ) 3-Y-0+ **£17,400** (£6,600; £3,300; £1,500) **Stalls** High

Form RPR

1120 **1** **Beneventa**[31] 2967 4-9-7 110........ SSanders 9 112
(JLDunlop) *b. off fore: hld up in tch: led over 2f out: styd on strly ins fnl f* **7/2**[2]

1112 **2** *3 ½* **Selebela**[24] 3210 3-8-4 93........ TPQueally 4 101
(LMCumani) *led over 9f: rdn and hung lft over 1f out: no ex ins fnl f* **4/1**[3]

1311 **3** *1 ½* **Portrait Of A Lady (IRE)**[14] 3528 3-8-4 87........ WRyan 3 99
(HRACecil) *lw: hld up: nt clr run over 2f out: hdwy over 1f out: rdn and no imp ins fnl f* **9/1**

31 **4** *2* **Goslar**$^{36}$ [2832] 3-8-4 87 TQuinn 6 95
(HCandy) *hld up: pushed along 5f out: hdwy over 2f out: wknd fnl f* **12/1**
2-1 **5** *¾* **Nuzooa (USA)**$^{37}$ [2805] 3-8-4 92 WSupple 5 94
(MPTregoning) *hld up: hdwy over 2f out: rdn and wknd over 1f out* **9/4**$^{1}$
316 **6** *1* **Feaat**$^{30}$ [2997] 3-8-4 94 KMcEvoy 2 93
(JHMGosden) *chsd ldrs tl wknd over 1f out* **9/1**
5126 **7** *nk* **Tawny Way**$^{28}$ [3078] 4-9-2 86 PRobinson 8 92
(WJarvis) *chsd ldrs tl wknd over 1f out* **33/1**
0054 **8** *25* **Qudrah (IRE)**$^{108}$ [1212] 4-9-2 85 JPMurtagh 7 52
(EJO'Neill) *hld up: wknd 2f out* **50/1**
1244 **9** *1 ¼* **Desert Royalty (IRE)**$^{8}$ [3716] 4-9-2 92 RMullen 1 50
(EALDunlop) *b: hld up: rdn over 3f out: wknd over 2f out* **14/1**

2m 28.47s (-4.49) **Going Correction** -0.10s/f (Good) **9** Ran SP% **112.3**
**WFA** 3 from 4yo 12lb
Speed ratings: **110,107,106,105,104 104,103,87,86**CSF £17.25 TOTE £4.30: £1.60, £1.70, £1.60; EX 17.90.
**Owner** Mrs J M Khan **Bred** R N And Mrs Khan **Trained** Arundel, W Sussex

**FOCUS**
The winner was the one with the solid form in this contest and made no mistake. The pace was strong.

**NOTEBOOK**
**Beneventa**, appreciated both the drop in class and step up in trip, winning with authority. Now she has proved she stays this far, there should be far more opportunities for her.
**Selebela** was far from disgraced on this step up in class and can certainly make her mark at this level.
**Portrait Of A Lady(IRE)** is an improving filly and may have done better still had she not had to switch to get a run.
**Goslar** looked to be thrown in at the deep end here, but she acquitted herself well and will certainly find easier openings.
**Nuzooa(USA)**, surprisingly preferred in the market to the winner, looked to find this trip beyond her.
**Feaat**, from the stable that took this last year, looked to run a little below her best.
**Desert Royalty(IRE)** *Official explanation: jockey said filly ran too free*

## 3945 GLEMSFORD H'CAP 5f
3:20 (3:20) (C ) (0-100,100) 3-Y-0+ **£9,490** (£2,920; £1,460; £730) **Stalls** High

Form RPR
2404 **1** **Connect**$^{15}$ [3480] 7-9-3 **85** (b) PRobinson 10 94
(MHTompkins) *chsd ldrs: r.o to ld post* **11/2**$^{2}$
113- **2** *nk* **First Order**$^{355}$ [3653] 3-10-0 **100** SSanders 5 108+
(SirMarkPrescott) *lw: trckd ldrs: racd keenly: rdn to ld ins fnl f: edgd lft and hdd post* **13/2**$^{3}$
6020 **3** *shd* **Cape Royal**$^{8}$ [3713] 4-9-5 **87** JPMurtagh 6 95
(MrsJRRamsden) *chsd ldrs: rdn and ev ch ins fnl f: r.o* **7/1**
0300 **4** *hd* **Prime Recreation**$^{23}$ [3227] 7-7-9 **66** oh5 LisaJones$^{(3)}$ 3 73
(PSFelgate) *b.: led: rdn and hdd ins fnl f: edgd lft: r.o* **25/1**
3003 **5** *nk* **Sir Desmond**$^{7}$ [3723] 6-8-9 **77** (p) EAhern 1 83
(RGuest) *hld up: pushed along 1/2-way: r.o ins fnl f* **11/2**$^{2}$
2406 **6** *nk* **Texas Gold**$^{7}$ [3723] 6-9-6 **88** RMullen 11 93
(WRMuir) *hld up: nt clr run over 1f out: swtchd lft: r.o ins fnl f: nt rch ldrs* **5/1**$^{1}$
4230 **7** *nk* **Further Outlook (USA)**$^{21}$ [3324] 10-9-2 **84** TQuinn 7 88
(DKIvory) *b.off fore: chsd ldr over 3f: styd on* **25/1**
3030 **8** *shd* **Henry Hall (IRE)**$^{15}$ [3480] 8-9-11 **93** KimTinkler 4 96
(NTinkler) *lw: chsd ldrs: rdn and ev ch ins fnl f: no ex towards fin* **12/1**
5046 **9** *hd* **Endless Summer**$^{20}$ [3339] 7-8-5 **73** PDoe 9 76
(AWCarroll) *hld up: outpcd over 1f out: running on whn nt clr run wl ins fnl f: nvr able to chal* **20/1**
0300 **10** *1* **Roses Of Spring**$^{34}$ [2909] 6-8-7 **80** (p) AQuinn$^{(5)}$ 2 79
(RMHCowell) *dwlt: hdwy 3f out: rdn and wknd fnl f* **20/1**
-100 **11** *nk* **Spliff**$^{11}$ [3598] 3-9-7 **93** (b$^{1}$) DSweeney 8 91
(HCandy) *hld up: rdn over 1f out: n.d* **10/1**
0530 **12** *3 ½* **Beauvrai**$^{10}$ [3645] 4-8-4 **72** (p) TPQueally 12 57
(VSmith) *s.s: a bhd* **11/1**

59.33 secs (-0.32) **Going Correction** +0.125s/f (Good)
**WFA** 3 from 4yo+ 4lb **12** Ran SP% **115.6**
Speed ratings: **107,106,106,106,105 105,104,104,104,102 102,96**CSF £37.54 CT £253.43 TOTE £6.80: £2.20, £2.10, £3.30; EX 49.80.
**Owner** Mrs P R Bowring **Bred** J A E Hobby **Trained** Newmarket, Suffolk

**FOCUS**
A competitive race of which the Handicapper can feel proud. The pace was solid.

**NOTEBOOK**
**Connect** found the drying ground in his favour and, with the early leader just rolling off the rails in the latter stages, just managed to squeeze through. He will go for the Hong Kong Jockey Club Handicap next weekend if the ground remains on the fast side.
**First Order** ◆ was always doing a little too much on this return to action and just got nailed on the line. Now the freshness has gone out of him he should have little difficulty gaining compensation.
**Cape Royal** confirmed himself in good form and will certainly find easier tasks than he faced here.
**Prime Recreation**, depsite his advancing years, still has plenty of zip. Had he been able to race of his correct mark, he must surely have gone close.
**Sir Desmond** was done no favours by having to race out wide and comes out of this with plenty of credit.
**Texas Gold** did not have the best of runs, but even so this was still a solid effort and did his Stewards Cup prospects no harm at all.
**Endless Summer** ◆, who is probably better suited by an extra furlong, had no luck in running, but can be rated as finishing up with the placed horses. His official age had been altered since his previous run, it having emerged that he was born in late 1997, rather than on January 2 1998. He faces disqualification from his two juvenile wins, in which case he would be eligible for maidens again.

## 3946 INVESCO PERPETUAL MAIDEN STKS 6f
3:55 (3:57) (D ) 2-Y-0 **£4,888** (£1,504; £752; £376) **Stalls** High

Form RPR
**1** **Camacho** 2-9-0 WRyan 11 84
(HRACecil) *well grown: compact: bkwd: w ldrs: led and hung lft over 2f out: rdn out* **2/1**$^{1}$
6 **2** *½* **Sign Writer (USA)**$^{10}$ [3643] 2-9-0 EAhern 6 83
(JNoseda) *lw: chsd ldrs: nt clr run over 1f out: rdn and ev ch ins fnl f: styd on* **5/1**$^{2}$
**3** *nk* **Fongtastic** 2-9-0 WSupple 3 82
(BJMeehan) *gd sort: lw: sn pushed along and prom: rdn 1/2-way: styd on u.p ins fnl f* **10/1**
**4** *1 ¼* **Diamonds And Dust** 2-9-0 PRobinson 9 78
(MHTompkins) *w'like: scope: hld up in tch: rdn over 1f out: styd on same pce ins fnl f* **33/1**
**5** *hd* **Desert Demon (IRE)** 2-9-0 MHills 8 77+
(BWHills) *gd sort: slowly in to stride: hld up: hdwy over 1f out: r.o* **10/1**
**6** *¾* **Pianoforte (USA)** 2-9-0 TPQueally 1 75
(DRLoder) *compact: scope: bkwd: led over 4f: wknd fnl f* **8/1**$^{3}$
**7** *2 ½* **Rebel Rebel (IRE)** 2-9-0 RMullen 2 68
(NACallaghan) *well grown: s.i.s: nvr nrr* **40/1**
**8** *nk* **Basic System (USA)** 2-9-0 BDoyle 12 67+
(SirMichaelStoute) *compact: scope: bkwd: s.i.s: hld up: hdwy and hung lft over 1f out: nvr trbld ldrs* **14/1**
**9** *¾* **Shrine Mountain (USA)** 2-8-11 J-PGuillambert$^{(3)}$ 7 64
(CEBrittain) *w'like: bkwd: w ldrs over 3f: wknd over 1f out* **50/1**
0 **10** *¾* **Never Away**$^{9}$ [3676] 2-8-9 JPMurtagh 10 57
(NACallaghan) *w ldrs 4f: wknd over 1f out* **16/1**
**11** *7* **Fighting Tom Cat (USA)** 2-9-0 (t) KMcEvoy 4 41
(SaeedBinSuroor) *w'like: scope: lw: prom: lost pl over 4f out: sn bhd* **5/1**$^{2}$
**12** *9* **Royal Mougins** 2-9-0 SSanders 5 14
(GWragg) *gd sort: s.s: outpcd* **25/1**

1m 14.62s (1.30) **Going Correction** +0.125s/f (Good) **12** Ran SP% **119.7**
Speed ratings: **96,95,94,93,93 92,88,88,87,86 76,64**CSF £11.17 TOTE £2.90: £1.70, £1.90, £2.70; EX 15.50.
**Owner** K Abdulla **Bred** Juddmonte Farms Ltd **Trained** Newmarket, Suffolk

**FOCUS**
Although the time was only ordinary, there were plenty of well-regarded animals on show.

**NOTEBOOK**
**Camacho** came into this with a big reputation, and although no more than workmanlike in victory, was very green and is open to plenty of improvement
**Sign Writer(USA)** had clearly learnt from his debut and showed enough to suggest he can win his maiden.
**Fongtastic**, out of dual five-furlong winning juvenile, looked very green and should have learnt plenty. However, he did have quite a hard race in the process.
**Diamonds And Dust**, a 6,000 gns yearling shaped quite nicely and is sure to have learnt plenty from this experience.
**Desert Demon(IRE)** ◆, a half-brother to Caustic Wit, took a while for the penny to drop and is certain to be all the wiser for the experience.
**Pianoforte(USA)** looked a bit more professional than some of his rivals and just got tired up the hill.

## 3947 DODSON AND HORRELL H'CAP 1m 6f 175y
4:30 (4:31) (D ) (0-85,83) 4-Y-0+ **£5,395** (£1,660; £830; £415) **Stalls** High

Form RPR
3-41 **1** **Bendarshaan**$^{11}$ [3608] 4-9-12 **83** SChin 5 92
(MJohnston) *lw: chsd ldrs: swtchd lft over 4f out: led over 3f out: rdn out* **10/3**$^{2}$
1-40 **2** *1 ¼* **Cara Fantasy (IRE)**$^{58}$ [2240] 4-9-8 **79** TQuinn 6 86
(JLDunlop) *lw: hld up in tch: nt clr wl over 1f out: r.o ins fnl f nt rch wnr* **4/1**$^{3}$
-610 **3** *½* **Balkan Knight**$^{14}$ [3521] 4-9-12 **83** (v) TPQueally 1 89
(DRLoder) *a.p: rdn and ev ch over 1f out: no ex wl ins fnl f* **4/1**$^{3}$
0-60 **4** *3* **Bobsleigh**$^{98}$ [1329] 5-9-1 **72** KDarley 3 74
(MrsAJPerrett) *trckd ldr: rdn over 1f out: wknd ins fnl f* **3/1**$^{1}$
0640 **5** *1 ¼* **Gallant Boy (IRE)**$^{7}$ [3731] 5-8-8 **68** (vt) FPFerris$^{(3)}$ 7 69
(PDEvans) *b.off fore: hld up: hdwy over 3f out: rdn over 2f out: wknd fnl f* **7/1**
26-0 **6** *7* **Lahob**$^{29}$ [3050] 4-8-4 **61** RMullen 4 53
(PHowling) *led: rdn and hdd over 3f out: wknd over 1f out* **33/1**
0-00 **7** *5* **Muskatsturm (GER)**$^{87}$ [1539] 5-8-13 **70** WRyan 2 55
(BJCurley) *hld up: plld hrd: wknd wl over 1f out* **14/1**

3m 12.58s (1.82) **Going Correction** -0.10s/f (Good) **7** Ran SP% **110.2**
Speed ratings: **91,90,90,88,87 84,81**CSF £15.72 TOTE £3.10: £1.90, £2.50; EX 14.20.
**Owner** Malih L Al Basti **Bred** The Duke Of Roxburghe's Stud, Beckhampton Stables **Trained** Middleham Moor, N Yorks
■ Stewards Enquiry : S Chin caution: careless riding

**FOCUS**
This was not that competitive, with most of the runners out of form and the pace only steady.

**NOTEBOOK**
**Bendarshaan** had too much pace for his rivals over this trip and won a shade more cosily than the verdict suggested. Now connections have found he does stay there should be plenty of opportunities for him.
**Cara Fantasy(IRE)** did not have the best of runs and found the winner had gone beyond recall when getting a run.
**Balkan Knight** had no excuses and although not beaten far, may have found this trip farther than ideal.
**Bobsleigh**, who stays much further than this, was not suited to the steady early pace.
**Gallant Boy(IRE)** has yet to prove he stays this far.

## 3948 DE NIRO'S NITECLUB LORD'S TAVERNERS MAIDEN STKS 7f
5:05 (5:05) (D ) 3-Y-0 **£5,434** (£1,672; £836; £418) **Stalls** High

Form RPR
**1** **Surreptitious** 3-8-9 TPQueally 7 64
(DRLoder) *gd sort: lw: a.p: rdn to ld over 1f out: r.o* **7/2**$^{3}$
2 **2** *nk* **Violet Park**$^{9}$ [3666] 3-8-9 KMcEvoy 4 67+
(BJMeehan) *trckd ldrs: plld hrd: n.m.r and hmpd over 1f out: r.o wl ins fnl f* **5/2**$^{1}$
6 **3** *½* **Polar Sun**$^{48}$ [2505] 3-9-0 JPMurtagh 1 67
(JRFanshawe) *kw: chsd ldrs: rdn and ev ch fr over 1f out: edgd lft ins fnl f: styd on* **5/1**
05 **4** *½* **Dream Easy**$^{28}$ [3094] 3-9-0 RPrice 3 66
(PLGilligan) *swtg: mde most over 5f: styd on* **12/1**
**5** *nk* **Mujawer (USA)** 3-9-0 WSupple 2 65
(MPTregoning) *gd sort: bkwd: hld up: hdwy over 1f out: sn rdn and ev ch: no ex towards fin* **3/1**$^{2}$
04 **6** *1 ¾* **Cazenove**$^{9}$ [3666] 3-9-0 KDarley 6 61
(MGQuinlan) *w ldr over 5f: no ex ins fnl f* **25/1**
U0 **7** *5* **Aljafliyah**$^{7}$ [3759] 3-8-2 AHamblett$^{(7)}$ 8 43
(LMCumani) *lw: s.s: hld up: rdn and wknd over 1f out* **33/1**
**8** *3* **Tides** 3-8-6 LisaJones$^{(3)}$ 9 35
(WJMusson) *s.i.s: sn prom: wknd over 1f out* **28/1**
0- **9** *24* **Painted Moon (USA)**$^{331}$ [4308] 3-8-6 J-PGuillambert$^{(3)}$ 5 —
(CEBrittain) *w ldrs 4f: sn rdn and wknd* **16/1**

1m 27.19s (0.42) **Going Correction** +0.125s/f (Good) **9** Ran SP% **116.3**
Speed ratings: **102,101,101,100,100 98,92,89,61**CSF £12.52 TOTE £3.60: £1.60, £1.50, £2.00; EX 10.20.
**Owner** Sheikh Mohammed **Bred** Darley **Trained** Newmarket, Suffolk

**FOCUS**
This did not look a strong maiden and the proximity of the sixth adds doubts as to the value of the form.

**NOTEBOOK**
**Surreptitious**, a half-sister to 12-furlong winners Nador and Quevilly, took adavantage of the trouble behind her to get off the mark at the first time of asking. While she probably did not achieve a great deal, she is open to improvement and will be suited by further in time.
**Violet Park** had no luck in running, and must surely have scored had she a clear run.
**Polar Sun** comes from a good family who get better as they get older.
**Dream Easy** does not look good enough to win a maiden, but should find plenty of opportunities in handicaps.
**Mujawer(USA)**, related to several winners, had his chance before lack of a previous outing found him out.

## 3949 GUNITE (EASTERN) LTD LORD'S TAVERNERS H'CAP 7f
5:35 (5:36) (D ) (0-80,79) 3-Y-O **£5,733** (£1,764; £882; £441) **Stalls** High

Form RPR
0251 **1** **Hazewind**[9] [3684] 3-7-12 **59**....(vt) FPFerris(3) 4 71
(PDEvans) *w ldrs tl led over 2f out: rdn clr ins fnl f: eased nr fin* **7/1**
3016 **2** *1 3/4* **Panshir (FR)**[27] [3135] 3-9-7 **79**.... RMullen 10 86+
(CFWall) *hld up: nt clr run over 1f out: r.o ins fnl f: no ch w wnr* **7/2**[1]
3464 **3** *1 1/2* **Ask The Clerk (IRE)**[19] [3384] 3-8-13 **71**.... MTebbutt 5 74
(VSmith) *chsd ldrs: rdn over 1f out: styd on same pce ins fnl f* **14/1**
0P40 **4** *3/4* **Molinia**[26] [3155] 3-7-9 **56**.... NMackay(3) 1 59+
(RMBeckett) *lw: started slowly: hld up: nt clr run over 1f out: r.o ins fnl f: nvr nrr* **25/1**
6450 **5** *1 1/4* **Carriacou**[23] [3230] 3-8-9 **67**.... TQuinn 8 65
(PWD'Arcy) *hld up: swtchd lft and hdwy over 2f out: sn rdn: styd on same pce ins fnl f* **20/1**
0000 **6** *nk* **Mount Vettore**[14] [3507] 3-9-0 **72**.... JPMurtagh 6 69
(MrsJRRamsden) *lw: led over 4f: wknd fnl f* **9/1**
4034 **7** *hd* **Spin King (IRE)**[14] [3527] 3-9-3 **75**.... KDarley 2 72
(MLWBell) *w ldrs: rdn over 2f out: ev ch wl over 1f out: wkng whn edgd rt ins fnl f* **4/1**[2]
5102 **8** *3/4* **Lorien Hill (IRE)**[21] [3306] 3-9-1 **73**.... MHills 11 68
(BWHills) *swtg: sn pushed along in rea: styd on ins fnl f: n.d* **11/2**[3]
6365 **9** *hd* **Dr Synn**[19] [3384] 3-8-9 **67**.... KMcEvoy 3 61
(JAkehurst) *b.: swtg: chsd ldrs: rdn over 2f out: wkng whn hmpd ins fnl f* **7/1**
0461 **10** *3/4* **Faith Healer (IRE)**[8] [3710] 3-7-6 **57**....(b) DFentiman(7) 9 49
(VSmith) *lw: chsd ldrs: rdn and hung rt over 1f out: wkng whn hmpd ins fnl f* **7/1**
00-0 **11** *1 1/2* **Carlburg (IRE)**[58] [2244] 3-8-7 **68**.... J-PGuillambert(3) 7 56
(CEBrittain) *prom: rdn over 2f out: wkng whn nt clr run ins fnl f* **33/1**

1m 25.98s (-0.79) **Going Correction** +0.125s/f (Good) **11 Ran SP% 123.3**
Speed ratings: **109,107,105,104,103 102,102,101,101,100 98**CSF £32.63 CT £352.68 TOTE £8.20: £2.50, £1.80, £3.90; EX 55.00 Place 6 £79.99, Place 5 £22.31.
**Owner** Waterline Racing Club **Bred** Gainsborough Stud Management Ltd **Trained** Pandy, Gwent

**FOCUS**
A modest contest and ordinary form, but the pace was sound.

**NOTEBOOK**
**Hazewind** won with something in hand and looks to be progressive.
**Panshir(FR)** never looked likely to peg back the winner having let him get first run.
**Ask The Clerk(IRE)** is well exposed and ran as well as he could have been expected to.
**Molinia** looked to be given plenty to do but would have been closer if a gap had come sooner. She has yet to score, but is not without ability.
**Carriacou** has become a disappointing and unreliable sort.
**Spin King(IRE)** was always seeing too much daylight from his outside draw.
T/Plt: £74.90 to a £1 stake. Pool: £69,223.65. 674.10 winning tickets. T/Qpdt: £9.20 to a £1 stake. Pool: £3,415.45. 272.90 winning tickets. CR

# 3582 RIPON (R-H)
Saturday, July 17

**OFFICIAL GOING: Soft**

## 3950 EBF SARAH ANN DANIELS 80TH BIRTHDAY MAIDEN FILLIES' STKS 5f
2:05 (2:08) (D ) 2-Y-O **£5,397** (£1,660; £830; £415) **Stalls** Low

Form RPR
4 **1** **Satin Finish (IRE)**[9] [3675] 2-8-11.... ACulhane 6 83
(MRChannon) *cl up: led over 1f out: rdn clr* **6/4**[1]
5 **2** *4* **Howards Princess**[16] [3445] 2-8-8.... TEaves(3) 1 69
(JSGoldie) *trckd ldrs: effrt and n.m.r wl over 1f out: swtchd rt ins last and styd on wl* **14/1**
**3** *1/2* **Pedlar Of Dreams (IRE)** 2-8-11.... MFenton 4 67
(TDBarron) *cl up: evc hance 2f out: sn rdn and one pce* **25/1**
3435 **4** *nk* **Ruby's Dream**[6] [3770] 2-8-11.... SWKelly 5 66
(JMBradley) *chsd ldrs: rdn wl over 1f out: kpt ons ame pce* **20/1**
34 **5** *1/2* **Elsie Wagg (USA)**[46] [2544] 2-8-11.... NCallan 3 64
(MJWallace) *led: rdn along 2f out: hdd over 1f out: one pce* **12/1**
24 **6** *hd* **Molly Marie (IRE)**[21] [3296] 2-8-11.... DAllan 9 64
(TDEasterby) *bmpd s: in rr: hdwy 2f out: swtchd rt and kpt on fnl f* **4/1**[2]
432 **7** *2* **Hillside Heather (IRE)**[12] [3583] 2-8-11.... FNorton 10 57
(ABerry) *in tch: rdn along 2f out: no imp* **10/1**[3]
**8** *1/2* **Algorithm** 2-8-11.... RWinston 2 55
(TDEasterby) *dwlt: a rr* **33/1**
**9** *hd* **Night Out (FR)** 2-8-11.... JFanning 7 54
(GCBravery) *chsd ldrs: rdn along 2f out: sn wknd* **33/1**
**10** *8* **Jasmine Hill** 2-8-11.... DeanMcKeown 11 26
(NBycroft) *wnt rt s: a rr* **80/1**
**11** *7* **Match Ball (USA)** 2-8-11.... JCarroll 8 —
(SaeedBinSuroor) *chsd ldrs: rdn along 2f out: sn wknd* **4/1**[2]

62.28 secs (2.08) **Going Correction** +0.525s/f (Yiel) **11 Ran SP% 119.2**
Speed ratings: **104,97,96,96,95 95,92,91,90,78 66**CSF £24.92 TOTE £2.50: £1.10, £4.10, £5.70; EX 32.50.
**Owner** Sheikh Mohammed **Bred** Darley **Trained** West Ilsley, Berks

**FOCUS**
A fair juvenile maiden, featuring three Lowther entries, run at a sound gallop.

**NOTEBOOK**
**Satin Finish(IRE)** , one of three Lowther entries in the field, confirmed the promise of her debut in a decent-looking Newmarket maiden and ran out a ready winner. She had no problems with this drop in trip, despite her breeding suggesting she needs much further, and this soft ground was right up her street. If she is to take a hand in the Lowther however, she will need to improve plenty once again.
**Howards Princess** improved on her debut effort and kept on for a clear second, but shaped as though a return to six furlongs would be more in her favour.
**Pedlar Of Dreams(IRE)** made a pleasing debut, showing good early pace, and will come on plenty for this. She will stay another furlong.
**Ruby's Dream** again ran her race and, as she is well exposed, is the benchmark for the form. She is well worth a switch to nurseries.
**Elsie Wagg(USA)** failed to lay up with the early gallop and found very little when asked to close on the leaders from halfway. This was again way below the form of her debut effort and connections will be hoping she can improve now she is eligible for handicaps.
**Match Ball(USA)** showed good early pace to race handily, but dropped out most tamely over two from home. This was a disappointing debut display, and although she should come on for this and could leave the form well behind on faster ground, her Lowther entry looks most optimistic. *Official explanation: jockey said filly was never travelling, possibly unsuited by the going*

## 3951 ALEXANDRE SAVILE ROW (S) STKS 6f
2:40 (2:40) (E ) 2-Y-O **£3,250** (£1,000; £500; £250) **Stalls** Low

Form RPR
5 **1** **Premier Times**[12] [3577] 2-8-11.... ACulhane 3 52
(MDHammond) *outpcd and pushed along after 1f: hdwy 1/2-way: rdn to ld ent last: styd on* **11/8**[1]
6333 **2** *2 1/2* **Danehill Fairy (IRE)**[10] [3620] 2-8-6....(b) JFanning 2 39
(MrsADuffield) *cl up: led 2f out: rdn and hdd ent last: kpt on same pce* **11/2**[3]
05 **3** *3/4* **Singhalongtasveer**[39] [2755] 2-8-11.... SWKelly 5 42
(WStorey) *dwlt: sn chsng ldrs: rdn 2f out and kpt on same pce* **25/1**
060 **4** *nk* **Tip Toes (IRE)**[4] [3824] 2-7-13.... BO'Neill(7) 1 39+
(MRChannon) *sn outpcd and bhd: hdwy 1/2wy: swtchd rt 2f out: rdn and kpt on ins last* **8/1**
0000 **5** *1 3/4* **Timmy**[14] [3506] 2-8-8....(b[1]) TEaves(3) 6 36
(MESowersby) *led: rdn along and hdd 2f out: wknd ent last* **40/1**
0606 **6** *1/2* **Miss Good Time**[16] [3444] 2-8-6.... MFenton 7 29
(JGGiven) *dwlt: sn pushed along and in tch on outer: rdn 2f out and sn btn* **9/4**[2]
5005 **7** *14* **Northern Revoque (IRE)**[8] [3709] 2-8-6....(b[1]) RWinston 4 —
(ABerry) *chsd ldrs: rdn along over 2f out: sn wknd* **20/1**

1m 19.28s (6.38) **Going Correction** +0.525s/f (Yiel) **7 Ran SP% 110.4**
Speed ratings: **78,74,73,73,70 70,51**CSF £8.66 TOTE £2.60: £1.60, £2.60; EX 9.20.The winner was bought in for 8,000gns.
**Owner** Pentland Times Partnership **Bred** Mrs M Lingwood **Trained** Middleham, N Yorks

**FOCUS**
A dire juvenile seller that saw the field finish well strung out, and the time was very moderate, even for this low level.

**NOTEBOOK**
**Premier Times** , dropping in class, showed the benefit of his debut and relished this extra furlong. He did his job nicely and may be capable back up in grade, but was beating very little this time and he looks only modest.
**Danehill Fairy(IRE)** held every chance, but could not go with the winner late on. She is well exposed and sets the standard for the form.
**Singhalongtasveer** was staying on best of all having made a sluggish start. This was her best effort to date and she is now eligible to run in nurseries.
**Tip Toes(IRE)** improved on her latest effort on this easy ground, but is short of acceleration and may appreciate a longer trip.
**Miss Good Time** ran a very poor race and has now run out of excuses.

## 3952 LEEDS HOSPITAL FUND H'CAP 1m 2f
3:15 (3:15) (D ) (0-80,79) 3-Y-O+ **£5,850** (£1,800; £900; £450) **Stalls** High

Form RPR
2314 **1** **Olivia Rose (IRE)**[21] [3327] 5-9-13 **79**.... NCallan 7 89
(JPearce) *trckd ldrs: hdwy 3f out: rdn and squeezed through on inner to ld ent last: r.o* **13/2**
5-45 **2** *1 1/2* **Nevada Desert (IRE)**[52] [2410] 4-9-5 **71**.... DeanMcKeown 10 78
(RMWhitaker) *keen: led: rdn along 2f out: edgd lft over 1f out: hdd ent last: kpt on same pce* **11/2**[3]
4252 **3** *2 1/2* **Tedsdale Mac**[8] [3714] 5-8-5 **57**.... FNorton 6 60
(NBycroft) *trckd ldrs: effrt over 2f out: sn rdn and satyed on ins last* **7/1**
0-24 **4** *1 1/4* **Strider**[49] [2472] 3-9-1 **77**.... RWinston 1 78
(SirMichaelStoute) *keen: cl up: rdn over 2f out: drvn and wknd over 1f out* **7/2**[1]
1612 **5** *1 1/2* **Rotuma (IRE)**[14] [3534] 5-9-4 **73**....(b) LEnstone(3) 3 71
(MDods) *trckd ldrs: hdwy 3f out: rdn 2f out: sn one pce* **9/2**[2]
2003 **6** *3* **Megan's Magic**[31] [2982] 4-9-2 **68**.... SWKelly 2 61
(WStorey) *dwlt: sn in tch: effrt 3f out: rdn 2f out and sn no imp* **9/2**[2]
32-0 **7** *8* **Fanling Lady**[53] [2392] 3-8-11 **73**.... ANicholls 8 52
(DNicholls) *a rr* **33/1**
0000 **8** *5* **Broadway Score (USA)**[15] [3470] 6-8-13 **70**....(b[1]) PMulrennan(5) 5 41
(MWEasterby) *chsd ldng pair: rdn along 4f out: sn wknd and bhd fnl 2f* **14/1**
4250 **9** *3/4* **Champain Sands (IRE)**[30] [3005] 5-7-12 **55**.... BSwarbrick(5) 4 25
(WMBrisbourne) *keen: hld up in tch: hdwy on outer 4f out: rdn along 3f out and sn wknd* **16/1**

2m 12.32s (4.32) **Going Correction** +0.525s/f (Yiel)
**WFA** 3 from 4yo+ 10lb **9 Ran SP% 115.3**
Speed ratings: **103,101,99,98,97 95,88,84,84**CSF £41.99 CT £258.74 TOTE £5.00: £1.90, £2.50, £2.10; EX 60.10.
**Owner** A Watford **Bred** Dermot Cantillon **Trained** Newmarket, Suffolk

**FOCUS**
A modest affair run at just a steady gallop.

**NOTEBOOK**
**Olivia Rose(IRE)** won tidily and produced a personal best to score. She has been in excellent form since her reappearance this year and is obviously much improved, with all ground seemingly coming alike to her. This game mare may have more to offer still.
**Nevada Desert(IRE)** again turned in a sound effort, but lost his chance by racing too freely early and then hanging under pressure late in the day. He has been running well of late without winning and, despite being high enough in the weights, he can find a similar event.
**Tedsdale Mac** was not disgraced, but lacked a change of gear when it mattered over this longer trip.
**Strider**, disappointing on his handicap debut last time, again ran below expectations and is clearly limited.
**Rotuma(IRE)** could only find the one pace late on and ran as though he is now weighted to the hilt.
**Megan's Magic**, third behind the winner off this mark last time, was unsuited by the lack of early pace and never threatened. She can do better, but needs everything to fall right in her races.
**Champain Sands(IRE)** *Official explanation: jockey said gelding was unsuited by the going*

## 3953 RIPON BELL-RINGER STKS (H'CAP) 1m 4f 60y
3:45 (3:46) (D ) (0-85,85) 3-Y-O+ **£13,780** (£4,240; £2,120; £1,060) **Stalls** High

Form RPR
2231 **1** **Lets Roll**[13] [3561] 3-8-7 **76**.... DeanMcKeown 6 89
(CWThornton) *hld up: smooth hdwy over 3f out: led ent last: pushed clr* **3/1**[1]

1101 **2** *2* **Party Ploy**[5] 3794 6-8-8 **68** 5ex........................................ LEnstone(3) 4 78
(KRBurke) *cl up: led 31/2f out and sn pushed clr: rdn 2f out: hdd ent last: kpt on: no ch w wnr* **7/1**[3]
0056 **3** *7* **Dunaskin (IRE)**[8] 3716 4-9-5 **81**........................................ PMulrennan(5) 7 81
(DEddy) *led: rdn along 4f out: sn hdd and drvn: kpt on same pce fnl 2f* **8/1**
0544 **4** *1/2* **Sporting Gesture**[24] 3199 7-9-4 **75**........................................ DaleGibson 8 75
(MWEasterby) *chsd ldrs: rdn along 3f out: kpt ons ame pce fnl 2f* **10/1**
2043 **5** *3* **Aleron (IRE)**[7] 3731 6-9-1 **72**........................................(p) NCallan 2 67
(JJQuinn) *trckd ldrs: effrt 4f out: sn rdn along and wknd wl over 2f out* **7/1**[3]
0343 **6** *2 1/2* **Stallone**[35] 2895 7-8-13 **73**........................................ TEaves(3) 10 65
(NWilson) *dwlt: bhd and pushed along 1/2-way: sme hdwy u.p 3f out: nvr a factor* **14/1**
3520 **7** *7* **Northside Lodge (IRE)**[9] 3678 6-9-5 **76**........................................ MFenton 9 58
(PWHarris) *a towards rr* **12/1**
3-23 **8** *1 1/2* **Magnetic Pole**[62] 2144 3-9-2 **85**........................................ RWinston 1 65
(SirMichaelStoute) *keen hld: dwlt: sn chsng ldrs: rdn along over 3f out and sn btn* **9/2**[2]
4024 **9** *1/2* **Rutters Rebel (IRE)**[12] 3584 3-7-12 **72**........................................ BSwarbrick(5) 5 51
(GASwinbank) *in tch: rdn along over 4f out and sn wknd* **20/1**
4002 **10** *dist* **Baileys Dancer**[22] 3274 3-8-6 **75**........................................(b[1]) JFanning 3 —
(MJohnston) *chsd ldrs: rdn along over 4f out and sn btn* **10/1**

2m 42.71s (2.81) **Going Correction** +0.525s/f (Yiel)
**WFA** 3 from 4yo+ 12lb **10** Ran SP% **116.6**
Speed ratings: **111,109,105,104,102 101,96,95,95,**—CSF £24.13 CT £153.40 TOTE £4.10: £1.70, £3.40, £2.50; EX 32.70.
**Owner** A Crute and Partners **Bred** G G A Gregson **Trained** Middleham Moor, N Yorks

**FOCUS**
A good contest for the grade run at a solid pace in which the first two came clear.

**NOTEBOOK**
**Lets Roll** followed up his recent Redcar success off this 3lb higher mark and won readily. He has been much improved since stepping up in trip and won this in the style of a progressive sort, so would be very hard to pass if going for the hat-trick under a penalty.
**Party Ploy** ran freely up with the pace and got the run of the race, but had no chance with the winner. He still ran with credit and finished a clear second best, yet will find life tougher now however, off his higher future mark.
**Dunaskin(IRE)** dictated as he prefers, but was readily brushed aside by the first two, and may need to drop back in trip before he enters the winner's enclosure once again.
**Sporting Gesture** ran his race on ground less than ideal, but left the impression he needs some respite from the Handicapper.
**Magnetic Pole** was far too keen after missing the break and found nil under pressure some way from home. This was a disappointing handicap debut, but he may be capable of better in time.

## 3954 HEUSTON HOSPITALITY MAIDEN H'CAP STKS 6f
**4:20** (4:21) (E ) (0-70,70) 3-Y-0+ **£4,225** (£1,300; £650; £325) **Stalls** Low

Form RPR
0062 **1** **Red Monarch (IRE)**[33] 2932 3-8-13 **55**........................................ NCallan 8 63
(PABlockley) *mde virtually all stands side: rdn clr and edgd rt ent last: styd on* **6/1**[3]
5003 **2** *2* **Uhuru Peak**[10] 3624 3-8-7 **54**........................................ PMulrennan(5) 10 56
(MWEasterby) *trckd ldrs stands side: hdwy 2f out: rdn to chse wnr ins last: kpt on* **12/1**
3000 **3** *hd* **Pride Of Kinloch**[28] 3098 4-9-4 **55**........................................ FNorton 12 56
(JHetherton) *chsd ldrs stands side: rdn and swtchd lft over 1f out: kpt on u.p ins last* **7/1**
0022 **4** *3/4* **Lord Baskerville**[2] 3877 3-8-7 **54**........................................ MLawson(5) 20 53
(WStorey) *c lose up far side: rdn to ld that gp 2f out: kpt on* **5/1**[1]
5U30 **5** *1/2* **Killerby Nicko**[15] 3471 3-8-5 **47** ow1........................................(b) JCarroll 19 45
(TDEasterby) *prom far side: rdn 2f out: kpt on* **9/1**
630 **6** *hd* **Pure Imagination (IRE)**[15] 3487 3-9-8 **64**........................................ DeanMcKeown 5 61
(JMBradley) *cl up stands side: rdn 2f out: one pce appr last* **16/1**
50-0 **7** *1 3/4* **Fleet Anchor**[15] 3486 3-9-4 **60**........................................ RFfrench 18 52
(JMBradley) *chsd ldrs far side: rdn 2f out: kpt on same pce* **25/1**
0-00 **8** *1/2* **Fizzy Lizzy**[19] 3381 4-7-5 **35** oh1........................................ LeanneKershaw(7) 7 25
(JeddO'Keeffe) *chsd ldrs stands side: rdn 2f out: grad wknd* **25/1**
5036 **9** *3/4* **Firebird Rising (USA)**[14] 3517 3-9-5 **61**........................................ MFenton 4 49
(TDBarron) *hld up stands side: hdwy 2f out: sn rdn and no imp* **8/1**
/000 **10** *nk* **Dispol Verity**[8] 3710 4-8-3 **40**........................................ PMQuinn 3 27
(WMBrisbourne) *chsd ldrs stands side: rdn along 2f out: sn wknd* **28/1**
000- **11** *1/2* **Rue De Paris**[312] 4792 4-8-4 **44** ow2........................................ TEaves(3) 13 30
(JohnAHarris) *led far side gp: rdn along and hdd 2f out: sn wknd* **66/1**
-536 **12** *1 1/4* **Palvic Moon**[8] 3711 3-9-4 **60**........................................ JFanning 1 42
(CSmith) *cl up stands side: rdn alon g 2f out: sn wknd* **16/1**
-000 **13** *1/2* **Sujosise**[10] 3624 3-8-0 **42**........................................ PFessey 17 22
(JJQuinn) *chsd ldrs far side: rdn along 2f out: sn wknd* **25/1**
035 **14** *1/2* **Ice Planet**[77] 1771 3-9-13 **69**........................................ RWinston 9 48
(DNicholls) *in tch stands side: rdn along over 2f out: sn wknd* **16/1**
0-56 **15** *nk* **Scooby Dooby Do**[22] 3267 3-9-4 **60**........................................ VHalliday 16 38
(RMWhitaker) *chsd ldrs far side: rdn along over 2f out: sn wknd* **20/1**
0022 **16** *1* **Beaver Diva**[19] 3364 3-7-7 **40**........................................ BSwarbrick(5) 15 15
(WMBrisbourne) *hld up far side: hdwy whn nt clr run 2f out: sn rdn and btn* **11/2**[2]
0000 **17** *17* **Tanaffus**[103] 1268 4-8-10 **47**........................................(b[1]) ACulhane 11 —
(DWChapman) *racd stands side: bhd fr 1/2-way* **50/1**

1m 16.08s (3.18) **Going Correction** +0.525s/f (Yiel)
**WFA** 3 from 4yo 5lb **17** Ran SP% **133.7**
Speed ratings: **99,96,96,95,94 94,91,91,90,89 89,87,86,86,85 84,61**CSF £77.52 CT £541.89 TOTE £6.60: £2.30, £2.50, £2.20, £2.10; EX 69.60.
**Owner** Bigwigs Bloodstock III **Bred** Michael Dalton **Trained** Southwell, Notts

**FOCUS**
A weak event which saw the field split into two groups and the stands' side came out on top.

**NOTEBOOK**
**Red Monarch(IRE)** won well under a positive ride and made amends for his narrow defeat at Brighton last time, when making his handicap debut. This softer ground very much suited, and it would be a surprise if he was not placed to score again while at this end of the handicap.
**Uhuru Peak** put up another improved display and finished his race well. This ground was no problem and he looks to be nearing that elusive first success.
**Pride Of Kinloch** turned in a sound effort from his draw, but could not quicken when it mattered. He is an in-and-out performer who may need a drop into a lower grade before scoring.
**Lord Baskerville** came out the best of those to race on the far side and was far from disgraced. He is better on faster ground and is in good form at present.
**Killerby Nicko** improved a touch for this drop in trip and easier surface.
**Firebird Rising(USA)** *Official explanation: jockey said filly missed the break*
**Palvic Moon** *Official explanation: jockey said saddle slipped*
**Ice Planet** *Official explanation: jockey said colt hung right handed*

**Beaver Diva**, who looked quirky when finishing second at Ayr last time, would have finished closer but for meeting trouble two from home, but still found nil for pressure when in the clear, and was slightly disappointing.

## 3955 DOBSON GASKETS C & J ANNIVERSARY MEDIAN AUCTION MAIDEN STKS 1m 1f
**4:55** (4:57) (F ) 3-Y-0 **£4,225** (£1,300; £650; £325) **Stalls** High

Form RPR
2522 **1** **My Paris**[11] 3610 3-9-0 80........................................ NCallan 4 73+
(KARyan) *cl up: led wl over 4f out: pushed clr 3f out: easily* **10/11**[1]
466 **2** *5* **Aston Lad**[10] 3625 3-8-9 45........................................ PMulrennan(5) 3 63
(MDHammond) *dwlt and bhd: hdwy 4f out: styd on fnl 2f: no ch w wnr* **66/1**
0050 **3** *8* **Rigonza**[13] 3561 3-9-0 65........................................ DAllan 7 47
(TDEasterby) *chsd ldrs: hdwy to chse wnr 3f out: sn rdn and one pce* **25/1**
0-40 **4** *5* **Vamose (IRE)**[64] 2093 3-9-0 66........................................ MFenton 5 37
(MissGayKelleway) *led: rdnalong and hdd wl over 4f out: sn wknd* **10/1**[3]
0-3 **5** *13* **Bien Good**[10] 3625 3-8-6........................................ TEaves(3) 8 6
(MrsMReveley) *s.i.s: a bhd* **20/1**
0-00 **6** *1 3/4* **Chicago Bond (USA)**[15] 3473 3-8-9 63........................................ DMcGaffin 1 3
(BSmart) *a bhd* **50/1**
4423 **7** *dist* **Little Bob**[21] 3297 3-9-0 75........................................ JFanning 6 —
(JDBethell) *trckd ldng pair: cocked jaw and rn out home turn: virtually p.u after* **6/4**[2]

1m 58.98s (5.13) **Going Correction** +0.525s/f (Yiel) **7** Ran SP% **113.5**
Speed ratings: **98,93,86,82,70 68,**—CSF £77.31 TOTE £1.90: £1.20, £10.50; EX 36.60 Place 6 £57.53, Place 5 £29.82.
**Owner** J And A Spensley **Bred** J And A Spensley **Trained** Hambleton, N Yorks

**FOCUS**
A maiden lacking any strength in depth and the form looks unreliable.

**NOTEBOOK**
**My Paris**, who has had more seconds than Oliver Twist this year, was left with a simple task when his main rival lost all chance on the home turn, but still did his job well and gained a deserved success. His confidence will be high now and he proved he can go on soft ground, but is not the best treated on a mark of 80, so is not one to lump on for a follow-up bid back in handicaps.
**Aston Lad** is flattered by his finishing position, but still ran on to take a clear second and at least showed a bit more for this drop back in trip. He will fare better when he enters a handicap over this trip.
**Rigonza**, who played up at the start in a first-time visor last time, was a never dangerous third and is another flattered by her finishing position.
**Chicago Bond(USA)** *Official explanation: jockey said filly was unsuited by the ground*
**Little Bob** gave himself no chance when cocking his jaw and completely failing to handle the home turn. Although he ran well at this track on his reappearance in April, he will best kept to left-handed tracks, and is well worth another chance in something similar.
T/Plt: £43.20 to a £1 stake. Pool: £36,816.95. 620.75 winning tickets. T/Qpdt: £17.60 to a £1 stake. Pool: £2,158.10. 90.55 winning tickets. JR

3956 - 3958a (Foreign Racing) - See Raceform Interactive

# 3349 CURRAGH (R-H)
Saturday, July 17

**OFFICIAL GOING: Good**

## 3959a LADBROKES.COM INTERNATIONAL STKS (GROUP 3) 1m
**4:00** (4:01) 3-Y-0 **£34,383** (£10,088; £4,806; £1,637)

RPR
**1** **Red Feather (IRE)**[14] 3547 3-8-11 106........................................(t) NGMcCullagh 7 109
(EdwardLynam, Ire) *sn led: rdn clr fr 1 1/2f out: styd on wl fnl f* **8/1**
**2** *2 1/2* **Trefflich (GER)**[21] 3334 3-9-0........................................ MJKinane 5 106
(JohnMOxx, Ire) *trckd ldr in 2nd: rdn fr 1 1/2f out: sn no imp: kpt on same pce* **7/1**[3]
**3** *2* **Wathab (IRE)**[104] 1256 3-9-0 115........................................(t) PJSmullen 3 102
(DKWeld, Ire) *chsd ldrs: mainly 4th: rdn and wnt 3rd 1f out: no imp and kpt on same pce fnl f* **6/1**[2]
**4** *1* **Jazz Scene (IRE)**[14] 3542 3-9-0........................................ KJManning 4 99
(MRChannon) *trckd ldrs in 3rd: rdn fr over 2f out: sn no imp: 4th fr 1f out* **10/1**
**5** *3/4* **One Cool Cat (USA)**[77] 1764 3-9-7 118........................................ JPSpencer 2 105
(APO'Brien, Ire) *rr: impr into 4th and rdn 1 1/2f out: sn no imp: hmpd cl home* **1/2**[1]
**6** *hd* **Alexander Duchess (IRE)**[21] 3328 3-8-11 100........................................ DJCondon 6 94
(JGBurns, Ire) *chsd ldrs: mainly 5th: rdn and no imp fr under 2f out* **16/1**
**7** *4* **Kanisfluh**[55] 2328 3-8-11 89........................................(bt) WMLordan 1 85
(TStack, Ire) *chsd ldrs: mainly 6th: rdn in rr and no imp fr 3f out* **20/1**

1m 41.0s **Going Correction** +0.075s/f (Good) **7** Ran SP% **124.3**
Speed ratings: **112,109,107,106,105 105,105**CSF £67.18 TOTE £11.60: £2.40, £2.80; DF 51.00.
**Owner** Lady O'Reilly **Bred** Michael Dalton **Trained** Dunshaughlin, Co Meath

**FOCUS**
A fair time for the grade, but very much a tactical affair in which the first two were first and second throughout.

**NOTEBOOK**
**Red Feather(IRE)** was given a canny front-running ride and was not going to be caught when quickening from a furlong and a half down.
**Trefflich(GER)** built on an ordinary maiden win here. He ran second throughout and still managed a bit more pace inside the last.
**Wathab(IRE)** has yet to reproduce his juvenile form but there is plenty of time for him to peak, although he does not look worth anything like his 115 rating.
**Jazz Scene(IRE)** was making no impression on the first pair from two furlongs down.
**One Cool Cat(USA)** performed dismally, missing the kick and never at any stage looking likely to get involved. He was said to have a much slower than normal heartbeat when examined after the race, and his future is now in the balance, with retirement looking the likely option. He was an outstanding juvenile but could hardly have been more disappointing this year.

## 3961a LADBROKE ROCKINGHAM H'CAP (PREMIER HANDICAP) 5f
**5:00** (5:02) 3-Y-0+ **£42,323** (£13,450; £6,408; £2,183)

RPR
**1** **Osterhase (IRE)**[20] 3350 5-10-1 110........................................(b) FMBerry 13 119
(JEMulhern, Ire) *trckd across towards rail and led sn after 1 f: rdn and strly pressed over 1f out: styd on wl fnl f* **3/1**[1]
**2** *1 1/2* **Jacks Estate (IRE)**[20] 3351 9-8-4 92........................................ CPGeoghegan(7) 15 96
(AdrianMcguinness, Ire) *chsd ldrs: 4th 1/2-way: rdn in 2nd over 1f out: sn no imp: kpt on same pce* **20/1**

3 1 1/2 **Majestic Times (IRE)**[20] 3351 4-8-2 83 NGMcCullagh 17 81
(LiamMcateer, Ire) *chsd ldrs: rdn in 4th over 1f out: no imp and kpt on same pce fnl f* **14/1**

4 1 **Lone Plainsman**[7] 3762 3-7-7 83 DJMoran(5) 1 78
(PFO'Donnell, Ire) *sn led on rail: hdd after 1 f: rdn in 3rd over 1f out: kpt on one pce fnl f* **14/1**

5 hd **Moon Unit (IRE)**[20] 3350 3-9-3 102 DMGrant 5 96
(HRogers, Ire) *chsd ldrs: rdn in 5th and kpt on same pce fr over 1f out* **8/1**[3]

6 1/2 **Step Back (IRE)**[22] 3285 11-8-7 88 PJSmullen 6 80
(GerardKeane, Ire) *chsd ldrs: 6th 1/2-way: rdn and no imp fr 2f out* **14/1**

7 shd **Libras Child (IRE)**[20] 3351 5-8-4 85 ow1 MJKinane 4 77
(PDelaney, Ire) *chsd ldrs: 8th and rdn fr 1 1/2f out: kpt on wout threatening fnl f* **7/1**[2]

8 nk **Budelli (IRE)**[20] 3351 7-7-9 83 (b) RPCleary(7) 9 74
(MHalford, Ire) *towards rr: kpt on wout threatening fnl f* **14/1**

9 3/4 **Tubbertown Rose (IRE)**[10] 3646 6-7-9 79 (b) CatherineGannon(3) 14 67
(PeterCasey, Ire) *prom: mid-div bef 1/2-way: rdn and no imp fr 2f out* **16/1**

10 hd **Tigim (IRE)**[10] 3646 5-8-1 85 MCHussey(3) 18 72
(PeterHenley, Ire) *chsd ldrs and outer: rdn and no imp fr 1/2-way* **12/1**

11 hd **Assigh Lady (IRE)**[20] 3351 6-7-9 83 BSHughes(7) 2 70
(DesmondMcdonogh, Ire) *mid-div: 9th and rdn fr 2f out: sn no imp and kpt on same pce* **16/1**

12 nk **Halmahera (IRE)**[22] 3266 9-9-3 98 (b) JPSpencer 8 83
(KARyan) *mid-div: rdn fr 2f out: sn no imp* **7/1**[2]

13 hd **Galloway Boy (IRE)**[10] 3646 7-7-7 79 (tp) HelenKeohane(5) 7 64
(SJMahon, Ire) *a towards rr: nvr a threat* **25/1**

14 nk **Serov (IRE)**[22] 3285 6-8-3 84 (b) WMLordan 12 68
(TStack, Ire) *mid-div best: no imp fr 2f out* **12/1**

15 3/4 **Cupids Ray (IRE)**[17] 3431 3-7-12 83 TPO'Shea 11 64
(MHalford, Ire) *a towards rr: nvr a threat* **12/1**

16 nk **Raining**[22] 3285 6-8-3 84 JAHeffernan 3 64
(TGMccourt, Ire) *chsd ldrs: rdn and no imp fr 2f out* **12/1**

17 1/2 **Lupine (IRE)**[10] 3646 5-8-7 88 KJManning 10 66
(GWRobinson, Ire) *mid-div best: nvr a threat: no imp fr over 1f out* **16/1**

18 1/2 **Mombassa (IRE)**[10] 3648 4-9-5 100 DPMcDonogh 16 76
(EdwardLynam, Ire) *chsd ldrs: 5th and rdn fr 2f out: wknd fnl f* **14/1**

58.60 secs **Going Correction** -0.15s/f (Firm)
**WFA** 3 from 4yo+ 4lb **18** Ran SP% **151.5**
Speed ratings: **117,114,112,110,110 109,109,109,109,109 109,109,109,109,109 109,109,109**CSF £89.92 CT £631.04 TOTE £3.70: £1.80, £4.00, £4.10, £4.90; DF 225.20.
**Owner** Michael Rosenfeld **Bred** E Kopica & M Rosenfeld **Trained** the Curragh, Co Kildare

**FOCUS**
A decent sprint and a fine performance from the winner in a good time.

**NOTEBOOK**
**Osterhase(IRE)** underlined just what an improved sprinter he is. Soon in front on the inner from a high draw, he ran on strongly inside the last for what will be his final run as a handicapper.
**Jacks Estate(IRE)** also came from a bad draw but was in contention from halfway. For his age he showed plenty of zest inside the last, although never seriously threatening the winner.
**Majestic Times(IRE)** has done well for a 5,000 gns cast-off out of Tim Easterby's, and ran on strongly inside the last furlong.
**Lone Plainsman** improved on his maiden win the previous weekend.
**Halmahera(IRE)** was under pressure two furlongs down and found nothing inside the last.

3960 - 3962a (Foreign Racing) - See Raceform Interactive

## 3863 MAISONS-LAFFITTE (R-H)
Saturday, July 17

**OFFICIAL GOING: Good**

### 3963a PRIX MAURICE DE NIEUIL (GROUP 2) 1m 7f
3:20 (4:00) 4-Y-0+ **£44,736** (£16,268; £7,764; £5,176)

RPR

1 **Forestier (FR)**[55] 2337 4-9-2 C-PLemaire 1 111
(EDanel, France) *made all, pressed 2f out, ridden and ran on well to line 1 1/2f out* 1

2 2 **Royal Fantasy (GER)**[258] 5901 4-8-13 WMongil 4 106
(HSteinmetz, Germany) *unruly start, raced in 2nd, disputing 2nd straight, effort to press leader 2f out, kept on one pace*

3 shd **Clear Thinking**[20] 3358 4-8-12 CSoumillon 5 105
(AFabre, France) *racd in 3rd, tk cl order app str, disp 2nd str, rdn 2f out & outpcd, rallied & styd on fr 1f out, just missed 2nd* 3

4 1 1/2 **Risk Seeker**[47] 2533 4-9-2 OPeslier 3 108
(ELellouche, France) *held up in last, effort 2f out, never in challenging position* 2

3m 26.6s **4** Ran SP% **122.1**
Speed ratings: .
**Owner** Mme R-J Wattinne **Bred** Mme Rene Wattinne **Trained** France

**FOCUS**
The distance of this race was increased from 1m 6f to 1m 7f following concern over the state of the home turn following the first race.

**NOTEBOOK**
**Forestier(FR)** benefited from an uncontested lead, but was probably the best horse in the race anyway. Still very much on the upgrade, he will next be seen in the Group Two Prix Kergorlay at Deauville on August 22.
**Royal Fantasy(GER)** has given trouble at the start before, and did so here on her first run this season. Produced an effort early in the straight, but could make no impression on the winner.
**Clear Thinking** was doing all his best work in the closing stages after being outpaced two furlongs from home. However the finishing distances flattered him, as he was never really a factor in the race.
**Risk Seeker** was held up in last, and was never put into the race with any conviction. He is capable of far better form given a more positive approach.

3964 - (Foreign Racing) - See Raceform Interactive

## 3956 CURRAGH (R-H)
Sunday, July 18

**OFFICIAL GOING: Good to firm (good on sprint track)**

### 3965a DUBAI DUTY FREE ANGLESEY STKS (GROUP 3) 6f 63y
2:40 (2:40) 2-Y-0 **£34,383** (£10,088; £4,806; £1,637)

RPR

1 **Oratorio (IRE)**[33] 2954 2-9-0 JAHeffernan 4 109
(APO'Brien, Ire) *cl up in 2nd: led 2f out: rdn clr fr over 1f out: kpt on wl* **9/1**

2 1 **Cougar Cat (USA)**[31] 2996 2-9-0 JPSpencer 3 106
(APO'Brien, Ire) *hld up in rr: hdwy under 2f out: 4th 1f out: kpt on wl wout troubling wnr* **9/2**[3]

3 nk **Indesatchel (IRE)**[23] 3283 2-9-0 KFallon 5 105
(DavidWachman, Ire) *hld up in tch: 5th 1/2-way: prog 2f out: 2nd 1f out: kpt on same pce u.p* **2/1**[1]

4 1 1/2 **Turnkey**[33] 2954 2-9-0 TEDurcan 8 101
(MRChannon) *trckd ldrs on far side: 4th 2f out: kpt on same pce* **7/2**[2]

5 3 1/2 **Kay Two (IRE)**[10] 3685 2-9-0 PJSmullen 2 90
(MsFMCrowley, Ire) *led: hdd 2f out: no ex fr over 1f out* **14/1**

6 1/2 **Slip Dance (IRE)**[22] 3316 2-8-11 KMcEvoy 6 86
(EamonTyrrell, Ire) *chsd ldrs in 3rd: rdn 2f out: sn no ex* **13/2**

7 2 1/2 **Dance Night (IRE)**[31] 2996 2-9-0 LDettori 1 81
(BAMcmahon) *chsd ldrs on stands rail: 4th halway: wknd fr 2f out* **14/1**

8 1/2 **Rare Cross (IRE)**[24] 3253 2-8-11 FMBerry 7 77
(JosephGMurphy, Ire) *chsd ldrs to over 2f out: sn no ex and wknd* **25/1**

1m 15.7s **Going Correction** -0.25s/f (Firm) **8** Ran SP% **114.3**
Speed ratings: **102,100,100,98,93 92,89,88**CSF £48.99 TOTE £17.60: £4.20, £1.90, £1.10; DF 50.60.
**Owner** Mrs John Magnier **Bred** Barronstown Stud & Orpendale **Trained** Ballydoyle, Co Tipperary

**FOCUS**
A race dominated by the O'Brien pair run in a decent time and the form look solid.

**NOTEBOOK**
**Oratorio(IRE)**, arguably with slight better form than his stable companion Cougar Cat, always had the call over the shorter priced Ballydoyle runner. In front over two furlongs out, he ran on strongly to improve on his Coventry Stakes running. He looks progressive.
**Cougar Cat(USA)** was out the back from the start. Making headway on the outer after failing to get the clearest of runs, he ran on well enough and he too confirmed he was better than his Royal Ascot run.
**Indesatchel(IRE)** had been impressive on his debut over seven furlongs here but was unable to find the pace to trouble the winner from a furlong out and wilted near the finish. He will appreciate another step up in trip.
**Turnkey** could not build on his Coventry fifth and was just a one-paced fourth from two furlongs down. He may have found the ground a bit too fast for him.
**Kay Two(IRE)** took them along until the winner went by.
**Slip Dance(IRE)** found this a lot hotter than when winning at Newmarket.
**Dance Night(IRE)** was readily outpaced over the last two furlongs.

### 3967a EMIRATES AIRLINE MINSTREL STKS (GROUP 3) 7f
3:40 (3:40) 4-Y-0+ **£36,619** (£10,704; £5,070; £1,690)

RPR

1 **Trade Fair**[22] 3318 4-9-0 RHughes 6 116
(RCharlton) *settled 3rd: hdwy under 2f out: led 1f out: r.o wl: comf* **13/8**[1]

2 1 1/2 **One More Round (USA)**[84] 1647 6-9-0 108 PJSmullen 3 112
(DKWeld, Ire) *sn 4th: prog 2f out: 2nd and chal 1f out: kpt on wl without troubling wnr* **10/1**

3 1/2 **Millennium Force**[8] 3730 6-9-0 TEDurcan 5 111
(MRChannon) *chsd ldrs: 6th and rdn under 3f out: styd on wl fr over 1f out* **9/1**

4 1 **Naahy**[22] 3318 4-9-3 106 LDettori 4 111
(MRChannon) *led: strly pressed 1 1/2f out: hdd 1f out: no ex cl home* **8/1**

5 3/4 **Latino Magic (IRE)**[21] 3355 4-9-0 106 RMBurke 1 106
(RJOsborne, Ire) *hld up: 5th and rdn 2 1/2f out: no imp: kpt on same pce* **13/2**[3]

6 1 1/2 **Tout Seul (IRE)**[45] 2623 4-9-0 SCarson 9 102
(RFJohnsonHoughton) *sn towards rr: no imp fr 3f out* **10/1**

7 4 **Sea Dart (USA)**[105] 1254 4-9-6 107 MJKinane 2 97
(JohnMOxx, Ire) *sn 2nd: rdn to chal 3f out: wknd fr over 2f out* **14/1**

8 nk **Avorado (IRE)**[21] 3351 6-9-3 103 KJManning 8 93
(JSBolger, Ire) *a bhd* **16/1**

9 7 **Abunawwas (IRE)**[46] 2603 4-9-0 109 DPMcDonogh 7 71
(KevinPrendergast, Ire) *a bhd* **11/2**[2]

1m 21.5s **Going Correction** -0.575s/f (Hard) **9** Ran SP% **118.7**
Speed ratings: **113,111,110,109,108 107,102,102,94**CSF £20.00 TOTE £3.00: £1.50, £4.50, £2.90; DF 67.70.
**Owner** K Abdulla **Bred** Juddmonte Farms **Trained** Beckhampton, Wilts

**FOCUS**
This was a fast run race, the time only eclipsed by Hawk Wing's record time.

**NOTEBOOK**
**Trade Fair** had an easy task on paper but was made work for it after leading just inside the last. Well on top at the line, he can go on again from this.
**One More Round(USA)**, without a win since September 2002, looked a serious threat early inside the last but failed to carry it through. Defeat was no disgrace but he is not going to be easy to place.
**Millennium Force**, third in this last season, is another that finds it difficult to win but he really got going all too late this time. The ability is still there.
**Naahy** did a solid job of front running , keeping on well when headed but just being pipped by his stable companion for third place on the line.
**Latino Magic(IRE)** found this a bit much although he was running on again at the finish.
**Tout Seul(IRE)** is still a long way from reproducing his old form and never looked a possibility.
**Sea Dart(USA)** dropped away in the last furlong and a half.
**Abunawwas(IRE)** was reported as being in "repiratory distress." *Official explanation: vet said colt finished distressed*

### 3968a DARLEY IRISH OAKS (GROUP 1) (FILLIES) 1m 4f
4:15 (4:15) 3-Y-0 **£167,042** (£54,366; £26,197; £9,295)

RPR

1 **Ouija Board**[44] 2640 3-9-0 KFallon 4 117
(EALDunlop) *dwlt: settled 5th: 4th and hdwy ent st: rdn to ld over 1 1/2f out: styd on wl: eased nr fin* **4/7**[1]

2 1 **Punctilious**[31] 2997 3-9-0 (t) LDettori 6 114
(SaeedBinSuroor) *chsd ldrs in 4th: 3rd into st: led 2f out: hdd over 1 1/2f out: kpt on u.p* **5/1**[3]

3 3/4 **Hazarista (IRE)**[65] 2102 3-9-0 100 MJKinane 5 113
(JohnMOxx, Ire) *hld up towards rr: 5th into st: 3rd and kpt on fr under 2f out* **20/1**

4 7 **All Too Beautiful (IRE)**[44] 2640 3-9-0 110 JPSpencer 7 102
(APO'Brien, Ire) *led: hdd after 4f: regained ld ent st: hdd & wknd qckly 2f out* **4/1**[2]

5 4 **Marinnette (IRE)**[23] 3288 3-9-0 79 JAHeffernan 1 95?
(MPSunderland, Ire) *nvr a factor: kpt on one pce st* **200/1**

6 4 **Danelissima (IRE)**[15] 3519 3-9-0 105 (b) KJManning 3 89
(JSBolger, Ire) *prom: led after 4f: clr 1/2-way: hdd ent st: wknd qckly* **16/1**

7 4 **Royal Tigress (USA)**[15] 3547 3-9-0 105 (b[1]) CO'Donoghue 2 83
(APO'Brien, Ire) *chsd ldrs in 3rd: wknd fr 4f out: trailing st* **50/1**

2m 28.2s **Going Correction** -0.475s/f (Firm) **7** Ran SP% **113.4**
Speed ratings: **117,116,115,111,108 105,103**CSF £3.83 TOTE £1.70: £1.10, £2.90; DF 4.70.

**Owner** Lord Derby **Bred** Stanley Estate And Stud Co **Trained** Newmarket, Suffolk

**FOCUS**

A fast-run race and a clear cut winner completing the Oaks double, having scored at Epsom.

**NOTEBOOK**

**Ouija Board** was not as visually impressive as at Epsom but there was only one winner from early in the straight. Pushed to the front with over a furlong and a half to race, she had it sewn up soon afterwards and was eased close home. She may now take on the colts in the Juddmonte at York.

**Punctilious** found nine lengths with the winner compared with Epsom. She appeared a lot happier on this more conventional track and acquitted herself well, but just was not able to match the winner's toe.

**Hazarista(IRE)** stepped up considerably on her Gowran and Cork successes but did not enjoy the clearest of runs before finishing strongly. The Yorkshire Oaks would be a possibility for her.

**All Too Beautiful(IRE)** was made plenty of use of and did not run anywhere near her Epsom form.

**Marinnette(IRE)**, a 79-rated maiden handicapper, ran the race of her career to date, staying on dourly without ever threatening.

**Danelissima(IRE)** was not ridden to her strengths and is better with more patient tactics. She dropped out very quickly in the straight.

**Royal Tigress(USA)** was no threat over the last quarter mile.

## 3969a KILBOY ESTATE STKS (LISTED RACE) (F&M) 1m 1f

**4:50** (4:52) 3-Y-O+ **£27,507** (£8,070; £3,845; £1,309)

RPR

1 **Tropical Lady (IRE)**[15] [3547] 4-9-11 112 ......... KJManning 12 109
(JSBolger, Ire) *hld up: 8th early st: hdwy 2f out: 4th whn swtchd over 1f out: 2nd under 1f out: sn led: drawing clr whn veered rt cl home* **4/5**[1]

2 1 ½ **Noahs Ark (IRE)**[46] [2604] 3-8-11 99 ......... PJSmullen 2 101
(DKWeld, Ire) *led: hdd briefly 2f out: regained ld over 1 1/2f out: hdd wl ins fnl f: no ex* **8/1**[3]

3 ½ **Kisses For Me (IRE)**[44] [2640] 3-8-11 95 ......... JPSpencer 8 100
(APO'Brien, Ire) *prom: 4th into st: 3rd 2f out: sltly hmpd over 1f out: kpt on* **9/1**

4 ¾ **Leonor Fini (IRE)**[32] [2993] 3-8-11 95 ......... DPMcDonogh 3 99
(KevinPrendergast, Ire) *prom: 3rd into st: dropped to 5th under 2f out: kpt on ins fnl f* **10/1**

5 2 **Treasure The Lady (IRE)**[91] [1485] 3-8-11 97 ......... MJKinane 5 95
(JohnMOxx, Ire) *trckd ldr in 2nd: led briefly 2f out: hdd over 1 1/2f out: wknd ins fnl f* **4/1**[2]

6 hd **Misty Mountain (IRE)**[25] [3214] 3-8-11 ......... WJO'Connor 11 94
(EdwardPHarty, Ire) *chsd ldrs in 6th: kpt on one pced st* **25/1**

7 shd **Jummana (FR)**[239] [6050] 4-9-6 ......... FMBerry 6 89
(NoelMeade, Ire) *chsd ldrs in 7th: wknd fr 2f out* **25/1**

8 2 ½ **Mollyputtheketelon (USA)**[11] [3649] 3-8-11 75 ......... TPO'Shea 10 89
(MHalford, Ire) *hld up in rr: kpt on one pced st* **25/1**

9 ¾ **Blue Reema (IRE)**[85] [1634] 4-9-6 96 ......... (tp) JAHeffernan 9 87
(MHalford, Ire) *towards rr: no imp st* **20/1**

10 1 ½ **Perfecto (IRE)**[16] [3501] 3-8-11 ......... KFallon 4 84
(DavidWachman, Ire) *chsd ldrs in 5th: wknd early st* **9/1**

11 ½ **Caldy Dancer (IRE)**[329] [4412] 3-8-11 ......... TEDurcan 1 83
(MRChannon) *a bhd* **10/1**

1m 50.4s **Going Correction** -0.475s/f (Firm)
**WFA** 3 from 4yo+ 9lb **11** Ran SP% **141.1**
Speed ratings: **116,114,114,113,111 111,109,109,108,107 106**CSF £10.66 TOTE £1.80: £1.20, £2.50, £2.90; DF 13.00.
**Owner** George J Kent **Bred** John Boden & Willie Kane **Trained** Coolcullen, Co Carlow

**NOTEBOOK**

**Tropical Lady(IRE)** continued her notable rate of progression through the ranks, making it five in a row. She had an easy task on official ratings and came through with a sustained run. She inconvenienced Kisses For Me over a furlong out and then, after leading inside the last, edged right onto the runner-up when in control.

**Noahs Ark(IRE)**tried to make all and kept coming back for more on two occasions when headed. She had to be snatched up close home but the Stewards did not give her the benefit of the doubt.

**Kisses For Me(IRE)** was struggling to hold her own position, let alone keep the winner hemmed in, when slightly hampered over a furlong down. She is improving.

**Leonor Fini(IRE)** needs further.

**Treasure The Lady(IRE)** flattered briefly two furlongs out but had not the pace to capitalise.

**Caldy Dancer(IRE)** was always struggling in the rear.

3970 - 3971a (Foreign Racing) - See Raceform Interactive

# 1656 FRANKFURT (L-H)

Sunday, July 18

**OFFICIAL GOING: Good**

## 3972a LOTTO HESSEN-POKAL (GROUP 3) 1m 2f

**3:45** (3:45) 3-Y-O+ **£22,535** (£9,155; £4,577; £2,465)

RPR

1 **Soldier Hollow**[31] [3030] 4-9-1 ......... ASuborics 3 113
(PSchiergen, Germany) *raced in 3rd, improved on turn to lead entering straight ( 2 1/2f out), comfortably.* 1

2 2 ½ **Anolitas (GER)**[28] [3134] 4-9-1 ......... (b) IFerguson 7 108
(UOstmann, Germany) *always close up in 4th, went 3rd 3f out, chased winner final 1 1/2f out, no impression*

3 ¾ **Winning Dash (GER)**[49] [2508] 4-9-1 ......... THellier 1 107
(WKujath, Germany) *set steady pace til headed by winner 2 1/2f out, kept on one pace.* 2

4 ½ **Morbidezza (GER)**[28] [3134] 4-8-11 ......... LHammer-Hansen 4 102
(MTrinker, Germany) *held up in rear, 6th straight, ran on final 2f, nearest at finish.*

5 1 **Near Honor (GER)**[21] [3357] 6-8-13 ......... JBojko 2 102
(TimGibson, Germany) *tracked leader to well over 2f out, 5th straight, one pace.*

6 ½ **Lotta (GER)**[56] [2341] 3-7-12 ......... NRichter 5 96
(AWohler, Germany) *always close up, 4th straight, no extra from 1 1/2f out.* 3

7 nk **Willingly (GER)**[28] [3134] 5-8-13 ......... KKerekes 6 101
(MTrybuhl) *always in last two.*

8 2 ½ **Fruhtau (GER)**[21] [3357] 7-8-13 ......... MO'Reilly 8 96
(HHorwart, Germany) *last most of way*

2m 10.16s (2.68)
**WFA** 3 from 4yo+ 10lb **8** Ran SP% **112.7**
Speed ratings: .
**Owner** Gestut Park Wiedingen **Bred** Car Colston Hall Stud **Trained** Germany



# KREFELD (R-H)

Sunday, July 18

**OFFICIAL GOING: Soft**

## 3973a WETTEN LEIP - GROSSER STUTENPREIS (LISTED) (F&M) 1m 3f

**4:05** (4:16) 3-Y-O+ **£8,451** (£3,099; £1,690; £845)

RPR

1 **Mariella (GER)** 3-8-7 ......... PRoberts 2 —
(CVonDerRecke, Germany)

2 6 **Top Call (GER)**[63] [2157] 3-8-7 ......... AStarke 11 —
(ASchutz, Germany) 2

3 ½ **Antique Rose (GER)**[24] 4-9-6 ......... WMongil 5 —
(HSteinmetz, Germany)

4 shd **Golden Rose (GER)** 4-9-6 ......... ADeVries 7 —
(HHesse, Germany)

5 3 ½ **La Sabana (FR)**[288] [5387] 4-9-6 ......... MAndrouin 1 —
(H-APantall, France)

6 2 **Kastoria (GER)**[16] [3504] 5-9-6 ......... ABoschert 9 —
(AWohler, Germany)

7 nk **Gymera (GER)** 3-8-7 ......... FilipMinarik 4 —
(ATrybuhl, Germany)

8 ¾ **Fleurie Domaine**[16] [3504] 5-9-6 ......... AGoritz 10 —
(MarioHofer, Germany)

9 6 **Quetena (GER)** 4-9-6 ......... AHelfenbein 8 —
(PRau, Germany) 1

10 23 **Nadeszhda**[11] [3638] 4-9-6 ......... FJohansson 6 —
(SirMarkPrescott) *raced in 3rd, 4th straight, soon ridden & beaten, eased final f.* 3

2m 21.17s
**WFA** 3 from 4yo+ 11lb **10** Ran SP% **131.4**
Speed ratings: .
**Owner** R Paulick **Bred** L & R Paulick **Trained** Germany

**NOTEBOOK**

**Nadeszhda** was all at sea on the soft ground and was eased right down in the closing stages.

# 3793 AYR (L-H)

Monday, July 19

**OFFICIAL GOING: Good to firm**

Wind: fresh across Weather: cloudy, bright

## 3974 FERGIE'S 50TH EUROPEAN BREEDERS FUND MAIDEN STKS 7f 50y

**2:15** (2:16) (D ) 2-Y-O **£5,525** (£1,700; £850; £425) **Stalls** Low

Form RPR

625 1 **Ballycroy Girl (IRE)**[10] [3718] 2-8-9 ......... EAhern 1 72
(ABailey) *hld up in tch: hdwy to ld appr fnl f: r.o wl* **20/1**

5 2 2 **Venetian King (USA)**[37] [2898] 2-9-0 ......... RWinston 5 72
(JHowardJohnson) *plld hrd: in tch: smooth hdwy to ld wl over 1f out: rdn and hdd appr fnl f: one pce ins last* **11/4**[2]

56 3 1 ¾ **Shujune Al Hawaa (IRE)**[17] [3476] 2-8-9 ......... ACulhane 3 63
(MRChannon) *stdd in tch: effrt 2f out: kpt on fnl f: nvr rchd ldrs* **7/1**[3]

4 nk **Highest Return (USA)** 2-9-0 ......... JFanning 6 67
(MJohnston) *chsd ldrs: led briefly 2f out: sn one pce* **11/4**[2]

622 5 1 ¾ **Tom Forest**[21] [3373] 2-9-0 ......... DHolland 7 63
(ACrook) *led 3f: cl up tl rdn and no ex fr 2f out* **2/1**[1]

6 6 5 **Geojimali**[7] [3793] 2-8-11 ......... NMackay[(3)] 4 51
(JSGoldie) *stdd s: nvr rchd ldrs* **66/1**

46 7 4 **King Henrik (USA)**[19] [3406] 2-9-0 ......... KDarley 2 41
(ACrook) *plld hrd: led after 3f to 2f out: sn btn* **33/1**

1m 33.49s (1.02) **Going Correction** -0.30s/f (Firm) **7** Ran SP% **108.4**
Speed ratings: **82,79,77,77,75 69,65**CSF £67.00 TOTE £19.10: £7.20, £2.10; EX 73.30.
**Owner** R T Collins **Bred** Martin Francis **Trained** Little Budworth, Cheshire

**FOCUS**

Not an easy maiden to assess with the time being slow, but the winner showed improved form.

**NOTEBOOK**

**Ballycroy Girl(IRE)** came with a steady run to score decisively and ought to stay a mile on this evidence. Her best previous effort came over this course and distance and the return to fast ground appeared to suit.

**Venetian King(USA)** was a bit on his toes in the paddock and was keen in the early stages. Not appearing to be helping his rider once in front, he is bred to stay this trip but might prove best back at six for now.

**Shujune Al Hawaa(IRE)** , stepping up another furlong in trip, was keeping on late in the day. She looks a nursery type.

**Highest Return(USA)**is the first foal of a mare who won at up to ten furlongs. After striking the front he was soon run down, but he looks capable of winning races with the experience behind him.

**Tom Forest**, runner-up to a couple of useful Mark Johnston juveniles in Spirit Of France and Leo's Lucky Star, was disappointing over this longer trip but would not have won back at six.

**Geojimali** was never in the hunt but looks the type to improve with experience.

**King Henrik(USA)**, the stable's second string, sweated up at the start and was much too keen in the race.

## 3975 KWIK KEG 0800 3280508 NURSERY 6f

**2:45** (2:49) (C ) 2-Y-O **£8,060** (£2,480; £1,240; £620) **Stalls** High

Form RPR

2134 1 **The Crooked Ring**[10] [3703] 2-8-8 78 ......... RWinston 6 83
(PDEvans) *hld up in tch: hdwy to ld appr fnl f: edgd rt: r.o fnl f* **8/1**

4123 2 1 **Doctor Hilary**[23] [3290] 2-9-7 91 ......... KFallon 4 93+
(MLWBell) *chsd ldrs: effrt over 1f out: chsd wnr ins fnl f: kpt on cl home* **7/2**[1]

51 3 ¾ **Generous Option**[9] [3741] 2-9-3 87 ......... JFanning 1 87
(MJohnston) *led to appr fnl f: kpt on same pce* **4/1**[2]

0533 4 3 **Monash Lad (IRE)**[4] [3876] 2-8-10 80 ......... PRobinson 7 71
(MHTompkins) *chsd ldrs tl rdn and one pce fr over 1f out* **7/1**[3]

1041 5 2 **Nova Tor (IRE)**[10] [3704] 2-8-12 82 ......... EAhern 5 70+
(NPLittmoden) *trckd ldrs: nt clr run over 2f to over 1f out: sn outpcd* **10/1**

210 6 2 **Bold Marc (IRE)**[34] [2959] 2-9-7 91 ......... DarrenWilliams 3 70
(KRBurke) *chsd ldrs tl rdn and wknd wl over 1f out* **10/1**

1321 7 5 **Speed Dial Harry (IRE)**[9] [3736] 2-9-2 86 ......... (v) KDalgleish 2 50
(KRBurke) *cl up to 2f out: sn rdn and btn* **16/1**



The Form Book, Raceform Ltd, Compton, RG20 6NL

001 **8** *6* **Rancho Cucamonga (IRE)**[16] 3532 2-8-5 **75**........................ KDarley 8 21
(TDBarron) *hld up in tch: rdn whn hmpd 1/2-way: sn btn* **7/2**[1]
1m 11.97s (-1.75) **Going Correction** -0.40s/f (Firm) **8** Ran SP% **112.1**
Speed ratings: **95,93,92,88,86 83,76,68**CSF £34.70 CT £129.23 TOTE £9.90: £2.40, £1.80, £1.90; EX 45.00.
**Owner** J R Salter **Bred** W H R John And Partners **Trained** Pandy, Gwent

**FOCUS**
This included some useful sorts and looks fairly decent form. The figures shown as 'official ratings' are estimates for guidance only.

**NOTEBOOK**
**The Crooked Ring** had looked fully exposed but this was his best effort yet. Back over his optimum trip, he came from off the pace to secure victory and this is probably the way to ride him.
**Doctor Hilary**, back over six furlongs, came through to take second but was always being held. He can improve on this but gave the impression that he could do with the visor back on.
**Generous Option** did well to get across and bag the rail from her low draw. The way she kept on suggests she will stay a seventh furlong, but while she handled this ground she might prefer some give.
**Monash Lad(IRE)**, again rather keen early on, promises to stay seven furlongs if he can settle better.
**Nova Tor(IRE)** appeared to see out the sixth furlong but may prove best being allowed to bowl along over five.
**Bold Marc(IRE)**, out of his depth at Royal Ascot, did not shape as if six furlongs was what he wanted.
**Rancho Cucamonga(IRE)** was hampered on the rail at halfway but had already started to throw out distress signals. Her rider looked down afterwards as if something might have been amiss, and this run can be ignored. She probably needs easier ground. *Official explanation: jockey said filly was in season*

## 3976 LAND O'BURNS FILLIES' STKS (LISTED RACE) 5f
**3:15** (3:16) (A ) 3-Y-O+ **£17,400** (£6,600; £3,300; £1,500) **Stalls** High

Form RPR
-660 **1** **Airwave**[11] 3674 4-8-13 110........................ DHolland 2 105+
(HCandy) *chsd ldrs on outside: led over 1f out: pushed out* **4/6**[1]
12L0 **2** *1 1/4* **Forever Phoenix**[38] 2857 4-8-13 92........................ EAhern 6 100+
(RMHCowell) *hld up in tch: hdwy over 1f out: chsd wnr ins last: r.o* **16/1**
0002 **3** *1 1/4* **Proud Boast**[7] 3795 6-8-13 89........................ KDarley 3 95
(DNicholls) *in tch on outside: effrt over 1f out: one pce ins fnl f* **16/1**
0003 **4** *nk* **Dragon Flyer (IRE)**[9] 3732 5-8-13 98........................ RWinston 11 94
(MQuinn) *trckd ldrs tl rdn and nt qckn fnl f* **20/1**
3000 **5** *hd* **Dame De Noche**[18] 3453 4-8-13 82........................ ACulhane 8 93
(JGGiven) *trckd ldrs: rdn whn carried lft ins fnl f: one pce* **50/1**
-123 **6** *shd* **Autumn Pearl**[30] 3092 3-8-9 98........................ PRobinson 5 93
(MAJarvis) *led to over 1f out: sn outpcd* **9/2**[2]
-405 **7** *hd* **Needles And Pins (IRE)**[44] 2685 3-8-9 92........................ KFallon 10 92+
(MLWBell) *in tch ins: nt clr run over 2f out: r.o fnl f: no imp* **12/1**[3]
5-45 **8** *1* **Curfew**[9] 3732 5-8-13 92........................ WSupple 4 95+
(JRFanshawe) *dwlt: hld up: nt clr run fr 2f out: hmpd ins fnl f: nt rcvr* **16/1**
6400 **9** *1* **Bali Royal**[16] 3537 6-8-13 98........................ JFanning 9 84
(MSSaunders) *prom tl rdn and wknd fr 2f out* **20/1**
-000 **10** *5* **Blue Crush (IRE)**[42] 2744 3-8-9........................ DarrenWilliams 1 64
(KRBurke) *cl up: rdn and lost pl whn hmpd 1f out* **100/1**
57.49 secs (-2.94) **Going Correction** -0.40s/f (Firm)
**WFA** 3 from 4yo+ 4lb **10** Ran SP% **116.0**
Speed ratings: **107,105,103,102,102 102,101,100,98,90**CSF £12.97 TOTE £1.70: £1.02, £4.50, £3.80; EX 19.50.
**Owner** Henry Candy & Partners **Bred** R T And Mrs Watson **Trained** Wantage, Oxon
■ The first running of the Land O'Burns Stakes in this form.
■ Stewards Enquiry : R Winston two-day ban: careless riding (Jul 31-Aug 1)

**FOCUS**
Airwave had plenty in hand on the ratings and won comfortably, although this was still 12lb below the pick of her form last year. This is decent form for the grade and the time was only 0.29 sec outside the track record.

**NOTEBOOK**
**Airwave**, down in grade having been racing mainly at the top level, recorded her first victory since last season's Temple Stakes. Partnered by Holland for the first time and ridden much more handily, she was a very comfortable winner and will now take on the colts again in the Nunthorpe.
**Forever Phoenix** ran on well late in the day but the favourite was too good. Still improving, she proved she handles a quick surface and deserves to pick up a race of this nature.
**Proud Boast** ran another sound race and is clearly in fine heart at present.
**Dragon Flyer(IRE)** ran a solid race once more but she remains difficult to win with.
**Dame De Noche** is a winner over a mile and has never run over the minimum trip before. This was a good effort and she would have finished a bit closer had she not been carried left by Dragon Flyer.
**Autumn Pearl** has plenty of natural pace but did not see out her race as well as she has been doing.
**Needles And Pins(IRE)**, who has been racing over six furlongs, ran respectably on ground that was probably faster than ideal.
**Curfew**, who was slow to go as she often is, met with trouble in running and this performance can be written off. This trip is too sharp for her in any case. *Official explanation: jockey said mare was denied a clear run*

## 3977 GILES INSURANCE STKS (H'CAP) 1m
**3:45** (3:46) (C ) (0-95,88) 3-Y-O+ **£9,509** (£2,926; £1,463; £731) **Stalls** Low

Form RPR
3200 **1** **Top Dirham**[26] 3198 6-8-8 **70**........................ KFallon 3 77
(MWEasterby) *prom: rdn to ld 1f out: hld on wl* **3/1**[1]
0530 **2** *hd* **Vicious Warrior**[9] 3756 5-9-10 **86**........................ DeanMcKeown 6 93
(RMWhitaker) *chsd ldrs: led 2f to 1f out: rallied: jst hld* **5/1**[3]
-130 **3** *3/4* **Penrith (FR)**[19] 3415 3-9-4 **88**........................ JFanning 2 93+
(MJohnston) *hld up: nt clr run over 2f to over 1f out: r.o fnl f: no imp* **8/1**
3304 **4** *4* **Cherished Number**[9] 3745 5-8-12 **74**........................(v) DHolland 7 70
(ISemple) *hld up in tch: rdn over 2f out: r.o fnl f* **9/2**[2]
2652 **5** *hd* **Stoic Leader (IRE)**[7] 3797 4-9-7 **83**........................ RWinston 4 79
(RFFisher) *hld up in tch: nt clr run fr over 2f out: rdn over 1f out: no imp* **8/1**
0100 **6** *shd* **Sea Storm (IRE)**[29] 3119 6-9-2 **81**........................ THamilton[(3)] 9 76
(DRMacleod) *cl up: led briefly over 2f out: rdn and nt qckn* **20/1**
2120 **7** *2 1/2* **Countykat (IRE)**[22] 3347 4-8-10 **72**........................(v) DarrenWilliams 5 62
(KRBurke) *chsd ldrs tl rdn and outpcd fr 2f out* **10/1**
0646 **8** *shd* **Ballyhurry (USA)**[30] 3079 7-8-4 **69**........................ NMackay[(3)] 1 58
(JSGoldie) *hld up: effrt over 2f out: btn over 1f out* **8/1**
3335 **9** *nk* **Sarraaf (IRE)**[25] 3235 8-8-7 **69**........................ WSupple 8 58
(JSGoldie) *led to over 2f out: btn over 1f out* **16/1**
1m 39.85s (-3.27) **Going Correction** -0.30s/f (Firm)
**WFA** 3 from 4yo+ 8lb **9** Ran SP% **110.9**
Speed ratings: **104,103,103,99,98 98,96,96,95**CSF £16.62 CT £124.64 TOTE £3.90: £1.70, £2.30, £2.40; EX 25.10 Trifecta £180.20 Pool: £1,487.81 - 5.86 winning units..
**Owner** Steve Hull **Bred** Whitsbury Manor Stud **Trained** Sheriff Hutton, N Yorks

**FOCUS**
A reasonable handicap run at just an ordinary pace for the grade but the form is fair.

**NOTEBOOK**
**Top Dirham** ◆, 2lb lower than when last successful over a year previously, has had his excuses in recent outings but, re-united with Fallon, there were no problems this time around and he is probably value for a little more than the winning margin. The two previous occasions he gained a win off the back of a defeat, he has followed up.
**Vicious Warrior** has not won since September 2002 and is still 4lb higher than when gaining that success. He kept on really gamely when headed and was closing on the eventual winner right the way to the line, but he will go up again for not winning.
**Penrith(FR)**, the only three-year-old in the field, would have been closer had he not had to wait for a gap. He was clear of the remainder and is still progressing.
**Cherished Number** is beginning to look quite well handicapped, but he remains below his best.
**Stoic Leader(IRE)**, a really tough sort, has been kept very busy lately and was below his best.

## 3978 DAILY RECORD SCOTTISH DERBY (GROUP 2) 1m 2f
**4:15** (4:15) (A ) 3-Y-O+ **£58,000** (£22,000; £11,000; £5,000) **Stalls** Low

Form RPR
-213 **1** **Kalaman (IRE)**[16] 3540 4-9-2 116........................ KFallon 4 121+
(SirMichaelStoute) *chsd clr ldr: shkn up and hung lft fr over 2f out: led over 1f out: kpt on wl* **5/6**[1]
0312 **2** *1* **Gateman**[9] 3724 7-9-2 113........................ KDalgleish 6 117+
(MJohnston) *led and sn clr: rdn over 2f out: hdd over 1f out: hmpd ins last: kpt on towards fin* **8/1**
6236 **3** *1 1/4* **Ikhtyar (IRE)**[16] 3540 4-9-2 116........................(v[1]) RHills 5 115
(JHMGosden) *prom chsng gp: effrt over 2f out: kpt on fnl f* **7/2**[2]
3403 **4** *nk* **Checkit (IRE)**[8] 3792 4-9-2 112........................ ACulhane 2 114
(MRChannon) *hld up: effrt over 2f out: r.o fnl f: no imp* **16/1**
3305 **5** *7* **Scott's View**[33] 2968 5-9-2 115........................ SChin 7 101
(MJohnston) *hld up: rdn over 2f out: sn btn* **13/2**[3]
0566 **6** *2 1/2* **Kelucia (IRE)**[16] 3541 3-8-3 97........................ WSupple 8 93
(JSGoldie) *hld up: rdn over 2f out: sn btn* **100/1**
1-51 **7** *3/4* **Fruhlingssturm**[11] 3661 4-9-5 112........................ PRobinson 1 98
(MAJarvis) *chsd ldrs: rdn over 2f out: btn over 1f out* **16/1**
2m 4.90s (-7.29) **Going Correction** -0.30s/f (Firm)
**WFA** 3 from 4yo+ 10lb **7** Ran SP% **114.0**
Speed ratings: **117,116,115,114,109 107,106**CSF £8.55 TOTE £1.90: £1.20, £2.40; EX 6.30.
**Owner** H H Aga Khan **Bred** His Highness The Aga Khan's Studs S C **Trained** Newmarket, Suffolk

**FOCUS**
A controversial race with the result standing after a Stewards' enquiry. Runner-up Gateman set a sound pace and this is decent form for the grade.

**NOTEBOOK**
**Kalaman(IRE)** gained a belated first Group-race win, although he did not have to be at his best to score. Steadily reducing Gateman's clear lead, he struck the front going well, but hung over to the rail and tightened up that rival. He was the winner on merit, and the Stewards made the correct decision in allowing him to keep the race. The Juddmonte International is likely to be his next port of call.
**Gateman** was allowed to do his own thing in front and was ten lengths clear at one stage, but was headed by Kalaman in the straight. Having to be snatched up briefly, costing him momentum, when that rival went across him inside the last, he was closing when back on an even keel but did not have sufficient time to mount one of his trademark rallies. In all likelihood the Stewards called it right, but he should not be long in finding compensation especially as he proved he stays this longer trip.
**Ikhtyar(IRE)** travelled well in the first-time visor but did not find a great deal in the latter stages. Even so, he finished slightly closer to Kalaman than he had in the Eclipse.
**Checkit(IRE)** was running on at the end, but perhaps his rider should have got after him a bit earlier. He did not appear to find ten furlongs a problem on his first run at the trip, but will continue to prove tricky to place.
**Scott's View**, who started a shorter price than stablemate Gateman, is normally admirably consistent but was below-par on this occasion.
**Kelucia(IRE)** has been sent off at 100/1 three times now this season and
**Fruhlingssturm** faced a stiff task under a 3lb penalty for winning a Hamburg Group Two last September.

## 3979 GILES INSURANCE RATED STKS (H'CAP) 6f
**4:45** (4:48) (D ) (0-80,77) 3-Y-O+ **£7,038** (£2,165; £1,082; £541) **Stalls** High

Form RPR
-000 **1** **Machinist (IRE)**[23] 3299 4-9-5 **75**........................ AlexGreaves 6 92+
(DNicholls) *trckd ldrs: rdn to ld ins fnl f: r.o strly* **7/1**
1110 **2** *3* **Foley Millennium (IRE)**[8] 3772 6-8-10 **66**........................ RWinston 7 74
(MQuinn) *led to ins fnl f: nt pce of wnr* **10/1**
0466 **3** *1/2* **Highland Warrior**[18] 3446 5-9-2 **72**........................ WSupple 2 79
(JSGoldie) *dwlt: hld up: nt clr run over 2f out: effrt over 1f out: one pce fnl f* **9/2**[1]
0103 **4** *3/4* **Sharoura**[9] 3735 8-8-5 **64**........................ THamilton[(3)] 8 68+
(RAFahey) *chsd ldrs: nt clr run 1/2-way: rdn and kpt on fnl f* **6/1**[3]
0103 **5** *2* **Sir Don (IRE)**[12] 3623 5-8-10 **66**........................(v) ANicholls 3 64
(DNicholls) *cl up tl rdn and outpcd over 1f out* **8/1**
1356 **6** *shd* **College Maid (IRE)**[12] 3623 7-8-0 **63** oh2........................ JCurrie[(7)] 4 61
(JSGoldie) *in tch: rdn over 2f out: sn no ex* **20/1**
-010 **7** *2* **Prince Dayjur (USA)**[12] 3645 5-9-7 **77**........................(v) KFallon 5 69
(MJWallace) *cl up tl wknd wl over 1f out* **9/2**[1]
0000 **8** *nk* **Seafield Towers**[3] 3901 4-9-3 **73**........................(p) DHolland 9 64
(MissLAPerratt) *dwlt: plld hrd in rr: n.m.r 1/2-way: sn rdn and no imp* **5/1**[2]
2510 **9** *5* **Under My Spell**[16] 3523 3-9-1 **76**........................ EAhern 1 52
(PDEvans) *prom tl rdn and wknd over 1f out* **10/1**
69.88 secs (-3.84) **Going Correction** -0.40s/f (Firm)
**WFA** 3 from 4yo+ 5lb **9** Ran SP% **113.9**
Speed ratings: **109,105,104,103,100 100,97,97,90**CSF £73.10 CT £350.68 TOTE £8.70: £2.10, £3.90, £1.70; EX 189.70 Place 6 £37.94, Place 5 £8.23.
**Owner** M J Pipe **Bred** Ballymacoll Stud Farm Ltd **Trained** Sessay, N Yorks

**FOCUS**
This is fair form, with the winner putting in an improved effort. The time was good for the grade and the form looks solid.

**NOTEBOOK**
**Machinist(IRE)** ◆, who has been edging down the weights, was running over six furlongs for only the second time since his racecourse debut. He travelled well in behind before scooting clear to win in good style, and there should be plenty more to come from him now that his trainer knows he has another sprinter on his hands.
**Foley Millennium(IRE)** was able to lead and bounced back to form, although proving no match for the winner. This was his first run over six furlongs for more than three years.
**Highland Warrior** missed the break once again but was keeping on from the rear. 6lb higher than when last successful, he is capable of scoring again but will require things to drop right.
**Sharoura** ◆ was trapped on the rails at halfway before keeping on nicely. She remains one to be interested in.
**Sir Don(IRE)**, a stablemate of the winner, was 5lb higher than when tasting victory at Hamilton last month.

**Prince Dayjur(USA)** needs to have things his own way out in front. *Official explanation: jockey said gelding lost its action*
**Seafield Towers** *Official explanation: jockey said gelding ran too freely*
T/Jkpt: Not won. T/Plt: £71.20 to a £1 stake. Pool: £55,964.75. 573.15 winning tickets. T/Qpdt: £8.70 to a £1 stake. Pool: £4,501.10. 382.00 winning tickets. RY

# $^{3817}$BEVERLEY (R-H)
## Monday, July 19

**OFFICIAL GOING: Good to soft (good in places)**
After two dry days the jockeys described the ground as 'almost good but showing signs of wear and tear after a busy spell'.
Wind: Almost nil. Weather: Fine.

## 3980 OLD GRAVEL PITS ALLERTHORPE CLAIMING STKS — 5f
6:35 (6:35) (F) 2-Y-O — £3,297 (£942; £471) Stalls High

Form — RPR
56 **1** **Baymist**$^{6}$ 3818 2-8-11 ............ TLucas 6 60
(MWEasterby) *trckd ldr: led over 2f out: r.o wl fnl f* **9/2**$^{2}$
5305 **2** 1 ½ **Procrastinate (IRE)**$^{34}$ 2960 2-8-6 ............ RFfrench 8 50
(RFFisher) *chsd ldrs: swtchd lft over 1f out: styd on wl ins last to take 2nd nr line* **9/2**$^{2}$
0004 **3** hd **Roko**$^{6}$ 3818 2-8-6 ............(b$^{1}$) PMulrennan$^{(5)}$ 5 54
(MWEasterby) *swvd lft s: sn trcking ldrs: rdn 2f out: kpt on ins last* **17/2**
6331 **4** 2 **Von Wessex**$^{40}$ 2773 2-8-6 ............ CHaddon$^{(7)}$ 9 49
(WGMTurner) *led tl over 2f out: wknd 1f out* **6/4**$^{1}$
04U0 **5** 1 ¼ **Fold Walk**$^{60}$ 2248 2-7-11 ............ RThomas$^{(5)}$ 4 34
(MWEasterby) *s.i.s: outpcd and bhd: sme hdwy 2f out: hung rt: nvr rchd ldrs* **40/1**
0 **6** 1 **Hopelessly Devoted**$^{18}$ 3444 2-8-10 ............ GFaulkner 7 38
(PCHaslam) *chsd ldrs: hung lft and lost pl over 2f out* **8/1**
50 **7** 3 ½ **Magic Genie (IRE)**$^{18}$ 3444 2-8-8 ............ DaleGibson 3 24
(MWEasterby) *sn chsng ldrs: rdn over 2f out: sn btn* **13/2**$^{3}$

65.06 secs (1.06) **Going Correction** +0.025s/f (Good) **7** Ran SP% **113.8**
Speed ratings: **92,89,89,86,84 82,76**CSF £24.60 TOTE £6.80: £2.20, £2.30; EX 37.70.
**Owner** Mrs M E Curtis **Bred** Bearstone Stud **Trained** Sheriff Hutton, N Yorks
■ Veteran Terry Lucas's first winner for nine months.

**FOCUS**
With the favourite well below form this claimer took little winning, but Baymist looks likely to progress and make her mark in nursery company.

**NOTEBOOK**
**Baymist**, having her third run, still has a bit to learn but in the end was right on top. This hopefully sets her up for a nursery success.
**Procrastinate(IRE)**, outpointed by Von Wessex here, stayed on to snatch second spot almost on the line, appreciating the easier ground.
**Roko**, who finished two places ahead of the winner here a week earlier, wore first-time blinkers and did not look straightforward. A seller would be more his cup of tea.
**Von Wessex**, absent for six weeks, had the plum draw but, after making the running, he dropped right away. This was not his true form.
**Fold Walk**, on her toes beforehand, ducked and dived and looks a bit of a madam.
**Hopelessly Devoted**, very edgy beforehand, at least showed a fraction more than on her debut two weeks earlier.

## 3981 I. J. BLAKEY HAULAGE H'CAP — 1m 1f 207y
7:05 (7:05) (E) (0-75,75) 3-Y-O — £4,992 (£1,536; £768; £384) Stalls High

Form — RPR
5130 **1** **Futoo (IRE)**$^{6}$ 3819 3-8-9 **63** ow2 ............ FLynch 7 70
(GMMoore) *led: qcknd over 3f out: edgd lft fnl f: jst hld on* **7/1**$^{3}$
4020 **2** ½ **Pay Attention**$^{56}$ 2355 3-8-3 **57** ............ DAllan 13 63
(TDEasterby) *chsd ldrs: outpcd and nt clr run over 2f out: swtchd lft over 1f out: styd on wl ins last* **13/2**$^{2}$
0006 **3** 1 ¼ **Joey Perhaps**$^{6}$ 3822 3-7-10 **55** oh2 ow3 ............ RThomas$^{(5)}$ 6 59
(JRBest) *trckd ldrs: wnt rt over 2f out: styd on same pce fnl f* **16/1**
0230 **4** 2 ½ **Magic Amigo**$^{13}$ 3614 3-9-7 **75** ............ KDarley 1 74
(JRJenkins) *chsd ldrs: kpt on same pce fnl 2f* **9/1**
0000 **5** 1 **Super King**$^{6}$ 3819 3-8-5 **59** ............ DeanMcKeown 11 57
(NBycroft) *dwlt: hld up on wd outside: effrt 3f out: styd on fnl f* **12/1**
0464 **6** nk **Orion Express**$^{8}$ 3780 3-8-3 **62** ............ PMulrennan$^{(5)}$ 8 59
(MWEasterby) *hld up and bhd: kpt on fnl 2f: nvr nr ldrs* **6/1**$^{1}$
0351 **7** hd **Come What July (IRE)**$^{10}$ 3707 3-7-12 **55** ............(b) LisaJones$^{(3)}$ 9 52
(MrsNMacauley) *hld up; hdwy on inner over 2f out: nt clr run over 1f out: styd on* **9/1**
0042 **8** hd **Munaawesh (USA)**$^{14}$ 3581 3-8-2 **56** ............(b) JBramhill 2 52
(DWChapman) *swtchd rt after s: t.k.h in rr: effrt over 2f out: hung lft: nvr nr ldrs* **7/1**$^{3}$
0205 **9** ¾ **Impulsive Bid (IRE)**$^{16}$ 3517 3-8-8 **62** ............ MFenton 10 57
(JeddO'Keeffe) *mid-div: t.k.h: effrt over 3f out: nvr nr ldrs* **22/1**
0060 **10** 1 ¾ **Chisel**$^{20}$ 3401 3-8-3 **57** ............ RFfrench 12 49
(MJohnston) *mid-div: hdwy 4f out: wknd over 1f out* **16/1**
6010 **11** 3 ½ **Miss Eloise**$^{9}$ 3746 3-8-2 **63** ............ AMullen$^{(7)}$ 5 48
(TDEasterby) *in tch: effrt over 2f out: sn lost pl* **15/2**
0-40 **12** ¾ **River Line (USA)**$^{14}$ 3581 3-7-5 **52** oh5 ............ DFentiman$^{(7)}$ 4 36
(CWFairhurst) *chsd ldrs: lost pl over 1f out* **33/1**
5000 **13** 19 **Farnborough (USA)**$^{55}$ 2379 3-7-10 **55** ............ BSwarbrick$^{(5)}$ 3 5
(RJPrice) *tk fierce hold on outer: chsd ldrs: lost pl over 3f out: sn bhd* **14/1**

2m 7.63s (0.43) **Going Correction** +0.025s/f (Good) **13** Ran SP% **117.8**
Speed ratings: **99,98,97,95,94 94,94,94,93,92 89,88,73**CSF £51.24 CT £709.63 TOTE £6.50: £2.10, £3.40, £4.40; EX 59.30.
**Owner** M K Roddis **Bred** John Bernard O'Connor **Trained** Middleham Moor, N Yorks

**FOCUS**
A moderate race and modest form in a tactical affair with the winner dictating things from the front.

**NOTEBOOK**
**Futoo(IRE)**, well backed in the offices, had his own way in front and in the end did just enough. His stamina just lasted out and he will go hurdling sooner rather than later.
**Pay Attention**, suited by the easier ground, found herself in trouble through her lack of basic speed. Eventually making her way to the outside, she would have prevailed in a few more strides and will be suited by a slightly stiffer test. She came back with plenty of cuts and bruises.
**Joey Perhaps**, unplaced in eight previous starts, was just out of the handicap. At long last he seems to be getting the hang of things.
**Magic Amigo**, happy to be back on turf, looked light and was warm beforehand. This is as good as he is.
**Super King**, 6lb lower, found himself an in impossible position. Making ground on the wide outside, he was staying on to some purpose at the finish and looks capable of better.
**Orion Express** keeps running well but as a result receives no relief whatsoever.
**Impulsive Bid(IRE)** *Official explanation: jockey said filly suffered interference in the early stages*

## 3982 MKM BUILDING SUPPLIES H'CAP — 7f 100y
7:35 (7:35) (D) (0-80,76) 3-Y-O+ — £6,851 (£2,108; £1,054; £527) Stalls High

Form — RPR
0163 **1** **Zanjeer**$^{3}$ 3895 4-8-13 **66** ............ PMulrennan$^{(5)}$ 2 77+
(NWilson) *trckd ldr: t.k.h: edgd rt and led 1f out: hld on towards fin* **5/1**$^{2}$
2516 **2** ½ **Young Mr Grace (IRE)**$^{4}$ 3869 4-9-7 **76** ............ AMullen$^{(7)}$ 6 82
(TDEasterby) *mid-div: effrt over 2f out: n.m.r over 1f out: styd on wl ins last* **5/1**$^{2}$
1003 **3** ¾ **St Savarin (FR)**$^{6}$ 3819 3-9-3 **72** ............ NPollard 9 76
(JRBest) *led: qcknd over 3f out: hdd 1f out: no ex whn sltly hmpd and swtchd lft ins last* **9/2**$^{1}$
0-25 **4** 1 **Eddies Jewel**$^{14}$ 3586 4-7-5 **46** oh11 ............ DFentiman$^{(7)}$ 5 48?
(JSWainwright) *hld up and bhd: styd on fnl 2f: nt rch ldrs* **40/1**
2200 **5** nk **Carlton (IRE)**$^{45}$ 2666 10-8-6 **59** ............ RThomas$^{(5)}$ 7 60
(CRDore) *trckd ldrs: effrt on ins over 2f out: nt clr run jst ins last: kpt on* **10/1**
0433 **6** 2 **Riska King**$^{16}$ 3516 4-9-5 **67** ............ GParkin 3 63
(RAFahey) *sn trcking ldrs: t.k.h: wknd and eased jst ins last* **11/2**$^{3}$
2401 **7** 1 ½ **Time To Regret**$^{3}$ 3921 4-8-5 **56** 6ex ............ TEaves$^{(3)}$ 1 48
(JSWainwright) *chsd ldrs: effrt over 3f out: lost pl over 1f out* **10/1**
0-00 **8** 3 **Pearl Pride (USA)**$^{55}$ 2390 3-8-13 **68** ............ RFfrench 4 53
(MJohnston) *rr-div: effrt 4f out: rdn and edgd rt 2f out: sn lost pl* **20/1**
0002 **9** ¾ **Qualitair Wings**$^{11}$ 3660 5-9-10 **72** ............(b$^{1}$) KDarley 8 55
(JHetherton) *rel to r: bhd: sme hdwy whn hung rt and n.m.r 2f out: nvr a factor* **9/2**$^{1}$

1m 33.86s (-0.44) **Going Correction** +0.025s/f (Good)
**WFA** 3 from 4yo+ 7lb **9** Ran SP% **110.5**
Speed ratings: **103,102,101,100,100 97,96,92,91**CSF £28.09 CT £113.10 TOTE £5.70: £2.50, £1.80, £1.90; EX 35.80.
**Owner** Malcom Wilson **Bred** D J Deer **Trained** Malton, N Yorks

**FOCUS**
In effect a 0-76 handicap run at no great pace and the form is ordinary and not all that sound.

**NOTEBOOK**
**Zanjeer** took a keen grip as a result of the steady pace. He dived right when taking charge and in the end did just enough.
**Young Mr Grace(IRE)**, 2lb higher than Carlisle, had much less use made of him. Short of room at a crucial stage, he was reeling in the winner at the line.
**St Savarin(FR)**, who had the plum draw, dropped anchor in front. Forced to check when the winner went across him, he stuck on in game fashion and a slightly longer trip should not be beyond him.
**Eddies Jewel**, a maiden after 11 starts, was running from 11lb out of the handicap. He stayed on really well from off the pace but connections will be hoping the Handicapper does not take this at face value.
**Carlton(IRE)**, fresh and well after a seven-week break, was staying on in his own time up against the fence when left short of room inside the last. This was his 100th career start.
**Riska King**, closely matched with the runner-up on Carlisle running, was always doing too much due to the lack of any pace.
**Qualitair Wings**, in first-time blinkers, seemed to set off with the hand brake on. Under pressure he wanted to do nothing but hang right and this was an experiment unlikely to be repeated. *Official explanation: jockey said gelding hung right in home straight*

## 3983 EUROPEAN BREEDERS FUND UBC NOVICE STKS — 7f 100y
8:05 (8:05) (D) 2-Y-O — £4,953 (£1,524; £762; £381) Stalls High

Form — RPR
10 **1** **Where With All (IRE)**$^{30}$ 3071 2-9-5 ............ KMcEvoy 4 94+
(SaeedBinSuroor) *trckd ldrs: led 1f out: sn shkn up and qcknd clr* **5/2**$^{2}$
**2** 6 **Blue Prince (USA)** 2-8-8 ............ DSweeney 7 69
(RCharlton) *in tch: hdwy 4f out: led over 1f out: sn hdd: no ch w wnr* **10/1**
5 **3** 3 **Blackcomb Mountain (USA)**$^{11}$ 3679 2-8-2 ............ BSwarbrick$^{(5)}$ 8 61
(MFHarris) *trckd ldrs: t.k.h: one pce fnl 2f* **50/1**
1 **4** 3 **Comic Strip**$^{7}$ 3802 2-9-2 ............ SSanders 2 63
(SirMarkPrescott) *hdwy on wd outside over 4f out: drvn along to chse ldrs over 2f out: kpt on one pce* **5/4**$^{1}$
51 **5** ¾ **Dry Ice (IRE)**$^{22}$ 3336 2-9-2 ............ DaneO'Neill 6 61
(HCandy) *led: rdn over 2f out: hdd over 1f out: sn btn* **10/3**$^{3}$
0 **6** 2 **Nowaday (GER)**$^{23}$ 3313 2-8-12 ............ DaleGibson 3 52
(TPTate) *swtchd rt after s: sn outpcd end bhd: kpt on fnl 2f: nvr on terms* **100/1**
000 **7** shd **Doctor's Cave**$^{23}$ 3319 2-8-12 ............ KDarley 1 52
(CEBrittain) *sn trcking ldrs: chal 3f out: wknd over 1f out* **20/1**
**8** 25 **Moonfleet (IRE)** 2-8-3 ............ CCatlin 5 —
(MFHarris) *sn outpcd and bhd: hung lft and t.o 3f out* **100/1**

1m 33.65s (-0.65) **Going Correction** +0.025s/f (Good) **8** Ran SP% **113.9**
Speed ratings: **104,97,93,90,89 87,87,58**CSF £25.51 TOTE £3.60: £1.40, £2.20, £5.10; EX 21.90.
**Owner** Godolphin **Bred** Kilfrush Stud **Trained** Newmarket, Suffolk

**FOCUS**
A run-of -the mill contest, but quite an impressive winner in a good time who is well worth another try in much better company.

**NOTEBOOK**
**Where With All(IRE)**, a quality colt, travelled strongly on the outer. He tended to edge left, but when given one backhander quickened right away. This much easier ground was clearly in his favour and he is well worth another chance in a much higher grade.
**Blue Prince(USA)**, a March foal, is long in the back and was noisy in the paddock. On a track not easy for newcomers, he ran really well to finish clear second best behind a potentially very useful winner.
**Blackcomb Mountain(USA)**, very noisy beforehand, showed a moderate action and this may be as good as she is.
**Comic Strip** did not shine at all but may well be worth another chance on a much more orthodox track. He looked all at sea round the bend.
**Dry Ice(IRE)** found this much tougher and after working his way to the front he dropped right away.
**Nowaday(GER)** is still learning the ropes and looks capable of better given a lot more time.
**Moonfleet(IRE)** *Official explanation: jockey said filly hung right*

## 3984 SAILORS FAMILIES SOCIETY MAIDEN H'CAP STKS — 2m 35y
8:35 (8:35) (F) (0-55,55) 3-Y-O — £3,150 (£900; £450) Stalls High

Form — RPR
-523 **1** **Princess Kiotto**$^{17}$ 3479 3-9-6 **55** ............ DAllan 15 72+
(TDEasterby) *hld up: hdwy 5f out: wnt 2nd 1f out: styd on wl to ld nr fin* **11/2**$^{1}$
0300 **2** nk **Strangely Brown (IRE)**$^{32}$ 3026 3-9-1 **55** ............ PMakin$^{(5)}$ 7 72+
(SCWilliams) *hdwy 6f out: sn trcking ldrs: led over 1f out: hdd nr fin* **28/1**
-602 **3** 9 **Spring Breeze**$^{48}$ 2554 3-9-6 **55** ............(p) SWKelly 14 61
(MDods) *hdwy 6f out: sn chsng ldrs: one pce fnl 2f* **7/1**$^{2}$

0-00 **4** 1 ¾ **Habitual (IRE)**[108] [1226] 3-9-1 **50** ............ SSanders 12 54
(SirMarkPrescott) *chsd ldrs: led over 2f out: hdd over 1f out: sn wknd* **8/1**[3]

0-05 **5** 4 **Tell The Trees**[26] [3190] 3-9-3 **52** ............ FLynch 5 51
(RMBeckett) *sn bhd: kpt on fnl 3f* **14/1**

2543 **6** 1 ½ **Savannah River (IRE)**[5] [3837] 3-8-7 **42** ............(t) DeanMcKeown 1 39
(CWThornton) *sn chsng ldrs: wknd over 1f out* **9/1**

2430 **7** 3 **Romeo's Day**[48] [2554] 3-9-1 **50** ............ CCatlin 17 44
(MRChannon) *rr-div: hdwy over 3f out: nvr rchd ldrs* **16/1**

-005 **8** 1 ¼ **Adees Dancer**[17] [3473] 3-8-13 **55** ............ MStainton(7) 13 47
(BSmart) *chsd ldrs: outpcd 6f out: kpt on fnl 2f* **40/1**

0456 **9** 2 ½ **Morning Hawk (USA)**[95] [1405] 3-8-2 **44** ow2............ DerekNolan(7) 6 33
(JSMoore) *rr-div: drvn along over 4f out: nvr a factor* **10/1**

0-00 **10** 2 ½ **Introduction**[42] [2740] 3-8-6 **41** ow1............ MFenton 11 27
(RJPrice) *mid-div: effrt over 4f out: sn wknd* **14/1**

0603 **11** ½ **Northern Spirit**[48] [2554] 3-8-13 **48** ............(p) NCallan 3 34
(KARyan) *chsd ldr: reminders 10f out: led 6f out tl over 2f out: sn lost pl* **11/1**

5040 **12** 3 **Bollin Annabel**[17] [3479] 3-9-1 **50** ............ KMcEvoy 4 32
(TDEasterby) *chsd ldrs: hmpd 4f out: lost pl over 2f out* **14/1**

0-25 **13** 4 **Devito (FR)**[8] [3454] 3-9-4 **53** ............ VSlattery 2 30
(AKing) *in rr: bhd fnl 4f* **25/1**

0000 **14** 1 ½ **Barton Flower**[5] [3837] 3-8-12 **47** ............ TLucas 19 22
(MWEasterby) *chsd ldrs: lost pl 4f out* **50/1**

-300 **15** 3 ½ **Dawn Air (USA)**[17] [3479] 3-9-3 **52** ............ GParkin 10 23
(KARyan) *a in rr* **33/1**

0-54 **16** 14 **Over The Years (USA)**[73] [1947] 3-8-2 **37** ............ DaleGibson 18 —
(TPTate) *chsd ldrs: drvn along 7f out: lost pl over 4f out: sn bhd* **14/1**

0006 **17** 3 ½ **Flying With Eagles**[39] [2815] 3-8-7 **42** ............ DaneO'Neill 9 —
(JJay) *mid-div: sme hdwy 7f out: sn lost pl and bhd* **11/1**

0500 **18** 9 **Nafferton Heights (IRE)**[48] [2554] 3-8-6 **46** ............ PMulrennan(5) 20 —
(MWEasterby) *led tl 6f out: sn lost pl and bhd: eased fnl 2f* **20/1**

-002 **P** **Duncanbil (IRE)**[12] [3625] 3-8-10 **45** ............ RFfrench 8 —
(RFFisher) *t.o whn p.u over 2f out* **33/1**

00-0 **P** **Pattern Man**[66] [2090] 3-9-1 **50** ............ JBramhill 16 —
(JRNorton) *sn bhd and drvn along: eased over 7f out: wl t.o whn p.u over 2f out* **66/1**

3m 39.05s (-0.35) **Going Correction** +0.025s/f (Good) **20** Ran SP% **131.1**
Speed ratings: **101,100,96,95,93 92,91,90,89,88 87,86,84,83,81 74,73,68,—,—**CSF £173.71 CT £1133.47 TOTE £6.20: £2.20, £10.40, £2.50, £2.20; EX 359.30.

**Owner** Roy Matthews **Bred** R Matthews **Trained** Great Habton, N Yorks

**FOCUS**
A 0-55 maiden handicap, a seller in all but name, but run at a sound gallop and they came home well strung out, suggesting the form is reasonably solid.

**NOTEBOOK**
**Princess Kiotto** needed every yard of the two miles, opening her account at the seventh attempt.

**Strangely Brown(IRE)**, suited by the sound gallop, settled much better and in the end was only just worn down.

**Spring Breeze**, 4lb higher, finished a distant third ahead of plenty of deadwood.

**Habitual(IRE)**, unplaced in four previous starts over much shorter trips, started life from a plater's mark but was a big negative on the exchanges. After showing ahead he stamina seemed to give out completely.

**Tell The Trees**, taking a big step up in trip, stayed on past beaten and eased horses.

**Duncanbil(IRE)** *Official explanation: jockey said filly lost its action*

**Pattern Man** *Official explanation: jockey said colt lost its action*

## 3985 C D BRAMALL BEVERLEY FORD CLASSIFIED STKS 1m 1f 207y
**9:05** (9:05) (E) 3-Y-O+ **£3,861** (£1,188; £594; £297) **Stalls** High

Form RPR

0005 **1** **Prairie Wolf**[32] [3005] 8-9-7 74 ............ MFenton 6 82
(MLWBell) *led: qcknd over 4f out: jst hld on* **6/1**

1032 **2** *hd* **Hills Of Gold**[4] [3869] 5-8-13 71 ............ PMulrennan(5) 5 79
(MWEasterby) *hld up: wnt 2nd over 2f out: effrt over 1f out: hrd rdn and ev ch fnl f: jst hld* **7/4**[1]

31-0 **3** 2 ½ **Messe De Minuit (IRE)**[95] [1416] 3-8-12 75 ............ DSweeney 1 78
(RCharlton) *trckd ldrs: effrt 3f out: styd on same pce fnl 2f* **11/1**

5002 **4** *shd* **Jacaranda (IRE)**[11] [3662] 4-9-3 68 ............ DaneO'Neill 2 73
(MrsALMKing) *hld up: effrt 3f out: kpt on same pce fnl 2f* **9/2**[3]

0055 **5** 3 ½ **Internationalguest (IRE)**[14] [3591] 5-9-4 71 ............(b) SSanders 4 68
(GGMargarson) *trckd ldr: drvn along over 3f out: wknd 1f out* **4/1**[2]

0004 **6** 2 ½ **Derwent (USA)**[21] [3375] 5-9-3 69 ............(b) KMcEvoy 3 62
(JDBethell) *hld up: effrt over 3f out: sn wl outpcd and n.d* **13/2**

2m 9.57s (2.37) **Going Correction** +0.025s/f (Good)
**WFA** 3 from 4yo+ 10lb **6** Ran SP% **110.5**
Speed ratings: **91,90,88,88,85 83**CSF £16.46 TOTE £7.70: £2.90, £1.50; EX 17.90 Place 6 £157.01, Place 5 £58.70 .

**Owner** B J Warren **Bred** B J Warren **Trained** Newmarket, Suffolk

**FOCUS**
A fine tactical ride from the front and, although there was no pace, the form looks reasonable.

**NOTEBOOK**
**Prairie Wolf**, whose last win was from a mark of 88 in a handicap at Goodwood two years ago, looked back to his best beforehand and seemed to appreciate making the running. Under a fine tactical ride he did just enough. *Official explanation: trainer's representative said, regarding the improved form shown, gelding was better suited by making the running here and by today's slight drop in class*

**Hills Of Gold**, who has yet to prove his stamina, travelled strongly and went in pursuit of the winner. He never flinched but simply could not force his head in front.

**Messe De Minuit(IRE)**, absent since running poorly at Ripon in April, looked in good trim but never looked like raising his game sufficiently to trouble the first two.

**Jacaranda(IRE)** had a couple of pounds to find and could have done with a much stronger gallop.

**Internationalguest(IRE)**, tapped for toe when the winner went for home, found disappointingly little.

**Derwent(USA)**, who could have done with a much stronger pace, continues out of form.

T/Plt: £598.70 to a £1 stake. Pool: £46,713.10. 56.95 winning tickets. T/Qpdt: £17.20 to a £1 stake. Pool: £4,303.00. 184.80 winning tickets. WG

# 3823 BRIGHTON (L-H)
Monday, July 19

**OFFICIAL GOING: Good to firm**

## 3986 3663 FIRST FOR FOOD SERVICE MEDIAN AUCTION MAIDEN STKS 5f 59y
**2:30** (2:30) (F) 2-Y-O **£2,905** (£830; £415) **Stalls** Low

Form RPR

34 **1** **Louphole**[12] [3633] 2-9-0 ............ SSanders 1 81
(PJMakin) *led for 1f: rdn and led again appr fnl f: drvn clr ins last* **9/4**[1]

32 **2** 2 ½ **Dane's Castle (IRE)**[7] [3802] 2-9-0 ............ LDettori 7 72
(BJMeehan) *led after 1f: c alone over to stands' rail over 3f out: rdn and hdd appr fnl f: nt qckn ins last* **9/4**[1]

32S **3** 2 **Miss Cassia**[8] [3770] 2-8-9 ............ RSmith 2 60
(RHannon) *chsd ldrs: bmpd on bnd after 1f: rdn wl over 1f out: one pce after* **9/4**[1]

52 **4** ½ **Mulberry Lad (IRE)**[14] [3570] 2-9-0 ............ RMullen 5 63
(WRMuir) *pushed along in tch: a same pl: riddeand 2f out: one pce after* **8/1**[2]

03 **5** 6 **Artadi**[74] [1905] 2-8-9 ............ JQuinn 6 37
(PMPhelan) *slowly away: a bhd* **33/1**

05 **6** 8 **Three Aces (IRE)**[16] [3531] 2-8-10 ow1............ MTebbutt 3 10
(RMBeckett) *sn outpcd: a bhd* **20/1**[3]

62.72 secs (0.45) **Going Correction** -0.025s/f (Good) **6** Ran SP% **111.1**
Speed ratings: **95,91,87,87,77 64**CSF £7.26 TOTE £2.80: £1.90, £1.50; EX 9.60.

**Owner** Ten Of Hearts **Bred** Mrs P Harford **Trained** Ogbourne Maisey, Wilts

**FOCUS**
An average juvenile maiden in which the riders interestingly elected to come down the centre and stands' side in the home straight.

**NOTEBOOK**
**Louphole**, who had shown fair form in two previous outings, pinged out of the gates and was on the pace throughout, finding plenty under pressure from two out, to run out a ready winner. He appreciated this slight drop in trip, despite his pedigree suggesting he would be best over further, and could improve to land a nursery on this ground.

**Dane's Castle(IRE)** again showed good early speed from his wide stall and, after Dettori made an early switch to the stands rail entering the straight, he still held every chance until coming under maximum pressure two out. He may be better with a switch to nurseries, over another furlong.

**Miss Cassia**, who took a crashing fall on her last outing at Bath, ran her race and had no excuses, although her confidence may well have been dented. She has a bit to prove now and may need a switch to nurseries in order to score.

**Mulberry Lad(IRE)** struggled to go the early pace and he failed to quicken in the straight when the race got serious. He shaped as though he will fare better over further and is now eligible for nurseries.

## 3987 COMMERCIAL CATERING SUPPLIES NURSERY 6f 209y
**3:00** (3:02) (E) 2-Y-O **£3,437** (£1,057; £528; £264) **Stalls** Low

Form RPR

030 **1** **Whatatodo**[30] [3080] 2-8-4 **62** ............ JQuinn 4 63+
(MLWBell) *t.k.h: mde all: hung rt ent fnl f: r.o after* **8/1**

423 **2** 1 ½ **Wasalat (USA)**[32] [3014] 2-9-7 **79** ............ TEDurcan 9 76
(MRChannon) *a.p: chsd wnr fnl 3f: no imp ins fnl f* **6/1**[3]

51 **3** *nk* **He's A Diamond**[15] [3553] 2-9-6 **78** ............ LDettori 3 75
(TGMills) *in tch: rdn over 2f out: r.o wl fnl f* **2/1**[1]

0220 **4** ½ **Lakesdale (IRE)**[16] [3532] 2-7-13 **62** ............ HayleyTurner(5) 5 57
(MrsCADunnett) *trckd ldrs: rdn over 2f out: one pce ins fnl 2f* **33/1**

16 **5** 2 ½ **Treat Me Wild (IRE)**[11] [3679] 2-8-12 **70** ............ RLMoore 8 59
(RHannon) *towards rr: rdn 3f out: effrt 2f out: one pce appr fnl f* **10/1**

61 **6** 2 ½ **Nordhock (USA)**[18] [3458] 2-8-4 **62** ............ TPQueally 7 45
(NACallaghan) *hld up in tch: rdn over 2f out: wknd over 1f out* **9/2**[2]

6300 **7** 1 ½ **Gryskirk**[11] [3677] 2-8-9 **67** ............ PaulEddery 1 46
(PWD'Arcy) *v.s.a: efffort over 2f out: stmbld over 1f out: eased whn btn ins fnl f* **7/1**

0122 **8** 1 **Ronnies Lad**[20] [3390] 2-8-6 **64** ............(p) JFEgan 6 40
(AndrewReid) *prom: rdn 1/2-way: wknd 2f out* **14/1**

4332 **9** 1 **Aunty Euro (IRE)**[38] [2852] 2-8-11 **69** ............ SSanders 2 43
(EJO'Neill) *hld up in tch: rdn over 2f out: sn wknd* **16/1**

1m 24.19s (1.59) **Going Correction** -0.025s/f (Good) **9** Ran SP% **114.0**
Speed ratings: **89,87,86,86,83 80,78,77,76**CSF £54.49 CT £133.01 TOTE £12.00: £3.40, £1.80, £1.10; EX 87.30.

**Owner** M Talbot-Ponsonby & Partners **Bred** R And Mrs S J Turner **Trained** Newmarket, Suffolk

**FOCUS**
A potentially fair nursery with four of the nine runners having won previously. The pace was only steady, however, and the form seems just modest. The figures shown as 'official ratings' are estimates for guidance only.

**NOTEBOOK**
**Whatatodo**, who had shown definite promise on her second run, but disappointed last time, made virtually all the running to score under a well-judged ride. Being allowed to dictate just a steady gallop over this longer trip helped her, and this half-sister to the fair seven-furlong winner Cotosol could do better off a higher mark in this division, but got very much the run of the race on this occasion. *Official explanation: trainer's representative said, regarding the improved form shown, yard was out of form when filly disappointed last time out*

**Wasalat(USA)**, who had looked one paced over six furlongs at Ripon last time, improved a touch for this extra furlong and turned in a sound effort, but again failed to quicken late in the day and looks to have been allotted a fairly stiff mark.

**He's A Diamond** was well backed to follow up his recent course and distance maiden success but never really threatened to land the odds. This was disappointing, and although he may be capable of better in time, he has it all to prove now.

**Lakesdale(IRE)** improved to run her best race to date back on this faster ground and over this extra furlong, but her proximity at the finish sums up the form.

**Nordhock(USA)**, who had a hard race in landing a gamble when dropped into selling company last time, failed to sparkle and on this display looks to have been given a stiff mark. He may be capable of better on a more conventional track.

**Gryskirk**, not beaten far in a better nursery at Newmarket last time, completely missed the break and was up against it from then on. He recovered to join the pack entering the straight, but then stumbled badly and became unbalanced, and he should be capable of better back on a more conventional track.

## 3988 STOWELLS OF CHELSEA (S) STKS 6f 209y
**3:30** (3:30) (G) 3-5-Y-O **£2,606** (£744; £372) **Stalls** Low

Form RPR

-045 **1** **Majhool**[115] [1121] 5-9-5 60 ............ LDettori 4 54
(TGMills) *mde all: rdn over 1f out: jst hld on* **10/3**[1]

3200 **2** *hd* **Cargo**[16] 3533 5-8-12 46....................(tp) LTreadwell(7) 6 53
(BAPearce) *chse wnr thrght: rallied fnl f: jst failed* **10/1**

0520 **3** *shd* **Bahama Reef (IRE)**[15] 3554 3-8-12 57.................... MTebbutt 10 53
(BGubby) *a in tch: rdn over 2f out: rallied wl fnl f: kpt on* **10/1**

0450 **4** *½* **Barabella (IRE)**[8] 3772 3-8-4 58.................... JFMcDonald(3) 2 47
(RJHodges) *hld up in mid-div: hdwy 2f out: rdn and kpt on fnl f* **8/1**[3]

0100 **5** *1¼* **Rileys Dream**[16] 3533 5-9-6 40....................(p) SWhitworth 9 50
(BJLlewellyn) *towards rr: rdn and hdwy over 2f out: one pce fnl f* **20/1**

-000 **6** *hd* **Binnion Bay (IRE)**[10] 3689 3-8-12 67.................... RLMoore 11 48
(RHannon) *stdd s fr wd draw and sn brought over to far rail: kpt on fnl f but nvre on terms* **10/3**[1]

006 **7** *3½* **Love Of Life**[19] 3427 3-8-7 38.................... PDoe 7 34
(JulianPoulton) *towards rr: effrt on outside over 2f out: nvr nr to chal* **50/1**

3534 **8** *½* **Ivy Moon**[17] 3489 4-9-0 44.................... ADaly 3 33
(BJLlewellyn) *a in rr* **6/1**[2]

040- **9** *½* **Another Deal (FR)**[337] 4204 5-9-5 67.................... SDrowne 8 36
(RJHodges) *nvr bttr than mid-div: bhd fnl 2f* **8/1**[3]

3500 **10** *1½* **Rathmullan**[24] 3277 5-9-4 36....................(b) LiamJones(7) 5 39
(EAWheeler) *in tch tl rdn and wknd over 1f out* **33/1**

0060 **11** *¾* **Repeat (IRE)**[9] 3742 4-9-11 40.................... SSanders 1 37
(MissGayKelleway) *chsd ldrs tl rdn over 2f out: sn wknd* **20/1**

1m 23.21s (0.61) **Going Correction** -0.025s/f (Good)
**WFA** 3 from 4yo+ 7lb **11** Ran SP% **115.3**
Speed ratings: **95,94,94,94,92 92,88,87,87,85 84**CSF £35.70 TOTE £3.20: £1.80, £3.70, £2.60; EX 50.40.There was no bid for the winner. Bahama Reef and Barabella were the subject of friendly claims of £6,000.
**Owner** T G Mills **Bred** Gainsborough Stud Management Ltd **Trained** Headley, Surrey

**FOCUS**
A desperate affair that lacked any strength in depth, but it produced a thrilling finish. The time was ordinary and the form is not sure to work out.

**NOTEBOOK**
**Majhool**, who had recorded all of his previous wins on the Polytrack, made all of the running and scored all-out on this first run for new connections. He does have a liking for fast ground, stuck to his task gamely when challenged late on and did well to overcome an absence of 115 days.
**Cargo** was unable to dominate as he prefers, but ran a solid race and went down fighting. He got a touch outpaced, but rallied gamely and clearly got every yard of this trip, so looks well worth another chance.
**Bahama Reef(IRE)** , who only beat one home in a course and distance maiden last time, came there with every chance inside the last furlong, but could not get past the winner, try as he might. A drop back to six furlongs in this grade could see him score.
**Barabella(IRE)** looked a serious threat when coming with a challenge entering the final furlong, but could not quicken when it really mattered and struggled to see out the trip. This was an improved effort and she may do better back over shorter.
**Binnion Bay(IRE)**, joint top rated on official figures and dropping in grade, was given a fair bit to do from off the pace, but again turned in a disappointing effort and has clearly regressed from two to three.
**Ivy Moon** *Official explanation: jockey said filly was unsuited by the track*
**Another Deal(FR)** *Official explanation: jockey said gelding hung right*

## 3989 BLAKES BUTCHERS FILLIES' H'CAP 1m 3f 196y
4:00 (4:02) (E ) (0-75,73) 3-Y-O+ £3,382 (£1,040; £520; £260) **Stalls** High

Form RPR

3423 **1** **Blaze Of Colour**[21] 3383 3-9-0 71....................(v[1]) BDoyle 3 82
(SirMichaelStoute) *trckd ldr: rdn to ld over 1f out: drvn clr* **6/1**[3]

0433 **2** *3* **Bubbling Fun**[19] 3421 3-8-9 66.................... LDettori 8 72
(EALDunlop) *hld up: hdwy 4f out: rdn 2f out: kpt on one pce fnl f* **6/1**[3]

2365 **3** *hd* **Banningham Blaze**[4] 3885 4-8-5 50....................(v) RLMoore 5 56
(AWCarroll) *hld up in rr: hdwy over 2f out: styd on to go 3rd ins fnl f* **10/1**

66-2 **4** *1* **Our Emmy Lou**[5] 3837 3-8-2 59.................... JQuinn 1 63
(SirMarkPrescott) *led rieen and hdd over 1f out: wknd ins fnl f* **5/2**[1]

3061 **5** *2½* **Desert Island Disc**[15] 3557 7-10-0 73.................... GBaker 7 73
(JJBridger) *in tch: takened over to far rail and rdn 2f out: sn btn* **8/1**

2642 **6** *8* **High School**[28] 3156 3-9-1 72.................... TPQueally 4 60
(DRLoder) *a in rr* **8/1**

-432 **7** *6* **Kythia (IRE)**[15] 3557 3-9-2 73.................... SDrowne 6 51
(HMorrison) *in tch tl lost pl qckly 1/2-way: nvr on terms after* **3/1**[2]

30-6 **8** *½* **Armentieres**[198] 416 3-7-10 58....................(p) HayleyTurner(5) 2 35
(JLSpearing) *a struggling in rr* **50/1**

2m 29.38s (-2.72) **Going Correction** -0.025s/f (Good)
**WFA** 3 from 4yo+ 12lb **8** Ran SP% **115.4**
Speed ratings: **108,106,105,105,103 98,94,93**CSF £41.96 CT £354.88 TOTE £5.30: £2.30, £2.00, £2.80; EX 40.50.
**Owner** Maktoum Al Maktoum **Bred** Gainsborough Stud Management Ltd **Trained** Newmarket, Suffolk

**FOCUS**
A fair fillies' handicap, with some relatively unexposed performers on show, and the form looks reasonably solid. The early gallop was only steady but the overall time was reasonable and the field finished well strung out.

**NOTEBOOK**
**Blaze Of Colour** raced keenly in the first-time visor and took her time to get to the front, but really found her stride entering the final furlong and never looked in danger from that point on. She could build on this, if the headgear has the same effect next time.
**Bubbling Fun** , who shaped as though a step up in trip would suit last time, looked a threat when tracking the leaders approaching the home turn, but again found less than expected under maximum pressure and was made to look one paced.
**Banningham Blaze** stepped up on her latest outing, but was doing all of her best work all too late in the day. She is very hard horse to predict.
**Our Emmy Lou**, who had looked a little unlucky when only narrowly going down at Epsom on her handicap debut last time, this time had the run of the race in front, but disappointingly dropped out of contention with a furlong to run. She may be better with a more patient ride, but is not obviously well handicapped on this evidence.
**Kythia(IRE)** lost her place before four out and ran too badly to be true. Something was presumably amiss, but even so she has it all to prove now. *Official explanation: jockey said filly was unsuited by good to firm ground*

## 3990 BRAKES H'CAP 1m 1f 209y
4:30 (4:31) (F ) (0-55,59) 3-Y-O £2,975 (£850; £425) **Stalls** High

Form RPR

-211 **1** **Masafi (IRE)**[3] 3897 3-9-10 59 6ex.................... SSanders 1 82+
(SirMarkPrescott) *trckd leader: c over to stands' side over 3f out: led wl over 1f out: sn clr: easily* **8/13**[1]

0004 **2** *7* **Forge Lane (IRE)**[6] 3827 3-9-6 55....................(p) SWhitworth 11 59
(GLMoore) *hld up: hdwy over 2f out: drvn to chse clr wnr fnl f* **7/1**[2]

0002 **3** *½* **Waltzing Beau**[11] 3681 3-8-12 47.................... GBaker 2 50
(BGPowell) *a in tch: chsd ldrs 4f out: kpt on ins fnl 2f* **20/1**

3540 **4** *5* **Prince Valentine**[35] 2930 3-9-3 55.................... J-PGuillambert(3) 5 49
(DBFeek) *towards rea: rdn and hdwy 3f out: kpt on one pce fnl 2f* **50/1**

4302 **5** *hd* **Bretton**[12] 3637 3-8-8 43.................... TPQueally 12 36
(BAPearce) *mid-div: rdn 4f out: nvr nr to chal* **33/1**

6400 **6** *5* **Anisette**[2] 3932 3-8-10 45.................... PDoe 7 29
(JulianPoulton) *led: styd alone far side and hdd wl over 1f out: sn wknd* **66/1**

5026 **7** *shd* **Russalka**[6] 3827 3-8-11 53.................... MHalford(7) 3 36
(JulianPoulton) *mid-div: rdn over 2f out: sn btn* **16/1**

060- **8** *1½* **Allodarlin (IRE)**[240] 6046 3-8-13 53.................... NDeSouza(5) 6 34
(PFICole) *in tch tl rdn and wknd over 2f out* **40/1**

6251 **9** *¾* **Oktis Morilious (IRE)**[11] 3681 3-8-13 55.................... LTreadwell(7) 9 34
(AWCarroll) *in tch: rdn 3f out: wknd wl over 1f out* **15/2**[3]

00U3 **10** *2* **Don Argento**[6] 3827 3-8-5 40.................... DKinsella 10 15
(MrsAJBowlby) *slowly away: rdn and sme hdwy over 2f out: wknd over 1f out* **20/1**

6632 **11** *5* **Erte**[23] 3305 3-9-2 51.................... TEDurcan 8 17
(MRChannon) *hld up:: rdn 3f out: wknd 2f out* **9/1**

0000 **12** *23* **Kerristina**[23] 3303 3-8-0 35 oh5....................(v) JQuinn 4 —
(DJSFfrenchDavis) *trckd ldrs: wknd 4f out: eased over 1f out* **25/1**

2m 1.63s (-0.91) **Going Correction** -0.025s/f (Good) **12** Ran SP% **124.3**
Speed ratings: **102,96,96,92,91 87,87,86,85,84 80,61**CSF £5.14 CT £54.63 TOTE £1.70: £1.10, £2.00, £5.20; EX 6.70.
**Owner** G D Waters **Bred** G D Waters **Trained** Newmarket, Suffolk

**FOCUS**
A very weak handicap, with little strength in depth, and the field came home well and truly strung out, despite the time being nothing special.

**NOTEBOOK**
**Masafi(IRE)**, able to race off the same mark as when successful in a better contest last time, absolutely routed his rivals to land the quickfire hat-trick. He has progressed in leaps and bounds since stepping up to this trip, has the look of a typical improver from his ultra-shrewd yard, and will no doubts be turned out again quickly in search of the four-timer before his new mark takes effect.
**Forge Lane(IRE)** who finished fast last time over course and distance, stayed on to bag second close home, but was never a threat to the winner. He needs everything to fall right, but should be placed to exploit his current mark this summer.
**Waltzing Beau** was handy throughout and, although he lacked a change of gear when it mattered, ran another sound race and looks to be finding his form. He can get closer when upped in trip.
**Prince Valentine**, who has had his last three starts now over this course and distance, ran a touch better without the blinkers, but did not achieve a great deal.
**Bretton** was plugging on at the one pace in the straight and ran his best race to date on the turf.
**Don Argento** *Official explanation: trainer said gelding finished lame behind*
**Erte** *Official explanation: jockey said gelding was unsuited by track*

## 3991 GOURMET EXPRESS MAIDEN H'CAP (TO BE RIDDEN BY NATIONAL HUNT JOCKEYS) 5f 213y
5:00 (5:00) (F ) (0-55,55) 3-Y-O+ £2,975 (£850; £425) **Stalls** Low

Form RPR

2064 **1** **My Girl Pearl (IRE)**[6] 3828 4-11-6 45.................... SDurack 8 52
(MSSaunders) *in tch: ridden to ld 1f out: drvn out* **9/2**[1]

3654 **2** *nk* **Mr Uppity**[24] 3277 5-10-13 38....................(e) AProcter 6 44
(JulianPoulton) *hld up: rdn over 2f out: c over to stands' rail: fin fast fnl f to go cl 2nd nr fin* **6/1**[3]

0000 **3** *¾* **Dexileos (IRE)**[4] 3871 5-11-1 40....................(t) JMogford 2 44
(ADWPinder) *mid-div: hdwy over 2f out: ev ch ins fnl f: no ex nr fin* **9/1**

0000 **4** *2* **Confuzed**[21] 3378 4-11-4 43....................(b[1]) DRDennis 5 41
(DFlood) *hld up: hdwy and ev ch appr fnl f: fdd ins fnl f* **16/1**

0402 **5** *1¼* **Jasmine Pearl (IRE)**[24] 3260 3-11-4 48.................... LAspell 4 42
(TMJones) *towards rr: gd hdwy on ins 2f out: wknd ins fnl f* **11/2**[2]

0400 **6** *1½* **Costa Del Sol (IRE)**[5] 3844 3-10-10 40....................(b) BHitchcott 3 30
(JJBridger) *bhd and nvr on terms* **33/1**

0005 **7** *½* **Bahamian Belle**[11] 3668 4-11-1 40.................... JAMcCarthy 10 28
(PSMcentee) *towards rr: rdn 2f out: nvr on terms* **12/1**

0405 **8** *½* **Chatshow (USA)**[10] 3707 3-11-11 55.................... PFlynn 12 42
(LADace) *trckd ldr: hdd over 2f out: rdn and hdd 1f out: wknd* **8/1**

4400 **9** *1¼* **Bold Wolf**[38] 2836 3-11-3 47....................(p) JMMaguire 7 30
(JLSpearing) *led: hdd over 2f out: wknd over 1f out* **14/1**

2040 **10** *½* **Savernake Brave (IRE)**[27] 3175 3-10-13 43.................... RGreene 11 24
(MrsHSweeting) *slowly away and sn rdn: a bhd* **8/1**

0602 **11** *nk* **Blaise Wood (USA)**[20] 3391 3-11-8 52....................(p) PHide 9 32
(GLMoore) *a in rr* **7/1**

0506 **12** *7* **Moonglade (USA)**[27] 3175 4-10-6 31....................(b) MBatchelor 1 —
(MissJFeilden) *mid-div: rdn 1/2-way: wknd 2f out* **20/1**

1m 11.12s (1.02) **Going Correction** -0.025s/f (Good)
**WFA** 3 from 4yo+ 5lb **12** Ran SP% **120.5**
Speed ratings: **92,91,90,87,86 84,83,82,81,80 80,70**CSF £31.34 CT £242.01 TOTE £6.40: £2.40, £1.80, £3.50; EX 37.80 Place 6 £35.93, Place 5 £22.86.
**Owner** T A Godbert **Bred** Loan And Development Corporation **Trained** Haydon, Somerset

**FOCUS**
A dire event, and the form is poor despite the first three being clear.

**NOTEBOOK**
**My Girl Pearl(IRE)** dug deep under pressure late on to score all-out and appreciated this drop back in trip. This was a deserved success at the 28th time of asking, but she is certainly not one to lump on in a follow-up bid.
**Mr Uppity** , well backed throughout the day for this, struggled to go the pace early on, but was flying at the finish and was only just denied. This was his best effort to date on turf, but he is a fiendishly tricky ride who clearly has his quirks.
**Dexileos(IRE)** ran an improved race in third, holding every chance on this drop back in trip. He is capable of improving on his current mark.
**Confuzed** was only run out of contention late in the day after hanging to the far side, and improved for the application of blinkers.
**Jasmine Pearl(IRE)** looked very one paced in the straight and finished a never dangerous fifth.
T/Plt: £43.30 to a £1 stake. Pool: £39,409.25. 663.20 winning tickets. T/Qpdt: £35.90 to a £1 stake. Pool: £2,432.00. 50.10 winning tickets. JS

# 3805 WINDSOR (R-H)
Monday, July 19

**OFFICIAL GOING: Good to firm**

## 3992 EUROPEAN BREEDERS FUND MAIDEN FILLIES' STKS 6f
6:20 (6:20) (D ) 2-Y-O £5,265 (£1,620; £810; £405) **Stalls** High

Form RPR

336 **1** **Angel Sprints**[26] 3208 2-8-11.................... ADaly 5 83
(LGCottrell) *mde all: drvn along over 2f out: styd on wl to assert last half f* **7/2**[1]

43 **2** 1 ¼ **Gennie Bond**[10] 3693 2-8-11 RLMoore 1 79
(RHannon) *sn trcking ldr: upsides fr 3f out: rdn 2f out: nt qckn last half f* **9/2**[2]

30 **3** 1 ½ **Keep Baccknhit (IRE)**[8] 3770 2-8-6 AQuinn(5) 9 75
(GLMoore) *sn chsng ldrs: rdn and styd on same pce fnl 2f* **14/1**

0 **4** 3 ½ **Apple Of My Eye**[37] 2884 2-8-11 WRyan 6 64
(JRJenkins) *outpcd in rr: hdwy fr 2f out: kpt on ins last: nt pce to rch ldrs* **40/1**

**5** ½ **Lilting Prose (IRE)** 2-8-11 LDettori 3 63
(RHannon) *chsd ldrs: rdn over 2f out: wknd appr fnl f* **9/2**[2]

03 **6** 2 **Guinea A Minute (IRE)**[11] 3659 2-8-11 IMongan 7 57
(MLWBell) *bhd: sn pushed along: mod hdwy fnl f* **7/1**

**7** ¾ **Severely (FR)** 2-8-11 MHills 10 55
(BWHills) *t.k.h: a in rr* **5/1**[3]

**8** 1 ¼ **Sharp As A Tack (IRE)** 2-8-8 JFMcDonald(3) 4 51
(BJMeehan) *s.i.s: bhd: sme hdwy 3f out: rdn and hung lft over 2f out and sn lost tch* **12/1**

**9** 1 ¾ **Winter Moon** 2-8-11 SDrowne 2 46
(BRMillman) *s.i.s: hdwy to chse ldrs 1/2-way: sn wknd* **16/1**

64 **10** ¾ **Epitomise**[19] 3408 2-8-11 MTebbutt 8 43
(RMBeckett) *a outpcd* **16/1**

1m 12.54s (-1.33) **Going Correction** -0.25s/f (Firm) **10** Ran SP% **116.3**
Speed ratings: **98,96,94,89,89 86,85,83,81,80**CSF £18.97 TOTE £5.20: £2.40, £1.50, £4.30; EX 16.60.
**Owner** Mrs Lucy Halloran **Bred** Bishopswood Bloodstock And Trickledown Stud **Trained** Dulford, Devon

**FOCUS**
The first two dominated throughout and the form appears decent for the grade.

**NOTEBOOK**
**Angel Sprints**, the most experienced filly in the race, was quickly away, always in the right position and grabbed the rail, which was probably crucial, in the straight. The step up to six furlongs appeared to suit.
**Gennie Bond** has improved with every outing and showed her best form to date. She showed good speed form the outset, but the fact the favourite had the advantage of the rail probably acted against her. She is now eligible for handicaps.
**Keep Bacckinhit(IRE)** had an unfortunate experience at Bath last time but showed her true form this time. She finished nicely clear of the rest and is another who has now qualified for a mark.
**Apple Of My Eye**, a half-sister to Fruit Of Glory, struggled to go the early pace but kept on well enough in the closing stages. This was certainly a step up on her debut effort, and she is going to be suited by farther in time.
**Lilting Prose(IRE)**, a 45,000gns yearling, did best of the newcomers. She ran green and was not knocked about, and can be expected to come on for the run.

## 3993 COUNTRYSIDE ALLIANCE FILLIES' H'CAP 1m 67y
**6:50** (6:50) (E) (0-75,75) 3-Y-O **£3,591** (£1,105; £552; £276) **Stalls** High

Form RPR

0-02 **1** **Du Pre**[15] 3554 3-9-1 **69** SDrowne 11 80+
(MrsAJPerrett) *trckd ldr: rdn to ld ins fnl 2f: styd on wl u.p fnl f* **10/3**[2]

0005 **2** 1 **Filliemou (IRE)**[10] 3700 3-7-11 **54** FPFerris(3) 13 59
(AWCarroll) *led: rdn and hdd ins fnl 2f: styd on wl u.p to hold clr 2nd but nt pce of wnr ins last* **10/1**

0510 **3** 2 **Deign To Dance (IRE)**[10] 3700 3-8-7 **61** TEDurcan 8 61
(JGPortman) *bhd: hdwy on rails ins fnl 2f: r.o wl fnl f but nt rch ldrs* **8/1**

5-51 **4** nk **Hot Lips Page (FR)**[28] 3139 3-9-7 **75** RLMoore 1 74+
(RHannon) *hld up rr: hdwy over 2f out: swtchd lft and r.o to chse ldrs fnl f but no imp* **3/1**[1]

5053 **5** nk **Soviet Spirit**[19] 3427 3-7-12 **59** MHalford(7) 9 58
(CADwyer) *a chsng ldrs: rdn over 2f out: styd on same pce fnl f* **12/1**

062 **6** ¾ **Sea Of Gold**[20] 3392 3-9-4 **72** LDettori 10 69
(HJCyzer) *chsd ldrs: rdn over 2f out: styd on same pce* **6/1**[3]

-000 **7** 2 ½ **Hold Up**[13] 3603 3-8-6 **60** SWhitworth 6 51
(MissJFeilden) *chsd ldrs: rdn 3f out: wknd ins fnl 2f* **20/1**

004- **8** shd **Great Blasket (IRE)**[265] 5816 3-8-0 **54** JQuinn 4 45
(EJO'Neill) *chsd ldrs: chal fr over 3f out tl wknd ins fnl 2f* **25/1**

2-00 **9** 1 ½ **Flame Queen**[17] 3478 3-9-1 **69** TPQueally 5 56
(MissKBBoutflower) *chsd ldrs: racd on outside and t.k.h whn rn wd bnd 6f out and over 4f out: effrt ins fnl 3f: wknd 2f out* **20/1**

4000 **10** 3 **Snow Joke (IRE)**[11] 3684 3-7-10 **53** JFMcDonald(3) 7 34
(MrsPNDutfield) *unruly stalls: rdn 4f out: a bhd* **14/1**

00-4 **11** 2 **Pappy (IRE)**[193] 473 3-7-12 **52** oh2 SRighton 3 28
(AWCarroll) *chsd ldrs: t.k.h: rn wd bnd 6f out and over 4f out: wknd fr 3f out* **33/1**

030 **12** 9 **Burn**[14] 3592 3-8-10 **64** IMongan 2 19
(MLWBell) *prom whn rn wd bnd 6f out and over 4f out: chsd ldrs 3f out: wknd 2f out: eased whn no ch fnl f* **16/1**

1m 44.35s (-1.25) **Going Correction** -0.15s/f (Firm) **12** Ran SP% **119.1**
Speed ratings: **100,99,97,96,96 95,93,93,91,88 86,77**CSF £34.79 CT £252.24 TOTE £4.00: £1.40, £4.00, £2.80; EX 52.10.
**Owner** R A Grossman **Bred** C H Bothway **Trained** Pulborough, W Sussex

**FOCUS**
A moderate handicap and the gallop was only modest. The form is ordinary but fairly sound for the grade.

**NOTEBOOK**
**Du Pre** relished this extra furlong and produced a solid effort to get off the mark at the fifth attempt. She did not have to improve greatly to score on this handicap debut, but the manner of her victory suggests that she will stay farther and she could have more to offer this year.
**Filliemou(IRE)**, who has dropped 11lb in the ratings this year, ran a much more encouraging race and stayed on right to the line after being passed by the winner. She remains winless after 12 outings, but likes this trip and could capitalise on her tumble in the weights while her yard remains in good form.
**Deign To Dance(IRE)**, 4lb lower than when finishing well behind Filiiemou last time, ran a much better race, staying on well to the line, but she was never a serious threat.
**Hot Lips Page(FR)** found little when asked for maximum effort in the straight and ran as though the 6lb rise for her success in a weaker race last time had found her out.
**Soviet Spirit**, making her debut for her new connections, could not find a change of gear when it mattered, but she improved a touch on her latest third in a claimer.
**Sea Of Gold** did not improve for this handicap debut and was made to look very one paced in the straight. She looks to have been entered on a stiff mark.
**Flame Queen** *Official explanation: jockey said filly did not handle track.*
**Burn** *Official explanation: jockey said filly suffered interference and lost its action*

## 3994 RUTLAND MAIDEN STKS 1m 2f 7y
**7:20** (7:23) (D) 3-Y-O **£4,368** (£1,344; £672; £336) **Stalls** Low

Form RPR

6 **1** **Motorway (IRE)**[83] 1683 3-9-0 SDrowne 16 84
(RCharlton) *chsd ldrs: pushed along to ld jst ins fnl 2f: drvn and styd on wl whn chal fnl f* **7/2**[2]

02 **2** ¾ **News Sky (USA)**[18] 3447 3-9-0 MHills 14 83
(BWHills) *prom: chsd wnr ins fnl 2f: drvn to chal ins last: kpt on but no ex nr fin* **9/2**[3]

**3** 3 ½ **Day Of Reckoning** 3-8-9 BDoyle 5 71+
(SirMichaelStoute) *broke wl: stdd rr: pushed along and hdwy fr 3f out: r.o wl fr over 1f out but nt rch ldrs* **8/1**

434 **4** 1 ½ **Zangeal**[29] 3121 3-9-0 79 (t) RMullen 4 73
(CFWall) *chsd ldr tl led over 3f out: sn rdn and hung lft: hdd ins fnl 2f: sn btn* **10/3**[1]

6U **5** 1 ½ **Kilindini**[42] 2729 3-8-11 LPKeniry(3) 6 70
(MissECLavelle) *in tch whn rn wd bnd over 4f out: kpt on fr 3f out to chse ldrs over 2f out: sn one pce* **33/1**

00- **6** shd **Hat Trick Man**[278] 5571 3-9-0 RLMoore 11 70
(JAkehurst) *bhd: pushed along 3f out: styd on wl fnl 2f but nvr gng pce to rch ldrs* **20/1**

**7** 3 ½ **Aspired (IRE)** 3-8-9 OUrbina 8 63+
(JRFanshawe) *hld up mid-div: shkn up and effrt over 2f out: hung lft and green ins fnl 2f: sn wknd* **14/1**

45 **8** 5 **Rossall Point**[22] 3348 3-9-0 TQuinn 17 54+
(JLDunlop) *s.i.s: bhd: mod hdwy fr over 2f out* **8/1**

20 **9** 1 ¾ **Noble Mind**[17] 3487 3-9-0 DKinsella 3 51
(PGMurphy) *chsd ldrs tl wknd ins fnl 3f* **14/1**

00 **10** 3 ½ **Surface To Air**[35] 2950 3-9-0 RHavlin 15 44
(MrsPNDutfield) *s.i.s: a in rr* **66/1**

0 **11** 2 **Primeshade Promise**[14] 3592 3-8-9 RPrice 13 35
(DBurchell) *a in rr* **100/1**

00-0 **12** 7 **Sixtilsix (IRE)**[11] 3666 3-9-0 RLappin 2 27
(WJarvis) *sn led: hdd over 3f out: sn btn* **66/1**

00-0 **13** 5 **Gliding By**[12] 3630 3-8-9 JQuinn 7 12
(PRChamings) *chsd ldrs tl wknd ins fnl 3f* **33/1**

06 **14** 3 **Blaze The Trail**[18] 3454 3-8-9 TPQueally 1 —
(Jean-ReneAuvray) *chsd ldrs over 5f* **100/1**

**15** 10 **Start Of Authority** 3-9-0 TEDurcan 9 —
(JGallagher) *s.i.s: a bhd* **28/1**

2m 6.19s (-2.11) **Going Correction** -0.15s/f (Firm) **15** Ran SP% **118.1**
Speed ratings: **102,101,98,97,96 96,93,89,87,85 83,77,73,71,63**CSF £17.79 TOTE £3.60: £1.80, £1.60, £2.50; EX 13.30.
**Owner** Mountgrange Stud **Bred** Epona Bloodstock Ltd **Trained** Beckhampton, Wilts

**FOCUS**
Not a very competitive maiden, but the front two pulled clear of the promising newcomer Day Of Reckoning and the form looks reasonable.

**NOTEBOOK**
**Motorway(IRE)**, not seen since his debut at Bath 83 days earlier, confirmed that promise by getting off the mark. He took a while to get the better of News Sky in the straight, but always looked like getting on top and there should be more to come, especially over farther.
**News Sky(USA)** is progressing well and ran another promising race on this step up from a mile. He was clear of the remainder and is up to winning a similar race.
**Day Of Reckoning**, a half-sister to high-class middle-distance filly Phantom Gold, was very easy to back on course, but she made a pleasing debut. She never really looked like winning, but finished to good effect and came home best of the fillies. She can be expected to improve on this.
**Zangeal**, well backed on this first run in a tongue tie, travelled really well for much of the way, but hung badly when entering the straight and was unable to sustain his effort.
**Kilindini** stepped up on the form he showed on his debut and is clearly going the right way. He is now eligible for a handicap mark.

## 3995 CATLIN GROUP CLASSIFIED STKS 6f
**7:50** (7:51) (D) 3-Y-O **£6,870** (£2,114; £1,057; £528) **Stalls** High

Form RPR

133 **1** **Eisteddfod**[23] 3295 3-8-9 80 NDeSouza(5) 3 87
(PFICole) *trckd ldrs: rdn to ld jst ins fnl f: qcknd and kpt on strly cl home* **9/1**

1145 **2** 1 **Bohola Flyer (IRE)**[3] 3914 3-8-11 78 LDettori 7 81
(RHannon) *trckd ldrs tl outpcd over 2f out: drvn and styd on wl fnl f to take 2nd cl home: no imp on wnr* **9/2**[3]

6321 **3** ½ **Presto Shinko (IRE)**[38] 2839 3-9-3 83 RLMoore 2 86
(RHannon) *hld up in rr: hdwy: nt clr run and swtchd lft 1f out: styd on but nt pce to chal ins last* **11/4**[2]

3410 **4** shd **King's Caprice**[16] 3542 3-9-5 85 SCarson 1 87
(GBBalding) *stdd s: hld up in tch: hdwy to ld wl over 1f out: sn rdn: hdd jst ins last and sn one pce* **14/1**

0-26 **5** 2 ½ **Chance For Romance**[26] 3203 3-8-13 82 RMullen 5 74
(WRMuir) *sn led: hdd wl over 1f out: stl ev ch 1f out: wknd last half f* **25/1**

0-13 **6** 1 ¾ **Kschessinka (USA)**[23] 3317 3-8-12 81 MHills 4 67
(WJHaggas) *t.k.h: trckd ldrs: chal over 2f out tl over 1f out: wknd ins last* **5/4**[1]

4-00 **7** 3 ½ **Molly Moon (IRE)**[10] 3702 3-8-13 82 SDrowne 6 58
(MBlanshard) *rdn over 2f out: a outpcd and n.d* **25/1**

1m 12.52s (-1.35) **Going Correction** -0.25s/f (Firm) **7** Ran SP% **113.7**
Speed ratings: **99,97,97,96,93 91,86**CSF £48.06 TOTE £9.20: £2.80, £2.10; EX 37.40.
**Owner** Elite Racing Club **Bred** Elite Racing Club **Trained** Whatcombe, Oxon

**FOCUS**
A tight classified event, but an ordianry pace and only fair form.

**NOTEBOOK**
**Eisteddfod** took a competitive affair in good style, handling the quicker ground with little problem. He appreciated the drop back to six furlongs and once again confirmed himself a progressive sort. There looks to be more to come from him.
**Bohola Flyer(IRE)** had won on her previous two visits to the track and put in another good display, this time in defeat. She would not appear to have as much improvement in her as the winner, but should continue to run with credit.
**Presto Shinko(IRE)** had to be switched wide, which was not ideal, to be brought with his challenge. He finished fairly well but was not unlucky in any way.
**King's Caprice**, a course and distance winner last month, showed plenty of pace and had every chance. He hails from a family which usually benefits from some cut in the ground.
**Chance For Romance** has failed to build on her promising seasonal debut.
**Kschessinka(USA)**, unlucky in running last time out, was a well-backed favourite. She raced a touch keenly but it was disappointing to see her easily beaten off once the race got going in earnest. She is surely better than she showed here, but she has now been beaten twice at short odds, and presumably is losing her supporters fast.
**Molly Moon(IRE)** *Official explanation: vet said filly was distressed*

## 3996 COUNTRYSIDE ALLIANCE (S) STKS 1m 3f 135y
**8:20** (8:20) (E) 3-Y-O+ **£3,435** (£1,057; £528; £264) **Stalls** Low

Form RPR

330 **1** **Ambersong**[8] 3774 6-9-7 41 IMongan 8 59
(AWCarroll) *s.i.s: bhd: pushed along and hdwy 4f out: rdn 3f out: led ins fnl 2f: drvn clr fnl f* **4/1**[1]

6100 **2** 3 **Peruvian Breeze (IRE)**[21] 3379 3-9-0 58 TEDurcan 10 59
(JGallagher) *chsd ldrs: rdn: chal and edgd lft 2f out: styd on to chse wnr fr over 1f out but no imp* **13/2**

000- **3** 4 **Miss Woodpigeon**[131] 5377 8-9-2 SCarson 9 43
(JDFrost) *sn led: hdd after 2f: styd w ldr tl led again 5f out: rdn and hdd ins fnl 2f: sn btn* **16/1**

0564 **4** 3 1/2 **Blue Savanna**[7] 3809 4-9-12 40 (b) TJMurphy 4 47
(JGPortman) *pressed ldrs: rdn and ev ch over 2f out: wknd wl over 1f out* **6/1**[3]

0300 **5** 3/4 **Great Gidding**[17] 3479 3-8-9 55 SDrowne 3 41
(HMorrison) *pressed ldrs 3f: rdn and lost pl 4f out: n.d after* **4/1**[1]

6/0 **6** 1/2 **Devote**[69] 1687 6-9-7 (b) SWhitworth 6 40
(JDFrost) *s.i.s: slt ld after 2f tl hdd 5f out: wknd and bmpd 2f out* **33/1**

060/ **7** 1/2 **Lightning Star (USA)**[7] 3678 9-9-7 (b) RLMoore 1 39
(GLMoore) *prom: rdn 5f out: sn btn* **9/2**[2]

300 **8** 6 **Paddy Boy (IRE)**[25] 3245 3-8-9 48 TQuinn 5 30
(JRBoyle) *keen ho:d chsd ldrs 7f* **6/1**[3]

-460 **9** 3 1/2 **Keltic Rainbow (IRE)**[45] 2667 3-8-4 50 (p) PaulEddery 7 19
(DHaydnJones) *a in rr* **16/1**

2m 28.71s (-1.39) **Going Correction** -0.15s/f (Firm)
**WFA** 3 from 4yo+ 12lb 9 Ran SP% **114.8**
Speed ratings: **98,96,93,91,90 90,89,85,83**CSF £30.02 TOTE £5.90: £2.10, £1.90, £3.60; EX 31.60.There was no bid for the winner. Peruvian Breeze was claimed by R. Williams for £6,000.

**Owner** Pursuit Media **Bred** Miss K Rausing **Trained** Wixford, Warwicks

**FOCUS**
A poor race but, on paper, competitive nonetheless. The winner is not badly treated on his All-Weather form.

**NOTEBOOK**
**Ambersong**, second worst in at the weights, was nevertheless supported into joint-favouritism as he was at least in form and had been successful in the past. He won well enough but, outside of banded grade, will struggle to find another race as weak as this one.

**Peruvian Breeze(IRE)**, another who had a previous success to his name, was having his first outing for his new trainer. He plugged on for second but was never going to reel in the winner, and on this evidence his current rating flatters him.

**Miss Woodpigeon**, whose previous form on the Flat and over hurdles is poor, ran her best race to date on the level.

**Blue Savanna**, who does not find a lot under pressure, is not in the same form as he was in the spring.

**Great Gidding** was greatly flattered to finish third to New Morning at Leicester and his subsequent performances have confirmed that impression.

**Paddy Boy(IRE)** *Official explanation: jockey said gelding lost its action on the bend*

## 3997 SHARON BURROWS 40TH BIRTHDAY CELEBRATION H'CAP 1m 2f 7y
8:50 (8:50) (E) (0-70,65) 3-Y-O+ £3,571 (£1,099; £549; £274) Stalls Low

Form RPR

0003 **1** **Karaoke (IRE)**[5] 3842 4-9-10 **65** RLMoore 2 71
(SKirk) *mid-div: pushed along and hdwy 3f out: led appr fnl f: hrd drvn and hld on wl* **15/8**[1]

25-4 **2** nk **Malak Al Moulouk (USA)**[21] 3387 4-9-7 **65** LFletcher(3) 11 71
(JMPEustace) *in tch: hdwy over 3f out: drvn to chal 2f out: styd pressing wnr ins last tl no ex cl home* **6/1**[3]

0605 **3** 1 1/4 **Sir Haydn**[16] 3534 4-9-9 **64** (b) TEDurcan 12 67
(JRJenkins) *hld up in rr: hdwy over 2f out: str run ins fnl f but nt rch ldrs* **8/1**

5456 **4** 3/4 **Hilarious (IRE)**[10] 3710 4-7-10 **44** LucyRussell(7) 13 46
(DrJRJNaylor) *chsd ldrs: rdn to chal fr over 2f out: stl ev ch 1f out: outpcd ins last* **11/1**

50 **5** 3/4 **Latin Queen (IRE)**[17] 3490 4-8-4 **45** ADaly 10 46
(JDFrost) *chsd ldrs: led ins fnl 3f: rdn 2f out: hdd appr fnl f: wknd ins last* **16/1**

1600 **6** 1 1/4 **Stolen Song**[9] 3743 4-9-0 **55** SWhitworth 5 53
(MJRyan) *hld up in rr: gd hdwy 3f out: rdn to chal over 2f out: wknd fnl f* **16/1**

3030 **7** 2 1/2 **Rainbow World (IRE)**[5] 3844 4-9-3 **58** (p) JFEgan 7 51
(AndrewReid) *bhd: rdn over 3f out: nvr gng pce to rch ldrs* **5/1**[2]

0056 **8** 14 **Flying Treaty (USA)**[15] 3555 7-9-3 **58** (p) SDrowne 3 25
(JLSpearing) *chsd ldrs: rdn 5f out: sn btn* **12/1**

300- **9** nk **Curragh Gold (IRE)**[100] 5200 4-8-6 **54** AmyBaker(7) 4 20
(MrsPNDutfield) *a in rr* **25/1**

6-00 **10** nk **Major Blade (GER)**[58] 2302 6-8-13 **54** TQuinn 9 20
(BGPowell) *chsd ldrs tl wknd over 3f out* **25/1**

3000 **11** 3 1/2 **Spiders Web**[83] 1697 4-7-12 **39** oh10 (b) MHenry 8 —
(TKeddy) *chsd ldrs 6f* **50/1**

0100 **12** 13 **Senior Minister**[15] 3555 6-8-12 **60** LTreadwell(7) 1 —
(PWHiatt) *led: 8l clr after 3f: rdn 4f out: hdd ins fnl 3f: wknd qckly* **16/1**

2m 6.48s (-1.82) **Going Correction** -0.15s/f (Firm) 12 Ran SP% **120.2**
Speed ratings: **101,100,99,99,98 97,95,84,84,83 81,70**CSF £12.63 CT £76.13 TOTE £2.60: £1.20, £2.50, £2.80; EX 9.70 Place 6 £214.86, Place 5 £117.82.

**Owner** Speedlith Group **Bred** P F Headon **Trained** Upper Lambourn, Berks

**FOCUS**
Just a modest handicap and the winner did not need to run to his best to score.

**NOTEBOOK**
**Karaoke(IRE)** was not well drawn but, off a 2lb lower mark than when a creditable third at Kempton last time, showed good battling qualities to hold on in a tight finish. He has run a few decent races off marks in the mid-60s but is likely to struggle off a higher mark.

**Malak Al Moulouk(USA)** was having only his fifth-ever start, but the Handicapper did not look to have taken many chances with his handicap mark. He ran well off top weight though, and looks to be going the right way.

**Sir Haydn** has to be brought with a late run and has a poor strike-rate. He finished well with the blinkers back on instead of a visor, but we have seen this sort of performance before.

**Hilarious(IRE)** has dropped a fair way in the handicap over the last two years, but she continues to frustrate and remains a maiden.

**Latin Queen(IRE)** showed up well for a long way but appeared not to get home.

**Stolen Song** ran his best race of the current turf season but really needs farther than this.

T/Plt: £87.50 to a £1 stake. Pool: £51,971.50. 433.10 winning tickets. T/Qpdt: £12.80 to a £1 stake. Pool: £3,807.60. 219.10 winning tickets. ST

3998 - 4002a (Foreign Racing) - See Raceform Interactive

# 3974 AYR (L-H)
Tuesday, July 20

**OFFICIAL GOING: Good to firm**

## 4003 SHARP MINDS WINNERS WELCOME MEDIAN AUCTION MAIDEN STKS 6f
2:15 (2:15) (E) 2-Y-O £3,565 (£1,097; £548; £274) Stalls High

Form RPR

02 **1** **Madame Topflight**[15] 3577 2-8-6 NMackay(3) 5 80
(MrsGSRees) *mde all: pushed out fnl f* **12/1**

4 **2** 1 1/2 **Master Cobbler (IRE)**[28] 3176 2-9-0 KDarley 1 81
(GAButler) *keen: trckd ldrs: effrt 2f out: edgd rt and kpt on fnl f* **13/8**[2]

4 **3** shd **Love Angel (USA)**[13] 3643 2-9-0 JFanning 4 80
(MJohnston) *cl up: effrt over 1f out: kpt on same pce fnl f* **6/4**[1]

36 **4** 5 **Jerry's Girl (IRE)**[34] 2972 2-8-9 PHanagan 6 60
(MissLAPerratt) *in tch tl rdn and outpcd fr 2f out* **16/1**

**5** 6 **Bespoke** 2-9-0 SSanders 2 47
(SirMarkPrescott) *dwlt: sn outpcd: struggling fr 1/2-way* **10/1**[3]

**6** 3/4 **Quick Grand (IRE)** 2-8-9 RFfrench 7 40
(MissLAPerratt) *sn niggled in rr: struggling fr 1/2-way* **66/1**

**7** 6 **Compton Classic** 2-9-0 WSupple 3 27
(JSGoldie) *in tch to 1/2-way: sn rdn and btn* **33/1**

1m 12.52s (-1.20) **Going Correction** -0.35s/f (Firm) 7 Ran SP% **105.2**
Speed ratings: **94,92,91,85,77 76,68**CSF £27.07 TOTE £13.10: £3.10, £1.70; EX 32.10.

**Owner** P Bamford **Bred** Dandy's Farm **Trained** Sollom, Lancs

**FOCUS**
A modest juvenile ran at just a ordinary gallop, but the first three home were well clear of the rest and the form could prove to e better than rated.

**NOTEBOOK**
**Madame Topflight** pinged out to bag the lead and never really looked in danger from that point on. She has improved with each of her three starts to date and this extra furlong was right up her street, but she had the run of the race this time, and will probably need to improve again to take a nursery.

**Master Cobbler(IRE)** was much better away on than on his recent Newbury debut, but failed to improve on that form, and was always looking held by the winner. He raced a touch keenly over this extra furlong, and is not one to write off yet, especially as he has scope and is bred to do better over farther.

**Love Angel(USA)** could not quicken when it mattered, but shaped very much as though he will improve for another furlong. His short-term future looks to lie within nurseries.

**Jerry's Girl(IRE)** got outpaced when the race got serious, but now qualifies for nurseries, and she could fare a deal better in that division over further.

**Bespoke**, like a fair percentage of his stable's juveniles, was slow to break and never posed a serious threat on this racecourse debut. He is out of a dam who progressed with age over a bit farther, but his next run will tell us a lot more, and he could be capable of leaving this form well behind in due course.

## 4004 SHARP MINDS BETFAIR (S) STKS 7f 50y
2:45 (2:47) (F) 3-Y-O+ £3,438 (£1,058; £529; £264) Stalls Low

Form RPR

-166 **1** **Zhitomir**[60] 2260 6-9-11 49 SWKelly 2 59
(MDods) *prom: nt clr run and swtchd lft over 1f out: led ins fnl f: r.o wl* **13/2**[3]

3640 **2** 1/2 **Zahunda (IRE)**[11] 3697 5-9-0 37 KFallon 8 47
(WMBrisbourne) *led to ins fnl f: kpt on: hld towards fin* **11/1**

4332 **3** 1 1/4 **Wares Home (IRE)**[6] 3836 3-8-12 55 DarrenWilliams 5 48
(KRBurke) *plld hrd: cl up: effrt and hung lft fr over 1f out: no ex ins last* **7/2**[1]

0054 **4** 1 **Naughty Girl (IRE)**[8] 3807 4-9-0 50 (vt) EAhern 3 41
(PDEvans) *cl up: effrt and ev ch over 1f out: no ex ins fnl f* **7/1**

3060 **5** nk **Mount Pekan (IRE)**[17] 3520 4-9-5 41 WSupple 13 45
(JSGoldie) *hld up: hdwy over 1f out: hung lft: r.o fnl f: no imp* **25/1**

3000 **6** 2 1/2 **Zarin (IRE)**[14] 3615 6-9-5 54 ACulhane 14 39
(DWChapman) *hld up: hdwy and hung lft centre over 1f out: nvr rchd ldrs* **8/1**

-000 **7** 1 1/4 **Angel Isa (IRE)**[19] 3457 4-9-0 44 PHanagan 12 30
(RAFahey) *sn pushed along towards rr: effrt over 2f out: sn no imp* **12/1**

0-00 **8** 3/4 **Sandy Bay (IRE)**[103] 1318 5-9-5 37 PFessey 10 33
(ARDicken) *dwlt: bhd tl styd on fr over 1f out: n.d* **33/1**

0240 **9** 1 **Francis Flute**[32] 3039 6-9-0 51 PMulrennan(5) 7 31
(BMactaggart) *midfield on outside: effrt and hung lft over 2f out: btn over 1f out* **4/1**[2]

0006 **10** 1 3/4 **Pharaoh Hatshepsut (IRE)**[9] 3367 6-9-0 32 RFfrench 9 21
(JamesMoffatt) *cl up tl wknd fr 2f out* **100/1**

0360 **11** hd **Bargain Hunt (IRE)**[6] 3836 3-8-12 44 (v) JBramhill 6 26
(WStorey) *bhd: rdn 1/2-way: n.d* **33/1**

0000 **12** 2 1/2 **Blade's Edge**[10] 3734 3-8-12 50 (b) RLMoore 4 19
(ABailey) *hld up: effrt over 2f out: btn over 1f out* **25/1**

0000 **13** 1 1/4 **Needwood Bucolic (IRE)**[10] 3735 6-9-2 37 TEaves(3) 1 16
(RAllan) *hld up ins: rdn over 2f out: sn btn* **66/1**

0000 **14** 20 **Lion's Domane**[15] 3579 7-8-12 44 PPMathers(7) 11 —
(ABerry) *sn chsng ldrs: rdn and hung bdly lft over 2f out: faltered and qckly lost pl: virtually p.u ins last* **25/1**

1m 32.16s (-0.31) **Going Correction** -0.075s/f (Good)
**WFA** 3 from 4yo+ 7lb 14 Ran SP% **115.1**
Speed ratings: **98,97,96,94,94 91,90,89,88,86 86,83,81,58**CSF £67.33 TOTE £7.40: £3.00, £3.50, £1.10; EX 72.30.There was no bid for the winner

**Owner** M J K Dods **Bred** Serpentine Bloodstock Et Al **Trained** Piercebridge, Co Durham

**FOCUS**
This was poor on quality, but fairly competitive for the grade, and the pace was sound.

**NOTEBOOK**
**Zhitomir**, who won in this grade at Catterick on his reappearance under today's rider, had to wait for the gaps to appear approaching the final furlong but, when in the clear, readily extended away to score. This is clearly his level, his overall record would suggest he is best on a left-handed track and he could go in again granted similar conditions. There was no bid at the subsequent auction.

**Zahunda(IRE)** put up a sound effort at the weights, but again lacked a change of gear at the business end of the race. She is very hard to win with, yet seemed to enjoy making the running this time and is capable of a bit better back over a mile, when getting an easier surface.

**Wares Home(IRE)** looked to be travelling with ease turning for home, but paid for running too keenly through the early stages over this trip, and could not quicken off the bridle. She is probably better over six furlongs and, although she has her quirks, certainly has the ability to win at this level.

**Naughty Girl(IRE)** travelled like a winner, until finding nil off the bridle with a furlong to run, and again disappointed. She has regressed badly this year, but could be worth another drop back in distance, and the recent application of the visor has been a benefit.
**Mount Pekan(IRE)**, interestingly held up over this shorter trip, made good progress from off the pace in the straight, but looked to throw in the towel when asked for maximum effort late on.
**Francis Flute** spoilt his chance by hanging under pressure at a crucial point and ultimately proved disappointing on this drop in grade. He has only a 2002 maiden win to his name from 23 starts.

## 4005 SHARP MINDS BETFAIR : BEST ODDS H'CAP 1m 2f
3:15 (3:19) (E) (0-70,70) 3-Y-O+ £3,692 (£1,136; £568; £284) Stalls Low

Form RPR
4064 1 **Lennel**[3] 3929 6-9-8 64 (b) RLMoore 5 74
(ABailey) *hld up: hdwy to ld over 1f out: r.o strly* 11/2[3]
-006 2 2 **Jeepstar**[52] 2471 4-10-0 70 WSupple 6 76
(TDEasterby) *mde most to over 1f out: kpt on same pce fnl f* 7/2[1]
4552 3 ½ **Apache Point (IRE)**[10] 3738 7-8-12 54 KimTinkler 7 59
(NTinkler) *in tch: effrt over 2f out: kpt on fnl f* 6/1
0036 4 hd **Megan's Magic**[3] 3952 4-9-12 68 JBramhill 10 76+
(WStorey) *s.s: hdwy 1/2-way: nt clr run over 2f out: kpt on fnl f: nrst fin* 12/1
0360 5 ¾ **Sherwood Forest**[5] 3881 4-7-9 44 (v) LeanneKershaw(7) 11 47
(MissLAPerratt) *hld up: effrt centre over 2f out: no imp fnl f* 50/1
0052 6 3 **Forest Air (IRE)**[8] 3796 4-8-4 46 (p) RFfrench 4 44
(MissLAPerratt) *chsd ldrs: effrt and ev ch over 2f out: outpcd over 1f out* 11/1
0/45 7 ½ **Minstrel Hall**[8] 3796 5-8-5 50 TEaves(3) 1 47
(PMonteith) *hld up ins: hdwy and chsng ldrs whn n.m.r over 2f out: rdn and outpcd over 1f out* 20/1
0311 8 nk **Wahoo Sam (USA)**[10] 3738 4-9-6 67 PMakin(5) 3 63
(TDBarron) *keen: chsd ldrs: ev ch over 2f out: sn rdn and hung lft: wknd over 1f out* 8/1
2000 9 5 **Wilson Bluebottle (IRE)**[49] 2551 5-8-1 43 (b) DaleGibson 13 30
(MWEasterby) *prom outside tl wknd over 2f out* 25/1
0260 10 ¾ **Lucky Largo (IRE)**[8] 3794 4-8-10 57 (b) PMulrennan(5) 12 42
(MissLAPerratt) *hld up: rdn 3f out: nvr on terms* 33/1
-000 11 4 **Luxor**[10] 3731 7-7-12 47 DFentiman(7) 9 25
(MrsGSRees) *disp ld to 1/2-way: wknd over 2f out* 33/1
0500 12 5 **Repulse Bay (IRE)**[22] 3369 6-8-0 49 (b¹) JCurrie(7) 2 17
(JSGoldie) *hld up: rdn over 3f out: nvr on terms* 33/1
3453 13 9 **Templet (USA)**[8] 3794 4-9-9 65 (b) KFallon 8 16
(ISemple) *chsd ldrs: ev ch and rdn over 2f out: wandered and sn btn* 5/1[2]

2m 8.77s (-3.42) **Going Correction** -0.075s/f (Good) 13 Ran SP% 115.1
Speed ratings: **110,108,108,107,107 104,104,104,100,99 96,92,85**CSF £22.03 CT £119.37 TOTE £5.10: £1.10, £2.20, £3.60; EX 34.20.
**Owner** A Bailey **Bred** The Duke Of Sutherland **Trained** Little Budworth, Cheshire

**FOCUS**
This was run at just a modest gallop and the form is ordinary but solid.

**NOTEBOOK**
**Lennel**, winner of a course and distance seller almost exactly a year ago, showed a good turn of foot to settle the issue with a furlong to run. Although he has won on soft, he clearly appreciated the return to faster ground, and the way in which he went about his business suggests he could follow-up if in the same mood next time.
**Jeepstar** got his favoured lead and set the modest pace for most of the way, but could only find the one pace when challenged by the winner late on. He was very well backed for this, and did markedly improve on his previous three outings this season, so looks to be coming right and can score off this sort of mark.
**Apache Point(IRE)** again turned in an improved display and comprehensively reversed his recent form with Wahoo Sam on these slightly better terms. He is another to look fairly well-treated at present and could soon be winning over this trip.
**Megan's Magic** seemingly had a fair bit to do on turning for home, having badly missed the break, but really picked up well under pressure and would have finished closer with a better run two out. She is better than the bare form, and is clearly in fair form at present, but needs all to fall right in her races and is hard to predict.
**Sherwood Forest**, whose sole win came over another furlong at this track in 2003, ran one of his better races and clearly saves his best for this circuit.
**Wahoo Sam(USA)**, coming into this bidding for a hat-trick, ran far to freely and dropped out tamely in the straight. He proved very easy to back for this and was disappointing.
**Templet(USA)** dropped out alarmingly when holding a chance halfway up the straight, and something was presumably amiss. *Official explanation: trainer was unable to offer any explanation for poor form shown*

## 4006 SHARP MINDS BETFAIR : BACK AND LAY CLASSIFIED STKS 7f 50y
3:45 (3:46) (D) 3-Y-O+ £5,343 (£1,644; £822; £411) Stalls Low

Form RPR
-020 1 **Obrigado (USA)**[32] 3036 4-9-3 81 DHolland 6 92
(WJHaggas) *led after 2f: hdd over 2f out: hung lft and flashed tail: r.o to ld cl home* 11/2[3]
-603 2 nk **Winning Venture**[24] 3299 7-9-4 82 RLMoore 4 93?
(AWCarroll) *in tch: hdwy to ld over 2f out: hung lft: kpt on fnl fg: hdd cl home* 3/1[2]
0-10 3 1¾ **Flur Na H Alba**[31] 3079 5-9-2 83 (p) TEaves(3) 3 89
(ISemple) *trckd ldrs: rdn over 2f out: sn outpcd: r.o fnl f* 11/1
0565 4 17 **Telepathic (IRE)**[5] 3879 4-8-9 57 (t) PPMathers(7) 8 42
(ABerry) *in tch: hmpd 4f out: sn rdn and lost tch* 150/1
0502 B **Manaar (IRE)**[11] 3690 4-9-5 83 EAhern 2 —
(JNoseda) *trckd ldrs: b.d 4f out* 1/1[1]
0150 B **Atlantic Quest (USA)**[14] 3597 5-9-2 80 (p) KDarley 5 —
(GAHarker) *s.i.s: hld up in tch: b.d 4f out* 8/1
0000 F **Rosselli (USA)**[17] 3522 8-8-9 46 CEly(7) 1 —
(ABerry) *led 2f: chsd ldr: fell 4f out: broke leg: dead* 200/1

1m 31.42s (-1.05) **Going Correction** -0.075s/f (Good) 7 Ran SP% 111.0
Speed ratings: **103,102,100,81,— —,—**CSF £20.98 TOTE £6.50: £2.60, £3.00; EX 22.40.
**Owner** B Haggas **Bred** Bradyleigh Farms Inc **Trained** Newmarket, Suffolk

**FOCUS**
An incident-packed event that saw Rosselli fall and bring down Manaar and Atlantic Quest just past halfway. As such, the form has to be considered unreliable.

**NOTEBOOK**
**Obrigado(USA)**, who only beat one home in the Buckingham Palace Stakes last time, just prevailed under a strong ride. He rallied when headed two out, and despite twice flashing his tail, plus hanging badly under pressure, finished with real effect. He is clearly temperamental, and has been inconsistent in the main, but still has the scope to progress further this year.
**Winning Venture** looked set to end his long losing run when hitting the front, but hung slightly under maximum pressure, and could not hold off the fast finishing runner-up at the line. He did little wrong in defeat and has run into form of late, but is not one to place total faith in.
**Flur Na H Alba**, who had disappointed last time off this mark, kept on without looking a serious threat. This was a better showing, and he is best when allowed to dominate, but this inconsistent performer looks high in the weights now.
**Rosselli(USA)** fell when already beating a retreat and was tragically killed. He had badly regressed in his career, with his main purpose of late being as a schoolmaster for the stable's apprentices.However, he was a very smart performer on his day, and a decent winner of the Norfolk Stakes in 1998.
**Atlantic Quest(USA)** totally missed the kick and looked to have it all to do before he was brought down. He emerged without a scratch, but his confidence will have taken a knock for this.
**Manaar(IRE)**, whose latest form gave him an obvious chance in this, could do nothing when Rosselli fell and was very unlucky. The incident happened too early to tell how he would have fared and, if his confidence remains intact after this, he is certainly worthy of another chance.

## 4007 SHARP MINDS PHONE 0870 90 80 121 H'CAP 1m 7f
4:15 (4:19) (F) (0-55,55) 4-Y-O+ £3,380 (£1,040; £520; £260) Stalls Low

Form RPR
033- 1 **Gone Too Far**[20] 3055 6-8-11 46 (v) KDarley 2 57
(PMonteith) *led after 6f: mde rest: rdn and hld on wl fnl f* 6/1[3]
0-00 2 2½ **Liberty Seeker (FR)**[25] 2235 5-9-6 55 PHanagan 8 62
(PDNiven) *prom: smooth hdwy 3f out: effrt and chsd wnr over 1f out: edgd lft: kpt on same pce fnl f* 9/2[1]
5230 3 1 **Cosmic Case**[4] 3902 9-8-7 45 NMackay(3) 6 51
(JSGoldie) *hld up: hdwy over 2f out: kpt on fnl f: no imp* 7/1
4050 4 nk **Prince Of The Wood (IRE)**[16] 3564 4-8-10 45 (b¹) DHolland 5 51
(ABailey) *keen: cl up: effrt over 2f out: hung lft over 1f out: no ex* 9/2[1]
0001 5 5 **River Of Fire**[12] 3667 6-7-10 38 (v) NataliaGemelova(7) 1 37
(CNKellett) *hld up: outpcd 3f out: rallied 2f out: nvr rchd ldrs* 6/1[3]
64-0 6 ½ **Fly Kicker**[17] 3518 7-8-0 35 oh8 (p) JBramhill 3 33
(WStorey) *hld up: rdn 3f out: n.d* 20/1
2032 7 4 **Ipledgeallegiance (USA)**[8] 3803 8-7-7 35 oh5 (b) DFentiman(7) 7 28
(DWChapman) *hld up: rdn over 3f out: n.d* 5/1[2]
20/1 8 1¾ **Woodwind Down**[15] 3578 7-8-9 49 PMulrennan(5) 9 40
(MTodhunter) *prom tl rdn and wknd fr 2f out* 10/1
0500 9 8 **Mikasa (IRE)**[6] 3835 4-8-0 35 oh5 RFfrench 4 16
(RFFisher) *led 6f: rdn over 3f out: wknd over 2f out* 50/1

3m 20.27s (-2.20) **Going Correction** -0.075s/f (Good) 9 Ran SP% 109.9
Speed ratings: **102,100,100,99,97 97,94,93,89**CSF £30.55 CT £178.36 TOTE £6.40: £1.50, £1.60, £1.70; EX 24.70.
**Owner** D A Johnson **Bred** Worksop Manor Stud Farm **Trained** Rosewell, Midlothian

**FOCUS**
A dire event that was run at a steady gallop and the finish was dominated by two horses better known for their jumping exploits. The form looks moderate and no better than banded grade.

**NOTEBOOK**
**Gone Too Far**, better known for his expoits over the jumps, won decisively under a positive ride. He had disappointed under a penalty in a novice chase last time, and is considered too high in the ratings now, so this was a welcome result for connections. He could win more races on the Flat while at this end of the handicap.
**Liberty Seeker(FR)** went in pursuit of the winner in the straight, but could not find the necessary change of gear and was outstayed. He had looked useful when winning his first two novice chases recently and had seemed potentially well-in on his old Flat form, but failed to capitalise and may be best kept to chasing now.
**Cosmic Case** turned in an improved effort for this drop in grade, but was unsuited by the lack of early pace, and the trip may just stretch her nowadays.
**Prince Of The Wood(IRE)**, fitted with the first-time blinkers for this, again ran keenly and hung fire in the straight when under maximum pressure. He is a very tricky customer. *Official explanation: jockey said gelding hung right handed throughout*
**River Of Fire**, winner of a weaker race last time at Folkestone, got badly outpaced over this shorter trip and was well held. He will be better back over two miles, but looks to be in the Handicapper's grip now.
**Ipledgeallegiance(USA)** was never going and put in one of his moody efforts.

## 4008 SHARP MINDS BETFAIR : BET IN RUNNING H'CAP 1m
4:45 (4:49) (D) (0-80,74) 3-Y-O+ £5,512 (£1,696; £848; £424) Stalls Low

Form RPR
0603 1 **Harry Potter (GER)**[31] 3082 5-9-9 69 (v) DarrenWilliams 5 84
(KRBurke) *prom: hdwy 2f out: edgd lft: led ent fnl f: sn clr* 20/1
0001 2 6 **Parisian Playboy**[16] 3559 4-7-6 45 LeanneKershaw(7) 11 46
(JeddO'Keeffe) *racd wd: hld up: hdwy 1/2-way: kpt on fnl 2f: no ch w wnr* 20/1
0531 3 hd **Anthemion (IRE)**[4] 3903 7-8-10 56 6ex DMcGaffin 2 57
(MrsJCMcgregor) *led: rdn 3f out: hdd ent fnl f: sn outpcd* 7/2[1]
5445 4 nk **Pas De Surprise**[6] 3844 6-8-7 53 EAhern 8 53
(PDEvans) *hld up: hdwy over 2f out: no imp over 1f out* 8/1
0600 5 2 **Wessex (USA)**[31] 3079 4-9-9 72 TEaves(3) 6 67
(JamesMoffatt) *hld up: rdn over 3f out: styd on fnl f: n.d* 33/1
0061 6 nk **Wood Dalling (USA)**[4] 3895 6-8-7 58 6ex PMulrennan(5) 3 53
(ISemple) *prom: outpcd over 2f out: n.d after* 6/1[3]
-605 7 hd **Market Avenue**[10] 3738 5-9-1 61 PHanagan 9 55
(RAFahey) *hld up: hdwy 3f out: no imp over 1f out* 8/1
0200 8 nk **Argent**[33] 3002 3-7-12 52 oh2 (p) RFfrench 4 45
(MissLAPerratt) *chsd ldr tl outpcd wl over 1f out* 66/1
3442 9 ½ **Adobe**[9] 3771 9-9-1 66 BSwarbrick(5) 12 58
(WMBrisbourne) *hld up: rdn over 2f out: nvr rchd ldrs* 10/1
0000 10 1 **Arawan (IRE)**[18] 3470 4-8-11 57 (b) DaleGibson 7 47
(MWEasterby) *t.k.h in midfield: effrt over 2f out: hung lft and btn over 1f out* 9/2[2]
0024 11 4 **Regent's Secret (USA)**[21] 3401 4-9-1 61 WSupple 1 42
(JSGoldie) *hld up midfield: n.m.r over 2f out: sn btn* 10/1
2226 12 13 **Awesome Love (USA)**[14] 3610 3-9-6 74 (b¹) JFanning 10 25
(MJohnston) *trckd ldrs tl wknd fr 3f out* 16/1

1m 41.31s (-1.81) **Going Correction** -0.075s/f (Good)
**WFA** 3 from 4yo+ 8lb 12 Ran SP% 114.9
Speed ratings: **106,100,99,99,97 97,97,96,96,95 91,78**CSF £342.75 CT £1755.94 TOTE £19.60: £6.70, £7.90, £2.70; EX 403.80 Trifecta £1230.60 Part won. Pool £1,733.27 - 0.20 winning units. Place 6 £105.73, Place 5 £37.11.
**Owner** F Jeffers **Bred** Wilh Jackson **Trained** Middleham Moor, N Yorks

**FOCUS**
A modest race, but the pace was strong and resulted in an apparently improved effort from the winner, form which is not easy to take at face value.

**NOTEBOOK**
**Harry Potter(GER)**, with the blinkers swapped for a visor this time, ran out a comfortable winner. This was his best effort to date in this country and, although he will take a hike in the weights for this, he would have to be of interest if turned out under a penalty
**Parisian Playboy**, who stayed on to get off the mark in an apprentice race under today's rider last time, stayed on well without holding a chance with the winner. This confirmed he is improving, and he had no problems with this faster ground, but will doubtless go up again in the ratings now.
**Anthemion(IRE)**, who ended a four year losing run when making all decisively at Hamilton last time, paid late in the day for setting a strong early gallop. He was however, far from disgraced off this 6lb penalty.

**Pas De Surprise** came there with a chance about two furlongs out, but could only muster the one pace under pressure. He may be worth a try back over six furlongs, but is a very hard horse to win with nonetheless.
**Wessex(USA)** ran on all too late in the day, yet still bettered his previous efforts this season. He needs a further drop in the weights on this evidence, but looks the type to pop up when least expected.
**Wood Dalling(USA)** could not quicken at a crucial stage in the straight and proved slightly disappointing under his penalty.
**Arawan(IRE)**, subject of a gamble for this with the blinkers back on, ran too keen through the early stages and never threatened. He is clearly thought by connections to be better than his current rating, but will need to settle better, before he can exploit it.
T/Jkpt: Not won. T/Plt: £238.80 to a £1 stake. Pool: £67,757.65. 207.10 winning tickets. T/Qpdt: £43.00 to a £1 stake. Pool: £4,506.70. 77.40 winning tickets. RY

## 3834 CATTERICK (L-H)
Wednesday, July 21

**OFFICIAL GOING: Good to firm**

### 4009 LEVY BOARD MAIDEN STKS — 5f 212y
2:20 (2:21) (D) 2-Y-O — **£3,848** (£1,184; £592; £296) **Stalls Low**

Form — RPR
20 **1** **Golden Legacy (IRE)**[33] [3031] 2-8-9 ........ PHanagan 3 73+
(RAFahey) *trckd ldrs: led over 1f out: rdn clr fnl f: eased towards fin* **4/9**[1]
02 **2** 2 ½ **Rasa Sayang (USA)**[19] [3469] 2-8-9 ........ PMakin(5) 7 67
(TDBarron) *cl up: chsd wnr appr fnl f: r.o u.p: no imp* **4/1**[2]
0 **3** 2 ½ **Choreographic (IRE)**[19] [3469] 2-8-11 ........ THamilton(3) 6 60
(RAFahey) *in tch: keen early: pushed along 2f out: styd on fnl f: nvr able to chal* **16/1**
000 **4** ½ **Mister Buzz**[11] [3760] 2-9-0 ........ ACulhane 8 58
(MDHammond) *in tch: pushed along 2f out: no hdwy* **40/1**
**5** shd **Mary Gray** 2-8-9 ........ JFanning 5 53
(MJohnston) *s.i.s: towards rr: kpt on u.p fnl 2f: n.d* **8/1**[3]
40 **6** 2 **Zanderido**[11] [3760] 2-9-0 ........ DarrenWilliams 4 52?
(BSRothwell) *led tl hdd over 1f out: wknd fnl f* **100/1**
**7** 1 **Thornber Court (IRE)** 2-8-9 ........ FLynch 2 44
(ABerry) *dwlt: a rr* **50/1**
**8** 3 ½ **So Independent** 2-8-9 ........ RWinston 1 33
(CRWilson) *towards rr: effrt 1/2-way: sn bhd* **66/1**

1m 14.24s (0.24) **Going Correction** -0.15s/f (Firm) **8 Ran SP% 113.1**
Speed ratings: **92,88,85,84,84 81,80,75**CSF £2.41 TOTE £1.50: £1.02, £1.50, £2.20; EX 2.80.
**Owner** P N Devlin **Bred** E Tynan **Trained** Musley Bank, N Yorks

**FOCUS**
A fair maiden event which should throw up some winners in due course. The time was modest and the proximity of the sixth hold the form down.

**NOTEBOOK**
**Golden Legacy(IRE)**, who made a favourable impression when finishing fast on her debut and, not disgraced in the Albany Stakes last time, ran out a facile winner. This confirmed she is a useful filly, but will most likely have to step up to Listed company again, as she will be on a stiff mark for nurseries.
**Rasa Sayang(USA)** again found one too good, but was clear in second, despite not looking suited by this track. He ran with credit over this extra furlong, was well backed for this and now qualifies for nurseries, in which he can definitely find a race or two.
**Choreographic(IRE)**, slowly away on his debut behind the runner-up at Beverley last time, ran keen early on but still turned in an improved effort, and got a bit closer to Rasa Sayang this time over the extra furlong. It is unlikely that we will see the best of him until he tackles nurseries.
**Mister Buzz** improved a touch for this faster ground, but is going to struggle to win a maiden and will be better off in nurseries.
**Mary Gray** was very sluggish from the stalls and was up against it from then on. This debut experience will not be lost on this good-looking filly and she should be sharper next time.

### 4010 HALIFAX (S) STKS — 7f
2:50 (2:51) (G) 2-Y-O — **£2,618** (£748; £374) **Stalls Low**

Form — RPR
5065 **1** **Uredale (IRE)**[7] [3834] 2-8-11 ........ ACulhane 1 62
(MrsADuffield) *mde all: shkn up 2f out: r.o wl u.p fnl f* **5/1**[3]
6414 **2** 1 ½ **Mount Ephram (IRE)**[7] [3834] 2-9-3 ........ (b) PHanagan 8 64
(RFFisher) *slowly away: sn trcking ldrs: rdn to chse wnr over 1f out: no imp fnl f* **5/2**[1]
056 **3** 4 **Dartanian**[20] [3458] 2-8-11 ........ RWinston 3 48
(PDEvans) *prom: drvn along and ev ch over 2f out: no ex u.p* **6/1**
6154 **4** 1 ½ **Maureen's Lough (IRE)**[18] [3506] 2-8-7 ........ PMakin(5) 10 45
(TDBarron) *cl up: ev ch 2f out: sn rdn: no ex* **7/2**[2]
0 **5** 3 **Tewitfield Lass**[18] [3506] 2-7-13 ........ DFentiman(7) 13 32
(JRWeymes) *midfield: drvn along 1/2-way: no real hdwy* **66/1**
343 **6** ½ **Tonight (IRE)**[41] [2819] 2-8-6 ........ BSwarbrick(5) 11 36
(WMBrisbourne) *prom 2f: midfield and drvn along 1/2-way: no real hdwy* **10/1**
0050 **7** 1 ½ **Northern Revoque (IRE)**[4] [3951] 2-8-1 ........ (b) PPMathers(5) 2 27
(ABerry) *chsd ldrs: rdn over 2f out: sn btn* **25/1**
0 **8** 4 **Miss Trendsetter (IRE)**[20] [3444] 2-8-6 ........ GParkin 7 17
(KARyan) *midfield: drvn along 1/2-way: no hdwy* **16/1**
000 **9** 1 ½ **Tak's Girl**[20] [3444] 2-8-6 ........ RFitzpatrick 12 13
(PTMidgley) *towards rr most of way* **66/1**
040 **10** 2 **Lara's Girl**[14] [3632] 2-8-6 ........ TPQueally 6 8
(IAWood) *sn towards rr* **20/1**
**11** ½ **Specialise** 2-8-6 ........ RFfrench 9 7
(DWBarker) *s.s: a bhd* **12/1**
0000 **12** 1 ½ **Hollingwood Soul**[18] [3506] 2-8-6 ........ DeanMcKeown 4 3
(RonaldThompson) *s.s and early reminders: a bhd* **33/1**
000 **13** ½ **Black Combe Lady (IRE)**[23] [3366] 2-8-6 ........ PBradley 5 2
(ABerry) *sn bhd* **100/1**

1m 27.5s **Going Correction** -0.15s/f (Firm) **13 Ran SP% 119.9**
Speed ratings: **94,92,87,86,82 82,80,75,74,71 71,69,68**CSF £17.00 TOTE £6.00: £2.40, £1.10, £2.00; EX 16.30.The winner was bought in for 9,000gns.
**Owner** Miss B Duxbury & Mrs A Duffield **Bred** Denis McDonnell **Trained** Constable Burton, N Yorks

**FOCUS**
A weak event with little or no strength in depth. The pace was solid however, and the form looks reliable for the grade.

**NOTEBOOK**
**Uredale(IRE)** produced his best effort to date on this drop into the bottom grade, and reversed his recent maiden form with the runner-up under a positive ride. He is bred to do well at this trip and can pay his way back up in class, but is clearly has his limitations. He was bought in for 9,000gns.
**Mount Ephram(IRE)** looked to be going the best of all when tracking the leaders off the home turn, yet found less than expected off the bridle and was made to look one paced. He was still clear of the rest however, and can find another race at this level, but must learn to settle better if he is to progress.
**Dartanian** ran his best race to date back over this extra furlong and, although this is his level, he looks to be slowly going the right way.
**Maureen's Lough(IRE)** again ran her race, but could not quicken with the principals when it mattered and was well held. She is at least reliable, did the best of those drawn in double figures, and is the benchmark for the form.

### 4011 "GOODBYE & GOOD LUCK TRACEY" STKS (H'CAP) — 5f
3:20 (3:20) (D) (0-85,80) 3-Y-O+ — **£5,590** (£1,720; £860; £430) **Stalls Low**

Form — RPR
2306 **1** **Justalord**[31] [3126] 6-9-1 **67** ........ (b[1]) JEdmunds 2 76
(JBalding) *mde most: r.o u.p fnl f: all out* **11/2**[2]
0030 **2** nk **Sharp Hat**[18] [3524] 10-8-8 **60** ........ ACulhane 1 68
(DWChapman) *in tch: hdwy over 1f out: r.o u.p to go 2nd wl ins fnl f: clsng on wnr fin* **5/1**[1]
1100 **3** 1 ¼ **Maromito (IRE)**[47] [2663] 7-8-3 **55** ........ RFfrench 15 58+
(RBastiman) *w wnr: ev ch and rdn appr fnl f: no ex ins last* **33/1**
0000 **4** hd **Salviati (USA)**[5] [3920] 7-9-4 **77** ........ (p) CJDavies(3) 4 79+
(JMBradley) *s.s: bhd: hdwy 2f out: r.o u.p fnl f: nrst fin* **15/2**
0340 **5** nk **Strensall**[16] [3580] 7-9-8 **77** ........ TEaves(3) 3 78
(REBarr) *chsd ldrs: rdn over 1f out: no ex* **7/1**[3]
3545 **6** 1 **Amanda's Lad (IRE)**[18] [3512] 4-8-3 **55** ........ TPQueally 7 52
(MCChapman) *midfield: effrt 2f out: kpt on u.p fnl f* **25/1**
4602 **7** nk **Romany Nights (IRE)**[10] [3775] 4-9-8 **77** ........ (b) SHitchcott(3) 5 73
(JWUnett) *towards rr: hdwy 1/2-way: kpt on u.p fr over 1f out: n.d* **5/1**[1]
0022 **8** ½ **Boavista (IRE)**[10] [3772] 4-8-10 **62** ........ DeanMcKeown 8 56
(PDEvans) *s.i.s: sn midfield: effrt 2f out: no hdwy* **8/1**
2500 **9** 5 **Chairman Bobby**[15] [3606] 6-8-12 **69** ........ PMulrennan(5) 12 43
(DWBarker) *midfield: rdn 2f out: sn btn* **14/1**
0120 **10** 1 ¼ **Silver Mascot**[15] [3615] 5-8-7 **59** ow1 ........ RWinston 14 28
(ISemple) *dwlt: nvr bttr than mid-div* **10/1**
0000 **11** shd **Mr Spliffy (IRE)**[21] [3407] 5-7-12 **50** oh4 ........ PHanagan 11 18
(MCChapman) *chsd ldrs: rdn 2f out: sn btn* **28/1**
2100 **12** 5 **Dizzy In The Head**[11] [3732] 5-9-8 **79** ........ (b) NChalmers(5) 13 27
(PaulJohnson) *midfield to 1/2-way: sn bhd* **16/1**
-000 **13** 8 **Candleriggs (IRE)**[37] [2936] 8-8-8 **60** ........ ANicholls 6 —
(DNicholls) *towards rr: rdn 2f out: no hdwy: bhd and eased fnl f: fin lame* **14/1**

59.23 secs (-1.37) **Going Correction** -0.20s/f (Firm) **13 Ran SP% 122.6**
Speed ratings: **102,101,99,99,98 97,96,95,87,85 85,77,64**CSF £33.42 CT £878.20 TOTE £6.60: £1.90, £2.30, £9.80; EX 24.90.
**Owner** T H Heckingbottom **Bred** Mrs M S Teversham **Trained** Scrooby, Notts

**FOCUS**
A modest sprint run at a sound gallop, but those drawn low were at a definite advantage and the form is nothing out of the ordinary.

**NOTEBOOK**
**Justalord**, with the usual cheekpieces dispensed with for the first-time blinkers, showed his usual decent early speed to gamely make all. He is a better horse on the All-Weather, but is a likeable sort who is capable of holding his form, and he could be hard to peg back next time, provided the blinkers have the same effect.
**Sharp Hat**, second to Salviati in this race last season, was finishing fast, but again just found the line coming that bit too soon. This suggested he can score again off this mark, but he had a decent draw this time and does love this venue, having only once finished out of the frame in eight outings at the track.
**Maromito(IRE)** put in a much-improved display and did by far the best of those drawn in double figures. He is a better horse on the All-Weather, but he is particluary well-treated on last year's form, and on this display could be about to strike top form once more.
**Salviati(USA)**, winner of the corresponding race last year off a 5lb higher mark, ran his best race for a while and did well to finish fourth, having again lost ground at the start. He usually comes good at this time of year, so could be expected to improve again on this sound display.
**Strensall**, winner of this race in 2002 and third last year, held every chance. He had the draw in his favour this time, and looks held by the Handicapper at present.
**Romany Nights(IRE)** failed to land a blow and ran below par. He is a very frustrating horse to follow.
**Candleriggs(IRE)** *Official explanation: jockey said gelding finished lame*

### 4012 DARLINGTON OPERATIC SOCIETY "GUYS AND DOLLS" NURSERY — 7f
3:50 (3:51) (D) 2-Y-O — **£4,940** (£1,520; £760; £380) **Stalls Low**

Form — RPR
3522 **1** **Jane Jubilee (IRE)**[21] [3406] 2-9-6 **78** ........ JFanning 7 92+
(MJohnston) *trckd ldr: led 2f out: rdn 8 l clr ins fnl f: eased fnl 75yds* **7/4**[1]
020 **2** 5 **Dan's Heir**[21] [3406] 2-7-6 **57** ........ (p) DFentiman(7) 1 55
(PCHaslam) *midfield: hdwy 2f out: styd on to go 2nd jst ins fnl f: no ch w wnr* **16/1**
0523 **3** 3 **Brace Of Doves**[15] [3605] 2-8-7 **70** ........ PMakin(5) 2 61
(TDBarron) *hld up: drvn along and hdwy 2f out: nt clr run fr over 1f out tl jst ins fnl f: nvr able to chal* **9/2**[2]
404 **4** 1 ¼ **Sharp N Frosty**[31] [3124] 2-8-5 **68** ........ BSwarbrick(5) 3 55
(WMBrisbourne) *dwlt: bhd: hdwy 1/2-way: styd on fnl 2f: n.d* **25/1**
336 **5** 2 ½ **Twice Nightly**[28] [3196] 2-8-13 **74** ........ THamilton(3) 6 55
(JDBethell) *hld up: hung rt bnd 1/2-way: styd on fnl 2f: n.d* **12/1**
352 **6** nk **Regal Lustre**[11] [3736] 2-8-3 **61** ........ PHanagan 4 41
(JRWeymes) *midfield: no hdwy whn sltly hmpd 2f out* **25/1**
350 **7** shd **Paris Bell**[58] [2352] 2-8-10 **68** ........ DAllan 8 48
(TDEasterby) *keen early: sn trcking ldrs: ch over 2f out: wknd over 1f out* **28/1**
042 **8** ½ **Canary Dancer**[44] [2730] 2-8-6 **64** ........ GFaulkner 9 43
(PCHaslam) *chsd ldrs tl wknd 2f out* **10/1**
002 **9** 1 ½ **Jay (IRE)**[29] [3170] 2-7-12 **56** ........ (b) PMQuinn 10 31
(NACallaghan) *v.s.a: wl bhd tl sme late hdwy* **16/1**
232 **10** ¾ **Laconicos (IRE)**[26] [3259] 2-9-7 **79** ........ (v[1]) TPQueally 12 52
(DRLoder) *led tl hdd 2f out: sn wknd* **6/1**[3]
4021 **11** 1 ¾ **No Commission (IRE)**[5] [3898] 2-9-5 **77** 6ex ........ RWinston 11 46
(RFFisher) *midfield: drvn along 1/2-way: btn whn sltly hmpd 2f out* **13/2**
062 **12** 2 **Itsa Monkey (IRE)**[12] [3709] 2-7-12 **56** oh6 ........ RFfrench 5 20
(MJPolglase) *sn pushed along in rr* **66/1**

1m 27.22s (-0.28) **Going Correction** -0.15s/f (Firm) **12 Ran SP% 123.3**
Speed ratings: **95,89,85,84,81 81,81,80,78,77 75,73**CSF £35.23 CT £120.89 TOTE £2.50: £1.40, £5.00, £1.70; EX 55.90.
**Owner** Mrs Sheila Ramsden **Bred** Mrs S Ramsden **Trained** Middleham Moor, N Yorks
■ Stewards Enquiry : G Faulkner caution: careless riding

**FOCUS**
A modest nursery that saw the field finish well strung out behind the easy winner, who may be flattered by the bare form. The figures shown as 'official ratings' are estimates for guidance only.

**NOTEBOOK**

**Jane Jubilee(IRE)**, narrowly denied over course and distance in a maiden last time, ran out a most convincing winner on this nursery debut. She could not have won with much more authority and, although she may have beaten little this time, is obviously better than her current mark. A typically progressive sort for her powerful yard, she should have no trouble staying a mile and does look one to follow.

**Dan's Heir**, unplaced behind Jane Jubilee last time over this course and distance, ran on to bag the silver medal, but once again had no chance with the winner. This still respresented his best effort to date, he was a clear second best and could score off this low mark in a similar event.

**Brace Of Doves**, well supported in the betting ring, turned in another fair effort and had no problems with the trip. He may be better with a more prominent ride over this distance and should find a nursery this year in which to get off the mark.

**Sharp N Frosty** showed some promise on this nursery debut, and ran on late up the rail as if he already needs a stiffer test.

**Twice Nightly** was unable to go the early pace, but caught the eye finishing late on under a tender ride. He can do better.

**Laconicos(IRE)** went off too quickly in the first-time visor and can do better, but has something to prove now.

**No Commission(IRE)** ran well below the form of his recent success and could struggle now off his higher mark.

## 4013 BRADFORD H'CAP — 5f 212y

**4:20** (4:20) (E ) (0-70,69) 3-Y-O+ **£3,562** (£1,096; £548; £274) **Stalls** Low

Form / RPR

4-00 **1** **Northern Games**[36] 2965 5-8-12 **53**....................(b) GParkin 4 67
(KARyan) *rrd and s.s: bhd: drvn along and swtchd to outside wl over 1f out: styd on wl u.p to ld wl ins last* **25/1**

0560 **2** 1 1/4 **Nemo Fugat (IRE)**[32] 3082 5-9-3 **58**....................(v1) JFanning 10 68
(DNicholls) *sn trcking ldrs: chal over 1f out: ev ch ins last: no ex clsng stages* **12/1**

3230 **3** 1 **Kings College Boy**[18] 3509 4-9-5 **60**....................(b) PHanagan 14 67
(RAFahey) *midfield: hdwy u.p over 1f out: kpt on ins last: nvr able to chal* **16/1**

0331 **4** shd **Tancred Times**[7] 3836 9-9-6 **61** 6ex.................... FLynch 6 68
(DWBarker) *led tl hdd wl ins fnl f: eased and ct for 3rd cl home* **12/1**

0000 **5** 1 1/4 **Ballybunion (IRE)**[6] 3864 5-8-11 **52**.................... PMQuinn 3 55
(DNicholls) *in tch: effrt 2f out: kpt on same pce* **4/1**[1]

0400 **6** 1 1/2 **Mr Bountiful (IRE)**[21] 3409 6-8-9 **50**....................(tp) RWinston 12 48
(MDods) *towards rr: hdwy u.p into midfield over 1f out: kpt on same pce ins last* **14/1**

1321 **7** 1 1/4 **Compton Plume**[21] 3410 4-10-0 **69**.................... DaleGibson 1 64
(WHTinning) *in tch: effrt 2f out: sn btn* **8/1**

1035 **8** 3/4 **Sir Don (IRE)**[2] 3979 5-9-11 **66**....................(b1) AlexGreaves 7 58
(DNicholls) *cl up: rdn and ch over 2f out: wknd fnl f* **10/1**

0340 **9** 1 **Intellibet One**[9] 3810 4-8-10 **56**.................... PPMathers(5) 13 45
(PDEvans) *nvr bttr than mid-div* **12/1**

5550 **10** hd **Ronnie From Donny (IRE)**[15] 3606 4-9-5 **63**.................... TEaves(3) 9 52
(BEllison) *towards rr: sme hdwy over 2f out: sn rdn and btn* **20/1**

0040 **11** 1/2 **Toppling**[4] 3935 6-9-0 **55**....................(p) DeanMcKeown 11 42
(JMBradley) *cl up tl rdn and wknd over 1f out* **25/1**

1010 **12** nk **Massey**[11] 3735 8-8-9 **55**.................... PMakin(5) 2 41
(TDBarron) *midfield: drvn along over 2f out: sn btn* **7/1**[3]

3011 **13** nk **Mickledor (FR)**[11] 3735 4-8-8 **54**....................(p) PMulrennan(5) 8 40
(MDods) *sn bhd* **12/1**

4004 **14** 1 3/4 **Drury Lane (IRE)**[4] 3935 4-8-12 **53**....................(b) ACulhane 5 33
(DWChapman) *towards rr and drvn along 1/2-way: no hdwy* **9/2**[2]

1m 12.58s (-1.42) **Going Correction** -0.15s/f (Firm) **14** Ran SP% **126.7**

Speed ratings: **103,101,100,99,98 96,94,93,92,91 91,90,90,88**CSF £308.25 CT £5024.79 TOTE £35.40: £9.30, £4.80, £4.10; EX 421.10.

**Owner** R E Robinson **Bred** Mrs Wendy Robinson **Trained** Hambleton, N Yorks

■ Stewards Enquiry : F Lynch seven-day ban (reduced from 10 on appeal): failed to ride out for third place (Aug 1-7)

**FOCUS**

A moderate handicap run at a sound pace and the form looks reliable for the grade.

**NOTEBOOK**

**Northern Games**, with the blinkers back on after two poor efforts so far this term, produced an astonishing display to score. He lost plenty of ground as he reared coming out of the stalls and looked to have an impossible task, but responded gamely to pressure, and swept past the runner-up with ease close home. He has fallen in the weights, and was clearly well suited by the decent gallop, but his overall profile is far from consistent.

**Nemo Fugat(IRE)** produced an improved display and looked the most likely winner on turning for home, but could not quicken as looked likely under pressure and had no answer to the winner's late challenge. He has fallen in the weights this year, as he has badly regressed, yet it would be a suprise if he were not placed to go one better in this grade.

**Kings College Boy** ran his race, again finding a couple too good, and is the benchmark as to the strength of this form.

**Tancred Times**, who made all in a course and distance seller last time, had the run of the race in front, but was found out under her penalty in this better event. She was not disgraced and remains in good heart. *Official explanation: jockey said he had to check mare in anticipation of interference*

**Ballybunion(IRE)** , who boasts a decent strike rate at this track, has not been in the best of form recently and never looked a serious threat.

**Drury Lane(IRE)** was never going and ran too badly to be true. He has plummeted in the ratings this year, but has seemingly lost the plot and become very hard to predict. *Official explanation: trainer said gelding was unsuited by the undulating track*

## 4014 BATLEY CLAIMING STKS — 5f

**4:50** (4:51) (F) 3-Y-O+ **£2,996** (£856; £428) **Stalls** Low

Form / RPR

2356 **1** **Roxanne Mill**[11] 3744 6-8-13 74....................(p) PHanagan 9 69
(JMBradley) *cl up: led 1/2-way: drvn out fnl f* **11/10**[1]

L011 **2** 1 1/4 **Queen Of Night**[9] 3801 4-8-10 55.................... ACulhane 2 61
(DWChapman) *led tl hdd 1/2-way: kpt on u.p fnl f: no imp on wnr* **5/1**[2]

0003 **3** 1 1/4 **Loughlorien (IRE)**[7] 3836 5-8-9 44.................... THamilton(3) 6 58
(RAFahey) *towards rr: hdwy 2f out: kpt on u.p fnl f: nvr able to chal* **7/1**[3]

0000 **4** 2 **Tomthevic**[16] 3575 6-8-12 50.................... DaleGibson 1 50
(MrsPSly) *s.i.s: sn chsng ldrs: rdn 2f out: no ex* **12/1**

4044 **5** nk **Beyond Calculation (USA)**[11] 3742 10-8-11 53...(b) DeanMcKeown 11 48
(JMBradley) *towards rr: sme hdwy u.p over 1f out: n.d* **14/1**

35-0 **6** 3 1/2 **Risk Free**[11] 3734 7-8-9 59....................(v) PMulrennan(5) 7 37
(PDEvans) *sn rr div: rdn 2f out: no hdwy* **16/1**

5000 **7** 1 1/2 **African Spur (IRE)**[14] 3637 4-8-9 47.................... MLawson(5) 3 31
(DCarroll) *rr div: rdn 2f out: no hdwy* **50/1**

0060 **8** 1 1/2 **Vijay (IRE)**[11] 3735 5-8-10 49....................(b) RWinston 8 21
(ISemple) *chsd ldrs to 1/2-way: sn wknd* **33/1**

5255 **9** 1/2 **The Leather Wedge (IRE)**[23] 3378 5-8-9 40....................(b1) PPMathers(5) 5 23
(ABerry) *cl up tl wknd qckly wl over 1f out* **33/1**

59.09 secs (-1.51) **Going Correction** -0.20s/f (Firm)

**WFA** 3 from 4yo+ 4lb **9** Ran SP% **104.9**

Sbeedvinatiengwas**10t4,1n0e2d1t00,96,96**ila**90,88,85,85**CSF £5o19TOTE £2.00 £1.10, £1.30, £1.80; EX 9.50 £6,000.\n\x\x

**Owner** Dab Hand Racing **Bred** Highfield Stud Ltd **Trained** Sedbury, Gloucs

**FOCUS**

A fair claimer run at a true gallop and the form looks sound enough for the class.

**NOTEBOOK**

**Roxanne Mill**, who has been running well without winning so far this term, greatly appreciated this drop in grade and won as she was entitled to on official ratings. This will have done her confidence the world of good, and it will be interesting to see if she can put it together back up in class.

**Queen Of Night** did her best in defeat, but had no chance with the winner on official figures, and so it proved. This was another solid effort and her best on turf for some time.

**Loughlorien(IRE)** took time to find his full stride, but was closing at the finish and ran another sound race. He can certainly win at this level, but it is worth noting that he oftens saves his best for this track.

**Tomthevic** would have been closer but for a sluggish start, but still ran below his best.

**Beyond Calculation(USA)** is dropping in the handicap and is looking as if he is gradually coming back to form.

**Risk Free** *Official explanation: jockey said gelding hung left in final furlong*

## 4015 WILLIE CARSON - PINKER'S POND APPRENTICE H'CAP — 1m 3f 214y

**5:20** (5:20) (F ) (0-55,61) 3-Y-O+ **£3,010** (£860; £430) **Stalls** Low

Form / RPR

5051 **1** **Let It Be**[23] 3371 3-8-7 **46**.................... NeilBrown 8 56
(MrsMReveley) *trckd ldrs: led wl over 2f out: pushed clr fnl f* **12/1**

5035 **2** 5 **Dalriath**[6] 3380 5-8-11 **38**.................... PVarley 9 40
(MCChapman) *towards rr: hdwy 5f out: rdn to go 2nd over 1f out: styd on: no ch w wnr* **18/1**

0400 **3** 1/2 **Blue Venture (IRE)**[18] 3518 4-9-7 **48**.................... GBartley 19 49
(PCHaslam) *midfield: hdwy u.p 2f out: styd on fnl f: nvr able to chal* **50/1**

2560 **4** 1 1/2 **Danefonique (IRE)**[25] 3305 3-9-2 **55**.................... DanielleMcCreery 4 54
(DCarroll) *midfield whn bmpd rail after 4f: hdwy 2f out: styd on fnl f: nvr able to chal* **16/1**

0/14 **5** hd **Sovereign State (IRE)**[13] 3682 7-9-6 **47**....................(p) PJBenson 12 46
(DWThompson) *hld up: hdwy 1/2-way: trcking ldrs 4f out: ch and rdn over 2f out: no ex* **8/1**

1000 **6** 1 3/4 **Prairie Sun (GER)**[19] 3473 3-9-2 **55**....................(p) SArcher 2 51
(MrsADuffield) *s.i.s: bhd: hdwy over 2f out: styd on fnl f: n.d* **16/1**

0003 **7** 1 **Molly's Secret**[21] 3423 6-9-4 **45**....................(p) AshleighHorton 16 39
(CGCox) *towards rr whn n.m.r bnd after 3f: hdwy 2f out: styd on fnl f: n.d* **8/1**

-324 **8** 3/4 **Valeureux**[13] 3658 6-10-0 **55**.................... KPierrepont 7 48
(JHetherton) *trckd ldrs: outpcd whn hmpd 2f out: styd on fnl f* **15/2**[3]

1011 **9** 3/4 **Jackie Kiely**[5] 3917 3-9-8 **61** 6ex....................(t) JBrennan 14 53
(PSMcentee) *trckd ldrs: chal over 2f out: sn rdn: wknd over 1f out* **9/4**[1]

-200 **10** shd **Middleham Park (IRE)**[33] 3060 4-9-10 **51**.................... DWakenshaw 1 43
(PCHaslam) *in tch: effrt 3f out: sn btn* **25/1**

406- **11** 1 **Deekazz (IRE)**[509] 637 5-8-12 **39**.................... TO'Brien 11 29
(FWatson) *sn towards rr: sme late hdwy: n.d* **40/1**

0000 **12** 1 3/4 **Quay Walloper**[19] 3479 3-7-12 **37** oh2....................(v) TDean 18 24
(JRNorton) *midfield: effrt over 3f out: sn btn* **66/1**

0640 **13** nk **Hibernate (IRE)**[7] 3835 10-8-12 **39**.................... JaniceWebster 13 26
(CJTeague) *led tl hdd wl over 2f out: sn wknd* **40/1**

50-5 **14** 3/4 **Chevin**[23] 3369 5-9-1 **42**.................... AElliott 6 28
(RAFahey) *v.s.a: bhd: sme hdwy u.p 2f out: n.d* **7/1**[2]

0220 **15** hd **Cezzaro (IRE)**[27] 3247 6-8-12 **39**.................... MNem 5 24
(SRBowring) *cl up: ev ch over 2f out: sn wknd* **20/1**

0050 **16** 2 **Cryptogam**[5] 3919 4-8-12 **39**.................... SShaw 10 21
(MESowersby) *midfield: sme hdwy whn hmpd 2f out: wknd over 1f out* **50/1**

0030 **17** 2 **Margold (IRE)**[21] 3411 4-9-6 **47**.................... HFellows 3 26
(RHollinshead) *midfield tl wknd over 3f out* **20/1**

0260 **18** 12 **Miss Fleurie**[5] 3919 4-8-8 **35** oh3.................... SBushby 17 —
(RCraggs) *s.i.s: bhd: hdwy on outer and in tch 1/2-way: wknd over 3f out* **50/1**

00-0 **19** 28 **Fusillade (IRE)**[27] 3251 4-8-13 **40**.................... SusannahWileman 15 —
(AJLockwood) *sn towards rr: lost tch 5f out: t.o* **50/1**

-035 **U** **Iloveturtle (IRE)**[6] 2689 4-9-9 **50**.................... GEdwards 20 —
(MCChapman) *midfield whn sddle slipped and uns rdr over 7f out* **25/1**

2m 37.9s (-1.10) **Going Correction** -0.15s/f (Firm)

**WFA** 3 from 4yo+ 12lb **20** Ran SP% **133.4**

Speed ratings: **97,93,93,92,92 91,90,89,89,89 88,87,87,86,86 85,83,75,57,**—CSF £204.10 CT £10077.93 TOTE £12.90: £3.10, £3.70, £8.80, £4.10; EX 188.60 Place 6 £56.84, Place 5 £50.77.

**Owner** A Frame **Bred** Sir Eric Parker **Trained** Lingdale, N Yorks

■ A race restricted to apprentices who had never ridden a winner.

**FOCUS**

A modest handicap and not a race to dwell on, but the field came home well strung out and the winner may be able to follow up before being reassessed.

**NOTEBOOK**

**Let It Be** took the race by the scruff of the neck off the home bend, and readily followed up her recent success in a selling handicap off this 6lb higher mark. Although she effectively beat trees this time, she has really found her form now and will be hard to beat if turned out before the Handicapper has his say.

**Dalriath** held up to get this trip, ran on to the line, but never looked serious threat to the winner. She has yet to win on turf, but could get a bit closer when dropped back in trip.

**Blue Venture(IRE)** ran better for this drop in trip, but lacked the pace to threaten the principals.

**Danefonique(IRE)** can be rated slightly better than the bare form, and looks suited by this trip, but remains winless after 15 outings and is one to avoid.

**Sovereign State(IRE)**, a course and distance winner last month, seemed to have every chance before fading.

**Valeureux** has not built on his recent Pontefract second and was beaten when getting slightly hampered around the two-furlong marker.

**Jackie Kiely** made a move turning for home and looked a threat to all, but quickly fell in a hole and dropped out tamely. This has to go down as a missed opportunity and he will find life tougher from now on. *Official explanation: jockey said gelding was unsuited by the going*

**Chevin** lost all chance at the start and this run looks best ignored.

**Fusillade(IRE)** *Official explanation: trainer said gelding was later scoped and found to have a breathing problem*

T/Plt: £120.30 to a £1 stake. Pool: £34,258.10. 207.75 winning tickets. T/Qpdt: £74.20 to a £1 stake. Pool: £2,065.70. 20.60 winning tickets. JF

# 3882 LEICESTER (R-H)

Wednesday, July 21

**OFFICIAL GOING: Good to firm (good in places)**

The course looked in wonderful condition, but there was a bias towards those drawn low on the straght course.

Wind: Slight behind. Weather: Cloudy

## 4016 PRISCILLA BROWN DEBENHAMS LADIES NIGHT VIP MAIDEN AUCTION STKS — 7f 9y

**6:25** (6:27) (E) 2-Y-O — **£4,475** (£1,377; £688; £344) **Stalls** Low

Form — RPR

**1** **Lucky Red Pepper** 2-8-8 ........ JQuinn 4 — 73
(PWChapple-Hyam) *racd stands' side: chsd ldrs: rdn to ld over 1f out: r.o* **12/1**

04 **2** ¾ **Hallucinate**[24] 3343 2-8-5 ........ RMullen 2 — 68
(RHannon) *racd stands' side: chsd ldrs: rdn and ev ch over 1f out: r.o* **28/1**

0 **3** nk **Tumbleweed Galore (IRE)**[19] 3483 2-8-5 ........ JFMcDonald[(3)] 12 — 71
(BJMeehan) *racd stands' side: led 2f: remained handy: rdn and ev ch over 1f out: styd on* **100/1**

00 **4** hd **Mighty Empire (IRE)**[8] 3818 2-8-3 ........ PDoe 10 — 65
(MHTompkins) *racd stands' side: a.p: rdn over 2f out: ev ch over 1f out: styd on* **12/1**

**5** 2 **Chantaco (USA)** 2-8-5 ........ MartinDwyer 14 — 62
(AMBalding) *racd stands' side: dwlt: sn prom: led that gp 5f out: rdn and hdd over 1f out: no ex ins fnl f* **16/1**

05 **6** nk **High Dyke**[19] 3491 2-8-4 ........ PaulEddery 13 — 62+
(DHaydnJones) *racd far side: trckd ldrs: led that gp over 1f out: r.o: no ch w stands' side* **15/2**[2]

**7** shd **Penny Island (IRE)** 2-8-8 ow1 ........ JDSmith 17 — 64
(AKing) *racd far side: s.s: hld up: hdwy over 1f out: r.o* **25/1**

4 **8** 1 ¼ **Scarlet Invader (IRE)**[27] 3228 2-8-8 ........ TQuinn 19 — 61
(JLDunlop) *racd far side: w ldr: led that gp over 2f out: rdn and hdd over 1f out: wknd and eased ins fnl f* **15/8**[1]

54 **9** 1 ¾ **Louise Rayner**[29] 3164 2-7-13 ........ ANicholls 11 — 48
(MLWBell) *racd stands' side: s.i.s: hld up and bhd: hdwy and swtchd rt over 1f out: nvr nr to chal* **16/1**

0 **10** nk **Sea Map**[24] 3336 2-8-5 ........ WSupple 15 — 53
(SKirk) *racd stands' side: chsd ldrs over 5f* **100/1**

**11** nk **Daygar** 2-8-4 ........ JoannaBadger 5 — 51
(MGQuinlan) *racd stands' side: prom over 5f* **25/1**

**12** 1 ½ **Ifit (IRE)** 2-8-4 ........ CCatlin 8 — 47
(MRChannon) *racd stands' side: mid-div: rdn over 2f out: wknd over 1f out* **16/1**

0 **13** ¾ **Yeldham Lady**[13] 3676 2-7-12 ........ DKinsella 9 — 39
(JPearce) *racd stands' side: dwlt: hdwy over 2f out: rdn and wknd over 1f out* **9/1**[3]

04 **14** ½ **Missed A Beat**[43] 2761 2-7-13 ........ FNorton 20 — 39
(MBlanshard) *racd far side: hld up in tch: rdn over 1f out: sn wknd* **9/1**[3]

**15** 1 **Dudley Docker (IRE)** 2-8-5 ........ NPollard 6 — 43
(MHTompkins) *racd stands' side: s.s: outpcd* **100/1**

0 **16** 2 **David's Symphony (IRE)**[11] 3748 2-8-6 ........ RSmith 18 — 39
(RHannon) *racd far side: led that gp over 4f: wknd over 1f out* **66/1**

**17** 1 ¾ **Southern Tide (USA)** 2-8-9 ........ DSweeney 16 — 37
(JJSheehan) *s.s: racd far side: hdwy 5f out: wknd wl over 1f out* **33/1**

**18** 2 **Reference (IRE)** 2-8-8 ........ PDobbs 7 — 31
(RHannon) *racd stands' side: s.s: sn prom: wknd over 2f out* **20/1**

1m 25.4s (-0.70) **Going Correction** -0.275s/f (Firm) — **18** Ran SP% **122.9**

Speed ratings: **93,92,91,91,89 88,88,87,85,85 84,83,82,81,80 78,76,73**CSF £325.92 TOTE £8.70: £3.20, £11.50, £23.40; EX 343.20.

**Owner** Foreneish Racing **Bred** Roland Lerner **Trained** Newmarket, Suffolk

**FOCUS**

Only a fair maiden in which the field split into two, with those drawn on the stands' side having the advantage.

**NOTEBOOK**

**Lucky Red Pepper**, who is out of a mare that won over ten furlongs, looked as though the race would do him good. So with that in mind, he must have his fair share of ability.

**Hallucinate** is going the right way and was clearly suited by the step up in trip.

**Tumbleweed Galore(IRE)** proved better suited to this sounder surface and showed enough to suggest he can find a little race somewhere.

**Mighty Empire(IRE)** turned in his best effort to date and will have more options open to him now in nurseries.

**Chantaco(USA)**, who is out of a mare that won as a juvenile, was a little green and can be expected to improve for the experience.

**High Dyke**, who will stay further in time, did best of those to race on the far side.

**Penny Island(IRE)**, a half-brother to the smart Golden Rule, turned in a sound first effort and can be found an opening.

**Scarlet Invader(IRE)** was a shade disappointing even allowing for being drawn on the wrong side.

## 4017 DEBENHAMS LEICESTER LADIES NIGHT NURSERY — 5f 2y

**6:55** (6:55) (D) 2-Y-O — **£4,771** (£1,468; £734; £367) **Stalls** Low

Form — RPR

240 **1** **Brag (IRE)**[28] 3208 2-9-7 **72** ........ DSweeney 6 — 83+
(RCharlton) *trckd ldrs: rdn over 1f out: r.o to ld wl ins fnl f* **1/1**[1]

5412 **2** 1 **Straffan (IRE)**[6] 3883 2-8-5 **56** ........ ANicholls 1 — 60
(DNicholls) *led: hung rt thrght: clr 1/2-way: rdn over 1f out: hdd wl ins fnl f* **6/1**[3]

3106 **3** 2 ½ **Alsu (IRE)**[11] 3727 2-9-6 **71** ........ MartinDwyer 7 — 67
(AMBalding) *prom: rdn 1/2-way: edgd lft and no ex fnl f* **11/2**[2]

5004 **4** 5 **Next Time (IRE)**[19] 3491 2-8-9 **60** ........ TQuinn 4 — 38
(MJPolglase) *w ldr 2f: sn rdn: wknd over 1f out* **13/2**

0536 **5** 1 **Leonalto (IRE)**[11] 3729 2-8-6 **60** ........(b) JFMcDonald[(3)] 5 — 35
(BJMeehan) *w ldrs 2f: sn pushed along: wknd over 1f out* **12/1**

544 **6** 2 ½ **Missed Turn**[67] 2124 2-8-2 **53** ........ FNorton 2 — 19
(JMPEustace) *sn pushed along in rr: n.d* **14/1**

0002 **7** 3 **Comintrue (IRE)**[42] 2773 2-8-6 **57** ........ JQuinn 3 — 12
(EJO'Neill) *chsd ldrs 3f* **20/1**

59.48 secs (-1.45) **Going Correction** -0.275s/f (Firm) — **7** Ran SP% **112.1**

Speed ratings: **100,98,94,86,84 80,76**CSF £7.11 TOTE £1.70: £1.30, £1.80; EX 5.10.

**Owner** Lady Rothschild **Bred** Lord Rothschild **Trained** Beckhampton, Wilts

**FOCUS**

Probably not a great race, but the well-treated winner was well on top in the end and should be capable of adding to this.

**NOTEBOOK**

**Brag(IRE)** took a while to get on top, but won with authority in the end. There should be more to come from her.

**Straffan(IRE)**, having her first start for present connections, is a pacey filly, and although she has only a selling race to her name, looks sure to be found an opening at this level.

**Alsu(IRE)** looked to find this trip on the sharp side for her.

**Next Time(IRE)** is beginning to look exposed.

## 4018 FRED ARCHER 1885 (S) STKS — 1m 9y

**7:25** (7:26) (G) 3-Y-O — **£2,940** (£840; £420) **Stalls** Low

Form — RPR

0630 **1** **Kings Rock**[13] 3684 3-8-11 55 ........(b[1]) NCallan 14 — 55
(KARyan) *plld hrd and prom: jnd ldr 5f out: rdn to ld over 1f out : r.o* **7/1**[3]

003 **2** ½ **Magico**[22] 3391 3-8-11 44 ........(b) MartinDwyer 13 — 54
(PBurgoyne) *plld hrd and prom: rdn and wandered fr over 1f out: r.o* **20/1**

5020 **3** ½ **Red Rocky**[18] 3530 3-8-1 46 ........(p) StephanieHollinshead[(5)] 11 — 48
(RHollinshead) *led: rdn and hdd over 1f out: styd on* **16/1**

0-06 **4** 1 **Treason Trial**[6] 3875 3-8-11 62 ........ KimTinkler 4 — 51
(NTinkler) *hmpd s: hld up: hdwy and nt clr run 2f out: r.o* **9/2**[1]

5020 **5** ¾ **City General (IRE)**[14] 3626 3-8-4 50 ........(p) DerekNolan[(7)] 6 — 49
(JSMoore) *hld up: hdwy over 3f out: rdn over 1f out: styd on same pce* **9/1**

0002 **6** 1 ¾ **Elsinora**[18] 3513 3-8-6 45 ........(p) TPQueally 7 — 40
(HMorrison) *s.s: hld up: hdwy u.p over 2f out: edgd rt over 1f out: styd on same pce* **9/2**[1]

0060 **7** 1 **Wizard Looking**[4] 3932 3-8-11 60 ........ RSmith 10 — 43
(RHannon) *hld up in tch: rdn over 2f out: styd on same pce appr fnl f* **11/2**[2]

0000 **8** nk **Rumour Mill (IRE)**[24] 3348 3-8-8 40 ........(b[1]) SHitchcott[(3)] 8 — 42
(NEBerry) *hld up: rdn over 3f out: styd on same pce fnl 2f* **66/1**

0-25 **9** 5 **Go Free**[15] 3613 3-8-11 54 ........ ANicholls 12 — 30
(AMHales) *prom: rdn over 2f out: wknd over 1f out: eased* **16/1**

-000 **10** hd **Tshukudu**[4] 3932 3-8-6 38 ........ JQuinn 5 — 25
(MBlanshard) *edgd lft s: hld up: nvr trbld ldrs* **100/1**

-533 **11** 6 **Defana**[13] 3681 3-8-11 52 ........ JFanning 9 — 16
(MDods) *chsd ldrs: rdn over 2f out: sn wknd* **9/2**[1]

0000 **12** 2 ½ **Tamarina (IRE)**[34] 3008 3-8-6 45 ........(p) PDoe 1 — 5
(NEBerry) *sn outpcd and bhd* **100/1**

06-5 **13** 7 **Kilminchy Lady (IRE)**[22] 3392 3-8-6 45 ........ RMullen 3 — —
(WRMuir) *sn pushed along in rr: rdn and wknd over 3f out* **20/1**

0006 **14** 6 **Osla**[13] 3681 3-8-6 30 ........(b[1]) CCatlin 2 — —
(RBrotherton) *sn outpcd and bhd* **50/1**

1m 41.35s (-1.25) **Going Correction** +0.05s/f (Good) — **14** Ran SP% **119.2**

Speed ratings: **108,107,107,106,105 103,102,102,97,97 91,88,81,75**CSF £146.80 TOTE £10.20: £3.40, £4.10, £4.60; EX 96.30.The winner was bought in for 5,500gns.

**Owner** Miss Claire King and Peter McBride **Bred** M S Anderson **Trained** Hambleton, N Yorks

**FOCUS**

A poor seller in which it was beneficial to be up with the pace and the first three home had double-figure draws.

**NOTEBOOK**

**Kings Rock** was keen enough in the first-time blinkers, but he proved resolute in holding off the wayward Magico.

**Magico** did not look straightforward and may not be one to place too much faith in.

**Red Rocky** made the best of her way home from her high draw, and proved quite difficult to pass and, although she wears cheekpieces, does seem genuine enough.

**Treason Trial** done no favours at the start, never really looked like pegging back the leaders. He certainly has the ability to win at this level.

**City General(IRE)** is well exposed at this level.

**Elsinora** did not look that enthusiastic and is clearly one to treat with caution.

**Go Free** *Official explanation: jockey said gelding hung right-handed*

**Tshukudu** *Official explanation: jockey said filly did not handle the bend*

**Defana** *Official explanation: jockey said gelding lost its action*

**Osla** *Official explanation: jockey said filly had a breathing problem*

## 4019 GRAHAM PERCIVAL "PADDOCK TALK VIP WINNER" H'CAP — 1m 3f 183y

**8:00** (8:00) (D) (0-85,77) 3-Y-O+ — **£6,870** (£2,114; £1,057; £528) **Stalls** High

Form — RPR

1012 **1** **Party Ploy**[4] 3953 6-9-1 **68** 5ex ........ DarrenWilliams 6 — 76
(KRBurke) *mde all: rdn over 1f out: edgd lft ins fnl f: all out* **2/1**[1]

-510 **2** shd **Tender Falcon**[12] 3692 4-8-13 **69** ........ JFMcDonald[(3)] 4 — 77
(RJHodges) *chsd wnr: chal 4f out: rdn over 1f out: r.o* **9/1**

2044 **3** ¾ **Mexican Pete**[12] 3692 4-9-10 **77** ........ EAhern 5 — 84
(PWHiatt) *chsd ldrs: rdn and ev ch ins fnl f: unable qck nr fin* **9/2**[3]

-005 **4** ¾ **Best Be Going (IRE)**[21] 3415 4-9-9 **76** ........ TQuinn 3 — 82
(PWHarris) *hld up in tch: plld hrd: effrt and nt clr run over 1f out: styd on* **5/1**

20/1 **5** shd **Tiger Frog (USA)**[6] 3881 5-8-4 **60** 5ex ........(b) TEaves[(3)] 1 — 66
(JMackie) *a.p: stmbld 5f out: rdn over 3f out: styd on* **7/2**[2]

0602 **6** 4 **Aoninch**[11] 3752 4-8-8 **61** ........ NPollard 2 — 60
(MrsPNDutfield) *s.s: hld up: plld hrd: hdwy and hung rt fr over 1f out: wknd and eased ins fnl f* **8/1**

2m 37.42s (2.74) **Going Correction** +0.05s/f (Good) — **6** Ran SP% **111.5**

Speed ratings: **92,91,91,90,90 88**CSF £20.08 TOTE £2.80: £1.60, £3.90; EX 21.20.

**Owner** Ian A McInnes **Bred** I McInnes **Trained** Middleham Moor, N Yorks

**FOCUS**

This modest handicap was run at a crawl and the form needs treating with caution.

**NOTEBOOK**

**Party Ploy** had a soft time of things up front, but proved very game to hold on.

**Tender Falcon** stuck to his task well enough and put behind him a below-par effort last time.

**Mexican Pete**, 11lb higher than when last successful, would have been better suited by a stronger pace.

**Best Be Going(IRE)** got this trip well enough, but he did himself no favours by refusing to settle early on.

**Tiger Frog(USA)** under pressure some way out, stuck to his task well and would have preferred a stiffer test.

**Aoninch** given enough to do in what was a slowly-run race, did herself no favours by hanging into the rails late on.

## 4020 SOME ROBBIE SOME DAY FILLIES' H'CAP — 7f 9y

**8:30** (8:31) (D) (0-80,79) 3-Y-O — **£7,260** (£2,234; £1,117; £558) **Stalls** Low

Form — RPR

3361 **1** **Pickle**[6] 3874 3-8-11 **69** 6ex ........ MartinDwyer 9 — 81+
(SCWilliams) *prom: outpcd over 2f out: rallied over 1f out: led ins fnl f: rdn out* **3/1**[1]

3063 **2** 1 ¾ **Ela Paparouna**[28] 3209 3-8-12 **70** ........ DSweeney 13 — 77
(HCandy) *chsd ldrs: led over 2f out: rdn and hdd ins fnl f: unable qck* **5/1**[2]

0-60 **3** 1 **Scarlett Rose**[46] 2694 3-8-7 **65** CLowther 12 69
(DrJDScargill) *chsd ldrs: rdn and ev ch over 1f out: no ex ins fnl f* **33/1**

0-10 **4** nk **Hasayis**[68] 2097 3-8-10 **68** WSupple 3 71
(JLDunlop) *hld up: hdwy over 1f out: nt rch ldrs* **14/1**

5541 **5** 1 3/4 **Blaeberry**[14] 3636 3-8-2 **60** (b) ANicholls 11 59
(PLGilligan) *chsd ldrs: led 4f out: rdn and hdd over 2f out: no ex fnl f* **8/1**

-206 **6** 3/4 **Go Between**[29] 3178 3-9-7 **79** EAhern 2 76+
(EALDunlop) *hld up: hdwy 1/2-way: hmpd and lost pl wl over 1f out: styd on ins fnl f* **11/1**

0-00 **7** 2 1/2 **Beauty Of Dreams**[4] 3926 3-8-6 **71** LHarman(7) 4 61
(MRChannon) *s.i.s: hld up: rdn over 1f out: n.d* **66/1**

1146 **8** 1 3/4 **La Puce**[41] 2820 3-8-7 **65** ow1 FLynch 5 50
(MissGayKelleway) *chsd ldrs: rdn over 2f out: wknd over 1f out* **16/1**

6-03 **9** 1/2 **Moon Legend (USA)**[20] 3457 3-8-8 **66** TQuinn 1 50
(WJarvis) *s.i.s: nvr nrr* **11/2**[3]

2130 **10** 1/2 **Miss Judgement (IRE)**[7] 3849 3-8-6 **64** FNorton 10 47
(WRMuir) *hld up: hdwy over 2f out: wknd fnl f* **8/1**

0555 **11** 1 1/2 **Blue Daze**[13] 3684 3-8-7 **65** RMullen 6 44
(RHannon) *led 3f: wknd over 1f out* **16/1**

2034 **12** 1/2 **True (IRE)**[8] 3819 3-8-5 **63** JQuinn 8 40
(MrsSLamyman) *dwlt: sn prom: lost pl over 4f out: wknd over 2f out* **11/1**

41-0 **13** 5 **Hi Darl**[19] 3478 3-7-7 **56** oh2 BSwarbrick(5) 7 20
(WMBrisbourne) *prom: rdn over 4f out: lost pl 1/2-way: sn bhd* **80/1**

1m 23.55s (-2.55) **Going Correction** -0.275s/f (Firm) **13** Ran SP% **120.0**
Speed ratings: **103,101,99,99,97 96,93,91,91,90 88,88,82**CSF £16.99 CT £358.91 TOTE £3.30: £1.90, £1.50, £12.20; EX 20.00.
**Owner** S P Tindall **Bred** Simon Tindall **Trained** Newmarket, Suffolk

**FOCUS**
A competitive contest run at a good clip and fair form for the grade with a progressive winner.

**NOTEBOOK**
**Pickle** defied her penalty in fine style and looks a filly on the upgrade. Although she has yet to win beyond this seven furlongs, she does shape as though she really ought to stay further.
**Ela Paparouna** did not appear to do much wrong and deserves to find a race.
**Scarlett Rose**, who has struggled since making a promising debut at Newmarket last year, showed a bit more sparkle and should find opportunities off this mark.
**Hasayis** was doing her best work in the closing stages and looks to need a return to a mile.
**Blaeberry** could never get away from her field, as she had done at Lingfield, and was easily held.
**Go Between** had no luck in running and is probably value for finishing up with the placed horses.
**Moon Legend(USA)** *Official explanation: jockey said filly was slow away, lost her position and unlucky in running*

## 4021 WEATHERBYS INSURANCE SERVICES MEDIAN AUCTION MAIDEN STKS 5f 2y

**9:00** (9:00) (F) 3-Y-O **£3,406** (£1,048; £524; £262) **Stalls** Low

Form RPR

5622 **1** **True Magic**[28] 3201 3-8-9 69 TQuinn 1 70+
(JDBethell) *mde all: shkn up over 1f out: eased wl ins fnl f* **1/1**[1]

-020 **2** 3/4 **Harrison's Flyer (IRE)**[8] 3819 3-9-0 67 (b[1]) PHanagan 3 63
(RAFahey) *chsd ldrs: rdn over 1f out: r.o* **15/2**[3]

2 **3** 1 **Sokoke**[14] 3635 3-9-0 JQuinn 9 59
(RMBeckett) *bmpd s: a.p: rdn over 1f out: styd on same pce ins fnl f* **10/3**[2]

2-43 **4** hd **Fishlake Flyer (IRE)**[53] 2468 3-8-9 64 JFanning 4 53
(JGGiven) *hmpd s: chsd ldrs: rdn over 1f out: styd on same pce* **8/1**

0006 **5** 1 3/4 **Night Worker**[14] 3636 3-9-0 50 RSmith 7 51
(RHannon) *sn outpcd: swtchd rt and hdwy over 1f out: nvr trbld ldrs* **12/1**

4035 **6** 1/2 **Lakeside Guy (IRE)**[14] 3628 3-9-0 56 TPQueally 8 49
(PSMcentee) *edgd rt s: w wnr over 3f: wknd ins fnl f* **25/1**

5052 **7** 1 3/4 **Westborough (IRE)**[11] 3739 3-9-0 55 KimTinkler 5 42
(NTinkler) *s.i.s and bmpd s: sn pushed along in rr: n.d* **22/1**

3320 **8** 3 1/2 **Vittorioso (IRE)**[139] 963 3-9-0 54 (b) FLynch 6 28
(MissGayKelleway) *w wnr to 1/2-way: wknd over 1f out* **20/1**

-064 **9** 8 **Mind The Time**[120] 1089 3-9-0 35 MTebbutt 10 —
(JHetherton) *sn outpcd* **50/1**

59.60 secs (-1.33) **Going Correction** -0.275s/f (Firm) **9** Ran SP% **118.6**
Speed ratings: **99,97,96,95,93 92,89,83,71**CSF £9.17 TOTE £2.10: £1.20, £2.10, £1.40; EX 13.10 Place 6 £465.62, Place 5 £30.34.
**Owner** T R Lock **Bred** T R Lock **Trained** Middleham Moor, N Yorks

**FOCUS**
Not that competitive a maiden with the winner easing down in the latter stages and value for more than the official margin.

**NOTEBOOK**
**True Magic** had the best of the draw and won with more in hand than the official verdict.
**Harrison's Flyer(IRE)** took a while to get going in the first-time blinkers and may be better suited by a little further.
**Sokoke** lacked the experience of his rivals and was probably done no favours by his wide draw.
**Fishlake Flyer(IRE)** has had plenty of chances and is none to trustworthy.
**Night Worker** got going all to late and looks to appreciate a stiffer test than he faced here.
T/Plt: £423.70 to a £1 stake. Pool: £37,501.90. 64.60 winning tickets. T/Qpdt: £38.00 to a £1 stake. Pool: £3,829.50. 74.40 winning tickets. CR

# 3930 LINGFIELD (L-H)

Wednesday, July 21

**OFFICIAL GOING: Turf: good to firm aw: standard**
Wind: lt bhd Weather: fine but cloudy

## 4022 JAP KITCHEN CONTRACTS MEDIAN AUCTION MAIDEN STKS (DIV I) 7f (P)

**2:00** (2:03) (E) 2-Y-O **£3,513** (£1,081; £540; £270) **Stalls** Low

Form RPR

3 **1** **Raza Cab (IRE)**[32] 3093 2-9-0 KFallon 6 80
(CNAllen) *prom: effrt to ld wl over 1f out: rdn and in command fnl f* **5/1**

**2** 2 1/2 **Russian Consort (IRE)** 2-9-0 JDSmith 4 74
(AKing) *w'like: lw: s.s: wl in rr tl gd prog on wd outside fr 2f out: chsd wnr ins fnl f: kpt on but no imp* **40/1**

0 **3** 1 **Following Flow (USA)**[15] 3601 2-9-0 KDarley 3 71
(WJarvis) *cl up: rdn over 2f out: outpcd over 1f out: styd on again fnl f* **16/1**

0 **4** nk **Naval Force**[16] 3588 2-9-0 (t) SDrowne 13 71
(HMorrison) *prom: rdn to chal 2f out: ev ch over 1f out: one pce fnl f* **10/1**

52 **5** 3/4 **Seyaadi**[12] 3718 2-9-0 RHills 8 69
(EALDunlop) *b: b.hind: lw: trckd ldrs: nt clr run 2f out: shuffled along and one pce after* **5/2**[1]

**6** shd **Cupid's Glory** 2-9-0 SSanders 5 68+
(SirMarkPrescott) *str: bit bkwd: racd in midfield: prog on outer to press ldrs 2f out: rdn and cl up jst over 1f out: no ex and eased nr fin* **9/2**[3]

4 **7** hd **Fong Shui**[68] 2096 2-9-0 DSweeney 9 70+
(PJMakin) *dwlt: hld up in midfield: lost pl 3f out: nt clr run 2f out and over 1f out: styng on whn nt clr run again ins fnl f* **33/1**

2535 **8** 1 1/4 **Asian Tiger (IRE)**[13] 3677 2-9-0 DHolland 12 65
(RHannon) *mde most at stdy pce to wl over 1f out: sn wknd* **7/2**[2]

00 **9** 4 **Play Up Pompey**[14] 3633 2-9-0 ADaly 2 55
(JJBridger) *a in rr: rdn over 2f out: no prog* **66/1**

0056 **10** 1/2 **Elvina Hills (IRE)**[20] 3438 2-8-2 CHaddon(7) 10 49
(WGMTurner) *t.k.h: w ldr: ev ch wl over 1f out: wknd rapidly* **50/1**

3 **11** 1 **Keynes (JPN)**[23] 3377 2-9-0 JFortune 11 51
(JHMGosden) *t.k.h: prom: nt clr run 2f out: stl chsng ldrs whn nt clr run jst over 1f out: rdn and nt run on fnl f* **18/1**

00 **12** 6 **Beauchamp Twist**[19] 3491 2-8-9 SWKelly 7 31
(GAButler) *awkward s and hmpd sn after: a in rr: rdn 3f out: sn btn* **66/1**

**13** 1 **Eastwell Magic** 2-8-9 BDoyle 1 29
(JGGiven) *leggy: dwlt: a in last pair: wknd 3f out* **66/1**

1m 27.31s (1.37) **Going Correction** +0.10s/f (Slow) **13** Ran SP% **117.7**
Speed ratings: **96,93,92,91,90 90,90,89,84,83 82,75,74**CSF £201.73 TOTE £5.20: £1.50, £17.70, £4.40; EX 278.80.
**Owner** Alan Brazil Racing Club **Bred** Rathyork Stud **Trained** Newmarket, Suffolk

**FOCUS**
An interesting maiden which saw gambles on both Cupid's Glory and Naval Force, but both were floored. The form is difficult to gauge and messy with the main group bunched up.

**NOTEBOOK**
**Raza Cab(IRE)** was surprisingly weak in the market despite his debut form looking pretty strong in the context of this race. Prominent throughout, he burst through a gap between horses early in the straight and soon drew well clear. He is clearly going the right way and looks up to taking his chance in a conditions race. Connections believe he prefers a little cut in the ground, which is why they brought him here.
**Russian Consort(IRE)**, whose trainer does quite well with the few two-year-olds he runs, made a very promising debut, finishing well down the outside. By Groom Dancer out of a ten-furlong winner, he can be expected to improve with time as he steps up in trip.
**Following Flow(USA)** made his debut in a classy maiden at Newmarket and duly improved on his performance there in this easier company.
**Naval Force**, who was backed in from 20-1, was expected to come on for his eye-catching debut at Windsor. He ran well enough but just dropped out of the places close home.
**Seyaadi** had every chance and was just not good enough. He does now qualify for a handicap mark, however.
**Cupid's Glory** was heavily backed. A full-brother to Courting, who won four times as a juvenile over this trip, he was given every chance and just was not good enough.
**Fong Shui** was the one who caught the eye. Held up behind horses, he struggled to get a clear run, waiting in vain for a gap to appear, and he crossed the line having never been put under any pressure. He is probably a good deal better than this effort suggests.
**Asian Tiger(IRE)** had his limitations exposed.
**Keynes(JPN)** looks a difficult ride.

## 4023 JAP KITCHEN CONTRACTS MEDIAN AUCTION MAIDEN STKS (DIV II) 7f (P)

**2:30** (2:31) (E) 2-Y-O **£3,513** (£1,081; £540; £270) **Stalls** Low

Form RPR

4 **1** **Hypnotic**[7] 3847 2-9-0 SSanders 13 86+
(SirMarkPrescott) *trckd ldrs: led 3f out: shkn up and drew clr fr over 1f out: readily* **10/3**[1]

0302 **2** 5 **Flying Pass**[20] 3438 2-9-0 DaneO'Neill 6 69
(DJSFfrenchDavis) *hld up towards rr: prog to chse wnr over 2f out: no imp over 1f out* **7/2**[2]

**3** 1 1/4 **Saadigg (IRE)** 2-9-0 PRobinson 2 65
(MAJarvis) *unf: scope: bit bkwd: chsd ldrs: outpcd over 2f out: kpt on again fr over 1f out to take 3rd nr fin* **6/1**

00 **4** nk **King Of Blues (IRE)**[26] 3259 2-9-0 (t) EAhern 12 65
(MAMagnusson) *b: b.hind: towards rr: rdn 3f out: prog over 2f out: kpt on same pce fr over 1f out* **33/1**

**5** nk **Samson Quest** 2-9-0 MartinDwyer 3 64
(AMBalding) *w'like: bit bkwd: trckd ldrs: cl up over 2f out: outpcd wl over 1f out: one pce after* **12/1**

**6** 1/2 **Mystery Lot (IRE)** 2-8-9 JDSmith 11 58+
(AKing) *leggy: scope: bit bkwd: lengthy: s.s: wl in rr: prog over 2f out: rdn and styd on fr over 1f out: nrst fin* **33/1**

0 **7** 1 1/4 **Meditation**[20] 3456 2-8-9 KDarley 8 55
(IAWood) *prom: chsd wnr briefly wl over 2f out: hanging rt and fdd over 1f out* **25/1**

**8** 3/4 **Resplendent Prince** 2-9-0 DHolland 1 58
(PWHarris) *w'like: scope: bit bkwd: gd sort: chsd ldrs: outpcd over 2f out: no ch whn nt clr run 1f out* **6/1**

0 **9** 11 **Inchcape Rock**[69] 2058 2-9-0 SDrowne 10 30
(LGCottrell) *dwlt: rn v green and hanging bdly thrght: wl bhd fnl 3f* **20/1**

**10** 6 **Welsh Galaxy (IRE)** 2-8-9 RPrice 9 10
(PLGilligan) *leggy: a in rr: t.o over 2f out* **50/1**

0 **11** nk **Gallego**[19] 3476 2-9-0 (b[1]) RHavlin 4 14
(SLKeightley) *chsd ldrs to 1/2-way: wknd rapidly: t.o* **66/1**

04 **12** 3 1/2 **Sastre (IRE)**[13] 3659 2-8-9 JFEgan 5 —
(PMPhelan) *hmpd after 1f: sn chsd ldr to 3f out: wknd rapidly: t.o* **14/1**

06 **13** 8 **Fly To Dubai (IRE)**[32] 3080 2-9-0 KFallon 7 —
(EJO'Neill) *led to 3f out: wknd rapidly: t.o* **11/2**[3]

1m 27.45s (1.51) **Going Correction** +0.10s/f (Slow) **13** Ran SP% **121.6**
Speed ratings: **95,89,87,87,87 86,85,84,71,64 64,60,51**CSF £14.26 TOTE £5.20: £2.20, £1.80, £3.10; EX 20.40.
**Owner** Cheveley Park Stud **Bred** Cheveley Park Stud Ltd **Trained** Newmarket, Suffolk
■ Stewards Enquiry : K Fallon four-day ban: careless riding (Aug 1-4)

**FOCUS**
Only marginally the slower of the two divisions, but on paper certainly the weaker of the two, although the winner is much improved.

**NOTEBOOK**
**Hypnotic** travelled well throughout, picked up in good style in the straight and won as he liked. The step up to seven furlongs appeared to suit him well and he looks open to further improvment.
**Flying Pass** set a fair standard but, as he has shown before, he is vulnerable to anything with a bit more potential. He ran his race with no excuses.
**Saadigg(IRE)** shaped as though in need of the experience, taking a while to get the hang of things but running on well when it was all over. He should come on for the run.
**King Of Blues(IRE)**, for whom handicaps now beckon, should be seen to better effect in that sphere.
**Samson Quest** looked likely to take a hand turning in, but never quite got into the first three. He is entitled to come on for his debut, though.

**Mystery Lot(IRE)** is related to winners and shaped with some promise. Slowly away, she was never really in the race but stayed on in encouraging fashion. *Official explanation: jockey said filly missed the break*

**Resplendent Prince**, for whom there was some money beforehand, got knocked off his stride momentarily inside the last, but it made no real difference. *Official explanation: jockey said colt ran too free in the first half furlong and did not face kickback*

**Inchcape Rock** *Official explanation: jockey said colt did not face kickback*

**Sastre(IRE)** *Official explanation: jockey said filly suffered interference approaching the first bend and was eased*

## 4024 RATIONAL CLASSIFIED STKS — 7f (P)

**3:00** (3:00) (E) 3-Y-O — **£3,503** (£1,078; £539; £269) **Stalls** Low

Form — RPR

6-53 **1** **Grandalea**[9] 3807 3-9-0 75 ... KFallon 10 — 88
(SirMichaelStoute) *prom: chsd ldr 4f out: rdn to chal wl over 1f out: hrd drvn and forced ahd last 50yds* **11/4**[2]

1042 **2** *nk* **Eccentric**[7] 3849 3-9-3 75 ... JFEgan 11 — 90
(AndrewReid) *b: b.hind: led after 2f: clr w wnr fr 2f out: drvn fnl f: hdd last 50yds* **9/4**[1]

-060 **3** *7* **Sweetest Revenge (IRE)**[14] 3628 3-8-13 74 ... ADaly 5 — 68
(MDIUsher) *t.k.h: sn hld up in rr: outpcd over 2f out: hanging but kpt on over 1f out: tk modest 3rd wl ins fnl f* **14/1**

060 **4** *1 1/4* **Nikiforos**[20] 3448 3-8-12 67 ... SWhitworth 6 — 64
(JWHills) *hld up in last pair: outpcd 3f out: shuffled along and styd on fnl 2f: no ch* **66/1**

-231 **5** *hd* **Ragged Jack (IRE)**[11] 3739 3-9-0 72 ... SWKelly 2 — 65
(GABulter) *prom: rdn 3f out: sn outpcd: wknd over 1f out* **12/1**

-436 **6** *1 1/2* **La Landonne**[18] 3530 3-8-9 68 ... SSanders 1 — 57
(PMPhelan) *settled in midfield: outpcd wl over 2f out: no ch after* **12/1**

6000 **7** *shd* **Fools Entire**[54] 2457 3-8-9 67 ... FPFerris(3) 8 — 59
(JAGilbert) *prom: chsd ldng pair over 3f out: sn rdn: wknd rapidly over 1f out* **33/1**

34-5 **8** *5* **Christina's Dream**[14] 3622 3-8-11 72 ... DHolland 9 — 45
(PWHarris) *racd in midfield: rdn wl over 2f out: sn wknd* **6/1**[3]

-205 **9** *1 1/2* **Thara'A (IRE)**[49] 2577 3-8-9 69 ... SDrowne 7 — 39
(EALDunlop) *dwlt: wl in rr tl prog to chse ldrs over 2f out: wknd over 1f out* **10/1**

5043 **10** *8* **Wavertree Girl (IRE)**[28] 3211 3-8-9 68 ... (b) KDarley 3 — 19
(NPLittmoden) *s.s: wl in rr: brief effrt over 2f out: hanging and wknd rapidly wl over 1f out* **10/1**

4005 **11** *6* **Called Up**[25] 3322 3-8-12 68 ... DaneO'Neill 4 — 6
(HCandy) *led for 2f: wknd over 3f out: t.o* **20/1**

1m 25.91s (-0.03) **Going Correction** +0.10s/f (Slow) — **11** Ran SP% **121.2**
Speed ratings: **104,103,95,94,94 92,92,86,84,75 68**CSF £9.51 TOTE £3.20: £1.20, £1.80, £4.20; EX 8.90.
**Owner** Cheveley Park Stud **Bred** Cheveley Park Stud Ltd **Trained** Newmarket, Suffolk

**FOCUS**
A tight race on the ratings, but a fair time for the grade and in reality only two mattered from a long way out and they look progressive.

**NOTEBOOK**
**Grandalea** has not been getting home over a mile and the drop back to seven suited her, as well as being given a lead for once. It was over this course and distance that she finished runner-up to Sundrop last autumn, and clearly the track suits her style of running. Connections will no doubt be more than happy to have finally got a win out of this well-bred filly.

**Eccentric**, twice a course and distance winner, has also shown the pace for six around here and that speed was used to good effect on this occasion. She drew clear of the rest of the field but could not shake off the attentions of her main market rival, and in the end went down narrowly. This was a brave run in defeat.

**Sweetest Revenge(IRE)** brought home the rest of the field. She is rated 5lb higher on the All-Weather than on turf and appreciated the return to the artificial surface, seeing out her race well on her first attempt over seven furlongs.

**Nikiforos**, a handicap debutant, stayed on without getting competitive. His stable is in good form at present and this brother/half-brother to sprint winners is capable of better.

**Ragged Jack(IRE)** won over five furlongs last time and could make no impression on the leaders in the closing stages over this two-furlong longer trip.

**La Landonne** should have been suited by the return to seven, but she was unable to adopt her favoured prominent style of running with Eccentric in the field.

**Christina's Dream** was disappointing but did hang in the early stages. *Official explanation: jockey said filly had hung right early on*

**Thara'A(IRE)** *Official explanation: jockey said saddle slipped*

## 4025 WINTERHALTER FILLIES' H'CAP — 5f (P)

**3:30** (3:30) (F) (0-55,55) 3-Y-O+ — **£2,912** (£832; £416) **Stalls** High

Form — RPR

0004 **1** **Tender (IRE)**[13] 3680 4-9-2 49 ... (p) SDrowne 6 — 57
(MrsStefLiddiard) *b: mde virtually all: hung lft but def advantage over 1f out: hld on* **11/2**[3]

0020 **2** *nk* **Minimum Bid**[4] 3935 3-9-4 55 ... SSanders 8 — 62
(MissBSanders) *settled in rr: prog 2f out: hrd rdn and effrt on outer over 1f out: r.o wl to take 2nd last stride: too much to do* **7/1**

-243 **3** *shd* **Lucky Valentine**[16] 3575 4-9-2 49 ... (p) RLMoore 5 — 56
(GLMoore) *trckd ldng pair: effrt to press wnr jst over 1f out: ev ch ins fnl f: nt qckn* **11/4**[1]

00-0 **4** *1* **Inch By Inch**[39] 2875 5-9-1 48 ... (b) DHolland 10 — 51
(PJMakin) *trckd ldng pair: rdn and effrt over 1f out: ch ins fnl f: nt qckn* **9/2**[2]

6000 **5** *1 1/4* **Erracht**[10] 3772 6-9-4 51 ... GBaker 3 — 49
(MrsHSweeting) *w wnr to over 1f out: one pce fnl f* **6/1**

0500 **6** *1 1/4* **Averami**[14] 3636 3-8-11 55 ... (v) RJKilloran(7) 9 — 48
(AMBalding) *hld up in last: outpcd 1/2-way: modest late prog* **22/1**

0401 **7** *3/4* **Petana**[30] 3147 4-8-9 49 ... (p) NataliaGemelova(7) 7 — 39
(MDods) *s.i.s: chsd ldrs after 2f: no prog 2f out: fdd over 1f out* **10/1**

-040 **8** *shd* **Lady Justice**[39] 2875 4-9-8 55 ... KFallon 4 — 44
(WJarvis) *s.i.s: sn in midfield: drvn over 2f out: wknd over 1f out* **8/1**

0000 **9** *1 1/4* **Mannora**[4] 3935 4-9-3 50 ... KDarley 2 — 34
(PHowling) *s.i.s: a towards rr: struggling 2f out* **16/1**

-000 **10** *9* **Tikitano (IRE)**[24] 3344 3-8-8 52 ... MHoward(7) 1 — —
(DKIvory) *chsd ldrs to 1/2-way: wknd: t.o* **50/1**

60.43 secs (0.65) **Going Correction** +0.10s/f (Slow)
**WFA** 3 from 4yo+ 4lb — **10** Ran SP% **119.4**
Speed ratings: **98,97,97,95,93 91,90,90,88,74**CSF £44.94 CT £130.15 TOTE £7.00: £2.00, £2.20, £1.50; EX 33.30.
**Owner** Mrs Felicity Ashfield **Bred** M Ervine **Trained** Great Shefford, Berks

**FOCUS**
A moderate handicap run in an ordinary time and modest form.

**NOTEBOOK**
**Tender(IRE)** was tasting success for the first time in almost two years and won in gutsy style. She found seven furlongs too far on her previous visits here and sprinting is clearly her game. She looks ideal for a winter All-Weather campaign as she takes her racing particularly well.

**Minimum Bid** has run one or two races of promise and did best of the three-year-olds on this All-Weather debut, staying on steadily for second place. She looks capable of winning a little race.

**Lucky Valentine**, granted some better luck in running, might well have given the winner more to think about. She found her run blocked early in the straight but came home well once in the clear.

**Inch By Inch** is rated 8lb lower on the All-Weather than on turf and ran well enough, but her best form is over six.

**Erracht** showed plenty of pace but was cooked soon after turning in.

**Petana** could not repeat her Musselburgh performance off a higher mark on this different surface.

## 4026 LETHEBY & CHRISTOPHER H'CAP — 6f (P)

**4:00** (4:03) (E) (0-70,67) 3-Y-O+ — **£3,523** (£1,084; £542; £271) **Stalls** Low

Form — RPR

0-04 **1** **Woodbury**[120] 1087 5-9-0 53 ... GBaker 1 — 63
(MrsHSweeting) *b: mde all: rdn over 1f out: kpt on wl fnl f* **14/1**

2-00 **2** *1* **Salon Prive**[70] 2030 4-9-10 63 ... KFallon 2 — 70
(CACyzer) *prom: chsd wnr 1/2-way: hrd rdn to chal over 1f out: a hld* **10/1**

4-14 **3** *nk* **Chimali (IRE)**[10] 3777 3-9-9 67 ... EAhern 4 — 73
(JNoseda) *chsd wnr to 1/2-way: styd prom: rdn to chal over 1f out : unable qck* **4/1**[2]

5006 **4** *1 1/4* **Cormorant Wharf (IRE)**[11] 3747 4-10-0 67 ... (b[1]) JFEgan 6 — 69
(TEPowell) *b: lw: dwlt: hld up in rr: effrt 2f out: styd on wl fnl f: nvr able to chal* **9/1**

0040 **5** *1 1/4* **Illusive (IRE)**[15] 3606 7-9-5 58 ... (b) JFortune 8 — 57
(MWigham) *racd on outer: trckd ldrs: rdn 2f out: one pce over 1f out* **14/1**

2136 **6** *1/2* **Double M**[27] 3243 7-9-3 61 ... (v) RThomas(5) 7 — 58
(MrsLRichards) *hld up in midfield: effrt over 2f out: sn rdn and nt qckn: one pce after* **7/2**[1]

0003 **7** *nk* **Torquemada (IRE)**[21] 3420 3-8-13 60 ... FPFerris(3) 11 — 56
(WJarvis) *lw: dwlt: sn chsd ldrs: hrd rdn over 2f out: no prog over 1f out* **5/1**[3]

545- **8** *3* **The Baroness (IRE)**[323] 4636 4-9-4 57 ... SSanders 9 — 44
(EROertel) *hld up towards rr: prog to chse ldrs 2f out: wknd over 1f out* **25/1**

0200 **9** *1/2* **Zagala**[15] 3615 4-9-9 62 ... (t) PRobinson 5 — 48
(SLKeightley) *b.hind: chsd ldrs: u.p 1/2-way: wknd wl over 1f out* **7/1**

65-6 **10** *5* **Gameset'N'Match**[20] 3441 3-9-2 67 ... (b) CHaddon(7) 12 — 38
(WGMTurner) *sn pushed along: a wl in rr* **50/1**

0600 **11** *3 1/2* **Second Minister**[33] 3043 5-9-2 55 ... (b) DHolland 3 — 15
(DFlood) *b: s.s: settled in last: wl bhd fnl 2f* **16/1**

1m 13.52s (0.60) **Going Correction** +0.10s/f (Slow)
**WFA** 3 from 4yo+ 5lb — **11** Ran SP% **115.5**
Speed ratings: **100,98,98,96,94 94,93,89,89,82 77**CSF £144.06 CT £520.21 TOTE £15.40: £4.20, £4.10, £2.10; EX 185.40.
**Owner** P Sweeting **Bred** D R Tucker **Trained** Marlborough, Wilts

**FOCUS**
Just an ordinary handicap but sound enough for the grade.

**NOTEBOOK**
**Woodbury** had not won for almost two years but she showed plenty of dash from her low draw on this return from a four-month absence, and was always holding her rivals in the straight. Despite this win, she is arguably better handicapped on turf at present.

**Salon Prive**, who is lightly-raced, put up a better effort without the blinkers and with the Champion aboard. He stays farther than this and clearly acts on this surface perfectly well.

**Chimali(IRE)** did not look to have been favourably handicapped when allotted a rating of 67, and he once again ran a satisfactory race without suggesting that he is ready to strike off this sort of mark.

**Cormorant Wharf(IRE)** missed the break but stayed on well enough from the rear in the first-time blinkers. His style of running makes him difficult to win with, though. *Official explanation: jockey said gelding missed break*

**Illusive(IRE)** remains on a long losing run.

**Double M** was the disappointment of the race. He has been in good form this season but failed to run to his best back on a surface on which he has been successful many times in the past.

**Second Minister** *Official explanation: jockey said gelding missed break*

## 4027 EMH INTERNATIONAL H'CAP — 1m 3f 106y

**4:30** (4:30) (E) (0-75,75) 3-Y-O — **£4,355** (£1,340; £670; £335) **Stalls** High

Form — RPR

4640 **1** **Ellina**[21] 3421 3-8-11 63 ... KFallon 9 — 70
(JPearce) *lw: trckd ldrs: rdn and effrt over 2f out: drvn to ld ins fnl f: styd on wl* **14/1**

3641 **2** *1/2* **Velvet Waters**[16] 3572 3-8-7 59 ... SCarson 6 — 65
(RFJohnsonHoughton) *lw: trckd ldr: rdn to chal over 2f out: led wl over 1f out to ins fnl f: unable qck* **9/2**[2]

446 **3** *2* **Pope's Hill (IRE)**[21] 3417 3-9-7 73 ... DHolland 1 — 76+
(LMCumani) *lw: lost pl after 3f and racd in last trio after: rdn and prog over 2f out: edgd rt 1f out: kpt on to take 3rd ins fnl f* **6/1**

2041 **4** *1 1/4* **Ile Facile (IRE)**[7] 3837 3-9-9 75 7ex ... (t) KDarley 3 — 76
(NPLittmoden) *trckd ldrs: rdn 3f out: cl up over 1f out: one pce after* **5/1**[3]

3553 **5** *1/2* **Mustang Ali (IRE)**[16] 3572 3-9-3 69 ... JFEgan 7 — 69
(SKirk) *b.hind: sn settled in rr: effrt over 2f out: rdn and one pce after: nvr rchd ldrs* **7/2**[1]

00-0 **6** *1 1/2* **Optimal (IRE)**[10] 3773 3-8-10 62 ... SSanders 2 — 60
(SirMarkPrescott) *led to wl over 1f out: fdd u.p* **8/1**

0-44 **7** *3 1/2* **Papeete (GER)**[37] 2928 3-8-8 60 ... SDrowne 10 — 52
(MissBSanders) *settled in last pair: rdn 3f out: no prog* **14/1**

2410 **8** *hd* **Golden Empire (USA)**[30] 3160 3-9-6 72 ... TEDurcan 8 — 64
(EALDunlop) *rn in snatches: chsd ldrs: rdn and hanging rt over 2f out: wknd over 1f out* **16/1**

3324 **9** *4* **Desert Image (IRE)**[24] 3340 3-9-3 72 ... DCorby(3) 5 — 57
(CTinkler) *mostly trckd ldng pair tl wknd u.p over 2f out* **7/1**

**10** *8* **Team Tactics (IRE)**[299] 5205 3-8-7 59 ... SWhitworth 4 — 31
(LADace) *b: s.s: a last: rn wd bnd over 3f out: bhd after* **50/1**

2m 30.18s (0.66) **Going Correction** +0.15s/f (Good) — **10** Ran SP% **116.1**
Speed ratings: **103,102,101,100,99 98,96,96,93,87**CSF £75.72 CT £427.19 TOTE £19.10: £3.90, £2.30, £2.50; EX 171.70.
**Owner** The Exclusive Two Partnership **Bred** Lady Jennifer Green **Trained** Newmarket, Suffolk

**FOCUS**
A reasonable handicap run at a sound pace, but the form is unexceptional.

**NOTEBOOK**
**Ellina**, who has apparently needed time to mature mentally, took advantage of a 3lb drop in the weights to get off the mark. She should stay a little farther and it would not be a surprise to see her winning again.

**Velvet Waters** only went up a couple of pounds for her narrow Bath win and she made a bold bid to follow up. She was sticking to her task when headed and obviously has the right attitude.

**Pope's Hill(IRE)** shaped encouragingly on this handicap debut, staying on to some effect in the latter stages. Easier ground will suit him.
**Ile Facile(IRE)**, who hung both left and right, ran respectably under a 7lb penalty and is due to race off 3lb lower in future handicaps. *Official explanation: jockey said colt hung both ways*
**Mustang Ali(IRE)**, who was well supported, could never land a blow and finished further behind Velvet Waters than he had at Bath, despite being 1lb better off.
**Optimal(IRE)** tried a change in tactics, but was soon in trouble once collared and did not seem to see out this longer trip.

## 4028 COME RACING HERE ON SATURDAY EVENING MAIDEN STKS 1m 3f 106y
**5:00** (5:04) (D) 3-Y-O+ **£3,571** (£1,099; £549; £274) **Stalls** High

Form RPR

23 **1** **Light Of Morn**[54] 2460 3-8-8 ........ SSanders 10 86
(RGuest) *hld up in midfield: stdy prog fr 3f out: led over 1f out: shkn up and sn drew clr* **6/1**[2]

022 **2** *3 ½* **Idealistic (IRE)**[40] 2832 3-8-8 82 ........ DHolland 2 80
(LMCumani) *lw: trckd ldrs: effrt 3f out: prog to chal over 1f out: sn outpcd by wnr* **7/4**[1]

026 **3** *5* **Woman In White (FR)**[14] 3630 3-8-8 73 ........ JFortune 12 72
(JHMGosden) *led 9f out: rdn and def advantage over 2f out: hdd & wknd over 1f out* **12/1**[3]

03 **4** *1 ¼* **Wedding Cake (IRE)**[16] 3574 3-8-8 ........ KFallon 4 70
(SirMichaelStoute) *trckd ldrs: pushed along 5f out: nt handle downhill sn after: one pce and struggling fr over 2f out* **7/4**[1]

**5** *3 ½* **Cemgraft** 3-8-8 ........ SDrowne 1 64
(MissECLavelle) *unf: scope: lengthy: s.s: in tch in rr: outpcd 4f out: kpt on fnl 2f: no ch* **33/1**

03 **6** *shd* **Encompass (FR)**[15] 3608 3-8-8 ........ WRyan 7 64
(HRACecil) *trckd ldrs: rdn 3f out: sn btn: wknd over 1f out* **12/1**[3]

0 **7** *shd* **Enhancer**[50] 2562 6-9-10 ........ JFEgan 9 69
(MrsLCJewell) *trckd ldr 9f out: chal 4f out: ev ch 3f out: sn wknd* **33/1**

**8** *1 ¼* **Magical Quest** 4-9-10 ........ KDarley 13 67
(MrsAJPerrett) *w'like: s.s: racd in last pair: detached and pushed along over 3f out: styd on steadily fnl 2f: bttr for experience* **16/1**

**9** *hd* **Dual Purpose (IRE)** 9-9-10 ........ LVickers 3 67?
(CRoberts) *bit bkwd: led to 9f out: styd chsng ldrs tl wknd 3f out* **100/1**

40 **10** *1 ¾* **Lord Nellsson**[6] 3885 8-9-5 ........ HayleyTurner(5) 5 64?
(JSKing) *dwlt: racd in midfield: wknd over 2f out* **100/1**

**11** *hd* **Armatore (USA)**[280] 4-9-10 ........ SWhitworth 8 64?
(EROertel) *racd in midfield: rdn over 3f out: wknd over 2f out* **100/1**

0- **12** *5* **Whispering Valley**[378] 3099 4-9-5 ........ RLMoore 11 51
(MrsAJPerrett) *racd in midfield: rdn and struggling over 3f out: wknd over 2f out* **33/1**

5 **13** *5* **Chelsea's Diamond**[28] 3194 4-9-5 ........ (b) RPrice 14 43
(JAkehurst) *towards rr: prog 1/2-way: chsd ldrs 4f out: wknd rapidly 2f out* **100/1**

0 **14** *¾* **Little Gannet**[25] 3304 3-8-8 ........ DaneO'Neill 6 41
(SDow) *s.i.s: a in rr: detached over 3f out* **100/1**

2m 30.35s (0.83) **Going Correction** +0.15s/f (Good) **14** Ran SP% **124.0**
**WFA** 3 from 4yo+ 11lb
Speed ratings: **102,99,95,94,92 92,92,91,91,89 89,86,82,81**CSF £16.87 TOTE £7.90: £1.70, £1.10, £3.90; EX 18.40 Place 6 £209.11, Place 5 £32.21.
**Owner** Matthews Breeding And Racing **Bred** Matthews Breeding And Racing Ltd **Trained** Newmarket, Suffolk

**FOCUS**
A few well-bred animals on view here but most have been slow to come to hand. The overall form does not look that strong.

**NOTEBOOK**
**Light Of Morn**, who was considered a possible Oaks filly earlier in the season but is only now beginning to show her true ability, cruised up into contention and went nicely clear in the straight. While her immediate future lies in the hands of the Handicapper, connections hope to get her some black type in time.
**Idealistic(IRE)** caused odds-on punters to have their fingers burnt last time, but once again she headed the market. She had every chance and came clear of the rest, but is becoming a shade disappointing.
**Woman In White(FR)** may have been beaten on the stamina front but it is just as likely that she was simply outclassed, as she came into the race with a rating 9lb inferior to the runner-up.
**Wedding Cake(IRE)** struggled to handle the downhill section of the course but, once in line for home, picked up fairly well. She looks the type to do better now that she is eligible for a mark, and a longer trip should not inconvenience her.
**Cemgraft** did best of the newcomers, staying on well having been out the back for most of the race.
**Encompass(FR)** was slightly disappointing, but she is also now eligible to run in handicaps, and will be more interesting when she gets some cut underfoot.
**Magical Quest** was green and coltish in the paddock.
T/Plt: £202.80 to a £1 stake. Pool: £33,735.80. 121.40 winning tickets. T/Qpdt: £25.70 to a £1 stake. Pool: £2,572.40. 74.00 winning tickets. JN

# 3537 SANDOWN (R-H)
## Wednesday, July 21

**OFFICIAL GOING: Good to firm (good in places)**
It appeared hard to make up ground from off the pace on races run on the round course - the only exception being the mile six handicap.

## 4029 PANMURE GORDON EQUITIES APPRENTICE H'CAP 1m 2f 7y
**6:10** (6:11) (E) (0-75,74) 3-Y-O+ **£5,060** (£1,557; £778; £389) **Stalls** High

Form RPR

1110 **1** **A One (IRE)**[12] 3698 5-9-13 73 ........ FPFerris 9 86
(HJManners) *set str pce: travelling wl tl hrd drvn fr ins fnl 2f: styd on fnl f: hld on all out* **9/2**[3]

6500 **2** *shd* **Recount (FR)**[7] 3844 4-9-7 70 ........ MSavage(3) 8 83
(JRBest) *lw: t.k.h and stdd mid-div: hdwy 3f out: chsd wnr ins fnl 2f: styd on wl fnl f: edgd lft cl home: jst failed* **14/1**

3000 **3** *7* **Bluegrass Boy**[20] 3450 4-8-11 60 ........ RThomas(3) 2 60
(GBBalding) *bhd: pushed along over 2f out: styd on fr over 1f out to take 3rd ins fnl f but nvr nr ldrs* **12/1**

0306 **4** *hd* **Barry Island**[12] 3692 5-10-0 74 ........ LPKeniry 4 73
(DRCElsworth) *in tch: hdwy over 2f out: tk mod 3rd appr fnl f: wknd into 4th nr fin* **7/2**[1]

3363 **5** *1 ½* **Rebate**[16] 3573 4-8-9 60 ........ PGallagher(5) 6 56
(RHannon) *lw: in tch: pushed along 3f out: styd on same pce fnl 2f* **4/1**[2]

0200 **6** *1 ¼* **Movie King (IRE)**[32] 3097 5-9-3 63 ........ J-PGuillambert 7 57
(SGollings) *chsd wnr tl ins fnl 2f: sn btn* **12/1**

-001 **7** *1 ¾* **Factual Lad**[45] 2705 6-9-12 72 ........ ABeech 1 63
(BRMillman) *bhd: pushed along 3f out and nvr in contention* **8/1**

-530 **8** *½* **Cool Temper**[81] 1757 8-9-3 66 ........ NDeSouza(3) 10 56
(PFICole) *bhd: rdn and effrt 3f out: nvr in contention and wknd over 1f out* **8/1**

-600 **9** *8* **Glimmer Of Light (IRE)**[26] 3274 4-9-3 70 ........ MCoumbe(7) 5 45
(PWHarris) *lw: bhd most of way* **14/1**

250/ **10** *nk* **Jalons Star (IRE)**[361] 1326 6-8-6 59 ........ BO'Neill(7) 3 33
(MRChannon) *bhd: rdn and bried effrt 3f out: nvr in contention and sn rr* **16/1**

2m 8.76s (-1.42) **Going Correction** -0.125s/f (Firm) **10** Ran SP% **117.2**
Speed ratings: **100,99,94,94,92 91,90,90,83,83**CSF £65.90 CT £711.93 TOTE £5.20: £2.20, £3.10, £6.50; EX 101.10.
**Owner** H J Manners **Bred** Humphrey Okeke **Trained** Highworth, Wilts

**FOCUS**
With several of these out of form, this was not that competitive but, thanks to the eventual winner, they went a really good gallop and the first two home were able to pull nicely clear. This represents another big leap from an apparently exposed horse.

**NOTEBOOK**
**A One(IRE)** has won over as short as seven furlongs, but was below form when dropped back to that trip at Chepstow on his previous start and would appear better suited by this sort of distance these days. Racing off a mark 11lb higher than when last winning, he had nothing in hand of the runner-up at the line, but the pair were clear of the remainder and he will be hard to beat in turned out before he is reassessed, as he will escape a penalty. *Official explanation: trainer had no explanation for the improved form shown*
**Recount(FR)** ◆ emerges with a great deal of credit, for he was the only runner to get anywhere near the eventual winner and would have won in another stride. He will be 2lb lower in future handicaps before he is reassessed and will take a lot of beating if turned out in that period, although connections will hope to avoid today's winner next time.
**Bluegrass Boy** was given too much to do and could only plod on past beaten horses. More positive tactics may suit better.
**Barry Island** had his chance, but was woefully one paced. Claiming company may be more his level on this showing.
**Rebate** is 13lb lower than when last winning, but still not showing enough to suggest he is ready to strike.

## 4030 PANMURE GORDON INVESTMENT TRUST EBF MAIDEN STKS 7f 16y
**6:40** (6:48) (D) 2-Y-O **£5,304** (£1,632; £816; £408) **Stalls** High

Form RPR

6 **1** **Embossed (IRE)**[9] 3808 2-9-0 ........ RLMoore 15 96+
(RHannon) *lw: sn chsng ldr: pushed along over 3f out: led appr fnl 2f: kpt on wl to go steadily clr fnl f: readily* **7/2**[1]

2 **2** *4* **Woodsley House (IRE)**[11] 3749 2-9-0 ........ RHavlin 3 86
(MrsPNDutfield) *lw: sn ld: hdd over 2f out: rdn and styd on same pce fr over 1f out: no ch w wnr but r.o wl for clr 2nd* **5/1**[2]

**3** *1 ¼* **Surwaki (USA)** 2-9-0 ........ PRobinson 13 83
(CGCox) *neat: lw: prom: wnt 3rd 3f out: kpt on fr over 1f out but nvr gng pce of ldrs: one pce whn j. path last half f* **33/1**

**4** *1* **Windsor Knot (IRE)** 2-9-0 ........ JFortune 1 80
(JHMGosden) *rangy: bit bkwd: hld up in rr: stdy hdwy on outside fr 3f out: kpt on fr over 1f out but nvr gng pce to rch ldrs* **14/1**

**5** *1 ¾* **First Row (IRE)** 2-9-0 ........ SSanders 2 76
(BJMeehan) *str: lw: uns rdr and bolted 5f to s: in tch: rdn over 2f out: kpt on fr over 1f out but n.d* **20/1**

**6** *1 ¼* **Kingsholm** 2-9-0 ........ KFallon 14 73
(AMBalding) *tall: str: scope: uns rdr and bolted 5f to s: bhd: pushed along over 2f out: swtchd lft and hdwy appr fnl f: gng on cl home* **10/1**

0 **7** *3* **Velvet Heights (IRE)**[25] 3319 2-9-0 ........ SDrowne 5 65
(JLDunlop) *bhd: stdy hdwy on rails fnl 2f: nvr a danger* **16/1**

3 **8** *1 ¼* **Road To Heaven (USA)**[19] 3483 2-9-0 ........ DHolland 10 62
(EALDunlop) *chsd ldrs: rdn 3f out: wknd appr fnl f* **11/2**[3]

0 **9** *nk* **Guyana (IRE)**[20] 3451 2-9-0 ........ JFEgan 4 62
(SKirk) *chsd ldrs: rdn over 2f out: wknd over 1f out* **50/1**

4 **10** *1 ½* **Off Colour**[19] 3483 2-9-0 ........ KDarley 7 58
(MrsAJPerrett) *s.i.s: rdn 3f out: a in rr* **10/1**

0 **11** *hd* **Rawaabet (IRE)**[27] 3241 2-9-0 ........ DaneO'Neill 11 57
(MPTregoning) *chsd ldrs: rdn 3f out: wknd 2f out* **33/1**

**12** *shd* **Shahama (IRE)** 2-9-0 ........ ADaly 9 57
(MPTregoning) *w'like: bit bkwd: a in rr* **20/1**

0 **13** *½* **Northanger Abbey (IRE)**[11] 3749 2-9-0 ........ KMcEvoy 6 56
(JHMGosden) *s.i.s: a in rr* **33/1**

**14** *½* **Sendeed (USA)** 2-9-0 ........ (t) RHills 12 55
(SaeedBinSuroor) *cmpt: bit bkwd: rdn over 3f out: a bhd* **6/1**

0 **15** *3* **Swell Lad**[32] 3071 2-9-0 ........ SWKelly 8 47
(PFICole) *chsd ldrs: rn wd bnd over 3f out: sn rdn and green: wknd 2f out* **25/1**

1m 30.35s (-0.74) **Going Correction** -0.125s/f (Firm) **15** Ran SP% **123.4**
Speed ratings: **99,94,93,91,89 88,85,83,83,81 81,81,80,80,76**CSF £18.59 TOTE £5.30: £2.40, £2.20, £12.80; EX 20.40.
**Owner** Ms R Z Stephenson **Bred** Harron Eakin Farms **Trained** East Everleigh, Wilts

**FOCUS**
Hard to know what to make of this maiden, but the winner clearly showed improved form and looks a nice prospect. It proved hard to come from off the pace and several of these should be capable of better in time.

**NOTEBOOK**
**Embossed(IRE)** showed the benefit of his debut running to score an emphatic success on this step up from six furlongs. The bare form may flatter him, as quite a few, who were in need of the experience, did not get into this and he got the run of the race, but he is quite well regarded by connections, who will rightly look to step him up in grade next time.
**Woodsley House(IRE)**, a promising second on his debut at Salisbury, failed to show a great deal of improvement on that run and was readily brushed aside by the winner.
**Surwaki(USA)**, a 90,000euros yearling, half-brother to a juvenile placed over seven furlongs, made a pleasing debut. He travelled well just off the leaders and kept on right the way to the line, but just lacked a change of pace and should be capable of improvement.
**Windsor Knot(IRE)**, a 260,000euros purchase, out of a winner over a mile six, came from a very unpromising position to take fourth and never posed a threat to the principals. This experience should not be lost on him.
**First Row(IRE)**, a 220,000gns half-brother to nine-furlong winner Swift Tango, showed his inexperience when unseating his rider and bolting to the start. In the race itself he offered plenty of promise, and is another who looks capable of better.
**Kingsholm**, out of a dual Listed winner, also bolted to the start and ran well considering. Fallon was an interesting booking and he is probably capable of better. *Official explanation: jockey said saddle slipped*
**Road To Heaven(USA)**, $110,000 yearling, out of an unraced half-sister to a high-class to two-year-old in the US, and a multiple winner in Germany, attracted support but was well held. Given his breeding and the market move, he could yet be capable of better.

**Sendeed(USA)**, out of an unraced half-sister to a top-class performer in the US, was easy to back and interestingly partnered by Richard Hills, rather than Godolphin's employed jockey McEvoy, who was riding for John Gosden.

## 4031 LORD MCGOWAN H'CAP 7f 16y
7:10 (7:19) (C) (0-90,90) 3-Y-O **£10,348** (£3,184; £1,592; £796) **Stalls** High

Form RPR

0415 **1** **Peter Paul Rubens (USA)**[33] 3036 3-9-7 **90**........................ DHolland 8 112+
(PFICole) *lw: mde all: sn clr: shkn up over 1f out: unchal* **15/8**[1]

0106 **2** *6* **Flip Flop And Fly (IRE)**[11] 3750 3-9-1 **84**................................ JFEgan 4 87
(SKirk) *bhd:drvn and hdwy 2f out:swtchd lft then hung lft over 1f out: str run fnl f to take 2nd cl home but no ch w wnr* **12/1**

-600 **3** *nk* **Bentley's Ball (USA)**[18] 3542 3-9-5 **88**................................ RLMoore 6 90
(RHannon) *chsd ldrs: rdn and nt clr run jst ins fnl 2f: styd on to chse wnr jst ins last but no ch: lost 2nd cl home* **20/1**

-004 **4** *½* **Granato (GER)**[46] 2692 3-9-2 **85**................................ KFallon 3 86
(ACStewart) *t.k.h: in tch: pushed along 3f out: styd on fr over 1f out: kpt on cl home* **6/1**[3]

2110 **5** *1 ½* **Warden Complex**[12] 3690 3-9-3 **86**................................ OUrbina 7 83
(JRFanshawe) *in tch: hdwy on rails fr 3f out: chsd wnr over 1f out but no ch: wknd ins fnl f* **9/4**[2]

516- **6** *½* **Go Bananas**[297] 5250 3-9-4 **87**................................ JFortune 1 82
(BJMeehan) *s.i.s: bhd: pushed along and sme hdwy on rails fr 2f out: one pce fnl f* **16/1**

6020 **7** *½* **Colour Wheel**[12] 3690 3-9-7 **90**................................(t) SDrowne 9 84
(RCharlton) *lw: chsd ldrs in 3rd: rdn 2f out: wknd appr fnl f* **11/1**

4240 **8** *1 ¼* **Leaping Brave (IRE)**[18] 3527 3-8-5 **74**................................ SWKelly 5 65
(BRMillman) *chsd ldr tl ins fnl 2f: wknd qckly over 1f out* **66/1**

15 **9** *6* **Camberwell**[11] 3751 3-9-5 **88**................................ SSanders 2 62
(TGMills) *s.i.s: a in rr* **16/1**

1m 28.31s (-2.78) **Going Correction** -0.125s/f (Firm) 9 Ran SP% **113.9**
Speed ratings: **110,103,102,102,100 99,99,97,91**CSF £25.48 CT £343.01 TOTE £2.80: £1.70, £3.00, £4.00; EX 32.60 Trifecta £486.50 Pool: £4,111.36. 6.00 winning units..
**Owner** Richard Green (fine Paintings) **Bred** Mueller Farm **Trained** Whatcombe, Oxon

**FOCUS**
A decent event won decisively by an improving colt and the time was respectable for the grade, giving the form a sound look.

**NOTEBOOK**
**Peter Paul Rubens(USA)** ◆ simply routed this opposition and confirmed himself a colt of definite potential. He had only tired out of contention late on when fifth in the Buckingham Palace Stakes and was able to race off the same mark this time, so probably did not have to improve much to score. This looks to be his optimum trip, he remains open to plenty more improvement and is set to run under a penalty at Goodwood later this month. His style of running will be well favoured at that track, and granted he gets a high draw, he will take a world of beating.
**Flip Flop And Fly(IRE)** looked to have it all to do on entering the straight, but found his stride and was finishing best of all behind the decisive winner. On this display, he looks worth another try back at a mile, but still looks high enough in the weights at present.
**Bentley's Ball(USA)** posted a return to form and was not helped by meeting trouble two out. He could build on this now.
**Granato(GER)**, despite running keenly through the early stages, held every chance with two to run, but failed to find a change of gear under pressure. He must learn to settle better, but looks to be finding a bit of form and was better suited by this trip.
**Warden Complex** looked to be the chief threat to the winner when making a challenge approaching the final furlong, but found disappointingly little and finished well held. He had the look of a most progressive horse when winning back-to-back races in May and June respectively, but has smething to prove now and may be best watched.
**Go Bananas** ran very much as though this race was needed on this comeback from a 297-day absence. He should come on a fair bit for this.
**Colour Wheel** again put in a below-par display and is starting to run out of excuses.

## 4032 PANMURE GORDON CLASSIFIED STKS 1m 14y
7:45 (7:50) (D) 3-Y-O **£6,857** (£2,110; £1,055; £527) **Stalls** High

Form RPR

6304 **1** **Mr Jack Daniells (IRE)**[20] 3452 3-9-0 74................................ JFortune 9 83
(WRMuir) *trckd ldrs: drvn to chal over 1f out: slt ld jst ins last: hld on all out* **7/1**

231- **2** *nk* **Straw Bear (USA)**[319] 4735 3-9-2 77................................ SSanders 1 86+
(SirMarkPrescott) *wnt 2nd 5f out:slt ld ins fnl 2f: rdr dropped whip over 1f out :hdd jst ins last: styd chalng tl no ex cl home* **11/2**[3]

313 **3** *hd* **Habanero**[27] 3231 3-9-0 72................................ DHolland 6 82
(RHannon) *lw: led after 1f: rdn and hdd jst ins fnl 2f: str chal and edgd lft 1f out: edgd rt u.p cl home and no ex* **6/1**

-622 **4** *1* **Kibryaa (USA)**[8] 3819 3-9-3 78................................(p) PRobinson 7 86+
(MAJarvis) *t.k.h: led 1f: styd trcking ldrs: rdn and nt clr run appr fnl f: swtchd lft and kpt on wl ins last* **7/2**[2]

1404 **5** *¾* **Mission Man**[11] 3728 3-9-5 80................................ RLMoore 3 83
(RHannon) *lw: hld up in rr: rdn over 2f out: hdwy over 1f out: styd on fnl f but nt pce of ldrs* **12/1**

-050 **6** *shd* **Song Of Vala**[30] 3152 3-9-0 75................................(t) SDrowne 8 82+
(RCharlton) *lw: hld up in tch: hdwy on rails fr 2f out: effrt to chse ldrs 1f out: styng on wl whn bdly hmpd and snatched up fnl 100yds* **20/1**

2620 **7** *1* **King Of Diamonds**[32] 3086 3-8-9 74................................ MSavage[(5)] 5 75
(JRBest) *bhd: hdwy 2f out: n.m.r and effrt ins fnl 2f: swtchd lft and styd on same pce fnl f* **50/1**

5560 **8** *1 ¼* **Glebe Garden**[11] 3728 3-8-11 75................................ KDarley 2 69
(MLWBell) *b.hind: bhd: rdn over 2f out: styd on but nvr gng pce to rch ldrs* **50/1**

-331 **9** *1 ¾* **Secret Flame**[27] 3222 3-9-0 78................................ KFallon 10 68
(WJHaggas) *chsd ldrs: rdn 3f out: outpcd and no ch ins fnl 2f* **5/2**[1]

2-40 **10** *4* **Strawberry Fair**[16] 3592 3-8-11 73................................(t) KMcEvoy 4 54
(SaeedBinSuroor) *bhd most of way* **20/1**

1m 42.85s (-1.07) **Going Correction** -0.125s/f (Firm) 10 Ran SP% **114.1**
Speed ratings: **100,99,99,98,97 97,96,95,93,88**CSF £42.28 TOTE £8.30: £1.80, £2.10, £2.20; EX 76.20.
**Owner** Martin P Graham **Bred** Mick McGinn And James Waldron **Trained** Lambourn, Berks

**FOCUS**
A typically tight classified event with just 6lb separating the whole field on official ratings. There were a couple of hard-luck stories and they finished quite well bunched, but the form looks reasonably solid.

**NOTEBOOK**
**Mr Jack Daniells(IRE)** has been running well this season despite not always having things go his way, but he got a good trip this time around and made the most of it for a determined success. Although there was little in it at the line, he is quite well thought of and is the type of horse his trainer can do well with.
**Straw Bear(USA)**, not seen since winning a modest maiden at Wolverhampton 319 days previously, showed significant improvement on that effort and was just held - it may have been different had his rider not dropped his whip. It will be most disappointing if he does not go on from this and find a similar event.
**Habanero** was not inconvenienced by this drop back from ten furlongs and ran his race under a positive ride.
**Kibryaa(USA)**, in cheekpieces for the first time, was still there at the finish despite racing keenly, and would have gone very close indeed had he got a clear run inside the final furlong.
**Mission Man** kept on well enough, but just remains below his very best.
**Song Of Vala** has been tried at up to a mile and a half, but this trip appeared to suit and he would have gone very close to winning had he got a run up the rail close home.
**Secret Flame** was the disappointment of the race, finding nothing under pressure. *Official explanation: trainer said filly did not like being crowded between horses*

## 4033 PANMURE GORDON CORPORATE FINANCE H'CAP 1m 6f
8:15 (8:22) (D) (0-80,78) 4-Y-O+ **£6,857** (£2,110; £1,055; £527) **Stalls** Centre

Form RPR

0-06 **1** **Top Trees**[10] 3776 6-7-9 **49** oh4................................ NMackay[(3)] 6 55
(WSKittow) *rr but in tch: hdwy on outside fr 2f out: str run appr fnl f to ld cl home* **20/1**

2/02 **2** *½* **Coalition**[27] 3244 5-9-13 **78**................................ DaneO'Neill 11 83
(HCandy) *lw: in tch: hdwy whn nt clr run appr fnl 2f: swtchd lft and str run to ld jst ins fnl f: hdd cl home* **7/2**[1]

0-00 **3** *1 ¾* **Lillebror (GER)**[13] 3683 6-8-5 **56**................................ SWKelly 5 59
(BJCurley) *lw: hld up: hdwy on outside fr 5f out: trckd ldrs 2f out: kpt on wl and reminder ins last: nt pce of ldrs cl home* **14/1**

0355 **4** *½* **Rome (IRE)**[20] 3437 5-8-13 **64**................................ KFallon 3 66
(GPEnright) *chsd ldrs: rdn over 2f out: drvn to ld over 1f out: hdd jst ins last: no ex* **6/1**[2]

4/03 **5** *hd* **Saltango (GER)**[28] 3199 5-9-5 **73**................................ LPKeniry[(3)] 12 75
(AMHales) *bhd: hdwy and n.m.r over 2f out: drvn and hdwy over 1f out: chsd ldrs ins last and styd on one pce* **8/1**[3]

-000 **6** *½* **Larking About (USA)**[52] 2501 4-7-12 **52**................................ LisaJones[(3)] 8 53
(WJMusson) *swtg: bhd: hdwy on outside fr 2f out: kpt on ins last: gng on cl home* **25/1**

-504 **7** *¾* **Henry Island (IRE)**[13] 3683 11-8-10 **61**................................ SDrowne 7 61
(MrsAJBowlby) *swtg: hld up in rr: hdwy 3f out: chsd ldrs fr 2f out: outpcd ins fnl f* **14/1**

50-3 **8** *hd* **Gaelic Roulette (IRE)**[18] 3528 4-9-5 **70**................................ DHolland 9 70+
(PWHarris) *chsd ldrs: nt clr run 2f out: sn rdn: nvr gng pce to trble ldrs fnl f* **6/1**[2]

-500 **9** *1* **Sea Plume**[27] 3244 5-9-2 **67**................................(b[1]) JFortune 1 65
(LadyHerries) *chsd ldr tl slt ld over 2f out: hdd and appr fnl f: wknd ins last* **16/1**

1-56 **10** *nk* **Tilla**[31] 3120 4-8-12 **66**................................ LFletcher[(3)] 10 64+
(HMorrison) *bhd: rdn and hdwy 2f out: styng on whn nt clr run ins last: eased whn hld nr fin* **7/2**[1]

0 **11** *1 ¾* **Onward To Glory (USA)**[11] 3752 4-9-5 **70**................................ KMcEvoy 4 66
(JLDunlop) *lw: sn led: hdd appr fnl 2f: styd chalng tl wknd appr fnl f* **16/1**

3m 6.03s (1.66) **Going Correction** -0.125s/f (Firm) 11 Ran SP% **117.8**
Speed ratings: **90,89,88,88,88 88,87,87,86,86 85**CSF £89.23 CT £1044.11 TOTE £33.10: £5.80, £2.10, £8.10; EX 156.60.
**Owner** Mrs P E Hawkings **Bred** Mrs E Roberts **Trained** Blackborough, Devon

**FOCUS**
A modest staying handicap run at a reasonable pace. There were several hard-luck stories late on, and as such, the from looks misleading.

**NOTEBOOK**
**Top Trees**, 4lb out of the handicap for this, stayed on dourly to win a touch cosily and cause an upset. He had shown a bit more sparkle when sixth over two miles last time, but this course and distance looked right up his street, and he was given a fine ride by his very capable young jockeyr.
**Coalition** ◆, raised 3lb for a finishing second at Salisbury latest, looked booked for success when edging to the lead late on, but had no more to give when challenged by the eventual winner. This again confirmed that he has retained all of his ability after his lay-off in 2003, and he showed a fair turn of pace this time, so compensation surely awaits.
**Lillebror(GER)** ran his best race since switching from Germany and now looks to have slipped to a very favourable mark. He was not given a hard time of it late in the day, will be better over a slightly shorter trip and is one to respect when the market speaks in his favour.
**Rome(IRE)**, with the cheekpieces left off for this, looked to be holding every chance when making his move entering the straight and getting to the lead, but could only muster the one pace and will be better over slightly further. *Official explanation: jockey said gelding hung right handed*
**Gaelic Roulette(IRE)** was short of room halfway up the home straight when still full of running, but found little off the bridle once in the clear and looked a non-stayer over this trip. He is slightly better than this and could pick up a race when eased in distance.
**Tilla**, taken down steadily to post, suffered a troubled passage up the straight and can be rated a deal better than the bare form would indicate. *Official explanation: jockey said filly suffered interference in running*

## 4034 HARRY PANMURE GORDON H'CAP 5f 6y
8:45 (8:56) (D) (0-80,80) 4-Y-O+ **£7,036** (£2,165; £1,082; £541) **Stalls** High

Form RPR

1022 **1** **Jonny Ebeneezer**[7] 3841 5-8-1 **56**................................(b) NMackay[(3)] 8 70
(DFlood) *hld up in rr: rapid hdwy over 1f out: qcknd to ld fnl 100yds: sn clr: readily* **4/1**[1]

0420 **2** *1 ¼* **Domirati**[14] 3645 4-9-13 **79**................................ SDrowne 13 88
(RCharlton) *lw: in tch: gd hdwy fr 2f out: drvn to chal ins fnl f: kpt on but nt pce of wnr cl home* **11/2**[2]

0600 **3** *1* **Kathology (IRE)**[19] 3480 7-9-10 **79**................................ LPKeniry[(3)] 12 84
(DRCElsworth) *chsd ldrs tl led 1f out: sn hrd drvn: hdd and outpcd fnl 100yds* **20/1**

51 **4** *½* **Polar Impact**[25] 3326 5-9-9 **75**................................ JFortune 10 78
(GLMoore) *lw: bhd: hrd drvn 2f out: hdwy over 1f out: r.o wl but nt rch ldrs* **9/1**

3431 **5** *shd* **Jayanjay**[13] 3663 5-10-0 **80**................................ SSanders 2 83
(MissBSanders) *bhd: rdn 2f out: hdwy fr over 1f out: kpt on but nt rch ldrs* **12/1**

1153 **6** *½* **Aintnecessarilyso**[10] 3775 6-7-10 **55**................................ MHalford[(7)] 3 56
(NEBerry) *bhd: hdwy on stands side fnl f: fin strly* **20/1**

6010 **7** *nk* **Guns Blazing**[17] 3558 5-8-13 **72**................................(b) MHoward[(7)] 15 71
(DKIvory) *b: led tl hdd 1f out: sn one pce* **20/1**

4002 **8** *¾* **Seven No Trumps**[12] 3713 7-9-11 **77**................................(p) SWKelly 7 73
(JMBradley) *chsd ldrs: rdn 2f out: styd on same pce fnl f* **20/1**

4063 **9** *nk* **Currency**[14] 3645 7-9-11 **77**................................(p) RLMoore 14 72
(JMBradley) *swtg: b: bhd: sn rdn: kpt on fnl f but nvr a danger* **6/1**[3]

4362 **10** *1* **Law Maker**[31] 3126 4-7-12 **50** oh2................................(v) JBramhill 11 41
(MABuckley) *chsd ldrs tl wknd ins f* **33/1**

0206 **11** *1 ¼* **Taboor (IRE)**[17] 3558 6-8-0 **55**................................(b) LisaJones[(3)] 5 41
(JWPayne) *sn pushed along: nvr gng pce to rch ldrs* **25/1**

3000 **12** *hd* **Turibius**[14] 3645 5-9-11 **77** KFallon 9 62
(TEPowell) *bhd: pushed along 2f out: nvr gng pce of ldrs* **7/1**
3650 **13** *hd* **Ela Figura**[9] 3810 4-7-9 **50** oh1 (p) FPFerris(3) 4 35
(AWCarroll) *lw: bhd: effrt whn n.m.r over 1f out: n.d after* **33/1**
4102 **14** *1 1/4* **The Fisio**[25] 3326 4-9-9 **75** (v) KDarley 18 55
(SGollings) *s.i.s: outpcd in rr: mod prog fr over 1f out* **12/1**
504- **15** *2 1/2* **Flaran**[264] 5849 4-8-2 **61** LauraWells(7) 16 31
(ACStewart) *chsd ldrs tl wknd over 1f out* **33/1**
0600 **16** *5* **Margalita (IRE)**[20] 3440 4-8-11 **63** (t) JFEgan 1 13
(PMitchell) *lw: a outpcd* **50/1**
00-0 **17** *6* **Strathclyde (IRE)**[165] 703 5-9-13 **79** DaneO'Neill 17 5
(AMHales) *chsd ldr over 3f* **25/1**

60.55 secs (-1.64) **Going Correction** -0.20s/f (Firm) **17** Ran SP% **125.1**
Speed ratings: **105,103,101,100,100 99,99,97,97,95 93,93,93,91,87 79,69**CSF £21.31 CT £410.45 TOTE £4.20: £1.60, £2.60, £3.90, £3.10; EX 52.70 Place 6 £267.06, Place 5 £51.17.
**Owner** Mrs Ruth M Serrell **Bred** John Purcell **Trained** Upper Lambourn, Berks

**FOCUS**
A reasonable sprint handicap and it was no surprise to see them go a good pace. The form looks reliable.

**NOTEBOOK**
**Jonny Ebeneezer** is not as good as he was, but has taken really well to the fitting of blinkers and his current trainer has him in fine form. Racing off a mark 6lb lower than when runner-up on his two previous starts, he had an obvious chance and made the most of it, picking up well having been patiently ridden. He could be turned out under a penalty and is thriving on his racing.
**Domirati** is not very easy to win with and has never won on turf, but this was a solid-enough effort.
**Kathology(IRE)**, 5lb lower than when last successful, looked to have his conditions and showed real signs of a return to form.
**Polar Impact** probably just found things happening a little too quickly on ground fast enough for him.
**Jayanjay** was unable to follow up his Epsom success and just wins in his turn.
**Currency** got quite warm and was not at his best.
**Margalita(IRE)** *Official explanation: jockey said filly had lost her action*
T/Jkpt: Not won. T/Plt: £489.30 to a £1 stake. Pool: £66,467.00. 99.15 winning tickets. T/Qpdt: £61.00 to a £1 stake. Pool: £5,461.00. 66.20 winning tickets. ST

4035 - 4038a (Foreign Racing) - See Raceform Interactive

# VICHY
## Wednesday, July 21

**OFFICIAL GOING: Soft**

### 4039a GRAND PRIX DE VICHY (GROUP 3) 1m 2f
8:45 (8:56) 3-Y-O+ £25,704 (£10,282; £7,711; £5,141)

RPR
**1** **Bailador (IRE)**[34] 3030 4-9-2 CSoumillon 3 105
(AFabre, France) *held up, 11th straight, progress over 1 1/2f out, ridden to challenge over 1f out, led 100 yards out, ran on gamely, ridden* 1
**2** *1/2* **Demon Dancer (FR)**[45] 7-9-2 ELegrix 9 104
(YDeNicolay, France) *mid-division, headway over 1 1/2f out, pushed along & pressing leader over 1f out, every chance inside final furlong, staye*
**3** *1* **Mister Farmer (FR)**[24] 3359 3-8-6 SPasquier 2 102
(NBranchu, France) *held up in last, driven and stayed on from over 1f out to take 3rd close home*
**4** *hd* **Pont D'Or (IRE)**[90] 5-9-2 OPeslier 10 102
(DSepulchre, France) *mid-division, shaken up and headway straight, pressing leaders 1 1/2f out, pushed along to lead over 1f out, ridden & ran t*
**5** *snk* **Mocham Glen (FR)**[7] 7-9-2 SMaillot 4 102
(RobertCollet, France) *held up, ran on under pressure from 1 1/2f out, nearest at finish*
**6** *2* **Samando (FR)**[51] 2543 4-8-13 C-PLemaire 5 95
(FDoumen, France) *in touch on inside, disputing 3rd straight, soon pushed along, kept on at one pace under pressure* 2
**7** *3* **Jazz D'Allier (FR)**[97] 1435 7-9-2 IMendizabal 7 93
(EVagne, France) *never better than mid-division*
**8** *shd* **Nooska Tivoli (FR)**[11] 3768 3-8-6 (b) GBenoist 8 93
(PTual, France) *towards rear, pushed along 2f out, ridden 1 1/2f out, one pace*
**9** *nk* **Marshall (FR)**[21] 4-9-2 MBlancpain 6 92
(CLaffon-Parias, France) *in touch, effort 1 1/2f out, unable to quicken* 3
**10** *1/2* **Seraphine (GER)**[19] 3504 4-8-13 TGillet 12 88
(WHimmel, Germany) *prominent, 2nd straight, ridden and weakened from over 1f out*
**11** *1 1/2* **Prends Ton Temps (FR)**[34] 3030 7-9-2 DBoeuf 1 89
(DSmaga, France) *prominent, disputing 3rd straight, ridden over 1 1/2f out, weakened from 1f out*
**12** *7* **Last Empress (FR)**[115] 1163 4-8-13 OPlacais 11 74
(JJNapoli, France) *led, pushed along over 1 1/2f out, ridden and headed over 1f out, weakened*

2m 8.64s
**WFA** 3 from 4yo+ 10lb **12** Ran SP% **121.7**
Speed ratings: .
**Owner** Baron E De Rothschild **Bred** Ecurie Du Haras De Meautry **Trained** France

**NOTEBOOK**
**Bailador(IRE)** representing the Fabre yard, won this with a good effort from off the pace. Given a foreful ride in the final stages, he impressed with his attitude.
**Demon Dancer(FR)** continued his good run of form following a long layoff through injury. A winner of two Tierce handicaps previously, he would be well worth a try at early next month in the Listed Grand Handicap de Deauville over a mile.
**Mister Farmer(FR)** came from the rear and was staying on strongly at the finish. A step back up to a mile and a half would suit.

# 3770 BATH (L-H)
## Thursday, July 22

**OFFICIAL GOING: Good to firm (firm in places)**
Wind: nil Weather: isolated shower

### 4040 FISH BROTHERS RENAULT MEDIAN AUCTION MAIDEN STKS 5f 161y
2:20 (2:22) (F) 2-Y-O £3,164 (£904; £452) Stalls Low

Form RPR
056 **1** **Tight Circle**[26] 3290 2-8-9 FNorton 11 71
(MrsGHarvey) *mde all: rdn over 1f out: drvn out* **16/1**
2 **2** *1 1/2* **Goodwood Spirit**[22] 3414 2-9-0 TQuinn 9 71
(JLDunlop) *chsd ldrs: pushed along over 3f out: rdn over 2f out: kpt on ins fnl f: nt trble wnr* **1/2**[1]
5 **3** *1* **Cummiskey (IRE)**[108] 1269 2-9-0 SDrowne 7 68
(JAOsborne) *a.p: chsd wnr 2f out: rdn over 1f out: nt qckn* **5/1**[2]
**4** *1* **Tashyra (IRE)** 2-8-9 MartinDwyer 3 60
(AMBalding) *dwlt: hdwy on ins over 2f out: rdn wl over 1f out: one pce fnl f* **10/1**[3]
**5** *3/4* **Task's Muppet (IRE)** 2-8-6 JFMcDonald(3) 13 57
(JAOsborne) *bhd: rdn and hdwy over 2f out: one pce fnl f* **50/1**
**6** *shd* **Watchmyeyes (IRE)** 2-8-11 J-PGuillambert(3) 5 62
(NPLittmoden) *s.i.s: sn chsng ldrs: rdn over 2f out: one pce fnl f* **16/1**
35 **7** *2* **Trackattack**[10] 3802 2-9-0 RSmith 12 55
(JAOsborne) *s.i.s: bhd: rdn over 2f out: nvr nrr* **20/1**
**8** *3/4* **Makes Perfect (IRE)** 2-8-9 JFEgan 14 48
(SKirk) *bhd: hdwy on outside 2f out: wknd fnl f* **25/1**
00 **9** *6* **Gold Majesty**[8] 3840 2-8-9 CCatlin 10 28
(MRChannon) *bhd: rdn over 2f out: no rspnse* **40/1**
**10** *hd* **Theflyingscottie** 2-9-0 VSlattery 8 33
(JDFrost) *s.i.s: rdn over 2f out: a bhd* **66/1**
000 **11** *4* **Doughty**[17] 3588 2-9-0 (t) JoannaBadger 1 20
(DJWintle) *chsd wnr tl rdn and wknd 2f out* **100/1**
**12** *1* **Slite** 2-8-3 ow1 RKeogh(7) 2 13
(JAOsborne) *s.s: a wl bhd* **66/1**
000 **13** *8* **Pie Corner**[27] 3259 2-9-0 GBaker 6 —
(MMadgwick) *prom: rdn over 2f out: sn wknd* **100/1**

1m 12.43s (1.29) **Going Correction** +0.025s/f (Good) **13** Ran SP% **122.2**
Speed ratings: **92,90,88,87,86 86,83,82,74,74 68,67,56**CSF £24.30 TOTE £30.00: £3.60, £1.10, £1.50; EX 40.60.
**Owner** S A Cochrane **Bred** Wickfield Farm Partnership **Trained** Kingston Lisle, Oxon

**FOCUS**
An average juvenile maiden and the form looks suspect.

**NOTEBOOK**
**Tight Circle** stepped up markedly on her recent efforts to gamely make all. This extra furlong clearly suited and she is going the right way, but may have been slightly flattered by this, as she had very much the run of the race.
**Goodwood Spirit**, who created a favourable impression at Kempton on his debut, failed to improve on that effort and this has to go down as a missed opportunity. He now has it all to prove, but will be a better propostion over farther and is not one to be write off yet.
**Cummiskey(IRE)**, well-touted ahead of his slightly disappointing debut at Windsor in April, again ran green when holding every chance in the home straight. This was an improved effort, and he was not at all given a hard time late on, so could well leave this form behind when eligible for nurseries.
**Tashyra(IRE)**, a sister to a Group Two winning juvenile in Germany, did well to get involved late on having made a sluggish start on this debut. She should come on a fair bit for this.
**Task's Muppet(IRE)**, a cheaply-purchased filly who is bred for sprints, travelled nicely on this debut, but ran green under pressure and could only find the one pace late on. This experience will not have been lost on her and she was not disgraced.

### 4041 CITY MOTORS RENAULT/E.B.F. NOVICE STKS 5f 11y
2:55 (2:55) (D) 2-Y-O £4,332 (£1,333; £666; £333) Stalls Low

Form RPR
621 **1** **Lady Le Quesne (IRE)**[14] 3659 2-8-11 SDrowne 3 74+
(AMBalding) *a.p: rdn to ld 1f out: hdd ins fnl f: led again last strides* **4/6**[1]
0321 **2** *hd* **Bold Minstrel (IRE)**[12] 3729 2-9-2 FNorton 1 78
(MQuinn) *w ldr: rdn 2f out: led ins fnl f: hdd last strides* **10/3**[2]
31 **3** *1/2* **Westbrook Blue**[108] 1264 2-8-7 CHaddon(7) 4 74
(WGMTurner) *led: rdn 2f out: hdd 1f out: nt qckn cl home* **5/1**[3]
214 **4** *1 1/4* **Gee Bee Em**[22] 3414 2-9-0 CCatlin 2 70
(MRChannon) *hld up in tch: rdn 2f out: one pce* **14/1**

63.69 secs (1.19) **Going Correction** +0.025s/f (Good) **4** Ran SP% **106.4**
Speed ratings: **91,90,89,87**CSF £3.03 TOTE £1.60; EX 3.10.
**Owner** Coriolan Partnership V **Bred** Rozelle Bloodstock **Trained** Kingsclere, Hants

**FOCUS**
A fair novice event that saw each of the four runners in with a chance late on. Amodest time and form is slightly muddling.

**NOTEBOOK**
**Lady Le Quesne(IRE)** was all out to follow-up her recent maiden success over this shorter trip and back on fast ground. This was a laboured success, but she always looked like getting there in the final stages, and will surely be capable of better back over another furlong and looks useful.
**Bold Minstrel(IRE)**, off the mark at the fourth attempt last time, gave his all in defeat and was only just denied. He can be placed to score in nurseries over this trip.
**Westbrook Blue** had every chance and was far from disgraced on this return from an 108-day absence. He has another prize in him at the least and may be worth a shot over another furlong.
**Gee Bee Em** lacked the pace to get serious over this quick five furlongs, but was not beaten far and should be capable of improving back up in trip.

### 4042 A.K.S. YEOVIL RENAULT (S) STKS 1m 2f 46y
3:25 (3:25) (G) 4-Y-O+ £2,583 (£738; £369) Stalls Low

Form RPR
-000 **1** **Didoe**[9] 3827 5-8-11 **45** PDoe 6 48
(PWHiatt) *chsd ldr: led 3f out: rdn wl over 1f out: clr over 1f out: drvn out* **8/1**[2]
10-3 **2** *1* **Forbearing (IRE)**[7] 3885 7-9-2 **73** (v) CCatlin 4 52
(MCPipe) *hld up: rdn 4f out: hdwy over 2f out: styd on ins fnl f: nt rch wnr* **2/5**[1]
0600 **3** *3* **Rolex Free (ARG)**[5] 3934 6-9-2 **60** (v[1]) SWhitworth 1 46
(DFlood) *led: rdn and hdd 3f out: wknd ins fnl f* **25/1**
2060 **4** *shd* **Giust In Temp (IRE)**[16] 3607 5-9-2 **36** GBaker 2 46?
(PWHiatt) *dwlt: hld up in rr: hdwy over 2f out: rdn over 1f out: wknd ins fnl f* **33/1**
-655 **5** *shd* **Rojabaa**[30] 3173 5-9-2 **51** ADaly 8 46
(WGMTurner) *a.p: rdn over 2f out: chsd wnr over 1f out tl ins fnl f: wknd* **9/1**[3]

00-0 **6** *8* **Southampton Joe (USA)**[8] 3697 4-9-2 48........................(v[1]) VSlattery 7 31
(JGMO'Shea) *hld up: rdn 3f out: sn struggling* **28/1**
-000 **7** *3 1/2* **Lucky Archer**[20] 3489 11-9-2 45........................ JoannaBadger 5 25
(IanWilliams) *hld up: hdwy over 7f out: rdn and wknd over 2f out* **12/1**
**8** *3 1/2* **Saposcat (IRE)**[11] 4810 4-9-2 ........................(t) RSmith 3 19
(WGMTurner) *hld up: rdn and put hd in air 3f out: sn bhd* **66/1**
2m 10.93s (-0.07) **Going Correction** -0.05s/f (Good) **8** Ran SP% **112.0**
Speed ratings: **98,97,94,94,94 88,85,82**CSF £11.23 TOTE £7.70: £1.50, £1.02, £6.90; EX 14.80.There was no bid for the winner. Forbearing was claimed by Gary Roberts for £6,000.
**Owner** Mrs Marion Wickham **Bred** Mrs Wickham **Trained** Hook Norton, Oxon

**FOCUS**
A very weak event that was run at a modest gallop.

**NOTEBOOK**
**Didoe** won her first race at the 25th attempt under a well-judged ride from Doe. She would have been getting 28lb from the runner-up (who admittedly does look flattered by his mark) and deserves credit for sticking to her task late on over a track she clearly goes well at.
**Forbearing(IRE)**, with the visor back on after disappointing at Leicester last time, ran another moody race and proved a huge flop. He should have run all over this field according to official figures, but this seven-year-old has clearly fallen out of love with racing.
**Rolex Free(ARG)** showed a little more enthusiasm for the first-time visor, but was again readily held. He too is flattered by his current handicap mark.
**Giust In Temp(IRE)** improved a touch on his latest effort after a break, but never seriously threatened to break his duck.
**Rojabaa**

## 4043 WESTWARD RENAULT BATH H'CAP — 5f 11y
4:00 (4:00) (E ) (0-75,73) 3-Y-O **£4,134** (£1,272; £636; £318) **Stalls** Low

Form RPR
0556 **1** **Catch The Wind**[11] 3777 3-9-7 **73**........................(p) FNorton 3 88
(IAWood) *chsd ldr: rdn to ld over 1f out: r.o wl* **9/1**
6314 **2** *2 1/2* **Maluti**[18] 3562 3-8-1 **53**........................ CCatlin 1 59
(RGuest) *chsd ldrs: rdn over 2f out: kpt on ins fnl f: nt trble wnr* **6/4**[1]
0350 **3** *nk* **Rehia**[42] 2800 3-8-0 **52**........................ RSmith 5 57
(JWHills) *a.p: rdn 2f out: no ex ins fnl f* **16/1**
4666 **4** *1* **Mirasol Princess**[8] 3849 3-8-12 **71**........................ MHoward(7) 7 72
(DKIvory) *hld up in tch: rdn 2f out: one pce* **5/1**[3]
5436 **5** *1* **Melody King**[13] 3702 3-8-10 **67**........................(b) HayleyTurner(5) 4 65
(PDEvans) *bhd: rdn over 3f out: sme hdwy fnl f: nvr trbld ldrs* **4/1**[2]
0500 **6** *nk* **Peruvian Style (IRE)**[11] 3777 3-9-4 **73**........................(b[1]) J-PGuillambert(3) 2 70
(NPLittmoden) *led: rdn and hdd over 1f out: wknd ins fnl f* **5/1**[3]
-040 **7** *1 1/4* **Bahama Belle**[19] 3530 3-8-3 **55**........................(b[1]) MartinDwyer 6 47
(HSHowe) *rdn over 3f out: a bhd* **25/1**
62.31 secs (-0.19) **Going Correction** +0.025s/f (Good) **7** Ran SP% **113.1**
Speed ratings: **102,98,97,95,94 93,91**CSF £22.52 TOTE £10.10: £3.00, £1.90; EX 36.10.
**Owner** C S Tateson **Bred** J And Mrs S Cleeve **Trained** Upper Lambourn, Berks

**FOCUS**
A modest handicap, but the form looks fairly sound for the grade.

**NOTEBOOK**
**Catch The Wind**, who had not had things go her way so far this year, posted a welcome return to form and won this in good style. She was given a fine ride, and her confidence will have been greatly helped, largely due to the fact it was the first time she has passed a rival under pressure this season. The cheekpieces had a positive effect and she can win again, especially if turned out under a penalty.
**Maluti** was doing all of his best work too late in the day. That said, he was not disgraced against the winner and appreciated the better ground.
**Rehia** managed to improve on her most recent effort, but again looked very one paced and is a hard horse to catch right.
**Mirasol Princess** has now failed to build on her fair juvenile form in seven outings this year and looks to need further respite in the weights.
**Melody King** ran his race, but found his full stride all too late and never threatened.
**Peruvian Style(IRE)** was a sitting duck for the winner late on and dropped out tamely when headed. He ran way too freely in the first-time blinkers.

## 4044 RENAULT MASTER CLAIMING STKS — 5f 11y
4:35 (4:35) (F ) 3-Y-O+ **£3,115** (£890; £445) **Stalls** Low

Form RPR
6600 **1** **Byo (IRE)**[11] 3775 6-9-9 70........................ FNorton 8 69
(MQuinn) *mde all: rdn over 1f out: drvn out* **9/1**
0260 **2** *1* **Signor Panettiere**[25] 3344 3-9-3 69........................ SDrowne 7 63
(RHannon) *hld up in mid-div: hdwy over 1f out: running on whn hit on hd by winning jockey's whip wl ins fnl f* **7/2**[2]
6520 **3** *1/2* **Compton Banker (IRE)**[14] 3663 7-9-3 69........................(v) TQuinn 10 57
(GAButler) *s.i.s: bhd: swtchd rt and hdwy over 1f out: kpt on towards fin* **5/2**[1]
0401 **4** *1/2* **Jinksonthehouse**[24] 3364 3-8-5 56........................ HayleyTurner(5) 9 52
(MDIUsher) *chsd wnr: rdn and ev ch over 1f out: no ex towards fin* **9/1**
0000 **5** *1 3/4* **Bennanabaa**[17] 3575 5-9-2 40........................(t) BO'Neill(7) 2 54
(SCBurrough) *s.i.s: hdwy on ins 1f out: nt rch ldrs* **66/1**
0303 **6** *hd* **Diamond Ring**[11] 3772 5-8-9 40........................ NChalmers(5) 3 44
(MrsJCandlish) *bhd: swtchd rt and hdwy jst over 1f out: nvr trbld ldrs* **20/1**
0006 **7** *1/2* **Fiamma Royale (IRE)**[17] 3575 6-9-0 44........................ JFEgan 5 42
(MSSaunders) *chsd ldrs: rdn over 2f out: wknd 1f out* **8/1**
0312 **8** *shd* **Innclassic (IRE)**[10] 3801 3-9-2 65........................(b) VSlattery 1 48
(JaneSouthcombe) *prom: rdn 2f out: wknd ins fnl f* **7/1**[3]
-043 **9** *1* **Lake Verdi (IRE)**[14] 3668 5-9-5 53........................(t) MartinDwyer 4 43
(BHanbury) *towards rr: sme hdwy whn nt clr run on ins over 2f out: wknd over 1f out* **7/1**[3]
5660 **10** *1/2* **Captain Cloudy**[88] 1642 4-9-5 57........................ GBaker 11 41
(MMadgwick) *prom tl rdn and wknd over 1f out* **25/1**
00 **11** *1 1/2* **Till There Was You**[14] 3666 3-8-3 ........................ CHaddon(7) 6 30
(WGMTurner) *sn outpcd* **100/1**
62.52 secs (0.02) **Going Correction** +0.025s/f (Good)
**WFA** 3 from 4yo+ 4lb **11** Ran SP% **118.0**
Speed ratings: **100,98,97,96,94 93,92,92,91,90 87**CSF £39.66 TOTE £8.80: £3.40, £1.80, £1.50; EX 48.20.Compton Banker was claimed by David Evans for £7,000. Signor Panettiere was claimed by Jayne Smith £9,000.
**Owner** J G Dooley **Bred** E Johnston **Trained** Sparsholt, Oxon

**FOCUS**
A typically modest event for the grade and the first three on official figures were the first three home.

**NOTEBOOK**
**Byo(IRE)** pinged out from his wide draw and bravely made all. He was a big price for this, considering he often saves his best for the track and was dropping in grade, but may struggle off his current mark back in handicaps.
**Signor Panettiere** came there with every chance approaching the final furlong, but was outbattled by the winner. He was hit by the winner's whip late on and can gain compensation in this grade before long.
**Compton Banker(IRE)**, with the visor back on, was up against it after a sluggish start and was finishing all too late in the day. He has become a frustraing sort this year, was best in at the weights for this and it must go down as a missed opportunity.
**Jinksonthehouse**, winner of a seller over course and distance last time, ran her race with no excuses and is the benchmark for the form. She can find another race at this level.

## 4045 RENAULT TRAFIC FILLIES' H'CAP — 1m 2f 46y
5:10 (5:10) (E ) (0-70,65) 3-Y-O+ **£3,721** (£1,145; £572; £286) **Stalls** Low

Form RPR
0014 **1** **Donastrela (IRE)**[11] 3773 3-8-5 **57**........................(v) NChalmers(5) 8 69
(AMBalding) *hld up: smooth hdwy to ld over 2f out: sn shkn up and clr: rdn jst over 1f out: r.o wl* **6/1**[3]
-066 **2** *2 1/2* **Sienna Sunset (IRE)**[27] 3264 5-9-4 **55**........................ GBaker 2 63
(WMBrisbourne) *hld up: nt clr run over 2f out: rdn and hdwy wl over 1f out: chsd wnr fnl f: no imp* **20/1**
0000 **3** *3 1/2* **My Hope (IRE)**[13] 3700 3-9-3 **64**........................ SDrowne 1 65
(RCharlton) *hld up in tch: hdwy 3f out: rdn and ev ch 2f out: wknd ins fnl f* **14/1**
3132 **4** *1* **Ember Days**[6] 3917 5-10-0 **65**........................(p) TQuinn 9 64
(JLSpearing) *hld up: hdwy 3f out: rdn wl over 1f out: wknd ins fnl f* **2/1**[1]
0320 **5** *3* **Jessinca**[14] 3670 8-7-11 **39**........................ HayleyTurner(5) 5 32
(APJones) *hld up and bhd: plld out and hdwy 2f out: wknd fnl f* **10/1**
0000 **6** *3* **Margarets Wish**[13] 3697 4-8-5 **42**........................(b[1]) CCatlin 10 30
(TWall) *led: rdn and hdd 2f out: sn wknd* **50/1**
6 **7** *1 1/4* **Kalimenta (USA)**[8] 3852 3-9-4 **65**........................ JFEgan 6 50
(SKirk) *hd-butted rdr twice after s: rdn 3f out: a bhd* **13/2**
0044 **8** *3* **Bond May Day**[19] 3510 4-9-12 **63**........................ MartinDwyer 3 43
(BSmart) *plld hrd: sn prom: rdn over 2f out: wknd wl over 1f out* **8/1**
3030 **9** *1/2* **Nuzzle**[12] 3731 4-8-7 **44**........................ FNorton 4 23
(MQuinn) *chsd ldr: rdn over 3f out: wknd wl over 1f out* **5/1**[2]
1-15 **10** *10* **Lyrical Girl (USA)**[190] 522 3-8-12 **59**........................ SWhitworth 11 19
(HJManners) *prom tl rdn and wknd over 2f out* **14/1**
0-00 **11** *2 1/2* **Lady Redera (IRE)**[39] 2915 3-8-1 **48**........................(b[1]) DKinsella 7 3
(HSHowe) *dwlt: bhd: rdn 3f out: sn lost tch* **66/1**
2m 9.67s (-1.33) **Going Correction** -0.05s/f (Good)
**WFA** 3 from 4yo+ 10lb **11** Ran SP% **119.4**
Speed ratings: **103,101,98,97,95 92,91,89,88,80 78**CSF £120.48 CT £1619.01 TOTE £6.90: £1.70, £5.70, £3.60; EX 105.90 Place 6 £23.90, Place 5 £19.73.
**Owner** Guy Luck, Rosemary de Rougemont, Tom Cox **Bred** R H Thomas Cox And G William Robinson **Trained** Kingsclere, Hants

**FOCUS**
A moderate fillies' handicap that saw the field finish well strung out behind the decisive winner, suggesting the form is fair for the type of race.

**NOTEBOOK**
**Donastrela(IRE)** produced a personal best, showing a neat turn of foot, and won this comfortably. She has looked a much-improved performer (over this course and distance) since the visor was applied on her last three outings, and she can go in again while at this end of the handicap.
**Sienna Sunset(IRE)** ran her best race since resuming on the Flat this year and has clearly benefited from a drop in the weights. She was well held by the winner, but finished clear in second and could exploit this mark if able to maintain this form.
**My Hope(IRE)** turned in a much-improved effort over this longer trip, but lacked the change of gear to go with the winner. She could be worth another try back over a mile now she has found her form, as she looked to be running on empty close home over this ten furlongs.
**Ember Days** ran below par, even accounting for her big weight, and may be in need of a break now. She was again far from disgraced, however.
**Kalimenta(USA)** *Official explanation: jockey said he was hit in the face leaving the stalls*
**Nuzzle** is often the subject of support in the betting ring, as was the case this time, but never looked like breaking her duck on turf and remains a very frustrating filly.
T/Plt: £40.30 to a £1 stake. Pool: £26,140.50. 473.10 winning tickets. T/Qpdt: £20.70 to a £1 stake. Pool: £1,480.50. 52.90 winning tickets. KH

# 3864 DONCASTER (L-H)
Thursday, July 22

**OFFICIAL GOING: Good to firm, changing to good to soft after race 2 and soft race 4**

## 4046 GALAXY 105 & OUT IN PUBLISHING NURSERY — 5f
6:30 (6:31) (E ) 2-Y-O **£4,087** (£1,257; £628; £314) **Stalls** High

Form RPR
5226 **1** **Bibury Flyer**[5] 3938 2-9-4 **74**........................ SHitchcott(3) 4 81
(MRChannon) *hld up in rr: hdwy on outer 2f out: rdn to ld ins last: styd on* **11/4**[2]
4022 **2** *1* **I'm Aimee**[5] 3924 2-9-2 **72**........................ FPFerris(3) 1 75
(PDEvans) *chsd ldrs on outer: pushed along 1/2-way: hdwy wl over 1f out: rdn and ev ch ent last: sn rdn nd nt qckn* **4/1**[3]
0305 **3** *1 1/2* **Ryedane (IRE)**[16] 3605 2-8-12 **65**........................ DAllan 6 63
(TDEasterby) *hld up: pushed along and sltly outpcd 2f out: styng on whn nt m uch room over 1f out: kpt on ins last* **20/1**
4231 **4** *nk* **Forzeen**[5] 3930 2-9-12 **79** 6ex........................ DHolland 8 78+
(JAOsborne) *hld up in rr: gd hdwy on inner over 1f out tl hmpd ent last: swtchd lft and kpt on* **7/4**[1]
036 **5** *shd* **Skiddaw Wolf**[19] 3514 2-8-9 **62**........................ RWinston 3 58
(BSmart) *chsd ldr: hdwy 2f out: rdn to ld over 1f out: sn hung rt: hdd & wknd ins last* **12/1**
3303 **6** *3* **Chilali (IRE)**[12] 3729 2-8-4 **62**........................ PPMathers(5) 7 48
(ABerry) *cl up: rdn along and wandered wl over 1f out: sn wknd* **14/1**
5415 **7** *1/2* **Our Louis**[20] 3468 2-8-2 **55**........................ RFfrench 2 39
(JSWainwright) *led: rdn along 2f out: sn hung bdly lft: hdd & wknd* **20/1**
3531 **8** *6* **Eternally**[13] 3709 2-7-10 **52**........................(p) LisaJones(3) 5 15
(RMHCowell) *cl up: rdn along 2f out: sn wknd* **14/1**
61.21 secs (-0.21) **Going Correction** -0.075s/f (Good) **8** Ran SP% **113.6**
Speed ratings: **98,96,94,93,93 88,87,78**CSF £14.03 CT £176.40 TOTE £3.60: £1.40, £1.50, £4.20; EX 15.20.
**Owner** Ridgeway Downs Racing **Bred** Baydon House Stud **Trained** West Ilsley, Berks

**FOCUS**
There was a strong pace for this fairly modest nursery and the form looks solid. The figures shown as 'official ratings' are estimates for guidance only.

**NOTEBOOK**
**Bibury Flyer**, who ran well in the Super Sprint, finally got off the mark at the ninth time of asking. The fast pace suited her and she came from the back of the field to claim the race. She looks worth trying over six furlongs.
**I'm Aimee** has yet to win a race, but she is largely consistent and the rain before racing had turned the ground in her favour.

**Ryedane(IRE)**, despite the strong pace, struggled to go the early gallop but was putting in all his best work at the finish. He will be suited by a stiffer five or six furlongs.
**Forzeen** ran better than his finishing position suggests as he had to wait for a gap to appear next to the rail. He picked up well to take it, only for the door to be shut once again inside the final furlong. He would probably have finished at least third with a clear run. *Official explanation: jockey said colt was denied a clear run*
**Skiddaw Wolf** ran quite well considering she raced close to the fast pace for much of the way.
**Our Louis** paid the price for setting a strong pace in the early stages.

## 4047 GROLSCH CLASSIFIED STKS 6f
**7:00** (7:01) (D) 3-Y-O+ **£5,655** (£1,740; £870; £435) **Stalls** High

Form RPR
3232 **1** **Lord Of The East**[7] [3871] 5-9-1 75 JFanning 4 85
(DNicholls) *mde all: rdn clr over 1f out: drvn out* **9/1**
0023 **2** ¾ **Armagnac**[5] [3941] 6-9-3 77 DHolland 11 85
(MABuckley) *hld up towards rr: gd hdwy on inner over 1f out: styng wl whn n.m.r ins last: gng on nr fin* **3/1**[2]
3106 **3** 2 **Hiccups**[16] [3606] 4-9-6 80 (p) RWinston 7 82
(MrsJRRamsden) *hld up: hdwy wl over 1f out: rdn ent last and sn one pce* **8/1**[3]
0611 **4** ½ **Hartshead**[19] [3515] 5-9-1 72 DeanMcKeown 8 75
(GASwinbank) *trckd ldrs: effrt 2f out: sn rdn: hung rt ent last and sn btn* **15/8**[1]
6542 **5** 2½ **Soba Jones**[6] [3920] 7-9-1 69 JEdmunds 1 68
(JBalding) *cl up: ev ch 2f out: sn rdn and grad wknd* **12/1**
1103 **6** 2½ **Paddywack (IRE)**[6] [3920] 7-8-12 73 (b) LisaJones(3) 2 60
(DWChapman) *chsd ldrs on outer: rdn along 2f out: sn btn* **10/1**
2006 **7** 4 **Jalouhar**[12] [3730] 4-9-1 46 TWoodley 9 48
(BPJBaugh) *chsd ldrs: rdn along 1/2-way: sn wknd* **100/1**
3006 **8** 4 **Banjo Bay (IRE)**[23] [3399] 6-9-1 73 ANicholls 10 36
(DNicholls) *cl up: rdn over 2f out: sn wknd* **12/1**
0050 **9** nk **Smirfys Systems**[11] [3778] 5-9-2 76 DAllan 6 36
(WMBrisbourne) *a re* **20/1**
0005 **10** nk **Grey Cossack**[11] [3778] 7-9-1 73 RFitzpatrick 5 34
(PTMidgley) *dwlt: hdwy to chse ldrs 1/2-way: sn rdn and wknd* **16/1**
5654 **11** 8 **Telepathic (IRE)**[2] [4006] 4-8-10 57 (t) PPMathers(5) 3 10
(ABerry) *chasaed ldrs: rdn alonga nd hung lft after 2f out: sn lost pl and bhd* **100/1**

1m 13.08s (-1.20) **Going Correction** -0.075s/f (Good) **11** Ran SP% **118.0**
Speed ratings: **105,104,101,100,97 94,88,83,82,82 71**CSF £35.99 TOTE £10.40: £2.40, £1.40, £2.80; EX 30.80.
**Owner** The Wayward Lads **Bred** Catridge Farm Stud Ltd **Trained** Sessay, N Yorks

### FOCUS
A fair handicap but there are reservations over the form on deteriorating ground.

### NOTEBOOK
**Lord Of The East** has been in good form throughout the year. Best when allowed to dominate, he had his own way in front this time, which certainly helped. He has made all for four of his six career victories.
**Armagnac**, best in at the weights, has scored just once in each year he has been racing, and is clearly not the easiest to win with. Held up at the back, he came with a good late run, but he was never really ever going to catch the winner.
**Hiccups** could not be said to have benefited from the easing of the ground as his best form is all on top.
**Hartshead**, chasing the hat-trick, was slightly disappointing, and it remains to be seen whether he will be able to remain competitive back in handicap company off his new mark.
**Soba Jones** has not won on turf for over two years and, despite the fact that the rain had helped bring the ground in his favour, he dropped out tamely in the closing stages.
**Paddywack(IRE)** showed plenty of speed but found the sixth furlong too much.

## 4048 DC TRAINING & DEVELOPMENT SERVICES MAIDEN AUCTION STKS 6f
**7:30** (7:32) (E) 2-Y-O **£3,698** (£1,138; £569; £284) **Stalls** High

Form RPR
3 **1** **Cammies Future**[103] [1324] 2-8-12 WRyan 5 79+
(PWChapple-Hyam) *in tch: gd hdwy over 2f out: led over 1f out: styd on wl* **13/8**[1]
**2** 1 **Able Charlie (GER)** 2-8-11 RWinston 16 75
(MrsJRRamsden) *hld up in rr: hdwy over 2f out: swtchd outside over 1f out and styd on wl fnl f* **25/1**
5 **3** nk **Merchant (IRE)**[14] [3664] 2-8-11 ANicholls 18 74
(MLWBell) *in tch: hdwy over 2f out: rdn to chse wnr over 1f out: kpt on* **9/2**[3]
**4** 3½ **Methodical** 2-8-4 ow1 GGibbons 14 57
(IAWood) *towards rr: hdwy over 2f out: sn rdn and kpt on ins last: nrst fin* **33/1**
2 **5** 1½ **Tybalt**[15] [3632] 2-8-9 DHolland 12 57
(PWHarris) *midfield: swtchd lft and hdwy 2f out: rdn over 1f out: kpt on ins last* **10/3**[2]
**6** shd **Briannsta (IRE)** 2-8-6 SHitchcott(3) 15 57
(MRChannon) *bhd tl styd on wl fnl 2f: nrst fin* **20/1**
6004 **7** ¾ **Waterline Lover**[48] [2644] 2-8-3 FPFerris(3) 8 52
(PDEvans) *led: rdn along over 2f out: drvn and hdd wl over 1f out: sn wknd* **25/1**
**8** 3½ **Admittance (USA)** 2-8-6 LGoncalves 10 41
(MrsJRRamsden) *midfield: rdn along and outpcd 1/2-way: styd on appr last* **66/1**
0605 **9** hd **Desert Buzz (IRE)**[19] [3514] 2-8-8 MTebbutt 7 42
(JHetherton) *cl up: rdn over 2f out: sn drvn and wknd wl over 1f out* **25/1**
50 **10** 1 **Dover Street**[31] [3157] 2-8-11 PaulEddery 11 42
(PWD'Arcy) *midfield: pushed along halwfay: nvr a factor* **25/1**
6 **11** shd **Golden Squaw**[30] [3164] 2-8-3 DAllan 1 34
(TDEasterby) *prom on outer: rdn along 1/2-way: sn wknd* **33/1**
0 **12** nk **French Kisses**[45] [2730] 2-8-4 DeanMcKeown 6 34
(RonaldThompson) *bhd fr 1/2-way* **100/1**
00 **13** 1¼ **Wilford Maverick (IRE)**[10] [3802] 2-8-8 JFanning 2 35
(MJAttwater) *bhd fr 1/2-way* **33/1**
6 **14** 3 **Desert Phoenix (IRE)**[17] [3583] 2-8-5 PHanagan 9 23
(RAFahey) *bhd fr 1/2-way* **25/1**
**15** ½ **Shekan Star** 2-8-7 JEdmunds 17 23
(MrsMReveley) *a rr* **20/1**
**16** shd **Cala Fons (IRE)** 2-8-5 KimTinkler 3 21
(NTinkler) *dwlt: a rr* **100/1**
**17** hd **Plenty Cried Wolf** 2-8-7 THamilton(3) 13 25
(RAFahey) *a rr* **66/1**
**18** 12 **Orpen Wide (IRE)** 2-8-6 LisaJones(3) 4 —
(MCChapman) *sowly into stride: a bhd* **66/1**

1m 15.44s (1.16) **Going Correction** -0.075s/f (Good) **18** Ran SP% **123.4**
Speed ratings: **89,87,87,82,80 80,79,74,74,73 73,72,71,67,66 66,65,49**CSF £53.34 TOTE £2.40: £1.60, £4.90, £2.20; EX 45.30.
**Owner** Collins Deal Harrison-Allan Chapple-Hyam **Bred** D Brocklehurst **Trained** Newmarket, Suffolk

### FOCUS
A fair maiden and decent form from the front three, with a good performance from the winner, who bucked the draw bias.

### NOTEBOOK
**Cammies Future** won in good style and is surely a bit better than the bare form, as he overcame a poor draw and still won cosily. He had an unfortunate experience on his debut and this will have done his confidence some good. He clearly handles cut well.
**Able Charlie(GER)** stayed on well from the rear to claim the runner-up spot on this debut, and this German-bred looks sure to improve when stepped up in trip.
**Merchant(IRE)** had run well enough on his debut over seven furlongs and, from a good draw, showed he could handle this shorter distance, too.
**Methodical**, a half-sister to prolific sprint winner Palacegate Touch, appreciated the cut in the ground on her debut and stayed on well from the rear to finish a clear fourth. She might have got even closer had she not been blocked in her run approaching the final furlong, and she is open to improvement.
**Tybalt** was fairly drawn but ended up racing wide. He did not look happy on the rain-softened ground and should be given another chance back on a faster surface. *Official explanation: jockey said colt hung right from half way*
**Briannsta(IRE)**, a half-brother to three winners on the Flat, did not enjoy the best of runs inside the final two furlongs but kept on well enough.

## 4049 CARLING EXTRA COLD FILLIES' H'CAP 1m 2f 60y
**8:00** (8:02) (D) (0-85,77) 3-Y-O **£5,525** (£1,700; £850; £425) **Stalls** Low

Form RPR
3605 **1** **Rio De Jumeirah**[28] [3230] 3-9-5 **75** KFallon 1 86+
(CEBrittain) *trckd ldr: pushed along over 3f out: swtchd rt and hdwy to ld wl over 1f out: sn rdn clr: easily* **4/1**
-002 **2** 3½ **Eboracum (IRE)**[20] [3478] 3-8-7 **63** DAllan 3 68
(TDEasterby) *in rr and pushed along 1/2-way: hdwy over 3f out: swtchd rt and rdn wl over 1f out: styd on ins last: no ch w wnr* **10/3**[3]
0011 **3** 1½ **Trew Class**[16] [3610] 3-9-7 **77** DHolland 2 79+
(MHTompkins) *trckd ldrs: led after 2f: pushed along over 3f out: rdn wl over 2f out: drvn and hdd wl over 1f out: sn btn* **11/4**[1]
-554 **4** 3 **Appetina**[27] [3261] 3-8-9 **65** JFanning 5 62
(JGGiven) *led 2f: cl up and rdn along 3f out: drvn and wknd 2f out* **8/1**
62-6 **5** 14 **Serramanna**[97] [1440] 3-9-6 **76** WRyan 4 47
(HRACecil) *hld up in tch: pushed along over 4f out: sn rdn and btn 3f out* **3/1**[2]

2m 15.29s (3.53) **Going Correction** +0.10s/f (Good) **5** Ran SP% **105.9**
Speed ratings: **89,86,85,82,71**CSF £15.89 TOTE £4.30: £2.10, £2.00; EX 18.00.
**Owner** Abdullah Saeed Belhab **Bred** Darley **Trained** Newmarket, Suffolk

### FOCUS
Not that strong a race as only one of these fillies had tasted success before. Just a modest gallop to boot.

### NOTEBOOK
**Rio De Jumeirah** appreciated the return to ten furlongs and saw out the trip really well to get off the mark at the ninth attempt. She had not covered herself in glory on her only previous starts on soft ground, but she handled the easy conditions well on this occasion.
**Eboracum(IRE)** appreciates a little cut in the ground and, despite being 3lb higher than at Haydock last time, ran a decent race in defeat. Ridden to get the trip, she saw it out well off what was admittedly a modest gallop.
**Trew Class**, the only previous winner in the field, was chasing a hat-trick but found her chance compromised by the change in the going. She has done her winning on quicker ground and should not be written off on the basis of this effort. *Official explanation: jockey said filly was unsuited by good to soft ground*
**Appetina** travelled well throughout but found very little under pressure. This is not the first time she has flattered to deceive.
**Serramanna** ran another poor race and is beginning to look disappointing. The easy ground was not sufficient an excuse.

## 4050 EASTSIDE MAGAZINE H'CAP 1m (S)
**8:30** (8:30) (D) (0-80,80) 3-Y-O **£5,736** (£1,765; £882; £441) **Stalls** High

Form RPR
6240 **1** **Double Vodka (IRE)**[18] [3561] 3-8-4 **63** PHanagan 1 69
(MrsJRRamsden) *hld up in rr: gd hdwy 2f out: swtchd rt ent last: sn drvn and styd on wl to ld nr line* **3/1**[2]
4601 **2** hd **Charnock Bates One (IRE)**[19] [3507] 3-8-11 **70** RWinston 7 76
(TDEasterby) *trckd ldrs: hdwy to ld wl over 1f out: rdn ent last: drvn and hdd nr line* **4/1**[3]
0430 **3** hd **Bright Sun (IRE)**[17] [3585] 3-8-13 **72** KimTinkler 8 78
(NTinkler) *keen: trckd ldrs: hdwy 2f out: rdn to chal ins last and ev ch tl no ex nr fin* **12/1**
4405 **4** 2 **Honest Injun**[13] [3714] 3-9-1 **74** DHolland 6 79+
(BWHills) *hld up in tch: effrt on inner and nt clr run wl over 1f out: swtchd lft and rdn over 1f out: kpt on ins last* **5/2**[1]
4563 **5** ¾ **Foolish Groom**[11] [3780] 3-8-10 **69** (tp) ACulhane 4 69
(RHollinshead) *hld up in tch: hdwy on outer 2f out: sn rdn and ev ch over 1f out: drvn and wknd ent last* **13/2**
-146 **6** 9 **Cottingham (IRE)**[19] [3507] 3-8-1 **63** LisaJones(3) 9 45
(MCChapman) *cl up: rdn along over 2f out: drvn: wandered and wknd over 1f out* **14/1**
0425 **7** ½ **Heversham (IRE)**[16] [3610] 3-9-0 **73** MTebbutt 2 54
(JHetherton) *cl up: led after 1 1/2f: rdn along over 2f out: drvn and hdd over 1f out: sn wknd* **12/1**
0-50 **8** 1½ **Tyzack (IRE)**[65] [2217] 3-8-6 **65** JEdmunds 3 43
(JBalding) *a rr* **16/1**
4-00 **9** dist **Spartan Spear**[65] [2217] 3-8-4 **63** (p) JBramhill 10 —
(JBalding) *led 1 1/2f: sn pushed along and wkng whn hmpd 1/2-way and virtually p.u* **25/1**

1m 41.51s (-0.09) **Going Correction** +0.10s/f (Good) **9** Ran SP% **118.7**
Speed ratings: **104,103,103,101,100 91,91,89,—**CSF £16.03 CT £128.45 TOTE £3.90: £1.30, £1.90, £4.10; EX 14.00.
**Owner** Mrs Alison Iles **Bred** Daphne Davison **Trained** Sandhutton, N Yorks

### FOCUS
A fair handicap that developed into a bit of a sprint and luck in running played a part, and some doubts over the form being repeated.

**NOTEBOOK**
**Double Vodka(IRE)** had shown on a few occasions that a race was in him off this sort of mark, but his style of racing requires luck as he needs to be brought with a late run. While the favourite suffered an interrupted passage, the gaps appeared at the right time for him and he got up in the final strides.
**Charnock Bates One(IRE)**, who seems to act on any ground, was only denied in the shadow of the post. Clearly the Handicapper did not overreact when he put her up 7lb for winning at Beverley.
**Bright Sun(IRE)** looked a doubtful stayer beforehand but, despite racing keenly, saw it out in great fashion. Although the steady early pace may have suited him, this performance certainly opens up new options for him.
**Honest Injun**, trapped against the rail, could not get a run when he wanted it and in the end had to track the winner, who got first run, through. He would not have won, but he should have finished closer.
**Foolish Groom** had every chance entering the last but weakened inside it. He needs some help from the Handicapper.

## 4051 DONCASTER RACECOURSE SPONSORSHIP CLUB H'CAP 6f
**9:00** (9:02) (D) (0-85,90) 3-Y-O **£5,671** (£1,745; £872; £436) **Stalls** High

Form RPR
2261 **1** **Commando Scott (IRE)**[5] 3926 3-9-7 **84** 6ex FLynch 5 93
(ABerry) *mde all: edgd rt and rdn clr over 1f out: kpt on strly fnl f* **7/2**[1]
4111 **2** *2 ½* **Red Romeo**[8] 3845 3-9-13 **90** 6ex KFallon 7 92
(GASwinbank) *keen: trckd ldrs: hdwy to chse wnr ent last: sn drvn and hung rt: kpt on* **9/2**[3]
2110 **3** *1* **Cherokee Nation**[15] 3624 3-8-7 **70** DHolland 8 69+
(PWD'Arcy) *hld up: hdwy 2f out: sn rdn and kpt on fnl f* **5/1**
4512 **4** *¾* **Instant Recall (IRE)**[8] 3845 3-9-1 **78** (b) JFortune 12 74+
(BJMeehan) *in tch: hdwy to chse ldrs 2f out: sn rdn and one pce whn n.m.r ins last* **4/1**[2]
0350 **5** *½* **Ice Planet**[5] 3954 3-8-6 **69** RWinston 4 64
(DNicholls) *dwlt and hmpd s: bhd tl hdwy 2f out: rdn and styd on wl fnl f: nrst fin* **25/1**
-053 **6** *2 ½* **Ligne D'Eau**[33] 3085 3-7-10 **62** FPFerris(3) 9 49
(PDEvans) *chsd ldrs: rdn over 2f out: sn one pce* **10/1**
1-0 **7** *4* **Soliniki**[112] 1225 3-9-2 **79** VSlattery 11 54
(JAOsborne) *towards rr and rdn along 1/2-way: nvr a factor* **25/1**
3100 **8** *2* **Kabreet**[61] 2309 3-9-1 **78** WRyan 1 47
(EALDunlop) *wnt rt s: sn cl up: rdn along over 2f out: wknd wl over 1f out* **16/1**
6056 **9** *nk* **Compton Micky**[44] 2756 3-7-12 **61** oh5 (p) JBramhill 10 29
(JBalding) *in tch: rdn along over 2f out: sn wknd* **66/1**
3-65 **10** *½* **Abelard (IRE)**[40] 2877 3-8-2 **65** PHanagan 3 32
(RAFahey) *hmpd s: a rr* **13/2**
264- **11** *5* **Marysienka**[292] 5356 3-8-13 **76** JEdmunds 6 28
(JBalding) *in tch: rdn along 1/2-way and sn outpcd* **50/1**

1m 14.47s (0.19) **Going Correction** +0.10s/f (Good) **11** Ran SP% **116.5**
Speed ratings: **102,98,97,96,95 92,87,84,83,83 76**CSF £18.47 CT £78.49 TOTE £5.50: £2.30, £2.40, £1.70; EX 23.30 Place 6 £56.27, Place 5 £27.61.
**Owner** Mrs Ann Morris **Bred** Noel Finegan **Trained** Cockerham, Lancs

**FOCUS**
A fair handicap but there was not much pace on early and it paid to race near the front.

**NOTEBOOK**
**Commando Scott(IRE)**, who was 3lb well in, likes to race prominently and loves soft ground, so the fact that he was in front and was not pressed to go much of a gallop suited him down to the ground. A progressive sort, he won comfortably in the end.
**Red Romeo** has been in cracking form on faster ground of late and put up another good effort under his 6lb penalty under these very different conditions.
**Cherokee Nation** beat Commando Scott at Ripon earlier in the month and was better off at the weights on this occasion, but the ground was much slower this time and the way the race panned out did not suit this hold-up performer.
**Instant Recall(IRE)**, runner-up to Red Romeo last time, handles easy ground and was 8lb better off with that rival. He again finished behind him though, and is not progressing at the same rate.
**Ice Planet** was not suited by the steady early pace and looks capable of better when getting the race run to suit. He has yet to run on a quick surface in five starts and evidently a little ease in the ground is thought to suit him well.
**Ligne D'Eau**, who has shown his best form on a fast surface, was put up 5lb for his good run in a maiden last month.
T/Plt: £46.20 to a £1 stake. Pool: £47,442.80. 749.25 winning tickets. T/Qpdt: £12.80 to a £1 stake. Pool: £3,127.60. 180.20 winning tickets. JR

# 3664 FOLKESTONE (R-H)
Thursday, July 22
**OFFICIAL GOING: Good to firm (good in places)**
Wind: nil Weather: overcast; humid

## 4052 EVENING RACING AT FOLKESTONE RACECOURSE APPRENTICE H'CAP 6f
**6:15** (6:18) (F) (0-70,69) 3-Y-O **£3,059** (£874; £437) **Stalls** Low

Form RPR
050- **1** **Dave (IRE)**[271] 5746 3-8-4 **55** NDeSouza(3) 3 67
(JRBest) *rrd s: racd agains nr side rail: mde all: hrd rdn over 1f out: clr fnl f* **20/1**
-551 **2** *3* **Mugeba**[22] 3425 3-8-6 **59** (t) RachelCostello(5) 12 62+
(MissGayKelleway) *cl up far side: rdn to ld gp over 1f out: kpt on but no ch w nr side wnr* **8/1**
6332 **3** *nk* **Half A Handful**[10] 3798 3-9-3 **65** (v[1]) DCorby 1 67
(MJWallace) *trckd nr side ldrs: rdn 2f out: chsd wnr 1f out: no imp* **5/1**[2]
-060 **4** *¾* **Nebraska City**[17] 3589 3-8-7 **55** (t) LPKeniry 6 55
(PMitchell) *in tch nr side: rdn and struggling over 2f out: styd on fnl f: nrst fin* **33/1**
5000 **5** *1 ½* **Crewes Miss Isle**[41] 2849 3-9-0 **62** BReilly 10 57
(AGNewcombe) *racd far side: in tch: rdn to chse ldr 1f out: nt qckn and no imp* **12/1**
4025 **6** *hd* **Jasmine Pearl (IRE)**[3] 3991 3-7-9 **48** MHalford(5) 4 43
(TMJones) *mostly chsd wnr nr side to 1f out: wknd* **6/1**[3]
0006 **7** *¾* **Generous Spirit (IRE)**[71] 2029 3-9-0 **62** ABeech 5 54
(JAOsborne) *rrd s: racd nr side: detached in last of gp: hrd rdn and kpt on fr over 1f out: no ch* **8/1**
1640 **8** *1* **Arfinnit (IRE)**[11] 3772 3-8-5 **60** (v) TDean(7) 8 49
(MRChannon) *s.i.s: trckd far side ldrs: wknd fnl f* **6/1**[3]
3403 **9** *nk* **Bella Tutrice (IRE)**[8] 3849 3-9-7 **69** TPQueally 2 58
(IAWood) *prom nr side tl wknd 1f out* **4/1**[1]
3000 **10** *2 ½* **Kuringai**[55] 2444 3-9-0 **65** DFox(3) 11 46
(BWDuke) *led far side gp to 1/2-way: stl on terms over 1f out: wknd* **16/1**
0000 **11** *1 ¼* **Queen Of Bulgaria (IRE)**[38] 2942 3-7-11 **48** oh1 ow2 RThomas(3) 7 25
(JPearce) *racd nr side: struggling in rr 1/2-way: wl bhd over 1f out* **16/1**
0500 **12** *3* **Smokin Joe**[28] 3231 3-8-10 **61** ow1 (v[1]) MSavage(3) 9 29
(JRBest) *prom far side: led gp 1/2-way to over 1f out: wknd rapidly and eased* **12/1**

1m 13.61s (0.01) **Going Correction** -0.025s/f (Good) **12** Ran SP% **122.3**
Speed ratings: **98,94,93,92,90 90,89,88,87,84 82,78**CSF £177.33 CT £955.80 TOTE £19.00: £4.40, £2.60, £2.00; EX 465.40.
**Owner** M Folan,A Warner,D Giles,C Dennison **Bred** D Eataugh **Trained** Hucking, Kent

**FOCUS**
The field split into two groups with the winner coming from the seven who raced on the near side. This is modest form but it looks fairly sound.

**NOTEBOOK**
**Dave(IRE)** showed little in four runs over the minimum trip last season. He pitched leaving the stalls as the blindfold was whipped off and the promising de Souza did well to retain his balance, but was still able to make all. Likely to stay another furlong, he escapes a penalty for his win in this apprentice event and there should be further improvement in him. *Official explanation: trainer said, regarding the improved form shown, gelding had strengthened over the winter*
**Mugeba**, sold out of Willie Musson's yard after landing a seller, was fitted with a tongue-tie. She came out best of the five to race on the far side but the drop in trip did not do her any favours.
**Half A Handful** ran a decent race in the first-time visor and did not appear to do much wrong. Seven could be his best trip now.
**Nebraska City** settled better down in trip, having failed to stay a mile last time when too keen. He was keeping on when it was all over and maybe seven furlongs will prove best for him.
**Crewes Miss Isle** finished second best of the far-side quintet.
**Bella Tutrice(IRE)** is a filly who needs things her own way and, after half-missing the break, was unable to get to the front.

## 4053 EUROPEAN BREEDERS FUND MAIDEN FILLIES' STKS 7f (S)
**6:45** (6:49) (D) 2-Y-O **£5,408** (£1,664; £832; £416) **Stalls** Low

Form RPR
0 **1** **Hidden Chance**[15] 3627 2-8-6 RThomas(5) 12 69
(RHannon) *dwlt: racd in last trio and pushed along after 2f: swtchd to outer and rapid prog 2f out: str run to ld last stride* **5/1**[3]
**2** *hd* **Sweet Lorraine** 2-8-6 NDeSouza(5) 14 69
(TGMills) *pressed ldr: led 3f out: rdn 2l clr over 1f out: ct last stride* **16/1**
0 **3** *½* **Velveteen Rabbit**[14] 3675 2-8-11 LDettori 7 67
(SaeedBinSuroor) *prom: chsd wnr over 2f out: rdn and unable qck over 1f out: styd on* **5/2**[1]
**4** *nk* **Bongoali** 2-8-4 TDean(7) 3 67
(MRChannon) *dwlt: in tch: grad moved fr outer to inner 1/2-way: pushed along and styd on wl fnl 2f: nvr quite able to chal* **40/1**
**5** *hd* **Flaunting It (IRE)** 2-8-11 DSweeney 9 66
(JAOsborne) *trckd ldrs: lost pl 3f out: pushed along over 1f out: styd on wl fnl f: bttr for r* **50/1**
060 **6** *nk* **Imperial Miss (IRE)**[15] 3627 2-8-4 MHalford(7) 13 65
(BWDuke) *trckd ldrs gng wl: effrt over 2f out: rdn and unable qck over 1f out: kpt on same pce after* **25/1**
**7** *½* **Krumpet** 2-8-8 ABeech(3) 11 64
(GGMargarson) *dwlt: racd in last trio: pushed along and prog 2f out: styd on: nvr nrr* **66/1**
00 **8** *shd* **Romantic Gift**[54] 2481 2-8-8 LPKeniry(3) 4 64
(JMPEustace) *dwlt: towards rr: prog to chse ldrs 2f out: rdn and one pce fr over 1f out* **20/1**
**9** *1* **Issy Blue** 2-8-11 SWKelly 8 61
(JAOsborne) *trckd ldrs: rdn over 2f out: one pce and grad lost pl fnl f* **33/1**
0 **10** *1 ¼* **Sabbiosa (IRE)**[27] 3272 2-8-11 BDoyle 10 63+
(JLDunlop) *settled in last trio and rn green: sme prog 2f out: nt clr run ins fnl f and eased* **33/1**
**11** *3* **Fantaisiste** 2-8-11 SSanders 6 51
(SirMarkPrescott) *racd towards rr: effrt 3f out: sn rdn and struggling: wl btn over 1f out* **3/1**[2]
0 **12** *shd* **Resistance Heroine**[12] 3741 2-8-8 BReilly(3) 2 50
(EALDunlop) *racd in midfield: rdn over 2f out: sn struggling* **25/1**
0 **13** *6* **Entertain**[15] 3627 2-8-10 ow4 MSavage(3) 1 39
(MLWBell) *racd on outer and sn wl in tch: rdn over 3f out: rn green and sn wknd* **12/1**
0 **14** *4* **Georgina**[21] 3456 2-8-8 DCorby(3) 5 25
(MAJarvis) *trckd ldrs tl wknd 3f out* **8/1**
**15** *25* **French School** 2-8-11 TPQueally 15 —
(DRLoder) *mde most to 3f out: wknd rapidly and eased: t.o* **12/1**

1m 29.46s (1.66) **Going Correction** -0.025s/f (Good) **15** Ran SP% **126.8**
Speed ratings: **89,88,88,87,87 87,86,86,85,84 80,80,73,69,40**CSF £78.40 TOTE £6.40: £2.10, £3.40, £1.60; EX 115.50.
**Owner** Nicholas R Hodges **Bred** Miss K Rausing **Trained** East Everleigh, Wilts

**FOCUS**
The whole field went over to the far side. They finished in a heap and the form does not look up to much.

**NOTEBOOK**
**Hidden Chance** was last of all going to the two pole, but came with a strong flurry down the outer to snatch the race on the line. Another furlong will suit her.
**Sweet Lorraine** is out of an unraced half-sister to the Mills yard's Queen Elizabeth II Stakes winner Where Or When. She looked set to score entering the final furlong, but was denied right on the line.
**Velveteen Rabbit** is closely related to the stable's Dubai World Cup winner Moon Ballad. Up a furlong in trip from her debut, she kept on without mustering a change of pace having used up energy in tacking across from her low draw.
**Bongoali** is a sister to a couple of minor juvenile winners as well as useful middle-distance handicapper Pistol Pete. She showed ability despite appearing green.
**Flaunting It(IRE)**, a 40,000gns yearling, was keeping on quite nicely against the rail and should be capable of stepping up on this.
**Imperial Miss(IRE)** ran her best race to date but will remain vulnerable in this sort of company.
**Krumpet**, a half-sister to seven-furlong juvenile winner Bertocelli, was another keeping on at the death.
**Sabbiosa(IRE)**would have finished closer but for being eased when her path was blocked and ought to be capable of modest improvement. *Official explanation: jockey said filly ran out of room in the latter stages*
**Fantaisiste**, out of a half-sister to Gordon Stakes winner Germano, is bred to do better in time.
**French School** *Official explanation: jockey said filly lost her action*

## 4054 KENT AIR AMBULANCE TRUST (S) STKS 5f
**7:15** (7:15) (G) 2-Y-O **£2,863** (£818; £409) **Stalls** Low

Form RPR
6641 **1** **Piddies Pride (IRE)**[9] 3824 2-8-12 LDettori 5 64+
(PSMcentee) *w ldr: led 1/2-way: shkn up over 1f out: sn drew clr* **5/4**[1]
0210 **2** *5* **Keresforth**[5] 3930 2-9-3 (b) SSanders 4 52
(IAWood) *led to 1/2-way: chsd wnr after: no ch fnl f* **2/1**[2]

0 **3** *5* **His Majesty**[124] 1060 2-8-5 ........ StevenHarrison(7) 1 29
(NPLittmoden) *in tch: rdn 1/2-way: sn outpcd and struggling* **22/1**
44 **4** *9* **Cubic Confessions (IRE)**[110] 1240 2-8-7 ........ SWKelly 2 —
(JAOsborne) *s.i.s: in tch: shkn up 2f out: sn wknd: eased fnl f* **5/2**[3]
61.57 secs (0.87) **Going Correction** -0.025s/f (Good) **4** Ran SP% **110.7**
Speed ratings: **92,84,76,61**CSF £4.19 TOTE £1.70; EX 3.00.The winner was bought in for 13,500gns.
**Owner** Mrs B A McEntee **Bred** B Kennedy **Trained** Newmarket, Suffolk

**FOCUS**
A weakly-contested seller, but the winner is going the right way, although the form is worth treating with some caution.

**NOTEBOOK**
**Piddies Pride(IRE)**, claimed out of Ian Wood's yard after winning at Brighton, was much too good for her former stablemate. Unlikely to be inconvenienced by the return to six furlongs, she is improving and connections had to go to 13,500gns to buy her in.
**Keresforth**, back in selling company and with the blinkers reapplied, ran his race but was put in his place by the filly in the final furlong.
**His Majesty** had not run since finishing last in the first two-year-old race of the season at Lingfield back in March. He looks a very modest perfomer.
**Cubic Confessions(IRE)**, off the track since running in a couple of sand maidens in the spring, was beaten soon after halfway. She is not seeing out her races although she is bred to stay farther than this.

## 4055 COME BACK ON LADIES NIGHT H'CAP — 1m 4f
**7:45** (7:46) (F) (0-55,55) 3-Y-O — **£3,080** (£880; £440) **Stalls** Low

Form — RPR
0002 **1** **Bienheureux**[24] 3371 3-8-10 **45** ........ MFenton 13 51
(MissGayKelleway) *dwlt: settled in rr: sme prog 4f out: outpcd and rdn over 2f out: styd on strly u.p fnl f: led last stride* **10/1**
-056 **2** *hd* **Science Academy (USA)**[17] 3572 3-8-11 **51** ........ NDeSouza(5) 10 57
(PFICole) *led and set str pce: pressed 3f out: kicked 3l clr again over 1f out: hdd last stride* **14/1**
60-4 **3** *1 3/4* **A Monk Swimming (IRE)**[31] 3146 3-7-11 **35** oh3 ........ NMackay(3) 4 38
(JohnBerry) *chsd ldr to 8f out: styd prom: wnt 2nd again 2f out: sn rdn and no imp: one pce after* **9/1**
0053 **4** *hd* **Rinneen (IRE)**[14] 3669 3-8-11 **46** ........ (v) RLMoore 5 49
(RHannon) *racd in midfield: rdn 5f out: effrt u.p over 2f out: styd on fr over 1f out: nvr able to chal* **7/1**
2234 **5** *4* **Regal Performer (IRE)**[14] 3669 3-9-6 **55** ........ LDettori 14 51
(SKirk) *sn trckd ldrs: gng wl enough 3f out: rdn and nt qckn 2f out: fdd* **11/2**[3]
4024 **6** *3* **The King Of Rock**[17] 3572 3-9-3 **55** ........ LPKeniry(3) 9 47
(AGNewcombe) *t.k.h: chsd ldr 8f out to 2f out: wknd* **5/1**[2]
0000 **7** *3* **Venetian Romance (IRE)**[13] 3700 3-8-0 **40** ........ RThomas(5) 1 27
(APJones) *dwlt: wl in rr: lost tch 4f out: wl bhd over 2f out: rdn and styd on sn after: no ch* **33/1**
00 **8** *6* **Jango Malfoy (IRE)**[98] 1422 3-9-3 **52** ........ (t) ADaly 8 29
(BWDuke) *sn wl in rr: last and detached 7f out: wl bhd 4f out: rdn 2f out: plodded on* **80/1**
6-00 **9** *hd* **Cazisa Star (USA)**[21] 3459 3-9-6 **55** ........ EAhern 7 32
(PWHarris) *racd in midfield: lost pl and pushed along 5f out: brief effrt to chse clr ldng gp 2f out: no imp: wknd and eased* **25/1**
356 **10** *5* **Mrs Brown**[160] 760 3-9-6 **55** ........ SSanders 12 24
(SirMarkPrescott) *prom: rdn 5f out: stl chsng ldrs u.p over 2f out: wknd over 1f out: heavilt eased* **11/4**[1]
0363 **11** *3 1/2* **Vrisaki (IRE)**[21] 3461 3-8-8 **48** ........ DFox(5) 2 11
(MissDMountain) *t.k.h: trckd ldrs: rdn and in tch over 2f out: sn wknd: eased fnl f* **8/1**
006 **12** *13* **Scott**[22] 3422 3-9-6 **55** ........ TEDurcan 3 —
(JJay) *racd in midfield: lost pl and rdn 5f out: wl bhd fnl 3f* **20/1**
0 **13** *nk* **Newtown Chief**[15] 3636 3-8-7 **49** ........ StevenHarrison(7) 11 —
(NPLittmoden) *t.k.h: chsd ldrs for 5f: sn lost pl: wl bhd fnl 3f* **66/1**
-000 **14** *11* **Ocean Rock**[51] 2562 3-9-6 **55** ........ DaneO'Neill 6 —
(CAHorgan) *dwlt: a towards rr: wl bhd fnl 3f: t.o* **10/1**
2m 41.2s (0.80) **Going Correction** +0.025s/f (Good) **14** Ran SP% **131.5**
Speed ratings: **98,97,96,96,93 91,89,85,85,82 80,71,71,63**CSF £148.67 CT £1342.19 TOTE £13.00: £4.40, £4.70, £3.20; EX 327.20.
**Owner** Countrywide Classics Limited **Bred** N R Shields **Trained** Newmarket, Suffolk

**FOCUS**
A low-grade handicap run at a fair pace, and this is modest form.

**NOTEBOOK**
**Bienheureux**, previously with Willie Musson, confirmed the improvement he showed last time, with the horse who beat him at Pontefract having since franked the form. From a 5lb higher mark, he had plenty on his plate turning for home but stayed on well inside the last to snatch it on the line.
**Science Academy(USA)** , edging down the weights, was given a fine ride from the front by her Brazilian jockey who sent her for home off the turn. She looked to have it in the bag passing the furlong but was just caught.
**A Monk Swimming(IRE)** ran a decent race on this switch to a mile and a half, although he did not quite see it out after racing up with the pace. He is finding his way now and has plenty of room for improvement from his lowly mark.
**Rinneen(IRE)** again shaped as if she could be worth a try over 14 furlongs, although in all probability she is rather slow.
**Regal Performer(IRE)** ran his race again but did not really convince over this trip.
**Mrs Brown** stepped up in trip for her handicap bow after three runs on sand at up to a mile, was being ridden along and looked in trouble some way out. She was eased when finally seen off, accentuating the margin of defeat.

## 4056 GERALD LUKEHURST & SON FURNISHERS H'CAP — 1m 1f 149y
**8:15** (8:15) (D ) (0-80,77) 3-Y-O — **£5,508** (£1,695; £847; £423) **Stalls** Low

Form — RPR
2111 **1** **Masafi (IRE)**[3] 3990 3-8-3 **59** 6ex ........ SSanders 2 73+
(SirMarkPrescott) *led 7f out: mde rest: clr 4f out: 6l ahd 2f out: unchal and won w plenty in hand* **2/9**[1]
0640 **2** *3* **Little Eye (IRE)**[7] 3875 3-8-5 **61** ........ (v) TPQueally 3 64
(JRBest) *hld up in last pair: rdn and prog 3f out: chsd wnr 2f out: kpt on wl but no ch* **25/1**
5000 **3** *1 3/4* **Keepers Knight (IRE)**[17] 3589 3-8-1 **62** ........ NDeSouza(5) 6 62
(PFICole) *settled in detached last: prog 3f out: drvn to chse ldng pair over 1f out: kpt on wl* **33/1**
-555 **4** *13* **Mommkin**[29] 3213 3-9-1 **71** ........ TEDurcan 7 46
(MRChannon) *trckd ldrs: no imp 3f out: wknd 2f out: sn bhd* **14/1**[3]
0135 **5** *1 1/4* **Alfridini**[12] 3750 3-9-0 **73** ........ LPKeniry(3) 1 46
(DRCElsworth) *trckd ldrs: drvn over 3f out: effrt to dispute 2nd pl over 2f out: sn wknd* **9/1**[2]
3150 **6** *3 1/2* **Tannoor (USA)**[22] 3415 3-9-7 **77** ........ PRobinson 5 43
(MAJarvis) *led to 7f out: chsd wnr to 2f out: wknd: sn bhd* **16/1**
6063 **7** *4* **Bailaora (IRE)**[19] 3535 3-9-2 **72** ........ (b) RLMoore 4 31
(BWDuke) *trckd ldrs: wknd over 2f out: sn bhd* **20/1**
2m 3.22s (-1.94) **Going Correction** +0.025s/f (Good) **7** Ran SP% **115.9**
Speed ratings: **108,105,104,93,92 90,86**CSF £11.66 TOTE £1.20: £1.10, £10.90; EX 12.60.
**Owner** G D Waters **Bred** G D Waters **Trained** Newmarket, Suffolk

**FOCUS**
A moderate handicap and another victory for the progressive Masafi, in a time two seconds faster than the subsequent maiden over this trip.

**NOTEBOOK**
**Masafi(IRE)** made it four wins in 11 days and was able to race off the same mark as when landing the hat-trick. He went on after a couple of furlongs and, stepping up the pace, had all his rivals in trouble with half a mile to run. Value for far more than three lengths, with his rider looking over his shoulder on six occasions up the straight, he is another shining example of his trainer's mastery of the programme book.
**Little Eye(IRE)** kept on from the rear but is flattered to have finished as close to the winner as he did. He has had plenty of chances but is running well in the visor.
**Keepers Knight(IRE)**, some way off the pace for much of the way, kept on up the home straight for third, finishing well clear of the remainder. He does not look particularly well treated at present.
**Mommkin** turned around Salisbury form with Alfridini but the pair were well beaten.
**Alfridini**looks potentially a better horse on Polytrack.
**Tannoor(USA)** has been found wanting in handicaps since winning his maiden.

## 4057 COME EVENING RACING AGAIN ON AUGUST 5TH MEDIAN AUCTION MAIDEN STKS — 1m 1f 149y
**8:45** (8:46) (F ) 3-4-Y-O — **£2,961** (£846; £423) **Stalls** Low

Form — RPR
0330 **1** **Fuel Cell (IRE)**[17] 3589 3-8-11 **65** ........ RLMoore 7 71+
(RHannon) *chsd ldr: rdn to ld 3f out: looked reluctant but drvn clr over 1f out* **15/8**[1]
0 **2** *2* **Topkat (IRE)**[28] 3245 3-8-8 ........ LPKeniry(3) 5 67
(DRCElsworth) *s.s: racd in last pair: rdn and struggling 3f out: prog 2f out: chsd wnr 1f out: kpt on but nvr able to chal* **4/1**
-406 **3** *7* **Scarrabus (IRE)**[48] 2648 3-8-11 **69** ........ LDettori 4 54
(BGPowell) *chsd ldrs: rdn over 3f out: disp 2nd pl over 1f out: one pce and no imp* **3/1**[2]
00 **4** *4* **Sayrianna**[15] 3630 3-8-6 ........ TPQueally 1 41
(IAWood) *led to 3f out: chsd wnr to 1f out: wknd* **33/1**
006 **5** *1 1/4* **Preston Hall**[14] 3666 3-8-6 **50** ........ RThomas(5) 6 44
(MrsLCJewell) *trckd ldrs: rdn 3f out: wknd rapidly over 1f out* **66/1**
**6** *9* **Witching** 3-8-6 ........ EAhern 3 22
(DJDaly) *s.s: a in last pair: lost tch 3f out* **7/2**[3]
00- **P** **Tiz Molly (IRE)**[259] 5934 3-8-6 ........ TEDurcan 2 —
(MRChannon) *chsd ldrs tl p.u 7f out: broke down* **20/1**
2m 5.50s (0.34) **Going Correction** +0.025s/f (Good) **7** Ran SP% **111.2**
Speed ratings: **99,97,91,88,87 80,**—CSF £9.12 TOTE £2.70: £1.60, £2.30; EX 11.30 Place 6 £217.94, Place 5 £44.05.
**Owner** A F M (Holdings) Ltd **Bred** David Browne **Trained** East Everleigh, Wilts

**FOCUS**
A moderate event run at a decent pace, although the winner did not need to be at his best to score.

**NOTEBOOK**
**Fuel Cell(IRE)** took advantage of a good opportunity in this weak affair. After being ridden along to take command, he hung left quite badly early in the home straight but ran on well enough once straightened up to score decisively.
**Topkat(IRE)**, again slowly away, eventually found his stride in the final two furlongs and was closing on the winner at the end. He is learning with experience and needs one more run for a handicap mark.
**Scarrabus(IRE)**, ridden more prominently than he has been in recent races, had no real excuse.
**Sayrianna** ran her best race to date and is now eligible for handicaps.
**Preston Hall** faced a stiff task on these terms.
**Witching**, a half-sister to several winners abroad, was backed down from 8/1 for this debut but was always toiling after missing the break.
T/Plt: £207.80 to a £1 stake. Pool: £35,646.10. 125.20 winning tickets. T/Qpdt: £40.70 to a £1 stake. Pool: £2,599.60. 47.15 winning tickets. JN

# 4029 SANDOWN (R-H)
Thursday, July 22

**OFFICIAL GOING: Good to firm**

## 4058 KEITH PARKER "SUN-ICE AIR-CONDITIONING" MAIDEN AUCTION STKS — 5f 6y
**2:10** (2:12) (E ) 2-Y-O — **£4,163** (£1,281; £640; £320) **Stalls** High

Form — RPR
036 **1** **Pitch Up (IRE)**[17] 3588 2-9-0 ........ KFallon 8 77+
(TGMills) *lw: mde all: drvn and kpt finding ex thrght fnl f: readily* **7/2**[2]
2253 **2** *1/2* **Agent Kensington**[19] 3532 2-8-2 ........ RLMoore 5 63
(RHannon) *lw: rr but in tch: hdwy fr 2f out to chse wnr appr fnl f: kpt on but a hld* **7/2**[2]
**3** *1 1/4* **Cusoon** 2-8-7 ........ JFortune 7 64
(GLMoore) *leggy: scope: lw: s.i.s: bhd: rdn and hdwy over 1f out: kpt on wl fnl f but nt rch ldrs* **33/1**
066 **4** *nk* **Pennestamp (IRE)**[12] 3748 2-8-7 ........ RHavlin 2 63
(MrsPNDutfield) *wnt lft s: sn rcvrd and chsd wnr after 1f: rdn 2f out: outpcd fnl f* **33/1**
00 **5** *1/2* **Mister Aziz (IRE)**[16] 3611 2-8-7 ........ SSanders 1 61
(JMPEustace) *pushed lft s: sn in tch: rdn to chse ldrs over 1f out: one pce ins fnl f* **50/1**
2 **6** *3* **Sound That Alarm**[12] 3729 2-8-11 ........ SWKelly 3 54
(GAButler) *lw: chsd ldrs: rdn and edgd rt 2f out: wknd fnl f* **11/10**[1]
**7** *2* **Monashee Rose (IRE)** 2-8-2 ........ EAhern 9 38
(JSMoore) *wl-grwn: bit bkwd: s.i.s: a outpcd in rr* **40/1**
3 **8** *3 1/2* **Homme Dangereux**[41] 2852 2-8-9 ........ PRobinson 6 33
(CREgerton) *bit bkwd: chsd ldrs: rdn and hmpd on rails 2f out: sn wknd* **20/1**
**9** *5* **Floosie (IRE)** 2-8-4 ........ (t) TPQueally 4 11
(NPLittmoden) *str: bkwd: a outpcd* **12/1**[3]
61.72 secs (-0.47) **Going Correction** -0.25s/f (Firm) **9** Ran SP% **114.8**
Speed ratings: **93,92,90,89,88 84,80,75,67**CSF £15.13 TOTE £5.00: £1.10, £1.60, £8.00; EX 18.20.
**Owner** B G Chamley **Bred** Peter McCutcheon **Trained** Headley, Surrey

**FOCUS**
Only an ordinary maiden and it was left down to two relatively exposed runners to fight it out.

**NOTEBOOK**
**Pitch Up(IRE)** was smartly into his stride and took full advantage of his high draw, bagging the far rail and leading early before holding off all challenges to win with a little in hand. He had been disappointing prior to this, but seems to have got his act together and may be capable of winning in nursery company.
**Agent Kensington** ran another good race in defeat and pulled away from the third. He deserves to win a race.
**Cusoon** is bred to want another furlong or so in time and after taking time to find his stride, came home well to get up for third. This was a pleasing debut and he should find an ordinary maiden his for the taking.
**Pennestamp(IRE)** has run some fair races in defeat and may find life easier in handicaps if getting a decent mark. *Official explanation: jockey said colt hung right*
**Mister Aziz(IRE)** is now qualified for nurseries and will appreciate stepping back up in trip.
**Sound That Alarm** was a bitter disappointment, having run so well when second on his debut, but it is possible making his debut in a track like Chester threw him, as this was a contrasting test, and he deserves another chance. *Official explanation: trainer said colt was found to be slightly lame after the race*
**Homme Dangereux** *Official explanation: jockey said colt was unsuited by good to firm ground*

## 4059 SUNGARD SECURITIES FINANCE H'CAP — 5f 6y
**2:45** (2:46) (D) (0-85,85) 3-Y-O — **£6,971** (£2,145; £1,072; £536) **Stalls** High

Form — RPR
0-21 **1** **Royal Challenge**[19] 3511 3-8-11 **75**.......... SSanders 2 — 89+
(GAButler) *lw: trckd ldrs: chal: edgd rt and sn led 1f out: drvn out* **10/3**[1]
110 **2** ½ **Buy On The Red**[8] 3845 3-9-6 **84**.......... RHughes 10 — 91+
(WRMuir) *lw: trckd ldrs: squeezed through to chal ins fnl f: kpt on wl but nt pce of wnr cl home* **11/2**[2]
5310 **3** ½ **Treasure Cay**[11] 3777 3-9-1 **79**.......... (t) KDarley 8 — 84
(PWD'Arcy) *w ldr tl slt advantage fr 2f out: hdd 1f out: styd chalng tl no ex fnl 100yds* **11/2**[2]
00-1 **4** nk **Tregarron**[30] 3179 3-8-6 **70**.......... RLMoore 6 — 74
(RHannon) *chsd ldrs: rdn 2f out: kpt on same pce ins last* **8/1**
3661 **5** hd **Jadan (IRE)**[11] 3777 3-8-11 **75** 6ex.......... WSupple 5 — 78
(EJAlston) *chsd ldrs: rdn 2f out: styd on same pce ins fnl f* **7/1**[3]
6103 **6** ¾ **Divine Spirit**[13] 3702 3-9-7 **85**.......... ACulhane 1 — 86+
(MDods) *stdd s: hdwy and swtchd rt whn nt clr run 1f out: nt clr run after: nt rcvr and fin on bit* **10/1**
400- **7** nk **Morgan Lewis (IRE)**[364] 3529 3-7-10 **65** ow2.......... RThomas(5) 4 — 64+
(GBBalding) *h.d.w: lw: bhd: hdwy on ins whn bdly hmpd 1f out: nt rcvr* **14/1**
1043 **8** 3½ **Borzoi Maestro**[8] 3845 3-8-12 **76**.......... (p) KMcEvoy 9 — 63
(JLSpearing) *led tl narrowly hdd 2f out: wknd fnl f* **10/1**
4500 **9** 1 **Dolce Piccata**[29] 3203 3-8-13 **77**.......... (b) JFortune 7 — 60+
(BJMeehan) *s.i.s: bhd: hdwy on rails whn bdly hmpd 1f out: nt rcvr* **20/1**
02-0 **10** 14 **Sion Hill (IRE)**[6] 3920 3-9-0 **78**.......... (v[1]) KFallon 11 — 11
(SirMichaelStoute) *hung bdly rt thrght and nt keen* **12/1**

60.45 secs (-1.74) **Going Correction** -0.25s/f (Firm) **10** Ran SP% **114.8**
Speed ratings: **103,102,101,100,100 99,98,93,91,69**CSF £20.72 CT £99.22 TOTE £4.30: £1.50, £2.00, £3.00; EX 19.60.
**Owner** Cheveley Park Stud **Bred** Capt A L Smith-Maxwell **Trained** Blewbury, Oxon
■ Stewards Enquiry : A Culhane two-day ban: careless riding (Aug 2-3)

**FOCUS**
A competitive and decent sprint handicap although there were a couple of hard luck stories. It was won by a progressive sprinter and the form looks reasonably sound.

**NOTEBOOK**
**Royal Challenge** has the making of a real progressive sprinter and this was his second win on the bounce. Successful in his maiden at Beverley, he took this first step into handicap company in his stride and stayed on well to win despite getting a little warm. A rise in the weights will follow, but he looks up to defying it and could have a decent race in him before the season is out.
**Buy On The Red** had been on a roll prior to disappointing last time, and this was much more like his form. He continues to improve, but will need to if he is to defy his current mark.
**Treasure Cay**, unsuited by the good to soft ground when down the field at Haydock earlier in the month, came back to form on this faster surface and reversed form with Jadan in the process.
**Tregarron** beat Royal Challenge at Newbury last month - both making their seasonal debuts - but that one has progressed since and he could not confirm the form, although he still ran well.
**Jadan(IRE)** failed to confirm Haydock form with Treasure Cay under his 6lb penalty.
**Divine Spirit** was most unlucky, getting no run whatsoever throughout the final furlong or so and finishing full of running. He is likely to be underpriced next time as a result.
**Morgan Lewis(IRE)**, having his first run since this meeting last year - finished eighth in the opening maiden - was also unlucky not to get closer, having to switch out wide having been badly hampered. He too finished with plenty up his sleeve and is another going to be priced accordingly next time.
**Dolce Piccata** never had a chance to get involved, being badly hampered when trying to make ground.
**Sion Hill(IRE)** was hanging throughout in the first-time visor, and either has a physical problem or a mental one. *Official explanation: jockey said gelding lost his action*

## 4060 STAR STKS (LISTED RACE) (FILLIES) — 7f 16y
**3:15** (3:22) (A) 2-Y-O — **£17,400** (£6,600; £3,300; £1,500) **Stalls** High

Form — RPR
1 **1** **Queen Of Poland**[21] 3456 2-8-9.......... TPQueally 7 — 101
(DRLoder) *lw: in tch: hdwy over 2f out: chsd ldr over 1f out: rdn to chal ins last: asserted and kpt on wl fnl 100yds* **13/2**
21 **2** hd **Maids Causeway (IRE)**[29] 3202 2-8-9.......... KFallon 10 — 100
(BWHills) *lw: trckd ldrs: wnt 2nd 3f out: slt ld jst ins fnl 2f: rdn and kpt on fnl f: hdd and no ex fnl 100yds* **5/2**[1]
5213 **3** 3½ **Bentley's Bush (IRE)**[12] 3727 2-8-9.......... RHughes 1 — 91
(RHannon) *hld up in rr: hdwy fr 2f out: rdn fnl f: styd on wl cl home but nt pce to rch ldrs* **16/1**
1 **4** shd **Borthwick Girl (IRE)**[27] 3272 2-8-9.......... KDarley 2 — 91
(BJMeehan) *lw: sn chsng ldr: rdn and outpcd 2f out: styd on u.p fnl f but nt pce to rch ldrs* **16/1**
21 **5** ¾ **Park Law (IRE)**[15] 3627 2-8-9.......... JFortune 5 — 89
(JHMGosden) *sn led: hdd jst ins fnl f: wknd ins fnl f* **3/1**[2]
103 **6** ½ **Golden Anthem (USA)**[26] 3316 2-8-9.......... JQuinn 9 — 88
(JPearce) *t.k.h: chsd ldrs: rdn and effrt over 1f out: no imp: wknd ins last* **9/1**
314 **7** 1¾ **Shivaree**[16] 3599 2-8-9.......... TEDurcan 8 — 84
(MRChannon) *chsd ldrs: rdn 3f out: wknd fr 2f out* **5/1**[3]
301 **8** shd **Vondova**[14] 3676 2-8-9.......... DaneO'Neill 3 — 83
(RHannon) *bhd: rdn and effrt on outside over 2f out: nvr gng pce to rch ldrs* **20/1**
**9** ½ **Lady Pilot** 2-8-9.......... SSanders 4 — 82
(CEBrittain) *leggy: unf: rdn 3f out: a outpcd* **20/1**

1m 29.67s (-1.42) **Going Correction** -0.075s/f (Good) **9** Ran SP% **113.0**
Speed ratings: **105,104,100,100,99 99,97,97,96**CSF £22.58 TOTE £7.20: £1.60, £1.60, £2.30; EX 19.30.
**Owner** Sheikh Mohammed **Bred** Darley **Trained** Newmarket, Suffolk

**FOCUS**
Not a strong Listed race by any means - third placed horse held off a mark of 82 in a nursery earlier in the month - and the 'yardstick' with regards to the form ( Shivaree ) ran way below par.

**NOTEBOOK**
**Queen Of Poland** made a pleasing start to her career when winning at Yarmouth earlier in the month, and was well supported in the market on this first venture into Listed company. She came through to challenge Maids Causeway and took some time to get on top before going on and then having to hold off a renewed challenge from the favourite. She will stay a mile and should improve again.
**Maids Causeway(IRE)**, representing last season's winning trainer, struck the front around two furlongs out and kept running all the way to the line, just coming off worse in the battle. This is probabaly her grade and it will be a surprise if she is up to Group company.
**Bentley's Bush(IRE)** stepped up on her previous form in a nursery to just snatch third. She was well held by the front pair though and probably failed to achieve as much as it may look.
**Borthwick Girl(IRE)** stepped up on her debut form and was narrowly run out of third. She should stay further.
**Park Law(IRE)**, second behind Maids Causeway on her debut, has subsequently won her maiden and was evidently fancied. Having led she was easily passed and faded disappointingly. She is likely to be hard to place from now on.
**Golden Anthem(USA)** had her chance and is another difficult to place.
**Shivaree** was very disappointing as she set the standard on her fourth-place finish in the Cherry Hinton. She held a good early position but dropped away once coming under pressure.

## 4061 SANDOWN PARK RACING PLUS H'CAP — 1m 2f 7y
**3:50** (3:50) (C) (0-90,86) 3-Y-O+ — **£10,192** (£3,136; £1,568; £784) **Stalls** High

Form — RPR
P21- **1** **Sky Quest (IRE)**[275] 5695 6-9-10 **82**.......... (tp) RLMoore 4 — 93+
(PWHarris) *hld up rr but in tch:hdwy on rails over 1f out: drvn: squeezed through and qcknd to ld fnl 100yds* **8/1**
-021 **2** nk **Adaikali (IRE)**[45] 2732 3-9-4 **86**.......... KFallon 3 — 96+
(SirMichaelStoute) *lw: trckd ldr: led gng wl 3f out: shkn up 1f out: hdd: edgd lft and fnd no ex fnl 100yds* **10/11**[1]
5104 **3** nk **Whitsbury Cross**[19] 3543 3-8-12 **80**.......... DaneO'Neill 1 — 90+
(DRCElsworth) *lw: hld up rr but in tch: hdwy 2f out: chsd ldr appr fnl f: styng on but one pce whn bmpd fnl 100yds* **7/1**[3]
0034 **4** 6 **Stretton (IRE)**[20] 3482 6-9-8 **80**.......... (p) PRobinson 2 — 78
(JDBethell) *in tch: drvn to trck ldr 2f out: rdn over 1f out: wknd ins last* **11/4**[2]
5-00 **5** 2 **Great Scott**[19] 3542 3-9-2 **84**.......... SChin 5 — 79
(MJohnston) *led: 5l clr 7f out: hdd 3f out: wknd u.p over 1f out* **20/1**
00-0 **6** 7 **San Antonio**[80] 1840 4-9-7 **79**.......... ACulhane 6 — 60
(MrsPSly) *bit bkwd: in tch tl wknd 2f out* **50/1**

2m 9.11s (-1.07) **Going Correction** -0.075s/f (Good)
**WFA** 3 from 4yo+ 10lb **6** Ran SP% **109.4**
Speed ratings: **101,100,100,95,94 88**CSF £15.09 TOTE £7.60: £2.50, £1.60; EX 10.60.
**Owner** Colourful Band **Bred** Pendley Farm **Trained** Ringshall, Bucks

**FOCUS**
Probably not a bad little handicap and a seemingly improved performance from Sky Quest. The form looks reasonable and should work out.

**NOTEBOOK**
**Sky Quest(IRE)** looked to face a stiff task conceding the 10lb weight-for-age to the three-year-olds, and really needed to improve on his best to win. He seemingly did just that, nipping through on the rail late on to deny a couple of progressive colts. He will take a rise in the ratings for this and may need to improve again if he is to defy it.
**Adaikali(IRE)** came into this as a progressive colt, winning in gritty fashion at Pontefract last month, but he had no answer to the late burst of Sky Quest. This was still a good effort and, using the third as a form guide, this was an improved effort.
**Whitsbury Cross** has been in good form of late, stepping up on maiden form with his best run to date when fourth in a course and distance handicap earlier in the month. This was another sound effort and his racing style suggests he will get another couple of furlongs.
**Stretton(IRE)** ran a bit below form, folding tamely in the final furlong.
**Great Scott** was trying this trip for the first time and raced too keenly in the lead. He should continue to fall in the weights and will eventually get his act back together.

## 4062 SHARP MINDS BETFAIR H'CAP — 1m 6f
**4:25** (4:25) (D) (0-85,85) 3-Y-O — **£6,971** (£2,145; £1,072; £536) **Stalls** Centre

Form — RPR
3511 **1** **Peak Of Perfection (IRE)**[26] 3292 3-9-4 **82**.......... PRobinson 5 — 88+
(MAJarvis) *led 4f: styd trcking ldr: chal fr 3f out: rdn and styd on gamely to ld wl ins fnl f* **8/1**[2]
1210 **2** nk **Considine (USA)**[28] 3236 3-8-7 **71**.......... SSanders 9 — 76+
(JMPEustace) *swtg: chsd ldrs: chal 3f out tl led 2f out: styd on wl tl hdd and no ex wl ins last* **9/2**[1]
0023 **3** shd **Coventina (IRE)**[39] 2910 3-9-7 **85**.......... KDarley 4 — 90
(JLDunlop) *hld up in rr: nudged along on outside and styd on under hand driving but carried hd high ins fnl f: nt quite get up* **9/1**[3]
1400 **4** 1 **Man At Arms (IRE)**[10] 3806 3-9-0 **78**.......... RLMoore 6 — 82
(RHannon) *lw: mid-div: hdwy and rdn fr 2f out: chsd ldrs ins fnl f: nt qckn cl home* **20/1**
6561 **5** ½ **Hathlen (IRE)**[41] 2840 3-8-12 **76**.......... TEDurcan 2 — 79
(MRChannon) *bhd: rdn 3f out: hdwy over 1f out: styd on u.p fnl f: nt rch ldrs* **10/1**
-412 **6** hd **Bienvenue**[10] 3806 3-8-5 **69**.......... WSupple 10 — 72
(MPTregoning) *lw: chsd ldrs: rdn over 2f out: wknd wl ins fnl f* **9/2**[1]
-022 **7** 1¾ **Levitator**[15] 3629 3-8-6 **70**.......... KFallon 8 — 70
(SirMichaelStoute) *chsd ldrs: led 3f out: hdd 2f out: wknd fnl f* **9/2**[1]
433 **8** hd **Shongweni (IRE)**[25] 3348 3-8-3 **67**.......... (b[1]) JQuinn 11 — 67+
(PJMcbride) *chsd ldrs: rdn and effrt fr 2f out: chsd ldrs over 1f out: wknd ins fnl f* **9/1**[3]
1400 **9** 1 **Bukit Fraser (IRE)**[29] 3210 3-9-3 **81**.......... ACulhane 3 — 79
(PFICole) *bhd drvn along fr 3f out: styd on fr over 1f out but nvr nr ldrs* **16/1**
53-5 **10** ¾ **Salamba**[83] 1747 3-8-8 **72**.......... MHenry 12 — 69
(MHTompkins) *rdn 3f out: a in rr* **25/1**
0020 **11** ¾ **Master Wells (IRE)**[17] 3584 3-9-0 **78**.......... KMcEvoy 13 — 74
(JDBethell) *a in rr* **16/1**
3122 **12** 3 **Garston Star**[14] 3658 3-7-7 **62** oh2.......... BSwarbrick(5) 1 — 54
(JSMoore) *plld hrd: led after 4f: hdd 3f out: wknd rapidly ins fnl 2f* **25/1**

3m 3.92s (-0.45) **Going Correction** -0.075s/f (Good) **12** Ran SP% **119.0**
Speed ratings: **98,97,97,97,96 96,95,95,95,94 94,92**CSF £42.87 CT £333.00 TOTE £7.30: £2.80, £2.20, £2.90; EX 41.40 Trifecta £105.80 Pool: £1,639.33. 11.00 winning units..
**Owner** H R H Sultan Ahmad Shah **Bred** Hrh Sultan Ahmad Shah **Trained** Newmarket, Suffolk

**FOCUS**
A decent staying handicap and it was taken by a highly progressive gelding. Although the form not as strong as it might have been, the winner looks one to follow.

**NOTEBOOK**

**Peak Of Perfection(IRE)** came into this in good form - he had won his two most recent starts - but looked to be doing too much too early. However, this did not seem to affect him and, once Garston Star took the lead off him, he seemed to relax a little better. He picked up strongly in the straight and found plenty under pressure to deny Considine. A highly progressive gelding, there is no reason why he cannot improve again.

**Considine(USA)** got a little warm beforehand, but it did not appear to effect his performance and he went down fighting. He seemed suited to this drop back down in trip and should continue to pay his way.

**Coventina(IRE)** did not look too keen for pressure and would have won had she not carried her head so high. Whether she was feeling the ground, or simply did not want to go by, is open to question, but either way she did not look one to make a habit of backing.

**Man At Arms(IRE)** ran a fair enough race in defeat, plugging on at the one pace and could be worth trying over two miles.

**Hathlen(IRE)** is another for whom two miles will help as he has no change of pace.

**Bienvenue** seemingly failed to stay the trip and will be better suited by the return to a mile and a half.

**Levitator** looked a huge threat turning in but faded disappointingly. He is one to avoid.

## 4063 SHARP MINDS BETFAIR MAIDEN STKS — 1m 14y

5:00 (5:00) (D) 3-4-Y-O — £5,577 (£1,716; £858; £429) Stalls High

| Form | | | Horse | Jockey | RPR |
|---|---|---|---|---|---|
| 2 | 1 | | **Serre Chevalier (IRE)**[54] 2479 3-8-13 (PWHarris) *trckd ldr: chal 2f out: styd pressing challenging tl drvn to ld ins fnl f: kpt on wl to assert cl home* **4/7**[1] | EAhern 1 | 81 |
| 30 | 2 | hd | **Minority Report**[31] 3154 4-9-4 (LMCumani) *lw: trckd ldrs: drvn to take slt ld 2f out: hdd ins last: edgd lft but styd w wnr tl no ex home* **7/2**[2] | NMackay(3) 2 | 81 |
| 5/3 | 3 | 5 | **Silent Storm**[27] 3279 4-9-7 (HJCyzer) *led tl hdd 2f out: wknd appr fnl f* **9/2**[3] | FLynch 6 | 69 |
| 0 | 4 | 9 | **Chem's Legacy (IRE)**[33] 3085 4-9-7 (WRMuir) *lw: chsd ldrs: rdn 3f out: sn btn* **50/1** | SChin 3 | 48 |
| 0-00 | P | | **Curzon Lodge (IRE)**[41] 2833 4-9-7 (CTinkler) *a wl bhd: t.o whn wnt lame 2f out: p.u and dismntd ins fnl f* **50/1** | JQuinn 5 | — |

1m 44.0s (0.08) **Going Correction** -0.075s/f (Good)

**WFA** 3 from 4yo 8lb — **5** Ran SP% **108.0**

Speed ratings: **96,95,90,81,**—CSF £2.74 TOTE £1.50: £1.10, £1.60; EX 2.40 Place 6 £20.54, Place 5 £6.55.

**Owner** Mrs P W Harris **Bred** Ski Lodge Partnership **Trained** Ringshall, Bucks

**FOCUS**

A very ordinary maiden to close, with the winner probably running to similar level to sound debut form.

**NOTEBOOK**

**Serre Chevalier(IRE)** shaped with an abundance of promise when second on his debut at Kempton - albeit in a race that has not worked out - and he was rightly made a short-priced favourite. However, he made hard work of it, and it was only deep in the final furlong that he looked in control. He was made to panic late on as Minority Report tried to get back at him, but he was always just holding on.

**Minority Report** ran well in defeat and left behind a disappointing run at Nottingham. He is now qualified for handicaps.

**Silent Storm** ran a much better race than on his reappearance and should be suited by seven furlongs in a much lesser race.

**Curzon Lodge(IRE)** *Official explanation: jockey said gelding pulled up lame*

T/Jkpt: £118,905.80 to a £1 stake. Pool: £167,473.00. 1.00 winning ticket. T/Plt: £25.70 to a £1 stake. Pool: £60,464.80. 1,716.40 winning tickets. T/Qpdt: £5.10 to a £1 stake. Pool: £3,425.70. 496.80 winning tickets. ST

# 3456 YARMOUTH (L-H)

Thursday, July 22

**OFFICIAL GOING: Good (good to firm in places)**

Wind: almost nil Weather: fine & sunny

## 4064 BRITANNIA PIER THEATRE SUMMER SEASON MAIDEN STKS — 5f 43y

2:00 (2:01) (D) 2-Y-O — £3,354 (£1,032; £516; £258) Stalls High

| Form | | | Horse | Jockey | RPR |
|---|---|---|---|---|---|
| 6 | 1 | | **Rubyanne (IRE)**[59] 2370 2-8-9 (MJWallace) *settled 3rd: effrt 2f out: pushed ahd over 1f out: sn burst clr* **1/3**[1] | DHolland 5 | 84+ |
| | 2 | 4 | **Danehill Willy (IRE)** 2-9-0 (NACallaghan) *dwlt: rdn along: effrt and unbalanced 2f out: r.o stoutly ins fnl f to go 2nd cl home: will improve* **10/1**[3] | RMullen 6 | 68+ |
| 06 | 3 | 3/4 | **Il Pranzo**[10] 3805 2-9-0 (SKirk) *led: rdn 2f out: hdd over 1f out: onepced and demoted nr fin* **20/1** | MFenton 1 | 65 |
| 06 | 4 | 2 | **Chairman Rick (IRE)**[8] 3847 2-9-0 (DRLoder) *dwlt: rr div: effrt over 2f out: sn no imp* **28/1** | NPollard 3 | 58+ |
| 5 | 5 | 1 3/4 | **Dralion**[22] 3424 2-9-0 (JMPEustace) *pressed ldr 4f: wknd 1f out* **6/1**[2] | MHills 2 | 52 |
| | 6 | 6 | **In Rhubarb** 2-8-7 (IWMcinnes) *taken gingerly to s: s.i.s: effrt and rn green 2f out: sn wknd* **50/1** | (t) NataliaGemelova(7) 4 | 31 |

63.60 secs (0.90) **Going Correction** +0.05s/f (Good) — **6** Ran SP% **108.6**

Speed ratings: **94,87,86,83,80 70**CSF £3.87 TOTE £1.30: £1.10, £3.40; EX 3.70.

**Owner** H E Sheikh Rashid Bin Mohammed **Bred** Khorshed And Ian Deane And Eamonn Phelan **Trained** Newmarket, Suffolk

■ Stewards Enquiry : D Holland caution: careless riding

**FOCUS**

Not that strong a maiden and most of these are nursery types, but the winner is held in high regard and won very nicely.

**NOTEBOOK**

**Rubyanne(IRE)** would have gone close to beating the promising Pike Bishop on her debut at Windsor but for losing around ten lengths with a slow start, but had not been seen since due to some niggling problems, including ringworm. Racing for the first time in 59 days, she was able to confirm that initial promise with a most decisive success. Holland told connections afterwards she is the best filly he has sat on this year and it is all systems go for either the Molecomb or the Listed Roses Stakes at York.

**Danehill Willy(IRE)**, a 35,000gns yearling, half-brother to several winners, including a seven-furlong two-year-old winner, was nibbled at in the betting, but was no match for the winner. However, he will have learnt plenty from this and should improve, especially over a little further.

**Il Pranzo** ran respectably and does look to be going the right way, although he may be more of a nursery type.

**Chairman Rick(IRE)** made his debut over seven furlongs and is out of a winner over a mile three, so it was hardly surprising he found this trip a bit short. He is now qualified for a nursery mark and may do better in that field.

**Dralion** did not really build on his debut running, but is not one to give up on just yet. His sire showed a liking for soft ground, and so too did his half-brother Rapscallion, so he could be worth keeping in mind for when there is a bit of give in ground, possibly later in the season in nurseries.

## 4065 PETTITTS ANIMAL ADVENTURE PARK AT REEDHAM (S) STKS — 1m 2f 21y

2:35 (2:35) (G ) 3-Y-O+ — £2,562 (£732; £366) Stalls Low

| Form | | | Horse | Jockey | RPR |
|---|---|---|---|---|---|
| 0035 | 1 | | **Senor Eduardo**[20] 3489 7-9-5 48 (SGollings) *trckd ldrs gng wl: clsd to ld over 2f out: clr ins fnl f: readily* **5/1**[1] | NPollard 3 | 56 |
| 0500 | 2 | 4 | **Tata Naka**[24] 3380 4-9-1 37 ow1 (MrsCADunnett) *towards rr: hdwy over 2f out: n.m.r and swtchd lft ins fnl f: wnt 2nd cl home: no ch w wnr* **33/1** | TGMcLaughlin 5 | 44 |
| 6440 | 3 | 1/2 | **Jade Star (USA)**[14] 3670 4-9-6 50 (MissGayKelleway) *led: rdn 3f out: hdd over 2f out: outpcd by wnr ins fnl f and demoted nr fin* **5/1**[1] | MFenton 7 | 48 |
| 0400 | 4 | 1 1/2 | **Mystic Moon**[54] 2484 3-8-4 51 (JRJenkins) *scratchy to post: prom: rdn 3f out: ev ch 2f out: onepced fnl f* **16/1** | RMullen 8 | 39 |
| 0005 | 5 | shd | **Kyle Of Lochalsh**[24] 3367 4-9-5 49 (GGMargarson) *midfield: rdn 3f out: no imp or danger fnl 2f* **13/2**[3] | AMcCarthy 4 | 44 |
| 0000 | 6 | 1 1/2 | **Springalong (USA)**[11] 3087 4-9-5 56 (PDEvans) *pressed ldr tl rdn 3f out: lost pl tamely over 2f out* **5/1**[1] | NCallan 9 | 41 |
| 66 | 7 | hd | **Whenwillitwin**[10] 3809 3-8-2 (JSMoore) *dwlt: effrt outside over 3f out: sn drvn: btn 2f out* **12/1** | DerekNolan(7) 11 | 41 |
| 0000 | 8 | 1 | **Buckenham Stone**[15] 3637 5-9-0 30 (JPearce) *chsd ldrs: rdn 3f out: plodded on and n.d after* **100/1** | RPrice 2 | 34 |
| 3460 | 9 | hd | **Big Bad Burt**[16] 3613 3-8-2 62 (GCHChung) *s.s: bhd: btn 3f out* **12/1** | DeanWilliams(7) 1 | 39 |
| -000 | 10 | 2 | **Red Skelton (IRE)**[28] 3232 3-8-9 67 (WJHaggas) *dwlt: bhd: last and labouring 3f out* **11/2**[2] | (bt) DHolland 10 | 35 |
| 0330 | 11 | 8 | **Fitz The Bill (IRE)**[44] 2520 4-9-0 42 (NBKing) *dwlt: drvn up into midfield tl lost pl 1/2-way: last and nt keen over 2f out* **12/1** | (b) JMackay 6 | 15 |

2m 9.45s (1.48) **Going Correction** +0.075s/f (Good)

**WFA** 3 from 4yo+ 10lb — **11** Ran SP% **111.6**

Speed ratings: **97,93,93,92,92 90,90,89,89,88 81** CT £6.90 TOTE £2.30: £9.30, £1.80, £; EX293.30 1.The winner was bought in for 6,000gns. Jade Star was claimed by Mr P.Burgoyne for £6,000. Big Bad Burt was subject to a friendly

**Owner** R L Houlton **Bred** R L Houlton **Trained** Scamblesby, Lincs

**FOCUS**

A very moderate seller run in a slow time.

**NOTEBOOK**

**Senor Eduardo** improved on the form he showed in this grade on his two previous starts and was winning for the first time after 12 attempts on the Flat (he has run in bumpers and over hurdles). The stable's horses are running well and, now this one has got his head in front, he could well go in again.

**Tata Naka** had been tried over as short as six furlongs just two starts previously, but this trip appears to suit better and this was quite an encouraging effort. She will need to improve to win a similar race, but could do well in banded company when that starts up again.

**Jade Star(USA)**, with the cheekpieces left off this time, appreciated this drop in grade and has have no excuses.

**Mystic Moon**, still a maiden, ran respectably on this drop in grade and this is clearly her sort of level.

**Kyle Of Lochalsh**, with the blinkers left off this time, continues a long way below his best.

**Springalong(USA)**, beaten in a selling hurdle on his previous start, was supported into co-favouritism on this return to Flat, but showed little.

**Big Bad Burt** *Official explanation: jockey said gelding missed the break and subsequently hung right*

**Red Skelton(IRE)**, who had not beaten another horse home this season, was best off at the weights on this drop in grade but again showed nothing. He must have a problem and the tongue-tie and blinkers do not inspire confidence. *Official explanation: jockey said gelding hung right*

## 4066 WELLINGTON PIER & WINTER GARDENS FILLIES' H'CAP — 1m 3y

3:05 (3:07) (E ) (0-70,67) 3-Y-O+ — £3,799 (£1,169; £584; £292) Stalls High

| Form | | | Horse | Jockey | RPR |
|---|---|---|---|---|---|
| 2500 | 1 | | **Oh So Rosie (IRE)**[16] 3609 4-8-11 **53** (JSMoore) *hld up midfield: rdn 3f out: chsd ldr fnl 2f: sustained run after: drvn ahd nr fin* **12/1** | (p) DerekNolan(7) 8 | 64 |
| 5303 | 2 | hd | **Aesculus (USA)**[20] 3473 3-9-10 **67** (LMCumani) *moved wl to post: prom: led over 2f out: rdn and kpt on ins fnl f: jst ct* **13/2**[3] | DHolland 10 | 78 |
| 0323 | 3 | 1/2 | **Gabana (IRE)**[14] 3684 3-9-8 **65** (CFWall) *covered up in rr: hdwy over 1f out: rdn and put hd in air ins fnl f: n.g.t* **9/2**[1] | RMullen 13 | 74 |
| 2064 | 4 | 2 1/2 | **Ranny**[26] 3321 4-8-8 **48** (DrJDScargill) *chsd ldrs: drvn 2f out: wl hld fnl f* **9/2**[1] | PMakin(5) 6 | 52 |
| 0060 | 5 | 2 1/2 | **Balmacara**[16] 3609 5-8-6 **41** (MissKBBoutflower) *midfield: rdn over 2f out: sn no ch* **16/1** | NPollard 14 | 39 |
| 0006 | 6 | 1/2 | **Morag**[11] 3780 3-9-7 **64** (IAWood) *hld up towards rr: rdn 3f out: sn no imp* **18/1** | (p) JDSmith 7 | 61 |
| 60-0 | 7 | 5 | **Kama's Wheel**[34] 3060 5-7-7 **35** (JohnAHarris) *chsd ldrs tl 1/2-way: sn btn* **50/1** | DFentiman(7) 4 | 20 |
| 0050 | 8 | 5 | **Bint Royal (IRE)**[7] 3867 6-9-6 **55** (MissVHaigh) *chsd ldrs tl 1/2-way: rdn and btn 3f out* **12/1** | AMcCarthy 11 | 29 |
| 335 | 9 | shd | **Chertsey (IRE)**[20] 3486 3-9-5 **62** (CEBrittain) *led main gp: hdd over 2f out: hanging lft and lost pl qckly after* **14/1** | MHills 9 | 36 |
| 000 | 10 | 1 1/2 | **Acola (FR)**[50] 2594 4-9-3 **52** (RMHCowell) *stdd s: t.k.h in rr: racd awkwardly fr 1/2-way: no ch after* **40/1** | (v[1]) OUrbina 12 | 22 |
| -000 | 11 | 5 | **Tardis**[19] 3529 3-8-12 **55** (MLWBell) *chsd main ldr tl drvn and lost pl rapidly 3f out: t.o* **33/1** | JMackay 5 | 14 |
| 0544 | 12 | 10 | **Naughty Girl (IRE)**[2] 4004 4-9-1 **50** (PDEvans) *chsd tearaway far side ldr: rdn and wknd over 3f out: t.o and eased* **9/1** | (vt) NCallan 1 | — |
| 0030 | 13 | 1/2 | **Wodhill Be**[21] 3457 4-8-8 **43** (DMorris) *bhd: labouring 1/2-way: t.o* **40/1** | SCarson 2 | — |
| 0600 | 14 | 2 1/2 | **Classic Vision**[6] 3911 4-9-4 **53** (WJHaggas) *set breakneck pce w one pursuer on far side: clr tl 1/2-way: hdd over 2f out and nthing lft: t.o and eased* **5/1**[2] | (b) RHills 3 | — |

1m 39.69s (-0.01) **Going Correction** +0.05s/f (Good)

**WFA** 3 from 4yo+ 8lb — **14** Ran SP% **119.3**

Speed ratings: **102,101,101,98,96 95,90,85,85,84 79,69,68,66**CSF £85.41 CT £412.61 TOTE £15.00: £4.90, £3.10, £1.90; EX 138.50.

**Owner** J S Moore **Bred** Mark Commins **Trained** East Garston, Berks

**FOCUS**
Just a modest fillies' handicap in which the middle of the track proved the place to be - Naughty Girl and Classic Vision raced against the far-side rail and were beaten a mile.
**NOTEBOOK**
**Oh So Rosie(IRE)**, 7lb lower than at the beginning of the season and with the cheekpieces re-fitted, returned to form to end a losing run stretching back to her juvenile days. Given her recent winning record, she cannot be relied upon to repeat this next time, but this should have boosted her confidence and she is at the right end of the handicap. *Official explanation: trainer's representative had no explanation for the improved form shown*
**Aesculus(USA)** was not inconvenienced by this drop back from ten furlongs and was just held. She has a similar race in her.
**Gabana(IRE)** grabbed a place for the fourth successive race, but remains a maiden and did show a slightly awkward head carriage. There is a similar race in her, but she is probably not one to take too short a price about.
**Ranny** ran her race and will be even better on fast ground.
**Balmacara** ran one of her better races, but she is still looking for that first win.
**Naughty Girl(IRE)** *Official explanation: jockey said filly was hanging*
**Classic Vision** looked to go too fast on the apparently slower ground against the far rail.

## 4067 STANLEY M TREADWELL MEMORIAL H'CAP — 7f 3y
3:40 (3:44) (D) (0-85,84) 3-Y-0+ — £5,798 (£1,784; £892; £446) Stalls High

Form — RPR
0000 **1** **Will He Wish**[12] 3755 8-9-13 **84**........(b) IMongan 10 — 96
(SGollings) *hld up and bhd: vigorously drvn over 2f out: fnd stride late and clsd to ld 1f out: kpt on wl* **16/1**
2044 **2** 1 ½ **And Toto Too**[6] 3910 4-8-10 **67**........(b) NCallan 1 — 75
(PDEvans) *rr of midfield: drvn over 2f out: prog over 1f out: kpt on onepce to go 2nd fnl 100 yds* **12/1**
0-05 **3** ¾ **Bob's Buzz**[22] 3428 4-8-11 **68**........RMullen 3 — 74
(SCWilliams) *stdd s: plld hrd in rr: stl last over 2f out: hanging lft whn clsng after: hld ins fnl f* **4/1**[2]
0262 **4** ½ **Prince Hector**[43] 2789 5-9-9 **80**........RHills 5 — 85
(WJHaggas) *bhd: hanging lft fr 1/2-way: kpt on ins fnl f but nvr looking keen enough to win* **3/1**[1]
00-0 **5** hd **Rafferty (IRE)**[16] 3597 5-9-11 **82**........(b) DHolland 11 — 86
(CEBrittain) *racd freely in midfield: rdn and clsd to ld over 1f out: hanging bdly lft and sn hdd and fnd nil: onepced fnl 100 yds* **9/2**[3]
3-06 **6** 2 ½ **Morning After**[22] 3419 4-9-1 **72**........OUrbina 4 — 70
(JRFanshawe) *chsd ldrs tl rdn and no ex over 1f out* **12/1**
2200 **7** ¾ **Michelle Ma Belle (IRE)**[61] 2284 4-9-2 **73**........(b[1]) MHills 6 — 69
(SKirk) *keen and cl up: led over 2f out: hdd and pushed lft over 1f out: sn btn* **25/1**
0201 **8** nk **Ziet D'Alsace (FR)**[9] 3828 4-8-1 **58** 6ex........AMcCarthy 8 — 53
(AWCarroll) *prom: rdn and ev ch over 2f out: wkng whn checked over 1f out* **9/1**
0046 **9** 7 **Riva Royale**[34] 3047 4-9-9 **80**........(p) JDSmith 2 — 57
(IAWood) *cl up: rdn and ev ch over 2f out: wknd qckly: eased ins fnl f* **28/1**
6560 **10** 5 **Star Sensation (IRE)**[29] 3212 4-9-11 **82**........SCarson 7 — 46
(PWHarris) *chsd ldr over 4f: dropped out rapidly* **20/1**
3342 **11** 16 **Samuel Charles**[19] 3525 6-9-0 **71**........NPollard 9 — —
(WMBrisbourne) *led: hdd over 2f out: hanging lft and reluctant after: t.o* **8/1**

1m 25.33s (-1.17) **Going Correction** +0.05s/f (Good) — **11 Ran SP% 117.6**
Speed ratings: **108,106,105,104,104 101,100,100,92,86 68**CSF £188.83 CT £941.27 TOTE £16.00: £4.80, £2.70, £2.10; EX 167.50.
**Owner** Mrs D Dukes **Bred** Mrs C Buckland **Trained** Scamblesby, Lincs

**FOCUS**
A fair handicap in which those who raced up with the pace were nowhere to be seen at the finish, despite not appearing to go too fast, but the form looks fairly sound. The whole field raced up the centre of the track in the early stages, but the principals came home nearer the stands'-side rail.
**NOTEBOOK**
**Will He Wish**, five times a winner last season, gained his first win of this campaign off a mark 8lb lower than at the beginning of the year. He has an impressive strike-rate and is one to keep on the right side of, especially at Yarmouth where he is now two from two.
**And Toto Too** is still looking for her first win of the campaign, but she is running very creditably in defeat and will surely find a similar event soon enough.
**Bob's Buzz** is lightly raced this season, but this was a solid effort and he is in good form.
**Prince Hector** was unable to confirm the promise he showed at Newbury on his previous start and has now been a beaten favourite on his last three starts. Despite staying on, he never really looked like getting there and may do better back over a mile.
**Rafferty(IRE)** was unable to confirm the promise he showed on his belated reappearance at Newmarket, hanging under pressure when appearing to have every chance to win the race. *Official explanation: jockey said gelding hung left*

## 4068 EUROPEAN BREEDERS FUND CARLSBERG TETLEY FILLIES' CONDITIONS STKS — 7f 3y
4:15 (4:15) (C) 3-Y-0 — £9,210 (£3,405; £1,702; £774) Stalls High

Form — RPR
3-52 **1** **Lucky Pipit**[33] 3105 3-8-9 102........MHills 1 — 104+
(BWHills) *mde all: gng much the best 2f out: clr fnl f: pushed out: easily* **4/9**[1]
0-01 **2** 8 **Three Secrets (IRE)**[20] 3487 3-8-13 85........AMcCarthy 2 — 89+
(PWChapple-Hyam) *a 2nd: rdn over 2f out: one pce and wl hld after* **9/4**[2]
-300 **3** 1 ½ **Surf The Net**[7] 3867 3-8-9 92........DHolland 3 — 79
(RHannon) *sn pushed along and outpcd in 3rd: n.d fr 1/2-way* **14/1**[3]
**4** 13 **Tregenna** 3-8-6........OUrbina 5 — 43
(RMHCowell) *rn green in last: remote fr 1/2-way* **100/1**
0 **5** 21 **Lottie**[12] 3759 3-8-9........NPollard 6 — —
(MissVHaigh) *last pair and wl outpcd: t.o fr 1/2-way* **200/1**

1m 25.14s (-1.36) **Going Correction** +0.05s/f (Good) — **5 Ran SP% 108.2**
Speed ratings: **109,99,98,83,59**CSF £1.60 TOTE £1.40: £1.10, £1.20; EX 1.70.
**Owner** Maktoum Al Maktoum **Bred** Gainsborough Stud Management Ltd **Trained** Lambourn, Berks

**FOCUS**
An uncompetitive conditions race and they came home in market order.
**NOTEBOOK**
**Lucky Pipit**, successful in Listed company at two, had run well in that grade at Warwick on her previous start and, dropped in class, she found this much easier and ran out a very comfortable winner. This was a nice confidence boost and she deserves to try and gain some more black type.
**Three Secrets(IRE)**, off the mark in just an ordinary maiden at Warwick on her previous start, had 21lb to find with the winner at the weights and was unsurprisingly left behind by that one.
**Surf The Net** has not gone on at all from her encouraging reappearance. *Official explanation: jockey said filly was never travelling*
**Tregenna**, a 16,500gns yearling, full-sister to the smart ten-furlong dirt performer Zanay, had no chance.

## 4069 JARDINE LLOYD THOMPSON CORPORATE RISK MAIDEN STKS — 7f 3y
4:50 (4:50) (D) 3-Y-0 — £3,373 (£1,038; £519; £259) Stalls High

Form — RPR
5246 **1** **Go Yellow**[19] 3525 3-9-0 69........NCallan 5 — 76?
(PDEvans) *keen in last pair: effrt 2f out: rdn to ld over 1f out: battled on gamely fnl 100 yds* **14/1**[3]
3 **2** 1 **Lake Charlotte (USA)**[12] 3759 3-8-9........NPollard 6 — 68
(DRLoder) *keen in last pair: hld up tl drvn over 1f out: chal ins last f: a hld fnl 100 yds* **5/4**[2]
4- **3** 2 **Meneef (USA)**[293] 5345 3-9-0........RHills 4 — 68
(MPTregoning) *cl up: led over 3f out: drvn and hdd over 1f out: woefully onepced ins fnl f* **5/6**[1]
00 **4** 5 **Private Jessica**[83] 1749 3-8-9........OUrbina 3 — 50
(JRFanshawe) *chsd ldr: led 1/2-way: hdd over 3f out: wknd over 1f out* **50/1**
000 **5** dist **Hello Tiger**[16] 3613 3-8-7........(p) PGallagher[(7)] 2 — —
(JASupple) *led tl 1/2-way: sn dropped out: bdly t.o and eased* **250/1**

1m 26.94s (0.44) **Going Correction** +0.05s/f (Good) — **5 Ran SP% 108.0**
Speed ratings: **99,97,95,89,**—CSF £31.27 TOTE £12.40: £5.00, £1.10; EX 28.00.
**Owner** G R Price **Bred** Mrs C R M Pugh **Trained** Pandy, Gwent

**FOCUS**
With both Lake Charlotte and Meneef failing to show any progression from their first runs, it was left to the exposed handicapper Go Yellow to get off the mark. Not an easy race to rate.
**NOTEBOOK**
**Go Yellow** is exposed as just a fair handicapper, but he is battle-hardened and, despite racing quite keenly, made the most of the first two in the betting running below expectations. The handicapper should not put him up too much for this, if at all.
**Lake Charlotte(USA)**, beaten at even money when third at York on her debut in just a fair maiden, did not appear to improve on that effort.
**Meneef(USA)**, fourth in a really hot Newmarket maiden (beaten just a length and a half by Oujia Board) on his only start at two, was well fancied in the market on this first run in 293 days, but he ran a very lacklustre race. He may be capable of better, but has it all to prove now and one could afford to miss him if he wins.
**Private Jessica** is now qualified for a handicap mark and should find things easier in that sphere.

## 4070 SOUTH PIER LEISURE COMPLEX (LOWESTOFT) H'CAP — 1m 3f 101y
5:20 (5:20) (F) (0-55,61) 3-Y-0+ — £3,409 (£974; £487) Stalls Low

Form — RPR
-004 **1** **Inchpast**[8] 3837 3-9-4 **55**........(b) NCallan 1 — 67
(MHTompkins) *cl up: led 2f out: drvn clr ins fnl f* **7/2**[2]
0300 **2** 2 ½ **Muslin**[20] 3479 3-9-1 **52**........OUrbina 6 — 60
(JRFanshawe) *cl up: rdn and chsd wnr fnl 2f: wl hld ins fnl f* **11/1**
-006 **3** 1 **Genuinely (IRE)**[26] 3305 3-8-2 **39**........(v[1]) JMackay 5 — 45
(WJMusson) *midfield: drvn 3f out: clsd over 1f out: one pce u.p ins fnl f* **14/1**
2436 **4** 1 **Vanilla Moon**[24] 3383 4-9-6 **46**........(v) NPollard 3 — 51
(JRJenkins) *led: hdd 6f out: led again 4f out tl 2f out: rdn and plugged on fnl f* **10/1**
0100 **5** shd **Duc's Dream**[34] 3050 6-10-0 **54**........RMullen 11 — 59
(DMorris) *chsd ldr: led 6f out tl 4f out: drvn and wknd over 1f out* **10/3**[1]
6050 **6** shd **Compton Aviator**[11] 3774 8-9-8 **51**........(t) LFletcher[(3)] 10 — 55
(AWCarroll) *hld up midfield: rdn whn nt clr run 3f out: fnd nil and one pce after* **10/1**
0000 **7** 1 ¾ **Daimajin (IRE)**[6] 3921 5-9-7 **47**........LVickers 2 — 49
(MrsLucindaFeatherstone) *t.k.h towards rr: drvn over 2f out: nvr able to chal* **50/1**
-404 **8** ½ **Ellovamul**[17] 3578 4-9-5 **50**........PMakin[(5)] 4 — 51
(WMBrisbourne) *chsd ldrs: rdn 3f out: one pce fnl 2f* **7/1**
00 **9** 1 ½ **Perida (IRE)**[1] 3776 4-8-12 **45**........AHindley[(7)] 9 — 43
(BGPowell) *s.i.s: bhd: drvn 3f out: sn btn* **25/1**
0110 **10** 14 **Jackie Kiely**[1] 4015 3-9-10 **61** 6ex........(t) IMongan 8 — 37
(PSMcentee) *s.i.s: bhd: hdwy on outside fr 2f out: midfield but rdn and btn whn checked ins fnl f:virtually p.u* **9/2**[3]
0-60 **11** 25 **Pancake Role**[9] 3827 4-8-8 **34** oh2........AMcCarthy 7 — —
(AWCarroll) *rrd and s.s: wl t.o fnl 3f* **40/1**

2m 27.23s (-0.17) **Going Correction** +0.075s/f (Good)
**WFA** 3 from 4yo+ 11lb — **11 Ran SP% 117.4**
Speed ratings: **103,101,100,99,99 99,98,97,96,86 68**CSF £41.12 CT £484.84 TOTE £5.20: £1.90, £3.30, £3.30; EX 77.60 Place 6 £48.64, Place 5 £40.48.
**Owner** Marcoe Racing Welwyn **Bred** Stanley Estate And Stud Co **Trained** Newmarket, Suffolk

**FOCUS**
A pretty moderate handicap and a finish dominated by three-year-olds.
**NOTEBOOK**
**Inchpast** took well to the fitting of blinkers when fourth at Catterick on his previous start and confirmed his liking for the headgear with his first success to date. He may be forced to step up in grade next time, but is progressing.
**Muslin** showed little on her handicap debut over a mile six at Haydock but, dropped in trip, this was much better. She is on a fair mark and has the ability to win a similar contest.
**Genuinely(IRE)**, a lightly-raced maiden, ran well in a first-time visor. She only really had the one pace and promises to stay further.
**Vanilla Moon**, a long-standing maiden, posted another fair effort in defeat.
**Duc's Dream**, returned to the course and distance he gained his last success over, ran better than on his two most recent starts, but may do even better back on fast ground.
**Compton Aviator** found absolutely nothing under pressure.
**Jackie Kiely** stopped quite quickly a furlong out and looked to have a problem. *Official explanation: jockey said gelding missed the break*
**Pancake Role** *Official explanation: jockey said gelding reared at the start*
T/Plt: £50.20 to a £1 stake. Pool: £25,875.80. 376.20 winning tickets. T/Qpdt: £15.00 to a £1 stake. Pool: £1,734.90. 85.30 winning tickets. IM

4071 - 4073a (Foreign Racing) - See Raceform Interactive

# 3723 ASCOT (R-H)
Friday, July 23

**OFFICIAL GOING: Good to firm (good in places)**
Wind: lt against Weather: sunny; warm

## 4074 BRUNSWICK MAIDEN STKS (FILLIES) — 6f
2:15 (2:15) (D) 2-Y-0 — £5,395 (£1,660; £830; £415) Stalls Low

Form — RPR
**1** **Shohrah (IRE)** 2-8-11........RHills 3 — 91+
(MPTregoning) *str: scope: lw: dwlt: t.k.h and sn in tch: prog 1/2-way: shkn up to ld over 1f out: r.o wl: comf* **7/2**[2]
**2** 2 ½ **Epiphany** 2-8-11........LDettori 7 — 83
(EALDunlop) *leggy: scope: s.i.s: hld up in last pair: prog 2f out: chsd wnr jst over 1f out: styd on wl but no imp* **13/2**

2 **3** 3 1/2 **Dance Flower (IRE)**[14] 3693 2-8-11 .................................... TEDurcan 2 77+
(MRChannon) *lw: trckd ldrs: nt clr run wl over 2f out to 1f out: r.o to take 3rd nr fin: no ch* **11/4**[1]

002 **4** nk **Miss Malone (IRE)**[9] 3840 2-8-11 .................................... RHughes 5 72
(RHannon) *w ldrs: led 2f out to over 1f out: wknd fnl f* **6/1**[3]

23 **5** 1 **Secret History (USA)**[24] 3398 2-8-11 .................................... JFanning 1 69
(MJohnston) *disp ld to 2f out: rdn and sn btn* **7/1**

**6** 1 1/4 **Ghasiba (IRE)** 2-8-11 .................................... DHolland 6 65
(CEBrittain) *w'like: wnt rt s: racd in detached last and rn green: pushed along 2f out : kpt on fnl f* **16/1**

3 **7** 1 1/2 **Balletto**[33] 3123 2-8-11 .................................... DarrenWilliams 8 61
(KRBurke) *t.k.h: hld up bhd ldrs: shkn up 2f out: sn wknd* **12/1**

**8** 2 **Caona (USA)** 2-8-11 .................................... EAhern 4 55
(JNoseda) *gd sort: str: bkwd: disp ld to 2f out: sn wknd: eased fnl f* **8/1**

1m 16.53s (0.54) **Going Correction** +0.075s/f (Good) **8** Ran SP% **113.7**
Speed ratings: **99,95,91,90,89 87,85,82**CSF £26.08 TOTE £4.80: £1.70, £1.70, £1.30; EX 30.90.
**Owner** Hamdan Al Maktoum **Bred** Shadwell Estate Company Limited **Trained** Lambourn, Berks

**FOCUS**
A race won last year by subsequent Group One winner Carry On Katie. With the 'form' horses well held, this year's renewal looks pretty strong and should produce some nice sorts, not least the front two. The winning time was decent for the type of race.

**NOTEBOOK**
**Shohrah(IRE)**, a Giant's Causeway half-sister to a winner over ten furlongs, out of a half-sister to Irish Leger winner Ibn Bey and Yorkshire Oaks scorer Roseate Tern, is not exactly bred for this sort of trip but proved good enough to make a winning debut. She raced a little keenly after missing the break, but made up her ground easily when asked and pulled away nicely in the closing stages. The bookies reacted by making her a 25/1 shot for the Guineas and a 33/1 chance for the Oaks.
**Epiphany**, out of a 12-furlong winner, a half-sister to Irish 2000 Guineas winner Indian Haven, was also slow to leave the stalls and was no match for the winner in the closing stages, but she still managed to pull well clear of the remainder. She should have little bother in picking up a maiden, before stepping up in grade.
**Dance Flower(IRE)**, runner-up in just an ordinary course and distance maiden on her debut, was always going to be vulnerable to anything potentially smart and that is the way it worked out. She did not get the clearest of runs and could maybe have finished a little closer, but there can be no real excuses.
**Miss Malone(IRE)** looked to have her chance and was simply outclassed. She gives a reasonable guide to the strength of the form.
**Secret History(USA)**, beaten in a Hamilton maiden on her previous outing, was always going to find this even tougher. However, she is now qualified for nurseries and improvement cannot be ruled out.
**Ghasiba(IRE)**, a 54,000gns yearling, whose dam was placed over this trip at two and three, was never really going the pace, but kept on well enough in the closing stages and should have learnt from this. Being by Daylami, she is probably going to appreciate a little further.
**Balletto** found this tougher than the Pontefract maiden she made her debut in, but did not show a great deal of progression in any case.
**Caona(USA)** hails from the stable that took this last year with subsequent Group One winner Carry On Katie. This one however, a 170,000gns half-sister to a winner in the USA, was easy to back and readily held. It is interesting though that she made her debut at Ascot, so do not rule out improvement.

## 4075 JOHN GUEST BROWN JACK STKS (H'CAP) 2m 45y
**2:45** (2:45) (D ) (0-85,84) 3-Y-0+ **£9,532** (£2,933; £1,466; £733) **Stalls** High

Form RPR

5000 **1** **Mana D'Argent (IRE)**[13] 3725 7-9-13 **84** .................................... JFanning 14 94
(MJohnston) *lw: trckd ldrs: shkn up and effrt 3f out: rdn to ld over 1f out: jst hld on* **11/2**[3]

0300 **2** shd **Riyadh**[20] 3508 6-8-5 **62** .................................... (v) KDarley 8 72
(MJohnston) *lw: dwlt: t.k.h: hld up in rr: n.m.r 6f out: prog over 2f out: hanging bdly rt but r.o fnl f: jst failed* **9/1**

-445 **3** 3/4 **Akritas**[48] 2683 3-8-10 **84** .................................... TQuinn 4 93
(PFICole) *lw: t.k.h: prom: led 5f out to 4f out: styd pressing ldr: led 2f out to over 1f out: styd on fnl f: a jst hld* **9/2**[2]

-351 **4** 2 1/2 **Valance (IRE)**[16] 3644 4-9-9 **80** .................................... JPMurtagh 3 86
(CREgerton) *lw: t.k.h: prom: led 4f out and kicked on: hdd 2f out: wknd ins fnl f* **7/2**[1]

0053 **5** 1 1/4 **Beechy Bank (IRE)**[15] 3683 6-8-7 **64** ow1 .................................... DHolland 12 68
(MrsMaryHambro) *b: lw: hld up: last and detached 7f out: stl in last trio over 2f out: styd on wl fr over 1f out: no ch* **25/1**

0230 **6** hd **Red Scorpion (USA)**[22] 3449 5-8-7 **64** .................................... SWKelly 13 68
(WMBrisbourne) *t.k.h: trckd ldrs: rdn and unable qck over 2f out: one pce after* **25/1**

00-0 **7** 1 1/2 **Flamenco Bride**[13] 3752 4-8-12 **69** .................................... RHughes 11 71
(DRCElsworth) *trckd ldrs: pushed along and prog to chal 5f out: c wd bnd 3f out: sn lost pl: no imp ldrs after* **16/1**

0000 **8** 1 1/4 **Establishment**[38] 2958 7-8-10 **67** .................................... MartinDwyer 1 68
(CACyzer) *hld up in rr: rdn and effrt 3f out: prog 2f out: no imp over 1f out* **11/1**

1-05 **9** 2 1/2 **Astyanax (IRE)**[10] 3821 4-9-2 **73** .................................... JMackay 6 71
(SirMarkPrescott) *cl up: effrt 4f out: rdn and c wdst of all bnd 3f out: sn struggling* **11/1**

0-30 **10** 6 **Once (FR)**[38] 2958 4-9-2 **73** .................................... EAhern 2 64
(JAOsborne) *hld up in rr: rdn and no prog 3f out: bhd fnl 2f* **66/1**

-004 **11** 3/4 **Best Flight**[18] 3591 4-8-11 **68** .................................... MHills 7 58
(BWHills) *b.hind: lw: settled in midfield: effrt and cl enough 3f out: wknd 2f out* **25/1**

3336 **12** shd **High Point (IRE)**[16] 3644 6-9-8 **79** .................................... KFallon 5 69
(GPEnright) *hld up in midfield tl prog to ld after 4f: hdd and n.m.r 5f out: wknd over 2f out: eased* **9/1**

4P11 **13** 8 **Moonshine Beach**[12] 3776 6-8-9 **66** 4ex .................................... DaneO'Neill 9 46
(PWHiatt) *led at stdy pce for 4f: steadily lost pl fr 1/2-way: last over 3f out: eased: t.o* **10/1**

3m 36.94s (2.10) **Going Correction** +0.075s/f (Good)
**WFA** 3 from 4yo+ 17lb **13** Ran SP% **120.5**
Speed ratings: **97,96,96,95,94 94,93,93,91,88 88,88,84**CSF £52.72 CT £245.89 TOTE £6.90: £2.60, £2.90, £2.70; EX 25.80 Trifecta £357.40 Pool: £1,862.66. 3.70 winning units..
**Owner** Daniel A Couper **Bred** Daniel A Couper And George Hosie **Trained** Middleham Moor, N Yorks

**FOCUS**
A fair staying handicap, but the early pace was just ordinary and the winning time was slow. Some of these raced quite keenly, most notably both Akritas and Valance, but the form appears reasonably solid.

**NOTEBOOK**
**Mana D'Argent(IRE)** had not been seen at his best so far this year but, back down to the mark he last won off, he returned to form to gain his sixth career success at Ascot. He has never followed up a success, or won away from this place, so looks one to take on in his next intended target at Goodwood, but should be kept in mind for the Shergar Cup staying event, a race he won in 2002.
**Riyadh**, unlike his winning stablemate, did not make things easy for his rider and probably would have won this had he been more willing. Having said that, this was still an improvement on his recent efforts and, 26lb lower than when last successful in 2002, he will surely be placed to end that losing run.
**Akritas**, stepping up from a mile and a half, did not help his chance of seeing out this trip by racing quite keenly and was eventually outstayed. He will need to learn to settle better to prove fully effective over this sort of trip.
**Valance(IRE)**, 5lb higher than when successful at Newmarket on his previous start, was pretty keen and not looking to be enjoying the fast ground in the straight, despite having won on it twice.
**Beechy Bank(IRE)** was probably being ridden to get the trip, but the tactics were exaggerated and she could only stay on past beaten horses.
**Moonshine Beach** *Official explanation: jockey said gelding was unsuited by the good to firm, good in places ground*

## 4076 LADBROKES RATED STKS (H'CAP) 6f
**3:20** (3:20) (C ) (0-95,93) 3-Y-0+ **£8,659** (£3,201; £1,600; £727) **Stalls** Low

Form RPR

12-4 **1** **Khabfair**[22] 3453 3-9-2 **91** .................................... JPMurtagh 2 106+
(MrsAJPerrett) *lw: a gng wl: hld up in 4th: prog to ld over 1f out: rdn and in command fnl f* **7/4**[1]

0054 **2** 1 1/4 **Onlytime Will Tell**[45] 2750 6-9-7 **91** .................................... JFanning 6 102
(DNicholls) *hld up in last: prog 2f out: nt clr run over 1f out: chsd wnr ins fnl f: r.o but nvr able to chal* **4/1**[3]

000- **3** 4 **The Lord**[356] 3787 4-8-10 **87** .................................... CHaddon(7) 7 86
(WGMTurner) *t.k.h: led after 2f: bmpd along and hdd over 1f out: wknd ins fnl f* **20/1**

2641 **4** nk **Blackheath (IRE)**[7] 3901 8-9-1 **85** 3ex .................................... ANicholls 3 83
(DNicholls) *b: lw: led for 2f: rdn over 2f out: wknd over 1f out* **2/1**[2]

0600 **5** 1 **Nero's Return (IRE)**[21] 3482 3-9-4 **93** .................................... (b1) KDalgleish 5 88
(MJohnston) *trckd ldng pair: rdn wl over 2f out: struggling over 1f out* **6/1**

1m 14.87s (-1.12) **Going Correction** +0.075s/f (Good)
**WFA** 3 from 4yo+ 5lb **5** Ran SP% **108.7**
Speed ratings: **110,108,103,102,101**CSF £8.78 TOTE £2.40: £1.40, £2.00; EX 6.40.
**Owner** Star Pointe Ltd & Arlington Bloodstock **Bred** Peter Hodgson **Trained** Pulborough, W Sussex

**FOCUS**
An incredibly small field for a sprint handicap worth £14,000, probably as a result of it being a rated stakes. Still, a pretty smart performance from the lightly-raced Khabfair, who is progressing fast.

**NOTEBOOK**
**Khabfair** confirmed the promise he showed on his reappearance, running out a clear-cut winner. He is likely to face tougher opposition in future, but is clearly progressing and this was a nice confidence booster. He is in the Shergar Cup Sprint.
**Onlytime Will Tell** has not won since June 2002 and is still 11lb higher than when gaining that success. The winner got first run, but there can be no real excuses.
**The Lord**, the 2002 Brocklesby winner, had not been seen for 356 days. He raced quite keenly and did not get home, but this was still a pleasing return to action, especially considering connections stated before hand he was racing here to put him right for a Listed contest at Chester.
**Blackheath(IRE)**, 4lb well-in under his penalty for a recent Hamilton success, was below form and maintained his record of having never followed up.
**Nero's Return(IRE)**, tried over ten furlongs on his previous start, did not improve for the drop back in trip or the fitting of blinkers.

## 4077 WEATHERBYS EUROPEAN BREEDERS FUND VALIANT STKS (LISTED RACE) (F&M) 1m (R)
**3:50** (3:52) (A ) 3-Y-0+ **£17,400** (£6,600; £3,300; £1,500) **Stalls** High

Form RPR

-522 **1** **Coy (IRE)**[37] 2971 3-8-6 100 ow1 .................................... KFallon 3 107
(SirMichaelStoute) *lw: sn rousted along in last pair: prog u.p 2f out: squeezed through ins fnl f: led last strides* **6/4**[1]

2125 **2** nk **Celtic Heroine (IRE)**[16] 3641 3-8-9 97 .................................... KDarley 1 109
(MAJarvis) *lw: settled off the pce in 5th: pushed along and prog fr over 2f out: rdn to ld ins fnl f: hdd last strides* **5/1**[3]

-042 **3** 1/2 **Snow Goose**[20] 3541 3-8-5 103 .................................... TQuinn 2 104
(JLDunlop) *racd freely: led at gd pce: pressed wl over 1f out: hdd ins fnl f: kpt on wl* **5/1**[3]

-300 **4** 1 3/4 **Nataliya**[20] 3541 3-8-5 108 .................................... MartinDwyer 7 100
(JLDunlop) *lw: b.hind: trckd ldr: clsd 2f out: rdn to chal over 1f out: ev ch ent fnl f: wknd last 100yds* **8/1**

145 **5** 3/4 **Moon Dazzle (USA)**[20] 3541 3-8-5 106 .................................... RHills 5 98
(WJHaggas) *lw: settled in midfield: rdn and effrt over 2f out: no imp on ldrs over 1f out: one pce* **4/1**[2]

4144 **6** 1/2 **Brindisi**[20] 3541 3-8-5 95 .................................... MHills 4 97
(BWHills) *swtg: trckd ldng pair: shkn up and nt qckn 2f out: one pce after out* **25/1**

6230 **7** 3 1/2 **Kunda (IRE)**[20] 3541 3-8-5 96 .................................... DaneO'Neill 8 89
(RHannon) *b.hind: s.i.s: sn wl in tch: rdn and dropped to last over 2f out: no ch after* **25/1**

1m 40.92s (-2.12) **Going Correction** +0.075s/f (Good)
**WFA** 3 from 4yo 8lb **7** Ran SP% **112.1**
Speed ratings: **113,112,112,110,109 109,105**CSF £8.96 TOTE £2.20: £1.70, £2.50; EX 5.60 Trifecta £13.70 Pool: £1,545.10. 79.79 winning units..
**Owner** Cheveley Park Stud **Bred** Dr T A Ryan **Trained** Newmarket, Suffolk

**FOCUS**
A good, competitive Listed race and the pace was strong resulting in a smart time and decent form for the grade.

**NOTEBOOK**
**Coy(IRE)** was weighted to reverse Royal Ascot placings with Celtic Heroine, but it took a pretty special ride from Fallon for her to do so. She never really looked to be going that well, but received plenty of encouragement from the saddle and the Champion squeezed her through a small gap close home and forced her head in front on the line. Amazingly, she looked to win a shade cosily and is probably capable of even better yet.
**Celtic Heroine(IRE)** has not had things go her way since winning at Royal Ascot, but there was nothing wrong with this effort - she was simply not good enough to confirm placings with Coy on 8lb worse terms.
**Snow Goose** was pretty much allowed to do her own thing in front by both her jockey and the rest of the field, although stablemate and eventual fourth Nataliya did try to keep tabs on her. It suited well and she looked to run her race.
**Nataliya**, the best in at the weights, looked to have every chance if good enough, but she was just held. A slightly disappointing effort for a filly thought good enough to contest the Guineas.
**Moon Dazzle(USA)** has not gone on from her fine fourth to Attraction in the Coronation Stakes and this was a disappointing effort. She appeared to have her chance on the outside, but was unable to quicken.

## 4078 EUROPEAN BREEDERS FUND MAIDEN STKS 7f
4:25 (4:25) (D) 2-Y-0 £5,551 (£1,708; £854; £427) Stalls Low

Form RPR

0 **1** **Kamakiri (IRE)**[13] 3749 2-9-0 .................. RHughes 4 90+
(RHannon) *lw: hld up in last: stdy prog gng wl fr over 2f out: led over 1f out: pushed clr: comf* **10/1**

333 **2** *2* **Capable Guest (IRE)**[38] 2954 2-9-0 .................. TEDurcan 5 85
(MRChannon) *trckd ldng pair: rdn to chal and hanging 2f out: ev ch over 1f out: nt qckn and easily hld fnl f* **1/2**[1]

02 **3** *1¾* **Takhmin (IRE)**[29] 3248 2-9-0 .................. RHills 6 81
(MJohnston) *disp ld: def advantage 2f out: hdd over 1f out: sn outpcd* **7/1**[2]

**4** *1* **Bayeux De Moi (IRE)** 2-9-0 .................. JPMurtagh 1 79+
(MrsAJPerrett) *gd sort: str: bkwd: trckd ldrs: shkn up 2f out: swtchd rt over 1f out: outpcd and n.d fnl f* **9/1**[3]

0 **5** *6* **River Biscuit (USA)**[17] 3601 2-9-0 .................. RLMoore 2 64
(RHannon) *lw: disp ld to 2f out: rdn and wknd* **16/1**

**6** *nk* **Regal Attire (USA)** 2-9-0 .................. MartinDwyer 3 63
(AMBalding) *s.i.s: trckd ldrs: rdn 2f out: sn wknd* **14/1**

1m 30.13s (0.46) **Going Correction** +0.075s/f (Good) **6** Ran SP% **110.8**
Speed ratings: **100,97,95,94,87 87**CSF £15.31 TOTE £16.10: £3.90, £1.20; EX 35.90.

**Owner** Michael Pescod **Bred** South House Stud **Trained** East Everleigh, Wilts

**FOCUS**
Capable Guest did not appear to run to his Royal Ascot form, but this year's Coventry does not look that strong in any case (the second, fourth, fifth and sixth home were all beaten on their next start). The winner, whose stable took this last year with Fantastic View, created a good impression regardless of what level of form the runner-up ran to.

**NOTEBOOK**
**Kamakiri(IRE)** shaped with a good deal of promise on his debut at Salisbury and improved on that effort to get off the mark in style. He moved upsides the favourite going really well two out before readily brushing that one aside. A nice sort, he should go on again from this and looks well up to holding his own in a higher grade.

**Capable Guest(IRE)**, third in the Group Three Coventry Stakes at Royal Ascot on his previous start, was below form even allowing for the step up in trip (he had shaped as though seven furlongs would suit) and has now twice failed to land the odds in maiden company in his short career. The bare form of his third in Pattern company looks to flatter him and, although he will probably find a similar race, he has already shown he is not one to take a short price about.

**Takhmin(IRE)** found this tougher than the Thirsk maiden he was runner-up in on his previous start. He has a minor maiden in him, but connections may opt to go the nursery route with him now he is qualified for a mark.

**Bayeux De Moi(IRE)**, a half-brother to a juvenile placed over six and seven furlongs, out of a half-sister to an Irish Oaks winner, made a pleasing introduction. Given that he was making his debut at Ascot, he is clearly well thought of and should improve enough to win a maiden.

**River Biscuit(USA)**, in contrast to his winning stablemate, did not really improve on his debut outing, despite having the run of the race.

**Regal Attire(USA)**, a half-brother to Oaks winner Casual Look, offered some promise, but was ultimately well held. He is open to significant improvement.

## 4079 NEWSMITH CAPITAL OCTOBER CLUB H'CAP 1m 2f
5:00 (5:00) (D) (0-80,77) 3-Y-0 £5,447 (£1,676; £838; £419) Stalls High

Form RPR

-404 **1** **Iffy**[8] 3875 3-8-2 **58** .................. CCatlin 8 66
(PDCundell) *lw: mde all: steadily increased pce fr 6f out: drvn 2f out: r.o gamely fnl f: jst hld on* **9/2**[2]

00-4 **2** *nk* **Edgehill (IRE)**[29] 3251 3-8-4 **60** .................. TQuinn 7 71+
(CREgerton) *trckd ldrs: rdn 3f out: prog 2f out: chsd wnr jst over 1f out: str chal fnl f: ev ch: jst hld* **5/1**[3]

0314 **3** *2½* **Foxilla (IRE)**[25] 3383 3-7-11 **58** .................. RThomas(5) 3 61
(DRCElsworth) *hld up in rr: rdn 3f out: no prog tl r.o u.p over 1f out: tk 3rd nr fin* **13/2**

0020 **4** *¾* **Epaminondas (USA)**[14] 3689 3-8-10 **66** .................. RSmith 6 68
(RHannon) *trckd ldrs: effrt over 2f out: rdn and nt qckn wl over 1f out: one pce and btn after* **20/1**

0231 **5** *2½* **Vamp**[18] 3574 3-9-7 **77** .................. MartinDwyer 4 76+
(RMBeckett) *lw: trckd wnr 7f out: rdn 2f out: wknd jst over 1f out* **7/2**[1]

-130 **6** *¾* **Ali Deo**[27] 3312 3-9-6 **76** .................. RHills 1 71
(WJHaggas) *hld up in last: rdn and no prog wl over 2f out: n.d after* **10/1**

0054 **7** *½* **Desert Hawk**[16] 3631 3-8-13 **69** .................. RLMoore 5 63
(RHannon) *lw: chsd wnr to 7f out: styd chsng ldng pair: rdn over 3f out: wknd 2f out* **7/2**[1]

-633 **8** *½* **Turner**[27] 3294 3-9-2 **72** .................. SWKelly 2 66
(WMBrisbourne) *dwlt: t.k.h: hld up in rr: rdn and no prog 3f out: no ch after* **16/1**

2m 11.43s (2.70) **Going Correction** +0.075s/f (Good) **8** Ran SP% **112.4**
Speed ratings: **92,91,89,89,87 86,86,85**CSF £26.19 CT £143.04 TOTE £5.60: £1.70, £1.90, £2.30; EX 32.00 Place 6 £24.95, Place 5 £17.03.

**Owner** Nigel Johnson-Hill **Bred** D R Botterill **Trained** Compton, Berks

**FOCUS**
Just an ordinary handicap for the track, and a steady early pace resulting in a slow time means the form wants treating with a little caution.

**NOTEBOOK**
**Iffy**, stepping up from a mile, is usually held up but, with no pace on this time, he was able to dictate from the front and very much had things his own way. However, he still had to dig deep when challenged in the closing stages and ultimately ran out a very game winner. His stamina was not tested as much as it might have been, but the trip is basically not a problem and there are more races to be won with him at similar distances.

**Edgehill(IRE)**, stepping up from seven furlongs on this handicap debut, was the only one to give the winner a proper race and emerges with credit. He looks well up to winning a similar race.

**Foxilla(IRE)** ran well considering a stronger pace would have suited better.

**Epaminondas(USA)**, still a maiden, should not have been inconvenienced by this step back up in trip, but he ran disappointingly.

**Vamp**, off the mark at Bath on her previous start, should have appreciated the fast ground but was a long way below form.

**Desert Hawk** failed to confirm the promise he showed on his handicap debut and is better than this. He can be given another chance.

T/Jkpt: Not won. T/Plt: £34.80 to a £1 stake. Pool: £76,621.40. 1,605.15 winning tickets. T/Qpdt: £6.80 to a £1 stake. Pool: £4,333.80. 469.30 winning tickets. JN

# 3695 CHEPSTOW (L-H)
Friday, July 23

**OFFICIAL GOING: Good to firm (good in places)**
The ground had dried out a little during the day.
Wind: nil Weather: fine

## 4080 TINTERN AMATEUR RIDERS' H'CAP 1m 4f 23y
6:30 (6:31) (F) (0-70,70) 3-Y-0+ £3,101 (£886; £443) Stalls Low

Form RPR

6015 **1** **Theatre Lady (IRE)**[10] 3827 6-9-1 **46** 5ex.................. MissEFolkes(3) 9 57
(PDEvans) *hld up and bhd: hdwy on outside over 2f out: r.o to ld wl ins fnl f* **8/1**[2]

6434 **2** *1½* **Lazzaz**[12] 3774 6-9-0 **47**.................. MrsMarieKing(5) 17 56
(PWHiatt) *led: rdn over 2f out: hdd wl ins fnl f: nt qckn* **8/1**[2]

4356 **3** *1½* **Vandenberghe**[12] 3774 5-9-6 **48**.................. MissSBeddoes 3 58+
(JAOsborne) *hld up: stdy hdwy 4f out: swtchd lft 3f out: nt clr run on ins and swtchd rt over 1f out: r.o ins fnl f* **16/1**

0353 **4** *1* **Head To Kerry (IRE)**[6] 3942 4-9-8 **57**.................. MissAHockley(7) 16 62
(DJSFrenchDavis) *plld hrd: prom: wnt 2nd 6f out: no ex fnl f* **15/2**[1]

-056 **5** *nk* **Final Dividend (IRE)**[17] 3604 8-9-2 **47** ow3.......... MissJoannaRees(3) 5 52
(JMPEustace) *a.p: rdn and r.o one pce fnl f* **16/1**

6300 **6** *½* **Hashid (IRE)**[13] 3752 4-10-4 **65**.................. MrDavidTurner(5) 19 69
(PCRitchens) *prom: rdn and hung lft over 3f out: one pce fnl f* **66/1**

3204 **7** *5* **Sarn**[13] 3733 5-8-6 **41**.................. MissMMullineaux(7) 13 37
(MMullineaux) *bhd tl hdwy fnl 2f: nrst fin* **16/1**

/3-6 **8** *½* **Wizard Of Edge**[72] 463 4-10-11 **70**.................. MrJamesWhite(3) 12 65
(RJHodges) *hld up: rdn and hdwy over 2f out: no imp fnl f* **14/1**

-010 **9** *shd* **Burnt Copper (IRE)**[12] 3774 4-9-7 **54**.................. MissKManser(5) 8 49
(JRBest) *s.s: bhd tl hdwy over 2f out: n.d* **9/1**[3]

-313 **10** *1¼* **Critical Stage (IRE)**[155] 829 5-10-10 **66**.................. MissSBrotherton 6 59
(JDFrost) *prom: rdn over 2f out: wknd 1f out* **12/1**

6002 **11** *nk* **Milk And Sultana**[12] 3774 4-9-4 **49**.................. MrsSOwen(3) 1 41
(GAHam) *a bhd* **8/1**[2]

200- **12** *1½* **Eight (IRE)**[231] 5819 8-9-1 **50** ow3.................. MsTDzieciolowska(7) 2 40
(MRChannon) *hld up in mid-div: rdn over 2f out: no rspnse* **10/1**

/50- **13** *2½* **Black Swan (IRE)**[126] 5426 4-8-9 **40**.................. MrsSMoore(3) 7 26
(GAHam) *bhd fnl 4f* **66/1**

0/06 **14** *nk* **King Halling**[13] 3733 5-10-4 **60**.................. MissEJJones 10 45
(RFord) *w ldr 6f: rdn and wknd over 2f out* **33/1**

0003 **15** *3* **Somayda (IRE)**[13] 3747 9-8-5 **40**..................(p) JDoyle(7) 18 21
(MissJacquelineSDoyle) *hld up in tch: rdn 3f out: sn wknd* **33/1**

5550 **16** *7* **Silver Prophet (IRE)**[29] 3244 5-10-10 **66**..................(p) MrsSBosley 14 35
(MRBosley) *bhd most of way* **8/1**[2]

0/0- **17** *6* **Keep The Peace (IRE)**[24] 1566 6-9-1 **50**............(tp) MissHMLewis(7) 11 10
(KGWingrove) *bhd fnl 5f* **66/1**

0055 **18** *shd* **Duke's View (IRE)**[19] 3556 3-9-5 **62**..................(b) MissLJHarwood(3) 4 22
(MrsAJPerrett) *a bhd* **16/1**

30-0 **19** *21* **Beauchamp Ribbon**[25] 3383 4-10-0 **63**..................(p) MrGTumelty(7) 15 —
(AJChamberlain) *rel to r: a bhd: t.o* **33/1**

2m 38.27s (-0.23) **Going Correction** +0.05s/f (Good)
**WFA** 3 from 4yo+ 12lb **19** Ran SP% **126.5**
Speed ratings: **102,101,100,99,99 98,95,95,95,94 94,93,91,91,89 84,80,80,66**CSF £69.12 CT £1022.63 TOTE £7.60: £2.00, £2.40, £4.20, £2.30; EX 40.40.

**Owner** Waterline Racing Club **Bred** Terry Keaney **Trained** Pandy, Gwent

**FOCUS**
The first three had all met in a similar event at Bath 12 days earlier, giving the impression that the form is ordinary but sound.

**NOTEBOOK**
**Theatre Lady(IRE)** would have had another pound to carry had her new mark been in force. She was ridden to orders as her trainer reckons they always go off too fast in these events.
**Lazzaz**, 2lb higher than when third in this race last year, was meeting the winner on 3lb better terms than when beaten just over five lengths at Bath.
**Vandenberghe** was 5lb better off than when just over six lengths behind the winner at Bath. He would have finished closer with a trouble-free run, and the fact he is set to drop 2lb tomorrow augurs well for the near future.
**Head To Kerry(IRE)**, another set to drop a couple of pounds in future handicaps, ran too freely under his inexperienced rider.
**Final Dividend(IRE)** looked more at home back over a longer trip.
**Hashid(IRE)**, dropped 5lb, is not a straightforward ride but this was a much better effort with the headgear again left off.
**Silver Prophet(IRE)** *Official explanation: jockey said gelding lost its confidence when crowded*

## 4081 LETHEBY & CHRISTOPHER MAIDEN AUCTION STKS 6f 16y
7:00 (7:13) (E) 2-Y-0 £3,581 (£1,102; £551; £275) Stalls High

Form RPR

30 **1** **Sweet Coincidence**[20] 3532 2-8-2 .................. PDoe 12 66
(IAWood) *s.i.s: sn prom: bmpd over 4f out: rdn over 2f out: led jst over 1f out: rdn out* **9/1**

63 **2** *2* **Geisha Lady (IRE)**[12] 3770 2-8-1 ow4.................. NChalmers(5) 14 67+
(RMBeckett) *prom: carried lft over 4f out: rdn and ev ch over 1f out: nt qckn ins fnl f* **8/1**[3]

05 **3** *shd* **Barnbrook Empire (IRE)**[31] 3164 2-7-11 .................. DFox(5) 3 60
(IAWood) *led: rdn and hdd jst over 1f out: nt qckn* **66/1**

0 **4** *½* **Divine Diva**[7] 3904 2-8-4 .................. RLMoore 10 60
(RHannon) *outpcd: rdn over 2f out: hdwy fnl f: r.o* **20/1**

0 **5** *shd* **Kapaje**[44] 2786 2-8-2 .................. JoannaBadger 5 58
(PDEvans) *mid-div: rdn and swtchd lft over 2f out: hdwy over 1f out: kpt on towards fin* **66/1**

2 **6** *½* **Polar Dawn**[45] 2761 2-8-2 .................. AMcCarthy 4 56
(BRMillman) *s.i.s: sn prom: carried lft over 4f out: rdn over 2f out: one pce fnl f* **10/3**[1]

**7** *3* **Golden Applause (FR)** 2-8-1 .................. JFMcDonald(3) 15 49
(MrsALMKing) *mid-div: rdn over 2f out: no hdwy* **25/1**

0 **8** *1* **Before The Dawn**[20] 3532 2-8-2 .................. DKinsella 13 44
(AGNewcombe) *hld up in mid-div: swtchd lft over 2f out: sn shkn up: nvr nr to chal* **20/1**

**9** *¾* **Guildenstern (IRE)** 2-8-7 .................. SDrowne 16 47
(HMorrison) *prom: hung lft over 4f out: rdn over 2f out: wknd over 1f out* **9/2**[2]

0 **10** *5* **Mickey Pearce (IRE)**[18] 3588 2-8-7 .................. SRighton 1 32
(JGMO'Shea) *outpcd* **100/1**

**11** *nk* **Lord Of Dreams (IRE)** 2-8-9 .................. SCarson 9 33
(DWPArbuthnot) *sn bhd* **50/1**

36 **12** *1 ¼* **Mister Bell**$^{41}$ 2872 2-8-9 ........ DSweeney 8 30
(JGMO'Shea) *w ldr tl wknd 2f out* **25/1**

**13** *¾* **Arthurs Dream (IRE)** 2-9-0 ........ SWhitworth 11 32
(JGMO'Shea) *s.s: a in rr* **50/1**

1m 13.63s (1.43) **Going Correction** +0.05s/f (Good) **13** Ran SP% **87.5**
Speed ratings: **92,89,89,88,88 87,83,82,81,74 74,72,71**CSF £36.46 TOTE £7.90: £2.00, £1.60, £12.60; EX 30.40.
**Owner** S A Douch **Bred** Mrs M L Parry **Trained** Upper Lambourn, Berks

■ Diamond Josh (8/1, ref to ent stalls) & Sant Jordi (9/2, burst out of stalls & rn loose) were withdrawn. R4, deduct 25p in £.

■ Stewards Enquiry : J F McDonald £110 fine: passport irregularity
Natalia Gemelova £330 fine: vet found filly to be suffering from a contagious skin disease

**FOCUS**
An ordinary event with several horses stepping up promisingly on their debuts, but the form is weak overall.

**NOTEBOOK**
**Sweet Coincidence** continued the recent resurgence in form of her stable. Again losing ground at the start, she put her disappointing run at Nottingham behind her and will now probably go for nurseries.
**Geisha Lady(IRE)**, a half-sister to five juvenile winners, was not inconvenienced by this slightly longer trip.
**Barnbrook Empire(IRE)**, a stable companion of the winner, is a half-sister to a winner in Italy. Reverting back to six, she is going the right way.
**Divine Diva** ◆ finished much closer than seemed likely for much of the trip and is one to keep an eye on when stepped up in distance.
**Kapaje**, a half-sister to four winners, showed significant improvement on her debut for Mick Channon at Newbury last month. She is another who should appreciate further.
**Polar Dawn** had no real excuses and simply got tapped for toe.
**Before The Dawn** ◆ was not knocked about and gave the impression there might be better things to come.
**Guildenstern(IRE)**, out of a 13-furlong winner, caused a bit of havoc early on. His rider reported that he ducked away from some spectators on the rails causing his saddle to slip. *Official explanation: jockey said colt ducked away from spectators on the rails, causing saddle to slip*

## 4082 PIERCEFIELD CLAIMING STKS 2m 49y
7:30 (7:40) (F) 3-Y-O+ £2,961 (£846; £423) Stalls Low

Form RPR

10-6 **1** **Teorban (POL)**$^{45}$ 1010 5-9-10 58 ........ RLMoore 15 61
(MPitman) *hld up in tch: rdn over 3f out: led over 2f out: styd on wl* **10/3**$^{1}$

-003 **2** *5* **Simonovski (USA)**$^{20}$ 3529 3-8-10 63 ........ VSlattery 10 58
(JAOsborne) *hld up: stdy hdwy 8f out: rdn over 3f out: chsd wnr over 1f out: no imp* **9/2**$^{3}$

3405 **3** *3 ½* **Lord Lamb**$^{9}$ 3835 12-9-7 55 ........ JFortune 5 48
(MrsMReveley) *sn chsng ldr: led 10f out: rdn and hdd over 3f out: put hd in air 2f out: wknd fnl f* **4/1**$^{2}$

6000 **4** *2 ½* **Indian Chase**$^{13}$ 3752 7-9-2 40 ........ LucyRussell$^{(7)}$ 11 47
(DrJRJNaylor) *plld hrd: hdwy after 5f: rdn 3f out: wknd over 1f out* **20/1**

0662 **5** *1 ¾* **Buchanan Street (IRE)**$^{18}$ 3582 3-8-10 44 ........ DSweeney 7 49?
(JGMO'Shea) *hld up: hdwy on ins 4f out: sn rdn: wknd over 1f out* **16/1**

P0-6 **6** *hd* **Frixos (IRE)**$^{16}$ 3637 4-9-6 53 ........(b) SWhitworth 4 41
(MScudamore) *plld hrd: led early: prom: led again over 3f out: sn rdn: hdd over 2f out: wknd over 1f out* **33/1**

0363 **7** *2* **Our Imperial Bay (USA)**$^{11}$ 3803 5-9-13 52 ........(p) ADaly 8 46
(MrsJCandlish) *prom: stdd after 2f: sn mid-div: dropped rr 6f out: rdn over 3f out: hdwy over 2f out: n.d* **33/1**

-250 **8** *1 ¼* **Desert Quill (IRE)**$^{22}$ 3443 4-9-4 52 ........ SWKelly 12 36
(WMBrisbourne) *prom: rdn 9f out: wknd 2f out* **12/1**

/600 **9** *1 ¼* **Jazil**$^{8}$ 3885 9-9-6 50 ........(vt) GBaker 6 36
(KAMorgan) *sn led: hdd 10f out: rdn over 3f out: wknd 2f out* **40/1**

-000 **10** *8* **Ulshaw**$^{12}$ 3776 7-9-1 45 ........ SJDonohoe$^{(7)}$ 3 28
(BJLlewellyn) *a bhd* **15/2**

**11** *shd* **Somewin (IRE)**$^{9}$ 4-9-6 ........(p) AMcCarthy 13 26
(MissKMarks) *s.v.s: a in rr* **40/1**

4-30 **12** *22* **Gordy's Joy**$^{41}$ 2874 4-9-0 40 ........ JFMcDonald$^{(3)}$ 14 —
(GAHam) *hld up: hdwy 6f out: wknd over 4f out: t.o* **33/1**

U60- **13** *2 ½* **Fattaan (IRE)**$^{265}$ 5879 4-9-9 63 ........ RHavlin 2 —
(JGMO'Shea) *a bhd: t.o* **25/1**

-006 **14** *8* **Regal Repose**$^{49}$ 2662 4-8-10 45 ........ HayleyTurner$^{(5)}$ 9 —
(AJChamberlain) *plld hrd early: prom 6f: t.o* **66/1**

**15** *10* **Brazil Nut** 3-8-8 ........ PDoe 1 —
(MissKMarks) *a bhd: t.o fnl 5f* **40/1**

3m 40.01s (0.91) **Going Correction** +0.05s/f (Good) **15** Ran SP% **119.9**
**WFA** 3 from 4yo+ 17lb
Speed ratings: **99,96,94,93,92 92,91,90,90,86 86,75,73,69,64** CT £5.10 TOTE £2.10: £2.20, £1.30, £; EX18.80 1.The winner was claimed by Mark Duthie for £7,000. Simonovski was claimed by Deborah Helen Potter for £10,000. Indian
**Owner** Something In The City Partnership **Bred** Sk Golejewko **Trained** Upper Lambourn, Berks

**FOCUS**
They went no pace in this staying claimer and this is unlikely to provide much of a pointer to future events.

**NOTEBOOK**
**Teorban(POL)**, twice a winner over this trip at Wolverhampton, came here after one of his better efforts over hurdles. He was subsequently claimed for £7,000 after winning going away.
**Simonovski(USA)**, taking a big step up in trip, proved no match for the winner in the closing stages but did not seem to be beaten on the grounds of stamina.
**Lord Lamb** appeared to be hating every second of it in the final quarter of a mile.
**Indian Chase** eventually paid the penalty for proving to be too much of a handful for his young rider.
**Buchanan Street(IRE)** appeared to get found out by this much longer trip.
**Frixos(IRE)**, tackling two miles for the first time on the Flat, looked a doubtful stayer.
**Jazil** *Official explanation: jockey said gelding hung left throughout*
**Fattaan(IRE)** *Official explanation: jockey said saddle slipped*

## 4083 TOTESPORT H'CAP 7f 16y
8:00 (8:14) (E) (0-70,68) 3-Y-O+ £4,663 (£1,435; £717; £358) Stalls High

Form RPR

/000 **1** **Threezedzz**$^{35}$ 3043 6-9-1 58 ........(t) FPFerris$^{(3)}$ 6 66
(PDEvans) *racd far side: mde all: rdn over 2f out: drvn out* **25/1**

0406 **2** *nk* **Bishopstone Man**$^{12}$ 3771 7-9-12 66 ........ JFortune 8 73
(HCandy) *hld up towards rr: hdwy over 2f out: rdn over 1f out: r.o ins fnl f* **8/1**$^{3}$

0245 **3** *½* **Iphigenia (IRE)**$^{8}$ 3875 3-8-12 64 ........ HayleyTurner$^{(5)}$ 16 70
(PWHiatt) *a.p: rdn over 1f out: kpt on ins fnl f* **10/1**

U000 **4** *½* **The Gaikwar (IRE)**$^{14}$ 3698 5-9-2 61 ........(b) MSavage$^{(5)}$ 15 65
(NEBerry) *a.p: led stands' side and hung lft over 1f out: nt qckn towards fin* **20/1**

0003 **5** *1 ½* **Oases**$^{9}$ 3841 5-9-0 54 ........(v) SWhitworth 4 54
(DShaw) *dwlt: sn swtchd to stands' side gp: hld up: rdn and hdwy over 1f out: r.o ins fnl f* **20/1**

-022 **6** *hd* **Cyfrwys (IRE)**$^{14}$ 3711 3-9-4 65 ........ DKinsella 14 65
(BPalling) *led stands' side over 5f: wknd ins fnl f* **9/2**$^{1}$

1-10 **7** *½* **Gold Guest**$^{188}$ 559 5-9-5 66 ........ SJDonohoe$^{(7)}$ 17 65
(PDEvans) *mid-div: rdn and hdwy 2f out: wknd fnl f* **9/1**

0331 **8** *nk* **Over To You Bert**$^{12}$ 3771 5-8-2 45 6ex ........ JFMcDonald$^{(3)}$ 9 43
(RJHodges) *chsd ldrs: rdn over 3f out: wknd fnl f* **8/1**$^{3}$

1040 **9** *1 ¾* **Ballare (IRE)**$^{51}$ 2597 5-8-2 47 ........(v) RThomas$^{(5)}$ 2 40
(BobJones) *chsd wnr far side: rdn over 2f out: wknd over 1f out* **33/1**

0003 **10** *nk* **Baby Barry**$^{13}$ 3734 7-8-7 47 ........ AMcCarthy 3 39
(MrsGSRees) *racd far side: n.d* **14/1**

3200 **11** *shd* **Full Spate**$^{8}$ 3887 9-9-7 68 ........ CJDavies$^{(7)}$ 20 60
(JMBradley) *s.s: hld up: hdwy over 4f out: rdn 2f out: wknd over 1f out* **12/1**

0060 **12** *1 ¾* **Cotton Easter**$^{18}$ 3589 3-8-8 55 ........ PaulEddery 13 42
(MrsAJBowlby) *s.i.s: a bhd* **33/1**

4450 **13** *1 ½* **Lily Of The Guild (IRE)**$^{13}$ 3747 5-8-11 51 ........ SDrowne 10 34
(WSKittow) *s.s: a bhd* **9/1**

4600 **14** *1 ½* **Annijaz**$^{14}$ 3698 7-8-12 52 ........ RLMoore 19 31
(JMBradley) *a bhd* **6/1**$^{2}$

0000 **15** *nk* **Compton Arrow (IRE)**$^{27}$ 3298 8-8-11 51 ........ SRighton 12 29
(AWCarroll) *a bhd* **25/1**

0220 **16** *3* **Meelup (IRE)**$^{52}$ 2560 4-9-4 58 ........(p) VSlattery 7 28
(JaneSouthcombe) *prom: rdn over 2f out: sn wknd* **33/1**

00-0 **17** *2* **Scarpia**$^{21}$ 3487 4-8-5 45 ........ RSmith 18 10
(JCFox) *prom over 4f* **50/1**

000- **18** *½* **Vertedanz (IRE)**$^{197}$ 2055 4-8-4 49 ........ NChalmers$^{(5)}$ 5 12
(MissIECraig) *a bhd* **66/1**

0030 **19** *2 ½* **Danish Monarch**$^{31}$ 3180 3-9-3 64 ........ DSweeney 11 21
(ADWPinder) *prom tl rdn and wknd over 2f out* **33/1**

1m 22.82s (-0.38) **Going Correction** +0.05s/f (Good)
**WFA** 3 from 4yo+ 7lb **19** Ran SP% **130.6**
Speed ratings: **104,103,103,102,100 100,100,99,97,97 97,95,93,91,91 88,85,85,82**CSF £207.41 CT £2238.37 TOTE £42.70: £8.30, £2.20, £2.60, £5.80; EX 598.00.
**Owner** Steve Evans **Bred** Mrs R Pease **Trained** Pandy, Gwent

**FOCUS**
An ordinary handicap and reasonable form for the level. They split into two groups and there was little to choose between the two sides.

**NOTEBOOK**
**Threezedzz** was kept to the far side because he does not like being crowded and the plan worked perfectly.
**Bishopstone Man**, dropping back from a mile, was the first home on the stands' side but could not peg back the winner. The fact he is set to drop 2lb tomorrow augurs well for the near future.
**Iphigenia(IRE)** stuck to her task on this drop back to seven.
**The Gaikwar(IRE)**, dropped 4lb, ran much better than of late and would have gone even closer had he kept straight.
**Oases**, an habitual slow starter, again had the ground on the fast side for him.
**Cyfrwys(IRE)**, a springer in the market, has yet to prove she stays this trip.
**Danish Monarch** *Official explanation: jockey said gelding hung left*

## 4084 EUROPEAN BREEDERS FUND CLASSIFIED STKS 7f 16y
8:30 (8:40) (D) 3-Y-O+ £6,682 (£2,056; £1,028; £514) Stalls High

Form RPR

01-1 **1** **Alinda (IRE)**$^{20}$ 3525 3-8-6 75 ........ RLMoore 2 84
(PWHarris) *hld up: hdwy 2f out: rdn to ld cl home: r.o* **10/11**$^{1}$

2115 **2** *hd* **Goodenough Mover**$^{14}$ 3698 8-9-2 80 ........ HayleyTurner$^{(5)}$ 5 91
(JSKing) *a.p: led over 1f out: rdn and hdd cl home* **3/1**$^{2}$

3006 **3** *3* **Hilites (IRE)**$^{17}$ 3602 3-8-10 79 ........ SWhitworth 4 79
(JSMoore) *hld up: hdwy over 2f out: sn rdn: wknd ins fnl f* **16/1**

2011 **4** *nk* **Savile's Delight (IRE)**$^{12}$ 3779 5-9-8 74 ........ JFortune 1 83
(RBrotherton) *w ldr: led over 2f out: rdn and hdd over 1f out: wknd ins fnl f* **5/1**$^{3}$

00-0 **5** *2* **Elidore**$^{90}$ 1608 4-8-13 74 ........ DKinsella 7 69
(BPalling) *led: rdn and hdd over 2f out: wknd 1f out* **33/1**

21-0 **6** *5* **Bread Of Heaven**$^{81}$ 1829 3-8-8 77 ........(b$^{1}$) SDrowne 3 57
(MrsAJPerrett) *prom over 3f* **12/1**

100- **7** *8* **Gin 'N' Fonic (IRE)**$^{5}$ 4659 4-9-2 70 ........ RHavlin 6 37
(JDFrost) *sn wl bhd* **50/1**

1m 22.46s (-0.74) **Going Correction** +0.05s/f (Good)
**WFA** 3 from 4yo+ 7lb **7** Ran SP% **112.5**
Speed ratings: **106,105,102,102,99 94,84**CSF £3.64 TOTE £1.90: £1.50, £2.40; EX 4.10.
**Owner** Mrs P W Harris & E Jehu **Bred** Yeomanstown Stud **Trained** Ringshall, Bucks

**FOCUS**
This fair handicap was won in a highly respectable time and the form looks sound.

**NOTEBOOK**
**Alinda(IRE)**, held up by a throat infection prior to her win at Leicester, continues to progress and ought to get a mile.
**Goodenough Mover** again showed he does not have to dominate from the word go to be effective. There was no disgrace in this effort against a progressive younger rival.
**Hilites(IRE)** gave the impression she is better suited to six.
**Savile's Delight(IRE)** had something to find at the weights and also needs some cut in the ground to be seen at his best.
**Elidore** has not lived up to her two-year-old form and has been lightly raced.

## 4085 DENTS ORIGINALS FINE ART GALLERY OPENS TONIGHT H'CAP 5f 16y
9:00 (9:07) (E) (0-70,69) 3-Y-O+ £3,867 (£1,190; £595; £297) Stalls High

Form RPR

-062 **1** **Stagnite**$^{6}$ 3935 4-8-8 54 ........(p) NChalmers$^{(5)}$ 16 65
(MrsHSweeting) *w ldr tl led stands' side over 2f out: rdn over 1f out: r.o wl to take overall ld wl ins fnl f* **13/2**$^{3}$

0404 **2** *1 ¼* **Loch Inch**$^{11}$ 3810 7-8-10 51 ........(b) CCatlin 14 57
(JMBradley) *hld up: rdn and hdwy over 2f out: kpt on wl u.p ins fnl f* **8/1**

4020 **3** *hd* **Cerulean Rose**$^{31}$ 3178 5-9-10 68 ........ LFletcher$^{(3)}$ 9 73+
(AWCarroll) *chsd ldrs: rdn over 1f out: r.o ins fnl f: sddle slipped* **7/1**

1000 **4** *hd* **One Way Ticket**$^{8}$ 3887 4-10-0 69 ........(p) SWKelly 4 74
(JMBradley) *led far side: rdn and overall ldr over 1f out: hdd wl ins fnl f* **12/1**

6014 **5** *1 ¼* **Avit (IRE)**$^{34}$ 3084 4-7-12 39 ........ AMcCarthy 11 39
(PLGilligan) *a.p: rdn and edgd lft over 2f out: one pce fnl f* **14/1**

06-0 **6** *shd* **Moritat (IRE)**$^{36}$ 3025 4-8-9 53 ........ FPFerris$^{(3)}$ 6 53
(PDEvans) *racd far side: hld up: rdn and hdwy over 2f out: chsd ldr over 1f out: no ex wl ins fnl f* **10/1**

3633 **7** *¾* **Jazzy Millennium**$^{10}$ 3828 7-8-13 54 ........(b) SDrowne 10 51
(BRMillman) *hld up: rdn over 2f out: nvr nr to chal* **6/1**$^{2}$

4000 **8** *shd* **Yorkies Boy**[6] 3935 9-8-5 **51**........................................(p) RThomas(5) 17 48
(NEBerry) *hld up and bhd: rdn over 2f out: late hdwy: nvr nrr* **16/1**

4300 **9** *1* **So Sober (IRE)**[8] 3864 6-7-8 **40**........................................ HayleyTurner(5) 7 33
(DShaw) *racd far side: hld up: sme late hdwy: n.d* **33/1**

00-0 **10** *1* **Old Harry**[55] 2483 4-8-6 **47**........................................(t) DSweeney 1 36
(PCRitchens) *prom far side: rdn and wknd over 1f out* **66/1**

0-50 **11** *½* **Flapdoodle**[18] 3575 6-8-10 **51**........................................ PDoe 13 39
(AWCarroll) *led stands' side: rdn and hung lft over 2f out: sn hdd: wknd 1f out* **14/1**

0041 **12** *shd* **Coranglais**[12] 3772 4-9-10 **65** 7ex........................................(p) RLMoore 5 52
(JMBradley) *racd far side: a bhd* **11/2**[1]

0206 **13** *1 ½* **Indian Bazaar (IRE)**[12] 3772 8-8-7 **53**........................................ MSavage(5) 8 35
(NEBerry) *w ldr far side: rdn over 2f out: wknd over 1f out* **25/1**

0000 **14** *nk* **Arctic Burst (USA)**[16] 3623 4-9-0 **55**........................................(v) SWhitworth 12 36
(DShaw) *s.i.s: a in rr* **66/1**

420 **15** *5* **Comeraincomeshine (IRE)**[30] 3211 3-9-4 **63**........................................ JFortune 15 26
(TGMills) *prom: rdn over 2f out: lost action and eased jst over 1f out* **11/2**[1]

59.34 secs (-0.16) **Going Correction** +0.05s/f (Good)
**WFA** 3 from 4yo+ 4lb **15** Ran SP% **127.8**
Speed ratings: **103,101,100,100,98 98,97,96,95,93 92,92,90,89,81**CSF £59.84 CT £396.32 TOTE £8.90: £2.20, £3.10, £3.50; EX 41.40 Place 6 £207.73, Place 5 £72.53.
**Owner** P Sweeting **Bred** D A And Mrs Hicks **Trained** Marlborough, Wilts

**FOCUS**
There was again no advantage in the draw with the field racing on both sides of the course. This was ordinary form but is more solid than most.

**NOTEBOOK**
**Stagnite**, dropping back to the minimum trip, finally lived up to the way he works at home and broke his duck at the 32nd attempt.
**Loch Inch**, who ran into top form in August last year, produced another good effort but does go up a pound tomorrow.
**Cerulean Rose** was 26lb higher than when landing this race last season. She must have gone very close to following up had her saddle not slipped. *Official explanation: jockey said saddle slipped*
**One Way Ticket**, running over the minimum trip for the first time, did not have much to race with on the far side. This was a fine effort off a mark 7lb higher than when he won over six here last month.
**Avit(IRE)** turned in another creditable performance off a mark 4lb higher than when landing a weak handicap at Brighton in June.
**Moritat(IRE)** finished second of those who raced on the far side and seems to be coming to hand.
**Comeraincomeshine(IRE)** *Official explanation: jockey said filly lost its action inside the two furlong marker*
T/Plt: £167.00 to a £1 stake. Pool: £47,000.50. 205.35 winning tickets. T/Qpdt: £19.90 to a £1 stake. Pool: £3,718.70. 137.90 winning tickets. KH

# 3943 NEWMARKET (JULY) (R-H)
## Friday, July 23

**OFFICIAL GOING: Good to firm**
Wind: nil Weather: fine & sunny

## 4086 BOLLINGER CHAMPAGNE CHALLENGE SERIES H'CAP (FOR GENTLEMAN AMATEUR RIDERS) 1m 2f
**5:50** (5:51) (E) (0-75,75) 3-Y-0+ **£3,373** (£1,038; £519; £259) **Stalls** Centre

Form RPR

0024 **1** **Jacaranda (IRE)**[4] 3985 4-11-10 **68**........................................ MrSWalker 4 77
(MrsALMKing) *hld up towards rr: rdn and prog 2f out: checked and swtchd rt over 1f out: edgd lft after: led u.p nr fin* **7/1**

2123 **2** *nk* **Yankeedoodledandy (IRE)**[21] 3474 3-11-2 **75**.........(p) MrBHaslam(5) 9 83
(PCHaslam) *lw: chsd ldr: led over 6f out: 2l clr 1f out: drvn and edgd lft: jst ct* **4/1**[2]

3-30 **3** *1 ¼* **Kalou (GER)**[7] 3917 6-9-11 **48**........................................ MrDLQueally(7) 7 54
(BJCurley) *lw: stdd wl in rr: 10th and rdr motionless 2f out: urged frenetically after: styd on stoutly fnl 100 yds: given far too muc* **7/2**[1]

6534 **4** *1 ½* **Kylkenny**[13] 3752 9-12-0 **72**........................................(t) MrJRees 10 75
(HMorrison) *pressed ldrs: rdn over 1f out: nt qckn ins fnl f* **13/2**

0064 **5** *1 ½* **Forest Tune (IRE)**[7] 3917 6-10-3 **50**........................................ MrEDehdashti(3) 2 51
(BHanbury) *clo up: rdn 2f out: v one pced fnl f* **5/1**[3]

0032 **6** *¾* **Private Seal**[6] 3934 9-9-8 **45**........................................(t) MrAChahal(7) 6 44
(JulianPoulton) *stdd s: effrt over 2f out: no ch w ldrs fnl f* **20/1**

224- **7** *2* **Dramatic Quest**[426] 1833 7-11-7 **70**........................................(p) MrMichaelMurphy(5) 8 66
(IanWilliams) *b: chsd ldrs: rdn along 2f out: btn over 1f out* **14/1**

-404 **8** *2 ½* **Maria Bonita (IRE)**[18] 3573 3-10-4 **65**........................................(b) MrRVMoore(7) 5 56
(RMBeckett) *t.k.h towards rr: btn 2f out* **14/1**

5420 **9** *2* **Paso Doble**[23] 3412 6-10-6 **57**........................................ MrJMillman(7) 1 45
(BRMillman) *taken down early: bhd: effrt 4f out: rdn over 3f out: btn 2f out: eased fnl f* **14/1**

-000 **10** *dist* **Miss Hoofbeats**[27] 3305 3-9-5 **50** oh8........................................ MrSRees(5) 11 —
(MissJFeilden) *led over 3f: qckly dropped out: wl t.o fnl 2f* **33/1**

2m 7.13s (0.67) **Going Correction** -0.15s/f (Firm)
**WFA** 3 from 4yo+ 10lb **10** Ran SP% **112.4**
Speed ratings: **91,90,89,88,87 86,85,83,81,—**CSF £33.79 CT £113.70 TOTE £8.20: £2.60, £1.30, £1.80; EX 28.80.
**Owner** Touchwood Racing **Bred** The Near Miracle Syndicate **Trained** Wilmcote, Warwicks

**FOCUS**
An ordinary amateurs' event but sound for the grade, although many will feel aggrieved with the ride Mr Queally gave the favourite.

**NOTEBOOK**
**Jacaranda(IRE)** had arguably the best amateur in the race on board and had returned to form the last twice, so it came as no surprise to see him get get his head in front for the first time in over a year. If remaining in this sort of form he should be capable of finding a similar race.
**Yankeedoodledandy(IRE)** has yet to finish out of the three in eight starts as a three-year-old and holds his form well. This was another fine effort. *Official explanation: jockey said gelding saw too much daylight in running*
**Kalou(GER)** was set an almost impossible task by his inexperienced rider who gave him too much to do. He ultimately came home strongly and, although he looked a ready made winner, is likely to be under-priced next time.
**Kylkenny** has not won for well over a year but is still 4lb higher than when last winning on turf.
**Forest Tune(IRE)** has no change of gear and could only plod on.
**Maria Bonita(IRE)** does not stay this trip and it is surprising connections are persevering with her over it.

## 4087 NGK SPARK PLUGS MAIDEN STKS 1m 4f
**6:15** (6:19) (D) 3-Y-0 **£5,512** (£1,696; £848; £424) **Stalls** Centre

Form RPR

4-5 **1** **Daring Aim**[30] 3204 3-8-9........................................ KFallon 2 81
(SirMichaelStoute) *lw: reluctant to s and whirling tail: sn led: cajoled and looked awkward fr over 1f out: nursed along to hold persistent ch* **3/1**[2]

4 **2** *¾* **Articulation**[17] 3603 3-9-0........................................ RHughes 4 85
(HRACecil) *a 2nd: rdn to chal fr 2f out: n.g.t ins fnl f* **8/11**[1]

4 **3** *5* **Garnett (IRE)**[26] 3348 3-9-0........................................ DHolland 6 77
(AKing) *a 3rd: rdn over 2f out: plodded on and nvr making any imp* **8/1**[3]

3055 **4** *2* **Zuma (IRE)**[14] 3706 3-9-0 74........................................ EAhern 9 74
(RHannon) *lw: nvr bttr than 4th: rdn and outpcd over 3f out* **14/1**

0-5 **5** *15* **Patrixprial**[77] 1926 3-9-0........................................ PRobinson 1 50
(MHTompkins) *lw: midfield: rdn 4f out: sn struggling: t.o* **10/1**

**6** *22* **Ffizzamo Go** 3-9-0........................................(b[1]) JMackay 8 14
(RMBeckett) *cmpt: unf: bkwd: scrubbed along thrght in last pair: nvr gng: wl t.o fnl 3f* **50/1**

0 **7** *7* **Blue Track (IRE)**[8] 3882 3-9-0........................................ TGMcLaughlin 7 3
(MJAttwater) *b: bhd: drvn 4f out: sn wl t.o* **66/1**

2m 29.81s (-3.15) **Going Correction** -0.15s/f (Firm) **7** Ran SP% **113.2**
Speed ratings: **104,103,100,98,88 74,69**CSF £5.39 TOTE £3.30: £1.70, £1.30; EX 5.70.
**Owner** The Queen **Bred** The Queen **Trained** Newmarket, Suffolk

**FOCUS**
A fair maiden but the first two were clear and the form looks decent.

**NOTEBOOK**
**Daring Aim** looked in need of this step up in trip when plugging on on her seasonal reappearance at Kempton over a mile-two and, although she showed a fair amount of temperament - flashing her tail and not looking overly keen to get on with the job - proved good enough to hold the odds-on favourite. She was given an intelligent ride by Fallon, who used his initiative to take it up as a result of the slow gallop, and she ended up outstaying the favourite. She will now have to try her luck in handicaps.
**Articulation** was a skinny price on the basis of his sole start and he could not get by the winner who had the rail to race against. This was slightly disappointing and he looks only ordinary.
**Garnett(IRE)** is the type to do better once handicapped and racing over trips in excess of a mile six, being related to a hurdler.
**Zuma(IRE)** has become very disappointing and simply looks slow.
**Patrixprial** is now qualified for handicaps but will need further.

## 4088 CFX FOREX EBF NOVICE STKS 6f
**6:45** (6:45) (D) 2-Y-0 **£4,667** (£1,436; £718; £359) **Stalls** High

Form RPR

21 **1** **Crimson Sun (USA)**[55] 2470 2-9-5........................................ LDettori 4 95
(SaeedBinSuroor) *led gng wl: rdn and hdd ins fnl f: kpt on wl to regain advanage on line* **13/8**[1]

10 **2** *hd* **Kings Quay**[38] 2954 2-9-2........................................ DaneO'Neill 1 91
(RHannon) *hld up: effrt outside to ld ins fnl f: edgd sltly lft: drvn and jst ct* **5/2**[3]

2 **3** *2* **Yajbill (IRE)**[13] 3758 2-8-12........................................ KFallon 2 81
(MRChannon) *lw: pressed wnr: rdn over 2f out: ev ch 1f out: outpcd fnl 100 yds* **15/8**[2]

05 **4** *1* **Red Chairman**[17] 3601 2-8-12........................................ TPQueally 3 78
(DRLoder) *last pair: rdn 2f out: one pced after: a hld fnl f* **14/1**

1m 13.03s (-0.29) **Going Correction** -0.15s/f (Firm) **4** Ran SP% **108.1**
Speed ratings: **95,94,92,90**CSF £5.93 TOTE £2.20; EX 6.90.
**Owner** Godolphin **Bred** Darley **Trained** Newmarket, Suffolk

**FOCUS**
A good little novice stakes and the front pair are both smart. The tactical nature of the race governs the form.

**NOTEBOOK**
**Crimson Sun(USA)** was given a positive ride by Dettori and improved on the bare form of his maiden win with a narrow victory, rallying gamely to get back up in the dying strides. This was a decent effort conceding 3lb to Kings Quay, and another furlong should see further improvement, although connections are considering him for the Gimcrack.
**Kings Quay** ran below par on firm ground in the Coventry, having previously looked very good indeed when making a winning debut over five - a good effort considering his sire Montjeu was a middle-distance performer - and would have ideally preferred the going to be softer here as well. Despite this he looked certain to win when nosing ahead in the final furlong, only to get done on the line. He is sure to show improvement when finally getting some cut in the ground, and will also appreciate a seventh furlong.
**Yajbill(IRE)** came into this on the back of a second to the promising Visionist at York and showed a good deal of improvement, just being unable to match his more experienced rivals from the furlong pole. He should win his maiden.
**Red Chairman** is now handicapped and will do much better in nurseries.

## 4089 PORTLAND PLACE PROPERTIES NURSERY 7f
**7:15** (7:17) (D) 2-Y-0 **£4,832** (£1,487; £743; £371) **Stalls** High

Form RPR

2113 **1** **Silver Wraith (IRE)**[15] 3677 2-9-7 **91**........................................ JPMurtagh 4 94
(NACallaghan) *hld up midfield: effrt over 1f out: rdn and sustained run fnl f: led cl home: gamely* **7/2**[1]

0301 **2** *nk* **Whatatodo**[4] 3987 2-7-12 **68** 6ex........................................ JMackay 7 70
(MLWBell) *led: rdn over 2f out: kpt on wl fnl f: jst ct* **10/1**

0142 **3** *¾* **Sea Hunter**[15] 3677 2-8-12 **85**........................................ SHitchcott(3) 6 85
(MRChannon) *cl up: drvn over 2f out: ev ch ins fnl f: nt qckn last 50 yds: btn whn squeezed for room nr line* **7/2**[1]

5034 **4** *½* **Madam Caversfield**[22] 3438 2-8-1 **71**........................................ FNorton 11 70
(RHannon) *lw: midfield: rdn 3f out: outpcd 1f out: rallied and styng on nr fin* **16/1**

024 **5** *hd* **Alright My Son (IRE)**[56] 2439 2-8-6 **76**........................................ RMullen 9 75
(RHannon) *lw: drvn in rr: last and bdly outpcd 3f out: hdwy 1f out: kpt on v strly cl home* **10/1**

10 **6** *1 ½* **Heres The Plan (IRE)**[27] 3316 2-8-12 **82**........................................ LDettori 10 77
(MGQuinlan) *lw: keen: hld up and bhd: effrt and rdn over 2f out: one pce and unable to chal* **4/1**[2]

610 **7** *nk* **Don't Tell Trigger (IRE)**[8] 3886 2-7-9 **68** oh1........................................ LisaJones(3) 3 62
(JSMoore) *prom: rdn over 2f out: wknd 1f out* **20/1**

6251 **8** *shd* **Ballycroy Girl (IRE)**[4] 3974 2-8-4 **74** 6ex........................................ EAhern 8 68
(ABailey) *hld up: effrt outside 2f out: hanging lft fr over 1f out: sn btn* **7/1**[3]

2204 **9** *7* **Lakesdale (IRE)**[4] 3987 2-7-5 **68** oh6........................................ MHalford(7) 2 44
(MrsCADunnett) *chsd ldrs: rdn 2f out: wknd ins fnl f* **50/1**

5205 **10** *1 ½* **Clinet (IRE)**[13] 3727 2-7-13 **68** oh4 ow1........................................ JQuinn 5 42
(PMPhelan) *lw: rrd and s.s: plld hrd and prom after 3f: rdn and fdd over 1f out* **25/1**

041 **11** 1 3/4 **Time For You**[16] 3632 2-8-2 **72** PRobinson 1 40
(PJMcbride) *racd solo in centre: early spd: struggling fr 1/2-way: eased* **12/1**

1m 25.66s (-1.11) **Going Correction** -0.15s/f (Firm) **11** Ran SP% **119.3**
Speed ratings: **100,99,98,98,98 96,95,95,87,86 84**CSF £39.13 CT £133.60 TOTE £4.40: £2.00, £2.70, £1.90; EX 51.00.
**Owner** M Tabor **Bred** Mrs M Fox **Trained** Newmarket, Suffolk

**FOCUS**
A fair winning time and solid nursery form. The figures shown as 'official ratings' are estimates for guidance only.

**NOTEBOOK**
**Silver Wraith(IRE)** has shown himself to be a useful and reliable juvenile who always runs his race. He came into this on the back of a solid run in a course and distance nursery earlier in the month, and showed a good attitude in winning off top weight. He will need to keep on progressing if he is to win again.
**Whatatodo** showed improved form to make a successul nursery debut at Brighton, and progressed again to finish second here. She looked the most likely winner for a long way, and has plenty of speed so may be worth trying back at six furlongs.
**Sea Hunter** was 1lb worse off with Silver Wraith on the course and distance running and could not confirm the form. He ran a good race nonetheless, being squeezed up close home.
**Madam Caversfield** is pretty exposed but to her credit dug deep to try and get back at the principals. A mile should be within her compass.
**Alright My Son(IRE)** was struggling badly early on, but came home strongly and could ideally have done with another furlong. He had some half-decent form in maidens and as this was his first start since May, he can be expected to improve.
**Heres The Plan(IRE)** seemed more at home in this company - she ran in a Listed event latest - but could only plug on. She is high enough in the weights as her maiden win has not worked out.
**Time For You** *Official explanation: jockey said filly failed to stride out in latter stages*

## 4090 CORPORATE FX FOREIGN CURRENCY H'CAP 6f
7:45 (7:45) (C) (0-90,81) 3-Y-0+ **£9,431** (£2,902; £1,451; £725) **Stalls** High

Form RPR
0221 **1** **Jonny Ebeneezer**[2] 4034 5-8-10 **63** 7ex (b) LDettori 11 77
(DFlood) *hld up and bhd: smooth run fr 2f out: led jst ins fnl f: sn clr: easily* **2/1**[1]
2225 **2** 1 3/4 **Tony The Tap**[8] 3874 3-9-8 **80** DHolland 13 89
(NACallaghan) *cl 2nd tl led over 1f out: hdd 200 yds out: nt qckn w wnr but in clr command of rest* **9/2**[2]
0060 **3** 2 1/2 **Prince Cyrano**[54] 2503 5-9-5 **72** RMullen 4 73
(WJMusson) *lw: stdd in rr: rdn and passed btn horses ins fnl f: snatched 3rd but no threat to ldrs* **20/1**
4000 **4** nk **Juste Pour L'Amour**[7] 3911 4-9-5 **72** JPMurtagh 2 72
(PLGilligan) *bhd: rdn and prog over 1f out: sn making no imp* **14/1**
0-02 **5** hd **Golden Dixie (USA)**[12] 3778 5-9-13 **80** KFallon 9 80
(AMBalding) *prom: ev ch 1f out: drvn and sn outpcd: wknd to lose two pls nr fin* **13/2**
6430 **6** 2 **Indian Steppes (FR)**[7] 3914 5-8-6 **66** MHalford(7) 10 60
(JulianPoulton) *s.i.s: sn in midfield: rdn over 2f out: btn 1f out* **8/1**
0010 **7** 1 1/4 **Antonio Canova**[27] 3298 8-9-11 **78** FNorton 8 68
(BobJones) *lw: bhd: rdn 1/2-way: nvr in contention* **16/1**
0120 **8** 1 1/2 **Cape St Vincent**[22] 3439 4-9-7 **74** (v) RHughes 3 60
(HMorrison) *towards rr: n.m.r wl over 1f out: nvr gng wl after* **11/1**
000- **9** 1 **Barrantes**[226] 6162 7-9-7 **81** DerekNolan(7) 1 64
(MissSheenaWest) *led tl drvn and hdd over 1f out: dropped out rapidly* **20/1**
00 **10** nk **Mimic**[30] 3195 4-8-8 **68** RMills(7) 5 50
(RGuest) *prom tl rdn over 1f out: fading bdly ins fnl f* **66/1**
0-36 **11** shd **Semenovskii**[16] 3645 4-9-4 **71** SSanders 7 52
(PWD'Arcy) *chsd ldrs: rdn over 2f out: btn over 1f out* **6/1**[3]

1m 11.31s (-2.01) **Going Correction** -0.15s/f (Firm)
**WFA** 3 from 4yo+ 5lb **11** Ran SP% **122.1**
Speed ratings: **107,104,101,100,100 98,96,94,93,92 92**CSF £10.81 CT £147.71 TOTE £2.60: £1.50, £1.50, £15.30; EX 7.80.
**Owner** Mrs Ruth M Serrell **Bred** John Purcell **Trained** Upper Lambourn, Berks

**FOCUS**
A fair handicap and a good performance by Jonny Ebeneezer, who is improving at a rate of knots, and he showed he has plenty in hand with a cosy win.

**NOTEBOOK**
**Jonny Ebeneezer** has been in great form of late and was bidding to follow up his Sandown win from earlier in the week. He was given a nice ride by Dettori, who produced him with a perfectly-timed run to win as he liked. He takes his racing well, and it would come as no surprise to see him turned out quickly again in a hat-trick bid.
**Tony The Tap** has been progressive this season and ran another good race, pulling two and a half lengths clear of the third.
**Prince Cyrano** is without a win since his two-year-old days, but hinted at a little better with a staying on third. He is handicapped to win.
**Juste Pour L'Amour** has been running over further - tried over a mile two last month - and although running well in fourth, did not have the pace to make a serious challenge.
**Golden Dixie(USA)** has now run well the last twice but needs to come down the weights before he wins again.
**Indian Steppes(FR)** *Official explanation: trainer's representative said mare bled from the nose*
**Barrantes**, although capable of going well fresh, can be expected to leave this running behind in time.
**Semenovskii** ran below form and is better than this.

## 4091 VIBE FM CONDITIONS STKS 5f
8:15 (8:15) (C) 3-Y-0+ **£8,415** (£3,192; £1,596; £725) **Stalls** High

Form RPR
0000 **1** **Bahamian Pirate (USA)**[15] 3674 9-9-9 **105** KFallon 3 116
(DNicholls) *lw: scratchy to post: pushed along in rr: rdn and effrt over 1f out: kpt on gamely to ld fnl 50 yds* **6/1**[2]
20-3 **2** nk **Balmont (USA)**[15] 3674 3-9-1 **115** EAhern 4 111
(JNoseda) *h.d.w: swtg: hld up off pce: effrt over 1f out: sn rdn: kpt on but nvr quite gng wl enough ins fnl f: one pce cl home* **2/5**[1]
0034 **3** 1 1/4 **Dragon Flyer (IRE)**[4] 3976 5-8-3 **98** FNorton 5 90
(MQuinn) *lw: cl up: led over 1f out: drvn and hdd & wknd 50 yds out* **7/1**[3]
0-00 **4** 1 1/4 **Funfair Wane**[28] 3266 5-8-8 **93** ANicholls 2 90
(DNicholls) *cl up: drvn over 2f out: ev ch over 1f out: onepced after* **25/1**
5000 **5** 2 **Vita Spericolata (IRE)**[14] 3715 7-8-3 **81** JMackay 6 77
(JSWainwright) *led tl drvn and hdd over 1f out: hanging lft after and sn btn* **33/1**
5030 **6** 1 **Colonel Cotton (IRE)**[6] 3940 5-8-13 **100** WRyan 1 83
(NACallaghan) *sn bdly outpcd: styng on ins fnl f but nvr any ch* **14/1**
0-00 **7** 6 **Boleyn Castle (USA)**[34] 3074 7-8-8 **89** (p) TPQueally 7 54
(PSMcentee) *w ldr: hrd drvn 1/2-way: sn dropped out* **50/1**

57.84 secs (-1.81) **Going Correction** -0.15s/f (Firm)
**WFA** 3 from 5yo+ 4lb **7** Ran SP% **113.6**
Speed ratings: **108,107,105,103,100 98,89**CSF £8.77 TOTE £4.70: £1.80, £1.30; EX 8.20.
**Owner** Lucayan Stud **Bred** Trackside Farm & Liberation Farm & G A Seelbinder **Trained** Sessay, N Yorks

**FOCUS**
The form of this is likely to prove to be unreliable with the favourite disappointing, and Balmont deserves another chance to show his class.

**NOTEBOOK**
**Bahamian Pirate(USA)** came here appearing to be playing for second place - he had a lot of ground to find with hot favourite Balmont on July Cup running- but the nine-year-old had one of his better days and, with Balmont running below par, he was able to record his tenth career win. It is hard to see where he can go from here, and he will continue to struggle in all the top sprints.
**Balmont(USA)** looked a sprinter of immense potential when finishing third in the July Cup on his seasonal reappearance, and he was fully expected to go on from that with a victory. However, he looked very ordinary against nothing more than Listed company and it is possible that he 'bounced'. He is better than this and deserves another chance to prove himself a high-class sprinter.
**Dragon Flyer(IRE)** struggles to win these days and will continue to struggle.
**Funfair Wane** ran respectably at the minimum trip and is weighted to win again. He is one to watch out for back up in trip.
**Colonel Cotton(IRE)** is better in big field, strongly-run races.

## 4092 CORPORATE FX OVERSEAS PROPERTY H'CAP 1m
8:45 (8:46) (E) (0-75,73) 3-Y-0 **£4,241** (£1,305; £652; £326) **Stalls** High

Form RPR
3611 **1** **Pickle**[2] 4020 3-9-3 **69** 6ex SSanders 3 83+
(SCWilliams) *b.hind: midfield and gng wl: clsd 2f out: led 1f out: rdn and spurted clr: readily* **15/8**[1]
-011 **2** 2 1/2 **The Fun Merchant**[28] 3271 3-8-13 **65** JQuinn 5 74+
(JPearce) *trckd ldrs: effrt to ld 2f out: rdn and hdd 1f out: kpt on: no ch w wnr but remained clr of rest* **9/2**[2]
0300 **3** 4 **Louisiade (IRE)**[18] 3585 3-8-11 **63** TEDurcan 12 62
(TDEasterby) *lw: bhd: effrt 1/2-way: outpcd by ldng pair over 1f out: styd on steadily wout threatening* **20/1**
06-5 **4** 1/2 **Bright Fire (IRE)**[147] 906 3-7-11 **52** LisaJones(3) 8 50
(WJMusson) *lw: prom: rdn and ev ch over 1f out: one pce and sn btn* **12/1**
505 **5** shd **Dan Di Canio (IRE)**[22] 3447 3-8-13 **65** (t) DHolland 9 63
(PWHarris) *lw: keen and hld up: effrt to improve 2f out: hung lft and lost action briefly over 1f out: styd on whn stened fnl 100 yds* **10/1**
0060 **6** 1/2 **Cayman Calypso (IRE)**[9] 3852 3-8-13 **65** PRobinson 2 62
(MAJarvis) *chsd ldr 6f: outpcd by ldng pair over 1f out: wknd to lose three pls cl home* **25/1**
0340 **7** 1 **Bertocelli**[20] 3525 3-8-13 **65** JMackay 6 60
(GGMargarson) *lw: led: drvn and hdd 2f out: btn over 1f out* **14/1**
-060 **8** 1 3/4 **Chigorin**[7] 3312 3-9-2 **68** JPMurtagh 4 59
(JMPEustace) *stdd s: effrt and rdn 1/2-way: btn wl over 1f out* **13/2**[3]
0002 **9** 3 1/2 **Gallas (IRE)**[10] 3817 3-8-3 **55** (v) FNorton 13 37
(JSWainwright) *bhd: drvn and struggling 1/2-way* **25/1**
344 **10** 1 1/2 **Supamach (IRE)**[18] 3592 3-9-0 **66** KFallon 7 45
(PFICole) *cl up 5f: sn btn; eased ins fnl f* **13/2**[3]
65-5 **11** 2 1/2 **Miss Procurer (IRE)**[13] 3759 3-8-12 **69** (t) NDeSouza(5) 14 42
(PFICole) *swtchd lft after s to join rest of field: racd freely in midfield: wknd over 2f out* **20/1**
635- **12** shd **Broughton Bounty**[350] 3966 3-9-2 **68** RMullen 10 41
(WJMusson) *dropped out last: nvr a factor fr 1/2-way* **33/1**

1m 40.05s (-0.43) **Going Correction** -0.15s/f (Firm) **12** Ran SP% **123.2**
Speed ratings: **96,93,89,89,88 88,87,85,82,80 78,78**CSF £9.34 CT £137.57 TOTE £2.70: £1.30, £1.70, £8.60; EX 6.20 Place 6 £6.48, Place 5 £4.02.
**Owner** S P Tindall **Bred** Simon Tindall **Trained** Newmarket, Suffolk

**FOCUS**
A modest winning time for the grade, but couple of progressive horses dominated the outcome in a race. The form is sound and looks sure to produce future winners.

**NOTEBOOK**
**Pickle** was winning her first race in just over a week and did it in the style of a rapidly-improving filly. Although she is going to take another hike in the weights in future, she is in such form that the four-timer is likely.
**The Fun Merchant** can count himself unlucky to come up against such a progressive filly, as he destroyed the remainder by four lengths. He himself is improving and his winning has not stopped yet.
**Louisiade(IRE)** ran on for third without being able to get anywhere near the front two. This was his best effort for a while and he may be nearing a win.
**Bright Fire(IRE)** showed improved form on this handicap debut/step up in trip and will face less-demanding tasks.
**Dan Di Canio(IRE)** had things conspire against him and is on a fair mark. He did not look an easy ride, but is capable of winning a similar sort of race. *Official explanation: jockey said gelding had hung left down the hill*
**Supamach(IRE)** *Official explanation: jockey said filly made a noise*
T/Plt: £5.60 to a £1 stake. Pool: £43,646.90. 5,631.30 winning tickets. T/Qpdt: £4.50 to a £1 stake. Pool: £2,388.90. 389.70 winning tickets. IM

# 3799 SOUTHWELL (L-H)
### Friday, July 23

**OFFICIAL GOING: Standard**
The track appeared to be riding on the slower side with the majority of the races unfolding more towards the centre of the course.
Wind: Slight behind. Weather: Fine and sunny.

## 4093 ST BRIDGET'S DAY CLAIMING STKS 1m (F)
2:25 (2:31) (F) 3-Y-0+ **£2,975** (£850; £425) **Stalls** Low

Form RPR
4060 **1** **Book Matched**[34] 3102 3-9-1 **67** FNorton 10 74
(BSmart) *led 1f: remained handy tl led 3f out: rdn over 1f out: r.o* **14/1**
0050 **2** 2 1/2 **Sahaat**[20] 3536 6-9-10 **70** LFletcher(3) 11 73
(MJPolglase) *chsd ldrs: rdn and ev ch over 2f out: styd on same pce fnl f* **5/1**[3]
0005 **3** 3 **General**[15] 3658 7-9-11 **65** GGibbons 1 65
(NPLittmoden) *hld up: hmpd wl over 3f out: styd on u.p fnl 2f: nt trble ldrs* **9/1**

0002 **4** *hd* **Multiple Choice (IRE)**[14] 3707 3-8-12 65............(t) J-PGuillambert(3) 14 63
(NPLittmoden) *chsd ldrs: led 6f out: hdd 3f out: styd on same pce appr fnl f* **11/2**

0006 **5** *3/4* **Jaolins**[14] 3707 3-8-0 49.......................................... DKinsella 9 46
(PGMurphy) *s.i.s: hdwy 1/2-way: rdn over 2f out: styd on same pce appr fnl f* **33/1**

0040 **6** *1* **Fortune Point (IRE)**[31] 3177 6-9-9 61.................... IMongan 6 59
(AWCarroll) *led after 1f: hdd 6f out: rdn over 2f out: wknd fnl f* **11/1**

505 **7** *1* **Certain Justice (USA)**[8] 3871 6-9-13 70................................ JQuinn 7 61
(PFICole) *hld up: rdn 1/2-way: sme hdwy over 1f out: n.d* **7/2**[2]

2240 **8** *4* **Kustom Kit For Her**[131] 1022 4-8-10 45.......................(t) JBramhill 5 36
(SRBowring) *chsd ldrs: rdn over 3f out: wknd over 1f out* **50/1**

40-0 **9** *5* **Titian Flame (IRE)**[23] 3412 4-9-0 55............................... RHavlin 8 30
(MrsPNDutfield) *chsd ldrs to 1/2-way* **33/1**

6 **10** *9* **Invogue (FR)**[11] 3799 4-8-5 40.............................. THamilton(3) 13 6
(RAFahey) *s.i.s: sn outpcd* **40/1**

0004 **11** *hd* **Arabie**[8] 3871 6-9-9 ................................................... SSanders 4 21
(IanWilliams) *sn outpcd and bhd* **10/3**[1]

4200 **12** *8* **Colne Valley Amy**[26] 860 7-8-1 39............................ PPMathers(5) 12 —
(MrsSJSmith) *sn outpcd and bhd* **33/1**

0-60 **13** *1/2* **Pup's Pride**[160] 773 7-8-8 53..........................................(v) LisaJones(3) 3 —
(MrsNMacauley) *chsd ldrs to 1/2-way* **20/1**

0-00 **14** *1 1/4* **Cross Ash (IRE)**[20] 3525 4-9-13 66.................................[1] DaleGibson 2 5
(RHollinshead) *prom to 1/2-way* **33/1**

1m 45.71s (1.11) **Going Correction** +0.05s/f (Slow)
**WFA** 3 from 4yo+ 8lb **14 Ran SP% 123.3**
Speed ratings: **96,93,90,90,89 88,87,83,78,69 69,61,60,59**CSF £79.70 TOTE £24.40: £6.60, £1.50, £3.30; EX 127.80.Certain Justice was claimed by Mr W. Clifford for £12,000. General was claimed by Mr C. Dore for £11,000.
**Owner** Paul Darling **Bred** P A Darling **Trained** Hambleton, N Yorks

**FOCUS**
This looked a fair claimer on paper, but the time was slow and the form is not sure to work out.

**NOTEBOOK**
**Book Matched**, who gained his only other success on this surface, took advantage of the drop in grade and won with a little in hand.
**Sahaat** has been disappointing since coming over from France, and as a consequence has slipped to a 25lb lower mark. There was a bit more promise in this effort and connections should be able to find him an opening on this surface.
**General** looked to find this trip on the sharp side, but he may well have gone closer still had he not run into the back of the weakening Cross Ash on the turn into the home straight.
**Multiple Choice(IRE)** did not quite get home and may have had too much use made of him.
**Jaolins** has yet to convince she stays this far.
**Certain Justice(USA)** did not appear to face the kickback.
**Arabie** looked to be hating every minute of it and never went a yard. *Official explanation: trainer was unable to offer any explanation for poor form shown*

## 4094 LADBROKES.COM NURSERY 6f (F)
2:55 (3:02) (E) 2-Y-O **£3,721** (£1,145; £572; £286) **Stalls** Low

Form RPR

051 **1** **Diction (IRE)**[28] 3278 2-8-9 61.................................................. MFenton 7 64
(KRBurke) *mde all: rdn out* **10/3**[1]

0426 **2** *1/2* **Haroldini (IRE)**[8] 3886 2-9-5 71......................................... RHavlin 5 73
(MrsPNDutfield) *chsd ldrs: rdn and ev ch fr over 1f out: styd on* **11/1**

5030 **3** *3* **Amphitheatre (IRE)**[15] 3677 2-9-1 67.................................... SCarson 9 60
(RFJohnsonHoughton) *s.i.s: hld up: hdwy over 2f out: no imp fnl f* **14/1**

1410 **4** *3 1/2* **Lisa Mona Lisa (IRE)**[15] 3677 2-9-7 73................................ JQuinn 4 55
(VSmith) *chsd ldrs: rdn over 2f out: wknd over 1f out* **7/1**[3]

400 **5** *2 1/2* **Chicago Nights (IRE)**[50] 2617 2-7-9 50........................ LisaJones(3) 11 25
(PCHaslam) *chsd ldrs over 4f* **20/1**

1113 **6** *1* **Goldhill Prince**[31] 3170 2-9-0 71..................................(p) LTreadwell(5) 1 43
(WGMTurner) *chsd ldrs: rdn over 2f out: edgd rt and wknd over 1f out* **15/2**

4062 **7** *1 1/2* **Dane's Rock (IRE)**[50] 2622 2-8-7 66................................ RoryMoore(7) 8 33
(PCHaslam) *hld up in tch: rdn and hung rt over 3f out: sn bhd* **8/1**

036 **8** *shd* **Orpen Annie (IRE)**[15] 3665 2-9-1 67.................................... JMcAuley 6 34
(MissJFeilden) *sn pushed along: a in rr* **16/1**

0404 **9** *3/4* **Lord John**[8] 3886 2-8-11 63........................................... DaleGibson 10 27
(MWEasterby) *sn outpcd* **7/2**[2]

0040 **10** *6* **Ellis Cave**[11] 3802 2-8-1 56..........................................(v) THamilton(3) 3 —
(JJQuinn) *s.s: outpcd* **10/1**

6550 **11** *8* **Queen's Glory (IRE)**[8] 3886 2-9-5 71.................................. SSanders 2 —
(WRMuir) *hld up: wknd over 2f out* **12/1**

1m 18.2s (1.30) **Going Correction** +0.05s/f (Slow) **11 Ran SP% 123.1**
Speed ratings: **93,92,88,83,80 79,77,76,75,67 57**CSF £42.86 CT £471.12 TOTE £3.90: £1.50, £6.40, £4.90; EX 60.30.
**Owner** J C S Wilson **Bred** Heatherwold Stud **Trained** Middleham Moor, N Yorks

**FOCUS**
Not that competitive, but the front pair pulled nicely clear and the form may be better than rated. The figures shown as 'official ratings' are estimates for guidance only.

**NOTEBOOK**
**Diction(IRE)** had no trouble with the drop in trip and, although she had to dig deep to make sure, never really looked like getting beaten.
**Haroldini(IRE)** appreciated the step up in trip on this Fibresand debut and can be found an opening on this surface.
**Amphitheatre(IRE)** did himself no favours by falling out of the stalls, but showed enough to suggest he can make his mark on this surface.
**Lisa Mona Lisa(IRE)**, well placed to win a couple of sellers, was not disgraced under her big weight and may be better suited to an extra furlong now. *Official explanation: jockey said filly hung right*
**Dane's Rock(IRE)** *Official explanation: jockey said gelding would not face the kick back*
**Lord John** is better than he showed here and can reveal his true colours when facing a stiffer test. *Official explanation: jockey said colt was possibly unsuited by the surface*

## 4095 FIESTA DE SANTIAGO FILLIES' (S) STKS 7f (F)
3:30 (3:32) (G) 2-Y-O **£2,618** (£748; £374) **Stalls** Low

Form RPR

5 **1** **Vale De Lobo**[9] 3847 2-8-8 ........................................... SSanders 7 65+
(SirMarkPrescott) *w ldrs: led over 5f out: hdd over 4f out: led on bit over 2f out: rdn clr over 1f out: eased nr fin* **2/5**[1]

**2** *6* **Kumala Ocean (IRE)** 2-8-8 ........................................... GGibbons 11 45
(PABlockley) *broke wl: sn outpcd: stdy hdwy fnl 3f: no ch w wnr* **10/1**[2]

0005 **3** *nk* **Muestra (IRE)**[39] 2946 2-8-3 ......................................... PMakin(5) 8 44
(MrsPNDutfield) *hld up: hdwy over 2f out: nvr trbld ldrs* **25/1**

0 **4** *2* **Paris Tapis**[38] 2960 2-8-8 ................................................ GParkin 1 39
(KARyan) *w ldrs: led over 4f out: hdd over 2f out: sn rdn: wknd over 1f out* **14/1**

**5** *5* **Polesworth** 2-8-1 ......................................................... MHalford(7) 9 27
(CNKellett) *s.s: bhd tl styd on appr fnl f: nvr nrr* **14/1**

00 **6** *1 1/2* **Chin Dancer**[15] 3679 2-8-8 ...........................................(bt[1]) FNorton 4 23
(BRMillman) *sn outpcd and bhd: nvr nrr* **25/1**

0005 **7** *1 3/4* **Amalgam (IRE)**[8] 3883 2-8-8 ........................................ RHavlin 12 19
(MrsPNDutfield) *chsd ldrs: rdn 1/2-way: wknd over 1f out* **50/1**

50 **8** *3/4* **Web Racer (IRE)**[38] 2961 2-8-1 ..............................(b[1]) DFentiman(7) 10 17
(JRWeymes) *sn outpcd* **20/1**

00 **9** *1 3/4* **Fantastic Star**[66] 2213 2-8-8 ............................................ MFenton 6 12
(JGGiven) *chsd ldrs to 1/2-way* **14/1**

1005 **10** *6* **Bowland Bride (IRE)**[16] 3620 2-8-9 ........................(b) PPMathers(5) 13 3
(ABerry) *s.s: outpcd* **11/1**[3]

0000 **11** *5* **Black Combe Lady (IRE)**[2] 4010 2-8-8 .............................. PBradley 2 —
(ABerry) *led: hdd over 5f out: wknd 3f out* **50/1**

4030 **P** **Monashee Miss**[17] 3611 2-8-1 ..................................... RoryMoore(7) 3 —
(JAPickering) *chsd ldrs: wkng whn p.u over 2f out: lame* **25/1**

1m 33.18s (2.38) **Going Correction** +0.05s/f (Slow) **12 Ran SP% 129.1**
Speed ratings: **88,81,80,78,72 71,69,68,66,59 53,—**CSF £5.51 TOTE £1.30: £1.10, £3.70, £6.20; EX 11.90.The winner was sold to Tony Carroll for 20,000gns.
**Owner** B Haggas **Bred** J B Haggas **Trained** Newmarket, Suffolk

**FOCUS**
One-way traffic with the winner proving different class to her rivals. The form behind her is very poor.

**NOTEBOOK**
**Vale De Lobo** proved different class to her rivals and won pretty much as she liked. With improvement likely to come as she steps up in trip, the 20,000 guineas invested in her at the auction could prove money well spent.
**Kumala Ocean(IRE)** did just enough to secure second place without having to do too much.
**Muestra(IRE)** did not achieve a great deal in taking the minor honours.
**Paris Tapis** did her best to make sure the winner did not have things all her own way, but paid for her efforts late on.
**Amalgam(IRE)** *Official explanation: jockey said filly was possibly unsuited by the surface*

## 4096 LADBROKES.COM H'CAP 1m (F)
4:00 (4:02) (E) (0-75,72) 3-Y-O+ **£3,779** (£1,163; £581; £290) **Stalls** Low

Form RPR

1111 **1** **Masafi (IRE)**[1] 4056 3-8-8 59 6ex........................................ SSanders 2 80+
(SirMarkPrescott) *chsd ldrs: led over 1f out: rdn out* **2/7**[1]

-030 **2** *1 1/2* **Arran**[16] 3626 4-8-9 52......................................................... JQuinn 7 70
(VSmith) *hld up: hdwy over 3f out: led 2f out: sn rdn and hdd: styd on same pce fnl f* **40/1**

6511 **3** *3* **Downland (IRE)**[11] 3800 8-9-10 67 6ex.............................. KimTinkler 5 79
(NTinkler) *hld up in tch: racd keenly: rdn over 1f out: styd on same pce* **5/1**[2]

0222 **4** *2 1/2* **Midshipman**[17] 3614 6-9-3 60..........................................(vt) MFenton 1 67
(AWCarroll) *sn outpcd: bhd whn swtchd wd over 5f out: hdwy 3f out: hung lft over 1f out: sn wknd* **7/1**[3]

4055 **5** *3 1/2* **Brandy Cove**[28] 3282 7-9-4 61............................................... FLynch 4 61
(BSmart) *s.s: hld up: nvr trbld ldrs* **40/1**

0460 **6** *3* **Air Mail**[91] 1598 7-9-10 67.......................................... RFitzpatrick 8 61
(MrsNMacauley) *chsd ldrs: led over 3f out: hdd 2f out: sn rdn and wknd* **50/1**

1140 **7** *1 3/4* **Arms Acrossthesea**[33] 3128 5-9-4 61................................. JEdmunds 6 52
(JBalding) *hld up: nvr trbld ldrs* **40/1**

4415 **8** *8* **Danger Bird (IRE)**[17] 3615 4-9-0 57................................. DaleGibson 10 32
(RHollinshead) *sn pushed along and prom: wknd over 2f out* **40/1**

00-0 **9** *5* **Midmaar (IRE)**[17] 3614 3-8-9 60........................................ FNorton 3 25
(MWigham) *led: hdd over 6f out: wknd over 2f out* **100/1**

0010 **10** *6* **Bold Blade**[27] 3292 3-9-7 72..........................................(b) GGibbons 9 25
(MJPolglase) *unruly stalls: chsd ldrs: led over 6f out: hdd over 3f out: sn wknd* **50/1**

1m 42.75s (-1.85) **Going Correction** +0.05s/f (Slow)
**WFA** 3 from 4yo+ 8lb **10 Ran SP% 121.6**
Speed ratings: **111,109,106,104,100 97,95,87,82,76**CSF £29.53 CT £39.93 TOTE £1.40: £1.02, £6.90, £2.60; EX 24.10.
**Owner** G D Waters **Bred** G D Waters **Trained** Newmarket, Suffolk

**FOCUS**
A competitive contest with several in-form rivals taking part and it was run at a sound pace. The winning time was very smart for the grade and the form looks sound.

**NOTEBOOK**
**Masafi(IRE)** looked wonderfully well considering his busy schedule and, although he was made to work for his success, it will be a surprise if there is not more to come.
**Arran** ◆ did his best to make a fight of it, but was probably unlucky to bump into a progressive type. There will be other days for him.
**Downland(IRE)**, as usual on edge in the paddock, was taken down early. He did not have things quite go his way here, but is still clearly on good terms with himself.
**Midshipman** looked to find this trip too sharp for him nowadays.
**Brandy Cove** again made things difficult for himself by fluffing his lines at the start.

## 4097 ERNST & YOUNG MEDIAN AUCTION MAIDEN STKS 6f (F)
4:35 (4:37) (F) 3-Y-O **£3,283** (£938; £469) **Stalls** Low

Form RPR

0 **1** **Firenze**[31] 3179 3-8-9 ........................................................ OUrbina 1 77+
(JRFanshawe) *s.s: hld up: hdwy u.p over 1f out: styd on to ld wl ins fnl f* **2/1**[2]

02-2 **2** *3/4* **Stargem**[27] 3322 3-8-9 75....................................................... JQuinn 8 66
(JPearce) *chsd ldrs: rdn to ld and edgd lft over 1f out: hdd wl ins fnl f* **4/6**[1]

000 **3** *1 3/4* **Ragazzi (IRE)**[29] 3229 3-8-9 ........................................ PMakin(5) 3 66?
(TDBarron) *hld up: hdwy and hung rt over 3f out: rdn and hung lft over 1f out: styd on* **20/1**

4-44 **4** *1/2* **Troodos Jet**[21] 3486 3-9-0 65............................................. FNorton 6 64
(ABerry) *led over 4f out: rdn and hdd over 1f out: no ex ins fnl f* **5/1**[3]

0-60 **5** *3* **Coco Reef**[17] 3616 3-8-9 50............................................... MFenton 9 50
(BPalling) *led: hdd over 4f out: rdn over 2f out: wknd fnl f* **16/1**

00 **6** *3 1/2* **Bank Games**[28] 3279 3-9-0 ........................................... DaleGibson 4 45
(MWEasterby) *prom over 3f* **40/1**

03 **7** *2* **Festive Chimes (IRE)**[9] 3839 3-8-6 ................................ THamilton(3) 2 34
(JJQuinn) *dwlt: sn prom: wknd over 2f out* **12/1**

0-00 **8** *dist* **Luke Sharp**[25] 3368 3-9-0 33.............................................(b) GParkin 7 —
(KARyan) *sn outpcd* **66/1**

**9** *24* **Tanne Blixen** 3-8-6 ........................................................ LPKeniry(3) 5 —
(PSFelgate) *s.s: outpcd* **33/1**

1m 16.92s (0.02) **Going Correction** +0.05s/f (Slow) **9 Ran SP% 135.2**
Speed ratings: **101,100,97,97,93 88,85,—,—**CSF £4.34 TOTE £4.10: £1.10, £1.02, £7.20; EX 6.10.
**Owner** Mrs Jan Hopper **Bred** Mrs J P Hopper **Trained** Newmarket, Suffolk

**FOCUS**
A modest maiden although the runner-up had shown fair form in maidens coming into this. The proximity of third casts doubt on the value of the form.
**NOTEBOOK**
**Firenze** ◆ had clearly learnt plenty from her debut and won a shade more cosily than the margin suggested. There should be plenty more to come from her.
**Stargem** filled the runner-up spot for the third time, but did not appear to do anything wrong. All three of her previous runs have worked out well enough and she deserves a change of luck.
**Ragazzi(IRE)** showed his first signs of ability, although he looked a far from easy ride. Better will be seen of him in handicaps.
**Troodos Jet**, having his first taste of this surface, ran well enough but would be better off in handicaps.
**Luke Sharp** *Official explanation: jockey said gelding would not face the kick back*

## 4098 LADBROKES.COM APPRENTICE H'CAP 2m (F)
**5:10** (5:10) (G ) (0-55,49) 4-Y-O+ **£2,891** (£826; £413) **Stalls** Low

Form RPR
1542 **1** **Mercurious (IRE)**[14] 3712 4-8-11 **45** DerekNolan(5) 2 55
(JMackie) *a.p: chsd ldr over 3f out: rdn to ld over 1f out: styd on wl* **13/8**[1]
6220 **2** *5* **Doctor John**[59] 2385 7-8-11 **43** PMakin(3) 1 47
(AndrewTurnell) *hld up: hdwy 8f out: rdn over 2f out: styd on same pce* **7/4**[2]
460 **3** *1 ½* **Amusement**[16] 3637 8-9-1 **44** ABeech 6 46
(DGBridgwater) *led: rdn over 2f out: hdd over 1f out: no ex* **16/1**
-600 **4** *7* **African Dawn**[15] 3682 6-9-3 **46** (tp) LPKeniry 5 40
(LGCottrell) *prom: chsd ldr 5f out to over 3f out: sn wknd* **9/2**[3]
0-30 **5** *1* **Myrtus**[69] 2126 5-8-6 **40** DFentiman(5) 4 33
(JRWeymes) *chsd ldrs: rdn over 7f out: wknd over 4f out* **16/1**
00-0 **6** *dist* **Welsh And Wylde (IRE)**[78] 1426 4-9-6 **49** (p) J-PGuillambert 3 —
(BPalling) *chsd ldr 11f: sn rdn and wknd* **16/1**
3m 44.31s (-8.09) **Going Correction** +0.05s/f (Slow) **6** Ran SP% **110.3**
Speed ratings: **99,96,95,92,91** —CSF £4.57 TOTE £2.50: £1.10, £2.70; EX 3.30 Place 6 £14.31, Place 5 £3.02.
**Owner** Gwen K Dot.com **Bred** Miss Jill Finegan **Trained** Church Broughton, Derbys
■ Stewards Enquiry : A Beech two-day ban: used whip in an incorrect place (Aug 3-4)
**FOCUS**
An uncompetitive staying contest which little winning. The form is weak and effectively banded level.
**NOTEBOOK**
**Mercurious(IRE)**, whose form here last time behind Magic Red had been given a boost in the meantime, stays well and in the end that was good enough.
**Doctor John** is only slow, but he tries hard.
**Amusement**, who showed promise in a bumper a few years ago, is clearly of limited ability nowadays.
T/Plt: £55.60 to a £1 stake. Pool: £25,007.75. 328.15 winning tickets. T/Qpdt: £1.80 to a £1 stake. Pool: £1,695.20. 674.70 winning tickets. CR

# 3247 THIRSK (L-H)
Friday, July 23

**OFFICIAL GOING: Good to firm**

## 4099 EUROPEAN BREEDERS FUND JULY MAIDEN FILLIES' STKS 6f
**2:05** (2:07) (D ) 2-Y-O **£6,253** (£1,924; £962; £481) **Stalls** High

Form RPR
05 **1** **Top Form (IRE)**[10] 3823 2-8-11 RFfrench 3 80
(EALDunlop) *mde all: rdn 2f out: drvn ins last and hld on gamely* **16/1**
**2** *shd* **Honey Ryder** 2-8-11 TPQueally 7 79
(DRLoder) *trckd ldrs: effrt 2f out: rdn to chal and edgd lft ent last: rn green and kpt on* **7/2**[2]
25 **3** *shd* **Consider This**[20] 3532 2-8-11 PHanagan 13 79
(WMBrisbourne) *cl up: effrt 2f out: rdn over 1f out and ev ch tl drvn: edgd lft and nt qckn wlins last* **5/2**[1]
6 **4** *5* **Cerebus**[15] 3676 2-8-11 SChin 10 64
(NPLittmoden) *chsd ldrs: rdn along 2f out: sn onepce* **7/2**[2]
**5** *2* **Ignition** 2-8-6 BSwarbrick(5) 9 58
(WMBrisbourne) *s.i.s and bhd tl styd on fnl 2f* **50/1**
0 **6** *1 ¾* **Algorithm**[6] 3950 2-8-11 RWinston 5 53
(TDEasterby) *chsd ldrs on outer: rdn and hung rt 2f out: sn btn* **14/1**
**7** *½* **The Pen** 2-8-11 GFaulkner 2 51
(PCHaslam) *s.i.s and bhd tl sme late hdwy* **50/1**
06 **8** *1 ½* **Frogs' Gift (IRE)**[30] 3197 2-8-8 TEaves(3) 12 47
(GMMoore) *cl up: rdn along and wkng whn hmpd 2f out* **50/1**
0 **9** *1 ¼* **Molly Dancer**[9] 3840 2-8-11 ACulhane 1 43
(MRChannon) *dwlt: in tch on outer: effrt and pushed along whn sltly hmpd 2f out: nvr a factor* **7/1**[3]
**10** *1* **Calamari (IRE)** 2-8-11 MTebbutt 8 40
(MrsADuffield) *in tch: rdn along 1/2-way: sn wknd* **33/1**
34 **11** *1 ¾* **Witty Girl**[24] 3390 2-8-4 KGhunowa(7) 4 35
(MJPolglase) *s.i.s: a bhd* **25/1**
00 **12** *dist* **Princeable Lady (IRE)**[13] 3741 2-8-11 DAllan 6 —
(TDEasterby) *bhd fr 1/2-way: sddle slipped* **25/1**
1m 11.29s (-1.21) **Going Correction** -0.40s/f (Firm) **12** Ran SP% **114.6**
Speed ratings: **92,91,91,85,82 80,79,77,75,74 72,**—CSF £65.46 TOTE £20.10: £3.60, £1.50, £1.10; EX 33.60.
**Owner** ORS,Woods,Weatherby,Davies and Stone **Bred** Top Of The Form Syndicate **Trained** Newmarket, Suffolk
**FOCUS**
A fair maiden run at a decent pace but there was not much between the front three and the form behind those principals looks decidedly ordinary.
**NOTEBOOK**
**Top Form(IRE)**, easy to back, turned in an improved effort to defy her low draw and may well be capable of better in nursery company.
**Honey Ryder**, a 42,000gns half-sister to a high-class three-year-old in France/Germany, also to dual five-furlong juvenile winner Caxton Lad, showed ability despite her greenness on this racecourse debut, and looks capable of winning a similar event.
**Consider This** had the run of the race next to the stands' rail and ran right up to her best, despite hanging under pressure. She is in good hands and may be capable of better over further in nursery company.
**Cerebus** failed to build on an encouraging debut run, but looked ill-at-ease on these much quicker conditions. She may be capable of better over further when qualified for nurseries.
**Ignition**, a 6,200gns sister to multiple middle-distance winner TBM Can, was anything but disgraced on this debut and is sure to do better over further in modest handicaps in due course.
**Algorithm** ran to a similar level as on her debut but is likely to continue to look vulnerable in this grade.

**Princeable Lady(IRE)** *Official explanation: jockey said saddle slipped*

## 4100 HARROGATE NOVICE STKS 7f
**2:35** (2:39) (D ) 2-Y-O **£5,681** (£1,748; £874; £437) **Stalls** Low

Form RPR
1 **1** **Strawberry Dale (IRE)**[20] 3514 2-8-11 WSupple 4 88+
(JDBethell) *keen early: trckd ldrs: hdwy over 2f out: led over 1f out: pushed clr* **7/2**[2]
34 **2** *3* **Noorain**[12] 3770 2-8-7 ACulhane 5 75
(MRChannon) *chsd ldrs: hdwy to ld 3f out: sn rdn: hdd over 1f out: kpt ons ame pce* **14/1**[3]
**3** *1* **Thunderwing (IRE)** 2-8-8 PHanagan 2 73
(KRBurke) *hld up in tch: hdwy over 2f out: rdn and styd on fnl f* **40/1**
5412 **4** *2* **Fiefdom (IRE)**[13] 3727 2-9-2 RFfrench 7 76
(MJohnston) *led: pushed along and hdd 3f out: sn rdn and btn* **4/9**[1]
0 **5** *2 ½* **Zabeel Palace**[13] 3726 2-8-12 TPQueally 6 66
(DRLoder) *a rr* **14/1**[3]
**6** *4* **Dancing Shirl** 2-8-7 ow4 GFaulkner 1 51
(CWFairhurst) *chsd ldrs: rdn along 1/2-way:riven over3f out and sn wknd* **125/1**
3 **7** *1 ¾* **General Max (IRE)**[57] 2422 2-8-12 RWinston 3 51
(ACrook) *hld up in rr: sme hdwy 3f out: rdn and wknd over 2f out* **20/1**
1m 28.15s (1.05) **Going Correction** +0.125s/f (Good) **7** Ran SP% **112.8**
Speed ratings: **99,95,94,92,89 84,82**CSF £44.34 TOTE £5.90: £2.00, £2.90; EX 35.90.
**Owner** M J Dawson **Bred** Bryan Ryan **Trained** Middleham Moor, N Yorks
**FOCUS**
The pace soon steadied and this did not take as much winning as seemed likely, as the favourite was a long way below his recent best. Nevertheless the winner looks one to keep on the right side.
**NOTEBOOK**
**Strawberry Dale(IRE)** ◆, upped in trip, showed improved form to beat a reliable yardstick, and looks a bit better than the bare form as he took a good hold in the early stages. He is open to further improvement and looks one to keep on the right side.
**Noorain** is a reliable yardstick who ran his race over this longer trip. He looks vulnerable to progressive types over this trip but should continue to give a good account.
**Thunderwing(IRE)**, a 12,000 euro son of an Italian juvenile winner, showed more than enough on this racecourse debut for his in-form stable to suggest he will be capable of winning an ordinary event. *Official explanation: jockey said colt hung right handed throughout*
**Fiefdom(IRE)** looked the one to beat on his Ascot run over this trip but, although he had the run of the race, dropped away disappointingly once headed. He is better than this and is worth another chance.
**Zabeel Palace** was easy to back and failed to build on his debut effort. He is likely to continue to look vulnerable in this grade on this evidence.
**Dancing Shirl**, a half-sister to a couple of winners, only hinted at ability on this racecourse debut. She may do better in modest handicaps.

## 4101 MICHAEL J WOOD - CHANTRY CHEMICALS MAIDEN STKS 7f
**3:05** (3:06) (D ) 3-Y-O **£5,564** (£1,712; £856; £428) **Stalls** Low

Form RPR
5220 **1** **Wychbury (USA)**[42] 2847 3-8-11 **75** DCorby(3) 7 52+
(MJWallace) *cl up: led 3f out: pushed clr over 1f out* **4/6**[1]
5040 **2** *2* **Borodinsky**[20] 3517 3-8-11 **44** TEaves(3) 6 46
(REBarr) *trckd ldng pair: hdwy to chse wnr fnl 2f: sn rdn and kpt on same pce* **80/1**
0430 **3** *1 ½* **Gasparini (IRE)**[10] 3819 3-9-0 **59** DAllan 5 42+
(TDEasterby) *led: rdn along and hdd 3f out: sn one pce* **13/2**[3]
0340 **4** *shd* **Lord Wishingwell (IRE)**[29] 3234 3-8-9 **34** (v) MLawson(5) 4 42
(JSWainwright) *chsd ldrs: rdn along 3f out: drvn and kpt on same pce fnl 2f* **100/1**
0 **5** *¾* **Classic Lease**[22] 3447 3-9-0 ACulhane 8 40
(RHollinshead) *hld up: hdwy 3f out: rdn and hung lft wl over 1f out: sn no imp* **66/1**
634 **6** *shd* **Rosie Mac**[13] 3759 3-8-2 **62** SuzanneFrance(7) 3 35
(NBycroft) *towards rr: hdwy on outer over 2f out: sn rdn and kpt on fnl f: nrst fin* **10/1**
24- **7** *¾* **Dium Mac**[273] 5725 3-9-0 DeanMcKeown 9 38
(NBycroft) *chsd ldrs: rdn along 3f out: wkng whn hmpd wl over 1f out* **9/2**[2]
06 **8** *2 ½* **Pure Vintage (IRE)**[49] 2654 3-9-0 PHanagan 1 42+
(RAFahey) *hld up: effrt 3f out: sn rdn along: hld whn hmpd wl over 1f out* **20/1**
50 **9** *¾* **Dancer King (USA)**[18] 3587 3-9-0 RWinston 2 29
(TPTate) *a rr* **40/1**
1m 27.66s (0.56) **Going Correction** +0.125s/f (Good) **9** Ran SP% **111.5**
Speed ratings: **101,98,97,96,96 95,95,92,91**CSF £96.58 TOTE £1.80: £1.10, £12.30, £1.70; EX 91.30.
**Owner** Favourites Racing **Bred** Skymarc Farm **Trained** Newmarket, Suffolk
**FOCUS**
An uncompetitive maiden in which the winner did not have to improve to get off the mark. This bare form looks suspect.
**NOTEBOOK**
**Wychbury(USA)** looked the clear form pick and did not have to improve to get off the mark. However he is likely to struggle back in handicap company from his current mark in the mid-70s.
**Borodinsky**'s proximity confirms this race lackeds any strength and he is likely to continue to look vulnerable in this type of event.
**Gasparini(IRE)** had the run of the race but was below his best. He should be suited by the return to further, but he looks exposed and will invariably look vulnerable in this grade.
**Lord Wishingwell(IRE)**, back over this longer trip, was not disgraced in the face of another stiff task but it is hard to envisage him winning in this grade.
**Classic Lease** was not beaten far but the proximity of a couple of the placed horses confirms this bare form is modest at the very best. Low-grade handicaps will provide his best chance of success.
**Rosie Mac** looked to have fair claims in this company but proved disappointing and will not be easy to place successfully.
**Dium Mac** failed by a long chalk to confirm the bit of promise shown at two, and he will have to fare a good deal better to win in similar company.
**Dancer King(USA)** *Official explanation: trainer said gelding was unsuited by the ground*

## 4102 HUMBER (S) H'CAP 1m
**3:40** (3:40) (F ) (0-55,50) 3-Y-O **£3,477** (£1,070; £535; £267) **Stalls** Low

Form RPR
0034 **1** **Zonnebeke**[23] 3425 3-9-1 **45** RWinston 3 51
(KRBurke) *in tch: hdwy 3f out: rdn over 1f out: styd on u.p to ld nr line* **9/2**[1]
5603 **2** *hd* **Heathyards Joy**[10] 3817 3-7-12 **33** ow1 StephanieHollinshead(5) 8 39
(RHollinshead) *cl up: led after 3f: rdn along wl over 1f out: hdd nr fin* **9/2**[1]

0-00 **3** 1 1/4 **Weet An Haul**[49] 2667 3-9-5 **49**........................................(v[1]) PHanagan 9 52
(PABlockley) *trckd ldrs: effrt 3f out: rdn wl over 1f out: drvn and one pce fnl f* **10/1**[3]

3600 **4** 3/4 **Bargain Hunt (IRE)**[3] 4004 3-8-9 **44**................................ MLawson(5) 17 45
(WStorey) *in tch: hdwy on outer over 3f out: rdn and ev ch 2f out tl drvn and one pce ins last* **16/1**

0630 **5** 1/2 **Faraway Echo**[32] 3139 3-9-2 **49**....................................(v) NMackay(3) 11 49
(MLWBell) *dwlt: hdwy whn n.m.r bnd after 3f: swtchd outside and pushed along over 2f out: satyed on appr last: nrst fin* **12/1**

6000 **6** 1 1/2 **Mr Moon**[35] 3042 3-8-2 **32**..................................................(v[1]) PMQuinn 5 28
(MDHammond) *dwlt: hdwy on inner to chse ldrs after 3f: rdn along 3f out and sn one pce* **25/1**

0044 **7** hd **Chubbes**[20] 3513 3-9-1 **50**........................................(b[1]) PMulrennan(5) 13 46
(MDHammond) *stdd s and bhd: hdwy 2f out: styd on appr last: nrst fin* **11/2**[2]

6050 **8** 3 **Delta Lady**[29] 3229 3-8-12 **42**................................................ RFfrench 10 31
(RBastiman) *chsd ldrs: rdn along 3f out: wknd 2f out* **20/1**

0245 **9** 1/2 **Abrogate (IRE)**[5] 2176 3-9-3 **47**.......................................(p) GFaulkner 14 35
(PCHaslam) *prom:chsd ldr over 4f out: rdn over 2f out and grad wknd* **10/1**[3]

-000 **10** 3/4 **Alpha Zeta**[20] 3511 3-8-10 **40**........................................ DeanMcKeown 16 26
(CWThornton) *towards rr: hdwy whn nt clr run over 2f out: sn rdn and no imp* **50/1**

-000 **11** 1 3/4 **Svenson**[17] 3607 3-8-0 **30**........................................................ PFessey 12 12
(JSWainwright) *nvr a factor* **66/1**

0600 **12** nk **Wedowannagiveuthat (IRE)**[14] 3710 3-9-5 **49**........................ DAllan 1 30
(TDEasterby) *in tch on inner: rdn along 1/2-way and sn wknd* **16/1**

5050 **13** 1 1/2 **Knight To Remember (IRE)**[20] 3513 3-8-5 **38**.................. TEaves(3) 15 16
(REBarr) *a rr* **25/1**

0060 **14** 3 **Cottam Karminski**[10] 3822 3-8-10 **40**........................................ TLucas 7 11
(JSWainwright) *a rr* **33/1**

0000 **15** shd **Gemini Girl (IRE)**[11] 3798 3-8-12 **42**.................................... ACulhane 4 13
(MDHammond) *s.i.s: a bhd* **14/1**

-000 **16** 4 **Trinaree (IRE)**[29] 3229 3-8-8 **38**............................................... NPollard 2 —
(SGollings) *led 3f: rdn along 1/2-way and sn wknd* **25/1**

1m 41.63s (1.93) **Going Correction** +0.125s/f (Good) **16** Ran SP% **118.7**
Speed ratings: **95,94,93,92,92 90,90,87,87,86 84,84,82,79,79 75**CSF £20.68 CT £195.37 TOTE £5.00: £1.30, £1.50, £2.30, £3.90; EX 36.60.The winner was bought in for 5,200gns.
**Owner** John A Duffy **Bred** J A And Mrs Duffy **Trained** Middleham Moor, N Yorks

**FOCUS**
A low-grade event but one run at a sound pace but those racing up with the pace had the edge. This race is unlikely to be throwing up many winners.

**NOTEBOOK**
**Zonnebeke** has not proved entirely reliable, but looked to have fair claims in this poor race and elected to put her best foot forward under a typically-forceful Winston ride with the visor left off. She would not look an obvious one to follow up, though.
**Heathyards Joy** had been running creditably and, although she had the run of the race, did well given that she took a good hold in the early stages. She is due to go up 3lb in future handicaps, but should continue to go well in this grade.
**Weet An Haul**, an inconsistent performer, had the run of the race and was not disgraced over this longer trip in the first-time visor. However, his record suggests he would be no certainty to reproduce this next time.
**Bargain Hunt(IRE)** ran creditably and may be a bit better than the bare form, as he was forced to race widest of all from his wide draw. However his record of no wins from 22 starts and his inconsistency means he is one to tread carefully with.
**Faraway Echo** fared the best of those that attempted to come from off the pace, but this represents only poor form and the fact she is not the most consistent means she remains one to be cautious with.
**Mr Moon**, tried in the first-time visor, was not disgraced back over this shorter trip but does not look one to place any great faith in.
**Svenson** *Official explanation: jockey said colt hung right handed in home straight*

## 4103 ADRIAN TATE H'CAP 1m 4f
**4:10** (4:10) (D ) (0-80,79) 3-Y-O **£5,564** (£1,712; £856; £428) **Stalls** Low

Form RPR

032 **1** **Forged (IRE)**[27] 3297 3-9-4 **79**............................................ NMackay(3) 5 97+
(LMCumani) *trckd ldrs: hdwy to ld and hung lft 2f out: sn clr: easily* **13/8**[1]

0-00 **2** 9 **Classic Event (IRE)**[68] 2146 3-8-5 **63** ow1.......................... RWinston 3 62
(TDEasterby) *s.i.s: pushed along in rr over 5f out: rdn over 2f out: styd on fnl f: no ch w wnr* **33/1**

502- **3** 1 1/2 **Market Leader**[259] 5940 3-9-0 **72**............................................ WSupple 2 69
(MrsAJPerrett) *trckd ldr: effrt to chal 3f out: rdn and ev ch whn hmpd 2f out: sn drvn and one pce* **6/1**

3240 **4** 1 **Havetoavit (USA)**[19] 3561 3-8-3 **61** ow1.................................... SChin 6 56
(JDBethell) *led: rdn along over 3f out: drvn and hdd whn hmpd 2f out: sn btn* **11/2**[3]

3502 **5** 1 3/4 **Kristal's Dream (IRE)**[25] 3383 3-9-4 **76**................................ TPQueally 4 68
(JLDunlop) *trckd ldrs: effrt 3f out: sn rdn along swtchd ins and drvn 2f out: sn btn* **2/1**[2]

0500 **6** 6 **Auroville**[13] 3746 3-8-2 **60**......................................................(v) RFfrench 1 43
(MLWBell) *in tch: rdn along 5f out: wknd 3f out* **16/1**

2m 35.86s (0.66) **Going Correction** +0.125s/f (Good) **6** Ran SP% **109.9**
Speed ratings: **102,96,95,94,93 89**CSF £44.34 TOTE £2.90: £1.60, £5.20; EX 73.40.
**Owner** Gerard P Callanan **Bred** Gerard Callanan **Trained** Newmarket, Suffolk

**FOCUS**
Just an ordinary pace but an improved performance from the winner, who may be able to hold his own in stronger company, even after reassessment.

**NOTEBOOK**
**Forged(IRE)** ◆, back over this more suitable trip, showed improved form on this handicap debut and was value for at least a 12-length win. He will be up in the weights for this, but appeals as the type to progress again and can hold his own in stronger company.
**Classic Event(IRE)**, an habitual slow starter, ran his best race of the year and, while flattered a touch by his proximity to the very easy winner, may be capable of better, especially granted a stiffer test of stamina.
**Market Leader**, easy to back, was not disgraced given that he did not really settle on this handicap debut and reappearance and, on this evidence, may be better suited by the return to shorter in a more strongly-run race.
**Havetoavit(USA)**, attracted support and had the run of the race, but was beaten entirely on merit and will have to improve to get off the mark in this company.
**Kristal's Dream(IRE)** looked to have a fair bit in her favour and had the run of the race, but her response off the bridle was disappointing and, as she has been well below her best on two of her last three starts, may be one to tread carefully with.
**Auroville** was again well beaten in the visor and remains one to watch at present.

## 4104 STANLAND WARWICK DRYER FILLIES' H'CAP 6f
**4:45** (4:45) (D ) (0-80,72) 3-Y-O+ **£5,577** (£1,716; £858; £429) **Stalls** High

Form RPR

0065 **1** **Le Meridien (IRE)**[8] 3864 6-8-3 **48**.......................................(p) RFfrench 3 58
(JSWainwright) *sn prom on outer: hdwy to chal 2f out: led wl over 1f out: sn rdn and kpt on gamely ins last* **20/1**

1034 **2** shd **Sharoura**[4] 3979 8-9-5 **64**.......................................................... PHanagan 7 74
(RAFahey) *trckd ldrs: swtchd rt and hdwy over 1f out: rdn and ev ch ins last: jst hld* **7/1**[2]

3253 **3** 1/2 **Amelia (IRE)**[15] 3680 6-8-8 **58**........................................ BSwarbrick(5) 4 67
(WMBrisbourne) *trckd ldrs on outer: hdwy 2f out: rdn to chal over 1f out and ev ch tl no ex wl ins last* **12/1**

1241 **4** 1/2 **Estihlal**[20] 3530 3-9-8 **72**.............................................................. WSupple 5 79+
(EALDunlop) *bmpd s and bhd: gd hdwy on outer 2f out: rdn and ev ch ins last: drvn and no ex last 75 yds* **5/2**[1]

00-0 **5** 1 3/4 **Mitsuki**[13] 3754 5-9-4 **63**............................................................... SChin 1 65
(JDBethell) *towards rr: hdwy 2f out: sn rdn and kpt on ins last: nrst fin* **14/1**

3566 **6** 3/4 **College Maid (IRE)**[4] 3979 7-8-9 **61**............................(b) JCurrie(7) 12 61+
(JSGoldie) *hmpd s and bhd tl styd on appr last: nrst fin* **14/1**

305 **7** 1/2 **Roman Mistress (IRE)**[13] 3744 4-9-5 **64**..............................(b) DAllan 13 62
(TDEasterby) *wnt lft s: chsd ldrs: rdn along 2f out: no imp appr last* **15/2**[3]

2054 **8** 1 1/4 **Stokesies Wish**[8] 3887 4-9-4 **63**............................................. ACulhane 2 57
(JLSpearing) *racd alone far side: rdn along over 2f out: kpt on same pce* **14/1**

300 **9** shd **Island Spell**[9] 3838 3-9-0 **64**.................................................(p) PFessey 10 58
(CGrant) *cl up: rdn along 1/2-way: sn wknd* **80/1**

0041 **10** 1/2 **Shifty Night (IRE)**[14] 3708 3-7-10 **49**................................ NMackay(3) 15 41
(MrsCADunnett) *hld up: hdwy over 2f out: sn rdn and btn* **10/1**

5452 **11** 3/4 **College Queen**[15] 3668 6-9-5 **64**.........................................(b) NPollard 6 54
(SGollings) *wnt lft s: sn cl up: led 1/2-way tl rdn and hdd wl over 1f out: sn wknd* **15/2**[3]

0000 **12** 1 3/4 **Capetown Girl**[20] 3517 3-8-12 **62**....................................(v[1]) VHalliday 11 47
(KRBurke) *s.i.s: a rr* **25/1**

2-00 **13** 4 **Magic Music (IRE)**[48] 2670 5-9-10 **69**.................................. RWinston 9 42
(WMBrisbourne) *in tch: rdn along 1/2-way and sn wknd* **14/1**

0600 **14** hd **Safranine (IRE)**[23] 3407 7-9-2 **61**....................................... AnnStokell 8 33
(MissAStokell) *led to 1/2-way: sn rdn along and wknd* **33/1**

1m 11.06s (-1.44) **Going Correction** -0.40s/f (Firm)
**WFA** 3 from 4yo+ 5lb **14** Ran SP% **120.8**
Speed ratings: **93,92,92,91,89 88,87,85,85,85 84,81,76,76**CSF £150.75 CT £1782.86 TOTE £22.70: £5.90, £2.50, £3.40; EX 145.80.
**Owner** Miss S L Iggulden **Bred** John J Breslin **Trained** Kennythorpe, N Yorks

**FOCUS**
A run-of-the-mill handicap run at a sound pace and one in which all bar one of the runners raced on or towards the stands' rail. The form looks unexceptional.

**NOTEBOOK**
**Le Meridien(IRE)**, who is in foal, turned in her best effort of the year returned to this trip to record her first success away from Beverley. Impending motherhood has improved several mares, and she may well be capable of adding to her tally in the near future.
**Sharoura** is in good heart at present and gave it her best shot from her middle draw. She should continue to give a good account in this grade.
**Amelia(IRE)** fared well from her low draw after racing on the outside of the main group and she remains capable of winning a similar event from this sort of mark in the coming weeks.
**Estihlal** ◆ did not get the run of the race and consequently looks a bit better than the bare form. She is more than capable of winning a similar race in the near future, and is one to keep an eye on.
**Mitsuki**, who loves it at this course, fared much better than on her reappearance. She is on a fair mark, but her strike-rate in recent times suggests she may not be one to place maximum faith in.
**College Maid(IRE)** was not disgraced after meeting trouble at the start, but she is likely to continue to look vulnerable in handicap company from her current mark.
**Stokesies Wish** had nothing to race with on the far side and this placing is best ignored.

## 4105 LEVY BOARD APPRENTICE H'CAP 5f
**5:20** (5:20) (E ) (0-75,63) 3-Y-O+ **£4,182** (£1,287; £643; £321) **Stalls** High

Form RPR

-150 **1** **Playful Dane (IRE)**[35] 3038 7-8-13 **57**............................ KPierrepont(5) 9 72
(WSCunningham) *sn chsng ldr: hdwy to ld wl over 1f out: clr ins last: styd on* **10/1**

1215 **2** 3 1/2 **Soaked**[7] 3894 11-9-10 **63**.....................................................(b) BO'Neill 3 64
(DWChapman) *led and sn clr: pushed along 2f out: sn hdd: kpt on fnl f* **6/1**[3]

5456 **3** 1 **Amanda's Lad (IRE)**[2] 4011 4-9-2 **55**.................................. LiamJones 14 52
(MCChapman) *dwlt: sn in tch: rdn 2f out: satyed on ins last: nrst fin* **9/1**

0400 **4** 3/4 **Mystery Pips**[10] 3820 4-8-6 **45**............................................(v) RKeogh 11 39
(NTinkler) *midfield: hdwy 2f out: rdn to chse ldrs over 1f out: sn one pce* **10/1**

2044 **5** 3/4 **Bella Beguine**[10] 3820 5-8-1 **48**..............................(b) NatalieHassall(8) 4 39
(ABailey) *chsd ldrs: rdn 2f out: kpt on same pce* **10/1**

2500 **6** hd **American Cousin**[7] 3894 9-9-0 **58**.................................. PJBenson(5) 12 48
(DNicholls) *dwlt and bhd tl styd on ins last: nrst fin* **9/1**

0000 **7** shd **Danakim**[9] 3836 7-8-3 **42**.............................................. DonnaCaldwell 13 32
(JRWeymes) *chsd ldrs: rdn along 1/2-way: sn wknd* **20/1**

0000 **8** 1 1/2 **Mr Spliffy (IRE)**[2] 4011 5-8-7 **46**............................................ MStainton 6 30
(MCChapman) *bhd tl sme late hdwy* **16/1**

0001 **9** 3/4 **Rosie's Result**[8] 3864 4-8-12 **51** 6ex........................... JemmaMarshall 8 32
(MTodhunter) *in tch: effrt to chse ldrs 2f out: sn rdn and wknd* **5/1**[2]

0-04 **10** hd **Cellino**[49] 2661 3-8-2 **45**........................................................ KJackson 10 25
(AndrewTurnell) *bhd: drvn along 2f out: n.d* **33/1**

-050 **11** 5 **Matriarchal**[25] 3376 4-7-12 **45** oh7 ow8..................... JaniceWebster(8) 1 5
(DonEnricoIncisa) *racd wd: bhd fr 1/2-way* **100/1**

2004 **12** 3/4 **Kennington**[8] 3864 4-8-13 **52**..........................................(b) LauraPike 7 9
(MrsCADunnett) *s.i.s: a bhd* **9/2**[1]

0060 **13** nk **Star Applause**[20] 3524 4-7-12 **40**........................................ JCurrie(3) 2 —
(JSGoldie) *chsd ldrs on outer: rdn along 1/2-way: sn wknd* **66/1**

0150 **14** 1 1/2 **Blueberry Rhyme**[57] 2423 5-9-2 **58**..........................(v) StaceyRenwick(3) 5 8
(PABlockley) *in tch: rdn along 1/2-way: sn wknd* **12/1**

57.71 secs (-2.19) **Going Correction** -0.40s/f (Firm)
**WFA** 3 from 4yo+ 4lb **14** Ran SP% **120.2**
Speed ratings: **101,95,93,92,91 91,90,88,87,87 79,77,77,74**CSF £67.18 CT £588.38 TOTE £14.90: £4.00, £2.50, £2.20; EX 129.40 Place 6 £156.87, Place 5 £95.08.
**Owner** Ann And David Bell **Bred** Omicida Syndicate **Trained** Hutton Rudby, N Yorks

**FOCUS**
Another modest handicap, but run at a sound pace and the form should prove reliable at a similar level. The field raced stands' side.

**NOTEBOOK**

**Playful Dane(IRE)** made it four wins from his last 11 starts and proved his effectiveness over this trip. However, he did have the race teed up for him to a certain extent and will find life tougher after reassessment.

**Soaked** showed plenty of foot to get over to the stands'-side rail from his low draw, and gave it his best shot. He would have gone even closer from a more favourable draw and he is capable of further success from his current mark.

**Amanda's Lad(IRE)** ran creditably and is a fairly consistent sort, but the fact he has yet to win a race in 53 starts has to be a big concern.

**Mystery Pips**, with conditions to suit, had the run of the race from her favourable draw but was beaten on merit and this looks as good as she is.

**Bella Beguine** was not disgraced from her low draw and left the impression that the return to six furlongs would be in her favour. Her stable are back among the winners and she is one to keep an eye on.

**American Cousin** fared the best of those coming from off the pace and is on a fair mark at present, but he does need things to fall right and he is not one to place too much faith in.

**Kennington** attracted support but never figured after losing ground at the start.

T/Plt: £85.60 to a £1 stake. Pool: £28,431.90. 242.40 winning tickets. T/Qpdt: £17.50 to a £1 stake. Pool: £2,306.60. 97.15 winning tickets. JR

4106 - 4116a (Foreign Racing) - See Raceform Interactive

## 4074 ASCOT (R-H)

Saturday, July 24

**OFFICIAL GOING: Good to firm**

Wind: fresh against Weather: sunny; warm

### 4117 EUROPEAN BREEDERS FUND CROCKER BULTEEL MAIDEN STKS (C&G) 6f

**2:00** (2:06) (D ) 2-Y-O **£6,734** (£2,072; £1,036; £518) **Stalls** Low

Form RPR

1 **Nightfall (USA)** 2-8-11 ........................(t) LDettori 5 82
(SaeedBinSuroor) *cmpt: scope: bit bkwd: uns rdr and rn loose bef s: racd against nr side rail: mde virtually all: hrd pressed fr over 1f out* **4/1**[2]

2 *shd* **Moth Ball** 2-8-11 ........................ DHolland 4 82
(JAOsborne) *neat: lw: reluctant to enter stalls: trckd ldng trio: effrt over 1f out: jnd wnr ins fnl f: jst pipped* **11/2**

3 *1 ½* **Hallhoo (IRE)** 2-8-11 ........................ TEDurcan 1 77
(MRChannon) *leggy: unf: scope: hld up towards rr: effrt 2f out: hanging rt over 1f out: n.m.r ent fnl f: styd on to take 3rd nr fin* **7/1**

4 *½* **Prince Samos (IRE)** 2-8-11 ........................ KFallon 8 76
(RHannon) *wl-grwn: lw: s.i.s: sn pressed ldng pair: shkn up to press wnr 2f out: one pce fnl f* **7/2**[1]

5 *2* **Taj India (USA)** 2-8-11 ........................ JFanning 6 70
(MJohnston) *cmpt: pressed wnr to 2f out: stl ev ch over 1f out: fdd fnl f* **5/1**[3]

6 *hd* **Edge Of Blue** 2-8-11 ........................ DaneO'Neill 3 69
(RHannon) *lengthy: lw: dwlt: settled in rr: rdn over 2f out: one pce and no imp on ldrs* **7/1**

7 *3* **Antonio Stradivari (IRE)** 2-8-11 ........................ MartinDwyer 7 60
(AMBalding) *str: scope: bit bkwd: s.s: racd in last pair: rdn over 2f out: rn green and no prog wl over 1f out* **12/1**

8 *5* **San Deng** 2-8-11 ........................ SDrowne 9 45
(WRMuir) *leggy: unf: s.s and wnt rt: rcvrd and in tch 1/2-way: rdn over 2f out: rn green and wknd wl over 1f out* **25/1**

1m 18.0s (2.01) **Going Correction** +0.15s/f (Good) **8** Ran SP% **110.8**

Speed ratings: **92,91,89,89,86 86,82,75**CSF £24.48 TOTE £3.60: £1.80, £2.20, £2.10; EX 38.80.

**Owner** Godolphin **Bred** Gainsborough Farm Llc **Trained** Newmarket, Suffolk

■ Despite having had some good winners in the past, this maiden does not always work out.

**FOCUS**

This looked a good maiden on paper with many of the big juvenile trainers represented. However, this is not a maiden that always works out - last year's renewal being a prime example - and although likely to produce winners, there is nothing better than Listed class in the field.

**NOTEBOOK**

**Nightfall(USA)**, a Gimcrack entrant, jinked and unseated Dettori on his way down to the start, but this did not affect his performance. He was soon in the lead and bagged the stands' rail which helped him under pressure. He looked set to be passed a furlong out, and was indeed headed inside the final furlong before rallying to get back up on the line. Unlikely to be at the top of the stable's juvenile tree, connections reportedly have no great ambitions for him, but he was expected to improve for this and will be suited by a seventh furlong. He had a hard enough race in winning however, and is worth opposing next time when upped in grade.

**Moth Ball** was not over enthused about going into the stalls, but he was keen enough to race once coming out of them and looked set to score when edging into a narrow lead inside the furlong. However he was more towards the middle of the track and had nothing to race against and ultimately was nailed on the line. Still viewed as a 'big baby' by connections, he can be expected to improve on this and should win a run-of-the-mill maiden.

**Hallhoo(IRE)**, a 210,000gns purchase, did not seem at home on the ground and was reluctant to let himself down. He was hanging under pressure to boot and as a result this was a decent effort. Seven furlongs on good or softer ground will see him in a much better light and improvement can be expected.

**Prince Samos(IRE)** is bred for speed and with his stable's excellent record with juveniles and the fact Fallon was booked unsurprisingly saw him made favourite. He showed good speed having been slow to get going, but could not match the front pair when they went for home. Likely to benefit from the run - some of the stable's debutants have been improving for an outing - he can be expected better of in future.

**Taj India(USA)** ◆ comes from a stable with plenty of juvenile talent and this one, despite showing up well early, did not know his job as well as others. He will appreciate further and can leave this running behind in time.

**Edge Of Blue** was a well-supported stable companion of the favourite and ultimately proved disappointing. Sired by Bold Edge, who raced for the same connections, he may have just needed it and deserves another chance as better was clearly expected.

**Antonio Stradivari(IRE)** was not given a hard time and should have learned from this.

**San Deng** looks the sort to do better in time.

### 4118 SOLITARE DIAMOND RATED STKS (H'CAP) 1m 2f

**2:35** (2:35) (B ) (0-105,102) 3-Y-O+ **£17,400** (£6,600; £3,300; £1,500) **Stalls** High

Form RPR

1-21 1 **Mister Monet (IRE)**[9] 3878 3-8-8 **98**........................ JFanning 5 114+
(MJohnston) *lw: trckd ldng pair: nt clr run over 2f out: swtchd rt wl over 1f out: rdn to ld 1f out: r.o strly* **11/8**[1]

-350 2 *2* **Courageous Duke (USA)**[38] 2969 5-8-12 **92**........................ KFallon 9 102
(JNoseda) *racd in midfield: rdn and effrt over 2f out: ev ch over 1f out: r.o fnl f but no ch w wnr* **5/1**[2]

1155 3 *¾* **Fine Palette**[22] 3482 4-8-8 **88** oh2........................ WRyan 2 97
(HRACecil) *lw: s.i.s: sn plld hrd and trckd ldng trio: effrt to ld wl over 1f out: hdd 1f out: styd on* **16/1**

1236 4 *3 ½* **Swift Tango (IRE)**[21] 3521 4-9-6 **100**........................ LDettori 6 102
(EALDunlop) *dwlt: hld up in last trio: effrt over 2f out: styd on same pce fr over 1f out: nvr rchd ldrs* **5/1**[2]

60 5 *½* **Polygonal (FR)**[14] 3756 4-8-10 **88** oh1 ow2........................ OPeslier 8 91+
(MrsJRRamsden) *hld up in last trio: nt clr run over 2f out: shkn up and kpt on same pce fr over 1f out: no ch* **10/1**

0-03 6 *6* **Spuradich (IRE)**[34] 3118 4-8-11 **91**........................ JPMurtagh 4 81
(LMCumani) *lw: racd in midfield: shkn up over 2f out: no rspnse and sn btn: eased ins fnl f* **15/2**[3]

4560 7 *1 ½* **Forthright**[7] 3943 3-7-13 **89**........................(p) CCatlin 1 76
(CEBrittain) *t.k.h: trckd ldr to over 2f out: hrd rdn and wknd* **20/1**

1000 8 *5* **Putra Sandhurst (IRE)**[8] 3912 6-9-8 **102**........................ PRobinson 3 80
(MAJarvis) *b: led to wl over 1f out: pushed along and sn wknd* **25/1**

54-0 9 *1 ¾* **Weecandoo (IRE)**[22] 3484 6-8-10 **90**........................ GCarter 7 64
(CNAllen) *swtg: a in last: rdn and wl bhd 3f out* **25/1**

2m 7.31s (-1.42) **Going Correction** +0.15s/f (Good)

**WFA** 3 from 4yo+ 10lb **9** Ran SP% **114.6**

Speed ratings: **111,109,108,106,105 100,99,95,94**CSF £7.91 CT £71.84 TOTE £2.60: £1.60, £1.90, £3.00; EX 12.50 Trifecta £154.20 Pool of £1,707.92 - 7.86 winning units.

**Owner** Syndicate 2002 **Bred** Barronstown Stud, Orpendale And Mrs T Stack **Trained** Middleham Moor, N Yorks

**FOCUS**

A decent handicap although not a strong race for the prize, but it produced a most impressive winner in Mister Monet who looks destined for much better things.

**NOTEBOOK**

**Mister Monet(IRE)** was rated as one of his trainer's better juveniles last season, but only made his three-year-old debut 16 days previously, when he bolted up in a conditions event at Hamilton. Considered a Guineas prospect early in the season, he showed his class with an impressive display, quickening up smartly to win going away having found himself short of room until switched over a furlong out. Highly progressive, he has the speed for a mile and shapes as though a mile and a half is within his compass, so looks well up to winning a Group contest before the season is out.

**Courageous Duke(USA)** was stepping back up to this more favoured trip having finished down the field in the Hunt Cup and ran well, just being unable to cope with the raw pace of the winner.

**Fine Palette** is currently 9lb higher than when last winning and although running well, does not have a progressive enough profile to match his rating at present.

**Swift Tango(IRE)** found himself struggling for speed over this trip and will fare better back at a mile and a half.

**Polygonal(FR)** made no show from a bad draw in the John Smith's and ran much better here. He has yet to win on anything faster than good and will become interesting in the autumn.

**Spuradich(IRE)** ran a little disappointingly, not really going on from his promising third last time.

*Official explanation: jockey said he was unable to offer any explanation for the colt's poor performance*

### 4119 PRINCESS MARGARET STKS (GROUP 3) (FILLIES) 6f

**3:10** (3:10) (A ) 2-Y-O **£26,100** (£9,900; £4,950; £2,250) **Stalls** Low

Form RPR

12 1 **Soar**[38] 2970 2-8-9 ........................ JPMurtagh 4 104
(JRFanshawe) *lw: settled in 5th: stdy prog fr 2f out: shkn up to ld 1f out: r.o wl fnl f* **1/1**[1]

1 2 *1 ¾* **Valentin (IRE)**[15] 3693 2-8-9 ........................ DaneO'Neill 1 99
(RHannon) *lw: dwlt: racd in last and pushed along to stay in tch: rdn and effrt 2f out: styd on to take 2nd wl ins fnl f: no ch wnr* **9/2**[2]

516 3 *nk* **Kissing Lights (IRE)**[28] 3316 2-8-9 ........................ DHolland 5 98
(MLWBell) *led over 4f out to over 1f out: sn rdn and unable qck: styd on again fnl f* **25/1**

41 4 *1 ½* **Satin Finish (IRE)**[7] 3950 2-8-9 ........................ TEDurcan 3 93
(MRChannon) *cl up: effrt to ld over 1f out: hdd 1f out: fdd* **8/1**[3]

4122 5 *hd* **Right Answer**[14] 3753 2-8-9 ........................ KFallon 2 93
(APJarvis) *lw: trckd ldrs: rdn 2f out: sn unable qck: one pce fnl f* **9/2**[2]

41 6 *9* **Magical Romance (IRE)**[10] 3840 2-8-9 ........................ JFortune 6 66
(BJMeehan) *lw: wnt rt s: led to over 4f out: prom tl wknd 2f out* **12/1**

1m 15.6s (-0.39) **Going Correction** +0.15s/f (Good) **6** Ran SP% **109.0**

Speed ratings: **108,105,105,103,103 91**CSF £5.38 TOTE £1.90: £1.40, £2.30; EX 4.60.

**Owner** Cheveley Park Stud **Bred** Cheveley Park Stud Ltd **Trained** Newmarket, Suffolk

**FOCUS**

A very smart winning time, 2.4 seconds faster than the opener. Soar came into this as the one to beat on her Queen Mary form and handled the step up to six furlongs well.

**NOTEBOOK**

**Soar**, who found the smart Damson too hot to handle in the Queen Mary, was well suited to this step up to six furlongs and having travelled nicely came through to lead approaching the final furlong and ran right to the line. It could be argued she did not achieve as much as when second at the Royal meeting but remains progressive and will reportedly head to the Lowther Stakes from here.

**Valentin(IRE)** ran a similar race to when winning here on her debut, slightly outpaced in rear early before coming through with a good late run, only this time there was a good filly in the field and she could not reel her in. Seven furlongs is going to suit this filly and she can probably pick up a Listed race before the season is out, as physically she has some improving to do.

**Kissing Lights(IRE)** showed her Newmarket running to be all wrong with a game effort in third, sticking on well for pressure to rechallenge having been passed. She should stay seven furlongs, although does have plenty of speed.

**Satin Finish(IRE)** had won her maiden only the previous Saturday, and all her form prior to this had come on a softer surface. She ran well but fell a little short of what was required and will be seen to better effect in the autumn, when she is likely to be able to get her toe in a little.

**Right Answer**, representing last season's winning connections, had her chance but was not up to it. She had run in a nursery previously and may not be easy to place.

**Magical Romance(IRE)** came into this on the back of a Kempton maiden win and ran to bad to be true. This was surely not her form.

### 4120 TOTESPORT INTERNATIONAL STKS (HERITAGE H'CAP) 7f

**3:45** (3:48) (B ) 3-Y-O+ **£87,000** (£33,000; £16,500; £7,500) **Stalls** Low

Form RPR

3542 1 **Court Masterpiece**[16] 3673 4-9-2 **105**........................ KFallon 10 117
(EALDunlop) *lw: hld up: prog into midfield 4f out: trckd ldrs and nt clr run briefly over 1f out: drvn to ld last 150yds: styd on wl* **7/1**[2]

1-03 2 *nk* **Polar Way**[8] 3906 5-9-7 **110**........................ GaryStevens 9 121
(MrsAJPerrett) *hld up in midfield: swtchd rt 1/2-way: prog to ld wl over 1f out: hdd last 150yds: styd on wl but a hld* **20/1**

1100 3 *1* **Uhoomagoo**[36] 3036 6-8-3 **92**........................(b) JFEgan 23 101
(KARyan) *dwlt: wl in rr: swtchd sharply rt wl over 2f out: gd prog after: drvn to press ldrs ent fnl f: styd on wl* **33/1**

1302 4 *1 ½* **Vortex**[7] 3937 5-8-9 **98**........................(t) LDettori 6 103+
(MissGayKelleway) *b.hind: dwlt: hld up: in midfield 1/2-way: nt clr run over 2f out: swtchd and prog to chal 1f out: fdd ins fnl f* **4/1**[1]

/262 5 *3 ½* **St Andrews (IRE)**[21] 3539 4-8-3 **92**........................ PRobinson 11 88
(MAJarvis) *racd in midfield: bmpd 1/2-way: prog to chse ldrs 2f out: fdd jst over 1f out* **10/1**

-240 **6** *hd* **New Seeker**[14] 3724 4-9-0 **103**.......................................(b[1]) JPSpencer 18 98
(CGCox) *lw: trckd ldrs: prog to chal and ev ch wl over 1f out: wknd fnl f* **7/1**[2]

5222 **7** *1 ¼* **Digital**[14] 3755 7-7-5 **87**.......................................TDean(7) 16 79
(MRChannon) *hld up towards rr: sme prog over 2f out: pushed along and one pce after* **25/1**

0-00 **8** *½* **Tahirah**[36] 3052 4-7-12 **87** oh1.......................................MHenry 15 78+
(RGuest) *t.k.h: hld up wl in rr: nt clr run and swtchd sharply rt over 2f out: kpt on fr over 1f out: no ch* **40/1**

0146 **9** *1 ¾* **Royal Storm (IRE)**[16] 3673 5-8-10 **99**.......................................JPMurtagh 20 85+
(MrsAJPerrett) *lw: mde most to wl over 1f out: wknd* **12/1**

-511 **10** *1 ½* **Ettrick Water**[36] 3052 5-8-6 **95**.......................................(v) DHolland 4 77+
(LMCumani) *lw: trckd ldrs: lost pl and pushed along 3f out: no imp on ldrs after* **9/1**[3]

0-04 **11** *3 ½* **Capricho (IRE)**[57] 2466 7-9-1 **104**.......................................JFortune 12 77+
(JAkehurst) *hld up in rr: prog 1/2-way: chsd ldrs 2f out: pushed along and wknd jst over 1f out* **25/1**

1600 **12** *½* **Master Robbie**[16] 3673 5-8-2 **91**.......................................CCatlin 21 63
(MRChannon) *wl in rr: rdn and struggling 3f out: modest late prog* **25/1**

-000 **13** *¾* **Vicious Knight**[16] 3673 6-8-9 **98**.......................................ANicholls 26 68
(DNicholls) *hld up in rr: brief prog into midfield 3f out: sn no hdwy and btn* **25/1**

4203 **14** *1* **Greenslades**[16] 3673 5-8-6 **95**.......................................MartinDwyer 8 62
(PJMakin) *w ldr to over 2f out: sn wknd u.p* **20/1**

0150 **15** *2* **Taranaki**[15] 3690 6-7-10 **88**.......................................LisaJones(3) 1 50
(PDCundell) *trckd ldrs: cl up whn stmbld over 2f out: wknd sn after* **25/1**

-110 **16** *1 ½* **Autumn Glory (IRE)**[38] 2969 4-9-0 **103**.......................................SDrowne 13 61
(GWragg) *lw: nvr beyond midfield: no ch whn hmpd over 1f out* **20/1**

0660 **17** *1 ¾* **Binanti**[10] 3850 4-7-6 **88**.......................................(v[1]) CHaddon(7) 14 42
(PRChamings) *b: w ldrs: ev ch jst over 2f out: wknd rapidly* **66/1**

0300 **18** *¾* **Marshman (IRE)**[55] 2503 5-7-11 **89**.......................................FPFerris(3) 22 41
(MHTompkins) *n.m.r sn after s: a in rr: in last trio and struggling 3f out* **50/1**

6004 **19** *1 ¼* **Bahiano (IRE)**[38] 2966 3-8-10 **106** ow1.......................................OPeslier 27 54
(CEBrittain) *racd on outer: nvr gng wl and nvr on terms* **25/1**

0004 **20** *13* **El Coto**[16] 3673 4-8-11 **100**.......................................(b) SSanders 24 15
(BAMcmahon) *a wl in rr: hanging and wl btn over 2f out: t.o* **14/1**

20-5 **21** *3 ½* **Grizedale (IRE)**[16] 3673 5-8-5 **94**.......................................(t) JQuinn 17 —
(JAkehurst) *a wl in rr: wknd over 2f out: t.o* **14/1**

1m 27.54s (-2.13) **Going Correction** +0.15s/f (Good)
**WFA** 3 from 4yo+ 7lb **21 Ran SP% 131.3**
Speed ratings: **118,117,116,114,110 110,109,108,106,104 100,100,99,98,96 94,92,91,90,75 71**CSF £145.02 CT £4448.53 TOTE £5.80: £1.40, £6.50, £7.10, £1.90; EX 207.90 Trifecta £4684.90 Part won. Pool of £6,598.50 - 0.20 winning tickets..
**Owner** Maktoum Al Maktoum **Bred** Gainsborough Stud Management Ltd **Trained** Newmarket, Suffolk

**FOCUS**

A competitive, high-class handicap and a cracking winning time for the grade, 3.14 seconds faster than the ladies' race. It was surprising they did not split here as in recent meetings the far side had appeared to be on terms, if not held an advantage over this trip. A top performance from Court Masterpiece who now looks worthy of another try at Group level.

**NOTEBOOK**

**Court Masterpiece**, running off the same mark as when an unlucky second in the Bunbury Cup earlier in the month, momentarily found his way blocked, but he got out in plenty of time and simply stayed on too strongly for Polar Way. He had travelled sweetly in the race and looks well worth another try at Group level - he ran well in a Group Three at Newmarket last month - as he continues to progress.

**Polar Way** was not suited by the way the race was run when slightly disappointing at Newbury most recently, and was much more at home in this big field. It is quite possible he hit the front too soon as he does have a good change of pace, and a stiff seven furlongs was always going to push the limit of his stamina, especially under top-weight. This signalled a return to something like his best and, if going on from it, he is worthy of his place back in Group company.

**Uhoomagoo** came from a long way off the pace to run arguably his best race of the season so far, faring best of those drawn high. He is a very useful performer when things drop right, but will need to keep improving if he is to defy his current mark.

**Vortex** has had a most profitable season to date - winning six times on the All-Weather including a Listed race abroad - but he remains without a win on the turf. He has however run some cracking races in defeat and this featured among them. A tough horse who takes his racing well, a mile is his ideal trip and he simply seemed to struggle against this opposition off this mark.

**St Andrews(IRE)** has yet to run a bad race since coming back from injury, and should continue to perform well in all the decent mile handicaps.

**New Seeker** did not come into this in the same form as when successful last year - albeit he has been running in better races - and was racing off an 8lb higher mark to worsen matters. He had the first-time blinkers on in the hope they would bring about some improvement but, whilst he ran well, his progress has levelled out and he will now be hard to place as he is too high in the handicap and not quite up to Group level.

**Digital** takes his racing well and ran another sound race without threatening to win. He deserves to get his head in front again.

**Tahirah** was progressive at a low level for different connections last term and has not been disgraced in better races so far this year, this being another fine run. She is high enough in the weights for what she has achieved and is not well enough weighted to win this type of race at present. However, in a lesser race with a bigger weight, she looks capable of getting back on the winning trail.

**Royal Storm(IRE)** hides nothing from the Handicapper and found this too competitive.

**Ettrick Water** has been in good form in lesser events and was another who found this too competitive.

**Master Robbie** was in rear, out wide all the way and could never get involved.

**Autumn Glory(IRE)** has twice disappointed in competitive handicaps here this season, but both runs can be put down to the ground being too fast. Expect to see better from him in the autumn, and the Cambridgeshire looks an ideal target. *Official explanation: jockey said colt was unsuited by the good to firm ground*

**Grizedale(IRE)** *Official explanation: jockey said colt was unsuited by good to firm ground*

## 4121 KING GEORGE VI AND QUEEN ELIZABETH DIAMOND STKS (GROUP 1) 1m 4f

**4:25** (4:25) (A) 3-Y-0+ **£435,000** (£165,000; £82,500; £37,500) **Stalls** High

Form RPR

4-21 **1** **Doyen (IRE)**[35] 3072 4-9-7 124.......................................LDettori 5 131+
(SaeedBinSuroor) *b: lw: racd in 5th pl: eased out over 2f out: effrt to ld wl over 1f out: drew clr ent fnl f: impressive* **11/10**[1]

0-2 **2** *3* **Hard Buck (BRZ)**[21] 5-9-7.......................................GaryStevens 6 123
(KMcpeek, U.S.A) *leggy: lw: t.k.h: trckd ldr: led briefly 2f out: chsd wnr after: no ch fnl f but kpt on wl to hold on to 2nd nr fin* **33/1**

5-42 **3** *hd* **Sulamani (IRE)**[17] 3642 5-9-7 125.......................................(t) KMcEvoy 7 123
(SaeedBinSuroor) *hld up in 8th: plenty to do over 2f out: stdy prog fr wl over 1f out: r.o fnl f: jst failed to snatch 2nd pl* **7/1**

-211 **4** *1 ¾* **Gamut (IRE)**[20] 3567 5-9-7 117.......................................(t) KFallon 11 120+
(SirMichaelStoute) *lw: snatched up after 1f: racd in 6th: drvn and effrt over 2f out: chsd ldng pair over 1f out: no imp: lost 3rd last 150yd* **12/1**

1-43 **5** *1* **Vallee Enchantee (IRE)**[50] 2639 4-9-4.......................................OPeslier 4 115
(ELellouche, France) *racd on outer in 7th: drvn and effrt over 2f out: one pce and no imp on ldrs over 1f out* **6/1**[2]

24-3 **6** *¾* **Tycoon**[27] 3353 3-8-9.......................................JPSpencer 3 122+
(APO'Brien, Ire) *cmpt: str: scope: lw: hld up in last: rapid prog on inner whn rn into bk of wkng pcemaker 2f out: swtchd and kpt on: nt rcv* **16/1**

1101 **7** *nk* **Bandari (IRE)**[17] 3642 5-9-7 117.......................................RHills 2 117
(MJohnston) *settled in 9th pl: rdn and effrt on outer over 2f out: kpt on one pce fr over 1f out: nvr able to threaten ldrs* **12/1**

-423 **8** *2* **High Accolade**[17] 3642 4-9-7 116.......................................JPMurtagh 10 114
(MPTregoning) *racd in 10th pl: dropped to last and drvn over 3f out: struggling after: kpt on fnl f* **25/1**

5312 **9** *1 ¼* **Warrsan (IRE)**[21] 3540 6-9-7 120.......................................DHolland 9 112
(CEBrittain) *trckd ldng pair: rdn 3f out: wknd wl over 1f out* **13/2**[3]

1-66 **10** *2 ½* **Phoenix Reach (IRE)**[20] 3567 4-9-7 115.......................................(v) MartinDwyer 1 108
(AMBalding) *lw: b: t.k.h: trckd ldng trio: rdn wl over 2f out: wknd wl over 1f out: b.b.v* **33/1**

-300 **11** *dist* **Lunar Sovereign (USA)**[38] 2968 5-9-7 110.......................................(t) TEDurcan 8 —
(SaeedBinSuroor) *led: set stdy pce tl qcknd 4l clr 1/2-way: hdd & wknd 2f out: virtually p.u* **100/1**

2m 33.18s (-0.38) **Going Correction** +0.15s/f (Good)
**WFA** 3 from 4yo+ 12lb **11 Ran SP% 119.7**
Speed ratings: **107,105,104,103,103 102,102,101,100,98** —CSF £56.61 TOTE £2.20: £1.30, £5.00, £2.60; EX 63.00 Trifecta £335.50 Pool £6,946.74, 14.70 w/u.
**Owner** Godolphin **Bred** Sheikh Mohammed Bin Rashid Al Maktoum **Trained** Newmarket, Suffolk
■ Frankie Dettori's 2,000th domestic winner.

**FOCUS**

A desperately slow time for a King George, 1.09 seconds slower than the later 0-95 handicap, but that was down to the pace being modest and nothing should be taken away from Doyen, who has been rated value for a five-length win. It would be hard to assess the form any higher than the Hardwicke, and at this stage Doyen's form does not match that of a Daylami or Montjeu. Nevertheless, he is almost certainly capable of better still and looks exceptional.

**NOTEBOOK**

**Doyen(IRE)** came into this as a potential champion and produced a scintillating performance. An impressive winner of the Hardwicke Stakes at the Royal meeting, he faced much stronger opposition but disposed of them easily, quickening right away once asked for his effort off what was only a mediocre gallop set by his pacemaker Lunar Sovereign. The Irish Champion Stakes will reportedly be his next target and only a back-to-form Rakti could deny him completing the same double as former stable stars Swain and Daylami. The Arc - for which he has been cut to as short as even money, and Breeders' Cup Turf are both suitable targets for later in the year, with his turn of foot sure to stand him in good stead.

**Hard Buck(BRZ)**, an American raider, ran a blinder in second, confirming Dubai form from earlier in the year with Warrsan and denying Sulamani the runner-up spot for the second consecutive year. He tried to go with Doyen when he quickened, but was simply not good enough. He will no doubt reoppose Doyen if he turns up for the Breeders' Cup Turf.

**Sulamani(IRE)**, who looked to have run up a little light in the paddock, was not at ease on the ground but ran on bravely to just be denied second. He reversed Newmarket form with Bandari and is likely to have another go at the Arc - in which he was a slightly unlucky second two years ago - where he will be suited by the likely softer going.

**Gamut(IRE)** was only confirmed a definite starter a couple of hours before the race as there were significant worries about the ground. He showed what a good horse he is in finishing fourth on this ground, despite being messed around in the early stages, and he could well get closer to Doyen in the Arc.

**Vallee Enchantee(IRE)**, who looked so unlucky when third in the Coronation Cup at Epsom, had her chance this time and was not good enough. It is possible she would have preferred slightly softer going.

**Tycoon** ◆, coming into this on the back of a shock third in the Irish Derby and representing the three-year-olds, was blocked by the weakening Lunar Sovereign when making good headway up the inside rail from the back of the field, and he was unlucky not to get much closer. He surely has a good prize in him, and would be a likely sort for the St Leger, although connections are reportedly not committed to that route.

**Bandari(IRE)** beat Sulamani into second when winning the Princess of Wales Stakes at Newmarket earlier in the month but got warm beforehand - the ear plugs not having the same effect as at Newmarket - and came wide down the straight. He could not quicken under pressure and was ultimately disappointing. He continues to fall short of the top level, but is capable of winning a Group 1 on his day when he has favoured conditions - a small field and ground no faster than good.

**High Accolade** is not up to this level but had an off day and was always struggling in last place.

**Warrsan(IRE)** set the benchmark as he always runs his race and had beaten both Doyen and Vallee Enchantee at Epsom. A great effort to finish second in the Eclipse - clear of the third - most recently entitled him to take all the beating but he ran a rare bad race, connections blaming the run on the modest pace. He will be back.

**Phoenix Reach(IRE)** dropped right away after racing prominently and has yet to reproduce last year's classy form. He was found to have bled internally when scoped afterwards, so connections will consider campaigning him in the States, where medication is allowed. *Official explanation: trainer said colt had bled from the nose*

## 4122 STAR OF SOUTH AFRICA DIAMOND H'CAP (LADIES RACE) 7f

**5:00** (5:02) (C ) (0-90,87) 3-Y-0+ **£10,351** (£3,185; £1,592; £796) **Stalls** Low

Form RPR

0056 **1** **Hey Presto**[9] 3887 4-9-9 **69**.......................................MissNadineForde(5) 8 78
(CGCox) *hld up in midfield: prog over 2f out: led 1f out: jst hld on* **20/1**

0024 **2** *shd* **Treetops Hotel (IRE)**[11] 3825 5-8-9 **55**.......................................(p) MissJoeyEllis(5) 3 64
(BRJohnson) *hld up wl in rr: gd prog fr 2f out: r.o wl fnl f: jst failed* **33/1**

4000 **3** *¾* **Sawwaah (IRE)**[23] 3440 7-10-8 **80**.......................................MissKellyHarrison(3) 19 87
(DNicholls) *b: hld up wl in rr: prog over 2f out: clsd on wnr ins fnl f: nt qckn last 50yds* **33/1**

0632 **4** *½* **Spirit's Awakening**[44] 2806 5-9-3 **58**.......................................MissAElsey 24 64
(JAkehurst) *lw: prom: led over 2f out to 1f out: kpt on same pce* **20/1**

52 **5** *1 ¼* **Distant Country (USA)**[41] 2905 5-9-13 **71**.......(p) MissLAHourigan(3) 20 74
(MrsJRRamsden) *wl in rr: stdy prog fr over 2f out: rdn and styd on fnl f: nrst fin* **9/1**[2]

0440 **6** *shd* **What-A-Dancer (IRE)**[24] 3409 7-10-6 **75**.......................................MissSBrotherton 7 77
(GASwinbank) *swtg: hld up in tch: effrt whn squeezed out over 2f out: prog jst over 1f out: r.o wl nr fin* **16/1**

1566 **7** *nk* **Chateau Nicol**[7] 3941 5-10-8 **82**.......................................MrsRPowell(5) 12 83
(BGPowell) *hld up towards rr: stdy prog 2f out: clsd on wnr ins fnl f: wknd last 75yds* **12/1**

000 **8** *nk* **Lygeton Lad**[64] 2279 6-10-1 **70**.......................................(t) MissEJJones 14 71
(MissGayKelleway) *racd in midfield: rdn and effrt 2f out: one pce and no imp fnl f* **14/1**

0015 **9** *¾* **Mobo-Baco**[15] 3697 7-9-0 **55**.......................................MissLynseyHanna 21 54
(RJHodges) *taken down early: dwlt: wl in rr and r on outer: prog fr 2f out: no imp ldrs ins fnl f* **40/1**

6120 **10** *hd* **Brave Dane (IRE)**[42] [2881] 6-10-5 **74** MrsSBosley 17 72
(AWCarroll) *lw: settled wl in rr: stdy prog fr over 1f out: r.o wl fnl f: nvr nrr* **25/1**

0000 **11** *1* **Arctic Desert**[15] [3698] 4-10-4 **78** MissMSowerby(5) 6 74
(AMBalding) *b: racd in midfield: effrt whn bmpd on inner over 1f out: no imp after* **33/1**

2-20 **12** *1 1/4* **Capped For Victory (USA)**[63] [2295] 3-10-5 **86** MrsSEddery(5) 9 78+
(SirMichaelStoute) *lw: dwlt: hld up in midfield: effrt whn nt clr run wl over 1f out: nudged along and no ch after* **7/1**[1]

2001 **13** *3/4* **Graft**[24] [3412] 5-9-3 **63** (b) MrsCThompson(5) 23 53
(MrsPTownsley) *chsd ldrs: rdn and hanging lft fr 2f out: fdd over 1f out* **20/1**

0000 **14** *shd* **Colemanstown**[23] [3440] 4-9-2 **60** MissLEllison(3) 5 50
(BEllison) *taken down early: led to over 2f out: wknd over 1f out* **33/1**

6000 **15** *nk* **Gaelic Princess**[35] [3074] 4-10-10 **79** MissCHannaford 15 68
(AGNewcombe) *wl in rr: pushed along and effrt over 2f out: no hdwy over 1f out* **10/1**[3]

0052 **16** *hd* **Fiveoclock Express (IRE)**[10] [3850] 4-10-9 **78** (p) MsCWilliams 2 67
(MissGayKelleway) *b: b.hind: taken down early: hld up wl in rr: nt clr run on inner over 2f out: no ch after: eased* **14/1**

2135 **17** *1 1/4* **Cloud Dancer**[14] [3754] 5-10-8 **77** MissNCarberry 25 63
(KARyan) *racd on outer: towards rr: rdn and effrt over 2f out: wknd over 1f out* **7/1**[1]

2604 **18** *hd* **Magic Amour**[9] [3884] 6-9-2 **57** MissSBeddoes 10 42
(IanWilliams) *in tch: prog to chal 2f out: sn rdn and wknd* **33/1**

0500 **19** *2 1/2* **Bint Royal (IRE)**[2] [4066] 6-8-10 **56** oh2 ow1 MissFayeBramley(5) 4 35
(MissVHaigh) *chsd ldrs: wkng on inner whn bmpd over 1f out* **25/1**

5502 **20** *3* **Takes Tutu (USA)**[9] [3884] 5-10-7 **76** (b) MrsMMorris 22 47
(KRBurke) *taken down early: dwlt: sn w ldrs: wknd over 1f out* **11/1**

010- **21** *5* **Gems Bond**[112] 4-10-8 **80** MrsSMoore(3) 18 38
(JSMoore) *racd towards outer: a in rr* **40/1**

6424 **22** *1/2* **Quantum Leap**[16] [3663] 7-10-3 **72** (v) MissCO'Neill 11 28
(SDow) *swtg: b.hind: racd on wd outer in midfield: effrt to press ldrs over 2f out: wknd rapidly over 1f out* **25/1**

6000 **23** *nk* **Rainstorm**[18] [3604] 9-8-11 **55** oh15 MrsSOwen(3) 16 11
(WMBrisbourne) *pressed ldrs for 4f: wknd* **100/1**

0103 **24** *7* **Play Master (IRE)**[38] [2988] 3-9-6 **73** MissJFoster(5) 13 11
(DHaydnJones) *lw: pressed ldrs: rdn 3f out: sn wknd* **40/1**

21 **25** *10* **Mr Mistral**[29] [3268] 5-11-4 **87** MrsMCowdrey 1 —
(GWragg) *lw: b: taken down early: plld hrd: hld up: lost pl on inner 1/2-way: sn bhd and eased* **7/1**[1]

1m 30.68s (1.01) **Going Correction** +0.15s/f (Good)
**WFA** 3 from 4yo+ 7lb **25** Ran SP% **140.7**
Speed ratings: **100,99,99,98,97 96,96,96,95,95 94,92,91,91,91 91,89,89,86,83 77,76,76,68,57**CSF £574.94 CT £19547.27 TOTE £32.70: £6.70, £15.30, £11.00, £5.10; EX 1167.80.
**Owner** The Beechdown Flyers **Bred** Michael Edwards And John Parsons **Trained** Lambourn, Berks
■ Nadine Forde's first Flat winner.
■ Stewards Enquiry : Mrs C Thompson two-day ban: careless riding (Aug 4-5)

**FOCUS**
As always this was an ultra-competitive heat and there were plenty of hard luck stories in behind. The form however, is modest and not sure to work out.

**NOTEBOOK**
**Hey Presto** has been a frustrating sort this season, often unlucky in running and always coming home best when the race is all over. All his racing prior to this had been over five and six furlongs, and the step up to seven seemed just the trick as he raced in plenty of space and had every chance. Having taken it up around a furlong out, he only just managed to hold on from the fast-finishing Treetops Hotel and would have been beaten in another stride. Now connections have seemingly found his ideal trip, it will be interesting if he can build on this.
**Treetops Hotel(IRE)**, in contrast to the winner, has been running over further - fourth over a mile and a half latest - and as expected he was doing all his best work towards the end. He would have won in another stride and can be counted unfortunate.
**Sawwaah(IRE)** ran his best race for a while but remains plenty high enough in the weights.
**Spirit's Awakening** continues to run well without being able to get his head in front.
**Distant Country(USA)** came from a fair way back to challenge for the places but was out of luck. He will be best back at a mile.
**What-A-Dancer(IRE)** was a little unlucky not to finish closer and is on a winning mark at present.
**Chateau Nicol** is weighted up to his best at present and needs a drop in the weights.
**Brave Dane(IRE)** was keeping on from the rear at his own pace and may have found the ground a tad lively.
**Arctic Desert** tried to come with a run up the rail, but got into a barging match and that halted his progress.
**Capped For Victory(USA)** was slightly unlcuky not to finish closer and was only as short as he was in the betting due to connections. He remains a maiden.
**Graft** *Official explanation: jockey said gelding was struck into behind on both legs*
**Fiveoclock Express(IRE)** did not get the clearest of runs and could never get going. *Official explanation: jockey said gelding lost its action*
**Mr Mistral**, although made co-favourite, faced a pretty stiff task under top weight given this was only his third-ever start. He pulled far too hard on the inside and spoiled any chance he had, eventually being eased once beaten. *Official explanation: jockey said gelding was unsuited by the good to firm ground*

## 4123 SOUTH AFRICA ANNIVERSARY DIAMOND RATED STKS (H'CAP) 1m 4f
**5:35** (5:36) (C ) (0-95,94) 3-Y-O+ **£10,776** (£4,087; £2,043; £929) **Stalls** High

Form RPR

3153 **1** **Always Waining (IRE)**[16] [3678] 3-8-4 **86** JFanning 2 102+
(MJohnston) *lw: trckd ldr: led over 2f out: sn kicked clr: r.o wl and in n.d over 1f out* **11/2**[2]

-303 **2** *5* **Fort**[15] [3692] 3-8-5 **87** RHills 7 95
(MJohnston) *hld up in midfield: nt clr run briefly over 2f out: prog to chse wnr over 1f out: no imp* **9/2**[1]

31-6 **3** *3/4* **Argonaut**[109] [1286] 4-9-4 **88** KFallon 3 95
(SirMichaelStoute) *hld up in last trio: drvn on outer over 2f out: styd on fr over 1f out: tk 3rd wl ins fnl f* **9/2**[1]

/42- **4** *1/2* **It's The Limit (USA)**[427] [1835] 5-9-8 **92** SSanders 6 98
(MrsAJPerrett) *lw: settled in midfield: effrt 4f out: chsd ldrs 2f out: one pce after* **8/1**

004- **5** *hd* **Muhareb (USA)**[282] [5588] 5-9-10 **94** DHolland 5 100
(CEBrittain) *swtg: bit bkwd: trckd ldng trio: rdn and effrt over 2f out: one pce fr wl over 1f out* **20/1**

14-0 **6** *1 3/4* **Lodger (FR)**[15] [3716] 4-9-8 **92** WRyan 1 95
(JNoseda) *lw: dwlt: hld up in last: effrt 2f out: styd on: nvr nr ldrs* **16/1**

1-16 **7** *nk* **Grooms Affection**[28] [3325] 4-9-0 **84** JPMurtagh 10 86
(PWHarris) *lw: s.i.s: racd in midfield: rdn over 2f out: one pce and no imp over 1f out* **6/1**[3]

1125 **8** *1 1/4* **Bucks**[17] [3629] 7-8-10 **80** PRobinson 4 80
(DKIvory) *b: hld up in last trio: effrt whn hmpd on inner wl over 1f out: one pce after* **9/1**

-000 **9** *9* **Gallery God (FR)**[35] [3076] 8-9-6 **90** JFEgan 8 76
(SDow) *swtg: led to over 2f out: sn btn: eased fnl f* **25/1**

1132 **10** *2* **Court Of Appeal**[42] [2895] 7-9-3 **87** (t) KMcEvoy 9 70
(BEllison) *trckd ldng pair: rdn 3f out: wknd wl over 1f out* **11/2**[2]

2m 32.09s (-1.47) **Going Correction** +0.15s/f (Good)
**WFA** 3 from 4yo+ 12lb **10** Ran SP% **117.0**
Speed ratings: **110,106,106,105,105 104,104,103,97,96**CSF £30.61 CT £121.74 TOTE £7.00: £2.30, £2.10, £1.70; EX 14.90 Place 6 £190.01, Place 5 £53.59.
**Owner** The Always Trying Partnership **Bred** Barouche Stud Ireland Ltd **Trained** Middleham Moor, N Yorks

**FOCUS**
A strong handicap and a fair time for the class, but even though the time was 1.09 seconds faster than the King George, that comparison is a bit misleading as they went a truer pace here. A smart performance from the progressive Always Waining, who is set to reappear at Glorious Goodwood under a penalty.

**NOTEBOOK**
**Always Waining(IRE)** ◆ has been progressing with racing - typical for one of his stable's three-year-old handicappers - and came into this on the back of a solid third in a Newmarket handicap. He was unsuited by the easy going that day, but back on this faster surface he showed a decent change of pace to take lengths out of the opposition turning in. He galloped on strongly to lead home a one-two for the yard. A mile six should be within his compass and he looks the ideal type for the Melrose Stakes - the three-year-old version of the Ebor. In the meantime though he may reappear at Goodwood next week under a penalty and is sure to take some stopping.
**Fort** was the better fancied of the pair according to the betting, but was the second string on jockey bookings and proved no match for his stable companion. He has run some good races in defeat this season and may be better front-running over a mile two.
**Argonaut** unsuited by the soft ground when disappointing on his seasonal debut, fared well off what looked a stiffish mark on this handicap debut and will be suited by an extra couple of furlongs. He should improve with racing.
**It's The Limit(USA)** ◆ comes from a stable that is back in good shape having had a quiet first half to the season, and was nibbled at in the market for this seasonal debut. He had looked a good prospect when last seen over a year ago and made a pleasing comeback. Although two years older, he is as lightly raced and boasts a similar profile to the yard's Ebor winner of 2000 Give The Slip. He holds an entry in the race himself and will be of particular interest if taking his place in the line-up.
**Muhareb(USA)** was making his seasonal debut off a stiff-looking mark and ran as well as could have been expected. He should improve for this.
**Lodger(FR)** ◆ showed an improvement in form on his seasonal debut and was staying on nicely towards the end of the race. He was a quietly progressive colt last year and holds entries at both the Shergar Cup meeting and in the Ebor. It would come as no surprise to see him go well in one of those, if not both.
**Grooms Affection** failed to run his race and may have been feeling the ground. Although his win at Sandown was on a fast surface, he took a long time to get going there and may have been reluctant to let himself down. His maiden win came with a little juice in the ground and he is worth another chance back on going no faster than good.
**Bucks** was just starting a run when getting hampered. This knocked him off his stride and he could not get going after.
**Court Of Appeal** was well fancied by connections and clearly ran below expectations. He has been in good form and this run was not in keeping with his consistent season so far. *Official explanation: trainer said gelding was lame behind*
T/Plt: £355.70 to a £1 stake. Pool: £136,190.09. 279.50 winning tickets. T/Qpdt: £130.40 to a £1 stake. Pool: £6,891.70. 39.10 winning tickets. JN

# 4022 LINGFIELD (L-H)
### Saturday, July 24
**OFFICIAL GOING: Turf course - good to firm; all-weather - standard**

## 4124 PREMIER PENSIONS MANAGEMENT MAIDEN AUCTION STKS 5f
**6:05** (6:05) (F ) 2-Y-O **£3,297** (£942; £471) **Stalls** Centre

Form RPR

3322 **1** **Gifted Gamble**[8] [3900] 2-8-8 (b) PDobbs 8 72+
(KARyan) *trckd ldr: led 1/2-way: rdn out fnl f* **4/5**[1]

06 **2** *1 1/2* **Saucepot**[26] [3382] 2-8-3 ADaly 4 62
(MDIUsher) *a in tch: drvn out to chse wnr ins fnl f* **20/1**

2 **3** *hd* **Dispol In Mind**[17] [3620] 2-8-3 GGibbons 3 61
(IAWood) *s.i.s: hdwy 1/2-way: styd on fnl f: nvr nrr* **11/1**

6 **4** *hd* **Ne Oublie**[49] [2686] 2-8-8 EAhern 6 65
(JMackie) *a.p: ev ch appr fnl f: one pce after* **16/1**

5 **5** *nk* **Docklands Grace (USA)**[75] [2002] 2-8-4 RLMoore 1 60
(NPLittmoden) *in rr and outpcd: styd on fnl f: nvr nr to chal* **12/1**

**6** *1 3/4* **John Robie (USA)** 2-8-11 SWKelly 5 61
(GAButler) *slowly away: sn prom: wknd appr fnl f* **11/4**[2]

065 **7** *1* **Lowestoft Playboy**[24] [3413] 2-8-3 NChalmers(5) 2 55
(MrsCADunnett) *led to 1/2-way: rdn and wknd appr fnl f* **9/1**[3]

**8** *shd* **Manic** 2-8-2 ANicholls 7 48
(AndrewReid) *a outpcd in rr* **33/1**

59.18 secs (0.31) **Going Correction** -0.05s/f (Good) **8** Ran SP% **121.8**
Speed ratings: **95,92,92,91,91 88,87,86**CSF £23.83 TOTE £2.30: £1.10, £2.80, £2.60; EX 42.80.
**Owner** Margaret's Partnership **Bred** Mrs M Holdcroft And Mrs M Forsyth **Trained** Hambleton, N Yorks

**FOCUS**
A weak maiden run at a sound pace.

**NOTEBOOK**
**Gifted Gamble**, in the frame in all bar one of his previous outings to date, readily got off the mark at the seventh attempt. This was his easiest assignment so far and he may not have beaten a great deal this time, but the experience will have done his confidence a lot of good, and he can only improve when upped to six furlongs.
**Saucepot** turned in by far her best display to date. Her trainer has done fairly well with his juveniles so far this season and this speedily-bred sort will fare better now she is eligible for nurseries.
**Dispol In Mind** ran a promising race for her new connections and would have been closer but for a sluggish start. She has the ability to build on this, possibly over another furlong, and looks a likely sort for nurseries.
**Ne Oublie** , well supported at big odds in the betting ring beforehand, could not muster the change of gear to trouble the principals, but managed to improve a touch on his debut display.
**John Robie(USA)**, the first foal of a US turf winner, ran green on this debut and can be expected to step up on this form next time out.

## 4125 SHARP MINDS WINNERS WELCOME MEDIAN AUCTION MAIDEN STKS 7f

**6:35** (6:35) (F) 3-5-Y-O **£3,003** (£858; £429) **Stalls** Centre

Form RPR

-263 **1** **Desert Cristal (IRE)**[14] 3728 3-8-9 79 LDettori 11 67
(JRBoyle) *mde all: rdn over 2f out: kpt up to work fnl f* **4/6**[1]

20-0 **2** 1 ½ **Text**[16] 3684 3-9-0 60 ADaly 5 68
(MrsStefLiddiard) *in tch tl outpcd 1/2-way: swtchd lft to outside over 2f out: r.o to chse wnr ins fnl f* **25/1**

0 **3** 1 ½ **Witches Broom**[113] 1227 3-8-9 EAhern 8 59
(CACyzer) *t.k.h: a.p: kpt on one pce fnl f* **66/1**

5- **4** shd **Residential**[273] 5754 3-9-0 RLMoore 10 64+
(MrsAJPerrett) *s.i.s: sn chsd ldrs: rdn over 1f out: one pce after* **2/1**[2]

4654 **5** 1 **Fair Compton**[21] 3530 3-8-9 60 PDobbs 9 56
(RHannon) *plld hrd: w wnr tl rdn and wknd fnl f* **14/1**[3]

0604 **6** 3 **Nebraska City**[2] 4052 3-9-0 55 (t) NPollard 4 53
(PMitchell) *in tch tl wknd appr fnl f* **20/1**

23- **7** 3 **Assoon**[293] 3955 5-9-7 RBrisland 2 45
(GLMoore) *slowly away and in rr: nvr on terms* **20/1**

04 **8** 1 ¾ **Chem's Legacy (IRE)**[2] 4063 4-9-4 J-PGuillambert(3) 7 40
(WRMuir) *t.k.h: in tch tl rdn 1/2-way: sn bhd* **66/1**

0-00 **9** ½ **Lady Franpalm (IRE)**[95] 1519 4-8-9 52 CHaddon(7) 1 34
(MJHaynes) *trckd ldrs tl rdn 1/2-way: bhd fnl 2f* **66/1**

0 **10** 5 **Highland Lass**[28] 3322 3-8-4 NChalmers(5) 6 20
(MrsHSweeting) *hld up in mid-div: swtchd rt 1/2-way: wknd over 1f out* **25/1**

1m 23.84s (-0.37) **Going Correction** -0.05s/f (Good)
**WFA** 3 from 4yo+ 7lb **10** Ran SP% **121.7**
Speed ratings: **100,98,96,96,95 91,88,86,85,80**CSF £29.13 TOTE £1.80: £1.10, £6.40, £7.70; EX 47.90.
**Owner** John Hopkins (t/a South Hatch Racing) **Bred** Illuminatus Investments **Trained** Epsom, Surrey

**FOCUS**
An ordinary maiden, but the pace was solid and the form looks sound enough for the grade.

**NOTEBOOK**
**Desert Cristal(IRE)**, whose very best efforts gave her an obvious chance in this, made all to win as she was entitled to. This drop back to seven was not ideal, and she did not look totally at home on this track, but her confidence will have been boosted and she should continue to pay her way in handicaps.
**Text**, well held on his recent reappearance in a handicap at Warwick, turned in a much improved effort and was staying on well at the finish. A step back up to a mile and reverting to handicaps will be of benefit.
**Witches Broom**, who only beat one home on her debut in February on the Polytrack, would have finished closer but for running too freely through the early stages. This was a much improved effort and she can be expected to do better once handicapped and racing over farther.
**Residential**, who showed distinct promise in a fair Newbury maiden on his only start last year, ran disappointingly. He looked one-paced late on after travelling nicely, yet although he should do better for this outing and over slightly further, could have been expected to have finished slightly closer.
**Fair Compton**, despite running keen, did not stay this trip too well.
**Assoon** *Official explanation: jockey said gelding was unsuited by the good to firm going*

## 4126 SHARP MINDS BETFAIR H'CAP 7f

**7:05** (7:06) (D ) (0-85,84) 3-Y-O **£5,541** (£1,705; £852; £426) **Stalls** Centre

Form RPR

3440 **1** **Molcon (IRE)**[31] 3205 3-9-4 **81** JFEgan 7 90
(NACallaghan) *towards rr: rdn over 2f out: hdwy over 1f out: r.o u.p to ld last strides* **9/2**[3]

1503 **2** hd **Apex**[14] 3750 3-9-1 **78** KFallon 1 86
(EALDunlop) *a in tch:: rdn to ld 2f out: kpt on u.p: hdd last strides* **5/2**[1]

5220 **3** ½ **Pizazz**[37] 3001 3-9-5 **82** LDettori 6 89
(BJMeehan) *in tch: rdn 2f out: ev ch appr fnl f: kpt on one pce* **10/3**[2]

-000 **4** 2 ½ **I Won't Dance (IRE)**[14] 3750 3-8-12 **75** RLMoore 2 75
(RHannon) *prom: rdn over 2f out: one pce fnl f* **10/1**

4200 **5** 3 ½ **Best Desert (IRE)**[14] 3750 3-8-4 **67** ow2 NPollard 4 57
(JRBest) *c over to stands side and led early: styd prom but sn rdn: wknd wl over 1f out* **16/1**

0005 **6** shd **Convince (USA)**[28] 3295 3-9-5 **82** (p) SWKelly 3 72
(MABuckley) *c over to stands side and sn led: hdd 2f out: wknd over 1f out* **8/1**

0-10 **7** 2 ½ **Saristar**[63] 2309 3-9-7 **84** (t) DHolland 9 67
(PFICole) *a towards rr: rdn 3f out: nvr on terms* **6/1**

0000 **8** 10 **Knight Onthe Tiles (IRE)**[11] 3817 3-7-6 **62** (b) CHaddon(7) 8 18
(JRBest) *t.k.h: a bhd* **33/1**

0-06 **9** 5 **Sachin**[120] 1119 3-8-4 **67** EAhern 5 10
(JRBoyle) *towards rr: rdn 3f out: sn lost tch* **20/1**

1m 23.47s (-0.74) **Going Correction** -0.05s/f (Good) **9** Ran SP% **117.9**
Speed ratings: **102,101,101,98,94 94,91,79,74**CSF £16.55 CT £42.78 TOTE £7.10: £2.00, £1.70, £1.60; EX 24.80.
**Owner** Mark Venus **Bred** Noel O'Callaghan **Trained** Newmarket, Suffolk

**FOCUS**
A fair handicap run at a decent clip. The form looks solid enough for the grade.

**NOTEBOOK**
**Molcon(IRE)** really picked up strongly under pressure and got up near the line. He had looked to be going the wrong way, having made a bright start to the current campaign, but he has been freshened up recently and it has clearly done him the world of good. He can do even better with more cut in the ground. *Official explanation: trainer's representative said, regarding the improved form shown, gelding was probably feeling the effects of running three times in ten days when disappointing last time*
**Apex** ran another solid race and was only just denied. He is considered best with cut, and although he has a habit of finding one or two too good, is honest and can make amends in a similar event.
**Pizazz**, last seen when outclassed in the Britannia at Royal Ascot, showed his true colours and ran up to form. He is a touch high in the weights on this evidence, but is the benchmark for the form.
**I Won't Dance(IRE)**, who had not shown a great deal in three previous outings this year, broke smartly this time and held every chance if good enough. He could not quicken when it mattered, but his recent slide in the weights has helped and he appreciated this faster surface.
**Saristar** failed to go the early pace and ran way below her best over this extra furlong. This was her second consecutive disappointment and the tongue tie failed to bring about any improvement, so she has it all to prove now. *Official explanation: jockey said filly lost her action*
**Sachin** *Official explanation: jockey said gelding felt wrong behind.*

## 4127 SHARP MINDS BETFAIR: BEST ODDS CLASSIFIED STKS 7f 140y

**7:35** (7:37) (F) 3-Y-O+ **£3,087** (£882; £441) **Stalls** Centre

Form RPR

-336 **1** **Miss Madame (IRE)**[51] 2610 3-8-6 58 EAhern 2 67
(RGuest) *chsd ldr: led 3f out: drvn clr appr fnl f* **22/1**

3061 **2** 2 ½ **Lady Mo**[9] 3871 3-8-12 66 SSanders 1 66
(GGMargarson) *a.p: chsd wnr fnl 2f: nt qckn* **11/4**[1]

-625 **3** 1 ¼ **Choristar**[7] 3935 3-8-6 55 J-PGuillambert(3) 7 60
(WRMuir) *a in tch: rdn 2f out: kpt on fnl f* **14/1**

2000 **4** ½ **Jomus**[19] 3589 3-8-9 59 PDobbs 4 59
(LMontagueHall) *in rr and outpcd: hdwy over 1f out: styd on: nvr nrr* **33/1**

1053 **5** 1 **Londoner (USA)**[32] 3174 6-9-3 60 RLMoore 10 57
(SDow) *led tl hdd 3f out: rdn and fdd over 1f out* **6/1**[3]

0632 **6** hd **One Upmanship**[10] 3839 3-8-13 64 DHolland 8 60
(JGPortman) *hld up in rr: hdwy 2f out: nt pce to chal* **8/1**

-064 **7** nk **Violet Avenue**[22] 3478 3-8-8 58 ow2 MFenton 5 54
(JGGiven) *mid-div: rdn 3f out: wknd wl over 1f out* **14/1**

0453 **8** ¾ **Cuddles (FR)**[13] 3773 5-9-0 57 ANicholls 12 50
(KOCunningham-Brown) *s.i.s and outpcd: sme late hdwy: nvr on terms* **7/1**

-006 **9** ¾ **Pick A Berry**[22] 3486 3-8-6 57 JFEgan 6 49
(GWragg) *t.k.h: in tch tl wknd 2f out* **25/1**

4012 **10** 2 **Mister Clinton (IRE)**[11] 3828 7-9-3 59 ADaly 9 47
(DKIvory) *racd keenly: prom tl wknd 2f out* **7/1**

030 **11** 6 **Secam (POL)**[14] 3747 5-8-12 44 NChalmers(5) 3 32
(MrsPTownsley) *plld hrd: a in rr* **50/1**

0240 **12** 3 **Concubine (IRE)**[23] 3440 5-9-0 60 KFallon 11 21
(JRBoyle) *trckd ldrs: rdn 3f out: wknd 2f out: eased* **7/2**[2]

1m 31.43s (-0.03) **Going Correction** -0.05s/f (Good)
**WFA** 3 from 5yo+ 8lb **12** Ran SP% **125.7**
Speed ratings: **98,95,94,93,92 92,92,91,90,88 82,79**CSF £84.57 TOTE £25.60: £5.50, £1.50, £3.90; EX 245.90.
**Owner** Cosmic Greyhound Racing Partnership Iii **Bred** Gracelands Stud **Trained** Newmarket, Suffolk
■ Stewards Enquiry : E Ahern caution: used whip in an incorrect place

**FOCUS**
A moderate affair and very few managed to get into the argument. The form is ordinary but looks sound.

**NOTEBOOK**
**Miss Madame(IRE)**, who had spoilt her chances previously by pulling too hard, settled well this time and produced a tidy display to score over this longer trip. She has no problem getting this far, will be even better when covered up in her races and could score again while at this end of the handicap, as she looks fairly unexposed.
**Lady Mo**, winner of a claimer at Epsom last time out, ran another solid race in defeat. She is clearly in good heart and was clear in second.
**Choristar** ran better for this extra furlong and could exploit this current mark while his stable remain in fair form.
**Jomus** would have been better suited by a stronger gallop, yet still turned in his best display on turf this year. His win record of one from 16 is not inspiring however, and he is the type who needs all to fall right in his races.
**Londoner(USA)** had the run of the race in front, but was readily swept aside when headed approaching the final furlong. He was not disgraced and should be capable of better when dropped in trip. *Official explanation: jockey said gelding hung left*
**Pick A Berry** *Official explanation: jockey said filly was struck on nose by another rider's whip*
**Concubine(IRE)**, well backed for this easier assignment, dropped out most alarmingly and with something presumably amiss. *Official explanation: jockey said mare lost her action*

## 4128 SHARP MINDS BETFAIR: BACK AND LAY H'CAP 1m 2f (P)

**8:05** (8:07) (E) (0-55,59) 3-Y-O **£3,017** (£862; £431) **Stalls** Low

Form RPR

0-02 **1** **Quarrymount**[9] 3875 3-9-10 **59** SSanders 5 69+
(SirMarkPrescott) *a.p: rdn over 4f out: styd on u.p to ld post* **1/1**[1]

0043 **2** shd **Rubaiyat (IRE)**[28] 3305 3-9-1 **50** JFEgan 9 60
(GWragg) *led for 2f: led again 5f out: rdn over 2f out: hdd post* **8/1**[3]

-002 **3** shd **Willhego**[56] 2484 3-9-5 **54** NPollard 13 64
(JRBest) *s.i.s: in rr tl str hdwy 2f out: styd on wl and only jst failed to overhaul first 2* **14/1**

-656 **4** 5 **African Star**[23] 3461 3-9-4 **53** RLMoore 4 54
(MrsAJPerrett) *a.p: chal ldr clly 2f out tl wknd ins fnl f* **8/1**[3]

0615 **5** 1 ¼ **Cobalt Blue (IRE)**[14] 3746 3-9-3 **52** (b) DHolland 11 50
(WJHaggas) *hld up: rdn and hdwy to chse ldrs over 2f out: sn one pce* **8/1**[3]

050 **6** 5 **Stylish Dancer**[18] 3608 3-9-0 **49** IMongan 2 38
(MBlanshard) *mid-div: rdn and hdwy over 2f out: wknd over 1f out* **50/1**

4454 **7** 5 **Queen Lucia (IRE)**[22] 3473 3-9-6 **55** MFenton 10 34
(JGGiven) *chsd ldrs: rdn 3f out: wknd wl over 1f out* **20/1**

2300 **8** 2 ½ **Fox Hollow (IRE)**[37] 3026 3-9-1 **50** LDettori 1 24
(MJHaynes) *led after 2f: hdd 5f out: sn struggling in mid-div* **16/1**

-050 **9** hd **Macchiato**[13] 3773 3-9-3 **52** EAhern 8 26
(RFJohnsonHoughton) *in tch: rdn over 3f out: sn wknd* **33/1**

0106 **10** 2 ½ **Whiplash (IRE)**[7] 3932 3-9-3 **52** ANicholls 7 21
(KOCunningham-Brown) *a in rr* **40/1**

00 **11** nk **Newtown Chief**[2] 4055 3-9-0 **49** (p) GGibbons 12 18
(NPLittmoden) *in tch: rdn 4f out: wknd over 2f out* **40/1**

06-6 **12** 25 **Kinkozan**[23] 3447 3-9-2 **54** J-PGuillambert(3) 14 —
(NPLittmoden) *a bhd* **33/1**

4330 **13** 6 **Ask The Driver**[20] 3556 3-9-4 **53** KFallon 3 —
(DJSFfrenchDavis) *a bhd* **7/1**[2]

0000 **14** 23 **Pass Go**[40] 2932 3-9-6 **55** (t) SWKelly 6 —
(GAButler) *a bhd: eased wl over 1f out: t.o* **33/1**

2m 10.75s (2.90) **Going Correction** +0.375s/f (Slow) **14** Ran SP% **128.8**
Speed ratings: **103,102,102,98,97 93,89,87,87,85 85,65,60,42**CSF £9.67 CT £86.80 TOTE £2.20: £1.40, £2.50, £2.80; EX 10.10.
**Owner** Lady Fairhaven **Bred** Lord Fairhaven **Trained** Newmarket, Suffolk

**FOCUS**
A modest handicap which produced a thrilling finish and the first three came well clear, giving the form a sound look.

**NOTEBOOK**
**Quarrymount**, who showed his first worthwhile form when narrowly beaten at Epsom last time, gamely stuck his head out where it mattered to get up over this longer trip. He responded very well to maximum pressure and got every yard of this trip, so should improve again and will be hard to beat if turned out under a penalty.
**Rubaiyat(IRE)** took the race by the scruff of the neck early on and deserves credit for rallying when challenged inside the final furlong. This looks to be his optimum trip, he was only denied by the smallest of margins and he should soon be going one better at this level.
**Willhego** ◆ had it all do to after losing ground at the start, but really flew late on and in the end only just failed. He has markedly improved since being upped to this trip over course and distance the last twice and should soon make amends for this near miss.
**African Star** had every chance and improved on his recent efforts, but may be better over shorter.
**Cobalt Blue(IRE)** was held up to get the trip on this All-Weather bow, but could not find a change of pace and was well held. He may be best when allowed to dominate over shorter. *Official explanation: jockey said gelding missed break*

**Kinkozan** *Official explanation: jockey said colt did not enjoy the kick-back*

## 4129 SHARP MINDS PHONE 0870 90 80 121 H'CAP 2m (P)
8:35 (8:38) (E) (0-70,69) 3-Y-0+ **£3,493** (£1,075; £537; £268) **Stalls** Low

Form RPR
212 **1** **Belle Rouge**[10] 3851 6-9-8 **60** ... LDettori 11 70
(CAHorgan) *led after 2f: set stdy pce tl qcknd 2f out: rdn out* **13/8**[1]
6124 **2** *3/4* **Compton Eclaire (IRE)**[21] 3528 4-9-0 **52** ...(v) EAhern 5 61
(GAButler) *a in tch: hdwy after 6f: sn trckd wnr: rdn 2f out: no imp wl ins fnl f* **4/1**[2]
4504 **3** *4* **Most-Saucy**[9] 3873 8-9-3 **55** ... KFallon 9 59
(IAWood) *a in tch: rdn and hdwy 3f out: chsd first 2 over 1f out: but nt qckn* **4/1**[2]
-000 **4** *3* **Heart Springs**[22] 3488 4-8-7 **45** ... ADaly 12 46
(DrJRJNaylor) *in rr tl hdwy 3f out: styd on fnl 2f: nvr nr to chal* **33/1**
-004 **5** *1 1/4* **Bakhtyar**[33] 3160 3-8-3 **58** ...(b) JFEgan 8 57
(RCharlton) *in tch: rdn over 2f out: sn btn* **11/1**
-030 **6** *2* **Domenico (IRE)**[8] 2958 6-9-13 **65** ... DHolland 3 62
(JRJenkins) *plld hrd: in tch tl lost pl 4f out* **9/1**
545- **7** *3* **Betterware Boy**[186] 6131 4-9-7 **66** ... MHoward(7) 6 59
(PMPhelan) *hld up in rr: hdwy over 4f out: rdn and wknd wl over 1f out* **33/1**
/000 **8** *1 1/4* **Lady Jeannie**[16] 3670 7-7-9 **40** ... CHaddon(7) 7 32
(MJHaynes) *plld hrd: trckd ldrs: wknd over 2f out* **50/1**
2033 **9** *4* **Pay The Silver**[9] 3873 6-9-7 **59** ...(p) IMongan 2 46
(IAWood) *a bhd* **7/1**[3]
00-0 **10** *5* **Arctic Blue**[23] 3461 4-8-5 **50** ...(p) DerekNolan(7) 1 31
(MJGingell) *led for 2f: prom tl rdn over 3f out: sn wknd* **40/1**
340 **11** *2 1/2* **Watchful Witness**[27] 3348 4-9-3 **55** ...(v[1]) LVickers 4 33
(DrJRJNaylor) *mid-div tl lost pl over 5f out* **20/1**

3m 34.44s (5.86) **Going Correction** +0.375s/f (Slow)
**WFA** 3 from 4yo+ 17lb **11** Ran SP% **123.0**
Speed ratings: **100,99,97,96,95 94,93,92,90,87 86**CSF £8.14 CT £23.38 TOTE £2.30: £1.10, £2.00, £2.30; EX 12.10 Place 6 £9.14, Place 5 £5.56..
**Owner** Mrs B Woodford **Bred** Whitsbury Manor Stud **Trained** Ogbourne Maisey, Wilts

**FOCUS**
A moderate staying handicap run at a tactical pace and as such the form may be suspect, although the winner, second and fourth all ran to within a pound of their pre-race marks.

**NOTEBOOK**
**Belle Rouge** dominated from an early stage, dictated a stop-start gallop and won well. She is a most consistent mare and got this trip well, but had the benefit of a vintage Dettori ride this time and will go up in the weights again after this.
**Compton Eclaire(IRE)** could not peg back the winner try as she might, but semed to get the trip well and was clear in second. She looks a better horse with the visor on and, with a stonger gallop, could soon go one better off this mark on the sand.
**Most-Saucy** did not have the race run to suit and can do better. She has been crying out for this trip and remains weighted to win, but must have a strong gallop in order to shine.
**Heart Springs**, who has looked only plating-class to date, ran better for the longer trip and the return to this surface, but was never a serious threat.
T/Plt: £5.50 to a £1 stake. Pool: £35,323.10. 4,680.65 winning tickets. T/Qpdt: £3.10 to a £1 stake. Pool: £2,253.80. 528.00 winning tickets. JS

# 3308 NEWCASTLE (L-H)
Saturday, July 24

**OFFICIAL GOING: Good (good to firm in places)**
Wind: breezy, across Weather: cloudy

## 4130 BETFRED SPRINT SERIES FINAL H'CAP 6f
1:00 (1:01) (B) 3-Y-0+ **£11,945** (£4,530; £2,265; £1,029) **Stalls** Centre

Form RPR
0410 **1** **Fantasy Believer**[15] 3691 6-9-11 **91** ... THamilton(3) 15 102
(JJQuinn) *prom stands side: effrt over 2f out: led that gp ent fnl f: overall ldr wl ins last: hld on wl* **7/1**[3]
0350 **2** *nk* **Fair Shake (IRE)**[28] 3309 4-8-2 **65** ...(v[1]) PFessey 9 75
(DEddy) *dwlt: bhd stands side: rdn 1/2-way: gd hdwy over 1f out: kpt on wl: jst failed* **33/1**
0205 **3** *1/2* **Snow Bunting**[35] 3098 6-7-5 **61** oh3 ... DFentiman(7) 1 70
(JeddO'Keeffe) *hld up in tch far side: hdwy to and overall ldr over 1f out: hdd wl ins last: kpt on* **12/1**
4101 **4** *1 3/4* **Pinchbeck**[13] 3778 5-9-10 **87** ...(p) NCallan 6 90+
(MAJarvis) *swtchd stands side sn after s: hld up: hdwy over 1f out: kpt on: nrst fin* **9/2**[1]
0562 **5** *nk* **Yomalo (IRE)**[24] 3428 4-7-8 **64** ... MHalford(7) 13 66
(RGuest) *hld up stands side: hdwy and led that gp briefly appr fnl f: edgd lft: one pce ins last* **11/2**[2]
6330 **6** *nk* **Mr Malarkey (IRE)**[17] 3645 4-9-1 **78** ...(b) TGMcLaughlin 14 79
(MrsCADunnett) *disp ld stands side to appr fnl f: one pce* **11/1**
4430 **7** *nk* **Tally (IRE)**[8] 3894 4-7-12 **66** ... RThomas(5) 5 67
(MJPolglase) *prom far side: ev ch that gp over 1f out: one pce* **12/1**
1031 **8** *3/4* **Gone'N'Dunnett (IRE)**[20] 3558 5-7-7 **61** oh1 ...(v) BSwarbrick(5) 4 59
(MrsCADunnett) *w far side ldr: ev ch tl edgd lft and no ex over 1f out* **11/1**
0004 **9** *3/4* **Friar Tuck**[25] 3400 9-7-12 **61** oh10 ... RFfrench 10 57
(MissLAPerratt) *chsd stands side ldrs: rdn 1/2-way: no ex fr over 1f out* **50/1**
0600 **10** *nk* **A Teen**[9] 3887 6-7-12 **61** oh7 ... DKinsella 8 56
(PHowling) *hld up: rdn over 2f out: nvr rchd ldrs* **33/1**
0240 **11** *1 1/2* **Legal Set (IRE)**[8] 3901 8-7-7 **61** oh1 ...(t) DFox(5) 3 52
(MissAStokell) *led far side to over 1f out: sn outpcd* **20/1**
5326 **12** *hd* **Glencoe Solas (IRE)**[13] 3775 4-8-11 **74** ... KDalgleish 12 64
(SKirk) *disp ld stands side tl appr fnl f: sn btn* **12/1**
0005 **13** *nk* **William's Well**[23] 3446 10-7-12 **61** oh3 ...(b) DaleGibson 7 50
(MWEasterby) *chsd stands side ldrs: rdn and wknd over 1f out* **16/1**
3105 **14** *1/2* **Ulysees (IRE)**[21] 3515 5-8-8 **74** ... TEaves(3) 2 62
(ISemple) *trckd far side ldrs: lost pl over 2f out: n.d after* **10/1**
4663 **15** *7* **Highland Warrior**[5] 3979 5-8-9 **72** ... VHalliday 11 39
(JSGoldie) *missed break: hdwy into midfield stands side over 2f out: sn rdn and btn* **8/1**

1m 14.06s (-0.98) **Going Correction** 0.0s/f (Good) **15** Ran SP% **124.5**
Speed ratings: **106,105,104,102,102 101,101,100,99,99 97,96,96,95,86**CSF £234.95 CT £2798.98 TOTE £5.40: £2.10, £11.40, £3.20; EX 318.70.
**Owner** The Fantasy Fellowship B **Bred** John Khan **Trained** Settrington, N Yorks

**FOCUS**
A fair handicap run at a decent pace and the form is solid but, although the first two home raced on the stands' side, the proximity of the third home on the far side suggested there was little between the sides.

**NOTEBOOK**
**Fantasy Believer**, who got upset in the stalls prior to running poorly last time, showed that to be all wrong and ran as well has he ever has done. He looked value for a bit more than the winning margin and should continue to give a good account.
**Fair Shake(IRE)**, tried in a first-time visor, confirmed himself as good on fast ground as he is with cut with his best effort of the year. He is capable of winning a similar race, but his inconsistency prevents him from being one to get heavily involved with next time.
**Snow Bunting**, 3lb out of the handicap, fared best of those that raced on the far-side group and is also capable of winning races from his current mark. However his losing run, that stretches back nearly two years, highlights the fact he is not one to place maximum faith in.
**Pinchbeck**, 7lb higher than at Haydock, ran well but did leave the impression that he will continue to look vulnerable to well handicapped or progressive types from this mark in a similar grade.
**Yomalo(IRE)** ◆, who divided subsequent winners last time, may be a bit better than the bare form as she made up a good deal of ground in a short space of time on the outside of the stands'-side bunch and not surprisingly had little to offer late on. She is one to keep an eye on over this trip when dropped in grade.
**Mr Malarkey(IRE)** has not won for over a year but is a consistent sort who had the run of the race against the stands rail and gave it his best shot. He will get no respite though, and is likely to continue to look vulnerable in this grade.

## 4131 APPLEBY GROUP LIMITED MAIDEN AUCTION STKS (DIV I) 7f
1:35 (1:36) (F) 2-Y-0 **£3,290** (£940; £470) **Stalls** Centre

Form RPR
0 **1** **Skidrow**[27] 3336 2-8-11 ... DKinsella 7 83+
(MLWBell) *hld up: hdwy and swtchd lft over 2f out: led appr fnl f: pushed out: comf* **12/1**
032 **2** *4* **Bee Stinger**[17] 3633 2-8-7 ... NCallan 8 69
(IAWood) *keen: led to appr fnl f: kpt on same pce* **4/5**[1]
**3** *1/2* **Coconut Squeak** 2-8-4 ... SChin 3 65
(JGGiven) *a cl up: effrt over 1f out: sn one pce* **25/1**
0 **4** *1 3/4* **Jeune Loup**[14] 3758 2-8-13 ... GFaulkner 6 69
(PCHaslam) *trckd ldrs: effrt over 2f out: one pce fnl f* **12/1**
500 **5** *1* **Classic Style (IRE)**[18] 3611 2-7-13 ... AMullen(7) 5 60
(TDEasterby) *cl up tl rdn and outpcd over 1f out* **40/1**
05 **6** *4* **Scorpio Sally (IRE)**[25] 3398 2-8-4 ... RFfrench 9 48
(MDHammond) *in tch: rdn and outpcd over 2f out: n.d after* **20/1**
00 **7** *1/2* **Allstar Princess**[14] 3760 2-8-1 ow2 ... THamilton(3) 2 47
(RAFahey) *stdd rr: effrt over 2f out: sn rdn and btn over 1f out* **50/1**
0 **8** *3* **Morning Major (USA)**[30] 3233 2-8-9 ... PFessey 11 44
(TDBarron) *bhd and pushed along: shortlived effrt 2f out: nvr rchd ldrs* **25/1**
35 **9** *1* **Dancer's Serenade (IRE)**[20] 3560 2-8-13 ... DaleGibson 12 46
(TPTate) *cl up tl wknd over 2f out* **11/2**[2]
3034 **10** *1 1/4* **Llamadas**[18] 3611 2-8-8 ...(p) LEnstone(3) 1 41
(MDods) *hld up outside: effrt over 2f out: sn btn* **11/1**[3]
00 **11** *nk* **Negas (IRE)**[8] 3893 2-8-10 ... TEaves(3) 4 42
(JHowardJohnson) *dwlt: sn prom: rdn and wknd over 2f out* **20/1**
**12** *dist* **Trigony (IRE)** 2-8-11 ... KDalgleish 10 —
(TDEasterby) *s.v.s: sn t.o* **20/1**

1m 28.83s (0.81) **Going Correction** 0.0s/f (Good) **12** Ran SP% **121.0**
Speed ratings: **95,90,89,87,86 82,81,78,77,75 75,—**CSF £20.66 TOTE £10.90: £3.20, £1.10, £5.50; EX 32.40.
**Owner** Raymond Tooth & Miss Debbie Dove **Bred** P D Player **Trained** Newmarket, Suffolk

**FOCUS**
Just ordinary form behind the winner, who was showing much-improved form and looks capable of better. The pace was only fair and the field raced on the stands' side.

**NOTEBOOK**
**Skidrow** ◆, related to a couple of useful performers, notably sprinter Kastaway and mile and a quarter winner Skidmark, improved a good deal on his debut effort and, although the bare form behind him looks ordinary at best, he appeals as the type to progress again. He should stay a mile and can hold his own in stronger company.
**Bee Stinger** looks a fairly reliable yardstick and seemed to run his race, despite failing to settle early on, back over this longer trip. He is starting to look exposed but is capable of winning a small race up to this trip.
**Coconut Squeak**, a 7,000gns half-sister to dual mile winner Yalla, was easy to back but showed more than enough on this racecourse debut to suggest she can win an ordinary race in this grade. She should stay a mile and is open to improvement.
**Jeune Loup** bettered his debut effort over this longer trip and, given there is plenty of stamina in his pedigree, will be one to look out for in ordinary handicap company granted a stiffer test in due course.
**Classic Style(IRE)** is exposed as modest and her proximity confirms this bare form is nothing special. She is likely to continue to look vulnerable in this grade.
**Scorpio Sally(IRE)** achieved little and is another that is going to continue to look vulnerable in this type of event.

## 4132 PIMMS APPRENTICE CLAIMING STKS 7f
2:10 (2:10) (G) 3-Y-0+ **£2,660** (£760; £380) **Stalls** Centre

Form RPR
0400 **1** **Mehmaas**[18] 3612 8-8-11 43 ...(v) StevenHarrison(3) 6 62
(REBarr) *cl up far side: led 3f out: sn hrd pressed: hld on wl fnl f* **25/1**
-355 **2** *nk* **Killala (IRE)**[26] 3365 4-9-2 62 ... WHogg 3 63
(ISemple) *trckd far side ldrs: hdwy to chal over 2f out: kpt on: hld cl home* **11/4**[1]
0240 **3** *2 1/2* **Noble Pursuit**[18] 3604 7-8-9 50 ... LauraPike(5) 1 55
(REBarr) *prom far side: effrt over 2f out: edgd rt: kpt on same pce fnl f* **14/1**
-563 **4** *5* **Donna's Double**[8] 3903 9-9-3 54 ...(p) AMullen 9 45
(DEddy) *hld up stands side: hdwy over 1f out: kpt on fnl f: no imp* **9/2**[2]
3016 **5** *1 3/4* **Bailieborough (IRE)**[12] 3796 5-9-3 70 ...(v) PJBenson(7) 11 47
(DNicholls) *cl up stands side: led that gp 3f out: edgd lft and no imp fr over 1f out* **9/2**[2]
5000 **6** *9* **Give Him Credit (USA)**[10] 3836 4-9-1 52 ...(p) HPoulton 15 15
(MrsADuffield) *prom stands side: effrt 2f out: sn no imp* **33/1**
1461 **7** *1/2* **Tre Colline**[7] 3932 5-10-1 70 ... MHoward 8 27
(NTinkler) *prom stands side: lost pl after 3f: effrt over 2f out: nvr rchd ldrs* **5/1**[3]
0605 **8** *2 1/2* **Mount Pekan (IRE)**[4] 4004 4-8-10 41 ... JCurrie(5) 2 7
(JSGoldie) *missed break: a bhd far side* **25/1**
6540 **9** *1 3/4* **Niteowl Express (IRE)**[14] 3742 3-8-2 36 ... AReilly(3) 5 —
(JO'Reilly) *led far side to 3f out: sn btn* **66/1**
1534 **10** *2* **Countrywide Girl (IRE)**[18] 3612 5-8-4 39 ... KPierrepont(7) 12 —
(ABerry) *keen: prom stands side to 1/2-way: sn outpcd* **20/1**
/0-0 **11** *4* **Stormville (IRE)**[117] 1175 7-9-3 57 ... JDO'Reilly 14 —
(MBrittain) *led stands side 1f: cl up tl wknd over 2f out* **40/1**
-040 **12** *shd* **Tancred Arms**[37] 3006 8-8-3 38 ... DonnaCaldwell(5) 13 —
(DWBarker) *led after 1f stands side: hdd 3f out: sn btn* **22/1**

0330 **13** *6* **Summer Special**[19] 3579 4-9-1 44 (p) MHalford 10 —
(DWBarker) *in tch stands side: struggling fr 1/2-way* **20/1**
003 **14** *6* **Finger Of Fate**[12] 3801 4-8-13 42 (b) KGhunowa(3) 4 —
(MJPolglase) *cl up far side tl wknd fr 3f out* **14/1**
0200 **15** *16* **Leopard Creek**[11] 3820 3-8-1 53 (v[1]) AHamblett(5) 7 —
(MrsJRRamsden) *swtchd rt s: hld up in tch stands side: effrt 1/2-way: wknd qckly fr over 2f out* **14/1**

1m 28.44s (0.42) **Going Correction** 0.0s/f (Good)
**WFA** 3 from 4yo+ 7lb **15** Ran SP% **128.1**
Speed ratings: **97,96,93,88,86 75,75,72,70,68 63,63,56,49,31**CSF £91.06 TOTE £55.50: £10.20, £1.90, £7.90; EX 142.40.
**Owner** Cloughton Racing Partnership **Bred** Lady Richard Wellesley **Trained** Seamer, N Yorks

**FOCUS**
The usual mixed bag for this type of event and a decent pace. The far side held the edge but this race looks a dubious form guide.

**NOTEBOOK**
**Mehmaas**, an inconsistent sort, had not been in much form and faced a stiff task at the weights. He showed much more resilience than the runner-up but will be going up in the weights for this and would be no means certain to reproduce this next time. *Official explanation: trainer had no explanation for the improved form shown*
**Killala(IRE)** looked to have plenty in his favour regarding ground, trip and weights but, although he was not beaten far, he did not seem to be giving his best shot when put under pressure. He will find life tougher back in handicaps from his current mark.
**Noble Pursuit** was not disgraced but it is arguable whether he is the ideal sort of ride for an inexperienced apprentice, and his lengthy losing run means he is not one to place much faith in.
**Donna's Double**, dropped in trip, was not disgraced and fared the best of those that raced on the stands' side. The return to further and handicaps will help, but he does need things to fall right and he is not one to place too much faith in.
**Bailieborough(IRE)** looked to have a good chance at the weights down in trip, but was again below his best and may have been in front plenty soon enough for him. He did not look the ideal sort of ride for an inexperienced claimer.
**Give Him Credit(USA)** again offered little encouragement for the future.
**Tre Colline** looked to have fair claims on these terms but, although down in trip, ran poorly for no apparent reason.
**Finger Of Fate** *Official explanation: jockey said gelding bled from the nose*

## 4133 PIMMS SUMMER CLASSIC H'CAP 5f
2:45 (2:46) (D) (0-85,79) 3-Y-O+ **£7,000** (£2,154; £1,077; £538) **Stalls** Centre

Form RPR
1620 **1** **Awake**[8] 3920 7-9-10 **79** KDalgleish 1 93
(DNicholls) *stdd in tch far side: hdwy and swtchd 2f out: led ins fnl f: r.o wl* **5/1**[1]
0402 **2** *1 1/4* **Imperial Echo (USA)**[14] 3737 3-9-5 **78** (v) NCallan 3 88
(TDBarron) *keen: trckd far side ldrs: effrt 2f out: kpt on fnl f: nt rch ldr* **10/1**
0200 **3** *1/2* **Beyond The Clouds (IRE)**[15] 3713 8-9-3 **75** TEaves(3) 2 83
(JSWainwright) *cl up far side: led appr fnl f to ins last: one pce* **7/1**[3]
3205 **4** *1 3/4* **Winthorpe (IRE)**[8] 3920 4-8-13 **71** THamilton(3) 8 72
(JJQuinn) *hld up in tch far side: effrt on outside of that gp over 1f out: kpt on fnl f: no imp* **5/1**[1]
0-00 **5** *nk* **Strawberry Patch (IRE)**[19] 3580 5-8-0 **55** (p) PFessey 7 55
(MissLAPerratt) *prom far side: rdn over 2f out: one pce fnl f* **25/1**
0440 **6** *hd* **Pirlie Hill**[8] 3894 4-7-12 **53** oh2 DKinsella 6 53
(MissLAPerratt) *hld up far side: effrt 2f out: no imp fnl f* **25/1**
2303 **7** *nk* **Kings College Boy**[3] 4013 4-8-5 **60** (b) DaleGibson 10 59
(RAFahey) *trckd stands side ldrs: rdn to ld that gp over 1f out: kpt on: no ch w far side* **11/2**[2]
4300 **8** *3/4* **Viewforth**[8] 3894 6-8-11 **66** (b) VHalliday 13 62
(JSGoldie) *chsd stands side ldrs: rdn 1/2-way: kpt on u.p fnl f* **10/1**
5215 **9** *3/4* **Aahgowangowan (IRE)**[12] 3795 5-8-8 **63** (t) RFfrench 4 56
(MDods) *led far side to appr fnl f: wknd ins last* **11/2**[2]
0-00 **10** *1 1/2* **Trinity (IRE)**[77] 1971 8-7-12 **53** oh5 PMQuinn 9 41
(MBrittain) *w stands side ldr tl wknd over 1f out* **33/1**
3405 **11** *1/2* **Strensall**[3] 4011 7-9-5 **77** LEnstone(3) 12 63
(REBarr) *led stands side to over 1f out: sn btn* **9/1**
0565 **12** *6* **Linden's Lady**[8] 3923 4-7-9 **57** (be) DFentiman(7) 5 21
(JRWeymes) *keen: cl up far side tl wknd qckly 2f out* **33/1**

60.26 secs (-1.27) **Going Correction** 0.0s/f (Good)
**WFA** 3 from 4yo+ 4lb **12** Ran SP% **118.4**
Speed ratings: **110,108,107,104,103 103,103,101,100,98 97,87**CSF £52.62 CT £278.84 TOTE £6.00: £2.40, £3.80, £2.80; EX 68.50.
**Owner** Lucayan Stud & D Nicholls **Bred** Side Hill Stud **Trained** Sessay, N Yorks

**FOCUS**
A sound pace resulted in a decent time for the grade and the advantage lay with those that raced on the far side The form is solid, the winner is in good heart and may be capable of further success this summer.

**NOTEBOOK**
**Awake**, poorly drawn when below his best at Pontefract last time, showed what he was capable of with a fluent success and won with more in hand that the margin suggests. He is capable of winning again this summer.
**Imperial Echo(USA)**, back in trip and with the visor back on, ran creditably but, although the return to six furlongs should be in his favour, he may not be the most straightforward around.
**Beyond The Clouds(IRE)**, ran creditably back on a sound surface but, although capable of winning another race from his current mark when things fall right, his losing run that goes back to September 2002 has to be a concern.
**Winthorpe(IRE)**, who needs things to fall right, ran creditably given that he did not really get the run of the race, but he is not the sort to be making too many excuses about.
**Strawberry Patch(IRE)** has slipped a fair way in the weights and confirmed he retains ability with his best effort of the year. The return to six furlongs will suit and, although on a long losing run, he is one to keep an eye on.
**Pirlie Hill** was not disgraced but is likely to continue to look vulnerable in this grade.
**Kings College Boy** fared the best of the quartet that raced on the stands'-side but, although better than the bare result, is not one to place much faith in.

## 4134 TSG BEESWING RATED STKS (H'CAP) 7f
3:15 (3:16) (D) (0-85,81) 3-Y-O+ **£12,207** (£4,630; £2,315; £1,052) **Stalls** Centre

Form RPR
3031 **1** **True Night**[15] 3690 7-9-4 **81** TEaves(3) 13 90
(DNicholls) *hld up: hdwy whn n.m.r 2f out: edgd lft and led 1f out: r.o wl* **9/2**[1]
0402 **2** *nk* **Raphael (IRE)**[9] 3867 5-8-12 **79** AMullen(7) 8 87
(TDEasterby) *cl up: rdn to chal over 1f out: kpt on wl: jst hld* **12/1**
2131 **3** *nk* **Snap**[30] 3252 3-8-11 **78** RFfrench 6 85
(MJohnston) *towards rr: rdn 1/2-way: hdwy over 1f out: kpt on fnl f* **9/2**[1]
0300 **4** *shd* **Tidy (IRE)**[14] 3755 4-9-4 **78** KDalgleish 3 85
(MDHammond) *hld up: hdwy outside 2f out: kpt on u.p fnl f: no ex towards fin* **25/1**
1006 **5** *1 1/4* **Sea Storm (IRE)**[5] 3977 6-9-7 **81** (p) GFaulkner 11 85
(DRMacleod) *chsd ldrs: led 2f to 1f out: no ex* **20/1**
2001 **6** *shd* **Top Dirham**[5] 3977 6-8-13 **73** 3ex DaleGibson 9 76
(MWEasterby) *hld up: hdwy whn checked over 1f out: rdn and kpt on wl fnl f: nrst fin* **9/2**[1]
0-00 **7** *2 1/2* **Out For A Stroll**[77] 1968 5-9-1 **75** PFessey 10 72
(SCWilliams) *hld up: effrt 2f out: no ex ins fnl f* **7/1**[2]
U100 **8** *1 3/4* **Balakiref**[14] 3755 5-8-9 **69** NCallan 5 61
(MDods) *dwlt: hld up: hdwy over 1f out: no imp fnl f* **8/1**[3]
0516 **9** *5* **Sierra Vista**[14] 3754 4-9-4 **81** LEnstone(3) 12 60
(DWBarker) *cl up tl wknd appr fnl f* **14/1**
0 **10** *1* **Mobane Flyer**[14] 3755 4-8-4 **67** THamilton(3) 4 44
(RAFahey) *midfield: rdn over 2f out: wknd over 1f out* **40/1**
2006 **11** *2* **King Harson**[24] 3409 5-9-0 **79** (v) BSwarbrick(5) 7 51
(JDBethell) *led to 2f out: sn btn* **16/1**
2060 **12** *2* **Favour**[9] 3867 4-8-9 **69** LGoncalves 1 35
(MrsJRRamsden) *keen: in tch: lost pl after 2f: n.d after* **12/1**
3012 **13** *2* **Kirkby's Treasure**[21] 3516 6-9-0 **74** SChin 2 35
(ABerry) *prom tl wknd over 2f out* **14/1**

1m 27.26s (-0.76) **Going Correction** 0.0s/f (Good)
**WFA** 3 from 4yo+ 7lb **13** Ran SP% **123.8**
Speed ratings: **104,103,103,103,101 101,98,96,91,89 87,85,83**CSF £62.02 CT £273.51 TOTE £4.70: £2.50, £2.70, £1.80; EX 53.30.
**Owner** Benton And Partners **Bred** Crichel Farms Ltd **Trained** Sessay, N Yorks

**FOCUS**
A fair handicap run at a fair pace and the form should prove solid and reliable. The whole field raced on the far side.

**NOTEBOOK**
**True Night**, 3lb higher than his Ascot success, showed himself as good as ever with a gutsy success from his wide draw. He has been running well most of the year and should continue to give a good account in this type of event.
**Raphael(IRE)** is a model of consistency who ran right up to her best once again and looks a good guide to the worth of this form. She will get little respite from the Handicapper, but is likely to continue to give it her best shot.
**Snap ◆**, up in the weights and facing his toughest test to date, lost little in defeat but left the strong impression that the step up to a mile would be in his favour. He is open to further improvement and appeals as the type to win more races.
**Tidy(IRE)** seems better at this course than anywhere else and ran his race on ground that would have been plenty quick enough for him. He is likely to continue to look vulnerable in this type of race from his current mark, though.
**Sea Storm(IRE)** had the run of the race and ran his best race since winning at Musselburgh in May. He too is vulnerable to progressive or well handicapped types from this mark, though.
**Top Dirham ◆**, under a penalty and back in trip, did not get the rub of things shaped as though in better form than the bare result suggests. A more strongly-run race over a mile would suit and he looks capable of winning again from his new mark.
**Out For A Stroll**, with conditions to suit for the first time this year, shaped much better and will be one to keep a close eye on under similar conditions in the near future when the cash is down.

## 4135 APPLEBY GROUP LIMITED MAIDEN AUCTION STKS (DIV II) 7f
3:50 (3:50) (F) 2-Y-O **£3,283** (£938; £469) **Stalls** Centre

Form RPR
6 **1** **Arabian Ana (IRE)**[9] 3876 2-8-13 DMcGaffin 6 74
(BSmart) *dwlt: sn in tch: pushed along 1/2-way: led and rn green over 1f out: edgd lft ins last: kpt on* **6/1**[3]
03 **2** *1 1/2* **Spinnakers Girl**[33] 3145 2-7-9 DFentiman(7) 4 59
(JRWeymes) *cl up: led over 2f to over 1f out: 1l down whn n.m.r ins fnl f: one pce* **5/2**[1]
500 **3** *1 1/2* **Dixie Queen (IRE)**[16] 3679 2-8-6 NCallan 9 60
(MDods) *midfield: rdn over 2f out: kpt on fnl f: nt rch first two* **7/1**
0 **4** *shd* **Summer Silks**[11] 3818 2-8-1 ow2 THamilton(3) 11 57
(RAFahey) *hld up: effrt 2f out: kpt on fnl f: no imp* **9/1**
**5** *hd* **Askwith (IRE)** 2-8-6 BSwarbrick(5) 7 64
(JDBethell) *s.i.s: bhd tl styd on fr over 1f out: bttr for r* **12/1**
00 **6** *2 1/2* **Zando**[43] 2860 2-8-9 GFaulkner 1 56
(PCHaslam) *prom tl rdn and one pce fr 2f out* **7/1**
20 **7** *3* **Trickshot**[47] 2730 2-8-2 PMQuinn 5 41
(TDEasterby) *sn rdn in midfield: no imp fr 2f out* **9/2**[2]
00 **8** *3* **Mist Opportunity (IRE)**[39] 2961 2-8-4 RoryMoore(7) 8 43
(PCHaslam) *bhd: pushed along over 2f out: n.d* **50/1**
60 **9** *2 1/2* **For Nowt**[23] 3444 2-8-2 AMullen(7) 2 34
(TDEasterby) *keen: chsd ldrs to 2f out: sn btn* **14/1**
000 **10** *4* **Tillingborn Dancer (IRE)**[24] 3406 2-8-11 KDalgleish 10 26
(MDHammond) *led after 2f to over 2f out: sn btn* **25/1**
0 **11** *5* **Xaarist (IRE)**[30] 3233 2-8-11 DaleGibson 3 14
(TPTate) *keen: led 2f: wknd fr 3f out* **12/1**

1m 29.62s (1.60) **Going Correction** 0.0s/f (Good) **11** Ran SP% **123.9**
Speed ratings: **90,88,86,86,86 83,79,76,73,69 63**CSF £22.55 TOTE £10.50: £3.40, £1.60, £3.80; EX 60.50.
**Owner** H E Sheikh Rashid Bin Mohammed **Bred** Gabriel Bell **Trained** Hambleton, N Yorks

**FOCUS**
An ordinary maiden run at a fair pace and one in which the field again raced on the far side.

**NOTEBOOK**
**Arabian Ana(IRE)** left his debut form behind over this longer trip and, although this bare form is nothing special, he still looked in need of the experience. He should stay a mile and may be capable of better.
**Spinnakers Girl** probably ran to a similar level as on her latest start at Musselburgh and looks a fair guide to the worth of this form. She is going to continue to look vulnerable to anything progressive in this grade, though.
**Dixie Queen(IRE)** put a poor run at Warwick behind her and left the impression on this occasion that a further step up in trip will be in her favour. The handicap route is likely to offer her best chance of success, though.
**Summer Silks**, upped in trip, fared better than on her debut and left the impression that run of the mill handicaps and a stiffer test of stamina would see her in an even better light.
**Askwith(IRE) ◆**, who cost 15,000gns and is out of a nine-furlong winner, was easy to back but showed more than enough on this racecourse debut to suggest a similar race can be found, especially as he is likely to improve a fair bit for this run.
**Zando** was not disgraced but is another that is going to be seen to better effect in ordinary handicap company granted a stiffer test of stamina in due course.

## 4136 BELLWAY HOMES CLASSIFIED STKS 1m 2f 32y
4:20 (4:20) (D) 3-Y-O+ **£5,746** (£1,768; £884; £442) **Stalls** High

Form RPR
0563 **1** **Dunaskin (IRE)**[7] 3953 4-9-5 80 DKinsella 6 89
(DEddy) *set stdy pce to over 2f out: rallied to regain ld ins fnl f: r.o wl* **3/1**[3]
-330 **2** *3/4* **Mbosi (USA)**[9] 3869 3-8-12 83 RFfrench 1 91
(MJohnston) *pressed ldr: led over 2f out to ins fnl f: kpt on* **13/2**

3141 **3** *shd* **Olivia Rose (IRE)**[7] 3952 5-9-5 83 NCallan 4 88
(JPearce) *chsd ldrs: effrt over 1f out: chal ins fnl f: kpt on: hld cl home* **7/4**[1]

6612 **4** *1¼* **Scottish River (USA)**[9] 3872 5-9-2 82 BSwarbrick(5) 5 88
(MDIUsher) *missed break: keen in rr: effrt over 2f out: styd on fnl f: no imp* **5/2**[2]

3010 **5** *11* **Pawan (IRE)**[15] 3714 4-9-5 73 AnnStokell 3 66
(MissAStokell) *hld up in tch: outpcd 3f out: sn btn* **20/1**

204/ **6** *dist* **Axford Lord**[626] 5636 4-9-2 60 TEaves(3) 2 —
(ACWhillans) *prom to 4f out: sn lost tch* **40/1**

2m 13.55s (1.95) **Going Correction** +0.325s/f (Good) **6** Ran SP% **110.5**
**WFA** 3 from 4yo+ 10lb
Speed ratings: **105,104,104,103,94** —CSF £21.28 TOTE £4.30: £2.10, £3.10; EX 23.20 Place 6 £120.02, Place 5 £18.79.
**Owner** Mrs I Battla **Bred** J P And Miss M Mangan **Trained** Ingoe, Northumberland

**FOCUS**
An ordinary event in which the pace was on the steady side so, although it looks sound on paper, this bare form may not prove entirely reliable.

**NOTEBOOK**
**Dunaskin(IRE)**, who had a decent chance at the weights, got the run of the race over this shorter trip and showed the right attitude to regain the lead. He is a fair performer around this trip but is best when allowed to dominate.
**Mbosi(USA)** had a good chance at the weights, the run of the race and lost little in defeat over this longer trip. He is likely to find life tougher from his current mark back in competitive handicaps, though.
**Olivia Rose(IRE)** has been in tremendous heart this term and shaped well given that a stronger pace and easier ground would have been in her favour. She will be one to note granted more cut back in handicap company.
**Scottish River(USA)** deserves plenty of credit given that he did not enjoy the run of the race. A more strongly-run race would have suited but he is the type that needs things to fall just right.
**Pawan(IRE)** had a stiff task at the weights but was beaten before stamina became an issue over this trip and consistency is not his strongest suit.
**Axford Lord** ran poorly on this first start since November 2002.
T/Plt: £92.00 to a £1 stake. Pool: £42,525.45. 337.10 winning tickets. T/Qpdt: £15.40 to a £1 stake. Pool: £2,707.60. 130.10 winning tickets. RY

# 3741 NOTTINGHAM (L-H)
## Saturday, July 24

**OFFICIAL GOING: Good to firm**
Wind: Fresh against. Weather: Fine and sunny.

## 4137 CITY LIFE MAGAZINE MAIDEN FILLIES' STKS 6f 15y
**2:30** (2:31) (D) 2-Y-O **£4,946** (£1,522; £761; £380) **Stalls** High

Form RPR

222 **1** **Encanto (IRE)**[16] 3659 2-8-4 DerekNolan(7) 4 79
(JSMoore) *hld up: hdwy over 2f out: led over 1f out: rdn out* **7/2**[2]

0 **2** *1½* **Sharp As A Tack (IRE)**[5] 3992 2-8-8 JFMcDonald(3) 6 75
(BJMeehan) *dwlt: hld up: hdwy over 2f out: rdn and edgd rt over 1f out: r.o* **50/1**

3 **3** *1¼* **Ahdaaf (USA)**[16] 3676 2-8-11 WSupple 2 71
(JLDunlop) *a.p: led 2f out: sn rdn and hdd: no ex ins fnl f* **10/11**[1]

6 **4** *nk* **Casterossa**[43] 2837 2-8-11 TQuinn 10 70
(DHaydnJones) *s.s: hung lft and outpcd: hdwy over 1f out: r.o* **33/1**

6 **5** *hd* **Mitraillette (USA)**[28] 3296 2-8-11 BDoyle 8 69
(SirMichaelStoute) *hld up: pushed along over 3f out: swtchd lft and hdwy over 2f out: styd on same pce ins fnl f* **12/1**

5 **6** *3½* **Rapid Romance (USA)**[14] 3741 2-8-11 RMullen 9 59
(EALDunlop) *hld up: pushed along 1/2-way: n.d* **16/1**

2 **7** *1* **Scrooby Baby**[13] 3770 2-8-11 SWKelly 7 56
(JAOsborne) *sn pushed along and prom: wknd over 2f out* **5/1**[3]

6 **8** *shd* **Eukleia (USA)**[30] 3248 2-8-6 PMakin(5) 1 55
(TDBarron) *led: hung lft and hdd 2f out: wknd fnl f* **40/1**

**9** *14* **Shamrock Bay** 2-8-11 MFenton 3 13
(JGGiven) *chsd ldrs to 1/2-way* **20/1**

00 **10** *21* **Cadogen Square**[9] 3865 2-8-11 DarrenWilliams 5 —
(DWChapman) *s.i.s: sn prom: wknd over 2f out* **150/1**

1m 17.7s (2.90) **Going Correction** +0.40s/f (Good) **10** Ran SP% **117.6**
Speed ratings: **96,94,92,91,91 87,85,85,66,38**CSF £171.69 TOTE £4.00: £1.40, £13.30, £1.10; EX 150.40.
**Owner** Cistm Racing Club Ltd **Bred** Hadi Al Tajir **Trained** East Garston, Berks

**FOCUS**
An ordinary maiden and just fair form.

**NOTEBOOK**
**Encanto(IRE)**, whose rider continues to catch the eye, won a shade comfortably. She should stay seven furlongs, and was withdrawn from a Listed event over that trip two days earlier having bolted before the start.
**Sharp As A Tack(IRE)** was keeping on in the latter stages without really helping her rider, and flashed her tail more than once. She should stay a seventh furlong.
**Ahdaaf(USA)** was unable to build on the promise of her Newmarket debut and might have found this six a bit sharp.
**Casterossa** seemed set to finish at the back of the field until getting the hang of things late in the day. She is learning with experience.
**Mitraillette(USA)** made ground when switched to the outside but was making no further impression inside the last. She is bred to stay a bit farther than this.
**Rapid Romance(USA)**, who had shown a glimmer of promise on her debut over course and distance, was in trouble shortly after halfway.
**Scrooby Baby**, runner-up in a weak race on her debut, still looked green.
**Shamrock Bay** *Official explanation: jockey said filly got unbalanced*

## 4138 HAPPY BIRTHDAY MARK BEMROSE H'CAP 1m 1f 213y
**3:00** (3:00) (E) (0-70,68) 3-Y-O **£4,160** (£1,280; £640; £320) **Stalls** Low

Form RPR

5636 **1** **Rock Lobster**[26] 3379 3-8-13 **60** MFenton 12 70
(JGGiven) *hld up: hdwy over 2f out: rdn to ld over 1f out: r.o* **6/1**[3]

6024 **2** *1* **Scriptorium**[40] 2930 3-8-11 **61** NMackay(3) 6 69
(LMCumani) *s.i.s: sn chsng ldrs: rdn to ld over 2f out: hdd over 1f out: styd on same pce ins fnl f* **10/3**[2]

2532 **3** *½* **Pella**[10] 3844 3-9-2 **63** DSweeney 9 70
(MBlanshard) *hld up: hdwy over 2f out: rdn and ev ch ins fnl f: unable qck* **2/1**[1]

4450 **4** *2½* **Mambina (USA)**[57] 2442 3-8-13 **63** SHitchcott(3) 8 65
(MRChannon) *hld up in tch: rdn over 2f out: styd on same pce appr fnl f* **12/1**

3105 **5** *½* **Chara**[77] 1963 3-9-4 **65** RMullen 3 66
(JRJenkins) *s.i.s: bhd: hdwy over 1f out: nt clr run ins fnl f: nt rch ldrs* **16/1**

0216 **6** *hd* **Queen's Fantasy**[38] 2987 3-9-1 **62** (v) PaulEddery 16 63
(DHaydnJones) *chsd ldr 8f out: rdn to ld over 3f out: hdd over 2f out: wkng whn edgd lft 1f out* **10/1**

5550 **7** *1¾* **Snowed Under**[14] 3746 3-8-11 **58** TQuinn 5 56
(JDBethell) *sn led: rdn and hdd over 3f out: wknd over 1f out* **18/1**

5060 **8** *hd* **Imperial Royale (IRE)**[10] 3837 3-8-12 **59** (p) MTebbutt 13 56
(PLClinton) *chsd ldrs 8f* **28/1**

0-60 **9** *1* **Brooklands Lodge (USA)**[21] 3536 3-9-2 **63** IMongan 1 58
(MJAttwater) *hld up: rdn over 3f out: n.d* **33/1**

6004 **10** *½* **Canni Thinkaar (IRE)**[14] 3746 3-9-1 **62** JCarroll 14 56
(PWHarris) *chsd ldrs: rdn over 3f out: wknd over 2f out* **20/1**

-650 **11** *2* **Kalishka (IRE)**[8] 3921 3-8-13 **60** WSupple 4 51
(AndrewTurnell) *prom over 7f* **25/1**

50-0 **12** *¾* **Cheverak Forest (IRE)**[101] 1392 3-9-3 **64** KimTinkler 15 53
(DonEnricoIncisa) *a in rr* **25/1**

0045 **13** *5* **Magical Mimi**[8] 3897 3-9-0 **68** LeanneKershaw(7) 2 48
(JeddO'Keeffe) *s.s: a bhd* **25/1**

2m 10.2s (0.70) **Going Correction** +0.025s/f (Good) **13** Ran SP% **121.3**
Speed ratings: **98,97,96,94,94 94,92,92,91,91 89,89,85**CSF £24.16 CT £55.55 TOTE £8.00: £2.20, £2.00, £1.50; EX 38.90.
**Owner** A Clarke **Bred** Southill Stud **Trained** Willoughton, Lincs

**FOCUS**
An ordinary handicap, but the fairly modest form has a sound look.

**NOTEBOOK**
**Rock Lobster**, 13lb lower than at the start of the campaign, is currently rated higher on the All-Weather. Having his first run on fast ground, he came from off the pace to lead and appeared to idle a little once in front.
**Scriptorium** got to the front on the inside and stuck on when headed. He can win a little race but may need a mile and a half.
**Pella**, a well-backed favourite, delivered her challenge towards the centre of the track but was unable to find a change of gear. She has been running similar races over a little shorter of late and had edged back up the weights.
**Mambina(USA)** proved that she handles a sound surface but she may prove happiest back on soft ground.
**Chara**, a pound higher than when winning at Beverley in April, made late headway on this first run for 77 days without enjoying the clearest of passages.
**Queen's Fantasy**, who failed to stay 14 furlongs last time, tried to kick clear in the home straight but could never get away from the pack.

## 4139 JOHN WATKINS CELEBRATION (S) H'CAP 1m 6f 15y
**3:35** (3:35) (G) (0-55,53) 4-Y-O+ **£2,765** (£790; £395) **Stalls** Low

Form RPR

3653 **1** **Banningham Blaze**[5] 3989 4-8-13 **46** (v) IMongan 11 54
(AWCarroll) *hld up: hdwy over 2f out: rdn to ld 1f out: styd on wl* **3/1**[1]

0042 **2** *1¾* **Lunar Lord**[14] 3743 8-9-2 **49** JBramhill 5 55
(DBurchell) *trckd ldrs: led on bit over 3f out: rdn and hdd 1f out: styd on same pce* **10/3**[2]

6-05 **3** *1* **Pertemps Sia**[13] 3776 4-8-3 **36** WSupple 9 41
(ADSmith) *chsd ldrs: rdn over 2f out: no ex ins fnl f* **13/2**

0304 **4** *1½* **Border Terrier (IRE)**[12] 3794 6-8-3 **39** (b) NMackay(3) 10 42
(MDHammond) *plld hrd and prom: lost pl 6f out: hdwy 3f out: styd on same pce fnl f* **5/1**[3]

/204 **5** *1¼* **Cracow (IRE)**[9] 3885 7-8-8 **46** (p) PMakin(5) 6 47
(AMHales) *hld up: hdwy 6f out: rdn over 1f out: sn btn* **14/1**

0600 **6** *3* **Magic Charm**[26] 3369 6-7-7 **33** oh3 LeanneKershaw(7) 8 30
(JeddO'Keeffe) *s.i.s: hld up: hdwy 6f out: hung lft and wknd over 1f out* **20/1**

0062 **7** *½* **Think Quick (IRE)**[12] 3799 4-7-10 **36** ow1 RKennemore(7) 4 32
(RHollinshead) *hld up: hdwy over 4f out: edgd lft and wknd over 1f out* **9/1**

6000 **8** *12* **Grey Samurai**[22] 3490 4-7-7 **33** oh3 DeanWilliams(7) 7 12
(PTMidgley) *plld hrd: trckd ldr: rdn and wknd over 2f out* **100/1**

640/ **9** *shd* **Burning Truth (USA)**[90] 2361 10-9-6 **53** VSlattery 3 32
(MSheppard) *led over 10f: wknd over 1f out* **16/1**

0400 **10** *2* **Jack Durrance (IRE)**[13] 3776 4-8-3 **39** JFMcDonald(3) 1 15
(GAHam) *prom: rdn 4f out: wknd over 2f out* **12/1**

5600 **11** *1¼* **Lilian**[9] 3885 4-8-9 **42** (v) MFenton 12 16
(MissGayKelleway) *hld up: rdn 4f out: a bhd* **20/1**

000- **12** *dist* **Crispin House**[398] 2611 4-8-1 **34** KimTinkler 2 —
(RJPrice) *bhd fnl 11f* **66/1**

3m 7.10s (-0.10) **Going Correction** +0.025s/f (Good) **12** Ran SP% **120.3**
Speed ratings: **101,100,99,98,97 96,95,89,88,87 87,**—CSF £12.67 CT £61.83 TOTE £3.10: £1.30, £1.90, £2.30; EX 8.00.There was no bid for the winner.
**Owner** Dennis Deacon **Bred** D J And Mrs Deer **Trained** Wixford, Warwicks

**FOCUS**
A weak seller in which they went no pace in the early stages.

**NOTEBOOK**
**Banningham Blaze**, tackling a longer trip, cashed in on a 4lb drop in the weights to win this weak race a shade readily. *Official explanation: vet said filly suffered a slight cut on the inside leg*
**Lunar Lord** was 5lb higher than when runner-up over course and distance on his latest start. He was a little keen early on and the lack of a decent gallop did not do him any favours.
**Pertemps Sia**, the subject of a gamble, was once again plugging on at the end. This was the first time he has ever made the frame and he is not without hope. *Official explanation: jockey said colt pulled up lame*
**Border Terrier(IRE)**, who has plunged in the weights this term, was keeping on late over this longer trip.
**Cracow(IRE)**, fitted with cheekpieces, was going as well as anything until finding nothing when let down.

## 4140 LETHEBY & CHRISTOPHER RATED STKS (H'CAP) 1m 54y
**4:05** (4:05) (C) (0-90,89) 3-Y-O **£9,604** (£3,643; £1,821; £828) **Stalls** Centre

Form RPR

2050 **1** **Secretary General (IRE)**[16] 3671 3-9-6 **88** TQuinn 3 97+
(PFICole) *chsd ldrs: led over 2f out: rdn out* **5/2**[1]

0061 **2** *½* **Inchloss (IRE)**[14] 3745 3-8-9 **77** WSupple 8 85
(BAMcmahon) *hld up: swtchd rt and hdwy over 1f out: hung lft ins fnl f: r.o* **8/1**

-124 **3** *1* **Little Jimbob**[21] 3507 3-8-7 **75** GParkin 4 81
(RAFahey) *dwlt: sn prom: nt clr run over 1f out: styd on same pce towards fin* **9/1**

3-06 **4** *¾* **Naaddey**[64] 2276 3-9-3 **88** SHitchcott(3) 1 92
(MRChannon) *racd keenly and prom: outpcd over 2f out: rallied over 1f out: n.m.r ins fnl f: styd on same pce* **25/1**

-202 **5** ¾ **Hello It's Me**[22] [3477] 3-9-5 **87** MTebbutt 2 89
(HJCollingridge) *mde most over 5f: sn rdn: no ex ins fnl f* **9/2**[3]
1031 **6** 2 **Burley Flame**[11] [3819] 3-8-12 **80** MFenton 6 78
(JGGiven) *hld up: hdwy over 2f out: rdn over 1f out: no ex* **7/1**
1512 **7** ½ **Oasis Star (IRE)**[18] [3602] 3-9-7 **89** JCarroll 7 86+
(PWHarris) *trckd ldrs: rdn and ev ch fr over 2f out: looked hld whn n.m.r ins fnl f* **11/4**[2]
010 **8** 3 **Attune**[53] [2557] 3-8-9 **80** JFMcDonald(3) 5 70
(BJMeehan) *chsd ldrs: rdn over 2f out: wknd over 1f out* **25/1**

1m 46.15s (-0.25) **Going Correction** +0.025s/f (Good) **8** Ran SP% **114.7**
Speed ratings: **102,101,100,99,99 97,96,93**CSF £23.22 CT £152.06 TOTE £3.80: £1.30, £2.30, £2.60; EX 36.00.
**Owner** The Blenheim Partnership **Bred** Mrs C L Weld **Trained** Whatcombe, Oxon

**FOCUS**
Quite a competitive little handicap, but they went a muddling pace and several encountered traffic problems making the overall form somewhat messy.

**NOTEBOOK**
**Secretary General(IRE)**, who was beaten by the draw at Newmarket, enjoyed the run of the race and stuck his neck out willingly to score. There could be a little more to come.
**Inchloss(IRE)**, who goes well at Nottingham, was 3lb higher after winning on his last visit. He handled this fast ground but hung in the closing stages and probably prefers a bit of cut.
**Little Jimbob**, a consistent individual, ran well but did not have a lot of racing room in the last quarter-mile. A more strongly-run race will suit him.
**Naaddey** failed to beat a rival in two runs in the spring. This was more encouraging, but he did not really get the breaks and gave the impression that he might need the visor back on.
**Hello It's Me**, from a 2lb higher mark, set only a moderate pace and had been seen off entering the final furlong.
**Burley Flame**, 3lb higher, was not helped by being held up off a muddling pace.
**Oasis Star(IRE)** was going well when challenging on the outside, but did not find much off the bridle and appeared held when getting squeezed out inside the last. She has proved progressive this season and it may prove best to forgive her this.

## 4141 RACING UK MAIDEN FILLIES' STKS 1m 1f 213y
**4:35** (4:43) (D ) 3-Y-O **£5,005** (£1,540; £770; £385) **Stalls** Low

Form RPR
0-4 **1** **Castagna (USA)**[17] [3630] 3-8-11 TQuinn 9 83
(HRACecil) *chsd ldr 8f out: led 2f out: rdn clr* **11/4**[2]
2 **2** 8 **Autumn Wealth (IRE)**[17] [3630] 3-8-11 WSupple 10 69
(MrsAJPerrett) *chsd ldrs: rdn over 3f out: outpcd fnl 2f* **8/11**[1]
21-2 **3** 2 **Seeking A Way (USA)**[31] [3194] 3-8-11 RHavlin 8 65
(JHMGosden) *led 8f: wknd fnl f* **11/2**[3]
**4** 2 **Sovietta (IRE)** 3-8-11 MTebbutt 3 61
(RMBeckett) *s.i.s: hdwy over 3f out: edgd lft and wknd over 1f out* **33/1**
06 **5** 8 **Breaking The Rule (IRE)**[31] [3194] 3-8-11 JCarroll 6 47
(PRWebber) *s.i.s: a bhd* **66/1**
0 **6** hd **In Every Street (USA)**[10] [3848] 3-8-11 IMongan 4 47
(MAMagnusson) *chsd ldr 2f: remained handy tl wknd over 2f out* **25/1**
**7** dist **Kikis Girls (IRE)** 3-8-6 PMakin(5) 5 —
(MissMERowland) *s.i.s: a bhd* **80/1**

2m 9.97s (0.47) **Going Correction** +0.025s/f (Good) **7** Ran SP% **109.5**
Speed ratings: **99,92,91,89,83 82,**—CSF £4.66 TOTE £4.10: £1.70, £1.10; EX 6.50.
**Owner** Bloomsbury Stud **Bred** Bloomsbury Stud **Trained** Newmarket, Suffolk
■ Norma Hill (66/1, ref to ent stalls) & Pearnickety (100/1, unruly bhd stalls) were withdrawn. Rule 4 does not apply.

**FOCUS**
A weakly-contested maiden and not much confidence in the level of the form.

**NOTEBOOK**
**Castagna(USA)** took a little time to get on top but kept galloping for a clear-cut victory. Likely to stay farther, she gave the impression that she might appreciate easier ground.
**Autumn Wealth(IRE)** finished in front of Castagna at Kempton so this was disappointing. Still a little green, she was short of room early in the home straight before staying on to take a moderate second inside the last.
**Seeking A Way(USA)**, stepping down in trip, had no answers when headed and looks to have only the one pace. She is a winner of sorts, albeit in the now-discontinued Newmarket Challenge Cup.
**Sovietta(IRE)**, out of a fair middle-distance handicapper, is a half-sister to one-time decent juvenile Riverblue. She raced in the rear trio until making a little headway in the straight, but was beaten with two to run.
**In Every Street(USA)** *Official explanation: jockey said filly was unsuited by the good/firm ground*

## 4142 MIDLANDS RACING - 9 GREAT VENUES CLASSIFIED STKS 1m 54y
**5:10** (5:10) (E ) 3-Y-O+ **£3,672** (£1,130; £565; £282) **Stalls** Centre

Form RPR
6031 **1** **Harry Potter (GER)**[4] [4008] 5-10-0 69 (v) DarrenWilliams 5 83
(KRBurke) *hld up: hdwy 2f out: r.o to ld nr fin* **5/2**[1]
1130 **2** hd **Brazilian Terrace**[24] [3419] 4-9-5 75 HayleyTurner(5) 1 79
(MLWBell) *chsd ldrs: rdn over 2f out: led 1f out: sn edgd lft: hdd nr fin* **3/1**[2]
2101 **3** 1¼ **Nearly A Fool**[110] [1265] 6-9-6 71 (v) NMackay(3) 2 76+
(GGMargarson) *chsd ldrs: nt clr run and swtchd rt over 1f out: running on whn nt clr run wl ins fnl f* **11/2**
0010 **4** ½ **Aragon's Boy**[20] [3555] 4-9-8 70 DSweeney 8 73
(HCandy) *led: edgd lft over 1f out: sn hdd: kpt on* **20/1**
0L36 **5** 6 **Tagula Blue (IRE)**[8] [3921] 4-9-8 69 MTebbutt 6 59
(JAGlover) *hld up: hdwy over 2f out: wknd over 1f out* **12/1**
4435 **6** ½ **Summer Shades**[20] [3563] 6-9-5 67 TQuinn 3 55
(WMBrisbourne) *prom: chsd ldr 1/2-way tl wknd over 1f out* **9/1**
4420 **7** shd **Adobe**[4] [4008] 9-9-8 67 RMullen 7 58
(WMBrisbourne) *hld up: nt clr run over 2f out: n.d* **14/1**
0004 **8** 2 **Huxley (IRE)**[8] [3911] 5-9-8 70 (t) PMcCabe 9 53
(MGQuinlan) *hld up: plld hrd: rdn over 2f out: sn wknd* **4/1**[3]
6155 **9** 19 **Western Roots**[29] [3271] 3-9-5 75 WSupple 4 14
(KAMorgan) *hld up in tch: rdn and wknd over 2f out* **40/1**

1m 44.48s (-1.92) **Going Correction** +0.025s/f (Good)
**WFA** 3 from 4yo+ 8lb **9** Ran SP% **120.5**
Speed ratings: **110,109,108,108,102 101,101,99,80**CSF £10.65 TOTE £3.10: £1.40, £1.50, £3.30; EX 13.10 Place 6 £4.28, Place 5 £3.26.
**Owner** F Jeffers **Bred** Wilh Jackson **Trained** Middleham Moor, N Yorks
■ Stewards Enquiry : Darren Williams one-day ban: careless riding (Aug 4)

**FOCUS**
An ordinary handicap and a smart time for the grade, 1.67 seconds faster than the earlier 0 to 90 rated stakes for three-year-olds. The form looks sound.

**NOTEBOOK**
**Harry Potter(GER)**, a winner at Ayr four days earlier, hung fire but was persuaded to put his head in front near the line. He is a bit of a character, but is in fine heart at present.
**Brazilian Terrace**, best in on official figures, always runs well in this type of event and she did nothing wrong in defeat.
**Nearly A Fool** ◆, having his first outing since April, was twice stopped in his run in the latter stages although the line would have beaten him in any case. He is obviously capable of winning again on turf and another try at a mile should pay off.
**Aragon's Boy** won a weak maiden and he is not going to find it easy to supplement that.
**Tagula Blue(IRE)**, who was slow to go again, made his effort down the outside but had soon been seen off.
CR

# 3747 SALISBURY (R-H)
Saturday, July 24

**OFFICIAL GOING: Good to firm (firm in places on loop)**
Wind: Almost nil Weather: Fine and warm

## 4143 SAFFIE JOSEPH & SONS MAIDEN STKS 6f
**6:20** (6:20) (D ) 2-Y-O **£5,843** (£1,798; £899; £449) **Stalls** High

Form RPR
3 **1** **Motarassed**[24] [3424] 2-9-0 JFortune 8 86+
(JLDunlop) *chsd ldrs: effrt over 2f out: r.o to ld fnl 100 yds: rdn out* **5/2**[2]
5324 **2** 1½ **Marching Song**[16] [3677] 2-9-0 MartinDwyer 5 81
(RHannon) *chsd ldr: rdn to ld 1f out: hdd and nt qckn fnl 100 yds* **5/4**[1]
22 **3** 2 **Sunset Strip**[16] [3665] 2-9-0 TEDurcan 2 75
(MRChannon) *trckd ldng pair: swtchd rt and hmpd 2f out: plld wd: rn green and hd high: one pce fnl f* **5/1**[3]
**4** ½ **Palatinate (FR)** 2-9-0 DaneO'Neill 6 74+
(HCandy) *s.s: rn green and sn wl bhd: gd late hdwy: improve* **11/1**
**5** 1½ **Luciferous (USA)** 2-8-6 LisaJones(3) 4 64
(JaneSouthcombe) *led: rdn over 2f out: hdd & wknd 1f out* **50/1**
4 **6** nk **Diamond Hombre (USA)**[55] [2502] 2-9-0 MHills 7 68
(JWHills) *in tch: rdn to press ldrs over 2f out: wknd fnl f* **7/1**
30 **7** 1 **Celestial Arc (USA)**[14] [3749] 2-9-0 SDrowne 3 65
(PFICole) *dwlt: sn wl bhd: styd on fnl 2f* **20/1**
**8** 10 **Kolyma (IRE)** 2-8-9 CCatlin 1 30
(JLDunlop) *dwlt: sn t.o* **33/1**

1m 15.56s (0.62) **Going Correction** +0.175s/f (Good) **8** Ran SP% **120.2**
Speed ratings: **102,100,97,96,94 94,92,79**CSF £6.27 TOTE £4.10: £1.40, £1.10, £1.60; EX 5.90.
**Owner** Hamdan Al Maktoum **Bred** Shadwell Estate Company Limited **Trained** Arundel, W Sussex

**FOCUS**
A decent maiden probably containing a number of future winners, particularly the eyecatching Palatinate. A decent winning time for the type of race.

**NOTEBOOK**
**Motarassed** is progressing nicely and won readily. He runs as if he should get seven furlongs without a problem.
**Marching Song** looks at home at five, six and seven furlongs, so his versatility is not in doubt. All he needs now is to keep his head in front, for he deserves to get off the mark.
**Sunset Strip** did not get the best of runs, but neither was his finishing effort convincing. Relative lack of experience and the very fast ground may have contributed, but the jury is still out.
**Palatinate(FR)** ◆, a well-bred Desert Prince colt, has enough speed in his pedigree to have good prospects as a juvenile. This was a highly promising first effort from this good-looking sort, and he should come on a bundle for the experience.
**Luciferous(USA)**, a 10,000 guineas yearling with a good American pedigree, is weak at present. This was a satisfactory first outing and she can be expected to improve as she strengthens, though it will take time for her to fill out completely.
**Diamond Hombre(USA)** ought to have stayed this trip on the evidence of his breeding, but he ran more like a horse who would have preferred five furlongs at present.
**Celestial Arc(USA)** got himself into an impossible position and did well to finish as close as he did. Nurseries are looking an attractive option.
**Kolyma(IRE)** is on the small side, and showed nothing.

## 4144 FONTHILL STUD MAIDEN STKS 6f
**6:50** (6:50) (D ) 3-Y-O+ **£5,707** (£1,756; £878; £439) **Stalls** High

Form RPR
4 **1** **Kostar**[28] [3322] 3-8-12 RSmith 9 79
(CGCox) *unruly in stalls: dwlt: sn trcking ldng pair: disp ld over 1f out: drvn to ld nr fin* **3/1**[2]
0200 **2** hd **Bee Minor**[7] [3941] 3-8-7 73 MHills 2 73
(RHannon) *hld up in rr: swtchd outside and hdwy over 2f out: disp ld over 1f out: nt qckn fnl strides* **6/1**[3]
**3** 1¼ **Firebird** 3-8-4 LPKeniry(3) 4 69
(HCandy) *hld up towards rr: rdn and r.o fnl 2f: improve* **16/1**
0- **4** hd **Avessia**[267] [5850] 3-8-7 JFortune 6 69
(GLMoore) *chsd ldrs: rdn 1/2-way: styd on same pce* **13/2**
3-62 **5** nk **Anna Panna**[22] [3486] 3-8-7 71 DaneO'Neill 10 68
(HCandy) *led tl over 1f out: one pce* **11/8**[1]
000 **6** 1½ **Black Sabbeth**[22] [3487] 3-8-12 CCatlin 7 68
(PJMakin) *pressed ldr: ev ch wl over 1f out: no ex* **80/1**
000 **7** 1 **Heriot**[35] [3106] 3-8-12 (b) SCarson 8 65
(HCandy) *dwlt: sn in midfield: drvn along fr 1/2-way: 7th and no imp whn nt clr run ins fnl f* **80/1**
**8** hd **Miss Monza** 3-8-7 TEDurcan 3 60
(BRMillman) *dwlt: outpcd* **33/1**
**9** 5 **Inescapable (USA)** 3-8-12 SDrowne 1 50
(WRMuir) *mid-div tl wknd over 2f out* **25/1**
**U** **Conjuror** 3-8-12 MartinDwyer 5 —
(AMBalding) *s.s: in rr and refusing to gallop whn bucked rdr off after 100 yds* **7/1**

1m 15.35s (0.41) **Going Correction** +0.175s/f (Good) **10** Ran SP% **122.4**
Speed ratings: **104,103,102,101,101 99,98,97,91,**—CSF £22.22 TOTE £4.50: £1.50, £2.20, £3.50; EX 39.80.
**Owner** Mrs P Scott-Dunn And Mrs F J Ryan **Bred** Mrs P Scott-Dunn **Trained** Lambourn, Berks

**FOCUS**
A moderate maiden, with the runner-up now on a losing run of 13 but providing a sound-enough guide to the level. However, the winner and third home are less exposed and should progress.

**NOTEBOOK**
**Kostar** seems to have a problem with the stalls and has missed the break in both races to date. However, the manner in which he battled at the other end could not be faulted.
**Bee Minor** nearly got her head in front at long last, only to be pipped in the last 25 yards after a long battle. There is nothing wrong with her attitude despite a losing run of 13.
**Firebird** ◆, a 28,000 guineas daughter of Soviet Star, has plenty of speed in her pedigree but began to find her stride too late. However, it was a debut full of promise and, being a scopey sort, she should improve a good deal.
**Avessia** was with Roger Charlton last year but it would be a surprise if her new stable were unable to make hay with her following this sound seasonal debut, only her second appearance in all. She has speed in her pedigree but should stay another furlong on this evidence.

**Anna Panna**, one of three from her stable, was the best fancied in the betting and is running well enough to keep her connections optimistic. Six or seven furlongs are both an option on the evidence of recent runs.
**Black Sabbeth** had barely been sighted in his first three races, so this was something of a revelation. He could be interesting in run-of-the-mill handicap company.
**Conjuror** spent his brief time in the race impersonating a bucking bronco and soon succeeded in ejecting his rider. Still a bit weak but with some scope, he is from a good, speedy family, but now he must prove he is a racehorse

## 4145 MANOR FARM MEATS PREMIER CLAIMING STKS 1m
**7:20** (7:21) (D) 3-4-Y-O **£5,512** (£1,696; £848; £424) **Stalls** High

Form RPR
0602 **1** **Hoh Bleu Dee**[15] 3689 3-8-9 75....................(b[1]) DaneO'Neill 9 79
(SKirk) *plld hrd early: hld up in 5th: effrt 2f out: led 1f out: drvn out* **6/4**[1]
0050 **2** ½ **Top Spec (IRE)**[21] 3543 3-8-11 77.................... RSmith 8 80
(RHannon) *s.s: in rr on far rail: rdn 3f out: swtchd wd and hdwy 2f out: ev ch fnl f: r.o* **3/1**[2]
-000 **3** 1¼ **Atahuelpa**[44] 1066 4-9-5 77.................... TEDurcan 7 77
(AKing) *chsd ldng pair: led 3f out tl 1f out: one pce* **11/1**
3000 **4** 2½ **Love Triangle (IRE)**[14] 3750 3-9-1 76.................... LPKeniry(3) 3 78
(DRCElsworth) *t.k.h towards rr: hdwy to chse ldrs 2f out: one pce* **11/1**
2-03 **5** 4 **Queenstown (IRE)**[7] 3932 3-8-7 80....................(b) JFortune 1 58
(BJMeehan) *sn led and set gd pce: hdd 3f out: wknd wl over 1f out* **7/2**[3]
0255 **6** 1 **Rabitatit (IRE)**[16] 3670 3-8-5 62.................... SDrowne 2 54
(JGMO'Shea) *chsd ldr 5f: wknd 2f out* **8/1**
0000 **7** 20 **Awarding**[51] 2612 4-8-7 70.................... LucyRussell(7) 4 9
(DrJRJNaylor) *in tch tl wknd over 2f out* **28/1**

1m 43.34s (0.37) **Going Correction** +0.175s/f (Good)
**WFA** 3 from 4yo 8lb **7** Ran SP% **118.4**
Speed ratings: **105,104,103,100,96 95,75**CSF £6.59 TOTE £2.50: £1.80, £2.30; EX 11.00.
**Owner** D F Allport **Bred** Lord Halifax **Trained** Upper Lambourn, Berks

**FOCUS**
A reasonable claimer with some fair types who find it hard in handicap company at present. At first it looked as if there would be no pace, but Queenstown then went on and probably overdid it, setting up the race for the strong finishers, which offers doubts about the form.

**NOTEBOOK**
**Hoh Bleu Dee** was too headstrong in the first-time blinkers, so it helped when Queenstown went on to set a good pace. He looks at home in claimers but handicap success cannot be ruled out now he is back in form.
**Top Spec(IRE)** has been struggling in handicaps and this switch to claiming company nearly paid off, so it is obviously worth another go. He needs a lot of stoking but on this occasion kept responding.
**Atahuelpa** bounced back to form, with the drop to claiming company looking the most likely explanation. He is inconsistent, but useful at the right level when at his best.
**Love Triangle(IRE)** had a tough task at the weights and ran as well as could have been expected in the circumstances.
**Queenstown(IRE)** did the donkey work and probably went a shade too fast, since he merely set things up for the come-from-behind performers.
**Rabitatit(IRE)** was worst in at the weights, and any chance she had disappeared when she tried to chase the pacesetting Queenstown.

## 4146 APPROACH VAUXHALL H'CAP 1m 6f 15y
**7:50** (7:51) (E) (0-70,70) 3-Y-0+ **£3,627** (£1,116; £558; £279) **Stalls** Far side

Form RPR
-036 **1** **The Varlet**[23] 3437 4-9-9 68....................(p) SHitchcott(3) 3 77
(BICase) *bhd: hdwy and nt clr run over 2f out: eased outside: styd on to ld 1f out: drvn out* **22/1**
0404 **2** ½ **San Hernando**[10] 3851 4-10-0 70.................... DaneO'Neill 11 78
(DRCElsworth) *t.k.h in midfield: hdwy to ld over 2f out: hdd 1f out: kpt on* **7/1**
0630 **3** 1¾ **Claradotnet**[40] 2935 4-9-6 62.................... TEDurcan 13 68+
(MRChannon) *prom: outpcd 5f out: rallied and disputing cl 3rd whn hmpd on rail jst ins fnl f: one pce* **20/1**
30-0 **4** 1½ **Sir Alfred**[9] 3873 5-8-13 55.................... CCatlin 14 59+
(AKing) *reluctant to line up and w.r.s: lost 15 l: wl bhd tl rdn and hdwy over 2f out: nrst fin* **16/1**
0004 **5** ¾ **Cool Bathwick (IRE)**[13] 3776 5-7-13 44....................(t) LisaJones(3) 7 47
(BRMillman) *towards rr: hdwy 3f out: ev ch over 1f out: one pce* **10/1**
4612 **6** 1 **Winslow Boy (USA)**[22] 3479 3-8-4 60.................... JQuinn 12 61+
(CFWall) *hld up towards rr: effrt and nt clr run over 2f out: swtchd rt: one pce* **10/3**[2]
/506 **7** 1¼ **Greyfield (IRE)**[7] 3942 8-8-3 50.................... NDeSouza(5) 10 50
(KBishop) *t.k.h: prom: hrd rdn over 2f out: wknd over 1f out* **25/1**
-006 **8** 1¼ **Masterman Ready**[14] 3752 3-8-11 67.................... JFortune 5 65
(PWHarris) *mid-div: hdwy and ev ch over 2f out: wknd over 1f out* **11/1**
0040 **9** 10 **Sninfia (IRE)**[13] 3776 4-8-5 50.................... JFMcDonald(3) 2 34
(GAHam) *disp ld: led 6f out tl wknd over 2f out* **14/1**
130/ **10** 1¼ **Ash Hab (USA)**[829] 3796 6-9-1 60.................... LPKeniry(3) 9 42
(PBurgoyne) *mid-div tl wknd 5f out* **33/1**
060U **11** nk **Nick The Silver**[14] 3752 3-8-4 60.................... SCarson 8 42
(GBBalding) *t.k.h: disp ld tl 6f out: wknd 3f out* **25/1**
2151 **12** 6 **Diamond Orchid (IRE)**[24] 3429 4-8-11 56....................(v) FPFerris(3) 4 29
(PDEvans) *towards rr: mod effrt and hrd rdn 3f out: sn bhd: eased whn no ch over 1f out* **11/4**[1]
-165 **13** dist **Zalda**[22] 3479 3-8-5 61.................... SDrowne 6 —
(RCharlton) *reluctant to line up: blkd and lft 150 yds at s: a t.o* **11/2**[3]

3m 7.70s (1.70) **Going Correction** +0.175s/f (Good)
**WFA** 3 from 4yo+ 14lb **13** Ran SP% **127.3**
Speed ratings: **102,101,100,99,99 98,98,97,91,91 90,87,**—CSF £169.78 CT £3183.81 TOTE £47.80: £10.90, £2.80, £6.20; EX 179.00.
**Owner** Mrs A D Bourne **Bred** Mrs A D Bourne **Trained** Edgcote, Northants
■ Stewards Enquiry : N De SouzaD two-day ban: used whip with excessive frequency (Aug 4-5)

**FOCUS**
A low-grade staying race full of plodders, and some doubts over the form od a race in which they went a moderate pace until the two leaders quickened up at halfway.

**NOTEBOOK**
**The Varlet** was wearing cheekpieces for the first time and, in a driving finish, they may have made all the difference.
**San Hernando** was on a fair mark despite carrying top weight. He did his best and, though a largely disappointing horse, is in reasonable form at present.
**Claradotnet** obviously gets this trip well and ran as if two miles would be worth a go.
**Sir Alfred** finished remarkably close considering his antics at the start. He is not reliable but on a winning mark when in the mood.
**Cool Bathwick(IRE)**, wearing a tongue-tie for the first time, has little in the way of finishing speed, so this drop in trip was always going to be a problem.
**Winslow Boy(USA)** did not get an opening when he wanted it and, by the time the gap appeared, the moment was lost. It would be wrong to overstate the traffic problems, but they did not help. *Official explanation: jockey said gelding had suffered interference at the start*
**Greyfield(IRE)** had a hard race, which landed his rider an appearance in the Stewards' room.
**Masterman Ready** *Official explanation: trainer later said gelding was struck into*
**Diamond Orchid(IRE)** *Official explanation: jockey said filly lost her action in the final furlong*
**Zalda** was already thinking about refusing to race when Sir Alfred whipped round into her and made it certain. She was beaten around two furlongs, which is not significant; however her behaviour at the start was.

## 4147 WESTERN DAILY PRESS H'CAP 1m
**8:20** (8:24) (E) (0-70,70) 3-Y-O **£3,679** (£1,132; £566; £283) **Stalls** High

Form RPR
-650 **1** **Moscow Times**[15] 3689 3-9-4 70.................... LPKeniry(3) 6 76
(DRCElsworth) *stdd s: hld up in rr: smooth hdwy and swtchd outside 2f out: led over 1f out: rdn and styd on* **7/1**
0310 **2** ¾ **Knickyknackienoo**[19] 3589 3-8-10 59.................... SDrowne 3 66+
(AGNewcombe) *stdd s: hld up: rdn and hdwy whn nt clr run fr 2f out: cl 3rd whn no room fnl f: fin 3rd: plcd 2nd* **11/4**[1]
-650 **3** ½ **The Way We Were**[43] 2847 3-9-6 69.................... JFortune 2 74
(TGMills) *led after 1f tl over 2f out: rallied and ev ch ins fnl f: edgd rt and kpt on: fin 2nd: plcd 3rd* **5/1**[2]
1003 **4** 1 **Dagola (IRE)**[19] 3589 3-9-1 64.................... RSmith 11 65
(CGCox) *prom: rdn 3f out: cl 5th and hld whn nt clr run over 1f out: swtchd lft: styd on nr fin* **5/1**[2]
6004 **5** ¾ **Hana Dee**[12] 3798 3-8-8 57.................... TEDurcan 9 58+
(MRChannon) *sn pressing ldr: rdn 3f out: led 2f out tl over 1f out: 4th and hld whn hmpd ins fnl f* **9/1**
0100 **6** 4 **Balearic Star (IRE)**[21] 3543 3-9-5 68.................... GBaker 10 58
(BRMillman) *hld up in tch: led briefly over 2f out: wknd over 1f out* **6/1**[3]
040 **7** ¾ **Starmix**[12] 3806 3-9-0 68....................(b[1]) NDeSouza(5) 12 56
(PFICole) *mid-div: effrt 3f out: no imp* **8/1**
0-00 **8** shd **Turtle Patriarch (IRE)**[9] 3875 3-8-10 62.................... SHitchcott(3) 1 50
(MrsAJPerrett) *mid-div: effrt in centre 3f out: btn whn edgd rt 2f out* **16/1**
546- **9** 4 **Rumbling Bridge**[308] 5078 3-8-12 61.................... DaneO'Neill 4 40
(JLDunlop) *s.s: outpcd and bhd: n.d* **16/1**
6546 **10** 6 **Master Mahogany**[13] 3773 3-8-10 62.................... JFMcDonald(3) 8 27
(RJHodges) *led 1f: sn stdd towards rr: n.d fnl 3f* **12/1**
0-00 **11** 29 **Intitnice (IRE)**[178] 620 3-7-13 48....................(p) JQuinn 5 —
(MissKMGeorge) *t.k.h: sn prom: wknd over 2f out* **66/1**

1m 44.86s (1.89) **Going Correction** +0.175s/f (Good) **11** Ran SP% **128.8**
Speed ratings: **97,95,96,94,94 90,89,89,85,79 50**CSF £29.24 CT £113.08 TOTE £9.80: £3.20, £1.60, £2.20; EX 36.80.
**Owner** M Tabor **Bred** Lady Richard Wellesley **Trained** Whitsbury, Hants
■ Stewards Enquiry : L P Keniry two-day ban: careless riding (Aug 4-5)
J Fortune three-day ban: careless riding (Aug 4-6)

**FOCUS**
An ordinary handicap with some relatively unexposed performers and therefore a few potential improvers, though unlikely to be anything special. However, the winner is interesting and could do even better if benefiting from this first win.

**NOTEBOOK**
**Moscow Times**, patiently ridden, was only just doing enough in front but got off the mark at the seventh attempt. He is capable of even better if he feels like it, and this narrow victory was a good thing from a handicapping point of view. *Official explanation: trainer said, regarding the improved form shown, gelding had benefited from a drop in class*
**Knickyknackienoo** had a nightmare run through, though that is always a possibility because of the way he is ridden. When he has more luck, he will win again.
**The Way We Were** ran a game race and should be in contention again in similar company.
**Dagola(IRE)** saw his race out well, though he was clearly held and the intererence cannot be used as an excuse.
**Hana Dee** is back in form and close to a winning mark, with races over both seven furlongs and a mile an option.
**Balearic Star(IRE)** found disappointingly little after travelling smoothly. This was a below-par effort, because he stays a mile well.
**Starmix** was in first-time blinkers but they had a limited effect. He was dropped in trip, but it is hard to know what his best distance is because he looks a bit high in the weights.
**Master Mahogany** *Official explanation: jockey said gelding had been hanging*

## 4148 CITY CABS SALISBURY FILLIES' RATED STKS (H'CAP) 6f 212y
**8:50** (8:56) (D) (0-80,80) 3-Y-0+ **£6,214** (£2,357; £1,178; £535) **Stalls** Centre

Form RPR
0442 **1** **And Toto Too**[2] 4067 4-8-12 67....................(b) FPFerris(3) 3 75
(PDEvans) *dwlt: outpcd and bhd: drvn 1/2-way: swtchd rt and hdwy over 1f out: styd on to ld ins fnl f* **11/4**[2]
0120 **2** ¾ **In The Pink (IRE)**[23] 3457 4-9-3 72.................... SHitchcott(3) 8 78
(MRChannon) *dwlt: towards rr tl swtchd lft and hdwy 2f out: disp ld 1f out tl ins fnl f: kpt on* **7/1**
0-00 **3** shd **Kindlelight Debut**[8] 3910 4-9-8 74.................... JQuinn 7 80
(DKIvory) *trckd ldrs: hrd rdn ins fnl 2f: disp ld 1f out tl ins fnl f: kpt on* **20/1**
0246 **4** ¾ **Pink Sapphire (IRE)**[15] 3694 3-8-13 72.................... DaneO'Neill 9 76
(DRCElsworth) *chsd ldr: led over 2f out tl 1f out: styd on same pce* **11/2**
4003 **5** 1½ **Indiana Blues**[20] 3554 3-8-6 68.................... LPKeniry(3) 1 68
(AMBalding) *mid-div: effrt over 2f out: one pce appr fnl f* **8/1**
1200 **6** ½ **Shirley Oaks (IRE)**[11] 3828 6-8-2 57 oh8.................... JFMcDonald(3) 5 55
(MissZCDavison) *dwlt: outpcd and bhd: mod effrt and hrd rdn over 2f out: hmpd over 1f out: styd on fnl f* **25/1**
-010 **7** 3½ **Music Maid (IRE)**[15] 3690 6-8-13 65.................... SDrowne 4 54
(HSHowe) *dwlt: hld up towards rr: hdwy in centre over 2f out: no ex over 1f out* **5/1**[3]
000- **8** 3 **Bayonet**[378] 3216 8-8-2 57 oh17.................... LisaJones(3) 6 38
(JaneSouthcombe) *led tl over 2f out: wknd over 1f out* **66/1**
12-2 **9** dist **Search Mission (USA)**[23] 3457 3-9-7 80.................... JFortune 2 —
(MrsAJPerrett) *chsd ldng pair: wknd qckly over 2f out: bhd whn virtually p.u over 1f out* **2/1**[1]

1m 28.93s (-0.07) **Going Correction** +0.175s/f (Good)
**WFA** 3 from 4yo+ 7lb **9** Ran SP% **125.8**
Speed ratings: **107,106,106,105,103 102,98,95,**—CSF £24.31 CT £342.60 TOTE £4.40: £1.40, £1.70, £3.00; EX 33.20 Place 6 £116.13, Place 5 £100.46..
**Owner** Mrs S J Lawrence **Bred** Mrs M L Parry And P M Steele-Mortimer **Trained** Pandy, Gwent

**FOCUS**
A fair mares and fillies-only event at this level, and a useful winning time for the grade.

**NOTEBOOK**
**And Toto Too** finally got her reward for some good efforts, with the strong pace helping.
**In The Pink(IRE)** has been going up the weights but this fine effort showed she is still improving.
**Kindlelight Debut** had been shown a little mercy by the Handicapper and it nearly did the trick. Back in form, she will be there or thereabouts as long as she is not overburdened again as a result.
**Pink Sapphire(IRE)** is at home over this trip or a mile, but she was just done for finishing speed.

**Indiana Blues** ran a fair race on this handicap debut and should go close if dropped a few pounds. She runs over five furlongs to a mile, but this trip is probably as suitable as any.
**Shirley Oaks(IRE)**, raised in class, stayed on despite being hampered as the winner made her move. She was never getting there in time, but it was a good effort from out of the handicap.
**Search Mission(USA)** *Official explanation: jockey said filly had lost her action*
T/Plt: £119.00 to a £1 stake. Pool: £38,757.70. 237.75 winning tickets. T/Qpdt: £37.80 to a £1 stake. Pool: £2,517.70. 49.20 winning tickets. LM

## 3753 YORK (L-H)
### Saturday, July 24

**OFFICIAL GOING: Good to firm (firm in places)**

### 4149 PICKERINGS LIFTS 150TH ANNIVERSARY MAIDEN AUCTION STKS — 6f
**1:50** (1:50) (E ) 2-Y-O **£8,619** (£2,652; £1,326; £663) **Stalls** Centre

Form — RPR
42 **1** **Little Dalham**[14] 3748 2-8-9 .......... AMcCarthy 10 78+
(PWChapple-Hyam) *trckd ldrs: hdwy 2f out: led over 1f out: rdn and r.o wl fnl f* **4/5**[1]
0 **2** *2* **Viking Spirit**[12] 3808 2-8-9 .......... RLMoore 1 72
(PWHarris) *trckd ldrs: effrt 2f out: sn rdn: kpt on ins last* **8/1**[3]
0524 **3** *shd* **Campeon (IRE)**[11] 3823 2-8-10 .......... KDarley 2 73
(MJWallace) *led: rdn along 2f out: hdd over 1f out and kpt on same pce* **14/1**
**4** *½* **Wigwam Willie (IRE)** 2-8-7 .......... DCorby(3) 13 71
(MJWallace) *chsd ldrs: rdn along 2fd out: kpt on u.p fnl f* **20/1**
35 **5** *¾* **Claret And Amber**[14] 3758 2-8-9 .......... PHanagan 11 68+
(RAFahey) *hld up: hdwy and n.m.r over 2f out: rdn over 1f out:swtchd lft ent last and styd on: nrst fin* **13/2**[2]
**6** *¾* **Swift Oscar** 2-8-8 .......... EAhern 4 65
(JWHills) *bhd: hdwy 2f out: swtchd rt and styd on wl appr last: nrst fin* **13/2**[2]
**7** *1 ¾* **Etoile Russe (IRE)** 2-8-9 .......... DeanMcKeown 5 60
(PCHaslam) *in tch: effrt 2f out: sn rdn and no imp fnl f* **66/1**
**8** *2 ½* **Blushing Russian (IRE)** 2-8-8 .......... NPollard 9 52+
(PCHaslam) *n.d* **25/1**
**9** *1 ¼* **Kool Ovation** 2-8-9 ow5.......... ABeech(3) 8 52
(ADickman) *dwlt: in tch: switched lft and hdwy wl over 1f out: sn rdn and no impression* **33/1**
63 **10** *2 ½* **Underthemistletoe (IRE)**[14] 3736 2-8-3 .......... FNorton 7 36
(BSmart) *chsd ldrs: rdn along over 2f out: sn wknd* **40/1**
50 **11** *1 ¼* **Forest Viking (IRE)**[41] 2904 2-8-8 .......... RWinston 6 37
(JSWainwright) *prom: rdn along 1/2-way: sn wknd* **66/1**
00 **12** *shd* **Mill By The Stream**[43] 2860 2-8-9 .......... TPQueally 3 38
(APJarvis) *a rr* **40/1**
0 **13** *14* **Bahamian Bay**[15] 3718 2-8-3 ow1.......... DAllan 12 —
(MBrittain) *chsd ldrs to 1/2-way: sn wknd* **100/1**

1m 11.99s (-0.58) **Going Correction** -0.20s/f (Firm) **13** Ran SP% **120.4**
Speed ratings: **95,92,92,91,90 89,87,83,82,78 77,77,58**CSF £7.11 TOTE £2.00: £1.30, £2.60, £2.50; EX 10.10.
**Owner** Collins Deal Harrison-Allan Chapple-Hyam **Bred** S J Mear **Trained** Newmarket, Suffolk

**FOCUS**
A pretty ordinary maiden and the exposed Campeon gives a good guide to the strength of the form, which should prove reliable enough.

**NOTEBOOK**
**Little Dalham** confirmed the promise he showed on his two previous starts, finding plenty for pressure having travelled noticeably well throughout. His future looks to lie in the hands of the Handicapper.
**Viking Spirit** proved no match for the winner, but this was still an improvement on his debut running and he is going the right way.
**Campeon(IRE)** appreciated the return to six furlongs and ran his race. He just keeps finding a couple too good, but gives a guide to the strength of the form.
**Wigwam Willie(IRE)**, a 20,000gns yearling, out of a six-furlong two-year-old winner, was easy to back but made a pleasing debut. He is open to improvement.
**Claret And Amber** finished well from off the pace and would have been even closer with a clearer run. He is now qualified for a nursery mark and should do well in that grade, possibly over a little further.
**Swift Oscar**, a 6,000gns yearling, half-brother to numerous winners, including one over a mile, was never competitive and should leave this form behind in due course. *Official explanation: jockey said colt hung left in final two furlongs*
**Kool Ovation** *Official explanation: jockey said colt hung left throughout*

### 4150 SKYBET PRESS RED TO BET ON CHANNEL FOUR STKS (NURSERY) — 5f
**2:20** (2:20) (C ) 2-Y-O **£10,432** (£3,210; £1,605; £802) **Stalls** Centre

Form — RPR
6431 **1** **Mimi Mouse**[26] 3370 2-9-3 **82**.......... KDarley 6 86
(TDEasterby) *mde all: rdn over 1f out: kpt on wl fnl f* **4/1**[2]
2135 **2** *1 ½* **Katie Boo (IRE)**[15] 3704 2-8-8 **78**.......... PPMathers(5) 7 77
(ABerry) *trckd ldrs: hdwy 2f out: rdn to chse wnr ent last: sn drvn and kpt on* **13/2**
233 **3** *1* **Wise Wager (IRE)**[19] 3583 2-8-3 **68**.......... PHanagan 8 63
(RAFahey) *in tch:hdwy 2f out: rdn and kpt on fnl f* **4/1**[2]
0415 **4** *shd* **Nova Tor (IRE)**[5] 3975 2-9-3 **82**.......... TPQueally 3 77
(NPLittmoden) *chsd ldrs: rdn along 2f out: drvn and one pce fnl f* **13/2**
6205 **5** *¾* **Brut**[7] 3924 2-8-0 **65** ow1.......... FNorton 5 57
(DWBarker) *in tch: hdwy 2f out: sn rdn and kpt on same pce appr last* **20/1**
5215 **6** *nk* **Wonderful Mind**[14] 3753 2-8-9 **74**.......... RWinston 1 65
(TDEasterby) *cl up: rdn along 2f out: drvn and wknd appr last* **10/3**[1]
125 **7** *8* **Selkirk Storm (IRE)**[30] 3224 2-9-2 **86**.......... PMulrennan(5) 4 49
(MWEasterby) *dwlt: sn rdn along andf hung lft in rr: a bhd* **6/1**[3]

58.54 secs (-0.74) **Going Correction** -0.20s/f (Firm) **7** Ran SP% **108.8**
Speed ratings: **97,94,93,92,91 91,78**CSF £26.65 CT £97.25 TOTE £2.90: £2.00, £2.60; EX 19.80.
**Owner** Mrs Jean P Connew **Bred** Mrs P A Clark **Trained** Great Habton, N Yorks

**FOCUS**
Not as good a nursery as one might have expected for the grade or the prizemoney, but the form is still decent. The figures shown as 'official ratings' are estimates for guidance only.

**NOTEBOOK**
**Mimi Mouse** followed up her recent Pontefract maiden success in decisive fashion on this first venture into nursery company. In this sort of form, she could well complete the hat-trick.
**Katie Boo(IRE)** was below form on her handicap debut behind Nova Tor at Chester on her previous start, but this was much better. She has won over five furlongs, but is not all speed and may stay seven.
**Wise Wager(IRE)** did not really improve for the switch to nursery company and would not appear to be progressing.
**Nova Tor(IRE)** ran respectably on this drop back to five furlongs, but she did not show as much pace as when winning at Chester two starts previously and looks a shade flattered by that success.
**Brut** did little wrong, but probably just wants dropping in grade.
**Wonderful Mind**, again well backed, was again below form. Conditions appeared ideal, but he did not perform and has to be considered disappointing.

### 4151 SKYBET INTERACTIVE BETTING ON CHANNEL FOUR STKS (H'CAP) — 6f 217y
**2:50** (2:51) (C ) (0-90,88) 3-Y-O **£11,017** (£3,390; £1,695; £847) **Stalls** Low

Form — RPR
0333 **1** **Neon Blue**[7] 3926 3-7-10 **68**.......... HayleyTurner(5) 4 76
(RMWhitaker) *chsd ldrs: squeezed through on inner over 2f out: swtchd rt and rdn over 1f out: stayed on ins last to ld nr fin* **10/1**
2153 **2** *nk* **Distant Connection (IRE)**[14] 3755 3-9-1 **82**.......... TPQueally 3 89
(APJarvis) *led: rdn clr 2f out: drvn ins last: hdd and no ex nr fin* **10/3**[1]
0051 **3** *1 ½* **Mrs Moh (IRE)**[28] 3295 3-8-13 **80**.......... DAllan 7 83
(TDEasterby) *trckd leasders: hdwy to chse ldng pair over 1f out: sn rdn and kpt on* **6/1**[3]
5-62 **4** *2* **Rising Shadow (IRE)**[7] 3926 3-9-3 **84**.......... PHanagan 9 82+
(RAFahey) *hld up towards rr: hdwy on outer 2f out: sn rdn and kpt on ins last: nrst fin* **7/1**
-361 **5** *1 ¼* **Carry On Doc**[20] 3554 3-8-8 **75**.......... SWhitworth 2 69
(JWHills) *hld up in rr: hdwy and nt clr run wl over 2f out: swtchd rt and rdnwl over 1f out: kpt on: nrst fin* **15/2**
0010 **6** *nk* **Dark Day Blues (IRE)**[30] 3252 3-8-0 **67**.......... FNorton 8 60
(MDHammond) *chsd ldrs: rdn along over 2f out: sn drvn and wknd* **33/1**
0153 **7** *2* **Oddsmaker (IRE)**[7] 3943 3-9-7 **88**.......... DeanMcKeown 5 76
(PDEvans) *prom: pushed along whn hmpd 2f out: sn rdn and btn* **5/1**[2]
3600 **8** *1 ½* **Joshua's Gold (IRE)**[17] 3636 3-7-5 **65** oh14.......... DanielleMcCreery(7) 6 49
(DCarroll) *dwlt: a towards rr* **100/1**
2042 **9** *1 ¾* **Reidies Choice**[17] 3622 3-8-7 **74**.......... ACulhane 1 53+
(JGGiven) *hld up in rr: sme hdwy on inner over 2f out: sn rdn along and btn* **6/1**[3]
3-60 **10** *10* **Vademecum**[71] 2075 3-8-10 **77**.......... FLynch 10 29
(BSmart) *keen. cl up: rdn along 3f out: edgd lft and sn wknd* **16/1**
4360 **11** *1 ¾* **Elliot's Choice (IRE)**[15] 3708 3-7-13 **66**.......... JMackay 11 13
(DCarroll) *chsd ldrs: rdn along 3f out: sn wknd* **40/1**

1m 23.54s (0.23) **Going Correction** +0.15s/f (Good) **11** Ran SP% **113.9**
Speed ratings: **104,103,101,99,98 97,95,93,91,80 78**CSF £41.63 CT £220.18 TOTE £12.60: £3.80, £1.80, £2.00; EX 57.10.
**Owner** Country Lane Partnership **Bred** R And Mrs Watson And Mrs A J Ralli **Trained** Scarcroft, W Yorks

**FOCUS**
A reasonable handicap, although the form might want treating with a little caution as Distant Connection was able to dictate things from the front and several of these could not land a blow.

**NOTEBOOK**
**Neon Blue** does most of his racing over six furlongs and was well beaten on his only previous try over seven furlongs, but the trip proved no problem this time around, in fact he needed every yard of it. Now he has proved his stamina he has more options open to him and a follow-up could not be ruled out.
**Distant Connection(IRE)** had conditions to suit and only just failed to hang on under a fine front-running ride from Queally. He is 8lb higher than when last winning and will go up again for this, but he remains at the top of his game.
**Mrs Moh(IRE)** appeared to run her race, but was just found out by a 6lb rise in the weights for her recent Chester success.
**Rising Shadow(IRE)** never really posed a threat on this step back up in trip and probably would have preferred a stronger end-to-end gallop.
**Carry On Doc**, off the mark over a mile at Brighton on his previous start, did not have the race run to suit on this drop back in trip.
**Oddsmaker(IRE)** does most of his racing over a mile these days and was below form on this drop in trip.
**Reidies Choice** may have preferred a stronger all-round pace, but he was below form in any case.

### 4152 SKYBET DASH (HERITAGE H'CAP) — 6f
**3:25** (3:25) (B ) (0-105,100) 3-Y-O+ **£32,500** (£10,000; £5,000; £2,500) **Stalls** Centre

Form — RPR
0420 **1** **Mutawaqed (IRE)**[28] 3309 6-8-13 **85**.......... (t) RLMoore 8 96
(MAMagnusson) *towarsd rr and pushed along 1/2-way: gd hdwy over 1f out: rdn to ld ins last and hung bdly rt: drvn and kpt on* **13/2**[3]
0001 **2** *1* **Machinist (IRE)**[5] 3979 4-8-10 **82** 7ex.......... AlexGreaves 15 90+
(DNicholls) *hld up: gd hdwy on outer 2f out: rdn to chal and edgd lft ins last: ev ch tl no ex last 75 yds* **11/2**[2]
4422 **3** *½* **Ellens Academy (IRE)**[14] 3754 9-9-0 **86**.......... FNorton 9 93
(EJAlston) *towards rr: gd hdwy 2f out: rdn to chal 1f out and ev ch whn hmpd ins last: kpt on* **13/2**[3]
6413 **4** *shd* **Two Step Kid (USA)**[18] 3598 3-9-7 **98**.......... EAhern 5 106+
(JNoseda) *chsd ldr: hdwy to ld 2f out: rdn 1f out: ev ch whn bdly hmpd and hdd ins last: kpt on* **10/3**[1]
0105 **5** *1* **Loyal Tycoon (IRE)**[8] 3901 6-8-12 **89**.......... LTreadwell(5) 7 92
(DNicholls) *in tch: hdwy 2f out: sn rdn and kpt on same pce fnl f* **12/1**
2004 **6** *¾* **Simianna**[8] 3901 5-9-1 **92**.......... PPMathers(5) 4 93
(ABerry) *midfield: hdwy to chse ldrs 2 out sn rdn and kpt on same pce* **20/1**
5022 **7** *1 ½* **Talbot Avenue**[14] 3732 6-9-6 **92**.......... SRighton 12 88
(MMullineaux) *in tch: hdwy gng wl 1/2-way: rdn wl over 1f out and sn wknd* **12/1**
0120 **8** *1* **Bo McGinty (IRE)**[34] 3122 3-8-10 **87**.......... PHanagan 2 80
(RAFahey) *chsd ldrs: rdn along over 2f out and sn btn* **16/1**
6000 **9** *1* **Indian Spark**[14] 3754 10-8-10 **87**.......... PMulrennan(5) 10 77
(JSGoldie) *in tch: rdn along over 2f out: sn btn* **33/1**
2321 **10** *¾* **Lord Of The East**[2] 4047 5-8-10 **82** 7ex.......... SWhitworth 1 70
(DNicholls) *led: rdn along and hdd 2f out: sn wknd* **16/1**
1003 **11** *3* **River Falcon**[28] 3309 4-8-13 **85**.......... TPQueally 3 64
(JSGoldie) *chsd ldrs: rdn along over 2f out and sn wknd* **20/1**
0001 **12** *½* **Mine Behind**[13] 3775 4-8-7 **84**.......... MSavage(5) 11 62
(JRBest) *a rr* **25/1**
0000 **13** *nk* **Seafield Towers**[5] 3979 4-7-12 **70**.......... (p) JMackay 6 47
(MissLAPerratt) *dwlt: hdwy and in tch 1/2-way: sn rdn and wknd* **40/1**
6015 **14** *2* **Mister Sweets**[14] 3755 5-8-3 **75** ow2.......... RFitzpatrick 13 46
(DCarroll) *a rr* **33/1**

0-60 **15** *14* **Border Subject**[56] 2475 7-10-0 **100** KDarley 14 29
(RCharlton) *racd wd: pronient: rdn along wl over 2f out and sn wknd* **14/1**

69.95 secs (-2.62) **Going Correction** -0.20s/f (Firm)
**WFA** 3 from 4yo+ 5lb **15** Ran SP% **120.6**
Speed ratings: **109,107,107,106,105 104,102,101,99,98 94,94,93,91,72**CSF £38.01 CT £252.68 TOTE £7.90: £2.70, £3.20, £1.90; EX 74.70 Trifecta £252.80 Pool £1,460.32 - 4.10 winning tickets.
**Owner** East Wind Racing Ltd **Bred** Shadwell Estate Company Limited **Trained** Upper Lambourn, Berks
■ Stewards Enquiry : R L Moore three-day ban: careless riding (Aug 4-6)

**FOCUS**
A good, competitive sprint handicap and the form looks rock solid.

**NOTEBOOK**
**Mutawaqed(IRE)** had an excuse when below form at Newcastle on his previous start, but things worked out much better this time and he was good enough to gain his first success of the season. He could now go for the Stewards' Cup in which he will be forced to carry a 5lb penalty.
**Machinist(IRE)** ran well under a 7lb penalty for his recent Ayr success, but the winner was just too strong.
**Ellens Academy(IRE)**, still looking for his first win of the year, can be considered a little unlucky, for he got squeezed up when doing his best work close home.
**Two Step Kid(USA)**, in cracking form against his own age group, ran a fine race on this first run against his elders and will be worthy of respect if running in the Stewards' Cup, although he will need to improve.
**Loyal Tycoon(IRE)** ran a good race off a mark 10lb higher than when last successful, but he does look just a little high in the weights.

## 4153 HOVIS EBF FILLIES' H'CAP 1m 2f 88y
**4:00** (4:00) (C ) (0-95,95) 3-Y-0+ **£10,286** (£3,165; £1,582; £791) **Stalls** Low

Form RPR
5211 **1** **La Persiana**[27] 3345 3-8-10 **87** KDarley 1 105+
(WJarvis) *mde all: qcknd over 3f out: shkn up 2f out and styd on wl* **11/8**[1]
1232 **2** *3 ½* **Grey Clouds**[15] 3705 4-8-12 **79** DAllan 4 87
(TDEasterby) *traked wnr: pushed along over 2f out: rdn wl over 1f out: drvn and no imp appr last* **2/1**[2]
10/ **3** *10* **Rainbow Queen**[665] 4935 4-10-0 **95** FLynch 3 96+
(SirMichaelStoute) *hld up: hdwy 5f out: rdn along 3f out: btn and eased fnl 2f* **10/3**[3]
0065 **4** *8* **Rani Two**[14] 3731 5-8-4 **71** SWhitworth 2 45
(WMBrisbourne) *hld up: pushed along 5f out: sn rdn and wknd 4f out* **10/1**

2m 10.71s (1.27) **Going Correction** +0.275s/f (Good)
**WFA** 3 from 4yo+ 10lb **4** Ran SP% **107.6**
Speed ratings: **105,102,94,87**CSF £4.36 TOTE £2.00; EX 3.30.
**Owner** Plantation Stud **Bred** Plantation Stud **Trained** Newmarket, Suffolk

**FOCUS**
Only the front two ran their races and this was a very uncompetitive handicap for the money. The winner is progressive though, and should remain well treated after this.

**NOTEBOOK**
**La Persiana**, up 7lb for her recent Windsor success, completed the hat-trick in pretty straightforward fashion. Connections will now look to step her up to Listed company and the Virginia Stakes at Yarmouth could be on the cards.
**Grey Clouds**, a beaten favourite on her last two starts, was no match whatsoever for the winner and looks vulnerable off her current mark.
**Rainbow Queen**, not seen since disappointing behind Soviet Song in the Fillies' Mile 665 days previously, has been given a Yorkshire Oaks entry. She dropped out very tamely when the pace quickened and connections will be hoping this race brings her on significantly.
**Rani Two** had shaped as though about to hit form at Chester on her previous start, but this represented a step back.

## 4154 MR KIPLING EXCEEDINGLY GOOD CLAIMING STKS 6f
**4:45** (4:45) (D ) 3-Y-0+ **£5,720** (£1,760; £880; £440) **Stalls** Centre

Form RPR
3314 **1** **Tancred Times**[3] 4013 9-8-3 55 FNorton 5 57
(DWBarker) *mde all: rdn wl over 1f out: styd on gamely fnl f* **11/4**[2]
-020 **2** *1 ½* **Haulage Man**[20] 3559 6-9-4 57 (p) PHanagan 6 68
(DEddy) *trckd ldrs: smooth hdwy 2f out: rdn to chse wnr ent last: sn one pce* **8/1**
3050 **3** *1* **Pays D'Amour (IRE)**[24] 3409 7-8-11 62 SWhitworth 4 58
(DNicholls) *hld up: hdwy 2f out: rdn over 1f out: kpt on same pce* **7/1**
0000 **4** *1 ½* **African Spur (IRE)**[3] 4014 4-8-5 47 (v[1]) DTudhope[(7)] 8 54
(DCarroll) *cl up: rdn along 2f out: grad wknd* **33/1**
4345 **5** *½* **Border Artist**[8] 3895 5-9-1 64 AlexGreaves 2 56
(DNicholls) *trckd ldrs: smooth hdwy over 2f out: rdn wl over 1f out and sn btn* **4/1**[3]
5201 **6** *1 ¾* **Effective**[17] 3623 4-9-4 67 KDarley 1 53
(APJarvis) *trckd ldrs: hdwy 2f out: rdn over 1f out and sn btn* **9/4**[1]
1000 **7** *5* **Millfields Dreams**[7] 3941 5-8-12 59 MSavage[(5)] 3 37
(RBrotherton) *chsd ldrs: rdn along 1/2-way: sn wknd* **16/1**

1m 11.93s (-0.64) **Going Correction** -0.20s/f (Firm) **7** Ran SP% **109.9**
Speed ratings: **96,94,92,90,90 87,81**CSF £22.53 TOTE £3.10: £1.70, £3.60; EX 39.90.Tancred Times was claimed by David Allan for £5,000.
**Owner** D W Barker **Bred** W L Barker **Trained** Scorton, N Yorks

**FOCUS**
A pretty moderate claimer and the time was not great either, being two seconds slower than the handicap over the same trip. The form os held down bu the second and fourth.

**NOTEBOOK**
**Tancred Times**, best in at the weights on this drop in grade, ran out an emphatic winner from the front. She should be competitive back in handicaps whilst in this sort of form and was claimed for £5,000.
**Haulage Man** returned to form with a good effort, but the concession of over a stone to the winner proved too much.
**Pays D'Amour(IRE)** is not very consistent, but this was one of his better efforts.
**African Spur(IRE)** ran a little better than of late in a first-time visor, but remains very hard to win with.
**Border Artist** found disappointingly little under pressure.
**Effective** has won on this ground, but was not at his best on it this time. *Official explanation: jockey said gelding lost his action; trainer's representative said gelding was unsuited by the going*

## 4155 DUNCAN WILTSHIRE MEMORIAL RATED STKS (H'CAP) 1m 3f 198y
**5:20** (5:22) (D ) (0-80,75) 4-Y-0+ **£5,600** (£1,723; £861; £430) **Stalls** Low

Form RPR
0041 **1** **Jack Of Trumps (IRE)**[14] 3752 4-9-2 **70** FNorton 5 77
(GWragg) *trckd ldrs: hdwy on inner to ld 2f out: rdn over 1f out: styd on wl fnl f* **8/1**[3]
0652 **2** *hd* **Rajam**[9] 3873 6-9-7 **75** (v) AlexGreaves 7 82
(DNicholls) *trckd ldrs: hdwy 3f out: chal over 1f out: sn rdn and ev ch tl drvn and no ex nr fin* **33/1**
5444 **3** *shd* **Sporting Gesture**[7] 3953 7-9-1 **74** PMulrennan[(5)] 6 81
(MWEasterby) *in tch: swtchd rt and hdwy over 2f out: rdn over 1f out: drvn and kpt on wl fnl f* **11/2**[2]
4122 **4** *¾* **Danakil**[31] 3207 9-9-7 **75** TPQueally 1 81
(SDow) *prom: rdn along 2f out: drvn and kpt on fnl f* **10/1**
2211 **5** *1 ¾* **Inchnadamph**[14] 3740 4-8-9 **63** (t) RWinston 8 66
(TJFitzgerald) *hld up: hdwy over 2f out: sn rdna dn kpt on same pce appr last* **8/1**[3]
04/0 **6** *½* **Lawrence Of Arabia (IRE)**[10] 3844 4-8-4 **58** JMackay 9 65+
(SirMarkPrescott) *hld up in rr: wd st: hdwy 3f out: sn rdn and kpt on: nrst fin* **2/1**[1]
-452 **7** *1* **Nevada Desert (IRE)**[7] 3952 4-9-3 **71** DeanMcKeown 3 71
(RMWhitaker) *led: rdn along 3f out: hdd over 2f out and grad wknd* **14/1**
3436 **8** *½* **Stallone**[7] 3953 7-9-4 **72** PHanagan 13 72
(NWilson) *dwlt: hld up in rr: hdwy 3f out: rdn and kpt on fnl 2f: nt rch ldrs* **16/1**
4601 **9** *6* **Tomasino**[8] 3892 6-9-7 **75** (t) KDarley 2 65
(MrsMReveley) *hld up: hdwy 3f out: rdn 2f out and sn btn* **16/1**
/43- **10** *2 ½* **Timber Ice (USA)**[418] 2051 4-9-7 **75** DAllan 10 61
(HRACecil) *cl up: rdn along over 3f out: wknd over 2f out* **20/1**
P121 **11** *2 ½* **Merrymaker**[7] 3942 4-8-8 **67** PPMathers[(5)] 11 49
(WMBrisbourne) *hld up in rr: wd st: snm rdn along and no prog* **12/1**
1063 **12** *hd* **Maritime Blues**[9] 3866 4-8-10 **64** ACulhane 4 46
(JGGiven) *prom: rdn along 4f out: wknd over 2f out* **16/1**
430 **13** *2 ½* **Farne Isle**[19] 3587 5-9-2 **70** FLynch 12 48
(GAHarker) *a rr: wd st: sn bhd* **12/1**

2m 30.11s (1.25) **Going Correction** +0.275s/f (Good) **13** Ran SP% **127.4**
Speed ratings: **106,105,105,105,104 103,103,102,98,97 95,95,93**CSF £258.52 CT £1602.68 TOTE £6.70: £2.30, £9.50, £2.10; EX 374.30 Place 6 £111.68, Place 5 £78.21.
**Owner** Mollers Racing **Bred** Miss Susan Bates **Trained** Newmarket, Suffolk

**FOCUS**
A somewhat muddling affair, as the early pace was pretty steady before things quickened at the top of the straight, about half a mile from home. As a result, some of these were not seen to best effect and the form wants treating with a little caution.

**NOTEBOOK**
**Jack Of Trumps(IRE)**, 6lb higher than when successful at Salisbury on his previous start, defied the rise with a game success, keeping on really well having been well placed by the in-form Norton given the way the race was run. He should not go up too much for this and the hat-trick cannot be ruled out.
**Rajam** was a very big price considering the form he has been in lately and defied his odds with another solid effort.
**Sporting Gesture** would probably have appreciated a stronger end-to-end gallop and ran well in the circumstances.
**Danakil** appeared to run his race, but again gave the impression he is in the grip of the Handicapper.
**Inchnadamph**, 5lb higher than when successful at Hamilton on his previous start, lacked the pace to pose a serious threat given the way the race was run and is better than this.
**Lawrence Of Arabia(IRE)**, well backed to confirm the promise he showed on his return from a lay-off at Kempton on his previous start, was unsuited by the steady early pace and proved unable to get on terms when the pace quickened. A fair effort in the circumstances and he should be winning soon enough.
T/Plt: £30.50 to a £1 stake. Pool: £69,858.40. 1,669.55 winning tickets. T/Qpdt: £17.30 to a £1 stake. Pool: £4,319.60. 184.40 winning tickets. JR

4156 - 4157a (Foreign Racing) - See Raceform Interactive

3856

# LEOPARDSTOWN (L-H)
Saturday, July 24

**OFFICIAL GOING: Good to firm (good in places)**

## 4158a TYROS STKS (LISTED RACE) 7f
**6:45** (6:46) 2-Y-O **£22,922** (£6,725; £3,204; £1,091)

RPR
**1** **Elusive Double (IRE)**[44] 2824 2-9-0 PShanahan 6 100
(DKWeld, Ire) *hld up in rr: prog on outer appr st: led 150yds out: kpt on wl* **11/2**
**2** *1* **Lock And Key (IRE)**[6] 3970 2-8-11 CatherineGannon 7 95
(EdwardLynam, Ire) *s.i.s and hld up in tch: rdn early st: impr to chal 1f out: kpt on u.p* **10/1**
**3** *hd* **Amsterdam (IRE)**[52] 2599 2-9-0 JPSpencer 1 97
(APO'Brien, Ire) *led: strly pressed st: wandered abt u.p and hdd 150yds out: kpt on* **7/4**[1]
**4** *shd* **La Maitresse (IRE)**[10] 3859 2-8-11 TPO'Shea 3 94
(MHalford, Ire) *trckd ldrs in 4th: 3rd and chal over 1f out: kpt on same pce* **10/1**
**5** *1 ½* **Zelkova (IRE)**[48] 2708 2-9-0 FMBerry 8 93
(MsFMCrowley, Ire) *trckd ldr in 2nd: rdn ent st: ev ch 1 1/2f out: kpt on same pce* **9/2**[3]
**6** *shd* **Stagelight (IRE)**[21] 3544 2-9-0 PCosgrave 2 93
(APO'Brien, Ire) *hld up in tch: last appr st: effrt whn nt clr run and swtchd under 1f out: kpt on same pce* **11/4**[2]
**7** *2 ½* **Fearless Flyer (IRE)**[23] 3462 2-8-11 WMLordan 4 84
(TStack, Ire) *in tch: prog into 3rd and rdn appr st: wknd fr 2f out: eased ins fnl f* **12/1**

1m 29.1s **Going Correction** -0.175s/f (Firm) **7** Ran SP% **122.5**
Speed ratings: **110,108,108,108,106 106,103**CSF £61.40 TOTE £4.70: £2.80, £2.60; DF 19.90.
**Owner** Moyglare Stud Farm **Bred** Moyglare Stud Farm Ltd **Trained** The Curragh, Co Kildare

**NOTEBOOK**
**Elusive Double(IRE)** won an ordinary contest, coming from behind with a sustained run on the outer that saw him in front just over half a furlong out. He kept on strongly and will stay farther.
**Lock And Key(IRE)** won a six-furlong nursery last time out off 79. She gave away ground at the start but put in a sustained challenge inside the last, although she was always held.
**Amsterdam(IRE)** tried to make all but hung right under pressure inside the last and found little.
**La Maitresse(IRE)** was in third place and looking one-paced when edging right inside the last.
**Zelkova(IRE)** was possibly a bit unlucky. He was done no favours by the meanderings of his stablemate Amsterdam inside the last and might emerge best of these in time.

## 4159a IRISH STALLION FARMS EUROPEAN BREEDERS FUND SWEET MIMOSA STKS (LISTED RACE) (FILLIES) 6f

7:15 (7:15) 3-Y-O+ £32,091 (£9,415; £4,485; £1,528)

RPR

1 **Ulfah (USA)**[27] 3351 3-8-11 94 ........ DPMcDonogh 6 99
(KevinPrendergast, Ire) *led: strly pressed early st: hdd 1f out: rallied u.p to regain ld cl home* **4/1**[2]

2 *hd* **Shersha (IRE)**[27] 3349 5-9-2 92 ........ NGMcCullagh 4 98
(SJTreacy, Ire) *hld up in tch: 4th and hdwy ent st: led 1f out: sn drifted lft: hdd and drifted rt cl home* **9/1**[3]

3 *hd* **Ruby Rocket (IRE)**[15] 3715 3-9-0 ........ MJKinane 1 101
(HMorrison) *broke wl: settled 3rd: 2nd and chal early st: cl 3rd and ev ch fnl f: kpt on u.p* **8/15**[1]

4 *2* **Blue Dream (IRE)**[17] 3648 4-9-2 90 ........ CO'Donoghue 2 92
(DJSelvaratnam, Ire) *hld up: prog on inner ent st: 4th and no imp fr over 1f out* **20/1**

5 *2 1/2* **Anna Frid (GER)**[42] 2903 4-9-5 95 ........ PShanahan 10 87
(DKWeld, Ire) *chsd ldrs: impr into 3rd ent st: no ex fr over 1f out* **10/1**

6 *4* **Kanisfluh**[7] 3959 3-9-0 88 ........ (bt) WMLordan 3 75
(TStack, Ire) *dwlt: hld up in tch: no imp st* **16/1**

7 *2* **Follow (USA)**[21] 3547 3-8-11 91 ........ JPSpencer 5 66
(APO'Brien, Ire) *trckd ldrs: 5th 1/2-way: no imp st* **10/1**

8 *hd* **Aleida (IRE)**[28] 3328 3-8-11 83 ........ KJManning 7 66
(JSBolger, Ire) *sn 2nd: wknd ent st* **16/1**

1m 13.6s **Going Correction** +0.10s/f (Good)
**WFA** 3 from 4yo+ 5lb **8** Ran SP% **129.9**
Speed ratings: **110,109,109,106,103 98,95,95**CSF £45.16 TOTE £5.90: £2.00, £1.90, £1.10; DF 25.40.
**Owner** Hamdan Al Maktoum **Bred** Shadwell Farm Llc **Trained** Friarstown, Co Kildare

**NOTEBOOK**
**Ulfah(USA)** made virtually all and fought back tenaciously when joined inside the last.
**Shersha(IRE)** showed an improved level of form. She came through on the outer to have every chance from a furlong down but hung left and then edged out again when her rider changed his whip.
**Ruby Rocket(IRE)** looked more than good enough to take this but was disappointing. She had every chance between horses early in the straight but just did not pick up. She kept on at the one pace but showed little sparkle.
**Blue Dream(IRE)** ran her best race this season and should be up to winning a handicap.
**Anna Frid(GER)** had plenty to do at the weights but shaped as though she is coming back to form.
**Follow(USA)** never threatened at any stage.

## 4160a MELD STKS (GROUP 3) 1m 2f

7:45 (7:45) 3-Y-O+ £32,042 (£9,366; £4,436; £1,478)

RPR

1 **Latino Magic (IRE)**[6] 3967 4-9-7 106 ........ RMBurke 4 108
(RJOsborne, Ire) *hld up in rr: prog 3f out: 3rd and rdn ent st: cl 2nd and chal 1f out: styd on wl to ld on line* **6/1**

2 *shd* **Solskjaer (IRE)**[27] 3355 4-9-7 104 ........ JPSpencer 2 108
(APO'Brien, Ire) *mod 2nd: tk clsr order ent st: led over 1 1/2f out: strly pressed fnl f: kpt on wl: hdd on line* **5/1**[3]

3 *4* **Cache Creek (IRE)**[10] 3857 6-9-4 107 ........ FMBerry 5 97
(PHughes, Ire) *hld up: last appr st: kpt on to go mod 3rd ins fnl f* **10/3**[2]

4 *2* **Medicinal (IRE)**[45] 2796 3-8-11 107 ........ (b) PShanahan 3 96
(DKWeld, Ire) *mod 3rd: 4th and rdn ent st: sn no ex* **9/4**[1]

5 *3 1/2* **Big Bad Bob (IRE)**[37] 3030 4-9-10 ........ MJKinane 1 93
(JLDunlop) *led: sn wl clr: reduced advantage ent st: hdd over 1 1/2f out: wknd qckly* **9/4**[1]

2m 5.70s **Going Correction** -0.075s/f (Good)
**WFA** 3 from 4yo+ 10lb **5** Ran SP% **115.6**
Speed ratings: **115,114,111,110,107**CSF £35.07 TOTE £8.80: £2.80, £2.70; DF 48.50.
**Owner** Mrs P D Osborne **Bred** Ces Racing Ltd **Trained** Naas, Co Kildare
■ Stewards Enquiry : R M Burke caution: used whip with excessive frequency

**NOTEBOOK**
**Latino Magic(IRE)** was gaining his first success in eight starts this season. In second place from a furlong out, he got up on the line.
**Solskjaer(IRE)** went on with over a furlong and a half to race and looked the winner until pipped in the last few strides.
**Cache Creek(IRE)**, in foal to Barathea, stayed on for third but was never a serious challenger.
**Medicinal(IRE)** had dropped back to fourth before the straight and played no part over the last two furlongs.
**Big Bad Bob(IRE)** set an unsustainable pace and was beaten early in the straight.

4161 - 4162a (Foreign Racing) - See Raceform Interactive

# 4117 ASCOT (R-H)

Sunday, July 25

**OFFICIAL GOING: Good to firm**
Wind: lt against Weather: fine but cloudy

## 4163 FULLERTON TROPHY (CLASSIFIED STKS) 1m 2f

2:00 (2:00) (B) 3-Y-O+ £11,710 (£4,441; £2,220; £1,009) Stalls High

Form RPR

0011 1 **Wunderwood (USA)**[36] 3075 5-9-7 99 ........ SSanders 1 111+
(LadyHerries) *lw: trckd ldrs: effrt over 2f out: rdn to ld over 1f out: edgd rt then lft: drvn out* **7/4**[1]

11 2 *3/4* **Mutasallil (USA)**[35] 3118 4-9-6 98 ........ (t) RHills 5 109
(SaeedBinSuroor) *led: rdn and hdd over 1f out: kpt on wl fnl f: a hld* **4/1**[3]

0-1 3 *1 1/4* **Alphecca (USA)**[25] 3422 3-8-7 93 ........ KFallon 6 103+
(SirMichaelStoute) *trckd ldrs: hrd rdn wl over 2f out: styd on fnl f: nvr able to chal* **7/2**[2]

3400 4 *1* **Counsel's Opinion (IRE)**[22] 3521 7-9-8 100 ........ RMullen 7 106+
(CFWall) *hld up in last pair: gng wl 3f out: rdn and no rspnse 2f out: one pce after* **7/1**

0315 5 *1 1/4* **Vengeance**[16] 3716 4-9-6 98 ........ PDobbs 2 102
(MrsAJPerrett) *rousted along early: in tch: hrd rdn wl over 2f out: unable qck: one pce after* **10/1**

0060 6 *1* **Corriolanus (GER)**[37] 3034 4-9-3 94 ........ DHolland 4 97
(PMitchell) *lw: pressed ldr to 2f out: shkn up and grad fdd* **33/1**

5000 7 *16* **Bourgainville**[15] 3756 6-9-3 94 ........ (p) JFortune 3 67
(AMBalding) *s.s: a in last: wknd over 2f out: t.o* **12/1**

2m 9.15s (0.42) **Going Correction** +0.175s/f (Good)
**WFA** 3 from 4yo+ 10lb **7** Ran SP% **110.8**
Speed ratings: **105,104,103,102,101 100,88**CSF £8.32 TOTE £2.80: £2.00, £2.60; EX 10.70.
**Owner** Tony Perkins **Bred** Darley Stud Management, L L C **Trained** Angmering, W Sussex

**FOCUS**
A decent and competitive Classified event run at a fair gallop. The front three all look capable of further improvement and the form looks reliable.

**NOTEBOOK**
**Wunderwood(USA)** followed-up his win in the Duke Of Edinburgh Stakes at the Royal Meeting last time off this 7lb higher mark, and confirmed himself a highly progressive performer. He wandered about when in front late on, but the race was already in the bag at the time, and he had no problems with this shorter trip. Although the Ebor at York looks a logical target, he now gets a 7lb penalty for that, and connections were quick to suggest he may take his chance in the Melbourne Cup instead, a race in which he would be a fascinating contender.
**Mutasallil(USA)**, winner of both his previous outings in this country, made a bold bid from the front and stuck to his task well once headed by the winner late in the straight. He looks up to Listed Class on this evidence and would have little problem dropping back to a mile.
**Alphecca(USA)** ◆, who looked a colt of definite promise when making all in a Lingfield maiden last time, was far from disgraced in this much better grade. He still looked green under pressure, but ran on strongly after getting outpaced at the top of the straight. He will again learn from this and looks most progressive, so could well be up to winning a decent prize before the year is out, and will command plenty of respect when racing against his own age group once more.
**Counsel's Opinion(IRE)** ran his race, but could not quicken when it mattered and continues to look too high in the weights at present. He is reliable and sets the standard for the form.
**Vengeance** could not muster the pace over this shorter trip to trouble the principals and probably found this ground plenty quick enough. He will do better back over farther with more cut, but holds few secrets from the Handicapper, and is not easy to place.
**Bourgainville** was well backed to improve on his recent disappointments in the first-time cheekpieces, but never threatened after a slow start. He is starting to look regressive.

## 4164 CATHAY PACIFIC H'CAP 1m (R)

2:30 (2:30) (C) (0-90,89) 3-Y-O+ £9,782 (£3,010; £1,505; £752) Stalls High

Form RPR

031- 1 **Prince Of Thebes (IRE)**[360] 3710 3-9-4 87 ........ RMullen 7 97
(AMBalding) *h.d.w: lw: t.k.h: trckd ldr: rdn to ld over 1f out: drvn out and jst hld on* **20/1**

0021 2 *hd* **Welcome Stranger**[25] 3426 4-9-3 81 ........ LFletcher(3) 9 91
(JMPEustace) *trckd ldng pair: rdn and nt qckn over 2f out: styd on fr over 1f out: chsd wnr ins fnl f: gaining at fin* **8/1**

1111 3 *1* **Goodbye Mr Bond**[32] 3198 4-8-10 71 ........ FNorton 5 79
(EJAlston) *lw: settled in midfield: rdn wl over 2f out: no prog tl styd on fr over 1f out: nrst fin* **10/3**[1]

0603 4 *hd* **African Sahara (USA)**[10] 3869 5-9-3 78 ........ (t) GCarter 6 85
(MissDMountain) *hld up in last pair: rdn over 2f out: prog over 1f out: styd on fnl f: nrst fin* **8/1**

1106 5 *3/4* **Lifted Way**[32] 3205 5-9-4 79 ........ SDrowne 4 85
(PRChamings) *led to over 1f out: fdd ins fnl f* **10/1**

3331 6 *2* **Best Before (IRE)**[9] 3911 4-8-12 80 ........ SJDonohoe(7) 10 81
(PDEvans) *lw: trckd ldrs: hrd rdn over 2f out: nt qckn and no prog after* **7/2**[2]

114 7 *1* **A Woman In Love**[16] 3690 5-9-4 79 ........ SSanders 1 78
(MissBSanders) *hld up in last: rdn over 2f out: one pce and no imp* **4/1**[3]

465 8 *nk* **J R Stevenson (USA)**[26] 3397 8-8-11 72 ........ JFortune 8 70
(MWigham) *settled in last trio: pushed along 2f out: no prog and nvr nr ldrs* **20/1**

4465 9 *8* **Jools**[16] 3690 6-8-8 76 ........ MHoward(7) 2 56
(DKIvory) *b: racd wd in midfield: rdn over 2f out: sn wknd* **11/1**

1m 43.8s (0.76) **Going Correction** +0.175s/f (Good)
**WFA** 3 from 4yo+ 8lb **9** Ran SP% **114.5**
Speed ratings: **103,102,101,101,100 98,97,97,89**CSF £168.55 CT £675.43 TOTE £11.60: £2.40, £3.30, £1.70; EX 155.60 Trifecta £620.50 Pool: £1,748.07 - 2.00 winning tickets..
**Owner** N H Harris/Dr E Harris/Miss M Green **Bred** Mrs A Rothschild And London Thoroughbred Services **Trained** Kingsclere, Hants

**FOCUS**
Not as competitive as one might have expected - there were just nine runners in vast contrast to last year's renewal in which there were 21 - and, with the early pace just steady, it proved hard to come from far off the pace. As a result, several of these were not seen at their best.

**NOTEBOOK**
**Prince Of Thebes(IRE)**, not seen since winning just an ordinary Epsom maiden 260 days previously, defied both the lay-off and what looked a stiff handicap mark to make a winning return. It would be wrong to get carried away with this, for he did get the run of the race, but there should be more to come.
**Welcome Stranger**, 5lb higher than when successful at Yarmouth on his previous start, had conditions in his favour and ran his race, although a stronger pace may just have suited better.
**Goodbye Mr Bond**, in the form of his life this summer, winning his last four starts, did nothing wrong - he was simply unable to quicken up off the moderate gallop. He was racing off a mark 19lb higher than when starting his winning run, but there could yet be more to come granted a stronger-run race.
**African Sahara(USA)** ran very well considering the pace would not have been strong enough for him.
**Lifted Way** had the run of things in front, but had disappointingly little to offer inside the final furlong.
**Best Before(IRE)** hails from a stable in good form and has been in great heart himself but, 6lb higher than when winning at Newmarket on his previous start, he was not at his best.
**A Woman In Love** was pretty keen early on and could never get into it. She is better than this.
**Jools** *Official explanation: trainer said gelding finished distressed*

## 4165 HONG KONG JOCKEY CLUB SPRINT (HERITAGE H'CAP) 5f

3:00 (3:02) (B) 3-Y-O+ £40,600 (£15,400; £7,700; £3,500) Stalls Low

Form RPR

0-60 1 **Baltic King**[62] 2373 4-9-4 101 ........ (t) JFortune 21 112
(HMorrison) *lw: hld up far side: prog 1/2-way: rdn and effrt over 1f out: styd on wl to ld last 50yds* **9/1**[3]

-001 2 *nk* **Pivotal Point**[15] 3723 4-8-13 96 8ex ........ JPMurtagh 26 106
(PJMakin) *lw: disp ld far side: def advantage 1f out: worn down last 50yds* **16/1**

2L02 3 *1 1/4* **Forever Phoenix**[6] 3976 4-8-9 92 ........ BDoyle 3 97
(RMHCowell) *trckd nr side ldrs: effrt over 1f out: led gp ins fnl f: edgd rt: nt on terms w ldng pair far side* **9/1**[3]

4041 4 *hd* **Connect**[8] 3945 7-8-11 94 8ex ........ (b) PDoe 23 98
(MHTompkins) *chsd far side ldrs: hrd rdn 2f out: styd on fnl f: nvr able to chal* **33/1**

6414 5 *3/4* **Blackheath (IRE)**[2] 4076 8-8-7 90 8ex ........ PDobbs 13 91
(DNicholls) *b: taken down early: racd nr side: hld up in rr: prog on outer over 1f out: r.o wl fnl f: nrst fin* **33/1**

6023 6 *shd* **Corridor Creeper (FR)**[23] 3480 7-8-12 95 ........ (p) DHolland 5 96
(JMBradley) *mde most nr side to ins fnl f: edgd rt and no ex* **14/1**

5100 7 *nk* **Merlin's Dancer**[9] 3920 4-7-6 81 oh1 ow1 ........ MHalford(7) 20 81
(DNicholls) *disp ld far side: hung lft jst over 1f out: nt qckn and btn after* **40/1**

1636 **8** *nk* **Pic Up Sticks**[36] 3074 5-8-13 **96** ........ TEDurcan 4 94+
(MRChannon) *dwlt: hld up rr on nr side gp: gng easily but trapped bhd wall of horses fr 1/2-way to 1f out: r.o last 150yds: hopeless ta* **7/1**[1]

0000 **9** *½* **Whitbarrow (IRE)**[15] 3723 5-8-13 **96** ........ (p) RLMoore 11 92
(JMBradley) *lw: racd alone in centre: wl on terms w ldrs: fdd ins fnl f* **33/1**

1000 **10** *nk* **Pax**[9] 3901 7-8-0 **83** ........ PMQuinn 7 78
(DNicholls) *s.v.s: sn in tch at rr of nr side gp: effrt and swtchd to rail over 1f out: drvn and styd on: nrst fin* **40/1**

-530 **11** *nk* **Tychy**[36] 3074 5-8-9 **92** ........ SDrowne 9 86
(SCWilliams) *b: lw: w nr side ldrs tl wknd fnl f* **16/1**

0006 **12** *hd* **Malapropism**[13] 3795 4-8-1 **84** ........ CCatlin 15 77
(MRChannon) *racd nr side: trckd ldrs: rdn 2f out: unable qck and btn over 1f out: one pce* **50/1**

2000 **13** *½* **Danzig River (IRE)**[29] 3324 3-8-6 **93** ........ DaneO'Neill 2 84
(BWHills) *swtg: hld up wl in rr nr side: effrt over 1f out: kpt on but nvr rchd ldrs* **66/1**

0004 **14** *½* **Smokin Beau**[29] 3324 7-8-13 **96** ........ (b) TGMcLaughlin 14 85
(NPLittmoden) *dwlt: racd nr side: nvr on terms w ldrs: rdn and struggling 2f out* **33/1**

1014 **15** *shd* **Whistler**[15] 3723 7-8-9 **92** 8ex ........ (p) RHills 16 81
(JMBradley) *racd far side: towards rr of gp: rdn 2f out: no prog* **33/1**

0040 **16** *nk* **Atlantic Viking (IRE)**[30] 3266 9-8-10 **93** ........ MHenry 22 80
(DNicholls) *chsd far side ldrs: drvn wl over 1f out: wknd fnl f* **33/1**

3000 **17** *hd* **Nights Cross (IRE)**[8] 3940 3-9-3 **107** ........ SHitchcott(3) 8 94
(MRChannon) *w nr side ldrs over 3f: wknd fnl f* **33/1**

0023 **18** *1* **Proud Boast**[6] 3976 6-8-6 **89** ........ KDarley 1 72
(DNicholls) *taken down early: trckd nr side ldrs: pushed along 2f out: no prog and btn whn n.m.r over 1f out* **10/1**

-004 **19** *1* **Funfair Wane**[2] 4091 5-8-10 **93** ........ SWhitworth 10 72
(DNicholls) *taken down early: hld up wl in rr of nr side gp: no prog over 1f out* **28/1**

3155 **20** *½* **Green Manalishi**[16] 3702 3-8-4 **91** ........ JFEgan 12 68
(DWPArbuthnot) *w nr side ldrs over 3f: wknd* **16/1**

-602 **21** *1 ¾* **Plateau**[50] 2679 5-8-1 **84** ........ ANicholls 18 54
(DNicholls) *taken down early: racd far side: nvr on terms w ldrs: struggling 2f out* **9/1**[3]

13-2 **22** *3* **First Order**[8] 3945 3-8-13 **100** ........ SSanders 17 58
(SirMarkPrescott) *racd far side: nvr on terms w ldrs: wl btn 2f out* **8/1**[2]

0050 **23** *3 ½* **Little Edward**[23] 3480 6-8-2 **92** ........ AHindley(7) 24 36
(BGPowell) *s.s: racd far side: nvr able to rch ldrs: wknd over 1f out* **33/1**

0105 **24** *5* **Piccled**[18] 3645 6-8-0 **83** ........ FNorton 19 7
(EJAlston) *lw: virtually ref to r: a t.o* **20/1**

61.66 secs (-0.27) **Going Correction** +0.175s/f (Good)
**WFA** 3 from 4yo+ 4lb **24** Ran SP% **127.1**
Speed ratings: **109,108,106,106,105 104,104,103,103,102 102,101,101,100,100 99,99,97,96,95 92,87,82,74**CSF £123.69 CT £1375.26 TOTE £10.90: £3.00, £3.80, £3.00, £8.50; EX 195.80 Trifecta £4573.20 Pool: £12,238.38 - 1.90 winning tickets.
**Owner** Thurloe Thoroughbreds Viii **Bred** R F And Mrs Knipe **Trained** East Ilsley, Berks
■ Stewards Enquiry : B Doyle one-day ban: struck rival horse over head with whip twice (Aug 5)

**FOCUS**
A really competitive sprint handicap and rock-solid form. The field split into two groups (with the exception of Whitbarrow who raced on his own), although several horses drifted towards the centre of the track close home and the runners were spread all over the track at the line. The far side just had the edge.

**NOTEBOOK**
**Baltic King**, held on both his previous starts this term in a Group and Listed race, found this drop back into handicaps just what was required. The manner in which he did this suggests he could yet hold his own at a higher level, and connections may look for something abroad.
**Pivotal Point**, 3lb wrong at the weights under his 8lb penalty for his success in a much weaker race over course and distance on his previous start, ran a blinder in this better contest and was just held. He is open to further improvement, yet can race off a 5lb lower mark in the Stewards' Cup.
**Forever Phoenix**, runner-up toAirwave in a Listed contest at Ayr on her previous start, ran a cracker on this return to handicap company, winning her race on the near side. She may now be sent abroad in search for a Pattern victory.
**Connect** was raised just 2lb for his recent Newmarket success but because this was an early closer and had to carry an 8lb penalty. This was a fine effort in the circumstances.
**Blackheath(IRE)**, below form over six furlongs here two days previously, ran better on this drop in trip under his big penalty.
**Pic Up Sticks** can be rated much better than the bare form as he got no luck in running. As a result, he must be respected in the Stewards' Cup, but it is worth noting he is often 'unlucky in running'. *Official explanation: jockey said gelding suffered interference in running*
**First Order** was unable to confirm the promise he showed on his reappearance and this may have come a little too soon.
**Piccled** *Official explanation: jockey said gelding missed break*

## 4166 HONG KONG INTERNATIONAL SALE AUCTION STKS TROPHY (CONDITIONS RACE) 7f
**3:35** (3:37) (C) 2-Y-0 **£7,772** (£2,948; £1,474; £670) **Stalls** Low

Form RPR

12 **1** **Southern Africa (USA)**[23] 3481 2-8-13 ........ JFortune 4 89
(GAButler) *lw: t.k.h: trckd ldr: led wl over 1f out: hrd rdn fnl f: styd on wl* **11/2**[3]

542 **2** *1* **Group Captain**[17] 3679 2-8-7 ........ RLMoore 7 81
(SKirk) *hld up in tch: prog 3f out: drvn to chal over 1f out: ev ch ins fnl f: unable qck* **7/1**

511 **3** *shd* **Sacred Nuts (IRE)**[15] 3727 2-8-8 ........ DHolland 1 85+
(MLWBell) *lw: trckd ldrs: nt clr run 2f out tl swtchd and drvn ent fnl f: pressed ldrs last 100yds: unable qck nr fin* **10/11**[1]

31 **4** *4* **Ariodante**[18] 3633 2-8-7 ........ SSanders 8 71
(JMPEustace) *t.k.h: prom: rdn to chal wl over 1f out: ev ch 1f out: wknd rapidly last 100yds* **9/2**[2]

6506 **5** *1* **Im Spartacus**[17] 3677 2-8-7 ........ FNorton 3 68
(IAWood) *trckd ldrs: rdn 2f out: fdd over 1f out* **25/1**

0 **5** *dht* **Lady Luisa (IRE)**[8] 3931 2-8-2 ........ JFEgan 2 63
(JSMoore) *hld up in last: rdn over 2f out: brief effrt wl over 1f out: sn outpcd and btn* **66/1**

60 **7** *1 ¼* **Benedict Bay**[15] 3749 2-8-7 ........ SDrowne 6 65
(GBBalding) *a towards rr: rdn and no prog over 2f out* **66/1**

010 **8** *1* **John Forbes**[17] 3672 2-8-7 ........ DaneO'Neill 5 62
(BEllison) *led to wl over 1f out: wknd* **10/1**

1m 30.71s (1.04) **Going Correction** +0.175s/f (Good) **8** Ran SP% **114.4**
Speed ratings: **101,99,99,95,94 94,92,91**CSF £42.35 TOTE £6.00: £1.70, £2.00, £1.10; EX 37.50.
**Owner** The International Carnival Partnership **Bred** H Ahamdi And Michael Anderson **Trained** Blewbury, Oxon

**FOCUS**
A reasonable conditions event, although the pace was pretty steady early on.

**NOTEBOOK**
**Southern Africa(USA)**, runner-up to Polly Perkins in a five-furlong Listed race on his previous start, proved fully effective over these extra two furlongs and ran out a determined winner. Things would have been closer had the third got a better run, but there should yet be more to come and connections have a winter campaign in Dubai in mind for him.

**Group Captain** is still a maiden, but connections again ran him against previous winners and he again acquitted himself with credit. He travelled as well as anything on the outside of the field and kept on right the way to the line, suggesting he should have little trouble in winning his maiden.

**Sacred Nuts(IRE)**, successful in a six-furlong nursery here on his previous start, was a very unlucky loser on this step up in trip. A consistent sort, he should continue to go well, possibly back in nurseries, although he will probably be under-priced as a result of this run.

**Ariodante**, off the mark in a reasonable Lingfield maiden over six furlongs on his previous start, raced keenly on this step up in trip and did not get home.

**Im Spartacus** had it all to do on the book but ran a creditable race, especially considering a stronger pace would have suited.

**Lady Luisa(IRE)** stepped up on the form she showed on her debut and is going the right way.

## 4167 CATHAY PACIFIC HONG KONG INTERNATIONAL RACES H'CAP 1m 4f
**4:10** (4:10) (D) (0-85,84) 3-Y-O **£5,551** (£1,708; £854; £427) **Stalls** High

Form RPR

5-10 **1** **Vinando**[71] 2107 3-9-7 **84** ........ (t) SDrowne 5 98
(CREgerton) *lw: racd in 4th: rdn 4f out: no prog tl styd on fr 2f out to ld over 1f out: drvn clr* **8/1**

221- **2** *5* **Soulacroix**[268] 5847 3-9-7 **84** ........ SSanders 2 90
(MrsAJPerrett) *lw: led and set str pce: brief breather 5f out: rdn and hdd narrowly 2f out: ev ch over 1f out: sn outstyd by wnr* **11/4**[2]

6-12 **3** *½* **Mazuna (IRE)**[9] 3908 3-8-5 **68** ........ RLMoore 1 73
(CEBrittain) *swtg: trckd ldr: chal 4f out: led narrowly 2f out: hdd and outstyd over 1f out* **2/1**[1]

0042 **4** *5* **Uncle John**[12] 3825 3-7-12 **61** ........ CCatlin 3 58
(SKirk) *trckd ldng pair: drvn 3f out: no imp 2f out: wknd fnl f* **5/1**

4120 **5** *dist* **Swainson (USA)**[22] 3543 3-9-7 **84** ........ DHolland 4 —
(PMitchell) *dwlt: a last and nvr gng wl: lost tch 4f out: t.o* **7/2**[3]

2m 33.57s (0.01) **Going Correction** +0.175s/f (Good) **5** Ran SP% **110.0**
Speed ratings: **106,102,102,99,**—CSF £29.59 TOTE £9.00: £3.40, £2.00; EX 33.50.
**Owner** Mrs Evelyn Hankinson **Bred** Miss K Rausing **Trained** Chaddleworth, Berks

**FOCUS**
Not a very competitive race, but at least the pace was decent.

**NOTEBOOK**
**Vinando**, not seen since finishing well behind Pukka in a decent Newbury handicap 71 days previously, left that form well behind in a first-time tongue-tie, posting a career-best effort. Lightly raced, he is open to even more improvement and will stay further.

**Soulacroix**, off the mark over ten furlongs at Brighton when last seen 268 days previously, proved no match for the winner in the closing stages. He failed to prove himself fully effective over this trip, but probably just needed this.

**Mazuna(IRE)**, in fine form since being stepped up to middle distances, looked to have every chance but finished quite tamely. She has won over an extended mile three so this trip should not really have been a problem.

**Uncle John**, a five-length second to the highly-progressive Elusive Dream over this trip at Brighton on his previous start, ran a long way below form.

**Swainson(USA)**, racing on fast ground for the first time, was never going and this was most disappointing. *Official explanation: jockey said colt was never travelling*

## 4168 OWEN BROWN MAIDEN FILLIES' STKS 1m (R)
**4:45** (4:48) (D) 3-Y-O **£5,460** (£1,680; £840; £420) **Stalls** High

Form RPR

**1** **Tarfah (USA)** 3-8-11 ........ SSanders 2 83
(GAButler) *rangy: scope: lw: hld up in last: prog 2f out: chsd ldr over 1f out: pushed into ld last 150yds: styd on wl* **5/1**[3]

03 **2** *¾* **Arctic Silk**[9] 3916 3-8-11 ........ (t) TEDurcan 9 81
(SaeedBinSuroor) *b.hind: led: rdn over 1f out: hdd and unable qck last 150yds* **11/4**[2]

4 **3** *5* **Merwaha (IRE)**[51] 2647 3-8-11 ........ RHills 5 70+
(MPTregoning) *lw: settled in 5th: prog to chse ldr 2f out to over 1f out: wknd ins fnl f* **11/8**[1]

0 **4** *4* **Niobe's Way**[18] 3630 3-8-11 ........ SDrowne 6 60
(PRChamings) *chsd ldr to 2f out: wknd* **16/1**

00 **5** *1 ¼* **Lady Taverner**[18] 3630 3-8-11 ........ JFEgan 7 57
(HJCyzer) *prom tl wknd u.p 2f out* **33/1**

**6** *1 ½* **Paintbox** 3-8-11 ........ RLMoore 1 54
(MrsAJPerrett) *neat: bit bkwd: t.k.h: racd wd: in tch: c wd bnd 3f out: sn wknd* **12/1**

1m 43.76s (0.72) **Going Correction** +0.175s/f (Good) **6** Ran SP% **102.0**
Speed ratings: **103,102,97,93,92 90**CSF £15.32 TOTE £6.80: £2.20, £1.80; EX 16.80 Place 6 £ 99.47, Place 5 £60.74..
**Owner** Abdulla Al Khalifa **Bred** Sheik A Bin I Alkhalifa **Trained** Blewbury, Oxon

**FOCUS**
Not a very competitive fillies' maiden and the form looks ordinary, although the front two did at least pull clear of the remainder.

**NOTEBOOK**
**Tarfah(USA)**, out of a useful eight to ten-furlong winner, did not go off unsupported and was good enough to make a winning debut. She showed a good attitude to see off the eventual runner-up and the pair pulled well clear. She is quite well thought of, but will not be rushed.

**Arctic Silk** is progressing with racing and posted a solid effort in defeat. She is nothing special, but should win her maiden.

**Merwaha(IRE)**, fourth in just a fair Goodwood maiden on her debut, failed to build on that effort and this has to be considered disappointing. This ground may have been fast enough for her.

**Niobe's Way** looks more a handicap type.

**Lady Taverner** is now qualified for a handicap mark.

T/Jkpt: Not won. T/Plt: £145.10 to a £1 stake. Pool: £89,648.25. 450.75 winning tickets. T/Qpdt: £40.00 to a £1 stake. Pool: £5,197.50. 96.15 winning tickets. JN

# 4086 NEWMARKET (JULY) (R-H)

Sunday, July 25

**OFFICIAL GOING: Good**

Steady rain before racing turned the ground to good.

Wind: Slight across Weather: Rain prior to racing giving way to cloud

## 4169 NSPCC EBF MAIDEN STKS — 7f

**2:40** (2:42) (D) 2-Y-O — **£4,888** (£1,504; £752; £376) **Stalls** Low

Form — RPR

1 **Oude (USA)** 2-9-0 ... LDettori 8 — 91
(SaeedBinSuroor) *gd sort: leggy: chsd ldrs: shkn up over 1f out: r.o to ld wl ins fnl f* **6/4**[1]

2 *nk* **Shannon Springs (IRE)** 2-9-0 ... MHills 12 — 91
(BWHills) *neat: chsd ldrs: led 2f out: rdn and hdd wl ins fnl f* **11/2**[2]

4 — 3 *3* **Kharish (IRE)**[15] [3726] 2-9-0 ... EAhern 2 — 83
(JNoseda) *lw: w ldr: rdn and ev ch over 1f out: styd on same pce* **6/4**[1]

4 *1 1/2* **Dahman** 2-9-0 ... KMcEvoy 5 — 79
(SaeedBinSuroor) *gd sort: lw: s.i.s: hld up: hdwy 3f out: rdn over 1f out: styd on same pce* **25/1**

5 *2* **Mutamaasek (USA)** 2-9-0 ... WSupple 11 — 74
(JLDunlop) *cmpt: bkwd: mid-div: hdwy 1/2-way: wknd over 1f out* **20/1**[3]

6 *hd* **Eltizaam (USA)** 2-9-0 ... NPollard 9 — 74
(EALDunlop) *gd sort: scope: s.s: hld up: styd on ins fnl f: nvr nr to chal* **33/1**

7 *3* **Sand Repeal (IRE)** 2-8-11 ... BReilly(3) 6 — 66
(MissJFeilden) *leggy: scope: chsd ldrs: rdn and ev ch 2f out: sn wknd* **100/1**

0 — 8 *1 1/4* **Rebel Rebel (IRE)**[8] [3946] 2-9-0 ... WRyan 4 — 63
(NACallaghan) *lw: hld up: a in rr* **28/1**

9 *hd* **Fu Manchu** 2-9-0 ... TPQueally 7 — 63
(DRLoder) *gd sort: leggy: hld up: a in rr* **20/1**[3]

10 *1/2* **Furl Away** 2-9-0 ... JQuinn 3 — 61
(JWPayne) *w'like: scope: hld up in tch: racd keenly: rdn over 2f out: sn wknd* **100/1**

0 — 11 *3* **Little Indy**[13] [3805] 2-9-0 ... IMongan 1 — 54
(RBrotherton) *led 5f: sn wknd* **100/1**

12 *nk* **Oneshottwolions (IRE)** 2-9-0 ... MTebbutt 10 — 53
(EALDunlop) *w'like: leggy: s.s: a bhd* **33/1**

1m 28.22s (1.45) **Going Correction** +0.075s/f (Good) — **12** Ran SP% **121.1**

Speed ratings: **94,93,90,88,86 86,82,81,80,80 76,76**CSF £10.24 TOTE £2.70: £1.30, £2.00, £1.20; EX 13.40.

**Owner** Godolphin **Bred** Darley And Stonerside Stable **Trained** Newmarket, Suffolk

**FOCUS**

A slow time, but there were some well-regarded types on show and the race should throw up winners.

**NOTEBOOK**

**Oude(USA)**, a half-brother to several winners in the USA, showed a smart turn of foot to win a shade cosily. A likeable sort, he is clearly open to plenty of improvement, and impressed leading layers sufficiently to give him a 25/1 quote for next year's Guineas.

**Shannon Springs(IRE)**, who is out of an unraced mare, turned in a solid effort from his wide draw and should have little trouble paying his way.

**Kharish(IRE)** had the edge in experience, but time may tell he was taking on two above-average colts.

**Dahman**, a half-brother to the useful State Dilemma as well as winning hurdler Brave Dane, was very green and can be expected to improve as he steps up in trip.

**Mutamaasek(USA)**, a brother to juvenile winner Madaeh was another who looked as though the experience would do him good.

**Eltizaam(USA)**, a half-brother to the top-class Harayir, as well as ten-furlong winners Min Ahraar and Nasaayem, shaped quite nicely under a considerate ride and can repay the kindness shown in due course.

**Oneshottwolions(IRE)** *Official explanation: jockey said colt gurgled and choked*

## 4170 RECTANGLE GROUP CLASSIFIED STKS — 1m 2f

**3:10** (3:12) (E) 3-Y-O — **£4,104** (£1,263; £631; £315) **Stalls** Centre

Form — RPR

0111 — 1 **Doctored**[11] [3852] 3-9-1 71 ... (b) KFallon 8 — 76
(PDEvans) *lw: hld up: hdwy 4f out: sn rdn: ev ch fr over 1f out: edgd rt ins fnl f: r.o to ld nr fin* **3/1**[1]

U012 — 2 *hd* **Hatch A Plan (IRE)**[16] [3706] 3-9-2 72 ... JQuinn 7 — 77
(RMBeckett) *hld up: hdwy and nt clr run over 1f out: swtchd rt: rdn to ld and hung lft ins fnl f: hdd nr fin* **9/2**[2]

2304 — 3 *4* **Magic Amigo**[6] [3981] 3-9-5 75 ... LDettori 1 — 78+
(JRJenkins) *a.p: rdn to ld over 1f out: hdd and hmpd ins fnl f: nt rcvr* **7/1**

0-53 — 4 *1 1/2* **Fort Churchill (IRE)**[53] [2595] 3-9-2 72 ... MHills 3 — 67
(MHTompkins) *lw: led 7f: edgd rt over 1f out: no ex* **11/2**[3]

0630 — 5 *1 1/2* **Bailaora (IRE)**[3] [4056] 3-9-2 72 ... (b) KMcEvoy 2 — 64
(BWDuke) *chsd ldr: led 3f out: rdn and hdd over 1f out: wknd ins fnl f* **25/1**

0050 — 6 *6* **Haydn (USA)**[25] [3428] 3-9-0 65 ... IMongan 5 — 50
(CNAllen) *hld up: racd keenly: rdn over 2f out: wknd over 1f out* **25/1**

50-0 — 7 *3 1/2* **Belisco (USA)**[89] [1683] 3-9-3 73 ... WSupple 6 — 47
(MrsAJPerrett) *lw hld up in tch: rdn and wknd over 1f out* **14/1**

-312 — 8 *1 3/4* **Munaawashat (IRE)**[26] [3397] 3-8-12 71 ... DarrenWilliams 4 — 38
(KRBurke) *swtg: trckd ldrs: plld hrd: rdn and wknd over 1f out* **3/1**[1]

2m 7.11s (0.65) **Going Correction** +0.075s/f (Good) — **8** Ran SP% **110.4**

Speed ratings: **100,99,96,95,94 89,86,85**CSF £15.38 TOTE £3.30: £1.50, £1.70, £1.70; EX 12.90.

**Owner** Treble Chance Partnership **Bred** Wickfield Farm Partnership **Trained** Pandy, Gwent

**FOCUS**

An ordinary contest with the field racing down the centre of the course once in line for home. There was plenty of trouble in the latter stages, but the form looks sound.

**NOTEBOOK**

**Doctored** has a willing attitude and is standing his racing well. Connections intend turning him out under a penalty at Nottingham later in the week.

**Hatch A Plan(IRE)**, even allowing for not having the best of runs, did not impress with his attitude and is clearly one to have reservations about.

**Magic Amigo** was still battling away when almost brought down by the winner and runner-up in the latter stages.

**Fort Churchill(IRE)** won the battle for the early lead, but was easily brushed aside when the race began in earnest.

**Bailaora(IRE)** had no excuses, he just was not good enough.

**Munaawashat(IRE)**could not get her own way in front and dropped away tamely in the dip.

## 4171 ATOS ORIGINS H'CAP — 1m

**3:45** (3:46) (C) (0-90,86) 3-Y-O — **£9,204** (£3,491; £1,745; £793) **Stalls** Low

Form — RPR

5-31 — 1 **Tableau (USA)**[55] [2519] 3-9-5 84 ... MHills 5 — 89
(BWHills) *lw: mde all: qcknd 3f out: rdn out* **10/1**

0441 — 2 *shd* **Momtic (IRE)**[18] [3631] 3-9-6 85 ... LDettori 6 — 90
(WJarvis) *lw: edgd rt s: chsd wnr: rdn over 1f out: edgd rt ins fnl f: r.o* **5/1**

3105 — 3 *3/4* **Alshawameq (IRE)**[17] [3671] 3-9-7 86 ... WSupple 2 — 92+
(JLDunlop) *hld up: hmpd over 1f out: nt clr run ins fnl f: r.o* **3/1**[2]

0034 — 4 *hd* **Ermine Grey**[30] [3280] 3-8-6 71 ... (v) PaulEddery 3 — 74
(DHaydnJones) *chsd ldrs: rdn over 2f out: hmpd over 1f out: styng on whn hmpd towards fin* **25/1**

2136 — 5 *1/2* **Maclean**[54] [2558] 3-8-12 77 ... (v[1]) KFallon 4 — 79
(SirMichaelStoute) *lw: hld up: hdwy and hung lft fr over 1f out: nt run on* **15/8**[1]

2511 — 6 *hd* **Hazewind**[8] [3949] 3-7-9 65 ... (vt) HayleyTurner(5) 1 — 66
(PDEvans) *chsd ldrs: rdn over 1f out: styd on* **7/2**[3]

1m 40.32s (-0.16) **Going Correction** +0.075s/f (Good) — **6** Ran SP% **111.6**

Speed ratings: **103,102,102,101,101 101**CSF £56.61 TOTE £9.20: £3.00, £2.30; EX 53.30.

**Owner** K Abdulla **Bred** Juddmonte Farms Inc **Trained** Lambourn, Berks

**FOCUS**

A competitive handicap, but the early pace was only steady and it turned into a three-furlong sprint.

**NOTEBOOK**

**Tableau(USA)**was in the right place in a steadily-run contest, and although the margin was only a narrow one, never really looked like getting beaten.

**Momtic(IRE)** stuck to his task well enough, but like several of these, would have preferred a stronger pace.

**Alshawameq(IRE)** did not have things go his way with the steady pace, and then almost getting knocked over by the errant Maclean.

**Ermine Grey** has yet to strike on turf, and the rain prior to racing was certainly in his favour. However, he was still going as well as any when almost knocked over by Maclean, not once, but twice.

**Maclean**, visored for the first time, has become disappointing and did everything but bark.

**Hazewind** was not disgraced in this much better contest, and back in his right grade is worthy of interest.

## 4172 BALLYGALLON STUD MEDIAN AUCTION MAIDEN STKS — 6f

**4:20** (4:21) (E) 2-Y-O — **£4,192** (£1,290; £645; £322) **Stalls** Low

Form — RPR

5 — 1 **Lubeck**[15] [3760] 2-9-0 ... TPQueally 8 — 79
(DRLoder) *mde all: rdn and edgd rt over 1f out: all out* **7/2**[2]

5 — 2 *nk* **Disguise**[13] [3808] 2-9-0 ... KFallon 2 — 78
(BWHills) *lw: chsd wnr: rdn over 1f out: r.o* **4/5**[1]

3 *nk* **Salinja (USA)** 2-9-0 ... WSupple 6 — 77
(MrsAJPerrett) *w'like: bit bkwd: chsd ldrs: rdn over 1f out: r.o* **7/1**[3]

4 *2 1/2* **Maneki Neko (IRE)** 2-9-0 ... LDettori 9 — 70
(MHTompkins) *cmpt: bkwd: mid-div: hdwy 1/2-way: rdn over 1f out: styd on same pce* **11/1**

5 *6* **Easy Mover (IRE)** 2-8-9 ... JQuinn 4 — 47
(RGuest) *w'like: scope: sn outpcd* **25/1**

5 — 6 *2 1/2* **Bespoke**[5] [4003] 2-9-0 ... JMackay 5 — 44
(SirMarkPrescott) *s.s: effrt 1/2-way: wknd 2f out* **12/1**

7 *2 1/2* **Lola Sapola (IRE)** 2-8-9 ... WRyan 3 — 32
(NACallaghan) *leggy: scope: lw: sn outpcd* **25/1**

8 *3 1/2* **Mambazo** 2-9-0 ... EAhern 1 — 26
(SCWilliams) *cmpt: scope: bkwd: s.s: hld up: wknd over 2f out* **33/1**

1m 14.77s (1.45) **Going Correction** +0.075s/f (Good) — **8** Ran SP% **116.9**

Speed ratings: **93,92,92,88,80 77,74,69**CSF £6.69 TOTE £4.90: £1.02, £1.50, £2.30; EX 7.50.

**Owner** Sheikh Mohammed **Bred** C J Mills **Trained** Newmarket, Suffolk

**FOCUS**

Another slowly-run contest with very few getting into it, but fairly decent maiden form nonetheless.

**NOTEBOOK**

**Lubeck** looked to have matters well in hand going into the dip, but he stuck his head in the air and had little to spare at the line. Whether it was greenness or temperament, we shall have to wait and see.

**Disguise** gave the impression another furlong would not come amiss.

**Salinja(USA)**, a half-brother to a sprint winner in the States, looked a little green and can only improve for the experience.

**Maneki Neko(IRE)**, an early foal, shaped with a degree of promise and looks as though he will appreciate an extra furlong in time.

## 4173 NSPCC FAMILY DAY RATED STKS (H'CAP) — 1m 2f

**4:55** (4:57) (C) (0-95,92) 3-Y-O+ — **£12,203** (£4,628; £2,314; £1,052) **Stalls** Centre

Form — RPR

2-10 — 1 **King Of Dreams (IRE)**[101] [1414] 3-8-9 89 ... SChin 1 — 103+
(MJohnston) *a.p: chsd ldr over 3f out: rdn to ld over 1f out: r.o* **16/1**

2231 — 2 *1 3/4* **Anna Pallida**[18] [3630] 3-8-1 81 ow1 ... WSupple 6 — 91+
(PWHarris) *hld up: hdwy over 2f out: rdn and ev ch over 1f out: edgd lft: styd on same pce* **5/1**[3]

1116 — 3 *1/2* **Polar Jem**[15] [3756] 4-9-8 92 ... AMcCarthy 2 — 95
(GGMargarson) *lw: led after 1f: rdn and hdd over 1f out: styd on* **5/2**[2]

3100 — 4 *3/4* **Credit (IRE)**[17] [3671] 3-8-5 85 ... JQuinn 8 — 87
(RHannon) *hld up in tch: rdn over 3f out: styd on same pce fnl f* **14/1**

41 — 5 *1/2* **Double Aspect (IRE)**[31] [3245] 3-8-8 88 ... KFallon 5 — 89
(SirMichaelStoute) *lw: hld up in tch: rdn over 1f out: styd on same pce* **9/4**[1]

4321 — 6 *29* **Barking Mad (USA)**[16] [3705] 6-9-0 84 ... IMongan 4 — 30
(MLWBell) *led 1f: chsd ldr to over 3f out: wknd over 2f out* **15/2**

1400 — 7 *dist* **Zero Tolerance (IRE)**[15] [3756] 4-9-6 90 ... EAhern 7 — —
(TDBarron) *lw: hld up: sn bhd* **6/1**

2m 4.77s (-1.69) **Going Correction** +0.075s/f (Good)

**WFA** 3 from 4yo+ 10lb — **7** Ran SP% **114.6**

Speed ratings: **109,107,107,106,106 83,—**CSF £92.76 CT £271.81 TOTE £13.80: £5.00, £2.60; EX 68.80.

**Owner** Saeed Buhaleeba **Bred** David Jamison Bloodstock And G Roddick **Trained** Middleham Moor, N Yorks

**FOCUS**

A competitive handicap run at a good pace.

**NOTEBOOK**

**King Of Dreams(IRE)**, who had returned sore after disappointing last time, appreciated this easier ground and won in the style of an improving colt.

**Anna Pallida** is a tough filly and was far from disgraced on this first venture into handicap company.

**Polar Jem** deserves plenty of credit for having set a searching gallop, and kept battling to the line.

**Credit(IRE)** stayed this longer trip well enough, he just needs a little respite from the Handicapper.

**Double Aspect(IRE)** lacked the experience of his rivals, but he will certainly have learnt plenty from this.
**Barking Mad(USA)** could never get to the front and dropped away tamely.
**Zero Tolerance(IRE)** was reported to have suffered with a slipped saddle. *Official explanation: jockey said saddle slipped*

## 4174 RICHARD WADDINGTON & SAINSBURY'S H'CAP 1m 6f 175y
5:25 (5:26) (D) (0-85,82) 3-Y-0+ £6,760 (£2,080; £1,040; £520) Stalls Centre

Form RPR
-000 **1** **High Action (USA)**[15] 3725 4-9-11 **82**....(t) KFallon 5 96+
(IanWilliams) *chsd ldrs: led 2f out: clr 1f out: styd on wl* **9/4**[1]
0460 **2** *5* **Dovedon Hero**[17] 3678 4-9-1 **72**....(b) MHills 6 77
(PJMcbride) *lw: hld up: hdwy over 2f out: styd on same pce fnl f* **8/1**
-000 **3** *nk* **Skye's Folly (USA)**[50] 2684 4-9-1 **72**.... KMcEvoy 3 76
(JGGiven) *lw: chsd ldrs: rdn over 2f out: styd ons ame pce fnl f* **14/1**
2216 **4** *nk* **Twofan (USA)**[23] 3485 3-8-8 **80**.... SChin 2 84
(MJohnston) *led: rdn and hdd 2f out: no ex fnl f* **4/1**[3]
3050 **5** *8* **The Ring (IRE)**[9] 3902 4-8-11 **68**.... LDettori 7 62
(MrsMReveley) *lw: hld up: hdwy over 2f out: wknd over 1f out* **3/1**[2]
/002 **6** *9* **Weet For Me**[15] 3733 8-9-3 **74**.... WSupple 4 56
(RHollinshead) *chsd ldr tl rdn over 2f out: wknd over 1f out* **11/1**
0200 **7** *nk* **King Flyer (IRE)**[18] 3644 8-9-6 **77**....(b) SWhitworth 1 59
(MissJFeilden) *hld up: rdn over 3f out: wknd 2f out* **6/1**

3m 9.72s (-1.04) **Going Correction** +0.075s/f (Good)
**WFA** 3 from 4yo+ 15lb **7** Ran SP% **116.2**
Speed ratings: **105,102,102,102,97 92,92**CSF £21.62 TOTE £3.40: £2.10, £3.00; EX 33.90 Place 6 £198.83, Place 5 £169.65.
**Owner** C N Barnes **Bred** Harold Harrison **Trained** Portway, Warwicks

**FOCUS**
An uncompetitive contest and the runners again came up the centre once in line for home.

**NOTEBOOK**
**High Action(USA)**, who did not quite last the two miles at Ascot, was more at home over this trip and won with plenty in hand. He has an entry in the Ebor, although he is far from certain to make the cut.
**Dovedon Hero** is probably better suited to a sounder surface.
**Skye's Folly(USA)**, 3lb lower than when last successful, had no excuses and looks to have something to prove now.
**Twofan(USA)** had no excuses, he just lacks a change of gear.
**The Ring(IRE)** appears to have two ways of running and is not one to rely on.
**Weet For Me** *Official explanation: trainer said gelding finished distressed*
T/Plt: £210.10 to a £1 stake. Pool: £51,490.60. 178.90 winning tickets. T/Qpdt: £60.70 to a £1 stake. Pool: £2,044.90. 24.90 winning tickets. CR

# [3918] PONTEFRACT (L-H)
Sunday, July 25

**OFFICIAL GOING: Good to firm**

## 4175 TOLENT CONSTRUCTION MAIDEN STKS 5f
2:15 (2:16) (D) 2-Y-0 £5,577 (£1,716; £858; £429) Stalls Low

Form RPR
43 **1** **Witchry**[56] 2502 2-9-0 .... PRobinson 6 84+
(MAJarvis) *trckd ldr: hdwy to ld appr last: sn clr* **1/4**[1]
**2** *4* **Graze On** 2-9-0 .... RWinston 10 70
(JJQuinn) *wnt rt s and bhd: hdwy 1/2-way: styd on wl fnl f* **25/1**
**3** *2 1/2* **Zomerlust** 2-9-0 .... JFanning 2 61
(JJQuinn) *chsd ldr: rdn along 2f out: styd on fnl f* **14/1**
**4** *1/2* **Harrys House** 2-9-0 .... PHanagan 5 60
(JJQuinn) *midfield: hdwy 2f out: styd on fnl f* **25/1**
002 **5** *nk* **Niteowl Lad (IRE)**[9] 3893 2-8-7 .... JDO'Reilly(7) 3 58
(JO'Reilly) *sn led: rdn along 2f out: sn hung rt: hdd over 1f out and sn wknd* **11/1**[2]
**6** *1 3/4* **Asadara** 2-8-2 .... SuzanneFrance(7) 1 47
(NBycroft) *s.i.s andbhd tl styd on appr last* **100/1**
**7** *1* **Tyrone Sam** 2-9-0 .... NCallan 4 49
(KARyan) *midfield: pushed along 1/2-way: nvr a factor* **12/1**[3]
50 **8** *3 1/2* **Waggledance (IRE)**[12] 3818 2-9-0 .... GParkin 8 37
(JSWainwright) *chsd ldng pair: wd st and grad wknd* **33/1**
0 **9** *3 1/2* **Eskdale (IRE)**[70] 2141 2-9-0 .... SRighton 9 24
(RFFisher) *sn outpcd and bhd fr 1/2-way* **66/1**
**10** *2* **Apetite** 2-8-7 .... AReilly(7) 7 17
(NBycroft) *s.i.s: a bhd* **100/1**

64.06 secs (0.26) **Going Correction** +0.125s/f (Good) **10** Ran SP% **116.8**
Speed ratings: **102,95,91,90,90 87,85,80,74,71**CSF £15.83 TOTE £1.30: £1.02, £3.10, £3.30; EX 9.20.
**Owner** Sheikh Mohammed **Bred** Darley **Trained** Newmarket, Suffolk

**FOCUS**
A smart winning time for the grade, but nonetheless this was not a strong maiden and Witchry faced a simple task in bidding to lose his maiden tag.

**NOTEBOOK**
**Witchry** was turned over at odds on when last seen back in May - his jockey reporting him to be very coltish - and as a result he had been gelded. It seemed to do the trick and, although not having to beat anything of note, he did it well enough in the end. The step back up to six furlongs will suit now and he is likely to pay his way in nurseries.
**Graze On** was only a cheap purchase, but he shaped with promise on this racecourse debut, faring best of the Quinn trio. Six furlongs will suit and he does not need to improve a great deal to win an ordinary maiden.
**Zomerlust** is related to some smart performers - In The Groove and Harmonic Way - and he shaped with enough promise to suggest he can sneak a weak race.
**Harrys House** came off third best of the Quinn trio but did not run without hope for the future, staying on to claim fourth.
**Niteowl Lad(IRE)** needs a drop into claiming or selling company if he is to win a race.
**Tyrone Sam**, a 34,000 gns purchase, should be capable of better in time.
**Waggledance(IRE)** *Official explanation: jockey said bit slipped*

## 4176 L & J WINDOWS CLASSIFIED STKS 1m 4f 8y
2:50 (2:51) (D) 3-Y-0+ £5,421 (£1,668; £834; £417) Stalls Low

Form RPR
0512 **1** **Astrocharm (IRE)**[17] 3678 5-9-5 83.... PRobinson 5 96+
(MHTompkins) *in tch: pushed along over 3f out: gd hdwy 2f out: led over 1f out and sn clr* **6/4**[1]
-411 **2** *4* **Bendarshaan**[8] 3947 4-9-12 87.... RFfrench 1 92
(MJohnston) *trckd ldng pair: hdwy to ld 3f out: rdn and hdd over 1f out sn btn* **2/1**[2]
4210 **3** *9* **Horner (USA)**[32] 3210 3-8-4 82....(b[1]) NDeSouza(5) 6 73
(PFICole) *led: rdn along 4f out: hdd 3f out and sn wknd* **15/2**
00-0 **4** *14* **Fourth Dimension (IRE)**[16] 3716 5-9-8 83.... AlexGreaves 2 51
(DNicholls) *sn trcking ldr: hdwy to chal 4f out: rdn 3f out and sn btn* **7/1**[3]
0540 **5** *dist* **Qudrah (IRE)**[8] 3944 4-9-7 85.... JCarroll 3 —
(EJO'Neill) *reminders sn after s: in tch tl rdn along 1/2-way: sn lost tch and bhd* **25/1**
10-0 **R** **Conquering Love (IRE)**[16] 3716 6-9-5 83.... THamilton(3) 4 —
(BEllison) *drvn fr s and ref to r after 100 yds* **10/1**

2m 40.94s (0.89) **Going Correction** +0.125s/f (Good)
**WFA** 3 from 4yo+ 12lb **6** Ran SP% **110.5**
Speed ratings: **102,99,93,84,—** —CSF £4.55 TOTE £2.10: £1.10, £1.80; EX 3.00.
**Owner** Mystic Meg Limited **Bred** Miss D J Merson **Trained** Newmarket, Suffolk

**FOCUS**
This featured two progressive handicappers and the pair filled the first two placings, with Astrocharm coming out on top.

**NOTEBOOK**
**Astrocharm(IRE)** came into this on the back of a good second in a Newmarket handicap that is working out well - the third placed horse Always Waining won the last at Ascot the previous day - and once coming through to take it up, stayed on strongly to win as she pleased. She is in tremendous form and should go close to following up.
**Bendarshaan** showed an improvement in form for the step up to a mile seven when winning at Newmarket and was unsuited by this drop in trip. When stepping up to two miles he will be winning again.
**Horner(USA)** was done no favours by the first-time blinkers and was readily passed.
**Qudrah(IRE)** *Official explanation: jockey said filly hung right throughout*

## 4177 GRAHAM ROCK MEMORIAL H'CAP 1m 2f 6y
3:20 (3:20) (D) (0-85,81) 3-Y-0 £6,825 (£2,100; £1,050; £525) Stalls Low

Form RPR
0013 **1** **Mr Tambourine Man (IRE)**[24] 3442 3-9-2 **81**.... NDeSouza(5) 3 87
(PFICole) *led: rdn along over 2f out: drvn and hdd over 1f out: rallied u.str driving to ld wl ins last: jst hld on* **6/4**[1]
0000 **2** *hd* **Royal Distant (USA)**[23] 3473 3-8-5 **65**.... DaleGibson 1 70
(MWEasterby) *in tch and pushed along 1/2-way: rdn and hdwy 2f out: drvn and styd on wl fnl f: jst failed* **16/1**
2364 **3** *shd* **Tytheknot**[22] 3535 3-8-12 **72**.... PHanagan 5 77
(JeddO'Keeffe) *trckd wnr: hdwy 3f out: rdn to ld over 1f out: drvn and hdd wl ins last: no ex nr fin* **5/1**[3]
3052 **4** *8* **Third Empire**[9] 3897 3-8-7 **67**.... RWinston 4 57
(CGrant) *chsd ldng pair: ridden along over 4f out: wknd wl over 2f out* **5/1**[3]
-030 **5** *7* **Whispered Promises (USA)**[17] 3678 3-9-6 **80**....(b[1]) RFfrench 2 57
(MJohnston) *chsd ldrs: drvn along bef 1/2-way: sn outpcd and bhd* **5/2**[2]

2m 16.18s (2.27) **Going Correction** +0.125s/f (Good) **5** Ran SP% **107.8**
Speed ratings: **95,94,94,88,82**CSF £22.01 TOTE £1.90: £1.20, £4.50; EX 21.70.
**Owner** C Wright & The Hon Mrs J M Corbett **Bred** Stratford Place Stud **Trained** Whatcombe, Oxon

**FOCUS**
An average heat that saw a thrilling finish, but it produced a modest winning time for the grade.

**NOTEBOOK**
**Mr Tambourine Man(IRE)** rallied gamely once headed and stuck his head out to get back up on the line. He may not have been best suited to making the early running, on this evidence will stay further and could be a bit better than the bare form suggests.
**Royal Distant(USA)** went down fighting and ran by far her best race for current connections. This was close to the form she showed as a juvenile for John Gosden last year, and she can be placed to advantage off this mark by her shrewd stable.
**Tytheknot** could not find any more after making a bold bid for home entering the last furlong. This was another solid effort, he was suited by this faster surface and will find a race if able maintain this form.
**Third Empire** ran disappointingly, dropping away without putting up any sort of fight.
**Whispered Promises(USA)**, tried in the first-time blinkers, showed little over this shorter trip but it will all fall back into place one day and he is not one to give up on yet.

## 4178 POMFRET RATED STKS (H'CAP) 1m 4y
3:55 (3:55) (B) (0-100,100) 3-Y-0+ £12,069 (£4,578; £2,289; £1,040) Stalls Low

Form RPR
3000 **1** **Wing Commander**[15] 3756 5-8-11 **90**.... PHanagan 5 102
(RAFahey) *trckd ldrs: hdwy to c hallenge over 1f out: rdn to ld ins last: styd on wl* **11/2**[3]
5302 **2** *3* **Vicious Warrior**[6] 3977 5-8-7 **86**.... DeanMcKeown 10 91
(RMWhitaker) *chsd ldr: hdwy to ld 2f out: sn rdn: hdd ins last and kpt on same pce* **8/1**
0020 **3** *3/4* **Calcutta**[22] 3539 8-9-4 **97**.... PRobinson 2 100
(BWHills) *hld up in tch: effrt and nt clr run 2f out: hdwy over 1f out: sn rdn and kpt on ins last* **9/1**
1062 **4** *2* **Flighty Fellow (IRE)**[16] 3717 4-9-1 **94**.... DAllan 6 93
(TDEasterby) *hld up: hdwy 3f out: rdn and edgd lft wl over 1f out: drvn and kpt on same pce aproachinglast* **10/1**
1303 **5** *nk* **Penrith (FR)**[6] 3977 3-8-1 **88**.... JFanning 7 86
(MJohnston) *hld up in rr: hdwy whn nt clr run over 2f out and again over 1f out: sn rdn and kpt on: nt rch ldrs* **10/3**[2]
0025 **6** *1 3/4* **Cripsey Brook**[29] 3299 6-8-8 **87**.... KimTinkler 1 81
(DonEnricoIncisa) *hld up and bhd: hdwy over 1f out: rdn and kpt on ins last: nvr nr ldrs* **20/1**
0011 **7** *2* **Everest (IRE)**[8] 3937 7-8-4 **86**.... TEaves(3) 8 75
(BEllison) *hld up in rr: hdwy whn n.m.r over 2f out: rdn wl over 1f out: no imp* **5/2**[1]
002- **8** *6* **Roskilde (IRE)**[374] 3342 4-9-7 **100**.... ACulhane 9 76
(MRChannon) *chsd ldrs: rdn along 3f out: drvn and wknd 2f out* **14/1**
5310 **9** *3* **Little Venice (IRE)**[19] 3597 4-8-4 **86**.... LisaJones(3) 3 55
(CFWall) *hld up: rdn along 3f out: hdd 2f out and sn wknd* **28/1**
0000 **10** *13* **Tough Love**[85] 1773 5-8-7 **86**.... RWinston 4 25
(TDEasterby) *hld up towards rr: swtchd rt and rdn wl over 2f out: sn btn* **12/1**

1m 45.2s (-0.40) **Going Correction** +0.125s/f (Good)
**WFA** 3 from 4yo+ 8lb **10** Ran SP% **119.8**
Speed ratings: **107,104,103,101,100 99,97,91,88,75**CSF £50.48 CT £405.23 TOTE £7.00: £2.00, £3.60, £3.30; EX 81.00.
**Owner** Steve Ryan **Bred** P And Mrs Venner **Trained** Musley Bank, N Yorks

**FOCUS**
A welcome win for Wing Commander.

**NOTEBOOK**
**Wing Commander** was winning his first race since his maiden back in 2001 and it was a deserved victory at that. He has run many good races in defeat - his staying on eighth in the John Smith's last time being a prime example - and, now he has got his head in front again, may be capable of improving further.

**Vicious Warrior** could not confirm York form with the winner from 2lb worse terms, but ran well nonetheless. He has been in good form and is threatening to get his head in front again.
**Calcutta** was unsuited by the ease in the going at Sandown recently, and this a better effort. He was slightly unlucky not to finish closer and is on a winning mark.
**Flighty Fellow(IRE)** stayed on from off the pace to claim third, but was never getting there quick enough.
**Penrith(FR)**, although slightly unlucky again, has not gone on from his seasonal reappearance success and is becoming a little disappointing. He has been held up in his races of late and it will be interesting to see him back front-running - he made all when winning on his sole start at two.
**Everest(IRE)** saw his good recent run come to an end off a career-high mark. He did not get the breaks this time and is better suited to a bigger field over a straight mile.

## 4179 TOTEPLACEPOT H'CAP — 6f
**4:30** (4:30) (C ) (0-90,90) 3-Y-0+ — **£9,326** (£3,537; £1,768; £804) **Stalls** Low

Form — RPR
0444 **1** — **Undeterred**[19] 3606 8-8-8 **70** ... NCallan 8 — 81
(TDBarron) *trckd ldrs: hdwy 2f out: rdn to ld 1f out: edgd rt ins last: hld on* — **5/1**[2]
2400 **2** ½ **Legal Set (IRE)**[1] 4130 8-7-7 **60** ... (t) DFox(5) 2 — 69
(MissAStokell) *trckd ldrs on inner: nt clr run and swtchd rt 1f out: rdn and styd on wl fnl f* — **20/1**
4104 **3** 1 ¼ **Cd Flyer (IRE)**[15] 3755 7-9-6 **87** ... PMulrennan(5) 1 — 92
(BEllison) *hld up: hdwy 2f out: rdn and styd on fnl f* — **6/1**[3]
4112 **4** 1 ¼ **Never Without Me**[10] 3887 4-7-10 **61** ... JFMcDonald(3) 4 — 63
(JFCoupland) *cl up: led 2f out: rdn and hdd 1f out: wknd ins last* — **5/1**[2]
1003 **5** 2 ½ **H Harrison (IRE)**[24] 3440 4-9-5 **81** ... RFfrench 3 — 75
(IWMcinnes) *led: rdn along and hdd 2f out: sn wknd* — **10/1**
3223 **6** nk **Time N Time Again**[14] 3778 6-8-7 **69** ... (p) DAllan 6 — 62
(EJAlston) *s.i.s and in rr: hdwy wl over 1f out: sn rdn and no imp* — **5/1**[2]
0000 **7** 5 **Hit's Only Money (IRE)**[31] 3235 4-10-0 **90** ... DeanMcKeown 7 — 68
(PABlockley) *cl up: rdn along over 2f out and sn wknd* — **4/1**[1]
0051 **8** ½ **Marshallspark (IRE)**[10] 3887 5-8-4 **66** ... PHanagan 5 — 43
(RAFahey) *trckd ldrs: effrt 2f out: sn rdn and wknd* — **5/1**[2]

1m 16.86s (-0.44) **Going Correction** +0.125s/f (Good) — **8** Ran SP% **114.8**
Speed ratings: **107,106,104,103,99 99,92,91**CSF £94.17 CT £616.81 TOTE £6.30: £2.20, £4.60, £2.90; EX 69.60.
**Owner** P D Savill **Bred** Deerfield Farm **Trained** Maunby, N Yorks

**FOCUS**
Not the strongest of Class C handicaps.

**NOTEBOOK**
**Undeterred** is back on a good mark and took advantage of it with a game victory. He is still capable of winning decent races and should not go up much for this.
**Legal Set(IRE)** has had a busy time of it this season but takes his racing extremely well and bounced right back to something like his best after a couple of below par efforts. He should continue to pay his way.
**Cd Flyer(IRE)** has been in good form but is still 4lb higher than when last winning and may need to drop a couple of pound before scoring again.
**Never Without Me** has yet to win on turf but was a little disappointing nonetheless, fading under pressure late on.
**H Harrison(IRE)** is better over seven furlongs and could not go the pace when it quickened up.
**Hit's Only Money(IRE)** remains a long way below his best.

## 4180 SUNDAY FUNDAY MAIDEN STKS — 1m 4y
**5:05** (5:06) (D ) 3-Y-0 — **£5,460** (£1,680; £840; £420) **Stalls** Low

Form — RPR
0 **1** — **Choir Leader**[92] 1612 3-9-0 ... SWKelly 7 — 97+
(WJHaggas) *mde all: qcknd clr 2f out: unchal* — **10/11**[1]
00 **2** 9 **Killmorey**[57] 2479 3-9-0 ... RFfrench 6 — 68+
(SCWilliams) *chsd ldrs: rdn along over 3f out: drvn and no ch w wnr fnl 2f* — **4/1**[2]
-050 **3** 4 **Speed Racer**[18] 3624 3-8-9 55 ... KimTinkler 9 — 54
(DonEnricoIncisa) *chsd ldng pair: rdn along over 3f out: kpt on same pce* — **25/1**
5 **4** ½ **Kyber**[18] 3625 3-9-0 ... RWinston 1 — 58?
(RFFisher) *bhd: hdwy 3f out: rdn along and kpt on fnl 2f* — **25/1**
00 **5** shd **Dalmarnock (IRE)**[33] 3168 3-9-0 ... FLynch 8 — 58?
(BSmart) *chsd ldrs: rdn along 4f out: drvn and plugged ons ame pce fnl 2f* — **20/1**
**6** 4 **Mount Cottage** 3-8-9 ... ACulhane 2 — 43
(JGGiven) *in tch: hdwy 3f out: rdn along and btn 2f out* — **13/2**[3]
3 **7** 26 **Banana Grove (IRE)**[10] 3878 3-8-9 ... PPMathers(5) 3 — —
(ABerry) *s.i.s: a bhd* — **7/1**
-006 **8** dist **Kalush**[42] 2906 3-9-0 58 ... NCallan 5 — —
(RonaldThompson) *chsd wnr: rdn along over 3f out and sn wknd* — **16/1**
**9** 20 **Mardonicdeclare** 3-9-0 ... GParkin 4 — —
(PSFelgate) *sn outpcd and wl bhd fr 1/2-way* — **40/1**

1m 46.7s (1.10) **Going Correction** +0.125s/f (Good) — **9** Ran SP% **119.0**
Speed ratings: **99,90,86,85,85 81,55,—,—**CSF £4.58 TOTE £2.00: £1.10, £1.40, £6.80; EX 7.00.
**Owner** Cheveley Park Stud **Bred** Cheveley Park Stud Ltd **Trained** Newmarket, Suffolk

**FOCUS**
A shocking event and it would be unwise to get carried away with the winner's performance, but the Handicapper may not go overboard as a result.

**NOTEBOOK**
**Choir Leader** was a bitter disappointment on his debut back in April - being beaten 25 lengths - and showed his true colours here, making all and powering away to win easily. It was a poor affair but he could do no more than win the way he did and it will be interesting to see what he turns up in next.
**Killmorey**, although finishing second, probably did not improve on previous form but is now qualified for handicaps and better can be expected when he makes the transition.
**Speed Racer** is poor and does nothing for the form.
**Kyber** is unlikely to be seen to best effect until running in staying handicaps.
**Dalmarnock(IRE)** can now run in low-grade handicaps.
**Mount Cottage** is clearly a horse of modest ability.
**Kalush** *Official explanation: jockey said gelding moved badly throughout*

## 4181 FAMILY DAY H'CAP — 5f
**5:40** (5:40) (E ) (0-70,70) 3-Y-0+ — **£4,260** (£1,311; £655; £327) **Stalls** Low

Form — RPR
0005 **1** — **Ballybunion (IRE)**[4] 4013 5-8-7 **49** ... JFanning 5 — 61
(DNicholls) *trckd ldrs: hdwy wl over 1f out: rdn ent last: styd on to ld last 50 yds* — **7/2**[1]
0424 **2** ½ **Blue Maeve**[22] 3511 4-8-9 **51** ... SRighton 4 — 61
(JHetherton) *led: pushed along and hdd over 2f out: rdn to ld over 1f out: drvn ins last: hdd and no ex last 100 yds* — **16/1**
3003 **3** ¾ **Tantric**[9] 3923 5-8-8 **57** ow2 ... JDO'Reilly(7) 2 — 64+
(JO'Reilly) *in tch: hdwy on inner 2f out: effrt and n.m.r over 1f out:# sn rdn and styd on ins last: nrest fi nish* — **14/1**
-100 **4** ½ **Molotov**[34] 3151 4-7-10 **45** ... NataliaGemelova(7) 13 — 50
(IWMcinnes) *cl up: led over 2f out tl rdn and hdd over 1f out: drvn: edgd rt and one pce ins last* — **40/1**
3541 **5** nk **Blessed Place**[13] 3810 4-8-9 **51** ... (t) PHanagan 7 — 55
(DJSFfrenchDavis) *chsd ldrs: rdn wl over 1f out: drvn and hld whn carried rt ins last* — **8/1**[3]
5250 **6** ½ **Laurel Dawn**[9] 3920 6-9-2 **61** ... JFMcDonald(3) 6 — 63
(IWMcinnes) *in tch: hdwy and n.m.r over 1f out: swtchd rt ent last and styd on wl towards fin* — **15/2**[2]
0004 **7** 1 **Port St Charles (IRE)**[11] 3836 7-8-11 **58** ... RThomas(5) 10 — 56
(CRDore) *towards rr: hdwy wl over 1f out: sn rdn and kpt on ins last nrst fin* — **25/1**
0651 **8** ½ **Le Meridien (IRE)**[2] 4104 6-8-13 **55** 6ex ... (p) RWinston 3 — 51
(JSWainwright) *bhd: hdwy wl over 1f out: sn rdn and kpt on ins last: nrst fin* — **9/1**
0510 **9** hd **Fairgame Man**[9] 3894 6-8-5 **47** ... (p) GParkin 15 — 42
(JSWainwright) *in tch: rdn along wl over 1f out and sn one pce* — **10/1**
0255 **10** 2 **Brigadier Monty (IRE)**[13] 3810 6-8-11 **53** ... ACulhane 8 — 40
(MrsSLamyman) *bhd tl sme late hdwy* — **10/1**
0002 **11** ½ **Rectangle (IRE)**[9] 3923 4-9-11 **67** ... AlexGreaves 17 — 52+
(DNicholls) *prom on outer: rdn along 2f out: grad wknd* — **10/1**
0000 **12** 1 ¾ **Arctic Burst (USA)**[2] 4085 4-8-13 **55** ... (v) NCallan 1 — 33
(DShaw) *bhd tl sme hdwy on inner 2f out: rdn over 1f out and no imp* — **50/1**
0020 **13** 2 **One Last Time**[35] 3126 4-9-4 **60** ... RFfrench 12 — 30
(RBastiman) *stdd and swtchd lft s: a rr* — **20/1**
3504 **14** hd **Fox Covert (IRE)**[10] 3877 3-8-10 **56** ... FLynch 18 — 25
(DWBarker) *racd wd: in tch tl rdn and wknd 2f out* — **33/1**
3620 **15** shd **Law Maker**[4] 4034 4-8-6 **48** ... (v) JBramhill 9 — 17
(MABuckley) *in tch: rdn along over 2f out: sn wknd* — **33/1**
1405 **16** 3 ½ **Game Flora**[18] 3624 3-8-5 **54** ... TEaves(3) 16 — 9
(MESowersby) *in tch on outer: rdn along 1/2-way: sn wknd* — **66/1**
2100 **17** ¾ **Flying Tackle**[9] 3894 6-8-9 **51** ... (p) SWKelly 14 — 3
(MDods) *a towards rr* — **20/1**
0001 **18** 3 ½ **Izmail (IRE)**[9] 3894 5-9-9 **70** ... LTreadwell(5) 11 — 8
(DNicholls) *prom: pushed along 1/2-way: sn wknd* — **11/1**

63.31 secs (-0.49) **Going Correction** +0.125s/f (Good)
**WFA** 3 from 4yo+ 4lb — **18** Ran SP% **128.4**
Speed ratings: **108,107,106,105,104 103,102,101,101,98 97,94,91,90,90 85,83,78**CSF £60.35 CT £541.11 TOTE £5.10: £1.70, £3.70, £2.60, £9.80; EX 88.20 Place 6 £42.80, Place 5 £35.80..
**Owner** I Blakey, M Gosse, D Nicholls **Bred** La Pescaia S A S Di Miuta Pontello **Trained** Sessay, N Yorks

**FOCUS**
A decent winning time for the grade. Those who raced up with the pace were at an advantage here and nothing really got into it that raced from off the pace.

**NOTEBOOK**
**Ballybunion(IRE)** was last successful in a handicap off 62 and was racing here off a 13lb lower mark. He had an ideal run through and stayed on strongly. He is more than capable of winning again, and it will be interesting to see where he turns up next.
**Blue Maeve** remains a maiden but ran arguably his best race, battling away strongly to get back into the lead before the winner swooped. His winning turn is not far off.
**Tantric** is coming right back to form and it will not be long before he is winning again.
**Molotov** ran better than his price entitled him to from a moderate draw and it was only in the final furlong he cried enough. This was far and away his best effort for a long time, but the way the race panned out seemed to suit those who raced prominently.
**Blessed Place** was unable to supplement his Windsor win off a 4lb higher mark.
**Laurel Dawn** did not get the clearest of runs and was unlucky not to finish closer.
**Le Meridien(IRE)** was doing her best work at the death having been off the pace.
**Rectangle(IRE)** ran disappointingly having come back to form at the course earlier in the month, but is ideally suited by a little cut in the ground and is worth looking out for when getting his toe in.
**Arctic Burst(USA)** *Official explanation: jockey said gelding lost a front shoe*
**Izmail(IRE)** reportedly ran 'flat' and can be given another chance. *Official explanation: jockey said gelding ran flat*
T/Plt: £61.80 to a £1 stake. Pool: £38,078.60. 449.40 winning tickets. T/Qpdt: £26.20 to a £1 stake. Pool: £1,921.70. 54.25 winning tickets. JR

# 1983 DUSSELDORF (R-H)
Sunday, July 25

**OFFICIAL GOING: Soft**

## 4183a WEST LB DEUTSCHLANDPREIS (GROUP 1) — 1m 4f
**3:45** (3:49) 3-Y-0+ — **£63,380** (£24,648; £11,972; £5,986)

RPR
**1** — **Albanova**[273] 5782 5-9-2 ... THellier 6 — 111
(SirMarkPrescott) *always in touch, 3rd on inside straight, soon went 2nd, hard ridden over 1f out, driven to lead well inside final f, ran on* — **114/10**
**2** nk **Dayano (GER)**[21] 3565 3-8-6 ... AStarke 4 — 113
(AWohler, Germany) *always close up, 4th on outside straight, ran on under pressure to take 2nd close home* — **59/10**
**3** ¾ **Rotteck (GER)**[28] 3357 4-9-6 ... JPalik 1 — 114
(HSteguweit, Germany) *led, hard ridden & 2l up over 1f out, caught well inside final f, no extra* — **42/10**[2]
**4** 2 ½ **El Tiger (GER)**[21] 3565 3-8-6 ... ASuborics 3 — 108
(PSchiergen, Germany) *held up, 6th straight, driven to go 4th over 1f out, kept on one pace* — **51/10**[3]
**5** 2 ½ **Brian Boru**[38] 2998 4-9-6 ... JPSpencer 7 — 106
(APO'Brien, Ire) *pressed leader, 2nd straight, ridden & beaten well over 1f out* — **11/10**[1]
**6** 5 **La Ina (GER)**[49] 2723 3-8-1 ... WMLordan 5 — 92
(ATrybuhl, Germany) *held up, last straight, always behind* — **42/10**[2]
**7** 14 **Senex (GER)**[35] 3136 4-9-6 ... WMongil 9 — 78
(HBlume, Germany) *held up, headway to go 3rd 4f out, 5th straight, soon weakened* — **106/10**

2m 33.29s
**WFA** 3 from 4yo+ 12lb — **7** Ran SP% **133.7**
Speed ratings: .
**Owner** Miss K Rausing **Bred** Miss K Rausing **Trained** Newmarket, Suffolk

**NOTEBOOK**
**Albanova** will have delighted connections with this win. Ground conditions came in her favour, and she looked slightly overpriced considering she had won first time out for the previous three years.
**Dayano(GER)** was best performer of the trio of three-year-olds on the day. On this evidence he will struggle to top this effort in all aged company.
**Rotteck(GER)** in good form of late, was a reluctant leader but turned in another good effort. He should continue in this vein for a while yet.
**Brian Boru** must be considered very disappointing. He boasted the best form coming into the race, and this looked an ideal opportunity, but he failed to fire.

## 3963 MAISONS-LAFFITTE (R-H)
Sunday, July 25

**OFFICIAL GOING: Good**

### 4184a PRIX ROBERT PAPIN (GROUP 2) (C&F) 5f 110y
2:15 (2:14) 2-Y-0 £42,148 (£16,268; £7,764; £5,176)

RPR
1 **Divine Proportions (USA)**[27] [3388] 2-8-13 C-PLemaire 4 103+
(PBary, France) *close 3rd on outside, driven to lead just inside final f, pushed out* 1
2 1 **Shifting Place**[28] [3362] 2-8-13 DVargiu 6 100
(RMenichetti, Italy) *led, ridden & hung right well over 1f out, headed just inside final f, kept on same pace*
3 ¾ **Portrayal (USA)**[13] 2-8-13 GaryStevens 7 97
(AFabre, France) *closed up to track winner on outside after 2f, ridden over 1f out, one pace* 2
4 nse **Great Blood (FR)**[27] [3388] 2-8-13 OPeslier 2 97
(XThomas-Demeaulte, France) *raced on rails, pressed leader, every chance well over 1f out, soon outpaced, rallied under pressure closing stages* 3
5 1 **Salut Thomas (FR)**[27] [3388] 2-9-2 (b) CSoumillon 3 97
(RobertCollet, France) *close up til outpaced well over 1f out*
6 2½ **Sunny Sky (FR)**[34] 2-9-2 TThulliez 1 88
(MZilber, France) *close up on rails til weakened 2f out*
7 1½ **Molto Bello (USA)**[27] 2-9-2 DBoeuf 8 83
(YDeNicolay, France) *always outpaced*
8 3 **Gold Marie (IRE)**[28] [3362] 2-8-13 MDemuro 5 69
(BGrizzetti, Italy) *always outpaced*
64.80 secs **Going Correction** -0.125s/f (Firm) 8 Ran SP% **116.5**
Speed ratings: **105,103,102,102,101 97,95,91.**
**Owner** Niarchos Family **Bred** Flaxman Holding Ltd **Trained** France

**NOTEBOOK**
**Divine Proportions(USA)**, who needed a few smacks from her jockey a furlong and a half out, quickened up well and dominated the latter stages of this Group Two event. She is now unbeaten in three races and is improving with every outing. She will now take on an international field in the Prix Morny, and the extra half furlong in the race will be an advantage.
**Shifting Place** looked very well in the paddock. Smartly into her stride, she led from the start and looked the likely winner at the furlong marker, but she could not quicken in the latter stages and was caught by the odds-on favourite. It was a decent effort from this Italian filly and her jockey felt that she is still learning the game.
**Portrayal(USA)** could not quicken when things warmed up a furlong and a half out. Nevertheless, she stayed on well and is certain to be suited by a longer trip in the future. A Group event looks within her grasp later in the season.
**Great Blood(FR)** was one of the leaders and was still well there at the furlong marker, but her stamina gradually ran out and she was just pipped for third place on the line. A game little filly, she is now finding the competition a little warm after an excellent start to the season.

## 4093 SOUTHWELL (L-H)
Monday, July 26

**OFFICIAL GOING: Standard**
Race times suggested the track was riding fast. The inside of the track seemed to be riding slower and it was hard to make up ground from off the pace.
Wind: nil Weather: fine becoming sunny

### 4185 AT THE RACES COMMITTED TO RACING CLAIMING STKS 6f (F)
2:45 (2:47) (F) 3-Y-0+ £3,073 (£878; £439) Stalls Low

Form RPR
6500 1 **Branston Tiger**[15] [3779] 5-9-4 62 (b) SSanders 10 61
(JGGiven) *mid-div: rdn and hdwy on outside over 2f out: led 1f out: r.o* 4/1[1]
0040 2 1 **Travelling Times**[16] [3735] 5-9-0 40 (v) DAllan 11 54?
(JSWainwright) *chsd ldrs: sn rdn along: ev ch 1f out: nt qckn* 50/1
1343 3 1 **On The Trail**[13] [3820] 7-9-0 56 ACulhane 12 51
(DWChapman) *hld up in tch: rdn and ev ch 1f out: no ex towards fin* 9/2[2]
1632 4 nk **Mallia**[20] [3616] 11-8-3 46 PMakin(5) 9 44
(TDBarron) *s.i.s: sn mid-div: rdn and hdwy over 2f out: one pce fnl f* 5/1[3]
4004 5 1¾ **Bond Shakira**[14] [3801] 3-8-4 49 FNorton 5 40
(BSmart) *led: rdn and hdd 1f out: wknd ins fnl f* 20/1
0000 6 ¾ **Wilson Bluebottle (IRE)**[6] [4005] 5-8-12 48 (b) DaleGibson 13 41
(MWEasterby) *bhd tl hdwy fnl f: nvr nrr* 20/1
0120 7 nk **Cornwallis**[21] [3589] 3-8-4 57 HayleyTurner(5) 8 42
(JSKing) *chsd ldrs: sn rdn along: wknd fnl f* 11/2
6500 8 3½ **Spy Master**[16] [3742] 6-8-3 31 ow2 (tp) DTudhope(7) 2 27
(JParkes) *bhd: sme hdwy on ins 2f out: n.d* 66/1
0-40 9 ½ **High Esteem**[181] [612] 8-8-12 53 (vt[1]) VSlattery 4 28
(MABuckley) *w ldr: rdn and ev ch 2f out: wknd jst over 1f out* 33/1
0000 10 shd **Its Ecco Boy**[11] [3887] 6-8-12 55 RWinston 6 27
(PHowling) *mid-div: pushed along over 3f out: sn lost pl* 9/1
0004 11 ½ **Confuzed**[7] [3991] 4-8-12 43 (e) SWhitworth 7 26
(DFlood) *s.i.s: a bhd* 20/1
0003 12 ½ **Pedro Jack (IRE)**[31] [3260] 7-9-3 70 PMulrennan(5) 3 34
(MABuckley) *s.i.s: a bhd* 8/1
6000 13 2½ **Second Minister**[5] [4026] 5-9-9 55 (b) LPKeniry(3) 1 31
(DFlood) *dwlt: a in rr* 25/1
1m 15.64s (-1.26) **Going Correction** -0.25s/f (Stan) 13 Ran SP% **115.9**
**WFA** 3 from 4yo+ 5lb
Speed ratings: **98,96,95,94,92 91,91,86,85,85 85,84,81**CSF £215.87 TOTE £5.90: £2.30, £14.40, £1.80; EX 238.10.The winner was bought by Diamond Racing Ltd for £8,000. Cornwallis was claimed by Nigel Shields for £6,000.
**Owner** J David Abell **Bred** Branston Stud Ltd **Trained** Willoughton, Lincs

**FOCUS**
A fairly routine Fibresand claimer in which they went a good early pace, but appeared to slow up towards the end. Despite the proximity of the first left-hand bend, which in theory should have favoured the low numbers, the five drawn widest of all finished in the first six. This suggests the bias away from the inside rail was still very much in evidence.
**NOTEBOOK**
**Branston Tiger**, who has been tumbling down the handicap this year, was still one of those best in on adjusted official ratings. This drop into claiming company enabled him to return to form, and being brought with his effort widest of all was also a help to him given the way the track was riding.
**Travelling Times** is a long way below the horse he once was, but has gone well here in the past and ran way above his official mark considering he would have been 18lb better off with the winner in a handicap.
**On The Trail**, held up from his wide draw, had every chance but was unable to quicken where it mattered. He is retaining his form well.
**Mallia** may be at the veteran stage, but he has a wonderful record under these conditions and ran right up to his best recent form.
**Bond Shakira** was given a positive ride, especially over a trip at which she is yet to convince, but she was given no peace by High Esteem and eventually ran out of fuel.
**Wilson Bluebottle(IRE)**, usually likes to race near the front, but he was held up on this dramatic drop in trip and he did not have the time to get into the race.
**Cornwallis** was up there early, but raced closer to the inside rail than most down the home straight and failed to get home.
**High Esteem** *Official explanation: jockey said gelding lost a front shoe*
**Pedro Jack(IRE)**, best in at the weights, fluffed the start and never got competitive.

### 4186 AT THE RACES FROM 9A.M. NURSERY 7f (F)
3:15 (3:16) (E) 2-Y-0 £3,818 (£1,175; £587; £293) Stalls Low

Form RPR
624 1 **Caitlin (IRE)**[14] [3802] 2-8-1 64 FNorton 8 66
(BSmart) *hld up in tch: rdn and edgd lft 2f out: r.o u.p to ld last stride* 14/1
21 2 hd **Prize Fighter (IRE)**[20] [3611] 2-9-7 84 AMcCarthy 6 85
(PWChapple-Hyam) *a.p: led 2f out: sn rdn and hung lft: hdd last stride* 2/5[1]
510 3 2 **Snookered Again**[20] [3605] 2-8-5 73 PMulrennan(5) 4 69
(MWEasterby) *s.i.s: bhd: rdn 4f out: hdwy over 1f out: fin wl* 14/1
61 4 ¾ **Pauline's Prince**[28] [3377] 2-8-8 71 DSweeney 5 65
(RHollinshead) *t.k.h: hdwy over 3f out: rdn over 2f out: one pce fnl f* 9/1[3]
0622 5 nk **Chutney Mary (IRE)**[20] [3611] 2-8-8 71 SSanders 2 64
(JGPortman) *led: rdn and hdd 2f out: sltly hmpd jst over 1f out: wknd ins fnl f* 8/1[2]
3320 6 3½ **Aunty Euro (IRE)**[7] [3987] 2-8-6 69 JCarroll 7 54
(EJO'Neill) *prom: rdn over 2f out: wknd over 1f out* 66/1
2125 7 9 **Unlimited**[52] [2655] 2-9-1 78 ACulhane 9 40
(MrsADuffield) *sn outpcd* 20/1
5144 8 nk **Indibraun (IRE)**[35] [3145] 2-9-4 81 GFaulkner 3 42
(PCHaslam) *s.i.s: sn mid-div: rdn over 3f out: wknd over 2f out* 12/1
5653 9 2½ **Dusty Dane (IRE)**[22] [3553] 2-8-3 71 PMakin(5) 1 26
(WGMTurner) *mid-div: rdn over 3f out: wknd over 2f out* 16/1
003 10 12 **Dishdasha (IRE)**[37] [3100] 2-7-12 61 oh5 JBramhill 10 —
(CRDore) *in tch: rdn over 3f out: sn wknd* 66/1
1m 29.81s (-0.99) **Going Correction** -0.25s/f (Stan) 10 Ran SP% **127.2**
Speed ratings: **95,94,92,91,91 87,77,76,73,60**CSF £21.78 CT £112.95 TOTE £12.60: £3.60, £1.10, £4.20; EX 47.10.
**Owner** EKOS Pinnacle Partnership **Bred** Shadwell Estate Company Limited **Trained** Hambleton, N Yorks

**FOCUS**
A competitive nursery in which the pace was solid without being breakneck. It looks fair form. The 'official ratings' are only an estimate and are for guidance only.
**NOTEBOOK**
**Caitlin(IRE)** had shown some ability in maiden company on this surface, but it was the seventh furlong every bit as much as a lenient mark which enabled her to show improved form, and she stayed on in dour fashion to nail the favourite near the line. She should eventually get a mile and still has a little scope.
**Prize Fighter(IRE)** was very heavily backed despite opening at odds-on and ended up a very short price in a handicap. He was always in the ideal position to strike, but once he hit the front he hung left under the whip, ending up in the slower ground next to the inside rail, and was mugged near the line. He has questions to answer now.
**Snookered Again ◆**, a winner on his only previous visit here, was out the back early and, given how difficult it is to make up appreciable ground on this surface, did remarkably well to finish as close as he did. Stamina appears to be his forte and there should be another race in him when conditions are suitable.
**Pauline's Prince**, winner of a course-and-distance maiden last time, took quite a hold early but stayed on down the straight in a way that suggested he will be suited by an even greater test of stamina.
**Chutney Mary(IRE)** was able to dominate this time, but she also stuck close to the inside rail and that did not help her get home. She was already beaten when the runner-up went across her.

### 4187 EUROPEAN BREEDERS FUND MAIDEN STKS 5f (F)
3:45 (3:47) (D) 2-Y-0 £4,160 (£1,280; £640; £320) Stalls High

Form RPR
20 1 **Safsoof (USA)**[41] [2959] 2-9-0 LDettori 2 83
(SaeedBinSuroor) *mde all: drew clr fnl f: v easily* 1/10[1]
43 2 8 **Sister Gee (IRE)**[14] [3802] 2-8-9 JBramhill 6 50
(RHollinshead) *a.p: rdn and wnt 2nd jst over 2f out: wknd ins fnl f* 11/1[2]
3 shd **Game Lad** 2-9-0 DAllan 1 55
(TDEasterby) *s.i.s: sn in tch: rdn over 2f out: kpt on ins fnl f* 12/1[3]
0066 4 1½ **Serene Pearl (IRE)**[26] [3408] 2-8-6 (t) TEaves(3) 3 44
(GMMoore) *w wnr tl rdn jst over 2f out: wknd fnl f* 40/1
30 5 3 **Homme Dangereux**[4] [4058] 2-8-9 NDeSouza(5) 7 39
(CREgerton) *s.i.s: outpcd and bhd: sme late hdwy* 12/1[3]
6 hd **All A Dream** 2-8-9 SSanders 5 33
(RGuest) *s.i.s: sn in tch: rdn over 2f out: wknd over 1f out* 16/1
59.81 secs (-0.59) **Going Correction** -0.20s/f (Stan) 6 Ran SP% **122.9**
Speed ratings: **96,83,83,80,75 75**CSF £3.62 TOTE £1.10: £1.02, £3.10; EX 2.50.
**Owner** Godolphin **Bred** Westwood Thoroughbreds, Sez Who Racing Et Al **Trained** Newmarket, Suffolk

**FOCUS**
A very uncompetitive maiden with a predictable outcome. This was rare sight for Southwell, a Godolphin winner, but the form behind the long odds-on favourite looks moderate.
**NOTEBOOK**
**Safsoof(USA)**, taking a huge step down in class, is bred for sand and the race was over as soon as the stalls opened. He should have found this a happy experience and if he returns to sand later in his career, it is likely to be at a much higher level.

**Sister Gee(IRE)**, whose two previous outings had both been here, did her best to hang on to the tail of the favourite over this shorter trip, but the effort eventually burst her and she only just held on for second.
**Game Lad**, out of a winning half-sister to Missile, is bred to need further and should do better in time.
**Serene Pearl(IRE)** is exposed as moderate and achieved very little.

## 4188 SKY 415, NTL 908, TELEWEST 534 H'CAP 6f (F)
**4:15** (4:16) (E) (0-75,75) 3-Y-0+ **£3,721** (£1,145; £572; £286) **Stalls** Low

Form RPR
4300 **1** **Tally (IRE)**[2] 4130 4-9-0 **59** .... LFletcher[(3)] 5 69
(MJPolglase) *a.p: rdn over 2f out: led over 1f out: hung lft ins fnl f: r.o* **10/1**[3]
3062 **2** 1 ½ **Headland (USA)**[23] 3533 6-8-9 **51** .... (be) ACulhane 4 56
(DWChapman) *led: rdn and hdd over 1f out: nt qckn ins fnl f* **16/1**
2523 **3** ½ **Tsarbuck**[14] 3800 3-8-12 **59** .... (v[1]) GFaulkner 1 63
(RMHCowell) *a.p: rdn 2f out: nt qckn fnl f* **12/1**
2211 **4** 1 ¾ **Jonny Ebeneezer**[3] 4090 5-9-10 **66** 6ex .... (b) LDettori 2 64
(DFlood) *s.i.s: hdwy over 2f out: swtchd rt over 1f out: no ex fnl f* **10/11**[1]
0046 **5** 2 **Irusan (IRE)**[20] 3615 4-9-5 **61** .... PHanagan 6 53
(JeddO'Keeffe) *bhd: rdn over 3f out: late hdwy: nrst fin* **33/1**
2231 **6** 1 **Extra Cover (IRE)**[17] 3711 3-10-0 **75** .... (b) DSweeney 7 64
(RCharlton) *s.i.s: hdwy 2f out: wknd fnl f* **7/2**[2]
0000 **7** ¾ **St Ivian**[14] 3800 4-9-8 **64** .... (v) RFitzpatrick 8 51
(MrsNMacauley) *prom: rdn 3f out: wknd over 1f out* **33/1**
0010 **8** 1 ½ **Commander Bond**[23] 3517 3-9-10 **71** .... FLynch 9 54
(BSmart) *hld up in tch: rdn over 2f out: wknd over 1f out* **10/1**[3]
0-04 **9** 1 **Lord Arthur**[17] 3711 3-8-9 **56** .... DaleGibson 3 36
(MWEasterby) *w ldr tl rdn over 2f out: sn wknd* **33/1**

1m 15.34s (-1.56) **Going Correction** -0.25s/f (Stan)
**WFA** 3 from 4yo+ 5lb **9** Ran SP% **115.2**
Speed ratings: **100,98,97,95,92 91,90,88,86**CSF £148.42 CT £1925.16 TOTE £9.40: £2.50, £3.10, £2.30; EX 117.40.
**Owner** General Sir Geoffrey Howlett **Bred** D Twomey **Trained** Southwell, Notts

**FOCUS**
A fair handicap in which it paid to race close to the pace and not many got into it.

**NOTEBOOK**
**Tally(IRE)**, 11lb lower than for his last handicap on this surface, was never far away and had the race won after hitting the front despite hanging under pressure.
**Headland(USA)**, not the easiest to win with these days, was given a good ride from the front despite not winning this. He stayed mid-track on reaching the straight and that probably helped him hang on for as long as he did.
**Tsarbuck** runs consistently well on this track and put in another solid effort in the first-time visor. He may not have been helped by racing closer to the inside rail than those that finished around him.
**Jonny Ebeneezer** came here in great form after two recent wins on turf for which he had a 6lb penalty, but although he has won here his overall form on sand is not quite as good and he could never pick up sufficiently to threaten the leaders.
**Irusan(IRE)**, who is yet to make the frame, ran as though needing an extra furlong but failed to stay when tried over it here last time so this effort may be misleading.
**Extra Cover(IRE)** had plenty on giving weight to his elders, but more relevant was that over the last couple of furlongs he did not look to be fancying it at all.

## 4189 AT THE RACES DEDICATED RACING CHANNEL H'CAP 1m 4f (F)
**4:45** (4:46) (F) (0-55,55) 3-Y-0+ **£3,094** (£884; £442) **Stalls** Low

Form RPR
6003 **1** **Rolex Free (ARG)**[4] 4042 6-9-12 **53** .... (v) LDettori 13 64
(DFlood) *led after 1f: rdn 4f out: hdd 3f out: led again and edgd rt over 1f out: all out* **11/2**[3]
1500 **2** 1 **Antony Ebeneezer**[8] 3423 5-8-3 **35** .... HayleyTurner[(5)] 11 45
(CRDore) *t.k.h in rr: hdwy over 4f out: rdn and edgd lft over 1f out: styd on ins fnl f* **11/2**[3]
0513 **3** shd **Salut Saint Cloud**[27] 3393 3-9-0 **53** .... SWhitworth 1 63
(GLMoore) *hld up in tch: rdn and outpcd over 4f out: rallied over 1f out: styd on wl ins fnl f* **6/1**
-404 **4** 1 **Ela Re**[9] 2816 5-9-2 **43** .... JBramhill 10 51
(CRDore) *hld up in mid-div: hdwy over 5f out: led 3f out: rdn 2f out: hdd over 1f out: no ex wl ins fnl f* **5/1**[2]
3605 **5** 11 **Kentucky Bullet (USA)**[14] 3799 8-8-7 **37** .... (p) LPKeniry[(3)] 4 29
(AGNewcombe) *led 1f: hld up in tch: rdn 4f out: wknd over 2f out* **8/1**
2600 **6** ¾ **Western Command (GER)**[14] 3799 8-8-8 **35** oh10..(p) JoannaBadger 8 25
(MrsNMacauley) *hld up in mid-div: rdn over 4f out: sn wknd* **50/1**
3000 **7** shd **Paddy Boy (IRE)**[7] 3996 3-8-9 **48** .... DSweeney 14 38
(JRBoyle) *s.i.s: sn prom: rdn 4f out: wknd over 2f out* **20/1**
4545 **8** 6 **Disabuse**[16] 3743 4-9-9 **55** .... (b) PMulrennan[(5)] 5 36
(MWEasterby) *prom: rdn 4f out: sn wknd* **9/2**[1]
2200 **9** 5 **Cezzaro (IRE)**[5] 4015 6-8-3 **35** oh5 .... (t) BSwarbrick[(5)] 12 9
(SRBowring) *hld up and bhd: hdwy over 5f out: rdn over 4f out: sn wknd* **20/1**
3000 **10** shd **Spanish Star**[14] 3799 7-8-9 **43** .... SarahSayer[(7)] 6 17
(MrsNMacauley) *a bhd* **20/1**
1030 **11** 1 ½ **Seraph**[29] 2408 4-8-13 **40** .... (p) SSanders 3 11
(JohnAHarris) *a bhd* **12/1**
0-52 **12** 2 **White Park Bay (IRE)**[14] 3809 4-9-8 **54** .... LTreadwell[(5)] 7 22
(MissSuzySmith) *s.i.s: a bhd* **12/1**
0404 **13** 11 **Banners Flying (IRE)**[14] 3799 4-9-9 **50** .... ACulhane 9 2
(DWChapman) *a bhd* **33/1**
00-0 **14** dist **Legion Of Honour (IRE)**[60] 2426 5-9-4 **50** .... AQuinn[(5)] 2 —
(MissSJWilton) *s.i.s: sn prom: wknd 6f out: t.o* **66/1**

2m 39.54s (-2.56) **Going Correction** -0.25s/f (Stan)
**WFA** 3 from 4yo+ 12lb **14** Ran SP% **127.1**
Speed ratings: **98,97,97,96,89 88,88,84,81,81 80,78,71,**—CSF £34.99 CT £196.85 TOTE £8.90: £2.90, £2.20, £1.50; EX 56.30.
**Owner** Mrs Ruth M Serrell **Bred** Firmamento Corporation **Trained** Upper Lambourn, Berks

**FOCUS**
A modest handicap run at an ordinary pace and there is little to get excited about outside of the front four.

**NOTEBOOK**
**Rolex Free(ARG)**, on whom Dettori was a late replacement, was racing off a 17lb lower mark than for his last handicap on sand. Well backed, his rider was very keen to get to the front early and he particularly impressed with the way he battled back after losing the lead early in the straight.
**Antony Ebeneezer**, back on the same mark as when winning over course and distance back in March, came from off the pace and had every chance halfway up the home straight, but his rider elected to challenge on the inside of the winner, and given the way the track was riding that may not have helped his chance.
**Salut Saint Cloud**, inclined to run in snatches, had every chance and was not stopping at the end. In fact it looked as if he would get even further.
**Ela Re**, who has given mixed signals over his ability to stay this trip on the Flat, had every chance turning in but lack of finishing pace looks his greatest handicap on the level.
**Kentucky Bullet(USA)** probably achieved little as he was well beaten by the front four.
**Disabuse** is proven on the surface and should have done better, but it was noticeable how he started to struggle as soon as he was switched right over to the inside rail starting the turn for home.

## 4190 AT THE RACES ON NTL, IRELAND H'CAP 1m (F)
**5:15** (5:17) (F) (0-55,55) 3-Y-0+ **£3,178** (£908; £454) **Stalls** Low

Form RPR
0302 **1** **Arran**[3] 4096 4-9-11 **52** .... SSanders 8 65+
(VSmith) *hld up in mid-div: hdwy whn n.m.r over 2f out: rdn over 1f out: edgd lft and led ins fnl f: rdn out* **1/1**[1]
-035 **2** 1 ½ **Miss Glory Be**[167] 737 6-9-8 **49** .... (p) ANicholls 5 59+
(EROertel) *hld up in tch: rdn over 2f out: kpt on ins fnl f* **14/1**
0010 **3** 2 ½ **Reversionary**[13] 3822 3-9-0 **49** .... (b) DaleGibson 2 54
(MWEasterby) *a.p: rdn over 2f out: hung lft jst over 1f out: no ex towards fin* **33/1**
4210 **4** nk **Bulawayo**[14] 3804 7-9-6 **52** .... (b) BSwarbrick[(5)] 4 56
(AndrewReid) *w ldr: led over 4f out: rdn 2f out: hdd ins fnl f: no ex towards fin* **10/1**[3]
-006 **5** 1 ½ **Desert Fury**[54] 2597 7-8-11 **43** .... PMulrennan[(5)] 1 44
(RBastiman) *hld up and bhd: hdwy on ins over 3f out: rdn over 2f out: swtchd rt 1f out: one pce* **9/1**[2]
1100 **6** ¾ **Rocinante (IRE)**[11] 2879 4-9-10 **51** .... RWinston 14 51
(JJQuinn) *prom: lost pl 3f out: rdn and rallied over 1f out: one pce fnl f* **16/1**
1000 **7** 1 ½ **Qobtaan (USA)**[91] 1681 5-9-12 **53** .... GBaker 3 50
(MRBosley) *hld up and bhd: hdwy on ins 2f out: sn rdn: no imp fnl f* **25/1**
004 **8** ¾ **Petrolina (IRE)**[20] 3613 3-9-3 **55** .... LFletcher[(3)] 11 50
(HMorrison) *prom: rdn over 3f out: wknd over 1f out* **14/1**
0030 **9** 2 **Dubonai (IRE)**[42] 2943 4-9-12 **53** .... JCarroll 16 44
(AndrewTurnell) *hld up: effrt on outside over 3f out: rdn and no hdwy fnl 2f* **14/1**
0034 **10** hd **Rocky Reppin**[14] 3804 4-8-11 **45** .... KPierrepont[(7)] 13 36
(JBalding) *bhd: rdn over 3f out: n.d* **16/1**
0300 **11** 1 ½ **Secam (POL)**[2] 4127 5-9-3 **44** .... (b) ACulhane 10 32
(MrsPTownsley) *hld up: hdwy on outside over 4f out: rdn and wknd 2f out* **33/1**
4010 **12** 4 **Super Dominion**[14] 3804 7-9-6 **47** .... (p) DSweeney 9 27
(RHollinshead) *rdn over 3f out: a bhd* **20/1**
000- **13** 1 ¾ **Warren Place**[354] 3931 4-9-2 **43** .... SRighton 6 20
(JHetherton) *sn led: hdd over 4f out: sn rdn: wknd 2f out* **50/1**
0466 **14** 2 **Inmom (IRE)**[24] 3473 3-9-6 **55** .... JBramhill 12 28
(SRBowring) *mid-div: lost pl 4f out: sn bhd* **20/1**
4403 **15** 1 ½ **Jade Star (USA)**[4] 4065 4-9-7 **53** .... DFox[(5)] 15 23
(PBurgoyne) *prom: rdn over 3f out: wknd over 2f out* **12/1**
1620 **16** 19 **Amethyst Rock**[51] 2689 6-8-13 **40** .... FLynch 7 —
(PLGilligan) *sn outpcd: t.o fnl 4f* **25/1**

1m 43.0s (-1.60) **Going Correction** -0.25s/f (Stan)
**WFA** 3 from 4yo+ 8lb **16** Ran SP% **133.6**
Speed ratings: **98,96,94,93,92 91,89,89,87,87 85,81,79,77,76 57**CSF £17.11 CT £367.07 TOTE £2.00: £1.02, £3.20, £13.20, £3.20; EX 22.50 Place 6 £60.28, Place 5 £34.16.
**Owner** The Three Amigos **Bred** The Overbury Stud **Trained** Exning, Suffolk

**FOCUS**
A low-grade if competitive handicap run at a solid early pace. The winner looks progressive, and the runner-up is fairly handicapped now.

**NOTEBOOK**
**Arran ◆**, all the rage after his cracking effort against the bang-in-form Masafi here three days earlier, had to work a bit in order to score but should be given extra credit as he had the door shut on him at a crucial stage, yet still showed a useful turn of foot and was well on top at the line. He looks capable of more.
**Miss Glory Be**, making her debut for the yard on this first start since February, is proven on this surface even though she has yet to win here and she ran a decent race in defeat. She is well handicapped on her best form and will not always come up against a progressive sort.
**Reversionary** ran well enough on this sand debut, but he just seemed to want to hang over to the inside rail passing the furlong pole and looks the sort who needs everything to fall just right.
**Bulawayo**, a Fibresand veteran, was given his usual positive ride but gave the inside rail away to no-one, so he probably did well to finish where he did.
**Desert Fury**, a shadow of the horse he once was, has not won for three years and faced an uphill struggle in trying to come from way off the pace.
**Rocinante(IRE)**, out of form since a couple of soft-ground turf victories in the spring, has won on Fibresand and was not totally disgraced.
**Qobtaan(USA)** could never get into the race from off the pace, but he is proven on Fibresand and is slipping back to a reasonable mark.
**Inmom(IRE)** *Official explanation: jockey said filly ran without declared tongue-strap, which had come adrift and could not be re-fitted*
**Amethyst Rock** *Official explanation: jockey said gelding would not face kickback and was never travelling*
T/Plt: £131.10 to a £1 stake. Pool: £40,243.25. 224.00 winning tickets. T/Qpdt: £23.50 to a £1 stake. Pool: £2,452.00. 76.90 winning tickets. KH

# 3992 WINDSOR (R-H)
Monday, July 26

**OFFICIAL GOING: Good to firm**
Wind: almost nil Weather: sunny

## 4191 CANNONS STOKE POGES MAIDEN STKS 5f 10y
**6:15** (6:17) (D) 2-Y-0 **£5,161** (£1,588; £794; £397) **Stalls** High

Form RPR
4 **1** **Clove (USA)**[33] 3208 2-8-9 .... MHills 2 71
(BWHills) *prom: trckd ldr 2f out: shkn up and narrow ld over 1f out: rdn out* **4/5**[1]
**2** ¾ **Middle Earth (USA)** 2-9-0 .... MartinDwyer 3 74+
(AMBalding) *s.i.s: sn trckd ldrs: effrt over 1f out: rn green but styd on ins fnl f to take 2nd nr fin* **11/4**[2]
40 **3** nk **Our Fugitive (IRE)**[24] 3491 2-9-0 .... JFortune 6 73
(AWCarroll) *led to over 1f out: kpt on wl u.p fnl f* **50/1**
53 **4** nk **Cummiskey (IRE)**[4] 4040 2-9-0 .... SDrowne 9 72+
(JAOsborne) *trckd ldrs: nt clr run on inner over 1f out and again ent fnl f: styng on whn nt clr run nr fin* **10/1**
4 **5** hd **Ninja Storm (IRE)**[14] 3805 2-9-0 .... RLMoore 7 71
(GLMoore) *dwlt: sn rcvrd to chse ldrs: pushed along over 1f out: kpt on fnl f: nvr quite able to chal* **9/1**[3]

3 **6** *3* **Great Belief (IRE)**[14] 3805 2-9-0 TQuinn 4 61
(TDMccarthy) *t.k.h: chsd ldr to 2f out: wknd fnl f* **12/1**
**7** *5* **Regal Dream (IRE)** 2-9-0 EAhern 1 43
(JWHills) *racd in midfield: outpcd fr 1/2-way: no ch fr over 1f out* **25/1**
060 **8** *5* **Whistling Along**[71] 2141 2-9-0 DaneO'Neill 8 26
(JMBradley) *outpcd and pushed along over 3f out: a bhd* **66/1**
6 **9** *2* **Just Bonnie**[45] 2831 2-9-0 TPQueally 10 19
(JMBradley) *outpcd and pushed along over 3f out: a bhd* **66/1**
**10** *2 1/2* **Eden Star (IRE)** 2-8-9 DHolland 5 —
(DKIvory) *sn outpcd: a bhd* **50/1**

60.29 secs (-0.91) **Going Correction** -0.275s/f (Firm) **10** Ran SP% **119.8**
Speed ratings: **96,94,94,93,93 88,80,72,69,65**CSF £3.08 TOTE £1.90: £1.10, £1.30, £9.50; EX 4.40.
**Owner** K Abdulla **Bred** Juddmonte Farms Inc **Trained** Lambourn, Berks

**FOCUS**
A fair maiden and the first five finished clear, although the winner was only workmalike in success.

**NOTEBOOK**
**Clove(USA)** had run well on the wrong side at Salisbury on her debut and showed plenty of pace from her low draw. Her future is in the hands of the Handicapper now, and while she should get six furlongs in time, this trip appears to suit for the time being.
**Middle Earth(USA)**, a $100,000 yearling, is out of a mare who was a smart older sprinter in the US. He was the subject of good support throughout the day and ran a promising race on his debut. There should be better to come.
**Our Fugitive(IRE)** ran his best race to date, showing decent pace throughout. This effort makes him eligible for a handicap mark.
**Cummiskey(IRE)** kept finding his run blocked and finished with a lot left in the tank. He might have given the winner something to think about with a clear passage, but he is now eligible to run in nurseries, and it is for a race in that sphere that he should be kept in mind. *Official explanation: jockey said he was unable to get a run in closing stages*
**Ninja Storm(IRE)** kept on steadily and finished clear of the rest, reversing his debut form with Great Belief in the process.
**Great Belief(IRE)** would have finished closer had he been pushed out, but he would still have finished sixth.
**Eden Star(IRE)** *Official explanation: jockey said filly was in season*

## 4192 WINDSOR-RACECOURSE.CO.UK H'CAP — 1m 2f 7y
**6:45** (6:47) (E) (0-75,75) 3-Y-O+ **£3,620** (£1,114; £557; £278) **Stalls Low**

Form RPR
1101 **1** **A One (IRE)**[5] 4029 5-9-9 **73** FPFerris(3) 14 89+
(HJManners) *mde all: drew 4l clr 4f out: rdn over 1f out: eased ins fnl f: unchal* **2/1**[1]
0020 **2** *2* **El Chaparral (IRE)**[12] 3841 4-9-2 **63** DaneO'Neill 3 73
(DKIvory) *dwlt: hld up wl in rr: rn wd bnd over 5f out: rdn and prog on outer over 2f out: chsd wnr over 1f out: no real imp* **12/1**
5002 **3** *nk* **Recount (FR)**[5] 4029 4-9-2 **68** MSavage(5) 4 77+
(JRBest) *led to post: t.k.h and hld up in rr: prog to midfield 1/2-way: rdn and styd on fnl 2f: uns jockey after fin* **7/1**[3]
6405 **4** *3 1/2* **Gallant Boy (IRE)**[9] 3947 5-9-5 **66** (vt) JFortune 6 69
(PDEvans) *s.i.s: hld up wl in rr: plenty to do over 3f out: rdn and prog over 2f out: styd on to take 4th nr fin* **6/1**[2]
0410 **5** *shd* **Our Destiny**[18] 3682 6-8-11 **58** RLMoore 12 61
(AWCarroll) *racd in midfield: rdn 3f out: unable qck over 2f out: one pce after* **14/1**
6043 **6** *3/4* **Pacific Ocean (ARG)**[24] 3490 5-8-6 **53** (t) FNorton 11 54
(MrsStefLiddiard) *t.k.h: hld up bhd ldrs: rdn 3f out: nt qckn and btn 2f out* **16/1**
/230 **7** *3 1/2* **Cosi Fan Tutte**[13] 3825 6-9-2 **63** (vt) DHolland 17 58
(MCPipe) *hld up but sn in midfield: effrt on inner whn nt clr run briefly 3f out: one pce after* **8/1**
5402 **8** *hd* **Leighton (IRE)**[11] 3880 4-10-0 **75** SCarson 9 69
(RMStronge) *prom: chsd wnr over 3f out: no imp: wknd and lost 2nd over 1f out* **16/1**
0300 **9** *3/4* **Rainbow World (IRE)**[7] 3997 4-8-10 **57** (tp) JFEgan 8 50
(AndrewReid) *prom: drvn 4f out: disp 2nd pl over 2f out: sn wknd* **16/1**
002- **10** *1/2* **Efrhina (IRE)**[50] 5501 4-9-4 **65** SDrowne 13 57
(MrsStefLiddiard) *hld up in midfield: snatched up bnd 6f out: no prog over 3f out: no ch after* **25/1**
**11** *1* **Icarus Dream (IRE)**[34] 3184 3-8-8 **70** NChalmers(5) 2 60
(PRHedger) *a towards rr: rdn and struggling 4f out: n.d after* **33/1**
0063 **12** *hd* **Piquet**[19] 3637 6-7-12 **45** oh3 JMackay 18 34
(JJBridger) *hld up in last: detached fr remainder over 3f out: nudged along and kpt on steadily fnl 2f: nvr nr ldrs* **33/1**
0-00 **13** *6* **Victory Venture (IRE)**[10] 3909 4-9-8 **69** TQuinn 7 47
(IanWilliams) *chsd ldrs: u.p and losing pl over 4f out: bhd fnl 2f* **33/1**
0000 **14** *1 1/4* **Nabtat Saif**[10] 3910 3-8-6 **63** PDobbs 15 39
(RHannon) *a towards rr: shkn up and struggling 4f out: wl bhd fnl 2f* **33/1**
6-06 **15** *1/2* **Celtic Star (IRE)**[21] 3573 6-8-11 **58** (b[1]) JPMurtagh 5 33
(MissKMGeorge) *chsd wnr tl hung lft 4f out: nt run on* **25/1**
0-0 **16** *10* **Outside Investor (IRE)**[12] 3850 4-10-0 **75** TPQueally 10 31
(TPMcgovern) *prom: rdn to chse wnr 4f out to over 3f out: wknd rapidly* **33/1**
1324 **17** *8* **Ember Days**[4] 4045 5-9-6 **67** (p) EAhern 1 8
(JLSpearing) *prom in chsng gp: rdn over 3f out: no ch but stl chsng ldrs whn lost action over 1f out: heavily eased* **12/1**

2m 5.45s (-2.85) **Going Correction** -0.275s/f (Firm)
**WFA** 3 from 4yo+ 10lb **17** Ran SP% **133.3**
Speed ratings: **100,98,98,95,95 94,91,91,91,90 89,89,84,83,83 75,69**CSF £28.15 CT £149.95 TOTE £2.80: £1.50, £2.30, £2.10, £2.00; EX 42.60.
**Owner** H J Manners **Bred** Humphrey Okeke **Trained** Highworth, Wilts

**FOCUS**
A fair handicap, although not that competitive. Another good performance from A One, who has thrived since changing stables.

**NOTEBOOK**
**A One(IRE)** was able to race off the same mark as when successful at Sandown on his latest start and, employing the tactics which have proven so successful of late, set a decent pace and had his rivals in trouble a fair way out. Despite having a busy time of it, he is holding his form well, and he is in again at Nottingham on Friday.
**El Chaparral(IRE)** ran well over a mile on his previous visit, and his breeding suggested he was worth a go over this longer distance. He made up a lot of ground from the rear and, although he could not peg back the in-form winner, he is certainly worth another try over this trip.
**Recount(FR)** had run the favourite very close at Sandown on his latest start, but he stayed on well at that stiff track and his winning form is over a mile and a half, so this sharper ten furlongs was unlikely to suit him ideally. His performance in the race confirmed that impression.
**Gallant Boy(IRE)**, whose handicap mark has dropped 8lb this turf season, shaped with a bit more promise, but he has a poor strike-rate.
**Our Destiny** was tackling better opposition than he normally competes against, and in the circumstances he did not run badly.
**Pacific Ocean(ARG)** usually runs his race but he has yet to break his maiden tag.
**Rainbow World(IRE)** *Official explanation: jockey said colt was never travelling*
**Piquet** *Official explanation: jockey said mare suffered interference and lost action*
**Celtic Star(IRE)** *Official explanation: jockey said gelding hung left*

## 4193 TRI HOSPITALITY CONSULTING MAIDEN STKS — 6f
**7:15** (7:17) (D) 2-Y-O **£5,369** (£1,652; £826; £413) **Stalls High**

Form RPR
2 **1** **Persian Rock (IRE)**[121] 1128 2-9-0 DHolland 9 80
(JAOsborne) *w ldr: rdn to ld wl over 1f out: drvn out and hld on wl* **7/4**[1]
0 **2** *1/2* **Cool Panic (IRE)**[57] 2502 2-9-0 JPMurtagh 6 79
(MLWBell) *trckd ldng pair: effrt 2f out: drvn to chse wnr fnl f: a jst hld* **8/1**
0 **3** *1 1/4* **Cape Quest**[20] 3601 2-9-0 PDobbs 13 75
(RHannon) *mde most to wl over 1f out: one pce u.p* **5/1**[3]
**4** *1/2* **Enforcer** 2-9-0 SDrowne 2 73
(WRMuir) *dwlt: outpcd and wl off the pce: rdn and prog 2f out: styd on strly fnl f: nrst fin* **33/1**
**5** *shd* **Pollito (IRE)** 2-9-0 JFortune 8 73
(BJMeehan) *chsd ldng pair: pushed along over 3f out: effrt u.p over 1f out: one pce* **20/1**
**6** *1/2* **Red Rudy** 2-9-0 KFallon 4 71
(RMBeckett) *chsd ldrs: taken to wd outside and effrt over 2f out: rdn and no imp jst over 1f out: one pce after* **5/1**[3]
**7** *nk* **Lady Londra** 2-8-4 ow2 MHoward(7) 11 68
(DKIvory) *dwlt: outpcd in midfield: prog over 2f out: pushed along to chse ldrs over 1f out: no imp fnl f* **66/1**
0 **8** *2* **Rum Creek**[16] 3749 2-9-0 JFEgan 5 65
(SKirk) *off the pce in midfield and pushed along 4f out: nvr on terms* **50/1**
40 **9** *hd* **Darko Karim**[37] 3071 2-9-0 TPQueally 10 64
(DRLoder) *wl off the pce towards rr: reminder 4f out: looked reluctant after and nvr on terms* **4/1**[2]
0 **10** *3 1/2* **Coombe Centenary**[19] 3632 2-8-9 DaneO'Neill 12 48
(SDow) *dwlt: outpcd and a struggling* **100/1**
**11** *3 1/2* **Sonntag Blue (IRE)** 2-9-0 TQuinn 1 43
(JAOsborne) *outpcd and sn wl bhd: nvr a factor* **33/1**
**12** *8* **Paddys Tern** 2-8-11 DCorby(3) 7 19
(NMBabbage) *sn outpcd and bhd: wknd 2f out* **100/1**
**13** *1/2* **Moon Bird** 2-8-9 EAhern 3 12
(CACyzer) *dwlt: outpcd and a wl bhd* **16/1**

1m 12.93s (-0.94) **Going Correction** -0.275s/f (Firm) **13** Ran SP% **122.8**
Speed ratings: **95,94,92,92,91 91,90,88,87,83 78,67,67**CSF £16.94 TOTE £2.50: £1.50, £2.40, £2.00; EX 18.00.
**Owner** Waney Racing Group Inc & Karmaa Racing **Bred** Mrs Noelle Walsh **Trained** Upper Lambourn, Berks

**FOCUS**
This looked an ordinary maiden.

**NOTEBOOK**
**Persian Rock(IRE)** had been off the track since his debut in March, but he made light of his absence and battled on well to hold on by half a length. He is in the Gimcrack, but this bare form suggests he is short of the class required to take a hand there. Nurseries look likely to be his game.
**Cool Panic(IRE)**, a half-brother to five winners including smart performers Inzar's Best and Ruby Rocket, improved on his effort in a decent Newmarket maiden two months earlier. He looks to be progressing along the right lines.
**Cape Quest**, who made his debut in a hot Newmarket maiden, made good use of his high draw and forced the pace for much of the way. This was a fair effort and he looks to be going the right way.
**Enforcer** is a brother to juvenile winner Lord Of The Inn and half-brother to a two-year-old winner in Italy. This was a promising effort on his debut and, as his brother was best on soft ground, a little cut in the ground may help him in future.
**Pollito(IRE)**, a half-brother to two winners, is already a gelding. He had his chance on his debut as he had the rail to help in the straight.
**Red Rudy** *Official explanation: jockey said colt hung left*
**Lady Londra**, whose dam is a half-sister to top-class hurdler Cardinal Hill, was not knocked about in a lost cause and should benefit from the experience.
**Rum Creek** *Official explanation: jockey said filly hung violently left*
**Sonntag Blue(IRE)** *Official explanation: jockey said colt hung left throughout*
**Moon Bird** *Official explanation: jockey said filly lost her action*

## 4194 TOTESPORT FILLIES' H'CAP — 6f
**7:45** (7:50) (D) (0-80,80) 3-Y-O+ **£7,202** (£2,216; £1,108; £554) **Stalls High**

Form RPR
345 **1** **Wunderbra (IRE)**[31] 3279 3-7-12 **55** (t) JMackay 8 65
(MLWBell) *trckd ldr: led wl over 1f out: urged along and in command fnl f* **20/1**
3200 **2** *1 1/4* **Ballinger Express**[45] 2836 4-8-10 **62** (b) MartinDwyer 9 68
(AMBalding) *led: rdn and hdd wl over 1f out: kpt on same pce after* **16/1**
0600 **3** *nk* **Miss George**[19] 3645 6-10-0 **80** DHolland 6 85
(DKIvory) *s.i.s: hld up in last pair: stdy prog fr 2f out: rdn and unable qck jst over 1f out: styd on to take 3rd* **11/2**[2]
1356 **4** *nk* **Maddie's A Jem**[51] 2670 4-9-7 **73** KFallon 4 77
(JRJenkins) *racd in midfield: drvn and effrt 2f out: kpt on one pce u.p fr over 1f out* **7/1**
06-0 **5** *3/4* **Darla (IRE)**[11] 3874 3-8-11 **68** JPMurtagh 12 70
(JWPayne) *t.k.h: trckd ldng pair: rdn and nt qckn wl over 1f out: one pce after* **16/1**
0540 **6** *1* **Stokesies Wish**[3] 4104 4-8-12 **64** KMcEvoy 7 63
(JLSpearing) *trckd ldrs: shuffled along 2f out: one pce and no imp fnl f* **6/1**[3]
-405 **7** *hd* **Zwadi (IRE)**[30] 3306 3-9-0 **71** DaneO'Neill 11 69
(HCandy) *racd in last pair: rdn over 2f out: kpt on fnl f: n.d* **14/1**
5100 **8** *3/4* **Under My Spell**[7] 3979 3-8-12 **76** SJDonohoe(7) 5 72
(PDEvans) *racd in midfield: u.p over 2f out: no hdwy* **16/1**
1000 **9** *3/4* **Hagley Park**[21] 3575 5-7-9 **50** oh5 FPFerris(3) 13 44
(MissKMGeorge) *racd in midfield: hrd rdn 2f out: no prog over 1f out* **25/1**
5-00 **10** *1/2* **Officer's Pink**[51] 2670 4-8-11 **68** (t) NDeSouza(5) 3 60
(PFICole) *a towards rr: in last trio and rdn over 2f out: struggling after* **33/1**
1452 **11** *shd* **Bohola Flyer (IRE)**[7] 3995 3-9-7 **78** RLMoore 2 70
(RHannon) *racd on wd outside: nvr on terms w ldrs: no prog u.p 2f out* **4/1**[1]
0201 **12** *shd* **Kallista's Pride**[16] 3747 4-8-9 **61** NPollard 10 53
(JRBest) *dwlt: sn in midfield: hrd rdn over 2f out: fdd fnl f* **10/1**
1553 **13** *nk* **I Wish**[34] 3178 6-8-4 **59** ow2 LPKeniry(3) 14 50
(MMadgwick) *trckd ldrs: rdn and lost pl 2f out: n.d after* **11/2**[2]

1m 11.46s (-2.41) **Going Correction** -0.275s/f (Firm)
**WFA** 3 from 4yo+ 5lb **13** Ran SP% **122.5**
Speed ratings: **105,103,102,102,101 100,99,98,97,97 97,97,96**CSF £310.16 CT £2016.71 TOTE £17.90: £3.90, £5.20, £2.10; EX 341.20 Trifecta £899.10 Part won..

**Owner** Fitzroy Thoroughbreds **Bred** J F Tuthill And Mrs A Whitehead **Trained** Newmarket, Suffolk

**FOCUS**

An ordinary event won by a handicap debutante, and a race which does not strike as being packed with future winners.

**NOTEBOOK**

**Wunderbra(IRE)** had run well enough on her turf debut but been a beaten favourite on both starts on Fibresand since. As a result she had been given a moderate mark, and she took advantage of that back on grass. Clearly the green stuff suits her better than the artificial surface, and she starts her handicap career at the right end of the weights.

**Ballinger Express** made a bold bid from the front, grabbing the valuable stands'-side rail in the straight. She was unlucky to run into a well-handicapped rival and can clearly win a race off this sort of mark.

**Miss George**, for whom the draw does not matter, as she likes to challenge from way off the pace, came with her usual late run. She won this race last year off a mark of 76 but could not repeat the feat off a 4lb higher mark.

**Maddie's A Jem** ran a decent race from a low draw and on ground plenty quick enough for her.

**Darla(IRE)**, who had a good draw, has yet to recapture her two-year-old best.

**Stokesies Wish** has only one win from 26 starts to her name.

**Zwadi(IRE)** looks tripless.

## 4195 COME RACING NEXT MONDAY-LADIES NIGHT MAIDEN STKS 1m 67y

**8:15** (8:20) (D) 3-Y-O **£4,264** (£1,312; £656; £328) **Stalls** High

Form RPR

23 **1** **Nouveau Riche (IRE)**[43] [2911] 3-8-9 RLMoore 12 69
(HMorrison) *pressed ldr: led 5f out: rdn and hdd jst over 1f out: led again ins fnl f: styd on wl* **11/4**[2]

5 **2** 3/4 **Sea Nymph (IRE)**[10] [3916] 3-8-9 KFallon 18 68
(SirMichaelStoute) *prom: effrt 2f out: rdn to ld jst over 1f out: hanging and hdd ins fnl f: nt qckn* **5/2**[1]

22 **3** 2 **Violet Park**[9] [3948] 3-8-9 JFortune 9 63
(BJMeehan) *t.k.h: trckd ldrs: rdn 2f out: hanging bdly lft and nt qckn over 1f out: tk 3rd nr fin* **11/4**[2]

06 **4** 1/2 **Alenushka**[21] [3592] 3-8-9 DaneO'Neill 7 62
(HCandy) *prom: rdn and cl up 2f out: outpcd over 1f out* **14/1**

0-5 **5** 2 1/2 **Fisby**[12] [3846] 3-9-0 JFEgan 2 61
(SKirk) *settled wl in rr: prog on wd outside fr over 2f out: shkn up and chsd ldrs over 1f out: no hdwy after* **66/1**

0-0 **6** nk **Richie Boy**[46] [2808] 3-9-0 MHenry 6 60
(MAJarvis) *chsd ldrs: rdn 3f out: outpcd 2f out: kpt on ins fnl f* **40/1**

0 **7** 3/4 **Ceylon Round (FR)**[22] [3554] 3-8-6 DCorby(3) 17 54
(MJWallace) *trckd ldng gp: gng wl enough 3f out: rdn and outpcd 2f out : no ch after* **66/1**

-000 **8** nk **Tartiruga (IRE)**[17] [3695] 3-9-0 45 FNorton 8 58?
(LGCottrell) *led to 5f out: styd pressing ldrs tl wknd wl over 1f out* **66/1**

60 **9** 2 1/2 **Grand Rapide**[32] [3251] 3-8-9 KMcEvoy 11 47
(JLSpearing) *racd in midfield: shkn up and effrt over 3f out: no imp on ldrs fnl 2f* **33/1**

**10** 3/4 **Constructor** 3-9-0 TPQueally 3 51
(CACyzer) *chsd ldrs: rdn over 3f out: fdd fnl 2f* **50/1**

00-6 **11** 1/2 **Monash Girl (IRE)**[27] [3391] 3-8-4 30 NChalmers(5) 14 44?
(BRJohnson) *s.i.s: hld up in midfield: rdn and no prog 3f out* **66/1**

3 **12** 1 1/4 **Go Garuda**[25] [3447] 3-9-0 TQuinn 4 46
(DWPArbuthnot) *wl in rr: rdn over 3f out: effrt on outer 2f out: wknd over 1f out* **7/1**[3]

00 **13** 3/4 **Medica Boba**[21] [3592] 3-8-9 SDrowne 5 40
(HMorrison) *settled towards rr: pushed along 3f out: nvr nr ldrs* **50/1**

0 **14** 1 3/4 **Anna Gayle**[12] [3843] 3-8-9 SCarson 13 36
(MrsAJPerrett) *a in rr: rdn and struggling 3f out* **50/1**

000 **15** 1 1/4 **Crimson Star (IRE)**[48] [2765] 3-8-9 EAhern 15 33
(CTinkler) *settled wl in rr: pushed along and no prog 3f out* **66/1**

000- **16** 5 **Ballet Ruse**[262] [5938] 3-8-9 JMackay 10 21
(SirMarkPrescott) *dwlt: a wl in rr* **33/1**

0 **17** 13 **Sylvaticus (IRE)**[65] [2301] 3-9-0 PDobbs 1 —
(RHannon) *sn bhd in last: t.o fnl 3f* **66/1**

1m 43.47s (-2.13) **Going Correction** -0.275s/f (Firm) **17** Ran SP% **124.2**

Speed ratings: **99,98,96,95,93 92,92,91,89,88 88,86,86,84,83 78,65**CSF £9.48 TOTE £4.00: £1.70, £1.50, £1.40; EX 8.30.

**Owner** Nicholas Cooper **Bred** Bodfari Stud Ltd **Trained** East Ilsley, Berks

**FOCUS**

The first three home all had their supporters but the race lacked much strength in depth.

**NOTEBOOK**

**Nouveau Riche(IRE)**, up there from the start, came good at the third time of asking. She had the advantage of the rail in the straight, but it was still a good performance to come back and take the race after being headed by the favourite approaching the final furlong. Connections are now keen on gaining some black type for her, but she will have to improve if she is to realise those hopes.

**Sea Nymph(IRE)** got her head in front approaching the furlong marker, but she hung under pressure and the winner came back at her. Being by Spectrum, she might be suited by easier ground.

**Violet Park** was another who hung under pressure on this, the quickest ground she had ever raced on. She got the trip well enough though, and handicaps are now an option for her.

**Alenushka** is improving with every run and is now eligible for handicaps. She came clear of the rest and her future is in the hands of the Handicapper.

**Fisby** shaped with plenty more promise this time, staying on steadily down the outside. He looks one to note when moving into handicap company.

**Richie Boy** improved on his previous performances on this step up in trip.

**Go Garuda** was not without his supporters in the market, but he let them down badly. He is surely capable of better than this.

## 4196 VERITAS H'CAP 1m 3f 135y

**8:45** (8:50) (E ) (0-70,67) 3-Y-0+ **£3,659** (£1,126; £563; £281) **Stalls** Low

Form RPR

4251 **1** **Pont Neuf (IRE)**[14] [3809] 4-9-0 60 (t) SJDonohoe(7) 8 69
(PDEvans) *settled wl in rr: prog fr 3f out: drvn to ld 1f out: styd on wl* **11/2**[3]

0020 **2** 2 **Milk And Sultana**[3] [4080] 4-9-0 53 EAhern 2 59
(GAHam) *settled in midfield and off the pce: prog over 3f out: led over 2f out : drvn and hdd 1f out: no ex* **20/1**

6006 **3** nk **Stolen Song**[7] [3997] 4-9-2 55 SWhitworth 12 60
(MJRyan) *hld up in last trio and wl off the pce: rdn and prog on outer fr 3f out: kpt on u.p to take 3rd ins fnl f* **14/1**

-021 **4** 1 1/4 **Absinther**[27] [3393] 7-8-11 50 GBaker 16 53
(MRBosley) *dwlt: hld up in last and wl off the pce: prog on wd outside fr 3f out: styd on same pce fnl f* **7/1**

3210 **5** 4 **Anyhow (IRE)**[19] [3638] 7-10-0 67 JPMurtagh 9 64
(MissKMGeorge) *settled in midfield and off the pce: prog 4f out: chsd ldrs 2f out: wknd fnl f* **10/1**

0060 **6** 2 1/2 **Traveller's Tale**[21] [3573] 5-9-6 59 SDrowne 10 52
(PGMurphy) *settled towards rr and wl off the pce: prog over 3f out: chsd ldrs 2f out: wknd over 1f out* **25/1**

104- **7** shd **Smoothie (IRE)**[31] [6190] 6-9-10 63 RLMoore 1 56
(IanWilliams) *trckd clr ldrs: rdn 3f out: wknd 2f out* **14/1**

-066 **8** 3/4 **Tasneef (USA)**[25] [3450] 5-9-4 57 (b) TPQueally 14 49
(TDMccarthy) *racd freely: led after 2f: clr 1/2-way: wknd and hdd over 2f out* **14/1**

3240 **9** 1 **Bakiri (IRE)**[25] [3450] 6-9-7 60 JFEgan 5 50
(AndrewReid) *trckd clr ldrs: prog over 3f out: chsng ldrs whn hmpd on inner over 2f out: sn wknd* **18/1**

1005 **10** 1/2 **Duc's Dream**[4] [4070] 6-9-1 54 DHolland 15 43
(DMorris) *prom bhd clr ldrs: chsd clr ldr over 3f out: sn wknd* **5/1**[2]

6053 **11** 1 1/4 **Sir Haydn**[7] [3997] 4-9-11 64 (v) KFallon 6 51
(JRJenkins) *hld up wl in rr and off the pce: prog fr 4f out: drvn to chse ldrs over 2f out: sn wknd and eased* **9/2**[1]

0406 **12** 3 1/2 **Petite Colleen (IRE)**[14] [3806] 3-8-11 62 (p) FNorton 4 44
(DHaydnJones) *racd in midfield: lost pl 5f out: sn struggling in rr* **14/1**

-406 **13** 1 3/4 **Maximinus**[29] [3348] 4-8-13 55 LPKeniry(3) 7 34
(MMadgwick) *racd in midfield: lost pl on bnd over 6f out: rdn and struggling over 4f out* **12/1**

4-30 **14** 4 **Frangipani (IRE)**[29] [3348] 3-9-0 65 (t) TQuinn 11 37
(PFICole) *chsd clr ldrs: wknd over 3f out* **20/1**

030- **15** 9 **Veneziana**[270] [5834] 3-8-7 63 NDeSouza(5) 3 21
(PFICole) *led for 2f: chsd ldr to over 3f out: wknd rapidly* **25/1**

2m 26.83s (-3.27) **Going Correction** -0.275s/f (Firm)

**WFA** 3 from 4yo+ 12lb **15** Ran SP% **128.7**

Speed ratings: **99,97,97,96,93 92,92,91,91,90 89,87,86,83,77**CSF £121.79 CT £1494.35 TOTE £7.30: £2.10, £5.50, £4.80; EX 204.00 Place 6 £57.78, Place 5 £46.37.

**Owner** Mrs S J Lawrence **Bred** Mull Enterprises Ltd **Trained** Pandy, Gwent

**FOCUS**

There was a fair pace on here and the principals came from way off the pace. Only ordinary form, though.

**NOTEBOOK**

**Pont Neuf(IRE)** had been dropped 5lb since winning a seller over the course and distance last time out and her new trainer won with her at the first time of asking, despite the ground being quicker on this occasion. She could be capable of going in again while in this mood.

**Milk And Sultana** is not particularly consistent, but she has run a couple of races this term which suggest that she can win a race of this nature.

**Stolen Song** once again found the distance inadequate. The decent pace brought him into the equation late on but really he could have done with another quarter mile.

**Absinther**, who won this race last year off a 2lb lower mark, came here in top form having won at Brighton last time out. Having been held up in rear, he came with a sweeping run in the straight, but his progress was just not quick enough. He has never won more than one race in a season.

**Anyhow(IRE)** looks held by the Handicapper off her current mark.

**Traveller's Tale** has dropped 12lb in the handicap since the start of the turf season, but it has been warranted as he has struggled to recapture his best form.

**Tasneef(USA)** used up too much energy too early in the race.

T/Jkpt: £9,230.50 to a £1 stake. Pool: £32,502.00. 2.50 winning tickets. T/Plt: £35.60 to a £1 stake. Pool: £65,023.15. 1,329.95 winning tickets. T/Qpdt: £28.30 to a £1 stake. Pool: £3,259.30. 85.20 winning tickets. JN

# 4064 YARMOUTH (L-H)

Monday, July 26

**OFFICIAL GOING: Good to firm**

Wind: Slight against. Weather: Fine and sunny

## 4197 MILLS & REEVE NOVICE FILLIES' AUCTION STKS 5f 43y

**6:00** (6:01) (E ) 2-Y-O **£3,477** (£1,070; £535; £267) **Stalls** High

Form RPR

4145 **1** **Smiddy Hill**[9] [3930] 2-8-6 RFfrench 2 83
(RBastiman) *mde all: clr over 1f out: rdn out* **6/4**[1]

**2** 3 **Farthing (IRE)** 2-8-8 WSupple 7 75
(GCBravery) *a.p: wnt 2nd 1f out: r.o: no ch w wnr* **12/1**

1440 **3** 3 1/2 **High Chart**[40] [2970] 2-8-6 CCatlin 4 60
(GGMargarson) *chsd wnr 4f: no ex* **5/2**[2]

1200 **4** 3 **Evanesce**[9] [3938] 2-8-5 SHitchcott(3) 1 52
(MRChannon) *hld up: rdn 1/2-way: n.d* **4/1**[3]

00 **5** 1/2 **Ariane Star (IRE)**[23] [3532] 2-8-5 PRobinson 5 47
(MAJarvis) *prom to 1/2-way* **8/1**

00 **6** 1/2 **Sherbourne**[62] [2382] 2-8-2 PaulEddery 3 42
(MGQuinlan) *s.i.s: outpcd* **100/1**

63.48 secs (0.78) **Going Correction** +0.175s/f (Good) **6** Ran SP% **108.4**

Speed ratings: **100,95,89,84,84 83**CSF £18.69 TOTE £2.60: £1.30, £2.90; EX 27.00.

**Owner** I B Barker **Bred** I B Barker **Trained** Cowthorpe, N Yorks

**FOCUS**

A very decent time for a race of its type. The winner is clearly well suited to dominating on fast ground.

**NOTEBOOK**

**Smiddy Hill** bowled along in front and was never seriously challenged, scoring in a good time. All speed, she will be kept to the minimum trip, but the handicapper is likely to punish her for this.

**Farthing(IRE)** is a half-sister to six and seven-furlong winner Tidy. She made late progress when getting the hang of things and the experience should not be lost on her.

**High Chart**, out of her depth in the Queen Mary Stakes on her most recent start, chased the pacey favourite in vain to the furlong pole before losing second spot.

**Evanesce** was not disgraced in the Weatherbys Super Sprint but she found this too sharp and was never in a challenging position.

**Ariane Star(IRE)**

**Sherbourne** *Official explanation: jockey said filly hung right*

## 4198 PERTWEE & BACK FORD DRIVE FOR VALUE MAIDEN AUCTION STKS 7f 3y

**6:30** (6:32) (F ) 2-Y-O **£2,961** (£846; £423) **Stalls** High

Form RPR

2 **1** **Active Asset (IRE)**[73] [2095] 2-8-10 TEDurcan 4 75+
(MRChannon) *stmbld s: sn chsng ldrs: rdn and ev ch fr over 2f out: styd on u.p to ld post* **2/1**[2]

**2** shd **Double Kudos (FR)** 2-8-10 IMongan 7 75
(JGGiven) *s.i.s: outpcd: hdwy over 2f out: rdn to ld ins fnl f: hdd post* **14/1**

0 **3** 1 1/2 **Daisy Bucket**[37] [3083] 2-8-2 RFfrench 8 63
(DMSimcock) *chsd ldrs: led over 2f out: rdn and hdd ins fnl f: unable qck* **25/1**

**4** nk **Call Me Max** 2-8-10 WSupple 1 70
(EALDunlop) *hld up: hdwy over 2f out: rdn and edgd rt over 1f out: styd on* **14/1**

0 **5** 3/4 **Captain Margaret**[18] 3675 2-8-5 ....(t) JQuinn 10 63
(JPearce) *s.i.s: hld up: hdwy over 1f out: nt rch ldrs* **40/1**

0 **6** *nk* **Fadael (IRE)**[24] 3491 2-8-5 .... PaulEddery 13 63
(PWD'Arcy) *s.i.s: hld up: plld hrd: nt clr run over 1f out: r.o ins fnl f: nvr nrr* **18/1**

0 **7** *1* **Musical Day**[10] 3905 2-8-6 ow1 .... NCallan 12 61
(BJMeehan) *mid-div: rdn 1/2-way: nt clr run over 1f out: styd on: nt pce to chal* **15/2**[3]

0 **8** 1 1/4 **Pride Of London (IRE)**[23] 3532 2-8-2 .... DKinsella 6 54
(IAWood) *led: hdd over 4f out: rdn over 1f out: styd on same pce* **100/1**

5 **9** 3 1/2 **Ringarooma**[18] 3676 2-8-2 .... PRobinson 14 45
(MHTompkins) *hld up in tch: plld hrd: wknd over 1f out* **7/4**[1]

60 **10** 1 1/4 **Liameliss**[19] 3627 2-7-9 .... MHalford(7) 2 42
(MAAllen) *hld up: pushed along 1/2-way: n.d* **80/1**

0635 **11** 1 3/4 **Be Bop Aloha**[22] 3553 2-7-13 .... JFMcDonald(3) 3 38
(IAWood) *w ldr: plld hrd: led over 4f out: hdd over 2f out: wknd over 1f out* **16/1**

**12** *shd* **Gibraltar Bay (IRE)** 2-8-5 .... CCatlin 5 41
(GGMargarson) *s.i.s: outpcd* **40/1**

06 **13** *1* **Marians Maid (IRE)**[19] 3632 2-8-2 .... RMullen 11 35
(JSMoore) *chsd ldrs over 5f* **25/1**

**14** *22* **Prophet's Calling (IRE)** 2-8-4 .... J-PGuillambert(3) 9 —
(MissDAMchale) *started slowly: outpcd* **100/1**

1m 28.38s (1.88) **Going Correction** +0.175s/f (Good) **14** Ran SP% **121.7**
Speed ratings: **96,95,94,93,92 92,91,90,86,84 82,82,81,56**CSF £29.58 TOTE £3.30: £1.50, £3.80, £8.90; EX 45.40.
**Owner** aAIM Racing Syndicate **Bred** Rathasker Stud **Trained** West Ilsley, Berks

**FOCUS**

The runners came down the centre of the track. The form might prove a little dubious with several in behind the first two showing improvement.

**NOTEBOOK**

**Active Asset(IRE)** battled willingly to put his head in front on the line. He appreciated the extra furlong and there should be further improvement in him over a mile.

**Double Kudos(FR)** is a half-brother to Devil River Peek, a German-trained Group One winner, as well as Tulipa, winner of the Group Two Prix de Royallieu for Godolphin. Running on down the outside to put his head in front, he was just denied but is sure to go one better soon, perhaps over a mile.

**Daisy Bucket**, who was doing her best work at the finish on her debut, knew more this time, but after taking a narrow lead she could not see off the two colts.

**Call Me Max**, who was a little keen through the first part of the race, stayed on at the one pace once brought under pressure. Out of a mare who won over a mile at three, he may need a little more time.

**Captain Margaret** was equipped with a tongue strap. She faded to finish tailed off on her debut, but was ridden differently on this second outing and put in a better run. *Official explanation: jockey said filly stumbled shortly after the start*

**Fadael(IRE)**, stepping up two furlongs in trip from her debut, was keeping on quite nicely once the leaders had gone for home and looks to be learning.

**Ringarooma** was keen both going to post and early on in the race. Having travelled well, she found nothing once coming under pressure and she will have to settle better.

## 4199 HALLS GROUP H'CAP 7f 3y

7:00 (7:02) (E ) (0-70,69) 3-Y-O+ £3,945 (£1,214; £607; £303) Stalls High

Form RPR

0234 **1** **Concer Eto**[75] 2030 5-9-13 **69** ....(p) WSupple 9 82
(SCWilliams) *racd centre: hld up: hdwy over 1f out: r.o to ld wl ins fnl f* **7/2**[1]

4021 **2** 1/2 **Balerno**[12] 3841 5-9-3 **59** .... NDay 2 71
(RIngram) *racd centre: hld up in tch: rdn to ld 1f out: hdd wl ins fnl f* **5/1**[3]

0-00 **3** 1 1/2 **Sister Sophia (USA)**[12] 3841 4-9-6 **62** .... RMullen 6 70
(WJMusson) *s.i.s: racd centre: hld up: hdwy over 1f out: r.o* **40/1**

0000 **4** 1/2 **Iced Diamond (IRE)**[12] 3841 5-8-10 **52** .... CCatlin 11 59
(WMBrisbourne) *racd centre: hld up: hdwy over 1f out: styd on* **8/1**

1500 **5** 1/2 **Artistry**[12] 3841 4-8-13 **58** .... JFMcDonald(3) 7 63
(BJMeehan) *racd centre: chsd ldr tl led 3f out: sn rdn: hdd 1f out: styd on same pce* **25/1**

5224 **6** *nk* **Smith N Allan Oils**[10] 3895 5-8-12 **54** ....(p) SWKelly 4 58
(MDods) *racd centre: chsd ldrs: rdn and ev ch over 1f out: no ex* **5/1**[3]

0640 **7** 1 1/2 **Jedeydd**[10] 3895 7-8-8 **53** ....(t) LEnstone(3) 5 53
(MDods) *racd centre: chsd ldrs: rdn over 1f out: no ex* **14/1**

5050 **8** *5* **Warlingham (IRE)**[26] 3428 6-9-0 **56** .... PaulEddery 12 43
(PHowling) *racd alone stands' side: w ldrs: rdn and edgd lft over 1f out: wknd fnl f* **12/1**

150- **9** *4* **Kind Emperor**[313] 4998 7-9-8 **64** .... AMackay 3 40
(PLGilligan) *racd centre: led 4f: wknd over 1f out* **12/1**

0032 **10** 1 1/4 **Yashin (IRE)**[11] 3874 3-8-11 **60** .... PRobinson 10 33
(MHTompkins) *racd centre: hld up in tch: wknd wl over 1f out* **9/2**[2]

-000 **11** *5* **Kew The Music**[74] 2064 4-9-3 **59** .... TEDurcan 8 18
(MRChannon) *racd centre: prom over 5f* **40/1**

0010 **12** *10* **Albadi**[30] 3321 3-8-1 **50** ....(b) JQuinn 1 —
(CEBrittain) *racd centre: chsd ldrs: rdn 1/2-way: wknd over 2f out* **20/1**

1m 27.08s (0.58) **Going Correction** +0.175s/f (Good)
**WFA** 3 from 4yo+ 7lb **12** Ran SP% **120.4**
Speed ratings: **103,102,100,100,99 99,97,91,87,85 80,68**CSF £20.17 CT £606.37 TOTE £4.90: £2.80, £2.20, £7.70; EX 21.40.
**Owner** Bainey Racing Partnership **Bred** Lloyd Bros **Trained** Newmarket, Suffolk

**FOCUS**

The whole field came down the centre with the exception of Warlingham. This looks decent form for the grade.

**NOTEBOOK**

**Concer Eto**, returning from a break, had gained his last win at this track in August from a 5lb lower mark. Left with work to do when slightly short of room with over two to run, he made up ground quickly to challenge but hung left and showed an awkward head carriage before asserting.

**Balerno**, raised 5lb after Kempton, battled on well and only gave best in the final 50 yards. He is in top form at present.

**Sister Sophia(USA)** half reared as the stalls opened, losing ground, and did well to reach her final position. From a mark 6lb lower than at the start of the season, this was her best run for this yard but she does not look entirely straightforward.

**Iced Diamond(IRE)** is slipping in the weights and this was another solid run. He might be ready for another crack at a mile.

**Artistry**, having her second run back after a break, finished closer to Balerno but slightly further behind Iced Diamond than she had at Kempton from a 2lb lower mark.

**Smith N Allan Oils** is running creditably at the moment but appears held off his current turf mark.

**Yashin(IRE)** *Official explanation: jockey said gelding became upset in the stalls*

## 4200 PERTWEE & BACK FORD STREETKA (S) STKS 6f 3y

7:30 (7:32) (G ) 2-Y-O £2,541 (£726; £363) Stalls High

Form RPR

0014 **1** **Tipsy Lillie**[11] 3883 2-8-11 .... NCallan 1 51
(JulianPoulton) *racd centre: chsd ldrs: rdn to ld over 1f out: hdd ins fnl f: rallied to ld post* **7/1**

0020 **2** *shd* **Jay (IRE)**[5] 4012 2-8-6 .... PRobinson 4 46
(NACallaghan) *s.s: racd centre: hdwy u.p over 1f out: led ins fnl f: hdd post* **7/2**[2]

5432 **3** 1 1/4 **General Nuisance (IRE)**[13] 3824 2-8-4 ....(b[1]) DerekNolan(7) 7 47
(JSMoore) *racd centre: plld hrd: w ldr tl led over 3f out: rdn and hdd over 1f out: styd on u.p* **5/2**[1]

0605 **4** *nk* **Ahaz**[27] 3390 2-8-11 ....(b) IMongan 6 46
(IAWood) *racd centre: hld up in tch: rdn over 2f out: styd on u.p: nvr able to chal* **20/1**

0604 **5** *nk* **Tip Toes (IRE)**[9] 3951 2-7-13 .... TDean(7) 5 40
(MRChannon) *led centre: hdd over 4f out: rdn over 1f out: kpt on* **14/1**

455 **6** 1 3/4 **Sapphire Princess**[21] 3571 2-8-6 .... PDoe 2 35
(IAWood) *racd centre: plld hrd and prom: lost pl over 4f out: rdn whn hmpd over 1f out: nvr able to chal* **8/1**

0 **7** *nk* **Herencia (IRE)**[32] 3248 2-8-11 .... DeanMcKeown 8 39
(PABlockley) *chsd ldr stands' side: rdn over 2f out: n.d* **8/1**

2102 **8** *1* **Keresforth**[4] 4054 2-8-13 ....(b) LEnstone(3) 9 41
(IAWood) *led stands' side duo: rdn over 1f out: sn btn* **9/2**[3]

1m 17.55s (3.95) **Going Correction** +0.175s/f (Good) **8** Ran SP% **115.1**
Speed ratings: **80,79,78,77,77 75,74,73**CSF £31.96 TOTE £8.90: £2.30, £1.50, £1.30; EX 28.60.The winner was bought in for 7,000gns.
**Owner** Mrs A C Guinle **Bred** Southill Stud **Trained** Kentford, Suffolk

**FOCUS**

A pedestrian winning time, even for a poor race like this. The two to race alone on the stands' side finished at the back of the field.

**NOTEBOOK**

**Tipsy Lillie**, back over six furlongs, kept battling away and just got there. She has won two sellers now so will not be able to run in any more this season.

**Jay(IRE)** , with the blinkers left off, was slow to leave the stalls and went away to her left. She looked an awkward ride, but responded to pressure to get her head in front only to be touched off. She will do well to find an easier opportunity.

**General Nuisance(IRE)**, tried in blinkers after three runs in cheekpieces, kept trying but is fully exposed.

**Ahaz** benefited from the change of tactics and came out on top of Ian Wood's three runners.

**Tip Toes(IRE)** again hinted that she needs seven furlongs.

**Keresforth**, one of two to race up the stands' rail, did not stay the sixth furlong.

## 4201 COCKRILL GLASS FILLIES' H'CAP 1m 2f 21y

8:00 (8:02) (E ) (0-70,68) 3-Y-O+ £3,818 (£1,175; £587; £293) Stalls Low

Form RPR

4040 **1** **Ellovamul**[4] 4070 4-8-9 **50** .... PMakin(5) 9 58
(WMBrisbourne) *hld up: hdwy over 3f out: rdn and hung lft wl over 1f out: sn led: styd on* **6/1**[3]

1002 **2** 3/4 **Estimate**[20] 3609 4-9-2 **52** ....(v) DeanMcKeown 10 59
(JohnAHarris) *hld up: hdwy u.p and hung lft fr over 1f out: r.o* **5/1**[1]

4505 **3** 1/2 **Carriacou**[9] 3949 3-9-4 **64** .... PRobinson 6 70
(PWD'Arcy) *s.s: hld up: hdwy over 1f out: styd on* **13/2**

1060 **4** 3/4 **Sunset Mirage (USA)**[18] 3670 3-9-8 **68** ....(v[1]) TEDurcan 3 72
(EALDunlop) *chsd ldrs: led 3f out: rdn and hdd over 1f out: n.m.r ins fnl f: no ex towards fin* **10/1**

5015 **5** *3* **Hula Ballew**[10] 3921 4-9-10 **60** ....(p) SWKelly 13 59+
(MDods) *hld up: hdwy over 3f out: rdn and ev ch over 1f out: no ex ins fnl f* **11/2**[2]

06-0 **6** *2* **Legality**[184] 602 4-8-8 **51** .... MHalford(7) 14 46
(JulianPoulton) *hld up: styd on appr fnl f: nvr nrr* **40/1**

6600 **7** *5* **Nassiria**[10] 3919 3-9-2 **65** .... J-PGuillambert(3) 8 50
(CEBrittain) *chsd ldr: rdn and ev ch 3f out: wknd over 1f out* **33/1**

2104 **8** 1/2 **Joint Destiny (IRE)**[40] 2974 3-8-0 **49** .... LisaJones(3) 5 33
(EJO'Neill) *hld up: hdwy over 4f out: sn rdn: wknd over 3f out* **10/1**

-560 **9** 3/4 **Absolutely Soaked (IRE)**[77] 1998 3-8-13 **59** .... CLowther 1 42
(DrJDScargill) *hld up in tch: plld hrd: rdn and ev ch over 2f out: wkng whn hmpd wl over 1f out* **11/1**

6-65 **10** 1/2 **Eboracum Lady (USA)**[17] 3710 4-8-12 **48** .... CCatlin 4 30
(JDBethell) *chsd ldrs: rdn over 2f out: wkng whn n.m.r over 1f out* **10/1**

0-06 **11** *11* **Dry Wit (IRE)**[14] 3807 3-8-13 **59** .... JQuinn 11 20
(RMBeckett) *chsd ldrs over 6f* **20/1**

0-00 **12** *1* **Carla Moon**[23] 3530 3-9-0 **60** .... RMullen 12 19
(CFWall) *hld up in tch: wknd over 3f out* **40/1**

-023 **13** *15* **Boogie Magic**[14] 3809 4-9-10 **60** .... IMongan 7 —
(CNAllen) *led 7f: sn wknd* **10/1**

2m 8.67s (0.70) **Going Correction** +0.175s/f (Good)
**WFA** 3 from 4yo+ 10lb **13** Ran SP% **116.9**
Speed ratings: **104,103,103,102,100 98,94,94,93,93 84,83,71**CSF £33.89 CT £201.04 TOTE £8.10: £2.80, £2.00, £2.90; EX 44.00.
**Owner** Clayfields Racing **Bred** Joseph Hogan **Trained** Great Ness, Shropshire

**FOCUS**

An ordinary fillies' handicap.

**NOTEBOOK**

**Ellovamul** was beaten here four days earlier but had gained her last win at this track from the same mark in September. She liked the faster ground and scored despite not helping her rider when going to the front.

**Estimate**, back up in trip, stayed on but hung in behind the winner and did not look too enthusiastic about putting her head in front. Successful in a seller at this course in May, she is capable of winning again but might be happier finishing second.

**Carriacou** was having her second attempt at this trip, the first having come in a Listed race last backend. She was staying on at the end but always that bit too late.

**Sunset Mirage(USA)**, visored for the first time, was just held when done no favours by the hanging winner inside the last.

**Hula Ballew** had today's runner-up behind her when winning at Pontefract but was 9lb worse off here. She travelled well, but could not find a change of gear once let down.

**Legality**, who has dropped to a handy mark, made an encouraging return to the track after six months off.

**Absolutely Soaked(IRE)** travelled strongly for some way before running out of steam, and gave the impression that she should prove capable of better over a mile.

**Dry Wit(IRE)** *Official explanation: jockey said filly hung during the race*

**Boogie Magic** *Official explanation: jockey said filly had no more to give once headed*

## 4202 LITTLEWOODS BET DIRECT H'CAP — 2m

8:30 (8:30) (F) (0-55,53) 4-Y-0+ — £3,297 (£942; £471) Stalls Low

Form — RPR

0004 **1** **Annakita**[26] 3429 4-7-13 **37** ........ LisaJones(3) 6 — 47
(WJMusson) *hld up: hmpd after 3f: hdwy over 4f out: led over 2f out: rdn out* **4/1**[2]

-016 **2** ½ **Oops (IRE)**[9] 3928 5-8-8 **43** ........ WSupple 5 — 52
(JFCoupland) *a.p: chsd ldr 5f out: rdn over 2f out: styd on* **8/1**

0402 **3** 1 **Circus Maximus (USA)**[15] 3776 7-9-4 **53** ........ (p) TEDurcan 8 — 61
(IanWilliams) *prom: outpcd 5f out: hdwy over 1f out: r.o* **3/1**[1]

**3** *dht* **Super Fellow (IRE)**[29] 4909 10-7-8 **36** ow1 ........ MHalford(7) 10 — 44
(CNKellett) *s.s: sn given reminders: hld up: r.o ins fnl f: nt rch ldrs* **10/1**

4145 **5** 1¼ **Royale Pearl**[19] 3638 4-8-5 **40** ........ CCatlin 11 — 47
(RIngram) *hld up: hmpd over 6f out: hdwy over 3f out: no ex ins fnl f* **8/1**

0015 **6** 4 **River Of Fire**[6] 4007 6-7-10 **38** ........ (v) NataliaGemelova(7) 7 — 40
(CNKellett) *led: rdn and hdd over 2f out: wknd over 1f out* **13/2**

2033 **7** 1 **Galandora**[15] 3776 4-8-10 **52** ........ LucyRussell(7) 4 — 53
(DrJRJNaylor) *prom: hmpd after 3f: rdn over 2f out: wknd over 1f out* **6/1**[3]

0000 **8** 19 **Vanbrugh (FR)**[40] 2987 4-7-13 **41** ........ (tp) MNem(7) 1 — 19
(MissDAMchale) *chsd ldrs: rdn over 3f out: wknd over 2f out* **20/1**

3300 **9** 9 **Fitz The Bill (IRE)**[4] 4065 4-8-0 **42** ........ (t) DerekNolan(7) 2 — 9
(NBKing) *chsd ldrs: rdn adn wknd 3f out* **66/1**

-P00 **10** 2½ **Polanski Mill**[15] 3776 5-9-3 **52** ........ PaulEddery 9 — 16
(CAHorgan) *dwlt: hld up: a bhd: lost tch fnl 4f* **16/1**

0660 **11** 1½ **Promote**[12] 3851 8-8-5 **40** ........ (t) JQuinn 3 — —
(MsAEEmbiricos) *hld up: hdwy over 3f out: sn wknd* **33/1**

0-60 **12** ¾ **Lord Lahar**[56] 2525 5-7-12 **40** ........ TDean(7) 12 — —
(MRChannon) *s.s: hld up: plld hrd: hdwy after 3f: sn chsng ldr : wknd over 4f out* **66/1**

3m 34.67s (4.67) **Going Correction** +0.175s/f (Good) **12** Ran SP% **120.5**
Speed ratings: **95,94,94,94,93 91,91,81,77,75 75,74**CSF £35.73 TOTE £4.90: £1.10, £2.90; EX 46.50 TRIFECTA PL: CM £1.10, SF £1.40; TRICAST: A/O/CM £55.28, A/O/SF £151.90; Place 6 £35.28, Place 5 £18.03.

**Owner** N A Rooney **Bred** K L West, W J Musson And Broughton Bloodstock **Trained** Newmarket, Suffolk

**FOCUS**

A low-grade handicap and a modest winning time.

**NOTEBOOK**

**Annakita**, tackling two miles for only the second time, took advantage of a drop in the weights. She was in front plenty soon enough but was always going to hold on.

**Oops(IRE)** continues to run well and went down fighting. He is a versatile sort in terms of ground conditions.

**Circus Maximus(USA)** was left with a lot to do after losing his pitch turning out of the back straight. It was only in the final furlong that he really found his stride, but the effort came too late.

**Super Fellow(IRE)** had four runs on the Flat in Ireland, the latest in 2000, and is much better known as a chaser. After falling out of the stalls, he looked set to stay at the back of the field until flying home when it was too late. Having run over an extended four miles on his latest chase run, he probably thought he had to go round again.

**Royale Pearl** seemed to stay this longer trip and was only run out of third place near the line.

**River Of Fire**, raised 6lb after Folkestone, adopted similar front-running tactics but had no answers when tackled.

**Promote** *Official explanation: jockey said gelding made a noise*

T/Plt: £30.20 to a £1 stake. Pool: £38,495.20. 928.55 winning tickets. T/Qpdt: £9.90 to a £1 stake. Pool: £3,546.20. 264.10 winning tickets. CR

4203 - 4206a (Foreign Racing) - See Raceform Interactive

# 3980 BEVERLEY (R-H)

Tuesday, July 27

**OFFICIAL GOING: Good to firm (firm in places in home straight)**

## 4207 NATIONAL FESTIVAL CIRCUS (S) H'CAP — 1m 4f 16y

2:20 (2:20) (F) (0-55,51) 3-Y-O — £3,415 (£1,051; £525; £262) Stalls High

Form — RPR

6030 **1** **Northern Spirit**[8] 3984 3-9-1 **48** ........ (b1) NCallan 9 — 54
(KARyan) *trckd ldrs: hdwy to chse ldr wl over 1f out: rdn ent last: styd on to ld last 100 yds* **2/1**[1]

-064 **2** *nk* **Oniz Tiptoes (IRE)**[22] 3582 3-8-2 **35** ........ (v1) CCatlin 6 — 41
(JSWainwright) *keen: sn led and clr: rdn along 2f out: drvn ins last: hdd last 100 yds: kpt on* **12/1**

4005 **3** 2½ **Campbells Lad**[24] 3513 3-8-7 **40** ........ FNorton 4 — 42
(ABerry) *hld up towards rr: hdwy over 2f out: rdn to chse ldng pair whn hung rt ins last: one pce* **7/1**[3]

0644 **4** 2½ **Frambo (IRE)**[9] 3305 3-8-4 **40** ........ (tp) LisaJones(3) 7 — 38
(JGPortman) *chsd ldrs: rdn along over 2f out: sn drvn and one pce* **15/2**

3030 **5** 1¼ **Bonjour Bond (IRE)**[14] 3822 3-9-0 **47** ........ (v1) DMcGaffin 8 — 43
(BSmart) *hld up in tch: hdwy over 5f out: rdn along over 2f out and sn no imp* **10/1**

5000 **6** 1 **Nafferton Heights (IRE)**[8] 3984 3-8-13 **46** ........ (b1) TLucas 3 — 40
(MWEasterby) *chsd ldr: rdn along over 2f out: drvn and wknd wl over 1f out* **14/1**

6320 **7** 1¾ **Erte**[8] 3990 3-9-4 **51** ........ ACulhane 2 — 43
(MRChannon) *bhd tl rdn along and sme late hdwy* **9/2**[2]

2650 **8** 3½ **Royal Upstart**[29] 3371 3-7-5 **31** oh1 ........ DFentiman(7) 1 — 17
(WMBrisbourne) *bhd fr 1/2-way* **14/1**

-060 **9** 9 **Dame Nova (IRE)**[10] 3026 3-8-2 **42** ........ RoryMoore(7) 10 — 14
(PCHaslam) *s.i.s: a rr* **25/1**

0530 **10** 5 **Tancred Imp**[72] 2146 3-8-8 **41** ........ PHanagan 5 — 5
(DWBarker) *chsd ldrs: rdn along 5f out: wknd 3f out* **14/1**

2m 40.66s (1.36) **Going Correction** +0.075s/f (Good) **10** Ran SP% **116.4**
Speed ratings: **98,97,96,94,93 92,91,89,83,80**CSF £28.12 CT £144.12 TOTE £3.00: £1.40, £3.80, £3.10; EX 40.60.The winner was sold to C Moore for 6,200gns. Erte was claimed by J. B. Walton for £6,000.

**Owner** Ralph Murray **Bred** R Murray **Trained** Hambleton, N Yorks

**FOCUS**

A very poor heat run at a tactical gallop. The first two were clear.

**NOTEBOOK**

**Northern Spirit**, well-backed for this drop into selling company in the first-time blinkers, found plenty under pressure late on and won his first race at the tenth time of asking. This drop in trip and a return to quick ground was ideal, but he could struggle off a higher mark back up in grade in the future. He was sold for 6,200gns at the subsequent auction.

**Oniz Tiptoes(IRE)**, with the blinkers swapped for the first-time visor this time, paid late on for running keenly at the head of affairs, but was only just denied and was clear in second. He is edging closer in this grade, may be slightly better back over ten furlongs and can find a similar event this summer.

**Campbells Lad** did not stay this trip too well and spoilt any chance of closing on the leaders by hanging under pressure. However, it was his best effort to date.

**Frambo(IRE)** again did little to suggest she gets the trip and could only keep on at the same pace throughout on this return to the Flat.

**Erte** was never in it and turned in another frustrating display. He looks to be going the wrong way again. *Official explanation: jockey said gelding stumbled about 6f out*

## 4208 EUROPEAN BREEDERS FUND HOLDERNESS PONY CLUB MAIDEN STKS — 7f 100y

2:55 (2:57) (D) 2-Y-O — £4,940 (£1,520; £760; £380) Stalls High

Form — RPR

44 **1** **Banknote**[34] 3197 2-9-0 ........ KDarley 4 — 75
(AMBalding) *trckd ldrs: hdwy 2f out: rdn over 1f out: styd on to ld ins last* **4/1**[3]

05 **2** ¾ **Ball Boy**[12] 3870 2-9-0 ........ ACulhane 9 — 73
(MRChannon) *trckd ldrs: hdwy 2f out: rdn to ld 1f out: hdd and no ex ins last* **7/2**[2]

03 **3** ¾ **Tumbleweed Galore (IRE)**[6] 4016 2-8-11 ........ JFMcDonald(3) 7 — 71
(BJMeehan) *in tch: hdwy 2f out: swtchd lft over 1f out: sn rdn and kpt on wl fnl f: nrst fin* **16/1**

4 **4** 1½ **Miss Rosie**[59] 2470 2-8-9 ........ DAllan 10 — 62
(TDEasterby) *sn led: rdn along 2f out: drvn and hdd 1f out: wknd ins last* **11/2**

606 **5** 1 **Mirage Prince (IRE)**[30] 3336 2-8-9 ........ BSwarbrick(5) 5 — 65
(WMBrisbourne) *cl up: rdn along 2f out: wknd aproaching last* **66/1**

6 **6** 2½ **Chinese Puzzle**[17] 3749 2-9-0 ........ (t) WRyan 8 — 59
(HRACecil) *hld up: hdwy 3f out: rdn along wl over 1f out and sn no imp* **2/1**[1]

**7** 2 **Fenrir** 2-9-0 ........ GHind 6 — 55
(JRWeymes) *dwlt and bhd tl sme late hdwy* **100/1**

066 **8** *nk* **Forpetesake**[24] 3506 2-9-0 ........ FNorton 11 — 54
(MsDeborahJEvans) *towards rr: pushed along 1/2-way: rdn along 2f out: n.d* **66/1**

43 **9** 3½ **Lodgician (IRE)**[18] 3718 2-9-0 ........ PHanagan 2 — 46
(JJQuinn) *chsd ldrs on outer: pushed along wl over 2f out: rdn and hung rt over 1f out: sn btn* **12/1**

4 **10** *shd* **Eborarry (IRE)**[24] 3505 2-9-0 ........ JQuinn 12 — 45
(TDEasterby) *s.i.s: a rr* **50/1**

**11** 1 **Terminate (GER)** 2-9-0 ........ JMackay 1 — 43
(SirMarkPrescott) *dwlt: sn in tch on outer: n.m.r and shuffled bk 1/2-way: bhd after* **10/1**

1m 35.27s (0.97) **Going Correction** +0.075s/f (Good) **11** Ran SP% **119.5**
Speed ratings: **97,96,95,93,92 89,87,86,82,82 81**CSF £18.71 TOTE £5.20: £1.80, £1.30, £3.00; EX 16.90.

**Owner** The Queen **Bred** Exors Of The Late Queen Elizabeth **Trained** Kingsclere, Hants

**FOCUS**

A fair maiden run at a sound enough gallop. The winner always looked likely to be better than pre-race form suggested.

**NOTEBOOK**

**Banknote**, who disappointed over five furlongs when missing the break at Carlisle last time, broke smartly and showed a good attitude under pressure to record a tidy first success over this longer trip. His future is now in the hands of the Handicapper and he will stay a bit further in time.

**Ball Boy ◆**, well-supported in the ring to improve on his previous two outings, did just that, but could not hold off the winner when challenged late on. This stiffer test proved ideal, and although he could find a small maiden, he looks the type to prosper from a switch to nurseries.

**Tumbleweed Galore(IRE)**, third at 100/1 in a Leicester maiden last time, ran another sound race and now qualifies for nurseries, where he should fare a deal better. This looked about as far as he would want to go, an opinion his pedigree backs up.

**Miss Rosie** proved very easy to back on this second outing, and failed to improve as expected on her debut effort over this longer trip, having enjoyed the run of the race in front. She looks a likely type for nurseries

**Mirage Prince(IRE)**, who had shown little in three previous starts, looks to be slowly getting the hang of things and again looked suited by a test of stamina. His proximity at the finish drags the form down a little, however.

**Chinese Puzzle** looked very one paced and failed to find the normal improvement on this second career start. She already looks in need of a mile, and may be better back on easier ground, so should not be written off just yet.

**Lodgician(IRE)** *Official explanation: jockey said colt became upset in the stalls and was hanging right-handed from the turn into the straight*

**Terminate(GER)** was easy to back for this debut and, like a fair number of his stable's two-year-olds, was up against it after a slow start. This relation to juvenile winners can be expected to leave this form behind in due course.

## 4209 TOTEEXACTA H'CAP — 1m 100y

3:30 (3:30) (D) (0-80,80) 3-Y-0+ — £6,938 (£2,135; £1,067; £533) Stalls High

Form — RPR

6-00 **1** **Splodger Mac (IRE)**[22] 3586 5-7-13 **51** oh12 ow1 ........ JQuinn 8 — 61
(NBycroft) *mde all: qcknd clr over 2f out: ridden over 1f out: drvn and kpt on gamely towards fin* **66/1**

2523 **2** *nk* **Tedsdale Mac**[10] 3952 5-8-5 **57** ........ FNorton 10 — 66
(NBycroft) *trckd ldng pair: effrt on inner wl over 1f out: rdn ent last and styd on: jst hld* **3/1**[1]

0400 **3** *shd* **Gifted Flame**[11] 3911 5-8-9 **61** ........ DarrenWilliams 3 — 70
(TDBarron) *dwlt: sn in tch on inner: swed lft and hdwy over 1f out: rdn to chse wnr ins last: sn drvn and kpt on* **4/1**[2]

0016 **4** 4 **Cryfield**[18] 3714 7-8-10 **62** ........ KimTinkler 7 — 63
(NTinkler) *chsd ldr: rdn along 2f out: grad wknd appr last* **11/2**[3]

0364 **5** *nk* **Tedstale (USA)**[12] 3879 6-10-0 **80** ........ KDarley 4 — 80
(TDEasterby) *towards rr: pushed along over 3f out: rdn 2f out: kpt on same pce* **6/1**

10 **6** *nk* **First Dynasty (USA)**[73] 1845 4-9-6 **77** ........ AQuinn(5) 9 — 76
(MissSJWilton) *chsd ldrs: rdn along 3f out: wknd over 2f out* **14/1**

100 **7** 3 **Sedge (USA)**[11] 3921 4-8-5 **57** ........ RFitzpatrick 2 — 50
(PTMidgley) *wnt lft s and bhd: hdwy on inner 2f out: sn rdn and no imp* **33/1**

1000 **8** ¾ **Prince Of Gold**[17] 3731 4-9-0 **66** ........ (p) NCallan 5 — 57
(RHollinshead) *in tch: rdn along over 2f out: sn wknd* **8/1**

-265 **9** *nk* **Wrenlane**[14] 3819 3-8-4 **64** ........ PHanagan 1 — 55
(RAFahey) *bmpd s: a rr* **7/1**

150B **10** 3½ **Atlantic Quest (USA)**[7] 4006 5-9-9 **80** ........ PMulrennan(5) 6 — 63
(GAHarker) *chsd ldrs on outer: rdn along 3f out: sn btn* **14/1**

1m 47.6s (0.30) **Going Correction** +0.075s/f (Good)
**WFA** 3 from 4yo+ 8lb **10** Ran SP% **116.0**
Speed ratings: **101,100,100,96,96 96,93,92,91,88**CSF £257.06 CT £1038.37 TOTE £143.00: £14.60, £1.30, £2.80; EX 188.10.

**Owner** N Bycroft **Bred** John Brady **Trained** Brandsby, N Yorks

■ Stewards Enquiry : A Quinn one-day ban: careless riding (Aug 7)

**FOCUS**
A modest affair that produced just an ordinary time for the grade. The winner looks flaterred by being able to dominate a tactical affair.
**NOTEBOOK**
**Splodger Mac(IRE)** made all under a fine ride from Quinn to score a first win at the 11th attempt. This was a remarkable performance from 12lb out of the handicap (plus he carried 1lb overweight) and he deserves credit for holding on at the finish, but he will take a hike in the weights now, and is far from certain to follow-up on this. *Official explanation: trainer said, regarding the improved form shown, gelding was a difficult animal to train and everything had to go right for him in a race*
**Tedsdale Mac** just failed to reel in his stablemate, try as he might. This drop in trip suited and he again produced a solid effort, but remains winless since 2002, and is not one to place total faith in.
**Gifted Flame**, well-backed to improve on his recent efforts, did himself no favours by running keen early on at the back of the pack, but still held every chance if good enough late on. He was only just denied, and can score in a similar event, but his tendency to miss the break is becoming very frustrating.
**Cryfield** ran his race with no excuses, but looks held by his current mark at present.
**Tedstale(USA)** continues to look badly handicapped, but would have been better served by a stronger gallop.

## 4210 GEO. HOULTONS 125TH ANNIVERSARY H'CAP — 1m 4f 16y
4:05 (4:05) (E) (0-70,70) 3-Y-O+ £3,848 (£1,184; £592; £296) Stalls High

Form — RPR
4353 **1** **Shotley Dancer**[11] 3919 5-7-13 **41** oh6 ow1 ........ FNorton 5 48
(NBycroft) *in tch: hdwy to join ldr 1/2-way: led over3f out: rdn wl over 1f out: drvn and r.o gamely fnl f* **20/1**
0635 **2** ¾ **East Cape**[25] 3472 7-8-0 **42** ........ KimTinkler 2 48
(DonEnricoIncisa) *hld up and bhd: hdwy 5f out: effrt wl over 1f out: sn rdn: swtchd rt and styd on wl fnl f* **12/1**
0/00 **3** 1 **Lady Stratagem**[21] 3604 5-8-0 **42** ........ PFessey 7 46
(EWTuer) *trckd ldrs: hdwy over 3f out: rdn to chal over 1f out and ev ch tl drvn and no ex wl ins last* **50/1**
4022 **4** nk **Red River Rebel**[19] 3682 6-8-13 **55** ........ DarrenWilliams 6 59
(JRNorton) *trckd ldng pair: effrt and n.m.r 3f out: rdn along 2f out: drvn and kpt on ins last* **4/5**[1]
-254 **5** ½ **Eddies Jewel**[8] 3982 4-7-13 **41** oh5 ow1 ........ CCatlin 10 44
(JSWainwright) *in tch: rdn along 3f out: drvn and kpt on fnl f* **14/1**
035U **6** ½ **IlovetURTLE (IRE)**[6] 4015 4-8-5 **50** ........ LisaJones(3) 12 52
(MCChapman) *hld up and bhd: hdwy on outer 2f out: sn rdn: swtchd rt ins fnl f: styd on: nrst fin* **20/1**
0600 **7** ½ **Zan Lo (IRE)**[12] 3866 4-8-4 **51** ........ PMulrennan(5) 9 53
(BSRothwell) *in tch: effrt on inner over 2f out: sn rdn along and kpt on same pce* **66/1**
13-0 **8** 1¾ **Turn Of Phrase (IRE)**[30] 743 5-9-3 **59** ........ (b) PHanagan 8 58
(RAFahey) *hld up in midfield: hdwy over 3f out: sn rdn along and no imp* **11/1**[3]
0034 **9** ½ **Fleetfoot Mac**[15] 3806 3-8-12 **66** ........ NCallan 1 64
(PDEvans) *led: rdn along 4f out: sn hdd & wknd over 2f out* **9/1**[2]
0352 **10** ¾ **Dalriath**[6] 4015 5-7-7 **40** oh2 ........ DFox(5) 4 37
(MCChapman) *s.i.s: a rr* **16/1**
1046 **11** 12 **Little Task**[12] 3881 6-7-9 **44** oh5 ow4 ........ AReilly(7) 11 22
(JSWainwright) *a bhd* **20/1**
-224 **12** 5 **Sadler's Pride (IRE)**[53] 2652 4-10-0 **70** ........ JCarroll 13 40
(AndrewTurnell) *hld up: hdwy on outer and in tch 1/2-way: rdn along over 4f out sn wknd* **14/1**
2000 **13** 6 **Miss Ocean Monarch**[22] 3578 4-7-5 **40** oh5 ........ (be) DFentiman(7) 3 —
(DWChapman) *a bhd* **66/1**

2m 39.45s (0.15) **Going Correction** +0.075s/f (Good)
**WFA** 3 from 4yo+ 12lb — **13** Ran SP% **120.0**
Speed ratings: **102,101,100,100,100 99,99,98,98,97 89,86,82**CSF £228.37 CT £11258.61 TOTE £20.30: £4.00, £2.90, £10.90; EX 189.40.
**Owner** J A Swinburne **Bred** J A And Mrs Duffy **Trained** Brandsby, N Yorks
**FOCUS**
A moderate race run at a decent gallop, but the form looks suspect with a long-standing maiden winning.
**NOTEBOOK**
**Shotley Dancer**, who showed improved form when upped to this trip last time, produced a personal best to score a first-ever success at the 35th time of asking. She was 6lb out of the handicap, and had to carry 1lb overweight, so has clearly found her niche and could step up on this again.
**East Cape** stepped up on his effort over course and distance last time and was finishing best of all behind the winner. He is on a fair mark and looks capable of expoliting it with a more prominent ride over this trip.
**Lady Stratagem** ran a much improved race and was only run out of contention late on. She is hard to predict however, remains winless on the Flat, and cannot be certain to repeat this form next time.
**Red River Rebel** had every chance to repeat last year's win in this race off the same mark, but could not quicken when it mattered and was slightly disappointing.
**Fleetfoot Mac** *Official explanation: jockey said gelding was unsuited by the ground*

## 4211 LADIES DAY HERE ON 11TH AUGUST CLASSIFIED STKS — 5f
4:40 (4:41) (E) 3-Y-O+ £3,786 (£1,165; £582; £291) Stalls High

Form — RPR
3005 **1** **Distant Times**[10] 3926 3-9-2 74 ........ DAllan 10 84
(TDEasterby) *chsd ldrs: hdwy 2f out: sn rdn: led ins last and drvn out* **5/1**
4060 **2** nk **Trick Cyclist**[29] 3384 3-8-7 72 ........ TBlock(7) 6 81
(AMBalding) *in tch: hdwy 2f out: rdn and ev ch ins last: kpt on* **10/1**
0220 **3** 2½ **Boavista (IRE)**[6] 4011 4-8-13 62 ........ NCallan 4 66
(PDEvans) *bolted to s: led: rdn along 2f out: drvn ent last: sn hdd & wknd* **14/1**
2054 **4** ¾ **Winthorpe (IRE)**[3] 4133 4-9-0 71 ........ THamilton(3) 7 67
(JJQuinn) *cl up: rdn along wl over 1f out: sn drvn and wknd* **3/1**[1]
6000 **5** 1½ **Percy Douglas**[12] 3864 4-9-2 40 ........ (t) AnnStokell 9 60?
(MissAStokell) *wnt lft s: sn chsng ldrs: rdn wl over 1f out and sn btn* **50/1**
3000 **6** 1¼ **Sunley Sense**[18] 3713 8-9-6 74 ........ (v) ACulhane 5 59
(MRChannon) *chsd ldrs: rdn wl over 1f out: sn btn* **9/2**[3]
-000 **7** 9 **Miss Ceylon**[12] 3864 4-8-13 39 ........ (b[1]) JMcAuley 3 16
(SPGriffiths) *sn outpcd and bhd fr 1/2-way* **66/1**
0100 **8** 12 **Tommy Smith**[11] 3920 6-9-3 71 ........ (b) DarrenWilliams 8 —
(JSWainwright) *wnt rt: bmpd s and rdr lost iron: a bhd* **10/3**[2]
1020 **9** 1¾ **The Fisio**[6] 4034 4-9-7 75 ........ (v) KDarley 1 —
(SGollings) *stl blindfolded whn stalls open: v.s.a and a bhd* **15/2**
0000 **L** **General Smith**[53] 2656 5-8-11 50 ........ PMulrennan(5) 2 —
(GAHarker) *rrd and stuck in stalls s: tk no part* **50/1**

62.76 secs (-1.24) **Going Correction** -0.20s/f (Firm)
**WFA** 3 from 4yo+ 4lb — **10** Ran SP% **115.9**
Speed ratings: **101,100,96,95,92 90,76,57,54,**—CSF £53.10 TOTE £6.50: £2.00, £2.70, £2.80; EX 80.20.
**Owner** Times Of Wigan **Bred** Times Of Wigan Ltd **Trained** Great Habton, N Yorks
**FOCUS**
An eventful classified stakes that saw three of the field lose all chance at the start. As such, the form looks worth treating with a degree of caution.
**NOTEBOOK**
**Distant Times**, with the visor left off this time, stayed on well up the rising ground to record a gritty success. He appreciated the return to this faster ground and the fast pace over this shorter trip was very much in his favour. Although he has struggled off a higher mark in the past, he could be worth keeping to the minimum trip, and may build on this.
**Trick Cyclist** was finishing with real effect, but the line came too soon. This was his most worthwhile form for a while, but his ability to reproduce this next time must be taken on trust.
**Boavista(IRE)**, who bolted to start, could find no more late on after showing good early pace to get to the far rail and lead. This was not a bad effort at the weights and she deserves credit.
**Winthorpe(IRE)** had every chance if good enough and is starting to run out of excuses.
**Sunley Sense**, the subject of strong support in the betting ring, ran his race and can have no excuses on this drop in grade.
**Tommy Smith** had an impossible task after he was bumped and his rider lost an iron at the start. This run is best forgotten. *Official explanation: jockey said saddle slipped and he lost an iron in the first furlong*
**The Fisio** lost all chance at the start and this run should be ignored. *Official explanation: jockey said gelding missed the break after blind was removed late due to the behaviour of General Smith in the next stall*

## 4212 KEN MAGEE LIFETIME IN RACING MAIDEN AUCTION FILLIES' STKS — 5f
5:15 (5:16) (F) 2-Y-O £3,396 (£1,045; £522; £261) Stalls High

Form — RPR
4620 **1** **Withering Lady (IRE)**[10] 3938 2-8-5 ........ RHavlin 8 77
(MrsPNDutfield) *trckd ldrs: hdwy to ld 2f out: rdn ins last and kpt on* **4/9**[1]
4320 **2** 1¼ **Hillside Heather (IRE)**[10] 3950 2-8-2 ........ FNorton 4 70
(ABerry) *a.p: shkn up to chse ldr ent last: son rdn and edgd rt: kpt on* **6/1**[2]
00 **3** 6 **Emeraude Du Cap**[24] 3532 2-8-2 ........ JMackay 9 49
(MLWBell) *hld up: hdwy 2f out: rdn and edgd lft ent last: one pce* **25/1**
**4** ¾ **Rainbow Iris** 2-8-9 ........ DMcGaffin 1 53
(BSmart) *cl up on outer: rdn along 2f out: sn one pce* **20/1**
02 **5** nk **Russian Servana (IRE)**[24] 3526 2-8-2 ........ JQuinn 6 45
(JPearce) *in tch: rdn along 2f out: edgd rt 1f out: no imp* **12/1**[3]
0 **6** hd **Jasmine Hill**[10] 3950 2-8-2 ........ CCatlin 10 44
(NBycroft) *cl up: rdn along and lost pl 1/2-way: drvn and edgd lft ent last* **16/1**
5 **7** 1 **Sunny Times (IRE)**[20] 3633 2-7-13 ........ LisaJones(3) 2 41
(JWPayne) *in tch on outer: pushed along 1/2-way: no hdwy* **20/1**
00 **8** 7 **Star Of Kildare (IRE)**[25] 3469 2-8-2 ........ KimTinkler 11 16
(NTinkler) *led: rdn along and hdd 2f out: sn wknd and bhd whn bdly hmpd ins last* **50/1**
**9** 21 **Blissphilly** 2-8-9 ........ PHanagan 5 —
(RAFahey) *s.i.s: a wl bhd* **25/1**
0 **B** **Peaceful Frontier**[14] 3818 2-8-3 ow1 ........ RFitzpatrick 7 —
(CSmith) *pushed along in rr: rdn wl over 1f out: hmpd and b.d ins last* **100/1**

63.74 secs (-0.26) **Going Correction** -0.20s/f (Firm) — **10** Ran SP% **117.3**
Speed ratings: **94,92,82,81,80 80,78,67,34,**—CSF £2.85 TOTE £1.60: £1.10, £1.60, £2.00; EX 1.80.
**Owner** Salter, Wilson and Oakes **Bred** R P Michaelson And D Allport **Trained** Axmouth, Devon
**FOCUS**
A pretty ordinary maiden in which Withering Lady was able to confirm her recent improvement. The front two were well clear.
**NOTEBOOK**
**Withering Lady(IRE)** has showed improved form lately - she finished runner-up in a reasonable Salisbury maiden before a very creditable seventh in the Super Sprint - and was too good for these. Things will be harder in future, but she could just be the type to run well in a Sales race later in the year.
**Hillside Heather(IRE)** had not appeared to be progressing in recent outings, but this was an improved effort. She was clear of the remainder and there is a minor event in her if she goes the right way.
**Emeraude Du Cap** had shown little on her first two starts but, dropped a furlong in trip, she showed her first signs of ability. She is now qualified for a nursery mark and could do well in that grade.
**Rainbow Iris**, a 14,000gns half-sister to five-furlong two-year-old winner Oro Verde, made a respectable debut and is open to improvement.
**Russian Servana(IRE)**, well supported on her debut for new connections, found this tougher than the seller she contested on her previous start.

## 4213 DOROTHY LAIRD MEMORIAL TROPHY (LADIES RACE) (HANDICAP STKS) — 1m 1f 207y
5:50 (5:51) (E) (0-75,69) 3-Y-O+ £3,991 (£1,228; £614; £307) Stalls High

Form — RPR
4524 **1** **Oscar Pepper (USA)**[11] 3903 7-10-9 **64** ........ (v) AlexGreaves 16 77
(TDBarron) *in tch: hdwy 3f out: rdn to ld over 1f out: drvn and kpt on* **8/1**[3]
0000 **2** 3 **Rainstorm**[3] 4122 9-8-13 **40** ........ MrsSOwen 12 47
(WMBrisbourne) *stdd s and bhd: swed outside and hdwy 2f out: styd on ins last* **12/1**
3510 **3** nk **Come What July (IRE)**[8] 3981 3-9-4 **55** ........ (b) MrsMMorris 19 62
(MrsNMacauley) *hld up towards rr: hdwy on inner 1/2-way: rdn to chse ldrs wl over 1f out: kpt on ins last* **16/1**
1122 **4** nk **Yenaled**[17] 3731 7-11-0 **69** ........ MissNCarberry 18 75
(KARyan) *hld up towards rr: hdwy over 3f out: rdn over 1f out: styd on fnl f* **11/4**[1]
3060 **5** ½ **Beneking**[17] 3734 4-9-10 **51** ........ StephanieHollinshead 8 56
(RHollinshead) *midfield: hdwy 1/2-way: chsd ldrs wl over 1f out: sn rdn and one pce ent last* **50/1**
4342 **6** 2½ **Lazzaz**[4] 4080 6-9-1 **47** ........ MrsMarieKing(5) 9 47
(PWHiatt) *cl up: rdn over 2f out: drvn and wknd over 1f out* **6/1**[2]
0026 **7** 1 **Late Arrival**[15] 3804 7-8-13 **40** ........ (b) LisaJones 17 39
(MDHammond) *hld up towards rr: swed rt and hdwy over 2f out: rdn wl over 1f out: kpt on ins last: nt rch ldrs* **12/1**
-000 **8** ¾ **Shalbeblue (IRE)**[36] 3149 7-9-1 **42** ........ (b) MissLEllison 11 39
(BEllison) *chsd ldrs: rdn wl over 2f out and grad wknd* **33/1**
6300 **9** ½ **Uno Mente**[11] 3921 5-9-10 **51** ........ KimTinkler 6 47
(DonEnricoIncisa) *hld up and bhd: hdwy 3f out: rdn and kpt on appr last: nt rch ldrs* **25/1**
0151 **10** 1 **Theatre Lady (IRE)**[4] 4080 6-9-11 **52** 5ex ........ MissEFolkes 4 46
(PDEvans) *b ehind tl styd on fnl 2f* **12/1**
1500 **11** ½ **Littleton Zephir (USA)**[19] 3670 5-9-1 **47** ........ MrsCThompson(5) 1 40
(MrsPTownsley) *in tch on outer: wd st: rdn along 3f out: grad wknd* **40/1**

146- **12** ½ **Emperor's Well**[285] [5596] 5-10-2 **57**........................(b) MissSBrotherton 15 49
(MWEasterby) *led: rdn along 3f out: drvn and hdd over 1f out: sn wknd* **40/1**

00-0 **13** 2½ **Eight (IRE)**[4] [4080] 8-9-1 **47**.................................... MsTDzieciolowska(5) 3 35
(MRChannon) *in tch: rdn along 3f out: grad wknd* **50/1**

2/03 **14** ¾ **Awwal Marra (USA)**[11] [3899] 4-9-4 **45**............................ MsCWilliams 14 31
(EWTuer) *a towards rr* **22/1**

06-0 **15** *nk* **Deekazz (IRE)**[6] [4015] 5-9-0 **44** ow7.................. MissVictoriaCasey(5) 13 32
(FWatson) *midfield: pushed along 4f out and sn wknd* **66/1**

0442 **16** 1¼ **Holly Rose**[19] [3670] 5-9-12 **53**....................................(v[1]) HayleyTurner 10 36
(DECantillon) *bhd fr 1/2-way* **10/1**

2112 **17** 1¼ **Santiburi Lad (IRE)**[16] [3781] 7-10-13 **68**.......................... MrsNWilson 2 49
(NWilson) *trckd ldrs: effrt and swtchd ins 2f out: sn rdn and btn* **8/1**[3]

-060 **18** 3½ **Wuxi Venture**[10] [3470] 9-10-3 **63**.............................. MissVTunnicliffe(5) 7 37
(RAFahey) *a rr* **20/1**

-400 **19** 27 **Cadeaux Rouge (IRE)**[56] [2546] 3-8-13 **55**................. MissAWallace(5) 5 —
(MrsPNDutfield) *cl up: rdn along 4f out: wknd qckly and sn bhd* **50/1**

2m 6.92s (-0.28) **Going Correction** +0.075s/f (Good)
**WFA** 3 from 4yo+ 10lb **19** Ran SP% **129.4**
Speed ratings: **104,101,101,101,100 98,97,97,96,96 95,95,93,92,92 91,90,87,66**CSF £95.74 CT £1541.39 TOTE £9.80: £2.10, £4.10, £4.80, £1.10; EX 79.00 Place 6 £537.10, Place 5 £315.23.
**Owner** Ian Armitage **Bred** Carlos Perez **Trained** Maunby, N Yorks

**FOCUS**
A strong pace to this ladies' race and it suited those to be rideen off the gallop. Once again a high draw proved crucial.

**NOTEBOOK**
**Oscar Pepper(USA)** responded gamely to pressure in the sraight and in the end ran out a ready winner. He has been consistent this year, but is was his first win since June 2003 and he did have the benefit of a high draw this time, so may struggle in the future if the Handicapper reacts literally to this.
**Rainstorm** finished best of all behind the winner and ran his best race for sometime. He does go well in this type of event and is weighted to win at present, but may need a slight drop in trip.
**Come What July(IRE)** had the plum draw and ran on well enough under pressure in the straight, but never really looked like scoring. This goes down as another sound effort, but he remains a maiden on turf.
**Yenaled** got going a bit too late from his decent draw and could only muster the one pace when asked for maximum effort. This was slightly disappointing, but he may just be weighted to his best at present, and was not disgraced.
**Lazzaz** could not get to the front from his moderate draw and ran below par as a result. He rarely wins, but is a good yardstick in this division and is capbale of slightly better, back on a more conventional track.
**Holly Rose** *Official explanation: jockey said mare did not face the visor*
T/Plt: £1,000.40 to a £1 stake. Pool: £43,651.35. 31.85 winning tickets. T/Qpdt: £287.10 to a £1 stake. Pool: £3,647.50. 9.40 winning tickets. JR

# 3043 GOODWOOD (R-H)

Tuesday, July 27

**OFFICIAL GOING: Good (good to firm in places on round course)**
Wind: nil Weather: fine but cloudy

## 4214 STERLING INSURANCE SUMMER STKS (HERITAGE H'CAP) 1m 1f 192y
**2:05** (2:06) (B ) 4-Y-O+ **£29,000** (£11,000; £5,500; £2,500) **Stalls** Low

Form RPR

32-0 **1** **Coat Of Honour (USA)**[17] [3756] 4-8-12 **92**......................... SSanders 11 105+
(SirMarkPrescott) *trckd ldr: led 2f out: wandered u.p 1f out: drvn and kpt on wl nr fin* **10/1**

2605 **2** *nk* **Impeller (IRE)**[10] [3937] 5-8-6 **86**......................................... SDrowne 16 95
(WRMuir) *lw: hld up in midfield: prog and swtchd sharply lft 2f out: str run to press wnr last 100yds: nt qckn nr fin* **9/1**

2055 **3** ½ **Bonecrusher**[19] [3661] 5-9-10 **104**....................................(v) TPQueally 14 114+
(DRLoder) *dwlt: hld up in rr: prog whn hmpd 2f out: swtchd lft and rapid hdwy fnl f: fin strly: unlucky* **25/1**

2060 **4** 1 **Anani (USA)**[39] [3034] 4-9-8 **102**............................................ TQuinn 13 108
(EALDunlop) *prom: effrt over 2f out: drvn to chse wnr jst over 1f out tl ins fnl f: nt qckn* **25/1**

0511 **5** *hd* **Spanish Don**[13] [3842] 6-8-12 **95**...................................... LPKeniry(3) 8 101
(DRCElsworth) *lw: t.k.h: hld up bhd ldrs: effrt over 2f out: rdn and nt qckn over 1f out: kpt on fnl f* **11/2**[2]

-042 **6** *nk* **Windy Britain**[18] [3694] 5-8-8 **88**............................................. DHolland 4 93+
(LMCumani) *lw: hld up in rr: prog on inner whn nt clr run over 1f out: styd on fnl f: nrst fin* **7/1**[3]

0000 **7** *nk* **Sir George Turner**[39] [3034] 5-9-1 **95**.............................. KDalgleish 10 100+
(MJohnston) *pushed along in rr early: effrt over 2f out: chsng ldrs whn nt clr run over 1f out: styd on ins fnl f* **50/1**

121- **8** 1¾ **Fantastic Love (USA)**[404] [2482] 4-9-8 **102**..........................(t) LDettori 15 103
(SaeedBinSuroor) *prom: rdn to chal over 2f out: unable qck wl over 1f out: fdd fnl f* **9/2**[1]

0051 **9** *nk* **Prairie Wolf**[8] [3985] 8-7-9 **78** 4ex...................................... NMackay(3) 1 79
(MLWBell) *trckd ldrs: rdn whn n.m.r 2f out: sn btn* **12/1**

004 **10** ¾ **Chinkara**[27] [3415] 4-8-10 **90**................................................ JFortune 9 89
(BJMeehan) *hld up in midfield: prog on outer over 2f out: nt qckn over 1f out : wknd fnl f* **10/1**

0136 **11** *hd* **Krugerrand (USA)**[13] [3842] 5-8-4 **84**................................... GCarter 17 83+
(WJMusson) *dwlt: racd in last pair: effrt on inner whn nt clr run 2f out: no ch after* **25/1**

5620 **12** *nk* **Alrafid (IRE)**[34] [3212] 5-8-6 **86**............................................. RLMoore 7 84+
(GLMoore) *wl in rr: effrt on inner whn nt clr run 2f out: swtchd sharply lft wl over 1f out: no real prog* **12/1**

4630 **13** 1¼ **Blythe Knight (IRE)**[17] [3756] 4-9-9 **103**.................................. KFallon 5 99+
(EALDunlop) *hld up towards rr: shkn up and effrt whn hmpd 2f out: nt rcvr and eased* **12/1**

0000 **14** 1 **Telemachus**[18] [3716] 4-8-6 **86**............................................(b[1]) MFenton 12 80
(JGGiven) *led to 2f out: wknd* **22/1**

-066 **15** 2 **Foodbroker Founder**[25] [3482] 4-9-3 **97**............................... DaneO'Neill 6 87
(DRCElsworth) *trckd ldrs tl lost pl and btn over 3f out* **33/1**

2m 6.61s (-1.07) **Going Correction** +0.05s/f (Good) **15** Ran SP% **118.1**
Speed ratings: **106,105,105,104,104 104,103,102,102,101 101,101,100,99,97**CSF £86.41 CT £2190.12 TOTE £13.90: £4.10, £3.50, £6.80; EX 188.20 Trifecta £1739.20 Part won..
**Owner** E B Rimmer-Osborne House **Bred** Makio Shimoyashiki **Trained** Newmarket, Suffolk

**FOCUS**
A good, competitive handicap, but an unspectacular time for the class of race, and some scrimmaging in the straight led to several runners having hard-luck stories.

**NOTEBOOK**
**Coat Of Honour(USA)**, an improver in 2003 when fitted with blinkers, showed the benefit of his recent run at York and, given a positive ride, was just able to hold on. He had the headgear left off on this occasion, but did run around in front before responding when challenged; it would be no surprise to see the blinkers re-applied at some stage. Although he is likely to be raised a few pounds for this, no doubt connections will find a suitable opportunity for him, and a race such as the Courage Handicap at Newbury springs to mind.
**Impeller(IRE)**, returning to this longer trip, likes this track and, getting a good run through on the inside, had every chance before the winner responded. Late summer is his time of year, and it would be no surprise to see him try to repeat last season's success in the nine-furlong handicap at the September meeting.
**Bonecrusher ♦**, with the visor back on, missed the break and was one of the worst sufferers in the scrimmaging halfway up the straight. He finished strongly once in the clear and deserves to pick up a similar race after being touched off at Epsom earlier in the year. He will be interesting if finding an opportunity on Newmarket's July course, where he has scored on both previous appearances.
**Anani(USA)**seemed to run his race but has suffered for his efforts in Pattern company last season. Although he is slipping in the handicap, he needs to drop a few pounds more in order to get his head in front.
**Spanish Don**, attempting the hat-trick but up in class and racing off a 7lb higher mark, had his chance and stuck to his task without being good enough. He remains a progressive sort and may be seen to better effect back on a flatter track.
**Windy Britain**, who was settled at the back from her high draw, got a run through near the rail and, although slightly held up in her run, cannot be said to be particularly unlucky. She will appreciate the return to a stiffer track and can add to her score before long.
**Sir George Turner**, without the visor that was fitted last time, missed the break and was struggling from an early stage. He ran on in the closing stages, following the runner-up through, without ever looking likely to reach the principals. He is slipping in the handicap and at least this suggested he may be on the way back.
**Fantastic Love(USA)**, making his debut for Godolphin and having his first outing since Royal Ascot last year, is now a gelding. Despite that and the drop in trip, he was made favourite, but after racing close to the pace was in trouble once the winner kicked for home. Nevertheless, the outing should bring him on, a step up in trip will be in his favour and he may be the sort for a race such as the Ebor.
**Prairie Wolf**, who has a terrific record in this race, having won it in 2002, ran his race but is not quite as good as he used to be and faded in the closing stages.
**Krugerrand(USA)** *Official explanation: jockey said gelding suffered interference 1 1/2f out*
**Blythe Knight(IRE)** was travelling well when becoming sandwiched during the scrimmaging early in the straight, which effectively ended his chance. He is not an easy horse to win with and needs to be produced just right, but is clearly a lot better than this bare result suggests. *Official explanation: jockey said colt suffered interference 1 1/2f out*
**Telemachus**, fitted with blinkers for the first time, had to be pushed to get to the front but, once there, probably ran a little too free and did not get home.

## 4215 ABN AMRO STKS (REGISTERED AS THE GORDON STAKES) (GROUP 3) 1m 4f
**2:40** (2:40) (A ) 3-Y-O **£29,000** (£11,000; £5,500; £2,500) **Stalls** Low

Form RPR

4-22 **1** **Maraahel (IRE)**[40] [2999] 3-8-10 **103**.............................................. RHills 8 116
(SirMichaelStoute) *lw: trckd ldrs: smooth prog to ld over 2f out: rdn over 1f out: styd on wl* **9/4**[2]

-3 **2** 1½ **Go For Gold (IRE)**[75] [2068] 3-8-10 ........................................... KFallon 7 114
(APO'Brien, Ire) *settled in rr: prog 3f out: chsd wnr over 1f out: drvn and no imp fnl f: kpt on* **25/1**

1 **3** 1½ **Remaadd (USA)**[74] [2085] 3-8-10 **100**................................ MartinDwyer 6 111
(MPTregoning) *bit bkwd: led for 2f: styd prom: unable qck and lost pl 2f out: styd on again ins fnl f* **5/1**[3]

1-4 **4** *nk* **Mikado**[31] [3333] 3-8-10 ............................................................ JPMurtagh 3 111
(APO'Brien, Ire) *neat: led after 2f: rdn over 3f out: hdd over 2f out: one pce after* **11/1**

-121 **5** 3½ **Duke Of Venice (USA)**[39] [3035] 3-8-13 **114**.........................(t) LDettori 4 108
(SaeedBinSuroor) *restless in stalls: wl in tch: effrt 3f out: chsd wnr briefly wl over 1f out: sn outpcd and btn* **13/8**[1]

3 **6** ¾ **Lyonels Glory**[30] [3359] 3-8-10 ............................................... DHolland 1 104
(USuter, Germany) *w'like: settled in last: effrt on outer wl over 2f out: one pce and nvr able to rch ldrs* **20/1**

0201 **7** 4 **Massif Centrale**[26] [3454] 3-8-10 **100**.................................... DaneO'Neill 2 98
(DRCElsworth) *lw: w ldr after 2f to wl over 2f out: sn wknd* **14/1**

-510 **8** ¾ **Manyana (IRE)**[51] [2722] 3-8-10 **106**....................................(t) WSupple 5 97
(MPTregoning) *t.k.h: hld up: rdn 3f out: sn btn* **16/1**

2m 36.01s (-2.92) **Going Correction** +0.05s/f (Good) **8** Ran SP% **115.0**
Speed ratings: **111,110,109,108,106 105,103,102**CSF £54.55 TOTE £3.50: £1.50, £2.10, £2.00; EX 76.00 Trifecta £338.20 Pool of £2,172.61 - 4.56 winning units..
**Owner** Hamdan Al Maktoum **Bred** Shadwell Estate Company Limited **Trained** Newmarket, Suffolk

**FOCUS**
The pace was only moderate for this traditional St Leger trial, but it looked an up-to-scratch renewal. An average winning time for a race of its class, though.

**NOTEBOOK**
**Maraahel(IRE)** successfully stepped out of handicap company, quickening nicely to lead and always holding the runner-up. Set to go for the St Leger now, he promises to stay the extra distance at Doncaster and easier ground will not inconvenience him.
**Go For Gold(IRE)** failed to give his running when well beaten at York in May. Ridden more conservatively, he improved for this longer trip and, as a half-brother to Leger winner Milan, should have no problem staying at Doncaster.
**Remaadd(USA) ♦** looked to be carrying some condition, as he had on his debut. He lost his pitch with a quarter of a mile to run and was shuffled back to sixth place, but came home in taking style. He looks sure to win a nice race, but will need supplementing for the St Leger.
**Mikado**, dropped in trip, made a lot of the running and battled on when headed, although he was running out of steam near the line.
**Duke Of Venice(USA)** was conceding 3lb all round due to his Queen's Vase win. Although not entirely disgraced, neither the track nor the drop in trip from two miles were in his favour. *Official explanation: jockey said colt did not handle the track*
**Lyonels Glory**, a German raider, is a really big colt. He might have found the ground too fast and remains a maiden.
**Massif Centrale** was found wanting on his return to Group company. This track probably did not suit him.
**Manyana(IRE)** *Official explanation: jockey said colt had a breathing problem*

## 4216 BETFAIR CUP (REGISTERED AS THE LENNOX STKS) (GROUP 2) 7f
**3:15** (3:15) (A ) 3-Y-O+ **£58,000** (£22,000; £11,000; £5,000) **Stalls** High

Form RPR

1-30 **1** **Byron**[42] [2956] 3-8-7 **111**........................................................(t) KMcEvoy 5 117
(SaeedBinSuroor) *lw: trckd ldng trio: effrt to ld jst over 1f out: qcknd 2l clr ins fnl f: rdn out* **16/1**

2140 **2** ¾ **Suggestive**[17] [3724] 6-9-0 **109**.....................................................(b) MHills 1 115
(WJHaggas) *hld up in midfield: rdn and unable qck wl over 1f out: r.o fnl f to chse wnr last 50yds: clsng fin but a hld* **25/1**

0-10 **3** 3/4 **Kheleyf (USA)**[19] 3674 3-8-7 112 LDettori 7 113
(SaeedBinSuroor) *lw: settled in midfield: angled out and effrt wl over 1f out: chsd wnr ins fnl f: nt pce to chal: lost 2nd last 50yds* **9/4**[1]

1104 **4** 1 1/2 **Naahy**[9] 3967 4-9-0 106 SHitchcott 8 109
(MRChannon) *led at fast pce: rdn 2f out: hdd jst over 1f out: one pce* **14/1**

-332 **5** hd **Crystal Castle (USA)**[38] 3073 6-9-0 (t) KFallon 6 109
(JEHammond, France) *hanging and racd in last pair: effrt over 2f out: kpt on same pce and nvr able to chal* **11/4**[2]

-031 **6** nk **Trade Fair**[9] 3967 4-9-0 117 SDrowne 2 108
(RCharlton) *trckd ldng pair: poised to chal 2f out: rdn and nt qckn over 1f out: fdd last 100yds* **7/2**[3]

3104 **7** hd **So Will I**[10] 3940 3-8-7 108 RHills 9 107
(MPTregoning) *racd in last pair: effrt on inner 2f out: nt clr run and eased out 1f out: r.o: no ch* **16/1**

3531 **8** 1 **Vanderlin**[17] 3730 5-9-0 109 MartinDwyer 4 105
(AMBalding) *mostly chsd ldr to over 1f out: wknd ins fnl f* **8/1**

1m 25.67s (-2.36) **Going Correction** +0.05s/f (Good)
**WFA** 3 from 4yo+ 7lb **8** Ran SP% **113.0**
Speed ratings: **115,114,113,111,111 111,110,109**CSF £321.49 TOTE £14.70: £2.60, £4.90, £1.40; EX 264.70 Trifecta £798.50 Pool of £2,654.28 - 2.36 winning units..
**Owner** Godolphin **Bred** Cheveley Park Stud Ltd **Trained** Newmarket, Suffolk

**FOCUS**
A truly-run race but probably not a great Group Two. The winning time was bang on par for a race of this class, though.

**NOTEBOOK**
**Byron** was tackling this trip for the first time, having run all his races as a juvenile for David Loder over six furlongs and failed to quite see out the mile in two runs this term. He showed a bright turn of foot to put his stamp on the race and although his lead was being reduced near the line he was always going to hold on.
**Suggestive**, who likes it here, had the strong pace he needs but was not helped by his draw. He had lost his pitch and was near the back of the field passing the furlong pole, but really found his stride inside the last and finished strongly.
**Kheleyf(USA)**, who found the six furlongs of the July Cup too sharp, was the Godolphin number one. He had his chance but was just unable to peg back his stablemate and was caught for second near the line.
**Naahy**, who has a good record at Goodwood, had plenty to find with some of these but ran a typically gutsy race from the front.
**Crystal Castle(USA)** might have finished a little closer had he not been slightly short of room in the latter stages, but in truth he was never really going. The seven furlongs was not a problem but the track was.
**Trade Fair** had ground and trip to suit but his regular rider Richard Hughes was absent with a back problem. Failing to pick up when well placed, he has become somewhat disappointing this season, his Curragh win apart.
**So Will I**, back over seven furlongs, suffered a frustrating run. He had nowhere to go when attempting to improve on the rails and by the time he could be pulled out the race was all but over.
**Vanderlin** was found out in this better grade but despite finishing last he was only beaten around four and a half lengths.

## 4217 BETFAIR MOLECOMB STKS (GROUP 3) 5f
3:50 (3:51) (A) 2-Y-O £23,200 (£8,800; £4,400; £2,000) Stalls Low

Form RPR

220 **1** **Tournedos (IRE)**[10] 3938 2-8-12 TEDurcan 1 102
(MRChannon) *racd on inner: hld up in last pair: nt clr run 2f out tl swtchd rt 1f out: rapid prog fnl f: rdn to ld last strides* **14/1**

3131 **2** nk **Mary Read**[30] 3346 2-8-9 FLynch 13 98
(BSmart) *pressed ldrs: drvn to ld 1f out: edgd lft ins fnl f: collared last strides* **25/1**

134 **3** 2 **Safari Sunset (IRE)**[18] 3696 2-8-12 PDoe 9 94
(PWinkworth) *w ldr: led 2f out to 1f out: stl cl up whn hmpd and snatched up ins fnl f: kpt on* **66/1**

1240 **4** shd **Bigalos Bandit**[18] 3703 2-8-12 RWinston 10 94
(JJQuinn) *b.hind pressed ldrs: rdn and unable qck 2f out: n.m.r sn after: kpt on u.p fnl f* **66/1**

21 **5** 1 **Roodeye**[29] 3382 2-8-9 KFallon 6 87
(RFJohnsonHoughton) *racd in midfield: shkn up 2f out: no prog whn hmpd 1f out: kpt on* **11/2**[3]

1160 **6** shd **Dance Night (IRE)**[9] 3965 2-8-12 GGibbons 3 90
(BAMcmahon) *racd in midfield: rdn wl over 1f out: kpt on same pce: nvr able to chal* **66/1**

513 **7** hd **Skywards**[40] 2996 2-8-12 LDettori 11 89
(SaeedBinSuroor) *lw: racd towards outer: trckd ldrs gng wl: shkn up over 1f out: hanging and fnd nil: btn fnl f* **5/2**[1]

1101 **8** hd **Siena Gold**[10] 3938 2-8-9 JFortune 2 85
(BJMeehan) *racd on inner towards rr: effrt 2f out: keeping on one pce whn forced to switch rt ins fnl f* **6/1**

1211 **9** nk **Beckermet (IRE)**[18] 3703 2-8-12 RFfrench 4 87
(RFFisher) *hit side of stalls s: racd in last pair: stmbld over 3f out: nt clr run 2f out: hmpd 1f out: running on at fin: nvr had a c* **3/1**[2]

541 **10** 1 1/4 **Theatre Of Dreams**[59] 2489 2-8-12 ANicholls 5 83
(DNicholls) *mde most to 2f out: wl hld whn hmpd ins fnl f* **50/1**

1120 **11** 4 **Royal Island (IRE)**[42] 2959 2-8-12 JFanning 12 69
(MJohnston) *racd on outer: on terms to 2f out: sn btn* **14/1**

610 **12** 2 1/2 **Spree (IRE)**[40] 2996 2-8-9 RLMoore 7 57
(RHannon) *racd in midfield: lost pl 1/2-way: bhd fr over 1f out* **10/1**

212 **13** 5 **Kwame**[18] 3696 2-8-9 SWKelly 14 40
(MissECLavelle) *dwlt: racd on outer: on terms to 2f out: wknd* **50/1**

58.54 secs (-0.51) **Going Correction** -0.10s/f (Good) **13** Ran SP% **117.9**
Speed ratings: **100,99,96,96,94 94,94,93,93,91 84,80,72**CSF £324.41 TOTE £16.80: £3.80, £4.20, £5.80; EX 383.80 TRIFECTA Not won..
**Owner** Ridgeway Downs Racing **Bred** Pat Grogan **Trained** West Ilsley, Berks

**FOCUS**
A competitive race on paper, but a fairly modest winning time for a juvenile Group Three and one or two hard-luck stories.

**NOTEBOOK**
**Tournedos(IRE)**, who disappointed slightly when not getting cover in the sales race at Newbury, had the rail draw but had to switch to the outside to get a run. He was fortunate in that the gaps opened for him, but once in the clear he produced a good turn of foot to settle the issue. He could go for the Roses Stakes at York and the Flying Childers at Doncaster.
**Mary Read** who is all speed and was well suited by the track, ran another game race from her wide draw and improved significantly, only being caught near the line. She seems likely to re-oppose the winner at York and Doncaster.
**Safari Sunset(IRE)**, another speedy sort who got worked up before disappointing last time, ran his race, showing plenty of toe. He was a couple of pounds below his Ascot form with the winner, and it may be worth giving him a confidence booster in a lower grade before taking on the first two again.
**Bigalos Bandit** ran close to previous Beverley form with the winner but does not look quite up to this grade. He has shown form on soft ground, and one of the autumn sales races may provide his best chance of getting back on the winning trail.
**Roodeye**, stepping up in class, did not get the best of runs and was doing her best work in the closing stages. Although she is in the Lowther, that looks to be aiming a little high, and re-opposing several of these in the Roses Stakes looks a better option.
**Dance Night(IRE)**, returning to the minimum trip, ran his race before fading in the last half-furlong. A drop in grade and easy ground may help him return to winning ways.
**Skywards**, third in the Norfolk Stakes at Royal Ascot, had every chance and came to win his race but faded disappointingly late on. He had looked better than this previously and may have had an excuse.
**Siena Gold**, who made all in the Weatherbys Super Sprint, could not get to the front on this occasion and never landed a blow. Evidence suggests she is not up to Pattern class.
**Beckermet(IRE)** was the unlucky horse in the race, as he missed the break and then appeared to clip heels at the bottom of the hill. He then suffered as the runners bunched over a furlong out and was only finding his stride at the finish. This run should be ignored.

## 4218 TATLER SUMMER SEASON STKS (HERITAGE H'CAP) 1m 6f
4:25 (4:27) (B ) (0-105,100) 3-Y-O+ £29,000 (£11,000; £5,500; £2,500) Stalls High

Form RPR

0511 **1** **Mephisto (IRE)**[19] 3678 5-9-4 92 DHolland 16 109+
(LMCumani) *hld up in midfield: n.m.r over 5f out: effrt and nt clr run over 2f out to over 1f out: str run fnl f to ld last 75yds* **7/2**[1]

0351 **2** 1/2 **Sergeant Cecil**[16] 3692 5-9-1 89 JFortune 3 99
(BRMillman) *lw: hld up wl in rr: smooth prog 3f out: plld out and effrt to ld over 1f out: edgd rt but 2l clr ins fnl f: hdd last 75y* **16/1**

11-0 **3** 1/2 **Jagger**[31] 3310 4-9-9 97 EAhern 9 107+
(GABulter) *lw: racd in midfield: effrt whn bmpd over 2f out and lost pl: swtchd lft wl over 1f out: r.o strly fnl f: nrst fin* **9/2**[2]

0500 **4** 1/2 **Santando**[17] 3757 4-9-2 90 (v) KFallon 4 99
(CEBrittain) *settled towards rr: rdn and prog 3f out: chsd ldr over 1f out to ins fnl f: one pce* **25/1**

0/06 **5** 3/4 **Self Defense**[17] 3725 7-9-12 100 JPMurtagh 1 108+
(PRChamings) *lw: settled towards rr: n.m.r over 5f out: nt clr run on inner over 2f out to over 1f out: r.o wl fnl f: nrst fin* **25/1**

0-35 **6** 2 1/2 **Big Moment**[38] 3076 6-9-9 97 LDettori 6 102
(MrsAJPerrett) *hld up wl in rr: prog on outer 3f out: drvn to chse ldrs 2f out: edgd rt and nt qckn over 1f out* **12/1**

0-04 **7** 1/2 **Fourth Dimension (IRE)**[2] 4176 5-8-9 83 ANicholls 10 87
(DNicholls) *dwlt and stdd s: hld up in last: effrt on wd outside over 3f out: prog to chse ldrs 2f out: no hdwy after* **50/1**

-011 **8** 3/4 **Dorothy's Friend**[17] 3725 4-9-0 88 SDrowne 13 91
(RCharlton) *lw: trckd ldrs: effrt over 2f out: no prog whn n.m.r over 1f out: one pce* **11/2**[3]

4112 **9** nk **Bendarshaan**[2] 4176 4-8-13 87 KDalgleish 8 89+
(MJohnston) *hld up wl in rr: trying to make prog on inner whn nt clr run 2f out: swtchd lft jst over 1f out: rdn and kpt on: no ch* **14/1**

-422 **10** shd **Nawamees (IRE)**[31] 3325 6-9-2 90 (p) RLMoore 2 92
(GLMoore) *trckd ldrs: prog to ld over 2f out: hdd & wknd over 1f out* **33/1**

-004 **11** 1/2 **Mamcazma**[17] 3757 6-9-2 90 MTebbutt 11 91+
(DMorris) *trckd ldrs: lost pl and rdn over 3f out: effrt again 2f out: n.m.r over 1f out: no ch after: eased ins fnl f* **25/1**

0 **12** 1 1/2 **Almah (SAF)**[17] 3725 6-9-2 90 RWinston 15 89
(MissVenetiaWilliams) *chsd ldng pair to 3f out: wknd 2f out* **100/1**

6044 **13** 12 **Hambleden**[24] 3521 7-9-10 98 PRobinson 5 81
(MAJarvis) *sn led and set str pce: hdd & wknd rapidly over 2f out* **11/1**

0402 **14** 9 **Anticipating**[22] 3590 4-8-11 85 MartinDwyer 14 55
(AMBalding) *racd in midfield: rdn and edgd rt over 2f out: no prog and btn whn hmpd over 1f out: eased* **14/1**

-000 **15** 6 **Morson Boy (USA)**[17] 3757 4-9-4 92 JFanning 12 54
(MJohnston) *pressed ldr to 3f out: wknd* **7/1**

3m 1.35s (-2.40) **Going Correction** +0.05s/f (Good) **15** Ran SP% **121.0**
Speed ratings: **108,107,107,107,106 105,105,104,104,104 104,103,96,91,87**CSF £57.73 CT £263.39 TOTE £4.70: £2.60, £4.40, £2.60; EX 96.40.
**Owner** Mrs Angie Silver **Bred** Shadwell Estate Company Limited **Trained** Newmarket, Suffolk

**FOCUS**
A strong, competitive handicap in which it paid to come from off the pace. The time was sound for a race of its type, and the form should stand up well. Indeed it could prove a crucial trial for the Ebor.

**NOTEBOOK**
**Mephisto(IRE)** ◆, who did not start racing until he was four, is progressing really well this season and the step up in trip and grade did not stop him. He looked full of running when trapped on the inside rail, and once he found an opening he picked up impresssively and was always going to get there. He looks an ideal sort for the Ebor, and may have enough in hand to defy a 7lb penalty.
**Sergeant Cecil**, 3lb higher than for his win at Ascot, seems to settle better when held up at the back, and looked sure to score when sweeping to the front entering the final furlong. It was no disgrace to be collared by the winner and he looks well capable of picking up another decent handicap, possibly at Sandown, a track that suits him well.
**Jagger** ◆, whose win at this meeting last year was the first leg of a hat-trick, was more unlucky than most. He was on the heels of the leaders and looking for a run when squeezed out and shuffled back to almost last over a quarter of a mile from home. However, he picked up really well when in the clear and was closing down on the first two all the way to the line. He looks set to re-oppose the winner on 7lb better terms in the Ebor and is sure to get closer given better fortune at York.
**Santando** was another to run well having missed the break, but did not quite have the pace of the principals. He looks worth a try over two miles and has slipped to a reasonable mark.
**Self Defense** has been running really well in competitive staying handicaps, and did so again despite not getting the clearest of runs. The Shergar Cup stayers' race looks to offer a better chance of him winning a decent handicap than the Ebor.
**Big Moment**, a course and distance winner who was making his third appearance in this race, performed quite well over a trip that is probably on the short side for him nowadays. He looks worth another crack at the Cesarewitch, especially if dropped a few more pounds.
**Fourth Dimension(IRE)**, who has been running over shorter trips this season, missed the break but ran his best race for his current trainer. He should find better opportunities in a slightly lower grade.
**Dorothy's Friend** was given a positive ride, but gave the impression that this trip was on the short side for him on such a sharp track. He has risen a fair amount in the weights, but at this stage appeals as a Cesarewitch type if he can hold his form.
**Almah(SAF)** chased the leading pair for some way before fading and could be of interest off a lower mark with the blinkers re-applied. *Official explanation: jockey said mare was hanging left*
**Hambleden**, well backed, got in a battle for the lead with Morson Boy which ultimately cost both of them.
**Anticipating** was involved in a barging match with Jagger halfway up the straight and was eased as if something was amiss. *Official explanation: jockey said gelding lost its action*
**Morson Boy(USA)** lost out on the early battle for the lead and is struggling for form at present *Official explanation: jockey said saddle slipped*

## 4219 EVENING STANDARD EBF MAIDEN STKS (C&G) 6f
5:00 (5:00) (D) 2-Y-O £8,248 (£2,538; £1,269; £634) Stalls Low

Form RPR
0000 1 **Doctor's Cave**[8] 3983 2-8-11 .................... SSanders 8 89
(CEBrittain) *w ldr: led after 2f: narrowly hdd 2f out: rallied fnl f to ld last 75yds* **50/1**
2 *nk* **Rajwa (USA)** 2-8-11 .................... (t) LDettori 10 88
(SaeedBinSuroor) *str: trckd ldrs: smooth prog to ld narrowly 2f out: rdn fnl f: hdd last 75yds* **1/1**[1]
3222 3 *2* **Mceldowney**[11] 3898 2-8-11 .................... KDalgleish 2 82
(MJohnston) *led for 2f: styd pressing ldrs: rdn 2f out: kpt on ins fnl f* **6/1**[3]
34 4 *1 1/4* **Councellor (FR)**[31] 3319 2-8-11 .................... KFallon 5 78
(RHannon) *lw: wnt rt s: in tch towards rr: swtchd rt and rdn 2f out: chsd ldrs 1f out: one pce after* **6/1**[3]
5 *nk* **One Putra (IRE)** 2-8-11 .................... PRobinson 9 77
(MAJarvis) *w'like: bit bkwd: trckd ldrs: edgd lft over 2f out: cl up over 1f out: one pce after* **16/1**
6 *3 1/2* **Ocean Gift** 2-8-11 .................... DaneO'Neill 7 67
(DRCElsworth) *w'like: bit bkwd: s.v.s: bhd tl prog on outer 1/2-way: chsd ldrs but nt on terms over 1f out: no imp after* **28/1**
7 *3 1/2* **Toshi (USA)** 2-8-11 .................... JFanning 3 56
(MJohnston) *w'like: w ldrs: lost pl and rdn over 2f out: wknd over 1f out* **11/2**[2]
8 *5* **Grigorovitch (IRE)** 2-8-11 .................... MHills 6 41
(BWHills) *w'like: s.v.s: plld hrd and rn green: rcvrd to chse ldrs after 2f: wknd rapidly over 1f out* **16/1**
9 *1 3/4* **Wembury Point (IRE)** 2-8-11 .................... SWhitworth 1 36
(BGPowell) *w'like: s.s: outpcd and a bhd* **50/1**
0 10 *nk* **Superstitious (IRE)**[17] 3760 2-8-11 .................... GGibbons 4 35
(BAMcmahon) *trckd ldrs: rdn whn squeezed out over 2f out: wknd and eased* **33/1**

1m 12.38s (-0.46) **Going Correction** -0.10s/f (Good) **10 Ran SP% 116.0**
Speed ratings: **99,98,95,94,93 89,84,77,75,75**CSF £99.69 TOTE £68.60: £10.10, £1.40, £1.90; EX 192.80.
**Owner** A J Richards **Bred** Tweenhills Stud And Genesis Green Stud **Trained** Newmarket, Suffolk

**FOCUS**
A shock winner, but a creditable time for a race of its type and the form looks solid enough, although there were probably no stars on show.

**NOTEBOOK**
**Doctor's Cave**, down in trip, has been a slow learner but this was his fifth run and he knew his job now. He showed the right attitude to get on top near the finish after eyeballing the favourite and there appeared no fluke about it.
**Rajwa(USA)**, who looked a nice type in the paddock, is the first son of Dubai Millennium to be beaten. Just unable to shake off his more experienced rival, he does not look one of the stable's stars but will have no problem winning his maiden.
**Mceldowney** continues to find a couple too good. He may need to step up to seven furlongs back in a nursery.
**Councellor(FR)** went right leaving the gate and was unable to lead, as he had done on his first two runs. He should be able to step up on this back at seven furlongs.
**One Putra(IRE)** is a half-brother to ten-furlong winner Rondelet. Withdrawn at Ascot over the weekend as the ground was too fast, he shaped with promise and can win an ordinary maiden.
**Ocean Gift** is out of a dam who won over seven furlongs, herself a daughter of smart sprinter Night At Sea. He looked in need of the outing beforehand and gave himself too much to do after falling out of the stalls, but there were signs that he is capable of a fair bit of improvement.
**Toshi(USA)** is a half-brother to six winners out of a mare from the family of White Muzzle and Almutawakel. He was well backed, but lost his place in a bit of scrimmaging and could not recover. He should be capable of better.
**Grigorovitch(IRE)** *Official explanation: jockey said colt ran very free early on*
**Superstitious(IRE)** *Official explanation: jockey said colt was hampered at the 2f marker*

## 4220 DARNLEY STKS (H'CAP) 1m
5:35 (5:36) (D) (0-85,85) 3-Y-O+ £8,560 (£2,634; £1,317; £658) Stalls High

Form RPR
2211 1 **Pango**[18] 3698 5-9-7 **81** .................... LFletcher(3) 17 93
(HMorrison) *lw: prom: trckd ldr 4f out: effrt to ld over 1f out: drvn and hrd pressed fnl f: hld on wl* **5/1**[1]
1-00 2 *1/2* **Ringsider (IRE)**[52] 2676 3-8-12 **77** .................... TPQueally 19 88
(GAButler) *racd in midfield: rdn 3f out: prog wl over 1f out: r.o to press wnr wl ins fnl f: a jst hld* **16/1**
0040 3 *shd* **Highland Reel**[10] 3937 7-10-0 **85** .................... TQuinn 9 96
(DRCElsworth) *hld up towards rr: rdn and effrt wl over 1f out: r.o wl fnl f: gaining at fin* **20/1**
4301 4 *1/2* **Freeloader (IRE)**[13] 3844 4-9-6 **77** .................... RHills 18 87
(JWHills) *trckd ldrs: eased to outer and effrt over 2f out: rdn to press wnr 1f out: kpt on same pce* **5/1**[1]
4406 5 *3/4* **What-A-Dancer (IRE)**[3] 4122 7-9-4 **75** .................... KFallon 11 83
(GASwinbank) *racd in midfield: rdn and effrt over 2f out: prog to press ldrs over 1f out: nt qckn fnl f* **6/1**[2]
411 6 *nk* **Pintle**[12] 3884 4-9-3 **74** .................... KMcEvoy 16 81
(JLSpearing) *cl up: effrt on inner 2f out: one pce fr over 1f out* **8/1**[3]
6032 7 *hd* **Winning Venture**[7] 4006 7-9-11 **82** .................... DHolland 14 89
(AWCarroll) *led at gd pce: hdd and wandered over 1f out: one pce u.p* **14/1**
6122 8 *1/2* **Evaluator (IRE)**[17] 3750 3-9-4 **83** .................... JFortune 3 89
(TGMills) *settled towards rr: rdn and effrt on outer over 2f out: styd on wl fr over 1f out: nt rch ldrs* **12/1**
3635 9 *1 1/4* **Rebate**[6] 4029 4-8-3 **60** .................... (t) RSmith 13 63
(RHannon) *lw: trckd ldrs: cl up 2f out: sn nt qckn: one pce after* **33/1**
0210 10 *nk* **Omaha City (IRE)**[21] 3597 10-9-2 **73** .................... MTebbutt 10 75
(BGubby) *sn in rr: nt clr run briefly over 2f out: hanging bdly and nt qckn over 1f out: kpt on* **16/1**
0600 11 *nk* **Atlantic Ace**[12] 3869 7-8-8 **65** .................... FLynch 7 67
(BSmart) *b: dwlt: t.k.h: swtchd to inner and hld up wl in rr: rdn and effrt over 2f out: one pce and n.d* **25/1**
2200 12 *2 1/2* **Ephesus**[13] 3850 4-9-9 **80** .................... (v) WSupple 2 76
(MissGayKelleway) *settled wl in rr: effrt over 2f out: one pce and no ch whn hmpd 1f out* **50/1**
4454 13 *nk* **Pas De Surprise**[7] 4008 6-7-9 **55** oh2 .................... FPFerris(3) 15 50
(PDEvans) *chsd ldr to 4f out: styd prom: ev ch 2f out: sn wknd* **20/1**
0150 14 *nk* **Just Tim (IRE)**[36] 3159 3-8-13 **78** .................... (t) RLMoore 8 72
(RHannon) *prom on outer tl rdn and steadily lost pl fr wl over 2f out* **40/1**
0035 15 *hd* **Mythical Charm**[20] 3626 5-7-5 **55** oh6 .................... (t) NataliaGemelova(7) 5 49
(JJBridger) *dwlt: t.k.h and hld up in rr: effrt on inner 2f out: no prog* **33/1**
-655 16 *2* **Lucayan Dancer**[24] 3510 4-8-1 **58** .................... ANicholls 4 47
(DNicholls) *racd towards rr: rdn and effrt 3f out: sn no prog and btn* **50/1**
111- 17 *shd* **Compton Drake**[214] 6239 5-8-9 **66** .................... LDettori 6 55
(GAButler) *lw: hld up wl in rr: rdn over 2f out: no prog* **10/1**
0000 18 *15* **Learned Lad (FR)**[13] 3844 6-7-12 **55** oh7 .................... DKinsella 1 10
(JamiePoulton) *a wl in rr: t.o fnl 3f* **100/1**
5500 19 *3* **Terraquin (IRE)**[20] 3631 4-8-10 **67** .................... (p) GBaker 12 15
(JJBridger) *b: chsd ldrs: wknd 3f out: eased over 1f out: t.o* **33/1**

1m 39.22s (-1.05) **Going Correction** +0.05s/f (Good)
**WFA** 3 from 4yo+ 8lb **19 Ran SP% 123.5**
Speed ratings: **107,106,106,105,105 104,104,104,102,102 102,99,99,99,99 97,96,81,78**CSF £76.36 CT £1536.08 TOTE £6.00: £2.50, £5.50, £4.10, £2.40; EX 168.00 Place 6 £2,725.72, Place 5 £410.53.
**Owner** Pangfield Partners **Bred** T J Billington **Trained** East Ilsley, Berks

**FOCUS**
High draws were favoured in this ordinary, but competitive, handicap. A fair winning time for the grade.

**NOTEBOOK**
**Pango** has found notable improvement at the age of five and completed the hat-trick from a mark 9lb higher than the first of those victories. He had no problem with the return to a mile and held off several challngers inside the last furlong in gritty style.
**Ringsider(IRE)** showed little in two runs earlier in the season when his yard was out of form. Staying on stoutly under pressure, although he was well beaten over ten furlongs last time he looks worth another try over that sort of trip.
**Highland Reel** goes well here and was racing off the same mark as when scoring over course and distance in May. He was not helped by his draw and his strong finishing burst came that bit too late.
**Freeloader(IRE)**, from a 5lb higher mark, ran another good race but the furlong-shorter trip was not ideal.
**What-A-Dancer(IRE)**, making a quick reappearance, stayed on under plenty of driving but never quite looked like picking up the leaders.
**Pintle**, from a 5lb higher mark, ran a decent race but this longer trip eventually told.
**Winning Venture** is without a win since September 2001, but he is running creditably at the moment and is 15lb lower than when last successful.
**Evaluator(IRE)**, who has gone up 8lb after good runs in defeat on his last two starts, had a big task from his low draw and was staying on all too late.
T/Jkpt: Not won. T/Plt: £2,417.90 to a £1 stake. Pool: £174,556.59. 52.70 winning tickets. T/Qpdt: £127.20 to a £1 stake. Pool: £10,165.40. 59.10 winning tickets. JN

4221 - 4225a (Foreign Racing) - See Raceform Interactive

# 4214 GOODWOOD (R-H)
Wednesday, July 28

**OFFICIAL GOING: Good (good to firm in places)**
Wind: almost nil Weather: sunny and warm

## 4226 GOODWOOD STKS (H'CAP) 2m 5f
2:05 (2:05) (C) (0-95,95) 3-Y-O+ £23,200 (£8,800; £4,400; £2,000) Stalls Far side

Form RPR
50-4 1 **Alrida (IRE)**[11] 3236 5-7-12 **65** .................... PHanagan 9 75+
(RAFahey) *a wl plcd: gng easily 4f out: led 3f out: rdn and pressed fnl 2f: a holding rivals* **11/2**[2]
00-0 2 *nk* **Stance**[43] 2958 5-8-8 **75** .................... (p) RLMoore 1 85
(GLMoore) *lw: hld up towards rr: prog over 4f out: chsd ldrs 2f out: swtchd lft jst over 1f out: drvn to press wnr last 100yds: a hld* **14/1**
4200 3 *1 3/4* **Distant Prospect (IRE)**[18] 3725 7-9-9 **90** .................... MartinDwyer 2 98+
(AMBalding) *prom: lost pl 7f out: outpcd whn n.m.r over 4f out: rallied 3f out: r.o wl fnl f to snatch 3rd on line* **25/1**
0040 4 *shd* **Almizan (IRE)**[43] 2958 4-8-13 **80** .................... (v[1]) TEDurcan 8 88
(MRChannon) *hld up in midfield: prog 6f out: effrt to chse wnr over 2f out: sn chalng: hld 1f out: wknd last 100yds* **33/1**
0001 5 *1* **Mana D'Argent (IRE)**[5] 4075 7-9-6 **87** 3ex .................... JFanning 6 94
(MJohnston) *settled wl in rr: plenty to do 5f out: gd prog on outer fr 3f out: pressed ldrs and looked dangerous over 1f out: one pce a* **12/1**
-604 6 *1/2* **Bobsleigh**[11] 3947 5-8-4 **71** .................... PRobinson 11 78
(MrsAJPerrett) *led for 5f: styd prom: sltly outpcd over 4f out: kpt on same pce fr over 2f out* **16/1**
6250 7 *5* **Kristensen**[18] 3725 5-8-13 **80** .................... (p) DHolland 16 82
(DEddy) *led after 5f to 7f out: sn lost pl: effrt again over 3f out: fdd fr over 1f out* **18/1**
3514 8 *3* **Valance (IRE)**[5] 4075 4-8-13 **80** .................... JPMurtagh 4 79
(CREgerton) *t.k.h: hld up in rr: prog into midfield 3f out: sn no imp on ldrs: plodded on* **20/1**
5211 9 *3 1/2* **Quedex**[11] 3928 8-8-6 **76** .................... JFMcDonald(3) 5 71
(RJPrice) *hld up towards rr: n.m.r after 6f: outpcd 5f out: effrt over 3f out: no ch w ldrs fnl 2f: plodded on* **14/1**
6102 10 *4* **Tiyoun (IRE)**[21] 3621 6-9-4 **85** .................... JPSpencer 19 76
(JeddO'Keeffe) *hld up in rr: brief effrt over 3f out: sn no prog and wl btn* **33/1**
2660 11 *2* **Teresa**[21] 3644 4-8-8 **75** .................... MJKinane 3 64
(JLDunlop) *hld up in midfield: prog to press ldrs 11f out: wknd 3f out: eased fnl 2f* **20/1**
4440 12 *3/4* **Redspin (IRE)**[21] 3644 4-7-12 **65** .................... CCatlin 17 53
(JSMoore) *lw: s.s: a wl in rr: last over 6f out: plodded on u.p fr over 3f out* **25/1**
10-3 13 *4* **Ten Carat**[21] 3644 4-10-0 **95** .................... LDettori 7 79
(MrsAJPerrett) *trckd ldrs: lost pl over 4f out: wknd over 2f out* **9/2**[1]
6-40 14 *1* **Galleon Beach**[15] 3821 7-7-9 **65** oh5 .................... NMackay(3) 18 48
(BDLeavy) *s.s: a wl in rr: no ch fnl 4f* **66/1**
522- 15 *shd* **Albanov (IRE)**[249] 6053 4-10-0 **95** .................... (b) KDalgleish 15 78
(MJohnston) *prom: led 7f out to 6f out: wknd over 3f out* **16/1**
3002 16 *1/2* **Riyadh**[5] 4075 6-7-12 **65** oh3 .................... (v) RFfrench 14 48
(MJohnston) *s.s: rcvrd to chse ldrs after 5f: wknd over 4f out* **8/1**
/00- 17 *3 1/2* **One For Me**[17] 3649 6-7-9 **65** oh26 .................... LisaJones(3) 10 44
(Jean-ReneAuvray) *a wl in rr: last and losing tch 5f out* **100/1**
0204 18 *11* **Promoter**[18] 3725 4-9-8 **89** .................... EAhern 12 57
(JNoseda) *lw: t.k.h: trckd ldrs: led 6f out to 3f out: wknd alarmingly* **13/2**[3]
0053 19 *dist* **Dance Light (IRE)**[25] 3508 5-7-12 **65** oh7 .................... JQuinn 13 —
(TTClement) *a towards rr: n.m.r 13f out: wknd rapidly u.p over 3f out: t.o* **66/1**

4m 32.1s **19 Ran SP% 123.1**
Speed ratings: CSF £70.80 CT £1805.05 TOTE £7.30: £2.50, £4.60, £6.10, £6.20; EX 142.50 TRIFECTA Not won..
**Owner** Mark Russell & Friends **Bred** Stone Farms **Trained** Musley Bank, N Yorks

**FOCUS**
A flip start was used and the race hand-timed. A really competitive staying handicap, although the early pace was just steady, even allowing for the marathon distance. No speed figures have been produced for this contest as not enough races have been run over the trip from which to calculate a reliable median time.

**NOTEBOOK**

**Alrida(IRE)**, who showed much improved form when winning the Summer Hurdle at Market Rasen on his previous start, was able to race off a mark 10lb lower than when last winning on the Flat. Always travelling ominously strongly, he probably got there a little too soon and looked to idle slightly in front, but he pulled out more when challenged by the eventual runner-up and was never going to be pegged back. He can win again, as he should not go up too much for this and will be effective back over slightly shorter.

**Stance** had been kept in training for this very race rather than being given a break, and justified the decision with a fine effort in defeat. He just lacked the tactical pace of the winner and proved unable to get into a position to get one continuous run, which ultimately cost him the race.

**Distant Prospect(IRE)** relishes a proper stamina test and ran a fine race, especially considering he did not get the clearest of runs, and would have preferred easier ground.

**Almizan(IRE)**, 8lb higher than when last successful, has been threatening to hit form this season and ran respectably in a first-time visor. It can only be taken on trust that the headgear will continue to have a positive effect.

**Mana D'Argent(IRE)** looked to run his race, but just lacked a decisive finishing kick and has never won beyond two miles. He also remains without a win away from Ascot and must therefore be kept in mind for the Shergar Cup staying event back at his favourite course.

**Ten Carat** shaped with a good deal of promise on his reappearance when a little unlucky at Newmarket, but he was unable to build on that effort and was beaten before his stamina was tested. He has yet to show he is fully effective in big fields. *Official explanation: jockey said colt had been unsuited by the track and ground*

**Riyadh** has won over two and a half miles and should not have been inconvenienced by this trip, but he was unable to confirm the promise of his recent Ascot second to stablemate Mana D'Argent and is quite simply disappointing.

**Promoter** had been in good form without winning so far this season, including when runner-up in the Ascot Stakes over two and a half miles. He was still looked to be going pretty well entering the straight, despite having raced keenly, but he weakened very quickly when put under pressure and something could well have been amiss.

**Dance Light(IRE)** *Official explanation: trainer said mare was found to be lame after the race*

## 4227 VEUVE CLICQUOT VINTAGE STKS (GROUP 2) — 7f

**2:40** (2:43) (A ) 2-Y-O **£40,600** (£15,400; £7,700; £3,500) **Stalls** High

Form — RPR

1 **1** **Shamardal (USA)**[16] 3793 2-8-11 .................. JFanning 10 114+
(MJohnston) *lw: mde all: pushed along and drew clr fr 2f out: in n.d after: impressive* **8/13**[1]

0133 **2** *2 1/2* **Wilko (USA)**[20] 3672 2-8-11 .................. EAhern 7 103
(JNoseda) *chsd ldrs: rdn and effrt over 2f out: chsd wnr over 1f out: kpt on wl but no imp* **7/1**[2]

214 **3** *1 1/4* **Fox**[20] 3672 2-8-11 .................. KFallon 3 100
(CEBrittain) *t.k.h: hld up in last: hanging and rdn over 3f out: effrt on outer 2f out: drvn to take 3rd last stride* **10/1**[3]

010 **4** *shd* **Destinate (IRE)**[20] 3672 2-8-11 .................. PDobbs 4 100
(RHannon) *lw: settled in rr: rdn and outpcd over 2f out: styd on fnl f* **66/1**

162 **5** *hd* **Berkhamsted (IRE)**[18] 3726 2-8-11 .................. LDettori 9 99
(JAOsborne) *lw: s.i.s: sn trckd ldrs: rdn and lost pl 2f out: styd on again fnl f* **14/1**

1 **6** *hd* **Stagbury Hill (USA)**[40] 3051 2-8-11 .................. MHills 8 99
(JWHills) *lw: hld up towards rr: effrt over 2f out: sn rdn and outpcd: styd on ins fnl f* **25/1**

0 **7** *3/4* **Rowan Tree**[20] 3672 2-8-11 .................. JPSpencer 5 97
(APO'Brien, Ire) *chsd wnr to 2f out: sn outpcd: lost several pls nr fin* **20/1**

12 **8** *1* **Black Velvet**[12] 3907 2-8-11 ..................(b[1]) MartinDwyer 1 94
(MPTregoning) *prom: chsd wnr 2f out to over 1f out: wknd fnl f* **14/1**

1 **9** *3* **Solent (IRE)**[32] 3319 2-8-11 .................. DaneO'Neill 6 87
(RHannon) *hld up in rr: rdn and struggling over 2f out: no prog* **16/1**

4116 **10** *2* **Dahteer (IRE)**[17] 3790 2-8-11 ..................(v[1]) TEDurcan 2 82
(MRChannon) *hld up in rr: rdn and struggling over 2f out: no ch whn squeezed out over 1f out* **50/1**

1m 27.41s (-0.62) **Going Correction** +0.05s/f (Good) **10** Ran SP% **114.8**
Speed ratings: **105,102,100,100,100 100,99,98,94,92**CSF £4.78 TOTE £1.70: £1.30, £1.80, £1.90; EX 6.40 Trifecta £43.60 Pool £2,437.29 - 39.63 winning units..

**Owner** Abdulla Buhaleeba **Bred** Brilliant Stable **Trained** Middleham Moor, N Yorks

**FOCUS**

Shamardal was most impressive again and recorded the best juvenile performance of the season so far, having been rated value for another couple of lengths. The form is solid with Wilko, Fox and Destinate all running right up to Superlative Stakes form and, as a result, both the Johnston and Godolphin camps have a line on the form - Dubawi won the Newmarket race. The winning time was unexceptional, but perfectly acceptable for a race of this grade.

**NOTEBOOK**

**Shamardal(USA)** ◆ is held in the highest regard by connections and duly justified cramped odds with a display of sheer quality, having his rivals beaten before he had even come off the bridle. Once asked to go and seal victory he sprinted clear, showing a smart change of pace. Mark Johnston, who won this with Lucky Story for the same owner last year, is keen to head straight for a Group One now, as he missed the chance with Lucky Story at two, and the logical target would be the National Stakes at The Curragh, as the Dewhurst is still a fair way off. The best we have seen so far from the first crop of Giant's Causeway, he has plenty of physical scope and at this stage is justifiably favourite for next year's Guineas - his trainer won this race with Mister Baileys before that one went on to win the Guineas.

**Wilko(USA)** set the standard as he had shown a solid level of form when third in the Superlative Stakes at Newmarket. Always well placed, he simply could not go with the winner but he stuck on well for second. He may always find one or two too good in this grade, and will be more at home back in Group Three and Listed company.

**Fox** ran a very good race to come from where he was positioned, as he raced keenly and hung in rear. He ran to the pound with Wilko on Newmarket form, and he too is probably more of a Group Three/Listed-class horse.

**Destinate(IRE)** ran a personal best, leaving behind a disappointing effort at Newmarket and staying on well from the back. He ideally wants a mile and can improve for it.

**Berkhamsted(IRE)** failed to improve for the step up to this trip at Ascot earlier in the month but ran a much better race.

**Stagbury Hill(USA)** is an interesting one for the future as he got warm beforehand and raced too keenly in the early part of the race. He found himself a fair way behind when the tempo was raised but stayed on well in the closing stages. He had previously made a successful debut - a rarity for one of his trainer's juveniles - and he looks capable of improving on this next time, when he will hopefully relax a bit more.

**Rowan Tree** was the only one who failed to run up to his Newmarket form. He travelled well just off the leader before being unable to quicken, and was swamped late on.

**Black Velvet** looks Listed class at best and the blinkers failed to improve him.

**Solent(IRE)** won in good style on his debut last month but was taking a sharp rise in class. He found himself behind the whole way and struggling to go the pace. His sire was at his best with some cut in the ground, and this fellow will improve for the combination of softer going and a mile.

**Dahteer(IRE)** is not up to this company and failed to improve for the fitting of a visor.

## 4228 CANTOR ODDS SUSSEX STKS (GROUP 1) — 1m

**3:15** (3:27) (A ) 3-Y-O+ **£174,000** (£66,000; £33,000; £15,000) **Stalls** High

Form — RPR

3121 **1** **Soviet Song (IRE)**[22] 3600 4-9-4 115.................. JPMurtagh 5 124
(JRFanshawe) *settled in midfield: n.m.r over 2f out: prog sn after: led and qcknd jst over 1f out: rdn out: hld on wl* **3/1**[2]

2-30 **2** *nk* **Nayyir**[20] 3674 6-9-7 .................. MJKinane 11 126
(GABButler) *lw: hld up towards rr: nt clr run briefly wl over 1f out: angled out to chse wnr ent fnl f: str chal last 100yds: jst hld* **12/1**

11-4 **3** *2* **Le Vie Dei Colori**[73] 2155 4-9-7 .................. DHolland 7 121
(LMCumani) *w'like: str: trckd ldrs: shkn up to ld 2f out: hdd jst over 1f out: outpcd fnl f* **12/1**

4304 **4** *2* **Norse Dancer (IRE)**[25] 3540 4-9-7 116..................(b) TQuinn 1 117
(DRCElsworth) *lw: hld up in last pair: effrt on outer over 2f out: rdn and prog over 1f out: fnd nil ins fnl f* **20/1**

2530 **5** *nk* **Antonius Pius (USA)**[20] 3674 3-8-13 ..................(vt[1]) JPSpencer 10 116
(APO'Brien, Ire) *trckd ldrs gng wl: nt clr run over 2f out to jst over 1f out: fnd nthing whn in the clr fnl f* **8/1**

30-5 **6** *shd* **Tillerman**[43] 2957 8-9-7 117.................. OPeslier 6 116
(MrsAJPerrett) *stdd s: hld up in rr: effrt over 2f out: rdn and one pce fr over 1f out* **20/1**

1503 **7** *2* **Hurricane Alan (IRE)**[18] 3724 4-9-7 114.................. KFallon 3 111
(RHannon) *restless stalls: dwlt: racd in rr: pushed along 3f out: nt clr run briefly 2f out: one pce and n.d* **40/1**

4034 **8** *2* **Checkit (IRE)**[9] 3978 4-9-7 112.................. ACulhane 2 107
(MRChannon) *hld up in last pair: nt clr run over 2f out: styng on but no ch whn bdly hmpd jst ins fnl f: nt rcvr* **100/1**

-114 **9** *3/4* **Haafhd**[43] 2956 3-8-13 122.................. RHills 8 105
(BWHills) *prom: ev ch jst over 2f out: wknd over 1f out: no ch whn hmpd jst ins fnl f* **9/2**[3]

60-1 **10** *2* **Passing Glance**[53] 2678 5-9-7 118.................. MartinDwyer 4 100
(AMBalding) *sn led: hdd over 3f out: losing pl whn hmpd over 2f out* **16/1**

0011 **11** *6* **Refuse To Bend (IRE)**[25] 3540 4-9-7 121..................(t) LDettori 9 87
(SaeedBinSuroor) *trckd ldr: led over 3f out: rdn and hdd 2f out: wkng whn bdly hmpd jst ins fnl f* **11/4**[1]

1m 36.98s (-3.29) **Going Correction** +0.05s/f (Good)
**WFA** 3 from 4yo+ 8lb **11** Ran SP% **115.2**
Speed ratings: **118,117,115,113,113 113,111,109,108,106 100**CSF £36.10 TOTE £3.90: £1.60, £3.50, £2.50; EX 45.90 Trifecta £948.80 Pool £4,811.07 - 3.60 winning units..

**Owner** Elite Racing Club **Bred** Elite Racing Club **Trained** Newmarket, Suffolk

**FOCUS**

This looked like a top-class renewal of the Sussex Stakes, and although neither Haafhd nor Refuse To Bend ran their races the form is still well in line with the average for the race. Confirmed front-runner Passing Glance took long enough to get to the front and did not exactly go flat to the boards, but the pace was decent enough and the winning time was as you would expect for a race like this.

**NOTEBOOK**

**Soviet Song(IRE)** had her summer break put on hold to come here and fully justified the decision by following up her Falmouth Stakes success. Always well placed, she showed a similar change of pace to that shown when winning at Newmarket and stuck her neck out determinedly when challenged. The form looks solid, and Murtagh feels she is up there with the best milers he has ridden. She will now be freshened up ahead of a tilt at the Matron Stakes and the Queen Elizabeth II Stakes. She was beaten in the latter race last year, but James Fanshawe is not concerned as he feels she was not right at the time.

**Nayyir** did not have things go his way when below form in the July Cup on his previous start, but bounced back with a career-best effort, despite having to be switched out for a run. Being a gelding, he should have many racing days left in him yet and could well pick up a much-deserved first Group One, although the Celebration Mile is the immediate target. Connections have ruled out the Breeders' Cup and could instead send him back to Dubai and give him plenty of time to settle down there.

**Le Vie Dei Colori**, the 2003 Italian Guineas winner, was making his British debut on his first start for Luca Cumani and ran a fine race despite carrying some condition. He was beaten fair and square by the front two, but his new trainer expects improvement, in which case he should be a real force in similar events from now on.

**Norse Dancer(IRE)** ran yet another fine race on the figures, but again found a few to beat him. He has the ability to win a Group One - he has shown that time and time again - but where or when is anyone's guess.

**Antonius Pius(USA)** has had a nightmare season and has already been written off by many, but he can be forgiven what was another luckless run. Racing in a visor for the first time, he travelled as well as anything into the straight and was still hard on the bridle when the below-form pair Haafhd and Refuse to Bend were going backwards, but he could not get a run and the race was all over when the gaps finally appeared. It could be argued that he did not find much when in the clear, but in fairness some of the best milers in the world had long got first run.

**Tillerman**, fifth in the Queen Anne on his previous start, ran a similar race and falls just short of this level in this country.

**Hurricane Alan(IRE)** is not up to this level.

**Checkit(IRE)** can be considered unlucky not to have finished closer as he enjoyed very little luck in running, but he is quite simply a very hard horse to win with. Also, he is arguably not quite up to Group One class.

**Haafhd**, not seen since running a below-par fourth in the St James' Palace Stakes at Royal Ascot, again failed to run up to his best. He was edgy beforehand and had to be re-shod at the start, which would not have helped his chance, but it is hard to use that as the main excuse. The track could also have been to blame, but he was quite simply disappointing. Something else may come to light in time, but even so, he still has to prove he can do it against his elders. *Official explanation: jockey said colt lost its action*

**Passing Glance** had quite a task at this level, but looked to run below his best in any case.

**Refuse To Bend(IRE)** has been as good as ever this season with wins in the Queen Anne and Eclipse but, chasing a hat-trick of Group Ones, he was a long way below form. Dettori said he was simply unable to switch him off and there was nothing left at the finish. *Official explanation: jockey had no explanation for the poor form shown*

## 4229 CANTORODDS.COM STKS (HERITAGE H'CAP) — 1m 4f

**3:50** (4:01) (B ) (0-105,105) 3-Y-O **£49,300** (£18,700; £9,350; £4,250) **Stalls** Low

Form — RPR

3162 **1** **Cutting Crew (USA)**[19] 3692 3-8-8 **92**.................. DHolland 14 105
(PWHarris) *mde all: gng wl 3f out: drvn 2l clr 1f out: a holding on after* **12/1**

-231 **2** *3/4* **Larkwing (IRE)**[67] 2312 3-8-0 **84**.................. FNorton 8 96
(GWragg) *lw: hld up in midfield: rdn over 2f out: prog u.p wl over 1f out: r.o to chse wnr ins fnl f: clsng at fin* **20/1**

1-02 **3** *3/4* **Always First**[13] 3878 3-8-11 **95**.................. KFallon 9 106
(SirMichaelStoute) *hld up towards rr: rdn over 2f out: prog on outer over 1f out: r.o fnl f: nrst fin* **8/1**

2-10 **4** *1/2* **Odiham**[41] 2999 3-8-1 **85**.................. JFEgan 3 95
(HMorrison) *trckd ldrs: rdn over 2f out: chsd wnr over 1f out to ins fnl f: one pce* **11/1**

461 **5** *1 ¼* **Stage Right**[28] 3417 3-8-1 **85** .......... MartinDwyer 16 93
(DRCElsworth) *trckd ldrs: sltly outpcd 3f out: rdn and nt clr run briefly 2f out: styd on fr over 1f out* **33/1**

1531 **6** *¾* **Always Waining (IRE)**[4] 4123 3-8-9 **93** 7ex .......... JFanning 6 100
(MJohnston) *trckd ldng pair tl chsd wnr over 2f out: no imp and lost 2nd over 1f out: kpt on* **4/1**[1]

3606 **7** *2 ½* **Red Lancer**[11] 3927 3-9-2 **105** .......... LTreadwell(5) 10 108
(RJPrice) *hld up wl in rr: outpcd 3f out: rdn and styd on fr over 2f out: nvr able to rch ldrs* **66/1**

1-55 **8** *½* **Prime Powered (IRE)**[53] 2676 3-8-4 **88** .......... (p) RLMoore 13 90
(GLMoore) *lw: trckd ldrs: rdn 3f out: one pce and hld 2f out: wknd fnl f* **25/1**

4125 **9** *½* **Zeitgeist (IRE)**[19] 3692 3-8-3 **87** .......... TPQueally 4 88
(LMCumani) *lw: hld up wl in rr: rdn 3f out: prog on wd outside over 1f out: no ch* **12/1**

3032 **10** *½* **Fort**[4] 4123 3-8-3 **87** .......... RFfrench 5 88
(MJohnston) *mostly chsd wnr to over 2f out: wknd rapidly over 1f out* **16/1**

0131 **11** *1* **Admiral (IRE)**[41] 2999 3-7-13 **86** .......... NMackay(3) 1 85
(SirMichaelStoute) *t.k.h: sn prom: rdn 3f out: wknd wl over 1f out* **7/1**[3]

0214 **12** *¾* **Le Tiss (IRE)**[41] 2999 3-8-2 **89** .......... SHitchcott(3) 12 87
(MRChannon) *lw: hld up in rr: rdn 3f out: sme prog over 2f out: no imp wl over 1f out: sn wknd* **10/1**

4301 **13** *3* **Settlement Craic (IRE)**[16] 3806 3-8-7 **91** .......... JFortune 7 84
(TGMills) *swtg: a wl in rr: struggling and u.p over 3f out* **20/1**

1205 **14** *hd* **Swainson (USA)**[3] 4167 3-8-0 **84** .......... JQuinn 2 77
(PMitchell) *s.s: a wl in rr: wl btn fnl 3f* **100/1**

1213 **15** *3 ½* **Etmaam**[41] 2999 3-8-10 **94** .......... RHills 11 81
(MJohnston) *settled in rr: rdn 4f out: no rspnse and btn over 3f out* **9/2**[2]

4014 **16** *15* **Protective**[11] 3927 3-8-4 **88** .......... WSupple 15 51
(JGGiven) *trckd ldrs: rdn over 3f out: wknd rapidly over 2f out: t.o* **66/1**

2m 35.72s (-3.21) **Going Correction** +0.05s/f (Good) 16 Ran SP% **120.8**
Speed ratings: **112,111,111,110,109 109,107,107,107,106 106,105,103,103,101 91**CSF £237.19 CT £2042.78 TOTE £14.40: £3.10, £2.70, £1.80, £3.30; EX 292.00 Trifecta £3299.30 Pool £14,870.19 - 3.20 winning units..
**Owner** Mrs P W Harris **Bred** P W Harris **Trained** Ringshall, Bucks

**FOCUS**
A strong handicap that should throw up winners, and a smart winning time for a race of its type. The first five all showed improved form. Royal Ascot's King George V looked the key to the race, but Admiral, Etmaam and Le Tiss all finished well down the field and that race may have taken more out of them than had first appeared. If so, Maraahel's Gordon Stakes win looks all the better, as he finished second in that race.

**NOTEBOOK**
**Cutting Crew(USA)** was smartly into his stride and allowed a soft lead, so he had time for a breather before the run for home began. His assured stamina stood him in good stead and, although not the biggest, he kept finding, fending off several challenges. He will go up again for this and will need to keep progressing to defy a new mark, but he is a hearty character who will always give one hundred per cent.
**Larkwing(IRE)** ◆ came into this on the back of a maiden win from ordinary opposition at Newmarket and showed a sizeable amount of improvement in finishing second, going on well close home having looked awkward under pressure with a high head carriage. This was his first start since May and only fifth in all, so he can be expected to progress again. With an extra couple of furlongs sure to suit, the Melrose Stakes at York's Ebor meeting looks a plausible target.
**Always First** has progressed with each run this season and relished this step up in trip. Unable to cope with the pace of the impressive Mister Monet in a virtual match at Hamilton, the extra three furlongs and move into handicaps saw him in a much better light and he was finishing to good effect. He holds an engagement in the Great Voltigeur, but is not up to that level at present and is best kept to handicaps for the time being.
**Odiham** was allowed to take his chance despite there being concerns over his ability to handle the ground. The decision was justified, despite him possibly not being seen at his best. He is an improving three-year-old who still has more to give, and another two furlongs should see him in an even better light.
**Stage Right** ◆ was another who could have done with easier going but he too performed with great credit. He was momentarily denied a clear run and that did him no favours as he is a big, galloping sort who grinds away. The Melrose Stakes also looks an ideal target for him as the long straight at York should ensure he gets a clean crack at things, and the extra distance will play to his strengths, too.
**Always Waining(IRE)**, so impressive when winning a less competitive race the previous Saturday, ran well under his 7lb penalty but found this tougher and never looked a likely winner. Maybe he found the race coming too soon, but he remains a likely sort for similar races for the remainder of the campaign.
**Red Lancer** ran well for a 66-1 shot and came back to something like his early-season form, staying on from well off the pace.
**Prime Powered(IRE)** looked a doubtful stayer beforehand and so it proved. He had previously been progressive at ten furlongs despite looking a tad high in the weights, and can do better back down in trip.
**Zeitgeist(IRE)** is not as progressive as some may have thought and he ran as well as could have been expected.
**Fort** is likely to be best suited by a strongly-run ten furlongs, as he does not see this trip out that well. He weakened disappointingly having raced up with the pace, but can be given another chance under more suitable conditions.
**Admiral(IRE)** ran way below the form of his King George V win at the Royal meeting off a 4lb higher mark. He is better than this and should be given another chance.
**Le Tiss(IRE)**, another coming into this having run well in the King George V, also ran disappointingly and was way below his best.
**Settlement Craic(IRE)** was always trailing and failed to run his race.
**Swainson(USA)** has become disappointing and not gone on from his promising early-season efforts.
**Etmaam**, third in the King George V handicap, ran a flat race and was never going. He is better than this. *Official explanation: trainer had no explanation for the poor form shown*
**Protective** was hopelessly tailed off, stopping as though something was amiss. *Official explanation: jockey said colt had been unsuited by the good, good to firm in places going*

## 4230 WEATHERBYS BANK FILLIES' RATED STKS (H'CAP) 1m 1f
**4:25** (4:34) (C) (0-90,89) 3-Y-O+ **£9,251** (£3,509; £1,754; £797) **Stalls** Low

Form RPR

1211 **1** **Diamond Lodge**[11] 3943 3-9-8 **87** .......... EAhern 2 100+
(JNoseda) *lw: t.k.h: prom: trckd ldr 3f out: led 2f out: drvn and hrd pressed over 1f out: styd on wl* **11/4**[1]

5221 **2** *½* **Wee Dinns (IRE)**[12] 3908 3-9-3 **82** .......... JFEgan 6 94+
(SKirk) *racd in midfield: nt clr run and swtchd lft 3f out: prog 2f out: drvn to chal fnl f: a jst hld* **3/1**[2]

3043 **3** *1 ½* **Spring Goddess (IRE)**[19] 3694 3-9-2 **81** .......... KFallon 7 87
(APJarvis) *hld up in midfield: prog on outer over 2f out: drvn to chal and ev ch jst over 1f out: nt qckn ins fnl f* **9/2**[3]

323- **4** *2 ½* **Petrosa (IRE)**[317] 4937 4-9-0 **70** .......... TQuinn 5 71
(DRCElsworth) *hld up in rr: rdn 3f out: sme prog u.p fnl 2f: nvr rchd ldrs* **33/1**

2610 **5** *¾* **Tuscarora (IRE)**[12] 3910 5-8-7 **63** oh7 .......... TPQueally 9 63
(AWCarroll) *dwlt: t.k.h and hld up towards rr: prog on inner 3f out: cl up whn nt clr run 2f out to over 1f out: nt rcvr* **20/1**

02-0 **6** *1 ½* **Why Dubai (USA)**[109] 1327 3-9-10 **89** .......... RLMoore 10 86
(RHannon) *lw: prom: rdn over 3f out: stl cl up 2f out: fdd over 1f out* **12/1**

311- **7** *1 ¼* **Taminoula (IRE)**[290] 5503 3-9-1 **80** .......... DaneO'Neill 11 74
(MrsAJPerrett) *dwlt: sn trckd ldrs: rdn 3f out: losing pl whn squeezed out 2f out: n.d after* **7/1**

2641 **8** *1 ½* **Lara Falana**[11] 3933 6-8-12 **68** .......... JQuinn 8 59
(MissBSanders) *led: kicked on 4f out: hdd & wknd 2f out* **14/1**

0063 **9** *2 ½* **Hilites (IRE)**[5] 4084 3-9-0 **79** .......... SWhitworth 3 65
(JSMoore) *stdd s: hld up in last pair: shuffled along over 2f out: nvr nr ldrs* **33/1**

43-6 **10** *hd* **Honorine (IRE)**[59] 2504 4-9-10 **80** .......... PRobinson 4 66
(JWPayne) *t.k.h: hld up in last pair: shuffled along over 2f out: nvr nr ldrs* **16/1**

0405 **11** *3* **Totally Yours (IRE)**[13] 3867 3-9-8 **87** .......... MartinDwyer 12 67
(WRMuir) *racd in midfield: effrt and chsd ldrs jst over 2f out: wknd wl over 1f out* **33/1**

5510 **12** *1* **Dark Raider (IRE)**[12] 3908 3-8-5 **73** ow3 .......... DCorby(3) 1 51
(APJones) *chsd ldr to 3f out: wknd* **33/1**

1m 55.75s (-1.11) **Going Correction** +0.05s/f (Good)
**WFA** 3 from 4yo+ 9lb 12 Ran SP% **119.1**
Speed ratings: **106,105,104,102,101 100,98,97,95,95 92,91**CSF £10.34 CT £34.39 TOTE £3.70: £1.80, £1.80, £2.00; EX 9.90.
**Owner** Mrs J Harris **Bred** Chippenham Lodge Stud Ltd **Trained** Newmarket, Suffolk
■ Stewards Enquiry : E Ahern two-day ban: used whip in an incorrect place (Aug 9-10)

**FOCUS**
The proximity of Tuscarora from 7lb out of the handicap holds the form down a little, but a fair winning time for the grade and another good performance by Diamond Lodge, who continues to progress and has earned herself a crack at pattern company.

**NOTEBOOK**
**Diamond Lodge** has only met with defeat once since her debut - when caught out by a fine tactical ride at Sandown in June - and was recording her third straight win, and fourth of the season all told. She always held a good pitch and showed a good attitude in holding off Wee Dinns when that rival threw down a challenge. She has earned herself a crack at Listed company and should be able to gain some black type.
**Wee Dinns(IRE)** has been steadily progressing at a lower level and stepped up on all previous form here, as she was running off a 7lb higher mark than when winning at Newbury. She could well have another similar race in her still.
**Spring Goddess(IRE)** always seems to want for pace in the latter stages of her races, and she could not go on with the front pair from the furlong pole. She had to come wide with her challenge and did not look at ease under pressure. Although not bred to stay a mile and a half, she may be worth chancing over it.
**Petrosa(IRE)** did not go on from her initial promise last season, looking very reluctant on occasions, but this was more encouraging. She is entitled to improve on this seasonal debut, but might benefit from a confidence-boosting win in a maiden before running again in this type of race.
**Tuscarora(IRE)** ran well from out of the handicap and was unlucky not to finish closer, having been denied a clear run by the tiring Lara Falana. She remains in good form.
**Why Dubai(USA)** raced prominently from her good draw but did not see the race out. She is high enough in the weights and needs to drop a few pounds before winning.
**Taminoula(IRE)** was making her seasonal debut and had run her race when getting squeezed out. She was racing here off a high mark for what she had actually achieved at two - two wins from moderate opposition - and a drop in the weights is needed before she wins again.
**Hilites(IRE)** could never get into it and tried to come from too far off the pace.

## 4231 FINDON MAIDEN FILLIES' STKS 6f
**5:00** (5:05) (D) 2-Y-O **£10,432** (£3,210; £1,605; £802) **Stalls** Low

Form RPR

**1** **Suez** 2-8-11 .......... PRobinson 3 91+
(MAJarvis) *str: bit bkwd: led for 1f: led again over 2f out: shkn up over 1f out: r.o wl: promising* **9/2**[3]

**2** *2 ½* **Clear Impression (IRE)** 2-8-11 .......... JFortune 7 84+
(PWChapple-Hyam) *lengthy: unf: scope: n.m.r sn after s: in tch: stdy prog on outer 1/2-way: shkn up to chse wnr wl over 1f out: r.o but no i* **7/4**[1]

6 **3** *4* **Toffee Vodka (IRE)**[14] 3840 2-8-11 .......... RHills 6 72
(JWHills) *squeezed out s: racd in last pair and wl off the pce: stdy prog fr 2f out: styd on to take 3rd nr fin* **16/1**

230 **4** *½* **On The Waterline (IRE)**[71] 2208 2-8-11 .......... NCallan 8 70
(PDEvans) *prom: rdn over 2f out: unable qck wl over 1f out: one pce after* **40/1**

03 **5** *shd* **Madhavi**[12] 3904 2-8-11 .......... PDobbs 5 70
(RHannon) *towards rr: rdn and outpcd 1/2-way: styd on fr over 1f out: no ch* **7/1**

62 **6** *½* **Unreal**[20] 3675 2-8-11 .......... MHills 2 68
(BWHills) *trckd ldrs: rdn over 2f out: outpcd and btn over 1f out* **9/4**[2]

0 **7** *5* **Starlight River (IRE)**[25] 3531 2-8-11 .......... MartinDwyer 4 53
(WRMuir) *led after 1f to over 2f out: wknd wl over 1f out* **100/1**

0 **8** *3* **Corniche Dancer**[12] 3905 2-8-8 .......... SHitchcott(3) 9 44
(MRChannon) *s.s: outpcd and a struggling* **100/1**

1m 10.99s (-1.85) **Going Correction** -0.275s/f (Firm) 8 Ran SP% **108.1**
Speed ratings: **101,97,92,91,91 90,84,80**CSF £11.35 TOTE £5.60: £1.50, £1.30, £1.90; EX 14.80.
**Owner** Sheikh Mohammed **Bred** Meon Valley Stud **Trained** Newmarket, Suffolk

**FOCUS**
Two potentially classy fillies dominated the finish of a race that was run in a very smart time for a maiden. Suez can step straight up to Group company, while Clear Impression is a ready-made maiden winner.

**NOTEBOOK**
**Suez** ◆, a 480,000gns purchase, is bred on the dam's side to want a mile plus, but her sire was more of a speed influence and she was supported into 9-2 from an opening 6-1. Always well placed after a good start, she really hit top stride when getting back to the front, and stayed on too strongly for the well-touted Clear Impression. There is plenty of physical improvement to come and she will stay further. She looks well worth her place in Group company and connections are aiming her at the Lowther Stakes, where she is sure to go well.
**Clear Impression(IRE)** ◆ came here with good things expected of her and did not disappoint, beating the remainder easily and simply being unable to cope with a winner who looked well above average. She too looks smart, and she should have no trouble winning her maiden before going on to better things.
**Toffee Vodka(IRE)** stayed on takingly for third without being given a hard time, and improved on her debut effort. Her stable is going well and she should win her maiden..
**On The Waterline(IRE)** does not do much for the form but she was beaten far enough by the principals for it not to matter. She should do better once running in nurseries.

**Madhavi** will appreciate a seventh furlong and is now eligible to run in nurseries, a sphere in which she should enjoy success.

**Unreal** failed to run up to the form that saw her finish second at Newmarket and was readily held. She too looks more of a nursery sort.

## 4232 ZUHAIR STKS (H'CAP) (PREVIOUSLY KNOWN AS THE CHARLTON STAKES) 5f

**5:35** (5:36) (D ) (0-80,80) 4-Y-O+ **£10,985** (£3,380; £1,690; £845) **Stalls** Low

Form RPR

1366 **1** **Double M**[7] 4026 7-8-1 **58**......(v) RThomas(5) 10 70
(MrsLRichards) *lw: trckd nr side ldrs: prog to ld jst over 1f out: clr fnl f: comf* **28/1**

6000 **2** *2* **Time To Remember (IRE)**[12] 3895 6-8-3 **55**...... WSupple 6 60
(DNicholls) *racd in midfield nr side: effrt 2f out: swtchd rt jst over 1f out : r.o to snatch 2nd on line* **25/1**

113 **3** *shd* **Lady Protector**[45] 2909 5-8-3 **55**...... JFanning 11 59
(JBalding) *prom nr side: led wl over 1f out to jst over 1f out: no ch w wnr fnl f: lost 2nd on line* **25/1**

1000 **4** *3/4* **Merlin's Dancer**[3] 4165 4-9-13 **79**...... ANicholls 14 81
(DNicholls) *pressed far side ldrs: rdn to ld gp ins fnl f: no ch w wnr* **13/2**[2]

0004 **5** *shd* **Salviati (USA)**[7] 4011 7-9-2 **75**......(p) CJDavies(7) 21 76
(JMBradley) *lw: s.s: wl in rr far side: prog 2f out: str run fnl f: fin wl* **11/2**[1]

3000 **6** *1/2* **Roses Of Spring**[11] 3945 6-9-7 **78**......(p) AQuinn(5) 13 78
(RMHCowell) *chsd far side ldrs: rdn 2f out: styd on fnl f: unable to chal* **16/1**

1554 **7** *shd* **Devise (IRE)**[21] 3645 5-10-0 **80**...... TEDurcan 4 79
(MSSaunders) *racd nr side: s.i.s: outpcd and bhd: prog in centre 2f out: styd on fnl f* **16/1**

0621 **8** *1/2* **Stagnite**[5] 4085 4-8-5 **62** 7ex......(p) NChalmers(5) 22 59
(MrsHSweeting) *racd against far side rail: chsd ldrs: rdn 2f out: kpt on ins fnl f: nvr able to chal* **10/1**

0533 **9** *hd* **Playtime Blue**[12] 3894 4-8-5 **60**...... DCorby(3) 12 57
(MrsHSweeting) *lw: racd far side: chsd ldrs: u.p 1/2-way: kpt on fr over 1f out* **16/1**

3100 **10** *hd* **Polish Emperor (USA)**[51] 2739 4-9-11 **77**......(e) NCallan 18 73
(PWHarris) *pressed far side ldr: wknd ins fnl f* **10/1**

5000 **11** *shd* **Online Investor**[12] 3894 5-8-12 **64**...... ACulhane 16 60
(DNicholls) *racd far side: outpcd and wl off the pce: effrt and nt clr run over 1f out and ins fnl f: styd on* **10/1**

5415 **12** *shd* **Blessed Place**[3] 4181 4-7-10 **51**......(t) JFMcDonald(3) 8 46
(DJSFfrenchDavis) *prom nr side: led gp after 2f to wl over 1f out: wknd fnl f* **33/1**

0100 **12** *dht* **Guns Blazing**[7] 4034 5-8-13 **72**......(b) MHoward(7) 20 67
(DKIvory) *b: b.hind: led far side gp tl ins fnl f: wknd* **16/1**

6500 **14** *3/4* **Ela Figura**[7] 4034 4-7-9 **50** oh2...... LisaJones(3) 5 43
(AWCarroll) *lw: chsd nr side ldrs: rdn and no prog wl over 1f out* **100/1**

0203 **15** *hd* **Cerulean Rose**[5] 4085 5-9-2 **68**...... RLMoore 2 60
(AWCarroll) *racd nr side: outpcd and wl in rr: nvr on terms* **9/1**[3]

1100 **16** *hd* **Willhewiz**[27] 3453 4-9-13 **79**......(v) KDalgleish 15 70
(RMStronge) *prom far side: hanging and wkng ent fnl f: no ch whn hmpd last 75yds* **25/1**

4003 **17** *shd* **Redwood Star**[36] 3175 4-8-3 **55** ow1......(e) RPrice 17 46
(PLGilligan) *racd far side: off the pce and sn pushed along: effrt over 1f out: nt clr run ins fnl f: no ch* **9/1**[3]

0-04 **18** *nk* **Inch By Inch**[7] 4025 5-8-4 **56**......(b) MartinDwyer 7 46
(PJMakin) *led nr side gp for 2f: wknd over 1f out* **50/1**

0500 **18** *dht* **Madrasee**[27] 3439 6-9-4 **70**...... PDobbs 9 60
(LMontagueHall) *racd nr side: nvr on terms w ldrs: no prog fnl 2f* **25/1**

0-00 **20** *nk* **Sir Edwin Landseer (USA)**[11] 3941 4-9-9 **75**...... VHalliday 19 64
(ChristianWroe, UAE) *s.v.s: racd far side: wl bhd tl kpt on ins fnl f* **33/1**

3400 **21** *1* **Intellibet One**[7] 4013 4-8-3 **55**...... PHanagan 3 40
(PDEvans) *racd nr side: nvr on terms* **50/1**

0006 **22** *6* **Super Song**[14] 3841 4-8-1 **53**......(t) JoannaBadger 1 16
(PDEvans) *lw: racd nr side: outpcd and bhd fr 1/2-way* **100/1**

57.64 secs (-1.41) **Going Correction** -0.275s/f (Firm) **22** Ran SP% **130.1**
Speed ratings: **100,96,96,95,95 94,94,93,93,92 92,92,92,91,91 90,90,90,90,89 88,78**CSF £608.45 CT £16274.18 TOTE £28.60: £4.60, £5.60, £3.10, £2.10; EX 925.20 Place 6 £83.01, Place 5 £19.27.

**Owner** Bryan Mathieson **Bred** M G Tebbitt **Trained** Funtington, W Sussex

■ Stewards Enquiry : C J Davies one-day ban: careless riding (Aug 8)

**FOCUS**
A really competitive sprint handicap in which the field split into two groups. The near-side group just had the edge, providing the first three home. The time was fairly modest for the grade considering the conditions.

**NOTEBOOK**
**Double M** was very disappointing on the Polytrack just seven days previously, but left that effort well behind with a most emphatic success on this drop in trip and return to turf. This is the highest mark he has ever won off, but he will take quite a rise in the weights for this and would therefore be of interest under a penalty, although he does tend to need things to go his way.

**Time To Remember(IRE)**, 14lb lower than when last winning, ran his best race of the season so far according to RPR's. If this can be built on, he should be able to end a losing run stretching back over a year.

**Lady Protector** continues in good heart and did nothing wrong.

**Merlin's Dancer** has only ever won over six furlongs but, in winning his race on the far side, showed himself fully effective over this trip.

**Salviati(USA)** ◆, 2lb lower than in future handicaps, confirmed the promise of his recent Catterick effort in finishing a short-head second on the far side. He is 13lb lower than when last winning, and back in form, can surely find a similar event.

**Devise(IRE)** was surprisingly outpaced for a horse who has won over this trip four times, but he finished to good effect and remains in good heart.

**Online Investor** *Official explanation: jockey said gelding had been denied a clear run*

**Willhewiz** *Official explanation: jockey said colt had hung right*

**Redwood Star** got little luck in running and can be rated better than the bare form.

T/Jkpt: £27,436.80 to a £1 stake. Pool: £38,643.50. 0.50 winning tickets. T/Plt: £128.90 to a £1 stake. Pool: £164,005.50. 928.40 winning tickets. T/Qpdt: £25.80 to a £1 stake. Pool: £7,657.00. 219.05 winning tickets. JN

# 3840 KEMPTON (R-H)
## Wednesday, July 28

**OFFICIAL GOING: Good to firm**

## 4233 SHARP MINDS BETFAIR APPRENTICE H'CAP 1m 4f

**6:05** (6:05) (E ) (0-75,73) 3-Y-O+ **£4,036** (£1,242; £621; £310) **Stalls** High

Form RPR

0615 **1** **Desert Island Disc**[9] 3989 7-10-0 **73**...... ABeech 5 84
(JJBridger) *chsd clr lear: rdn to ld over 1f out: kpt up to work: comf* **7/1**

3534 **2** *1 3/4* **Head To Kerry (IRE)**[5] 4080 4-8-7 **55**......(t) PGallagher(3) 3 63
(DJSFfrenchDavis) *lw: sn led and clr: rdn and hdd over 1f out: kpt on wl but no imp fnl f* **11/2**[3]

5043 **3** *hd* **Most-Saucy**[4] 4129 8-8-10 **55**...... FPFerris 6 63
(IAWood) *trckd ldng pair: rdn over 2f out: styd on fnl f to press 2nd cl home* **4/1**[2]

0023 **4** *1 1/2* **Recount (FR)**[2] 4192 4-9-9 **68**...... MSavage 2 73
(JRBest) *lw: hld up in rr. hdwy 4f out: rdn 2f out: fdd ins fnl f* **2/1**[1]

4316 **5** *2 1/2* **Sudden Flight (IRE)**[14] 3851 7-9-8 **70**...... SJDonohoe(3) 7 71
(PDEvans) *racd in mid-div: rdn over 3f out and sn in rr* **9/1**

3435 **6** *4* **Escalade**[19] 3695 7-7-11 **47**......(p) DeanWilliams(5) 1 42
(WMBrisbourne) *hld up in rr: nvr on terms fnl 3f* **12/1**

4023 **7** *1 1/2* **Great View (IRE)**[15] 3825 5-9-6 **65**......(v) LPKeniry 4 58
(MrsALMKing) *lw: in tch in mid-div: rdn 3f out: sn btn* **7/1**

2m 35.88s (0.88) **Going Correction** +0.075s/f (Good) **7** Ran SP% **111.4**
Speed ratings: **100,98,98,97,96 93,92**CSF £42.17 TOTE £6.90: £2.00, £3.80; EX 46.10.

**Owner** W Wood **Bred** Southill Stud **Trained** Liphook, Hants

**FOCUS**
A fair apprentice race that was run at a solid pace and the form looks sound.

**NOTEBOOK**
**Desert Island Disc**, who won this last year and finished second in 2002, advertised her clear liking for this track and won tidily under top weight. She was 11lb higher than when successful last season, so this goes down as a personal best, and she had the race run to suit this time. She comes good at this time of year, but may need to reappear under a penalty in order to follow-up, as she can expect another rise in the weights now.

**Head To Kerry(IRE)** ◆ settled better in the lead this time and ran a game race from the front. He has run into form, having dropped in the weights of late, and can certainly exploit this mark before long, especially if upped in trip once again.

**Most-Saucy** ran her usual game race and is never far away, but may not have been ideally suited by this drop back in trip. She has slipped markedly in the weights this year, but really does need a very strong gallop to be seen at her best over this trip, and can get closer with a step back up in distance.

**Recount(FR)** has had a busy time of late, but still could have been expected to finish a bit closer over this more suitable trip. He may need a slight break now, but is due to go up 8lb in the future, and life will be a lot tougher as a result.

## 4234 EUROPEAN BREEDERS FUND MAIDEN FILLIES' STKS 7f (J)

**6:35** (6:35) (D ) 2-Y-O **£4,971** (£1,529; £764; £382) **Stalls** High

Form RPR

**1** **Hachita (USA)** 2-8-11...... WRyan 8 81
(HRACecil) *cmpt: lw: hld up in rr: gd hdwy on outside 2f out: r.o strly to ld ins fnl f* **12/1**

**2** *1 1/4* **Innocent Splendour** 2-8-11...... EAhern 2 77
(EALDunlop) *leggy: scope: lw: a in tch: rdn and ev ch ins fnl f: nt pce of wnr* **25/1**

0 **3** *3/4* **She's My Outsider**[21] 3627 2-8-11...... FNorton 5 76
(IAWood) *t.k.h in mid-div: rdn over 2f out: styd on wl fnl f* **40/1**

2 **4** *hd* **Arbella**[21] 3627 2-8-11...... DHolland 7 78+
(PWHarris) *lw: hld up in rr: hdwy 2f out and switche rt appr fnl f: r.o* **11/4**[2]

64 **5** *1 3/4* **Mulberry Wine**[20] 3665 2-8-11...... DSweeney 13 71
(MBlanshard) *led tl tl rdn and hdd ins fnl f: fdd* **33/1**

5 **6** *1 3/4* **Autumn Melody (FR)**[21] 3627 2-8-11......(t) LDettori 1 68+
(SaeedBinSuroor) *in cl tch w ldr tl rdn and wknd over 1f out* **11/2**

06 **7** *1/2* **Spinning Coin**[21] 3627 2-8-11...... DaneO'Neill 10 65
(JGPortman) *slowly away: in rr tl passed sme btn horses fnl f* **50/1**

**8** *1 1/4* **Balletomaine (IRE)** 2-8-4...... KMay(7) 12 62
(BWHills) *leggy: scope: bit bkwd: chsd ldrs: rdn and wkng whn sltly hmpd 1f out* **33/1**

4 **9** *3* **Heat Of The Night**[21] 3627 2-8-11...... TQuinn 3 54
(JLDunlop) *lw: fly-jmpd s: sn prom: rdn 2f out: sn btn* **9/2**[3]

02 **10** *1/2* **Great Opinions (USA)**[27] 3456 2-8-11...... KFallon 11 53
(JHMGosden) *lw: s.i.s: sn chsd ldrs: rdn and wknd 2f out* **9/4**[1]

0606 **11** *3/4* **Imperial Miss (IRE)**[6] 4053 2-8-11...... ADaly 4 51
(BWDuke) *trckd ldrs tl rdn and wknd 2f out* **50/1**

**12** *2 1/2* **Alpine Gold (IRE)** 2-8-11...... SDrowne 6 45
(JLDunlop) *str: bit bkwd: scope: slowly away: a bhd* **40/1**

05 **13** *3/4* **Victory Hymn (IRE)**[30] 3366 2-8-11...... CCatlin 9 43
(MRChannon) *a struggling in rr* **50/1**

1m 27.93s (0.66) **Going Correction** +0.075s/f (Good) **13** Ran SP% **119.2**
Speed ratings: **99,97,96,96,94 92,91,90,87,86 85,82,81**CSF £274.59 TOTE £12.90: £3.00, £5.00, £11.40; EX 142.60.

**Owner** K Abdulla **Bred** Juddmonte Farms Inc **Trained** Newmarket, Suffolk

**FOCUS**
A fair fillies' maiden that could be rated higher and should throw up its share of winners as it produced a smart winning time.

**NOTEBOOK**
**Hachita(USA)**, whose dam is half-sister to the top-class performers Zafonic and Zamindar, showed a neat turn of foot late on and won this going away. It was a very pleasing debut effort, especially as she looked green through the early parts, and she should come on a fair bit for the experience.

**Innocent Splendour** shaped with definite promise on this debut and was bang there until greenness found her out in the final furlong. She will stay further, will be sharper next time and looks to have a future.

**She's My Outsider** broke much better than on her recent course and distance debut, and despite running keenly, ran on well late in the day and showed significant improvement. Although her future looks to lie in handicaps, she can find a maiden over this trip.

**Arbella** failed to confirm her debut form with the third placed filly and paid for running too freely early on. That said, she again showed ability and was not helped by having to switch for a run late in the straight. She is far from one to write off.

**Mulberry Wine**, who had shown just moderate form in two previous outings, ran her best race to date and will no doubt fare better now she is eligible for nurseries.

**Autumn Melody(FR)** ran very much to her debut form with Arbella and failed to improve as expected. Although she is bred in the purple, she is clearly no star.

**Heat Of The Night**, closely matched with a few of these on her debut form, spoilt her chance at the start and can be expected to leave this form behind in the future. *Official explanation: jockey said filly tried to go under gates just before they opened*

**Great Opinions(USA)**, whose latest second looked to give her an obvious chance in this, was slow to break, but still recovered to hold every chance. This was a disappointing effort. *Official explanation: trainer had no explanation for the poor form shown*

## 4235 SHANGRI-LA HOTEL SINGAPORE NURSERY 6f

7:05 (7:06) (E) 2-Y-O **£4,173** (£1,284; £642; £321) **Stalls** Centre

Form RPR

1341 **1** **The Crooked Ring**[9] [3975] 2-9-1 **83** 6ex SJDonohoe(7) 5 89
(PDEvans) *hld up in rr: rdn and hdwy appr fnl f: r.o to ld wl ins last: all out* **5/1**[2]

450 **2** ½ **Ridder**[18] [3748] 2-8-9 **70** EAhern 6 75
(DJCoakley) *lw: mid-div: rdn to ld ins fnl f: no ex and hdd nr fin* **20/1**

6411 **3** ¾ **Piddies Pride (IRE)**[6] [4054] 2-8-4 **68** 6ex FPFerris(3) 3 70
(PSMcentee) *sn rdn along in rr: hdwy over 1f out: r.o wl fnl f: nvr nrr* **7/1**[3]

011 **4** 1½ **Island Swing (IRE)**[47] [2858] 2-9-7 **82** LDettori 4 80
(JLSpearing) *b: led stands side gp. ev ch appr fnl f: one pce ins* **9/2**[1]

3410 **5** ½ **Lateral Thinker (IRE)**[11] [3938] 2-8-8 **69** SDrowne 2 65
(JAOsborne) *chsd ldrs stand side:: fdd ent fnl f* **10/1**

250 **6** ¾ **Arthur Wardle (USA)**[23] [3588] 2-8-10 **71** DHolland 11 65
(MLWBell) *slowly away and rdn to keep in tch on outside: wknd over 1f out* **7/1**[3]

3250 **7** nk **Grand Option**[11] [3938] 2-9-0 **75** ADaly 10 68
(BWDuke) *overall ldr on far side: briefly hdd 1/2-way: hdd & wknd ins fnl f* **20/1**

453 **8** nk **Royal Orissa**[16] [3808] 2-9-2 **77** PaulEddery 8 69
(DHaydnJones) *hld up on far side: hdwy and ev ch appr fnl f: wknd ins* **9/2**[1]

2144 **9** 2 **Gee Bee Em**[6] [4041] 2-9-0 **75** CCatlin 7 61
(MRChannon) *lw: chsd ldrs tl rdn and wknd wl over 1f out* **16/1**

2061 **10** ½ **Colonel Bilko (IRE)**[13] [3886] 2-8-10 **71** FNorton 9 56
(BRMillman) *prom on far side: led briefly 1/2-way: wknd over 1f out* **9/1**

1m 12.35s (-0.72) **Going Correction** -0.25s/f (Firm) **10** Ran SP% **112.5**

Speed ratings: **94,93,92,90,89 88,88,87,85,84**CSF £94.95 CT £691.97 TOTE £5.00: £2.20, £3.00, £2.40; EX 175.40.

**Owner** J R Salter **Bred** W H R John And Partners **Trained** Pandy, Gwent

**FOCUS**

A decent nursery for the grade. The field split into two groups and the satnds' side came out on top, so as such the form has to be treated with a degree of caution. The figures shown as 'official ratings' are estimates for guidance only.

**NOTEBOOK**

**The Crooked Ring** followed-up his recent Ayr success under a 6lb penalty in typically gritty fashion. He has improved with almost every outing this season and is a very genuine sort, yet although he will take another rise in the weights, should continue to pay his way in this sphere.

**Ridder**, who had shown fair form on his debut over course and distance in May, had every chance, but got outbattled by the winner on this nursery bow. This was by far his best effort to date, he should improve again, and is the type his trainer does well with.

**Piddies Pride(IRE)**, who came into this on the back of two selling wins over the minimum trip, ran her best race to date in defeat under her penalty. She can find a nursery or two this summer and seems best suited by this sixth furlong.

**Island Swing(IRE)** again showed good early pace to lead, but had nothing left when challenged entering the final stages in this better race. He was not disgraced, but looks to have been given a stiff mark on this evidence.

**Arthur Wardle(USA)** did not have things go his way on this nursery debut and should be capable of better when getting some cover. *Official explanation: jockey said colt was never travelling*

**Royal Orissa**, had shown fair form in his three starts prior to this, but could not get on terms having been held up on the far side. He should be capable of improving, but would not be one to place total faith in.

**Colonel Bilko(IRE)** *Official explanation: jockey said gelding hung left in the final 2f*

## 4236 COMMITMENTS LIVE HERE NEXT WEDNESDAY RATED STKS (H'CAP) 7f (J)

7:35 (7:36) (D) (0-85,82) 3-Y-O **£7,276** (£2,759; £1,379; £627) **Stalls** High

Form RPR

2203 **1** **Pizazz**[4] [4126] 3-9-7 **82** (b[1]) JFortune 3 97
(BJMeehan) *lw: mde all: rdn clr over 1f out: unchal* **6/1**

0413 **2** 5 **Dumnoni**[19] [3698] 3-9-5 **80** NCallan 4 82
(JulianPoulton) *chsd wnr thrght: rdn over 1f out and readily outpcd* **9/2**[3]

2323 **3** 1¾ **Farewell Gift**[35] [3203] 3-9-7 **82** KFallon 2 79
(RHannon) *lw: mid-div: wnt 3rd over 2f out: but no ch w first 2* **3/1**[2]

1650 **4** ½ **River Treat (FR)**[30] [3384] 3-9-5 **80** DHolland 7 76
(GWragg) *hld up in rr: styd on ins fnl 2f but nvr nr to chal* **10/1**

0056 **5** 1¼ **Convince (USA)**[4] [4126] 3-9-7 **82** SDrowne 5 74
(MABuckley) *stdd s and hld up in rr: nvr on terms* **20/1**

0162 **6** 1½ **Panshir (FR)**[11] [3949] 3-9-6 **81** RMullen 1 70
(CFWall) *s.i.s: hdwy on oustide 3f out but sn wl hld* **15/8**[1]

043 **7** 22 **Memory Man**[14] [3848] 3-8-6 **67** FNorton 6 —
(WRMuir) *lw: chassd first 2 tl wknd qckly over 2f out: eased whn wl btn over 1f out* **20/1**

1m 26.08s (-1.19) **Going Correction** +0.075s/f (Good) **7** Ran SP% **110.9**

Speed ratings: **109,103,101,100,99 97,72**CSF £30.78 TOTE £6.60: £2.40, £2.80; EX 22.10.

**Owner** Mrs Susan Roy **Bred** Mrs D O Joly **Trained** Upper Lambourn, Berks

**FOCUS**

A smart winning time for the grade and the field were well stung out behind the decisive winner who put up an improved performance in the blinkers.

**NOTEBOOK**

**Pizazz** pinged out to grab the lead and never looked like being caught at any stage. This was his first win at the ninth attempt and the first-time blinkers certainly had a positive effect. He could well go on from this, but will face will rise in the weights.

**Dumnoni** was readily held by the winner, but again ran with credit and is becoming a consistent performer. However, he has no secrets from the Handicapper now.

**Farewell Gift**, who has not run a bad race all season despite not winning, could not land a blow over this extra furlong. He has the ability, but looks in need of respite from the Handicapper before he can lose his maiden tag in this division.

**River Treat(FR)** was not suited by being held up and was staying on too late. He looks too high in the weights at present.

**Panshir(FR)** , who came into this in the form of his life, showed little and ran well below par. This leaves him with a lot to prove now.

## 4237 "SURREY HERALD" CLASSIFIED STKS 1m (J)

8:05 (8:06) (D) 3-Y-O+ **£6,808** (£2,095; £1,047; £523) **Stalls** High

Form RPR

0212 **1** **Welcome Stranger**[3] [4164] 4-9-1 81 LFletcher(3) 3 92
(JMPEustace) *hld up in tch: wnt 2nd over 2f out: led over 1f out: edgd lft but sn clr: easily* **7/4**[2]

4021 **2** 3½ **Arkholme**[19] [3689] 3-8-9 80 (b) SDrowne 1 83
(PWinkworth) *trckd ldr clly: led 3f out: rdn and hdd over 1f out: nt pce of wnr* **7/2**[3]

-005 **3** 1¾ **Sweet Indulgence (IRE)**[11] [3943] 3-8-12 83 KFallon 5 82
(DrJDScargill) *lw: t.k.h: in tch tl one pce ins fnl 2f* **13/8**[1]

0525 **4** shd **Vienna's Boy (IRE)**[14] [3845] 3-8-12 83 DaneO'Neill 4 82
(RHannon) *stdd s and hld up: sme hdwy 2f out but nvr nr to chal* **12/1**

-500 **5** 9 **Ryan's Future (IRE)**[13] [3872] 4-9-3 79 CCatlin 2 58
(JAkehurst) *led tl hdd 3f out: wknd over 2f out* **16/1**

1m 39.36s (-0.26) **Going Correction** +0.075s/f (Good)

**WFA** 3 from 4yo 8lb **5** Ran SP% **110.3**

Speed ratings: **104,100,98,98,89**CSF £8.22 TOTE £2.70: £1.40, £2.10; EX 6.20.

**Owner** H R Moszkowicz **Bred** Henry And Mrs Rosemary Moszkowicz **Trained** Newmarket, Suffolk

**FOCUS**

A tight looking classified event that saw the field strung out behind the easy winner and the form looks sound.

**NOTEBOOK**

**Welcome Stranger**, who had looked a little unlucky at Ascot in a better race last time, confirmed his current rude health with a facile success. He looks to be still improving, and on this display, is well worth a crack in better company now.

**Arkholme** ran his race in second, but was made to look pedestrian by the winner. This was a fair debut for his new connections and, although he has his quirks, can pay his way off this sort of mark.

**Sweet Indulgence(IRE)**, not disgraced in three competitive handicaps at Newmarket previously this year, was well-backed in the ring, but disappointed and never got into the argument. He could well be capable of better back in handicaps, but has it all to prove now, and looks a tricky ride.

**Vienna's Boy(IRE)** did little to convince that he gets this trip. He looks too high in the weights at present.

## 4238 SHARP MINDS BETFAIR H'CAP 1m (J)

8:35 (8:37) (E) (0-75,73) 3-Y-O+ **£4,231** (£1,302; £651; £325) **Stalls** High

Form RPR

6223 **1** **Todlea (IRE)**[14] [3844] 4-9-12 **73** LDettori 7 82
(JAOsborne) *lw: a.p: wnt 2nd 2f out and sn led: rdn clr* **5/2**[1]

6360 **2** 1½ **Fleetwood Bay**[19] [3698] 4-9-6 **67** (t) JFortune 12 73
(BRMillman) *lw: led after 1f. hdd over 1f out: kpt on wl but nt pce of wnr* **12/1**

0004 **3** ½ **The Gaikwar (IRE)**[5] [4083] 5-8-9 **61** (b) MSavage(5) 1 65
(NEBerry) *b: hld up in rr: hdwy over 2f out: styd on fnl f but nvr nr to chal* **14/1**

0300 **4** shd **Zafarshah (IRE)**[19] [3698] 5-8-13 **60** (v) KFallon 11 64
(PDEvans) *t.k.h: a in tch: kpt on fnl f but nvr chal for ld* **9/2**[2]

1604 **5** 2½ **My Maite (IRE)**[14] [3844] 5-7-13 **46** (tp) CCatlin 3 44
(RIngram) *lw: in rr: styd on ins fnl 2f but nvr nr to chal* **8/1**

5-30 **6** ½ **Pending (IRE)**[18] [3745] 3-9-3 **72** (p) JPMurtagh 6 69
(JRFanshawe) *lw: prom: rdn 2f out: wknd appr fnl f* **11/2**[3]

0051 **7** shd **Little Englander**[25] [3536] 4-8-11 **58** DaneO'Neill 4 55
(HCandy) *lw: b.hind: hld up in rr: kpt on fnl f but nvr on terms* **8/1**

0055 **8** ½ **Esperance (IRE)**[20] [3662] 4-7-9 **45** oh1 FPFerris(3) 8 41
(JAkehurst) *led for 1f: chsd ldr tl 2f out: wknd over 1f out* **33/1**

0-16 **9** ¾ **Hollywood Henry (IRE)**[20] [3660] 4-8-9 **56** (p) ADaly 2 50
(JAkehurst) *a bhd* **10/1**

5300 **10** ½ **Cool Temper**[7] [4029] 8-9-0 **66** (b[1]) NDeSouza(5) 9 59
(PFICole) *mid-div tl rdn and wknd 2f out* **20/1**

4643 **11** shd **Nautical**[15] [3826] 6-8-3 **50** RMullen 5 43
(AWCarroll) *swtg: s.i.s: effrt on outside over 2f out: sn btn* **10/1**

1000 **12** dist **Senior Minister**[9] [3997] 6-8-13 **60** EAhern 10 —
(PWHiatt) *chsd ldrs tl rdn 4f out: wknd rapidly: t.o* **33/1**

1m 40.68s (1.06) **Going Correction** +0.075s/f (Good)

**WFA** 3 from 4yo+ 8lb **12** Ran SP% **127.5**

Speed ratings: **97,95,95,94,92 91,91,91,90,90 89,—**CSF £37.51 CT £377.88 TOTE £3.70: £1.60, £4.30, £4.50; EX 38.90 Place 6 £4,726.93, Place 5 £1,040.23.

**Owner** Lynn Wilson Giles Wilson Martin Landau **Bred** Irish National Stud **Trained** Upper Lambourn, Berks

**FOCUS**

A modest winning time for the class of contest, but the form looks solid with the placed horses running to form.

**NOTEBOOK**

**Todlea(IRE)** gained a deserved success and relished this drop in trip. He is an honest sort, but will go up in the weights for this and may struggle as a result.

**Fleetwood Bay**, dropped 10lb since his reappearance in April, ran a brave race form the front. He improved for the application of the tongue-tie and does look best at this trip.

**The Gaikwar(IRE)** ran on late to grab third over this extra furlong and has clearly dropped to a winning mark.

**Zafarshah(IRE)** ran very keenly through the early parts, but stayed on well enough in the straight and improved on recent efforts. *Official explanation: jockey said gelding did not feel right in the straight and pecked on the run to the line, so he held gelding together to the line*

**Pending(IRE)**, making his handicap debut, failed to improve for the application of cheekpieces and looked very one paced.

**Senior Minister** *Official explanation: jockey said gelding finished lame*

T/Plt: £3,109.90 to a £1 stake. Pool: £38,129.30. 8.95 winning tickets. T/Qpdt: £28.30 to a £1 stake. Pool: £4,433.50. 115.60 winning tickets. JS

# 4016 LEICESTER (R-H)

## Wednesday, July 28

**OFFICIAL GOING: Good (good to firm in places)**

Unlike the last couple of meetings where large fields on the straingth course split into two groups, they all elected to race on the stands' side.

Wind: Slight behind. Weather: Overcast and humid.

## 4239 EBF CRIMEBEAT CHARITY RACENIGHT MAIDEN STKS 5f 218y

6:20 (6:21) (D) 2-Y-O **£5,447** (£1,676; £838; £419) **Stalls** Low

Form RPR

2 **1** **Army Of Angels (IRE)**[21] [3643] 2-9-0 (t) KMcEvoy 6 94+
(SaeedBinSuroor) *w ldr tl led over 2f out: rdn clr fnl f* **2/13**[1]

53 **2** 8 **Avertigo**[15] [3823] 2-9-0 KDarley 4 70
(WRMuir) *led: rdn and hdd over 2f out: outpcd over 1f out* **15/2**[2]

0 **3** 1½ **Storm Fury (USA)**[18] [3749] 2-9-0 AMcCarthy 2 65
(PWChapple-Hyam) *chsd ldrs: rdn 1/2-way: outpcd over 1f out* **20/1**[3]

0 **4** 5 **Allizam**[11] [3925] 2-9-0 GCarter 5 50
(BAMcmahon) *s.i.s: sn prom: outpcd fnl 4f* **80/1**

**5** 1¾ **Beau Marche** 2-9-0 IMongan 1 45
(IAWood) *sn outpcd and bhd* **33/1**

6 5 **Layed Back Rocky** 2-9-0 .................................................. SRighton 3 30
(MMullineaux) *s.s: outpcd* **66/1**

1m 11.04s (-2.36) **Going Correction** -0.30s/f (Firm) **6** Ran SP% **108.9**
Speed ratings: **103,92,90,83,81 74**CSF £1.44 TOTE £1.10: £1.02, £1.80; EX 1.50.
**Owner** Godolphin **Bred** Gerard Callanan **Trained** Newmarket, Suffolk

**FOCUS**
A straightforward task for the winner, but he still recorded a smart winning time for a race of its type and could be rated higher.

**NOTEBOOK**
**Army Of Angels(IRE)** was still a little green in the preliminaries, but looked to face a simple task, and so it proved. However, it was nice to see him kept up to his work in an effort to teach him something. He holds an entry in the Gimcrack but, while that may just be flying a bit high, he does look the sort to have a nice prize in him.
**Avertigo** was easily put in his place when the winner went on and, while he may not be quite up to winning a maiden, he should find a nursery somewhere.
**Storm Fury(USA)** is still on the leggy side at present and should do better when facing a stiffer task.
**Beau Marche**, a half-brother to the useful sprinter Smokin Beau, was too green to do himself justice.

## 4240 SAMWORTH BROTHERS H'CAP 1m 1f 218y
**6:50** (6:50) (D) (0-80,77) 3-Y-0+ **£6,968** (£2,144; £1,072; £536) **Stalls** High

Form RPR
2110 **1** **Realism (FR)**[11] 3942 4-9-10 **74** .................................... DarrenWilliams 2 87
(PWHiatt) *a.p: led over 2f out: rdn over 1f out: styd on wl* **5/1**[3]
221 **2** *5* **Fortune's Princess**[12] 3922 3-9-3 **77** .................................... KDarley 7 81
(MJWallace) *hld up: hdwy over 3f out: rdn and ev ch over 1f out: wknd ins fnl f* **3/1**[1]
106- **3** *nk* **Royal Bathwick (IRE)**[301] 5305 4-9-9 **73** .................................... GBaker 1 76
(BRMillman) *s.i.s: hld up: rdn over 1f out: r.o ins fnl f: nt rch ldrs* **14/1**
324- **4** *1/2* **Young Rooney**[396] 2778 4-9-5 **69** .................................... TPQueally 5 71
(MMullineaux) *led: rdn and hdd over 2f out: styd on same pce appr fnl f* **28/1**
0320 **5** *1/2* **Summer Bounty**[18] 3731 8-9-12 **76** .................................... SWKelly 3 77
(FJordan) *s.i.s: hld up: hdwy over 2f out: rdn over 1f out: wknd ins fnl f* **7/2**[2]
-040 **6** *1* **Colophony (USA)**[26] 3474 4-9-7 **71** .................................... (t) MFenton 8 70
(KAMorgan) *s.i.s: hld up: hdwy over 3f out: hung rt and wknd over 1f out* **11/1**
0011 **7** *3/4* **Zeis (IRE)**[13] 3885 4-9-4 **68** .................................... (t) JFEgan 4 66
(AndrewReid) *chsd ldrs: rdn 1/2-way: wknd over 1f out* **7/2**[2]
6630 **8** *3/4* **Active Account (USA)**[17] 3781 7-8-10 **60** .................................... IMongan 6 56
(MrsHDalton) *chsd ldr tl rdn over 3f out: wknd over 1f out* **8/1**

2m 5.64s (-2.76) **Going Correction** -0.15s/f (Firm)
**WFA** 3 from 4yo+ 10lb **8** Ran SP% **115.7**
Speed ratings: **105,101,100,100,99 99,98,97**CSF £20.68 CT £197.00 TOTE £6.30: £2.30, £1.10, £4.20; EX 16.80.
**Owner** Miss Maria McKinney **Bred** Darley Stud Management Co Ltd **Trained** Hook Norton, Oxon
■ Stewards Enquiry : S W Kelly two-day ban: careless riding (Aug 8-9)

**FOCUS**
An ordinary race although quite competitive on paper, but it was won in runaway fashion in a fair time.

**NOTEBOOK**
**Realism(FR)**, who disappointed last time when tried over further, proved well suited to the strong pace back over his optimum trip. He is still clearly progressing. *Official explanation: trainer said, regarding the improved form shown, gelding appeared to benefit from stronger handling by today's full jockey - ran in apprentice race last time*
**Fortune's Princess** did her best to ensure the winner did not have things all his own way, but she paid for those efforts late on and finished weakly.
**Royal Bathwick(IRE)** making a belated return to action, stayed on when the race was all but over. She will certainly strip sharper for the outing.
**Young Rooney**, off the course for over a year, took his rivals along at a fair clip and deserves some credit for not falling away. Although yet to score, he will certainly find easier openings than he faced here.
**Summer Bounty** had the sound pace he needs, but was most disappointing with no apparent excuse.

## 4241 EVERARDS BREWERY CLAIMING STKS 7f 9y
**7:20** (7:20) (E) 3-Y-0 **£3,552** (£1,093; £546; £273) **Stalls** Low

Form RPR
0004 **1** **Stevedore (IRE)**[19] 3707 3-9-3 70 .................................... GBaker 11 70
(JohnAHarris) *chsd ldrs: led over 2f out: rdn out* **5/1**[2]
-000 **2** *1 1/2* **Blue Java**[13] 3875 3-8-13 59 .................................... MFenton 15 63
(HMorrison) *s.i.s: sn prom: led 1/2-way: hdd over 2f out: rdn and ev ch fr over 1f out tl no ex wl ins fnl f* **9/2**[1]
0026 **3** *1 3/4* **Elsinora**[7] 4018 3-8-0 43 .................................... (b[1]) DKinsella 2 45
(HMorrison) *chsd ldrs: rdn and ev ch over 2f out: styd on same pce appr fnl f* **10/1**
5-50 **4** *hd* **Miss Procurer (IRE)**[5] 4092 3-8-12 69 .................................... JQuinn 5 56
(PFICole) *s.i.s: hld up: hdwy over 1f out: rdn and edgd lft ins fnl f: styd on same pce* **14/1**
0203 **5** *1 3/4* **Red Rocky**[7] 4018 3-7-13 46 .................................... (p) StephanieHollinshead[(5)] 4 44
(RHollinshead) *led to 1/2-way: rdn over 2f out: styng on same pce whn faltered ins fnl f* **9/1**
-150 **6** *1 1/2* **Lyrical Girl (USA)**[6] 4045 3-8-7 59 .................................... DFox[(5)] 7 48
(HJManners) *sn pushed along in rr: styd on fnl f: nvr nrr* **12/1**
0000 **7** *nk* **Chiqitita (IRE)**[19] 3710 3-7-11 51 .................................... HayleyTurner[(5)] 9 37
(MissMERowland) *mid-div: rdn 1/2-way: styd on fnl f: n.d* **100/1**
0100 **8** *shd* **Pererin**[48] 2803 3-8-5 46 .................................... (b) TPQueally 3 40
(IAWood) *chsd ldrs: rdn 1/2-way: wknd wl over 1f out* **20/1**
0510 **9** *nk* **Shinko Femme (IRE)**[21] 3622 3-8-8 53 .................................... KimTinkler 13 42
(NTinkler) *mid-div: rdn 1/2-way: wknd over 1f out* **9/1**
0006 **10** *5* **Lupine Howl**[23] 3582 3-9-3 44 .................................... (p) GGibbons 8 38
(BAMcmahon) *chsd ldrs over 4f* **66/1**
0060 **11** *6* **Sworn To Secrecy**[21] 3628 3-8-4 57 .................................... (b) KMcEvoy 1 10
(SKirk) *s.s: outpcd* **11/2**[3]
4100 **12** *4* **Fizzy Lady**[19] 3700 3-8-8 60 .................................... (t) RSmith 12 3
(NEBerry) *prom over 4f* **25/1**
0535 **13** *8* **Soviet Spirit**[9] 3993 3-8-7 59 .................................... MHalford[(7)] 14 —
(CADwyer) *prom over 4f* **10/1**
2000 **14** *8* **Maybe Someday**[28] 3425 3-8-9 52 .................................... (b) IMongan 6 —
(JBalding) *n.d* **50/1**
-630 **15** *8* **Delusion**[41] 3002 3-8-5 53 ow1 .................................... KDarley 10 —
(TDEasterby) *sn bhd* **9/1**

1m 24.66s (-1.44) **Going Correction** -0.30s/f (Firm) **15** Ran SP% **125.8**
Speed ratings: **96,94,92,92,90 88,88,87,87,81 74,70,61,52,42**CSF £27.78 TOTE £5.60: £2.30, £2.30, £3.00; EX 54.00.Stevedore was claimed by Rod Millman for £10,000.
**Owner** Cleartherm Ltd **Bred** C J Foy **Trained** Eastwell, Leics

**FOCUS**
An ordinary seller, but run at a fair pace and very few got into it. The form is basically weak.

**NOTEBOOK**
**Stevedore(IRE)**, having his first race for new connections, was without the headgear this time. He saw his race out honestly enough, but will again have new surroundings as he was claimed afterwards by Rod Millman.
**Blue Java**, done no favours by his wide draw, has found his level and should have no trouble scoring in this grade.
**Elsinora** again left the impression she is far from an easy ride.
**Miss Procurer(IRE)** is clearly flattered by her current mark, but should be able to make her presence felt at this level. *Official explanation: jockey said filly had a breathing problem*
**Red Rocky** showed her customary early pace, but she folded rather tamely in the latter stages.
**Lyrical Girl(USA)** found this trip too sharp for her. In foal to Kier Park, she will not get many more chances.
**Sworn To Secrecy** *Official explanation: jockey said filly had lost her action*
**Maybe Someday** *Official explanation: jockey said gelding lost its action*
**Delusion** *Official explanation: jockey said filly had lost her action*

## 4242 NEXT H'CAP 1m 9y
**7:50** (8:04) (E) (0-70,70) 3-Y-0 **£7,299** (£2,246; £1,123; £561) **Stalls** High

Form RPR
1311 **1** **She's Our Lass (IRE)**[41] 3004 3-9-6 **69** .................................... KMcEvoy 4 77
(DCarroll) *hld up: hdwy over 2f out: r.o to ld wl ins fnl f* **7/1**[3]
6-00 **2** *2* **Burlington Place**[14] 3849 3-8-11 **60** .................................... JFEgan 12 63
(SKirk) *chsd ldr tl led over 6f out: rdn over 1f out: hdd wl ins fnl f* **25/1**
3003 **3** *nk* **Louisiade (IRE)**[5] 4092 3-9-0 **63** .................................... MFenton 13 65
(TDEasterby) *a.p: rdn to chse ldr and hung rt over 1f out: styd on same pce ins fnl f* **12/1**
0545 **4** *2* **Stanley Crane (USA)**[14] 3848 3-8-10 **59** .................................... (t) BDoyle 5 57
(BHanbury) *hld up: nt clr run over 2f out: r.o ins fnl f: nvr trbld ldrs* **16/1**
3103 **5** *3/4* **Knickyknackienoo**[4] 4147 3-8-10 **59** .................................... SWhitworth 11 55
(AGNewcombe) *s.i.s: hld up: plld hrd: hdwy over 3f out: rdn over 1f out: edgd rt and no ex fnl f* **9/2**[2]
2040 **6** *1 1/4* **Phluke**[25] 3527 3-9-7 **70** .................................... SCarson 14 63
(RFJohnsonHoughton) *led: hdd over 6f out: rdn over 2f out: wknd fnl f* **16/1**
0112 **7** *1* **The Fun Merchant**[5] 4092 3-9-2 **65** .................................... JQuinn 2 56
(JPearce) *hld up: hdwy over 3f out: rdn and hung rt over 1f out: wknd fnl f* **7/4**[1]
0010 **8** *2* **Mister Trickster (IRE)**[17] 3180 3-8-13 **62** .................................... SRighton 9 48
(RDickin) *plld hrd and prom: rdn over 3f out: wknd 2f out* **16/1**
1 **9** *5* **Komoto**[14] 3848 3-9-7 **70** .................................... TPQueally 6 45
(GAButler) *s.i.s: hld up: rdn over 4f out: a in rr* **9/1**
0032 **10** *6* **Mr Belvedere**[44] 2928 3-8-7 **56** .................................... JMackay 8 17
(AJLidderdale) *chsd ldrs: rdn over 3f out: wknd over 2f out* **25/1**
3323 **11** *1 1/4* **Half A Handful**[6] 4052 3-9-3 **66** .................................... (v) KDarley 7 24
(MJWallace) *hld up in tch: hmpd over 5f out: rdn over 3f out: wknd over 2f out* **12/1**

1m 41.41s (-1.19) **Going Correction** -0.15s/f (Firm) **11** Ran SP% **117.8**
Speed ratings: **99,97,96,94,93 92,91,89,84,78 77**CSF £166.15 CT £2071.23 TOTE £5.80: £2.90, £5.90, £3.30; EX 236.10.
**Owner** We-Know Partnership **Bred** Illuminatus Investments **Trained** Warthill, N Yorks

**FOCUS**
A competitive race for the grade, but the pace was only steady which serves to devalue the form slightly.

**NOTEBOOK**
**She's Our Lass(IRE)** continues to progress and showed a smart turn of foot to score with something in hand. Although 15lb higher than when last successful in a handicap, there still looks more to come from her.
**Burlington Place** had something of a soft lead and could well be flattered by this effort.
**Louisiade(IRE)** had no excuses and looked a far from easy ride.
**Stanley Crane(USA)** did well to finish as close as he did, for he was in the wrong place in a slowly-run race.
**Knickyknackienoo** did himself no favours by refusing to settle.
**The Fun Merchant** was not suited by the steady pace and is better than he showed. *Official explanation: trainer had no explanation for the poor form shown other than that gelding may have suffered from being drawn on the outer*
**Half A Handful** *Official explanation: jockey said colt had a breathing problem*

## 4243 EBF HIGH SHERIFFS' MEDIAN AUCTION MAIDEN FILLIES' STKS 5f 218y
**8:20** (8:28) (E) 2-Y-0 **£4,212** (£1,296; £648; £324) **Stalls** Low

Form RPR
002 **1** **Good Wee Girl (IRE)**[15] 3823 2-8-11 .................................... JFEgan 12 71
(SKirk) *chsd ldrs: rdn to ld 1f out: r.o* **12/1**
64 **2** *1* **Cerebus**[5] 4099 2-8-11 .................................... IMongan 13 68
(NPLittmoden) *chsd ldrs: rdn over 1f out: styd on* **10/1**
5 **3** *1/2* **Subyan Dreams**[19] 3693 2-8-11 .................................... AMcCarthy 1 66
(PWChapple-Hyam) *chsd ldrs: rdn 1/2-way: r.o* **7/4**[1]
**4** *2 1/2* **Heartsonfire (IRE)**[77] 2048 2-8-11 .................................... MFenton 11 58
(PWD'Arcy) *led 5f: hung rt and wknd ins fnl f* **20/1**
3 **5** *shd* **Sambarina (IRE)**[26] 3476 2-8-11 .................................... RSmith 15 58
(CGCox) *s.i.s: sn prom: rdn over 2f out: styd on same pce fnl f* **3/1**[2]
0 **6** *2 1/2* **Lady Hen**[20] 3675 2-8-11 .................................... KDarley 8 50
(MJWallace) *mid-div: rdn over 2f out: nvr trbld ldrs* **9/2**[3]
**7** *hd* **Lake Wakatipu** 2-8-11 .................................... SRighton 4 50
(MMullineaux) *s.s: outpcd: styd on ins fnl f: nvr nrr* **80/1**
4354 **8** *1 1/2* **Ruby's Dream**[11] 3950 2-8-11 .................................... DeanMcKeown 14 45
(JMBradley) *chsd ldrs to 1/2-way* **12/1**
**9** *4* **Succession** 2-8-11 .................................... JMackay 5 33
(SirMarkPrescott) *s.i.s: outpcd* **25/1**
0 **10** *11* **Floosie (IRE)**[6] 4058 2-8-8 .................................... (t) J-PGuillambert[(3)] 2 —
(NPLittmoden) *chsd ldrs over 3f* **33/1**
**11** *2* **Frida** 2-8-11 .................................... SWhitworth 6 —
(PDCundell) *s.s: hld up: plld hrd: wknd over 2f out* **40/1**
0 **12** *5* **Katie Killane**[25] 3531 2-8-11 .................................... VSlattery 9 —
(MWellings) *chsd ldrs to 1/2-way: bhd whn hung rt over 1f out* **100/1**
**13** *12* **Isle Of Light (IRE)** 2-8-11 .................................... JQuinn 3 —
(WRMuir) *hld up: plld hrd: wknd over 2f out* **66/1**
**14** *5* **Little Waltham** 2-8-11 .................................... SCarson 10 —
(KAMorgan) *s.i.s: outpcd* **100/1**

1m 12.77s (-0.63) **Going Correction** -0.30s/f (Firm) **14** Ran SP% **122.7**
Speed ratings: **92,90,90,86,86 83,82,80,75,60 58,51,35,28**CSF £121.63 TOTE £8.00: £2.60, £2.20, £1.20; EX 75.80.
**Owner** E Power & M Kavanagh **Bred** Auriga Partnership **Trained** Upper Lambourn, Berks

**FOCUS**
Although they all raced in one group those drawn high filled four of the first five places. The time was ordinary which serves to hold the form down.
**NOTEBOOK**
**Good Wee Girl(IRE)** confirmed recent Brighton promise, and this effort should ensure she does not start life off on too stiff a mark in nurseries.
**Cerebus** stuck to her task well enough and gave the impression another furlong would not come amiss.
**Subyan Dreams** took a bit of winding up and should do better when facing a stiffer task.
**Heartsonfire(IRE)**, who had shown promise in a couple of ordinary maidens in Ireland, gave the impression that trip looked beyond her, although it is possible she may have needed this after a break.
**Sambarina(IRE)** does not do anything quickly and may have appreciated a stronger pace.
**Lady Hen** should do better when stepping up in trip.
**Isle Of Light(IRE)** *Official explanation: jockey said filly had run too freely*

## 4244 CRIMEBEAT CHARITY RACENIGHT CLASSIFIED STKS — 5f 218y
**8:50** (8:52) (E) 3-Y-O+ — **£4,036** (£1,242; £621; £310) **Stalls** Low

| Form | | | | RPR |
|---|---|---|---|---|
| 3540 | **1** | | **Mistral Sky**[14] 3841 5-9-2 64 ....(v) JFEgan 4<br>(MrsStefLiddiard) *hld up: rdn 1/2-way: hdwy over 2f out: styd on u.p to ld nr fin* **7/2**[3] | 75 |
| 2341 | **2** | *shd* | **High Ridge**[12] 3923 5-9-2 69 ....(p) DeanMcKeown 1<br>(JMBradley) *chsd ldrs: led 1f out: rdn and hdd nr fin* **15/8**[1] | 75 |
| 500 | **3** | *3* | **Prince Of Blues (IRE)**[19] 3705 6-9-2 59 ....(b) SRighton 5<br>(MMullineaux) *led 5f: no ex* **40/1** | 66 |
| 2461 | **4** | *1* | **Go Yellow**[6] 4069 3-9-3 69 .... IMongan 2<br>(PDEvans) *chsd ldrs: rdn and ev ch over 1f out: wknd ins fnl f* **11/2** | 69 |
| 1103 | **5** | *1 1/4* | **Cherokee Nation**[6] 4051 3-8-11 70 .... KDarley 6<br>(PWD'Arcy) *s.i.s: hld up: plld hrd: hdwy over 2f out: rdn and wknd over 1f out* **11/4**[2] | 59 |
| 1065 | **6** | *1/2* | **Generous Gesture (IRE)**[33] 3280 3-8-11 73 ....(v) MFenton 3<br>(MLWBell) *hld up: hdwy over 2f out: wknd over 1f out* **8/1** | 58 |
| 6030 | **7** | *4* | **Xsynna**[23] 3575 8-8-11 34 .... HayleyTurner(5) 7<br>(MissMERowland) *chsd ldrs over 3f* **100/1** | 46? |

1m 12.12s (-1.28) **Going Correction** -0.30s/f (Firm)
**WFA** 3 from 5yo+ 5lb — **7** Ran SP% **113.6**
Speed ratings: **96,95,91,90,88 88,82**CSF £10.36 TOTE £4.40: £3.40, £1.50; EX 22.80 Place 6 £54.26, Place 5 £46.77.
**Owner** Shefford Valley Stud **Bred** Peter Nelson **Trained** Great Shefford, Berks
**FOCUS**
An ordinary contest and a steady pace which resulted in a moderate winning time for the class, giving the form an unreliable appearance.
**NOTEBOOK**
**Mistral Sky**, who has been running with credit over further, did not really have the strong pace he needs at this trip, but he is game and stuck to his task well to get his head in front in the shadow of the post.
**High Ridge** came in to this in good form, and had no excuses having got first run on the winner.
**Prince Of Blues(IRE)** had a soft time of things up front and may have been slightly flattered by the result.
**Go Yellow** had plenty to find with the winner on these terms compared with their running here earlier in the month.
**Cherokee Nation**, who proved very weak in the market, took a fierce grip having missed a beat at the start and it was hardly surprising he failed to see his race out. He is better than he showed here.
**Generous Gesture(IRE)**, a dual-winner on the Fibresand, has yet to strike on turf.
T/Plt: £94.00. Pool of £33,211.65 - 257.90 winning units. T/Qpdt: £38.00. Pool of £2,228.70 - 43.40 winning units. CR

# 3576 MUSSELBURGH (R-H)
### Wednesday, July 28
**OFFICIAL GOING: Good to firm (firm in places)**

## 4245 EUROPEAN BREEDERS FUND MEDIAN AUCTION MAIDEN FILLIES' STKS — 5f
**2:30** (2:30) (E) 2-Y-O — **£4,351** (£1,339; £669; £334) **Stalls** Low

| Form | | | | RPR |
|---|---|---|---|---|
| 364 | **1** | | **Jerry's Girl (IRE)**[8] 4003 2-8-11 .... SSanders 6<br>(MissLAPerratt) *chsd ldrs: rdn along 2f out: styd on u.p ent last to ld last 75 yds* **11/4**[2] | 61 |
| 0 | **2** | *3/4* | **Ducal Diva**[34] 3248 2-8-4 .... DFentiman(7) 1<br>(JRWeymes) *cl up: n.m.r on rail after 1f: rdn to ld wl over 1f out: edgd rt ins last: hdd and no ex last 75 yds* **5/2**[1] | 58 |
| | **3** | *1 3/4* | **Folga** 2-8-11 .... DeanMcKeown 2<br>(RPElliott) *cl up: edgd lft after 1f: rdn along 2f out: ev ch tl drvn and one pce ent last* **5/1** | 52 |
| | **4** | *3/4* | **Bond Babe** 2-8-11 .... FLynch 4<br>(BSmart) *bmpd s and bhd tl styd on fnl f* **3/1**[3] | 50 |
| | **5** | *1* | **One Of Each (IRE)** 2-8-4 .... DTudhope(7) 7<br>(DCarroll) *led: rdn along 2f out: sn hdd and drvn: wknd ent last* **14/1** | 46 |
| 6 | **6** | *1/2* | **Quick Grand (IRE)**[8] 4003 2-8-11 .... RWinston 3<br>(MissLAPerratt) *wnt rt s: a rr* **14/1** | 44 |

61.08 secs (0.68) **Going Correction** -0.075s/f (Good) — **6** Ran SP% **110.2**
Speed ratings: **91,89,87,85,84 83**CSF £9.66 TOTE £2.90: £2.00, £1.50; EX 10.10.
**Owner** Jerry Ryan **Bred** Joe O'Leary **Trained** Ayr, Strathclyde
**FOCUS**
A weak event, not much better than a seller.
**NOTEBOOK**
**Jerry's Girl(IRE)** broke her duck at the fourth attempt in this weak affair. She only got on top in the last half furlong and won despite, not because of, the drop in trip.
**Ducal Diva**, a well-backed favourite, had the rail to race against. Having got to the front, she appeared to hang away from the fence a little and was cut down towards the finish.
**Folga** is a half-sister to six winners out of a mare who was a decent sprinter. She showed pace on this debut and is entitled to improve. *Official explanation: jockey said filly ran very green*
**Bond Babe ◆** is a half-sister to four winners, including smart sprinter Baltic King. Receiving a bump leaving the stalls and outpaced at the back of the field, she was still last passing the furlong pole but then found her feet and came home in good style. A much more prominent showing can be expected next time. *Official explanation: jockey said filly suffered interference at the start*
**One Of Each(IRE)**, out of a six-furlong winner, showed good early pace and ought to be capable of lasting longer next time.
**Quick Grand(IRE)** was always at the back of the field, but she did finish closer to stablemate Jerry's Girl than she had at Ayr.

## 4246 LINKS H'CAP — 1m
**3:00** (3:00) (F) (0-55,55) 3-Y-O+ — **£2,996** (£856; £428) **Stalls** Low

| Form | | | | RPR |
|---|---|---|---|---|
| 1620 | **1** | | **Son Of Thunder (IRE)**[20] 3684 3-9-2 55 .... LEnstone(3) 4<br>(MDods) *stdd s and bhd: swtchd outside and hdwy over 2f out: rdn to ld jst ins last: styd on* **9/1**[3] | 70 |
| 00-0 | **2** | *2* | **Loner**[24] 3559 6-9-5 50 ....(p) THamilton(3) 9<br>(RAFahey) *dwlt and reminders s: bhd:swtchd outside and gd hdwy over 2f out: led over 1f out: sn rdn: edgd lft and hdd ins last* **6/1**[2] | 60 |
| 0600 | **3** | *2 1/2* | **Penwell Hill (USA)**[12] 3921 5-9-4 51 .... PMakin(5) 12<br>(TDBarron) *chsd ldrs: rdn along over 2f out: styd on un der press fnl f* **10/1** | 55 |
| 0450 | **4** | *1* | **Otago (IRE)**[21] 3626 3-9-0 55 .... BSwarbrick(5) 5<br>(JRBest) *bhd: hdwy over 2f out: sn rdn and kpt on fnl f: nrst fin* **14/1** | 57 |
| -002 | **5** | *1/2* | **Islands Farewell**[12] 3899 4-9-11 53 .... AlexGreaves 3<br>(DNicholls) *prom: rdn along over 2f out: drvnand wknd appr last* **12/1** | 54 |
| 0060 | **6** | *3/4* | **Mon Secret (IRE)**[49] 2776 6-9-9 51 .... FLynch 10<br>(BSmart) *hld up and behund: hdwy on inner and nt clr run wl over 2f out: swtchd lft over 1f out: kpt on ins last: nt rch ldrs* **16/1** | 50 |
| 0000 | **7** | *hd* | **Hoh's Back**[18] 3734 5-9-5 54 ....(p) NataliaGemelova(7) 8<br>(PaulJohnson) *a midfield: rdn along 3f out: sn no imp* **25/1** | 53 |
| 0033 | **8** | *1/2* | **Shamwari Fire (IRE)**[12] 3921 4-9-7 49 .... DAllan 14<br>(IWMcinnes) *chsd ldrs: rdn over 2f out: drvn and wandered wl over 1f out: sn wknd* **6/1**[2] | 46 |
| -040 | **9** | *2 1/2* | **Expected Bonus (USA)**[22] 3604 5-9-5 47 ....(b) DaleGibson 7<br>(SCWilliams) *led: rdn along 3f out: hdd and drvn 2f out: sn btn* **5/1**[1] | 39 |
| 4010 | **10** | *nk* | **Time To Regret**[9] 3982 4-9-6 53 .... PMulrennan(5) 6<br>(JSWainwright) *chsd ldrs: rdn along over 2f out: grad wknd* **10/1** | 44 |
| 4-60 | **11** | *3/4* | **Scramble (USA)**[65] 2368 6-9-8 50 ....(tp) GParkin 13<br>(BEllison) *a rr* **12/1** | 39 |
| -020 | **12** | *1/2* | **Canlis**[26] 3471 5-9-5 47 .... RWinston 2<br>(DWThompson) *cl up: rdn to ld briefly 2f out: sn hdd & wknd* **16/1** | 35 |
| 4400 | **13** | *7* | **Shifty**[23] 3586 5-8-12 47 .... DFentiman(7) 11<br>(DNicholls) *in tch on inner: rdn along 3f out: sn wknd* **6/1**[2] | 19 |

1m 39.97s (-2.73) **Going Correction** -0.15s/f (Firm)
**WFA** 3 from 4yo+ 8lb — **13** Ran SP% **125.4**
Speed ratings: **107,105,102,101,101 100,100,99,97,96 96,95,88**CSF £65.35 CT £588.15 TOTE £10.50: £5.30, £2.00, £3.20; EX 55.90.
**Owner** Russ Mould **Bred** Sentinel Bloodstock And B Stewart **Trained** Piercebridge, Co Durham
**FOCUS**
An ordinary handicap but a decent time and fair form for the grade. The first two both came from off the pace.
**NOTEBOOK**
**Son Of Thunder(IRE)**, suited by the faster ground, overcame a low draw to score back at his favourite track. He is improving. *Official explanation: trainer had no explanation for the improved form shown*
**Loner**, with the cheekpieces back on, ran a much better race on this second outing for the Fahey yard but he has never had much stomach for a fight. He is fairly treated at present.
**Penwell Hill(USA)**, who has been easing in the weights, ran a better race, albeit from a decent draw.
**Otago(IRE)**, tackling a mile for the first time, was keeping on well at the line. He was the least experienced member of the field and probably has improvement in him.
**Islands Farewell** was put up 8lb for chasing home a 1/9 shot at Hamilton and that was sufficient to anchor him, although he was not disgraced.
**Mon Secret(IRE)**, who is best over seven furlongs, kept on after encountering a troubled passage. *Official explanation: jockey said gelding never got a run*
**Expected Bonus(USA)**, back in the blinkers, made the running as usual but did not offer much resistance when headed. He is well handicapped but not running well enough at present to take advantage.
**Time To Regret** *Official explanation: jockey said gelding was never travelling*
**Canlis** *Official explanation: jockey said gelding hung left*

## 4247 STEWARTS TURF (S) STKS — 5f
**3:35** (3:35) (E) 3-Y-O+ — **£3,464** (£1,066; £533; £266) **Stalls** Low

| Form | | | | RPR |
|---|---|---|---|---|
| 0660 | **1** | | **Bettys Pride**[12] 3894 5-8-9 49 .... RWinston 1<br>(MDods) *hld up in rr: swtchd rt and hdwy wl over 1f out: str run to ld ins last: styd on* **5/1**[3] | 53 |
| 4000 | **2** | *1/2* | **Joyce's Choice**[13] 3864 5-8-9 45 ....(p) MLawson(5) 3<br>(JSWainwright) *chsd ldrs: swtchd lft and hdwy over 1f out: sn rdn and kpt on* **25/1** | 56 |
| 2152 | **3** | *2* | **Soaked**[5] 4105 11-9-5 63 ....(b) SSanders 8<br>(DWChapman) *cl up on outer: effrt to chal 2f out: rdn to ld briefly 1f out: sn hdd and one pce* **1/1**[1] | 53 |
| 0000 | **4** | *nk* | **Danakim**[5] 4105 7-8-12 40 .... DFentiman(7) 4<br>(JRWeymes) *cl up: rdn 2f out: drvn whn n ot much room over 1f out: kpt on ins last* **33/1** | 52 |
| 1016 | **5** | *1* | **Wendy's Girl (IRE)**[14] 3838 3-8-7 63 ....(b) THamilton(3) 6<br>(RPElliott) *cl up: rdn along 2f out: drvna nd wknd ent last* **10/3**[2] | 43 |
| 5006 | **6** | *shd* | **American Cousin**[5] 4105 9-9-5 55 .... AlexGreaves 2<br>(DNicholls) *towards rr: pushed along and hdwy 2f out: swtchd rt and rdn over 1f out: sn one pce* **13/2** | 47 |
| 400- | **7** | *1* | **Alfie Lee (IRE)**[266] 5924 7-9-0 43 ....(tp) JMcAuley 7<br>(DANolan) *led: rdn along 2f out: hdd & wknd over 1f out* **50/1** | 38 |
| 000- | **8** | *15* | **Louis Prima**[289] 5535 3-8-10 38 ....(b) DMcGaffin 5<br>(MissLAPerratt) *remindesr after s: in tch tlr idden along 1/2-way and sn wknd* **100/1** | — |

59.21 secs (-1.19) **Going Correction** -0.075s/f (Good)
**WFA** 3 from 5yo+ 4lb — **8** Ran SP% **112.8**
Speed ratings: **106,105,102,101,99 99,98,74**CSF £103.35 TOTE £6.20: £1.40, £3.80, £1.10; EX 51.40.There was no bid for the winner.
**Owner** Betty's Brigade **Bred** Raffin Stud And Raimon Bloodstock **Trained** Piercebridge, Co Durham
■ Stewards Enquiry : M Lawson two-day ban: careless riding (Aug 8-9)
**FOCUS**
A fair time for a seller, albeit quite a valuable one. The form looks a little suspect.
**NOTEBOOK**
**Bettys Pride**, minus the cheekpieces, came from last to first. From a yard enjoying a good spell, she is well handicapped at present and there could be more to come now that she has recaptured some form.
**Joyce's Choice** , with cheekpieces replacing blinkers, had plenty on at the weights, and this was a surprise return to form after a long time in the doldrums.
**Soaked**, dropped into selling comapny, was unable to have things his own way in front from his wide draw. This was a long way below the form he has shown in his last couple of runs.
**Danakim** had a lot on his plate based on official ratings and ran respectably.
**Wendy's Girl(IRE)** seems best when allowed to dominate over six furlongs.

**4248** **GERRARD WEALTH MANAGEMENT FILLIES' H'CAP** **7f 30y**
4:10 (4:10) (D ) (0-80,79) 3-Y-O+ £6,708 (£2,064; £1,032; £516) Stalls Low

Form RPR
2066 1 **Go Between**[7] 4020 3-10-0 **79**............ SSanders 4 92
(EALDunlop) *dwlt: sn in tch: hdwy 2f out: swtchd outside and rdn to ld 1f out: styd on* **5/2**[1]
5000 2 1 3/4 **Bint Royal (IRE)**[4] 4122 6-8-4 **53**............ PMakin(5) 5 61
(MissVHaigh) *cl: led 1/2-way: rdn and hdd wl over 1f out: kpt on ins last* **11/2**[3]
0000 3 shd **Cut Ridge (IRE)**[22] 3609 5-7-5 **42** oh4............ DFentiman(7) 3 50
(JSWainwright) *trckd ldrs: hdwy over 2f out: rdn to ld wl over 1f out: drvn and hdd ent last: one pce* **12/1**
6402 4 3 **Zahunda (IRE)**[8] 4004 5-7-7 **42** oh5............ BSwarbrick(5) 1 42
(WMBrisbourne) *led to 1/2-way: cl up tl rdn along and wknd fnl 2f* **5/1**[2]
0544 5 nk **Graceful Air (IRE)**[13] 3878 3-8-6 **57**............ GHind 6 56
(JRWeymes) *rdn along in rr 1/2-way: sme late hdwy* **9/1**
5666 6 nk **College Maid (IRE)**[5] 4104 7-8-10 **61**............ JCurrie(7) 8 59
(JSGoldie) *chsd ldrs: rdn along 3f out: sn wknd* **11/2**[3]
-003 7 1 3/4 **Tokewanna**[19] 3701 4-8-8 **52**............ RWinston 2 46
(WMBrisbourne) *plld hrd: chsd ldrs on outer tl rdn: edgd rt and wknd over 2f out* **9/1**
0050 8 3 **Alice Blackthorn**[21] 3623 3-8-8 **59**............ DMcGaffin 7 45
(BSmart) *s.i.s: a rr* **16/1**

1m 28.46s (-1.07) **Going Correction** -0.15s/f (Firm)
**WFA** 3 from 4yo+ 7lb **8** Ran SP% **109.6**
Speed ratings: **100,98,97,94,94 93,91,88**CSF £14.75 CT £122.59 TOTE £2.10: £1.70, £1.60, £2.40; EX 24.10.
**Owner** Ahmed Buhaleeba **Bred** John Ellis **Trained** Newmarket, Suffolk

**FOCUS**
Not a strong handicap, in which the early pace was only modest and the form looks relatively weak.

**NOTEBOOK**
**Go Between** was slowly away again, but it did not make much difference as she came from off the speed to win going away. She will find things tougher from a revised mark in the 80s.
**Bint Royal(IRE)**, who wins infrequently, ran well enough to prove that the cheekpieces are not essential, although she is still below her best at present.
**Cut Ridge(IRE)** ran well from out of the handicap and this could prove her optimum trip.
**Zahunda(IRE)**, who was 5lb out of the handicap, again made the running but was comfortably seen off. She has a poor strike rate.
**Tokewanna**, without the tongue tie which seemed to bring about improvement at Chester, was too keen for her own good in the early stages.

**4249** **EDINBURGH EVENING NEWS H'CAP** **1m 1f**
4:45 (4:45) (E ) (0-75,75) 3-Y-O £5,424 (£1,669; £834; £417) Stalls Low

Form RPR
1111 1 **Masafi (IRE)**[5] 4096 3-9-13 **75** 6ex............ SSanders 1 97+
(SirMarkPrescott) *mde all: qcknd clr wl over 1f out: easily* **4/9**[1]
0063 2 7 **Joey Perhaps**[9] 3981 3-7-9 **48**............ BSwarbrick(5) 3 54
(JRBest) *hld up in tch: hdwy to chse wnr 2f out: sn rdn and kpt on: no ch w wnr* **9/2**[2]
4134 3 2 **Charlie Tango (IRE)**[16] 3796 3-9-1 **68**............ PMulrennan(5) 5 70
(NTinkler) *trckd ldrs: effrt over 2f out: sn rdn and kpt on same pce* **11/1**[3]
0420 4 nk **Munaawesh (USA)**[9] 3981 3-8-1 **56**............(b) DFentiman(7) 6 57
(DWChapman) *cl up: effrt to chse wnr over 3f out: sn rdn along and btn* **20/1**
1040 5 5 **Mission Affirmed (USA)**[17] 3780 3-9-1 **63**............ DaleGibson 4 54
(TPTate) *chsd wnr: rdn along over 3f out and sn wknd* **25/1**
0330 6 24 **Four Kings**[33] 3271 3-9-1 **63**............(t) RWinston 2 6
(RAllan) *outpcd and bhd fr 1/2-way* **33/1**

1m 51.95s (-1.25) **Going Correction** -0.15s/f (Firm) **6** Ran SP% **107.3**
Speed ratings: **99,92,91,90,86 64**CSF £2.26 TOTE £1.40: £1.10, £1.60; EX 2.60.
**Owner** G D Waters **Bred** G D Waters **Trained** Newmarket, Suffolk

**FOCUS**
An uncompetitive affair but Masafi continues to improve and gained his sixth handicap win in the space of 17 days, still looking to have a fair amount in hand.

**NOTEBOOK**
**Masafi(IRE)** had no problem completing the six-timer, despite being 16lb higher than for his latest win. He won pretty easily and could still be a step ahead of the Handicapper, by as much as a stone on this evidence.
**Joey Perhaps** ran another decent race but had a thankless task against the fast-improving winner. He is finding his way but is set to go up 7lb in future handicaps.
**Charlie Tango(IRE)**, formerly with Mick Channon, did not shape as if the drop in trip was what he needed.
**Munaawesh(USA)**ran his race but remains a frustrating maiden.
**Mission Affirmed(USA)**, a better horse on Fibresand, was having his first race on fast ground.
**Four Kings** was previously with James Eustace. *Official explanation: jockey said colt had a breathing problem*

**4250** **RECTANGLE GROUP APPRENTICE H'CAP** **1m 5f**
5:20 (5:20) (F ) (0-55,53) 4-Y-O+ £2,968 (£848; £424) Stalls High

Form RPR
2303 1 **Cosmic Case**[8] 4007 9-8-6 **44**............ PMulrennan(3) 5 53
(JSGoldie) *trckd ldrs: pushed long over 3f out: rdn to ld wl over 1f out: kpt on* **7/4**[1]
/145 2 3/4 **Sovereign State (IRE)**[7] 4015 7-8-12 **47**............(p) LEnstone 2 55
(DWThompson) *hld up in rr: hdwy 3f out: rdn along 2f out: styd on to chse wnr ins last: no imp towards fin* **4/1**[3]
2225 3 5 **Ellway Heights**[18] 3740 7-9-1 **53**............ BSwarbrick(3) 1 54
(WMBrisbourne) *hld up: hdwy 3f out: rdn 2f out: edgd rt and one pce over 1f out* **11/4**[2]
0456 4 2 1/2 **Smarter Charter**[20] 3658 11-7-11 **37**............ KristinStubbs(5) 3 34
(MrsLStubbs) *t.k.h: hld up tl rapid hdwy to ld 1/2-way: rdn along 3f out: hdd 2f out and sn wknd* **12/1**
6400 5 1 1/2 **Hibernate (IRE)**[7] 4015 10-8-2 **37**............ THamilton 7 32
(CJTeague) *set stdy pce tl hdd 1/2-way: rdn along over 3f out: sn wknd* **20/1**
0000 6 1 **Daimajin (IRE)**[6] 4070 5-8-7 **47**............(p) DTudhope(5) 6 41
(MrsLucindaFeatherstone) *prom: rdn along 3f out: wknd 2f out* **20/1**
0320 7 5 **Ipledgeallegiance (USA)**[8] 4007 8-7-7 **33** oh3............(b) DFentiman(5) 4 20
(DWChapman) *reminders in rr after s: bhd tl rapid hdwy to chse ldrs 1/2-way: rn wd home bnd: sn b ehind* **7/1**

2m 51.1s course record **7** Ran SP% **112.7**
Speed ratings: CSF £8.80 TOTE £2.50: £1.10, £3.70; EX 11.70 Place 6 £16.42, Place 5 £10.65.
**Owner** The Cosmic Cases **Bred** V H Rowe **Trained** Uplawmoor, E Renfrews

**FOCUS**
No speed figures have been produced for this contest as not enough races have been run over the trip from which to calculate a reliable median time. The field went no pace until picking things up at around halfway. This is modest form.

**NOTEBOOK**
**Cosmic Case**, tackling a more suitable trip, regained winning ways despite the lack of the true gallop she is happiest with. Her rider's claim in open races will be cut to 3lb after this win.
**Sovereign State(IRE)** stayed on under pressure in the last couple of furlongs without getting to the winner. He is not well treated at present.
**Ellway Heights** was held up as usual and the lack of pace in the first half of the contest did not help his cause. *Official explanation: jockey said gelding bled from the nose*
**Smarter Charter** rushed up to lead at halfway, but was put in his place with two to run and extended his losing sequence to 26.
T/Plt: £18.20 to a £1 stake. Pool: £25,216.50. 1,010.25 winning tickets. T/Qpdt: £4.10 to a £1 stake. Pool: £1,605.50. 287.55 winning tickets. JR

4221 **GALWAY** (R-H)
Wednesday, July 28

**OFFICIAL GOING: Good to firm (firm in places)**

**4251a** **HP SOFTWARE PUBLISHING SERVICES H'CAP** **7f**
3:00 (3:00) (40-70,67) 3-Y-O £6,569 (£1,530; £675; £389)

RPR
1 **General Feeling (IRE)**[37] 3158 3-9-5 65............ PBBeggy(7) 12 79
(SKirk) *towards rr: last 3f out: swtchd to outer 2 1/2f out: hdwy ent st: 9th 1f out: r.o strly to ld 100yds out: sn clr* **10/1**
2 3 1/2 **Premier Prospect (USA)**[11] 3960 3-8-10 56............(p) RPCleary(7) 17 61
(WPBrowne, Ire) *led and disp: slt advantage fr 1/2-way: strly pressed fr over 2f out: kpt on wl: hdd 100yds out* **7/1**[2]
3 shd **Nok Twice (IRE)**[18] 3764 3-9-9 62............(p) DPMcDonogh 2 67
(JCHayden, Ire) *mid-div on outer: impr into 6th after 1/2-way: 3rd and chal early st: kpt on same pce* **14/1**
4 1 **String Serenade (IRE)**[40] 3066 3-9-8 61............ PCosgrave 3 63
(JCHarley, Ire) *chsd ldrs: 5th after 1/2-way: 4th and chal ent st: no imp fnl f* **10/1**
5 shd **Silver Harbour (USA)**[14] 3855 3-8-9 51............ DJCondon(3) 8 53
(JGBurns, Ire) *hld up: prog on outer appr st: 6th over 1f out: kpt on* **16/1**
6 1 **Duchess Of Ross (IRE)**[15] 3829 3-9-11 64............(b[1]) PJSmullen 5 63
(DKWeld, Ire) *mid-div: hdwy 2 1/2f out: 4th and swtchd to inner 2f out: rdn to chal ent st: no ex fnl f* **9/1**[3]
7 1 **Sean Nos (IRE)**[14] 3860 3-9-3 63............ JEMoriarty(7) 1 60
(ThomasCooper, Ire) *slowly away and bhd: styd on wl fr 2f out* **12/1**
8 nk **Endless Peace (IRE)**[51] 2746 3-8-13 55............(t) MCHussey(3) 11 51
(MGHolden, Ire) *mid-div thrght: kpt on one pced st* **14/1**
9 2 1/2 **Homegrown (IRE)**[87] 1808 3-10-0 67............ JAHeffernan 10 56
(PatrickTallis, Ire) *sn cl up on outer: 3rd and chal 2f out: no ex st* **14/1**
10 nk **Meadow**[22] 3617 3-9-7 60............ WMLordan 15 49
(PFCashman, Ire) *cl up: 2nd and chal fr 3f out: wknd ent st* **12/1**
11 nk **Spanish Cove (IRE)**[19] 3721 3-8-10 52............ CatherineGannon(3) 14 40
(TJO'Mara, Ire) *prom early: no imp fr over 2f out* **20/1**
12 1/2 **Jinx Johnson (IRE)**[14] 3855 3-9-4 57............ RMBurke 7 44
(MPSunderland, Ire) *towards rr: kpt on one pced fr 2f out* **12/1**
13 nk **Karramalu (IRE)**[6] 4072 3-10-0 67............ TPO'Shea 6 53
(DanielMarkLoughnane, Ire) *nvr a factor* **13/2**[1]
14 nk **Our Kid**[61] 2452 3-9-7 60............ NGMcCullagh 4 45
(TGMccourt, Ire) *s.i.s and nvr a factor* **33/1**
15 1/2 **Taylors Tree Rock (IRE)**[63] 2417 3-8-7 53............ MACleere(7) 9 37
(TGMccourt, Ire) *nvr a factor* **33/1**
16 3 **Charlottine (IRE)**[26] 3500 3-9-3 56............(b[1]) KJManning 16 32
(MPSunderland, Ire) *mid-div: wknd over 2f out* **10/1**
17 6 **Miss Chapman (IRE)**[18] 3764 3-8-7 53............ DGHogan(7) 18 13
(JarlathPFahey, Ire) *chsd ldrs on inner: 5th 1/2-way: wknd 2 1/2f out* **33/1**
18 3 **Ostopet (IRE)**[5] 4113 3-9-2 55............ FMBerry 13 7
(JEMulhern, Ire) *cl up and disp ld: hdd 1/2-way: wknd under 3f out: eased fnl f* **20/1**

1m 28.6s **18** Ran SP% **130.4**
Speed ratings: CSF £77.54 CT £1032.31 TOTE £13.80: £3.00, £1.70, £5.10, £2.00; DF 180.00.
**Owner** The So Long Partnership **Bred** John Graham And Leslie Laverty **Trained** Upper Lambourn, Berks

**NOTEBOOK**
**General Feeling(IRE)** absolutely trotted up here, quickening right away inside the last.

4252 - 4255a (Foreign Racing) - See Raceform Interactive

3892 **CARLISLE** (R-H)
Thursday, July 29

**OFFICIAL GOING: Home straight - firm (good to firm in places); remainder - good to firm (firm in places)**

**4256** **VIACOM MAIDEN AUCTION STKS** **5f 193y**
2:15 (2:15) (E ) 2-Y-O £3,835 (£1,180; £590; £295) Stalls High

Form RPR
0 1 **Toby's Dream (IRE)**[35] 3228 2-8-11............ SChin 4 77
(MJohnston) *mde all: drvn out* **33/1**
53 2 3/4 **Merchant (IRE)**[7] 4048 2-8-9............ JMackay 13 73
(MLWBell) *dwlt: keen and sn chsng ldrs: rdn over 2f out: r.o fnl f* **13/8**[1]
04 3 nk **Naval Force**[8] 4022 2-8-11............(t) SSanders 5 74
(HMorrison) *midfield: rdn 1/2-way: swtchd lft and hdwy over 1f out: r.o fnl f* **9/2**[2]
4 1 **Rainbow Rising (IRE)** 2-9-0............ RWinston 3 74
(JHowardJohnson) *keen: chsd ldrs: effrt 2f out: one pce fnl f* **9/2**[2]
5 5 nk **Crocodile Kiss (IRE)**[15] 3840 2-8-6............ SWKelly 1 65
(JAOsborne) *chsd ldrs: rdn over 2f out: one pce fnl f* **9/2**[2]
005 6 1 1/4 **Davy Crockett**[13] 3918 2-8-7............ ACulhane 2 62
(MrsJRRamsden) *hld up: shkn up over 2f out: kpt on fnl f: nrst fin* **10/1**[3]
7 shd **Nasseem Dubai (USA)** 2-9-0............ GHind 6 69
(MrsADuffield) *s.i.s: effrt over 1f out: nrst fin* **33/1**
40 8 1 1/2 **Favouring (IRE)**[82] 1960 2-8-7............ PHanagan 9 57
(RAFahey) *bhd: shkn up over 2f out: sme late hdwy: n.d* **25/1**
9 3/4 **Hannah's Tribe (IRE)** 2-8-2............ AMcCarthy 8 50
(BSmart) *bhd: pushed along 1/2-way: n.d* **25/1**

3 **10** *1 ¼* **Lovelorn**[49] 2812 2-8-7 TLucas 10 51
(MWEasterby) *plld hrd: disp ld over 3f out: wknd over 1f out* **20/1**

0 **11** *10* **So Independent**[8] 4009 2-8-2 ow3 THamilton(3) 7 19
(CRWilson) *prom to over 3f out: sn wknd* **100/1**

0004 **12** *12* **Toldo (IRE)**[19] 3736 2-8-7 (b) JCarroll 11 —
(ABerry) *missed break: nvr on terms* **100/1**

1m 13.91s (-0.29) **Going Correction** -0.15s/f (Firm) **12** Ran SP% **122.0**
Speed ratings: **95,94,93,92,91 90,90,88,87,85 72,56**CSF £86.23 TOTE £33.10: £5.70, £1.50, £1.60; EX 121.90.

**Owner** Lawrence Wosskow **Bred** Rathasker Stud **Trained** Middleham Moor, N Yorks

**FOCUS**
Although there were a couple of interesting performances, the fact that only six lengths covered the first ten home suggests that this form is nothing special. The pace was fair and the form should stand up at a similar level.

**NOTEBOOK**
**Toby's Dream(IRE)**, well beaten after a slow start on his debut, jumped out much quicker this time and posted a much-improved effort. He has plenty of physical scope and looks a likely candidate for nurseries. He should stay seven furlongs.
**Merchant(IRE)** ran creditably on this first start on fast ground, and again left the impression that the return to seven furlongs will suit. He looks capable of winning a small event.
**Naval Force**, again in the tongue-tie, ran creditably and looks a fair guide as to the level of this form. He shaped as though the return to seven furlongs would suit and he looks sure to win an ordinary event in due course.
**Rainbow Rising(IRE)** ◆ is not a bad sort on looks and shaped well on this racecourse debut. The step up to seven furlongs will suit, both on the evidence of this run and on his pedigree, and he looks sure to win a race for a stable that has plenty of talent in the juvenile department.
**Crocodile Kiss(IRE)**, who showed ability on her debut, was relatively easy to back but again showed promise. The step up to seven furlongs is going to be in her favour and she is also the type that may fare better in nurseries.
**Davy Crockett** caught the eye from his low draw and again shaped as though the step up to seven furlongs would be in his favour. All his best efforts have been on a sound surface and he may be capable of winning an ordinary race.
**Lovelorn**, who shaped well at Southwell on his debut, had been off the course since but will have to settle better if he is to progress.

## 4257 TOTE NEIL WYATT GROUNDSTAFF AWARD CLAIMING STKS 5f 193y
**2:50** (2:51) (F) 3-Y-O+ **£3,220** (£920; £460) **Stalls** High

Form RPR

-000 **1** **Fizzy Lizzy**[12] 3954 4-7-10 32 LeanneKershaw(7) 7 43
(JeddO'Keeffe) *bhd: hdwy on outside to ld 2f out: hld on wl* **11/1**

0600 **2** *1* **Vijay (IRE)**[8] 4014 5-8-9 49 RWinston 9 46
(ISemple) *towards rr: hdwy over 1f out: kpt on fnl f* **9/2**[3]

0000 **3** *hd* **Angel Isa (IRE)**[9] 4004 4-8-10 44 PHanagan 5 46
(RAFahey) *trckd ldrs: effrt and ev ch ent fnl f: one pce* **5/1**

4006 **4** *nk* **Mr Bountiful (IRE)**[8] 4013 6-9-7 50 (tp) SWKelly 3 57
(MDods) *hld up: effrt over 2f out: chsd ldrs over 1f out: no ex ins last* **7/2**[2]

0004 **5** *4* **Pilgrim Princess (IRE)**[71] 2227 6-8-8 40 DAllan 10 32
(EJAlston) *cl up tl outpcd over 1f out* **10/3**[1]

0-00 **6** *¾* **Cayman Mischief**[34] 3269 4-8-10 25 JBramhill 8 31
(JamesMoffatt) *bhd tl sme late hdwy: nvr on terms* **66/1**

0 **7** *hd* **Wild Tide**[24] 3587 5-8-2 ow2 THamilton(3) 12 26
(DWThompson) *bhd: pushed along 1/2-way: sme late hdwy* **50/1**

00-0 **8** *1 ¼* **Bishops Bounce**[42] 3002 3-8-6 55 DaleGibson 11 28
(TAKCuthbert) *in tch tl wknd fr over 2f out* **7/1**

0-00 **9** *5* **Always Daring**[17] 3800 5-7-11 31 (p) NataliaGemelova(7) 1 6
(CJTeague) *led to 2f out: sn rdn and btn* **50/1**

000/ **10** *2 ½* **Jumbo's Flyer**[508] 3107 7-8-6 PMulrennan(5) 6 5
(FPMurtagh) *cl up tl wknd 1/2-way* **50/1**

1m 13.33s (-0.87) **Going Correction** -0.15s/f (Firm)
**WFA** 3 from 4yo+ 5lb **10** Ran SP% **108.4**
Speed ratings: **99,97,97,97,91 90,90,88,82,78**CSF £53.62 TOTE £16.40: £2.90, £1.50, £1.70; EX 92.40.Fizzy Lizzy was claimed by Gerald Ham for £2,500.

**Owner** Only For Fun Partnership **Bred** J Johnson **Trained** Middleham Moor, N Yorks

■ Stewards Enquiry : Natalia Gemelova one-day ban: careless riding (Aug 9)

**FOCUS**
A sound pace but a race concerning unreliable types and this does not look a reliable form guide.

**NOTEBOOK**
**Fizzy Lizzy**, a poor and inconsistent performer, turned in an improved effort to beat some unreliable rivals and get off the mark at the 17th attempt. She may be a bit better than the bare form but her record suggests she is not an obvious one to follow up.
**Vijay(IRE)** was not beaten far but was still below his best and remains one to tread carefully with.
**Angel Isa(IRE)** ran her best race for some time but is another who is less than reliable and, although the return to seven furlongs may help, she is not one to place too much faith in.
**Mr Bountiful(IRE)** had a bit to find strictly at the weights but even so was disappointing in this company. Seven furlongs suits him better but he does need things to fall just right.
**Pilgrim Princess(IRE)** had the run of the race from her favourable draw but showed exactly why she has not won for such a long time. She is one to tread carefully with.
**Cayman Mischief** showed her first worthwhile form in the face of a stiff task but, although she left the impression that a stiffer test would suit, she will have to show more before she is a betting proposition. *Official explanation: jockey said filly lost a hind shoe*

## 4258 ST. JAMES SECURITY CLASSIFIED STKS 1m 1f 61y
**3:25** (3:25) (E) 3-Y-O+ **£3,558** (£1,095; £547; £273) **Stalls** High

Form RPR

1111 **1** **Masafi (IRE)**[1] 4249 3-9-0 69 SSanders 3 89+
(SirMarkPrescott) *keen: mde all: rdn and r.o strly fr 2f out* **4/6**[1]

1113 **2** *2 ½* **Goodbye Mr Bond**[4] 4164 4-9-4 71 DAllan 5 79
(EJAlston) *sn pushed along in rr: hdwy outside 3f out: chsd wnr ins last: no imp* **11/4**[2]

4463 **3** *½* **Millagros (IRE)**[14] 3880 4-9-2 72 (v[1]) DMcGaffin 9 76
(ISemple) *prom: effrt over 2f out: one pce ins fnl f* **25/1**

2036 **4** *½* **Fossgate**[38] 3152 3-8-8 70 (p) PHanagan 8 76
(JDBethell) *chsd wnr: rdn over 2f out: edgd rt over 1f out: sn no ex* **16/1**

0230 **5** *¾* **Just A Fluke (IRE)**[14] 3872 3-8-13 75 SChin 6 79+
(MJohnston) *hld up in tch: effrt over 2f out: edgd rt over 1f out: no imp fnl f* **9/1**[3]

2520 **6** *10* **Compton Dragon (USA)**[19] 3731 5-9-7 74 (v) AlexGreaves 1 59
(DNicholls) *s.i.s: hld up: rdn over 3f out: n.d* **25/1**

0006 **7** *5* **Gala Sunday (USA)**[25] 3563 4-9-3 70 DaleGibson 7 45
(MWEasterby) *hld up in tch: rdn over 3f out: sn btn* **50/1**

-530 **8** *1 ¼* **Gwen John (USA)**[13] 3908 3-8-7 72 (b[1]) ACulhane 2 41
(HMorrison) *chsd ldrs tl rdn and wknd fr over 2f out* **28/1**

6005 **9** *2* **Wessex (USA)**[9] 4008 4-9-5 72 RWinston 4 40
(JamesMoffatt) *in tch on outside: rdn over 3f out: wknd over 2f out* **33/1**

1m 54.15s (-3.88) **Going Correction** -0.10s/f (Good)
**WFA** 3 from 4yo+ 9lb **9** Ran SP% **115.1**
Speed ratings: **113,110,110,109,109 100,95,94,93**CSF £2.30 TOTE £1.80: £1.10, £1.10, £3.90; EX 3.00.

**Owner** G D Waters **Bred** G D Waters **Trained** Newmarket, Suffolk

■ A record seventh win in just seventeen days for Masafi, who took two days off Chaplins Club's previous record set in 1988.

**FOCUS**
Another win from the progressive and durable Masafi, who scored with a bit more in hand than the official margin suggests. The pace was sound, the time was excellent, and this form should stand up.

**NOTEBOOK**
**Masafi(IRE)** ◆, turned out after his run the previous day, came through his stiffest test to date with his recent unbeaten record intact. Given the keen hold he took early on, he may be better than the bare form and this highly progressive sort remains one to keep on the right side.
**Goodbye Mr Bond**, who ran creditably in a race that was not run to suit last time, did not travel with his usual fluency but seemed to give it his best shot and ran right up to his best against a highly progressive rival. He may be capable of further success away from progressive sorts.
**Millagros(IRE)**, had conditions to suit and ran creditably in the first-time visor, but she is likely to continue to look vulnerable to progressive sorts in this type of event or in handicaps from her current mark.
**Fossgate**, tried in cheekpieces, was not disgraced in terms of form but left the impression that he is not the most straightforward of individuals. He has yet to win and may be one to tread carefully with.
**Just A Fluke(IRE)** ran well over this course and distance in June and put a below-par run at Epsom behind him. He shaped as though a stiffer test of stamina would have been in his favour.
**Compton Dragon(USA)** faced a stiff task at the weights but ran poorly even so back over this trip. He has not won for over two years and will not be easy to place successfully in handicaps from his current mark.
**Gala Sunday(USA)** continues to disappoint.

## 4259 PHIL COOK 70TH BIRTHDAY H'CAP 7f 200y
**4:00** (4:00) (F) (0-55,55) 3-Y-O **£3,290** (£940; £470) **Stalls** High

Form RPR

6000 **1** **Joshua's Gold (IRE)**[5] 4151 3-8-7 51 DTudhope(7) 2 56
(DCarroll) *cl up: led over 2f out: hld on wl* **14/1**

00-1 **2** *nk* **Boppys Princess**[16] 3822 3-8-6 43 PHanagan 7 48
(RAFahey) *hld up midfield: rdn and effrt whn no room over 2f out: r.o wl fnl f* **6/1**[3]

3134 **3** *¾* **Roman The Park (IRE)**[24] 3581 3-8-5 42 DAllan 17 45
(TDEasterby) *trckd ldrs: effrt over 2f out: kpt on fnl f: hld cl home* **5/1**[2]

-554 **4** *hd* **Shibumi**[22] 3636 3-9-1 52 ACulhane 18 55
(HMorrison) *cl up: led over 3f to over 2f out: rallied: one pce ins fnl f* **4/1**[1]

06-6 **5** *2 ½* **Midnight Prince**[22] 3622 3-8-9 51 PMulrennan(5) 15 48
(MWEasterby) *trckd ldrs tl rdn and nt qckn over 1f out* **15/2**

0-05 **6** *½* **Grele (USA)**[20] 3701 3-8-5 47 PMakin(5) 9 43
(RHollinshead) *hld up: hdwy over 2f out: kpt on: no imp fnl f* **20/1**

0215 **7** *shd* **Delcienne**[16] 3822 3-8-9 46 AMcCarthy 3 41
(GGMargarson) *dwlt: sn in tch on outside: effrt over 2f out: sn no ex* **9/1**

0224 **8** *2 ½* **Lord Baskerville**[12] 3954 3-9-3 54 JBramhill 14 44
(WStorey) *keen: cl up tl wknd wl over 1f out* **10/1**

0000 **9** *1* **Alpha Zeta**[6] 4102 3-8-3 40 DaleGibson 13 27
(CWThornton) *hld up: effrt and swtchd lft 2f out: nvr rchd ldrs* **25/1**

U550 **10** *nk* **Dalida**[51] 2766 3-8-10 47 GFaulkner 12 34
(PCHaslam) *midfield: rdn over 2f out: sn outpcd* **25/1**

0006 **11** *½* **Ricky Martan**[45] 2931 3-8-12 49 JMackay 10 35
(GCBravery) *bhd: rdn over 3f out: n.d* **33/1**

0-05 **12** *1 ½* **Polar Galaxy**[38] 3146 3-8-8 45 SWKelly 6 27
(CWFairhurst) *in tch tl wknd fr 2f out* **50/1**

0600 **13** *nk* **Koodoo**[24] 3581 3-8-9 46 RWinston 16 27
(ACrook) *missed break: nvr on terms* **10/1**

0020 **14** *shd* **Gallas (IRE)**[6] 4092 3-8-13 53 (v) THamilton(3) 5 34
(JSWainwright) *bhd: rdn over 3f out: nvr on terms* **25/1**

0005 **15** *3 ½* **Trysting Grove (IRE)**[16] 3817 3-8-6 43 GParkin 11 16
(KARyan) *bhd: rdn 1/2-way: sn btn* **12/1**

0-60 **16** *2* **Plumpie Mac (IRE)**[16] 3817 3-8-7 44 DKinsella 4 13
(NBycroft) *led to over 3f out: wknd over 2f out* **33/1**

0000 **17** *1 ½* **Farnborough (USA)**[10] 3981 3-8-13 55 BSwarbrick(5) 1 20
(RJPrice) *a bhd* **20/1**

0000 **18** *½* **Gemini Girl (IRE)**[6] 4102 3-8-3 40 PMQuinn 8 4
(MDHammond) *a bhd* **40/1**

1m 39.51s (-0.49) **Going Correction** -0.10s/f (Good) **18** Ran SP% **136.6**
Speed ratings: **98,97,96,96,94 93,93,91,90,89 89,87,87,87,83 81,80,79**CSF £94.83 CT £518.20 TOTE £19.70: £3.30, £1.80, £1.90, £1.50; EX 432.00.

**Owner** K H Taylor Limited **Bred** M G Masterson **Trained** Warthill, N Yorks

**FOCUS**
A run-of-the-mill handicap and not strong form, but the winner did well to overcome a low draw, although the unlucky one was runner-up Boppys Princess, who remains one to keep on the right side.

**NOTEBOOK**
**Joshua's Gold(IRE)** overcame a low draw to record his best effort for a while and showed the right attitude to notch his first win. He would be no certainty to confirm placings with the runner-up should the pair meet again, but should not be going up too much for this win and may be capable of better.
**Boppys Princess** confirmed her recent improvement and looked an unlucky loser as she ran out of room when just starting to make her effort. She fared easily the best of those coming from off the pace and appeals strongly as the type to win more races in this company.
**Roman The Park(IRE)** is a reliable sort who had the rub of things from his favourable draw and he looks a good guide to the level of this form. He should continue to give a good account.
**Shibumi** looked to have plenty in her favour regarding ground, trip and draw and she ran right up to her best. She is sure to be placed to best advantage by current connections in due course.
**Midnight Prince**, who had the draw and conditions in his favour, ran to a similar level as on his reappearance over this longer trip for the first time. He may be capable of winning a similar race.
**Grele(USA)** was not disgraced on this handicap debut, given this race suited those racing prominently, and this lightly-raced sort may be capable of better granted a stiffer test of stamina.
**Lord Baskerville** pulled too hard to give himself any chance of lasting home over this trip but, although the return to sprinting will suit, his record of no wins from 17 starts is a bit of a concern.
**Koodoo** *Official explanation: trainer said gelding reared just before the stalls opened and missed the break*
**Plumpie Mac(IRE)** *Official explanation: jockey said filly ran too free and had no more to give*



The Form Book, Raceform Ltd, Compton, RG20 6NL

## 4260 MCCALLUM BUILDERS FILLIES' H'CAP 6f 192y
4:35 (4:35) (E) (0-75,75) 3-Y-O+ £3,688 (£1,135; £567; £283) Stalls High

Form RPR
0002 1 **Bint Royal (IRE)**[1] 4248 6-8-1 **53**... PPMathers(5) 9 63
(MissVHaigh) *prom: effrt 2f out: styd on to ld wl ins fnl f* **5/1**[2]
0003 2 1/2 **Cut Ridge (IRE)**[1] 4248 5-7-5 **45** oh7... DFentiman(7) 1 54
(JSWainwright) *keen: cl up: led over 3f out: hdd wl ins fnl f: kpt on* **8/1**
-330 3 hd **Mistress Twister**[22] 3622 3-8-8 **67**... PMakin(5) 6 75
(TDBarron) *towards rr: rdn 3f out: kpt on strly fnl f* **8/1**
0342 4 nk **Sharoura**[6] 4104 8-9-3 **64**... PHanagan 11 71
(RAFahey) *trckd ldrs: rdn whn hit by rivals whip over 2f out: squeezed through wl over 1f out: kpt on fnl f: hld towards fin* **7/4**[1]
0030 5 2 **Blonde En Blonde (IRE)**[21] 3680 4-8-5 **52**...(b) JBramhill 5 54
(NPLittmoden) *bhd: rdn 1/2-way: hdwy over 1f out: flashed tail ins last: r.o* **11/2**[3]
0053 6 nk **Spring Dancer**[55] 2667 3-7-12 **52** oh2...(t) AMcCarthy 8 53
(TJFitzgerald) *bhd: hdwy over 1f out: no imp ins fnl f* **16/1**
0040 7 1 **Efimac**[37] 3169 4-7-12 **45** oh7... DKinsella 2 44
(NBycroft) *bhd: rdn and effrt on outside over 3f out: nvr rchd ldrs* **16/1**
00/0 8 3 1/2 **Midnight Arrow**[19] 3734 6-7-11 **49** ow4... RThomas(5) 3 39
(ABerry) *bhd: rdn 3f out: n.d* **66/1**
0060 9 2 1/2 **Pharaoh Hatshepsut (IRE)**[9] 4004 6-7-12 **45** oh13..(b[1]) DaleGibson 12 28
(JamesMoffatt) *led to over 3f out: wknd 2f out* **66/1**
0650 10 9 **Gaiety Girl (USA)**[27] 3478 3-8-3 **57**...(b[1]) DAllan 4 17
(TDEasterby) *keen: w ldr tl wknd 2f out* **14/1**
-006 11 25 **Devine Light (IRE)**[13] 3892 4-8-6 **56**...(p) THamilton(3) 7 —
(BMactaggart) *cl up tl wknd over 3f out* **33/1**
000- 12 3 1/2 **Perfect Love**[225] 6208 4-10-0 **75**... SWKelly 10 —
(EJAlston) *midfield: hung rt fr 1/2-way: sn lost pl and eased* **11/1**

1m 26.03s (-1.07) **Going Correction** -0.10s/f (Good)
**WFA** 3 from 4yo+ 7lb **12** Ran SP% **123.3**
Speed ratings: **102,101,101,100,98 98,97,93,90,79 51,47**CSF £46.51 CT £327.37 TOTE £8.80: £2.20, £3.90, £1.70; EX 54.80.
**Owner** Miss V Haigh **Bred** Gainsborough Stud Management Ltd **Trained** Bawtry, S Yorks

**FOCUS**
An ordinary fillies' handicap in which the pace was sound, but the first two had been beaten the previous day suggesting the form is not all that strong.

**NOTEBOOK**
**Bint Royal(IRE)**, turned out quickly after her Musselburgh run, confirmed that return to form and again showed she is just as good without the cheekpieces. She is not the most reliable, but is capable of winning again this summer when in the mood.
**Cut Ridge(IRE)** ◆, worse off at the weights with Bint Royal that at Musselburgh the previous day, bettered that effort from 7lb out of the handicap and looks better than the bare result, as she took a good hold and raced three deep for much of the way. She can win races from her current mark.
**Mistress Twister**, easy to back, showed her Catterick run from a wide draw to be all wrong and showed more than enough to suggest she can win a similar event this summer. She will stay a mile on this evidence.
**Sharoura** was not beaten through lack of stamina tried over a stiff seven furlongs for the first time. She had previously run well over an easy seven, and may be better than the bare result as she was hit over the head by a rival's whip at a crucial stage. She should continue to give a good account.
**Blonde En Blonde(IRE)**, back over a more suitable trip, was not disgraced in terms of form but is not the most consistent and did not impress when flashing her tail for pressure in the closing stages. She needs things to fall just right.
**Spring Dancer**, tried in a tongue-tie for the first time, ran her best race for some time on this first start for new connections but, although a stiffer test of stamina may help, her record suggests she is one to tread carefully with.
**Perfect Love** *Official explanation: jockey said saddle slipped jumping out of the stalls*

## 4261 TOM CONNORS "LIFETIME IN RACING" APPRENTICE H'CAP 1m 6f 32y
5:10 (5:10) (F) (0-55,52) 4-Y-O+ £3,248 (£928; £464) Stalls High

Form RPR
0-60 1 **Little Tobias (IRE)**[90] 1754 5-9-4 **50**... RThomas 7 61
(AndrewTurnell) *cl up: effrt over 2f out: led ent fnl f: styd on wl* **11/1**
006 2 3/4 **Bravely Does It (USA)**[23] 3607 4-9-6 **52**... BSwarbrick 10 62
(WMBrisbourne) *set stdy pce: led to ent fnl f: kpt on* **10/1**
3563 3 3 **Vandenberghe**[6] 4080 5-8-9 **46**... RKeogh(5) 4 52
(JAOsborne) *hld up: hdwy on outside over 4f out: ch wl over 1f out: edgd rt and outpcd ins fnl f* **3/1**[2]
1000 4 1 1/2 **Fletcher**[47] 2874 10-8-1 **38**...(p) TBlock(5) 1 42
(HMorrison) *cl up tl rdn and outpcd fr wl over 1f out* **8/1**
00/5 5 1 **Mr Midaz**[12] 3929 5-8-8 **45**... AMullen(5) 5 48
(DWWhillans) *bhd: struggling over 4f out: styd on wl fnl f: n.d* **10/1**
0-62 6 3/4 **Prize Ring**[18] 3782 5-9-3 **52**... MLawson(3) 9 54
(GMMoore) *in tch: pushed along 1/2-way: effrt over 2f out: btn fnl f* **9/4**[1]
0110 7 1 3/4 **Court One**[47] 2893 6-8-13 **48** ow1... LTreadwell(3) 2 47
(RJPrice) *hld up: effrt over 2f out: wknd appr fnl f* **6/1**[3]
0400 8 8 **Sninfia (IRE)**[5] 4146 4-8-13 **50**... WHogg(5) 8 38
(GAHam) *plld hrd in tch: effrt over 3f out: wknd wl over 1f out* **11/1**
060- 9 13 **Caper**[391] 2952 4-8-6 **45**... HFellows(7) 6 15
(RHollinshead) *keen: hld up in tch: rdn over 3f out: sn btn* **25/1**
3-50 10 2 1/2 **Karyon (IRE)**[17] 3803 4-8-0 **35**... RoryMoore(3) 3 1
(MissKateMilligan) *prom tl wknd over 3f out* **20/1**

3m 6.61s (-0.69) **Going Correction** -0.10s/f (Good) **10** Ran SP% **124.6**
Speed ratings: **97,96,94,94,93 93,92,87,80,78**CSF £123.45 CT £423.07 TOTE £7.10: £2.10, £3.20, £1.30; EX 58.40 Place 6 £77.09, Place 5 £49.68.
**Owner** Mrs Claire Hollowood **Bred** Paradime Ltd **Trained** Malton, N Yorks
■ Stewards Enquiry : R Thomas three-day ban: used whip with excessive frequency and in the wrong place (Aug 9-10, Oct 12)

**FOCUS**
A low-grade handicap and the steady pace meant that those racing close to the pace had the edge over those held up. Consequently this does not look a result to take at face value.

**NOTEBOOK**
**Little Tobias(IRE)** had conditions to suit on this first start since April and, after enjoying the run of the race, showed the right attitude to win his third race from his last seven Flat starts. Consistency is not his strongest suit and he did have the rub of things, but he will be suited by the return to two miles and can win again in ordinary company.
**Bravely Does It(USA)**, upped in trip for this handicap debut, looked to have a stiff task at the weights but turned in a much-improved effort. He did have the run of the race to a large degree, but is in good hands and may be capable of better.
**Vandenberghe** looks better than the bare result, given that he was dropped out in a steadily run race and gave the outside to no-one. A more strongly-run race would have suited, but he again left the impression that he is not the most straightforward.
**Fletcher**, a poor stayer nowadays, ran his best race for some time but this race did favour those racing close to the steady pace and, given his inconsistency, would not be one to lump on next time.
**Mr Midaz**, upped markedly in trip, did well to finish as close as he did in this slowly-run race, especially as he had plenty to do half a mile out. A stronger pace over this trip would have suited, but he is not the most reliable around.
**Prize Ring** looked to have fair claims in this company on his latest Haydock run but was below that level. A more strongly-run race would have been in his favour.
T/Plt: £146.00 to a £1 stake. Pool: £25,242.40. 126.20 winning tickets. T/Qpdt: £9.10 to a £1 stake. Pool: £2,002.30. 161.20 winning tickets. RY

# 3870 EPSOM (L-H)
### Thursday, July 29

**OFFICIAL GOING: Good to firm**

## 4262 BETFRED "THE BONUS KING" APPRENTICE H'CAP 1m 2f 18y
6:05 (6:07) (E) (0-75,75) 3-Y-O+ £4,715 (£1,451; £725; £362) Stalls Low

Form RPR
1011 1 **Cristoforo (IRE)**[28] 3437 7-9-5 **66**... TPQueally 3 81+
(BJCurley) *s.i.s and hld up in rr: rdn and hdwy over 2f out: styd on to ld ins fnl f* **7/4**[1]
6111 2 1 1/4 **Burgundy**[12] 3934 7-8-12 **59**...(b) LPKeniry 7 69
(PMitchell) *slowly away: in rr tl hdwy on outside over 2f out: r.o wl to go 2nd ins fnl f* **3/1**[2]
0140 3 2 1/2 **Katiypour (IRE)**[14] 3872 7-10-0 **75**... LisaJones 8 80
(MissBSanders) *t.k.h: a.p: led over 1f out: rdn and hdd ins fnl f: no ex* **7/1**
3030 4 2 **Icannshift (IRE)**[16] 3827 4-8-6 **53**... RMiles 4 54
(SDow) *mde most tl hdd over 1f out: sn wknd* **7/2**[3]
-036 5 3 1/2 **My Galliano (IRE)**[21] 3662 8-9-0 **66**... AHindley(5) 6 61
(BGPowell) *trckd ldr: led briefly over 3f out: rdn and wknd over 1f out* **9/1**
0040 6 6 **Kingston Town (USA)**[170] 735 4-9-2 **63**...(b) J-PGuillambert 2 46
(NPLittmoden) *mid-div: rdn over 2f out: sn lost tch* **20/1**
50/0 7 3 **Jalons Star (IRE)**[8] 4029 6-8-6 **60**... TO'Brien(7) 9 38
(MRChannon) *mid-div: rdn over 3f out: sn btn* **25/1**
050 8 9 **Vicat Cole**[29] 3417 3-8-13 **70**... AQuinn 1 31
(MrsLJMongan) *in tch rdn and wknd 3f out* **20/1**
0-00 9 5 **Beauchamp Ribbon**[6] 4080 4-9-2 **63**...(b) FPFerris 5 14
(AJChamberlain) *in tch tl wknd over 2f out* **33/1**

2m 6.66s (-2.04) **Going Correction** -0.25s/f (Firm)
**WFA** 3 from 4yo+ 10lb **9** Ran SP% **122.4**
Speed ratings: **98,97,95,93,90 85,83,76,72**CSF £7.23 CT £30.84 TOTE £2.90: £1.80, £1.30, £1.80; EX 7.10.
**Owner** P Byrne **Bred** Bill Dwan And Tom Lynch **Trained** Newmarket, Suffolk

**FOCUS**
Just a modest handicap, but reasonably competitive with the in-form pair Cristoforo and Burgundy going head-to-head. The pace appeared decent enough and the form is ordinary but solid.

**NOTEBOOK**
**Cristoforo(IRE)**, 6lb higher than when winning by just a short head over a mile and a half here on his previous start, coped well with this drop back in trip and gained his seventh win from his last eight Flat starts with authority. Further success cannot be ruled out, as he will avoid a penalty for this if turned out before he is reassessed, and connections may send him to Windsor next.
**Burgundy** is nowhere near as good as he was (he was racing off a mark 20lb lower than when last winning a handicap), and has not always been the easiest to predict. However, his confidence is on a high after racking up a hat-trick in a claimer and two sellers, and he ran creditably on this step up in grade. He again took plenty of time to find his stride after the start, but was simply beaten by a better horse. Clear of the remainder, he looks up to winning a similar race.
**Katiypour(IRE)** ran better than he did over this course and distance on his previous outing, but was up against some bang in-form horses and does look a little high in the weights.
**Icannshift(IRE)**, a beaten favourite on his last two starts, can have no excuses and has just one to his name since his juvenile days. *Official explanation: jockey said gelding had a breathing problem*
**My Galliano(IRE)** continues out of form.

## 4263 LONDON FOCUS EBF MAIDEN STKS 7f
6:35 (6:36) (D) 2-Y-O £6,841 (£2,105; £1,052; £526) Stalls Low

Form RPR
1 **Red Peony** 2-8-9... TPQueally 1 89+
(SirMarkPrescott) *mde all: pushed clr appr fnl f: comf* **4/1**[1]
6 2 3 1/2 **Hadrian (IRE)**[33] 3313 2-9-0... KDalgleish 6 82
(MJohnston) *chsd wnr thrght: r.o wl and clr 2nd ins fnl 2f but no ch w wnr* **8/1**
34 3 1 1/2 **Bounty Quest**[27] 3476 2-9-0... PDobbs 5 78
(RHannon) *racd 4th tl styd on to chse first 2 ins fnl 2f* **13/2**
25 4 2 **Mastman (IRE)**[12] 3939 2-9-0...(t) JFortune 8 73
(BJMeehan) *towards rr: rdn and sme hdwy over 2f out: styd on but nvr on terms* **5/1**[2]
0 5 1 1/4 **Basic System (USA)**[12] 3946 2-9-0... BDoyle 7 70
(SirMichaelStoute) *t.k.h: in tch tl rdn and wknd 2f out* **6/1**[3]
04 6 hd **Discomania**[14] 3870 2-9-0... SDrowne 3 69
(RCharlton) *bhd: sme hdwy over 2f out: rdn and sn btn* **6/1**[3]
506 7 1 **Zolash (IRE)**[22] 3633 2-8-7... DerekNolan(7) 4 67
(JSMoore) *a outpcd in rr* **40/1**
6 8 1 1/2 **Della Salute**[21] 3675 2-8-6... LPKeniry(3) 9 58
(AMBalding) *t.k.h: chsd wnrs tl rdn and wknd 2f out* **16/1**
4232 9 16 **Wasalat (USA)**[10] 3987 2-8-9... CCatlin 2 18
(MRChannon) *rrd up s and lost several l: c home in own time* **4/1**[1]

1m 21.3s (-2.65) **Going Correction** -0.25s/f (Firm) 2y crse rec **9** Ran SP% **118.0**
Speed ratings: **105,101,99,97,95 95,94,92,74**CSF £37.44 TOTE £4.60: £1.60, £2.00, £2.30; EX 34.80.
**Owner** Cheveley Park Stud **Bred** Cheveley Park Stud Ltd **Trained** Newmarket, Suffolk

**FOCUS**
As is so often the case for Epsom maidens, this was not a particularly strong heat. However, Red Peony was clear and looks pretty smart with the form behind appearing solid, the time was especially smart. The first two home were in the first two throughout.

**NOTEBOOK**
**Red Peony** ◆, out of a seven-furlong two-year-old winner who was successful over ten furlongs at three, justified significant market support with a winning debut. There really was a lot to like about this performance, not least her enthusiastic attitude and, although she should improve on this, she did not look in need of the experience and could be ready for Pattern company already.
**Hadrian(IRE)** was pretty green on his debut but knew more this time and duly showed improved form. He should progress and has a similar event in him, although his long-term future lies in the hands of the Handicapper.
**Bounty Quest**, in three runs, has now been tried over five, six and seven furlongs. He keeps finding a couple too good and may be more do better at lesser track, or in nurseries.
**Mastman(IRE)**, in a tongue-tie for the first time, has not really gone on from his promising debut but can be given another chance on a more conventional track. *Official explanation: jockey said colt was unsuited by the track*

**Basic System(USA)** appeared to step up on his debut running and, although nothing special, is going the right way.
**Discomania** *Official explanation: jockey said, regarding the apparent tender ride, his orders were to jump out just in behind the leaders, to do his best but not to raise his stick because the colt had been tricky at home, adding that colt could not go the early pace and would probably benefit from a longer trip*
**Wasalat(USA)** lost all chance at the start. *Official explanation: jockey said filly reared as the stalls opened*

## 4264 BETFRED "WE PAY DOUBLE RESULT" FILLIES' H'CAP — 1m 114y

**7:05** (7:08) (D) (0-80,74) 3-Y-0+ — **£8,131** (£2,502; £1,251; £625) **Stalls** Low

| Form | | | | RPR |
|---|---|---|---|---|
| 5221 | **1** | | **Dami (USA)**[30] [3394] 3-9-10 **74**.....(p) SSanders 5<br>(CEBrittain) *chsd ldr: pushed along over 2f out and rdn to ld 1f out: all out* **4/1**[2] | 84 |
| 0220 | **2** | *nk* | **Kindness**[16] [3827] 4-8-7 **48**..... CCatlin 2<br>(ADWPinder) *led rdn and hdd 1f out: rallied wl fnl f* **12/1** | 57 |
| 5131 | **3** | *3* | **Kryssa**[20] [3700] 3-9-8 **72**..... JFortune 6<br>(GLMoore) *hld up in tch: rdn 2f out: kpt on one pce: no ch w first 2* **1/1**[1] | 75 |
| 0233 | **4** | *1 1/2* | **Archerfield (IRE)**[14] [3875] 3-8-12 **62**..... SDrowne 3<br>(JWHills) *stdd s: hld up: effrt over 2f out: one pce after* **6/1**[3] | 62 |
| 2255 | **5** | *4* | **Marnie**[18] [3771] 7-8-8 **49**..... JQuinn 1<br>(JAkehurst) *chsd ldrs tl rdn and wknd 2f out* **7/1** | 40 |
| 1040 | **6** | *3/4* | **Joint Destiny (IRE)**[3] [4201] 3-7-10 **49**..... NMackay(3) 4<br>(EJO'Neill) *a bhd: lost tch 2f out* **14/1** | 39 |

1m 43.66s (-2.08) **Going Correction** -0.25s/f (Firm)
**WFA** 3 from 4yo+ 9lb — **6 Ran SP% 111.1**
Speed ratings: **99,98,96,94,91 90**CSF £45.08 TOTE £5.10: £2.90, £3.40; EX 37.60.
**Owner** Saeed Manana **Bred** Newgate Stud Farm Inc **Trained** Newmarket, Suffolk

**FOCUS**
Just a modest handicap in which - like in the previous race - it proved hard to come from off the pace. However, the form should hold up in similar company.

**NOTEBOOK**
**Dami(USA)**, off the mark over ten furlongs at Brighton on her previous start, did not appear suited by this drop back in trip, but was just good enough to defy a 4lb rise in the weights. With the favourite below form, it is hard to know what she achieved, but there should be more to come when returned to further.
**Kindness**, dropped back in trip from ten furlongs, posted a game effort from the front and was only just denied her first-ever success. She has a similar race in her, but has had plenty of chances in lower grades and it would be unwise to get carried away with this performance.
**Kryssa** was unable to follow up her recent Chepstow success off a 6lb higher mark and was not at her best. In a race in which it proved hard to come from off the pace, she can be forgiven this.
**Archerfield(IRE)** had the tongue-tie left off this time, but it made little difference.
**Marnie** is not running up to her best at the moment.

## 4265 RUBBING HOUSE CLAIMING STKS — 7f

**7:35** (7:36) (E) 3-Y-0+ — **£4,725** (£1,454; £727; £363) **Stalls** Low

| Form | | | | RPR |
|---|---|---|---|---|
| 1403 | **1** | | **Scarrottoo**[47] [2886] 6-9-2 55..... RLMoore 11<br>(SCWilliams) *hld up towards rr: rdn and hdwy on outside 2f out: r.o to ld wl ins fnl f* **11/4**[3] | 65 |
| 0612 | **2** | *1/2* | **Lady Mo**[5] [4127] 3-8-10 66..... SSanders 12<br>(GGMargarson) *drawn wd: hdwy on outside 1/2-way: rdn to ld appr fnl f: hdd wl ins last* **2/1**[1] | 65 |
| 3000 | **3** | *3* | **Instinct**[56] [2614] 3-8-10 59..... PDobbs 9<br>(RHannon) *slowly away and in rr tl hdwy over 1f out: r.o fnl f to go 3rd cl home* **20/1** | 57+ |
| 5-60 | **4** | *nk* | **Gameset'N'Match**[8] [4026] 3-8-8 67.....(p) ADaly 6<br>(WGMTurner) *chsd ldr: led over 2f out: hdd appr fnl f: one pce and lost 3rd cl home* **50/1** | 54 |
| | **5** | *5* | **La Calera (GER)**[11] 3-8-3.....(v[1]) CCatlin 1<br>(MFHarris) *chsd ldrs: rdn and wknd appr fnl f* **25/1** | 36 |
| -600 | **6** | *nk* | **Bad Intentions (IRE)**[21] [3680] 4-9-0 65..... GCarter 5<br>(MissDMountain) *chsd ldrs tl rdn and wknd over 1f out* **20/1** | 39 |
| 6324 | **7** | *2* | **Newcorr (IRE)**[77] [2051] 5-8-13 32.....(p) TPQueally 2<br>(JJBridger) *mid-div tl wknd 2f out* **33/1** | 33 |
| 0000 | **8** | *3 1/2* | **Mutabari (USA)**[51] [2762] 10-8-3 30..... AmyMyatt(7) 8<br>(JLSpearing) *a towards rr* **66/1** | 21 |
| 50 | **9** | *1* | **Chelsea's Diamond**[8] [4028] 4-8-12.....(p) VSlattery 10<br>(JAkehurst) *slowly away: a bhd* **33/1** | 20 |
| 1600 | **10** | *2* | **Gilly's General (IRE)**[42] [3024] 4-8-12 44..... SWhitworth 3<br>(JWUnett) *led tl hdd over 2f out: sn wknd* **33/1** | 15 |
| 0451 | **11** | *20* | **Majhool**[10] [3988] 5-8-8 60..... RMiles(3) 7<br>(TGMills) *s.i.s: sn mid-div: rdn and wknd qckly 2f out: eased fnl f* **9/4**[2] | — |

1m 21.64s (-2.31) **Going Correction** -0.25s/f (Firm)
**WFA** 3 from 4yo+ 7lb — **11 Ran SP% 116.4**
Speed ratings: **103,102,99,98,92 92,90,86,85,82 60**CSF £7.65 TOTE £4.50: £1.60, £1.40, £3.70; EX 9.80.Majhool was claimed by I W McInnes for £4,000.
**Owner** Michael Peacock **Bred** Freedom Farm Stud **Trained** Newmarket, Suffolk

**FOCUS**
Just a modest claimer, and the form does not look that strong.

**NOTEBOOK**
**Scarrottoo** had 10lb to find with the runner-up at the weights, but he had conditions in his favour and was given a good ride by Moore, who timed his challenge well and got one continuous run. He should be competitive back in handicaps, but may just take a rise in the weights for this.
**Lady Mo** should have beaten the winner going strictly by official ratings, as she had 10lb in hand of that one at the weights. She did not appear to do anything wrong and finished well clear of the remainder, showing herself still in good form.
**Instinct** appreciated the drop in grade and would have been even closer had he broken on terms.
**Gameset'N'Match**, with cheekpieces replacing blinkers, was up a furlong in trip and fared best of those to race up with the speed. He got a little tired late on and may just prove better over six furlongs.
**La Calera(GER)**, a winner over seven furlongs on dirt in Germany, offered little promise on his British debut over hurdles. Switched to the Flat, this was a little better.
**Gilly's General(IRE)** *Official explanation: jockey said gelding did not handle the track*
**Majhool**, off the mark on his debut for Terry Mills at Brighton on his previous start, had a claiming price of just £4,000 and connections were obviously not worried about losing him. Despite running a shocker, he was indeed claimed. *Official explanation: jockey said gelding finished distressed*

## 4266 RECTANGLE GROUP H'CAP — 1m 114y

**8:05** (8:05) (D) (0-80,79) 3-Y-0 — **£8,092** (£2,490; £1,245; £622) **Stalls** Low

| Form | | | | RPR |
|---|---|---|---|---|
| 133 | **1** | | **Habanero**[8] [4032] 3-9-0 **72**..... RLMoore 5<br>(RHannon) *mde all: rdn and kpt on gamely whn chal ins fnl f* **3/1**[2] | 84 |
| 6111 | **2** | *1/2* | **Pickle**[6] [4092] 3-9-2 **74** 6ex..... SSanders 4<br>(SCWilliams) *hld up: swtchd rt and hdwy over 2f out: wnt 2nd ent fnl f to chal wnr clly: no ex nr fin* **11/8**[1] | 85 |
| 0335 | **3** | *5* | **Go Solo**[27] [3475] 3-9-5 **77**..... MHills 6<br>(BWHills) *a.p: chsd wnr 5f out tl ent fnl f: eased whn clrly hld by first 2* **7/1**[3] | 80+ |
| 0630 | **4** | *3* | **Hilites (IRE)**[1] [4230] 3-9-0 **79**..... DerekNolan(7) 1<br>(JSMoore) *slowly away: hdwy on ins 2f out: sn one pce* **25/1** | 73 |
| 6501 | **5** | *1* | **Malibu (IRE)**[16] [3826] 3-9-6 **78**..... KFallon 3<br>(SDow) *chsd ldr for over 3f: wknd wl over 1f out* **3/1**[2] | 70 |
| 0030 | **6** | *6* | **Scientist**[28] [3452] 3-9-0 **72**..... JFortune 7<br>(JHMGosden) *in tch tl rdn and wknd over 2f out* **14/1** | 51 |
| 0004 | **7** | *9* | **Jomus**[5] [4127] 3-7-12 **59**..... NMackay(3) 2<br>(LMontagueHall) *slowly away: a bhd* **20/1** | 20 |

1m 42.88s (-2.86) **Going Correction** -0.25s/f (Firm) — **7 Ran SP% 119.9**
Speed ratings: **102,101,97,94,93 88,80**CSF £8.09 TOTE £5.20: £2.40, £1.80; EX 10.00.
**Owner** The Waney Racing Group Inc **Bred** Eric Puerari, Oceanic Bloodstock And Haras De Etre **Trained** East Everleigh, Wilts

**FOCUS**
A fair handicap, despite the small field, and a good match between Habanero and Pickle who are both still improving.

**NOTEBOOK**
**Habanero**, 2lb lower than in future handicaps, is often at his best when gaining an uncontested lead and, although not entirely left alone, he did enjoy things up front and found plenty when challenged by the in-form Pickle. Things will obviously be tougher in future, but he should continue to go well in similar events.
**Pickle**, 4lb lower than in future handicaps under her penalty, had every chance but found the winner just too strong. She was well clear of the remainder and this was a fine effort in defeat, but she could be one to take on off her new mark.
**Go Solo**, beaten in a claimer over ten furlongs on his previous start, was left behind by the front two but did at least beat the rest well enough.
**Hilites(IRE)**, 3lb higher than in future handicaps, never threatened and failed to prove her stamina.
**Malibu(IRE)**, 5lb higher than when successful at Brighton on his previous start, found this tougher but was below form in any case.

## 4267 BETTER BUSINESS H'CAP — 6f

**8:35** (8:35) (D) (0-80,80) 3-Y-0 — **£8,190** (£2,520; £1,260; £630) **Stalls** High

| Form | | | | RPR |
|---|---|---|---|---|
| 2252 | **1** | | **Tony The Tap**[6] [4090] 3-9-7 **80**..... KFallon 10<br>(NACallaghan) *outpcd in rr: strly rdn and hdwy over 1f out: r.o u.p to ld fnl 50yds* **11/8**[1] | 86 |
| 0-14 | **2** | *nk* | **Tregarron**[7] [4059] 3-8-11 **70**..... RLMoore 1<br>(RHannon) *led tl hdd over 2f out: rdn to ld again ins fnl f: hdd fnl 50yds* **5/1**[3] | 75 |
| 4643 | **3** | *3/4* | **Ask The Clerk (IRE)**[12] [3949] 3-8-12 **71**..... MTebbutt 4<br>(VSmith) *a prominet: ev ch ins fnl f: nt qckn nr fin* **8/1** | 74 |
| 3100 | **4** | *nk* | **Emtilaak**[29] [3420] 3-9-3 **76**..... WSupple 5<br>(BHanbury) *hld up in rr: hdwy on ins whn nt clr run appr fnl f: r.o ins* **10/1** | 78 |
| 5006 | **5** | *nk* | **Peruvian Style (IRE)**[7] [4043] 3-8-11 **70**..... TPQueally 9<br>(NPLittmoden) *a in tch. hdwy over 1f out to hold ev ch ins fnl f: kpt on* **16/1** | 71 |
| 3000 | **6** | *1 1/2* | **Imperium**[15] [3849] 3-8-12 **71**..... SDrowne 3<br>(MrsStefLiddiard) *mid-div: hdwy to ld over 2f out: hdd ins fnl f: fdd* **16/1** | 67 |
| 3222 | **7** | *3/4* | **Intriguing Glimpse**[47] [2889] 3-9-5 **78**..... SSanders 6<br>(MissBSanders) *hld up: hdwy 2f out: rdn and wknd ins fnl f* **7/2**[2] | 72 |
| 0050 | **8** | *1 1/4* | **Black Oval**[36] [3211] 3-7-9 **57** oh8..... LisaJones(3) 2<br>(SDow) *chsd ldr: wknd over 1f out* **33/1** | 47 |
| 0100 | **9** | *9* | **Alizar (IRE)**[15] [3849] 3-7-13 **58**..... CCatlin 7<br>(SDow) *prom tl wknd qckly over 2f out* **33/1** | 21 |

69.02 secs (-1.61) **Going Correction** -0.25s/f (Firm) — **9 Ran SP% 118.8**
Speed ratings: **100,99,98,98,97 95,94,93,81**CSF £8.87 CT £40.48 TOTE £2.20: £1.40, £1.70, £2.20; EX 11.00 Place 6 £32.69, Place 5 £22.41.
**Owner** K J Mercer **Bred** K J Mercer **Trained** Newmarket, Suffolk

**FOCUS**
A really competitive sprint handicap and the field were well bunched at the line, although the winner is capable of better and had a little in hand.

**NOTEBOOK**
**Tony The Tap**, 3lb lower than in future handicaps off the back of a recent second at Newmarket, found himself with plenty to do in the straight and appeared inclined to hang into the camber, but Fallon's persistence eventually paid off. He was declared to run the following day under a 7lb penalty at Newmarket.
**Tregarron** continues in good form, but was unable to resist the well-handicapped winner's challenge. This was just his third start of the year and there should be more to come.
**Ask The Clerk(IRE)** again ran his race, but he just keeps finding a couple too good.
**Emtilaak**, below form on his two previous starts, ran much better and this track probably just gave him something to think about.
**Peruvian Style(IRE)**, with the blinkers left off this time, posted a better effort.
**Intriguing Glimpse** has been holding his form well this season, but has done most of his racing (and all of his winning) over five furlongs and was not good enough to take the gaps over this extra furlong.

T/Plt: £33.60 to a £1 stake. Pool: £43,226.30. 938.50 winning tickets. T/Qpdt: £9.10 to a £1 stake. Pool: £3,233.10. 261.60 winning tickets. JS

# 4226 GOODWOOD (R-H)

### Thursday, July 29

**OFFICIAL GOING: Good to firm (good in places)**

The false rail, present for the first two days of the meeting and positioned on the far side of the straight, was taken down before racing.
Wind: almost nil Weather: sunny, becoming cloudy

## 4268 ALBERT STKS (H'CAP) — 7f

**2:05** (2:08) (C) (0-100,97) 3-Y-0 — **£26,100** (£9,900; £4,950; £2,250) **Stalls** High

| Form | | | | RPR |
|---|---|---|---|---|
| 4151 | **1** | | **Peter Paul Rubens (USA)**[8] [4031] 3-9-6 **96** 6ex..... RLMoore 8<br>(PFICole) *lw: mde all: clr w runner-up 2f out: rdn and styd on wl* **3/1**[2] | 114+ |
| 0521 | **2** | *1 1/2* | **Compton's Eleven**[19] [3737] 3-8-7 **86**..... SHitchcott(3) 6<br>(MRChannon) *t.k.h: pressed wnr: clr of remainder 2f out: drvn and styd on: a hld* **20/1** | 100 |
| -111 | **3** | *1* | **Peeress**[23] [3602] 3-9-4 **94**..... KFallon 18<br>(SirMichaelStoute) *b.off hind: lw: n.m.r on inner after 1f: hld up in midfield: gng wl over 2f out: prog to chse ldng pair 1f out: r.o: no ch* **9/4**[1] | 105+ |
| 2-11 | **4** | *2 1/2* | **Take A Bow**[19] [3750] 3-9-0 **90**..... JQuinn 4<br>(PRChamings) *forced to r wd: bmpd after 1f: towards rr: effrt over 2f out: r.o fr over 1f out: nrst fin* **16/1** | 95 |
| 0255 | **5** | *hd* | **Free Trip**[42] [3001] 3-8-13 **89**..... LDettori 16<br>(JHMGosden) *racd in midfield and off the pce: pushed along 1/2-way: drvn and styd on fnl 2f: nvr nrr* **5/1**[3] | 93 |

6012 **6** ½ **Mahmoom**[23] [3598] 3-9-2 **92** TEDurcan 17 95
(MRChannon) *wl in tch: chsd clr ldng pair 2f out: hanging and no imp: one pce fnl f* **10/1**

0026 **7** nk **Bettalatethannever (IRE)**[15] [3850] 3-8-9 **85** DaneO'Neill 12 87
(SDow) *lw: racd towards rr: n.m.r after 1f: rdn 3f out: styd on fnl 2f: n.d* **50/1**

0332 **8** nk **Jedburgh**[19] [3751] 3-9-7 **97** TQuinn 3 99
(JLDunlop) *wl in rr: pushed along 1/2-way: taken to outer and drvn 2f out: styd on: n.d* **25/1**

0300 **9** 1¼ **Fancy Foxtrot**[15] [3850] 3-8-13 **89** JFortune 1 87
(BJMeehan) *swtchd fr outside draw and hld up in detached last: effrt on inner over 2f out: one pce and no ch w ldrs* **50/1**

1532 **10** ½ **Distant Connection (IRE)**[5] [4151] 3-8-6 **82** KMcEvoy 14 79
(APJarvis) *mostly chsd ldng pair to 2f out: wknd* **12/1**

5060 **11** ¾ **Desert Dreamer (IRE)**[33] [3295] 3-8-12 **88** MHills 11 83
(BWHills) *dwlt: hld up in rr: gng wl enough 3f out: shuffled along 2f out: nvr on terms* **33/1**

0420 **12** 3½ **Mister Saif (USA)**[20] [3691] 3-8-11 **87** PDobbs 5 73
(RHannon) *chsd ldrs tl wknd 2f out* **66/1**

0422 **13** nk **Eccentric**[8] [4024] 3-7-13 **75** ow1 FNorton 9 60
(AndrewReid) *b: b.hind: swtg: prom tl wknd 2f out: eased ins fnl f* **33/1**

61-0 **14** hd **Dvinsky (USA)**[20] [3702] 3-8-12 **88** (b[1]) JPMurtagh 2 73
(GAButler) *chsd ldrs tl wknd 2f out* **28/1**

-120 **15** 1½ **Invasian (IRE)**[12] [3943] 3-8-11 **87** WRyan 10 68
(HRACecil) *racd in midfield: rdn and no prog over 2f out: sn wknd* **33/1**

0000 **16** 1¾ **Parkview Love (USA)**[42] [3001] 3-9-4 **94** KDalgleish 13 70
(MJohnston) *a in rr: rdn and struggling 3f out* **25/1**

-400 **17** 1¼ **Lord Links (IRE)**[19] [3728] 3-8-6 **82** MartinDwyer 7 55
(RHannon) *t.k.h: hld up in rr: drvn 3f out: sn btn* **33/1**

1m 25.4s (-2.63) **Going Correction** -0.05s/f (Good) **17** Ran SP% **128.2**
Speed ratings: **113,111,110,107,107 106,106,105,104,103 102,98,98,98,96 94,93**CSF £70.14 CT £173.90 TOTE £4.30: £1.80, £5.00, £1.50, £3.00; EX 111.90 Trifecta £255.70 Pool of £2,773.68 - 7.70 winning units..
**Owner** Richard Green (fine Paintings) **Bred** Mueller Farm **Trained** Whatcombe, Oxon

**FOCUS**
Despite the numbers, only three horses were seriously fancied. The winner, making all, clocked the quickest time of the three races run over this distance, and very few got into it from off the pace.

**NOTEBOOK**
**Peter Paul Rubens(USA)**, who won so impressively at Sandown eight days earlier, was 7lb well in. He overcame his moderate stall position with a fast start and, once in the lead, never looked back. He maintained a strong gallop throughout and this performance suggests he is well up to taking his place in Listed grade.
**Compton's Eleven** is more exposed than the winner but came here in top form. He too was quickly away, negating his poor draw in the process, and was the only one who ever threatened the winner. Another hike in the handicap is now inevitable.
**Peeress** was chasing the four-timer and, being ideally drawn, was unsurprisingly strong in the market. She got stuck in behind horses though, and although she finished well down the ouside once in the clear, the bird had flown. Things just did not work out as planned on this occasion, and a return to a mile will help her in future.
**Take A Bow**, whose successes have come on easier ground, did not appear inconvenienced by this quicker surface. He was forced to race wide, which did not help, and there is more to come from this lightly-raced type.
**Free Trip** was popular in the market but failed to make use of his favourable draw. All his best work was being done in the latter stages but the overall impression is that the Handicapper has his measure for the time being.
**Mahmoom**, another who was well-drawn, went up another 3lb for his Newmarket effort last time, and he too looks to have his work cut out off his current rating.
**Bettalatethannever(IRE)**, who has done his winning on the All-Weather, ran one of his best races on turf.
**Jedburgh** is also high enough in the weights. He shaped as though a step back up to a mile will suit, but he has appeared not to get home over the distance in the past.
**Desert Dreamer(IRE)** had to wait a good while for a gap to appear, but he did not really pick up when it did eventually arrive.
**Dvinsky(USA)** *Official explanation: jockey said colt lost its action*

## 4269 KING GEORGE STKS (GROUP 3) 5f
**2:40** (2:41) (A) 3-Y-0+ **£29,000** (£11,000; £5,500; £2,500) **Stalls** Low

Form RPR

3424 **1** **Ringmoor Down**[20] [3715] 5-8-11 **106** TQuinn 12 112
(DWPArbuthnot) *hld up in rr: prog on outer 2f out: chsd ldr fnl f: drvn ahd last strides* **10/1**

2164 **2** hd **Boogie Street**[26] [3537] 3-8-10 **110** (t) JFortune 9 114
(RHannon) *lw: w ldr: led over 2f out: drvn and hung rt fnl f: hdd last strides* **15/2**[3]

3410 **3** ¾ **The Tatling (IRE)**[26] [3537] 7-9-8 **115** RLMoore 7 119
(JMBradley) *hld up in rr: prog over 1f out: r.o to chse ldng pair wl ins fnl f: jst unable to chal* **8/1**

-215 **4** 1 **Avonbridge**[40] [3073] 4-9-8 **114** SDrowne 8 116
(RCharlton) *settled in midfield: effrt to chse ldr over 1f out: unable qck: kpt on same pce fnl f* **13/2**[2]

5300 **5** ½ **Tychy**[4] [4165] 5-8-11 **92** MartinDwyer 10 103
(SCWilliams) *led to over 2f out: sn rdn: kpt on again ins fnl f* **50/1**

0001 **6** nk **Bahamian Pirate (USA)**[6] [4091] 9-9-0 **105** EAhern 6 105
(DNicholls) *b.off hind: lw: racd in midfield: rdn 1/2-way: struggling after: styd on ins fnl f* **14/1**

0110 **7** ½ **Celtic Mill**[33] [3308] 6-9-0 **107** LEnstone 3 103
(DWBarker) *prom on nr side: rdn and unable qck over 2f out: one pce after* **9/1**

61-5 **8** nk **Majestic Missile (IRE)**[44] [2955] 3-8-10 **116** KFallon 13 102
(WJHaggas) *hld up bhd ldrs: effrt 2f out: hanging rt and nt qckn over 1f out: btn fnl f* **2/1**[1]

1060 **9** 1¼ **If Paradise**[44] [2955] 3-8-10 **102** DaneO'Neill 5 98
(RHannon) *chsd ldrs: rdn over 2f out: struggling fr wl over 1f out* **66/1**

0330 **10** hd **Bishops Court**[19] [3732] 10-9-0 **107** LDettori 1 97
(MrsJRRamsden) *hld up in last: shuffled along 2f out: nt qckn and no ch* **12/1**

0343 **11** nk **Dragon Flyer (IRE)**[6] [4091] 5-8-11 **98** FNorton 4 93
(MQuinn) *chsd ldrs: rdn 3f out: struggling fnl 2f* **50/1**

3401 **12** 5 **Fire Up The Band**[19] [3732] 5-9-0 **99** ANicholls 2 78
(DNicholls) *prom early: rdn and struggling 3f out: wl btn over 1f out* **20/1**

1236 **13** ¾ **Autumn Pearl**[10] [3976] 3-8-7 **98** PRobinson 11 72
(MAJarvis) *racd on wd outside: spd over 3f: sn wknd* **33/1**

56.73 secs (-2.32) **Going Correction** -0.125s/f (Firm)
**WFA** 3 from 4yo+ 4lb **13** Ran SP% **116.1**
Speed ratings: **113,112,111,109,109 108,107,107,105,105 104,96,95**CSF £77.34 TOTE £12.80: £3.70, £2.50, £2.60; EX 85.70 Trifecta £435.90 Pool of £2,517.74 - 4.10 winning units..
**Owner** Prof C D Green **Bred** Pigeon House Stud **Trained** Upper Lambourn, Berks

**FOCUS**
A fairly competitive Group Three in which the form of the King's Stand Stakes at Royal Ascot proved the key. Tychy's proximity a slight concern, but good efforts nevertheless from the third and fourth under their 8lb penalties.

**NOTEBOOK**
**Ringmoor Down** needs a strong gallop, as she likes to be held up and come with a late rattle. She did not get the breaks at Ascot and the ground was not quick enough on her next two starts, but everything fell right this time as she got to the front in the final strides. She is not in the Nunthorpe, but she may still get a crack at a Group One later in the season in the Abbaye.
**Boogie Street** is all speed and this track looked sure to bring out the best in him, especially with the ground riding quick. He helped set a decent pace and looked the likeliest winner a furlong out, but in the end he was just edged out. Still relatively lightly-raced, there is surely improvement to come, this year and especially next, and his first Group race success is just around the corner.
**The Tatling(IRE)**, who won the race last year, ran a super race under his 8lb penalty. He too is ideally suited by coming off a fast pace, and emerges as the best of these at the weights. He has been installed as favourite for the Nunthorpe on the back of this, a race in which he finished runner-up last season.
**Avonbridge**, for whom the ground was probably quicker than ideal, was another to race well under a Group Two penalty. He remains high on the short-list for the Abbaye, when hopefully he will get some give underfoot.
**Tychy** showed plenty of speed to make the running to halfway, and it is to her credit that she kept on to finish a very honourable fifth. This was a personal best.
**Bahamian Pirate(USA)**, who was scratchy to post, is difficult to catch right and this sharp five furlongs on quick ground did not play to his strengths.
**Celtic Mill** lacked the pace over this shorter trip and in this company.
**Majestic Missile(IRE)** had run well from a poor draw at Ascot and looked to hold every chance here. He did not help his rider by carrying his head high and hanging, though, and never really looked happy. He now has questions to answer.
**Fire Up The Band** did not move to post well and was struggling before halfway.
**Autumn Pearl** *Official explanation: jockey said filly was unsuited by the good to firm ground*

## 4270 LADY O GOODWOOD CUP (GROUP 2) 2m
**3:15** (3:15) (A) 3-Y-0+ **£58,000** (£22,000; £11,000; £5,000) **Stalls** High

Form RPR

-613 **1** **Darasim (IRE)**[42] [2998] 6-9-4 **115** (v) JFanning 8 116
(MJohnston) *mde all: set stdy pce tl kicked on over 3f out: urged along and drew clr fr 2f out: unchal* **11/8**[1]

5044 **2** 2½ **Royal Rebel**[26] [3538] 8-9-4 **110** (v) JPMurtagh 1 113
(MJohnston) *racd towards rr: hrd rdn over 4f out: prog u.p over 2f out: chsd wnr jst ins fnl f: no imp* **14/1**

2603 **3** ¾ **Misternando**[26] [3538] 4-9-4 **108** (v) SHitchcott 5 112
(MRChannon) *lw: settled in midfield: prog 4f out: drvn to dispute 2nd pl 2f out tl ent fnl f: kpt on same pce* **11/1**

0015 **4** 1 **Double Obsession**[19] [3725] 4-9-4 **95** (v) JFEgan 4 111
(MJohnston) *trckd ldng pair: rdn to chse wnr over 2f out tl jst ins fnl f: no imp: one pce after* **12/1**

-331 **5** ½ **Romany Prince**[26] [3538] 5-9-4 **110** DaneO'Neill 9 110
(DRCElsworth) *lw: s.s: hld up in last pair: gng easily over 3f out: rdn and effrt over 2f out: styd on fnl f: no ch* **11/1**

-332 **6** nk **Silver Gilt**[26] [3538] 4-9-4 **110** LDettori 7 110
(JHMGosden) *t.k.h early: trckd ldrs: rdn and effrt 3f out: nt clr run over 1f out: no hdwy after* **15/2**[3]

1-04 **7** ½ **Supremacy**[13] [3912] 5-9-4 **104** KFallon 6 109
(SirMichaelStoute) *hld up in midfield: lost pl over 5f out: rdn 3f out: no prog tl kpt on fnl f* **8/1**

-113 **8** 8 **Anak Pekan**[33] [3310] 4-9-4 **105** PRobinson 2 100+
(MAJarvis) *chsd wnr to over 2f out: sn wknd* **7/1**[2]

30P5 **9** 7 **Hilbre Island**[59] [2533] 4-9-4 **110** MHills 3 91
(BJMeehan) *hld up in last pair: rdn over 3f out: wknd over 2f out* **16/1**

3m 26.93s (-3.73) **Going Correction** -0.05s/f (Good) **9** Ran SP% **114.4**
Speed ratings: **107,105,105,104,104 104,104,100,96**CSF £22.68 TOTE £2.50: £1.30, £3.50, £3.50; EX 18.60 Trifecta £109.60 Pool of £3,051.66 - 19.76 winning units..
**Owner** Markus Graff **Bred** His Highness The Aga Khan's Studs S C **Trained** Middleham Moor, N Yorks

**FOCUS**
Not a vintage renewal, but the Gold Cup form was upheld even if Darasim did not need to run up to his best to win. The early gallop was sedate and the time was moderate.

**NOTEBOOK**
**Darasim(IRE)**, who had 5lb and upwards in hand of the rest according to official ratings, could also boast a great course record, having been successful at this meeting the previous two years and finished second and third on his only other two starts at the track. His rider gave him a textbook ride from the front, kicking on early in the straight when the challenges began to emerge. He won easily enough, as his form suggested he should, and the Melboune Cup could now be on the cards.
**Royal Rebel**, who won this race in 2000, finds two miles on the short side these days. He did not race as lazily this time and, as a consequence, less was required of his rider in the first half of the race. He stayed on well for second place in the straight, and his performance, together with the winner's, helps uphold the Gold Cup form.
**Misternando** had the ground more in his favour this time and put up a decent effort. He came to challenge two furlongs out but the winner just kicked away and he was unable to match him. The more galloping track at Doncaster ought to suit him better.
**Double Obsession**, the Ascot Stakes winner, ran well on his first outing in Group company, only tiring out of second place inside the last. He is clearly going the right way, although his rating is bound to go up for this effort against higher-rated rivals.
**Romany Prince**needs producing late and is hard to win with but should have been ridden with a bit more urgency in a race run at just a steady pace. His effort came too late and he ought too have finished closer.
**Silver Gilt** had never run on ground quicker than good before, and this performance probably explains why.
**Supremacy** has yet to confirm that he stays two miles properly, as this race was run at a steady pace early on, and his win at Ascot was gained when he himself set a pedestrian early gallop.
**Anak Pekan**, stepping into Pattern company for the first time, found the ground much too quick for his liking. *Official explanation: jockey said gelding was unsuited by the good to firm ground*
**Hilbre Island** *Official explanation: jockey said colt was unsuited by the track*

## 4271 LADBROKES.COM STKS (H'CAP) 1m 1f 192y
**3:50** (3:53) (B) (0-110,104) 3-Y-0 **£43,500** (£16,500; £8,250; £3,750) **Stalls** Low

Form RPR

14-2 **1** **Art Trader (USA)**[13] [3915] 3-8-10 **93** JPMurtagh 11 108+
(MrsAJPerrett) *trckd clr ldrs: eased to outer gng wl 3f out: prog to ld 2f out: edgd rt and drvn over 1f out: styd on wl* **7/2**[1]

0142 **2** 1¼ **Fine Silver (IRE)**[12] [3943] 3-8-10 **93** TQuinn 7 105
(PFICole) *hld up in midfield: hrd rdn 3f out: prog 2f out: hanging rt but chsd wnr ins fnl f: no imp last 100yds* **12/1**

0126 **3** 1½ **Watamu (IRE)**[36] [3210] 3-8-1 **84** (v[1]) JQuinn 14 94+
(PJMakin) *lw: hld up in rr: effrt on inner and rdn 3f out: nt clr run 2f out to 1f out: swtchd lft: r.o wl last 150yds: nrst fin* **14/1**

3330 **4** *shd* **Mutafanen**[19] 3756 3-9-6 **103** RHills 6 112
(EALDunlop) *hld up wl in rr: stdy prog on outer fr 3f out: rdn and hanging rt fr 2f out: chsd ldrs 1f out: styd on same pce* **12/1**

1-43 **5** *hd* **Warrad (USA)**[15] 3850 3-8-5 **88** EAhern 15 97
(GAButler) *lw: prom: effrt to ld 3f out and rdn: hdd 2f out: one pce fnl f* **9/1**[3]

4222 **6** *3* **Royal Warrant**[22] 3641 3-8-10 **93** MartinDwyer 5 96
(AMBalding) *lw: sn prom: rdn 3f out: cl up but hld whn n.m.r over 1f out: wknd ins fnl f* **10/1**

6612 **7** *¾* **Woody Valentine (USA)**[14] 3879 3-7-13 **82** RFfrench 4 84
(MJohnston) *prom: hrd rdn over 3f out: chal and ev ch 2f out: stl chsng ldrs but hld whn n.m.r over 1f out: wknd* **14/1**

1106 **8** *hd* **Gatwick (IRE)**[42] 3000 3-9-4 **104** SHitchcott[(3)] 3 105
(MRChannon) *hld up in midfield: hrd rdn and struggling over 3f out: styd on one pce fnl 2f: n.d* **8/1**[2]

1141 **9** *1 ¼* **Gavroche (IRE)**[20] 3706 3-8-3 **89** J-PGuillambert[(3)] 2 91+
(CADwyer) *hld up in rr: prog and swtchd to inner over 2f out: chsd ldrs over 1f out: nt clr run sn after: wknd* **20/1**

1350 **10** *5* **Gold History (USA)**[12] 3937 3-9-3 **100** JFanning 8 90
(MJohnston) *hld up in last trio: rdn over 3f out: no prog and btn sn after* **40/1**

1124 **11** *hd* **Dancing Lyra**[54] 2676 3-8-7 **90** MHills 1 79
(JWHills) *mostly chsd ldr to over 3f out: wkng whn n.m.r over 2f out* **12/1**

1-00 **12** *3* **Seneschal**[88] 1799 3-7-11 **87** TDean[(7)] 10 71
(MRChannon) *swtg: racd v freely: led: clr 6f out: hdd 3f out: wknd 2f out* **66/1**

1530 **13** *5* **Oddsmaker (IRE)**[5] 4151 3-8-5 **88** DeanMcKeown 13 62
(PDEvans) *t.k.h: hld up in rr: rdn over 3f out: no prog: sn wknd* **33/1**

1-52 **14** *1 ¼* **Kingsword (USA)**[39] 3118 3-9-0 **97** KFallon 16 69
(SirMichaelStoute) *hld up in midfield: rdn and no prog over 3f out: eased whn wl btn 2f out* **9/1**[3]

6312 **15** *shd* **Lucayan Legend (IRE)**[42] 3001 3-8-11 **94** LDettori 9 65
(RHannon) *dwlt: racd in last and nvr gng wl: rdn and brief effrt 4f out: sn wknd* **9/1**[3]

1-43 **16** *8* **Mutawassel (USA)**[83] 1924 3-9-3 **100** (b[1]) WSupple 12 56
(BWHills) *t.k.h: hld up in midfield: rdn 4f out: sn wknd and bhd* **40/1**

2m 5.31s (-2.37) **Going Correction** -0.05s/f (Good) **16** Ran SP% **122.9**
Speed ratings: **107,106,104,104,104 102,101,101,100,96 96,93,89,88,88** 82CSF £44.49 CT £542.61 TOTE £4.50: £1.70, £3.70, £4.90, £4.20; EX 64.90 Trifecta £835.20 Pool of £7,764.10 - 6.60 winning units..
**Owner** Matthew Green & Oliver Simmons **Bred** R H Thomson **Trained** Pulborough, W Sussex

**FOCUS**
A quality handicap run at a strong pace, and a finish dominated by progressive types. The form should hold up.

**NOTEBOOK**
**Art Trader(USA)** was well backed, got to the lead travelling strongly and, although he edged right towards the rail under pressure, responded well to his rider's urgings to win quite comfortably. He looked beforehand as though he could be made even fitter, so there is likely to be even better to come.
**Fine Silver(IRE)** had no trouble at all with the extra distance and simply met a better-handicapped rival. He is progressive, having already climbed 10lb in the ratings since the beginning of the season, and it is unfortunate that he only has one win to his name this year.
**Watamu(IRE)** ◆ had raced closer to the pace when twice running well here in May, but he was racing over farther then, and he may have found things happening a bit too quick over this shorter trip. Having said that, given that his ambitious run up the inside in the straight failed so badly and the first two got first run on him, it was quite an achievement to finish a fast-finishing third. There is a nice race to be won with him.
**Mutafanen** showed improved form under his big weight, staying on well down the outside in the straight. He prefers a bit of give in the ground, and is entitled to consideration in Listed grade on his best form.
**Warrad(USA)**, who like the winner had had only three previous outings, had every chance and it is possible that his stamina gave out over this longer trip.
**Royal Warrant** has gone up 10lb without winning since the beginning of the turf campaign, and things are not going to get any easier soon.
**Woody Valentine(USA)** ran a fair race back up in grade, but it might just be that he needs a bit of give underfoot to produce his best.
**Gatwick(IRE)** could be difficult to place from now on.
**Gavroche(IRE)** did not get the best of runs next to the far-side rail, and is probably a bit better than his finishing position suggests.
**Lucayan Legend(IRE)** *Official explanation: jockey said colt was unsuited by the track and the good to firm ground*
**Mutawassel(USA)** was edgy in the preliminaries.

## 4272 EUROPEAN BREEDERS FUND NEW HAM MAIDEN FILLIES' STKS 7f
4:25 (4:32) (D) 2-Y-0 **£10,465** (£2,415; £2,415; £805) **Stalls** High

Form RPR

4 **1** **Miss L'Augeval**[13] 3904 2-8-11 KDarley 9 76
(GWragg) *lw: trckd ldrs: pushed along over 2f out: effrt over 1f out: wandered but led jst ins fnl f: rdn out* **10/3**[1]

**2** *½* **Love Affair (IRE)** 2-8-11 RLMoore 12 75
(RHannon) *lengthy: w'like: scope: dwlt: racd in midfield: shkn up over 2f out: styd on wl fr over 1f out: jst hld* **7/1**[3]

0 **2** *dht* **Kalmini (USA)**[13] 3905 2-8-11 TEDurcan 6 75
(MRChannon) *trckd ldrs: pushed along 3f out: effrt over 1f out: styd on wl fnl f: jst hld* **16/1**

**4** *hd* **Miss Sharapova (IRE)** 2-8-11 KFallon 10 74
(GAButler) *w'like: scope: t.k.h early: hld up in midfield: pushed along 3f out: unable qck 2f out: styd on wl again fnl f* **9/2**[2]

**5** *shd* **Ellens Princess (IRE)** 2-8-11 PDobbs 2 74
(RHannon) *leggy: dwlt: hld up wl in rr: nudged along and sme prog on outer 2f out: reminder and kpt on wl fnl f* **33/1**

0 **6** *1* **Midcap (IRE)**[13] 3904 2-8-11 MHills 4 72
(BWHills) *trckd ldr: led over 2f out: rdn and hdd jst ins fnl f: lost several pls nr fin* **33/1**

**7** *hd* **Rumbalara** 2-8-11 JFortune 13 71
(JHMGosden) *w'like: sn in midfield: effrt over 2f out: nt clr run over 1f out: rdn and flashed tail ent fnl f: fly-jmpd 150yds out: nt* **10/1**

**8** *1* **Ceiriog Valley** 2-8-11 RHills 7 69
(BWHills) *w'like: scope: bit bkwd: dwlt: wl in rr: shkn up and rn green 2f out: no prog tl styd on ins fnl f* **33/1**

5 **9** *nk* **Gwyneth**[36] 3202 2-8-11 TQuinn 11 68
(JLDunlop) *trckd ldrs: shkn up over 2f out: no imp 1f out: fdd fnl f* **12/1**

4 **10** *½* **Something Exciting**[13] 3905 2-8-11 NPollard 3 67
(DRCElsworth) *hld up wl in rr: rdn over 2f out: no prog tl styd on ins fnl f* **9/1**

5 **11** *shd* **Mary Gray**[8] 4009 2-8-11 JFanning 8 66
(MJohnston) *led to over 2f out: wknd fnl f* **25/1**

3 **12** *¾* **Sharaby (IRE)**[22] 3627 2-8-11 LDettori 5 64
(EALDunlop) *lw: racd on outer: hld up in tch: shkn up over 2f out: looked reluctant and hanging over 1f out: sn btn* **9/2**[2]

**13** *5* **Casual Glance** 2-8-11 MartinDwyer 1 52+
(AMBalding) *w'like: leggy: wnt sharply lft s: a in detached last: allowed to complete in own time* **20/1**

1m 29.18s (1.15) **Going Correction** -0.05s/f (Good) **13** Ran SP% **122.0**
Speed ratings: **91,90,90,90,90 88,88,87,87,86 86,85,79** TOTE £4.20: £1.80 TRIFECTA PL: K £5.50, LA £32.40; EX: ML/K £33.20, ML/LA £16.40; CSF: ML/K £28.70, ML/LA £12.79.
**Owner** J L C Pearce **Bred** J L C Pearce **Trained** Newmarket, Suffolk

**FOCUS**
They finished in something of a heap and the form is probably nothing special.

**NOTEBOOK**
**Miss L'Augeval** had run a promising race on her debut at Newbury and was sure to appreciate the seventh furlong. She was all out to hold on from a steadily closing bunch, though, and the form is probably not very strong. That said, she is likely to do better when able to race over a mile.
**Love Affair(IRE)**, a half-sister to Glockenbach, a multiple winner in Germany, and to multiple Italian winner Royal Partners, came in for support in the market on her debut and ran a fairly promising race, dead-heating for the runner-up spot.
**Kalmini(USA)** finished in mid-division in another Newbury maiden on her debut and will not be seen to full advantage until she gets to race over middle distances. She was staying on well at the finish and is another who will appreciate a mile this year.
**Miss Sharapova(IRE)**, a half-sister to four winners, had her chance and was staying on again at the finish, suggesting that she too will appreciate a mile in time.
**Ellens Princess(IRE)**, who looks quite weak at present, ran green but finished well on the outside. She is a half-sister to four winners, notably Ellens Lad and Ellens Academy, and looks sure to improve with racing.
**Midcap(IRE)**, who is quite a nice type, was swamped inside the last but had run well up until then. This was a marked improvement on her debut effort.
**Rumbalara**, who is a bit on the leg at the moment, did not get the clearest of runs, but she also flashed her tail under pressure.
**Sharaby(IRE)** was on her toes beforehand. *Official explanation: jockey said filly was unsuited by the good to firm ground*
**Casual Glance**, a half-sister to five useful performers, including Hidden Meadow, Kingsclere and Passing Glance, is not very robust.

## 4273 DE BOER EUROPEAN BREEDERS FUND CLASSIFIED STKS 7f
5:00 (5:04) (B) 3-Y-0+ **£12,296** (£4,664; £2,332; £1,060) **Stalls** High

Form RPR

2-03 **1** **Golden Sahara (IRE)**[19] 3751 3-8-9 95 (t) LDettori 12 102
(SaeedBinSuroor) *lw: prom: trckd ldr gng easily 2f out: rdn to chal 1f out: r.o gamely to ld last 75yds* **8/1**[3]

0111 **2** *½* **Material Witness (IRE)**[21] 3673 7-9-6 99 MartinDwyer 10 105
(WRMuir) *led at gd pce: rdn 2f out: hrd pressed 1f out: r.o gamely: hdd last 75yds* **5/1**[2]

4000 **3** *nk* **Boston Lodge**[26] 3539 4-9-2 95 (v[1]) JPMurtagh 9 102+
(GAButler) *s.s: hld up off the pce: smooth prog over 2f out: nt clr run over 1f out: swtchd lft and stl no room: r.o nr fin* **8/1**[3]

2002 **4** *½* **Moonlight Man**[13] 3906 3-9-0 100 RLMoore 3 103
(RHannon) *lw: racd towards rr: rdn 3f out: prog u.p to chal 2f out: edgd rt over 1f out: styd on same pce* **14/1**

2605 **5** *1 ½* **Wizard Of Noz**[20] 3717 4-9-5 98 KFallon 7 97+
(JNoseda) *hld up in midfield and off the pce: nt clr run briefly wl over 2f out: rdn wl over 1f out: kpt on ins fnl f: n.d* **8/1**[3]

-003 **6** *¾* **Quiet Storm (IRE)**[52] 2733 4-8-13 93 JFEgan 5 89
(GWragg) *chsd ldng quartet: pushed along 1/2-way: rdn to chal 2f out: fdd ins fnl f* **25/1**

0344 **7** *hd* **Sew'N'So Character (IRE)**[12] 3943 3-8-9 94 (b[1]) DSweeney 4 92
(MBlanshard) *prom: rdn and beginning to lose pl whn n.m.r over 1f out: fdd* **16/1**

2220 **8** *½* **Digital**[5] 4120 7-9-2 90 SHitchcott 8 91
(MRChannon) *hld up in last pair: rdn 3f out: no prog tl kpt on fr over 1f out* **10/1**

5320 **9** *½* **Maghanim**[21] 3673 4-9-5 98 RHills 2 92
(JLDunlop) *hld up in last pair and wl off the pce: shuffled along over 2f out: kpt on same pce: no ch* **9/1**

0000 **10** *3 ½* **Vicious Knight**[5] 4120 6-9-2 95 ANicholls 6 80
(DNicholls) *racd wl in rr: drvn 3f out: no prog and struggling sn after* **16/1**

11 **11** *¾* **Kehaar**[21] 3671 3-8-9 93 EAhern 1 78
(MAMagnusson) *racd wd: hld up in rr: rdn and hanging 3f out: fnd nil and sn btn* **7/2**[1]

2100 **12** *nk* **Makfool (FR)**[21] 3673 3-8-11 97 TEDurcan 11 79
(MRChannon) *mostly chsd ldr to 2f out: wknd* **14/1**

1m 25.81s (-2.22) **Going Correction** -0.05s/f (Good)
**WFA** 3 from 4yo+ 7lb **12** Ran SP% **120.3**
Speed ratings: **110,109,109,108,106 105,105,105,104,100 99,99**CSF £48.46 TOTE £6.40: £2.10, £2.20, £3.90; EX 40.50.
**Owner** Godolphin **Bred** Gainsborough Stud Management Ltd **Trained** Newmarket, Suffolk
■ Stewards Enquiry : R L Moore one-day ban: careless riding (Aug 9)

**FOCUS**
Despite the fact that Material Witness set a good pace in front, the final time was 0.41sec slower than the handicap won by Peter Paul Rubens earlier on the card. The first three home were drawn in the top four boxes.

**NOTEBOOK**
**Golden Sahara(IRE)**, well drawn and back on fast ground, enjoyed a good trip throughout and came to challenge going well approaching the final furlong. He did not stride clear as had looked possible but he always looked likely to take the leader's measure. He looks up to challenging for honours in Listed grade.
**Material Witness(IRE)**, who is a seven-furlong specialist, set a decent pace in front from his good draw and would not go down without a fight. Given his rating, he is likely to have to try his hand in Listed grade before long.
**Boston Lodge**, visored for the first time, did not get the gap on the rail he was waiting for and had to be switched out to challenge. He lost momentum and finished all too late. He is a frustrating character but he is very effective between seven furlongs and a mile, and he should continue to run well now that his stable is back in form.
**Moonlight Man** was not as well drawn as the first three home but he enjoyed a clear run down the outside of the track, and he appeared to run his race.
**Wizard Of Noz** has been disappointing this season, but on the plus side his rating is steadily dropping.
**Quiet Storm(IRE)** was narrowly best in at these weights but her recent form is over farther.
**Maghanim** likes to make the running but that was always unlikely from trap two, and with the well-drawn Material Witness in opposition. The change in tactics did not suit and this run should be forgiven.
**Kehaar** was poorly drawn, raced wide throughout and never looked happy on the track. This was not his true form and he should be given another chance back on a more conventional course.

## 4274 VALDOE RATED STKS (H'CAP) 1m 6f
5:35 (5:35) (C) (0-95,95) 3-Y-O £9,613 (£3,646; £1,823; £828) **Stalls** High

Form RPR
4113 **1** **Lochbuie (IRE)**[36] 3210 3-9-2 **90** JFEgan 7 104+
(GWragg) *hld up in cl tch: rdn and effrt over 2f out: led over 1f out: edgd rt u.p fnl f: hld on wl* **7/2**[1]
-311 **2** ¾ **Yoshka**[22] 3621 3-8-13 **87** RFfrench 3 100+
(MJohnston) *narrow: trckd ldrs: effrt to ld 3f out: hrd rdn and hdd over 1f out: rallied fnl f: a jst hld* **7/2**[1]
-011 **3** 1 ¾ **Tungsten Strike (USA)**[15] 3851 3-8-7 **81** MartinDwyer 10 92
(MrsAJPerrett) *lw: cl up: rdn 3f out: chsd ldrs u.p over 1f out: styd on but nvr able to chal* **7/2**[1]
0310 **4** 2 ½ **Anousa (IRE)**[12] 3927 3-9-7 **95** KFallon 9 103+
(PHowling) *hld up in last pair: rdn 3f out: prog u.p to chse ldrs over 1f out: no ex fnl f* **8/1**[2]
2164 **5** 3 **Twofan (USA)**[4] 4174 3-8-6 **80** JFanning 4 84
(MJohnston) *lw: mostly chsd ldr: ev ch 3f out: wknd over 1f out* **12/1**[3]
4004 **6** nk **Man At Arms (IRE)**[7] 4062 3-8-4 **78** oh3 RLMoore 1 82
(RHannon) *s.i.s: hld up in last pair: rdn over 3f out: sme prog over 1f out: fdd fnl f* **16/1**
331 **7** nk **Leg Spinner (IRE)**[36] 3194 3-8-5 **79** ow1 KDarley 2 82
(MRChannon) *hld up in tch: rdn over 3f out: struggling over 2f out: fdd fnl f* **8/1**[2]
0410 **8** 11 **Red Birr (IRE)**[26] 3543 3-8-8 **82** LDettori 8 71
(AMBalding) *led to 3f out: wknd 2f out* **16/1**
4-10 **9** 7 **Waziri (IRE)**[14] 3872 3-8-4 **78** oh1 KMcEvoy 6 58
(HMorrison) *t.k.h: cl up: lost pl 5f out: wknd u.p wl over 2f out* **14/1**

3m 0.78s (-2.97) **Going Correction** -0.05s/f (Good) **9** Ran SP% **115.0**
Speed ratings: **106,105,104,103,101 101,101,94,90**CSF £14.78 CT £45.10 TOTE £4.90: £2.00, £1.80, £1.90; EX 20.40 Place 6 £108.41, Place 5 £74.08.
**Owner** Mollers Racing **Bred** M Fahy **Trained** Newmarket, Suffolk

**FOCUS**
A decent staying handicap featuring a few progressive types. The first three home all look capable of going on to better things.

**NOTEBOOK**
**Lochbuie(IRE)** had shaped as though he would get this extra two furlongs and he really saw it out well, despite the ground riding quicker than possibly would be ideal. A progressive type, there is surely more to come, and while at this stage his chances of getting into the Ebor look slim, the Melrose Handicap looks an ideal target.
**Yoshka**, a progressive Mark Johnston-trained stayer, went for home three furlongs out and soon had most of his rivals in trouble. The winner proved too much over this mile six distance, though, and although he is perfectly able over this trip, he gives the impression that a step back up to two miles will be ideal.
**Tungsten Strike(USA)** was racing off a 10lb higher mark than at Lingfield and ran really well, staying on strongly at the finish and suggesting that he too will do better when returned to two miles.
**Anousa(IRE)** was raised 13lb for his Listed-grade win having previously been beaten in handicaps a number of times off marks in the low 80s, albeit over middle distances rather than staying trips. He looks likely to struggle off this sort of mark.
**Twofan(USA)** is rather one-paced and this quicker ground, on which he had never raced before, probably did not play to his strengths.
**Man At Arms(IRE)**, 3lb wrong at the weights, never threatened.
**Leg Spinner(IRE)** came in for some market support but never quite had the pace to challenge.
**Waziri(IRE)** looked dull in his coat in the paddock.
T/Jkpt: £28,248.50 to a £1 stake. Pool: £39,786.74. 0.50 winning tickets. T/Plt: £175.40 to a £1 stake. Pool: £164,183.75. 683.05 winning tickets. T/Qpdt: £32.20 to a £1 stake. Pool: £6,242.85. 143.45 winning tickets. JN

# 4245 MUSSELBURGH (R-H)
Thursday, July 29

**OFFICIAL GOING: Good to firm (firm in places)**

## 4275 FAMOUS GROUSE H'CAP STKS (AMATEUR RIDERS) 2m
6:20 (6:20) (F) (0-55,51) 4-Y-O+ £3,373 (£1,038; £519; £259) **Stalls** Low

Form RPR
00 **1** **Regal Fantasy (IRE)**[29] 3411 4-9-4 **32** MissFayeBramley(5) 3 38
(PABlockley) *in tch: hdwy over 3f out: rdn over 1f out: styd on to ld ins last* **10/1**
3605 **2** ¾ **Sherwood Forest**[9] 4005 4-10-5 **42** (v) MissSBrotherton 5 47
(MissLAPerratt) *midfield: hdwy over 3f out: rdn along 2f out: kpt on u.p fnl f: nrst fin* **10/1**
0506 **3** 1 ½ **Mr Fortywinks (IRE)**[12] 3576 10-10-5 **45** MissLEllison(3) 8 49
(BEllison) *led 5f: close up tl led again 4f out: rdn clr 2f out: drvn over 1f out: hdd & wknd ins last* **11/2**[2]
2040 **4** nk **Sarn**[6] 4080 5-9-11 **41** MissMMullineaux(7) 2 44
(MMullineaux) *hld up and way bhd: hdwy on inner 3f out: rdn over 1f out: kpt on: nrst fin* **9/2**[1]
00-1 **5** 2 ½ **Peter's Imp (IRE)**[15] 3835 9-11-0 **51** MrDJewett 10 51
(ABerry) *hld up: hdwy over 6f out: effrt on wd outside over 2f out: sn rdn and no imp fnl f* **12/1**
16/6 **6** 3 ½ **Welsh Dream**[31] 3363 7-10-9 **46** MrCStorey 1 42
(MissSEForster) *in tch: hdwy over 6f out: rdn along 3f out: sn drvn and no hdwy* **12/1**
5000 **7** 7 **Repulse Bay (IRE)**[9] 4005 6-10-12 **49** MsCWilliams 4 37
(JSGoldie) *midfield: sme hdwy over 4f out: sn rdn along and wknd over 2f out* **15/2**[3]
04-6 **8** 3 ½ **Double Blade**[14] 2214 9-10-0 **40** MrsNWilson(3) 11 23
(NWilson) *cl up: led after 5f tl rdn along and hdd over 4f out: sn wknd* **9/2**[1]
040/ **9** 2 **San Dimas (USA)**[285] 3137 7-9-7 **35** (v) MissJRiding(5) 12 16
(RAllan) *chsd ldng pair: rdn along 6f out: wknd over 4f out* **14/1**
0000 **10** dist **Outward (USA)**[23] 3604 4-10-3 **45** MissRBastiman(5) 7 —
(RBastiman) *jinked bdly lft s: plld hrd: a rr* **40/1**
00-0 **11** dist **Waterline Spirit**[18] 3774 4-9-10 **40** MissABevan(7) 9 —
(PDEvans) *in tch: rdn along over 6f out: sn wknd* **33/1**

3m 35.2s (1.50) **Going Correction** -0.05s/f (Good) **11** Ran SP% **109.1**
Speed ratings: **95,94,93,93,92 90,87,85,84,—** —CSF £97.25 CT £554.59 TOTE £12.20: £2.60, £2.40, £1.40; EX 180.90.
**Owner** M J Wiley **Bred** W G McKinley **Trained** Southwell, Notts

**FOCUS**
A poor race in which two of the runners set a strong pace clear of the remainder. The form is weak.

**NOTEBOOK**
**Regal Fantasy(IRE)**, an ex-Irish filly, came home the best to win for the first time. The step up to two miles was in her favour, along with a 4lb drop in the weights *Official explanation: trainer said, regarding the improved form shown, filly had benefited from the use of a different bit*
**Sherwood Forest**, who ran over ten furlongs last time, had no problem with this big step up in trip and was staying on at the end.
**Mr Fortywinks(IRE)** is without a win since landing this event a year ago from a 6lb lower mark. Again given a positive ride, he was clear with two to run but was inclined to wander in front and was cut down inside the last.
**Sarn** had been set too much to do over 12 furlongs at Chepstow, and it was a similar story back over two miles.
**Peter's Imp(IRE)**, a comeback ride for Dale Jewett, was officially rated just 25 when winning a claimer first time out.
**Double Blade**, a winner over fences earlier in the month, was soon clear along with one rival, but was the first of the pair to crack.
**Outward(USA)** *Official explanation: jockey said gelding was too keen and finished very tired*
**Waterline Spirit** *Official explanation: jockey said gelding had no more to give*

## 4276 GREENGAUGE HOME TURF CLAIMING STKS 1m
6:50 (6:50) (F) 3-Y-O+ £3,513 (£1,081; £540; £270) **Stalls** Low

Form RPR
0165 **1** **Bailieborough (IRE)**[5] 4132 5-9-11 70 (v) AlexGreaves 6 68
(DNicholls) *hld up in tch: smooth hdwy over 2f out: rdn to ld ent last: kpt on* **4/1**[3]
3552 **2** 1 **Killala (IRE)**[5] 4132 4-9-4 62 RWinston 10 59
(ISemple) *stdd s and bhd: hdwy over 3f out: rdn to chse ldrs over 1f out: sn drvn and one pce* **5/2**[1]
3420 **3** 1 ½ **Tojoneski**[26] 3520 5-9-5 46 (p) ACulhane 2 56?
(IWMcinnes) *cl up: led over 3f out: rdn along 2f out: drvn and hdd ent last: one pce* **8/1**
3040 **4** 1 ½ **Alafzar (IRE)**[48] 2834 6-9-2 58 (t) SJDonohoe(7) 8 57
(PDEvans) *trckd ldrs: rdn along over 2f out: drvn and one pce appr last* **9/1**
3350 **5** 2 ½ **Sarraaf (IRE)**[10] 3977 8-9-4 69 PMulrennan(5) 4 51
(JSGoldie) *hld up towards rr: hdwy wl over 2f out: sn rdn and no imp* **7/2**[2]
-600 **6** 7 **Scramble (USA)**[1] 4246 6-9-2 50 (tp) GParkin 7 28
(BEllison) *led: rdn along and hdd over 3f out: sn wknd* **25/1**
500/ **7** ¾ **Society Times (USA)**[1253] 350 11-9-7 16 (t) JMcAuley 1 31?
(DANolan) *a rr* **150/1**
2600 **8** 1 **Lucky Largo (IRE)**[9] 4005 4-9-3 55 (b) DMcGaffin 9 25
(MissLAPerratt) *in tch: rdn along 3f out: drvn and btn 2f out* **25/1**
0000 **9** 6 **Environmentalist**[31] 3367 5-8-9 40 (t) CHaddon(7) 3 10
(DANolan) *slowl into stride: a rr* **100/1**
50 **10** 16 **Sharabad (FR)**[23] 3607 6-9-7 VHalliday 5 —
(MrsLBNormile) *chsd ldrs and sn rdn along: drvn 1/2-way and sn wknd* **100/1**
3323 **11** ¾ **Wares Home (IRE)**[9] 4004 3-8-13 55 (p) DarrenWilliams 11 —
(KRBurke) *dwlt: sn chsng ldrs on inner: rdn along and wkng whn hung bdly lft 2f out* **12/1**

1m 39.66s (-3.04) **Going Correction** -0.05s/f (Good)
**WFA** 3 from 4yo+ 8lb **11** Ran SP% **109.9**
Speed ratings: **105,104,102,101,98 91,90,89,83,67 67**CSF £12.95 TOTE £4.70: £1.70, £1.10, £2.00; EX 18.00.Killala was claimed by R N Bevis for £7,000.
**Owner** Middleham Park Racing Xviii **Bred** Churchtown Stud **Trained** Sessay, N Yorks

**FOCUS**
An ordinary claimer in which the early gallop was not strong and the form does not look sound.

**NOTEBOOK**
**Bailieborough(IRE)** is a decent performer at this level and battled on well to score, turning around Newcastle form with Killala over this extra furlong.
**Killala(IRE)** had finished in front of tonight's winner when runner-up at Newcastle. Tackling a mile for the first time, he appeared to stay but lacked the commitment of the winner under pressure.
**Tojoneski** remains in good order but a win is proving elusive.
**Alafzar(IRE)**, who is not the most consistent, ran a fair race minus the usual headgear.
**Sarraaf(IRE)** could not capitalise on a drop into claiming company and continues to frustrate.
**Wares Home(IRE)** *Official explanation: jockey said gelding hung left-handed throughout*

## 4277 DAILY RECORD MAIDEN AUCTION STKS 7f 30y
7:20 (7:22) (E) 2-Y-O £3,380 (£1,040; £520; £260) **Stalls** Low

Form RPR
632 **1** **Coleorton Dane**[15] 3834 2-8-6 NCallan 2 69
(KARyan) *mde all: qcknd clr over 2f out: rdn over 1f out: drvn ins last: hld on* **13/8**[1]
04 **2** ¾ **Heybrook Boy (USA)**[13] 3918 2-8-10 SChin 4 71
(MJohnston) *chsd ldrs: pushed along and outpcd 2f out: sn rdn: styd on wl u.p fnl f* **7/2**[3]
03 **3** shd **Cava Bien**[31] 3366 2-8-4 PHanagan 6 65
(JGGiven) *chsd ldrs: rdn along and outpcd 2f out: drvn and styd on wl fnl f* **3/1**[2]
53 **4** ½ **Blackcomb Mountain (USA)**[10] 3983 2-7-13 JMackay 5 61+
(MFHarris) *chsd wnr: rdn along 2f out: styng on whn hung bdly lft 1f out: nt rcvr* **9/1**
2 **5** 1 **Kumala Ocean (IRE)**[6] 4095 2-7-13 JBramhill 8 56
(PABlockley) *towards rr: pushed along 1/2-way: rdn over 2f out: kpt on fnl f: nrst fin* **16/1**
05 **6** 7 **Isitloveyourafter (IRE)**[42] 3003 2-8-1 ow3 THamilton(3) 3 44
(RPElliott) *chsd ldrs: rdn along and hung lft home turn: sn bhd* **100/1**
0 **7** 3 ½ **Lightening Fire (IRE)**[13] 3918 2-8-6 DKinsella 7 37
(TJEtherington) *dwlt: sn pushed along in rr: wd in home st and sn bhd* **25/1**
**8** 10 **Fly Me To Dunoon (IRE)** 2-8-5 DarrenWilliams 1 12
(KRBurke) *stmbld s: a rr* **25/1**

1m 30.92s (1.39) **Going Correction** -0.05s/f (Good) **8** Ran SP% **109.9**
Speed ratings: **91,90,90,89,88 80,76,64**CSF £6.76 TOTE £2.50: £1.20, £1.80, £1.20; EX 7.80.
**Owner** Coleorton Moor Racing **Bred** A Holmes **Trained** Hambleton, N Yorks

**FOCUS**
A fair maiden and reliable despite the modest time. Coleorton Dane stole a decisive advantage when kicking clear two out.

**NOTEBOOK**
**Coleorton Dane** has been steadily progressive and seemed well suited to this more aggressive ride, leading throughout and just finding enough to hold off several finishers having gone clear. The form is not overly strong, but he is the type to progress again and he can pay his way in nurseries.
**Heybrook Boy(USA)** is another progressing with racing but he could not cope when the winner quickened clear. He stayed on nicely towards the end though and will be well suit by a mile when handicapping.
**Cava Bien** is learning with experience and yet another who will be seen to better effect in nurseries.

**Blackcomb Mountain(USA)** did not quite run up to the level of form that saw him finish third behind a useful Godolphin juvenile at Beverley - flattered, but a decent effort nonetheless - and she looked awkward under pressure. There is a small race in her. *Official explanation: jockey said filly hung badly left-handed in the straight*
**Kumala Ocean(IRE)** stepped up on her debut effort - second in an All-Weather seller - and can win a race in that grade on turf.
**Lightening Fire(IRE)** *Official explanation: jockey said gelding ran green and hung badly left-handed in the straight*

## 4278 SCOTTISH EQUITABLE/JOCKEY ASSOCIATION NURSERY 7f 30y
**7:50** (7:50) (D) 2-Y-O **£8,141** (£2,505; £1,252; £626) **Stalls** Low

Form RPR
5221 **1** **Jane Jubilee (IRE)**[8] [4012] 2-9-11 **83** 7ex.................. SChin 1 92+
(MJohnston) *racd wd: trckd ldrs: shkn up and ushed along 2f out: rdn to ld ent last: hung rt and kpt on* **8/15**[1]
5233 **2** *2* **Brace Of Doves**[8] [4012] 2-8-5 **68**.................. PMakin(5) 3 69
(TDBarron) *led: rdn along 2f out: hdd and edgd lft ent last: kpt on same pce* **8/1**[3]
5210 **3** *6* **Windy Prospect**[42] [2996] 2-9-7 **79**.................. NCallan 2 65
(PABlockley) *chsd ldng pair: rdn along over 2f out: drvn and one pce over 1f out* **7/1**[2]
1113 **4** *nk* **Princely Vale (IRE)**[14] [3886] 2-8-8 **73**..................(p) CHaddon(7) 5 58
(WGMTurner) *hld up: hdwy over 2f out: sn rdn along and one pce* **14/1**
0511 **5** *6* **Diction (IRE)**[6] [4094] 2-8-8 **66** 7ex.................. DarrenWilliams 4 36
(KRBurke) *a rr* **16/1**
51 **6** *3 1/2* **Premier Times**[12] [3951] 2-8-0 **58**.................. DaleGibson 6 20
(MDHammond) *chsd ldr: rdn along over 2f out: sn btn* **8/1**[3]

1m 29.15s (-0.38) **Going Correction** -0.05s/f (Good) **6** Ran SP% **112.5**
Speed ratings: **101,98,91,91,84 80**CSF £5.62 TOTE £1.40: £1.10, £2.70; EX 3.60.
**Owner** Mrs Sheila Ramsden **Bred** Mrs S Ramsden **Trained** Middleham Moor, N Yorks

**FOCUS**
Jane Jubilee had little trouble following up her recent demolition job and remains progressive. The time was decent.

**NOTEBOOK**
**Jane Jubilee(IRE)** bolted up off a 5lb lower mark at Catterick last week and although shouldering a big weight, she had little trouble following up. She hung to her right under pressure, but seemed happy enough and obviously needs stepping up in grade.
**Brace Of Doves**, behind Jane Jubilee at Catterick, got closer this time as he was entitled to at the weights, but was never going to beat her.
**Windy Prospect** was more at home in this company - he competed at Group level last time - but was still not up to the task. He may be one to watch out for when getting some cut in the ground as his sole win to date was on the Fibresand.
**Princely Vale(IRE)** plugged on from the rear without ever threatening.

## 4279 ROSSLEIGH LAND ROVER H'CAP (FOR THE ROSSLEIGH LAND ROVER TROPHY) 5f
**8:20** (8:27) (E) (0-70,69) 3-Y-O+ **£6,968** (£2,144; £1,072; £536) **Stalls** Low

Form RPR
5000 **1** **Catch The Cat (IRE)**[13] [3920] 5-9-13 **69**..................(v) GParkin 7 79
(JSWainwright) *wnt lft s: chsd ldrs: rdn along 2f out: swtchd rt and hdwy to ld ins last: drvn out* **8/1**[2]
2405 **2** *1/2* **Valiant Romeo**[16] [3820] 4-8-6 **53**.................. PMulrennan(5) 9 61
(RBastiman) *chsd ldrs: rdn along wl over 1f out: hdwy ent last: kpt on* **10/1**[3]
6-06 **3** *1* **Moritat (IRE)**[6] [4085] 4-8-11 **53**.................. NCallan 11 57
(PDEvans) *towards rr: gd hdwy 2f out: sn rdn and styd on strly fnl f* **12/1**
00-0 **4** *1 3/4* **Alfie Lee (IRE)**[1] [4247] 7-7-8 **43**..................(tp) CHaddon(7) 12 40
(DANolan) *chsd ldrs: rdn wl over 1f out: kpt on ins last* **33/1**
4406 **5** *nk* **Pirlie Hill**[5] [4133] 4-8-9 **51**.................. DKinsella 10 47
(MissLAPerratt) *dwlt and bhd: hdwy wl over 1f out: swtchd rt and rdn ent last: nrst fin* **16/1**
3600 **6** *shd* **He's A Rocket (IRE)**[25] [3562] 3-9-0 **60**..................(b) DarrenWilliams 4 55
(KRBurke) *chsd ldrs: rdn over 3f out: drvn and kpt on ins last* **14/1**
0020 **7** *hd* **Rectangle (IRE)**[4] [4181] 4-9-11 **67**.................. AlexGreaves 14 62
(DNicholls) *chsd ldrs: rdn wl over 1f out: kpt on same pce* **12/1**
5002 **8** *nk* **Peters Choice**[13] [3894] 3-9-6 **66**..................(b) RWinston 2 59
(ISemple) *led: rdn and edgd rt over 1f out: hdd & wknd ent last* **7/1**[1]
3150 **9** *hd* **Champagne Cracker**[22] [3624] 3-9-2 **65**.................. THamilton(3) 3 58
(MissLAPerratt) *chsd ldrs: rdn 2f out: wknd appr last* **33/1**
-500 **10** *1 1/2* **Sea Fern**[15] [3838] 3-8-1 **47**.................. PHanagan 6 34+
(DEddy) *squeezed out s and bhd tl sme late hdwy* **50/1**
-005 **11** *1/2* **Strawberry Patch (IRE)**[5] [4133] 5-8-13 **55**..................(p) SChin 5 40+
(MissLAPerratt) *bdly hmpd after 100 yds: bhd tl sme late hdwy* **10/1**[3]
0112 **12** *shd* **Queen Of Night**[8] [4014] 4-9-4 **60**.................. ACulhane 16 44
(DWChapman) *racd wd: in touc h: rdn along 2f out and no imp* **16/1**
1000 **13** *2 1/2* **Feu Duty (IRE)**[13] [3894] 3-9-5 **65**.................. DMcGaffin 15 39
(TJEtherington) *racd wd: in tch: rdn along 2f out and sn wknd* **50/1**
-606 **14** *1/2* **Mutayam**[24] [3580] 4-8-1 **43**..................(t) JMcAuley 8 15
(DANolan) *wnt lft s and sn cl up: rdn along 2f out: sn wknd* **66/1**
0600 **15** *4* **Star Applause**[6] [4105] 4-7-12 **40**.................. JMackay 13 —
(JSGoldie) *a rr* **100/1**

58.98 secs (-1.42) **Going Correction** -0.20s/f (Firm)
**WFA** 3 from 4yo+ 4lb **15** Ran SP% **87.9**
Speed ratings: **103,102,100,97,97 97,96,96,96,93 92,92,88,87,81**CSF £41.73 CT £334.98 TOTE £6.00: £2.50, £2.90, £3.70; EX 70.90.
**Owner** T W Heseltine **Bred** Mrs Jill M Harley **Trained** Kennythorpe, N Yorks
■ Dave (9/4 fav) was withdrawn after bursting out of the stalls. Rule 4 applies, deduct 30p in the £.
■ Stewards Enquiry : D Kinsella one-day ban: used whip without giving filly time to respond (Aug 9)

**FOCUS**
Ordinary form but a decent gallop and the form look solid for the level.

**NOTEBOOK**
**Catch The Cat(IRE)** was unable to grab the lead after going left from the gates, but came through to settle it inside the final furlong. He likes this track and was racing off the same mark as when successful here in May.
**Valiant Romeo** ran another sound race despite the absence of the usual visor. He has raced exclusively over the minimum trip in the last couple of seasons, but could be worth another try over six furlongs.
**Moritat(IRE)**, done no favours by the draw again, was keeping on strongly late in the day.
**Alfie Lee(IRE)** has run two decent races here in as many days now, but is it is more than five years since he last won.
**Pirlie Hill**, who is edging down the weights, had plenty on her plate after a slow start but was keeping on stoutly.
**Peters Choice** again showed good pace but was unable to last home. *Official explanation: jockey said gelding hung right-handed in the final furlong*

**Feu Duty(IRE)** *Official explanation: jockey said filly hung right-handed throughout and was unsuited by the going*

## 4280 BRIDGEWELL SECURITIES H'CAP 7f 30y
**8:50** (8:54) (D) (0-80,80) 3-Y-O+ **£6,773** (£2,084; £1,042; £521) **Stalls** Low

Form RPR
0033 **1** **St Savarin (FR)**[10] [3982] 3-8-13 **73**.................. MSavage(5) 4 81
(JRBest) *led 2f: cl up tl led again 3f out: rdn clear 2f out: kpt on ins last* **4/1**[3]
0120 **2** *3/4* **Kirkby's Treasure**[5] [4134] 6-9-12 **74**.................. FLynch 3 80+
(ABerry) *bhd: hdwy when nt clr run and hit in face w whip wl over 1f out: squeezed though and hung bdly lft ins last: fin strly* **7/2**[2]
0240 **3** *2* **Regent's Secret (USA)**[9] [4008] 4-8-8 **61**.................. PMulrennan(5) 10 62
(JSGoldie) *hld up in tch: hdwy on inner over 2f out: sn rdn and kpt on fnl f* **10/1**
**4** *1/2* **Mister Marmaduke**[87] [1851] 3-9-11 **80**.................. DMcGaffin 1 80
(ISemple) *hld up and bhd: swtchd outside and gd hdwy 3f out: rdn to chse ldrs over 1f out: drvn ent last and one pce* **33/1**
0106 **5** *hd* **Dark Day Blues (IRE)**[5] [4151] 3-8-12 **67**.................. DarrenWilliams 7 66
(MDHammond) *keen: chsd ldrs: rdn along over 2f out: drvn and one pce over 1f out* **12/1**
5000 **6** *shd* **Blythe Spirit**[23] [3606] 5-9-4 **66**.................. PHanagan 8 65
(RAFahey) *trckd ldrs: hdwy over 2f out: rdn over 1f out and sn btn* **3/1**[1]
5-06 **7** *nk* **Risk Free**[8] [4014] 7-8-11 **59**..................(v) RWinston 9 57
(PDEvans) *cl up: led after 2f tl rdn along and hdd 3f out: sn wknd* **14/1**
00-0 **8** *6* **Procreate (IRE)**[26] [3550] 4-7-12 **46** oh4.................. JMcAuley 2 28
(MissAMWinters, Ire) *s.i.s: rapid hdwy to join ldrs after 2f: rdn along wl over 2f out: drvn and wkng whn hmpd ent last* **33/1**
0206 **9** *1* **Silver Seeker (USA)**[13] [3895] 4-8-3 **54**.................. THamilton(3) 6 34
(ARDicken) *s.i.s: a rr* **14/1**
3220 **10** *3/4* **Whippasnapper**[61] [2492] 4-8-12 **67**.................. CHaddon(7) 5 45
(JRBest) *dwlt: sn in tch: rdn along 1/2-way and sn wknd* **7/1**

1m 28.86s (-0.67) **Going Correction** -0.05s/f (Good)
**WFA** 3 from 4yo+ 7lb **10** Ran SP% **115.7**
Speed ratings: **102,101,98,98,98 97,97,90,89,88**CSF £18.26 CT £130.06 TOTE £3.50: £2.60, £1.50, £1.90; EX 11.50 Place 6 £26.81, Place 5 £8.49.
**Owner** D S Nevison **Bred** F W Holtkotter **Trained** Hucking, Kent
■ Stewards Enquiry : F Lynch one-day ban: careless riding (Aug 9)

**FOCUS**
The gallop was not particularly strong but the proximity of the reliable runner-up gives the form a reasonably solid look.

**NOTEBOOK**
**St Savarin(FR)**, always in the front rank, struck for home with a quarter of a mile to run and battled on well. He is an honest sort.
**Kirkby's Treasure** remains in good heart. Things did not go his way, as he received a smack over the face from a rival jockey's whip when looking for a gap. Despite hanging to his left when in the clear, as he has done before, he finished well.
**Regent's Secret(USA)** remains a maiden but certainly has the ability to pick up a race from what has become a useful mark.
**Mister Marmaduke**, an ex-Irish gelding who has been off for three months, shaped encouragingly on his first run for this yard.
**Blythe Spirit**, 9lb lower than at the start of the season, was a disappointment over this longer trip.
T/Plt: £66.90 to a £1 stake. Pool: £33,359.85. 363.65 winning tickets. T/Qpdt: £7.80 to a £1 stake. Pool: £3,059.60. 286.70 winning tickets. JR

4281 - 4283a (Foreign Racing) - See Raceform Interactive

# [3388]CHANTILLY (R-H)
Thursday, July 29

**OFFICIAL GOING: Good**

## 4284a PRIX DAPHNIS (GROUP 3) (C&G) 1m 1f
**2:35** (2:35) 3-Y-O **£25,704** (£10,282; £6,426; £6,426)

RPR
**1** **Cacique (IRE)**[32] [3360] 3-8-9.................. GaryStevens 1 113+
(AFabre, France) *made all, shaken up 2f out, pushed clear over 1f out, eased close home, easily* 1
**2** *1 1/2* **Ershaad (USA)**[53] [2721] 3-8-9.................. CSoumillon 3 110
(JEHammond, France) *in touch, 4th straight, pushed along to chase leader 1 1/2f out, outpaced closing stages but easily held 2nd* 2
**3** *1 1/2* **High Flash (IRE)**[31] [3389] 3-8-9.................. TThulliez 5 107
(PBary, France) *held up, last straight, pushed along over 1 1/2f out, stayed on steadily but never dangerous* 3
**3** *dht* **Apeiron (GER)**[25] [3565] 3-8-12.................. J-PCarvalho 2 110
(MarioHofer, Germany) *raced in 2nd, pushed along in straight & lost place, kept on one pace*
**5** *hd* **Charmo (FR)**[38] [3163] 3-8-9.................. SPasquier 4 107
(PDemercastel, France) *in touch, 5th straight, outpaced 2f out, never dangerous*
**6** *5* **Kensington (GER)**[109] [1350] 3-8-9..................(b) TJarnet 6 98
(AJunk, France) *raced towards outside, 3rd straight, outpaced from well over 1f out*

1m 54.9s **Going Correction** +0.45s/f (Yiel) **6** Ran SP% **124.0**
Speed ratings: **103,101,100,100,100 95**.
**Owner** K Abdulla **Bred** Juddmonte Farms **Trained** France

**NOTEBOOK**
**Cacique(IRE)**, runner-up to Bago on his last two starts, won without turning a hair. A full-brother to Banks Hill, Dansili and Intercontinental, he clearly has a good deal of ability, and a third clash with Bago in the Juddmonte International could be on the cards.
**Ershaad(USA)** finished one place behind Cacique in the Prix Jean Prat and had to settle for a minor role again.

## [4268]GOODWOOD (R-H)

Friday, July 30

**OFFICIAL GOING: Good to firm**

The false rail on the lower bend was taken down overnight.

Wind: lt hlf against Weather: fine/sunny

### 4285 GLORIOUS STKS (LISTED RACE) 1m 4f

**2:05** (2:06) (A) 4-Y-O+ **£17,400** (£6,600; £3,300; £1,500) **Stalls** Low

Form RPR

2-21 **1** **Alkaased (USA)**[27] 3521 4-8-12 105 ........ JFortune 9 114
(LMCumani) *lw: trckd ldng pair: effrt to ld wl over 1f out: drvn and hrd pressed fnl f: r.o strly and hld on wl* **11/4**[1]

0-01 **2** *nk* **First Charter**[34] 3315 5-9-1 109 ........ KFallon 8 117
(SirMichaelStoute) *trckd ldng trio: effrt 2f out: chsd wnr over 1f out: str chal fnl f: r.o wl but a jst hld* **3/1**[2]

4104 **3** *6* **Alkaadhem**[28] 3484 4-9-1 108 ........ RHills 2 107
(MPTregoning) *lw: hld up in midfield: clsd on ldrs 3f out: gng wl whn nt clr run 2f out: effrt to go 3rd jst ins fnl f but easily outpcd* **9/1**

6335 **4** *1 1/2* **Persian Majesty (IRE)**[23] 3642 4-8-12 113 ........ JPMurtagh 4 102
(PWHarris) *s.i.s: hld up in last pair: rdn over 2f out: outpcd and btn over 1f out* **7/2**[3]

2506 **5** *hd* **Compton Bolter (IRE)**[28] 3484 7-9-1 107 ........ EAhern 6 105
(GAButler) *led for 1f: trckd ldr after: chal over 4f out: upsides 2f out: sn outpcd and btn* **12/1**

4414 **6** *1 1/4* **Persian Lightning (IRE)**[42] 3034 5-8-12 107 ........ SDrowne 3 100
(JLDunlop) *swtg: hld up in last pair: rdn over 2f out: no prog and wl btn over 1f out: fdd* **14/1**

5040 **7** *3 1/2* **Tizzy May (FR)**[27] 3538 4-8-12 100 ........ DaneO'Neill 7 94
(RHannon) *hld up in last trio: rdn over 3f out: sn struggling* **66/1**

250- **8** *1 3/4* **Millstreet**[269] 5921 5-8-12 110 ........ (t) LDettori 5 91
(SaeedBinSuroor) *lw: pushed up to ld after 1f: rdn and hdd wl over 1f out: wknd rapidly fnl f* **12/1**

0501 **P** **Eastern Breeze (IRE)**[14] 3912 6-8-12 105 ........ (e) PaulEddery 1 —
(PWD'Arcy) *settled in midfield: in tch whn p.u over 3f out: dead* **20/1**

2m 34.4s (-4.53) **Going Correction** -0.05s/f (Good) **9** Ran SP% **112.2**
Speed ratings: **113,112,108,107,107 106,104,103,—**CSF £10.68 TOTE £3.70: £1.50, £1.50, £3.20; EX 11.90 Trifecta £60.40 Pool of £2,216.10 - 26.04 winning units.
**Owner** M R Charlton **Bred** Clovelly Farms **Trained** Newmarket, Suffolk

**FOCUS**
They were well strung out in the early stages as Millstreet, accompanied by Compton Bolter, set a strong gallop. The first two pulled well clear and posted career bests.

**NOTEBOOK**
**Alkaased(USA)** had hacked up in the Old Newton Cup last time out and was well supported into favouritism on this first try in Listed company. Having quickened up past the leading duo inside the final quarter mile, he found extra when tackled by the eventual runner-up, and on this evidence he looks capable of making the grade in Group company (his trainer does not favour running in the Ebor under top-weight).
**First Charter** tracked the winner through inside the final quarter mile and had every chance to pick him up if good enough, but he had to accept he was second-best on the day. A solid performer at this sort of level, he loves fast ground and stays farther than this, so there should be other days for him. The result must have been slightly galling for Stoute, as he trained the winner up until this season.
**Alkaadhem**did not convince over this longer trip. This was his first attempt over a mile and a half and the pace was strong, so it was a true test. He travelled well but had to wait to get a run between two furlongs out and a furlong and a half out, during which time the winner and runner-up got first run on him. When he eventually did get out, though, he failed to make any inroads on their lead. Indeed, he actually lost ground, suggesting the distance was too far.
**Persian Majesty(IRE)** was the highest rated of these and his form when attempting to give Gold Cup winner Papineau 10lb over this course and distance earlier in the year, and his performance behind Doyen at Royal Ascot, looked to give him every chance in this grade. He was fairly weak in the market, though, and never really got a look in, only staying on steadily in the closing stages. He appears to be regressing.
**Compton Bolter(IRE)** paid for mixing it with the trail-blazing Millstreet.
**Persian Lightning(IRE)** never got in a blow for his out-of-form stable. He looks tricky to place off his current mark.
**Millstreet** had been off the track since the Melbourne Cup and weakened quickly after forcing a strong pace

### 4286 OAK TREE STKS (GROUP 3) (F&M) 7f

**2:40** (2:41) (A) 3-Y-O+ **£29,000** (£11,000; £5,500; £2,500) **Stalls** High

Form RPR

1-65 **1** **Phantom Wind (USA)**[13] 3940 3-8-6 98 ........ SDrowne 7 109
(JHMGosden) *hld up in midfield: prog on inner 2f out: plld out ins fnl f: drvn and qcknd to ld nr fin* **16/1**

-255 **2** *1/2* **Nyramba**[54] 2720 3-8-6 107 ........ JFortune 11 107
(JHMGosden) *prom: trckd ldr over 1f out: rdn to ld last 150yds: hdd nr fin* **13/2**

1-60 **3** *1 1/4* **Chic**[44] 2967 4-8-13 97 ........ KFallon 10 104
(SirMichaelStoute) *swtg: racd in rr: effrt 2f out: squeezed through 1f out: rdn and r.o to take 3rd nr fin: too much to do* **10/3**[1]

2110 **4** *1* **Gonfilia (GER)**[44] 2967 4-9-2 103 ........ (t) LDettori 12 104
(SaeedBinSuroor) *lw: led: kicked on 2f out: hdd last 150yds: wkng nr fin* **5/1**[2]

1310 **5** *2* **Golden Nun**[21] 3715 4-9-2 101 ........ (b) KDarley 6 99
(TDEasterby) *t.k.h early: hld up bhd ldrs: rdn over 2f out: kpt on same pce fr over 1f out* **25/1**

11-1 **6** *nk* **Silk Fan (IRE)**[27] 3542 3-8-6 95 ........ DHolland 5 95
(PWHarris) *racd in midfield: effrt on outer over 2f out: unable qck wl over 1f out: one pce after* **5/1**[2]

1100 **7** *1 1/4* **Enchanted**[48] 2903 5-8-13 94 ........ JPMurtagh 1 92
(NACallaghan) *hld up in rr: stl in last trio but gng wl enough 2f out: hmpd 1f out: no ch* **40/1**

-521 **8** *3/4* **Lucky Pipit**[8] 4068 3-8-6 102 ........ MHills 4 90
(BWHills) *s.i.s: sn chsd ldrs: rdn and unable qck wl over 1f out: fdd* **16/1**

6041 **9** *1/2* **Grey Pearl**[35] 3275 5-8-13 86 ........ MFenton 3 88
(MissGayKelleway) *pressed ldr: rdn wl over 1f out: lost pl over 1f out: wkng whn hmpd ins fnl f* **66/1**

15 **10** *1* **Saint Etienne (IRE)**[69] 2308 3-8-6 90 ........ MartinDwyer 9 86
(AMBalding) *a in rr: rdn and struggling wl over 2f out* **25/1**

5463 **11** *1/2* **Dowager**[13] 3940 3-8-6 100 ........ DaneO'Neill 8 84
(RHannon) *a in rr: rdn 3f out: no prog and btn after* **14/1**

2111 **12** *2* **Lucky Spin**[41] 3105 3-8-6 104 ........ RLMoore 2 79
(RHannon) *lw: racd towards rr: rdn 4f out: brief effrt u.p over 2f out: sn wknd* **11/2**[3]

1m 26.1s (-1.93) **Going Correction** -0.05s/f (Good)
**WFA** 3 from 4yo+ 7lb **12** Ran SP% **115.2**
Speed ratings: **109,108,107,105,103 103,101,100,100,99 98,96**CSF £109.83 TOTE £22.80: £5.00, £2.50, £1.50; EX 142.70 Trifecta £1081.60 Pool of £2,742.23 - 1.80 winning tickets..
**Owner** K Abdulla **Bred** Juddmonte Farms Inc **Trained** Manton, Wilts

**FOCUS**
A decent Group Three in which it paid to race next to the far-side rail. Much improved form from Phantom Wind, whose prominence in the market when withdrawn from the 1000 Guineas owed more to potential than achievement.

**NOTEBOOK**
**Phantom Wind(USA)** ◆ was fancied by many as a possible 1000 Guineas winner earlier in the season, but her ordinary performance in the Fred Darling dented those expectations and she was pulled out of the Classic on the morning of the race. It is only now that this well-bred filly has come to herself, and she showed here that she has plenty of ability, quickening up well once switched and winning a shade cosily. Fast ground looks essential to her, she should get a mile, and further success in Group company should be expected.
**Nyramba**, the better fancied of the Gosden duo, enjoyed a nice trip throughout, tracking the leader on the rail. She had just taken the leader's measure when her stable-companion went by her, and this trip probably suits her better than a mile.
**Chic**, who was luckless and almost fell at Royal Ascot, was well supported into favouritism. Her rider did not make very good use of her high draw, though, dropping well back in the pack, which resulted in him having to hope for a gap to appear in the straight. By the time it came and she went in pursuit of the leaders inside the final furlong, the first two had gone beyond recall. Two of her three victories to date have come when tracking the leader, so it is not as if she has to be ridden like this.
**Gonfilia(GER)** did what she does best, which is to set out to make all. She had the draw to assist her in that and ran a solid race under her penalty on ground quicker than ideal.
**Golden Nun** has never won over seven furlongs, although she has run well over the trip on a number of occasions. She had a tough task here under her penalty and in the circumstances this was not a bad effort.
**Silk Fan(IRE)** came to have her chance on the outside but she failed to pick up like the principals. She was stepping up from handicap company and can be given another chance in a slightly lesser grade.
**Enchanted** did not get a clear run just inside the final furlong and would surely have finished closer had she enjoyed an uninterrupted passage. She is difficult to place off her current rating.
**Lucky Spin** was the morning favourite but she could not be given away in the ring and failed to run her race. Her previous efforts suggest she should be forgiven this run and given another chance in Group company.

### 4287 WILLIAM HILL MILE (HERITAGE H'CAP) 1m

**3:15** (3:19) (B) 3-Y-O+ **£58,000** (£22,000; £11,000; £5,000) **Stalls** High

Form RPR

22 **1** **Ancient World (USA)**[58] 2588 4-9-10 **103** ........ LDettori 20 117+
(SaeedBinSuroor) *a wl plcd: eased off rail and qcknd to ld 1f out: rdn out* **9/2**[1]

6052 **2** *1 1/4* **Impeller (IRE)**[3] 4214 5-8-8 **87** ........ SDrowne 19 98
(WRMuir) *lw: trckd ldrs: n.m.r 2f out: prog over 1f out: rdn to chse wnr ins fnl f: no imp* **10/1**

0000 **3** *2* **Tuning Fork**[27] 3539 4-8-10 **89** ........ DHolland 2 95
(JAkehurst) *led: rdn and hdd 1f out: sn outpcd: kpt on* **80/1**

0040 **4** *hd* **El Coto**[6] 4120 4-9-7 **100** ........ SSanders 15 106
(BAMcmahon) *trckd ldrs: rdn 2f out: styd on u.p fnl f* **33/1**

3000 **5** *3/4* **Definite Guest (IRE)**[13] 3937 6-8-2 **80** ow1 ........ JFEgan 4 89+
(RAFahey) *swtchd to inner after s and hld up in last: gd prog on inner over 2f out: nt clr run 1f out: wl hld whn nt clr run nr fin* **66/1**

0024 **6** *nk* **Audience**[13] 3937 4-8-11 **90** ........ (p) JQuinn 14 94
(JAkehurst) *trckd ldng gp: effrt and n.m.r briefly 2f out: styd on same pce fnl f* **14/1**

1003 **7** *3/4* **Uhoomagoo**[6] 4120 6-8-13 **92** ........ (b) NCallan 12 94
(KARyan) *racd in midfield on outer: u.p over 3f out: kpt on gamely fnl 2f: nrst fin* **10/1**

1306 **8** *1/2* **Mystical Girl (USA)**[23] 3641 3-8-7 **94** ........ RFfrench 9 95
(MJohnston) *trckd ldr: rdn whn bmpd 1f out: wknd ins fnl f* **14/1**

6014 **9** *shd* **Pentecost**[20] 3724 5-9-5 **98** ........ MartinDwyer 13 98+
(AMBalding) *t.k.h: n.m.r s and hld up wl in rr: nowhere to to 3f out to over 1f out: fin strly* **10/1**

0013 **10** *1/2* **Unshakable (IRE)**[27] 3539 5-9-1 **94** ........ FNorton 21 93+
(BobJones) *lw: b.hind: hld up in midfield: nt clr run fr over 2f out to jst over 1f out: styd on ins fnl f* **7/1**[2]

3106 **11** *1/2* **Putra Kuantan**[21] 3717 4-9-7 **100** ........ PRobinson 17 103+
(MAJarvis) *lw: chsd ldrs: rdn and cl up 2f out: fdd fnl f: no ch whn bdly hmpd last strides* **9/1**[3]

0240 **12** *1* **Amandus (USA)**[22] 3673 4-9-2 **95** ........ TPQueally 16 91+
(DRLoder) *dwlt: hld up wl in rr: nt clr run over 2f out and again over 1f out: no ch after* **14/1**

2100 **13** *3/4* **Omaha City (IRE)**[3] 4220 10-7-12 **77** oh3 ........ DKinsella 10 71
(BGubby) *pressed ldrs: rdn over 2f out: wknd fnl f* **66/1**

0141 **14** *nk* **Flowerdrum (USA)**[37] 3212 4-8-8 **87** ........ EAhern 11 80
(WJHaggas) *trckd ldng gp: rdn over 2f out: wknd fnl f* **16/1**

0003 **15** *2* **Sawwaah (IRE)**[6] 4122 7-8-1 **80** ........ ANicholls 22 69+
(DNicholls) *b.: t.k.h: hld up in midfield: nt clr run over 2f out: hmpd over 1f out: nt rcvr: hmpd again ins fnl f: eased* **14/1**

0001 **16** *2* **Wing Commander**[5] 4178 5-9-3 **96** 5ex ........ PHanagan 7 80+
(RAFahey) *a towards rr: pushed along over 2f out: keeping on one pce whn nt clr run 1f out: nvr nr ldrs* **20/1**

0000 **17** *1* **Convent Girl (IRE)**[44] 2969 4-8-12 **91** ........ RHavlin 18 73+
(MrsPNDutfield) *t.k.h: hld up wl in rr: nt clr fr over 2f out: no prog fnl f* **100/1**

30-3 **18** *hd* **Battle Chant (USA)**[13] 3937 4-9-9 **102** ........ KFallon 6 83
(MrsAJPerrett) *lw: reluctant to go to post: hld up wl in rr: pushed along over 2f out: no prog* **12/1**

5300 **19** *2 1/2* **Finished Article (IRE)**[27] 3539 7-8-10 **89** ........ DaneO'Neill 1 65
(DRCElsworth) *lw: hld up in rr: effrt on wd outside 3f out: sn rdn and no prog* **33/1**

5020 **20** *4* **Takes Tutu (USA)**[6] 4122 5-7-9 **77** oh3 ........ (b) JFMcDonald(3) 5 43
(KRBurke) *taken down early: racd wd: a in rr: struggling fnl 3f* **100/1**

0020 **21** *12* **Serieux**[13] 3937 5-8-11 **90** ........ KDarley 8 29+
(MrsAJPerrett) *chsd ldrs: rdn and wknd over 2f out: no ch whn squeezed out over 1f out* **50/1**

1m 38.15s (-2.12) **Going Correction** -0.05s/f (Good)
**WFA** 3 from 4yo+ 8lb **21** Ran SP% **127.0**
Speed ratings: **108,106,104,104,103 103,102,102,102,101 101,100,99,99,97 95,94,93,91,87 75**CSF £45.74 CT £3285.67 TOTE £5.40: £2.30, £3.60, £10.20, £6.80; EX 63.70 Trifecta £3810.40 Pool of £5,366.82 - 0.20 winning tickets..

**Owner** Godolphin **Bred** Darley Stud Management, L L C **Trained** Newmarket, Suffolk
■ Stewards Enquiry : J Quinn one-day ban: careless riding (Aug 10)
L Dettori one-day ban: careless riding (Aug 10)

**FOCUS**
One for the draw bores, with the importance of a high-numbered stall and a prominent position once again proving critical over this distance. Ancient World was well placed to avoid the traffic problems that are inevitable in big fields around here and outclassed his rivals, looking a Group horse. Definite Guest and Pentecost are among those who ran much better than their finishing positions.

**NOTEBOOK**
**Ancient World(USA)** had been entered in Group One races earlier this year but his efforts at Windsor and Nottingham had let the stable down and he failed to take up those engagements. Gelded since, he was well drawn and ran out a good winner under top weight, confirming his credentials as a Group-class performer. He handled the quick ground perfectly well despite his best form in France being on softer going.
**Impeller(IRE)** is a tricky horse to win with but this course winner usually runs well here and, from a good draw, he repeated his performance at the track earlier in the week by finishing runner-up again.
**Tuning Fork** has dropped 11lb since joining his new stable this season and this was the first time he has shown his form this year. Getting to the lead from stall two was quite an achievement and preserving enough energy to keep on for third was another. His trainer has a Group Two race in Germany in mind for him now.
**El Coto** does not really want the ground as fast as this and, although he held a good position next to the rail, he was unable to pick up on the quick surface. It was still a good effort under his big weight, though, confirming once again that this type of race brings out the best in him.
**Definite Guest(IRE)** ◆ was poorly drawn and got absolutely no run inside the final two furlongs, finishing the race having never been put under pressure. He would surely have gone close with a clear run and, as he is due to drop 2lb in the handicap, connections will no doubt be on the lookout for an opportunity in the coming days.
**Audience** was another who found the ground quicker than ideal, and he is due to go up 3lb in future handicaps so things are not going to get any easier.
**Uhoomagoo** was forced to challenge wide in the straight, which was not the place to be, but at least he enjoyed an uninterrupted run.
**Mystical Girl(USA)** could not get to the front, where she likes to be, in this big field. *Official explanation: jockey said filly slipped on the bend*
**Pentecost** finished his race with plenty still to offer, having enjoyed no luck in running. He showed enough to suggest that he should remain competitive in handicap company, even off a 2lb higher mark.
**Unshakable(IRE)**, another happier on easier ground, failed to take advantage of his good draw. He should be happier back on a more galloping track, although given the number of times he has been well fancied for these big handicaps, he has to be regarded as something of an unerachiever.
**Amandus(USA)** did not enjoy much luck, although as a rule he is not one for whom excuses should be made.
**Sawwaah(IRE)** was continuously hampered and squeezed up inside the final two furlongs and never got a chance to show what he could do. His style of running does mean that this will happen to him from time to time, though.

## 4288 RICHMOND STKS (GROUP 2) (C&G) 6f
**3:50** (3:51) (A ) 2-Y-O **£40,600** (£15,400; £7,700; £3,500) **Stalls** Low

Form RPR
1 **1** **Montgomery's Arch (USA)**[22] [3664] 2-8-11 ........................ JFortune 5 108
(PWChapple-Hyam) *w'like: scope: sn led: rdn over 1f out: hdd jst ins fnl f: rallied u.p to ld last strides* **13/2**
2123 **2** *nk* **Mystical Land (IRE)**[23] [3640] 2-8-11 ........................ LDettori 4 107
(JHMGosden) *lw: trckd ldr: rdn to ld jst ins fnl f: styd on: hdd last strides* **11/4**[2]
1131 **3** *2* **Silver Wraith (IRE)**[7] [4089] 2-8-11 ........................ JPMurtagh 7 101
(NACallaghan) *hld up and sn in last: plenty to do 2f out: rdn and r.o to take 3rd ins fnl f: nt rch ldng pair* **9/1**
1 **4** *1 ½* **Stetchworth Prince**[23] [3643] 2-8-11 ........................ TPQueally 6 97
(DRLoder) *hld up in tch: effrt 2f out: rdn and one pce over 1f out* **15/2**
212 **5** *2* **Amazin**[21] [3703] 2-8-11 ........................ KFallon 8 91
(RHannon) *t.k.h: trckd ldng pair: rdn 2f out: nt qckn and btn over 1f out* **5/1**[3]
1111 **6** *1 ¾* **Blue Dakota (IRE)**[43] [2996] 2-9-0 ........................ EAhern 1 88
(JNoseda) *lw: plld hrd and restrained bhd ldrs: effrt 2f out: cl enough over 1f out: wknd and eased* **9/4**[1]
0514 **7** *3* **Alpaga Le Jomage (IRE)**[13] [3938] 2-8-11 ........................ JFEgan 2 76
(BJMeehan) *plld hrd: hld up: in tch 2f out: sn wknd* **80/1**
1414 **U** **Obe Gold**[13] [3939] 2-8-11 ........................(v[1]) TEDurcan 3 —
(MRChannon) *lw: t.k.h: hld up in last pair: stmbld and uns rdr after 1f* **33/1**

1m 12.81s (-0.03) **Going Correction** -0.05s/f (Good) **8** Ran SP% **113.4**
Speed ratings: **98,97,94,92,90 87,83,**—CSF £24.31 TOTE £7.90: £2.10, £1.40, £2.10; EX 36.60 Trifecta £112.30 Pool of £2,209.86 - 13.96 winning tickets.
**Owner** Franconson Partners **Bred** Sycamore Hall Farm Llc **Trained** Newmarket, Suffolk
■ Stewards Enquiry : J Fortune caution: used whip without giving colt time to respond

**FOCUS**
The early pace was not strong and that led to one or two, including the favourite, failing to settle. The winning time was therefore moderate for the class. Montgomery's Arch has been rated a little below the average for the race's recent winners but was nevertheless showing much improved form.

**NOTEBOOK**
**Montgomery's Arch(USA)** had won his maiden impressively but the drop back in trip had to be a worry. On the other hand, though, the faster ground looked sure to suit. Sent into the lead, he set his own pace in front and, although headed by the eventual runner-up inside the final furlong, he battled back well to reclaim the race in the last strides. He will surely appreciate a return to seven furlongs, and a step up to a mile in time.
**Mystical Land(IRE)** has improved for the step up to six furlongs but prefers a little ease in the ground, so this surface was probably on the quick side for him. He got to the front inside the last but in the end was just edged out by the rallying winner. He is now likely to head for the Prix Morny, where the ground should be suitable.
**Silver Wraith(IRE)**, a winner of a seven-furlong nursery last time, came from way off the pace to pick up third place prize money. He fully deserves his place in Pattern company now and a return to seven furlongs will clearly be of benefit.
**Stetchworth Prince**, like the winner, came into this race on the back of a debut win in a maiden. He ran a solid enough race without threatening to win, and he will find races at a slightly lower level.
**Amazin** was supported in the market but raced a touch freely and could never land a blow. A faster pace would have suited him but it might just be that he is not up to this class.
**Blue Dakota(IRE)** was held up to get this longer trip but the pace was not strong and as a result he raced keenly in the early stages. He found little at the business end, and the conclusion must be that he is a pure speedball who will be at his best making the running back over the minimum trip.
**Alpaga Le Jomage(IRE)** has plenty of ability but was out of his depth in this grade.

## 4289 TURF CLUB RATED STKS (H'CAP) 5f
**4:25** (4:28) (C ) (0-90,90) 3-Y-O **£9,494** (£3,601; £1,800; £818) **Stalls** Low

Form RPR
0012 **1** **Jimmy Ryan (IRE)**[20] [3723] 3-9-5 **88** ........................ TQuinn 1 101
(TDMcCarthy) *chsd nr side ldrs: drvn to ld jst over 1f out: hanging rt but in command fnl f* **12/1**
3103 **2** *1 ½* **Treasure Cay**[8] [4059] 3-8-10 **79** ........................(t) KDarley 18 87
(PWD'Arcy) *racd in centre: chsd ldrs: rdn over 1f out: r.o to chse wnr ins fnl f: no imp* **20/1**
5560 **3** *1 ¾* **Handsome Cross (IRE)**[29] [3455] 3-8-11 **80** ........................ DaneO'Neill 3 82
(HMorrison) *racd against nr side rail: wl in tch: hrd rdn to chal over 1f out: styd on same pce* **25/1**
1410 **4** *hd* **Icenaslice (IRE)**[16] [3838] 3-8-4 **73** oh7 ........................ RFfrench 5 74
(JJQuinn) *mde most on nr side to over 1f out: nt qckn* **66/1**
-050 **5** *1 ½* **Skyharbor**[27] [3523] 3-8-6 **75** ........................ JFanning 6 71
(DNicholls) *racd nr side: chsd ldrs: rdn and hanging rt fr over 1f out: styd on* **25/1**
-211 **6** *½* **Royal Challenge**[8] [4059] 3-8-7 **76** 3ex ........................ KFallon 21 70
(GAButler) *s.i.s: racd towards rr of centre gp: shkn up 2f out: styd on fnl f: nvr able to chal* **2/1**[1]
0624 **7** *hd* **Rydal (USA)**[13] [3926] 3-9-1 **84** ........................(b) LDettori 9 77
(GAButler) *b.hind: racd nr side in midfield: rdn and kpt on fr over 1f out: n.d* **20/1**
0044 **8** *hd* **Incise**[35] [3273] 3-9-0 **83** ........................ JFortune 19 75
(BJMeehan) *racd centre: prom in gp: rdn and one pce over 1f out* **20/1**
-500 **9** *nk* **Fiddle Me Blue**[53] [2741] 3-8-4 **73** oh1 ........................ JQuinn 22 64
(HMorrison) *racd alone towards far side: on terms to over 1f out: kpt on fnl f* **20/1**
1550 **10** *nk* **Green Manalishi**[5] [4165] 3-9-7 **90** ........................ TEDurcan 20 80
(DWPArbuthnot) *lw: racd centre: hld up bhd ldrs: effrt over 1f out: nt qckn sn after* **13/2**[2]
5000 **11** *hd* **Dolce Piccata**[8] [4059] 3-8-5 **77** ........................(b) JFMcDonald[(3)] 15 66
(BJMeehan) *dwlt and squeezed out sn after s: wl in rr in centre gp: nvr on terms: kpt on* **66/1**
1102 **12** *nk* **Buy On The Red**[8] [4059] 3-8-12 **84** ........................ RMiles[(3)] 16 72
(WRMuir) *racd centre: chsd ldrs: rdn and one pce over 1f out* **10/1**
1036 **13** *hd* **Divine Spirit**[8] [4059] 3-9-2 **85** ........................(p) JFEgan 10 73
(MDods) *racd nr side: in rr: outpcd 1/2-way: styd on ins fnl f: no ch* **12/1**
3043 **14** *nk* **Lualua**[19] [3777] 3-8-6 **75** ........................ PHanagan 8 62
(TDBarron) *lw: s.s: racd nr side: rcvrd to chse ldrs 1/2-way: one pce over 1f out* **33/1**
0055 **15** *1 ¼* **Spanish Ace**[13] [3941] 3-9-4 **87** ........................(v) MartinDwyer 12 69
(AMBalding) *disp ld in centre gp to over 1f out: fdd* **9/1**[3]
0310 **16** *shd* **Silver Prelude**[19] [3777] 3-9-1 **84** ........................ PRobinson 11 66
(DKIvory) *racd mostly in centre: wl on terms tl fdd over 1f out* **25/1**
4022 **17** *nk* **Imperial Echo (USA)**[6] [4133] 3-8-9 **78** ........................(v) NCallan 4 59
(TDBarron) *s.s: racd nr side: nvr on terms w ldrs* **11/1**
-435 **18** *2 ½* **Sessay**[73] [2217] 3-8-4 **73** oh4 ........................ ANicholls 17 45
(DNicholls) *disp ld in centre gp to over 1f out: wknd* **66/1**
0006 **19** *shd* **Imperium**[1] [4267] 3-8-4 **73** oh2 ........................ FNorton 14 44
(MrsStefLiddiard) *racd in centre: outpcd and struggling 3f out: n.d after* **33/1**
3010 **20** *hd* **Hello Roberto**[14] [3894] 3-8-4 **73** oh1 ........................ EAhern 7 44
(MJPolglase) *prom on nr side to 2f out: wknd* **50/1**
0340 **21** *nk* **Harry Up**[48] [2897] 3-9-4 **87** ........................ MFenton 2 56
(JGGiven) *s.i.s: racd nr side: a outpcd* **33/1**

58.05 secs (-1.00) **Going Correction** -0.05s/f (Good) **21** Ran SP% **135.3**
Speed ratings: **106,103,100,100,98 97,96,96,96,95 95,94,94,94,92 91,91,87,87,86 86**CSF £241.65 CT £5936.08 TOTE £12.80: £2.40, £3.60, £7.40, £16.20; EX 345.40.
**Owner** James Ryan **Bred** Barronstown Stud And Orpendale **Trained** Godstone, Surrey

**FOCUS**
There was a bias towards the near-side runners, although those drawn high did not help themselves by failing to tack over to the far rail. The form looks questionable.

**NOTEBOOK**
**Jimmy Ryan(IRE)** has been in great form of late, finishing runner-up to Pivotal Point on his most recent start. He finished strongly to run out a clear winner and, while it is true he had the best of the draw, his profile suggests he is progressive, and he should continue to run well in these cavalry charges.
**Treasure Cay** is a consistent sort. He did well from his moderate draw and was one of only two (the other was the favourite) who got into the first seven from a double-figure stall.
**Handsome Cross(IRE)** enjoyed the advantage of racing next to the stands'-side rail throughout. He kept on well for third and is undoubtedly at his best over the minimum trip. His record over five furlongs currently reads 412323, while over six furlongs or farther it reads 7325560.
**Icenaslice(IRE)** ran a blinder from 7lb out of the handicap, but she is likely to pay for her effort with another rise in the weights.
**Skyharbor** has dropped 13lb in the weights this season and finally put up a more promising effort, although it was disconcerting to see him hang badly right under pressure.
**Royal Challenge**, who was heavily backed, looked to have plenty going for him off just a 1lb higher mark than when successful at Sandown last time. He lost ground with a slow start, though, and although he finally came through to finish second-best of those drawn high, he was never a threat to the principals. A stiffer track may be required, but he will also have to improve as he is due to go up another 4lb.
**Rydal(USA)** found everything happening too quickly over this sharp five furlongs on this quick ground.
**Green Manalishi** seems to have lost his form of late.
**Divine Spirit** had the cheekpieces, which he has worn to success twice before, back on. He has run well on sharp tracks in the past but on this occasion he found everything happening too quickly.
**Imperium** *Official explanation: jockey said gelding lost a shoe*

## 4290 EUROPEAN BREEDERS FUND TRUNDLE MAIDEN STKS (COLTS & GELDING) 7f
**5:00** (5:02) (D ) 2-Y-O **£10,692** (£3,290; £1,645; £822) **Stalls** High

Form RPR
4 **1** **Jonquil (IRE)**[29] [3451] 2-8-11 ........................ JFortune 11 91+
(JHMGosden) *lw: w ldr: led over 4f out: drew clr 2f out: 4l up jst over 1f out: rdn out nr fin: unchal* **7/2**[2]
**2** *1 ½* **Looks Could Kill (USA)** 2-8-11 ........................ KFallon 4 87
(GAButler) *w'like: scope: bkwd: racd in midfield: prog over 2f out: chsd wnr over 1f out: styd on fnl f but nvr able to chal* **11/2**
**3** *hd* **Silent Jo (JPN)** 2-8-11 ........................ LDettori 3 87+
(SaeedBinSuroor) *wlike: bit bkwd: s.i.s: settled in rr: nt clr run and swtchd rt jst over 2f out: r.o to dispute 2nd pl fnl f: nrst fin* **9/2**[3]
**4** *6* **Zamboozle (IRE)** 2-8-11 ........................ DaneO'Neill 5 72
(DRCElsworth) *wlike: scope: bit bkwd: dwlt: wl in rr: effrt on wd outside over 2f out: styd on steadily to take modest 4th ins fnl f* **50/1**

6 **5** 3½ **Silverleaf**[34] [3319] 2-8-11 .......... TEDurcan 8 63
(MRChannon) *chsd ldrs: pushed along 1/2-way: rn green 2f out: wknd over 1f out* **14/1**

**6** 1 **King Marju (IRE)** 2-8-11 .......... AMcCarthy 2 61
(PWChapple-Hyam) *wlike: racd freely: led to over 4f out: chsd wnr to over 1f out: wknd rapidly ins fnl f* **12/1**

**7** shd **My Rascal (IRE)** 2-8-11 .......... RLMoore 6 60
(MJWallace) *wlike: scope: wl in rr: pushed along and struggling 3f out: no ch after* **50/1**

**8** ½ **Election Seeker (IRE)** 2-8-6 .......... AQuinn(5) 12 59
(GLMoore) *str: wlike: rn green in rr: reminder over 2f out: sme prog wl over 1f out: wknd sn after* **50/1**

2 **9** 1½ **Ground Rules (USA)**[28] [3483] 2-8-11 .......... PRobinson 9 55
(BWHills) *lw: squeezed out s: sn chsd ldrs: pushed along 3f out: no prog 2f out: wknd* **11/4**[1]

**10** 4 **Art Elegant** 2-8-11 .......... MartinDwyer 10 45
(BWHills) *unf: tall: chsd ldng pair tl wknd rapidly 2f out* **14/1**

4 **11** 5 **Highest Return (USA)**[11] [3974] 2-8-11 .......... JFanning 1 33
(MJohnston) *edgy: chsd ldng pair tl wknd rapidly 2f out* **16/1**

**12** 13 **Primed Up (IRE)** 2-8-11 .......... EAhern 7 —
(GLMoore) *leggy: dwlt: a wl bhd: t.o* **50/1**

1m 28.07s (0.04) **Going Correction** -0.05s/f (Good) **12 Ran SP% 117.2**
Speed ratings: **97,95,95,88,84 83,82,82,80,76 70,55**CSF £22.51 TOTE £5.10: £1.90, £2.20, £1.70; EX 28.60.
**Owner** Sheikh Mohammed **Bred** Ballygallon Stud **Trained** Manton, Wilts

**FOCUS**
Almost certainly strong maiden form, and the first three, who pulled nicely clear, will not need to improve much to hold their own in Listed company.

**NOTEBOOK**
**Jonquil(IRE)** had the benefit of previous racecourse experience and a good draw to boot. He made plenty of use of it, too, racing towards the fore from the off. It is true that he got first run on the eventual second and third, but he won well enough, and one can see why his trainer is planning to step him up to Listed company next.
**Looks Could Kill(USA)**, whose dam was a smart mile to ten-furlong performer, was well backed for his debut. He stayed on well to finish runner-up to a colt with previous experience, and should not be long in going one better.
**Silent Jo(JPN)** ◆, who cost the equivalent of £365,000 when bought as a yearling in Japan, shaped with a good deal of promise, running on well for third having had his challenge delayed and been forced to race wide. He was weak in the market beforehand, suggesting this run was expected to bring him on, and there is almost certainly more to come.
**Zamboozle(IRE)**, whose dam is a half-sister to high-class middle-distance stayers Azzilfi and Khamaseen, is going to appreciate a mile this year. He was putting in some nice work at the finish and will improve with racing.
**Silverleaf**, who is still green, could be a nursery type after one more run.
**King Marju(IRE)**, whose dam is a half-sister to high-class juvenile sprinter Cayman Kai (later placed in the Irish 2000 Guineas), raced freely in front and showed promise for the future. He might be worth dropping back to six.
**Ground Rules(USA)**, whose stable is not really firing at present, could not build on his promising debut, which came on easier ground, and failed to land a blow.

## 4291 STEWARDS' SPRINT STKS (H'CAP) 6f
5:35 (5:37) (B) 3-Y-0+ **£13,108** (£4,972; £2,486; £1,130) **Stalls Low**

Form RPR

0004 **1** **Merlin's Dancer**[2] [4232] 4-9-5 **80** .......... ANicholls 5 96
(DNicholls) *swtg: b.hind: racd against nr side rail: mde virtually all: clr fnl f: drvn out* **10/1**

3412 **2** 1¼ **High Ridge**[2] [4244] 5-8-7 **68** .......... (p) FNorton 4 80
(JMBradley) *racd against nr side rail: wl in rr of gp: rdn over 2f out: prog over 1f out: styd on strly to take 2nd nr fin* **9/1**[3]

0005 **3** ½ **Dame De Noche**[11] [3976] 4-9-10 **85** .......... NCallan 2 96
(JGGiven) *cl up nr side: chsd wnr 1/2-way: no imp 1f out: flashed tail ins fnl f: lost 2nd nr fin* **16/1**

6103 **4** 1¼ **Albashoosh**[31] [3400] 6-8-9 **70** .......... TEDurcan 26 77+
(DNicholls) *dwlt: racd far side: in rr tl prog 1/2-way: led gp wl over 1f out: clr fnl f: no ch w ldn trio nr side* **12/1**

6020 **5** ½ **Romany Nights (IRE)**[9] [4011] 4-9-3 **78** .......... (b) DSweeney 11 83
(JWUnett) *trckd nr side ldrs: rdn 2f out: hanging and nt qckn over 1f out: styd on ins fnl f* **40/1**

1330 **6** ¾ **Hard To Catch (IRE)**[19] [3778] 6-9-0 **80** .......... (b) MSavage(5) 1 83
(DKIvory) *racd nr side: wl in rr of gp: rdn over 2f out: r.o fr jst over 1f out: nrst fin* **40/1**

0051 **7** 1½ **Ballybunion (IRE)**[5] [4181] 5-7-12 **59** oh6 .......... PHanagan 25 58+
(DNicholls) *racd in midfield of far side gp: hrd rdn to chse gp ldr over 1f out: no imp fnl f: kpt on* **16/1**

0503 **8** 1½ **Pays D'Amour (IRE)**[6] [4154] 7-8-3 **64** .......... (t) PDoe 13 58
(DNicholls) *racd on outer of nr side gp: in tch: edgd rt fnl 2f: one pce fnl f* **66/1**

0230 **9** hd **Idle Power (IRE)**[13] [3941] 6-9-2 **77** .......... (p) MartinDwyer 21 70+
(JRBoyle) *dwlt: racd far side: trckd ldrs: one pce fr over 1f out* **14/1**

0000 **10** shd **Online Investor**[2] [4232] 5-8-3 **64** .......... EAhern 3 57
(DNicholls) *racd nr side: wl in rr: swtchd rt 2f out: nt clr run over 1f out: drvn and kpt on fnl f* **12/1**

0630 **11** ½ **Currency**[9] [4034] 7-9-1 **76** .......... (b[1]) JFEgan 15 68
(JMBradley) *b. trckd nr side ldrs: cl up 2f out: sn nt qckn u.p : fdd fnl f* **33/1**

4441 **12** shd **Undeterred**[5] [4179] 8-8-13 **74** 3ex .......... KDarley 19 65+
(TDBarron) *towards rr of far side gp: effrt 2f out: one pce and nvr able to chal* **13/2**[2]

0060 **13** ½ **Attorney**[15] [3864] 6-7-12 **59** oh13 .......... (v) DKinsella 8 49
(DShaw) *racd in midfield nr side: rdn and nt qckn 2f out: no prog after* **66/1**

1310 **14** ¾ **Parkside Pursuit**[14] [3920] 6-9-0 **75** .......... RLMoore 24 63+
(JMBradley) *wl in rr far side: effrt 2f out: chsd ldrs over 1f out: no prog fnl f* **25/1**

0002 **15** shd **Time To Remember (IRE)**[2] [4232] 6-7-12 **59** oh2 .......... RFfrench 6 46
(DNicholls) *b.hind: swtg: chsd wnr nr side to 1/2-way: wknd over 1f out* **10/1**

0000 **16** shd **Pax**[5] [4165] 7-9-8 **83** .......... AlexGreaves 7 70
(DNicholls) *s.s: racd nr side and sn in midfield: outpcd over 2f out: effrt and nt clr run over 1f out: no ch after* **33/1**

3210 **17** 1¼ **Lord Of The East**[6] [4152] 5-8-13 **74** .......... JFanning 23 57+
(DNicholls) *mde most on far side to wl over 1f out: grad wknd* **16/1**

604 **18** hd **Obe One**[14] [3920] 4-8-2 **68** .......... PPMathers(5) 12 51
(ABerry) *racd in midfield nr side: hrd rdn over 2f out: hanging rt and wknd over 1f out* **20/1**

2240 **19** ¾ **Devon Flame**[13] [3941] 5-8-11 **75** .......... JFMcDonald(3) 18 55+
(RJHodges) *lw: w far side ldr tl wknd wl over 1f out* **33/1**

6020 **20** nk **Plateau**[5] [4165] 5-9-9 **84** .......... JFortune 20 63+
(DNicholls) *restless stalls: racd in rr of far side gp: no reel prog fnl 2f* **16/1**

6000 **21** ½ **Long Weekend (IRE)**[48] [2885] 6-7-12 **59** oh16 .......... JoannaBadger 10 37
(DShaw) *racd nr side: wl in rr of gp: hanging rt fr 2f out: no prog* **100/1**

1055 **22** shd **Loyal Tycoon (IRE)**[6] [4152] 6-9-2 **82** 3ex .......... LTreadwell(5) 17 60+
(DNicholls) *w far side ldrs for 4f: nt qckn over 1f out: eased ins fnl f* **6/1**[1]

003 **23** 1½ **Prince Of Blues (IRE)**[2] [4244] 6-7-12 **59** .......... (b) SRighton 16 32+
(MMullineaux) *w far side ldrs for 4f: wknd* **66/1**

0350 **24** ½ **Sir Don (IRE)**[9] [4013] 5-8-3 **67** ow1 .......... (v) LPKeniry(3) 14 39
(DNicholls) *dwlt: racd on outer of nr side gp: chsd ldrs tl wknd 2f out* **66/1**

0050 **25** 8 **Landing Strip (IRE)**[26] [3558] 4-8-11 **72** .......... DaneO'Neill 9 20
(JMPEustace) *s.s: racd nr side: a in rr: hanging rt and wknd over 1f out* **66/1**

0000 **26** 2 **Turibius**[9] [4034] 5-8-12 **78** .......... AQuinn(5) 22 20+
(TEPowell) *trckd far side ldrs tl wknd over 1f out: heavily eased ins fnl f* **33/1**

1m 11.47s (-1.37) **Going Correction** -0.05s/f (Good) **26 Ran SP% 135.1**
Speed ratings: **107,105,104,103,102 101,99,97,97,96 96,96,95,94,94 94,92,92,91,90 90,90,88,87,76 74**CSF £91.46 CT £933.90 TOTE £10.00: £2.20, £3.50, £4.80, £5.40; EX 129.90 Place 6 £425.57, Place 5 £275.60.
**Owner** Chalfont Foodhalls Ltd **Bred** Cheveley Park Stud Ltd **Trained** Sessay, N Yorks

**FOCUS**
As in the five-furlong race earlier on the card, it proved an advantage to be drawn low, with three of the five bottom stalls filling the first three places, although once again those drawn high failed to race right next to the far rail, where the ground traditionally rides quicker. The form looks strong.

**NOTEBOOK**
**Merlin's Dancer**, who 'won' the race on the far side in the five-furlong sprint earlier in the week, is more effective over this trip, and on this occasion he had been handed a better draw. Bagging the valuable near-side rail, he made almost all the running to run out a clear winner, and he is clearly in top form at present.
**High Ridge** followed the winner through on the stands'-side rail, putting in his best work at the finish as usual. He has been running well all season and is clearly well suited by a quick surface.
**Dame De Noche**, another to benefit from being drawn low and racing towards the stands' side, ran well under her big weight and looks to be returning to form.
**Albashoosh** ◆, first home on the far side, 'won' his race by a fair margin. He was rated in the mid 80s in the spring of last year and has dropped to a mark which can now be exploited. He will soon be winning.
**Romany Nights(IRE)**, although largely consistent, has proved time and time again that he is very difficult to win with.
**Hard To Catch(IRE)**, a Brighton specialist, has a mixed record here. He stayed on without ever troubling the leaders on this occasion.
**Ballybunion(IRE)** finished second-best on the far side. He came here in good form, having won last time out, but he had to race from 6lb out of the handicap, and in the circumstances this was a good effort.
**Online Investor** travelled well but was taken towards the centre of the track in search of a gap inside the final two furlongs. It did not come and he was hampered when attempting to squeeze through. He finished well afterwards, though, and he still remains of interest for a contest of this nature.
**Undeterred**, last year's winner off a 1lb lower mark, found himself drawn on the wrong side, but he was still disappointing.
**Loyal Tycoon(IRE)** *Official explanation: jockey said gelding ran flat*
**Landing Strip(IRE)** *Official explanation: jockey said gelding mised the break*
T/Jkpt: Not won. T/Plt: £438.20 to a £1 stake. Pool: £167,653.84. 279.25 winning tickets. T/Qpdt: £158.40 to a £1 stake. Pool: £7,258.15. 33.90 winning tickets. JN

# 4169 NEWMARKET (JULY) (R-H)
## Friday, July 30

**OFFICIAL GOING: Good to firm**
A hot day ensured the ground was on the fast side, although, most of the races were slowly run.
Wind: Slight across Weather: Hot and sunny

## 4292 TURFTOURS.COM MEDIAN AUCTION MAIDEN STKS 7f
6:05 (6:06) (E) 2-Y-O **£3,516** (£1,082; £541; £270) **Stalls High**

Form RPR

3 **1** **Fongtastic**[13] [3946] 2-9-0 .......... DHolland 17 85
(BJMeehan) *mde all stands' side: rdn over 1f out: r.o* **9/2**[2]

**2** 2 **Spear (IRE)** 2-8-11 .......... ABeech(3) 1 80
(DRLoder) *racd far side: hld up: hdwy over 2f out: hung rt over 1f out: r.o* **14/1**

2 **3** nk **Frith (IRE)**[24] [3601] 2-9-0 .......... MHills 3 79
(BWHills) *led far side: rdn over 1f out: styd on* **10/11**[1]

**4** ¾ **House Martin** 2-8-9 .......... RMullen 16 72
(AMBalding) *racd stands' side: s.i.s: hld up: nt clr run over 2f out: swtchd lft and hdwy over 1f out: nt rch ldrs* **25/1**

56 **5** 1½ **Traianos (USA)**[14] [3913] 2-8-9 .......... NDeSouza(5) 8 73
(PFICole) *chsd ldr far side: rdn over 1f out: styd on same pce* **25/1**

**6** ½ **Kristinor (FR)** 2-9-0 .......... JPMurtagh 14 72
(JRFanshawe) *racd stands' side: hld up: swtchd lft and hdwy over 2f out: hung lft over 1f out: hung rt ins fnl f: nvr trbld ldrs* **11/2**[3]

**7** 1¼ **Fantasy Ride** 2-9-0 .......... RPrice 10 69
(JPearce) *racd stands' side: chsd ldrs: rdn over 2f out: wknd over 1f out* **66/1**

2 **8** 1 **Danehill Willy (IRE)**[8] [4064] 2-9-0 .......... PDobbs 6 67
(NACallaghan) *racd far side: hld up: r.o ins fnl f: nvr nrr* **12/1**

**9** 2½ **Akraan** 2-8-9 .......... RHills 15 55
(EALDunlop) *racd stands' side: chsd ldrs over 5f* **16/1**

**10** 1¾ **Mink Mitten** 2-8-9 .......... (t) SWhitworth 5 51
(DJDaly) *racd far side: dwlt: hld up: hdwy over 2f out: wknd over 1f out* **50/1**

0 **11** shd **Hows That**[14] [3918] 2-8-9 .......... GCarter 11 51
(PJMcbride) *racd stands' side: chsd ldrs: rdn over 2f out: sn wknd* **66/1**

4 **12** nk **Tombola (FR)**[36] [3241] 2-9-0 .......... TQuinn 12 55
(JLDunlop) *racd stands' side: hld up in tch: rdn 1/2-way: wknd wl over 1f out* **16/1**

0 **13** 2 **Royal Abigail (IRE)**[27] [3532] 2-8-9 .......... WRyan 4 45
(EALDunlop) *racd far side: chsd ldrs over 5f* **66/1**

**14** 6 **Patau** 2-8-11 .......... DCorby(3) 9 35
(MJWallace) *racd stands' side: chsd ldrs: rdn 1/2-way: wknd over 2f out* **33/1**

0 **15** 9 **Bregaglia**[35] [3259] 2-8-9 .......... MHenry 7 7
(RMHCowell) *racd far side: chsd ldrs over 4f* **66/1**

16 *nk* **Assured (IRE)** 2-8-9 ........................ PaulEddery 13 7
(PWD'Arcy) *racd stands' side: dwlt: outpcd* **50/1**

1m 26.73s (-0.04) **Going Correction** +0.10s/f (Good) **16** Ran SP% **132.6**
Speed ratings: **104,101,101,100,98 98,96,95,92,90 90,90,88,81,70 70**CSF £67.78 TOTE £6.20: £1.90, £3.30, £1.30; EX 103.20.
**Owner** Stephen Dartnell **Bred** F C T Wilson **Trained** Upper Lambourn, Berks

**FOCUS**
This looked quite a hot heat for the grade and represents decent maiden form. The field split into two equal groups, but there was no bias.

**NOTEBOOK**
**Fongtastic** had clearly learnt from his debut and was very professional this time. A scopey colt, he looks sure to add to this.
**Spear(IRE)** ◆, who is out of a mare that won over 12 furlongs, was very green and looks sure to have learnt plenty from the experience.
**Frith(IRE)** was far from disgraced, and with improvement to come over a mile, should find plenty of opportunities in the coming months.
**House Martin**, whose dam won over five furlongs as a three-year-old, didn't have the best of runs and can be expected to find plenty of improvement from this.
**Traianos(USA)** was again found wanting, but will have more options open to him now in nurseries.
**Kristinor(FR)**, from the same family as the high-class Pursuit Of Love, was edgy and colty in the preliminaries and looked far from a straightforward ride.
**Fantasy Ride** didn't shape at all badly and will certainly find easier openings than he faced here.
**Danehill Willy(IRE)** was doing his best work in the closing stages and already looks to need a mile. There are races to be won with him.

## 4293 TURFTOURS.COM GO RACING IN PARIS H'CAP 1m
**6:35** (6:35) (D) (0-80,78) 3-Y-O+ **£5,460** (£1,680; £840; £420) **Stalls** High

Form RPR
0435 **1** **Habshan (USA)**[27] [3536] 4-9-1 **67** ........................ DHolland 9 77
(NAGraham) *chsd ldrs: nt clr run over 1f out: hmpd 1f out: r.o to ld towards fin* **7/2**[1]
0020 **2** *nk* **Qualitair Wings**[11] [3982] 5-9-6 **72** ........................ DMcGaffin 6 81
(JHetherton) *s.s: hld up: racd keenly: hdwy over 2f out: rdn: hung rt and led 1f out: hdd towards fin* **10/1**
6034 **3** *1* **African Sahara (USA)**[5] [4164] 5-9-12 **78** ........................ (t) GCarter 7 85
(MissDMountain) *hld up: nt clr run over 1f out: r.o ins fnl f: nt rch ldrs* **7/2**[1]
6265 **4** *½* **Topton (IRE)**[15] [3869] 10-9-11 **77** ........................ (b) JPMurtagh 8 83
(PHowling) *trckd ldrs: rdn over 2f out: nt clr run and stmbld 1f out: styd on same pce ins fnl f* **5/1**[3]
0200 **5** *3 ½* **Tiber Tiger (IRE)**[24] [3597] 4-9-9 **78** ........................ (b) J-PGuillambert[(3)] 5 76
(NPLittmoden) *hld up: racd keenly: outpcd 3f out: nt clr run over 1f out: n.d* **13/2**
0231 **6** *nk* **Boundless Prospect (USA)**[14] [3910] 5-9-11 **77** ........................ MHills 3 74
(JWHills) *chsd ldr: rdn and ev ch whn bdly hmpd 1f out: nt rcvr* **4/1**[2]
06/0 **7** *¾* **Garden Society (IRE)**[41] [3090] 7-9-4 **70** ........................ WRyan 1 65
(WAO'Gorman) *prom: ev ch 2f out: hmpd over 1f out: sn wknd* **25/1**
430 **8** *hd* **Kabeer**[28] [3487] 6-9-4 **70** ........................ RMullen 4 65
(PSMcentee) *set stdy pce: qcknd 3f out: hung lft and hdd 1f out: sn btn* **20/1**

1m 41.99s (1.51) **Going Correction** +0.10s/f (Good) **8** Ran SP% **112.1**
Speed ratings: **96,95,94,94,90 90,89,89**CSF £37.19 CT £128.69 TOTE £4.40: £1.70, £3.40, £1.70; EX 52.10.
**Owner** Alan & Jill Smith **Bred** Darley Stud Management, L L C **Trained** Newmarket, Suffolk

**FOCUS**
A messy contest with no pace on and plenty of trouble in the dip. Unreliable form.

**NOTEBOOK**
**Habshan(USA)** confirmed recent promise, but not without a few anxious moments and would have been an unlucky loser. With his trainer giving up shortly he is set to join Chris Wall.
**Qualitair Wings**, without the headgear this time, showed a bit more sparkle but, he lacks consistency.
**African Sahara(USA)** didn't have the strong pace he needs and had no luck in running.
**Topton(IRE)** was unsuited by the lack of pace and was done no favours by running into the back of Boundless Prospect in the dip.
**Tiber Tiger(IRE)** wasn't suited to the lack of pace and never got competitive.
**Boundless Prospect(USA)** was still in with a shout when almost brought down entering the final furlong.

## 4294 BREEDERS CUP IN TEXAS WITH TURFTOURS H'CAP 6f
**7:05** (7:08) (C) (0-90,89) 3-Y-O+ **£9,548** (£2,938; £1,469; £734) **Stalls** High

Form RPR
2114 **1** **Jonny Ebeneezer**[4] [4188] 5-8-10 **71** 7ex ........................ (b) LDettori 6 86+
(DFlood) *trckd ldrs: plld hrd: nt clr run over 1f out: qcknd to ld wl ins fnl f* **13/8**[1]
5300 **2** *1 ¼* **Beauvrai**[13] [3945] 4-8-11 **72** ........................ (p) MTebbutt 10 80
(VSmith) *hld up: nt clr run over 1f out: sn rdn and ev ch: r.o* **20/1**
2053 **3** *hd* **Snow Bunting**[6] [4130] 6-7-5 **59** oh1 ........................ LeanneKershaw[(7)] 3 66
(JeddO'Keeffe) *hld up: hdwy over 3f out: rdn to ld ins fnl f: sn hdd: kpt on* **6/1**[3]
-000 **4** *2* **Boleyn Castle (USA)**[7] [4091] 7-9-11 **89** ........................ LFletcher[(3)] 4 90
(PSMcentee) *set stdy pce: qcknd 1/2-way: hdd and no ex ins fnl f* **50/1**
4500 **5** *shd* **Fearby Cross (IRE)**[34] [3321] 8-8-3 **64** ........................ RMullen 8 65
(WJMusson) *hld up: hdwy fnl f: nt trble ldrs* **9/1**
210/ **6** *½* **Desert Lord**[650] [5370] 4-9-9 **84** ........................ JPMurtagh 5 83
(SirMichaelStoute) *hld up in tch: outpcd 1/2-way: effrt over 1f out: nt trble ldrs* **6/1**[3]
0004 **7** *hd* **Juste Pour L'Amour**[7] [4090] 4-8-9 **70** ........................ DHolland 2 69
(PLGilligan) *chsd ldrs: rdn over 2f out: wknd ins fnl f* **16/1**
0054 **8** *nk* **Starbeck (IRE)**[15] [3867] 6-9-8 **83** ........................ PMcCabe 7 81
(PHowling) *s.s: hld up: hdwy 2f out: rdn over 1f out: wknd ins fnl f* **20/1**
2521 **9** *½* **Tony The Tap**[1] [4267] 3-9-2 **87** 7ex ........................ DFox[(5)] 9 83
(NACallaghan) *trckd ldrs: nt clr run fr over 1f out: nvr able to chal* **7/2**[2]
-010 **10** *1* **Corps De Ballet (IRE)**[24] [3598] 3-9-8 **88** ........................ TQuinn 1 81
(JLDunlop) *chsd ldr: rdn and ev ch over 1f out: looked hld whn bmpd ins fnl f* **16/1**

1m 12.26s (-1.06) **Going Correction** +0.10s/f (Good)
**WFA** 3 from 4yo+ 5lb **10** Ran SP% **122.1**
Speed ratings: **111,109,109,106,106 105,105,104,104,102**CSF £43.99 CT £177.50 TOTE £2.50: £1.20, £5.40, £2.10; EX 72.70.
**Owner** Mrs Ruth M Serrell **Bred** John Purcell **Trained** Upper Lambourn, Berks

**FOCUS**
They didn't appear to go that quick here, but the overall time looked respectable and the form is fair.

**NOTEBOOK**
**Jonny Ebeneezer** is much happier on turf and bounced back with an impressive turn of foot. He is rocketing back up the handicap, but when he is in this sort of form his style of running makes him hard to get to grips with. He goes particularly well for Dettori, who rides him with plenty of confidence.
**Beauvrai**, who has yet to stike on turf, didn't have the best of runs, but still turned in a solid effort.
**Snow Bunting** was caught wide from his low draw and was a little keen with no cover. In the circumstances this was a fine effort and he is clearly on good terms with himself at present.
**Boleyn Castle(USA)**, who two years ago was winning off a 19lb higher mark, had no excuse.
**Fearby Cross(IRE)** would have preferred a stronger pace over this trip.
**Desert Lord**, last seen in the Dewhurst almost two years ago, looked a little ring-rusty. He must have given the right signs at home to have been kept in training and, providing he remains sound, should be capable of making his mark off his current rating.
**Tony The Tap**, none the worse for winning at Epsom the previous night, was all dressed up with nowhere to go and can be rated as having finished among the places. *Official explanation: jockey said gelding never got a run*
**Corps De Ballet(IRE)** *Official explanation: jockey said saddle slipped*

## 4295 TURFTOURS.COM FOR SPORTING HOSPITALITY CONDITIONS STKS 7f
**7:35** (7:40) (C) 2-Y-O **£7,273** (£2,758; £1,379; £627) **Stalls** High

Form RPR
112 **1** **Brecon Beacon**[41] [3071] 2-9-1 ........................ JPMurtagh 2 101
(PFICole) *mde all: rdn and hung lft fr over 1f out: r.o* **5/2**[1]
1 **2** *¾* **Perfectperformance (USA)**[36] [3240] 2-9-1 ........................ LDettori 8 99
(SaeedBinSuroor) *trckd ldrs: rdn over 2f out: r.o ins fnl f* **5/2**[1]
21 **3** *1 ¼* **In The Fan (USA)**[15] [3870] 2-8-11 ........................ TQuinn 1 92
(JLDunlop) *trckd wnr: rdn over 2f out: styd on* **8/1**
1 **4** *nk* **Visionist (IRE)**[20] [3758] 2-8-11 ........................ DHolland 4 91
(JAOsborne) *a.p: rdn and ev ch over 1f out: no ex towards fin* **6/1**[3]
3 **5** *¾* **Bunny Rabbit (USA)**[32] [3373] 2-8-11 ........................ MHills 6 89
(BJMeehan) *hld up: nt clr run and outpcd over 1f out: styd on ins fnl f: nt trble ldrs* **40/1**
010 **6** *1 ¼* **Perfect Choice (IRE)**[41] [3071] 2-9-1 ........................ WRyan 3 90
(BJMeehan) *a.p: rdn over 1f out: no ex ins fnl f* **33/1**
**7** *1 ¼* **Diktatorial** 2-8-9 ........................ RMullen 9 81
(AMBalding) *hld up: rdn over 2f out: n.d* **50/1**
1 **8** *¾* **Liakoura (GER)**[20] [3749] 2-9-1 ........................ KDarley 5 85
(MrsAJPerrett) *hld up: rdn over 2f out: wknd over 1f out* **11/4**[2]

1m 25.89s (-0.88) **Going Correction** +0.10s/f (Good) **8** Ran SP% **116.5**
Speed ratings: **109,108,106,106,105 104,102,101**CSF £9.17 TOTE £3.50: £1.20, £1.50, £2.00; EX 6.80.
**Owner** Elite Racing Club **Bred** Elite Racing Club **Trained** Whatcombe, Oxon

**FOCUS**
This looked a useful contest, with six of the eight runners having already won, and it was run in 0.84 seconds faster than the earlier maiden. The form looks reasonably solid, with the winner reproducing his Ascot form and the runner-up improving a couple of lengths on his Salisbury debut.

**NOTEBOOK**
**Brecon Beacon** had something of a soft time up front, but showed the right attitude at the business end. With improvement to come over an extra furlong he should find other openings.
**Perfectperformance(USA)**, who wore a rug for stalls entry, was loaded early and was probably in the stalls for the best part of seven minutes. He lacked the experience of the winner, but he stuck to his task well and already looks to need a stiffer test.
**In The Fan(USA)** got warm at the start and gave trouble loading into the stalls. He was a little keen early on and would have preferred a stronger pace, but he stayed on well enough up the hill in a manner which suggested he will have no trouble staying an extra furlong.
**Visionist(IRE)** left the impression this trip was far enough for him at this stage of his career.
**Bunny Rabbit(USA)** looked to face a stiff task, but he comes out of this with plenty of credit and may have done better still had he anything like a clear run. A maiden should be a formality. *Official explanation: jockey said colt never got a clear run*
**Perfect Choice(IRE)** didn't quite see this trip out and may be better at six furlongs for the time being.
**Diktatorial**faced a very stiff introduction, and it can't have helped that he was in the stalls for about seven minutes.
**Liakoura(GER)** was difficult to load and ran no sort of race. This effort can be forgotten. *Official explanation: trainer had no explanation for the poor form shown*

## 4296 TURFTOURS.COM GO RACING IN BARBADOS EBF MAIDEN STKS 6f
**8:05** (8:05) (D) 2-Y-O **£4,745** (£1,460; £730; £365) **Stalls** High

Form RPR
**1** **Sun Kissed (JPN)** 2-9-0 ........................ LDettori 2 85+
(SaeedBinSuroor) *chsd ldrs: rdn to ld wl ins fnl f* **3/1**[2]
2 **2** *nk* **Daniel Thomas (IRE)**[34] [3319] 2-9-0 ........................ KDarley 3 84+
(MrsAJPerrett) *chsd ldr: rdn to ld 1f out: hdd wl ins fnl f* **5/6**[1]
35 **3** *1* **My Princess (IRE)**[44] [2972] 2-8-4 ........................ DFox[(5)] 1 75
(NACallaghan) *led 5f: styd on same pce* **16/1**
**4** *¾* **Haunting Memories (IRE)** 2-9-0 ........................ PRobinson 4 77
(MAJarvis) *hld up in tch: nt clr run ins fnl f: nvr able to chal* **8/1**
**5** *7* **Walkonthewildside** 2-9-0 ........................ TPQueally 5 53
(DRLoder) *hld up: wknd over 2f out* **11/2**[3]

1m 15.7s (2.38) **Going Correction** +0.10s/f (Good) **5** Ran SP% **111.9**
Speed ratings: **88,87,86,85,75**CSF £6.07 TOTE £2.80: £1.50, £1.30; EX 4.30.
**Owner** Godolphin **Bred** Gainsborough Stud Management Ltd **Trained** Newmarket, Suffolk

**FOCUS**
As was the norm for much of the evening, a slowly run contest. The form may well prove misleading.

**NOTEBOOK**
**Sun Kissed(JPN)**, who is from the same family as the high-class Commander Collins, showed a nice turn of foot to wear down the favourite in the closing stages. Bred to stay further the race was hardly run to suit, but he is clearly a useful colt with a bright future.
**Daniel Thomas(IRE)** hardly had the race run to suit on this drop in trip.
**My Princess(IRE)** had a soft time of things up front and is flattered by this effort. She should have more luck in nurseries.
**Haunting Memories(IRE)**, who is out of a mare that enjoyed plenty of success in Italy, didn't shape at all badly and will certainly be wiser next time.
**Walkonthewildside**, who is out of a mare that won a Group 1 as a juvenile, looks as though he will need time.

## 4297 TURFTOURS.COM PRIX DE L'ARC DE TRIOMPHE H'CAP 1m 4f
**8:35** (8:36) (D) (0-80,80) 3-Y-O+ **£5,421** (£1,668; £834; £417) **Stalls** Centre

Form RPR
0223 **1** **Stolen Hours (USA)**[22] [3658] 4-8-11 **63** ........................ JQuinn 3 72
(JAkehurst) *hld up in tch: jnd ldr over 5f out: led over 3f out: styd on wl* **11/4**[2]
030 **2** *1 ½* **Gift Voucher (IRE)**[14] [3922] 3-9-2 **80** ........................ (t) KFallon 5 86+
(SirMichaelStoute) *sn led: hdd over 3f out: sn rdn: outpcd over 1f out: styd on ins fnl f* **2/1**[1]
6230 **3** *nk* **Piri Piri (IRE)**[35] [3274] 4-9-1 **67** ........................ SWhitworth 1 73
(PJMcbride) *hld up: hdwy to chse wnr over 2f out: rdn over 1f out: no ex ins fnl f* **7/2**

5300 **4** *2* **Distant Cousin**[34] [3300] 7-8-6 **58**..........(v) RMullen 4 61
(MABuckley) *prom: rdn over 2f out: wknd fnl f* **9/1**

260- **5** *7* **Jasmick (IRE)**[273] [5852] 6-9-7 **76**.......... LFletcher(3) 2 71+
(HMorrison) *chsd ldr over 8f: rdn over 1f out: wknd fnl f* **10/3**[3]

2m 38.03s (5.07) **Going Correction** +0.10s/f (Good)
**WFA** 3 from 4yo+ 12lb **5** Ran SP% **115.3**
Speed ratings: **87,86,85,84,79**CSF £9.16 TOTE £3.90: £1.60, £1.60; EX 7.40 Place 6 £5.27, Place 5 £4.03.
**Owner** A D Spence **Bred** Allen E Paulson **Trained** Epsom, Surrey

**FOCUS**
This didn't look the strongest of races and the pace was moderate.

**NOTEBOOK**
**Stolen Hours(USA)** wasn't winning out of turn and got first run on his rivals, which made the difference in the end.
**Gift Voucher(IRE)** was making his handicap debut. He may do better with some cover in a strongly run race, so deserves another chance to confirm the promise he showed at Kempton on his second start.
**Piri Piri(IRE)** again failed to get home and has become a disappointing filly.
**Distant Cousin** continues to struggle, despite his declining mark.
**Jasmick(IRE)** ran as though the race was needed.
T/Plt: £6.40 to a £1 stake. Pool: £42,715.00. 4,804.05 winning tickets. T/Qpdt: £3.00 to a £1 stake. Pool: £2,611.80. 642.90 winning tickets. CR

## 4137 NOTTINGHAM (L-H)
Friday, July 30

**OFFICIAL GOING: Good to firm (good in places)**

### 4298 EUROPEAN BREEDERS FUND MAIDEN FILLIES' STKS 5f 13y
**6:20** (6:20) (D ) 2-Y-O **£5,655** (£1,740; £870; £435) **Stalls** High

Form RPR

4 **1** **All For Laura**[55] [2690] 2-8-11 .......... TPQueally 1 86
(DRLoder) *wnt lft s: sn cl up: led 2f out: pushed clr over 1f out: kpt on* **3/1**[2]

**2** *3* **Rasseem (IRE)** 2-8-11 .......... KMcEvoy 2 76
(SaeedBinSuroor) *led: rdn along and hdd 2f out: kpt on u.p fnl f* **8/1**

**3** *shd* **Regina** 2-8-11 .......... BDoyle 4 75+
(SirMichaelStoute) *dwlt: sn trcking ldng pair: effrt 2f out: sn rdn: edgd lft ins last: kpt on same pce* **9/2**[3]

**4** *1/2* **Neverletme Go (IRE)** 2-8-11 .......... SDrowne 5 73+
(GWragg) *trckd ldng pair: effrt over 2f out: sn shkn up and briefly outpcd: swtchd lft ins last and kpt on nr fin* **8/11**[1]

63.80 secs (2.00) **Going Correction** +0.20s/f (Good) **4** Ran SP% **112.2**
Speed ratings: **92,87,87,86**CSF £21.49 TOTE £3.60; EX 10.90.
**Owner** Lord Lloyd-Webber **Bred** Watership Down Stud **Trained** Newmarket, Suffolk

**FOCUS**
Although small on numbers, this boasted some well-bred fillies' who all look to have a future. The newcomers all look to have claims of reversing form with the winner in due course.

**NOTEBOOK**
**All For Laura**, the only runner with the benefit of previous experience, confirmed the promise of her debut fourth at Newmarket in June and ran out a ready winner. The drop back a furlong proved ideal and she showed a neat turn of foot when quickening. She is worth a chance in decent company.
**Rasseem(IRE)**, the first foal of a dam who won over this trip as a juvenile, looked sharp for this debut. She was smart form the gates and held every chance, but her inexperience found her out late in the day. She is entitled to improve on this, and should have no trouble winning a similar event.
**Regina**, a well-related daughter of Green Desert, ran distinctly green on this racecourse bow and can be expected to leave this form behind in due course. She will get six furlongs.
**Neverletme Go(IRE)** ◆, the first foal out of her stable's top-class sprinter Cassandra Go, is highly regarded and was well backed to open her account at the first time of asking, but when push came to shove she was betrayed by her lack of experience. She will come on plenty for this experience and another furlong will help. A Lowther entry, she should leave this form well behind in time.

### 4299 96 TRENT FM JO & TWIGGY'S CLASSIFIED STKS 5f 13y
**6:50** (6:51) (E ) 3-Y-O+ **£3,721** (£1,145; £572; £286) **Stalls** High

Form RPR

1102 **1** **Foley Millennium (IRE)**[11] [3979] 6-9-2 66.......... NPollard 9 81+
(MQuinn) *sn led: rdn clr over 1f out: kpt on* **9/2**[1]

5561 **2** *1 1/2* **Catch The Wind**[8] [4043] 3-9-5 70..........(p) SSanders 2 81
(IAWood) *trckd ldrs: hdwy to chse wnr wl over 1f out: sn rdn and no imp fnl f* **9/2**[1]

2203 **3** *1 3/4* **Boavista (IRE)**[3] [4211] 4-8-9 62.......... SHitchcott(3) 3 63
(PDEvans) *dwlt: sn in tch: rdn along to chse ldrs 2f out: drvn and one pce appr last* **17/2**

3001 **4** *nk* **Tally (IRE)**[4] [4188] 4-9-3 66.......... RThomas(5) 6 72
(MJPolglase) *sn pushed along in rr: hdwy 2f out: swtchd lft and rdn 1f out: kpt on ins last: nrst fin* **7/1**[2]

5066 **5** *1/2* **Dunn Deal (IRE)**[18] [3810] 4-8-10 62.......... BSwarbrick(5) 5 63
(WMBrisbourne) *in tch tl rdn along and outpcd 1/2-way: hdwy over 1f out: drvn and kpt on fnl f* **11/1**

2010 **6** *hd* **Kallista's Pride**[4] [4194] 4-8-12 61.......... IMongan 7 60
(JRBest) *chsd ldrs: rdn 2f out: sn one pce* **25/1**

3061 **7** *3/4* **Justalord**[9] [4011] 6-9-9 67..........(b) JEdmunds 4 68
(JBalding) *cl up: shkn up 2f out: sn rdn and btn* **8/1**[3]

0040 **8** *2* **Twice Upon A Time**[14] [3920] 5-8-12 65.......... ACulhane 12 50
(BSmart) *towards rr: hdwy and in tch 1/2-way: sn rdn and wknd* **9/2**[1]

1440 **9** *2 1/2* **Shrink**[53] [2741] 3-8-8 65.......... JMackay 10 41
(MLWBell) *dwlt and hmpd s: bhd tl swtchd outside and sme hdwy 2f out: sn rdn and wknd* **14/1**

0000 **10** *3* **Kuringai**[8] [4052] 3-8-11 65.......... ADaly 1 33
(BWDuke) *in tch on outer: rdn along 1/2-way: sn wknd* **66/1**

3004 **11** *1/2* **Prime Recreation**[13] [3945] 7-8-13 66.......... LisaJones(3) 8 32
(PSFelgate) *cl up: rdn along after 2f out: sn wknd* **11/1**

4365 **U** **Melody King**[8] [4043] 3-8-10 67..........(b) FPFerris(3) 11 —
(PDEvans) *bmpd and uns rdr s* **33/1**

61.86 secs (0.06) **Going Correction** +0.20s/f (Good)
**WFA** 3 from 4yo+ 4lb **12** Ran SP% **120.3**
Speed ratings: **107,104,101,101,100 100,99,95,91,87 86,—**CSF £23.49 TOTE £6.50: £2.20, £3.20, £3.00; EX 31.60.
**Owner** Mrs S G Davies **Bred** Elperefa Bloodstock **Trained** Sparsholt, Oxon

**FOCUS**
A typically tight Classified stakes, run at a solid gallop. Fair form.

**NOTEBOOK**
**Foley Millennium(IRE)** took advantage of his favourable draw and made all the running to win in good style. He enjoyed this drop back to five furlongs, and was winning off a 21lb higher mark than when first successful this term, in a Banded event at Kempton in May. He loves to be out in the lead, should not be troubled by stepping back up another furlong, and still looks well treated on his juvenile form.
**Catch The Wind**, who bounced back to form when successful at Bath last time, ran with credit from her modest draw. The recent application of cheekpieces, and a drop in the weights, have helped bring about improvement, but she is due to go up to a mark of 80 in the future and may struggle as a result.
**Boavista(IRE)** again ran a sound race, and deserves credit to finish as close as she did from her poor draw, having lost ground at the start. She has just the one win from 31 outings to date, but is a genuine filly who could be placed to advantage again off her current mark.
**Tally(IRE)** was unable to go the pace over this shorter trip and never looked like following up on his recent All-Waether success. He can do better back over a sixth furlong, but does look a touch high in the weights at present.
**Twice Upon A Time** has to be considered disappointing. She has dropped in the weights this year, on account of her loss of form, but did not look a serious threat at any stage and she continues to frustrate.

### 4300 CAMPBELL'S HOMEPRIDE SAUCES H'CAP 1m 1f 213y
**7:20** (7:20) (C ) (0-90,80) 3-Y-O **£10,803** (£3,324; £1,662; £831) **Stalls** Low

Form RPR

341 **1** **Nordwind (IRE)**[16] [3846] 3-9-2 **75**.......... IMongan 6 80+
(PWHarris) *in tch: hdwy 4f out: effrt 2f out: rdn to chal over 1f out: sn rdn: kpt on to ld post* **5/2**[2]

5-63 **2** *hd* **Night Spot**[24] [3610] 3-9-7 **80**.......... SDrowne 5 84
(RCharlton) *chsd clr ldr: hdwy 5f out: led 2f out: sn jnd and rdn: drvn ins last: hdd on post* **4/1**[3]

1111 **3** *nk* **Doctored**[5] [4170] 3-8-11 **77** 6ex..........(b) SJDonohoe(7) 1 81?
(PDEvans) *in tch: pushed along and outpcd 4f out: rdn and hdwy 2f out: swtchd rt and drvn ent last: styd on wl nr fin* **7/1**

-412 **4** *1* **Spring Jim**[23] [3631] 3-9-6 **79**.......... KMcEvoy 3 81
(JRFanshawe) *hld up in rr: hdwy 5f out: rdn and ch over 1f out: sn drvn and kpt on same pce ins last* **15/8**[1]

0414 **5** *9* **Ile Facile (IRE)**[9] [4027] 3-8-13 **72**..........(t) GGibbons 2 57
(NPLittmoden) *led and sn clr: rdn along over 4f out: hdd 2f out and sn wknd* **14/1**

4510 **6** *28* **Zaffeu**[37] [3210] 3-8-11 **70**.......... SSanders 4 2
(NPLittmoden) *s.i.s and bhd: hdwy 1/2-way: rdn along 3f out and sn wknd* **9/1**

2m 10.87s (1.37) **Going Correction** +0.05s/f (Good) **6** Ran SP% **112.5**
Speed ratings: **96,95,95,94,87 65**CSF £12.91 TOTE £3.50: £2.00, £2.70; EX 13.00.
**Owner** Mrs P W Harris **Bred** Christoph Berglar **Trained** Ringshall, Bucks

**FOCUS**
An interesting handicap, despite the small field. It was run at a decent gallop and the form looks sound.

**NOTEBOOK**
**Nordwind(IRE)**, off the mark in a Polytrack maiden last time, followed up with a gritty success on this handicap debut. Although he took his time to get past the runner-up, he always looked like doing so, and this longer trip played to his strengths. He remains unexposed, is the type his trainer excels with and could prove a deal better than his current official rating.
**Night Spot** went down fighting and showed more than enough to suggest he can find a race over this trip or a bit further.
**Doctored**, who has been a revelation this season, responded gamely to pressure and was only just denied under his penalty. This was his best run to date in defeat, and while he remains in this mood a seventh win of the season can not be ruled out.
**Spring Jim**, who looked unlucky when narrowly going down at Kempton last time, ran his race with no obvious excuses off this 4lb higher mark. He may do better in a bigger field and should not be written off on this display.
**Zaffeu** *Official explanation: jockey said gelding was never travelling*

### 4301 KONICA EAST DIRECT H'CAP 1m 54y
**7:50** (7:50) (E ) (0-75,75) 3-Y-O+ **£3,818** (£1,175; £587; £293) **Stalls** Centre

Form RPR

4356 **1** **Summer Shades**[6] [4142] 6-9-1 **67**.......... BSwarbrick(5) 3 76
(WMBrisbourne) *trckd ldrs: n.m.r and swtchd rt wl over 2f out: hdwy to chal over 1f out: drvn ins last: styd on to ld nr fin* **11/1**

0044 **2** *1/2* **Newcorp Lad**[14] [3921] 4-8-12 **59**.......... ACulhane 9 67
(MrsGSRees) *trckd ldrs: gd hdwy 3f out: led 2f out: rdn over 1f out: drvn ins last: hdd and no ex nr fin* **15/2**

0000 **3** *2 1/2* **Hilltime (IRE)**[26] [3559] 4-8-4 **51**.......... WSupple 5 53
(JJQuinn) *chsd ldr: hdwy to ld 3f out: rdn and hdd 2f out: drvn and one pce fnl f* **14/1**

1013 **4** *1 3/4* **Nearly A Fool**[6] [4142] 6-9-10 **71**..........(v) NPollard 7 69
(GGMargarson) *hld up towards rr: swtchd outside and hdwy wl over 2f out: rdn and hung lft ent last: kpt on same pce* **3/1**[1]

000- **5** *1/2* **New Wish (IRE)**[280] [5724] 4-9-5 **66**.......... DaleGibson 2 63
(MWEasterby) *keen: trckd ldrs: effrt 3f out: rdn over 2f out and btn wl over 1f out* **10/3**[2]

3060 **6** *3/4* **Arry Dash**[16] [3842] 4-9-11 **75**.......... SHitchcott(3) 6 70
(MRChannon) *s.i.s and bhd: hdwy on inner over 2f out: sn rdn and kpt on: nrst fin* **13/2**

/5-0 **7** *3* **Polish Spirit**[16] [3844] 9-9-4 **65**.......... SDrowne 8 53
(BRMillman) *hld up towards rr: effrt and sme hdwy on outer over 2f out: sn rdn and btn* **12/1**

1000 **8** *3* **Tatweer (IRE)**[22] [3663] 4-8-6 **53**..........(v) SWKelly 1 35
(DShaw) *s.i.s: a rr* **50/1**

3220 **9** *1 1/2* **Blue Mariner**[23] [3631] 4-9-9 **70**.......... IMongan 4 48
(PWHarris) *led: rdn along 4f out: hdd 3f out and sn wknd* **10/1**

3004 **10** *7* **Zafarshah (IRE)**[2] [4238] 5-8-10 **60**..........(v) FPFerris(3) 10 22
(PDEvans) *chsd ldrs: rdn along over 3f out: sn wknd* **5/1**[3]

1m 45.65s (-0.75) **Going Correction** +0.05s/f (Good) **10** Ran SP% **123.6**
Speed ratings: **105,104,102,100,99 99,96,93,91,84**CSF £96.31 CT £1210.54 TOTE £20.70: £4.90, £1.90, £7.10; EX 131.20.
**Owner** K Bennett **Bred** C A And R M Cyzer **Trained** Great Ness, Shropshire

**FOCUS**
A modest handicap, but it was run at a sound pace.

**NOTEBOOK**
**Summer Shades** really picked up when switched to make her challenge approaching two out and gamley stayed on to get up close home. She had been running well without success this year, but this was by far her best effort, and she readily reversed recent course and distance form with the third placed horse on these same terms.
**Newcorp Lad** ◆ ran his best race of the season and was a clear second best. He is more than capable of expoliting this fair looking mark.
**Hilltime(IRE)** turned in an improved effort and could be placed to score a first win on the Flat off this mark. However, he may just need a slight drop in trip.

**Nearly A Fool** spoilt his chance by hanging under pressure and could only muster the one pace late on. He failed to confirm recent course and distance form with the winner and ran below par. A drop back to seven furlongs could bring about improvement, however.
**New Wish(IRE)** was not disgraced on this first start for 280 days and is entitled to improve a fair bit. He was rated 92 as a three-year-old, and is one to respect when the market speaks in his favour, although he sometimes compromises his chance by running too keen in the early stages.

## 4302 LETHEBY & CHRISTOPHER H'CAP 2m 9y
8:20 (8:20) (F) (0-55,55) 3-Y-O £3,332 (£952; £476) Stalls Low

| Form | | | | RPR |
|---|---|---|---|---|
| 3002 | 1 | | **Strangely Brown (IRE)**[11] 3984 3-9-4 **55** SSanders 3 (SCWilliams) *trckd ldrs: smooth prog 4f out: led 2f out: sn clr: easily* **13/8**[1] | 74+ |
| 6023 | 2 | 9 | **Spring Breeze**[11] 3984 3-9-4 **55** (b[1]) SWKelly 10 (MDods) *led: rdn along over 3f out: hdd 2f out: drvn and kpt on: no ch w wnr* **7/1**[3] | 63+ |
| 6444 | 3 | 5 | **Frambo (IRE)**[3] 4207 3-8-0 **40** (b) NMackay(3) 11 (JGPortman) *in tch: hdwy to chse ldrs 1/2-way: rdn along over 3f out: sn drvn and one pce fnl 2f* **20/1** | 42 |
| 4560 | 4 | ½ | **Morning Hawk (USA)**[11] 3984 3-8-0 **42** (b[1]) RThomas(5) 14 (JSMoore) *towards rr: hdwy on outer over 4f out: rdn along wl over 2f out: kpt on same pce appr last* **33/1** | 43 |
| 0021 | 5 | 3 | **Bienheureux**[8] 4055 3-8-13 **50** 5ex MFenton 8 (MissGayKelleway) *hld up towards rr: hdwy over 5f out: rdn along on outer wl over 2f out: nvr nr ldrs* **4/1**[2] | 48 |
| 004 | 6 | ½ | **Twilight Years**[23] 3625 3-8-8 **45** WSupple 9 (TDEasterby) *prom: chsd ldr after 6f: rdn along over 3f out: grad wknd* **16/1** | 42 |
| 0063 | 7 | 3 | **Genuinely (IRE)**[8] 4070 3-8-2 **39** (v) JMackay 13 (WJMusson) *bhd: hdwy over 4f out: sn rdn along and nvr nr ldrs* **9/1** | 33 |
| 4300 | 8 | 1 | **Romeo's Day**[11] 3984 3-8-10 **50** (v[1]) SHitchcott(3) 5 (MRChannon) *chsd ldrs: rdn along over 4f out: sn wknd* **20/1** | 42 |
| 5620 | 9 | 14 | **Cunning Pursuit**[28] 3479 3-8-9 **46** ACulhane 16 (MLWBell) *prom: rdn along over 5f out: wknd 4f out* **14/1** | 22 |
| 0016 | 10 | 3 | **Mister Completely (IRE)**[24] 3612 3-8-9 **46** IMongan 4 (JRBest) *bhd: sme hdwy on inner over 3f out: sn rdn along and nvr a factor* **18/1** | 18 |
| 0103 | 11 | 8 | **Illeana (GER)**[23] 3638 3-8-13 **55** PMakin(5) 6 (WRMuir) *a rr* **9/1** | 17 |
| 000 | 12 | 6 | **Jango Malfoy (IRE)**[8] 4055 3-9-1 **52** (t) ADaly 15 (BWDuke) *midfield: sme hdwy 1/2-way: rdn along and wknd over 5f out: bhd whn hung bdly lft over 2f out* **50/1** | 7 |
| 0-00 | 13 | 6 | **Snow Chance (IRE)**[21] 3707 3-7-7 **35** oh1 BSwarbrick(5) 12 (WMBrisbourne) *a rr: drvn along 1/2-way and sn bhd* **66/1** | — |
| 3005 | 14 | 1¼ | **Great Gidding**[11] 3996 3-9-4 **55** (b[1]) SDrowne 2 (HMorrison) *prom: rdn along 1/2-way: sn wknd and bhd fnl 4f* **33/1** | 2 |

3m 35.83s (2.33) **Going Correction** +0.05s/f (Good) **14** Ran SP% **127.3**
Speed ratings: **96,91,89,88,87 87,85,85,78,76 72,69,66,65**CSF £13.06 CT £186.03 TOTE £2.10: £1.70, £2.20, £5.20; EX 13.90.
**Owner** J T and K Worsley **Bred** Barry Noonan **Trained** Newmarket, Suffolk

**FOCUS**
A dire event that saw the field finish well strung out behind facile winner Strangely Brown, who was entitled to win well.

**NOTEBOOK**
**Strangely Brown(IRE)**, whose latest second at Beverley off the same mark gave him an obvious chance here, ran very much to that form and registered a first ever success at the ninth attempt. He has really progressed the last twice since being stepped up to this trip and he had no problems with this faster surface. However, connections will be praying the Handicapper take the result too literally, as he was already due to go up 6lb, and could struggle off a much higher mark.
**Spring Breeze**, with the cheekpices left off in favour of first-time blinkers, ran very much up to recent form with the winner and was clear in second. He may not have been ideally suited by making the running and has a similar event within his compass.
**Frambo(IRE)**, unplaced in a selling handicap just three days previously, made hard work of finishing a never-dangerous third over this longer trip, but improved a touch.
**Morning Hawk(USA)**, tried in the first-time blinkers, again found little under pressure over this trip, and did little to suggest she can break her duck at this level.
**Bienheureux** failed to improve as expected over this longer distance and never looked looked like following up his recent success under his penalty. He can do better when eased again in trip, but has no secrets from the Handicapper now.
**Mister Completely(IRE)** *Official explanation: jockey said colt had no more to give*

## 4303 CITYLIFE MAGAZINE MEDIAN AUCTION MAIDEN STKS 1m 54y
8:50 (8:50) (F) 3-Y-O £3,304 (£944; £472) Stalls Centre

| Form | | | | RPR |
|---|---|---|---|---|
| 2 | 1 | | **Cashbar**[16] 3848 3-8-9 KMcEvoy 8 (JRFanshawe) *chsd clr ldr: hdwy to ld wl over 2f out: sn clr* **4/5**[1] | 81+ |
| 5 | 2 | 3 | **Marsh Orchid**[108] 1386 3-9-0 SDrowne 3 (WJarvis) *trckd ldrs: hdwy to chse wnr 2f out: sn rdn and kpt on same pce* **4/1**[2] | 74+ |
| | 3 | 4 | **Play Bouzouki** 3-8-6 NMackay(3) 4 (LMCumani) *s.i.s and bhd: hdwy 3f out: styd on fnl 2f: nrst fin* **5/1**[3] | 60+ |
| 3-00 | 4 | 1 | **My Michelle**[70] 2267 3-8-9 68 ACulhane 1 (BPalling) *hld up: hdwy on inner whn n.m.r over 2f out: sn rdn: swtchd rt and styd on ins last* **16/1** | 58 |
| 0420 | 5 | nk | **Oh Golly Gosh**[55] 2676 3-9-0 71 (v[1]) SSanders 6 (NPLittmoden) *led and sn clr: rdn along over 3f out: hdd wl over 2f out: sn wknd* **5/1**[3] | 62 |
| 6 | 6 | nk | **Port Sodrick**[16] 3848 3-9-0 ADaly 2 (MDIUsher) *s.i.s and bhd tl styd on fnl 2f: nrst fin* **33/1** | 61? |
| | 7 | 3½ | **Zoomiezando** 3-8-9 PMakin(5) 7 (MrsLucindaFeatherstone) *chsd ldrs: rdn along and hung lft over 2f out: sn wknd* **100/1** | 53? |
| 0 | 8 | 5 | **Through The Slips (USA)**[15] 3882 3-8-9 MFenton 9 (JGGiven) *chsd ldrs: rdn along 3f out: wknd fnl 2f* **20/1** | 37 |
| 0-00 | 9 | 6 | **Fifth Column (USA)**[38] 3168 3-9-0 WSupple 5 (JRFanshawe) *bhd fr 1/2-way* **25/1** | 28 |

1m 46.83s (0.43) **Going Correction** +0.05s/f (Good) **9** Ran SP% **127.3**
Speed ratings: **99,96,92,91,90 90,86,81,75**CSF £4.90 TOTE £2.00: £1.30, £1.30, £1.80; EX 2.20 Place 6 £261.87, Place 5 £57.61.
**Owner** Barford Bloodstock **Bred** Mrs C Handscombe **Trained** Newmarket, Suffolk

**FOCUS**
A maiden full of late-maturing types run at a fair gallop. The first three are unexposed and can probably all rate a bit higher than the bare form.

**NOTEBOOK**
**Cashbar**, a late-maturing filly, confirmed the promise of her recent debut on the Polytrack with a decisive success. It will be interesting to see where her in-form yard send her next, as she looks the type to improve with experience and she should get a bit further.
**Marsh Orchid**, who shaped with some ability on his debut back in April, improved on that effort, but held no chance with the winner. He was a clear second and will no doubt fare better when handicapped.
**Play Bouzouki**, half-sister to the smart Alkaadem, blew her chance at the start on this racecourse bow, but was staying on well at the finish, and shaped with a degree of promise. She will be a lot sharper next time.
**My Michelle** is starting to look fairly exposed and is probably flattered a little by her current BHB rating.
**Oh Golly Gosh**, tried in the first-time visor, dropped out tamely having set the pace over this shorter trip. He is one to avoid.
T/Plt: £147.30 to a £1 stake. Pool: £33,848.05. 167.65 winning tickets. T/Qpdt: £23.80 to a £1 stake. Pool: £2,684.00. 83.40 winning tickets. JR

# 4099 THIRSK (L-H)
Friday, July 30

**OFFICIAL GOING: Good to firm (firm in places)**
The jockeys described the going as on the fast side of good but loose in the back straight and on the home turn.
Wind: Moderate 1/2 behind. Weather: Overcast.

## 4304 COSTA CLAIMING STKS 7f
2:30 (2:31) (E) 2-Y-O £3,672 (£1,130; £565; £282) Stalls Low

| Form | | | | RPR |
|---|---|---|---|---|
| 1544 | 1 | | **Maureen's Lough (IRE)**[9] 4010 2-7-12 NMackay(3) 9 (TDBarron) *w ldr: led 3f out: rdn clr ent last* **7/4**[1] | 47 |
| 000 | 2 | 2½ | **Countrywide Sun**[22] 3665 2-8-13 (p) TGMcLaughlin 8 (NPLittmoden) *led tl 3f out: kpt on same pce appr fnl f* **7/1**[3] | 53 |
| 6 | 3 | nk | **Dancing Shirl**[7] 4100 2-8-6 GFaulkner 3 (CWFairhurst) *chsd ldrs: effrt 3f out: swtchd rt 1f out: kpt on same pce* **8/1** | 45 |
| 0500 | 4 | nk | **Lanas Turn**[27] 3532 2-8-5 WSupple 7 (TDEasterby) *chsd ldrs: rdn 3f out: sn outpcd: edgd rt and kpt on fnl f* **16/1** | 44 |
| 1136 | 5 | ½ | **Goldhill Prince**[7] 4094 2-8-4 (p) CHaddon(7) 5 (WGMTurner) *chsd ldrs: effrt 3f out: styd on same pce* **11/4**[2] | 48 |
| 604 | 6 | nk | **Faithful Flash**[17] 3824 2-8-3 (b[1]) BReilly(3) 4 (CADwyer) *hld up towards rr: hmpd and lost pl over 4f out: styd on fnl 2f* **16/1** | 43 |
| 053 | 7 | ½ | **Singhalongtasveer**[13] 3951 2-8-7 JBramhill 10 (WStorey) *rr-div: hdwy over 2f out: styng on whn n.m.r jst ins last* **20/1** | 42 |
| 0620 | 8 | 5 | **Itsa Monkey (IRE)**[9] 4012 2-8-0 (p) KGhunowa(7) 2 (MJPolglase) *s.i.s: sn bhd and drvn along* **25/1** | 30 |
| 05 | 9 | 5 | **Tewitfield Lass**[9] 4010 2-7-11 DFentiman(7) 1 (JRWeymes) *in tch: outpcd over 3f out: sn lost pl* **20/1** | 14 |
| | 10 | ¾ | **Gunnerbergkamp** 2-8-11 ACulhane 11 (MDHammond) *s.i.s: sn bhd* **20/1** | 19 |
| 0 | P | | **Specialise**[9] 4010 2-8-2 DaleGibson 6 (DWBarker) *s.i.s: hung rt thrght: bhd and rn wd bnd over 4f out: sn t.o and p.u and dismntd* **25/1** | — |

1m 28.48s (1.38) **Going Correction** +0.075s/f (Good) **11** Ran SP% **120.4**
Speed ratings: **95,92,91,91,90 90,89,84,78,77** —CSF £13.51 TOTE £2.60: £1.60, £1.60, £2.70; EX 15.50.The winner was bought by M C Chapman for £5,000.
**Owner** Oghill House Stud **Bred** Paul Hyland **Trained** Maunby, N Yorks

**FOCUS**
Very modest form, and the winner did not need to be anywhere near her best.

**NOTEBOOK**
**Maureen's Lough(IRE)**, put in to be claimed for just £5,000 and with her rider taking off 3lb, looked to hold outstanding claims and she did not have to be anywhere near her best to take this with the minimum of fuss. She was claimed and now joins Michael Chapman's stable.
**Countrywide Sun**, who gave problems leaving the paddock, wore cheekpieces rather than blinkers. On his toes beforehand, he was backed at long odds and possibly appreciating the much quicker ground, ran easily his best race so far.
**Dancing Shirl**, who made her debut in stronger company here just a week earlier, has a round action. She will appreciate a mile and slightly easier ground.
**Lanas Turn**, who is not in love with the starting stalls, jumped off on terms this time. A seller might be more her mark.
**Goldhill Prince**, warm beforehand, did not impress at all going to post and looks to have gone off the boil for the time being.
**Faithful Flash**, in first time blinkers, did well in the end after being knocked out of her stride rounding the final turn.
**Singhalongtasveer**, a late foal, is improving with every outing and a selling nursery could be his cup of tea.
**Specialise** *Official explanation: jockey said filly failed to handle the bend and lost her action*

## 4305 SKELTON CASTLE H'CAP 7f
3:00 (3:02) (E) (0-70,66) 3-Y-O+ £3,857 (£1,187; £593; £296) Stalls Low

| Form | | | | RPR |
|---|---|---|---|---|
| 0622 | 1 | | **Headland (USA)**[4] 4188 6-8-10 **51** (be) ACulhane 7 (DWChapman) *rr-div: hdwy on outer 3f out: styd on to ld jst ins fnl f: hld on wl* **8/1**[2] | 59 |
| 5320 | 2 | ¾ | **Bollin Edward**[24] 3606 5-9-8 **63** (v) DAllan 6 (TDEasterby) *mid-div: effrt over 3f out: n.m.r 2f out: styd on fnl f* **4/1**[1] | 69 |
| 6020 | 3 | nk | **Saros (IRE)**[23] 3622 3-8-9 **57** FLynch 10 (BSmart) *sn bhd and drvn along: hdwy on outside 3f out: styd on wl fnl f* **12/1** | 62 |
| 5000 | 4 | 1¼ | **Roman Maze**[15] 3884 4-9-5 **60** SWKelly 13 (WMBrisbourne) *mid-div: hdwy over 2f out: edgd lft and led over 1f out: hdd jst ins fnl f: no ex* **8/1**[2] | 62 |
| 0106 | 5 | ¾ | **Flashing Blade**[15] 3867 4-9-11 **66** (t) GGibbons 9 (BAMcmahon) *chsd ldrs: effrt over 2f out: styd on same pce* **12/1** | 66 |
| 3100 | 6 | hd | **Jubilee Street (IRE)**[28] 3470 5-9-1 **56** GHind 2 (MrsADuffield) *in tch: effrt over 2f out: n.m.r over 1f out: kpt on* **8/1**[2] | 55 |
| 00-0 | 7 | 1½ | **Zap Attack**[73] 2219 4-9-6 **66** MLawson(5) 4 (JParkes) *mid-div: nt clr run and swtchd rt 2f out: kpt on* **25/1** | 61 |
| 6500 | 8 | ½ | **Flying Edge (IRE)**[27] 3516 4-9-0 **55** WSupple 14 (EJAlston) *prom: effrt over 2f out: no imp* **16/1** | 49 |
| 0400 | 9 | 1 | **Toppling**[9] 4013 6-8-12 **53** (p) CCatlin 11 (JMBradley) *t.k.h: led over 1f: wkng whn n.m.r over 2f out* **33/1** | 44 |
| 6400 | 10 | nk | **Jedeydd**[4] 4199 7-8-9 **53** (bt[1]) LEnstone(3) 12 (MDods) *s.i.s: hdwy whn nt clr run 2f out: n.d after* **12/1** | 43 |
| -441 | 11 | 1¾ | **Thornaby Green**[15] 3877 3-8-11 **64** PMakin(5) 5 (TDBarron) *w ldr: led over 2f out: hdd over 1f out: sn wknd* **4/1**[1] | 50 |
| 1466 | 12 | 5 | **Cottingham (IRE)**[8] 4050 3-9-1 **63** KDalgleish 3 (MCChapman) *led over 5f out tl over 2f out: lost pl and eased over 1f out* **25/1** | 35 |

000- **13** *15* **Iron Temptress (IRE)**[288] 5590 3-8-12 **65**.................... PMulrennan(5) 8 —
(GMMoore) *bhd: eased fnl 2f* **66/1**

1m 26.33s (-0.77) **Going Correction** +0.075s/f (Good)
**WFA** 3 from 4yo+ 7lb **13** Ran SP% **122.8**
Speed ratings: **107,106,105,104,103 103,101,101,99,99 97,91,74**CSF £35.28 CT £336.31 TOTE £8.60: £2.70, £2.40, £3.50; EX 28.00.
**Owner** Harold D White **Bred** O J Martinez **Trained** Stillington, N Yorks

**FOCUS**
In effect just a 0-66 handicap, with a fair bit of trouble in running. Ordinary form.

**NOTEBOOK**
**Headland(USA)** made ground from the rear down the outside, avoiding the traffic problems on his inner.
**Bollin Edward** looked at his very best beforehand. His rider had to sit and suffer for a few strides, otherwise he would have given the winner even more to do. The fact remains however that his strike rate now is just one from 26.
**Saros(IRE)** struggled to go the pace but was picking up ground in good style at the end. He really needs the full mile.
**Roman Maze**, drawn one from the outside, moved poorly to post. He dived left when he hit the front causing traffic problems for them on his inside.
**Flashing Blade** looked at his best and is slipping to a lenient mark. A mile suits him slightly better.
**Jubilee Street(IRE)**, hard to predict, ran one of his better races and was unfortunate not to finish a bit closer.
**Zap Attack**, absent for 10 weeks and having just his second outing, is a keen type. Forced to pull wide, he was staying on in his own time at the death and this was a lot more encouraging.
**Thornaby Green**, 3lb higher, went on but did not see out the extra furlong.
**Iron Temptress(IRE)** *Official explanation: jockey said filly cocked her jaw round the home bend*

## 4306 DEEPDALE SOLUTIONS NSPCC MAIDEN STKS 1m
3:35 (3:36) (D) 3-Y-O+ **£5,616** (£1,728; £864; £432) **Stalls** Low

Form RPR
4-2 **1** **Triple Jump**[25] 3587 3-8-13 .................................... WSupple 4 68+
(TDEasterby) *trckd ldrs: led over 2f out: drvn along and styd on* **8/13**[1]
-325 **2** *1* **River Nurey (IRE)**[26] 3554 3-8-13 **70**.................................. ACulhane 10 66+
(BWHills) *trckd ldrs: effrt 3f out: styd on fnl f: no real imp* **2/1**[2]
56- **3** *2 1/2* **The Number**[340] 4453 3-8-13 ........................................ KDalgleish 9 60+
(ISemple) *trckd ldrs: hung lft over 1f out: kpt on same pce* **25/1**[3]
06- **4** *1 1/2* **Smirfys Dance Hall (IRE)**[476] 1011 4-9-2 ................ TGMcLaughlin 12 52+
(WMBrisbourne) *hld up in rr: hdwy 3f out: kpt on wl fnl f* **100/1**
00 **5** *2 1/2* **Dee En Ay (IRE)**[25] 3587 3-8-6 ...................................... AMullen(7) 8 51
(TDEasterby) *w ldr: led over 3f out tl over 2f out: fdd appr fnl f* **100/1**
0 **6** *6* **Java Dancer**[29] 3447 3-8-13 .............................................. DAllan 7 37
(TDEasterby) *sn in rr: kpt on fnl 2f: nvr on terms* **33/1**
00- **7** *3/4* **St Jude**[276] 5815 4-9-7 ................................................ JBramhill 3 35
(JBalding) *trckd ldrs: lost pl over 2f out* **100/1**
0 **8** *1 1/4* **Coco Point Breeze**[16] 3846 3-8-8 ...................................... SChin 11 27
(JGGiven) *rr-div: sme hdwy over 2f out: nvr a factor* **66/1**
0 **9** *nk* **Jidiya (IRE)**[76] 2133 5-9-7 ............................................... CCatlin 2 32
(SGollings) *s.i.s: a towards rr* **33/1**
00 **10** *1/2* **Trinity Fair**[23] 3630 3-8-8 ......................................... DeanMcKeown 5 26
(JGGiven) *led tl over 3f out: sn lost pl* **50/1**
00-0 **11** *5* **Ballet Ruse**[4] 4195 3-8-8 ................................................ JMackay 1 14
(SirMarkPrescott) *s.i.s: a bhd* **33/1**

1m 40.52s (0.82) **Going Correction** +0.075s/f (Good)
**WFA** 3 from 4yo+ 8lb **11** Ran SP% **114.3**
Speed ratings: **98,97,94,93,90 84,83,82,82,81 76**CSF £1.71 TOTE £1.80: £1.02, £1.10, £4.30; EX 2.30.
**Owner** Mr and Mrs J D Cotton **Bred** Mrs G Slater **Trained** Great Habton, N Yorks

**FOCUS**
An ordinary maiden, lacking any strength in depth, and they bet 25/1 bar the first two, neither of whom were at their best.

**NOTEBOOK**
**Triple Jump**, 8lb top on RPR, wore a cross noseband. He travelled strongly and had simply to be kept up to his work. His future depends on a realistic handicap mark.
**River Nurey(IRE)**, an unfurnished-type, was given a much more patient ride. Despite his rider throwing everything at him he was never going to seriously trouble the winner.
**The Number**, absent for a year, had just a couple of runs at two. A keen type, he hung badly, and although he is now qualified for handicaps he looks anything but straightforward.
**Smirfys Dance Hall(IRE)**, who had a couple of outings last spring, stayed on steadily and looks capable of something better now he is qualified for handicaps.
**Dee En Ay(IRE)**, a moderate mover, showed a lot more and this third outing opens up the handicap route.
**Java Dancer**, never in the contest, needs another trip to the races to qualify for a handicap mark.

## 4307 CRAYKE FILLIES' H'CAP 1m 4f
4:10 (4:10) (E) (0-70,67) 3-Y-O **£3,750** (£1,154; £577; £288) **Stalls** Low

Form RPR
-125 **1** **Richtee (IRE)**[26] 3561 3-9-4 **67**.................................. THamilton(3) 10 74
(RAFahey) *trckd ldrs: led 2f out: hld on towards fin* **11/2**[2]
6412 **2** *3/4* **Velvet Waters**[9] 4027 3-8-13 **59**....................................... SCarson 1 65
(RFJohnsonHoughton) *in tch: effrt over 3f out: styd on wl fnl f* **13/2**[3]
0141 **3** *hd* **Donastrela (IRE)**[8] 4045 3-8-12 **63** 6ex...................(v) NChalmers(5) 3 69
(AMBalding) *hld up towards rr: effrt over 3f out: plld wd over 1f out: styd on wl ins last* **11/2**[2]
2600 **4** *1 1/4* **On Cloud Nine**[22] 3670 3-8-13 **64**............................. HayleyTurner(5) 11 68
(MLWBell) *in tch: effrt 3f out: styd on same pce fnl f* **25/1**
0511 **5** *shd* **Let It Be**[9] 4015 3-8-0 **46**................................................. CCatlin 2 50+
(MrsMReveley) *mid-div: effrt on ins over 3f out: n.m.r over 1f out: kpt on same pce* **9/4**[1]
5006 **6** *shd* **Prelude**[21] 3706 3-9-0 **60**................................................ SWKelly 13 63
(WMBrisbourne) *trckd ldrs: effrt over 2f out: nt qckn appr fnl f* **66/1**
0002 **7** *1 1/4* **Royal Distant (USA)**[5] 4177 3-9-5 **65**............................. DaleGibson 6 66
(MWEasterby) *sn bhd: hdwy over 2f out: kpt on same pce* **20/1**
-350 **8** *3/4* **Silver Rhythm**[44] 2977 3-8-5 **51** ow1......................... DeanMcKeown 16 51
(KRBurke) *chsd ldrs: one pce fnl 2f* **33/1**
640 **9** *1 1/4* **Zuri (IRE)**[25] 3592 3-9-2 **65**.......................................... NMackay(3) 4 63
(LMCumani) *in tch: effrt over 2f out: kpt on one pce* **12/1**
0006 **10** *1 1/4* **Prairie Sun (GER)**[9] 4015 3-8-9 **55**...................................(p) GHind 8 51
(MrsADuffield) *bhd: hdwy 3f out: hung lft: nvr nr ldrs* **20/1**
0022 **11** *1 1/4* **Eboracum (IRE)**[8] 4049 3-9-3 **63**........................................ DAllan 5 57
(TDEasterby) *bhd: hdwy over 3f out: nvr rchd ldrs* **12/1**
-020 **12** *3 1/2* **Plausabelle**[79] 2038 3-8-6 **52**............................................ WSupple 12 41
(TDEasterby) *a towards rr* **25/1**
0-60 **13** *2* **Power Nap**[20] 3759 3-8-1 **47**......................................(t) KimTinkler 7 32
(NTinkler) *a in rr* **100/1**
0-40 **14** *3* **Land Of Nod (IRE)**[14] 3908 3-8-11 **62**.....................(b[1]) PMulrennan(5) 14 43
(GAButler) *t.k.h: led 2f: led over 3f out tl 2f out: sn wknd* **16/1**
0323 **15** *2* **Lucky Arthur (IRE)**[21] 3695 3-9-0 **60**................................ JMackay 9 37
(JGMO'Shea) *sn bhd* **14/1**
0050 **16** *23* **Adees Dancer**[11] 3984 3-8-9 **55**.......................................... FLynch 15 —
(BSmart) *dwlt: hdwy on outer to ld after 2f: hung rt after: rn wd bnd and hdd over 3f out: sn bhd and eased* **66/1**

2m 36.69s (1.49) **Going Correction** +0.075s/f (Good) **16** Ran SP% **126.9**
Speed ratings: **98,97,97,96,96 96,95,95,94,93 92,90,88,86,85 70**CSF £39.37 CT £215.28 TOTE £7.30: £1.60, £2.70, £2.20, £5.40; EX 43.80.
**Owner** Terence Elsey and Richard Mustill **Bred** Niall Farrell **Trained** Musley Bank, N Yorks

**FOCUS**
An ordinary handicap, not run at a strong pace, but the winner improved again and the placed horses seemed to run to their marks.

**NOTEBOOK**
**Richtee(IRE)**, stepping up in distance, stole first run. In the end this game and improving sort did just enough.
**Velvet Waters**, due to race from a 3lb higher mark in future, stuck to her task in willing fashion and was chipping away the winner's advantage at the line.
**Donastrela(IRE)**, under her penalty, seemed to be ridden with the extra two furlongs in mind. Forced to pull outside, she finished to some purpose.
**On Cloud Nine**, having just her fifth career start, is learning to settle better and she may well improve again.
**Let It Be**, unpenalised for a Catterick win that earned her a 10lb rise, was very edgy beforehand. Making her effort on the inner, she was left slightly short of room but in the end it was lack of basic speed that brought about her downfall.
**Prelude**, down 3lb since her handicap debut, shaped much better and stamina was definitely not an issue.
**Eboracum(IRE)** *Official explanation: jockey said filly was unsuited by the ground*

## 4308 PETER BELL MEMORIAL STKS (H'CAP) 6f
4:45 (4:45) (D) (0-80,79) 3-Y-O+ **£5,590** (£1,720; £860; £430) **Stalls** High

Form RPR
6114 **1** **Hartshead**[8] 4047 5-9-7 **72**........................................ DeanMcKeown 6 84
(GASwinbank) *hld up: stdy hdwy over 2f out: led last 150yds: r.o wl* **10/3**[1]
0500 **2** *3/4* **Smirfys Systems**[8] 4047 5-9-7 **72**.............................. TGMcLaughlin 12 82
(WMBrisbourne) *trckd ldr: led over 1f out: hdd and no ex ins last* **7/1**
4042 **3** *1/2* **Loch Inch**[7] 4085 7-8-1 **52**............................................(b) CCatlin 10 60
(JMBradley) *chsd ldrs: nt qckn ins last* **9/1**
0500 **4** *shd* **Inter Vision (USA)**[19] 3778 4-9-9 **79**............................ PMulrennan(5) 7 87
(ADickman) *in tch: effrt over 2f out: styd on fnl f: no ex last 100yds* **13/2**[3]
5602 **5** *shd* **Nemo Fugat (IRE)**[9] 4013 5-8-7 **58**..................................(v) JCarroll 4 66
(DNicholls) *dwlt: bhd: hdwy on outside 2f out: styd on ins last* **7/1**
3230 **6** *1 1/2* **Brantwood (IRE)**[15] 3884 4-8-8 **59**.....................................(t) GGibbons 1 62
(BAMcmahon) *crossed over to stands' side 1st f: led tl over 1f out: hung lft and fdd ins last* **20/1**
2506 **7** *3/4* **Laurel Dawn**[5] 4181 6-8-10 **61**.............................................. DAllan 2 62
(IWMcinnes) *chsd ldrs on outer: nt qckn appr fnl f* **20/1**
0-05 **8** *shd* **Mitsuki**[7] 4104 5-8-12 **63**.................................................. WSupple 11 64
(JDBethell) *hld up: effrt on inner 2f out: nvr a real threat* **9/2**[2]
2163 **9** *hd* **Climate (IRE)**[39] 3159 5-9-12 **77**..........................................(b) GParkin 3 77
(KARyan) *sn bhd and rdn along: swtchd lft and styd on fnl f* **14/1**
0000 **10** *nk* **Mr Spliffy (IRE)**[7] 4105 5-7-12 **49** oh3.............................. JBramhill 5 48
(MCChapman) *hld up towards rr: hdwy 2f out: sn rdn and nvr on terms* **50/1**
0040 **11** *1 1/2* **Drury Lane (IRE)**[9] 4013 4-7-11 **53**.........................(b) HayleyTurner(5) 8 48
(DWChapman) *in rr fnl 2f* **14/1**

1m 11.57s (-0.93) **Going Correction** +0.05s/f (Good)
**WFA** 3 from 4yo+ 5lb **11** Ran SP% **114.4**
Speed ratings: **108,107,106,106,106 104,103,102,102,102 100**CSF £25.13 CT £194.27 TOTE £3.50: £2.10, £2.00, £2.30; EX 36.90.
**Owner** B Valentine Swinbank **Bred** Gainsborough Stud Management Ltd **Trained** Melsonby, N Yorks
■ Trainer Alan Swinbank's 100th career success.
■ Stewards Enquiry : C Catlin caution: used whip without giving gelding time to respond
D Allan one-day ban: failed to keep straight from stalls (Aug 10)
G Gibbons one-day ban: failed to keep straight from stalls (Aug 20)

**FOCUS**
Solid form, the winner improving a bit more and the second, who looked well treated on 2003 form, recording his best effort this year.

**NOTEBOOK**
**Hartshead**, much happier on this quick ground, was given a confident ride and in the end scored in most convincing fashion. He is still on the up.
**Smirfys Systems**, who took this a year ago from a 4lb lower mark, returned to form but met a sprinter on the up.
**Loch Inch** again ran well but looks weighted to the limit, 1lb higher than his last winning mark.
**Inter Vision(USA)**, 1lb lower than his last win, showed a return to form, sticking on in willing fashion.
**Nemo Fugat(IRE)**, with the visor on again, gave away ground at the start and never looked to be enjoying his work. Even so he put in some fine late work and a seventh furlong will be in his favour.
**Brantwood(IRE)**, warm beforehand, moved poorly to post. Drawn one, he was soon racing towards the stands' side rail and his rider deserves to have his knuckles rapped.

## 4309 TELETEXT "HANDS AND HEELS" APPRENTICE MAIDEN H'CAP 6f
5:20 (5:21) (E) (0-70,65) 3-Y-O+ **£3,809** (£1,172; £586; £293) **Stalls** High

Form RPR
-506 **1** **Oeuf A La Neige**[56] 2656 4-9-12 **61**.............................. DeanWilliams 19 71
(GCHChung) *racd stands' side: chsd ldrs: n.m.r 2f out: styd on to ld last 75yds* **10/1**[3]
0003 **2** *1/2* **Pride Of Kinloch**[13] 3954 4-9-6 **55**...................................... MHalford 15 63
(JHetherton) *racd stands' side: chsd ldrs: led over 1f out: hdd and no ex ins last* **10/1**[3]
4563 **3** *1 3/4* **Amanda's Lad (IRE)**[7] 4105 4-9-3 **55**.......................... LucyRussell(3) 14 58
(MCChapman) *racd stands' side: chsd ldrs: led over 2f out tl over 1f out: kpt on ins last* **12/1**
4606 **4** *1 1/4* **Trojan Flight**[14] 3897 3-9-3 **60**.......................................... AHamblett(3) 4 59
(MrsJRRamsden) *racd far side: chsd ldrs: led that gp over 1f out: edgd rt and no ex* **18/1**
045- **5** *1* **M For Magic**[330] 4681 5-8-3 **41**........................................ KPierrepont(3) 2 37
(CWFairhurst) *racd far side: w ldr: that that gp over 2f out tl over 1f out: unable qckn* **33/1**
0052 **6** *1/2* **Sir Loin**[16] 3838 3-9-0 **57**................................................ KGhunowa(3) 6 52
(NTinkler) *rdr lost iron leaving stalls: racd far side: chsd ldrs: nt qckn appr fnl f* **10/1**[3]
-040 **7** *1/2* **Cellino**[7] 4105 3-8-2 **45**.................................................... KJackson(3) 8 38
(AndrewTurnell) *racd far side: chsd ldrs: outpcd 2f out: kpt on ins last* **66/1**
0302 **8** *1/2* **Orangino**[20] 3735 6-8-3 **43**........................................... RKennemore(5) 12 35
(JSHaldane) *racd stands' side: chsd ldrs: one pce fnl 2f* **10/1**[3]

0-00 **9** *nk* **Fleet Anchor**[13] [3954] 3-9-0 **57** ........ CJDavies(3) 1 48
(JMBradley) *racd far-side: mid-div: kpt on fnl 2f* **20/1**
5006 **10** *shd* **Averami**[9] [4025] 3-8-7 **50** ........ (v) RJKilloran(3) 7 40
(AMBalding) *racd far side: hld up towards rr: kpt on fnl 2f: nvr rchd ldrs* **16/1**
-504 **11** *nk* **Megabond**[21] [3708] 3-9-0 **57** ........ MStainton(3) 5 46
(BSmart) *racd far side: sn bhd: kpt on appr fnl f* **20/1**
4303 **12** *1 ½* **Gasparini (IRE)**[7] [4101] 3-9-4 **58** ........ AMullen 20 43
(TDEasterby) *racd stands' side: chsd ldrs: edgd lft and outpcd fnl 2f* **9/1**[2]
0032 **13** *hd* **Uhuru Peak**[13] [3954] 3-9-1 **55** ........ MHoward 11 39
(MWEasterby) *racd stands' side: chsd ldrs: hung lft 2f out: sn outpcd* **10/1**[3]
0330 **14** *1 ½* **Bells Boy's**[59] [2556] 5-7-13 **37** ........ (p) DonnaCaldwell(3) 16 17
(KARyan) *led stands' side tl over 2f out: wknd and eased ins last* **16/1**
0202 **15** *1 ¼* **Harrison's Flyer (IRE)**[9] [4021] 3-9-8 **65** ........ (b) BO'Neill(3) 10 41
(RAFahey) *dwlt: bhd stands' side: hung lft over 2f out: nvr on terms* **8/1**[1]
0450 **16** *1 ½* **Dark Champion**[14] [3894] 4-9-8 **57** ........ (p) JDO'Reilly 9 29
(REBarr) *racd far side: chsd ldrs: fdd over 1f out* **25/1**
05-5 **17** *½* **Aggi Mac**[162] [828] 3-8-4 **44** ........ SuzanneFrance 13 14
(NBycroft) *v free and uns rdr gng to s: mid-div: outpcd fnl 2f* **50/1**
0-00 **18** *nk* **Sweet Talking Girl**[91] [1750] 4-7-9 **35** ow2 ........ (tp) HazelBoyd(5) 3 4
(JMBradley) *racd far side: led that gp tl over 2f out: wknd over 1f out* **66/1**
-500 **19** *10* **Caribbean Blue**[36] [3234] 3-8-2 **45** ........ JemmaMarshall(3) 18 —
(RMWhitaker) *racd stands' side: mid-div: lost pl 2f out: eased* **14/1**
6306 **20** *dist* **Pure Imagination (IRE)**[13] [3954] 3-9-8 **62** ........ HPoulton 17 —
(JMBradley) *rrd s: racd stands' side: bhd and sddle slipped: virtually p.u: t.o* **11/1**

1m 12.84s (0.34) **Going Correction** +0.05s/f (Good)
**WFA** 3 from 4yo+ 5lb **20** Ran SP% **127.5**
Speed ratings: **99,98,96,94,93 92,91,91,90,90 90,88,87,85,84 82,81,81,67,**—CSF £101.37 CT £1241.26 TOTE £12.20: £4.10, £4.40, £3.50, £5.90; EX 125.00 Place 6 £66.73, Place 5 £46.64.
**Owner** G C H Chung **Bred** Gainsborough Stud Management Ltd **Trained** Newmarket, Suffolk

**FOCUS**
A 0-61 'hands and heels' apprentice maiden handicap, a seller in all but name.

**NOTEBOOK**
**Oeuf A La Neige** who has slipped down the ratings, made it 12th time lucky, sticking on well after being left short of room hard up against the stands' side running rail. It was a change of luck for his trainer and the boy, aboard his 10th winner, looks to have a future.
**Pride Of Kinloch**, on her 21st start, worked her way to the front but in the end just missed out.
**Amanda's Lad(IRE)**, having his 54th start, has now been placed eight times.
**Trojan Flight**, one of eight to set off racing towards the far side, edged right once in front on that side and in the end joined those racing on the other wing.
**M For Magic**, reappearing with 19 previous starts under his belt, has been tried at up to 11 furlongs in the past.
**Sir Loin**, stepping up to six for the first time, did well considering his rider had to cope with just one iron throughout. *Official explanation: jockey said he lost an iron on leaving the stalls*
**Harrison's Flyer(IRE)**, very edgy beforehand, made a tardy start and wanted to do nothing but hang left.
**Pure Imagination(IRE)** *Official explanation: jockey said saddle slipped*
T/Plt: £78.20 to a £1 stake. Pool: £31,606.85. 294.95 winning tickets. T/Qpdt: £24.40 to a £1 stake. Pool: £2,036.90. 61.55 winning tickets. WG

4310 - 4314a (Foreign Racing) - See Raceform Interactive

# 4046 DONCASTER (L-H)
## Saturday, July 31

**OFFICIAL GOING: Good to firm**

## 4315 LITTLE CHEF EBF MAIDEN STKS 7f
**1:00** (1:03) (D) 2-Y-O **£4,992** (£1,536; £768; £384) **Stalls** High

Form RPR
**1** **Le Corvee (IRE)** 2-9-0 ........ JDSmith 11 91+
(AKing) *trckd ldrs: hdwy to ld wl over 1f out: sn qcknd clr* **66/1**
5 **2** *3* **Mister Genepi**[21] [3749] 2-9-0 ........ MartinDwyer 9 83
(WRMuir) *pushed lft s: sn trcking ldrs: hdwy and ev ch 2f out: sn rdn and nt match pce of wnr* **9/2**[3]
3 **3** *1 ¼* **Eqdaam (USA)**[35] [3319] 2-9-0 ........ RHills 2 80
(JHMGosden) *trckd ldrs: hdwy to chal over 2f out and ev ch tl rdn and one pce over 1f out* **2/1**[1]
**4** *nk* **Singhalese** 2-8-9 ........ SWKelly 10 74
(JAOsborne) *wnt lft s: sn led: rdn along 3f out: hdd wl over 1f out: sn one pce* **14/1**
**5** *5* **Mobarhen (USA)** 2-8-11 ........ NMackay(3) 4 67
(SirMichaelStoute) *in tch: pushed along and outpcd 1/2-way: styd on appr last* **10/1**
4 **6** *¾* **Desert Commander (IRE)**[21] [3749] 2-9-0 ........ JCarroll 5 65
(SaeedBinSuroor) *trckd ldrs: hdwy to chal 3f out and ev ch tl rdn and wknd wl over 1f out* **11/4**[2]
**7** *6* **Coeur Courageux (FR)** 2-9-0 ........ JPMurtagh 3 50
(DFlood) *s.i.s and bhd: hdwy 1/2-way: rdn and in tch whn hung lft 2f out: sn btn and eased* **8/1**
**8** *hd* **Fantorini (USA)** 2-9-0 ........ RHavlin 8 49
(JHMGosden) *cl up: pushed along 1/2-way: rdn wl over 2f out and sn wknd* **25/1**
**9** *shd* **Robinzal** 2-9-0 ........ DAllan 6 49
(TDEasterby) *a rr* **66/1**
6 **10** *shd* **Zoripp (IRE)**[22] [3718] 2-9-0 ........ MFenton 1 49
(JGGiven) *wnt lft s: sn pushed along and bhd fr 1/2-way* **66/1**

1m 28.34s (0.53) **Going Correction** +0.05s/f (Good) **10** Ran SP% **113.4**
Speed ratings: **98,94,93,92,87 86,79,79,79,78**CSF £333.46 TOTE £67.30: £10.00, £1.70, £1.20; EX 469.10.
**Owner** David Mason **Bred** Forenaghts Stud And David O'Reilly **Trained** Barbury Castle, Wilts

**FOCUS**
Probably a fair maiden despite the winner being returned at 66-1 and the form looks fairly strong.

**NOTEBOOK**
**Le Corvee(IRE)**, whose stable does not have many two-year-olds but has had a fair degree of success with those it has run, was friendless in the market, but there looked no fluke about this win. He travelled well behind the pace and, when sent about his business, went on to record a smooth victory. He should not be underestimated when stepping up in grade.
**Mister Genepi**, who lost his action on his debut at Salisbury, comprehensively turned the form around with Desert Commander on this quicker ground. He looks to be going the right way.
**Eqdaam(USA)**, third in a Newmarket maiden first time out, comes from a stable whose juveniles usually improve a good deal for their debut outings. He ran a similar race though, and might turn out to be a nursery type.
**Singhalese**, a half-sister to two winners, showed plenty of pace, suggesting she will be happier over six furlongs for the time being.
**Mobarhen(USA)**, a half-brother to high-class American three-year-old Royal Assault, was the Hamdan second string on jockey bookings. He got agitated in the stalls and struggled to go the pace in the race itself, but should benefit from the experience.
**Desert Commander(IRE)** looks to have gone backwards since his debut and another performance like this will ensure he will not be racing in the Godolphin Blue for long.
**Coeur Courageux(FR)**, who was not unfancied, was fractious in the stalls and slowly away. He made good progress to chase the leaders though, and was not knocked about once his chance had gone. There looks to be much better to come from this son of a dual five-furlong Listed winner. *Official explanation: jockey said colt was unruly in stalls, hit him in the face and was never travelling*

## 4316 TRADE UNION UNISON YOUR FRIEND AT WORK MAIDEN STKS 7f
**1:35** (1:35) (D) 3-Y-O+ **£5,558** (£1,710; £855; £427) **Stalls** High

Form RPR
4 **1** **Literatim**[89] [1820] 4-9-4 ........ NMackay(3) 6 87
(LMCumani) *trckd ldr: led 1/2-way: rdn and hdd over 2f out: swtchd lft and rallied to ld ins last* **3/1**[2]
32 **2** *½* **Kauri Forest (USA)**[15] [3916] 3-9-0 ........ (t) JPMurtagh 1 86
(JRFanshawe) *trckd ldng pair: smooth hdwy to ld over 2f out: pushed along and edgd rt 1 1/2f out: sn rdn: put hd in air and hdd ins last* **4/9**[1]
03-6 **3** *10* **Zazous**[35] [3322] 3-9-0 70 ........ VSlattery 4 60
(AKing) *in tch: hdwy 1/2-way: rdn along wl over 2f out and kpt on same pce* **10/1**[3]
05 **4** *7* **Lottie**[9] [4068] 3-8-9 ........ SChin 3 37
(MissVHaigh) *led: pushed along and hdd 1/2-way: sn wknd* **66/1**
4 **5** *15* **Tregenna**[9] [4068] 3-8-9 ........ MHenry 5 —
(RMHCowell) *sn outpcd and bhd fr 1/2-way* **66/1**
**6** *5* **Ollijay** 3-9-0 ........ MartinDwyer 2 —
(MrsHDalton) *s.i.s: a bhd* **14/1**

1m 27.74s (-0.07) **Going Correction** +0.05s/f (Good)
**WFA** 3 from 4yo 7lb **6** Ran SP% **113.0**
Speed ratings: **102,101,90,82,64 59**CSF £4.73 TOTE £5.00: £1.80, £1.10; EX 7.50.
**Owner** Aston House Stud **Bred** Aston House Stud **Trained** Newmarket, Suffolk

**FOCUS**
An uncompetitive event and a match in all but name.

**NOTEBOOK**
**Literatim** took advantage of the favourite's mental frailties and rallied past him. He probably did not achieve that much in terms of form, but at least he showed the right attitude.
**Kauri Forest(USA)** looked sure to go on and win comfortably when cruising into the lead approaching the two-furlong marker, but it would seem that he is not that keen on being in front, as he put his head in the air and let his chief market rival come back at him. He is now eligible for handicaps, and presumably his challenge will be delayed until the last possible moment in future.
**Zazous** never really got in a blow at the principals, but he shapes as though he will do better when moved into handicap company and granted a stiffer test.
**Lottie** showed some early pace but was soon put in her place.

## 4317 UNISON TRADE UNION POSITIVELY PUBLIC CONDITIONS STKS 6f
**2:10** (2:10) (C) 3-Y-O+ **£8,631** (£3,274; £1,637; £744) **Stalls** High

Form RPR
2266 **1** **Mac Love**[14] [3940] 3-8-9 103 ........ GCarter 7 111
(JAkehurst) *hld up in rr: swtchd lft and hdwy 2f out: rdn and styd on srongly ins last to ld nr fin* **5/1**[3]
2003 **2** *nk* **Lochridge**[22] [3715] 5-8-12 102 ........ MartinDwyer 6 108
(AMBalding) *led: rdn and qcknd wl over 1f out: drvn ins last: hdd and no ex nr fin* **5/4**[1]
-250 **3** *2* **Milk It Mick**[91] [1764] 3-9-3 108 ........ SWKelly 1 112
(JAOsborne) *trckd ldrs: hdwy to chse ldr over 1f out and ev ch tl rdn and nt qckn ins last* **5/2**[2]
5-53 **4** *3* **Tedburrow**[58] [2625] 12-9-0 88 ........ JPMurtagh 3 95
(EJAlston) *hld up: hdwy 2f out: rdn and kpt on fnl f* **12/1**
10-0 **5** *2 ½* **Tashkil (IRE)**[45] [2966] 3-8-9 103 ........ RHills 4 88
(JHMGosden) *sn chsng ldr: rdn along over 2f out: sn wknd* **13/2**
6000 **6** *7* **Safranine (IRE)**[8] [4104] 7-8-9 61 ........ AnnStokell 2 62
(MissAStokell) *in tch on outer: sn rdn along and outpcd fr 1/2-way* **125/1**
6540 **7** *2* **Telepathic (IRE)**[9] [4047] 4-9-0 57 ........ PBradley 5 61
(ABerry) *prom to 1/2-way:sn outpcd and bhd* **100/1**
0060 **8** *2 ½* **Jalouhar**[9] [4047] 4-9-0 46 ........ TWoodley 8 53
(BPJBaugh) *chsd ldrs: rdn along 1/2-way and sn wknd* **200/1**

1m 13.01s (-1.27) **Going Correction** +0.05s/f (Good)
**WFA** 3 from 4yo+ 5lb **8** Ran SP% **113.0**
Speed ratings: **110,109,106,102,99 90,87,84**CSF £11.42 TOTE £4.90: £1.10, £1.20, £1.70; EX 13.80.
**Owner** Vimal Khosla **Bred** Kingwood Bloodstock **Trained** Epsom, Surrey

**FOCUS**
A decent race made up mostly of 'twilight' horses, something reflected in the lack of recent winning form. However, the pace was decent and the form looks fairly sound.

**NOTEBOOK**
**Mac Love**, officially joint best in at the weights, appreciated the drop in grade and fast pace, and came from last to first to win for the first time in the best part of a year. Hopefully this will have done his confidence some good, as he is likely to have to step back up into Pattern company now.
**Lochridge** looked to have been found the perfect opportunity to get off the mark for the season, but although she was given a fine ride and quickened up in good style when asked, she was eventually narrowly denied. There will be other days, and races confined to her own sex will provide the greatest opportunities.
**Milk It Mick**, having his first outing since the Guineas, had not raced over a distance as short as this for over a year. Giving weight all round, he ran well over a trip short of his best, and he is sure to come on for this first run in three months.
**Tedburrow** ran a decent race given that at the ratings he had plenty to find with the principals.
**Tashkil(IRE)** was a smart juvenile but he has now run poorly on both starts this year. He now has questions to answer.

## 4318 JUST TRAYS FILLIES' H'CAP 1m (R)
**2:40** (2:40) (D) (0-85,84) 3-Y-O **£5,605** (£1,724; £862; £431) **Stalls** High

Form RPR
0-11 **1** **Perle D'Or (IRE)**[51] [2820] 3-8-11 **74** ........ ACulhane 6 87+
(WJHaggas) *trckd ldrs on inner: effrt 2f out: swtchd rt and rdn 1f out: styd on strly to ld ins last* **5/2**[1]
6012 **2** *1 ¾* **Charnock Bates One (IRE)**[9] [4050] 3-8-7 **70** ........ DAllan 4 79
(TDEasterby) *hld up: hdwy 3f out: led wl over 1f out: sn rdn and edgd lft: drvn and hdd ins last* **3/1**[3]
0010 **3** *2 ½* **Keeper's Lodge (IRE)**[14] [3926] 3-8-7 **70** ........ GGibbons 5 73
(BAMcmahon) *hld up: hdwy 3f out: rdn and ev ch 2f out tl drvn and one pce ent last* **9/1**

6611 **4** *1* **Keyaki (IRE)**[35] [3306] 3-9-3 **80** .......... JPMurtagh 7 81
(CFWall) *cl up: effrt to ld wl over 2f out: sn rdn and hdd wl over 1f out: drvn and weaked enering last* **11/4**[2]
0450 **5** *10* **Magical Mimi**[7] [4138] 3-7-11 **67** .......... LeanneKershaw(7) 3 45
(JeddO'Keeffe) *hld up: hdwy on outer 4f out: sn rdn and btn 3f out* **20/1**
0-36 **6** *½* **Have Faith (IRE)**[30] [3452] 3-9-7 **84** .......... MHills 2 61
(BWHills) *set stdy pce: qcknd over 3f out: rdn and hdd over 2f out and sn wknd* **9/2**

1m 42.16s (1.61) **Going Correction** +0.35s/f (Good) **6** Ran SP% **113.2**
Speed ratings: **105,103,100,99,89 89**CSF £10.51 TOTE £3.10: £2.10, £2.00; EX 13.00.
**Owner** The Perle d'Or Partnership **Bred** J Bowdren **Trained** Newmarket, Suffolk

**FOCUS**
A fair race but there was a slow early pace to this race and it turned into something of a sprint. However, the first two look progressive and can rate higher.

**NOTEBOOK**
**Perle D'Or(IRE)** found the best turn of foot to mow down her rivals in the straight after they had gone just a steady early pace. She was racking up the hat-trick here and is certainly progressing along the right lines.
**Charnock Bates One(IRE)** is as consistent as they come and once again ran a solid race in defeat.
**Keeper's Lodge(IRE)** found six furlongs too short last time and appreciated the return to a mile, although a stronger all-round gallop would have probably suited her.
**Keyaki(IRE)** did not appear to get home over this longer trip despite the steady early pace.
**Magical Mimi** has dropped 12lb in the handicap this season and this performance did little to suggest she is on the way back.
**Have Faith(IRE)** had the benefit of making the pace in a steadily-run race, but she still shaped like a non-stayer.

## 4319 WEATHERBYS BANK SUMMER CUP (H'CAP) 1m 2f 60y
**3:15** (3:15) (D) (0-85,85) 3-Y-0+ **£22,834** (£7,026; £3,513; £1,756) **Stalls** Low

Form RPR
4215 **1** **Opening Ceremony (USA)**[20] [3781] 5-8-12 **72** .......... THamilton(3) 9 80
(RAFahey) *trckd ldrs: hdwy to ld 2 1/2f out: rdn over 1f out: drvn ins last: hld on gamely* **11/1**[3]
5232 **2** *shd* **Tedsdale Mac**[4] [4209] 5-7-11 **57** .......... NMackay(3) 1 65
(NBycroft) *trckd ldrs on inner: pushed along 2f out: rdn ent last: styd on wl nr fin: jst failed* **7/1**[1]
-005 **3** *hd* **Great Scott**[9] [4061] 3-8-13 **80** .......... SChin 13 88
(MJohnston) *cl up: effrt over 2f out and ev ch tl drvn and no ex nr fin* **25/1**
2460 **4** *hd* **Go Tech**[22] [3714] 4-9-2 **73** .......... GGibbons 4 80
(TDEasterby) *hld up: hdwy over 3f out: rdn wl over 1f out: drvn and kpt on ins last: nrst fin* **14/1**
1360 **5** *nk* **Krugerrand (USA)**[4] [4214] 5-9-13 **84** .......... GCarter 2 91+
(WJMusson) *hld up and bhd: hdwy over 3f out: rdn over 1f out: kpt on ins last: nrst fin* **12/1**
0213 **6** *¾* **Les Arcs (USA)**[29] [3470] 4-9-6 **77** .......... ACulhane 7 82
(RCGuest) *in tch: pushed along and outpcd wl over 2f out: rdn over 1f out: kpt on ins last: nrst fin* **7/1**[1]
2321 **7** *nk* **Rondelet (IRE)**[16] [3872] 3-9-0 **81** .......... MartinDwyer 10 86
(RMBeckett) *trckd ldrs: effrt 3f out: rdn 2f out: drvn and kpt on same pce ent last* **8/1**[2]
5010 **8** *shd* **War Owl (USA)**[21] [3731] 7-9-2 **73** .......... JPMurtagh 15 77+
(IanWilliams) *s.i.s and bhd: hdwy on inner 3f out: rdn and styng on whn n.m.r ent last: kpt on* **7/1**[1]
3006 **9** *¾* **Alekhine (IRE)**[15] [3915] 3-9-1 **82** ..........(e[1]) RHills 11 85+
(PWHarris) *hld up and bhd: hdwy over 2f out: sn rdn along and nt rch ldrs* **7/1**[1]
5206 **10** *nk* **Compton Dragon (USA)**[2] [4258] 5-9-3 **74** ..........(v) MHills 3 76
(DNicholls) *s.i.s: a towards rr* **25/1**
0300 **11** *3 ½* **Swift Alchemist**[17] [3841] 4-8-0 **57** ow1 .......... ADaly 6 53
(MrsHSweeting) *a towards rr* **50/1**
3010 **12** *nk* **Intricate Web (IRE)**[29] [3477] 8-9-12 **83** .......... DAllan 14 78
(EJAlston) *hld up towards rr: hdwy on outer over 3f out: rdn along 2 out and sn btn* **14/1**
0105 **13** *5* **Pawan (IRE)**[7] [4136] 4-9-1 **72** .......... AnnStokell 5 58
(MissAStokell) *midfield: pushed along over 3f out: nvr a factor* **66/1**
3302 **14** *1* **Mbosi (USA)**[7] [4136] 3-9-3 **84** .......... JFanning 12 68
(MJohnston) *led: rdn along over 3f out: hdd 2 1/2f out and sn wknd* **11/1**[3]
6-26 **15** *17* **Solo Flight**[56] [2671] 7-9-11 **85** .......... LFletcher(3) 8 37
(HMorrison) *chsd ldrs on outer: rdn along 3f out: sn wknd* **8/1**[2]

2m 14.99s (3.23) **Going Correction** +0.35s/f (Good) **15** Ran SP% **121.1**
**WFA** 3 from 4yo+ 10lb
Speed ratings: **101,100,100,100,100 99,99,99,98,98 95,95,91,90,77**CSF £83.52 CT £1906.53 TOTE £16.10: £4.90, £2.20, £7.70; EX 94.40.
**Owner** H Hurst **Bred** Juddmonte Farms Inc **Trained** Musley Bank, N Yorks
■ Stewards Enquiry : S Chin two-day ban: used whip with excessive force (Aug 11-12)

**FOCUS**
A good prize for this fair handicap but a bunch finish to a race run at a steady early pace, and the form leaves something to be desired.

**NOTEBOOK**
**Opening Ceremony(USA)**, only 2lb higher than when last winning at Chester, was perfectly positioned to take advantage of the steady early pace, going to the front with over a quarter mile to run and holding on well under pressure.
**Tedsdale Mac** only has a maiden win to his name but he is a consistent performer in this sort of grade over a variety of distances, and this was another good effort.
**Great Scott**, 4lb lower, appears to be returning to form and is now on a mark his trainer can exploit.
**Go Tech** has not won since his two-year-old days, but he has dropped 12lb this season and he gave more encouragement this time, especially as the steady pace did not suit him as a hold-up horse.
**Krugerrand(USA)** got the trip well in this more steadily-run race, although his style of running demands a quicker pace.
**Les Arcs(USA)** could have done with a stronger all-round gallop.
**War Owl(USA)** *Official explanation: jockey said he could not get a run*
**Compton Dragon(USA)** *Official explanation: jockey said he could not get a run*

## 4320 UNION IN FRONT IS UNISON H'CAP 5f
**3:50** (3:51) (E) (0-70,70) 3-Y-0 **£4,321** (£1,329; £664; £332) **Stalls** High

Form RPR
-325 **1** **Bella Boy Zee (IRE)**[159] [865] 3-8-8 **57** .......... GGibbons 11 63
(PABlockley) *chsd ldr: led wl over 1f out: sn rdn: drvn ins last: jst hld on* **14/1**
0124 **2** *shd* **Short Chorus**[17] [3838] 3-8-3 **52** ..........(p) DAllan 5 58
(JBalding) *prom: rdn along over 1f out: drvn and styd on ins last: jst failed* **7/1**[3]
0100 **3** *hd* **Piccleyes**[16] [3871] 3-8-11 **60** ..........(b) MHills 10 65
(RHannon) *hld up: hdwy 2f out: swtchd lft and rdn ent last: styd on wl nr fin* **8/1**
44-4 **4** *½* **Kamenka**[36] [3267] 3-9-4 **70** .......... THamilton(3) 3 73
(RAFahey) *chsd ldrs: effrt and ev ch over 1f out: drvn ins last and no ex nr fin* **12/1**
0200 **5** *½* **Piccolo Prince**[28] [3523] 3-9-4 **67** .......... JPMurtagh 6 68
(EJAlston) *midfield: hdwy and nt clr run over 1f out: swtchd rt ins last and kpt on towards fin* **9/1**
6211 **6** *¾* **Nanna (IRE)**[17] [3838] 3-9-6 **69** .......... ACulhane 4 70+
(RHollinshead) *chsd ldrs: effr 2f out: sn rdn and wknd ins last* **9/4**[1]
0-50 **7** *nk* **Hamaasy**[28] [3511] 3-8-12 **61** .......... JFanning 9 58
(DNicholls) *chsd ldrs: rdn o ver 1f out: wknd ent last* **25/1**
5043 **8** *1* **Obe Bold (IRE)**[17] [3838] 3-8-10 **59** .......... PBradley 12 52
(ABerry) *towards rr: hdwy 2f out: sn rdn and no imp fnl f* **6/1**[2]
-030 **9** *2 ½* **Fitzwarren**[20] [3777] 3-9-5 **68** ..........(v) MartinDwyer 7 51
(NBycroft) *s.i.s and behind tl styd on appr last* **11/1**
3500 **10** *½* **Smart Starprincess (IRE)**[16] [3887] 3-8-5 **57** ..........(b) NMackay(3) 8 38
(MJAttwater) *led: rdn and hdd over 1f out: sn wknd* **14/1**
00-0 **11** *1 ¼* **First Eclipse (IRE)**[17] [3838] 3-8-3 **52** ow2 .......... JEdmunds 2 28
(JBalding) *chsd ldrs: rdn along 1/2-way: sn wknd* **28/1**
3053 **12** *1 ½* **Only If I Laugh**[33] [3364] 3-8-11 **60** ..........(b) GParkin 1 30
(PABlockley) *a rr* **10/1**

62.00 secs (0.58) **Going Correction** +0.05s/f (Good) **12** Ran SP% **124.4**
Speed ratings: **97,96,96,95,94 93,93,91,87,86 84,82**CSF £114.19 CT £871.72 TOTE £21.30: £4.80, £2.40, £2.60; EX 148.60 Place 6 £41.47, Place 5 £23.18.
**Owner** Transbuild **Bred** Humphrey Okeke **Trained** Southwell, Notts

**FOCUS**
A modest handicap although the form looks fairly reliable for the level.

**NOTEBOOK**
**Bella Boy Zee(IRE)**, a five-furlong specialist, shrugged off a five-month absence to score in battling style. She had a good draw on this occasion though, and it remains to be seen whether she can build on it.
**Short Chorus** has been running well this season and only narrowly failed to win his second race of the year. She was not as well drawn as the winner or third.
**Piccleyes** ran well over a distance which looked too short for her. She will appreciate a return to six furlongs.
**Kamenka** was another who will be happier over six. This was not a bad run on her handicap debut.
**Piccolo Prince** prefers a bit of give in the ground and has been doing his recent winning over six furlongs. He was staying on well at the finish.
**Nanna(IRE)**, who has made all on each of the three occasions he has won, could not get to the front on this occasion.
**Smart Starprincess(IRE)** showed good early speed. *Official explanation: jockey said filly was unsuited by the ground*
T/Plt: £35.60 to a £1 stake. Pool: £42,203.95. 863.80 winning units. T/Qpdt: £38.50 to a £1 stake. Pool: £2,630.90. 50.55 winning units. JR

# 4285 GOODWOOD (R-H)
## Saturday, July 31

**OFFICIAL GOING: Good to firm**
Wind: lt hlf against Weather: sunny and warm

## 4321 VODAFONE FILLIES' STKS (REGISTERED AS THE LILLIE LANGTRY STAKES) (GROUP 3) 1m 6f
**2:00** (2:02) (A) 3-Y-0+ **£29,000** (£11,000; £5,500; £2,500) **Stalls** High

Form RPR
5121 **1** **Astrocharm (IRE)**[6] [4176] 5-9-6 83 .......... NCallan 7 102
(MHTompkins) *hld up in 5th: clsd on ldrs 4f out: nt clr run 3f out: plld out and effrt 2f out: rdn to ld last 100yds: styd on wl* **12/1**
-311 **2** *¾* **Pongee**[28] [3519] 4-9-11 107 .......... JFortune 5 106
(LMCumani) *hld up in 6th: prog to ld 3f out: rdn and hdd 2f out: sn led again: hrd rdn and hdd last 100yds: kpt on* **11/8**[1]
-326 **3** *4* **Summitville**[28] [3519] 4-9-6 104 .......... LDettori 2 95
(JGGiven) *lw: hld up in last: rapid prog over 3f out: shkn up to ld narrowly 2f out: sn hdd and fnd nil: wknd ins fnl f* **3/1**[2]
3166 **4** *2* **Feaat**[14] [3944] 3-8-6 90 .......... KMcEvoy 6 93
(JHMGosden) *lw: trckd ldr: squeezed out 8f out and sn lost pl: effrt again to ld briefly over 3f out: rdn and btn over 2f out* **20/1**
4-51 **5** *3* **Daring Aim**[8] [4087] 3-8-6 .......... KFallon 4 88
(SirMichaelStoute) *swtg: reluctant to enter stalls: in tch: trckd ldr 6f out: chal over 3f out: sn nt qckn: flashed tail u.p 2f out whn btn* **10/1**
3113 **6** *dist* **Portrait Of A Lady (IRE)**[14] [3944] 3-8-6 93 .......... WRyan 3 —
(HRACecil) *led at str pce: hdd over 3f out: wknd rapidly over 2f out: t.o* **9/2**[3]
31/5 **7** *dist* **Ballerina Suprema (IRE)**[35] [3327] 4-9-6 85 .......... DHolland 1 —
(CREgerton) *t.k.h: prom: pushed up to press ldr 8f out where no room: wknd over 3f out: sn wl t.o* **33/1**

3m 0.27s (-3.48) **Going Correction** -0.025s/f (Good)
**WFA** 3 from 4yo+ 14lb **7** Ran SP% **109.8**
Speed ratings: **108,107,105,104,102** —,—CSF £26.81 TOTE £15.00: £4.90, £1.60; EX 31.60.
**Owner** Mystic Meg Limited **Bred** Miss D J Merson **Trained** Newmarket, Suffolk
■ Stewards Enquiry : K McEvoy one-day ban (reduced from two on appeal): careless riding (Aug 11)

**FOCUS**
A weak Group Three, but the pace was strong, and the first two came clear. Pongee was a little below her best but Astrocharm has nevertheless clearly improved again and the Newmarket handicap in which she was second behind Mephisto could hardly be working out better.

**NOTEBOOK**
**Astrocharm(IRE)** was taking a big step up in class after winning a 0-80 classified stakes at Pontefract only six days previously, but she is in terrific form and stayed on dourly over the extra two furlongs. This was much improved form, and she could be rated a little better, as she was momentarily stopped in her run three out. However, she is unlikely to find another Group race as weak as this and will struggle back in handicaps when she has been reassessed.
**Pongee** looked booked for success when winning the battle with Summitville and hitting the front approaching the final furlong, but that took its toll and she had no more to give under her penalty when the eventual winner challenged. She got this trip well enough and looks a Park Hill type, but before that she will probably bid to maintain her trainer's excellent record in the Galtres Stakes at York.
**Summitville** was entitled to get closer to Pongee on these 5lb better terms and on this faster ground, but she found little after edging narrowly ahead two out, looking the likely winner. This was another below-par display, but the trip may have found her out.
**Feaat** ran her race and was far from disgraced at these weights. She did not see out this trip, and can be expected to get closer when reverting to shorter, at a more realistic level. *Official explanation: jockey said filly slipped on the top bend*
**Daring Aim** played up at the start and during the race, giving Fallon a very hard time. She has talent, but is still to fully mature and is not one to place any faith in.

**Portrait Of A Lady(IRE)**, who has started to fulfil her potential this year, suprisingly made the early running over this longer trip and paid for setting too strong a pace. She is capable of better than this.

**Ballerina Suprema(IRE)** was not done any favours early on, but ran too keen over this longer trip and was tailed off at the finish. She is useful, but only has a juvenile maiden win to her name, and will be found wanting if tried at this level again.

## 4322 VODAFONE THOROUGHBRED STKS (LISTED RACE) 1m
**2:30** (2:33) (A) 3-Y-O **£20,300** (£7,700; £3,850; £1,750) **Stalls** High

Form RPR

1 **1** **Fong's Thong (USA)**[15] 3906 3-8-12 108 ........ JFortune 9 113
(BJMeehan) *h.d.w: lw: mde all at gd pce: 2l clr 2f out: rdn and styd on strly fr over 1f out: impressive* **6/4**[1]

-421 **2** *2* **Mandobi (IRE)**[44] 3001 3-8-12 102 ........ LDettori 6 108
(ACStewart) *hld up in midfield: nt clr run over 2f out: plld out wl over 1f out: prog to chse wnr ins fnl f: no imp* **5/2**[2]

3040 **3** *shd* **Kings Point (IRE)**[23] 3673 3-8-12 98 ........ DaneO'Neill 8 108?
(RHannon) *lw: trckd ldng pair: rdn to chse wnr over 1f out to ins fnl f: kpt on* **33/1**

-604 **4** *3* **Resplendent One (IRE)**[23] 3671 3-8-12 97 ........ RMiles 5 101
(TGMills) *t.k.h: pressed wnr: rdn over 2f out: lost 2nd pl over 1f out: fdd fnl f* **33/1**

2440 **5** *1* **Jack Sullivan (USA)**[43] 3036 3-8-12 98 ........(bt[1]) EAhern 2 99
(GAButler) *t.k.h: hld up in rr: rdn over 2f out: one pce and n.d fr wl over 1f out* **25/1**

5666 **6** *shd* **Kelucia (IRE)**[12] 3978 3-8-7 97 ........ RFfrench 1 94
(JSGoldie) *s.i.s: hld up in last: rdn over 2f out: one pce and n.d* **25/1**

2030 **7** *3 ½* **Thyolo (IRE)**[28] 3539 3-8-12 99 ........ RSmith 3 91
(CGCox) *hld up towards rr: rdn 3f out: no prog over 2f out: btn after* **9/1**

4-40 **8** *4* **Auditorium**[45] 2966 3-8-12 109 ........ KFallon 7 81
(SirMichaelStoute) *chsd ldng trio: rdn over 2f out: btn wl over 1f out: eased ins fnl f* **5/1**[3]

0040 **9** *dist* **Bahiano (IRE)**[7] 4120 3-8-12 105 ........ DHolland 4 —
(CEBrittain) *nvr gng wl: a in rr: struggling 3f out: eased 2f out: t.o* **20/1**

1m 37.81s (-2.46) **Going Correction** -0.025s/f (Good) **9** Ran SP% **113.6**
Speed ratings: **111,109,108,105,104 104,101,97,—**CSF £4.72 TOTE £2.60: £1.20, £1.20, £5.70; EX 5.50 Trifecta £62.60 Pool of £2,301.95 - 26.10 winning units.
**Owner** Joe L Allbritton **Bred** W A Hamilton **Trained** Upper Lambourn, Berks

**FOCUS**
A decent contest run at a strong gallop. The winner has obvious Group race potential, but the form behind him should possibly be treated with a degree of caution.

**NOTEBOOK**
**Fong's Thong(USA)**, who had looked colt of real potential when scoring on his British debut at Newbury, confirmed that promise with another impressive success. Racing over an extra furlong, he once again made all of the running and did well to quicken twice in the straight. He has really improved since being switched to the turf from the US this year, and he certainly looks worthy of his chance in Group company. Brian Meehan may aim as high as the Queen Elizabeth II Stakes, but the Celebration Mile, back at this venue, would provide a good stepping stone.
**Mandobi(IRE)** ◆, who produced his best effort when winning the Britannia at Royal Ascot last time, was pulled out to have a chance entering the final furlong, but could not get to the winner, try as he might. This was another improved effort, nevertheless, and he should find a race at this level before the season is out.
**Kings Point(IRE)**, who won his maiden at this track as a juvenile, is inconsistent but appeared to turn in an improved display, doing all of his best work late on. He relished this faster ground, and although he does look exposed, could be placed to find a race over the trip at this level.
**Resplendent One(IRE)** again ran keen through the early parts and has his quirks, but turned in another sound effort at the weights.
**Jack Sullivan(USA)** failed to run up to form with Kings Point in the first-time blinkers. He is a very tricky ride and looks too high in the ratings at present.
**Kelucia(IRE)** lost ground at the start from her wide draw and was up against it from then on. She has not really gone on from her successful juvenile campaign and will probably remain hard to place.
**Thyolo(IRE)** again turned in a disappointing display and could be going the wrong way. He had his conditions on this occasion and has it all to prove now.
**Auditorium** was hard at it from some way out and turned in a very poor effort. He had looked very smart last year, but injury struck, and he has yet to prove that he is over his problems.
**Bahiano(IRE)** again looked moody and was never going. *Official explanation: jockey said colt moved badly throughout*

## 4323 VODAFONE NASSAU STKS (GROUP 1) (F&M) 1m 1f 192y
**3:05** (3:06) (A) 3-Y-O+ **£116,000** (£44,000; £22,000; £10,000) **Stalls** High

Form RPR

5-16 **1** **Favourable Terms**[25] 3600 4-9-2 112 ........ KFallon 2 115
(SirMichaelStoute) *hld up in tch: plld out and effrt over 2f out: shkn up to ld over 1f out: hrd rdn and edgd rt ins fnl f: jst hld on* **11/2**[3]

1202 **2** *shd* **Silence Is Golden**[29] 3484 5-9-2 101 ........ JFortune 1 115
(BJMeehan) *lw: hld up in last: effrt 3f out: drvn 2f out: r.o wl fnl f: jst failed* **12/1**

3-11 **3** *nk* **Chorist**[35] 3331 5-9-2 112 ........ DHolland 4 114
(WJHaggas) *trckd ldr: led 3f out: hrd rdn and hdd over 1f out: pressed wnr after: hld whn n.m.r and lost 2nd nr fin* **6/4**[1]

5-3 **4** *7* **Zosima (USA)**[45] 2971 3-8-6 107 ........(t) LDettori 3 101
(SaeedBinSuroor) *swtg: b.hind: hld up in tch: shkn up 3f out: no prog and sn btn* **2/1**[2]

1-44 **5** *1 ¼* **Echoes In Eternity (IRE)**[70] 2318 4-9-2 107 ........(t) KMcEvoy 6 99
(SaeedBinSuroor) *led to 3f out: wknd over 1f out* **9/1**

0210 **6** *¾* **Menhoubah (USA)**[48] 2925 3-8-6 106 ........(p) SSanders 5 97
(CEBrittain) *trckd ldng pair: hrd rdn to chal over 2f out: wknd over 1f out* **20/1**

2m 5.70s (-1.98) **Going Correction** -0.025s/f (Good)
**WFA** 3 from 4yo+ 10lb **6** Ran SP% **111.2**
Speed ratings: **106,105,105,100,99 98**CSF £60.73 TOTE £5.50: £2.70, £2.20; EX 60.40.
**Owner** Maktoum Al Maktoum **Bred** Gainsborough Stud Management Ltd **Trained** Newmarket, Suffolk
■ Stewards Enquiry : K Fallon one-day ban: careless riding (Aug 11)

**FOCUS**
A poor renewal of this Group One and the older horses dominated the finish. The winning time was very modest for a race of its type.

**NOTEBOOK**
**Favourable Terms** put a disappointing effort at Newmarket last time firmly behind her, to win all out over this longer trip. She had looked likley to win a touch cosily when hitting the front late on, but was made to pull out all the stops by Chorist, and then had to dig very deep to stick her head out on the line when the runner-up came to challenge. She is almost certainly better at a mile, and deserves great credit for this victory, but is not the soundest of fillies, and does not appeal as one to follow-up in a Group One.
**Silence Is Golden** absolutely flew at the death, having looked to have it all to do two from home, and only lost out by the most narrow of margins. This was by far her best display to date (she had won on her reappearance this year off a mark of 95) and she is very smart on her day, but she is in foal and looks to have made her last appearance on a racecourse. Her paddock value will now have been greatly enhanced.
**Chorist**, who came into this in the form of her life having won a Group One in Ireland last time, was not beaten far, but still ran below par. She is well-suited to this trip and had her ground, but could not fend off the challengers late on, so was disappointing in the circumstances.
**Zosima(USA)**, third off top weight in a handicap at Royal Ascot on her British debut last time, never seriously threatened over the longer trip in this much better company. She was a short price for this and is worthy of another chance back at a mile, when racing at a more realistic level.
**Echoes In Eternity(IRE)**, winner of the Sun Chariot in 2003, set the race up for the first three home. She is a decent filly in her own right and deserves to take her chance in a Group Two contest.
**Menhoubah(USA)** failed to improve as expected for this faster ground and ran a tame race. She has it all to prove at this level now.

## 4324 VODAFONE STEWARDS' CUP (HERITAGE H'CAP) 6f
**3:35** (3:46) (B) 3-Y-O+ **£58,000** (£22,000; £11,000; £5,000) **Stalls** Low

Form RPR

0012 **1** **Pivotal Point**[6] 4165 4-8-11 **91** 3ex ........ SSanders 1 106+
(PJMakin) *s.i.s: sn trckd nr side ldrs: gng easily 2f out: rdn to ld over 1f out: edgd rt but in command fnl f* **7/1**[1]

4101 **2** *1 ¼* **Fantasy Believer**[7] 4130 6-8-9 **89** 5ex ........ DHolland 24 100+
(JJQuinn) *lw: dwlt: last of far side gp early: prog whn nt clr run over 1f out: str run fnl f to ld gp last strides* **10/1**[3]

3630 **3** *nk* **High Reach**[30] 3453 4-8-11 **91** ........ KFallon 28 101
(TGMills) *lw: led far side gp and racd against rail: 2l clr and drvn 1f out: nt on terms w wnr after: lost ld fnl strides* **7/1**[1]

4134 **4** *½* **Two Step Kid (USA)**[7] 4152 3-8-10 **95** ........ EAhern 6 104
(JNoseda) *trckd nr side ldrs: effrt 2f out: rdn to chse wnr fnl f: edgd rt and no imp* **9/1**[2]

0046 **5** *hd* **Simianna**[7] 4152 5-8-8 **93** ........(p) PPMathers[(5)] 10 101
(ABerry) *lw: wl in rr nr side: rdn over 2f out: styd on wl fnl f: nrst fin* **40/1**

6050 **6** *nk* **Halmahera (IRE)**[14] 3961 9-9-4 **98** ........ NCallan 29 105
(KARyan) *cl up far side: chsd ldr over 1f out: no imp ins fnl f: kpt on* **40/1**

1001 **7** *shd* **Artie**[22] 3713 5-8-6 **86** 3ex ........ BDoyle 9 93
(TDEasterby) *w nr side ldr: ev ch over 1f out: one pce after* **50/1**

4110 **8** *½* **Raccoon (IRE)**[56] 2679 4-8-10 **90** ........(v) KDarley 2 95
(TDBarron) *b.hind: led nr side gp to over 1f out: nt qckn fnl f* **20/1**

1112 **9** *hd* **Material Witness (IRE)**[2] 4273 7-9-0 **94** 5ex ........ LDettori 4 99
(WRMuir) *swtg: chsd nr side ldrs: rdn and struggling 2f out: styd on wl last 150yds: nrst fin* **14/1**

0006 **10** *nk* **Cd Europe (IRE)**[15] 3901 6-8-9 **89** ........(p) WRyan 30 93
(KARyan) *hld up wl in rr far side: hmpd on inner 1/2-way: swtchd lft 2f out: rdn and styd on fr over 1f out: nt rcvr* **66/1**

0230 **11** *nk* **Proud Boast**[6] 4165 6-8-9 **89** ........ KMcEvoy 27 92
(DNicholls) *chsd far side ldrs: rdn and hanging over 1f out: kpt on same pce fnl f* **25/1**

4066 **12** *shd* **Texas Gold**[14] 3945 6-8-9 **89** ........ RMullen 25 92
(WRMuir) *lw: hld up in rr far side: n.m.r over 2f out: prog to chse ldrs over 1f out: one pce ins fnl f* **14/1**

0211 **13** *shd* **Caribbean Coral**[36] 3266 5-9-9 **103** ........ RWinston 8 105
(JJQuinn) *dwlt: last of nr side gp: rdn and struggling over 2f out: styd on wl fnl 150yds: nvr nrr* **16/1**

1460 **14** *1* **Royal Storm (IRE)**[7] 4120 5-9-5 **99** ........ JFortune 26 98
(MrsAJPerrett) *lw: pressed far side ldr to over 1f out: wknd ins fnl f* **16/1**

0040 **15** *¾* **Smokin Beau**[6] 4165 7-9-2 **96** ........ TGMcLaughlin 5 93
(NPLittmoden) *chsd nr side ldrs: rdn 1/2-way: lost pl and struggling over 2f out: modest late prog* **40/1**

4201 **16** *hd* **Mutawaqed (IRE)**[7] 4152 6-8-10 **90** 5ex ........(t) RLMoore 14 86
(MAMagnusson) *b: b.hind:hld up in rr far side: nt clr run over 2f out: kpt on fr over 1f out: nt pce to rch ldrs* **10/1**[3]

6360 **17** *1 ¼* **Pic Up Sticks**[6] 4165 5-9-2 **96** ........ TEDurcan 11 89
(MRChannon) *lw: hld up in rr of nr side gp: prog on outer 2f out: shkn up and fnd nil over 1f out* **7/1**[1]

0236 **18** *¾* **Corridor Creeper (FR)**[6] 4165 7-9-1 **95** ........(p) CCatlin 22 85
(JMBradley) *pressed far side ldrs tl wknd wl over 1f out* **50/1**

1003 **19** *hd* **Native Title**[21] 3754 6-8-7 **87** ........ NPollard 23 77
(DNicholls) *settled in rr far side: rdn and no real prog wl over 1f out* **25/1**

3020 **20** *1 ½* **Marsad (IRE)**[35] 3324 10-8-8 **88** ........ PDoe 13 73
(JAkehurst) *racd on outer of nr side gp: chsd ldrs: struggling and btn wl over 1f out* **100/1**

0000 **21** *¾* **Whitbarrow (IRE)**[6] 4165 5-9-2 **96** ........(p) DaneO'Neill 15 79
(JMBradley) *racd on wd outside of nr side gp: in tch 4f: sn btn* **66/1**

0105 **22** *½* **Circuit Dancer (IRE)**[28] 3522 4-9-2 **96** ........ RFfrench 12 78
(ABerry) *chsd nr side ldrs for 4f: sn wknd* **100/1**

4145 **23** *3 ½* **Blackheath (IRE)**[6] 4165 8-8-4 **87** 5ex ........ LPKeniry[(3)] 7 58
(DNicholls) *chsd nr side ldrs for 4f: wknd* **28/1**

0352 **24** *nk* **Dazzling Bay**[28] 3522 4-9-8 **102** ........ JFEgan 18 72
(TDEasterby) *ref to go to post tl dismntd and led to s: reluctant to enter stalls: chsd far side ldrs 4f: no ch whn hmpd over 1f out* **20/1**

0020 **25** *5* **Coconut Penang (IRE)**[23] 3673 4-9-2 **96** ........(b[1]) SWhitworth 17 51
(PWChapple-Hyam) *racd on outer of far side gp: chsd ldrs over 3f: no ch whn bdly hmpd by loose horse over 1f out* **20/1**

0000 **26** *12* **Stormont (IRE)**[15] 3906 4-9-10 **104** ........(v) JQuinn 20 23
(HJCollingridge) *dwlt: racd far side: a in rr: eased over 1f out: t.o* **66/1**

0040 **27** *1 ½* **Funfair Wane**[6] 4165 5-8-13 **93** ........ ANicholls 21 8
(DNicholls) *sn rdn to chse far side ldrs: wknd and eased 2f out: t.o* **50/1**

2000 **U** **Peruvian Chief (IRE)**[63] 2475 7-8-12 **95** ........(v) J-PGuillambert[(3)] 19 —
(NPLittmoden) *swvd and uns rdr s* **100/1**

1m 10.78s (-2.06) **Going Correction** -0.025s/f (Good)
**WFA** 3 from 4yo+ 5lb **28** Ran SP% **136.9**
Speed ratings: **112,110,109,109,109 108,108,107,107,107 106,106,106,105,104 103,102,101,100,98 97,97,92,92,85** CSF £65.31 CT £538.30 TOTE £10.10: £3.20, £3.30, £2.50, £3.70; EX 111.30 Trifecta £986.80 Pool of £23,073.95 - 16.60 winning units.
**Owner** R A Bernard **Bred** T R Lock **Trained** Ogbourne Maisey, Wilts

**FOCUS**
Not a vintage field, but strong handicap form nevertheless. The stands' side group were favoured, defying the historical bias but continuing a trend that had prevailed in sprints all week. The form looks solid in the main, and those placed on the far side can be rated slightly better than their finishing positions suggest.

**NOTEBOOK**
**Pivotal Point**, who had recently hit form with a vengeance over five furlongs, produced an excellent turn of foot to quicken into the lead and win going away, on the favoured stands' side. He was slow to break this time, but it proved to his advantage over this extra furlong, as he was travelling with ease before asked to go and win his race. Rapidly improving, he looks a sprinter capable of going places this year, as the division is notably weak and his stable excels with this type. It is interesting that his trainer cited the Prix de L'Abbaye at Longchamp as a possible target, as he saddled Imperial Beauty to finish a short-head runner-up in 1999 and obviously holds this gelding in similarly high esteem.
**Fantasy Believer** was not helped by his sluggish start and had to overcome trouble in running as he made his way from the back of the far-side group. He flew at the finish to 'win' his race, but Pivotal Point was beyond recall. He is in the form of his life but was already due a 6lb rise.
**High Reach**, who boasts some solid form in this division, showed very good early pace to lead on the far side, but could do nothing when the eventual winner went past on the stands' side and eventually lost second near the line. He ran better than the bare form would suggest, and surely has a big handicap within his grasp.
**Two Step Kid(USA)**, the only three-year-old in the field, looked a threat entering the last two furlongs, but quickly came under maximum pressure and could not quicken with the principals when it really mattered. He still turned in a blinding effort against his elders, and although already due a 4lb rise even before this, he has youth on his side and is open to plenty more improvement.
**Simianna**, sixth in the corresponding race last season, ran very much up to that form this time around. She responded gamely to heavy pressure over two out and was finishing with real effect. Granted a favourable draw in an event such as the Ayr Gold Cup in September, she appeals as the type to go well at decent odds.
**Halmahera(IRE)**, with the blinkers left off for this, registered by far his best display of the current campaign. He has slipped to a favourable mark, and will be entitled to go very close if bidding for his third straight win in the Portland Handicap at Doncaster in September.
**Artie** produced a sterling effort, on much faster ground than he ideally prefers. He looks capable of taking a decent prize off this sort of mark, when able to get his toe into the ground once again.
**Raccoon(IRE)** showed his customary early pace, but was there to be shot at over this distance, and will greatly appreciate a return to the minimum trip. He left the impression his best is yet to come.
**Material Witness(IRE)** has been in excellent form this season and was runner-up over seven furlongs at this track two days previously, but he could not get to the front over this shorter trip. He was finishing with purpose, and is clearly best over the extra furlong, but he will be weighted to the hilt for the foreseeable future and will need to improve again.
**Cd Europe(IRE)** suffered a nightmare passage from halfway and would have finished a lot closer with a clear run. He appreciated the re-application of the cheekpieces, and although he will always need luck in running this effort suggest he may have another prize in him before the year is out.
**Mutawaqed(IRE)**, under a 5lb penalty for winning impressively at York recently, was interestingly switched to race off the pace on the unfavoured far side, but lost ground in doing so, and was unable to muster his usual strong finish.
**Pic Up Sticks** had things go his way this time, but found less than looked likely off the bridle. This was disappointing.
**Coconut Penang(IRE)** was already well beaten whe he was hampered by the loose horse. He has not built on his excellent second in the Wokingham in June and is one to treat with caution at present. *Official explanation: jockey said colt was eased after being hampered by a loose horse*
**Stormont(IRE)** *Official explanation: jockey said colt lost its action*
**Funfair Wane** *Official explanation: jockey said gelding lost its action*

## 4325 VODAFONE RACEGOERS CLUB NURSERY STKS (H'CAP) 6f
4:10 (4:17) (C) 2-Y-O £10,822 (£3,330; £1,665; £832) Stalls Low

Form RPR
334 **1** **Easy Feeling (IRE)**[56] 2686 2-8-8 **79** ........ RLMoore 7 83
(RHannon) *lw: trckd ldrs: shkn up and edgd lft wl over 1f out: rdn and r.o to ld jst ins fnl f: sn clr* **13/2**
2261 **2** *2 ½* **Bibury Flyer**[9] 4046 2-8-10 **84** ........ SHitchcott(3) 3 84+
(MRChannon) *lw: hld up in rr: nt clr run over 2f out: swtchd rt wl over 1f out: sn rdn and nt qckn: styd on to take 2nd nr fin* **10/3**[1]
526 **3** *nk* **Come Good**[54] 2736 2-8-1 **72** ........ RSmith 2 68
(RHannon) *pressed ldrs to 1/2-way: sn outpcd and drvn: wl in rr 2f out: nt clr run over 1f out: styd on wl again fnl f* **14/1**
140 **4** *nk* **Talcen Gwyn (IRE)**[14] 3930 2-8-10 **81** ........ JFEgan 4 76
(MFHarris) *b: led: rdn over 1f out: hdd & wknd jst ins fnl f* **14/1**
3221 **5** *1* **Gifted Gamble**[7] 4124 2-8-13 **84** ........(b) NCallan 8 76
(KARyan) *lw: wnt lft s: mostly pressed ldr: hrd rdn 2f out: ev ch over 1f out: nt qckn* **6/1**[3]
1534 **6** *½* **Empire's Ghodha**[21] 3753 2-9-5 **90** ........ JFortune 5 80
(BJMeehan) *hld up in rr: prog to chse ldrs 2f out: n.m.r and nt qckn 1f out: one pce after* **11/2**[2]
0010 **7** *10* **Rancho Cucamonga (IRE)**[12] 3975 2-8-5 **76** ........ KDarley 9 36
(TDBarron) *wnt rt s: racd on outer: chsd ldrs: wknd rapidly and eased jst over 1f out* **15/2**
130 **8** *1* **Gortumblo**[37] 3242 2-9-7 **92** ........ SSanders 6 49
(DJSFfrenchDavis) *hld up in rr: effrt over 2f out: wknd rapidly over 1f out* **8/1**
6010 **9** *6* **Blue Marble**[21] 3753 2-8-6 **77** ........ KFallon 1 16
(CEBrittain) *pushed along early: prom 4f: wkng whn nt clr run over 1f out: eased* **7/1**

1m 12.35s (-0.49) **Going Correction** -0.025s/f (Good) **9** Ran SP% **114.8**
Speed ratings: **102,98,98,97,96 95,82,81,73**CSF £28.27 CT £295.42 TOTE £7.30: £1.90, £1.70, £3.00; EX 21.40.
**Owner** Speedlith Group **Bred** P E Banahan **Trained** East Everleigh, Wilts

**FOCUS**
A decent nursery, but rather a messy race and so it remains to be seen how reliable the form is. The winner has been assessed as having improved 12lb, and the runner-up is a bit better than the bare facts suggest. The 'official ratings' are only an estimate and are for guidance only.

**NOTEBOOK**
**Easy Feeling(IRE)** quickened up nicely when in the clear entering the final furlong to run out a comfortable winner. She had shown definite promise in her three previous outings, but this was by far her best display to date, and she clearly relished the step back up to this trip. She will now probably head to Ireland, where she will have every chance of maintaining her yard's outstanding record in the valuable sales race in August.
**Bibury Flyer**, finally off the mark at the tenth attempt last time, was trying another furlong and had to wait for the gaps to appear two out. She found less than looked likely under pressure when in the clear, and never looked a serious threat to the winner, but she is yet to run a bad race and gives the form a solid look.
**Come Good** , who disappointed when a beaten favourite in a weak maiden at Windsor last time, stepped up on that form and ran his best race to date. He got outpaced this time, and shaped as though he will do better over another furlong, but can certainly be placed to score off this sort of mark before the year is out.
**Talcen Gwyn(IRE)** showed good early pace to tow the field along, but had no more in the locker when challenged approaching the last furlong. He improved on his recent efforts however, and a drop back to the minimum trip would be to his advantage.
**Gifted Gamble** did not improve as expected over this extra furlong and finished well held after showing good early pace. He had been a model of consistency in maidens prior to this and may be worth another chance at this trip on a more conventional track, but has a bit to prove now.
**Empire's Ghodha** ran with credit over this extra furlong, but does look high enough in the weights, on the overall balance of his form.

## 4326 VODAFONE NURSERY STKS (H'CAP) 7f
4:45 (4:46) (C) 2-Y-O £10,968 (£3,375; £1,687; £843) Stalls High

Form RPR
303 **1** **Keep Bacckinhit (IRE)**[12] 3992 2-8-3 **77** ........ LisaJones(3) 7 81
(GLMoore) *lw: hld up in midfield: nt clr run briefly over 2f out: prog over 1f out: rdn to ld last 75yds: jst hld on* **20/1**
1103 **2** *shd* **Justaquestion**[23] 3679 2-8-13 **84** ........ KFallon 4 87
(IAWood) *hld up in last pair: nt clr run over 2f out: swtchd to inner and prog jst over 1f out: r.o nr fin: jst failed* **7/1**
051 **3** *1* **Lady Chef**[42] 3083 2-8-5 **76** ........ TEDurcan 8 77
(BRMillman) *trckd ldrs: effrt to ld on inner wl over 1f out: kpt on fnl f: hdd last 75yds* **8/1**
501 **4** *2 ½* **Al Garhoud Bridge**[31] 3406 2-9-4 **92** ........ SHitchcott(3) 6 87+
(MRChannon) *h.d.w: lw: hld up bhd ldrs: n.m.r 1/2-way: prog to chal 2f out : rdn and ev ch over 1f out: fdd fnl f* **7/4**[1]
230 **5** *5* **Exit Smiling**[14] 3938 2-8-5 **76** ........ RFfrench 5 58
(MJohnston) *chsd ldr to 2f out: wknd* **6/1**[3]
5106 **6** *nk* **Elisha (IRE)**[14] 3930 2-7-9 **71** ........ DFox(5) 9 52
(DMSimcock) *led to wl over 1f out: wkng whn squeezed out 1f out* **12/1**
541 **7** *½* **Emerald Penang (IRE)**[30] 3438 2-8-9 **80** ........ SWhitworth 3 60
(PWChapple-Hyam) *trckd ldrs: lost pl 3f out: sn rdn and struggling: hung rt and wknd 2f out* **4/1**[2]
155 **8** *1 ½* **Trempjane**[24] 3643 2-8-11 **82** ........ DaneO'Neill 1 58
(RHannon) *lw: a in last pair: u.p and no prog over 2f out* **33/1**
0024 **9** *¾* **Miss Malone (IRE)**[8] 4074 2-8-11 **82** ........ RLMoore 2 56
(RHannon) *in tch: hrd rdn wl over 2f out: sn wknd* **16/1**

1m 28.43s (0.40) **Going Correction** -0.025s/f (Good) **9** Ran SP% **115.5**
Speed ratings: **96,95,94,91,86 85,85,83,82**CSF £152.70 CT £1237.73 TOTE £19.40: £3.20, £1.90, £2.00; EX 125.90.
**Owner** Pleasure Palace Racing **Bred** Thomas And Nora Russell **Trained** Woodingdean, E Sussex
■ A landmark for Lisa Jones, who joins Emma O'Gorman and Alex Greaves as the only girls to ride out their claims.
■ Stewards Enquiry : S Hitchcott one-day ban: careless riding (Aug 11)

**FOCUS**
A useful field to a nursery that was run at sound pace, and the first three finished clear, all showing improved form. However, it was a messy affair, and the form might not be entirely reliable.

**NOTEBOOK**
**Keep Bacckinhit(IRE)** found a neat turn of foot when quickening clear approaching the final furlong and did well to hold off the fast finishing Justaquestion at the line. She got first run on the rather unlucky runner-up, but still turned in a much improved display over this longer trip, and is entitled to improve again on this first ever win.
**Justaquestion ◆** , making her nursery debut, suffered constant traffic problems in the straight, but flew home when in the clear would have won in another couple of strides. She has really improved since being stepped up to this trip, but the ground was plenty fast enough for her. She should have no trouble going one better in this sphere.
**Lady Chef**, off the mark when upped to this trip last time, held every chance if good enough on this nursery debut. She was far from disgraced in defeat and will be seen to better effect when racing on a more conventional track.
**Al Garhoud Bridge** was another to suffer trouble in running and is better than the bare form. He looks fairly treated and is worth another chance.
**Emerald Penang(IRE)** failed to build on his recent Epsom maiden success and ran disappointingly.

## 4327 VODAFONE APPRENTICE STKS (H'CAP) 1m 1f
5:20 (5:22) (D) (0-80,78) 3-Y-O+ £10,692 (£3,290; £1,645; £822) Stalls High

Form RPR
-002 **1** **Ringsider (IRE)**[4] 4220 3-9-2 **77** ........ LisaJones 5 89+
(GAButler) *lw: hld up wl in rr: prog on inner fr over 2f out: rdn to ld last 100yds: sn clr* **4/1**[1]
0045 **2** *1 ¾* **Ocean Of Storms (IRE)**[15] 3909 9-9-10 **76** ........(t) SHitchcott 12 84
(ChristianWroe, UAE) *s.s: sn rcvrd to midfield: rdn and prog over 2f out: led briefly ins fnl f: sn outpcd by wnr* **33/1**
6001 **3** *1 ½* **Artistic Style**[26] 3579 4-8-11 **63** ........ TEaves 2 68
(BEllison) *hld up in rr: rdn 3f out: prog 2f out: hanging over 1f out: styd on to take 3rd nr fin* **10/1**
0203 **4** *nk* **Voice Mail**[22] 3705 5-9-5 **78** ........ TBlock(7) 4 82
(AMBalding) *t.k.h early: prom: trckd ldr over 2f out and gng wl: led over 1f out: hdd & wknd ins fnl f* **14/1**
0511 **5** *2 ½* **Parnassian**[16] 3869 4-9-2 **71** ........ RThomas(3) 8 70
(GBBalding) *trckd ldrs: effrt over 2f out: cl up and rdn jst over 1f out: wknd ins fnl f* **5/1**[2]
4030 **6** *1* **Hail The Chief**[85] 1927 7-9-4 **73** ........ NChalmers(3) 13 70
(JAkehurst) *led at gd pce: hdd and wknd over 1f out* **12/1**
-560 **7** *shd* **Dont Call Me Derek**[134] 1057 3-7-12 **62** ........ DFox(3) 10 59
(SCWilliams) *bit bkwd: b.hind: stdd s: hld up in detached last: c wd bnd 4f out: rdn 3f out: kpt on fnl f: no ch* **9/1**
2204 **8** *1 ½* **Say What You See (IRE)**[17] 3842 4-8-12 **71** ........(v) HGemberlu(7) 6 65
(JWHills) *lw: hld up in midfield: gng wl enough over 2f out: rdn and fnd nil wl over 1f out* **7/1**[3]
6410 **9** *1 ¼* **Baker Of Oz**[28] 3525 3-8-6 **72** ........ PGallagher(5) 1 64
(RHannon) *settled in rr: rdn 3f out: no prog* **16/1**
0554 **10** *½* **Mad Carew (USA)**[43] 3048 5-9-3 **76** ........(be) HPoulton(5) 7 65
(GLMoore) *hld up towards rr: rdn whn n.m.r over 2f out: no ch after* **12/1**
2013 **11** *nk* **Wind Chime (IRE)**[24] 3626 7-9-0 **66** ........ LPKeniry 3 56
(AGNewcombe) *chsd ldrs tl wknd 2f out* **7/1**[3]
1454 **12** *¾* **Low Cloud**[21] 3731 4-9-5 **76** ........ LTreadwell(5) 11 65
(DNicholls) *s.i.s: t.k.h and sn trckd ldr to over 2f out: wknd over 1f out* **20/1**

1m 56.02s (-0.84) **Going Correction** -0.025s/f (Good)
**WFA** 3 from 4yo+ 9lb **12** Ran SP% **116.4**
Speed ratings: **102,100,99,98,96 95,95,94,93,92 92,91**CSF £138.99 CT £1257.81 TOTE £4.90: £2.00, £6.30, £4.70; EX 123.60 Place 6 £582.24, Place 5 £309.14.
**Owner** S A O'Donoghue & M V Deegan **Bred** Airlie Stud **Trained** Blewbury, Oxon

**FOCUS**
The pace was strong, but by the meeting's standards this is ordinary form.

**NOTEBOOK**
**Ringsider(IRE)**, runner-up over a mile at the track just four days previously, quickened up nicely inside the last furlong to win going away, showing improved form again. He is somewhat headstrong, so the strong pace was very much to his advantage, and although he will go up in the weights for this he looks worth a chance in a better race.
**Ocean Of Storms(IRE)** came there to win his race entering the final furlong, but had no answer to the winner when challenged late on. He again did himself no favours with a sluggish start, and although he is not the easiest horse to win with, this was his best effort in Britain to date and the drop back in trip was ideal.

**Artistic Style**, off the mark at the tenth attempt last time when winning a Musselburgh seller, improved on that form and stayed on well in the straight. He is clearly on good terms at present.
**Voice Mail** ran too keen early on, but still held every chance if good enough, until finding less than looked likely in the straight. He is weighted to his best on this evidence.
**Parnassian** was up another 10lb for his latest win at Doncaster and also racing on quicker ground over an extra furlong. A combination of those factors found him out.
**Hail The Chief** did well to finish as close as he did, considering he led at a strong pace for most of the contest. He may have been revitalised by another change of scenery and has more races in him when returning to the All-Weather.
**Low Cloud** *Official explanation: jockey said gelding was unsuited by the good to firm going*
T/Plt: £338.80 to a £1 stake. Pool: £142,328.16. 306.60 winning tickets. T/Qpdt: £93.60 to a £1 stake. Pool: £5,464.90. 43.20 winning tickets. JN

# 3898 HAMILTON (R-H)
Saturday, July 31

**OFFICIAL GOING: Good to firm (firm in places)**
Wind: almost nil Weather: hot, sunny

## 4328 REAL RADIO APPRENTICES H'CAP (ROUND 3) 1m 4f 17y
6:20 (6:20) (E) (0-70,60) 3-Y-O+ £4,078 (£1,255; £627; £313) Stalls High

Form RPR
3053 **1** **Easibet Dot Net**[20] 3781 4-9-10 **60**.....(p) WHogg 5 72
(ISemple) *mde all: drew clr fr over 2f out: unchal* **7/2**[2]
3031 **2** *6* **Cosmic Case**[3] 4250 9-8-10 **51** 6ex..... KPierrepont(5) 4 53
(JSGoldie) *hld up in tch: hdwy on outside over 4f out: outpcd 3f out: kpt on fnl f: no ch w wnr* **5/2**[1]
5634 **3** *2* **Donna's Double**[7] 4132 9-9-2 **52**.....(p) JDO'Reilly 2 51
(DEddy) *hld up: smooth hdwy 4f out: rdn and hung lft over 2f out: no imp fnl f* **9/2**[3]
0422 **4** *3 1/2* **Spree Vision**[15] 3892 8-8-8 **51**..... HFellows(7) 3 45
(PMonteith) *in tch: effrt over 3f out: outpcd wl over 1f out* **7/2**[2]
6000 **5** *dist* **Howards Dream (IRE)**[21] 3740 6-7-8 **35** oh9 ow1.(t) DonnaCaldwell(5) 1 —
(DANolan) *cl up: rdn 1/2-way: wknd fr 4f out* **12/1**
200- **6** *10* **Bridge Pal**[269] 5928 4-9-3 **56**..... AReilly(3) 6 —
(PMonteith) *chsd wnr to 4f out: sn wknd: t.o* **10/1**
2m 34.84s (-4.36) **Going Correction** -0.275s/f (Firm) **6** Ran SP% **108.0**
Speed ratings: **103,99,97,95,—** —CSF £11.64 TOTE £4.40: £2.30, £1.40; EX 16.00.
**Owner** www.easibet dot net **Bred** L A C Ashby Newhall Estate Farm **Trained** Carluke, S Lanarks
■ Stewards Enquiry : J D O'Reilly three-day ban: used whip with excessive frequency (Aug 11-13)
W Hogg caution: used whip above shoulder height

**FOCUS**
A low-grade event run at just a modest pace and one in which the winner very much had the rub of things. This bare form may not prove entirely reliable.

**NOTEBOOK**
**Easibet Dot Net**, back up in trip and back on a sound surface, enjoyed the rub of things in a weak race at a course that suits front-runners to notch his first win on turf. However, he will find life much tougher after reassessment in a more competitive race.
**Cosmic Case** extended her run of creditable efforts under her penalty, but once again demonstrated her vulnerability in races run at a less than true gallop. She has been consistent though, and should continue to give a good account.
**Donna's Double**, up markedly in trip, travelled strongly for much of the way in this steadily-run race, but did not find anywhere near as much as anticipated when asked for an effort. He is on a fair mark and will be seen to much better effect over a mile and a quarter in a truly-run race.
**Spree Vision**, with the usual visor omitted, would have been ideally suited by more of a test but he is not the most consistent and his losing run of over two years means he is not really one to place much faith in.
**Howards Dream(IRE)** looked to face a stiff task from 9lb out of the weights, but ran poorly even after attracting a bit of support. His course and distance win last summer seems a very long time away.
**Bridge Pal**, a modest middle-distance maiden, ran a shocker on this reappearance and this first start for current connections. However, she is in good hands and would not be one to write off just yet.

## 4329 IAN SORBIE MEMORIAL NOVICE AUCTION STKS 6f 5y
6:50 (6:50) (E) 2-Y-O £4,127 (£1,270; £635; £317) Stalls Low

Form RPR
4 **1** **Hansomelle (IRE)**[15] 3893 2-8-2..... DaleGibson 5 65
(BMactaggart) *prom on outside: rdn over 2f out: led ins fnl f: r.o wl* **14/1**
4 **2** *1/2* **Invertiel (USA)**[16] 3876 2-8-13..... GHind 1 74
(ISemple) *dwlt: sn prom: nt clr run fr 1/2-way tl swtchd rt and hdwy over 1f out: r.o: nt rch wnr* **8/1**[3]
1221 **3** *3/4* **Melalchrist**[29] 3468 2-9-5..... PHanagan 3 78
(JJQuinn) *cl up: led over 1f out to ins fnl f: no ex* **4/6**[1]
3210 **4** *3 1/2* **Speed Dial Harry (IRE)**[12] 3975 2-8-13..... DarrenWilliams 4 61
(KRBurke) *cl up: ev ch over 1f out: wknd ins fnl f* **3/1**[2]
2000 **5** *8* **Kristikhab (IRE)**[15] 3893 2-8-11..... FLynch 2 35
(ABerry) *led: hdd whn n.m.r over 1f out: sn btn* **25/1**
1m 13.29s (0.19) **Going Correction** -0.20s/f (Firm) **5** Ran SP% **106.6**
Speed ratings: **90,89,88,83,73**CSF £97.78 TOTE £12.80: £6.10, £3.10; EX 95.20.
**Owner** Corsby Racing **Bred** J Beckett **Trained** Hawick, Borders

**FOCUS**
Just an ordinary event run at a fair gallop and, with the two market leaders disappointing, this race took less winning than seemed likely and the value of the form is hard to gauge. The runner-up looked an unlucky loser.

**NOTEBOOK**
**Hansomelle(IRE)** confirmed the bit of promise shown on her debut and proved well suited by the step up to this trip. She should not be going up too much for this success, should stay seven furlongs and, although she may have been fortunate to beat the runner-up this time, she may well be capable of better.
**Invertiel(USA)** ◆, who again took the eye in the paddock, looked an unlucky loser as he had no room for much of the last half of the contest and the winner had got first run when he did get clear. There is plenty of room for improvement and he appeals as the type to win a similar race at the very least.
**Melalchrist**, having his first run over six furlongs, looked to have strong claims in an ordinary event, despite his penalty, but did not seem beaten through lack of stamina. On this evidence he is going to find life tough in competitive nursery company.
**Speed Dial Harry(IRE)**, persevered with over this trip but with the visor left off this time, showed his customary speed and left the strong impression that the return to five furlongs would be in his favour.
**Kristikhab(IRE)**, an inconsistent maiden, looked to have a stiff task back over this trip, but in any case ran poorly and does not look one to place too much faith in.

## 4330 ROBERT WISEMAN DAIRIES "THE ONE" NURSERY 6f 5y
7:20 (7:20) (D) 2-Y-O £5,187 (£1,596; £798; £399) Stalls Low

Form RPR
603 **1** **Borderlescott**[18] 3818 2-7-12 **64** oh1..... PHanagan 5 67
(RBastiman) *prom: rdn to ld 1f out: kpt on wl* **11/2**[3]
2103 **2** *1/2* **Windy Prospect**[2] 4278 2-9-2 **82**..... DeanMcKeown 4 83
(PABlockley) *cl up: effrt and ev ch 1f out: kpt on towards fin* **6/1**
31 **3** *3* **Propellor (IRE)**[16] 3876 2-9-2 **87**..... PMakin(5) 2 79
(ADickman) *dwlt: sn chsng ldrs: n.m.r 1/2-way: led 2f to 1f out: outpcd ins last* **1/1**[1]
561 **4** *5* **Baymist**[12] 3980 2-7-13 **65**..... DaleGibson 3 42
(MWEasterby) *trckd ldrs tl outpcd fr 2f out* **5/1**[2]
0504 **5** *5* **Ochil Hills Dancer (IRE)**[16] 3868 2-7-11 **68**..... BSwarbrick(5) 1 30
(ACrook) *led to 2f out: sn outpcd* **12/1**
3526 **6** *3 1/2* **Regal Lustre**[10] 4012 2-7-5 **64** oh5..... DFentiman(7) 6 16
(JRWeymes) *prom on outside tl wknd wl over 1f out* **20/1**
1m 12.64s (-0.46) **Going Correction** -0.20s/f (Firm) **6** Ran SP% **108.8**
Speed ratings: **95,94,90,83,77 72**CSF £34.56 TOTE £8.00: £2.60, £2.10; EX 32.30.
**Owner** Border Rail & Plant Limited **Bred** James Clark **Trained** Cowthorpe, N Yorks

**FOCUS**
A run-of-the-mill event in which the pace was sound, but another race where the two market leaders were a shade disappointing. The 'official ratings' are only an estimate and are for guidance only.

**NOTEBOOK**
**Borderlescott**, who was sweating in the preliminaries on what was admittedly a warm evening, showed improved form to get off the mark on his first run over this trip. He should stay further and may well be capable of better.
**Windy Prospect** back in trip, had the run of the race and ran creditably. He has proved consistent over sprint distances, but he is likely to remain vulnerable to progressive types in this type of event.
**Propellor(IRE)**, who is not very big, ran creditably on this nursery debut but will almost certainly need a bit of leniency from the Handicapper if he is to return to winning ways.
**Baymist** run of progressive efforts came to an abrupt end on this nursery debut, and it may be that this first run on very quick ground was the cause of this below-par effort. She is worth another chance on easier ground.
**Ochil Hills Dancer(IRE)** ran creditably over this trip early last month, but has been a long way below that level since and again ran poorly. She will have to show more before she is worth a bet.
**Regal Lustre** is only a modest performer and was again soundly beaten from out of the handicap.

## 4331 EUROPEAN BREEDERS FUND FILLIES' H'CAP 5f 4y
7:50 (7:50) (D) (0-85,81) 3-Y-O+ £6,792 (£2,090; £1,045; £522) Stalls Low

Form RPR
1305 **1** **Baron Rhodes**[20] 3777 3-9-9 **76**..... DMcGaffin 6 83
(JSWainwright) *trckd ldrs: rdn over 2f out: led ins fnl f: r.o wl* **9/1**
3561 **2** *1* **Roxanne Mill**[10] 4014 6-9-10 **73**.....(p) FLynch 7 77
(PABlockley) *led to ins fnl f: kpt on same pce* **5/1**[2]
0210 **3** *hd* **Scottish Exile (IRE)**[17] 3838 3-9-4 **71**.....(v) DarrenWilliams 5 74
(KRBurke) *in tch: effrt 2f out: r.o fnl f* **12/1**
050 **4** *1/2* **Roman Mistress (IRE)**[8] 4104 4-8-13 **62**..... DAllan 4 63
(TDEasterby) *trckd ldrs: effrt 1/2-way: kpt on same pce ins fnl f* **13/2**
515 **5** *3/4* **Robwillcall**[40] 3147 4-8-1 **50**..... DaleGibson 1 49
(ABerry) *cl up: rdn and hung rt over 2f out: kpt on same pce fr over 1f out* **16/1**
-063 **5** *dht* **Dispol Katie**[21] 3744 3-9-9 **81**..... PMakin(5) 3 80
(TDBarron) *prom: rdn over 2f out: no imp tl r.o fnl f* **2/1**[1]
6601 **7** *nk* **Bettys Pride**[3] 4247 5-8-7 **56** 7ex..... PHanagan 8 53
(MDods) *in tch on outside: rdn and outpcd fr 2f out* **13/2**
2533 **8** *19* **Amelia (IRE)**[8] 4104 6-8-5 **59**..... BSwarbrick(5) 2 —
(WMBrisbourne) *bhd: rdn 1/2-way: sn lost tch:bbv* **6/1**[3]
59.75 secs (-1.51) **Going Correction** -0.20s/f (Firm)
**WFA** 3 from 4yo+ 4lb **8** Ran SP% **114.5**
Speed ratings: **104,102,102,101,100 100,99,69**CSF £53.39 CT £544.94 TOTE £8.70: £2.00, £3.40, £2.90; EX 34.90.
**Owner** I Barran & P Rhodes **Bred** E Smith **Trained** Kennythorpe, N Yorks

**FOCUS**
A run-of-the-mill handicap in which the pace was sound and the form should stand up at a similar level. The whole field raced stands side.

**NOTEBOOK**
**Baron Rhodes**, usually a consistent sort, had the race run to suit and put a couple of below-par efforts firmly behind her. She showed the right attitude and should continue to give a good account away from progressive types.
**Roxanne Mill**, having her first run for her new stable, showed bags of foot and may be a bit better than the bare form as she did set a strong gallop after tacking over from her wide draw. She is a consistent sort who remains likely to win a similar event.
**Scottish Exile(IRE)**, not at her best from a poor draw at Catterick last time, showed much more like her true form this time, despite being ridden with a bit more patience than is usually the case. She too should continue to go well.
**Roman Mistress(IRE)** is a consistent sort who again ran creditably back in trip, but the fact that she has only won once in the last two years has to be a concern to win-only punters.
**Robwillcall** looked in tremendous condition and was not disgraced after enjoying the run of the race, but looked anything but an easy ride as she just wanted to hang to her right. *Official explanation: jockey said filly hung right throughout*
**Dispol Katie** won twice over this trip on fast ground last year, but left the impression that the return to six furlongs would be in her favour. She is likely to remain vulnerable to progressive sorts from her current mark, though.
**Bettys Pride** *Official explanation: jockey said mare did not handle the hill*
**Amelia(IRE)** looked to have fair claims in an ordinary event, but was soundly beaten and reportedly broke a blood vessel. *Official explanation: trainer said mare bled from the nose*

## 4332 VARIETY CLUB OF SCOTLAND MAIDEN STKS 1m 1f 36y
8:20 (8:22) (D) 3-Y-O £6,181 (£1,902; £951; £475) Stalls High

Form RPR
2-53 **1** **Notable Guest (USA)**[15] 3915 3-9-0 87..... FLynch 1 60+
(SirMichaelStoute) *cl up: led 1/2-way: pushed along over 2f out: r.o strly fnl f* **1/10**[1]
2000 **2** *5* **Argent**[11] 4008 3-9-0 48.....(p) DarrenWilliams 7 50
(MissLAPerratt) *trckd ldrs: effrt and ev ch 2f out: hung rt: sn one pce* **33/1**
6 **3** *1 1/2* **Reem Two**[22] 3701 3-8-6..... LEnstone(3) 6 42
(DMccain) *prom: effrt over 2f out: sn one pce* **12/1**[2]
0 **4** *11* **Dalkeys Lass**[15] 3899 3-8-9..... VHalliday 5 20
(MrsLBNormile) *hld up in tch: rdn and outpcd fr 3f out* **50/1**
0 **5** *shd* **Danettie**[89] 1842 3-8-4..... BSwarbrick(5) 4 20+
(WMBrisbourne) *cl up tl wknd over 3f out* **50/1**
0 **6** *1/2* **After Lent (IRE)**[6] 2519 3-9-0..... DeanMcKeown 2 24+
(PABlockley) *hld up: shkn up over 3f out: n.d* **16/1**[3]
000 **7** *6* **Raybers Magic**[18] 3817 3-8-9..... GHind 8 7
(JRWeymes) *led to 1/2-way: wknd over 3f out* **50/1**

8 24 **Betfred** 3-9-0 ............ DaleGibson 3 —
(ABerry) *sn wl bhd* **33/1**

1m 58.95s (-0.65) **Going Correction** -0.275s/f (Firm) **8** Ran SP% **116.2**
Speed ratings: **91,86,85,75,75 74,69,48**CSF £12.61 TOTE £1.10: £1.02, £4.30, £3.20; EX 4.40.
**Owner** K Abdulla **Bred** Juddmonte Farms Inc **Trained** Newmarket, Suffolk

**FOCUS**
A one horse race on paper and, although the winner was well on top at the end, he did not have to be anywhere near his pre-race mark. The winning time was very modest.

**NOTEBOOK**
**Notable Guest(USA)** did not have to be at his best to win a most uncompetitive maiden in workmanlike fashion. However he will find things much tougher from his mark in the 80s back in handicap company.
**Argent**, a fully exposed and inconsistent performer, seemed to run well in the face of a very stiff task but connections will be hoping he is rated on his proximity to the rest of the field rather than to the winner. His record suggests he will be one to take on next time.
**Reem Two** bettered her debut form but is another that is best rated by her proximity to the placed horses rather than to the winner. She will continue to look vulnerable in this grade.
**Dalkeys Lass** is likely to be seen to better effect granted a stiffer test of stamina in low-grade handicaps in due course.
**Danettie** achieved little and is another that is going to continue to look vulnerable in this type of event. *Official explanation: jockey said filly hung left-handed throughout*
**After Lent(IRE)** was not knocked about and will be seen to better effect in modest handicap company in due course.

## 4333 SCOTTISH RACING H'CAP (A QUALIFIER FOR THE TOTEPOOL HANDICAP SERIES FINAL) 1m 1f 36y
**8:50** (8:50) (E) (0-75,73) 3-Y-0+ **£4,907** (£1,510; £755; £377) **Stalls** High

Form RPR
3110 **1** **Wahoo Sam (USA)**[11] 4005 4-9-2 **67** ............ PMakin[(5)] 1 79+
(TDBarron) *mde all: rdn over 2f out: kpt on wl fnl f* **5/1**[2]
5313 **2** 1 **Anthemion (IRE)**[11] 4008 7-9-0 **60** ............ DMcGaffin 10 67
(MrsJCMcgregor) *chsd wnr: rdn and outpcd over 2f out: r.o fnl f: nt rch wnr* **5/1**[2]
1404 **3** ½ **Jordans Elect**[32] 3397 4-9-13 **73** ............ GHind 9 79
(ISemple) *trckd ldrs: effrt over 2f out: kpt on same pce fnl f* **8/1**
5-06 **4** hd **Kristiansand**[15] 3903 4-9-1 **64** ............ LEnstone[(3)] 8 71+
(PMonteith) *hld up: effrt whn n.m.r over 1f out: r.o fnl f* **33/1**
6002 **5** ¾ **Encounter**[15] 3903 8-8-1 **47** ow2 ............ DAllan 5 52
(JHetherton) *hld up. rdn over 3f out: kpt on fnl f: no imp* **6/1**[3]
0040 **6** 1 ½ **Basinet**[15] 3921 6-8-7 **53** ............ (p) PHanagan 3 55
(JJQuinn) *hld up: nt clr run 3f out: rdn whn n.m.r appr fnl f: nvr rchd ldrs* **7/1**
3044 **7** 7 **Cherished Number**[12] 3977 5-9-12 **72** ............ (v) DarrenWilliams 7 60
(ISemple) *chsd ldrs tl wknd over 2f out* **11/4**[1]
1052 **8** nk **Zawrak (IRE)**[15] 3921 5-8-9 **62** ............ (v) WHogg[(7)] 2 49
(IWMcinnes) *hld up: rdn over 3f out: sn btn* **9/1**
2400 **9** 7 **Francis Flute**[11] 4004 6-8-4 **55** ow6 ............ PMulrennan[(5)] 6 28
(BMactaggart) *prom to 1/2-way: sn lost pl* **16/1**

1m 55.69s (-3.91) **Going Correction** -0.275s/f (Firm) **9** Ran SP% **116.7**
Speed ratings: **106,105,104,104,103 102,96,96,89**CSF £30.57 CT £198.28 TOTE £6.20: £2.40, £2.20, £2.60; EX 30.30 Place 6 £641.30, Place 5 £381.69.
**Owner** C A Washbourn **Bred** Stonereath Farms Inc **Trained** Maunby, N Yorks
■ Stewards Enquiry : L Enstone six-day ban (up from five days after an unsuccessful appeal): careless riding (Aug 11-16)

**FOCUS**
An ordinary handicap but the form appears reasonably sound. The modest pace ensured those that raced up with the pace held a big edge over those held up.

**NOTEBOOK**
**Wahoo Sam(USA)** showed plenty of early dash to overcome a low draw and was given a tactically astute ride by his promising young rider, who seems a good judge of pace. This was his third course win and he is always likely to be seen to best effect when allowed to dominate.
**Anthemion(IRE)** continues in good heart but left the impression that a stiffer test of stamina over this trip would have been in his favour. He will continue to be of interest at this course when it looks as though he may get an easy lead.
**Jordans Elect**, always well placed in a race run at a less than true gallop, ran creditably at a course where he has already won twice this season. He is another that would have been suited by a more end-to-end gallop.
**Kristiansand ◆** ran his best race for his current stable and may be a bit better than the bare result, as he fared the best of those that attempted to come from off the pace. He is in very capable hands and is one to keep an eye on.
**Encounter** was not disgraced with his rider putting up a couple of pounds overweight, especially as he would have been much better suited by a better gallop. However, he is the sort that needs things to fall just right.
**Basinet**, with the cheekpieces back on, looks better than the bare result as this race favoured those racing close to the pace and he did not get anything like a good run through on the rails. However his record suggests he is not one to take a short price about next time.
T/Plt: £329.30 to a £1 stake. Pool: £32,299.25. 71.60 winning tickets. T/Qpdt: £11.90 to a £1 stake. Pool: £2,640.10. 163.85 winning tickets. RY

# 4124 LINGFIELD (L-H)
Saturday, July 31
**OFFICIAL GOING: Turf course - good to firm; all-weather - standard**

## 4334 EUROPEAN BREEDERS FUND MAIDEN STKS 5f (P)
**6:05** (6:05) (D) 2-Y-0 **£4,212** (£1,296; £648; £324) **Stalls** High

Form RPR
**1** **Sumora (IRE)** 2-8-9 ............ JFortune 9 82+
(GAButler) *mde all: rdn clr fnl f: promising* **5/1**[3]
3 **2** 2 **Countdown**[15] 3900 2-9-0 ............ SSanders 4 80
(SirMarkPrescott) *s.i.s: hdwy on outside 2f out: strly rdn to go 2nd cl home* **9/4**[2]
4 **3** nk **Bahamian Magic**[21] 3758 2-9-0 ............ TPQueally 2 79
(DRLoder) *chsd wnr: rdn over 1f out: no ex and lost 2nd cl home* **11/2**
62 **4** 7 **Sign Writer (USA)**[14] 3946 2-9-0 ............ EAhern 7 54
(JNoseda) *chsd ldrs on outside: rdn and wknd over 1f out* **5/4**[1]
0 **5** 5 **Global Banker (IRE)**[26] 3588 2-9-0 ............ (t) OUrbina 3 37
(GCHChung) *in tch tl rdn and wknd over 1f out* **50/1**
**6** ½ **General Haigh** 2-8-9 ............ MSavage[(5)] 5 35
(JRBest) *s.i.s: bhd and a outpcd* **33/1**
600 **7** 2 ½ **Dancing Moonlight (IRE)**[24] 3632 2-8-2 ............ (p) CHaddon[(7)] 6 21
(MrsNMacauley) *a outpcd in rr* **66/1**
0 **8** 9 **A Qui Le Tour**[19] 3805 2-9-0 ............ CCatlin 8 —
(MRHoad) *outpcd thrght* **66/1**

60.54 secs (0.76) **Going Correction** +0.175s/f (Slow) **8** Ran SP% **115.2**
Speed ratings: **100,96,96,85,77 76,72,57**CSF £16.68 TOTE £7.10: £2.90, £1.40, £1.90; EX 27.70.
**Owner** Sangster Family **Bred** King Bloodstock And Swettenham Stud **Trained** Blewbury, Oxon

**FOCUS**
The time was decent for the grade and this appears fairly strong maiden form which should produce future winners.

**NOTEBOOK**
**Sumora(IRE)** is out of an unraced half-sister to Derby winner Dr Devious. Smartly away and able to cross over from her high draw, she was always travelling well in front. This was a bright start and she should be capable of stepping up on this.
**Countdown** was slow to go and again showed signs of greenness. Staying on to claim second inside the last, he is capable of better as he gains experience.
**Bahamian Magic**, down a furlong in trip from his debut, was bustled along leaving the stalls to chase the eventual winner. Collared for second near the line, he might improve back over six.
**Sign Writer(USA)**, tackling the Polytrack for the first time, was left behind by the principals in the home straight.
**Global Banker(IRE)**, equipped with a tongue tie for this second run, showed more than he had on his debut.

## 4335 DEREK BURRIDGE RACING & GOLF TROPHIES MEDIAN AUCTION MAIDEN STKS 7f 140y
**6:35** (6:36) (F) 2-Y-0 **£3,786** (£1,165; £582; £291) **Stalls** Centre

Form RPR
00 **1** **Triple Zero (IRE)**[24] 3627 2-8-9 ............ SSanders 9 65
(APJarvis) *trckd ldr: led 2f out: rdn out and styd on wl fnl f* **25/1**
30 **2** ½ **Keynes (JPN)**[10] 4022 2-9-0 ............ (v[1]) JFortune 7 69
(JHMGosden) *led tl hdd 2f out: rallied and ev ch ins fnl f: kpt on* **14/1**
0 **3** 1 ½ **Young Mick**[25] 3601 2-9-0 ............ AMcCarthy 2 66
(GGMargarson) *a.p: outpcd over 2f out: styd on wl fnl f* **20/1**
4 **4** ¾ **Jazrawy**[44] 3014 2-9-0 ............ DHolland 3 64
(LMCumani) *in tch: rdn 4f out: outpcd over 2f out: styd on fnl f* **11/4**[2]
**5** ¾ **Sir Monty (USA)** 2-9-0 ............ RLMoore 5 62
(MrsAJPerrett) *mid-div: ridden and hung rt 3f out: styd on wl fnl f* **9/1**
000 **6** ½ **Beauchamp Twist**[10] 4022 2-8-9 ............ (b[1]) CCatlin 4 56
(GAButler) *in rr tl hdwy ins fnl 2f: nvr nrr* **33/1**
3 **7** 1 **Flag Point (IRE)**[37] 3240 2-9-0 ............ TQuinn 15 59
(JLDunlop) *in tch tl rdn and one pce fnl 3f* **9/4**[1]
0 **8** ½ **Danger Zone**[19] 3808 2-9-0 ............ EAhern 14 58
(MrsAJPerrett) *prom: rdn 1/2-way: wknd appr fnl f* **6/1**[3]
0 **9** 2 ½ **Blue Spectrum (IRE)**[14] 3931 2-9-0 ............ JDSmith 10 52
(JSMoore) *slowly away: a bhd* **66/1**
**10** 1 ½ **Cordier** 2-9-0 ............ TPQueally 1 48
(DRLoder) *mid-div: rdn 1/2-way: wknd over 2f out* **7/1**
**11** 1 ¾ **Pearl's A Singer (IRE)** 2-8-9 ............ RMullen 13 39
(MLWBell) *mid-div: rdn 4f out: wknd over 2f out* **14/1**
**12** 3 ½ **Speedie Rossini (IRE)** 2-9-0 ............ OUrbina 12 36
(SCWilliams) *swvd lft s: a bhd* **25/1**
0 **13** 3 ½ **Rhoslan (IRE)**[15] 3913 2-9-0 ............ JFEgan 8 28
(CADwyer) *in tch tl rdn and wknd over 2f out* **33/1**
**14** 14 **Hursley** 2-8-9 ............ DaneO'Neill 16 —
(SKirk) *a bhd* **25/1**

1m 32.84s (1.38) **Going Correction** -0.05s/f (Good) **14** Ran SP% **131.2**
Speed ratings: **91,90,89,88,87 87,86,85,83,81 79,76,72,58**CSF £345.31 TOTE £66.00: £14.40, £3.90, £4.20; EX 455.60.
**Owner** Quadrillian Partnership **Bred** Martyn J McEnery **Trained** Twyford, Bucks
■ A remarkable 44th winner in July for Seb Sanders, who had won the Stewards' Cup earlier in the day.

**FOCUS**
Few got into this weak maiden and the bare form is modest.

**NOTEBOOK**
**Triple Zero(IRE)** had shown next to nothing on her first two starts. Grabbing the rail, she was always in the first two and showed the right attitude to hold on.
**Keynes(JPN)** benefited from the application of a visor, although he was a little free in the early stages. He went down fighting and is now qualified for handicaps.
**Young Mick** was unable to go with the first two a quarter of a mile out but was keeping on inside the final furlong. A little farther should suit him.
**Jazrawy** was being niggled along before halfway and, while he was staying on, he never looked like catching the leaders. He is still learning the game.
**Sir Monty(USA)**, related to a smart juvenile in the United States called Sandy Lady, caught the eye on this debut. He was hanging with three to run but stayed on nicely in the closing stages, and should be able to build on this sympathetic introduction.
**Beauchamp Twist**, blinkered for the first time, stayed on when it was all over.
**Flag Point(IRE)** *Official explanation: jockey said colt ran too free to post*
**Danger Zone**, who was backed in from 14/1, was being ridden along from halfway but only faded inside the last.
**Rhoslan(IRE)** *Official explanation: jockey said colt ran too free during the race*

## 4336 PLAY A ROUND AT LINGFIELD CLUB H'CAP 6f
**7:05** (7:09) (F) (0-55,55) 3-Y-0+ **£3,122** (£892; £446) **Stalls** Centre

Form RPR
-063 **1** **United Spirit (IRE)**[24] 3636 3-9-4 **55** ............ (b[1]) EAhern 3 69
(MAMagnusson) *mid-div: hdwy over 2f out: led ins fnl f: r.o wl* **8/1**
0405 **2** 1 ¾ **Cold Climate**[17] 3841 9-9-8 **54** ............ JFEgan 7 63
(BobJones) *mid-div: gd hdwy over 1f out and ev ch ins fnl f: nt pce of wnr* **6/1**[3]
0210 **3** nk **Enjoy The Buzz**[14] 3935 5-9-4 **50** ............ CCatlin 15 58
(JMBradley) *towards rr: outpcd over 2f out: r.o strly fnl f* **5/1**[2]
6330 **4** ½ **Jazzy Millennium**[8] 4085 7-7-7 **53** ............ (b) DHolland 13 60+
(BRMillman) *hld up: rdn over 2f out: nt clr run and swtchd rt over 1f out: r.o strly fnl f: nvr nrr: unfortunate* **7/2**[1]
00-0 **5** ¾ **Pretty Kool**[40] 3154 4-9-3 **49** ............ OUrbina 11 53+
(SCWilliams) *mid-div: outpcd 1/2-way: hdwy appr fnl f: kpt on wl* **10/1**
0023 **6** nk **Jagged (IRE)**[14] 3935 4-9-9 **55** ............ (b) TPQueally 2 58
(JRJenkins) *in tch: led wl over 1f out: hdd and no ex ins fnl f* **5/1**[2]
0430 **7** shd **Lake Verdi (IRE)**[9] 4044 5-9-6 **52** ............ (t) DaneO'Neill 14 55
(BHanbury) *rrd up s: effrt and hung rt 2f out: kpt on fnl f* **16/1**
0240 **8** shd **Astrac (IRE)**[16] 3884 13-9-3 **49** ............ SDrowne 4 52
(MrsALMKing) *in rr: rdn over 2f out: r.o fnl f* **14/1**
2060 **9** 1 **Indian Bazaar (IRE)**[8] 4085 8-9-2 **51** ............ RMiles[(3)] 10 51
(NEBerry) *trckd ldrs tl rdn and wknd over 1f out* **20/1**
0000 **10** 1 ½ **St Ivian**[5] 4188 4-9-2 **55** ............ (v) CHaddon[(7)] 12 50
(MrsNMacauley) *in tch on ins: nt clr run over 2f out but kpt on fnl f* **33/1**
0-00 **11** nk **Pirouettes (IRE)**[15] 3911 4-9-0 **49** ............ (b[1]) DCorby[(3)] 1 43
(EROertel) *s.i.s: nvr on terms* **66/1**

3050 **12** *nk* **Tappit (IRE)**[26] 3575 5-8-12 **49** ........ MSavage(5) 5 43
(NEBerry) *prom: rdn over 2f out: wknd fnl f* **33/1**

6046 **13** *5* **Nebraska City**[7] 4125 3-9-3 **54** ........ SWhitworth 6 33
(PMitchell) *outpcd and a bhd* **50/1**

0000 **14** *3* **Mayzin (IRE)**[49] 2885 4-9-3 **49** ........(p) TQuinn 16 19
(RMFlower) *prom on stands' side: rdn whn hmpd over 1f out: nt rcvr* **10/1**

0500 **15** *½* **Boanerges (IRE)**[16] 3864 7-9-5 **51** ........(b[1]) RLMoore 8 19
(JMBradley) *chsd ldrs tl rdn and wknd over 2f out* **14/1**

-000 **16** *1 ½* **Perfect Hindsight (IRE)**[29] 3486 3-9-4 **55** ........(b[1]) JFortune 9 19
(CGCox) *led tl rdn and hdd wl over 1f out: wknd qckly* **25/1**

1m 11.08s (-0.57) **Going Correction** -0.05s/f (Good)
**WFA** 3 from 4yo+ 5lb **16** Ran SP% **136.3**
Speed ratings: **101,98,98,97,96 96,96,95,94,92 92,91,85,81,80 78**CSF £58.80 CT £291.95 TOTE £9.50: £2.40, £2.30, £1.80, £1.70; EX 85.70.
**Owner** East Wind Racing Ltd **Bred** Atlantic Racing Limited **Trained** Upper Lambourn, Berks

**FOCUS**
A moderate handicap and ordinary form, although solid enough for the grade.

**NOTEBOOK**
**United Spirit(IRE)**, equipped with blinkers instead of cheekpieces, came with a good run on the outside to win going away. She is improving, and a return to seven furlongs would not go amiss.
**Cold Climate**, 4lb lower than when winning at this track in December, was suited by the return to six furlongs.
**Enjoy The Buzz** looked set to finish nearer last than first with two furlongs to run, but really found his stride when switched to the outside and finished strongly.
**Jazzy Millennium** ◆ met with trouble and finished full of running. A pound lower than when last successful, he is capable of gaining compensation if getting the breaks.
**Pretty Kool**, making her handicap debut, has been running over further and this drop in trip brought about a better performance.
**Jagged(IRE)** had to work hard to get to the lead and he had nothing in reserve when tackled inside the last.

## 4337 PLEASURE HOUSE PLAY AFTER RACING MAIDEN STKS 6f
7:35 (7:37) (D) 3-Y-0+ £3,532 (£1,087; £543; £271) Stalls Centre

Form RPR

0000 **1** **Mr Hullabalou (IRE)**[16] 3874 3-9-0 61 ........ EAhern 1 63
(RIngram) *a.p on outside: led wl over 1f out: rdn out fnl f* **10/1**

**2** *1 ½* **Kool Acclaim** 3-8-9 ........ OUrbina 6 54
(SCWilliams) *hld up in rr: hdwy 1/2-way: r.o to chse wnr fnl f: no imp* **12/1**

3 **3** *2 ½* **Bold Bunny**[48] 2908 3-8-9 ........ DaneO'Neill 4 46
(SCWilliams) *led tl hdd wl over 1f out: hung lft and fdd ins fnl f* **7/1**[3]

4 **4** *1 ¼* **Sylva Royal (IRE)**[122] 1202 3-8-9 ........ SSanders 8 42
(CEBrittain) *trckd ldrs: rdn 1/2-way: wknd fnl f* **3/1**[2]

0-00 **5** *2 ½* **Paradise Breeze**[23] 3666 3-8-6 ........ LisaJones(3) 7 35
(CAHorgan) *trckd ldr: rdn over 3f out: wknd wl over 1f out* **25/1**

432- **6** *1* **Thomas Lawrence (USA)**[384] 3241 3-9-0 93 ........ DHolland 2 37
(PFICole) *prom: rdn 1/2-way: wknd 2f out* **10/11**[1]

0-00 **7** *½* **Court Chancellor**[48] 2915 3-9-0 43 ........(b[1]) RLMoore 3 35
(PMitchell) *in tch tl rdn 1/2-way: sn bhd* **33/1**

0 **8** *6* **Inescapable (USA)**[7] 4144 3-9-0 ........ SDrowne 10 17
(WRMuir) *in tch on ins: rdn 1/2-way: sn wknd* **20/1**

0 **9** *½* **Just Dashing**[37] 3245 5-8-12 ........ NataliaGemelova(7) 9 16
(JELong) *towards rr: rdn over 3f out: nvr on terms* **66/1**

060 **10** *½* **Mantel Mini**[14] 3932 5-8-11 30 ........(v[1]) BReilly(3) 5 9
(BAPearce) *slowly away: a bhd* **66/1**

1m 11.54s (-0.11) **Going Correction** -0.05s/f (Good)
**WFA** 3 from 5yo 5lb **10** Ran SP% **121.2**
Speed ratings: **98,96,92,91,87 86,85,77,77,76**CSF £115.98 TOTE £15.40: £2.30, £4.50, £1.40; EX 372.70.
**Owner** Hullbran Bros **Bred** Brian Killeen **Trained** Epsom, Surrey

**FOCUS**
This took little winning with Thomas Lawrence disappointing, and the form is only modest.

**NOTEBOOK**
**Mr Hullabalou(IRE)** has been found wanting in handicaps, but this represented an easier opportunity and he took it in willing fashion. He may struggle back in handicap company.
**Kool Acclaim** , out of a five-furlong winner, is a half-sister to two winning sprinters as well as to Pretty Kool, who finished fifth in the previous race. This was a promising start, albeit in a weak maiden.
**Bold Bunny** travelled nicely in front, if racing a little freely, but did not find a great deal when tackled. She has the ability to win a small race provided she settles better.
**Sylva Royal(IRE)**, who bolted going to the start at Ascot last week and was withdrawn, is not very big. She did not shape as if this drop in trip was the answer.
**Thomas Lawrence(USA)** split Peak To Creek and Mandobi on his final run at two, but that was over a year ago and he has presumably had his problems since. He was beaten with two furlongs to run and a watching brief is advised. *Official explanation: jockey said gelding was never travelling*

## 4338 SHARP MINDS BETFAIR H'CAP 7f
8:05 (8:07) (E) (0-75,75) 3-Y-0 £4,459 (£1,372; £686; £343) Stalls Centre

Form RPR

5415 **1** **Blaeberry**[10] 4020 3-8-6 **60** ........(b) JFEgan 5 67
(PLGilligan) *mid-div: hdwy 3f out: led over 1f out: edgd lft fnl f: jst hld on* **13/2**[3]

5654 **2** *hd* **Head Boy**[16] 3874 3-7-12 **55** ........ LisaJones(3) 6 61
(SDow) *a.p: led 2f out: hdd over 1f out: rallied fnl f: jst failed* **5/1**[2]

5203 **3** *2* **Bahama Reef (IRE)**[12] 3988 3-8-1 **55** ........ CCatlin 7 56
(BGubby) *chsd ldrs tl one pce fnl f* **14/1**

050 **4** *hd* **Glencalvie (IRE)**[15] 3916 3-8-5 **59** ........ EAhern 2 59
(JNoseda) *in tch: hdwy 1/2-way to chse ldrs: one pce fnl f* **7/2**[1]

2201 **5** *1 ¼* **Wychbury (USA)**[8] 4101 3-9-4 **75** ........ DCorby(3) 8 72
(MJWallace) *led tl hdd 2f out: fdd ins fnl f* **5/1**[2]

0410 **6** *1 ¼* **Shifty Night (IRE)**[8] 4104 3-7-12 **52** oh5 ........ AMcCarthy 11 46
(MrsCADunnett) *in tch: rdn 1/2-way: kpt on one pce ins fnl 2f* **20/1**

P404 **7** *2* **Molinia**[14] 3949 3-8-1 **55** ........ JQuinn 1 44
(RMBeckett) *prom on outside: rdn 3f out: no hdwy after* **13/2**[3]

6040 **8** *nk* **Acuzio**[20] 3780 3-8-7 **61** ........ TEDurcan 4 49
(WMBrisbourne) *in tch: rdn 1/2-way: sn wknd* **25/1**

-606 **9** *2 ½* **Regal Flight (IRE)**[27] 3554 3-7-11 **56** oh2 ow4 ........ RThomas(5) 10 37
(JMBradley) *rrd up s: plld hrd: a in rr* **33/1**

401- **10** *nk* **Model Figure (USA)**[320] 4946 3-9-3 **71** ........ DHolland 9 52
(BWHills) *in tch: rdn 1/2-way: sn btn* **13/2**[3]

4366 **11** *7* **La Landonne**[10] 4024 3-8-12 **66** ........ SWKelly 13 28
(PMPhelan) *prom: rdn 1/2-way: wknd wl over 1f out* **12/1**

0-00 **12** *1* **Carlburg (IRE)**[14] 3949 3-8-7 **64** ........ J-PGuillambert(3) 12 24
(CEBrittain) *a bhd* **25/1**

6040 **13** *shd* **Must Be So**[39] 3175 3-7-5 **52** oh20 ........(t) CHaddon(7) 3 11
(JJBridger) *trckd ldrs tl rdn and wknd qckly 1/2-way* **66/1**

1m 22.96s (-1.25) **Going Correction** -0.05s/f (Good) **13** Ran SP% **126.8**
Speed ratings: **105,104,102,102,100 99,97,96,93,93 85,84,84**CSF £39.28 CT £460.16 TOTE £9.20: £1.80, £2.10, £3.80; EX 30.20.
**Owner** Lady Bland **Bred** Lady Bland **Trained** Newmarket, Suffolk

**FOCUS**
Another moderate handicap in which the field fanned out across the track. This is not strong form, with the third horse having been beaten in a seller last time.

**NOTEBOOK**
**Blaeberry** was 5lb higher than when landing a similar event here earlier in the month, when she had United Spirit, a winner earlier on this card, back in third. A change in tactics did the trick and she was always just about holding the runner-up, the pair of them edging left under pressure.
**Head Boy** went down narrowly, but appeared to be hanging in front and then edged left under pressure, as did the winner, as he rallied.
**Bahama Reef(IRE)** kept on to take third place on the line. He was beaten in a seller last time which puts this form into context.
**Glencalvie(IRE)**, on his handicap bow, was not helped by racing on the outside of the field from his low draw. After working his way into contention, he lost third spot in the last few strides. A return to a mile should suit him.
**Wychbury(USA)** stumbled on a poor maiden at Thirsk and was found wanting on this return to handicap company.

## 4339 COME BACK NEXT SATURDAY FILLIES' H'CAP 1m 2f (P)
8:35 (8:36) (F) (0-55,55) 3-Y-0+ £2,968 (£848; £424) Stalls Low

Form RPR

0630 **1** **Piquet**[5] 4192 6-9-8 **46** ........ TPQueally 6 53
(JJBridger) *a.p: shkn up 2f out: styd on to ld fnl 50yds* **14/1**

3300 **2** *½* **Semelle De Vent (USA)**[35] 3305 3-9-4 **52** ........(v[1]) JFortune 12 58
(JHMGosden) *hld up in mid-div: hdwy over 3f out: led wl over 1f out: rdn and hdd fnl 50yds* **8/1**

0352 **3** *nk* **Miss Glory Be**[5] 4190 6-9-11 **49** ........(p) DHolland 11 54
(EROertel) *mid-div: rdn 3f out: clsd on ldr 2f out: kpt on fnl f but no imp on ldng pair* **5/2**[1]

0/0- **4** *5* **Flaming Spirt**[564] 305 5-9-12 **50** ........ JDSmith 1 46
(JSMoore) *trckd ldrs: rdn 3f out: one pce fnl 2f* **14/1**

3560 **5** *½* **Mrs Brown**[9] 4055 3-9-7 **55** ........ SSanders 2 50
(SirMarkPrescott) *s.i.s: sn trckd ldrs: led briefly over 2f out: wknd over 1f out* **5/1**[2]

1363 **6** *2 ½* **Cumbrian Princess**[42] 3088 7-9-2 **45** ........ RThomas(5) 9 35
(MBlanshard) *sn mid-div but nvr impr on that* **10/1**

2060 **7** *1* **Madame Marie (IRE)**[23] 3670 4-9-8 **49** ........ LisaJones(3) 13 37
(SDow) *a towards rr* **12/1**

0401 **8** *¾* **Ellovamul**[5] 4201 4-9-10 **53** 6ex ........ MSavage(5) 7 40
(WMBrisbourne) *mid-div: rdn 4f out: nvr on terms after* **8/1**

4564 **9** *hd* **Hilarious (IRE)**[12] 3997 4-8-13 **44** ........(p) LucyRussell(7) 14 31
(DrJRJNaylor) *a in rr* **25/1**

3200 **10** *2* **Ryan's Bliss (IRE)**[29] 3490 4-9-3 **44** ........ RMiles(3) 10 27
(TDMccarthy) *prom on outside: rdn over 2f out: sn btn* **16/1**

0022 **11** *3* **Estimate**[5] 4201 4-9-7 **45** ........(v) SWhitworth 8 22
(JohnAHarris) *s.i.s: a bhd* **11/2**[3]

50-0 **12** *4* **Artzola (IRE)**[129] 1102 4-9-12 **50** ........ EAhern 4 19
(RIngram) *led tl hdd over 2f out: wknd qckly* **33/1**

4420 **13** *18* **Holly Rose**[4] 4213 5-9-12 **50** ........ JFEgan 3 —
(DECantillon) *sn trckd ldr: rdn and wknd qckly over 3f out* **7/1**

0005 **14** *7* **Figura**[14] 3934 6-10-0 **52** ........ SWKelly 5 —
(RIngram) *hld up: rdn and wknd 4f out* **16/1**

2m 10.37s (2.52) **Going Correction** +0.175s/f (Slow)
**WFA** 3 from 4yo+ 10lb **14** Ran SP% **144.0**
Speed ratings: **96,95,95,91,90 88,88,87,87,85 83,80,65,60**CSF £145.38 CT £394.24 TOTE £21.50: £4.50, £3.30, £1.60; EX 301.20 Place 6 £2,860.06, Place 5 £1,612.86.
**Owner** J J Bridger **Bred** D E And Mrs J Cash **Trained** Liphook, Hants

**FOCUS**
A moderate fillies' handicap run at a steady pace and this is very ordinary form.

**NOTEBOOK**
**Piquet** likes it here and she ran out a cosy winner of a weak event. She did not need to improve on the level of form she showed when third over course and distance earlier in the month.
**Semelle De Vent(USA)**, fitted with a visor instead of blinkers, has been running over a mile and a half. She was rushed around horses to lead off the home turn and grabbed the rail, but was cut down close home.
**Miss Glory Be** ran her race and finished clear of the remainder, but while she does stay this trip she is probably best at a mile.
**Flaming Spirt** is well treated on the pick of her 2002 form, but was well below par in the latter half of that year and this was her first outing since January 2003.
**Mrs Brown** was slowly away, as she has been before, but was soon in a prominent position. She plugged on as if a return to a mile and a half might suit her.
**Cumbrian Princess** passed beaten rivals but could never land a blow.
**Madame Marie(IRE)** was staying on when it was too late on this All-Weather bow.
T/Plt: £1,209.80 to a £1 stake. Pool: £36,874.40. 22.25 winning tickets. T/Qpdt: £49.30 to a £1 stake. Pool: £3,587.20. 53.80 winning tickets. JS

# 4292 NEWMARKET (JULY) (R-H)
Saturday, July 31

**OFFICIAL GOING: Good to firm**
Another dry night followed by a hot, humid day, ensured the ground remained on the fast side.
Wind: Slight across Weather: Sunny and humid

## 4340 HELEN ROLLASON CANCER CARE CENTRE APPEAL H'CAP 7f
1:45 (1:45) (D) (0-80,77) 3-Y-0 £6,838 (£2,104; £1,052; £526) Stalls Low

Form RPR

100 **1** **Attune**[7] 4140 3-9-4 **77** ........(b[1]) JFMcDonald(3) 5 89
(BJMeehan) *lw: trckd ldr tl led over 2f out: drvn clr ins fnl f* **14/1**

1660 **2** *3* **Granston (IRE)**[48] 2907 3-9-5 **75** ........ TQuinn 4 79
(JDBethell) *sn pushed along and prom: rdn to chse wnr and hung lft over 1f out: no ex ins fnl f* **7/2**[1]

-603 **3** *shd* **Scarlett Rose**[10] 4020 3-8-9 **65** ........ CLowther 1 69
(DrJDScargill) *a.p: rdn 1/2-way: n.m.r over 1f out: styd on* **9/2**[3]

4303 **4** *¾* **Bright Sun (IRE)**[9] 4050 3-9-2 **72** ........ KimTinkler 3 74
(NTinkler) *lw: s.i.s: sn pushed along and prom: outpcd over 2f out: nt clr run over 1f out: styd on* **4/1**[2]

5400 **5** *5* **Geller**[16] 3875 3-8-9 **65** ........ PDobbs 2 53
(RHannon) *chsd ldrs: nt clr run over 2f out: wknd fnl f* **10/1**

0340 **6** *2 ½* **Spin King (IRE)**[14] 3949 3-9-4 **74**.....................(v[1]) JMackay 6 55
(MLWBell) *sn led: rdn and hdd over 2f out: wknd over 1f out* **7/2**[1]

1460 **7** *nk* **La Puce**[10] 4020 3-7-13 **62**.....................(t) RachelCostello(7) 7 43
(MissGayKelleway) *lw: dwlt: a in rr* **20/1**

-020 **8** *nk* **Mind Alert**[28] 3523 3-8-11 **67**..................... WSupple 8 47
(TDEasterby) *hld up: rdn over 2f out: wknd over 1f out* **8/1**

1m 23.84s (-2.93) **Going Correction** -0.25s/f (Firm) **8** Ran SP% **114.3**
Speed ratings: **106,102,102,101,95 93,92,92**CSF £62.48 CT £262.91 TOTE £18.80: £3.80, £1.60, £1.30; EX 59.10.
**Owner** Wyck Hall Stud **Bred** Wyck Hall Stud Ltd **Trained** Upper Lambourn, Berks

**FOCUS**
A race full of disappointing types and ordinary form for the track, although it was soundly run.

**NOTEBOOK**
**Attune** travelled much better in the first-time blinkers, and showed a nice attitude when asked to go and win her race.
**Granston(IRE)** was never travelling with any fluency and may be better suited to a mile.
**Scarlett Rose** turned in another solid effort, but she does not do anything quickly and may be worth a try over a mile.
**Bright Sun(IRE)** has been disappointing since winning his maiden last year, but this was not a bad effort and he still has time on his side.
**Geller** continues to struggle and did not improve any for the drop in trip.
**Spin King(IRE)** was keen enough in the first-time visor, and connections must be running out of ideas with him now.

## 4341 FANTASY ISLAND THEMED FAMILY RESORT ATTRACTION EBF STUBBS STKS (LISTED RACE) 1m

**2:20** (2:20) (A) 4-Y-0+ **£19,040** (£7,040; £3,520; £1,600) **Stalls** Low

Form RPR

25-0 **1** **Pawn Broker**[133] 1062 7-8-12 **105**..................... WSupple 1 110
(DRCElsworth) *hld up: gd hdwy over 1f out: r.o to ld wl ins fnl f* **9/1**

3115 **2** *1* **Mine (IRE)**[28] 3539 6-8-12 **108**.....................(v) TQuinn 5 107
(JDBethell) *lw: hld up: hdwy to chse ldr over 4f out: led over 1f out: rdn and hdd wl ins fnl f* **6/4**[1]

1040 **3** *1 ¼* **Sublimity (FR)**[56] 2678 4-9-2 **110**.....................(t) SDrowne 2 108
(SirMichaelStoute) *swtg: led: rdn and hdd over 1f out: no ex towards fin* **7/2**[2]

0041 **4** *hd* **Always Esteemed (IRE)**[17] 3850 4-8-12 **95**..................... FNorton 3 104
(GWragg) *swtg: chsd ldr over 3f: rdn over 2f out: styd on* **6/1**[3]

34-0 **5** *1* **Tarjman**[35] 3323 4-8-12 **111**..................... TPQueally 4 102
(ACStewart) *hld up in tch: rdn over 1f out: nt run on* **7/2**[2]

1m 39.61s (-0.87) **Going Correction** -0.25s/f (Firm) **5** Ran SP% **108.7**
Speed ratings: **94,93,91,91,90**CSF £22.57 TOTE £9.10: £2.60, £1.30; EX 16.80.
**Owner** Raymond Tooth **Bred** R J McAlpine And D O Pickering **Trained** Whitsbury, Hants

**FOCUS**
A useful contest somewhat ruined by the lack of a decent gallop, which suggests the form is not that reliable.

**NOTEBOOK**
**Pawn Broker**, over a trip short of his best, hardly had the race run to suit, but he showed plenty of resolution on meeting the rising ground to gain his first success over this trip since his juvenile days.
**Mine(IRE)**, who is better suited to larger fields and a strong pace, had neither. However, it was still a surprise to see him go in pursuit of the winner before halfway, and take up the running some way out, which left him something of a sitting duck for the rest of them.
**Sublimity(FR)** has made the running in the past, but is ideally suited to having a lead.
**Always Esteemed(IRE)** was far from disgraced on these terms, but with only a moderate pace being set, it is possible he was slightly flattered.
**Tarjman** should have been suited by the way the race was run, but his attitude left something to be desired when asked to pick up.

## 4342 SIEMENS SMART HOME TECHNOLOGY NURSERY 6f

**2:50** (2:50) (B) 2-Y-0 **£13,754** (£4,232; £2,116; £1,058) **Stalls** Low

Form RPR

321 **1** **Transaction (IRE)**[21] 3760 2-8-13 **87**..................... SDrowne 5 91
(JMPEustace) *hld up: hdwy over 1f out: rdn to ld ins fnl f: hung lft towards fin: r.o* **10/1**

4113 **2** *hd* **Piddies Pride (IRE)**[3] 4235 2-7-9 **72**..................... FPFerris(3) 10 75
(PSMcentee) *sn led: hdd over 3f out: led over 2f out: rdn and hdd ins fnl f: r.o: edgd rt nr fin* **12/1**

3213 **3** *1 ¼* **Space Shuttle**[44] 3011 2-8-13 **87**.....................(b) WSupple 4 87
(TDEasterby) *b.near hind: lw: hld up: plld hrd: hdwy over 1f out: styng on same pce whn n.m.r nr fin* **15/2**

221 **4** *½* **Encanto (IRE)**[7] 4137 2-8-4 **85**..................... DerekNolan(7) 7 83
(JSMoore) *hld up: hdwy u.p over 1f out: styd on same pce ins fnl f* **10/1**

5113 **5** *1 ¼* **Sacred Nuts (IRE)**[6] 4166 2-9-7 **95**..................... JMackay 8 89
(MLWBell) *hld up in tch: chsd ldr 2f out: sn rdn: no ex fnl f* **3/1**[1]

054 **6** *1* **Red Chairman**[8] 4088 2-8-10 **84**..................... TPQueally 6 75
(DRLoder) *chsd ldr tl led over 3f out: hdd over 2f out: wknd ins fnl f* **4/1**[2]

1600 **7** *shd* **Norcroft**[21] 3727 2-8-5 **82**..................... JFMcDonald(3) 11 73
(NACallaghan) *dwlt: hld up: rdn over 2f out: styd on ins fnl f: edgd lft: nvr trbld ldrs* **40/1**

4403 **8** *1 ¾* **High Chart**[5] 4197 2-8-10 **84**..................... AMcCarthy 2 70
(GGMargarson) *chsd ldrs: rdn over 2f out: wknd fnl f* **33/1**

0301 **9** *5* **Prospect Court**[25] 3605 2-8-11 **85**..................... TQuinn 3 56
(JDBethell) *chsd ldrs over 4f* **8/1**

3342 **10** *¾* **Safendonseabiscuit**[16] 3886 2-8-6 **80**.....................(b[1]) FNorton 1 48
(SKirk) *chsd ldrs: rdn 1/2-way: wknd 2f out* **14/1**

432 **11** *nk* **Gennie Bond**[12] 3992 2-8-7 **81**..................... PDobbs 9 49
(RHannon) *lw: chsd ldrs over 4f* **7/1**[3]

1m 12.56s (-0.76) **Going Correction** -0.25s/f (Firm) **11** Ran SP% **118.3**
Speed ratings: **95,94,93,92,90 89,89,86,80,79 78**CSF £124.58 CT £976.52 TOTE £11.60: £3.20, £3.60, £2.80; EX 142.10.
**Owner** George Darling **Bred** George Darling **Trained** Newmarket, Suffolk
■ Stewards Enquiry : S Drowne one-day ban: careless riding (Aug 11)

**FOCUS**
A competitive nursery run at a good clip in which the form looks solid going to an unexposed winner.The 'official ratings' are only an estimate and are for guidance only.

**NOTEBOOK**
**Transaction(IRE)** proved well suited to the strong pace and continues on an upward curve. He was bought at the Doncaster St Leger sales and that bonus race in September is his target.
**Piddies Pride(IRE)** is a tough filly and stayed on bravely having looked likely to be swamped.
**Space Shuttle** did himself no favours by refusing to settle early on, despite the strong pace. However, there is no doubt he does have his fair share of ability.
**Encanto(IRE)** seemed to run her race and had no excuses.
**Sacred Nuts(IRE)** unlucky at Ascot, was made a short price to atone. However, he had no excuses this time and could be difficult to place off his current mark.
**Red Chairman**, tackling handicappers for the first time, looks to need some respite if he is going to trouble the judge.

## 4343 LAWSHALL H'CAP 1m 2f

**3:25** (3:27) (C) (0-90,87) 3-Y-O+ **£13,624** (£4,192; £2,096; £1,048) **Stalls** Centre

Form RPR

3064 **1** **Barry Island**[10] 4029 5-8-13 **73**..................... JMackay 10 84
(DRCElsworth) *chsd ldrs: rdn to ld over 1f out: r.o* **14/1**

0062 **2** *½* **Jeepstar**[11] 4005 4-8-11 **71**..................... WSupple 7 81
(TDEasterby) *led: rdn: hung lft and hdd over 1f out: r.o* **9/2**[2]

0110 **3** *1 ½* **Silvaline**[22] 3692 5-8-13 **80**..................... CHaddon(7) 4 87
(TKeddy) *chsd ldr: rdn and ev ch over 1f out: no ex ins fnl f* **14/1**

2025 **4** *½* **Hello It's Me**[7] 4140 3-9-2 **86**..................... MTebbutt 1 92
(HJCollingridge) *swtg: a.p: rdn over 3f out: styd on u.p* **16/1**

-120 **5** *½* **Trueno (IRE)**[42] 3097 5-9-10 **84**..................... TPQueally 5 89
(LMCumani) *hld up: plld hrd: rdn over 1f out: styd on: nt pce to chal* **16/1**

3414 **6** *hd* **Ken's Dream**[15] 3909 5-9-8 **82**..................... PMcCabe 6 87
(MsAEEmbiricos) *hld up: hdwy over 2f out: nt clr run over 1f out: edgd lft and no ex ins fnl f* **7/1**[3]

0031 **7** *2* **Karaoke (IRE)**[12] 3997 4-8-8 **68**..................... FNorton 9 69
(SKirk) *hld up: rdn over 2f out: nvr trbld ldrs* **12/1**

0344 **8** *1* **Stretton (IRE)**[9] 4061 6-9-4 **78**..................... TQuinn 2 77
(JDBethell) *lw: hld up: hdwy over 1f out: wknd ins fnl f* **8/1**

0212 **9** *2* **Adaikali (IRE)**[9] 4061 3-9-3 **87**..................... SDrowne 3 82
(SirMichaelStoute) *hld up: plld hrd: hdwy over 1f out: wknd ins fnl f* **2/1**[1]

1413 **10** *3* **Olivia Rose (IRE)**[7] 4136 5-9-9 **83**..................... PDobbs 8 73
(JPearce) *hld up in tch: rdn over 1f out: sn wknd* **12/1**

2m 5.44s (-1.02) **Going Correction** +0.025s/f (Good)
**WFA** 3 from 4yo+ 10lb **10** Ran SP% **115.6**
Speed ratings: **105,104,103,103,102 102,100,100,98,96**CSF £75.37 CT £911.98 TOTE £20.60: £3.80, £2.20, £4.50; EX 85.90.
**Owner** Matthew Green **Bred** The Lavington Stud **Trained** Whitsbury, Hants
■ Stewards Enquiry : C Haddon caution: careless riding

**FOCUS**
A 0-84 in effect and the way this was run suited those racing close to the pace. Despite this the form looks sound.

**NOTEBOOK**
**Barry Island** was always in the right place and got first run on his rivals, which made the difference. This was his first success on turf.
**Jeepstar** had something of a soft lead, but did himself no favours by continually hanging left, although he did keep plugging away.
**Silvaline** continues in good form, although it looks as though the Handicapper may well have hold of him for the time being.
**Hello It's Me** stuck to his task well enough, but never really looked like taking a hand. *Official explanation: jockey said gelding hung right*
**Trueno(IRE)** did best of the hold-up horses and may be worth another try over a bit further.
**Ken's Dream**, who can take a grip, settled well enough, but would have preferred a stronger pace.
**Adaikali(IRE)** was always seeing too much daylight on the outside of the field and dropped away tamely up the hill. He is better than he showed here. *Official explanation: vet said colt finished distressed*

## 4344 HOTEL FELIX CAMBRIDGE EBF MAIDEN FILLIES' STKS 7f

**4:00** (4:01) (D) 2-Y-O **£4,813** (£1,481; £740; £370) **Stalls** Low

Form RPR

3 **1** **Road Rage (IRE)**[15] 3913 2-8-11..................... TQuinn 2 75
(EALDunlop) *chsd ldr tl led 2f out: hrd rdn and hung rt ins fnl f: r.o* **8/11**[1]

**2** *shd* **Elizabethan Age (FR)** 2-8-11..................... TPQueally 4 75
(DRLoder) *gd sort: lw: chsd ldrs: rdn and ev ch whn edgd rt ins fnl f: r.o* **9/2**[2]

**3** *1 ¼* **Crystalline** 2-8-8..................... ABeech(3) 5 72
(DRLoder) *compact: scope: bit bkwd: hld up: hdwy over 1f out: r.o* **8/1**

**4** *shd* **Mokaraba** 2-8-11..................... SWKelly 1 71
(JLDunlop) *w'like: scope: s.i.s: sn prom: rdn over 2f out: r.o* **16/1**

**5** *shd* **Thakafaat (IRE)** 2-8-11..................... WSupple 6 71
(JLDunlop) *leggy: scope: s.s: hld up: hdwy over 1f out: r.o* **7/1**[3]

**6** *shd* **Tohama** 2-8-11..................... SDrowne 3 71
(JLDunlop) *gd sort: scope: bit bkwd: prom: hmpd and lost pl over 5f out: hdwy over 2f out: r.o* **16/1**

0 **7** *1* **Garance**[30] 3451 2-8-11..................... PDobbs 7 68
(RHannon) *led over 5f: no ex wl ins fnl f* **16/1**

1m 27.93s (1.16) **Going Correction** +0.025s/f (Good) **7** Ran SP% **117.3**
Speed ratings: **94,93,92,92,92 92,90**CSF £4.62 TOTE £1.60: £1.40, £2.20; EX 5.30.
**Owner** Cliveden Stud **Bred** Cliveden Stud Ltd **Trained** Newmarket, Suffolk

**FOCUS**
Some well-bred fillies on show, but the race was slowly run and three-lengths covered the seven home, making the form looks unreliable.

**NOTEBOOK**
**Road Rage(IRE)** was made to work hard for her victory and still looked pretty green. The slow pace would have been against her, and she looks the sort to do better as she steps up in trip. *Official explanation: jockey said filly ran green*
**Elizabethan Age(FR)**, out of a mare that stayed 12-furlongs, would not have been ideally suited by the steady pace, but is open to improvement especially when facing a stiffer test.
**Crystalline**, a half-sister to 12-furlong winner Balkan Knight, took a while to grasp what was required and is sure to have learnt from the experience.
**Mokaraba**, who is from the same family as the high-class Salsabil, was very green and can only be wiser for the experience.
**Thakafaat(IRE)**, whose dam won over six furlongs as a juvenile, was very green and should step up on this effort in time.
**Tohama**, a half-sister to Group Two winner Azzilfi, was another unsuited by the lack of pace and should improve for for the experience.

## 4345 HELEN ROLLASON LIVE WELL EXPERIENCE CLASSIFIED STKS 1m 4f

**4:35** (4:35) (C) 3-Y-O+ **£9,470** (£2,914; £1,457; £728) **Stalls** Centre

Form RPR

1260 **1** **Tawny Way**[14] 3944 4-9-1 **86**..................... TQuinn 4 93
(WJarvis) *lw: led 9f: rdn to ld over 1f out: all out* **14/1**

0011 **2** *hd* **Wait For The Will (USA)**[36] 3276 8-8-13 **90**.....................(b) AQuinn(5) 6 96
(GLMoore) *chsd ldrs: led over 2f out: hdd over 1f out: r.o* **7/2**[1]

0245 **3** *1* **Highland Games (IRE)**[42] 3075 4-9-4 **87**..................... WSupple 1 94
(JGGiven) *chsd ldrs: led 3f out: sn rdn and hdd: styd on same pce ins fnl f* **9/2**[2]

4-06 **4** *¾* **Lodger (FR)**[7] 4123 4-9-5 **91**..................... SWKelly 2 94
(JNoseda) *lw: prom: lost pl 3f out: rallied fnl f: nt pce to chal* **8/1**

0110 **5** *3* **Millville**[108] 1401 4-9-4 **85**..................... MTebbutt 3 88
(MAJarvis) *lw: hld up: hdwy over 3f out: sn rdn: wknd ins fnl f* **9/2**[2]

6531 **6** *¾* **Gold Ring**[15] 3909 4-9-5 **91**..................... SCarson 7 88
(GBBalding) *chsd ldr: rdn and ev ch fr over 2f out: tl wknd fnl f* **5/1**[3]

1-63 **7** ½ **Argonaut**[7] [4123] 4-9-4 89 ........ SDrowne 5 86
(SirMichaelStoute) *lw: hld up: hdwy over 4f out: rdn over 2f out: no ex* **9/2**[2]

/00- **8** nk **Halland**[96] [1367] 6-8-11 82 ........ StevenHarrison(7) 8 86
(NPLittmoden) *hld up: hdwy over 3f out: wknd over 1f out* **28/1**

2m 31.83s (-1.13) **Going Correction** +0.025s/f (Good) **8** Ran SP% **114.7**
Speed ratings: **104,103,103,102,100 100,99,99**CSF £62.79 TOTE £18.90: £2.70, £1.30, £1.70; EX 70.90.
**Owner** Rams Racing Club **Bred** K P Seow **Trained** Newmarket, Suffolk

**FOCUS**
Quite a tight classified race on the figures, but the pace looked no more than ordinary. However, the first three ran close to previous marks, giving the form a sound look.

**NOTEBOOK**
**Tawny Way** had the run of the race and showed plenty of resolution to hold on.
**Wait For The Will(USA)** looked all over the winner, but did not find as much off the bridle as looked likely.
**Highland Games(IRE)** is running well enough at present, but he has gone quite a while now without getting his head in front.
**Lodger(FR)** does not do anything quickly and, while a stronger pace would have seen him in a better light, he may be worth another try over further.
**Millville** ran as though just needing the outing.
**Gold Ring**, who had every chance, may have found the ground on the lively side. *Official explanation: jockey said gelding was unsuited by the ground*
**Argonaut** did not move that well to post and was one of the first beaten.

## 4346 POSLINGFORD H'CAP 1m 4f
**5:10** (5:10) (E) (0-70,67) 3-Y-O **£3,549** (£1,092; £546; £273) **Stalls** Centre

Form RPR

040- **1** **Worcester Lodge**[268] [5932] 3-9-2 **62** ........ SDrowne 15 78+
(RCharlton) *b: a.p: rdn over 3f out: led ins fnl f: styd on wl* **8/1**

0041 **2** 2 **Inchpast**[9] [4070] 3-8-11 **62** ........ (b) AQuinn(5) 3 67+
(MHTompkins) *chsd ldrs: nt clr run over 1f out: r.o ins fnl f* **9/2**[1]

0-40 **3** shd **Jolizero**[21] [3746] 3-8-4 **57** ........ DerekNolan(7) 7 62
(PWChapple-Hyam) *lw: chsd ldrs: led over 2f out: hdd and unable qck ins fnl f* **6/1**[2]

4063 **4** 1 **Scarrabus (IRE)**[9] [4057] 3-9-5 **65** ........ GBaker 9 68
(BGPowell) *hld up: hdwy 3f out: ev chnce over 1f out: sn rdn and edgd rt: no ex ins fnl f* **25/1**

1055 **5** 1 ¼ **Chara**[7] [4138] 3-9-2 **65** ........ JFMcDonald(3) 13 66
(JRJenkins) *lw: hld up: nt clr run over 3f out: hdwy over 1f out: nt rch ldrs* **16/1**

6-00 **6** ¾ **Trilemma**[21] [3746] 3-9-2 **62** ........ JMackay 10 62+
(SirMarkPrescott) *lw: hld up: hdwy over 2f out: r.o* **20/1**

5530 **7** nk **Siegfrieds Night (IRE)**[17] [3837] 3-8-13 **62** ........ ABeech(3) 17 62
(MCChapman) *hld up in tch: rdn over 1f out: styd on same pce* **9/1**

00 **8** ½ **Sharadi (IRE)**[27] [3561] 3-9-0 **60** ........ MTebbutt 4 59+
(VSmith) *chsd ldr: rdn and ev ch fr over 2f out: edgd lft and hmpd over 1f out: wknd and eased wl ins fnl f* **10/1**

-305 **9** 6 **Pangloss (IRE)**[38] [3210] 3-9-7 **67** ........ (b[1]) PDobbs 14 56
(GLMoore) *hld up: plld hrd: rdn over 2f out: sn wknd* **14/1**

6401 **10** ½ **Ellina**[10] [4027] 3-9-7 **67** ........ RPrice 8 55
(JPearce) *s.i.s: hld up: hdwy over 3f out: wknd over 2f out* **10/1**

3-03 **11** 7 **Polar Dancer**[17] [3852] 3-8-13 **59** ........ WSupple 1 36
(MrsAJPerrett) *hld up: hmpd over 7f out: hdwy over 5f out: wknd 2f out* **7/1**[3]

60U0 **12** hd **Nick The Silver**[7] [4146] 3-8-11 **57** ........ SCarson 16 34
(GBBalding) *hld up in tch: plld hrd: rdn and wknd 3f out* **33/1**

6410 **13** ½ **It's Blue Chip**[19] [3806] 3-9-5 **65** ........ PaulEddery 2 41
(PWD'Arcy) *s.s: hld up: a in rr* **14/1**

3-40 **14** nk **Devious Ayers (IRE)**[89] [1830] 3-9-3 **63** ........ SWKelly 12 39
(GAButler) *led over 9f: wknd over 1f out* **11/1**

0-40 **15** 1 ½ **Greek Star**[49] [2888] 3-8-2 **48** ........ FNorton 11 21
(KAMorgan) *hld up: wknd over 2f out* **22/1**

5436 **16** 22 **Savannah River (IRE)**[12] [3984] 3-7-13 **45** ........ (t) DKinsella 5 —
(CWThornton) *hld up: rdn over 5f out: sn wknd* **14/1**

3630 **17** dist **Vrisaki (IRE)**[9] [4055] 3-7-11 **46** ........ FPFerris(3) 6 —
(MissDMountain) *s.i.s: hld up: hdwy over 5f out: wknd and eased over 2f out* **28/1**

2m 33.03s (0.07) **Going Correction** +0.025s/f (Good) **17** Ran SP% **137.8**
Speed ratings: **100,98,98,97,97 96,96,96,92,91 87,86,86,86,85 70,**—CSF £46.24 CT £250.56 TOTE £11.50: £2.70, £2.10, £2.50, £8.70; EX 45.00 Place 6 £256.36, Place 5 £111.80.
**Owner** Lady Rothschild **Bred** Lord Rothschild **Trained** Beckhampton, Wilts
■ Stewards Enquiry : Derek Nolan one-day ban: careless riding

**FOCUS**
A moderate contest, but the winner is unexposed and looks capable of better.

**NOTEBOOK**
**Worcester Lodge** showed his true colours on this first venture into handicap company over a more suitable trip. He is open to any amount of improvement
**Inchpast** made a bold effort to follow up his Yarmouth victory, and would surely have gone close with anything like a clear run.
**Jolizero** found improvement for this step up in trip and should find a race in due course.
**Scarrabus(IRE)**, dropped out in the early stages, came through to have every chance before not quite getting up the hill. He does have a little ability, but may just need dropping a little in trip.
**Chara** did not have much luck in running, but showed enough to merit consideration in a similar contest.
**Trilemma** does not do anything quickly and may appreciate further still.
**It's Blue Chip** *Official explanation: jockey said colt was unsuited by the ground*
**Devious Ayers(IRE)** *Official explanation: jockey said gelding was too keen*
**Savannah River(IRE)** *Official explanation: jockey said filly was unsuited by the ground*
**Vrisaki(IRE)** *Official explanation: jockey said colt ran too keenly early in the race*
T/Plt: £337.20 to a £1 stake. Pool: £53,977.05. 116.85 winning tickets. T/Qpdt: £31.90 to a £1 stake. Pool: £3,020.80. 70.00 winning tickets. CR

# 4304 THIRSK (L-H)
Saturday, July 31

**OFFICIAL GOING: Firm**
The going was described as 'very fast but with a good cover of grass'.
Wind: Almost nil. Weather: Fine and sunny.

## 4347 EUROPEAN BREEDERS FUND THOMAS LORD MAIDEN STKS 5f
**2:05** (2:07) (D) 2-Y-O **£6,214** (£1,912; £956; £478) **Stalls** High

Form RPR

32 **1** **Turnaround (GER)**[35] [3313] 2-9-0 ........ IMongan 6 84+
(MrsJRRamsden) *trckd ldr: led appr fnl f: pushed out: comf* **4/7**[1]

**2** 2 ½ **Carnivore** 2-9-0 ........ DarrenWilliams 3 71
(TDBarron) *leggy: unf: scope: s.i.s: hld up: hdwy over 1f out: wnt 2nd ins fnl f: no imp on wnr* **11/2**[2]

0 **3** ½ **Peters Delite**[29] [3476] 2-9-0 ........ PHanagan 7 70
(RAFahey) *chsd ldrs: rdn wl over 1f out: kpt on same pce* **16/1**

3036 **4** 2 **Chilali (IRE)**[9] [4046] 2-8-9 ........ DaleGibson 4 58
(ABerry) *led tl hdd appr fnl f: no ex* **14/1**

06 **5** 2 **Algorithm**[8] [4099] 2-8-9 ........ PMQuinn 2 51
(TDEasterby) *towards rr: sme hdwy 1/2-way: rdn wl over 1f out: no further prog* **20/1**

0 **6** 3 **Kerny (IRE)**[77] [2125] 2-9-0 ........ GHind 1 45
(JJQuinn) *chsd ldrs tl wknd appr fnl f* **66/1**

5 **7** nk **Wayward Shot (IRE)**[29] [3469] 2-9-0 ........ TLucas 5 44
(MWEasterby) *dwlt: a towards rr* **12/1**[3]

**8** 1 ½ **Halla San** 2-9-0 ........ LGoncalves 8 39
(MrsJRRamsden) *rangy: unf: dwlt: a bhd* **25/1**

**9** 29 **Feel The Need** 2-8-9 ........ PMulrennan(5) 9 —
(MABarnes) *leggy: unf: dwlt: slways bhd: lost tch fnl 2f: t.o* **33/1**

58.68 secs (-1.22) **Going Correction** -0.25s/f (Firm) **9** Ran SP% **112.3**
Speed ratings: **99,95,94,91,87 83,82,80,33**CSF £3.32 TOTE £1.40: £1.02, £2.20, £1.80; EX 3.70.
**Owner** J Musgrave **Bred** Gestut Brummerhof **Trained** Sandhutton, N Yorks

**FOCUS**
Just an ordinary maiden but the form looks sound. The winner will progress especially over six and the placed horses can do better.

**NOTEBOOK**
**Turnaround(GER)** travelled strongly and took this with the minimum of fuss. He took some pulling up and will be suited by six in nursery company.
**Carnivore**, a May foal, is on the leg but is quite an athletic type. Given a patient ride, in the end he was asked to do just enough to secure second spot. He will improve a fair bit given a little more time.
**Peters Delite**, a March foal, is on the leg but has a powerful action. He showed a lot more than on his debut but still gave the impression he has something to learn.
**Chilali(IRE)**, having her eighth start and only third in a seller, was on her toes beforehand. She showed plenty of pace but tended to hang away from the running rail and in the end was put in her place.
**Algorithm**, on her toes beforehand, was dropping back in trip on her third outing. Never able to go the pace, she will need to return to six plus in nurseries.
**Kerny(IRE)**, absent for 11 weeks, had made his debut on the All-Weather.

## 4348 HERTEL NURSERY 5f
**2:35** (2:36) (C) 2-Y-O **£9,704** (£2,986; £1,493; £746) **Stalls** High

Form RPR

2333 **1** **Wise Wager (IRE)**[7] [4150] 2-8-4 **68** ........ PHanagan 1 72
(RAFahey) *led after 1f: rdn over 1f out: kpt on wl fnl f* **7/1**

1352 **2** 1 ¼ **Katie Boo (IRE)**[7] [4150] 2-9-2 **80** ........ GHind 9 80
(ABerry) *s.i.s: sn midfield: nt clr run briefly 2f out: sn rdn: r.o wl to go 2nd wl ins fnl f* **6/1**

2401 **3** 1 ¼ **Brag (IRE)**[10] [4017] 2-9-4 **82** ........ DSweeney 8 83+
(RCharlton) *in tch: nt clr run 2f out: r.o wl fnl f: nrst fin* **15/8**[1]

111 **4** hd **Key Secret**[21] [3753] 2-9-0 **83** ........ HayleyTurner(5) 3 78
(MLWBell) *towards rr: hdwy over 1f out: edgd lft u.p fnl f: nvr able to chal* **5/1**[3]

414 **5** shd **African Breeze**[30] [3445] 2-9-5 **83** ........ DeanMcKeown 6 77
(RMWhitaker) *s.i.s: rr: hdwy to chse ldrs ent fnl f: hung lft u.p and no ex ins last* **14/1**

41 **6** 1 **Pro Tempore**[15] [3893] 2-8-8 **72** ........ IMongan 5 63
(MrsJRRamsden) *chsd ldrs: rdn over 1f out: fdd fnl f* **14/1**

2314 **7** ½ **Forzeen**[9] [4046] 2-9-7 **85** ........ MFenton 4 74
(JAOsborne) *towards rr: hdwy 2f out: sn rdn: no further prog fnl f* **4/1**[2]

4150 **8** 3 ½ **Our Louis**[9] [4046] 2-7-12 **62** oh6 ........ PMQuinn 10 39
(JSWainwright) *led 1f: remained prom tl hung lft and wknd over 1f out* **66/1**

2100 **9** 7 **Town House**[14] [3924] 2-8-11 **75** ........ DaleGibson 7 27
(BPJBaugh) *cl up tl wknd qckly 2f out* **20/1**

020 **10** 4 **Noodles**[15] [3918] 2-8-11 **75** ........ JCarroll 2 13
(TDEasterby) *slowly away: a bhd* **33/1**

58.81 secs (-1.09) **Going Correction** -0.25s/f (Firm) **10** Ran SP% **120.8**
Speed ratings: **98,96,94,93,93 91,91,85,74,67**CSF £49.60 CT £114.28 TOTE £9.30: £2.00, £1.70, £1.50; EX 35.40.
**Owner** P Timmins & J Rhodes **Bred** David Brickley **Trained** Musley Bank, N Yorks

**FOCUS**
A decent nursery which appears fairly solid formwise. The 'official ratings' are only an estimate and are for guidance only.

**NOTEBOOK**
**Wise Wager(IRE)**, drawn one, is all speed and was in front against the stands' side rail at halfway. She should continue to give a good account of herself.
**Katie Boo(IRE)**, closely matched with the winner on York running, made a tardy start. She finished to some effect but too late to get in a blow.
**Brag(IRE)**, from a much stiffer mark, impressed going to post but on the way back she had little luck, otherwise she would have given the winner much more to do.
**Key Secret**, from a much higher mark, showed a moderate action and failed completely to go the pace. Always tending to hang left, she put in some solid late work on the wide outside and is worth a try over six. *Official explanation: jockey said filly hung left*
**African Breeze** made a tardy start and struggled to keep up. Closer at the line than anywhere before, she must be worth another try over six.
**Pro Tempore**, who has more size and scope than many of these, still has a bit to learn and her handicap mark looks on the stiff side.
**Forzeen**, who has been put up in the ratings, wore a cross noseband and did not impress going down. He never figured.
**Our Louis** almost bolted going to post then hung away from the running rail after showing ahead early on. *Official explanation: jockey said filly hung left*

## 4349 EKOS CONSULTING H'CAP 1m
**3:10** (3:10) (C) (0-95,92) 3-Y-O+ **£9,587** (£2,950; £1,475; £737) **Stalls** Low

Form RPR

5354 **1** **Efidium**[20] [3779] 6-8-2 **68** ........ PHanagan 3 76
(NBycroft) *hld up: hdwy 3f out: rdn to ld jst ins fnl f: styd on* **9/1**

4022 **2** 1 **Raphael (IRE)**[7] [4134] 5-8-7 **80** ........ AMullen(7) 8 86
(TDEasterby) *cl up: led over 2f out: rdn over 1f out: hdd jst ins fnl f: no ex* **5/2**[1]

1146 **3** 1 **Alchemist Master**[16] [3884] 5-8-6 **72** ........ (p) DeanMcKeown 6 75
(RMWhitaker) *trckd ldrs: rdn 2f out: kpt on fnl f* **9/1**

4200 **4** hd **Adobe**[7] [4142] 9-7-9 **66** ........ BSwarbrick(5) 2 69
(WMBrisbourne) *hld up in rr: effrt over 2f out: rdn wl over 1f out: styd on ins fnl f: nvr able to chal* **9/1**

0311 **5** ½ **Harry Potter (GER)**[7] 4142 5-9-0 **80**..........(v) DarrenWilliams 4 82
(KRBurke) *hld up: hmpd 1/2-way: effrt 3f out: styd on u.p fnl 2f: n.d* **7/2**[2]

0065 **6** *1* **Sea Storm (IRE)**[7] 4134 6-8-10 **79**..........(p) LEnstone(3) 1 78
(DRMacleod) *chsd ldrs: rdn and outpcd 2f out: n.d after* **8/1**

0542 **7** 3½ **Onlytime Will Tell**[8] 4076 6-9-11 **91**.......... JCarroll 5 82+
(DNicholls) *led tl hdd over 2f out: wknd fnl f* **9/2**[3]

10-0 **8** *9* **Montmartre (IRE)**[21] 3757 4-9-7 **92**.......... PMulrennan(5) 7 63
(JHowardJohnson) *prom tl wknd qckly over 2f out* **16/1**

1m 39.56s (-0.14) **Going Correction** -0.05s/f (Good) **8** Ran SP% **116.0**
Speed ratings: **98,97,96,95,95 94,90,81**CSF £32.35 CT £215.33 TOTE £11.90: £2.30, £1.70, £2.70; EX 21.70.
**Owner** Hambleton Racing Partnership **Bred** T Umpleby **Trained** Brandsby, N Yorks

**FOCUS**
A 0-92 handicap run at just a steady pace until in line for home, the form is ordinary for the grade.

**NOTEBOOK**
**Efidium**, 4lb higher than when he won at York in May, made it eight career wins on his 63rd start.
**Raphael(IRE)**, who is blooming, ran right up to her best and went down with all guns blazing from a career high mark.
**Alchemist Master**, 15lb higher than when breaking his duck four outings ago, looked very fit indeed and could have done with a stronger early pace.
**Adobe**, attempting his third win in this race, likes to come from off a strong pace and this was certainly not run to suit him.
**Harry Potter(GER)**, hoisted 11lb, was warm beforehand and was on the back foot after being left short of room at halfway.
**Sea Storm(IRE)**, back on a winning mark, was left short of room on the inner rounding the home turn and could never get back into the firing line.
**Onlytime Will Tell**, very warm beforehand, found himself in front. Doing a bit too much he did not see out the mile.

## 4350 WHITBY (S) H'CAP (LADIES RACE) 6f
3:45 (3:45) (F) (0-55,54) 3-Y-0+ **£4,241** (£1,305; £652; £326) **Stalls** High

Form RPR

0056 **1** **Zietzig (IRE)**[17] 3836 7-9-11 **40**.......... MissKellyHarrison(3) 13 55
(DNicholls) *edgd rt s: sn prom stands side: led jst ins fnl f: r.o wl* **7/1**[2]

0004 **2** 2½ **Danakim**[3] 4247 7-9-13 **39**.......... MsCWilliams 19 47
(JRWeymes) *racd stands side: led: rdn 2f out: hdd jst ins fnl f: kpt on: no ch w wnr* **13/2**[1]

6050 **3** ¾ **Frimley's Mattery**[27] 3559 4-10-3 **50**.......... MissVBarr(7) 18 55
(REBarr) *in tch stands side: drvn along over 2f out: styd on fnl f: nvr able to chal* **33/1**

2160 **4** *nk* **Redoubtable (USA)**[15] 3895 13-10-8 **53**.......... MissHCuthbert(5) 4 57
(DWChapman) *hld up far side: hdwy 1/2-way: disp gp ld over 1f out: kpt on ins last* **11/1**

0633 **5** *shd* **Ace-Ma-Vahra**[19] 3804 6-10-0 **40**..........(b) MissSBrotherton 2 44
(SRBowring) *trckd ldrs far side: disp gp ld fnl 2f: kpt on ins fnl f* **14/1**

0004 **6** 3½ **African Spur (IRE)**[7] 4154 4-10-2 **47**..........(v) MissDAllman(5) 17 41
(DCarroll) *cl up stands side: fdd appr fnl f* **10/1**

0000 **7** ½ **Grand View**[21] 3742 8-9-5 **36**..........(p) MissDawnRankin(5) 16 28
(JRWeymes) *towards rr stands side: hdwy 1/2-way: hung lft over 1f out: no further prog* **33/1**

0120 **8** *nk* **Torrent**[18] 3820 9-11-0 **54**..........(b) MissLynseyHanna 14 45
(DWChapman) *in tch stands side: effrt 2f out: no hdwy* **7/1**[2]

0016 **9** ½ **Sabana (IRE)**[14] 3935 6-10-7 **47**..........(p) MissEJJones 5 37
(JMBradley) *trckd ldrs far side: chal for gp ld 2f out: sn rdn and btn* **8/1**[3]

0050 **10** ¾ **Zamyatina (IRE)**[21] 3734 5-9-13 **39**.......... MissAElsey 7 26
(PLClinton) *in tch far side: kpt on same pce fnl 2f* **20/1**

0445 **11** *1* **Beyond Calculation (USA)**[10] 4014 10-10-11 **51**.....(b) MrsSBosley 12 35
(JMBradley) *chsd ldrs stands side: rdn over 1f out: sn btn* **10/1**

2000 **12** 1¼ **The Gambler**[40] 3148 4-10-5 **48**..........(p) MissLEllison(3) 8 29
(PaulJohnson) *in tch far side: chal for gp ld 2f out: sn rdn and btn* **25/1**

0055 **13** ¾ **Old Bailey (USA)**[17] 3836 4-10-0 **43**..........(p) MrsNWilson(3) 3 21
(TDBarron) *racd far side: n.d* **10/1**

-000 **14** 3½ **Blues Princess**[28] 3524 4-9-13 **44**..........(b) MissVTunnicliffe(5) 9 12
(RAFahey) *led far side most of way tl hdd 2f out: sn wknd* **20/1**

3300 **15** *6* **Bells Boy's**[1] 4309 5-9-11 **37**..........(p) MissCO'Neill 10 —
(KARyan) *in tch stands side: rdn 2f out: sn wknd* **16/1**

650- **16** *4* **Distant King**[358] 3953 11-10-1 **48** ow5.......... MissJCoward(7) 1 —
(GPKelly) *chsd ldrs far side tl wknd over 2f out* **33/1**

0006 **17** *hd* **Wilheheckaslike**[67] 2389 3-9-1 **39** oh4..........(b) MissWGibson(7) 15 —
(WStorey) *racd stands side: hmpd and slowly away: a wl bhd* **66/1**

0000 **18** *14* **Blade's Edge**[11] 4004 3-9-7 **45**..........(v[1]) DrHMcCarthy(7) 20 —
(ABailey) *s.v.s: a t.o* **25/1**

1m 12.56s (0.06) **Going Correction** -0.25s/f (Firm)
**WFA** 3 from 4yo+ 5lb **18** Ran SP% **125.1**
Speed ratings: **89,85,84,84,84 79,78,78,77,76 75,73,72,68,60 54,54,35**CSF £47.09 CT £1446.97 TOTE £7.60: £2.20, £2.40, £10.40, £2.00; EX 31.00.There was no bid for the winner.
**Owner** Mrs C L Swiers **Bred** Liam Queally **Trained** Sessay, N Yorks

**FOCUS**
A poor ladies' handicap in which the runners covered every inch of the track. In the end the first three were on the stands' side, but the form looks sound for the level.

**NOTEBOOK**
**Zietzig(IRE)**, with one of the better riders aboard, in the end scored in clear-cut fashion.
**Danakim**, on one of his better days, led them a merry dance on the stands' side but he had no answer when the winner swept by.
**Frimley's Matterry**, suited by this much quicker ground, was reaching a place for the second time in 18 starts.
**Redoubtable(USA)**, a winner of 20 races, was having his 160th start and is a great testament to his trainer's skill.
**Ace-Ma-Vahra**, drawn one from the far side, was given a fine ride and came out best of the few who stuck to that flank. This trip looks her bare minimum.
**African Spur(IRE)**, on a long losing run, travels strongly but finds little.

## 4351 SKIPTON CASTLE MAIDEN FILLIES' STKS 7f
4:20 (4:21) (D) 3-Y-0+ **£5,590** (£1,720; £860; £430) **Stalls** Low

Form RPR

-030 **1** **Moon Legend (USA)**[10] 4020 3-8-9 **66**.......... HayleyTurner(5) 8 68
(WJarvis) *hld up: hdwy 3f out: rdn into 3rd 2f out: hung lft over 1f out: r.o wl to ld ins fnl f: styd on* **4/1**[3]

**2** *nk* **Fascination Street (IRE)**[23] 3-9-0 **69**.......... MHenry 7 67
(MAJarvis) *prom: rdn into slt ld 2f out: hdd ins fnl f: styd on* **8/1**

0 **3** *5* **Eltihaab (USA)**[30] 3447 3-9-0 .......... JCarroll 2 54
(SaeedBinSuroor) *led after 1f: rdn and hdd 2f out: wknd fnl f* **5/4**[1]

3- **4** *5* **Magari**[304] 5296 3-9-0 .......... MFenton 5 40
(JGGiven) *cl up: ev ch and rdn over 2f out: sn outpcd by first 3* **6/1**

-600 **5** 1½ **Pay Time**[58] 2620 5-9-2 34.......... PMulrennan(5) 6 36
(REBarr) *hld up: effrt 3f out: sn rdn: no hdwy* **100/1**

**6** *3* **Fizzy Pop**[140] 5-9-4 .......... LEnstone(3) 10 28
(WSCunningham) *hld up in rr: lost tch 1/2-way: n.d* **50/1**

000 **7** *nk* **Estoille**[28] 3512 3-8-7 ..........(t) AndrewWebb(7) 4 27
(MrsSLamyman) *trckd ldrs: effrt 3f out: sn rdn and btn* **66/1**

0 **8** *11* **Miss Chancelot**[31] 3410 3-9-0 .......... RLappin 3 —
(SPGriffiths) *keen: led 1f: remained prom tl wknd 3f out: t.o* **66/1**

55-6 **L** **Elusive Kitty (USA)**[203] 490 3-9-0 69..........(t) IMongan 1 —
(GABulter) *ref to r: tk no part* **7/2**[2]

1m 27.33s (0.23) **Going Correction** -0.05s/f (Good)
**WFA** 3 from 5yo 7lb **9** Ran SP% **118.0**
Speed ratings: **96,95,89,84,82 79,78,66,—**CSF £35.81 TOTE £5.80: £1.30, £2.90, £1.10; EX 25.50.
**Owner** Eugene Lismonde **Bred** Reavill Farm **Trained** Newmarket, Suffolk

**FOCUS**
A very modest maiden with the first two seemingly fully exposed.

**NOTEBOOK**
**Moon Legend(USA)**, given a patient ride, took a fair bit of organising but did just enough in the end. A more galloping track will suit her better.
**Fascination Street(IRE)**, quite a tall filly, had shown limited ability in four starts in France. After working hard to put her head in front, she narrowly missed out in the end.
**Eltihaab(USA)**, a lengthy-type, is a lazy walker. She had her own way in front but folded tamely when challenged. She is starting to look a major disappointment.
**Magari**, well beaten third in one backend outing at two, moved upsides halfway up the home straight but she did not see it out.
**Pay Time**, having her 15th start, is rated just 34 and puts a cap on the overall value of the form.
**Elusive Kitty(USA)**, who is only small, dug her toes in when the gates opened and put her rider on the ground.

## 4352 RICHMOND CASTLE H'CAP 2m
4:55 (4:56) (E) (0-75,72) 4-Y-0+ **£4,114** (£1,266; £633; £316) **Stalls** Low

Form RPR

016 **1** **Best Port (IRE)**[37] 3236 8-8-12 **62**.......... MLawson(5) 9 71
(JParkes) *hld up: hdwy 3f out: chsng ldrs and rdn over 1f out: styd on to ld clsng stages: all out* **9/2**[2]

-206 **2** *hd* **Most Definitely (IRE)**[27] 3564 4-8-8 **60**.......... AMullen(7) 7 69
(TDEasterby) *hld up: nt clr run over 2f out: hdwy u.p over 1f out: disp ld wl ins last: no ex clsng stages* **10/1**

P110 **3** *hd* **Moonshine Beach**[8] 4075 6-9-1 **63**.......... LFletcher(3) 3 72
(PWHiatt) *cl up: led over 3f out: styd on u.p: hdd clsng stages* **7/1**

0014 **4** *2* **Sonoma (IRE)**[21] 3743 4-8-12 **62**.......... HayleyTurner(5) 4 68
(MLWBell) *chsd ldrs: rdn over 2f out: ch over 1f out: no ex ins last* **4/1**[1]

0300 **5** *4* **Greenwich Meantime**[18] 3821 4-9-13 **72**.......... LGoncalves 10 74
(MrsJRRamsden) *prom: ch and rdn 2f out: wknd appr fnl f* **16/1**

4033 **6** *8* **Blackthorn**[59] 2584 5-8-12 **57**.......... IMongan 8 49
(MrsJRRamsden) *s.i.s: hld up: drvn along 3f out: sn btn* **11/2**[3]

0060 **7** *8* **Freedom Now (IRE)**[41] 2935 6-9-9 **68**.......... MFenton 1 50
(MDHammond) *led tl hdd over 3f out: sn wknd* **20/1**

60-3 **8** *22* **Celtic Blaze (IRE)**[18] 3821 5-8-6 **56**..........(tp) PMulrennan(5) 2 12
(BSRothwell) *hld up: drvn along and wknd over 3f out: t.o* **10/1**

0-20 **9** *1* **Academy (IRE)**[54] 2731 9-8-12 **57**.......... JCarroll 6 12
(AndrewTurnell) *rr: lost tch 1/2-way: t.o* **11/1**

3144 **P** **Paddy Mul**[15] 3902 7-8-3 **48**..........(t) JBramhill 5 —
(WStorey) *in tch: effrt over 2f out: sn rdn and btn: eased appr fnl f: p.u lame ins last* **11/2**[3]

3m 26.96s (-4.24) **Going Correction** -0.05s/f (Good) **10** Ran SP% **118.6**
Speed ratings: **108,107,107,106,104 100,96,85,85,—**CSF £49.87 CT £315.19 TOTE £5.20: £2.30, £2.40, £3.00; EX 47.90 Place 6 £37.86, Place 5 £31.99.
**Owner** M Wormald **Bred** Lord Harrington **Trained** Upper Helmsley, N Yorks
■ Stewards Enquiry : L Fletcher one-day ban: used whip above shoulder height (Aug 11)

**FOCUS**
A 0-72 handicap run at a sound pace, making the form ordinary but sound enough.

**NOTEBOOK**
**Best Port(IRE)**, suited by the quick ground and sound pace, did just enough to record his ninth career success.
**Most Definitely(IRE)**, another suited by the quick ground, overcame traffic problems to throw down a strong challenge but at the line this maiden had to settle for second spot for the seventh time.
**Moonshine Beach** kicked for home off what had been a generous pace. He never flinched but in the end just missed out.
**Sonoma(IRE)**, in the firing line throughout, had no excuse.
**Greenwich Meantime** is slipping down the ratings but he hardly looks a winner waiting to happen.
**Blackthorn**, who is only small, may be better employed in claiming company over shorter.
**Paddy Mul** went lame and was dismounted. *Official explanation: jockey said horse finished lame*
T/Plt: £35.50 to a £1 stake. Pool: £34,697.05. 712.80 winning tickets. T/Qpdt: £18.00 to a £1 stake. Pool: £2,015.50. 82.50 winning tickets. JF

4353 - 4355a (Foreign Racing) - See Raceform Interactive

# 3790 DEAUVILLE (R-H)
Saturday, July 31

**OFFICIAL GOING: Turf course - good to soft; all-weather - standard**

## 4356a PRIX DE LA CALONNE (LISTED) (FILLIES) 1m
2:40 (2:40) 3-Y-0 **£15,845** (£6,338; £4,754; £3,169)

RPR

**1** **Petit Calva (FR)**[55] 2720 3-9-2 .......... TJarnet 5 105
(RGibson, France)

**2** *hd* **Polyfirst (FR)**[51] 2830 3-8-12 .......... OPeslier 10 101
(MmeCHead-Maarek, France)

**3** *hd* **Secret Melody (FR)**[75] 2193 3-8-12 .......... C-PLemaire 4 101
(H-APantall, France)

**4** 1½ **Life (FR)**[23] 3-8-12 .......... SPasquier 7 98
(MmeCHead-Maarek, France)

**5** *shd* **Sogna Di Me**[27] 3569 3-8-12 .......... MDemuro 6 97
(BGrizzetti, Italy)

**6** *shd* **Super Bobbina (IRE)**[55] 2720 3-9-2 .......... ACorniani 9 101
(IBugattella, Italy)

**7** *shd* **Tulipe Royale (FR)**[76] 2160 3-8-12 .......... ELegrix 8 97
(J-MBeguigne, France)

**8** ½ **Tolzey (USA)**[23] 3688 3-8-12 ..........(b) YTake 13 96
(H-APantall, France)

**9** *snk* **Risque De Verglas (FR)**[34] 3-8-12 .......... IMendizabal 2 96
(MmeR-WAllen, France)

**10** ¾ **Bright Abundance (USA)**[37] 3258 3-8-12 .......... MBlancpain 3 94
(CLaffon-Parias, France)

11 **Aricia (IRE)**[43] [3033] 3-8-12 .......... CSoumillon 11 94
(JHMGosden) *held up in rear, 11th straight, ridden on outside over 2f out, unable to quicken*

12 **Bits Of Paradise (FR)**[23] [3688] 3-8-12 .......... GaryStevens 1 94
(AFabre, France)

1m 41.1s **Going Correction** +0.075s/f (Good) **12** Ran
Speed ratings: **113,112,112,111,111 110,110,110,110,109 109,109.**
**Owner** Mrs A G Kavanagh **Bred** Classic Breeding Sarl And Maurice Hassan **Trained** France

**NOTEBOOK**
**Aricia(IRE)**, held up in the early stages, she made a move forward on the outside at the entrance to the straight but she did not quicken in the latter stages and finished 12th. The first ten past the post were separated by under three lengths in a race without much pace.

## 4357a PRIX DU CERCLE (LISTED) 5f
**3:20** (3:19) 3-Y-O+ **£15,845** (£6,338; £4,754; £3,169)

RPR

1 **Ratio**[308] [5211] 6-9-0 .......... TGillet 6 114
(JEHammond, France) 2

2 *hd* **Miss Emma (IRE)**[21] [3769] 4-8-11 .......... OPeslier 11 110
(JEHammond, France)

3 *1* **Blanche (FR)**[21] [3769] 5-8-11 .......... DBonilla 7 106
(JRossi, France)

4 *1 ½* **Raffelberger (GER)**[28] [3552] 3-9-0 .......... ASuborics 1 108
(MarioHofer, Germany) *finished 5th, placed 4th* 1

5 *shd* **Dobby Road (FR)**[40] [3162] 5-9-0 .......... FSpanu 8 103
(MlleVDissaux, France) *finished 6th, placed 5th*

6 *hd* **Villadolide (FR)**[92] [1756] 3-8-6 .......... C-PLemaire 5 99
(MmeCHead-Maarek, France) *finished 4th, disqualified, placed 6th*

7 *nse* **Together (FR)**[40] [3162] 4-8-11 .......... DSicaud 4 100
(MmeCBoqueho-Vergne, France)

8 *½* **Swedish Shave (FR)**[21] [3769] 6-9-4 .......... TJarnet 2 105
(RGibson, France)

9 *1 ½* **Rue La Fayette (SWE)**[28] [3552] 4-8-11 .......... ODoleuze 3 93
(FReuterskiold, Sweden)

10 *shd* **Sister Moonshine (FR)**[40] [3162] 3-8-6 .......... SPasquier 13 91
(RPritchard-Gordon, France) 3

11 **Jefferson** 3-8-10 ..........(b) VVion 9 95
(BruceHellier, Germany)

12 **Banjo's Spirit (IRE)**[20] 3-8-10 .......... IMendizabal 10 95
(GBindella, Spain)

13 **Curfew**[12] [3976] 5-8-11 .......... TThulliez 12 92
(JRFanshawe) *always towards rear on outside*

57.00 secs
**WFA** 3 from 4yo+ 4lb **13** Ran SP% **21.5**
Speed ratings: ..
**Owner** Mrs John Davall **Bred** R F And S D Knipe **Trained** France

**NOTEBOOK**
**Curfew** was slowly into her stride and made no show. She is certainly better than this.

# [3729] CHESTER (L-H)
Sunday, August 1

**OFFICIAL GOING: Good to firm**

## 4358 WARWICK INTERNATIONAL NURSERY STKS (H'CAP) 6f 18y
**2:20** (2:21) (D) 2-Y-O **£4,841** (£1,489; £744; £372) **Stalls** High

Form RPR

201 1 **Golden Legacy (IRE)**[11] [4009] 2-9-7 **87** .......... PHanagan 10 94
(RAFahey) *s.i.s: hdwy after 2f: nt clr run 1/2-way: sn swtchd rt: led over 1f out: r.o wl* **8/1**

0222 2 *3 ½* **I'm Aimee**[10] [4046] 2-8-9 **78** .......... FPFerris(3) 7 75
(PDEvans) *chsd ldrs: sn pushed along: styd on to take 2nd ins fnl f: no imp on wnr* **8/1**

230 3 *1* **Mytton's Bell (IRE)**[15] [3925] 2-8-6 **72** .......... DAllan 9 66
(ABailey) *bhd: rdn and hdwy 2f out: styd on wl fnl f: nvr nrr* **16/1**

5313 4 *nk* **Missperon (IRE)**[22] [3753] 2-8-13 **79** .......... NCallan 3 72
(KARyan) *prom: nt clr run over 1f out: sn rdn and lost pl: kpt on one pce fnl f* **10/3**[1]

021 5 *1* **Madame Topflight**[12] [4003] 2-8-13 **82** .......... NMackay(3) 1 72
(MrsGSRees) *led: rdn and hdd over 1f out: wknd ins fnl f* **7/2**[2]

345 6 *½* **Elsie Wagg (USA)**[15] [3950] 2-8-7 **73** .......... KDarley 5 61
(MJWallace) *sn pushed along towards rr: effrt over 1f out: no imp* **10/1**

4011 7 *½* **Make Us Flush**[15] [3924] 2-8-9 **75** .......... FNorton 4 62
(ABerry) *sn outpcd: styng on whn nt clr run ins fnl f: sn eased and no ch* **7/1**[3]

4154 8 *2 ½* **Nova Tor (IRE)**[8] [4150] 2-9-2 **82** .......... IMongan 8 61
(NPLittmoden) *chsd ldrs: pushed along whn nt clr run over 2f out: wknd over 1f out: eased ins fnl f* **16/1**

1045 9 *8* **Tiviski (IRE)**[23] [3703] 2-8-13 **79** .......... MHills 2 34
(EJAlston) *prom: rdn 2f out: sn wknd: eased fnl f* **8/1**

1m 14.52s (-1.36) **Going Correction** -0.10s/f (Good) **9** Ran SP% **112.0**
Speed ratings: **105,100,99,98,97 96,95,92,81**CSF £67.22 CT £989.80 TOTE £10.40: £2.10, £1.70, £5.10; EX 81.20.
**Owner** P N Devlin **Bred** E Tynan **Trained** Musley Bank, N Yorks

**FOCUS**
A cracking winning time for the type of race and the form looks sound. The 'official ratings' are only an estimate and are for guidance only.

**NOTEBOOK**
**Golden Legacy(IRE)**, despite being drawn on the outside and forfeiting ground at the start, won as she pleased and made a mockery of her current mark, posting a cracking time in the process. She had shown plenty of ability in her three previous outings, so this performance off top weight confirmed that she is improving rapidly, and deserved of another chance back up at Listed level.
**I'm Aimee** runner-up on her three previous starts, again found one too good. She has trouble quickening at the end of her races, but always gives her all, and got this trip well. She is a reliable benchmark as to the form.
**Mytton's Bell(IRE)** ran much better on this return to quicker ground, and deserves extra credit from her wide draw. She should be capable of progressing further, when faced with a stiffer test.
**Missperon(IRE)** was tight for room over one out on the rail, but found less than looked likely off the bridle on turning for home when in the clear. She seemed to appreciate this extra furlong and did best of those that raced prominently.
**Madame Topflight** led at a decent gallop from her plum draw and was still in with every chance entering the straight, but fell in a hole thereafter and finished well held. On this evidence, she looks to have been allotted a fairly stiff mark.
**Elsie Wagg(USA)** looked to be feeling this fast ground and failed to improve for this nursery bow. She could prove better served by an easier surface, but looks too high in the weights nonetheless.
**Tiviski(IRE)** *Official explanation: trainer said filly was unsuited by the good to firm going*

## 4359 CHESHIRE COUNTY COUNCIL FOSTER CARE EBF MAIDEN STKS 7f 2y
**2:50** (2:51) (D) 2-Y-O **£4,841** (£1,489; £744; £372) **Stalls** Low

Form RPR

6 1 **Love And Laughter (IRE)**[15] [3925] 2-8-9 .......... DAllan 2 72
(TDEasterby) *trckd ldrs: pushed along 3f out: led ins fnl f: r.o* **2/1**[1]

0 2 *2* **Wizardmicktee (IRE)**[15] [3925] 2-9-0 .......... JFanning 4 72
(ABailey) *led: rdn over 1f out: hdd ins fnl f: no ex cl home* **14/1**

3 *1 ½* **Oxford Street Pete (IRE)** 2-9-0 .......... VSlattery 8 68+
(ABailey) *s.s: hld up: hdwy 4f out: nt clr run and rn green over 1f out: r.o ins fnl f: promising* **20/1**

6 4 *nk* **Watchmyeyes (IRE)**[10] [4040] 2-8-11 .......... J-PGuillambert(3) 12 68
(NPLittmoden) *prom: rdn and ev ch over 1f out: nt qckn ins fnl f* **4/1**[2]

0 5 *nk* **Swallow Falls (IRE)**[22] [3729] 2-8-6 .......... LEnstone(3) 3 62
(DMccain) *prom: rdn over 1f out: styd on same pce* **16/1**

4 6 *1 ¼* **Zantero**[65] [2453] 2-8-11 .......... THamilton(3) 11 64
(RPElliott) *midfield: rdn and hdwy over 1f out: rn green: one pce ins fnl f* **10/1**

7 *1 ¼* **Kristalchen** 2-8-9 .......... MFenton 10 56
(JGGiven) *s.s: pushed along thrght: bhd: kpt on fnl f: nvr trbld ldrs* **7/1**[3]

6000 8 *5* **Den Perry**[23] [3703] 2-8-9 .......... PPMathers(5) 5 48
(ABerry) *in tch: rdn over 2f out: wknd over 1f out* **33/1**

0000 9 *11* **Lord Chalfont (IRE)**[34] [3377] 2-9-0 ..........(p) DHolland 1 21
(MJPolglase) *a bhd* **16/1**

10 *3* **Laurollie** 2-8-2 .......... LucyRussell(7) 7 8
(DrJRJNaylor) *s.s: a bhd* **40/1**

11 *2* **Benny The Bus** 2-9-0 .......... ACulhane 9 8
(MrsGSRees) *sn pushed along: nvr on terms* **7/1**[3]

1m 28.48s (0.19) **Going Correction** -0.10s/f (Good) **11** Ran SP% **116.0**
Speed ratings: **94,91,90,89,89 87,86,80,68,64 62**CSF £31.73 TOTE £2.50: £1.30, £2.30, £3.70; EX 28.40.
**Owner** Gold Star Partners **Bred** Roundhill Stud And Nicholas Stringer **Trained** Great Habton, N Yorks

**FOCUS**
An ordinary maiden run at a fair pace and the field came home well strung out. The bare form is modest but can rate higher.

**NOTEBOOK**
**Love And Laughter(IRE)** showed the benefit of her debut experience and responded gamely to pressure, when again running green at halfway, to register a workmanlike first success. She did not look to be doing much in front late on, so could be value for more than the official winning margin, and looks the type to progress over further.
**Wizardmicktee(IRE)** broke much better this and showed good early toe to bag the lead. He enjoyed this quicker ground, but ran very much up to his debut form with the winner, and therefore did not obviously show much improvement. Although he just looks modest at this early stage, he will fare better when handicapped, and can find a race this year.
**Oxford Street Pete(IRE)** ◆ made a pleasing debut and shaped with definite promise. He travelled well in behind the leaders, would have been closer with a clear run in the straight, and will be a lot sharper next time.
**Watchmyeyes(IRE)** did well to lay up with the early pace from his wide stall, but that took its toll late on, and he had no more to offer when it mattered. This was a fair effort and he got the trip well enough.
**Swallow Falls(IRE)**, never dangerous over the minimum trip at this track on his debut last time, improved markedly on that form over this longer trip. He is entitled to improve again.
**Zantero**, who shaped with some promise when a modest fourth on his debut in May, again ran green through the early stages but was slowly getting the hang of things late on. He can do better when racing on a more galloping track and looks a likely nursery type.
**Kristalchen** was never going the pace on this debut, but kept on well enough under pressure when the race was effectively over. She will appreciate further in time and this experience will not have been lost on her.

## 4360 HALLIWELL JONES BMW - MILE H'CAP 7f 122y
**3:25** (3:27) (C) (0-90,88) 3-Y-O+ **£9,724** (£2,992; £1,496; £748) **Stalls** Low

Form RPR

0023 1 **Nashaab (USA)**[75] [2201] 7-9-11 **88** .......... FPFerris(3) 1 99
(PDEvans) *dwlt: rdn along and bhd: gd hdwy on outside 2f out: led 1f out: hdd wl ins fnl f: rallied to regain ld post* **5/1**[1]

0004 2 *shd* **Roman Maze**[2] [4305] 4-8-0 **60** .......... FNorton 8 71+
(WMBrisbourne) *hld up: nt clr run over 2f out: rdn and swtchd rt over 1f out: r.o to ld wl ins fnl f: hdd post* **10/1**[3]

0311 3 *nk* **True Night**[8] [4134] 7-9-9 **83** .......... DHolland 13 93
(DNicholls) *in tch: n.m.r and hmpd 2f out: edgd lft over 1f out: r.o and ev ch ins fnl f: hld fnl strides* **5/1**[1]

0004 4 *3 ½* **Iced Diamond (IRE)**[6] [4199] 5-7-5 **58** oh6..........(t) DFentiman(7) 12 59
(WMBrisbourne) *midfield: pushed along over 2f out: hdwy whn bmpd over 1f out: styd on same pce fnl f* **33/1**

0000 5 *1 ½* **No Grouse**[25] [3623] 4-8-8 **68** ..........(p) PHanagan 11 66
(RAFahey) *midfield: n.m.r and hmpd jst over 2f out: sn rdn: one pce fnl f* **25/1**

1124 6 *nk* **Waterside (IRE)**[31] [3439] 5-9-8 **82** .......... IMongan 10 79
(GLMoore) *prom: led over 3f out: rdn and hdd 1f out: no ex ins fnl f* **14/1**

1631 7 *3 ½* **Zanjeer**[13] [3982] 4-8-7 **70** .......... THamilton(3) 4 58
(NWilson) *trckd ldrs: n.m.r 2f out: sn lost pl: n.d after* **11/2**[2]

0035 8 *nk* **H Harrison (IRE)**[7] [4179] 4-9-7 **81** .......... RFfrench 14 68
(IWMcinnes) *in tch: rdn to chse ldrs over 2f out: wknd fnl f* **16/1**

5635 9 *1* **Foolish Groom**[10] [4050] 3-8-1 **68** ..........(tp) DaleGibson 2 53
(RHollinshead) *hld up: rdn over 2f out: nvr on terms* **14/1**

0212 10 *2* **Merdiff**[20] [3800] 5-7-8 **59** .......... BSwarbrick(5) 7 39
(WMBrisbourne) *prom: rdn 2f out: wknd over 1f out* **11/2**[2]

0203 11 *5* **Flying Express**[50] [2891] 4-9-11 **85** .......... MHills 5 52
(BWHills) *led: rdn and hdd over 3f out: wknd over 1f out* **11/2**[2]

5006 12 *12* **Sugar Cube Treat**[38] [3225] 8-7-12 **58** oh27.......... SRighton 9 —
(MMullineaux) *rdn along thrght: a bhd* **100/1**

1m 32.86s (-11.89) **Going Correction** -0.10s/f (Good)
**WFA** 3 from 4yo+ 7lb **12** Ran SP% **115.6**
Speed ratings: **105,104,104,101,99 99,95,95,94,92 87,75**CSF £52.87 CT £266.49 TOTE £6.50: £2.50, £3.90, £1.90; EX 67.20 Trifecta £1192.70 Part won. Pool of £1,679.90 - 0.90 winning units..
**Owner** M W Lawrence **Bred** Shadwell Farm Inc **Trained** Pandy, Gwent
■ Stewards Enquiry : D Holland caution: used whip down the shoulder in the forehand position

**FOCUS**
A decent handicap, and despite it being a rough race, the form looks sound. The pace was strong and it suited those to be held up.

**NOTEBOOK**

**Nashaab(USA)** ◆ blew his chance of capitalising on the plum draw with a tardy start and, despite looking to have it all to do at halfway, responded gamely to strong pressure and came there going easily approaching two out. He then idled when in front and had to vigorously ridden to hold off his challengers at the line. This was a remarkable performance in the circumstances, and his first success since landing this event in 2001, so he is clearly in excellent order at present.

**Roman Maze** ran by far his best race of the current campaign and recorded a personal best on turf. He has slipped in the weights this year, on account of his poor form, but can be placed to score off this sort of mark and clearly enjoyed the strong gallop.

**True Night** gave his all from an impossible-looking draw and deserves extra credit for this narrow defeat. He has again been expertly placed this summer and should continue to pay his way, but has yet to win off this sort of mark, and will need to improve again in order to score.

**Iced Diamond(IRE)**, racing in the first-time tongue tie and from 6lb out of the handicap, ran a blinder from his wide stall and would have been a touch closer but for meeting trouble in the straight. He was aided by his rider's claim, but still ran his best race of the season, and looks to be on a favourable mark.

**No Grouse** ran better than the bare form would indicate. He was stopped in his run approaching two out and could not recover to trouble the principals, but still turned in an improved effort from his tricky draw. However, he often saves his best for this circuit. *Official explanation: jockey said gelding had hung right-handed throughout*

**Waterside(IRE)** fared best of those to force the decent pace and again turned in a sound effort, but does look high in the weights now.

**Zanjeer** got shuffled back when in contention two from home and lost all chance as a result. He has gone up in the weights recently, due to his improved form, but is still relatively unexposed and is worthy of another chance. *Official explanation: jockey said gelding never got a run*

**Merdiff** paid for racing on the strong pace, but still dropped out tamely in the straight, and has it all to prove off this mark on turf now.

**Flying Express** dropped out in the straight having raced fiercely early on, in an attempt to capitalise on his decent draw. He does look high in the weights on the balance of his overall form, but dropping back to six furlongs could help him find improvement.

## 4361 SPORTINGOPTIONS.CO.UK (BETTING EXCHANGE) CURZON PARK RATED STKS (H'CAP) — 2m 2f 147y

**4:00** (4:00) (B) (0-105,85) 4-Y-0+ **£13,694** (£4,496; £2,248) **Stalls High**

Form — RPR

0001 **1** **High Action (USA)**[7] [4174] 4-9-4 **85** 3ex.............................(t) DHolland 2 — 95
(IanWilliams) *mde all: qcknd pce over 4f out: rdn over 1f out: styd on gamely* **5/4**[2]

0313 **2** *3/4* **Thewhirlingdervish (IRE)**[22] [3725] 6-9-2 **83**............................ KDarley 1 — 92
(TDEasterby) *trckd wnr: rdn and lost 2nd whn n.m.r 3f out: regained 2nd and ev ch ins fnl f: nt qckn cl home* **1/1**[1]

1-05 **3** *1* **Coup De Chance (IRE)**[75] [2210] 4-9-3 **84**................(b) DeanMcKeown 3 — 92
(PABlockley) *hld up in last pl: wnt 2nd 3f out: ev ch fr 2f out tl rdn: flashed tail and lost 2nd ins fnl f: sn btn* **7/1**[3]

4m 18.2s (12.82) **Going Correction** -0.10s/f (Good) **3** Ran SP% **106.9**

Speed ratings: **69,68,68**CSF £2.86 TOTE £2.20; EX 2.60.

**Owner** C N Barnes **Bred** Harold Harrison **Trained** Portway, Warwicks

**FOCUS**

A poor turn out for the prizemoney. The steady gallop produced a pedestrian winning time and the form is worth treating with caution.

**NOTEBOOK**

**High Action(USA)** dictated a stop-start pace throughout, and found plenty under pressure in the straight to see off his two rivals under his 3lb penalty. This did not conclusively prove he truly gets this far, but he is clearly in great heart at present, and could have more to offer still. He will most likely now head to the Ebor under a 7lb penalty, and it is very interesting that last year's winner of this race, Sun Bird, finished runner-up in that event, also under a 7lb penalty.

**Thewhirlingdervish(IRE)**, the one definite stayer in this line-up, would have been much better suited by making the running and ensuring a decent test of stamina. He has been a good servant to his stable and, granted a truly-run two miles next time, can go one better off this mark.

**Coup De Chance(IRE)** looked a real threat on turning for home, but needs to be asked for her challenge as late as possible, and probably went for home too soon this time. She was suited by the steady gallop over this much longer trip, and still has to prove she gets this far, but improved on recent efforts nonetheless.

## 4362 CHESHIRE LIFE QUEENSFERRY STKS (LISTED RACE) — 6f 18y

**4:35** (4:35) (A) 3-Y-0+ **£17,850** (£6,600; £3,300; £1,500) **Stalls High**

Form — RPR

1-40 **1** **Rum Shot**[71] [2294] 3-8-10 100................................................ DSweeney 2 — 100+
(HCandy) *trckd ldrs: qcknd to ld wl ins fnl f: r.o* **4/1**[2]

0220 **2** *1/2* **Talbot Avenue**[8] [4152] 6-9-0 92........................................... DHolland 1 — 98
(MMullineaux) *prom: led over 1f out: sn rdn: hdd wl ins fnl f: nt qckn* **5/2**[1]

0000 **3** *1 1/2* **Nights Cross (IRE)**[7] [4165] 3-8-10 105.............................. KDarley 3 — 94
(MRChannon) *trckd ldrs: pushed along over 2f out: styd on same pce fnl f* **5/2**[1]

1505 **4** *nk* **Goldeva**[23] [3715] 5-8-13 100.........................................(t) ACulhane 5 — 92
(RHollinshead) *hld up: rdn over 1f out: nt pce to chal* **5/1**[3]

0005 **5** *2* **Vita Spericolata (IRE)**[9] [4091] 7-8-9 81.............................. RFfrench 4 — 82
(JSWainwright) *led: pushed along over 2f out: rdn and hdd over 1f out: wknd ins fnl f* **5/1**[3]

1m 12.94s (-2.94) **Going Correction** -0.10s/f (Good)

**WFA** 3 from 5yo+ 4lb **5** Ran SP% **110.5**

Speed ratings: **115,114,112,111,109**CSF £14.32 TOTE £5.80: £2.10, £1.90; EX 18.80.

**Owner** H R Mould **Bred** Mossborough Stud Company Ltd **Trained** Wantage, Oxon

■ Stewards Enquiry : D Sweeney caution: used whip without giving colt time to respond

**FOCUS**

The form is below average for the class, but it was still a decent time for a Listed race.

**NOTEBOOK**

**Rum Shot**, given a break since disappointing on his latest outing, won going away and produced a career-best effort in the process. He had looked a bright prospect as a juvenile and this was much more like his true form, yet it was his first time racing around a bend and, as he is still very lightly-raced, should build on this and take higher order in this divison before the season is out.

**Talbot Avenue** improved, and ran very much up to the form of his second over course and distance on his penultimate outing, though he had no answer to the winner's challenge late on. He looks best over this trip now, but will most likely continue to find life tough off his current mark when returning to handicaps.

**Nights Cross(IRE)** had every chance on official figures but, although he was not disgraced in defeat, looks to be going the wrong way and is best watched for the time being.

**Goldeva** was a little disappointing, but looked to be feeling the ground, and is worthy of another chance when able to get her toe in.

**Vita Spericolata(IRE)** dropped out having set the decent gallop she prefers, and has not won since taking this event back in 2002. Although she has retained her pace this year, she does look to be regressing.

## 4363 ALDFORD GLASS & HOPE HOUSE H'CAP — 1m 4f 66y

**5:05** (5:05) (C) (0-90,80) 3-Y-0+ **£9,490** (£2,920; £1,460; £730) **Stalls Low**

Form — RPR

2123 **1** **Sualda (IRE)**[17] [3881] 5-9-0 **70**................................................ PHanagan 8 — 78
(RAFahey) *hld up: pushed along 3f out: hdwy over 1f out: led ins fnl f: drvn out* **5/1**[3]

0435 **2** *1/2* **Aleron (IRE)**[15] [3953] 6-9-1 **71**...............................................(p) DHolland 2 — 78
(JJQuinn) *in tch: hdwy over 2f out: led 1f out: edgd lft and hdd ins fnl f: nt qckn* **9/2**[2]

0641 **3** *1 1/2* **Lennel**[12] [4005] 6-8-12 **68**.......................................................(b) MFenton 5 — 73
(ABailey) *hld up: rdn over 2f out: r.o ins fnl f: nrst fin* **11/2**

4054 **4** *3/4* **Gallant Boy (IRE)**[6] [4192] 5-8-7 **66**..................................(vt) FPFerris(3) 1 — 70
(PDEvans) *hld up: pushed along over 3f out: hdwy over 1f out: kpt on u.p ins fnl f* **9/2**[2]

1154 **5** *1/2* **Ben Hur**[23] [3705] 5-9-5 **75**........................................................ SWKelly 7 — 78
(WMBrisbourne) *led: pushed along over 3f out: edgd rt over 1f out: sn hdd: no ex ins fnl f* **7/1**

4443 **6** *1/2* **Sporting Gesture**[8] [4155] 7-9-4 **77**................................ PMulrennan(3) 4 — 79
(MWEasterby) *chsd ldr: pushed along 4f out: lost 2nd over 1f out: no ex ins fnl f* **4/1**[1]

0000 **7** *5* **Financial Future**[16] [3909] 4-9-5 **75**........................................ JFanning 6 — 70
(MJohnston) *prom: rdn over 2f out: wknd over 1f out* **8/1**

0-00 **8** *10* **Nopekan (IRE)**[30] [3475] 4-9-5 **80**........................................ PMakin(5) 3 — 60
(MissKMarks) *hld up: lft bhd 3f out* **20/1**

2m 37.68s (-2.84) **Going Correction** -0.10s/f (Good) **8** Ran SP% **116.8**

Speed ratings: **105,104,103,103,102 102,99,92**CSF £28.37 CT £128.96 TOTE £6.50: £2.30, £2.30, £2.20; EX 33.00 Place 6 £273.25, Place 5 £50.06.

**Owner** J H Tattersall **Bred** St Simon Foundation **Trained** Musley Bank, N Yorks

**FOCUS**

A fair handicap, the pace was solid, and the form looks sound for the grade.

**NOTEBOOK**

**Sualda(IRE)** prospered from the generous gallop and responded gamely to pressure to register a gritty success. Since his reappearance in June he has hit the frame in all of his outings, and this rates his best form, but life will be tougher off a higher mark in the future, and connections will be keen to turn him out under a penalty.

**Aleron(IRE)** ran a game race and enjoyed this strong gallop, but could find no more when challenged by the eventual winner. He was clear in second and does hold his form well enough, but on this evidence, looks to be in the Handicapper's grip.

**Lennel**, raised 4lb for a comfortable win at Ayr last time, ran his race and got the trip well. He has found his form and can find a race over this distance. *Official explanation: jockey said gelding slipped on the bend*

**Gallant Boy(IRE)** stayed on well in the straight, having been set a fair bit to do, and did enough to suggest he can be placed to advantage off this mark. However, he has a poor win record.

**Ben Hur** was given a suprisingly positive ride over this longer trip, and will be seen to a better effect when ridden with more patience. However, he does look too high in the weights now.

**Sporting Gesture** dropped out quickly in the straight, having raced up with the strong pace from the start. He can do better when ridden with more restraint, but hardly appeals as well-handicapped at present.

T/Plt: £142.70 to a £1 stake. Pool: £58,484.40. 299.05 winning tickets. T/Qpdt: £32.50 to a £1 stake. Pool: £3,482.60. 79.15 winning tickets. DO

# 3936 NEWBURY (L-H)

### Sunday, August 1

**OFFICIAL GOING: Good to firm**

## 4364 ROCK CAPITAL GROUP EBF MAIDEN FILLIES' STKS — 6f 8y

**2:00** (2:07) (D) 2-Y-0 **£6,188** (£1,904; £952; £476) **Stalls High**

Form — RPR

35 **1** **Swan Nebula (USA)**[16] [3905] 2-8-9 ........................................(t) LDettori 11 — 80
(SaeedBinSuroor) *disp ld: rdn to chal fr over 1f out: led last hlf f: drvn out* **3/1**[2]

0 **2** *1* **County Clare**[64] [2481] 2-8-9 ............................................... RMullen 2 — 77
(AMBalding) *pressed ldr: chal 3f out: rdn and outpcd 2f out: styd on u.p fnl f to take 2nd last strides* **12/1**

0 **3** *shd* **Encouragement**[60] [2585] 2-8-9 ........................................... RLMoore 1 — 77
(RHannon) *slt advantage: rdn 2f out: hdd and one pce last half f* **20/1**

**4** *1 3/4* **Nazaaha (USA)** 2-8-9 ........................................................ RHills 8 — 71
(JLDunlop) *tall: well grown: s.i.s: bhd: pushed along and hdwy fr 2f out: kpt on fnl f but nt rch ldrs* **11/1**

23 **5** *1* **Dance Flower (IRE)**[9] [4074] 2-8-9 ........................................ CCatlin 12 — 68
(MRChannon) *lw: in tch: rdn to chse ldrs 1/2-way: styd on u.p fnl f but nvr gng pce to chal* **9/4**[1]

**6** *nk* **Piper's Ash (USA)** 2-8-9 ................................................... SDrowne 7 — 68+
(RCharlton) *w'like: s.i.s: sn rcvrd and in tch: pushed along and hdwy to chse ldrs ins fnl 2f: no ex ins last* **4/1**[3]

0 **7** *3 1/2* **Miss Patricia**[21] [3770] 2-8-9 ................................................ EAhern 15 — 57
(JGPortman) *s.i.s: sn rcvrd: drvn to chse ldrs 1/2-way: outpcd appr fnl f* **25/1**

0 **8** *1* **Ifit (IRE)**[11] [4016] 2-8-9 ........................................................ JPMurtagh 10 — 54
(MRChannon) *bhd: rdn over 2f out: styd on fnl f but nvr gng pce to rch ldrs* **33/1**

**9** *nk* **Manorshield Minx** 2-8-9 ........................................................ JFortune 9 — 53
(SKirk) *w'like: bkwd: bhd: pushed along 1/2-way: styd on fr over 1f out: nt a danger* **25/1**

0 **10** *1 1/2* **The Keep**[25] [3633] 2-8-9 ......................................................... PDobbs 4 — 49
(RHannon) *chsd ldrs: rdn 3f out: wknd ins fnl 2f* **14/1**

00 **11** *3/4* **Sukuma (IRE)**[46] [2985] 2-8-4 ................................................. NChalmers(5) 6 — 46
(AMBalding) *unruly bef s: plld hrd and chse ldrs over 3f* **66/1**

**12** *5* **Doitforreel (IRE)** 2-8-9 ........................................................... TPQueally 3 — 31
(IAWood) *compact: chsd ldrs tl wknd over 2f out* **100/1**

0 **13** *3* **Mina Alsalaam**[22] [3741] 2-8-9 ................................................ SWhitworth 13 — 22
(MRChannon) *sn in tch: wknd over 2f out* **66/1**

6 **14** *3/4* **Tamora**[23] [3693] 2-8-9 ............................................................... PDoe 16 — 20
(APJarvis) *a in rr* **11/1**

1m 13.04s (-1.33) **Going Correction** -0.275s/f (Firm) **14** Ran SP% **126.2**

Speed ratings: **97,95,95,93,91 91,86,85,85,83 82,75,71,70**CSF £38.73 TOTE £3.90: £1.60, £3.50, £5.10; EX 58.90.

**Owner** Godolphin **Bred** Darley **Trained** Newmarket, Suffolk

**FOCUS**

This was an ordinary maiden by the course standards, won by one of the Godolphin lesser lights, and the form is difficult to assess at this stage.

**NOTEBOOK**

**Swan Nebula(USA)** had shown promise in two starts without suggesting she is one of her powerful stable's better prospects and was dropping back a furlong in trip having weakened tamely over seven furlongs most recently; she wears a tongue tie and seemingly has breathing difficulties. Ridden handily throughout, she stayed on well enough once getting to the front and was always holding the placed horses. She should not be given too stiff a mark and nurseries are her best chance of future success.

**County Clare** made her debut in a Lingfield maiden that is churning out winners and she herself nearly added to the list. Green and inexperienced on her debut, she knew more this time and stayed on well to get up for second having been outpaced when the tempo quickened. She should win her maiden and will improve for seven furlongs.

**Encouragement** was reported to have lost her action when disappointing on her debut in a race won by the useful Gloved Hand, and this presumably was much more like what was expected. No great shakes, she is entitled to improve for this and can land an average heat.

**Nazaaha(USA)**is sired by is trainers former top-class sprinter Elnadim, but there is stamina on the dam's side and she shaped as though an extra furlong would not go amiss. This was a promising debut as, having been slow to get going, she stayed on nicely without being given a hard time and was closing gradually at the line. She is the one to take from the race and a maiden success should not be hard to come about.

**Dance Flower(IRE)** had shown useful form in two starts prior to this, but was disappointing and is beginning to have an exposed look to her. She is now qualified for nurseries however and may be capable of better in that sphere.

**Piper's Ash(USA)** comes from a stable who can have first-time-up winners, but this one shaped as though the run would do her good. Bred to stay a mile, she should improve for the experience and much better can be expected next time.

**Miss Patricia** showed improved form from her debut and should improve again when moving into nurseries.

**Ifit(IRE)** was well held over seven on her debut and shaped better here. The step back up in trip helped and she is another likely to be seen at her best in nurseries.

**Manorshield Minx** shaped with promise and is entitled to improve for the outing.

**Tamora** shaped with plenty of promise on her debut, but failed to run a race and was never striding out in rear having been a bit slow to get going. She is better than this and is one to watch out for in nurseries.

## 4365 RSA SECURITY & BACYP NURSERY 7f (S)

**2:30** (2:36) (D) 2-Y-O **£5,824** (£1,792; £896; £448) **Stalls** High

| Form | | | | RPR |
|---|---|---|---|---|
| 004 | **1** | | **King Of Blues (IRE)**[11] 4023 2-8-8 **73**....(t) EAhern 4<br>(MAMagnusson) *lw: trckd ldrs: rdn to ld 1f out: styd on wl u.p ins last* **10/1** | 74 |
| 464 | **2** | *½* | **Musico (IRE)**[27] 3588 2-8-9 **74**.... GBaker 2<br>(BRMillman) *in tch: hdwy 3f out: pressed wnr over 1f out: kpt on wl fnl f but nt pce of wnr cl home* **8/1** | 74 |
| 0533 | **3** | *nk* | **Caly Dancer (IRE)**[54] 2761 2-8-13 **78**.... SSanders 12<br>(DRCElsworth) *lw: s.i.s: t.k.h and sn rcvrd to ld over 5f out: rdn and hdd 1f out: rallied ins last but no ex fnl 150yds* **6/1**[2] | 77 |
| 4100 | **4** | *1½* | **Alta Petens**[15] 3938 2-9-1 **80**.... JMackay 8<br>(MLWBell) *t.k.h early: trckd ldrs 1/2-way: n.m.r on stands rails over 1f out: kpt on ins last but nt pce to trble ldrs* **6/1**[2] | 75 |
| 530 | **5** | *1* | **Fortnum**[55] 2736 2-8-2 **67**.... RLMoore 10<br>(RHannon) *pressed ldrs: rdn and ev ch over 1f out: wknd ins last* **18/1** | 60 |
| 040 | **6** | *nk* | **He's A Star**[41] 3157 2-7-13 **64**.... RSmith 3<br>(RHannon) *bhd: hdwy over 2f out: sn rdn: kpt on same pce ins fnl f* **10/1** | 56 |
| 5325 | **7** | *2½* | **Simplify**[17] 3886 2-9-0 **79**....(b) TPQueally 5<br>(DRLoder) *chsd ldrs: hrd rdn over 2f out: one pce u.p appr fnl f* **10/1** | 65 |
| 513 | **8** | *2* | **He's A Diamond**[13] 3987 2-9-0 **79**.... JFortune 9<br>(TGMills) *led tl hdd over 5f out: styd pressing ldr tl wknd 2f out* **9/2**[1] | 60 |
| 563 | **9** | *5* | **Shujune Al Hawaa (IRE)**[13] 3974 2-8-7 **72**.... CCatlin 11<br>(MRChannon) *in tch: rdn 4f out: sn btn* **12/1** | 40 |
| 350 | **10** | *2½* | **Trackattack**[10] 4040 2-8-12 **77**.... LDettori 7<br>(JAOsborne) *s.i.s: a outpcd in rr* **7/1**[3] | 39 |
| 013 | **11** | *12* | **Three Pennies**[29] 3505 2-8-11 **76**.... SDrowne 1<br>(MDods) *b.hind: t.k.h in rr: effrt 3f out: sn wknd* **16/1** | 8 |

1m 25.35s (-1.87) **Going Correction** -0.275s/f (Firm) **11** Ran SP% **116.5**

Speed ratings: **99,98,98,96,95 94,92,89,84,81 67**CSF £86.79 CT £536.66 TOTE £13.40: £3.50, £2.70, £2.60; EX 223.80.

**Owner** East Wind Racing Ltd **Bred** Robert Wilson **Trained** Upper Lambourn, Berks

**FOCUS**

Quite a decent nursery with the third providing the level of the form, and one that should produce future winners. The 'official ratings' are only an estimate and are for guidance only.

**NOTEBOOK**

**King Of Blues(IRE)** stepped up on previous efforts to make a winning nursery debut. Reportedly a relaxed individual, he had shown promise on his three previous starts and is clearly improving with racing.

**Musico(IRE)** came into this on a very fair mark given he had run behind some useful sorts, but the winner is clearly the more progressive. He has a similar race in him.

**Caly Dancer(IRE)** unsurprisingly improved for this step up in trip - his dam won over a mile four - and should progress again for a mile. His form over shorter is ordinary, but he has a race in him at this sort of distance.

**Alta Petens** has disappointed in stiff company over shorter the last twice and seemed well suited to this step up in trip and drop in grade. She is high enough in the weights for what she has actually achieved.

**Fortnum** showed a slight improvement in form for this nursery debut and can land a small race.

**He's A Star** has a similar profile to stable companion Fortnum and can also land a small race.

**He's A Diamond** ran disappointingly without any apparent excuse. He is better than this and may appreciate softer going.

**Three Pennies** *Official explanation: jockey said filly suffered an injury in running*

## 4366 STONES THE PRINTERS H'CAP 5f 34y

**3:05** (3:06) (C) (0-95,91) 3-Y-O+ **£9,841** (£3,028; £1,514; £757) **Stalls** High

| Form | | | | RPR |
|---|---|---|---|---|
| 0045 | **1** | | **Salviati (USA)**[4] 4232 7-9-0 **77**....(p) RLMoore 7<br>(JMBradley) *lw: s.i.s: in tch: rdn: swtchd lft and hdwy over 1f out: str run to ld last half f: drvn out* **9/2**[1] | 90 |
| 0203 | **2** | *1* | **Cape Royal**[15] 3945 4-9-11 **88**.... JPMurtagh 15<br>(MrsJRRamsden) *swtg: awkward stalls and s.i.s: gd hdwy on rails fr 2f out: drvn to ld 1f out: hdd and nt qckn last half f* **6/1**[3] | 97 |
| 0140 | **3** | *¾* | **Whistler**[7] 4165 7-10-0 **91**....(p) RHills 10<br>(JMBradley) *hld up on rails but in tch: hdwy over 1f out but n.m.r: styd on wl last half f: nt rch ldrs* **20/1** | 97 |
| 0060 | **4** | *nk* | **Malapropism**[7] 4165 4-8-12 **82**.... BO'Neill[(7)] 3<br>(MRChannon) *bhd: hdwy fr 2f out: chsd ldrs 1f out: kpt on ins last: one pce nr fin* **25/1** | 87 |
| 6003 | **5** | *nk* | **Kathology (IRE)**[11] 4034 7-9-2 **79**.... TQuinn 8<br>(DRCElsworth) *w ldrs: chal fr 3f out tl 1f out: outpcd ins last* **12/1** | 83 |
| 0060 | **6** | *½* | **Nivernais**[16] 3910 5-8-8 **71**.... DaneO'Neill 11<br>(HCandy) *drvn fr stalls to press ldrs: led ins fnl 2f: hdd 1f out: one pce u.p ins last* **12/1** | 73 |
| 00-3 | **7** | *shd* | **The Lord**[9] 4076 4-9-0 **84**.... CHaddon[(7)] 2<br>(WGMTurner) *chsd ldrs: ev chnace appr fnl f: one pce ins last* **16/1** | 86 |
| 0414 | **8** | *shd* | **Connect**[7] 4165 7-9-10 **87**....(b) PDoe 4<br>(MHTompkins) *lw: b.hind: s.i.s: bhd: rdn and effrt 2f out: styng on whn n.m.r 1f out: kpt on same pce* **11/2**[2] | 89 |
| 0145 | **9** | *shd* | **Dancing Mystery**[22] 3723 10-9-5 **82**.... SCarson 13<br>(EAWheeler) *trckd ldrs: rdn over 1f out: styd on same pce* **16/1** | 83 |
| 2300 | **10** | *½* | **Further Outlook (USA)**[15] 3945 10-9-7 **84**.... JFortune 1<br>(DKIvory) *racd alone in centre crse and up w pce: rdn and stl ev ch whn c to join main gp over 1f out: wknd ins last* **33/1** | 83 |
| -000 | **11** | *2* | **Sir Edwin Landseer (USA)**[4] 4232 4-8-7 **75**.... RThomas[(5)] 9<br>(ChristianWroe, UAE) *rrd stalls: bhd: hdwy whn hmpd over 1f out: nt rcvr* **20/1** | 67 |
| 0004 | **12** | *nk* | **Danehill Stroller (IRE)**[15] 3941 4-9-6 **83**....(p) SSanders 5<br>(RMBeckett) *chsd ldrs tl wknd qckly over 1f out* **7/1** | 74 |
| 0500 | **13** | *2* | **Little Edward**[7] 4165 6-9-10 **90**.... LPKeniry[(3)] 14<br>(BGPowell) *sn slt ld on stands rails: hdd ins fnl 2f: sn btn* **25/1** | 74 |
| 4202 | **14** | *7* | **Domirati**[11] 4034 4-9-5 **82**.... SDrowne 6<br>(RCharlton) *chsd ldrs: rdn and one pce whn hmpd over 1f out: eased whn no ch* **13/2** | 41 |

60.15 secs (-2.50) **Going Correction** -0.275s/f (Firm) **14** Ran SP% **121.0**

Speed ratings: **109,107,106,105,105 104,104,104,103,103 99,99,96,85**CSF £28.21 CT £515.33 TOTE £5.60: £2.70, £2.80, £3.80; EX 49.60.

**Owner** J M Bradley **Bred** Cyril Humphris **Trained** Sedbury, Gloucs

■ Stewards Enquiry : R L Moore caution: careless riding

**FOCUS**

A competitive sprint handicap as one would expect, and the form is solid for the grade.

**NOTEBOOK**

**Salviati(USA)** can often lose his race at the start - as seen when beaten at Goodwood last week - but he was away on terms with them and came with a strong run to win comfortably. Clearly in good form, he should continue to pay his way.

**Cape Royal** got himself a little warm beforehand but it seemingly did not affect his performance. He came through with what momentarily looked a winning run but was claimed by Salviati in the final half furlong.

**Whistler** stayed on well from the rear but was never going to get there. He is 7lb higher than when last successful, and probably needs to drop a few pounds before winning again.

**Malapropism** ◆ is coming back to form and ran his best race for a while. He is one to keep an eye on in the coming weeks.

**Kathology(IRE)** is on a winning mark but always seems to find at least one too good.

**Nivernais** has been disappointing this season and was never going at any point.

**The Lord** was a very useful juvenile and looks to be coming back to something like his best.

**Connect** was a little unlucky not to finish closer having met with interference.

**Domirati** *Official explanation: trainer said gelding was wrong behind*

## 4367 EUROPEAN BREEDERS FUND CHALICE STKS (LISTED RACE) (F&M) 1m 4f 5y

**3:40** (3:40) (A) 3-Y-O+ **£17,400** (£6,600; £3,300; £1,500) **Stalls** High

| Form | | | | RPR |
|---|---|---|---|---|
| 2222 | **1** | | **Sahool**[29] 3519 3-8-4 107.... RHills 2<br>(MPTregoning) *trckd ldrs: wnt 2nd 3f out: rdn to take slt ld over 1f out: idled u.p ins last: asserted cl home* **4/6**[1] | 101 |
| 1163 | **2** | *nk* | **Polar Jem**[7] 4173 4-9-1 92.... AMcCarthy 1<br>(GGMargarson) *led: rdn and narrowly hdd appr fnl f: rallied u.p to chal ins last: no ex nr fin* **12/1** | 101 |
| 1122 | **3** | *1¾* | **Selebela**[15] 3944 3-8-4 95.... TPQueally 5<br>(LMCumani) *chsd ldrs: rdn and outpcd 3f out: styd on u.p fr 2f out: r.o wl fnl f but nt rch ldrs* **5/1**[2] | 98+ |
| 231 | **4** | *3* | **Light Of Morn**[11] 4028 3-8-5 ow1.... SSanders 4<br>(RGuest) *hld up in rr: hdwy 3f out: styd on to chse ldrs over 2f out: no imp and wknd over 1f* **14/1** | 94 |
| 511 | **5** | *3* | **Light Wind**[27] 3590 3-8-4 86.... RLMoore 6<br>(MrsAJPerrett) *s.i.s: hdwy on outside 4f out: rdn and effrt 3f out: nvr gng pce to trble ldrs: wknd fr 2f out* **11/1** | 89 |
| -451 | **6** | *2* | **Mocca (IRE)**[51] 2848 3-8-4 87.... EAhern 10<br>(DJCoakley) *hld up in rr: pushed along over 3f out: a bhd* **25/1** | 85 |
| 1034 | **7** | *3½* | **Tidal**[17] 3872 5-9-1 84.... JFortune 3<br>(AWCarroll) *chsd ldr to 3f out: wknd qckly over 2f out* **40/1** | 80 |
| 2-1 | **8** | *6* | **Well Known**[80] 2060 3-8-4 92.... SDrowne 8<br>(RCharlton) *plld hrd: hld up in rr: rdn 3f out: sn btn* **10/1**[3] | 70 |
| -405 | **9** | *9* | **Doctrine**[23] 3699 3-8-4 93.... RHavlin 9<br>(JHMGosden) *t.k.h: chsd ldrs tl wknd fr 3f out* **33/1** | 56 |

2m 30.29s (-6.00) **Going Correction** -0.275s/f (Firm)

**WFA** 3 from 4yo+ 11lb **9** Ran SP% **117.7**

Speed ratings: **109,108,107,105,103 102,99,95,89**CSF £10.41 TOTE £1.60: £1.10, £2.40, £1.80; EX 12.00.

**Owner** Hamdan Al Maktoum **Bred** John Davis **Trained** Lambourn, Berks

**FOCUS**

Not a strong Listed event but a deserved win for Sahool, who has been knocking on the door in Group races, and did not need to run to her best to score.

**NOTEBOOK**

**Sahool** has been running her heart out in defeat in Group contests and deserved a win. This drop in grade presented her with an ideal opportunity but she still made hard enough work of it, only really getting on top in the final half furlong.

**Polar Jem** has had a profitable season, winning four times, and this was a career-best effort. She has been running well off a now too high a mark in handicaps, and this grade represents her best chance of future success - there are enough weak backend Listed races for her to run in.

**Selebela** was struggling when the pace quickened, but stayed on well through tiring horses to claim third. She remains in good form and is probably worth trying in the Park Hill Stakes at Doncaster, where the extra couple of furlongs will suit.

**Light Of Morn** travelled sweetly throughout on this rise in grade but found nothing off the bridle and was ultimately disappointing. She undoubtedly has ability, and can do better in time.

**Light Wind** could have done with the ground being a little easier and never really let herself down. She has been highly progressive prior to this and is another likely type for the Park Hill Stakes next month.

**Well Known** never really settled and was beaten a long way. A drop in trip should see her in a better light.

## 4368 JOHN NIKE LEISURESPORT FILLIES' H'CAP 1m 2f 6y

**4:15** (4:15) (D) (0-85,85) 3-Y-O **£7,247** (£2,230; £1,115; £557) **Stalls** High

| Form | | | | RPR |
|---|---|---|---|---|
| -010 | **1** | | **Portmanteau**[32] 3415 3-9-7 **85**.... JPMurtagh 4<br>(SirMichaelStoute) *lw: t.k.h: trckd ldrs: drvn to ld appr fnl 2f: rdn clr 1f out: readily* **8/1** | 93 |

3143 **2** 1 3/4 **Foxilla (IRE)**[9] 4079 3-7-7 **62** oh4 ................................. HayleyTurner(5) 1 66
(DRCElsworth) *in tch: rdn 3f out and outpcd: swtchd rt to outside 2f out: str run appr fnl f: fin wl: nt rch wnr* **8/1**

-021 **3** 1 **Du Pre**[13] 3993 3-8-10 **74** ................................. SDrowne 2 76
(MrsAJPerrett) *swtg: chsd ldrs: hrd drvn fr 3f out: styd on fr over 1f out but nvr gng pce to trble wnr* **9/2**[2]

21 **4** hd **Apsara**[26] 3607 3-9-2 **80** ................................. (v) WRyan 11 82+
(HRACecil) *rel to r:lost 14l s:in tch main gp 7f out:hung lft on rails 3f out:swtchd outside 2f out:str run ins last:fin wl* **3/1**[1]

-040 **5** 1 **Lady Blade (IRE)**[16] 3919 3-7-5 **62** oh5 ................................. CHaddon(7) 7 62
(BHanbury) *t.k.h in rr: hdwy 3f out: chsd ldrs fr 2f out: rdn over 1f out: one pce fnl f* **40/1**

5233 **6** 1 1/4 **Tree Tops**[16] 3908 3-8-8 **72** ................................. JFortune 10 70
(JHMGosden) *trckd ldr: led 4f out: rdn and hdd over 2f out: wknd appr fnl f* **11/2**[3]

0240 **7** 5 **Powerful Parrish (USA)**[16] 3908 3-8-10 **74** ................................. (t) TQuinn 9 62
(PFICole) *lw: bhd: hdwy 3f out: wkng whn n.m.r 2f out* **20/1**

-000 **8** 1 **Persian Genie (IRE)**[18] 3843 3-7-10 **65** ow2 ................................. RThomas(5) 8 51
(GBBalding) *lw: a in rr* **16/1**

00 **9** 1 1/4 **Live Wire Lucy (USA)**[17] 3867 3-9-7 **85** ................................. RMullen 5 69
(CTinkler) *led tl hdd 4f out: wknd qckly ins fnl 3f* **50/1**

4042 **10** 12 **Saffron Fox**[22] 3728 3-9-1 **79** ................................. RLMoore 6 40
(JGPortman) *rdn 4f out: a in rr* **9/2**[2]

2m 6.58s (-2.13) **Going Correction** -0.275s/f (Firm) **10** Ran SP% **114.0**
Speed ratings: **97,95,94,94,93 92,88,88,87,77**CSF £67.32 CT £323.33 TOTE £8.30: £3.10, £2.60, £1.70; EX 76.30.
**Owner** Maktoum Al Maktoum **Bred** Newgate Stud Co **Trained** Newmarket, Suffolk
■ Stewards Enquiry : Hayley Turner one-day ban: careless riding (Aug 12)

**FOCUS**
Only an average fillies' handicap where the story of the race was the unlucky run of Apsara, who lost 14 lengths at the start and was only beaten just under three. The form does not look that strong.

**NOTEBOOK**
**Portmanteau** disappointed last time having previously lost her maiden tag at Pontefract, but she bounced right back to form with a cosy win. Always well placed, she came through to lead around two out and was never going to be caught. Clearly not the most consistent, she is not neccessarily one to bank on for a follow up. *Official explanation: trainer's representative had no explanation for the improved form shown other than that filly had benefited from the good to firm ground*
**Foxilla(IRE)** ran well off a 4lb higher mark than when third at Ascot the other week and is evidently still progressing. She chased the winner the best she could, but was never getting to her.
**Du Pre** got a little warm beforehand which would not have done her chances any good, but she still ran well off her 5lb higher mark.
**Apsara** blew the race at the start, losing around 14 lengths having looked far from keen to get on with the job. She did mightily well to get involved and was only just run out of a place. She looked awkward under pressure and because of how unlucky she looked is likely to be underpriced next time, so it may be worth taking her on.
**Lady Blade(IRE)** remains an exposed maiden, although this was a slightly improved effort.
**Tree Tops** failed to run up to the level that saw her finish third here earlier in the month.
**Saffron Fox** ran no sort of race and would have found this ground way to fast for her. *Official explanation: jockey said filly was unsuited by the ground*

## 4369 SFI MAIDEN STKS 1m 1f
**4:45** (4:46) (D ) 3-Y-O **£6,006** (£1,848; £924; £462) **Stalls** High

Form RPR

**1** **Tahtheeb (IRE)** 3-8-9 ................................. RHills 2 71
(MPTregoning) *str: scope: bit bkwd: s.i.s: bhd: rdn and green 3f out: hung lft and plld to outside 2f out: continued to hang but str run* **9/2**[2]

00 **2** 1 1/4 **Ogilvy (USA)**[26] 3603 3-9-0 ................................. JFortune 13 74
(JHMGosden) *chsd ldr: chal over 4f out: rdn to ld over 1f out: hdd and one pce fnl 100yds* **8/1**

3 **3** 1 3/4 **Red Sail**[57] 2693 3-8-9 ................................. JPMurtagh 1 65+
(JRFanshawe) *b.hind: slowly away and lost 5l s: rdn 3f out: hdwy fr 2f out: styd on wl fnl f but nt rch ldrs* **15/8**[1]

6 **4** hd **Coppice (IRE)**[111] 1371 3-9-0 ................................. TPQueally 8 70
(LMCumani) *chsd ldrs: rdn 3f out: disp 2nd over 1f out: styd on same pce fnl f* **14/1**

02 **5** nk **Topkat (IRE)**[10] 4057 3-8-11 ................................. LPKeniry(3) 6 69
(DRCElsworth) *in tch: outpcd 3f out: pushed along 2f out: kpt on wl fnl f: gng on cl home* **7/1**[3]

00 **6** 1 3/4 **Gay Romance**[27] 3592 3-8-9 ................................. WRyan 3 61
(BWHills) *led tl hdd over 4f out: styd pressing ldrs to 2f out:wknd appr fnl f* **40/1**

0 **7** 1 1/4 **Charmed By Fire (USA)**[18] 3843 3-9-0 ................................. RLMoore 12 63
(MrsAJPerrett) *chsd ldrs: led over 4f out: rdn over 2f out: hdd over 1f out and sn wknd* **25/1**

000 **8** 3/4 **Tipsy Lady**[49] 2911 3-8-9 ................................. DaneO'Neill 10 57
(DRCElsworth) *bhd: kpt on wl fnl 2f: nvr rchd ldrs* **33/1**

- **9** nk **Sunshine On Me** 3-8-9 ................................. RMullen 4 56
(CFWall) *bhd: rdn 4f out: styd on fr over 1f out but n.d* **50/1**

0-00 **10** 4 **Bonsai (IRE)**[61] 2562 3-8-9 ................................. EAhern 5 48
(RTPhillips) *s.i.s: hdwy into mid-div 6f out: wknd over 2f out* **33/1**

**11** nk **Big Hurry (USA)** 3-8-9 ................................. SDrowne 14 47
(RCharlton) *in tch tl wknd fr 3f out* **12/1**

5 **12** 2 1/2 **Mujawer (USA)**[15] 3948 3-9-0 ................................. PDobbs 7 47
(MPTregoning) *chsd ldrs 6f* **10/1**

0- **13** 1 **Sweep The Board (IRE)**[417] 2271 3-9-0 ................................. SSanders 11 45
(APJarvis) *a in rr* **33/1**

0 **14** 7 **Danze Romance**[16] 3916 3-8-9 ................................. TQuinn 9 26
(JLDunlop) *chsd ldrs tl n.m.r and wknd 3f out* **16/1**

1m 53.38s (-0.97) **Going Correction** -0.275s/f (Firm) **14** Ran SP% **123.0**
Speed ratings: **93,91,90,90,89 88,87,86,86,82 82,80,79,73**CSF £38.76 TOTE £6.20: £2.60, £3.70, £1.40; EX 66.80 Place 6 £94.14, Place 5 £29.93.
**Owner** Hamdan Al Maktoum **Bred** Shadwell Estate Company Limited **Trained** Lambourn, Berks

**FOCUS**
A modest maiden for the track and a moderate winning time for the grade, but a smart winning debut by Tahtheeb nonetheless.

**NOTEBOOK**
**Tahtheeb(IRE)** was nothing to get over-excited about on breeding, but she made a most pleasing winning debut, winning with plenty in hand. Despite running green, and hanging continually under pressure, she showed a decent change of pace to come through and win, albeit from moderate opposition. She should come on for the experience and is worth her place in a higher-grade event.
**Ogilvy(USA)** has shown himself to be nothing special but this was his best effort to date. He will be better off handicapping.
**Red Sail** lost precious ground at the start that may have cost her the race. She stayed on well in the end but it was too late and she had to settle for third. She has a maiden in her.
**Coppice(IRE)** showed the benefit of his debut, albeit back in April, and he plugged on to claim fourth. Another for whom handicaps are likely to represent the best winning chance, he will appreciate the step up in trip and should progress again.
**Topkat(IRE)** is now eligible for handicaps and will appreciate a greater stamina test.
**Charmed By Fire(USA)** ran better than his finishing position may suggest and needs only one more run to qualify for a mark.
**Mujawer(USA)**, a stablemate of the winner, showed promise on his debut in an average Newmarket maiden, but seems to have gone completely the wrong way.
**Danze Romance** *Official explanation: jockey said filly ran too free*
T/Jkpt: £40,841.90 to a £1 stake. Pool: £57,523.85. 0.50 winning tickets. T/Plt: £209.80 to a £1 stake. Pool: £63,627.50. 221.35 winning tickets. T/Qpdt: £11.00 to a £1 stake. Pool: £4,315.30. 289.20 winning tickets. ST

4370 - (Foreign Racing) - See Raceform Interactive

# 4353 GALWAY (R-H)
Sunday, August 1

**OFFICIAL GOING: Good to firm**

## 4371a MICHAEL MCNAMARA & CO. BUILDERS H'CAP (PREMIER HANDICAP) 7f
**4:20** (4:23) 3-Y-0+ **£45,845** (£13,450; £6,408; £2,183)

RPR

**1** **Amourallis (IRE)**[5] 4222 3-7-4 87 ................................. CDHayes(10) 3 98
(GMLyons, Ire) *bhd: hdwy between horses 2f out: 6th into st: 2nd ins fnl f: r.o wl to ld cl home* **7/1**[2]

**2** 1/2 **Senator's Alibi**[5] 4222 6-8-8 89 ................................. PShanahan 11 99
(TJO'Mara, Ire) *mid-div: hdwy on outer 2 1/2f out: cl 3rd appr st: rdn to ld over 1f out: kpt on wl: hdd cl home* **10/1**[3]

**3** 2 **Majestic Times (IRE)**[15] 3961 4-8-1 82 ................................. NGMcCullagh 1 87
(LiamMcateer, Ire) *hld up: rdn and styd on wl fr 2f out* **16/1**

**4** 3/4 **Mainly Mine (IRE)**[26] 3617 5-8-1 82 ................................. RMBurke 13 85
(CCollins, Ire) *dwlt: sn chsd ldrs: 7th bef 1/2-way: hdwy into 2nd 2f out: led appr st: hdd over 1f out: no ex* **10/1**[3]

**5** 1 1/2 **King Jock (USA)**[35] 3351 3-8-2 89 ................................. TPO'Shea 6 88
(DKWeld, Ire) *chsd ldrs: 4th and rdn 3f out: 5th 2f out: kpt on st* **11/1**

**6** 3/4 **Marfooq (USA)**[2] 4313 4-7-8 81 ow1 ................................. DAMurphy(7) 12 79
(MMcdonagh, Ire) *towards rr: kpt on fr over 2f out* **20/1**

**7** 3/4 **Sheer Tenby (IRE)**[35] 3351 7-9-0 95 ................................. (bt) JAHeffernan 4 89
(PaulARoche, Ire) *chsd ldrs: 3rd 1/2-way: rdn over 2f out: no ex st* **14/1**

**8** 1 **Master Robbie**[8] 4120 5-8-8 89 ................................. PJSmullen 15 81
(MRChannon) *hld up: kpt on one pce fr 2f out* **7/1**[2]

**9** 1/2 **Assigh Lady (IRE)**[15] 3961 6-7-9 81 ................................. HelenKeohane(5) 10 71
(DesmondMcdonogh, Ire) *nvr a factor: sme late prog* **20/1**

**10** hd **Hanabad (IRE)**[35] 3350 4-9-10 105 ................................. MJKinane 9 95
(JohnMOxx, Ire) *mid-div: 9th and effrt on outer over 2f out: 6th appr st: sn no ex* **11/4**[1]

**11** 3/4 **Mombassa (IRE)**[15] 3961 4-9-0 95 ................................. DPMcDonogh 2 83
(EdwardLynam, Ire) *bhd: last 3f out: sme late prog* **20/1**

**12** 1 **Jemmy John (IRE)**[67] 2415 4-7-7 81 ................................. (p) PBBeggy(7) 8 66
(GMLyons, Ire) *cl up: led over 3f out: strly pressed 2f out: hdd appr st: sn wknd* **16/1**

**13** 2 **Libras Child (IRE)**[15] 3961 5-8-1 82 ................................. DMGrant 17 62
(PDelaney, Ire) *nvr a factor* **16/1**

**14** 3/4 **Twogoodreasons (IRE)**[281] 5761 4-7-12 82 ................................. (b) DKinsella(3) 5 60
(NoelMeade, Ire) *nvr a factor* **14/1**

**15** 1 **Jacks Estate (IRE)**[15] 3961 9-8-6 94 ................................. CPGeoghegan(7) 14 69
(AdrianMcguinness, Ire) *chsd ldrs: 5th 1/2-way: wknd fr 2 1/2f out* **10/1**[3]

**16** 1/2 **Due Respect (IRE)**[8] 4157 4-7-8 82 ................................. RPCleary(7) 16 56
(DTHughes, Ire) *chsd ldrs in 6th: wknd over 2f out* **14/1**

**17** 7 **Frosty Wind (IRE)**[18] 3858 6-8-12 93 ................................. FMBerry 18 48
(MissITOakes, Ire) *led: hdd over 3f out: sn wknd: eased st* **14/1**

**S** **Danecare (IRE)**[46] 2995 4-8-6 90 ................................. DJCondon(3) 7 —
(JGBurns, Ire) *towards rr whn rn off bnd and uns rdr bef 1/2-way* **16/1**

1m 27.5s
**WFA** 3 from 4yo+ 6lb **18** Ran SP% **151.8**
Speed ratings: CSF £75.84 CT £953.21 TOTE £9.10: £2.20, £2.20, £3.90, £4.00; DF 91.90.
**Owner** Mrs Christine Kiernan **Bred** Shane Moroney **Trained** Dunsany, Co. Meath
■ Stewards Enquiry : D J Condon seven-day ban: accepted ride when unable to do weight and tried to weigh out without back protector (Aug 11-16,18)

**NOTEBOOK**
**Amourallis(IRE)** was well in compared with the Handicapper's reassessment of her after an earlier run in the week and overcame traffic problems to get in front near the finish.
**Master Robbie** had not the pace to challenge in the straight, just keeping on without quickening.
**Mombassa(IRE)** *Official explanation: vet said gelding was suffering a degree of heat exhaustion post race*
**Jacks Estate(IRE)** *Official explanation: vet said gelding was suffering a degree of heat exhaustion post race*

4376 - (Foreign Racing) - See Raceform Interactive

# 2926 COLOGNE (R-H)
Sunday, August 1

**OFFICIAL GOING: Good**

## 4377a GLOBETROTTER TROPHY (LISTED) 1m 3f
**2:40** (2:41) 3-Y-0+ **£9,155** (£2,817; £1,408; £704)

RPR

**1** **Foreign Affairs**[91] 1802 6-9-6 ................................. JQuinn 6 110
(SirMarkPrescott) *trckd ldr, pushed along over 3f out, rdn to chal ins fnl f, led 50y out, went a hd up, just held on (47/10)* 2

**2** nse **Epalo (GER)**[77] 2156 5-9-6 ................................. THellier 8 110
(ASchutz, Germany) *led til caught by winner 50y out, fought on well (3/10)* 1

**3** 9 **Absolut Power (GER)** 3-8-9 ow2 ................................. EPedroza 3 95
(AWohler, Germany)

**4** 1 1/2 **Lysuna (GER)**[32] 3434 4-9-2 ................................. ABoschert 5 89
(ATrybuhl, Germany)

**5** 5 **Tempelwachter (GER)**[287] 5659 10-9-6 ................................. (b) ADeVries 7 85
(HHesse, Germany)

**6** 3 1/2 **Oakboy (GER)**[28] 3565 3-8-7 ................................. (b) PHeugl 9 77
(HSteinmetz, Germany)

7 *5* **Linux (GER)** 5-9-6 ........ ABest 1 72
(WBauermeister, Germany)

2m 15.39s
**WFA** 3 from 4yo+ 10lb **7** Ran SP% **17.5**
Speed ratings: .
**Owner** Charles C Walker - Osborne House **Bred** Miss K Rausing **Trained** Newmarket, Suffolk

**NOTEBOOK**
**Foreign Affairs** seems to have improved at the age of six and took the notable scalp of Epalo here, although the runner-up may have been short of full fitness. Off the bridle three furlongs out, he looked unlikely to get on terms with the leader but showed a great attitude to battle his way to the front and then hold off a renewed challenge.
**Epalo(GER)** did not disappoint his trainer despite this long odds-on reverse as he was returning from a long lay-off. This should put him spot on for the Arlington Million, in Chicago on August 14, where this habitual front-runner\n\x\x will prove hard to pass.

## 4378a GLOBETROTTER MEILE (GROUP 3) 1m
**3:55** (4:01) 3-Y-0+ **£22,535** (£7,042; £3,251; £2,113)

RPR

1 **Pepperstorm (GER)**[36] [3335] 3-8-7 ........ ABoschert 6 111
(UOstmann, Germany) *mid-division, improved from 4f out to go 4th straight, strong run to lead well over 1f out, ran on well* 2

2 *nk* **Eagle Rise (IRE)**[36] [3335] 4-9-2 ........ THellier 7 112
(ASchutz, Germany) *held up, good headway on outside from over 1f out, finished well* 3

3 *3/4* **Tahreeb (FR)**[29] [3539] 3-8-9 ........ MartinDwyer 14 111
(MPTregoning) *raced in 3rd to straight, challenged 1 1/2f out, every chance inside final f, kept on same pace last 150y out* 1

4 *5* **Lazio (GER)**[36] [3335] 3-8-9 ow2........ ADeVries 8 101
(ATrybuhl, Germany) *mid-division, 6th straight, ran on one pace* 2

5 *nk* **Bear King (GER)**[21] [3792] 7-9-4 ........ NRichter 5 102
(CSprengel, Germany) *held up, headway final 2f, never nearer*

6 *nk* **Horeion Directa (GER)**[35] [3361] 5-9-2 ........ WMongil 12 99
(AndreasLowe, Germany) *mid-division, kept on one pace final 2f*

7 *1/2* **Tartuffo (GER)**[658] [5269] 4-9-2 ........ JBojko 9 98
(PRau, Germany) *towards rear to straight, some late progress, never a factor*

8 *1 1/2* **Rajpute (GER)**[42] [3134] 4-9-0 ........ ABest 2 93
(DrABolte, Germany) *held up in rear, last straight, never nearer*

9 *1 1/2* **Arlecchina (GER)**[21] [3792] 4-8-11 ........ TMundry 11 87
(UStoltefuss, Germany) *in rear to straight, kept on one pace*

10 *3* **Berber (GER)**[254] [6044] 6-9-2 ........ WPanov 15 86
(WFigge, Germany) *always towards rear*

11 *nse* **Forever Free (GER)**[36] [3335] 4-9-0 ........ ASchikora 3 84
(DKRichardson, Germany) *mid-division, beaten 2f out*

12 *1* **Sambaprinz (GER)**[21] [3792] 5-9-4 ........ EPedroza 10 86
(HHorwart, Germany) *mid-division, 7th straight, soon beaten*

13 *3 1/2* **Peppercorn (GER)**[36] [3335] 7-9-6 ........ PHeugl 4 81
(UOstmann, Germany) *prominent, 2nd straight, led well over 2f out to well over 1f out, weakened quickly*

14 *4* **Ibisco (GER)**[57] 4-9-0 ........(b) AGoritz 1 67
(GSybrecht, Germany) *led to well over 2f out, weakened quickly*

1m 34.2s
**WFA** 3 from 4yo+ 7lb **14** Ran SP% **130.8**
Speed ratings: .
**Owner** Gestut Hony-Hof **Bred** P A Battel Et Al **Trained** Germany

**NOTEBOOK**
**Tahreeb(FR)** performed well under his 2lb penalty. Close up throughout, he was the only one to go with Pepperstorm when the winner hit the front a furlong and a half out and, having stayed on gamely, only lost second in the closing stages.

# COPENHAGEN (L-H)
Sunday, August 1

**OFFICIAL GOING: Good**

## 4379a TUBORG CLASSIC 3-ARS MILE 1m
**1:53** (12:00) 3-Y-0 **£1,703** (£851; £426; £255)

RPR

1 **Soap Watcher (IRE)**[292] [5557] 3-8-7 ow2........ MSantos 7 —
(LReuterskiold, Sweden)

2 *shd* **Tiger Tiger (FR)**[39] [3210] 3-9-6 ........ JFEgan 3 —
(JamiePoulton) *raced in 3rd or 4th, led 1f out, headed close home (7/10F)* 1

3 *1* **Thai Express (DEN)** 3-8-5 ........ CathrineWeilby 6 —
(BOlsen, Norway)

4 *2* **Tzatziki (DEN)** 3-8-8 ow1........ LHammer-Hansen 4 —
(SJensen, Denmark)

5 *1/2* **Flirting Groom** 3-8-9 ........ FJohansson 9 —
(BHallencreutz, Sweden)

6 *1 1/2* **Star Quest (DEN)** 3-8-9 ow2........ KAndersen 5 —
(BOlsen, Norway)

1m 36.4s **6** Ran SP% **58.8**
Speed ratings: .
**Owner** Stall Lodder & Reuterskiold Hb **Bred** Yeomanstown Stud **Trained** Sweden

**NOTEBOOK**
**Tiger Tiger(FR)** hit the front with a furlong to run but was not at home on ground that was much faster than the official description and was run out of it in the last few strides.

## 4380a SCANDINAVIAN OPEN CHAMPIONSHIP (GROUP 3) 1m 4f
**3:10** (12:00) 3-Y-0+ **£28,500** (£9,502; £4,751; £2,851)

RPR

1 **Crocodile Dundee (IRE)**[30] [3484] 3-8-5 ........ JFEgan 8 103
(JamiePoulton) *raced in 5th, headway to go 3rd entering straight, soon every chance, hard ridden to lead close home* 2

2 *shd* **Maktub (ITY)**[29] [3540] 5-9-6 ........ GMosse 4 107
(MAJarvis) *raced in 2nd til led narrowly over 2f out, ran on gamely when challenged from over 1f out, headed close home* 1

3 *1* **Mity Dancer (GER)**[30] [3504] 4-8-11 ........ LHammer-Hansen 2 96
(DKRichardson, Germany) *raced in 3rd or 4th, ridden 2f out, stayed on*

4 *1* **Dano-Mast**[231] [6188] 8-9-4 ........ FSanchez 6 102
(FPoulsen, France) *behind, driven along over 2f out, stayed on gamely down outside to take 4th closing stages, nearest finish* 3

5 *1* **The Khamsin (DEN)**[13] 5-9-2 ........ JJohansen 3 98
(MsCErichsen, Norway) *in touch, every chance over 1 1/2f out, kept on same pace*

6 *1/2* **Alpino Chileno (ARG)**[31] 5-9-2 ........(b) FDiaz 9 97
(RuneHaugen, Norway) *close up, effort and one pace from 2f out*

7 *shd* **Binary File (USA)**[338] [4568] 6-9-2 ........ NCordrey 5 97
(SJensen, Denmark) *close up til weakened final f*

8 *3* **Santiago Matias (CHI)** 5-9-2 ........(b) MSantos 10 93
(FCastro, Sweden) *never dangerous*

9 *2* **Albaran (GER)**[322] [4926] 11-9-2 ........ MLarsen 11 90
(MsCErichsen, Norway) *always towards rear*

10 *2* **Royal Experiment (USA)**[273] [5901] 5-9-4 ........ FJohansson 7 89
(WidoNeuroth, Norway) *always towards rear*

11 *3* **Peruginos Flyer (IRE)**[33] 5-9-2 ........ SaraSlot 1 82
(JTandari, Germany) *led to over 2f out, weakened*

2m 26.8s
**WFA** 3 from 4yo+ 11lb **11** Ran SP% **125.6**
Speed ratings: .
**Owner** R W Huggins **Bred** T J Pabst **Trained** Telscombe, E Sussex

**FOCUS**
A first Pattern-race success for Jamie Poulton.

**NOTEBOOK**
**Crocodile Dundee(IRE)** was the only three-year-old in the field yet showed resolution beyond his years to catch Maktub in the shadow of the post. Silence Is Golden franked his Sandown win in the Nassau and this fast-improving colt may return to Scandinavia for next month's Stockholm Cup.
**Maktub(ITY)** stalked the leader before taking it up on the home turn. He fought on gamely to repel a number of challengers only to be undone by the winner's last-gasp effort.

# 4356 DEAUVILLE (R-H)
Sunday, August 1

**OFFICIAL GOING: Good**

## 4382a PRIX DE CABOURG (GROUP 3) 6f
**2:15** (2:16) 2-Y-0 **£25,704** (£10,282; £7,711; £5,141)

RPR

1 **Layman (USA)**[22] 2-8-11 ........ GaryStevens 2 115+
(AFabre, France) *made all, ridden clear 1f out, ran on strongly* 2

2 *5* **Inhabitant**[21] [3790] 2-8-11 ........ ODoleuze 3 100
(MmeCHead-Maarek, France) *hld up in rr early, disp 4th half-way, rdn 2f out, chsd wnr under str pressure last 150yds, no imp* 3

3 *1* **Salut Thomas (FR)**[7] [4184] 2-8-11 ........(b) CSoumillon 6 97
(RobertCollet, France) *plld early, restrained in rr & swtchd to rail, last to 1 1/2f out, styd on under pressure to reach 3rd 80yds out, nvr nrr*

4 *1 1/2* **Lady Weasley (FR)**[34] [3388] 2-8-8 ........ FSpanu 4 89
(MlleVDissaux, France) *tracked 3rd on outside, improved to dispute 2nd 1f out, one pace*

5 *1/2* **Osidy (USA)**[34] 2-8-11 ........ ELegrix 5 91
(XNakkachdji, France) *pulled early, raced in 3rd to 1 1/2f out, weakened final f*

6 *4* **Million Wishes**[39] 2-8-8 ........ TGillet 1 76
(JEPease, France) *tracked winner on rails, beaten 2f out* 1

7 *2* **Beautifix (GER)**[34] 2-8-8 ........ OPeslier 7 70
(CLaffon-Parias, France) *raced 2nd on outside, every chance well over 1f out, weakened from distance, eased*

1m 10.9s **Going Correction** -0.175s/f (Firm) **7** Ran SP% **122.6**
Speed ratings: **107,100,99,97,96 91,88.**
**Owner** Sheikh Mohammed **Bred** Darley **Trained** France

**NOTEBOOK**
**Layman(USA)** was soon in command, taking the field along at a pace which quickened running into the final two furlongs. At this point he had the race won and the others struggling in his wake. The colt drew clear to win by five lengths. He is the best of his sex to be seen out in France this season and will be very difficult to beat in the Prix Morny later in the month.
**Inhabitant** went into pursuit of the winner from one and a half out but never got in a blow. It was an honest run and he should manage to win at this level later in the season.
**Salut Thomas(FR)** was last for much of this race and then brought with a late challenge near the rail. He did not quite get home and will now be raced over a shorter distance.
**Lady Weasley(FR)**, one of the pack following the winner, she stayed on without quickening and lost third place inside the final furlong.

## 4383a PRIX D'ASTARTE (GROUP 1) (F&M) (STRAIGHT COURSE) 1m
**3:20** (3:21) 3-Y-0+ **£80,479** (£32,197; £16,099; £8,042)

RPR

1 **Marbye (IRE)**[46] [2967] 4-9-0 ........ MDemuro 5 112
(BGrizzetti, Italy) *held up in 6th, edged outside & headway 2f out, ridden over 1f out, led 120yds out, driven out* **118/10**

2 *1/2* **Majestic Desert**[29] [3547] 3-8-7 ........ TEDurcan 1 111
(MRChannon) *hld up bhd ldrs on rails, swtchd towards outside wl over 1f out, driven to go 2nd wl ins fnl f, ran on* **52/10**[3]

3 *3/4* **Nebraska Tornado (USA)**[47] [2957] 4-9-0 ........ GaryStevens 3 110
(AFabre, France) *led 1f, led again over 2f out to 1 1/2f out, outpaced, rallied under pressure to regain 3rd final strides* **11/10**[1]

4 *snk* **Monturani (IRE)**[26] [3600] 5-9-0 ........ OPeslier 6 109
(GWragg) *always close up on outside, challenged 2f out, every chance distance, one pace* **122/10**

5 *shd* **Martha Stewart (IRE)**[52] [2830] 3-8-7 ........ CSoumillon 8 109
(RGibson, France) *held up in rear, headway on outside over 2f out, led 1 1/2f out, hard ridden & headed 120yds out, one pace* **91/10**

6 *hd* **Cattiva Generosa**[38] [3258] 3-8-7 ........ TJarnet 2 109
(RGibson, France) *tracked leaders, outpaced 2f out, rallied inside final f, nearest at finish* **15/1**

7 *nk* **Denebola (USA)**[24] [3688] 3-8-7 ........ C-PLemaire 7 108
(PBary, France) *hld up in rr on rails, hdwy well over 1f out, driven through gap on rails 150yds out, no extra final 100yds* **5/2**[2]

8 *10* **Rumba Loca (IRE)**[70] [2341] 3-8-7 ........ YTake 4 88
(BGrizzetti, Italy) *led after 1f, headed over 2f out, soon weakened* **118/10**

1m 36.7s **Going Correction** -0.45s/f (Firm)
**WFA** 3 from 4yo+ 7lb **8** Ran SP% **131.7**
Speed ratings: **114,113,112,112,112 112,112,102.**
**Owner** Teruya Yoshida **Bred** Curtasse Snc **Trained** Italy



The Form Book, Raceform Ltd, Compton, RG20 6NL

**NOTEBOOK**

**Marbye(IRE)** was given a waiting ride as her stable mate set a moderate pace. Switched to the outside one and a half out, she quickened well and took the lead with 100 yards left to run. The filly was third in this race a year ago and has certainly improved as a four-year-old. She will be in the line up for the Jacques Le Marois on August 15.

**Majestic Desert**, from her number one draw, she was always on the rail and going well. She had to be extracted and go around the horses before making her challenge one and a half out but could not accelerate as well as the winner. It was another game effort from this filly and she may also come back for the Jacques Le Marois.

**Nebraska Tornado(USA)** was simply beaten for a lack of pace - her best form all coming over trips in excess of this. She was always well up on the rail but outpaced when things quickened up on the final stages. She then ran on again as the race came to an end, with her jockey regretting he had not made all the running. Much better things can be expected of back up in trip.

**Monturani(IRE)** was always up with the pace and she looked the likely winner one and a half out but did not quicken under pressure. She was given every chance and it was a very game effort. There are no plans for the moment.

## [2541] MUNICH (L-H)

Sunday, August 1

**OFFICIAL GOING: Good**

### 4385a GROSSER DALLMAYR-PREIS BAYERISCHES ZUCHTRENNEN (GROUP 1) 1m 2f

3:40 (3:46) 3-Y-O+ **£64,085** (£25,352; £12,676; £7,042)

RPR

1 **Intendant (GER)**[28] 3565 3-8-9 JPalik 7 116
(FrauABertram, Germany) *held up in 6th, 7th straight, ran on well from distance to lead 100y out, ran on strongly* **153/10**

2 1 1/2 **Powerscourt**[29] 3540 4-9-6 JPSpencer 3 115
(APO'Brien, Ire) *set strong pace, headed 100y out, one pace* **3/5**[1]

3 1 **Imperial Dancer**[29] 3540 6-9-6 SHitchcott 5 114
(MRChannon) *held up, 8th straight, headway to go 3rd inside final f, kept on* **20/1**

4 1 1/4 **Scott's View**[13] 3978 5-9-6 SChin 8 112
(MJohnston) *always close up, 5th straight, went 2nd briefly approaching final f, one pace* **87/10**

5 2 **Deva (GER)**[42] 3137 5-9-2 J-PCarvalho 6 104
(DRonge, Germany) *held up, last straight, kept on from 2f out, never nearer* **8/1**

6 5 **Gentle Tiger (GER)**[28] 3565 3-8-9 ASuborics 2 97
(PSchiergen, Germany) *mid-division, 6th straight, no extra from 2f out* **46/10**[2]

7 1/2 **Serenus (GER)**[302] 5388 6-9-6 (b) TO'Sullivan 4 98
(WFigge, Germany) *mid-division, headway to go 4th approaching straight, soon weakened* **31/1**

8 5 **Next Gina (GER)**[30] 3504 4-9-2 AStarke 9 86
(ASchutz, Germany) *disputed 2nd, 2nd straight, slightly hampered over 2f out, soon beaten* **63/10**[3]

9 18 **Egerton (GER)**[28] 3565 3-8-9 AHelfenbein 1 56
(PRau, Germany) *tracked leader, 3rd straight, weakened quickly* **149/10**

2m 4.27s
**WFA** 3 from 4yo+ 9lb **9** Ran SP% **135.8**
Speed ratings: .
**Owner** F Leve **Bred** F Leve **Trained** Germany

**NOTEBOOK**

**Intendant(GER)** left his previous form well behind with this shock win. However, as a son of Lando, it was no surprise that he improved a good deal on fast ground.

**Powerscourt**, despite accounting for all his market rivals, had no answer to the winner's late burst. The Arlington Million is one of a number of possible future targets.

**Imperial Dancer** stayed on from the rear to take third. This was his best effort since the spring, suggesting that he should be capable of winning this type of race on soft ground.

**Scott's View** gave chase to Powerscourt approaching the furlong pole but his run petered out in the closing stages.

## [4256] CARLISLE (R-H)

Monday, August 2

**OFFICIAL GOING: Firm (good to firm in places)**

### 4386 RED MILLS IRISH HORSEFEEDS LADY AMATEUR RIDERS' H'CAP 7f 200y

6:20 (6:21) (E) (0-70,61) 3-Y-O+ **£3,786** (£1,165; £582; £291) **Stalls High**

Form RPR

4003 1 **Gifted Flame**[6] 4209 5-11-0 **61** MissEJJones 6 73
(TDBarron) *slowly away: hld up: hdwy 2f out: rdn to ld ins fnl f: r.o* **5/1**[1]

0012 2 1 3/4 **Pepper Road**[17] 3895 5-10-1 **53** MissRBastiman(5) 5 61
(RBastiman) *prom: led 2f out: hdd ins fnl f: no ex* **5/1**[1]

0632 3 1 1/4 **Joey Perhaps**[5] 4249 3-9-10 **55** MissKManser(5) 15 60
(JRBest) *slowy away: sn midfield: hdwy and in tch over 2f out: rdn over 1f out: styd on ins last* **8/1**[3]

1434 4 1/2 **Kelseas Kolby (IRE)**[39] 3247 4-10-3 **55** (v) MissFayeBramley(5) 2 59
(PABlockley) *in tch: effrt over 2f out: kpt on fr over 1f out* **20/1**

223- 5 1 **Firozi**[209] 4542 5-9-11 **49** MissVTunnicliffe(5) 8 51
(RAFahey) *midfield: kpt on fnl 2f: n.d* **14/1**

0-00 6 shd **Kama's Wheel**[11] 4066 5-8-10 **32** MissKellyHarrison(3) 3 33
(JohnAHarris) *chsd ldrs: rdn 2f out: no ex* **33/1**

-010 7 shd **Night Market**[35] 3375 6-10-2 **52** MrsNWilson(3) 12 53
(NWilson) *slowly away: sn in tch: chsng ldrs 2f out: no further prog* **9/1**

0002 8 nk **Rainstorm**[6] 4213 9-9-4 **40** MrsSOwen(3) 4 41
(WMBrisbourne) *slowly away: hld up midfield: hdwy to join ldrs over 2f out: ev ch 2f out: wknd appr fnl f* **5/1**[1]

5001 9 1 1/2 **Oh So Rosie (IRE)**[11] 4066 4-10-5 **55** (p) MrsSMoore(3) 16 52
(JSMoore) *slowly away: bhd: hdwy into midfield 3f out: no further prog* **13/2**[2]

0000 10 nk **Mutared (IRE)**[27] 3604 6-9-6 **42** (p) MrsEmmaLittmoden(3) 1 38
(NPLittmoden) *nvr bttr than mid-div* **33/1**

0000 11 1 **Dark Cut (IRE)**[27] 3604 4-8-13 **37** MissDawnRankin(5) 9 31
(HAlexander) *sn towards rr: n.d* **33/1**

2403 12 2 **Noble Pursuit**[9] 4132 7-9-10 **50** MissVBarr(7) 13 39
(REBarr) *slowly away: bhd most of way* **16/1**

00/0 13 1/2 **Thwaab**[45] 3040 12-8-12 **38** (v) MissVictoriaCasey(7) 14 26
(FWatson) *sn towards rr* **50/1**

0-20 14 1 **Hebenus**[54] 2779 5-9-7 **45** MissHCuthbert(5) 10 31
(TAKCuthbert) *prom tl rdn and wknd 2f out* **25/1**

00-0 15 nk **The Spook**[35] 3367 4-9-6 **39** MrsSBosley 7 24
(WMBrisbourne) *slowly away: bhd most of way* **40/1**

3405 16 1 1/4 **Magic Mamma's Too**[39] 3247 4-10-1 **48** MsCWilliams 11 30
(JRWeymes) *led tl rdn and hdd 2f out: sn wknd* **20/1**

1m 41.69s (1.69) **Going Correction** 0.0s/f (Good)
**WFA** 3 from 4yo+ 7lb **16** Ran SP% **123.6**
Speed ratings: **91,89,88,87,86 86,86,86,84,84 83,81,80,79,79 78**CSF £26.01 CT £211.61 TOTE £6.30: £1.60, £1.30, £2.20, £7.60; EX 19.50.
**Owner** Raymond Miquel **Bred** Taker Bloodstock **Trained** Maunby, N Yorks

**FOCUS**

A moderate amateur riders' handicap that saw many runners lose their chance with a slow start. However, the form looks reasonably sound with the first three running close to their marks.

**NOTEBOOK**

**Gifted Flame** yet again missed the break and took a keen hold early, but still had enough up his sleeve to take this contest in ready fashion. This was a deserved success and he is on top of his game at present, but his tendency to start slowly means he will always need things to fall right in his races, and he is not one to lump on in a follow-up bid.

**Pepper Road** held every chance back over this extra furlong, and turned in another solid effort, but could not match the winner late on. He has recently found his form at this track the last three times and is capable of making amends off this sort of mark.

**Joey Perhaps**, eased in trip, lost his chance at the start and was coming home all too late. He has recently found his level of late and looks to be edging closer to that first success.

**Kelseas Kolby(IRE)** ran his race and turned in a sound display, but looked very one paced late on over this trip. He has yet to win outside of selling company.

**Firozi**, not seen since finishing tailed off over hurdles in January, produced a pleasing comeback and is entitled to improve on this display.

**Rainstorm**, winner of this race last year off a 4lb higher mark, was forced to race wide after his sluggish start and that cost him.

**Oh So Rosie(IRE)** was another to miss the kick and failed to take advantage of her inside draw. She can do better, but is a very hard horse to predict.

### 4387 BEADLE AND HILL CLAIMING STKS 6f 192y

6:50 (6:53) (F) 3-Y-O **£3,164** (£904; £452) **Stalls High**

Form RPR

0440 1 **Chubbes**[10] 4102 3-7-13 48 (b) HayleyTurner(5) 8 51
(MDHammond) *midfield: drvn along 1/2-way: hdwy over 1f out: r.o wl u.p to ld clsng stages* **13/2**[3]

0060 2 nk **Love Of Life**[14] 3988 3-8-0 38 LisaJones(3) 2 49
(JulianPoulton) *s.i.s: hld up: hdwy on outer 2f out: edgd rt and styd on u.p to chal wl ins last: no ex cl home* **16/1**

5 3 3/4 **La Calera (GER)**[4] 4265 3-8-3 65 (v) ANicholls 7 47
(MFHarris) *led: hdd 3f out: remained cl up: styd on u.p to ld again jst ins fnl f: hdd clsng stages: no ex* **12/1**

0360 4 1/2 **Firebird Rising (USA)**[16] 3954 3-8-2 58 NMackay(3) 1 48
(TDBarron) *sn trcking ldrs: led 3f out: rdn and hdd jst ins fnl f: no ex clsng stages* **3/1**[1]

1005 5 5 **Garnock Venture (IRE)**[24] 3708 3-8-10 52 (b) SSanders 4 39
(ABerry) *cl up: ev ch 3f out: sn rdn: fdd fnl 2f* **15/2**

0024 6 1 1/2 **Multiple Choice (IRE)**[10] 4093 3-8-8 64 (t) J-PGuillambert(3) 12 36
(NPLittmoden) *prom: ev ch 3f out: fdd* **7/2**[2]

6300 7 1 1/2 **Delusion**[5] 4241 3-8-2 53 DAllan 3 23
(TDEasterby) *towards rr: sn drvn along: sme late hdwy: n.d* **10/1**

4536 8 2 1/2 **Compassion (IRE)**[21] 3798 3-7-13 46 (p) PHanagan 13 13
(MissLAPerratt) *in tch: rdn over 2f out: sn btn* **13/2**[3]

0220 9 3 1/2 **Beaver Diva**[16] 3954 3-7-6 40 DFentiman(7) 10 4
(WMBrisbourne) *hld up: keen early: drvn along 1/2-way: sn btn* **10/1**

0006 10 hd **Mr Moon**[10] 4102 3-7-12 29 (b[1]) PPMathers(5) 6 7
(MDHammond) *towards rr most of way* **20/1**

11 8 **Blackpool Jack** 3-8-2 ow1 THamilton(3) 11 —
(FPMurtagh) *s.i.s: a bhd* **33/1**

1m 27.17s (0.07) **Going Correction** 0.0s/f (Good) **11** Ran SP% **125.1**
Speed ratings: **99,98,97,97,91 89,88,85,81,81 71**CSF £112.12 TOTE £9.00: £2.70, £3.10, £4.30; EX 165.10.La Calera was claimed by Mr G. Chung for £8,000.
**Owner** Garden Shed Racing 1 **Bred** Hascombe And Valiant Studs **Trained** Middleham, N Yorks

**FOCUS**

A dire contest, full of disappointing types, run at a fair pace, but the form is poor.

**NOTEBOOK**

**Chubbes** responded gamely to his rider's urgings in the straight, and found a different gear entering the last furlong to get up in the dying strides. He was unable to go the early pace over this shorter trip, but the track suited and the race was in effect run to suit. This was his best performance of the current campaign, and it was a solid effort at the weights.

**Love Of Life** did herself no favours with a sluggish start, but only just went down in the end and ran by far her best race to date. She faced a stiff task at the weights, but ran above her current rating, and an extra furlong could see her go one better at this level.

**La Calera(GER)** could not find a change of pace when it mattered over this shorter trip, but still turned in a sound effort and could find a race at this level, most likely back over seven furlongs.

**Firebird Rising(USA)** was handy throughout and travelled best of all, until she looked to throw in the towel when asked to win her race late on. She has ability, but also her quirks, and is one to avoid.

**Multiple Choice(IRE)** failed to find anything under maximum pressure on this drop back in trip. He had shown a bit more in this grade on the All-Weather the last twice, but has badly regressed since his juvenile season, and is one to leave alone at present.

### 4388 LLOYD BMW MAIDEN AUCTION STKS 5f

7:20 (7:21) (E) 2-Y-O **£3,477** (£1,070; £535; £267) **Stalls High**

Form RPR

0 1 **Monashee Rose (IRE)**[11] 4058 2-7-13 NMackay(3) 4 74
(JSMoore) *cl up: led over 1f out: r.o wl u.p ins last* **10/1**[3]

4 2 2 **Bond Babe**[5] 4245 2-8-4 FNorton 5 69
(BSmart) *s.i.s: sn in tch: hdwy 2f out: rdn to chal ent fnl f: no imp on wnr ins last* **7/1**[2]

2 3 1 3/4 **Breaking Shadow (IRE)**[20] 3818 2-8-9 PHanagan 6 68
(RAFahey) *led tl hdd over 1f out: sn rdn and btn* **2/5**[1]

P63 4 1 **Shatin Leader**[17] 3893 2-8-2 RFfrench 3 57
(MissLAPerratt) *prom: rdn 2f out: hung rt over 1f out: kpt on same pce* **14/1**

00 5 2 **Cree**[97] 1686 2-8-8 (b[1]) SSanders 1 56
(WRMuir) *rr but in tch: rdn 2f out: sn btn* **16/1**

6 5 **Hits Only Cash** 2-8-10 DeanMcKeown 2 41
(PABlockley) *s.i.s: rr but in tch: rdn 1/2-way: sn wknd* **12/1**

60.72 secs (-0.78) **Going Correction** -0.30s/f (Firm) **6** Ran SP% **113.3**
Speed ratings: **94,90,88,86,83 75**CSF £74.52 TOTE £12.20: £3.10, £1.90; EX 60.00.
**Owner** The Fairway Connection **Bred** Mrs Eithne Thompson **Trained** East Garston, Berks

**FOCUS**
An ordinary juvenile maiden run at a sound pace. Although the form is hard to gauge, it may throw up a few winners over this trip before the season is out.
**NOTEBOOK**
**Monashee Rose(IRE)** broke much better than on her recent Sandown debut and found a neat turn of pace to settle the argument entering the final furlong. This was a much-improved effort, and she was well supported in the betting ring, so she could be capable of better when tackling nurseries.
**Bond Babe ◆**, as on her debut, was slow to go from the gates and mounted her finishing challenge all too late. She must learn to break better, but no doubt has ability, and it would be no surprise should this half-sister to the smart sprinter Baltic King, leave this form well behind in due course.
**Breaking Shadow(IRE)** looked to be hating this ground, but was still disappointing all the same. He had caught a tartar when shaping with promise on his recent debut at Beverley, and can be given another chance when reverting to a softer surface. *Official explanation: jockey said colt was unsuited by the fast ground*
**Shatin Leader** ran her race, but again hung right under pressure, and is beginning to a difficult ride.

## 4389 COORS BREWERS H'CAP — 1m 3f 206y
**7:50** (7:51) (D ) (0-80,76) 3-Y-O — **£5,772** (£1,776; £888; £444) **Stalls** Low

Form — RPR
0020 **1** **Baileys Dancer**[16] 3953 3-9-6 **75** ........ JFanning 1 82
(MJohnston) *trckd ldr: led over 2f out: styd on wl: eased clsng stages* **9/2**[3]
2131 **2** 1 1/2 **Charlotte Vale**[17] 3919 3-9-4 **73** ........ MFenton 4 78
(MDHammond) *hld up in tch: hdwy to chal 2f out: sn rdn: no imp on wnr fnl f* **3/1**[2]
314- **3** 1/2 **Aurelia**[294] 5544 3-9-7 **76** ........ SSanders 2 80
(SirMarkPrescott) *s.i.s: hld up: hdwy to chse first 2 wl over 1f out: rdn ent fnl f: no further prog* **11/10**[1]
0130 **4** 3 1/2 **Ego Trip**[19] 3837 3-7-13 **54** ........ DaleGibson 5 53
(MWEasterby) *slowly away: hld up: keen early: effrt 3f out: sn btn* **10/1**
1220 **5** 1 **Garston Star**[11] 4062 3-8-2 **57** ........ FNorton 3 54
(JSMoore) *keen: led: 6 l clr 1/2-way: hdd over 2f out: sn wknd* **6/1**
2m 31.97s (-0.43) **Going Correction** 0.0s/f (Good) **5** Ran SP% **114.2**
Speed ratings: **101,100,99,97,96**CSF £18.69 TOTE £4.40: £2.00, £1.40; EX 16.30.
**Owner** G R Bailey Ltd (baileys Horse Feeds) **Bred** P And Mrs Venner **Trained** Middleham Moor, N Yorks
**FOCUS**
A fair handicap, run at a solid pace, and the form looks sound.
**NOTEBOOK**
**Baileys Dancer**, with the blinkers left off this time, relished this return to fast ground and ran out a ready winner, over a trip she was not certain to stay. She has taken time to find her feet this season, but has slipped in the weights as a result, and may well be able to score again off a higher mark, as she is still unexposed over this distance. *Official explanation: trainer's representative said, regarding the improved form shown, filly may have been unsuited by wearing blinkers for the first time at Ripon on her previous run*
**Charlotte Vale ◆**, who came into this in the form of her life, travelled best of all until finding little on this firm ground when asked to win her race. Her recent 5lb rise in the weights does not look harsh on this evidence, she still has the scope to progress and will do better when reverting to an easier surface.
**Aurelia**, who showed fair form last year as a juvenile, was well-backed for this seasonal debut, but ran as though the race was just needed and is far from one to write off.
**Ego Trip** could not go with the principals when the race got serious and paid for running too keen through the early stages. He looks a non-stayer over this distance.
**Garston Star** found nil off the bridle having run way too freely at the head of affairs for most of the contest. *Official explanation: jockey said gelding ran too free*

## 4390 BANK OF SCOTLAND CLASSIFIED STKS — 6f 192y
**8:20** (8:22) (F ) 3-Y-O+ — **£3,150** (£900; £450) **Stalls** High

Form — RPR
2005 **1** **Best Desert (IRE)**[9] 4126 3-8-13 63 ........ NPollard 7 68
(JRBest) *towards rr: drvn along over 2f out: hdwy to chse first 2 over 1f out: r.o wl u.p to ld post* **11/1**
6025 **2** shd **Nemo Fugat (IRE)**[3] 4308 5-9-2 60 ........(v) ANicholls 4 65
(DNicholls) *w ldr: rdn to ld over 1f out: styd on: ct post* **7/2**[3]
**3** 1 **Musical Top (USA)**[71] 2328 4-8-10 60 ........ LFletcher(3) 8 59
(HMorrison) *mde most tl rdn and hdd over 1f out: kpt on same pce* **16/1**
-001 **4** 6 **Northern Games**[12] 4013 5-9-2 59 ........(b) GParkin 1 46
(KARyan) *bhd and sn drvn along: kpt on fnl 2f: n.d* **7/1**
5061 **5** nk **Oeuf A La Neige**[3] 4309 4-8-10 61 ........ DeanWilliams(7) 6 46
(GCHChung) *chsd ldrs: drvn along 3f out: wknd 2f out* **10/3**[2]
6340 **6** nk **Waltzing Wizard**[17] 3895 5-8-11 51 ........ PPMathers(5) 2 44
(ABerry) *towards rr: drvn along 1/2-way: no hdwy* **16/1**
0203 **7** 6 **Saros (IRE)**[3] 4305 3-8-10 57 ........ DMcGaffin 5 28
(BSmart) *chsd ldrs tl rdn and wknd over 2f out* **9/1**
-344 **8** 6 **Pure Folly (IRE)**[19] 3849 3-8-7 57 ........ SSanders 3 9
(SirMarkPrescott) *hld up: effrt over 2f out: sn rdn and btn* **3/1**[1]
1m 26.64s (-0.46) **Going Correction** 0.0s/f (Good)
**WFA** 3 from 4yo+ 6lb **8** Ran SP% **112.9**
Speed ratings: **102,101,100,93,93 93,86,79**CSF £48.11 TOTE £13.40: £2.40, £1.40, £4.20; EX 64.30.
**Owner** Paul Hudson **Bred** Mull Enterprizes **Trained** Hucking, Kent
■ Stewards Enquiry : N Pollard caution: used whip in the incorrect place
**FOCUS**
A modest affair that produced a nail-biting finish. The first three came well clear, but the form does not look that strong.
**NOTEBOOK**
**Best Desert(IRE)**, who looked to have a good chance at the weights, just prevailed in the bobbing finish to win his first race at the 11th attempt. He could progress, while in this current form, but is a horse who needs all to fall right in his races.
**Nemo Fugat(IRE) ◆** was only just denied. He looked most likely to score when hitting the front, but this stiff seven found him out, and he had no answer to the winner's late challenge. A sharper test can see him deservedly go one better.
**Musical Top(USA)**, making her British debut, had the run of the race from the front, but tired out of it late on over this longer trip. She is entitled to come on a fair bit for this and can be placed to advantage before the season's end.
**Northern Games**, who bounced back to form when beating Nemo Fugat at Catterick recently, was well held off this 6lb higher mark. This longer trip did not suit, but he looks in the Handicapper's grip now all the same.
**Oeuf A La Neige**, who escaped penalty for finally getting off the mark at Thirsk three days previously under today's rider, never looked happy and turned in a disappointing effort over this extra furlong.
**Pure Folly(IRE)** ran too badly to be true. Something may well have been amiss.

## 4391 LLOYD MINI H'CAP — 5f 193y
**8:50** (8:50) (F ) (0-55,54) 3-Y-O — **£3,234** (£924; £462) **Stalls** High

Form — RPR
0400 **1** **Dellagio (IRE)**[26] 3636 3-9-0 **50** ........ FNorton 2 57
(CADwyer) *in tch gng wl: hdwy to ld wl over 1f out: r.o u.p fnl f* **11/4**[2]
0043 **2** 1/2 **Bowling Along**[18] 3887 3-9-1 **54** ........ THamilton(3) 12 59
(MESowersby) *dwlt: sn midfield: hdwy 2f out: wnt 2nd ent fnl f: r.o u.p ins last: clsng on wnr fin* **5/2**[1]
0045 **3** 3 **Royal Nite Owl**[62] 2556 3-8-4 **40** ........ DAllan 6 36
(JO'Reilly) *cl up: rdn and ev ch 2f out: kpt on same pce* **8/1**
050 **4** 1 3/4 **From The North (IRE)**[29] 3562 3-8-13 **52** ........(v) ABeech(3) 5 43
(ADickman) *chsd ldrs: rdn and outpcd over 2f out: styd on fr over 1f out* **12/1**
-004 **5** hd **Royal Awakening (IRE)**[19] 3839 3-8-12 **51** ........ TEaves(3) 1 41
(REBarr) *rr div and sn drvn along: hdwy 2f out: styd on fnl f: nvr able to chal* **20/1**
4050 **6** 1/2 **Game Flora**[8] 4181 3-9-1 **54** ........ PMulrennan(3) 10 43
(MESowersby) *led tl hdd over 3f out: sn drvn along: fdd fnl 2f* **14/1**
2000 **7** nk **Leopard Creek**[9] 4132 3-9-0 **50** ........ SSanders 4 38
(MrsJRRamsden) *towards rr: sme hdwy u.p 2f out: no further prog fnl f* **5/1**[3]
00-0 **8** 1/2 **Louis Prima**[5] 4247 3-8-2 **38** ........ RFfrench 9 24
(MissLAPerratt) *cl up: led over 3f out: rdn and hdd wl over 1f out: sn btn* **33/1**
0040 **9** 1 1/4 **Aguilera**[19] 3836 3-8-4 **40** ........ VHalliday 11 23
(MDods) *rr div: drvn along over 2f out: sn btn* **33/1**
0-02 **10** 7 **Tiz Wiz**[95] 1719 3-8-7 **43** ........ JBramhill 7 5
(WStorey) *sn drvn along in rr* **9/1**
0650 **11** 1 1/2 **Lavish Times**[21] 3801 3-8-2 **43** ........ PPMathers(5) 8 —
(ABerry) *sn drvn along in rr* **14/1**
-000 **12** 1 1/4 **Yorke's Folly (USA)**[18] 3877 3-9-0 **50** ........ GFaulkner 3 3
(CWFairhurst) *chsd ldrs tl wknd 2f out: no ch whn eased ins last* **33/1**
1m 12.79s (-1.41) **Going Correction** -0.30s/f (Firm) **12** Ran SP% **127.6**
Speed ratings: **97,96,92,90,89 89,88,88,86,77 75,73**CSF £10.55 CT £50.96 TOTE £4.00: £1.40, £1.60, £3.40; EX 14.60 Place 6 £671.70, Place 5 £304.26.
**Owner** Mrs J Parvizi **Bred** Scuderia Toro **Trained** Newmarket, Suffolk
**FOCUS**
A moderate sprint handicap and the form is poor, although the first two came clear.
**NOTEBOOK**
**Dellagio(IRE)** produced by far his best display of the current campaign and won this a touch cosily. He has fallen over two stone in the weights since joining his new connections at the start of the season and, now he has found his form, should be able to build on this off a higher mark.
**Bowling Along** was staying on all too late in the day, and would have given the winner more to think about, but for losing ground at the start. She is best when dominating, looks to be coming right and deserves another chance in a similar event.
**Royal Nite Owl** dropped 6lb for this, lacked a change of gear under pressure when holding every chance. He is only plating class, but turned in an improved effort, and is entitled to improve on this.
**From The North(IRE)**, down 4lb in the ratings after her latest poor display, found this ground much more to her liking and was not disgraced in defeat.
**Leopard Creek**, with the headgear left off for this, again showed little and looks a moody character.
**Tiz Wiz** *Official explanation: jockey said filly was unsuited by the fast ground*
**Yorke's Folly(USA)** *Official explanation: jockey said filly lost her action*
T/Plt: £820.30 to a £1 stake. Pool: £41,015.90. 36.50 winning tickets. T/Qpdt: £31.50 to a £1 stake. Pool: £3,021.10. 70.90 winning tickets. JF

# 3950 RIPON (R-H)
Monday, August 2

**OFFICIAL GOING: Good to firm**
As in most meetings here, it was crucial to race on or close to the pace. Race times suggested the ground was easier than the official description.

## 4392 BBC RADIO YORK SANDIE DUNLEAVY EBF NOVICE STKS — 6f
**2:15** (2:15) (D ) 2-Y-O — **£5,387** (£1,657; £828; £414) **Stalls** Low

Form — RPR
120 **1** **Imperial Sound**[16] 3938 2-9-5 ........ SSanders 2 90+
(TDBarron) *mde all: shkn up wl over 1f out: sn clr* **2/9**[1]
0 **2** 5 **Wolf Hammer (USA)**[29] 3560 2-8-9 ........ PMulrennan(3) 3 63
(JHowardJohnson) *wnt rt s: sn trcking ldng pair: hdwy to chse wnr 4f out: rdn over 2f out: kpt on same pce* **25/1**
1250 **3** 3 1/2 **Unlimited**[7] 4186 2-9-0 ........ JFanning 1 55
(MrsADuffield) *chsd wnr: pushed along after 2f: rdn 1/2-way and sn outpcd* **20/1**[3]
**4** dist **Rockpiler** 2-8-8 ........ RWinston 4 —
(JHowardJohnson) *wnt rt s: a rr: nt striding out and virtually p.u fnl 2f* **11/2**[2]
1m 15.35s (2.45) **Going Correction** +0.325s/f (Good) **4** Ran SP% **105.8**
Speed ratings: **96,89,84,**—CSF £6.75 TOTE £1.20; EX 6.50.
**Owner** J Stephenson **Bred** R Burton **Trained** Maunby, N Yorks
**FOCUS**
An uncompetitive event in which the order hardly changed and the winner proved completely different class.
**NOTEBOOK**
**Imperial Sound**, tenth in the Weatherbys Super Sprint, was well backed despite opening at long odds-on. He found this somewhat easier and never had a moment's worry, whilst the extra furlong proved well within his compass. He looks worth another try in better company.
**Wolf Hammer(USA)**, dropping back a furlong and racing on much faster ground than on his debut, faced a very stiff task in taking on a decent sort such as the winner, but he was not disgraced and any further improvement on this should enable him to find a race at his own level.
**Unlimited** was struggling at halfway and seems to have gone backwards since showing fair form on Fibresand in his first two starts.
**Rockpiler**, a 300,000euros yearling and first foal of the useful sprinter Emma Peel, was expected to fare a good deal better than his stable companion according to the market, but he came out of the stalls sideways and hardly went a yard. He is surely capable of much better than this.

## 4393 BBC RADIO YORK COLIN HAZELDEN (S) H'CAP — 5f
**2:45** (2:45) (F ) (0-55,55) 3-Y-O — **£3,250** (£928; £464) **Stalls** Low

Form — RPR
3503 **1** **Rehia**[11] 4043 3-9-1 **52** ........ MHills 8 57
(JWHills) *a.p: hdwy to ld over 1f out: sn rdn and kpt on* **7/2**[1]
0020 **2** nk **Burkees Graw (IRE)**[20] 3820 3-8-8 **45** ........ RWinston 3 49
(MrsSLamyman) *trckd ldrs: hdwy 2f out: sn rdn and kpt on wl fnl f* **13/2**

5400 **3** 1 1/2 **Barras (IRE)**$^{26}$ 3636 3-9-1 **52**...(v) MFenton 4 50
(MissGayKelleway) *led: rdn along 2f out: hdd over 1f out: kpt on same pce* **4/1$^{2}$**

0000 **4** 3 1/2 **Designer City (IRE)**$^{33}$ 3410 3-8-2 **39**... FNorton 1 23
(ABerry) *towards rr: hdwy 2f out: sn rdn along and kpt on ins last: nt rch ldrs* **14/1**

006 **5** 1 **Bank Games**$^{10}$ 4097 3-8-8 **48**... PMulrennan$^{(3)}$ 2 28
(MWEasterby) *chsd ldrs: rdn along 2f out: kpt on same pce appr last* **6/1$^{3}$**

-560 **6** 3 **Scooby Dooby Do**$^{16}$ 3954 3-9-4 **55**...(p) VHalliday 6 23
(RMWhitaker) *in tch: sn rdn along: outpcd and bhd fr 1/2-way* **10/1**

3044 **7** 1 1/2 **Vaudevire**$^{35}$ 3364 3-8-2 **39**...(b) JFanning 7 1
(RPElliott) *cl up: rdn along 2f out: sn wknd* **13/2**

0000 **8** 1 1/4 **Gemini Girl (IRE)**$^{4}$ 4259 3-7-10 **36**...(v$^{1}$) NMackay$^{(3)}$ 5 —
(MDHammond) *a rr* **7/1**

0-00 **9** 6 **Rusty Boy**$^{17}$ 3892 3-7-8 **38**... DFentiman$^{(7)}$ 9 —
(ACrook) *prom on outer: rdn along 1/2-way: sn wknd* **50/1**

62.11 secs (1.91) **Going Correction** +0.325s/f (Good) **9** Ran SP% **113.4**
Speed ratings: **97,96,94,88,86 82,79,77,68**CSF £25.95 CT £93.72 TOTE £4.30: £1.60, £2.30, £2.10; EX 21.50.There was no bid for the winner.
**Owner** G And Mrs L Woodward **Bred** David John Brown **Trained** Upper Lambourn, Berks

**FOCUS**
A routine seller run at an average pace and, although the front three came clear, the form is poor.

**NOTEBOOK**
**Rehia** probably only needed to repeat her Bath effort to win this and managed to do so after having been given a positive ride, but she did not have much to spare at the line. Given her overall record, she is likely to struggle outside this grade.
**Burkees Graw(IRE)**, back under probably his best conditions, nearly pulled the race out of the fire but will need to find an equally modest event in order to double his winning record.
**Barras(IRE)**, back under similar conditions to those on which he gained his only previous win, was dropping in grade. He managed to get over to the stands' rail and made most of the running, but found the front pair too strong.
**Designer City(IRE)**, badly out of form this year and who bled last time, did not improve much for the drop into a seller.
**Bank Games**, unplaced in three maidens including two on Fibresand, did not improve for the switch to selling handicap company nor the drop to the minimum trip.

## 4394 ARMSTRONG MEMORIAL RATED STKS (H'CAP) 6f
**3:15** (3:15) (C ) (0-95,92) 3-Y-0+ **£10,499** (£3,982; £1,991; £905) **Stalls** Low

Form RPR

1345 **1** **Bygone Days**$^{37}$ 3309 3-8-9 **84**... MHills 1 98
(WJHaggas) *mde virtually all: rdn wl over 1f out: drvn ins last: jst hld on* **2/1$^{1}$**

5004 **2** shd **Inter Vision (USA)**$^{3}$ 4308 4-8-8 **79**... RWinston 2 93
(ADickman) *chsd ldrs: pushed along 1/2-way: hdwy 2f out: sn rdn and styng on whn edgd lft ins last: sn drvn and jst failed* **9/2$^{2}$**

0205 **3** 3 1/2 **Romany Nights (IRE)**$^{3}$ 4291 4-8-7 **81**...(b) SHitchcott$^{(3)}$ 4 85
(JWUnett) *chsd ldrs: hdwy 2f out: sn ridden and kpt on same pce fnl f* **6/1$^{3}$**

1200 **4** 5 **Bo McGinty (IRE)**$^{9}$ 4152 3-8-11 **86**... PHanagan 9 75
(RAFahey) *towards rr and rdn along after 2f: sme hdwy fnl 2f: nvr a factor* **8/1**

-100 **5** 1 1/4 **Bonne De Fleur**$^{30}$ 3523 3-9-1 **90**... DMcGaffin 6 75
(BSmart) *in tch: rdn along 1/2-way: drvn and wknd over 2f out* **33/1**

0000 **6** shd **Indian Spark**$^{9}$ 4152 10-8-9 **83**... NMackay$^{(3)}$ 8 67
(JSGoldie) *a towards rr* **16/1**

5100 **7** 1/2 **Times Review (USA)**$^{30}$ 3523 3-8-8 **83**... KDarley 7 66
(TDEasterby) *a towards rr* **33/1**

536- **8** nk **Impressive Flight (IRE)**$^{388}$ 3187 5-9-2 **92**... PMakin$^{(5)}$ 10 74
(TDBarron) *s.i.s: a bhd* **16/1**

0053 **9** 2 1/2 **Dame De Noche**$^{3}$ 4291 4-9-0 **85**... IMongan 3 60
(JGGiven) *cl up: rdn along 1/2-way: wknd over 2f out* **9/2$^{2}$**

1m 13.49s (0.59) **Going Correction** +0.325s/f (Good)
**WFA** 3 from 4yo+ 4lb **9** Ran SP% **112.7**
Speed ratings: **109,108,104,97,95 95,95,94,91**CSF £10.50 CT £43.81 TOTE £3.20: £1.10, £1.80, £1.90; EX 13.80 Trifecta £86.40 Pool: £1,498.33. 12.30 winning units..
**Owner** J Hanson **Bred** J A E Hobby **Trained** Newmarket, Suffolk

**FOCUS**
A race run at a cracking gallop with the winner and Dame De Noche taking each other on from the start. There was a decent gap between the second and fourth and the form looks solid, whilst the draw played its part with the front three coming from the four lowest stalls.

**NOTEBOOK**
**Bygone Days**, a consistent sort, had the perfect draw and made full use of it from the off. He managed to fend off the attentions of Dame De Noche some way out, but only just held off the runner-up and would have been beaten in another stride.
**Inter Vision(USA)** ◆ is running progressively better as he slips down the handicap, and so strongly was he finishing that he would have got up in another stride. He will not be long in winning.
**Romany Nights(IRE)** could never get on terms with the front pair despite doing his best, though he did pull right away from the fourth. The problem is that he finds himself back on a career-high mark despite having gone 26 races without a win.
**Bo McGinty(IRE)** never got into the race and seems to have gone off the boil for the time being. He may prefer easier ground.
**Bonne De Fleur** paid dearly for winning a weak Listed contest here in the spring, and needs to come down a good deal more in the weights yet. In any case her long-term future as a broodmare is assured.
**Impressive Flight(IRE)** lost all chance at the start. *Official explanation: jockey said mare missed the break*
**Dame De Noche** tried to match strides with the winner from the start and ultimately paid for it. *Official explanation: jockey said filly was unsuited by the going*

## 4395 TOMMY SHEDDEN CHALLENGE TROPHY H'CAP 1m 2f
**3:45** (3:47) (D ) (0-85,82) 3-Y-0 **£6,825** (£2,100; £1,050; £525) **Stalls** High

Form RPR

2401 **1** **Double Vodka (IRE)**$^{11}$ 4050 3-8-3 **64**... PHanagan 5 74
(MrsJRRamsden) *hld up: hdwy on inner over 2f out: swtchd lft and rdn ent last: styd on to ld last 50 yds* **9/4$^{1}$**

6051 **2** 1/2 **Rio De Jumeirah**$^{11}$ 4049 3-9-7 **82**... SSanders 6 91
(CEBrittain) *trckd ldrs: hdwy to chal over 2f out: rdn to ld over 1f out: drvn ins last: hdd and no ex last 50 yds* **13/2**

1301 **3** 2 1/2 **Futoo (IRE)**$^{14}$ 3981 3-8-0 **66**... BSwarbrick$^{(5)}$ 4 70
(GMMoore) *led: rdn along over 2f out: drvn and hdd over 1f out: kpt on same pce* **5/1**

0053 **4** 5 **Great Scott**$^{2}$ 4319 3-9-5 **80**... SChin 3 75
(MJohnston) *trckd ldrs: effrt 3f out: sn rdn along and btn wl over 1f out* **3/1$^{2}$**

3-41 **5** 1 3/4 **Game Dame**$^{42}$ 3142 3-9-3 **78**... MHills 1 69
(BWHills) *cl up: rdn along over 2f out: drvn and wknd over 1f out* **9/2$^{3}$**

6346 **6** 3 1/2 **Rosie Mac**$^{10}$ 4101 3-8-0 **61** ow2... FNorton 2 46
(NBycroft) *bhd fr 1/2-way* **14/1**

2m 7.93s (-0.07) **Going Correction** +0.225s/f (Good) **6** Ran SP% **110.6**
Speed ratings: **109,108,106,102,101 98**CSF £16.57 TOTE £2.80: £2.10, £2.70; EX 21.00.
**Owner** Mrs Alison Iles **Bred** Daphne Davison **Trained** Sandhutton, N Yorks

**FOCUS**
A decent handicap run at a sound pace and a smart time for the grade, 2.3 seconds faster than the later maiden. The first two are improvers.

**NOTEBOOK**
**Double Vodka(IRE)** was always travelling well and the only question was whether he would get a run. Pulled out in plenty of time, he quickened up nicely, which was just as well as the runner-up did not give up lightly. He had no problem seeing out the trip on this faster ground.
**Rio De Jumeirah**, raised 7lb for her Doncaster victory, ran a fine race on this faster ground and battled back well when the winner went past. She should not be long in winning again.
**Futoo(IRE)**, raised 3lb, attempted the same tactics as when successful on easier ground at Beverley, but this was a better race and he was unable to last home.
**Great Scott** was comfortably held, but he does look much better when able to dominate from the front.
**Game Dame** found life much tougher on this switch to handicap company and was struggling some way out.

## 4396 BLACK SHEEP BREWERY MAIDEN STKS 1m 2f
**4:15** (4:15) (D ) 3-Y-0+ **£4,461** (£1,372; £686; £343) **Stalls** High

Form RPR

0- **1** **Payola (USA)**$^{346}$ 4347 3-8-7... SSanders 3 69
(CEBrittain) *trckd ldrs: hdwy on outer 3f out: rdn along 2f out: styd on to ld over 1f out: drvn ins last: hld on wl* **13/2$^{2}$**

00 **2** 1/2 **Jidiya (IRE)**$^{3}$ 4306 5-9-7... IMongan 1 73?
(SGollings) *cl up: pushed along 3f out: rdn 2f out and ev ch: drvn ins last: no ex last 75 yds* **28/1$^{3}$**

022 **3** 4 **News Sky (USA)**$^{14}$ 3994 3-8-12 80... MHills 2 65
(BWHills) *led: rdn along over 2f out: hdd over 1f out: sn hrd drvn and wknd* **1/6$^{1}$**

00 **4** 12 **Rouge Et Noir**$^{17}$ 3899 6-9-0... NeilBrown$^{(7)}$ 6 43
(MrsMReveley) *hld up in tch: effrt 4f out: sn rdn along and nvr a factor* **28/1$^{3}$**

500 **5** 5 **Blue Nun**$^{69}$ 2392 3-8-7 47... JFanning 4 28
(MrsADuffield) *trckd ldrs on inner: rdn along 4f out: sn wknd* **100/1**

0-00 **6** dist **Alethea Gee**$^{17}$ 3896 6-8-13... TEaves$^{(3)}$ 5 —
(MrsMReveley) *a rr: bhd fnl 4f* **100/1**

2m 10.23s (2.23) **Going Correction** +0.225s/f (Good)
**WFA** 3 from 5yo+ 9lb **6** Ran SP% **107.9**
Speed ratings: **100,99,96,86,82** —CSF £79.23 TOTE £6.20: £2.10, £9.40; EX 85.90.
**Owner** Sheikh Marwan Al Maktoum **Bred** Darley **Trained** Newmarket, Suffolk

**FOCUS**
A modest maiden and a real shock with the long odds-on favourite finishing only third, and as a result the form is hard to assess. The time was modest for the grade though, 2.3 seconds slower than the earlier handicap.

**NOTEBOOK**
**Payola(USA)**, not seen since her racecourse debut 11 months ago, was brought widest with her effort and battled on gamely to score a shock victory. She still has scope for improvement, but with the red-hot favourite running so poorly it is probably better to measure this performance through the runner-up.
**Jidiya(IRE)**, winner of a bumper in his native Ireland, ran his best race under either code since coming here, especially as he was off the bridle some way out, and he never stopped trying. The form may not add up to much, but he has the option of going back over hurdles so there should be race of some sort in him.
**News Sky(USA)** should have beaten this bunch hollow, especially as he had the run of the race out in front, but he capitulated tamely when the front pair came to challenge. This was far too bad to be true. *Official explanation: trainer's representative had no explanation for the poor form shown*
**Rouge Et Noir** was quickly left behind, but he has finished runner-up in three bumpers so will probably be much better off over hurdles.

## 4397 CHILDREN'S DAY H'CAP 1m 4f 60y
**4:45** (4:45) (E ) (0-70,68) 3-Y-0+ **£3,746** (£1,152; £576; £288) **Stalls** High

Form RPR

1512 **1** **Hearthstead Dream**$^{18}$ 3881 3-9-5 **68**...(b) JFanning 8 77
(JDBethell) *trckd ldrs: smooth hdwy 4f out: led 21/2f out: rdn over 1f out and styd on strly ins last* **5/1$^{3}$**

5000 **2** 1 **Hernando's Boy**$^{16}$ 3561 3-8-4 **55** ow1... TEaves$^{(3)}$ 10 63
(MrsMReveley) *trckd ldrs: effrt and n.m.r on inner wl over 1f out: sn rdn and nt clr run ent last: styd on* **11/1**

0/15 **3** hd **Tiger Frog (USA)**$^{12}$ 4019 5-9-3 **62**...(b) DerekNolan$^{(7)}$ 4 69
(JMackie) *in tch: hdwy 4f out: effrt to chse wnr wl over 1f out: sn rdn and kpt on same pce fnl f* **3/1$^{1}$**

3531 **4** 1 1/4 **Shotley Dancer**$^{6}$ 4210 5-8-2 **40** 6ex... FNorton 9 45
(NBycroft) *hld up and bhd: hdwy on outer 3f out: rdn wl over 1f out: kpt on ins last: nrst fin* **4/1$^{2}$**

0215 **5** hd **Archirondel**$^{18}$ 3881 6-9-3 **58**... PMulrennan$^{(3)}$ 7 63
(MDHammond) *hld up and bhd: hdwy over 2f out: rdn to chse ldrs over 1f out: sn drvn and one pce* **13/2**

00/6 **6** 9 **All Bleevable**$^{17}$ 3608 7-8-7 **45**... RWinston 5 35
(MrsSLamyman) *prom: rdn along and wkng whn n.m.r on inner 3f out: sn bhd* **14/1**

0045 **7** 3/4 **Turftanzer (GER)**$^{41}$ 3165 5-7-12 **36** oh6...(t) KimTinkler 6 25
(DonEnricoIncisa) *led: rdn along 4f out: hdd 21/2f out and grad wknd* **28/1**

3520 **8** 7 **Dalriath**$^{6}$ 4210 5-7-8 **39**... DeanWilliams$^{(7)}$ 2 17
(MCChapman) *a rr* **16/1**

6000 **9** 2 1/2 **Zan Lo (IRE)**$^{6}$ 4210 4-8-13 **51**... MFenton 1 25
(BSRothwell) *chsd ldr: rdn along and wkng whn hung rt 3f out: sn bhd* **33/1**

6210 **10** 5 **Trusted Mole (IRE)**$^{31}$ 3492 6-9-1 **58**... BSwarbrick$^{(5)}$ 3 24
(WMBrisbourne) *in tch: effrt on outer 4f out: sn rdn along and wknd over 2f out* **8/1**

2m 41.6s (1.70) **Going Correction** +0.225s/f (Good)
**WFA** 3 from 4yo+ 11lb **10** Ran SP% **113.4**
Speed ratings: **103,102,102,101,101 95,94,90,88,85**CSF £56.98 CT £191.38 TOTE £4.70: £2.00, £3.20, £1.50; EX 62.50 Place 6 £53.92, Place 5 £42.87.
**Owner** S A B Dinsmore **Bred** G And Mrs Middlebrook **Trained** Middleham Moor, N Yorks

**FOCUS**
An ordinary but competitive little handicap but the early pace was nothing special. As a result not many got into the race from off the speed.

**NOTEBOOK**
**Hearthstead Dream** remains in good form. Never far away, he took over inside the last three furlongs and bravely held on from there to record his first win outside claiming company. He goes on any ground, but a rise in the handicap will leave him vulnerable.

**Hernando's Boy**, unplaced in seven previous outings on the Flat, was back on the level following a decent effort on his hurdling debut and carried the improvement back on to the Flat. He did not get the clearest of passages down the straight, but it would be hard to say it cost him victory. Nonetheless, he now seems to be getting it together and has the ability to win a race.
**Tiger Frog(USA)** ran another creditable race on the Flat considering he would have preferred a stronger gallop, but he was not alone there.
**Shotley Dancer**, who was actually racing off a 1lb lower mark than when successful at Beverley last time, did as well as could be expected considering she was trying to come from off the pace in a moderately-run race on a track that suits front runners.
**Archirondel** again did not have the race run to suit and his effort was never enough. Things will fall right for him again one day.
**All Bleevable**, who has shown very little in three previous outings on the Flat, has often made the running with some success over hurdles so it was surprising that not more use was made of him.
T/Plt: £189.50 to a £1 stake. Pool: £36,608.10. 141.00 winning tickets. T/Qpdt: £78.70 to a £1 stake. Pool: £1,883.20. 17.70 winning tickets. JR

## 4191 WINDSOR (R-H)
### Monday, August 2

**OFFICIAL GOING: Good to firm**
Wind: almost nil Weather: fine and very warm

## 4398 BOLLINGER CHAMPAGNE CHALLENGE SERIES H'CAP (FOR GENTLEMAN AMATEUR RIDERS) 1m 3f 135y
**6:05** (6:06) (E) (0-75,74) 3-Y-0+ **£3,513** (£1,081; £540; £270) **Stalls** Low

Form RPR
0111 **1** **Cristoforo (IRE)**[4] 4262 7-10-13 **66** MrDLQueally(7) 12 87+
(BJCurley) *s.s: sn rcvrd: jnd chsng gp 7f out: cruised up to ld over 1f out: easily* **5/4**[1]
0063 **2** *3* **Stolen Song**[7] 4196 4-10-8 **54** MrSWalker 14 62
(MJRyan) *wl plcd in chsng gp: pushed along over 3f out: led 2f out to over 1f out: no ch w wnr after* **11/2**[2]
-046 **3** *3/4* **Redi (ITY)**[50] 2915 3-10-10 **67** MrGArizkorreta 4 74
(LMCumani) *prom in chsng gp: rdn over 3f out: kpt on same pce u.p fnl 2f* **14/1**
016- **4** *1/2* **Precious Mystery (IRE)**[102] 5376 4-10-4 **57** MrGTumelty(7) 3 63
(AKing) *racd in midfield and off the pce by 1/2-way: pushed along 4f out: hung rt but kpt on fnl 2f: n.d* **20/1**
0441 **5** *hd* **Skylarker (USA)**[31] 3492 6-12-0 **74** MrLJefford 8 80
(WSKittow) *prom in chsng gp: pushed up to ld over 3f out: hdd and one pce 2f out* **11/1**[3]
0030 **6** *1 1/2* **Somayda (IRE)**[10] 4080 9-9-3 **42** oh2 JDoyle(7) 11 45
(MissJacquelineSDoyle) *pressed ldr and sn clr of rest: led 5f out: rdn and hdd over 3f out: kpt on u.p* **66/1**
2511 **7** *1 1/4* **Pont Neuf (IRE)**[7] 4196 4-11-2 **65** 5ex (t) MrLNewnes(3) 6 66+
(PDEvans) *s.s: hld up in rr: wl bhd 4f out: pushed along and kpt on fr over 2f out: no ch* **11/2**[2]
0-02 **8** *10* **Bhutan (IRE)**[20] 3827 9-9-11 **46** MrJJBest(3) 10 31
(GBBalding) *dwlt: hld up wl in rr: plenty to do over 3f out but gng wl enough : shkn up and fnd nil 2f out* **14/1**
50-0 **9** *hd* **Saddler's Quest**[16] 3929 7-10-11 **60** MrEDehdashti(3) 13 45
(BPJBaugh) *chsd clr ldng pair to 4f out: wknd u.p 3f out* **50/1**
4200 **10** *2* **Paso Doble**[10] 4086 6-10-2 **55** MrJMillman(7) 9 37
(BRMillman) *a off the pce and wl in rr: rdn and struggling 4f out* **33/1**
45-0 **11** *1 3/4* **Betterware Boy**[9] 4129 4-11-7 **72** MrJMorgan(5) 2 51
(PMPhelan) *nvr on terms w ldrs: rdn in midfield and no ch over 3f out* **33/1**
24-0 **12** *2* **Dramatic Quest**[10] 4086 7-11-8 **73** ow3 (p) MrMichaelMurphy(5) 5 49
(IanWilliams) *nvr on terms: bmpd along towards rr and no ch over 3f out* **20/1**
0/00 **13** *10* **Jalons Star (IRE)**[4] 4262 6-10-6 **57** MrMWalford(5) 1 17
(MRChannon) *led and clr w one rival: hdd 5f out: ev ch over 3f out: wknd rapidly* **50/1**
510/ **14** *23* **Dr Cool**[647] 5458 7-11-2 **69** MrSGascoyne(7) 7 —
(JAkehurst) *s.s: a wl in rr: wl bhd in last pair 4f out: eased fnl 2f: t.o* **33/1**

2m 28.33s (-1.77) **Going Correction** -0.075s/f (Good)
**WFA** 3 from 4yo+ 11lb **14** Ran SP% **120.6**
Speed ratings: **102,100,99,99,99 98,97,90,90,89 87,86,79,64**CSF £6.94 CT £69.83 TOTE £2.40: £1.60, £1.50, £5.20; EX 12.60.
**Owner** P Byrne **Bred** Bill Dwan And Tom Lynch **Trained** Newmarket, Suffolk
■ The first winner for Declan Queally, 16-year-old brother of Tom Queally who won on Cristoforo at Epsom last week.

**FOCUS**
A moderate amateurs' handicap in which Jalons Star and Somayda went off rather fast in front and were largely ignored by the rest of the field. However, this resulted in a decent time and the winner is value for more than the official margin.

**NOTEBOOK**
**Cristoforo(IRE)** had no problem making it eight wins from his last nine Flat starts, without including a victory in a charity race at Newbury. Unpenalised for landing an apprentice event last week, he was settled well off the pace and came through to win with a great deal in hand under his inexperienced rider. He can score again on the level, although may be switched back to hurdles now.
**Stolen Song** had no chance with the favourite once headed but did stick on. He reversed recent course form with Pont Neuf on these revised terms.
**Redi(ITY)** ran a better race over this more suitable trip, and there could be a little more improvement in him.
**Precious Mystery(IRE)**, last seen in action over hurdles in April, stayed on in the last quarter-mile and this should have blown away any cobwebs.
**Skylarker(USA)**, from a 5lb higher mark, was collared with two to run and had nothing more to offer under his welter burden.
**Somayda(IRE)** kept on quite well considering she and one other had gone off pretty fast.
**Pont Neuf(IRE)**, bidding for a hat-trick over course and distance, made late headway from the back of the field but was never in the hunt.
**Dramatic Quest** *Official explanation: jockey said gelding lost its action*
**Jalons Star(IRE)**Jalons Star and Somayda went off too fast and the remainder let them go.

## 4399 EUROPEAN BREEDERS FUND MAIDEN FILLIES' STKS 6f
**6:35** (6:38) (D) 2-Y-O **£5,447** (£1,676; £838; £419) **Stalls** High

Form RPR
04 **1** **Apple Of My Eye**[14] 3992 2-8-11 WRyan 16 79
(JRJenkins) *racd in midfield: trckd ldrs and nt clr run 2f out: led jst over 1f out: rdn and edgd lft fnl f: styd on wl* **14/1**
**2** *1* **Amica** 2-8-11 RLMoore 8 76
(GLMoore) *dwlt: rn green in last and wl off the pce: gd prog fr 2f out: styd on wl to take 2nd wl ins fnl f* **50/1**
**3** *3/4* **Flying Dancer** 2-8-11 JDSmith 13 74
(AKing) *rn green towards rr and pushed along: prog 2f out: styd on fnl f: nrst fin* **8/1**
64 **4** *1 1/2* **Casterossa**[9] 4137 2-8-11 PaulEddery 7 69
(DHaydnJones) *trckd ldr: led wl over 1f out to jst over 1f out: fdd ins fnl f* **16/1**
0 **5** *1 1/4* **Caona (USA)**[10] 4074 2-8-11 EAhern 14 65
(JNoseda) *prom: drvn 2f out: ev ch jst over 1f out: fdd fnl f* **7/1**[3]
0 **6** *1/2* **Night Out (FR)**[16] 3950 2-8-11 DHolland 12 64
(GCBravery) *chsd ldrs: rdn 2f out: u.p but ch jst over 1f out: fdd* **33/1**
**7** *shd* **Zonic** 2-8-11 BDoyle 1 63
(SirMichaelStoute) *v s.i.s and wnt lft s: racd in rr: sme prog 2f out: nt clr run ins fnl f: styd on* **14/1**
**8** *nk* **Red Finesse** 2-8-11 PRobinson 5 63
(MAJarvis) *racd on outer: trckd ldrs: rdn and unable qck 2f out: btn over 1f out* **2/1**[1]
5 **9** *1 1/2* **Blazing View (USA)**[28] 3588 2-8-11 WSupple 3 58
(EALDunlop) *racd in midfield: rdn and no prog over 2f out* **4/1**[2]
**10** *3 1/2* **Gramada (IRE)** 2-8-11 SDrowne 4 48
(MJWallace) *a towards rr: struggling over 2f out* **25/1**
4 **11** *1/2* **Veritable**[81] 2058 2-8-11 JFEgan 2 46
(SKirk) *led to wl over 1f out: wknd rapidly fnl f* **12/1**
**12** *1* **Lighted Way** 2-8-6 NChalmers(5) 15 43
(AMBalding) *dwlt: sn rcvrd and prom: wknd over 2f out* **25/1**
**13** *3* **Night Club Queen (IRE)** 2-8-11 TQuinn 10 34
(JWHills) *a in rr: rdn and struggling 1/2-way* **20/1**

1m 14.69s (0.82) **Going Correction** +0.025s/f (Good) **13** Ran SP% **121.2**
Speed ratings: **95,93,92,90,89 88,88,87,85,81 80,79,75**CSF £601.23 TOTE £14.10: £3.70, £15.00, £2.70; EX 544.70.
**Owner** R B Hill **Bred** The Buy And Sell Partnership **Trained** Royston, Herts

**FOCUS**
Only a fair maiden with the fourth providing the level of the form.

**NOTEBOOK**
**Apple Of My Eye** burst through to lead when a gap opened and soon had the race sewn up, although she might have struck the front a little soon and her lead was being reduced near the line. The race in which she finished fourth here last time is working out.
**Amica**, who makes little appeal on breeding, stayed on well from the back of the field and obviously has ability, although she held an alternative entry in a sand seller this week which tempers enthusiasm for her prospects.
**Flying Dancer** is out of a decent sprint handicapper, runner-up in both the Wokingham and the Ayr Gold Cup, who has produced three juvenile winners. She was doing her best work at the finish and will know what is required of her next time.
**Casterossa** had been outpaced after a slow start on her previous outing but had learnt from that and showed plenty of pace to go with the leaders. Nurseries are an option now.
**Caona(USA)** showed more than she had on her debut at Ascot but is beginning to look an expensive buy at 170,000 gns.
**Night Out(FR)** kept on in a manner which suggests she will get seven furlongs in time.
**Zonic**, who found herseft at the back of the field after missing the break, was in the process of staying on when running out of room inside the final furlong. A half-sister to three winners, notably Injaaz, she should be capable of better.
**Red Finesse** is a half-sister to last year's juvenile winner Rising Shadow. She failed to pick up after travelling well but was not helped by having to deliver her challenge on the outside.
**Blazing View(USA)**, backed down from 7/1, did not improve on her debut effort.

## 4400 LIVE VIDEO ON WWW.ATTHERACES.CO.UK H'CAP 5f 10y
**7:05** (7:07) (E) (0-70,69) 3-Y-0+ **£3,493** (£1,075; £537; £268) **Stalls** High

Form RPR
3444 **1** **Davids Mark**[51] 2885 4-8-9 **50** LDettori 11 59
(JRJenkins) *mde all and sn racd against nr side rail: drvn and hrd pressed fnl f: jst hld on* **11/2**[3]
3661 **2** *shd* **Double M**[5] 4232 7-9-5 **65** 7ex (v) RThomas(5) 6 74
(MrsLRichards) *hld up towards rr: nt clr run briefly 2f out: prog over 1f out: str chal ins fnl f: jst failed* **9/2**[2]
0423 **3** *nk* **Loch Inch**[3] 4308 7-8-11 **52** (b) RLMoore 16 60+
(JMBradley) *racd in rr: nt clr run 2f out: prog wl over 1f out: drvn to chal ins fnl f: nt qckn nr fin* **7/2**[1]
0000 **4** *1 1/2* **Yorkies Boy**[10] 4085 9-8-0 **48** (p) MHalford(7) 13 51
(NEBerry) *racd in rr: nt clr run fr over 2f out to over 1f out: r.o ins fnl f: nrst fin* **20/1**
5300 **5** *nk* **Pulse**[21] 3810 6-9-5 **60** (p) DHolland 8 62
(JMBradley) *prom gng wl: trckd wnr wl over 1f out: rdn and edgd lft jst over 1f out: fnd nil* **14/1**
1302 **6** *2 1/2* **Harbour House**[29] 3558 5-8-5 **46** ADaly 4 39
(JJBridger) *s.i.s: mostly last: rdn and nt clr run 2f out: styd on fnl f: n.d* **16/1**
4150 **7** *hd* **Blessed Place**[5] 4232 4-8-10 **51** TQuinn 12 43
(DJSFfrenchDavis) *trckd ldrs: rdn and effrt over 1f out: wknd ins fnl f* **9/1**
0005 **8** *3/4* **Erracht**[12] 4025 6-9-6 **61** GBaker 7 50
(MrsHSweeting) *racd towards outer: chsd ldrs: lost pl 2f out: effrt again over 1f out: wknd fnl f* **20/1**
2002 **9** *1 1/2* **Ballinger Express**[7] 4194 4-9-7 **62** (b) MartinDwyer 2 46
(AMBalding) *racd on outer: chsd ldrs: wl in tch over 1f out: sn wknd* **14/1**
4000 **10** *shd* **Intellibet One**[5] 4232 4-8-13 **54** NCallan 14 37
(PDEvans) *trckd ldrs: rdn to chal 2f out: n.m.r sn after: lost pl and btn over 1f out* **11/1**
0145 **11** *shd* **Avit (IRE)**[10] 4085 4-7-12 **39** oh1 AMcCarthy 15 22
(PLGilligan) *prom: u.p 2f out: wknd over 1f out* **10/1**
0000 **12** *3/4* **Tripti (IRE)**[99] 1642 4-8-5 **49** JFMcDonald(3) 9 29
(JJBridger) *racd towards rr: rdn whn nt clr run 2f out: no prog* **33/1**
0041 **13** *1/2* **Tender (IRE)**[12] 4025 4-8-11 **52** (p) SDrowne 5 30
(MrsStefLiddiard) *racd towards outer: chsd ldrs tl wknd over 1f out* **16/1**
-500 **14** *1/2* **Flapdoodle**[10] 4085 6-8-7 **48** TPQueally 3 25
(AWCarroll) *chsd ldrs tl wknd rapidly over 1f out* **20/1**
6664 **15** *2 1/2* **Mirasol Princess**[11] 4043 3-9-11 **69** DaneO'Neill 1 37
(DKIvory) *racd on wd outside: wl in tch tl wknd over 1f out* **20/1**
3000 **16** *2* **Catchthebatch**[35] 3378 8-8-6 **47** SCarson 10 7
(EAWheeler) *mostly chsd wnr to 2f out: wknd* **33/1**

60.67 secs (-0.53) **Going Correction** -0.075s/f (Good)
**WFA** 3 from 4yo+ 3lb **16** Ran SP% **133.2**
Speed ratings: **101,100,100,97,97 93,93,91,89,89 89,88,87,86,82 79**CSF £30.08 CT £108.71 TOTE £7.50: £1.90, £1.90, £1.50, £6.10; EX 48.30.
**Owner** Miss C Roylance **Bred** D Lowe **Trained** Royston, Herts

**FOCUS**
An ordinary sprint handicap in which a high draw was favoured. The form looks solid enough for the grade.

**NOTEBOOK**
**Davids Mark** travelled well against the rail and Dettori only went for his whip approaching the furlong pole. Just holding the runner-up's late burst, he relished the quick ground.
**Double M**, penalised for his win at Glorious Goodwood, only just failed to follow up. He was looking for room in the straight but finished strongly down the centre of the track when in the clear. The draw beat him as much as anything.
**Loch Inch** was well drawn, but found himself behind horses on the rail once in line for home. Following the winner through, he ran on but could not quite get his head in front. He is on a handy mark now and this is his time of year.
**Yorkies Boy** ran his best race since joining this yard, albeit from a favourable draw. His last win, back in May 2001, was off a mark of 100 which shows how much he has deteriorated, but there could still be another win in him.
**Pulse** travelled well but did not pick up when push came to shove.
**Harbour House** was slow to go but made good headway under pressure. He is still in good heart.
**Blessed Place**, without the tongue tie this time, has been held three times off this mark since winning here last month.

## 4401 SLOUGH ESTATES H'CAP — 1m 67y
7:35 (7:35) (D) (0-85,85) 3-Y-O+ — £5,492 (£1,690; £845; £422) Stalls High

| Form | | | | RPR |
|---|---|---|---|---|
| 5124 | 1 | | **Fen Gypsy**[19] [3841] 6-8-12 **65** .... NCallan 6 *(PDEvans) cl up: rdn over 2f out: led over 1f out: hrd drvn fnl f: hld on* **13/2**[3] | 73 |
| 6430 | 2 | nk | **Nautical**[5] [4238] 6-7-13 **52** oh1 ow1 .... CCatlin 4 *(AWCarroll) dwlt: t.k.h and hld up: prog 3f out: hrd rdn to chal fnl f: nt qckn nr fin* **20/1** | 59 |
| 0-05 | 3 | hd | **Rafferty (IRE)**[11] [4067] 5-10-0 **81** .... DHolland 1 *(CEBrittain) hld up in rr: effrt over 2f out: hrd rdn over 1f out: styd on ins fnl f: nt rch ldng pair* **7/2**[2] | 88 |
| 5020 | 4 | 1 1/4 | **Johannian**[19] [3844] 6-9-4 **71** .... RLMoore 7 *(JMBradley) prom: led over 2f out to over 1f out: nt qckn and btn fnl f* **12/1** | 75 |
| 1011 | 5 | 3 | **A One (IRE)**[7] [4192] 5-10-1 **85** 6ex .... FPFerris(3) 8 *(HJManners) led to over 2f out: sn lost pl and btn: kpt on again nr fin* **9/4**[1] | 82 |
| 1364 | 6 | 1/2 | **Maclean**[8] [4171] 3-9-3 **77** .... (v) LDettori 5 *(SirMichaelStoute) trckd ldr: ev ch over 2f out: nt qckn over 1f out: eased whn btn* **7/2**[2] | 73 |
| 00-0 | 7 | 1/2 | **Barrantes**[10] [4090] 7-9-7 **79** .... NChalmers(5) 2 *(MissSheenaWest) trckd ldrs: lost pl over 2f out: hanging lft and nt qckn over 1f out: wknd fnl f* **25/1** | 74 |
| 4650 | U | | **Jools**[8] [4164] 6-9-9 **76** .... TQuinn 3 *(DKIvory) hld up: 6th whn slipped and uns rdr over 4f out* **11/1** | — |

1m 43.85s (-1.75) **Going Correction** -0.075s/f (Good)
**WFA** 3 from 5yo+ 7lb — **8** Ran SP% **113.2**
Speed ratings: **105,104,104,103,100 99,99,**—CSF £117.49 CT £528.10 TOTE £7.60: £1.80, £3.80, £1.60; EX 178.40.
**Owner** P D Evans **Bred** Juddmonte Farms **Trained** Pandy, Gwent

**FOCUS**
Quite a competitive little handicap and, although the time was reasonable, the form does not look particularly solid.

**NOTEBOOK**
**Fen Gypsy**, off the same mark as when runner-up at Chester two starts ago, showed a willing attitude under pressure. This extended mile is as far as he wants to go.
**Nautical**, whose rider put up a pound overweight, travelled well, if a little keenly, and went down narrowly. He gave the impression that some headgear might have a positive effect, having worn a visor on his racecourse debut in the UAE back in 2001.
**Rafferty(IRE)** was without the blinkers he has been wearing of late. At the back of the field when obliged to sidestep the fallen jockey with over half a mile to run, he was staying on well in the final furlong but the line was always going to beat him. He can be counted as a little unlucky.
**Johannian** is certainly weighted to win off this sort of mark but is proving unable to get his head in front, although it is not for want of trying.
**A One(IRE)** was rated no less than 34lb higher than when successful in a claimer in June. Although his winning run came to a halt, he was keeping on again near the line over a trip short of his best and it could pay to give him another chance if he is freshened up by a break.
**Maclean** again looked less than enthusiastic about exerting himself.

## 4402 ROUSE & CO MAIDEN STKS — 1m 2f 7y
8:05 (8:06) (D) 3-Y-O — £4,290 (£1,320; £660; £330) Stalls Low

| Form | | | | RPR |
|---|---|---|---|---|
| 2- | 1 | | **Poise (IRE)**[318] [5040] 3-8-9 .... LDettori 6 *(SirMichaelStoute) t.k.h early: trckd ldng pair: pushed into ld wl over 1f out: drew clr fnl f: comf* **1/3**[1] | 87+ |
| 4326 | 2 | 5 | **Michabo (IRE)**[19] [3843] 3-9-0 78 .... DaneO'Neill 9 *(DRCElsworth) led: rdn over 2f out: hdd wl over 1f out: kpt on but no ch w wnr* **10/1**[3] | 77 |
| -605 | 3 | 3 | **Laabbij (USA)**[70] [2361] 3-9-0 75 .... (b[1]) MartinDwyer 4 *(MPTregoning) dwlt: rcvrd to chse ldng trio after 3f: rdn over 2f out: outpcd wl over 1f out: one pce after* **8/1**[2] | 71 |
| | 4 | 2 1/2 | **Pleasant** 3-8-9 .... JFEgan 8 *(LGCottrell) rn green in last: wl bhd 1/2-way: sme prog 3f out: pushed along and kpt on fnl 2f* **33/1** | 61 |
| 0 | 5 | 2 | **Celebre Citation (IRE)**[112] [1371] 3-9-0 .... (t) OUrbina 3 *(JRFanshawe) hld up in tch: shuffled along over 2f out: sn outpcd* **16/1** | 62 |
| 00 | 6 | nk | **Ceylon Round (FR)**[7] [4195] 3-8-6 .... DCorby(3) 7 *(MJWallace) chsd ldr to over 2f out: wknd over 1f out* **33/1** | 57 |
| | 7 | 1 1/4 | **Stage Secret (IRE)** 3-9-0 .... SDrowne 2 *(MissECLavelle) t.k.h: hld up in midfield: effrt 3f out: rdn 2f out: wknd over 1f out* **25/1** | 60 |
| | 8 | 17 | **One Of Distinction** 3-8-9 .... WSupple 1 *(EALDunlop) hld up in rr: wknd 3f out: wl bhd fnl 2f* **16/1** | 22 |
| | 9 | 19 | **Its My Son** 3-9-0 .... ADaly 5 *(LGCottrell) a in rr: wknd 3f out: t.o* **33/1** | — |

2m 7.13s (-1.17) **Going Correction** -0.075s/f (Good) — **9** Ran SP% **119.7**
Speed ratings: **101,97,94,92,91 90,89,76,60**CSF £4.70 TOTE £1.40: £1.10, £1.90, £2.50; EX 3.50.
**Owner** Cheveley Park Stud **Bred** Strawhill Farm **Trained** Newmarket, Suffolk

**FOCUS**
A fair maiden but easy pickings for the highly-regarded Poise, who had little to beat and should rate higher.

**NOTEBOOK**
**Poise(IRE)** was once thought of as an Oaks filly, but she has been slow to come to hand. She was much too classy for this opposition and it would be no surprise to see her shooting for some black type sooner rather than later.
**Michabo(IRE)** settled satisfactorily in front but carried his head a little high when collared. He was no match for the filly but was easily second best.
**Laabbij(USA)** wore first-time blinkers back in maiden company for this first run in over two months. He was merely best of the rest and a mark in the 70s will not help him back in handicaps..
**Pleasant** is the first foal of a winning hurdler who was placed twice on the Flat over ten furlongs. This was a nice introduction but she is likely to need more time.
**Celebre Citation(IRE)**, off the track since his debut in April, was equipped with a tongue strap. He needs one more run for a mark.
**Ceylon Round(FR)** is now eligible for handicaps. A step back in trip may suit her.
**One Of Distinction** is a half-sister to mile winners Man Of Distinction and Him Of Distinction out of a mare who won the Group Three Anglesey Stakes as a juvenile. She was always struggling at the back of the field on this debut.

## 4403 COME RACING THIS SUNDAY FAMILY FUN DAY H'CAP — 6f
8:35 (8:37) (E) (0-70,70) 3-Y-O+ — £3,649 (£1,123; £561; £280) Stalls High

| Form | | | | RPR |
|---|---|---|---|---|
| 2000 | 1 | | **Michelle Ma Belle (IRE)**[11] [4067] 4-10-0 **70** .... (b) JFEgan 6 *(SKirk) hld up in midfield: prog on wd outside fr 1/2-way: led over 1f out: drvn and styd on wl* **25/1** | 82 |
| 2000 | 2 | 1 | **Full Spate**[10] [4083] 9-9-10 **66** .... RLMoore 18 *(JMBradley) trckd ldrs: rdn 2f out: hanging lft 1f out: styd on fnl f to take 2nd nr fin* **8/1**[3] | 75 |
| 0236 | 3 | nk | **Jagged (IRE)**[2] [4336] 4-8-13 **55** .... (v) LDettori 14 *(JRJenkins) trckd ldrs: effrt 2f out: rdn and nt qckn over 1f out: styd on same pce fnl f* **11/2**[2] | 63 |
| 4122 | 4 | nk | **High Ridge**[3] [4291] 5-9-13 **69** .... (p) DaneO'Neill 13 *(JMBradley) racd in last pair: swtchd to outside and prog 2f out: drvn and styd on fnl f: nrst fin* **9/4**[1] | 76+ |
| 5000 | 5 | hd | **B A Highflyer**[57] [2703] 4-9-2 **58** .... CCatlin 5 *(MRChannon) racd towards rr: hrd rdn and prog on outer 2f out: styd on u.str.p fnl f* **25/1** | 65 |
| 3631 | 6 | 1/2 | **Adantino**[16] [3935] 5-9-1 **57** .... (b) TPQueally 16 *(BRMillman) trckd ldrs: rdn to chal and ev ch over 1f out: one pce* **11/2**[2] | 62 |
| 0000 | 7 | 3/4 | **Mayzin (IRE)**[2] [4336] 4-8-7 **49** .... (p) EAhern 15 *(RMFlower) w ldr to over 1f out: one pce ins fnl f* **20/1** | 52 |
| 1536 | 8 | nk | **Aintnecessarilyso**[12] [4034] 6-8-6 **55** .... MHalford(7) 12 *(NEBerry) racd in rr: rdn over 2f out: kpt on fr over 1f out: n.d* **10/1** | 57 |
| 0500 | 9 | 3/4 | **Warlingham (IRE)**[7] [4199] 6-9-0 **56** .... SDrowne 10 *(PHowling) a in midfield: shkn up and no imp ldrs over 1f out* **25/1** | 56 |
| 0006 | 10 | nk | **Pink Supreme**[20] [3817] 3-8-6 **52** ow1 .... NCallan 3 *(IAWood) a in midfield: rdn and swtchd lft over 1f out: no prog* **50/1** | 51 |
| 0001 | 11 | 1/2 | **Threezedzz**[10] [4083] 6-8-12 **61** .... (t) SJDonohoe(7) 4 *(PDEvans) pressed ldrs tl wknd 1f out* **16/1** | 58 |
| 5010 | 12 | 1 1/4 | **Firework**[25] [3663] 6-9-6 **62** .... (p) DHolland 19 *(JAkehurst) mde most to over 1f out: wkng whn n.m.r ins fnl f* **8/1**[3] | 55 |
| 0505 | 13 | shd | **Formalise**[23] [3747] 4-8-10 **57** .... RThomas(5) 11 *(GBBalding) restless in stalls: wnt rt s: racd in midfield: lost pl and btn over 1f out* **20/1** | 50 |
| 0203 | 14 | 3/4 | **Semper Paratus (USA)**[35] [3381] 5-8-12 **54** .... (b) MTebbutt 2 *(VSmith) detached in last and sn pushed along: nvr a factor* **33/1** | 45 |
| 000- | 15 | 1/2 | **Nathan Detroit**[247] [6094] 4-9-0 **56** .... DSweeney 17 *(PJMakin) outpcd and a in last trio* **33/1** | 45 |
| -041 | 16 | 1 1/2 | **Woodbury**[12] [4026] 5-9-6 **62** .... GBaker 9 *(MrsHSweeting) chsd ldrs to 2f out: wknd over 1f out* **20/1** | 47 |
| 0203 | 17 | nk | **Night Cap (IRE)**[51] [2885] 5-8-1 **46** ow3 .... RMiles(3) 7 *(TDMccarthy) prom: wkng whn sltly hmpd over 1f out* **12/1** | 30 |

1m 13.35s (-0.52) **Going Correction** +0.025s/f (Good)
**WFA** 3 from 4yo+ 4lb — **17** Ran SP% **140.1**
Speed ratings: **104,102,102,101,101 100,99,99,98,98 97,95,95,94,94 92,91**CSF £219.51 CT £1354.00 TOTE £24.80: £4.40, £2.30, £1.70, £1.40; EX 256.70 Place 6 £119.89, Place 5 £85.06.

**Owner** Bill Allan & Mrs Michelle Cousins **Bred** Snowdrop Stud Co Ltd **Trained** Upper Lambourn, Berks

**FOCUS**
An ordinary sprint handicap which produced a good gallop and the form looks sound.

**NOTEBOOK**
**Michelle Ma Belle(IRE)** defied topweight and a modest draw to score on her second run in blinkers. The change to hold-up tactics clearly made a difference.
**Full Spate**, who likes it here, ran well from a favourable draw, but despite some solid recent efforts he is without a win this term and the handicapper looks to have his measure.
**Jagged(IRE)** keeps running well but that first win remains elusive. It could be that he needs to be produced late.
**High Ridge**, only a pound higher than when runner-up at Glorious Goodwood, remains in good form.
**B A Highflyer**, returning from a break, was a pound lower than when last getting his head in front and this was a decent run.
**Adantino** needs everything to fall right and was held off a 3lb higher mark.
T/Jkpt: Not won. T/Plt: £120.80 to a £1 stake. Pool: £65,143.00. 393.40 winning tickets. T/Qpdt: £9.00 to a £1 stake. Pool: £4,849.20. 396.70 winning tickets. JN

# 4106 CORK (R-H)
Monday, August 2

**OFFICIAL GOING: Sprint course - firm; remainder - good to firm (firm in places)**

## 4405a KING CHARLEMAGNE PLATINUM STKS (LISTED RACE) — 1m
3:10 (3:10) 3-Y-O+ — £27,507 (£8,070; £3,845; £1,309)

| | | | RPR |
|---|---|---|---|
| 1 | | **Caradak (IRE)**[6] [4225] 3-9-0 .... MJKinane 3 *(JohnMOxx, Ire) trckd ldr in 2nd: dropped to 3rd fr under 5f out: rdn to chal in 2nd fr under 2f out: led over 1f out: styd on wl fnl f* **9/4**[2] | 110+ |
| 2 | 1 1/2 | **One More Round (USA)**[15] [3967] 6-9-7 109 .... PJSmullen 1 *(DKWeld, Ire) led: hdd fr 5f out: led again under 2f out: strly pressed and hdd over 1f out: kpt on same pce u.p fnl f* **8/13**[1] | 107 |
| 3 | 2 1/2 | **Shersha (IRE)**[9] [4159] 5-9-4 98 .... NGMcCullagh 4 *(SJTreacy, Ire) rr: rdn fr over 2f out: no imp fr 1 1/2f out: kpt on wout threatening into 3rd fnl f* **5/1**[3] | 98 |
| 4 | 3 | **Peace Offering (IRE)**[36] [3351] 4-9-7 98 .... JPSpencer 2 *(DeclanGillespie, Ire) trckd ldrs: impr to ld fr under 5f out: strly pressed and hdd under 2f out: no ex and dropped to last ins fnl f: eased cl h* **12/1** | 94 |

1m 36.8s
**WFA** 3 from 4yo+ 7lb — **4** Ran SP% **117.0**
Speed ratings: CSF £4.48 TOTE £3.80; DF 4.30.
**Owner** H H Aga Khan **Bred** H H Aga Khan's Studs S C **Trained** Currabeg, Co Kildare

**NOTEBOOK**
**Caradak(IRE)** was impressive when winning his maiden at Galway six days earlier and beat these older rivals very smoothly. His trainer rates him highly and he will be stepping up into Group company next.
**One More Round(USA)** should have dealt with a maiden winner on these terms and it looks as if his 109 rating rather flatters him. He has not won since September 2002 and, although this looked like a spot of clever placing, he came up against something of a tartar.
**Shersha(IRE)** possibly finds this trip a bit too far.
**Peace Offering(IRE)** has not won since his two-year-old days.

## 4406a IRISH STALLION FARMS EUROPEAN BREEDERS FUND GIVE THANKS STKS (LISTED RACE) (F&M) 1m 4f
3:40 (3:40) 3-Y-0+ **£32,091** (£9,415; £4,485; £1,528)

RPR
1 **My Renee (USA)**68 2416 4-9-10 103 NGMcCullagh 2 107
(MJGrassick, Ire) *trckd ldrs: t.k.h early: rdn to ld 1 1/2f out: strly pressed and hdd briefly over 1f out: sn in front again: styd on wl fnl* **4/1**3
2 *nk* **Tarakala (IRE)**47 2993 3-8-10 98 (b1) MJKinane 1 104
(JohnMOxx, Ire) *chsd ldrs: mainly 5th: rdn to chal and briefly in front over 1f out: kpt on same pce u.p fnl f* **7/2**2
3 1 1/2 **Kisses For Me (IRE)**15 3969 3-8-10 99 JPSpencer 6 101
(APO'Brien, Ire) *trckd ldrs: mainly 4th: swtchd to outer and rdn fr 1 1/2f out: 3rd and kpt on same pce wout rching ldrs fnl f* **11/4**1
4 3/4 **Leonor Fini (IRE)**15 3969 3-8-10 97 DPMcDonogh 5 100
(KevinPrendergast, Ire) *rr: rdn fr under 2f out: kpt on wl wout threatening fr over 1f out* **8/1**
5 3 **Rich Sense (USA)**5 4252 3-8-10 92 PJSmullen 4 95
(DKWeld, Ire) *trckd ldr in 2nd: rdn to chal and on terms fr early st: no ex u.p fr 1 1/2f out* **11/2**
6 1/2 **Valentina Guest (IRE)**19 3862 3-8-10 99 JAHeffernan 8 94
(PeterCasey, Ire) *racd mainly in 6th: rdn and kpt on same pce u.p fr 1 1/2f out* **11/2**
7 2 1/2 **Somethingforsunday (IRE)**6 4222 4-9-7 88 (t) RMBurke 7 90
(MissITOakes, Ire) *sn led: strly pressed fr early st: hdd over 1 1/2f out: sn no ex* **20/1**

2m 34.7s
**WFA** 3 from 4yo 11lb 7 Ran SP% **115.5**
Speed ratings: CSF £18.78 TOTE £5.10: £2.60, £2.10; DF 17.90.
**Owner** Miss P F O'Kelly **Bred** Kilcarn Stud **Trained** Pollardstown, Co Kildare

**NOTEBOOK**
**My Renee(USA)** repelled all challenges, coming back for more each time and finally asserting well inside the last.
**Tarakala(IRE)**, blinkered for the first time, was duelling with the winner from over a furlong out but had to concede inside the last half furlong.
**Kisses For Me(IRE)** found traffic problems with less than two furlongs to race, picked up nicely after being switched, but found only the one pace inside the last. She might have preferred a bit of give in the ground.
**Leonor Fini(IRE)** stayed on without quickening.
**Rich Sense(USA)** had her chances in the straight but was very one-paced from over a furlong out.

4407 - 4412a (Foreign Racing) - See Raceform Interactive

# 3986 BRIGHTON (L-H)
Tuesday, August 3

**OFFICIAL GOING: Firm**
A warm day and, despite overnight watering, the ground was riding very fast.
Wind: almost nil Weather: hazy sun

## 4413 RACING'S BIG DAY OUT FOR NSPCC MEDIAN AUCTION MAIDEN STKS 5f 213y
2:15 (2:17) (E) 2-Y-O **£3,367** (£1,036; £518; £259) **Stalls** Low

Form RPR
3 1 **Cusoon**12 4058 2-9-0 RLMoore 6 82+
(GLMoore) *sn swtchd to ins rail: hld up in tch: led over 2f out: rdn clr: readily* **11/8**1
524 2 6 **Mulberry Lad (IRE)**15 3986 2-9-0 68 (b1) MartinDwyer 3 63
(WRMuir) *bmpd s: w ldrs: outpcd by wnr ins fnl 2f: 2nd and hld whn edgd lft fnl f* **8/1**3
22 3 1 **Connotation**34 3418 2-8-9 DHolland 5 55
(PWD'Arcy) *wd: hld up in 5th: rdn 1/2-way: carried hd high: hung lft and flashed tail over 1f out: nt rch ldrs* **13/8**2
3400 4 1 3/4 **Majestical (IRE)**17 3930 2-9-0 58 SDrowne 1 54
(WRMuir) *w ldr: led over 3f out tl over 2f out: wknd over 1f out* **25/1**
05 5 4 **Worth A Grand (IRE)**24 3748 2-9-0 PDoe 2 42
(JWMullins) *led over 2f: wknd over 2f out* **10/1**
0 6 *shd* **Makes Perfect (IRE)**12 4040 2-8-9 JFEgan 4 37
(SKirk) *wnt lft s: sn outpcd in rr* **12/1**

69.52 secs (-0.58) **Going Correction** -0.10s/f (Good) 6 Ran SP% **111.9**
Speed ratings: **99,91,89,87,82 81**CSF £12.92 TOTE £2.50: £1.30, £3.00; EX 7.80.
**Owner** The Winning Hand **Bred** Mrs Dare Wigan And Dominic Wigan **Trained** Woodingdean, E Sussex

**FOCUS**
Not a great maiden but a creditable winning time for the grade and the form looks solid-enough for the level.

**NOTEBOOK**
**Cusoon** ran out an authoritative winner, drawing well clear in the closing stages. He had shaped as though the step up to six furlongs would suit on his debut at Sandown, and had clearly learnt plenty from that experience. While the rest of the field came down the middle of the track, he raced more towards the far-side rail, and although that may have been an advantage, he was clearly the best horse in the race.
**Mulberry Lad(IRE)**, blinkered for the first time, had the benefit of previous course experience and ran a solid-enough race. He will have a better chance of getting his head in front in nursery company.
**Connotation** was the morning favourite and also had experience of this track, and her performance must be regarded as disappointing. Despite the race being run over an extra furlong to that she had raced over before, she found herself outpaced and was only running on when it was all over. She is at least now eligible for nurseries.
**Majestical(IRE)** did not appear to see out this longer trip.
**Worth A Grand(IRE)**, who drifted badly on the exchanges beforehand despite having posted a decent effort in a better race at Salisbury on his previous start, is another now eligible for a mark.
**Makes Perfect(IRE)** *Official explanation: vet said filly finished lame behind*

## 4414 THE TOTE SUPPORTS THE NSPCC FILLIES' H'CAP 6f 209y
2:45 (2:45) (E) (0-70,66) 3-Y-0+ **£5,499** (£1,692; £846; £423) **Stalls** Low

Form RPR
02-0 1 **Icecap**22 3804 4-8-6 49 CHaddon(7) 6 58
(WGMTurner) *t.k.h: prom: led over 2f out: drvn out* **12/1**
5530 2 1 1/2 **I Wish**8 4194 6-9-7 57 GBaker 7 62
(MMadgwick) *stdd s: plld hrd in rr: hrd rdn and hdwy over 1f out: r.o to take 2nd on line* **6/1**
6122 3 *shd* **Lady Mo**5 4265 3-9-10 66 AMcCarthy 3 71
(GGMargarson) *mid-div: swtchd rt and effrt over 2f out: kpt on fnl f* **7/2**2
2010 4 *nk* **Ziet D'Alsace (FR)**12 4067 4-9-10 60 RLMoore 2 64
(AWCarroll) *mid-div: hdwy to chse wnr 2f out: one pce: lost 2nd nr fin* **9/4**1
3350 5 1 1/2 **Chertsey (IRE)**12 4066 3-9-3 59 EAhern 9 59
(CEBrittain) *chsd ldrs: hrd rdn over 1f out: no ex* **14/1**
0305 6 1 **Blonde En Blonde (IRE)**5 4260 4-9-2 52 (b) DHolland 4 49
(NPLittmoden) *in rr: rdn 1/2-way: hdwy 2f out: no imp* **9/2**3
5433 7 1 3/4 **Stagecoach Ruby**91 1864 3-7-7 40 oh1 HayleyTurner(5) 10 33
(GLMoore) *w ldrs: hung rt over 2f out: wknd wl over 1f out* **14/1**
0-00 8 2 1/2 **Averlline**53 2839 3-9-4 65 NChalmers(5) 5 51
(BDeHaan) *dwlt: sn in midfield: rdn and btn over 2f out* **20/1**
1-66 9 1 1/4 **Tictactoe**105 1517 3-8-12 54 CCatlin 11 36
(DJDaly) *wd: chsd ldrs over 4f* **14/1**
-000 10 10 **Moscow Mary**50 2942 3-8-8 50 SWhitworth 8 5
(AGNewcombe) *led tl over 2f out: sn wknd* **33/1**

1m 21.72s (-0.88) **Going Correction** -0.10s/f (Good)
**WFA** 3 from 4yo+ 6lb 10 Ran SP% **120.9**
Speed ratings: **101,99,99,98,97 95,93,91,89,78**CSF £85.30 CT £313.33 TOTE £17.40: £3.60, £2.60, £1.40; EX 116.00.
**Owner** Mrs Anna L Sanders **Bred** Cheveley Park Stud Ltd **Trained** Sigwells, Somerset

**FOCUS**
This looked quite an open fillies' handicap, but the time was ordinary. The form looks modest but reasonably reliable for the grade.

**NOTEBOOK**
**Icecap**, on whom there was a bit of a gamble, was making her debut for Bill Turner, having failed to get her head in front for her two previous trainers. A 40-1 shot in the morning, she was backed down to 12-1, showed good speed throughout and, clinging to the far-side rail in the straight, held off the closing pack in good style.
**I Wish** missed the break and did not settle very well in the early stages, but she came home strongly. She is equally effective over six and seven furlongs and put a rare poor performance last time behind her.
**Lady Mo** appears well suited by undulating tracks as she has run well here more than once, and won at Epsom and Lingfield in the past.
**Ziet D'Alsace(FR)** has a good record over this course and distance, and she looked booked for second before weakening inside the last. Her current rating looks a tad high, being 7lb higher than her last winning mark.
**Chertsey(IRE)**, who is lightly raced, showed decent pace for a long way but did not appear to see out the trip.
**Blonde En Blonde(IRE)** has never been the easiest to win with, and merely plugged on from the rear at the one pace.

## 4415 DAILY MAIL SUPPORTS THE NSPCC BRIGHTON DASH (H'CAP) 5f 59y
3:15 (3:16) (D) (0-80,80) 3-Y-0+ **£6,662** (£2,050; £1,025; £512) **Stalls** Low

Form RPR
2060 1 **Taboor (IRE)**13 4034 6-8-1 53 (bt) MartinDwyer 6 62
(JWPayne) *rdn along in rr: hdwy and edgd lft over 1f out: str run to ld fnl 50 yds* **14/1**
4315 2 *nk* **Jayanjay**13 4034 5-10-0 80 DHolland 3 88
(MissBSanders) *towards rr: effrt and nt clr run 2f out: eased outside and hdwy over 1f out: ev ch fnl 50 yds: r.o* **7/2**1
6001 3 3/4 **Byo (IRE)**12 4044 6-9-3 69 RLMoore 8 74
(MQuinn) *chsd ldrs: drvn to ld 1f out: hdd and nt qckn fnl 50 yds* **12/1**
0030 4 1 **Redwood Star**6 4232 4-8-4 56 ow2 (e) JFEgan 7 58
(PLGilligan) *chsd ldrs: n.m.r over 1f out: ev ch ins fnl f: one pce* **11/2**3
0310 5 1 1/4 **Gone'N'Dunnett (IRE)**10 4130 5-8-8 60 (v) DaneO'Neill 5 57
(MrsCADunnett) *mde most tl 1f out: no ex* **6/1**
0040 6 *nk* **Port St Charles (IRE)**9 4181 7-8-1 58 (b1) RThomas(5) 1 54
(CRDore) *dwlt: hdwy and in tch whn n.m.r over 1f out: no imp* **7/1**
0006 7 1 1/4 **Roses Of Spring**6 4232 6-9-7 78 (p) AQuinn(5) 9 70
(RMHCowell) *dwlt: sn in midfield: effrt over 2f out: squeezed for room and btn 1f out* **11/2**3
6210 8 1/2 **Stagnite**6 4232 4-8-2 59 (p) NChalmers(5) 4 49
(MrsHSweeting) *w ldrs tl wknd 1f out* **9/2**2
0005 9 9 **Tamarella (IRE)**29 3575 4-7-12 50 oh3 (b) AMcCarthy 2 7
(GGMargarson) *w ldrs to 1/2-way* **25/1**

61.10 secs (-1.17) **Going Correction** -0.10s/f (Good) 9 Ran SP% **116.2**
Speed ratings: **105,104,103,101,99 97,97,96,82**CSF £63.05 CT £623.51 TOTE £15.40: £3.60, £1.60, £3.10; EX 63.10.
**Owner** T W Morley **Bred** Rathasker Stud **Trained** Newmarket, Suffolk

**FOCUS**
Just an ordinary handicap, but the leaders went plenty quick enough and the race played into the hands of the hold-up horses. However, the form appears sound enough.

**NOTEBOOK**
**Taboor(IRE)**, running off a career-low mark, appreciated the fast pace and fairly flew up the hill in the last furlong. A lot of his best form has been on stiff tracks, and he would be one to keep an eye on should he return to a track with an uphill finish.
**Jayanjay** had a troubled run approaching the final furlong, but he was in the clear early enough to have every chance. This was a fair performance under his big weight, and he clearly loves switchback tracks. He is likely to continue to suffer at the hands of the Handicapper for his consistency, though.
**Byo(IRE)** often makes the running, but could never get to the lead from his wide draw. However, he did hold his position well enough and came to win his race a furlong out, only to get swamped by the first two. This was a good effort back in handicap company after winning a claimer last time, and he will be of interest if returning to that sort of grade.
**Redwood Star** is another who likes a trip to Brighton and ran a solid-enough race. Held up just behind the pacesetter, she did not get a perfect run but got the vital gap coming into the last furlong and had every chance. She does seem to show her best form at this time of year, but is probably a touch high in the weights at the moment.
**Gone'N'Dunnett(IRE)** helped to force a furious pace and was unsurprisingly a spent force inside the last furlong. Perhaps a flatter track would enable him to get home better, but he has won here before so it is more likely that he is a shade high in the handicap at present.
**Port St Charles(IRE)**, blinkered for the first time, missed the break and sat in behind the pace. He did not really have a lot of luck in running and was not overly persevered with when his chance was gone. His mark is now lower than for his last turf success, but he remains difficult to win with.

## 4416 TOTESPORT.COM BRIGHTON CHALLENGE CUP (H'CAP) 1m 3f 196y
3:45 (3:47) (D ) (0-80,78) 3-Y-0+ £13,650 (£4,200; £2,100; £1,050) Stalls High

Form RPR

6151 **1** **Desert Island Disc**[6] 4233 7-9-5 **72** ... JFMcDonald(3) 3 82
(JJBridger) *mid-div: hrd rdn 3f out: hdwy over 1f out: led ins fnl f: pushed out: jst hld on* **9/1**

6413 **2** *shd* **Lennel**[2] 4363 6-9-4 **68** ... (b) MFenton 13 78
(ABailey) *dwlt: bhd: rdn 4f out: gd hdwy fnl 2f: jst failed* **10/1**

0214 **3** *2 ½* **Absinther**[8] 4196 7-7-9 **50** ... HayleyTurner(5) 4 56
(MRBosley) *dwlt: towards rr: swtchd outside and hrd rdn 3f out: styd on fnl 2f: nrst fin* **10/1**

4231 **4** *nk* **Blaze Of Colour**[15] 3989 3-9-2 **77** ... (v) BDoyle 8 83+
(SirMichaelStoute) *t.k.h: led: 3l clr 6f out to 2f out: hrd rdn and tired over 1f out: hdd and no ex ins fnl f* **4/1**[1]

0310 **5** *3* **Karaoke (IRE)**[3] 4343 4-9-4 **68** ... JFEgan 2 69
(SKirk) *hdwy 6f out: chsd ldr 2f out: hrd rdn and hung lft over 1f out: no ex fnl f* **16/1**

4160 **6** *1 ¾* **Mostarsil (USA)**[27] 3629 6-9-4 **68** ... (p) RLMoore 12 66
(GLMoore) *chsd ldrs: hrd rdn over 2f out: one pce* **7/1**[3]

0121 **7** *¾* **Party Ploy**[13] 4019 6-9-6 **70** ... DarrenWilliams 1 67
(KRBurke) *prom tl wknd over 1f out* **7/1**[3]

0422 **8** *½* **Antigiotto (IRE)**[19] 3882 3-9-3 **78** ... DHolland 11 74
(LMCumani) *in tch: rdn 5f out: outpcd fnl 2f* **66/1**

4204 **9** *2 ½* **Dispol Evita**[17] 3933 5-7-12 **48** ... AMcCarthy 5 40
(JamiePoulton) *in rr: mod effrt and hrd rdn 3f out: nvr trbld ldrs* **33/1**

0433 **10** *1 ¼* **Most-Saucy**[6] 4233 8-8-4 **54** ... PDoe 10 44
(IAWood) *chsd ldr 7f: wknd over 1f out* **10/1**

5200 **11** *3* **Northside Lodge (IRE)**[17] 3953 6-9-11 **75** ... MartinDwyer 14 60
(PWHarris) *rdn 7f out: a bhd* **5/1**[2]

2013 **12** *3* **Orinocovsky (IRE)**[99] 1677 5-8-9 **59** ... EAhern 9 39
(NPLittmoden) *in tch: outpcd 4f out: grad lost pl* **10/1**

00-6 **13** *29* **Honor Rouge (IRE)**[20] 2305 5-9-6 **70** ... VSlattery 6 4
(DGBridgwater) *in tch: wknd over 5f out: sn bhd: eased whn no ch over 2f out* **16/1**

0330 **P** **Pay The Silver**[10] 4129 6-9-0 **64** ... (p) IMongan 7 —
(IAWood) *mid-div: rdn 5f out: sn lost pl: eased 3f out: t.o whn p.u 50 yds fr line: dismntd* **20/1**

2m 28.4s (-3.70) **Going Correction** -0.10s/f (Good)
**WFA** 3 from 4yo+ 11lb **14** Ran SP% **129.0**
Speed ratings: **108,107,106,106,104 102,102,102,100,99 97,95,76,—**CSF £101.59 CT £946.46 TOTE £10.00: £2.70, £2.70, £4.00; EX 115.60 Trifecta £1035.00 Pool £, w/u.
**Owner** W Wood **Bred** Southill Stud **Trained** Liphook, Hants

**FOCUS**
A valuable handicap for the track, rewarded with a competitive field. The race was run at a strong pace and the principals all came from off the pace, giving the form a sound and reliable appearance.

**NOTEBOOK**
**Desert Island Disc**, already twice a winner over this course and distance, finished best of all to gain a narrow victory. As the race she won at Kempton six days earlier was an apprentices' event, she avoided a penalty in this race, in fact she ran off a mark 1lb lower than at the Sunbury track. Things are likely to become decidedly more difficult once her new mark kicks in.
**Lennel** was making a quick reappearance following a decent effort at Chester at the weekend. He has done most of his winning over ten furlongs but it is surely only a matter of time before he wins over this trip, as he does not lack in stamina. A strong pace, however, does look essential given his style of running.
**Absinther**, another with good previous course form, ran a decent race, coming from well off the pace in a contest which was run to suit, although it is a long time since he won off a mark in the 50s.
**Blaze Of Colour** was successful over the course and distance when fitted with a visor for the first time. The headgear was on again on this occasion and she showed plenty of early pace. Indeed, she appeared to have stolen a decisive advantage turning for home - she was matched at very short prices in-running - only to hit the wall inside the last.
**Karaoke(IRE)**, for whom a mile and a half was a venture into the unknown, came there to have his chance but appeared not to get home, although his rider later reported that the gelding had a breathing problem. *Official explanation: jockey said gelding had a breathing problem*
**Antigiotto(IRE)** *Official explanation: jockey said gelding ran in snatches*
**Most-Saucy**, having her 100th start, was ridden more prominently than usual and was a spent force with a quarter mile to run.
**Orinocovsky(IRE)** *Official explanation: jockey said gelding did not handle the track or the firm ground*
**Honor Rouge(IRE)** *Official explanation: jockey said mare was unsuited by the firm ground*
**Pay The Silver** *Official explanation: jockey said gelding was unsuited by the firm ground*

## 4417 VIDEO MEETING COMPANY SUPPORTS THE NSPCC MAIDEN STKS 1m 1f 209y
4:15 (4:17) (D ) 3-Y-0+ £4,017 (£1,236; £618; £309) Stalls High

Form RPR

-034 **1** **Thirteen Tricks (USA)**[18] 3908 3-8-5 74 ... RLMoore 2 61+
(MrsAJPerrett) *cl up: led over 2f out: rdn clr: easily* **1/10**[1]

00-0 **2** *5* **So Determined (IRE)**[54] 2808 3-8-10 ... EAhern 6 57+
(GAButler) *hld up in tch: smooth effrt on outside over 3f out: wnt 2nd and ev ch 2f out: nt pce of wnr* **11/1**[2]

0000 **3** *12* **Dash For Glory**[32] 3490 5-9-0 29 ... HayleyTurner(5) 1 34
(JSKing) *cl up: rdn and outpcd 1/2-way: btn whn hung lft 2f out* **33/1**[3]

0 **4** *5* **West End Wonder (IRE)**[38] 3297 5-9-2 ... DCorby(3) 5 25
(MJWallace) *led tl over 2f out: sn wknd* **33/1**[3]

2m 1.44s (-1.10) **Going Correction** -0.10s/f (Good)
**WFA** 3 from 4yo+ 9lb **4** Ran SP% **105.1**
Speed ratings: **100,96,86,82**CSF £1.61 TOTE £1.10; EX 1.70.
**Owner** Cheveley Park Stud **Bred** Calumet Farm **Trained** Pulborough, W Sussex

**FOCUS**
An uncompetitive maiden, and the winner did not need to run to her best to win easily.

**NOTEBOOK**
**Thirteen Tricks(USA)** enjoyed a nice confidence booster. She had plenty in hand of her three rivals on her form to date and duly won without being put under undue pressure. The Handicapper only dropped her 1lb for her latest Newbury fourth though, and a little more mercy may be required before she is capable of winning in handicap company.
**So Determined(IRE)** was pushed out to finish a clear second, although well behind the easy winner. He is clearly only of moderate ability.
**Dash For Glory** is rated just 29, but he earned his owners £618 for finishing third.

## 4418 CLASSIC FM SUPPORTS THE NSPCC CLASSIFIED STKS 7f 214y
4:45 (4:46) (F ) 3-Y-0+ £4,104 (£1,263; £631; £315) Stalls Low

Form RPR

0120 **1** **Mister Clinton (IRE)**[10] 4127 7-9-3 59 ... DHolland 3 68
(DKIvory) *hld up in rr: effrt and nt clr run over 2f out: hmpd and swtchd rt over 1f out: r.o to ld on line* **5/2**[1]

0535 **2** *shd* **Londoner (USA)**[10] 4127 6-9-3 60 ... RLMoore 4 68
(SDow) *chsd ldrs: led ins fnl f: hrd rdn and kpt on: hdd on line* **11/2**[3]

0630 **3** *1 ¾* **Liberty Royal**[34] 3412 5-9-7 64 ... (p) DSweeney 1 68
(PJMakin) *chsd ldrs: drvn to chal over 1f out: nt qckn ins fnl f* **5/1**[2]

1215 **4** *1 ½* **Prime Offer**[30] 3559 8-9-1 65 ... CHaddon(7) 7 66
(JJay) *sn led: hrd rdn and hdd ins fnl f: no ex* **6/1**

-000 **5** *2* **Florian**[20] 3841 6-9-0 59 ... RMiles(3) 8 56
(TGMills) *stdd s: plld hrd in rr: hdwy and nt clr run wl over 1f out: eased out: one pce* **14/1**

4105 **6** *2 ½* **Our Destiny**[8] 4192 6-9-3 58 ... IMongan 9 50
(AWCarroll) *hld up in rr: rdn over 2f out: nt pce to chal* **13/2**

3630 **7** *3 ½* **Poppyline**[21] 3828 4-9-0 51 ... (b[1]) SDrowne 5 39
(WRMuir) *chsd ldrs: hrd rdn over 2f out: sn wknd: eased whn wl btn 1f out* **16/1**

-002 **8** *30* **Burlington Place**[6] 4242 3-8-10 60 ... JFEgan 2 —
(SKirk) *w ldr: rdn and lost action over 2f out: qckly lost pl* **13/2**

1m 33.54s (-1.46) **Going Correction** -0.10s/f (Good)
**WFA** 3 from 4yo+ 7lb **8** Ran SP% **114.1**
Speed ratings: **103,102,101,99,97 95,91,61**CSF £16.30 TOTE £2.90: £1.20, £1.80, £1.90; EX 15.90.
**Owner** J B Waterfall **Bred** C N Hart **Trained** Radlett, Herts

**FOCUS**
A moderate handicap and not particularly strong form. With three confirmed front-runners in the field, this looked sure to be run at a furious gallop. However, Florian was held up and Londoner only tracked the pace, which left pace-setting duties to Prime Offer and Burlington Place. They still went quick enough, though.

**NOTEBOOK**
**Mister Clinton(IRE)**, who rarely runs a bad race here and needs to be brought with a late challenge, had the race run to suit. He did not enjoy the clearest of runs and had to be switched a couple of times, but found enough under pressure to get up close home. Everything fell right this time and he would not appeal as an obvious choice to follow up.
**Londoner(USA)** likes to front run but was restrained just in behind the pace on this occasion. A tricky ride, he responded well to pressure and was only just denied. *Official explanation: jockey said gelding hung left*
**Liberty Royal** had the race run to suit and stayed on well enough for third. He never really looked like winning, though.
**Prime Offer** probably did not appreciate being taken on for the lead as three of her four wins have come when making every yard.
**Florian** did not appreciate being restrained.
**Our Destiny** was simply disappointing as he had the race run to suit.
**Burlington Place** *Official explanation: jockey said gelding was unsuited by the track and hung right*

## 4419 PIGGYBANKKIDS APPRENTICE MAIDEN H'CAP 6f 209y
5:15 (5:19) (F ) (0-55,55) 3-Y-0+ £2,975 (£850; £425) Stalls Low

Form RPR

4-04 **1** **Brandywine Bay (IRE)**[82] 2052 4-8-4 **38** ... (p) TBlock(5) 5 46
(APJones) *towards rr: hdwy 2f out: r.o to ld fnl strides* **11/2**[2]

-030 **2** *hd* **Growler**[19] 3875 3-9-6 **55** ... (v[1]) WHogg 9 62
(JLDunlop) *prom: led and swvd lft over 2f out: drvn 2l clr whn hit rail over 1f out: no ex and hdd fnl strides* **7/2**[1]

6600 **3** *½* **Captain Cloudy**[12] 4044 4-9-10 **53** ... RLucey-Butler 7 59
(MMadgwick) *hld up in tch: effrt over 2f out: styd on fnl f* **8/1**

0004 **4** *2 ½* **Johnny Alljays (IRE)**[17] 3391 3-7-8 **36** ... (p) LauraReynolds(7) 2 35
(JSMoore) *prom: disputing 2nd whn n.m.r ins fnl f: one pce* **10/1**

5000 **5** *2* **Benjamin (IRE)**[23] 3774 6-8-6 **35** ... (bt) DeanWilliams 6 29
(JaneSouthcombe) *led: hdd and hmpd over 2f out: wknd over 1f out* **11/2**[2]

0256 **6** *shd* **Jasmine Pearl (IRE)**[12] 4052 3-8-11 **46** ... MHalford 11 39
(TMJones) *hld up in midfield: shkn up and r.o over 1f out: gng on at fin* **6/1**[3]

6020 **7** *3* **Blaise Wood (USA)**[15] 3991 3-8-7 **47** ... (b) JJones(5) 8 32
(GLMoore) *t.k.h towards rr: swtchd wd and effrt 3f out: nvr rchd ldrs* **9/1**

0000 **8** *2* **Bunkhouse**[20] 3848 4-8-13 **47** ... (p) BO'Neill(5) 4 27
(WGMTurner) *dwlt: bhd: hrd rdn fnl 2f: nt trble ldrs* **20/1**

4006 **9** *1 ¼* **Costa Del Sol (IRE)**[15] 3991 3-7-11 **37** ... (b) LucyRussell(5) 10 13
(JJBridger) *prom on outside over 4f* **25/1**

0000 **10** *3* **Blade's Edge**[3] 4350 3-8-3 **45** ... NatalieHassall(7) 3 13
(ABailey) *s.s: a bhd* **16/1**

000- **11** *shd* **Guard**[267] 5973 4-8-8 **37** ... (t) StevenHarrison 1 5
(NPLittmoden) *in tch 4f* **14/1**

0-40 **12** *½* **Mrs Boz**[39] 3261 4-7-13 **33** oh4 ... KJackson(5) 13 —
(AWCarroll) *mid-div tl wknd 3f out* **33/1**

1m 22.78s (0.18) **Going Correction** -0.10s/f (Good)
**WFA** 3 from 4yo+ 6lb **12** Ran SP% **121.6**
Speed ratings: **94,93,93,90,88 87,84,82,80,77 77,76**CSF £25.11 CT £158.72 TOTE £7.80: £2.70, £1.10, £3.60; EX 35.40 Place 6 £121.77, Place 5 £64.35.
**Owner** Mrs K T Pilkington **Bred** Rathasker Stud **Trained** Eastbury, Berks
■ Stewards Enquiry : W Hogg one-day ban: careless riding (Aug 14)

**FOCUS**
A desperate affair, no better than a seller, and a modest winning time for the grade. However, the first three ran close to their marks giving the form a sound if very moderate look.

**NOTEBOOK**
**Brandywine Bay(IRE)**, whose connections were worried that the ground may be too fast for her, handled the conditions well and came from off the fast pace to get up in the final strides. A thoroughly exposed performer she may be, but she had form off higher marks than this last year and clearly her three-month break had done her some good.
**Growler** looked set for victory before the hill eventually found him out. His stable is in the doldrums at the moment and this was a fair run in the circumstances.
**Captain Cloudy** appreciated the return to seven furlongs having been found out over the minimum trip lately.
**Johnny Alljays(IRE)** appeared happier back on the level after failing to cut much ice on his debut over hurdles last time.
**Benjamin(IRE)**, who was available at 25-1 early doors, was the subject of a gamble in the morning and the money continued to come for him on course. He appeared to go too quick in the early stages though, and began to weaken out of contention with over two furlongs to run.
**Jasmine Pearl(IRE)** was surprisingly staying on at the finish of this seven-furlong contest having previously looked to find six furlongs on the far side. *Official explanation: jockey said filly lost her shoe and cut her knee*
T/Jkpt: Not won. Pool £134,303.42 T/Plt: £97.10 to a £1 stake. Pool: £69,772.65. 524.15 winning tickets. T/Qpdt: £25.30 to a £1 stake. Pool: £3,930.70. 114.55 winning tickets. LM

# 4009 CATTERICK (L-H)

Tuesday, August 3

**OFFICIAL GOING: Good to firm (firm in places)**

## 4420 "REDCAR" MAIDEN STKS — 7f

2:30 (2:31) (D) 2-Y-O — £4,238 (£1,304; £652; £326) Stalls Low

Form — RPR

03 **1** **Following Flow (USA)**[13] [4022] 2-9-0 .......... PHanagan 6 79
(WJarvis) *trckd ldrs: led jst ins fnl f: drvn out* **5/1**[3]

00 **2** 1 1/2 **Tcherina (IRE)**[38] [3296] 2-8-9 .......... DAllan 2 70
(TDEasterby) *slowly away: hld up in rr: pushed along over 2f out: rdn over 1f out: r.o wl ins fnl f: wnt 2nd cl home: nt trble wnr* **100/1**

624 **3** shd **Mozafin**[17] [3925] 2-9-0 88 .......... TEDurcan 4 75
(MRChannon) *cl up: drvn along 1/2-way: ev ch and rdn 1f out: no ex ins last* **2/1**[1]

**4** nk **Jaamid** 2-9-0 .......... JFanning 3 74
(MJohnston) *led: rdn over 1f out: hdd jst ins fnl f: no ex* **2/1**[1]

**5** 1 1/4 **Varenka (IRE)** 2-8-9 .......... SSanders 5 66
(SirMarkPrescott) *s.i.s: sn prom: rdn wl over 1f out: stl cl up whn nt clr run ent fnl f: no ex ins last* **9/2**[2]

**6** 3 **Fasylitator (IRE)** 2-9-0 .......... SWKelly 8 64
(JAOsborne) *in tch: effrt over 2f out: btn over 1f out* **12/1**

**7** 8 **Si Si Si** 2-8-9 .......... NCallan 7 39
(JGGiven) *slowly away: rr: lost tch fnl 2f* **25/1**

1m 27.36s (-0.14) **Going Correction** -0.075s/f (Good) **7** Ran SP% **114.0**

Speed ratings: **97,95,95,94,93 89,80**CSF £237.39 TOTE £6.30: £2.40, £16.20; EX 186.20.

**Owner** Sales Race 2001 Syndicate **Bred** Villiers Syndicate **Trained** Newmarket, Suffolk

**FOCUS**

The pace was only ordinary and the presence of a 100/1 shot in second does not enhance the form.

**NOTEBOOK**

**Following Flow(USA)** gave a boost to the form of the maiden won by Belenus at the Newmarket July meeting. He is improving and should stay a mile, and the fact that he acts on Polytrack increases his options.

**Tcherina(IRE)** stood still in the stalls and forfeited a lot of ground, but flew home to snatch second. The seventh furlong brought about improvement and she is now eligible for nurseries.

**Mozafin** came under pressure some way out, but stuck on to have his chance. He stayed this longer trip but might need a return to easier underfoot conditions.

**Jaamid**, a 60,000 gns yearling, is a half-brother to useful performers Highest Cool and Heezapistol, the latter also a winning jumper. A drifter in the maket, he ran respectably without appearing at home on the track's undulations, and should improve on a more conventional track.

**Varenka(IRE)** is out of a half-sister to Listed winer Hill Hopper and useful stayer Prairie Falcon. She was just held when a gap closed on her at the furlong pole, which ended her chance. There should be better to come.

**Fasylitator(IRE)** is a 36,000 gns yearling out of a mare who won over six furlongs at two. He was not helped by his wide draw but will have to improve on this if he is to make his mark.

**Si Si Si** was always struggling. Callan had been unseated going to post and he gave up his later rides due to an injured shoulder.

## 4421 "DONCASTER" (S) STKS — 1m 7f 177y

3:00 (3:00) (G) 3-5-Y-O — £2,863 (£818; £409) Stalls Low

Form — RPR

-055 **1** **Tell The Trees**[15] [3984] 3-8-2 48 .......... JMackay 1 58+
(RMBeckett) *trckd ldr: led 2f out: pushed clr: eased ins fnl f: comf* **6/4**[1]

0100 **2** 4 **Bold Blade**[11] [4096] 3-8-10 60 .......... LFletcher(3) 4 63+
(MJPolglase) *led tl rdn and hdd 2f out: styd on: no ch w wnr* **5/1**

-005 **3** 1 1/2 **House Of Blues**[31] [3529] 3-8-7 57 .......... SWKelly 7 54
(JAOsborne) *hld up: keen: drvn along and outpcd over 4f out: rallied 3f out: wnt 3rd over 1f out: styd on: nvr able to chal* **9/2**[3]

2500 **4** 7 **Desert Quill (IRE)**[11] [4082] 4-8-12 47 .......... BSwarbrick(5) 2 41
(WMBrisbourne) *trckd ldrs: effrt 4f out: sn rdn and btn* **4/1**[2]

3400 **5** 1/2 **Abuelos**[119] [1279] 5-9-8 43 .......... PHanagan 6 45
(DWThompson) *hld up: drvn along over 3f out: no hdwy* **22/1**

5000 **6** 10 **Mikasa (IRE)**[14] [4007] 4-9-8 25 .......... (b[1]) SSanders 8 33
(RFFisher) *hld up in tch: keen: hdwy to go 3rd 3f out: no imp on first 2: rdn and wknd 2f out* **12/1**

00 **7** 16 **Smeorach**[55] [2783] 3-8-2 .......... RFfrench 5 9
(JamesMoffatt) *trckd ldrs: drvn along 4f out: wknd qckly: t.o* **40/1**

P **Green Conversion (IRE)** 3-8-2 .......... PMakin(5) 9 —
(GFierro) *slowly away: rr: lost tch 6f out: wl t.o whn p.u and dismntd 2f out* **33/1**

3m 33.25s (1.85) **Going Correction** -0.075s/f (Good)

**WFA** 3 from 4yo+ 15lb **8** Ran SP% **112.3**

Speed ratings: **92,90,89,85,85 80,72,**—CSF £8.85 TOTE £2.20: £1.10, £1.90, £2.10; EX 8.80.The winner was sold to Mr S Mercer for 12,600gns

**Owner** Major R P Thorman **Bred** Major R P Thorman And P P Thorman **Trained** Lambourn, Berks

**FOCUS**

A modest winning time, even for a seller, and there are doubts over the form, but Tell The Trees was a comfortable winner.

**NOTEBOOK**

**Tell The Trees**, ridden more prominently on this second start at the trip, stayed on strongly for a clear-cut win. Martin Pipe liked what he saw and it is easy to envisage her making her mark in early-season juvenile hurdles.

**Bold Blade**, who did not wear his customary blinkers, ran over half this trip on his previous start. He did not relinquish the lead without a fight, but had to concede that the filly was too strong for him in the last two furlongs.

**House Of Blues** had not tackled further than 12furlongs before, but stayed on quite strongly in the latter stages and obviously has plenty of stamina. He is not a straightforward ride, however.

**Desert Quill(IRE)**, taking another drop in grade, was comprehensively beaten. She does act on Fibresand and that could be her best option.

**Green Conversion(IRE)** *Official explanation: trainer said gelding pulled up lame*

## 4422 EAT, SLEEP AT THE NAG'S HEAD, PICKHILL H'CAP — 5f

3:30 (3:31) (F) (0-55,55) 3-Y-O+ — £4,472 (£1,376; £688; £344) Stalls Low

Form — RPR

4242 **1** **Blue Maeve**[9] [4181] 4-9-3 51 .......... SRighton 1 72
(JHetherton) *led after 1f: mde rest: rdn over 1f out: drew clr fnl f* **11/2**[1]

0000 **2** 4 **Mr Spliffy (IRE)**[4] [4308] 5-8-6 43 .......... J-PGuillambert(3) 2 49
(MCChapman) *led 1f: remained cl up: ev ch and rdn over 1f out: outpcd by wnr fnl f* **10/1**

4004 **3** nk **Mystery Pips**[11] [4105] 4-8-9 43 .......... (v) KimTinkler 6 48
(NTinkler) *chsd ldrs: rdn 2f out: kpt on fnl f* **14/1**

0033 **4** shd **Loughlorien (IRE)**[13] [4014] 5-9-2 50 .......... (v) PHanagan 16 55+
(RAFahey) *towards rr: hdwy u.p into midfield 2f out: kpt on fnl f* **13/2**[2]

050 **5** 1/2 **Dane Rhapsody (IRE)**[38] [3322] 3-8-7 47 ow3 .......... SHitchcott(3) 5 50
(BPalling) *chsd ldrs: rdn 1/2-way: kpt on fnl f* **25/1**

0002 **6** 3/4 **Joyce's Choice**[6] [4247] 5-8-6 45 .......... (p) MLawson(5) 3 45
(JSWainwright) *dwlt: towards rr: hdwy into midfield 1/2-way: kpt on u.p fnl f: n.d* **15/2**[3]

1200 **7** nk **Torrent**[3] [4350] 9-9-1 54 .......... (b) PMakin(5) 11 53
(DWChapman) *trckd ldrs: effrt 2f out: rdn and btn 1f out* **14/1**

1003 **8** 1/2 **Maromito (IRE)**[13] [4011] 7-9-7 55 .......... RFfrench 15 52
(RBastiman) *chsd ldrs: rdn 2f out: btn 1f out* **10/1**

5633 **9** 1 **Amanda's Lad (IRE)**[4] [4309] 4-9-5 53 .......... SWKelly 17 47
(MCChapman) *in tch: drvn along 2f out: no hdwy* **9/1**

4010 **10** 1 3/4 **Petana**[13] [4025] 4-8-12 49 .......... (p) LisaJones(3) 10 37
(MDods) *nvr bttr than mid-div* **20/1**

0010 **11** 3/4 **Rosie's Result**[11] [4105] 4-9-2 50 .......... JFanning 14 35
(MTodhunter) *nvr bttr than mid-div* **12/1**

304 **12** 1/2 **Good Time Bobby**[18] [3896] 7-8-10 51 .......... JDO'Reilly(7) 7 34
(JO'Reilly) *s.i.s: bhd most of way* **33/1**

0000 **13** hd **Rum Destiny (IRE)**[19] [3864] 5-8-8 42 .......... (b) GParkin 9 24
(JSWainwright) *bhd most of way* **25/1**

3006 **14** nk **Count Cougar (USA)**[34] [3407] 4-9-6 54 .......... DaleGibson 4 35
(SPGriffiths) *chsd ldrs: rdn 2f out: sn wknd: no ch whn eased clsng stages* **25/1**

6210 **15** 3 1/2 **Cleveland Way**[57] [2735] 4-8-10 44 .......... (v) RWinston 12 13
(JO'Reilly) *sn towards rr* **25/1**

3234 **16** 1 1/4 **Valazar (USA)**[36] [3378] 5-8-12 46 .......... SSanders 13 10
(DWChapman) *bhd most of way* **9/1**

000- **17** 2 **Solar Prince (IRE)**[284] [5723] 3-9-4 55 .......... RLappin 8 12
(JosephQuinn, Ire) *sn bhd* **50/1**

58.72 secs (-1.88) **Going Correction** -0.35s/f (Firm)

**WFA** 3 from 4yo+ 3lb **17** Ran SP% **124.7**

Speed ratings: **101,94,94,93,93 91,91,90,89,86 85,84,83,83,77 75,72**CSF £54.94 CT £527.06 TOTE £7.10: £1.80, £3.00, £3.10, £2.10; EX 46.50.

**Owner** R G Fell **Bred** P J And Mrs Nolan **Trained** Malton, N Yorks

**FOCUS**

A run-of-the-mill sprint handicap in which the draw played a major part with stall one beating stall two.

**NOTEBOOK**

**Blue Maeve** was ideally drawn for a front runner. Smartly away and soon in command, he was kept up to his work in the final furlong to rout the opposition. While the draw was a big help on this occasion, he is clearly on the upgrade.

**Mr Spliffy(IRE)** was well berthed in stall two, but the favourite was drawn better. He was in second place for most of the way and this was something of a return to form.

**Mystery Pips** is 6lb lower than when successful at Goodwood last September and is certainly capable of winning from this mark, but her strike rate is not good.

**Loughlorien(IRE)**, with the visor refitted, stayed on late in the day. This was a decent effort from a bad draw.

**Dane Rhapsody(IRE)**, who failed to make the frame in three maidens, ran a creditable race on this handicap debut, albeit from a favourable draw.

**Count Cougar(USA)** *Official explanation: jockey said gelding lost its action*

**Valazar(USA)** *Official explanation: jockey said gelding lost its action*

## 4423 "WETHERBY STEEPLECHASES" CLAIMING STKS — 1m 3f 214y

4:00 (4:00) (F) 3-Y-O+ — £3,474 (£1,069; £534; £267) Stalls Low

Form — RPR

0325 **1** **Platinum Charmer (IRE)**[18] [3892] 4-9-4 55 .......... (p) LEnstone(3) 13 56
(KRBurke) *towards rr: drvn along 4f out: hdwy 2f out: styd on wl u.p to ld wl ins fnl f* **9/2**[2]

1235 **2** 1/2 **Eton (GER)**[19] [3872] 8-9-12 73 .......... AlexGreaves 14 60
(DNicholls) *prom: led over 9f out: 3 l clr 1f out: rdn and hdd wl ins fnl f: no ex* **4/5**[1]

0-15 **3** 2 1/2 **Peter's Imp (IRE)**[5] [4275] 9-9-2 51 .......... PPMathers(5) 4 51
(ABerry) *hld up in rr: hdwy 2f out: styd on fnl f: nrst fin* **12/1**[3]

0620 **4** nk **Think Quick (IRE)**[10] [4139] 4-8-6 32 .......... StephanieHollinshead(5) 9 41
(RHollinshead) *hld up: hdwy into midfield 3f out: styd on u.p fnl f: nvr able to chal* **22/1**

2000 **5** 1/2 **Cezzaro (IRE)**[8] [4189] 6-8-11 36 .......... LisaJones(3) 7 43
(SRBowring) *led tl hdd over 9f out: chsd ldr after: ev ch 2f out: no ex* **25/1**

6032 **6** 2 1/2 **Balalaika Tune (IRE)**[20] [3835] 5-8-10 34 .......... (t) JBramhill 5 35
(WStorey) *hld up: hdwy 3f out: in tch and rdn over 1f out: no further prog* **14/1**

0200 **7** 2 **Canlis**[6] [4246] 5-9-0 47 .......... PHanagan 3 36
(DWThompson) *in tch: pushed along whn nt clr run over 3f out: hmpd over 2f out: nvr able to chal* **16/1**

060- **8** nk **Dabus**[2] [5013] 9-8-11 28 .......... J-PGuillambert(3) 10 35
(MCChapman) *prom tl rdn and wknd 2f out* **33/1**

0005 **9** 2 1/2 **Stepastray**[19] [3880] 7-9-4 41 .......... TEaves(3) 8 38
(REBarr) *chsd ldrs: rdn 3f out: sn btn* **25/1**

/060 **10** 1/2 **Norma Speakman (IRE)**[34] [3411] 4-8-4 40 .......... AMullen(7) 12 27
(EWTuer) *rr: effrt over 3f out: sn btn* **100/1**

-000 **11** nk **Sandy Bay (IRE)**[14] [4004] 5-9-3 35 .......... SSanders 6 33
(ARDicken) *midfield: sme hdwy and in tch 3f out: sn rdn and btn* **40/1**

**12** 6 **Miss De Bois** 7-8-9 .......... SWKelly 2 15
(WMBrisbourne) *chsd ldrs tl rdn and wknd over 3f out* **20/1**

0600 **13** 3 1/2 **Grady**[25] [3695] 5-8-9 30 .......... BSwarbrick(5) 1 15
(WMBrisbourne) *midfield tl rdn and wknd 4f out* **66/1**

40-0 **14** dist **Marton Mere**[20] [3835] 8-9-0 32 .......... RWinston 11 —
(AJLockwood) *in tch tl wknd qckly over 3f out: t.o* **50/1**

2m 37.59s (-1.41) **Going Correction** -0.075s/f (Good) **14** Ran SP% **120.6**

Speed ratings: **101,100,99,98,98 96,95,95,93,93 93,89,86,**—CSF £7.54 TOTE £6.00: £1.50, £1.10, £2.40; EX 11.10.The winner was the subject of a friendly claim

**Owner** Spigot Lodge Partnership **Bred** F Hinojosa **Trained** Middleham Moor, N Yorks

**FOCUS**

An ordinary claimer run at an average pace, with a somewhat controversial finish, but the form is weak.

**NOTEBOOK**

**Platinum Charmer(IRE)** had a valid excuse for a below-par effort at Carlisle. Under a well-judged ride, he cut down the favourite, whose rider was slow to pick up her stick, and won a shade cosily.

**Eton(GER)** had 13lb in hand on official ratings and for a long way things were going to plan as he travelled well in front. His rider had taken three looks over her shoulder before picking up her stick inside the last, but he failed to find a great deal for pressure and was cut down by the strongly-finishing winner. With hindsight, Greaves might have got after her mount a little earlier.

**Peter's Imp(IRE)** stayed on from the back of the field but could never land a blow. A more strongly-run race is what he needs.

**Think Quick(IRE)**, a poor maiden, failed to stay 14 furlongs at Nottingham but this was a better effort.

**Cezzaro(IRE)** was always in the front rank and only lost third spot inside the last.

## 4424 CATTERICKBRIDGE.CO.UK H'CAP 1m 5f 175y
4:30 (4:30) (E) (0-70,67) 3-Y-O+ £4,251 (£1,308; £654; £327) Stalls Low

Form RPR

0-50 **1** **Chevin**[13] 4015 5-8-0 **41** .......... PHanagan 5 50
(RAFahey) *hld up: hdwy 4f out: led over 1f out: styd on wl u.p* **5/1**[2]

4-06 **2** 2½ **Majestic Vision**[24] 3743 3-8-13 **67** .......... JFanning 4 73
(PWHarris) *led tl rdn and hdd over 1f out: styd on* **7/1**

5033 **3** 1½ **Red Forest (IRE)**[18] 3902 5-8-13 **61** .......... (t) DerekNolan(7) 2 64
(JMackie) *in tch: hmpd 4f out: chsng ldrs and rdn 2f out: styd on* **4/1**[1]

0520 **4** ½ **Theatre Tinka (IRE)**[32] 3488 5-9-2 **57** .......... (p) SSanders 8 60
(RHollinshead) *prom: rdn and ch over 2f out: kpt on same pce* **11/2**[3]

3426 **5** 2 **Lazzaz**[7] 4213 6-8-6 **47** .......... JoannaBadger 9 47
(PWHiatt) *sn cl up: rdn and ch over 2f out: fdd fr over 1f out* **15/2**

0060 **6** hd **Prairie Sun (GER)**[4] 4307 3-7-12 **52** .......... JMackay 1 52
(MrsADuffield) *chsd ldrs: hmpd and lost pl 4f out: n.d after* **20/1**

5000 **7** ¾ **Prince Holing**[19] 3866 4-9-10 **65** .......... (t) RWinston 7 64
(MTodhunter) *hld up and bhd: gd hdwy to trck ldrs 4f out: rdn 3f out: sn btn* **16/1**

2346 **8** 5 **Next Flight (IRE)**[22] 3803 5-8-4 **48** .......... PMulrennan(3) 6 40
(REBarr) *wnt lft and s.s: hld up in rr: nt clr run 4f out and over 2f out: n.d* **15/2**

/003 **9** 13 **Lady Stratagem**[7] 4210 5-8-1 **42** .......... RFfrench 3 15
(EWTuer) *in tch tl wknd over 3f out: t.o* **16/1**

0404 **10** 9 **Perestroika (IRE)**[17] 3782 6-8-8 **52** .......... TEaves(3) 10 13
(BEllison) *in tch: drvn along 1/2-way: dropped rr 5f out: sn lost tch: t.o* **9/1**

3m 1.84s (-2.66) **Going Correction** -0.075s/f (Good)
**WFA** 3 from 4yo+ 13lb **10** Ran SP% **114.6**
Speed ratings: **104,102,101,101,100 100,99,96,89,84**CSF £39.18 CT £152.83 TOTE £5.80: £2.10, £2.40, £1.90; EX 32.90.
**Owner** D M Beresford **Bred** D M Beresford **Trained** Musley Bank, N Yorks

**FOCUS**
They went just a fair pace in this 0-70 handicap, in which the topweight ran off 65. The form is ordinary but could rate a little higher.

**NOTEBOOK**
**Chevin** lost all chance at the start here last time under an inexperienced apprentice. This longer trip suited her and now that she has found her form she could follow up, having won two on the bounce off a 2lb higher mark than this last summer.
**Majestic Vision**, who is still learning the game, stuck on well when headed and should be capable of further improvement.
**Red Forest(IRE)** did not enjoy the best luck in running but that cannot be really used as an excuse. He appears to stay this trip but 12 furlongs could be his optimum.
**Theatre Tinka(IRE)**, who is not the most consistent, ran a better race after failing to stay 1m 7f at Warwick.
**Lazzaz**, back up in trip, was unable to get his own way out in front.
**Next Flight(IRE)** *Official explanation: jockey said gelding was never travelling*
**Perestroika(IRE)** *Official explanation: trainer said gelding was found to have a throat infection*

## 4425 "CATTERICK BRIDGE" H'CAP 7f
5:00 (5:01) (F) (0-55,57) 3-Y-O+ £4,719 (£1,452; £726; £363) Stalls Low

Form RPR

1006 **1** **Jubilee Street (IRE)**[4] 4305 5-9-10 **55** .......... GHind 9 64
(MrsADuffield) *in tch: hdwy u.p 2f out: led jst ins fnl f: all out* **11/1**

0030 **2** shd **Baby Barry**[11] 4083 7-9-1 **46** .......... SSanders 6 55
(MrsGSRees) *midfield: hdwy 2f out: rdn to chal ent fnl f: disp ld ins last: no ex clsng stages* **10/1**

3500 **3** nk **Golden Spectrum (IRE)**[18] 3921 5-9-10 **55** .......... (v[1]) AlexGreaves 14 63
(DNicholls) *midfield: hdwy 2f out: r.o wl u.p fnl f: clsng on first 2 nr fin* **40/1**

0001 **4** 1 **Joshua's Gold (IRE)**[5] 4259 3-8-13 **57** 6ex .......... (v[1]) DTudhope(7) 16 62
(DCarroll) *trckd ldrs on outer: led 2f out: hung rt: hdd jst ins fnl f: no ex* **12/1**

5650 **5** 2 **Linden's Lady**[10] 4133 4-9-8 **53** .......... RWinston 15 53
(JRWeymes) *hld up in rr: hdwy u.p over 1f out: styd on fnl f: nvr able to chal* **66/1**

0035 **6** ¾ **Oases**[11] 4083 5-9-6 **54** .......... (v) THamilton(3) 17 52
(DShaw) *s.s: bhd: hdwy 3f out: rdn 2f out: styd on fnl f: nvr able to chal* **14/1**

2246 **7** 1 **Smith N Allan Oils**[8] 4199 5-9-9 **54** .......... (p) SWKelly 13 49
(MDods) *sn towards rr and drvn along: styd on fnl 2f: nvr able to chal* **7/1**[2]

4451 **8** shd **Miss Wizz**[39] 3269 4-8-7 **45** .......... (p) RoryMoore(7) 18 40
(WStorey) *hld up: hdwy into midfield 3f out: rdn 2f out: no further prog* **25/1**

0-02 **9** 1¾ **Loner**[6] 4246 6-9-5 **50** .......... (p) PHanagan 8 40
(RAFahey) *midfield: pushed along 1/2-way: sme hdwy and in tch over 1f out: no further prog fnl f: b.b.v* **3/1**[1]

0-00 **10** 1 **Bowlegs Billy**[31] 3511 4-9-0 **45** .......... JEdmunds 4 32
(JBalding) *chsd ldrs: rdn 2f out: fdd* **50/1**

1604 **11** ¾ **Redoubtable (USA)**[3] 4350 13-9-3 **53** .......... PMakin(5) 2 38
(DWChapman) *midfield: drvn along 2f out: no hdwy* **12/1**

0020 **12** shd **Time To Remember (IRE)**[4] 4291 6-9-10 **55** .......... ANicholls 7 40
(DNicholls) *sn led: hdd 2f out: wknd appr fnl f: no ch whn eased ins last* **11/1**

0064 **13** 1 **Mr Bountiful (IRE)**[5] 4257 6-9-0 **48** .......... (bt[1]) LisaJones(3) 3 30
(MDods) *s.i.s: nvr bttr than mid-div* **9/1**[3]

064- **14** ½ **Star Ovation (IRE)**[383] 3343 7-9-9 **54** .......... RLappin 1 35
(MsRebeccaBowden, Ire) *cl up tl rdn and wknd 2f out* **50/1**

0100 **15** 5 **Massey**[13] 4013 8-9-7 **52** .......... JFanning 5 20
(TDBarron) *in tch to 1/2-way: sn towards rr* **14/1**

6050 **16** 1 **Parker**[61] 2614 7-9-7 **55** .......... (b) SHitchcott(3) 10 20
(BPalling) *chsd ldrs tl wknd 3f out* **25/1**

0062 **17** nk **Blunham**[29] 3586 4-8-13 **47** .......... J-PGuillambert(3) 12 11
(MCChapman) *led early: cl up tl wknd 2f out* **10/1**

1500 **18** 2½ **Only One Legend (IRE)**[20] 3836 6-9-3 **48** .......... (b) GParkin 11 5
(KARyan) *sn bhd* **20/1**

1m 26.85s (-0.65) **Going Correction** -0.075s/f (Good)
**WFA** 3 from 4yo+ 6lb **18** Ran SP% **131.4**
Speed ratings: **100,99,99,98,96 95,94,94,92,90 90,89,88,88,82 81,80,78**CSF £117.25 CT £4415.30 TOTE £14.60: £3.20, £2.80, £19.30, £3.80; EX 178.60 Place 6 £231.42, Place 5 £18.04.
**Owner** D W Holdsworth & J A McMahon **Bred** My Firebird Syndicate **Trained** Constable Burton, N Yorks

■ The first winner in Britain this year for Gary Hind, who is currently based in the Czech Republic.

**FOCUS**
A routine handicap run at a decent gallop. The form is modest but sound.

**NOTEBOOK**
**Jubilee Street(IRE)**, who was a little unfortunate at Thirsk, put his head in front inside the last and just held on. He had his ideal conditions of fast ground and seven furlongs.
**Baby Barry** put a moderate effort at Chepstow behind him and went down fighting. He was 25lb higher when gaining his last win back in July 2002 and has worn headgear in all his victories.
**Golden Spectrum(IRE)** wore a visor for the first time although he has been tried in blinkers and cheekpieces before. He was keeping on late in the day from a low draw but the line beat him.
**Joshua's Gold(IRE)**, under a 6lb penalty, wore a first-time visor. He ducked right soon after hitting the front and was unable to hold on, but this was still a decent effort from a moderate stalls position.
**Linden's Lady**, without the headgear, was keeping on at the end on this return to seven furlongs.
**Oases** missed the break as usual and did well to reach his final position. *Official explanation: jockey said gelding missed the break*
**Loner**, who was well backed, had a valid excuse. *Official explanation: vet said gelding had bled from the nose*
**Time To Remember(IRE)** *Official explanation: jockey said gelding had no more to give once headed*
T/Plt: £559.60 to a £1 stake. Pool £47,108.00. 61.45 winning tickets T/Qpdt: £30.10 to a £1 stake. Pool £4,608.00. 113.10 winning tickets JF

4426 - 4429a (Foreign Racing) - See Raceform Interactive

# 4381 DEAUVILLE (R-H)
Tuesday, August 3

**OFFICIAL GOING: Turf course - good to soft; all-weather - standard**

## 4430a PRIX DE PSYCHE (GROUP 3) (FILLIES) 1m 2f
2:20 (2:29) 3-Y-O £25,704 (£10,282; £7,711; £5,141)

RPR

**1** **Quilanga (GER)**[93] 1805 3-8-12 .......... GaryStevens 11 107
(AWohler, Germany) *always close up towards outside, 3rd straight, led 1 1/2f out, ran on well*

**2** 1 **Kinnaird (IRE)**[25] 3699 3-8-12 .......... KDarley 12 106
(PCHaslam) *prominent, 2nd straight pressing leader, every chance 1 1/2f out, stayed on at same pace* **3**

**3** ½ **Cloon (USA)**[40] 3258 3-8-12 .......... (b) C-PLemaire 10 105
(NClement, France) *held up on outside, 9th straight, headway down outside to go 3rd inside final f, ran on, nearest finish*

**4** 1½ **Love And Bubbles (USA)**[40] 3258 3-9-2 .......... IMendizabal 4 106
(RobertCollet, France) *held up on inside, 8th straight, good headway to go 3rd 1 1/2f out, one pace final f* **2**

**5** 2 **Green Way (FR)**[30] 3-8-12 .......... ELegrix 2 99
(MDelzangles, France) *held up in rear, 10th straight, headway on inside 2f out, kept on to take 5th closing stages*

**6** ¾ **Asti (IRE)**[51] 2925 3-8-12 .......... OPeslier 3 97
(ELellouche, France) *pulled hard early, in touch, 5th straight tracking leaders, effort and one pace from 1 1/2f out* **1**

**7** 2 **Via Milano (FR)**[79] 2160 3-8-12 .......... CSoumillon 7 94
(MmeJLaurent-JoyeRossi, France) *midfield, 6th straight, pushed along and one pace final 1 1/2f*

**8** snk **Bay Tree (IRE)**[48] 2971 3-8-12 .......... TPQueally 6 93
(DRLoder) *held up in rear, last straight, still last when hard ridden 1 1/2f out, modest late headway*

**9** ¾ **Kayak**[72] 2341 3-8-12 .......... TThulliez 5 92
(PBary, France) *11th straight, always in rear*

**10** 1½ **Give Me Five (GER)**[32] 3504 3-8-12 .......... DBoeuf 9 89
(FrauEMader, Germany) *set steady pace til headed 1 1/2f out, weakened*

**11** **Buoyant (IRE)**[30] 3566 3-8-12 .......... DBonilla 1 89
(FHead, France) *prominent on inside racing keenly, 7th straight, soon weakened*

**12** **Shoko**[72] 2341 3-8-12 .......... MDemuro 8 89
(BGrizzetti, Italy) *prominent on inside, 4th straight, weakened quickly 2f out*

2m 8.00s **Going Correction** -0.05s/f (Good) **12** Ran SP% **121.6**
Speed ratings: **110,109,108,107,106 105,103,103,103,101 101,101.**
**Owner** Stiftung Gestut Fahrhof **Bred** Stiftung Gestut Fahrhof **Trained** Germany

**NOTEBOOK**
**Quilanga(GER)** is now unbeaten in four races outside of the country she is trained in. Quilanga quickly took the advantage in the straight and easily fought off her only challenger, the British-trained Kinnaird. This filly will probably go next for a Group 3 in Bremen later in the month and maybe back to France for the Vermeille in September.
**Kinnaird(IRE)** ran a good race in defeat, just being unable to match the winner for speed in the final furlong. The jockey reported that the filly needs softer ground and she may well be coming back for the Prix de la Nanette depending on the going.
**Cloon(USA)** settled in behind Quilanga at the entrance to the straight but was unable to accelerate as well as the front pair. However she battled on to easily take third place.
**Love And Bubbles(USA)** was ridden under waiting tactics and she managed to close in on the rest of the group in the straight but was never a real threat.
**Bay Tree(IRE)** played a waiting game but was never really travelling well and did not have enough to give when asked to quicken by Queally in the final stages.

# 4413 BRIGHTON (L-H)
Wednesday, August 4

**OFFICIAL GOING: Firm**
Wind: almost nil Weather: fine

## 4432 CHAPLIN'S BAR AT BURGESS HILL MAIDEN AUCTION STKS 6f 209y
2:40 (2:40) (E) 2-Y-O £3,421 (£1,052; £526; £263) Stalls Low

Form RPR

353 **1** **My Princess (IRE)**[5] 4296 2-8-7 .......... LDettori 8 75+
(NACallaghan) *prom: drvn to ld 1f out: edgd lft: sn clr: comf* **2/1**[2]

5 **2** 2½ **Chantaco (USA)**[14] 4016 2-8-9 .......... MartinDwyer 6 71
(AMBalding) *sn led: rdn and hdd 1f out: one pce* **15/8**[1]

6304 **3** 2½ **Azuree (IRE)**[21] 3840 2-8-9 **77** .......... (b) PDobbs 3 64
(RHannon) *prom: hrd rdn over 1f out: no ex* **7/1**[3]

0 **4** ¾ **Busaco**[44] 3157 2-8-9 .......... IMongan 7 62
(JLDunlop) *in tch: drvn along over 2f out: one pce* **16/1**

**5** nk **Bold Counsel (IRE)** 2-8-8 .......... SSanders 5 60
(BJMeehan) *dwlt: hdwy 4f out: one pce fnl 2f* **7/1**[3]

**6** 5 **Sweeney Todd (IRE)** 2-8-9 .......... RHavlin 2 48
(JGPortman) *dwlt: a bhd* **40/1**

7 1 1/4 **Wandering Act (IRE)** 2-8-11 ............ TPQueally 4 47
(MJWallace) *bhd fnl 3f* **7/1**[3]

1m 22.04s (-0.56) **Going Correction** -0.05s/f (Good) **7** Ran SP% **113.9**
Speed ratings: **101,98,95,94,94 88,86**CSF £6.12 TOTE £2.40: £1.70, £2.30; EX 6.30.
**Owner** T Mohan **Bred** J Sheehan **Trained** Newmarket, Suffolk

**FOCUS**
A modest maiden auction event run at an ordinary pace early, though the time was 0.25 seconds faster than the all-aged classified stakes. The form looks sound enough for the grade.

**NOTEBOOK**
**My Princess(IRE)** had a couple of fair placed efforts to her name and was an expensive failure in between, though she may have had excuses there. It was interesting that she was kept to maidens rather than going the nursery route and she won in clear-cut style, despite not looking totally at ease on the track. The extra furlong proved no problem at all, and she appears to like good ground or faster. *Official explanation: had a couple of fair placed efforts to her name and was an expensive failure in between, though she may have had excuses there. It was interesting that she was kept to maidens rather than going the nursery route and she won in clear-cut style, despite not looking totally at ease on the track. The extra furlong proved no problem at all, and she appears to like good ground or faster.*
**Chantaco(USA)** stepped up on his Leicester debut under a positive ride and lasted longer in front this time. However, he did not seem to quite get home. He may need to drop a furlong. *Official explanation: stepped up on his Leicester debut under a positive ride and lasted longer in front this time. However, he did not seem to quite get home. He may need to drop a furlong.*
**Azuree(IRE)**, the most experienced in the field, did not improve for the extra furlong and now looks totally exposed. She appears to like a fast surface and will probably need to find a weakish nursery to put her head in front. *Official explanation: , the most experienced in the field, did not improve for the extra furlong and now looks totally exposed. She appears to like a fast surface and will probably need to find a weakish nursery to put her head in front.*
**Busaco** improved marginally from his debut without looking a winner waiting to happen. *Official explanation: improved marginally from his debut without looking a winner waiting to happen.*
**Wandering Act(IRE)** was subject of a gamble on this debut, but he never gave his supporters much hope. A late foal, he may need more time. *Official explanation: was subject of a gamble on this debut, but he never gave his supporters much hope. A late foal, he may need more time.*

## 4433 SEAVIEW AT EAST PRESTON (S) H'CAP — 1m 3f 196y
**3:10** (3:12) (G) (0-55,54) 3-Y-O+ — **£3,321** (£1,022; £511; £255) **Stalls** High

Form / RPR

2205 **1** **Mr Whizz**[17] [3667] 7-8-5 **34** ............ (p) DerekNolan(7) 7 48
(APJones) *dwlt: gd hdwy on outside 5f out: wnt to ins rail and hrd rdn over 2f out: led over 1f out: styd on* **10/1**

5644 **2** *3* **Blue Savanna**[16] [3996] 4-9-1 **40** ............ (b) NMackay(3) 4 49
(JGPortman) *prom: led 5f out tl over 1f out: sn outpcd* **8/1**[3]

6531 **3** *3* **Banningham Blaze**[11] [4139] 4-10-0 **50** ............ (v) IMongan 3 54
(AWCarroll) *dwlt: hdwy 4f out: hrd rdn 2f out: one pce* **11/4**[1]

0031 **4** *1* **Rolex Free (ARG)**[9] [4189] 6-10-4 **54** 6ex ............ (v) LDettori 1 57
(DFlood) *led tl 5f out: sn rdn and outpcd: same pl fnl 3f* **7/2**[2]

20-0 **5** *7* **Blue Streak (IRE)**[33] [3088] 7-9-12 **48** ............ (b) DaneO'Neill 2 39
(GLMoore) *chsd ldrs 7f* **10/1**

2345 **6** *10* **Regal Performer (IRE)**[13] [4055] 3-9-5 **52** ............ JFEgan 6 27
(SKirk) *hld up in 6th: hrd rdn 4f out: wknd 3f out* **7/2**[2]

0-00 **7** *18* **Gliding By**[16] [3994] 3-9-5 **52** ............ SSanders 8 —
(PRChamings) *bhd fnl 5f* **16/1**

2045 **8** *20* **Cracow (IRE)**[11] [4139] 7-9-9 **45** ............ (p) MartinDwyer 5 —
(AMHales) *prom over 7f* **8/1**[3]

2m 33.24s (1.14) **Going Correction** -0.05s/f (Good)
**WFA** 3 from 4yo+ 11lb **8** Ran SP% **117.4**
Speed ratings: **94,92,90,89,84 78,66,52**CSF £88.25 CT £283.28 TOTE £11.20: £3.60, £2.40, £1.30; EX 117.00.The winner was bought in for 4,200gns. Banningham Blaze was subject to a friendly claim.
**Owner** The Milk Sheiks **Bred** K D Linsley **Trained** Eastbury, Berks

**FOCUS**
A poor contest and something of a surprise winner. The time was moderate, even for a seller and the form does not look reliable.

**NOTEBOOK**
**Mr Whizz** has been mixing Flat racing, hurdling and chasing in recent months. The gelding saw the trip out better than he has done in the past, but will be fortunate to find another race like this. Connections always have the option of putting him back over obstacles.
**Blue Savanna** looked the likely winner when passing the front-running Rolex Free over half a mile from home, but he started to hang in the later stages and the gap he left next to the inside rail allowed the winner through. This looks as good as he is now.
**Banningham Blaze** , who usually goes well here, tried to come from off the pace. Despite some strong driving she wasn't making any impression on the front pair inside the last furlong. She may need farther these days and does appear to like these sharp tracks.
**Rolex Free(ARG)** made much of the running, but folded rather tamely after losing the lead some way from home and was unable to carry his improved Fibresand effort back on to turf. *Official explanation: jockey said gelding was unsuited by the firm ground*
**Gliding By** *Official explanation: trainer said filly was struck into*
**Cracow(IRE)** *Official explanation: jockey said gelding was unsuited by the firm ground*

## 4434 EBONY ROOM BRIGHTON SPRINT (H'CAP) — 5f 213y
**3:40** (3:40) (D) (0-80,80) 3-Y-O — **£6,656** (£2,048; £1,024; £512) **Stalls** Low

Form / RPR

0602 **1** **Who's Winning (IRE)**[38] [3338] 3-8-7 **66** ............ SSanders 5 73
(BGPowell) *trckd ldng pair: led 2f out: hrd rdn fnl f: jst hld on* **13/2**[3]

0065 **2** *shd* **Peruvian Style (IRE)**[6] [4267] 3-8-11 **70** ............ TPQueally 7 77
(NPLittmoden) *hld up in tch: effrt whn n.m.r over 2f out and wl over 1f out: str run fnl f: jst failed* **7/1**

2414 **3** *1/2* **Estihlal**[12] [4104] 3-9-0 **73** ............ WSupple 3 79
(EALDunlop) *dwlt: hld up in rr: hdwy over 2f out: edgd lft: hrd rdn and ev ch fnl f: nt qckn nr fin* **1/1**[1]

-500 **4** *2 1/2* **Ace Club**[35] [3420] 3-8-8 **67** ............ LDettori 4 65
(WJHaggas) *chsd ldrs: effrt and nt clr run wl over 1f out: swtchd rt: styd on same pce* **4/1**[2]

4504 **5** *2* **Barabella (IRE)**[16] [3988] 3-7-9 **57** oh2 ............ JFMcDonald(3) 2 49
(RJHodges) *t.k.h in rr: effrt and nt clr run over 2f out: swtchd rt and hmpd wl over 1f out: nvr rchd ldrs* **16/1**

1226 **6** *3 1/2* **Emaradia**[128] [1178] 3-7-12 **57** oh3 ............ LisaJones 1 39
(AWCarroll) *led 1f: prom tl wknd over 1f out* **20/1**

-265 **7** *5* **Chance For Romance**[16] [3995] 3-9-7 **80** ............ (v[1]) MartinDwyer 6 47
(WRMuir) *led after 1f tl 2f out: wkng whn short of room and bmpd sn after* **8/1**

69.37 secs (1.89) **Going Correction** -0.05s/f (Good) **7** Ran SP% **117.6**
Speed ratings: **102,101,101,97,95 90,83**CSF £52.13 TOTE £8.70: £2.80, £3.20; EX 38.90.
**Owner** Mrs Rachel A Powell **Bred** Colin Kennedy **Trained** Morestead, Hants
■ Stewards Enquiry : S Sanders one-day ban: used whip with excessive frequency (Aug 15)

**FOCUS**
A decent sprint handicap and a blanket finish.

**NOTEBOOK**
**Who's Winning(IRE)** was making his debut for Brendan Powell after being claimed out of a Warwick claimer. He did get first run on his two nearest rivals, but showed great courage in the closing stages to just hang on and record his first victory since his racecourse debut. He has run well off much higher marks than this in the past, so might be capable of following up despite the narrow winning margin. *Official explanation: was making his debut for Brendan Powell after being claimed out of a Warwick claimer. He did get first run on his two nearest rivals, but showed great courage in the closing stages to just hang on and record his first victory since his racecourse debut. He has run well off much higher marks than this in the past, so might be capable of following up despite the narrow winning margin.*
**Peruvian Style(IRE)** ◆ finished fastest of all and would have won in another stride. This was his best effort on turf so far this year, especially considering he lost his off-fore plate, and it should not be long before he goes one better. *Official explanation: finished fastest of all and would have won in another stride. This was his best effort on turf so far this year, especially considering he lost his off-fore plate, and it should not be long before he goes one better.*
**Estihlal** had ground to make up following a tardy start, but she was close enough if good enough inside the last furlong and the winner was always holding her. She had previously shown good form in larger fields and is not one to dismiss on the back of this slightly disappointing effort. *Official explanation: had ground to make up following a tardy start, but she was close enough if good enough inside the last furlong and the winner was always holding her. She had previously shown good form in larger fields and is not one to dismiss on the back of this slightly disappointing effort.*
**Ace Club** was more lightly raced than his rivals, but he had run moderately in his last two starts and this was only marginally better. His best two runs have been on stiff course, and maybe a return to that kind of track will suit him better. *Official explanation: was more lightly raced than his rivals, but he had run moderately in his last two starts and this was only marginally better. His best two runs have been on stiff course, and maybe a return to that kind of track will suit him better.*
**Barabella(IRE)** is now a maiden after 12 starts and was beaten in a seller last time, but she deserves some credit as she didn't get the clearest of passages, so may still be capable of winning a modest event. *Official explanation: is now a maiden after 12 starts and was beaten in a seller last time, but she deserves some credit as she didn't get the clearest of passages, so may still be capable of winning a modest event.*
**Chance For Romance** *Official explanation: trainer said filly was unsuited by the first-time visor*

## 4435 JOHN SMITH'S BRIGHTON MILE CHALLENGE TROPHY (RATED STKS) (H'CAP) — 7f 214y
**4:10** (4:10) (D) (0-80,79) 3-Y-O+ — **£18,966** (£7,194; £3,597; £1,635) **Stalls** Low

Form / RPR

3032 **1** **Aesculus (USA)**[13] [4066] 3-8-1 **68** ............ NMackay(3) 10 78
(LMCumani) *in tch: effrt over 2f out: styd on to ld nr fin* **12/1**

2400 **2** *nk* **Flint River**[63] [2575] 6-8-11 **71** ............ LFletcher(3) 7 80
(HMorrison) *prom: led over 1f out: hung lft: hrd rdn and hdd ins fnl f: kpt on* **16/1**

0200 **3** *1/2* **Takes Tutu (USA)**[5] [4287] 5-9-5 **76** ............ (b) SWhitworth 2 84
(KRBurke) *stdd s: hld up and bhd: smooth hdwy 2f out: led ins fnl f: hdd and nt qckn nr fin* **33/1**

1403 **4** *1/2* **Katiypour (IRE)**[6] [4262] 7-9-4 **75** ............ LisaJones 14 82
(MissBSanders) *s.i.s: t.k.h towards rr: hdwy on outside 2f out: nrst fin* **25/1**

1111 **5** *3/4* **Masafi (IRE)**[6] [4258] 3-9-1 **79** 3ex ............ SSanders 11 84
(SirMarkPrescott) *prom: ev ch over 2f out: hrd rdn: one pce* **4/5**[1]

650U **6** *2* **Jools**[2] [4401] 6-9-5 **76** ............ WSupple 12 76
(DKIvory) *mid-div: rdn over 2f out: kpt on fnl f* **25/1**

065 **7** *hd* **Dance On The Top**[21] [3850] 6-9-8 **79** ............ (t) MartinDwyer 13 79
(JRBoyle) *chsd ldr: led over 2f out tl over 1f out: one pce* **25/1**

2034 **8** *1/2* **Voice Mail**[4] [4327] 5-9-0 **78** ............ TBlock(7) 3 77
(AMBalding) *mid-div: drvn to chse ldrs ins fnl 2f: one pce appr fnl f* **20/1**

6021 **9** *2* **Hoh Bleu Dee**[11] [4145] 3-8-11 **75** ............ JFEgan 5 69
(SKirk) *chsd ldrs 3f: rdn and dropped towards rr: rallied and nt clr run over 1f out: one pce* **16/1**

0010 **10** *nk* **Factual Lad**[14] [4029] 6-9-1 **72** ............ SWKelly 4 65
(BRMillman) *mid-div: rdn 2f out: no imp* **33/1**

0104 **11** *6* **Aragon's Boy**[11] [4142] 4-8-12 **69** ............ DaneO'Neill 6 49
(HCandy) *led tl over 2f out: wknd over 1f out* **33/1**

5352 **12** *hd* **Londoner (USA)**[1] [4418] 6-8-5 **62** oh2 ............ CCatlin 15 41
(SDow) *chsd ldrs: drvn along 3f out: sn wknd and hung lft* **20/1**

2231 **13** *shd* **Todlea (IRE)**[7] [4238] 4-9-5 **76** 3ex ............ LDettori 8 55
(JAOsborne) *dwlt: a bhd* **9/2**[2]

2060 **14** *3 1/2* **Borrego (IRE)**[33] [3477] 4-9-5 **76** ............ SCarson 1 47
(CEBrittain) *chsd ldrs 5f* **50/1**

140 **15** *1 3/4* **A Woman In Love**[10] [4164] 5-9-8 **79** ............ TPQueally 9 46
(MissBSanders) *dwlt: plld hrd in rr: mod effrt on outside 3f out: rdn and no rspnse* **15/2**[3]

1m 33.21s (-1.79) **Going Correction** -0.05s/f (Good)
**WFA** 3 from 4yo+ 7lb **15** Ran SP% **136.8**
Speed ratings: **106,105,105,104,103 101,101,101,99,98 92,92,92,89,87**CSF £186.25 CT £6272.78 TOTE £17.20: £3.40, £7.50, £6.90; EX 203.60 Trifecta £1259.70 Pool: £1,774.33. 0.30 winning tickets..
**Owner** Duke Of Devonshire **Bred** Lord Hartington **Trained** Newmarket, Suffolk

**FOCUS**
A decent prize on offer for this fair handicap and a thrilling finish. The form is decent for the grade.

**NOTEBOOK**
**Aesculus(USA)** ◆ recorded her first win on turf under a fine ride from Nicky Mackay. Her previous form was nothing to write home about despite only just getting caught last time, but she did not see the racecourse until October and this victory strongly suggests she is improving.
**Flint River** has recorded most of his recent victories at Wolverhampton, but he did win here last term. He returned to form with a fine effort to finish second after having a short break since his last outing. He has a good record at Brighton, one win and a second, and would be interesting if returning to this course before going back to the All-Weather this coming winter.
**Takes Tutu(USA)** is on a lengthy losing run and this was one of his better recent effort. He does not have a consistent profile, so whether he will repeat it next time is anyone's guess.
**Katiypour(IRE)** stayed on well down the outside in the closing stages, but still looks a shade too high in the weights. He would be interesting if they stepped him down into a claimer again, as he has a three from three record in those events.
**Masafi(IRE)** was bidding to win his eighth race on the bounce. Despite racing off a 4lb higher mark than he has ever won off before, he was still well in as he is due to go up another 13lb from Saturday. He came with every chance and it may be that his recent exertions have finally taken their toll. It also worth noting that his two wins over this trip came on Fibresand so he may have found the mile on a track like this too sharp. The jockey reported that the ground was too quick for him as well.
**Todlea(IRE)** *Official explanation: jockey said gelding was unsuited by the firm ground*

## 4436 CORAL GREYHOUND STADIA H'CAP 1m 1f 209y
4:40 (4:42) (E) (0-70,65) 3-Y-O+ £5,408 (£1,664; £832; £416) Stalls High

Form RPR
3265 1 **Kirkham Abbey**[19] 3903 4-9-9 63 SSanders 8 74
(MAJarvis) *hld up towards rr: rdn and hdwy on outside 4f out: jnd ldr 2f out: drvn to ld ins fnl f* 7/2[2]
0406 2 1 ½ **Fortune Point (IRE)**[12] 4093 6-9-2 56 (v) WSupple 3 64
(AWCarroll) *led: jnd by wnr 2f out: hrd rdn and hdd ins fnl f: kpt on* 14/1
3200 3 7 **Fantasy Crusader**[19] 3911 5-8-8 48 (p) DaneO'Neill 9 43
(JAGilbert) *chsd ldrs: rdn over 4f out: n.m.r and outpcd 2f out: btn whn hung lft over 1f out* 11/1
3310 4 nk **Over To You Bert**[12] 4083 5-8-1 44 JFMcDonald(3) 5 38
(RJHodges) *prom: hrd rdn and btn 2f out* 7/1[3]
5130 5 shd **Husky (POL)**[17] 2053 6-8-5 45 (p) ADaly 7 39
(RMHCowell) *s.s: bhd: rdn 3f out: nrst fin* 20/1
1056 6 1 **Our Destiny**[1] 4418 6-8-11 58 DerekNolan(7) 2 50
(AWCarroll) *chsd ldrs: outpcd over 2f out: sn btn* 8/1
2110 7 2 ½ **Kernel Dowery (IRE)**[34] 3459 4-9-10 64 (e) MartinDwyer 6 51
(PWHarris) *prom over 7f* 7/2[2]
542- 8 ¾ **Second Of May**[259] 6026 4-9-11 65 JFEgan 4 51
(PRChamings) *dwlt: hld up in tch: lost pl 5f out: n.d after* 10/1
0042 9 shd **Forge Lane (IRE)**[16] 3990 3-8-6 55 (b[1]) SWhitworth 1 41
(GLMoore) *s.s: hld up towards rr: hrd rdn over 2f out: sn bhd* 10/3[1]

2m 0.92s (-1.62) **Going Correction** -0.05s/f (Good)
**WFA** 3 from 4yo+ 9lb 9 Ran SP% 120.0
Speed ratings: **104,102,97,96,96 96,94,93,93**CSF £53.31 CT £500.04 TOTE £3.10: £1.50, £4.40, £4.00; EX 66.80.
**Owner** P D Savill **Bred** Highclere Stud Ltd **Trained** Newmarket, Suffolk

**FOCUS**
A modest handicap in which the front pair pulled a very long way clear of the others, and the form is ordinary outside the front two.

**NOTEBOOK**
**Kirkham Abbey** has a good record here and bounced back to form under a determined ride to score off a career-high mark. He was without headgear for the first time in well over a year, which might have been a contributory factor. From his record this appears to be his level, as he has yet to win above a Grade E race.
**Fortune Point(IRE)** tried to make all and fought back bravely after being headed. This was a better effort than in his last few outings on turf and the reapplication of a visor, after over a year without them on, would seem a valid reason for the improvement.
**Fantasy Crusader** often runs well here but is very hard to win with. He is now back to a winning mark and should be noted back at Brighton or Lingfield.
**Over To You Bert** ran with a little credit without convincing he stays this trip on the level. Another slight drop in the handicap may see him more competitive.
**Husky(POL)** was never closer than at the line and has the option of going back over hurdles.
**Kernel Dowery(IRE)** disappointed again and looks like he is still slightly high in the handicap.
**Forge Lane(IRE)** had looked progressive before this, but never got into the race and the first-time blinkers didn't seem to help. *Official explanation: had looked progressive before this, but never got into the race and the first-time blinkers didn't seem to help.*

## 4437 CLUB AND INSTITUTE UNION CLASSIFIED STKS 6f 209y
5:10 (5:10) (E) 3-Y-O+ £3,328 (£1,024; £512; £256) Stalls Low

Form RPR
3420 1 **Samuel Charles**[13] 4067 6-9-3 70 SWKelly 6 78
(WMBrisbourne) *mde all: rdn and carried hd high fr over 2f out: drvn clr over 1f out: styd on wl* 9/2
1200 2 2 ½ **Brave Dane (IRE)**[11] 4122 6-9-7 74 WSupple 1 76+
(AWCarroll) *hld up in rr: rdn over 2f out: hdwy and nt clr run over 1f out: swtchd rt: r.o to take 2nd nr fin* 7/2[3]
3615 3 ½ **Carry On Doc**[11] 4151 3-9-2 75 SWhitworth 2 75
(JWHills) *chsd ldrs: rdn over 2f out: styd on same pce* 9/4[1]
0145 4 ½ **Franksalot (IRE)**[31] 3555 4-9-3 69 SSanders 4 69
(MissBSanders) *t.k.h: chsd wnr: rdn over 2f out: one pce: lost 2nd ins fnl f* 5/2[2]
6000 5 2 ½ **Our Gamble (IRE)**[42] 3211 3-8-8 70 DaneO'Neill 3 59
(RHannon) *hld up in rr: effrt on outside 3f out: edgd lft: no ex fnl 2f* 12/1
0104 6 5 **Ziet D'Alsace (FR)**[1] 4414 4-9-0 60 ADaly 5 46
(AWCarroll) *stdd s: t.k.h: cl up: wkng whn n.m.r over 2f out* 8/1

1m 22.29s (-0.31) **Going Correction** -0.05s/f (Good)
**WFA** 3 from 4yo+ 6lb 6 Ran SP% 118.5
Speed ratings: **99,96,95,95,92 86**CSF £21.79 TOTE £6.40: £2.40, £2.10; EX 26.10 Place 6 £2,187.34, Place 5 £1,524.59.
**Owner** J F Thomas **Bred** Sheikh Mohammed Obaid Al Maktoum **Trained** Great Ness, Shropshire

**FOCUS**
A tight little classified stakes with just 3lb covering five of the six runners on adjusted official ratings. The time was modest for the grade, 0.25 seconds slower than the earlier juvenile maiden, but the form looks fairly reasonable.

**NOTEBOOK**
**Samuel Charles** had been running consistently well up until a poor effort at Yarmouth last time. He had the luxury of a soft lead here and made full use of it. He did show his usual high head-carriage in the closing stages, but already had the race won by then and ran right to the line. Trainer Mark Brisbourne reported that on his last outing he had run his race before even getting to the start and during the race he merely set it up for the other runners. *Official explanation: had been running consistently well up until a poor effort at Yarmouth last time. He had the luxury of a soft lead here and made full use of it. He did show his usual high head-carriage in the closing stages, but already had the race won by then and ran right to the line. Trainer Mark Brisbourne reported that on his last outing he had run his race before even getting to the start and during the race he merely set it up for the other runners.*
**Brave Dane(IRE)**was always likely to find this too sharp and that appeared to be the case, though he did stay on to snatch second. A step up in trip will surely be on the cards next time, and there is always the option of a return to hurdles *Official explanation: was always likely to find this too sharp and that appeared to be the case, though he did stay on to snatch second. A step up in trip will surely be on the cards next time, and there is always the option of a return to hurdles*
**Carry On Doc** probably needs an extra furlong and could never land a blow. *Official explanation: probably needs an extra furlong and could never land a blow.*
**Franksalot(IRE)** was always up there and had every chance, but his efforts to get on terms with the winner eventually took their toll and he lost two places in the final 50 yards. He is still slightly higher than his last winning mark and probably needs a slight drop in the weights. *Official explanation: was always up there and had every chance, but his efforts to get on terms with the winner eventually took their toll and he lost two places in the final 50 yards. He is still slightly higher than his last winning mark and probably needs a slight drop in the weights.*
**Ziet D'Alsace(FR)** goes well here and was running for the second time in 24 hours. She had a bit to find with her five rivals on adjusted official ratings and ran accordingly. *Official explanation: goes well here and was running for the second time in 24 hours. She had a bit to find with her five rivals on adjusted official ratings and ran accordingly.*
T/Jkpt: Not won. T/Plt: £1,887.70 to a £1 stake. Pool: £59,605.25. 23.05 winning tickets. T/Qpdt: £538.40 to a £1 stake. Pool: £2,328.40. 3.20 winning tickets. LM

# [4233]KEMPTON (R-H)
Wednesday, August 4

**OFFICIAL GOING: Good to firm (good in places)**
The ground appeared to be quicker against the stands rail in the home straight.
Wind: nil Weather: very warm

## 4438 THE COMMITMENTS LIVE TONIGHT APPRENTICE H'CAP 1m (J)
6:00 (6:01) (E) (0-75,72) 3-Y-O+ £4,124 (£1,269; £634; £317) Stalls High

Form RPR
1112 1 **Burgundy**[6] 4262 7-9-0 59 (b) TPQueally 2 66
(PMitchell) *dwlt: racd in last: rdn over 3f out: sustained prog on outer fnl 2f: led nr fin* 9/2[2]
0043 2 ¾ **The Gaikwar (IRE)**[7] 4238 5-9-2 61 (b) MSavage 6 66
(NEBerry) *b.hind: lw: s.i.s: sn in midfield: prog 3f out: rdn to ld over 1f out: hdd nr fin* 7/1
6501 3 ½ **Moscow Times**[11] 4147 3-9-3 72 NataliaGemelova(3) 5 76
(DRCElsworth) *s.i.s: hld up in rr: stdy prog over 2f out: rdn to chal fnl f: upsides last 75yds: edgd rt and nt qckn* 8/1
1241 4 ¾ **Fen Gypsy**[2] 4401 6-9-9 71 6ex SJDonohoe(3) 1 73
(PDEvans) *racd on outer: trckd ldrs: lost pl and rdn 1/2-way: effrt u.p over 2f out: styd on: nt quite pce to chal* 11/2[3]
0212 5 ½ **Balerno**[9] 4199 5-9-0 59 DCorby 4 60
(RIngram) *settled in rr: prog over 2f out: hrd rdn and kpt on fr over 1f out: nvr able to chal* 7/2[1]
3602 6 ¾ **Fleetwood Bay**[7] 4238 4-9-8 67 (t) NChalmers 11 66
(BRMillman) *lw: trckd ldr: led over 2f out to over 1f out: one pce after* 8/1
0102 7 1 ½ **Gran Clicquot**[35] 3412 9-8-0 48 CHaddon(3) 7 44
(GPEnright) *racd in midfield: rdn over 3f out: effrt to chse ldrs over 1f out: no ex ins fnl f* 12/1
0/0 8 1 ¼ **Lizarazu (GER)**[25] 3745 5-9-13 72 RMiles 8 65
(FJordan) *w'like: hld up in rr: prog to trck ldrs 3f out: rdn and nt qckn over 1f out: fdd fnl f* 20/1
0040 9 3 **Catch The Fox**[28] 3631 4-7-7 43 oh1 LucyRussell(5) 10 29
(JJBridger) *swtg: chsd ldrs: rdn 3f out: wknd over 1f out* 33/1
5046 10 5 **Espada (IRE)**[20] 3871 8-8-2 52 (b) RKeogh(5) 9 26
(JAOsborne) *led: edgd lft and hdd over 2f out: wknd wl over 1f out* 20/1
50-1 11 1 ¾ **Listen To Reason (IRE)**[21] 3839 3-8-13 65 BReilly 3 35
(JGGiven) *lw: trckd ldrs: rdn 3f out: sn wknd* 14/1

1m 40.9s (1.28) **Going Correction** +0.125s/f (Good)
**WFA** 3 from 4yo+ 7lb 11 Ran SP% 117.3
Speed ratings: **98,97,96,96,95 94,93,92,89,84 82**CSF £34.95 CT £246.90 TOTE £4.90: £1.90, £2.60, £2.50; EX 56.00.
**Owner** Mrs S Sheldon **Bred** Cheveley Park Stud Ltd **Trained** Epsom, Surrey

**FOCUS**
A modest but competitive handicap and, although the proximity of the fifth anchors the form. The field raced far side to middle in the straight, with the winner coming up the middle.

**NOTEBOOK**
**Burgundy**, 4lb lower than in future handicaps off the back of his second to Cristoforo at Epsom on his previous start, had no such well-handicapped horses to contend with this time and showed himself still at the top of his game, gaining his fourth win from his last five outings. In this sort of form, he could well go in again.
**The Gaikwar(IRE)** remains in good heart, again showing enough to suggest a similar race will come his way this season.
**Moscow Times**, just 2lb higher than when successful at Salisbury on his previous start, did not appear to have excuses and remains in good heart.
**Fen Gypsy** has never followed up and was unable to add to his recent Windsor success under a 6lb penalty. Likely to be kept busy, he should continue to run well in similar events and should win again in his turn.
**Balerno** looked to have conditions to suit but was unable to take advantage of racing off a mark 3lb lower than in future.

## 4439 O'CALLAGHAN HOTELS NURSERY 6f
6:30 (6:32) (E) 2-Y-O £4,163 (£1,281; £640; £320) Stalls Centre

Form RPR
165 1 **Treat Me Wild (IRE)**[16] 3987 2-8-5 68 RSmith 4 69
(RHannon) *lw: cl up: trckd ldng pair wl over 1f out: rdn and styd on wl fnl f: led last stride* 14/1
3411 2 shd **The Crooked Ring**[7] 4235 2-9-3 87 6ex SJDonohoe(7) 3 88
(PDEvans) *lw: hld up in tch: smooth prog 1/2-way: led 2f out: rdn fnl f: tired and hdd last stride* 6/5[1]
3230 3 1 ½ **Edge Fund**[18] 3938 2-9-2 79 KMcEvoy 7 76
(BRMillman) *w ldr: led 1/2-way to 2f out: hrd rdn and one pce fr over 1f out* 6/1[3]
0664 4 2 **Pennestamp (IRE)**[13] 4058 2-8-5 68 RHavlin 5 59
(MrsPNDutfield) *racd freely: led to 1/2-way: cl up u.p 2f out: hanging and nt qckn over 1f out* 9/1
166 5 8 **King After**[91] 1878 2-9-2 84 MSavage(5) 6 51
(JRBest) *pressed ldrs: lost pl bef 1/2-way: u.p and wl btn 2f out* 10/1
640 6 5 **Epitomise**[16] 3992 2-8-6 69 MartinDwyer 1 21
(RMBeckett) *racd on outer: hld up: effrt and in tch 1/2-way: sn shkn up and btn: eased over 1f out: t.o* 14/1
064 7 ¾ **Chairman Rick (IRE)**[13] 4064 2-8-3 66 (v[1]) TPQueally 2 15
(DRLoder) *nvr gng wl: u.p and struggling bef 1/2-way: wl bhd 2f out: t.o* 4/1[2]

1m 13.94s (0.87) **Going Correction** -0.025s/f (Good) 7 Ran SP% 112.2
Speed ratings: **93,92,90,88,77 70,69**CSF £30.31 TOTE £9.30: £2.90, £1.60; EX 25.00.
**Owner** The Old Downton Partnership **Bred** David John Brown **Trained** East Everleigh, Wilts

**FOCUS**
Not that strong a nursery in which the field raced down the centre of the track.

**NOTEBOOK**
**Treat Me Wild(IRE)** had been tried over seven furlongs on her two starts since winning a claimer over five furlongs on her debut but, dropped in trip, she returned to form with a career-best effort. She is an ideal type for this sort of grade and could yet stay seven furlongs.
**The Crooked Ring**, 4lb well-in under his penalty, should have won this strictly on form, but could never quite get away from his field under his big weight. Things will be tougher off his new mark and he could just be one to take on at this level from now on.
**Edge Fund**, back up in trip with the cheekpieces left off this time, ran his race but did not look good enough.
**Pennestamp(IRE)** did not appear to get home and may be worth another try over five furlongs.
**King After**, racing for the first time in 91 days, looked on a ridiculously high mark for this handicap debut and was well beaten.
**Epitomise** *Official explanation: jockey said filly lost her action*
**Chairman Rick(IRE)**, fitted with a visor for the first time for this handicap debut, was well supported but showed little.

## 4440 RELAY TECHNICAL TRANSPORT MAIDEN STKS 5f
7:00 (7:00) (D) 3-Y-O+ £5,369 (£1,652; £826; £413) Stalls Centre

Form RPR
4- 1 **Elvina**[233] 6191 3-8-9 ................ LDettori 9 59
(AGNewcombe) *racd alone against far side rails: on terms w main gp: def advantage 1f out: drvn and jst hld on* **9/1**
63 2 *hd* **Millinsky (USA)**[43] 3179 3-8-9 ................ DHolland 7 58
(RGuest) *hld up bhd ldrs: nt clr run wl over 1f out: plld out to ld main gp ins fnl f: r.o wl nr fin: jst failed* **8/11**[1]
-000 3 *2 ½* **Ryan's Quest (IRE)**[43] 3175 5-8-9 39 ................ RMiles(3) 3 48
(TDMccarthy) *prom: led main gp 1/2-way to jst ins fnl f: one pce* **20/1**
0050 4 *¾* **Scarlett Breeze**[28] 3628 3-8-9 46 ................ MHills 6 45
(JWHills) *w ldrs: rdn and ev ch over 1f out: fdd fnl f* **15/2**[3]
5 *¾* **Heavens Walk** 3-9-0 ................ SSanders 1 47
(PJMakin) *w'like: str: sn trckd ldrs: cl up 2f out: shkn up and unable qck over 1f out: fdd fnl f* **11/4**[2]
3404 6 *6* **Lord Wishingwell (IRE)**[12] 4101 3-9-0 37 ................(v) CCatlin 4 23
(JSWainwright) *in tch for 2f: sn struggling and bhd* **25/1**
0000 7 *3* **Diaphanous**[23] 3810 6-8-12 35 ................(b) SCarson 8 6
(EAWheeler) *t.k.h: led main gp to 1/2-way: wknd rapidly over 1f out* **33/1**
0 8 *1* **Imperial Wizard**[196] 574 3-9-0 ................ ADaly 5 7
(MDIUsher) *bit bkwd: wl bhd after 2f: kpt on fnl f* **50/1**
000- 9 *6* **Angel Maid**[285] 5735 3-8-9 ................ RHavlin 2 —
(GBBalding) *sn wl bhd* **33/1**

60.46 secs (-0.75) **Going Correction** -0.025s/f (Good)
**WFA** 3 from 5yo+ 3lb 9 Ran SP% **122.8**
Speed ratings: **105,104,100,99,98 88,83,82,72**CSF £16.56 TOTE £6.00: £1.60, £1.10, £4.20; EX 11.10.
**Owner** Patel, Thomas, Eagle & Capel **Bred** M Patel And G I Thomas **Trained** Yarnscombe, Devon

**FOCUS**
A very moderate sprint maiden and the overall level of the form is poor. The winner raced away from the main group against the far rail and could well be flattered by this.

**NOTEBOOK**
**Elvina**, not seen since finishing fourth in a weak Fibresand maiden 233 days previously, left that form behind to get off the mark. She raced away from the remainder against the far rail and as a result it is hard to know what she achieved.
**Millinsky(USA)** came clear of all bar the winner, who raced alone against the far rail. She is now qualified for a handicap mark, and should get just a modest rating.
**Ryan's Quest(IRE)** was well held and will need to find improvement to win a similar race.
**Scarlett Breeze** may find things easier in selling company.
**Heavens Walk**, a first foal, out of a half-sister to winners, showed just moderate ability but could improve.

## 4441 MCGEE GROUP H'CAP 1m 6f 92y
7:30 (7:30) (D) (0-85,85) 3-Y-O+ £8,229 (£2,532; £1,266; £633) Stalls High

Form RPR
0-22 1 **Mr Ed (IRE)**[33] 3485 6-9-3 74 ................(p) LDettori 3 86+
(PBowen) *hld up wl in rr: stdy prog fr 4f out: plld out and rdn over 2f out: hdwy to ld over 1f out: idled in front: drvn out* **3/1**[1]
4152 2 *¾* **Masked (IRE)**[18] 3942 3-8-5 75 ................ KMcEvoy 11 83
(JWHills) *lw: settled in midfield: prog to trck ldrs over 2f out: rdn and nt qckn wl over 1f out: styd on to press wnr last 100yds:a* **9/1**
0-00 3 *¾* **Flamenco Bride**[12] 4075 4-8-10 67 ................ JFEgan 6 74
(DRCElsworth) *lw: hld up: prog 7f out: effrt to ld jst over 2f out: hdd over 1f out: kpt on ins fnl f* **16/1**
5342 4 *6* **Head To Kerry (IRE)**[7] 4233 4-7-9 55 ................(t) JFMcDonald(3) 8 54
(DJSFfrenchDavis) *t.k.h: hld up in midfield: gng easily 4f out: prog to chal 2f out: wknd fnl f* **7/1**
4000 5 *½* **Bukit Fraser (IRE)**[13] 4062 3-8-9 79 ................ SSanders 10 77
(PFICole) *trckd ldrs: prog to chse ldr 5f out: rdn and ev ch 2f out: wknd jst over 1f out* **11/2**[3]
1-10 6 *8* **Ocean Avenue (IRE)**[46] 3075 5-9-12 83 ................ DHolland 7 70
(CAHorgan) *led at gd pce: 4l clr 6f out: drvn and hdd jst over 2f out: wknd* **4/1**[2]
60-5 7 *3* **Jasmick (IRE)**[5] 4297 6-9-2 76 ................ LFletcher(3) 9 59
(HMorrison) *settled towards rr: rdn 4f out: sn struggling: wl bhd fnl 2f* **11/1**
3165 8 *7* **Sudden Flight (IRE)**[7] 4233 7-8-13 70 ................ RHavlin 5 43
(PDEvans) *hld up in rr: shkn up 4f out: no prog and sn wl btn* **16/1**
0013 9 *1* **Cantrip**[53] 2893 4-7-12 55 oh4 ................ LisaJones 2 26
(MissBSanders) *prom: rdn 6f out: disp 2nd pl briefly 5f out: wknd 4f out* **20/1**
0112 10 *1 ½* **Darn Good**[27] 3683 3-8-1 71 ................(b) MartinDwyer 12 40
(RHannon) *prom: pushed along bef 1/2-way: lost pl and struggling over 5f out: sn no ch* **10/1**
2000 11 *2 ½* **Western (IRE)**[25] 3752 4-9-3 74 ................ DaneO'Neill 1 40
(JAkehurst) *dwlt: a in rr: shkn up and no prog over 4f out: bhd after* **50/1**
351/ 12 *dist* **Fait Le Jojo (FR)**[74] 3967 7-10-0 85 ................ JPMurtagh 4 —
(PJHobbs) *chsd ldr to 5f out: wknd rapidly: t.o 3f out: eased* **14/1**

3m 6.93s (-3.73) **Going Correction** -0.125s/f (Firm)
**WFA** 3 from 4yo+ 13lb 12 Ran SP% **125.5**
Speed ratings: **105,104,104,100,100 95,94,90,89,88 87,—**CSF £32.95 CT £391.95 TOTE £3.70: £1.90, £3.00, £4.10; EX 28.50.
**Owner** Gwilym J Morris **Bred** P E Banahan **Trained** Letterston, Pembrokes

**FOCUS**
No better than fair form, but it was competitive enough and they went a good pace, setting it up for the closers. The action took place down the middle of the track in the straight.

**NOTEBOOK**
**Mr Ed(IRE)** was beaten quite a way into second over this trip at Sandown on his previous start, but stepped up on that effort under a fine waiting from Dettori. His immediate future could lie back over hurdles for a race at Newton Abbot but, judged on this performance, he could gain further success on the Flat.
**Masked(IRE)** appeared to improve for the step up from a mile and a half, showing there is a similar race in him with a good effort in defeat. He ought to get two miles.
**Flamenco Bride** ran her best race of the season so far and looks to be running into form.
**Head To Kerry(IRE)**, not for the first time this season, just failed to see out his race.
**Bukit Fraser(IRE)** was 7lb lower than when making his handicap debut earlier in the season, but was readily held and failed to convince he wants this sort of trip.
**Ocean Avenue(IRE)**, the winner of this race last year off a mark of 75, proved unable to sustain the good early gallop he set.
**Sudden Flight(IRE)** *Official explanation: trainer said gelding was unsuited by the ground*
**Fait Le Jojo(FR)** *Official explanation: vet said gelding finished sore in front*

## 4442 BYRNE GROUP CLASSIFIED STKS 1m (J)
8:00 (8:02) (C) 3-Y-O+ £11,128 (£3,424; £1,712; £856) Stalls High

Form RPR
-215 1 **Dawn Surprise (USA)**[29] 3602 3-8-11 89 ................(t) LDettori 9 103+
(SaeedBinSuroor) *trckd ldr: effrt to ld 2f out: rdn and styd on wl fr over 1f out* **11/4**[1]
2121 2 *1 ½* **Welcome Stranger**[7] 4237 4-9-6 81 ................ LFletcher(3) 8 99
(JMPEustace) *s.i.s: sn chsd ldrs: rdn and effrt 3f out: styd on wl to chse wnr ins fnl f: no imp* **5/1**[3]
0001 3 *½* **Will He Wish**[13] 4067 8-9-7 89 ................(b) JFEgan 4 96
(SGollings) *trckd ldrs: effrt over 2f out: chsd wnr over 1f out to ins fnl f: kpt on same pce* **14/1**
0403 4 *1 ¾* **Highland Reel**[8] 4220 7-9-3 85 ................ DaneO'Neill 7 88
(DRCElsworth) *settled in midfield: rdn over 2f out: one pce fr wl over 1f out* **9/1**
2111 5 *nk* **Diamond Lodge**[7] 4230 3-9-1 87 ................ SWKelly 6 92
(JNoseda) *lw: trckd ldrs: effrt to chal 2f out: sn rdn and nt qckn: fdd ins fnl f* **3/1**[2]
0-40 6 *2* **Dubrovsky**[39] 3299 4-9-3 84 ................(t) JPMurtagh 2 83
(JRFanshawe) *hld up towards rr: drvn over 2f out: no prog and btn wl over 1f out* **5/1**[3]
0-30 7 *shd* **Sharplaw Venture**[21] 3850 4-9-3 88 ................ DHolland 3 82
(WJHaggas) *racd freely: led at str pce: hdd 2f out: sn btn* **25/1**
0200 8 *3 ½* **Serieux**[5] 4287 5-9-6 88 ................ SSanders 1 77
(MrsAJPerrett) *lw: hld up in last pair: rdn 3f out: no prog* **9/1**
5440 9 *6* **Our Teddy (IRE)**[32] 3539 4-9-3 85 ................(b) MartinDwyer 5 60
(AMBalding) *hld up in last pair: rdn over 3f out: wknd over 2f out* **20/1**

1m 39.15s (-0.47) **Going Correction** +0.125s/f (Good)
**WFA** 3 from 4yo+ 7lb 9 Ran SP% **120.3**
Speed ratings: **107,105,105,103,102 100,100,97,91**CSF £17.77 TOTE £4.20: £1.60, £1.70, £4.10; EX 24.20.
**Owner** Godolphin **Bred** Gainsborough Stud Management Llc **Trained** Newmarket, Suffolk

**FOCUS**
A decent enough classified event and a tight race on the figures, with just 5lb separating the entire field. The form looks basically good. The field raced towards the stands'-side rail in the straight.

**NOTEBOOK**
**Dawn Surprise(USA)** was ideally suited by this return to a mile and won convincingly, showing she does not need to lead in the process. She lightly raced and open to more improvement, possibly over a little further.
**Welcome Stranger** had his ideal conditions, but the winner was just too strong. This was still a good effort in defeat and he remains in cracking order.
**Will He Wish** was unproven beyond seven furlongs and is fully effective over six, but he showed he stays a mile, if not ideally suited by it.
**Highland Reel** did not run a bad race, but he seems at his very best in big-field handicaps.
**Diamond Lodge** looked highly progressive when completing the hat-trick at Goodwood on her previous start, but this was a little disappointing. She can be given another chance to show she is better than this.
**Sharplaw Venture** *Official explanation: jockey said filly hung badly left throughout*

## 4443 MCARDLE GROUP H'CAP 1m 2f (J)
8:30 (8:34) (E) (0-75,77) 3-Y-O £4,212 (£1,296; £648; £324) Stalls Centre

Form RPR
6402 1 **Little Eye (IRE)**[13] 4056 3-8-8 62 ................(v) LDettori 10 68
(JRBest) *racd in midfield: prog 3f out: drvn to chse ldr over 1f out: led ins fnl f: hld on wl* **7/2**[1]
0-00 2 *½* **American Duke (USA)**[32] 3543 3-8-10 64 ................ PaulEddery 1 69
(BJMeehan) *settled in rr: rdn and prog wl over 2f out: drvn to press wnr wl ins fnl f: jst hld* **14/1**
4041 3 *1 ¼* **Iffy**[12] 4079 3-8-9 63 ................ CCatlin 14 66
(PDCundell) *led: styd on inner fr 7f out whn rest of field racd wd: drvn 2f out: hdd and no ex ins fnl f* **5/1**[3]
0-51 4 *1 ½* **Desert Reign**[20] 3875 3-9-3 71 ................ TPQueally 8 71
(APJarvis) *lw: racd in midfield: nt clr run and swtchd lft over 2f out: drvn and styd on fr over 1f out: nrst fin* **6/1**
-600 5 *1 ¼* **La Professoressa (IRE)**[51] 2949 3-8-5 59 ................ RHavlin 4 56
(MrsPNDutfield) *prom: chsd ldr over 2f out: ev ch over 1f out: fdd ins fnl f* **25/1**
6-54 6 *nk* **Bright Fire (IRE)**[12] 4092 3-7-12 52 oh2 ................ LisaJones 12 49
(WJMusson) *racd in midfield: rdn and effrt over 2f out: chsd ldrs over 1f out: one pce after* **14/1**
0520 7 *1 ½* **Sharaab (USA)**[19] 3922 3-9-2 70 ................(t) DHolland 6 64
(BHanbury) *mostly chsd ldr to over 2f out: fdd over 1f out* **20/1**
3640 8 *shd* **Anduril**[51] 2949 3-8-10 64 ................ JFEgan 15 58
(JMPEustace) *rrd bdly s: hld up in last trio: prog on inner 4f out: rdn to chse ldrs over 1f out: fdd fnl f: eased* **25/1**
000- 9 *1 ½* **Circassian (IRE)**[299] 5467 3-8-7 61 ................ SSanders 3 52
(SirMarkPrescott) *trckd ldrs: rdn over 2f out: sn lost pl: n.d over 1f out* **7/1**
1113 10 *½* **Doctored**[5] 4300 3-9-2 77 6ex ................(b) SJDonohoe(7) 13 67
(PDEvans) *racd in midfield: effrt 3f out: sme prog in centre 2f out: wknd fnl f* **9/2**[2]
0-40 11 *1* **Spring Adieu**[33] 3473 3-8-10 64 ................ JPMurtagh 11 52
(MrsAJPerrett) *chsd ldrs: rdn and unable qck over 2f out: fdd over 1f out* **25/1**
4454 12 *½* **Cartronageeraghlad (IRE)**[29] 3610 3-9-7 75 ................ DaneO'Neill 9 62
(JAOsborne) *a in rr: rdn and no prog over 2f out* **8/1**
-440 13 *1 ¾* **Papeete (GER)**[14] 4027 3-8-2 56 ................ SCarson 7 40
(MissBSanders) *a in rr: rdn and struggling 3f out* **33/1**
2006 14 *1 ½* **Midshipman Easy (USA)**[20] 3866 3-9-2 70 ................(e1) SWKelly 5 51
(PWHarris) *lw: a in last trio: rdn 4f out: struggling after* **25/1**

2m 5.65s (-0.49) **Going Correction** +0.125s/f (Good) 14 Ran SP% **131.4**
Speed ratings: **106,105,104,103,102 102,100,100,99,99 98,98,96,95**CSF £55.13 CT £262.22 TOTE £4.30: £1.80, £5.70, £2.10; EX 136.60 Place 6 £48.49, Place 5 £13.86.
**Owner** Mr & Mrs R Dawbarn **Bred** Mrs Dare Wigan **Trained** Hucking, Kent

**FOCUS**
Just a modest handicap in which the field raced towards the stands'-side rail in the straight. The form looks sound for the grade.

**NOTEBOOK**
**Little Eye(IRE)** has taken well to the fitting of a visor in recent outings and was able to gain his first success at the 20th attempt. Now he has got his head in front, he should go on from this for his in-form yard.
**American Duke(USA)**, racing off a mark 10lb lower than when first contesting a handicap, showed himself on a reasonable rating with a solid effort. He is still a maiden, but looks up to winning a similar race. *Official explanation: jockey said saddle slipped*
**Iffy**, 5lb higher than when off the mark in a weak race at Ascot on his previous start, ran respectably and these conditions clearly suit well.


The Form Book, Raceform Ltd, Compton, RG20 6NL

**Desert Reign**, 6lb higher than when landing a gamble over an extended mile on his previous start at Epsom, would have been closer with a clearer run on this step up in trip.
**La Professoressa(IRE)** did not run a bad race, but her optimum remains unclear.
**Anduril** *Official explanation: jockey said colt did not handle the track*
**Doctored**, successful on six of his last eight starts, was simply not at his best but, if any horse can be forgiven a bad run, he can.
T/Plt: £34.60 to a £1 stake. Pool: £49,647.80. 1,045.95 winning tickets. T/Qpdt: £9.50 to a £1 stake. Pool: £4,389.80. 338.70 winning tickets. JN

# 4130 NEWCASTLE (L-H)
## Wednesday, August 4

**OFFICIAL GOING: Good to soft (good in places)**
Wind: light, half behind Weather: overcast

## 4444 "JAZZY" GEOFF AINSLEY SUPPORTS NSPCC MAIDEN STKS — 1m 1f 9y
2:30 (2:32) (D) 3-Y-O+ — £3,435 (£1,057; £528; £264) Stalls Centre

Form — RPR
4230 **1** **Little Bob**[18] 3955 3-8-13 75 ... TEDurcan 9 — 71+
(JDBethell) *hld up in tch: hdwy to chse ldrs after 3f: led and edgd lft over 2f out: edgd rt ins fnl f: hld on wl* **11/10**[1]
4 **2** ½ **St Barchan (IRE)**[35] 3422 3-8-13 ... KDarley 1 — 70+
(WJarvis) *dwlt: keen and sn chsng ldrs: n.m.r over 2f out: effrt and pressed wnr over 1f out: r.o: hld towards fin* **11/4**[2]
54 **3** 6 **Kyber**[10] 4180 3-8-13 ... RWinston 8 — 58
(RFFisher) *prom: effrt over 2f out: edgd lft: sn outpcd* **10/1**
0503 **4** nk **Rigonza**[18] 3955 3-8-13 62 ... DAllan 6 — 57
(TDEasterby) *hld up in tch: rdn and outpcd 3f out: rallied over 1f out: no imp* **5/1**[3]
0000 **5** 4 **The Loose Screw (IRE)**[32] 3520 6-9-2 35 ... (p) BSwarbrick(5) 2 — 49?
(GMMoore) *led to over 2f out: sn btn* **33/1**
0 **6** 12 **High Class Pet**[30] 3587 4-9-2 ... GFaulkner 7 — 20
(FPMurtagh) *hld up in tch: effrt over 3f out: rdn and wknd over 2f out* **100/1**
0-0 **7** ½ **Red Mountain**[33] 3475 3-8-10 ... LEnstone(3) 4 — 24
(DWBarker) *chsd ldrs to 3f out: sn btn* **33/1**
5005 **8** 7 **Blue Nun**[2] 4396 3-8-8 47 ... GGibbons 3 — 5
(MrsADuffield) *chsd ldrs tl wknd fr 3f out* **33/1**
0- **9** 4 **Distinctlythebest**[436] 1877 4-9-2 ... (t) PMakin(5) 5 — 2
(FWatson) *bhd: struggling fr 4f out* **100/1**

1m 58.63s (0.83) **Going Correction** +0.25s/f (Good)
**WFA** 3 from 4yo+ 8lb — **9** Ran SP% **110.8**
Speed ratings: **106,105,100,99,96 85,85,79,75**CSF £3.79 TOTE £2.30: £1.10, £1.20, £1.60; EX 6.00.
**Owner** Robert Gibbons **Bred** R F Gibbons **Trained** Middleham Moor, N Yorks

**FOCUS**
An uncompetitive maiden in which the pace was only fair and a race in which the two market leaders pulled clear in the last quarter mile. The form behind the front two looks very ordinary.

**NOTEBOOK**
**Little Bob**, who cocked his jaw and ran out at Ripon last time, looked to have solid claims on his previous Doncaster run (form working out well) and he showed the right attitude to beat a less exposed rival. He will find things tougher back in handicaps, though.
**St Barchan(IRE)** was easy to back but bettered his debut effort and left the impression that a stiffer test of stamina would have been in his favour. He looks capable of winning a similar event away from progressive types.
**Kyber** again had the run of the race and was not disgraced. He is likely to continue to look vulnerable in this grade but may do better over further in handicaps and, as a half-brother to hurdles winner Hamadeenah, will be of interest for current connections when sent over timber.
**Rigonza**, back on a sound surface, was not totally disgraced but again did not look the easiest of rides and, although a stiffer test of stamina may help, he does not look one to place much faith in.
**The Loose Screw(IRE)** looked to face a very stiff task at the weights and, given he had the rub of this steadily-run race, is almost certainly flattered by his proximity. He is likely to find things tough going.
**High Class Pet** was again soundly beaten and will continue to look vulnerable in this grade.

## 4445 MOWDEN PARK ESTATES SUPPORTS NSPCC NURSERY — 7f
3:00 (3:00) (E) 2-Y-O — £3,818 (£1,175; £587; £293) Stalls Low

Form — RPR
5503 **1** **Lady Misha**[43] 3164 2-7-12 62 ... JMackay 9 — 65
(JeddO'Keeffe) *prom: rdn 1/2-way: led 1f out: styd on wl* **16/1**
13 **2** 1 **Sir Anthony (IRE)**[20] 3865 2-9-7 85 ... DMcGaffin 18 — 86
(BSmart) *hld up: hdwy on outside 2f: kpt on fnl f: hld towards fin* **5/1**[2]
2332 **3** 1½ **Brace Of Doves**[6] 4278 2-8-5 69 ... KDarley 3 — 66
(TDBarron) *keen: cl up: led over 2f out to 1f out: one pce* **11/4**[1]
032 **4** ½ **Spinnakers Girl**[11] 4135 2-8-6 70 ... RWinston 12 — 66
(JRWeymes) *hld up midfield: effrt 2f out: one pce ins fnl f* **14/1**
0663 **5** 1¾ **Mitchelland**[18] 3924 2-8-7 74 ... TEaves(3) 11 — 65
(JamesMoffatt) *s.i.s: bhd: n.m.r over 2f out: r.o fnl f: no imp* **12/1**
1313 **6** ½ **Society Music (IRE)**[21] 3834 2-8-13 80 ... LEnstone(3) 10 — 70
(MDods) *keen: hld up: rdn 2f out: no imp fnl f* **10/1**
4040 **7** 2 **Lord John**[12] 4094 2-8-0 64 ... DaleGibson 8 — 49
(MWEasterby) *prom: rdn along 1/2-way: one pce over 1f out* **16/1**
266 **8** nk **Skippit John**[52] 2904 2-8-8 72 ... DeanMcKeown 15 — 56
(RonaldThompson) *keen: cl up tl outpcd wl over 1f out* **25/1**
3365 **9** hd **Twice Nightly**[14] 4012 2-8-2 69 ... THamilton(3) 5 — 53
(JDBethell) *bhd: rdn over 2f out: nvr rchd ldrs* **10/1**
106 **10** hd **Heres The Plan (IRE)**[12] 4089 2-9-2 80 ... PMcCabe 14 — 63
(MGQuinlan) *led to over 2f out: btn fnl f* **6/1**[3]
400 **11** ¾ **Master Joseph**[46] 3083 2-8-0 64 ... PMQuinn 1 — 46
(MRChannon) *hld up: nt clr run over 2f out: n.d* **16/1**
6104 **12** hd **Mytton's Dream**[29] 3605 2-7-12 62 oh2 ... JBramhill 2 — 43
(ABailey) *midfield: rdn over 2f out: wknd over 1f out* **20/1**
0651 **13** 9 **Uredale (IRE)**[14] 4010 2-8-4 68 ... GGibbons 13 — 27
(MrsADuffield) *in tch tl wknd over 2f out* **12/1**

1m 29.06s (1.04) **Going Correction** 0.0s/f (Good) — **13** Ran SP% **124.1**
Speed ratings: **94,92,91,90,88 88,85,85,85,84 84,83,73**CSF £97.78 CT £297.84 TOTE £23.20: £6.60, £1.90, £1.60; EX 230.50.
**Owner** Allen, Kelly & Moore **Bred** Bishop's Down Farm **Trained** Middleham Moor, N Yorks

**FOCUS**
An ordinary nursery which was run at only a fair gallop and a race in which the whole field raced on the far side. The form looks solid. The 'official ratings' are estimated and for guidance only.

**NOTEBOOK**
**Lady Misha** turned in an improved effort to get off the mark for a stable that has been going well in recent times. She should prove equally effective over a mile and should continue to give a good account.
**Sir Anthony(IRE)** ◆, a lightly raced sort, turned in his best effort on this first run over seven furlongs and did well as he fared easily the best of those that was held up off the ordinary gallop. He may be a bit better than the bare form and looks sure to win more races.
**Brace Of Doves** is a consistent sort who had the run of the race and looks the best guide to the level of this form. He should continue to give a good account but left the impression that the step up to a mile would be in his favour.
**Spinnakers Girl** is a reliable sort who ran right up to her best on this first run on easy ground and this nursery debut. She is likely to be vulnerable to progressive types in this grade but should continue to go well and should stay a mile.
**Mitchelland** up a fair bit in trip, did not fail through lack of stamina and looks better than the bare form as he met trouble when attempting to make ground from an uncompromising position. He is one to keep an eye on.
**Society Music(IRE)**, ridden with more restraint this time, failed to settle but was anything but disgraced on ground he handles. His provisional rating looks plenty high enough, though and he is likely to remain vulnerable to progressive types.

## 4446 LLOYDS TSB SUPPORTS NSPCC MEDIAN AUCTION MAIDEN STKS — 6f
3:30 (3:32) (F) 2-Y-O — £3,052 (£872; £436) Stalls Low

Form — RPR
2 **1** **Spy King (USA)**[20] 3876 2-9-0 ... KDarley 13 — 88
(MJohnston) *chsd far side ldrs: effrt over 2f out: led 1f out: hld on wl* **9/2**[3]
F **2** ½ **Stretford End (IRE)**[23] 3793 2-9-0 ... DMcGaffin 17 — 86+
(BSmart) *led and clr stands side: rdn over 2f out: r.o wl fnl f: jst hld by far side wnr* **4/1**[2]
2220 **3** 1 **Tagula Sunrise (IRE)**[18] 3938 2-8-6 85 ... THamilton(3) 12 — 78
(RAFahey) *led after 2f far side to 1f out: one pce fnl f* **3/1**[1]
3 **4** 1¼ **Game Lad**[9] 4187 2-9-0 ... DAllan 16 — 79+
(TDEasterby) *chsd stands side ldr: rdn 1/2-way: kpt on fnl f* **25/1**
05 **5** 2 **Profit's Reality (IRE)**[67] 2470 2-9-0 ... DeanMcKeown 2 — 73
(PABlockley) *in tch far side: effrt over 2f out: no imp fnl f* **10/1**
223 **6** 2 **Sunset Strip**[11] 4143 2-9-0 78 ... TEDurcan 11 — 67
(MRChannon) *led 2f far side: cl up tl one pce fr 2f out* **9/2**[3]
40 **7** nk **Union Jack Jackson (IRE)**[33] 3476 2-9-0 ... JBramhill 15 — 66
(JGGiven) *in tch far side: rdn over 2f out: no imp fnl f* **66/1**
**8** 2 **River Liffey** 2-9-0 ... RMullen 18 — 60+
(MLWBell) *dwlt: rdn along bhd stands side ldrs 1/2-way: no imp fnl f* **20/1**
0000 **9** 1¾ **Fantasy Defender (IRE)**[46] 3083 2-9-0 ... GFaulkner 10 — 55?
(JJQuinn) *hld up far side: rdn over 2f out: sn n.d* **100/1**
0 **10** nk **Succession**[7] 4243 2-8-9 ... JMackay 1 — 49
(SirMarkPrescott) *bhd far side: pushed along 1/2-way: n.d* **40/1**
**11** shd **Balgarth (USA)** 2-8-9 ... PMakin(5) 14 — 54
(TDBarron) *hld up midfield far side: shkn up 2f out: sn outpcd* **20/1**
0 **12** 1¼ **Shekan Star**[13] 4048 2-8-9 ... DaleGibson 5 — 45
(MrsMReveley) *a bhd far side* **100/1**
20 **13** 3 **As Handsome Does**[25] 3758 2-9-0 ... (t) KimTinkler 6 — 41
(NTinkler) *bhd and pushed along 1/2-way far side: sn n.d* **66/1**
0 **14** 3 **Plenty Cried Wolf**[13] 4048 2-8-11 ... PMulrennan(3) 3 — 32
(RAFahey) *in tch far side tl wknd over 2f out* **66/1**
05 **15** 4 **Detroit Dancer**[22] 3818 2-9-0 ... GGibbons 4 — 20
(RonaldThompson) *prom far side: rdn and wknd fr over 2f out* **100/1**
**16** 10 **Azahara** 2-8-6 ... LEnstone(3) 8 — —
(MrsMReveley) *sn bhd far side: no ch fr 1/2-way* **66/1**
**17** ½ **Kashtanka (IRE)** 2-9-0 ... RWinston 7 — —
(JJQuinn) *a bhd far side* **50/1**
**18** dist **Perrywinkle** 2-8-6 ... TEaves(3) 9 — —
(JamesMoffatt) *missed break: sn t.o far side* **100/1**

1m 15.28s (0.24) **Going Correction** 0.0s/f (Good) — **18** Ran SP% **118.2**
Speed ratings: **98,97,96,94,91 89,88,85,83,83 83,81,77,73,68 54,54,—**CSF £19.75 TOTE £4.80: £2.30, £2.10, £1.30; EX 24.20.
**Owner** P D Savill **Bred** Russell S Davis **Trained** Middleham Moor, N Yorks

**FOCUS**
A fair race of its type and one in which the bulk of the runners raced on the far side. However the proximity of the stands'-side quartet suggests there was little or no advantage/disadvantage in the draw. The winning time was very decent for the grade and the form looks strong.

**NOTEBOOK**
**Spy King(USA)** duly improved for his debut run and appreciated the stiffer test of stamina this race had to offer to get off the mark. He should stay seven furlongs and is likely to fare better again.
**Stretford End(IRE)** ◆, well backed before falling on his debut, proved himself none the worse for that experience and showed he was capable of fair form. Whether he would have beaten the winner had he been drawn on the far side is a matter for debate but he is a fair sort on looks who is open to further improvement and is sure to win a similar event.
**Tagula Sunrise(IRE)**, tried over this trip and on easy ground for the first time, ran creditably and, although she has now been placed in four of her five starts, she has done nothing wrong and is capable of picking up a small event.
**Game Lad** ◆ bettered the form of his All-Weather debut on this first start on turf and left the impression that the step up to seven furlongs would be in his favour. He too looks the type to win an ordinary race.
**Profit's Reality(IRE)** shaped as though retaining all his ability on this first start since May and will be an interesting proposition at up to seven furlongs in nursery company in due course.
**Sunset Strip** may not be the most straightforward and will have to improve to win a competitive nursery but shaped as though the return to seven furlongs would be in his favour.

## 4447 YUILL HOMES SUPPORTS NSPCC H'CAP — 7f
4:00 (4:02) (E) (0-75,71) 3-Y-O+ — £4,056 (£1,248; £624; £312) Stalls Low

Form — RPR
0012 **1** **Parisian Playboy**[15] 4008 4-7-9 45 ... LeanneKershaw(7) 9 — 59+
(JeddO'Keeffe) *hld up and bhd: hdwy over 1f out: led ins fnl f: edgd lft: r.o wl* **9/2**[1]
0-00 **2** ½ **Stormville (IRE)**[11] 4132 7-8-4 52 ow2 ... MLawson(5) 11 — 61
(MBrittain) *in tch: effrt over 2f out: kpt on fnl f: nt rch wnr* **25/1**
0000 **3** 1 **Bond Playboy**[43] 3167 4-9-3 60 ... DMcGaffin 18 — 67
(BSmart) *led: clr over 1f out: hdd and no ex ins fnl f* **33/1**
0400 **4** 1 **Tancred Arms**[11] 4132 8-7-5 41 oh6 ... (v) DonnaCaldwell(7) 8 — 45
(DWBarker) *prom tl rdn and nt qckn fnl f* **100/1**
2046 **5** ½ **Noble Penny**[30] 3586 5-7-10 46 ... AElliott(7) 16 — 49
(MrsKWalton) *bhd and sn rdn along: hdwy over 1f out: nrst fin* **12/1**
0-00 **6** hd **Inchdura**[25] 3755 6-9-10 67 ... KimTinkler 7 — 70
(NTinkler) *bhd: rdn 1/2-way: kpt on fnl f: nrst fin* **9/1**[3]
0260 **7** 2 **Mallard (IRE)**[25] 3734 6-9-3 60 ... KDarley 13 — 58
(JGGiven) *hld up: effrt over 2f out: shkn up and sn one pce* **9/2**[1]
6050 **8** 1¼ **Mount Pekan (IRE)**[11] 4132 4-7-12 41 ... JMackay 10 — 35
(JSGoldie) *bhd: rdn 1/2-way: nvr rchd ldrs* **33/1**
2005 **9** ½ **Carlton (IRE)**[16] 3982 10-8-10 58 ... RThomas(5) 17 — 51
(CRDore) *trckd ldrs tl rdn and wknd fnl f* **9/1**[3]
-010 **10** 1 **Stellite**[86] 1993 4-8-2 48 ow1 ... THamilton(3) 14 — 39
(JSGoldie) *cl up tl wknd over 1f out* **13/2**[2]

-103 **11** *hd* **Tancred Miss**[29] 3612 5-7-13 **42**.......... JMcAuley 12 32
(DWBarker) *midfield: rdn over 2f out: sn btn* **25/1**

4-00 **12** *2* **The Wizard Mul**[102] 1620 4-9-3 **60**.......... JBramhill 15 45
(WStorey) *w wnr early: cl up tl wknd over 1f out* **16/1**

4001 **13** *nk* **Mehmaas**[11] 4132 8-8-10 **56**..........(v) TEaves(3) 4 40
(REBarr) *prom 3f: sn lost pl: n.d after* **12/1**

000- **14** *1 ½* **Piper**[335] 4687 4-7-7 **41** oh5.......... BSwarbrick(5) 5 22
(DWBarker) *chsd ldrs tl rdn and wknd over 2f out* **66/1**

0100 **15** *¾* **Libre**[19] 3895 4-9-2 **59**..........(bt) DeanMcKeown 2 38
(RCGuest) *hld up: rdn over 2f out: sn btn* **16/1**

3306 **16** *13* **Four Kings**[7] 4249 3-8-9 **63**.......... PPMathers(5) 3 9
(RAllan) *in tch 3f: sn lost pl* **33/1**

4250 **17** *11* **Heversham (IRE)**[13] 4050 3-9-5 **71**.......... LEnstone(3) 1 —
(JHetherton) *bhd: rdn 1/2-way: nvr on terms* **20/1**

1m 28.42s (0.40) **Going Correction** 0.0s/f (Good)
**WFA** 3 from 4yo+ 6lb **17** Ran SP% **120.6**
Speed ratings: **97,96,95,94,93 93,91,89,89,87 87,85,85,83,82 67,55**CSF £126.42 CT £3425.41 TOTE £6.20: £1.90, £4.90, £5.50, £22.50; EX 252.60.
**Owner** Playboy Partnership **Bred** Paul Scholes **Trained** Middleham Moor, N Yorks
■ Stewards Enquiry : T Eaves two-day ban: careless riding (Aug 15-16)

**FOCUS**
A run-of-the-mill event comprising several unreliable sorts, but a sound pace and the winner is on the upgrade, albeit at a modest level. He appeals as the type to win more races, but the overall form is not that solid.

**NOTEBOOK**
**Parisian Playboy** ◆ is getting his act together and notched his second win from his last three starts to extend the yard's good recent run. He fared the best of those that came from off the pace and appeals as the type to win again, especially on his favoured easy ground and back over a mile.
**Stormville(IRE)** seems to go well at this course and, although very lightly raced in recent times, confirmed he retains ability. Whether this will be reproduced next time remains to be seen, though.
**Bond Playboy** has not won on turf for some time and is not the most consistent but showed he retains enough ability to win a similar race from this sort of mark. However he is another that is not sure to put it all in next time.
**Tancred Arms**, whose form has been patchy since her Ayr win last year, was not disgraced from 6lb out of the handicap but, although capable of winning a similar event, is not one to place too much faith in.
**Noble Penny** did well to finish as close as she did given her wide draw and her uncompromising position at halfway but the fact that she is unreliable and has yet to win in 20 starts has to be a big worry.
**Inchdura** has not won for some time but has plummeted in the weights and confirmed he retains ability. The return to a mile should suit and he will be one to keep an eye on in similar company.
*Official explanation: jockey said gelding suffered interference in the first furlong*

## 4448 TBI WEALTH MANAGEMENT SUPPORTS NSPCC H'CAP 2m 19y
**4:30** (4:30) (E) (0-75,75) 3-Y-O+ **£3,789** (£1,166; £583; £291) **Stalls** Centre

Form RPR

2451 **1** **Toni Alcala**[37] 3363 5-9-9 **73**.......... PMulrennan(3) 4 79
(RFFisher) *in tch: effrt over 2f out: led appr fnl f: kpt on wl* **13/2**[3]

0020 **2** *hd* **Riyadh**[7] 4226 6-9-5 **66**.......... KDarley 5 72
(MJohnston) *hld up in tch: niggled over 4f out: hdwy and ev ch over 1f out: kpt on but a hld* **7/2**[1]

0-40 **3** *4* **Fantastico (IRE)**[35] 2615 4-8-13 **60**..........(p) RWinston 9 61
(MrsKWalton) *prom: led over 2f to appr fnl f: no ex ins last* **10/1**

1540 **4** *3* **Colorado Falls (IRE)**[19] 3902 6-9-11 **75**.......... LEnstone(3) 3 73
(PMonteith) *hld up: effrt over 2f out: r.o fnl f: nrst fin* **13/2**[3]

4330 **5** *½* **Shongweni (IRE)**[13] 4062 3-8-3 **65**.......... RMullen 7 62
(PJMcbride) *prom: rdn and n.m.r over 2f out: sn one pce* **15/2**

-540 **6** *1 ½* **Simple Ideals (USA)**[23] 3803 10-7-12 **45** oh10.......... KimTinkler 2 40
(DonEnricoIncisa) *bhd: pushed along over 3f out: n.d* **10/1**

-000 **7** *½* **Allez Mousson**[18] 3928 6-7-12 **45**..........(b) JBramhill 8 40
(ABailey) *hld up: rdn 4f out: n.d* **16/1**

0403 **8** *½* **Calomeria**[18] 3928 3-8-0 **62**..........(b) JMackay 12 56
(RMBeckett) *cl up: ev ch over 2f out: wknd over 1f out* **10/1**

6666 **9** *7* **Lebenstanz**[19] 3919 4-9-4 **65**.......... DaleGibson 11 51
(LMCumani) *keen: led to over 2f out: sn btn* **11/2**[2]

-400 **10** *7* **River Line (USA)**[16] 3981 3-7-7 **60** oh13.......... BSwarbrick(5) 10 37
(CWFairhurst) *sn chsng ldrs: rdn and wknd over 2f out* **33/1**

3m 40.33s (5.30) **Going Correction** +0.25s/f (Good)
**WFA** 3 from 4yo+ 15lb **10** Ran SP% **112.1**
Speed ratings: **96,95,93,92,92 91,91,90,87,83**CSF £28.27 CT £223.22 TOTE £5.50: £2.50, £1.60, £3.40; EX 14.70.
**Owner** Alan Willoughby **Bred** Mrs Agnes Steele Moore **Trained** Ulverston, Cumbria

**FOCUS**
A run-of-the-mill handicap run at an ordinary gallop and a modest winning time. The first two did well to pull clear in the closing stages and both are running well of late.

**NOTEBOOK**
**Toni Alcala** is a much more reliable sort these days and showed too much fighting spirit for a less than hearty rival to notch his fourth success of the year. He should continue to give a good account.
**Riyadh** is capable of winning in this grade but, although showing his Goodwood run to be all wrong, again left the impression that he is saving something for himself. He remains one to tread carefully with.
**Fantastico(IRE)**, last seen when winning over hurdles in first-time cheekpieces in June, ran creditably in the same headgear, especially as she may have preferred a sounder surface. She looks capable of winning over this trip back on fast ground.
**Colorado Falls(IRE)**, over this trip for the first time on the Flat, was not totally disgraced and did not fail through lack of stamina, but did not really leave the impression that he is about to return to winning ways from his current mark.
**Shongweni(IRE)**, with the headgear left off this time, did not improve for the step up to this trip, although he did meet a bit of trouble and he may be suited by a more strongly-run race over shorter.
**Simple Ideals(USA)** was not disgraced from 10lb out of the handicap but given he is on a long losing run and is not the most consistent, he would not be one to lump on from his proper rating next time.
**Allez Mousson** *Official explanation: jockey said gelding was unsuited by the slow early pace*
**Lebenstanz**, closely related to high-class stayer Boreas, failed to settle on this first start over this trip and ran poorly. She is not one to write off just yet but looks unlikely to be emulating her illustrious relative.

## 4449 J & G ARCHIBALD SUPPORTS NSPCC CHAMPAGNE APPRENTICE CLASSIFIED STKS 1m 2f 32y
**5:00** (5:00) (G) 3-Y-O+ **£2,623** (£749; £374) **Stalls** High

Form RPR

0202 **1** **Pay Attention**[16] 3981 3-8-5 60.......... DAllan 1 70
(TDEasterby) *trckd ldrs: led 1f out: rdn out* **4/1**[1]

5123 **2** *2 ½* **Melodian**[84] 2039 9-9-0 62..........(b) MLawson(5) 8 71
(MBrittain) *cl up: led 1/2-way: hdd over 1f out: one pce* **5/1**[3]

5001 **3** *1* **Fairlie**[22] 3817 3-8-5 59.......... TEaves 9 64
(MrsMReveley) *hld up: rdn and hdwy over 1f out: nrst fin* **12/1**

6361 **4** *½* **Rock Lobster**[11] 4138 3-8-9 64.......... PMakin(3) 7 70
(JGGiven) *hld up in tch: hdwy to chsd ldrs whn n.m.r 2f out: sn rdn: kpt on ins last* **4/1**[1]

2513 **5** *½* **Pearl Of York (DEN)**[19] 3897 3-8-8 63.......... LEnstone 6 65
(RGuest) *chsd ldrs: rdn to ld over 1f out: sn hdd: outpcd towards fin* **9/2**[2]

4646 **6** *2 ½* **Orion Express**[16] 3981 3-8-5 60.......... PMulrennan(3) 4 61
(MWEasterby) *hld up: effrt and rdn 2f out: sn no imp* **12/1**

033- **7** *½* **Beamish Prince**[147] 3527 5-9-0 59.......... BSwarbrick(3) 5 60
(GMMoore) *keen: cl up: effrt over 2f out: sn btn* **16/1**

060 **8** *27* **Pure Vintage (IRE)**[12] 4101 3-8-8 58.......... THamilton 2 14
(RAFahey) *in tch tl rdn and wknd over 3f out* **6/1**

00-0 **9** *3* **North Landing (IRE)**[40] 1915 4-8-10 40.......... AReilly(7) 3 9
(RCGuest) *led to 1/2-way: wknd 3f out* **66/1**

2m 14.32s (2.72) **Going Correction** +0.25s/f (Good)
**WFA** 3 from 4yo+ 9lb **9** Ran SP% **111.9**
Speed ratings: **99,97,96,95,95 93,93,71,69**CSF £23.00 TOTE £3.60: £2.10, £1.90, £1.90; EX 21.40 Place 6 £35.84, Place 5 £29.61.
**Owner** Ryedale Partners No 6 **Bred** M H Easterby **Trained** Great Habton, N Yorks

**FOCUS**
An ordinary event run at just a fair gallop and those that raced close to the pace held the edge. However, the form looks sound for the grade.

**NOTEBOOK**
**Pay Attention**, who shaped as though coming to hand at Beverley last time, had conditions to suit and fully confirmed that promise. Now she has got her head in front, she may well be capable of better.
**Melodian** had conditions to suit on this first start for nearly three months and looks a good guide to the level of this form. He is vulnerable to progressive sorts but should continue to give a good account on his favoured easy ground.
**Fairlie**, having her first run for new connections, proved her effectiveness over this trip to fare the best of those held up and she left the impression that a stiffer test of stamina would be in her favour.
**Rock Lobster** has won over this trip and has form on easy ground but, although not disgraced, was another that left the impression that a stiffer test of stamina over this trip would have suited.
**Pearl Of York(DEN)** ran creditably and may be a bit better than the bare form. She will remain of interest in a similar grade back on a sound surface.
**Orion Express** is an inconsistent maiden who was not totally disgraced in the face of a stiff task but he will have to improve to win from his current mark in handicap company.
T/Plt: £36.70 to a £1 stake. Pool: £37,306.55. 740.55 winning tickets. T/Qpdt: £22.10 to a £1 stake. Pool: £1,843.10. 61.50 winning tickets. RY

# 4175 PONTEFRACT (L-H)
### Wednesday, August 4

**OFFICIAL GOING: Good to firm (good in places)**
The going was described by the jockeys as ' on the quick side of good but cut up against the far side rail in the home straight' - hence they came wide.
Wind: Slight 1/2 against. Weather: Fine and humid.

## 4450 BOLLINGER CHAMPAGNE CHALLENGE SERIES H'CAP (FOR GENTLEMAN AMATEUR RIDERS) 1m 2f 6y
**2:20** (2:23) (E) (0-80,79) 3-Y-O+ **£4,732** (£1,456; £728; £364) **Stalls** Low

Form RPR

2344 **1** **Night Sight (USA)**[20] 3866 7-10-11 **67**.......... MrJMorgan(5) 5 76
(MrsSLamyman) *hld up in tch: tk clsr order on bit over 1f out: shkn up to ld ins fnl f: styd on* **11/2**[3]

1250 **2** *½* **Bucks**[11] 4123 7-11-9 **79**.......... MrMichaelMurphy(5) 1 87
(DKIvory) *hld up in rr: hdwy over 1f out: ev ch ins fnl f: no ex clsng stages* **8/1**

2006 **3** *2 ½* **Movie King (IRE)**[14] 4029 5-10-4 **62**.......... MrTFWoodside(7) 3 65
(SGollings) *led: hrd pressed 2f out: rdn and hdd ins fnl f: sn btn* **14/1**

5241 **4** *3* **Oscar Pepper (USA)**[8] 4213 7-11-4 **69** 5ex..........(v) MrSWalker 2 67
(TDBarron) *trckd ldrs: reminders 4f out: rdn and wknd appr fnl f* **4/1**[2]

1101 **5** *3 ½* **Realism (FR)**[7] 4240 4-11-11 **79** 5ex.......... MrLNewnes(3) 6 70
(PWHiatt) *trckd ldr: chal 2f out: rdn appr fnl f: wknd ins last* **11/8**[1]

0046 **6** *2* **Derwent (USA)**[16] 3985 5-10-13 **67**..........(b) MrJJBest(3) 4 54
(JDBethell) *hld up: keen early: effrt over 2f out: rdn and wknd over 1f out* **6/1**

2m 18.58s (4.67) **Going Correction** +0.325s/f (Good) **6** Ran SP% **109.6**
Speed ratings: **94,93,91,89,86 84**CSF £43.58 TOTE £6.90: £3.50, £5.30; EX 41.90.
**Owner** David Fravigar-Alan Mann **Bred** Costello, Davis, Dolan And Ryan **Trained** Louth, Lincs
■ Stewards Enquiry : Mr T F Woodside three-day ban: used whip without allowing gelding time to respond and in the wrong place (Aug 18,20,24)

**FOCUS**
Just a steady gallop to halfway. This is ordinary form.

**NOTEBOOK**
**Night Sight(USA)**, back over his best trip, ended a two-year drought under a highly competent and confident ride.
**Bucks**, 5lb higher than his last win, ambled out of the stalls and was not helped by the lack of early pace. He drew almost level inside the last but was never going to be anything but second best. This trip is his bare minimum.
**Movie King(IRE)** was partnered by a rider who has experience in Irish points but was making his debut in this country. Allowed a soft lead, he seemed to curl up inside the last - not surprising as Woodside's use of the stick was brutal and rightly earned him a three-day ban.
**Oscar Pepper(USA)**, under his penalty, was under pressure fully half a mile from home and he dropped away coming to the final furlong. The gallop was not nearly as strong this time.
**Realism(FR)**, under his penalty, tired noticeably inside the last, unsuited by the loose ground on the inner. *Official explanation: jockey said gelding was unsuited by the going*
**Derwent(USA)**, who has been dropped more than a stone this season, is on a lengthy losing run but as a result of the lack of pace he was far too keen.

## 4451 DEM WINDOW SOLUTIONS KBE H'CAP 1m 4y
**2:50** (2:50) (E) (0-70,69) 3-Y-O **£4,299** (£1,323; £661; £330) **Stalls** Low

Form RPR

4241 **1** **Silverhay**[24] 3780 3-9-6 **68**.......... NCallan 4 75+
(TDBarron) *cl up: led over 3f out: rdn over 1f out: hung bdly rt and rdr lost whip appr fnl f: styd on* **9/4**[1]

0034 **2** *½* **Dagola (IRE)**[11] 4147 3-9-2 **64**.......... PRobinson 9 70
(CGCox) *in tch: racd far rail after 2f: ev ch and rdn over 1f out: ch whn nt clr run jst ins fnl f: styd on* **4/1**[2]

0045 **3** *3 ½* **Hana Dee**[11] 4147 3-8-5 **56**.......... SHitchcott(3) 10 54
(MRChannon) *dwlt: rr div: hdwy u.p over 2f out: chsng first 2 whn hung rt appr fnl f: no imp ins last* **14/1**

0000 **4** 1 3/4 **Mr Midasman (IRE)**[76] 2239 3-8-12 **60** DSweeney 6 54
(RHollinshead) *towards rr: hdwy u.p 2f out: kpt on fnl f: n.d* **40/1**

1065 **5** 1 3/4 **Dark Day Blues (IRE)**[6] 4280 3-9-4 **66** ACulhane 1 56
(MDHammond) *midfield: hdwy u.p over 2f out: no further prog fr over 1f out* **7/1**

0-56 **6** 1 3/4 **Sierra**[19] 3922 3-9-3 **65** RHills 11 51
(CEBrittain) *dwlt: hckd up in rr: effrt 3f out: sn rdn: kpt on fnl 2f: n.d* **16/1**

-035 **7** 1 1/2 **Queenstown (IRE)**[11] 4145 3-9-7 **69** (b) DHolland 7 51
(BJMeehan) *led tl hdd over 3f out: fdd fnl 2f* **8/1**

0-00 **8** nk **Orpenberry (IRE)**[63] 2589 3-9-0 **62** MFenton 2 44
(EJAlston) *chsd ldrs: rdn over 2f out: wknd over 1f out* **40/1**

0030 **9** 9 **Acca Larentia (IRE)**[22] 3817 3-7-11 **50** DFox(5) 5 11
(RMWhitaker) *in tch: drvn along 1/2-way: wknd 3f out* **33/1**

0003 **10** 2 1/2 **My Hope (IRE)**[13] 4045 3-9-1 **63** SDrowne 3 18
(RCharlton) *towards rr: rdn over 2f out: no hdwy* **6/1**[3]

2050 **11** 17 **Impulsive Bid (IRE)**[16] 3981 3-8-12 **60** PHanagan 8 —
(JeddO'Keeffe) *in tch: rdn over 2f out: sn wknd: t.o* **20/1**

0006 **12** 1 **Nafferton Heights (IRE)**[8] 4207 3-7-12 **46** oh4 RFfrench 12 —
(MWEasterby) *chsd ldrs tl wknd 3f out: t.o* **25/1**

1m 48.27s (2.67) **Going Correction** +0.325s/f (Good) **12** Ran SP% **117.6**
Speed ratings: **99,98,95,93,91 89,88,87,78,76 59,58**CSF £9.89 CT £100.96 TOTE £3.00: £1.60, £1.90, £3.20; EX 11.20.
**Owner** D C Rutter P J Huntbach **Bred** Major W R Hern And W H Carson **Trained** Maunby, N Yorks
■ Stewards Enquiry : N Callan caution: careless riding

**FOCUS**
The first two ended up against the outside running rail. The form is not strong.

**NOTEBOOK**
**Silverhay**, just 2lb higher, hung badly and his rider dropped his stick just inside the last. He went across the runner-up on the wide outside but the result quite rightly stood.
**Dagola(IRE)**chose the wide outside route in glorious isolation after the first two furlongs. The winner went across him and forced him to switch inside the last but at the line he was definitely second best.
**Hana Dee**, a big negative on the exchanges, is slipping to a lenient mark but she has so far managed just two places now from 11 starts.
**Mr Midasman(IRE)**, down 12lb this term, was back in action after a 11-week break. He looks likely to benefit from a step back up in trip.
**Dark Day Blues(IRE)**, well backed at long odds, was just 3lb higher than when winning at Redcar in June. A keen type, he was settled in midfield but never really looked like picking up sufficiently to take a hand.
**Sierra**, unplaced in three previous starts, looks to have started life in handicap company from a stiff mark.

## 4452 CHAPLINS CLUB H'CAP 5f
3:20 (3:21) (E) (0-75,76) 3-Y-0+ £6,906 (£2,125; £1,062; £531) Stalls Low

Form RPR

3433 **1** **On The Trail**[9] 4185 7-7-13 **46** ANicholls 13 56
(DWChapman) *trckd ldrs: rdn over 1f out: r.o wl u.p to ld wl ins fnl f* **20/1**

1124 **2** nk **Never Without Me**[10] 4179 4-9-0 **61** DHolland 7 70
(JFCoupland) *prom: rdn over 1f out: ev ch wl ins fnl f: no ex cl home* **6/1**[2]

3030 **3** nk **Kings College Boy**[11] 4133 4-8-13 **60** (b) PHanagan 14 68
(RAFahey) *trckd ldrs: bmpd over 2f out: rdn into narrow ld main gp appr fnl f: no ex ins last* **6/1**[2]

0300 **4** 1 **Consensus (IRE)**[60] 2670 5-10-0 **75** PRobinson 1 79+
(MBrittain) *racd far rail: led tl rdn: wknd and hdd wl ins fnl f* **11/1**

1120 **5** 2 1/2 **Queen Of Night**[6] 4279 4-8-13 **60** JCarroll 15 55
(DWChapman) *dwlt: rr: hdwy u.p over 1f out: kpt on ins last: nvr able to chal* **25/1**

0500 **6** 1 1/4 **Vigorous (IRE)**[35] 3407 4-8-13 **67** AMullen(7) 12 58
(MTodhunter) *dwlt: towards rr: rdn 2f out: kpt on fnl f: nvr able to chal* **33/1**

5330 **7** 1 **Playtime Blue**[7] 4232 4-8-13 **60** GBaker 10 47
(MrsHSweeting) *cl up: rdn 2f out: no ex* **15/2**[3]

0001 **8** 1 1/4 **Catch The Cat (IRE)**[6] 4279 5-10-1 **76** 7ex (v) GParkin 6 59
(JSWainwright) *midfield: hdwy to chse ldr 1/2-way: fdd fr over 1f out* **12/1**

1000 **9** hd **Karminskey Park**[19] 3920 5-9-3 **64** JFanning 9 46
(TJEtherington) *sn towards rr: n.d* **12/1**

0042 **10** 1 1/4 **Danakim**[4] 4350 7-7-5 **45** oh6 DFentiman(7) 16 22
(JRWeymes) *prom tl rdn and wknd wl over 1f out* **33/1**

0005 **11** 1 **Percy Douglas**[8] 4211 4-7-7 **45** oh5 (t) DFox(5) 2 19
(MissAStokell) *sn bhd: n.d* **22/1**

5031 **12** 3/4 **Midnight Parkes**[19] 3920 5-9-11 **72** (p) MHenry 8 43
(EJAlston) *chsd ldrs to 1/2-way: sn wknd* **8/1**

3210 **13** nk **Compton Plume**[14] 4013 4-9-6 **67** VHalliday 5 37
(WHTinning) *in tch to 1/2-way: sn wknd* **20/1**

1523 **14** 3 1/2 **Soaked**[7] 4247 11-9-2 **63** (b) ACulhane 4 20
(DWChapman) *chsd ldrs tl wknd over 1f out* **10/1**

4052 **15** 2 **Valiant Romeo**[6] 4279 4-8-6 **53** RFfrench 3 3
(RBastiman) *bhd fr 1/2-way* **11/2**[1]

63.91 secs (0.11) **Going Correction** +0.325s/f (Good) **15** Ran SP% **123.2**
Speed ratings: **112,111,111,109,105 103,101,99,99,97 95,94,94,88,85**CSF £128.30 CT £847.43 TOTE £25.80: £5.70, £2.60, £2.30; EX 205.70.
**Owner** J M Chapman **Bred** Ian Bellamy **Trained** Stillington, N Yorks
■ A second success for David Chapman in a race re-named in 1993 to mark his record-breaker Chaplins Club.

**FOCUS**
A very fast winning time for the grade. The form is ordinary but looks solid.

**NOTEBOOK**
**On The Trail**, whose 12 previous wins were achieved on the All-Weather, stuck his neck out to land the spoils for Adrian Nicholls, whose father David rode Chaplins Club on a regular basis.
**Never Without Me**, whose three wins have been on the All-Weather, was just held and is clearly very effective over the minimum trip.
**Kings College Boy**, a winner of just one of his previous 27 starts, took a bump on the home turn. Hanging right, in the end he just missed out. *Official explanation: jockey said gelding hung right throughout*
**Consensus(IRE)**, back after a two-month break, is slipping down the ratings. Her rider, who started the trend to go wide in the previous race, had no option but to ride to the draw from stall one this time and after leading overall she missed out to the first three, who raced on the stands' side, near the line.
**Queen Of Night**, one of her trainer's three runners in a race run in honour of his record breaker, was drawn one from the outside and took a hefty bump on the home turn. Unfortunately for her Southwell's Fibresand track is out of commission at present.
**Vigorous(IRE)**, down 6lb this time, was having her first outing for her new stable.
**Valiant Romeo** ran badly for no apparent reason. *Official explanation: trainer had no explanation for the poor form shown*

## 4453 TONY SYKES SOUND H'CAP 1m 4f 8y
3:50 (3:50) (D) (0-85,80) 3-Y-O+ £9,303 (£3,528; £1,764; £802) Stalls Low

Form RPR

4430 **1** **Flotta**[33] 3485 5-9-7 **80** SHitchcott(3) 3 88
(MRChannon) *hld up: hdwy 3f out: led 2f out: sn rdn: hld on wl fnl f: all out* **10/3**[2]

0443 **2** 1/2 **Mexican Pete**[14] 4019 4-9-8 **78** ACulhane 5 85
(PWHiatt) *hld up: hdwy to dispute ld 2f out: sn rdn: ev ch fnl f: no ex wl ins fnl f* **10/3**[2]

0120 **3** 3 1/2 **Sahem (IRE)**[25] 3725 7-9-10 **80** PHanagan 4 81
(DEddy) *trckd ldr: led 3f out: rdn and hdd 2f out: wknd ent fnl f* **3/1**[1]

6522 **4** 5 **Rajam**[11] 4155 6-9-8 **78** (v) AlexGreaves 1 71
(DNicholls) *prom: chal over 2f out: sn rdn: wknd appr fnl f* **7/2**[3]

1200 **5** 11 **Hip Hop Harry**[78] 2210 4-9-10 **80** WRyan 6 56
(EALDunlop) *hld up: effrt over 2f out: sn lost tch* **15/2**

40/0 **6** 9 **The Roundsills**[18] 3929 10-7-12 **54** oh19 SRighton 2 15
(MMullineaux) *led tl rdn and hdd 3f out: sn wknd: lost tch over 1f out* **100/1**

2m 42.83s (2.78) **Going Correction** +0.325s/f (Good) **6** Ran SP% **106.1**
Speed ratings: **103,102,100,97,89 83**CSF £13.06 TOTE £4.90: £2.40, £2.50; EX 13.50.
**Owner** W G R Wightman **Bred** W G R Wightman **Trained** West Ilsley, Berks

**FOCUS**
In effect a 0-80 handicap run at a steady gallop in the early stages, but in the end the first two came clear. Fair form, rated through the runer-up

**NOTEBOOK**
**Flotta**, back to his last winning mark, did just enough.
**Mexican Pete**, without a win for a year, keeps climbing up the ratings and in the end just missed out.
**Sahem(IRE)**, 7lb higher than when winning at Carlisle, did not have things his own way this time and found the first two leaving him for dead inside the last.
**Rajam**, 3lb higher, would have preferred much quicker ground.
**Hip Hop Harry**, absent for 11 weeks, seems much more effective on the All-Weather.
**The Roundsills**, without a win on the level for five years, was 19lb 'wrong' at the weights.

## 4454 BIRDSALL FARMS MAIDEN STKS 6f
4:20 (4:22) (D) 2-Y-O £5,603 (£1,724; £862; £431) Stalls Low

Form RPR

6 **1** **Reqqa**[25] 3760 2-9-0 RHills 13 90+
(MJohnston) *trckd ldrs: led over 1f out: rdn clr fnl f* **6/5**[1]

23 **2** 5 **Yajbill (IRE)**[12] 4088 2-9-0 ACulhane 12 75
(MRChannon) *led 1f: cl up: ev ch 2f out: sn rdn: styd on to go 2nd ins fnl f: no ch w wnr* **11/4**[2]

0 **3** 3/4 **Along The Nile**[19] 3918 2-9-0 LGoncalves 5 73
(MrsJRRamsden) *dwlt: hld up: hdwy 1/2-way: rdn to chse wnr jst ins fnl f: no ex* **28/1**

**4** 3 **Street Ballad (IRE)** 2-8-9 PHanagan 6 59
(MrsJRRamsden) *rangy: unf: slowly away: bhd: hdwy 2f out: styd on fnl f: nvr nrr* **25/1**

0 **5** 1 1/4 **Imperial Dynasty (USA)**[41] 3248 2-8-11 SHitchcott(3) 14 60
(TDBarron) *led after 1f tl rdn and hdd over 1f out: fdd* **33/1**

0 **6** 2 1/2 **Yorkshire Lad (IRE)**[132] 1105 2-8-7 DTudhope(7) 11 53
(DCarroll) *in tch: no imp on ldrs fnl 2f* **25/1**

4 **7** 1 3/4 **Cutlass Gaudy**[57] 2749 2-8-9 StephanieHollinshead(5) 3 47
(RHollinshead) *prom: wnt 2nd over 1f out: no imp on wnr: wknd fnl f* **33/1**

25 **8** shd **Tybalt**[13] 4048 2-9-0 DHolland 10 47
(PWHarris) *in tch tl wknd 2f out* **8/1**[3]

56 **9** 4 **Bespoke**[10] 4172 2-8-7 SArcher(7) 8 35
(SirMarkPrescott) *slowly away: a bhd* **40/1**

**10** 1 1/2 **Rock Haven (IRE)** 2-9-0 NCallan 2 30
(PWHarris) *leggy: unf: s.i.s: a bhd* **40/1**

6 **11** 6 **Pevensey (IRE)**[61] 2651 2-9-0 SDrowne 4 12
(JHMGosden) *sn bhd* **10/1**

3 **12** shd **Queue Up**[52] 2904 2-9-0 MFenton 9 12
(JGGiven) *in tch to 1/2-way: sn wknd* **16/1**

**13** 8 **Come To Daddy (IRE)** 2-9-0 DKinsella 7 —
(FJordan) *lengthy: unf: s.v.s: a wl bhd* **100/1**

1m 19.28s (1.98) **Going Correction** +0.325s/f (Good) **13** Ran SP% **121.1**
Speed ratings: **99,92,91,87,85 82,80,79,74,72 64,64,53**CSF £3.88 TOTE £2.30: £1.20, £1.50, £9.20; EX 3.90.
**Owner** Hamdan Al Maktoum **Bred** R T And Mrs Watson **Trained** Middleham Moor, N Yorks

**FOCUS**
25/1 bar four but the winner looks a good prospect, possibly at Listed level.

**NOTEBOOK**
**Reqqa**, a major positive on the exchanges, travelled best but had to be kept up to his work to pull clear. Up in the air, he still has a fair bit to learn but can only go the one way.
**Yajbill(IRE)**, a negative on the exchanges, came across a winner of some potential and deserves to find a race.
**Along The Nile** improved on his debut effort and will appreciate a step up to seven.
**Street Ballad(IRE)**, a March foal, stands over a fair amount of ground but she looks as though she needs more time yet. It was a pleasing bow and she looks capable of better in due course.
**Imperial Dynasty(USA)**, drawn on the wide outside, showed a lot more than on his debut six week earlier and this rangy type will improve again.
**Yorkshire Lad(IRE)** has been absent since showing some ability first time on the opening day of the turf Flat season.
**Tybalt** *Official explanation: jockey said colt hung right-handed in the closing stages*

## 4455 MATTY BOWN MEMORIAL MAIDEN STKS 1m 4y
4:50 (4:52) (D) 3-Y-O+ £5,395 (£1,660; £830; £415) Stalls Low

Form RPR

30 **1** **Clipperdown (IRE)**[19] 3916 3-9-0 NCallan 1 80
(PWHarris) *trckd ldrs: rdn over 1f out: led ins fnl f: styd on* **5/2**[2]

23 **2** 1 1/4 **Zathonia**[30] 3592 3-8-9 SDrowne 6 72
(RCharlton) *trckd ldr: led appr fnl f: rdn and hdd ins last: no ex* **5/2**[2]

0 **3** 2 **Royal Lustre**[19] 3916 3-9-0 RHills 3 72
(JHMGosden) *led: qcknd 3f out: rdn and hdd appr fnl f: sn btn* **11/8**[1]

**4** 9 **Perrywinkle Boy** 3-9-0 ACulhane 2 52?
(MDHammond) *hld up: effrt 3f out: grad lost tch* **33/1**

24-0 **5** dist **Dium Mac**[12] 4101 3-9-0 **70** PHanagan 5 —
(NBycroft) *dwlt: hld up: effrt over 3f out: sn outpcd and lost tch: t.o* **9/1**[3]

1m 51.65s (6.05) **Going Correction** +0.325s/f (Good)
**WFA** 3 from 7yo 7lb **5** Ran SP% **112.2**
Speed ratings: **82,80,78,69,—**CSF £9.33 TOTE £3.00: £1.70, £2.10; EX 7.00.
**Owner** Mrs G Godfrey & Mrs A Horner **Bred** Newsells Park Stud Limited **Trained** Ringshall, Bucks

**FOCUS**
A fair maiden run at just a steady gallop and a very slow winning time. The first three pulled clear.

**NOTEBOOK**
**Clipperdown(IRE)** is going the right way and showed a much better attitude than the runner-up. His future depends on a realistic handicap mark.
**Zathonia** went on travelling best but tended to hang left in front and the winner seemed to outbattle her.
**Royal Lustre**, just behind today's winner first time, was a major positive on the exchanges but this regally-bred individual, who has a moderate action, was very disappointing and looked totally paceless after trying to steal it from the front.
**Perrywinkle Boy**, bred for speed, is a weak-looking newcomer and once the gallop was stepped up he was soon toiling.
**Dium Mac** ran badly and eventually completed in his own time.

## 4456 AUGUST CLASSIFIED STKS — 6f

5:20 (5:21) (E) 3-Y-O — £4,085 (£1,257; £628; £314) Stalls Low

| Form | | | Horse | Jockey | RPR |
|---|---|---|---|---|---|
| 42-5 | 1 | | **Out After Dark**[98] 1702 3-9-5 75 | PRobinson 7 | 82 |
| | | | (CGCox) *mde virtually all: hld on wl u.p fnl f* | **5/2**[1] | |
| 2240 | 2 | *nk* | **Flying Bantam (IRE)**[20] 3877 3-9-0 68 | PHanagan 6 | 76 |
| | | | (RAFahey) *hld up: drvn along and hdwy over 1f out: wnt 2nd ent fnl f: ch and rdn ins last: styd on* | **13/2** | |
| 0300 | 3 | *5* | **Fitzwarren**[4] 4320 3-9-0 68 | NCallan 9 | 61 |
| | | | (NBycroft) *w wnr: rdn 2f out: wknd ent fnl f* | **12/1** | |
| 0-00 | 4 | *¾* | **Key Of Gold (IRE)**[34] 3446 3-9-0 70 | RHills 5 | 59 |
| | | | (DCarroll) *trckd ldrs: rdn over 1f out: kpt on same pce* | **12/1** | |
| 64-0 | 5 | *3* | **Marysienka**[13] 4051 3-8-7 73 | KPierrepont(7) 1 | 50 |
| | | | (JBalding) *trckd ldrs: effrt wl over 1f out: sn rdn and btn* | **16/1** | |
| 2316 | 6 | *1 ¼* | **Extra Cover (IRE)**[9] 4188 3-9-5 75 | (b) DSweeney 4 | 51 |
| | | | (RCharlton) *hld up: effrt 2f out: sn rdn: no hdwy* | **4/1**[3] | |
| 6433 | 7 | *5* | **Ask The Clerk (IRE)**[6] 4267 3-9-1 71 | MTebbutt 8 | 32+ |
| | | | (VSmith) *hmpd sn after s: hld up in tch: smooth hdwy to trck ldrs whn hmpd over 1f out: nt rcvr: rr whn eased ins last* | **11/4**[2] | |
| 0100 | 8 | *5* | **Commander Bond**[9] 4188 3-9-1 71 | JCarroll 2 | 17 |
| | | | (BSmart) *s.i.s: hld up in rr: effrt 2f out: sn btn: bhd and eased ins fnl f* | **20/1** | |

1m 17.74s (0.44) **Going Correction** +0.325s/f (Good) — **8** Ran SP% **114.6**
Speed ratings: **110,109,102,101,97 96,89,82**CSF £19.36 TOTE £4.10: £1.60, £2.00, £2.80; EX 14.60 Place 6 £84.65, Place 5 £16.76.
**Owner** The Night Owls **Bred** C J Mills **Trained** Lambourn, Berks
■ Stewards Enquiry : N Callan two-day ban: careless riding (Aug 15-16)
P Robinson two-day ban: careless riding (Aug 15-16)

**FOCUS**
A rough race with the field tightening up turning in. The winning time was very smart for the grade and the form is fair.

**NOTEBOOK**
**Out After Dark**, a positive on the exchanges, looked in tip-top trim. He went wide early on, getting in the way of the horse drawn on his outside, and in the end did just enough.
**Flying Bantam(IRE)**, dwarfed by the winner, was well supported in the ring. Flat out at halfway, in the end he made the winner pull out all the stops.
**Fitzwarren**, by no means a model of consistency, was keen to grab the stands'-side rail turning in. With his stamina at a low ebb, he tired noticeably in the final furlong and pulled up minus one front shoe.
**Key Of Gold(IRE)**, whose sole win at two was on the All-Weather, showed a lot more than on his first two runs this year.
**Marysienka**, last of 11 on her return two weeks earlier, appreciated the much quicker ground but she will struggle in handicap company unless her rating is slashed.
**Extra Cover(IRE)**, driven along in the early stages, ran a lifeless race.
**Ask The Clerk(IRE)**, knocked sideways by the winner early on, was travelling strongly when badly hampered turning in. He was heavily eased and did not look sound. This was an unhappy experience to say the very least. *Official explanation: jockey said gelding suffered interference in running and lost its action*
**Commander Bond** seemed to lose his action and was heavily eased in the closing stages. *Official explanation: jockey said gelding was never travelling*
T/Plt: £109.00 to a £1 stake. Pool: £36,326.90. 243.10 winning tickets. T/Qpdt: £17.70 to a £1 stake. Pool: £2,474.80. 103.20 winning tickets. JF

# 4197 YARMOUTH (L-H)

Wednesday, August 4

**OFFICIAL GOING: Good to firm (firm in places)**
Yarmouth had missed the rain affecting the country so the ground remained on the fast side, although, there was a good covering of grass and no jar.
Wind: Slight across Weather: Sunny and humid

## 4457 31ST RUNNING OF THE BOTTON BROTHERS H'CAP (LADIES RACE) — 1m 6f 17y

5:45 (5:45) (F) (0-75,72) 3-Y-O+ — £2,905 (£830; £415) Stalls Low

| Form | | | Horse | Jockey | RPR |
|---|---|---|---|---|---|
| -050 | 1 | | **Astyanax (IRE)**[12] 4075 4-11-0 72 | MsCWilliams 1 | 79 |
| | | | (SirMarkPrescott) *led 2f: led over 6f out: rdn out* | **4/1**[3] | |
| 5300 | 2 | *1* | **Siegfrieds Night (IRE)**[4] 4346 3-9-5 62 | MissSBrotherton 4 | 68 |
| | | | (MCChapman) *hld up: hdwy 5f out: rdn to chse wnr over 1f out: styd on* | **9/1** | |
| 6046 | 3 | *5* | **Bobsleigh**[7] 4226 5-10-10 71 | MissLJHarwood(3) 2 | 70 |
| | | | (MrsAJPerrett) *chsd ldrs: outpcd 6f out: rdn over 3f out: styd on ins fnl f* | **9/4**[1] | |
| 0-00 | 4 | *¾* | **Eight (IRE)**[8] 4213 8-8-13 50 ow3 | MsTDzieciolowska(7) 8 | 48 |
| | | | (MRChannon) *mid-div: hdwy 1/2-way: chsd wnr 4f out tl rdn over 1f out: no ex* | **40/1** | |
| 5040 | 5 | *2* | **Makarim (IRE)**[24] 3776 8-8-11 41 | (p) MrsSBosley 9 | 36 |
| | | | (MRBosley) *hld up: styd on fnl 2f: :n.d* | **14/1** | |
| 1510 | 6 | *1* | **Theatre Lady (IRE)**[8] 4213 6-9-2 49 | MissEFolkes(3) 5 | 43 |
| | | | (PDEvans) *hld up: hdwy over 4f out: wknd 2f out* | **8/1** | |
| 0514 | 7 | *9* | **Euippe**[18] 3928 3-9-12 69 | MissEJJones 6 | 50 |
| | | | (JGGiven) *hld up: hdwy over 4f out: rdn and wknd over 2f out* | **7/2**[2] | |
| 4400 | 8 | *6* | **Redspin (IRE)**[7] 4226 4-10-4 65 | MrsSMoore(3) 7 | 38 |
| | | | (JSMoore) *chsd ldrs tl wknd over 2f out* | **16/1** | |
| 01-0 | P | | **Mischief**[48] 3018 8-8-5 40 oh4 | MissJoeyEllis(5) 3 | — |
| | | | (KBell) *s.s: sn prom: led 12f out: hdd over 6f out: sn wknd: t.o whn p.u over 2f out* | **33/1** | |

3m 5.83s (0.63) **Going Correction** +0.05s/f (Good)
**WFA** 3 from 4yo+ 13lb — **9** Ran SP% **112.0**
Speed ratings: **100,99,96,96,95 94,89,85,—**CSF £38.02 CT £97.72 TOTE £5.50: £1.90, £2.80, £1.50; EX 48.90.
**Owner** Lady Katharine Watts **Bred** P D Player **Trained** Newmarket, Suffolk

**FOCUS**
An ordinary contest full of exposed types and the form is modest.

**NOTEBOOK**
**Astyanax(IRE)**, 6lb higher than when landing this last year, had plenty of use made of him and just outstayed the runner-up.
**Siegfrieds Night(IRE)** proved he stays this trip with a fine effort, although he does lack a change of gear.
**Bobsleigh**was on and off the bridle throughout and may benefit from some form of headgear.
**Eight(IRE)** turned in his best effort for a while, but he is inconsistent and cannot be relied upon to reproduce this.
**Makarim(IRE)** is on a long losing run and despite his plunging mark, never looked likely to take a hand.
**Mischief** *Official explanation: jockey said gelding lost its action*

## 4458 CONSTITUTION MOTORS HYUNDAI CLAIMING STKS — 1m 2f 21y

6:15 (6:15) (F) 3-Y-O+ — £2,933 (£838; £419) Stalls Low

| Form | | | Horse | Jockey | RPR |
|---|---|---|---|---|---|
| 1400 | 1 | | **Arms Acrossthesea**[12] 4096 5-9-5 57 | JEdmunds 2 | 55 |
| | | | (JBalding) *a.p: rdn over 1f out: r.o to ld post* | **7/1**[3] | |
| /15- | 2 | *shd* | **Morahib**[413] 2460 6-9-11 88 | GCarter 1 | 61 |
| | | | (WJMusson) *led: shkn up over 1f out: rdn ins fnl f: hdd post* | **11/4**[1] | |
| 0326 | 3 | *½* | **Private Seal**[12] 4086 9-8-8 43 | (t) MHalford(7) 5 | 50 |
| | | | (JulianPoulton) *hld up: rdn over 1f out: r.o ins fnl f: nt rch ldrs* | **14/1** | |
| 4600 | 4 | *1* | **Big Bad Burt**[13] 4065 3-8-3 59 | DeanWilliams(7) 4 | 52 |
| | | | (GCHChung) *dwlt: sn prom: rdn over 1f out: styd on* | **8/1** | |
| 2000 | 5 | *1* | **Ivory Coast (IRE)**[24] 3773 3-8-7 59 | JQuinn 6 | 47 |
| | | | (WRMuir) *chsd ldr: rdn and ev ch over 2f out: no ex fnl f* | **9/2**[2] | |
| 0351 | 6 | *1 ½* | **Senor Eduardo**[13] 4065 7-9-5 54 | NPollard 3 | 47 |
| | | | (SGollings) *hld up in tch: rdn over 3f out: no imp fnl f* | **11/4**[1] | |
| 0406 | 7 | *1 ¼* | **Kingston Town (USA)**[6] 4262 4-9-3 63 | (b) J-PGuillambert(3) 7 | 46 |
| | | | (NPLittmoden) *hld up: rdn over 2f out: n.d* | **10/1** | |

2m 11.72s (3.75) **Going Correction** +0.05s/f (Good)
**WFA** 3 from 4yo+ 9lb — **7** Ran SP% **110.9**
Speed ratings: **87,86,86,85,84 83,82**CSF £24.93 TOTE £7.40: £2.40, £2.20; EX 31.10.
**Owner** J Carter **Bred** Miss Mandy Jane Barber **Trained** Scrooby, Notts

**FOCUS**
A very moderate contest in which the runner-up was well below his official rating. This form needs treating with caution for it was a slowly-run contest.

**NOTEBOOK**
**Arms Acrossthesea** did well to land this for he stays further and would not have been suited by the steady pace.
**Morahib**, a useful handicapper last term, has clearly had his problems in the meatime and looked a long way below his best.
**Private Seal** was flattered to finish so close.
**Big Bad Burt** did not prove conclusively that he stays this far, for the way the race was run hardly put the emphasis on stamina.
**Ivory Coast(IRE)** had no excuses, and does not look as good on turf as she is on the Polytrack. *Official explanation: jockey said filly hung right*
**Senor Eduardo** would have been better suited by a stronger pace.

## 4459 BANHAM POULTRY H'CAP — 6f 3y

6:45 (6:45) (D) (0-80,77) 3-Y-O+ — £5,720 (£1,760; £880; £440) Stalls High

| Form | | | Horse | Jockey | RPR |
|---|---|---|---|---|---|
| 3306 | 1 | | **Mr Malarkey (IRE)**[11] 4130 4-9-9 77 | (bt) HayleyTurner(5) 8 | 88 |
| | | | (MrsCADunnett) *racd stands' side: mde all: rdn and hung lft fr over 1f out: r.o* | **4/1**[2] | |
| 5401 | 2 | *1 ¼* | **Mistral Sky**[7] 4244 5-9-7 70 6ex | (v) FNorton 5 | 77 |
| | | | (MrsStefLiddiard) *racd centre: chsd ldrs tl led that gp and hung rt over 1f out: carried lft ins fnl f: unable qck towards fin* | **11/2**[3] | |
| 3141 | 3 | *hd* | **Tancred Times**[11] 4154 9-8-12 61 | JQuinn 4 | 68 |
| | | | (CFWall) *led centre over 4f: styd on* | **7/1** | |
| 00-5 | 4 | *1 ¼* | **Asbo**[20] 3887 4-8-4 60 | MHalford(7) 9 | 63 |
| | | | (DrJDScargill) *racd stands' side: prom: chsd wnr and hung lft fr over 1f out: no ex ins fnl f* | **14/1** | |
| 6300 | 5 | *2* | **Currency**[5] 4291 7-9-6 76 | (p) CJDavies(7) 2 | 73 |
| | | | (JMBradley) *racd centre: bhd: rdn over 1f out: nvr trbld ldrs* | **9/1** | |
| 5625 | 6 | *1 ¼* | **Yomalo (IRE)**[11] 4130 4-9-1 64 | EAhern 1 | 57 |
| | | | (RGuest) *racd centre: bhd: hung lft over 2f out: hdwy over 1f out: wknd ins fnl f* | **11/4**[1] | |
| 0410 | 7 | *1 ¼* | **Coranglais**[12] 4085 4-8-11 63 | (p) FPFerris(3) 10 | 52 |
| | | | (JMBradley) *racd stands' side: chsd wnr over 4f: sn btn* | **15/2** | |
| 3000 | 8 | *¾* | **Night Wolf (IRE)**[21] 3841 4-8-6 62 | BO'Neill(7) 3 | 49 |
| | | | (MRChannon) *swtchd to r stands' side over 4f out: a in rr* | **33/1** | |
| 2-22 | 9 | *2* | **Stargem**[12] 4097 3-9-6 73 | RPrice 6 | 54 |
| | | | (JPearce) *plld hrd: trckd ldr centre 4f: sn wknd* | **11/1** | |

1m 12.3s (-1.30) **Going Correction** -0.025s/f (Good)
**WFA** 3 from 4yo+ 4lb — **9** Ran SP% **114.3**
Speed ratings: **107,105,105,103,100 99,97,96,93**CSF £25.99 CT £147.99 TOTE £6.10: £1.50, £1.70, £1.90; EX 42.70.
**Owner** T S Child **Bred** Mrs C A Dunnett **Trained** Hingham, Norfolk

**FOCUS**
A competitive handicap in which the field split into two groups, with no advantage to either group. he form is ordinary but sound.

**NOTEBOOK**
**Mr Malarkey(IRE)**, who was equipped with a tongue-tie for the first time, again did his best to throw victory away, but lucky for him there was nothing good enough to take advantage. *Official explanation: jockey said gelding hung left*
**Mistral Sky** turned in sound effort under his penalty, despite coming off a straight line.
**Tancred Times** was far from disgraced in this better contest and, although she is getting no younger, still has plenty of zip.
**Asbo** may have still just needed this to put an edge on her.
**Currency**, who had the cheekpieces back on, never threatened to get competitive.
**Yomalo(IRE)** raced widest of all and never really looked like getting on terms. She is worth another chance.

## 4460 "ENJOY A NIGHT AT THE OCEAN ROOMS" (S) H'CAP — 1m 3y

7:15 (7:15) (G) (0-55,52) 3-4-Y-O — £2,653 (£758; £379) Stalls High

| Form | | | Horse | Jockey | RPR |
|---|---|---|---|---|---|
| 00P0 | 1 | | **Taiyo**[63] 2597 4-9-1 42 | EAhern 6 | 52 |
| | | | (JWPayne) *racd centre: chsd ldrs: lft in ld over 2f out: edgd rt ins fnl f: rdn out* | **14/1** | |
| 0341 | 2 | *2* | **Zonnebeke**[12] 4102 3-9-0 48 | (v) TGMcLaughlin 4 | 53 |
| | | | (KRBurke) *racd centre: hld up: hdwy over 3f out: chsd wnr over 1f out: sn rdn and no imp* | **3/1**[1] | |
| 4006 | 3 | *½* | **Anisette**[16] 3990 3-8-0 41 | MHalford(7) 2 | 45 |
| | | | (JulianPoulton) *racd centre: prom: rdn over 2f out: styd on* | **6/1**[3] | |

0400 **4** *2* **Danifah (IRE)**[30] 3575 3-8-5 **42**.............................. FPFerris(3) 1 41
(PDEvans) *racd centre: chsd ldrs: rdn over 2f out: styd on same pce fnl f* **9/1**

0550 **5** *½* **Esperance (IRE)**[7] 4238 4-9-3 **44**.............................. GCarter 12 42
(JAkehurst) *s.s: racd stands' side: outpcd: styd on ins fnl f: nvr nrr* **4/1**[2]

6000 **6** *nk* **Lilian**[11] 4139 4-8-4 **38**.............................. (b[1]) RachelCostello(7) 13 35
(MissGayKelleway) *racd stands' side: chsd ldrs: rdn over 2f out: wknd over 1f out* **25/1**

0300 **7** *1 ½* **Lenwade**[22] 3822 3-8-1 **35**.............................. AMcCarthy 5 29
(GGMargarson) *racd centre: bhd and rdn 5f out: hdwy u.p over 1f out: wknd ins fnl f* **20/1**

0046 **8** *2 ½* **Leitrim Rock (IRE)**[26] 3697 4-9-1 **42**.............................. FNorton 10 30
(AGNewcombe) *s.s: racd centre: outpcd* **4/1**[2]

3340 **9** *15* **Roving Vixen (IRE)**[35] 3427 3-8-1 **40**.............................. (b) HayleyTurner(5) 11 —
(JLSpearing) *led centre: hung rt over 3f out: hdd over 2f out: sn wknd* **12/1**

6-50 **10** *2 ½* **Kilminchy Lady (IRE)**[14] 4018 3-8-6 **40**.............................. NPollard 9 —
(WRMuir) *racd centre: bhd fr 1/2-way* **50/1**

000 **11** *1* **Newtown Chief**[11] 4128 3-8-6 **43**.............................. (b[1]) J-PGuillambert(3) 7 —
(NPLittmoden) *racd centre: chsd ldrs over 5f* **66/1**

1m 40.28s (0.58) **Going Correction** -0.025s/f (Good)
**WFA** 3 from 4yo 7lb **11 Ran SP% 115.7**
Speed ratings: **96,94,93,91,91 90,89,86,71,69 68**CSF £53.39 CT £287.19 TOTE £21.60: £4.40, £1.50, £2.30; EX 99.90.The winner was bought in for 7,600gns. Zonnebeke was claimed by Christine Dunnett for £6,000.
**Owner** Mrs J Morley **Bred** Downclose Stud **Trained** Newmarket, Suffolk

**FOCUS**
The field again split into two with the centre group coming out best. A typical seller, full of iffy customers, and the form is poor.

**NOTEBOOK**
**Taiyo** finally got her head in front, but it was probabaly down to the reluctance of the runner-up to go by as much as anything.
**Zonnebeke** travelled far and away the best for much of the trip, but not for the first time found precious little when push came to shove.
**Anisette** stuck on willingly enough, but she is exposed as moderate.
**Danifah(IRE)** did not quite see this trip out.
**Esperance(IRE)**, who missed the break, came from a mile back and did best of those to race up the stands' side.
**Leitrim Rock(IRE)** blew his chance at the start.

## 4461 CUSTOM KITCHENS NOVICE STKS 7f 3y
**7:45** (7:46) (D) 2-Y-O **£3,334** (£1,026; £513; £256) **Stalls** High

Form RPR
1332 **1** **Wilko (USA)**[7] 4227 2-9-5 **100**.............................. EAhern 2 81+
(JNoseda) *led 1f: trckd ldr: shkn up to ld over 1f out: r.o* **1/6**[1]

0 **2** *½* **Shrine Mountain (USA)**[18] 3946 2-8-9 .............................. J-PGuillambert(3) 3 73
(CEBrittain) *plld hrd: led 6f out: qcknd over 2f out: hdd over 1f out: r.o* **33/1**

**3** *2 ½* **Linngari (IRE)** 2-8-8 .............................. GCarter 1 61
(SirMichaelStoute) *chsd ldrs: shkn up over 1f out: no ex* **13/2**[2]

05 **4** *1 ¾* **Zabeel Palace**[12] 4100 2-8-12 .............................. NPollard 4 60
(DRLoder) *hld up: plld hrd: rdn over 1f out: nvr trbld ldrs* **20/1**[3]

1m 28.7s (2.20) **Going Correction** -0.025s/f (Good) **4 Ran SP% 106.7**
Speed ratings: **86,85,82,80**CSF £7.48 TOTE £1.10; EX 6.10.
**Owner** Mrs Susan Roy **Bred** Ro Parra **Trained** Newmarket, Suffolk

**FOCUS**
A pedestrian winning time for the class, and with the long odds-on favourite winning only narrowly the form has a suspect look.

**NOTEBOOK**
**Wilko(USA)** looked to make hard work of what should have been an easy task. However, the slow pace would have hardly played to his strengths.
**Shrine Mountain(USA)**, a nice, rangy individual, has a good action but only set a moderate pace. While he may have been flattered to finishing so close to the winner, there is no doubt there is better to come from him, especially with another year on his back.
**Linngari(IRE)**, who is out of a mare that won over 12 furlongs, would not have been suited to the steady pace.
**Zabeel Palace** did himself no favours by refusing to settle. However, he will have more options open to him now in nurseries.

## 4462 BET365 08000 322365 H'CAP 7f 3y
**8:15** (8:15) (E) (0-75,75) 3-Y-0+ **£3,750** (£1,154; £577; £288) **Stalls** High

Form RPR
0010 **1** **Threezedzz**[2] 4403 6-8-11 **61**.............................. (t) FPFerris(3) 1 78
(PDEvans) *mde all: rdn clr fnl f: eased nr fin* **9/2**[3]

0500 **2** *5* **Hand Chime**[114] 1358 7-9-4 **72**.............................. DanielleDeverson(7) 4 76
(WJHaggas) *hld up: hdwy 1/2-way: ev ch wl over 1f out: wknd ins fnl f* **8/1**

500/ **3** *2 ½* **Hammer Of The Gods (IRE)**[746] 3171 4-7-8 **48**.............................. (t) MHalford(7) 3 46
(JulianPoulton) *trckd wnr over 4f: edgd lft and wknd ins fnl f* **50/1**

000 **4** *½* **Lygeton Lad**[11] 4122 6-9-7 **68**.............................. (t) MFenton 2 64
(MissGayKelleway) *chsd ldrs: rdn over 2f out: wknd fnl f* **5/2**[2]

-053 **5** *2* **Bob's Buzz**[13] 4067 4-9-7 **68**.............................. TGMcLaughlin 5 59
(SCWilliams) *hld up: plld hrd: rdn over 2f out: n.d* **5/4**[1]

0010 **6** *8* **Invader**[21] 3842 8-9-11 **75**.............................. (t) J-PGuillambert(3) 6 45
(CEBrittain) *hld up: rdn over 2f out: sn wknd* **10/1**

1m 25.2s (-1.30) **Going Correction** -0.025s/f (Good) **6 Ran SP% 113.4**
Speed ratings: **106,100,97,96,94 85**CSF £38.45 TOTE £4.70: £2.90, £4.90; EX 34.80 Place 6 £107.20, Place 5 £67.72 .
**Owner** Steve Evans **Bred** Mrs R Pease **Trained** Pandy, Gwent

**FOCUS**
A moderate handicap and the form probably needs treating with some caution, for most of these needed cover and the winner had his own way up front.

**NOTEBOOK**
**Threezedzz** with most of his rivals keen to have some cover, he ended up with a soft lead and never really looked like being overhauled.
**Hand Chime**, a fair performer at his best, is beginning to slip down the weights.
**Hammer Of The Gods(IRE)**, tackling handicappers for the first time, ran as though he needed this outing.
**Lygeton Lad** is not as good on turf as he is on the All-Weather surfaces.
**Bob's Buzz** gave himself no chance by refusing to settle. *Official explanation: jockey said gelding ran too free*
T/Plt: £69.80 to a £1 stake. Pool: £31,386.40. 328.15 winning tickets. T/Qpdt: £11.80 to a £1 stake. Pool: £2,481.80. 155.60 winning tickets. CR

4463 - 4466a (Foreign Racing) - See Raceform Interactive

# [4432]BRIGHTON (L-H)
Thursday, August 5

**OFFICIAL GOING: Firm**

## 4467 PLEASURE PALACE RACING LADY RIDERS SERIES CLAIMING STKS 1m 3f 196y
**5:55** (5:56) (F) 3-Y-0+ **£3,341** (£1,028; £514; £257) **Stalls** High

Form RPR
0565 **1** **Final Dividend (IRE)**[13] 4080 8-9-10 **44**.............................. MissJoannaRees(3) 5 56
(JMPEustace) *trckd ldr: led wl over 1f out: rdn out fnl f* **7/2**[3]

5313 **2** *nk* **Banningham Blaze**[1] 4433 4-9-10 **50**.............................. MrsSBosley 1 53
(AWCarroll) *stdd s: wl in rr tl hdwy over 2f out: fin wl to take clsng 2nd in fnl f* **10/3**[2]

5133 **3** *2 ½* **Salut Saint Cloud**[10] 4189 3-9-1 **53**.............................. MissHayleyMoore(5) 6 56
(GLMoore) *wl in rr tl swtchd rt over 2f out: sn mde hdwy: fin wl: nvr nrr* **13/8**[1]

0000 **4** *½* **Joely Green**[28] 3667 7-9-8 **39**.............................. MrsEmmaLittmoden(3) 3 49
(NPLittmoden) *a abt same pl: rdn over 3f out: one pce ins fnl 2f* **12/1**

1456 **5** *4* **Fiddles Music**[28] 3669 3-8-10 **43**.............................. MsDGoad(5) 4 44
(MissSheenaWest) *led tl hdd wl over 1f out: sn wknd* **25/1**

0550 **6** *¾* **Duke's View (IRE)**[13] 4080 3-9-1 **58**.............................. MissLJHarwood(3) 7 46
(MrsAJPerrett) *chsd ldrs tl wknd over 1f out* **11/2**

00/6 **7** *12* **Little Fox (IRE)**[31] 3590 9-10-1 **45** ow12.............................. MissDonnaHandley(7) 2 33
(JJBridger) *slowly away: a wl bhd* **25/1**

2m 34.21s (2.11) **Going Correction** -0.05s/f (Good)
**WFA** 3 from 4yo+ 11lb **7 Ran SP% 114.2**
Speed ratings: **90,89,88,87,85 84,76**CSF £15.53 TOTE £4.90: £2.30, £2.70; EX 20.70.
**Owner** Charles Curtis **Bred** Dan Daly **Trained** Newmarket, Suffolk

**FOCUS**
A dire contest in which the first two home came clear.

**NOTEBOOK**
**Final Dividend(IRE)** responded gamely to his rider's vigorous urgings and was all out to hold off the winner at the line. This drop into claiming company was much to his advantage and he could win again in this grade, although he looks in decline, as this was his first success since scoring over course and distance in 2003, when he was rated 19lb higher.
**Banningham Blaze**, with the visor left off this time, again got going all too late. She had finished third over course and distance just 24 hours previously, and that effort may have taken its toll late on, but she is hard to win with nonetheless.
**Salut Saint Cloud** was well backed for this, but failed to pick up under maximum pressure when it mattered. He has been in fair form of late for his current connections, at this sort of level, and could return to winning ways when reverting to a more conventional track.
**Joely Green** improved on his most recent efforts, but is better over further.
**Duke's View(IRE)**, with the blinkers dispensed with after his latest dismal display, failed to improve for this drop in class and looks a very moody character.

## 4468 CHAPEL DOWN ENGLISH WINE MEDIAN AUCTION MAIDEN FILLIES' STKS 6f 209y
**6:25** (6:26) (E) 2-Y-O **£3,382** (£1,040; £520; £260) **Stalls** Low

Form RPR
**1** **Favourita** 2-8-6 .............................. J-PGuillambert(3) 3 71+
(CEBrittain) *s.i.s: in rr tl hdwy over 2f out: strly rdn to ld nr fin* **16/1**

6225 **2** *½* **Chutney Mary (IRE)**[10] 4186 2-8-6 **72**.............................. ABeech(3) 7 70
(JGPortman) *trckd ldr: strly rdn to ld wl ins fnl f: hdd cl home* **9/2**[3]

0 **3** *¾* **Fantaisiste**[14] 4053 2-8-9 .............................. SCarson 5 68
(SirMarkPrescott) *led tl rdn and hdd wl ins fnl f: no ex* **11/4**[1]

0 **4** *½* **Grandma's Girl**[24] 3808 2-8-9 .............................. RBrisland 1 67
(RGuest) *t.k.h: a.p: rdn over 1f out: kpt on one pce* **20/1**

4 **5** *1 ¼* **Bongoali**[14] 4053 2-8-6 .............................. SHitchcott(3) 10 64
(MRChannon) *swtchd to ins fr wd draw and in rr: rdn and hdwy over 2f out: styd on* **10/3**[2]

0344 **6** *shd* **Madam Caversfield**[13] 4089 2-8-2 **71**.............................. PGallagher(7) 8 63
(RHannon) *towards rr tl hdwy 1/2-way: kpt on one pce fnl 2f* **10/3**[2]

00 **7** *3 ½* **Georgina**[14] 4053 2-8-9 .............................. MHenry 9 54
(MAJarvis) *trckd ldrs: rdn and wknd over 1f out* **16/1**

05 **8** *9* **Blue Line**[60] 2702 2-8-9 .............................. GBaker 6 31+
(MMadgwick) *t.k.h: rdn over 4f out: wknd over 1f out* **16/1**

1m 23.04s (0.44) **Going Correction** -0.05s/f (Good) **8 Ran SP% 113.4**
Speed ratings: **95,94,93,93,91 91,87,77**CSF £84.80 TOTE £20.50: £4.30, £2.00, £2.20; EX 70.60.
**Owner** Wyck Hall Stud **Bred** Wyck Hall Stud Ltd **Trained** Newmarket, Suffolk
■ Stewards Enquiry : A Beech caution: used whip with excessive frequency

**FOCUS**
A fair fillies' maiden that saw the first four pull clear. The winner can be rated better than the bare form.

**NOTEBOOK**
**Favourita**, half-sister to smart middle-distance stayer Time Zone, ran green through from the start, but responded really well for pressure approaching two out to score in workmanlike fashion. There was a lot to like about this debut success, and as she can be expected to improve for the experience, should do even better in time with a stiffer test.
**Chutney Mary(IRE)** had no more to offer when challenged by the winner late on, but posted a solid effort, and could go one better when reverting to nurseries. This looks about as far as she wants to go and she is the yardstick for the form.
**Fantaisiste** showed significant improvement from her recent debut and had every chance. She was suprisingly finding little late on, as on breeding, she should relish every yard of this trip. A more galloping track would be to her advantage, and she should win races, but will no doubt make a better three-year-old.
**Grandma's Girl** ran too keen early on and paid for it late in the day, but still turned in a much improved effort over this longer trip and much faster ground. She is the type to do better once handicapped.
**Bongoali** did not show much improvement on this second outing, and failed to confirm debut form with the Fantaisiste, but kept on under pressure and would appreciate a more conventional track next time.
**Madam Caversfield** looked to be doing her rider no favours when asked for maximum effort and was disappointing. She is becoming frustrating, and is totally exposed now, so could struggle to win a maiden this summer.
**Blue Line** ran way too freely early on and finished well beaten, but did not look totally happy on this track and now qualifies for nurseries.

## 4469 KARMA BRIGHTON MARINA (S) H'CAP — 5f 213y
6:55 (6:55) (G) (0-55,51) 3-Y-O+ £2,923 (£835; £417) Stalls Low

Form — RPR

1005 **1** **Rileys Dream**[17] 3988 5-8-11 **43**....(p) DCorby[(3)] 8 — 53
(BJLlewellyn) *hld up: hdwy over 2f out: rdn to ld jst ins fnl f: kpt up to work* **11/2**[3]

2002 **2** *1 1/4* **Cargo**[17] 3988 5-9-3 **46**....(tp) SSanders 4 — 52
(BAPearce) *trckd ldr: led 2f out: rdn and hdd jst ins fnl f: nt qckn* **5/2**[1]

-050 **3** *3* **Bandbox (IRE)**[38] 3376 9-8-3 **32**....(p) MHenry 5 — 29
(MSalaman) *trckd ldrs: rdn 1/2-way: short of room 2f out: kpt on fnl f* **8/1**

5000 **4** *nk* **Rathmullan**[17] 3988 5-8-7 **36**....(b) SCarson 1 — 32
(EAWheeler) *rdn along in rr: sme hdwy over 1f out: kpt on one pce* **20/1**

0400 **5** *1 1/4* **Must Be So**[5] 4338 3-7-6 **32**....(t) LucyRussell[(7)] 7 — 25
(JJBridger) *trckd leders: rdn over 2f out: wknd ent fnl f* **25/1**

2433 **6** *nk* **Lucky Valentine**[15] 4025 4-9-5 **51**....(b) SHitchcott[(3)] 3 — 43
(GLMoore) *hld up in tch: wknd fnl f* **3/1**[2]

4330 **7** *8* **Stagecoach Ruby**[2] 4414 3-8-6 **39**.... JQuinn 2 — 7
(GLMoore) *led tl hdd 2f out: sn wknd* **3/1**[2]

69.76 secs (-0.34) **Going Correction** -0.05s/f (Good)
**WFA** 3 from 4yo+ 4lb — **7** Ran SP% **113.7**
Speed ratings: **100,98,94,93,92 91,81**CSF £19.42 CT £108.55 TOTE £6.60: £2.90, £1.90; EX 25.90.There was no bid for the winner.
**Owner** Greg Robinson And A N Jay **Bred** R Olley **Trained** Fochriw, Caerphilly

**FOCUS**
A poor race won in decent style by Rileys Dream.

**NOTEBOOK**
**Rileys Dream** won with a little bit in hand. She is in good form and should continue to pay her way.
**Cargo** has been running consistently of late but remains without a win for over two years. He had every chance but was unable to cope with the winner in the closing stages.
**Bandbox(IRE)** was pressed for room at a vital stage and could only plug on.
**Rathmullan** was always struggling to go the pace could make no impression in the latter stages. *Official explanation: jockey said gelding lost its shoe*
**Lucky Valentine** proved disappointing and none of the headgear she has been tried in of late seems to make a difference.
**Stagecoach Ruby**, a stable companion of Lucky Valentine, dropped out tamely having showed up well early and also ran below par.

## 4470 VENTURE LIFESTYLE PHOTOGRAPHY H'CAP — 7f 214y
7:25 (7:25) (E) (0-70,71) 3-Y-O £3,993 (£1,228; £614; £307) Stalls Low

Form — RPR

3041 **1** **General Feeling (IRE)**[8] 4251 3-9-13 **71** 6ex.... JFEgan 6 — 83+
(SKirk) *hld up in tch: hdwy 1/2-way: hung lft but led 1f out: rdn out* **6/4**[1]

3361 **2** *1 1/4* **Miss Madame (IRE)**[12] 4127 3-9-7 **65**.... SSanders 4 — 74
(RGuest) *trckd ldr rdn and ev ch 1f out: nt qckn fnl 100yds* **11/4**[2]

0003 **3** *1 1/2* **Instinct**[7] 4265 3-8-8 **59**.... PGallagher[(7)] 5 — 65
(RHannon) *hld up in rr: hdwy on outside over 2f out: hung lft appr fnl f: r.o ins* **11/2**

0052 **4** *1* **Filliemou (IRE)**[17] 3993 3-8-12 **56**.... GBaker 7 — 59
(AWCarroll) *sn led: rdn and hdd 1f out: wknd* **5/1**[3]

4450 **5** *1 3/4* **Even Easier**[23] 3827 3-8-8 **52**....(b) RBrisland 1 — 51
(GLMoore) *hld up in tch: swtchd rt over 2f out: wknd fnl f* **12/1**

4610 **6** *12* **Faith Healer (IRE)**[19] 3949 3-8-11 **55**....(b) JQuinn 2 — 27
(VSmith) *trckd ldrs: rdn over 2f out and sn bhd: eased ins fnl f* **15/2**

1m 34.54s (-0.46) **Going Correction** -0.05s/f (Good) — **6** Ran SP% **118.2**
Speed ratings: **100,98,97,96,94 82**CSF £6.33 TOTE £2.90: £1.90, £1.70; EX 7.20.
**Owner** The So Long Partnership **Bred** John Graham And Leslie Laverty **Trained** Upper Lambourn, Berks

**FOCUS**
A pretty uncompetitive affair and the two that were expected to dominate did so, with the favourite coming out on top.

**NOTEBOOK**
**General Feeling(IRE)** was a successful raider at the Galway Festival and proved good enough to follow up under a 6lb penalty. He hung under pressure, but that may have been down to the very fast ground, and he won with a little more in hand than it may have appeared. He will have to improve further if he is defy a new mark though.
**Miss Madame(IRE)** did it well enough at Lingfield on her most recent outing and ran well in a follow-up bid, just being unable to match the winner in the final furlong. A drop in trip may see her winning again.
**Instinct** is not up to much and remains a maiden, but has a small race in him.
**Filliemou(IRE)**, who ran well when front-running on her previous outing, tried the same tactics again but was brushed aside.

## 4471 GLEESON CLASSIC HOMES APARTMENTS PALMEIRA GRANDE FILLIES' H'CAP — 1m 1f 209y
7:55 (7:58) (E) (0-70,70) 3-Y-O+ £4,056 (£1,248; £624; £312) Stalls High

Form — RPR

0-06 **1** **Optimal (IRE)**[15] 4027 3-8-10 **61**....(b[1]) SSanders 1 — 67
(SirMarkPrescott) *trckd ldr: tk narrow ld over 2f out: drvn out fnl f* **7/2**[3]

0604 **2** *3/4* **Sunset Mirage (USA)**[10] 4201 3-9-3 **68**....(v) JFEgan 5 — 73
(EALDunlop) *hld up in tch: rdn 2f out: r.o to go 2nd ins fnl f* **5/2**[2]

6000 **3** *3/4* **Nassiria**[10] 4201 3-8-11 **65**....(p) J-PGuillambert[(3)] 3 — 69
(CEBrittain) *led: hdd over 2f out: ev ch ent fnl f: one pce and lost 2nd ins* **20/1**

0662 **4** *7* **Sienna Sunset (IRE)**[14] 4045 5-8-13 **55**.... GBaker 6 — 45
(WMBrisbourne) *plld hard: hld up in tch: hdwy over 3f out: wknd over 1f out* **2/1**[1]

0444 **5** *1 3/4* **Magic Verse**[27] 3710 3-8-1 **52**.... JQuinn 2 — 39
(RGuest) *trckd ldrs tl rdn and wknd over 1f out* **10/1**

464- **6** *5* **Maid For Life (IRE)**[264] 6005 4-8-11 **56**.... DCorby[(3)] 8 — 33
(MJWallace) *slowly away: wl in rr tl hdwy on outside 4f out: swtchd lft to ins over 2f out: no imp after* **13/2**

0 **7** *7* **Jahia (NZ)**[74] 1284 5-9-7 **70**.... RLucey-Butler[(7)] 4 — 34
(MMadgwick) *rrd s: a bhd* **33/1**

6301 **8** *28* **Piquet**[5] 4339 6-8-7 **49** 7ex.... DarrenWilliams 7 — —
(JJBridger) *trckd leaers tl rdn and outpcd 4f out: sn wknd and eased whn btn: t.o* **8/1**

2m 1.92s (-0.62) **Going Correction** -0.05s/f (Good)
**WFA** 3 from 4yo+ 9lb — **8** Ran SP% **125.4**
Speed ratings: **100,99,98,93,91 87,82,59**CSF £14.17 CT £161.78 TOTE £4.60: £1.10, £1.70, £4.50; EX 19.90.
**Owner** Lady O'Reilly **Bred** Dr A J O'Reilly And Skymarc Farm **Trained** Newmarket, Suffolk

**FOCUS**
Just ordinary form, but the winner is not badly handicapped and the front three were well clear of the remainder.

**NOTEBOOK**
**Optimal(IRE)** ◆ looked a typical well-handicapped Prescott horse at the beginning of the season but had disappointed on her first two starts. Dropped back in trip with blinkers fitted for the first time, she did what was required. She should not go up to much for this and can win again - her half-brother One Off was well beaten on his first start at three before winning his next six.
**Sunset Mirage(USA)** had conditions in her favour and she looked to run her race, although the winner was just too strong.
**Nassiria**, with cheekpieces on for the first time, posted a most respectable effort in pulling well clear of all bar the front two. She is still a maiden, but does look to have a similar race in her.
**Sienna Sunset(IRE)** was unable to build on the promise of her recent Bath outing. *Official explanation: trainer said mare was unsuited by the track on today's firm ground*
**Magic Verse** had been in reasonable form on Fibresand recently but, returned to turf, was well beaten.
**Piquet** *Official explanation: trainer said mare did not travel down the hill on the firm ground*

## 4472 CURIOUS GRAPE ENGLISH WINE CLASSIFIED STKS — 5f 59y
8:25 (8:25) (E) 3-Y-O+ £3,993 (£1,228; £614; £307) Stalls Low

Form — RPR

0602 **1** **Trick Cyclist**[9] 4211 3-9-2 72.... SSanders 3 — 80
(AMBalding) *wnt rt s: mde all: hung lft appr fnl f: rdn out* **2/1**[2]

0060 **2** *1 1/2* **Imperium**[6] 4289 3-9-1 71.... JFEgan 1 — 73
(MrsStefLiddiard) *trckd wnr thrght: rdn over 1f out: no imp ins* **9/2**

3002 **3** *5* **Beauvrai**[6] 4294 4-9-5 72....(p) MTebbutt 5 — 54
(VSmith) *bmpd s: plld hrd: nt clr run over 1f out: wknd fnl f: b.b.v* **7/4**[1]

2103 **4** *nk* **Scottish Exile (IRE)**[5] 4331 3-8-12 71....(v) DarrenWilliams 7 — 49
(KRBurke) *trckd ldrs rdn 1/2-way: wknd over 1f out* **7/2**[3]

0005 **5** *1 1/4* **Run On**[25] 3772 6-9-3 46.... SRighton 6 — 46
(DGBridgwater) *a bhd: effrt over 1f out: but sn btn* **25/1**

61.57 secs (-0.70) **Going Correction** -0.05s/f (Good)
**WFA** 3 from 4yo+ 3lb — **5** Ran SP% **113.9**
Speed ratings: **103,100,92,92,90**CSF £11.58 TOTE £2.40: £1.90, £1.90; EX 13.20 Place 6 £60.43, Place 5 £28.15.
**Owner** Park House Partnership **Bred** Simon And Helen Plumbly **Trained** Kingsclere, Hants

**FOCUS**
A fair sprint but just ordinary form, with just the first two running near to their marks.

**NOTEBOOK**
**Trick Cyclist** had just a novice race success as a two-year-old coming into this but, under a determined ride from the in-form Seb Sanders who rides this track better than anyone, he ended a losing run stretching back to May 2003. He should continue to go well in similar events, but is obviously not a prolific winner.
**Imperium** appreciated the drop in grade and pulled clear of all bar the winner. He goes well here.
**Beauvrai** did not find as much as had looked likely, hardly surprising considering he broke a blood-vessel. *Official explanation: trainer said gelding had bled from the nose*
**Scottish Exile(IRE)** had conditions in her favour, but was beaten far enough.
**Run On** was well held and has not won for over two years.
T/Plt: £56.50. Pool of £34,647.85 - 446.95 winning units. T/Qpdt: £11.80. Pool of £3,212.50 - 200.70 winning units. JS

# [4080]CHEPSTOW (L-H)
### Thursday, August 5

**OFFICIAL GOING: Good to firm**
Wind: nil Weather: sunny and very warm

## 4473 COCA-COLA H'CAP — 1m 4f 23y
2:20 (2:20) (F) (0-55,55) 3-Y-O+ £3,136 (£896; £448) Stalls Low

Form — RPR

520U **1** **Royal Axminster**[35] 3450 9-8-8 **40**.... AmyBaker[(7)] 5 — 50
(MrsPNDutfield) *mde all: clr after 2f: pushed along 3f out: hld on wl fnl f* **20/1**

-051 **2** *hd* **Danebank (IRE)**[28] 3682 4-9-5 **51**....(p) DerekNolan[(7)] 17 — 61
(JMackie) *a.p: rdn 3f out: ev ch ins fnl f: r.o* **6/1**[2]

0030 **3** *nk* **Molly's Secret**[15] 4015 6-9-5 **44**....(p) JFEgan 19 — 53
(CGCox) *hld up in mid-div: rdn and hdwy over 3f out: ev ch ins fnl f: r.o* **9/1**

3453 **4** *1 3/4* **Bojangles (IRE)**[28] 3682 5-9-10 **49**.... DHolland 13 — 55
(RBrotherton) *prom: lost pl over 5f out: rdn 4f out: rallied over 2f out: styd on ins fnl f* **9/2**[1]

505 **5** *hd* **Latin Queen (IRE)**[17] 3997 4-9-3 **45**.... FPFerris[(3)] 16 — 51
(JDFrost) *chsd wnr: rdn over 2f out: ev ch 1f out: no ex towards fin* **20/1**

33-5 **6** *1 1/2* **Marrel**[18] 3851 6-9-3 **42**.... JoannaBadger 2 — 46
(DBurchell) *dwlt: hld up: rdn 4f out: swtchd rt and hdwy over 1f out: nt rch ldrs* **15/2**[3]

0036 **7** *1/2* **Java Dawn (IRE)**[28] 3667 4-8-10 **40**.... AQuinn[(5)] 1 — 43
(TEPowell) *s.s: wl bhd tl hdwy and swtchd lft jst over 1f out: nrst fin* **25/1**

0422 **8** *nk* **Lunar Lord**[12] 4139 8-9-11 **50**.... JBramhill 18 — 52
(DBurchell) *hld up: hdwy over 5f out: wnt 2nd over 4f out tl rdn over 3f out: wknd fnl f* **10/1**

-055 **9** *3/4* **Chanfron**[28] 3683 3-9-5 **55**.... PaulEddery 11 — 56
(BRMillman) *prom: rdn over 3f out: wknd over 1f out* **11/1**

0-66 **10** *1* **Frixos (IRE)**[13] 4082 4-9-11 **50**....(b) VSlattery 12 — 50
(MScudamore) *mid-div: rdn 4f out: no rspnse* **33/1**

5060 **11** *3/4* **Greyfield (IRE)**[12] 4146 8-9-3 **45**.... RMiles[(3)] 14 — 43
(KBishop) *s.s: nvr nr ldrs* **8/1**

4424 **12** *nk* **Tom Bell (IRE)**[28] 3667 4-9-5 **49**....(v) NChalmers[(5)] 7 — 47
(JGMO'Shea) *s.i.s: hdwy whn slipped bnd wl over 4f out: n.d after* **10/1**

-600 **13** *1* **Lord Lahar**[10] 4202 5-9-1 **40**.... RLappin 6 — 36
(MRChannon) *hld up: hdwy over 5f out: rdn over 4f out: wknd over 3f out* **33/1**

020/ **14** *hd* **Stafford King (IRE)**[229] 3712 7-9-1 **40**.... DKinsella 8 — 36
(JGMO'Shea) *a bhd* **50/1**

0526 **15** *1* **Mr Dip**[19] 3929 4-9-9 **48**.... NPollard 10 — 42
(AWCarroll) *a bhd* **14/1**

0000 **16** *2 1/2* **Royal Trigger**[25] 3776 4-10-0 **53**....(bt) ADaly 15 — 43
(IanWilliams) *prom tl rdn and wknd over 2f out* **16/1**

00-0 **17** *2* **Rainsborough Hill**[91] 1911 3-8-9 **48**.... JFMcDonald[(3)] 9 — 35
(AKing) *dwlt: a bhd* **40/1**

0000 **18** *10* **Tatweer (IRE)**[6] 4301 4-10-0 **53**....(v) SWhitworth 4 — 24
(DShaw) *s.v.s: a in rr* **33/1**

060/ **19** *dist* **Hobart Junction (IRE)**[403] 546 9-8-5 **37**.... TBlock[(7)] 3 — —
(JATDeGiles) *mid-div: rdn and lost pl over 4f: sn bhd: t.o* **50/1**

2m 39.44s (0.94) **Going Correction** +0.075s/f (Good)
**WFA** 3 from 4yo+ 11lb — **19** Ran SP% **133.0**
Speed ratings: **99,98,98,97,97 96,96,95,95,94 94,93,93,93,92 90,89,82,—**CSF £134.34 CT £1203.17 TOTE £63.10: £8.80, £1.10, £2.20, £1.60; EX 351.60.
**Owner** Axminster Carpets Ltd **Bred** Meon Valley Stud **Trained** Axmouth, Devon

**FOCUS**
A weak race in which Royal Axminster was allowed to make all for a hard-fought success.
**NOTEBOOK**
**Royal Axminster** was allowed the lead and had built up around a 15-length advantage by half way. He came right back to them in the straight though but this may have helped him as he is best when in company at the end of his races and was only just doing enough in front. He is not the most consistent and is going to struggle to follow up.
**Danebank(IRE)** was a winner at Warwick on a softer surface last time and he ran well on this quicker surface. The first-time cheekpieces did not seem to have much effect on him, but he should continue to pay his way.
**Molly's Secret** continues to hint at a return to the winners enclosure, being beaten under half a length.
**Bojangles(IRE)** was 3lb better off with Danebank on Warwick form and it was disappointing he could not get any closer.
**Latin Queen(IRE)** plugged on steadily and but lacked to pace to throw down a serious challenge.
**Marrel** would have found this too sharp and better can be expected granted a stiffer test.
**Java Dawn(IRE)** is another who would have found this an insufficient test and she was doing all her best work at the finish.
**Lunar Lord** *Official explanation: jockey said gelding was very keen*
**Tom Bell(IRE)** *Official explanation: jockey said gelding slipped on the bend turning ino the home straight*
**Tatweer(IRE)** *Official explanation: jockey said gelding slipped on the bend turning ino the home straight*
**Hobart Junction(IRE)** *Official explanation: jockey said gelding had a breathing problem*

## 4474 GUINNESS MEDIAN AUCTION MAIDEN STKS — 5f 16y
**2:50** (2:52) (E) 2-Y-0 — **£3,523** (£1,084; £542; £271) **Stalls** High

Form — RPR
20 **1** **Lucky Emerald (IRE)**[24] 3805 2-8-6 .................................. FPFerris(3) 4 — 69
(BPalling) *a.p: rdn over 2f out: hung lft ins fnl f: r.o to ld towards fin* **12/1**
403 **2** ½ **Our Fugitive (IRE)**[10] 4191 2-9-0 .................................. NPollard 6 — 72
(AWCarroll) *led: rdn and hung lft over 1f out: swvd rt jst ins fnl f: hdd towards fin* **7/1**[3]
2 **3** *shd* **Dancing Rose (IRE)**[24] 3805 2-8-9 .................................. RSmith 11 — 67
(CGCox) *chsd ldrs: pushed along over 2f out: r.o ins fnl f* **5/2**[2]
2532 **4** *nk* **Agent Kensington**[14] 4058 2-8-9 67 .................................. DHolland 12 — 66
(RHannon) *in tch: rdn over 2f out: r.o ins fnl f* **6/4**[1]
063 **5** *1* **Il Pranzo**[14] 4064 2-9-0 72 .................................. JFEgan 7 — 67
(SKirk) *chsd ldr: rdn over 1f out: nt qckn ins fnl f* **12/1**
**6** *2* **Tanning** 2-8-6 .................................. JFMcDonald(3) 5 — 55
(HMorrison) *outpcd: nvr nrr* **16/1**
30 **7** ¾ **Blakeshall Hope**[24] 3802 2-9-0 .................................. JoannaBadger 8 — 57
(PDEvans) *chsd ldrs: rdn over 2f out: wknd wl over 1f out* **33/1**
**8** *5* **Sartaena (IRE)** 2-8-4 .................................. NChalmers(5) 2 — 35
(RMBeckett) *racd alone far side: spd over 3f* **33/1**
**9** *1 ¾* **Starduster** 2-8-9 .................................. PaulEddery 9 — 29
(BRMillman) *s.i.s: sn wl bhd* **25/1**
00 **10** *1 ½* **Secret Diva (IRE)**[58] 2761 2-8-9 .................................. DKinsella 3 — 24
(MrsPNDutfield) *outpcd* **66/1**
**11** *dist* **Will The Till** 2-9-0 .................................. SWhitworth 1 — —
(JMBradley) *wnt lft s: sn lost action and t.o* **33/1**
0 **12** *10* **Theflyingscottie**[14] 4040 2-9-0 .................................. VSlattery 10 — —
(JDFrost) *sn wl bhd: t.o whn virtually p.u over 2f out* **66/1**

60.69 secs (1.19) **Going Correction** +0.075s/f (Good) **12** Ran SP% **118.0**
Speed ratings: **93,92,92,91,89 86,85,77,74,72** —,—CSF £87.70 TOTE £12.40: £2.50, £2.40, £1.40; EX 97.10.
**Owner** T Clarke **Bred** Dr John Waldron **Trained** Tredodridge, Vale Of Glamorgan
**FOCUS**
An average maiden, but the form should prove very reliable. It should have been won by Our Fugitive, but he threw it away by swerving right at the furlong pole.
**NOTEBOOK**
**Lucky Emerald(IRE)** got a little warm beforehand and did not pick up immediately after coming under pressure, but once getting going she came through to lead and stuck on well. She reportedly blew her chance before the start at Windsor when disappointing and although not the biggest, she should pay her way in nurseries.
**Our Fugitive(IRE)** was still going best and had the lead when swerving right. He was still only run out of it close home and, while nothing special and not one to be taking too short a price about, he is capable of winning.
**Dancing Rose(IRE)** was never really going with any great zest and could not obtain a good early pitch from her draw. She came home well though once hitting top stride and will be well suited by another furlong.
**Agent Kensington**, despite being well exposed, was the one to beat and ran disappointingly. She is one to avoid.
**Il Pranzo** was a little unlucky not to get closer, as he was denied a clear run when just starting to pick up and could make no real impression after. He is up to winning in nursery company.
**Tanning** will do better in time, and this relatively late foal will appreciate an extra furlong.
**Will The Till** *Official explanation: jockey said gelding dived left after leaving the stalls and knocked itself*
**Theflyingscottie** *Official explanation: jockey said gelding knocked itself coming out of the stalls and he thought it had gone lame*

## 4475 LETHEBY & CHRISTOPHER NURSERY — 6f 16y
**3:20** (3:20) (E) 2-Y-0 — **£4,173** (£1,284; £642; £321) **Stalls** High

Form — RPR
653 **1** **Dove Cottage (IRE)**[31] 3570 2-8-5 **60** .................................. DKinsella 5 — 60
(WSKittow) *w ldr: rdn to ld 2f out: sn edgd lft: r.o* **14/1**
21 **2** ¾ **Godsend**[34] 3491 2-9-5 **74** .................................. DHolland 1 — 75+
(RHannon) *a.p: rdn and ev ch 1f out: nt qckn towards fin* **8/11**[1]
4200 **3** *1* **Gavioli (IRE)**[21] 3886 2-8-10 **65** .................................. (t) SWhitworth 7 — 60
(JMBradley) *a.p: rdn over 1f out: kpt on u.p ins fnl f* **33/1**
632 **4** *1* **Geisha Lady (IRE)**[13] 4081 2-9-2 **76** .................................. NChalmers(5) 2 — 68
(RMBeckett) *bhd: swtchd rt over 4f out: late hdwy: nvr nrr* **8/1**[3]
0021 **5** ¾ **Good Wee Girl (IRE)**[8] 4243 2-9-5 **74** 7ex .................................. JFEgan 6 — 64
(SKirk) *prom: rdn over 2f out: wknd ins fnl f* **4/1**[2]
0040 **6** *shd* **Waterline Lover**[14] 4048 2-8-1 **59** .................................. FPFerris(3) 8 — 48
(PDEvans) *led: rdn and hdd 2f out: wknd wl ins fnl f* **12/1**
4323 **7** *2* **General Nuisance (IRE)**[10] 4200 2-8-2 **60** .................................. (p) JFMcDonald(3) 3 — 43
(JSMoore) *sn bhd: rdn over 2f out: no rspnse* **20/1**
4226 **8** *nk* **Glasson Lodge**[23] 3824 2-8-0 **55** .................................. JoannaBadger 4 — 38
(PDEvans) *prom: rdn and lost pl over 3f out: sn bhd* **20/1**

1m 13.13s (0.93) **Going Correction** +0.075s/f (Good) **8** Ran SP% **115.8**
Speed ratings: **96,95,93,92,91 91,88,88**CSF £24.73 CT £369.46 TOTE £14.10: £2.60, £1.10, £5.60; EX 66.60.
**Owner** Reg Gifford **Bred** D R Tucker **Trained** Blackborough, Devon
■ Stewards Enquiry : D Kinsella caution: used whip without giving colt time to respond
**FOCUS**
A straightforward success for Dove Cottage, but just fair nursery form.
**NOTEBOOK**
**Dove Cottage(IRE)** had been running over five furlongs and this extra furlong allowed him to show improved form. Always well placed, he took it up around two furlongs out and stayed on well. Connections believe he will be well served by some juice in the ground, and there should be more to come from him.
**Godsend** was sent off at cramped odds - due to connections - and had her chance. She had to race wide, which would not have helped, and she can do better, but she will need to, otherwise she will continue to be vulnerable.
**Gavioli(IRE)** improved on previous form hinted at better to come. He can win down in grade.
**Geisha Lady(IRE)** ideally wants farther and can improve on this when stepping up to seven.
**Good Wee Girl(IRE)** had her chance and failed to run up to her winning maiden form.
**Waterline Lover** led for over half the race but was oon in trouble and faded disappointingly.

## 4476 COORS BREWERS (S) STKS — 1m 2f 36y
**3:50** (3:50) (G) 3-Y-0+ — **£2,653** (£758; £379) **Stalls** Low

Form — RPR
0502 **1** **Go Green**[27] 3697 3-8-2 46 .................................. (t) FPFerris(3) 4 — 53
(PDEvans) *hld up: hdwy 5f out: rdn over 2f out: led jst over 1f out: r.o* **7/2**[3]
2300 **2** *hd* **Cosi Fan Tutte**[10] 4192 6-9-5 63 .................................. (vt) DHolland 8 — 58
(MCPipe) *a.p: rdn to ld over 2f out: hdd jst over 1f out: r.o* **7/4**[1]
-002 **3** *5* **Relative Hero (IRE)**[21] 3885 4-9-0 51 .................................. (v[1]) AQuinn(5) 7 — 48
(MissSJWilton) *t.k.h: a.p: rdn over 3f out: wknd fnl f* **8/1**
3301 **4** *7* **Ambersong**[17] 3996 6-9-3 51 .................................. DerekNolan(7) 1 — 40
(AWCarroll) *s.i.s: rdn and hdwy 4f out: wknd over 2f out* **10/3**[2]
0000 **5** *1* **Tamarina (IRE)**[15] 4018 3-8-2 38 .................................. (b) JFMcDonald(3) 9 — 28
(NEBerry) *t.k.h: w ldr: led over 5f out: rdn and hdd over 2f out: wknd wl over 1f out* **100/1**
6600 **6** *1 ¾* **My Country Club**[26] 3742 7-8-12 43 .................................. GBartley(7) 6 — 30
(AGJuckes) *hld up in tch: lost pl over 5f out: n.d after* **40/1**
00-3 **7** *nk* **Miss Woodpigeon**[17] 3996 8-9-0 40 .................................. VSlattery 11 — 24
(JDFrost) *hld up in tch: rdn and edgd lft over 3f out: sn wknd* **12/1**
0000 **8** *2 ½* **Rumour Mill (IRE)**[15] 4018 3-8-7 40 .................................. (b) RMiles(3) 10 — 24
(NEBerry) *bhd: hdwy over 3f out: wknd 2f out* **25/1**
0000 **9** ¾ **Manikato (USA)**[52] 2939 10-8-12 26 .................................. KirbyHarris(7) 5 — 23
(KGWingrove) *a bhd* **25/1**
0000 **10** *5* **Kerristina**[17] 3990 3-8-5 30 .................................. SWhitworth 3 — 8
(DJSFrenchDavis) *rdn 4f out: a in rr* **50/1**
000/ **11** *dist* **Artists Retreat**[707] 4284 5-9-0 37 .................................. JBramhill 2 — —
(BDLeavy) *led: hdd over 5f out: rdn and wknd qckly over 4f out: t.o* **50/1**

2m 9.74s (0.14) **Going Correction** +0.075s/f (Good)
**WFA** 3 from 4yo+ 9lb **11** Ran SP% **115.5**
Speed ratings: **102,101,97,92,91 90,89,87,87,83** —CSF £9.32 TOTE £4.00: £2.40, £1.10, £2.00; EX 13.60.The winner was bought in for 6,800gns.
**Owner** P D Evans **Bred** Mrs C R M Pugh **Trained** Pandy, Gwent
**FOCUS**
A weak event, and an unlikely source of future winners.
**NOTEBOOK**
**Go Green** was among the better treated at the weights and proved well suited by this step up in trip, running on strongly all the way to the line. She is evidently a tough sort and can win again at this level.
**Cosi Fan Tutte** is not easy to win with, but went down fighting. He pulled five lengths clear of the third.
**Relative Hero(IRE)** found a mile and a half too far most recently and raced too keenly in the first-time visor back down in trip.
**Ambersong** ran below form without an apparent excuse.
**Rumour Mill(IRE)** *Official explanation: jockey said colt was unsuited by the downhill parts of the course*

## 4477 FOOD PARTNERS FILLIES' H'CAP — 1m 14y
**4:20** (4:20) (E) (0-70,65) 3-Y-0+ — **£3,965** (£1,220; £610; £305) **Stalls** High

Form — RPR
6105 **1** **Tuscarora (IRE)**[8] 4230 5-9-5 **56** .................................. RMiles(3) 4 — 66
(AWCarroll) *hld up: sltly hmpd sn after s: smooth hdwy on outside to ld 2f out: rdn and edgd rt jst over 1f out: r.o* **15/8**[1]
5440 **2** *shd* **Naughty Girl (IRE)**[14] 4066 4-8-7 **44** .................................. (vt) FPFerris(3) 7 — 54
(PDEvans) *hld up: hdwy over 2f out: rdn over 1f out: r.o ins fnl f* **12/1**
5055 **3** *3 ½* **Trois Etoiles (IRE)**[22] 3852 3-8-9 **57** .................................. DerekNolan(7) 2 — 59
(JWHills) *a.p: led 3f out to 2f out: sn rdn: wknd fnl f* **4/1**[2]
4004 **4** *3* **Danifah (IRE)**[1] 4460 3-8-1 **42** .................................. JoannaBadger 9 — 37
(PDEvans) *led early: prom: rdn and nt clr run over 2f out: sn swtchd lft: wknd over 1f out* **16/1**
5340 **5** *3* **Ivy Moon**[17] 3988 4-8-9 **43** .................................. SWhitworth 6 — 31
(BJLlewellyn) *bmpd sn after s: plld hrd early in rr: swtchd lft 1f out: n.d* **11/1**
0640 **6** *1 ½* **Young Love**[29] 3636 3-8-8 **52** .................................. (v[1]) JFMcDonald(3) 8 — 37
(MissECLavelle) *t.k.h: prom: rdn and ev ch over 2f out: wknd wl over 1f out* **12/1**
-110 **7** *hd* **Toccata Aria**[20] 3919 6-9-5 **53** .................................. DHolland 3 — 37
(JMBradley) *sn led: rdn and hdd 3f out: wknd 2f out* **4/1**[2]
6000 **8** *2 ½* **Annijaz**[13] 4083 7-9-3 **51** .................................. DKinsella 1 — 29
(JMBradley) *hld up: hdwy over 3f out: rdn and ev ch over 2f out: wknd over 1f out* **9/1**[3]

1m 35.6s (-0.30) **Going Correction** +0.075s/f (Good)
**WFA** 3 from 4yo+ 7lb **8** Ran SP% **114.4**
Speed ratings: **104,103,100,97,94 92,92,90**CSF £26.50 CT £82.60 TOTE £2.20: £1.80, £2.60, £2.50; EX 28.70.
**Owner** Pursuit Media **Bred** Yeomanstown Stud **Trained** Wixford, Warwicks
**FOCUS**
Ordinary form. Tuscarora stood out on her Goodwood run.
**NOTEBOOK**
**Tuscarora(IRE)** was a stand out on her Glorious Goodwood form - ran well from 7lb out of the handicap behind Diamond Lodge - and as a result of that was effectively off a 7lb lower mark here. She only just got the better of the duel but always just does enough and will continue to run well.
**Naughty Girl(IRE)** could only manage fourth in a seller on her penultimate outing, but she is capable on her day, as she showed with this narrow defeat. She is not one to rely on.
**Trois Etoiles(IRE)** is becoming disappointing and was readily held.
**Danifah(IRE)** had her chance but never looked like winning.
**Ivy Moon** raced too keenly and was reported to have hung. *Official explanation: jockey said colt hung right-handed throughout*
**Toccata Aria** has been below par the last twice now and looks one best left alone until showing more.

## 4478 MERBURY CATERING MAIDEN STKS — 7f 16y
**4:50** (4:50) (D) 3-Y-0+ — **£3,474** (£1,069; £534; £267) **Stalls** High

Form — RPR
223 **1** **Violet Park**[10] 4195 3-8-5 .................................. JFMcDonald(3) 4 — 70
(BJMeehan) *w ldr: rdn to ld 2f out: drew clr fnl f: readily* **9/4**[2]

-220 **2** 7 **Taqaah**[22] 3845 3-8-13 80 ADaly 7 56
(MPTregoning) *dwlt: t.k.h: hdwy over 3f out: rdn 2f out: wnt 2nd ins fnl f: no ch w wnr* **11/8**[1]

00 **3** ½ **Primeshade Promise**[17] 3994 3-8-8 JBramhill 1 50
(DBurchell) *led: rdn and hdd 2f out: one pce* **100/1**

0604 **4** ½ **Nikiforos**[15] 4024 3-8-13 65 SWhitworth 3 54
(JWHills) *hld up: edgd lft on outside over 4f out: hdwy over 2f out: rdn and wnt 2nd briefly 1f out: no ex* **20/1**

0- **5** 1¼ **Homeward (IRE)**[286] 5735 3-8-8 DKinsella 2 45
(AMBalding) *w ldrs tl rdn and wknd over 2f out* **33/1**

0536 **6** 4 **Ligne D'Eau**[14] 4051 3-8-10 59 FPFerris(3) 5 39
(PDEvans) *hld up in tch: rdn 3f out: sn wknd* **12/1**

046 **7** ¾ **Cazenove**[19] 3948 3-8-13 PaulEddery 8 37
(MGQuinlan) *prom: rdn over 3f out: wknd over 2f out* **20/1**

**8** ¾ **Irish Playwright (IRE)** 4-9-5 VSlattery 6 35
(DGBridgwater) *s.s and wnt lft: sn wl bhd: sme late hdwy* **50/1**

3-63 **9** hd **Zazous**[5] 4316 3-8-13 70 DHolland 10 35
(AKing) *a bhd* **9/2**[3]

00 **10** 7 **Homebred Star**[28] 3666 3-8-8 NChalmers(5) 9 16
(PBowen) *a bhd* **40/1**

1m 23.18s (-0.02) **Going Correction** +0.075s/f (Good)
**WFA** 3 from 4yo 6lb **10** Ran SP% **116.6**
Speed ratings: **103,95,94,93,92 87,87,86,85,77**CSF £5.29 TOTE £3.30: £1.10, £1.50, £18.70; EX 6.50.
**Owner** Mrs J Cash **Bred** D E And Mrs J Cash **Trained** Upper Lambourn, Berks

**FOCUS**
Despite a couple or reasonable ratings, this was a moderate maiden - the winner apart - well advertised by the placing of Primeshade Promise, who had shown nothing previously.

**NOTEBOOK**
**Violet Park** deserved to get her head in front. She had been unlucky when beaten only a neck at Newmarket on her second start, but made up for it here in good style - possibly winning too well from a handicapping point of view, although with key rivals running below par/going the wrong way, she did not achieve as much as first impressions suggest.
**Taqaah** is not the most willing and struggled to get the better of the rank outsider for second. He remains one to avoid.
**Primeshade Promise** left her two previous runs behind with a shock third at 100/1. Although seemingly improving, she will struggle to find a weak enough maiden to win, and finishing so close to a Shiekh Ahmed 80-rated horse looks bad news from a handicapping point of view.
**Nikiforos** will be better off back in handicaps.
**Homeward(IRE)** is a horse of minor ability.
**Zazous** ran no sort of race and is better than this.

## 4479 LETHEBY & CHRISTOPHER STKS (H'CAP) (LADIES RACE) 1m 14y
5:20 (5:21) (E) (0-70,70) 3-Y-0+ £3,857 (£1,187; £593; £296) Stalls High

Form RPR
3020 **1** **Lord Chamberlain**[27] 3697 11-9-9 50 (b) MissKellyHarrison(3) 9 60
(JMBradley) *hld up: hdwy over 2f out: rdn to ld 1f out: r.o* **12/1**

0040 **2** 1½ **Adalar (IRE)**[25] 3771 4-9-13 58 MissABevan(7) 14 65
(PDEvans) *led: hdd 1f out: nt qckn* **8/1**[3]

0064 **3** 1 **Cormorant Wharf (IRE)**[15] 4026 4-10-7 66 MissJPowell(7) 13 70
(TEPowell) *s.i.s: hld up in rr: hdwy over 1f out: r.o ins fnl f* **11/1**

2060 **4** nk **Smoothly Does It**[38] 3386 3-9-12 64 MsTDzieciolowska(7) 10 68
(MrsAJBowlby) *hld up in tch: ev ch over 1f out: nt qckn fnl f* **10/1**

0020 **5** 1¾ **Rainstorm**[3] 4386 9-8-13 40 MrsSOwen(3) 12 40
(WMBrisbourne) *prom: chsd ldr over 4f out: ev ch over 1f out: wknd fnl f* **6/1**[2]

3130 **6** ½ **Critical Stage (IRE)**[13] 4080 5-10-11 63 MissSBrotherton 7 61
(JDFrost) *prom: rdn over 2f out: wknd 1f out* **10/1**

4540 **7** 1¼ **Pas De Surprise**[9] 4220 6-9-11 52 MissEFolkes(3) 1 48
(PDEvans) *hld up: swtchd rt sn after s: rdn and hdwy over 2f out: no further prog* **12/1**

0003 **8** ¾ **Daydream Dancer**[27] 3700 3-8-13 49 (b) MissNadineForde(5) 6 43
(CGCox) *hld up: rdn over 3f out: no hdwy fnl 2f* **14/1**

2400 **9** 1½ **Leaping Brave (IRE)**[15] 4031 3-10-11 70 MissEJJones 11 60
(BRMillman) *chsd ldr over 3f: rdn over 2f out: wknd wl over 1f out* **10/1**

2016 **10** 3 **Chandelier**[20] 3910 4-9-13 51 MsCWilliams 5 34
(MSSaunders) *s.s and swtchd to stands' side: a bhd* **5/1**[1]

0-00 **11** 1 **Ark Admiral**[7] 3747 5-10-6 61 MissCTizzard(3) 8 42
(CLTizzard) *bhd fnl 4f* **33/1**

0010 **12** nk **Oh So Rosie (IRE)**[3] 4386 4-10-0 55 (p) MrsSMoore(3) 2 35
(JSMoore) *bhd: hdwy over 3f out: rdn over 2f out: wknd wl over 1f out* **6/1**[2]

3460 **13** ¾ **Magic Warrior**[47] 3088 4-9-9 52 MissSarah-JaneDurman(5) 4 31
(JCFox) *prom tl wknd over 1f out* **33/1**

1506 **14** 1 **Lyrical Girl (USA)**[8] 4241 3-9-9 59 MissJoeyEllis(5) 3 35
(HJManners) *a bhd* **20/1**

1m 36.32s (0.42) **Going Correction** +0.075s/f (Good)
**WFA** 3 from 4yo+ 7lb **14** Ran SP% **124.7**
Speed ratings: **100,98,97,97,95 94,93,92,91,88 87,87,86,85**CSF £106.51 CT £1106.25 TOTE £14.40: £3.80, £4.10, £4.70; EX 186.20 Place 6 £14.64, Place 5 £6.05.
**Owner** W C Harries **Bred** Dragon's Stud **Trained** Sedbury, Gloucs

**FOCUS**
A poor quality affair. As usual over a mile here, there was a strong bias towards those drawn high.

**NOTEBOOK**
**Lord Chamberlain** - often the bridesmaid, never the bride - was winning his first race on turf in over two years. He is frustrating and, at the age of 11, not one to place total faith in.
**Adalar(IRE)** attempted to make all and managed to lead on the stands' rail. He stuck on well to keep second and may be worth trying back over farther.
**Cormorant Wharf(IRE)** was held up and failed to take advantage of his good draw. He kept on well in the closing stages to reach a place without actually threatening to win.
**Smoothly Does It** looked a big danger at one point but could offer no more, having got into a good challenging position.
**Rainstorm**, off a 4lb lower mark than when last successful, proved unable to take advantage of it. Despite being nine, he is on a winnable mark and can probably pick up a small event.
**Chandelier** reportedly tried to duck under the stalls and lost the blindfold in the process. He shied at the blind that was on the floor when coming out of the stalls and it resulted in him being slowly away. This may well explain the bad effort. *Official explanation: jockey said gelding shied at the blind that was on the ground as the stalls opened and lost ground as a result*
T/Plt: £19.20 to a £1 stake. Pool: £31,010.05. 1,176.20 winning tickets. T/Qpdt: £2.60 to a £1 stake. Pool: £1,896.50. 533.20 winning tickets. KH

# 4052 FOLKESTONE (R-H)
## Thursday, August 5

**OFFICIAL GOING: Good to firm (firm in places)**
Wind: almost nil Weather: overcast and humid, drizzle races 3 and 4

## 4480 LOUIS'S TRIUMPH MEDIAN AUCTION MAIDEN STKS 7f (S)
5:40 (5:41) (F) 2-Y-0 £3,521 (£1,006; £503) Stalls Low

Form RPR
4 **1** **Querido (USA)**[26] 3760 2-9-0 LDettori 9 81+
(SaeedBinSuroor) *mde all: stretched clr over 2f out: easily* **1/3**[1]

**2** 4 **Mansiya** 2-8-9 KMcEvoy 5 63
(CEBrittain) *trckd ldrs: shkn up to chse wnr over 1f out: no imp* **16/1**

**3** nk **Haatmey** 2-9-0 TEDurcan 1 67
(MRChannon) *prom: chsd wnr 3f out: sn outpcd: lost 2nd over 1f out: kpt on* **14/1**[3]

00 **4** 3 **Lord Normacote**[32] 3553 2-9-0 RHavlin 3 60
(CADwyer) *chsd wnr to 3f out: sn outpcd: rdn and plugged on* **66/1**

**5** ¾ **Knightsbridge Hill (IRE)** 2-9-0 JDSmith 4 58
(AKing) *settled in rr: outpcd wl over 2f out: pushed along and one pce after* **20/1**

056 **6** nk **Merrymadcap (IRE)**[28] 3664 2-9-0 DSweeney 6 57
(MBlanshard) *settled in rr: shkn up and outpcd wl over 2f out: one pce after* **25/1**

3 **7** 7 **Jamaaron**[28] 3664 2-9-0 PDobbs 2 40
(RHannon) *dwlt: in tch: effrt 3f out: wknd rapidly 2f out* **7/1**[2]

**8** ¾ **Raffish** 2-8-11 LFletcher(3) 7 38
(JMPEustace) *dwlt: in tch: pushed along 1/2-way: wknd over 2f out* **40/1**

0 **9** ¾ **Speedie Rossini (IRE)**[5] 4335 2-9-0 VHalliday 8 36
(SCWilliams) *prom: rdn 1/2-way: wknd over 2f out* **66/1**

1m 28.09s (0.29) **Going Correction** -0.075s/f (Good) **9** Ran SP% **114.1**
Speed ratings: **95,90,90,86,85 85,77,76,75**CSF £6.34 TOTE £1.50: £1.10, £2.60, £1.80; EX 7.80.
**Owner** Godolphin **Bred** Darley **Trained** Newmarket, Suffolk

**FOCUS**
A decent performance from Querido, who had run fourth in a decent York maiden on his debut and found this opposition much less taxing.

**NOTEBOOK**
**Querido(USA)**, fourth on his debut in a reasonably strong York maiden, found this much easier and simply outclassed his rivals. There should be plenty more to come and he will be worthy of respect in a higher grade.
**Mansiya**, a half-sister to four winners, including a couple of seven-furlong juvenile scorers, out of a seven-furlong two-year-old winner, was nibbled at in the betting and made a respectable debut. She was not good enough to go with the winner, but kept on steadily for pressure and should benefit from the run.
**Haatmey**, a half-brother to an eight-furlong two-year-old winner, out of a 12-furlong scorer, looked as though the outing would bring him on and posted a good effort considering.
**Lord Normacote**, well beaten in just ordinary events on his two previous starts, showed much improved form and is now qualified for a mark. He should find things easier in nurseries.
**Knightsbridge Hill(IRE)**, an 11,000gns purchase, is a half-brother to three winners, including a winner four times over five furlongs at two. He was well held but hails from a stable that does well with its select bunch of juveniles and could improve.
**Jamaaron**, third to subsequent Richmond winner Montgomery's Arch over course and distance on his debut (good to soft), ran as though something was amiss. The faster ground is the obvious explanation, but it was also reported that he had kicked the stalls.

## 4481 CHAPEL DOWN MAIDEN STKS 6f
6:10 (6:10) (D) 2-Y-0 £4,173 (£1,284; £642; £321) Stalls Low

Form RPR
3242 **1** **Marching Song**[12] 4143 2-9-0 85 PDobbs 1 81+
(RHannon) *mde virtually all: drew clr fr 2f out: easily* **11/10**[1]

5 **2** 6 **Averting**[31] 3570 2-9-0 DSweeney 2 63
(RFJohnsonHoughton) *cl up: chsd wnr jst over 2f out: sn outpcd: kpt on* **25/1**

0 **3** ¾ **San Deng**[12] 4117 2-9-0 KMcEvoy 4 61
(WRMuir) *wl in tch: shkn up and outpcd 2f out: kpt on fr over 1f out* **50/1**

00 **4** ¾ **Royal Pardon**[26] 3741 2-8-9 MFenton 6 54
(MLWBell) *hld up in last: outpcd over 2f out: shuffled along over 1f out: r.o to snatch 4th nr fin* **33/1**

5 **5** ½ **Insignia (IRE)**[79] 2208 2-9-0 RHavlin 7 57
(JHMGosden) *w wnr to 1/2-way: shkn up and fdd wl over 1f out* **3/1**[2]

0 **6** 2½ **Lama Albarq (USA)**[31] 3588 2-9-0 LDettori 3 50
(SaeedBinSuroor) *hld up in last pair: pushed along over 2f out: no rspnse and sn btn* **10/3**[3]

0 **7** 1 **Valios (IRE)**[24] 3808 2-9-0 TEDurcan 5 47
(LMCumani) *t.k.h: cl up to over 2f out: wknd over 1f out* **20/1**

1m 13.57s (-0.03) **Going Correction** -0.075s/f (Good) **7** Ran SP% **109.2**
Speed ratings: **97,89,88,87,86 83,81**CSF £31.68 TOTE £2.00: £1.40, £4.90; EX 16.20.
**Owner** The Queen **Bred** The Queen **Trained** East Everleigh, Wilts

**FOCUS**
An uncompetitive maiden in which Marching Song ran just below his best, despite winning easily.

**NOTEBOOK**
**Marching Song** was faced with his easiest task to date and gained a deserved first success in good style. Pat Dobbs feels he is improving and he should be competitive back in better company.
**Averting** stepped up on his debut running, but was still left behind by the winner and is probably more of a handicap type.
**San Deng** found this less competitive than the Ascot maiden in which he made his debut and was able to get in the money, but his long-term future lies in handicaps.
**Royal Pardon** caught the eye running on when it was all over. She is now qualified for a rating and could be capable of better in nurseries.
**Insignia(IRE)** offered some promise behind subsequent Royal Ascot winner Chateau Istana on his debut 79 days previously, but showed no improvement and was most disappointing.
**Lama Albarq(USA)** showed next to nothing once again.

## 4482 CURIOUS GRAPE NURSERY 7f (S)
6:40 (6:42) (D) 2-Y-0 £5,590 (£1,720; £860; £430) Stalls Low

Form RPR
4104 **1** **Lisa Mona Lisa (IRE)**[13] 4094 2-9-0 70 TEDurcan 3 70
(VSmith) *mde virtually all: drvn 2f out: jnd fnl f: hld on wl* **5/1**

031 **2** shd **Rowan Lodge (IRE)**[23] 3823 2-9-7 77 LDettori 2 77
(MHTompkins) *uns rdr and bolted bef s: t.k.h: trckd wnr: chal and upsides fnl f: nt qckn last strides* **6/4**[1]

042 **3** ½ **Hallucinate**[15] 4016 2-8-13 69 PDobbs 1 68
(RHannon) *trckd ldrs: gng wl enough over 2f out: rdn and nt qckn over 1f out: styd on ins fnl f* **7/2**[3]



The Form Book, Raceform Ltd, Compton, RG20 6NL

5065 **4** 1/2 **Im Spartacus**[11] 4166 2-8-12 **68**.............................................. MFenton 5 65
(IAWood) *pressed ldng pair: rdn and unable qck 2f out: kpt on again last 100yds* **3/1**[2]

620 **5** 1 **Megell (IRE)**[43] 3196 2-8-12 **68**.............................................. PMcCabe 4 63
(MGQuinlan) *dwlt: hld up in last pair: gng wl 2f out: rdn and nt qckn over 1f out: fdd nr fin* **14/1**

035 **6** 13 **Artadi**[17] 3986 2-8-1 **57**.............................................. (e[1]) AMcCarthy 6 19
(PMPhelan) *s.s: t.k.h: hld up in last pair: wknd 2f out* **25/1**

1m 29.47s (1.67) **Going Correction** -0.075s/f (Good) **6** Ran SP% **114.4**
Speed ratings: **87,86,86,85,84 69**CSF £13.38 TOTE £6.60: £2.60, £1.50; EX 18.10.
**Owner** Stephen Dartnell **Bred** A Geraghty **Trained** Exning, Suffolk

**FOCUS**
Not great form, but pretty competitive nonetheless and this race should produce winners at a similar level. They went just a steady early pace and as a result the winning time was very slow for the grade.

**NOTEBOOK**
**Lisa Mona Lisa(IRE)** appreciated the return to seven furlongs to gain her first success outside of selling company. She has progressed with racing and could well defy a rise in the weights to pick up another nursery before the season is out.
**Rowan Lodge(IRE)** got loose beforehand but did not look to take much out of himself. He is improving and only just failed to follow up his Brighton maiden success. This was his first run over seven furlongs, but the trip was not a problem.
**Hallucinate** looked to have been given a very fair mark for his nursery debut and ran well. There is a similar race in him.
**Im Spartacus**, due to be raised 4lb off the back of his fifth in a reasonable event at Ascot, just lacked the pace to take the gaps, but was flying at the finish. His new mark will make things tougher.
**Megell(IRE)**, trying this trip for the first time, would have appreciated a stronger pace.

## 4483 BARRETTS OF ASHFORD LAND ROVER H'CAP 7f (S)
**7:10** (7:11) (E) (0-70,65) 3-Y-O **£3,503** (£1,078; £539; £269) **Stalls** Low

Form RPR
2453 **1** **Iphigenia (IRE)**[13] 4083 3-9-7 **65**.............................................. LisaJones 7 76
(PWHiatt) *prom: led 3f out: clr 2f out: in n.d after: rdn out* **3/1**[2]

0004 **2** 5 **Trifti**[22] 3848 3-9-0 **58**.............................................. KMcEvoy 3 56
(CACyzer) *trckd ldrs: nt clr run over 2f out: sn outpcd: rdn and styd on to take 2nd ins fnl f: no ch w wnr* **20/1**

3206 **3** 2 **Princess Galadriel**[36] 3421 3-9-1 **59**.............................................. NPollard 4 52
(JRBest) *dwlt: racd in last pair: pushed along 1/2-way: u.p whn nt clr run over 1f out: styd on fnl f to take 3rd nr fin* **4/1**[3]

0320 **4** nk **Yashin (IRE)**[10] 4199 3-9-2 **60**.............................................. LDettori 5 52
(MHTompkins) *taken steadily to post: pressed ldr to 3f out: sn rdn: wnt 2nd again over 1f out to ins fnl f: fdd* **11/4**[1]

-000 **5** 1 **Beauty Of Dreams**[15] 4020 3-9-7 **65**.............................................. TEDurcan 8 54
(MRChannon) *wl in tch: outpcd and rdn over 2f out: one pce after* **20/1**

3400 **6** shd **Bertocelli**[13] 4092 3-9-5 **63**.............................................. AMcCarthy 1 52
(GGMargarson) *racd on outer: in rr: rdn and struggling over 2f out: no prog* **8/1**

5600 **7** nk **Dont Call Me Derek**[5] 4327 3-9-4 **62**.............................................. VHalliday 2 50
(SCWilliams) *s.s: sn in tch: rdn 3f out: nt qckn and btn 2f out : one pce after* **11/2**

4600 **8** 1 1/4 **La Puce**[5] 4340 3-9-4 **62**.............................................. MFenton 6 47
(MissGayKelleway) *racd freely: led to 3f out: jinked over 2f out: chsd wnr to over 1f out: wknd* **16/1**

1m 27.42s (-0.38) **Going Correction** -0.075s/f (Good) **8** Ran SP% **113.6**
Speed ratings: **99,93,91,90,89 89,89,87**CSF £57.60 CT £242.11 TOTE £3.80: £1.10, £4.90, £1.80; EX 42.20.
**Owner** Clive Roberts **Bred** Mrs Ellen Maye **Trained** Hook Norton, Oxon

**FOCUS**
A most uncompetitive handicap.

**NOTEBOOK**
**Iphigenia(IRE)** got off the mark in emphatic style, but it does not say much for the opposition that she was able to win like this. This will have provided a nice confidence boost, but unless she is turned out under a penalty, a follow up will depend on how the Handicapper rates this performance.
**Trifti** did not appear to stay a mile at Lingfield on his previous start, but he just lacked the necessary pace on this drop in trip.
**Princess Galadriel** is from a stable in good form and ran a little better than the bare facts indicate.
**Yashin(IRE)** looked to have conditions to suit but was below form for the second race running.
**Beauty Of Dreams** continues out of form.
**Dont Call Me Derek** was trying this trip for the first time, but showed little.

## 4484 SEAHOLME MARQUEES MEDIAN AUCTION MAIDEN STKS 5f
**7:40** (7:40) (E) 3-4-Y-O **£3,347** (£1,030; £515; £257) **Stalls** Low

Form RPR
03 **1** **Dance To The Blues (IRE)**[64] 2586 3-8-9.............................................. PDobbs 2 64
(BDeHaan) *cl up: led on inner wl over 1f out: pushed clr fnl f: readily* **9/4**[1]

0356 **2** 1 3/4 **Lakeside Guy (IRE)**[15] 4021 3-9-0 56.............................................. LDettori 3 63
(PSMcentee) *led: rdn and hdd wl over 1f out: one pce fnl f* **3/1**[2]

00-0 **3** 3 **Saccharine**[41] 3271 3-8-2.............................................. KGhunowa(7) 5 47
(MJPolglase) *pushed along in rr after 2f: wl outpcd and rdn 2f out: kpt on ins fnl f* **50/1**

0006 **4** 1 **Black Sabbeth**[12] 4144 3-9-0 69.............................................. DSweeney 6 48
(PJMakin) *in tch: outpcd and rdn 1/2-way: struggling after* **7/2**[3]

3200 **5** 1 1/2 **Vittorioso (IRE)**[15] 4021 3-9-0 51.............................................. (b) MFenton 4 43
(MissGayKelleway) *prom to 1/2-way: sn outpcd u.p* **11/1**

0400 **6** hd **Lady Justice**[15] 4025 4-8-12 50.............................................. LisaJones 7 37
(WJarvis) *racd alone on far side: nvr on terms* **3/1**[2]

59.79 secs (-0.91) **Going Correction** -0.075s/f (Good)
**WFA** 3 from 4yo 3lb **6** Ran SP% **113.3**
Speed ratings: **104,101,96,94,92 92**CSF £9.50 TOTE £3.00: £1.70, £2.00; EX 8.50.
**Owner** Mrs D Vaughan **Bred** R P Killoran **Trained** Lambourn, Berks

**FOCUS**
A weak maiden, although the winner is progressing.

**NOTEBOOK**
**Dance To The Blues(IRE)** is improving with racing and gained a clear-cut success. With a 56-rated performer in second, she should not be too harshly treated and can be competitive in handicaps.
**Lakeside Guy(IRE)** looked to run his race and can have no real excuses. Low grade handicaps may suit better.
**Saccharine**, last in a claimer over a mile on her previous start, ran better dropped in trip but may just prove better at around six furlongs.
**Black Sabbeth** got his rating of 69 off the back of what appeared a promising run at Salisbury on his previous start, but this effort would suggest that run flatters him.
**Lady Justice**, for some reason raced alone over the far side. She can be given another chance.

## 4485 WINE FOR HOME H'CAP 1m 1f 149y
**8:10** (8:10) (F) (0-55,55) 3-Y-O+ **£3,122** (£892; £446) **Stalls** Low

Form RPR
3600 **1** **Royal Racer (FR)**[20] 3911 6-9-7 **48**.............................................. (b[1]) NPollard 14 56
(JRBest) *led to over 5f out: trckd ldr tl led again 2f out: drvn 2l clr ins fnl f: jst hld on* **9/1**

000/ **2** nk **Serraval (FR)**[710] 2960 6-10-0 **55**.............................................. RHavlin 10 62
(GBBalding) *hld up wl in rr: last 3f out: gd prog 2f out: r.o wl fnl f: jst failed* **20/1**

0645 **3** 1 3/4 **Forest Tune (IRE)**[13] 4086 6-9-7 **48**.............................................. (b) LDettori 11 52
(BHanbury) *t.k.h: cl up: led over 5f out: rdn and hdd 2f out: nt qckn* **4/1**[1]

6 **4** nk **Prairie Law (GER)**[20] 3917 4-9-1 **42**.............................................. LisaJones 8 46
(IanWilliams) *racd in midfield: outpcd over 2f out: prog over 1f out: hung lft ins fnl f: styd on* **8/1**

0000 **5** 1/2 **Silistra**[23] 3828 5-8-6 **40**.............................................. (p) NataliaGemelova(7) 13 43
(MrsLCJewell) *wl in tch: rdn to chse ldng pair 2f out: sn one pce and no imp* **66/1**

0436 **6** 1 1/4 **No Chance To Dance (IRE)**[20] 3911 4-9-6 **47**.............................................. (t) TEDurcan 9 47
(HJCollingridge) *hld up in rr: shkn up 3f out: kpt on fr over 1f out: n.d* **12/1**

0060 **7** 1/2 **Ursa Major**[20] 3917 10-9-4 **45**.............................................. KMcEvoy 5 44
(TKeddy) *hld up in midfield: rdn and outpcd 2f out: no imp ldrs after* **20/1**

0604 **8** 2 **Giust In Temp (IRE)**[14] 4042 5-8-13 **40**.............................................. MFenton 12 35
(PWHiatt) *chsd ldr to 6f out: styd prom tl wknd 2f out* **25/1**

0100 **9** hd **Burnt Copper (IRE)**[13] 4080 4-9-6 **52**.............................................. (v[1]) MSavage(5) 15 47
(JRBest) *s.v.s: rchd midfield after 4f: rdn and struggling 3f out* **6/1**[3]

0042 **10** 1/2 **Tintawn Gold (IRE)**[34] 3490 4-9-7 **48**.............................................. DSweeney 2 42
(SWoodman) *cl up: trckd ldng pair over 3f out to 2f out: sn wknd* **4/1**[1]

6045 **11** 1 **My Maite (IRE)**[8] 4238 5-9-5 **46**.............................................. (tp) NDay 3 38
(RIngram) *hld up in rr: rdn and no prog over 2f out: n.d after* **5/1**[2]

0055 **12** 7 **Kyle Of Lochalsh**[14] 4065 4-9-5 **46**.............................................. AMcCarthy 7 25
(GGMargarson) *hld up in midfield: rdn and wknd 3f out* **20/1**

0000 **13** 13 **Night Driver (IRE)**[36] 3423 5-9-4 **45**.............................................. (p) PDobbs 1 —
(GLMoore) *racd wd: in tch: wknd over 3f out: t.o* **25/1**

2m 4.42s (-0.74) **Going Correction** -0.075s/f (Good)
**WFA** 3 from 4yo+ 9lb **13** Ran SP% **123.2**
Speed ratings: **99,98,97,97,96 95,95,93,93,93 92,86,76**CSF £184.32 CT £846.04 TOTE £11.60: £3.60, £9.20, £1.90; EX 484.80 Place 6 £25.40, Place 5 £20.84.
**Owner** Mr & Mrs R Dawbarn **Bred** Mme Renee Geffroy **Trained** Hucking, Kent

**FOCUS**
A moderate handicap. The winner was back to his earlier course and distance form.

**NOTEBOOK**
**Royal Racer(FR)**, with blinkers replacing a visor, was just 1lb higher than when successful over this course and distance earlier in the season. He was relatively unproven on fast ground, but handled it well under the usual positive ride and ran out a narrow winner. This is very much his level.
**Serraval(FR)** was last seen running over hurdles 710 days previously but, 12lb lower than when last winning on the Flat, she made a most encouraging return to action. Good performances off the back of breaks are not always repeated on the following run, so although this effort suggests she has a similar race in her, it may not be next time.
**Forest Tune(IRE)**, with the blinkers back on, ran another solid race in defeat and can win a similar event in this sort of form.
**Prairie Law(GER)** confirmed the promise he showed on his British debut at Newmarket and looks to be going the right way for his new trainer.
**Silistra**, a long-standing maiden, posted one of his better recent efforts.
**Burnt Copper(IRE)** was slowly away in the first-time visor and could never get into it.
**Tintawn Gold(IRE)**, a beaten favourite on her previous start, had been off for the track for over a month since and was not at her best.
**My Maite(IRE)** had been running respectably, but this was disappointing.
T/Plt: £18.20. Pool of £28,581.30 - 1,143.80 winning units. T/Qpdt: £11.80. Pool of £2,286.60 - 143.20 winning units. JN

# 3924 HAYDOCK (L-H)
Thursday, August 5

**OFFICIAL GOING: Good (good to soft in places)**
Wind: almost nil Weather: humid

## 4486 GATEHOUSE H'CAP 1m 3f 200y
**2:10** (2:11) (D) (0-80,80) 3-Y-O+ **£5,746** (£1,768; £884; £442) **Stalls** High

Form RPR
5144 **1** **Dallool**[61] 2683 3-9-9 **80**.............................................. PRobinson 2 92+
(MAJarvis) *sn led: pushed along over 2f out: rdn over 1f out: kpt on wl fnl f* **3/1**[1]

4056 **2** 1/2 **Maxilla (IRE)**[28] 3670 4-9-6 **69**.............................................. NMackay(3) 7 80
(LMCumani) *held up and bhd: gd hdwy 3f out: rdn over 1f out:d riven and styd on wl fnl f* **10/1**

2311 **3** 2 1/2 **Dickie Deadeye**[21] 3866 7-9-4 **69**.............................................. RThomas(5) 1 76
(GBBalding) *trckd ldrs: hdwy to chse wnr over 2f out: rdn and no imp ent last* **7/2**[2]

3302 **4** 3 **Dr Cerullo**[31] 3584 3-9-3 **74**.............................................. EAhern 12 76
(CTinkler) *chsd ldrs: rdn along and outpcd 1/2-way: styd on fnl 2f* **14/1**

4213 **5** hd **Smart John**[25] 3782 4-9-5 **70**.............................................. BSwarbrick(5) 4 72
(WMBrisbourne) *in tch: effrt on outer over 3f out: rdn along over 2f out and sn btn* **5/1**[3]

04-0 **6** 2 1/2 **Smoothie (IRE)**[10] 4196 6-9-3 **63**.............................................. SDrowne 11 61
(IanWilliams) *bhd tl sme late hdwy* **50/1**

-430 **7** 1 **Irish Blade (IRE)**[39] 3345 3-9-4 **75**.............................................. DaneO'Neill 9 71
(HCandy) *chsd ldrs: rdn along over 3f out: wknd fnl 2f* **12/1**

1210 **8** 6 **Merrymaker**[12] 4155 4-9-7 **67**.............................................. SWKelly 6 54
(WMBrisbourne) *s.i.s: hdwy to join ldrs after 4f: rdn along 4f out and sn wknd* **11/1**

4045 **9** 5 **Transcendantale (FR)**[24] 3807 6-7-5 **44** oh2.............................................. DFentiman(7) 5 23
(MrsSLamyman) *in tch: rdn along 4f out: sn wknd* **33/1**

4530 **10** 1 **Templet (USA)**[16] 4005 4-9-4 **64**.............................................. RWinston 3 41
(ISemple) *hld up: hdwy to chse ldrs 1/2-way: rdn along over 3f out: wknd over 2f out* **25/1**

24-4 **11** 3 **Young Rooney**[8] 4240 4-9-9 **69**.............................................. WSupple 10 41
(MMullineaux) *prom:rdn along over 4f out and sn wknd* **25/1**

5-35 **P** **Trullitti (IRE)**[33] 3535 3-9-2 **73**.............................................. KDarley 8 —
(JLDunlop) *chsd ldrs: pushed along and lost pl bef 1/2-way: bhd whn p.u lame and dismntd over 3f out* **16/1**

2m 31.63s (-3.53) **Going Correction** -0.20s/f (Firm)
**WFA** 3 from 4yo+ 11lb **12** Ran SP% **114.1**
Speed ratings: **103,102,101,99,98 97,96,92,89,88 86,—**CSF £30.90 CT £108.42 TOTE £4.00: £2.10, £3.20, £1.70; EX 32.90.

**Owner** Sheikh Ahmed Al Maktoum **Bred** Plantation Stud **Trained** Newmarket, Suffolk

**FOCUS**

A decent handicap, run at an even pace and won by a progressive sort. Solid and reliable form.

**NOTEBOOK**

**Dallool**, one of the more progressive sorts in the field and dropping back in grade, soon found himself in front and had the right man on board to set the right pace. He only had to get serious entering the final furlong, but never looked like being caught and the best of him is probably still to be seen.

**Maxilla(IRE)** stayed on all the way to the line without ever looking like getting to the winner, but certainly saw this trip out much better than she did earlier in her career and looks well worth another try.

**Dickie Deadeye** appeared to be going every bit as well as the winner racing down the home straight, but did not find as much off the bridle as had looked likely. This was still a fair effort off a 12lb higher mark.

**Dr Cerullo**, raised 2lb despite getting beaten last time, lacked the pace to get on terms but was not disgraced and could be very interesting when he can get his toe in.

**Smart John** has a very good record here and ran his race, but looks held off this sort of mark.

**Young Rooney** *Official explanation: jockey said gelding ran too free early on*

**Trullitti(IRE)** reportedly lost her action and was pulled up soon after turning for home. *Official explanation: jockey said filly lost her action behind*

## 4487 HAYDOCK PARK ANNUAL BADGEHOLDERS CLUB MAIDEN AUCTION STKS (DIV I) 6f

**2:40** (2:41) (E ) 2-Y-O **£3,601** (£1,108; £554; £277) **Stalls** Centre

Form RPR

2 **1** **Throw The Dice**[19] 3925 2-8-9 NCallan 2 80+
(KARyan) *trckd ldrs: smooth hdwy to ld wl over 1f out: edgd rt and rdn clr ins last* **11/4**[1]

042 **2** *1 1/4* **Persian Carpet**[20] 3918 2-8-2 70 FNorton 7 63
(IAWood) *cl up: effrt 2f out and ev ch tl rdn and kpt on same pce ent last* **7/1**

40 **3** *shd* **Phlaunt**[34] 3491 2-8-2 MartinDwyer 14 63
(RFJohnsonHoughton) *chsd ldrs: rdn along 2f out: styd on wl u.p fnl f* **14/1**

5 **4** *1* **Middle Eastern**[40] 3313 2-8-7 DeanMcKeown 10 65
(PABlockley) *chsd ldrs: effrt 2f out and ev ch tl rdn and one pce appr last* **25/1**

4 **5** *nk* **Turks Wood (IRE)**[72] 2376 2-8-7 PRobinson 9 64
(MHTompkins) *trckd ldrs: effrt 2f out and ch tl rdn and one pce appr last* **3/1**[2]

**6** *nk* **Chicken Soup** 2-8-11 SWKelly 1 67
(JAOsborne) *in tch: hdwy over 2f out: sn rdn and kpt on same pce appr last* **5/1**[3]

3440 **7** *2 1/2* **English Fellow**[21] 3886 2-8-7 76 GGibbons 6 55
(BAMcmahon) *led: rdn and hdd wl over 1f out: sn wknd* **10/1**

0 **8** *1/2* **Admittance (USA)**[14] 4048 2-8-4 LGoncalves 5 51
(MrsJRRamsden) *bhd tl sme late hdwy* **50/1**

**9** *shd* **Crimson Bow (GER)** 2-8-4 WSupple 12 51
(JGGiven) *a towards rr* **40/1**

0 **10** *nk* **Sonntag Blue (IRE)**[10] 4193 2-8-11 EAhern 4 57
(JAOsborne) *hld up: a rr* **50/1**

**11** *1* **Grandos (IRE)** 2-8-11 RWinston 11 54
(TDEasterby) *towards rr: hdwy on outer 1/2-way: sn rdn along and wknd 2f out* **12/1**

**12** *4* **Bella Plunkett (IRE)** 2-7-11 BSwarbrick[(5)] 3 33
(WMBrisbourne) *s.i.s and a rr* **80/1**

0 **13** *5* **Harry's Simmie (IRE)**[36] 3406 2-8-2 DaleGibson 13 18
(RHollinshead) *dwlt: hdwy on outer and in tch 1/2-way: sn rdn and wknd* **100/1**

**14** *1 1/4* **Phantom Song (IRE)** 2-8-2 DTudhope[(7)] 8 21
(DCarroll) *midfield: swtchd lft and hdwy 1/2-way: sn rdn along and wknd* **100/1**

1m 15.47s (0.58) **Going Correction** -0.05s/f (Good) **14** Ran SP% **117.7**

Speed ratings: **94,92,92,90,90 90,86,86,85,85 84,78,72,70**CSF £21.20 TOTE £3.40: £1.90, £1.90, £2.60; EX 24.60.

**Owner** Pendle Inn Partnership **Bred** N E Poole And Paul Trickey **Trained** Hambleton, N Yorks

**FOCUS**

The stall were in the centre and the field raced down the middle of the track. The winning time was 0.88 seconds slower than the second division, but was still acceptable for the grade. Throw The Dice has been judged value for another couple of lengths and could rate higher still.

**NOTEBOOK**

**Throw The Dice** confirmed the promise of his debut effort on softer ground here and showed a useful turn of foot to quicken away in the closing stages. There should be more to come.

**Persian Carpet**, with experience on her side, was always up with the pace. Her rider appeared to look down a couple of times passing the two-furlong pole, but she never stopped trying and was just beaten by a more progressive rival. She may be better off in nurseries now.

**Phlaunt**, appreciated the step back up in trip and looks as though she would get another furlong. She now qualifies for nurseries.

**Middle Eastern** improved from his debut effort on this better ground. He was the subject of some support at long odds and could be interesting when the money is really down.

**Turks Wood(IRE)**, off since his debut in May, ran with credit over this extra furlong and there should be a maiden in him. *Official explanation: jockey said colt ran green*

**Chicken Soup** ◆, a 32,000gns half-brother to a couple of winners including Radiant Bride, seems to held in some regard by his trainer and emerged best of the newcomers. He looks sure to improve and, as his half-sister won over two miles, a longer trip is also likely to suit him.

**English Fellow** had the edge in experience on his rivals but, after being given a positive ride, faded rather tamely. He is not progressing and his handicap mark does not look particularly lenient either.

## 4488 HAYDOCK PARK ANNUAL BADGEHOLDERS CLUB MAIDEN AUCTION STKS (DIV II) 6f

**3:10** (3:13) (E ) 2-Y-O **£3,588** (£1,104; £552; £276) **Stalls** Centre

Form RPR

0 **1** **Look At The Stars (IRE)**[24] 3808 2-8-9 KDarley 4 84
(CGCox) *trckd ldrs: pushed along 1/2-way: led over 1f out: drvn out* **16/1**

246 **2** *1* **Molly Marie (IRE)**[19] 3950 2-8-6 78 DAllan 10 78
(TDEasterby) *in tch: pushed along 1/2-way: hdwy over 1f out: r.o ins fnl f* **11/2**[3]

4 **3** *1* **Diamonds And Dust**[19] 3946 2-8-7 PRobinson 9 76
(MHTompkins) *trckd ldrs: nt clr run over 1f out: swtchd lft ent fnl f: kpt on* **2/1**[1]

0322 **4** *1* **Bee Stinger**[12] 4131 2-8-7 76 FNorton 5 73
(IAWood) *w ldr: rdn and ev ch over 1f out: styd on same pce* **4/1**[2]

0 **5** *1/2* **Flying Ridge (IRE)**[57] 2786 2-8-4 MartinDwyer 7 69
(AMBalding) *led: rdn and hdd over 1f out: flashed tail u.p: no ex ins fnl f* **25/1**

**6** *1/2* **Secret Cavern (USA)** 2-8-9 EAhern 3 78+
(JAOsborne) *midfield: pushed along 1/2-way: swtchd lft and hdwy ins fnl f: eased towards fin* **16/1**

2303 **7** *1/2* **Mytton's Bell (IRE)**[4] 4358 2-8-2 70 JFanning 12 64
(ABailey) *racd keenly: chsd ldrs: rdn over 1f out: no ex ins fnl f* **13/2**

0 **8** *3 1/2* **Issy Blue**[14] 4053 2-8-5 ow1 SWKelly 2 56
(JAOsborne) *sn pushed along in midfield: nt pce to chal* **25/1**

**9** *2* **Turn On The Style** 2-8-7 WSupple 11 52
(RPElliott) *towards rr: rdn 1/2-way: nvr trbld ldrs* **20/1**

03 **10** *shd* **Choreographic (IRE)**[15] 4009 2-8-8 THamilton[(3)] 1 56
(RAFahey) *a towards rr* **14/1**

**11** *6* **Globe Trekker (USA)** 2-8-4 RFfrench 6 31
(JamesMoffatt) *dwlt: sn outpcd* **66/1**

**12** *2 1/2* **Ms Three** 2-7-11 BSwarbrick[(5)] 8 21
(RFord) *a outpcd* **100/1**

**13** *7* **Mister Minty (IRE)** 2-8-7 DTudhope[(7)] 13 12
(DCarroll) *hld up: struggling fr 1/2-way* **33/1**

1m 14.59s (-0.30) **Going Correction** -0.05s/f (Good) **13** Ran SP% **118.4**

Speed ratings: **100,98,97,96,95 94,94,89,86,86 78,75,65**CSF £94.55 TOTE £14.90: £2.50, £2.10, £1.50; EX 140.50.

**Owner** S Barrow, A Parsons, P Stevenson **Bred** Broguestown Stud **Trained** Lambourn, Berks

**FOCUS**

Decent maiden form. The time was comfortably the fastest of the three races run over the trip on the day and good for the grade.

**NOTEBOOK**

**Look At The Stars(IRE)** ◆, who showed distinct signs of ability on his Windsor debut last month, confirmed it with a very game victory considering he was being nudged along some way out. The winning time suggests this was quite a decent maiden and he looks sure to go on improving.

**Molly Marie(IRE)** ran her best race since her debut, but came up against a more progressive rival. She should be competitive in nursery company off her current mark if maintaining this level of form.

**Diamonds And Dust**, promising on his debut, was forced to change directions a few times but it would be hard to say it cost him his chance. He still looks capable of winning an ordinary maiden.

**Bee Stinger**, back to six, ran his usual consistent race under a positive ride and looks an accurate yardstick for the form.

**Flying Ridge(IRE)** was much sharper than on her debut and made much of the running, but she showed her disgust at being hit with the whip and may not be totally straightforward.

**Secret Cavern(USA)** ◆, who fetched 22,000gns as a two-year-old, was noted staying on in taking style without being given at all a hard race and did easily best of the newcomers. He is very much one to keep an eye on and, as he is related to several winners in the US, could be interesting on sand at some point.

**Mytton's Bell(IRE)** showed up for a while before fading and may need genuinely fast ground. She would also probably be better off back in nurseries.

## 4489 JOAN AND RICHIE THOMAS GOLDEN WEDDING ANNIVERSARY H'CAP 6f

**3:40** (3:41) (E ) (0-70,67) 3-Y-O **£3,913** (£1,204; £602; £301) **Stalls** Centre

Form RPR

00-0 **1** **Morgan Lewis (IRE)**[14] 4059 3-8-12 63 RThomas[(5)] 17 77+
(GBBalding) *towards rr stands side: pushed along and hdwy over 2f out: rdn over 1f out: hung lft ent last: styd on to ld nr fin* **2/1**[1]

6060 **2** *1/2* **After The Show**[54] 2889 3-9-6 66 MartinDwyer 13 71
(JRJenkins) *cl up: led over 2f out: rdn clr over 1f out: drvn ins last: hdd and no ex nr fin* **20/1**

6064 **3** *shd* **Trojan Flight**[6] 4309 3-9-0 60 RWinston 1 65
(MrsJRRamsden) *towards rr far side: hdwy 2f out: rdn and styd on to chal ins last: ev ch tl drvn and no ex nr fin* **14/1**

-066 **4** *1 3/4* **Calculaite**[21] 3877 3-8-1 47 JFanning 7 46
(MrsGSRees) *cl up: led after 2f tl rdn and hdd over 2f out: drvn and kpt on same pce appr last* **25/1**

4410 **5** *nk* **Thornaby Green**[6] 4305 3-8-13 64 PMakin[(5)] 16 63
(TDBarron) *midfield: hdwy 2f out and sn rdn: drvn ent last and kpt on same pce* **11/1**[3]

2261 **6** *1 1/4* **Flash Ram**[20] 3896 3-9-7 67 (b) EAhern 20 62
(TDEasterby) *in tch: hdwy to chse ldrs over 2f out: sn rdn and no imp* **12/1**

6400 **7** *nk* **Arfinnit (IRE)**[14] 4052 3-8-12 58 (v) ACulhane 14 52
(MRChannon) *chsd ldrs towards stands side: rdn 2f out: drvn and one pce appr last* **12/1**

5021 **8** *1* **Musiotal**[24] 3798 3-8-6 55 NMackay[(3)] 11 46
(JSGoldie) *midfield: hdwy 2f out: sn rdn and no imp fnl f* **12/1**

5040 **9** *nk* **Dante's Devine (IRE)**[55] 2854 3-8-1 47 DaleGibson 19 37
(ABailey) *swtchd to r alone nr stands rail: midfield tl styd on fnl 2f: n.d* **66/1**

6003 **10** *3/4* **Turkish Delight**[21] 3877 3-8-13 59 JEdmunds 12 47
(JBalding) *towards rr: hdwy 2f out: sn rdn and no imp* **14/1**

664 **11** *1 1/2* **Intavac Boy**[33] 3512 3-9-0 60 DeanMcKeown 3 43
(CWThornton) *dwlt and towards rr far side tl sme late hdwy* **25/1**

0005 **12** *1/2* **Smart Danny**[21] 3877 3-7-12 44 RFfrench 10 26
(JJQuinn) *slowly into stride and bhd: rdn along 1/2-way and sme late hdwy* **25/1**

0514 **13** *1 3/4* **Shamrock Tea**[31] 3585 3-8-10 59 THamilton[(3)] 9 36
(RAFahey) *s.i.s: sn in tch: rdn along 1/2-way and wknd 2f out* **6/1**[2]

00-0 **14** *3 1/2* **O'l Lucy Broon**[97] 1742 3-8-5 54 TEaves[(3)] 15 20
(JSGoldie) *nvr nr ldrs* **100/1**

2330 **15** *1/2* **Weakest Link**[150] 983 3-8-12 58 WSupple 5 23
(EJAlston) *a towards rr* **25/1**

0205 **16** *8* **La Fonteyne**[27] 3711 3-8-2 48 JMcAuley 2 —
(CBBBooth) *a rr* **50/1**

4400 **17** *3 1/2* **Orchestration (IRE)**[39] 3344 3-8-13 59 (b[1]) ANicholls 6 —
(JWUnett) *led 2f: rdn along 1/2-way: sn wknd* **33/1**

0000 **18** *7* **Disco Diva**[54] 2875 3-8-11 57 NCallan 4 —
(MBlanshard) *a rr* **33/1**

1m 15.26s (0.37) **Going Correction** -0.05s/f (Good) **18** Ran SP% **122.8**

Speed ratings: **95,94,94,91,91 89,89,88,87,86 84,84,81,77,76 65,61,51**CSF £49.36 CT £487.05 TOTE £2.90: £1.60, £5.80, £2.50, £9.50; EX 42.10.

**Owner** Mrs G Smith **Bred** Isaac Morgan **Trained** Kimpton,Hants

**FOCUS**

A modest winning time for the grade, 0.67 seconds slower than the second division of the juvenile maiden. The overall form looks modest, although the winner looks one to sollow in this sort of company.

**NOTEBOOK**

**Morgan Lewis(IRE)**, a real eye-catcher at Sandown, started a very short price but his supporters must have been very nervous, as for a long time he was being pushed along at the back of the field and apparently going nowhere. However, the penny eventually dropped and he dourly stayed on to lead near the line. He should not be raised much for this and has further improvement in him, as he is still not the finished article.

**After The Show** was always up with the pace and looked likely to win a furlong out until the winner came out of the clouds. He should find a race before too long, especially with more cut in the ground.
**Trojan Flight** is still a maiden and has not always looked straightforward, but arguably put in his best effort yet. He may need softer ground.
**Calculaite** ran his best race so far on his seventh start. Now that he has earned himself a basement handicap mark, it may be worth putting him back on Fibresand.
**Thornaby Green** did not run badly on this return to six, but could have done with the ground staying fast.
**Flash Ram** probably finds this trip on the sharp side, but looks high enough in the weights based on what he has actually achieved.
**Smart Danny** *Official explanation: jockey said gelding missed the break*
**Shamrock Tea** *Official explanation: vet said gelding was struck into and lost its action*
**Orchestration(IRE)** *Official explanation: jockey said gelding was eased in the last 110yds and had no more to give*
**Disco Diva** *Official explanation: jockey said filly hung left throughout*

## 4490 DIANE MURPHY 40TH BIRTHDAY H'CAP 1m 30y
**4:10** (4:12) (C) (0-90,88) 3-Y-O **£10,205** (£3,140; £1,570; £785) **Stalls** Low

Form RPR
0513 **1** **Mrs Moh (IRE)**[12] 4151 3-8-13 **80** DAllan 3 90
(TDEasterby) *trckd ldrs: rdn to ld over 1f out: kpt on wl* **12/1**
0612 **2** ¾ **Inchloss (IRE)**[12] 4140 3-8-12 **79** JFanning 2 87
(BAMcmahon) *midfield: rdn 2f out: swtchd rt over 1f out: edgd lft ins fnl f: r.o u.p* **9/1**
1-00 **3** 1 ¼ **Border Music**[111] 1437 3-8-10 **77** MartinDwyer 7 82
(AMBalding) *hld up: rdn and hdwy over 1f out: styd on ins fnl f* **16/1**
0006 **4** nk **Iskander**[19] 3926 3-8-6 **73** (b) JCarroll 13 77+
(KARyan) *hld up: hdwy over 2f out: nt clr run over 1f out: sn swtchd rt: styd on ins fnl f* **33/1**
6224 **5** nk **Kibryaa (USA)**[15] 4032 3-8-13 **80** (p) PRobinson 1 84
(MAJarvis) *prom: n.m.r over 1f out: rdn whn n.m.r and hmpd ins fnl f: sn lost pl: kpt on cl home* **11/4**[1]
-150 **6** ½ **Baffle**[34] 3478 3-8-7 **74** KDarley 9 76
(JLDunlop) *led: rdn over 2f out: hdd over 1f out: no ex ins fnl f* **33/1**
14- **7** 2 ½ **Familiar Affair**[282] 5822 3-9-1 **82** DMcGaffin 11 79
(BSmart) *racd keenly: prom: rdn over 2f out: 4th and hld whn n.m.r and hmpd ins fnl f: n.d after* **25/1**
6346 **8** 3 ½ **Weet A Head (IRE)**[58] 2751 3-8-10 **77** ACulhane 6 66
(RHollinshead) *behind: rdn 4f out: sme hdwy over 1f out: nvr able to chal* **16/1**
1 **9** 3 ½ **Balavista (USA)**[35] 3447 3-9-3 **84** SDrowne 5 65
(RCharlton) *midfield: rdn over 2f out: no imp: wknd fnl f* **7/2**[2]
1100 **10** 3 ½ **Ace Coming**[20] 3903 3-8-2 **69** (b) PFessey 12 42
(DEddy) *racd keenly: trckd ldrs tl rdn and wknd over 2f out* **50/1**
1020 **11** 2 **Key Partners (IRE)**[79] 2207 3-9-1 **82** DeanMcKeown 8 50
(PABlockley) *a bhd* **25/1**
0440 **12** 3 ½ **Golden Grace**[49] 2999 3-9-7 **88** WSupple 4 48
(EALDunlop) *trckd ldrs early: lost pl and rdn over 4f out: n.d after* **13/2**[3]

1m 43.22s (-2.33) **Going Correction** -0.20s/f (Firm) **12 Ran SP% 107.2**
Speed ratings: **103,102,101,100,100 99,97,93,90,86 84,81**CSF £88.09 CT £1289.64 TOTE £12.20: £2.60, £2.40, £3.30; EX 71.90 Trifecta £789.20 Pool of £2,556.73 - 2.30 winning units..
**Owner** Salifix **Bred** James Gleeson **Trained** Great Habton, N Yorks

**FOCUS**
A decent handicap run at a solid pace. A worthy winner, though a bit of trouble for a few in behind.

**NOTEBOOK**
**Mrs Moh(IRE)**, trying this trip for the first time, was always going well just behind the leaders and quickened up nicely when asked. She was a deserved winner, though a couple of her nearest pursuers did not get the run of the race.
**Inchloss(IRE)** could have done with even easier conditions than this, but was arguably unlucky not to go even closer as he had to switch positions on more than one occasion in order to get a run. On the other hand, he also contributed to his own problems by tending to hang under pressure.
**Border Music ◆**, off since April, would probably have preferred faster ground but stayed on well in the closing stages and looks capable of winning a similar race on turf.
**Iskander ◆**, switched off out the back, tried for an audacious run up the inside rail down the home straight but was stopped in his tracks over a furlong from home. Switched wide, he stayed on well but the damage had been done. He has dropped 20lb since the start of the season and is very much one to keep on the right side.
**Kibryaa(USA)** raced prominently, but never saw much daylight and got into all sorts of trouble in the last furlong or so. He can be considered a couple of lengths better than his finishing position.
**Baffle** set the pace for over six furlongs before dropping away. His stable remains quiet.
**Familiar Affair** stalked the leader for much of the way, but was already under pressure and going nowhere when getting a hefty bump a furlong from home.
**Balavista(USA)**, the form of whose debut victory here has taken several knocks in the meantime, looks to have been given a very harsh handicap mark judged on this effort.
**Golden Grace** *Official explanation: jockey said colt had no more to give*

## 4491 SWAN WITH TWO NECKS MAIDEN CLAIMING STKS 1m 30y
**4:40** (4:41) (F) 3-Y-O **£3,010** (£860; £430) **Stalls** Low

Form RPR
6326 **1** **One Upmanship**[12] 4127 3-8-10 64 NCallan 4 64
(JGPortman) *trckd ldrs: smooth hdwy 3f out: shkn up over 1f out: rdn ins last: styd on to ld last 50 yds* **11/2**[3]
0606 **2** nk **Cayman Calypso (IRE)**[13] 4092 3-8-10 62 PRobinson 3 63
(MAJarvis) *led: rdn along over 2f out: drvn ins last: hdd and no ex last 50 yds* **4/1**[1]
-064 **3** 3 **Treason Trial**[15] 4018 3-8-7 57 KDarley 2 53
(NTinkler) *hld up in tch: hdwy 3f out: sn rdn: kpt on same pce fnl 2f* **5/1**[2]
6-30 **4** nk **Soviet Sceptre (IRE)**[77] 2236 3-9-0 70 (t) ACulhane 6 60
(MissDMountain) *hld up: hdwy on outer over 2f out: rdn over 1f out: one pce fnl f* **7/1**
-504 **5** 2 ½ **Miss Procurer (IRE)**[8] 4241 3-8-5 64 (t) SDrowne 8 45
(PFICole) *dwlt and bhd tl styd on fnl 2f: n.d* **13/2**
005 **6** 2 ½ **Dee En Ay (IRE)**[6] 4306 3-8-12 DAllan 9 46
(TDEasterby) *in tch: effrt 3f out: sn rdn and no imp* **20/1**
-300 **7** 5 **Frangipani (IRE)**[10] 4196 3-8-9 65 JFanning 1 32
(PFICole) *chsd ldng pair: rdn along over 3f out: sn wknd* **12/1**
30-0 **8** 2 ½ **Veneziana**[10] 4196 3-8-7 63 EAhern 10 24
(PFICole) *in tch: effrt over 3f out: sn rdn and wknd* **12/1**
504- **9** 5 **Big Tom (IRE)**[92] 1892 3-8-7 62 DTudhope[(7)] 5 19
(DCarroll) *chsd ldr: rdn along over 3f out: sn wknd* **10/1**
30 **P** **Banana Grove (IRE)**[11] 4180 3-8-9 PPMathers[(5)] 7 19
(ABerry) *a rr: sddle slipped over 3f out and sn p.u* **20/1**

1m 44.17s (-1.38) **Going Correction** -0.20s/f (Firm) **10 Ran SP% 111.9**
Speed ratings: **98,97,94,94,91 89,84,81,76,76**CSF £26.54 TOTE £7.10: £1.70, £1.90, £1.60; EX 25.60.
**Owner** M J Vandenberghe **Bred** Red House Stud **Trained** Compton, Berks

**FOCUS**
An ordinary claimer, though the pace was solid and the front pair pulled clear. The form has been rated through the runner-up.

**NOTEBOOK**
**One Upmanship**, trying his longest trip to date, could be seen travelling best a long way from home, but in the end had to dig deep in order to get the better of the determined runner-up and record his first win at the 17th attempt.
**Cayman Calypso(IRE)**, unplaced in five previous starts and dropped into a claimer for the first time, made a bold bid to make all and fought back really well when headed. He should be able to win a similar event.
**Treason Trial** looks a very hard ride, as he was off the bridle at halfway and only consented late to run on and snatch third. He might find some improvement for a longer trip.
**Soviet Sceptre(IRE)**, making his debut for the yard and off since May, was back up to a mile after a couple of runs over six. He had every chance, but his best trip remains unknown and his best previous effort came on soft ground.
**Miss Procurer(IRE)** made up some ground from off the pace but did not look to be completely exerting herself.
**Banana Grove(IRE)** *Official explanation: jockey said saddle slipped*

## 4492 LCCC DEVELOPMENT ASSOCIATION 10TH ANNIVERSARY MAIDEN STKS 1m 2f 120y
**5:10** (5:11) (D) 3-Y-O+ **£5,746** (£1,768; £884; £442) **Stalls** High

Form RPR
42 **1** **Articulation**[13] 4087 3-9-0 WRyan 8 88
(HRACecil) *prom: led over 2f out: rdn and hdd narrowly over 1f out: rallied to gamely regain ld towards fin* **15/8**[1]
6 **2** hd **Countrywide Luck**[20] 3916 3-9-0 JFanning 11 88
(NPLittmoden) *in tch: hdwy 4f out: rdn to ld narrowly over 1f out: hdd towards fin* **9/2**[3]
244 **3** 6 **Chanteloup**[38] 3374 3-8-10 89 ow1 JPMurtagh 5 73
(JRFanshawe) *midfield: rdn 4f out: hdwy 3f out: rdn to chse ldrs over 1f out: one pce* **9/2**[3]
532 **4** 3 ½ **Mikao (IRE)**[30] 3603 3-9-0 80 PRobinson 1 72
(MHTompkins) *prom: led over 3f out: rdn and hdd over 2f out: wknd over 1f out* **7/2**[2]
00 **5** 3 **Baranook (IRE)**[20] 3922 3-9-0 EAhern 9 66
(PWHarris) *midfield: rdn 1/2-way: kpt on one pce fnl f: nvr able to chal* **66/1**
5 **6** 1 ¼ **Rollswood (USA)**[163] 871 4-9-10 KDarley 6 64
(PRHedger) *hld up: effrt 3f out: no imp* **40/1**
**7** 4 **Mith Hill** 3-9-0 WSupple 4 57
(EALDunlop) *rdn along early: in tch: n.m.r over 3f out: sn rdn: wknd over 2f out* **25/1**
**8** 3 ½ **Dream Alive** 3-9-0 (t) NCallan 10 52
(MBlanshard) *hld up: rdn over 3f out: nvr on terms* **100/1**
000 **9** 4 **Hoops And Blades**[20] 3916 3-9-0 TGMcLaughlin 13 45
(NPLittmoden) *dwlt: a bhd* **100/1**
0 **10** 1 **Cugina Nicola**[22] 3843 3-8-9 SDrowne 7 38
(GBBalding) *a bhd* **66/1**
6 **11** 12 **Ben's Revenge**[21] 3885 4-9-5 LTreadwell[(5)] 3 23
(MWellings) *t.k.h: in tch: rdn 4f out: wknd over 2f out* **100/1**
50 **12** 9 **Jordans Spark**[49] 3015 3-9-0 RWinston 2 7
(ISemple) *led: rdn and hdd over 3f out: wknd over 2f out* **66/1**

2m 14.7s (-3.03) **Going Correction** -0.20s/f (Firm)
**WFA** 3 from 4yo 10lb **12 Ran SP% 107.1**
Speed ratings: **103,102,98,95,93 92,89,87,84,83 75,68**CSF £8.58 TOTE £2.20: £1.10, £1.60, £1.90; EX 16.00.
**Owner** K Abdulla **Bred** Juddmonte Farms **Trained** Newmarket, Suffolk

**FOCUS**
There may have been 12 runners, but only four had a chance according to the market and so it proved. The winning time compared favourably to the closing handicap and they finished well strung out, but there was little promise from those outside the front quartet.

**NOTEBOOK**
**Articulation** is no world-beater, but he had the form to win this and fought back very bravely when headed. His future is now totally in the hands of the Handicapper.
**Countrywide Luck** improved for the step up in trip and looked like winning when taking over a furlong from home, but the favourite was in no mood to give in and worried him out of it. He is still learning and there was a decent gap back to the third, so he should be up to finding a similar event.
**Chanteloup** does not appear to be progressing and was well beaten by the front pair. She is likely to continue to be hard to place, especially as her current handicap mark looks stiff enough judged on her last two efforts.
**Mikao(IRE)** had every chance and is another who does not appear to be progressing.
**Baranook(IRE)** did best of the long shots and may do better in handicaps.
**Jordans Spark** *Official explanation: jockey said gelding ran green and had no more to give*

## 4493 ST HELENS H'CAP 1m 2f 120y
**5:45** (5:45) (E) (0-75,72) 3-Y-O+ **£3,705** (£1,140; £570; £285) **Stalls** High

Form RPR
1232 **1** **Melodian**[1] 4449 9-8-13 **62** (b) MLawson[(5)] 1 72
(MBrittain) *prom: rdn to ld over 3f out: hdd over 1f out: rallied to regain ld wl ins fnl f: r.o* **13/2**
2440 **2** 1 ¼ **Trouble Mountain (USA)**[50] 2982 7-9-10 **68** RWinston 7 76
(MWEasterby) *towards rr: rdn over 3f out: hdwy over 2f out: styd on ins fnl f* **10/1**
4132 **3** hd **Lennel**[2] 4416 6-9-5 **68** (b) PMakin[(5)] 14 76
(ABailey) *midfield: pushed along and hdwy over 3f out: styd on ins fnl f* **4/1**[2]
-330 **4** hd **Ma Yahab**[49] 3020 3-9-1 **72** NMackay[(3)] 8 79
(LMCumani) *midfield: hdwy 3f out: led over 1f out: hdd wl ins fnl f: hld towards fin* **8/1**
0040 **5** 1 ¾ **Band**[19] 3929 4-8-11 **55** DaneO'Neill 11 59
(BAMcmahon) *hld up: hdwy over 3f out: rdn and ev ch over 1f out: no ex ins fnl f* **12/1**
3124 **6** 1 ½ **Scurra**[26] 3740 5-8-8 **55** PMulrennan[(3)] 10 57
(ACWhillans) *trckd ldrs: rdn 4f out: kpt on same pce fr over 1f out* **14/1**
1060 **7** ¾ **Sinjaree**[20] 3917 6-7-5 **42** oh2 DFentiman[(7)] 2 43
(MrsSLamyman) *midfield: rdn over 2f out: kpt on fnl f: nvr able to chal* **40/1**
4504 **8** nk **Mambina (USA)**[12] 4138 3-8-8 **62** ACulhane 5 62
(MRChannon) *trckd ldrs: rdn and ev ch wl over 1f out: wknd ins fnl f* **20/1**
040- **9** 11 **Petrolero (ARG)**[234] 6193 5-8-0 **44** RFfrench 4 25
(JamesMoffatt) *racd keenly: midfield: rdn and wknd 3f out* **66/1**
066 **10** nk **Phone Tapping**[31] 3587 3-8-2 **55** ow1 PRobinson 6 37
(MHTompkins) *in tch: rdn over 3f out: sn wknd* **7/2**[1]
-452 **11** 7 **Santa Caterina (IRE)**[26] 3746 3-9-3 **71** KDarley 12 40
(JLDunlop) *led: rdn and hdd over 3f out: wknd over 2f out* **6/1**[3]

5605 **12** *10* **Fit To Fly (IRE)**[27] 3689 3-9-2 **70** ................ NCallan 9 22
(MrsJCandlish) *midfield: lost pl 1/2-way: n.d after* **33/1**

0405 **13** *11* **Belshazzar (USA)**[25] 3780 3-9-0 **68** ................ JEdmunds 3 1
(TPTate) *a bhd* **33/1**

510P **14** *18* **Our Little Rosie**[62] 2665 3-8-6 **60** ................ FNorton 13 —
(MBlanshard) *a bhd* **40/1**

2m 15.6s (-2.13) **Going Correction** -0.20s/f (Firm)
**WFA** 3 from 4yo+ 10lb **14** Ran SP% **121.4**
Speed ratings: **99,98,97,97,96 95,94,94,86,86 81,74,66,53**CSF £66.07 CT £299.03 TOTE £8.70: £3.10, £3.30, £2.40; EX 103.20 Place 6 £60.29, Place 5 £42.76.
**Owner** Mel Brittain **Bred** Northgate Lodge Stud Ltd **Trained** Warthill, N Yorks

**FOCUS**
An ordinary handicap and something of a war of attrition down the home straight, but solid enough form. A modest winning time for the grade, 0.9 seconds slower than the earlier maiden.

**NOTEBOOK**
**Melodian**, making a quick reappearance after finishing runner-up at Newcastle just 24 hours earlier, took over some way from home but showed real guts to hold off several challengers in the closing stages. This was a fine effort considering he would have preferred softer ground.
**Trouble Mountain(USA)**, was minus the blinkers this time. Held up as usual, he came with his customary late dash only to find one had gone beyond recall. He is a horribly difficult ride and connections must be pulling their hair out by now.
**Lennel**, racing for the third time in five days, made late progress down the outside but this effort does suggest he really needs 12 furlongs these days.
**Ma Yahab**, still a maiden, ran a good deal better than at Ripon. He looked likely to score when taking it up against the inside rail a furlong out, but did not get home. He has the ability to win a race, but does not look straightforward.
**Band** remains a maiden after 15 attempts, but put in one of his better recent efforts and has slipped 19lb since the start of the season.
**Phone Tapping**, making his handicap debut and stepping up in trip, was very well backed but dropped out disappointingly over the last couple of furlongs. He apparently blew very hard afterwards and is obviously thought capable of much better. *Official explanation: vet said gelding was blowing hard after race*
**Fit To Fly(IRE)** *Official explanation: trainer said gelding was unsuited by the ground*
T/Jkpt: £268,642.91 to a £1 stake. Pool: £567,555.44. 1.50 winning tickets. T/Plt: £110.70 to a £1 stake. Pool: £69,066.70. 455.10 winning tickets. T/Qpdt: £57.20 to a £1 stake. Pool: £2,276.30. 29.40 winning tickets. DO

# 4457 YARMOUTH (L-H)
Thursday, August 5

**OFFICIAL GOING: Good to firm (firm in places)**
Wind: Moderate behind Weather: Overcast and humid

## 4494 EUROPEAN BREEDERS FUND MAIDEN STKS — 6f 3y
2:30 (2:31) (D) 2-Y-0 — **£4,748** (£1,461; £730; £365) **Stalls** High

Form RPR

**1** **Ghurra (USA)** 2-8-9 ................ RHills 2 73
(EALDunlop) *chsd ldr tl led 2f out: hdd over 1f out: r.o to ld post* **12/1**

**2** *hd* **Munaddam (USA)** 2-9-0 ................ LDettori 3 78
(SaeedBinSuroor) *s.i.s: sn trcking ldrs: led over 1f out: rdn and hdd post* **4/9**[1]

00 **3** *hd* **Wise Dennis**[35] 3438 2-9-0 ................ EStack 5 77
(APJarvis) *chsd ldrs: outpcd 2f out: edgd lft and r.o ins fnl f* **50/1**

**4** *2* **Windermere Island** 2-8-9 ................ RMullen 6 66
(MLWBell) *hld up: outpcd over 2f out: r.o ins fnl f: nt rch ldrs* **20/1**

**5** *nk* **Santa Fe (IRE)** 2-9-0 ................ KFallon 7 70
(SirMichaelStoute) *dwlt: sn prom: rdn over 2f out: styd on same pce fnl f* **5/1**[2]

**6** *hd* **Love Thirty** 2-8-9 ................ CCatlin 1 65
(MRChannon) *sn outpcd: hdwy over 2f out: styd on same pce fnl f* **40/1**

**7** *1 3/4* **Royal Wedding** 2-9-0 ................ TPQueally 4 64
(DRLoder) *led 4f: wkng whn hmpd ins fnl f* **9/1**[3]

1m 13.91s (0.31) **Going Correction** -0.15s/f (Firm) **7** Ran SP% **112.8**
Speed ratings: **91,90,90,87,87 87,84**CSF £17.65 TOTE £16.00: £4.50, £1.10; EX 23.00.
**Owner** Hamdan Al Maktoum **Bred** Shadwell Farm Llc **Trained** Newmarket, Suffolk

**FOCUS**
A potentially useful field, but an impossible race to rate with confidence. The winning time was moderate for the class and the form should be treated cautiously to begin with.

**NOTEBOOK**
**Ghurra(USA)**, a half-sister to 1997 Middle Park winner Hayil, registered a very pleasing debut success. Always up with the pace, she stuck to her task really well in the late stages, winning gamely. She will no doubt relish another furlong and her entry in the Group one Cheveley Park confirms she is highly thought of. She will have learnt plenty and has a bright future.
**Munaddam(USA)**, a regally-bred son of unbeaten two-year-old Aljabr, was the subject of serious support. He did himself no favours with a sluggish start and saw little cover in the first half of the race, yet he still looked like winning inside the last furlong, until he could find no more when challenged. He was only just denied, and this will have taught him plenty, so expect him to be hard to beat next time, en-route to tackling a rise in class.
**Wise Dennis**, who had shown only modest ability in two previous outings, was motoring close home and may well have got up with another half furlong. This was a big improvement and he can score over farther in nurseries, but his proximity does raise a question about the form.
**Windermere Island** is a half-sister to high class Nevsion Lad, who won the July Stakes for the stable in 2003, and she made a promising debut. She was outpaced at half-way, mainly due to greeness, but was gradually getting the hang of things late on and can be expected to step up on this next time.
**Santa Fe(IRE)**, an imposing newcomer, ran distinctly green throughout, but shaped with promise nonetheless and can be expected to leave this form behind in due course. There is plenty of stamina on his dam's side and he will no doubt do well over a mile plus next year.
**Royal Wedding**, a 140,000gns purchase and a half-brother to ten-furlong Listed winner Lagudin, showed plenty of pace to lead, before dropping out disappointingly late on. He should do better over farther in time, but will have to show an enormous improvement if he is to justify his Group Two Champagne Stakes entry.

## 4495 BENNETTS ELECTRICAL TOSHIBA CLAIMING STKS — 6f 3y
3:00 (3:00) (F) 3-Y-0+ — **£2,877** (£822; £411) **Stalls** High

Form RPR

0-00 **1** **Fort McHenry (IRE)**[50] 2976 4-9-5 70 ................ (p) LDettori 5 68
(NACallaghan) *mde all: rdn out* **15/8**[2]

4300 **2** *nk* **Lake Verdi (IRE)**[5] 4336 5-8-9 52 ................ (t) RHills 6 57
(BHanbury) *chsd wnr: rdn over 1f out: r.o* **8/1**[3]

3230 **3** *1 1/4* **Wares Home (IRE)**[7] 4276 3-8-1 50 ow1 ................ SBushby(7) 4 56
(KRBurke) *trckd ldrs: rdn and hung lft ins fnl f: no ex towards fin* **16/1**

0620 **4** *5* **Blue Knight (IRE)**[71] 2399 5-9-4 73 ................ KFallon 3 47
(APJarvis) *sn pushed along in rr: hdwy u.p over 2f out: wknd fnl f* **6/5**[1]

0000 **5** *1* **Night Wolf (IRE)**[1] 4459 4-9-1 62 ................ CCatlin 1 41
(MRChannon) *sn outpcd: effrt over 2f out: wknd over 1f out* **14/1**

0400 **6** *5* **Pardon Moi**[33] 3530 3-8-1 47 ................ HayleyTurner(5) 2 21
(MrsCADunnett) *s.i.s: outpcd: hdwy u.p over 2f out: sn wknd* **20/1**

1m 12.46s (-1.14) **Going Correction** -0.15s/f (Firm)
**WFA** 3 from 4yo+ 4lb **6** Ran SP% **108.7**
Speed ratings: **101,100,98,92,90 84**CSF £15.58 TOTE £2.80: £1.50, £3.20; EX 12.40.Blue Knight (IRE) was claimed by Paul Howling for £15,000. Lake Verdi (IRE) was claimed by J. T. Billson for £6,000.
**Owner** M Tabor **Bred** Somerville Stud **Trained** Newmarket, Suffolk

**FOCUS**
An event full of disappointing types. The first two came clear, but the winner did not need to be at his best.

**NOTEBOOK**
**Fort McHenry(IRE)**, with the cheekpieces re-applied for the first time since winning in them in 2003, won a touch cosily on this drop into claiming company. He always looked to be holding the runner-up late on and this headgear obviously has the desired effect. He could do better back up in grade, now his confidence has been boosted.
**Lake Verdi(IRE)** turned in his best effort in a while and made the winner work late on. He had a very difficult task at these weights and, although far from consistent, looks worth a chance back in a handicap off this declining mark.
**Wares Home(IRE)**, who ran poorly in the cheekpieces last time, put that effort behind him with a solid effort at the weights. He is hard to win with, but deserves to be rewarded for his consistency at this level.
**Blue Knight(IRE)**, off for 71 days after finishing lame last time at Goodwood, again ran too badly to be true and this must rate a missed opportunity. He was beaten a long way out and looks to be regressing. *Official explanation: trainer said gelding was unsuited by the good to firm, firm in places surface*

## 4496 NSPCC FILLIES' H'CAP — 7f 3y
3:30 (3:32) (E) (0-75,72) 3-Y-0 — **£3,867** (£1,190; £595; £297) **Stalls** High

Form RPR

5600 **1** **Glebe Garden**[15] 4032 3-9-5 **70** ................ LDettori 10 76
(MLWBell) *racd stands' side: mde virtually all: rdn out* **4/1**[2]

5512 **2** *1* **Mugeba**[14] 4052 3-8-9 **60** ................ (t) IMongan 5 64+
(MissGayKelleway) *hld up in tch: racd centre fnl 5f: rdn and ev ch fr over 1f out: r.o* **3/1**[1]

4050 **3** *hd* **Zwadi (IRE)**[10] 4194 3-9-6 **71** ................ CCatlin 4 74
(HCandy) *racd centre fnl 5f: chsd ldr: rdn to ld that gp over 1f out : r.o* **8/1**

-000 **4** *1 3/4* **Flame Queen**[17] 3993 3-9-1 **66** ................ GHind 1 64
(MissKBBoutflower) *led centre gp over 5f: no ex ins fnl f* **14/1**

0655 **5** *1 1/4* **Beautiful Noise**[29] 3636 3-8-1 **52** ................ JMackay 11 47
(DMorris) *racd stands' side: chsd ldrs: rdn over 1f out: styd on same pce* **5/1**[3]

00-5 **6** *3/4* **Fabuloso**[78] 2231 3-7-7 **49** oh8 ................ DFox(5) 9 42
(VSmith) *racd stands' side: bhd: styd on ins fnl f: nvr nrr* **33/1**

05-0 **7** *3/4* **Annie Miller (IRE)**[33] 3530 3-9-0 **65** ................ KFallon 6 56
(MJWallace) *racd stands' side: chsd wnr: rdn over 2f out: sn hung lft: wknd fnl f* **5/1**[3]

0000 **8** *1/2* **Hold Up**[17] 3993 3-8-3 **57** ................ BReilly(3) 8 47
(MissJFeilden) *racd stands' side: chsd ldrs: rdn over 2f out: wknd over 1f out* **14/1**

0000 **9** *5* **Fragrant Star**[26] 3728 3-9-7 **72** ................ RHills 7 48
(CEBrittain) *racd stands' side: chsd ldrs 5f* **12/1**

-000 **10** *2 1/2* **Carla Moon**[10] 4201 3-8-9 **60** ................ RMullen 3 29
(CFWall) *racd centre fnl 5f: hld up: rdn over 2f out: wknd over 1f out* **50/1**

-000 **11** *9* **Shebaan**[45] 3158 3-7-7 **49** oh4 ................ HayleyTurner(5) 2 —
(PSMcentee) *prom centre tl hung lft and wknd fnl 3f* **50/1**

1m 25.25s (-1.25) **Going Correction** -0.15s/f (Firm) **11** Ran SP% **117.3**
Speed ratings: **101,99,99,97,96 95,94,93,88,85 75**CSF £16.19 CT £92.67 TOTE £4.10: £2.10, £1.10, £2.50; EX 17.00.
**Owner** Christopher Wright & W H Carson **Bred** Minster Enterprises Ltd **Trained** Newmarket, Suffolk

**FOCUS**
A modest fillies' handicap run at a sound gallop. The field split into two groups, but there was no obvious bias.

**NOTEBOOK**
**Glebe Garden** appreciated the drop to this trip and returned to form under a well-judged ride form Dettori. She was not disgraced early in the season in the face of some stiff tasks and had dropped in the ratings after some poor recent efforts. She has found her level again.
**Mugeba** ran her race and can have no excuses. She has been in fine form on the turf since winning a seller over course and distance in June, and should be able to win another race over the trip off this sort of mark.
**Zwadi(IRE)** ran her race, but failed to confirm her Lingfield form with the winner on these revised terms. She is struggling to find her optimum trip, but has found some form recently.
**Flame Queen** showed good early speed, but could only muster the one pace in the final furlong and was well held. She has not progressed since finishing runner-up in a fair maiden at Leicester in 2003, but this was her best effort since that effort. A drop back to six furlongs could see her get closer.
**Beautiful Noise** is always there or thereabouts, but again could not quicken when it mattered, and still shows no sign of capitalising on her declining mark.
**Annie Miller(IRE)** did not make the improvement one might have expected from her seasonal appearance in July and was slightly disappointing. However, she did not seem to stay this trip and could do with dropping back a furlong.

## 4497 GREAT YARMOUTH GLASS (S) H'CAP — 1m 3y
4:00 (4:02) (G) (0-55,55) 3-Y-0 — **£2,590** (£740; £370) **Stalls** High

Form RPR

0205 **1** **City General (IRE)**[15] 4018 3-8-12 **49** ................ (p) SChin 11 56
(JSMoore) *chsd ldrs: rdn to ld 1f out: edgd lft wl ins fnl f: r.o* **4/1**[2]

6301 **2** *1 1/2* **Kings Rock**[15] 4018 3-9-4 **55** ................ (b) KFallon 8 59
(KARyan) *chsd ldrs: rdn over 3f out: ev ch fr over 1f out: styng on same pce whn n.m.r towards fin* **5/4**[1]

1000 **3** *shd* **Pererin**[8] 4241 3-8-9 **46** ................ (b) TPQueally 1 49
(IAWood) *s.i.s: sn prom: rdn to ld over 1f out: sn hdd: edgd rt ins fnl f: styd on same pce* **17/2**[3]

3000 **4** *4* **Lenwade**[1] 4460 3-7-7 **35** ................ DFox(5) 4 29
(GGMargarson) *dwlt: bhd: rdn over 3f out: styd on ins fnl f: nvr nrr* **16/1**

0000 **5** *hd* **Diverted**[43] 3193 3-7-6 **36** ................ NicolPolli(7) 12 30
(MGQuinlan) *chsd ldrs: rdn over 2f out: hung lft over 1f out: styd on same pce* **40/1**

0000 **6** *1 1/2* **Tardis**[14] 4066 3-8-12 **49** ................ RMullen 5 39
(MLWBell) *chsd ldr tl led over 5f out: hung rt over 2f out: rdn and hdd over 1f out: wknd ins fnl f* **9/1**

6600 **7** *3 1/2* **Brother Cadfael**[27] 3707 3-7-8 **36** ................ HayleyTurner(5) 6 18
(JohnAHarris) *chsd ldrs over 5f* **25/1**

6650 **8** *6* **David's Girl**[36] 3425 3-8-1 **38** ................ JMackay 13 6
(DMorris) *sn pushed along in rr: wknd over 2f out* **9/1**

0010 **9** *1 1/4* **Stonor Lady (USA)**[122] 1267 3-8-9 **46** ................ CCatlin 9 11
(PWD'Arcy) *hld up: rdn 1/2-way: wknd over 2f out* **12/1**

0-00 **10** *14* **Variety Club**[27] 3697 3-9-1 **52**....................(b[1]) RHills 2 —
(AMBalding) *led: hdd over 5f out: wknd 1/2-way* **20/1**

1m 39.71s (0.01) **Going Correction** -0.15s/f (Firm) **10** Ran SP% **119.6**
Speed ratings: **93,91,91,87,87 85,82,76,74,60**CSF £9.39 CT £42.27 TOTE £5.90: £1.60, £1.10, £2.30; EX 12.20.The winner was bought for 3,600gns.
**Owner** A D Crook **Bred** Brendan Morrin **Trained** East Garston, Berks

**FOCUS**
A weak event, but a fair gallop and the first three came clear. The third is probably the best yardstick.

**NOTEBOOK**
**City General(IRE)** responded well to pressure when hitting the front over one out and ran on strongly to score. However, he is inconsistent in the main.
**Kings Rock** could only muster the one pace when holding every chance late on and failed to confirm recent form with the winner on these 6lb worse terms.
**Pererin**, down in class, was not helped by a sluggish start, but still recovered to hold every chance one out and ran his best race for some time. This proves he gets the trip and he can score in this grade, although not the easiest of rides.
**Lenwade** was staying on all too late, having lost ground at the start. She was not disgraced and will be suited by a step back up in trip.

## 4498 EVENTGUARD MAIDEN AUCTION STKS 1m 3y
4:30 (4:32) (E) 2-Y-O £3,406 (£1,048; £524; £262) Stalls High

Form RPR
2 **1** **Baradore (IRE)**[20] 3913 2-8-7 .................... TPQueally 4 87
(MGQuinlan) *mde all centre: rdn and edgd rt over 1f out: r.o* **5/2**[2]
0 **2** *1 1/2* **Silver Highlight (CAN)**[20] 3905 2-8-7 .................... RMullen 2 84
(AMBalding) *racd centre: hld up in tch: rdn over 1f out: styd on* **10/1**[3]
265 **3** *1 1/4* **Arabian Dancer**[30] 3599 2-8-2 **88**.................... CCatlin 9 76
(MRChannon) *racd stands' side: chsd ldrs: led that gp over 2f out: rdn over 1f out: no ex fnl f* **10/11**[1]
5060 **4** *12* **Zolash (IRE)**[7] 4263 2-8-8 .................... SChin 1 56
(JSMoore) *racd centre: chsd ldrs over 5f* **25/1**
0 **5** *3/4* **Champagne Rossini (IRE)**[24] 3805 2-8-7 .................... GHind 3 53
(MCChapman) *racd centre: s.i.s: chsd ldrs over 5f* **66/1**
000 **6** *2 1/2* **Mill By The Stream**[12] 4149 2-8-9 .................... EStack 6 49
(APJarvis) *racd stands' side: led that gp over 5f: sn wknd* **80/1**
**7** *3* **Hallowed Dream (IRE)** 2-8-5 ow1.................... RHills 7 39
(CEBrittain) *s.s: racd stands' side: n.d* **12/1**
0 **8** *1 3/4* **Spence Appeal (IRE)**[26] 3758 2-8-11 .................... KFallon 5 41
(KARyan) *racd stands' side: chsd ldr tl wknd over 2f out* **14/1**
**9** *3 1/2* **Caribbean Diamond (IRE)** 2-8-2 .................... PDoe 10 24
(IAWood) *racd stands' side: in rr: rdn 1/2-way: sn wknd* **66/1**
000 **10** *7* **Amanderica (IRE)**[33] 3506 2-7-11 ....................(t) DFox(5) 8 —
(MCChapman) *racd stands' side: sn outpcd* **100/1**

1m 38.62s (-1.08) **Going Correction** -0.15s/f (Firm) **10** Ran SP% **113.5**
Speed ratings: **99,97,96,84,83 81,78,76,72,65**CSF £25.69 TOTE £3.90: £1.20, £2.30, £1.10; EX 16.90.
**Owner** L Cashman **Bred** Rathbarry Stud **Trained** Newmarket, Suffolk

**FOCUS**
A decent winning time for the grade and the first three came well clear. The winner could be rated a fair bit higher.

**NOTEBOOK**
**Baradore(IRE)** confirmed the promise of her recent debut at Newmarket to run out a ready winner. She was there to be shot at approaching the final furlong, but found plenty in front. Highly regarded by her up and coming yard, she has plenty of scope and deserves a crack in decent company.
**Silver Highlight(CAN)**, who looked badly in need of her recent debut at Newbury, stayed on to emerge as the main danger to the eventual winner one out, but again ran green under pressure. She was readily held, but this was a much improved effort, nevertheless. She she will do much better in time over further, but should find a maiden this year.
**Arabian Dancer** came into this as the clear form choice on her previous efforts, but found very little off the bridle late on and was disappointing. This longer trip found her out, and she may be better back over shorter, but she has it all to prove now.
**Zolash(IRE)** ran his race, but did not find much under pressure over this longer trip. A switch to nurseries and a sharper test, could bring about improvement.
**Mill By The Stream** *Official explanation: jockey said colt hung left throughout*
**Spence Appeal(IRE)** *Official explanation: jockeys said colt lost its action*
**Caribbean Diamond(IRE)** *Official explanation: jockey said filly hung left*

## 4499 BBC RADIO NORFOLK MAIDEN H'CAP 1m 3f 101y
5:00 (5:01) (F) (0-55,54) 3-Y-O+ £3,038 (£868; £434) Stalls Low

Form RPR
0562 **1** **Science Academy (USA)**[14] 4055 3-10-0 **54**.................... KFallon 4 70+
(PFICole) *a.p: led over 1f out: edgd lft: rdn clr* **3/1**[2]
5002 **2** *3 1/2* **Tata Naka**[14] 4065 4-9-8 **43**.................... HayleyTurner(5) 8 49
(MrsCADunnett) *hld up: hdwy over 2f out: styd on: no ch w wnr* **12/1**
0060 **3** *nk* **Scott**[14] 4055 3-9-3 **50**.................... CHaddon(7) 6 56
(JJay) *hld up: plld hrd: hdwy over 2f out: rdn over 1f out: styd on* **50/1**
0-00 **4** *1* **Royal Starlet**[31] 3572 3-9-9 **49**.................... IMongan 14 53
(MrsAJPerrett) *w ldrs tl led over 2f out: rdn and hdd over 1f out: no ex* **20/1**
-004 **5** *3 1/2* **Habitual (IRE)**[17] 3984 3-9-10 **50**.................... JMackay 7 48
(SirMarkPrescott) *prom: rdn over 2f out: wknd over 1f out* **5/2**[1]
4364 **6** *nk* **Vanilla Moon**[14] 4070 4-10-0 **44**....................(v) SChin 1 42
(JRJenkins) *led over 1f: remained handy: rdn over 3f out: wknd over 1f out* **8/1**
0-43 **7** *2 1/2* **A Monk Swimming (IRE)**[14] 4055 3-8-9 **35**.................... GCarter 9 29
(JohnBerry) *hld up: hdwy over 3f out: wknd over 1f out* **9/2**[3]
6000 **8** *3/4* **Kalamansi (IRE)**[50] 2974 3-9-5 **50**.................... DFox(5) 12 43
(NACallaghan) *hld up: nvr nrr* **40/1**
0500 **9** *3/4* **Macchiato**[12] 4128 3-9-9 **49**.................... RHills 2 40
(RFJohnsonHoughton) *led 10f out: hdd over 2f out: wknd over 1f out* **50/1**
000- **10** *1 1/2* **Inspector Blue**[377] 3557 6-9-5 **35**.................... PDoe 3 24
(TKeddy) *hld up in tch: rdn and wknd over 2f out* **66/1**
000- **11** *3 1/2* **Its A Mystery (IRE)**[56] 5848 5-9-9 **39**....................(t) GHind 13 22
(RJSmith) *hld up: rdn over 3f out: n.d* **50/1**
60-0 **12** *1/2* **Allodarlin (IRE)**[17] 3990 3-9-10 **50**.................... RMullen 5 33
(PFICole) *chsd ldrs: rdn over 4f out: wknd over 2f out* **40/1**
-000 **13** *6* **Mad Maurice**[75] 2298 3-9-5 **45**....................(p) TPQueally 10 18
(BJCurley) *hld up: wknd over 3f out* **12/1**
6300 **14** *nk* **Vrisaki (IRE)**[5] 4346 3-9-6 **46**.................... OUrbina 11 19
(MissDMountain) *s.s: hld up: hdwy over 3f out: rdn and wknd over 2f out* **14/1**

2m 28.39s (0.99) **Going Correction** +0.125s/f (Good)
**WFA** 3 from 4yo+ 10lb **14** Ran SP% **121.9**
Speed ratings: **101,98,98,97,94 94,92,92,91,90 88,87,83,83**CSF £37.58 CT £1532.66 TOTE £2.90: £2.10, £3.10, £5.90; EX 32.00 Place 6 £18.60, Place 5 £14.19.
**Owner** Sir Martyn Arbib **Bred** M Arbib **Trained** Whatcombe, Oxon

**FOCUS**
A reasonable gallop, but a weak affair. The first two came clear and the winner has been rated value for more than the bare margin.

**NOTEBOOK**
**Science Academy(USA)**, just denied at Folkestone last time off a 3lb lower mark, gained deserved compensation in good style and lost her maiden tag at the eighth attempt. She was always travelling well in behind the pace and responded gamely when asked to win the race. This was a decent effort under her big weight and she is clearly going the right way, so would be of definite interest if turned out under a penalty.
**Tata Naka** turned in another improved effort and showed enough to suggest she can get off the mark in a small race over the trip, when given a slightly more positive ride.
**Scott**, beaten out of sight by the winner at Folkestone last time, got a lot closer this time. This was a personal best and he looks to be slowly getting the hang of things.
**Royal Starlet** showed her best form to date and only tired out of contention late on. A slight drop in trip can see her get closer.
**Habitual(IRE)** , who failed to stay two miles when a beaten favourite on his handicap debut last time, looked very one paced when push came to shove and was well beaten. He does not look one of his trainer's more progressive inmates at this stage.
**A Monk Swimming(IRE)** failed to run up to his recent form with the winner and was disappointing. He is a tricky ride. *Official explanation: trainer said gelding was unsuited by the good to firm, firm in places surface; trainer later said gelding was found to have pulled its gluteal muscles*
T/Plt: £22.90. Pool of £30,221.60 - 962.70 winning units. T/Qpdt: £4.20. Pool of £1,997.50 - 350.20 winning units. CR

4500 - 4506a (Foreign Racing) - See Raceform Interactive

# 4486 HAYDOCK (L-H)
Friday, August 6

**OFFICIAL GOING: Good**
The track had escaped the storms and the going had dried out and was described by the riders as 'just on the slow side of good'.
Wind: Almost nil. Weather: Fine and sunny.

## 4507 RECTANGLE GROUP E B F MAIDEN STKS 5f
6:10 (6:10) (D) 2-Y-O £4,901 (£1,508; £754; £377) Stalls Centre

Form RPR
32 **1** **Countdown**[6] 4334 2-9-0 .................... SSanders 5 80+
(SirMarkPrescott) *prom: led 2f out: r.o wl* **4/9**[1]
**2** *1 1/2* **One Great Idea (IRE)** 2-9-0 .................... NCallan 4 75+
(TDBarron) *in tch: rdn to chse wnr over 1f out: r.o* **4/1**[2]
0 **3** *4* **Kool Ovation**[13] 4149 2-8-11 .................... ABeech(3) 6 61
(ADickman) *led: rdn and hdd 2f out: wknd ins fnl f* **66/1**
0 **4** *1 3/4* **Lucy Parkes**[112] 1449 2-8-9 .................... MHenry 7 50
(EJAlston) *chsd ldrs: rdn and outpcd 1/2-way: styd on ins fnl f* **28/1**
0 **5** *nk* **Diktatit**[81] 2177 2-8-6 .................... SHitchcott(3) 11 49
(MRChannon) *hld up: pushed along 2f out: hdwy and hung lft over 1f out: kpt on: nt pce to chal* **11/1**[3]
0 **6** *shd* **Marlenes Girl (IRE)**[24] 3818 2-8-4 .................... PPMathers(5) 10 48
(ABerry) *hld up: rdn 1/2-way: hdwy over 1f out: nvr able to chal* **100/1**
6 **7** *1/2* **Hits Only Cash**[4] 4388 2-9-0 .................... DeanMcKeown 3 51
(PABlockley) *bmpd s: bhd: sme hdwy over 1f out: nvr trbld ldrs* **33/1**
000 **8** *shd* **Slate Grey**[21] 3893 2-9-0 .................... DarrenWilliams 9 51
(KRBurke) *dwlt: hld up: rdn 1/2-way: nvr trbld ldrs* **66/1**
000 **9** *2* **Princeable Lady (IRE)**[14] 4099 2-8-9 .................... DAllan 1 39
(TDEasterby) *towards rr: effrt 2f out: no imp: wknd 1f out* **22/1**
0 **10** *1 3/4* **Benny The Bus**[5] 4359 2-9-0 .................... ACulhane 8 38
(MrsGSRees) *prom tl rdn and wknd 2f out* **66/1**

62.02 secs (-0.05) **Going Correction** -0.05s/f (Good) **10** Ran SP% **113.8**
Speed ratings: **98,95,89,86,85 85,84,84,81,78**CSF £2.08 TOTE £1.50: £1.10, £1.40, £5.80; EX 3.20.
**Owner** Cheveley Park Stud **Bred** Lady Fairhaven **Trained** Newmarket, Suffolk

**FOCUS**
No strength in depth, but Countdown and well-backed newcomer One Great Idea came clear. Both can do better, but the rest look moderate.

**NOTEBOOK**
**Countdown** was kept right up to his work and was well on top at the finish. His form figures now live up to his name, three, two, one.
**One Great Idea(IRE)** ◆, a March foal, is quite a tall type. Well backed, he kept the winner up to his work and looks sure to go one better.
**Kool Ovation**, who hung left on his debut, showed bags of toe but in the end the first two ran right away from him.
**Lucy Parkes**, last of eight in a better race first time, put in some solid late work after getting outpaced and will benefit from a step up to six.
**Diktatit**, hopelessly green first time, has had three months to learn but she still looks very short of experience.
**Marlenes Girl(IRE)**, last of 15 on her debut, showed a fair bit more here.
**Hits Only Cash**, knocked out of his stride at the start, showed a bit more than on his debut despite a tendency to hang left. *Official explanation: jockey said colt suffered interference coming out of the stalls*
**Benny The Bus** *Official explanation: jockey said gelding hung left-handed*

## 4508 COUNTRYWIDE FREIGHT NURSERY 5f
6:40 (6:40) (E) 2-Y-O £3,614 (£1,112; £556; £278) Stalls Centre

Form RPR
5614 **1** **Baymist**[6] 4330 2-8-3 **63**.................... RFfrench 3 67
(MWEasterby) *hld up: rdn and hdwy over 1f out: led ins fnl f: r.o* **25/1**
0110 **2** *1* **Make Us Flush**[5] 4358 2-8-13 **73**.................... FNorton 11 73
(ABerry) *hld up: rdn and hdwy over 1f out: r.o ins fnl f* **11/1**
1063 **3** *shd* **Alsu (IRE)**[16] 4017 2-8-11 **71**.................... SSanders 4 71
(AMBalding) *midfield: hdwy 1/2-way: led over 1f out: hdd ins fnl f: kpt on* **8/1**[3]
2221 **4** *3/4* **Distinctly Game**[56] 2860 2-9-7 **81**.................... NCallan 7 78
(KARyan) *midfield: hdwy over 1f out: styd on ins fnl f* **13/8**[1]
5243 **5** *1 1/2* **Campeon (IRE)**[13] 4149 2-9-0 **74**.................... KDarley 1 66
(MJWallace) *led: rdn and hdd over 1f out: no ex ins fnl f* **10/1**
1605 **6** *1/2* **Handsome Lady**[41] 3290 2-9-3 **77**....................(v[1]) PHanagan 6 67
(ISemple) *prom: rdn over 1f out: fdd ins fnl f* **11/1**
3053 **7** *1* **Ryedane (IRE)**[15] 4046 2-8-5 **65**.................... DAllan 2 52
(TDEasterby) *towards rr: pushed along 1/2-way: styd on fr over 1f out: nt pce to chal* **7/1**[2]
2610 **8** *3* **Chilly Cracker**[22] 3886 2-8-11 **71**.................... DaleGibson 9 47
(RHollinshead) *prom: rdn 2f out: sn wknd* **66/1**
0100 **9** *1 1/4* **Flossytoo**[65] 2568 2-8-7 **74**.................... JDO'Reilly(7) 5 46
(JO'Reilly) *dwlt: sn chsd ldrs: rdn and wknd over 1f out* **33/1**
1406 **10** *1 3/4* **Apologies**[20] 3924 2-9-2 **76**.................... GGibbons 8 42
(BAMcmahon) *chsd ldrs for 2f: sn outpcd* **16/1**

062 **11** 1 **Saucepot**[13] 4124 2-8-5 **65** SCarson 10 27
(MDIUsher) *in tch: rdn 1/2-way: sn wknd* **16/1**

4122 **12** 1 3/4 **Straffan (IRE)**[16] 4017 2-8-0 **60** ANicholls 12 16
(DNicholls) *hld up: effrt 1/2-way: no imp* **11/1**

62.16 secs (0.09) **Going Correction** -0.05s/f (Good) **12** Ran SP% **115.8**
Speed ratings: **97,95,95,94,91 90,89,84,82,79 78,75**CSF £269.26 CT £2442.42 TOTE £39.40: £7.50, £2.00, £2.70; EX 324.30.
**Owner** Mrs M E Curtis **Bred** Bearstone Stud **Trained** Sheriff Hutton, N Yorks

**FOCUS**
Reliable form, with the second, third and fourth all close to their pre-race marks.

**NOTEBOOK**
**Baymist**, soon flat to the boards, came from almost last to first and clearly appreciated the slight give underfoot.
**Make Us Flush**, successful here two outings ago, put in all his best work at the finish and will relish a return to six furlongs.
**Alsu(IRE)**, well backed, worked hard to get her head in front but in the end was simply not good enough. A return to six looks on the cards.
**Distinctly Game**, back after an eight-week break, travelled strongly on his nursery bow. He was clawing back the first three at the line and deserves to find another race.
**Campeon(IRE)**, back over the minimum trip, showed bags of toe but could not find enough to keep his head in front on his eighth start.
**Handsome Lady**, in a first-time visor, showed bags of toe but had no more to give inside the last. She hasn't progressed at all since winning on her debut.
**Ryedane(IRE)**, who made a tardy start, stayed on when it was all over and needs a sixth furlong.
**Saucepot** *Official explanation: jockey said filly hung right-handed in the closing stages*

## 4509 PREMIER WEALTH MANAGEMENT LTD CLAIMING STKS 6f
**7:10** (7:10) (F) 3-Y-O+ **£3,031** (£866; £433) **Stalls** Centre

Form RPR

4000 **1** **Jedeydd**[7] 4305 7-9-1 **53** (bt) RWinston 6 62
(MDods) *hld up in rr: hdwy 2f out: swtchd rt ins fnl f: sn led: r.o* **14/1**

5030 **2** 3/4 **Pays D'Amour (IRE)**[7] 4291 7-8-11 **60** (t) AlexGreaves 8 56
(DNicholls) *chsd ldrs: rdn 2f out: ev ch ins fnl f: nt qckn cl home* **2/1**[1]

0-00 **3** shd **White Ledger (IRE)**[31] 3615 5-8-9 **50** (v) PHanagan 13 53
(RAFahey) *led: rdn over 1f out: hdd wl ins fnl f: hld cl home* **12/1**

-050 **4** 2 1/2 **Polar Galaxy**[8] 4259 3-8-6 **45** GFaulkner 14 47
(CWFairhurst) *chsd ldrs: rdn 2f out: styd on same pce* **33/1**

0066 **5** hd **American Cousin**[9] 4247 9-8-7 **55** ANicholls 7 43
(DNicholls) *in rr: rdn and hdwy over 2f out: ch ins fnl f: no ex cl home* **5/1**[2]

0410 **6** 1 1/2 **King Nicholas (USA)**[27] 3742 5-8-8 **53** (tp) MLawson(5) 9 45
(JParkes) *midfield: rdn and outpcd 1/2-way: styd on ins fnl f: nt pce to chal* **11/2**[3]

00 **7** 3 **Wild Tide**[8] 4257 5-8-2 RFfrench 11 25
(DWThompson) *chsd ldrs tl rdn 1/2-way: outpcd after* **100/1**

6324 **8** 5 **Mallia**[11] 4185 11-8-2 **44** PMakin(5) 2 15
(TDBarron) *in tch: rdn and wknd 2f out* **6/1**

0500 **9** 1 1/2 **Matriarchal**[14] 4105 4-8-2 **30** KimTinkler 10 5
(DonEnricoIncisa) *s.i.s: a bhd* **100/1**

0000 **10** nk **Buthaina (IRE)**[34] 3520 4-8-11 **45** TEaves(3) 3 16
(THCaldwell) *in touch: rdn and wknd over 2f out* **50/1**

5340 **11** 1 1/2 **Countrywide Girl (IRE)**[13] 4132 5-8-1 **35** PPMathers(5) 1 4
(ABerry) *chsd ldrs: rdn and wandered 2f out: sn wknd* **25/1**

6000 **12** 3 **Cloudless (USA)**[43] 3227 4-8-5 **43** SHitchcott(3) 4 —
(JWUnett) *prom tl rdn and wknd over 2f out* **20/1**

0060 **U** **Sugar Cube Treat**[5] 4360 8-7-13 **31** PVarley(7) 12 —
(MMullineaux) *rrd and uns rdr s* **33/1**

1m 15.46s (0.57) **Going Correction** -0.05s/f (Good) **13** Ran SP% **112.5**
**WFA** 3 from 4yo+ 4lb
Speed ratings: **94,93,92,89,89 87,83,76,74,74 72,68,**—CSF £37.69 TOTE £13.80: £3.20, £2.10, £4.10; EX 35.90.Pays D'Amour was claimed by Lynda Perrett for £6,000.
**Owner** Neil Harrison **Bred** Aziz Merza **Trained** Piercebridge, Co Durham

**FOCUS**
A moderate time for the grade. The winner was back to his best but the favourite was around a stone off form.

**NOTEBOOK**
**Jedeydd**, who took a walk in the market, ran out of racing room soon after halfway. Making his way to the stands' side, he nailed a rival who on official figures was rated a stone ahead of him.
**Pays D'Amour(IRE)**, clear top-rated on official figures, travelled strongly but in the end was just edged out.
**White Ledger(IRE)** showed bags of toe and this was easily his best effort for his present trainer. A drop back to five might suit.
**Polar Galaxy**, led down all the way to the start, seems to find this trip her bare minimum.
**American Cousin**, clear second-best on official figures, is not easy to predict these days.
**King Nicholas(USA)**, with cheekpieces on again, struggled to go the gallop and really needs more give underfoot.

## 4510 MTB GROUP CLASSIFIED STKS 6f
**7:40** (7:41) (C) 3-Y-O+ **£9,236** (£2,842; £1,421; £710) **Stalls** Centre

Form RPR

0030 **1** **River Falcon**[13] 4152 4-9-0 **84** NMackay(3) 2 96
(JSGoldie) *trckd ldr on far side: overall ld over 3f out: rdn and clr over 1f out: all out* **12/1**

5212 **2** hd **Compton's Eleven**[8] 4268 3-8-11 **86** SHitchcott(3) 5 96+
(MRChannon) *prom in centre: led gp 1/2-way: rdn over 2f out: edgd lft over 1f out: r.o: jst failed* **3/1**[1]

0013 **3** 1 **Pieter Brueghel (USA)**[21] 3901 5-9-4 **86** RWinston 10 93
(DNicholls) *led centre gp to 1/2-way: ridden over 2f out: styd on ins fnl f* **9/1**

4104 **4** nk **King's Caprice**[18] 3995 3-8-13 **85** SCarson 11 91
(GBBalding) *hld up in centre: hdwy over 2f out: r.o ins fnl f* **12/1**

4223 **5** 1/2 **Ellens Academy (IRE)**[13] 4152 9-9-4 **86** WSupple 3 91
(EJAlston) *hld up in centre: rdn and hdwy over 2f out: r.o ins fnl f* **6/1**[3]

1014 **6** 7 **Pinchbeck**[13] 4130 5-9-5 **87** (p) PRobinson 4 71
(MAJarvis) *in tch in centre: rdn over 2f out: wknd over 1f out* **7/2**[2]

0000 **7** nk **Hit's Only Money (IRE)**[12] 4179 4-9-8 **90** DeanMcKeown 9 73
(PABlockley) *in tch in centre: rdn and wknd over 2f out* **25/1**

5400 **8** 1 1/2 **Telepathic (IRE)**[6] 4317 4-8-12 **55** PPMathers(5) 6 63
(ABerry) *hld up in centre: rdn over 2f out: nvr on terms* **200/1**

0-53 **9** 4 **Sophrano (IRE)**[53] 2941 4-9-3 **60** GFaulkner 12 51
(PABlockley) *chsd ldrs in centre: rdn and wknd 1/2-way* **150/1**

21-5 **10** nk **Partners In Jazz (USA)**[76] 2309 3-9-2 **88** NCallan 7 53
(TDBarron) *s.i.s: sn prom in centre: rdn over 2f out: sn wknd* **7/2**[2]

0600 **11** 1/2 **Jalouhar**[6] 4317 4-9-3 **46** TWoodley 1 49
(BPJBaugh) *racd far-side: led overall tl over 3f out: wknd over 2f out* **200/1**

1m 13.81s (-1.08) **Going Correction** -0.05s/f (Good)
**WFA** 3 from 4yo+ 4lb **11** Ran SP% **114.6**
Speed ratings: **105,104,103,103,102 93,92,90,85,84 84**CSF £46.81 TOTE £15.00: £4.50, £1.70, £2.60; EX 87.80.
**Owner** F Brady, E Bruce & S Bruce **Bred** Manor Farm Packers Ltd **Trained** Uplawmoor, E Renfrews
■ Stewards Enquiry : N Mackay one-day ban: failed to keep straight from stalls (Aug 20)
T Woodley one-day ban: failed to keep straight from stalls (Aug 20)

**FOCUS**
Decent form. The first two ended up hard against the far side running rail.

**NOTEBOOK**
**River Falcon**, suited by the bit of ease in the ground, was one of two to make a bee-line for the far side rail. In the end the post came just in time.
**Compton's Eleven**, hoisted 4lb after Goodwood, showed ahead in the centre at halfway. He hung left and continued to do so even after his rider changed his whip. In the end he was just denied.
**Pieter Brueghel(USA)** showed bags of toe and kept on all the way to the line despite a tendency to hang left-handed under severe pressure.
**King's Caprice** travelled strongly and was putting in all his best work at the finish. He is progressing nicely.
**Ellens Academy(IRE)**, held right up off the pace, stayed on in good style inside the last but had lain too far out of his ground.
**Pinchbeck** was under pressure some way out and dropped away in disappointing fashion. This was not his true running.
**Partners In Jazz(USA)**, very warm at the start, was restless in the stalls. After a tardy start he was soon chasing the leaders, but he dropped right away soon after half way. He is clearly a bit of a tricky customer.

## 4511 SPROSTON ANNIVERSARY H'CAP 1m 30y
**8:10** (8:11) (E) (0-70,67) 3-Y-O+ **£3,848** (£1,184; £592; £296) **Stalls** Low

Form RPR

2162 **1** **Double Ransom**[38] 3401 5-9-8 **61** (b) PHanagan 3 72
(MrsLStubbs) *chsd ldrs: rdn over 3f out: r.o to ld wl ins fnl f* **7/1**[3]

0-40 **2** 1/2 **Explode**[88] 1993 7-8-10 **49** SSanders 7 58
(MissLCSiddall) *prom: led wl over 4f out: hdd wl ins fnl f* **33/1**

2403 **3** 1 1/2 **Regent's Secret (USA)**[8] 4280 4-9-3 **59** NMackay(3) 6 65
(JSGoldie) *hld up: swtchd rt and hdwy over 1f out: r.o ins fnl f* **12/1**

0442 **4** hd **Newcorp Lad**[7] 4301 4-9-6 **59** ACulhane 5 65
(MrsGSRees) *in tch: rdn over 2f out: ev ch ins fnl f: no ex cl home* **9/2**[1]

5523 **5** 1 3/4 **Apache Point (IRE)**[17] 4005 7-9-1 **54** KimTinkler 8 56
(NTinkler) *chsd ldrs: rdn over 2f out: kpt on fnl f* **15/2**

0022 **6** shd **Quicks The Word**[21] 3911 4-9-2 **55** KDarley 10 56
(CWThornton) *in tch: rdn over 3f out: kpt on fnl f* **6/1**[2]

0-10 **7** 1 1/4 **Mount Hillaby (IRE)**[197] 588 4-9-3 **59** PMulrennan(3) 17 57
(MWEasterby) *midfield: rdn over 2f out: styd on ins fnl f* **16/1**

620 **8** hd **Route Sixty Six (IRE)**[41] 3301 8-8-8 **47** DaleGibson 2 45
(JeddO'Keeffe) *in rr: rdn over 2f out: swtchd rt 1f out: styd on wl fnl f: nrst fin* **25/1**

0025 **9** nk **Encounter**[6] 4333 8-8-6 **45** DAllan 4 42
(JHetherton) *midfield: rdn and nt clr run over 2f out and again over over 1f out: styd on ins fnl f* **12/1**

0-00 **10** 1 **Maureen Ann**[35] 3471 4-8-12 **51** JBramhill 9 46
(TJFitzgerald) *racd keenly: midfield: rdn over 2f out: one pce fnl f* **50/1**

6206 **11** 3 1/2 **Vermilion Creek**[34] 3536 5-8-7 **51** StephanieHollinshead(5) 14 38
(RHollinshead) *s.i.s: in rr: kpt on fnl f: nvr able to chal* **25/1**

2200 **12** shd **Meelup (IRE)**[14] 4083 4-9-3 **56** (p) VSlattery 15 43
(JaneSouthcombe) *led for 1f: remained prom: rdn over 2f out: wknd fnl f* **66/1**

5/33 **13** nk **Silent Storm**[15] 4063 4-9-9 **67** NChalmers(5) 16 53
(HJCyzer) *led after 1f: hdd wl over 4f out: rdn over 2f out: wknd over 1f out* **16/1**

0121 **14** 1 3/4 **Parisian Playboy**[2] 4447 4-8-5 **51** 6ex LeanneKershaw(7) 13 33
(JeddO'Keeffe) *a bhd* **6/1**[2]

2002 **15** nk **Rymer's Rascal**[34] 3520 12-8-10 **49** WSupple 18 30
(EJAlston) *midfield: rdn over 2f out: wknd over 1f out* **16/1**

0000 **16** 1/2 **Kew The Music**[11] 4199 4-9-3 **59** SHitchcott(3) 1 39
(MRChannon) *midfield: rdn over 2f out: wknd over 1f out* **33/1**

0000 **17** 10 **Qobtaan (USA)**[11] 4190 5-9-0 **53** GBaker 12 10
(MRBosley) *a bhd* **100/1**

1m 43.5s (-2.05) **Going Correction** -0.10s/f (Good) **17** Ran SP% **122.1**
Speed ratings: **106,105,104,103,102 101,100,100,100,99 95,95,95,93,93 92,82**CSF £232.08 CT £2734.91 TOTE £7.80: £2.00, £9.40, £3.70, £1.80; EX 391.00.
**Owner** Tyme Partnership **Bred** Limestone Stud **Trained** Malton, N. Yorks
■ Stewards Enquiry : S Sanders caution: used whip without giving gelding time to respond

**FOCUS**
A strong pace, but plenty encountered traffic problems and a low draw was vital. The form overall looks modest.

**NOTEBOOK**
**Double Ransom**, 3lb higher, never left the inner and in the end did just enough. On the face of it, this looks improved form.
**Explode**, having his first outing for eleven weeks, never left the inside. Having shown ahead once in line for home he just missed out, but this was best effort for some time. He has slipped a long way in the handicap.
**Regent's Secret(USA)** has to be held up and therefore needs luck in running, which he definitely did not enjoy here. Pulled wide coming to the final furlong he finished best of all.
**Newcorp Lad** is in good form and was just found lacking inside the last. He is rated to the very limit now.
**Apache Point(IRE)** was always tending to race a bit wide and though sticking to his task he never really threatened.
**Quicks The Word**, drawn in double figures, could never get tucked in and some solid late work was to no avail.
**Encounter** *Official explanation: jockey said gelding was continually denied a run*
**Parisian Playboy**, drawn in double figures, took the widest route of all and was never on terms.

## 4512 NORTH WEST RACING CLUB SILVER JUBILEE H'CAP 1m 6f
**8:40** (8:40) (D) (0-85,84) 3-Y-O+ **£5,648** (£1,738; £869; £434) **Stalls** Low

Form RPR

5221 **1** **Magic Combination (IRE)**[26] 3782 11-9-6 **79** PMulrennan(3) 6 89
(LLungo) *hld up: swtchd rt and hdwy over 2f out: led ins fnl f: styd on wl* **9/2**[3]

-560 **2** 2 **Tilla**[16] 4033 4-8-10 **66** SSanders 3 73
(HMorrison) *hld up: hdwy 4f out: rdn to ld over 1f out: hdd ins fnl f: one pce cl home* **2/1**[1]

1232 **3** 1 1/4 **Yankeedoodledandy (IRE)**[14] 4086 3-8-1 **77** RoryMoore(7) 7 82
(PCHaslam) *trckd ldrs: rdn to ld over 2f out: hdd over 1f out: no ex cl home* **9/2**[3]

| | | | | RPR |
|---|---|---|---|---|
| 4 | hd | **Pilgrims Progress (IRE)**[95] [2809] 4-9-3 **73** RWinston 2 | 78 |
| | | (DWThompson) *in tch: rdn over 2f out: styd on cl home* **50/1** | |
| 0026 | 5 | 3/4 | **Weet For Me**[12] [4174] 8-9-4 **74** NCallan 5 | 78 |
| | | (RHollinshead) *led: rdn and hdd over 2f out: styd on same pce* **22/1** | |
| 1210 | 6 | 1/2 | **Dr Sharp (IRE)**[27] [3725] 4-9-10 **80** DaleGibson 1 | 83 |
| | | (TPTate) *trckd ldrs: lost pl over 3f out: rallied over 2f out: one pce over 1f out* **7/2[2]** | |
| 340/ | 7 | 9 | **Leopard Spot (IRE)**[650] [2741] 6-7-12 **54** oh4 PFessey 10 | 45 |
| | | (ISemple) *s.s: in rr: effrt over 3f out: no imp* **50/1** | |
| 3-50 | 8 | nk | **Salamba**[15] [4062] 3-8-2 **71** ow1 PRobinson 8 | 61 |
| | | (MHTompkins) *prom: rdn 3f out: sn wknd* **12/1** | |
| -626 | 9 | 7 | **Prize Ring**[8] [4261] 5-7-7 **54** oh2 BSwarbrick(5) 9 | 34 |
| | | (GMMoore) *midfield: hdwy after 6f: rdn and wknd 3f out* **12/1** | |

3m 4.21s (-1.94) **Going Correction** -0.10s/f (Good)
**WFA** 3 from 4yo+ 13lb **9 Ran SP% 115.6**
Speed ratings: **101,99,99,99,98 98,93,93,89**CSF £13.74 CT £41.66 TOTE £4.60: £1.80, £1.50, £1.30; EX 14.50 Place 6 £242.71, Place 5 £112.24.
**Owner** Sw Transport (swindon) Ltd & R J Gilbert **Bred** William J O'Regan **Trained** Carruthertown, D'fries & G'way

**FOCUS**
In effect a 0-80 handicap. It was run at just a steady pace, but the winner still came from second last turning in. The form is nothing special but should work out.

**NOTEBOOK**
**Magic Combination(IRE)**, 7lb higher, was given a very patient ride. Pulled outside, he finished with real relish to in the end win going away. In his twelfth year, he is showing his best form ever on the Flat and is a credit to his trainer.
**Tilla**, led to the start, travelled strongly but possibly saw too much daylight on the outer, for after taking it up plenty soon enough, she found the winner much too determined. She is definitely on a winning mark when everything falls into place.
**Yankeedoodledandy(IRE)**, attempting a new trip, ran another tip-top race but he is now 12lb higher than his last success.
**Pilgrims Progress(IRE)**, having his first outing since May, kept on surprisingly well considering how keenly he raced due to the lack of serious pace.
**Weet For Me**, who finished distressed 12 days previously, dropped anchor in front. Stepping up the gallop starting the home turn, he was ultimately simply not quick enough.
**Dr Sharp(IRE)**, sticking to the inner, ran a bit flat and will benefit from a short break.
T/Plt: £83.30 to a £1 stake. Pool: £51,527.55. 451.10 winning tickets. T/Qpdt: £7.70 to a £1 stake. Pool: £3,588.20. 343.75 winning tickets. DO

# 4334 LINGFIELD (L-H)
## Friday, August 6

**OFFICIAL GOING: Turf course - firm (good to firm in places); all-weather course - standard**
Wind: almost nil Weather: sunny and hot

## 4513 LINGFIELD GOLF CLUB MAIDEN STKS — 1m 6f
**2:10** (2:10) (D) 3-Y-0+ **£3,591** (£1,105; £552; £276) **Stalls High**

| Form | | | | RPR |
|---|---|---|---|---|
| 0 | 1 | | **Magical Quest**[16] [4028] 4-9-11 JPMurtagh 6 | 89+ |
| | | | (MrsAJPerrett) *led after 3f: pushed along 5f out: rdn clr over 2f out: unchal after* **6/1[3]** | |
| 222- | 2 | 6 | **Red Damson (IRE)**[297] [5557] 3-8-12 **80** SSanders 5 | 81+ |
| | | | (SirMarkPrescott) *led for 3f: chsd wnr tl rdn and dropped bk to 3rd over 5f out: kpt on to chse wnr again 2f out: no imp* **8/11[1]** | |
| 43 | 3 | 6 | **Garnett (IRE)**[14] [4087] 3-8-12 DHolland 9 | 75+ |
| | | | (AKing) *cl up: rdn to chse wnr over 5f out: no imp over 2f out: sn lost 2nd and wl btn* **3/1[2]** | |
| 50 | 4 | 9 | **My True Love (IRE)**[21] [3912] 5-9-11 SDrowne 1 | 46 |
| | | | (RJBaker) *dwlt: hld up in rr: lost tch w ldrs over 5f out: no ch after: plodded on* **20/1** | |
| 50-0 | 5 | 2 | **Black Swan (IRE)**[14] [4080] 4-9-11 **35** JQuinn 3 | 43? |
| | | | (GAHam) *wl in rr: struggling over 6f out: sn no ch: plodded on* **66/1** | |
| 0 | 6 | 5 | **Dual Purpose (IRE)**[16] [4028] 9-9-11 LVickers 2 | 36 |
| | | | (CRoberts) *dwlt: outpcd over 5f out: fdd fnl 3f* **25/1** | |
| 000- | 7 | 1 1/4 | **Icey Run**[315] [5201] 4-9-11 SRighton 8 | 34 |
| | | | (DGBridgwater) *bkwd: chsd ldrs: outpcd over 5f out: wknd u.p over 2f out* **100/1** | |
| 00-0 | 8 | 10 | **Lysander's Quest (IRE)**[75] [2324] 6-9-11 **37** NDay 10 | 20 |
| | | | (RIngram) *in tch to 6f out: sn wknd: t.o* **50/1** | |
| 0-0 | 9 | 1 1/2 | **Whispering Valley**[16] [4028] 4-9-6 DaneO'Neill 4 | 13 |
| | | | (MrsAJPerrett) *prom tl wknd 5f out: t.o* **33/1** | |
| 00-0 | 10 | dist | **Russian Icon**[20] [3934] 3-8-7 SWhitworth 7 | — |
| | | | (LADace) *dwlt: a in rr: t.o fr 1/2-way* **100/1** | |

3m 6.62s (-0.30) **Going Correction** +0.05s/f (Good)
**WFA** 3 from 4yo+ 13lb **10 Ran SP% 114.2**
Speed ratings: **102,98,95,90,88 86,85,79,78,—**CSF £10.21 TOTE £5.50: £1.10, £1.10, £1.30; EX 15.00.
**Owner** K Abdulla **Bred** Juddmonte Farms **Trained** Pulborough, W Sussex

**FOCUS**
With Red Damson below form, this was a weak maiden. Nevertheless, Magical Quest is progressing, and the first three can all be seen to better effect in a more strongly run race

**NOTEBOOK**
**Magical Quest** was green on his debut here and clearly benefited from both that experience and the step up in trip. His immediate future will depend on how the Handicapper views this six-length beating of an 80-rated performer, but he is at least progressing.
**Red Damson(IRE)**, three times runner-up over a mile off a mark in the 70s last season, got outpaced when things quickened and did not run to his current rating of 80 on this step up in trip and first run in 297 days. A stronger pace would have suited and he should not be written off.
**Garnett(IRE)** did not improve as anticipated for the step up in trip but is now qualified for handicaps and that will give connections more options.
**My True Love(IRE)** was beaten a long way, but is at least now qualified for a handicap mark.

## 4514 ARTHUR GODDARD MEMORIAL NOVICE STKS — 5f (P)
**2:40** (2:41) (D) 2-Y-0 **£3,474** (£1,069; £534; £267) **Stalls High**

| Form | | | | RPR |
|---|---|---|---|---|
| 0361 | 1 | | **Pitch Up (IRE)**[15] [4058] 2-9-2 **81** KFallon 6 | 95 |
| | | | (TGMills) *lw: mde all: kicked 2l clr 2f out: drvn fnl f: kpt on wl* **9/2[3]** | |
| 1 | 2 | 1 1/2 | **Sundance (IRE)**[25] [3805] 2-9-2 JQuinn 5 | 90 |
| | | | (HJCollingridge) *lw: sn chsd wnr: rdn and unable qckn wl over 1f out: no imp after* **11/8[1]** | |
| 1445 | 3 | 1 | **Canton (IRE)**[20] [3938] 2-9-2 **95** DaneO'Neill 8 | 87 |
| | | | (RHannon) *s.i.s: sn rcvrd: rdn to chse ldng pair over 2f out: kpt on same pce fr over 1f out* **5/2[2]** | |
| 313 | 4 | 4 | **Westbrook Blue**[15] [4041] 2-8-7 **81** CHaddon(7) 9 | 71 |
| | | | (WGMTurner) *chsd ldrs: rdn and outpcd over 2f out: no imp after* **20/1** | |
| 5212 | 5 | hd | **Russian Rocket (IRE)**[20] [3930] 2-8-11 **80** HayleyTurner(5) 3 | 72 |
| | | | (MrsCADunnett) *chsd ldng pair to over 2f out: sn outpcd and btn* **10/1** | |
| 45 | 6 | 1 1/2 | **Ninja Storm (IRE)**[11] [4191] 2-8-12 EAhern 2 | 63 |
| | | | (GLMoore) *s.s: hld up in last of main gp: nt clr run wl over 1f out to ins fnl f: no ch: do bttr* **14/1** | |
| 46 | 7 | hd | **Diamond Hombre (USA)**[13] [4143] 2-8-12 RHills 7 | 62 |
| | | | (JWHills) *racd in midfield: rdn 1/2-way: hanging and btn wl over 1f out* **33/1** | |
| 6000 | 8 | 3/4 | **Misty Princess**[27] [3741] 2-8-0 KGhunowa(7) 1 | 54 |
| | | | (MJPolglase) *racd in midfield: rdn 1/2-way: sn struggling* **100/1** | |
| 04 | 9 | 1 1/4 | **Tartatartufata**[100] [1709] 2-8-7 SWhitworth 10 | 50 |
| | | | (DShaw) *racd wd: in tch to 1/2-way: sn btn* **100/1** | |
| | 10 | 13 | **Chantelle's Dream** 2-8-4 PDoe 4 | — |
| | | | (IAWood) *w'like: bkwd: s.s: a wl bhd: t.o* **100/1** | |

59.87 secs (0.09) **Going Correction** +0.275s/f (Slow) **10 Ran SP% 115.3**
Speed ratings: **110,107,106,99,99 96,96,95,93,72**CSF £10.72 TOTE £3.60: £1.50, £1.30, £1.30; EX 14.80.
**Owner** B G Chamley **Bred** Peter McCutcheon **Trained** Headley, Surrey

**FOCUS**
A decent novice event run in an outstanding time in which the first five were all previous winners. If the fifth horse ran to within a few pounds of his best (there is little reason to suggest he did not) then this is particularly solid form, and it was a fine effort from the winner, although horses racing up with the pace were favoured and it was hard to come from behind.

**NOTEBOOK**
**Pitch Up(IRE)** appreciated the drop back to five furlongs when winning his maiden at Sandown on his previous start and again showed bundles of pace to follow up on his nursery debut. He could well win again in this grade, but his main aim is a valuable Sales race at Newmarket in October.
**Sundance(IRE)**, a comfortable debut winner of just an ordinary Windsor maiden, ran well on this step up in class but just lacked the pace of the winner. Connections reckon he may prove even better back on turf and, with only two runs under his belt, there should be more to come.
**Canton(IRE)**, fifth in the Super Sprint on his previous start, had an excellent chance on the ratings but was slowly away and could never really get on terms with the winner. He fared best of those to race off the pace and it was a reasonable effort in the circumstances.
**Westbrook Blue** was never really a danger and, unless he improves for another furlong, he may just continue to find a few too good.
**Russian Rocket(IRE)**, a course and distance maiden winner and runner-up in a nursery on the turf track here on his previous start, gives the form a very solid look if he ran to within a few pounds of his best.
**Ninja Storm(IRE)** ◆ lost a significant amount of ground with a slow start and was waited with thereafter. Still on the bridle at the top of the straight, he got stuck in behind a wall of horses and should have finished much closer. This run qualifies him for a handicap mark and he must be looked at closely in nursery company. *Official explanation: jockey said colt threw its head up in the air on leaving the stalls and was slowly away*
**Diamond Hombre(USA)** is now qualified for a handicap mark and improvement next time cannot be ruled out.

## 4515 TOTETRIFECTA RATED STKS (H'CAP) — 6f (P)
**3:10** (3:11) (D) (0-80,79) 3-Y-0 **£7,202** (£2,216; £1,108; £554) **Stalls Low**

| Form | | | | RPR |
|---|---|---|---|---|
| 1000 | 1 | | **Finders Keepers**[61] [2704] 3-9-0 **72** EAhern 6 | 81 |
| | | | (EALDunlop) *stdd s: hld up towards rr gng wl: prog over 1f out: hanging rt but led ins fnl f: in command after* **10/1** | |
| -406 | 2 | 3/4 | **The Jobber (IRE)**[23] [3845] 3-9-6 **78** KFallon 5 | 85 |
| | | | (MBlanshard) *trckd ldrs: rdn and effrt to ld ins fnl f: sn hdd and outpcd by wnr* **6/1[2]** | |
| 0603 | 3 | 1 1/2 | **Sweetest Revenge (IRE)**[16] [4024] 3-9-0 **72** ADaly 3 | 74 |
| | | | (MDIUsher) *w ldr: led 2f out to ins fnl f: one pce* **8/1** | |
| 1004 | 4 | 1/2 | **Emtilaak**[8] [4267] 3-9-4 **76** RHills 10 | 77 |
| | | | (BHanbury) *b: lw: trckd ldrs: gng wl enough 2f out: rdn and nt qckn over 1f out: one pce after* **9/2[1]** | |
| 4213 | 5 | shd | **Here To Me**[22] [3874] 3-9-0 **72** DaneO'Neill 1 | 72 |
| | | | (RHannon) *mde most to 2f out: hrd rdn and one pce* **9/2[1]** | |
| 2315 | 6 | 1/2 | **Ragged Jack (IRE)**[16] [4024] 3-8-12 **70** SWKelly 2 | 69 |
| | | | (GAButler) *taken down early: trckd ldrs: drvn 2f out: unable qck over 1f out: one pce after* **11/1** | |
| 1100 | 7 | 1 1/4 | **Toronto Heights (USA)**[113] [1408] 3-9-2 **79** ThomasYeung(5) 9 | 74 |
| | | | (PWChapple-Hyam) *settled towards rr: effrt on outer wl over 1f out: no imp ldrs* **8/1** | |
| 5000 | 8 | 2 | **Smokin Joe**[15] [4052] 3-8-7 **65** oh3 (v) NPollard 11 | 54 |
| | | | (JRBest) *racd in last pair: rdn on wd outside wl over 1f out: no prog* **25/1** | |
| 0000 | 9 | nk | **Fools Entire**[16] [4024] 3-8-7 **65** oh2 JQuinn 4 | 53 |
| | | | (JAGilbert) *w ldr to 2f out: wknd fnl f* **25/1** | |
| 0100 | 10 | 1 | **Hello Roberto**[7] [4289] 3-8-7 **72** KGhunowa(7) 8 | 57 |
| | | | (MJPolglase) *a towards rr: pushed along and no prog 2f out* **12/1** | |
| 4645 | 11 | 1 1/4 | **Cut And Dried**[23] [3849] 3-8-7 **65** MartinDwyer 7 | 46 |
| | | | (DMSimcock) *t.k.h: hld up in last pair: rdn and no prog 2f out* **7/1[3]** | |

1m 13.61s (0.69) **Going Correction** +0.275s/f (Slow) **11 Ran SP% 118.2**
Speed ratings: **106,105,103,102,102 101,99,97,96,95 93**CSF £69.28 CT £506.45 TOTE £12.60: £3.50, £2.70, £2.80; EX 89.00 Trifecta £858.10 Pool: £1,208.73. 0.40 winning tickets..
**Owner** Maktoum Al Maktoum **Bred** Gainsborough Stud Management Ltd **Trained** Newmarket, Suffolk

**FOCUS**
A fair sprint handicap run in a decent time and the form looks up to scratch for the grade.

**NOTEBOOK**
**Finders Keepers** has been out of sorts on the turf recently but, returned to a surface that suits well, he benefited from a confident ride from Eddie Ahern to gain his first handicap success. This should have boosted his confidence and he could well follow up - he would be of particular interest back on Polytrack.
**The Jobber(IRE)**, making his debut on Polytrack, was beaten fairly by the winner but this was still a personal best. He is quite lightly raced and looks up to winning a similar race this season.
**Sweetest Revenge(IRE)** travelled really well into the straight, but was left behind by the front two inside the last furlong. She is a course and distance winner, but showed plenty of early pace and could yet prove fully effective over the minimum trip.
**Emtilaak** could well be a bit of a thinker, but this was a respectable enough effort.
**Here To Me** did not run badly, but was ultimately readily held on this Polytrack debut.

## 4516 GOLF AND GAMBLE FILLIES' (S) STKS — 6f (P)
**3:40** (3:41) (G) 2-Y-0 **£2,940** (£840; £420) **Stalls Low**

| Form | | | | RPR |
|---|---|---|---|---|
| 4556 | 1 | | **Sapphire Princess**[11] [4200] 2-8-11 **51** PDoe 5 | 54 |
| | | | (IAWood) *trckd ldng trio: rdn over 2f out: drvn to ld jst over 1f out: kpt on one pce to draw clr* **16/1** | |
| 00 | 2 | 2 | **Yeldham Lady**[16] [4016] 2-8-11 JQuinn 4 | 48 |
| | | | (JPearce) *outpcd and rdn in last after 1f: sme prog fr 1/2-way: styd on u.p to take 2nd nr fin* **9/4[1]** | |
| 3653 | 3 | 1/2 | **Concert Time**[34] [3526] 2-8-6 **46** RThomas(5) 7 | 46 |
| | | | (CRDore) *t.k.h: mde most to jst over 1f out: nt qckn and btn fnl f* **12/1** | |

6403 **4** *5* **Turtle Magic (IRE)**[22] 3883 2-8-6 **54**....................(p) AQuinn(5) 9 31
(WGMTurner) *prom: jnd ldr 1/2-way to over 1f out: fnd nil: wknd fnl f* **5/1**

06 **5** *2* **Petite Noire**[42] 3278 2-8-11....................(t) EAhern 6 25
(JGPortman) *n.m.r after 1f: wl in rr: brief effrt on wd outside over 2f out: sn wknd* **20/1**

5500 **6** *3/4* **Queen's Glory (IRE)**[14] 4094 2-8-11 **66**....................(v[1]) DHolland 8 23
(WRMuir) *n.m.r and snatched up after 1f: sn in tch: rdn to press ldrs 2f out: wknd rapidly fnl f* **10/3**[2]

4025 **7** *9* **Alice King (IRE)**[65] 2593 2-8-4 **50**.................... CHaddon(7) 1 —
(WGMTurner) *mounted on crse: reluctant to enter stalls: outpcd and rdn 4f out: bhd after* **10/1**

01 **8** *9* **Marcela Zabala**[22] 3883 2-9-2 **55**.................... MFenton 2 —
(JGGiven) *lw: pressed ldr: rdn whn bdly hmpd on inner over 2f out: nt rcvr and eased* **9/2**[3]

1m 17.24s (4.32) **Going Correction** +0.275s/f (Slow) **8** Ran SP% **116.1**
Speed ratings: **82,79,78,72,69 68,56,44**CSF £53.17 TOTE £26.80: £2.90, £1.30, £2.50; EX 62.80.There was no bid for the winner. Yeldham Lady was subject to a friendly claim.
**Owner** Sporting Occasions **Bred** R S Cockerill (farms) Ltd **Trained** Upper Lambourn, Berks
■ Stewards Enquiry : R Thomas one-day ban: careless riding (Aug 20)
A Quinn two-day ban: careless riding (Aug 20-21)

**FOCUS**
A moderate seller run in a slow time.

**NOTEBOOK**
**Sapphire Princess** was a little disappointing on her first try at this trip, but she left that form behind with a smooth success. Things will be tougher under a penalty, but she does at least appear to be going the right way.
**Yeldham Lady**, dropped in class and distance, was well backed. She was badly outpaced soon after the start and did well to finish second in the circumstances. On this evidence, a return to seven furlongs will suit.
**Concert Time**, up a furlong, was a little keen and did not really get home. Five furlongs may yet prove to be her optimum trip.
**Turtle Magic(IRE)**, with cheekpieces replacing a visor, did not find a great deal under pressure and has now had nine chances.
**Petite Noire** did not show enough.
**Queen's Glory(IRE)**, in a visor for the first time, had a great chance at the weighs but stopped very quickly in the straight and something may have been amiss.
**Marcela Zabala** had quite a task under a penalty for a recent selling success over five furlongs, but she was not out of it when badly hampered with about two to go. *Official explanation: jockey said filly had a breathing problem*

## 4517 CHRIS WOTTON CUP FILLIES' H'CAP 7f (P)

4:10 (4:12) (F) (0-55,61) 3-Y-0+ **£3,003** (£858; £429) **Stalls** Low

Form RPR

0631 **1** **United Spirit (IRE)**[6] 4336 3-9-10 **61** 6ex....................(b) EAhern 14 72
(MAMagnusson) *dwlt: sn rcvrd to chse ldrs: rdn to chse ldr over 2f out: styd on wl to ld nr fin* **5/1**[2]

-504 **2** *nk* **Dixie Dancing**[20] 3932 5-9-10 **55**.................... MartinDwyer 12 65
(CACyzer) *trckd ldr: led over 2f out: kicked 2l clr wl over 1f out: hdd nr fin* **13/2**

0-05 **3** *2 1/2* **Pretty Kool**[6] 4336 4-9-4 **49**.................... KMcEvoy 11 53
(SCWilliams) *trckd ldrs: rdn and effrt 2f out: chsd ldng pair fnl f: no imp* **11/2**[3]

0030 **4** *nk* **Tokewanna**[9] 4248 4-9-2 **47**....................(t) SWKelly 6 50
(WMBrisbourne) *t.k.h: hld up in midfield: prog 2f out: styd on one pce fr over 1f out* **20/1**

0644 **5** *hd* **Ranny**[15] 4066 4-9-3 **51**.................... RMiles(3) 3 53
(DrJDScargill) *wl in rr: prog on outer over 2f out: drvn and kpt on fr over 1f out: nvr rchd ldrs* **4/1**[1]

5063 **6** *2* **Wanna Shout**[20] 3933 6-9-9 **54**.................... LisaJones 10 51
(RDickin) *prom: rdn over 2f out: nt qckn wl over 1f out: fdd fnl f* **11/2**[3]

0-00 **7** *2 1/2* **Artzola (IRE)**[6] 4339 4-9-5 **50**.................... DHolland 7 41
(CAHorgan) *sn wl in rr: rdn over 2f out: one pce and n.d* **16/1**

4150 **8** *1/2* **Bells Beach (IRE)**[34] 3533 6-9-8 **53**.................... SDrowne 13 42
(PHowling) *racd on outer and sn towards rr: effrt over 2f out: wknd fnl f* **16/1**

-500 **9** *3* **Emmervale**[57] 2823 5-9-0 **45**....................(v) JPMurtagh 8 26
(RMHCowell) *led to over 2f out: wknd over 1f out* **8/1**

0000 **10** *1* **Dream Of Dubai (IRE)**[28] 3700 3-9-4 **55**.................... JFEgan 5 34
(PMitchell) *hld up in midfield: effrt on inner over 2f out: no ch whn nt clr run 1f out* **20/1**

0 **11** *1 1/4* **Team Tactics (IRE)**[16] 4027 3-9-4 **55**.................... ADaly 1 31
(LADace) *dwlt: racd mostly in last: nvr a factor* **50/1**

4050 **12** *4* **Soul Provider (IRE)**[24] 3817 3-9-1 **52**....................(b[1]) PDoe 4 17
(MJAttwater) *racd in rr: rdn on outer and effrt 3f out: wknd 2f out* **25/1**

/0-0 **13** *3* **Guardian Spirit**[83] 2122 5-8-11 **45**.................... J-PGuillambert(3) 2 2
(DShaw) *no room on inner after 1f and dropped to rr: nvr able to rcvr* **66/1**

0400 **14** *1* **Bahama Belle**[15] 4043 3-9-1 **52**....................(b) DaneO'Neill 9 7
(HSHowe) *chsd ldrs on outer tl wknd wl over 2f out* **33/1**

1m 28.36s (2.42) **Going Correction** +0.275s/f (Slow)
**WFA** 3 from 4yo+ 6lb **14** Ran SP% **123.4**
Speed ratings: **97,96,93,93,93 90,88,87,84,82 81,76,73,72**CSF £35.52 CT £163.94 TOTE £6.20: £2.20, £2.00, £2.70; EX 38.90.
**Owner** East Wind Racing Ltd **Bred** Atlantic Racing Limited **Trained** Upper Lambourn, Berks

**FOCUS**
Reasonable form in its own context and no reason it should not work out.

**NOTEBOOK**
**United Spirit(IRE)**, racing under a 6lb penalty for her success over six furlongs on the turf track here on her previous start, needed all of this seven furlongs to follow up switched to the Polytrack. Although she was all out to win this, she is still progressing and the hat-trick cannot be ruled out.
**Dixie Dancing ◆**, 9lb lower than when winning over a mile on this track in December 2002, travelled really well into the straight and only just failed to justify market support. She was clear of the remainder and is up to winning a similar race whilst in this sort of form.
**Pretty Kool** has been tried over as far as ten furlongs and over as short as six. Racing over this trip for just the second time, she was no match for the winner but was gaining her best placing to date and connections look to be finding the key to her.
**Tokewanna**, making her Polytrack debut, appeared to appreciate the re-fitting of a tongue-tie and ran respectably. However, she is not helping her chance by racing keenly.
**Ranny** gained her only previous win over a mile and was given quite a bit to do on this drop back to seven furlongs.
**Wanna Shout** looks to find this trip just on the short side these days.
**Soul Provider(IRE)** *Official explanation: trainer said filly was found to be suffering from heat stress after the arec*

## 4518 CELEBRATE YOUR WEDDING AT LINGFIELD RACECOURSE H'CAP 1m 3f 106y

4:40 (4:40) (E) (0-75,73) 3-Y-0+ **£4,238** (£1,304; £652; £326) **Stalls** High

Form RPR

4225 **1** **La Petite Chinoise**[23] 3837 3-8-13 **70**.................... JPMurtagh 6 79
(RGuest) *lw: trckd ldr: led 3f out: rdn and pressed 2f out: styd on wl: drew clr ins fnl f* **7/1**

4342 **2** *1 3/4* **Carrowdore (IRE)**[36] 3459 4-9-9 **70**.................... IMongan 7 76
(GAHuffer) *wl in tch: chsd wnr over 2f out: rdn to chal wl over 1f out: nt qckn and btn fnl f* **9/4**[1]

0003 **3** *1 3/4* **Atahuelpa**[13] 4145 4-9-12 **73**.................... EAhern 8 76
(AKing) *hld up towards rr: prog 4f out: chsd ldng pair over 2f out: no imp over 1f out* **7/1**

0063 **4** *3* **Persian King (IRE)**[36] 3437 7-9-0 **61**.................... SDrowne 4 59
(JABOld) *settled in last pair: outpcd 5f out: rdn 3f out: kpt on fnl 2f: nt rch ldrs* **11/2**[3]

0000 **5** *2* **The Violin Player (USA)**[34] 3535 3-8-12 **72**.................... J-PGuillambert(3) 3 67
(HJCollingridge) *chsd ldng pair to over 4f out: lost pl: nt qckn and btn over 2f out: fdd* **20/1**

5535 **6** *2* **Mustang Ali (IRE)**[16] 4027 3-8-9 **66**.................... DHolland 2 58
(SKirk) *lw: settled in rr: outpcd 5f out: struggling fnl 3f* **5/2**[2]

0600 **7** *nk* **Sovereign Dreamer (USA)**[48] 3095 4-9-7 **73**.................... NDeSouza(5) 1 65
(PFICole) *led to 3f out: wknd* **12/1**

-600 **8** *27* **Brooklands Lodge (USA)**[13] 4138 3-8-3 **60**.................... SRighton 5 8
(MJAttwater) *t.k.h: hld up in last: lost tch 5f out: t.o* **33/1**

2m 28.55s (-0.97) **Going Correction** +0.05s/f (Good)
**WFA** 3 from 4yo+ 10lb **8** Ran SP% **115.1**
Speed ratings: **105,103,102,100,98 97,97,77**CSF £23.35 CT £115.69 TOTE £7.10: £1.30, £1.20, £3.00; EX 20.90.
**Owner** N Elsass **Bred** Burton Agnes Stud Co Ltd **Trained** Newmarket, Suffolk

**FOCUS**
A weak race and very ordinary form.

**NOTEBOOK**
**La Petite Chinoise** looked pretty exposed going into this but gained a much-deserved first success in game fashion. She now heads to Denmark for their Oaks.
**Carrowdore(IRE)**, making his debut for a new stable and back up to a mile and a half, found the winner too strong. He has just one win to his name.
**Atahuelpa**, third in a reasonable claimer over a mile on his debut for Alan King, was able to confirm that promise on this step up in trip with another solid effort, although he does look a little high in the weights.
**Persian King(IRE)** was supported in the ring but again shaped as though in need of further.
**Mustang Ali(IRE)** could have gone very close on the best of his form, but he is a frustrating sort. *Official explanation: jockey said gelding did not act coming down the hill*
**Brooklands Lodge(USA)** *Official explanation: jockey said filly was found to be suffering from heat stress after the race*

## 4519 COME RACING AT LINGFIELD H'CAP 1m 2f

5:10 (5:10) (F) (0-55,54) 3-Y-0+ **£3,185** (£910; £455) **Stalls** Low

Form RPR

2003 **1** **Fantasy Crusader**[2] 4436 5-9-8 **48**....................(p) DaneO'Neill 4 57
(JAGilbert) *chsd ldr: rdn over 2f out: led jst ins fnl f: drvn clr* **9/2**[1]

0001 **2** *2* **Didoe**[15] 4042 5-9-7 **47**.................... PDoe 2 52
(PWHiatt) *led: rdn and pressed over 2f out: hdd jst ins fnl f: wknd and jst hld on for 2nd* **11/2**[2]

0450 **3** *shd* **My Maite (IRE)**[1] 4485 5-9-6 **46**....................(tp) NDay 13 51
(RIngram) *hld up towards rr: effrt over 3f out: rdn and nt qckn over 2f out: styd on fr over 1f out: nrst fin* **13/2**[3]

1305 **4** *shd* **Husky (POL)**[2] 4436 6-9-5 **45**....................(p) ADaly 14 50
(RMHCowell) *hld up in last: sme prog 3f out: hanging and reluctant fr over 2f out tl r.o ins fnl f: nvr nrr* **9/1**

2000 **5** *1 3/4* **Ryan's Bliss (IRE)**[6] 4339 4-8-12 **41**.................... J-PGuillambert(3) 11 42
(TDMccarthy) *hld up towards rr: rdn and effrt on outer 3f out: one pce and nvr rchd ldrs* **20/1**

6-00 **6** *shd* **Deekazz (IRE)**[10] 4213 5-8-9 **35**....................(v) EAhern 1 36
(FWatson) *trckd ldrs: rdn and effrt over 2f out: cl up over 1f out: one pce after* **25/1**

0436 **7** *2 1/2* **Pacific Ocean (ARG)**[11] 4192 5-9-13 **53**....................(t) SDrowne 6 50
(MrsStefLiddiard) *trckd ldrs: wnt 3rd 4f out and gng wl: rdn to chal over 2f out: fnd nil and sn btn* **9/2**[1]

4356 **8** *5* **Escalade**[9] 4233 7-9-7 **47**....................(v) SWKelly 7 34
(WMBrisbourne) *nvr beyond midfield: rdn and no prog over 2f out: wknd* **13/2**[3]

44-0 **9** *5* **Zuleta**[46] 3143 3-9-5 **54**.................... DSweeney 10 32
(MBlanshard) *racd in midfield: wknd over 2f out* **33/1**

006 **10** *1 1/2* **Miss Shangri La**[38] 3392 3-9-0 **49**.................... DHolland 5 24
(GWragg) *prom: hrd rdn over 5f out: nt run on and sn lost pl: bhd fnl 2f* **11/1**

0600 **11** *6* **Estrella Levante**[33] 3555 4-9-8 **48**.................... LisaJones 3 11
(RMFlower) *trckd ldng pair to 4f out: wknd* **33/1**

2m 9.77s (0.17) **Going Correction** +0.05s/f (Good)
**WFA** 3 from 4yo+ 9lb **11** Ran SP% **111.2**
Speed ratings: **101,99,99,99,97 97,95,91,87,86 81**CSF £25.69 CT £153.37 TOTE £4.10: £1.40, £2.80, £1.80; EX 14.90 Place 6 £39.78, Place 5 £38.42.
**Owner** The Fantasy Fellowship **Bred** J R C And Mrs Wren **Trained** Hargrave, Suffolk

**FOCUS**
A moderate handicap in which it proved hard to come from off the pace.

**NOTEBOOK**
**Fantasy Crusader** had conditions to suit and, just 1lb higher than when winning the corresponding race last year, scored convincingly. He should continue to go well in similar low-class events.
**Didoe**, finally off the mark in a Bath seller on her previous start, looked to run her race.
**My Maite(IRE)** came from on an unpromising position to grab third, but was never a threat to the winner. An inconsistent sort, he is far from sure to confirm this next time.
**Husky(POL)** struggled to land a serious blow and may be worth another try over further. *Official explanation: jockey said gelding had hung right-handed*
**Ryan's Bliss(IRE)** did not run badly, but she remains a maiden.
**Pacific Ocean(ARG)** found disappointingly little and is proving incredibly hard to win with.
T/Jkpt: Not won. T/Plt: £102.90 to a £1 stake. Pool: £41,105.90. 291.40 winning tickets. T/Qpdt: £61.60 to a £1 stake. Pool: £1,783.40. 21.40 winning tickets. JN

# [4340] NEWMARKET (JULY) (R-H)

Friday, August 6

**OFFICIAL GOING: Good to firm**

Another very warm day ensured the ground was on the fast side, despite heavy watering during the week.

Wind: Almost nil Weather: Fine, but humid

## 4520 STUART AND DAVE'S H'CAP — 1m 2f

5:55 (5:55) (C) (0-95,95) 3-Y-O+ — £9,568 (£2,944; £1,472; £736) Stalls Centre

| Form | Pos | Dist | Horse / comment | Jockey | RPR |
|---|---|---|---|---|---|
| 605 | 1 | | **Polygonal (FR)**[13] [4118] 4-9-6 **85** (MrsJRRamsden) *lw: chsd ldrs: led over 1f out: r.o wl* **6/1**[3] | GMosse 3 | 101 |
| 21 | 2 | 6 | **Elmustanser**[49] [3054] 3-9-7 **95** (t) (SaeedBinSuroor) *b.off fore: led: hung lft and hdd over 1f out: wknd ins fnl f* **5/2**[2] | LDettori 5 | 100 |
| 502 | 3 | 1 | **Courageous Duke (USA)**[13] [4118] 5-10-0 **93** (JNoseda) *lw: chsd ldr: rdn and ev ch over 1f out: wknd ins fnl f* **5/4**[1] | KFallon 4 | 96 |
| -100 | 4 | 1 | **First Centurion**[62] [2683] 3-8-9 **83** (JWHills) *chsd ldrs: rdn over 2f out: wknd over 1f out* **12/1** | MHills 6 | 84 |
| 0100 | 5 | 3 | **Lilli Marlane**[22] [3872] 4-8-7 **72** (NACallaghan) *hld up: effrt over 1f out: sn wknd* **16/1** | WRyan 2 | 67 |
| -000 | 6 | 3 | **Liquid Form (IRE)**[23] [3842] 4-9-1 **80** (BHanbury) *hld up: rdn over 2f out: wknd over 1f out* **10/1** | TEDurcan 1 | 69 |

2m 4.46s (-2.00) **Going Correction** +0.05s/f (Good)
**WFA** 3 from 4yo+ 9lb — **6** Ran SP% **110.0**
Speed ratings: **110,105,104,103,101 98**CSF £20.45 TOTE £6.70: £2.40, £1.80; EX 30.60.
**Owner** R C Thompson **Bred** Ecurie Ferdane **Trained** Sandhutton, N Yorks

**FOCUS**
A strongly run contest in which the front three filled those positions throughout. Decent form despite the small field.

**NOTEBOOK**
**Polygonal(FR)**, who had shown his best form in France when there was plenty of give underfoot, showed a smart turn of foot on this faster surface to win with plenty in hand.
**Elmustanser** lacked the experience of some of these, but left his maiden form behind and was far from disgraced. He can be found easier opportunities.
**Courageous Duke(USA)** had his optimum conditions but folded tamely up the hill.
**First Centurion**, off the bridle some way out, looked to find this surface too quick.
**Lilli Marlane** found this company too hot.
**Liquid Form(IRE)** stays further than this and should have been suited to the fast pace, but this was stronger company than he is used to. He is beginning to get some respite from the Handicapper and is worth a look at a lower level.

## 4521 MINERAL STAR (S) STKS — 7f

6:25 (6:25) (E) 2-Y-O — £4,085 (£1,257; £628; £314) Stalls Low

| Form | Pos | Dist | Horse / comment | Jockey | RPR |
|---|---|---|---|---|---|
| 100 | 1 | | **Don't Tell Trigger (IRE)**[14] [4089] 2-8-11 65 (JSMoore) *lw: mde all stands' side: rdn over 2f out: styd on u.p* **5/1**[2] | JDSmith 11 | 66 |
| 2040 | 2 | 1 3/4 | **Lakesdale (IRE)**[14] [4089] 2-8-1 60 (MrsCADunnett) *racd far side: chsd ldrs: led that gp wl ins fnl f: r.o* **25/1** | HayleyTurner(5) 1 | 57 |
| 0303 | 3 | 3/4 | **Amphitheatre (IRE)**[14] [4094] 2-8-11 66 (RFJohnsonHoughton) *racd far side: chsd ldr tl led that gp over 2f out: hdd wl ins fnl f* **11/2**[3] | KFallon 5 | 60 |
| 0360 | 4 | nk | **Orpen Annie (IRE)**[14] [4094] 2-8-3 65 (MissJFeilden) *b. near fore: chsd ldrs far side: rdn over 2f out: styd on* **20/1** | BReilly(3) 3 | 54 |
| 00 | 5 | hd | **Ladruca**[36] [3444] 2-8-6 (RHannon) *b.off hind: racd far side: hld up: hdwy 2f out: r.o* **25/1** | RSmith 10 | 54 |
| 1 | 6 | 3/4 | **Pon My Soul (IRE)**[34] [3506] 2-9-2 (MGQuinlan) *chsd wnr stands' side: rdn over 1f out: no ex* **6/1** | PDobbs 12 | 62 |
| 4262 | 7 | hd | **Haroldini (IRE)**[14] [4094] 2-8-11 70 (MrsPNDutfield) *led far side: over 4f: no ex ins fnl f* **4/1**[1] | RHavlin 4 | 57 |
| 0202 | 8 | 1 1/2 | **Jay (IRE)**[11] [4200] 2-8-6 52 (b) (NACallaghan) *racd far side: dwlt: sn pushed along and prom: nt clr run and lost pl over 2f out: styd on ins fnl f* **12/1** | TPQueally 2 | 48 |
| 5441 | 9 | 7 | **Maureen's Lough (IRE)**[7] [4304] 2-8-11 57 (JHetherton) *racd far side: prom: racd keenly: rdn over 2f out: wknd fnl f* **5/1**[2] | LDettori 6 | 35 |
| 00 | 10 | 2 | **Blue Spectrum (IRE)**[6] [4335] 2-8-4 (JSMoore) *racd far side: s.i.s: hld up: rdn and wknd over 2f out* **66/1** | DerekNolan(7) 7 | 30 |
| 005 | 11 | nk | **Ariane Star (IRE)**[11] [4197] 2-8-6 (MAJarvis) *racd far side: chsd ldrs over 4f* **11/1** | MHills 9 | 25 |
| 6045 | 12 | nk | **Tip Toes (IRE)**[11] [4200] 2-8-6 45 (MRChannon) *racd far side: hld up: rdn and wknd over 2f out* **33/1** | TEDurcan 8 | 24 |

1m 28.96s (2.19) **Going Correction** +0.05s/f (Good) — **12** Ran SP% **115.9**
Speed ratings: **89,87,86,85,85 84,84,82,74,72 72,71**CSF £129.39 TOTE £7.00: £2.20, £6.90, £1.80; EX 87.70.The winner was bought in for 9,500gns. Haroldini was bought by John Balding for £10,000.
**Owner** Bigwigs Bloodstock Racing Club V **Bred** Park Place International Ltd **Trained** East Garston, Berks
■ Stewards Enquiry : J D Smith one-day ban: failed to keep straight from stalls (Aug 20)

**FOCUS**
This looked a strongish seller, albeit slowly run in a moderate time. The field split into two, with the winner and one other electing to race up the stands' side. There didn't appear to be any great advantage in the draw.

**NOTEBOOK**
**Don't Tell Trigger(IRE)**, dropped in company after a couple of promising efforts in nurseries, made a bee line for the stands' side soon after the stalls opened, a move which was to win her the race. However, the stewards decided that her jockey didn't ride to his draw and banned him for a day.
**Lakesdale(IRE)**, who sported the same colours as the winner, made it a one-two for their owners when 'winning' her race on the far side. She should have little trouble landing a similar event.
**Amphitheatre(IRE)** stayed this trip well enough and should have a similar contest in him.
**Orpen Annie(IRE)** showed a bit more on this drop in class and shaped as though she will stay further.
**Ladruca** has found her level. She is a half-sister to a mile winner and may be suited by a stiffer test.
**Pon My Soul(IRE)**, facing different conditions to those he encountered on his debut, probably didn't run too badly under his penalty.
**Haroldini(IRE)** had plenty of use made of him, but didn't quite get home.

## 4522 BERNARD LLOYD/HOLE IN THE WALL H'CAP — 6f

6:55 (6:56) (D) (0-80,77) 3-Y-O+ — £5,616 (£1,728; £864; £432) Stalls Low

| Form | Pos | Dist | Horse / comment | Jockey | RPR |
|---|---|---|---|---|---|
| -360 | 1 | | **Semenovskii**[14] [4090] 4-9-4 **69** (PWD'Arcy) *swtchd to r stands' side 5f out: mde virtually all: swvd lft 2f out: all out* **6/1**[3] | DHolland 8 | 80 |
| 4052 | 2 | nk | **Cold Climate**[6] [4336] 9-8-3 **54** (BobJones) *lw: swtchd to r stands' side 5f out: chsd wnr: rdn and ev ch fr over 1f out: styd on* **11/2**[2] | JQuinn 11 | 64 |
| 3306 | 3 | 1 1/4 | **Hard To Catch (IRE)**[7] [4291] 6-9-7 **77** (b) (DKIvory) *b.off fore: racd far side: dwlt: hld up: hdwy to ld that gp over 1f out: r.o* **9/1** | MSavage(5) 1 | 83 |
| 0533 | 4 | nk | **Snow Bunting**[7] [4294] 6-8-11 **62** (JeddO'Keeffe) *swtg: swtchd to r stands' side 5f out: hld up: hdwy over 1f out: r.o* **4/1**[1] | MFenton 12 | 67 |
| 0603 | 5 | shd | **Prince Cyrano**[14] [4090] 5-9-6 **71** (WJMusson) *dwlt: swtchd to r stands' side 5f out: hld up: hdwy over 2f out: rdn and ev ch over 1f out: no ex ins fnl f* **7/1** | RMullen 10 | 76 |
| -002 | 6 | 4 | **Salon Prive**[16] [4026] 4-8-9 **60** (CACyzer) *lw: swtchd to r stands' side 5f out: prom: hung lft over 2f out: sn wknd* **7/1** | LDettori 7 | 53 |
| 0040 | 7 | hd | **Juste Pour L'Amour**[7] [4294] 4-9-5 **70** (PLGilligan) *racd far side: w ldr of that gp: rdn and ev ch over 1f out: wknd ins fnl f* **11/1** | JFEgan 4 | 62 |
| 4000 | 8 | 2 | **Multahab**[37] [3428] 5-7-10 **50** (t) (PSMcentee) *swtchd to r stands' side 5f out: chsd ldrs: rdn over 2f out: wknd over 1f out* **20/1** | FPFerris(3) 13 | 36 |
| 00 | 9 | 1/2 | **Mimic**[14] [4090] 4-8-5 **63** (RGuest) *racd far side: chsd ldrs: rdn over 2f out: wknd fnl f* **20/1** | RMills(7) 2 | 48 |
| 0004 | 10 | 1/2 | **Yorkies Boy**[4] [4400] 9-7-10 **52** oh1 ow3 (p) (NEBerry) *b: racd far side: chsd ldrs over 4f* **14/1** | RThomas(5) 6 | 35 |
| 1566 | 11 | 5 | **Silver Chime**[36] [3439] 4-9-3 **68** (DMSimcock) *racd far side: edgd rt s: chsd ldrs over 4f* **14/1** | MartinDwyer 3 | 36 |
| 0-00 | 12 | 6 | **Strathclyde (IRE)**[16] [4034] 5-9-10 **75** (AMHales) *led far side over 4f: wknd ins fnl f* **25/1** | CCatlin 5 | 25 |

1m 13.9s (0.58) **Going Correction** +0.05s/f (Good) — **12** Ran SP% **119.7**
Speed ratings: **98,97,95,95,95 90,89,87,86,85 79,71**CSF £38.22 CT £304.94 TOTE £8.20: £3.10, £1.70, £2.80; EX 46.20.
**Owner** Peter Beaton-Brown **Bred** J P Coggan **Trained** Newmarket, Suffolk

**FOCUS**
The field again split into two and the stands' side had the best of it. Ordinary form and a moderate time for the grade.

**NOTEBOOK**
**Semenovskii** had what turned out to be the best of the draw. He is a bit of an in and out performer, but he is clearly useful at this level when things go his way.
**Cold Climate** is running well at present, although there were signs he wasn't that keen to go by. He has worn cheekpieces in the past and may benefit from them again.
**Hard To Catch(IRE)** turned in a soild effort under his big weight, from what looked a difficult draw.
**Snow Bunting** took an age to pick up and found the leaders beyond recall when he finally got going. Raised 3lb for getting beaten here last week, he isn't going to find things any easier. *Official explanation: jockey said gelding jumped out of the stalls awkwardly*
**Prince Cyrano** was a little unlucky in that he was caught out wide. This was another fair effort.
**Salon Prive** didn't look an easy ride.

## 4523 MYKAL INDUSTRIES MAIDEN STKS — 7f

7:25 (7:26) (D) 2-Y-O — £4,842 (£1,490; £745; £372) Stalls Low

| Form | Pos | Dist | Horse / comment | Jockey | RPR |
|---|---|---|---|---|---|
| 4 | 1 | | **Windsor Knot (IRE)**[16] [4030] 2-9-0 (JHMGosden) *lw: mde all: shkn up ins fnl f: r.o* **4/5**[1] | JPMurtagh 13 | 91+ |
| | 2 | 2 | **Monsoon Rain (USA)** 2-9-0 (SaeedBinSuroor) *leggy: scope: chsd ldrs: rdn over 2f out: styd on* **4/1**[2] | LDettori 15 | 83 |
| 4 | 3 | 3/4 | **Golden Fury**[54] [2904] 2-9-0 (JLDunlop) *hld up in tch: plld hrd: rdn over 1f out: styd on* **11/1** | GMosse 11 | 81 |
| | 4 | 3/4 | **Given A Choice (IRE)** 2-9-0 (JGGiven) *well grown: lw: hld up: nt clr run over 1f out: r.o ins fnl f: nt rch ldrs* **16/1** | IMongan 10 | 82+ |
| | 5 | 3/4 | **Wotchalike (IRE)** 2-9-0 (DRCElsworth) *compact: str: bkwd: chsd wnr: rdn over 2f out: no ex ins fnl f* **66/1** | NPollard 5 | 77 |
| | 6 | hd | **Dubai Venture** 2-9-0 (SirMichaelStoute) *gd sort: leggy: sn pushed along in rr: styd on fnl f: nvr trbld ldrs* **8/1**[3] | KFallon 9 | 77 |
| 0 | 7 | 1 | **The Coires (IRE)**[21] [3913] 2-9-0 (RHannon) *lw: edgd rt s: chsd ldrs: rdn over 2f out: wknd ins fnl f* **50/1** | DaneO'Neill 1 | 74 |
| | 8 | nk | **Ebtikaar (IRE)** 2-9-0 (JLDunlop) *w'like: scope: s.i.s: hld up: sme hdwy over 1f out: n.d* **14/1** | RHills 8 | 74 |
| | 9 | 3 1/2 | **Desert Classic** 2-8-9 (EALDunlop) *gd sort: bkwd: prom: rdn over 2f out: wknd fnl f* **33/1** | EAhern 12 | 60 |
| | 10 | 1 1/2 | **Wingman (IRE)** 2-9-0 (JWHills) *w'like: scope: s.i.s and hmpd s: hld up: hdwy over 2f out: wknd over 1f out* **20/1** | MHills 2 | 61 |
| 0 | 11 | 2 | **South O'The Border**[55] [2890] 2-8-11 (TGMills) *lw: prom tl hung lft and wknd over 1f out* **50/1** | RMiles(3) 6 | 56 |
| 006 | 12 | 3 | **Sherbourne**[11] [4197] 2-8-9 (MGQuinlan) *s.i.s: a bhd* **66/1** | PaulEddery 3 | 44 |
| | 13 | hd | **King Zafeen (IRE)** 2-9-0 (MRChannon) *w'like: s.i.s: hld up: effrt over 2f out: wknd over 1f out* **33/1** | TEDurcan 14 | 48 |
| 30 | 14 | 2 1/2 | **Mr Kalandi (IRE)**[62] [2674] 2-9-0 (PWD'Arcy) *lw: prom 5f* **25/1** | DHolland 4 | 42 |

1m 27.25s (0.48) **Going Correction** +0.05s/f (Good) — **14** Ran SP% **128.9**
Speed ratings: **99,96,95,95,94 93,92,92,88,86 84,81,80,77**CSF £3.96 TOTE £2.10: £1.30, £1.80, £3.50; EX 6.50.
**Owner** Sheikh Mohammed **Bred** Tally-Ho Stud **Trained** Manton, Wilts

**FOCUS**
Hard to know what to make of this, especially as the winner had the benefit of experience and the run of the race. Although the stalls were on the far side, the field elected to race on the stands' side.

**NOTEBOOK**
**Windsor Knot(IRE)** quickly bagged the rails from his high draw and was nicely on top in the end. There will be more to come from him as he steps up in trip.
**Monsoon Rain(USA)** was a $550,000 yearling and is related to to Estimraar, a Group 3 winner in the UAE. He wasn't knocked around on this racecourse debut and looks sure to pay his way in time.
**Golden Fury** proved well suited by this step up in trip and similar improvement should see him getting off the mark.

**Given A Choice(IRE)** ◆, a half-brother to the high-class middle-distance performer Bandari, was very green during the early part of the race but picked up in fine style late on. He will have no trouble getting off the mark.

**Wotchalike(IRE)**, a half-brother to stayer Coquette Rouge showed plenty of pace, and as he is from a yard whose newcomers normally come on a bundle for their first outing, he looks set to pay his way in due course.

**Dubai Venture**, a brother to 12-furlong winner Affirmative Action, took a while for the penny to drop and should find improvement when stepped up in trip.

**Wingman(IRE)**, a half-brother to Charlie Tango, didn't have the best of draws as it turned out, with the field electing to race over on the stands' side. He didn't shape too badly and can be expected to improve on this effort.

**South O'The Border** *Official explanation: jockey said colt was unsuited by the good to firm ground*

## 4524 FIRESTONE PRODUCTS NURSERY 7f

**7:55** (7:55) (D ) 2-Y-O **£4,754** (£1,463; £731; £365) **Stalls** Low

| Form | | | | RPR |
|---|---|---|---|---|
| 004 | **1** | | **Mighty Empire (IRE)**[16] 4016 2-8-7 **66** LDettori 5<br>(MHTompkins) *trckd ldrs: plld hrd: led ins fnl f: rdn clr* **9/4**[1] | 74+ |
| 0245 | **2** | *3 ½* | **Alright My Son (IRE)**[14] 4089 2-9-3 **76** DaneO'Neill 7<br>(RHannon) *lw: led: hung lft over 1f out: hdd and no ex ins fnl f* **5/2**[2] | 75 |
| 616 | **3** | *½* | **Nordhock (USA)**[18] 3987 2-7-10 **60** DFox(5) 4<br>(NACallaghan) *sn pushed along and prom: outpcd over 2f out: styd on ins fnl f* **16/1** | 58 |
| 043 | **4** | *1* | **Burton Ash**[27] 3741 2-9-1 **74** MFenton 6<br>(JGGiven) *w ldr: rdn and ev ch over 1f out: no ex ins fnl f* **12/1** | 70 |
| 3022 | **5** | *1 ¼* | **Flying Pass**[16] 4023 2-9-2 **75** DHolland 1<br>(DJSFfrenchDavis) *prom: jnd ldrs 1/2-way: rdn over 1f out: wknd ins fnl f* **11/2**[3] | 67 |
| 036 | **6** | *¾* | **Guinea A Minute (IRE)**[18] 3992 2-8-8 **67** RMullen 3<br>(MLWBell) *prom: jnd ldrs 1/2-way: rdn over 2f out: wknd fnl f* **7/1** | 58 |
| 342 | **7** | *18* | **Noorain**[14] 4100 2-9-7 **80** TEDurcan 2<br>(MRChannon) *lw: plld hrd: sn w ldrs: hmpd and lost pl over 2f out: sn bhd* **7/1** | 26 |

1m 28.05s (1.28) **Going Correction** +0.05s/f (Good) **7 Ran SP% 113.3**
Speed ratings: **94,90,89,88,86 86,65**CSF £7.97 TOTE £3.20: £1.90, £1.60; EX 5.50.

**Owner** The Mighty Empire Partnership **Bred** John Martin McLoughney **Trained** Newmarket, Suffolk

**FOCUS**

A slowly run contest in which most of the field pulled too hard for their own good. Again they came to race over on the stands' side.

**NOTEBOOK**

**Mighty Empire(IRE)**, making his nursery debut, showed his true colours and won with plenty in hand.

**Alright My Son(IRE)**, who had the benefit of the rails to help, did nothing but hang in the latter stages, leaving a gap for the winner to shoot through.

**Nordhock(USA)** would have appreciated a stronger pace. Although she has only a selling victory to her name, she looks capable of adding to that at this level

**Burton Ash** was always doing a little too much and didn't quite get home.

**Flying Pass** is looking more and more exposed, and had no excuses here.

**Noorain** pulled far too hard and will need to learn to settle if she is to progress. *Official explanation: jockey had no explanation for the poor form shown*

## 4525 BEXHILL CONDITIONS STKS 1m 2f

**8:25** (8:25) (C ) 3-Y-O+ **£8,398** (£3,185; £1,592; £724) **Stalls** Centre

| Form | | | | RPR |
|---|---|---|---|---|
| 0606 | **1** | | **Corriolanus (GER)**[12] 4163 4-8-13 94 DHolland 5<br>(PMitchell) *hld up: hdwy over 1f out: rdn to ld ins fnl f: r.o* **20/1** | 104 |
| -026 | **2** | *1 ¾* | **Elshadi (IRE)**[20] 3936 3-8-7 104 (b) MartinDwyer 1<br>(MPTregoning) *lw: set str pce: rdn and hdd ins fnl f: no ex* **6/1**[3] | 104 |
| 1-36 | **3** | *¾* | **Carini**[21] 3912 3-7-13 94 CCatlin 4<br>(HCandy) *chsd ldrs: rdn over 2f out: nt clr run over 1f out: styd on* **20/1** | 94 |
| 1-22 | **4** | *¾* | **Imtiyaz (USA)**[29] 3661 5-9-2 108 (t) LDettori 3<br>(SaeedBinSuroor) *lw: hld up: hdwy over 3f out: rdn over 1f out: nt run on* **4/6**[1] | 101 |
| 0400 | **5** | *1 ½* | **Tizzy May (FR)**[7] 4285 4-8-13 100 DaneO'Neill 2<br>(RHannon) *hld up: hdwy over 2f out: sn rdn: wknd fnl f* **5/1**[2] | 95 |
| 246- | **6** | *dist* | **Island Sound**[280] 5853 7-8-13 102 KFallon 6<br>(DRCElsworth) *chsd ldr: rdn over 4f out: wknd over 1f out* **7/1** | — |

2m 3.79s (-2.67) **Going Correction** +0.05s/f (Good)
**WFA** 3 from 4yo+ 9lb **6 Ran SP% 113.0**
Speed ratings: **112,110,110,109,108** —CSF £129.68 TOTE £19.40: £5.00, £3.20; EX 194.30 Place 6 £62.16, Place 5 £55.10.

**Owner** Richard J Cohen **Bred** Gestut Schlenderhan **Trained** Epsom, Surrey

**FOCUS**

A hot contest, worthy of Listed status, and run at a furious pace in a smart time. Corriolanus has been rated back to near his German best, but the form is not straightforward to assess, with Elshadi and Imtiyaz both below form

**NOTEBOOK**

**Corriolanus(GER)** was the last to play his cards, and with the front-running Elshadi already drained, having fought off first Island Sound and then Imtiyaz, he powered clear to win with the minimum of fuss.

**Elshadi(IRE)** was never left alone up front and fought off one after another. However, those efforts had taken their toll in the closing stages and he just couldn't respond when the winner came by.

**Carini** is a tough filly and didn't have the best of runs. However, it would be stretching it a bit to say she was unlucky.

**Imtiyaz(USA)** ridden with a bit more restraint than normal, came through to have his chance, but carried his head on one side and didn't appear to go through with his effort.

**Tizzy May(FR)** again flattered only to decieve.

**Island Sound** could never get his own way in front and dropped away tamely.

T/Plt: £455.70 to a £1 stake. Pool: £48,511.90. 77.70 winning tickets. T/Qpdt: £34.20 to a £1 stake. Pool: £3,837.30. 82.95 winning tickets. CR

# 4163 ASCOT (R-H)

Saturday, August 7

**OFFICIAL GOING: Good (good to soft in places)**

The fifth renewal held at Ascot of the Shergar Cup, won this year by the Rest of the World team. Both six-furlong races were run on the round course.

Wind: nil Weather: sunny and hot

## 4526 PRINCE'S TRUST SHERGAR CUP DISTAFF (RATED STKS H'CAP) (F&M) 6f (R)

**1:40** (1:43) (B ) (0-100,100) 3-Y-O+ **£22,550** (£7,892; £3,608; £2,818) **Stalls** High

| Form | | | | RPR |
|---|---|---|---|---|
| 3005 | **1** | | **Tychy**[9] 4269 5-9-3 **92** GMosse 7<br>(SCWilliams) *lw: b.front: prom: chsd ldr over 2f out: drvn to chal over 1f out: led ins fnl f: kpt on wl* **11/4**[1] | 101 |
| 4214 | **2** | *1* | **Fruit Of Glory**[22] 3914 5-9-5 **94** LDettori 10<br>(JRJenkins) *lw: trckd ldrs: effrt 2f out: rdn and styd on fnl f to take 2nd nr fin* **11/2** | 100 |
| 0010 | **3** | *nk* | **Caveral**[63] 2685 3-9-2 **95** WCMarwing 8<br>(RHannon) *t.k.h: hld up: last 1/2-way: prog 2f out: r.o wl fnl f to take 3rd last stride* **20/1** | 100 |
| 2300 | **4** | *hd* | **Speed Cop**[53] 2955 4-9-6 **95** JPMurtagh 5<br>(AMBalding) *led: gng wl 2f out: rdn and hdd ins fnl f: fnd nil* **12/1** | 100 |
| 0003 | **5** | *hd* | **Fanny's Fancy**[22] 3914 4-8-13 **88** KDarley 1<br>(CFWall) *b.hind: racd on outer: chsd ldrs: rdn 2f out: styd on fnl f: nt rch ldrs* **5/1**[3] | 92 |
| 2300 | **6** | *½* | **Proud Boast**[7] 4324 6-9-1 **90** KFallon 9<br>(DNicholls) *s.s: wl in rr: prog on inner 2f out: styd on fnl f: nvr able to chal* **8/1** | 92 |
| L023 | **7** | *3 ½* | **Forever Phoenix**[13] 4165 4-9-3 **92** DHolland 3<br>(RMHCowell) *hld up in last trio: prog into midfield 1/2-way: rdn and nt qckn 2f out: one pce after* **9/2**[2] | 84 |
| 0- | **8** | *½* | **Mrs St George (IRE)**[15] 4107 3-8-6 **85** DVargiu 2<br>(JGBurns, Ire) *str: lw: racd in last trio: rdn and no prog over 2f out: one pce after* **16/1** | 75 |
| 0-00 | **9** | *7* | **Barrantes**[5] 4401 7-8-9 **84** oh3 MJKinane 4<br>(MissSheenaWest) *b: rdn to press ldr: wknd over 2f out* **40/1** | 53 |
| 4000 | **10** | *2 ½* | **Bali Royal**[19] 3976 6-9-9 **98** DMOliver 6<br>(MSSaunders) *t.k.h: hld up in midfield: wknd over 2f out* **33/1** | 60 |

1m 14.73s
**WFA** 3 from 4yo+ 4lb **10 Ran SP% 111.7**
Speed ratings: CSF £16.50 CT £212.46 TOTE £3.90: £1.90, £1.60, £5.10; EX 25.30 Trifecta £450.80 Pool: £635.02. 0.90 winning tickets..

**Owner** P Ellinas **Bred** L Ellinas **Trained** Newmarket, Suffolk

**FOCUS**

A decent handicap and the first of two six-furlong races run on the round course on the day. It paid not to be drawn low and the form does not look outstanding for the grade. Because of the unusual course arrangement due to building works, there is no median time for the round six furlongs so no speed figures can be calculated.

**NOTEBOOK**

**Tychy** was last seen finishing fifth in Group Three company at Glorious Goodwood, and this represented a distinct drop in class. Allowed to run off the same mark of 92 - due to go up 5lb in future - she was always well positioned under Mosse and came with her winning challenge a furlong out, getting the better of early leader Speed Cop before holding on well from the finishers. She is evidently in top form at present and connections are reportedly looking to a Listed event at Pontefract on the 15th prior to a crack at the Haydock Sprint Cup.

**Fruit Of Glory** takes her racing well and ran another sound race. She had every chance but could not pick up in time. Still 5lb higher than when last winning, she seems to be progressing well enough to defy it.

**Caveral** ◆ is the one to take from the race. Unable to make an impact in Listed company when last seen in June, she had previously beaten Fruit Of Glory by three lengths at Windsor and was over-priced at 20/1. Unable to take advantage of her good draw, she found herself stone last turning in and could not make the ground up in time - flying home to just get third. She is progressive and should make her mark at Listed level before the season is out.

**Speed Cop** is all pace and was always going to find this stiff six furlongs stretching her. She had not run since June but got the lead and it was only in the final half furlong she emptied. Better can be expected of her next time back at the minimum.

**Fanny's Fancy** had the beating of Fruit Of Glory on their recent Newmarket form, but was towards the outer for most of the way - as a result of her poor draw - and never picked up well enough down the straight. She gives every indication that seven furlongs will suit.

**Proud Boast** was beaten only four lengths in the Stewards' Cup last week and again ran well. She is still high enough in the weights but will be better suited by softer going.

**Forever Phoenix** ran a rare bad race and could never get into it. She is better than this. *Official explanation: jockey said filly did not handle the bend*

## 4527 PORTHAULT SHERGAR CUP JUVENILE (AUCTION RACE) 7f (R)

**2:10** (2:13) (B ) 2-Y-O **£22,550** (£7,892; £3,608; £2,818) **Stalls** High

| Form | | | | RPR |
|---|---|---|---|---|
| 1032 | **1** | | **Justaquestion**[7] 4326 2-8-10 82 LDettori 5<br>(IAWood) *lw: hld up in last pair: rapid prog on outer fr 2f out: drvn to ld last 50yds* **10/1** | 92 |
| 2106 | **2** | *hd* | **Beaver Patrol (IRE)**[22] 3907 2-9-6 95 MJKinane 8<br>(RFJohnsonHoughton) *racd in midfield: rdn and effrt 2f out: r.o to chal wl ins fnl f: jst pipped* **14/1** | 101 |
| 11 | **3** | *nk* | **Lamh Eile (IRE)**[24] 3834 2-8-7 DVargiu 7<br>(TDBarron) *lw: prom: trckd ldr over 2f out: rdn to chal over 1f out and rdr unbalanced: led ins fnl f: hdd last 50yds* **11/2** | 87 |
| 0104 | **4** | *½* | **Destinate (IRE)**[10] 4227 2-9-1 95 DHolland 4<br>(RHannon) *b.hiind: trckd ldrs: lost pl bnd 3f out and rdn: effrt u.p 2f out: hrd drvn and r.o fnl f: nt rch ldrs* **9/2**[2] | 94 |
| 2212 | **5** | *1* | **Spirit Of France (IRE)**[32] 3605 2-9-2 95 JPSpencer 10<br>(MJohnston) *led: rdn 2f out: hdd and fdd ins fnl f* **4/1**[1] | 93 |
| 61 | **6** | *½* | **Embossed (IRE)**[17] 4030 2-9-1 YTake 9<br>(RHannon) *s.i.s: hld up in last pair: prog on inner 2f out: running on whn nt clr run nr fin* **5/1**[3] | 90 |
| 03 | **7** | *5* | **Kandidate**[21] 3939 2-8-12 GMosse 6<br>(CEBrittain) *lw: racd in last trio: rdn over 2f out: no prog and wl btn over 1f out* **10/1** | 75 |
| 5422 | **8** | *3 ½* | **Group Captain**[13] 4166 2-8-12 80 JPMurtagh 2<br>(SKirk) *racd in midfield: rdn 3f out: wknd 2f out* **12/1** | 66 |
| 10 | **9** | *1 ¼* | **Street Cred**[22] 3907 2-9-1 DMOliver 3<br>(AMBalding) *chsd ldr to over 2f out: wknd* **33/1** | 66 |



The Form Book, Raceform Ltd, Compton, RG20 6NL

2223 **10** 7 **Mceldowney**[11] 4219 2-8-12 77........................................ KDarley 1 45
(MJohnston) *trckd ldrs: wl in tch over 2f out: sn wknd rapidly* **20/1**

1m 28.3s **10** Ran SP% **110.5**

Speed ratings: CSF £131.74 TOTE £7.20: £1.70, £2.80, £2.50; EX 114.70 Trifecta £617.40 Pool: £869.59. 0.30 winning tickets..

**Owner** Christopher Shankland **Bred** A S Reid **Trained** Upper Lambourn, Berks

**FOCUS**

This looked a fair juvenile event that should produce future winners, despite being below the recent standard for the race. With no median time for the round seven furlongs, no speed figures can be calculated.

**NOTEBOOK**

**Justaquestion** was beaten in a nursery at Glorious Goodwood most recently - albeit slightly unlucky - and had something to find with the likes of Destinate and Spirit Of France at the weights. Dettori was content to sit last on her until making his move around the field turning in and she picked up strongly for her rider, edging ahead in the closing stages. This represented a marked improvement and, although the Group Three Prestige Stakes back at Goodwood looks a big ask, her stable trained Protectorate to finish second in the 2001 renewal and she too may be capable of sneaking a place.

**Beaver Patrol(IRE)** has struggled in Group and Listed contests the last twice and seemed well served by this drop in grade/step up in trip. He was badly in at the weights, which makes the run look all the better, and is worth his place over this trip back in Listed company now he has returned to something like his best.

**Lamh Eile(IRE)** was taking a significant step up in grade having bolted up in much lesser events, but was well in at the weights and proved up to it. She was up there throughout and held her chance but was unable to repel to late challengers. This was only her third run and there should be more to come from her.

**Destinate(IRE)** was the one to beat on the form of his fourth behind the best two-year-old colt seen out so far this season Shamardal in the Vintage Stakes, but he lost his good early position and never looked happy. He kept on well for pressure and was not beaten far in the end, but would still have disappointed connections.

**Spirit Of France(IRE)** was surprisingly made favourite ahead of Destinate - he like the winner had been beaten in a nursery last time - and having led for most of the journey found himself unable to go again when the pack came at him. His a big colt who will make up into a better three-year-old.

**Embossed(IRE)** was a most impressive scorer at Sandown last month - a race that has produced winners - but he never got involved - being out the back and choosing to try his luck towards the inside. He was staying on when denied a clear run and is better than he showed.

**Kandidate** came into this on the back of only two runs and, as neither had been a winning one, could be given little chance. He did not prove good enough and will be more at home back in maiden company.

**Mceldowney**

## 4528 MURPHY'S FASTFLOW SHERGAR CUP MILE (RATED STKS H'CAP) 1m (R)

**2:45** (2:48) (B) (0-100,103) 4-Y-0+ **£22,550** (£7,892; £3,608; £2,818) **Stalls** High

Form RPR

0140 **1** **Pentecost**[8] 4287 5-9-7 **100**........................................ KFallon 6 113+
(AMBalding) *lw: hld up in last quartet: stdy prog over 2f out: shkn up to ld last 150yds: in command after* **9/2**[1]

3024 **2** 1 1/4 **Vortex**[14] 4120 5-9-10 **103**........................................(t) YTake 5 113
(MissGayKelleway) *lw: b.hind: trckd clr ldng pair: clsd 2f out: led over 1f out: rdn and hdd last 150yds: outpcd* **6/1**[3]

0010 **3** 1 **Wing Commander**[8] 4287 5-9-0 **93** 3ex........................................ DVargiu 7 101
(RAFahey) *lw: trckd clr ldrs: clsd 2f out: effrt over 1f out: styd on same pce fnl f* **9/1**

0-36 **4** 1 **Colisay**[35] 3539 5-9-7 **100**........................................(v[1]) JPSpencer 4 106
(EFVaughan) *hld up in last pair: effrt 2f out: rdn and r.o fnl f: nt rch ldrs* **10/1**

0130 **5** 1 1/4 **Unshakable (IRE)**[8] 4287 5-9-1 **94**........................................ LDettori 8 97
(BobJones) *b: lw: hld up in midfield: shkn up 2f out: nt clr run over 1f out: one pce after* **11/2**[2]

2030 **6** 1 1/4 **Greenslades**[14] 4120 5-9-3 **96**........................................ GMosse 2 96
(PJMakin) *chsd clr ldr: led jst ins fnl 2f: hdd & wknd over 1f out* **8/1**

2625 **7** hd **St Andrews (IRE)**[14] 4120 4-9-2 **95**........................................ WCMarwing 9 94
(MAJarvis) *hld up in midfield: clsd 2f out: nt clr run 1f out: shuffled along and lost pl ins fnl f* **11/2**[2]

4500 **8** 2 **Camp Commander (IRE)**[21] 3937 5-9-1 **94**........................................(t) DHolland 3 89
(CEBrittain) *hld up in last pair: rdn 3f out: no prog and btn 2f out* **8/1**

0203 **9** 1 1/4 **Calcutta**[13] 4178 8-9-4 **97**........................................ KDarley 10 89
(BWHills) *hld up in last trio: rdn over 2f out: no prog* **20/1**

4004 **10** 15 **Selective**[24] 3850 5-9-0 **93**........................................ JPMurtagh 1 50
(EFVaughan) *led at fast pce: hdd jst ins fnl 2f: wknd: t.o* **16/1**

1m 41.14s (-1.90) **Going Correction** +0.10s/f (Good) **10** Ran SP% **115.2**

Speed ratings: **113,111,110,109,108 107,107,105,103,88**CSF £30.74 CT £232.65 TOTE £3.70: £1.80, £2.40, £3.20; EX 16.50 Trifecta £131.80 Pool: £1,281.57. 6.90 winning tickets..

**Owner** J C, J R And S R Hitchins **Bred** Miss S N Ralphs **Trained** Kingsclere, Hants

■ Stewards Enquiry : K Fallon caution: careless riding

**FOCUS**

A strong handicap in which they went a fast gallop thanks to the efforts of Selective, and Pentecost came through to win the race for the second consecutive year. The form looks solid for the grade.

**NOTEBOOK**

**Pentecost**, 8lb higher than when successful in this race last term, has been in better form this time around - winning at Sandown and being beaten only a length in Group company on his penultimate outing. He was given a patient ride as he likes to come at horses, and came through with a strong run to win going away. Connections are keen to return to Group company with the improving five-year-old, and have a Group Three at Salisbury pencilled in as his next target.

**Vortex** has been beaten no more than two lengths in each of his last six outings - some of which have been in the most competitive handicaps of the season - and he ran another blinder. He has been on the go since January but shown no signs of losing his form and was running off a career high mark of 103.

**Wing Commander** had little chance from his single-figure stall in the William Hill Mile most recently, and this represented a return to form. He is not the most consistent but useful on his day and is sure to play a hand in a decent handicap before the year is out.

**Colisay**, sporting the first-time visor, got beaten further by the winner than he had at Sandown despite being 7lb better off, and the headgear evidently failed to make much difference. He remains too high in the handicap to win at present.

**Unshakable(IRE)** disappointed from his plum draw in the William Hill Mile and again would have let his supporters down. He simply seems handicapped up to his best at present; he has never won off a mark in the 90s.

**Greenslades** was running off an 11lb higher mark than when last successful back in August 2003. He has run many good races in defeat since then but simply finds it hard going off this mark, and did too much early in chasing the clear early leader.

**St Andrews(IRE)** has run some big races in defeat this season since returning from injury, and maybe this fourth race in just over six weeks took its toll. He is better than this and one to bear in mind for a good backend handicap.

**Camp Commander(IRE)** is a frustrating character who often runs really well in defeat, but he could not even manage that. He has been off form the last twice now and looks best left along for the time being.

**Calcutta** is not up to this kind of race at the bigger courses any more, and is going to be hard to place off his rating for a horse who is no longer on the up.

**Selective** is usually restrained but went on and set a decent gallop. As a result he failed to run his race and the question has to be asked as to whether he was doing a 'job' for the 'team' as Pentecost likes a good pace.

## 4529 SODEXHO SHERGAR CUP STAYERS (RATED STKS H'CAP) 2m 45y

**3:20** (3:21) (B) (0-100,100) 4-Y-0+ **£22,550** (£7,892; £3,608; £2,818) **Stalls** High

Form RPR

0110 **1** **Dorothy's Friend**[11] 4218 4-8-9 **88**........................................ MJKinane 6 100+
(RCharlton) *lw: hld up in last pair: rdn 3f out: gd prog on outer 2f out: led last 150yds: styd on stoutly* **11/4**[1]

0154 **2** 1 **Double Obsession**[9] 4270 4-9-2 **95**........................................(v) DMOliver 4 105+
(MJohnston) *trckd ldrs: effrt over 2f out: rdn to ld over 1f out: hdd and one pce last 150yds* **3/1**[2]

2453 **3** 2 **Highland Games (IRE)**[7] 4345 4-8-8 **87**........................................ YTake 8 95
(JGGiven) *trckd ldrs: lost pl steadily fr 7f out: in rr 3f out: plld wd over 2f out: rdn and r.o over 1f out: nvr able to chal* **10/1**

3-60 **4** 1 3/4 **Gold Medallist**[35] 3538 4-9-7 **100**........................................ WCMarwing 3 106
(DRCElsworth) *trckd ldr and sn clr of rest: rdn to ld over 3f out: hdd and one pce over 1f out* **25/1**

34/3 **5** 1 3/4 **Penny Pictures (IRE)**[53] 2958 5-8-8 **87**........................................ KFallon 2 91
(MCPipe) *dwlt: t.k.h: hld up in rr: prog 6f out: rdn to join ldr 2f out: nt qckn and btn over 1f out* **9/2**[3]

00 **6** 1 1/2 **Almah (SAF)**[11] 4218 6-8-11 **90**........................................ KDarley 7 92
(MissVenetiaWilliams) *hld up in last: effrt 3f out: rdn and one pce fnl 2f* **25/1**

0000 **7** hd **Morson Boy (USA)**[11] 4218 4-8-13 **92**........................................ DHolland 10 94
(MJohnston) *led and sn clr w one rival: hdd over 3f out: wknd over 1f out* **7/1**

22-0 **8** 6 **Albanov (IRE)**[10] 4226 4-9-2 **95**........................................ JPSpencer 9 90
(MJohnston) *hld up towards rr: effrt 3f out: hrd rdn and no imp 2f out: wknd: eased* **14/1**

5004 **9** 1 1/2 **Santando**[11] 4218 4-8-11 **90**........................................(v) GMosse 1 83
(CEBrittain) *wl in tch: trckd clr ldng pair 10f out to over 4f out: wknd 2f out: eased* **7/1**

460/ **10** 16 **Nostradamus (USA)**[139] 1841 5-9-0 **93**........................................ DVargiu 5 67
(KJBurke, Ire) *dwlt: in tch to over 4f out: wknd: t.o* **40/1**

3m 32.72s (-2.12) **Going Correction** +0.10s/f (Good) **10** Ran SP% **120.7**

Speed ratings: **109,108,107,106,105 105,104,101,101,93**CSF £11.38 CT £73.53 TOTE £3.30: £1.20, £1.60, £2.90; EX 7.70 Trifecta £89.40 Pool: £1,196.40. 9.50 winning tickets..

**Owner** Mountgrange Stud **Bred** Floors Farming And Christopher J Heath **Trained** Beckhampton, Wilts

**FOCUS**

They went a good clip thanks in a race that is likely to work out, despite not appearing as solid as it might have been, with several horses in the line-up having the potential to make their mark at Pattern level, and those that do not, hinting at better to come for later in the season.

**NOTEBOOK**

**Dorothy's Friend** disappointed when dropped to a mile six at Goodwood most recently, and the step back up to two miles saw a return to winning ways. He did not get going until late, and it was only in the last furlong he looked like getting Double Obsession. He was winning off a 26lb higher mark than when first successful last year, and there is no reason why he can not progress further and make up into a Pattern performer in time.

**Double Obsession**, although not favourite, was the one to beat on the back of his gallant fourth in the Goodwood Cup and set a tall standard. He looked set to score when taking it up, but the winner had his move covered. He is due to go up 10lb in future and that will makes things an awful lot tougher in handicaps, so connections will have to hope he improves enough to claim status as a resident Cup horse. He could be an interesting contender for the Prix Du Cadran if getting his beloved fast ground, as his useful change of pace over that sort of trip will stand him in good stead.

**Highland Games(IRE)** ◆ showed improved form for the step up to this trip and was edging closer all the time at the line. He is sure to go up a couple of pounds for this, but is sure remain on a winning mark and could be an interesting contender in the Ebor off a feather weight.

**Gold Medallist** ◆ had been beaten a total of 52 lengths in his two runs prior to this in 2004, and this was a welcome return to form. He chased clear early leader Morson Boy, but kept going when that one cried enough and momentarily looked as though he may cause an upset. Those early exertions took their toll but it was still an excellent effort under top-weight. As he proved at three, he is up to Pattern level and, with connections reknowed for doing well with their stayers, Group races look the way to go.

**Penny Pictures(IRE)** had not run since being hammered by Double Obsession at Ascot and reduced the deficit on much better terms. He is exposed, but probably capable of a bold showing in something like the Cesarewitch - a race his trainer usually targets a few at.

**Almah(SAF)** is going the right way and was plugging on at her own pace. She won in blinkers in her native South Africa, and may be one to watch out for if or when the headgear is refitted.

**Morson Boy(USA)** ran another disappointing race, dropping away having made the running until turning in. It was reported the saddle slipped - as it had done at Goodwood last time - and it may be down to the fact he is such a big horse. Still only a four-year-old, he should be dropped a further few pounds and will get it all together again one day when filling his huge frame. *Official explanation: jockey said saddle slipped*

**Albanov(IRE)** needed the outing on his first start of the season and for the stable at Goodwood, and he still looked a little ring-rusty. Backend races on soft ground will be much more his bag.

**Santando** *Official explanation: jockey said colt stumbled leaving the stalls and got tired in the closing stages*

## 4530 CARVILL SHERGAR CUP CHALLENGE (RATED STKS H'CAP) 1m 4f

**3:50** (3:55) (B) (0-100,100) 4-Y-0+ **£22,550** (£7,892; £3,608; £2,818) **Stalls** High

Form RPR

0240 **1** **Desert Quest (IRE)**[28] 3756 4-8-13 **92**........................................(b) JPSpencer 1 103
(AMBalding) *hld up in last: stl last over 2f out: prog on inner over 1f out: squeezed through fnl f: drvn and r.o wl to ld last strides* **14/1**

4004 **2** nk **Counsel's Opinion (IRE)**[13] 4163 7-9-7 **100**........................................ WCMarwing 3 111
(CFWall) *lw: dwlt: hld up in rr: prog on outer over 2f out: led jst over 1f out : r.o fnl f: hdd last strides* **12/1**

2364 **3** nk **Swift Tango (IRE)**[14] 4118 4-9-7 **100**........................................ DMOliver 2 111
(EALDunlop) *lw: hld up in midfield: plld out and effrt 2f out: rdn to chal 1f out: fnd nil and hld nr fin* **12/1**

-112 **4** 1/2 **Hawridge Prince**[24] 3842 4-9-2 **95**........................................ JPMurtagh 8 105
(LGCottrell) *lw: hld up in midfield: effrt over 2f out: nt clr run over 1f out: styd on ins fnl f* **7/1**[3]

1-13 **5** 3/4 **Starry Lodge (IRE)**[28] 3756 4-9-3 **96**........................................ LDettori 9 105
(LMCumani) *trckd ldrs: effrt over 2f out: rdn to ld briefly over 1f out: one pce ins fnl f* **6/4**[1]

0440 **6** nk **Hambleden**[11] 4218 7-9-5 **98**........................................ KFallon 6 106
(MAJarvis) *led: rdn over 2f out: hdd over 1f out: one pce* **5/1**[2]

2440 **7** 3/4 **Desert Royalty (IRE)**[21] 3944 4-8-13 **92**........................................ DHolland 4 99
(EALDunlop) *b.front: trckd ldrs: rdn to chal 2f out: wknd ins fnl f* **22/1**

0000 **8** *1 3/4* **Sir George Turner**[11] [4214] 5-9-2 **95** ........ MJKinane 5 99
(MJohnston) *racd in last pair: rdn over 3f out: sme prog over 1f out: hanging and looked reluctant: nvr rchd ldrs* **10/1**

04-5 **9** *10* **Muhareb (USA)**[14] [4123] 5-9-1 **94** ........ YTake 10 82
(CEBrittain) *swtg: prom: cl up wl over 1f out: wknd rapidly fnl f* **20/1**

120 **10** *10* **Akash (IRE)**[98] [1762] 4-8-12 **91** ........ GMosse 7 63
(MJohnston) *mostly trckd ldr to 2f out: losing pl whn hmpd sn after: wknd and eased* **14/1**

2m 34.22s (0.66) **Going Correction** +0.10s/f (Good) **10** Ran SP% **116.1**
Speed ratings: **101,100,100,100,99 99,99,97,91,84**CSF £169.19 CT £2073.45 TOTE £19.70: £5.60, £3.00, £2.70; EX 200.10 TRIFECTA Not won..
**Owner** Ballygallon Stud Ltd **Bred** Ballygallon Stud **Trained** Kingsclere, Hants

**FOCUS**
Another good handicap and solid enough form, although it was a very modest time considering the class of race.

**NOTEBOOK**
**Desert Quest(IRE)** was last seen running down the field in the John Smith's Cup, but his earlier form entitled him to respect - most notably his fast-finishing second to Persian Lightning on Oaks Day. He is not the easiest of rides and has his quirks, but had the ideal partner for his style of running and weaved his way through on the inner to get up in the closing stages. This is how he likes to be ridden and he will not always get the breaks. *Official explanation: trainer's representative had no explanation for the improved form shown other than that gelding is a quirky character*
**Counsel's Opinion(IRE)** had gained his last two wins at this course and he looked set to make it three when striking the front, but the stiff finish caught him out and he was collared by Desert Quest on the line. Those two wins here had come over a mile two and, although running off a 3lb higher mark, he is in good form and can win back down in trip.
**Swift Tango(IRE)** has not run a bad race all season and was suited to this step back up in trip, having been short of pace over a mile two here last month. He is 10lb higher than when winning at Newbury in May, and may need to drop a few pounds before he is winning again.
**Hawridge Prince** is still unexposed and proved suited by this step up in trip. He has been progressive over a mile and a quarter - going up 19lb since the start of the season - and there looks to be more to come at this trip as he was a little unlucky not to get closer.
**Starry Lodge(IRE)** set the standard on the back of his third in the John Smith's Cup and proved disappointing. He held the ideal position throughout and came with his challenge, but could not sustain the run.
**Hambleden** ran his usual race from the front and was readily outpaced when the challengers came. He hides nothing from the Handicapper.
**Sir George Turner** looked as though he was on his way back at Goodwood after a long spell in the wilderness but, having been held up right at the back, did not pick up and looked far from in love with the game. He undoubtedly has plenty of ability and is on a good mark, but is clearly a tricky customer.
**Muhareb(USA)** shaped with promise on his seasonal return last month, but failed to run up to anything like that form and ended up well beaten. He is better than this but is clearly one to treat with caution.
**Akash(IRE)** could be given a chance on early-season form, but he had not been seen since disappointing at the Guineas meeting and dropped away tamely having raced in second for most of the way, although admittedly he was hampered when weakening. He is not one to give up on though, as his best form is on soft ground, and there is sure to be a decent handicap in him towards to end of the season.

## 4531 DUBAI DUTY FREE SHERGAR CUP SPRINT (RATED STKS H'CAP) 6f (R)
4:20 (4:30) (B ) (0-100,97) 3-Y-O £22,550 (£7,892; £3,608; £2,818) **Stalls** High

Form RPR

-042 **1** **Paradise Isle**[28] [3744] 3-9-1 **91** ........ WCMarwing 4 105
(CFWall) *mde all: drew clr fnl 2f: unchal* **14/1**

2141 **2** *3* **Alderney Race (USA)**[32] [3598] 3-9-7 **97** ........ KDarley 5 102+
(RCharlton) *hld up in midfield: nt clr run 2f out: prog over 1f out: r.o to chse wnr last 100yds: no ch* **3/1**[1]

2-41 **3** *1/2* **Khabfair**[15] [4076] 3-9-4 **94** 3ex ........ DVargiu 9 98
(MrsAJPerrett) *trckd ldrs: rdn and effrt 2f out: chsd wnr 1f out to last 100yds: kpt on* **7/2**[2]

3004 **4** *1 1/2* **Glaramara**[28] [3730] 3-9-7 **97** ........ KFallon 8 96
(ABailey) *settled in last trio: brought wd and drvn over 2f out: styd on fr over 1f out: nt rch ldrs* **14/1**

2611 **5** *nk* **Commando Scott (IRE)**[16] [4051] 3-9-0 **90** 3ex ........ MJKinane 1 88
(ABerry) *lw: prom: chsd wnr over 2f out: no imp: lost 2nd and fdd 1f out* **11/1**

122 **6** *1/2* **Doitnow (IRE)**[21] [3941] 3-8-13 **89** ........ LDettori 10 86
(RAFahey) *s.i.s: racd on inner in rr: effrt over 2f out: no hdwy over 1f out* **3/1**[1]

6005 **7** *1 3/4* **Nero's Return (IRE)**[15] [4076] 3-9-3 **93** ........ YTake 3 84
(MJohnston) *racd in midfield: rdn and effrt 2f out: wknd fnl f* **25/1**

3600 **8** *1/2* **High Voltage**[32] [3598] 3-9-4 **94** ........ DMOliver 7 84
(KRBurke) *chsd wnr to over 2f out: wknd over 1f out* **20/1**

0442 **9** *2* **Valjarv (IRE)**[22] [3914] 3-9-2 **92** ........(v[1]) JPMurtagh 2 76
(NPLittmoden) *dwlt and drvn s: nvr gng wl: a in last pair* **7/1**[3]

0000 **10** *4* **Danzig River (IRE)**[13] [4165] 3-9-3 **93** ........ JPSpencer 6 65
(BWHills) *a in rr: rdn and no prog over 2f out* **25/1**

1m 14.37s **10** Ran SP% **118.8**
Speed ratings: CSF £55.71 CT £188.56 TOTE £15.00: £3.10, £1.90, £1.80; EX 81.90 Trifecta £291.20 Pool: £1,599.72. 3.90 winning tickets. Place 6 £579.47, Place 5 £258.93.
**Owner** The Equema Partnership **Bred** Jeremy Green And Sons **Trained** Newmarket, Suffolk
■ The first winner in this country for South African rider Weichong Marwing.

**FOCUS**
No median time for the round six furlongs, so no speed figures can be calculated. A decent sprint, but the winner dictated the pace and, running well above previous marks, gives the form a suspect look.

**NOTEBOOK**
**Paradise Isle** owes much of her success to a fine tactical ride by Marwing. Having broken smartly, she was soon in the lead and settled well enough under her pilot, who reduced the pace to only a modest one, and in doing so caused all those in behind to fight for their heads. He sat quietly on her until about a furlong and a half out where she quickened away before staying on strongly to win comfortably. She had been doing all her racing this season over five, and the return to six furlongs brought about an improved performance. There may be more to come from her.
**Alderney Race(USA)** was racing off a 6lb higher mark than when winning a competitive sprint at Newmarket last month, and was a little unlucky not to get closer but would never have beaten the winner. He remains progressive and, as he would have been unsuited by the way race was run, better can be expected of him back in big-field sprint on a straight course.
**Khabfair** did it nicely at the course last month and again ran well, simply being unable to cope with the winner's burst of speed. He is lightly raced, going the right way, and has similar preferences to the second, needing a big-field sprint on a straight course.
**Glaramara** did well to finish as close as he did, as his best form is over seven furlongs and he was in the wrong place considering the pace they went. He has not won this season, but has run several good races and will get his turn again despite remaining high enough in the weights.
**Commando Scott(IRE)** was bidding to land a hat-trick having won in soft ground at Haydock and Doncaster, but could not defy a 6lb higher mark under these livlier conditions.
**Doitnow(IRE)** proved disappointing as he had previously been progressive. He can be given another chance, as the race may not have been run to suit.
**Nero's Return(IRE)** ran one of his better races, but has still to prove he has trained on and questions remain unanswered over the best trip for him. He is still too high in the weights.
**High Voltage** is firmly in the grip of the Handicapper and has struggled of late.
**Valjarv(IRE)** was never going in the first-time visor and proved disappointing.
**Danzig River(IRE)** continues out of form. *Official explanation: jockey said colt was hanging left throughout*
T/Plt: £267.70 to a £1 stake. Pool: £89,431.30. 243.85 winning tickets. T/Qpdt: £28.90 to a £1 stake. Pool: £5,201.00. 133.10 winning tickets. JN

# 4003 AYR (L-H)
Saturday, August 7
**OFFICIAL GOING: Good to firm (good in places)**

## 4532 ADVERTISINGWORKS EUROPEAN BREEDERS FUND MAIDEN STKS 6f
6:05 (6:05) (D ) 2-Y-O £5,460 (£1,680; £840; £420) **Stalls** Low

Form RPR

2 **1** **Epiphany**[15] [4074] 2-8-9 ........ SSanders 1 74+
(EALDunlop) *led to appr fnl f: rallied to ld ins last: all out* **4/11**[1]

**2** *shd* **Mintlaw** 2-8-9 ........ RWinston 4 74+
(ISemple) *missed break: hdwy and prom over 3f out: rdn to ld appr fnl f: hdd ins last: rallied: jst hld* **33/1**

**3** *3* **Branston Lily** 2-8-9 ........ PHanagan 6 65
(GASwinbank) *trckd ldrs: rdn over 2f out: one pce fnl f* **12/1**[3]

**4** *shd* **Emerald Bay (IRE)** 2-9-0 ........ JFanning 7 70
(MJohnston) *disp ld: rdn over 2f out: one pce fr over 1f out* **7/2**[2]

66 **5** *8* **Geojimali**[19] [3974] 2-8-7 ........ JCurrie(7) 5 46
(JSGoldie) *bhd and sn outpcd: sme late hdwy: nvr on terms* **66/1**

66 **6** *3 1/2* **Quick Grand (IRE)**[10] [4245] 2-8-9 ........ RFfrench 3 30
(MissLAPerratt) *sn outpcd: nvr on terms* **100/1**

000 **7** *6* **The Terminator (IRE)**[44] [3233] 2-9-0 ........(p) PBradley 2 17
(ABerry) *prom tl rdn and wknd 2f out* **100/1**

1m 13.01s (-0.71) **Going Correction** -0.225s/f (Firm) **7** Ran SP% **109.6**
Speed ratings: **95,94,90,90,80 75,67**CSF £18.03 TOTE £1.30: £1.02, £11.70; EX 12.30.
**Owner** Cliveden Stud **Bred** Cliveden Stud Ltd **Trained** Newmarket, Suffolk

**FOCUS**
An run-of-the-mill event that did not unfold the way the betting suggested it might. Although the bare form is ordinary, the principals look capable of better and the race may well throw up a winner or two.

**NOTEBOOK**
**Epiphany** looked the one to beat on her Ascot run, but was made to work very hard by a rival that may well have prevailed had she had the benefit of experience. The step up to seven furlongs may help but she may have to improve to win in nursery company.
**Mintlaw ♦**, who is related to three juvenile winners over sprint distances, is on the leg at present but showed more than enough after losing ground at the start to suggest she can win a similar race with this experience behind her.
**Branston Lily**, related to three-time juvenile winner over sprint distances Branston Pickle, ran creditably on this racecourse debut and looks sure to come on for the experience.
**Emerald Bay(IRE)**, related to a mile and a quarter winner, showed more than enough on this racecourse debut to suggest he can win a race, especially granted a stiffer test of stamina.
**Geojimali** was again soundly beaten, but remains the sort likely to do better in low-grade handicaps over further in due course.
**Quick Grand(IRE)** is likely to continue to look vulnerable in this grade.

## 4533 TOTESPORT.COM CLASSIFIED STKS 1m 2f
6:35 (6:35) (D ) 3-Y-O+ £5,336 (£1,642; £821; £410) **Stalls** Low

Form RPR

-536 **1** **Bessemer (JPN)**[40] [3365] 3-8-9 81 ........ RWinston 4 92+
(ISemple) *prom: smooth hdwy to press ldr over 1f out: shkn up to ld ins fnl f: comf* **4/1**[3]

3216 **2** *1 1/4* **Barking Mad (USA)**[13] [4173] 6-9-7 84 ........ SSanders 1 89
(MLWBell) *led: rdn over 2f out: hdd ins fnl f: no ch w wnr* **7/4**[1]

3020 **3** *14* **Mbosi (USA)**[7] [4319] 3-8-12 84 ........ JFanning 2 62
(MJohnston) *pressed ldr tl wknd 2f out* **15/8**[2]

-431 **4** *14* **On Every Street**[48] [3129] 3-8-8 77 ........(v) RFfrench 3 32
(RBastiman) *cl up tl wknd fr over 2f out* **11/2**

2m 6.75s (-5.44) **Going Correction** -0.225s/f (Firm)
**WFA** 3 from 6yo 9lb **4** Ran SP% **106.5**
Speed ratings: **112,111,99,88**CSF £10.99 TOTE £5.40; EX 13.40.
**Owner** Clarke Boon **Bred** Darley Stud **Trained** Carluke, S Lanarks

**FOCUS**
An uncompetitive event run at an apparently steady early pace, but the time was very decent for the grade. Although the winner had more in hand than the margin suggests, this bare form may not prove entirely reliable as only the first two showed their form.

**NOTEBOOK**
**Bessemer(JPN)**, having his first run for his new stable, won with a bit more in hand than the official margin suggests to extend his unbeaten record at this course. However this was not much of a race and he will face a stiffer test back in handicap company.
**Barking Mad(USA)** had the run of the race and did nothing wrong but is another that will face a much stiffer task back in competitive handicap company from his current mark.
**Mbosi(USA)** had a good chance at the weights and had the run of the race, but was again a long way below his very best and remains one to tread carefully with.
**On Every Street**, with the tongue-strap left off on this first start for new connections, ran poorly and looks one to tread carefully with in the near future.

## 4534 DM HALL H'CAP 6f
7:05 (7:06) (E ) (0-70,69) 3-Y-O+ £5,512 (£1,696; £848; £424) **Stalls** Low

Form RPR

0510 **1** **Marshallspark (IRE)**[13] [4179] 5-9-9 **65** ........ PHanagan 5 77
(RAFahey) *prom: rdn to ld over 1f out: r.o strly* **4/1**[2]

0050 **2** *1 1/2* **Strawberry Patch (IRE)**[9] [4279] 5-8-10 **52** ........(p) SSanders 6 60
(MissLAPerratt) *sn niggled in rr: hdwy over 1f out: kpt on: nt rch wnr* **6/1**

1034 **3** *1* **Albashoosh**[8] [4291] 6-9-13 **69** ........ AlexGreaves 1 74
(DNicholls) *hld up in tch: hdwy whn n.m.r over 1f out: r.o same pce wl ins fnl f* **7/4**[1]

6000 **4** *3/4* **Star Applause**[9] [4279] 4-7-9 **40** oh5 ........ NMackay(3) 7 42
(JSGoldie) *in tch: effrt centre over 1f out: no imp fnl f* **33/1**

6666 **5** *1 1/4* **College Maid (IRE)**[10] [4248] 7-8-10 **59** ........(v) JCurrie(7) 8 58
(JSGoldie) *disp ld to over 1f out: outpcd ins last* **9/1**

0600 **6** *1* **Pharaoh Hatshepsut (IRE)**[9] [4260] 6-7-12 **40** oh14 ........(b) PFessey 4 36
(JamesMoffatt) *trckd ldrs tl rdn and wknd over 1f out* **66/1**



The Form Book, Raceform Ltd, Compton, RG20 6NL

0404 **7** 1 ½ **Tuscan Flyer**22 3894 6-9-5 **61**....(b) RFfrench 2 52
(RBastiman) *mde most to over 1f out: sn btn* **9/2**3

0420 **8** 1 ¾ **Danakim**3 4452 7-7-5 **40**.... DFentiman(7) 3 26
(JRWeymes) *trckd ldrs tl wknd over 1f out* **10/1**

1m 11.87s (-1.85) **Going Correction** -0.225s/f (Firm) **8** Ran SP% **112.4**
Speed ratings: **103,101,99,98,97 95,93,91**CSF £27.06 CT £55.36 TOTE £5.10: £1.90, £1.40, £1.10; EX 17.70.
**Owner** J J Staunton **Bred** Mrs Teresa Bergin **Trained** Musley Bank, N Yorks
■ Stewards Enquiry : R Ffrench one-day ban: careless riding (Aug 20)

**FOCUS**
An ordinary event in which Albashoosh disappointed at short odds for the third time in his last four starts. This bare form is ordinary and may not prove entirely reliable.

**NOTEBOOK**
**Marshallspark(IRE)** had disappointed at Pontefract on his previous start but showed that form to be all wrong with a fluent win. He had the run of the race though, and may look vulnerable in a more competitive event after reassessment.
**Strawberry Patch(IRE)** ran his best race of the year returned to this trip and, although on a long losing run, may be able to pick up a small event away from progressive performers from this current mark. He seems best on a sound surface.
**Albashoosh**'s Goodwood run looked to give him solid claims in this company but he found this less-truly run race a different ballgame and was below that level after meeting trouble. A strongly-run race over this trip where the leaders come back to him suits his requirements these days, but he is not really one to be lumping on at short odds.
**Star Applause**, having her first start for new connections, was not disgraced from 5lb out of the handicap having made ground on the outside of the main group, and so may be a bit better than the bare form. She shaped as though worth a try over a bit further.
**College Maid(IRE)** has struggled from marks in the low 60s since winning over seven at this course in May, and she will have to show a bit more before she is a betting proposition once again.
**Pharaoh Hatshepsut(IRE)**, down in trip, was not totally disgraced but did not really shape as though she was a winner waiting to happen.

## 4535 JOHN CONROY (BATCHELOR) CLAIMING STKS 7f 50y
7:35 (7:36) (E) 3-Y-0+ **£3,559** (£1,095; £547; £273) **Stalls** Low

Form RPR

1651 **1** **Bailieborough (IRE)**9 4276 5-9-9 68....(v) AlexGreaves 6 75
(DNicholls) *hld up in tch: smooth hdwy to ld over 2f out: rdn and edgd rt ins fnl f: r.o* **7/4**1

3505 **2** ½ **Sarraaf (IRE)**9 4276 8-9-3 65.... NMackay(3) 8 71
(JSGoldie) *hld up in tch: hdwy outside to press wnr over 1f out: r.o ins last* **9/4**2

5360 **3** 7 **Compassion (IRE)**5 4387 3-8-2 46....(p) RFfrench 9 41
(MissLAPerratt) *chsd ldrs: effrt 2f out: sn outpcd* **20/1**

400P **4** 1 **Puri**36 3490 5-9-4 50....(v1) JFanning 4 48
(JGGiven) *prom: rdn over 2f out: sn no ex* **25/1**

4024 **5** nk **Zahunda (IRE)**10 4248 5-8-8 40.... SSanders 2 37
(WMBrisbourne) *led to over 2f out: wknd over 1f out* **4/1**3

6002 **6** 2 **Vijay (IRE)**9 4257 5-8-13 45.... RWinston 5 37
(ISemple) *prom: effrt over 2f out: btn over 1f out* **6/1**

0000 **7** 5 **Needwood Bucolic (IRE)**18 4004 6-8-6 33....(b1) DFentiman(7) 1 24
(RAllan) *hld up: rdn 3f out: sn btn* **100/1**

0000 **8** 3 **Lion's Domane**18 4004 7-9-1 44.... PHanagan 3 18
(ABerry) *w ldr tl wknd over 2f out* **33/1**

0-00 **9** dist **The Spook**5 4386 4-8-10 39.... PMulrennan(3) 7 —
(WMBrisbourne) *missed break: sn lost tch* **50/1**

1m 31.16s (-1.31) **Going Correction** -0.225s/f (Firm)
**WFA** 3 from 4yo+ 6lb **9** Ran SP% **115.9**
Speed ratings: **98,97,89,88,87 85,79,76,—**CSF £5.60 TOTE £2.90: £1.20, £1.30, £3.80; EX 6.40.
**Owner** Middleham Park Racing Xviii **Bred** Churchtown Stud **Trained** Sessay, N Yorks

**FOCUS**
A low-grade event in which the market leaders came to the fore and the pace seemed sound. This bare form should prove reliable, with the second being the yardstick.

**NOTEBOOK**
**Bailieborough(IRE)** has not always looked entirely reliable, but he is a fair sort in this grade and is effective from seven to nine furlongs. He notched his fourth win from his last eight starts and should continue to go well in this company.
**Sarraaf(IRE)**, who had a good chance at the weights, did not do much wrong on the face of it, and may be a bit better than the bare form as he made his ground on the outside. However he is not one to place too much faith in.
**Compassion(IRE)** was not disgraced in the face of a stiff task, but he is not the most consistent and the fact she has yet to win a race has to be a concern.
**Puri**, tried in a first-time visor, is another that was not totally disgraced in the face of a stiff task but, on this evidence, is not going to be one that will be easy to place successfully.
**Zahunda(IRE)** was disappointing, even allowing for the fact she had something to find at the weights, and she was not helped by being taken on in the early stages. She is capable of winning a small race, but a record of one win from 35 starts inspires little confidence.
**Vijay(IRE)** is essentially a disappointing sort that did not improve for the return to this trip. He is not one to place too much faith in.

## 4536 TOTEQUADPOT H'CAP 1m 2f 192y
8:05 (8:07) (E) (0-70,70) 3-Y-0 **£3,575** (£1,100; £550; £275) **Stalls** Low

Form RPR

0240 **1** **Rutters Rebel (IRE)**21 3953 3-9-4 **70**.... PMulrennan(3) 3 77
(GASwinbank) *in tch: effrt over 2f out: led wl ins fnl f: r.o* **15/2**3

-021 **2** ½ **Quarrymount**14 4128 3-9-0 **63**.... SSanders 1 69
(SirMarkPrescott) *led: rdn over 2f out: hdd wl ins fnl f: one pce* **11/8**1

1251 **3** ½ **Richtee (IRE)**8 4307 3-9-7 **70**.... PHanagan 2 75
(RAFahey) *keen: cl up: effrt over 2f out: kpt on ins fnl f* **7/4**2

0034 **4** ½ **Saameq (IRE)**23 3881 3-8-0 **49**.... PFessey 5 53
(ISemple) *hld up: effrt over 2f out: kpt on fnl f: no imp* **10/1**

1343 **5** 1 ¼ **Charlie Tango (IRE)**10 4249 3-9-5 **68**.... RWinston 7 70
(NTinkler) *prom: effrt over 2f out: one pce fnl f* **9/1**

0066 **6** ¾ **Prelude**8 4307 3-8-11 **60**.... JFanning 4 61
(WMBrisbourne) *hld up in tch: rdn over 2f out: one pce over 1f out* **16/1**

045 **7** 17 **Columbian Emerald (IRE)**51 3013 3-8-3 **52**.... RFfrench 6 24
(TJEtherington) *cl up to 3f out: sn rdn and wknd* **50/1**

2m 20.01s (-3.31) **Going Correction** -0.225s/f (Firm) **7** Ran SP% **117.2**
Speed ratings: **103,102,102,101,101 100,88**CSF £19.07 TOTE £10.80: £4.30, £1.30; EX 43.00.
**Owner** Mrs Michele Rutter **Bred** Epona Bloodstock Ltd **Trained** Melsonby, N Yorks

**FOCUS**
Another ordinary handicap in which the runner-up was allowed to dictate. The field finished in a bunch and this bare form may prove less than reliable.

**NOTEBOOK**
**Rutters Rebel(IRE)** proved well suited by the return to a sound surface and elected to put his best foot forward. A stronger pace should suit and, as he should not be going up too much for this win, may be capable of further success away from progressive sorts.
**Quarrymount**, upped in trip for the return to turf, ran creditably having enjoyed very much the run of the race. However, with the benefit of hindsight, may have been better served by making this a stronger test of stamina. He is capable of winning again in this grade.
**Richtee(IRE)** ran creditably but did not do her prospects much good by taking a keen grip in the early stages, and would almost certainly have been suited by a stronger gallop. She is worth another chance when the emphasis is more on stamina.
**Saameq(IRE)** looked in good shape and fared the best of those that came from off the steady pace. Consequently he looks a bit better than the bare form, and can win a small event in the 0-55 bracket granted a stiffer test of stamina.
**Charlie Tango(IRE)** was not totally disgraced up in trip, but left the impression that a more strongly-run race over shorter would have been in his favour.
**Prelude**, weighted to get closer to Richtee on recent evidence, was not totally disgraced and is another from this race that may have been better served by a stiffer test. However, she will have to improve to win from her current mark.

## 4537 KIDZPLAY H'CAP 1m 1f 20y
8:35 (8:38) (E) (0-70,68) 3-Y-0+ **£3,645** (£1,121; £560; £280) **Stalls** Low

Form RPR

500- **1** **Royal Indulgence**320 5126 4-8-7 **43**.... JFanning 10 55
(WMBrisbourne) *dwlt: keen in rr: stdy hdwy over 2f out: led ins fnl f: r.o wl: comf* **33/1**

0506 **2** 1 ¾ **Skiddaw Jones**65 2618 4-8-11 **47**.... RFfrench 8 56
(MissLAPerratt) *prom: rdn to ld over 1f out: hdd ins fnl f: kpt on: no ch w wnr* **9/1**

0164 **3** nk **Cryfield**11 4209 7-9-10 **60**.... KimTinkler 4 68
(NTinkler) *trckd ldrs: rdn over 2f out: sn outpcd: kpt on fnl f* **6/1**3

0031 **4** ½ **Gifted Flame**5 4386 5-10-4 **68** 6ex.... SSanders 9 75
(TDBarron) *dwlt: hld up: hdwy on outside over 2f out: effrt and ch 1f out: sn rdn and nt qckn* **3/1**1

6050 **5** ¾ **Market Avenue**18 4008 5-9-8 **58**.... PHanagan 1 64
(RAFahey) *keen: hld up in tch: effrt over 2f out: one pce fnl f* **4/1**2

0616 **6** 5 **Wood Dalling (USA)**18 4008 6-9-6 **56**.... RWinston 5 52
(ISemple) *led 3f: cl up: disp ld over 2f to over 1f out: sn no ex* **4/1**2

0526 **7** ¾ **Forest Air (IRE)**18 4005 4-8-10 **46**....(p) PBradley 7 40
(MissLAPerratt) *keen: led after 3f to over 1f out: sn btn* **11/1**

0400 **8** shd **Colloseum**44 3231 3-8-10 **54**.... DMcGaffin 11 48
(TJEtherington) *hld up: effrt over 2f out: btn over 1f out* **33/1**

-006 **9** 1 **Howards Rocket**22 3899 3-8-0 **47**.... NMackay(3) 3 39
(JSGoldie) *in tch tl wknd over 2f out* **10/1**

00/0 **10** 1 **Society Times (USA)**9 4276 11-7-5 **34** oh10....(t) DFentiman(7) 12 24
(DANolan) *racd wd: hld up: hdwy over 3f out: wknd 2f out* **100/1**

600/ **11** 9 **Zandeed (IRE)**662 5276 6-9-7 **60**.... PMulrennan(3) 2 32
(MissLAPerratt) *keen: trckd ldrs tl wknd over 2f out* **25/1**

0000 **12** ¾ **Environmentalist**9 4276 5-7-12 **34** oh4....(bt) PFessey 6 4
(DANolan) *prom to 3f out: sn wknd* **100/1**

1m 56.68s (0.14) **Going Correction** -0.225s/f (Firm)
**WFA** 3 from 4yo+ 8lb **12** Ran SP% **118.4**
Speed ratings: **90,88,88,87,87 82,81,81,80,80 72,71**CSF £298.88 CT £2045.62 TOTE £38.70: £5.50, £2.90, £2.80; EX 422.90 Place 6 £127.56, Place 5 £94.14..
**Owner** P G Evans **Bred** P V And J P Jackson **Trained** Great Ness, Shropshire

**FOCUS**
A very moderate handicap and a less than true gallop resulted in a very slow time for the grade. The form appears reasonably sound, but the winner looks a bit better than the bare form, as he came from a most uncompromising position, and he is one to keep an eye on.

**NOTEBOOK**
**Royal Indulgence** ◆ turned in a fluent display on this first start for new connections and looks a bit better than the bare form as he made up plenty of ground off the steady pace. He looks the type to win again for his shrewd stable.
**Skiddaw Jones** seems to reserve his best efforts for this course and ran creditably. He did have the run of the race though, and would be no certainty to reproduce this next time.
**Cryfield** was not disgraced but left the impression that a stiffer test of stamina over this trip would have been in his favour.
**Gifted Flame** ran creditably under his penalty and may be better than the bare form, as he made up his ground wide of the field but was another in this field, to leave the impression that a much stiffer test over this trip would have suited.
**Market Avenue** is another that would have been suited by a stronger pace over this trip. However, she is becoming expensive to follow and may not be one to place maximum faith in.
**Wood Dalling(USA)** had the run of the race but was again below the form of his Carlisle win. He does not look one to place too much faith in.
T/Plt: £103.00 to a £1 stake. Pool: £31,158.00. 220.70 winning tickets. T/Qpdt: £10.00 to a £1 stake. Pool: £2,467.20. 180.80 winning tickets. RY

# 4507 HAYDOCK (L-H)
Saturday, August 7

**OFFICIAL GOING: Good**
The ground was faster than it was the previous night after a drying day, but seemed rather dead and few horses were able to challenge from off the pace.

## 4538 CORAL.CO.UK H'CAP 5f
1:55 (1:57) (C) (0-100,94) 3-Y-0+ **£17,862** (£5,496; £2,748; £1,374) **Stalls** Centre

Form RPR

0400 **1** **Smokin Beau**7 4324 7-9-9 **93**.... JFanning 17 104
(NPLittmoden) *mde most on stands' side: rdn over 1f out: r.o wl* **25/1**

5540 **2** ½ **Devise (IRE)**10 4232 5-8-6 **79**.... RMiles(3) 8 88
(MSSaunders) *w ldr centre: rdn 1/2-way: styd on ins fnl f* **11/1**

2360 **3** ¾ **Corridor Creeper (FR)**7 4324 7-9-10 **94**....(p) FNorton 2 101
(JMBradley) *chsd ldrs far side: rdn over 1f out: styd on* **22/1**

1403 **4** ½ **Whistler**6 4366 7-9-6 **90**....(p) RHills 1 95
(JMBradley) *bhd far side: n.m.r 2f out: swtchd rt over 1f out: r.o fnl f: nrst fin* **12/1**

0016 **5** nk **Zarzu**22 3920 5-8-4 **79**.... RThomas(5) 16 83+
(CRDore) *bhd stands' side: rdn over 2f out: hdwy over 1f out: r.o* **25/1**

0004 **6** shd **Maktavish**26 3795 5-8-11 **81**....(p) PHanagan 10 84
(ISemple) *w ldr stands' side: rdn 2f out: kpt on same pce* **20/1**

1100 **7** shd **Raccoon (IRE)**7 4324 4-9-6 **90**....(v) SSanders 20 93
(TDBarron) *in tch stands' side: rdn 2f out: styd on fnl f* **10/3**1

1450 **8** 1 **Dancing Mystery**6 4366 10-8-12 **82**.... SCarson 14 81
(EAWheeler) *hld up stands' side: rdn over 2f out: styd on fnl f* **50/1**

0604 **9** ½ **Malapropism**6 4366 4-8-11 **81**.... ACulhane 6 79
(MRChannon) *sn led far side gp: rdn over 1f out: fdd ins fnl f* **16/1**

0005 **10** 1 **Matty Tun**36 3480 5-9-3 **87**.... WSupple 11 81
(JBalding) *s.i.s: sn chsd ldrs stands' side: rdn 1/2-way: wknd 1f out* **20/1**

4140 **11** ½ **Connect**6 4366 7-9-10 **94**....(b) PRobinson 18 86
(MHTompkins) *bhd on stands' side: rdn 1/2-way: nvr trbld ldrs* **20/1**

1450 **12** *shd* **Blackheath (IRE)**[7] 4324 8-8-13 **88** ............ LTreadwell(5) 13 80
(DNicholls) *bhd on stands' side: nvr on terms* **25/1**
6201 **13** *nk* **Awake**[14] 4133 7-9-1 **85** ............ ANicholls 4 76
(DNicholls) *chsd ldr far side: outpcd fnl f* **12/1**
0500 **14** *1* **Local Poet**[32] 3598 3-8-13 **86** ............ (t) GGibbons 9 73
(BAMcmahon) *prom stands' side: wknd over 1f out* **66/1**
0300 **15** *3/4* **Henry Hall (IRE)**[21] 3945 8-9-9 **93** ............ KimTinkler 19 77
(NTinkler) *a bhd on stands' side* **33/1**
0010 **16** *hd* **Artie**[7] 4324 5-9-3 **87** ............ RWinston 3 71
(TDEasterby) *led early on far side: rdn 2f out: wknd ins fnl f* **10/1**
2032 **17** *hd* **Cape Royal**[6] 4366 4-9-4 **88** ............ JFortune 7 71
(MrsJRRamsden) *t.k.h: hld up on far side: nvr trbld ldrs* **9/1**[3]
0451 **18** *nk* **Salviati (USA)**[6] 4366 7-8-13 **83** 6ex ............ (p) EAhern 15 65+
(JMBradley) *dwlt: bhd on stands' side: rdn 2f out: n.m.r 1f out: sn eased* **15/2**[2]
0651 **19** *2* **Ptarmigan Ridge**[26] 3795 8-9-2 **86** ............ MFenton 5 61
(MissLAPerratt) *in rr on far side: hmpd over 1f out: n.d* **20/1**
1050 **L** **Piccled**[13] 4165 6-8-13 **83** ............ DAllan 12 —
(EJAlston) *ref to r: tk no part* **33/1**

59.24 secs (-2.83) **Going Correction** -0.40s/f (Firm)
**WFA** 3 from 4yo+ 3lb **20** Ran SP% **127.8**
Speed ratings: **106,105,104,103,102 102,102,100,100,98 97,97,96,95,94 93,93,93,89,**—CSF £245.03 CT £6190.13 TOTE £29.30: £5.10, £3.90, £4.80, £2.70; EX 748.50.
**Owner** Turf 2000 Limited **Bred** Alan Spargo **Trained** Newmarket, Suffolk

**FOCUS**
A very competitive handicap and the form looks solid. The field split into two groups, one on the far side and the other in the centre-to-stands' side which was favoured. Few got into it from off the pace.

**NOTEBOOK**
**Smokin Beau** gained his first win since October 2002, when he was 17lb higher than he was here, and will still be well treated after this. Despite stumbling as he exited the stalls, he was always to the fore and the change of tactics did the trick.
**Devise(IRE)** showed good pace in the centre of the track and was keeping on at the finish. An intermediate trip of five and a half furlongs could prove his optimum.
**Corridor Creeper(FR)**, back at the minimum trip after fading in the Stewards' Cup, ran well on the unfavoured flank. He is still 9lb higher than when last winning.
**Whistler**, successful in this valuable event a year ago from a 12lb lower mark, ran well from a low draw and would have finished closer had he not met trouble with a quarter of a mile to run.
**Zarzu** finished well from off the pace, and although 7lb higher than when scoring at Musselburgh he is still competitive off this mark.
**Maktavish** showed his customary dash on the stands' side and only faded out of the places inside the final furlong.
**Raccoon(IRE)**, who had run well in the Stewards' Cup over six, appeared to find this a bit too sharp and was unable to take advantage of a good draw.
**Malapropism**showed good speed to lead the far-side group until inside the final furlong.
**Salviati(USA)**, under a 6lb penelty, was unable to overcome his regular slow start on this occasion.
**Ptarmigan Ridge** *Official explanation: jockey said horse lost its action behind*

## 4539 PETROS ROSE OF LANCASTER STKS (GROUP 3) 1m 2f 120y
**2:30** (2:34) (A) 3-Y-0+ **£37,700** (£14,300; £7,150; £3,250) **Stalls** High

Form RPR
-211 **1** **Mister Monet (IRE)**[14] 4118 3-8-7 106 ............ JFanning 6 124+
(MJohnston) *led early: chsd ldr: led over 3f out: rdn over 2f out: clr and edgd lft over 1f out: kpt on* **1/1**[1]
-011 **2** *1 1/2* **Muqbil (USA)**[21] 3936 4-9-3 114 ............ RHills 4 119
(JLDunlop) *hld up in tch: impr to chse wnr over 2f out: hung lft ins fnl f: styd on towards fin* **5/2**[2]
0340 **3** *5* **Checkit (IRE)**[10] 4228 4-9-3 112 ............ ACulhane 2 111
(MRChannon) *hld up: rdn over 2f out: kpt on fnl f: no imp on ldrs* **13/2**[3]
10-4 **4** *1 3/4* **Franklins Gardens**[105] 1622 4-9-3 108 ............ PRobinson 5 108
(MHTompkins) *hld up: effrt over 2f out: nvr able to chal* **14/1**
1-00 **5** *1* **Lateen Sails**[53] 2957 4-9-3 110 ............ (t) KMcEvoy 3 106
(SaeedBinSuroor) *sn led: hdd over 3f out: wknd 2f out* **12/1**
1000 **6** *3/4* **Chancellor (IRE)**[35] 3540 6-9-7 110 ............ JFortune 1 109
(JLDunlop) *chsd ldrs: rdn over 3f out: wknd over 2f out* **40/1**

2m 10.4s (-7.33) **Going Correction** -0.40s/f (Firm)
**WFA** 3 from 4yo+ 10lb **6** Ran SP% **108.7**
Speed ratings: **110,108,105,104,103 102**CSF £3.35 TOTE £2.00: £1.10, £2.00; EX 3.20.
**Owner** Syndicate 2002 **Bred** Barronstown Stud, Orpendale And Mrs T Stack **Trained** Middleham Moor, N Yorks

**FOCUS**
Quite a decent pace but the winning time was no more than ordinary for the grade. The runners made for the centre of the track once in line for home. Both the first and second are better than this grade.

**NOTEBOOK**
**Mister Monet(IRE)** successfully made the big jump from handicaps to Group Three company. He quickened well to take up the running, but edged over to the far rail and idled quite markedly in front, pricking his ears and looking as if he might pull himself up near the line. He is clearly still green and there is plenty more to come from him as he gains experience, with the Champion Stakes at Newmarket his end-of-season target.
**Muqbil(USA)** hung when giving chase to the progressive winner and was unable to get to him, although he was running on near the line. He finished clear of the rest and remains capable of winning another race at this level.
**Checkit(IRE)** put in another creditable effort but this run merely underlines how hard a horse he is to place.
**Franklins Gardens** had a difficult task trying to come from off the pace but did pass a couple of rivals. The return to a mile and a half could pay off.
**Lateen Sails** settled well enough in front but did not have any answers when headed. Front-running tactics worked well on his final start of last season but he has been picked off each time this year and a different approach might be required.
**Chancellor(IRE)**, saddled with a Group Three penalty for his win in the Gordon Richards Stakes in April, has failed to beat a single rival in four runs since.

## 4540 TOTESPORT STKS (HERITAGE H'CAP) 1m 2f 120y
**3:00** (3:03) (B) (0-105,106) 3-Y-0+ **£43,500** (£16,500; £8,250; £3,750) **Stalls** High

Form RPR
5631 **1** **Dunaskin (IRE)**[14] 4136 4-8-6 **83** ............ DKinsella 2 95
(DEddy) *mde all: clr 4f out: kpt on wl ins fnl f* **50/1**
2-01 **2** *1* **Coat Of Honour (USA)**[11] 4214 4-9-6 **97** ............ SSanders 11 107
(SirMarkPrescott) *a.p: rdn over 2f out: chalng ins fnl f: no ex towards fin* **5/1**[2]
3233 **3** *nk* **Shahzan House (IRE)**[36] 3482 5-9-5 **96** ............ (p) PRobinson 14 106
(MAJarvis) *chsd ldrs: rdn over 2f out: styd on* **14/1**
3304 **4** *1 1/2* **Mutafanen**[9] 4271 3-9-2 **103** ............ (v[1]) WSupple 12 110+
(EALDunlop) *hld up: rdn over 3f out: hdwy over 1f out: styd on ins fnl f* **14/1**
-101 **5** *1 1/4* **King Of Dreams (IRE)**[13] 4173 3-8-7 **94** ............ RFfrench 4 99
(MJohnston) *chsd ldrs: rdn over 3f out: kpt on ins fnl f* **9/2**[1]
0553 **6** *1 1/4* **Bonecrusher**[11] 4214 5-9-12 **106** ............ (v) ABeech(3) 3 109+
(DRLoder) *hld up: rdn over 3f out: hdwy over 2f out: styd on* **9/1**[3]
112 **7** *nk* **Mutasallil (USA)**[13] 4163 4-9-9 **100** ............ (t) RHills 8 102
(SaeedBinSuroor) *midfield: rdn over 3f out: kpt on one pce fnl 2f* **9/1**[3]
0426 **8** *1/2* **Windy Britain**[11] 4214 5-8-11 **88** ............ JFortune 18 90
(LMCumani) *s.s: hld up: hdwy over 3f out: n.m.r over 1f out: styd on* **10/1**
1-16 **9** *3/4* **Ski Jump (USA)**[45] 3207 4-8-8 **85** ............ (v[1]) PHanagan 13 85
(RAFahey) *towards rr: outpcd over 3f out: kpt on fr 2f out* **33/1**
1103 **10** *2* **Silvaline**[7] 4343 5-8-3 **80** ............ PDoe 17 77
(TKeddy) *bhd: hdwy over 3f out: no imp on ldrs* **33/1**
2220 **11** *1/2* **James Caird (IRE)**[21] 3937 4-8-9 **86** ............ MHenry 16 82
(MHTompkins) *in tch: rdn over 2f out: no imp* **25/1**
0256 **12** *nk* **Cripsey Brook**[13] 4178 6-8-8 **85** ............ KimTinkler 19 81
(DonEnricoIncisa) *towards rr: rdn over 3f out: nvr trbld ldrs* **33/1**
6425 **13** *1/2* **Ofaraby**[24] 3842 4-8-13 **90** ............ KMcEvoy 15 85
(MAJarvis) *racd keenly: in tch: n.m.r 3f out: rdn and n.m.r again over 2f out: no imp fnl f* **25/1**
0000 **14** *1/2* **Telemachus**[11] 4214 4-8-6 **83** ............ (b) MFenton 6 77
(JGGiven) *in tch: rdn and hdwy over 3f out: wknd over 1f out* **50/1**
0100 **15** *1/2* **Intricate Web (IRE)**[7] 4319 8-8-4 **81** ............ FNorton 1 74
(EJAlston) *hld up: rdn over 3f out: n.d* **33/1**
0624 **16** *1 3/4* **Flighty Fellow (IRE)**[13] 4178 4-9-3 **94** ............ (b) DAllan 9 84
(TDEasterby) *racd keenly: in tch: rdn and wknd over 3f out* **33/1**
6124 **17** *shd* **Scottish River (USA)**[14] 4136 5-8-0 **82** ............ HayleyTurner(5) 5 72
(MDIUsher) *dwlt: racd keenly: hld up: rdn over 2f out: no imp* **50/1**
1010 **18** *hd* **Ionian Spring (IRE)**[28] 3756 9-9-4 **95** ............ EAhern 10 85
(CGCox) *s.s: bhd: hdwy over 4f out: rdn and n.m.r over 2f out: eased fnl f* **20/1**
1553 **19** *4* **Fine Palette**[14] 4118 4-8-11 **88** ............ PaulEddery 20 71
(HRACecil) *prom: effrt over 4f out: wknd over 2f out* **16/1**
3035 **20** *4* **Penrith (FR)**[13] 4178 3-8-1 **88** ............ JFanning 7 64
(MJohnston) *racd keenly: midfield: rdn and wknd over 2f out* **10/1**

2m 11.58s (-6.15) **Going Correction** -0.40s/f (Firm)
**WFA** 3 from 4yo+ 10lb **20** Ran SP% **125.3**
Speed ratings: **106,105,105,103,103 102,101,101,101,99 99,98,98,98,97 96,96,96,93,90**CSF £263.55 CT £3753.82 TOTE £72.70: £11.90, £2.80, £3.40, £4.10; EX 804.60 TRIFECTA Not won..
**Owner** Mrs I Battla **Bred** J P And Miss M Mangan **Trained** Ingoe, Northumberland
■ The biggest career success so far for both Don Eddy and David Kinsella.

**FOCUS**
A very competitive handicap on paper, but a falsely-run affair as the winner was able to dictate in front. The form might not hold up as a result. Few got into it from off the pace.

**NOTEBOOK**
**Dunaskin(IRE)**, from a 3lb higher mark, was given a fine ride by Kinsella, who dictated a steady pace before quickening the tempo approaching the straight. With plenty still left in the tank, he held on well, but he will not always be able to dominate in this manner.
**Coat Of Honour(USA)** chased the eventual winner throughout but could not quite get past him. This was a sound effort from a 5lb higher mark and another nice handicap could come his way.
**Shahzan House(IRE)** came there looking a big danger but did not quite pick up. He is a consistent individual but he has no secrets from the handicapper.
**Mutafanen**, visored for the first time, was the only one of the principals to come from off the pace and this was a very creditable effort in the circumstances.
**King Of Dreams(IRE)**, racing from a 5lb higher mark, had no real excuse but it could be that he will prove just as effective over twelve furlongs.
**Bonecrusher**, raised a couple of pounds after his unfortunate Goodwood defeat, came from the rear as usual but the lack of a true gallop counted against him. He remains in good form but is the type who needs everything to fall right.
**Mutasallil(USA)** has been making all in small-field conditions events and was ridden differently on this handicap debut. He could never land a telling blow and may be a couple of pounds too high.
**Windy Britain** faced a thankless task trying to come from the rear in this falsely-run affair and should be given another chance.
**Ski Jump(USA)**, with a visor replacing blinkers, soon lost a prominent early pitch but was keeping on quite strongly from the rear in the latter stages.
**Ofaraby** *Official explanation: jockey said gelding suffered a cut leg*
**Ionian Spring(IRE)** *Official explanation: trainer said gelding was unsuited by the loose ground*

## 4541 SODEXHO EUROPEAN BREEDERS FUND NOVICE FILLIES' STKS 6f
**3:35** (3:36) (D) 2-Y-0 **£5,018** (£1,544; £772; £386) **Stalls** Centre

Form RPR
10 **1** **Satin Kiss (USA)**[32] 3599 2-9-2 90 ............ KMcEvoy 2 85
(SaeedBinSuroor) *mde all: r.o fnl f* **2/1**[1]
45 **2** *1 1/4* **Indiena**[22] 3904 2-8-9 ............ JFortune 1 74
(BJMeehan) *racd keenly: trckd ldrs: rdn to chse wnr 1f out: styd on* **3/1**[2]
**3** *1 1/4* **Rashida** 2-8-5 ............ EAhern 5 67
(JNoseda) *dwlt: in rr: styd on fnl f: nvr able to chal* **4/1**[3]
2160 **4** *nk* **Sapphire Dream**[50] 3031 2-9-2 84 ............ RWinston 4 77
(ABailey) *prom: rdn 2f out: no ex fnl f* **7/1**
1 **5** *3/4* **Bridge T'The Stars**[27] 3770 2-8-11 ............ SCarson 6 69
(RFJohnsonHoughton) *hld up: rdn over 2f out: rn green: no imp* **5/1**

1m 14.2s (-0.69) **Going Correction** -0.40s/f (Firm) **5** Ran SP% **107.5**
Speed ratings: **88,86,84,84,83**CSF £7.76 TOTE £2.60: £1.50, £2.60; EX 9.20.
**Owner** Godolphin **Bred** Darley **Trained** Newmarket, Suffolk

**FOCUS**
Comfortable for Satin Kiss, but a modest time for the grade and the form is nothing special.

**NOTEBOOK**
**Satin Kiss(USA)** set her own pace and, despite running green, won a shade comfortably. She was out of her depth in the Cherry Hinton last time and the ground at Newmarket was faster than she would have liked too.
**Indiena** adopted different tactics and was a little keen, but she stayed on well enough after being pulled out to chase the winner. There should be a small race for her.
**Rashida** is out of an unraced half-sister to Irish 1000 Guineas winner Tarascon. She was keeping on nicely when it was all over after missing the kick and then racing rather up in the air through greenness.
**Sapphire Dream**, having her first run since Royal Ascot, is likely to prove hard to place from a mark in the 80s.
**Bridge T'The Stars** won a poor maiden first time and was found wanting in this company, although she still looked green.

## 4542 ALAN'S 60TH BIRTHDAY H'CAP 6f
**4:10** (4:11) (E) (0-70,70) 4-Y-0+ **£3,809** (£1,172; £586; £293) **Stalls** Centre

Form RPR
0002 **1** **Full Spate**[5] 4403 9-9-10 **66** ............ FNorton 16 79
(JMBradley) *hld up: hdwy over 1f out: rdn to ld ins fnl f: r.o* **7/1**[2]
613 **2** *1/2* **Fonthill Road (IRE)**[27] 3779 4-10-0 **70** ............ JFortune 8 81
(RAFahey) *bhd: rdn 1/2-way: hdwy over 1f out: r.o ins fnl f* **10/3**[1]

-000 **3** *1* **Smirfys Party**[37] 3446 6-8-6 **48**............................(v) ANicholls 19 56
(DNicholls) *prom: led over 2f out: hdd ins fnl f: nt qckn* **25/1**

5000 **4** *3/4* **Flying Edge (IRE)**[8] 4305 4-8-11 **53**.............................. WSupple 12 59
(EJAlston) *midfield: rdn over 2f out: hdwy and hung lft 1f out: styd on ins fnl f* **14/1**

/000 **5** *hd* **Smirfys Night**[25] 3820 5-8-8 **50**........................................ PDoe 15 55
(DNicholls) *led: rdn and hdd over 2f out: styd on same pce fnl f* **33/1**

0050 **6** *1 1/4* **William's Well**[14] 4130 10-9-1 **57**..........................(b) DaleGibson 9 58
(MWEasterby) *in tch: rdn 2f out: styd on u.p ins fnl f* **16/1**

0040 **7** *nk* **Friar Tuck**[14] 4130 9-8-6 **51**................................ ABeech(3) 13 52
(MissLAPerratt) *bhd: rdn over 2f out: hdwy over 1f out: styd on fnl f* **25/1**

0400 **8** *nk* **Drury Lane (IRE)**[8] 4308 4-8-9 **51**..............................(b) EAhern 18 51
(DWChapman) *hld up: rdn over 2f out: hdwy over 1f out: kpt on fnl f* **12/1**

0202 **9** *nk* **Haulage Man**[14] 4154 6-9-4 **60**..............................(p) PRobinson 3 59
(DEddy) *dwlt: sn chsd ldrs: rdn 2f out: wknd ins fnl f* **7/1**[2]

5360 **10** *nk* **Aintnecessarilyso**[5] 4403 6-8-6 **55**.............................. MHalford(7) 17 53
(NEBerry) *bhd: styd on u.p fnl f: nvr nrr* **10/1**

-040 **11** *3/4* **Indian Maiden (IRE)**[27] 3775 4-9-5 **66**.............................. PMakin(5) 7 62
(MSSaunders) *hld up: rdn 2f out: nvr trbld ldrs* **33/1**

3000 **12** *1 3/4* **Viewforth**[14] 4133 6-9-8 **64**..............................(b) VHalliday 20 54
(JSGoldie) *in tch: rdn over 2f out: sn wknd* **9/1**[3]

4065 **13** *shd* **Pirlie Hill**[9] 4279 4-8-2 **49**.............................. HayleyTurner(5) 6 39
(MissLAPerratt) *towards rr: hdwy over 2f out: rdn over 1f out: wknd ins fnl f* **25/1**

0-05 **14** *hd* **Elidore**[15] 4084 4-9-13 **69**..............................(v[1]) ACulhane 10 58
(BPalling) *prom: rdn over 2f out: sn wknd* **40/1**

2056 **15** *1* **Lucius Verrus (USA)**[32] 3616 4-8-7 **49**..................(v) DarrenWilliams 2 35
(DShaw) *hld up: rdn 1/2-way: no imp* **40/1**

000 **16** *1/2* **Indian Shores**[70] 2473 5-8-6 **48**.............................. MHenry 11 33
(MMullineaux) *a bhd* **40/1**

-502 **17** *hd* **Calusa Lady (IRE)**[28] 3747 4-8-11 **53**.............................. SCarson 4 37
(GBBalding) *midfield: outpcd fr 1/2-way* **16/1**

2306 **18** *1/2* **Brantwood (IRE)**[8] 4308 4-9-2 **58**..............................(t) GGibbons 14 41
(BAMcmahon) *prom: rdn 2f out: wknd over 1f out* **16/1**

-000 **19** *3/4* **Trinity (IRE)**[14] 4133 8-8-6 **48**.............................. DAllan 1 29
(MBrittain) *chsd ldrs: rdn over 2f out: wknd over 1f out* **25/1**

1500 **20** *hd* **Blueberry Rhyme**[15] 4105 5-9-0 **56**..............................(v) MFenton 5 36
(PABlockley) *midfield: rdn over 2f out: sn wknd* **40/1**

1m 12.46s (-2.43) **Going Correction** -0.40s/f (Firm) **20** Ran SP% **130.2**
Speed ratings: **100,99,98,97,96 95,94,94,93,93 92,90,90,89,88 87,87,86,85,85**CSF £28.31 CT £584.75 TOTE £7.30: £2.00, £1.90, £4.60, £4.80; EX 29.40.
**Owner** E A Hayward **Bred** Juddmonte Farms **Trained** Sedbury, Gloucs

**FOCUS**
An ordinary sprint in which high numbers were favoured. Again, few got involved from off the pace. The form looks sound enough on paper.

**NOTEBOOK**
**Full Spate** has a good cruising speed and he travelled well before sealing victory inside the last. He has now won every season since 1999 but he will go up a bit for this.
**Fonthill Road(IRE)** was running on well at the line and this was a sound effort off topweight. He appeared to find seven furlongs stretching him here last month but could be worth another chance at that trip. This run will not have helped his handicap mark.
**Smirfys Party** was towed along by his stablemate until striking the front and stuck on quite well once headed. He is on a decent mark these days.
**Flying Edge(IRE)**, 7lb lower than when last getting his head in front a year ago, was doing his best work at the finish after hanging fire with a furlong to run.
**Smirfys Night** showed good pace to lead towards the near side and was just run out of the places. This was his best run since returning from a season's abence and he is well treated now.
**William's Well**, who ran well here two starts back, was 7lb higher at the start of the campaign and could be ready to strike.
**Friar Tuck** half-reared as the stalls opened and did well to reach his finishing position.

## 4543 LESTER PIGGOTT RATED STKS (H'CAP) 1m 30y
4:40 (4:42) (C) (0-90,86) 3-Y-0+ £10,179 (£3,132; £1,566; £783) Stalls Low

Form RPR

5162 **1** **Young Mr Grace (IRE)**[19] 3982 4-8-11 **78**.............................. DAllan 3 88
(TDEasterby) *trckd ldrs: rdn over 3f out: led over 2f out: kpt on* **9/2**[2]

0030 **2** *1* **Sawwaah (IRE)**[8] 4287 7-9-0 **81**.............................. ANicholls 9 89
(DNicholls) *in tch: rdn over 2f out: hung lft and hdwy over 1f out: styd on towards fin* **5/1**[3]

0-04 **3** *shd* **Impersonator**[92] 1938 4-8-9 **76**.............................. PDoe 6 83
(JLDunlop) *prom: led over 3f out: hdd over 2f out: styd on* **11/1**

1001 **4** *shd* **Langford**[23] 3879 4-9-5 **86**.............................. PRobinson 4 93
(MHTompkins) *racd keenly: in tch: hdwy over 2f out: rdn over 1f out: styd on* **3/1**[1]

0000 **5** *3* **Tough Love**[13] 4178 5-9-3 **84**.............................. WSupple 5 84
(TDEasterby) *hld up: effrt over 1f out: kpt on one pce fnl f* **15/2**

1100 **6** *2 1/2* **Acomb**[23] 3872 4-8-10 **77**.............................. EAhern 2 72
(MWEasterby) *racd keenly: hld up in tch: hdwy over 2f out: sn rdn and wknd* **11/2**

6000 **7** *2* **Namroud (USA)**[40] 3365 5-8-13 **80**.............................. JFortune 7 70
(RAFahey) *hld up: rdn over 2f out: nvr on terms* **9/1**

6-20 **8** *6* **Soller Bay**[92] 1927 7-8-8 **75**.............................. DarrenWilliams 8 51
(KRBurke) *led: rdn and hdd over 3f out: wknd 2f out* **12/1**

1m 41.21s (-4.34) **Going Correction** -0.40s/f (Firm) **8** Ran SP% **113.0**
Speed ratings: **105,104,103,103,100 98,96,90**CSF £26.52 CT £230.99 TOTE £4.50: £1.70, £2.00, £3.20; EX 30.90 Place 6 £114.29, Place 5 £29.74.
**Owner** Norman Jackson **Bred** Michael Greany **Trained** Great Habton, N Yorks

**FOCUS**
A decent handicap in which they went a fair pace and again came down the centre in the home straight. The form does not look all that strong for the grade.

**NOTEBOOK**
**Young Mr Grace(IRE)**, a largely consistent individual, battled willingly to hold on to his lead. The mile was not a problem and there could be a bit more to come from him at this trip.
**Sawwaah(IRE)** hung in behind the eventual third when coming with his challenge but was running on at the line. He is in good form at present but is a frustrating individual.
**Impersonator** went without the blinkers on this first start in three months. This was a sound run on ground that was faster than he would have wanted.
**Langford** travelled well, if racing a little keenly, but was never quite able to challenge despite plugging on.
**Tough Love**, a stablemate of the winner, has had excuses on his last couple of starts but was beaten fair and square on this occasion. He is one to be wary of at the moment.
**Acomb**, a keen individual, has been in the handicapper's grip since back-to-back wins earlier in the season.
**Namroud(USA)**, with the blinkers left off, was rather keen in rear and was never within striking distance. *Official explanation: jockey said gelding ran too free early on*
**Soller Bay** was unable to get his own way in front and after being harried for the lead he dropped out pretty quickly once headed.

T/Plt: £161.10 to a £1 stake. Pool: £58,232.45. 263.80 winning tickets. T/Qpdt: £12.90 to a £1 stake. Pool: £2,959.60. 169.70 winning tickets. DO

# 4513 LINGFIELD (L-H)
Saturday, August 7

**OFFICIAL GOING: Turf course - good to firm (firm in places); all-weather course - standard**

## 4544 LINGFIELD-RACECOURSE.CO.UK MAIDEN STKS 1m (P)
5:50 (5:52) (D) 2-Y-O £3,896 (£1,199; £599; £299) Stalls High

Form RPR

2 **1** **Russian Consort (IRE)**[17] 4022 2-9-0 .............................. JDSmith 6 83+
(AKing) *t.k.h: a in tch: rdn to ld 2f out: pushed clr fnl f* **5/2**[1]

6 **2** *2 1/2* **Zalaal (USA)**[21] 3931 2-9-0 .............................. RLMoore 8 76
(SaeedBinSuroor) *a in tch: rdn to chse wnr fnl f* **3/1**[2]

**3** *2 1/2* **Elrafa Mujahid** 2-8-9 .............................. ADaly 2 65
(JulianPoulton) *led: hdd 2f out: kpt on one pce* **50/1**

3 **4** *2 1/2* **Saadigg (IRE)**[17] 4023 2-9-0 .............................. NCallan 3 65
(MAJarvis) *trckd ldrs: rdn over 3f out: no hdwy ins fnl 2f* **4/1**[3]

6 **5** *nk* **Eltizaam (USA)**[13] 4169 2-9-0 .............................. NPollard 4 64
(EALDunlop) *trckd ldrs: rdn over 2f out: wknd over 1f out* **5/1**

**6** *4* **Just Do It (UAE)** 2-9-0 .............................. TEDurcan 12 55
(MRChannon) *slowly away: racd wd: btn 2f out* **16/1**

0 **7** *5* **Terminate (GER)**[11] 4208 2-9-0 .............................. JQuinn 10 44
(SirMarkPrescott) *t.k.h: in tch: hdwy 3f out: wknd wl over 1f out* **7/1**

**8** *7* **Loitokitok** 2-9-0 .............................. CCatlin 5 29
(PDCundell) *v.s.a: a bhd* **50/1**

**9** *shd* **Krasivi's Boy (USA)** 2-9-0 .............................. LisaJones 7 28
(GLMoore) *a in rr* **33/1**

0 **10** *24* **Little Waltham**[10] 4243 2-8-9 .............................. DSweeney 9 —
(KAMorgan) *sn struggling in rr: t.o* **100/1**

**11** *17* **Louise Paris (IRE)** 2-8-9 .............................. SRighton 1 —
(MJAttwater) *plld hrd: w ldr tl wknd qckly 3f out: t.o* **100/1**

1m 41.58s (2.03) **Going Correction** +0.20s/f (Slow) **11** Ran SP% **117.5**
Speed ratings: **97,94,92,89,89 85,80,73,73,49 32**CSF £9.94 TOTE £4.00: £1.40, £1.80, £17.80; EX 12.30.
**Owner** Four Mile Racing **Bred** Gestut Gorlsdorf **Trained** Barbury Castle, Wilts

**FOCUS**
A fair maiden, full of potential staying types, that saw the field finish strung out behind the winner, who can rate higher. This should throw up its share of winners.

**NOTEBOOK**
**Russian Consort(IRE)**, despite taking a keen hold early on, confirmed the promise of his recent debut second at this track and readily went one better over this extra furlong. He will come on again for this experience and he deserves to have a crack at decent company over this trip.
**Zalaal(USA)** ◆ improved on his debut effort over this extra furlong, but was firmly put in his place by the winner. This extra furlong suited and he was a clear second best, so should have little trouble in going one better in this division.
**Elrafa Mujahid**, a cheaply-bought daughter of Mujahid, showed definite promise on this racecourse bow and will have learnt plenty from the experience. She was smart from the gates, looked well suited by this trip and should get further in time.
**Saadigg(IRE)**, who had shaped with promise on his debut on this surface 17 days previously, failed to show significant improvement from his debut over this longer trip, but still turned in a sound-enough effort. It would be no surprise were he to leave this form behind in due course, and appeals as the type to progress over middle distances as a three-year-old.
**Eltizaam(USA)** failed to build on his fair debut effort at Newmarket recently and may have been found out by this extra furlong. He should be capable of better, but this Derby entry has a bit to prove now.

## 4545 WHIPS & TEES MEDIAN AUCTION MAIDEN STKS 1m 2f (P)
6:20 (6:22) (F) 3-4-Y-O £2,982 (£852; £426) Stalls Low

Form RPR

3- **1** **Exterior (USA)**[341] 4611 3-8-12 .............................. RLMoore 9 86+
(MrsAJPerrett) *t.k.h: trckd ldrs: pushed along 4f out: hdwy to lead 2f out: rdn clr appr fnl f* **11/10**[1]

04 **2** *12* **Disparity (USA)**[23] 3882 3-8-7 ..............................(t) TEDurcan 5 57+
(JRFanshawe) *trckd ldr: losing 2nd whn squeezed out over 2f out: styd on ins fnl 2f to take poor 2nd cl home* **7/1**[3]

5460 **3** *hd* **Brough Supreme**[28] 3743 3-8-12 65.............................. SDrowne 6 62
(HMorrison) *led tl hdd 2f out: rdn and one pce after: lost 2nd cl home* **3/1**[2]

66 **4** *2* **Port Sodrick**[8] 4303 3-8-12 .............................. ADaly 8 58?
(MDIUsher) *in rr tl hdwy 4f out: rdn 2f out: kpt on one pce* **10/1**

4030 **5** *9* **Shalati Princess**[42] 3305 3-8-4 41.............................. LPKeniry(3) 4 36
(JCFox) *mid-div: rdn 4f out: no ch fnl 2f* **16/1**

00- **6** *2* **Dingley Lass**[381] 3503 4-9-2 .............................. JQuinn 3 32
(HMorrison) *rdn 1/2-way and a in rr* **33/1**

46 **7** *1* **The Nibbler**[24] 3846 3-8-12 .............................. GBaker 7 35
(GCHChung) *stdd s and in rr tl hdwy 4f out: rdn and wknd 2f out* **16/1**

00 **8** *dist* **Blue Track (IRE)**[15] 4087 3-8-12 .............................. NCallan 1 —
(MJAttwater) *trckd ldrs: rdn 4f out: wknd qckly: t.o* **50/1**

2m 9.59s (1.74) **Going Correction** +0.20s/f (Slow)
**WFA** 3 from 4yo 9lb **8** Ran SP% **110.9**
Speed ratings: **101,91,91,89,82 80,80,**—CSF £8.87 TOTE £1.90: £1.10, £1.90, £1.60; EX 4.90.
**Owner** K Abdulla **Bred** Juddmonte Farms Inc **Trained** Pulborough, W Sussex

**FOCUS**
Very little strength in depth to this maiden and the field came home well strung out behind the facile winner. The third and fifth provide the level of the form.

**NOTEBOOK**
**Exterior(USA)** , off since his promising debut as a juvenile in 2003, showed he has done well physically since his break and posted a commanding display to get off the mark. He had no problems with this trip, should get 12 furlongs without a fuss, and it will be interesting to see where his connections pitch him in next, as he looks promising.
**Disparity(USA)** was firmly put in her place behind the winner, and did not look the easiest of rides this time, but will no doubt fare better now she is eligible for handicaps.
**Brough Supreme** had the run of the race in front, but was made to look pedestrian when the winner went past and could only muster the same pace from then on. He failed to stay 14 furlongs last time, but may be capable of getting closer back in handicaps over this trip.
**Port Sodrick** never looked a threat over this longer distance, but now qualifies for handicaps, and should do better as a result. He would also benefit from dropping back to a mile.
**Blue Track(IRE)** *Official explanation: jockey said colt returned lame*

## 4546 LINGFIELD GOLF CLUB H'CAP 7f 140y

**6:50** (6:51) (F) (0-55,59) 3-Y-O+ **£3,185** (£910; £455) **Stalls** Centre

Form RPR

0032 **1** **Cut Ridge (IRE)**[9] 4260 5-9-2 **46**........................................ DHolland 5 57
(JSWainwright) *racd alone centre: a in tch: led wl over 1f out: sn clr* **11/2**[3]

0404 **2** *2 ½* **Enna (POL)**[21] 3934 5-9-1 **45**........................................ SDrowne 15 50
(MrsStefLiddiard) *towards rr on stands'rail: rdn and hdwy over 2f out: r.o to go 2nd ins fnl f* **16/1**

2033 **3** *nk* **Bahama Reef (IRE)**[7] 4338 3-9-4 **55**........................................ CCatlin 6 59
(BGubby) *a in tch: rdn over 3f out: kpt on u.p* **20/1**

0201 **4** *½* **Lord Chamberlain**[2] 4479 11-9-5 **56** 6ex........................(b) CJDavies[(7)] 13 59
(JMBradley) *towards rr: rdn and styd on ins fnl 2f: nvr nrr* **10/1**

4031 **5** *½* **Scarrottoo**[9] 4265 6-9-11 **55**........................................ RLMoore 16 57+
(SCWilliams) *hld up in rr: mde sme late hdwy* **4/1**[1]

0150 **6** *shd* **Mobo-Baco**[14] 4122 7-9-10 **54**........................................ VSlattery 9 55
(RJHodges) *slowly away: sn mid-div: rdn 3f out: kpt on one pce* **14/1**

2006 **7** *shd* **Shirley Oaks (IRE)**[14] 4148 6-9-1 **50**........................................ NChalmers[(5)] 11 51
(MissZCDavison) *towards rr: nvr nr to chal* **14/1**

6542 **8** *nk* **Head Boy**[7] 4338 3-9-8 **59**........................................ LisaJones 1 59
(SDow) *nvr bttr than mid-div* **6/1**

4203 **9** *¾* **Tojoneski**[9] 4276 5-8-13 **46**........................................(p) JFMcDonald[(3)] 7 44
(IWMcinnes) *led: hdd wl over 1f out: fdd fnl f* **5/1**[2]

0000 **10** *1 ¼* **Mayzin (IRE)**[5] 4403 4-9-3 **47**........................................ DSweeney 3 42
(RMFlower) *stdd s: sn mid-div: swtchd lft over 3f out: sn rdn and no further hdwy* **16/1**

4600 **11** *3* **Kinsman (IRE)**[46] 3174 7-9-4 **51**........................................(b) J-PGuillambert[(3)] 12 39
(TDMccarthy) *slowly away: a in rr* **16/1**

1060 **12** *10* **Whiplash (IRE)**[14] 4128 3-8-13 **53**........................................ LPKeniry[(3)] 8 16
(KOCunningham-Brown) *w ldr: rdn and wknd 2f out: eased whn btn* **33/1**

5000 **13** *nk* **Wood Fern (UAE)**[22] 3910 4-9-8 **52**........................................ TEDurcan 14 14
(MRChannon) *in tch: rdn over 2f out: wknd over 1f out* **20/1**

4000 **14** *1* **Toppling**[8] 4305 6-9-6 **50**........................................(p) NCallan 2 10
(JMBradley) *prom: rdn 3f out: sn wknd* **16/1**

0006 **15** *13* **Easily Averted (IRE)**[76] 2322 3-8-12 **56** ow3.......... RLucey-Butler[(7)] 10 —
(PButler) *mid-div tl wknd qckly 3f out: t.o* **33/1**

1m 30.24s (-1.22) **Going Correction** -0.40s/f (Firm)
**WFA** 3 from 4yo+ 7lb **15** Ran **SP%** **127.7**
Speed ratings: **90,87,87,86,86 86,86,85,84,83 80,70,70,69,56**CSF £91.33 CT £1705.10 TOTE £5.70: £2.10, £6.20, £4.50; EX 172.40.
**Owner** Mrs Chris Harrington **Bred** Mrs Chris Harrington **Trained** Kennythorpe, N Yorks

**FOCUS**
A poor event, run at a modest pace, and form is not worth a great deal.

**NOTEBOOK**
**Cut Ridge(IRE)**, who had recently run into form, confirmed her current well-being with a comfortable success. She was kept wide of the pack throughout, which seemed to suit her, and this extra distance played to her strengths. Although she is in great heart at present, she is largely inconsistent and does not appeal greatly as one to follow-up.
**Enna(POL)**, dropping back from ten furlongs, stayed on well for a never-dangerous second, but his proximity at the death sums up the form.
**Bahama Reef(IRE)** looked very one paced when push came to shove, but still turned in another fair effort and has now hit the frame in his last three outings, so could be placed to advantage before long.
**Lord Chamberlain**, who ended a long losing run on the turf when scoring at Chepstow two days previously, was not at all disgraced but was found out by his 6lb penalty.
**Scarrottoo**, a winner off this mark at Epsom last time out, did not get the breaks on this occasion from off the pace, but was still slightly disappointing nonetheless. *Official explanation: trainer said gelding was unlucky in running*
**Tojoneski**, third in a claimer last time, dropped out tamely having had the run of the race in front. He is a moody character and one to avoid outside of plating-class.

## 4547 PLAY GOLF AND COME RACING CLASSIFIED STKS 6f

**7:20** (7:21) (F) 3-Y-O+ **£3,601** (£1,108; £554; £277) **Stalls** Low

Form RPR

1300 **1** **Miss Judgement (IRE)**[17] 4020 3-8-6 **62**........................................ RMiles[(3)] 6 72
(WRMuir) *in tch: rdn and edgd rt bef led appr fnl f: drvn out* **10/1**

4012 **2** *¾* **Mistral Sky**[3] 4459 5-9-9 **72**........................................(v) SDrowne 4 80
(MrsStefLiddiard) *rrd up leaving stalls: sn in tch: rdn over 2f out: r.o to go 2nd ins fnl f* **15/8**[1]

5406 **3** *¾* **Stokesies Wish**[12] 4194 4-8-13 **62**........................................ LisaJones 1 68
(JLSpearing) *sn prom: ev ch whn carried rt appr fnl f: kpt on* **8/1**

1021 **4** *2 ½* **Foley Millennium (IRE)**[8] 4299 6-9-10 **73**........................................ NPollard 5 71
(MQuinn) *led tl rdn and hdd appr fnl f: wknd ins* **5/2**[2]

6545 **5** *1 ¼* **Fair Compton**[14] 4125 3-8-9 **60**........................................ RLMoore 8 57
(RHannon) *outpcd thrght* **14/1**

0-24 **6** *shd* **Sweet Pickle**[48] 3125 3-8-13 **69**........................................ DHolland 2 60
(DJCoakley) *prom: rdn over 2f out: wknd wl over 1f out* **4/1**[3]

6450 **7** *6* **Cut And Dried**[1] 4515 3-8-9 **65**........................................ LPKeniry[(3)] 7 41
(DMSimcock) *chsd ldrs tl wknd over 1f out* **25/1**

69.45 secs (-2.20) **Going Correction** -0.40s/f (Firm)
**WFA** 3 from 4yo+ 4lb **7** Ran **SP%** **114.1**
Speed ratings: **98,97,96,92,91 90,82**CSF £29.10 TOTE £13.80: £3.50, £2.40; EX 47.30.
**Owner** Double D Partnership **Bred** Yeomanstown Stud **Trained** Lambourn, Berks
■ Stewards Enquiry : R Miles caution: careless riding

**FOCUS**
A modest but competitive classified event run at a sound gallop and the first three came clear. The form is just average but solid enough.

**NOTEBOOK**
**Miss Judgement(IRE)** responded well to pressure in the straight and ran out a ready winner. She had not built on her success at Nottingham in June in three subsequent outings, but this drop back in grade worked the oracle and she looks to have found her level now. *Official explanation: trainer's representative said, regarding the improved form shown, the race was a drop in trip and class for the filly*
**Mistral Sky** did himself no favours when rearing at the start and was up against it from then on. He has taken his racing well of late, is capable of better and deserves credit for finishing as close as he did.
**Stokesies Wish** ran her race, but is hard to win with and could do with some respite from the Handicapper.
**Foley Millennium(IRE)** has been in terrific form this season, improving over two stone in the ratings since his first success, but he was well held this time and the Handicapper may now have his measure.
**Sweet Pickle** had every chance if good enough and ran below her best. She has a few questions to answer now.

## 4548 FURLONGS AND FAIRWAYS H'CAP 6f

**7:50** (7:52) (F) (0-55,55) 3-Y-O+ **£3,206** (£916; £458) **Stalls** Centre

Form RPR

3304 **1** **Jazzy Millennium**[7] 4336 7-9-7 **53**........................................(v) DHolland 2 62
(BRMillman) *a in tch on outside: rdn 2f out: r.o u.p to ld last strides* **7/2**[1]

2103 **2** *nk* **Enjoy The Buzz**[7] 4336 5-9-4 **50**........................................ RLMoore 13 58
(JMBradley) *hld up: hdwy 1/2-way: r.o strly to snatch 2nd last stride* **7/2**[1]

6510 **3** *shd* **Le Meridien (IRE)**[13] 4181 6-9-5 **51**........................................ NPollard 10 59
(JSWainwright) *a.p: led 2f out: rdn and hdd nr fin* **10/1**

2030 **4** *1* **Night Cap (IRE)**[5] 4403 5-8-8 **43**........................................ J-PGuillambert[(3)] 8 48
(TDMccarthy) *mid-div: swtchd rt over 2f out: kpt on fnl f: nt qckn fnl 50yds* **9/1**

-063 **5** *nk* **Moritat (IRE)**[9] 4279 4-9-8 **54**........................................ NCallan 7 58
(PDEvans) *mid-div: rdn 3f out: kpt on one pce fnl f* **11/2**[2]

3026 **6** *1* **Harbour House**[5] 4400 5-9-0 **46**........................................ ADaly 1 47
(JJBridger) *mid-div on outside: styd on fnl f: nvr nrr* **10/1**

0641 **7** *hd* **My Girl Pearl (IRE)**[19] 3991 4-8-13 **48**........................................ RMiles[(3)] 11 48
(MSSaunders) *led: hdd 2f out: wknd appr fnl f* **8/1**[3]

4000 **8** *2 ½* **Bold Wolf**[19] 3991 3-8-8 **44**........................................ SWhitworth 4 37
(JLSpearing) *in tch: rdn 3f out: sn outpcd* **33/1**

0005 **9** *3 ½* **Cedric Coverwell**[31] 3635 4-8-9 **41**........................................(b[1]) JQuinn 14 23
(DKIvory) *s.i.s: sn prom: rdn 2f out: sn wknd* **33/1**

4050 **10** *nk* **Chatshow (USA)**[19] 3991 3-9-3 **53**........................................(t) AMcCarthy 3 34
(LADace) *slowly away: a towards rr* **25/1**

0500 **11** *½* **Black Oval**[9] 4267 3-8-13 **49**........................................(v[1]) LisaJones 6 29
(SDow) *prom to 1/2-way* **25/1**

0000 **12** *1 ¼* **Knight Onthe Tiles (IRE)**[14] 4126 3-9-5 **55**........................................(b) GBaker 5 31
(JRBest) *mid-div: lost pl 1/2-way: sn bhd* **25/1**

0-00 **13** *hd* **Old Harry**[15] 4085 4-8-10 **42**........................................(t) CCatlin 9 17
(PCRitchens) *a in rr* **33/1**

0065 **14** *1* **Night Worker**[17] 4021 3-9-0 **50**........................................ TEDurcan 12 22
(RHannon) *mid-div: rdn 1/2-way: sn bhd* **16/1**

0500 **15** *2 ½* **Tappit (IRE)**[7] 4336 5-8-9 **46**........................................ MSavage[(5)] 15 11
(NEBerry) *in tch: rdn over 2f out: wknd qckly* **33/1**

69.85 secs (-1.80) **Going Correction** -0.40s/f (Firm)
**WFA** 3 from 4yo+ 4lb **15** Ran **SP%** **128.3**
Speed ratings: **96,95,95,94,93 92,92,88,84,83 83,81,81,79,76**CSF £14.22 CT £116.07 TOTE £3.80: £1.90, £1.70, £3.50; EX 9.20.
**Owner** Millennium Millionaires Partnership **Bred** Dunchurch Lodge Stud Co **Trained** Kentisbeare, Devon

**FOCUS**
A moderate event run at a fair pace. The form looks sound for the class with the first three close to their marks.

**NOTEBOOK**
**Jazzy Millennium**, an unlucky fourth over course and distance last time, proved game late on by sticking his head out where it mattered to win all-out. This is his level, and he should continue to pay his way over this trip, which looks to be his optimum nowadays.
**Enjoy The Buzz**, having his third consecutive run over the course and distance, got going a bit too late this time and was only just denied. This was yet another solid effort and he should not be long in going one better off this sort of mark.
**Le Meridien(IRE)** made a bold bid for home two out, but could not fend off the front pair close home. This was a decent effort, and she was not beaten at all far this time, so could go one better in a similar event, but is not the easiest to win with.
**Night Cap(IRE)** ran another sound race over a course and distance he likes, but again found little at the business end of the race. He remains winless after 18 starts.
**Moritat(IRE)** failed to quicken over this extra furlong, but was not disgraced and would appreciate dropping back to the minimum trip.

## 4549 LINGFIELD RACECOURSE H'CAP 7f (P)

**8:20** (8:24) (D) (0-85,83) 3-Y-O+ **£5,736** (£1,765; £882; £441) **Stalls** Low

Form RPR

1220 **1** **Harrison Point (USA)**[32] 3597 4-9-12 **83**........................................ AMcCarthy 5 93+
(PWChapple-Hyam) *in tch: hdwy over 2f out: edgd lft appr fnl f: sn led: drvn out* **3/1**[1]

0535 **2** *1 ¼* **Bob's Buzz**[3] 4462 4-8-11 **68**........................................ ADaly 11 75
(SCWilliams) *s.i.s: hld up in rr: hdwy on outside over 2f out: styd on to go 2nd ins fnl f* **10/1**

0-50 **3** *½* **Last Appointment (USA)**[64] 2646 4-9-7 **78**........................................ DHolland 14 84
(JMPEustace) *led after 1f: rdn over 2f out: bmpd appr fnl f and sn hdd: lost 2nd ins fnl f* **7/1**

0404 **4** *¾* **Alafzar (IRE)**[9] 4276 6-8-5 **62**........................................(vt) NCallan 3 66
(PDEvans) *mid-div: hdwy over 2f out: styd on: nvr nrr* **20/1**

003 **5** *¾* **Kentucky King (USA)**[23] 3872 4-9-7 **81**........................................ RMiles[(3)] 12 83
(PWHiatt) *in rr tl styd on ins fnl 2f* **20/1**

4610 **6** *nk* **Tre Colline**[14] 4132 5-9-8 **79**........................................ GBaker 2 80
(NTinkler) *mid-div: rdn 3f out: kpt on one pce fnl 2f* **14/1**

3056 **7** *½* **Blonde En Blonde (IRE)**[4] 4414 4-8-8 **68**........................(b) J-PGuillambert[(3)] 9 68
(NPLittmoden) *in tch: rdn 3f out: ev ch appr fnl f: one pce after* **14/1**

60-2 **8** *hd* **Zariano**[21] 3932 4-9-0 **74**........................................ LPKeniry[(3)] 13 73
(RMStronge) *chsd ldr: rdn over 2f out: one pce after* **16/1**

0-10 **9** *2* **Gallery Breeze**[22] 3910 5-8-13 **70**........................................ VSlattery 8 64
(JLSpearing) *mid-div: rdn 3f out: no imp after* **20/1**

0331 **10** *nk* **St Savarin (FR)**[9] 4280 3-8-13 **76**........................................ NPollard 7 69
(JRBest) *led for 1f: rdn 3f out: wknd wl over 1f out* **5/1**[3]

2000 **11** *3 ½* **Cheese 'n Biscuits**[29] 3698 4-9-9 **80**........................................(p) RLMoore 10 64
(GLMoore) *a in rr* **9/1**

1500 **12** *6* **Taranaki**[14] 4120 6-9-4 **75**........................................ SWhitworth 6 44
(PDCundell) *in tch on ins tl rdn and hmpd on bnd 2f out: nt rcvr* **9/2**[2]

3200 **13** *hd* **Have Some Fun**[27] 3771 4-8-2 **59**........................................ JQuinn 6 27
(PRChamings) *mid-div: rdn over 3f out: sn wknd* **40/1**

1m 27.38s (1.44) **Going Correction** +0.20s/f (Slow)
**WFA** 3 from 4yo+ 6lb **13** Ran **SP%** **127.4**
Speed ratings: **99,97,97,96,95 94,94,94,91,91 87,80,80**CSF £34.89 CT £213.15 TOTE £4.30: £2.40, £3.60, £2.70; EX 46.30 Place 6 £47.26, Place 5 £27.00..
**Owner** Sangster Family, M O'Donovan, F Cook **Bred** Creston Farm **Trained** Newmarket, Suffolk
■ Stewards Enquiry : N Pollard three-day ban: careless riding (Aug 18-20)

**FOCUS**
A fair handicap run in a modest time and the form is nothing special. There were plenty of runners tightened for room on the final bend and the form may be worth treating with a degree of caution as a result.

**NOTEBOOK**
**Harrison Point(USA)** , far from disgraced when unplaced in a much better race at Newmarket last time, got back to winning ways in good style. He has a decent record on the Polytrack, has been running well all season, and showed enough this time to suggest he may have more to offer.

**Bob's Buzz**, bitterly disappointing at Yarmouth three days previously, settled better this time and showed his true colours in defeat. He is clearly a quirky sort, but has ability and can be placed to make amends off this sort of mark, although he may want a mile now.
**Last Appointment(USA)** was not helped by getting bumped by the winner in the straight, and can be rated slightly better than the bare form, but it made no difference to the result. This was a more encouraging effort, and this lightly-raced colt should not be long in scoring again, if able to maintain this form.
**Alafzar(IRE)**, with the visor back on, ran another fair race, but looks firmly in the Handicapper's grip at present.
**St Savarin(FR)**, a winner last time off a 3lb lower mark at Musselburgh, dropped out tamely in the straight and has to be considered disappointing. *Official explanation: jockey said gelding ran flat having had three races in quick succession*
**Taranaki** lost all chance when hampered on the turn for home and this run is best forgotten.
T/Plt: £127.70 to a £1 stake. Pool: £33,963.80. 194.10 winning tickets. T/Qpdt: £61.90 to a £1 stake. Pool: £2,133.80. 25.50 winning tickets. JS

# 4520 NEWMARKET (JULY) (R-H)

## Saturday, August 7

**OFFICIAL GOING: Good to firm (firm in places)**
After another dry night and a scorching hot day the day was getting quicker all the time. There appeared little advantage in the draw.
Wind: Almost nil Weather: Hot and sunny

## 4550 CHAMPIONS HEALTH CLUB H'CAP — 2m 24y

1:45 (1:47) (C) (0-90,89) 3-Y-0+ £13,676 (£4,208; £2,104; £1,052) Stalls High

| Form | | | | | RPR |
|---|---|---|---|---|---|
| 0233 | 1 | | **Coventina (IRE)**[16] 4062 3-8-10 **86** (JLDunlop) *chsd ldrs: led over 1f out: edgd rt: rdn out* 8/1[3] | RLMoore 11 | 95 |
| 0113 | 2 | 1 1/4 | **Tungsten Strike (USA)**[9] 4274 3-8-7 **83** (MrsAJPerrett) *sn led: rdn and hdd over 1f out: styd on same pce* 2/1[1] | MartinDwyer 2 | 90+ |
| /022 | 3 | 3 | **Coalition**[17] 4033 5-9-6 **81** (HCandy) *lw: hld up: hdwy over 2f out: sn rdn: nt rch ldrs* 7/1[2] | DaneO'Neill 6 | 85 |
| 1231 | 4 | 1/2 | **Sualda (IRE)**[6] 4363 5-9-0 **75** 5ex (RAFahey) *hld up: hdwy over 3f out: rdn over 1f out: styd on same pce* 16/1 | GParkin 8 | 78 |
| 2306 | 5 | hd | **Red Scorpion (USA)**[15] 4075 5-7-12 **64** (WMBrisbourne) *hld up in tch: rdn 4f out: styd on same pce fnl f* 33/1 | BSwarbrick(5) 7 | 67 |
| 3132 | 6 | hd | **Thewhirlingdervish (IRE)**[6] 4361 6-9-8 **83** (TDEasterby) *chsd ldrs: rdn over 1f out: no ex* 9/1 | JQuinn 10 | 86 |
| 4602 | 7 | 5 | **Dovedon Hero**[13] 4174 4-8-11 **72** (PJMcbride) *hld up: effrt over 2f out: no imp appr fnl f* 20/1 | (b) MHills 12 | 69 |
| 40-1 | 8 | 1/2 | **Jack Dawson (IRE)**[21] 2491 7-9-1 **76** (JohnBerry) *lw: chsd ldrs: rdn over 2f out: wknd over 1f out: eased ins fnl f* 9/1 | TEDurcan 4 | 72 |
| 0002 | 9 | 20 | **Random Quest**[28] 3725 6-9-11 **86** (BJLlewellyn) *hld up: plld hrd: hdwy over 6f out: rdn and wknd over 2f out* | SWhitworth 1 | 58 |
| 0361 | 10 | 1/2 | **The Varlet**[14] 4146 4-8-6 **70** (BICase) *hld up: racd keenly: hdwy over 3f out: rdn and wknd over 2f out* 33/1 | (p) SHitchcott(3) 3 | 41 |
| 0040 | 11 | 3 | **Mamcazma**[11] 4218 6-10-0 **89** (DMorris) *prom: racd keenly: wknd 3f out* 16/1 | MTebbutt 5 | 57 |

Time Not Taken
**WFA** 3 from 4yo+ 15lb **11** Ran **SP% 110.5**
Speed ratings: CSF £21.36 CT £100.70 TOTE £10.50: £2.80, £1.30, £2.50; EX 22.80.
**Owner** Capt J Macdonald-Buchanan **Bred** The Lavington Stud **Trained** Arundel, W Sussex

**FOCUS**
A fair handicap and quite a competitive race, but the pace appeared only moderate. No race time was recorded so no speed figures could be calculated.

**NOTEBOOK**
**Coventina(IRE)** appreciated the step up in trip and was well on top in the end. There should be more to come from her.
**Tungsten Strike(USA)** did nothing wrong and was just beaten by an unexposed sort at this trip. There will be other days for him.
**Coalition** was not suited by the lack of early pace, and got going far too late.
**Sualda(IRE)** appeared to stay this longer trip well enough, but was just found out by his penalty.
**Red Scorpion(USA)**, caught a little flat-footed as the pace lifted, stayed on gamely and will find easier openings than he faced here.
**Thewhirlingdervish(IRE)** is game and consistent, but could have done with a stronger pace.
**Random Quest** *Official explanation: jockey said gelding lost its near fore plate*

## 4551 TEAM EVENTS FILLIES' H'CAP — 1m

2:15 (2:17) (D) (0-85,84) 3-Y-0+ £6,760 (£2,080; £1,040; £520) Stalls High

| Form | | | | | RPR |
|---|---|---|---|---|---|
| 3215 | 1 | | **Golden Island (IRE)**[29] 3694 3-9-10 **83** (JWHills) *lw: chsd ldrs: led and edgd rt over 1f out: rdn out* 11/2[1] | MHills 1 | 92 |
| 3561 | 2 | nk | **Summer Shades**[8] 4301 6-8-13 **70** (WMBrisbourne) *hld up: swtchd lft and hdwy over 1f out: r.o wl* 11/2[1] | BSwarbrick(5) 6 | 78 |
| 0632 | 3 | 1 1/4 | **Ela Paparouna**[17] 4020 3-8-13 **72** (HCandy) *swtg: edgd rt s: sn led: rdn and hdd 2f out: no ex ins fnl f* 11/2[1] | DaneO'Neill 9 | 77 |
| 5041 | 4 | 3 | **Scotland The Brave**[23] 3867 4-9-4 **70** (JDBethell) *swtg: w ldr tl led 2f out: hdd over 1f out: no ex ins fnl f* 6/1[3] | (p) MartinDwyer 8 | 68 |
| 116- | 5 | 1 1/2 | **Russian Ruby (FR)**[281] 5851 3-9-11 **84** (NACallaghan) *trckd ldrs: plld hrd: wknd fnl f* 16/1 | JFEgan 5 | 79 |
| -003 | 6 | nk | **Sister Sophia (USA)**[12] 4199 4-8-10 **62** (WJMusson) *s.i.s: hld up: rdn over 1f out: n.d* 14/1 | RMullen 7 | 56 |
| 1202 | 7 | 1 3/4 | **In The Pink (IRE)**[14] 4148 4-9-3 **72** (MRChannon) *hld up: hdwy u.p over 2f out: wknd fnl f* 11/2[1] | SHitchcott(3) 4 | 62 |
| -514 | 8 | 5 | **Hot Lips Page (FR)**[19] 3993 3-9-1 **74** (RHannon) *lw: prom: rdn over 3f out: wknd over 1f out* 13/2[2] | RLMoore 3 | 53 |
| -003 | 9 | 28 | **Kindlelight Debut**[14] 4148 4-9-8 **74** (DKIvory) *b: plld hrd and prom: wknd and eased 2f out* 8/1 | NCallan 2 | — |

1m 39.46s (-1.02) **Going Correction** -0.025s/f (Good)
**WFA** 3 from 4yo+ 7lb **9** Ran **SP% 112.8**
Speed ratings: **104,103,102,99,97 97,95,90,62**CSF £34.51 CT £173.41 TOTE £6.80: £2.50, £2.50, £1.90; EX 40.50.
**Owner** D M Kerr And N Brunskill **Bred** Barouche Stud Ireland Ltd **Trained** Upper Lambourn, Berks

**FOCUS**
Quite a competitive fillies' handicap, but they didn't appear to go that quick. The form looks ordinary but sound for the grade.

**NOTEBOOK**
**Golden Island(IRE)**, unlike most of her rivals, is still open to a little improvement. She made light of her wide draw, and although the runner-up was bearing down on her at the line, she never really looked like being reeled in. Connections intend stepping up to Listed class next time with the Virginia Stakes at Yarmouth the target.
**Summer Shades** had her favoured fast ground, but did not have the best of luck in running. However, this confirmed she is at the top of her game at present.
**Ela Paparouna**, stepping up in trip, did not quite get home as well as she might have and may appreciate less use being made of her.
**Scotland The Brave** was always in the right place, but she has yet to convince over this trip.
**Russian Ruby(FR)**, making a belated return to action, was very fresh and should be all the better for the outing.
**Kindlelight Debut** *Official explanation: jockey said saddle slipped*

## 4552 SWYNFORD PADDOCKS HOTEL SWEET SOLERA STKS (GROUP 3) (FILLIES) — 7f

2:50 (2:51) (A) 2-Y-O £23,200 (£8,800; £4,400; £2,000) Stalls High

| Form | | | | | RPR |
|---|---|---|---|---|---|
| 212 | 1 | | **Maids Causeway (IRE)**[16] 4060 2-8-8 98 (BWHills) *trckd ldrs: led over 1f out: rdn out* 5/1[2] | SDrowne 10 | 100 |
| 416 | 2 | 1 1/4 | **Slip Dance (IRE)**[20] 3965 2-8-11 (EamonTyrrell, Ire) *lw: hld up: hdwy over 1f out: r.o* 10/1 | JFEgan 2 | 100 |
| 215 | 3 | 1/2 | **Park Romance (IRE)**[50] 3031 2-8-8 90 (BJMeehan) *hld up: outpcd 1/2-way: hdwy over 1f out: r.o* 10/1 | RLMoore 9 | 96 |
| 24 | 4 | nk | **Arbella**[10] 4234 2-8-8 (PWHarris) *lw: chsd ldrs: rdn and ev ch over 1f out: styd on same pce* 9/1[3] | MartinDwyer 6 | 95 |
| 0513 | 5 | 1 3/4 | **Indiannie Star**[22] 3907 2-8-8 87 (MRChannon) *chsd ldr tl led over 2f out: rdn and hdd over 1f out: no ex* 50/1 | SHitchcott 3 | 91 |
| 1 | 6 | hd | **Windscreamer**[22] 3905 2-8-8 (JWHills) *hld up: hdwy over 2f out: one pce fnl f* 3/1[1] | MHills 7 | 90 |
| 12 | 7 | hd | **Royal Alchemist**[42] 3316 2-8-8 (MDIUsher) *s.i.s: hld up: swtchd rt over 1f out: r.o ins fnl f: nt trble ldrs* 14/1 | ADaly 1 | 90 |
| 12 | 8 | 3 | **Valentin (IRE)**[14] 4119 2-8-8 (RHannon) *lw: plld hrd and prom: wknd fnl f* 5/1[2] | DaneO'Neill 5 | 82 |
| 11 | 9 | shd | **Strawberry Dale (IRE)**[15] 4100 2-8-8 (JDBethell) *hld up: plld hrd: nt clr run over 1f out: nvr able to chal* 9/1[3] | TEDurcan 11 | 82 |
| 6103 | 10 | nk | **Extreme Beauty (USA)**[32] 3599 2-8-8 93 (CEBrittain) *chsd ldrs: rdn 1/2-way: wknd over 1f out* 10/1 | JQuinn 8 | 81 |
| 1132 | 11 | 6 | **Piddies Pride (IRE)**[7] 4342 2-8-8 70 (PSMcentee) *led over 4f: wknd over 1f out* 66/1 | FPFerris 4 | 66 |

1m 25.5s (-1.27) **Going Correction** -0.025s/f (Good) **11** Ran **SP% 115.7**
Speed ratings: **106,104,104,103,101 101,101,97,97,97 90**CSF £53.38 TOTE £5.20: £1.70, £3.80, £3.10; EX 65.00.
**Owner** Lady Richard Wellesley **Bred** The Vallee Des Reves Syndicate **Trained** Lambourn, Berks
■ Stewards Enquiry : F P Ferris one-day ban: failed to keep straight from stalls (Aug 20)
S Hitchcott one-day ban: failed to keep straight from stalls (Aug 20)

**FOCUS**
This did not look the strongest of Group Threes and the early pace was only ordinary, but the winning time was fair for the grade and the form looks reasonably solid.

**NOTEBOOK**
**Maids Causeway(IRE)** took this step up in class in her stride, although it has to be said this didn't look the most competitive of contests. However, she is well thought of and should continue to improve, especially as she looks sure to appreciate a step up in trip.
**Slip Dance(IRE)** appreciated being back amongst her own sex and was far from disgraced under her Listed penalty.
**Park Romance(IRE)** was doing her best work in the closing stages, having looked to face a hopeless task at halfway. This trip held no fears for her, and she should certainly make her presence felt at Listed level at least.
**Arbella** left her maiden form well behind and, with improvement to come as she steps up in trip, looks to have a bright future.
**Indiannie Star**, who is out of a mare that won twice over this trip, was always in the right place, but she just was not good enough at this level.
**Windscreamer**, who was well supported, was somewhat disappointing with no apparent excuse. Impressive when winning her maiden, she is surely better than this. *Official explanation: trainer said filly was found to be coughing on returning home*
**Royal Alchemist** again gave a hint of better to come after not having the best of runs. She will have no trouble staying an extra furlong, and looks sure to give her small yard some fun at this level during the autumn.
**Valentin(IRE)**, already proven at this level, was always doing too much on the outside of the field. She may be better over six furlongs for the time being.
**Strawberry Dale(IRE)** travelled well at the back of the field, but could never find a run through. She is certainly worth another try at this level.
**Extreme Beauty(USA)** had shaped as though this trip might suit when staying on into third in the Cherry Hinton, but she folded tamely and was some way below her best.
**Piddies Pride(IRE)** was simply outclassed.

## 4553 TOTESPORT SILVER SALVER STKS (H'CAP) — 7f

3:25 (3:27) (B) (0-105,102) 3-Y-0+ £19,500 (£6,000; £3,000; £1,500) Stalls High

| Form | | | | | RPR |
|---|---|---|---|---|---|
| 10/6 | 1 | | **Desert Lord**[8] 4294 4-8-7 **82** (SirMichaelStoute) *lw: racd stands' side: hld up in tch: shkn up over 1f out: r.o wl to ld post* 6/1[1] | MartinDwyer 19 | 92+ |
| 4600 | 2 | shd | **Royal Storm (IRE)**[7] 4324 5-9-8 **97** (MrsAJPerrett) *lw: racd stands' side: chsd ldrs: rdn to ld wl ins fnl f: hdd post* 13/2[2] | SDrowne 18 | 107 |
| 0232 | 3 | nk | **Armagnac**[16] 4047 6-8-4 **79** (MABuckley) *racd stands' side: hld up: hdwy over 1f out: rdn and ev ch ins fnl f: r.o* 14/1 | ADaly 6 | 88 |
| 4065 | 4 | 1/2 | **What-A-Dancer (IRE)**[11] 4220 7-7-10 **74** (GASwinbank) *racd stands' side: trckd ldrs: led over 1f out: hung lft and hdd wl ins fnl f* 11/1[3] | JFMcDonald(3) 13 | 82 |
| 6055 | 5 | 3/4 | **Wizard Of Noz**[9] 4273 4-9-6 **95** (JNoseda) *racd stands' side: hld up in tch: rdn and ev ch over 1f out: sn hung lft and nt run on* 14/1 | (v[1]) SWKelly 9 | 101 |
| 000- | 6 | shd | **Folio (IRE)**[315] 5217 4-8-12 **87** (WJMusson) *racd stands' side: hld up in tch: rdn and nt clr run ins fnl f: styd on* 50/1 | RMullen 17 | 93+ |
| 3631 | 7 | nk | **Look Here's Carol (IRE)**[28] 3755 4-9-2 **91** (BAMcmahon) *racd stands' side: chsd ldrs: rdn over 2f out: styd on* 14/1 | GCarter 15 | 96 |
| 4401 | 8 | nk | **Molcon (IRE)**[14] 4126 3-8-3 **84** (NACallaghan) *racd stands' side: mid-div: rdn over 2f out: styd on* 16/1 | JFEgan 11 | 88 |
| 5354 | 9 | 1/2 | **Kool (IRE)**[41] 3337 5-9-0 **89** (PFICole) *swtg: racd far side: trckd ldr tl led that gp over 1f out: no ch w stands' side* 12/1 | RLMoore 2 | 92 |

-040 **10** *shd* **Capricho (IRE)**[14] 4120 7-9-13 **102** JQuinn 10 105
(JAkehurst) *racd stands' side: hld up: hdwy 1f out: nt rch ldrs* **14/1**

0540 **11** *½* **Starbeck (IRE)**[8] 4294 6-8-6 **81** NCallan 16 82
(PHowling) *b: racd stands' side: hld up: hdwy and hung lft fnl f: nvr trbld ldrs* **25/1**

3000 **12** *hd* **Marshman (IRE)**[14] 4120 5-8-11 **86** MHills 14 87
(MHTompkins) *lw: racd stands' side: hld up: r.o ins fnl f: nvr nrr* **14/1**

5000 **13** *hd* **Watching**[29] 3713 7-8-5 **80** GParkin 20 80+
(RAFahey) *lw: racd stands' side: hld up: n.d* **25/1**

0406 **14** *1* **Kareeb (FR)**[28] 3755 7-7-12 **73** CCatlin 7 71
(WJMusson) *racd stands's side: hld u in tch: rdn over 2f out: no ex fnl f* **12/1**

0000 **15** *hd* **Master Robbie**[6] 4371 5-8-11 **89** (v[1]) SHitchcott(3) 1 86
(MRChannon) *lw: racd far side: hld up: rdn over 1f out: n.d* **14/1**

1246 **16** *1 ½* **Waterside (IRE)**[6] 4360 5-8-7 **82** SWhitworth 8 75
(GLMoore) *led stands' side over 5f: sn wknd* **25/1**

0200 **17** *½* **Mysterinch**[29] 3717 4-9-1 **90** IMongan 3 82
(JeddO'Keeffe) *led far side: rdn over 2f out: hdd over 1f out: sn wknd* **33/1**

6050 **18** *nk* **Atavus**[30] 3673 7-8-13 **88** AMcCarthy 5 79
(GGMargarson) *racd stands' side: chsd ldr tl led wl over 1f out: sn hdd: wknd ins fnl f* **25/1**

0561 **19** *2* **Hey Presto**[14] 4122 4-7-12 **73** LisaJones 4 59
(CGCox) *racd far side: chsd ldrs: hung rt 2f out: wknd over 1f out* **12/1**

-000 **20** *28* **Tahirah**[14] 4120 4-8-10 **85** TEDurcan 12 —
(RGuest) *racd stands' side: chsd ldrs: rdn over 3f out: wknd over 1f out* **14/1**

1m 24.88s (-1.89) **Going Correction** -0.025s/f (Good)
**WFA** 3 from 4yo+ 6lb **20** Ran SP% **131.9**
Speed ratings: **109,108,108,107,107 107,106,106,105,105 105,104,104,103,103 101,100,100,98,66**CSF £41.83 CT £563.97 TOTE £7.90: £2.10, £2.60, £4.50, £3.00; EX 39.70 Trifecta £686.50 Pool: £967.00. 0.90 winning tickets..

**Owner** Cheveley Park Stud **Bred** Cheveley Park Stud Ltd **Trained** Newmarket, Suffolk

**FOCUS**

A typically competitive handicap run at a good clip with those drawn high having the advantage. The form looks strong for the grade and solid.

**NOTEBOOK**

**Desert Lord** confirmed recent promise when producing a storming late run to collar the runner-up on the line. With plenty of improvement to come, especially with an extra furlong likely to suit, he looks one to keep on the right side of.

**Royal Storm(IRE)** looked to have done everything just right until collared on the line. A tough and genuine type, he should continue to give a good account.

**Armagnac**, who has yet to score at this trip, turned in one of his best efforts from a poor draw.

**What-A-Dancer(IRE)** is not the easiest horse to win with and, he did not look to give it all he might have done.

**Wizard Of Noz**, wearing a visor for the first time, did not impress with his attitude and looks one to have reservations about.

**Folio(IRE)**, who was making a belated return to action, has not won since his juvenile days, but there was enough promise in this effort to give connections plenty of encouragement for the future.

**Look Here's Carol(IRE)**, who would have found the ground quicker than she likes, is a consistent filly and looked to run somewhere close to her mark again.

**Tahirah** *Official explanation: jockey said filly was moving very badly during the race; vet said filly was in season*

## 4554 ANDROMEDA MAIDEN STKS — 1m 4f

4:00 (4:01) (D ) 3-Y-0+ **£5,629** (£1,732; £866; £433) **Stalls** High

Form RPR

22 **1** **Mandatum**[22] 3922 3-8-10 MartinDwyer 9 79+
(LMCumani) *w ldr tl led over 7f out: rdn and hung lft ins fnl f: all out* **9/4**[1]

203 **2** *½* **Turnstile**[28] 3752 3-8-10 72 RLMoore 10 78
(RHannon) *a.p: rdn to chse wnr over 1f out: sn ev ch: edgd lft: styd on* **9/2**[3]

0- **3** *1 ¾* **Day One**[255] 6074 3-8-10 JFEgan 6 75
(GWragg) *h.d.w: hld up: hdwy 1/2-way: rdn over 1f out: styd on same pce* **14/1**

2220 **4** *1 ½* **Ganymede**[22] 3915 3-8-10 77 RMullen 4 73
(MLWBell) *chsd ldrs: rdn over 2f out: no ex fnl f* **6/1**

22 **5** *13* **Jayer Gilles**[32] 3608 4-9-7 DaneO'Neill 1 52
(HCandy) *chsd ldrs over 9f* **7/2**[2]

0-66 **6** *17* **Simon's Seat (USA)**[49] 3095 5-9-7 62 MHills 12 25
(PHowling) *dwlt: hld up: n.d* **20/1**

6-06 **7** *¾* **Lahob**[21] 3947 4-9-7 58 SWKelly 11 24
(PHowling) *led over 4f: hmpd over 3f out: sn wknd* **66/1**

43 **8** *5* **Wodhill Hope**[37] 3460 4-9-2 MTebbutt 8 11
(DMorris) *s.s: hld up: rdn over 4f out: sn wknd* **100/1**

5 **9** *8* **Cemgraft**[17] 4028 3-8-6 ow1 SDrowne 7 —
(MissECLavelle) *lw: prom: lost pl after 2f: rdn and wknd over 3f out* **11/1**

0 **10** *¾* **Jacobin (USA)**[56] 2888 3-8-10 SWhitworth 2 2
(PJMcbride) *prom over 8f* **66/1**

**11** *dist* **Riviera Red (IRE)** 4-9-7 AMcCarthy 5 —
(LMontagueHall) *well grown: dwlt: sn bhd: eased fnl 3f* **66/1**

- **12** *dist* **Grand Music (IRE)** 4-9-7 IMongan 3 —
(JJSheehan) *w'like: s.s: a t.o* **50/1**

2m 30.22s (-2.74) **Going Correction** -0.025s/f (Good)
**WFA** 3 from 4yo+ 11lb **12** Ran SP% **112.6**
Speed ratings: **108,107,106,105,96 85,85,81,76,75** —,—CSF £11.15 TOTE £2.50: £1.70, £1.80, £3.00; EX 10.50.

**Owner** Aston House Stud **Bred** Aston House Stud **Trained** Newmarket, Suffolk

**FOCUS**

An ordinary maiden, but it was run at a sound pace and the front four pulled nicely clear. The runner-up provides the best guide to the level of the form.

**NOTEBOOK**

**Mandatum** proved better suited by this trip and, although a narrow winner, never really looked like being passed. This effort should ensure he does not start off on too stiff a mark when going handicapping.

**Turnstile** has become a little frustrating and, although doing nothing wrong, it was the same story here. *Official explanation: jockey said colt was hanging*

**Day One** shaped well enough under tender handling, and is one to keep an eye on for a similar contest.

**Ganymede** again flattered only to deceive, and the slight nudge he received off Turnstile in the dip made no difference whatsoever.

**Jayer Gilles** dropped away tamely and was clearly below the form he had previously shown. However, he will have more options open to him now in handicaps.

**Grand Music(IRE)** *Official explanation: jockey said colt was never travelling*

## 4555 LONG MELFORD MAIDEN STKS — 6f

4:30 (4:31) (D ) 3-Y-0 **£5,434** (£1,672; £836; £418) **Stalls** High

Form RPR

U **1** **Conjuror**[14] 4144 3-8-7 RJKilloran(7) 8 79+
(AMBalding) *trckd ldrs: rdn to ld ins fnl f: r.o* **16/1**

050 **2** *1 ¼* **Imtalkinggibberish**[52] 2966 3-9-0 85 MartinDwyer 3 76
(JRJenkins) *led: rdn and hdd ins fnl f: styd on same pce* **3/1**[2]

3233 **3** *shd* **Farewell Gift**[10] 4236 3-9-0 81 RLMoore 2 75
(RHannon) *lw: chsd ldrs: rdn and ev ch over 1f out: edgd rt: nt qckn* **6/4**[1]

4-30 **4** *1 ¾* **Tropical Storm (IRE)**[44] 3251 3-9-0 70 SWKelly 1 70
(JNoseda) *w ldr over 3f: sn rdn: styd on same pce fnl f* **8/1**

4 **5** *nk* **Rachel's Verdict**[49] 3085 3-8-9 DaneO'Neill 5 64
(JRFanshawe) *plld hrd and prom: styd on same pce appr fnl f* **7/2**[3]

0 **6** *7* **Tides**[21] 3948 3-8-9 RMullen 4 43
(WJMusson) *in tch: sn pushed along: wknd over 1f out* **50/1**

6 **7** *3* **Classic Expression**[43] 3279 3-8-9 GCarter 7 34
(BAMcmahon) *sn outpcd* **33/1**

**8** *3* **Bird Key** 3-8-9 JFEgan 6 25
(RGuest) *w'like: bkwd: scope: s.i.s: outpcd* **14/1**

1m 12.99s (-0.33) **Going Correction** -0.025s/f (Good) **8** Ran SP% **115.8**
Speed ratings: **101,99,99,96,96 87,83,79**CSF £64.65 TOTE £19.70: £4.20, £1.60, £1.10; EX 92.40.

**Owner** Kennet Valley Thorougbreds I **Bred** Tedwood Bloodstock Ltd And Partners **Trained** Kingsclere, Hants

**FOCUS**

A decent maiden on paper and they set off pretty quick in this, but the overall time looked only fair and the form may not prove particularly strong.

**NOTEBOOK**

**Conjuror**, who took no time in getting rid of his rider on his debut, was on his best behaviour here. He was always travelling well on the heels of the leaders and showed a nice turn of foot when asked. There should be plenty more to come from him.

**Imtalkinggibberish** was keen to lead, but with Tropical Storm for company probably did a bit too much too soon.

**Farewell Gift** continues to frustrate and did not look to try that hard.

**Tropical Storm(IRE)** does not look good enough to win a maiden and would have more of a shout in handicaps.

**Rachel's Verdict** will need to learn to settle if she is to progress.

## 4556 NEWMARKETRACECOURSES.CO.UK H'CAP — 1m 2f

5:00 (5:00) (E ) (0-70,70) 3-Y-0+ **£4,153** (£1,278; £639; £319) **Stalls** High

Form RPR

0-10 **1** **Wellington Hall (GER)**[87] 2032 6-9-6 **62** AMcCarthy 10 68
(PWChapple-Hyam) *chsd ldrs: led 2f out: edgd rt nr fin: rdn out* **11/4**[1]

2303 **2** *shd* **Piri Piri (IRE)**[8] 4297 4-9-11 **67** SWhitworth 2 73
(PJMcbride) *s.i.s: hld up: hdwy over 1f out: rdn and ev ch ins fnl f: edgd rt nr fin: r.o* **11/2**[2]

1100 **3** *1 ½* **Jackie Kiely**[16] 4070 3-8-11 **65** (t) FPFerris(3) 3 68
(PSMcentee) *lw: slowly in to stride: hld up: hdwy 1/2-way: rdn and ev ch ins fnl f: styng on same pce whn n.m.r nr fin* **10/1**

-000 **4** *hd* **Iftikhar (USA)**[21] 3929 5-8-10 **52** SWKelly 7 55
(WMBrisbourne) *lw: s.i.s: hld up: hdwy over 1f out: r.o* **20/1**

6350 **5** *shd* **Rebate**[11] 4220 4-9-2 **58** (t) JFEgan 5 61
(RHannon) *hld up: plld hrd: hdwy over 1f out: r.o* **8/1**[3]

0450 **6** *½* **Galey River (USA)**[22] 3917 5-7-6 **41** oh2 ow1 DeanWilliams(7) 13 43
(JJSheehan) *lw: chsd ldrs: rdn over 4f out: nt clr run and lost pl over 2f out: r.o ins fnl f* **25/1**

004 **7** *2* **Rajayoga**[24] 3852 3-8-8 **59** MHills 12 57
(MHTompkins) *hld up: plld hrd: hmpd 8f out: swtchd lft over 2f out: hdwy over 1f out: no imp fnl f* **10/1**

-055 **8** *5* **Welcome Signal**[22] 3917 4-9-9 **65** (p) DaneO'Neill 9 53
(JRFanshawe) *lw: chsd ldr tl led over 3f out: rdn and hdd 2f out: wknd fnl f* **11/2**[2]

**9** *3* **Darab (POL)**[32] 4-9-9 **65** MartinDwyer 11 48
(RMHCowell) *s.i.s: sn prom: lost pl 5f out: wknd over 1f out* **20/1**

0006 **10** *2 ½* **Daimajin (IRE)**[10] 4250 5-8-0 **42** JMcAuley 8 20
(MrsLucindaFeatherstone) *prom: rdn and ev ch over 2f out: wknd over 1f out* **25/1**

0630 **11** *1 ¼* **Maritime Blues**[14] 4155 4-9-6 **62** RMullen 4 38
(JGGiven) *led over 6f: wknd over 1f out* **11/1**

0506 **12** *dist* **Haydn (USA)**[13] 4170 3-8-13 **64** IMongan 6 —
(GAHuffer) *hld up: racd keenly: rdn and wknd over 2f out* **20/1**

2m 7.75s (1.29) **Going Correction** -0.025s/f (Good)
**WFA** 3 from 4yo+ 9lb **12** Ran SP% **117.0**
Speed ratings: **93,92,91,91,91 91,89,85,83,81 80**,—CSF £15.06 CT £128.77 TOTE £3.30: £2.10, £1.70, £2.70; EX 20.80 Place 6 £35.43, Place 5 £23.72.

**Owner** Allan Darke & Tom Matthews **Bred** Baron G Von Ullmann **Trained** Newmarket, Suffolk

■ Stewards Enquiry : Dean Williams one-day ban: careless riding (Aug 20)

**FOCUS**

An ordinary handicap and a very slow winning time for the class, but competitive nonetheless and may rate higher.

**NOTEBOOK**

**Wellington Hall(GER)**, awash with sweat, proved very game and is clearly at his best when fresh.

**Piri Piri(IRE)**, much better suited by this trip looked to have timed it just right and only lost out on the nod. While she does find it hard to win, she certainly has the ability. *Official explanation: jockey said saddle slipped*

**Jackie Kiely** continues in good form despite his busy schedule.

**Iftikhar(USA)** has slipped to a handy mark and it will be a surprise if his handler cannot place him to good effect.

**Rebate** has now slipped to his lowest mark ever and is one to keep an eye on, despite his poor win-to-run ratio.

**Galey River(USA)** must have gone close with anything like a clear run.

**Darab(POL)** *Official explanation: jockey said gelding was unsuited by the firm ground*

T/Plt: £32.20 to a £1 stake. Pool: £63,260.00. 1,432.15 winning tickets. T/Qpdt: £13.00 to a £1 stake. Pool: £2,999.85. 169.65 winning tickets. CR

# 3559 REDCAR (L-H)

Saturday, August 7

**OFFICIAL GOING: Good to firm**

## 4557 COME RACING TOMORROW H'CAP 6f

**2:00** (2:00) (F) (0-55,58) 3-Y-0+ **£4,121** (£1,268; £634; £317) **Stalls** Centre

Form RPR

0503 **1** **Frimley's Matterry**[7] 4350 4-8-13 **49** TEaves(3) 4 58
(REBarr) *midfield far side: hdwy 2f out: sn rdn and styd on strly ent last to ld last 50 yds* **20/1**

3036 **2** 1/2 **Diamond Ring**[16] 4044 5-8-12 **45** GHind 11 53
(MrsJCandlish) *bhd: swtchd rt and hdwy 2f out: rdn over 1f out: styd on strly ins last* **22/1**

2066 **3** shd **Royal Windmill (IRE)**[33] 3579 5-8-9 **45** PMulrennan(3) 15 52
(MDHammond) *midfield: gd hdwy wl over 1f out: styd on strly ins last* **14/1**

6506 **4** nk **Levelled**[23] 3864 10-8-8 **41** DeanMcKeown 10 47
(DWChapman) *led: rdn wl over 1f out: drvn ins last: hdd and no ex last 50 yds* **25/1**

006 **5** 1 **Xanadu**[22] 3894 8-9-4 **51** (p) JMackay 19 54
(MissLAPerratt) *racd towards stands side: chsd ldrs: rdn wl over 1f out: kpt on u.p ins last* **12/1**

0032 **6** nk **Pride Of Kinloch**[8] 4309 4-9-11 **58** WRyan 12 60
(JHetherton) *s.i.s and bhd: hdwy stands side 2f out: sn rdn: styd on wl fnl f* **10/1**

0334 **7** hd **Loughlorien (IRE)**[4] 4422 5-9-0 **50** THamilton(3) 2 52
(RAFahey) *hld up in midfield: smooth hdwy to trck ldrs 2f out: rdn and ch over 1f out: sn drvn and nt qckn* **11/2**[1]

0110 **8** 3/4 **Mickledor (FR)**[17] 4013 4-9-0 **54** (p) DTudhope(7) 9 54
(MDods) *bhd and swtchd lft after 2f: hdwy and in tch 2f out: sn rdn along and kpt on same pce* **14/1**

0-30 **9** hd **Joshuas Boy (IRE)**[78] 2260 4-8-9 **42** (p) JCarroll 6 41
(KARyan) *chsd ldrs: rdn along and outpcd 2f out: kpt on u.p ins last* **18/1**

0561 **10** nk **Zietzig (IRE)**[7] 4350 7-8-7 **47** PJBenson(7) 7 45
(DNicholls) *prom: rdn along 2f out: grad wknd* **15/2**[3]

4510 **11** 1/2 **Miss Wizz**[4] 4425 4-8-5 **45** (p) RoryMoore(7) 17 42
(WStorey) *in tch stands side: rdn along 2f out: kpt on same pce* **10/1**

5003 **12** shd **Golden Spectrum (IRE)**[4] 4425 5-9-8 **55** (v) AlexGreaves 3 51
(DNicholls) *in tch far side: hdwy 2f out: sn rdn along and no imp* **6/1**[2]

2100 **13** 1 3/4 **Cleveland Way**[4] 4422 4-8-11 **44** (v) JBramhill 16 35
(JO'Reilly) *chsd ldrs: rdn along 1/2-way: sn wknd* **33/1**

0432 **14** hd **Bowling Along**[5] 4391 3-9-3 **54** DMcGaffin 20 44
(MESowersby) *s.i.s and bhd tl styd on fnl 2f* **6/1**[2]

3040 **15** hd **Good Time Bobby**[4] 4422 7-8-11 **51** JDO'Reilly(7) 8 41
(JO'Reilly) *in tch: rdn along over 2f out: sn btn* **40/1**

0046 **16** 1 1/4 **African Spur (IRE)**[7] 4350 4-8-5 **45** (v) DanielleMcCreery(7) 14 31
(DCarroll) *a rr* **25/1**

-000 **17** 2 **Lakelands Lady (IRE)**[144] 1033 4-9-7 **54** JEdmunds 18 34
(JBalding) *chsd ldr: rdn along over 2f out: sn wknd* **22/1**

00-0 **18** nk **Warren Place**[12] 4190 4-8-6 **42** ow2 LEnstone(3) 5 21
(JHetherton) *chsd ldrs: rdn along after 2f: sn wknd* **100/1**

0050 **19** nk **Percy Douglas**[3] 4452 4-8-12 **45** (t) AnnStokell 1 23
(MissAStokell) *in tch far side: rdn along over 2f out: sn wknd* **16/1**

-060 **20** 9 **New Day Dawning**[59] 2778 3-8-10 **47** RFitzpatrick 13 —
(CSmith) *sn in rr:bhd fr 1/2-way* **100/1**

1m 12.43s (0.73) **Going Correction** +0.05s/f (Good)
**WFA** 3 from 4yo+ 4lb **20** Ran SP% **133.2**
Speed ratings: **97,96,96,95,94 94,93,92,92,92 91,91,89,88,88 86,84,83,83,71**CSF £401.37 CT £6374.91 TOTE £40.60: £6.50, £10.00, £3.60, £10.80; EX 1022.30.
**Owner** Mrs R E Barr **Bred** T P Lyons **Trained** Seamer, N Yorks

**FOCUS**
A 0-58 handicap, a seller in all but name, and the form may only be relevant in that grade.

**NOTEBOOK**
**Frimley's Matterry**, third in a seller at Thirsk, broke his duck at the 19th attempt.
**Diamond Ring**, who has not won since her juvenile days, is in good form at present.
**Royal Windmill(IRE)**, with the cheekpieces left off, found this trip on the sharp side.
**Levelled** led them a merry dance and was only worn down in the closing stages.
**Xanadu** showed himself to be in good heart, but his last three wins have been much nearer home at Hamilton.
**Pride Of Kinloch**, 3lb higher, gave away far more ground at the start than she was eventually beaten by.
**Loughlorien(IRE)**, making a quick reappearance, again showed himself in good form, though he prefers less-firm ground than he encountered on this occasion.
**Bowling Along** *Official explanation: jockey said filly was denied a clear run*

## 4558 TETLEY'S IMPERIAL ALE RATED STKS (H'CAP) 1m

**2:35** (2:36) (D) (0-85,84) 3-Y-0+ **£18,297** (£5,630; £2,815; £1,407) **Stalls** Centre

Form RPR

0343 **1** **African Sahara (USA)**[8] 4293 5-9-2 **78** (t) OUrbina 2 89
(MissDMountain) *hld up far side: hdwy 1/2-way: effrt 2f out: rdn to ld over 1f out: drvn ins last: styd on wl* **7/1**[3]

3541 **2** hd **Efidium**[7] 4349 6-8-9 **71** DeanMcKeown 3 82
(NBycroft) *hld up far side: hdwy 1/2-way: rdn to chal over 1f out: drvn ins last and ev ch tl no ex nr fin* **14/1**

3645 **3** 1 1/4 **Tedstale (USA)**[11] 4209 6-9-2 **78** (b) WRyan 9 86
(TDEasterby) *trckd ldrs: nt clr run 2f out: swtchd rt over 1f out: sn rdn and styd on stringly ins last: nrst fin* **16/1**

50B0 **4** 1/2 **Atlantic Quest (USA)**[11] 4209 5-9-1 **77** (p) JCarroll 12 84
(GAHarker) *hld up and bhd stands side: gd hdwy over 2f out: rdn and ch whn hung bdly lft ent last: kpt on same pce* **25/1**

2005 **5** nk **Tiber Tiger (IRE)**[8] 4293 4-9-0 **76** (b) TGMcLaughlin 5 82
(NPLittmoden) *hld up far side: hdwy over 2f out: rdn over 1f out: kpt on ins last: nrst fin* **25/1**

0006 **6** 1 **Mount Vettore**[21] 3949 3-8-0 **69** JMackay 7 73
(MrsJRRamsden) *hld up and bhd: hdwy over 2f out: swtchd rt and rdn over 1f out: kpt on ins last: nrst fin* **20/1**

6120 **7** 1/2 **Woody Valentine (USA)**[9] 4271 3-8-13 **82** SChin 6 84
(MJohnston) *prom: rdn along over 2f out: drvn wl over 1f out and sn one pce* **10/1**

0202 **8** nk **Qualitair Wings**[8] 4293 5-8-10 **72** DMcGaffin 10 74
(JHetherton) *towards rr: hdwy over 2f out: sn rdn and kpt on: nvr rch rch ldrs* **20/1**

0201 **9** 1 1/2 **Obrigado (USA)**[18] 4006 4-9-6 **82** (v[1]) TPQueally 8 80
(WJHaggas) *puleld hrd: led after 1f: rdn along over 2f out: hdd & wknd wl over 1f out* **12/1**

0005 **10** 1 1/2 **Definite Guest (IRE)**[8] 4287 6-9-2 **81** THamilton(3) 1 76
(RAFahey) *midfield: smooth hdwy to trck ldrs 3f out: rdn 2f out: sn n.m.r and wknd wl over 1f out* **11/2**[2]

2161 **11** shd **Tony Tie**[26] 3797 8-9-5 **84** PMulrennan(3) 4 79
(JSGoldie) *trckd ldrs: effrt over 2f out: sn rdn and wkng whn hmpd over 1f out* **14/1**

3113 **12** 1 1/2 **True Night**[6] 4360 7-9-4 **83** TEaves(3) 13 74
(DNicholls) *in tch: pushed along over 2f out: sn rdn and wknd* **4/1**[1]

25 **13** 1 1/2 **Distant Country (USA)**[14] 4122 5-8-9 **71** (p) LGoncalves 16 59
(MrsJRRamsden) *hld up in rr: stdy hdwy on outer over 2f out: rdn to chse ldrs over 1f out: n.m.r and sn wknd* **15/2**

1050 **14** 3/4 **Pawan (IRE)**[7] 4319 4-8-8 **70** AnnStokell 15 56
(MissAStokell) *chsd ldrs stands side: rdn along over 2f out: sn wknd* **50/1**

1200 **15** 12 **Beltane**[40] 3386 6-7-12 **67** oh25 CHaddon(7) 11 25
(WDeBest-Turner) *led 1f: prom tl rdn along 1/2-way and sn wknd* **200/1**

0222 **16** 7 **Raphael (IRE)**[7] 4349 5-8-11 **80** AMullen(7) 14 22
(TDEasterby) *in tch: pushed along 1/2-way: sn wknd and bhd whn eased fnl 2f* **8/1**

1m 37.33s (-0.37) **Going Correction** +0.05s/f (Good)
**WFA** 3 from 4yo+ 7lb **16** Ran SP% **126.4**
Speed ratings: **103,102,101,101,100 99,99,98,97,95 95,94,92,92,80 73**CSF £97.15 CT £1602.71 TOTE £9.00: £2.50, £3.10, £4.60, £4.50; EX 147.00.
**Owner** Miss Debbie Mountain **Bred** Chris Nolan **Trained** Newmarket, Suffolk
■ Stewards Enquiry : W Ryan caution: careless riding

**FOCUS**
A fair handicap run at just a steady pace in the early stages. The form looks reasonably solid.

**NOTEBOOK**
**African Sahara(USA)**, who won twice in August last year, came from off the pace and showed a good attitude in a tight finish.
**Efidium**, on a career-high mark, is in the form of his life and in the end was only just held at bay.
**Tedstale(USA)**, who could have done with a stronger early pace, met trouble before finishing strongly. He is back on the same mark now as his last win.
**Atlantic Quest(USA)**, 3lb lower than when successful here in October, ran a lot better than of late.
**Tiber Tiger(IRE)**, who prefers straight tracks, stuck to the far rail and ran one of his better races this time.
**Mount Vettore**, who has been out of form, ran a lot better and has slipped to a lenient mark
**Definite Guest(IRE)**, out of luck at Goodwood, moved up looking a real threat but, after being tightened up slightly, he dropped right away in disappointing fashion. He is becoming hard to predict.
**True Night**, who is being kept very busy, ran a rare disappointing race.
**Raphael(IRE)**, on her 50th start, was struck into and sadly this winner of six races had to be destroyed.

## 4559 REDCARRACING.CO.UK (S) STKS 6f

**3:05** (3:06) (G) 2-Y-O **£3,017** (£862; £431) **Stalls** Centre

Form RPR

0 **1** **The Pen**[15] 4099 2-8-6 GFaulkner 4 51
(PCHaslam) *dwlt: sn in tch: hdwy 2f out: sn rdn: styd on strly ins last to ld last 50 yds* **5/1**[2]

04 **2** 1/2 **Paris Tapis**[15] 4095 2-8-6 JCarroll 16 49
(KARyan) *chsd ldr: hdwy to ld over 1f out: sn rdn: drvn ins last hdd and no ex last 50 yds* **6/1**[3]

5540 **3** 1 3/4 **Frisby Ridge (IRE)**[35] 3506 2-7-13 43 (b) AMullen(7) 2 44
(TDEasterby) *led: rdn along and edgd rt 2f out: hdd over 1f out: kpt on same pce* **9/1**

000 **4** 1/2 **Cadogen Square**[14] 4137 2-8-6 DeanMcKeown 3 43
(DWChapman) *chsd ldng pair: effrt and ev ch 2f out: sn rdn and kpt on same pce ins last* **33/1**

6066 **5** 1 1/2 **Miss Good Time**[21] 3951 2-8-6 (b[1]) JBramhill 9 38
(JGGiven) *s.i.s and b ehind: hdwy halfway: rdn and hung bdly lft over 1f out: kpt on ins last: nrst fin* **8/1**

0 **6** 2 1/2 **Blissphilly**[11] 4212 2-8-3 THamilton(3) 8 31
(RAFahey) *dwlt and b ehind tl styd on fnl 2f* **14/1**

516 **7** 3/4 **Premier Times**[9] 4278 2-9-0 59 PMulrennan(3) 17 39
(MDHammond) *bhd tl styd on fnl 2f* **5/1**[2]

0 **8** nk **Keyalzao (IRE)**[44] 3233 2-8-6 ow3 LEnstone(3) 5 30
(ACrook) *chsd ldrs: rdn along 2f out: wknd over 1f out* **25/1**

0 **9** 3/4 **Apetite**[13] 4175 2-8-4 SuzanneFrance(7) 10 30
(NBycroft) *s.i.s and bhd tl sme late hdwy* **33/1**

600 **10** 1 1/4 **For Nowt**[14] 4135 2-8-11 WRyan 14 26
(TDEasterby) *towards rr: effrt and edgd lft 2f out: sn rdn and no hdwy* **7/1**

0 **11** 3 **Gunnerbergkamp**[8] 4304 2-8-11 PMQuinn 7 17
(MDHammond) *bhd fr 1/2-way* **33/1**

3332 **12** 1 3/4 **Danehill Fairy (IRE)**[21] 3951 2-8-6 47 (b) GHind 6 —
(MrsADuffield) *chsd ldrs: rdn over 2f out: sn drvn and wknd* **9/2**[1]

0006 **13** 6 **Hunipot**[31] 3620 2-8-8 ow2 DMcGaffin 13 —
(MESowersby) *a rr* **50/1**

0B **14** nk **Peaceful Frontier**[11] 4212 2-8-6 RFitzpatrick 12 —
(CSmith) *in tch: rdn along 1/2-way: sn wknd* **33/1**

0005 **15** 1 3/4 **Timmy**[21] 3951 2-8-8 (b) TEaves(3) 1 —
(MESowersby) *bhd fr 1/2-way* **66/1**

1m 13.08s (1.38) **Going Correction** +0.05s/f (Good) **15** Ran SP% **125.1**
Speed ratings: **92,91,89,88,86 83,82,81,80,78 74,72,64,64,61**CSF £34.31 TOTE £6.80: £2.50, £2.60, £3.50; EX 37.50.The winner was bought in for 9,000gns.
**Owner** Middleham Park Racing XXVIII **Bred** Mrs R D Peacock **Trained** Middleham Moor, N Yorks

**FOCUS**
A very modest race even by selling-race standards.

**NOTEBOOK**
**The Pen**, a negative on the exchanges, again started slowly. She can improve again and looks a likely type for a low-grade nursery over seven furlongs plus.
**Paris Tapis**, dropping back in trip, came off a straight line otherwise she would have given the winner slightly more to do.
**Frisby Ridge(IRE)** made the running, but hung badly under pressure and was run out of it inside the last.
**Cadogen Square**, tailed off on her first three starts, ran considerably better.
**Miss Good Time**, suited by this much quicker ground, wore first-time blinkers but all she wanted to do was hang. She is losing the plot.
**Blissphilly** again gave away ground at the start. She showed some ability and, showing nothing at home, will improve again.
**Premier Times**, a positive on the exchanges, was back in the right grade but was never in the hunt.

## 4560 EUROPEAN BREEDERS FUND MAIDEN FILLIES' STKS 7f
**3:40** (3:40) (D) 2-Y-O **£4,342** (£1,336; £668; £334) **Stalls** Centre

Form RPR

3 **1** **Dubai Surprise (IRE)**[22] 3905 2-8-11 ........................... TPQueally 6 78+
(DRLoder) *trckd ldrs: smooth hdwy over 2f out: led over 1f out: rdn ins last and styd on* **10/11**[1]

**2** *1 1/4* **Aldente** 2-8-11 ........................... JMackay 4 72
(SirMarkPrescott) *trckd ldrs: hdwy over 2f out: sn rdn and ev ch tl drvn and nt qckn ins last* **8/1**[3]

00 **3** *3/4* **Resistance Heroine**[16] 4053 2-8-11 ........................... OUrbina 3 70
(EALDunlop) *hld up in tch: hdwy over 2f out: rdn over 1f out: kpt on same pce ins last* **25/1**

05 **4** *3* **Patxaran (IRE)**[23] 3876 2-8-11 ........................... GFaulkner 1 63
(PCHaslam) *chsd ldrs: rdn along 2f out: wknd over 1f out* **66/1**

56 **5** *1* **Autumn Melody (FR)**[10] 4234 2-8-11 ...........................(t) JCarroll 7 60
(SaeedBinSuroor) *sn led: pushed along wl over 2f out: rdn and hdd over 1f out: sn wknd* **9/1**

30 **6** *1 1/4* **African Gift**[29] 3693 2-8-11 ........................... SChin 2 57
(JGGiven) *cl up: rdn and hung bdly lft wl over 1f out: sn wknd* **16/1**

**7** *6* **Love Me Tender** 2-8-11 ........................... WRyan 5 42
(HRACecil) *hld up in rr: shkn up over 2f out and no rspnse* **5/2**[2]

1m 25.64s (0.74) **Going Correction** +0.05s/f (Good) **7** Ran SP% **113.3**
Speed ratings: **97,95,94,91,90 88,81**CSF £9.19 TOTE £2.30: £1.10, £2.20; EX 8.30.
**Owner** Dr Ali Ridha **Bred** James F Hanly **Trained** Newmarket, Suffolk

**FOCUS**
A decent maiden on paper but no gallop in the early stages and the form may prove only fair.

**NOTEBOOK**
**Dubai Surprise(IRE)** travelled strongly and took this with the minimum of fuss. She will improve again and will be suited by a mile.
**Aldente**, an April foal, was well backed to make a winning debut. Outpaced and driven along at halfway, she stuck to her guns in willing fashion and is sure to improve and find a race or two.
**Resistance Heroine** ran much better than on her first two starts, but as a result will not start life in nurseries from anything like a lenient mark.
**Patxaran(IRE)**, the big-priced outsider, shaped better than on her first two starts and connections will be hoping for a realistic handicap mark.
**Autumn Melody(FR)** has engaged reverse gear since making a satisfactory debut.
**African Gift**, disappointing on her second start, wanted to do nothing but hang violently left.
**Love Me Tender**, a positive on the exchanges, took a walk in the market and was soon struggling. She must be better than she showed here.

## 4561 MARY REVELEY RACING CLUB CLAIMING STKS 1m 6f 19y
**4:15** (4:15) (E) 3-Y-0+ **£3,347** (£1,030; £515; £257) **Stalls** Low

Form RPR

3306 **1** **Righty Ho**[24] 3835 10-8-9 43........................... KristinStubbs(7) 5 50
(WHTinning) *trckd ldrs: rapid prog to ld 3f out and sn clr: rdn and kpt on appr last* **4/1**[3]

1516 **2** *1* **Life Is Beautiful (IRE)**[36] 3472 5-9-2 53........................... TEaves(3) 3 52
(WHTinning) *led: stdd 4f out: hdd 3f out: shkn up over 2f out: sn rdn and kpt on same pce* **1/1**[1]

0310 **3** *1 1/4* **Crackleando**[36] 3479 3-8-8 60........................... StevenHarrison(7) 1 59
(NPLittmoden) *chsd ldr: rdn along 3f out: drvn and one pce fnl 2f* **5/2**[2]

6 **4** *11* **Ffizzamo Go**[15] 4087 3-8-5 ...........................(b) JMackay 6 33
(RMBeckett) *dwlt: rapid hdwy to chse ldr after 6f: rdn along over 3f out and sn btn* **10/1**

0000 **5** *13* **Steppenwolf**[27] 3771 3-8-0 37........................... CHaddon(7) 4 17
(WDeBest-Turner) *keen: chsd ldrs tl lost pl over 5f out and sn bhd* **25/1**

0060 **6** *dist* **Wilheheckaslike**[7] 4350 3-8-3 30........................... JBramhill 7 —
(WStorey) *a rr* **33/1**

3m 7.42s (2.42) **Going Correction** +0.05s/f (Good)
**WFA** 3 from 5yo+ 13lb **6** Ran SP% **114.4**
Speed ratings: **95,94,93,87,80** —CSF £8.71 TOTE £7.00: £2.60, £1.20; EX 12.60.
**Owner** W H Tinning **Bred** B J Warren **Trained** Thornton-le-Clay, N Yorks

**FOCUS**
A weak claimer and no gallop to halfway. The time was consequently modest for the grade and the form is of little consequence.

**NOTEBOOK**
**Righty Ho**, pushed along when the pace increased at halfway, went on past his stablemate and never really looked in any danger of being overhauled.
**Life Is Beautiful(IRE)**, who had 7lb in hand of her stablemate on official figures, has yet to shine over this trip. A negative on the exchanges, she seemed to be beaten to the punch and, though sticking to her task, never really looked like getting in a telling blow.
**Crackleando**, who had 5lb in hand of the winner on official figures, was a positive on the exchanges. He was struggling to keep up halfway up the straight and did not look to be striding out fully.
**Ffizzamo Go**, making just his second start and again sporting blinkers, moved up rapidly to join issue but dropped out just as quickly.
**Steppenwolf**, who would not settle, is a maiden now after 13 starts and looks likely to remain one.

## 4562 GO RACING IN YORKSHIRE MAIDEN H'CAP 1m 2f
**4:50** (4:51) (E) (0-75,72) 3-Y-0+ **£4,745** (£1,460; £730; £365) **Stalls** Low

Form RPR

2404 **1** **Havetoavit (USA)**[15] 4103 3-8-10 **58**........................... TPQueally 4 71+
(JDBethell) *mde all: qcknd clr 3f out: styd on* **5/1**[2]

4204 **2** *6* **Munaawesh (USA)**[10] 4249 3-8-8 **56**...........................(b) DeanMcKeown 7 57
(DWChapman) *hld up: hdwy 5f out:rdn to chse wnr 2f out: drvn and no imp appr last* **8/1**

5454 **3** *6* **Stanley Crane (USA)**[10] 4242 3-8-9 **57**...........................(t) GHind 10 47
(BHanbury) *hld up: hdwy 1/2-way: rdn along to chse ldrs 3f out: drvn and one pce fnl 2f* **7/1**[3]

0220 **4** *2 1/2* **Eboracum (IRE)**[8] 4307 3-8-8 **63**...........................(b[1]) AMullen(7) 8 48
(TDEasterby) *trckd ldrs: hdwy on inner 1/2-way: rdn along 3f out and sn one pce* **10/1**

600- **5** *1* **Rhetorical**[299] 5532 3-8-9 **57**........................... JMackay 9 40
(SirMarkPrescott) *sn rdn along in rr: drvn and sme hdwy over 2f out: nvr a factor* **5/1**[2]

4332 **6** *nk* **Bubbling Fun**[19] 3989 3-9-4 **66**........................... WRyan 6 48
(EALDunlop) *chsd wnr: rdn along 3f out: sn wknd* **7/4**[1]

0-00 **7** *4* **Zarneeta**[27] 3773 3-7-9 **50**........................... CHaddon(7) 2 25
(WDeBest-Turner) *sn outpcd and rdn along: a bhd* **100/1**

0600 **8** *9* **Chisel**[19] 3981 3-8-7 **55**........................... SChin 5 13
(MJohnston) *chsd ldrs: rdn along 4f out: sn wknd* **14/1**

-600 **9** *hd* **Power Nap**[8] 4307 3-7-12 **46** oh6...........................(vt[1]) JoannaBadger 11 3
(NTinkler) *chsd ldrs on outerm: rdn along over 4f out: sn wknd* **66/1**

2-00 **10** *5* **Fanling Lady**[21] 3952 3-9-10 **72**........................... JCarroll 1 20
(DNicholls) *towards rr: rdn along 4f out: sn struggling and b ehind whn eased fnl 2f* **10/1**

2m 5.72s (-1.08) **Going Correction** +0.05s/f (Good)
**WFA** 3 from 4yo 9lb **10** Ran SP% **120.6**
Speed ratings: **106,101,96,94,93 93,90,82,82,78**CSF £46.42 CT £286.26 TOTE £5.80: £2.30, £2.60, £1.90; EX 27.60 Place 6 £476.81, Place 5 £69.60.
**Owner** John E Lund **Bred** Irish National Stud **Trained** Middleham Moor, N Yorks

**FOCUS**
A modest handicap run at a sound pace and a decisive winner who looked in total command from the final turn. A couple of disappointing efforts by well-fancied horses tends to weaken the form.

**NOTEBOOK**
**Havetoavit(USA)**, dropping back in trip, was given his own way in front. He stepped up the gallop once in line for home and was soon clear with the race in the bag. The Handicapper will take a dim view.
**Munaawesh(USA)**, given a patient ride, went in pursuit of the winner but his cause was a hopeless one.
**Stanley Crane(USA)** settled better but he does not look by any means straightforward.
**Eboracum(IRE)** had blinkers on for the first time but would have preferred easier ground.
**Rhetorical**, weak in the market, was flat out from start to finish.
**Bubbling Fun**, well backed, went in pursuit of the winner but found nothing at all under pressure.
*Official explanation: trainer's representative had no explanation for the poor form shown*
**Fanling Lady** *Official explanation: jockey said filly hung right throughout*
T/Plt: £705.00 to a £1 stake. Pool: £29,362.60. 30.40 winning tickets. T/Qpdt: £22.00 to a £1 stake. Pool: £2,103.50. 70.50 winning tickets. JR

4563 - 4565a (Foreign Racing) - See Raceform Interactive

# 4430 DEAUVILLE (R-H)
### Saturday, August 7

**OFFICIAL GOING: Good to soft**

## 4566a PRIX DE POMONE (GROUP 2) (F&M) 1m 4f 110y
**3:30** (3:29) 3-Y-0+ **£42,148** (£16,268; £7,764; £5,176)

RPR

**1** **Lune D'Or (FR)**[34] 3566 3-8-11 ........................... TJarnet 5 112
(RGibson, France) *raced in 6th, close 5th on inside straight, went 2nd 2f out, ridden over 1f out, ran on steadily to lead well inside final* 2

**2** *1/2* **Hidden Hope**[35] 3519 3-8-6 ........................... DBonilla 8 106
(GWragg) *raced in 3rd, led 2 1/2f out, driven 2l up over 1f out, no extra & caught well inside final f*

**3** *nk* **Sweet Stream (ITY)**[92] 1952 4-9-4 ........................... TGillet 9 106
(JEHammond, France) *held up in rear, 10th on inside straight, headway to go 3rd over 1f out, kept on under pressure*

**4** *3/4* **Walkamia (FR)**[55] 2924 4-9-4 ........................... ELegrix 12 105
(AFabre, France) *raced in 7th, closing up on outside & 6th straight, came wide & stayed on steadily under pressure final 2f*

**5** *shd* **Royal Fantasy (GER)**[21] 3963 4-9-4 ........................... WMongil 10 105
(HSteinmetz, Germany) *held up, 9th straight, headway 2f out, ran on final f, nearest at finish* 2

**6** *1* **Whortleberry (FR)**[21] 4-9-4 ........................... CSoumillon 1 103
(FRohaut, France) *held up in mid-division, close 8th straight, 3rd well over 1f out, no extra final f* 3

**7** *shd* **Visorama (IRE)**[34] 3567 4-9-4 ........................... GaryStevens 4 103
(AFabre, France) *held up in rear, last straight, some progress from 2f out, never near to challenge* 1

**8** *2* **Dream Play (IRE)**[34] 3566 3-8-7 ow1........................... OPeslier 11 101
(AFabre, France) *raced in 5th, 7th straight, one pace final 2f*

**9** *10* **Rave Reviews (IRE)**[51] 2997 3-8-6 ........................... ODoleuze 13 85
(JLDunlop) *raced in 4th to straight, ridden & beaten well over 1f out*

**10** *3/4* **Beneventa**[21] 3944 4-9-4 ........................... TThulliez 2 84
(JLDunlop) *led to 2 1/2f out, 3rd straight, weakened quickly*

**11** *hd* **Baranquilla**[20] 3-8-6 ........................... C-PLemaire 3 84
(H-APantall, France) *held up towards rear, 11th straight, always behind*

**12** *4* **Ile Rousse**[458] 4-9-4 ........................... SHamel 6 78
(H-APantall, France) *tracked leader, 2nd straight, weakened quickly* 2

2m 38.9s **Going Correction** -0.30s/f (Firm)
**WFA** 3 from 4yo 11lb **12** Ran SP% **150.1**
Speed ratings: **111,110,110,110,109 109,109,108,101,101 101,98.**
**Owner** Mme P De Moussac **Bred** Haras De Mezeray S A **Trained** France

**NOTEBOOK**
**Lune D'Or(FR)** is definitely going the right way. Never far from the leading group she came with a run up the centre of the track to take the lead inside the final furlong. She stayed on well and further improvement must be expected . She was winning her second Group Two of the season and one in the top category looks within her grasp. She now goes for the Prix Vermeille and may well be supplemented into the Arc de Triomphe.
**Hidden Hope** was given a great ride. Always well placed, she slipped through on the inside and built up a lead of a couple of lengths by the two-furlong marker. However, although she tried gallantly she could not hold the winner. She may return to Deauville for the Prix Minerve later in the month.
**Sweet Stream(ITY)**left a disappointing Chantilly run behind. She made up late ground on the far rail and was putting in her best work in the latter stages. This was a promising effort.
**Walkamia(FR)** made a forward move at the beginning of the straight but then stayed on at one pace. An even longer trip may be to her advantage.
**Visorama(IRE)** could never get into it and is better than the bare form.
**Rave Reviews(IRE)**well up in the early stages and rounding the final turn she was a beaten force early in the straight. She should have done better but perhaps the softer conditions did not suit.
**Beneventa**, another Dunlop inmate, ran a rare bad race and stopped sharply. Made much of the early running and appeared to be going easily rounding the final turn. Her jockey said she was never on the right leg. She is better than this and had been progressive, so can be given another chance when/if her stable return to form.

# 4239 LEICESTER (R-H)
### Sunday, August 8

**OFFICIAL GOING: Good to firm**
Wind: Fresh across Weather: Sunny and humid

## 4567 EBF JOHN VIRGO MAIDEN STKS 7f 9y
**2:20** (2:22) (D) 2-Y-O **£5,798** (£1,784; £892; £446) **Stalls** Low

Form RPR

3332 **1** **Capable Guest (IRE)**[16] 4078 2-9-0 100........................... JFanning 16 86+
(MRChannon) *chsd ldrs tl led 1/2-way: shkn up over 1f out: r.o* **5/4**[1]

6 **2** 1 ½ **Pianoforte (USA)**[22] [3946] 2-9-0 .............................. TPQueally 2 83
(DRLoder) *a.p: rdn over 1f out: r.o* **14/1**

**3** *nk* **Banchieri** 2-9-0 .............................. KMcEvoy 18 82
(SaeedBinSuroor) *a.p: chsd wnr 3f out: styd on same pce ins fnl f* **11/2**[2]

5 **4** *3* **Walkonthewildside**[9] [4296] 2-8-11 .............................. ABeech[(3)] 7 74
(DRLoder) *hld up: hdwy over 2f out: nt trble ldrs* **25/1**

**5** 1 ½ **Humourous (IRE)** 2-9-0 ..............................(t) KDarley 9 71
(SaeedBinSuroor) *chsd ldrs: rdn over 1f out: styd on same pce* **11/1**

0 **6** *1* **Penny Island (IRE)**[18] [4016] 2-9-0 .............................. JDSmith 17 68
(AKing) *hld up in tch: rdn over 2f out: styd on same pce appr fnl f* **16/1**

**7** *nk* **Mostashaar (FR)** 2-9-0 .............................. RHills 10 67
(SirMichaelStoute) *dwlt: styd on appr fnl f: nvr nrr* **13/2**[3]

4 **8** ¾ **Baddam**[48] [3150] 2-9-0 .............................. IMongan 8 65
(JLDunlop) *mid-div: rdn 1/2-way: n.d* **40/1**

66 **9** 1 ¾ **Chinese Puzzle**[12] [4208] 2-9-0 ..............................(t) WRyan 12 61
(HRACecil) *prom over 5f* **16/1**

0 **10** *5* **Wujood**[23] [3913] 2-9-0 .............................. WSupple 6 49
(JLDunlop) *hld up: rdn ahlfway: n.d* **25/1**

50 **11** *1* **Arc Of Light (IRE)**[27] [3808] 2-9-0 .............................. MHills 4 46
(BWHills) *free to post: plld hrd and prom: lost pl over 4f out: wknd over 2f out* **25/1**

**12** ¾ **Mothecombe Dream (IRE)** 2-8-11 .............................. JFMcDonald[(3)] 3 44
(BJMeehan) *dwlt: sn prom: n.m.r 1/2-way: sn wknd* **33/1**

**13** *2* **Imperioli** 2-9-0 .............................. DeanMcKeown 11 39
(PABlockley) *s.s: outpcd* **66/1**

0030 **14** *nk* **Dishdasha (IRE)**[13] [4186] 2-8-9 55 .............................. RThomas[(5)] 15 38
(CRDore) *chsd ldr tl led over 4f out: hdd 1/2-way: wknd over 2f out* **200/1**

**15** *5* **Mytori** 2-8-9 .............................. SWhitworth 14 21
(DShaw) *s.s: outpcd* **125/1**

**16** *12* **Preskani** 2-9-0 .............................. RFitzpatrick 1 —
(MrsNMacauley) *sn led: hdd over 4f out: wknd 1/2-way* **125/1**

1m 23.36s (-2.74) **Going Correction** -0.375s/f (Firm) **16** Ran SP% **120.4**
Speed ratings: **100,98,97,94,92 91,91,90,88,82 81,80,78,78,72 58**CSF £19.03 TOTE £2.10: £1.10, £3.20, £2.70; EX 14.30.
**Owner** John Guest **Bred** Mountarmstrong Stud **Trained** West Ilsley, Berks

**FOCUS**
A decent maiden although the winner did not need to run to his best to score. The field raced towards the stands' side and the time was fair.

**NOTEBOOK**
**Capable Guest(IRE)** has twice been turned over at odds on, but he was well backed to make amends. Well suited by the seven furlongs and positive tactics, he scored pretty comfortably and Fanning did not have to get serious with him. Easier ground could benefit him and he will go for a Listed event at Deauville now.
**Pianoforte(USA)** built on his debut effort and had no problem with the extra furlong, staying on to steal second near the line.
**Banchieri** did his best to give the favourite a race, but was held in the final furlong and lost second place near the line. A half-brother to high-class filly Dazzle, he will come on for the run. *Official explanation: jockey said colt was slowly into its stride*
**Walkonthewildside**, last of five on his debut, is going the right way and he appreciated this extra furlong.
**Humourous(IRE)**, the Godolphin second string, was being niggled along shortly after halfway. He is in the Royal Lodge and is a half-brother to a mile winner, so another furlong ought to suit him.
**Penny Island(IRE)** has now run decent two races in maidens at this track and is a likely sort for handicaps next term.
**Mostashaar(FR)** is a half-brother to the yard's St Leger fancy Maraahel. He did not shape badly on this debut but is going to have to improve if he is to live up to some big-race entries.

## 4568 LEICESTER TIGERS (S) STKS — 7f 9y
2:50 (2:50) (G) 3-4-Y-0 — £2,968 (£848; £424) Stalls Low

Form RPR

5100 **1** **Shinko Femme (IRE)**[11] [4241] 3-8-10 53 .............................. WRyan 11 51
(NTinkler) *hld up: hdwy over 2f out: rdn to ld ins fnl f: jst hld on* **12/1**

4344 **2** *shd* **Kelseas Kolby (IRE)**[6] [4386] 4-9-7 55 ..............................(v) DeanMcKeown 12 56
(PABlockley) *hld up in tch: nt clr run over 1f out: squeezed through ins fnl f: r.o* **7/2**[3]

030 **3** *1* **Finger Of Fate**[15] [4132] 4-9-2 42 ..............................(b) GGibbons 7 48
(MJPolglase) *led: rdn over 1f out: hdd and unable qck ins fnl f* **20/1**

5522 **4** *shd* **Killala (IRE)**[10] [4276] 4-9-2 58 .............................. KDarley 10 48
(RNBevis) *prom: rdn 1/2-way: ev ch fr over 1f out: no ex towards fin* **2/1**[1]

00-0 **5** 2 ½ **Rue De Paris**[22] [3954] 4-8-13 40 .............................. THamilton[(3)] 4 41
(JohnAHarris) *chsd ldrs: rdn and ev ch fr over 1f out: wknd towards fin* **33/1**

0000 **6** ¾ **Chiqitita (IRE)**[11] [4241] 3-8-0 47 .............................. BSwarbrick[(5)] 9 34
(MissMERowland) *chsd ldr to 1/2-way: rdn over 2f out: sn outpcd* **33/1**

0600 **7** 1 ¼ **Sworn To Secrecy**[11] [4241] 3-8-2 54 .............................. JFMcDonald[(3)] 3 31
(SKirk) *chsd ldrs: rdn 1/2-way: sn outpcd* **11/1**

0300 **8** *2* **Wodhill Be**[17] [4066] 4-8-11 40 .............................. MTebbutt 14 25
(DMorris) *hld up: hdwy u.p over 1f out: wknd ins fnl f* **20/1**

4300 **9** *6* **Luke After Me (IRE)**[48] [3148] 4-9-2 52 .............................. KMcEvoy 1 14
(GASwinbank) *hld up: hmpd 3f out: n.d* **5/2**[2]

0546 **R** **Princess Ismene**[59] [2822] 3-8-10 45 ..............................(b) IMongan 8 —
(PABlockley) *ref to r* **12/1**

1m 24.43s (-1.67) **Going Correction** -0.375s/f (Firm)
**WFA** 3 from 4yo 6lb **10** Ran SP% **123.3**
Speed ratings: **94,93,92,92,89 88,87,85,78,—** CT £13.20 TOTE £3.10: £1.30, £3.80, £; EX34.10 1.There was no bid for the winner. Kelseas Kolby was claimed by Mr P. Butler for £6,000. Killala was subject to a friendly claim.e
**Owner** The Penniless Partnership **Bred** Rathbarry Stud **Trained** Langton, N Yorks

**FOCUS**
A modest time, even for a seller and the level of form is weak.

**NOTEBOOK**
**Shinko Femme(IRE)**, down in grade, took a narrow lead and held on by the skin of her teeth from the unfortunate runner-up.
**Kelseas Kolby(IRE)**, who has gained both his career wins over course and distance, nearly made it three. Squeezing through when a gap finally appeared, he finished fast but needed one more stride.
**Finger Of Fate** grabbed the rail and appeared to enjoy bowling along in front. He stuck on when headed and obviously stays this trip, but has enough pace to handle a drop back to six furlongs.
**Killala(IRE)** could not capitalise on the drop into the bottom grade and appeared to have no real excuse. He looks one to be wary of.
**Rue De Paris**, having only his second run of the season, was slightly squeezed out as the runner-up came past him inside the last, but was held at the time.
**Luke After Me(IRE)** could never get into the race after running out of room with three furlongs to race, but the fact that he seemed to give up pretty easily and the way he carried his head suggests caution is advisable.

## 4569 COALVILLE GLASS & GLAZING H'CAP — 1m 9y
3:20 (3:20) (D) (0-85,80) 3-Y-0+ — £6,987 (£2,150; £1,075; £537) Stalls Low

Form RPR

-600 **1** **Giocoso (USA)**[25] [3842] 4-9-10 **76** .............................. KDarley 10 88
(BPalling) *mde all: rdn clr over 1f out: eased nr fin* **11/1**

2341 **2** 1 ½ **Concer Eto**[13] [4199] 5-9-7 **73** ..............................(p) WSupple 12 82
(SCWilliams) *hld up: hdwy over 2f out: rdn to chse wnr 1f out: styd on* **7/2**[1]

2000 **3** 1 ½ **Ephesus**[12] [4220] 4-9-12 **78** ..............................(v) IMongan 14 84
(MissGayKelleway) *a.p: rdn to chse wnr over 1f out: styd on same pce fnl f* **10/1**

5115 **4** 2 ½ **Parnassian**[8] [4327] 4-9-0 **71** .............................. RThomas[(5)] 6 71
(GBBalding) *hld up: hdwy over 2f out: hung rt ins fnl f: nt rch ldrs* **6/1**[3]

0440 **5** *shd* **Cherished Number**[8] [4333] 5-9-1 **70** .............................. THamilton[(3)] 8 70
(ISemple) *chsd wnr over 6f: no ex* **10/1**

3210 **6** *nk* **Mr Velocity (IRE)**[29] [3755] 4-9-6 **72** .............................. TPQueally 9 71
(EFVaughan) *a.p: rdn over 2f out: styd on same pce* **4/1**[2]

2654 **7** ½ **Topton (IRE)**[9] [4293] 10-9-10 **76** ..............................(b) RHills 4 74
(PHowling) *hld up: styd on appr fnl f: nvr nrr* **9/1**

2004 **8** ½ **Adobe**[8] [4349] 9-8-8 **65** .............................. BSwarbrick[(5)] 2 62
(WMBrisbourne) *hld up: rdn over 2f out: nvr nrr* **10/1**

0030 **9** ¾ **Sheriff's Deputy**[22] [3929] 4-9-0 **66** .............................. SWhitworth 7 61
(JWUnett) *chsd ldrs: rdn over 3f out: wknd over 1f out* **20/1**

0000 **10** 2 ½ **Prince Of Gold**[12] [4209] 4-8-12 **64** ..............................(b[1]) JFanning 3 53
(RHollinshead) *hld up: rdn over 2f out: n.d* **20/1**

0/00 **11** *6* **Lizarazu (GER)**[4] [4438] 5-9-3 **72** .............................. RMiles[(3)] 5 47
(FJordan) *hld up: a in rr* **20/1**

0-06 **12** *12* **San Antonio**[17] [4061] 4-9-7 **73** .............................. WRyan 1 21
(MrsPSly) *mid-div: rdn over 3f out: wknd over 2f out* **33/1**

1m 39.44s (-3.16) **Going Correction** -0.15s/f (Firm) **12** Ran SP% **119.3**
Speed ratings: **109,107,106,103,103 103,102,102,101,98 92,80**CSF £47.04 CT £331.87 TOTE £13.30: £4.40, £2.00, £2.80; EX 64.30.
**Owner** W Devine & P Morgan **Bred** J F And Mrs Demeo,Joe Mullholland Jr & John Mull **Trained** Tredodridge, Vale Of Glamorgan

**FOCUS**
A fair handicap in which the winner was allowed to dictate a moderate pace before winding things up in the straight. However, the time was decent for the grade and the form looks solid.

**NOTEBOOK**
**Giocoso(USA)**, who began the season on a 9lb higher mark, was given a fine ride from the front by Darley. Winding things up in the straight, he stayed on strongly and was never going to be caught despite changing his legs as if the ground was faster than ideal.
**Concer Eto**, from a 4lb higher mark, ran a decent race but the enterprisingly-ridden winner always had his measure.
**Ephesus**, who did not get the breaks at Goodwood, was always well enough placed in this easier company but lacked the pace to get to the eventual winner.
**Parnassian** was back at a more suitable trip, but although staying on was never able to land a blow. The way this race was run did not suit those who tried to come from behind, and the ground was too fast for him as well.
**Cherished Number**, the visor dispensed with, ran a fair race off a mark 11lb lower than at the start of the season.
**Mr Velocity(IRE)** was found out by the lack of a true gallop and it might pay to give him another chance.
**Lizarazu(GER)** *Official explanation: jockey said horse was unsuited by the firm ground*

## 4570 LEICESTER CITY FOOTBALL CLUB RATED STKS (H'CAP) — 7f 9y
3:50 (3:50) (B) (0-100,100) 3-Y-0 — £12,414 (£4,708; £2,354; £1,070) Stalls Low

Form RPR

5221 **1** **My Paris**[22] [3955] 3-8-4 **83** oh3 .............................. JFanning 6 91
(KARyan) *mde all: qcknd 2f out: eased nr fin* **10/1**

0024 **2** *1* **Moonlight Man**[10] [4273] 3-9-7 **100** .............................. PDobbs 1 105
(RHannon) *chsd wnr: rdn over 1f out: kpt on* **8/1**[3]

-411 **3** 2 ½ **Royal Prince**[57] [2880] 3-8-10 **89** .............................. OUrbina 7 87
(JRFanshawe) *trckd ldrs: plld hrd: rdn over 1f out: styd on same pce* **4/5**[1]

16-6 **4** *nk* **Go Bananas**[18] [4031] 3-8-4 **86** .............................. JFMcDonald[(3)] 4 83
(BJMeehan) *plld hrd and prom: rdn over 1f out: styd on same pce* **16/1**

4166 **5** ½ **Appalachian Trail (IRE)**[22] [3943] 3-8-10 **89** ..............................(v[1]) IMongan 3 85
(ISemple) *hld up: effrt over 1f out: nvr trbld ldrs* **9/2**[2]

-624 **6** 3 ½ **Rising Shadow (IRE)**[15] [4151] 3-8-5 **84** .............................. WSupple 5 71
(RAFahey) *hld up: rdn over 2f out: wknd fnl f* **12/1**

11-5 **7** *10* **Firebelly**[162] [913] 3-9-2 **95** .............................. KDarley 2 55
(MJWallace) *chsd ldrs: rdn over 2f out: sn wknd* **25/1**

1m 23.13s (-2.97) **Going Correction** -0.375s/f (Firm) **7** Ran SP% **111.4**
Speed ratings: **101,99,97,96,96 92,80**CSF £79.91 TOTE £11.10: £5.10, £3.50; EX 67.90.
**Owner** J And A Spensley **Bred** J And A Spensley **Trained** Hambleton, N Yorks

**FOCUS**
A decent handicap on paper, but another race where the winner made his own running, and a modest time for the grade, which raises doubt about the value of the form.

**NOTEBOOK**
**My Paris** set a moderate gallop before injecting some pace with a quarter of a mile to run and was always in command from then on. He belatedly got off the mark last time and that appears to have done his confidence good.
**Moonlight Man** was in second place throughout and stuck on against the rail, but the winner was nicely in command. He is likely to remain hard to place from this sort of mark.
**Royal Prince**, who went up 11lb after winning over this course and distance in June, did not settle in the first part of the race and was unable to quicken when the tempo lifted. He might need a mile.
**Go Bananas**, having his second run back, was disadvantaged by the false pace and failed to settle.
**Appalachian Trail(IRE)**, in a first-time visor, was another caught out by the lack of a true gallop.

## 4571 STUART PEARCE H'CAP — 1m 1f 218y
4:20 (4:20) (D) (0-85,79) 3-Y-0+ — £6,948 (£2,138; £1,069; £534) Stalls High

Form RPR

6125 **1** **Rotuma (IRE)**[22] [3952] 5-9-0 73 ..............................(b) DTudhope[(7)] 1 82
(MDods) *chsd ldr tl led over 2f out: hdd briefly over 1f out: r.o* **6/1**

1121 **2** *hd* **Burgundy**[4] [4438] 7-8-11 63 ..............................(b) TPQueally 4 72
(PMitchell) *s.i.s: hld up: hdwy over 3f out: rdn to ld briefly over 1f out: r.o* **5/2**[1]

0241 **3** *2* **Jacaranda (IRE)**[16] [4086] 4-9-5 71 .............................. JFanning 8 76
(MrsALMKing) *chsd ldrs: rdn over 1f out: styd on same pce ins fnl f* **4/1**[3]

0360 **4** *5* **Giunchiglio**[25] [3844] 5-8-12 64 .............................. KMcEvoy 6 60
(WMBrisbourne) *prom: rdn over 2f out: wknd over 1f out* **6/1**

2151 **5** *1* **Opening Ceremony (USA)**[8] [4319] 5-9-6 75 .............................. THamilton[(3)] 2 69
(RAFahey) *hld up: hdwy over 3f out: wknd over 1f out* **3/1**[2]

/10- **6** 2 ½ **Theatre Time (USA)**[439] [1901] 4-9-13 79 .............................. PDobbs 5 68
(IanWilliams) *sn led: hdd over 2f out: wknd over 1f out* **11/1**

2m 7.67s (-0.73) **Going Correction** -0.15s/f (Firm) **6** Ran SP% **110.5**
Speed ratings: **96,95,94,90,89 87**CSF £20.64 CT £62.64 TOTE £9.40: £3.30, £2.00; EX 29.30.

**Owner** Denton Hall Racing Ltd **Bred** Sean Twomey **Trained** Piercebridge, Co Durham

**FOCUS**

Another slowly-run affair which developed into a sprint in the last two furlongs. A very moderate winning time for the grade and the form is ordinary.

**NOTEBOOK**

**Rotuma(IRE)** always had the leader covered before going on and showed the right attitude in a good tussle with the favourite. He is better on easy ground according to connections.

**Burgundy**, from a 4lb higher mark, got a nice run along the rail and briefly nosed ahead, but was just outpointed in a duel to the line. The lack of pace was against him and he remains in good form.

**Jacaranda(IRE)**, raised 3lb for his win in an amateurs' event, was unable to quicken with the first two when the pace hotted up.

**Giunchiglio** was outpaced by the principals in a slowly-run affair.

**Opening Ceremony(USA)**, 3lb higher, took advantage of a steadily-run race when scoring at Doncaster, but a similar scenario worked against her here.

**Theatre Time(USA)** set a modest gallop, but unlike the previous two winners on the card could never get away and had no answers when headed.

## 4572 PETER EBDON CLASSIFIED STKS — 1m 3f 183y

4:50 (4:50) (D) 3-Y-0+ — £5,414 (£1,666; £833; £416) Stalls High

Form — RPR

3310 **1** — **Leg Spinner (IRE)**$^{10}$ [4274] 3-8-8 77 ... KDarley 4 — 82
(MRChannon) *chsd ldr tl led over 2f out: rdn over 1f out: hung lft ins fnl f: all out* **7/2**$^{2}$

56-3 **2** shd **Albavilla**$^{103}$ [1684] 4-9-0 75 ... IMongan 2 — 77
(PWHarris) *hld up: hdwy and hung rt fr over 2f out: rdn and ev ch ins fnl f: r.o* **5/1**$^{3}$

4020 **3** 1 3/4 **Leighton (IRE)**$^{13}$ [4192] 4-9-3 74 ... TPQueally 8 — 77
(RMStronge) *chsd ldrs: nt clr run over 1f out: rdn and ev ch ins fnl f: looked hld whn hmpd towards fin* **20/1**

0122 **4** shd **Hatch A Plan (IRE)**$^{14}$ [4170] 3-8-6 74 ... KMcEvoy 3 — 77
(RMBeckett) *hld up: swtchd lft over 1f out: r.o ins fnl f: nt trble ldrs* **7/2**$^{2}$

300- **5** 1/2 **Seeyaaj**$^{25}$ [5724] 4-9-8 80 ... WRyan 5 — 81
(JonjoO'Neill) *led over 9f: no ex ins fnl f* **9/1**

4432 **6** nk **Mexican Pete**$^{4}$ [4453] 4-9-6 78 ... JFanning 7 — 79
(PWHiatt) *hld up in tch: rdn over 1f out: btn whn hmpd ins fnl f* **2/1**$^{1}$

05-5 **7** 23 **Taffrail**$^{75}$ [1212] 6-9-1 80 ... DerekNolan$^{(7)}$ 1 — 44
(DBurchell) *chsd ldrs over 9f* **20/1**

2m 31.34s (-3.34) **Going Correction** -0.15s/f (Firm)

**WFA** 3 from 4yo+ 11lb — 7 Ran SP% **114.0**

Speed ratings: **105,104,103,103,103 103,87**CSF £21.05 TOTE £4.90: £2.50, £2.70; EX 29.00 Place 6 £701.30, Place 5 £511.92.

**Owner** P D Savill **Bred** Steven Nolan **Trained** West Ilsley, Berks

■ Stewards Enquiry : K Darley two-day ban: careless riding (Aug 20-21)

**FOCUS**

A fair and typically tight classified event, but again there was no pace on, and this was quite a rough race.

**NOTEBOOK**

**Leg Spinner(IRE)**, down two furlongs in trip, showed a commendably brave attitude to hold on to his lead, although he did edge left under pressure. There should be more to come

**Albavilla** has apparently had her problems and had not run since April. Edging right as she made her challenge on the outside, she ran up against a very determined rival and just missed out.

**Leighton(IRE)** had his chance, but was held when having to be snatched up near the line. He just lacks a change of gear.

**Hatch A Plan(IRE)**, put up for finishing second in his last two runs, met with trouble and had to be switched round the outside before finishing strongly, just failing to get up for third.

**Seeyaaj**, who has developed into a fair hurdler since joining this yard, set a modest pace and stuck on quite well when headed.

**Mexican Pete** again shaped as if held by the Handicapper, but could have done with a stronger gallop.

T/Plt: £702.80 to a £1 stake. Pool: £38,945.60. 40.45 winning tickets. T/Qpdt: £43.60 to a £1 stake. Pool: £2,153.10. 36.50 winning tickets. CR

# $^{4557}$REDCAR (L-H)

Sunday, August 8

**OFFICIAL GOING: Firm (good to firm in places)**

The going was reckoned to be 'very firm' by the riders.

Wind: Fresh 1/2 against. Weather: Fine and sunny.

## 4573 TFM ROADSHOW IS HERE TODAY MEDIAN AUCTION MAIDEN STKS — 1m 1f

2:40 (2:41) (E) 3-4-Y-0 — £3,623 (£1,115; £557; £278) Stalls Low

Form — RPR

30P **1** — **Banana Grove (IRE)**$^{3}$ [4491] 3-8-7 ... PPMathers$^{(5)}$ 5 — 62
(ABerry) *in tch: hdwy over 3f out: led 2f out: kpt on wl* **33/1**

52 **2** 3/4 **Marsh Orchid**$^{9}$ [4303] 3-8-12 ... PHanagan 7 — 60
(WJarvis) *rn in snatches: drvn along and hung lft over 4f out: hdwy 3f out: edgd lft and wnt 2nd over 1f out: no real imp* **1/2**$^{1}$

4205 **3** 3 1/2 **Oh Golly Gosh**$^{9}$ [4303] 3-8-12 69 ... (p) TGMcLaughlin 1 — 53
(NPLittmoden) *sn chsng ldrs: led over 4f out: hung rt and hdd 2f out: fdd appr fnl f* **5/1**$^{2}$

0402 **4** 3 1/2 **Borodinsky**$^{16}$ [4101] 3-8-9 44 ... TEaves$^{(3)}$ 6 — 46
(REBarr) *chsd ldrs: outpcd 5f out: kpt on fnl 2f* **10/1**

0-0 **5** 4 **Wonder Wolf**$^{56}$ [2908] 3-8-7 ... GParkin 2 — 33
(RAFahey) *s.i.s: kpt on fnl 2f: nvr a factor* **25/1**

6 **6** 2 1/2 **Alpha Juliet (IRE)**$^{45}$ [3251] 3-8-7 ... RFfrench 3 — 28
(GMMoore) *w ldrs: drvn along 4f out: sn lost pl* **8/1**$^{3}$

0 **7** 9 **Zoomiezando**$^{9}$ [4303] 3-8-7 ... PMakin$^{(5)}$ 4 — 15
(MrsLucindaFeatherstone) *sn chsng ldrs: lost pl over 3f out: sn bhd* **66/1**

0-0 **8** 5 **Distinctlythebest**$^{4}$ [4444] 4-9-3 ... PMulrennan$^{(3)}$ 8 — 5
(FWatson) *led tl over 4f out: lost pl 3f out: sn bhd* **80/1**

1m 53.9s (0.50) **Going Correction** -0.025s/f (Good)

**WFA** 3 from 4yo 8lb — 8 Ran SP% **113.0**

Speed ratings: **96,95,92,89,85 83,75,70**CSF £50.07 TOTE £26.00: £5.70, £1.02, £1.70; EX 75.50.

**Owner** Alan Berry **Bred** Gordan Woodworth **Trained** Cockerham, Lancs

**FOCUS**

A modest time for a very modest race and the form is unlikely to work out.

**NOTEBOOK**

**Banana Grove(IRE)** had shown absolutely nothing in three previous starts - saddle slipped latest - and it was surprising he was only a 33/1 chance. However, he found dramatic improvement from out of nowhere and got the better of the hot favourite. Quite where he will go from here is open to debate as he will struggle in handicaps, and he will probably just make up the numbers in conditions events where he can pick up some prizemoney here and there.

**Marsh Orchid** looked to face a simple task against poor rivals in a bid to break his duck but never looked happy, being niggled and hanging under pressure at halfway. It is possible he was unsuited by the ground and, although not up to much, can be given another chance in low-grade handicaps. *Official explanation: jockey said gelding stumbled shortly after the start and was never travelling thereafter*

**Oh Golly Gosh** remains a maiden after ten starts and was also hanging under pressure. He can afford to be missed when or if he finally manages to win.

**Borodinsky** plugged on at his own pace and never posed a threat.

## 4574 FUNFAIR IS HERE TODAY CLASSIFIED STKS — 1m

3:10 (3:10) (E) 3-Y-0+ — £3,662 (£1,127; £563; £281) Stalls Centre

Form — RPR

0251 **1** — **Sharp Needle**$^{53}$ [2974] 3-8-13 70 ... EAhern 5 — 75+
(JNoseda) *trckd ldrs: edgd lft and reminders over 1f out: led last 75yds: readily* **13/8**$^{1}$

4151 **2** 3/4 **Blaeberry**$^{8}$ [4338] 3-8-8 65 ... (b) ANicholls 4 — 69
(PLGilligan) *w ldr: led and hung lft over 2f out: hdd and no ex ins last* **11/2**$^{3}$

2414 **3** nk **Oscar Pepper (USA)**$^{4}$ [4450] 7-9-6 67 ... (v) AlexGreaves 11 — 73
(TDBarron) *hld up: effrt 3f out: hrd rdn and hung lft over 1f out: swtchd rt ins last: kpt on* **3/1**$^{2}$

0-00 **4** 7 **Zap Attack**$^{9}$ [4305] 4-9-4 64 ... RFfrench 3 — 55
(JParkes) *trckd ldrs: wknd fnl 2f* **9/1**

2000 **5** 3/4 **Beltane**$^{1}$ [4558] 6-8-11 42 ... CHaddon$^{(7)}$ 1 — 53?
(WDeBest-Turner) *in tch on outside: rdn 3f out: sn wl outpcd* **33/1**

0060 **6** 3/4 **Gala Sunday (USA)**$^{10}$ [4258] 4-9-7 68 ... (b$^{1}$) DaleGibson 7 — 54
(MWEasterby) *led tl over 2f out: sn lost pl* **7/1**

-600 **7** 1 1/2 **Attacca**$^{86}$ [2075] 3-9-2 70 ... DAllan 6 — 53
(JRWeymes) *hld up: hdwy over 2f out: sn rdn and btn* **25/1**

0/00 **8** 4 **Thwaab**$^{6}$ [4386] 12-9-1 38 ... (v) PMulrennan$^{(3)}$ 2 — 39
(FWatson) *chsd ldrs: lost pl over 2f out: sn bhd* **100/1**

-006 **9** 8 **Chicago Bond (USA)**$^{22}$ [3955] 3-8-8 60 ... DMcGaffin 9 — 17
(BSmart) *sn trcking ldrs: rdn 3f out: sn lost pl and bhd* **28/1**

1m 38.02s (0.32) **Going Correction** -0.025s/f (Good)

**WFA** 3 from 4yo+ 7lb — 9 Ran SP% **112.2**

Speed ratings: **97,96,95,88,88 87,85,81,73**CSF £10.21 TOTE £2.20: £1.20, £2.40, £1.30; EX 7.80.

**Owner** Arashan Ali **Bred** Sentinel Bloodstock And Arashan Ali **Trained** Newmarket, Suffolk

**FOCUS**

A fair handicap but a moderate winning time for the grade. The form is ordinary although the winner should rate higher.

**NOTEBOOK**

**Sharp Needle** scraped home on her handicap debut at Hamilton but was much more convincing here and won with a bit in hand. She beat an in-form filly into second and should not be left on too stiff a mark after this, so may well be capable of completing a hat-trick.

**Blaeberry** showed a determined attitude when winning at Lingfield towards the end of last month, and did her best to give the winner a race here. She is still on a fair-enough mark and should continue to run well.

**Oscar Pepper(USA)** has a good record at the course and stayed on for pressure to claim third despite hanging a little to his left. He finished well clear of the fourth. *Official explanation: jockey said gelding hung left in the closing stages*

**Zap Attack** could not go with the front trio when things really heated up and folded into fourth.

**Beltane** ran well for one of his price but was not entitled to get so close on official ratings and does little for those around him.

**Gala Sunday(USA)** dropped away in the first-time blinkers having led for three quarters of the way. He remains frustrating.

## 4575 TOTEEXACTA NURSERY STKS (H'CAP) — 6f

3:40 (3:40) (C) 2-Y-0 — £10,481 (£3,225; £1,612; £806) Stalls Centre

Form — RPR

355 **1** — **Claret And Amber**$^{15}$ [4149] 2-8-6 71 ... PHanagan 1 — 84+
(RAFahey) *in rr: drvn along over 2f out: hdwy and nt clr run over 1f out: swtchd lft: styd on strly to ld last 75yds* **9/2**$^{2}$

1032 **2** 1 1/4 **Windy Prospect**$^{8}$ [4330] 2-9-5 84 ... MFenton 8 — 90
(PABlockley) *trckd ldrs: styd on to ld ins last: sn hdd and nt qckn* **13/2**$^{3}$

2133 **3** 1 **Space Shuttle**$^{8}$ [4342] 2-9-7 86 ... DAllan 5 — 89
(TDEasterby) *trckd ldrs: outpcd over 2f out: styd on strly fnl f* **9/2**$^{2}$

3202 **4** 1 1/4 **Hillside Heather (IRE)**$^{12}$ [4212] 2-8-4 69 ... FNorton 4 — 68
(ABerry) *led: wandered over 1f out: hdd & wknd ins last* **12/1**

2643 **5** 2 1/2 **Taras Treasure (IRE)**$^{39}$ [3406] 2-8-5 73 ... PMulrennan$^{(3)}$ 2 — 65
(JJQuinn) *dwlt: sn trcking ldrs: effrt over 2f out: wknd over 1f out* **12/1**

022 **6** 1/2 **Rasa Sayang (USA)**$^{18}$ [4009] 2-8-0 68 ... NMackay$^{(3)}$ 10 — 58
(TDBarron) *sn trcking ldrs: effrt over 2f out: wknd over 1f out* **9/2**$^{2}$

3206 **7** 1 **Lady Dan (IRE)**$^{29}$ [3753] 2-8-5 70 ... DaleGibson 3 — 57
(MWEasterby) *w ldrs: rdn over 2f out: lost pl over 1f out* **10/1**

3641 **8** 3 **Jerry's Girl (IRE)**$^{11}$ [4245] 2-8-7 72 ... RFfrench 6 — 50
(MissLAPerratt) *sn bhd and drvn along* **25/1**

2612 **9** 3/4 **Bibury Flyer**$^{8}$ [4325] 2-9-5 84 ... EAhern 9 — 60
(MRChannon) *sn trcking ldrs: lost pl over 1f out* **4/1**$^{1}$

1m 11.38s (-0.32) **Going Correction** -0.025s/f (Good) — 9 Ran SP% **116.2**

Speed ratings: **101,99,98,96,93 92,91,87,86**CSF £34.04 CT £140.04 TOTE £5.10: £1.50, £3.00, £2.30; EX 55.70 Trifecta £384.60 Pool: £10,184.22. 18.80 winning units..

**Owner** The Matthewman Partnership **Bred** D R Tucker **Trained** Musley Bank, N Yorks

**FOCUS**

A competitive nursery and the winner confirmed earlier promise to win going away. The form, rated through second and third, looks pretty solid.

**NOTEBOOK**

**Claret And Amber** had shaped with promise in three starts in maidens and was running off a fair enough mark of 71. He struggled to go the early pace, but really got going once getting into the clear and won going away. He will stay seven furlongs and looks to have more to offer.

**Windy Prospect** takes his racing well and ran another solid race in defeat. He remains winless on turf but will his turn will come.

**Space Shuttle** ran well in a better-grade contest at Newmarket last week and had the blinkers he has been wearing dispensed with. He finished strongly having got tapped for toe and may be worth trying over seven.

**Hillside Heather(IRE)** was trying this trip for the first-time and, having shown up well early, did not get home. A drop back to the minimum will see her in a better light.

**Taras Treasure(IRE)** was unsuited by this drop in trip, not having the pace to cope.

**Rasa Sayang(USA)** sweated up beforehand and was reported to have finished lame. *Official explanation: jockey said colt finished lame*

**Bibury Flyer** ran a rare bad race, wanting to do nothing but hang left-handed, and something may have been amiss. *Official explanation: jockey said filly hung left throughout*

## 4576 FAMILY FUNDAY H'CAP 6f
**4:10** (4:11) (D) (0-85,83) 3-Y-O **£7,026** (£2,162; £1,081; £540) **Stalls** Centre

Form RPR

0430 **1** **Obe Bold (IRE)**[8] 4320 3-8-0 **62** oh1 ow2 FNorton 5 68
(ABerry) *hld up: hdwy over 2f out: led over 1f out: r.o wl* **12/1**

64 **2** ¾ **Nistaki (USA)**[47] 3168 3-8-8 **70** DAllan 3 74+
(TDEasterby) *dwlt: hld up: stmbld over 3f out: effrt 2f out: styd on wl ins last: nt rch wnr* **13/8**[1]

0220 **3** 1¼ **Imperial Echo (USA)**[9] 4289 3-8-13 **80** (v) PMakin(5) 7 80
(TDBarron) *chsd ldrs: kpt on same pce fnl f* **5/1**[3]

0204 **4** ½ **Celtic Thunder**[25] 3845 3-9-7 **83** DMcGaffin 8 82
(TJEtherington) *led: hung bdly lft and hdd over 1f out: eased towards fin* **7/1**

-650 **5** 1¾ **Abelard (IRE)**[17] 4051 3-8-0 **62** PHanagan 1 55
(RAFahey) *chsd ldrs on outer: rdn over 2f out: sn outpcd* **7/2**[2]

3003 **6** 1 **Fitzwarren**[4] 4456 3-8-5 **67** EAhern 6 57
(NBycroft) *chsd ldrs: wknd over 1f out* **12/1**

0045 **7** 1 **Royal Awakening (IRE)**[6] 4391 3-7-5 **60** oh9 DFentiman(7) 2 47
(REBarr) *chsd ldrs: sn drvn along: wl outpcd fnl 2f* **40/1**

3251 **8** 3½ **Bella Boy Zee (IRE)**[8] 4320 3-7-12 **60** DaleGibson 4 37
(PABlockley) *in tch: effrt over 2f out: lost pl over 1f out: eased* **10/1**

1m 10.61s (-1.09) **Going Correction** -0.025s/f (Good) **8** Ran SP% **116.4**
Speed ratings: **106,105,103,102,100 99,97,93**CSF £32.64 CT £116.54 TOTE £14.70: £2.20, £1.80, £1.70; EX 52.60.
**Owner** Alan Berry **Bred** Saud Bin Saad **Trained** Cockerham, Lancs

**FOCUS**
A ctight little heat run at a decent pace and the form looks ordinary but sound.

**NOTEBOOK**
**Obe Bold(IRE)** left a slightly disappoitning run at Doncaster behind to win her first handicap. She is well exposed but can win in her turn.
**Nistaki(USA)** was a little unlucky, stumbling when just getting going and losing momentum, only to fly home when it was all too late. He had been running over a mile in maidens and, although coping with this trip, could ideally do with a return to seven.
**Imperial Echo(USA)** was dropping in grade having contested a hot handicap at Goodwood, and was slightly disappointing as his form prior to that entitled him to do better.
**Celtic Thunder** is another that has been contesting better-class races and, having led for most of the way, he hung badly to his left losing his action. Eventually eased, he is better than the form suggests. *Official explanation: jockey said gelding hung left and lost its action in the closing stages*
**Abelard(IRE)** ran better back on this faster surface but was still well held.

## 4577 NATIONAL FESTIVAL CIRCUS IS HERE H'CAP 7f
**4:40** (4:41) (D) (0-80,79) 3-Y-O+ **£7,260** (£2,234; £1,117; £558) **Stalls** Centre

Form RPR

1105 **1** **Yorkshire Blue**[23] 3910 5-8-2 **57** NMackay(3) 15 67+
(JSGoldie) *hld up: hdwy over 2f out: led last 150yds: hld on wl: sddle slipped* **7/2**[1]

-001 **2** ¾ **Splodger Mac (IRE)**[12] 4209 5-8-1 **53** FNorton 10 61
(NBycroft) *mde most: hdd ins last: kpt on wl* **25/1**

250 **3** hd **Distant Country (USA)**[1] 4558 5-9-5 **71** (p) MFenton 14 78+
(MrsJRRamsden) *s.i.s: hld up: hdwy over 2f out: nt clr run over 1f out: swtchd rt: styd on wl* **7/1**[3]

0656 **4** ½ **Sea Storm (IRE)**[8] 4349 6-9-12 **78** (p) RFfrench 12 84
(DRMacleod) *w ldrs: rdn over 2f out: kpt on wl fnl f* **20/1**

0055 **5** ½ **Tiber Tiger (IRE)**[1] 4558 4-9-10 **76** TGMcLaughlin 11 81
(NPLittmoden) *bhd: hdwy over 2f out: kpt on wl fnl f* **10/1**

0654 **6** ½ **What-A-Dancer (IRE)**[1] 4553 7-9-5 **74** PMulrennan(3) 5 78
(GASwinbank) *in tch: effrt over 2f out: hung lft over 1f out: nt qckn* **11/2**[2]

3202 **7** ½ **Bollin Edward**[9] 4305 5-8-13 **65** (v) DAllan 2 67+
(TDEasterby) *hld up: hdwy over 3f out: keeping on same pce whn sltly hmpd jst ins last* **9/1**

0060 **8** ¾ **Banjo Bay (IRE)**[17] 4047 6-9-4 **70** AlexGreaves 3 70
(DNicholls) *chsd ldrs: one pce whn bmpd jst ins last* **25/1**

00-5 **9** 1 **New Wish (IRE)**[9] 4301 4-8-12 **64** DaleGibson 9 62
(MWEasterby) *mid-div: rdn over 3f out: kpt on: nvr a real threat* **12/1**

0042 **10** hd **Inter Vision (USA)**[6] 4394 4-9-10 **79** TEaves(3) 4 76
(ADickman) *dwlt: sn trcking ldrs: hrd rdn over 1f out: kpt on same pce* **8/1**

0010 **11** ½ **Mehmaas**[4] 4447 8-7-13 **56** (v) PPMathers(5) 1 52
(REBarr) *racd alone far side: w ldrs: one pce fnl 2f* **50/1**

4002 **12** 1½ **Legal Set (IRE)**[14] 4179 8-8-6 **63** (t) DFox(5) 7 55
(MissAStokell) *chsd ldrs: effrt over 2f out: fdd over 1f out* **20/1**

5113 **13** nk **Downland (IRE)**[16] 4096 8-9-3 **69** KimTinkler 13 60
(NTinkler) *sn in rr* **20/1**

0005 **14** nk **No Grouse**[7] 4360 4-9-2 **68** (p) PHanagan 16 58
(RAFahey) *racd towards stands' side: in rr: hdwy u.p over 2f out: nvr on terms* **12/1**

0003 **15** nk **Hilltime (IRE)**[9] 4301 4-7-12 **50** PFessey 17 40
(JJQuinn) *racd towards stands' side: bhd: sme hewady over 2f out: nvr on terms* **28/1**

6040 **16** 2½ **Magic Amour**[15] 4122 6-8-3 **55** EAhern 6 38
(IanWilliams) *w ldrs: wknd and eased over 1f out* **20/1**

1m 23.46s (-1.44) **Going Correction** -0.025s/f (Good) **16** Ran SP% **127.8**
Speed ratings: **107,106,105,105,104 104,103,102,101,101 100,99,98,98,98 95**CSF £106.16 CT £613.93 TOTE £5.70: £2.10, £5.80, £3.30, £5.00; EX 125.90.
**Owner** John Mc C Hodge **Bred** R T And Mrs Watson **Trained** Uplawmoor, E Renfrews
■ Stewards Enquiry : P P Mathers one-day ban: failed to keep straight from stalls (Aug 20)

**FOCUS**
Another tight handicap and the field finished well bunched. The time was reasonable and the form appears solid.

**NOTEBOOK**
**Yorkshire Blue** was slightly unlucky not to finish closer at Newbury when last seen, but everything fell into place - apart from his saddle slipping in the closing stages - and he won a shade cosily. These are his ideal conditions and there should be more to come.
**Splodger Mac(IRE)** caused a shock when winning at Beverley last time and nearly pulled it off again, just finding one too good. He is evidently in good form and as he is still on a good mark, only 2lb higher here than when winning, has another small race in him.
**Distant Country(USA)**, well down the field at the course the previous day, was unlucky not to be at least second; being slow to get going and blocked when trying to come with a run. He is better than the bare form but does not win very often.
**Sea Storm(IRE)** is probably best at a mile these days and simply could not get going in time.
**Tiber Tiger(IRE)** was another to have run here the previous day and failed to confirm form with Distant Country.
**What-A-Dancer(IRE)** failed to run up to the form that saw him finish fourth at Newmarket the previous day and was disappointing, albeit not beaten far.
**New Wish(IRE)** is on a good mark and nearing a win.

## 4578 REDCAR CRICKET CLUB STKS (H'CAP) 2m 4y
**5:10** (5:10) (E) (0-75,79) 3-Y-O+ **£3,643** (£1,121; £560; £280) **Stalls** Low

Form RPR

4123 **1** **Spitting Image (IRE)**[35] 3564 4-8-11 **59** TEaves(3) 4 67
(MrsMReveley) *trckd ldr: qcknd and led over 4f out: hdd over 2f out: styd on gamely to ld last 150yds: jst hld on* **5/2**[1]

6303 **2** nk **Claradotnet**[15] 4146 4-9-3 **62** EAhern 5 70
(MRChannon) *trckd ldrs: effrt over 4f out: styd on ins last: jst hld* **10/3**[2]

0003 **3** 1 **Skye's Folly (USA)**[14] 4174 4-9-13 **72** (b[1]) MFenton 1 78
(JGGiven) *trckd ldrs: led over 2f out: hrd rdn over 1f out: hdd jst ins last: wknd nr fin* **4/1**

-153 **4** 4 **Peter's Imp (IRE)**[5] 4423 9-7-12 **48** PPMathers(5) 2 50
(ABerry) *hld up: hdwy 4f out: sn chsng ldrs: wknd 1f out* **6/1**

4511 **5** nk **Toni Alcala**[4] 4448 5-10-3 **79** 6ex PMulrennan(3) 7 80
(RFFisher) *hld up in last pl: hdwy on ins 4f out: rdn and edgd rt 2f out: sn wknd* **7/2**[3]

0005 **6** dist **Steppenwolf**[1] 4561 3-7-8 **61** oh21 ow3 CHaddon(7) 3 —
(WDeBest-Turner) *led: hdd over 4f out: sn lost pl and bhd: t.o* **66/1**

3m 29.48s (-2.02) **Going Correction** -0.025s/f (Good)
**WFA** 3 from 4yo+ 15lb **6** Ran SP% **109.7**
Speed ratings: **104,103,103,101,101** —CSF £10.54 TOTE £3.20: £1.80, £2.30; EX 9.80 Place 6 £12.69, Place 5 £10.51.
**Owner** The Mary Reveley Racing Club **Bred** Denis McDonnell **Trained** Lingdale, N Yorks

**FOCUS**
An ordinary staying handicap producing a good finish, with the principals running close to the expected level.

**NOTEBOOK**
**Spitting Image(IRE)** has been in good form of late and was recording her second career success. She did it the hard way, grinding out the result having taken it up half a mile out, and there is no reason why, off what is still a fair-looking mark, she cannot win again.
**Claradotnet** has not won in nine starts since landing her maiden, but this was a better run. She chased the winner hard but just failed to get there in time, and can pick up small race now back to form.
**Skye's Folly(USA)** returned to form at Newmarket and again ran well, although the blinkers failed to make any difference. He may be better without them and still has improvement in him.
**Toni Alcala** has been in great heart of late - winning the last twice - but ran most disappointingly here in his hat-trick bid.
T/Jkpt: Not won. T/Plt: £24.20 to a £1 stake. Pool: £42,687.60. 1282.85 winning tickets. T/Qpdt: £22.50 to a £1 stake. Pool: £2,084.50. 68.50 winning tickets. WG

# 4398 WINDSOR (R-H)
Sunday, August 8

**OFFICIAL GOING: Good to firm**
Wind: almost nil Weather: fine and hot, humid

## 4579 DINE IN THE CASTLE RESTAURANT TODAY MAIDEN AUCTION STKS (DIV I) 1m 67y
**2:30** (2:31) (E) 2-Y-O **£3,484** (£1,072; £536; £268) **Stalls** High

Form RPR

05 **1** **Blaise Hollow (USA)**[22] 3931 2-9-0 SDrowne 6 83
(RCharlton) *t.k.h: prom: led wl over 1f out: clr fnl f: pushed out* **11/4**[1]

**2** 3 **Lithos** 2-9-0 LDettori 5 76
(JAOsborne) *in tch: hmpd bnd 5f out and dropped to rr: rdn and prog over 2f out: chsd wnr jst over 1f out: no imp* **7/1**

06 **3** 4 **Fadael (IRE)**[13] 4198 2-8-9 JFortune 8 63
(PWD'Arcy) *led to wl over 1f out: grad wknd* **4/1**[2]

0 **4** 1½ **Gibraltar Bay (IRE)**[13] 4198 2-8-6 AMcCarthy 9 56
(GGMargarson) *s.i.s: sn chsd ldrs: rdn over 3f out: outpcd and btn wl over 1f out* **25/1**

**5** ½ **Maktu** 2-8-7 RLMoore 11 56
(PFICole) *dwlt: wl in rr: outpcd and bhd 5f out: kpt on fnl 2f: n.d* **13/2**[3]

35 **6** ½ **Hawridge King**[42] 3336 2-8-7 SCarson 2 55
(WSKittow) *plld v hrd: chsd ldrs: hung bdly lft bnd 5f out: effrt in centre 2f out: no prog over 1f out* **4/1**[2]

**7** 13 **Cross My Shadow (IRE)** 2-8-11 (t) DaneO'Neill 3 31
(MFHarris) *chsd ldr after 2f to over 3f out: wknd and eased* **33/1**

00 **8** 1½ **David's Symphony (IRE)**[18] 4016 2-9-0 RSmith 7 30
(RHannon) *chsd ldr for 2f: rdn over 3f out: sn wknd and eased* **16/1**

0000 **9** 7 **Lord Chalfont (IRE)**[7] 4359 2-8-0 (b) KGhunowa(7) 10 —
(MJPolglase) *outpcd early: rcvrd and in tch whn bdly hmpd bnd 5f out: no ch after* **100/1**

00 **10** 3 **Corniche Dancer**[11] 4231 2-8-3 ow1 LHarman(7) 4 —
(MRChannon) *s.v.s: plld hrd and sn in tch: hanging lft and hmpd bnd 5f out: effrt to chse ldrs 3f out: wknd rapidly* **16/1**

00 **U** **Sea Map**[18] 4016 2-8-11 RMullen 1 —
(SKirk) *veered lft and uns rdr s* **25/1**

1m 45.81s (0.21) **Going Correction** -0.125s/f (Firm) **11** Ran SP% **115.9**
Speed ratings: **93,90,86,84,84 83,70,69,62,59** —CSF £21.39 TOTE £2.90: £1.70, £2.10, £1.70; EX 23.30.
**Owner** D J Deer **Bred** Newbiggin Ltd **Trained** Beckhampton, Wilts

**FOCUS**
Not a very strong maiden, but decent enough performances from the front two. The winning time was marginally slower than the second division.

**NOTEBOOK**
**Blaise Hollow(USA)** appreciated the step up in trip and ran out a comfortable winner. It is hard to be sure just what he achieved and his immediate future looks to lie in the hands of the Handicapper, but he is progressing.
**Lithos**, a 27,000euros purchase, out of a three-year-old winner in France, was easy enough to back on course despite the eye-catching booking of Dettori, but made a very pleasing debut. He would have been much closer had he not been carried wide on the bend, and looks well up to winning a similar event.
**Fadael(IRE)** made her debut over five furlongs and failed to prove her stamina for this sort of trip. She is now qualified for a handicap mark and should find things easier in that sphere.
**Gibraltar Bay(IRE)** was ultimately well beaten, but this was an improvement on her debut running and she is clearly going the right way.
**Maktu**, a 4,000gns purchase, out of a ten-furlong three-year-old winner, made a promising-enough debut. He never once threatened after a slow start, but stayed on to the line and looks capable of improvement.
**Hawridge King** was far too keen on this step up in trip and hung badly on the bend just over half a mile from home. Judged on his first two starts, he is better than this. *Official explanation: jockey said gelding hung badly left throughout*

## 4580 ATTHERACES.COM FILLIES' H'CAP 1m 67y
**3:00** (3:02) (E ) (0-75,72) 3-Y-O **£3,601** (£1,108; £554; £277) **Stalls** High

Form RPR

1313 **1** **Kryssa**[10] 4264 3-9-7 **72** RLMoore 1 81
(GLMoore) *hld up in rr: prog on outer fr 3f out: drvn to ld jst ins fnl f: hld on gamely* **4/1**[2]

5103 **2** *nk* **Deign To Dance (IRE)**[20] 3993 3-8-9 **60** LDettori 5 68
(JGPortman) *hld up in midfield: prog wl over 1f out: drvn and str chal ins fnl f: jst hld* **7/2**[1]

5-6L **3** *1 1/4* **Elusive Kitty (USA)**[8] 4351 3-9-4 **69** (t) SRighton 12 74
(GAButler) *sed v awkwardly: wl in rr: prog over 2f out: swtchd lft jst over 1f out: drvn and styd on ins fnl f* **20/1**

0524 **4** *3/4* **Filliemou (IRE)**[3] 4470 3-8-2 **56** FPFerris(3) 6 59
(AWCarroll) *t.k.h: pressed ldr to 5f out: styd prom: chsd ldr again over 2f out to over 1f out: one pce* **10/1**

-625 **5** *1/2* **Anna Panna**[15] 4144 3-9-6 **71** DaneO'Neill 11 73
(HCandy) *trckd ldrs: rdn and effrt 2f out: cl up jst over 1f out: one pce* **8/1**

1306 **6** *nk* **Night Frolic**[37] 3478 3-8-12 **63** PRobinson 8 65
(JWHills) *mde most to jst ins fnl f: wknd* **13/2**[3]

4-10 **7** *shd* **Farriers Charm**[85] 2112 3-8-12 **63** JFortune 2 64+
(DJCoakley) *sn in last: adrift at 1/2-way: effrt 3f out: rdn and styng on whn bmpd 1f out: nt clr run sn after: kpt on* **14/1**

5323 **8** *shd* **Pella**[15] 4138 3-8-12 **63** JQuinn 9 64
(MBlanshard) *trckd ldrs: shkn up 3f out: nt clr run on inner wl over 1f out: fnd little fnl f* **4/1**[2]

2600 **9** *5* **Sonderborg**[26] 3827 3-8-1 **52** (b) LisaJones 4 42
(MissAMNewton-Smith) *racd in rr: effrt on inner whn no room and snatched up over 2f out: no ch after* **25/1**

0500 **10** *hd* **Gentle Raindrop (IRE)**[30] 3700 3-8-11 **62** RMullen 3 51
(SKirk) *chsd ldrs: rdn 3f out: wknd over 1f out* **25/1**

6040 **11** *2* **La Vie Est Belle**[46] 3211 3-9-3 **68** GBaker 7 53
(BRMillman) *t.k.h: prom: chsd ldr 5f out to over 3f out: wknd* **20/1**

1m 44.3s (-1.30) **Going Correction** -0.125s/f (Firm) **11** Ran SP% **119.6**
Speed ratings: **101,100,99,98,98 97,97,97,92,92 90**CSF £17.65 CT £252.55 TOTE £4.60: £1.60, £1.90, £5.60; EX 11.40.
**Owner** D J Deer **Bred** D J And Mrs Deer **Trained** Woodingdean, E Sussex
■ Stewards Enquiry : S Righton one-day ban: careless riding (Aug 19)

**FOCUS**
Just a modest fillies' handicap in which the consistent Kryssa was gaining her fourth win of the campaign. The form is ordinary and not particularly solid.

**NOTEBOOK**
**Kryssa**, a really tough sort, has only ever been out of the first three twice in her ten-race career and gained her fourth win of the season in determined fashion. She was racing off a career-high mark and things will be tougher when she is reassessed, but she nearly always gives her running.
**Deign To Dance(IRE)** got much closer to the winner than she did at Chepstow two starts previously and is clearly in better form now.
**Elusive Kitty(USA)**, who refused to race on her previous start, did not look a particularly straightforward ride. She clearly has the ability to win a race, but is still a maiden and does not look like one to trust.
**Filliemou(IRE)** remains in good form without managing to gain that elusive first success.
**Anna Panna**, racing beyond seven furlongs for the first time, had not shaped as though in need of this sort of trip but ran respectably.
**Pella** had been in good form recently without managing to get her head in front, but this was disappointing. She did not get the clearest of runs, but can hardly be considered unlucky.

## 4581 IAN HUTCHINSON MEMORIAL CONDITIONS STKS 6f
**3:30** (3:31) (D ) 2-Y-O **£7,026** (£2,162; £1,081; £540) **Stalls** High

Form RPR

1 **1** **Caesar Beware (IRE)**[66] 2609 2-8-10 DaneO'Neill 2 107+
(HCandy) *trckd ldrs: rdn to ld wl over 1f out: sn drew rt away: eased fnl 100yds* **11/10**[1]

5105 **2** *6* **Al Qudra (IRE)**[23] 3907 2-8-12 90 JFortune 1 89
(BJMeehan) *pushed along in last to stay in tch: effrt on outer 2f out: styd on u.p to take modest 2nd nr fin* **33/1**

1 **3** *nk* **Josh**[22] 3925 2-8-12 PRobinson 5 88
(MAJarvis) *restless stalls: sn trckd ldrs: effrt to chse wnr jst over 1f out: no ch: lost 2nd nr fin* **7/2**[2]

11 **4** *1 1/2* **Aastral Magic**[42] 3343 2-8-5 87 RLMoore 7 77
(RHannon) *led to over 3f out: outpcd 2f out: one pce after* **9/1**

1232 **5** *3/4* **Doctor Hilary**[20] 3975 2-8-10 93 RMullen 3 79
(MLWBell) *pressed ldr: led over 3f out: hrd rdn and hdd wl over 1f out: wknd fnl f* **8/1**

1 **6** *2* **Nightfall (USA)**[15] 4117 2-8-12 (t) LDettori 6 75
(SaeedBinSuroor) *trckd ldrs: pushed along 1/2-way: rdn and fnd nil wl over 1f out* **4/1**[3]

1m 12.24s (-1.63) **Going Correction** -0.25s/f (Firm) **6** Ran SP% **113.9**
Speed ratings: **100,92,91,89,88 85**CSF £38.70 TOTE £2.10: £1.70, £8.40; EX 53.90.
**Owner** Mill House Partnership **Bred** Glending Bloodstock **Trained** Wantage, Oxon

**FOCUS**
This looked like a strong conditions event - well up to scratch with last year's running won by Pastoral Pursuits - and Caesar Beware showed himself a high-class prospect with a very impressive success. With the previously unbeaten Aastral Magic appearing to run her race in fourth, the form looks very solid.

**NOTEBOOK**
**Caesar Beware(IRE)** ◆ beat subsequent Listed winner Don Pele three lengths easily on his debut at Chepstow and followed up in impressive fashion. He will take all the beating in the St Leger Yearling Stakes at Doncaster, his next intended target, before a possible tilt at the Mill Reef. He is a top-class prospect.
**Al Qudra(IRE)**, fifth behind Don Pele in Listed company on his previous start, simply bumped into a very smart performer.
**Josh** created a good impression when winning on his debut in a Haydock maiden that is beginning to work out, but that was on soft ground and he was unable to go on from that under these much quicker conditions.
**Aastral Magic**, successful on her first two starts, including over course and distance on her previous start, was faced with her toughest test to date and was well held. She appeared to run her race and, if she did, this is very solid form.
**Doctor Hilary**, a slightly unlucky second off an estimated mark of 91 in a nursery on her previous start, did not appear to run to his rating.
**Nightfall(USA)**, off the mark on his debut at Ascot, was disappointing on this step up in grade. He can be given another chance to show he is better than this.

## 4582 WINDSOR-RACECOURSE.CO.UK RATED STKS (H'CAP) 1m 2f 7y
**4:00** (4:01) (D ) (0-85,88) 3-Y-O **£6,975** (£2,146; £1,073; £536) **Stalls** Low

Form RPR

1004 **1** **Credit (IRE)**[14] 4173 3-9-6 **84** RLMoore 5 91+
(RHannon) *dwlt: sn trckd ldr: rdn over 2f out: led over 1f out: styd on wl* **4/1**[3]

0101 **2** *1 1/2* **Portmanteau**[7] 4368 3-9-10 **88** 3ex LDettori 6 92+
(SirMichaelStoute) *trckd ldng pair: effrt over 2f out: drvn to chse wnr ins fnl f: no imp* **3/1**[2]

-000 **3** *3/4* **Breathing Sun (IRE)**[36] 3543 3-8-12 **76** (t) RMullen 2 79
(WJMusson) *s.i.s: hld up in last pair: prog on outer 3f out: drvn to dispute 2nd pl ins fnl f: one pce* **11/1**

3221 **4** *1 3/4* **Arrgatt (IRE)**[23] 3899 3-9-5 **83** PRobinson 4 82
(MAJarvis) *t.k.h: led: rdn and hdd over 1f out: wknd fnl f* **13/2**

61 **5** *3* **Motorway (IRE)**[20] 3994 3-9-5 **83** SDrowne 1 77
(RCharlton) *trckd ldrs: rdn over 2f out: wknd over 1f out* **11/4**[1]

3043 **6** *1/2* **Magic Amigo**[14] 4170 3-8-11 **75** NPollard 3 68
(JRJenkins) *hld up in tch: rdn over 2f out: wknd over 1f out* **16/1**

-002 **7** *3 1/2* **American Duke (USA)**[4] 4443 3-8-4 **68** oh4 PaulEddery 7 54
(BJMeehan) *t.k.h: hld up in last pair: outpcd 3f out: shuffled along and nvr on terms after* **8/1**

2m 6.69s (-1.61) **Going Correction** -0.125s/f (Firm) **7** Ran SP% **110.3**
Speed ratings: **101,99,99,97,95 95,92**CSF £15.19 TOTE £5.40: £2.70, £1.70; EX 19.50.
**Owner** Highclere Thoroughbred Racing XV **Bred** G J Cullinan **Trained** East Everleigh, Wilts

**FOCUS**
A fairly decent handicap, featuring some unexposed three-year-olds, and the form looks sound although not outstanding.

**NOTEBOOK**
**Credit(IRE)** responded gamely to his rider's urgings in the straight, and despite taking time to hit full stride, ran out a cosy winner. He proved in no uncertain terms that he stays this trip, is still lightly-raced and did enough on this occasion to suggest that the best is yet to come.
**Portmanteau** turned in another solid effort, but was anchored by her 3lb penalty, and could not go with the winner late on. She remains open to improvement and can find another race this level during the summer.
**Breathing Sun(IRE)** has taken time to make his mark this season, having enjoyed success last year as a juvenile, and again hinted that a return to top form is imminent.
**Arrgatt(IRE)** ran too freely in the lead on this handicap debut and paid for that when the challengers loomed up in the straight. He can do better, but looks high enough in the weights on this evidence.
**Motorway(IRE)**, off the mark at the second attempt in a course and distance maiden last time, was disappointing. He failed to improve from that effort, and looks to have been allotted a stiff mark, but is very lightly-raced, so may prove this form to be wrong in the future.

## 4583 BOOK YOUR DISCOUNTED TICKETS ON-LINE MAIDEN FILLIES' STKS 1m 2f 7y
**4:30** (4:32) (D ) 3-Y-O+ **£4,251** (£1,308; £654; £327) **Stalls** Low

Form RPR

0 **1** **Boot 'n Toot**[131] 1186 3-8-12 LDettori 4 75
(CACyzer) *trckd ldrs: clsd fr over 2f out: drvn and styd on wl to ld nr fin* **12/1**

003 **2** *nk* **Uig**[76] 2374 3-8-12 77 DaneO'Neill 1 74
(HSHowe) *racd freely: led and sn clr: pushed along and pressed over 2f out: kpt on wl tl hdd nr fin* **8/1**[3]

42 **3** *nk* **Plummet (USA)**[25] 3843 3-8-12 JFortune 8 73
(JHMGosden) *trckd clr ldr: clsd over 2f out: rdn to chal wl over 1f out: nt qckn and hld nr fin* **8/15**[1]

0 **4** *shd* **Samaria (GER)**[42] 3348 3-8-12 RMullen 3 73
(CFWall) *hld up in rr and wl off the pce: pushed along and prog on outer 3f out: shkn up and styd on fnl f: nvr nrr* **33/1**

35 **5** *1 1/2* **Safirah**[25] 3843 3-8-12 PRobinson 10 70
(MAJarvis) *hld up in rr and wl off the pce: prog 3f out: reminders over 1f out: kpt on same pce* **7/1**[2]

**6** *3* **Ismahaan**[118] 5-9-7 RLMoore 5 65
(GWragg) *racd in midfield: pushed along over 4f out: nvr able to rch ldrs but plugged on fnl 2f* **16/1**

02-0 **7** *3/4* **Efrhina (IRE)**[13] 4192 4-9-7 63 SDrowne 11 63+
(MrsStefLiddiard) *chsd ldrs: pushed along over 3f out: no imp 2f out: eased whn btn ins fnl f* **12/1**

**8** *22* **Patterson (IRE)** 3-8-12 GBaker 9 21
(JMMadgwick) *s.s: a wl in rr: t.o over 2f out* **33/1**

00 **9** *6* **Pearnickity**[58] 2832 3-8-12 PDoe 6 10
(AWCarroll) *dwlt: a wl in rr: rdn over 4f out: t.o over 2f out* **50/1**

000 **10** *1/2* **Lookouthereicome**[42] 3348 3-8-12 JQuinn 2 9
(TTClement) *s.s: rcvrd to chse ldrs after 3f: wknd rapidly 3f out: t.o* **20/1**

0-00 **11** *1 1/2* **Cloud Catcher (IRE)**[72] 2454 3-8-12 SRighton 7 6
(MAppleby) *a in rr: rdn 1/2-way: tailing off whn hung bdly lft 3f out* **100/1**

2m 6.91s (-1.39) **Going Correction** -0.125s/f (Firm)
**WFA** 3 from 4yo+ 9lb **11** Ran SP% **123.7**
Speed ratings: **100,99,99,99,98 95,95,77,72,72 71**CSF £104.41 TOTE £8.10: £2.60, £2.60, £1.02; EX 128.70.
**Owner** Mrs Charles Cyzer **Bred** C A Cyzer **Trained** Maplehurst, W Sussex

**FOCUS**
An ordinary fillies' maiden with the favourite below form.

**NOTEBOOK**
**Boot 'n Toot** showed absolutely nothing when second last on her debut on good to soft ground at Folkestone, but Dettori was booked and she left that form well behind. The form is not easy to assess but, with more improvement a distinct possibility, she should not be underestimated next time.
**Uig**, not seen since finishing a close third in a course and distance maiden 76 days previously, showed that effort was no fluke with another solid performance. The Handicapper has taken no chances putting her on a mark of 77, and her best chance of success is probably in this grade.
**Plummet(USA)**, two and a half lengths behind today's runner-up on her debut, managed to get closer but was simply not good enough to reverse the placings. She has a maiden in her, but is nothing special.
**Samaria(GER)** improved significantly on her debut running and should go on again from this.
**Safirah** ran a satisfactory race. She is now qualified for handicaps and should do well in that sphere over further.
**Cloud Catcher(IRE)** *Official explanation: jockey said filly hung left turning into the home straight*

## 4584 NATIONAL HUNT RACING RETURNS TO WINDSOR MAIDEN AUCTION STKS (DIV II) 1m 67y
**5:00** (5:03) (E ) 2-Y-O **£3,474** (£1,069; £534; £267) **Stalls** High

Form RPR

3 **1** **Glorious Step (USA)**[38] 3456 2-8-9 LDettori 7 82+
(JHMGosden) *mde all: jinked bnd 5f out and again over 3f out: in command 1f out: pushed out* **1/1**[1]

33 **2** *1 ½* **Little Miss Gracie**$^{35}$ [3560] 2-8-3 ........................................ LPKeniry(3) 9 74
(PBurgoyne) *dwlt: sn rcvrd and prom: effrt over 2f out: rdn and styd on to take 2nd ins fnl f: no imp on wnr* **9/2**$^{3}$

4 **3** *¾* **Call Me Max**$^{13}$ [4198] 2-9-0 ........................................ JFortune 8 80
(EALDunlop) *chsd wnr: hrd rdn 2f out: no imp 1f out: lost 2nd ins fnl f* **4/1**$^{2}$

000 **4** *1 ½* **Fair Along (GER)**$^{75}$ [2382] 2-8-7 ........................................ PRobinson 4 70
(WJarvis) *t.k.h: hld up bhd ldrs: effrt 3f out: shkn up and no imp 2f out: kpt on* **16/1**

6 **5** *nk* **Briannsta (IRE)**$^{17}$ [4048] 2-8-11 ........................................ DaneO'Neill 1 73
(MRChannon) *hld up in last pair: pushed along and styd on steadily fr 3f out: nvr nrr* **9/1**

**6** *5* **Tranquilizer** 2-8-2 ........................................(t) JQuinn 2 53
(DJCoakley) *s.i.s: hld up in last: sme prog over 2f out: reminder over 1f out: no hdwy after* **25/1**

**7** *½* **Arch Folly** 2-8-7 ........................................ RMullen 10 57
(JGPortman) *dwlt: racd in rr: nt clr run briefly 3f out: shkn up 2f out: sn btn* **50/1**

6350 **8** *¾* **Be Bop Aloha**$^{13}$ [4198] 2-8-2 58........................................(p) PDoe 3 50
(IAWood) *rn green: hld up in midfield: effrt over 3f out: rdn and wknd 2f out* **40/1**

00 **9** *3 ½* **Looking Great (USA)**$^{27}$ [3808] 2-9-0 ........................................ SCarson 6 55
(RFJohnsonHoughton) *chsd ldrs: rdn 1/2-way: wknd wl over 2f out* **20/1**

000 **10** *9* **Pips Pearl (IRE)**$^{29}$ [3748] 2-8-2 ........................................ AMcCarthy 11 23
(MrsPNDutfield) *racd in midfield: rdn and struggling 1/2-way: sn wknd* **50/1**

1m 45.68s (0.08) **Going Correction** -0.125s/f (Firm) **10** Ran SP% **119.0**
Speed ratings: **94,92,91,90,89 84,84,83,80,71**CSF £5.51 TOTE £1.90: £1.10, £1.30, £1.50; EX 4.80.
**Owner** Saif Ali **Bred** Classic Lines Partnership **Trained** Manton, Wilts

**FOCUS**
A fair maiden that produced a marginally faster time than the first division, but one you would expect for the grade and the form looks reasonable.

**NOTEBOOK**
**Glorious Step(USA)** pinged out of the gates and, although there to be shot at approaching two out, always looked to have enough in the locker to hold off her nearest rivals. This confirmed the promise of her Yarmouth debut, in what looked a decent maiden, and should have learnt a great deal from this experience. Her entry in the Group One Fillies' Mile at Ascot in September confirms she is held in high regard, and she looks to have a bright future.
**Little Miss Gracie** ran another improved race, and despite not able to get near the winner, lost nothing in defeat. She got every yard of this trip, and now qualifies for nurseries, but has run well in defeat against some promising types so far, and will have again done her future mark no favours.
**Call Me Max** looked a threat to the winner before two out, but could not quicken and just kept on at the same pace thereafter. This was however, another solid effort and he had looked suited but this extra furlong, so should find a race and will no doubt fare better when handicapped.
**Fair Along(GER)** ran very keen at this first try over a mile, and paid for that late on, but still improved significantly to run his best race to date. He is slowly getting the hang of things, but may be best over slightly shorter for now. *Official explanation: jockey said gelding was too keen early on*
**Briannsta(IRE)**, whose debut effort over six furlongs suggested a step up in trip would suit, again ran green through the early stages but was doing his best work late on. This experience will not have been lost on him and he looks a likely nursery type.

## 4585 COME RACING AGAIN TOMORROW NIGHT H'CAP 5f 10y
**5:30** (5:32) (E ) (0-75,75) 3-Y-O **£3,838** (£1,181; £590; £295) **Stalls** High

Form RPR

6640 **1** **Mirasol Princess**$^{6}$ [4400] 3-9-1 **69**........................................ DaneO'Neill 11 76
(DKIvory) *s.i.s: outpcd and rdn: prog on outer 2f out: led ins fnl f: styd on wl* **8/1**

4014 **2** *1 ¼* **Jinksonthehouse**$^{17}$ [4044] 3-7-11 **56**........................................ HayleyTurner(5) 1 58
(MDIUsher) *sn chsd ldrs: rdn 2f out: effrt to chal 1f out: nt pce of wnr ins fnl f* **16/1**

3451 **3** *nk* **Wunderbra (IRE)**$^{13}$ [4194] 3-8-6 **60**........................................(t) JMackay 3 61
(MLWBell) *pressed ldr: led wl over 1f out: sn hrd rdn: hdd and fdd ins fnl f* **4/1**$^{2}$

000- **4** *1* **King Egbert (FR)**$^{327}$ [4957] 3-8-6 **60**........................................ PDoe 4 57
(AWCarroll) *dwlt and sltly hmpd s: chsd ldrs over 3f out: effrt on outer 2f out: one pce fnl f* **40/1**

0430 **5** *nk* **Borzoi Maestro**$^{17}$ [4059] 3-9-7 **75**........................................(p) LDettori 2 71
(JLSpearing) *led to wl over 1f out: sn hrd rdn: wknd ins fnl f* **6/1**$^{3}$

1003 **6** *1* **Piccleyes**$^{8}$ [4320] 3-8-7 **61**........................................(b) RLMoore 7 53
(RHannon) *stmbld bdly s: struggling in last: kpt on fnl f: nt rcvr* **6/1**$^{3}$

0652 **7** *1* **Peruvian Style (IRE)**$^{4}$ [4434] 3-9-1 **69**........................................ JFortune 10 57
(NPLittmoden) *chsd ldrs: rdn 1/2-way: no imp over 1f out: wknd fnl f* **5/2**$^{1}$

3033 **8** *2* **Blue Moon Hitman (IRE)**$^{32}$ [3635] 3-8-3 **60**........................................ FPFerris(3) 9 40
(RBrotherton) *chsd ldrs: hrd rdn 1/2-way: wknd over 1f out* **12/1**

6006 **9** *2* **He's A Rocket (IRE)**$^{10}$ [4279] 3-8-0 **59** ow1........................................(b) NChalmers(5) 8 31
(KRBurke) *outpcd and rdn after 2f: struggling fnl 2f* **15/2**

60.35 secs (-0.85) **Going Correction** -0.25s/f (Firm) **9** Ran SP% **116.0**
Speed ratings: **96,94,93,91,91 89,88,85,81**CSF £125.61 CT £591.65 TOTE £9.70: £3.00, £3.10, £1.80; EX 194.80 Place 6 £9.11, Place 5 £5.72.
**Owner** Anthony W Parsons **Bred** Bearstone Stud **Trained** Radlett, Herts

**FOCUS**
Just a modest sprint, but competitive enough and the form looks ordinary.

**NOTEBOOK**
**Mirasol Princess** forfeited her good draw against the rail with a slow start, but was still good enough to gain her first win of the year. She won off a mark of 76 last year, so should be competitive when reassessed. *Official explanation: trainer said filly was unsuited by the low draw and slow early pace last time*
**Jinksonthehouse**, in good form in selling and claiming company recently, ran well in this higher grade and looks up to winning a small handicap.
**Wunderbra(IRE)**, off the mark over six furlongs here on her handicap debut on her previous outing, may not have been ideally suited by this drop in trip and was unable to follow up.
**King Egbert(FR)** offered some promise in four runs for John Dunlop last season, but was last seen finishing last in blinkers in a Salisbury maiden. Racing for the first time in 327 days, he ran a most encouraging race and can win a similar race given normal improvement.
**Borzoi Maestro** is high enough in the weights.
**Piccleyes** lost his race at the start and is better than this. *Official explanation: jockey said gelding stumbled on leaving the stalls*
**Peruvian Style(IRE)** was unable to build on the promise of his recent Brighton second and could be best watched until returning to Polytrack.
T/Plt: £20.20 to a £1 stake. Pool: £40,824.15. 1,473.90 winning tickets. T/Qpdt: £7.60 to a £1 stake. Pool: £2,007.90. 194.40 winning tickets. JN

4586 - (Foreign Racing) - See Raceform Interactive

# 3964 CURRAGH (R-H)
Sunday, August 8

**OFFICIAL GOING: Good to firm**
The "good to firm" ground was very much on the easy side in the straight.

## 4587a ROYAL WHIP STKS (GROUP 2) 1m 2f
**2:45** (2:46) 3-Y-O+ **£54,929** (£17,394; £8,239; £2,746)

RPR

**1** **Solskjaer (IRE)**$^{15}$ [4160] 4-9-6 108........................................ JPSpencer 4 109
(APO'Brien, Ire) *mde all: qcknd pce ent st: strly pressed fr over 1f out: kpt on wl u.p: all out* **9/4**$^{2}$

**2** *hd* **Tropical Lady (IRE)**$^{21}$ [3969] 4-9-3 112........................................ MJKinane 5 106
(JSBolger, Ire) *trckd ldrs in 4th: nt clr run on inner fr 2f out: swtchd to chal wl ins fnl f: r.o wl: jst failed* **11/8**$^{1}$

**3** *nk* **Medicinal (IRE)**$^{15}$ [4160] 3-8-11 107........................................(b) PJSmullen 7 108
(DKWeld, Ire) *trckd ldr in 2nd: 3rd under 2f out: kpt on u.p fnl f* **7/1**

**4** *nk* **Trefflich (GER)**$^{22}$ [3959] 3-8-11 ........................................ FMBerry 1 107
(JohnMOxx, Ire) *trckd ldrs in 3rd: hdwy travelling wl 2f out: cl 2nd and chal over 1f out: ev ch: no ex cl home* **10/1**

**5** *2* **Media Puzzle (USA)**$^{642}$ [5642] 7-9-6 ........................................ PShanahan 6 104
(DKWeld, Ire) *hld up in rr: 5th and no imp st: kpt on fnl f* **20/1**

**6** *nk* **Latino Magic (IRE)**$^{15}$ [4160] 4-9-6 109........................................ RMBurke 3 103
(RJOsborne, Ire) *racd keenly in 5th: rdn and no imp early st: kpt on same pce fr 2f out* **5/1**$^{3}$

2m 2.90s **Going Correction** -0.50s/f (Hard)
**WFA** 3 from 4yo+ 9lb **6** Ran SP% **115.9**
Speed ratings: **106,105,105,105,103 103**CSF £6.02 TOTE £4.00: £1.70, £1.50; DF 5.60.
**Owner** Mrs A M O'Brien **Bred** Orpendale **Trained** Ballydoyle, Co Tipperary

**NOTEBOOK**
**Solskjaer(IRE)** made all in a very tactical race, quickening the pace twice in the straight. It looked a messy race behind him and he was all out to hold on. Ligament injuries have seen him lightly campaigned but he has done nothing wrong this season and this trip was no problem. He could take his chance in the Irish Champion Stakes.
**Tropical Lady(IRE)**, whose bid for six in a row was thwarted by a luckless run up the inner from two furlongs down, got daylight between horses all too late and could be considered unlucky.
**Medicinal(IRE)** never looked as though he was going to catch the winner and was instrumental in Tropical Lady's misfortunes. He ran on strongly over the last half furlong, though, and this was a big improvement on his Leopardstown run behind Latino Magic and Solskjaer.
**Trefflich(GER)** travelled well to challenge over a furlong out but could not raise his effort inside the last half furlong.
**Media Puzzle(USA)** ran an absolute cracker on his first appearance since his Melbourne Cup win almost two years ago. He kept on encouragingly over the last two furlongs without ever threatening over this inadequate trip, and his next outing will be interesting.
**Latino Magic(IRE)** did not run up to his Leopardstown form but this was his ninth appearance of the season.

## 4588a WEDGWOOD H'CAP 1m 2f
**3:15** (3:17) (50-90,90) 3-Y-O+ **£11,461** (£3,362; £1,602; £545)

RPR

**1** **Soliza (IRE)**$^{6}$ [4404] 3-8-10 81........................................ PShanahan 1 89
(CCollins, Ire) *sn prom: 2nd 1/2-way: rdn st: chal fr over 1f out: styd on wl to ld cl home* **7/2**$^{1}$

**2** *nk* **Newlands North (IRE)**$^{11}$ [4252] 3-8-0 71........................................ TPO'Shea 7 78
(MJPO'Brien, Ire) *attempted to make all: rdn and styd on wl st: hdd cl home* **6/1**$^{2}$

**3** *3 ½* **Victram (IRE)**$^{5}$ [4429] 4-8-2 71........................................ CPGeoghegan(7) 4 72
(AdrianMcguinness, Ire) *rr of mid-div: hdwy on outer ent st: 5th 2f out: kpt on fnl f* **12/1**

**4** *½* **Orpailleur**$^{16}$ [4111] 3-8-1 75........................................ MCHussey(3) 10 75
(MsJoannaMorgan, Ire) *hld up in mid-div: 8th after 1/2-way: 4th into st: mod 3rd whn veered rt 1f out: sn no ex* **12/1**

**5** *½* **Stormy Larissa (IRE)**$^{9}$ [4313] 4-8-6 68........................................ JAHeffernan 9 67
(EdwardPHarty, Ire) *hld up in rr: hdwy on outer early st: 7th 1 1/2f out: kpt on* **16/1**

**6** *2* **Saintly Rachel (IRE)**$^{21}$ [3964] 6-7-4 62........................................ CDHayes(10) 6 57
(CFSwan, Ire) *s.i.s: progess on outer 1/2-way: 6th 2f out: sn no ex* **10/1**$^{3}$

**7** *¾* **Shaykhan (IRE)**$^{11}$ [4254] 6-8-1 70........................................ SHunter(7) 5 64
(JamesLeavy, Ire) *trckd ldrs in 4th: 3rd and rdn early st: no imp: wknd ins fnl f* **10/1**$^{3}$

**8** *¾* **Man Of Aran**$^{5}$ [4429] 4-8-6 75........................................ RPCleary(7) 2 67
(MHalford, Ire) *towards rr: kpt on one pce st* **14/1**

**9** *hd* **Imdina (IRE)**$^{22}$ [3958] 3-8-5 76 ow1........................................ MJKinane 17 68
(JohnMOxx, Ire) *mid-div: pushed along 1/2-way: no imp st* **12/1**

**10** *1* **Littleton Telchar (USA)**$^{34}$ [3591] 4-9-2 78........................................ KFallon 15 68
(MJRyan) *mid-div: rdn appr st: sn no ex* **12/1**

**11** *hd* **Battle Games (IRE)**$^{91}$ [1978] 3-9-1 86........................................(b$^{1}$) FMBerry 12 76
(DeclanGillespie, Ire) *mid-div: 8th 1/2-way: no imp fr 3f out* **10/1**$^{3}$

**12** *½* **Trouville (IRE)**$^{17}$ [4072] 5-7-4 62........................................ AmyKathleenParsons(10) 18 51
(GerardO'Leary, Ire) *towards rr fr 4f out* **25/1**

**13** *4* **On The Horizon (IRE)**$^{9}$ [4310] 4-9-0 76........................................ PJSmullen 13 57
(DKWeld, Ire) *prom: 3rd early: 6th and rdn ent st: wknd 2f out* **12/1**

**14** *nk* **Marfinca (IRE)**$^{15}$ [4161] 3-9-0 85........................................ DPMcDonogh 11 65
(KevinPrendergast, Ire) *chsd ldrs: 5th 1/2-way: rdn and wknd fr 3f out* **10/1**$^{3}$

**15** *10* **Monsignor Phil (IRE)**$^{25}$ [3858] 4-9-5 86........................................(b) DJMoran(5) 8 47
(JSBolger, Ire) *chsd ldrs: 7th hlafway: no ex and wknd st* **10/1**$^{3}$

**16** *½* **Sat Nam (IRE)**$^{6}$ [4411] 3-7-7 71........................................ PBBeggy(7) 16 32
(NNelson, Ire) *nvr a factor* **20/1**

**17** *6* **Irish Empire (IRE)**$^{78}$ [2319] 6-9-6 82........................................ NGMcCullagh 3 31
(MJGrassick, Ire) *a bhd* **12/1**

2m 2.20s **Going Correction** -0.50s/f (Hard)
**WFA** 3 from 4yo+ 9lb **17** Ran SP% **149.3**
Speed ratings: **108,107,104,104,104 102,101,101,101,100 100,99,96,96,88 88,83**CSF £27.94 CT £262.03 TOTE £3.50: £1.40, £2.60, £3.20, £4.90; DF 21.70.
**Owner** Mrs H D McCalmont **Bred** Mrs H D McCalmont **Trained** The Curragh, Co Kildare
■ Stewards Enquiry : T P O'Shea two-day ban: used whip with excessive force and frequency (Aug 18-19)

**NOTEBOOK**
**Soliza(IRE)**, upped 2lb after a luckless effort at Cork last time, gained compensation here.
**Littleton Telchar(USA)**, who was denied a run at Galway due to a passport difficulty, was going nowhere under pressure before the straight.

## 4589a INDEPENDENT WATERFORD WEDGWOOD PHOENIX STKS (GROUP 1) (ENTIRE COLTS & FILLIES) 6f

**3:45** (3:45) 2-Y-O **£127,183** (£40,563; £19,436; £6,760)

RPR

1 **Damson (IRE)**[53] 2970 2-8-11 ........ KFallon 1 110
(DavidWachman, Ire) *a in tch: 3rd and rdn over 2f out: impr to chal 1 1/2f out: led under 1f out: styd on wl* **8/11**[1]

2 ¾ **Oratorio (IRE)**[21] 3965 2-9-0 ........ JAHeffernan 2 111
(APO'Brien, Ire) *prom: 2nd bef 1/2-way: 3rd u.p 1 1/2f out: kpt on ins fnl f* **15/2**[3]

3 ½ **Russian Blue (IRE)**[42] 3352 2-9-0 ........ JPSpencer 4 110
(APO'Brien, Ire) *broke wl and led: rdn and strly pressed 1 1/2f out: hdd under 1f out: no ex whn drifted rt u.p cl home* **9/4**[2]

4 5 **Billet (IRE)**[8] 4353 2-8-11 ........ FMBerry 3 92?
(AnthonyMullins, Ire) *hld up: prog into mod 4th over 2f out: no imp: kpt on same pce* **50/1**

5 9 **Camouflage (FR)**[18] 4036 2-9-0 ........ DPMcDonogh 6 68
(KevinPrendergast, Ire) *4th early: 5th and lost tch over 2f out: sn wknd* **10/1**

6 1 **Premier Dane (IRE)**[16] 4112 2-9-0 ........ JBowman 5 65
(KevinPrendergast, Ire) *chsd ldrs early: wknd fr 1/2-way* **20/1**

1m 13.2s **Going Correction** -0.025s/f (Good) **6** Ran SP% **116.3**
Speed ratings: **109,108,107,100,88 87**CSF £7.81 TOTE £1.70: £1.20, £3.30; DF 9.50.
**Owner** Mrs John Magnier **Bred** Epona Bloodstock Ltd **Trained** Carrick on Shore, Co Tipperary

**NOTEBOOK**
**Damson(IRE)** does not exactly catch the eye but she has matured into a very high-class filly already. Fallon was able to switch her off early, so much so that he had to get after her at halfway to quicken. She challenged between horses to lead early inside the last and went on. It was not exactly a display of blinding speed but she did everything that was asked of her and did not have a hard race. The Cheveley Park would appear to be at her mercy.
**Oratorio(IRE)** ran on better than his more fancied stable-companion but never really threatened once the winner went on.
**Russian Blue(IRE)** attracted plenty of market support and tried to make all, but he was no match for the winner when she went by and was beaten when edging right close home.
**Billet(IRE)** stayed on in fourth without playing any active part.
**Camouflage(FR)** did not build on his initial Naas promise.

## 4590a PATRICK P. O'LEARY MEMORIAL PHOENIX SPRINT STKS (GROUP 3) 6f

**4:15** (4:16) 3-Y-O+ **£34,330** (£10,035; £4,753; £1,584)

RPR

1 **One Cool Cat (USA)**[22] 3959 3-9-8 111........ JPSpencer 7 123+
(APO'Brien, Ire) *hld up in rr: in tch travelling easily over 1f out: qcknd to ld 150yds out: drvn clr: easily* **3/1**[1]

2 1 **The Kiddykid (IRE)**[22] 3940 4-9-7 ........ PJSmullen 6 114
(PDEvans) *a.p: 3rd and rdn 2f out: led 1f out: hdd 150yds out: kpt on wl u.p* **8/1**

3 ¾ **Nights Cross (IRE)**[7] 4362 3-9-0 ........(b[1]) ACulhane 2 109
(MRChannon) *hld up: 6th and hdwy 2f out: 4th under 1f out: kpt on* **10/1**

4 1 ½ **Osterhase (IRE)**[22] 3961 5-9-4 118........(b) FMBerry 10 104
(JEMulhern, Ire) *led: strly pressed 1 1/2f out: hdd 1f out: sn no ex* **10/3**[2]

5 hd **Ulfah (USA)**[15] 4159 3-8-11 99........ DPMcDonogh 3 101
(KevinPrendergast, Ire) *in tch on stand's rail: 3rd 1/2-way: rdn and one pce fr 2f out* **9/1**

6 hd **Desert Fantasy (IRE)**[42] 3351 5-9-4 108........(bt) JAHeffernan 8 103
(CRoche, Ire) *chsd ldrs on outer: rdn and one pce fr 1 1/2f out* **4/1**[3]

7 1 **Simianna**[8] 4324 5-9-1 ........(p) PShanahan 5 97
(ABerry) *chsd ldrs: 5th after 1/2-way: swtchd to chal under 2f out: sn no ex* **20/1**

8 hd **Hanabad (IRE)**[7] 4371 4-9-4 103........(b[1]) MJKinane 4 99
(JohnMOxx, Ire) *hld up in tch: rdn and no imp fr under 2f out* **10/1**

9 2 **Moon Unit (IRE)**[22] 3961 3-8-11 101........ DMGrant 9 90
(HRogers, Ire) *prom: 2nd and rdn 1/2-way: wknd fr 1 1/2f out* **20/1**

L **Grand Reward (USA)**[32] 3648 3-9-0 106........ CO'Donoghue 1 —
(APO'Brien, Ire) *ref to r* **10/1**

1m 12.7s **Going Correction** -0.025s/f (Good)
**WFA** 3 from 4yo+ 4lb **10** Ran SP% **126.0**
Speed ratings: **112,110,109,107,107 107,105,105,102,**—CSF £30.40 TOTE £2.70: £1.50, £3.70, £6.50; DF 45.20.
**Owner** Mrs John Magnier **Bred** WinStar Farm Llc **Trained** Ballydoyle, Co Tipperary

**NOTEBOOK**
**One Cool Cat(USA)** has probably found his correct trip and certainly justified his trainer's faith in him. Switched off in the rear, he cruised through to lead well inside the last and drew clear, possibly being value for three lengths. He has plenty of time left to build into a top sprinter and the Nunthorpe, followed by Haydock, could be the next stepping stones now that the right key has been found.
**The Kiddykid(IRE)** might be a bit flattered by the bare result but kept on quite well and has run to form with the third horse. Successful in the Group Three Greenlands Stakes here in May, he seems to like this track.
**Nights Cross(IRE)** made good progress over the last furlong but was never a real challenger to the winner.
**Osterhase(IRE)** came over to the rail from his outside draw and tried to make all, but he was headed by the runner-up a furlong out and found nothing extra. He is better suited by the minimum these days.
**Ulfah(USA)** could find only the one pace after being in touch throughout.
**Desert Fantasy(IRE)**, well supported, could not quicken after racing with the pace on the outer.
**Simianna** had no difficulty going the pace but, after switching to make her effort, found nothing from a furlong and a half down.
**Hanabad(IRE)** again disappointed.
**Grand Reward(USA)** sat back in the stalls and bobbed his jockey over his head when they opened.

## 4592a ROBERT H. GRIFFIN DEBUTANTE STKS (GROUP 2) (FILLIES) 7f

**5:15** (5:16) 2-Y-O **£59,507** (£17,394; £8,239; £2,746)

RPR

1 **Silk And Scarlet**[25] 3859 2-8-11 ........ JPSpencer 4 102+
(APO'Brien, Ire) *hld up in rr: hdwy 1 1/2f out: 2nd under 1f out: pushed out to ld 100yds out: drvn nr fin: easily* **13/8**[1]

2 ½ **Luas Line (IRE)**[6] 4407 2-8-11 ........ KFallon 1 96
(DavidWachman, Ire) *trckd ldrs: 4th 1/2-way: rdn to ld over 1f out: hdd 100yds out: kpt on wl wout troubling wnr* **3/1**[2]

3 2 **Chelsea Rose (IRE)**[60] 2791 2-8-11 ........ PShanahan 7 91
(CCollins, Ire) *disp ld: hdd under 2f out: kpt on u.p* **7/2**[3]

4 1 **National Swagger (IRE)**[25] 3859 2-8-11 ........ MJKinane 8 88
(JSBolger, Ire) *chsd ldrs on far rail: 5th and rdn 2f out: kpt on same pce* **12/1**

5 1 ½ **Alexander Icequeen (IRE)**[25] 3859 2-8-11 ........ PJSmullen 3 85
(DKWeld, Ire) *hld up in tch: rdn and no imp fr 2f out: one pce* **6/1**

6 1 **Right Key (IRE)**[12] 4223 2-8-11 ........ DPMcDonogh 5 82
(KevinPrendergast, Ire) *chsd ldrs: 6th and rdn over 2f out: no imp* **10/1**

7 ½ **Sweet Gypsy Rose (IRE)**[29] 2-8-11 ........ JAHeffernan 2 81
(DavidWachman, Ire) *cl up and disp ld: hdd under 2f out: sn no ex* **12/1**

8 2 **Desert Tigress (USA)**[16] 4106 2-8-11 ........ PCosgrave 6 76
(APO'Brien, Ire) *disp ld: slt advantage under 2f out: hdd over 1f out: no ex* **10/1**

1m 25.4s **Going Correction** -0.125s/f (Firm) **8** Ran SP% **133.2**
Speed ratings: **109,108,106,105,103 102,101,99**CSF £8.19 TOTE £3.10: £1.20, £2.00, £1.50; DF 7.70.
**Owner** Mrs John Magnier **Bred** Juddmonte Farms **Trained** Ballydoyle, Co Tipperary

**NOTEBOOK**
**Silk And Scarlet** put up another useful performance, leading under half a furlong out to win very easily. She will try the Group One Moyglare Stud Stakes next.
**Luas Line(IRE)** finished 13 lengths behind the winner in a Listed event at Leopardstown, but she had since landed the odds in a Cork maiden and has improved. She got in front a furlong out but was readily outpaced in the end.
**Chelsea Rose(IRE)** had beaten the winner two lengths when the pair finished first and second in a Leopardstown maiden in June. She might not have made the same progress in the interim but this was still a smart performance. In hindsight, taking on the Ballydoyle pacemaker Desert Tigress might not have been the most effective tactics.
**National Swagger(IRE)**, still a maiden after four starts, was closer to the winner on this occasion than last time.
**Alexander Icequeen(IRE)**, a length and a half behind the winner on their previous encounter, was just one-paced from two furlongs down.

4593 - 4594a (Foreign Racing) - See Raceform Interactive

# 4566 DEAUVILLE (R-H)

Sunday, August 8

**OFFICIAL GOING: Turf course - good to soft; all-weather - standard**

## 4595a PRIX MAURICE DE GHEEST (GROUP 1) 6f 110y(S)

**2:50** (2:54) 3-Y-O+ **£80,479** (£32,197; £16,099; £8,042)

RPR

1 **Somnus**[31] 3674 4-9-2 ........ GaryStevens 2 120
(TDEasterby) *trckd ldr on stands rail til jnd main grp halfway, pushed along to ld 3f out, hld on gamely under pressure* **12/1**

2 nk **Whipper (USA)**[99] 1764 3-8-12 ........ CSoumillon 10 121+
(RobertCollet, France) *held up, headway 2f, ridden 1f out, ran on but not reach winner* **9/2**[2]

3 nk **Dolma (FR)**[31] 3688 3-8-8 ........ C-PLemaire 4 116?
(NClement, France) *led small stands rail group til raced alone from halfway, stayed on gamely under pressure final f* **25/1**

4 hd **Ashdown Express (IRE)**[31] 3674 5-9-2 ........ SSanders 6 118
(CFWall) *held up, headway over 2f out to go 2nd 1f out, one pace final f* **12/1**

5 1 **The Trader (IRE)**[29] 3769 6-9-2 ........(b) DSweeney 15 115
(MBlanshard) *held up in last, switched left and headway 2f out, ridden and jinked left 1f out, ran on, nearest finish* **8/1**[3]

6 2 **Lucky Strike**[36] 3552 6-9-2 ........ ADeVries 5 110
(ATrybuhl, Germany) *always prominent, every chance over 1f out, one pace* **20/1**

7 ¾ **Golden Nun**[9] 4286 4-8-13 ........(b) RWinston 8 105
(TDEasterby) *held up in rear, headway over 1f out, stayed on final f, nearest finish* **50/1**

8 hd **Dexterity (USA)**[64] 6-9-2 ........ TJarnet 7 107?
(H-APantall, France) *midfield, chasing leaders 1 1/2f out, one pace final f* **50/1**

9 shd **Monsieur Bond (IRE)**[31] 3674 4-9-2 ........ FLynch 19 107
(BSmart) *close up on outside, ridden and one pace final 2f* **14/1**

10 nk **Frizzante**[31] 3674 5-8-13 ........ JPMurtagh 18 103
(JRFanshawe) *held up in rear on outside, effort and unable to quicken over 1f out* **3/1**[1]

11 hd **Brunel (IRE)**[54] 2956 3-8-12 ........ DHolland 12 108
(WJHaggas) *led after 1f to 3f out, remained prominent til weakened 1 1/2f out* **12/1**

12 nk **Royal Millennium (IRE)**[43] 3308 6-9-2 ........ TEDurcan 11 105
(MRChannon) *in touch, ridden and hung right 1 1/2f out, soon beaten* **20/1**

13 ¾ **Charming Groom (FR)**[42] 3361 5-9-2 ........ OPeslier 20 103
(FHead, France) *mid-division, ridden and unable to quicken from 1 1/2f out* **20/1**

14 3 **Porlezza (FR)**[31] 3674 5-8-13 ........ DBoeuf 3 92
(YDeNicolay, France) *held up in small stands side group til joined main group halfway, effort and hung left 2f out, never a factor* **10/1**

15 nse **Seeking The Dia (USA)**[31] 3674 3-8-12 ........ YTake 9 97
(HideyukiMori, Japan) *close up in 4th til weakened over 1 1/2f out* **33/1**

16 6 **Vasywait (FR)**[29] 3769 5-9-2 ........ FSpanu 16 80
(J-LGay, France) *in touch til weakened quickly 2f out* **33/1**

17 nk **Crystal Castle (USA)**[12] 4216 6-9-2 ........ TGillet 13 79
(JEHammond, France) *broke out of stalls and had to be reloaded, always in rear* **16/1**

18 2 ½ **Dorubako (IRE)**[29] 3732 3-8-12 ........ NYokoyama 17 74
(HideyukiMori, Japan) *led 1f out, weakened quickly over 2f out* **40/1**

1m 16.0s **Going Correction** +0.075s/f (Good)
**WFA** 3 from 4yo+ 4lb **18** Ran SP% **129.4**
Speed ratings: **116,115,115,115,113 111,110,110,110,110 109,109,108,105,105 98,98,95.**
**Owner** Legard Sidebottom & Sykes **Bred** Lady Legard **Trained** Great Habton, N Yorks

**NOTEBOOK**
**Somnus** certainly appreciated the good to soft ground. He broke well with a small group on the rails before rejoining the pack up the centre of the track at the halfway stage. He led one out and stayed on well to fend off all challenges. When conditions are right he is a top-class performer and now goes for back-to-back victories in the Stanley Leisure Sprint at Haydock.
**Whipper(USA)**, who was heavily backed before the race, was in mid-division before beginning a dangerous-looking challenge at the furlong marker. He quickened but was held by the winner in the final 50 yards. It was a terrific performance by a three-year-old, especially as he had not been out for three months, and there are many possibilities for him now.

**Dolma(FR)** ran a fine race and was always leading the little group on the rail. She was left on her own for the last two furlongs and battled on gamely to the line. A filly who was bought out of a claimer, she looks capable of winning a Group race and will now be trained for the Prix de la Foret.
**Ashdown Express(IRE)**, in mid-division early, came with a dangerous-looking run from one out but was slightly one-paced in the closing stages. He is a gelding who always runs his heart out.
**The Trader(IRE)**still had plenty to do at the two-furlong marker, but ran on really well despite hanging when making his challenge. However, he never quite made it to the leading group and maybe this distance is just beyond his best trip.
**Golden Nun** made up some late ground but never looked like finishing in the frame.
**Monsieur Bond(IRE)**, never far from the leading group, he came with a run on the far side but it petered out when things really warmed up at the furlong marker.
**Frizzante** produced a most disappointing effort and her connections were at a loss to explain why she did not repeat the July Cup form. She was never really in the hunt and did not quicken in the latter stages, as she usually does, and the fact she did not have the clearest of runs made little difference. This effort is best forgotten and she is now likely to go for the Stanley Leisure Sprint.
**Brunel(IRE)** was up with the leading group from the start and ran well until the furlong marker, where his stride began to shorten. His jockey felt that the distance might have been a little sharp for him.
**Royal Millennium(IRE)**, who acts in the conditions and came into this in good form, delivered a run on the outside of the pack from one and a half out, and then gradually dropped back inside the final furlong.

## 3792 HOPPEGARTEN (R-H)

Sunday, August 8

**OFFICIAL GOING: Good**

### 4596a GROSSER PREIS VON BERLIN (GROUP 3) 6f 110y
**3:35** (3:50) 3-Y-O+ **£22,535** (£9,155; £4,577; £2,465)

RPR
1 **Felicity (GER)**[31] 3688 3-8-7 ........ ABoschert 1 106
(PRau, Germany) *held up, strong run from 2f out to lead 150yds out, ran on well* 3
2 ¾ **Key To Pleasure (GER)**[73] 2438 4-9-5 ........ J-PCarvalho 3 110
(MarioHofer, Germany) *always close up, led 2f out, headed 150yds out, one pace* 2
3 2 ½ **Gold Type (IRE)**[36] 3552 5-9-5 ........ AHelfenbein 6 102
(KWoodburn) *held up, ran on strongly from over 1f out to take 3rd closing stages*
4 ½ **Areias (GER)**[36] 3552 6-9-5 ........ AStarke 2 101
(ASchutz, Germany) *held up, stayed on steadily final 2f*
5 1 ½ **Barrichello (GER)**[280] 5904 4-9-5 ........(b) PAJohnson 4 96
(PSchiergen, Germany) *in rear, kept on from over 1f out but never near leaders*
6 shd **Naahy**[12] 4216 4-9-5 ........ SHitchcott 11 96
(MRChannon) *broke well, brought to centre and disputed lead, headed 2f out, weakened over 1f out* 1
7 ½ **Matrix (GER)**[84] 2158 3-8-11 ........ IFerguson 7 92
(WBaltromei, Germany) *prominent 4f*
8 2 **Fiepes Shuffle (GER)**[36] 3552 4-9-5 ........ PHeugl 10 88
(MarioHofer, Germany) *close up til weakened 2f out*
9 shd **Toylsome**[301] 5528 5-9-5 ........(b) ASuborics 8 88
(PSchiergen, Germany) *disputed lead til headed 2f out, weakened quickly*
10 5 **Furioso Directa (GER)**[43] 3335 4-9-5 ........(b) JPalik 9 73
(AndreasLowe, Germany) *never a factor*
11 12 **Bodyguard Of Spain (GER)**[36] 3552 5-9-5 ........ MTimpelan 5 37
(CZschache, Germany) *prominent to halfway*

1m 16.8s
**WFA** 3 from 4yo+ 4lb **11** Ran SP% **128.2**
Speed ratings: .
**Owner** Gestut Ittlingen **Bred** Gestut Hof Ittlingen **Trained** Germany

**NOTEBOOK**
**Felicity(GER)** was a solid third behind top fillies Dolma and Denebola in France on her previous start. This was a weak Group Three, but she did it well and should continue to progress.
**Naahy** had the worst of the draw and, with a number of other front-runners in the field, was unable to dictate. He is better than the bare form suggests.

## LA TESTE DE BUCH (R-H)

Sunday, August 8

**OFFICIAL GOING: Good**

### 4597a CRITERIUM DU BEQUET (LISTED) 6f
**3:20** (3:20) 2-Y-O **£15,845** (£6,338; £4,754; £3,169)

RPR
1 **Corsario (FR)**[27] 2-9-2 ........ MBlancpain 9 103
(CLaffon-Parias, France)
2 2 **Toupie**[15] 2-8-13 ........ J-BEyquem 1 94
(FRohaut, France)
3 3 **Songoku (IRE)** 2-9-2 ........ CNora 4 88
(RMartin-Sanchez, Spain)
4 2 **Enticer (FR)** 2-9-2 ........ PSogorb 3 82
(DGuillemin, France)
5 nk **Medigating (FR)**[28] 3790 2-9-2 ........ IMendizabal 5 81
(MRoussel, France)
6 ¾ **Michelucci (FR)** 2-9-2 ........ NathalieDesoutter 8 79
(RAvialLopez, France)
7 1 **Polly Alexander (IRE)**[33] 3599 2-8-13 ........ DMorrison 2 73
(MJWallace) *close up til weakened from over 1f out*
8 ½ **Royal Mistress**[28] 3790 2-8-13 ........ SPasquier 10 71
(RGibson, France)
9 ¾ **Flower Bowl (FR)** 2-8-13 ........ F-XBertras 6 69
(FRohaut, France)
10 5 **Centifolia (FR)**[22] 2-8-13 ........ J-RDubosc 7 54
(DSoubagne, France)

1m 10.6s **10** Ran
Speed ratings: .
**Owner** J R Lomba **Bred** C Laffon-Parias **Trained** France

**NOTEBOOK**
**Polly Alexander(IRE)**, with a local rider replacing Callan, was up with the pace from the start, but was unable maintain her effort as the pace quickened in the closing stages.

## 4544 LINGFIELD (L-H)

Monday, August 9

**OFFICIAL GOING: Standard**
Wind: nil Weather: overcast, humid

### 4598 LINGFIELD-RACECOURSE.CO.UK EBF MEDIAN AUCTION MAIDEN STKS (DIV I) 6f (P)
**2:00** (2:02) (F) 2-Y-O **£3,555** (£1,094; £547; £273) **Stalls** Low

Form RPR
6 1 **Cupid's Glory**[19] 4022 2-9-0 ........ SSanders 4 87+
(SirMarkPrescott) *trckd ldrs: effrt 2f out: shkn up to ld jst ins fnl f: sn clr* **4/5**[1]
20 2 3 **Scrooby Baby**[16] 4137 2-8-9 ........ DHolland 7 73
(JAOsborne) *pressed ldr: rdn and ev ch 1f out: kpt on same pce* **8/1**[3]
322 3 1 ½ **Dane's Castle (IRE)**[21] 3986 2-9-0 75 ........ JFortune 6 73
(BJMeehan) *led: rdn 2f out: hdd jst ins fnl f: one pce* **5/1**[2]
6 4 3 **Icing**[30] 3741 2-8-9 ........ KFallon 2 59
(WJHaggas) *wnt rt s: chsd ldng gp: shkn up 2f out: one pce fr over 1f out* **5/1**[2]
50 5 ½ **Rosapenna (IRE)**[30] 3741 2-8-9 ........ GBaker 5 58
(CFWall) *pressed ldrs: rdn and rn wd bnd 2f out: sn outpcd* **25/1**
6 1 **Penang Sapphire** 2-9-0 ........ TPQueally 1 60
(GAButler) *prom: rdn over 2f out: fdd over 1f out* **8/1**[3]
20 7 nk **Bogaz (IRE)**[70] 2522 2-9-0 ........ MartinDwyer 11 59
(RMBeckett) *pressed ldrs: ev ch 2f out: wknd over 1f out* **12/1**
8 3 **Duroob** 2-9-0 ........ RHills 10 65+
(EALDunlop) *dwlt: racd in last trio: sme prog whn nt clr run over 1f out: eased w jockey looking down fnl f* **10/1**
00 9 6 **Sonntag Blue (IRE)**[4] 4487 2-9-0 ........ VSlattery 9 32
(JAOsborne) *outpcd and sn pushed along: nvr a factor* **25/1**
10 22 **Time Traveller** 2-8-7 ........ MHalford(7) 8 —
(TMJones) *dwlt: outpcd and rdn w much tail swishing: t.o* **50/1**

1m 13.47s (0.55) **Going Correction** +0.075s/f (Slow) **10** Ran SP% **137.5**
Speed ratings: **99,95,93,89,88 87,86,82,74,45**CSF £10.85 TOTE £1.80: £1.10, £4.10, £1.10; EX 15.60.
**Owner** Hesmonds Stud **Bred** Cheveley Park Stud Ltd **Trained** Newmarket, Suffolk

**FOCUS**
A solid pace and decent time for the grade, nearly half a second faster than the second division. The form looks strong and should work out.

**NOTEBOOK**
**Cupid's Glory ◆**, the form of whose debut effort here is working out well, improved from that and, despite the drop in trip, quickened up very nicely in the closing stages to score with ease. His pedigree suggests a mile will eventually be his best trip and he should carry on improving.
**Scrooby Baby** arguably put up her best effort yet and was just beaten by a potentially-useful rival. Her future may lie in nurseries.
**Dane's Castle(IRE)** did his best under a positive ride, but yet again lack of pace at the business end proved his undoing. He is likely to remain vulnerable to an improver in races like this.
**Icing** cannoned into the eventual winner at the start, but nonetheless had every chance turning for home before getting left behind. She will need to find a modest maiden in order to get off the mark, but a win of any sort is probably the only goal for her.
**Rosapenna(IRE)** showed up for a while, but will probably be better off in nurseries eventually.
**Penang Sapphire**, first foal of a Listed winner, did best of the newcomers and is entitled to improve from this.
**Duroob** *Official explanation: jockey said bit slipped through colt's mouth*

### 4599 LINGFIELD-RACECOURSE.CO.UK EBF MEDIAN AUCTION MAIDEN STKS (DIV II) 6f (P)
**2:30** (2:32) (F) 2-Y-O **£3,549** (£1,092; £546; £273) **Stalls** Low

Form RPR
3 1 **Wedding Party**[26] 3840 2-8-9 ........ KFallon 8 83+
(MrsAJPerrett) *restless in stalls: prom: trckd ldr 4f out: rdn and rn wd bnd 2f out: led 1f out: styd on wl* **11/10**[1]
2 4 **Mutanabi (USA)** 2-9-0 ........ LDettori 9 73
(SaeedBinSuroor) *led after 1f: clr w wnr over 2f out: rdn and hdd 1f out: wknd* **7/4**[2]
00 3 ¾ **Guyana (IRE)**[19] 4030 2-9-0 ........ JFEgan 10 71+
(SKirk) *dwlt: sn in midfield: chsd clr ldng pair over 2f out: kpt on one pce* **20/1**
4 2 ½ **Bob Baileys** 2-9-0 ........ JQuinn 5 63
(PRChamings) *outpcd and wl in rr: prog 2f out: reminder 1f out: kpt on steadily* **33/1**
5 ½ **Danescourt (IRE)** 2-9-0 ........ MartinDwyer 4 62
(JAOsborne) *led for 1f: chsd ldng pair to over 2f out: fdd* **14/1**
6 hd **Brooklime (IRE)** 2-9-0 ........ DHolland 3 61
(JAOsborne) *dwlt: racd towards rr: effrt over 2f out: no ch w ldrs: fdd fnl f* **7/1**[3]
00 7 1 **Aspen Ridge (IRE)**[84] 2177 2-8-9 ........ SDrowne 6 53
(CTinkler) *sn pushed along in midfield: outpcd 1/2-way: no ch after* **10/1**
8 7 **Killena Boy (IRE)** 2-9-0 ........ JFortune 1 37
(WJarvis) *s.v.s: wl in rr: no ch 2f out: wknd fnl f* **16/1**
0 9 6 **Winter Mist**[39] 3444 2-8-6 ........ J-PGuillambert(3) 7 14
(NPLittmoden) *reluctant to go to post and enter stalls: outpcd and early reminders: u.str.p and wl bhd 1/2-way* **50/1**
10 1 ¼ **Autumn Daze** 2-8-9 ........ MHenry 2 10
(MJRyan) *chsd ldrs to 1/2-way: wknd rapidly* **100/1**

1m 13.96s (1.04) **Going Correction** +0.075s/f (Slow) **10** Ran SP% **128.8**
Speed ratings: **96,90,89,86,85 85,84,74,66,65**CSF £3.55 TOTE £2.40: £1.10, £1.10, £6.60; EX 5.00.
**Owner** Cheveley Park Stud **Bred** Cheveley Park Stud Ltd **Trained** Pulborough, W Sussex

**FOCUS**
A race dominated by the two market principals and a winning time nearly half a second slower than the first division, but still creditable for the grade.

**NOTEBOOK**
**Wedding Party ◆** confirmed the promise of her debut in a race that basically became a match from the off. She powered right away down the home straight though, and was well on top at the line. She remains a nice prospect.
**Mutanabi(USA)**, who cost $1,600,000 as a two-year-old, is bred to appreciate this surface. She lacked the previous experience of her market rival but, even though that is not normally a problem with the stable's runners, it appeared to be the case here so there is probably much better to come.
**Guyana(IRE)**, well beaten on his first two starts, showed his first sign of form on this drop back in trip and switch to sand. With the runner-up appearing to blow up the result may flatter him a little, as he was always about the same distance behind the winner, but he obviously has some ability and it will be interesting to see what nursery mark he gets.

**Bob Baileys ◆**, a relatively cheap purchase out of a winning half-sister to several juvenile winners, was noted staying on quite nicely towards the end and is worth keeping in mind.
**Danescourt(IRE)**, who cost 14,000gns as a two-year-old, is a half-brother to seven winners and managed to keep tabs on the principals for some time before blowing up. Better should follow.
**Brooklime(IRE)**, a 50,000euros colt, is from the same family as Attraction and Lord Of Men. He never managed to get into the race, but it would be no surprise to see him improve a good deal from this.

## 4600 COME EVENING RACING ON 21ST AUGUST (S) STKS — 1m 4f (P)
3:00 (3:00) (G) 3-Y-0+ — £2,569 (£734; £367) Stalls Low

Form — RPR

0314 **1** **Rolex Free (ARG)**[5] 4433 6-9-12 57 (v) LDettori 4 — 63
*(DFlood) led after 2f: kicked on 4f out: hrd rdn 2f out: styd on* **3/1**[1]

3002 **2** *4* **Cosi Fan Tutte**[4] 4476 6-9-7 63 (vt) KFallon 1 — 51
*(MCPipe) trckd ldrs: effrt to chse wnr over 2f out: drvn and no imp wl over 1f out* **3/1**[1]

0004 **3** *4* **One Alone**[33] 3637 3-8-5 39 (b[1]) MartinDwyer 12 — 40
*(Jean-ReneAuvray) s.v.s: racd in last pair to 5f out: prog to chse clr ldng trio over 3f out: kpt on to take 3rd last 100yds* **14/1**

0230 **4** *2* **Boogie Magic**[14] 4201 4-9-2 57 (p) IMongan 6 — 37
*(GAHuffer) prom: chsd wnr over 4f out to over 2f out: fdd* **11/1**

0020 **5** *3* **Another Con (IRE)**[63] 2740 3-8-10 60 RMullen 10 — 37
*(PHowling) racd in midfield: drvn and outpcd 4f out: no ch after: plugged on* **11/2**[2]

6442 **6** *18* **Blue Savanna**[5] 4433 4-9-12 50 (b) DHolland 9 — 13
*(JGPortman) racd wd: hld up: wnt prom over 5f out: wknd over 3f out: eased fnl f* **11/2**[2]

0200 **7** *1* **Golden Dual**[7] 1463 4-9-0 56 (b) CHaddon(7) 5 — 7
*(CLTizzard) s.s: sn rdn and nvr gng wl: t.o 4f out: plodded on* **10/1**[3]

6000 **8** *8* **El Magnifico**[29] 2546 3-8-10 42 (b[1]) SSanders 11 — —
*(PDCundell) racd in midfield: reminder over 6f out: wknd 4f out: t.o* **25/1**

0000 **9** *1 3/4* **Buckenham Stone**[18] 4065 5-9-2 30 RPrice 8 — —
*(JPearce) prom: chsd wnr 7f out to over 4f out: wknd: t.o* **66/1**

0000 **10** *1 3/4* **Night Driver (IRE)**[4] 4485 5-9-7 62 (be) JFortune 3 — —
*(GLMoore) led for 2f: wknd 1/2-way: t.o* **16/1**

0000 **11** *5* **Harry Came Home**[62] 2766 3-8-10 30 AMcCarthy 7 — —
*(JCFox) a towards rr: t.o over 3f out* **50/1**

1605 **12** *nk* **Regulated (IRE)**[33] 3637 3-9-1 63 DaneO'Neill 2 — —
*(DBFeek) s.i.s: a in rr: t.o over 3f out* **11/1**

2m 35.8s (1.56) **Going Correction** +0.075s/f (Slow)
**WFA** 3 from 4yo+ 11lb — **12** Ran SP% **126.4**
Speed ratings: **97,94,91,90,88 76,75,70,69,68 64,64**CSF £11.75 TOTE £3.30: £1.60, £1.10, £6.10; EX 8.30.The winner was bought in for 7,200gns.
**Owner** Mrs Ruth M Serrell **Bred** Firmamento Corporation **Trained** Upper Lambourn, Berks

**FOCUS**
A moderate seller, but at least a solid pace. The future does not look bright for most of these.

**NOTEBOOK**
**Rolex Free(ARG)**, happier back on sand after failing to run his race on Brighton's undulations the previous week, soon established his usual position out in front. He made a bid for glory starting down the false straight and none of his rivals were good enough to cut into the advantage. There should be plenty more opportunities for him at this sort of level on sand.
**Cosi Fan Tutte** tried his best to get on terms with the winner over the final couple of furlongs, but could never make any impression. He may be better over ten furlongs, but still has the ability to win a race like this.
**One Alone**, wearing blinkers for the first time rather than a visor, lost about as much ground at the start as she was eventually beaten by the runner-up, so deserves some credit especially as she had plenty to find with most of these at the weights. She seems to have improved since being stepped up to middle distances.
**Boogie Magic** did not improve for the drop in grade and will do well to find a race.
**Another Con(IRE)** had the form to go very close in this and has won on this surface, but she was off the bridle after just half a mile and it was a struggle from then on. She may have her own ideas about the game.
**Blue Savanna**, who had finished in front of the winner at Brighton the previous week, dropped out very tamely and his rider reported that he ran flat. *Official explanation: jockey said gelding ran flat*

## 4601 LINGFIELD LEISURE CLUB NURSERY — 7f (P)
3:30 (3:33) (E) 2-Y-0 — £3,857 (£1,187; £593; £296) Stalls Low

Form — RPR

41 **1** **Hypnotic**[19] 4023 2-9-12 88 SSanders 3 — 93+
*(SirMarkPrescott) mde virtually all: shkn up and in command 1f out: r.o wl* **5/6**[1]

4105 **2** *2 1/2* **Lateral Thinker (IRE)**[12] 4235 2-8-7 69 LDettori 8 — 68
*(JAOsborne) racd in midfield: prog 2f out: rdn and nt qckn over 1f out: styd on wl fnl f to take 2nd nr fin* **7/1**[3]

3000 **3** *nk* **Gryskirk**[21] 3987 2-8-2 64 AMcCarthy 12 — 62
*(PWD'Arcy) trckd ldrs: prog to chse wnr wl over 1f out: no imp: lost 2nd nr fin* **10/1**

534 **4** *1/2* **Blackcomb Mountain (USA)**[11] 4277 2-8-8 70 DHolland 5 — 67
*(MFHarris) racd towards outer: pressed wnr: ev ch 2f out: drvn and one pce over 1f out* **25/1**

16 **5** *2* **Sky Crusader**[30] 3726 2-9-8 84 SDrowne 1 — 77+
*(RIngram) pressed wnr to jst over 2f out: fdd over 1f out* **11/4**[2]

040 **6** *1/2* **Our Choice (IRE)**[79] 2310 2-8-3 65 TPQueally 10 — 56
*(NPLittmoden) pushed along in rr: rdn and effrt over 2f out: one pce and nvr rchd ldrs* **20/1**

0563 **7** *3/4* **Dartanian**[19] 4010 2-7-9 60 oh2 FPFerris(3) 2 — 49
*(PDEvans) towards rr: rdn 3f out: no imp 2f out: kpt on* **33/1**

300 **8** *3* **Bint Il Sultan (IRE)**[26] 3840 2-8-4 66 ow3 JFEgan 11 — 50+
*(EALDunlop) pushed along in last early: rchd midfield over 2f out: no hdwy after: eased ins fnl f* **20/1**

540 **9** *2 1/2* **Louise Rayner**[19] 4016 2-7-12 60 oh2 JMackay 9 — 35
*(MLWBell) a in rr: last and drvn 4f out: no ch after* **16/1**

400 **10** *5* **Perianth (IRE)**[63] 2736 2-8-3 65 MartinDwyer 6 — 28
*(BJMeehan) racd on outer: pressed wnr tl wknd rapidly 2f out* **20/1**

003 **11** *1 1/2* **Bellalou**[27] 3824 2-7-7 60 oh5 DFox(5) 7 — 19
*(NACallaghan) a in rr: last and wl bhd over 2f out* **25/1**

16 **12** *5* **Elgin Marbles**[25] 3865 2-9-8 84 DaneO'Neill 4 — 30
*(RHannon) pressed wnr tl wknd rapidly over 2f out* **12/1**

1m 28.22s (2.28) **Going Correction** +0.075s/f (Slow) — **12** Ran SP% **141.3**
Speed ratings: **89,86,85,85,82 82,81,78,75,69 67,62**CSF £8.97 CT £52.59 TOTE £2.00: £1.10, £3.90, £6.70; EX 8.90.
**Owner** Cheveley Park Stud **Bred** Cheveley Park Stud Ltd **Trained** Newmarket, Suffolk

**FOCUS**
A fair nursery in which they appeared to go hard early, but must have paid for it late on as the time was moderate for the grade. However, the form rated through the third and fourth looks reasonably solid

**NOTEBOOK**
**Hypnotic** technically just about made all the running, although he never had an easy lead with a whole host of rivals up alongside him for much of the way, but he saw his race out much better than them. On only his third-ever start, this was a big weight for a two-year-old to carry successfully, which suggests he looks well worth a try in Pattern company.
**Lateral Thinker(IRE)**, trying her longest trip to date, stayed on to take the runner-up spot and is certainly consistent but, with several paying late on for trying to go with the favourite from the off, she may be a little bit flattered by the bare result.
**Gryskirk** broke on terms this time and ran up to his best, but is still to truly convince that he stays this trip.
**Blackcomb Mountain(USA)**, making her nursery debut, tried to keep tabs with the favourite for much of the way, but did not see her race out quite so well. She still has a little bit of scope.
**Sky Crusader** was another to race up with the pace from the start, but the way he did not get home reinforces the view that he may be suited by a drop to six.
**Our Choice(IRE)**, making both his handicap and sand debuts as well as stepping up in trip, made up some ground from off the pace in the second half of the contest. He still has some scope and his breeding suggests he will get further.
**Perianth(IRE)**, making his handicap and sand debuts and stepping up in trip, was another that paid for trying to go with the pace from the start.
**Elgin Marbles**, making his handicap and sand debuts and stepping up in trip on only his third-ever start, was involved in a five-way battle for the early lead and it eventually finished him.

## 4602 SPONSOR A RACE AT LINGFIELD H'CAP — 7f (P)
4:00 (4:02) (E) (0-75,76) 3-Y-0+ — £3,906 (£1,202; £601; £300) Stalls Low

Form — RPR

1454 **1** **Franksalot (IRE)**[5] 4437 4-9-8 69 SSanders 9 — 81
*(MissBSanders) settled in midfield: prog over 2f out: rdn to ld ins fnl f: sn clr* **12/1**

5005 **2** *3* **Artistry**[14] 4199 4-9-0 61 DaneO'Neill 10 — 65
*(BJMeehan) trckd ldrs: effrt to chse ldr 2f out: rdn and unable qck over 1f out: kpt on nr fin* **16/1**

521 **3** *hd* **Ali Bruce**[42] 3376 4-9-3 64 IMongan 5 — 68
*(GLMoore) prom: led 3f out: kicked on over 1f out: hdd & wknd ins fnl f* **11/2**[2]

2120 **4** *2* **Merdiff**[8] 4360 5-9-2 63 DHolland 13 — 61
*(WMBrisbourne) racd wd: settled in rr: prog 2f out: rdn and kpt on fr over 1f out* **10/1**

4300 **5** *1 3/4* **Kabeer**[10] 4293 6-9-5 66 RMullen 11 — 60
*(PSMcentee) hld up wl in rr: prog 2f out: rdn and kpt on same pce: no ch* **33/1**

0000 **6** *nk* **Arctic Desert**[16] 4122 4-10-0 75 (v) MartinDwyer 14 — 68
*(AMBalding) hld up in last pair: nt clr run 3f out to 2f out: n.d after* **11/2**[2]

0101 **7** *1/2* **Threezedzz**[5] 4462 6-9-3 67 6ex (t) FPFerris(3) 2 — 59
*(PDEvans) restless in stalls: led to 3f out: wknd over 1f out* **5/1**[1]

0134 **8** *2* **Nearly A Fool**[10] 4301 6-9-5 66 (v) NPollard 3 — 53
*(GGMargarson) chsd ldrs: rdn bef 1/2-way: lost pl and struggling over 2f out* **5/1**[1]

3021 **9** *1 3/4* **Arran**[14] 4190 4-8-11 58 GCarter 7 — 40
*(VSmith) hld up towards rr: nt clr run on inner over 2f out: no ch after* **7/1**[3]

/330 **10** *1 1/4* **Silent Storm**[3] 4511 4-9-6 67 (v[1]) KFallon 8 — 46
*(HJCyzer) chsd ldrs: rdn 3f out: no prog 2f out: fdd* **14/1**

2200 **11** *nk* **Whippasnapper**[11] 4280 4-9-3 69 MSavage(5) 12 — 47
*(JRBest) a towards rr: rdn and no prog wl over 2f out* **12/1**

-001 **12** *5* **Fort McHenry (IRE)**[4] 4495 4-10-1 76 6ex (p) LDettori 4 — 41
*(NACallaghan) pressed ldr to 3f out: sn wknd* **12/1**

2000 **13** *8* **Have Some Fun**[2] 4549 4-8-12 59 (b[1]) JQuinn 6 — 3
*(PRChamings) s.s: a wl in rr: drvn and struggling 1/2-way* **33/1**

0005 **14** *4* **Fulvio (USA)**[23] 3932 4-8-9 56 PDoe 1 — —
*(JamiePoulton) chsd ldrs to 3f out: wknd rapidly* **16/1**

1m 25.93s (-0.01) **Going Correction** +0.075s/f (Slow) — **14** Ran SP% **133.1**
Speed ratings: **103,99,99,97,95 94,94,91,89,88 88,82,73,68**CSF £210.40 CT £1203.24 TOTE £18.80: £4.30, £5.80, £2.00; EX 150.10.
**Owner** Peter Crate, Jane Byers, Roger Knight **Bred** J P Hardiman **Trained** Epsom, Surrey

**FOCUS**
A competitive, if modest handicap and a decent pace. The form is ordinary but could rate a little higher.

**NOTEBOOK**
**Franksalot(IRE)** had shown nothing in his only previous try on this surface almost two years ago, but he came into this in good form on turf. Given a patient ride, he picked up really well when asked and booted right away from his field in the closing stages. His stable do well with their handicappers here and he looks worth persevering with on Polytrack.
**Artistry**, a course-and-distance winner on her last visit back in April, was never far away but could not match strides with the winner down the home straight. She might be suited by an extra furlong on this surface.
**Ali Bruce**, claimed after winning over this trip at Southwell in June, moved to the front on the turn for home and looked the one to beat, but he did not get home. Stamina ought not to have been an issue, and it is more likely he was just found out in this better race on his handicap debut.
**Merdiff** stayed on from off the pace over the last couple of furlongs, but could never get on terms with the front three and looks better suited by Fibresand.
**Kabeer**, usually makes the running, but was held up this time and did make some late progress. He may be worth stepping back up in trip if ridden this way.
**Arctic Desert**, who has dropped 15lb since the start of the season, had to wait for a while to find a path through from the back of the field, but was close enough a furlong from home had he been good enough.
**Threezedzz**, carrying a 6lb penalty for his Yarmouth victory, set the pace until past halfway before dropping out. To be fair to him, he apparently does not like being crowded, so being drawn close to the inside on this track was probably not ideal.
**Nearly A Fool** was off the bridle at halfway and, even though he was short of room turning for home, it made little difference to the result. He is currently 11lb above his highest winning handicap mark on sand.
**Arran**, who showed nothing in three outings on this track last autumn, came into this in good form on Fibresand, However, he never managed to get a clear run so he still has to prove himself here. *Official explanation: jockey said gelding ran short of room turning into the home straight*
**Fort McHenry(IRE)**, carrying a 6lb penalty for his Yarmouth win, looked nothing like so effective when unable to dominate from the front and folded tamely.
**Have Some Fun** *Official explanation: jockey said gelding pecked leaving the stalls*

## 4603 PLAY GOLF AND COME RACING H'CAP — 2m (P)
4:30 (4:33) (F) (0-55,55) 4-Y-0+ — £2,954 (£844; £422) Stalls Low

Form — RPR

5-30 **1** **Tommy Carson**[36] 3461 9-8-3 38 PDoe 5 — 46
*(JamiePoulton) prom: pushed along 6f out: chsd ldr 4f out: drvn to ld wl over 1f out: jst hld on* **10/1**

1510 **2** *nk* **Diamond Orchid (IRE)**[16] 4146 4-8-10 45 (v) TEDurcan 8 — 53
*(PDEvans) settled in midfield: prog over 3f out: rdn to chse wnr fnl f: clsd nr fin: jst failed* **4/1**[2]



The Form Book, Raceform Ltd, Compton, RG20 6NL

5633 **3** *1* **Vandenberghe**[11] 4261 5-8-9 **51** ............ RKeogh(7) 3 58
(JAOsborne) *settled in midfield: prog to chse ldng pair 3f out: hmpd 2f out and nt clr run over 1f out: styd on: nt rcvr* **9/1**

0-11 **4** *3/4* **Magic Red**[28] 3803 4-9-4 **53** ............ IMongan 6 59
(MJRyan) *led for 4f: chsd ldr: drvn bnd 9f out: led over 4f out: hdd and no ex wl over 1f out* **9/4**[1]

0004 **5** *3 1/2* **Heart Springs**[16] 4129 4-8-7 **42** ............ ADaly 12 44
(DrJRJNaylor) *dwlt: hld up in last: stl last but gng wl 5f out: prog after: chsd clr ldrs over 1f out: no imp: hopeless task* **16/1**

2044 **6** *4* **Mandoob**[44] 3303 7-9-6 **55** ............ (t) NPollard 9 52
(BRJohnson) *hld up wl in rr: prog 5f out: chsd ldrs over 2f out: no imp after* **13/2**[3]

20/- **7** *15* **Saorsie**[139] 3898 6-8-0 **40** ............ DFox(5) 7 19
(JCFox) *prom: pushed along 5f out: nt clr run over 3f out: wknd over 2f out* **25/1**

0004 **8** *3 1/2* **Indian Chase**[17] 4082 7-8-6 **41** ow1 ............ DSweeney 11 16
(DrJRJNaylor) *a towards rr: rdn and struggling over 4f out: sn no ch* **14/1**

6040 **9** *3* **Ribbons And Bows (IRE)**[24] 3919 4-9-6 **55** ............ SWhitworth 1 26
(CACyzer) *racd in midfield: rdn 6f out: sn struggling and bhd* **25/1**

P000 **10** *5* **Polanski Mill**[14] 4202 5-9-1 **50** ............ (tp) SCarson 10 15
(CAHorgan) *led after 4f to over 4f out: wknd 3f out: wl bhd* **50/1**

0/60 **11** *14* **Little Fox (IRE)**[4] 4467 9-8-11 **49** ............ ABeech(3) 2 —
(JJBridger) *dwlt: a in rr: t.o fnl 2f* **50/1**

0130 **12** *2 1/2* **Cantrip**[5] 4441 4-9-2 **51** ............ SSanders 13 —
(MissBSanders) *prom tl wknd 5f out: t.o* **8/1**

1455 **13** *10* **Royale Pearl**[14] 4202 4-8-5 **40** ............ GCarter 4 —
(RIngram) *racd in midfield tl wknd 5f out: t.o* **7/1**

3m 29.6s (1.02) **Going Correction** +0.075s/f (Slow) **13** Ran SP% **131.0**
Speed ratings: **100,99,99,98,97 95,87,85,84,81 74,73,68**CSF £53.38 CT £395.25 TOTE £13.30: £4.80, £1.70, £2.10; EX 81.40.
**Owner** J Logan **Bred** W H F Carson **Trained** Telscombe, E Sussex

**FOCUS**
A very moderate handicap, though the pace was fair and they finished well strung out and the form looks reliable at a low level.

**NOTEBOOK**
**Tommy Carson** had only ever won over fences before this, but he has run well off this mark here before. Despite being shoved along some way out, he never stopped trying and his stamina just about saw him home. He will do well to find another opportunity like this on the level.
**Diamond Orchid(IRE)**, trying this trip for the first time on the Flat, is well handicapped on her turf form and very nearly got there. She is well worth another try at the trip.
**Vandenberghe**, whose two previous victories had come at Wolverhampton, had no problem with the trip this time and was almost certainly unlucky not to win this. He had every chance when repeatedly getting into all sorts of trouble from the final bend, yet was beaten little more than a length. Unfortunately, his overall strike-rate does not make him one to lump on to gain compensation next time.
**Magic Red**, beaten out of sight in his only previous try here, was off a 6lb higher mark after his two impressive victories on Fibresand. However, on this occasion he was off the bridle before halfway and even though he forged his way to the front half a mile from home, he was never convincing in front and was swamped down the home straight. The generous view is that he is just not so effective here and a return to a more testing surface should tell us more.
**Heart Springs** ◆, still a maiden, again ran with credit over course and distance despite being given an awful lot to do. She gives the impression she has the ability to win a small race under similar conditions.
**Mandoob** has dropped to a mark 10lb lower than for his last win on sand, but that is because he has been disappointing since showing good form on Fibresand earlier in the year.
**Cantrip** *Official explanation: jockey said filly was never travelling after halfway*
**Royale Pearl** *Official explanation: jockey said filly ran lethargically*

## 4604 LINGFIELD GOLF CLUB APPRENTICE H'CAP — 1m 2f (P)
**5:00** (5:02) (F) (0-55,55) 3-Y-0+ — **£3,024** (£864; £432) **Stalls** Low

Form RPR

6-00 **1** **Music Mix (IRE)**[46] 3231 3-9-7 **55** ............ HPoulton 6 70
(EALDunlop) *hld up in rr: stdy prog over 3f out: led wl over 1f out: rdn clr* **7/1**

00/6 **2** *5* **Zeloso**[23] 3934 6-8-12 **42** ............ (v) RKeogh(5) 13 47
(MFHarris) *hld up in rr: rdn and prog over 2f out: styd on to take 2nd ins fnl f* **16/1**

3523 **3** *nk* **Miss Glory Be**[9] 4339 6-9-6 **52** ............ (p) CharlotteKerton(7) 1 56
(EROertel) *in tch: effrt to chse ldng pair 3f out: chsd ldr over 1f out to ins fnl f: one pce* **7/1**

4506 **4** *3* **Galey River (USA)**[2] 4556 5-8-11 **41** ............ (p) BO'Neill(5) 2 40
(JJSheehan) *racd in midfield: hmpd 3f out and dropped to rr: rdn and styd on again fr over 1f out* **3/1**[2]

0-00 **5** *1* **Scarpia**[17] 4083 4-8-10 **40** ............ KJackson(5) 11 37
(JCFox) *s.v.s: wl in rr: kpt on fnl 2f: no ch* **33/1**

6323 **6** *hd* **Joey Perhaps**[7] 4386 3-9-7 **55** ............ DeanWilliams 8 51
(JRBest) *t.k.h: trckd ldr: led gng easily 3f out: fnd nil in front : hdd & wknd wl over 1f out* **11/4**[1]

3010 **7** *3 1/2* **Piquet**[4] 4471 6-9-6 **50** ............ LucyRussell(5) 5 40
(JJBridger) *hld up in midfield: effrt to chse ldrs 3f out: wknd fnl f* **6/1**

5605 **8** *1 1/4* **Mrs Brown**[9] 4339 3-9-0 **55** ............ SArcher(7) 7 42
(SirMarkPrescott) *n.m.r after 1f: hld up: rdn and prog on outer over 2f out: wknd over 1f out* **8/1**

-000 **9** *1/2* **Pirouettes (IRE)**[9] 4336 4-9-1 **45** ............ (t) JemmaMarshall(5) 14 31
(EROertel) *led to 3f out: wknd 2f out* **33/1**

3606 **10** *1* **Indian Blaze**[26] 3844 10-9-11 **50** ............ MHalford 3 35
(AndrewReid) *racd in midfield: effrt 3f out: no imp on ldrs over 1f out: wknd* **7/2**[3]

0200 **11** *8* **Blaise Wood (USA)**[6] 4419 3-8-8 **47** ............ JJones(5) 4 16
(GLMoore) *a in rr: rdn and struggling over 4f out* **12/1**

0-00 **12** *5* **Midmaar (IRE)**[17] 4096 3-9-2 **55** ............ LauraPike(5) 9 15
(MWigham) *racd wd: hld up: effrt over 3f out: wknd over 2f out* **33/1**

00-0 **13** *9* **Guard**[6] 4419 4-9-2 **41** ............ (t) StevenHarrison 10 —
(NPLittmoden) *prom tl wknd over 3f out* **25/1**

2m 9.52s (1.67) **Going Correction** +0.075s/f (Slow)
**WFA** 3 from 4yo+ 9lb **13** Ran SP% **150.5**
Speed ratings: **96,92,91,89,88 88,85,84,84,83 77,73,65**CSF £138.56 CT £863.40 TOTE £10.60: £3.90, £6.60, £2.30; EX 707.30 Place 6 £59.52, Place 5 £43.36.
**Owner** Khalifa Sultan **Bred** Gainsborough Stud Management Ltd **Trained** Newmarket, Suffolk

**FOCUS**
A moderate contest and a modest winning time for the grade, though the winner does have a little scope.

**NOTEBOOK**
**Music Mix(IRE)** ◆ had been disappointing since showing promise on his debut here last autumn, but was less exposed than his rivals and bounded clear for an easy win. He avoids a penalty for this, so would be very interesting if turned out again quickly.
**Zeloso** was never able to get anywhere near the winner, but still ran better than on his recent comeback from a long layoff and should now be cherry-ripe for a return to hurdling.
**Miss Glory Be**, rather harshly raised 3lb since her last start despite not winning, ran her usual consistent race but still gives the impression she is a bit better on Fibresand.
**Galey River(USA)** was certainly unlucky not to finish much closer as he completely lost his place after getting badly hampered passing the three-furlong pole, yet was staying on very well at the end. He deserves compensation, but his moderate strike-rate is rather off-putting.
**Scarpia**, unplaced in all his nine previous starts, did well to reach his final position on this sand debut as he gave away several lengths at the start. He is not completely without hope.
**Joey Perhaps** looked to have a great chance of finally breaking his duck when cruising to the front on the bridle turning for home, but he quickly went from one extreme to the other and had already appeared to throw in the towel when his rider lost his whip passing the furlong pole.
**Indian Blaze** had conditions to suit, but was very disappointing and there seemed no real excuse.
T/Plt: £24.30 to a £1 stake. Pool: £36,549.40. 1,096.85 winning tickets. T/Qpdt: £22.40 to a £1 stake. Pool: £1,948.80. 64.30 winning tickets. JN

# 4347 THIRSK (L-H)
### Monday, August 9

**OFFICIAL GOING: Good to soft changing to soft after 8.00 (race 5)**
After over 1/2" rain during the day the going was desrcibed as 'soft' at the start of the night and it deteriorated further over the last three as heavy rain fell.
Wind: Almost nil. Weather: Overcast and humid, heavy rain last three races.

## 4605 SINNINGTON (S) H'CAP — 1m
**6:00** (6:00) (F) (0-55,54) 3-Y-0+ — **£3,248** (£928; £464) **Stalls** Low

Form RPR

3100 **1** **Dara Mac**[24] 3921 5-9-3 **53** ............ SuzanneFrance(7) 6 67
(NBycroft) *hld up and bhd: swtchd outside and gd hdwy over 2f out: led over 1f out: rdn clr* **6/1**[1]

0006 **2** *5* **Zarin (IRE)**[20] 4004 6-9-6 **49** ............ ACulhane 3 53
(DWChapman) *led: rdn along 2f out: hdd over 1f out: sn drvn and one pce* **10/1**[3]

01-0 **3** *1 1/4* **Millkom Elegance**[3] 3411 5-9-2 **45** ............ (b) NCallan 16 46
(KARyan) *in tch: hdwy on outer wl over 2f out: effrt and ev ch over 1f out: sn rdn and one pce* **14/1**

3060 **4** *3/4* **Donegal Shore (IRE)**[28] 3804 5-9-0 **43** ............ (vt) KMcEvoy 14 42
(MrsJCandlish) *hld up and bhd: hdwy on outer over 2f out: sn rdn: kpt on u.p fnl f: nrst fin* **16/1**

2000 **5** *1* **Canlis**[6] 4423 5-9-2 **45** ............ PHanagan 10 42
(DWThompson) *towards rr: hdwy over 2f out: sn rdn and kpt on ins last: nrst fin* **20/1**

0020 **6** *1/2* **Rymer's Rascal**[3] 4511 12-9-6 **49** ............ WSupple 5 45
(EJAlston) *towards rr: hdwy inner 2f out: sn rdn and kpt on same pce* **6/1**[1]

3300 **7** *nk* **Summer Special**[16] 4132 4-8-10 **42** ............ (p) LEnstone(3) 8 38
(DWBarker) *chsd ldrs: rdn along wl over 2f out: drvn and wknd over 1f out* **33/1**

0100 **8** *1 1/4* **Super Dominion**[14] 4190 7-8-13 **47** ............ (p) StephanieHollinshead(5) 2 40
(RHollinshead) *cl up: rdn along 3f out: wknd fnl 2f* **33/1**

4030 **9** *hd* **Noble Pursuit**[7] 4386 7-9-4 **50** ............ TEaves(3) 15 42
(REBarr) *midfield: pushed along over 3f out: rdn over 2f out and no hdwy* **16/1**

0-06 **10** *1/2* **Alpine Hideaway (IRE)**[14] 3471 11-9-2 **45** ............ (p) DAllan 12 36
(JSWainwright) *cl up: rdn along 3f out: wknd 2f out* **20/1**

555- **11** *3* **Eastern Scarlet (IRE)**[46] 2027 4-8-12 **41** ............ FNorton 13 26
(VSmith) *slowlyinto stride: a rr* **6/1**[1]

0536 **12** *shd* **Spring Dancer**[11] 4260 3-8-10 **49** ............ (t) PMulrennan(3) 7 34
(TJFitzgerald) *chsd ldrs: rdn along 3f out: sn drvn and wknd* **12/1**

0330 **13** *shd* **Shamwari Fire (IRE)**[12] 4246 4-9-5 **48** ............ RFfrench 9 33
(IWMcinnes) *chsd ldrs: rdn along 3f out: sn wknd* **15/2**[2]

6335 **14** *5* **Ace-Ma-Vahra**[9] 4350 6-8-11 **40** ............ JBramhill 1 14
(SRBowring) *bhd fr 1/2-way* **12/1**

0060 **15** *20* **Thumamah (IRE)**[60] 2811 5-9-0 **43** ............ (t) DarrenWilliams 4 —
(BPJBaugh) *a bhd* **50/1**

0620 **16** *1* **Blunham**[6] 4425 4-9-4 **47** ............ RWinston 11 —
(MCChapman) *bhd fr 1/2-way* **16/1**

00-0 **17** *25* **Magenta Rising (IRE)**[14] 581 4-9-4 **54** ............ RoryMoore(7) 18 —
(DWThompson) *cl up on outer: rdn along over 3f out: sn wknd* **33/1**

1m 44.52s (4.82) **Going Correction** +0.625s/f (Yiel)
**WFA** 3 from 4yo+ 7lb **17** Ran SP% **123.7**
Speed ratings: **100,95,93,93,92 91,91,89,89,89 86,86,86,81,61 60,35**CSF £59.82 CT £851.29 TOTE £8.30: £2.60, £3.40, £3.00, £4.70; EX 114.40.There was no bid for the winner.
**Owner** N Bycroft **Bred** N Bycroft And G Allison **Trained** Brandsby, N Yorks

**FOCUS**
A weak seller run at an even pace throughout.

**NOTEBOOK**
**Dara Mac**, runner-up in this race last year off a 3lb lower mark, went one place better with a most emphatic success, thanks in no small part to a really well-judged ride from Suzanne France. He seemed to relish the easy surface and should continue to go well in similarly moderate company when there is cut in the ground.
**Zarin(IRE)** posted a good effort considering he tried to make all, and the eventual winner raced in last for much of the way. He should be able to pick up a similar race for his talented trainer.
**Millkom Elegance** returned home lame after being pulled over hurdles just three days previously, but she showed herself back in good heart returned to the Flat with a solid effort.
**Donegal Shore(IRE)** has not won since scoring on his debut for Barry Hills back in September 2001. He was next to the winner at the top of the straight, but lacked that one's pace and could be worth a try at around ten furlongs.
**Canlis**, dropped half a mile in trip, shaped as though a return to slightly further would suit.
**Rymer's Rascal** would probably have been placed with a better run.
**Eastern Scarlet(IRE)** had been successful in this country over five furlongs back in 2002, but was last seen well beaten over hurdles at Tipperary. Making his debut for a new trainer, he was really well backed but showed little to justify the confidence.

## 4606 BEATRICE STEPHENSON MAIDEN AUCTION STKS — 7f
**6:30** (6:33) (E) 2-Y-0 — **£3,750** (£1,154; £577; £288) **Stalls** Low

Form RPR

3 **1** **Thunderwing (IRE)**[17] 4100 2-8-10 ............ DarrenWilliams 9 80+
(KRBurke) *in tch: hdwy on outer over 2f out: rdn to ld and hung lft over 1f out: styd on wl* **6/1**

**2** *2 1/2* **King's Account (USA)** 2-8-10 ............ JFanning 10 67
(MJohnston) *rangy: unf: scope: towards rr: stdy hdwy 3f out: rdn to chse ldrs over 1f out: kpt on wl fnl f* **12/1**

0 **3** ¾ **Robinzal**[9] [4315] 2-8-10 ............ KDarley 13 65
(TDEasterby) *sn led: rdn along over 2f out: hdd over 1f out: drvn and one pce fnl f* **33/1**

0 **4** 1½ **Comical Errors (USA)**[24] [3918] 2-8-3 ............ RoryMoore(7) 8 61
(PCHaslam) *bhd: hdwy over 2f out: styd on wl appr last: nrst fin* **66/1**

3 **5** ¾ **Good Investment**[24] [3918] 2-8-10 ............ GFaulkner 2 59
(PCHaslam) *cl up: rdn and ev ch 2f out: drvn and one pce appr last* **9/2**[2]

2 **6** ¾ **Able Charlie (GER)**[18] [4048] 2-8-10 ............ RWinston 14 57
(MrsJRRamsden) *keen: chsd ldrs: hung rt 1/2-way: effrt and ev ch over 2f out: sn rdn and wknd wl over 1f out* **9/4**[1]

44 **7** hd **Miss Rosie**[13] [4208] 2-8-8 ............ DAllan 4 55
(TDEasterby) *prom on inner: pushed along 1/2-way: rdn over 2f out and grad wknd* **5/1**[3]

**8** 9 **Andy Mal** 2-8-2 ............ PHanagan 3 26
(RAFahey) *leggy: unf: bhd tl sme late hdwy* **25/1**

0 **9** 2 **Hannah's Tribe (IRE)**[11] [4256] 2-8-2 ............ FNorton 6 21
(BSmart) *a rr* **50/1**

0 **10** 1 **My Rascal (IRE)**[10] [4290] 2-8-10 ............ NCallan 5 27
(MJWallace) *prom: rdn along 3f out: wknd 2f out* **7/1**

**11** ¾ **Liability (IRE)** 2-8-2 ............ KimTinkler 7 17
(NTinkler) *leggy: unf: s.i.s: a rr* **100/1**

04 **12** shd **Summer Silks**[16] [4135] 2-8-2 ............ RFfrench 11 17
(RAFahey) *in tch on outer: rdn along 3f out: sn wknd* **18/1**

**13** 2½ **Smiling Starduster (IRE)** 2-8-2 ow2 ............ DTudhope(7) 1 17
(DCarroll) *neat: in tch on inner: hdwy to chse ldrs 3f out: rdn and wknd over 2f out* **66/1**

**R** **Continental Flyer (IRE)** 2-8-5 ............ VHalliday 12 —
(MDods) *leggy: unf: lft in stalls: ref to r* **66/1**

1m 32.44s (5.34) **Going Correction** +0.625s/f (Yiel) **14** Ran SP% **119.6**
Speed ratings: **94,91,90,88,87 86,86,76,74,72 72,71,69,**—CSF £72.57 TOTE £6.00: £2.30, £4.10, £6.10; EX 109.90.
**Owner** Market Avenue Racing Club Ltd **Bred** Agricola Del Parco **Trained** Middleham Moor, N Yorks

**FOCUS**
Just an ordinary maiden auction, but decent enough performances from the front two.

**NOTEBOOK**
**Thunderwing(IRE)**, an encouraging third in a reasonable novice event on fast ground here on his debut, was well suited by this easier ground and was able to build on that initial promise. His trainer has always thought a bit of him, and he will be worthy of respect in a higher grade.
**King's Account(USA)** is a 15,000gns half-brother to three winners, including a smart juvenile in the USA. He looked weak in the paddock and showed real signs of inexperience beforehand, unseating his rider and running loose. In the race itself, he got going all too late and was no match for the winner, but he will surely improve for the outing and can win a similar event.
**Robinzal** was pretty keen early on, but still improved significantly on his debut and is going the right way.
**Comical Errors(USA)** looked the stable second string on both the market and jockey bookings but ran above himself, improving on what he showed first time up.
**Good Investment** shaped well when third on fast ground on his debut at Pontefract, but was unable to build on that on this much easier surface.
**Able Charlie(GER)** can be forgiven this as he was stuck outside from his poor draw, and raced far too keenly to ever get home.
**Miss Rosie** was not at her best on this first run on easy ground, but she is at least now qualified for a handicap mark.
**My Rascal(IRE)** did not progress from his debut running and may be more of a nursery type.

## 4607 EBF CALVERTS CARPETS MEDIAN AUCTION MAIDEN STKS 5f
**7:00** (7:05) (E) 2-Y-O **£4,192** (£1,290; £645; £322) **Stalls** High

Form RPR

4440 **1** **Coleorton Dancer**[31] [3704] 2-9-0 65 ............ NCallan 7 77
(KARyan) *cl up: led over 1f out: rdn clr ins last* **16/1**[3]

00 **2** 4 **Oceanico Dot Com (IRE)**[37] [3532] 2-8-9 ............ FNorton 8 58
(ABerry) *cl up: rdn and ev ch wl over 1f out: kpt on same pce ins last* **40/1**

64 **3** 2 **Ne Oublie**[16] [4124] 2-9-0 ............ DaleGibson 2 56
(JMackie) *chsd ldrs on outer: rdn along 2f out: kpt on same pce appr last* **25/1**

4220 **4** hd **Chiselled (IRE)**[23] [3938] 2-9-0 85 ............ DarrenWilliams 12 55
(KRBurke) *swtg: wnt lft s: sn led: rdn 2f out: sn hdd and btn* **4/9**[1]

5 **5** ½ **One Of Each (IRE)**[12] [4245] 2-8-2 ............ DTudhope(7) 10 49
(DCarroll) *chsd ldrs: rdn 2f out: kpt on same pce appr last* **40/1**

**6** ¾ **Coconut Moon** 2-8-9 ............ PHanagan 4 46
(RAFahey) *cmpt: s.i.s and bhd: hdwy 2f out: styng on whn nt clr run ent last: kpt on* **20/1**

06 **7** 5 **Jasmine Hill**[13] [4212] 2-8-9 ............ RWinston 13 28
(NBycroft) *bhd tl styd on appr last: nrst fin* **66/1**

00 **8** ¾ **Herencia (IRE)**[14] [4200] 2-9-0 ............ DeanMcKeown 3 31
(PABlockley) *bhd tl sme late hdwy* **100/1**

3 **9** hd **Folga**[12] [4245] 2-8-9 ............ WSupple 11 25
(RPElliott) *hmpd s: a rr* **20/1**

6050 **10** hd **Desert Buzz (IRE)**[18] [4048] 2-9-0 ............ MTebbutt 1 29
(JHetherton) *in tch on outer: rdn along over 2f out and sn wknd* **80/1**

30 **11** 2 **Liwa's Lake (USA)**[42] [3382] 2-8-9 ............ KMcEvoy 6 17
(SaeedBinSuroor) *in tch to 1/2-way: sn rdn along and wknd* **11/2**[2]

000 **12** 3 **Star Of Kildare (IRE)**[13] [4212] 2-8-9 ............ KimTinkler 9 7
(NTinkler) *bhd fr 1/2-way* **100/1**

62.03 secs (2.13) **Going Correction** +0.35s/f (Good) **12** Ran SP% **113.5**
Speed ratings: **96,89,86,86,85 84,76,74,74,74 71,66**CSF £478.95 TOTE £19.90: £3.20, £6.50, £3.60; EX 1471.30.
**Owner** Coleorton Moor Racing **Bred** A Holmes **Trained** Hambleton, N Yorks

**FOCUS**
With both Chiselled and Liwa's Lake below form this was a weak maiden that did not take a lot of winning, but Coleorton Dancer was still quite impressive and appears an improved performer.

**NOTEBOOK**
**Coleorton Dancer** ◆ had shown ability on his previous starts but would often race keenly and not get home. However, gelded since his last run, he settled well and really saw his race out, winning impressively. He would be hard to beat in a nursery if turned out under a penalty.
**Oceanico Dot Com(IRE)** had been well beaten on her two previous starts but, racing on soft ground for the first time, she showed improved form. Given the winner is rated just 65, she should not be rated too harshly.
**Ne Oublie** stayed on well enough seems to be going the right way. He is now qualified for a handicap mark and should do better in that sphere, possibly over another furlong.
**Chiselled(IRE)** had shown promise in maiden company before running a creditable ninth in the Super Sprint, but he got very warm beforehand and had little to offer in the race when it mattered. *Official explanation: jockey said colt was unsuited by the good to soft going*
**One Of Each(IRE)** did not really build on his debut promise.
**Coconut Moon**, a half-sister to a seven-furlong placed juvenile, showed her inexperience beforehand but ran creditably and would have been closer with better luck. She should improve.
**Liwa's Lake(USA)**, a tall, narrow-type, was on edge beforehand and proved very easy to back. She has not gone on at all from her close debut third to subsequent Listed and Group winner Jewel In The Sand.

## 4608 WEATHERBYS PRINTING SERVICES H'CAP 5f
**7:30** (7:33) (D) (0-80,80) 3-Y-O **£5,538** (£1,704; £852; £426) **Stalls** High

Form RPR

6221 **1** **True Magic**[19] [4021] 3-8-10 **69** ............ JFanning 13 79
(JDBethell) *trckd ldrs: hdwy to chal over 1f out: rdn to ld ins last: kpt on* **7/1**[2]

0643 **2** hd **Trojan Flight**[4] [4489] 3-8-0 **59** ............ FNorton 7 69+
(MrsJRRamsden) *trckd ldrs: hdwy and nt clr run over 1f out:swtchd rt and sddle slipped ins last: styd on wl* **6/1**[1]

3051 **3** 1 **Baron Rhodes**[9] [4331] 3-9-4 **80** ............ TEaves(3) 12 86
(JSWainwright) *cl up: led 2f out: sn rdn: hdd and nt qckn ins last* **7/1**[2]

4-44 **4** 1¾ **Kamenka**[9] [4320] 3-8-11 **70** ............ PHanagan 14 70
(RAFahey) *in tch and sn pushed along: hdwy 2f out: sn rdn and kpt on fnl f* **12/1**

0165 **5** ½ **Wendy's Girl (IRE)**[12] [4247] 3-8-3 **62** ............(b) RFfrench 9 60
(RPElliott) *in rr: swtchd lft and rdn wl over 1f out: styd on u.p fnl furlon g: nrst fin* **28/1**

0400 **6** hd **Baylaw Star**[51] [3077] 3-8-10 **69** ............(p) NCallan 10 66
(KARyan) *led: rdn along 1/2-way: hdd 2f out and sn drvn: wknd over 1f out* **33/1**

2116 **7** hd **Nanna (IRE)**[9] [4320] 3-8-10 **69** ............ ACulhane 15 65
(RHollinshead) *cl up: rdn along 2f out: grad wknd* **7/1**[2]

0526 **8** ½ **Sir Loin**[10] [4309] 3-7-12 **57** ............ KimTinkler 8 52
(NTinkler) *cl up: rdn over 2f out: grad wknd* **16/1**

4-05 **9** ½ **Marysienka**[5] [4456] 3-9-0 **73** ............ JEdmunds 17 66
(JBalding) *chsd ldrs: rdn 2f out: sn wknd* **40/1**

6615 **10** ¾ **Jadan (IRE)**[18] [4059] 3-9-2 **75** ............ WSupple 11 65
(EJAlston) *towards rr: hdwy 2f out: sn rdn and no imp* **15/2**[3]

6450 **11** 1 **Tizzy's Law**[45] [3273] 3-8-5 **64** ............ JBramhill 2 51
(MABuckley) *chsd ldrs: rdn 2f out: sn wknd* **14/1**

3600 **12** hd **Elliot's Choice (IRE)**[16] [4151] 3-8-4 **63** ............ KMcEvoy 16 49
(DCarroll) *hld up: hdwy and nt clr run 2f out and over 1f out: nvr a factor* **16/1**

0430 **13** 2½ **Lualua**[10] [4289] 3-9-0 **73** ............(v[1]) DarrenWilliams 5 50
(TDBarron) *s.i.s: bhd and swtchd rt after 1f: rdn along and sme hdwy whn bdly hmpd over 1f out: nt rcvr* **8/1**

2510 **14** 1¼ **Bella Boy Zee (IRE)**[1] [4576] 3-7-8 **60** ............ DFentiman(7) 6 32
(PABlockley) *in tch on outer: rdn along 1/2-way and sn wknd* **14/1**

-500 **15** 1½ **Hamaasy**[9] [4320] 3-8-1 **60** ............ ANicholls 4 27
(DNicholls) *in tch on outer: rdn along 1/2-way: sn wknd* **25/1**

61.62 secs (1.72) **Going Correction** +0.35s/f (Good) **15** Ran SP% **120.1**
Speed ratings: **100,99,98,95,94 94,93,93,92,91 89,89,85,83,80**CSF £46.36 CT £317.80 TOTE £8.20: £2.90, £1.90, £2.70; EX 39.20.
**Owner** T R Lock **Bred** T R Lock **Trained** Middleham Moor, N Yorks

**FOCUS**
Just a modest sprint handicap, but there were a couple to take from the race. The form is fair for the grade.

**NOTEBOOK**
**True Magic**, off the mark in just a modest maiden on fast ground at Leicester on her previous start, proved equally effective on this easier surface, but was a very fortunate winner as she would have been caught by the eventual runner-up had that one's saddle not slipped.
**Trojan Flight** ◆ would have won had his saddle not slipped - his jockey had to show tremendous balance just to stay on the horse, let alone get it to within ahead of the winner. The money was down tonight, but he should be able to gain compensation. *Official explanation: jockey said saddle slipped in the closing stages*
**Baron Rhodes** was just found out by a 4lb rise for his recent Hamilton success. She has yet to finish out of the three at Thirsk.
**Kamenka** ◆ ran a good race in defeat but once again shaped as though in need of further. One to look out for when she is stepped up in trip.
**Wendy's Girl(IRE)** gained both her previous wins on fast ground, but she seemed to handle these conditions well, running a solid race over a trip just short of her best.
**Elliot's Choice(IRE)** *Official explanation: jockey said gelding lost his position at the start and was continually denied a run*

## 4609 BLACK SHEEP BREWERY STKS (H'CAP) 2m
**8:00** (8:01) (F) (0-55,50) 4-Y-O+ **£3,484** (£1,072; £536; £268) **Stalls** Low

Form RPR

3 **1** **Super Fellow (IRE)**[14] [4202] 10-8-4 **36** ............ JBramhill 8 45
(CNKellett) *hld up in rr: pushed along over 2f out: swtchd rt and rdn wl over 1f out: str run to ld wl ins last: sn clr* **7/1**

5421 **2** 1¾ **Mercurious (IRE)**[17] [4098] 4-8-9 **41** ............ DaleGibson 5 48
(JMackie) *trckd ldrs: hdwy on outer 3f out: rdn to ld over 1f out: sn drvn and wandered: hdd and nt qckn wl ins last* **7/1**

0162 **3** nk **Oops (IRE)**[14] [4202] 5-8-12 **44** ............ WSupple 11 51
(JFCoupland) *cl up: led wl over 2f out: sn rdn: hdd and drvn over 1f out: kpt on u.p ins last* **7/2**[1]

2202 **4** 1½ **Doctor John**[17] [4098] 7-8-8 **43** ............(p) DCorby(3) 13 48
(AndrewTurnell) *hld up: hdwy 3f out: swtchd lft and rdn wl over 1f out: styd on to chal ent last: sn drvn and one pce* **10/1**

001 **5** 3½ **Regal Fantasy (IRE)**[11] [4275] 4-8-4 **36** ............ DeanMcKeown 2 37
(PABlockley) *hld up in tch: stdy hdwy 6f out: rdn and ch 2f out: sn drvn and wknd* **6/1**[3]

35U6 **6** 7 **Iloveturtle (IRE)**[8] [4210] 4-9-0 **46** ............ RWinston 1 38
(MCChapman) *trckd ldrs: effrt 3f out: rdn over 2f out and sn btn* **9/2**[2]

5406 **7** 3½ **Simple Ideals (USA)**[5] [4448] 10-8-3 **35** ............ KimTinkler 3 23
(DonEnricoIncisa) *hld up: hdwy on inner to trck ldrs 1/2-way: lost pl over 4f out: rdn along and hdwy on over 2f out: sn rdn and wknd* **8/1**

1452 **8** 3½ **Sovereign State (IRE)**[12] [4250] 7-9-4 **50** ............(p) FNorton 6 34
(DWThompson) *hld up and bhd: hdwy 4f out: rdn along and btn over 2f out* **8/1**

4040 **9** 10 **Banners Flying (IRE)**[14] [4189] 4-9-4 **50** ............ ACulhane 10 22
(DWChapman) *led: rdn along 4f out: hdd & wknd wl over 2f out* **33/1**

020- **10** dist **Golden Fields (IRE)**[7] [5972] 4-8-12 **44** ............ NCallan 12 —
(MrsJCandlish) *hld up and bhd: hdwy on outer over 5f out: hung bdly rtbnd over 4f out and virtually p.u* **50/1**

3m 47.12s (15.92) **Going Correction** +1.025s/f (Soft) **10** Ran SP% **115.9**
Speed ratings: **101,100,99,99,97 93,92,90,85,**—CSF £54.94 CT £201.38 TOTE £10.00: £2.60, £2.10, £2.40; EX 181.70.
**Owner** A M Egan **Bred** Gerard McClure **Trained** Swadlincote, Derbys

**FOCUS**
A very moderate handicap and a real test of stamina, which suited the winner, and the form looks sound enough.

**NOTEBOOK**

**Super Fellow(IRE)**, better known as a hurdler and most recently a chaser, including in Ireland, was able to build on the promise he had shown on his return to the Flat at Yarmouth on his previous start. A winner over three miles two over fences, this trip is short enough for him and he needed plenty of driving to pick up from quite a way off the pace. He will always be one to take on unless a real stamina test is guaranteed.

**Mercurious(IRE)**, 4lb lower than when winning over this trip on the Southwell Fibresand on her previous start, can have no excuses.

**Oops(IRE)** handled conditions well enough and ran his race, but he was unable to confirm recent placings with the winner.

**Doctor John**, with the cheekpieces back on, did not look to have an excuse and this is as good as he is.

**Iloveturtle(IRE)** did not see out the trip on this ground.

**Golden Fields(IRE)** *Official explanation: jockey said filly cocked her jaw and would not go round the bend*

## 4610 URE H'CAP 1m

8:30 (8:31) (E ) (0-75,74) 3-Y-O **£3,682** (£1,133; £566; £283) **Stalls** Low

Form RPR

3111 **1** **She's Our Lass (IRE)**[12] 4242 3-9-7 **74** KMcEvoy 9 85+
(DCarroll) *hld up: wd st and oushed along 3f out: gd hdwy 2f out: led over 1f out and rdn clr* **7/2**[2]

4660 **2** *1 1/2* **Cottingham (IRE)**[10] 4305 3-8-1 **59** StephanieHollinshead(5) 5 64
(MCChapman) *trckd ldrs: hdwy to ld 2f out: sn rdn and hdd over 1f out: kpt on same pce* **16/1**

500 **3** *3/4* **Dancer King (USA)**[17] 4101 3-7-12 **51** RFfrench 8 55
(TPTate) *hld up in tch: hdwy over 2f out: swtchd lft and rdn over 1f out: kpt on* **10/1**

2650 **4** *2* **Wrenlane**[13] 4209 3-8-10 **63** PHanagan 6 63
(RAFahey) *a.p: effrt 3f out and ev ch tl rdn and one pce over 1f out* **7/2**[2]

0560 **5** *1/2* **Compton Micky**[18] 4051 3-8-2 **55** (p) JBramhill 10 54
(JBalding) *hld up and bhd: hdwy over 2f out: rdn and hung lft over 1f out: sn one pce* **20/1**

0320 **6** *1 3/4* **Uhuru Peak**[10] 4309 3-8-2 **55** DaleGibson 7 50
(MWEasterby) *in tch: hdwy 1/2-way: rdn over 2f out and sn btn* **7/1**[3]

0033 **7** *hd* **Louisiade (IRE)**[12] 4242 3-8-9 **62** DAllan 1 57
(TDEasterby) *led: rdn along 3f out: hdd 2f out and grad weakned* **11/4**[1]

006 **8** *3* **Bold Phoenix (IRE)**[34] 3603 3-9-6 **73** KDarley 4 62
(EFVaughan) *in tch: rapid hdwy to join ldr after 2f: cl up tl rdn and wknd over 2f out* **11/1**

0-00 **9** *7* **Cheverak Forest (IRE)**[16] 4138 3-8-9 **62** KimTinkler 2 37
(DonEnricoIncisa) *a rr* **20/1**

1m 50.0s (10.30) **Going Correction** +1.30s/f (Soft) **9** Ran SP% **116.4**
Speed ratings: **100,98,97,95,95 93,93,90,83**CSF £57.80 CT £507.33 TOTE £2.90: £2.00, £2.90, £2.20; EX 80.00 Place 6 £3,461.20, Place 5 £1,101.25.
**Owner** We-Know Partnership **Bred** Illuminatus Investments **Trained** Warthill, N Yorks

**FOCUS**

A moderate handicap with not much strength in depth, but there was a lot to like about the way She's Our Lass went about gaining her fifth win of the campaign

**NOTEBOOK**

**She's Our Lass(IRE)** gained her fifth win of the campaign off a mark 20lb higher than when gaining her first success, and she won in a manner that suggests there could yet be even more to come.

**Cottingham(IRE)** only has a regional maiden win to his name, but this was a decent-enough effort.

**Dancer King(USA)** was well held in three runs in maiden company, but this was a promising handicap debut and he looks on a fair-enough mark.

**Wrenlane** attracted some interesting market support but was well held and remains a maiden.

**Compton Micky** did not run badly on this first try over a mile.

**Louisiade(IRE)** was not at his best and this ground probably failed to suit.

**Cheverak Forest(IRE)** *Official explanation: jockey said gelding was unsuited by the soft ground*

T/Plt: £2,640.40 to a £1 stake. Pool: £41,596.00. 11.50 winning tickets. T/Qpdt: £254.70 to a £1 stake. Pool: £3,786.50. 11.00 winning tickets. JR

# 4579 WINDSOR (R-H)

## Monday, August 9

**OFFICIAL GOING: Good to soft (good in places)**

The rain had eased the ground sufficiently to encourage the riders to race towards the far side in the straight.

## 4611 GUINNESS MAIDEN STKS 6f

5:45 (5:51) (D ) 2-Y-O **£5,343** (£1,644; £822; £411) **Stalls** High

Form RPR

5 **1** **One Putra (IRE)**[13] 4219 2-9-0 PRobinson 5 91
(MAJarvis) *mde virtually all: pushed along 2f out: drvn and r.o wl fnl f: readily* **10/3**[2]

**2** *1 1/2* **Rebuttal (USA)** 2-9-0 JFortune 8 87
(BJMeehan) *s.i.s: sn rcvrd to chse ldrs: rdn to go 2nd 1f out: styd on but nt pce of wnr ins last* **8/1**

2 **3** *1 1/4* **Moth Ball**[16] 4117 2-9-0 DHolland 9 83
(JAOsborne) *w wnr: ev ch and drvn 2f out: no imp and lost 2nd 1f out: kpt on one pce* **9/2**[3]

**4** *1/2* **Sudden Dismissal (IRE)** 2-9-0 TPQueally 14 82
(GAButler) *chsd ldrs: rdn and effrt 2f out: no ex fnl f* **33/1**

4 **5** *2* **Enforcer**[14] 4193 2-9-0 SDrowne 18 76
(WRMuir) *in tch: drvn along over 2f out: kpt on fr over 1f out but nvr gng pce of ldrs* **10/1**

0 **6** *2* **Go Mo (IRE)**[60] 2804 2-9-0 JFEgan 1 70
(SKirk) *in tch: outpcd over 2f out: kpt on again ins last* **66/1**

4 **7** *1/2* **Prince Samos (IRE)**[16] 4117 2-9-0 KFallon 17 68
(RHannon) *chsd ldrs: rdn over 2f out: wknd fnl f* **3/1**[1]

**8** *1/2* **Bolodenka (IRE)** 2-9-0 RMullen 12 67
(WJMusson) *in tch: outpcd 1/2-way: kpt on again fnl f* **33/1**

0 **9** *1/2* **Lady Londra**[14] 4193 2-8-4 ow2 MHoward(7) 4 62
(DKIvory) *in tch: rdn 1/2-way: wknd ins fnl 2f* **66/1**

**10** *1 1/4* **One Good Thing (USA)** 2-9-0 LDettori 11 61
(SaeedBinSuroor) *mid-div: sn reminders: nvr in contention* **13/2**

0 **11** *1 1/4* **Southern Tide (USA)**[19] 4016 2-9-0 MFenton 16 58
(JJSheehan) *nvr bttr than mid-div* **66/1**

**12** *3/4* **Come On Jonny (IRE)** 2-8-9 NChalmers(5) 13 55
(RMBeckett) *v.s.a: sn rdn: sme hdwy fnl 2f but n.d* **50/1**

**13** *nk* **Ruby Murray** 2-8-9 JQuinn 2 49
(BJMeehan) *outpcd* **50/1**

**14** *6* **Kirkhammerton (IRE)** 2-9-0 VSlattery 3 36
(JAOsborne) *s.i.s: sn in tch: wknd 2f out* **66/1**

55 **15** *1 1/4* **Dralion**[18] 4064 2-8-11 LFletcher(3) 10 33
(JMPEustace) *rdn 1/2-way: a outpcd* **50/1**

0 **16** *5* **Reference (IRE)**[19] 4016 2-9-0 PDobbs 6 18
(RHannon) *a outpcd in rr* **66/1**

**17** *7* **My Gacho (IRE)** 2-9-0 RHavlin 15 —
(MrsPNDutfield) *slowly away: a outpcd in rr* **33/1**

0 **18** *nk* **Eden Star (IRE)**[14] 4191 2-8-9 DaneO'Neill 7 —
(DKIvory) *chsd ldrs to 1/2-way* **66/1**

1m 13.31s (-0.56) **Going Correction** -0.10s/f (Good) **18** Ran SP% **123.5**
Speed ratings: **99,97,95,94,92 89,88,88,87,85 84,83,82,74,72 66,56,56**CSF £28.08 TOTE £5.50: £1.60, £2.20, £2.10; EX 39.10.
**Owner** H R H Sultan Ahmad Shah **Bred** Mount Coote Stud,Richard Pegum And M Bell Racing **Trained** Newmarket, Suffolk

**FOCUS**

A decent-looking maiden in which the first two home are both well entered up. The form looks fairly strong for the grade.

**NOTEBOOK**

**One Putra(IRE)** had run promisingly at Goodwood on his debut and this son of Indian Ridge looked sure to appreciate the rain-softened ground. Well supported, his rider immediately headed for the far side and that proved a wise move. He made almost all the running and won with a bit up his sleeve, and a conditions race looks the next logical step.

**Rebuttal(USA)** ◆, who cost $400,000 at one of the US breeze-ups, is out of a multiple sprint winner, and is clearly well regarded, as he is entered in the Gimcrack, Champagne and Middle Park Stakes. This was a pleasing debut and, as his trainer's runners usually improve a good deal for their debuts, he should not be long in going one better.

**Moth Ball**, coltish beforehand, was again troublesome at the start. Narrowly beaten on his debut, he ran well again, although he may have run into a couple of decent performers here, and his time will surely come.

**Sudden Dismissal(IRE)**, whose stable is emerging from the doldrums, shaped well on his debut. His normally advantageous high draw proved a handicap on this rain-softened ground so this effort was probably better than it looks on paper.

**Enforcer** has not enjoyed much luck with the draw so far, as he was drawn low on his debut here when the ground was riding fast, and found himself drawn on the opposite side this time, only to find the whole field tacking over to the far side on the softish ground.

**Go Mo(IRE)** stepped up considerably on his debut effort from his good low draw. He looks a nursery type.

**Prince Samos(IRE)** was sent off favourite again but his draw was a handicap on this occasion with the ground riding slow. He could be more of a nursery type and will be eligible for handicaps after one more run.

**One Good Thing(USA)**, who cost $550,000 as a yearling, is a half-brother to several US winners. He was not particularly strong in the market for a Godolphin newcomer and was never a threat in the race itself, running green in the early stages. There should be better to come, and faster ground may suit.

**Ruby Murray** *Official explanation: jockey said filly stumbled about 1 1/2f out*

## 4612 NICHOLAS CUNNINGHAM MEMORIAL FILLIES' AUCTION NURSERY 6f

6:15 (6:18) (E ) 2-Y-O **£4,264** (£1,312; £656; £328) **Stalls** High

Form RPR

016 **1** **Tequila Sheila (IRE)**[24] 3898 2-9-2 **78** KFallon 7 81
(KRBurke) *hld up in rr: hdwy and pushed along ins fnl 2f: str run over 1f out to ld fnl 100yds: styd on wl* **7/1**[3]

253 **2** *1* **Consider This**[17] 4099 2-9-3 **79** SSanders 6 79
(WMBrisbourne) *w ldrs: rdn to ld wl over 1f out: kpt on u.p tl hdd and nt qckn fnl 100yds* **9/1**

5040 **3** *shd* **Ivana Illyich (IRE)**[25] 3886 2-8-8 **70** JFEgan 8 70
(SKirk) *bhd: hdwy on ins fr 2f out: nt clr run 1f out: swtchd rt to outside and kpt on fnl f: fin wl* **16/1**

154 **4** *1 1/4* **Alvarinho Lady**[46] 3242 2-8-12 **74** PaulEddery 2 70
(DHaydnJones) *w ldrs: str chal fr 2f out: stl ev ch 1f out: outpcd ins last* **10/1**

214 **5** *3/4* **Encanto (IRE)**[9] 4342 2-9-0 **83** DerekNolan(7) 3 77
(JSMoore) *bhd: hdwy on ins over 2f out: squeezed through to chal 1f out: fnd no ex u.p ins last* **7/1**[3]

4030 **6** *3* **High Chart**[9] 4342 2-9-0 **76** (t) AMcCarthy 9 61
(GGMargarson) *chsd ldrs: rdn 1/2-way: outpcd fnl 2f* **16/1**

002 **7** *3/4* **Debs Broughton**[56] 2946 2-7-12 **60** oh4 LisaJones 4 42
(WJMusson) *sn in tch: rdn 1/2-way: hung lft fr 2f out: n.m.r over 1f out and sn wknd* **25/1**

6201 **8** *3/4* **Withering Lady (IRE)**[13] 4212 2-9-4 **80** RHavlin 5 60
(MrsPNDutfield) *t.k.h: chsd ldrs 4f* **8/1**

035 **9** *3 1/2* **Madhavi**[12] 4231 2-8-13 **75** PDobbs 11 45
(RHannon) *a outpcd* **4/1**[1]

2004 **10** *1/2* **Evanesce**[14] 4197 2-8-12 **74** CCatlin 12 42
(MRChannon) *pressed ldrs 3f: wknd 2f out* **14/1**

0114 **11** *3/4* **Island Swing (IRE)**[12] 4235 2-9-6 **82** LDettori 1 48
(JLSpearing) *led: hdd wl over 1f out: wkng on rails whn squeezed 1f out: eased whn no ch* **5/1**[2]

360 **12** *dist* **Baileys Applause**[23] 3930 2-7-11 **64** (b) HayleyTurner(5) 10 —
(CADwyer) *a outpcd: sddle slipped over 2f out: t.o* **20/1**

1m 14.38s (0.51) **Going Correction** -0.10s/f (Good) **12** Ran SP% **118.9**
Speed ratings: **92,90,90,88,87 83,82,81,77,76 75,—**CSF £68.91 CT £982.36 TOTE £5.80: £2.10, £3.20, £6.70; EX 52.90.
**Owner** Lee Westwood **Bred** Martyn J McEnery **Trained** Middleham Moor, N Yorks

**FOCUS**

A fair nursery in which once again the whole field tacked over to race towards the far-side rail in the straight. The form appears sound.

**NOTEBOOK**

**Tequila Sheila(IRE)** continues to look as though this trip is on the short side, but the rain-softened ground helped on this occasion and, under a strong ride from the champion, she ran out a deserved winner.

**Consider This**, who was prominent throughout, ran well on her handicap debut despite her stiff-enough mark, and appears to be progressing with racing.

**Ivana Illyich(IRE)** did not get the best of runs, but finished her race well and looks sure to capitalise on her current mark sooner rather than later.

**Alvarinho Lady** allayed any fears that this softer ground would not be in her favour and ran a perfectly good race.

**Encanto(IRE)**, one of the more experienced fillies in the line-up, ran a fair race under top weight, but she looks open to less improvement than one or two of her rivals.

**High Chart** has gone backwards since her debut win here back in April.

**Withering Lady(IRE)** *Official explanation: jockey said filly did not handle the good to soft, good in places ground*

**Madhavi**, who needed the rain to be given the go-ahead to run, was a very disappointing favourite and surely she is capable of better than this.

**Island Swing(IRE)** showed plenty of early pace but was beaten a fair way out and perhaps the ground was too slow, although she looks to be on a high-enough mark, too.

**Baileys Applause** *Official explanation: jockey said saddle slipped*

## 4613 TALKSPORT 1089/1053AM "PORKY" PARRY CLASSIFIED STKS 1m 67y
6:45 (6:46) (D) 3-Y-O+ £5,492 (£1,690; £845; £422) Stalls High

Form RPR
1 **1** **Tarfah (USA)**[15] 4168 3-8-9 82 SSanders 2 102+
(GAButler) *trckd ldr: chal over 3f out: led ins fnl 2f: pushed clr appr fnl f: easily* **11/4**[2]
035 **2** *5* **Kentucky King (USA)**[2] 4549 4-9-3 80 LDettori 6 86
(PWHiatt) *chsd ldrs in 4th: rdn and hdwy 3f out: styd on wl to take 2nd last half f but no ch w wnr* **9/2**
51 **3** *1 1/2* **Cut Short (USA)**[66] 2647 3-8-7 80 JFortune 4 86+
(JHMGosden) *led: pushed along 3f out: hdd ins fnl 2f: no ch w wnr over 1f out: wknd and lost 2nd last half f* **9/4**[1]
-053 **4** *3* **Rafferty (IRE)**[7] 4401 5-9-4 81 DHolland 5 78
(CEBrittain) *chsd ldrs in 3rd: rdn 3f out: wknd qckly 2f out* **7/2**[3]
4064 **5** *1* **Lining Wine (IRE)**[61] 2789 8-9-4 81 SCarson 3 75
(BGPowell) *in tch: rdn 3f out: hung lft and carried hdd high fr 2f out: nt run on* **16/1**
0-00 **6** *4* **Jewel Of India**[177] 768 5-9-3 80 SDrowne 7 66
(MrsALMKing) *rdn over 3f out: a bhd and n.d* **33/1**
50U6 **7** *14* **Jools**[5] 4435 6-9-3 75 DaneO'Neill 1 37
(DKIvory) *a bhd: lost tch fnl 3f* **10/1**

1m 46.1s (0.50) **Going Correction** +0.40s/f (Good)
**WFA** 3 from 4yo+ 7lb **7** Ran **SP% 115.8**
Speed ratings: **113,108,106,103,102 98,84**CSF £15.97 TOTE £3.50: £2.00, £2.70; EX 18.40.
**Owner** Abdulla Al Khalifa **Bred** Sheik A Bin I Alkahlifa **Trained** Blewbury, Oxon

**FOCUS**
A decent classified contest and a cracking time for the grade with an impressive performance from the winner. The form looks good for the grade and can rate higher

**NOTEBOOK**
**Tarfah(USA)** ◆ ran out an impressive winner on only her second career start, turning what had looked a fairly tight race into a procession. Her stable is coming out of a lean spell and she looks good enough to take her chance in Listed company, although her immediate aim will no doubt be geared by the Handicapper's reaction to this success. She should get farther than this, and she has already shown that she is adaptable ground-wise.
**Kentucky King(USA)**, proven with give in the ground, posted a very respectable effort. He had no chance with the impressive winner, who is clearly better than an 80-rated animal, and could have done no more than finish a clear runner-up.
**Cut Short(USA)** looked set for a battle with the winner inside the final quarter mile, but she gave way fairly tamely. The ground may well have found her out and she deserves another chance back on a faster surface.
**Rafferty(IRE)** has won on good to soft in the past and his last-time-out effort here would have been better had he not been hampered, so this performance has to go down as slightly disappointing.
**Lining Wine(IRE)** is still winless on turf from 17 starts.
**Jools** *Official explanation: jockey said gelding lost a shoe*

## 4614 TOTEQUADPOT H'CAP 6f
7:15 (7:16) (C) (0-100,98) 3-Y-O+ £12,504 (£4,743; £2,371; £1,078) Stalls High

Form RPR
1141 **1** **Jonny Ebeneezer**[10] 4294 5-8-9 79 (b) LDettori 12 92+
(DFlood) *racd far side: hld up in tch: qcknd to ld ins fnl f: easily* **3/1**[1]
3152 **2** *1 1/2* **Jayanjay**[6] 4415 5-8-10 80 SSanders 5 88
(MissBSanders) *racd far side: chsd ldrs: rdn and kpt on fr over 1f out: tk 2nd ins last half f but no ch w wnr* **7/1**
0030 **3** *2* **Crimson Silk**[23] 3940 4-9-8 92 (b[1]) PaulEddery 6 94
(DHaydnJones) *racd far side: w ldrs: led jst ins fnl 2f: hdd ins fnl f: one pce whn hung lft: hit rail and lost 2nd last half f* **16/1**
3213 **4** *1/2* **Presto Shinko (IRE)**[21] 3995 3-8-9 83 KFallon 13 84
(RHannon) *racd far side: in tch: pushed along 3f out: styd on fr over 1f out but nvr gng pce to rch ldrs* **11/2**[2]
5000 **5** *shd* **Little Edward**[8] 4366 6-9-1 88 LPKeniry[(3)] 1 88
(BGPowell) *racd far side: s.i.s: sn rcvrd and in tch: rdn 2f out: kpt on same pce fr over 1f out* **25/1**
3000 **6** *1 1/4* **Further Outlook (USA)**[8] 4366 10-9-0 84 DHolland 7 80
(DKIvory) *racd far side: mde most tl hdd ins fnl 2f: wknd ins fnl f* **25/1**
4010 **7** *hd* **Zilch**[32] 3673 6-10-0 98 RMullen 11 94
(MLWBell) *racd far side: bhd: rdn over 2f out: kpt on fr over 1f out and r.o ins last: nt rch ldrs* **12/1**
0200 **8** *nk* **Marsad (IRE)**[9] 4324 10-9-2 86 PDoe 3 81
(JAkehurst) *racd far side: bhd: rdn 1/2-way: kpt on fr over 1f out: nt rch ldrs* **14/1**
0004 **9** *3 1/2* **Boleyn Castle (USA)**[10] 4294 7-9-0 87 LFletcher[(3)] 2 71
(PSMcentee) *racd far side: pressed ldr over 3f: wknd over 1f out* **25/1**
0014 **10** *2 1/2* **Tally (IRE)**[10] 4299 4-7-12 68 oh1 JMackay 8 45
(MJPolglase) *racd far side: unruly stalls and slowly away: rdn and effrt 1/2-way: styd on same pce fr over 1f out* **20/1**
6003 **11** *3/4* **Miss George**[14] 4194 6-8-11 81 DaneO'Neill 10 56
(DKIvory) *racd far side:s.i.s: outpcd* **12/1**
1220 **12** *4* **Caustic Wit (IRE)**[23] 3941 6-8-12 85 (p) RMiles[(3)] 18 48
(MSSaunders) *led stands side gp thrght: no ch w far side fnl 2f* **6/1**[3]
0001 **13** *3/4* **Michelle Ma Belle (IRE)**[7] 4403 4-8-6 76 6ex (b) JFEgan 16 36
(SKirk) *racd stands side: chsd ldrs: no ch w far side fnl 2f* **10/1**
3510 **14** *1/2* **Willheconquertoo**[28] 3810 4-7-8 69 (t) BSwarbrick[(5)] 17 28
(AndrewReid) *racd stands side: chsd ldrs: no ch w far side fnl 2f: hmpd 1f out* **16/1**
5203 **15** *shd* **Compton Banker (IRE)**[18] 4044 7-7-9 68 oh1 FPFerris[(3)] 14 27
(PDEvans) *racd far side: outpcd* **33/1**
0010 **16** *8* **Mine Behind**[16] 4152 4-8-8 83 MSavage[(5)] 15 18
(JRBest) *racd stands side: chsd ldrs: no ch w far side fnl 2f* **20/1**

1m 12.52s (-1.35) **Going Correction** -0.10s/f (Good)
**WFA** 3 from 4yo+ 4lb **16** Ran **SP% 134.1**
Speed ratings: **105,103,100,99,99 97,97,97,92,89 88,82,81,81,81 70**CSF £23.32 CT £318.33 TOTE £3.40: £1.80, £2.00, £3.50, £1.90; EX 17.50 TRIFECTA Not won..
**Owner** Mrs Ruth M Serrell **Bred** John Purcell **Trained** Upper Lambourn, Berks
■ Stewards Enquiry : R Miles one-day ban: careless riding (Aug 20)

**FOCUS**
A good quality handicap and the winner did well to defy his double-figure draw. The form looks solid.

**NOTEBOOK**
**Jonny Ebeneezer** has been in terrific form of late and continues to defy the Handicapper, this time scoring off a mark 23lb higher than that which he won off when beginning his winning run 20 days earlier. He overcame a fairly bad draw, travelled well and won with plenty in hand, suggesting there is even more to come, and the Great St Wilfrid, under a 4lb penalty, is a possibility. Clearly he is as happy on easy ground as he is on a fast surface.
**Jayanjay** once again posted a sound effort in defeat, finding only the rapidly-improving winner too strong. Already due to go up 2lb, he will take yet another hike for this performance.
**Crimson Silk** runs his best races here for some reason and can now boast a course record which reads 31133. He was wearing blinkers for the first time on this occasion and they certainly did not hurt his performance.
**Presto Shinko(IRE)**, the only three-year-old in the field, was not well drawn as it turned out and again found himself finishing well but without being able to reach the leaders.
**Little Edward** was well drawn but he has never won beyond five and a half furlongs.
**Further Outlook(USA)** tends to run well at this course but he is poorly handicapped at present.
**Zilch** is another who has plenty on his plate now off marks in the high 90s.
**Marsad(IRE)** needs a little help from the Handicapper.
**Miss George** *Official explanation: jockey said mare spread a plate*
**Caustic Wit(IRE)** brought home the stands'-side quartet, but they finished a long way behind the far-side group.

## 4615 READING EVENING POST MAIDEN STKS 1m 67y
7:45 (7:47) (D) 3-Y-O+ £4,251 (£1,308; £654; £327) Stalls High

Form RPR
52 **1** **Sea Nymph (IRE)**[14] 4195 3-8-9 KFallon 8 71+
(SirMichaelStoute) *hld up in tch: led ins fnl 2f: pushed clr fnl f: easily* **4/7**[1]
**2** *1 3/4* **Newnham (IRE)** 3-8-11 NMackay[(3)] 6 73+
(LMCumani) *bhd: hdwy 3f out: styd on wl to go 2nd ins fnl f but no ch w wnr* **14/1**
6 **3** *2 1/2* **Paintbox**[15] 4168 3-8-9 SSanders 7 62+
(MrsAJPerrett) *bhd: pushed along 3f out: r.o fr over 1f out and fin wl but no ch w ldrs* **10/1**[3]
05 **4** *1 1/2* **Danettie**[9] 4332 3-8-4 BSwarbrick[(5)] 11 59
(WMBrisbourne) *chsd ldrs: chal 3f out: chsd wnr over 1f out but no ch: wknd fnl f* **66/1**
0-50 **5** *2 1/2* **Second Warning**[58] 2883 3-9-0 60 LDettori 12 59
(DJDaly) *chsd ldrs: chal 3f out: styng on one pce whn bmpd ins fnl 2f: nvr a danger after* **20/1**
0-0 **6** *hd* **Sweep The Board (IRE)**[8] 4369 3-9-0 TPQueally 14 59
(APJarvis) *led: kpt slt ld fr 3f out: edgd lft u.p 2f out:hdd sn after: sn wknd* **66/1**
0-0 **7** *1 1/4* **Lasser Light (IRE)**[46] 3245 4-9-7 SRighton 5 56
(DGBridgwater) *chsd ldrs: rdn to chal 3f out: styd on one pce fnl 2f* **50/1**
3-4 **8** *nk* **Magari**[9] 4351 3-8-9 MFenton 2 50
(JGGiven) *bhd: rdn 3f out: nvr in contention* **25/1**
**9** *1 1/4* **Russian Applause** 4-9-7 JQuinn 1 53
(PRChamings) *in tch: rdn 3f out: wknd over 2f out* **33/1**
0202 **10** *nk* **El Chaparral (IRE)**[14] 4192 4-9-7 68 DaneO'Neill 13 52
(DKIvory) *v.s.a: plld hrd: hdwy 4f out: chal 3f out: sn rdn: wknd over 2f out* **9/2**[2]
000 **11** *2* **Medica Boba**[14] 4195 3-8-9 SDrowne 10 43
(HMorrison) *bhd most of way* **50/1**
**12** *3 1/2* **Rabbit** 3-8-9 VSlattery 9 36
(MrsALMKing) *slowly away: a in rr* **50/1**
04 **13** *14* **Spes Bona (USA)**[35] 3587 3-9-0 DHolland 3 11
(WJHaggas) *a bhd* **20/1**

1m 47.61s (2.01) **Going Correction** +0.40s/f (Good)
**WFA** 3 from 4yo 7lb **13** Ran **SP% 122.8**
Speed ratings: **105,103,100,99,96 96,95,95,93,93 91,87,73**CSF £9.50 TOTE £1.60: £1.10, £4.10, £2.30; EX 12.80.
**Owner** Ballymacoll Stud **Bred** Ballymacoll Stud Farm Ltd **Trained** Newmarket, Suffolk

**FOCUS**
A modest, uncompetitive maiden, although the first three should rate better than the bare form.

**NOTEBOOK**
**Sea Nymph(IRE)** had the form in the book to win this modest maiden and duly scored in good style. The easier ground may well have been in her favour and the Handicapper should not overburden her if taking this form literally.
**Newnham(IRE)**, who has already been gelded, ran a promising race on his debut. Bred for middle distances, the conditions brought his stamina into play and he picked up the runner-up prize inside the last. There should be better to come as he steps up in distance.
**Paintbox**, whose dam is from the family of middle-distance stars Colorpsin, Kayf Tara and Opera House, settled better this time and saw her race out well.
**Danettie** ran her best race to date and is now eligible for handicaps, in which sphere she should pay her way.
**Second Warning** has had a few chances and probably ran up to form.
**Russian Applause** *Official explanation: jockey said gelding was hanging and stumbled during the race*
**El Chaparral(IRE)** used up too much energy trying to make up the ground lost with a poor start.

## 4616 COME RACING ON SATURDAY EVENING 28TH AUGUST H'CAP 1m 3f 135y
8:15 (8:15) (E) (0-70,70) 3-Y-O+ £3,532 (£1,087; £543; £271) Stalls Low

Form RPR
2400 **1** **Bakiri (IRE)**[14] 4196 6-8-13 55 JFEgan 12 66
(AndrewReid) *chsd ldrs: rdn to ld wl over 1f out: r.o wl: collapsed after line: dead* **20/1**
5110 **2** *3/4* **Pont Neuf (IRE)**[7] 4398 4-9-2 65 SJDonohoe[(7)] 11 74
(PDEvans) *mid-div: rdn and hdwy 2f out: styd on strly ins fnl f but nt rch wnr* **5/1**[2]
2143 **3** *1 1/2* **Absinther**[6] 4416 7-8-2 49 HayleyTurner[(5)] 8 56
(MRBosley) *s.i.s: bhd: rapid hdwy 3f out: slt ld appr fnl 2f: hdd wl over 1f out: one pce ins last* **13/2**
/0-4 **4** *nk* **Flaming Spirt**[9] 4339 5-8-2 51 ow1 DerekNolan[(7)] 13 58
(JSMoore) *sn chsng ldrs: rdn over 2f out: kpt on fr over 1f out: one pce ins last* **33/1**
0502 **5** *1 1/2* **Sahaat**[17] 4093 6-9-11 70 LFletcher[(3)] 4 74
(MJPolglase) *led after 1f: hdd after 2f: styd chsng ldrs u.p: one pce fr over 1f out* **33/1**
0632 **6** *3/4* **Stolen Song**[7] 4398 4-8-13 55 SWhitworth 2 58
(MJRyan) *w ldrs: rdn to chal 3f out: one pce fnl 2f* **11/1**
3000 **7** *shd* **Swift Alchemist**[9] 4319 4-8-13 55 (p) GBaker 9 58
(MrsHSweeting) *bhd: rdn over 3f out: sn edgd lft: styd on fr over 1f out but n.d* **50/1**
6215 **8** *nk* **Man The Gate**[25] 3873 5-9-3 59 SSanders 14 61
(PDCundell) *bhd: hdwy and rdn 3f out: styng on whn n.m.r over 1f out: nt trble ldrs* **6/1**[3]
-303 **9** *3/4* **Kalou (GER)**[17] 4086 6-8-6 48 TPQueally 17 49
(BJCurley) *in tch: chsd ldrs and rdn 3f out: one pce 2f out: no ch w ldrs whn stmbld appr fnl f* **11/4**[1]
0-04 **10** *nk* **Sir Alfred**[16] 4146 5-8-13 55 TEDurcan 1 56
(AKing) *bhd: hdwy 4f out: pressed ldrs and rdn 3f out: wknd fr 2f out* **20/1**
5-42 **11** *1* **Malak Al Moulouk (USA)**[21] 3997 4-9-11 67 DHolland 3 66
(JMPEustace) *trckd ldrs: led 3f out: hdd appr fnl 2f: wknd over 1f out* **6/1**[3]
1050 **12** *1 3/4* **Private Benjamin**[30] 3752 4-8-4 46 PDoe 7 42
(JamiePoulton) *bhd: hdwy 3f out: chsd ldrs over 2f out: sn wknd* **25/1**

230/ **13** ½ **Desert Air (JPN)**[128] 4830 5-9-13 **69** JFortune 15 64
(MCPipe) *led after 2f: hdd 3f out: wknd 2f out* **20/1**

0555 **14** 1 ½ **Internationalguest (IRE)**[21] 3985 5-10-0 **70** (p) NPollard 6 63
(GGMargarson) *mid-div: effrt to chse ldrs over 2f out: wknd over 1f out* **14/1**

/-65 **15** nk **Saspys Lad**[33] 2619 7-8-13 **60** BSwarbrick(5) 10 53
(WMBrisbourne) *a in rr* **33/1**

-000 **16** 7 **Victory Venture (IRE)**[14] 4192 4-9-9 **65** CCatlin 5 46
(IanWilliams) *plld hrd: led 1f: wknd 3f out* **66/1**

2m 34.8s (4.70) **Going Correction** +0.40s/f (Good)
**WFA** 3 from 4yo+ 11lb **16** Ran SP% **130.6**
Speed ratings: **100,99,98,98,97 96,96,96,96,95 95,94,93,92,92 87**CSF £115.22 CT £758.44 TOTE £29.40: £4.50, £1.80, £1.80, £8.70; EX 197.10 Place 6 £140.84, Place 5 £78.46.
**Owner** A S Reid **Bred** His Highness The Aga Khan's Studs S C **Trained** Mill Hill, London NW7

**FOCUS**
A modest handicap with a tragic end for the connections of the winner. The form is ordinary but fairly reliable.

**NOTEBOOK**
**Bakiri(IRE)**, whose handicap mark had dropped 20lb since the beginning of the turf season, found the easier conditions bringing about an improved performance. He found plenty under pressure to win by three-quarters of a length, but sadly suffered a fatal heart attack soon after the line.
**Pont Neuf(IRE)** was putting in all her best work at the finish and looks to have further improvment in her. A rating of just 55 on the All-Weather is begging to be exploited.
**Absinther** once again showed that he is in great form at the moment, but he is not the easiest to win with.
**Flaming Spirt** had run a promising race on the Polytrack on her return from an 18-month absence last time, and it was good to see that she had not gone backwards from that.
**Sahaat** has seen his handicap mark fall 25lb since his arrival in this country 18 months ago, but he remains winless on these shores.
**Stolen Song** has never finished in the first four on ground as soft as this.
**Kalou(GER)** is currently well handicapped and had run as though ready to strike last time out but, having been in the perfect position, he failed to produce a telling challenge on this occasion. The ground may have been against him, and he remains of interest off his current mark. *Official explanation: jockey said gelding ran too free in the early stages*
T/Jkpt: Not won. T/Plt: £136.40 to a £1 stake. Pool: £59,563.90. 318.75 winning tickets. T/Qpdt: £18.30 to a £1 stake. Pool: £4,050.50. 163.50 winning tickets. ST

# 4040 BATH (L-H)
## Tuesday, August 10

**OFFICIAL GOING: Good to firm**

## 4617 SALTWELLSIGNS.CO.UK CLAIMING STKS — 5f 161y
**2:15** (2:15) (E) 3-Y-0+ **£4,114** (£1,266; £633; £316) **Stalls** Low

Form RPR

0400 **1** **Atlantic Viking (IRE)**[16] 4165 9-9-5 **91** RWinston 13 77
(DNicholls) *drawn wd: hdwy over 2f out: led appr fnl f: r.o* **1/1**[1]

4000 **2** 1 **Arfinnit (IRE)**[5] 4489 3-8-4 58 ow1 (v) SHitchcott(3) 14 66
(MRChannon) *slowly away: rdn over 3f out: hdwy u.p over 1f out: snatched 2nd cl home* **20/1**

6021 **3** hd **Trick Cyclist**[5] 4472 3-9-0 72 MartinDwyer 6 72
(AMBalding) *chsd ldr: led 2f out: rdn and hdd appr fnl f: one pce and lost 2nd cl home* **3/1**[2]

0013 **4** shd **Byo (IRE)**[7] 4415 6-8-10 69 FNorton 4 64
(MQuinn) *a.p: rdn over 2f out: no ex ins fnl f* **15/2**[3]

5410 **5** ½ **Cayman Breeze**[71] 2528 4-8-8 57 RLMoore 8 60
(JMBradley) *in rr: rdn and mde late hdwy on outside: nvr nrr* **20/1**

0000 **6** 1 ¾ **Millfields Dreams**[17] 4154 5-8-4 57 BSwarbrick(5) 2 56
(RBrotherton) *in tch: rdn 3f out: no imp ins fnl 2f* **40/1**

0040 **7** hd **Man Crazy (IRE)**[24] 3935 3-7-12 54 (b) JMackay 11 48
(RMBeckett) *led tl hdd 2f out: wknd over 1f out* **28/1**

365U **8** 3 ½ **Melody King**[11] 4299 3-8-0 65 (b) FPFerris(3) 7 41
(PDEvans) *prom tl wknd over 2f out* **16/1**

0040 **9** 2 **Confuzed**[15] 4185 4-8-7 40 (be) GHannon 9 35
(DFlood) *prom: rdn 1/2-way: wknd 2f out* **66/1**

-605 **10** ½ **Coco Reef**[18] 4097 3-7-12 47 DKinsella 12 28
(BPalling) *in rr whn bmpd over 4f out: nvr on terms* **66/1**

0000 **11** ½ **Ridicule**[38] 3533 5-8-7 44 (bt) SDrowne 10 31
(JGPortman) *mid-div: rdn 1/2-way: sn btn* **66/1**

**12** 3 ½ **Java Gold** 3-7-11 CHaddon(7) 3 21
(WGMTurner) *mid-div whn stmbld over 4f out: sn bhd* **100/1**

0005 **13** 6 **Bennanabaa**[19] 4044 5-8-7 46 (t) BO'Neill(7) 1 7
(SCBurrough) *slowly away: a bhd* **80/1**

1m 10.52s (-0.62) **Going Correction** -0.15s/f (Firm)
**WFA** 3 from 4yo+ 4lb **13** Ran SP% **114.8**
Speed ratings: **98,96,96,96,95 93,93,88,85,85 84,79,71**CSF £28.87 TOTE £2.00: £1.20, £5.20, £1.10; EX 29.50.
**Owner** David Faulkner **Bred** Kilcarn Stud **Trained** Sessay, N Yorks

**FOCUS**
An ordinary claimer and a modest winning time for the grade. The form is held down by the proximity of the second and fifth.

**NOTEBOOK**
**Atlantic Viking(IRE)**, whose stable has won the last two renewals of this event, scored fairly comfortably. Rated 19lb superior to his closest rival in the field, he was sent into the lead two furlongs out and the race was as good as over from there, although he did slightly idle in front. This outing confirms the talent is still there, and hopefully will have given the horse confidence. David Nicholls is now aiming him for a race at Epsom later this month, a track he has run well at in the past.
**Arfinnit(IRE)** missed the break, as is often the case, but finished well to get up for second. His cause was helped by a decent pace up front and the leaders tying up. All his wins have come at six furlongs, and a similar contest at a stiff track may enable him to get his head in front.
**Trick Cyclist** helped to cut out a fast pace up front, and it was not until approaching the last furlong that those efforts took their toll. To his credit he stuck his head out all the way to the line. He is competitive off this kind of mark and, from his racing style, a return to a sharp downhill course could see him go pretty close next time.
**Byo(IRE)** was always up with the pace, but could not quicken inside the last furlong. It was a slightly disappointing effort on the back of a fair run in a handicap last time out. He will continue to run his race, but may need less competitive races in order to regain the winning thread.
**Cayman Breeze** travelled pretty well during the race and encountered some slight interference at a crucial point. He would never have won the race but may well have reached a place. However, he does appear to travel with his head raised a touch and may not be one to place a lot of faith in.
**Bennanabaa** *Official explanation: trainer said gelding was slowly away and sulked*

## 4618 SALTWELL SIGNS H'CAP — 1m 3f 144y
**2:45** (2:45) (E) (0-75,75) 3-Y-O **£3,565** (£1,097; £548; £274) **Stalls** Low

Form RPR

4122 **1** **Velvet Waters**[11] 4307 3-8-7 **61** SCarson 2 73
(RFJohnsonHoughton) *trckd ldr: rdn to ld over 2f out: kpt up to work: styd on wl* **5/1**[3]

0220 **2** 3 ½ **Principessa**[25] 3908 3-9-0 **68** JFortune 6 74
(BPalling) *led tl hdd over 2f out: styd on wl but no imp after* **10/1**

1413 **3** nk **Donastrela (IRE)**[11] 4307 3-8-4 **63** (v) NChalmers(5) 11 69
(AMBalding) *hld up in rr: styd on fnl 2f: nvr nrr* **4/1**[2]

2510 **4** 2 ½ **Oktis Morilious (IRE)**[22] 3990 3-7-7 **54** CHaddon(7) 8 56
(AWCarroll) *in tch: rdn over 3f out: one pce after* **20/1**

-000 **5** 1 ½ **Autumn Flyer (IRE)**[27] 3852 3-8-3 **57** RLMoore 12 57
(CGCox) *hld up: rdn over 3f out: one pce after* **33/1**

1-03 **6** 2 ½ **Messe De Minuit (IRE)**[22] 3985 3-9-7 **75** SDrowne 10 71
(RCharlton) *towards rr: rdn over 4f out: nvr nr to chal* **12/1**

3240 **7** nk **Desert Image (IRE)**[20] 4027 3-8-13 **70** DCorby(3) 9 65
(CTinkler) *t.k.h: in rr tl hdwy 5f out: wknd over 3f out* **14/1**

4126 **8** 2 ½ **Bienvenue**[19] 4062 3-9-5 **73** MartinDwyer 5 64
(MPTregoning) *in rr: rdn over 3f out: nvr on terms* **3/1**[1]

5554 **9** ½ **Mommkin**[19] 4056 3-9-0 **68** (v[1]) TEDurcan 1 58
(MRChannon) *chsd ldrs: rdn over 2f out: wknd over 1f out* **20/1**

10 **10** 2 **Komoto**[13] 4242 3-8-13 **67** TPQueally 4 54
(GAButler) *t.k.h: hld up in rr and nvr on terms* **14/1**

5106 **11** 3 ½ **Zaffeu**[11] 4300 3-8-12 **69** J-PGuillambert(3) 3 51
(NPLittmoden) *t.k.h: mid-div whn short of room after 4f: sn bhd and nvr on terms after* **20/1**

6305 **12** ¾ **Bailaora (IRE)**[16] 4170 3-9-1 **69** (b) KFallon 7 49
(BWDuke) *chsd ldrs tl rdn 3f out: sn btn* **14/1**

2m 27.94s (-2.36) **Going Correction** -0.15s/f (Firm) **12** Ran SP% **115.7**
Speed ratings: **101,98,98,96,95 94,93,92,91,90 88,87**CSF £49.41 CT £219.39 TOTE £6.10: £1.70, £3.50, £1.90; EX 76.50.
**Owner** R Crutchley **Bred** R E Crutchley **Trained** Blewbury, Oxon

**FOCUS**
A modest handicap in which very few got into the race from off the pace. Despite this the form is fair and looks sound for the grade.

**NOTEBOOK**
**Velvet Waters**, a course and distance winner here last month, had run well in defeat since and, despite being 4lb higher than for her victory, put up another brave effort under a positive ride. She will go up a fair amount for this, but should continue to be competitive at a modest level, especially if returning to this track.
**Principessa**, dropped back to this grade but trying her longest trip to date, set the pace and, although no match for the winner, kept on well to hold on to second place. She is yet to win a race but seems to give of her best, and should be able to pick up a small handicap, possibly against her own sex, before the season is out.
**Donastrela(IRE)**, twice a winner over ten furlongs of this track, was settled at the back. She went in pursuit of the leaders but the winner had already flown, and then her effort appeared to flatten out in the last furlong, as she could not go past the runner-up. A return to ten furlongs should be in her favour, although she may now be a couple of pounds too high in the handicap.
**Oktis Morilious(IRE)**, who finished runner-up to Donastrela here in June, was 3lb better off with that rival but finished a length further behind. He seemed to run his race, but looks to be in the Handicapper's grip at present.
**Autumn Flyer(IRE)**, dropped 5lb, was held up this time having made the running on his previous outing. He seemed to perform better without ever looking likely to get into the argument, but is relatively inexperienced and may improve given time.
**Messe De Minuit(IRE)**, whose form has been on easy ground and Polytrack, was held up at the back and ran on without ever looking likely to reach the front rank. He should drop a few pounds as a result of this, and will be more interesting on easy ground this autumn.
**Desert Image(IRE)**, who had run well on all his previous visits to the track, was held up at the back and, as the race panned out, that was not the place to be.
**Bienvenue**, dropping back in trip, was another that was held up at the back. However, this was a somewhat lacklustre effort. *Official explanation: jockey said filly was hampered on the last bend and never got back into the race*
**Bailaora(IRE)** *Official explanation: jockey said colt had no more to give in the closing stages*

## 4619 MISS HUCKLEBRIDGE H'CAP — 1m 5y
**3:15** (3:16) (E) (0-70,70) 3-Y-O **£4,498** (£1,384; £692; £346) **Stalls** Low

Form RPR

0250 **1** **Raysoot (IRE)**[26] 3874 3-8-7 **56** (t) KFallon 12 68
(EFVaughan) *mde all rdn 3f out: kpt on u.p* **9/2**[2]

5400 **2** 2 ½ **Jarvo**[26] 3875 3-8-8 **60** J-PGuillambert(3) 2 66
(NPLittmoden) *chsd wnr thrght: kpt on but no imp fnl 2f* **50/1**

5460 **3** 1 ½ **Master Mahogany**[17] 4147 3-8-11 **60** SDrowne 5 63
(RJHodges) *a in tch: styd on one pce fnl 2f to go 3rd ins fnl f* **14/1**

0342 **4** nk **Dagola (IRE)**[6] 4451 3-9-1 **64** JFortune 11 66
(CGCox) *hld up in tch. rdn over 3f out: kpt on one pce u.p* **13/8**[1]

0041 **5** nk **Stevedore (IRE)**[13] 4241 3-9-7 **70** GBaker 4 71
(BRMillman) *in tch: rdn 3f out: kpt on one pce* **8/1**[3]

0044 **6** ½ **Danifah (IRE)**[5] 4477 3-7-9 **47** oh5 FPFerris(3) 9 47
(PDEvans) *t.k.h: chsd first 2: rdn over 3f out: wknd ins fnl f* **16/1**

0006 **7** 8 **Binnion Bay (IRE)**[22] 3988 3-8-10 **59** RLMoore 6 41
(RHannon) *a towards rr* **12/1**

0-00 **8** ½ **My Sunshine (IRE)**[59] 2900 3-8-13 **62** MHills 7 42
(BWHills) *mid-div: rdn over 3f out: sn bhd* **11/1**

0453 **9** nk **Hana Dee**[6] 4451 3-8-4 **56** SHitchcott(3) 8 36
(MRChannon) *slowly away: a bhd* **10/1**

-565 **10** 1 **Amber Fox (IRE)**[54] 3019 3-7-12 **47** JoannaBadger 10 24
(PDEvans) *a in rr* **66/1**

1350 **11** ¾ **Rowan Pursuit**[171] 845 3-9-1 **64** (b) TPQueally 1 40
(JAkehurst) *mid-div: rdn 1/2-way: sn bhd* **10/1**

-106 **12** 5 **Count Dracula**[55] 2988 3-9-1 **64** MartinDwyer 3 28
(Jean-ReneAuvray) *a bhd* **33/1**

1m 39.72s (-1.28) **Going Correction** -0.15s/f (Firm) **12** Ran SP% **120.5**
Speed ratings: **100,97,96,95,95 94,86,86,86,85 84,79**CSF £218.46 CT £2970.33 TOTE £6.50: £2.30, £13.80, £4.90; EX 341.50 Trifecta £1284.30 Pool £1,808.88, 0.20 winning units - part won..
**Owner** Sheikh Ahmed Al Maktoum **Bred** Kazushi Takayama **Trained** Newmarket, Suffolk
■ A first winner as a trainer for Ed Vaughan, who took over the licence following the death of Alec Stewart.

**FOCUS**
A modest handicap and ordinary form, but won in impressive style and the form looks sound.

**NOTEBOOK**

**Raysoot(IRE)** ◆, who gave new trainer Ed Vaughan a first winner, was give a very positive ride from an outside draw. He managed to get over to the rail and had a lot of the field in trouble from a long way out. Fitted with the first-time tongue tie, he fairly ran away from them in the final furlong. As is the case with the stable's horses in the past he can improve again, and providing the Handicapper does not over-react he will have every chance of following up. The trainer stated the horse is unsuited by undulating tracks.

**Jarvo** has not been running that well recently and this was one of his better efforts this season. Always traveling well behind the eventual easy winner, he kept on soundly for the last two furlongs. Although he is inconsistent, a repeat of this effort in maiden handicap company may offer his best chance of success.

**Master Mahogany** is gradually finding a little form since being dropped back to a mile. He stayed on steadily after travelling well during the race but was never going to bother the front two. He is open to more improvement, but will probably need a fairly weak grade of race in which to gain a first success.

**Dagola(IRE)** was held up in the middle of the field and did not make much impression on the leaders at the business end. This was a disappointing effort considering his previous form, with no apparent reason for it apart from maybe a busy recent schedule.

**Stevedore(IRE)** is still on the same mark as when scoring last time, and ran well enough over a longer trip. He appears to enjoy seven furlongs and an undulating track and would be of interest given those conditions in the near future.

**Danifah(IRE)** was keen in the early stages and paid the penalty at the business end.

## 4620 TIPTO TWO-YEAR-OLD (S) STKS — 5f 11y

3:45 (3:47) (G) 2-Y-O — **£2,548** (£728; £364) **Stalls** Low

Form — RPR

1 **Arbors Little Girl** 2-8-6 ........ SDrowne 7 — 55
(BRMillman) *outpcd and in rr: rdn and gd hdwy over 1f out: r.o strly to ld post* — **8/1**

4004 2 *shd* **Majestical (IRE)**[7] 4413 2-8-11 58 ........ MartinDwyer 9 — 60
(WRMuir) *a.p: sn chsd ldr: rdn and led ins fnl f: hdd post* — **11/2**[3]

00 3 *2 ½* **Ruby Muja**[29] 3805 2-8-6 ........ RLMoore 1 — 46
(RHannon) *led after 1f: rdn and hdd ins fnl f: wknd* — **11/2**[3]

300 4 *4* **Blakeshall Hope**[5] 4474 2-8-11 ........ (v[1]) RWinston 10 — 37
(PDEvans) *sn rdn: towards rr: passed btn horses fnl f* — **5/1**[2]

5561 5 *hd* **Sapphire Princess**[4] 4516 2-8-6 50 ........ BSwarbrick(5) 6 — 37
(IAWood) *towards rr and nvr on terms* — **9/1**

6654 6 *shd* **Zachy Boy**[36] 3571 2-8-4 58 ........ (b) DerekNolan(7) 8 — 36
(JSMoore) *wnt lft s: in tch tl wknd over 1f out* — **16/1**

05 7 *1 ½* **Diktatit**[4] 4507 2-8-4 ow1 ........ SHitchcott(3) 5 — 27
(MRChannon) *in tch: rdn 1/2-way: one pce after* — **9/2**[1]

5365 8 *7* **Leonalto (IRE)**[20] 4017 2-8-11 59 ........ (b) JFortune 3 — 6
(BJMeehan) *led for 1f: rdn 2f out: wknd qckly over 1f out* — **5/1**[2]

9 *5* **Tinker's First** 2-7-13 ........ CHaddon(7) 4 — —
(WGMTurner) *outpcd thrght* — **20/1**

62.45 secs (-0.05) **Going Correction** -0.15s/f (Firm) — **9** Ran SP% **114.0**

Speed ratings: **94,93,89,83,83 82,80,69,61**CSF £50.80 TOTE £6.70: £1.60, £3.00, £2.60; EX 67.50.The winner was bought in for 4,400gns. Majestical was the subject of a friendly claim.

**Owner** Dr Ian R Shenkin **Bred** Mrs M Shenkin **Trained** Kentisbeare, Devon

**FOCUS**

A very modest seller, but a well-backed debut winner and the first three came clear.

**NOTEBOOK**

**Arbors Little Girl**, a debutante who had failed to enter the stalls on her intended first outing, came from well off the pace to land a gamble. She was retained at the subsequent auction and, with some decent winners on her dam's side, may prove capable of scoring again.

**Majestical(IRE)**, who has shown ability in maidens, was dropping in grade and very nearly got off the mark. He appeared to have matters in hand when taking the advantage inside the last, but had the race snatched away in the line. He is more than capable of gaining compensation in this grade.

**Ruby Muja**, another taking a drop in grade, soon got to the front but was overhauled by the winner inside the last. She is clearly nothing special, but seems to be gradually progressing and may have a small race in her, possibly a selling nursery.

**Blakeshall Hope**, dropped into a seller for the first time, was very unsettled in the first-time visor and only ran on in the closing stages. His dam was a prolific winner on sand, and perhaps that is where his future lies.

**Diktatit**, another dropped in grade, showed up in the early stages but was somewhat disappointing in the end.

## 4621 WICK MAIDEN AUCTION FILLIES' STKS — 5f 161y

4:15 (4:15) (E) 2-Y-O — **£3,584** (£1,103; £551; £275) **Stalls** Low

Form — RPR

05 1 **Rosiella**[50] 3157 2-8-4 ........ FNorton 7 — 70
(MBlanshard) *a in tch: hdwy to go 2nd over 1f out: drvn out to ld fnl 75yds* — **10/1**[3]

5324 2 *nk* **Agent Kensington**[5] 4474 2-8-3 67 ........ RLMoore 6 — 68
(RHannon) *mid-div: swtchd rt 2f out: kpt on to press wnr clly wl ins fnl f* — **9/4**[2]

022 3 *¾* **Shososola (IRE)**[38] 3532 2-8-3 72 ........ JFMcDonald(3) 4 — 69
(BJMeehan) *led after 1f: rdn and hdd 75 yds out: no ex* — **13/8**[1]

050 4 *3 ½* **Mabella (IRE)**[27] 3840 2-8-7 ........ SDrowne 1 — 59
(BRMillman) *outpcd: rdn and r.o fnl f: nvr nr to chal* — **14/1**

0 5 *1* **Cabin Fever**[25] 3904 2-8-4 ........ RSmith 11 — 53
(JCFox) *in tch tl rdn and wknd appr fnl f* — **20/1**

6 *¾* **Purple Door** 2-8-4 ........ MartinDwyer 3 — 50
(RMBeckett) *slowly away: in rr: passed sme btn horses fnl f* — **33/1**

053 7 *3* **Barnbrook Empire (IRE)**[18] 4081 2-8-4 72 ........ TPQueally 9 — 41
(IAWood) *sn chsd ldr: wknd over 1f out* — **10/1**[3]

8 *3 ½* **Ferrara Flame (IRE)** 2-8-5 ........ CCatlin 8 — 30
(JAOsborne) *s.i.s: a bhd* — **50/1**

530 9 *3 ½* **Feminist (IRE)**[59] 2872 2-8-13 74 ........ TEDurcan 5 — 27
(MRChannon) *led for 1f: wknd over 2f out* — **20/1**

6 10 *2* **Ribbons Of Gold**[125] 1299 2-8-8 ........ SWKelly 10 — 16
(JAOsborne) *in tch for 2f: sn bhd* — **12/1**

11 *¾* **Miss Sudbrook (IRE)** 2-8-4 ........ PaulEddery 2 — 9
(DHaydnJones) *slowly away: a bhd* — **40/1**

1m 11.03s (-0.11) **Going Correction** -0.15s/f (Firm) — **11** Ran SP% **118.3**

Speed ratings: **94,93,92,87,86 85,81,76,72,69 68**CSF £31.26 TOTE £11.50: £2.90, £1.20, £1.20; EX 30.90.

**Owner** Mrs R Wellman, B McAllister, D Hampson **Bred** Chippenham Lodge Stud Ltd **Trained** Upper Lambourn, Berks

**FOCUS**

Probably a good maiden for the track in which the first three may well prove fair performers. The form looks sound for the grade.

**NOTEBOOK**

**Rosiella** had shown a glimpse of talent last time out at Windsor and took this race in determined fashion. She sat just behind the pace-setters and when asked to quicken did so in good style.When in front she held on bravely to deny the late challenge of the runner up. This was a good effort considering that she had been suffering from a cough since her last appearance, and she may able to progress with this under her belt.

**Agent Kensington** ran another good race in defeat and reversed Nottingham placings with Shosolosa despite being on 5lb worse terms. Some may question her resolution given her placed efforts, but her overall form reads well and she will surely pick up a race soon, and off her current mark nurseries may provide the best option.

**Shososola(IRE)** attempted to run her rivals into the ground, and only gave best entering the last furlong. This was a decent effort and she would be of interest if dropping back to five furlongs on a sharper track.

**Mabella(IRE)** sat in midfield for most of the race, and surprisingly for a thrice-raced animal appeared to still run a little green. She was never going to catch the three principals but did stay on steadily from two out. She maybe interesting if stepped up to seven furlongs in a weak nursery.

**Cabin Fever** dropped in grade for her second outing, again showed some ability and is likely to do better when quailfied for a handicap mark.

**Purple Door**, by a sire who has done well with his juveniles, showed a fair amount of promise on this debut considering she missed the break. She will be better for the experience.

**Barnbrook Empire(IRE)** should have run better than this judged on official ratings, but ran her best race when making the running and may need to dominate. The Handicapper is likely to drop her a few pounds after this.

## 4622 HOSPITALITY AT BATH FILLIES' H'CAP — 5f 11y

4:45 (4:45) (E) (0-75,70) 3-Y-O+ — **£3,545** (£1,091; £545; £272) **Stalls** Low

Form — RPR

5000 1 **Fiddle Me Blue**[11] 4289 3-10-0 70 ........ SDrowne 2 — 79
(HMorrison) *trckd ldrs: rdn to ld 1f out: r.o wl* — **7/2**[2]

1450 2 *1 ½* **Avit (IRE)**[8] 4400 4-7-13 38 ........ AMcCarthy 10 — 42
(PLGilligan) *hld up on outside: rdn after 2f: hdwy over 1f out: r.o to go 2nd ins fnl f* — **12/1**

133 3 *½* **Lady Protector**[13] 4232 5-9-4 57 ........ DaleGibson 3 — 59
(JBalding) *outpcd in rr: hdwy 2f out: strly rdn and r.o wl fnl f: nvr nrr* — **5/2**[1]

0142 4 *½* **Jinksonthehouse**[2] 4585 3-8-9 56 ........ HayleyTurner(5) 12 — 56
(MDIUsher) *in tch: led wl over 1f out: edgd lft and hdd ent fnl f: no ex* — **13/2**

0000 5 *1* **Hagley Park**[15] 4194 5-8-3 45 ........ JFMcDonald(3) 8 — 42
(MissKMGeorge) *in tch: short of room and swtchd rt over 1f out: nt qckn* — **20/1**

2033 6 *hd* **Boavista (IRE)**[11] 4299 4-9-1 61 ........ SJDonohoe(7) 6 — 57
(PDEvans) *s.i.s: sn in tch: wknd appr fnl f* — **5/1**[3]

0410 7 *hd* **Tender (IRE)**[8] 4400 4-8-13 52 ........ (p) FNorton 4 — 47
(MrsStefLiddiard) *sn outpcd: nvr on terms* — **10/1**

2266 8 *1* **Emaradia**[6] 4434 3-8-12 54 ........ RLMoore 9 — 46
(AWCarroll) *a outpcd* — **20/1**

3120 9 *2 ½* **Innclassic (IRE)**[19] 4044 3-9-7 63 ........ (b) VSlattery 5 — 46
(JaneSouthcombe) *prom on ins: led after 2f: hdd wl over 1f out: wknd fnl f* — **33/1**

0020 10 *½* **Ballinger Express**[8] 4400 4-9-11 64 ........ (b) MartinDwyer 11 — 45
(AMBalding) *led for 2f: rdn and wknd wl over 1f out* — **8/1**

3-00 11 *6* **Royal Supremacy (IRE)**[85] 2166 3-8-5 47 ........ (t) CCatlin 7 — 6
(JMBradley) *prom tl rdn 2f out: wknd qckly* — **33/1**

61.59 secs (-0.91) **Going Correction** -0.15s/f (Firm)

**WFA** 3 from 4yo+ 3lb — **11** Ran SP% **124.1**

Speed ratings: **101,98,97,97,95 95,94,93,89,88 78**CSF £45.26 CT £127.62 TOTE £4.70: £1.80, £3.90, £1.80; EX 75.30 Place 6 £65.46, Place 5 £53.06.

**Owner** David Dobson **Bred** Wickfield Farm Partnership **Trained** East Ilsley, Berks

**FOCUS**

A moderate fillies' sprint in which the top weight benefited from a drop in grade. The form is modest but could rate a little higher.

**NOTEBOOK**

**Fiddle Me Blue**, who has performed with credit in better company, particularly from an outside draw at Goodwood last time, appreciated the drop in grade. She got a good lead, and took advantage of the opening when it appeared to score cosily. This should have helped her confidence, and it will not be the biggest surprise if she follows up.

**Avit(IRE)**, who had a wide draw, was settled off the pace and ran on late without ever threatening the winner. She is very modest but is holding her form reasonably well and may find further opportunities when banded racing restarts in the autumn.

**Lady Protector**, despite being 12lb higher than when winning in May, has held her form well. She was outpaced in the early stages, but kept on to good effect. If she can hold her place early on, she may have another race in her.

**Jinksonthehouse**, runner-up in a similar race at Windsor two days previously, made a bold bid to overcome her outside draw, and briefly looked the winner when hitting the front before being run down. She is capable of winning again off her current mark.

**Hagley Park**, having her second outing for her new trainer, showed some promise in finishing on the heels of the placed horses. All her wins have been on Fibresand, mainly at Wolverhampton (which is replacing its surface with Polytrack), and her best opportunities lie in sellers.

**Boavista(IRE)** is generally consistent and has run well on all her previous visits to this track. She was not helped on this occasion by a slow start.

**Tender(IRE)** *Official explanation: jockey said saddle slipped*

T/Jkpt: Not won. T/Plt: £199.20 to a £1 stake. Pool £66,391.50. 243.30 winning tickets T/Qpdt: £60.40 to a £1 stake. Pool £3,380.90. 41.40 winning tickets JS

# 4207 BEVERLEY (R-H)

## Wednesday, August 11

**OFFICIAL GOING: Good to soft**

## 4624 WATS ON CLAIMING STKS — 1m 100y

2:10 (2:12) (E) 3-Y-O+ — **£3,571** (£1,099; £549; £274) **Stalls** High

Form — RPR

-060 1 **Alpine Hideaway (IRE)**[2] 4605 11-9-2 45 ........ (p) DAllan 8 — 53
(JSWainwright) *trckd ldrs: hdwy 2f out: rdn and styd on to ld ins last: drvn out* — **12/1**

6062 2 *hd* **Cayman Calypso (IRE)**[6] 4491 3-9-5 62 ........ NCallan 13 — 63
(MAJarvis) *trckd ldrs: hdwy 2f out: rdn to ld over 1f out: drvn and hdd ins last: kpt on* — **4/1**[1]

0-00 3 *1 ½* **Gem Bien (USA)**[63] 2789 6-9-8 76 ........ ACulhane 10 — 55
(DWChapman) *bhd: gd hdwy over 2f out: rdn over 1f out: kpt on wl fnl f: nrst fin* — **4/1**[1]

000/ 4 *hd* **Ash Bold (IRE)**[1309] 5421 7-8-7 28 ........ TEaves(3) 11 — 43
(BEllison) *cl up: rdn 2f out and ev ch tld drvn and one pce fnl f* — **100/1**

**Clarinch Claymore**, who took this two years ago, was below his best being unsuited by the lack of serious pace. He will bounce back.
**Greenwich Meantime** is right off the boil.

## 4628 EAST RIDING MAIL H'CAP — 1m 1f 207y
4:10 (4:10) (E) (0-70,68) 3-Y-O — £3,731 (£1,148; £574; £287) Stalls High

Form — RPR

006- **1** **Can Can Flyer (IRE)**[247] 6145 3-8-12 **59** ........ RFrench 6 68+
(MJohnston) *chsd ldrs: rdn along and outpcd 2f out: drvn and styd on ent last to ld last 50 yds* **14/1**

0005 **2** ½ **Super King**[23] 3981 3-8-12 **59** ........ EAhern 8 67
(NBycroft) *in tch: hdwy over 3f out: chal over 1f out: rdn to ld enteri ng last: sn drvn: hdd and no ex last 50 yds* **9/1**[3]

1103 **3** *2* **Magic Sting**[33] 3706 3-9-2 **68** ........ HayleyTurner(5) 2 72
(MLWBell) *keen: sn cl up: led 1/2-way:rdn wl over 1f out: hdd ent last: no ex* **9/2**[2]

3013 **4** *hd* **Futoo (IRE)**[9] 4395 3-9-0 **66** ........ BSwarbrick(5) 12 70
(GMMoore) *led to 1/2-way: cl up tl rdn and outpcd wl over 1f out: drvn and kpt on fnl f* **5/2**[1]

4662 **5** *nk* **Aston Lad**[25] 3955 3-8-3 **50** ........ FNorton 7 53+
(MDHammond) *hld up and wl bhd: hdwy over 2f out: swtchd rt and rdn over 1f out: styd on strly ins last: nrst fin* **9/1**[3]

5103 **6** *1 ½* **Come What July (IRE)**[15] 4213 3-8-8 **55** ........ (b) RFitzpatrick 1 56
(MrsNMacauley) *stdd s and bhd: hdwy on outer 3f out: rdn 2f out: kpt on same pce appr last* **12/1**

0-60 **7** *1 ½* **Armentieres**[23] 3989 3-8-8 **55** ........ (b) GHind 10 53
(JLSpearing) *chsd ldrs: rdn over 2f out: sn one pce* **33/1**

6-65 **8** *13* **Midnight Prince**[13] 4259 3-8-2 **49** ........ DaleGibson 9 24
(MWEasterby) *bhd fr 1/2-way* **11/1**

0100 **9** *2* **Miss Eloise**[23] 3981 3-9-0 **61** ........ (b[1]) WSupple 4 32
(TDEasterby) *midfield: effrt over 3f out: sn rdn along and btn* **12/1**

-066 **10** *2* **Saida Lenasera (FR)**[54] 3050 3-9-3 **64** ........ ANicholls 3 31
(MrsPSly) *chsd ldrs: rdn along 3f out: sn wknd* **20/1**

06-0 **11** *13* **Abbeygate**[32] 3746 3-9-3 **64** ........ NCallan 5 8
(TKeddy) *a rr* **16/1**

5604 **12** *12* **Danefonique (IRE)**[21] 4015 3-8-3 **50** ........ DAllan 11 —
(DCarroll) *chsd ldrs on inner: rdn along 4f out: sn wknd* **10/1**

2m 11.11s (3.91) **Going Correction** +0.375s/f (Good) **12** Ran SP% **119.8**
Speed ratings: **99,98,97,96,96 95,94,83,82,80 70,60**CSF £135.85 CT £668.81 TOTE £15.80: £3.80, £2.80, £2.70; EX 284.40.
**Owner** A W Robinson **Bred** I Robinson & A W Robinson **Trained** Middleham Moor, N Yorks

**FOCUS**
A modest handicap in which the form looks sound and the winner could improve on this.

**NOTEBOOK**
**Can Can Flyer(IRE)**, having only his fourth career start and only his second on turf, was making his handicap bow from a plater's mark. He stuck to his guns and will be even better suited by a slightly stiffer test. *Official explanation: trainer said this was colt's first run in a handicap and he did not consider that the colt had shown any improvement in form*
**Super King**, from a stable riding the crest of a wave, was just edged out near the line.
**Magic Sting**, drawn one from the outside, was far too keen. Sent to the front, in the end he did not see it out anywhere near as well as the first two.
**Futoo(IRE)**, 3lb higher than when winning here two outings ago, had the plum draw. After looking well held he came again near the line, and now may be the right time to give hurdling a try.
**Aston Lad**, possibly well treated on his handicap bow, was given a very negative ride and in the circumstances did well to finish so close.
**Come What July(IRE)**, whose two wins were on the All-Weather, did well trying to come from off the back towards the outside. This will set him up for when Southwell re-opens.
**Saida Lenasera(FR)** *Official explanation: jockey said filly was unsuited by the good to soft ground*
**Danefonique(IRE)** *Official explanation: jockey said filly lost her action*

## 4629 HULL DAILY MAIL MAIDEN STKS — 1m 1f 207y
4:40 (4:40) (D) 3-Y-O — £4,392 (£1,255; £627) Stalls High

Form — RPR

0 **1** **Mith Hill**[6] 4492 3-9-0 ........ EAhern 3 78
(EALDunlop) *hld up: outpcd and rdn along 4f out: hdwy wl over 1f out: styd on u.p to ld wl ins last* **5/2**[2]

5040 **2** *2* **Mambina (USA)**[6] 4493 3-8-9 62 ........ CCatlin 2 69
(MRChannon) *led: rdn along 3f out: drvn 2f out: hdd and no ex wl ins last* **4/1**[3]

44 **3** *4* **Premier Rouge**[41] 3448 3-9-0 ........ NCallan 1 67
(EFVaughan) *cl up: effrt over 2f out: sn rdn: drvn over 1f out: wknd ent last* **11/8**[1]

0 **P** **Aspired (IRE)**[23] 3994 3-8-9 ........ RFrench 4 —
(JRFanshawe) *chse ldng pair: hung bdly lft and rn v wd home turn: p.u and dismntd over 2f out* **4/1**[3]

2m 12.59s (5.39) **Going Correction** +0.375s/f (Good) **4** Ran SP% **110.7**
Speed ratings: **93,91,88,—**CSF £12.01 TOTE £4.00; EX 9.60.
**Owner** Mohammed Jaber **Bred** Floors Farming, Hmh Management Ltd And John Warren **Trained** Newmarket, Suffolk

**FOCUS**
A poor maiden with the winner seeing out the trip in the end much better than the other two. the time was slow and the form may prove unreliable.

**NOTEBOOK**
**Mith Hill**, having his second career outing after making his debut just six days earlier, made very heavy weather of it but in the end his superior stamina seemed to carry the day. Hopefully he can build on this in handicap company over a fair bit further.
**Mambina(USA)**, having her tenth career start, is officially rated just 62.
**Premier Rouge** was disappointing, but at least this sets him up for a try in handicap company.
**Aspired(IRE)** failed completely to handle the turn and with there seemingly being a problem with her tack, she was finally pulled up and dismounted. *Official explanation: jockey said filly hung severely left-handed*

## 4630 DOWNEY'S DIARY CLASSIFIED STKS — 1m 4f 16y
5:10 (5:10) (F) 3-Y-O+ — £3,339 (£954; £477) Stalls High

Form — RPR

0412 **1** **Inchpast**[11] 4346 3-8-10 64 ........ (b) NCallan 8 73
(MHTompkins) *trckd ldrs: hdwy on inner 2f out: rdn over 1f out: styd on to ld ins last: drvn and kpt on* **6/1**[2]

-403 **2** ½ **Jolizero**[11] 4346 3-8-1 59 ........ ThomasYeung(5) 1 68
(PWChapple-Hyam) *led: rdn and hung lft 2f out: drvn over 1f out: hdd ins last: kpt on* **9/1**

6004 **3** *1 ¼* **On Cloud Nine**[12] 4307 3-8-2 64 ........ HayleyTurner(5) 10 67
(MLWBell) *hld up towards rr: hdwy on inenr 3f out: rdn to chse ldrs over 1f out: swtchd rt ent last and kpt on u.p* **7/1**

2021 **4** *nk* **Pay Attention**[7] 4449 3-8-3 60 ........ DAllan 4 63
(TDEasterby) *hld up: hdwy on outer over 4f out: rdn to chal and sltly hmpd 2f out: sn drvn and wandered: one pce ent last* **13/8**[1]

6-24 **5** *9* **Our Emmy Lou**[23] 3989 3-8-5 62 ........ EAhern 7 51
(SirMarkPrescott) *hld up: gd hdwy on outer over 3f out: rdn 2f out and sn btn* **13/2**[3]

0023 **6** *5* **Relative Hero (IRE)**[6] 4476 4-8-12 51 ........ (v) AQuinn(5) 6 45
(MissSJWilton) *prom: rdn along 3f out: drvn 2f out and sn wknd* **40/1**

4100 **7** ½ **It's Blue Chip**[11] 4346 3-8-10 64 ........ JCarroll 5 48
(PWD'Arcy) *dwlt: a rr* **14/1**

066- **8** ½ **Brave Knight**[283] 5013 7-9-3 32 ........ FNorton 9 43
(NBycroft) *bhd fr 1/2-way* **66/1**

3534 **9** *2 ½* **Saxe-Coburg (IRE)**[25] 3942 7-8-12 56 ........ BSwarbrick(5) 11 39
(GAHam) *chsd ldrs: rdn along 4f out: sn wknd* **7/1**

-000 **10** *23* **Pearl Pride (USA)**[23] 3982 3-8-6 63 ........ RFrench 2 5
(MJohnston) *chsd ldr: rdn along 3f out: sn wknd* **20/1**

2545 **11** *3* **Eddies Jewel**[15] 4210 4-9-0 39 ........ THamilton(3) 3 —
(JSWainwright) *midfield: hdwy and in tch 4f out: rdn 3f out and sn wknd* **40/1**

2m 43.55s (4.25) **Going Correction** +0.375s/f (Good)
**WFA** 3 from 4yo+ 11lb **11** Ran SP% **118.5**
Speed ratings: **100,99,98,98,92 89,88,88,86,71 69**CSF £57.39 TOTE £6.80: £2.00, £3.90, £1.90; EX 69.90 Place 6 £321.61, Place 5 £172.64.
**Owner** Marcoe Racing Welwyn **Bred** Stanley Estate And Stud Co **Trained** Newmarket, Suffolk
■ Stewards Enquiry : Thomas Yeung seven-day ban: used whip with excessive frequency, without giving gelding time to respond and down the shoulder in the forehand position (Aug 22-28)

**FOCUS**
A modest handicap but fair form for the grade.

**NOTEBOOK**
**Inchpast**, weak in the market, never left the inner and in the end did just enough.
**Jolizero**, whose apprentice rider rode five winners in Hong Kong during their season, proved very game in front. Hanging left, his rider immediately switched his whip hand, but his over-reliance on the stick put him in hot water.
**On Cloud Nine** stayed on from off the pace and, after being switched, lacked the pace to get in a telling blow.
**Pay Attention**, always tending to race on the outer, wandered and was always making very hard work of it. She is better than she showed on this day.
**Our Emmy Lou**, who looked very fit indeed, was totally unpopular in the betting. She tended to edge left and in the end was well beaten off. *Official explanation: jockey said filly was unsuited by the going*
T/Plt: £409.20 to a £1 stake. Pool: £38,986.70. 69.55 winning tickets. T/Qpdt: £170.00 to a £1 stake. Pool: £1,999.50. 8.70 winning tickets. JR

# 4328 HAMILTON (R-H)
### Wednesday, August 11

**OFFICIAL GOING: Soft**
Weather: rain after race 3, easing before race 6

## 4631 LANARKSHIRE EXTRA CLAIMING STKS — 1m 1f 36y
5:55 (5:55) (E) 3-Y-O+ — £4,208 (£1,295; £647; £323) Stalls High

Form — RPR

31-1 **1** **The Prince**[42] 3427 10-9-4 84 ........ SSanders 2 61+
(IanWilliams) *trckd ldrs: shkn up to ld ins fnl f: comf* **1/3**[1]

5300 **2** *3 ½* **Templet (USA)**[6] 4486 4-10-0 64 ........ (b) RWinston 4 64
(ISemple) *trckd ldr: led over 3f out: rdn over 2f out: hdd ins fnl f: no ch w wnr* **10/1**[3]

6300 **3** *6* **Wings Of Morning (IRE)**[47] 3280 3-8-6 65 ........ (v[1]) JBramhill 3 38
(PABlockley) *led to over 3f out: sn outpcd* **6/1**[2]

0000 **4** ½ **Sandy Bay (IRE)**[8] 4423 5-8-11 35 ........ PFessey 5 34
(ARDicken) *dwlt: sn prom: rdn and wknd fr 3f out* **80/1**

06 **5** *8* **Charlie George**[40] 3475 3-8-11 ........ PMulrennan(3) 1 29
(PMonteith) *keen: in tch tl wknd fr 4f out* **14/1**

2m 1.75s (2.15) **Going Correction** +0.225s/f (Good)
**WFA** 3 from 4yo+ 8lb **5** Ran SP% **106.3**
Speed ratings: **99,95,90,90,83**CSF £3.98 TOTE £1.20: £1.02, £3.20; EX 3.40.
**Owner** Patrick Kelly **Bred** Bottisham Heath Stud **Trained** Portway, Warwicks

**FOCUS**
An uncompetitive race run at just an ordinary pace and a straightforward task for the winner, who is a fair sort for this grade and was well below last year's form in winning.

**NOTEBOOK**
**The Prince** had plenty in his favour in an uncompetitive race, and did not have to improve to win his fourth race from his last six starts. He is likely to struggle in handicaps from his current mark but is a fair tool in this grade.
**Templet(USA)**, down in trip, had a stiff task at the weights and, although he did not do much wrong on this occasion, does not look one to place too much faith in.
**Wings Of Morning(IRE)** did not get home in the first-time visor and, although this inconsistent sort will be suited by the return to shorter distances, he is not one to place much faith in.
**Sandy Bay(IRE)** faced a stiff task on these terms and is flattered by his proximity.
**Charlie George** gave trouble at the start and ran poorly. Although he is now qualified for handicaps, he will have to improve to win even a modest event.

## 4632 TNT INTERNATIONAL NOVICE STKS (A QUALIFIER FOR THE HAMILTON PARK 2-Y-O SERIES FINAL) — 6f 5y
6:25 (6:25) (D) 2-Y-O — £5,531 (£1,702; £851; £425) Stalls High

Form — RPR

21 **1** **Spy King (USA)**[7] 4446 2-9-0 ........ KDarley 2 88+
(MJohnston) *mde all: shkn up 2f out: r.o strly* **4/6**[1]

1 **2** *1 ¾* **Buddy Brown**[53] 3081 2-9-5 ........ RWinston 1 88+
(JHowardJohnson) *dwlt: outpcd: hdwy over 1f out: kpt on: nt rch wnr* **9/1**

414U **3** *nk* **Obe Gold**[12] 4288 2-9-5 97 ........ ACulhane 5 87
(MRChannon) *w wnr tl rdn and one pce appr fnl f* **7/2**[2]

055 **4** *shd* **Profit's Reality (IRE)**[7] 4446 2-8-12 ........ DeanMcKeown 4 80
(PABlockley) *chsd ldrs: shkn up and outpcd 2f out: kpt on fnl f: no imp* **20/1**

6635 **5** *10* **Mitchelland**[7] 4445 2-9-0 74 ........ SSanders 3 52
(JamesMoffatt) *trckd ldrs tl wknd fr 2f out* **8/1**[3]

1m 14.09s (0.99) **Going Correction** +0.225s/f (Good) **5** Ran SP% **108.1**
Speed ratings: **102,99,99,99,85**CSF £7.08 TOTE £1.50: £1.10, £2.40; EX 6.00.
**Owner** P D Savill **Bred** Russell S Davis **Trained** Middleham Moor, N Yorks

**FOCUS**
Not many runners, but an interesting event in which the pace was sound and an improved performance from Spy King, who remains one to keep on the right side. The time was smart for the grade, but the form behind does not look that solid.

**NOTEBOOK**
**Spy King(USA)** ◆, who travelled better in these conditions than he had on his two previous outings, turned in his best effort yet and showed the right attitude for pressure. He is getting better all the time, should prove as effective over seven and remains one to keep on the right side.

6000 **5** 3/4 **Lord Lahar**[6] 4473 5-9-6 37 .......... CCatlin 14 51
(MRChannon) *chsd ldrs on inner: rdn along 2f out: drvn and kpt on same pce fnl f* **40/1**

00 **6** nk **Mobane Flyer**[18] 4134 4-9-12 63 .......... PHanagan 4 57
(RAFahey) *midfield: hdwy over 2f out: rdn over 1f out: kpt on ins last: nrst fin* **5/1**[3]

500/ **7** 2 **Dee Pee Tee Cee (IRE)**[687] 4863 10-9-12 46 .......... TLucas 12 53
(MWEasterby) *led: rdn along over 2f out: drvn and hdd over 1f out: grad wknd* **20/1**

5030 **8** 1 3/4 **Erupt**[37] 3579 11-8-11 40 .......... THamilton(3) 7 37
(REBarr) *s.i.s and bhd tl styd on fnl 2f* **25/1**

02 **9** 1/2 **Flying Spud**[29] 3822 3-8-13 50 .......... DeanMcKeown 16 42
(JLSpearing) *chsd ldrs: rdn along 2f out: sn btn* **9/2**[2]

6040 **10** shd **Giust In Temp (IRE)**[6] 4485 5-8-12 40 .......... DarrenWilliams 9 34
(PWHiatt) *chsd ldrs: rdn over 2f out: drvna nd wknd over 1f out* **20/1**

0050 **11** nk **Stepastray**[8] 4423 7-9-4 41 .......... (v) GParkin 1 39
(REBarr) *s.i.s and bhd tl sme late hdwy* **33/1**

0400 **12** 1 1/4 **Efimac**[13] 4260 4-8-10 38 .......... AReilly(7) 2 35
(NBycroft) *a towards rr* **33/1**

0000 **13** 1 1/2 **Dark Cut (IRE)**[9] 4386 4-8-13 37 .......... RKeogh(7) 15 35
(HAlexander) *in tch on inner: rdn along 3f out: sn wknd* **50/1**

-000 **14** hd **Moon Royale**[148] 1031 6-8-6 34 .......... HayleyTurner(5) 6 26
(MrsNMacauley) *in tch on outer: hdwy 3f out: sn rdn and wknd 2f out* **66/1**

0- **15** 2 **Mazram**[483] 1076 5-8-6 .......... NataliaGemelova(7) 3 24
(IWMcinnes) *bhd fr 1/2-way* **100/1**

0200 **16** nk **Gallas (IRE)**[13] 4259 3-8-9 49 .......... (v) RFfrench 5 26
(JSWainwright) *a rr* **9/1**

1m 50.63s (3.33) **Going Correction** +0.375s/f (Good)
**WFA** 3 from 4yo+ 7lb **16** Ran SP% **119.7**
Speed ratings: **98,97,96,96,95 95,93,91,90,90 90,89,87,87,85 85**CSF £53.53 TOTE £15.90: £4.00, £2.00, £2.00; EX 70.20.
**Owner** Peter Easterby **Bred** Roseberry Ltd **Trained** Kennythorpe, N Yorks
■ A third success in six years in this race for Alpine Hideaway.

**FOCUS**
A very moderate claimer and a modest time, with the runner-up providing the line to the form

**NOTEBOOK**
**Alpine Hideaway(IRE)**, having his second outing in three days, showed real battling qualities to take this for the second year running and the third time in all.
**Cayman Calypso(IRE)** had 9lb in hand of the winner on official figures but, after working hard to get to the head of affairs, in the end he just missed out.
**Gem Bien(USA)**, having his first outing for his new trainer, had over a stone in hand on official figures but he has been bang out of form. Given a lot to do, he seemed to be here on a fact-finding mission and hopefully his rating will be slashed.
**Ash Bold(IRE)** was last seen in action over hurdles on New Year's Day 2001. Unfortunately his decent effort may mean that his rating will soar.
**Lord Lahar**, who had an impossible task, has been bang out of form.
**Mobane Flyer**, having his third outing here, ran better and his one win in Ireland was on firm ground.
**Dee Pee Tee Cee(IRE)**, now a veteran, was having his first outing for almost two years,
**Flying Spud** was disappointing considering he had the ground in his favour.

## 4625 EUROPEAN BREEDERS FUND JOURNAL MAIDEN STKS 7f 100y
**2:40** (2:43) (D ) 2-Y-O **£5,577** (£1,716; £858; £429) **Stalls** High

Form RPR

5 **1** **Varenka (IRE)**[8] 4420 2-8-9 .......... SSanders 12 90+
(SirMarkPrescott) *mde all: rdn 2f out: styd on strly fnl f* **3/1**[2]

**2** 5 **Brahminy Kite (USA)** 2-9-0 .......... RFfrench 2 83
(MJohnston) *in tch:effrt and rn green over 2f out: hdwy over 1f out: styd on ins last* **12/1**

02 **3** 1 **Gone Fishing (IRE)**[38] 3560 2-8-9 .......... NCallan 8 76
(MAJarvis) *trckd ldrs: hdwy to chse wnr over 2f out: rdn and hung rt over 1f out: sn drvn and one pce* **5/2**[1]

4 **4** 6 **Etaar**[26] 3913 2-9-0 .......... WSupple 10 67
(NAGraham) *cl 4th whn stmbld and lost 3 l bnd after 2f: sn pushed along: chsdldrs over 3f out: rdn over 2f out: sn btn* **5/1**[3]

**5** 1 1/4 **Red Riot (USA)** 2-9-0 .......... KDarley 9 64
(DRLoder) *towards rr: hdwy over 2f out: kpt on appr last* **5/1**[3]

06 **6** 1 **Nowaday (GER)**[23] 3983 2-9-0 .......... EAhern 6 62
(TPTate) *bhd tl styd on fnl 2f* **50/1**

0 **7** shd **Balletomaine (IRE)**[14] 4234 2-8-9 .......... MHills 1 56
(BWHills) *cl up: rdn along 1/2-way: wknd over 2f out* **8/1**

**8** 1/2 **Just Waz (USA)** 2-9-0 .......... PHanagan 3 60
(RMWhitaker) *s.i.s: a rr* **25/1**

**9** 8 **Viable** 2-9-0 .......... ACulhane 11 41
(MrsPSly) *s.i.s: a bhd* **50/1**

40 **10** 1/2 **Eborarry (IRE)**[15] 4208 2-9-0 .......... DAllan 7 40
(TDEasterby) *bhd fr 1/2-way* **50/1**

00 **11** 8 **Metolica**[87] 2141 2-8-9 .......... RFitzpatrick 4 16
(CSmith) *a rr* **100/1**

1m 36.67s (2.37) **Going Correction** +0.375s/f (Good) **11** Ran SP% **116.4**
Speed ratings: **101,95,94,87,85 84,84,84,74,74 65**CSF £36.62 TOTE £3.70: £1.50, £3.30, £1.40; EX 44.70.
**Owner** Lady Roborough **Bred** Dr Dean Harron **Trained** Newmarket, Suffolk
■ Etaar was Neil Graham's last runner as a trainer before joining the Godolphin set-up.

**FOCUS**
A fair maiden in which the winner set just a steady pace until picking up the gallop once in line for home. The time was creditable for the grade.

**NOTEBOOK**
**Varenka(IRE)** had clearly learnt plenty on her debut and was very professional. She kept up the gallop in relentless fashion and will be even better suited by the full mile. She looks very useful.
**Brahminy Kite(USA)** ◆, an April foal, was a negative on the exchanges. He looked very inexperienced but there was much to like about the way he picked up late on to snatch second spot. He will improve a good deal and will make an even better three-year-old.
**Gone Fishing(IRE)**, absent for five weeks, went in pursuit of the winner but did not see it out anywhere near as well.
**Etaar** was on the back foot after stumbling leaving the back straight, and after that there was never going to be a fairytale end for his trainer.
**Red Riot(USA)**, well supported, took an age to grasp the nettle. He will know a lot more next time.

## 4626 TOTEPLACEPOT H'CAP 5f
**3:10** (3:11) (D ) (0-80,80) 3-Y-O+ **£8,417** (£2,590; £1,295; £647) **Stalls** High

Form RPR

6432 **1** **Trojan Flight**[2] 4608 3-8-7 59 .......... FNorton 17 73
(MrsJRRamsden) *squeezed out s and bhd on far rail: swtchd lft and hdwy 2f out: rdn over 1f out and str run to ld ins last* **3/1**[1]

-136 **2** 1 1/2 **Hout Bay**[188] 680 7-8-7 56 .......... PHanagan 11 65
(RAFahey) *in tch: hdwy 2f out: rdn to ld 1f out and hung rt: hdd and drvn ins last: nt qckn* **20/1**

1036 **3** 1 **Paddywack (IRE)**[20] 4047 7-9-10 73 .......... (b) ACulhane 13 78
(DWChapman) *hld up in midfield: hdwy 2f out: rdn and styd on ins last* **7/1**

0033 **4** 1 **Tantric**[17] 4181 5-8-9 58 .......... SSanders 20 60+
(JO'Reilly) *chsd ldrs: nt clr run and swtchd lft over 1f out: sn rdn and kpt on* **6/1**[2]

2421 **5** 1 1/4 **Blue Maeve**[8] 4422 4-8-12 61 7ex .......... SRighton 8 58+
(JHetherton) *chsd ldrs: rdn over 1f out: kpt on same pce fnl f* **12/1**

3004 **6** 3/4 **Consensus (IRE)**[7] 4452 5-9-12 75 .......... KDarley 15 70
(MBrittain) *led: rdn along 2f out: hdd 1f out and sn wknd* **12/1**

2003 **7** 1 **Beyond The Clouds (IRE)**[18] 4133 8-9-13 76 .......... GParkin 4 67+
(JSWainwright) *towards rr: hdwy 2f out: sn rdn and kpt on fnl f: nrst fin* **20/1**

5100 **8** 3/4 **Fairgame Man**[17] 4181 6-7-12 47 oh1 .......... (p) PMQuinn 1 35+
(JSWainwright) *racd stands side: in tch: hdwy 1/2-way: sn rdn and no imp fnl f* **33/1**

5425 **9** 1/2 **Soba Jones**[20] 4047 7-9-9 72 .......... JEdmunds 19 59
(JBalding) *chsd ldrs far side: rdn along 2f out: drvn and wknd over 1f out* **13/2**[3]

0020 **10** 1/2 **Seven No Trumps**[21] 4034 7-9-6 76 .......... (p) CJDavies(7) 6 61
(JMBradley) *bhd tl styd on appr last* **20/1**

560 **11** 1 **Musical Fair**[30] 3795 4-9-13 76 .......... EAhern 18 57
(JAGlover) *in tch far side: rdn along 2f out: grad wknd* **16/1**

0406 **12** 1/2 **Port St Charles (IRE)**[8] 4415 7-8-2 56 .......... (b) HayleyTurner(5) 9 35
(CRDore) *midfield: pushed along 1/2-way: no hdwy* **25/1**

0000 **13** shd **Chico Guapo (IRE)**[42] 3407 4-9-9 72 .......... WSupple 16 51
(JAGlover) *cl up: rdn 2f out: drvn and wknd over 1f out* **20/1**

5060 **14** 3/4 **Laurel Dawn**[12] 4308 6-8-11 60 .......... RFfrench 2 36
(IWMcinnes) *swtchd rt s: a rr* **33/1**

6000 **15** 3/4 **Elliot's Choice (IRE)**[2] 4608 3-8-4 63 .......... DTudhope(7) 10 37
(DCarroll) *chsd ldrs: rdn along 1/2-way: sn wknd* **33/1**

0000 **16** 1 **Miss Ceylon**[15] 4211 4-7-12 47 oh8 .......... (b) JMcAuley 12 17
(SPGriffiths) *bhd fr 1/2-way* **100/1**

0051 **17** 5 **Distant Times**[15] 4211 3-9-10 76 .......... DAllan 3 28+
(TDEasterby) *racd stands side: in tch tl rdn along 1/2-way: sn wknd* **20/1**

0635 **18** 6 **Dispol Katie**[11] 4331 3-10-0 80 .......... NCallan 14 10
(TDBarron) *chsd ldrs: rdn whn hmpd wl over 1f out: sddle slipped and virtually p.u* **9/1**

63.57 secs (-0.43) **Going Correction** +0.05s/f (Good)
**WFA** 3 from 4yo+ 3lb **18** Ran SP% **133.9**
Speed ratings: **105,102,101,99,97 96,94,93,92,91 90,89,89,88,86 85,77,67**CSF £74.40 CT £424.16 TOTE £4.30: £1.60, £5.20, £1.70, £1.70; EX 98.10 Trifecta £3061.60 Part won. Pool: £4,312.19. 0.60 winning units..
**Owner** Timothy O'Gram **Bred** L C And Mrs A E Sigsworth **Trained** Sandhutton, N Yorks
■ Stewards Enquiry : J Edmunds two-day ban: careless riding (Aug 22,23)

**FOCUS**
An ordinary but competitive handicap run at a reasonable pace for the grade and the form looks solid.

**NOTEBOOK**
**Trojan Flight**, hampered at the start, was left with a lot to do and in the end had to make his final effort towards the centre of the track. He really buckled down and in the end won going right away, a richly-deserved first success after his misfortune two days earlier.
**Hout Bay**, absent for six months, had no answer to the winner's very late surge. In the past he has won from a 2lb higher mark.
**Paddywack(IRE)**, 5lb higher than when he recorded his 15th career success here in April, was having his 110th start and is a testimony to his trainer's skills.
**Tantric**, who has never won over less than seven furlongs, showed himself to be in very good heart and was unlucky not to finish even closer.
**Blue Maeve**, hoisted 8lb after Catterick, ran a blinder from a poor draw, racing wide of the main body of the field throughout.
**Consensus(IRE)** as usual showed bags of toe from a favourable draw, but she is finding it very hard to keep her head in front.
**Beyond The Clouds(IRE)**, who has not won for almost two years, did really well from a very poor draw but his rating seems static.
**Fairgame Man** was one of just two to elect to race against the stands'-side rail.
**Musical Fair**, who prefers much quicker ground, collected a hefty bump from Soba Jones.
**Dispol Katie** *Official explanation: jockey said saddle slipped*

## 4627 CHARLES ELSEY MEMORIAL CHALLENGE TROPHY (H'CAP) 2m 35y
**3:40** (3:40) (E ) (0-75,72) 3-Y-O+ **£4,134** (£1,272; £636; £318) **Stalls** High

Form RPR

1103 **1** **Moonshine Beach**[11] 4352 6-9-7 65 .......... DarrenWilliams 1 75
(PWHiatt) *led 6f: cl up: rdn 2f out: drvn to chal and hung rt ent last: styd on to ld last 100 yds.* **5/1**[3]

5314 **2** 1 **Shotley Dancer**[9] 4397 5-8-0 44 ow2 .......... FNorton 2 53
(NBycroft) *trckd ldr: led after 6f: qcknd 3f out: rdn wl over 1f out: drvn ins last: hdd and no ex last 100 yds* **8/1**

0064 **3** 3 1/2 **Vicars Destiny**[29] 3821 6-8-12 63 .......... AndrewWebb(7) 6 68
(MrsSLamyman) *hld up in tch: hdwy over 2f out: rdn wl over 1f out: drvn and same pce appr last* **5/1**[3]

3320 **4** 1 3/4 **Wing Collar**[38] 3561 3-8-7 66 .......... WSupple 3 69
(TDEasterby) *keen: trckd ldrs: puashed along 3f out: rdn 2f out and sn one pce* **11/4**[2]

0531 **5** 3/4 **Clarinch Claymore**[29] 3821 8-9-11 72 .......... TEaves(3) 7 74
(JMJefferson) *hld up: hdwy over 5f out: effrt 3f out: sn rdn and btn wl over 1f out* **5/2**[1]

3005 **6** 3 **Greenwich Meantime**[11] 4352 4-9-12 70 .......... LGoncalves 4 68
(MrsJRRamsden) *hld up: hdwy 3f out: rdn 2f out and sn btn* **9/1**

3m 43.79s (4.39) **Going Correction** +0.375s/f (Good)
**WFA** 3 from 4yo+ 15lb **6** Ran SP% **109.7**
Speed ratings: **104,103,101,100,100 99**CSF £39.88 TOTE £6.40: £2.30, £2.50; EX 23.20.
**Owner** Ken Read **Bred** Lawrence Shepherd **Trained** Hook Norton, Oxon

**FOCUS**
A fair handicap run at a stop-start pace. Nothing got into the race from behind and the form is not sure to work out.

**NOTEBOOK**
**Moonshine Beach** hung fire under strong pressure, but his rider was at his most determined and persuaded him to really stretch out near the line. He is a fine advert for his trainer.
**Shotley Dancer**, stepping up in trip, would not settle so her rider let her stride on in front. Kicking for home straightening up, in the end she was just edged out.
**Vicars Destiny**, suited by the give underfoot, made her effort on the wide outside and could never get near the first two.
**Wing Collar**, still a maiden, would not settle over this extended trip and in the end his stamina seemed to give out altogether.

**Buddy Brown** ◆, who took the eye in the preliminaries, did not look entirely happy at this course but bettered his debut run and left the strong impression that the return to seven furlongs would suit. He looks sure to win another race.
**Obe Gold**, back on a soft surface, had the run of the race and seemed beaten on merit. He is not going to be the easiest to place in handicaps or this type of event on this evidence.
**Profit's Reality(IRE)** got closer to the winner than he had done at Newcastle last week, and left the impression that a stiffer test of stamina would have been in his favour. He is in capable hands and, although this will not have done his prospective handicap mark any good, he is one to note when upped to seven furlongs.
**Mitchelland** faced a stiff task at the weights but goes particularly well on a soft surface, so this has to go down as a disappointing effort. However the return to ordinary handicap company will suit and she is not one to write off yet.

## 4633 AZURE E.B.F MAIDEN STKS 1m 65y
6:55 (6:56) (D) 2-Y-O £6,890 (£2,120; £1,060; £530) Stalls High

Form RPR
2 **1** **Looks Could Kill (USA)**[12] 4290 2-9-0 SSanders 5 89+
(GAButler) *in tch: smooth hdwy and ev ch over 1f out: rdn and led ins fnl f: r.o wl* **8/11**[1]
2 **2** *1 1/2* **Love Palace (IRE)**[39] 3505 2-9-0 KDarley 2 86+
(MJohnston) *led at stdy pce: shkn up 2f out: hdd ins fnl f: one pce* **7/2**[2]
4 **3** *8* **Jackadandy (USA)**[33] 3718 2-9-0 RWinston 4 66
(JHowardJohnson) *prom: rdn 3f out: one pce fr 2f out* **14/1**
**4** *shd* **Haiban** 2-9-0 PHanagan 1 68+
(GAButler) *wnt lft s: outpcd tl hdwy over 1f out: nvr rchd ldrs* **16/1**
052 **5** *3* **Ball Boy**[15] 4208 2-9-0 75 ACulhane 3 59
(MRChannon) *cl up tl rdn and outpcd fr over 2f out* **7/1**[3]
0 **6** *3 1/2* **Balthasar**[72] 2522 2-9-0 DeanMcKeown 6 52
(PABlockley) *chsd ldrs tl rdn and wknd over 2f out* **100/1**

1m 50.0s (0.70) **Going Correction** +0.225s/f (Good) **6** Ran SP% **106.2**
Speed ratings: **105,103,95,95,92 88**CSF £2.97 TOTE £1.70: £1.10, £2.00; EX 2.40.
**Owner** It's A Breeze **Bred** Maple Leaf Farm **Trained** Blewbury, Oxon

**FOCUS**
Little strength in depth and only a modest early pace, but the first two eventually pulled clear of the remainder and the winning time was very smart indeed for the grade and the form is strong for the type of race. The winner, who looks a bit better than the bare form, appeals as the type to win more races.

**NOTEBOOK**
**Looks Could Kill(USA)** ◆ fully confirmed debut promise over this longer trip on much softer ground, and showed the right attitude to beat a rival who very much enjoyed the run of the race. He should stay further and appeals as the type to win more races.
**Love Palace(IRE)** ◆, whose debut form had taken a few knocks, very much had the run of the race this time and is a strong sort who looks just the type to improve again for current connections. He is sure to win a similar event at the very least.
**Jackadandy(USA)** again hinted at ability but left the impression that a stiffer test of stamina and the step into nursery company would be in his favour, and he will be one to look out for when handicapped granted a suitable test.
**Haiban** was easy to back but hinted at ability on this racecourse debut. He may fare better in ordinary handicap company in due course.
**Ball Boy** had progressed steadily with every outing but was a long way below his best on this first start away from fast ground. He will be worth another chance away from progressive sorts back on a sound surface.
**Balthasar** again offered little immediate promise and is likely to continue to look vulnerable in this grade.

## 4634 CAPTAIN J. C. STEWART RATED STKS (H'CAP) 1m 1f 36y
7:30 (7:30) (C) (0-90,84) 3-Y-0+ £12,168 (£4,615; £2,307; £1,049) Stalls High

Form RPR
0050 **1** **Danelor (IRE)**[33] 3714 6-9-3 **80** PHanagan 2 93+
(RAFahey) *pressed ldr: effrt over 2f out: led ins fnl f: r.o wl* **11/2**
1101 **2** *1 3/4* **Wahoo Sam (USA)**[11] 4333 4-8-2 **70** PMakin(5) 6 80+
(TDBarron) *led: rdn over 1f out: hdd ins fnl f: one pce* **4/1**[2]
0020 **3** *6* **Allied Victory (USA)**[31] 3781 4-8-10 **73** DeanMcKeown 7 71
(EJAlston) *stmbld s: sn chsng ldrs: rdn and outpcd 3f out: n.d after* **14/1**
0100 **4** *5* **War Owl (USA)**[11] 4319 7-8-10 **73** SSanders 5 61
(IanWilliams) *hld up: rdn over 3f out: edgd rt and sn no imp* **10/3**[1]
2322 **5** *1 1/4* **Grey Clouds**[18] 4153 4-9-2 **79** RWinston 1 64
(TDEasterby) *hld up in tch: pushed along over 3f out: nvr rchd ldrs* **9/2**[3]
1610 **6** *1/2* **Tony Tie**[4] 4558 8-9-4 **84** PMulrennan(3) 4 68
(JSGoldie) *sn bhd: hmpd after 2f: nvr on terms* **11/2**
0105 **7** *28* **Hiawatha (IRE)**[46] 3291 5-8-9 **72** KDarley 3 —
(PABlockley) *keen: cl up tl rdn and wknd fr 3f out* **10/1**

1m 59.82s (0.22) **Going Correction** +0.225s/f (Good) **7** Ran SP% **107.8**
Speed ratings: **108,106,101,96,95 95,70**CSF £24.38 TOTE £7.10: £2.70, £3.10; EX 27.90.
**Owner** Mark A Leatham **Bred** Barronstown Stud And Orpendale **Trained** Musley Bank, N Yorks
■ Stewards Enquiry : R Winston caution: careless riding

**FOCUS**
An open event on paper but a steady pace meant that nothing got into this race from off the pace and, as such, the bare form may not prove that reliable.

**NOTEBOOK**
**Danelor(IRE)** had not won since landing his maiden over three years ago but had the run of the race and showed the right attitude to beat a progressive rival who was allowed an easy lead. This bare form may not prove reliable though, and he will have more to do back in a competitive handicap after reassessment.
**Wahoo Sam(USA)** had been in tremendous form at this course and ran his best race yet in this stronger grade, despite again being allowed his own way in front. He was clear of the remainder and should continue to go well when allowed to dominate.
**Allied Victory(USA)**, who wisely raced close to the steady pace, was again below his best and he does not look one to place too much faith in.
**War Owl(USA)** who had been the victim of poor draws on his last two starts, was again not seen to best effect in these conditions given the way the race unfolded and is by no means one to write off yet. A more strongly-run race on a sound surface over a mile and a quarter will suit, and he is one to keep an eye on.
**Grey Clouds**, usually a model of consistency, ran a rare poor race but, given this race was not really run to suit and the fact she may not have been ideally suited by this track, she is well worth another chance.
**Tony Tie** had been in tremendous heart and is a proven performer both at this course and on soft ground, but ran poorly for no apparent reason. This run is best overlooked. *Official explanation: jockey said gelding suffered interference and lost its action as a result*
**Hiawatha(IRE)** *Official explanation: jockey said gelding had a breathing problem*

## 4635 DA LUCIANO CLASSIFIED STKS 6f 5y
8:00 (8:00) (D) 3-Y-0+ £5,343 (£1,644; £822; £411) Stalls High

Form RPR
1000 **1** **Dizzy In The Head**[21] 4011 5-9-2 77 (b) PHanagan 8 77
(PaulJohnson) *mde all: clr over 1f out: drvn out* **7/2**[2]
0000 **2** *5* **Abbajabba**[114] 1500 8-9-3 78 JBramhill 7 63
(CWFairhurst) *chsd ldrs: outpcd 2f out: r.o fnl f: no ch w wnr* **7/2**[2]
-530 **3** *nk* **Sophrano (IRE)**[5] 4510 4-9-0 60 DeanMcKeown 1 59
(PABlockley) *racd centre: cl up: rdn and one pce fr 2f out* **20/1**
0020 **4** *1/2* **Legal Set (IRE)**[3] 4577 8-8-9 63 (t) PMakin(5) 5 58
(MissAStokell) *cl up: rdn over 2f out: edgd rt and sn no ex* **9/2**[3]
4000 **5** *1 3/4* **Telepathic (IRE)**[5] 4510 4-8-9 55 PPMathers(5) 2 52
(ABerry) *prom tl rdn and outpcd fr 2f out* **50/1**
0500 **6** *3/4* **Percy Douglas**[4] 4557 4-8-7 45 (t) SuzanneFrance(7) 6 50
(MissAStokell) *sn outpaced: nvr on terms* **66/1**
1050 **7** *3/4* **Ulysees (IRE)**[18] 4130 5-9-0 73 RWinston 3 48
(ISemple) *sn outpcd: nvr rchd ldrs* **13/8**[1]
04/6 **8** *4* **Axford Lord**[18] 4136 4-8-11 55 PMulrennan(3) 4 36
(ACWhillans) *sn bhd: nvr on terms* **100/1**

1m 14.3s (1.20) **Going Correction** +0.225s/f (Good) **8** Ran SP% **109.9**
Speed ratings: **101,94,93,93,90 89,88,83**CSF £14.64 TOTE £3.60: £1.50, £1.90, £1.80; EX 11.50.
**Owner** P And Mrs D M Johnson **Bred** Bearstone Stud And T Herbert Jackson **Trained** White-le-Head, Co Durham

**FOCUS**
An ordinary event but a race full of unreliable types, suggesting the form is not strong, and the winner is going to struggle in handicaps after reassessment if the assessor takes this win at face value.

**NOTEBOOK**
**Dizzy In The Head**, who had valid excuses for his last three below-par efforts, won an uncompetitive race with plenty in hand at a course that suits this style of racing. His short-term future in handicaps depends on how the assessor views this result, though.
**Abbajabba** had conditions to suit and a good chance at the weights, but showed exactly why he has become such an unreliable betting proposition. He has not won for nearly three years and remains one to tread carefully with.
**Sophrano(IRE)**, who had something to find at the weights, was not disgraced and may well be a bit better than the bare result as he raced furthest away from the far rail. The return to seven furlongs will suit but, as consistency has not been his strongest suit so far, he would not be one to lump on next time.
**Legal Set(IRE)**, who won over course and distance in June, was not disgraced back over this trip but he may well be happier back on a sound surface.
**Telepathic(IRE)** was not disgraced in the face of this latest stiff task but, given he is usually asked to compete on unfavourable terms, is not one to be interested in.
**Percy Douglas** faced a stiff task at the weights and offered little encouragement.
**Ulysees(IRE)**, a course and distance winner in April who attracted plenty of support, could have been expected to fare considerably better than he did and he remains one to tread carefully with at present.

## 4636 SYTNER FERRARI OWNERS TRACK DAY H'CAP 1m 4f 17y
8:30 (8:30) (D) (0-85,84) 3-Y-O £6,870 (£2,114; £1,057; £528) Stalls Low

Form RPR
2513 **1** **Richtee (IRE)**[4] 4536 3-8-7 **70** PHanagan 3 78
(RAFahey) *trckd ldrs: effrt over 2f out: led ins fnl f: drvn out* **5/2**[3]
1423 **2** *hd* **Obay**[37] 3590 3-9-7 **84** SSanders 2 92
(EALDunlop) *pressed ldr: effrt over 2f out: disp ld ins fnl f: kpt on: jst hld* **15/8**[1]
1312 **3** *1 1/4* **Charlotte Vale**[9] 4389 3-8-10 **73** ACulhane 4 79
(MDHammond) *trckd ldrs: drvn along over 3f out: rallied over 1f out: no ex ins fnl f* **2/1**[2]
1002 **4** *hd* **Bold Blade**[8] 4421 3-7-11 **65** oh1 ow4 PPMathers(5) 1 71?
(MJPolglase) *set stdy pce: rdn over 3f out: edgd lft 2f out: hdd ins fnl f: sn btn* **7/1**

2m 44.5s (5.30) **Going Correction** +0.225s/f (Good) **4** Ran SP% **109.2**
Speed ratings: **91,90,90,89**CSF £7.56 TOTE £3.20; EX 7.10 Place 6 £41.78, Place 5 £34.46.
**Owner** Terence Elsey and Richard Mustill **Bred** Niall Farrell **Trained** Musley Bank, N Yorks

**FOCUS**
An ordinary handicap in which the lack of a decent gallop means this bare form may not be entirely reliable. The winner is a genuine sort though, who should continue to give a good account.

**NOTEBOOK**
**Richtee(IRE)** is a consistent sort who reversed recent soft ground placings with Charlotte Vale. She shapes as though the step up to a mile and three quarters will be within her range and she should continue to give a good account.
**Obay** has had his resolution questioned but, with the blinkers left off, did nothing wrong this time. However, a further small rise is on the cards and he is likely to be found out in a competitive handicap after reassessment.
**Charlotte Vale** is a most consistent sort who again ran creditably but left the impression that a stiffer test of stamina would have been in her favour. She goes on any ground and should continue to give a good account.
**Bold Blade**, 4lb out of the handicap, ran creditably back on a soft surface, but it is worth bearing in mind that he very much had the rub of things at a course that favours front-runners and this bare form may flatter him to an extent.
T/Plt: £34.60 to a £1 stake. Pool: £28,966.85. 609.60 winning tickets. T/Qpdt: £34.30 to a £1 stake. Pool: £2,332.80. 50.20 winning tickets. RY

# 4143 SALISBURY (R-H)
Wednesday, August 11

**OFFICIAL GOING: Good to firm (good in places on straight course)**

## 4637 CARMEN WINES EBF MAIDEN STKS 6f
2:30 (2:30) (D) 2-Y-O £5,902 (£1,816; £908; £454) Stalls High

Form RPR
03 **1** **Cape Quest**[16] 4193 2-9-0 RLMoore 11 85
(RHannon) *lw: scope: mde virtually all: rdn 2f out: hrd drvn fnl f: styd on wl cl home* **7/2**[2]
**2** *3/4* **Nota Bene** 2-8-11 LPKeniry(3) 6 83+
(DRCElsworth) *w'like: scope: bit bkwd: bmpd s: bhd: hdwy over 2f out: swtchd lft over 1f out: rn green but kpt on wl fnl f: gng on cl hom* **8/1**
**3** *1 1/2* **Sound The Drum (USA)** 2-9-0 JFortune 3 78+
(JHMGosden) *w'like: scope: bit bkwd: s.i.s: sn rcvrd: chsd ldrs 4f out: wnt 2nd and rdn 2f out: no imp on wnr and lost 2nd fnl f* **7/1**[3]
**4** *3* **Tiggers Touch** 2-8-9 JFanning 1 64
(BRMillman) *w'like: pressed wnr 3f: rdn and lost 2nd 2f out: wknd fnl f* **20/1**
032 **5** *6* **Rusky Dusky (USA)**[37] 3588 2-9-0 79 PDobbs 5 51
(RHannon) *t.k.h: cl up: rdn over 2f out: wknd ins fnl quarter m* **7/2**[2]
**6** *1 1/4* **Desert Moonbeam (IRE)** 2-8-9 RHavlin 2 43
(RJHodges) *bit bkwd: bhd: sme hdwy fr over 1f out but nvr a danger* **50/1**

522 **7** *1* **African Storm (IRE)**[42] 3413 2-9-0 81 ........................ LDettori 9 45
(SKirk) *swtg: chsd ldrs: plld hrd: rdn 2f out: sn wknd: eased whn no ch ins fnl f* **5/2**[1]

**8** *nk* **Pussy Cat** 2-8-9 ........................ DaneO'Neill 7 39
(KOCunningham-Brown) *leggy: weak: bit bkwd: s.i.s: sn pushed along a in rr* **50/1**

040 **9** *2 ½* **Make It Happen Now**[56] 2970 2-8-9 50 ........................ ADaly 10 31
(SCBurrough) *chsd ldrs 1/2-way: sn btn* **66/1**

**10** *nk* **Granita** 2-8-9 ........................ DSweeney 4 30
(MBlanshard) *leggy: w'like: bit bkwd: t.k.h: in tch over 3f* **16/1**

4500 **11** *6* **Iam Foreverblowing**[57] 2959 2-8-2 45 ........................ BO'Neill(7) 8 12
(SCBurrough) *wnt lft s: sn chsng ldrs: hung lft and wknd over 2f out* **100/1**

1m 15.28s (0.34) **Going Correction** +0.075s/f (Good) **11** Ran SP% **113.7**
Speed ratings: **100,99,97,93,85 83,82,81,78,77 69**CSF £29.18 TOTE £4.60: £1.60, £2.70, £2.30; EX 34.30.
**Owner** Malih L Al Basti **Bred** Major C R And Mrs Philipson **Trained** East Everleigh, Wilts

**FOCUS**
By no means a great maiden, but the winner is progressing and the second and third both made encouraging debuts.

**NOTEBOOK**
**Cape Quest** continued his progression with an all-the-way success, soon grabbing the rail from his high draw and keeping on well when challenged. His future depends much on how the Handicapper rates this performance and things are likely to be tougher from now on, but he has improved with each run so far and could well do so again.
**Nota Bene ◆** is a half-brother to the smart Tarjman but cost just 14,000gns. He looked very much in need of the experience, wandering around when put under pressure and not totally concentrating on the job, but he finished to good effect and offered plenty of promise. He should improve significantly for the experience and can win a maiden.
**Sound The Drum(USA)**, a $200,000 yearling (the most expensive runner in the field), out of an unraced half-sister to several winners in the USA, has a Mill Reef entry. He recovered well enough from a slow start to race close to the pace, but was stuck out wide with no cover for much of the way and can be expected to improve on this form next time.
**Tiggers Touch**, who looked fit for this debut, is not exactly bred for speed given that her dam was unraced at two and later won over hurdles, but she broke well from the lowest stall of all and was soon showing plenty of dash. However, she seemed to know her job and may not improve as much as some of these.
**Rusky Dusky(USA)** did not get home after racing keenly and may benefit from more positive tactics and a drop back to five furlongs.
**African Storm(IRE)**, racing beyond five furlongs for the first time, was on her toes in the paddock and was never going to get home after pulling hard. *Official explanation: jockey said colt ran too free*

## 4638 BEMBRIDGE CLAIMING STKS 6f 212y
3:00 (3:04) (E) 2-Y-O £3,562 (£1,096; £548; £274) Stalls Centre

Form RPR

005 **1** **Ladruca**[5] 4521 2-8-2 ........................ RSmith 2 54
(RHannon) *small: lw: trckd ldrs: led wl over 1f out: drvn clr ins last* **7/2**[2]

0 **2** *5* **Slite**[20] 4040 2-8-5 ow1 ........................ SWKelly 9 44
(JAOsborne) *chsd ldrs: led over 3f out: rdn and hdd wl over 1f out: no ch w wnr fnl f: jst hld on for 2nd* **20/1**

0400 **3** *shd* **Lara's Girl**[21] 4010 2-8-2 40 ........................ PDoe 4 41
(IAWood) *chsd ldrs: rdn over 2f out: styd on u.p fr over 1f out: chal for 2nd last strides but no ch w wnr* **20/1**

0604 **4** *¾* **Zolash (IRE)**[6] 4498 2-9-1 ........................ MartinDwyer 8 52
(JSMoore) *bhd: rdn 3f out: styd on u.p fnl 2f: gng on cl home but nvr a danger* **3/1**[1]

50 **5** *nk* **Listen To Me**[99] 1853 2-8-7 ........................ RHavlin 1 43
(DHaydnJones) *sn led: hdd over 3f out: sn rdn: one pce fnl 2f* **20/1**

6054 **6** *3 ½* **Ahaz**[16] 4200 2-8-7 55 ........................ (p) MFenton 12 34
(IAWood) *in tch: rdn 3f out: wknd ins fnl 2f* **10/1**

000 **7** *2* **Secret Diva (IRE)**[6] 4474 2-7-13 ........................ JFMcDonald(3) 11 24
(MrsPNDutfield) *t.k.h: chsd ldrs tl rdn and outpcd 1/2-way: n.d after* **33/1**

6 **8** *1 ¾* **Sweeney Todd (IRE)**[7] 4432 2-9-3 ........................ RLMoore 13 35
(JGPortman) *bhd: hdwy into mid-div 1/2-way: nvr gng pce to rch ldrs* **7/1**

0053 **9** *nk* **Muestra (IRE)**[19] 4095 2-8-0 54 ow1 ........................ RMiles(3) 5 20
(MrsPNDutfield) *nvr bttr than mid-div* **6/1**[3]

006 **10** *½* **Chin Dancer**[19] 4095 2-7-11 ow2 ........................ (bt) RThomas(5) 6 18
(BRMillman) *lw: chsd ldrs tl wknd qckly over 2f out* **33/1**

0030 **11** *½* **Joe Ninety (IRE)**[58] 2946 2-8-9 47 ........................ JDSmith 10 24
(JSMoore) *lw: a in rr* **14/1**

0 **12** *9* **Ardasnails (IRE)**[47] 3259 2-8-6 ........................ LPKeniry(3) 3 1
(PBurgoyne) *a in rr* **100/1**

**13** *1 ¼* **Jules Lee** 2-8-10 ........................ CHaddon(7) 7 5
(WGMTurner) *w'like: neat: rdn and veered bdly rt 3f out: a bhd* **20/1**

1m 30.32s (1.32) **Going Correction** +0.075s/f (Good) **13** Ran SP% **115.7**
Speed ratings: **95,89,89,88,87 83,81,79,79,78 78,67,66**CSF £74.64 TOTE £4.60: £1.70, £7.50, £9.10; EX 84.00.The winner was claimed by G Margarson for £5,000. Slite was claimed by R Hodges £6,000.
**Owner** R Hannon **Bred** Plantation Stud **Trained** East Everleigh, Wilts

**FOCUS**
A very moderate claimerand, the winner apart, likely to have little bearing on future events

**NOTEBOOK**
**Ladruca**, who looked very fit, found this easier than the Newmarket seller she contested on her previous start and won well. She was claimed for £5,000, but could struggle outside of this grade.
**Slite**, well beaten in a Bath maiden on her debut, looked to improve on that effort but did appear to carry her head slightly awkwardly, possibly through greenness, and just failed to get home. She is bred for speed and may just prove better over shorter. She will now join Ron Hodges.
**Lara's Girl** ran her best race to date and may have a similarly moderate contest in her, possibly over a mile.
**Zolash(IRE)** did not appear to really get home over a mile on his previous start, but that was in maiden company and he simply got going too late on this drop in trip and grade.
**Listen To Me**, stepping up from five furlongs on this first run in 99 days, did not get home.
**Ahaz** failed to prove he gets this trip.
**Sweeney Todd(IRE)**, well beaten in a Brighton maiden on his debut, failed to build on that dropped in grade.
**Muestra(IRE)** was below the moderate form she showed when third in a seven-furlong Fibresand seller on her previous start.

## 4639 WEATHERBYS STONEHENGE STKS (LISTED RACE) 1m
3:30 (3:32) (A) 2-Y-O £20,100 (£6,600; £3,300) Stalls High

Form RPR

12 **1** **Perfectperformance (USA)**[12] 4295 2-8-11 ........................ LDettori 2 104+
(SaeedBinSuroor) *lw: trckd ldrs in 3rd: hdwy 3f out: led ins fnl 2f: rdn and edgd rt 1f out: pushed clr: readily* **4/5**[1]

511 **2** *3* **Grand Marque (IRE)**[25] 3939 2-8-11 100 ........................ JFortune 1 97+
(RHannon) *lw: w ldr:slt advantage 4f out: rdn 3f out: hdd ins fnl 2f: one pce u.p whn crossed and swtchd lft 1f out: sn btn* **13/8**[2]

21 **3** *5* **Minnesota (USA)**[25] 3931 2-8-11 83 ........................ DaneO'Neill 3 83
(HCandy) *lw: led tl hdd 4f out: no ch fr ins fnl 3f* **13/2**[3]

1m 43.53s (0.56) **Going Correction** +0.075s/f (Good) **3** Ran SP% **107.0**
Speed ratings: **100,97,92**CSF £2.37 TOTE £1.50; EX 2.20.
**Owner** Godolphin **Bred** Brushwood Stable **Trained** Newmarket, Suffolk

**FOCUS**
A small but select Listed affair, run at a reasonable pace. Each of the runners had previously won, and the form looks sound, but is hard to gauge at this stage.

**NOTEBOOK**
**Perfectperformance(USA)**, who had more scope than the other two, improved as expected over this extra furlong and ran out a convincing winner. He has taken time to mature, but has done precious little wrong in three outings to date and should improve again on this success. Entered in the Champagne Stakes and the Royal Lodge, this half-brother to top-class filly Russian Rhythm looks worthy of taking his chance in Group company and has a very bright future.
**Grand Marque(IRE)**, who had improved significantly in winning his two outings, could not go with the winner when challenged and finished well held. However, time may tell there was little disgrace in this defeat, he should be placed to win again and will stay further in time. *Official explanation: jockey said colt hung left throughout*
**Minnesota(USA)**, a ready winner of a fair Lingfield maiden when upped to seven furlongs last time, was firmly put in his place by the first two. He was not given a hard time late on, seemed to just about get this trip and should find easier opportunities this year.

## 4640 EUROPEAN BREEDERS FUND UPAVON FILLIES' STKS (LISTED RACE) 1m 1f 198y
4:00 (4:00) (A) 3-Y-O+ £26,100 (£9,900; £4,950; £2,250) Stalls High

Form RPR

2145 **1** **New Morning (IRE)**[39] 3519 3-8-5 104 ........................ PRobinson 6 109+
(MAJarvis) *lw: mde all: set modest early pce: pushed along and qcknd fr 3f out: styd on wl and in n.d fnl 2f* **6/4**[1]

1 **2** *1 ¾* **Tahtheeb (IRE)**[10] 4369 3-8-5 ........................ RHills 8 106+
(MPTregoning) *scope: lw: bhd: pushed along and hdwy fr 4f out: styd on wl to chse wnr 1f out: gng on cl home but a hld* **13/2**[3]

0423 **3** *2 ½* **Snow Goose**[19] 4077 3-8-5 103 ........................ JFanning 9 101
(JLDunlop) *chsd ldrs: wnt 2nd 4f out: sn rdn: nvr gng pce of wnr and lost 2nd 1f out* **7/2**[2]

0-12 **4** *3 ½* **Mango Mischief (IRE)**[46] 3327 3-8-5 92 ........................ RLMoore 10 94
(JLDunlop) *bhd: swtchd lft ins fnl 3f: kpt on fnl 2f but nvr a danger* **16/1**

**5** *2 ½* **Bayberry (UAE)**[304] 4-9-0 ........................ WRyan 7 90
(HRACecil) *w'like: angular: b.hind: chsd ldrs: rdn 3f out: wknd fr 2f out* **40/1**

0314 **6** *3* **Incheni (IRE)**[33] 3699 3-8-9 100 ........................ TEDurcan 3 88
(GWragg) *chsd ldrs: edgd rt and wknd 3f out* **11/1**

54 **7** *6* **La Hermana**[24] 3-8-5 ........................ ASuborics 2 72
(AWohler, Germany) *bhd: rdn and effrt on outside 3f out: n.d and sn wknd* **12/1**

1-04 **8** *3* **Top Romance (IRE)**[68] 2641 3-8-5 100 ........................ MartinDwyer 4 67
(SirMichaelStoute) *in tch: rdn to chse ldrs over 3f out: sn wknd* **8/1**

2-10 **9** *8* **Well Known**[10] 4367 3-8-6 92 ow1 ........................ DaneO'Neill 5 53
(RCharlton) *plld hrd: chsd wnr to 4f out: wknd qckly ins fnl 3f* **25/1**

4530 **10** *6* **Cuddles (FR)**[18] 4127 5-9-0 57 ........................ LPKeniry 1 40
(KOCunningham-Brown) *a bhd* **200/1**

2m 5.39s (-2.93) **Going Correction** +0.075s/f (Good)
**WFA** 3 from 4yo+ 9lb **10** Ran SP% **115.4**
Speed ratings: **114,112,110,107,105 103,98,96,89,85**CSF £11.45 TOTE £2.20: £1.40, £2.50, £1.80; EX 14.10.
**Owner** N R A Springer **Bred** Ballymacoll Stud Farm Ltd **Trained** Newmarket, Suffolk

**FOCUS**
This had the look of just an ordinary Listed contest, but very promising performances from the front two who should rate higher. With New Morning allowed her own way out in front, the pace was reasonable enough and the final time was smart, but nothing could get to her when she quickened and the field finished well strung out.

**NOTEBOOK**
**New Morning(IRE)**, fourth in the Ribblesdale and fifth in the Lancashire Oaks on her two outings since winning a maiden, got things her own way on this drop in grade and scored most decisively. A full-sister to both Islington and Greek Dance, this will have significantly boosted her paddock value, but she is set to stay in training at four and promises to improve again. She will be worthy of respect when stepping back up to Group company.
**Tahtheeb(IRE)**, off the mark on her debut in a nine-furlong Newbury maiden, acquitted herself creditably on this step up in class, finishing well from quite a way off the pace without managing to land a blow. She should be able to progress again and could make her mark in Pattern company.
**Snow Goose**, who looked fit but did not look that good in her coat, was racing beyond a mile for the first time. She was ridden with a little more restraint than is often the case and appeared to just about get the trip. This is about as good as she is.
**Mango Mischief(IRE)**, runner-up in a Windsor handicap off a mark of 85 on her previous start, had quite a bit to do at the weights but ran respectably. She looks capable of gaining some black type, possibly abroad.
**Bayberry(UAE)**, a maiden winner for Andre Fabre in France last season, was racing for the first time in 304 days and did not post a bad effort. She should improve for the run, but may just need to go on her travels once more to gain some black type.
**Incheni(IRE)** has not gone on at all from her Newbury Listed success two starts back, despite appearing to have conditions in her favour.
**La Hermana**, a German raider, whose form includes a fifth in the German Guineas three starts back, was below form on her British debut and may not have been suited by the fast ground.
**Top Romance(IRE)** is bred for this sort of trip but failed to last home. *Official explanation: jockey said filly hung left and lost her action in the straight*
**Well Known**, dropped back from a mile and a half, again failed to settle and see out the trip.
**Cuddles(FR)** was a long way out of her depth.

## 4641 VIOLET APPLIN CHALLENGE CUP H'CAP 1m 1f 198y
4:30 (4:31) (E) (0-70,70) 3-Y-O+ £3,828 (£1,178; £589; £294) Stalls High

Form RPR

0003 **1** **Bluegrass Boy**[21] 4029 4-8-12 **59** ........................ RThomas(5) 3 70
(GBBalding) *hld up in rr: hdwy on outside fr 3f out: hrd rdn and r.o fr over 1f out to ld cl home: all out* **8/1**

11-0 **2** *½* **Compton Drake**[15] 4220 5-9-10 **66** ........................ ASuborics 13 76
(GAButler) *lw: trckd ldrs: chal on ins fr 3f out tl ld 1f out: kpt on u.p: hdd and no ex cl home* **9/2**[3]

2-00 **3** *1 ½* **Efrhina (IRE)**[3] 4583 4-9-7 **63** ........................ RHavlin 12 70
(MrsStefLiddiard) *chsd ldrs: drvn and outpcd 3f out: styd on again u.p fr over 1f out: gng on cl home* **20/1**

5344 **4** *½* **Kylkenny**[19] 4086 9-10-0 **70** ........................ (t) RLMoore 6 76
(HMorrison) *bhd: hdwy 4f out: chal 3f out: led wl over 2f out: sn rdn: hdd 1f out and sn one pce* **4/1**[2]

23-4 **5** *½* **Petrosa (IRE)**[14] 4230 4-9-11 **70** ........................ LPKeniry(3) 10 75
(DRCElsworth) *lw: bhd: hdwy over 2f out: styng on whn nt clr run jst ins fnl f: one pce after* **7/2**[1]

5-00 **6** *nk* **Polish Spirit**[12] 4301 9-9-4 **60** JFanning 9 65
(BRMillman) *chsd ldrs: ev ch fr 3f out tl one pce fr ins fnl 2f* **14/1**
6400 **7** *6* **Zuri (IRE)**[12] 4307 3-8-12 **63** JPMurtagh 1 56
(LMCumani) *in tch: rdn over 2f out: no imp: wknd over 1f out* **17/2**
0005 **8** *4* **Mamore Gap (IRE)**[26] 3911 6-9-5 **68** PGallagher(7) 7 54
(RHannon) *bhd: rdn and effrt on outside fr 3f out: nvr nr ldrs* **8/1**
46-0 **9** *hd* **Rumbling Bridge**[18] 4147 3-8-8 **59** PDoe 8 44
(JLDunlop) *bhd: rdn 4f out: no ch whn hmpd on rails 2f out* **25/1**
-060 **10** *3 ½* **Dry Wit (IRE)**[16] 4201 3-8-6 **57** MartinDwyer 5 36
(RMBeckett) *chsd ldr after 2f: slt ld ins fnl 3f: hdd sn after: wknd 2f out* **33/1**
600- **11** *½* **Mark Your Way**[387] 3471 4-8-8 **55** NChalmers(5) 14 33
(PRChamings) *lw: a in rr* **50/1**
0000 **12** *3 ½* **Dusty Carpet**[93] 2000 6-9-4 **60** JoannaBadger 4 31
(MJWeeden) *a in rr* **33/1**
4360 **13** *1 ½* **Pacific Ocean (ARG)**[5] 4519 5-8-10 **52** (p) ADaly 2 20
(MrsStefLiddiard) *racd wd bnd after 3f: chsd ldrs: chal 4f out to 3f out: wknd rapidly* **16/1**
**14** *23* **Richmond Lodge (IRE)**[348] 4565 4-9-0 **56** GBaker 11 —
(MMadgwick) *swtg: led: hdd jst ins fnl 3f: wknd qckly* **33/1**

2m 8.90s (0.58) **Going Correction** +0.075s/f (Good)
**WFA** 3 from 4yo+ 9lb **14** Ran SP% **125.1**
Speed ratings: **100,99,98,98,97 97,92,89,89,86 86,83,82,63**CSF £42.51 CT £722.99 TOTE £9.80: £3.40, £2.10, £6.90; EX 58.00.
**Owner** Supreme Team **Bred** J And Mrs Bowtell **Trained** Kimpton,Hants

**FOCUS**
A modest handicap run at a solid gallop. The form looks questionable, but the first six were well clear.

**NOTEBOOK**
**Bluegrass Boy** stayed on dourly in the final furlong to get the better of the runner-up and win all-out. It was his first success in 15 attempts, and the Handicapper has given him a chance of late, so he may be able to build on this and should be of interest if turned out under a penalty.
**Compton Drake**, the subject of good support in the betting ring, looked likely to score when hitting the front, but had no more in the locker when the eventual winner came with his late challenge. He showed the benefit of his recent comeback effort and, although he is on a career-high mark, did enough to suggest there are further prizes to be won with him.
**Efrhina(IRE)** ran in snatches and was staying again on all too late, but improved on her effort in a Windsor maiden three days previously. She is lightly-raced and, if able to maintain this form, could be placed to advantage off this modest mark.
**Kylkenny** could not find a change of gear when challenged for the lead late on and just kept on at the same pace thereafter. He is very well treated on the best of his previous form, but shows little sign of capitalising and could be regressing.
**Petrosa(IRE)** did not enjoy the best of runs late on, but it made little difference to the result. The form of her comeback run at Goodwood last time gave her an obvious chance in this, but she again ran below her best, and is a very frustrating performer.

## 4642 GOLDRING SECURITY SERVICES FILLIES' H'CAP 1m 4f
**5:00** (5:00) (D) (0-80,80) 3-Y-0+ **£7,384** (£2,272; £1,136; £568) **Stalls** High

Form RPR
2-21 **1** **Asaleeb**[41] 3460 3-9-6 **80** RHills 11 91+
(EFVaughan) *trckd ldrs: slt ld fr 3f out: rdn fr over 1f out: hld on gamely u.p* **4/1**[2]
6026 **2** *nk* **Aoninch**[21] 4019 4-8-11 **60** JFanning 7 70
(MrsPNDutfield) *hld up in rr: stdy hdwy fr 3f out: pressing wnr whn ct by whip 1f out: u.p but no ex cl home* **12/1**
06-3 **3** *¾* **Royal Bathwick (IRE)**[14] 4240 4-9-10 **73** GBaker 12 82
(BRMillman) *s.i.s: hld up in rr: hdwy on rails fr 4f out to press ldrs fr 3f out: stl ev ch 1f out: one pce ins last* **16/1**
5020 **4** *6* **Keep On Movin' (IRE)**[27] 3873 3-8-13 **73** GCarter 5 72
(TGMills) *mid-div: drvn 3f out: styd on to chse ldrs fr over 1f out but nvr a danger* **16/1**
2105 **5** *2 ½* **Anyhow (IRE)**[16] 4196 7-8-13 **65** DNolan(3) 4 60
(MissKMGeorge) *in tch: hdwy over 4f out: chsd ldrs 3f out: sn rdn: wknd qckly over 1f out* **10/1**
0263 **6** *1 ¼* **Woman In White (FR)**[21] 4028 3-8-13 **73** RHavlin 8 66
(JHMGosden) *t.k.h: chsd ldrs: rdn 3f out: wknd 2f out* **16/1**
/000 **7** *5* **Enchanted Ocean (USA)**[25] 3942 5-7-13 **53** RThomas(5) 9 38
(GBBalding) *bhd: hdwy to chse ldrs over 3f out: sn wknd* **33/1**
1122 **8** *2 ½* **Prenup (IRE)**[38] 3561 3-9-2 **76** JPMurtagh 6 57
(LMCumani) *lw: t.k.h: chsd ldr tl led 5f out: narrowly hdd 3f out: sn rdn: wknd fr 2f out* **7/4**[1]
2040 **9** *5* **Dispol Evita**[8] 4416 5-7-10 **48** JFMcDonald(3) 1 21
(JamiePoulton) *lw: s.i.s: bhd: hdwy 5f out: effrt 3f out: sn wknd* **25/1**
0-30 **10** *1 ½* **Gaelic Roulette (IRE)**[21] 4033 4-9-7 **70** RLMoore 2 41
(PWHarris) *chsd ldrs: rdn 4f out: wknd fr 3f out* **11/2**[3]
05-0 **11** *12* **Opera Babe (IRE)**[100] 1823 3-8-12 **72** SCarson 10 24
(HSHowe) *a in rr: no ch fnl 4f* **66/1**
5025 **12** *dist* **Kristal's Dream (IRE)**[19] 4103 3-9-2 **76** (t) IMongan 3 —
(JLDunlop) *led tl hdd 5f out: wknd qckly fr 4f out: t.o fnl 2f* **20/1**

2m 36.14s (-0.21) **Going Correction** +0.075s/f (Good)
**WFA** 3 from 4yo+ 11lb **12** Ran SP% **119.2**
Speed ratings: **103,102,102,98,96 95,92,90,87,86 78,—**CSF £49.47 CT £703.89 TOTE £4.80: £2.00, £3.10, £3.50; EX 54.60 Place 6 £161.39, Place 5 £65.48.
**Owner** Hamdan Al Maktoum **Bred** Shadwell Estate Company Limited **Trained** Newmarket, Suffolk

**FOCUS**
A modest fillies' handicap run at a fair gallop and the first three came well clear, suggesting the form may hold up.

**NOTEBOOK**
**Asaleeb**, a facile winner of her maiden at Yarmouth last time, followed-up gamely on this handicap debut. She has been much improved since stepping up to this trip, and remains unexposed and open to further improvement, but beat little this time and it would be wise not to get too carried away with this form.
**Aoninch** came there to win her race inside the final furlong and held every chance, but got outbattled by the winner close home. This was a solid effort however, and although yet to win off a mark this high, she deserves to find a similar event.
**Royal Bathwick(IRE)**, third on her recent seasonal reappearance at Leicester, produced another sound effort under her big weight. She was not helped by a slow start and seemed to get this trip, but although she was clear of the rest in third, remains vulnerable to an improver off this mark.
**Keep On Movin'(IRE)** ran his race, but continues to look high enough in the weights at present, and has not really built on his sole success as a juvenile last year in five outings this term.
**Prenup(IRE)**, for the first time this season, ran very keenly through the early stages and was beaten some way out. This has to rate a disappointment and, although she has looked progressive this season, she has also now been a beaten favourite on her last three outings. *Official explanation: trainer's representative had no explanation for the poor form shown*
**Gaelic Roulette(IRE)**, who ran better than her finishing postion suggests at Sandown last time, ran poorly with no obvious excuses on this drop back in trip.
**Kristal's Dream(IRE)** *Official explanation: jockey said filly had a breathing problem*

T/Jkpt: £5,455.00 to a £1 stake. Pool: £88,357.00. 11.50 winning tickets. T/Plt: £418.80 to a £1 stake. Pool: £45,898.95. 80.00 winning tickets. T/Qpdt: £36.70 to a £1 stake. Pool: £2,686.80. 54.10 winning tickets. ST

# 4058 SANDOWN (R-H)
### Wednesday, August 11

**OFFICIAL GOING: Good to firm (good in places)**
Wind: almost nil Weather: overcast becoming bright, warm

## 4643 PLATINUM SECURITY MEDIAN AUCTION MAIDEN STKS 5f 6y
**5:40** (5:41) (E ) 2-Y-O **£4,085** (£1,257; £628; £314) **Stalls** High

Form RPR
6 **1** **Piper's Ash (USA)**[10] 4364 2-8-9 JFortune 6 95+
(RCharlton) *lw: mde all: easily drew rt away fr over 1f out* **5/6**[1]
**2** *7* **Killington (IRE)** 2-9-0 SWKelly 3 72
(GAButler) *lw: scope: str: rrd stalls: dwlt: t.k.h and in tch: chsd wnr 2f out: no ch: tired last 100yds* **12/1**
6 **3** *¾* **Edge Of Blue**[18] 4117 2-9-0 PDobbs 5 69
(RHannon) *lw: chsd wnr for 2f: outpcd 2f out: kpt on again nr fin* **6/1**[3]
2 **4** *shd* **Farthing (IRE)**[16] 4197 2-8-9 LDettori 4 64
(GCBravery) *cl up: chsd wnr 3f out to 2f out: u.p and btn after* **9/4**[2]
05 **5** *1* **Kingsgate Bay (IRE)**[42] 3418 2-9-0 NPollard 1 65
(JRBest) *lw: hld up: outpcd and rdn 1/2-way: no prog tl styd on last 150yds* **25/1**
**6** *3* **Bold Maggie** 2-8-9 SWhitworth 2 50
(GLMoore) *unf: scope: s.v.s: a in last pair: wl btn fnl 2f* **25/1**

61.99 secs (-0.20) **Going Correction** -0.175s/f (Firm) **6** Ran SP% **115.0**
Speed ratings: **94,82,81,81,79 75**CSF £13.18 TOTE £1.80: £1.60, £3.00; EX 16.40.
**Owner** K Abdulla **Bred** Juddmonte Farms Inc **Trained** Beckhampton, Wilts

**FOCUS**
Just the six runners, but a maiden that should work out, with the winner potentially Pattern class.

**NOTEBOOK**
**Piper's Ash(USA)** ◆ shaped with promise on her debut over six furlongs and, with the benefit of that experience, she appreciated the drop in trip and put up a really smart performance. She looks Listed class at the very least and must be respected in a higher grade.
**Killington(IRE)**, a half-brother to a couple of two-year-old winners out of a five-furlong juvenile winner, was fairly well supported in the ring. He was no match whatsoever for the winner after racing keenly, but came home best of the rest and should win a maiden given normal improvement, although it would help if he settled better.
**Edge Of Blue**, sixth on his debut over a furlong further at Ascot, was not suited by this drop in trip as he simply lacked the pace of the front two. He should be able to find an ordinary maiden back up in trip.
**Farthing(IRE)** shaped with promise when a well-held second in an ordinary race at Yarmouth on her debut, but failed to improve on that.
**Kingsgate Bay(IRE)** again offered encouragement and should not be overlooked next time now he is qualified for a handicap mark.
**Bold Maggie**, a half-sister to a six-furlong three-year-old winner, out of a seven-furlong juvenile winner, was very slowly away but showed speed to make up some of the lost ground before dropping away. With this experience under her belt, she should be capable of better.

## 4644 LONDON STOCK EXCHANGE MAIDEN FILLIES' STKS 1m 14y
**6:10** (6:11) (D) 3-Y-O+ **£5,512** (£1,696; £848; £424) **Stalls** High

Form RPR
2 **1** **Liberty Flag (USA)**[37] 3592 3-8-11 JFortune 4 71+
(JHMGosden) *racd in 4th: rdn 3f out: struggling tl r.o u.p over 1f out: led ins fnl f: drvn out* **8/11**[1]
064 **2** *¾* **Alenushka**[16] 4195 3-8-11 65 DaneO'Neill 1 69
(HCandy) *sn trckd ldr: rdn 2f out: led over 1f out: hdd and unable qck ins fnl f* **15/2**
**3** *nk* **Batik (IRE)** 3-8-4 AHamblett(7) 8 68+
(LMCumani) *str: scope: bit bkwd: s.s: hld up in last pair: wl bhd 3f out: rapid prog over 1f out: gaining fast at fin: promising* **20/1**
43 **4** *1 ½* **Merwaha (IRE)**[17] 4168 3-8-11 (b[1]) TEDurcan 5 65
(MPTregoning) *s.i.s: t.k.h: hld up: prog 3f out: rdn to chal and looked dangerous 1f out: fnd nil and immediately btn* **5/1**[2]
0000 **5** *1 ½* **Tipsy Lady**[10] 4369 3-8-11 NPollard 7 61
(DRCElsworth) *b: led: kicked on 3f out: rdn and hdd over 1f out: fdd fnl f* **20/1**
03 **6** *8* **Witches Broom**[18] 4125 3-8-11 LDettori 6 43
(CACyzer) *sn trckd ldng pair: rdn over 3f out: wknd over 2f out* **11/2**[3]
00 **7** *5* **Coco Point Breeze**[12] 4306 3-8-11 MFenton 3 32
(JGGiven) *nvr beyond midfield: rdn and wl bhd over 2f out* **100/1**
**8** *6* **Gentle Warning** 4-8-11 DFentiman(7) 2 18
(MAppleby) *lengthy: unf: a in last pair: wl bhd fnl 3f* **100/1**

1m 43.95s (0.03) **Going Correction** -0.20s/f (Firm)
**WFA** 3 from 4yo 7lb **8** Ran SP% **113.2**
Speed ratings: **91,90,89,88,86 78,73,67**CSF £6.51 TOTE £1.80: £1.10, £2.00, £3.50; EX 5.20.
**Owner** W S Farish **Bred** G Watts Humphrey Jr And William S Farish **Trained** Manton, Wilts

**FOCUS**
A modest maiden run at a fair early gallop though the final time was modest. The form provides the giuide to the level in what is a weak race.

**NOTEBOOK**
**Liberty Flag(USA)** , about two lengths ahead of the runner-up on her Windsor debut, responded gamely to her rider's urgings up the run-in and outstayed her rivals close home. This confirmed the promise of her fast-finishing debut last time, and as she again ran green on this occasion, should benefit from the experience once more.
**Alenushka** ran pretty much up to her Windsor form with the winner and only tired out of contention late on. She is clearly limited, but looks well worth a switch to handicaps, while on this modest current mark.
**Batik(IRE)** ◆, making her belated debut, lost ground at the start, but was really motoring late on and finished best of all. This was an eye-catching debut, and she certainly looks the one to take from the race with a view to the future, so should have little trouble in winning her maiden.
**Merwaha(IRE)** lost ground with a slow start and ran very freely in the first-time blinkers, but still held every chance if good enough up the run-in. She is temperamental, but has ability, and now qualifies for handicaps, where she should fare better.
**Tipsy Lady** had the run of the race in front, before dropping out when meeting the rising ground in the straight. This offered a little more encouragement and she would prosper from a switch to handicaps.
**Witches Broom** ran well below the form of her latest outingand was disappointing, but now becomes eligible for handicaps.

## 4645 LONDON STOCK EXCHANGE CONDITIONS STKS — 7f 16y
**6:40** (6:41) (C ) 2-Y-O — **£7,886** (£2,798; £1,399; £636) **Stalls** High

Form — RPR

01 **1** — **Kamakiri (IRE)**[19] 4078 2-9-2 ........ RLMoore 3 — 98+
(RHannon) *trckd ldr: shkn up to ld 2f out: styd on strly* **6/4**[1]

21 **2** 2 1/2 **Active Asset (IRE)**[16] 4198 2-8-11 85 ........ TEDurcan 2 — 87
(MRChannon) *led: rdn and hdd 2f out: kpt on same pce after* **12/1**[3]

1 **3** 2 1/2 **Hachita (USA)**[14] 4234 2-8-11 ........ WRyan 4 — 81
(HRACecil) *t.k.h: hld up in 3rd: shkn up and nt qckn over 2f out: one pce after* **7/2**[2]

12 **4** 8 **Blues And Royals (USA)**[25] 3939 2-9-2 ........ LDettori 1 — 66
(SaeedBinSuroor) *lw: s.i.s: hld up in last: pushed along and struggling 3f out: wknd over 1f out* **6/4**[1]

1m 32.15s (1.06) **Going Correction** -0.20s/f (Firm) — **4** Ran SP% **109.9**
Speed ratings: **85,82,79,70**CSF £16.22 TOTE £2.70; EX 16.80.
**Owner** Michael Pescod **Bred** South House Stud **Trained** East Everleigh, Wilts

**FOCUS**
Blues And Royals was obviously below form and Hachita did not appear to improve on her debut running, but still a pretty decent performance from Kamakiri. The pace was just steady and the final time was very slow.

**NOTEBOOK**
**Kamakiri(IRE)** followed up his Ascot maiden success with another taking performance. He was a touch keen early on, but that can be put down to the steady early pace and he travelled really strongly into the straight, before pulling away when asked. He looks ready for another step up in grade and should not be underestimated if going straight for the Royal Lodge.
**Active Asset(IRE)**, off the mark with just a short-head to spare in an ordinary Yarmouth maiden, looked to improve on that effort but was still no match for the winner. He would appear to be progressing, but will not be easy to place off his current sort of mark.
**Hachita(USA)**, off the mark on her debut over this trip at Kempton, did not really build on that and has to be considered a little disappointing.
**Blues And Royals(USA)**, runner-up in this grade at Newbury on his previous start, ran a shocker and connections could offer no explanation. Interestingly, he was awkward on leaving the stalls, rearing slightly as the gates opened.

## 4646 LONDON STOCK EXCHANGE H'CAP — 7f 16y
**7:15** (7:16) (C ) (0-90,90) 3-Y-O — **£10,608** (£3,264; £1,632; £816) **Stalls** High

Form — RPR

-114 **1** — **Take A Bow**[13] 4268 3-9-7 90 ........ JQuinn 5 — 107+
(PRChamings) *lw: hld up in midfield: prog on inner over 2f out: led wl over 1f out: clr fnl f: impressive* **3/1**[1]

2555 **2** 3 **Free Trip**[13] 4268 3-9-5 88 ........ JFortune 2 — 94+
(JHMGosden) *hld up towards rr: rdn over 2f out: prog over 1f out: r.o to chse wnr last 100yds: no imp* **4/1**[2]

1020 **3** nk **Lorien Hill (IRE)**[25] 3949 3-8-4 73 ........ MartinDwyer 10 — 78
(BWHills) *prom: ev ch wl over 1f out: chsd wnr after tl lost 2nd last 100yds* **20/1**

2410 **4** 1 1/4 **Dr Thong**[29] 3819 3-9-0 83 ........ PDobbs 12 — 85
(PFICole) *lw: mde most: edgd lft and hdd wl over 1f out: one pce after* **13/2**[3]

1062 **5** shd **Flip Flop And Fly (IRE)**[21] 4031 3-9-2 85 ........ LDettori 9 — 86+
(SKirk) *hld up in last pair: rdn over 2f out: prog on inner jst over 1f out: r.o ins fnl f: nvr nrr* **4/1**[2]

-060 **6** 1 **Jath**[71] 2557 3-8-13 82 ........ NPollard 3 — 81
(JulianPoulton) *settled towards rr: rdn over 2f out: prog to chse ldrs over 1f out: hld whn sltly hmpd 1f out* **50/1**

0316 **7** 1/2 **Burley Flame**[18] 4140 3-8-11 80 ........ MFenton 11 — 77
(JGGiven) *hld up towards rr: rdn 3f out: no prog and struggling 2f out: one pce after* **20/1**

0260 **8** shd **Bettalatethannever (IRE)**[13] 4268 3-9-1 84 ........ DaneO'Neill 1 — 81
(SDow) *lw: racd wd: hld up in midfield: prog 2f out: drvn to dispute 2nd over 1f out: hanging bdly rt and sn wknd* **12/1**

150 **9** 3 1/2 **Camberwell**[21] 4031 3-8-13 85 ........ RMiles(3) 8 — 73+
(TGMills) *hld up in detached last: shuffled along over 2f out: nvr nr ldrs* **25/1**

4614 **10** shd **Go Yellow**[14] 4244 3-7-7 69 ........ DFentiman(7) 4 — 56
(PDEvans) *chsd ldng pair: rdn 3f out: wknd 2f out* **25/1**

431 **11** 6 **Corky (IRE)**[34] 3666 3-8-9 78 ........ RLMoore 6 — 49+
(RHannon) *trckd ldrs: rdn wl over 2f out: btn whn hmpd over 1f out: wknd and eased* **8/1**

-000 **12** 7 **First Candlelight**[36] 3602 3-8-9 78 ........ IMongan 7 — 30
(JGGiven) *racd freely: w ldr to over 2f out: losing pl quikcly whn hmpd jst over 1f out* **40/1**

1m 27.8s (-3.29) **Going Correction** -0.20s/f (Firm) — **12** Ran SP% **118.8**
Speed ratings: **110,106,106,104,104 103,102,102,98,98 91,83**CSF £13.33 CT £208.68 TOTE £3.90: £1.80, £2.20, £7.10; EX 18.70.
**Owner** Mrs J E L Wright **Bred** Heatherwold Stud **Trained** Baughurst, Hants
■ Stewards Enquiry : Dane O'Neill one-day ban: careless riding (Aug 22)

**FOCUS**
A decent handicap that produced a very smart winning time for the grade. The form looks strong and solid.

**NOTEBOOK**
**Take A Bow** confirmed himself a rapidly-improving handicapper with a decisive success. Far from disgraced from a poor draw at Goodwood last time in a better race, he showed a neat turn of foot to score this time and could be rated value for more than the official winning margin. He looks to have plenty more improvement in him, and deserves a crack at a Listed contest over this trip, or back up at a mile.
**Free Trip**, closely matched with the winner on their recent Goodwood form, ran very much as though a return to a mile would see him get closer. He remains worthy of another chance, and time may tell he was far from disgraced.
**Lorien Hill(IRE)** turned in a better effort and showed her true colours, but held no chance with the winner. She is well worth stepping back up to a mile.
**Dr Thong** had the run of the race in front, but was a sitting duck and looked one paced when he was challenged entering the final furlong. This was an improvement on his latest effort however, and he should find easier opportunities, but has a bit to prove off this current rating.
**Flip Flop And Fly(IRE)**, a fast-finishing second over course and distance in a similar event last time, again ran on all too late in the day. He looks to be crying out for the step back up to a mile and is reasonably handicapped at present.
**Bettalatethannever(IRE)**, not far behind the front pair at Goodwood last time, looked to hang fire when under pressure but was in with every chance approaching two out. He needs producing as late as possible and, although he looks a better horse on the Polytrack, is worth another chance.
**Camberwell** *Official explanation: jockeys said gelding hung badly right*
**Corky(IRE)** ran below expectations and was already beating a retreat when he got bumped over one out. He has it all to prove now.

## 4647 SHARP MINDS BETFAIR H'CAP — 2m 78y
**7:45** (7:47) (D ) (0-80,74) 3-Y-O+ — **£5,486** (£1,688; £844; £422) **Stalls** High

Form — RPR

0021 **1** — **Strangely Brown (IRE)**[12] 4302 3-8-0 65 ........ MartinDwyer 10 — 82+
(SCWilliams) *lw: trckd ldr to 9f out: wnt 2nd again 2f out: shkn up to ld over 1f out: styd on wl* **2/1**[1]

121 **2** 2 1/2 **Belle Rouge**[18] 4129 6-9-1 65 ........ LDettori 5 — 73
(CAHorgan) *led: rdn and hdd over 1f out: styd on same pce* **11/2**[2]

4523 **3** 1 1/4 **Race The Ace**[32] 3743 3-8-5 70 ........ JQuinn 1 — 76
(JLDunlop) *lw: hld up in last: rapid prog to chse ldr 9f out: rdn over 2f out: one pce over 1f out* **11/2**[2]

4463 **4** 1 1/4 **Pope's Hill (IRE)**[21] 4027 3-8-7 72 ........ DHolland 3 — 77+
(LMCumani) *settled in midfield: rdn 3f out: kpt on fr over 2f out: nt pce to rch ldrs* **12/1**

-061 **5** 1 **Top Trees**[21] 4033 6-8-0 53 ........ NMackay(3) 4 — 56
(WSKittow) *racd in midfield: rdn 3f out: one pce and no imp ldrs after* **10/1**

1120 **6** 3/4 **Darn Good**[7] 4441 3-8-6 71 ........ (b) RLMoore 2 — 73
(RHannon) *racd in midfield: lost pl and rdn over 3f out: effrt on outer over 2f out: no hdwy over 1f out* **16/1**

0-61 **7** hd **Teorban (POL)**[19] 4082 5-8-8 58 ........ SWhitworth 6 — 60
(DJSFfrenchDavis) *hld up in rr: in last pair and rdn over 3f out: one pce after* **20/1**

4042 **8** 1 1/4 **San Hernando**[18] 4146 4-9-6 70 ........ DaneO'Neill 11 — 71
(DRCElsworth) *lw: hld up: last fr 1/2-way tl effrt 3f out: hanging rt and kpt on one pce fnl 2f* **9/1**[3]

0-50 **9** 2 1/2 **Jasmick (IRE)**[7] 4441 6-9-10 74 ........ JFortune 14 — 72
(HMorrison) *trckd ldrs: rdn over 2f out: wknd wl over 1f out* **16/1**

5040 **10** 3 1/2 **Henry Island (IRE)**[21] 4033 11-8-10 60 ........ TEDurcan 9 — 53
(MrsAJBowlby) *swtg: trckd ldrs: rdn and wknd 2f out* **33/1**

-003 **11** 2 **Lillebror (GER)**[21] 4033 6-8-7 57 ........ SWKelly 13 — 48
(BJCurley) *racd in midfield: pushed along and wknd over 2f out* **9/1**[3]

-004 **12** 5 **Song Of The Sea**[41] 3454 3-7-9 63 oh1 ........ (t) JFMcDonald(3) 7 — 48
(JWHills) *sed awkwardly: t.k.h: hld up in rr: brief effrt 3f out: sn wknd* **25/1**

3m 39.75s (1.52) **Going Correction** -0.20s/f (Firm)
**WFA** 3 from 4yo+ 15lb — **12** Ran SP% **124.2**
Speed ratings: **88,86,86,85,85 84,84,83,82,80 79,77**CSF £12.80 CT £56.35 TOTE £3.00: £1.60, £2.10, £2.10; EX 13.50.
**Owner** J T and K Worsley **Bred** Barry Noonan **Trained** Newmarket, Suffolk

**FOCUS**
A modest handicap that was tactical and it produced a very slow winning time for the class. Those racing handily were at an advantage, although on paper the form appears sound.

**NOTEBOOK**
**Strangely Brown(IRE)** followed-up his facile Nottingham success in similarly decisive fashion off a 10lb higher mark. He has readily improved for racing over this trip of late and looks to have more improvement in him, but this was run to suit, and connections will again hoping the Handicapper is none too harsh on him.
**Belle Rouge** set the stop-start pace for most of the way and had the run of the race, but could not go with the winner when challenged in the straight. She is a model of consistency and should win again in this grade during the summer.
**Race The Ace** did best of those to come from off the pace and improved again for this step up in distance. He remains unexposed, looks the type to do better with more experience and should find races before the year is out.
**Pope's Hill(IRE)** ◆ was staying on without threatening the principals and showed her best form to date. This was a big step up in trip, and it very much suited, so with positive tactics over this distance and slightly more cut, this unexposed son of Sadler's Wells should get off the mark.
**Top Trees** never threatened to follow-up his recent course success, off this 4lb higher mark, and could do with a drop back in trip.
**Teorban(POL)** *Official explanation: jockey said gelding had lost both front shoes*
**San Hernando** again looked a fiendishly tricky ride and ran below his best.
**Lillebror(GER)** failed to build on his recent improved effort at the course last time over this longer distance. A better all-round gallop will possibly see him in a better light, and he is not one to be writing off just yet.

## 4648 SHARP MINDS BETFAIR RATED STKS (H'CAP) — 1m 2f 7y
**8:15** (8:19) (D ) (0-80,80) 3-Y-O — **£6,211** (£2,356; £1,178; £535) **Stalls** High

Form — RPR

14 **1** — **Hasaiyda (IRE)**[33] 3694 3-9-2 75 ........ JFortune 2 — 91+
(SirMichaelStoute) *lw: trckd ldrs: rdn to chal 2f out: drvn ahd jst ins fnl f: styd on* **9/4**[1]

3411 **2** 1 **Nordwind (IRE)**[12] 4300 3-9-4 77 ........ IMongan 10 — 89+
(PWHarris) *lw: trckd ldrs: rdn to chal 2f out: hung both ways and ref to overtake* **5/2**[2]

3301 **3** 3/4 **Fuel Cell (IRE)**[20] 4057 3-8-11 70 ........ (b[1]) RLMoore 6 — 76
(RHannon) *trckd ldr: rdn to ld 3f out: hrd pressed 2f out: kpt on tl hdd and no ex jst ins fnl f* **14/1**

3041 **4** 1 1/2 **Mr Jack Daniells (IRE)**[21] 4032 3-9-2 75 ........ MartinDwyer 1 — 78
(WRMuir) *lw: hld up towards rr: gng wl enough over 2f out: hrd rdn and effrt over 1f out: kpt on same pce* **7/2**[3]

0004 **5** 1 1/2 **Love Triangle (IRE)**[18] 4145 3-8-13 75 ........ LPKeniry(3) 7 — 75
(DRCElsworth) *hld up in last: effrt over 2f out: rdn and kpt on same pce fr over 1f out* **25/1**

1130 **6** 5 **Doctored**[7] 4443 3-9-4 77 ........ (b) LDettori 3 — 68
(PDEvans) *settled in rr: rdn and prog over 2f out: wknd jst over 1f out* **8/1**

1003 **7** 3 **Jackie Kiely**[4] 4556 3-8-6 65 ........ (t) SWKelly 9 — 50
(PSMcentee) *settled in rr: effrt 3f out: no prog 2f out: wknd over 1f out* **12/1**

00-6 **8** 5 **Hat Trick Man**[23] 3994 3-8-13 72 ........ DaneO'Neill 4 — 48
(JAkehurst) *t.k.h: racd wd hld up: rdn and fnd nil over 2f out: sn wknd* **16/1**

0212 **9** 7 **Arkholme**[14] 4237 3-9-7 80 ........ PDoe 8 — 42
(PWinkworth) *led to 3f out: wknd rapidly 2f out* **12/1**

2m 9.50s (-0.68) **Going Correction** -0.20s/f (Firm) — **9** Ran SP% **124.5**
Speed ratings: **94,93,92,91,90 86,83,79,74**CSF £8.88 CT £67.19 TOTE £3.40: £1.70, £2.00, £3.40; EX 10.00 Place 6 £11.16, Place 5 £6.85.
**Owner** H H Aga Khan **Bred** His Highness The Aga Khan's Studs S C **Trained** Newmarket, Suffolk

**FOCUS**
A fair, quite competitive handicap, but a slow winning time. The first two are progressive but the third holds the form down.

**NOTEBOOK**
**Hasaiyda(IRE)**, not beaten far on her handicap debut at Ascot, improved on that effort under a good, strong ride from Jimmy Fortune. Clearly progressing, she could well defy another rise and promises to stay a little further.

**Nordwind(IRE)** was chasing the hat-trick off a mark just 2lb higher than when winning his handicap debut at Nottingham, but he showed a most disappointing attitude under pressure, hanging to both his left and right and proving reluctant to go past horses under pressure. He cannot be followed off the back of this, but hopefully it is something connections can correct. *Official explanation: jockey said colt hung left on the way up the home straight*
**Fuel Cell(IRE)**, off the mark in ordinary company at Folkestone on his debut, ran respectably in this better contest fitted with first-time blinkers.
**Mr Jack Daniells(IRE)**, racing beyond a mile for the first time, did not find as much as had looked likely and failed to prove he truly stayed.
**Love Triangle(IRE)** posted a reasonable effort on this first run over ten furlongs, but he was never really a threat.
**Doctored** was again below form and his recent busy spell could be catching up with him.
**Arkholme** *Official explanation: jockey said gelding stopped quickly in the home straight*
T/Plt: £26.90 to a £1 stake. Pool: £40,966.25. 1109.00 winning tickets. T/Qpdt: £11.00 to a £1 stake. Pool: £3,153.30. 210.55 winning tickets. JN

# 4494 YARMOUTH (L-H)

## Wednesday, August 11

**OFFICIAL GOING: Good to firm (good in places)**
Wind: slt against Weather: hot & sunny

### 4649 EUROPEAN BREEDERS FUND MAIDEN STKS — 6f 3y
2:20 (2:20) (D) 2-Y-O — £4,715 (£1,451; £725; £362) Stalls High

Form — RPR
46 **1** **Desert Commander (IRE)**[11] 4315 2-9-0 ........................(t) TPQueally 6 81
(SaeedBinSuroor) *prom: led wl over 1f out: edgd lft: drvn out* **17/2**[3]
03 **2** 1 1/4 **Wavertree Warrior (IRE)**[32] 3758 2-8-11 ................ J-PGuillambert(3) 7 77
(NPLittmoden) *hld up: rdn and outpcd 2f out: rallied ins fnl f: wnt 2nd cl home* **16/1**
224 **3** 1 1/2 **Juantorena**[57] 2959 2-9-0 95.................................................. DHolland 3 73
(MLWBell) *led: drvn and hdd wl over 1f out: wknd and lost 2nd wl ins fnl f* **4/11**[1]
**4** 1/2 **King's Kama** 2-9-0 ........................................................... FLynch 5 71
(SirMichaelStoute) *bhd: drvn 1/2-way: btn 2f out: plugged on* **15/2**[2]
45 **5** shd **Turks Wood (IRE)**[6] 4487 2-9-0 ............................................ MHenry 2 71
(MHTompkins) *disp 2nd tl rdn 1/2-way: no imp fnl 2f* **25/1**
0 **6** 2 **Fighting Tom Cat (USA)**[25] 3946 2-9-0 .............................(t) RMullen 1 65
(SaeedBinSuroor) *s.i.s: effrt 1/2-way: rdn 2f out: sn btn* **20/1**
**7** 14 **Three Boars** 2-9-0 .................................................... MTebbutt 4 23
(WJarvis) *s.i.s: pushed along after 2f: sn struggling: eased and t.o* **100/1**
1m 16.52s (2.92) **Going Correction** +0.475s/f (Yiel) **7** Ran SP% **111.1**
Speed ratings: **99,97,95,94,94 91,73**CSF £108.60 TOTE £11.10: £3.80, £2.90; EX 45.70.
**Owner** Godolphin **Bred** Gainsborough Stud Management Ltd **Trained** Newmarket, Suffolk
**FOCUS**
Probably not a great maiden as the favourite disappointed.
**NOTEBOOK**
**Desert Commander(IRE)** had not been getting home over seven furlongs and appreciated the drop back to sprinting. Fitted with a tongue-tie this time, he travelled strongly and picked up well when asked to go and win his race, and although the disappointing run of the favourite casts doubt on the value of the form, this half-brother to Lucky Pipit looks open to improvement.
**Wavertree Warrior(IRE)**, Proud Native's half-brother, appears to be progressing with racing. He was doing all his best work in the closing stages on this occasion and nurseries are now open to him.
**Juantorena**, having run well in each of his three previous starts, including in the Windsor Castle Stakes at Royal Ascot, looked to have been found the ideal opportunity to get off the mark. However, things did not pan out as expected, as he was eventually well held in third. It is difficult to suggest that lack of stamina was the only cause for his defeat as the winner had his measure with at least two furlongs to run, and it might be that he just needed this race following an almost two-month absence. Nevertheless, a drop back to five looks likely next time.
**King's Kama** was found out by greenness. He was weak in the market beforehand despite holding Group race entries and should be capable of better in time.
**Turks Wood(IRE)** has a Middle Park entry but that looks very optimistic on the evidence of this run, and nurseries look like being more his thing.

### 4650 PARKLANDS LEISURE HOLIDAY CARAVANS FILLIES' H'CAP — 6f 3y
2:50 (2:51) (E) (0-70,67) 3-Y-O — £3,838 (£1,181; £590; £295) Stalls High

Form — RPR
0120 **1** **Rise**[25] 3926 3-9-4 64.............................................................(b) JFEgan 12 74
(AndrewReid) *mde all on stands' rail: drvn and kpt on gamely fnl f: all out* **4/1**[2]
6-05 **2** 1 1/2 **Darla (IRE)**[16] 4194 3-9-7 67.................................................. TPQueally 2 73
(JWPayne) *hld up gng wl: effrt 2f out: ev ch 1f out: rdn and no imp* **15/2**[3]
4400 **3** 2 1/2 **Shrink**[12] 4299 3-9-2 62.............................................................(t) RMullen 14 60
(MLWBell) *chsd ldrs: rdn 2f out: nt qckn fnl f* **16/1**
0030 **4** 1 1/4 **Urban Rose**[65] 2741 3-9-3 63.......................................................(t) MHenry 1 57
(RMHCowell) *midfield: ch 2f out: no ex 1f out: wkng cl home* **25/1**
6555 **5** 1/2 **Beautiful Noise**[6] 4496 3-8-6 52.................................................(b[1]) JQuinn 3 45
(DMorris) *s.i.s: hdwy to midfield 1/2-way: hrd drvn 2f out: nt qckn* **9/1**
3505 **6** hd **Chertsey (IRE)**[8] 4414 3-8-10 59................................. J-PGuillambert(3) 7 51
(CEBrittain) *sn cl up: rdn over 2f out: no imp after* **11/1**
5122 **7** nk **Mugeba**[6] 4496 3-9-0 60...........................................................(bt[1]) DHolland 9 51
(MissGayKelleway) *cl up: rdn over 2f out: little rspnse: btn 1f out* **3/1**[1]
2050 **8** hd **Indrani**[27] 3877 3-7-7 46 oh2 ow2.......................................... MHalford(7) 5 37
(JohnAHarris) *plld hrd and prom: rdn over 2f out: btn over 1f out* **33/1**
4006 **9** 1 1/4 **Pardon Moi**[6] 4495 3-8-1 47.................................................. DKinsella 10 34
(MrsCADunnett) *bhd: rdn 1/2-way: btn 2f out* **33/1**
4106 **10** nk **Shifty Night (IRE)**[11] 4338 3-7-8 47........................ DeanWilliams(7) 8 33
(MrsCADunnett) *midfield: drvn and btn 2f out* **11/1**
0430 **11** 1/2 **Wavertree Girl (IRE)**[21] 4024 3-9-7 67....................(b) TGMcLaughlin 13 52
(NPLittmoden) *s.i.s: a bhd* **20/1**
1400 **12** 11 **Party Princess (IRE)**[39] 3530 3-9-2 62..................................... JMackay 4 14
(JAGlover) *prom: drvn and wknd over 2f out: eased and t.o* **12/1**
3210 **13** 1/2 **Mitzi Caspar**[44] 3380 3-8-6 52.............................................. AMcCarthy 6 —
(PLGilligan) *drvn 1/2-way: struggling after: eased and t.o* **33/1**
0030 **14** dist **Turkish Delight**[6] 4489 3-8-13 59...................................... LisaJones 11 —
(JBalding) *hld up in midfield: rdn and btn 2f out: sddle slipped fnl f and virtually p.u* **12/1**
1m 16.24s (2.64) **Going Correction** +0.475s/f (Yiel) **14** Ran SP% **122.1**
Speed ratings: **101,99,95,94,93 93,92,92,90,90 89,75,74,—**CSF £32.41 CT £445.84 TOTE £5.20: £1.80, £2.90, £7.70; EX 53.10.
**Owner** A S Reid **Bred** Cheveley Park Stud Ltd **Trained** Mill Hill, London NW7
**FOCUS**
An ordinary fillies' handicap in which the first and third raced close to the stands'-side rail, although there looked no draw bias. The form looks ordinary and not strong.
**NOTEBOOK**
**Rise** runs her best races when getting away from the gate quickly and gaining a prominent position, and she did that here. Hard up against the rail throughout, she always looked likely to hold off her challengers, and is clearly in good heart at present. It would not be a surprise to see her back on the All-Weather soon, as her rating on the sand is far lower than on turf, and she won on the Polytrack off 78 this time last year.
**Darla(IRE)**, one of the more lightly-raced runners in the field, built on the promise of her Windsor effort and looks capable of soon going one better in similar company.
**Shrink** put a couple of below-par performances behind her, but was unable to match the pace of her stands'-side companion Rise in the closing stages.
**Urban Rose** ran a fair race without suggesting she is about to strike.
**Beautiful Noise**, in first-time blinkers, raced on the wide outside throughout and could never quite get to the leaders. *Official explanation: jockey said filly was slowly into her stride*
**Mugeba** *Official explanation: jockey said filly hung*
**Indrani**, whose best form is on an easier surface, did not run too badly in the cicumstances, especially as she was running from 2lb out of the handicap, carried 2lb overweight and pulled very hard in the early stages.
**Turkish Delight** *Official explanation: jockey said saddle slipped*

### 4651 BET365 08000 322365 (S) STKS — 6f 3y
3:20 (3:21) (G) 2-Y-O — £2,520 (£720; £360) Stalls High

Form — RPR
2020 **1** **Jay (IRE)**[5] 4521 2-8-7 53.................................................(b) DHolland 2 48
(NACallaghan) *v.s.i.s: styd on 2f out: chal and hung fire fnl f: cajoled to ld reluctantly cl home* **2/1**[1]
03 **2** 3/4 **His Majesty**[20] 4054 2-8-5 ......................................... StevenHarrison(7) 5 51
(NPLittmoden) *settled 3rd: clsd to ld 1f out: drvn along: hdd cl home* **14/1**
3230 **3** 3 **General Nuisance (IRE)**[6] 4475 2-8-5 59.................(b) DerekNolan(7) 3 42
(JSMoore) *led: drvn and hdd 1f out: wknd fnl 100 yds* **4/1**[3]
2260 **4** shd **Glasson Lodge**[6] 4475 2-8-4 55.......................................(v) FPFerris(3) 4 36
(PDEvans) *settled 4th: drvn over 2f out: one pce and sn btn* **4/1**[3]
025 **5** 6 **Russian Servana (IRE)**[15] 4212 2-8-7 52................................ JQuinn 1 18
(JPearce) *chsd ldr: rdn over 2f out: wknd 1f out: eased* **9/4**[2]
1m 18.62s (5.02) **Going Correction** +0.475s/f (Yiel) **5** Ran SP% **110.8**
Speed ratings: **85,84,80,79,71**CSF £25.90 TOTE £2.40: £2.10, £2.90; EX 28.70.There was no bid for the winner.
**Owner** G C Hartigan **Bred** Mrs J Gittins **Trained** Newmarket, Suffolk
**FOCUS**
A very modest race and a moderate time even for a juvenile seller, but exciting nonetheless. The winner is rated as having run to his best.
**NOTEBOOK**
**Jay(IRE)** has a habit of losing ground at the start, but on this occasion she lost a good six lengths. However, her rider did not panic and, with the leaders hitting the wall having gone too quickly early, he brought her through with a perfectly-timed run to lead close home. She is clearly not short of ability, but unfortunately she is also far from keen on the job and needs plenty of driving, so would not appeal as the type to follow up.
**His Majesty** was well beaten in a Folkestone seller last time and this was more encouraging. He also took advantage of the leaders folding up in front and looked set to score until the favourite nailed him inside the last.
**General Nuisance(IRE)** paid for going off too fast in the early stages.
**Glasson Lodge** has had a number of chances in this grade and was once again found wanting, although on this occasion the vet reported that she was lame after the race. *Official explanation: jockey said filly finished lame*
**Russian Servana(IRE)** *Official explanation: trainer said filly was found to have sore shins on returning home*

### 4652 BENNETTS ELECTRICAL TOSHIBA H'CAP — 7f 3y
3:50 (3:51) (D) (0-80,78) 3-Y-O+ — £5,512 (£1,696; £848; £424) Stalls High

Form — RPR
3612 **1** **Miss Madame (IRE)**[6] 4470 3-8-7 65........................................ TPQueally 3 76
(RGuest) *led centre quintet tl over 2f out: rallied to ld again wl ins fnl f: styd on wl* **3/1**[1]
4100 **2** 1 1/4 **Warden Warren**[54] 3052 6-9-7 73..............................(p) TGMcLaughlin 2 81
(MrsCADunnett) *racd centre: led over 2f out: kpt on wl tl drvn and hdd fnl 100 yds: no ex* **17/2**
0035 **3** 2 **Ammenayr (IRE)**[126] 1294 4-9-12 78.......................................... DHolland 4 81
(TGMills) *racd centre: effrt 2f out: hd high: drvn and wl hld fnl f* **7/2**[2]
4421 **4** 1 1/4 **And Toto Too**[18] 4148 4-9-0 69........................................(v) FPFerris(3) 1 69
(PDEvans) *dwlt: drvn over 2f out: n.d to ldrs fnl f* **3/1**[1]
0100 **5** 2 **Antonio Canova**[19] 4090 8-9-10 76.......................................... JFEgan 5 70
(BobJones) *std in last of centre gp: rdn 2f out: sn btn* **8/1**
004 **6** nk **Lygeton Lad**[7] 4462 6-9-2 68........................................................(t) RMullen 7 62
(MissGayKelleway) *taken down early: led stands' pair and prom over 4f: btn 2f out: wandering fnl f* **11/2**[3]
50-0 **7** 5 **King Of Music (USA)**[70] 2596 3-8-10 68.................................... JMackay 6 49
(GProdromou) *chsd stands' side ldr: jnd him 3f out: rdn and btn 2f out: eased ins fnl f* **33/1**
1m 29.7s (3.20) **Going Correction** +0.475s/f (Yiel)
**WFA** 3 from 4yo+ 6lb **7** Ran SP% **112.2**
Speed ratings: **100,98,96,94,92 92,86**CSF £27.53 TOTE £2.90: £1.50, £4.20; EX 32.40.
**Owner** Cosmic Greyhound Racing Partnership Iii **Bred** Gracelands Stud **Trained** Newmarket, Suffolk
**FOCUS**
A pretty competitive handicap on paper and the field split into two, with the bulk of the runners racing down the centre of the track while Lygeton Lad and King Of Music stuck to the stands'-side rail. The centre group came out on top, and the form looks reasonably reliable.
**NOTEBOOK**
**Miss Madame(IRE)** did not find the drop back to seven furlongs from a mile any problem and, having raced prominently throughout, responded well to pressure and won going away. She might be due a break now following three runs fairly close together.
**Warden Warren**, last year's winner, made a bold bid to repeat the trick off a 4lb higher mark. He runs his best races in small fields - he has won six times from 13 starts in single-figure fields - and this was another solid effort.
**Ammenayr(IRE)** ran a promising race under top weight on his return from a four-month absence, and he should come on for the outing.
**And Toto Too**, who likes to come with a late rattle, would have been suited by a stronger pace.
**Antonio Canova** is happier on easier ground over six furlongs.

### 4653 MUNCHIES CAFE MAIDEN FILLIES' STKS — 6f 3y
4:20 (4:20) (D) 3-Y-O — £3,380 (£1,040; £520; £260) Stalls High

Form — RPR
2 **1** **Kool Acclaim**[11] 4337 3-8-11 ............................................... OUrbina 8 76+
(SCWilliams) *hld up in midfield: hdwy 2f out: led ins fnl f: hung lft and drvn out* **8/1**[3]
00 **2** 3/4 **Antigua Bay (IRE)**[81] 2311 3-8-11 ...................................... LisaJones 6 74+
(JARToller) *last pair: bustled along and bdly outpcd 1/2-way: styd on wl fnl f to take 2nd fnl strides* **9/1**

32 **3** *hd* **Lake Charlotte (USA)**[20] 4069 3-8-11 ................................ TPQueally 7 73
(DRLoder) *led and gng wl: rdn 1f out: sn hdd and nt qckn: lost 2nd fnl strides* **4/5**[1]

03 **4** *6* **Eltihaab (USA)**[11] 4351 3-8-11 ........................................(t) DHolland 3 55
(SaeedBinSuroor) *s.i.s: bhd: effrt 1/2-way: sn rdn: struggling over 1f out* **3/1**[2]

0-0 **5** *5* **Noble Desert (FR)**[91] 2046 3-8-11 ...................................... JMackay 5 40
(RGuest) *cl up: rdn over 2f out: sn wknd* **40/1**

44 **6** *hd* **Sylva Royal (IRE)**[11] 4337 3-8-8 .............................. J-PGuillambert(3) 1 40
(CEBrittain) *chsd ldr: drvn and fdd tamely 2f out* **20/1**

0060 **7** *6* **Pick A Berry**[18] 4127 3-8-11 55 ................................................ JFEgan 4 22
(GWragg) *sn rdn: nvr gng wl: struggling over 2f out* **20/1**

06 **8** *3* **Tides**[4] 4555 3-8-11 .................................................................. RMullen 2 13
(WJMusson) *keen early: towards rr: drvn and wl btn over 2f out: eased fnl f* **100/1**

1m 15.38s (1.78) **Going Correction** +0.475s/f (Yiel) **8** Ran SP% **114.6**
Speed ratings: **107,106,105,97,91 90,82,78**CSF £69.74 TOTE £8.00: £2.40, £2.30, £1.02; EX 40.30.
**Owner** Carol Shekells & Associates **Bred** Old Mill Stud **Trained** Newmarket, Suffolk

**FOCUS**
Not a strong maiden, but a decent time and the first two in the betting appeared to have been priced up based on their connections rather than their actual achievements on the racecourse. Despite this the time was reasonable and the form may prove sound.

**NOTEBOOK**
**Kool Acclaim** was not without her supporters in the ring and successfully built on the promise of her debut outing at Lingfield. She quickened well to pick up the leader but idled a little once in front, so there should be better to come. Connections will be hoping the Handicapper does not overreact to this win.
**Antigua Bay(IRE)** had shaped with promise on her debut but had disappointed badly on her next outing. Returning from almost three months off, she found six furlongs on the sharp side and will be suited by a step back up in trip now that she is eligible for handicaps. Softer ground may also suit this daughter of Turtle Island.
**Lake Charlotte(USA)** set out to make every yard on this drop back in trip, but she was found out for speed. The fact that she was coming back at the winner at the end suggests that seven furlongs is probably more her trip.
**Eltihaab(USA)** had the tongue-tie fitted this time following two disappointing efforts, but she once again failed to run up to market expectations. She is becoming disappointing.
**Noble Desert(FR)** is now eligible for a mark and should have better opportunities in handicap company.
**Pick A Berry** *Official explanation: jockey said filly as unsuited by today's good to firm, good in places ground*

## 4654 VAUXHALL HOLIDAY PARK CLAIMING STKS 1m 2f 21y
4:50 (4:50) (F) 3-Y-O **£2,898** (£828; £414) **Stalls** Low

Form RPR

0643 **1** **Treason Trial**[6] 4491 3-8-9 57 ................................................ OUrbina 3 59
(NTinkler) *cl up: rdn over 2f out: led over 1f out: pushed out: comf* **11/4**[1]

5006 **2** *2* **Auroville**[19] 4103 3-9-1 57 ................................................... RMullen 5 62
(MLWBell) *trckd ldrs: drvn to chse wnr 1f out: fnd little: wl hld whn edgd lft ins fnl f* **9/2**[3]

0000 **3** *3 ½* **Tshukudu**[21] 4018 3-8-0 38 .................................................. DKinsella 8 40
(MBlanshard) *t.k.h: led: jst hdd 3f out: remained w ldrs tl wknd over 1f out* **40/1**

5350 **4** *2 ½* **Soviet Spirit**[14] 4241 3-8-7 55 ................................................ BReilly(3) 4 45
(CADwyer) *midfield and rdn 4f out: sn outpcd: no ch fnl 2f* **16/1**

0004 **5** *½* **Lenwade**[6] 4497 3-8-2 35 ................................................. AMcCarthy 10 36
(GGMargarson) *prom: rdn 3f out: btn 2f out* **20/1**

0260 **6** *nk* **Russalka**[23] 3990 3-8-1 51 ................................................ MHalford(7) 7 42
(JulianPoulton) *s.i.s: keen and awkward in rr: last st: nvr nr ldrs* **7/1**

4004 **7** *3* **Mystic Moon**[20] 4065 3-8-12 48 ................................................ JFEgan 9 40
(JRJenkins) *pressed ldr: tk slt ld 2f out tl over 1f out: dropped out v tamely: eased ins fnl f* **16/1**

400 **8** *2* **Starmix**[18] 4147 3-9-11 65 .................................................. DHolland 2 49
(PFICole) *a bhd: struggling fnl 4f* **9/2**[3]

0005 **9** *1 ¼* **Ivory Coast (IRE)**[7] 4458 3-9-0 59 ........................................ TPQueally 11 36
(WRMuir) *keen in rr: rdn and brief effrt over 3f out: sn labouring* **4/1**[2]

0005 **10** *1 ¼* **Diverted**[6] 4497 3-8-0 36 ................................................... JMackay 1 19
(MGQuinlan) *drvn along early: midfield: rdn and wknd over 3f out* **40/1**

2m 10.77s (2.80) **Going Correction** +0.175s/f (Good) **10** Ran SP% **116.9**
Speed ratings: **95,93,90,88,88 87,85,83,82,81**CSF £14.89 TOTE £2.50: £1.60, £2.40, £12.40; EX 34.00.
**Owner** Elite Racing Club **Bred** A Pereira, Arnstein Stud **Trained** Langton, N Yorks

**FOCUS**
There was not much of a gallop on early for this modest claimer, and the principals all raced close to the pace. The form looks weak.

**NOTEBOOK**
**Treason Trial** was best in according to adjusted official ratings and looked sure to be suited by the step up to ten furlongs. Always well positioned, he was angled out with a quarter mile to run and stayed on really well to the line. This was not much of a race, but he is fairly lightly raced, and there could be more to come as he steps up even farther in distance. He was subsequently claimed by Stef Liddiard.
**Auroville** had shown little in the visor on his last two starts, and so the headgear was dispensed with this time. Dropping into claiming company for the first time brought about improvement, and he finished nicely clear of the third.
**Tshukudu**, the early leader, was responsible for setting the steady gallop, and her reward was to hold on for third place. Despite hanging right, this was a step up on her previous efforts, but she could well be flattered. *Official explanation: jockey said filly hung right-handed*
**Soviet Spirit** ran a bit better than the bare form suggests as she had to make up ground from midfield, and that was difficult following the slow early pace.
**Lenwade**, another who benefited from racing prominently, is struggling to find her best trip.
**Russalka** was disadvantaged by being held up at the rear in a slowly-run race.
**Ivory Coast(IRE)** *Official explanation: jockey said filly hung right-handed*
**Diverted** *Official explanation: jockey said filly was unsuited by today's good to firm, good in places ground*

## 4655 LONG BAR CLASSIFIED STKS 1m 2f 21y
5:20 (5:21) (F) 3-Y-O+ **£3,031** (£866; £433) **Stalls** Low

Form RPR

00-1 **1** **Barton Sands (IRE)**[110] 1590 7-9-3 60 ...................................... OUrbina 9 73
(JJay) *hld up last early: hdwy 3f out: rdn to ld wl over 1f out: sn spurted clr: easily* **14/1**

-050 **2** *5* **Patrixtoo (FR)**[53] 3089 3-8-8 57 ............................................ MHenry 2 63
(MHTompkins) *hld up: pushed along 4f out: hmpd wl over 2f out and relegated to last: plld outside and r.o wl fnl f: no ch w wnr* **33/1**

3526 **3** *shd* **General Flumpa**[32] 3746 3-8-12 64 ........................................ RMullen 5 67
(CFWall) *midfield: rdn and outpcd 3f out: styd on ins fnl f: unable to chal* **8/1**

50-0 **4** *½* **Kind Emperor**[16] 4199 7-9-5 62 ................................................ AMackay 4 64
(PLGilligan) *set brisk pce: rdn and hdd over 1f out: edgd rt after: lost 2 pls nr fin* **10/1**

0502 **5** *3 ½* **Golden Drift**[28] 3852 3-8-5 60 ................................................ JFEgan 3 52
(GWragg) *midfield: rdn over 5f out: boxed in fnl 3f: kpt on ins fnl f but no ch* **9/2**[3]

4001 **6** *nk* **Arms Acrossthesea**[7] 4458 5-9-9 57 ...................................... TPQueally 6 61
(JBalding) *prom: drvn 2f out: wknd 1f out* **11/1**

5053 **7** *1 ½* **Carriacou**[16] 4201 3-8-2 64 .............................................. DerekNolan(7) 8 53
(PWD'Arcy) *str hold towards rr: effrt on ins 3f out: sn rdn and no imp* **7/2**[2]

0242 **8** *½* **Scriptorium**[18] 4138 3-8-10 62 ............................................ DHolland 10 53
(LMCumani) *chsd ldrs: effrt 3f out: rdn 2f out: sn btn* **11/4**[1]

4500 **9** *shd* **King Of Knight (IRE)**[54] 3050 3-8-3 62 .................................. MHalford(7) 7 53
(GProdromou) *sn pushed along in rr: effrt on ins 3f out: drvn and wknd over 1f out* **20/1**

5600 **10** *1* **Absolutely Soaked (IRE)**[16] 4201 3-8-5 57 ............................ LisaJones 11 46
(DrJDScargill) *t.k.h: pressed ldrs: wknd wl over 1f out* **20/1**

00-4 **11** *11* **Dreams Forgotten (IRE)**[75] 2446 4-9-0 57 ............................ AMcCarthy 1 25
(GGMargarson) *chsd ldr: rdn 3f out: lost pl qckly: eased and t.o* **14/1**

2m 8.64s (0.67) **Going Correction** +0.175s/f (Good)
**WFA** 3 from 4yo+ 9lb **11** Ran SP% **121.4**
Speed ratings: **104,100,99,99,96 96,95,94,94,94 85**CSF £418.48 TOTE £18.00: £5.40, £6.20, £2.30; EX 898.80 Place 6 £463.46, Place 5 £30.23.
**Owner** I N Chinn **Bred** Patrick Cassidy **Trained** Newmarket, Suffolk

**FOCUS**
In contrast to the claimer, there was a good pace for this classified race and the form may prove fair for the grade.

**NOTEBOOK**
**Barton Sands(IRE)**, formerly with Martin Pipe, cost only 2,000gns when he was bought out of a seller in April, and his new stable look to have got a bargain, as he absolutely bolted up. He completed a treble on the card for Urbina and clearly the gelding retains plenty of ability, but on previous evidence it would be dangerous to assume he will repeat this performance next time.
**Patrixtoo(FR)** did not enjoy the best of runs and ended up being shuffled back to last just as he should have been making a forward move. He finished well though, and the return to this trip clearly suited.
**General Flumpa** would have appreciated more give in the ground and stays farther than this.
**Kind Emperor**, last year's winner, as usual attempted to make all the running. Given that he looked likely to be swamped at the two-furlong marker, he kept on surprisingly well to finish fourth.
**Golden Drift** was continually denied a run and can be rated better than her finishing position. She could be one to look out for in a fillies'-only handicap.
**Carriacou** is rather a disappointing sort who has had a number of chances.
**Scriptorium** was well enough placed if good enough, but could find no extra at the business end. His rider reported that the colt hung left-handed in the home straight. *Official explanation: jockey said colt hung left-handed down the home straight*

T/Plt: £339.40 to a £1 stake. Pool: £30,508.45. 65.60 winning tickets. T/Qpdt: £12.80 to a £1 stake. Pool: £3,068.80. 176.50 winning tickets. IM

4656 - 4662a (Foreign Racing) - See Raceform Interactive

# 4624 BEVERLEY (R-H)
Thursday, August 12

**4663 Meeting Abandoned** - Waterlogged

# 4473 CHEPSTOW (L-H)
Thursday, August 12

**OFFICIAL GOING: Good to soft**
The ground was softer than forecast after torrential rain at lunchtime and again just before the start of racing.
Wind: nil Weather: sunny spells and showers

## 4669 ARGUS COUNTY OF MONMOUTHSHIRE FAMILY DAY APPRENTICE H'CAP 1m 2f 36y
5:45 (5:46) (G) (0-55,50) 3-Y-O+ **£2,709** (£774; £387) **Stalls** Low

Form RPR

5300 **1** **Got To Be Cash**[26] 3929 5-9-13 **50** ................................ BSwarbrick(3) 11 58
(WMBrisbourne) *hld up: hdwy 4f out: led over 2f out: rdn clr fnl f: pushed out* **10/3**[1]

0- **2** *2 ½* **Black Legend (IRE)**[14] 1433 5-9-2 **42** ..........................(t) SJDonohoe(3) 6 42
(RLee) *hld up: hdwy over 2f out: rdn over 1f out: styd on ins fnl f: nt trble wnr* **15/2**

04-6 **3** *7* **Tomsk (IRE)**[87] 2185 4-8-7 **35** ................................................ WHogg(5) 7 22
(MissKMGeorge) *s.i.s: hld up: hdwy over 3f out: rdn over 2f out: wknd ins fnl f* **25/1**

0500 **4** *1* **Zalkani (IRE)**[34] 3697 4-9-5 **47** ............................................ AHindley(5) 12 33
(BGPowell) *s.i.s: hld up: hdwy on ins over 3f out: sn rdn: nt clr run and swtchd rt ins fnl f: n.d* **16/1**

/00- **5** *hd* **Street Games**[416] 2640 5-8-7 **35** ................................ JemmaMarshall(5) 5 20
(DGBridgwater) *s.i.s: hld up and bhd: hdwy on outside over 3f out: ev ch over 2f out: wknd ins fnl f* **50/1**

5640 **6** *1 ½* **Hilarious (IRE)**[12] 4339 4-9-1 **43** ......................................(p) HPoulton(5) 2 26
(DrJRJNaylor) *a.p: rdn and ev ch over 2f out: wknd fnl f* **7/1**[3]

3240 **7** *3 ½* **Newcorr (IRE)**[14] 4265 5-8-9 **32** ................................................(p) DFox 15 8
(JJBridger) *s.i.s: bhd: rdn over 3f out: nvr nr ldrs* **12/1**

0006 **8** *hd* **Margarets Wish**[21] 4045 4-9-0 **40** ..........................(b) StephanieHollinshead(3) 1 16
(TWall) *hld up in tch: led over 5f out: rdn and hdd over 2f out: wknd fnl f* **14/1**

20/0 **9** *8* **Stafford King (IRE)**[7] 4473 7-8-12 **40** ........................ StevenHarrison(5) 14 1
(JGMO'Shea) *a bhd* **20/1**

0630 **10** *1 ¼* **Coolfore Jade (IRE)**[47] 3303 4-9-4 **41** ...................................... MSavage 13 —
(NEBerry) *hld up in tch: rdn over 3f out: wknd over 2f out* **11/1**

0-30 **11** *23* **Nassau Street**[143] 1077 4-8-9 **37** ........................................ TBlock(5) 10 —
(DJSFfrenchDavis) *prom: rdn over 3f out: sn wknd: t.o* **12/1**

0-00 **12** *shd* **Silver Island**[48] 3279 3-8-10 **45** .......................................... DerekNolan(3) 9 —
(RMHCowell) *hld up: rdn over 4f out: sn bhd: t.o* **14/1**

0535 **13** *20* **Saucy**[38] 3581 3-8-11 **46** ..................................................(b) ThomasYeung(3) 3 —
(BJMeehan) *t.k.h: led: hdd over 5f out: wknd over 3f out: eased whn btn fnl 2f: t.o* **13/2**[2]



The Form Book, Raceform Ltd, Compton, RG20 6NL

0000 **14** 1 ¾ **Bunkhouse**[9] 4419 4-9-10 **47**.................................(v[1]) AQuinn 4 —
(WGMTurner) *sn chsng ldr: lost 2nd over 5f out: rdn over 4f out: wknd over 3f out: t.o* **33/1**

2m 17.42s (7.82) **Going Correction** +0.675s/f (Yiel)
**WFA** 3 from 4yo+ 9lb **14** Ran SP% **117.1**
Speed ratings: **95,93,87,86,86 85,82,82,75,74 56,56,40,39**CSF £24.94 CT £539.07 TOTE £3.60: £1.50, £2.70, £7.90; EX 44.00.
**Owner** Mrs B Penton **Bred** Penton Haulage **Trained** Great Ness, Shropshire

**FOCUS**
A moderate heat - only five of these had won a race before and the form is very weak.

**NOTEBOOK**
**Got To Be Cash** appreciated the give in the ground and proved good enough to give weight all round in this moderate contest. She will go up a few pounds for this though, and could struggle off her revised mark.
**Black Legend(IRE)** has been doing his recent running over hurdles and this was only his second start on the Flat in this country. He finished well from off the pace and was nicely clear of the third at the line. A step up to a mile and a half should suit.
**Tomsk(IRE)** has changed stables and ran a more promising race for his new trainer. He is of very limited ability, though.
**Zalkani(IRE)** once again hindered his chance of success by failing to get away on terms. He remains a maiden after 12 starts.
**Street Games**, returning from a 416-day absence and making his debut for his new stable, ran his best race to date, although this was also his easiest task so far.
**Hilarious(IRE)**, a long-standing maiden, does not stay ten furlongs.

## 4670 JACK BROWN BOOKMAKERS MEDIAN AUCTION MAIDEN FILLIES' STKS 5f 16y
6:15 (6:15) (F) 2-Y-O £2,933 (£838; £419) Stalls High

Form RPR
33 **1** **Trim Image**[38] 3577 2-8-11 ........................................ RLappin 6 69
(WJarvis) *w ldr: led 3f out: rdn over 1f out: jst hld on* **7/2**[3]
2 **2** nk **Amica**[10] 4399 2-8-11 ........................................ DHolland 2 68+
(GLMoore) *s.i.s: sn pushed along: hdwy on outside over 2f out: rdn and r.o fnl f: jst failed* **5/2**[2]
00 **3** 3 **Starlight River (IRE)**[15] 4231 2-8-11 .............................. DKinsella 3 57
(WRMuir) *a.p: wnt 2nd over 2f out: rdn wl over 1f out: no ex fnl f* **20/1**
4 **4** ¾ **Tashyra (IRE)**[21] 4040 2-8-11 .............................. MartinDwyer 5 55
(AMBalding) *outpcd after 2f: sn rdn: swtchd lft and hdwy jst over 1f out: one pce fnl f* **7/4**[1]
5 **5** ½ **Task's Muppet (IRE)**[21] 4040 2-8-11 .............................. PDoe 8 53
(JAOsborne) *rdn and hdwy 3f out: wknd over 1f out* **10/1**
**6** 5 **Edged In Gold** 2-8-11 ........................................ DSweeney 4 36
(PJMakin) *bhd: effrt whn n.m.r 2f out: n.d after* **16/1**
0 **7** 1 ½ **Sartaena (IRE)**[7] 4474 2-8-8 .............................. FPFerris(3) 7 30
(RMBeckett) *led 2f: rdn over 2f out: wknd wl over 1f out* **25/1**
4060 **8** ¾ **Ms Polly Garter**[26] 3930 2-8-11 **52**.............................. JFEgan 1 28
(JMBradley) *chsd ldrs tl wknd 1f out* **40/1**

63.85 secs (4.35) **Going Correction** +0.50s/f (Yiel) **8** Ran SP% **113.2**
Speed ratings: **85,84,79,78,77 69,67,66**CSF £12.24 TOTE £4.70: £1.30, £1.30, £7.30; EX 9.10.
**Owner** Ms I Bristow **Bred** Whitsbury Manor Stud And Stuart McPhee Bloodstock **Trained** Newmarket, Suffolk

**FOCUS**
A modest maiden, highlighted by the performance of the third and the form is far from solid.

**NOTEBOOK**
**Trim Image**, one of the most experienced in the line-up, showed good pace from the off and, crucially, had the advantage of the rail in the latter stages. She had looked fairly exposed prior to this, so the race probably did not take that much winning.
**Amica** had stayed on well over six on her debut so the drop back to five was not sure to suit. Having been slowly away, she struggled to go the early pace, but was predictably doing her best work at the finish. A step back up in trip will suit.
**Starlight River(IRE)** had not shown much on her first two starts but this was an improved effort. This daughter of Spectrum clearly enjoyed the ground.
**Tashyra(IRE)** was not suited by the drop back in trip and will be more interesting when racing over six furlongs. She might be more of a nursery type, though. *Official explanation: jockey said filly stumbled*
**Task's Muppet(IRE)** failed to build on the promise of her debut effort on this easier ground.
**Ms Polly Garter** *Official explanation: jockey said filly was unsuited by the good to soft ground*

## 4671 WEATHERBYS BANK NURSERY 6f 16y
6:45 (6:47) (E) 2-Y-O £4,488 (£1,381; £690; £345) Stalls High

Form RPR
21 **1** **Persian Rock (IRE)**[17] 4193 2-9-7 **82**.............................. DHolland 3 82
(JAOsborne) *mde all: rdn over 1f out: edgd rt wl ins fnl f: r.o* **15/8**[1]
5263 **2** ½ **Come Good**[12] 4325 2-8-9 **70**.............................. RLMoore 1 69
(RHannon) *blindfolded tl mounted in paddock: w wnr: rdn and ev ch 2f out: r.o* **3/1**[3]
4642 **3** 1 **Musico (IRE)**[11] 4365 2-8-11 **72**.............................. SDrowne 2 74+
(BRMillman) *s.s: bhd: rdn over 2f out: hdwy on stands' rail wl over 1f out: running on whn nt clr run wl ins fnl f* **9/4**[2]
0410 **4** 1 ¾ **Time For You**[20] 4089 2-8-8 **69**.............................. ADaly 6 59
(PJMcbride) *hld up: rdn 3f out: kpt on fnl f: nvr trbld ldrs* **12/1**
2003 **5** 3 ½ **Gavioli (IRE)**[7] 4475 2-8-4 **65**.............................. (t) JFEgan 4 45
(JMBradley) *trckd ldrs: rdn jst over 2f out: sn wknd* **9/1**
5006 **6** 5 **Queen's Glory (IRE)**[6] 4516 2-8-5 **66**.............................. MartinDwyer 5 31
(WRMuir) *t.k.h: sn w ldrs: rdn over 2f out: wknd over 1f out* **33/1**

1m 17.36s (5.16) **Going Correction** +0.50s/f (Yiel) **6** Ran SP% **111.2**
Speed ratings: **85,84,83,80,76 69**CSF £7.69 TOTE £2.20: £1.40, £2.10; EX 8.00.
**Owner** Waney Racing Group Inc & Karmaa Racing **Bred** Mrs Noelle Walsh **Trained** Upper Lambourn, Berks

**FOCUS**
A very poor winning time for the grade which means the form is only fair, but the winner is probably a bit better than the form suggests.

**NOTEBOOK**
**Persian Rock(IRE)** bagged the stands'-side rail and made every yard. This was a good performance as he was probably not at his best on the softish surface. The fact that he was entered in the Gimcrack gives an indication of the regard in which his trainer holds him, and he could be capable of a bit more than this bare form suggests. His late-season target is the big sales race at the St Leger meeting.
**Come Good** is clearly not the most straightforward of animals as he had to blindfolded beforehand, but he ran well in the race itself and had no excuse.
**Musico(IRE)** had run well over seven last time so it did not help him that he was slowly away over this shorter trip. Running on at the finish, he might have challenged for the runner-up spot with a clear passage, and a return to seven ought to see him enter the winner's enclosure.
**Time For You**, who had never previously run on anything but good to firm ground, never really got competitive on this slower surface.
**Gavioli(IRE)** was one of the more exposed performers in the line-up. *Official explanation: jockey said colt had a breathing problem*

## 4672 JACK BROWN BOOKMAKERS H'CAP 1m 14y
7:15 (7:16) (D) (0-80,82) 3-Y-O+ £6,929 (£2,132; £1,066; £533) Stalls High

Form RPR
1010 **1** **Threezedzz**[3] 4602 6-8-12 **67** 6ex.............................. (t) FPFerris(3) 5 88
(PDEvans) *mde all: rdn over 1f out: drew clr fnl f: r.o wl* **7/1**[3]
3000 **2** 7 **Cool Temper**[15] 4238 8-8-10 **62**.............................. SSanders 1 68
(PFICole) *a.p: wnt 2nd over 4f out: rdn over 2f out: btn over 1f out* **11/1**
0432 **3** 2 **The Gaikwar (IRE)**[8] 4438 5-8-6 **61**.............................. (b) RMiles(3) 6 63
(NEBerry) *s.i.s: hld up: hdwy on outside over 3f out: rdn jst over 2f out: one pce* **9/2**[2]
6001 **4** ¾ **Giocoso (USA)**[4] 4569 4-10-2 **82** 6ex.............................. DHolland 11 83
(BPalling) *w wnr over 3f: rdn over 2f out: one pce* **9/4**[1]
6540 **5** ¾ **Topton (IRE)**[4] 4569 10-9-10 **76**.............................. (b) SWKelly 4 75
(PHowling) *s.i.s: bhd: reminder over 4f out: rdn over 2f out: r.o fnl f: n.d* **16/1**
0204 **6** 2 ½ **Johannian**[10] 4401 6-9-5 **71**.............................. SDrowne 10 65
(JMBradley) *a bhd* **8/1**
2060 **7** 1 ¾ **Oakley Rambo**[62] 2838 5-9-10 **76**.............................. RLMoore 7 66
(RHannon) *prom: rdn over 2f out: sn wknd* **11/1**
0160 **8** 2 ½ **Chandelier**[7] 4479 4-7-13 **51**.............................. AMcCarthy 8 36
(MSSaunders) *s.i.s: hld up: hdwy over 3f out: rdn over 2f out: wknd over 1f out* **12/1**
10-0 **9** 4 **Gems Bond**[19] 4122 4-9-4 **77**.............................. DerekNolan(7) 9 53
(JSMoore) *hld up: rdn and sme hdwy whn swtchd lft over 2f out: wknd wl over 1f out* **33/1**
1000 **10** 27 **Under My Spell**[17] 4194 3-9-1 **74**.............................. JFortune 12 —
(PDEvans) *a in rr: t.o* **25/1**
3104 **11** dist **Premier Dream (USA)**[38] 3586 3-8-10 **69**.............................. DSweeney 3 —
(JGMO'Shea) *prom tl rdn and wknd over 3f out: t.o* **20/1**
0/0- **P** **Russian Comrade (IRE)**[161] 3843 8-9-1 **67**.............................. VSlattery 2 —
(JCTuck) *rel to r: sn p.u* **40/1**

1m 39.0s (3.10) **Going Correction** +0.50s/f (Yiel)
**WFA** 3 from 4yo+ 7lb **12** Ran SP% **116.8**
Speed ratings: **104,97,95,94,93 91,89,86,82,55 —,—**CSF £76.50 CT £392.64 TOTE £7.30: £2.90, £2.60, £2.30; EX 96.70.
**Owner** Steve Evans **Bred** Mrs R Pease **Trained** Pandy, Gwent

**FOCUS**
An ordinary handicap, but the winner confirmed himself ahead of the Handicapper, although there is not much strength in depth to the form.

**NOTEBOOK**
**Threezedzz** appreciated the return to turf after running below par on Polytrack last time. Quickly into the lead, he made every yard, bagging the stands'-side rail from halfway. He ran out a most decisive winner, is clearly versatile regarding ground, and will no doubt be out again soon before the Handicapper gets a chance to react.
**Cool Temper**, racing off a mark 2lb lower than when last successful, at this track in fact, shaped with more encouragement this time, running well from his poor draw and beating the rest well enough.
**The Gaikwar(IRE)** is performing with a degree of consistency at the moment, but he usually finds one or two to beat him. *Official explanation: jockey said horse was unsuited by the good to soft ground*
**Giocoso(USA)**, making a quick reappearance under a 6lb penalty, had his favoured front-running role usurped by the winner and, although he had the rail to help, he was struggling from a fair way out. To his credit he kept plugging away, though. *Official explanation: jockey said colt was unsuited by the good to soft ground*
**Topton(IRE)** has been held off this sort of mark all season and ran a typical race.
**Johannian** *Official explanation: jockey said gelding was unsuited by the good to soft ground*
**Gems Bond** *Official explanation: jockey said gelding ducked as the stalls opened and missed the break*
**Premier Dream(USA)** *Official explanation: jockey said colt had a breathing problem*

## 4673 BET DIRECT ON 0800 211222 MEDIAN AUCTION MAIDEN STKS 1m 4f 23y
7:45 (7:47) (F) 3-4-Y-O £2,905 (£830; £415) Stalls Low

Form RPR
0463 **1** **Redi (ITY)**[10] 4398 3-8-10 **67**.............................. DHolland 5 74
(LMCumani) *led early: chsd ldr: rdn and edgd rt 1f out: hrd rdn to ld cl home* **5/6**[1]
6053 **2** nk **Laabbij (USA)**[10] 4402 3-8-10 **75**.............................. (b) MartinDwyer 1 74
(MPTregoning) *sn led: hrd rdn fnl f: hdd cl home* **7/4**[2]
005 **3** 11 **Bayou Princess**[28] 3882 3-8-5 **62**.............................. AMcCarthy 4 52
(BDeHaan) *hld up: hdwy over 5f out: rdn and wknd over 3f out* **50/1**
**4** 6 **Lyes Green** 3-8-10 .............................. SSanders 3 48
(RMBeckett) *prom: rdn and lost pl over 5f out: bhd fnl 4f* **11/1**[3]
60 **5** 12 **Ben's Revenge**[7] 4492 4-9-7 .............................. VSlattery 2 30
(MWellings) *a bhd: rdn over 4f out: sn struggling* **100/1**
60 **P** **Chapelco**[42] 3454 3-8-10 .............................. JFortune 6 —
(JLDunlop) *prom 6f: t.o 4f out: p.u ins fnl f* **16/1**
6060 **P** **Unintentional**[78] 2402 3-8-2 **52**.............................. (v[1]) FPFerris(3) 7 —
(RBrotherton) *hld up: hdwy over 5f out: rdn over 3f out: wknd over 2f out: p.u and dismntd ins fnl f* **50/1**

2m 45.16s (6.66) **Going Correction** +0.675s/f (Yiel)
**WFA** 3 from 4yo 11lb **7** Ran SP% **110.0**
Speed ratings: **104,103,96,92,84 —,—**CSF £2.23 TOTE £1.90: £1.10, £1.60; EX 2.40.
**Owner** Equibreed S.R.L. **Bred** Rz Pian Del Lago Di Fattoria Marcianella Srl **Trained** Newmarket, Suffolk

**FOCUS**
A weak race, although the first three ran to form on paper. It was a two-horse race according to the betting, and that's how it worked out.

**NOTEBOOK**
**Redi(ITY)** is pretty exposed as a mid-60s performer, but he found a weak maiden and saw the trip out just the best to narrowly get the better of his only serious rival. He needed plenty of driving to get his head in front but he clearly stays well.
**Laabbij(USA)** looks high in the handicap on what he has achieved, and getting beaten by a 67-rated performer at level weights confirmed that impression.
**Bayou Princess** could never strike a blow at the first two and was always only chasing third-place prizemoney.
**Lyes Green** is a half-brother to winning hurdler Winsley.
**Unintentional** *Official explanation: trainer said filly had lost her action*

## 4674 MONMOUTHSHIRE SHOW THURSDAY 26TH AUGUST H'CAP 7f 16y
8:15 (8:18) (F) (0-55,55) 3-Y-O £3,360 (£960; £480) Stalls High

Form RPR
0446 **1** **Danifah (IRE)**[2] 4619 3-8-2 **42**.............................. FPFerris(3) 2 66
(PDEvans) *mde all: rdn over 2f out: clr wl over 1f out: readily* **6/1**[2]
-000 **2** 8 **Fleet Anchor**[13] 4309 3-9-3 **54**.............................. JFEgan 3 57
(JMBradley) *a.p: rdn and chsd wnr over 3f out to 2f out: wnt 2nd again ins fnl f: no ch w wnr* **16/1**

0-40 **3** *2* **Pappy (IRE)**[24] 3993 3-8-11 **48** PDoe 12 46
(AWCarroll) *t.k.h: a.p: rdn and chsd wnr 2f out tl no ex ins fnl f* **14/1**

600 **4** *1* **Grand Rapide**[17] 4195 3-9-0 **51** SDrowne 6 46
(JLSpearing) *hld up: rdn and hdwy over 2f out: one pce fnl f* **20/1**

0000 **5** *5* **Tartiruga (IRE)**[17] 4195 3-8-8 **45** DKinsella 13 27
(LGCottrell) *chsd ldrs: rdn and no hdwy fnl 2f* **12/1**

0600 **6** *4* **Whiplash (IRE)**[5] 4546 3-8-11 **53** (b[1]) ThomasYeung(5) 1 25
(KOCunningham-Brown) *chsd wnr over 3f: rdn and wknd 2f out* **33/1**

0-66 **7** *1* **Comic Tales**[29] 3839 3-8-12 **49** (b[1]) AMcCarthy 4 18
(MMullineaux) *s.i.s: rdn and hdwy over 2f out: wknd over 1f out* **33/1**

**8** *1 1/2* **Primatech (IRE)**[24] 4000 3-8-11 **48** DHolland 18 14
(MichaelCunningham, Ire) *hld up: rdn and no imp fnl 2f* **6/1**[2]

0505 **9** *shd* **Dane Rhapsody (IRE)**[9] 4422 3-8-8 **45** ow1 SSanders 19 10
(BPalling) *t.k.h: rdn and short-lived effrt over 2f out* **6/1**[2]

0650 **10** *3/4* **Night Worker**[5] 4548 3-8-13 **50** RLMoore 11 13
(RHannon) *hld up: rdn over 3f out: short-lived effrt 2f out* **10/1**[3]

00-0 **11** *3/4* **Webbington Lass (IRE)**[119] 1405 3-8-3 **40** (v[1]) ADaly 9 1
(DrJRJNaylor) *prom tl wknd over 2f out* **40/1**

0-40 **12** *hd* **Maid The Cut**[162] 955 3-9-0 **51** VSlattery 7 12
(ADSmith) *a bhd* **33/1**

1-00 **13** *hd* **Hi Darl**[22] 4020 3-8-8 **50** BSwarbrick(5) 15 10
(WMBrisbourne) *hld up: rdn over 3f out: bhd fnl 2f* **20/1**

2051 **14** *4* **City General (IRE)**[7] 4497 3-8-11 **55** 6ex (p) DerekNolan(7) 17 5
(JSMoore) *racd alone under stands' rail: spd 3f* **4/1**[1]

0-40 **15** *2* **Bold Trump**[102] 1796 3-9-4 **55** MartinDwyer 16 —
(Jean-ReneAuvray) *bhd fnl 3f* **16/1**

006 **16** *7* **Collada (IRE)**[65] 2765 3-9-2 **53** JFortune 10 —
(JHMGosden) *prom 3f: eased whn no ch ins fnl f* **10/1**[3]

-000 **17** *7* **Intitnice (IRE)**[19] 4147 3-8-3 **40** JoannaBadger 20 —
(MissKMGeorge) *a bhd* **40/1**

0-00 **18** *nk* **Lola Lola (IRE)**[34] 3710 3-8-6 **43** DaneO'Neill 14 —
(JLDunlop) *a bhd* **20/1**

1m 25.29s (2.09) **Going Correction** +0.50s/f (Yiel) **18 Ran SP% 135.1**
Speed ratings: **108,98,96,95,89 85,84,82,82,81 80,80,80,75,73 65,57,56**CSF £97.73 CT £1374.57 TOTE £6.90: £2.20, £3.80, £5.10, £9.50; EX 148.20 Place 6 £67.30, Place 5 £30.37.
**Owner** E A R Morgans **Bred** Rocklow Stud **Trained** Pandy, Gwent

**FOCUS**
A very decent winning time for the grade which suggests the form is solid, although some caution may be necessary. Those who raced towards the far side held the call from a long way out.

**NOTEBOOK**
**Danifah(IRE)** won a nursery here at around this time last year off a mark of 67, but she has been on a downward spiral since, and was racing off a 25lb lower mark on this ocassion. She appreciated the drop back to seven and had the best of the draw, but she won so easily that she would probably have scored wherever she had been drawn. Her trainer will no doubt be looking for a race in the next few days where she can run under a penalty, as the Handicapper is likely to put her up quite a bit for this wide-margin win.
**Fleet Anchor** had shaped as though in need of a step up in distance, and he put up his best performance on his first run over seven furlongs, finishing clear of the rest.
**Pappy(IRE)** once again proved difficult to settle, and that trait continues to hamper her finishing effort.
**Grand Rapide**, making her handicap debut off a moderate mark, ran well enough from what was a good low draw.
**Tartiruga(IRE)** had less to do in this company and posted a better effort as a result, although he was still beaten a long way by the winner.
**Comic Tales** *Official explanation: jockey said gelding was unsuited by the good to soft ground*
**City General(IRE)** found himself drawn on the wrong side and this run can be ignored.
T/Plt: £70.00 to a £1 stake. Pool: £38,043.70. 396.35 winning tickets. T/Qpdt: £22.00 to a £1 stake. Pool: £3,540.50. 119.00 winning tickets. KH

## 4538 HAYDOCK (L-H)
### Thursday, August 12

**OFFICIAL GOING: Heavy**
The ground was heavy after plenty of overnight rain and the meeting had to pass a morning inspection before being given the go ahead.
Wind: almost nil Weather: lt shower during evening; mainly dry

### 4675 KEALSHORE CLAIMING STKS — 5f
**6:00** (6:01) (F) 2-Y-O — **£3,052** (£872; £436) **Stalls** Centre

Form — RPR

06 **1** **Hopelessly Devoted**[24] 3980 2-7-11 RoryMoore(7) 4 55
(PCHaslam) *prom: hung rt and lost pl 1/2-way: rallied over 1f out: led ins fnl f: r.o* **16/1**

042 **2** *3/4* **Paris Tapis**[5] 4559 2-8-6 ow1 NCallan 5 55
(KARyan) *prom: led 2f out: sn rdn: hdd ins fnl f: nt qckn* **3/1**[1]

0043 **3** *2* **Roko**[24] 3980 2-8-10 59 TLucas 7 53
(MWEasterby) *prom: rdn 2f out: hung lft ins fnl f: styd on same pce* **5/1**[2]

3320 **4** *1* **Danehill Fairy (IRE)**[5] 4559 2-7-12 47 (v) NMackay(3) 2 41
(MrsADuffield) *chsd ldrs: rdn 1/2-way: kpt on same pce* **11/2**[3]

**5** *1/2* **Weet N Measures** 2-9-1 ACulhane 9 54
(RHollinshead) *dwlt and bmpd s: bhd: rn green: edgd lft and styd on fnl f: nrst fin* **16/1**

3314 **6** *1 1/2* **Von Wessex**[24] 3980 2-8-3 63 (t) CHaddon(7) 3 44
(WGMTurner) *led: rdn and hdd 2f out: sn hung rt: wknd fnl f* **8/1**

**7** *1 1/4* **Beaumont Girl (IRE)** 2-8-5 DeanMcKeown 1 35
(GASwinbank) *wnt lft s: bhd: sn hung lft: nt pce to chal* **15/2**

0005 **8** *1 1/4* **Kristikhab (IRE)**[12] 4329 2-8-10 62 (p) FNorton 6 37
(ABerry) *sed slwoly: bhd: hdwy 2f out: wknd and eased ins fnl f* **8/1**

05 **9** *6* **Carmania (IRE)**[33] 3729 2-8-8 THamilton(3) 10 20
(RPElliott) *prom: rdn and wkng whn n.m.r over 1f out* **14/1**

00 **10** *2 1/2* **Gallego**[22] 4023 2-8-4 (v[1]) SRighton 8 5
(SLKeightley) *wnt rt s: chsd ldrs tl rdn and wknd 1/2-way* **100/1**

64.70 secs (2.63) **Going Correction** +0.275s/f (Good) **10 Ran SP% 110.5**
Speed ratings: **89,87,84,83,82 79,77,75,66,62**CSF £59.81 TOTE £18.20: £3.60, £1.60, £1.80; EX 58.40.
**Owner** T E Pocock **Bred** T E Pocock **Trained** Middleham Moor, N Yorks

**FOCUS**
A most uncompetitive claimer and the form is no better than selling class.

**NOTEBOOK**
**Hopelessly Devoted** is a tricky ride, but found plenty for pressure and was going away at the line. The form is unlikely to amount to much, as it has the look of a moderate race.
**Paris Tapis**, on her first start over the minimum trip, ran a fair race and could win a similarily modest contest.
**Roko** was in front of the winner on his previous start but appears to be regressing.
**Danehill Fairy(IRE)** is thoroughly exposed but showed more than on her previous start
**Weet N Measures** was hampered at the start and showed a glimmer of ability on this debut. He may be capable of better. *Official explanation: jockey said colt was bumped at the start and hung left throughout*
**Von Wessex** moved poorly to post, then raced prominently and did not get home.
**Kristikhab(IRE)**, from a stable in form, was slowly away and ran poorly. He appears to be regressing quickly and looks out of love with racing. *Official explanation: jockey said gelding missed the break*

### 4676 COMMHOIST.CO.UK NURSERY — 6f
**6:30** (6:30) (E) 2-Y-O — **£3,581** (£1,102; £551; £275) **Stalls** Centre

Form — RPR

1102 **1** **Make Us Flush**[6] 4508 2-9-0 **73** FNorton 3 73
(ABerry) *hld up: hdwy over 2f out: rdn to ld over 1f out: hld on wl* **3/1**[2]

3510 **2** *nk* **Monsieur Mirasol**[37] 3605 2-9-4 **77** NCallan 7 76
(KARyan) *hld up: rdn and hdwy over 1f out: r.o ins fnl f* **2/1**[1]

2222 **3** *nk* **I'm Aimee**[11] 4358 2-9-3 **76** ACulhane 2 75
(PDEvans) *led 1f: remained prom: rdn over 1f out: ev ch ins fnl f: nt qckn cl home* **10/3**[3]

3500 **4** *3/4* **Paris Bell**[22] 4012 2-8-5 **64** DAllan 1 61
(TDEasterby) *hld up in rr: rdn and hdwy over 1f out: styd on fnl f: nt pce of ldrs* **10/1**

1134 **5** *1* **Princely Vale (IRE)**[14] 4278 2-8-6 **72** (p) CHaddon(7) 4 66
(WGMTurner) *led after 1f: rdn whn hung rt and hdd over 1f out: kpt on same pce* **14/1**

625 **6** *1* **Ming Vase**[37] 3611 2-8-5 **64** GGibbons 8 56
(DCarroll) *chsd ldrs: rdn over 2f out: one pce fr over 1f out* **8/1**

1m 17.11s (2.22) **Going Correction** +0.275s/f (Good) **6 Ran SP% 108.3**
Speed ratings: **96,95,95,94,92 91**CSF £8.71 CT £16.67 TOTE £3.60: £1.80, £2.30; EX 11.20.
**Owner** The Bath Tub Boys **Bred** Bearstone Stud **Trained** Cockerham, Lancs

**FOCUS**
A run-of-the-mill nursery in which the pace was fair and the form is solid at a modest level.

**NOTEBOOK**
**Make Us Flush**, representing a trainer in form, has only ever won at this track. She showed a good attitude and found just enough to see off the runner-up. She could follow up but will find it harder, as she is bound to be raised.
**Monsieur Mirasol** was supported in the market and may have been a touch unlucky, as he did not get the clearest of runs when trapped momentarily behind I'm Aimee. He clearly enjoys testing conditions and may be worth a try over slightly further.
**I'm Aimee** ran well enough while at the same time not quite seeming to get home.
**Paris Bell** ran in snatches and does not look one to trust.

### 4677 COMMHOIST LOGISTICS H'CAP — 6f
**7:00** (7:00) (C) (0-90,84) 3-Y-O+ — **£9,854** (£3,032; £1,516; £758) **Stalls** Centre

Form — RPR

**1** **Sahara Prince (IRE)**[16] 4224 4-9-1 **74** KDarley 4 88
(MichaelCunningham, Ire) *chsd ldr: rdn to ld 1f out: r.o* **10/1**

132 **2** *nk* **Fonthill Road (IRE)**[5] 4542 4-8-11 **70** PHanagan 8 83
(RAFahey) *chsd ldrs: rdn over 1f out: wnt 2nd ins fnl f: sn struck by rival's whip: r.o* **8/11**[1]

030 **3** *4* **Prince Of Blues (IRE)**[13] 4291 6-8-0 **59** (b) SRighton 1 60
(MMullineaux) *led: rdn and hdd 1f out: no ex ins fnl f* **25/1**

0400 **4** *1* **Marker**[34] 3698 4-8-12 **76** RThomas(5) 6 74
(GBBalding) *hld up: rdn over 2f out: nvr able to chal* **9/2**[2]

1000 **5** *nk* **Balakiref**[19] 4134 5-8-9 **68** RWinston 2 65
(MDods) *dwlt: bhd: rdn 1/2-way: nvr trbld ldrs* **13/2**[3]

0-30 **6** *5* **The Lord**[11] 4366 4-9-4 **84** CHaddon(7) 5 66
(WGMTurner) *t.k.h: chsd ldrs: rdn 1/2-way: wknd over 1f out* **12/1**

1m 15.47s (0.58) **Going Correction** +0.275s/f (Good) **6 Ran SP% 110.0**
Speed ratings: **107,106,101,99,99 92**CSF £17.30 CT £168.11 TOTE £5.80: £2.80, £1.10; EX 8.70.
**Owner** Herb M Stanley **Bred** Patrick H Dillon **Trained** Navan, Co Meath

**FOCUS**
A modest handicap run at a decent pace with the front two finishing well clear, giving the form a sound look.

**NOTEBOOK**
**Sahara Prince(IRE)**, the Irish raider, got his head in front for the first time. All his recent form was over seven furlongs, and he was well suited by the strong pace and testing conditions. He got first run after travelling sweetly in second throughout, and was always holding the runner-up.
**Fonthill Road(IRE)** was heavily supported in the market and was the only challenger to the winner under a strong ride. He never really looked like winning and may have been flattered to his proximity to the winner.
**Prince Of Blues(IRE)** took them along at a good pace and ran well, but is on a long losing run.
**The Lord** is normally ridden up with the pace but was heavily restrained throughout. The change of tactics clearly did not suit and he is far better than he showed.

### 4678 COMMHOIST LIFTING SOLUTIONS H'CAP — 1m 2f 120y
**7:30** (7:30) (D) (0-80,78) 3-Y-O+ — **£5,687** (£1,750; £875; £437) **Stalls** High

Form — RPR

4402 **1** **Trouble Mountain (USA)**[7] 4493 7-9-3 **68** RWinston 4 75
(MWEasterby) *hld up: rdn and hdwy over 2f out: burst through gap to ld ins fnl f: r.o* **7/2**[3]

-604 **2** *1 1/4* **Alpine Special (IRE)**[37] 3614 3-7-13 **67** RoryMoore(7) 1 72
(PCHaslam) *t.k.h: trckd ldrs: rdn over 2f out: led 1f out: hdd ins fnl f: nt qckn* **11/2**

4020 **3** *1* **Devant (NZ)**[37] 3597 4-9-13 **78** PRobinson 5 81
(MAJarvis) *hld up: rdn over 3f out: styd on fnl f: nvr nrr* **3/1**[2]

5132 **4** *1 1/4* **Pure Mischief (IRE)**[26] 3929 5-9-2 **72** RThomas(5) 2 73
(CRDore) *led early: chsd ldr: rdn 2f out: ev ch ins fnl f: no ex towards fin* **9/4**[1]

0050 **5** *2 1/2* **Slalom (IRE)**[27] 3911 4-9-7 **72** (p) MFenton 3 69
(MissGayKelleway) *sn led: qcknd 4f out: rdn over 3f out: edgd rt over 1f out: sn hdd: wknd ins fnl f* **7/1**

2m 24.07s (6.34) **Going Correction** +0.325s/f (Good)
**WFA** 3 from 4yo+ 10lb **5 Ran SP% 105.9**
Speed ratings: **89,88,87,86,84**CSF £19.84 TOTE £4.00: £1.40, £2.60; EX 17.50.
**Owner** Mrs Jean Turpin **Bred** Robert B Berger **Trained** Sheriff Hutton, N Yorks

**FOCUS**
A fair handicap but a very slow time indeed for the grade. No pace early resulted in a sprint to the line and less than six lengths covered the whole field at the finish. This race should be ignored as a form guide.

**NOTEBOOK**
**Trouble Mountain(USA)** had run well when finishing second on his previous start over course and distance, and went one better under a well-judged ride. He was always well placed given the way the race was run and ran on all the way to the line.
**Alpine Special(IRE)** was very keen early, refusing to settle, and would have preferred a stronger pace.

**Devant(NZ)** has not won for over a year and she seems to have her own ideas about the game. She took a long time to find top gear by which point the race was all over.
**Pure Mischief(IRE)** needed a stronger pace.

## 4679 COMMHOIST LIFTING CONTRACTORS MAIDEN STKS 1m 30y
**8:00** (8:00) (D) 3-Y-O+ **£5,655** (£1,740; £870; £435) **Stalls** Low

Form RPR
433 **1** **Aperitif**[27] [3896] 3-9-0 77 PHanagan 1 73+
(WJHaggas) *t.k.h: chsd ldrs: rdn over 2f out: led over 1f out: sn edgd lft and clr: eased towards fin* **4/6**[1]
3252 **2** *7* **River Nurey (IRE)**[13] [4306] 3-9-0 70 KDarley 6 53+
(BWHills) *led: rdn and hdd over 2f out: one pce fnl f* **7/4**[2]
05 **3** *nk* **Classic Lease**[20] [4101] 3-9-0 ACulhane 3 52
(RHollinshead) *towards rr: hdwy 4f out: swtchd rt over 1f out: kpt on ins fnl f* **33/1**
6 **4** *2* **Mount Cottage**[18] [4180] 3-8-9 MFenton 2 43
(JGGiven) *niggled along towards rr: rn green: hdwy 4f out: outpcd and hung lft over 2f out: styd on towards fin* **11/1**[3]
0 **5** *hd* **Start Of Authority**[24] [3994] 3-9-0 NCallan 4 48
(JGallagher) *t.k.h: chsd ldr: led over 2f out: rdn and hdd over 1f out: wknd ins fnl f* **33/1**
0- **6** *dist* **Whitkirk Star (IRE)**[316] [5295] 3-9-0 JMcAuley 5 —
(SPGriffiths) *s.i.s: bhd: lost tch 3f out: t.o* **100/1**

1m 48.12s (2.57) **Going Correction** +0.325s/f (Good)
**WFA** 3 from 4yo 7lb **6** Ran SP% **111.6**
Speed ratings: **100,93,92,90,90** —CSF £2.01 TOTE £1.70: £1.30, £1.10; EX 2.20.
**Owner** Stretton Manor Stud **Bred** A B Barraclough **Trained** Newmarket, Suffolk

**FOCUS**
An ordinary maiden, where half the field had little chance and the winner was a stone below his best in victory.

**NOTEBOOK**
**Aperitif** was unruly in the stalls and was very keen early, fly-jumping throughout the first two furlongs. He hit a flat spot two furlongs out and momentarily looked in trouble but, switched for a clear run, he soon picked up and quickened away to score readily.
**River Nurey(IRE)** had no excuses and may need to be dropped into selling company if he is going to get his head in front.
**Classic Lease** is now handicapped and is improving slowly. He could be interesting if given a mark of around 50.
**Whitkirk Star(IRE)** moved poorly to post and has no ability.

## 4680 COMMHOIST SUPER SKYRIG H'CAP 1m 30y
**8:30** (8:31) (E) (0-70,68) 3-Y-O **£3,669** (£1,129; £564; £282) **Stalls** Low

Form RPR
0-12 **1** **Boppys Princess**[14] [4259] 3-7-12 **45** PHanagan 3 61+
(RAFahey) *midfield: hdwy over 3f out: led over 1f out: r.o* **5/2**[1]
6000 **2** *2 ½* **Dont Call Me Derek**[7] [4483] 3-9-0 **61** DAllan 1 72
(SCWilliams) *t.k.h: a.p: rdn over 3f out: ev ch over 1f out: styd on: nt pce of wnr* **8/1**
4400 **3** *5* **Rare Coincidence**[33] [3738] 3-9-1 **65** (p) DNolan(3) 12 66
(RFFisher) *a.p: rdn over 2f out: no ex ins fnl f* **25/1**
6400 **4** *2 ½* **Anduril**[8] [4443] 3-9-3 **64** FNorton 5 60
(JMPEustace) *s.i.s: midfield: rdn over 3f out: one pce* **13/2**
0400 **5** *2* **Acuzio**[12] [4338] 3-8-11 **58** RWinston 8 50
(WMBrisbourne) *led: rdn over 2f out: hdd over 1f out: wknd ins fnl f* **25/1**
-220 **6** *2* **Sabrina Brown**[27] [3910] 3-8-12 **64** RThomas(5) 11 52
(GBBalding) *hld up: clipped rival's heels over 6f out: hdwy over 2f out: wknd fnl f* **3/1**[2]
1-02 **7** *nk* **Almond Willow (IRE)**[32] [3780] 3-9-5 **66** KDarley 2 53
(JNoseda) *flashed tail several times: towards rr: rdn 4f out: nvr trbld ldrs* **6/1**[3]
336- **8** *1* **Miss Ladybird (USA)**[297] [5671] 3-9-2 **63** MFenton 6 48
(JGGiven) *in tch: rdn over 3f out: sn wknd* **25/1**
05-0 **9** *½* **Mr Lewin**[56] [3004] 3-8-10 **57** DarrenWilliams 10 41
(RAFahey) *hld up: rdn over 3f out: nvr on terms* **25/1**
0-05 **10** *1* **Stephano**[51] [3168] 3-9-1 **62** ACulhane 4 44
(BWHills) *chsd ldrs tl rdn and lost pl over 4f out: n.d after* **9/1**

1m 47.02s (1.47) **Going Correction** +0.325s/f (Good) **10** Ran SP% **117.7**
Speed ratings: **105,102,97,95,93 91,90,89,89,88**CSF £22.16 CT £401.29 TOTE £3.70: £1.60, £2.80, £4.10; EX 51.20 Place 6 £22.81, Place 5 £11.95.
**Owner** Mrs S Bond **Bred** Mrs Sylvia Bond **Trained** Musley Bank, N Yorks

**FOCUS**
A run-of-the-mill handicap run at a good pace and a decent winning time for the grade, 1.1 seconds faster than the maiden, suggesting the form is fair for the grade.

**NOTEBOOK**
**Boppys Princess** has now won two of her last three and has clearly improved since last season. She quickened well off a good pace to score cosily. She is progressing and should win again.
**Dont Call Me Derek**, heavily supported in the market, ran a career best and connections were unlucky to come up against such a progressive winner. He looks sure to win off his current mark.
**Rare Coincidence** has never won on the turf but showed a return to form after a desperate run last time.
**Anduril** missed the break and merely ran on past beaten rivals.
**Acuzio** sweated up beforehand and did too much early on. He looks a horse who lives on his nerves and needs to learn to settle.
**Sabrina Brown** clipped heels over six furlongs out and the apprentice rider did well to stay aboard. This run can be ignored.
T/Plt: £20.70 to a £1 stake. Pool £42,753.60. 1,506.45 winning tickets T/Qpdt: £8.20 to a £1 stake. Pool £3,085.30. 276.80 winning tickets DO

# 4637 SALISBURY (R-H)
### Thursday, August 12

**OFFICIAL GOING: Good to soft**
Despite the winners of the first and last races racing on the far side, the majority of runners throughout the card opted to race towards the stands' side.

## 4681 DOWNS MAIDEN AUCTION STKS (DIV I) 6f 212y
**2:00** (2:00) (E) 2-Y-O **£3,601** (£1,108; £554; £277) **Stalls** Centre

Form RPR
02 **1** **Sharp As A Tack (IRE)**[19] [4137] 2-8-9 JFortune 14 84
(BJMeehan) *racd far side: mde all that gp and def advantage overall wl over 1f out: drvn out* **5/1**[2]
6 **2** *1 ½* **Mystery Lot (IRE)**[22] [4023] 2-8-2 DKinsella 8 73+
(AKing) *lw: racd stands side:chsd ldr:led gp and ev ch w far side ins fnl 2f:kpt on but nt pce of wnr far side fnl f* **12/1**
**3** *1 ½* **Foxhaven** 2-9-0 MartinDwyer 9 81
(PRChamings) *w'like: str: bit bkwd: racd far side: in tch: styd on to chse wnr ins fnl f but no imp* **50/1**
26 **4** *nk* **Polar Dawn**[20] [4081] 2-8-2 AMcCarthy 12 69
(BRMillman) *racd far side and chsd wnr: one pce fr over 1f out and no imp: wknd and lost 2nd that side ins last* **7/1**
00 **5** *2* **Danger Zone**[12] [4335] 2-8-7 SDrowne 3 68
(MrsAJPerrett) *racd stands side: chsd ldrs: rdn and one pce fnl 2f* **20/1**
0 **6** *4* **Just A Try (USA)**[26] [3939] 2-9-0 PDobbs 7 65
(RHannon) *racd stands side: in tch: wknd fr 2f out* **12/1**
6 **7** *1* **Swift Oscar**[19] [4149] 2-8-7 DHolland 6 56
(JWHills) *lw: racd stand side: in tch: pushed along over 2f out: soke hdwy fr over 1f out but n.d* **4/1**[1]
**8** *3* **Boracay Dream (IRE)** 2-8-9 JQuinn 11 50
(PWChapple-Hyam) *w'like: bit bkwd: racd stands side: s.i.s: outpcd fr 1/2-way* **10/1**
03 **9** *1 ¼* **Dahliyev (IRE)**[26] [3931] 2-9-0 JPMurtagh 4 52
(PWHarris) *lw: racd stands side and sn led: hdd ins fnl 2f: sn wknd* **11/2**[3]
**10** *1 ¼* **Eva Soneva So Fast (IRE)** 2-8-9 DaneO'Neill 13 44
(JLDunlop) *w'like: leggy: bit bkwd: racd far side: s.i.s: a bhd* **25/1**
00 **11** *1 ½* **Issy Blue**[7] [4488] 2-8-4 JFEgan 2 35
(JAOsborne) *racd stands side: in tch 4f* **33/1**
00 **12** *1* **Pride Of London (IRE)**[17] [4198] 2-8-2 PDoe 1 30
(IAWood) *racd stands side: chsd ldrs over 4f* **33/1**
00 **13** *nk* **Mickey Pearce (IRE)**[20] [4081] 2-8-2 DFox(5) 16 35
(JGMO'Shea) *racd far side: in tch to 1/2-way* **100/1**
**14** *15* **Whitland** 2-8-7 (t) NPollard 15 —
(MrsPNDutfield) *unf: bit bkwd: racd far side: a bhd* **20/1**
**15** *shd* **Backstreet Lad** 2-8-11 GBaker 5 —
(BRMillman) *leggy: bit bkwd: v.s.a: a bhd* **50/1**
**16** *1* **Volitio** 2-8-9 LDettori 10 —
(SKirk) *w'like: bit bkwd: racd stands side: a bhd* **14/1**

1m 29.09s (0.09) **Going Correction** +0.10s/f (Good) **16** Ran SP% **119.9**
Speed ratings: **103,101,99,99,96 92,91,87,86,84 83,82,81,64,64 63**CSF £56.62 TOTE £4.90: £1.80, £4.00, £12.10; EX 108.20.
**Owner** P Minikes **Bred** David John Brown **Trained** Upper Lambourn, Berks

**FOCUS**
Not easy to assess the value of the form given that the field split into two groups, but it looked a reasonable contest beforehand and, with several offering promise, it should produce winners. Three of the first four home, including the winner, raced far side. The winning time was very decent time for the grade of contest, 0.51 seconds faster than the other division and 0.15 seconds faster than the three-year-old maiden, giving the race a sound look.

**NOTEBOOK**
**Sharp As A Tack(IRE)** showed the benefit of her experience on this step up in trip, getting off the mark in decisive fashion under a positive ride. Given she raced in the smaller group on the far side, it is hard to know what she achieved, but she is at least going the right way and should be competitive in nurseries.
**Mystery Lot(IRE)** offered some promise on her debut in a Polytrack maiden and, switched to turf, she was able to confirm that and win the race on the stands' side. She was clear of the remainder should soon pick up a maiden.
**Foxhaven**, a 40,000gns yearling out of a seven-furlong two-year-old winner, made a very pleasing debut, coming out second best on the far-side group. With normal improvement, he should find a maiden.
**Polar Dawn** has not really built on the promise she showed when going down by just a short head here on her debut, and appeals as one to take on in similar company.
**Danger Zone** looks to be going the right way and could do even better now he is qualified for a handicap mark.
**Swift Oscar** failed to build on the promise he showed on his debut at York and now just needs one more run for a handicap mark.
**Boracay Dream(IRE)** *Official explanation: jockey said bit slipped through colt's mouth*
**Dahliyev(IRE)** offered some promise at Lingfield on his previous start but this represented a step backwards. However, he is now qualified for a handicap mark. *Official explanation: jockey said colt hung left*

## 4682 DOWNS MAIDEN AUCTION STKS (DIV II) 6f 212y
**2:30** (2:31) (E) 2-Y-O **£3,588** (£1,104; £552; £276) **Stalls** Centre

Form RPR
**1** **Joint Aspiration** 2-8-9 TEDurcan 5 84
(MRChannon) *w'like: leggy: racd stands side: s.i.s: bhd: rdn and hdwy fr 3f out: chsd ldrs 2f out: led ins fnl f: drvn out* **6/1**
40 **2** *3* **Scarlet Invader (IRE)**[22] [4016] 2-8-11 JPMurtagh 7 78
(JLDunlop) *lw: racd stands side and led overall: rdn appr fnl 2f: hdd ins fnl f and sn outpcd* **9/2**[2]
**3** *2* **Gitche Manito (IRE)** 2-8-11 JDSmith 4 73
(AKing) *w'like: scope: bit bkwd: racd stands side: chsd ldr: rdn and effrt fr over 2f out: wknd over 1f out* **16/1**
40 **4** *3 ½* **Seasons Estates**[107] [1686] 2-8-4 AMcCarthy 11 57
(BRMillman) *racd stands side: chsd ldrs: rdn 3f out: wknd over 1f out* **20/1**
**5** *½* **Silsong (USA)** 2-8-2 RSmith 12 54
(BRMillman) *w'like: racd stands side: in tch: rdn 3f out: sn outpcd* **66/1**
5 **6** *1 ¼* **Sir Monty (USA)**[12] [4335] 2-8-11 SDrowne 16 60
(MrsAJPerrett) *lw: racd far side: led: clr of sole rival over 2f out but nvr gng pce of stands side* **10/3**[1]
**7** *hd* **Captain Johnno (IRE)** 2-8-9 LDettori 2 57
(DRLoder) *racd stands side: t.k.h: in tch: pushed along and n.m.r ins fnl 2f: wknd appr fnl f* **5/1**[3]
5 **8** *4* **Flaunting It (IRE)**[21] [4053] 2-8-9 DHolland 9 47
(JAOsborne) *racd stands side: in tch tl rdn 3f out and sn btn* **6/1**
**9** *nk* **Nip Nip (IRE)** 2-7-11 DFox(5) 13 39
(ADSmith) *leggy: racd stands side but wd: rdn over 3f out and sn bhd* **66/1**
**10** *10* **Monad (IRE)** 2-7-9 AmyBaker(7) 3 14
(MrsPNDutfield) *w'like: bit bkwd: v.s.a: a bhd* **50/1**
**11** *8* **Thorny Mandate** 2-8-9 SCarson 14 —
(RFJohnsonHoughton) *unf: scope: lengthy: racd far side and chsd sole opponent tl lft bhd appr fnl 2f* **12/1**

1m 29.6s (0.60) **Going Correction** +0.10s/f (Good) **11** Ran SP% **109.8**
Speed ratings: **100,96,94,90,89 88,88,83,83,71 62**CSF £29.96 TOTE £7.40: £2.10, £1.50, £3.60; EX 33.60.
**Owner** Ridgeway Downs Racing **Bred** Messinger Stud Ltd **Trained** West Ilsley, Berks

**FOCUS**
Despite that fact three of the first four home in the first division of this race raced towards the far side of the track, all bar two elected to come stands' side and had the call by some way. This looked like a pretty ordinary maiden, the winning time was 0.51 seconds slower than the first division, but still respectable for the grade and the form should prove fair enough.

**NOTEBOOK**

**Joint Aspiration**, a 36,000gns purchase, out of a 12-furlong three-year-old winner, has been entered in a couple of valuable sales races and the Fillies' Mile. An athletic type, she picked up well from quite a way off the pace to make a winning debut in decent enough style. The time was not great in comparison to the first division, but this was her first run and, held in high regard by her trainer, she should improve and be competitive in a higher grade.

**Scarlet Invader(IRE)** failed to build on a promising debut when a disappointing favourite at Leicester on his previous start and, although this was better, he was readily brushed aside by the winner and will remain vulnerable in this grade. He may find things easier in handicaps.

**Gitche Manito(IRE)**, a 26,000gns purchase, half-sister to a winning miler in Germany, out of an unraced sister to the smart Rainbow Heights, hails from a stable that does well with its juveniles and this one made a promising debut.

**Seasons Estates**, racing beyond five furlongs for the first time, ran respectably without really proving his stamina for this sort of trip.

**Silsong(USA)**, a 9,000gns yearling, half-sister to three winners, including a multiple scorer in the USA, is a stablemate of the fourth. This was a satisfactory debut, but she will need to improve to win a similar race.

**Sir Monty(USA)** ◆ was one of just two to race on the far side and as a result had no chance. He annihilated the only other horse to stay his side and can be given another chance.

**Captain Johnno(IRE)**, a 20,000gns purchase, out of a three-times winner over a mile six, is entered in a couple of sales races. He was never really going well enough to pose a threat, but hinted at ability and should be better for the experience. *Official explanation: jockey said mount was behaving in a coltish manner*

**Flaunting It(IRE)** failed to build on his debut effort on this easier ground and needs just one more run for a nursery mark.

## 4683 SOVEREIGN WINDOWS & CONSERVATORIES MAIDEN STKS 6f 212y

**3:05** (3:06) (D) 3-Y-O **£5,804** (£1,786; £893; £446) **Stalls** Centre

Form RPR

03- **1** **Cape Vincent**[337] 4818 3-9-0 .......... JFortune 6 91+
(JHMGosden) *h.d.w: chsd ldrs: pushed along over 2f out: led wl over 1f out: drvn clr ins last: readily* **4/6**[1]

200- **2** *4* **Patterdale**[392] 3348 3-9-0 86 .......... LDettori 9 75
(WJHaggas) *in tch: hdwy over 2f out: styd on to chse wnr ins fnl f but no ch* **9/1**

6- **3** *2* **Mrs Shilling**[301] 5587 3-8-9 .......... OUrbina 4 65+
(JRFanshawe) *lw: tall: chsd ldrs: rdn over 2f out: one pce whn swtchd rt ins last* **15/2**[3]

-202 **4** *shd* **Noora (IRE)**[33] 3759 3-8-9 75 .......... WSupple 10 65
(MPTregoning) *chsd ldr: led over 2f out: sn rdn: hdd wl over 1f out: sn btn* **5/1**[2]

0000 **5** *3* **Snow Joke (IRE)**[24] 3993 3-8-9 49 .......... NPollard 7 57
(MrsPNDutfield) *broke wl: and c lft to ld on stands rail: rdn 3f out: hdd over 2f out: sn btn* **100/1**

**6** *3/4* **Encora Bay** 3-8-9 .......... JQuinn 2 55
(PRChamings) *w'like: bit bkwd: broke wl: stdd rr: pushed along 3f out: kpt on fr over 1f out but nvr a danger* **50/1**

**7** *1/2* **Mister Muja (IRE)** 3-9-0 .......... (t) IMongan 11 59
(PWHarris) *w'like: str: bit bkwd: rdn 3f out: a in rr* **33/1**

23- **8** *1/2* **Mindset (IRE)**[381] 3638 3-8-9 .......... DHolland 1 52
(LMCumani) *trckd ldrs tl wknd qckly 2f out* **10/1**

**9** *5* **Superfling** 3-9-0 .......... PDobbs 5 44
(RHannon) *unf: bit bkwd: bhd: pushed along:green and hung rt over 2f out* **33/1**

**10** *1 1/2* **Kajul** 3-8-9 .......... SDrowne 8 36
(CAHorgan) *w'like: bit bkwd: slowly away: a bhd: hung rt and green 3f out* **66/1**

**11** *9* **Dine 'N' Dash** 3-8-11 .......... LPKeniry(3) 3 17
(AGNewcombe) *w'like: sn bhd: rdn and no ch fr 1/2-way* **66/1**

1m 29.24s (0.24) **Going Correction** +0.10s/f (Good) **11** Ran SP% **119.3**

Speed ratings: **102,97,95,95,91 90,90,89,83,82 71**CSF £7.63 TOTE £1.70: £1.10, £2.40, £1.90; EX 13.90.

**Owner** Sheikh Mohammed **Bred** Cuadra Asturias **Trained** Manton, Wilts

**FOCUS**

Very little strength in depth to this maiden, but promising performances from the front three. The whole field raced stands' side and the form is fair, with the fifth providing the level.

**NOTEBOOK**

**Cape Vincent** offered plenty of promise on both his starts as a juvenile, and was able to confirm that promise having done very well physically from two to three. Given that this was his first run in 337 days, there should be plenty more to come and he should not be underestimated in a higher grade.

**Patterdale** was tried in Listed company last season and finished his two-year-old campaign with a rating of 86. Racing for the first time in 392 days, he posted a respectable effort without running up to her rating. It remains to be seen how good he is, but he should pick up a maiden with normal improvement.

**Mrs Shilling**, well beaten behind Phantom Wind on her sole start last season, was quite well supported on course for this first run in 301 days and made a reasonable return to action. This was just her second run and she should progress.

**Noora(IRE)** was left behind when the pace quickened and is beginning to look exposed. The ground should not have been a problem.

**Snow Joke(IRE)**, dropped back in trip, showed plenty of pace but was totally outclassed in the closing stages. She should find things easier in and handicaps and sellers.

**Encora Bay** *Official explanation: jockey said filly lost her action*

## 4684 STELLA ARTOIS FILLIES' H'CAP 1m

**3:40** (3:40) (D) (0-85,85) 3-Y-0+ **£7,124** (£2,192; £1,096; £548) **Stalls** High

Form RPR

0-00 **1** **Zweibrucken (IRE)**[61] 2887 3-9-7 **80** .......... JFEgan 6 86
(SKirk) *trckd ldr: chal ins fnl 3f: rdn to ld appr fnl f: pushed clr ins last* **8/1**[3]

231 **2** *1 1/2* **Nouveau Riche (IRE)**[17] 4195 3-9-4 **77** .......... SDrowne 3 80
(HMorrison) *lw: led: rdn over 2f out: hdd appr fnl f: one pce ins last* **7/4**[2]

0-40 **3** *2 1/2* **Enford Princess**[26] 3943 3-9-12 **85** .......... JFortune 1 83
(RHannon) *chsd ldrs: rdn over 2f out: swtchd rt fnl f and kpt on same pce* **8/1**[3]

1662 **4** *2* **Red Sahara (IRE)**[31] 3807 3-9-7 **80** .......... LDettori 5 73
(WJHaggas) *hld up rr but in tch: hdwy on outside to chse ldrs 3f out: rdn over 2f out: no imp and wknd over 1f out* **5/4**[1]

10-0 **5** *1* **Betty Stogs (IRE)**[124] 1327 3-9-8 **84** .......... LPKeniry(3) 4 75
(DRCElsworth) *trckd ldrs: n.m.r 4f out: rdn and effrt over 2f out: wknd appr fnl f* **20/1**

1m 44.98s (2.01) **Going Correction** +0.10s/f (Good)

**WFA** 3 from 4yo+ 7lb **5** Ran SP% **107.8**

Speed ratings: **93,91,89,87,86**CSF £21.55 TOTE £7.10: £2.60, £1.60; EX 22.70.

**Owner** Eddie Tynan **Bred** E Tynan **Trained** Upper Lambourn, Berks

**FOCUS**

Just the five runners, but possibly reasonable form. The time was very modest for the grade and all the runners raced towards the stands' side.

**NOTEBOOK**

**Zweibrucken(IRE)** had been quite highly tried on her two previous runs this season and this drop in grade clearly suited. It is also worth noting this is just the second time she has raced on ground with soft in the description - she won on her only previous try on it - and she must be respected when faced with similar conditions.

**Nouveau Riche(IRE)**, off the mark in a Windsor maiden on her previous start, found this tougher but acquitted herself with credit in pulling clear of the remainder. This is her sort of level and she should continue to go well.

**Enford Princess**, 5lb lower than at the beginning of the season and dropped in grade, ran respectably but will need to go on again to get her head in front.

**Red Sahara(IRE)** proved unable to build on the promise she showed when upped to this trip at Windsor on her previous start and was a little disappointing.

**Betty Stogs(IRE)** again failed to prove her effectiveness on this sort of ground.

## 4685 TOTESPORT SOVEREIGN STKS (GROUP 3) (C&G) 1m

**4:15** (4:16) (A ) 3-Y-0+ **£34,800** (£13,200; £6,600; £3,000) **Stalls** High

Form RPR

3044 **1** **Norse Dancer (IRE)**[15] 4228 4-9-0 115 .......... JFEgan 12 116
(DRCElsworth) *lw: bhd: pushed along 4f out: hdwy on outside fr 3f out: chsd ldrs 1f out: str run ins last: carried rt and led last stride* **3/1**[2]

111- **2** *shd* **Lucky Story (USA)**[335] 4863 3-8-7 118 .......... DHolland 9 116
(MJohnston) *in tch:nudged along 4f out:hdwy over 2f out: drvn to ld 1f out edgd lft u.p ins last: edgd rt and hdd last strides* **9/2**[3]

5030 **3** *2* **Hurricane Alan (IRE)**[15] 4228 4-9-5 114 .......... PDobbs 2 117
(RHannon) *trckd ldrs: rdn over 2f out: swtchd rt 1f out: kpt on wl fnl f but nt pce of ldrs* **25/1**

0-10 **4** *shd* **Passing Glance**[15] 4228 5-9-5 118 .......... MartinDwyer 7 117
(AMBalding) *lw: sn led: rdn and styd on whn chal fr 2f out: hdd 1f out: one pce whn n.m.r ins last* **12/1**

1121 **5** *1* **Shot To Fame (USA)**[33] 3724 5-9-3 111 .......... JPMurtagh 11 113
(PWHarris) *chsd ldrs: hrd drvn to chal fr 2f out: stl ev ch over 1f out: wknd ins last* **12/1**

1100 **6** *1/2* **Autumn Glory (IRE)**[19] 4120 4-9-0 102 .......... SDrowne 1 109
(GWragg) *lw: chsd ldrs: rdn over 2f out: styd on same pce* **16/1**

1104 **7** *1* **African Dream**[29] 3863 3-8-10 112 .......... JQuinn 3 110
(PWChapple-Hyam) *trckd ldrs: rdn over 2f out: no imp over 1f out: wknd ins last* **16/1**

221 **8** *3/4* **Ancient World (USA)**[13] 4287 4-9-0 110 .......... LDettori 8 105
(SaeedBinSuroor) *hld up in rr: hdwy on outside fr 3f out: effrt over 2f out: nvr gng pce to ldrs and wknd appr fnl f* **5/2**[1]

1401 **9** *nk* **Pentecost**[5] 4528 5-9-0 100 .......... LPKeniry 4 104
(AMBalding) *hld up mid-div: rdn and effrt over 2f out: wknd fnl f* **16/1**

1006 **10** *6* **Tout Seul (IRE)**[25] 3967 4-9-0 107 .......... SCarson 6 92
(RFJohnsonHoughton) *in tch early: rdn and bhd fnl 4f* **33/1**

0403 **11** *hd* **Sublimity (FR)**[12] 4341 4-9-0 108 .......... (t) JFortune 10 91
(SirMichaelStoute) *s.i.s: rdn 1/2-way: a in rr* **40/1**

0066 **12** *3 1/2* **Lago D'Orta (IRE)**[26] 3937 4-9-0 100 .......... DaneO'Neill 5 84
(CGCox) *a in rr* **50/1**

1m 41.63s (-1.34) **Going Correction** +0.10s/f (Good)

**WFA** 3 from 4yo+ 7lb **12** Ran SP% **116.0**

Speed ratings: **110,109,107,107,106 106,105,104,104,98 98,94**CSF £15.96 TOTE £4.10: £1.40, £2.30, £4.10; EX 17.90 Trifecta £370.10 Pool of £6,443.14 - 12.36 winning units..

**Owner** J C Smith **Bred** Ralph Ergnist And Bruno Faust **Trained** Whitsbury, Hants

■ Stewards Enquiry : D Holland caution: careless riding

**FOCUS**

A classy field for this Group Three and a good result form-wise, with Norse Dancer and Lucky Story, both proven at a higher level, dominating the finish. The pace was reasonable, and sound without being really strong, and the time was only ordinary for the grade. All the runners raced towards the stands'-side rail.

**NOTEBOOK**

**Norse Dancer(IRE)** has proved most frustrating at the top level both this season and last, showing on more than one occasion he has the ability to win a Group One but continually finding a few too good. However, with the blinkers left off, this drop in grade was just what he needed and he did enough to end a losing run stretching back to his juvenile days. This could have boosted his confidence and a horse of his ability deserves to be racing at the highest level, but this win does not erase the memory of previous defeats in top races and he still has it to prove. Connections were eyeing a quick reappearance in the International Stakes at York.

**Lucky Story(USA)**, twice a Group winner last season, including when beating subsequent Guineas winner Haafhd into third in the Champagne Stakes on his last outing, had his reappearance delayed through injury but looked big and well in the paddock. In the race itself, he made a most pleasing return, only just failing to get the better of a consistent Group One performer. The Queen Elizabeth II Stakes at Ascot could be the plan, and he must be a leading player in that given normal improvement.

**Hurricane Alan(IRE)** found this easier than the Group One Sussex Stakes he contested on his previous outing and ran creditably - the front two are simply better horses.

**Passing Glance** was successful in this race last year, but it has since been given Group Three status and he found this year's renewal tougher.

**Shot To Fame(USA)** has improved significantly this season and landed a Group Three at Ascot on his previous start, but he was just held under his penalty.

**African Dream**, dropped back from ten furlongs, ran better than his finishing position suggests, for he got stuck in behind horses and could not quite get in the clear when looking for a run. He is not one to give up on just yet.

**Ancient World(USA)** was always going to find this tougher than the handicap (albeit ultra competitive) he won at Goodwood on his previous start, but did not look as well in the paddock as he did last time and was below form. *Official explanation: jockey said gelding was unsuited by the good to soft ground*

**Sublimity(FR)** got warm beforehand, but he has been worse.

## 4686 MATTHEW CLARK H'CAP 1m 6f 15y

**4:50** (4:50) (E) (0-70,69) 3-Y-0+ **£3,867** (£1,190; £595; £297) **Stalls** Far side

Form RPR

1650 **1** **Zalda**[19] 4146 3-8-6 **61** .......... (v[1]) SDrowne 6 73
(RCharlton) *sn chsng ldr: led 3f out: sn rdn: narrowly hdd last half f: rallied to ld again last stride* **11/1**

5602 **2** *shd* **Tilla**[6] 4512 4-9-10 **66** .......... JPMurtagh 10 78
(HMorrison) *hld up in rr:hdwy 4f out:chsd wnr ins fnl 2f:rdn to take slt advantage last half f: hdd and no ex last stride* **5/2**[1]

3640 **3** *7* **Typhoon Tilly**[124] 1329 7-9-13 **69** .......... LDettori 9 71
(CREgerton) *lw: slowly away: bhd: hdwy fr 3f out: chsd ldrs fr 2f out but nvr gng pce to rch ldrs* **7/2**[2]

1242 **4** *1 3/4* **Compton Eclaire (IRE)**[19] 4129 4-9-5 **61** .......... (v) JFortune 1 61
(GAButler) *hld up in rr: hdwy on outside and hung rt 3f out: nvr gng pce to rch ldrs: edgd lft 1f out* **5/1**[3]

45-6 **5** 1 **Javelin**[41] 3492 8-8-7 **49**....................(p) TEDurcan 7 47
(IanWilliams) *chsd ldrs: rdn fr 4f out: lost pl 3f out: edgd rt and styd on again appr fnl f but nvr a danger* **20/1**

1260 **6** 6 **Red Sun**[49] 3236 7-9-4 **60**....................(t) WSupple 4 50
(JMackie) *led to 3f out: wknd fr 2f out* **9/1**

-203 **7** 4 **Resonance**[127] 1297 3-8-9 **64**.................... VSlattery 5 48
(NATwiston-Davies) *in tch: rdn and hdwy 4f out: wknd fr 3f out* **7/1**

6230 **8** 1 3/4 **Giko**[32] 3776 10-7-13 **41** oh3 ow1.................... MHenry 11 23
(JaneSouthcombe) *chsd ldrs: rdn 4f out: wknd 2f out: no ch whn hmpd 1f out* **25/1**

500/ **9** 20 **Kwaheri**[15] 3874 6-8-3 **45**.................... NPollard 3 —
(MrsPNDutfield) *in tch: rdn 5f out: sn wknd* **66/1**

6-00 **10** 1 **Vin Du Pays**[27] 3909 4-8-8 **50**.................... IMongan 2 3
(MBlanshard) *chsd ldrs: rdn: wknd and rdr dropped whip over 3f out* **33/1**

3m 6.83s (0.83) **Going Correction** +0.10s/f (Good)
**WFA** 3 from 4yo+ 13lb **10** Ran SP% **111.3**
Speed ratings: **101,100,96,95,95 91,89,88,77,76**CSF £35.65 CT £114.79 TOTE £9.40: £2.40, £1.40, £1.50; EX 35.20.
**Owner** D J Deer **Bred** D J And Mrs Deer **Trained** Beckhampton, Wilts

**FOCUS**
Just a modest staying handicap in which the front two pulled clear and resulting in fair form for the grade.

**NOTEBOOK**
**Zalda** was reluctant to race when beaten a mile here on her previous start so full credit must go to connections for sweetening her up, and the fitting of a visor clearly had a very positive effect. She looked beaten when challenged by Tilla, but she battled back particularly gamely. If the headgear continues to have a positive effect, she looks up to winning more races.
**Tilla** came to win her race and very nearly managed it, she just had no answer to Zalda's late thrust. Well clear of the remainder, she should soon be winning.
**Typhoon Tilly** had been off the track for 124 days but looked fit enough. He was simply unable to quicken out of this ground and is better suited to a decent surface.
**Compton Eclaire(IRE)**, 9lb higher than when runner-up on Polytrack on her previous start, failed to prove her effectiveness with cut in the ground but is better treated on the All-Weather in any case.
**Javelin**, in declared cheekpieces for the first time, was never really a threat when it mattered but he did look as though the run would do him good.

## 4687 AXMINSTER CARPETS APPRENTICE H'CAP 6f

**5:20** (5:21) (E) (0-80,77) 3-Y-O+ **£3,627** (£1,116; £558; £279) **Stalls** High

Form RPR

00 **1** **Mimic**[6] 4522 4-8-4 **63**.................... RMills(10) 12 76
(RGuest) *racd far side and led sole opponent that side: a up w pce stands side: def ld 1f out: rdn and hld on ins last* **14/1**

3005 **2** 3/4 **Currency**[8] 4459 7-9-3 **74**.................... CJDavies(8) 5 85
(JMBradley) *b: racd stands side: in tch:led that gp and chal for overall ld over 1f out: kpt on but nt pce of wnr far side ins fnl f* **8/1**

0606 **3** 1 3/4 **Nivernais**[11] 4366 5-9-0 **71**.................... CCavanagh(8) 6 77
(HCandy) *racd stands side: led that gp tl hdd over 1f out: styd on same pce* **3/1**[1]

0005 **4** shd **B A Highflyer**[10] 4403 4-8-1 **58**.................... BO'Neill(8) 9 63
(MRChannon) *in tch: hdwy centre crse 2f out: hung rt to far side over 1f out: styd on same pce ins last* **11/2**[3]

0000 **5** hd **Gaelic Princess**[19] 4122 4-9-11 **77**.................... LTreadwell(3) 4 82
(AGNewcombe) *racd stands side: wnt lft 4f out: rdn 3f out: r.o fr over 1f out but nt pce to rch ldrs* **7/1**

5000 **6** 2 **Tappit (IRE)**[5] 4548 5-7-7 **47** oh1.................... KJackson(5) 15 46
(NEBerry) *racd far side: chsd wnr tl wknd wl over 1f out* **33/1**

5002 **7** 1/2 **Hand Chime**[8] 4462 7-8-13 **72**.................... DanielleDeverson(10) 3 69
(WJHaggas) *racd stands side: bhd: sme hdwy fr over 1f out: nvr nr ldrs* **5/1**[2]

0050 **8** 2 **Bennanabaa**[2] 4617 5-7-7 **47** oh1....................(t) DonnaCaldwell(5) 8 38
(SCBurrough) *racd stands side: pressed ldrs over 4f* **50/1**

0030 **9** 1/2 **Torquemada (IRE)**[22] 4026 3-8-1 **59**.................... DeanWilliams(5) 10 49
(WJarvis) *racd stands side: pressed ldrs 4f: wknd over 1f out* **10/1**

0600 **10** 2 **Indian Bazaar (IRE)**[12] 4336 8-7-9 **49**....................(p) MHalford(5) 1 33
(NEBerry) *racd stands side: chsd ldrs over 3f* **33/1**

0050 **11** nk **Fulvio (USA)**[3] 4602 4-7-13 **53**....................(v) LiamJones(5) 13 36
(JamiePoulton) *racd stands side: sn outpcd* **33/1**

000- **12** shd **Fly More**[279] 5941 7-9-13 **76**.................... NChalmers 14 58
(JMBradley) *bit bkwd: racd towards stands side: bhd: sme hdwy in centre crse over 2f out: sn wknd* **20/1**

0460 **13** 3 **Nebraska City**[12] 4336 3-7-13 **52**....................(v) AMedeiros 7 25
(BGubby) *racd stands side: a bhd* **50/1**

-060 **14** 1 1/2 **Golden Bounty**[43] 3416 5-8-9 **68**.................... WBurton(10) 11 37
(RHannon) *lw: racd stands side: pressed ldrs 4f* **16/1**

0000 **15** 5 **Awarding**[19] 4145 4-8-6 **63**....................(bt[1]) LucyRussell(8) 2 17
(DrJRJNaylor) *racd stands side: hmpd 4f out: sn lost tch* **25/1**

1m 15.8s (0.86) **Going Correction** +0.10s/f (Good)
**WFA** 3 from 4yo+ 4lb **15** Ran SP% **123.7**
Speed ratings: **98,97,93,90,87 87,87,87,87,87 87,87,87,87,87**CSF £116.47 CT £444.92 TOTE £16.50: £3.30, £3.90, £1.60; EX 158.80 Place 6 £94.34, Place 5 £24.54.
**Owner** C J Mills **Bred** W H Joyce **Trained** Newmarket, Suffolk
■ Stewards Enquiry : L Treadwell one-day ban: careless riding (Aug 23)

**FOCUS**
A modest sprint handicap and messy form. Only two horses raced against the far side from the start, but that pair included the winner.

**NOTEBOOK**
**Mimic** was one of just two runners who raced over the far side from the start and the tactics worked a treat. Her three previous wins came on fast ground, but she handled this softer surface well. She would avoid a penalty if turned out before she is reassessed, but should not go up much in any case and can remain competitive in similar company.
**Currency** had the headgear left off this time and posted a really good effort for a horse who has gained all of his previous wins on good to firm or faster, winning his race on the stands' side. He has not won for well over a year, but is on a fair mark and looks up to taking a similar event.
**Nivernais** did not look to have any excuses but is simply proving hard to win with this season.
**B A Highflyer**, 1lb lower than when last successful, had conditions in his favour and would have been closer but for hanging from the stands' side to the far side under pressure.
**Gaelic Princess** ran well on ground that may have been a little softer than ideal.
**Hand Chime** should not have been inconvenienced by the ground but was below form and has to be considered disappointing.
**Fly More** looked as though the run would do him good.
**Awarding** *Official explanation: jockey said gelding had a breathing problem*
T/Jkpt: Not won. T/Plt: £82.30 to a £1 stake. Pool: £46,156.35. 409.40 winning tickets. T/Qpdt: £11.20 to a £1 stake. Pool: £3,600.10. 236.85 winning tickets. ST

# 4643 SANDOWN (R-H)

Thursday, August 12

**OFFICIAL GOING: Good to soft**
With the ground softening, the vast majority of the runners came over to the stands' side in the home straight.
Wind: lt across Weather: heavy rain before meeting and after race 1

## 4688 SHARP MINDS BETFAIR H'CAP 5f 6y

**2:20** (2:25) (D) (0-85,84) 3-Y-O **£6,841** (£2,105; £1,052; £526) **Stalls** High

Form RPR

6240 **1** **Rydal (USA)**[13] 4289 3-9-6 **83**....................(v[1]) SWKelly 8 91
(GAButler) *hld up in cl tch: eased out to chse ldr ovedr 1f out: hrd rdn and r.o to ld last stride* **9/2**[3]

5612 **2** shd **Catch The Wind**[13] 4299 3-9-3 **80**....................(p) SSanders 6 88
(IAWood) *mde most: hrd rdn fnl f: hdd last stride* **9/1**

0360 **3** 1 1/4 **Divine Spirit**[13] 4289 3-9-7 **84**.................... RWinston 7 88
(MDods) *lw: hld up bhd ldrs: n.m.r over 1f out: chsd ldng pair fnl f: styd on* **7/2**[2]

1242 **4** 3/4 **Short Chorus**[12] 4320 3-7-12 **61** oh7....................(p) JBramhill 5 62
(JBalding) *settled in last pair: effrt on outer wl over 1f out: styd on fnl f: unable to chal* **12/1**

1141 **5** 2 **Ivory Lace**[70] 2610 3-9-0 **77**.................... DSweeney 1 71
(SWoodman) *stdd s: hld up in last: effrt over 1f out: one pce and nvr rchd ldrs* **14/1**

1032 **6** 2 1/2 **Treasure Cay**[13] 4289 3-9-5 **82**....................(t) KFallon 4 67
(PWD'Arcy) *t.k.h: hld up bhd ldrs: rdn 2f out: wknd fnl f* **2/1**[1]

0000 **7** 1/2 **Dolce Piccata**[13] 4289 3-8-8 **74**....................(b) JFMcDonald(3) 3 57
(BJMeehan) *w ldr to wl over 1f out: wknd u.p fnl f* **12/1**

1000 **8** 7 **Kabreet**[21] 4051 3-8-11 **74**....................(v[1]) EAhern 2 32
(EALDunlop) *lw: racd on outer: chsd ldrs to 2f out: wknd* **12/1**

63.15 secs (0.96) **Going Correction** +0.25s/f (Good) **8** Ran SP% **113.5**
Speed ratings: **102,101,99,98,95 91,90,79**CSF £43.22 CT £143.27 TOTE £5.80: £1.60, £2.20, £1.80; EX 51.70.
**Owner** Mr & Mrs G Middlebrook **Bred** Gary And Mrs Middlebrook **Trained** Blewbury, Oxon
■ Stewards Enquiry : S W Kelly two-day ban: careless riding (Aug 23,24)

**FOCUS**
A fair handicap run at only an ordinary pace. The draw played its part with the four highest stalls beating the four lowest, nevertheless the form looks sound.

**NOTEBOOK**
**Rydal(USA)**, with the plum draw, travelled very well just behind the leaders but rather had to ease the eventual third out of the way in order to get a run. Once in the clear, he did seem to hang fire for a few strides but managed to put in a late thrust which took him to the front right on the line. This stiff five on rain-softened ground appeared to suit.
**Catch The Wind** could probably have done without the rain and had a 7lb rise to contend with, but she very much had the run of the race out in front and was unluckily denied right on the post.
**Divine Spirit**, another who could have done with the ground remaining fast, was still in there battling away when the winner gave him a nudge over a furlong from home and he could never make much impression after that. The interference may have cost him a little impetus, but not enough for his final placing to have been affected.
**Short Chorus** ◆, with being 7lb out of the handicap, was racing off a stone higher mark than for her last win. She was finishing in good style and this was a most commendable effort, but the Handicapper will have noticed so it would probably be wise to get her out again quickly.
**Ivory Lace**, switched over from her wide draw, trailed the field for most of the way and could never land a blow.
**Treasure Cay**, raised another 3lb for his Goodwood effort, pulled far too hard to give himself any chance of lasting home.
**Kabreet** *Official explanation: jockey said colt was unsuited by the ground*

## 4689 E B F MANSELL PLC & RUDDLE WILKINSON ARCHITECTS MAIDEN STKS 1m 14y

**2:50** (2:58) (D) 2-Y-O **£5,512** (£1,696; £848; £424) **Stalls** High

Form RPR

00 **1** **Velvet Heights (IRE)**[22] 4030 2-9-0 .................... GCarter 2 81
(JLDunlop) *lw: prom: c wd in home st and wl on terms: def advantage ins fnl f: r.o wl* **33/1**

43 **2** 2 **Kharish (IRE)**[18] 4169 2-9-0 .................... EAhern 1 77
(JNoseda) *prom: led 3f out: rdn over 1f out: hdd ins fnl f: no ex* **11/4**[1]

6 **3** 1 3/4 **Kingsholm**[22] 4030 2-9-0 .................... KFallon 8 73
(AMBalding) *chsd ldr to 1/2-way: lost pl: rdn over 2f out: kpt on fr over 1f out* **10/3**[2]

6 **4** 1 **William Tell (IRE)**[26] 3939 2-8-11 .................... SHitchcott(3) 3 71
(MRChannon) *towards rr: rdn 3f out: kpt on fnl 2f: nvr able to chal* **50/1**

**5** nk **Majestic Movement (USA)** 2-9-0 .................... RHavlin 4 70
(JHMGosden) *bit bkwd: cmpt: str: scope: cl up: chsd ldr over 2f out: no imp over 1f out: fdd fnl f* **25/1**

**6** 2 1/2 **Figaro's Quest (IRE)** 2-9-0 .................... JFanning 9 65
(PFICole) *str: bit bkwd: sn struggling in last: wl bhd 1/2-way: c wd in st: kpt on fnl 2f* **16/1**

22 **7** shd **Chapter (IRE)**[49] 3241 2-9-0 .................... RLMoore 10 65
(RHannon) *trckd ldrs: rdn 3f out: effrt 2f out: one pce and no imp over 1f out* **11/2**

0 **8** shd **Asaateel (IRE)**[26] 3931 2-9-0 .................... MHills 7 65
(JLDunlop) *bit bkwd: settled wl in rr: shuffled along and sme prog 2f out: no hdwy after* **16/1**

4 **9** 7 **Creative Character (USA)**[26] 3931 2-8-9 .................... NDeSouza(5) 11 50
(PFICole) *lw: led to 3f out: wknd 2f out* **16/1**

40 **10** 5 **Art Legend**[89] 2111 2-9-0 .................... SSanders 6 39
(DRCElsworth) *stdd s: plld hrd and hld up: hanging and nt look keen over 2f out: sn no ch* **33/1**

4 **11** dist **Dahman**[18] 4169 2-9-0 .................... KMcEvoy 12 —
(SaeedBinSuroor) *trckd ldrs tl wknd rapidly over 2f out: t.o* **7/2**[3]

1m 47.74s (3.82) **Going Correction** +0.10s/f (Good) **11** Ran SP% **116.7**
Speed ratings: **84,82,80,79,78 76,76,76,69,64** —CSF £119.26 TOTE £42.20: £9.20, £1.30, £1.80; EX 244.20.
**Owner** Windflower Overseas Holdings Inc **Bred** Windflower Overseas **Trained** Arundel, W Sussex

**FOCUS**
A very modest time for the grade, but several of these are bred for stamina and probably need more time. The winner was the only one to race down the stands' side in the home straight, and that set the trend for the rest of the afternoon.

**NOTEBOOK**

**Velvet Heights(IRE)**, who showed little in two previous starts, improved no end for the extra furlong and more testing conditions, but being the only one brought over to the stands' side in the home straight that effectively won him the race. The slow time sounds a note of caution, but being out of a two-mile winner he is entitled to carry on improving as he develops.

**Kharish(IRE)**, up in trip and racing on easier ground, came to win his race at just the right time and the only thing he did wrong was stay on the far side whilst the winner did a solo wide. He should have an ordinary maiden in him, but does qualify for a nursery mark now.

**Kingsholm** was well supported in the ring, but despite having every chance looked rather one paced in the latter stages. His stamina gives mixed signals over his ideal trip, but he is beginning to look more of a stayer.

**William Tell(IRE)** was a bit more gathered than he was on his debut, but ran as though he would appreciate an even greater test of stamina than this.

**Majestic Movement(USA)**, out of a half-sister to Ramruma, showed some ability and did best of the newcomers. He can be expected to come on a lot for this.

**Figaro's Quest(IRE)**, a half-brother to Saddler's Quest and Seren Hill, is bred to need middle distances in time and ran accordingly.

**Chapter(IRE)** does not seem to be progressing, though this was his first attempt on easy ground.

**Dahman** suddenly dropped out with two furlongs to run as though something was amiss. *Official explanation: jockey said colt lost its action in the good to soft ground*

## 4690 RECTANGLE GROUP H'CAP — 7f 16y

**3:25** (3:29) (C ) (0-90,90) 3-Y-0+ — **£10,634** (£3,272; £1,636; £818) **Stalls** High

Form — RPR

-530 **1** **Presumptive (IRE)**[37] 3597 4-9-1 **77** ........ KFallon 2 — 89+
(RCharlton) *settled in rr: plenty to do 3f out: prog over 2f out: clsd to ld last 75yds: drvn out* — **2/1**[1]

6324 **2** *1* **Spirit's Awakening**[19] 4122 5-7-12 **60** oh2 ........ JMackay 6 — 69
(JAkehurst) *lw: chsd clr ldr: clsd 2f out: led ent fnl f: hdd and outpcd last 75yds* — **13/2**[2]

0400 **3** *1* **Norton (IRE)**[50] 3212 7-9-11 **90** ........ RMiles(3) 3 — 96
(TGMills) *chsd ldng pair: rdn to cl 2f out: chal 1f out: kpt on same pce* — **13/2**[2]

1065 **4** *3/4* **Lifted Way**[18] 4164 5-9-2 **78** ........ JFanning 7 — 82
(PRChamings) *led and sn clr: 5l up 3f out: grad c bk to rivals: hdd and one pce 1f out* — **7/1**[3]

6600 **5** *1 1/2* **Binanti**[19] 4120 4-9-9 **85** ........ EAhern 1 — 86
(PRChamings) *racd wd thrght: hld up in last: effrt over 2f out: kpt on: n.d* — **12/1**

0013 **6** *shd* **Will He Wish**[8] 4442 8-9-13 **89** ........ (b) SWKelly 9 — 89
(SGollings) *lw: chsd clr ldrs: rdn over 3f out: no real imp fr over 1f out* **8/1**

0420 **7** *1* **Blue Trojan (IRE)**[26] 3937 4-9-3 **86** ........ JDWalsh(7) 5 — 84
(SKirk) *racd in midfield: rdn over 2f out: no imp over 1f out: n.d after* **10/1**

2-52 **8** *2 1/2* **Point Of Dispute**[27] 3910 9-9-6 **82** ........ (v) SSanders 4 — 73
(PJMakin) *dwlt: hld up in last pair: rdn 2f out: no rspnse* — **7/1**[3]

1m 30.33s (-0.76) **Going Correction** +0.10s/f (Good) — **8** Ran SP% **112.9**

Speed ratings: **108,106,105,104,103 103,101,99**CSF £14.79 CT £70.18 TOTE £3.00: £1.40, £1.70, £2.10; EX 19.60.

**Owner** Ecurie Pharos **Bred** Dr T A Ryan **Trained** Beckhampton, Wilts

**FOCUS**

A race run at a true gallop and the whole field came over to the stands' side in the home straight. The form is fair but not outstanding for the grade.

**NOTEBOOK**

**Presumptive(IRE)** finally rewarded his connections' patience having been well backed. He came from a long way back to get on top in the closing stages, but also gave the impression that even at his age there is still a bit of improvement in him.

**Spirit's Awakening** has form on soft ground and looked to have hit the front at just the right time, but frustratingly again found one to come and beat him. His consistency means he gets no help from the Handicapper.

**Norton(IRE)** has dropped to a 1lb lower mark than when winning the 2002 Hunt Cup and ran much better without the visor. There should be a similar contest in him.

**Lifted Way**, who goes in the ground, was quickly sent into a clear lead, and the fact that he stayed in there fighting for so long and was not beaten far earns him credit.

**Binanti**, kept wide of his field from the stalls, never landed a blow but he has become well handicapped and is better on faster ground.

**Will He Wish**, returning to probably his best trip, was another whose best form is on faster ground and he was in trouble some way out.

## 4691 SHARP MINDS BETFAIR CLASSIFIED STKS — 1m 1f

**4:00** (4:00) (D ) 3-Y-0+ — **£6,841** (£2,105; £1,052; £526) **Stalls** High

Form — RPR

-244 **1** **Strider**[26] 3952 3-8-10 **76** ........ KFallon 8 — 84
(SirMichaelStoute) *prom: shkn up 3f out: clsd on ldr 1f out: hrd drvn to ld last 100yds: hung lft: hld on* — **7/1**[3]

5005 **2** *nk* **Ryan's Future (IRE)**[15] 4237 4-9-0 **74** ........ SHitchcott(3) 2 — 82
(JAkehurst) *dwlt: racd in last pair: rdn over 3f out: prog 2f out: styd on wl fnl f: jst failed* — **25/1**

31-2 **3** *shd* **Straw Bear (USA)**[22] 4032 3-8-11 **77** ........ SSanders 9 — 84
(SirMarkPrescott) *lw: trckd ldrs: rdn over 2f out: clsd and ch 1f out: nt qckn u.p* — **1/1**[1]

600 **4** *3/4* **Cello**[56] 3001 3-8-12 **78** ........ (t) RLMoore 6 — 84
(RHannon) *hld up in midfield: prog to ld over 2f out: 2l clr over 1f out: hdd & wknd last 100yds* — **5/1**[2]

4034 **5** *1/2* **Katiypour (IRE)**[8] 4435 7-9-3 **75** ........ LisaJones 5 — 80
(MissBSanders) *hld up in rr: shuffled along 2f out: no imp ldrs over 1f out: styd on ins fnl f* — **12/1**

1545 **6** *1* **Ben Hur**[11] 4363 5-9-3 **75** ........ SWKelly 10 — 78
(WMBrisbourne) *trckd ldr: led 1/2-way: rdn and hdd over 2f out: one pce u.p* — **25/1**

5015 **7** *5* **Malibu (IRE)**[14] 4266 3-8-12 **78** ........ EAhern 3 — 71
(SDow) *a in rr: rdn and no prog 3f out* — **33/1**

221- **8** *2 1/2* **Electrique (IRE)**[186] 4756 4-9-5 **80** ........ LFletcher(3) 7 — 68
(JAOsborne) *lw: chsd ldrs: rdn 3f out: wknd 2f out* — **40/1**

032 **9** *17* **Arctic Silk**[18] 4168 3-8-8 **77** ........ (t) KMcEvoy 1 — 28
(SaeedBinSuroor) *lw: led to 1/2-way: wknd over 2f out: t.o* — **7/1**[3]

1m 57.34s (1.23) **Going Correction** +0.10s/f (Good)

**WFA** 3 from 4yo+ 8lb — **9** Ran SP% **112.4**

Speed ratings: **98,97,97,96,96 95,91,88,73**CSF £158.30 TOTE £8.90: £2.00, £4.70, £1.20; EX 220.30.

**Owner** Cheveley Park Stud **Bred** Arnfin Lund And John James **Trained** Newmarket, Suffolk

**FOCUS**

A rather messy affair and a modest time for the grade, but the form looks fairly sound on paper. Again the whole field raced wide up the straight.

**NOTEBOOK**

**Strider** had started to look disappointing, but managed to pull what had looked a lost cause out of the fire under a power-packed ride despite hanging badly left in the closing stages. The way this race was run raises questions over the value of the form though, and he will be fortunate to find another opportunity like this.

**Ryan's Future(IRE)** ◆ has dropped to a reasonable mark and came from off the pace to finish a very close second despite the ground probably being softer than ideal. He seems to be returning to form.

**Straw Bear(USA)** may have started so short in the market because of connections and though he was not beaten far, he had every chance and did not really step up on his reappearance.

**Cello**, very well backed, seemed likely to land the gamble when coming through on the stands' side to hit the front halfway up the straight, but no sooner had he got there then he started to hang right under pressure and basically threw it away. He has plenty of questions to answer now.

**Katiypour(IRE)** was coming home well enough on ground that would have been softer than ideal.

**Malibu(IRE)** *Official explanation: jockey said gelding was unsuited by the good to soft ground*

**Arctic Silk**, making her handicap debut, ran a shocker.

## 4692 DAVERT BANKS H'CAP — 1m 6f

**4:35** (4:35) (D ) (0-80,80) 3-Y-0 — **£7,003** (£2,155; £1,077; £538) **Stalls** Centre

Form — RPR

0220 **1** **Levitator**[21] 4062 3-8-9 **68** ........ KFallon 1 — 80
(SirMichaelStoute) *hld up: wnt prom 10f out: chsd ldr over 2f out: rdn to ld over 1f out: 1l up ins fnl f: all out* — **7/2**[2]

000 **2** *shd* **Sharadi (IRE)**[12] 4346 3-8-0 **59** ........ JoannaBadger 6 — 71
(VSmith) *lw: cl up: led 5f out: rdn and hdd over 1f out: kpt on wl again ins fnl f: jst failed* — **20/1**

6126 **3** *5* **Winslow Boy (USA)**[19] 4146 3-8-1 **60** ........ LisaJones 3 — 65
(CFWall) *dwlt: hld up in rr: prog but outpcd over 2f out: kpt on one pce to take 3rd fnl f* — **5/1**[3]

5 **4** *2* **Fire Dragon (IRE)**[13] 3292 3-9-7 **80** ........ (p) FMBerry 9 — 82
(JonjoO'Neill) *cl up: led 7f out to 5f out: ev ch over 2f out: hung lft and rt: fnd nil* — **7/1**

3326 **5** *5* **Vicario**[29] 3837 3-8-4 **63** ........ JMackay 8 — 58
(MLWBell) *in tch: rdn 5f out: sn bhd and struggling* — **12/1**

2102 **6** *1 1/4* **Considine (USA)**[21] 4062 3-8-13 **72** ........ KMcEvoy 5 — 65
(JMPEustace) *lw: led after 3f and stdd the pce: hdd 7f out: rdn over 4f out: wknd over 2f out* — **5/2**[1]

1-23 **7** *3* **Seeking A Way (USA)**[19] 4141 3-8-11 **70** ........ RHavlin 7 — 59
(JHMGosden) *trckd ldrs: lost tch over 4f out: rdn and no ch 3f out* **16/1**

2645 **8** *6* **Absolutelythebest (IRE)**[31] 3806 3-9-7 **80** ........ EAhern 10 — 61
(EALDunlop) *lw: led for 3f: cl up after: 5th and rdn whn styd far side in st : sn no ch* — **10/1**

0555 **9** *16* **Chara**[12] 4346 3-8-2 **64** ........ JFMcDonald(3) 2 — 22
(JRJenkins) *hld up in rr: lost tch and rdn 5f out: wknd 3f out: t.o* — **10/1**

3m 6.09s (1.72) **Going Correction** +0.10s/f (Good) — **9** Ran SP% **116.5**

Speed ratings: **99,98,96,94,92 91,89,86,77**CSF £69.96 CT £352.08 TOTE £4.80: £1.60, £4.60, £2.30; EX 88.30.

**Owner** K Abdulla **Bred** Juddmonte Farms **Trained** Newmarket, Suffolk

**FOCUS**

A fair staying handicap run at an even pace and fair form for the grade. All but one of the field came over to the stands' side in the home straight and they finished well strung out.

**NOTEBOOK**

**Levitator** put his poor showing on this track last time behind him on this easier ground, but it was a close-run thing and the champion had to be at his strongest to get him home. He does not look anything special and it would be no surprise to see him snapped up by the jumping boys in the autumn.

**Sharadi(IRE)**, no closer than fourth in seven previous starts, is tumbling down the weights and ran by far his best race so far over this longer trip. Never far away, he kept on coming back when it looked as though he was going to drop away and very nearly snatched the verdict. A small staying handicap can be found.

**Winslow Boy(USA)** has shown his best form on faster ground and his effort was too little too late.

**Fire Dragon(IRE)**, back on the level after a victory over hurdles, had every chance but did not look all that happy over the last couple of furlongs. He looks to be on a stiff mark on what he has achieved on the Flat.

**Vicario** was struggling out the back rounding the home turn and only reached his final position because others did not get home.

**Considine(USA)** has decent form on soft ground, but was in trouble turning for home and this was disappointing.

**Absolutelythebest(IRE)** stayed alone on the far side after turning for home and it did not help. *Official explanation: jockey said colt was unsuited by the good to soft ground*

## 4693 ELMBRIDGE MAIDEN STKS — 1m 2f 7y

**5:10** (5:11) (D ) 3-Y-0 — **£5,395** (£1,660; £830; £415) **Stalls** High

Form — RPR

3262 **1** **Michabo (IRE)**[10] 4402 3-9-0 **78** ........ SSanders 5 — 79
(DRCElsworth) *mde all: rdn and jnd over 1f out: hanging rt sn after: kpt on to assert last 100yds* — **7/4**[2]

5 **2** *1 1/2* **Wait For Spring (USA)**[36] 3630 3-8-9 ........ KFallon 4 — 71
(JHMGosden) *lw: cl up: rdn to chal over 1f out: jnd wnr ent fnl f: flashed tail and fnd nil* — **4/5**[1]

04 **3** *1 3/4* **Niobe's Way**[18] 4168 3-8-9 ........ EAhern 2 — 68
(PRChamings) *lw: hld up in 4th: gng wl enough 2f out: reminder over 1f out: kpt on steadily* — **14/1**

6U5 **4** *1 1/2* **Kilindini**[24] 3994 3-9-0 ........ RHavlin 1 — 70
(MissECLavelle) *t.k.h early: hld up in last: rdn and unable qck 2f out: one pce after* — **40/1**

00 **5** *hd* **Charmed By Fire (USA)**[11] 4369 3-9-0 ........ JFanning 3 — 70
(MrsAJPerrett) *bit bkwd: s.i.s: sn trckd wnr: upsides and gng wl over 1f out : rdn and wknd tamely sn after* — **12/1**[3]

2m 13.57s (3.39) **Going Correction** +0.10s/f (Good) — **5** Ran SP% **108.7**

Speed ratings: **90,88,87,86,86**CSF £3.38 TOTE £2.80: £1.20, £1.10; EX 3.40 Place 6 £15.99, Place 5 £5.45.

**Owner** Mrs Michael Meredith **Bred** Gestut Gorlsdorf **Trained** Whitsbury, Hants

**FOCUS**

A modest pace early and it developed into a sprint up the home straight. The winning time was moderate for the grade and does not appear to be that solid. Once again the whole field came wide.

**NOTEBOOK**

**Michabo(IRE)** may have been the most exposed in the field, but had the form to win this. Given a patient ride in front, he looked in some trouble when things quickened up in the home straight, but saw his race out much more resolutely than his rivals. The victory was welcome, but further opportunities will not be easy to find.

**Wait For Spring(USA)**, on easier ground than on her debut, ranged alongside the leader coming to the last furlong, but the tail went when she was put under pressure and she did not fancy it.

**Niobe's Way** never landed a blow, but has more options now that she qualifies for handicaps.

**Kilindini** inclined to take a hold early, stayed in the race thanks to the modest early gallop but was found wanting when the pace quickened. Handicaps look a better option for him.



The Form Book, Raceform Ltd, Compton, RG20 6NL

**Charmed By Fire(USA)** seemed to be going the best of the quintet coming to the last furlong, but quickly went from one extreme to the other and has questions to answer.
T/Plt: £61.20 to a £1 stake. Pool: £53,129.75. 632.90 winning tickets. T/Qpdt: £19.30 to a £1 stake. Pool: £4,319.40. 164.80 winning tickets. JN

4697 - (Foreign Racing) - See Raceform Interactive

## 4420 CATTERICK (L-H)

Friday, August 13

**OFFICIAL GOING: Soft (heavy in places)**

The going did not seem as testing as the official version despite more than 4" rain and the meeting surviving a morning inspection.
Wind: Slight 1/2 against. Weather: Fine.

### 4698 I.R.M. AMATEUR RIDERS' H'CAP — 1m 3f 214y
6:00 (6:00) (F) (0-75,71) 3-Y-O+ — £2,996 (£856; £428) Stalls High

Form — RPR

1352 **1** **Romil Star (GER)**[49] 3281 7-9-7 **50**....(v) MissKellyBurke(7) 4 — 58
(KRBurke) *stmbld s: rr: hdwy 2f out: styd on strly fnl f: led cl home* **16/1**

-534 **2** ½ **Fort Churchill (IRE)**[19] 4170 3-10-3 **71**....(b[1]) MrSWarren(7) 12 — 78
(MHTompkins) *trckd ldrs: led wl over 1f out: styd on u.p: hdd cl home* **20/1**

1102 **3** hd **Pont Neuf (IRE)**[4] 4616 4-10-12 **65**....(t) MissKellyHarrison(3) 3 — 72
(PDEvans) *rr: hdwy on outer 2f out: styd on wl u.p fnl f: no ex clsng stages* **9/2[1]**

0260 **4** ½ **Late Arrival**[17] 4213 7-8-11 **40**.... MissWGibson(7) 14 — 46
(MDHammond) *towards rr: prog into midfield 1/2-way: hdwy to chse ldr appr fnl f: styd on: no ex ins last* **33/1**

2505 **5** 1½ **Bramantino (IRE)**[33] 3782 4-9-12 **53**....(b) MissVTunnicliffe(5) 6 — 57
(RAFahey) *rr: hdwy 2f out: styd on fnl f: nvr nrr* **10/1**

5651 **6** 5 **Final Dividend (IRE)**[8] 4467 8-9-10 **49** 5ex.... MissJoannaRees(3) 15 — 46
(JMPEustace) *chsd ldrs: outpcd and lost pl 4f out: styd on fnl 2f* **14/1**

3251 **7** nk **Platinum Charmer (IRE)**[10] 4423 4-10-7 **60** 5ex....(p) MrSDobson(3) 8 — 57
(KRBurke) *midfield: sme hdwy and in tch 2f out: no further prog* **8/1**

6 **8** ½ **Bushido (IRE)**[27] 3782 5-10-1 **56**.... MissFayeBramley(5) 7 — 52
(MrsSJSmith) *rr: styd on fnl 2f: n.d* **15/2[3]**

-004 **9** 1 **Eight (IRE)**[9] 4457 8-9-2 **45**.... MsTDzieciolowska(7) 16 — 40
(MRChannon) *midfield: effrt 3f out: no hdwy* **20/1**

6315 **10** shd **Dash Of Magic**[55] 3099 6-9-4 **40**.... MrsSBosley 11 — 35
(JHetherton) *slowly away: sn midfield: hdwy on outside to ld 3f out: c wd home st: rdn and hdd 2f out: sn wknd* **14/1**

0000 **11** 7 **Shalbeblue (IRE)**[17] 4213 7-9-3 **42**....(b) MissLEllison(3) 17 — 27
(BEllison) *cl up: led 1/2-way: hdd 3f out: slt loead again 2f out: sn hdd & wknd* **20/1**

-301 **12** hd **Mr Mischief**[161] 971 4-11-1 **70**.... MissAArmitage(5) 10 — 54
(PCHaslam) *led tl hdd 1/2-way: outpcd and lost pl 4f out* **9/1**

0600 **13** 1 **Imperial Royale (IRE)**[20] 4138 3-9-8 **60** ow5....(p) MrDWeekes(5) 9 — 43
(PLClinton) *midfield to 1/2-way: sn drvn along towards rr* **66/1**

5544 **14** nk **Appetina**[22] 4049 3-10-1 **62**.... MsCWilliams 5 — 45
(JGGiven) *midfield: hdwy to chse ldrs 4f out: wknd 2f out* **25/1**

0-60 **15** ¾ **Chapter House (USA)**[42] 3492 5-10-11 **68**.... MrOGreenall(7) 18 — 50
(MWEasterby) *prom tl wknd 3f out* **50/1**

4416 **16** 6 **Isa'Af (IRE)**[29] 3873 5-11-0 **69**.... MrsMarieKing(5) 2 — 42
(PWHiatt) *midfield tl wknd 4f out* **13/2[2]**

3060 **17** dist **Four Kings**[9] 4447 3-9-8 **60**....(t) MissJRiding(5) 13 — —
(RAllan) *bhd fr 1/2-way: t.o* **50/1**

2m 45.93s (6.93) **Going Correction** +0.525s/f (Yiel) — **17** Ran SP% **119.2**
**WFA** 3 from 4yo+ 11lb
Speed ratings: **97,96,96,96,95 91,91,91,90,90 85,85,85,84,84 80,**—CSF £306.34 CT £1686.93 TOTE £24.20: £4.20, £3.10, £1.20, £6.10; EX 355.70.
**Owner** Mrs Elaine M Burke **Bred** J H A Baggen **Trained** Middleham Moor, N Yorks
■ A winner on her first ride in public for Kelly Burke, daughter of the winning trainer.

**FOCUS**

A 0-71 amateur riders' handicap run at a furious early pace, but the overall time and the form are both modest.

**NOTEBOOK**

**Romil Star(GER)**, whose four previous wins in this country were on the All-Weather, has scored from a 16lb higher mark in the past. With just a couple behind him turning in, he made it without his rider ever picking up the stick.
**Fort Churchill(IRE)**, whose rider has yet to taste success, never left the inner. Under severe pressure he was picked off near the line. His rider should drop his leathers a couple of holes and rely less on the stick.
**Pont Neuf(IRE)**, put to sleep at the rear, made her effort on the wide outside and was only found lacking near the line. Both her wins have been at Windsor.
**Late Arrival**, who takes time to get going, ran one of his better races suited seemingly by the step up in distance and the softer ground.
**Bramantino(IRE)**, suited by the soft ground, stayed on from an impossible position.
**Appetina** *Official explanation: jockey said filly finished tired*

### 4699 ENTER TONIGHT'S RACECARD COMPETITION (S) STKS — 7f
6:30 (6:31) (G) 2-Y-O — £2,632 (£752; £376) Stalls Low

Form — RPR

5630 **1** **Dartanian**[4] 4601 2-8-11 58.... RWinston 7 — 56
(PDEvans) *w ldr: led over 2f out: styd on wl* **5/1[3]**

0040 **2** 3½ **Toldo (IRE)**[15] 4256 2-8-11 45.... FLynch 6 — 47
(ABerry) *hld up in rr: hdwy 1/2-way: rdn to chse wnr ent fnl f: kpt on: no imp* **33/1**

0402 **3** ½ **Lakesdale (IRE)**[7] 4521 2-8-3 60.... NMackay(3) 10 — 41
(MrsCADunnett) *trckd ldrs: effrt over 1f out: sn chsng wnr and rdn: no ex fnl f* **9/4[1]**

0500 **4** 3 **Northern Revoque (IRE)**[23] 4010 2-8-1.... PPMathers(5) 13 — 34
(ABerry) *chsd ldrs: drvn along 3f out: no hdwy whn hung lft appr fnl f* **66/1**

0006 **5** ¾ **Lane Marshal**[29] 3883 2-8-8....(b) TEaves(3) 1 — 37
(MESowersby) *sn led: hdd over 2f out: kpt on same pce u.p* **66/1**

0450 **6** 3 **Tip Toes (IRE)**[7] 4521 2-7-13 49.... TO'Brien(7) 3 — 24
(MRChannon) *midfield: kpt on u.p fnl 2f: n.d* **20/1**

00 **7** 1¾ **Belton**[76] 2470 2-8-11.... GGibbons 9 — 25
(RonaldThompson) *s.i.s: towards rr: styd on fnl 2f: n.d* **7/1**

5160 **8** 1¾ **Premier Times**[6] 4559 2-8-11 59.... ACulhane 4 — 20
(MDHammond) *midfield: drvn along 1/2-way: no hdwy* **9/2[2]**

0620 **9** 1 **Dane's Rock (IRE)**[21] 4094 2-8-11 65....(b) GFaulkner 8 — 18
(PCHaslam) *prom: hung rt bnd 4f out: fdd fnl 2f* **10/1**

06 **10** 3 **Highbury Lass**[66] 2755 2-7-13.... RoryMoore(7) 2 — 5
(PCHaslam) *s.i.s: towards rr most of way* **33/1**

050 **11** 3 **Tewitfield Lass**[14] 4304 2-7-13.... DFentiman(7) 11 — —
(JRWeymes) *nvr bttr than mid-div* **66/1**

604 **12** ½ **Cash Time**[37] 3620 2-8-6 44.... RFitzpatrick 5 — —
(JO'Reilly) *s.i.s: sn chsng ldrs: drvn along 1/2-way: wknd 2f out* **25/1**

6000 **13** 5 **For Nowt**[6] 4559 2-8-11.... DAllan 15 — —
(TDEasterby) *midfield: drvn along 1/2-way: wknd 2f out* **20/1**

00 **14** 1¼ **Gunnerbergkamp**[6] 4559 2-8-11.... PMQuinn 14 — —
(MDHammond) *s.i.s: a bhd* **100/1**

00 **15** nk **Miss Trendsetter (IRE)**[23] 4010 2-8-6....(p) JCarroll 12 — —
(KARyan) *midfield to 1/2-way: sn wknd* **40/1**

1m 31.68s (4.18) **Going Correction** +0.525s/f (Yiel) — **15** Ran SP% **114.4**
Speed ratings: **97,93,92,89,88 84,82,80,79,76 72,72,66,65,64**CSF £160.18 TOTE £7.50: £2.30, £7.90, £1.30; EX 260.80.The winner was bought in for 4,400gns. Lakesdale was claimed by Miss D. Mountain for £6,000.
**Owner** Garry Gardiner **Bred** L And Mrs C R M Gardiner **Trained** Pandy, Gwent

**FOCUS**

Not a bad time given the grade and the conditions and a clear cut winner, although the form is no better than modest.

**NOTEBOOK**

**Dartanian** found the underfoot conditions no problem and ran out a most decisive winner of this very modest seller.
**Toldo(IRE)** is at long last learning to run in a straight line and ran easily his best race yet.
**Lakesdale(IRE)**, having her eighth start, did not seem inconvenienced by the totally different ground.
**Northern Revoque(IRE)** ran to the same level of form as when about six lengths in arrears of the winner here two outings ago.
**Lane Marshal**, having his seventh start, was soon leading them a merry dance but could not fully sustain his effort all the way to the line.
**Tip Toes(IRE)**, having her seventh start, seems likely to continue to struggle even at this rock-bottom level.
**Belton** *Official explanation: jockey said colt ran green*

### 4700 R.M.C. MATERIALS NURSERY — 5f 212y
7:00 (7:00) (D) 2-Y-O — £4,823 (£1,484; £742; £371) Stalls Low

Form — RPR

0312 **1** **Rowan Lodge (IRE)**[8] 4482 2-9-4 **77**.... NMackay(3) 4 — 81+
(MHTompkins) *in tch: hdwy over 1f out: r.o u.p to ld ins fnl f* **3/1[3]**

400 **2** nk **Favouring (IRE)**[15] 4256 2-8-8 **64**.... PHanagan 2 — 67+
(RAFahey) *towards rr: hdwy 1/2-way: chal and edgd lft jst ins fnl f: r.o* **11/4[2]**

3433 **3** 2 **Angelofthenorth**[28] 3898 2-8-12 **68**.... ACulhane 7 — 65
(JDBethell) *mde most tl rdn and hdd ins fnl f: no ex* **8/1**

0400 **4** 2 **Lord John**[9] 4445 2-8-6 **62**.... DaleGibson 9 — 53
(MWEasterby) *prom: rdn 2f out: kpt on same pce* **20/1**

6355 **5** 1¼ **Mitchelland**[2] 4632 2-9-1 **74**....(v[1]) TEaves(3) 6 — 61
(JamesMoffatt) *sn cl up: rdn and ev ch over 1f out: wknd fnl f* **12/1**

305 **6** 1¼ **Strathtay**[57] 3014 2-8-13 **69**.... DeanMcKeown 8 — 53
(PCHaslam) *dwlt: sn chsng ldrs: rdn 2f out: fdd* **10/1**

423 **7** 1 **Secret Pact (IRE)**[29] 3870 2-9-5 **75**.... RFfrench 1 — 56
(MJohnston) *bhd and drvn along 1/2-way: n.d* **5/2[1]**

6064 **8** ½ **Justenjoy Yourself**[41] 3526 2-7-5 **54** oh12.... NataliaGemelova(7) 3 — 33
(CADwyer) *s.i.s: n.d* **66/1**

2660 **9** 1¾ **Skippit John**[9] 4445 2-9-2 **72**.... GGibbons 5 — 46
(RonaldThompson) *chsd ldrs: rdn 2f out: sn btn* **25/1**

1m 18.09s (4.09) **Going Correction** +0.525s/f (Yiel) — **9** Ran SP% **118.2**
Speed ratings: **93,92,89,87,85 83,82,81,79**CSF £11.80 CT £60.24 TOTE £3.90: £1.90, £1.10, £1.70; EX 21.70.
**Owner** The Rowan Stud and Clique Partnership **Bred** M P B Bloodstock Ltd **Trained** Newmarket, Suffolk

**FOCUS**

A modest nursery but strong form from the front pair for the grade.

**NOTEBOOK**

**Rowan Lodge(IRE)**, a negative on the exchanges, settled better in this more strongly-run race over a furlongs less. He always looked like doing just enough.
**Favouring(IRE)**, on his handicap bow, came in for plenty of market support. Soon behind and pushed along, despite a tendency to hang left in the end he came off just second best. This will have taught him something.
**Angelofthenorth**, whose best previous effort was here, made this a true test and seemed well suited by both the trip and the ground.
**Lord John** proved suited by the return to grass but is starting to look fully exposed.
**Mitchelland**, in a first-time visor, was having her second outing in three days and was not at her very best.
**Strathtay** did not improve for the give underfoot and has to build on the promise of her first run.
**Secret Pact(IRE)**, absent for four weeks, was very ring rusty and never went a yard. He can surely do a lot better than this. *Official explanation: trainer had no explanation for the poor form shown*

### 4701 SIMON BAILES PEUGEOT CLAIMING STKS — 5f
7:30 (7:30) (F) 3-Y-O+ — £3,031 (£866; £433) Stalls Low

Form — RPR

-003 **1** **White Ledger (IRE)**[7] 4509 5-8-11 50....(v) PHanagan 16 — 56
(RAFahey) *in tch: hdwy whn nt clr run appr fnl f: burst through to ld clsng stages* **9/2[2]**

0060 **2** 1 **He's A Rocket (IRE)**[5] 4585 3-8-13 58....(p) GFaulkner 13 — 58
(KRBurke) *prom: slt ld and rdn ins fnl f: hdd clsng stages* **20/1**

5230 **3** nk **Soaked**[9] 4452 11-8-10 62....(b) ACulhane 8 — 51
(DWChapman) *led tl rdn and hdd ins fnl f: kpt on* **11/2[3]**

000- **4** nk **Outeast (IRE)**[314] 5374 4-8-3 44.... RFfrench 15 — 43
(GAHarker) *chsd ldrs: ev ch and rdn ins fnl f: no ex clsng stages* **50/1**

3000 **5** hd **So Sober (IRE)**[21] 4085 6-8-8 37.... RWinston 4 — 48
(DShaw) *midfield: hmpd ins first f: hdwy u.p appr fnl f: kpt on ins last* **50/1**

0306 **6** 1½ **Shielaligh**[53] 3158 3-8-8 70....(p) MFenton 14 — 46
(MissGayKelleway) *s.i.s: sn midfield: hdwy u.p appr fnl f: kpt on ins last* **10/1**

0665 **7** 1¾ **American Cousin**[7] 4509 9-8-10 52.... ANicholls 9 — 40
(DNicholls) *dwlt: towards rr: kpt on fr over 1f out: n.d* **12/1**

-006 **8** 1¾ **Cayman Mischief**[15] 4257 4-8-3 27.... JBramhill 5 — 28
(JamesMoffatt) *rr div: kpt on fr over 1f out: n.d* **100/1**

5612 **9** hd **Roxanne Mill**[13] 4331 6-9-0 74....(p) FLynch 11 — 38
(PABlockley) *w ldr: rdn over 1f out: wknd fnl f* **7/4[1]**

6006 **10** ½ **Pharaoh Hatshepsut (IRE)**[6] 4534 6-8-5 26....(b) PFessey 12 — 28
(JamesMoffatt) *dwlt: rr div most of way* **100/1**

0045 **11** 1 **Bond Shakira**[18] 4185 3-8-3 47.... DAllan 10 — 26
(BSmart) *chsd ldrs tl wknd over 1f out* **50/1**

0400 **12** 1¾ **Aguilera**[11] 4391 3-8-6 40 ow3.... VHalliday 7 — 23
(MDods) *a rr div* **100/1**

0010 **13** shd **Cash**[90] 2130 6-9-2 59....(p) NMackay(3) 1 — 33
(PaulJohnson) *nvr bttr than mid-div* **28/1**

-400 **14** nk **High Esteem**[18] 4185 8-8-3 47....(b[1]) PMakin(5) 3 — 21
(MABuckley) *prom tl wknd 2f out* **100/1**

1000 **15** *hd* **Alastair Smellie**[38] 3616 8-8-3 45..............................(v) DFentiman(7) 2 22
(SLKeightley) *dwlt: a rr div* **33/1**

3102 **16** *1 1/4* **Blue Power (IRE)**[49] 3270 3-8-10 60.............................. PMulrennan(3) 6 25
(KRBurke) *sn rr div* **8/1**

61.56 secs (0.96) **Going Correction** +0.225s/f (Good)
**WFA** 3 from 4yo+ 3lb **16** Ran SP% **118.8**
Speed ratings: **101,99,98,98,98 95,92,90,89,89 87,84,84,83,83 81**CSF £95.43 TOTE £6.90: £2.40, £6.70, £2.10; EX 164.80.Outeast was claimed by Mrs K. Pilkington for £4,000.
**Owner** Castlemead Developments Limited **Bred** E Tynan **Trained** Musley Bank, N Yorks
■ Stewards Enquiry : P Mulrennan one-day ban: careless riding (Aug 24)

**FOCUS**
A modest claimer in which the form is weak and not particularly reliable. They all came across to race towards the stands' side.

**NOTEBOOK**
**White Ledger(IRE)**, drawn 16 of 16, had plenty to find on official figures. Despite running out of racing room and having to switch, then being hit over the head with a whip, he burst through to show ahead near the finish.
**He's A Rocket(IRE)**, in cheekpieces rather than blinkers, appreciated the give in the ground and showed a return to form, only being picked off by the winner near the line.
**Soaked** showed all his old dash and was only edged out of it inside the last.
**Outeast(IRE)**, making a belated return, showed a return to form considering how badly she fared in the second half of last term. Her rider's use of the whip was not appreciated by the winner.
**So Sober(IRE)** had a mountain to climb and his four wins have been on the All-Weather.
**Roxanne Mill** had the best chance on official figures, but she dropped away disappointingly in the final furlong for no apparent reason.

## 4702 TENNANTS ANTIQUE AND FINE ART AUCTIONEERS H'CAP 7f
**8:00** (8:00) (E) (0-70,71) 3-Y-O+ **£3,708** (£1,141; £570; £285) **Stalls** Low

Form RPR

00-3 **1** **Pertemps Magus**[48] 3301 4-9-3 57.............................. PHanagan 4 71
(RAFahey) *in tch: hdwy over 2f out: rdn to ld ins fnl f: r.o wl* **4/1**[1]

4531 **2** *3* **Iphigenia (IRE)**[8] 4483 3-9-6 71 6ex.............................. PMakin(5) 3 77
(PWHiatt) *led tl rdn and hdd ins fnl f: no ex* **9/1**[3]

5010 **3** *1 1/2* **Boisdale (IRE)**[38] 3616 6-8-2 49.............................. DFentiman(7) 10 51
(SLKeightley) *prom: rdn over 1f out: kpt on same pce* **20/1**

1335 **4** *nk* **Roman Empire**[32] 3800 4-8-11 51..............................(b) GParkin 5 53
(KARyan) *midfield: hdwy over 2f out: rdn over 1f out: kpt on same pce* **10/1**

6221 **5** *1 1/2* **Headland (USA)**[14] 4305 6-9-1 55..............................(be) ACulhane 6 53
(DWChapman) *chsd ldrs: rdn over 1f out: no hdwy* **10/1**

1661 **6** *1/2* **Zhitomir**[24] 4004 6-8-9 52.............................. PMulrennan(3) 13 49
(MDods) *s.i.s: sn midfield: kpt on u.p fnl 2f: n.d* **9/1**[3]

3604 **7** *3* **Firebird Rising (USA)**[11] 4387 3-8-9 58.............................. NMackay(3) 1 47
(TDBarron) *midfield: drvn along 1/2-way: kpt on fnl f: n.d* **16/1**

0302 **8** *shd* **Baby Barry**[10] 4425 7-8-6 46.............................. DaleGibson 17 35
(MrsGSRees) *towards rr: nt clr run over 2f out: kpt on fr over 1f out: n.d* **12/1**

2000 **9** *1/2* **Thunderclap**[95] 1993 5-8-12 55.............................. THamilton(3) 2 43
(JJQuinn) *prom tl rdn and wknd over 1f out* **25/1**

0356 **10** *nk* **Oases**[10] 4425 5-9-0 54..............................(v) FLynch 8 41
(DShaw) *slowly away: bhd: hdwy into midfield 2f out: no further prog* **11/2**[2]

0040 **11** *1 1/2* **Pharoah's Gold (IRE)**[48] 3321 6-8-8 51.............................. TEaves(3) 14 34
(DShaw) *s.i.s: towards rr most of way* **33/1**

0445 **12** *1 1/2* **Bella Beguine**[21] 4105 5-8-7 47..............................(b) MFenton 11 26
(ABailey) *in tch tl wknd 2f out* **14/1**

-060 **13** *hd* **Risk Free**[15] 4280 7-9-2 56..............................(v) RWinston 16 35
(PDEvans) *midfield tl wknd over 2f out* **16/1**

0030 **14** *2 1/2* **Golden Spectrum (IRE)**[6] 4557 5-9-1 55..............................(v) JCarroll 15 28
(DNicholls) *sn bhd* **16/1**

0252 **15** *1 1/4* **Nemo Fugat (IRE)**[11] 4390 5-9-6 60..............................(v) ANicholls 9 29
(DNicholls) *keen: midfield whn bmpd 4f out: wknd 2f out* **10/1**

1m 29.7s (2.20) **Going Correction** +0.525s/f (Yiel)
**WFA** 3 from 4yo+ 6lb **15** Ran SP% **126.2**
Speed ratings: **108,104,102,102,100 100,96,96,96,95 94,92,92,89,87**CSF £40.13 CT £685.39 TOTE £4.90: £2.00, £4.90, £7.10; EX 75.00.
**Owner** The Spinal Injuries Association **Bred** Pertemps Group P L C **Trained** Musley Bank, N Yorks

**FOCUS**
A modest handicap run at a strong gallop and a fair time given the conditions.

**NOTEBOOK**
**Pertemps Magus**, from a stable riding the crest of a wave, was having her first outing for seven weeks and just her second start in ten months. Suited by the give underfoot, she ran out a most decisive winner.
**Iphigenia(IRE)**, raised 10lb after Folkestone, had just a 6lb penalty but, after setting a strong pace, she had no answer when the winner swept by.
**Boisdale(IRE)**, absent for over five weeks, seems more effective on the All-Weather - his last four wins have been on the artificial surfaces.
**Roman Empire**, who usually plies his trade on the All-Weather, has been on the sidelines for a month and this will set him up for a return to sand.
**Headland(USA)**, 4lb higher, was a negative on the exchanges and is better on much quicker ground.
**Nemo Fugat(IRE)** *Official explanation: jockey said gelding was denied a run from 2f out*

## 4703 CHARITY NIGHT MAIDEN STKS 1m 3f 214y
**8:30** (8:31) (D) 3-Y-O+ **£3,435** (£1,057; £528; £264) **Stalls** High

Form RPR

4303 **1** **Gironde**[32] 3806 3-8-13 88..............................(v[1]) FLynch 5 85+
(SirMichaelStoute) *hld up: smooth hdwy to ld over 3f out: drew clr over 1f out: easily* **1/8**[1]

5034 **2** *15* **Rigonza**[9] 4444 3-8-13 62.............................. DAllan 3 59
(TDEasterby) *hld up: hdwy to dispute 2nd 3f out: kpt on fnl f: no ch w wnr* **16/1**[3]

543 **3** *1 3/4* **Kyber**[9] 4444 3-8-13.............................. RWinston 1 57
(RFFisher) *prom: dropped rr but stl in tch 1/2-way: hung lft 4f out: hdwy to dispute 2nd 3f out: no further prog* **14/1**[2]

0 **4** *dist* **Transkei**[39] 3587 3-8-8.............................. RFfrench 4 —
(MrsLStubbs) *cl up: plld hrd early: wknd qckly 3f out: t.o* **50/1**

**5** *13* **Wizards Princess**[92] 4-9-0.............................. PPMathers(5) 2 —
(DWThompson) *sn led: hdd over 3f out: wknd qckly: t.o* **66/1**

2m 46.36s (7.36) **Going Correction** +0.525s/f (Yiel)
**WFA** 3 from 4yo 11lb **5** Ran SP% **104.9**
Speed ratings: **96,86,84,—,—**CSF £2.54 TOTE £1.10: £1.10, £3.20; EX 3.30 Place 6 £55.92, Place 5 £17.57.
**Owner** The Celle Syndicate Incorporated **Bred** Ridgecourt Stud **Trained** Newmarket, Suffolk

**FOCUS**
A one-sided contest and a modest winning time for the grade, even allowing for the conditions. The form is very weak and the winner did not need to be near best to win as he liked.

**NOTEBOOK**
**Gironde** had almost two stone in hand on official ratings and went well clear in effortless fashion coming off the home turn. His trainer showed little charity dispatching him north for this!
**Rigonza** followed the winner home at a respectable distance.
**Kyber** gave his rider desperate problems, hanging violently right from the halfway mark. *Official explanation: jockey said gelding hung left throughout*
**Transkei**, keen early, has been beaten out of sight on both her starts now.
**Wizards Princess**, who had her trainer at the start, had finished beaten out of sight on her previous visit to the track.
T/Plt: £112.80 to a £1 stake. Pool: £40,584.10. 262.60 winning tickets. T/Qpdt: £28.00 to a £1 stake. Pool: £3,565.00. 94.20 winning tickets. JF

# 4480 FOLKESTONE (R-H)
Friday, August 13

**OFFICIAL GOING: Good (good to soft in places) changing to good to soft after 2.50 (race 3)**
The ground became increasingly softer as the meeting progressed. Most of the runners in the sprint races went far side, but there seemed to be no great bias.
Wind: fresh bhd Weather: frequent heavy showers

## 4704 KENTISH EXPRESS "I'VE WON A COMPETITION" MAIDEN AUCTION STKS 5f
**1:50** (1:51) (F) 2-Y-O **£2,926** (£836; £418) **Stalls** Low

Form RPR

040 **1** **Grand Place**[27] 3938 2-8-11 73.............................. DaneO'Neill 1 79
(RHannon) *chsd ldr: rdn to ld over 1f out: sn clr* **5/6**[1]

005 **2** *4* **Cree**[11] 4388 2-8-9..............................(b) SSanders 6 63
(WRMuir) *led to over 1f out: no ch w wnr fnl f* **10/1**

55 **3** *1 1/2* **Docklands Grace (USA)**[20] 4124 2-8-4.............................. JMackay 4 53
(NPLittmoden) *pressed ldrs: outpcd wl over 1f out: no imp after* **5/1**[3]

6 **4** *2* **General Haigh**[13] 4334 2-8-13.............................. NPollard 3 55
(JRBest) *pushed along to stay in tch: one pce and no imp over 1f out* **14/1**

**5** *3* **Cayenne (GER)** 2-8-8.............................. MartinDwyer 7 39
(DMSimcock) *restless stalls: s.s: wl bhd: kpt on fnl f: no ch* **9/2**[2]

0 **6** *8* **Chantelle's Dream**[7] 4514 2-8-2.............................. PDoe 2 5
(IAWood) *rel to r: a wl bhd* **40/1**

0 **7** *10* **Aleshanee**[39] 3583 2-8-6.............................. NCallan 5 —
(JRBest) *pressed ldrs for 2f: wknd rapidly: t.o* **20/1**

60.12 secs (-0.58) **Going Correction** -0.15s/f (Firm) **7** Ran SP% **112.4**
Speed ratings: **98,91,89,86,81 68,52**CSF £10.09 TOTE £1.70: £1.10, £4.20; EX 8.50.
**Owner** Mrs J K Powell **Bred** R G Percival And Miss S M Rhodes **Trained** East Everleigh, Wilts

**FOCUS**
A moderate maiden lacking strength in depth and little to excited about amongst the beaten horses. The winner was different class, which explains why the winning time was decent for the grade. The whole field stayed stands' side.

**NOTEBOOK**
**Grand Place** found this rather easier then the Weatherbys Super Sprint. He had to be shaken up before halfway, but the further they went the more he was in control and he completed the task with the minimum of fuss. Nurseries under similar conditions look the best option.
**Cree** soon bagged the stands' rail and made a bold bid to lead the whole way, but the winner was far too classy. He may need to drop down a grade.
**Docklands Grace(USA)** was always being taken along a stride too quickly. Nursery company and a longer trip, as well as possibly a return to Fibresand, may be her best options.
**General Haigh**, as on his debut, struggled to go the pace. His dam was a sprinter, but his half-sister Ambersong has won over 12 furlongs so he could be interesting in modest company over further.
**Cayenne(GER)**, an 18,000gns filly related to winners in Germany, was the only newcomer in the field and did not show much except that she looked badly in need of the experience.

## 4705 EUROPEAN BREEDERS FUND MAIDEN FILLIES' STKS (DIV I) 7f (S)
**2:20** (2:21) (D) 2-Y-O **£5,174** (£1,592; £796; £398) **Stalls** Low

Form RPR

**1** **Ratukidul (FR)** 2-8-11.............................. DHolland 4 73+
(SirMichaelStoute) *s.i.s: wl off the pce in last trio: stdy prog on outer over 2f out: rdn fnl f: r.o to ld last stride* **10/1**

6 **2** *shd* **Ghasiba (IRE)**[21] 4074 2-8-11.............................. SSanders 7 73
(CEBrittain) *chsd ldng pair: rdn wl over 2f out: styd on u.p to ld wl ins fnl f: hdd last stride* **4/1**[2]

0 **3** *1 1/4* **Northern Secret**[38] 3601 2-8-11.............................. MartinDwyer 3 70
(AMBalding) *pressed ldr: chal over 2f out: stl upsides wl ins fnl f: no ex nr fin* **8/1**

5 **4** *nk* **Ellens Princess (IRE)**[15] 4272 2-8-11.............................. PDobbs 1 69
(RHannon) *trckd ldng pair: pushed along over 2f out: rdn to chal 1f out: ev ch: fdd nr fin* **6/1**

6 **5** *1/2* **Entertaining**[54] 3116 2-8-11.............................. DaneO'Neill 9 68
(HCandy) *led: hrd pressed fr over 2f out: kpt on wl tl hdd & wknd wl ins fnl f* **5/1**[3]

0 **6** *1 1/4* **Big Hoo Hah**[37] 3627 2-8-11.............................. DSweeney 8 65
(CACyzer) *racd in midfield: lost pl and wl in rr 3f out: shkn up and styd on again fr over 1f out* **100/1**

2 **7** *1* **Sweet Lorraine**[22] 4053 2-8-8.............................. RMiles(3) 6 62
(TGMills) *wl in rr: prog to chse clr ldrs 3f out: rn green over 2f out : no imp after* **7/2**[1]

00 **8** *3/4* **Sabbiosa (IRE)**[22] 4053 2-8-11.............................. NCallan 10 60
(JLDunlop) *chsd ldrs: rdn 3f out: sn outpcd: kpt on fnl f* **33/1**

0 **9** *2* **Krumpet**[22] 4053 2-8-11.............................. AMcCarthy 12 55
(GGMargarson) *dwlt: a in rr: shkn up 1/2-way: no imp on ldrs* **16/1**

0 **10** *nk* **Hursley**[13] 4335 2-8-11.............................. VSlattery 5 55
(SKirk) *racd in midfield: pushed along 1/2-way: lost pl and wl btn over 2f out* **100/1**

020 **11** *hd* **Great Opinions (USA)**[16] 4234 2-8-11 75..............................(b[1]) RHavlin 11 54
(JHMGosden) *a towards rr: rdn and struggling 3f out: no prog* **9/1**

**12** *hd* **Legend Of Dance** 2-8-11.............................. TEDurcan 2 54
(BJMeehan) *s.s: rn green in last and sn bhd: kpt on fnl f* **33/1**

1m 27.63s (-0.17) **Going Correction** -0.15s/f (Firm) **12** Ran SP% **117.1**
Speed ratings: **94,93,92,92,91 90,88,88,85,85 85,85**CSF £48.58 TOTE £11.80: £3.90, £1.90, £3.50; EX 61.20.
**Owner** Niarchos Family **Bred** Suc S Niarchos **Trained** Newmarket, Suffolk

**FOCUS**
Just a fair maiden and the time was only average for the type of race despite being 0.47 seconds faster than the second division. The form is only fair but a few of these are open to a bit more improvement. Over this longer trip, the whole field moved across to race far side.

**NOTEBOOK**
**Ratukidul(FR)**, a half-sister to Hernando and Johann Quatz, was given a very patient ride and only had one behind her at halfway, but she made relentless progress down the outside of the field in the second half of the contest and maintained her effort to get up right on the line. The form as it stands is nothing special, but she is likely to progress a good deal and should develop into a fair middle-distance filly next season.
**Ghasiba(IRE)**, well backed to confirm the promise of her Ascot debut, did everything right and was mugged right on the line. She can be counted rather unlucky to have run into such a well-bred rival in a Folkestone maiden.
**Northern Secret** was given a much more positive ride than on her debut and deserves credit for hanging in there for as long as she did. She should be able to win an ordinary maiden.
**Ellens Princess(IRE)** looked a likely winner when delivering her challenge a furlong from home, but the principals were finishing more strongly down the middle of the track and there was nothing she could do about it.
**Entertaining** made much of the running, but was swamped inside the final furlong and did not appear to improve for the longer trip.
**Big Hoo Hah** ran a bit better than her price suggested she would.
**Sweet Lorraine** appeared to disappoint, but this was probably a stronger maiden than the one she was second in here on her debut. *Official explanation: jockey said filly was unsuited by the good, good to soft in places ground*
**Great Opinions(USA)** ran a stinker and looks to be going the wrong way.

## 4706 EUROPEAN BREEDERS FUND MAIDEN FILLIES' STKS (DIV II) 7f (S)
**2:50** (2:52) (D) 2-Y-O **£5,161** (£1,588; £794; £397) **Stalls** Low

| Form | | | | | RPR |
|---|---|---|---|---|---|
| 02 | 1 | | **Kalmini (USA)**[15] 4272 2-8-11 ... TEDurcan 6 *(MRChannon) sn pushed along in midfield: str reminders over 4f out: prog over 2f out: drvn to ld ins fnl f: styd on* **9/2**[3] | | 72 |
| 03 | 2 | 3/4 | **Velveteen Rabbit**[22] 4053 2-8-11 ... KMcEvoy 3 (SaeedBinSuroor) *trckd ldrs: shkn up to chal 2f out: led over 1f out: hdd and fnd nil ins fnl f* **5/1** | | 70 |
| | 3 | 1/2 | **Hashima (USA)** 2-8-8 ... J-PGuillambert(3) 4 (CEBrittain) *rn green in rr: last of main gp and struggling over 2f out: gd prog over 1f out: clsng nr fin* **16/1** | | 69 |
| 65 | 4 | 2 | **Mitraillette (USA)**[20] 4137 2-8-11 ... DHolland 7 (SirMichaelStoute) *led to 1/2-way: styd chsng ldrs: unable qck over 2f out: one pce after* **4/1**[2] | | 64 |
| 0 | 5 | 1 1/4 | **Kolyma (IRE)**[20] 4143 2-8-11 ... NCallan 11 (JLDunlop) *chsd ldrs: rdn 3f out: cl up over 1f out: one pce u.p* **66/1** | | 61 |
| | 6 | nk | **Marchetta** 2-8-11 ... NPollard 10 (PWHarris) *racd in midfield: effrt over 2f out: hrd rdn and one pce over 1f out* **20/1** | | 60 |
| 0 | 7 | shd | **Akraan**[14] 4292 2-8-11 ... WRyan 12 (EALDunlop) *settled in midfield: shkn up over 2f out: sme prog over 1f out: one pce fnl f* **16/1** | | 60 |
| 06 | 8 | 1 1/4 | **Midcap (IRE)**[15] 4272 2-8-11 ... MHills 5 (BWHills) *pressed ldr: led 1/2-way: rdn: hdd and flashed tail over 1f out: folded tamely* **6/1** | | 57 |
| 0 | 9 | hd | **Tomobel**[77] 2458 2-8-11 ... PDoe 1 (MHTompkins) *s.s: prog fr rr 3f out: rdn in midfield 2f out: no hdwy after* **50/1** | | 56 |
| 00 | 10 | 5 | **Musical Day**[18] 4198 2-8-11 ... PDobbs 2 (BJMeehan) *a towards rr: pushed along 1/2-way: struggling over 2f out* **14/1** | | 44 |
| 3 | 11 | 4 | **Crystalline**[13] 4344 2-8-11 ... SSanders 8 (DRLoder) *in tch: rdn 1/2-way: wknd over 2f out* **7/2**[1] | | 34 |
| | 12 | 3/4 | **The Chequered Lady** 2-8-8 ... RMiles(3) 9 (TDMccarthy) *s.s: a last: detached fr remainder 1/2-way* **66/1** | | 32 |

1m 28.1s (0.30) **Going Correction** -0.15s/f (Firm) **12** Ran **SP% 119.5**
Speed ratings: **92,91,90,88,86 86,86,84,84,79 74,73**CSF £26.91 TOTE £4.30: £1.70, £2.50, £5.40; EX 28.70.
**Owner** Sheikh Ahmed Al Maktoum **Bred** Darley **Trained** West Ilsley, Berks

**FOCUS**
The winning time was 0.47 seconds slower than the first division and the form is nothing special, but some are likely to improve in time. Again the whole field crossed over to race far side.

**NOTEBOOK**
**Kalmini(USA)** had to be pushed along and given reminders before halfway, but she responded to the pressure and gradually wore down her rivals. She now qualifies for nurseries, but looks a real stayer so a step up to a mile will certainly suit her.
**Velveteen Rabbit** ran a similar sort of race to her last outing here, again having to switch across from a low draw, but her lack of a change of gear where it matters was again evident. It will be a surprise if she is still in the care of Godolphin come next season.
**Hashima(USA)**, a $90,000 daughter of the Fillies' Mile winner Fairy Heights, looked to need the experience but was finishing in decent style and is likely to turn out the best of these in time.
**Mitraillette(USA)**, given a positive ride on this step up in trip, was not disgraced and may do better in nurseries, though she is obviously not one of the stable's better juveniles.
**Kolyma(IRE)** improved from her debut over this longer trip and ran with credit at a price. She will need to improve again a fair amount in order to get into the money though.
**Marchetta**, out of a winner over a mile, hinted at ability on this debut and the stable's representatives usually progress with time.
**Midcap(IRE)** did not confirm the promise of her Goodwood effort, despite a positive ride, and her attitude has to be called into question.
**Crystalline** ran appallingly considering the promise she showed on her debut, and something must have been amiss. *Official explanation: jockey said filly was never travelling*

## 4707 KMFM CLASSIFIED STKS 6f
**3:25** (3:25) (E) 3-Y-O+ **£3,360** (£1,034; £517; £258) **Stalls** Low

| Form | | | | RPR |
|---|---|---|---|---|
| 6420 | 1 | | **Sewmuch Character**[28] 3923 5-9-2 62 ... DSweeney 7 (MBlanshard) *mde all: drew 4l clr 2f out: tired and edgd lft ins fnl f: hld on* **5/1**[3] | 73 |
| -304 | 2 | nk | **Tropical Storm (IRE)**[6] 4555 3-9-3 70 ... SWKelly 4 (JNoseda) *chsd wnr: rdn and outpcd over 2f out: styd on u.p fnl f: clsng at fin* **8/1** | 77 |
| 6340 | 3 | 1 1/4 | **Dandouce**[72] 2577 3-8-6 67 ... ThomasYeung(5) 3 (PWChapple-Hyam) *chsd ldng pair: rdn and nt qckn 2f out: styd on fnl f but nvr able to chal* **7/2**[2] | 67 |
| 0350 | 4 | 1 1/4 | **Whistful (IRE)**[36] 3680 3-8-12 68 ... SSanders 5 (CFWall) *settled in rr: drvn and prog 2f out: kpt on same pce fnl f* **6/1** | 65 |
| 4100 | 5 | 5 | **Coranglais**[9] 4459 4-9-2 63 ... (p) NCallan 1 (JMBradley) *chsd ldrs: rdn and outpcd over 2f out: wknd fnl f* **8/1** | 50 |
| 0021 | 6 | 1 1/4 | **Full Spate**[6] 4542 9-9-9 66 ... DHolland 6 (JMBradley) *dwlt: sn trckd ldrs: rdn and outpcd over 2f out: wknd fnl f* **2/1**[1] | 53 |
| 0615 | 7 | 9 | **Oeuf A La Neige**[11] 4390 4-8-10 66 ... DeanWilliams(7) 8 (GCHChung) *a last: struggling fr 1/2-way: t.o* **14/1** | 20 |

1m 13.26s (-0.34) **Going Correction** +0.025s/f (Good)
**WFA** 3 from 4yo+ 4lb **7** Ran **SP% 115.4**
Speed ratings: **103,102,100,99,92 90,78**CSF £44.06 TOTE £8.00: £3.70, £2.50; EX 43.50.
**Owner** Aykroyd And Sons Ltd **Bred** Kingsmead Breeders **Trained** Upper Lambourn, Berks

**FOCUS**
A modest contest of its type run in deteriorating ground, though the pace was fair. There is little solid to go on form-wise and this race may prove a shade too high. The whole field were taken across to race far side.

**NOTEBOOK**
**Sewmuch Character**, who had a bit to find with most of his rivals at the weights, especially the three-year-olds, has form on easy ground and quickly bagged the far rail in front. A sudden injection of pace passing the two-furlong pole gained him a few lengths on his rivals, and given the winning margin that was to prove crucial.
**Tropical Storm(IRE)**, still a maiden, got caught out when the pace quickened passing the two-furlong pole and, though he tried his best, he could never quite claw back the leeway. He may be better over seven.
**Dandouce**, a maiden dropping back in trip, could never get any cover with her rider looking anxiously across at his rivals and that probably contributed to her downfall every bit as much as the trip appearing too sharp.
**Whistful(IRE)** is yet to win a race, but her best form has been on faster ground than this.
**Coranglais** has not built on his Bath victory and again showed little.
**Full Spate** has won on soft ground, but most of his best form has come on a faster surface. This was probably not his sort of race in any case, as all ten of his victories have come in double-figure fields.

## 4708 WHITE'S TRANSPORT 50 YEAR ANNIVERSARY FILLIES' H'CAP 6f
**4:00** (4:00) (F) (0-55,52) 3-Y-O+ **£3,017** (£862; £431) **Stalls** Low

| Form | | | | RPR |
|---|---|---|---|---|
| -053 | 1 | | **Pretty Kool**[7] 4517 4-9-5 48 ... SSanders 2 (SCWilliams) *led nr side pair: wl on terms w main gp: hrd rdn and edgd rt fnl f: gained upper hand nr fin* **11/4**[1] | 57 |
| 0321 | 2 | 1/2 | **Cut Ridge (IRE)**[6] 4546 5-9-9 52 6ex ... DHolland 6 (JSWainwright) *pressed far side ldr: led gp 1/2-way: edgd lft u.p over 1f out: jst hld by wnr nr fin* **7/2**[2] | 59 |
| 6410 | 3 | 1 3/4 | **My Girl Pearl (IRE)**[6] 4548 4-9-5 48 ... VSlattery 3 (MSSaunders) *cl up far side: chsd ldr over 1f out: hrd rdn and styd on same pce* **8/1**[3] | 50 |
| 0060 | 4 | nk | **Pink Supreme**[11] 4403 3-9-4 51 ... PDoe 1 (IAWood) *pressed wnr in nr side pair: no ex fnl f* **16/1** | 52 |
| -041 | 5 | nk | **Brandywine Bay (IRE)**[10] 4419 4-8-4 38 ... (p) HayleyTurner(5) 5 (APJones) *racd far side: sn outpcd and rdn: styd on fr over 1f out: nt rch ldrs ins fnl f* **8/1**[3] | 38 |
| 6300 | 6 | 2 | **Poppyline**[10] 4418 4-9-8 51 ... (b) KMcEvoy 12 (WRMuir) *trckd far side ldrs: rdn and cl up 2f out: fdd fnl f* **14/1** | 45 |
| 0600 | 7 | 1 3/4 | **Indian Lily**[41] 3530 3-9-3 50 ... (t) GBaker 8 (CFWall) *s.i.s: towards rr of far side gp: rdn over 2f out: no imp* **10/1** | 39 |
| 0050 | 8 | 3/4 | **Komena**[31] 3828 6-8-11 40 ... NCallan 4 (JWPayne) *wl in rr far side: rdn and sme prog over 1f out: wknd ins fnl f* **16/1** | 26 |
| 0500 | 9 | shd | **Indrani**[2] 4650 3-8-9 42 ... NPollard 11 (JohnAHarris) *led far side gp to 1/2-way: rdn and wknd over 1f out: eased ins fnl f* **14/1** | 28 |
| 0600 | 10 | 1 | **Akiramenai (USA)**[27] 3935 4-9-5 48 ... (b[1]) SWKelly 7 (MrsLStubbs) *racd far side: nvr gng wl: nvr on terms* **25/1** | 31 |
| 0060 | 11 | 2 | **Averami**[14] 4309 3-9-0 47 ... MartinDwyer 13 (AMBalding) *racd in midfield far side: effrt 2f out: wknd fnl f* **14/1** | 24 |
| -000 | 12 | 21 | **Sweet Talking Girl**[14] 4309 4-8-2 31 oh1 ... (tp) AMcCarthy 10 (JMBradley) *dwlt: rcvrd to chse far side ldrs: wknd rapidly over 2f out: t.o* **66/1** | — |

1m 13.58s (-0.02) **Going Correction** +0.025s/f (Good)
**WFA** 3 from 4yo+ 4lb **12** Ran **SP% 117.3**
Speed ratings: **101,100,98,97,97 94,92,91,91,89 87,59**CSF £11.69 CT £68.43 TOTE £3.70: £1.50, £1.70, £2.80; EX 14.00.
**Owner** Carol Shekells & Associates **Bred** Old Mill Stud **Trained** Newmarket, Suffolk

**FOCUS**
An average contest of its type, though the pace was fair and very few got into it. The form is modest but appears reliable. The pair drawn in stalls one and two decided to stay stands' side and, as they finished first and fourth, it certainly did them little harm.

**NOTEBOOK**
**Pretty Kool** decided to stay stands' side with just one other rival whilst the bulk of the field went far side, but she was always up with the pace. She drifted right under pressure in the final furlong, but with the runner-up hanging left at the same time, the pair ended up battling it out down the centre of the track in the last 50 yards and she saw her race out just the better.
**Cut Ridge(IRE)**, carrying a 6lb penalty for her Lingfield win, was given a positive ride in the far-side group. She eventually emerged best on that side, but hung left towards the winner inside the last furlong and was just worried out if it. This trip may be on the sharp side for her now.
**My Girl Pearl(IRE)** ran a prominent race in the far-side group and did little wrong, but she is not easy to win with and probably prefers faster ground.
**Pink Supreme** ◆ stayed against the stands' rail along with the winner and certainly put in a much-improved effort. This was the first time she had encountered easy ground since finishing runner-up in her sole start of last season, so it obviously suits, and she is dropping to a very exploitable mark.
**Brandywine Bay(IRE)** was not disgraced, but could have done with a longer trip and faster ground.
**Averami** *Official explanation: jockey said filly was unsuited by the good to soft ground*

## 4709 EUROPEAN BREEDERS FUND CLASSIFIED STKS 1m 1f 149y
**4:30** (4:30) (C) 3-Y-O **£8,195** (£3,108; £1,554; £706) **Stalls** Low

| Form | | | | RPR |
|---|---|---|---|---|
| 1200 | 1 | | **Invasian (IRE)**[15] 4268 3-8-13 86 ... WRyan 7 (HRACecil) *mde all: pushed 2l clr 2f out: styd on wl: readily* **14/1** | 101 |
| 0501 | 2 | 2 1/2 | **Secretary General (IRE)**[20] 4140 3-9-0 91 ... SSanders 6 (PFICole) *settled in 5th pl: effrt over 2f out: drvn to chse wnr ins fnl f: no imp* **5/1**[2] | 97 |
| 31-1 | 3 | 3 | **Prince Of Thebes (IRE)**[19] 4164 3-8-13 90 ... MartinDwyer 4 (AMBalding) *t.k.h early: trckd ldng pair: chsd wnr over 2f out: hung lft and fnd nil 1f out: sn lost 2nd and wknd* **5/1**[2] | 91 |
| 3440 | 4 | nk | **Sew'N'So Character (IRE)**[15] 4273 3-9-1 92 ... DSweeney 5 (MBlanshard) *hld up in last pair: effrt over 2f out: drvn and kpt on over 1f out: nvr rchd ldrs* **8/1** | 92 |
| 4412 | 5 | 1 1/4 | **Momtic (IRE)**[19] 4171 3-8-13 86 ... DHolland 2 (WJarvis) *trckd ldng trio: rdn over 2f out: sn one pce and btn* **6/1** | 88 |
| 1240 | 6 | 6 | **Dancing Lyra**[15] 4271 3-8-13 89 ... MHills 3 (JWHills) *hld up in last trio: rdn over 3f out: wknd 2f out* **3/1**[1] | 77 |
| 41-0 | 7 | 7 | **Rinjani (USA)**[47] 3345 3-8-13 90 ... (t) KMcEvoy 1 (SaeedBinSuroor) *t.k.h: trckd wnr tl wknd rapidly over 2f out* **12/1** | 64 |

1410 **8** *23* **Gavroche (IRE)**[15] 4271 3-8-10 89.............. J-PGuillambert(3) 8 23
(CADwyer) *hld up in last: prog into midfield 4f out: wknd rapidly over 2f out: t.o* **11/2**[3]

2m 5.21s (0.05) **Going Correction** +0.20s/f (Good) **8** Ran SP% **113.5**
Speed ratings: **107,105,102,102,101 96,90,72**CSF £80.80 TOTE £15.40: £3.20, £2.00, £1.40; EX 78.40.

**Owner** Dr Karen Sanderson **Bred** Dr Karen Monica Sanderson **Trained** Newmarket, Suffolk

**FOCUS**

A decent grade of contest for the track and the pace was a solid one, making the form decent for the grade. The ground on the round course appereaed a little easier than on the straight.

**NOTEBOOK**

**Invasian(IRE)**, was 4lb badly in with the majority of these on adjusted official ratings, but he had gained his only previous victory on an easy surface. With the ground in his favour, he proved well suited by the step in trip and, given a positive ride, never looked in any danger racing down the home straight. There may be a bit more to come from him under similar conditions.

**Secretary General(IRE)** had every chance turning for home, but could not make any impression on the winner. He just about handles these conditions, but is probably better on faster ground and this trip looked beyond his best.

**Prince Of Thebes(IRE)**, trying a longer trip and on an easy surface for the first time, did not help his chances of landing the hat-trick by pulling hard early, and when extra effort was required in the closing stages the response was limited.

**Sew'N'So Character(IRE)**, given a patient ride, made some late progress but it was laboured and he could never land a blow. He has paid for keeping some exalted company as a juvenile, but does look to be on a stiff mark based on what he has actually achieved.

**Momtic(IRE)** was the other one, along with the winner, who had a bit to find at the weights. He probably ran to form on ground that may have been softer than ideal. *Official explanation: jockey said colt was unsuited by the good to soft ground*

**Dancing Lyra** should have relished the conditions, but never picked up and was very disappointing.

**Rinjani(USA)** stopped very quickly having once again taken a good hold early. He does not look to have trained on.

**Gavroche(IRE)** put in a rare poor performance on his 13th outing of the year.

## 4710 EASTWELL MANOR H'CAP — 1m 4f

**5:00** (5:01) (F) (0-55,60) 3-Y-O **£3,010** (£860; £430) **Stalls** Low

Form RPR

5621 **1** **Science Academy (USA)**[8] 4499 3-9-6 60 6ex.............. NDeSouza(5) 9 70+
(PFICole) *hld up in tch: prog to chse ldr 3f out: led 2f out: rdn and styd on wl* **7/2**[2]

0006 **2** *2* **Top Achiever (IRE)**[57] 3002 3-9-6 55.............. SWKelly 6 62
(MrsLStubbs) *hld up in midfield: prog over 3f out: chsd wnr wl over 1f out: hung in bhd and nt qckn fnl f* **50/1**

0000 **3** *2* **Venetian Romance (IRE)**[22] 4055 3-7-11 37.............. HayleyTurner(5) 8 41
(APJones) *towards rr: pushed along over 5f out: prog 3f out: styd on u.p to take 3rd ins fnl f* **33/1**

-001 **4** *3/4* **Music Mix (IRE)**[4] 4604 3-9-6 55.............. WRyan 14 58
(EALDunlop) *hld up in rr: prog over 3f out: chsd ldrs 2f out: sn rdn and no imp* **13/8**[1]

-004 **5** *10* **Royal Starlet**[8] 4499 3-9-0 49.............. PDobbs 11 37
(MrsAJPerrett) *mostly chsd ldr to 3f out: hit rail sn after: wknd 2f out: eased ins fnl f* **12/1**

4-00 **6** *3* **Zuleta**[7] 4519 3-8-12 54.............. APutland(7) 3 37
(MBlanshard) *s.s: racd in detached last pair: rn wd bnd after 2f: passed wkng rivals fr 4f out: nvr nr ldrs* **33/1**

004 **7** *7* **Sayrianna**[22] 4057 3-9-0 49.............. PDoe 1 22
(IAWood) *t.k.h: led: rn wd bnd after 2f: drew 8l clr over 4f out: hdd & wknd 2f out* **33/1**

3000 **8** *21* **Romeo's Day**[14] 4302 3-8-10 45.............. MartinDwyer 5 —
(MRChannon) *s.s: racd in last pair: wknd over 3f out: t.o* **9/1**

6155 **9** *4* **Cobalt Blue (IRE)**[20] 4128 3-9-3 52..............(b) DHolland 7 —
(WJHaggas) *lost pl after 3f: in rr after: wknd over 3f out: t.o* **7/1**[3]

0642 **10** *17* **Oniz Tiptoes (IRE)**[17] 4207 3-8-5 40 ow1..............(v) NCallan 4 —
(JSWainwright) *t.k.h: disp 2nd pl to over 4f out: wknd rapidly over 3f out: t.o* **14/1**

-030 **11** *5* **Polar Dancer**[13] 4346 3-9-6 55.............. DaneO'Neill 12 —
(MrsAJPerrett) *t.k.h: trckd ldrs tl wknd rapidly over 3f out: t.o* **9/1**

0065 **12** *23* **Preston Hall**[22] 4057 3-9-0 49.............. NPollard 2 —
(MrsLCJewell) *t.k.h: trckd ldrs: rn wd bnd after 2f: wknd rapidly over 4f out: wl t.o* **50/1**

2m 43.23s (2.83) **Going Correction** +0.20s/f (Good) **12** Ran SP% **119.9**
Speed ratings: **98,96,95,94,88 86,81,67,64,53 50,34**CSF £184.34 CT £4922.14 TOTE £3.90: £1.40, £11.50, £6.70; EX 150.40.

**Owner** Sir Martyn Arbib **Bred** M Arbib **Trained** Whatcombe, Oxon

**FOCUS**

A poor contest, but the pace was decent and they finished spread out all over Kent. The form is modest but the winner is open to improvement. The decent early tempo caused a few to have a real problem negotiating the first turn.

**NOTEBOOK**

**Science Academy(USA)**, carrying a 6lb penalty for her fluent Yarmouth success, was on much easier ground but coped with it well under a very competent ride. She was always travelling sweetly and her rider did not panic when the leader went clear. Sent to the front starting up the home straight, her cause may have been slightly helped by her nearest challenger hanging in behind her, but she still won with plenty of authority.

**Top Achiever(IRE)**, unplaced in all five of his previous starts, improved a good deal on that and had every chance racing up the home straight, but he was inclined to duck in behind the winner and then had nothing more to give. He does not look the easiest of rides.

**Venetian Romance(IRE)**, whose record coming into this was one placing from 12 starts, made up a lot of ground over the last three furlongs to reach her final placing. She looks the ideal sort for a banded event under similar conditions.

**Music Mix(IRE)**, impressive winner of a moderate event on Polytrack four days earlier, tried to get into the race from the home turn but found the different surface and longer trip all too much.

**Royal Starlet**, 6lb better off with Science Academy for a five-length beating at Yarmouth, did not handle the different ground anything like as well as her old rival and it appeared to cause her stamina to give out.

**Zuleta**, trying this trip for the first time, gave away a lot of ground at the start and merely ran on past beaten horses.

**Sayrianna**, making her handicap debut and stepping up in trip, took a good hold early and had pulled herself into a big lead starting the turn for home, but the petrol then ran out completely.

**Preston Hall** *Official explanation: jockey said gelding had a breathing problem*

## 4711 KENT MESSENGER GROUP APPRENTICE H'CAP — 1m 1f 149y

**5:35** (5:35) (F) (0-75,75) 3-Y-O **£4,108** (£1,264; £632; £316) **Stalls** Low

Form RPR

0500 **1** **Nounou**[71] 2614 3-8-3 60.............. MHalford(3) 1 66
(DJDaly) *chsd clr ldr: clsd 3f out: rdn to ld over 1f out: kpt on wl* **7/1**

0436 **2** *1 1/4* **Magic Amigo**[5] 4582 3-9-0 75.............. JJeffrey(7) 4 79
(JRJenkins) *led and sn clr: c bk to field 3f out: hdd over 1f out: kpt on but hld ins fnl f* **3/1**[2]

6042 **3** *1 1/2* **Sunset Mirage (USA)**[8] 4471 3-9-2 70 ow2..............(v) LTreadwell 3 71
(EALDunlop) *hld up in last: smooth prog on inner 3f out: chal 2f out: rdn and nt qckn over 1f out* **9/4**[1]

-000 **4** *3/4* **Turtle Patriarch (IRE)**[20] 4147 3-8-4 58.............. ThomasYeung 2 58
(MrsAJPerrett) *chsd clr ldng pair: effrt 3f out: outpcd over 2f out: kpt on again fnl f* **5/1**

0003 **5** *5* **Keepers Knight (IRE)**[22] 4056 3-8-3 62.............. RJKilloran(5) 5 53
(PFICole) *hld up in 4th: effrt and clsd 3f out: wknd 2f out* **10/3**[3]

2m 9.25s (4.09) **Going Correction** +0.20s/f (Good) **5** Ran SP% **108.0**
Speed ratings: **91,90,88,88,84**CSF £26.53 TOTE £9.70: £3.50, £1.70; EX 43.30 Place 6 £184.82, Place 5 £124.75.

**Owner** Miss Anita Farrell **Bred** Downclose Stud **Trained** Newmarket, Suffolk

**FOCUS**

A tactical contest which basically turned into a three-furlong sprint. The winning time was modest for the grade and more than four seconds slower than the earlier classified event, despite this the form appears sound at a low level.

**NOTEBOOK**

**Nounou**, unplaced in all four of his previous starts, appreciated the return to a longer trip even though it was by no means a true test. He always had the winner in his sights and buckled down in good style when asked to go and win his race. The form probably does not mean a lot however. *Official explanation: trainer said colt had benefited from being schooled over hurdles the previous day*

**Magic Amigo**, whose only victory came under similar conditions over this course and distance, was able to establish a decent advantage by halfway without having to expend too much energy. As a result he was able to keep a bit in reserve for when the cavalry arrived, but even that was insufficient as the winner proved far too determined.

**Sunset Mirage(USA)**, switched off out the back, looked the likely winner when moving up on the inside of the front pair starting up the home straight, but she found less off the bridle than had seemed likely and is basically a disappointing performer.

**Turtle Patriarch(IRE)**, unplaced in all five of his previous starts, should have enjoyed the conditions judged on his breeding but just looks slow.

**Keepers Knight(IRE)** has shown his best form on Polytrack and probably wants faster ground, but even so this was a disappointing effort.

T/Plt: £254.50 to a £1 stake. Pool: £34,218.65. 98.15 winning tickets. T/Qpdt: £32.00 to a £1 stake. Pool: £3,745.60. 86.50 winning tickets. JN

# 4364 NEWBURY (L-H)

Friday, August 13

**OFFICIAL GOING: Good to soft**

## 4712 STANJAMESUK.COM EBF MAIDEN FILLIES' STKS (DIV I) — 6f 8y

**1:40** (1:42) (D) 2-Y-O **£5,642** (£1,736; £868; £434) **Stalls** Centre

Form RPR

**1** **Shanghai Lily (IRE)** 2-8-11.............. KFallon 6 85+
(SirMichaelStoute) *w'like: lengthy: scope: in tch: hdwy to chse ldrs and edgd rt over 2f out: led ins fnl 2f: pushed clr fnl f: easily* **3/1**[1]

**2** *4* **Ruby Wine** 2-8-6.............. RThomas(5) 11 73
(JMPEustace) *unf: scope: hld up in rr: effrt and n.m.r over 2f out: gd hdwy over 1f out: str run to take 2nd ins last but no ch w wnr* **12/1**

**3** *2* **Gold Queen** 2-8-11.............. CCatlin 8 67
(MRChannon) *w'like: led tl hdd ins fnl 2f: wknd fnl f but jst hld on for 3rd* **12/1**

**4** *nk* **Park Approach (IRE)** 2-8-11.............. EAhern 1 66
(JNoseda) *str: bit bkwd: t.k.h: trckd ldrs: rdn 2f out: wknd fnl f* **13/2**[3]

**5** *2* **Scent** 2-8-11.............. JQuinn 7 60+
(JLDunlop) *leggy: s.i.s: bhd: n.m.r over 2f out: kpt on wl fnl f but nvr gng pce to rch ldrs* **16/1**

**6** *nk* **Ponente** 2-8-11.............. SDrowne 5 59+
(BWHills) *w'like: leggy: bit bkwd: s.i.s: bhd: hdwy 2f out: sn one pce* **33/1**

**7** *nk* **This Is My Song** 2-8-11.............. JPMurtagh 9 58
(MrsAJPerrett) *w'like: bit bkwd: hld up in rr: hdwy over 2f out: nvr rch ldrs and wknd appr fnl f* **15/2**

**8** *1 1/2* **Romanova (IRE)** 2-8-11.............. TPQueally 4 54
(DRLoder) *w'like: bhd: pushed along 1/2-way: nvr gng pce of ldrs* **5/1**[2]

0 **9** *7* **Night Club Queen (IRE)**[11] 4399 2-8-11.............. JFEgan 10 33
(JWHills) *chsd ldrs: bmpd over 2f out and sn wknd* **20/1**

**10** *nk* **Alula** 2-8-11.............. RLMoore 3 32
(RHannon) *w'like: athletic: bit bkwd: bhd fr 1/2-way* **5/1**[2]

**11** *3 1/2* **Tanzanite (IRE)** 2-8-11.............. GCarter 2 21
(DWPArbuthnot) *unf: bit bkwd: s.i.s: sn rcvrd to mid-div: rdn 1/2-way: wknd 2f out* **50/1**

1m 15.41s (1.04) **Going Correction** +0.175s/f (Good) **11** Ran SP% **114.4**
Speed ratings: **100,94,92,91,88 88,88,86,76,76 71**CSF £39.01 TOTE £3.50: £1.70, £2.40, £2.80; EX 26.50.

**Owner** Cheveley Park Stud **Bred** Mrs Monica Hackett **Trained** Newmarket, Suffolk

**FOCUS**

A decent winning time for the class of race, more than a second faster than the second division. With this being virtually a newcomers' event it is difficult to weigh up the value of the form, but the winner looks a filly of some potential.

**NOTEBOOK**

**Shanghai Lily(IRE)** ◆, a 300,000euros half-sister to Eden Rock, was a well supported favourite on this debut. She showed plenty of pace to score with a fair amount in hand, and looks sure to go on to better things; she has been quoted as short as 25/1 for next year's 1000 Guineas.

**Ruby Wine** ◆, a first foal who is bred to stay middle distances at least, travelled well off the pace and kept on nicely in the closing stages, although being no match for the winner. She has scope and should be capable of winning her maiden at least.

**Gold Queen**, a 120,000gns first foal of a Listed winner, was keen going to the start. In the race she set off in front and, although swept aside by the winner, kept going to hold off the fourth, who had been snapping at her heels throughout. She should improve for the experience and may be more settled next time.

**Park Approach(IRE)**, a 140,000euros daughter of an unraced half-sister to a Middle Park winner, was green on the way to the start but showed plenty of ability, being up with the pace throughout. She got tired in the last furlong, but is likely to be better with this under her belt.

**Scent**, out of a decent miler, missed the break and ran as if the experience was needed. She was doing her best work at the finish and is another who will benefit from the outing.

**Ponente** was another that will be better for the experience, as she took time to find her stride before keeping on in the closing stages.

**This Is My Song**, out of an unraced half-sister to Predappio, will appreciate a longer trip than this in time.

**Romanova(IRE)** did not live up to market expectations on this debut.

**Alula**, a half-sister to Mind Games, was well backed but faded after showing early pace.

## 4713 AJA LADIES INVITATION FEGENTRI STKS (H'CAP) (IN HONOUR OF ELAIN MELLOR & SANDY MURPHY) 1m 2f 6y

2:10 (2:11) (F) (0-55,55) 3-Y-0+ £3,623 (£1,115; £557; £278) Stalls High

Form RPR
4534 1 **Bojangles (IRE)**[8] 4473 5-10-8 49........................ MissBDeGranvilliers 2 58
(RBrotherton) *trckd ldrs: led over 3f out: drvn and styd on wl fr over 1f out* **9/2**[1]
0-44 2 2 ½ **Flaming Spirt**[4] 4616 5-10-9 50........................ MissPFlierman 3 55
(JSMoore) *hld up in rr: hdwy over 4f out: chsd wnr fr ins fnl 3f: swtchd lft over 2f out: styd on fnl f but no imp* **6/1**[2]
64 3 ½ **Prairie Law (GER)**[8] 4485 4-10-1 42........................ MissAElsey 7 46
(IanWilliams) *bhd: hdwy 3f out: sn rdn: r.o wl fnl f and fin wl but nt rch ldrs* **6/1**[2]
0220 4 6 **Estimate**[13] 4339 4-10-12 53........................(v) MissSBrotherton 6 46
(JohnAHarris) *bhd: hdwy fr 5f out: chsd ldrs over 3f out: outpcd fnl 2f* **8/1**
5064 5 3 **Galey River (USA)**[4] 4604 5-9-11 38........................ MissEJohansson 12 26
(JJSheehan) *chsd ldrs: rdn 3f out: wknd 2f out* **7/1**[3]
1060 6 3 **Larad (IRE)**[27] 3190 3-9-12 48........................(b) MrsMMorris 8 30
(JSMoore) *bhd: rdn and effrt 3f out: nvr nr ldrs and sn btn* **16/1**
3104 7 5 **Over To You Bert**[9] 4436 5-10-3 44........................ MissEJJones 5 17
(RJHodges) *chsd ldrs over 6f* **7/1**[3]
00-0 8 4 **Cote Soleil**[211] 546 7-10-12 53........................ MissSJischa 4 19
(CREgerton) *chsd ldrs tl wknd fr 3f out* **20/1**
5055 9 3 **Latin Queen (IRE)**[8] 4473 4-10-4 45........................ MissEFolkes 9 6
(JDFrost) *sn led: hdd over 3f out: sn btn* **9/1**
0400 10 3 **Catch The Fox**[9] 4438 4-10-1 42........................ MrsSMoore 11 —
(JJBridger) *w ldr to 4f out: sn wknd* **25/1**
-600 11 5 **Pancake Role**[22] 4070 4-9-8 35 oh5........................ MissDLopez 1 —
(AWCarroll) *bhd most of way* **50/1**
4300 12 *dist* **Raheel (IRE)**[60] 2945 4-11-0 55........................(t) MissNVolz 10 —
(PMitchell) *virtually ref to r and a t.o* **14/1**

2m 11.52s (2.81) **Going Correction** +0.475s/f (Yiel)
**WFA** 3 from 4yo+ 9lb **12 Ran SP% 114.6**
Speed ratings: **107,105,104,99,97 95,91,87,85,83 79,—**CSF £28.70 CT £162.41 TOTE £4.40: £2.00, £2.10, £2.00; EX 25.70.
**Owner** Alan Solomon **Bred** C H Wacker Iii **Trained** Elmley Castle, Worcs

**FOCUS**
A moderate ladies' handicap run in not a bad time for a race of its type. The winner was the only one of those that raced prominently to finish in the frame and the form is very modest.

**NOTEBOOK**
**Bojangles(IRE)** had plenty of form at a similar level and the return to easy ground suited him. He settled behind the two leaders and, after taking the advantage some way from home, had to dig deep to hold on. He is fairly exposed and the Handicapper is unlikely to punish him too much for this effort.
**Flaming Spirt**, who was having her third race in a fortnight since returning from a long absence, was given a fine waiting ride and crept into contention looking likely to win. However, she was unable to find any more in the closing stages on ground which may have been a little soft for her. She may need a little time to get over her recent races, but retains her former ability and is 16lb below her last winning mark.
**Prairie Law(GER)** ran another decent race on this easier ground. He is an All-Weather winner in Germany, and will be one to watch out for on that surface, especially if blinkers are fitted.
**Estimate**, another who was given a decent waiting ride, has shown all her best form on fast ground, so may not have been favoured by the underfoot conditions.
**Galey River(USA)** has shown his form on the All-Weather tracks and also on fast ground and, after having a chance early in the straight, faded out of contention.
**Raheel(IRE)**, who is often slowly away, stood still when the stalls opened and had to be driven to take any part at all.

## 4714 STANJAMESUK.COM EBF MAIDEN FILLIES' STKS (DIV II) 6f 8y

2:40 (2:42) (D) 2-Y-0 £5,616 (£1,728; £864; £432) Stalls Centre

Form RPR
1 **Salamanca** 2-8-11........................ JFEgan 6 81+
(SKirk) *unf: scope: bhd: hdwy and nt clr run ins fnl 2f: drvn and qcknd to ld ins fnl: kpt on strly* **15/2**[3]
2 ¾ **Halle Bop** 2-8-11........................ LDettori 2 79+
(SaeedBinSuroor) *w'like: hld up in tch: nt clr run and swtchd lft ins fnl 2f: pushed along to chal 1f out: kpt on but nt pce of wnr ins last* **6/4**[1]
0 3 1 ¼ **Modraj**[28] 3904 2-8-11........................ WSupple 8 75
(JLDunlop) *bhd: hdwy 3f out: drvn to take slt ld 1f out: sn hdd: one pce ins last* **16/1**
00 4 1 **Miss Patricia**[12] 4364 2-8-11........................ TPQueally 9 72
(JGPortman) *bhd: hdwy 1/2-way: drvn to chse ldrs over 1f out: kpt on same pce ins last* **40/1**
5 ¾ **Blueberry Tart (IRE)** 2-8-11........................ SDrowne 5 70
(BJMeehan) *w'like: pressed ldrs: stl ev ch ins fnl 2f: wknd fnl f* **9/1**
6 1 **Missie Baileys** 2-8-8........................ LPKeniry[(3)] 7 67
(DRCElsworth) *w'like: athletic: slowly away: sn rcvrd: hdwy over 2f out: chsd ldrs over 1f out: wknd ins last* **33/1**
7 *shd* **Bailey Gate** 2-8-11........................ JFortune 3 66
(RHannon) *str: bit bkwd: w ldr tl slt advantage over 2f out: sn drvn: hdd 1f out: wknd ins last* **14/1**
8 *shd* **Montecito** 2-8-11........................ RLMoore 4 66
(RHannon) *unf: slt advantage tl narrowly hdd over 2f out: wknd appr fnl f* **20/1**
9 2 ½ **Desert Imp** 2-8-11........................ KFallon 10 59
(BWHills) *str: bit bkwd: s.i.s: sn rcvrd: swtchd lft after 2f: hdwy 3f out: pressed ldrs 2f out: wknd over 1f out* **4/1**[2]
05 10 *nk* **Caona (USA)**[11] 4399 2-8-11........................ EAhern 1 58
(JNoseda) *lw: chsd ldrs 4f* **10/1**

1m 16.43s (2.06) **Going Correction** +0.175s/f (Good) **10 Ran SP% 113.5**
Speed ratings: **93,92,90,89,88 86,86,86,83,82**CSF £18.22 TOTE £7.90: £2.50, £1.20, £3.50; EX 32.70.
**Owner** Wood Street Syndicate **Bred** D P Martin **Trained** Upper Lambourn, Berks

**FOCUS**
Another fillies' maiden, featuring few with racecourse experience, and an average time for the class, over a second slower than the first division. The form is difficult to gauge at this stage.

**NOTEBOOK**
**Salamanca**, a half-sister to a couple of seven-furlong juvenile winners, looked quite fit but was easy in the market. After being held up, she squeezed through to lead inside the final furlong and ran on well to hold the favourite a little cosily. She looked as if the experience will not be lost on her and, entered in a couple of sales races this autumn, may be able to improve sufficiently to figure in those.
**Halle Bop**, a medium-sized filly out of a high-class half-sister to the Derby winner Oath, was a slightly uneasy favourite. She travelled well on the heels of the leaders and, after being switched, seemed to have every chance but did not quite have the speed of the winner. She should be better for the run and can find a maiden over further.
**Modraj** stepped up on her debut effort over course and distance last month, and for a moment looked likely to score. She is another who will benefit from racing over a longer trip, and looks capable of picking up an ordinary maiden.
**Miss Patricia** had shown modest ability in a couple of maidens and looks to provide a key to the level of the form. She is now qualified for a handicap mark and can be placed to win a nursery.
**Blueberry Tart(IRE)** ◆ is by a sprinter, but out of a mare whose best form was over middle distances. She showed quite a bit of ability on this debut and, being from a yard whose juveniles often improve for an outing, can be expected to step up on this effort.
**Missie Baileys** missed the break and, in the circumstances, performed quite well to finish as close as she did.
**Bailey Gate**, a half-sister to Ringmoor Down, disputed the lead with her stable companion before fading.
**Montecito**, who is bred to appreciate further, kept her stable companion company throughout and will do better in time.
**Desert Imp**, a speedily-bred second foal of a juvenile winner, was well backed against the favourite. She missed the break and was then switched to the outside of her field before halfway. She got into contention before fading, and may give her supporters a chance to get compensation with this experience behind her. *Official explanation: jockey said filly was slowly away*

## 4715 STANJAMESUK.COM H'CAP 1m 5f 61y

3:15 (3:15) (C) (0-90,90) 3-Y-0+ £9,997 (£3,076; £1,538; £769) Stalls High

Form RPR
21-2 1 **Soulacroix**[19] 4167 3-8-11 85........................ JPMurtagh 5 98
(MrsAJPerrett) *in tch: rdn and styd over fr over 2f out: edgd rt over 1f out: squeezed through to ld fnl f: drvn and hld on wl* **11/2**[3]
6154 2 ¾ **Lost Soldier Three (IRE)**[28] 3915 3-8-13 87........................ KFallon 3 100+
(LMCumani) *lw: hld up in rr: rdn and hdwy over 2f out: styng on whn n.m.r 1f out and jst ins last: fin strly but a hld* **9/2**[2]
1236 3 1 ¾ **Meadaaf (IRE)**[40] 3561 3-8-6 80........................ SDrowne 1 89
(EFVaughan) *trckd ldrs: rdn over 3f out: chalng whn bmpd over 1f out: kpt on same pce ins last* **12/1**
4615 4 3 ½ **Stage Right**[16] 4229 3-8-8 85........................ LPKeniry[(3)] 7 89
(DRCElsworth) *lw: in tch: rdn fr over 3f out: styd on fr over 1f out but nvr gng pce to rch ldrs* **11/4**[1]
1120 5 1 ½ **Bendarshaan**[17] 4218 4-10-0 90........................ JFanning 4 92
(MJohnston) *trckd ldr: chal fr 4f out tl slt advantage and rdn ins fnl 3f: hdd 1f out and sn btn* **7/1**
0210 6 ½ **Shredded (USA)**[48] 3325 4-9-3 79........................(t) JFortune 2 80
(JHMGosden) *bit bkwd: led tl narrowly hdd ins fnl 3f: wknd ins fnl f* **10/1**
-160 7 3 ½ **Grooms Affection**[20] 4123 4-9-7 83........................ LDettori 6 79
(PWHarris) *bhd: hrd drvn fr 3f out: sme hdwy fr over 1f out but nvr a danger* **11/2**[3]
345- 8 1 **Gondolin (IRE)**[314] 5366 4-9-8 84........................ TPQueally 8 79
(GAButler) *bhd: rdn over 3f out: nvr raised pce to rch ldrs* **16/1**

2m 55.65s (4.66) **Going Correction** +0.475s/f (Yiel)
**WFA** 3 from 4yo 12lb **8 Ran SP% 110.8**
Speed ratings: **104,103,102,100,99 99,96,96**CSF £28.42 CT £269.70 TOTE £4.70: £2.00, £1.30, £3.30; EX 20.30 Trifecta £87.40 Pool: £1,342.50. 10.90 winning units..
**Owner** G C Stevens **Bred** D Bunn **Trained** Pulborough, W Sussex

**FOCUS**
A decent staying handicap run at just an ordinary gallop before the pace quickened early in the straight. Despite this the form looks sound enough.

**NOTEBOOK**
**Soulacroix**, an easy-ground maiden winner as a juvenile, showed the benefit of his recent outing and return to this surface by staying on stoutly to score. He is the sort the stable do well with and, although the Melrose Stakes next week may come a little too soon, he looks capable of winning again at around this trip during the autumn.
**Lost Soldier Three(IRE)**, another stepping up in trip, had two subsequent winners in front of him at Newmarket last time. He came from well back and did not get the best of runs, but was beaten on merit in the end. Having shown that he stays the trip, connections should be able to place him to win another race before long.
**Meadaaf(IRE)**, stepping up in trip and grade, was done no favours when the winner squeezed through a narrow opening, but it did not affect the result. He looks as if a shorter trip and faster ground will be more in his favour.
**Stage Right**, who should have appreciated this longer trip and more galloping track, did not have the strong gallop that would have suited and may not be quite as effective on an easy surface. He can be given a chance to show he is better than this, given his ideal conditions.
**Bendarshaan** got in a battle for the lead with Shredded early in the straight which ultimately cost both of them.
**Shredded(USA)** set the pace and kicked on early in the straight, but was taken on by Bendarshaan, and paid the penalty in the closing stages.

## 4716 STAN JAMES STKS (REGISTERED AS THE WASHINGTON SINGER STAKES) (LISTED RACE) 7f (S)

3:50 (3:51) (A) 2-Y-0 £14,875 (£5,500; £2,750; £1,250) Stalls Centre

Form RPR
102 1 **Kings Quay**[21] 4088 2-8-11 91........................ RLMoore 5 101
(RHannon) *disp cl 2nd tl drvn to ld ins fnl 2f: hung rt and then lft u.p ins last: hld on wl cl home* **3/1**[3]
3321 2 ½ **Wilko (USA)**[9] 4461 2-8-11 100........................ EAhern 1 100
(JNoseda) *lw: disp cl 2nd: rdn over 2f out: chsd wnr fnl f: kpt on but no imp cl home* **15/8**[2]
53 3 1 **Subyan Dreams**[16] 4243 2-8-7 ow1........................ JFortune 4 94
(PWChapple-Hyam) *hld up rr but wl in tch: rdn over 2f out: styd on u.p to take 3rd ins last but nt rch ldrs* **33/1**
1121 4 2 ½ **Brecon Beacon**[14] 4295 2-9-0 100........................ JPMurtagh 3 94
(PFICole) *lw: led: hdd ins fnl 2f: wknd ins fnl f: dismntd after fin* **11/8**[1]
5 ¾ **Rocamadour** 2-8-8........................ CCatlin 2 86
(MRChannon) *unf: scope: bit bkwd: in tch: rdn and outpcd over 2f out: kpt on u.p fnl f but n.d* **33/1**

1m 28.46s (1.24) **Going Correction** +0.175s/f (Good) **5 Ran SP% 107.8**
Speed ratings: **99,98,97,94,93**CSF £8.64 TOTE £4.20: £2.00, £1.60; EX 14.50.
**Owner** J R May **Bred** Newsells Park Stud Limited **Trained** East Everleigh, Wilts

**FOCUS**
A fair Listed contest, but an unspectacular time for the class of contest, although it was faster than the later maiden over the same trip, suggesting one or two may be flattered.

**NOTEBOOK**
**Kings Quay** finally got conditions that were expected to suit, cut in the ground and seven furlongs and, despite being keen early in the race, produced a turn of foot to get to the front and then held on despite wandering about. His previous form suggests he has done well to score at this level, but he gives the impression that he will improve with maturity.
**Wilko(USA)**, who has already been placed in a Group Two, again ran his race and looks a reliable yardstick as to the value of the form. He handles anything between fast and easy ground, and deserves to pick up a Pattern race before the season is out.
**Subyan Dreams**, who had been beaten in a couple of ordinary maidens, was well placed by connections to pick up some valuable black type. She was staying on well, will get further and should be able to pick up a race given a little give in the ground.

**Brecon Beacon**, who beat a subsequent Listed winner at Newmarket last time, was the disappointment of the race. He dictated the pace, but found little once the race began in earnest and faded tamely. He may have had excuses, but has already won on easy ground, so that should not be one of them.
**Rocamadour**, who is speedily-bred on his dam's side, had a stiff task on this debut but showed enough promise to suggest he can win races.

## 4717 STANJAMESCASINO.CO.UK H'CAP — 6f 8y

**4:20** (4:21) (D) (0-80,80) 3-Y-O — **£5,538** (£1,704; £852; £426) **Stalls** Centre

Form — RPR

5032 **1** — **Apex**[20] 4126 3-9-7 **80** ........ KFallon 14 — 93
(EALDunlop) *bhd: rdn 2f out: rapid hdwy over 1f out to ld ins fnl f: pushed clr: comf* — **3/1**[2]

4062 **2** *2* — **The Jobber (IRE)**[7] 4515 3-9-5 **78** ........ FNorton 13 — 85
(MBlanshard) *bhd: gd hdwy ins fnl 2f to take narrow ld 1f out: hdd ins last: kpt on but no ch w wnr* — **10/1**

0-01 **3** *1/2* — **Morgan Lewis (IRE)**[8] 4489 3-8-5 **69** 6ex ........ RThomas(5) 16 — 75
(GBBalding) *bhd: rdn and hdwy over 1f out: kpt on wl fnl f but nt pce of ldrs* — **2/1**[1]

2002 **4** *1 3/4* — **Bee Minor**[20] 4144 3-8-12 **71** ........ EAhern 8 — 71
(RHannon) *bhd: hdwy over 2f out: rdn to chse ldrs ins last: sn one pce* — **20/1**

4330 **5** *nk* — **Ask The Clerk (IRE)**[9] 4456 3-8-12 **71** ........ MTebbutt 6 — 70
(VSmith) *chsd ldrs: rdn over 1f out: one pce ins last* — **9/1**

-360 **6** *1 1/2* — **Chickado (IRE)**[29] 3887 3-7-10 **60** ........ DFox(5) 12 — 55
(DHaydnJones) *pressed ldrs: slt ld appr fnl f: sn hdd: wknd ins last* — **33/1**

5124 **7** *hd* — **Instant Recall (IRE)**[22] 4051 3-9-7 **80** ........(b) JFortune 11 — 74
(BJMeehan) *slt ld: rdn over 2f out: hdd appr fnl f: wknd ins last* — **6/1**[3]

-100 **8** *1/2* — **Beejay**[74] 2518 3-9-1 **74** ........ SDrowne 7 — 67
(PFICole) *chsd ldrs: outpcd whn hmpd over 1f out* — **33/1**

6304 **9** *nk* — **Hilites (IRE)**[15] 4266 3-8-10 **76** ........ DerekNolan(7) 2 — 68
(JSMoore) *s.i.s: sn rcvrd and in tch: drvn to chse ldrs 2f out: wknd ins fnl f* — **25/1**

0226 **10** *1/2* — **Cyfrwys (IRE)**[21] 4083 3-8-3 **62** ........ DKinsella 5 — 52
(BPalling) *pressed ldrs: ev ch appr fnl f: wknd ins last* — **14/1**

41 **11** *3/4* — **Kostar**[20] 4144 3-9-4 **77** ........ RSmith 4 — 65
(CGCox) *lw: chsd ldrs: rdn over 2f out: wknd over 1f out* — **14/1**

4305 **12** *2 1/2* — **Borzoi Maestro**[5] 4585 3-8-13 **75** ........ LPKeniry(3) 15 — 56
(JLSpearing) *lw: chsd ldrs: ev ch 2f out: wknd over 1f out* — **20/1**

60-0 **13** *shd* — **Saintly Place**[34] 3747 3-8-1 **60** ........ CCatlin 1 — 40
(MRChannon) *chsd ldrs tl wknd ins fnl 2f* — **66/1**

0-55 **14** *1 3/4* — **Fisby**[18] 4195 3-8-6 **65** ........ JFEgan 3 — 40
(SKirk) *in tch tl wknd 2f out* — **20/1**

140- **15** *1/2* — **Scarlet Empress**[275] 5979 3-9-3 **76** ........ RLMoore 10 — 50
(RHannon) *w ldr to 2f out: wknd sn after* — **50/1**

1m 14.52s (0.15) **Going Correction** +0.175s/f (Good) — **15** Ran SP% **132.5**
Speed ratings: **106,103,102,100,99 97,97,97,96,95 94,91,91,89,88**CSF £33.14 CT £79.52 TOTE £4.90: £1.80, £3.30, £1.70; EX 38.00.
**Owner** Patrick Milmo And Stuart Tilling **Bred** P D And Mrs C E Player And Jonathon Jay **Trained** Newmarket, Suffolk

**FOCUS**
A fair handicap that was run quicker than the two fillies' maidens earlier in the day and the form looks solid. Those drawn high and held up off the pace came out best.

**NOTEBOOK**
**Apex**, whose only win came on soft ground, was dropping back in trip. He had to be pushed along to keep up at one point, but once into his stride cut through the pack and won in good style. He is generally on an upward curve, and continued ease in the ground will be in his favour.
**The Jobber(IRE)**, another whose only win was on soft ground, was also held up and came through to lead briefly before the winner swept past. He is on a fair mark at present, and given his conditions looks capable of picking up a similar race.
**Morgan Lewis(IRE)**, carrying a 6lb penalty for his win on similar going at Haydock, followed the principals through to take third without ever looking likely to justify favouritism. He gives the impression a stiffer track or another furlong will be in his favour.
**Bee Minor** reversed Salisbury form with Kostar on 1lb better terms, but merely ran on past beaten rivals and was probably helped by switching to race nearer the stands' side.
**Ask The Clerk(IRE)**, who handles cut in the ground, appeared to have every chance but could not pick up.
**Chickado(IRE)** ran one of her best races on turf, but up to now her better performances have been on Fibresand.
**Instant Recall(IRE)** set the pace, but does not appear quite so effective with cut in the ground. His wins have both been on Polytrack.

## 4718 HAMLYN MILNE MAR-KEY MARQUEES MAIDEN FILLIES' STKS — 7f (S)

**4:50** (4:52) (D) 3-Y-O+ — **£5,798** (£1,784; £892; £446) **Stalls** Centre

Form — RPR

5- **1** — **Enrapture (USA)**[363] 4185 3-8-11 ........ KFallon 4 — 77+
(MrsAJPerrett) *lw: trckd ldrs: led over 2f out: pushed clr over 1f out: drvn and styd on wl cl home* — **6/5**[1]

**2** *1/2* — **Woodland Glade** 3-8-11 ........ JFortune 8 — 76
(RHannon) *w'like: narrow: in tch: hdwy 2f out: qcknd to chse wnr ins fnl f: swtchd lft and fin wl but a hld* — **10/1**

5 **3** *2 1/2* — **Tetcott (IRE)**[51] 3209 3-8-11 ........ WSupple 6 — 69
(MPTregoning) *in tch: hdwy over 2f out: chsd wnr over 1f out: no imp and outpcd fnl f* — **10/3**[2]

**4** *3/4* — **Future Deal** 3-8-11 ........ SCarson 7 — 67
(CAHorgan) *w'like: bit bkwd: chsd ldrs: chal fr 3f out and stl ev ch 2f out: no ex ins last* — **33/1**

33 **5** *1 3/4* — **Deuxieme (IRE)**[36] 3666 3-8-11 ........ SDrowne 9 — 63
(RCharlton) *s.i.s: plld hrd early: hdwy over 1f out: edgd lft whn rdn ins last and fnd no ex* — **7/2**[3]

00 **6** *2* — **Highland Lass**[20] 4125 3-8-6 ........ NChalmers(5) 5 — 57?
(MrsHSweeting) *chsd ldrs: slt advantage 3f out: hdd wl over 2f out: wknd over 1f out* — **50/1**

0 **7** *4* — **Under My Skin (IRE)**[37] 3630 3-8-11 ........(t) GCarter 10 — 47
(TGMills) *led 4f: wknd over 2f out* — **25/1**

00 **8** *1* — **Bonnetts (IRE)**[28] 3916 3-8-11 ........ CCatlin 3 — 44
(HCandy) *s.i.s: bhd: rdn flashed tail and no ch over 2f out* — **33/1**

U00 **9** *3/4* — **Aljafliyah**[27] 3948 3-8-4 ........ AHamblett(7) 2 — 42
(LMCumani) *s.i.s: bhd: hdwy 1/2-way: rdn: hung lft and wknd ins fnl 2f* — **33/1**

0 **10** *6* — **Miss Monza**[20] 4144 3-8-11 ........ FNorton 1 — 27
(BRMillman) *in tch over 4f* — **33/1**

1m 28.63s (1.41) **Going Correction** +0.175s/f (Good) — **10** Ran SP% **117.4**
Speed ratings: **98,97,94,93,91 89,84,83,82,76**CSF £13.90 TOTE £2.10: £1.10, £2.80, £1.10; EX 12.80.
**Owner** Cheveley Park Stud **Bred** Cheveley Park Stud **Trained** Pulborough, W Sussex

**FOCUS**
An ordinary fillies' maiden run slower than the earlier juvenile Listed race. The form is nothing special but appears reasonably sound.

**NOTEBOOK**
**Enrapture(USA)**, who showed promise on her sole appearance as a juvenile, was a short-priced favourite to overcome a year's absence. She burst to the front some way from home and went clear, but she began to tire in the closing stages and in the end had to battle to resist the late surge of the runner-up. Connections will no doubt be looking to gain some black type with her, but she will have to improve to attain that goal, although it is not out of the question that she can achieve it.
**Woodland Glade**, a half-sister to Baron's Pit, was making a belated debut and still looks weak. She travelled nicely off the pace and then picked up well in the closing stages to give the winner a race. She should come on for the outing and looks capable of picking up a maiden at least.
**Tetcott(IRE)**, out of a Brocklesby-winning sister to Brave Burt and Pip's Song, appeared to have every chance but could not find an extra gear in the closing stages. She gives the impression she will need a little further and may do better once qualified for handicaps.
**Future Deal**, whose dam won over this trip as a three-year-old, showed plenty of pace and stuck on well in the closing stages. She should improve for the experience and has a small race in her.
**Deuxieme(IRE)** missed the break and did not really settle out the back of the field. She ran on in the closing stages without ever looking likely to reach a challenging position, but at least now qualifies for a handicap mark.

## 4719 TOM MITCHELL "HALF CENTURY" BIRTHDAY CELEBRATION H'CAP — 1m 1f

**5:25** (5:25) (E) (0-75,75) 3-Y-O+ — **£4,127** (£1,270; £635; £317) **Stalls** High

Form — RPR

6043 **1** — **Didnt Tell My Wife**[28] 3911 5-9-5 **63** ........ KFallon 9 — 73
(CFWall) *hld up in tch: hdwy over 2f out: squeezed through to ld over 1f out: pushed out ins last: comf* — **15/8**[1]

0606 **2** *1 1/4* — **Arry Dash**[14] 4301 4-9-11 **72** ........ SHitchcott(3) 2 — 80
(MRChannon) *chsd ldrs: chal ins fnl 2f: chsd wnr fr over 1f out: no imp ins last* — **3/1**[2]

-100 **3** *3 1/2* — **Waziri (IRE)**[15] 4274 3-9-6 **75** ........ LFletcher(3) 11 — 76
(HMorrison) *bhd: hdwy on outside over 2f out: chsd ldr over 1f out: wknd ins last* — **7/1**

3-60 **4** *3 1/2* — **Wizard Of Edge**[21] 4080 4-9-9 **67** ........ FNorton 1 — 61
(RJHodges) *bhd: pushed along over 2f out: kpt on fnl f but nvr a danger* — **20/1**

4200 **5** *1* — **Phred**[44] 3412 4-9-2 **60** ........ SCarson 3 — 52
(RFJohnsonHoughton) *chsd ldrs: slt ld over 2f out: hdd over 1f out and sn wknd* — **10/1**

3636 **6** *1 1/2* — **Cumbrian Princess**[13] 4339 7-8-1 **45** ........ DKinsella 10 — 34
(MBlanshard) *bhd: hdwy over 3f out: chsd ldrs sn after: wknd ins fnl 2f* — **16/1**

3-60 **7** *2* — **How's Things**[41] 3520 4-9-2 **60** ........ RHavlin 6 — 45
(DHaydnJones) *chsd ldr: slt ld 3f out: hdd over 2f out: sn wknd* — **20/1**

0540 **8** *7* — **Desert Hawk**[21] 4079 3-9-2 **68** ........ JFortune 5 — 39
(RHannon) *chsd ldrs tl wknd over 2f out* — **5/1**[3]

00 **9** *3* — **Jahia (NZ)**[8] 4471 5-9-5 **70** ........ RLucey-Butler(7) 8 — 35
(MMadgwick) *sn ld: narrowly hdd 3f out: sn btn* — **50/1**

1m 57.92s (3.57) **Going Correction** +0.475s/f (Yiel)
**WFA** 3 from 4yo+ 8lb — **9** Ran SP% **115.4**
Speed ratings: **103,101,98,95,94 93,91,85,82**CSF £7.23 CT £31.09 TOTE £2.40: £1.20, £1.70, £2.00; EX 6.60 Place 6 £42.10, Place 5 £16.25.
**Owner** G D Newton **Bred** Mrs Frank Campbell **Trained** Newmarket, Suffolk
■ This completed a four-timer on the afternoon for Kieren Fallon.

**FOCUS**
A moderate handicap for the track run at an even pace, giving the form a straightforward and reliable look.

**NOTEBOOK**
**Didnt Tell My Wife**, who handles cut in the ground, was trying his longest trip to date. He travelled nicely just off the pace, and when eventually getting an opening soon put the result beyond doubt to give his jockey a four-timer. He has taken time to find his form this season, but he is on a reasonable mark and looks capable of supplementing this victory.
**Arry Dash**, like the winner travelled well just off the pace, and got a split on the rail at the same time. He came off second best but was clear of the rest and, 8lb lower than when last successful nearly 18 months ago, he seems suited by a flat track and could be weighted to score again.
**Waziri(IRE)**, who has been lightly raced, was taking a big drop in trip. He seemed to appreciate it and came from well back to chase the winner before his effort flattened out. He is now only a pound higher than when winning on his reappearance, and faster conditions may suit him better.
**Wizard Of Edge**, twice a winner over hurdles in the spring, ran on late in the day but presumably will be switching codes now the ground has shown signs of easing.
**Phred** ran well on this return from a short break, having apparently lost his form after some decent early-season efforts. He is 5lb lower than when winning last September, and will be interesting if re-appearing in the next couple of weeks.
**Desert Hawk**, a lightly-raced maiden, showed up for a fair way before fading. He looks high enough in the handicap for what he has achieved, and if dropped a few pound a maiden handicap may be his best option. *Official explanation: jockey had no explanation for the poor form shown*
T/Jkpt: Not won. T/Plt: £23.40 to a £1 stake. Pool: £45,651.90. 1,423.85 winning tickets. T/Qpdt: £7.30 to a £1 stake. Pool: £3,577.70. 362.30 winning tickets. ST

# 4444 NEWCASTLE (L-H)

Friday, August 13

**4720 Meeting Abandoned** - Waterlogged

# 4550 NEWMARKET (JULY) (R-H)

Friday, August 13

**OFFICIAL GOING: Good to soft changing to soft after 6.15 (race 2)**
After further rain the ground had become quite testing by Newmarket standards.
Wind: Fresh behind Weather: Raining

## 4726 LEARNDIRECT CLASSIFIED STKS — 1m

**5:45** (5:47) (E) 3-Y-O — **£4,241** (£1,305; £652; £326) **Stalls** High

Form — RPR

3034 **1** — **Bright Sun (IRE)**[13] 4340 3-9-2 72 ........ KimTinkler 2 — 81
(NTinkler) *racd stands' side: dwlt: sn prom: led 3f out: rdn and hung lft fr over 1f out: styd on* — **4/1**[1]

0230 **2** *1/2* — **Adorata (GER)**[29] 3875 3-8-11 67 ........ OUrbina 5 — 74
(JJay) *racd stands' side: hld up in tch: rdn and ev ch fr over 1f out: edgd lft ins fnl f: styd on* — **16/1**



The Form Book, Raceform Ltd, Compton, RG20 6NL

1 **3** *3 ½* **Surreptitious**[27] 3948 3-8-11 68 ............ TPQueally 8 67
(DRLoder) *lw: racd stands' side: chsd ldrs: rdn over 1f out: hung lft and styd on same pce* **4/1**[1]

1506 **4** *nk* **Tannoor (USA)**[22] 4056 3-9-5 75 ............(p) PRobinson 1 74
(MAJarvis) *racd alone far side: w ldrs: rdn over 1f out: no ex fnl f* **8/1**

054 **5** *1 ¼* **Dream Easy**[27] 3948 3-9-0 70 ............ RPrice 3 66
(PLGilligan) *swtg: racd stands' side: w ldrs over 3f: sn rdn: styd on same pce appr fnl f* **16/1**

-503 **6** *3* **Halabaloo (IRE)**[86] 2223 3-9-2 75 ............ JFEgan 4 62
(GWragg) *racd stands' side: hld up: rdn over 2f out: n.d* **5/1**[2]

4100 **7** *1* **Baker Of Oz**[13] 4327 3-9-2 72 ............ RLMoore 9 60
(RHannon) *lw: racd stands' side: w ldr tl led over 3f out: sn hdd: wknd fnl f* **8/1**

-306 **8** *3* **Pending (IRE)**[16] 4238 3-9-0 70 ............ JPMurtagh 10 52
(JRFanshawe) *racd stands' side: chsd ldrs: rdn over 2f out: wknd over 1f out* **6/1**[3]

0005 **9** *9* **Shaaban (IRE)**[48] 3294 3-8-11 69 ............ BReilly(3) 7 33
(MissJFeilden) *racd stands' side: chsd ldrs over 5f* **33/1**

3-50 **10** *10* **Negwa (IRE)**[110] 1640 3-8-11 70 ............ TEDurcan 6 9
(MRChannon) *racd stands' side: dwlt: hld up: wknd 3f out* **16/1**

-000 **11** *3 ½* **Mutassem (FR)**[52] 3180 3-9-0 69 ............ MHenry 12 4
(TKeddy) *b: led stands' side over 4f: sn wknd* **50/1**

1m 39.49s (-0.99) **Going Correction** -0.025s/f (Good) **11** Ran SP% **115.7**
Speed ratings: **103,102,99,98,97 94,93,90,81,71 67**CSF £69.39 TOTE £5.50: £1.70, £5.90, £1.60; EX 243.40.
**Owner** Leeds Plywood And Doors Ltd **Bred** Terence McDonald **Trained** Langton, N Yorks

**FOCUS**
A competitive event with the runners covered by 4lb on official ratings, but the form appears ordinary for the grade. Tannoor elected to race by himself on the far side.

**NOTEBOOK**
**Bright Sun(IRE)** handled conditions better than most, and now his trainer has found the right trip should be capable of scoring again.
**Adorata(GER)**, who failed to handle the undulations of Epsom last time, showed her true colours. While she has yet to get of the mark, she is not without ability.
**Surreptitious** did not appear to handle the rain-softened ground.
**Tannoor(USA)**, who stays further than this was probably done no favours by racing alone up the far rail.
**Dream Easy**, closely matched with Surreptitious on their running here last month, again hinted at having a little ability.
**Halabaloo(IRE)** never looked likely to take a hand at any stage and may need a faster surface to show her best.

## 4727 VIBE FM H'CAP 6f
6:15 (6:17) (D) (0-80,75) 3-Y-O+ **£5,538** (£1,704; £852; £426) **Stalls** High

Form RPR

0122 **1** **Mistral Sky**[6] 4547 5-9-7 **72** ............(v) JFEgan 5 82
(MrsStefLiddiard) *racd keenly: w ldr tl led over 1f out: drvn out* **4/1**[2]

0343 **2** *nk* **Albashoosh**[6] 4534 6-9-4 **69** ............ AlexGreaves 4 78
(DNicholls) *plld hrd: sn led: rdn and hdd over 1f out: r.o* **4/1**[2]

0-00 **3** *9* **Ben Lomand**[79] 2399 4-9-6 **71** ............ ADaly 1 53
(BWDuke) *lw: chsd ldrs tl wknd over 1f out* **25/1**

5005 **4** *hd* **Fearby Cross (IRE)**[14] 4294 8-8-11 **62** ............ RMullen 7 44
(WJMusson) *hld up: pushed along over 3f out: nvr trbld ldrs* **4/1**[2]

6000 **5** *½* **A Teen**[20] 4130 6-8-3 **54** ............ TPQueally 8 34
(PHowling) *b.hind: chsd ldrs over 4f* **20/1**

3002 **6** *1 ¼* **Lake Verdi (IRE)**[8] 4495 5-7-13 **50** ............(t) JMackay 6 26
(MissGayKelleway) *b: chsd ldrs over 4f* **8/1**[3]

1034 **7** *¾* **Scottish Exile (IRE)**[8] 4472 3-9-2 **71** ............(v) DarrenWilliams 2 45
(KRBurke) *hld up: rdn over 2f out: wknd over 1f out* **16/1**

021- **8** *3 ½* **St Austell**[401] 3103 4-9-8 **73** ............ LisaJones 3 37
(JARToller) *dwlt: sn prom: wknd over 1f out* **14/1**

0522 **9** *½* **Cold Climate**[7] 4522 9-8-4 **55** ............ JQuinn 9 17
(BobJones) *hld up in tch: rdn over 2f out: sn wknd* **7/2**[1]

1m 12.86s (-0.46) **Going Correction** -0.025s/f (Good)
**WFA** 3 from 4yo+ 4lb **9** Ran SP% **114.5**
Speed ratings: **102,101,89,89,88 87,86,81,80**CSF £20.21 CT £351.27 TOTE £4.70: £1.90, £1.80, £5.80; EX 21.30.
**Owner** Shefford Valley Stud **Bred** Peter Nelson **Trained** Great Shefford, Berks

**FOCUS**
An ordinary handicap, but not easy to rate with the weather taking a turn for the worse they finished well strung out, and the front pair filled those positions throughout. The early pace was pedestrian.

**NOTEBOOK**
**Mistral Sky** is a tough performer and really dug deep to fend off the runner-up. However, although the front pair pulled well clear of the remainder the form needs treating with caution, for they had the run of the race between them.
**Albashoosh**, proven in conditions, took a fierce grip and was a reluctant leader. He is much better with a lead.
**Ben Lomand** is better on a sounder surface and was easily left behind when they eventually quickened.
**Fearby Cross(IRE)** needs a flat out gallop over this trip, something he never got here.
**A Teen** has yet to shine on a soft surface.
**Cold Climate**, who has done most of his winning on a sound surface, was one of the first beaten.
*Official explanation: trainer said gelding needs things to go his own way and may have become unsettled tonight due to problems experienced in the starting stalls*

## 4728 LEARNDIRECT MAIDEN STKS 1m
6:45 (6:49) (D) 2-Y-O **£4,803** (£1,478; £739; £369) **Stalls** High

Form RPR

**1** **Motivator** 2-9-0 ............ KFallon 10 89+
(MLWBell) *neat: lw: hld up in tch: led over 1f out: sn clr* **3/1**[2]

**2** *6* **Sunday Symphony** 2-9-0 ............ KMcEvoy 4 74+
(SaeedBinSuroor) *gd sort: bit bkwd: chsd ldrs: rdn over 2f out: outpcd over 1f out* **9/2**[3]

033 **3** *¾* **Tumbleweed Galore (IRE)**[17] 4208 2-8-11 73 ............ JFMcDonald(3) 7 73
(BJMeehan) *w ldr tl led 5f out: rdn and hdd over 1f out: sn wknd* **10/1**

**4** *4* **Rosecliff** 2-9-0 ............ JPMurtagh 6 66
(AMBalding) *cmpt: s.s: hld up: hdwy over 2f out: nvr trbld ldrs* **16/1**

00 **5** *1 ½* **Rebel Rebel (IRE)**[19] 4169 2-9-0 ............ OUrbina 3 63
(NACallaghan) *lw: chsd ldrs over 6f* **50/1**

**6** *4* **Tamatave (IRE)** 2-9-0 ............(t) KDarley 11 56
(SaeedBinSuroor) *leggy: scope: prom: chsd ldr over 3f out: to over 2f out: wknd over 1f out* **10/1**

5 **7** *1 ¾* **Mutamaasek (USA)**[19] 4169 2-9-0 ............ WSupple 9 53
(JLDunlop) *hld up in tch: rdn and wknd wl over 1f out* **5/2**[1]

**8** *hd* **Notability (IRE)** 2-9-0 ............ PRobinson 1 52
(MAJarvis) *gd sort: scope: lw: hld up: hdwy 3f out: wknd 2f out* **9/1**

**9** *1 ¼* **Garhoud** 2-9-0 ............ EAhern 8 50
(EALDunlop) *w'like: scope: s.s: hld up: hdwy over 2f out: sn wknd* **20/1**

**10** *5* **Legally Fast (USA)** 2-9-0 ............ SDrowne 2 41
(PFICole) *w;like: scope: bkwd: led: hdd over 5f out: wknd over 3f out* **33/1**

60 **11** *nk* **Bibi Helen**[48] 3319 2-8-9 ............ RMullen 5 36
(NACallaghan) *lw: uns rdr and bolted to post: rrd and s.s: hdwy over 2f out: sn wknd* **66/1**

1m 41.11s (0.63) **Going Correction** +0.15s/f (Good) **11** Ran SP% **117.0**
Speed ratings: **102,96,95,91,89 85,84,83,82,77 77**CSF £16.32 TOTE £3.30: £1.50, £1.80, £2.70; EX 11.50.
**Owner** The Royal Ascot Racing Club **Bred** Deerfield Farm **Trained** Newmarket, Suffolk

**FOCUS**
The field raced more towards the centre of the track and produced a decent winning time for the grade. The winner was impressive and may eventually prove up to Pattern class.

**NOTEBOOK**
**Motivator**, a 75,000 gns yearling, absolutely bolted up without knowing he had done anything, and while some of his rivals may not have handled conditions, it would be churlish to take anything away from him. The Royal Lodge is his intended target.
**Sunday Symphony**, a half-brother to the useful Al Waffi and Made In Japan, was easily left trailing when the winner quickened up. However, he still looked green and is entitled to improve.
**Tumbleweed Galore(IRE)** did not get home on this rain-softened ground. However, there was still plenty of promise in this and he should be able to find an opening.
**Rosecliff**, a 150,000 gns yearling is out of a mare that won over six furlongs as a juvenile. Given time to get the hang of things, he can only improve for the experience.
**Rebel Rebel(IRE)**, a half-brother to Montmartre has faced some stiff tasks in his three runs to date. This was his best effort yet and he is one to keep an eye on when stepping into nurseries.
**Tamatave(IRE)**, a half-brother to middle-distance winner Manoubi, looks the sort to do better over further next year.
**Mutamaasek(USA)**, off the bridle some way out, failed to handle these testing conditions.

## 4729 JOE JENNINGS BOOKMAKERS H'CAP 1m 4f
7:15 (7:21) (C) (0-90,87) 3-Y-O+ **£9,665** (£2,974; £1,487; £743) **Stalls** Centre

Form RPR

2601 **1** **Tawny Way**[13] 4345 4-9-11 **87** ............ SDrowne 3 98
(WJarvis) *a.p: rdn to ld over 1f out: styd on wl* **14/1**

152 **2** *1 ¾* **Fling**[55] 3091 3-8-9 **82** ow1 ............ JPMurtagh 2 91
(JRFanshawe) *hld up: rdn over 2f out: r.o ins fnl f: nt rch wnr* **3/1**[2]

2231 **3** *nk* **Stolen Hours (USA)**[14] 4297 4-8-3 **65** ............ JQuinn 9 74
(JAkehurst) *lw: hld up: hdwy over 3f out: led over 2f out: sn hdd: rdn and ev ch over 1f out: styd on same pce* **14/1**

2135 **4** *1 ¼* **Smart John**[8] 4486 4-8-8 **70** ............ KFallon 5 77
(WMBrisbourne) *hld up in tch: outpcd over 2f out: styd on ins fnl f* **8/1**[3]

-210 **5** *1* **Reservoir (IRE)**[47] 3345 3-8-7 **80** ............ DHolland 6 85
(WJHaggas) *chsd ldr 5f: remained handy: rdn to ld 2f out: hdd over 1f out: no ex* **20/1**

1224 **6** *7* **Danakil**[20] 4155 9-9-1 **77** ............ RLMoore 8 73
(SDow) *hld up: hdwy over 1f out: wknd ins fnl f* **20/1**

4020 **7** *14* **Anticipating**[17] 4218 4-9-9 **85** ............ KDarley 7 61
(AMBalding) *dwlt: sn prom: chsd ldr over 5f out: rdn and ev ch fr over 2f out tl wknd over 1f out* **12/1**

1441 **8** *nk* **Dallool**[8] 4486 3-8-12 **85** 5ex ............ PRobinson 1 61
(MAJarvis) *lw: led over 9f: wknd over 1f out* **11/8**[1]

0201 **9** *16* **Baileys Dancer**[11] 4389 3-8-7 **80** 5ex ............ JFanning 4 33
(MJohnston) *prom: chsd ldr 7f out tl over 5f out: wknd over 2f out* **16/1**

2m 34.41s (1.45) **Going Correction** +0.15s/f (Good)
**WFA** 3 from 4yo+ 11lb **9** Ran SP% **114.6**
Speed ratings: **101,99,99,98,98 93,84,83,73**CSF £55.56 CT £605.76 TOTE £12.60: £3.20, £1.50, £3.70; EX 69.60.
**Owner** Rams Racing Club **Bred** K P Seow **Trained** Newmarket, Suffolk

**FOCUS**
A fair handicap in which the field elected to race on the far side once in line for home, and the form appears sound enough despite a modest time for the grade.

**NOTEBOOK**
**Tawny Way**, who had shown her best form on a sound surface, proved just as well suited by this easy ground. She is clearly on the upgrade and should continue to give a good account.
**Fling ◆** got going far too late, but at least proved she stays this far. There will be other days for her.
**Stolen Hours(USA)** was far from disgraced in this better race on ground which could well have been soft enough for him.
**Smart John** does not do anything quickly and may have done better with a stronger pace.
**Reservoir(IRE)**, stepping up in trip, did not quite get home in the testing ground.
**Danakil** found the ground had gone against him.
**Dallool**, who has made all to win twice before, was very disappointing and dropped away tamely.
*Official explanation: trainer said today's race may have come too soon after colt's previous run eight days ago*

## 4730 VIBE FM MEDIAN AUCTION MAIDEN STKS 7f
7:45 (7:50) (E) 2-Y-O **£4,338** (£1,335; £667; £333) **Stalls** High

Form RPR

0 **1** **Fu Manchu**[19] 4169 2-9-0 ............ TPQueally 14 84
(DRLoder) *lw: hld up in tch: rdn to ld wl ins fnl f: r.o* **12/1**

52 **2** *½* **Mister Genepi**[13] 4315 2-9-0 ............ SDrowne 20 83
(WRMuir) *lw: hld up: hdwy 1/2-way: led over 1f out: hdd wl ins fnl f* **4/1**[2]

3 **3** *1* **Fairmile**[36] 3665 2-9-0 ............ JPMurtagh 13 80
(PWHarris) *hld up: hdwy over 1f out: r.o* **11/2**

0 **4** *½* **Chief Scout**[27] 3925 2-9-0 ............ KFallon 4 79
(BJMeehan) *mde most over 5f: no ex ins fnl f* **5/1**[3]

**5** *hd* **Patronage** 2-9-0 ............ RMullen 10 79+
(MLWBell) *leggy: scope: dwlt: sn given reminders: hdwy 1/2-way: rdn and ev ch over 1f out: no ex ins fnl f* **20/1**

42 **6** *nk* **Coup D'Etat**[34] 3760 2-9-0 ............ KDarley 18 78
(JLDunlop) *hld up: hdwy u.p over 1f out: edgd lft ins fnl f: styd on* **11/4**[1]

**7** *5* **Press Express (IRE)** 2-9-0 ............ TEDurcan 17 66
(MRChannon) *leggy: scope: hld up: n.d* **50/1**

**8** *nk* **Atlantic Story (USA)** 2-9-0 ............ KMcEvoy 6 66
(SaeedBinSuroor) *w'like: scope: bkwd: chsd ldrs: rdn and ev ch over 1f out: sn wknd* **10/1**

**9** *1* **Scarp (USA)** 2-9-0 ............ EAhern 8 63
(JNoseda) *neat: hld up in tch: wknd over 1f out* **33/1**

00 **10** *1* **Succession**[9] 4446 2-8-9 ............ SSanders 11 56
(SirMarkPrescott) *chsd ldrs: hung lft and wknd 2f out* **25/1**

00 **11** *½* **Gurrun**[28] 3913 2-9-0 ............ OUrbina 3 60
(NACallaghan) *chsd ldrs over 5f* **66/1**

**12** *1 ¾* **Tiamo** 2-9-0 ............ DHolland 2 56
(MHTompkins) *w'like: s.i.s: outpcd* **33/1**

13 *shd* **Stancomb Wills (IRE)** 2-8-11 .......... FPFerris(3) 1 55
(MHTompkins) *w'like: bkwd: s.s: outpcd* **40/1**

0 14 *3 ½* **Election Seeker (IRE)**[14] 4290 2-8-9 .......... AQuinn(5) 15 47
(GLMoore) *hld up in tch: n.m.r and wknd over 2f out* **66/1**

15 *nk* **Stakhanov** 2-9-0 .......... SWKelly 16 47
(WJHaggas) *str: scope: s.s: a in rr* **50/1**

0 16 *1 ¼* **Sendeed (USA)**[23] 4030 2-9-0 .......... (t) WSupple 7 44
(SaeedBinSuroor) *s.i.s: sn chsng ldrs: wknd over 2f out* **20/1**

17 *1* **Archie Wright** 2-9-0 .......... RLMoore 9 41
(RHannon) *w'like: scope: prom over 4f* **33/1**

18 *15* **Cayuse** 2-8-9 .......... RPrice 12 1
(TTClement) *neat: s.i.s: outpcd* **100/1**

1m 27.49s (0.72) **Going Correction** +0.15s/f (Good) **18** Ran SP% **128.0**
Speed ratings: **101,100,99,98,98 98,92,92,90,89 89,87,87,83,82 81,80,63**CSF £55.39 TOTE £14.50: £3.20, £2.50, £2.30; EX 276.90.
**Owner** Egerton House Racing **Bred** Lord Vestey **Trained** Newmarket, Suffolk

**FOCUS**
Although the stalls were on the stands' side, the field raced more centre to far side, which gives the form a somewhat messy look. A smart winning time for the grade of contest.

**NOTEBOOK**
**Fu Manchu** had clearly learnt plenty from his debut and responded well under pressure to get the better of the runner-up. He should improve further still when facing an even stiffer test.
**Mister Genepi** with what should have been an ideal draw, probably had the worst of it with the runners electing to race more towards the far side.
**Fairmile** took a while to pick up, but showed enough to suggest he can make his mark, possibly when stepping up in trip.
**Chief Scout** may have found this trip, on the ground just stretching him.
**Patronage**, a 160,000gns yearling is out of a mare that stayed ten furlongs. Green as the stalls opened, he gradually got the hang of things before getting tired in the latter stages. Any amount of improvement can be expected.
**Coup D'Etat** did not look to be enjoying the ground and is certainly worth another chance.

## 4731 NEWMARKET NIGHTS FILLIES' RATED STKS (H'CAP) 7f
8:15 (8:18) (C) (0-95,88) 3-Y-0+ **£8,588** (£3,257; £1,628; £740) **Stalls** High

Form RPR

2231 1 **Violet Park**[8] 4478 3-8-0 **70** 3ex .......... JFMcDonald(3) 7 78
(BJMeehan) *trckd ldrs: racd keenly: rdn hung lft and ev ch fr over 1f out: styd on to ld post* **9/4**[1]

6020 2 *shd* **Cusco (IRE)**[38] 3602 3-9-7 **88** .......... RLMoore 3 96
(RHannon) *set stdy pce: qcknd over 2f out: rdn: hung lft and rt over 1f out: hdd post* **12/1**

2444 3 *2 ½* **Solar Power (IRE)**[38] 3602 3-9-3 **84** .......... JPMurtagh 1 86
(JRFanshawe) *lw: trckd ldr: plld hrd: rdn over 1f out: styd on same pce ins fnl f* **9/4**[1]

5400 4 *¾* **Starbeck (IRE)**[6] 4553 6-9-6 **81** .......... NCallan 5 81
(PHowling) *b: hld up in tch: rdn over 1f out: edgd lft and no ex ins fnl f* **10/1**

0000 5 *nk* **Cheese 'n Biscuits**[6] 4549 4-8-9 **70** .......... (p) KFallon 6 69
(GLMoore) *chsd ldrs: rdn whn hmpd over 1f out: styd on same pce* **8/1**

41-6 6 *2 ½* **Chanterelle (IRE)**[28] 3914 3-9-5 **86** .......... KDarley 8 79
(JLDunlop) *hld up: plld hrd: rdn over 2f out: wknd fnl f* **7/1**[3]

0661 7 *9* **Go Between**[16] 4248 3-9-4 **85** .......... SSanders 4 55
(EALDunlop) *hld up: plld hrd: wknd over 1f out* **13/2**[2]

1-00 8 *2 ½* **Zerlina (USA)**[91] 2089 3-8-13 **80** .......... CCatlin 2 44
(WJMusson) *lw: hld up: plld hrd: wknd over 1f out* **33/1**

1m 29.26s (2.49) **Going Correction** +0.15s/f (Good)
**WFA** 3 from 4yo+ 6lb **8** Ran SP% **118.2**
Speed ratings: **91,90,88,87,86 83,73,70**CSF £33.93 CT £68.87 TOTE £3.50: £1.70, £3.00, £1.50; EX 41.90 Place 6 £80.09, Place 5 £44.80.
**Owner** Mrs J Cash **Bred** D E And Mrs J Cash **Trained** Upper Lambourn, Berks

**FOCUS**
This was run in near darkness and run at a crawl which produced a very poor time for the class, 1.77 seconds slower than the preceding two-year-old maiden, giving the form a suspect look.

**NOTEBOOK**
**Violet Park** clearly has plenty of ability, but she is a far from easy ride.
**Cusco(IRE)** did a fair bit of running around in the latter stages, and only lost out on the nod. However, she had a soft lead and may be slightly flattered by this effort.
**Solar Power(IRE)** did herself no favours by refusing to settle.
**Starbeck(IRE)**, without a win since her juvenile days, again hinted that she may be returning to form.
**Cheese 'n Biscuits** was done no favours by the winner and runner-up as they squeezed her out in the dip.
T/Plt: £121.20 to a £1 stake. Pool: £50,198.15. 302.25 winning tickets. T/Qpdt: £29.30 to a £1 stake. Pool: £3,311.90. 83.40 winning tickets. CR

# 4182 ARLINGTON (L-H)
Friday, August 13

**OFFICIAL GOING: Fast**

## 4735a MARIAH'S STORM STKS (F&M) 1m 1f
12:17 (12:19) 3-Y-0+ £

RPR

1 **Tamweel (USA)**[35] 4-8-9 .......... RDouglas 6 —
(WCatalano, U.S.A) 1

2 *5* **Casual Attitude (USA)** 4-8-7 .......... ERazoJr 3 —
(SHobby, U.S.A)

3 *2* **Julie's Prize (USA)**[335] 4919 4-8-11 .......... (b) LSterling 2 —
(AnthonyMitchell, U.S.A) 2

4 *6* **Allspice (USA)**[496] 4-8-11 .......... (b) CEmigh 4 —
(GCilio, France)

5 *1 ¾* **Small Promises (CAN)** 6-8-6 ow1 .......... (b) EMartinJr 1 —
(BFlint, U.S.A)

6 *9* **Hennie's Song (USA)**[412] 4-8-7 .......... CMarquez 5 —
(SaeedBinSuroor) *last throughout* 3

1m 50.99s **6** Ran SP% **103.0**
Speed ratings: .
**Owner** Turf Express Inc & Darrell & Evelyn Yates Ltd **Bred** Shadwell Farm Llc **Trained** North America

**NOTEBOOK**
**Hennie's Song(USA)**, a front-runner having her first run for Saeed Bin Suroor, was always struggling on this occasion.

# 4321 GOODWOOD (R-H)
Saturday, August 14

**OFFICIAL GOING: Good (good to firm in places on round course)**

## 4736 BBCI APPRENTICE H'CAP 1m 3f
5:20 (5:20) (E) (0-75,71) 3-Y-0+ **£3,406** (£1,048; £524; £262) **Stalls** Low

Form RPR

2205 1 **Garston Star**[12] 4389 3-7-5 **55** .......... LauraReynolds(7) 8 72
(JSMoore) *led and sn clr: hdd over 2f out: rdn to ld again over 1f out: sn drew clr* **12/1**

0606 2 *7* **Traveller's Tale**[19] 4196 5-8-5 **55** .......... DerekNolan(3) 2 61
(PGMurphy) *chsd clr ldr and sn wl clr of rest: clsd 5f out: led over 2f out to over 1f out: wknd fnl f* **16/1**

00/2 3 *1 ¾* **Serraval (FR)**[9] 4485 6-8-12 **59** .......... RThomas 6 62
(GBBalding) *hld up in rr and wl off the pce: gng smoothly but stl plenty to do over 3f out: rdn to take 3rd over 1f out: no ch w wnr* **11/2**

-100 4 *shd* **Gold Guest**[22] 4083 5-9-1 **65** .......... SJDonohoe(3) 9 68
(PDEvans) *dwlt: hld up in rr and wl off the pce: rdn and swtchd rt over 2f out: styd on: no ch* **5/1**[3]

0500 5 *1 ¼* **Private Benjamin**[5] 4616 4-7-8 **46** .......... LiamJones(5) 4 47
(JamiePoulton) *t.k.h: hld up and wl off the pce: prog 4f out: c wd in st: one pce fnl 2f: no ch* **16/1**

3505 6 *1* **Rebate**[7] 4556 4-8-8 **58** .......... (t) PGallagher(3) 10 57
(RHannon) *s.v.s: hld up in last and wl off the pce: effrt on inner but no ch whn bmpd over 2f out: hmpd sn after: kpt on* **7/1**

-300 7 *2* **Once (FR)**[22] 4075 4-9-5 **71** .......... (b[1]) RKeogh(5) 3 67
(JAOsborne) *t.k.h: hld up and wl off the pce: chsd clr ldng trio over 4f out: no imp: wknd over 1f out* **25/1**

2150 8 *1* **Man The Gate**[5] 4616 5-8-12 **59** .......... NChalmers 7 54
(PDCundell) *hld up in rr and wl off the pce: effrt but no ch whn bdly hmpd over 2f out: nt rcvr* **7/2**[1]

0 9 *8* **Icarus Dream (IRE)**[19] 4192 3-8-8 **68** .......... (p) HMuya(3) 5 50
(PRHedger) *t.k.h: hld up in 3rd pl and sn wl bhd ldng pair: lost pl over 4f out: no ch whn hmpd over 2f out* **50/1**

0004 10 *4* **Sholay (IRE)**[36] 3695 5-7-12 **45** .......... DFox 1 20
(PMitchell) *t.k.h: hld up and wl off the pce: effrt 4f out: no ch: wkng whn hmpd over 2f out* **25/1**

0242 11 *2* **Treetops Hotel (IRE)**[21] 4122 5-8-6 **58** .......... (p) DeanWilliams(5) 11 30
(BRJohnson) *dwlt: hld up wl off the pce: prog to dispute modest 3rd pl 4f out: sn wknd* **4/1**[2]

2m 28.61s (2.50) **Going Correction** +0.10s/f (Good)
**WFA** 3 from 4yo+ 10lb **11** Ran SP% **115.9**
Speed ratings: **94,88,87,87,86 85,84,83,77,75 73**CSF £181.13 CT £1177.98 TOTE £12.60: £3.90, £5.30, £1.90; EX 199.00.
**Owner** East Garston Racing **Bred** Mrs P Lewis **Trained** East Garston, Berks
■ A first winner for apprentice Laura Reynolds.
■ Stewards Enquiry : S J Donohoe nine-day ban: careless riding (Aug 25-Sep 2)
R Keogh one-day ban: used whip with excessive frequency (Aug 25)

**FOCUS**
A modest apprentices' handicap and moderate winning time for the grade. The first two appeared to be given too much rope by the rest, which makes the form look questionable.

**NOTEBOOK**
**Garston Star**, whose only previous win was in a seller over course and distance, as usual set off like a scalded cat. Joined before the two pole, he responded well to his rider's urgings to draw away again and give her a comfortable first winner. Clearly suited by this track, unfortunately there are not many races of this grade here for him to take part in.
**Traveller's Tale**, who has dropped 16lb in the handicap since the start of the season, set off in pursuit of the leader and eventually closed him down to show in front just over two out. However, he had nothing in reserve with which to resist that rival's renewed challenge. He looks quite well treated at present, and a return to Epsom, where he gained his only success, may prove fruitful.
**Serraval(FR)**ran on from a long way back, but this second effort following nearly two years off suggests she remains in good heart. She is another who has been given a chance by the Handicapper.
**Gold Guest**, better known as an All-Weather performer, was another having his second outing after a break. He kept on well without ever looking likely to reach the principals, and will no doubt be back on Polytrack before long.
**Private Benjamin** was another who ran on from the back without ever looking likely to figure. He only needs to drop another pound to qualify for banded racing, but there is always the possibility of returning to hurdles.
**Man The Gate**, who beat the winner at Epsom last month, was settled at the back and then got squeezed out when looking for a run. As the race worked out he was too far back in any case, but he is better than this effort indicates.
**Treetops Hotel(IRE)**, back up in trip, was slow to get into his stride, but was one of the first to try to catch the clear leaders before dropping out halfway up the straight as if he does not stay this far. *Official explanation: vet said gelding finished lame on its right fore*

## 4737 BBC SOUTHERN COUNTIES RADIO H'CAP 1m 1f 192y
5:50 (5:53) (C) (0-90,90) 3-Y-0+ **£10,192** (£3,136; £1,568; £784) **Stalls** Low

Form RPR

21-1 1 **Sky Quest (IRE)**[23] 4061 6-10-0 **84** .......... (tp) DHolland 8 97+
(PWHarris) *hld up in rr: stdy prog on inner over 2f out: gng wl over 1f out: led last 150yds: sn rdn clr* **6/1**[3]

-550 2 *2* **Prime Powered (IRE)**[17] 4229 3-9-1 **85** .......... AQuinn(5) 4 92
(GLMoore) *trckd ldrs: effrt to chal over 2f out: rdn and unable qck wl over 1f out: styd on fnl f to take 2nd last stride* **7/1**

500 3 *shd* **Dream Magic**[31] 3842 6-9-3 **73** .......... MHenry 1 80
(MJRyan) *led after 3f: rdn and hdd over 2f out: led again over 1f out: hdd and one pce last 150yds* **22/1**

0000 4 *2* **Parkview Love (USA)**[16] 4268 3-9-11 **90** .......... SChin 6 93
(MJohnston) *led for 3f: rdn over 3f out: outpcd wl over 1f out: plugged on fnl f* **25/1**

1263 5 *nk* **Watamu (IRE)**[16] 4271 3-9-6 **85** .......... (v) GCarter 7 87
(PJMakin) *dwlt: hld up in rr: smooth prog over 3f out: jnd ldr gng easily over 2f out: rdn and fnd nil over 1f out: sn btn* **2/1**[1]

2212 6 *1 ½* **Wee Dinns (IRE)**[17] 4230 3-9-6 **85** .......... JFEgan 10 85
(SKirk) *trckd ldrs: effrt to ld over 2f out: hdd & wknd 1f out* **3/1**[2]

0452 7 *2 ½* **Ocean Of Storms (IRE)**[14] 4327 9-9-4 **79** .......... (t) RThomas(5) 5 74
(ChristianWroe, UAE) *s.v.s: racd in last: effrt and sme prog on outer over 2f out: wknd over 1f out* **16/1**

6040 8 *1* **Gig Harbor**[28] 3937 5-9-9 **79** .......... KMcEvoy 3 72
(MissECLavelle) *hld up in rr: wl in tch 3f out: rdn and no prog 2f out: sn wknd* **33/1**

0510 **9** *2* **Prairie Wolf**[18] 4214 8-9-0 **77**........................................ DerekNolan[(7)] 9 66
(MLWBell) *trckd ldrs: effrt on outer 3f out: rdn and hanging rt over 1f out: wknd* **8/1**

0-20 **10** *1 ¾* **Silver City**[29] 3909 4-9-11 **81**........................................ EAhern 2 67
(MrsAJPerrett) *prom: chsd ldr after 3f to over 3f out: sn wknd* **22/1**

2m 8.35s (0.67) **Going Correction** +0.10s/f (Good)
**WFA** 3 from 4yo+ 9lb **10** Ran SP% **117.6**
Speed ratings: **101,99,99,97,97 96,94,93,91,90**CSF £45.28 CT £870.50 TOTE £5.70: £2.30, £3.80, £7.10; EX 53.70.
**Owner** Colourful Band **Bred** Pendley Farm **Trained** Ringshall, Bucks

**FOCUS**
A decent handicap on paper, but a moderate winning time for the class of contest. The second sets the standard for the form.

**NOTEBOOK**
**Sky Quest(IRE)** ◆ has progressed well this season and, given an identical ride to when scoring on his reappearnce, got the gaps at the right time and won cosily. He looks to be ahead of the Handicapper at present and may not have finished winning yet, as long as underfoot conditions do not go against him.
**Prime Powered(IRE)** ◆ is relatively inexperienced but, always in about the right place, could not pick up immediately when asked and only stayed on in the closing stages. He gained his only win at Epsom, and there may be a race for him there at the Bank Holiday meeting.
**Dream Magic** has been struggling for form in the last year, but has now dropped to a reasonable mark and the switch to forcing tactics seemed to fire his enthusiasm. He was only run out of it late on, and a repeat of this effort, especially in a slightly lower grade, may work the oracle.
**Parkview Love(USA)**, another who has been struggling for form of late, has dropped a stone in the weights since April and showed signs of a revival. He seemed to stay this longer trip well enough.
**Watamu(IRE)**, favourite on the strength of a good effort over course and distance in July, again had the visor fitted and moved into a challenging position on the bridle. However, the response was minimal when he was asked for an effort and he looks one to have reservations about.
**Wee Dinns(IRE)** was always well placed but was a little keen early on. She looked a big threat when joining the leader halfway up the straight, but the effort petered out under pressure. She has done much of her racing against her own sex, and may be better off in that company.
**Prairie Wolf** was well backed returning to his favourite track, but failed to sparkle.

## 4738 BBC SOUTH TODAY STKS (H'CAP) 1m
6:20 (6:23) (D ) (0-80,78) 3-Y-O £5,499 (£1,692; £846; £423) Stalls High

Form RPR

0-30 **1** **Flying Adored**[42] 3527 3-8-12 **69**........................................ KFallon 6 78
(JLDunlop) *settled in rr: stdy prog on inner over 2f out: drvn to ld last 150yds: sn in command* **6/1**

-003 **2** *1 ½* **Border Music**[9] 4490 3-8-13 **77**........................................ TBlock[(7)] 9 83
(AMBalding) *hld up in last: stdy prog on outer over 2f out: rdn to chal 1f out: upsides ins fnl f: unable qck* **9/2**[2]

0333 **3** *nk* **Master Theo (USA)**[50] 3268 3-9-3 **74**........................................ DHolland 8 79
(HJCollingridge) *cl up: rdn to ld over 1f out: hdd and one pce last 150yds* **14/1**

4344 **4** *1 ¾* **Zangeal**[26] 3994 3-9-5 **76**........................................ RHills 2 77
(CFWall) *wl in tch: prog to chal 2f out: ev ch over 1f out: wknd fnl f* **4/1**[1]

2042 **5** *2* **On The Waterfront**[59] 2973 3-8-9 **66**........................................ EAhern 4 62
(JWHills) *w ldr: led after 3f: rdn and hdd over 1f out: wknd fnl f* **9/2**[2]

0-00 **6** *1 ¼* **Belisco (USA)**[20] 4170 3-9-1 **72**........................................(t) KMcEvoy 3 66
(MrsAJPerrett) *trckd ldrs: lost pl and rdn 2f out: n.d after* **16/1**

4000 **7** *2 ½* **Lord Links (IRE)**[16] 4268 3-9-7 **78**........................................ JFEgan 5 66
(RHannon) *hld up: effrt whn nowhere to go and snatched up over 2f out: nt rcvr* **11/2**[3]

4006 **8** *6* **Bertocelli**[9] 4483 3-8-3 **60**........................................ AMcCarthy 1 34
(GGMargarson) *led for 3f: wknd over 2f out* **12/1**

0042 **9** *3* **Trifti**[9] 4483 3-8-1 **58**........................................ JMackay 7 25
(CACyzer) *hld up in rr: rdn on outer over 3f out: wknd 2f out* **10/1**

1m 39.68s (-0.59) **Going Correction** +0.10s/f (Good) **9** Ran SP% **115.4**
Speed ratings: **106,104,104,102,100 99,96,90,87**CSF £33.11 CT £363.08 TOTE £6.00: £1.80, £1.60, £2.60; EX 23.50.
**Owner** Mrs Mark Burrell **Bred** Mrs M Burrell **Trained** Arundel, W Sussex

**FOCUS**
An ordinary handicap but run in a fair time for the class, and the principals came from off the pace. The form does not appear that sound.

**NOTEBOOK**
**Flying Adored** continued the gradual revival in fortunes of the Dunlop yard. Tucked in on the fence, she got a dream split at just the right time, and won in ready fashion. This will have done her confidence good and she may be capable of following up.
**Border Music**, who made a promising return earlier in the month, was given a confident ride and had every chance when challenging on the outside, but just found the winner too strong. He may have run into a well-handicapped rival, and should find another opportunity before long.
**Master Theo(USA)** appreciated this return to a sounder surface, and was another to have every chance. He was not good enough but there will be easier handicaps to be won this autumn.
**Zangeal**, with the tongue tie left off, was made favourite on this handicap debut, got into a challenging position, but lacked pace in the closing stages. A half-brother to High Accolade, he may appreciate some cut in the ground and could be worth making the running with.
**On The Waterfront**, up with the pace from the start, did not capitulate until late on. Less positive tactics may give him a better chance of lasting home.
**Lord Links(IRE)** *Official explanation: vet said gelding had been struck into on its near fore*

## 4739 EUROPEAN BREEDERS FUND CHICHESTER CITY MEDIAN AUCTION MAIDEN STKS 6f
6:55 (6:57) (E ) 2-Y-O £4,104 (£1,263; £631; £315) Stalls Low

Form RPR

23 **1** **Moth Ball**[5] 4611 2-9-0........................................ DHolland 1 84
(JAOsborne) *mde all: rdn over 1f out: hrd pressed fnl f: kpt on wl* **3/1**[2]

232 **2** *¾* **Yajbill (IRE)**[10] 4454 2-9-0 82........................................ TEDurcan 3 82
(MRChannon) *sn chsd ldr: shkn up to chal 1f out: fnd little and hld ins fnl f* **10/3**[3]

22 **3** *½* **Goodwood Spirit**[23] 4040 2-9-0........................................ KFallon 6 80
(JLDunlop) *hld up in rr: rdn 2f out: no prog tl r.o fnl f: nrst fin* **2/1**[1]

**4** *½* **Storm Silk (CAN)** 2-9-0........................................ KMcEvoy 2 79
(SaeedBinSuroor) *s.i.s: hld up in tch: shkn up and effrt 2f out: chsd ldrs ins fnl f: kpt on* **6/1**

**5** *2 ½* **Cordage (IRE)** 2-9-0........................................ TPQueally 5 71
(GAButler) *wl in tch: rdn and unable qck wl over 1f out: one pce after* **25/1**

30 **6** *5* **Transgress (IRE)**[35] 3749 2-9-0........................................ DaneO'Neill 7 56
(RHannon) *racd on outer: trckd ldrs: effrt over 2f out: wknd over 1f out* **8/1**

52 **7** *¾* **Averting**[9] 4481 2-9-0........................................ SCarson 9 54
(RFJohnsonHoughton) *racd in ldng trio tl wknd wl over 1f out* **28/1**

**8** *½* **Penkenna Princess (IRE)** 2-8-9........................................ SSanders 4 48
(RMBeckett) *s.i.s: in tch on outer: wknd over 1f out* **14/1**

**9** *3 ½* **Byron Bay** 2-8-9........................................ NChalmers[(5)] 8 42
(JJBridger) *s.i.s: rn green and a last: wknd 2f out* **66/1**

1m 12.88s (0.04) **Going Correction** +0.10s/f (Good) **9** Ran SP% **122.3**
Speed ratings: **103,102,101,100,97 90,89,89,84**CSF £14.23 TOTE £3.90: £1.80, £1.70, £1.10; EX 14.80.
**Owner** Mountgrange Stud **Bred** Stratford Place Stud **Trained** Upper Lambourn, Berks

**FOCUS**
A fair-looking juvenile maiden, and a very decent time for the type of contest, only fractionally slower than the following handicap for older fillies and the form looks solid.

**NOTEBOOK**
**Moth Ball**, who had run well in a couple of decent maidens prior to this, again showed immaturity beforehand. However, smartly away from the stalls, he put his experience to good use to make all, and kept finding extra when challenged. He looks capable of going on to better things.
**Yajbill(IRE)** was runner-up for the third time in four outings, but has come up against some useful sorts in that time. He did not look overly keen to go between the winner and the rail though, and may need some form of headgear fitted in order to enable him to get off the mark.
**Goodwood Spirit**, who had been placed in ordinary maidens, had to be stoked up in order to go about his business and was finishing best of all. He may be worth trying over another furlong, and looks well capable of landing an ordinary maiden.
**Storm Silk(CAN)**, a debutant with an American pedigree, was easy in the market, dwelt in the stalls and ran as if the experience will do him good. He is nothing out of the ordinary, but did best of the newcomers and should be capable of winning races.
**Cordage(IRE)** ◆, a debutant from the family of Oaks winner Bireme, showed distinct promise over a trip that will ultimately prove too short for him. He should benefit from the run and can find a race over further.
**Penkenna Princess(IRE)** caught the eye, showing speed after a tardy start on this debut and, despite dropping out in the closing stages, can be expected to do better in time.

## 4740 JILLY COOPER OBE FILLIES' STKS (H'CAP) 6f
7:30 (7:30) (D ) (0-85,79) 3-Y-O+ £6,825 (£2,100; £1,050; £525) Stalls Low

Form RPR

000 **1** **Canterloupe (IRE)**[28] 3941 6-9-4 **71**........................................ SSanders 3 84
(PJMakin) *hanging rt thrght: hld up in last: prog 2f out: hrd rdn and r.o to ld fnl strides* **5/1**[2]

3564 **2** *¾* **Maddie's A Jem**[19] 4194 4-9-6 **73**........................................ TEDurcan 10 84
(JRJenkins) *racd on outer: trckd ldrs: rdn over 1f out: led ins fnl f: nt qckn and hdd last strides* **9/1**

5042 **3** *1 ¼* **Dixie Dancing**[8] 4517 5-8-2 **55**........................................ JMackay 5 62
(CACyzer) *s.i.s: hld up in rr: prog over 2f out: rdn to ld wl over 1f out: edgd rt and hdd ins fnl f: one pce* **10/1**

0410 **4** *2* **Woodbury**[12] 4403 5-8-2 **60**........................................ NChalmers[(5)] 6 61
(MrsHSweeting) *mde most to 2f out: sn outpcd: kpt on ins fnl f* **25/1**

4143 **5** *hd* **Estihlal**[10] 4434 3-9-2 **73**........................................ RHills 8 74
(EALDunlop) *dwlt: sn rcvrd to trck ldrs: swtchd to wd outside jst over 1f out: nt qckn and btn sn after* **3/1**[1]

5000 **6** *2* **Madrasee**[17] 4232 6-9-0 **67**........................................ DHolland 4 62
(LMontagueHall) *trckd ldrs: gng wl 2f out: nt clr run over 1f out: fnd little whn in the clr fnl f* **12/1**

0350 **7** *½* **Mythical Charm**[18] 4220 5-7-7 **51** oh2........................................(t) DFox[(5)] 1 44
(JJBridger) *s.i.s: sn pushed along in rr: struggling whn nt clr run 2f out: kpt on* **25/1**

0004 **8** *½* **Craic Sa Ceili (IRE)**[44] 3455 4-8-7 **63**........................................ RMiles[(3)] 13 55
(MSSaunders) *prom on outer: rdn to ld briefly 2f out: wknd fnl f* **10/1**

0304 **9** *6* **Urban Rose**[3] 4650 3-8-6 **63**........................................(t) MHenry 9 37
(RMHCowell) *w ldr: upsides 2f out: sn wknd rapidly* **25/1**

2650 **10** *3 ½* **Chance For Romance**[10] 4434 3-9-8 **79**........................................ SChin 7 42
(WRMuir) *w ldrs to 1/2-way: sn lost pl and btn* **33/1**

0060 **11** *shd* **Roses Of Spring**[11] 4415 6-9-10 **77**........................................(p) EAhern 12 40
(RMHCowell) *racd on wd outside: in tch over 3f: wknd* **12/1**

4030 **12** *¾* **Bella Tutrice (IRE)**[23] 4052 3-8-12 **69**........................................ KFallon 11 30
(IAWood) *pressed ldrs: rdn to chal 2f out: wknd over 1f out: eased* **15/2**[3]

2400 **13** *¾* **Concubine (IRE)**[21] 4127 5-8-0 **58**........................................(b[1]) HayleyTurner[(5)] 2 16
(JRBoyle) *in tch over 3f: sn wknd* **12/1**

1m 12.81s (-0.03) **Going Correction** +0.10s/f (Good)
**WFA** 3 from 4yo+ 4lb **13** Ran SP% **119.2**
Speed ratings: **104,103,101,98,98 95,95,94,86,81 81,80,79**CSF £47.12 CT £454.41 TOTE £6.50: £2.70, £2.30, £3.10; EX 48.30.
**Owner** R A Ballin & The Billinomas **Bred** The Lavington Stud **Trained** Ogbourne Maisey, Wilts
■ Stewards Enquiry : S Sanders three-day ban: used whip with excessive frequency (Aug 25-27)

**FOCUS**
Effectively a 0-77 fillies' handicap in which the form is ordinary and the principals came from off the pace.

**NOTEBOOK**
**Canterloupe(IRE)** has been giving the impression her turn was not far away since coming back from a break. Dropped in the handicap and with a change of tactics, she was held up at the back early, but Sanders needed to be at his strongest to get her running. She followed the third through and, once into her stride, cut down her rivals late on to score going away. However, she may remember this and does not look a certainty to follow up.
**Maddie's A Jem** ◆ ran her second good race in a row from an unfavourable draw. She is close to a previous winning mark, will appreciate cut in the ground and, if getting a better stall next time, could make amends.
**Dixie Dancing** has done most of her racing of late on sand over longer trips. However, she ran well and came through strongly to hit the front before being run out of it by the winner, who followed her through. She has another race in her off her current mark.
**Woodbury**, another that has raced mostly on sand recently, helped set the pace but ran on again after looking beaten. She often runs her race but does not win all that regularly.
**Estihlal** missed the break slightly and had to come around her field to deliver her challenge. She faded in the closing stages and is beginning to looked held by the Handicapper off her current rating.
**Bella Tutrice(IRE)** ran quite well from her wide draw until fading.
**Concubine(IRE)** was keen in the first-time blinkers but got very little cover.

## 4741 RACING UK LIVE ON 425 MEDIAN AUCTION MAIDEN STKS 7f
8:00 (8:00) (E ) 3-4-Y-O £4,114 (£1,266; £633; £316) Stalls High

Form RPR

3 **1** **Majors Cast (IRE)**[43] 3487 3-8-12........................................ EAhern 5 79+
(JNoseda) *settled in 3rd: led jst over 2f out: sn clr: pushed out* **1/1**[1]

-225 **2** *2 ½* **Rangoon (USA)**[116] 1519 3-8-12 78........................................ KFallon 6 73
(MrsAJPerrett) *led to jst over 2f out: hung bdly lft after and lost all ch: kpt on fnl f* **2/1**[2]

0-02 **3** *1 ¾* **Text**[21] 4125 3-8-12 65........................................ JFEgan 2 68
(MrsStefLiddiard) *hld up in last: rdn and easily outpcd 2f out: kpt on fnl f* **6/1**[3]

00 **4** *6* **Inescapable (USA)**[14] 4337 3-8-12........................................ SSanders 3 52
(WRMuir) *t.k.h: hld up in 4th: rdn 3f out: wknd 2f out* **25/1**

030 **5** *5* **Khafayif (USA)**[52] [3209] 3-8-7 63 ........................ RHills 4 34
(BHanbury) *trckd ldr to over 2f out: sn shkn up and wknd* **14/1**

1m 27.93s (-0.10) **Going Correction** +0.10s/f (Good) **5** Ran SP% **108.1**
Speed ratings: **104,101,99,92,86**CSF £3.07 TOTE £1.90: £1.50, £1.50; EX 3.00 Place 6 £200.36, Place 5 £42.16..
**Owner** Mrs Susan Roy **Bred** Joe Fogarty **Trained** Newmarket, Suffolk

**FOCUS**
A modest maiden on paper but an easy winner in a fair time for the grade, with the third the guide to the level of the form.

**NOTEBOOK**
**Majors Cast(IRE)**, a nicely-bred colt who showed promise on his belated debut last month, justified favouritism in no uncertain terms. He got a split next to the rail over two out and swept into a clear lead before idling in the closing stages. In beating a 78-rated rival easily he is sure to get a mark in the mid-80s at least, and will need to improve again, although that may be possible.
**Rangoon(USA)**, who had done most of his racing on an easy surface, was returning from a four-month break. He set the pace but tended to drift left in the straight and let the winner up his inside. However, he ran on again in the closing stages to hunt up the winner, but the margin somewhat flatters him. However, he should be able to find a small race with this under his belt.
*Official explanation: jockey said colt hung left throughout*
**Text**, settled at the back, never landed a blow at the winner and was comfortably held by the runner-up. He is probably the best guide to the level of this form, but may be better off in handicaps off his current mark.
**Inescapable(USA)** has now been well held in three maidens and should qualify for a modest handicap mark.
**Khafayif(USA)** does not appear to be progressing and, despite having a decent pedigree, may well be going to the sales this autumn.
T/Plt: £123.80 to a £1 stake. Pool: £33,740.30. 198.90 winning tickets. T/Qpdt: £9.70 to a £1 stake. Pool: £3,735.40. 283.80 winning tickets. JN

## 4712 NEWBURY (L-H)
Saturday, August 14
**OFFICIAL GOING: Good (good to soft in places back straight)**

### 4742 STAN JAMES 08000 383384 RATED STKS (H'CAP) 7f (S)
**1:00** (1:02) (C) (0-95,95) 3-Y-O+ **£9,275** (£3,518; £1,759; £599) **Stalls** Centre

Form RPR
0302 **1** **Sawwaah (IRE)**[7] [4543] 7-8-7 **81** ........................ PDoe 14 91
(DNicholls) *b: lw: hld up in tch: n.m.r ins fnl 2f: swtchd lft and qcknd appr fnl f: r.o strly to ld fnl 75yds* **16/1**
3540 **2** *½* **Kool (IRE)**[7] [4553] 5-9-1 **89** ........................ DHolland 7 98
(PFICole) *lw: broke wl: sn bhd: nudged along 1/2-way: hdwy over 1f out: str run ins last: kpt on but nt pce of wnr fnl 75yds* **5/1**[1]
5000 **3** *hd* **Taranaki**[7] [4549] 6-8-9 **86** ........................ LPKeniry(3) 15 94
(PDCundell) *trckd ldrs: drvn to ld 1f out: kpt on wl tl hdd and no ex fnl 75yds* **20/1**
0000 **4** *½* **Craiova (IRE)**[36] [3690] 5-8-0 **81** oh4 ........................ KMay(7) 9 88
(BWHills) *lw: t.k.h: broke wl: stdd mid-div: hdwy over 2f out: drvn to chal 1f out: nt qckn ins last* **16/1**
3040 **4** *dht* **Jay Gee's Choice**[52] [3205] 4-8-9 **83** ........................ CCatlin 2 90
(MRChannon) *lw: trckd ldr tl slt ld ins fnl 2f: hdd 1f out: styd on same pce u.p* **33/1**
0306 **6** *1* **Greenslades**[7] [4528] 5-9-7 **95** ........................ KFallon 13 99
(PJMakin) *chsd ldrs: rdn and ev ch over 1f out: one pce u.p ins last* **5/1**[1]
2323 **7** *hd* **Armagnac**[7] [4553] 6-8-7 **81** oh1 ........................ ADaly 4 85
(MABuckley) *slowly away and lost 4l s: sn rcvrd and in tch: rdn 2f out: r.o u.p ins last and fin wl* **17/2**[3]
2200 **8** *hd* **Digital**[16] [4273] 7-9-2 **90** ........................ ACulhane 8 93
(MRChannon) *bhd: rdn over 2f out: ran on strly ins fnl f but nt pce to rch ldrs* **9/1**
6-60 **9** *shd* **Jazz Messenger (FR)**[94] [2044] 4-9-7 **95** ........................ RHughes 16 98
(GAButler) *stdd s and bhd: stl plenty to do 2f out: sn swtchd lft and kpt on fnl f: nvr gng pce to rch ldrs* **8/1**[2]
0000 **10** *¾* **Marshman (IRE)**[7] [4553] 5-8-10 **84** ........................ MHills 3 85
(MHTompkins) *bhd: rdn over 2f out: r.o wl fnl f: nt rch ldrs* **17/2**[3]
2316 **11** *nk* **Boundless Prospect (USA)**[15] [4293] 5-8-2 **81** oh4 ow2 DerekNolan(7) 12 83
(JWHills) *swtg: s.i.s: bhd: hrd drvn over 1f out: kpt on ins last but nvr rchd ldrs* **16/1**
0003 **12** *3* **Tuning Fork**[15] [4287] 4-9-1 **89** ........................ JQuinn 11 81
(JAkehurst) *led tl narrowly hdd ins fnl 2f: wknd ins fnl f* **10/1**
1000 **13** *1 ¼* **Willhewiz**[17] [4232] 4-8-7 **81** oh4 ........................ TPQueally 6 70
(RMStronge) *chsd ldrs tl wknd appr fnl f* **50/1**
0000 **14** *1 ½* **Master Robbie**[7] [4553] 5-9-0 **88** ........................ KMcEvoy 1 73
(MRChannon) *in tch: rdn over 2f out: sn btn* **25/1**
-000 **15** *3 ½* **King Carnival (USA)**[63] [2891] 3-8-7 **87** ........................ DaneO'Neill 10 63
(RHannon) *a in rr* **40/1**
3000 **16** *1 ¾* **Fancy Foxtrot**[16] [4268] 3-8-7 **87** ........................(b[1]) JFortune 5 59
(BJMeehan) *mid-div on outside: rdn and effrt 1/2-way: sn btn* **12/1**

1m 25.2s (-2.02) **Going Correction** -0.10s/f (Good)
**WFA** 3 from 4yo+ 6lb **16** Ran SP% **125.9**
Speed ratings: **107,106,106,105,105 104,104,104,103,103 102,99,97,96,92 90**CSF £92.38 CT £1727.22 TOTE £19.70: £3.90, £1.90, £4.90; EX 176.90 TRIFECTA PL: JGC £3.00 ,C £2.90.
**Owner** Fayzad Thoroughbred Limited **Bred** Shadwell Estate Company Limited **Trained** Sessay, N Yorks

**FOCUS**
A decent and very competitive handicap run at a solid pace and the field raced down the middle of the track. Despite this the form is not as strong on paper as it might have been.

**NOTEBOOK**
**Sawwaah(IRE)** needs everything to drop right, but even though he did not get the clearest of runs still managed to deliver his late effort with precision timing. This was the highest mark he has ever won off in proper handicap company, which is to the credit of all concerned.
**Kool(IRE)** delivered his effort at the same time as the winner, but with not quite the same effect. He has consistently been just missing out this term, but is 3lb below his last winning mark and running well enough to put that right.
**Taranaki**, running in this race for the third year in succession, put up his best effort in the contest so far and came with what looked a race-winning effort on the nearside a furlong from home, but he could not quite maintain it. He is not very consistent these days, but capable at this level on his day.
**Craiova(IRE)** ◆ moved up to hold every chance a furlong from home, but could not match the finishing pace of the principals. This was still his best performance for some time and he has become well handicapped.
**Jay Gee's Choice** ◆ is yet to win a handicap and without a victory in almost two years, but he ran well here under a positive ride and has dropped to a fair mark. This looks to be his best trip.
**Greenslades** probably ran up to his best, but unfortunately this effort probably means he is still unlikely to get any help from the Handicapper.
**Armagnac**, who has been creeping up the handicap of late despite not winning, did well to finish where he did considering how slowly he started.
**Digital**, who has risen 7lb in the handicap since June despite not winning, stayed on well in the closing stages but could not land a blow.
**Jazz Messenger(FR)** ◆, who trailed the field for much of the way, made some late progress after being switched without by any means being knocked about. This trip is too short for him now and he will be interesting back over further.
**Tuning Fork** racing over the shortest trip he has ever encountered, was given a positive ride but could not maintain the effort.
**Fancy Foxtrot** probably saw too much daylight on the outside of the field, but remains out of form.

### 4743 STAN JAMES SUPPORTING WESSEX HEARTBEAT EBF MAIDEN STKS (DIV I) 7f (S)
**1:40** (1:43) (D) 2-Y-O **£6,422** (£1,976; £988; £494) **Stalls** Centre

Form RPR
**1** **Etlaala** 2-9-0 ........................ RHills 6 89+
(BWHills) *gd sort: str: bit bkwd: mde virtually all: clr over 1f out: shkn up and styd on wl last half f: readily* **5/2**[1]
**2** *2 ½* **Count Kristo** 2-9-0 ........................ DaneO'Neill 11 83
(CGCox) *leggy: lw: s.i.s bhd: hdwy 2f out: drvn and r.o wl fnl f to take 2nd fnl 100yds: no ch w wnr: should improve* **25/1**
**3** *1 ¼* **Ameeq (USA)** 2-9-0 ........................ RHughes 10 80
(MPTregoning) *str: scope: stdd s:hld up rr but in tch:hdwy over 2f out:reminder over 1f out: chsd wnr but no imp ins last: lost 2nd fnl 1* **15/2**
6 **4** *1 ¾* **Ocean Gift**[18] [4219] 2-9-0 ........................ JFEgan 9 75
(DRCElsworth) *lw: chsd ldrs: wnt 2nd 3f out: rdn and no imression on wnr fr 2f out: outpcd ins last* **7/2**[2]
**5** *nk* **Wingspeed (IRE)** 2-9-0 ........................ DHolland 4 75
(MrsAJPerrett) *leggy: bit bkwd: chsd ldrs: rdn 2f out: outpcd appr fnl f* **9/1**
00 **6** *3* **Superstitious (IRE)**[18] [4219] 2-9-0 ........................ GGibbons 2 67
(BAMcmahon) *bit bkwd: sn in rr: rdn 3f out: effrt fr 2f out but nvr nr ldrs* **66/1**
03 **7** *3 ½* **Storm Fury (USA)**[17] [4239] 2-9-0 ........................ JQuinn 1 58
(PWChapple-Hyam) *w ldr early: lost 2nd 3f out: styd prom tl wknd appr fnl f* **14/1**
**8** *1 ¼* **Front Stage (IRE)** 2-9-0 ........................ KFallon 7 55
(SirMichaelStoute) *wl grwn: bit bkwd: rdn 3f out: nvr in contention* **5/1**[3]
**9** *shd* **Prince Vettori** 2-9-0 ........................ EAhern 3 55
(DJCoakley) *tall: scope: s.i.s: a outpcd* **33/1**
**10** *¾* **Bold Diktator** 2-9-0 ........................ MartinDwyer 8 53
(WRMuir) *rangy: scope: chsd ldrs tl wknd over 2f out* **50/1**

1m 27.14s (-0.08) **Going Correction** -0.10s/f (Good) **10** Ran SP% **106.1**
Speed ratings: **96,93,91,89,89 85,81,80,80,79**CSF £59.13 TOTE £3.00: £1.20, £3.90, £2.70; EX 72.00.
**Owner** Hamdan Al Maktoum **Bred** Matthews Breeding And Racing Ltd **Trained** Lambourn, Berks

**FOCUS**
Only an average time for the grade, despite being 0.71 seconds faster than the second division, but despite that the winner's form is strong and the front three all look worth following.

**NOTEBOOK**
**Etlaala** ◆, a 160,000gns full-brother to Selective and half-brother to Overspect, is out of a dam who won four times over the minimum trip. He certainly knew his job, making most of the running and forging nicely clear of his rivals inside the last furlong. He is sure to improve, but his breeding suggests he may not get much further than this and a crack at the Champagne Stakes is on the cards.
**Count Kristo** ◆, a 140,000euros yearling out of a full-sister to Quest For Fame, caught the eye with the way he came home from the rear of the field and is very much one to note, especially when stepped up in trip.
**Ameeq(USA)** ◆, a half-brother to Atwaar and Zulfaa, did his best to get on terms with the winner approaching the last two furlongs, but could never quite get there and got tired in the last half-furlong. This was a highly encouraging debut and, as his dam won over 12 furlongs, he should improve as he goes up in trip.
**Ocean Gift**, who had the advantage of previous experience, ran another promising race and, even though his breeding suggests this would be as far as he wants, his style of racing does not.
**Wingspeed(IRE)**, a 28,000gns half-brother to the useful Italian juvenile Pride Of Dingle, was not expected according to the market but this effort did offer some promise for the future.
**Superstitious(IRE)** has now faced stiff tasks in all three of his outings to date, but is obviously thought to have some ability and could be of interest in lesser company at one of the minor tracks.
**Storm Fury(USA)** did not improve for the extra furlong and is beginning to look exposed.
**Front Stage(IRE)**, a 65,000gns half-brother to First Fantasy out of a winning half-sister to Jeune, showed nothing on this debut though it is too early to write him off.

### 4744 STANJAMESUK.COM ST HUGH'S STKS (LISTED RACE) 5f 34y
**2:15** (2:16) (A) 2-Y-O **£14,500** (£5,500; £2,750; £1,250) **Stalls** Centre

Form RPR
1 **1** **Sumora (IRE)**[14] [4334] 2-8-8 ........................ JFortune 11 102
(GAButler) *lw: hld up in rr: rapid hdwy to ld jst over 1f out: edgd lft u.p ins last and r.o wl* **6/1**[3]
2021 **2** *1 ½* **Castelletto**[40] [3583] 2-8-8 85 ........................ GGibbons 4 97
(BAMcmahon) *swtg: chsd ldrs: rdn to chal over 1f out: kpt on ins last but no imp on wnr* **50/1**
1225 **3** *¾* **Right Answer**[21] [4119] 2-8-8 98 ........................ KFallon 12 94
(APJarvis) *lw: chsd ldrs: rdn to chal fr 2f out: stl upsides appr fnl f: one pce ins last* **5/1**[2]
1 **4** *shd* **Notjustaprettyface (USA)**[45] [3413] 2-8-8 ........................ RHughes 5 94
(HMorrison) *sn in tch: shkn up and chal appr fnl f: nt qckn ins last* **7/1**
41 **5** *½* **All For Laura**[15] [4298] 2-8-8 ........................ TPQueally 6 92
(DRLoder) *chsd ldrs tl rdn and outpcd 2f out: kpt on again u.p ins last: gng on nr fin* **10/1**
215 **6** *2* **Roodeye**[18] [4217] 2-8-8 94 ........................ MartinDwyer 10 85
(RFJohnsonHoughton) *outpcd in rr: rdn 1/2-way: kpt on fnl f but nvr gng pce to rch ldrs* **7/1**
13 **7** *1 ¾* **Oh Dara (USA)**[36] [3703] 2-8-8 90 ........................ DeanMcKeown 9 79
(PABlockley) *w ldrs: led 3f out: hdd appr fnl 2f: wknd appr fnl f* **50/1**
61 **8** *shd* **Rubyanne (IRE)**[23] [4064] 2-8-8 ........................ DHolland 3 78
(MJWallace) *lw: outpcd: pushed along fr 2f out: mod late prog* **7/1**
1312 **9** *nk* **Mary Read**[18] [4217] 2-8-13 100 ........................ FLynch 7 82
(BSmart) *led 2f: led again appr fnl 2f: hdd & wknd jst over 1f out* **8/1**
414 **10** *5* **Satin Finish (IRE)**[21] [4119] 2-8-8 98 ........................ ACulhane 2 60
(MRChannon) *outpcd most of way* **12/1**
215 **11** *8* **Sweet Royale**[35] [3736] 2-8-8 84 ........................ KMcEvoy 8 32
(MissLAPerratt) *b: swtg: spd to 1/2-way* **100/1**


The Form Book, Raceform Ltd, Compton, RG20 6NL

21 **12** *4* **Dance Away**93 2071 2-8-8 ........................................ JMackay 1 18
(MLWBell) *in tch: rdn 1/2-way: sn bhd* **9/2**1

61.23 secs (-1.42) **Going Correction** -0.10s/f (Good) **12** Ran SP% **119.4**
Speed ratings: **107,104,103,103,102 99,96,96,95,87 75,68**CSF £272.84 TOTE £7.60: £2.60, £8.30, £2.30; EX 241.30.
**Owner** Sangster Family **Bred** King Bloodstock And Swettenham Stud **Trained** Blewbury, Oxon

**FOCUS**

A very smart time for the type of race, 0.42 seconds faster than the later handicap for older horses. The apparently improved effort from the runner-up should in no way devalue the form, which otherwise looks sound.

**NOTEBOOK**

**Sumora(IRE)** ◆ maintained her unbeaten record with an impressive performance, showing a smart turn of foot to pass nearly all her rivals and win going away despite hanging right through greenness in the latter stages. She would not be the first smart representative from the yard to have made their debut on Polytrack, and now heads for the Flying Childers with a favourite's chance.

**Castelletto** ran a blinder on this step up in class and there is no reason to think this was a fluke. She is a very speedy filly and looks capable of winning a decent contest or two over this trip.

**Right Answer** had every chance and probably ran up to her best, but she may be better over the extra furlong now.

**Notjustaprettyface(USA)**, returning from a short break since her successful debut, had every chance and lost nothing in defeat on this step up in class against a field of mainly more experienced fillies.

**All For Laura** was not disgraced, but ran as though she needs to return to six.

**Roodeye** ◆ found everything happening too quickly for her, but was coming home well enough and looks to be crying out for an extra furlong. *Official explanation: jockey said filly was unsuited by the slow ground*

**Rubyanne(IRE)** *Official explanation: trainer said filly was unsuited by the slow ground*

**Mary Read** showed her usual early speed, but could not maintain the effort against a field of mostly more-progressive rivals.

**Satin Finish(IRE)** *Official explanation: jockey said filly hung left in the closing stages*

**Dance Away**, off since May, was never in the race and something must have been amiss. *Official explanation: jockey said filly was never travelling*

## 4745 STAN JAMES ONLINE HUNGERFORD STKS (GROUP 3) 7f (S)

**2:50** (2:52) (A ) 3-Y-0+ **£29,000** (£11,000; £5,500; £2,500) **Stalls** Centre

Form RPR

-603 **1** **Chic**15 4286 4-8-11 101 ........................................ KFallon 7 117
(SirMichaelStoute) *trckd ldrs: drvn to ld ins fnl 2f: edgd lft ins last but kpt on strly* **9/2**2

1402 **2** *1 ¾* **Suggestive**18 4216 6-9-0 111 ........................................(b) MHills 11 115+
(WJHaggas) *lw: hld up in rr: shkn up and hdwy appr fnl f: r.o fnl f to take 2nd cl home: nt trble wnr* **8/1**3

-401 **3** *¾* **Rum Shot**13 4362 3-8-8 100 ........................................ DaneO'Neill 6 113
(HCandy) *lw: chsd ldrs: led over 2f out: hdd ins fnl quarter m: styd chsng wnr but no imp: lost 2nd cl home* **20/1**

6355 **4** *¾* **Babodana**35 3724 4-9-0 108 ........................................ DHolland 13 111
(MHTompkins) *hld up in tch: rdn 2f out: gd hdwy over 1f out: chsd ldrs ins fnl f but nvr gng pce to chal* **9/2**2

1040 **5** *1 ¾* **So Will I**18 4216 3-8-8 108 ........................................ RHills 8 107
(MPTregoning) *hld up rr but in tch: rdn and hdwy over 2f out: chsd ldrs over 1f out: sn rdn: outpcd ins fnl f* **12/1**

651 **6** *hd* **Quito (IRE)**42 3522 7-9-0 108 ........................................(b) ACulhane 5 106+
(DWChapman) *hld up rr but in tch: rdn 2f out: styd on fr over 1f out but nvr gng pce to trble ldrs* **14/1**

15-0 **7** *¾* **Carrizo Creek (IRE)**122 1396 3-8-8 109 ........................................ JFortune 10 104
(BJMeehan) *t.k.h: pressed ldrs over 3f: styd prom tl wknd fnl f* **20/1**

4233 **8** *¾* **Millennium Force**27 3967 6-9-0 108 ........................................ CCatlin 12 102
(MRChannon) *bhd: drvn along fr 5f out: sme hdwy appr fnl f and kpt on ins last: n.d* **25/1**

-032 **9** *1 ½* **Polar Way**21 4120 5-9-0 114 ........................................ RHughes 9 98
(MrsAJPerrett) *lw: hld up rr but in tch: pushed along and hdwy ins fnl 2f: rdn and edgd lft fr 2f out: sn btn* **7/2**1

-205 **10** *½* **Duck Row (USA)**48 3355 9-9-0 106 ........................................ LisaJones 3 97
(JARToller) *pressed ldrs: rdn over 2f out: wknd over 1f out* **25/1**

1-00 **11** *1* **Just James**60 2957 5-9-5 113 ........................................ EAhern 4 99
(JNoseda) *in tch: swtchd lft to outside and rdn 2f out: wknd qckly over 1f out* **16/1**

0440 **12** *3 ½* **Country Reel (USA)**37 3674 4-9-0 110 ........................................(vt) KMcEvoy 1 85
(SaeedBinSuroor) *slt advantage tl hdd over 2f out: wknd qckly appr fnl f* **12/1**

5422 **13** *¾* **Makhlab (USA)**35 3730 4-9-0 108 ........................................(b) MartinDwyer 2 83
(BWHills) *lw: in tch: rdn to press ldrs 2f out: wknd qckly over 1f out* **16/1**

1m 23.99s (-3.23) **Going Correction** -0.10s/f (Good)
**WFA** 3 from 4yo+ 6lb **13** Ran SP% **120.7**
Speed ratings: **114,112,111,110,108 108,107,106,104,104 102,98,98**CSF £38.49 TOTE £5.10: £1.90, £2.90, £4.30; EX 40.80 Trifecta £664.60 Pool of £1,906.62 - 2.10 winning units..
**Owner** Cheveley Park Stud **Bred** Cheveley Park Stud Ltd **Trained** Newmarket, Suffolk

**FOCUS**

A decent pace for this Group Three and a winning time that was well up to standard for the grade. Despite this the form looks a little uneven.

**NOTEBOOK**

**Chic**, who has not had very much in the way of luck this term, found everything falling right for her this time, and once a gap appeared she was through it and away despite hanging left near the end. A return to a mile for the newly-elevated Sun Chariot Stakes is a possibility, and that could conceivably turn into a weak Group One.

**Suggestive** got the strong pace he needs but, as at Goodwood, he delivered a strong late challenge that was always going to be too late. The ability to win a race at this level is there, but timing his effort right is proving some task.

**Rum Shot** ◆, whose previous six outings have all been over six furlongs, ran a blinder on this step up in trip and class. There was no evidence that it was the extra furlong that beat him, and this gives his trainer plenty more options.

**Babodana** ran his race on this drop back in trip, but just appears held at this level.

**So Will I** appears to stay this trip despite his two wins to date coming over six. There seemed no excuses this time and it is interesting that he finished almost exactly the same distance behind Suggestive as he did at Goodwood.

**Quito(IRE)** had the strong pace he needs and did his best, but does not look up to this level.

**Carrizo Creek(IRE)** did not help his chances of lasting home by pulling hard early, but it remains to be seen whether he has trained on.

**Polar Way** ran disappointingly, but reportedly lost his action behind. *Official explanation: jockey said gelding lost its action behind 2f out*

**Country Reel(USA)** was given a positive ride on this first attempt at the trip, but folded rather tamely.

## 4746 STAN JAMES GEOFFREY FREER STKS (GROUP 2) 1m 5f 61y

**3:25** (3:25) (A ) 3-Y-0+ **£62,000** (£22,000; £11,000; £5,000) **Stalls** High

Form RPR

112- **1** **Mubtaker (USA)**314 5406 7-9-3 130 ........................................ RHills 4 121+
(MPTregoning) *bit bkwd: trckd ldr after 2f: impr fr 4f out to take slt ld ins fnl 3f: drvn and edgd lft over 1f out: forged clr: readily* **30/100**1

1402 **2** *2 ½* **Dubai Success**49 3333 4-9-3 112 ........................................ MHills 3 117
(BWHills) *lw: led tl narrowly hdd ins fnl 3f: rdn 2f out: kpt on fr over 1f out but no ch w wnr* **9/2**2

5065 **3** *1 ¾* **Compton Bolter (IRE)**15 4285 7-9-3 107 ........................................ RHughes 2 114
(GABulter) *hld up in 4th: hdwy on rails and clsd up 3f out: rdn 2f out: styd on same pce* **16/1**3

5-30 **4** *5* **The Great Gatsby (IRE)**38 3642 4-9-3 112 ........................................(b1) JFortune 1 107
(JHMGosden) *chsd ldr 2f: styd in 3rd: rdn and effrt 3f out: nvr gng pce of ldrs and wknd qckly ins fnl 2f* **16/1**3

2m 50.69s (-0.30) **Going Correction** +0.175s/f (Good) **4** Ran SP% **106.9**
Speed ratings: **107,105,104,101**CSF £1.91 TOTE £1.30; EX 1.60.
**Owner** Hamdan Al Maktoum **Bred** Warren W Rosenthal **Trained** Lambourn, Berks
■ Mubtaker was winning this race for the third successive year.

**FOCUS**

A race run at a crawl early and it basically turned into a four-furlong sprint. Despite the interest in Mubtaker's reappearance, it was a shame he scared off so many potential rivals and left this a very uncompetitive Group Two. The winning time was moderate for the class, but perhaps understandable with only four runners.

**NOTEBOOK**

**Mubtaker(USA)**, off since his cracking effort in last season's Arc, had little difficulty in seeing off his three rivals and he could have won by further had his rider really wanted. He did no more form-wise than he was entitled to, considering he had upwards of 18lb in hand of the others, but this will have blown the cobwebs away and he will now either go for the Grosser Preis von Baden or the September Stakes en-route to another crack at the Arc.

**Dubai Success**, who likes this track having won a Group Three here in the spring, found himself in front and set only a moderate pace, but was always a sitting duck for the favourite. He valiantly tried to fight back once the winner went past, but it proved a very unequal struggle. He has the ability to win back at Group Three level.

**Compton Bolter(IRE)**, switched off out the back, made a token effort halfway up the straight but it came to little. He has never won a Group race despite several attempts.

**The Great Gatsby(IRE)**, blinkered for the first time, saw plenty of daylight on the outside in the home straight which probably did not help, but even so looks a pale imitation of the horse that finished second in last year's Derby.

## 4747 STAN JAMES SUPPORTING WESSEX HEARTBEAT EBF MAIDEN STKS (DIV II) 7f (S)

**4:00** (4:01) (D ) 2-Y-0 **£6,396** (£1,968; £984; £492) **Stalls** Centre

Form RPR

3 **1** **Hallhoo (IRE)**21 4117 2-9-0 ........................................ ACulhane 2 81+
(MRChannon) *lw: mde all: rdn and c sharply rt to stands rail appr fnl f: drvn and hld on wl* **2/1**2

**2** *½* **Titian Time (USA)** 2-8-9 ........................................ JFortune 9 75+
(JHMGosden) *leggy: unf: lw: bhd: gd hdwy fr 2f out:chsng wnr whn hmpd and swtchd lft ins fnl f: kpt on but no imp on wnr cl home* **7/1**3

**3** *½* **Mayadeen (IRE)** 2-9-0 ........................................ MartinDwyer 8 79+
(MPTregoning) *unf: scope: bhd: hdwy over 1f out: drvn and kpt on wl fnl f: gng on cl home* **12/1**

**4** *hd* **Bertrose** 2-9-0 ........................................ EAhern 6 78+
(JLDunlop) *cmpt: bhd: drvn and hdwy fr 2f out: r.o wl fnl f: gng on nr fin* **25/1**

**5** *1 ½* **Spanish Ridge (IRE)** 2-9-0 ........................................ PDoe 7 74
(JLDunlop) *leggy: scope: s.i.s: bhd: hdwy fr 2f out: rdn and styd on wl fnl f: one pce nr fin* **33/1**

00 **6** *2 ½* **Swell Lad**24 4030 2-9-0 ........................................ TPQueally 1 68
(PFICole) *in tch: rdn to chse ldrs over 2f out: wknd fnl f* **33/1**

**7** *2 ½* **Sarem (USA)** 2-9-0 ........................................ RHills 3 62+
(MPTregoning) *w'like: lw: trckd ldr: rdn to chal 2f out: wknd qckly appr fnl f* **15/8**1

**8** *3 ½* **Rapid Flow** 2-9-0 ........................................ RHughes 4 53
(MrsAJPerrett) *lengthy: trckd ldrs: rdn 2f out: sn wknd* **12/1**

0 **9** *shd* **Golden Dynasty**51 3240 2-9-0 ........................................ PDobbs 5 53
(RHannon) *bkwd: t.k.h early: chsd ldrs over 4f* **25/1**

0 **10** *2* **Wembury Point (IRE)**18 4219 2-9-0 ........................................ DaneO'Neill 11 48
(BGPowell) *chsd ldrs tl wknd over 2f out* **33/1**

**11** *3* **Decoration** 2-9-0 ........................................ KFallon 10 40
(BJMeehan) *tall: str: bkwd: s.i.s: sn in tch: wknd qckly 2f out* **12/1**

1m 27.85s (0.63) **Going Correction** -0.10s/f (Good) **11** Ran SP% **120.2**
Speed ratings: **92,91,90,90,88 86,83,79,79,76 73**CSF £15.88 TOTE £3.00: £1.50, £1.90, £3.20; EX 21.10.
**Owner** Sheikh Ahmed Al Maktoum **Bred** Mrs Max Morris **Trained** West Ilsley, Berks

**FOCUS**

A modest time for the class, 0.71 seconds slower than the first division, but again some taking performances amongst the field. They tended to race more towards the stands' side of the track.

**NOTEBOOK**

**Hallhoo(IRE)**, with experience on his side, appreciated the extra furlong and slightly easier ground. Given a positive ride, he tended to hang right under pressure at around the furlong pole, doing the runner-up few favours, but was probably the winner on merit. Even softer ground would probably help him.

**Titian Time(USA)** ◆, a half-sister to a couple of winners including the Queen Mary winner Shining Hour, ran a debut full of promise. She was making significant progress against the stands' rail when the door was slammed in her face by the winner, and she then had insufficient time to make up the lost ground. It is not certain she would have won otherwise, but what is certain is that she is one to watch.

**Mayadeen(IRE)** ◆, out of a winning half-sister to Almutawakel, came from off the pace and finished in most taking style. He looks sure to improve a good deal and will get further.

**Bertrose** ◆, a half-brother to Ambrosine and Camrose, was very coltish and full of himself beforehand. Given a patient ride, he finished in great style and should improve a lot from this. His breeding suggests he will stay much further too.

**Spanish Ridge(IRE)** ◆, an Indian Ridge colt, started slowly and took a long time to realise what was required, but showed plenty of promise in the second half of the contest. His pedigree suggests softer ground will bring out the best in him.

**Sarem(USA)**, a $600,000 colt whose half-brother and dam were both winners in the USA, appeared to be the stable's first string on jockey bookings but, after showing prominently for a while, then dropped out. Better is to be expected.

## 4748 ANDREW STRODE-GIBBONS SUPPORTING WESSEX HEARTBEAT H'CAP 5f 34y
4:35 (4:36) (D ) (0-85,83) 3-Y-0+ £6,474 (£1,992; £996; £498) Stalls Centre

Form RPR

0502 **1** **Strawberry Patch (IRE)**[7] 4534 5-7-12 **53**......................(p) JMackay 11 65
(MissLAPerratt) *b: lw: chsd ldrs: sn pushed along:hrd drvn and r.o wl fnl f to ld last strides* **10/1**

-000 **2** *nk* **Brave Burt (IRE)**[38] 3645 7-9-11 **80**......................KFallon 4 91
(DNicholls) *b: lw: sn led: rdn 2f out: hung rt u.p fnl f: hdd last strides* **6/1**[3]

-000 **3** *1 ½* **Roman Quintet (IRE)**[140] 1131 4-8-5 **60**......................EAhern 3 66
(DWPArbuthnot) *trckd ldr: c rt and rdn ins fnl f: one pce whn hmpd fnl 100yds* **33/1**

0200 **4** *½* **Seven No Trumps**[3] 4626 7-9-7 **76**......................(p) DHolland 6 80
(JMBradley) *pressed ldrs: rdn 2f out: one pce ins fnl f* **10/1**

0006 **5** *nk* **Further Outlook (USA)**[5] 4614 10-10-0 **83**......................DaneO'Neill 9 86
(DKIvory) *b: b.hind: bhd: rdn 2f out: hdwy over 1f out: r.o ins last but nvr gng pce to rch ldrs* **20/1**

6040 **6** *hd* **Malapropism**[7] 4538 4-9-12 **81**......................ACulhane 13 83
(MRChannon) *lw: stdd s: t.k.h in rr: hdwy: rdn and hung lft fr over 1f out: kpt on cl home* **8/1**

0000 **7** *½* **Sir Edwin Landseer (USA)**[13] 4366 4-9-0 **69**......................GHind 12 69
(ChristianWroe, UAE) *bhd: rdn 2f out: hdwy over 1f out: styd on u.p ins last but nt rch ldrs* **16/1**

4500 **8** *¾* **Dancing Mystery**[7] 4538 10-9-11 **80**......................SCarson 10 78
(EAWheeler) *lw: stdd s: bhd: sme hdwy fnl f: kpt on cl home but nvr nr ldrs* **12/1**

6612 **9** *nk* **Double M**[12] 4400 7-8-11 **66**......................(v) RHughes 8 62
(MrsLRichards) *hld up in tch: pushed along 2f out: kpt on ins last but nvr a danger* **4/1**[1]

4510 **10** *nk* **Salviati (USA)**[7] 4538 7-9-7 **83**......................(p) CJDavies(7) 1 78
(JMBradley) *lw: bhd: hrd rdn 2f out: nvr gng pce to rch ldrs* **9/1**

2050 **11** *¾* **Sweet Cando (IRE)**[30] 3877 3-8-4 **62**......................(p) MartinDwyer 5 55
(MissLAPerratt) *b.hind: chsd ldrs: rdn 1/2-way: wknd fnl f* **33/1**

0165 **12** *1* **Zarzu**[7] 4538 5-9-7 **78**......................JFortune 7 67
(CRDore) *b.hind: pressed ldrs tl wknd fnl f* **9/2**[2]

-306 **13** *2* **The Lord**[2] 4677 4-9-13 **82**......................(p) ADaly 2 64
(WGMTurner) *pressed ldrs over 3f* **14/1**

61.65 secs (-1.00) **Going Correction** -0.10s/f (Good) **13** Ran SP% **122.6**
**WFA** 3 from 4yo+ 3lb
Speed ratings: **104,103,101,100,99 99,98,97,97,96 95,93,90**CSF £69.41 CT £1999.87 TOTE £11.40: £2.80, £2.00, £11.90; EX 79.80.
**Owner** Mrs Lucille Bone **Bred** Mrs G Doyle **Trained** Ayr, Strathclyde

**FOCUS**
A competitive handicap run at just an ordinary pace, but the form looks decent for the grade. The field split into two early with a smaller group of four staying far side, but the two groups came together late on and there seemed no great advantage.

**NOTEBOOK**
**Strawberry Patch(IRE)**, without a win in three years before this, was nonetheless well backed following his improved effort at Ayr seven days earlier. He did not let his supporters down, being produced with a well-timed effort on the nearside inside the last furlong to nail the runner-up in the dying strides. Now that he has found his form, he could win again.
**Brave Burt(IRE)**, who has dropped to a winning mark, appreciated the good ground and was given a positive ride in the far-side group. He looked like winning for most of the way, but he hung right under pressure in the closing stages and was worried out of it. He should be able to make amends off this mark, but the worry must be that he will be put up for this despite not winning.
**Roman Quintet(IRE)** ◆, who has just a solitary Polytrack maiden win to his name, was prominent in the far-side group but was continually carried right by the runner-up and his jockey had to stop riding when completely running out of room close to the line. It probably did not affect his finishing position, but this was still a decent effort and he remains comparatively unexposed on turf.
**Seven No Trumps** did best of the Bradley pair under a positive ride, but is an extremely hard horse to win with these days, as being 20lb lower than for his last victory will testify.
**Further Outlook(USA)** ran with credit, but is getting no help from the Handicapper and is unlikely to have any improvement in him at his age.
**Malapropism**, patiently ridden before making his effort on the nearside over a furlong from home, tended to hang into the whip despite a vigorous left-hand drive and is becoming frustrating.
**Double M** put in one of his more mediocre recent efforts, but has been kept very busy of late.

## 4749 STAN JAMES TELETEXT P630 H'CAP 1m 2f 6y
5:05 (5:10) (D ) (0-85,89) 3-Y-0 £6,610 (£2,034; £1,017; £508) Stalls High

Form RPR

-632 **1** **Night Spot**[15] 4300 3-9-3 **81**......................MartinDwyer 3 88
(RCharlton) *lw: sn led: hrd drvn fnl 2f: hld on gamely cl home* **13/2**

-123 **2** *nk* **Mazuna (IRE)**[20] 4167 3-8-4 **68**......................PDoe 13 75
(CEBrittain) *in tch: rdn over 2f out: str run u.p fr over 1f out: fin wl: nt quite get up* **12/1**

0041 **3** *nk* **Credit (IRE)**[6] 4582 3-9-11 **89** 5ex......................RHughes 12 95+
(RHannon) *lw: trckd ldrs: effrt and nt clr run 2f out and over 1f out: sn swtchd lft to rails: kpt on ins last: no ex cl home* **7/1**

1 **4** *½* **Hermitage Court (USA)**[29] 3916 3-9-6 **84**......................JFortune 8 89
(BJMeehan) *rangy: lw: trckd ldr: rdn to chal fr 3f out tl ins fnl 2f: styd on same pce u.p ins last* **4/1**[1]

1043 **5** *nk* **Whitsbury Cross**[23] 4061 3-8-13 **80**......................LPKeniry(3) 6 84
(DRCElsworth) *in tch: rdn 3f out: styd on wl fr over 1f out: kpt on cl home but nt rch ldrs* **8/1**

002 **6** *¾* **Killmorey**[20] 4180 3-7-12 **62**......................JMackay 1 65
(SCWilliams) *bhd: hdwy over 2f out: drvn and styd on fnl f but nt rch ldrs* **14/1**

0502 **7** *¾* **Top Spec (IRE)**[21] 4145 3-8-12 **76**......................PDobbs 7 78
(RHannon) *s.i.s: bhd: hdwy over 2f out: kpt on ins last but nvr gng pce to rch ldrs* **25/1**

5530 **8** *¾* **Winners Delight**[29] 3915 3-9-1 **79**......................KFallon 10 79
(APJarvis) *stdd s: hld up in rr: hdwy 3f out: styng on whn nt clr run over 1f out: n.d after* **11/2**[2]

0-40 **9** *½* **Donna Vita**[42] 3541 3-9-7 **85**......................JQuinn 2 84
(PWChapple-Hyam) *bhd: kpt on fnl 2f but nvr a danger* **40/1**

0120 **10** *1 ¼* **Hawkit (USA)**[50] 3271 3-8-7 **78**......................DTudhope(7) 9 75
(PDEvans) *hld up in rr: hdwy on outside and rdn fr 3f out: chsd ldrs 2f out: wknd over 1f out* **16/1**

4300 **11** *½* **Irish Blade (IRE)**[9] 4486 3-8-6 **70**......................DaneO'Neill 14 66
(HCandy) *b.hind: chsd ldrs tl wknd ins fnl 2f* **14/1**

0565 **12** *½* **Convince (USA)**[17] 4236 3-8-13 **77**......................ADaly 4 72
(MABuckley) *bhd most of way* **40/1**

0414 **13** *3* **Mr Jack Daniells (IRE)**[3] 4648 3-8-8 **75**......................RMiles(3) 15 64
(WRMuir) *chsd ldrs tl wknd qckly ins fnl 2f* **6/1**[3]

1000 **14** *2 ½* **Gretna**[52] 3206 3-8-13 **77**......................(b[1]) TPQueally 5 61
(JLDunlop) *chsd ldrs tl rdn and wknd qckly 3f out* **33/1**

2m 8.07s (-0.64) **Going Correction** +0.175s/f (Good) **14** Ran SP% **125.2**
Speed ratings: **109,108,108,108,107 107,106,106,105,104 104,103,101,99**CSF £83.11 CT £574.70 TOTE £8.10: £2.70, £4.80, £2.60; EX 38.30 Place 6 £149.03, Place 5 £48.18..
**Owner** D J Deer **Bred** D J And Mrs Deer **Trained** Beckhampton, Wilts

**FOCUS**
A decent pace and a smart winning time for the grade of contest. It paid to race close to the pace which may have had its effect formwise.

**NOTEBOOK**
**Night Spot** ◆ made sure there was no hanging about, quickly bagging the lead and then showing real grit and determination all the way down the home straight. He still seems to be progressing and can win again given similar conditions.
**Mazuna(IRE)** ran yet another fine race and though she was getting there slowly but surely, the post arrived just too soon. Despite the impression she might have given at Ascot, she does appear to need a bit further than this.
**Credit(IRE)**, carrying a 5lb penalty for his Windsor victory, was never far away and had to be switched to the inside rail in order to get a clear run. He had every chance though and stayed on all the way to the line, but was always just being held.
**Hermitage Court(USA)** ◆, who only made his debut last month, was given a positive ride over this longer trip and performed with plenty of credit against these much more experienced rivals. The Handicapper got his mark for this just about right, but he does have scope for improvement.
**Whitsbury Cross** stayed on well in the closing stages and would be very interesting over further.
**Killmorey**, making his handicap debut and stepping up a quarter of a mile in trip, was noted staying on nicely in the closing stages and is another that could be of interest over further, especially when the money is down.
**Top Spec(IRE)** stayed on in the latter stages without being able to land a blow, and would probably have preferred faster ground.
**Hawkit(USA)** may have seen too much daylight down the home straight.
**Mr Jack Daniells(IRE)** possibly saw too much daylight on the outside. Though close enough passing the three-furlong pole, he then had nothing more to offer.
T/Plt: £212.70 to a £1 stake. Pool: £64,700.40. 222.05 winning tickets. T/Qpdt: £18.90 to a £1 stake. Pool: £3,545.50. 138.45 winning tickets. ST

# 4726 NEWMARKET (JULY) (R-H)
Saturday, August 14

**OFFICIAL GOING: Good to soft**
After a dry night and a warm morning the ground had certainly dried out.
Wind: Slight across Weather: Sunny

## 4750 NGK SPARK PLUGS RATED STKS (H'CAP) 6f
2:05 (2:06) (B ) (0-105,101) 3-Y-0 £17,400 (£6,600; £3,300; £1,500) Stalls Low

Form RPR

1412 **1** **Alderney Race (USA)**[7] 4531 3-9-5 **99**......................SDrowne 6 108
(RCharlton) *chsd ldrs: rdn to ld ins fnl f: r.o* **4/1**[2]

0126 **2** *nk* **Mahmoom**[16] 4268 3-8-12 **92**......................TEDurcan 4 100
(MRChannon) *chsd ldrs: rdn over 1f out: r.o wl ins fnl f* **11/1**

0033 **3** *½* **Nights Cross (IRE)**[6] 4590 3-9-2 **99**......................(v[1]) SHitchcott(3) 13 106
(MRChannon) *chsd ldrs: rdn over 2f out: r.o* **17/2**

6003 **4** *½* **Bentley's Ball (USA)**[24] 4031 3-8-8 **88**......................RLMoore 11 93
(RHannon) *w ldr tl led over 2f out: rdn and edgd lft over 1f out: hdd and unable qck ins fnl f* **12/1**

4221 **5** *nk* **Flipando (IRE)**[42] 3523 3-8-6 **86**......................PHanagan 10 90
(TDBarron) *lw: led over 3f: rdn and edgd rt 1f out: styd on same pce* **5/1**[3]

-413 **6** *nk* **Khabfair**[7] 4531 3-9-1 **95**......................PRobinson 3 98+
(MrsAJPerrett) *chsd ldrs: nt clr run over 1f out: hmpd 1f out: styd on* **6/1**

0130 **7** *shd* **Traytonic**[39] 3598 3-9-7 **101**......................JPMurtagh 8 104+
(JRFanshawe) *lw: hld up: rdn over 2f out: r.o ins fnl f: nt rch ldrs* **7/2**[1]

4-50 **8** *1* **Botanical (USA)**[71] 2642 3-9-3 **97**......................(t) SSanders 1 97
(SaeedBinSuroor) *hld up: r.o ins fnl f: n.d* **20/1**

4420 **9** *nk* **Valjarv (IRE)**[7] 4531 3-8-9 **92**......................J-PGuillambert(3) 2 91
(NPLittmoden) *s.i.s: sn pushed along in rr: nvr nrr* **18/1**

040 **10** *2 ½* **Hatch**[31] 3850 3-8-8 **88**......................(t) RMullen 9 80
(RMHCowell) *lw: s.i.s: hld up: rdn over 1f out: n.d* **66/1**

1000 **11** *2* **Spliff**[28] 3945 3-8-11 **91**......................DSweeney 5 77
(HCandy) *s.s: hld up: a in rr* **14/1**

1m 13.2s (-0.12) **Going Correction** +0.075s/f (Good) **11** Ran SP% **117.9**
Speed ratings: **103,102,101,101,100 100,100,99,98,95 92**CSF £47.87 CT £366.65 TOTE £4.50: £1.60, £3.50, £2.50; EX 52.30 Trifecta £185.00 Pool of £703.90 - 2.70 winning units..
**Owner** Britton House Stud Ltd **Bred** Britton House Stud Inc **Trained** Beckhampton, Wilts

**FOCUS**
A competitive contest ruined somewhat by a lack of a decent gallop, and it favoured those racing up with the pace, and the proximity of the fourth tends to hold down the form.

**NOTEBOOK**
**Alderney Race(USA)** was always in the right place and poached enough of a lead to hold the fast-finishing Mahmoom. He continues on the upgrade and looks capable of breaking through into the Listed ranks.
**Mahmoom**, for one who stays further, hardly had the race run to suit.
**Nights Cross(IRE)**, who showed a bit more sparkle than of late when equipped with blinkers in Ireland, swopped those for a visor and was far from disgraced. He is beginning to get some respite from the Handicapper and is one to keep an eye on.
**Bentley's Ball(USA)** has struggled of late and, although not beaten far, he did have the run of things.
**Flipando(IRE)** was not disgraced in this better race and he can be found another opening at a lower level.
**Khabfair** did not have much luck in running and, although he is climbing up the weights, still has some improvement in him.
**Traytonic**, who got warm beforehand, was not suited to the steady pace.

## 4751 SPORTINGODDS.COM GREY HORSE H'CAP 6f
2:35 (2:35) (D ) (0-80,77) 3-Y-0+ £10,101 (£3,108; £1,554; £777) Stalls Low

Form RPR

0352 **1** **Middleton Grey**[34] 3779 6-9-1 **64**......................(b) JPMurtagh 5 74
(AGNewcombe) *hld up: hdwy over 1f out: rdn to ld ins fnl f: r.o* **4/1**[2]

1202 **2** *2* **Kirkby's Treasure**[16] 4280 6-9-13 **76**......................TEDurcan 2 80
(ABerry) *lw: sn pushed along in rr: r.o ins fnl f: nt rch wnr* **6/1**[3]

0040 **3** *nk* **Yorkies Boy**[8] 4522 9-7-9 **47** oh1......................(p) JFMcDonald(3) 10 50
(NEBerry) *b: hld up: hdwy over 1f out: r.o* **12/1**

0043 **4** *nk* **Nicholas Nickelby**[35] 3742 4-8-5 **54**......................(p) RLMoore 1 56
(MJPolglase) *lw: chsd ldrs: rdn and ev ch fr over 2f out: no ex ins fnl f* **33/1**

0-56 **5** *nk* **Mecca's Mate**[35] 3759 3-8-2 **55**......................PHanagan 4 56
(DWBarker) *lw: s.i.s: sn chsng ldrs: led 2f out: hdd and unable qck ins fnl f* **50/1**



The Form Book, Raceform Ltd, Compton, RG20 6NL

0035 **6** *1* **Sir Desmond**[28] 3945 6-10-0 **77**..........(p) SSanders 7 75
(RGuest) *mid-div: hdwy 1/2-way: nt clr run over 2f out: no ex fnl f* **9/4**[1]

4302 **7** *hd* **Nautical**[12] 4401 6-8-3 **52**.......... WSupple 8 50
(AWCarroll) *s.s: hld up: swtchd lft and hdwy over 1f out: nt clr run ins fnl f: nvr nr to chal* **14/1**

0600 **8** *nk* **Laurel Dawn**[3] 4626 6-8-4 **60**.......... NataliaGemelova(7) 12 57
(IWMcinnes) *chsd ldrs: rdn over 1f out: no ex* **25/1**

5660 **9** *1/2* **Silver Chime**[8] 4522 4-9-4 **67**.......... PRobinson 11 62
(DMSimcock) *chsd ldr tl led over 2f out: sn hdd: wknd fnl f* **22/1**

0520 **10** *1 3/4* **Fiveoclock Express (IRE)**[21] 4122 4-9-13 **76**..........(p) IMongan 3 66
(MissGayKelleway) *hld up: rdn over 1f out: n.d* **16/1**

0000 **11** *1 1/4* **Te Quiero**[36] 3690 6-8-12 **68**..........(t) RachelCostello(7) 6 54
(MissGayKelleway) *chsd ldrs over 4f* **25/1**

1200 **12** *6* **Silver Mascot**[24] 4011 5-8-8 **57**.......... RFfrench 9 25
(ISemple) *lw: racd keenly: led: hung rt and hdd over 2f out: wknd over 1f out* **6/1**[3]

1m 12.82s (-0.50) **Going Correction** +0.075s/f (Good)
**WFA** 3 from 4yo+ 4lb **12** Ran SP% **116.5**
Speed ratings: **106,103,102,102,102 100,100,100,99,97 95,87**CSF £25.81 CT £270.41 TOTE £5.50: £2.00, £1.80, £3.10; EX 31.20.
**Owner** Andy Beard **Bred** Mount Coote Stud **Trained** Yarnscombe, Devon

**FOCUS**
An ordinary contest for greys only, but it looked to be run at a sound pace. The form is modest but straightforward.

**NOTEBOOK**
**Middleton Grey** had the strong pace he needed over this trip to gain his first success on turf.
**Kirkby's Treasure** found this trip an inadequate test, but clearly remains on good terms with himself despite an increasing mark.
**Yorkies Boy**, although a long way below his best nowadays, still retains a little ability.
**Nicholas Nickelby** was not disgraced in this better race and does have the ability to win a little contest somewhere.
**Mecca's Mate** showed a bit more on this venture into handicap company, and did enough to suggest she should find a little race.
**Sir Desmond** did not have the best of runs, but that can hardly be used as an excuse.
**Nautical** *Official explanation: jockey said gelding failed to get a clear run in the latter stages*
**Silver Mascot** *Official explanation: jockey said gelding bolted to post and hung right throughout*

## 4752 BEDFORD LODGE HOTEL NURSERY 5f
**3:10** (3:11) (C ) 2-Y-O **£8,209** (£2,526; £1,263; £631) **Stalls** Low

Form RPR

1540 **1** **Nova Tor (IRE)**[13] 4358 2-8-10 **79**.......... IMongan 1 91
(NPLittmoden) *chsd ldrs: rdn to ld ins fnl f: r.o* **33/1**

3331 **2** *1 1/4* **Wise Wager (IRE)**[14] 4348 2-8-4 **73**.......... PHanagan 6 81
(RAFahey) *s.i.s: sn rcvrd to ld: edgd rt thrght: hdd and unable qck ins fnl f* **7/1**

4453 **3** *2* **Canton (IRE)**[8] 4514 2-9-7 **90**.......... RLMoore 12 91+
(RHannon) *hld up: nt clr run over 1f out: r.o ins fnl f: nvr trbld ldrs* **11/2**[3]

1114 **4** *3/4* **Key Secret**[14] 4348 2-8-12 **81**.......... JPMurtagh 7 79
(MLWBell) *lw: chsd ldrs: rdn over 1f out: no ex ins fnl f* **11/1**

3611 **5** *3/4* **Pitch Up (IRE)**[8] 4514 2-9-7 **90**.......... SSanders 2 86
(TGMills) *chsd ldrs: lost pl over 3f out: rallied over 1f out: no imp ins fnl f* **4/1**[1]

600 **6** *nk* **Baileys Applause**[5] 4612 2-7-7 **67** oh3..........(b) HayleyTurner(5) 13 62
(CADwyer) *lw: hld up: hdwy over 1f out: nt trble ldrs* **66/1**

431 **7** *1* **Witchry**[20] 4175 2-9-2 **85**.......... PRobinson 4 76
(MAJarvis) *s.i.s: hld up: n.m.r ins fnl f: n.d* **4/1**[1]

5346 **8** *shd* **Empire's Ghodha**[14] 4325 2-9-1 **87**..........(b) JFMcDonald(3) 5 78
(BJMeehan) *lw: hld up: rdn over 1f out: n.d* **14/1**

4013 **9** *3* **Brag (IRE)**[14] 4348 2-8-12 **81**.......... SDrowne 9 61
(RCharlton) *lw: chsd ldrs: rdn 1/2-way: wknd fnl f* **5/1**[2]

034 **10** *nk* **Lady Ann Summers (USA)**[36] 3693 2-8-7 **76**..........(b[1]) WSupple 14 55
(BJMeehan) *s.i.s: hld up: a in rr* **16/1**

4063 **11** *1* **Detonate**[36] 3704 2-8-6 **75**.......... RMullen 15 51
(IAWood) *b: chsd ldrs: rdn over 1f out: sn wknd* **25/1**

1534 **12** *3/4* **Monashee Prince (IRE)**[75] 2526 2-9-2 **85**.......... NPollard 11 58
(JRBest) *prom over 3f* **20/1**

3043 **13** *10* **Azuree (IRE)**[10] 4432 2-8-2 **71**..........(b) RSmith 8 9
(RHannon) *dwlt: outpcd* **33/1**

59.23 secs (-0.42) **Going Correction** +0.075s/f (Good) **13** Ran SP% **121.4**
Speed ratings: **106,104,100,99,98 97,96,96,91,90 89,88,72**CSF £244.54 CT £1542.39 TOTE £42.70: £9.70, £2.40, £3.30; EX 361.50 Trifecta £1542.39.
**Owner** Nigel Shields **Bred** Newlands House Stud **Trained** Newmarket, Suffolk

**FOCUS**
This was run at a fair clip and very few got competitive. The form looks strong with solid performers close up.

**NOTEBOOK**
**Nova Tor(IRE)** is a game filly and looked to put in a personal best, despite having had plenty of racing. She should continue to give a good account.
**Wise Wager(IRE)** did not break as well as she might have and tended to hang through the race, but she is clearly a pacy filly who will find other openings.
**Canton(IRE)** did not have the best of runs and shaped as though he really ought to appreciate an extra furlong. *Official explanation: jockey said colt hung left throughout*
**Key Secret**, 9lb higher than when winning at York, just looked to find this company a bit too hot for her.
**Pitch Up(IRE)** had the beating of the third on their running at Lingfield, but tended to run his race in snatches.
**Baileys Applause** was always seeing plenty of daylight on the outside of the field from her wide draw, but not for the first time was not disgraced. Her turn will come.
**Witchry** was always being taken along a little faster than ideal and may now need an extra furlong.

## 4753 HOOFBEATS TOURS MAIDEN FILLIES' STKS 7f
**3:40** (3:42) (D ) 2-Y-O **£5,707** (£1,756; £878; £439) **Stalls** Low

Form RPR

6 **1** **Cassydora**[29] 3905 2-8-11.......... SSanders 1 89+
(JLDunlop) *lw: led 6f out: clr 2f out: comf* **7/2**[1]

**2** *2 1/2* **Playful Act (IRE)** 2-8-11.......... RHavlin 13 82+
(JHMGosden) *gd sort: slowly in to stride: hld up: hdwy over 2f out: r.o: no ch w wnr* **7/1**[2]

02 **3** *2 1/2* **County Clare**[13] 4364 2-8-11.......... RMullen 7 76
(AMBalding) *lw: led 1f: chsd wnr: rdn over 2f out: sn outpcd* **7/2**[1]

**4** *nk* **Bahja (USA)** 2-8-11.......... WSupple 15 75
(JHMGosden) *gd sort: lw: s.i.s: hld up: swtchd rt and hdwy over 2f out: nt rch ldrs* **7/1**[2]

**5** *1 1/4* **Donyana** 2-8-11.......... PRobinson 8 72
(MAJarvis) *gd sort: lw: chsd ldrs: rdn over 2f out: wknd fnl f* **10/1**[3]

0 **6** *1* **Lunar Sky (USA)**[44] 3456 2-8-11.......... RLMoore 12 70
(CEBrittain) *s.i.s: hld up: hdwy over 2f out: hung lft over 1f out: nt trble ldrs* **14/1**

0 **7** *3* **Alpine Gold (IRE)**[17] 4234 2-8-11.......... IMongan 10 62
(JLDunlop) *lw: hld up: nvr nrr* **25/1**

**8** *1/2* **Allied Cause** 2-8-11.......... SDrowne 5 61
(LMCumani) *cmpt: scope: hld up: rdn over 2f out: wknd over 1f out* **7/1**[2]

0 **9** *1/2* **Lola Sapola (IRE)**[20] 4172 2-8-11.......... AMackay 11 60
(NACallaghan) *lw: hld up: shkn up over 1f out: nvr nr to chal* **50/1**

**10** *shd* **Moonmaiden** 2-8-11.......... TEDurcan 4 59
(MRChannon) *w'like: leggy: scope: s.s: outpcd: nvr nrr* **10/1**[3]

**11** *1/2* **Jenna Stannis** 2-8-11.......... DSweeney 3 58
(RMBeckett) *leggy: scope: prom: wkng whn hmpd over 2f out* **66/1**

000 **12** *nk* **Romantic Gift**[23] 4053 2-8-11.......... MTebbutt 2 57
(JMPEustace) *prom over 5f* **25/1**

00 **13** *1 1/2* **Never Away**[28] 3946 2-8-8.......... J-PGuillambert(3) 14 54
(NACallaghan) *hld up: hdwy 1/2-way: hung lft and wknd over 1f out* **25/1**

00 **14** *16* **Bregaglia**[15] 4292 2-8-11.......... OUrbina 9 14
(RMHCowell) *chsd ldrs over 4f* **100/1**

1m 27.0s (0.23) **Going Correction** +0.075s/f (Good) **14** Ran SP% **122.8**
Speed ratings: **101,98,95,94,93 92,88,88,87,87 87,86,85,66**CSF £27.13 TOTE £4.30: £1.50, £3.30, £1.50; EX 30.40.
**Owner** Hesmonds Stud **Bred** Hesmonds Stud Ltd **Trained** Arundel, W Sussex

**FOCUS**
This looked a fair maiden with plenty of well-bred types on show, and even though time was ordinary it looks sure to throw up plenty of winners in the future.

**NOTEBOOK**
**Cassydora** had clearly improved from her debut and looks a filly that is going places.
**Playful Act(IRE)** ◆, a sister to the useful Percussionist, as well as being a half-sister to Group Two winner Echoes In Eternity, has plenty to live up to, but there was plenty to like about this first effort and she looks to have a bright future.
**County Clare** had the edge in experience, but was easily left behind when the winner changed gear. Time may tell she was tackling a couple of above average types.
**Bahja(USA)** ◆, who is out of a mare that won the French Guineas, got going far too late, but is sure to have learnt plenty from the experience. She should not be too difficult to place.
**Donyana**, a half-sister to 1000 Guineas heroine Ameerat, just got tired up the hill. She is sure to improve on this and may well be better suited to a sounder surface.
**Lunar Sky(USA)** did not shape at all badly in what could prove to be quite a hot fillies' maiden.

## 4754 NATIONAL HORSERACING MUSEUM CLASSIFIED STKS 1m 2f
**4:15** (4:16) (D ) 3-Y-O+ **£5,486** (£1,688; £844; £422) **Stalls** Centre

Form RPR

1420 **1** **Boule D'Or (IRE)**[35] 3728 3-9-0 **85**.......... NDay 5 96
(RIngram) *lw: hld up: hdwy over 2f out: led over 1f out: rdn out* **6/1**

-260 **2** *2* **Solo Flight**[14] 4319 7-9-9 **85**.......... RLMoore 7 92
(HMorrison) *hld up: hdwy over 2f out: rdn over 1f out: styd on* **11/1**

3215 **3** *nk* **Marbush (IRE)**[35] 3728 3-8-12 **83**..........(t) PRobinson 4 89
(MAJarvis) *hld up: hdwy over 2f out: rdn and ev ch over 1f out: edgd lft and no ex ins fnl f* **6/1**

2-31 **4** *1 1/2* **Cellarmaster (IRE)**[35] 3746 3-8-9 **79**.......... SSanders 1 84
(EFVaughan) *lw: chsd ldrs: led 2f out: sn hdd: styd on same pce fnl f* **11/4**[1]

1205 **5** *1* **Trueno (IRE)**[14] 4343 5-9-6 **82**.......... SDrowne 3 84
(LMCumani) *hld up: plld hrd: hdwy over 3f out: rdn over 1f out: styd on same pce* **9/2**[2]

2162 **6** *4* **Barking Mad (USA)**[7] 4533 6-9-8 **84**.......... IMongan 8 79
(MLWBell) *led and sn clr: hdd 2f out: wknd fnl f* **13/2**

-406 **7** *6* **Dubrovsky**[10] 4442 4-9-6 **82**.......... JPMurtagh 2 66
(JRFanshawe) *lw: hld up: hdwy over 3f out: rdn and wknd over 1f out* **11/2**[3]

610- **8** *10* **Adjawar (IRE)**[294] 5738 6-9-7 **83**.......... PHanagan 6 49
(JJQuinn) *chsd ldr 4f: wknd over 2f out* **22/1**

2m 7.11s (0.65) **Going Correction** +0.075s/f (Good)
**WFA** 3 from 4yo+ 9lb **8** Ran SP% **114.8**
Speed ratings: **100,98,98,96,96 92,88,80**CSF £68.57 TOTE £8.40: £1.80, £2.80, £2.70; EX 83.30.
**Owner** Friends and Family **Bred** Major K R Thompson **Trained** Epsom, Surrey

**FOCUS**
A tight contest with just 1lb covering the field on adjusted ratings, and the form appears fair for the grade and sound. The field raced over the far side once in line for home.

**NOTEBOOK**
**Boule D'Or(IRE)**, whose disappointing effort last time was put down to the race coming too soon, bounced back to form having been freshened up. There could well be more to come from him.
**Solo Flight** takes a bit of knowing and looked to have been produced just right, but not for the first time, did not find what he might have.
**Marbush(IRE)**, who was fitted with a tongue-tie for the first time, had every chance, but did not quite get home on this easy ground.
**Cellarmaster(IRE)** was not disgraced in this better contest and should regain winning ways when his sights are lowered a little.
**Trueno(IRE)**, not for the first time, did himself no favours by refusing to settle.
**Barking Mad(USA)** dropped away tamely having established a healthy advantage to past halfway.
**Dubrovsky** *Official explanation: jockey said gelding had a breathing problem*

## 4755 NATIONAL STUD CONDITIONS STKS 1m 4f
**4:45** (4:45) (B ) 3-Y-O+ **£12,803** (£4,543; £2,271; £1,032) **Stalls** Centre

Form RPR

54-6 **1** **Orange Touch (GER)**[105] 1767 4-9-1 **101**.......... JPMurtagh 5 117+
(MrsAJPerrett) *lw: trckd ldr 7f: rdn over 3f out: led over 1f out: styd on wl* **7/1**[3]

13 **2** *6* **Remaadd (USA)**[18] 4215 3-8-7 **107**.......... SSanders 3 111
(MPTregoning) *led: rdn and hdd over 1f out: no ex* **4/7**[1]

-363 **3** *12* **Musanid (USA)**[28] 3936 4-9-1 **107**.......... WSupple 2 90
(SirMichaelStoute) *lw: prom: chsd ldr 5f out: rdn over 2f out: wknd over 1f out: eased* **9/4**[2]

006 **4** *dist* **Phoenix Nights (IRE)**[36] 3705 4-9-1 **52**.......... PPMathers 1 —
(ABerry) *b: hld up: rdn and wknd over 4f out* **66/1**

2m 34.18s (1.22) **Going Correction** +0.075s/f (Good)
**WFA** 3 from 4yo+ 11lb **4** Ran SP% **108.4**
Speed ratings: **98,94,86,**—CSF £11.92 TOTE £6.40; EX 15.50.
**Owner** Cheveley Park Stud **Bred** Gestut Auenquelle **Trained** Pulborough, W Sussex

**FOCUS**
An unsatisfactory contest in which they didn't appear to go a great pace. A surprise winner makes this difficult to rate, but the winner could be Group class if this form is true.

**NOTEBOOK**
**Orange Touch(GER)** settled much better than he did in the spring and showed a nice turn of foot to go clear. This trip appeared to bring about some improvement from him and, lightly-raced, there should be plenty more to come from him.

**Remaadd(USA)** was easily brushed aside and his St Leger entry looks wide of the mark on this display.
**Musanid(USA)** ran no sort of race and is clearly out of sorts at present.

## 4756 RUTLAND ARMS HOTEL RATED STKS (H'CAP) 1m
5:15 (5:15) (D) (0-85,81) 3-Y-O £5,025 (£1,906; £953; £433) Stalls Low

Form RPR
6200 **1** **King Of Diamonds**[24] 4032 3-8-10 **70**.................. WSupple 8 83+
(JRBest) *edgd rt s: hld up: hdwy 3f out: hung lft and led 2f out: r.o wl* **16/1**
4132 **2** *3* **Dumnoni**[17] 4236 3-9-6 **80**.................. IMongan 6 87
(JulianPoulton) *hld up: hdwy over 1f out: sn rdn: styd on* **6/1**
0506 **3** *1 3/4* **Song Of Vala**[24] 4032 3-9-1 **75**.................. SDrowne 5 78
(RCharlton) *chsd ldrs: rdn over 1f out: styd on same pce* **5/1**[2]
0053 **4** *1* **Sweet Indulgence (IRE)**[17] 4237 3-9-7 **81**.................. MTebbutt 7 82
(DrJDScargill) *chsd ldrs: rdn whn hmpd 2f out: styd on same pce appr fnl f* **14/1**
0051 **5** *shd* **Best Desert (IRE)**[12] 4390 3-8-7 **67** oh1.................. NPollard 4 68
(JRBest) *chsd ldrs: rdn over 2f out: styd on same pce appr fnl f* **16/1**
331 **6** *1 1/4* **Habanero**[16] 4266 3-9-5 **79**.................. RLMoore 1 77
(RHannon) *w ldr tl led over 6f out: rdn and hdd 2f out: wknd ins fnl f* **11/2**[3]
2245 **7** *2* **Kibryaa (USA)**[9] 4490 3-9-6 **80**..................(p) PRobinson 3 74
(MAJarvis) *led: hdd over 6f out: wknd fnl f* **3/1**[1]
21 **8** *2* **Cashbar**[15] 4303 3-9-3 **77**.................. JPMurtagh 2 67
(JRFanshawe) *chsd ldrs over 6f* **3/1**[1]

1m 40.11s (-0.37) **Going Correction** +0.075s/f (Good) **8** Ran SP% **114.8**
Speed ratings: **104,101,99,98,98 97,95,93**CSF £108.22 CT £557.15 TOTE £16.90: £2.80, £2.10, £2.20; EX 175.20 Place 6 £1,551.49, Place 5 £551.91..
**Owner** D Newland **Bred** D And Mrs Newland **Trained** Hucking, Kent

**FOCUS**
This didn't look that competitive and the form is ordinary but sound.

**NOTEBOOK**
**King Of Diamonds** got off the mark in fine style and won with plenty in hand. This was the first time he had encountered an easy surface and it clearly suited well.
**Dumnoni** found this trip well within her compass, but just came up against an unexposed sort.
**Song Of Vala** has been struggling to find a trip, and a return to this distance was of no help to him.
**Sweet Indulgence(IRE)** continues to frustrate and just has not built on a promising first effort.
**Best Desert(IRE)** gave the impression this trip may be too far for him.
**Habanero** was found out by a combination of a softer surface, and a 7lb higher mark than when successful at Epsom last time.
**Kibryaa(USA)**, who did not move that well to post, folded tamely up the hill.
**Cashbar** was very disappointing on ground which should have suited.
T/Plt: £1,758.20 to a £1 stake. Pool: £66,114.10. 27.45 winning tickets. T/Qpdt: £189.70 to a £1 stake. Pool: £2,896.90. 11.30 winning tickets. CR

# 4392 RIPON (R-H)
Saturday, August 14

**OFFICIAL GOING: Soft (heavy in places)**

## 4757 RIPON HORN BLOWER CONDITIONS STKS 6f
2:10 (2:11) (C) 2-Y-O £7,308 (£2,772; £1,386; £630) Stalls Low

Form RPR
2202 **1** **Dario Gee Gee (IRE)**[30] 3865 2-9-0 95.................. NCallan 7 95
(KARyan) *trckd ldrs: drvn to chal appr fnl f: r.o wl u.p to ld wl ins last* **9/4**[1]
4 **2** *1/2* **Rainbow Rising (IRE)**[16] 4256 2-8-11.................. RWinston 3 91
(JHowardJohnson) *led: drvn along 2f out: r.o wl u.p fnl f: hdd wl ins last: no ex* **7/1**
3140 **3** *5* **Shivaree**[23] 4060 2-8-11 92.................. JFanning 6 78
(MRChannon) *cl up: ev ch 2f out: sn rdn and btn* **11/4**[2]
313 **4** *2* **Propellor (IRE)**[14] 4330 2-8-13 85.................. ABeech(3) 2 78
(ADickman) *trckd ldrs: rdn over 2f out: sn btn* **11/2**
311 **5** *5* **Word Perfect**[30] 3868 2-9-2 93.................. DaleGibson 4 66
(MWEasterby) *dwlt: rr: sme hdwy 1/2-way: sn rdn and btn* **5/1**[3]
1 **6** *5* **El Rey Royale**[29] 3918 2-8-11.................. NMackay(3) 5 51
(MDHammond) *dwlt: in tch: rdn 1/2-way: sn wknd* **16/1**
0000 **7** *9* **Den Perry**[13] 4359 2-8-11.................. FNorton 1 26
(ABerry) *wl bhd fr 1/2-way* **200/1**

1m 15.3s (2.40) **Going Correction** +0.375s/f (Good) **7** Ran SP% **108.4**
Speed ratings: **99,98,91,89,82 75,63**CSF £16.46 TOTE £3.60: £1.50, £3.40; EX 21.90.
**Owner** Crewe And Nantwich Racing Club **Bred** John Malone **Trained** Hambleton, N Yorks
■ Stewards Enquiry : J Fanning one-day ban: failed to keep straight from stalls (Aug 25)

**FOCUS**
Probably a fair race with the front two pulling five lengths clear of the third. The winner was close to previous form and it looks a solid race on paper.

**NOTEBOOK**
**Dario Gee Gee(IRE)** has yet to run a bad race in six visits to the racecourse and was able to record his second win. This, on paper, was the easiest task he has faced since his debut and, although not finding it easy to get on top, he pulled out a little extra close home. He is not an easy one to place as he is not up to Pattern level and has too high a mark to get competitive in handicaps.
**Rainbow Rising(IRE)**, who is bred to be suited by farther, showed a big improvement on his debut when only fourth at Carlisle and kept battling away having tried to make all, pulling five lengths clear of the third. He will be suited by another furlong and will win his maiden.
**Shivaree** did not get home over seven furlongs at Sandown and appreciated this return to six, although she still failed to run up to the form that saw her finish fourth in the Cherry Hinton. She is another who is hard to place.
**Propellor(IRE)** ran as well as could have been expected at the weights. He will be better back in handicaps.
**Word Perfect** had won both races prior to this over five furlongs, but he was in trouble before stamina became an issue.

## 4758 DONAL & BERNADETTE MCWILLIAMS MEMORIAL MAIDEN STKS 5f
2:45 (2:52) (D) 3-Y-O+ £4,741 (£1,458; £729; £364) Stalls Low

Form RPR
-444 **1** **Troodos Jet**[22] 4097 3-9-0 64.................. FNorton 3 64
(ABerry) *mde all: r.o u.p fnl f* **2/1**[1]
0000 **2** *3/4* **Elliot's Choice (IRE)**[3] 4626 3-8-11 63..................(v[1]) DNolan(3) 2 62
(DCarroll) *trckd ldrs: nt clr run over 1f out: sn chsng wnr and rdn: no imp ins last* **7/2**[2]
**3** *8* **Ariesanne (IRE)** 3-8-9.................. GParkin 4 33
(RAFahey) *s.v.s: wl bhd: kpt on to take 3rd wl ins fnl f* **8/1**[3]
0 **4** *1 1/4* **Raetihi**[86] 2236 3-8-9.................. NCallan 5 29
(ASenior) *cl up tl rdn and wknd over 1f out* **33/1**

63.30 secs (3.10) **Going Correction** +0.375s/f (Good) **4** Ran SP% **69.6**
Speed ratings: **90,88,76,74**CSF £3.24 TOTE £1.80; EX 3.60.
**Owner** Anthony White **Bred** Auldyn Stud Ltd **Trained** Cockerham, Lancs
■ Harrison's Flyer (6/4F) was withdrawn (broke out of stalls). R4 applies, deduct 40p in the £.

**FOCUS**
A very moderate time for a very moderate race and the winner only needed to repeat previous efforts to score.

**NOTEBOOK**
**Troodos Jet** has not been beaten far in similar races this season and ran to form to finally get off the mark. Three-year-old plus sprint maidens are poor affairs at this time of year and he did not achieve much in winning, but now he has got his head in front, and may be up to landing a handicap.
**Elliot's Choice(IRE)** was having his 17th attempt at losing his maiden tag and again found one too strong. He should continue to be opposed.
**Ariesanne(IRE)** lost all chance at the gate when slowly away and should come on for the run.

## 4759 WILLIAM HILL GREAT ST WILFRID STKS (HERITAGE H'CAP) 6f
3:15 (3:20) (B) (0-105,101) 3-Y-O+ £29,000 (£11,000; £5,500; £2,500) Stalls Low

Form RPR
4001 **1** **Smokin Beau**[7] 4538 7-9-10 **98**.................. JFanning 11 116
(NPLittmoden) *racd far side: mde all: qcknd clr appr fnl f: r.o strly* **16/1**
0133 **2** *5* **Pieter Brueghel (USA)**[8] 4510 5-8-12 **86**.................. WRyan 5 89+
(DNicholls) *led stands side gp thrght: r.o wl: no ch w wnr* **16/1**
1063 **3** *1 1/4* **Hiccups**[23] 4047 4-8-5 **79**.................. PMQuinn 12 78
(DNicholls) *prom far side: rdn 2f out: edgd rt u.p ins fnl f: kpt on* **40/1**
0012 **4** *nk* **Machinist (IRE)**[21] 4152 4-8-9 **83**.................. ANicholls 20 81
(DNicholls) *rr div far side: hdwy 2f out: r.o wl u.p fnl f* **6/1**[2]
1043 **5** *1/2* **Cd Flyer (IRE)**[20] 4179 7-8-10 **87**.................. PMulrennan(3) 21 84
(BEllison) *in tch far side: rdn 2f out: kpt on same pce* **12/1**[3]
2200 **6** *1* **Hidden Dragon (USA)**[77] 2469 5-9-8 **96**.................. GFaulkner 19 90
(PABlockley) *prom far side: rdn 2f out: no ex whn hmpd ins fnl f* **20/1**
0100 **7** *hd* **Artie**[7] 4538 5-8-12 **86**.................. RWinston 6 79+
(TDEasterby) *chsd stands side ldr thrght: drvn along over 2f out: kpt on: no imp* **12/1**[3]
0002 **8** *2 1/2* **Abbajabba**[3] 4635 8-8-4 **78**.................. JBramhill 13 64
(CWFairhurst) *midfield far side: rdn 2f out: kpt on fnl f: n.d* **25/1**
0506 **9** *nk* **Halmahera (IRE)**[14] 4324 9-9-11 **99**.................. NCallan 4 84+
(KARyan) *in tch stands side: drvn along over 2f out: kpt on fnl f: n.d* **14/1**
0060 **10** *1* **Cd Europe (IRE)**[14] 4324 6-8-13 **87**..................(p) JCarroll 10 69
(KARyan) *prom far side: rdn 2f out: wknd fnl f* **22/1**
030 **11** *shd* **Bond Boy**[35] 3754 7-9-2 **90**.................. DMcGaffin 16 72
(BSmart) *midfield far side: rdn 2f out: no hdwy* **14/1**
36-0 **12** *1/2* **Impressive Flight (IRE)**[12] 4394 5-8-11 **90**.................. PMakin(5) 9 70
(TDBarron) *s.s: rr far side: styd on fr over 1f out: n.d* **50/1**
1-50 **13** *shd* **Partners In Jazz (USA)**[8] 4510 3-8-5 **86**.................. NMackay(3) 1 66+
(TDBarron) *prom stands side: drvn along 1/2-way: fdd fr over 1f out* **12/1**[3]
3520 **14** *1 1/2* **Dazzling Bay**[14] 4324 4-9-13 **101**..................(b) DAllan 18 76
(TDEasterby) *racd far side: dwlt: nvr bttr than mid-div* **28/1**
5160 **15** *1* **Sierra Vista**[21] 4134 4-8-3 **80**.................. TEaves(3) 3 52+
(DWBarker) *chsd ldrs stands side: drvn along 1/2-way: fdd fnl 2f* **25/1**
042 **16** *1* **Tom Tun**[29] 3901 9-9-6 **97**..................(b) THamilton(3) 14 66
(JBalding) *racd far side: s.i.s: a towards rr* **14/1**
1411 **17** *hd* **Jonny Ebeneezer**[5] 4614 5-8-9 **83** 4ex..................(b) SWKelly 17 52
(DFlood) *in tch far side: rdn 2f out: sn btn* **5/2**[1]
300- **18** *hd* **Resplendent Cee (IRE)**[280] 5953 5-9-12 **100**.................. MFenton 7 68+
(PWHarris) *in tch stands side: rdn 1/2-way: sn rr* **28/1**
05 **19** *2* **Kingscross**[37] 3663 6-8-3 **77**.................. FNorton 8 39+
(MBlanshard) *racd stands side: rr most of way* **20/1**

1m 13.65s (0.75) **Going Correction** +0.375s/f (Good)
**WFA** 3 from 4yo+ 4lb **19** Ran SP% **130.6**
Speed ratings: **110,103,101,101,100 99,99,95,95,93 93,93,93,91,89 88,88,87,85**CSF £232.01 CT £9903.99 TOTE £21.20: £3.90, £4.80, £8.00, £2.30; EX 654.70 TRIFECTA Not won..
**Owner** Turf 2000 Limited **Bred** Alan Spargo **Trained** Newmarket, Suffolk
■ Stewards Enquiry : P M Quinn two-day ban: careless riding (Aug 25,26)

**FOCUS**
A competitive race as ever on paper, but Smokin Beau destroyed the opposition under a good front-running ride from Fanning. There were no real hard-luck stories in behind, and the form appears strong with the winner looking well handicapped.

**NOTEBOOK**
**Smokin Beau** continued his revival with a scintillating display, making all having done well to get across to the far rail, and quickening away before powering clear. He has come down 14lb in the weights in the past year and seems to get on well with Fanning, so is capable of climbing back up the ladder and, in this kind of form, can probably make his mark again back at Listed level at least, as there is hardly anything between top handicap and Group sprinters.
**Pieter Brueghel(USA)** made all to win' the stands'-side race and deserves credit, for he would have been a good winner without Smokin Beau. He is very useful when on a going day and seems to be finding some consistency these days.
**Hiccups** was never far away and stuck on well for third. He is already a useful sprinter and, at the age of four, is in the right hands to keep on improving.
**Machinist(IRE)** made it a clean sweep of the minor placings for the Nicholls camp. He, like the third, is still unexposed and continues to go the right way.
**Cd Flyer(IRE)** ran his best race of the season so far from the highest draw of all. He has a good race in him before the season is out.
**Hidden Dragon(USA)**, winner of this race last season, was running off an identical mark, but did not come into this in quite the same form and has been off the track since May. He showed up well for most of the way before tiring and should come on for the run.
**Artie** had his chance stands' side on ground that suits.
**Abbajabba** was making late headway but not in enough time to make an impact.
**Partners In Jazz(USA)** has disappointed the last twice now and remains out of form.
**Jonny Ebeneezer** *Official explanation: trainer said gelding had boiled over during the preliminaries*

## 4760 EUROPEAN BREEDERS FUND FILLIES' H'CAP 1m 2f
3:50 (3:50) (D) (0-80,79) 3-Y-O+ £10,179 (£3,132; £1,566; £783) Stalls High

Form RPR
6624 **1** **Sienna Sunset (IRE)**[9] 4471 5-7-13 **55**.................. BSwarbrick(5) 6 64
(WMBrisbourne) *hld up in rr: rdn 3f out: gd hdwy over 1f out: styd on wl to ld wl ins fnl f* **12/1**
0122 **2** *nk* **Charnock Bates One (IRE)**[14] 4318 3-8-10 **70**.................. RWinston 1 78
(TDEasterby) *hld up in tch: effrt whn nt clr run over 2f out: hdwy u.p over 1f out: disp ld wl ins last: styd on* **9/2**[3]
1115 **3** *1 1/4* **Heneseys Leg**[28] 3933 4-9-12 **77**.................. KDarley 4 83
(JohnBerry) *cl up: led over 2f out: rdn and hdd wl ins fnl f: no ex* **13/2**
0654 **4** *1 1/2* **Rani Two**[21] 4153 5-8-12 **68**.................. PMakin(5) 7 71
(WMBrisbourne) *led tl rdn and hdd over 2f out: kpt on same pce* **12/1**
0512 **5** *hd* **Miss Pebbles (IRE)**[47] 3387 4-9-9 **74**..................(v) MFenton 3 77
(SCWilliams) *trckd ldrs: effrt over 2f out: rdn: hung rt: kpt on same pce* **4/1**[2]
200 **6** *2* **Route Sixty Six (IRE)**[8] 4511 8-7-12 **49** oh4.................. DaleGibson 5 49
(JeddO'Keeffe) *hld up in tch: effrt 3f out: sn rdn: no real hdwy* **16/1**

0420 **7** 8 **Saffron Fox**[13] [4368] 3-9-5 **79** NCallan 8 65
(JGPortman) *trckd ldrs: drvn along and outpcd over 2f out: rallying and in tch whn hmpd ins fnl f: no ch after and eased* **5/1**

0013 **8** 5 **Fairlie**[10] [4449] 3-7-10 **59** NMackay(3) 2 36
(MrsMReveley) *hld up: sme hdwy 3f out: sn rdn: wknd over 1f out* **7/2**[1]

2m 13.69s (5.69) **Going Correction** +0.65s/f (Yiel) **8** Ran SP% **111.7**
**WFA** 3 from 4yo+ 9lb
Speed ratings: **103,102,101,100,100 98,92,88**CSF £62.01 CT £379.73 TOTE £15.90: £3.50, £1.50, £2.20; EX 48.10.
**Owner** Ray Bailey **Bred** Knockeen Stud **Trained** Great Ness, Shropshire

**FOCUS**
A modest handicap and not much of a race and the winner was suited by the cut in the ground. The form looks reasonably sound.

**NOTEBOOK**
**Sienna Sunset(IRE)**, unsuited by the fast ground when disappointing at Brighton recently, was able to get her toe in and finished strongly to get up late on and win by a cosy neck. This was the first race she has won for over two years and, off her lowly mark, may be capable of winning again when getting her conditions.
**Charnock Bates One(IRE)** has put a consistent run of efforts together and was finishing second for the third consecutive run. Trying this trip for the first time, she was blocked in her run when trying to make ground but ultimately had every chance.
**Heneseys Leg**, reportedly upset by the delayed start when disappointing at Lingfield, returned to form on ground she has won on. She had her chance and is in the Handicapper's grip now.
**Rani Two** was tailed off at York last month and ran better, plugging on at the one pace under pressure.
**Miss Pebbles(IRE)** was hanging under pressure and did not look comfortable.
**Saffron Fox** was unlucky not to get closer as she was trying to make some inroads when hampered.
**Fairlie** proved a disappointment, running no race at all. She has been running in much lesser events, but even so should have performed better.

## 4761 RIPON-RACES.CO.UK MAIDEN AUCTION STKS 6f
**4:25** (4:29) (E) 2-Y-O **£5,023** (£1,545; £772; £386) **Stalls** Low

Form RPR

3 **1** **Zomerlust**[20] [4175] 2-8-7 RWinston 14 73
(JJQuinn) *cl up far side: rdn over 1f out: r.o wl u.p to ld clsng stages* **6/1**[2]

02 **2** hd **Wizardmicktee (IRE)**[13] [4359] 2-8-7 MFenton 12 73
(ABailey) *racd far side: led: rdn over 1f out: r.o wl u.p fnl f: hdd clsng stages* **8/1**[3]

**3** 5 **Bold Haze** 2-8-0 LeanneKershaw(7) 10 60
(MissSEHall) *racd far side: dwlt: sn in tch: gd hdwy to chse first 2 appr fnl f: no ex ins last* **66/1**

**4** nk **Boo** 2-8-11 DarrenWilliams 11 63
(KRBurke) *racd far side: trckd ldrs: rdn wl over 1f out: no ex fnl f* **12/1**

06 **5** 1 1/2 **Yorkshire Lad (IRE)**[10] [4454] 2-8-7 SWKelly 6 63+
(DCarroll) *cl up stands side: drvn along over 2f out: led gp ent fnl f: r.o u.p: no ch w far side ldrs* **12/1**

03 **6** 1/2 **Along The Nile**[10] [4454] 2-8-11 ABeech(3) 8 68+
(MrsJRRamsden) *chsd ldrs stands side: drvn along over 2f out: kpt on u.p fnl f: nvr able to chal* **9/2**[1]

00 **7** 2 **Hows That**[15] [4292] 2-7-13 NMackay(3) 9 51+
(PJMcbride) *rr stands side: styd on fnl 2f: n.d* **16/1**

**8** 1 **Mark Your Card** 2-8-2 DAllan 16 42
(TDEasterby) *racd far side: dwlt: sn midfield: effrt over 2f out: no hdwy* **14/1**

0000 **9** shd **Tillingborn Dancer (IRE)**[21] [4135] 2-8-9 JFanning 17 49
(MDHammond) *racd far side: slowly away: towards rr: styd on fnl 2f: n.d* **33/1**

00 **10** nk **Shekan Star**[10] [4446] 2-8-4 DaleGibson 7 50+
(MrsMReveley) *racd stands side: towards rr and drvn along over 2f out: n.d* **33/1**

00 **11** shd **Admittance (USA)**[9] [4487] 2-8-4 LGoncalves 19 43
(MrsJRRamsden) *towards rr far side: pushed along and no real hdwy whn nt clr run appr fnl f: n.d* **16/1**

30 **12** 1 1/2 **General Max (IRE)**[22] [4100] 2-8-11 GFaulkner 5 53+
(ACrook) *led stands side gp: rdn 2f out: lost gp ld and wknd fnl f* **33/1**

50 **13** 3 **Artic Fox**[35] [3758] 2-8-9 KDarley 3 43+
(TDEasterby) *chsd stands side ldrs: drvn along over 2f out: wknd appr fnl f* **9/2**[1]

6 **14** nk **Midnight In Moscow (IRE)**[78] [2447] 2-8-4 RoryMoore(7) 18 38
(PCHaslam) *keen: trckd ldrs far side: wknd 2f out* **16/1**

**15** 1 3/4 **Street Dancer (IRE)** 2-8-9 FNorton 13 31
(JJQuinn) *racd far side: dwlt: towards rr most of way* **20/1**

0200 **16** 3 **Noodles**[14] [4348] 2-8-11 **69** (b[1]) TEaves(3) 1 36+
(TDEasterby) *racd stands side: rr most of way* **20/1**

000 **17** 2 1/2 **Negas (IRE)**[21] [4131] 2-8-6 PMulrennan(3) 2 24+
(JHowardJohnson) *in tch stands side: rdn over 2f out: wknd over 1f out* **66/1**

**18** 17 **Judge Damuss (IRE)** 2-8-11 JCarroll 15 —
(ACrook) *rr far side: lost tch fnl 2f: t.o* **33/1**

1m 16.35s (3.45) **Going Correction** +0.375s/f (Good) **18** Ran SP% **125.7**
Speed ratings: **92,91,85,84,82 82,79,78,77,77 77,75,71,70,68 64,61,38**CSF £49.66 TOTE £8.00: £2.40, £3.10, £23.00; EX 45.20.
**Owner** P J Carr **Bred** The Lavington Stud **Trained** Settrington, N Yorks
■ Stewards Enquiry : R Winston three-day ban: used whip in the incorrect place (Aug 25-27)

**FOCUS**
Just a modest maiden in which the front pair pulled clear, and where it paid to race far side.

**NOTEBOOK**
**Zomerlust** ran with promise when third on his debut at Pontefract and was well suited by this extra furlong, needing every yard of it to get up in the final strides. He should not be given too harsh a mark, and can win a nursery when conditions are in his favour.
**Wizardmicktee(IRE)** showed this ground to be no inconvenience, and ran a game race from the front before being caught late on. He should make his mark in nurseries.
**Bold Haze** comes from an unfashionable juvenile stable, but held on for third having tried to go in pursuit of the front two and belied odds of 66/1. He should come on for this and may be overpriced next time due to connections.
**Boo** had his chance and made a pleasing debut. He, like the third, should benefit from the experience.
**Yorkshire Lad(IRE)** fared best of those on the stands' side and is now qualified for nurseries.
**Along The Nile** was on the wrong side and had no chance. He is better than this and now qualified for nurseries.
**Artic Fox** has not gone on from his promising debut and never got involved. He is now eligible for nurseries and it will be interesting to see how he fares.

## 4762 RIPON CATHEDRAL H'CAP 1m 4f 60y
**4:55** (4:58) (C) (0-90,79) 3-Y-O **£10,592** (£3,478; £1,739) **Stalls** High

Form RPR

0501 **1** **Hezaam (USA)**[42] [3543] 3-9-7 **79** KDarley 1 89
(JLDunlop) *hld up in tch: pushed along over 4f out: hdwy u.p over 1f out: styd on wl to ld clsng stages* **1/1**[1]

2323 **2** 1/2 **Yankeedoodledandy (IRE)**[8] [4512] 3-8-12 **77** RoryMoore(7) 2 86
(PCHaslam) *led: jnd 3f out: rdn 2f out: edgd lft u.p and hdd clsng stages: no ex* **3/1**[3]

5121 **3** 3 **Hearthstead Dream**[12] [4397] 3-8-13 **71** (b) JFanning 3 76
(JDBethell) *trckd ldr: jnd ldr 3f out: rdn and ev ch ent fnl f: no ex ins last: hld whn hmpd clsng stages* **9/4**[2]

2m 45.82s (5.92) **Going Correction** +0.65s/f (Yiel) **3** Ran SP% **105.8**
Speed ratings: **106,105,103**CSF £3.94 TOTE £1.70; EX 3.60 Place 6 £412.04, Place 5 £169.85..
**Owner** Hamdan Al Maktoum **Bred** Shadwell Farm Llc **Trained** Arundel, W Sussex
■ Stewards Enquiry : Rory Moore three-day ban: careless riding (Aug 25-27)

**FOCUS**
A fair handicap in which the runner-up is the best guide to the form. Hezaam made this look hard work but he will leave this form behind in a bigger field/better race.

**NOTEBOOK**
**Hezaam(USA)** has been waiting for this ground and was able to follow up his Sandown win from early last month. Stepping up two furlongs in trip, he looked in need of it and it was only late on he got going. There is more to come from him back in better races when he will get a true gallop.
**Yankeedoodledandy(IRE)** had every chance from the front but could not hold the late thrust of the winner. He is a very consistent gelding who will continue to pay his way.
**Hearthstead Dream** had run his race and was beaten when being hampered late on. He has been running consistently well and will be better back down in grade.
T/Plt: £203.10 to a £1 stake. Pool: £41,933.80. 150.70 winning tickets. T/Qpdt: £106.50 to a £1 stake. Pool: £2,232.60. 15.50 winning tickets. JF

4763 - 4765a (Foreign Racing) - See Raceform Interactive

# 4623 DEAUVILLE (R-H)
Saturday, August 14

**OFFICIAL GOING: Turf: holding; aw: standard**

## 4766a PRIX GONTAUT-BIRON LE ROYAL PALM HOTEL (GROUP 3) 1m 2f
**3:20** (3:19) 4-Y-O+ **£25,704** (£10,282; £7,711; £5,141)

RPR

**1** **Special Kaldoun (IRE)**[34] [3791] 5-8-11 DBoeuf 6 114
(DSmaga, France) *raced in 5th, headway to lead 150 yards out, ran on well*

**2** 1 **Demon Dancer (FR)**[24] [4039] 7-8-11 CSoumillon 2 112
(YDeNicolay, France) *held up in 6th, headway down outside from over 1f out to take 2nd close home* 2

**3** 1 **Mamool (IRE)**[284] [5921] 5-8-9 C-PLemaire 4 109
(SaeedBinSuroor) *set steady pace, headed entering straight, led again 1 1/2f out, headed 150 yards out, one pace* 1

**4** 1 1/2 **Pont D'Or (IRE)**[24] [4039] 5-8-9 OPeslier 7 106
(DSepulchre, France) *last to 1f out, stayed on well final f*

**5** 3/4 **Look Honey (IRE)**[58] [3030] 4-8-11 (b) YLerner 5 107
(CLerner, France) *raced in 3rd, 4th straight, hard ridden 1 1/2f out, one pace*

**6** 1/2 **Storm Trooper (GER)**[48] [3357] 4-8-11 (b) ASuborics 1 106
(ASchutz, Germany) *raced in 2nd til led narrowly entering straight, headed 1 1/2f out, weakened* 3

**7** 1 **Kalabar**[62] [2924] 4-8-9 TThulliez 3 102
(PBary, France) *raced in 4th, 3rd straight, effort and not quicken from over 1 1/2f out*

2m 13.2s **Going Correction** +0.525s/f (Yiel) **7** Ran SP% **122.2**
Speed ratings: **113,112,111,110,109 109,108.**
**Owner** Ecurie Chalhoub **Bred** Pontchartrain Stud & Alain Scemama **Trained** France

**NOTEBOOK**
**Special Kaldoun(IRE)**, back to ten furlongs for the first time since his juvenile days, the five year old impressed in this Group Three event. Mid-division early on, he came with a well-timed run up the centre of the track to lead a furlong out and revelled in the testing ground. He could now go for the La Coupe at Maisons-Laffitte.
**Demon Dancer(FR)** came with a strong late run from quite a way back but never looked like getting to the winner. This ex-handicapper appears to be improving with age.
**Mamool(IRE)**, racing for the first time in nine, made a very pleasing return. Asked to set just a moderate pace, he was outpaced early in the straight before staying on again towards the end.
**Pont D'Or(IRE)** never looked like threatening the first three past the post.

# 4735 ARLINGTON (L-H)
Saturday, August 14

**OFFICIAL GOING: Dirt - fast; turf - firm**

## 4767a BEVERLY D STKS (GRADE 1) (F&M) 1m 1f 110y(T)
**9:37** (9:38) 3-Y-O+ **£251,397** (£83,799; £41,899; £20,950)

RPR

**1** **Crimson Palace (SAF)**[59] [2967] 5-8-11 LDettori 9 113
(SaeedBinSuroor) *always close up on outside, 3rd straight, led 1f out, ran on strongly* **99/10**

**2** 1/2 **Riskaverse (USA)**[14] 5-8-11 PDay 1 112
(PatrickJKelly, U.S.A) *raced in 4th, stayed on under pressure from over 1f out* **84/10**

**3** hd **Necklace**[71] [2640] 3-8-5 JPSpencer 5 115
(APO'Brien, Ire) *raced in 6th on inside, switched right over 1f out, stayed on well final f, just missed 2nd* **254/10**

**4** nk **Musical Chimes (USA)**[21] 4-8-11 KDesormeaux 4 111
(NDrysdale, U.S.A) *reluctant leader for 3f, 2nd straight, ridden over 1f out, no extra final 70 yards* **21/10**[1]

**5** 3/4 **Bedanken (USA)**[21] 5-8-11 DPettinger 8 110
(DVonHemel, U.S.A) *held up in 10th, headway on outside to go 3rd 2 1/2f out, kept on at one pacve final 2f* **81/10**

**6** nk **Aubonne (GER)**[58] [3030] 4-8-11 EPrado 2 109
(ELibaud, France) *led after 3f, set slow pace, headed 1f out, no extra* **71/10**[3]

**7** 1/2 **Aud (USA)**[21] 4-8-11 ERazoJr 7 108
(AReinstedler, U.S.A) *held up in 9th, headway to go 7th over 1f out, one pace final f* **38/1**

8 1 **Shaconage (USA)**[21] 4-8-11 .................................. BBlanc 6 106
(MShirota, U.S.A) *held up in 8th, never a factor* **173/10**

9 1 **Commercante (FR)**[292] 5809 4-8-11 .................................. JDBailey 10 105
(RJFrankel, U.S.A) *raced in 7th, effort and not much room 2f out, beaten when slightly hampered over 1f out* **33/10**[2]

10 hd **Quero Quero (USA)**[34] 4-8-11 .................................. VEspinoza 11 104
(PLobo, U.S.A) *held up in last, always in rear* **24/1**

11 1/2 **Noches De Rosa (CHI)**[48] 6-8-11 ..................................(b) MESmith 3 103
(RichardEMandella, U.S.A) *raced in 5th til weakened over 1f out* **135/10**

1m 56.58s
**WFA** 3 from 4yo+ 8lb **11 Ran SP% 121.4**
Speed ratings: .
**Owner** Godolphin **Bred** Adv A P Joubert **Trained** Newmarket, Suffolk
■ Crimson Palace was winning in her fourth continent.

**FOCUS**
A reasonable renewal of the Beverly D Stakes and, although the pace was pretty modest, this provided us with some clues for the Breeders' Cup Filly & Mare Turf.

**NOTEBOOK**
**Crimson Palace(SAF)** was very disappointing at Ascot on her previous start (interestingly her first run on a straight track) but returned to form under a good ride from Frankie Dettori, who was had her well positioned. A really tough sort, she was winning on her fourth continent and will now be aimed at the Breeders' Cup Filly & Mare Turf, although the Flower Bowl at Belmont earlier in October may be on the cards.
**Riskaverse(USA)**, sixth in last year's Breeders' Cup behind Islington, pushed the winner all the way to the line but was just denied. She is likely to re-oppose the winner in Texas.
**Necklace** ◆, a slightly disappointing fourth in the Epsom Oaks on her previous start, raced against the rail for much of the way and had to wait for a gap but, when finally in the clear, she ran on well and was closing at the finish. This was arguably a career-best effort and she could worth keeping in mind for the E P Taylor Stakes at Woodbine before taking on the first two in the Breeders' Cup Filly & Mare Turf.
**Musical Chimes(USA)** was a shade disappointing and probably would gave preferred to get a lead.

## 4768a ARLINGTON MILLION XXII (GRADE 1) 1m 2f
10:35 (10:38) 3-Y-O+ **£335,196** (£111,732; £55,866; £27,933)

RPR

1 1 1/2 **Kicken Kris (USA)**[28] 4-9-0 .................................. KDesormeaux 4 123
(MMatz, U.S.A) *mid div, 5th str, staying on in 3rd whn badly hmpd against rail jst ins fnl f, recovered to fin 2nd, awarded race* **97/10**

2 1 **Magistretti (USA)**[28] 3936 4-9-0 ..................................(b) EPrado 12 119
(NACallaghan) *raced in 9th, headway 3f out, 7th straight, stayed on well final f to take 3rd close home, finished 3rd, placed 2nd* **24/1**

3 1/2 **Epalo (GER)**[13] 4377 5-9-0 .................................. AStarke 7 118+
(ASchutz, Germany) *raced in 3rd, led entering straight, headed and hampered 1f out, lost 3rd close home, finished 4th, placed 3rd* **41/10**[1]

4 **Powerscourt**[13] 4385 4-9-0 ..................................(v) JPSpencer 10 118
(APO'Brien, Ire) *hld up in 10th, hdwy around outside fr over 2f out, 4th on outside str, led and hung lft 1f out, ran on well, fin 1st, plcd 4th* **46/10**[2]

5 1 1/2 **Vangelis (USA)**[20] 5-9-0 ..................................(b) JValdiviaJr 9 115
(RJFrankel, U.S.A) *held up in 11th, stayed on down outside final 1 1/2f* **112/10**

6 3/4 **Mr O'Brien (IRE)**[42] 5-9-0 .................................. PDay 1 114+
(RobinLGraham, U.S.A) *5th on inside when stumbled halfway, 6th straight, one pace final 1 1/2f* **47/10**[3]

7 1/2 **Senor Swinger (USA)**[21] 4-9-0 .................................. BBlanc 8 113
(BBaffert, U.S.A) *held up in 8th, 9th straight on inside, switched right, kept on at one pace from over 1f out* **22/1**

8 3/4 **Sweet Return**[20] 4-9-0 .................................. JDBailey 3 112
(RMcanally, U.S.A) *raced in 4th til lost place over 2f out, 8th straight, no danger after* **53/10**

9 1 3/4 **Mobil (CAN)**[20] 4-9-0 .................................. JCJones 13 109
(MKeogh, Canada) *midfield, went 5th halfway, 10th and beaten entering straight* **20/1**

10 1/2 **Mystery Giver (USA)**[21] 6-9-0 .................................. RDouglas 6 108
(CBlock, U.S.A) *held up in rear, 12th straight, never a factor* **21/1**

11 2 3/4 **Sabiango (GER)**[63] 6-9-0 .................................. VEspinoza 5 103
(BBaffert, U.S.A) *raced in 2nd til led narrowly over 2f out, headed entering straight, weakened* **15/1**

12 2 **Vespone (IRE)**[28] 3936 4-9-0 ..................................(v) LDettori 2 100
(SaeedBinSuroor) *set fast pace til headed over 2f out, close 3rd straight, soon weakened* **19/2**

2m 0.80s **13 Ran SP% 123.6**
Speed ratings: .
**Owner** Brushwood Stables **Bred** Valerie Naify **Trained** USA
■ A controversial renewal of the Arlington Million with the first past the post demoted for the second year running.

**FOCUS**
The pace was good and the form looks reliable.

**NOTEBOOK**
**Kicken Kris(USA)** has to be considered a fortunate winner, as he would have been no better than a good second had the Stewards not intervened. However, he was badly hampered and benefited from Powerscourt's misdemeanour. He is improving all the time.
**Magistretti(USA)** had not been at his best so far this season but returned to form under his ideal conditions in first time blinkers, and may have been even closer with a better trip. He will now continue his career in the States and it would be no surprise to see him in the Breeders' Cup Turf, although the extra two furlongs would be a question mark.
**Epalo(GER)**, successful in the International Cup in Singapore earlier in the season, was beaten when hampered but would still have finished closer, and will continue to make his mark in these international events.
**Powerscourt** had not really gone on from his successful reappearance in the Tattersalls Gold Cup but, fitted with blinkers for the first time, he bounced right back to his best and was first past the most in most decisive fashion. It did not affect the result, but he caused interference to both Kicken Kris and Epalo at the top of the straight and the American Stewards placed him fourth - he would not have lost the race in this country. This was still a very good performance and he will be worthy of the utmost respect in a race like the Breeders' Cup Turf, or maybe even a race like the Canadian International.
**Sweet Return** had the promoted winner behind when successful in the Hollywood Derby last season and when runner-up in a Grade One this term, but he got a bump on turning in and was unable to quicken.
**Vespone(IRE)** was unable to sustain the good gallop he set.

## 4769a SECRETARIAT STKS (GRADE 1) 1m 2f
11:53 (12:00) 3-Y-O **£134,078** (£44,693; £22,346; £11,173)

RPR

1 **Kitten's Joy (USA)**[35] 3-8-11 .................................. JDBailey 1 120+
(DaleRomans, U.S.A) *dropped out in 6th, headway over 2f out, led 4-wide entering straight, drifted left while quickening clear* **9/10**[1]

2 3 1/4 **Greek Sun (USA)**[49] 3-8-9 .................................. EPrado 3 112
(RJFrankel, U.S.A) *held up in 5th, 5th straight on inside, switched right, hard ridden and stayed on final f to take 2nd last 50 yards* **29/10**[2]

3 1 1/4 **Moscow Ballet (IRE)**[48] 3353 3-8-7 .................................. JPSpencer 6 108
(APO'Brien, Ire) *raced in 3rd, hard ridden and every chance 1 1/2f out, went 2nd inside final f, lost 2nd final 50 yards* **74/10**[3]

4 1 **Simple Exchange (IRE)**[21] 4182 3-8-11 .................................. PJSmullen 7 110
(DKWeld, Ire) *raced in 4th, effort and every chance 1 1/2f out, one pace* **79/10**

5 3 **Cool Conductor (USA)**[21] 4182 3-8-7 .................................. PDay 5 101
(WMott, U.S.A) *set fast pace, 6 lengths clear 4f out, headed entering straight, weakened* **92/10**

6 1 1/4 **Hazyview**[31] 3863 3-8-7 .................................. LDettori 2 99
(NACallaghan) *chased clear leader, headway to press leader over 2f out, soon weakened* **9/1**

7 5 3/4 **Up Anchor (USA)**[21] 4182 3-8-7 .................................. RDouglas 4 89
(PMcgee, U.S.A) *trailed throughout* **53/1**

1m 59.65s **7 Ran SP% 123.1**
Speed ratings: .
**Owner** Kenneth L & Sarah K Ramsey **Bred** Kenneth L & Sarah K Ramsey **Trained** USA

**FOCUS**
A reasonable European challenge for the Secretariat, but they were left behind by the very impressive Kitten's Joy, who is very good if this form can be taken literally (there is little reason why in cannot). The pace was strong.

**NOTEBOOK**
**Kitten's Joy(USA)** ◆ followed up his Virginia Derby success in most impressive fashion, beating the time recorded by the winner of the Million. On a line through the European horses in third and fourth, he is very good and will be a threat to all if going for the Breeders' Cup Turf.
**Greek Sun(USA)**, unbeaten in three runs prior to this, was simply left behind by the winner, but this was still a good effort to see off the foreign challengers.
**Moscow Ballet(IRE)**, well beaten after setting the pace in the Irish Derby on his previous start, ran a respectable race but simply lacked the finishing kick of the winner. A confidence-boosting Group Three back in Europe may be of benefit.
**Simple Exchange(IRE)** found this tougher than the American Derby he won on his previous start and was unable to reverse Royal Ascot placings with Moscow Ballet.
**Hazyview** had improved significantly this season and promised to be suited by these conditions, but he found this toon hot and was not at his best.

# 4617 BATH (L-H)
Sunday, August 15

**OFFICIAL GOING: Good to firm**

## 4770 FERNDALE BAND CLUB MAIDEN AUCTION STKS 5f 11y
2:30 (2:30) (F) 2-Y-O **£3,349** (£957; £478) **Stalls Low**

Form RPR

23 1 **Dispol In Mind**[22] 4124 2-8-2 .................................. PDoe 11 64
(IAWood) *s.i.s: hdwy on outside 2f out: rdn to ld ent fnl f: r.o wl* **7/1**[3]

6 2 3/4 **Tanning**[10] 4474 2-7-13 .................................. JFMcDonald(3) 8 61
(HMorrison) *chsd ldrs: rdn over 1f out: r.o to go 2nd cl home* **8/1**

0620 3 shd **Saucepot**[9] 4508 2-7-11 63.................................. HayleyTurner(5) 7 61
(MDIUsher) *prom: rdn and led wl over 1f out: edgd lft and hdd ent fnl f: lost 2nd cl home* **9/1**

4 4 3/4 **Danzili Bay**[41] 3570 2-8-8 .................................. NChalmers(5) 2 69
(RMBeckett) *in tch: rdn whn carried lft ent fnl f: no ex ins* **16/1**

660 5 1 3/4 **Atsos (IRE)**[68] 2761 2-8-11 .................................. RLMoore 4 61
(RHannon) *outpcd: rdn and swtchd rt wl over 1f out: fin wl fnl f* **14/1**

4034 6 2 **Turtle Magic (IRE)**[9] 4516 2-7-9 53..................................(p) CHaddon(7) 5 45
(WGMTurner) *prom tl rdn and wknd fnl f* **20/1**

7 nk **Little Warning** 2-8-2 .................................. FNorton 12 44
(RMBeckett) *mid-div on outside: nvr nr to chal* **9/1**

5 8 nk **Beau Marche**[18] 4239 2-8-7 .................................. DSweeney 3 48
(IAWood) *bmpd s: a bhd* **33/1**

2303 9 nk **Edge Fund**[11] 4439 2-8-13 79.................................. SDrowne 6 67+
(BRMillman) *chsd ldrs: led briefly 2f out: wkng whn bdly hmpd ent fnl f: eased* **2/1**[1]

06 10 1 **Night Out (FR)**[13] 4399 2-8-6 .................................. DHolland 1 43
(GCBravery) *led tl hdd 2f out: sn wknd* **4/1**[2]

11 8 **Silver Creek** 2-8-7 .................................. CCatlin 9 16
(IAWood) *slowly away: outpcd and a wl bhd* **40/1**

62.52 secs (0.02) **Going Correction** -0.125s/f (Firm) **11 Ran SP% 119.6**
Speed ratings: **94,92,92,91,88 85,84,84,84,82 69**CSF £61.79 TOTE £6.30: £2.50, £2.70, £2.10; EX 61.00.
**Owner** Thomas & Susan Blane **Bred** Roseland Thoroughbreds Ltd **Trained** Upper Lambourn, Berks
■ Stewards Enquiry : N Chalmers two-day ban: careless riding (Aug 26-27)

**FOCUS**
A modest maiden in which the front four rather finished in a heap, but the early pace was fair and the third and sixth indicate the level of the form.

**NOTEBOOK**
**Dispol In Mind** does not help herself by starting slowly, but was brought with her effort widest of all and still proved good enough. An extra furlong and nurseries look her best option.
**Tanning** improved from her debut and was finishing in good style, again suggesting that she needs an extra furlong.
**Saucepot** was never far away and looked the one to beat when taking it up inside the last two furlongs, but was just run out of it. She is beginning to look exposed in contests like these and could probably have done without the rain.
**Danzili Bay** ran another fair race on this track, especially as he did not have much room to play with inside the final furlong, but he could really do with further.
**Atsos(IRE)** was not helped by the drop back in trip and could never get into the race. He has hinted at ability, but is really yet to confirm it.
**Edge Fund** was always close to the pace, but was already beaten when getting squeezed out against the inside rail entering the last furlong. He looks totally exposed and now has questions to answer.
**Night Out(FR)** *Official explanation: jockey said filly hung left*

## 4771 TOTESPORT.COM MILE FILLIES' H'CAP 1m 5y
3:00 (3:01) (E) (0-75,75) 3-Y-O+ **£5,239** (£1,612; £806; £403) **Stalls Low**

Form RPR

0012 1 **Didoe**[9] 4519 5-8-0 47.................................. JoannaBadger 7 55
(PWHiatt) *led for 1f: led over 2f out: sn clr: drvn out fnl f* **12/1**

1302 2 1 3/4 **Brazilian Terrace**[22] 4142 4-9-9 75.................................. HayleyTurner(5) 8 79
(MLWBell) *in tch on ins: styd on to go 2nd ins fnl f* **4/1**[1]

0005 3 1 **Beauty Of Dreams**[10] 4483 3-8-7 61.................................. CCatlin 15 63
(MRChannon) *racd wd in tch: styd on fnl f: nvr nrr* **25/1**

304 **4** *hd* **Hirayna**[37] [3701] 5-7-12 **50**................................ BSwarbrick(5) 9 51
(WMBrisbourne) *in tch: outpcd 3f out: hung lft appr fnl f: kpt on* **20/1**
0304 **5** *nk* **Tokewanna**[9] [4517] 4-8-3 **50**................................(t) DKinsella 3 51
(WMBrisbourne) *t.k.h: sn in tch: one pce appr fnl f* **25/1**
4032 **6** *¾* **Island Rapture**[33] [3826] 4-9-10 **71**................................ DHolland 11 70
(JARToller) *in tch: chsd wnr 2f out: wknd ins fnl f* **13/2**[2]
-104 **7** *½* **Hasayis**[25] [4020] 3-9-0 **68**................................ WSupple 5 66
(JLDunlop) *in rr: sme late hdwy: nvr nr to chal* **15/2**
2555 **8** *2* **Marnie**[17] [4264] 7-7-12 **48**................................ NMackay(3) 2 41
(JAkehurst) *hld up: rdn 1/2-way: n.d* **8/1**
4042 **9** *¾* **Enna (POL)**[8] [4546] 5-7-13 **46** ow1................................ FNorton 14 37
(MrsStefLiddiard) *s.i.s: a bhd* **7/1**[3]
0005 **10** *1* **Lark In The Park (IRE)**[40] [3609] 4-7-5 **45** oh5................ DFentiman(7) 4 34
(WMBrisbourne) *a bhd* **25/1**
2202 **11** *½* **Kindness**[17] [4264] 4-7-12 **50**................................ RThomas(5) 6 38
(ADWPinder) *sn chsd ldr: wknd 2f out* **11/1**
4402 **12** *2* **Naughty Girl (IRE)**[10] [4477] 4-7-10 **46**................(vt) FPFerris(3) 13 29
(PDEvans) *v.s.a: a bhd* **7/1**[3]
2-01 **13** *1* **Icecap**[12] [4414] 4-7-13 **53**................................ CHaddon(7) 10 34
(WGMTurner) *led after 1f: hdd over 2f out: wknd qckly* **12/1**
0000 **14** *1¼* **Annijaz**[10] [4477] 7-8-1 **48**................................ RLMoore 12 26
(JMBradley) *a bhd* **16/1**

1m 39.8s (-1.20) **Going Correction** +0.025s/f (Good)
**WFA** 3 from 4yo+ 7lb **14 Ran SP% 127.1**
Speed ratings: **107,105,104,104,103 103,102,100,99,98 98,96,95,94**CSF £59.96 CT £1238.45 TOTE £13.50: £2.80, £2.70, £8.30; EX 91.40.
**Owner** Mrs Marion Wickham **Bred** Mrs Wickham **Trained** Hook Norton, Oxon

**FOCUS**
A routine, but competitive, fillies' handicap run at a solid pace and the time was decent for the grade. As a result the form is ordinary but sound.

**NOTEBOOK**
**Didoe** only has a selling win to her name, but she does like it here and this victory was in no small part due to kicking on two furlongs out and establishing a decisive advantage whilst her opponents were getting in each other's way.
**Brazilian Terrace** goes well for Turner and held a good position just off the pace, but she ran into traffic just as the winner was skipping away and could not make up the ground once in the clear.
**Beauty Of Dreams** ran much better on this step back up to a mile. She has plummeted down the handicap and ran her best race for some time, so is worth keeping in mind.
**Hirayna**, making her handicap debut, was rather buried in traffic and shifted positions on a few occasions which may have partly been due to her hanging. She was staying on well at the line though and is not without hope.
**Tokewanna** ran alright, but is still a maiden after 19 attempts.
**Island Rapture** has been running better of late having tumbled down the handicap, but represented a backward step.
**Kindness** *Official explanation: jockey said filly hung left in the straight*

## 4772 BATHWICK TYRES LADY RIDERS' DERBY (RATED STKS) (H'CAP) 1m 3f 144y
3:30 (3:30) (C) (0-90,84) 3-Y-O+ **£16,250** (£5,000; £2,500; £1,250) **Stalls Low**

Form RPR
5102 **1** **Tender Falcon**[25] [4019] 4-9-8 **71**................................ MissCHannaford 15 86
(RJHodges) *hld up: gd hdwy 3f out: led wl over 1f out: sn clr* **20/1**
2502 **2** *5* **Bucks**[11] [4450] 7-9-13 **79**................................ MissLJHarwood(3) 2 86
(DKIvory) *slowly away: sn mid-div: stdy hdwy ins fnl 3f to go 2nd ins fnl f* **6/1**[3]
0340 **3** *3* **Voice Mail**[11] [4435] 5-9-9 **77**................................ MissMSowerby(5) 12 79
(AMBalding) *hld up: effrt on outside 2f out: styd on: nvr nr to chal* **12/1**
0544 **4** *1¼* **Gallant Boy (IRE)**[14] [4363] 5-9-1 **67** oh2................(vt) MissEFolkes(3) 6 67
(PDEvans) *mid-div: hmpd over 4f out and lost pl: kpt on one pce fnl 3f* **16/1**
3110 **5** *shd* **Sangiovese**[38] [3678] 5-9-13 **76**................................ MrsSBosley 3 76
(HMorrison) *trckd ldrs gng wl: led over 3f out: hdd wl over 1f out: wknd fnl f* **13/2**
2413 **6** *5* **Jacaranda (IRE)**[7] [4571] 4-9-8 **71**................................ MissNCarberry 11 63
(MrsALMKing) *mid-div: rdn over 2f out: nt pce to chal* **10/1**
51-0 **7** *½* **Barman (USA)**[71] [2671] 5-10-3 **80**................................(t) MsCWilliams 14 71
(PFICole) *sn trckd ldr: wknd wl over 1f out* **16/1**
5224 **8** *3* **Rajam**[11] [4453] 6-9-11 **77**................................(v) MissKellyHarrison(3) 13 63
(DNicholls) *chsd ldrs tl rdn and wknd over 2f out* **12/1**
-111 **9** *nk* **Flying Spirit (IRE)**[31] [3873] 5-9-13 **76**................................ MissEJJones 10 62
(GLMoore) *in tch: bhd fnl 3f* **11/2**[2]
0115 **10** *2* **A One (IRE)**[13] [4401] 5-10-6 **83**................................ MissSBrotherton 7 66
(HJManners) *led tl hdd over 3f out: sn wknd* **16/1**
0-14 **11** *nk* **Latalomne (USA)**[29] [3221] 10-9-10 **76**................................ MrsNWilson(3) 4 58
(NWilson) *hld up: nvr on terms* **20/1**
302 **12** *nk* **Minority Report**[24] [4063] 4-9-12 **78**................................ MrsSCumani(3) 5 60
(LMCumani) *a towards rr* **4/1**[1]
-053 **13** *2* **Coup De Chance (IRE)**[14] [4361] 4-10-2 **84**......(b) MissFayeBramley(5) 9 63
(PABlockley) *trckd ldrs tl wknd over 3f out* **20/1**
-000 **14** *7* **Barrantes**[8] [4526] 7-9-6 **74**................................ MsDGoad(5) 8 41
(MissSheenaWest) *v.s.a: a struggling in rr* **66/1**
352 **R** **Kentucky King (USA)**[6] [4613] 4-9-12 **80**................................ MrsMarieKing(5) 1 —
(PWHiatt) *ref to r* **25/1**

2m 27.97s (-2.33) **Going Correction** +0.025s/f (Good) **15 Ran SP% 124.8**
Speed ratings: **108,104,102,101,101 98,98,96,95,94 94,94,92,88,—**CSF £132.16 CT £1545.61 TOTE £23.80: £8.40, £2.90, £3.00; EX 173.00 Trifecta £4528.20 Pool £7,015.53 - 1.10 winning units..
**Owner** P E Axon **Bred** P E Axon **Trained** Charlton Adam, Somerset

**FOCUS**
A fair handicap that is the most valuable ladies' race in Europe. The leaders went off too fast and the principals came from the rear; so the winner may have been slightly flattered.

**NOTEBOOK**
**Tender Falcon** went up 2lb for a narrow defeat at Leicester. He was last but one turning into the straight, but the strong pace had played into his hands and he came with a good run down the outside to win decisively.
**Bucks** appreciated the return to this more suitable trip but, although staying on, could never trouble the winner.
**Voice Mail** appears to be in the Handicapper's grip and never looked like adding to his four course wins, although he was doing his best work at the finish and seemed to see out this longer trip.
**Gallant Boy(IRE)** ran up the back of a rival when beginning a forward move and could never really recover, although that cannot be used as an excuse. He is on a lengthy losing run and is 12lb lower than when last getting his head in front.
**Sangiovese** struck the front travelling well but could not contain the challengers coming from off the pace. Although 3lb higher than when scoring at Kempton, there could be a little more improvement to come from him.
**Flying Spirit(IRE)**, no less than 18lb higher than when scoring at Brighton in May, could never get into the action.
**A One(IRE)**, dropped 2lb, set a brisk pace. Soon on the retreat when headed, he is most effective at ten furlongs.
**Minority Report**, stepped up in trip for this handicap debut, never figured which was disappointing given that the race was run to suit those who avoided the fast early pace. This did not tell us whether he stayed or not.

## 4773 EUROPEAN BREEDERS FUND DICK HERN FILLIES' STKS (LISTED RACE) 1m 5y
4:00 (4:02) (A) 3-Y-O+ **£17,400** (£6,600; £3,300; £1,500) **Stalls Low**

Form RPR
1446 **1** **Brindisi**[23] [4077] 3-8-7 95................................ MHills 6 99
(BWHills) *hld up on outside: hdwy wl over 1f out: r.o to ld wl ins fnl f* **7/1**[3]
1455 **2** *1½* **Moon Dazzle (USA)**[23] [4077] 3-8-7 104................................ DHolland 2 96+
(WJHaggas) *s.i.s: in rr tl hdwy on ins then short of room 2f out: swtchd rt 1f out: fin fast to go 2nd post* **15/8**[1]
2-50 **3** *shd* **Zietory**[87] [2242] 4-9-0 99................................ DSweeney 8 95
(PFICole) *hld up: hdwy over 2f out: rdn and wnt 2nd over 1f out: lost 2nd post* **20/1**
3653 **4** *nk* **Ithaca (USA)**[43] [3541] 3-8-7 100................................ RHughes 9 95
(HRACecil) *led tl rdn and hdd wl ins fnl f: no ex* **7/2**[2]
1410 **5** *1* **Flowerdrum (USA)**[16] [4287] 4-9-0 86................................ SWKelly 5 92+
(WJHaggas) *a in tch: weakeneing whn hmpd jst ins fnl f* **8/1**
2-06 **6** *1½* **Why Dubai (USA)**[18] [4230] 3-8-7 89................................ RLMoore 4 89
(RHannon) *trckd ldrs: rdn 3f out: wknd fnl f* **14/1**
4214 **7** *½* **And Toto Too**[4] [4652] 4-9-0 69................................(b) FPFerris 11 88?
(PDEvans) *slowly away: in rr: rdn and effrt 2f out: nvr nr to chal* **25/1**
0000 **8** *1* **Tahirah**[8] [4553] 4-9-0 85................................ SDrowne 10 85
(RGuest) *mid-div: hdwy over 2f out: wknd appr fnl f* **28/1**
2151 **9** *1¾* **Golden Island (IRE)**[8] [4551] 3-8-7 83................................ SWhitworth 7 81
(JWHills) *slowly away: sn chsd ldrs: rdn 2f out: wknd over 1f out* **8/1**
2300 **10** *½* **Kunda (IRE)**[23] [4077] 3-8-7 94................................ PDobbs 1 80
(RHannon) *a bhd* **20/1**
25-0 **11** *nk* **Caldy Dancer (IRE)**[28] [3969] 3-8-7 105................................ CCatlin 3 80
(MRChannon) *slowly away and t.k.h in rr: snatched up and lost action after 3f and nvr on terms* **20/1**
4436 **12** *2½* **Cote Quest (USA)**[37] [3699] 4-9-0 92................................ WSupple 12 74
(SCWilliams) *chsd ldr tl wknd rapidly ins fnl 2f* **20/1**

1m 39.33s (-1.67) **Going Correction** +0.025s/f (Good)
**WFA** 3 from 4yo 7lb **12 Ran SP% 124.7**
Speed ratings: **109,107,107,107,106 104,104,103,101,100 100,98**CSF £19.31 TOTE £9.20: £2.40, £1.40, £4.90; EX 17.30.
**Owner** M H Dixon **Bred** Exors Of The Late R D Hollingsworth **Trained** Lambourn, Berks
■ Stewards Enquiry : D Sweeney one-day ban: careless riding (Aug 26)

**FOCUS**
A decent fillies' Listed contest run at a cracking gallop. The leaders probably went off too quick as the front three all came from the very back of the field, and the overall form is not that strong.

**NOTEBOOK**
**Brindisi**, who finished behind Moon Dazzle at Ascot last time, unlike that rival enjoyed the run of the race and was delivered with a storming late effort down the outside of the track. The breakneck gallop probably suited her.
**Moon Dazzle(USA)** had a nightmare. Breaking slowly may not have been that much of a problem given the way the race was run and the winner was in a similar position, but whilst her rival got an uninterrupted run, she met all sorts of traffic problems and by the time she was out in the clear it was too late. This was one that got away.
**Zietory**, off since May, was another to come from off the pace and this should have put her spot on. This looks to be her best trip and slightly easier ground would help her also.
**Ithaca(USA)** was responsible for the fast pace and deserves credit for hanging in there for as long as she did.
**Flowerdrum(USA)** had quite a bit to do stepping up in class considering the front four are rated upwards of 9lb superior to her, but was by no means disgraced. She would be better off back in handicap company provided the assessor does not take this at face value. *Official explanation: jockey said filly suffered interference in running*
**Why Dubai(USA)** continues to struggle this season as she looks badly handicapped, yet is not up to this class.
**And Toto Too** had a mountain to climb at this level and did as well as could reasonably be expected.
**Golden Island(IRE)** did not look happy on the track.
**Caldy Dancer(IRE)** *Official explanation: jockey said filly failed to handle the track*

## 4774 JOHN SMITHS EXTRA SMOOTH H'CAP 5f 161y
4:30 (4:32) (E) (0-75,73) 3-Y-O+ **£4,342** (£1,336; £668; £334) **Stalls Low**

Form RPR
0052 **1** **Currency**[3] [4687] 7-9-6 **72**................................ CJDavies(7) 17 86
(JMBradley) *bhd tl rdn and hdwy 2f out: led ent fnl f: drvn out* **11/2**[2]
2400 **2** *nk* **Devon Flame**[16] [4291] 5-10-0 **73**................................ SDrowne 8 86
(RJHodges) *hld up in tch: rdn to chse wnr over 1f out: kpt on* **7/1**
0510 **3** *2* **Ballybunion (IRE)**[16] [4291] 5-8-9 **54**................................ ANicholls 1 60
(DNicholls) *chsd ldrs: kpt on same pce fnl f* **4/1**[1]
0220 **4** *½* **Yorkie**[46] [3407] 5-8-8 **56**................................ FPFerris(3) 18 61
(PABlockley) *bhd tl rdn and hdwy on ins over 1f out: nvr nrr* **20/1**
3005 **5** *shd* **Pulse**[13] [4400] 6-8-13 **58**................................(p) FNorton 14 62
(JMBradley) *bhd: styd on fnl f* **10/1**
1500 **6** *1* **Blessed Place**[13] [4400] 4-8-5 **50**................................(t) SRighton 5 51
(DJSFfrenchDavis) *chsd ldrs tl wknd fnl f* **33/1**
6033 **7** *nk* **Sweetest Revenge (IRE)**[9] [4515] 3-9-4 **67**................(p) JDSmith 11 67
(MDIUsher) *bhd: rn wd on bnd over 3f out: nvr nr to chal* **16/1**
6316 **8** *shd* **Adantino**[13] [4403] 5-8-12 **57**................................(b) SWKelly 13 57
(BRMillman) *hld up in tch: ev ch over 1f out: rdn and rdr lost reins: wknd ins fnl f* **14/1**
5050 **9** *¾* **Formalise**[13] [4403] 4-8-5 **55**................................(p) RThomas(5) 12 52
(GBBalding) *trckd ldr: led 2f out: hdd ent fnl f: wknd qckly* **28/1**
3300 **10** *3½* **Playtime Blue**[11] [4452] 4-9-0 **59**................................ GBaker 7 45
(MrsHSweeting) *prom: rdn 2f out: sn wknd* **20/1**
6000 **11** *2* **Indian Bazaar (IRE)**[3] [4687] 8-8-1 **49**................(b) JFMcDonald(3) 9 28
(NEBerry) *led tl hdd 2f out: wknd qckly* **40/1**
1005 **12** *½* **Coranglais**[2] [4707] 4-9-2 **61**................................(p) RLMoore 3 39
(JMBradley) *slowly away: a bhd* **14/1**
00-0 **13** *13* **Nathan Detroit**[13] [4403] 4-8-6 **51**................................(p) DSweeney 2 —
(PJMakin) *slowly away: a bhd: lost tch over 2f out* **40/1**
0054 **B** **B A Highflyer**[3] [4687] 4-8-13 **58**................................ CCatlin 10 —
(MRChannon) *bhd whn b.d over 2f out: bdly lame* **7/1**
4233 **P** **Loch Inch**[13] [4400] 7-8-7 **52**................................(b) DHolland 19 —
(JMBradley) *bhd whn broke shoulder and p.u over 2f out: dead* **6/1**[3]

1m 10.23s (-0.91) **Going Correction** -0.125s/f (Firm)
**WFA** 3 from 4yo+ 4lb **15 Ran SP% 123.8**
Speed ratings: **101,100,97,97,97 95,95,95,94,89 86,86,68,—,—**CSF £41.00 CT £178.18 TOTE £7.40: £2.40, £3.10, £2.20; EX 56.80.

**Owner** Robert Bailey **Bred** Limestone Stud **Trained** Sedbury, Gloucs

**FOCUS**

A competitive if fairly modest handicap contested by sprinters who take each other on regularly, but the form looks reliable.

**NOTEBOOK**

**Currency** was without a win in over a year despite being kept busy, but had been hinting at a return to form and has become well handicapped. With the wide draw suiting his style of running, he was brought with a sweeping wide run but then had to withstand the late effort of the runner-up. Now that he has struck form he could well win again provided things fall right.

**Devon Flame** ran right up to his best and made sure the winner was not able to take things easy. He is only very slowly sliding back down the weights, but is still 5lb higher than his last winning mark and this effort means he probably will not go down any more for the time being.

**Ballybunion(IRE)**, runner-up in this last year, broke well and had the run of the race against the inside rail, holding a perfect position and just not proving good enough.

**Yorkie** ran up to his best under conditions that suit, but has still only ever won once on turf.

**Pulse** ran one of his better races, but is an expensive horse to follow. *Official explanation: jockey said gelding hung right*

**Sweetest Revenge(IRE)** probably did well to reach her finishing position as she missed the break and then raced very wide around the bend.

**Playtime Blue** *Official explanation: jockey said gelding lost its action in the final furlong*

## 4775 JACKIE COLES SURPRISE 40TH BIRTHDAY CELEBRATIONS MAIDEN STKS — 1m 3f 144y

**5:00** (5:03) (D ) 3-Y-O — **£3,740** (£1,151; £575; £287) **Stalls** Low

| Form | | | Horse | Jockey | RPR |
|---|---|---|---|---|---|
| 0222 | **1** | | **Idealistic (IRE)**[25] 4028 3-8-9 82 (LMCumani) *mde all: shkn up over 2f out: pushed clr: comf* **8/13**[1] | DHolland 6 | 53+ |
| 3-03 | **2** | 2 ½ | **Turn 'n Burn**[30] 3922 3-9-0 78 (CACyzer) *t.k.h: trckd ldrs: wnt 2nd over 4f out: no imp on wnr fnl 2f* **5/2**[2] | RLMoore 4 | 54+ |
| 4 | **3** | 1 | **Sovietta (IRE)**[22] 4141 3-8-6 (RMBeckett) *s.i.s: trckd wnr after 1f tl over 1f out: disp 2nd fnl 3f tl no ex ins last* **8/1**[3] | NMackay(3) 1 | 48+ |
| 0005 | **4** | 3 | **Nina Fontenail (FR)**[65] 2832 3-8-9 40 (BRMillman) *slowly away: plld hrd in rr: effrt over 3f out: no ch w first 3 after* **50/1** | FNorton 2 | 43 |
| 00 | **5** | 9 | **Anna Gayle**[20] 4195 3-8-9 (MrsAJPerrett) *in tch: rdn over 3f out: sn wknd* **25/1** | SDrowne 5 | 29 |
| | **6** | 1 ½ | **Montgomery** 3-8-9 (AGNewcombe) *slowly away: wl bhd fr 1/2-way* **25/1** | RThomas(5) 7 | 31 |
| -000 | **7** | 30 | **Cloud Catcher (IRE)**[7] 4583 3-8-9 (MAppleby) *plld hrd: in tch tl rdn and wknd over 3f out: t.o* **50/1** | SRighton 3 | — |

2m 32.01s (1.71) **Going Correction** +0.025s/f (Good) **7** Ran SP% **113.2**
Speed ratings: **95,93,92,90,84 83,63**CSF £2.24 TOTE £1.60: £1.10, £1.50; EX 1.70 Place 6 £154.33, Place 5 £32.74..

**Owner** Fittocks Stud **Bred** Fittocks Stud **Trained** Newmarket, Suffolk

**FOCUS**

A weak maiden in which basically only three had a realistic chance and the market got it right. The winning time was moderate for the class, more than four seconds slower than the ladies' race.

**NOTEBOOK**

**Idealistic(IRE)**, an expensive failure in her last two starts, appeared to face a straightforward task and, after setting the pace, only had to be nudged out to score. She only did as much as she was entitled to at the weights, so should be competitive in handicap company off this sort of mark.

**Turn 'n Burn** chased the winner home valiantly and did about as well as he was entitled to at the weights, but he is very one paced and also looks exposed now.

**Sovietta(IRE)** found the front pair too good, but was not disgraced and as this was only her second start she may have some improvement left.

**Nina Fontenail(FR)** is flattered to finish so close and her official mark is a more accurate measure of her ability.

T/Jkpt: Not won. T/Plt: £90.00 to a £1 stake. Pool: £45,142.40. 366.10 winning tickets. T/Qpdt: £12.70 to a £1 stake. Pool: £3,057.30. 176.90 winning tickets. JS

# 4450 PONTEFRACT (L-H)

### Sunday, August 15

**OFFICIAL GOING: Good to soft**

After 4" rain over the previous six days the riders reported the ground was a bit dead and sticky.

Wind: Slight 1/2 behind. Weather: Hot and humid.

## 4776 EUROPEAN BREEDERS FUND SUNDAY PLATE MAIDEN STKS — 5f

**2:10** (2:11) (D ) 2-Y-O — **£8,921** (£2,745; £1,372; £686) **Stalls** Low

| Form | | | Horse | Jockey | RPR |
|---|---|---|---|---|---|
| 2 | **1** | | **Graze On**[21] 4175 2-9-0 (JJQuinn) *trckd ldrs: led over 1f out: drvn out* **7/1**[3] | RWinston 7 | 81 |
| 4 | **2** | 1 | **Sentiero Rosso (USA)**[74] 2579 2-9-0 (BEllison) *chsd ldrs: ev ch ins last: no ex towards fin* **11/1** | JFortune 11 | 78 |
| 0 | **3** | 2 ½ | **Je Suis Belle**[41] 3588 2-8-9 (BWHills) *racd wd: chsd ldrs: edgd lft and kpt on wl fnl f* **11/2**[2] | RHills 17 | 64 |
| 60 | **4** | 2 | **Alexia Rose (IRE)**[53] 3196 2-8-9 (ABerry) *led tl 2f out: kpt on same pce* **100/1** | JBramhill 8 | 57 |
| | **5** | 1 | **Leslingtaylor (IRE)** 2-9-0 (JJQuinn) *leggy: unf: scope: chsd ldrs: fdd and eased ins last* **50/1** | GHind 3 | 59 |
| 22 | **6** | nk | **Hanseatic League (USA)**[71] 2686 2-9-0 (MJohnston) *w ldrs: led 2f out: sn hdd: wknd last 150yds* **8/11**[1] | JFanning 1 | 57 |
| 4 | **7** | 1 ½ | **Harrys House**[21] 4175 2-9-0 (JJQuinn) *racd wd early: sn outpcd: hdwy over 1f out: styd on wl ins last* **16/1** | PHanagan 18 | 52 |
| | **8** | nk | **Entailment** 2-9-0 (MrsJRRamsden) *w'like: rea-div: hdwy over 1f out: styd on towards fin* **40/1** | LGoncalves 13 | 51 |
| 0 | **9** | 1 ¼ | **Mickledo**[29] 3925 2-9-0 (ABailey) *cmpt: mid-div: kpt on fnl 2f: nvr nrr* **100/1** | MFenton 4 | 47 |
| 00 | **10** | ½ | **Apetite**[8] 4559 2-8-7 (NBycroft) *s.i.s: bhd tl sme hdwy fnl 2f* **150/1** | AReilly(7) 5 | 45 |
| 04 | **11** | ½ | **Lucy Parkes**[9] 4507 2-8-9 (EJAlston) *chsd ldrs: lost pl over 1f out* **40/1** | MHenry 2 | 38 |
| 50 | **12** | ½ | **Wayward Shot (IRE)**[15] 4347 2-9-0 (MWEasterby) *chsd ldrs: wknd over 1f out* **50/1** | TLucas 14 | 42 |
| 0 | **13** | 1 ½ | **Halla San**[15] 4347 2-8-11 (MrsJRRamsden) *sn outpcd and bhd* **66/1** | ABeech(3) 9 | 36 |
| 600 | **14** | ½ | **Paula Jo**[36] 3758 2-8-9 (JSWainwright) *mid-div: outpcd over 2f out: sn lost pl* **33/1** | GParkin 10 | 30 |
| 0 | **15** | 6 | **Phantom Song (IRE)**[10] 4487 2-9-0 (DCarroll) *racd wd early: sn bhd* **100/1** | EAhern 15 | 14 |
| 06 | **16** | 4 | **Marlenes Girl (IRE)**[9] 4507 2-8-4 (ABerry) *racd wd: bhd fnl 2f* **50/1** | PPMathers(5) 16 | — |
| | **17** | 6 | **Dolly Peel** 2-8-9 (GASwinbank) *leggy: unf: swvd bdly rt s: a wl bhd* **40/1** | DeanMcKeown 6 | — |
| 04 | **18** | ¾ | **Allizam**[18] 4239 2-9-0 (BAMcmahon) *s.i.s: sn wl bhd* **80/1** | GCarter 12 | — |

65.60 secs (1.80) **Going Correction** +0.30s/f (Good) **18** Ran SP% **122.5**
Speed ratings: **97,95,91,88,86 86,83,83,81,80 79,78,76,75,66 59,50,48**CSF £76.99 TOTE £6.10: £2.10, £2.30, £1.80; EX 69.40.

**Owner** J R Rowbottom **Bred** Mrs Sandra Cooper **Trained** Settrington, N Yorks

**FOCUS**

A fair maiden for the track, with the first two coming from races that are working out well.

**NOTEBOOK**

**Graze On** stepped up on his debut effort and showed a good attitude in a tight finish. He clearly handles easy ground and connections must now hope for a realistic nursery mark.

**Sentiero Rosso(USA)**, who cost 90,000gns, had clearly improved a good deal since his initial outing 74 days earlier. After a head-to-head battle he came off just second best. He will improve again and deserves to go one better.

**Je Suis Belle**, drawn one from the outside, raced wide but drifted left-handed in the home straight, eventually joining the first two on the far side. She will improve again.

**Alexia Rose(IRE)**, who finished last and showed a tendency to hang right on her first two starts, ran an awful lot better showing bags of speed to tow them along. She now qualifies for a nursery mark.

**Leslingtaylor(IRE)**, an April foal, is very much on the leg and looks weak at present. He showed a fair level of ability first time and was certainly not knocked about.

**Hanseatic League(USA)**, absent for ten weeks, took it up turning in but his stride shortened markedly inside the last.

**Harrys House**, three lengths behind the winner his stablemate first time, again showed ability but will need another day trip to qualify for a nursery mark.

**Entailment**, a March foal, is a keen type and seemed to be ridden on this debut with a view to teaching him to settle.

## 4777 RACECARD COMPETITION H'CAP — 1m 4f 8y

**2:40** (2:41) (C ) (0-100,88) 3-Y-O+ — **£9,372** (£3,555; £1,777; £808) **Stalls** Low

| Form | | | Horse | Jockey | RPR |
|---|---|---|---|---|---|
| 0622 | **1** | | **Jeepstar**[15] 4343 4-8-10 74 (TDEasterby) *mde all:r idden along 3f out: drvn over 1f out: kpt on gamely ins last* **10/1** | MFenton 8 | 85 |
| 0- | **2** | ¾ | **Pretty Star (GER)**[106] 4-9-10 88 (MJohnston) *trckd wnr: hdwy to chal over 2f out: sn rdn: drvn and ev ch ins last: no ex nr fin* **25/1** | JFanning 9 | 98 |
| 1203 | **3** | 1 | **Sahem (IRE)**[11] 4453 7-9-0 78 (DEddy) *trckd ldrs on inner: hdwy 2f out: rdn over 1f out: kpt on same pce ins last* **8/1** | PHanagan 4 | 86 |
| 415 | **4** | nk | **Double Aspect (IRE)**[21] 4173 3-8-11 86 (SirMichaelStoute) *in tch on inner: hdwy 3f out: swtchd rt and rdn ent last: sn drvn and one pce* **6/5**[1] | KFallon 1 | 94 |
| 4/00 | **5** | 1 | **Ranville**[36] 3757 6-9-8 86 (MAJarvis) *trckd ldrs: hdwy 4f out: rdn along and ch wl over 1f out: sn drvn and one pce* **16/1** | MHenry 5 | 92 |
| -500 | **6** | 6 | **Jasmick (IRE)**[4] 4647 6-8-8 72 (HMorrison) *hld up towards rr: hdwy to trck ldrs 1/2-way: effrt 3f out: rdn and wkng whn n.m.r over 1f out* **12/1** | TPQueally 3 | 69 |
| 1-00 | **7** | 1 | **Urowells (IRE)**[37] 3716 4-9-10 88 (EALDunlop) *hld up in rr: hdwy over 4f out: rdn over 2f out and sn no imression* **16/1** | JFortune 2 | 84 |
| 4352 | **8** | 9 | **Aleron (IRE)**[14] 4363 6-8-8 72 (JJQuinn) *in tch: effrt to chse ldrs over 4f out: sn rdn and wknd over 2f out* **7/1**[3] | (p) EAhern 6 | 54 |
| 0411 | **9** | dist | **Trance (IRE)**[57] 3078 4-9-4 87 (TDBarron) *in tch on outer: hdwy over 4f out: rdn and btn over 2f out* **11/2**[2] | PMakin(5) 7 | — |

2m 41.49s (1.44) **Going Correction** +0.30s/f (Good)
**WFA** 3 from 4yo+ 11lb **9** Ran SP% **116.8**
Speed ratings: **107,106,105,105,104 100,100,94,—**CSF £224.02 CT £2090.44 TOTE £8.00: £2.60, £3.80, £2.30; EX 124.60.

**Owner** Miss E Jeeps And Partners **Bred** P D And Mrs Player **Trained** Great Habton, N Yorks

**FOCUS**

A decent handicap in which the winner set a modest pace and only the favourite got into it from the rear. The first five finished clear and the form looks fair, although the proximity of the fifth raises doubts.

**NOTEBOOK**

**Jeepstar**, who has been edging up the weights in defeat, went off in front and held on grittily. He appreciated the step up in trip.

**Pretty Star(GER)**, a Listed winner over 11 furlongs in Germany last year, had been off the track since May and this was his debut for Johnston. In second place throughout, he was never able to get past a gutsy opponent. He has yet to run on ground faster than good.

**Sahem(IRE)** was unable to dominate with Jeepstar in opposition and was in a similar position throughout.

**Double Aspect(IRE)**, who just missed the break, took time to respond to Fallon's driving and did not look an easy ride, hanging in behind. He stayed this longer trip but might have preferred faster ground.

**Ranville** was tackling a trip short of his best but this was his best run since missing a season. He was still 5lb higher than when competing a four-timer in the latter part of 2002.

**Urowells(IRE)** *Official explanation: jockey said gelding hung left under pressure*

**Aleron(IRE)** *Official explanation: jockey said gelding ran flat*

**Trance(IRE)** *Official explanation: jockey said gelding failed to handle the track*

## 4778 SPORTINGOPTIONS.CO.UK (EXCHANGE BETTING) H'CAP — 2m 1f 22y

**3:10** (3:11) (E ) (0-65,64) 3-Y-O+ — **£5,772** (£1,776; £888; £444) **Stalls** Low

| Form | | | Horse | Jockey | RPR |
|---|---|---|---|---|---|
| 31 | **1** | | **Super Fellow (IRE)**[6] 4609 10-8-5 42 6ex (CNKellett) *hld up and bhd: pushed along 4f out: hdwy 3f out: rdn and str run over 1f out: styd on wl to ld last 100 yds* **13/2**[2] | JBramhill 4 | 51 |
| 3103 | **2** | 1 ¼ | **Crackleando**[8] 4561 3-8-3 58 (NPLittmoden) *cl up: led after 3f: rdn along 4f out: hdd wl over 1f out: drvna nd rallied to ld ent last: hdd and no ex last 100 yds* **20/1** | J-PGuillambert(3) 13 | 66 |
| 0643 | **3** | ½ | **Vicars Destiny**[4] 4627 6-9-12 63 (MrsSLamyman) *hld up and bhd: hdwy on outer 4f out: rdn to chse ldrs wl over 1f out: drvn and kpt on wl fnl f: nrst fin* **7/1**[3] | JFortune 18 | 70 |
| 0-12 | **4** | hd | **High Drama**[9] 3667 7-8-3 40 (PBowen) *trckd ldrs: effrt over 3f out: rdn along 2f out: drvn and edgd lft over 1f out: kpt on u.p fnl f* **7/1**[3] | TPQueally 1 | 47 |
| 1230 | **5** | ¾ | **Habitual Dancer**[44] 3479 3-8-6 58 (JeddO'Keeffe) *keen: led 3f: cl up: rdn along over 3f out: drvn and kpt on same pce fnl 2f* **25/1** | PHanagan 17 | 64 |

-042 **6** *hd* **Penny Stall**[29] 3928 3-8-11 **63** KFallon 15 69
(JLDunlop) *hld up in tch: smooth hdwy over 4f out: led wl over 1f out: sn rdn: drvn and hdd ent last: grad wknd* **7/4**[1]

054 **7** *8* **Molehill**[40] 3608 3-8-7 **59** MFenton 5 57
(JGGiven) *a.p: rdn along over 3f out: drvn 2f out and sn wknd* **16/1**

40/0 **8** *1 ½* **Leopard Spot (IRE)**[9] 4512 6-8-11 **48** PFessey 7 44
(ISemple) *hld up towards rr: hdwy over 3f out: rdn 2f out and sn no imp* **16/1**

0000 **9** *¾* **Allez Mousson**[11] 4448 6-8-4 **41** DAllan 14 37
(ABailey) *bhd: rdn along over 3f out: sme late hdwy* **14/1**

4000 **10** *nk* **Green 'N' Gold**[41] 3576 4-9-2 **53** ACulhane 2 48
(MDHammond) *bhd tl sme late hdwy* **20/1**

2051 **11** *3 ½* **Mr Whizz**[11] 4433 7-8-3 **40** (p) RFfrench 12 32
(APJones) *chsd ldrs: hdwy to dispute ld over 4f out: rdn along 3f out. drvn 2f out and sn wknd* **20/1**

-403 **12** *2 ½* **Fantastico (IRE)**[11] 4448 4-9-8 **59** (p) RWinston 9 48
(MrsKWalton) *midfield: rdn along over 4f out: sn wknd* **11/1**

0/00 **13** *shd* **Valdesco (IRE)**[35] 3781 6-9-8 **64** (b) PPMathers(5) 3 53
(MrsSJSmith) *chsd ldrs: rdn along 5f out: sn wknd* **20/1**

0306 **14** *1 ¾* **Domenico (IRE)**[6] 4129 6-9-12 **63** EAhern 6 50
(JRJenkins) *chsd ldrs: rdn along over 4f out: sn wknd* **33/1**

-060 **15** *dist* **Purr**[53] 3190 3-7-12 **50** oh1 MHenry 11 —
(TTClement) *in tch: hdwy on outer over 4f out: rdn along and wknd 3f out* **66/1**

345- **16** *dist* **Special Branch**[147] 3973 4-8-11 **48** JFanning 16 —
(JeddO'Keeffe) *chsd ldrs: rdn along over 6f out and sn wknd* **33/1**

/00- **R** **Jawwala (USA)**[25] 2839 5-9-8 **59** FLynch 10 —
(JRJenkins) *ref to r: tk no part* **66/1**

3m 58.82s (8.32) **Going Correction** +0.30s/f (Good)
**WFA** 3 from 4yo+ 15lb **17** Ran SP% **133.2**
Speed ratings: **92,91,91,91,90 90,86,86,85,85 84,82,82,81,— —,—**CSF £141.89 CT £972.10 TOTE £9.40: £2.50, £4.40, £1.80, £1.90; EX 310.90.
**Owner** A M Egan **Bred** Gerard McClure **Trained** Swadlincote, Derbys

**FOCUS**
A moderate handicap in which the pace was steady, resulting in a pedestrian winning time for the grade. The form however, is modest but sound for the grade.

**NOTEBOOK**
**Super Fellow(IRE)**, under a 6lb penalty for his win at Thirsk, was at the back of the field with a lot to do with under half a mile to run, but he responded to pressure and stayed on to win going away in the end. The greater the test of stamina the better for him, and he can win again at a lowly level provided he can be stoked up in time.
**Crackleando** dictated the pace and stuck on bravely against the fence to regain the lead, but was cut down in the last half-furlong. This easier ground suited.
**Vicars Destiny**, who was done no favours by the eventual winner as he squeezed past her, was never nearer than at the line. She remains a maiden on the level.
**High Drama**, whose latest outing was in a novice chase, has run two decent races from this mark since winning a ladies' race in June.
**Habitual Dancer**, well suited by give in the ground, appeared to see out this longer trip but could prove best at around two miles.
**Penny Stall** threw down a challenge to Crackleando in the straight, but found that rival too tough a nut to crack and her lead was shortlived. This looks as good as she is, although a stronger pace might have suited her.
**Molehill**, making her handicap debut, had promised to stay being out of a Cesarewitch winner, but she failed to see out the trip.
**Mr Whizz**, from a 6lb higher mark, was right in the mix turning for home but was found out by the trip in the end.

## 4779 SLATCH FARM STUD FLYING FILLIES' STKS (LISTED RACE) 6f
3:40 (3:41) (A) 3-Y-O+ £29,000 (£11,000; £5,500; £2,500) Stalls Low

Form RPR

5054 **1** **Goldeva**[14] 4362 5-9-4 97 ACulhane 8 104
(RHollinshead) *hld up in rr: smooth hdwy on ins over 2f out: shkn up to ld 150yds out: r.o wl* **20/1**

2142 **2** *2 ½* **Fruit Of Glory**[8] 4526 5-9-0 94 FLynch 4 93
(JRJenkins) *chsd ldrs: led over 1f out: hdd ins last: nt qckn* **10/1**[3]

4650 **3** *4* **Simianna**[7] 4590 5-9-0 94 (p) RWinston 6 81
(ABerry) *bhd: hdwy and n.m.r bnd over 2f out: styd on fnl f* **20/1**

0032 **4** *½* **Lochridge**[15] 4317 5-9-0 101 TPQueally 14 79
(AMBalding) *w ldrs: led over 3f out tl over 1f out: wknd fnl f* **7/2**[2]

2552 **5** *2* **Nyramba**[16] 4286 3-8-10 107 JFortune 1 73
(JHMGosden) *mid-div: effor and n.m.r over 2f out: nvr rchd ldrs* **5/2**[1]

0055 **6** *2* **Vita Spericolata (IRE)**[14] 4362 7-9-0 81 GParkin 9 67
(JSWainwright) *led over 2f: w ldrs tl wknd fnl f* **66/1**

4630 **7** *1 ¾* **Dowager**[16] 4286 3-8-10 100 DaneO'Neill 13 62
(RHannon) *sn outpcd and bhd: kpt on fnl 2f: nvr nr ldrs* **25/1**

0051 **8** *1* **Tychy**[8] 4526 5-9-0 97 KFallon 7 59
(SCWilliams) *chsd ldrs: hmpd and lost pl after 1f: hdwy on outer over 2f out: n.d* **5/2**[1]

1065 **9** *8* **Flashing Blade**[16] 4305 4-9-0 64 (t) GCarter 10 35
(BAMcmahon) *in rr: bhd fnl 2f* **100/1**

5103 **10** *3* **Le Meridien (IRE)**[8] 4548 6-9-0 51 (p) RFfrench 12 26
(JSWainwright) *chsd ldrs: lost pl over 2f out* **100/1**

3004 **11** *5* **Nataliya**[23] 4077 3-8-10 105 JFanning 5 11
(JLDunlop) *chsd ldrs: rdn and lost pl over 2f out* **10/1**[3]

-240 **12** *½* **Millybaa (USA)**[70] 2719 4-9-0 97 EAhern 2 9
(RGuest) *chsd ldrs: wkng whn hmpd over 2f out: sn bhd* **12/1**

1m 17.2s (-0.10) **Going Correction** +0.30s/f (Good)
**WFA** 3 from 4yo+ 4lb **12** Ran SP% **122.1**
Speed ratings: **112,108,103,102,100 97,95,93,83,79 72,71**CSF £201.58 TOTE £21.70: £3.90, £2.60, £3.40; EX 195.80.
**Owner** M Pyle & Mrs T Pyle **Bred** Longdon Stud Ltd **Trained** Upper Longdon, Staffs
■ Stewards Enquiry : T P Queally five-day ban: careless riding (Aug 26-30)

**FOCUS**
A rough renewal of this Listed race for fillies and, although the time was reasonable, the form is not outstanding for the level.

**NOTEBOOK**
**Goldeva**, giving weight away all round, was happy to sit off a strong pace. She enjoyed a dream run round the home turn and in the end took this in most decisive fashion, turning in a best-ever effort.
**Fruit Of Glory** mixed it throughout in a race run at a strong pace. She had no answer when the winner swept by, but deserves plenty of credit for finishing clear second best.
**Simianna**, fourth a year ago, met traffic problems on the turn in and, when she got into the clear, the first two had flown.
**Lochridge**, who took this a year ago, had a poor draw this time. She switched left after the first furlong knocking Tychy out of the contest. After helping set a very strong pace, she had no more to give straightening up. She prefers much quicker ground.
**Nyramba**, best in on official figures, met trouble on the turn but basically lacked the raw pace to be fully effective over this trip.
**Vita Spericolata(IRE)**, third last year, showed all her old speed, but she had a lot to find and tired badly in the final furlong.
**Tychy** lost all chance when knocked right back when Lochridge came right across at the end of the first furlong.

## 4780 WAKEFIELD UNISON QUALITY SERVICES FOR QUALITY PEOPLE H'CAP 1m 4y
4:10 (4:11) (C) (0-90,87) 3-Y-O £9,535 (£3,616; £1,808; £822) Stalls Low

Form RPR

4011 **1** **Double Vodka (IRE)**[13] 4395 3-8-1 **67** PHanagan 5 81+
(MrsJRRamsden) *hld up in tch: hdwy over 2f out: swtchd lft and squeezed through on inner to ld ins last: sn rdn and styd on wl* **3/1**[2]

1053 **2** *2 ½* **Alshawameq (IRE)**[21] 4171 3-9-6 **86** RHills 6 92
(JLDunlop) *pushed along s and bhd: hdwy 2f out: swtchd outside and rdn over 1f out: styd on wl fnl f* **6/1**[3]

01 **3** *¾* **Choir Leader**[21] 4180 3-9-5 **85** KFallon 3 89+
(WJHaggas) *trckd ldrs: pushed along over 2f out: rdn wl over 1f out: kpt on same pce u.p fnl f* **11/8**[1]

2411 **4** *3* **Silverhay**[11] 4451 3-8-7 **73** JFortune 4 71
(TDBarron) *chsd ldng pair: hdwy to ld 2f out: sn rdn: drvn and hdd ent last: wknd* **10/1**

4054 **5** *1* **Honest Injun**[24] 4050 3-8-8 **74** ACulhane 9 70
(BWHills) *hld up: hdwy over 2f out: sn rdn and kpt on appr last: nt rch ldrs* **14/1**

2222 **6** *1* **Riley Boys (IRE)**[36] 3745 3-9-1 **81** MFenton 7 75
(JGGiven) *hld up in tch: hdwy on outer wl over 1f out: sn rdn and no imp fnl f* **10/1**

4045 **7** *½* **Mission Man**[25] 4032 3-8-13 **79** DaneO'Neill 2 72
(RHannon) *cl up: rdn to ld over 2f out: sn hdd: drvn and wknd over 1f out* **20/1**

0100 **8** *15* **Rarefied (IRE)**[53] 3210 3-9-0 **80** RWinston 11 41
(TDEasterby) *a rr* **33/1**

5600 **9** *3 ½* **Forthright**[22] 4118 3-9-7 **87** (p) TPQueally 10 41
(CEBrittain) *chsd ldrs: rdn along 3f out: sn wknd* **25/1**

14-0 **10** *3* **Familiar Affair**[10] 4490 3-9-0 **80** FLynch 1 28
(BSmart) *led: rdn along 3f out: sn hdd & wknd* **25/1**

1m 46.48s (0.88) **Going Correction** +0.30s/f (Good) **10** Ran SP% **121.6**
Speed ratings: **107,104,103,100,99 98,98,83,79,76**CSF £21.35 CT £35.77 TOTE £4.80: £1.80, £2.40, £1.20; EX 31.50.
**Owner** Mrs Alison Iles **Bred** Daphne Davison **Trained** Sandhutton, N Yorks

**FOCUS**
Quite a well-contested handicap, run at a good pace, and the form looks solid.

**NOTEBOOK**
**Double Vodka(IRE)** was searching for room once in line for home, but a gap soon appeared and he took full advantage. Only 4lb higher than for his first win, he has more improvement in him and is a versatile sort who will not be troubled by a return to ten furlongs.
**Alshawameq(IRE)** stayed on from off the pace to go second inside the final furlong and clearly had no problem with the easy ground. His head carriage underlined that he is not entirely straightforward.
**Choir Leader** , easy winner of a soft maiden over course and distance, ran a solid race on this handicap debut but was slightly short of room at one stage in the straight and could not quicken up when in the clear. This ground probably did not suit him.
**Silverhay**, bidding for a hat-trick from a 5lb higher mark, had to work to get to the front and could not hold on inside the last. This was a decent effort given he raced close to the strong pace.
**Honest Injun** finished further behind Double Vodka than he had at Doncaster despite being 4lb better off.
**Riley Boys(IRE)** ran his usual honest race, but is 10lb higher than when last winning and the Handicapper looks to have him now.
**Familiar Affair** *Official explanation: jockey said saddle slipped*

## 4781 KIDS COME FREE MAIDEN STKS 1m 4y
4:40 (4:43) (D) 3-Y-O+ £8,921 (£2,745; £1,372; £686) Stalls Low

Form RPR

5 **1** **Stream Of Gold (IRE)**[40] 3603 3-8-12 KFallon 5 89+
(SirMichaelStoute) *trckd ldrs: smooth hdwy over 2f out: led ent last: sn clr: easily* **4/5**[1]

2- **2** *3* **Baboosh (IRE)**[333] 4986 3-8-7 RFfrench 3 73+
(JRFanshawe) *led: rdn along over 2f out: drvn and hdd ent last: kpt on: no ch w wnr* **4/1**[2]

**3** *¾* **Medalla (FR)** 4-9-5 TWilliams 12 76
(MBrittain) *midfield: hdwy over 2f out: sn rdn and kpt on appr last* **100/1**

0364 **4** *3 ½* **Fossgate**[17] 4258 3-8-12 70 (v[1]) JFanning 2 69
(JDBethell) *chsd ldr: rdn along 3f out: wknd fnl 2f* **8/1**[3]

04 **5** *5* **Capitole (IRE)**[40] 3607 3-8-12 PMcCabe 6 59
(EFVaughan) *chsd ldrs: effrt over 2f out: sn rdn and btn* **33/1**

0340 **6** *1* **True (IRE)**[25] 4020 3-8-0 63 AndrewWebb(7) 10 51
(MrsSLamyman) *in tch: rdn along over 3f out: nvr a factor* **12/1**

06 **7** *9* **Sonearsofar (IRE)**[30] 3896 4-9-0 MLawson(5) 11 38
(JParkes) *nvr nr ldrs* **100/1**

4 **8** *15* **Perrywinkle Boy**[11] 4455 3-8-12 ACulhane 9 6
(MDHammond) *a rr* **33/1**

**9** *½* **Thistle** 3-8-12 JFortune 7 5
(JHMGosden) *rangy: tall: chsd ldng pair tl rdn over 2f out and sn wknd* **9/1**

**10** *8* **Sinamay (USA)** 3-8-7 RWinston 14 —
(JJQuinn) *a bhd* **50/1**

00 **11** *26* **Dont Tell Simon**[16] 2555 3-8-12 GParkin 4 —
(MESowersby) *a outpcd and bhd* **100/1**

**12** *1* **City Lass** 4-8-11 PMulrennan(3) 8 —
(MESowersby) *s.i.s: a bhd* **100/1**

**P** **Rhum** 4-9-5 PHanagan 1 —
(ISemple) *slowly in to stride: bhd and v green: t.o and p.u 1/2-way* **25/1**

1m 47.88s (2.28) **Going Correction** +0.30s/f (Good)
**WFA** 3 from 4yo 7lb **13** Ran SP% **120.0**
Speed ratings: **100,97,96,92,87 86,77,62,62,54 28,27,—**CSF £3.78 TOTE £1.70: £1.20, £1.50, £12.30; EX 4.60.
**Owner** Ballymacoll Stud **Bred** Ballymacoll Stud Farm Ltd **Trained** Newmarket, Suffolk

**FOCUS**
A valuable maiden for the track, but a moderate time for the grade and a race containing a lot of dead wood. The first two should rate higher.

**NOTEBOOK**
**Stream Of Gold(IRE)**, half asleep in the paddock, showed a fluent action. Settling better than on his debut, he took a little time to warm to his task but ultimately ran out an easy winner, albeit of a weak race. A return to farther will not trouble him, but a likely mark in the mid-80s could make things difficult for him in handicaps.

**Baboosh(IRE)**, a lightly-made, smallish filly, put in a brave effort from the front but was easily brushed aside by the favourite passing the furlong pole. This was an encouraging return to action after an 11-month absence.
**Medalla(FR)** is out of a mare who won twice at up to a mile on easy ground. He shaped with plenty of promise on this debut but it remains to be seen whether it was a flash in the pan.
**Fossgate**, who has had plenty of chances, showed no real improvement in the first-time visor.
**Capitole(IRE)**, tackling easy ground for the first time, can run in handicaps now.
**Thistle**, on edge in the paddock on his debut, became very warm indeed behind the stalls. He is likely to need time and a longer trip. *Official explanation: jockey said colt boiled over before the start*
**City Lass** showed a good deal of temperament in the preliminaries.
**Rhum** *Official explanation: jockey said saddle slipped*

## 4782 GO RACING IN YORKSHIRE H'CAP — 5f
5:10 (5:12) (F) (0-55,55) 3-Y-O+ — £4,397 (£1,353; £676; £338) Stalls Low

Form — RPR
4331 **1** — **On The Trail**[11] 4452 7-9-0 **48** ........ ACulhane 3 — 61
(DWChapman) *mde all: clr 1f out: jst hld on* — **7/2**[2]
4441 **2** ½ **Davids Mark**[13] 4400 4-9-4 **52** ........ KFallon 18 — 63
(JRJenkins) *rr-div: hdwy on outer 2f out: wnt 2nd jst ins last: r.o wl: nt quite rch wnr* — **10/3**[1]
6100 **3** 1½ **Mister Mal (IRE)**[32] 3836 8-9-2 **53** ........ RMiles(3) 14 — 59
(BEllison) *bhd: hdwy on outer 2f out: styd on wl ins last* — **16/1**
0005 **4** hd **Smirfys Night**[8] 4542 5-9-1 **49** ........ JFanning 16 — 54
(DNicholls) *in rr: hdwy on wd outsider 2f out: kpt on wl fnl f* — **8/1**
0003 **5** 1¾ **Smirfys Party**[8] 4542 6-9-1 **49** ........ (v) PMQuinn 9 — 48
(DNicholls) *chsd ldrs: nt qckn fnl 2f* — **9/1**
0100 **6** ½ **Rosie's Result**[12] 4422 4-8-9 **50** ........ JemmaMarshall(7) 7 — 47
(MTodhunter) *chsd ldrs: kpt on same pce fnl 2f* — **20/1**
0-30 **7** ½ **Fenwicks Pride (IRE)**[89] 2219 6-9-7 **55** ........ PHanagan 5 — 50
(RAFahey) *bhd: hdwy whn nt clr run over 1f out: styd on ins last* — **7/1**[3]
1000 **8** shd **Fairgame Man**[4] 4626 6-8-12 **46** ........ (p) GParkin 1 — 41
(JSWainwright) *chsd ldrs: kpt on same pce fnl 2f* — **10/1**
0000 **9** nk **Lakelands Lady (IRE)**[8] 4557 4-9-1 **49** ........ JEdmunds 15 — 43
(JBalding) *chsd ldrs over one pce fnl 2f* — **40/1**
155 **10** 1¼ **Robwillcall**[15] 4331 4-8-10 **49** ........ PPMathers(5) 12 — 38
(ABerry) *chsd ldrs: one pce fnl 2f* — **16/1**
4450 **11** nk **Bella Beguine**[2] 4702 5-8-13 **47** ........ (b) MFenton 4 — 35
(ABailey) *mid-div: kpt on fnl 2f: nvr a threat* — **10/1**
0000 **12** hd **Arctic Burst (USA)**[21] 4181 4-9-1 **49** ........ (v) DarrenWilliams 17 — 36
(DShaw) *s.i.s: kpt on fnl 2f: nvr a threat* — **66/1**
0005 **13** 1¾ **Telepathic (IRE)**[4] 4635 4-9-7 **55** ........ PBradley 11 — 36
(ABerry) *mid-div: outpcd fnl 2f* — **20/1**
4500 **14** 1¼ **Dark Champion**[16] 4309 4-9-6 **54** ........ (v[1]) RWinston 2 — 30
(REBarr) *bhd: nt clr run over 1f out: nvr a factor* — **33/1**
100- **15** 2½ **Petite Mac**[334] 4969 4-8-12 **53** ........ AReilly(7) 8 — 20
(NBycroft) *in tch: lost pl over 2f out* — **50/1**
0400 **16** 1¼ **Good Time Bobby**[8] 4557 7-8-12 **46** ........ PMcCabe 10 — 9
(JO'Reilly) *sn bhd* — **50/1**
5360 **17** 7 **Palvic Moon**[29] 3954 3-9-4 **55** ........ (b[1]) RFitzpatrick 6 — —
(CSmith) *in tch: lost pl over 1f out: sn bhd and eased* — **66/1**
0-00 **18** 6 **Whinhill House**[59] 3010 4-9-0 **48** ........ FLynch 13 — —
(DWBarker) *w ldrs on outer: lost pl over 1f out: eased* — **66/1**

65.06 secs (1.26) **Going Correction** +0.30s/f (Good)
**WFA** 3 from 4yo+ 3lb — **18** Ran SP% **132.2**
Speed ratings: **101,100,97,97,94 93,93,92,92,90 89,89,86,84,80 78,67,58**CSF £15.45 CT £182.30 TOTE £4.60: £1.70, £1.70, £2.60, £3.20; EX 16.90 Place 6 £859.72, Place 5 £304.22..
**Owner** J M Chapman **Bred** Ian Bellamy **Trained** Stillington, N Yorks

**FOCUS**
A 0-55 handicap and the draw proved decisive. The form is fair for the grade and reliable.

**NOTEBOOK**
**On The Trail**, full of himself beforehand, seems to have developed speed with age and capitalised on a favourable draw.
**Davids Mark**, just 2lb higher, unlike the winner had a poor draw. He worked his way through the field to go in pursuit of the winner, and would have made it with a bit further to go.
**Mister Mal(IRE)**, absent for a month, finds the minimum trip on the sharp side.
**Smirfys Night**, drawn on the wide outside, has not tasted success for over two years but this was another encouraging effort.
**Smirfys Party**, very warm beforehand, was taken to post early. He rather lives on his nerves but six seems a better option.
**Rosie's Result** give a good account from a favourable draw.
**Fenwicks Pride(IRE)** has not won for over three years, but if this is any guide another success is just around the corner, especially if he is stepped up to six.
**Whinhill House** *Official explanation: trainer said gelding was found to have a back problem after the race*

T/Plt: £416.30 to a £1 stake. Pool: £44,261.55. 77.60 winning tickets. T/Qpdt: £26.20 to a £1 stake. Pool: £3,008.10. 84.90 winning tickets. JR

4783 - (Foreign Racing) - See Raceform Interactive

# 4156 LEOPARDSTOWN (L-H)
Sunday, August 15

**OFFICIAL GOING: Good to firm**

## 4784a BALLYROAN STKS (LISTED RACE) — 1m 4f
3:15 (3:15) 3-Y-O+ — £22,922 (£6,725; £3,204; £1,091)

RPR
**1** — **Foreign Affairs**[14] 4377 6-9-10 ........ JQuinn 7 — 110
(SirMarkPrescott) *mde virtually all: qcknd appr st: strly pressed ins fnl f: all out* — **7/1**
**2** nk **Vinnie Roe (IRE)**[81] 2416 6-10-0 117 ........ (b) PJSmullen 1 — 114
(DKWeld, Ire) *hld up in tch: 6th and drvn along 3f out: hdwy on inner st: 2nd ins fnl f: r.o wl cl home* — **1/1**[1]
**3** ¾ **Mkuzi**[50] 3333 5-9-12 110 ........ MJKinane 2 — 110
(JohnMOxx, Ire) *trckd ldrs in 4th: drvn along 4f out: bmpd under 2f out: kpt on wl u.p fnl f* — **9/2**[3]
**4** hd **Two Miles West (IRE)**[32] 3862 3-8-10 103 ........ JPSpencer 3 — 105
(APO'Brien, Ire) *hld up in rr: hdwy travelling best ent st: nt clr run and bmpd under 2f out: swtchd over 1f out: r.o wl* — **4/1**[2]
**5** 1½ **Lord Admiral (USA)**[38] 3686 3-8-10 98 ........ FMBerry 4 — 103
(CharlesO'Brien, Ire) *settled 3rd: 2nd and rdn st: no ex u.p ins fnl f* — **16/1**
**6** 8 **Faasel (IRE)**[20] 4206 3-8-10 98 ........ (b) DPMcDonogh 5 — 90
(KevinPrendergast, Ire) *trckd ldrs in 5th: rdn and outpcd early st: no ex fr 1 1/2f out* — **14/1**
**7** 1½ **Valentina Guest (IRE)**[13] 4406 3-8-7 99 ........ JAHeffernan 6 — 84
(PeterCasey, Ire) *sn 2nd: rdn fr 4f out: wknd early st: eased ins fnl f* — **12/1**

2m 34.3s **Going Correction** -0.50s/f (Hard)
**WFA** 3 from 5yo+ 11lb — **7** Ran SP% **120.9**
Speed ratings: **98,97,97,97,96 90,89**CSF £15.62 TOTE £10.10: £3.20, £1.40; DF 15.40.
**Owner** Charles C Walker - Osborne House **Bred** Miss K Rausing **Trained** Newmarket, Suffolk
■ Stewards Enquiry : J P Spencer three-day ban: careless riding (Aug 24-26)

**NOTEBOOK**
**Foreign Affairs** took his chance from the front and it paid off. Although his lead was being cut decisively over the last half furlong, the advantage he had built up early in the straight was all to much. He is tough but owed this to an enterprising pride.
**Vinnie Roe(IRE)** was going for a hat-trick in this particular event but was struggling and making no impression before the straight. He took hold of the bit again to go third over a furlong out and stayed on doggedly in second place with ever looking likely to peg back the winner. He may have sacrificed some of his speed with age but over the extra quarter mile of the Irish St Leger will still be a prime fancy to make it four in a row at the Curragh next month.
**Mkuzi** was seriously inconvenienced when bumped just under two furlongs out but gave as good as he got before staying on strongly towards the end.
**Two Miles West(IRE)** was involved in an incident with Mkuzi under two furlongs out with Spencer getting three days for "careless" riding. Once balanced again, he ran on well and might be considered a shade unlucky.
**Lord Admiral(USA)** stepped up a bit on previous efforts and is a potential improver.
**Faasel(IRE)** was struggling from early in the straight.
**Valentina Guest(IRE)** dropped right away over the last furlong.

## 4786a DESMOND STKS (GROUP 3) — 1m
4:15 (4:15) 3-Y-O+ — £32,042 (£9,366; £4,436; £1,478)

RPR
**1** — **Ace (IRE)**[22] 4162 3-8-13 ........ JPSpencer 4 — 118+
(APO'Brien, Ire) *trckd ldr in 2nd: impr to ld ent st: qcknd clr over 1 1/2f out: styd on wl: easily* — **5/4**[1]
**2** 2 **Hamairi (IRE)**[67] 2793 3-8-13 105 ........ MJKinane 1 — 110
(JohnMOxx, Ire) *hld up in rr: swtchd to outer early st: kpt on u.p to go 2nd ins fnl f: no ch w wnr* — **7/1**
**3** 1½ **Grand Passion (IRE)**[49] 3355 4-9-6 ........ JFEgan 3 — 107
(GWragg) *chsd ldrs in 3rd: rdn st: mod 2nd over 1f out: sn no ex* — **5/1**[3]
**4** 2½ **Latino Magic (IRE)**[7] 4587 4-9-9 109 ........ RMBurke 2 — 104
(RJOsborne, Ire) *led: rdn and hdd ent st: one pce* — **10/1**
**5** hd **Tropical Lady (IRE)**[7] 4587 4-9-6 112 ........ PShanahan 5 — 100
(JSBolger, Ire) *trckd ldrs in 4th: rdn and no imp early st: eased over 1f out* — **2/1**[2]

1m 37.3s **Going Correction** -0.50s/f (Hard)
**WFA** 3 from 4yo 7lb — **5** Ran SP% **116.0**
Speed ratings: **115,113,111,109,108**CSF £11.56 TOTE £2.50: £1.60, £3.10; DF 14.30.
**Owner** Mrs J Magnier,M Tabor,Mrs H McCalmont **Bred** Norelands Bloodstock **Trained** Ballydoyle, Co Tipperary

**NOTEBOOK**
**Ace(IRE)** stepped up on two minor successes and was backed to do so. In second place until going on early in the straight, he drew clear from well over a furlong down and the margin does not reflect his superiority. Ascot's Queen Elizabeth II Stakes is next on the agenda and he is smart.
**Hamairi(IRE)** switched out early in the straight and ran on from the rear to be nearest at the finish but was never on terms to deliver a challenge.
**Grand Passion(IRE)** found the younger colts much too strong over the last furlong.
**Latino Magic(IRE)** ran in front but had cried enough when the winner took over in the straight. These were not the right tactics for him.
**Tropical Lady(IRE)** was never travelling particularly well and her chance had gone turning for home. She has had a busy time and might appreciate a break.

4787 - 4793a (Foreign Racing) - See Raceform Interactive

# 4377 COLOGNE (R-H)
Sunday, August 15

**OFFICIAL GOING: Good**

## 4794a RHEINLAND-POKAL DER STADTSPARKASSE KOLN (GROUP 1) — 1m 4f
3:05 (3:09) 3-Y-O+ — £66,901 (£24,648; £11,972; £5,634)

RPR
**1** — **Albanova**[21] 4183 5-9-2 ........ THellier 7 — 111
(SirMarkPrescott) *cl 3rd to str, switched to rails & squeezed 1 1/2f out, switched out dist, qcknd to ld 100yds out, ran on wl* — **57/10**[3]
**2** ¾ **High Accolade**[22] 4121 4-9-6 ........ (v) MartinDwyer 6 — 114
(MPTregoning) *soon led, ridden over 2f out, hung right 1 1/2f out, caught 100yds out, ran on same pace* — **28/10**[2]
**3** 3 **Malinas (GER)**[42] 3565 3-8-8 ........ ASuborics 8 — 109
(PSchiergen, Germany) *tracked leader, 2nd straight, hard ridden & every chance well over 1f out, one pace* — **9/10**[1]
**4** nk **Simonas (IRE)**[56] 3136 5-9-6 ........ EPedroza 2 — 109
(AWohler, Germany) *held up in rear but always well in touch, last straight, some progress from over 1f out, never nearer* — **93/10**
**5** nk **Omikron (IRE)**[42] 3565 3-8-8 ........ ADeVries 3 — 108
(MarioHofer, Germany) *close 4th straight, one pace final 2f* — **10/1**
**6** 1½ **Well Made (GER)**[49] 3357 7-9-6 ........ WMongil 1 — 106
(HBlume, Germany) *mid division, close 6th straight, one pace* — **135/10**
**7** 20 **Rotteck (GER)**[21] 4183 4-9-6 ........ JPalik 4 — 76
(HSteguweit, Germany) *close up on outside, 5th straight, weakened quickly* — **69/10**

**WFA** 3 from 4yo+ 11lb — **7** Ran SP% **132.2**
Speed ratings: .
**Owner** Miss K Rausing **Bred** Miss K Rausing **Trained** Newmarket, Suffolk

# 4766 DEAUVILLE (R-H)

## Sunday, August 15

**OFFICIAL GOING: Aw: standard; turf: soft**

### 4795a PRIX FRESNAY-LE-BUFFARD-JACQUES LE MAROIS (GROUP 1) (C&F) 1m
2:55 (3:00) 3-Y-O+ £221,317 (£88,542; £44,271; £22,116)

RPR

1 **Whipper (USA)**[7] 4595 3-8-11 .................... CSoumillon 5 124
(RobertCollet, France) *mid-div, disp 6th half-way, pushed along to chase ldrs over 1 1/2f out, rdn to ld 1f out, ran on well, drvn out* **13/2[3]**

2 *1* **Six Perfections (FR)**[61] 2957 4-9-1 .................... TThulliez 3 119
(PBary, France) *mid-division, disputing 6th half-way, effort and ran on 1 1/2f out, went 2nd 100yds out, not catch winner* **13/8[1]**

3 *1 1/2* **My Risk (FR)**[63] 2923 5-9-4 .................... OPeslier 10 119
(J-MBeguigne, France) *raced in 3rd, disputing 3rd half-way, pushed along 2f out, ridden to lead briefly 1 1/2f out, stayed on* **8/1**

4 *1 1/2* **Majestic Desert**[14] 4383 3-8-8 .................... TEDurcan 6 113
(MRChannon) *in touch, disputing 3rd half-way, effort and led 1 1/2f out, ridden and ran on til headed 1f out, kept on one pace* **20/1**

5 *1/2* **Salselon**[36] 3724 5-9-4 .................... JPMurtagh 7 115
(LMCumani) *held up, took closer order over 3f out, ridden and stayed on at one pace from 2f out* **10/1**

6 *3* **Kheleyf (USA)**[19] 4216 3-8-11 .................... LDettori 4 109
(SaeedBinSuroor) *held up, some late headway but never dangerous* **16/1**

7 *2 1/2* **Baqah (IRE)**[40] 3600 3-8-8 .................... DBonilla 2 101
(FHead, France) *in touch til ridden and outpaced from over 1 1/2f out* **20/1**

8 *1* **Fomalhaut (USA)**[71] 5-9-4 .................... C-PLemaire 8 102
(PBary, France) *led, pushed along over 2f out ran on til headed 1 1/2f out* **150/1**

9 *2* **Byron**[19] 4216 3-8-11 .................... KMcEvoy 9 98
(SaeedBinSuroor) *mid-division, 5th half-way, unable to quicken from 2f out* **20/1**

10 *10* **Attraction**[40] 3600 3-8-8 .................... KDarley 1 75
(MJohnston) *raced in 2nd, pushed along half-way, lost place over 2f out, weakened* **11/4[2]**

1m 38.4s **Going Correction** +0.30s/f (Good)
**WFA** 3 from 4yo+ 7lb **10 Ran SP% 119.1**
Speed ratings: **118,117,115,114,113 110,108,107,105,95.**
**Owner** R C Strauss **Bred** Flaxman Holdings Ltd **Trained** France

**NOTEBOOK**
**Whipper(USA)** looked well in the preliminaries and did nothing wrong in the race. Having settled very well for Soumillon in the early stages, he ran on right the way to the line to conclusively prove his stamina for this sort of trip. A fine effort considering he had just a week to recover from his second in the Prix Maurice de Gheest. There are plenty of options for him now and they include the Moulin de Longchamp, Queen Elizabeth II Stakes and the Breeders' Cup Mile.
**Six Perfections(FR)** may not have acted as well as the winner in the conditions, as she was just a little one paced in the closing stages. Her next target could be a repeat bid in the Breeders' Cup Mile.
**My Risk(FR)** had every possible chance and galloped on resolutely, he was just unable to quicken like the front two.
**Majestic Desert** battled on gamely right the way to the line in ground that would have been soft enough. She may go for the Matron Stakes and has been invited for the Queen Elizabeth II Cup at Keeneland in October.
**Salselon** made some late progress but was never really dangerous. It was rather a disappointing effort and he may now be tried over a longer distance in something like the Coupe de Maisons-Laffitte.
**Kheleyf(USA)** came under pressure some way out and was never dangerous. He was apparently unsuited by the sticky ground.
**Byron** was a spent force one and a half out.
**Attraction** did not act at all on the ground. She was quickly at the head of affairs but never really looked at ease in the conditions and was well beaten by the two furlong marker. Her jockey looked after her in the closing stages and she will never be asked to run on soft ground again. Possible future targets include the Moulin, the Matron, the Queen Elizabeth II and the Breeders' Cup.

# 4467 BRIGHTON (L-H)

## Monday, August 16

**OFFICIAL GOING: Good to firm**
Wind: almost nil Weather: cloudy

### 4797 E.B.F./TOTEPOOL MEDIAN AUCTION MAIDEN STKS 5f 213y
2:30 (2:30) (F) 2-Y-O £2,947 (£842; £421) Stalls Low

Form RPR

5350 1 **Asian Tiger (IRE)**[26] 4022 2-9-0 83 .................... RLMoore 7 74
(RHannon) *in tch: effrt over 2f out: edgd lft 1f out: r.o to ld nr fin* **15/8[1]**

4 2 *nk* **Maneki Neko (IRE)**[22] 4172 2-8-11 .................... FPFerris(3) 1 73
(MHTompkins) *chsd ldrs: rdn 1/2-way: led ins fnl f: hdd and nt qckn nr fin* **9/2**

00 3 *1 1/2* **Molly Dancer**[24] 4099 2-8-9 .................... TEDurcan 2 63
(MRChannon) *plld hrd: trckd ldr: slt ld 2f out tl ins fnl f: one pce* **14/1**

202 4 *1/2* **Scrooby Baby**[7] 4598 2-8-9 .................... SWKelly 8 62
(JAOsborne) *led tl 2f out: rdn and ev ch 1f out: no ex* **4/1[3]**

5 5 *shd* **Easy Mover (IRE)**[22] 4172 2-8-9 .................... JMackay 3 62
(RGuest) *dwlt: rdn 1/2-way: hdwy on rail whn hmpd ins fnl 2f: swtchd wd ins fnl f: gng on at fin* **25/1**

5 6 *2* **Pollito (IRE)**[21] 4193 2-9-0 .................... JFortune 4 60
(BJMeehan) *prom: hmpd after 1f: hung lft and wknd ins fnl 2f: 5th and btn whn n.m.r 1f out* **3/1[2]**

0 7 *3 1/2* **Picot De Say**[56] 3157 2-9-0 .................... JFEgan 5 50
(JohnBerry) *t.k.h: in tch: outpcd 2f out: sn btn* **14/1**

8 *1/2* **Vino Venus** 2-8-9 .................... DSweeney 6 43
(MissSheenaWest) *t.k.h in rr: hrd rdn 2f out: nvr trbld ldrs* **66/1**

5446 9 *3 1/2* **Missed Turn**[26] 4017 2-8-4 49 .................... RThomas(5) 9 33
(JMPEustace) *stdd s: wd: t.k.h in rr: rdn and lost tch 2f out* **50/1**

1m 11.56s (1.46) **Going Correction** +0.05s/f (Good) **9 Ran SP% 118.6**
Speed ratings: **92,91,89,88,88 86,81,80,76**CSF £10.99 TOTE £3.00: £1.20, £2.40, £2.40; EX 12.00.
**Owner** The Waney Racing Group Inc **Bred** R P Ryan **Trained** East Everleigh, Wilts
■ Stewards Enquiry : F P FerrisE two-day ban: careless riding (Aug 27-28)

**FOCUS**
An ordinary maiden, with the winner below his best in getting off the mark, but one that is likely to produce future winners.
**NOTEBOOK**
**Asian Tiger(IRE)** had had plenty of chances prior to this to get off the mark, but in what was a slightly lesser race, just proved good enough to win. This stiff finish suited and he is probably worth trying over seven furlongs again in nursery company.
**Maneki Neko(IRE)** ran in a better race on his debut at Newmarket and went close to capitalising in this lesser event. He has speed to win over this trip, but will be suited by seven.
**Molly Dancer** ran well given she pulled hard in the early stages and is now qualified for nurseries. Her form entitles her to win one.
**Scrooby Baby** is beginning to look a little exposed although her form is good enough to win a maiden.
**Easy Mover(IRE)** was six lengths behind the second on her debut and showed improved form, arguably being unlucky not to get closer, making a slowish start and being hampered before running on. She has a maiden in her with further improvement anticipated at seven furlongs.
**Pollito(IRE)** was never happy after being hampered early on and deserves another chance. He is likely to be one for nurseries.
**Picot De Say** was supported in the ring but failed to improve on his debut form. One more run will see him qualified for a handicap mark.

### 4798 JIMMY HEAL MEMORIAL H'CAP 1m 1f 209y
3:00 (3:01) (F) (0-55,55) 3-Y-O £2,919 (£834; £417) Stalls High

Form RPR

0030 1 **Daydream Dancer**[11] 4479 3-8-12 **47** .................... (b) RSmith 9 53
(CGCox) *in tch: effrt over 2f out: styd on to ld fnl strides* **10/1**

0045 2 *hd* **Lenwade**[5] 4654 3-7-9 **35** oh2 .................... DFox(5) 10 40
(GGMargarson) *prom: rdn 4f out: drvn to ld wl ins fnl f: hdd fnl strides* **33/1**

1550 3 *1 1/4* **Cobalt Blue (IRE)**[3] 4710 3-9-3 **52** .................... (v[1]) JFEgan 11 55
(WJHaggas) *led: hrd rdn 2f out: hdd and nt qckn wl ins fnl f* **10/1**

5021 4 *3* **Go Green**[11] 4476 3-8-12 **54** .................... (t) SJDonohoe(7) 6 51
(PDEvans) *mid-div: outpcd 4f out: styd on fnl 2f* **3/1[1]**

0510 5 *nk* **City General (IRE)**[4] 4674 3-9-3 **52** .................... (p) SChin 2 49
(JSMoore) *t.k.h: chsd ldr: hrd rdn 2f out: no ex over 1f out* **10/1**

0023 6 *3/4* **Waltzing Beau**[28] 3990 3-8-11 **46** .................... GBaker 7 41
(BGPowell) *s.s: bhd: hrd rdn over 2f out: nrst fin* **8/1**

3002 7 *11* **Semelle De Vent (USA)**[16] 4339 3-9-6 **55** .................... (v) JFortune 1 29
(JHMGosden) *in tch: hrd rdn 2f out: sn wknd* **4/1[2]**

0420 8 *1* **Forge Lane (IRE)**[12] 4436 3-9-6 **55** .................... (b) RLMoore 3 28
(GLMoore) *towards rr: hrd rdn over 2f out: nvr nr ldrs* **11/2[3]**

0045 9 *3* **Royal Starlet**[3] 4710 3-8-13 **48** .................... (v[1]) PDobbs 4 15
(MrsAJPerrett) *prom to 1/2-way* **6/1**

060 10 *6* **Mary Carleton**[53] 3251 3-8-5 **40** .................... MHenry 12 —
(RMHCowell) *s.s: a bhd* **12/1**

0U30 11 *2* **Don Argento**[28] 3990 3-8-6 **41** ow1 .................... TEDurcan 8 —
(MrsAJBowlby) *s.s: hld up and bhd: nt clr run over 2f out: sn no ch* **33/1**

2m 3.51s (0.97) **Going Correction** +0.05s/f (Good) **11 Ran SP% 126.6**
Speed ratings: **98,97,96,94,94 93,84,84,81,76 75**CSF £310.51 CT £3381.18 TOTE £15.50: £4.00, £11.70, £4.20; EX 387.40.
**Owner** The Grey Lady Partnership **Bred** Haras Du Gazon **Trained** Lambourn, Berks

**FOCUS**
A low-grade handicap and poor form, but it did at least produce a good finish and looks sound enough for the grade.
**NOTEBOOK**
**Daydream Dancer** has looked tripless and not been seeing out her races out regardless of the trip, but she dug deep and got on top in the closing stages. She is nothing special, but has a very lowly mark and may win again if showing the same attitude.
**Lenwade** was recording a career best and was only narrowly denied the victory. She usually runs at a lesser level and can win back down in grade.
**Cobalt Blue(IRE)** ran a better race from the front in the first-time visor and, back down at a mile, should win a small race.
**Go Green** won a seller last time and was never quite going the pace. Back in a lesser race, possibly over farther, she can win again.
**City General(IRE)** had his chance but was running on empty in the final furlong.
**Waltzing Beau** is a big horse who still has growing to do and is the type who will be hurdling in a month or so.
**Semelle De Vent(USA)** looked a threat at one stage, but stopped quickly.
**Don Argento** *Official explanation: jockey said gelding was unsuited by the track*

### 4799 FENTON TIMBER CLAIMING STKS 1m 3f 196y
3:30 (3:30) (F) 4-Y-O+ £2,884 (£824; £412) Stalls High

Form RPR

060- 1 **Arabian Moon (IRE)**[10] 3406 8-9-2 71 .................... DNolan(3) 2 73
(RBrotherton) *trckd ldr: led over 3f out: rdn clr 1f out: readily* **4/1[3]**

3132 2 *5* **Banningham Blaze**[11] 4467 4-8-5 48 .................... (v) RThomas(5) 4 56
(AWCarroll) *hld up and bhd: hdwy to press wnr over 2f out: rdn and btn 1f out* **2/1[2]**

214- 3 *7* **Alaared (USA)**[69] 4949 4-9-5 83 .................... TEDurcan 1 54
(MRChannon) *hld up in 4th: hrd rdn over 2f out: no rspnse* **7/4[1]**

00/0 4 *1 3/4* **Shannon's Dream**[56] 3138 8-7-12 18 .................... JMackay 3 30
(PWHiatt) *chsd ldng pair: outpcd 4f out: n.d after* **50/1**

0-00 5 *2* **Gabor**[10] 2728 5-8-13 50 .................... (b) RLMoore 5 42
(GLMoore) *led tl over 3f out: wknd 2f out* **4/1[3]**

2m 32.12s (0.02) **Going Correction** +0.05s/f (Good) **5 Ran SP% 111.7**
Speed ratings: **101,97,93,91,90**CSF £12.61 TOTE £5.70: £2.70, £1.60; EX 20.60.
**Owner** Roy Brotherton **Bred** T Harris **Trained** Elmley Castle, Worcs

**FOCUS**
A poor race and modest form with the field finishing strung out.
**NOTEBOOK**
**Arabian Moon(IRE)** was a useful performer in his day and came into this in good form, having won over obstacles recently. He came through to lead inside the two pole and stayed on strongly to win easily. He will reportedly revert to the All-Weather now, and is up to winning in a similar grade.
**Banningham Blaze** looked a live threat at one stage but could make no further impression on the winner and was outstayed.
**Alaared(USA)** had the highest official rating of these but looked awkward on the track and was ultimately well beaten.
**Shannon's Dream** has an official rating of 18 and ran better than she was entitled to.
**Gabor** led at a decent pace early and suffered late on as a result.

### 4800 WEATHERBYS INSURANCE H'CAP 5f 59y
4:00 (4:01) (E) (0-75,69) 3-Y-O+ £0Stalls Low

Form RPR

3105 V *4* **Gone'N'Dunnett (IRE)**[13] 4415 5-9-2 **59** .................... (v) SChin 3 —
(MrsCADunnett) *anticipated s and hit gate: stall opened late and missed break: a bhd* **8/1**

3142 **V** *3* **Maluti**[25] [4043] 3-8-9 **54** JMackay 10 —
(RGuest) *stall opened late and s.i.s: hdwy on outside 3f out: wknd 2f out* **7/1**[3]

04-0 **V** *1 1/4* **Flaran**[26] [4034] 4-9-2 **59** KMcEvoy 11 —
(EFVaughan) *chsd wnr: hrd rdn over 1f out: one pce* **16/1**

0050 **V** *3/4* **Erracht**[14] [4400] 6-9-3 **60** GBaker 5 —
(MrsHSweeting) *prom over 3f* **14/1**

0000 **V** *3/4* **Kew The Music**[10] [4511] 4-8-2 **52** (v[1]) TO'Brien[(7)] 12 —
(MRChannon) *in tch: hung lft 2f out: kpt on fnl f* **20/1**

2204 **V** *1/2* **Yorkie**[1] [4774] 5-8-8 **56** PMakin[(5)] 7 —
(PABlockley) *stall opened late: towards rr: rdn and hdwy over 1f out: r.o fnl f* **9/2**[1]

0602 **V** *1/2* **Imperium**[11] [4472] 3-9-9 **68** JFEgan 6 —
(MrsStefLiddiard) *towards rr: hung lft 2f out: eased outside over 1f out: shkn up and r.o: nt rch ldrs* **5/1**[2]

5000 **V** *nk* **Boanerges (IRE)**[16] [4336] 7-8-2 **48** FPFerris[(3)] 9 —
(JMBradley) *stall opened late: sn outpcd towards rr* **16/1**

0601 **V** *nk* **Taboor (IRE)**[13] [4415] 6-8-10 **56** (bt) SHitchcott[(3)] 4 —
(JWPayne) *chsd ldrs: drvn along 1/2-way: no ex over 1f out* **8/1**

0304 **V** *nk* **Redwood Star**[13] [4415] 4-8-11 **54** (e) DSweeney 13 —
(PLGilligan) *hdwy 2f out: drvn to press wnr ins fnl f: r.o* **11/1**

0303 **V** *nk* **Finger Of Fate**[8] [4568] 4-7-8 **42** (b) DFox[(5)] 8 —
(MJPolglase) *stall opened late and s.i.s: bhd and rdn along: gd late hdwy* **16/1**

0000 **V** *shd* **Multahab**[10] [4522] 5-7-11 **45** (t) BSwarbrick[(5)] 2 —
(PSMcentee) *stall opened late: towards rr: nt clr run over 2f out tl wl over 1f out: eased outside: nvr nr to chal* **16/1**

0004 **V** **One Way Ticket**[24] [4085] 4-9-12 **69** (p) RLMoore 1 78
(JMBradley) *stall opened late: sn led: mde virtually all: drvn out* **7/1**[3]

**Owner Bred Trained**

**FOCUS**

The race was declared void as a result of seven of the stalls opening late. Runners are shown in finishing order. The 'winner' can feel hard done by.

**NOTEBOOK**

**One Way Ticket** can feel hard done by as he managed to make all the running despite his stall being one of the six to open late and him being one of those at a disadvantage. The race was subsequently voided.

**Flaran** ran well on ground that may have been a little lively at this trip and can win with a stiffer test.

**Yorkie** ran well the previous day and again went down fighting. He is evidently nearing a win and may appreciate slightly easier going.

**Imperium** finished well and was a little unfortunate not to get closer.

**Maluti** ran below par and can be given another chance as he has previously been progressive.

**Kew The Music** ran a better race in the first-time visor and stayed on despite not getting that much room. He is evidently not an easy ride and was hanging under pressure, but has the ability to win a similar race.

**Redwood Star** got away on terms and ran well without being able to get to him. She could ideally do with a stiffer test.

**Finger Of Fate** ran on well late having been slow to get going and is on a winning mark.

## 4801 ELVISTHEPOKERPLAYER.COM MEDIAN AUCTION MAIDEN STKS 5f 213y

**4:30** (4:30) (E) 3-4-Y-O **£3,367** (£1,036; £518; £259) **Stalls** Low

Form RPR

00-2 **1** **Patterdale**[4] [4683] 3-9-0 86 RLMoore 7 61
(WJHaggas) *trckd ldng pair: led 2f out: hung lft over 1f out: rdn out* **4/7**[1]

-050 **2** *1 3/4* **Cafe Americano**[34] [3828] 4-9-3 42 (e) DSweeney 3 56
(DWPArbuthnot) *stdd s: hdwy on outside 3f out: styd on to chse wnr ins fnl f* **33/1**

2 **3** *1 1/4* **Fascination Street (IRE)**[16] [4351] 3-8-9 65 MHenry 1 47
(MAJarvis) *pressed ldr: hrd rdn 2f out: one pce* **7/2**[2]

00-0 **4** *1/2* **Montana**[35] [3810] 4-9-3 44 KMcEvoy 4 51
(JLSpearing) *led tl 2f out: one pce* **10/1**

3006 **5** *3/4* **Poppyline**[3] [4708] 4-8-12 48 (b) SChin 5 44
(WRMuir) *towards rr: n.m.r on bnd over 4f out: hdwy 2f out: hrd rdn: no imp* **9/1**[3]

0-03 **6** *7* **Saccharine**[11] [4484] 3-8-2 44 KGhunowa[(7)] 6 23
(MJPolglase) *chsd ldrs over 3f* **20/1**

0000 **7** *9* **Philly Dee**[61] [2986] 3-8-4 42 (b) RThomas[(5)] 2 —
(NEBerry) *chsd ldrs: n.m.r on bnd over 4f out: wknd 2f out* **66/1**

69.91 secs (-0.19) **Going Correction** +0.05s/f (Good)

**WFA** 3 from 4yo 3lb **7** Ran SP% **114.2**

Speed ratings: **103,100,99,98,97 88,76**CSF £29.18 TOTE £1.40: £1.20, £11.60; EX 21.30.

**Owner** Mr & Mrs G Middlebrook **Bred** G And Mrs Middlebrook **Trained** Newmarket, Suffolk

**FOCUS**

A modest maiden in which Patterdale made hard enough work of beating a bunch who find it difficult to win, and needs to improve to defy his current mark in handicaps.

**NOTEBOOK**

**Patterdale**, who ran well at Royal Ascot as a juvenile, has since joined the Haggas yard - he was with Mark Johnston - and was bidding to build on his promising seasonal reappearance only days ago. He faced a simple task and got on top to win a shade comfortably, albeit from a poor rival. He is high in the weights and will need to improve to defy his mark of 86.

**Cafe Americano** has had his troubles but stayed on through tiring horses to claim second. He did not achieve as much as it may look and will continue to struggle to win.

**Fascination Street(IRE)** is modest and needs a return to handicapping.

**Montana** is another who finds it very hard to win and he raced keenly in the lead.

**Poppyline** was unlucky not to get closer and stayed on late in the day.

## 4802 CHAPEL DOWN ENGLISH WINE APPRENTICE H'CAP 7f 214y

**5:00** (5:00) (F) (0-70,67) 3-Y-O+ **£2,954** (£844; £422) **Stalls** Low

Form RPR

0400 **1** **Juste Pour L'Amour**[10] [4522] 4-9-11 **67** DFox 6 80
(PLGilligan) *mid-div: hdwy and sltly hmpd wl over 1f out: styd on to ld wl ins fnl f* **7/1**[3]

0402 **2** *1 1/2* **Adalar (IRE)**[11] [4479] 4-8-13 **58** SJDonohoe[(3)] 9 68
(PDEvans) *led: rdn and jnd 2f out: hdd and one pce wl ins fnl f* **5/1**[1]

3440 **3** *3/4* **Lucefer (IRE)**[75] [2573] 6-7-11 **44** DeanWilliams[(5)] 4 52
(GCHChung) *hld up and bhd: gd hdwy on outside 3f out: disp ld 2f out tl ins fnl f: one pce* **5/1**[1]

6303 **4** *nk* **Liberty Royal**[13] [4418] 5-9-6 **62** (p) AQuinn 12 70
(PJMakin) *towards rr: hdwy to press ldrs over 2f out: one pce fnl f* **5/1**[1]

0040 **5** *2* **Adobe**[8] [4569] 9-9-9 **65** BSwarbrick 5 68
(WMBrisbourne) *towards rr: hmpd over 3f out: effrt and briefly nt clr run wl over 1f out: nrst fin* **13/2**[2]

6445 **6** *1/2* **Ranny**[10] [4517] 4-8-1 **46** StephanieHollinshead[(3)] 11 48
(DrJDScargill) *mid-div: hrd rdn and hung lft 2f out: styd on same pce* **5/1**[1]

0005 **7** *hd* **Silistra**[11] [4485] 5-7-9 **40** oh1 (p) NataliaGemelova[(3)] 10 41
(MrsLCJewell) *chsd ldrs: no ex fnl 2f* **25/1**

0604 **8** *1 1/2* **Smoothly Does It**[11] [4479] 3-9-1 **63** RThomas 8 61
(MrsAJBowlby) *bhd: rdn and styd on fnl 2f: nvr nr to chal* **10/1**

0022 **9** *1* **Cargo**[11] [4469] 5-8-5 **47** (t) PMakin 3 43
(BAPearce) *chsd ldrs: hmpd 5f out: wknd over 1f out* **10/1**

0044 **10** *3* **Johnny Alljays (IRE)**[13] [4419] 3-7-5 **46** oh12 (p) LauraReynolds[(7)] 13 35
(JSMoore) *chsd ldrs: btn when carried lft wl over 1f out* **25/1**

0-00 **11** *1* **Allodarlin (IRE)**[11] [4499] 3-7-12 **46** oh1 NDeSouza 1 32
(PFICole) *prom over 3f: wknd qckly* **20/1**

6003 **12** *hd* **Captain Cloudy**[13] [4419] 4-8-11 **53** MSavage 7 39
(MMadgwick) *plld hrd: trckd ldr over 5f: sn hrd rdn and wknd* **12/1**

1m 35.11s (0.11) **Going Correction** +0.05s/f (Good)

**WFA** 3 from 4yo+ 6lb **12** Ran SP% **130.8**

Speed ratings: **101,99,98,98,96 95,95,94,93,90 89,89**CSF £45.49 CT £202.37 TOTE £10.50: £2.60, £1.90, £2.00; EX 67.20 Place 6 £152.91, Place 5 £77.76.

**Owner** Ian Marks **Bred** Ian Neville Marks **Trained** Newmarket, Suffolk

**FOCUS**

A modest handicap but fair form for the grade and a nice performance from Juste Pour L'Amour, who appreciated the return to this sort of trip.

**NOTEBOOK**

**Juste Pour L'Amour ◆** has been running over shorter and appreciated this drop in grade and return to farther. He won well despite being hampered and, as he was running off a 9lb lower mark than when last successful, can win again.

**Adalar(IRE)** ran his usual race from the front and will cling on to the lead long enough to win again one day.

**Lucefer(IRE)** did a lot of running to reach a challenging position and it took its toll late on. He should soon return to winning ways.

**Liberty Royal** was another who came from the back and could only plug on at the one pace.

**Adobe** has not won for over a year, but was unlucky not to get closer as, having been hampered, he was momentarily denied a clear run and ended up finishing well. He has a similar race in him in the not-too-distant future.

T/Plt: £233.20 to a £1 stake. Pool: £39,676.90. 124.20 winning tickets. T/Qpdt: £7.80 to a £1 stake. Pool: £3,491.20. 328.95 winning tickets. LM

# [4298]NOTTINGHAM (L-H)

Monday, August 16

**OFFICIAL GOING: Good (good to soft in palces)**

## 4803 RACING UK NURSERY 5f 13y

**2:15** (2:15) (E) 2-Y-O **£3,916** (£1,205; £602; £301) **Stalls** High

Form RPR

4401 **1** **Coleorton Dancer**[7] [4607] 2-8-1 **71** 6ex AMullen[(7)] 9 86+
(KARyan) *in touch: hdwy whn carried lft over 1f out: rdn and qcknd wl to ld ins last: sn clr* **5/4**[1]

2304 **2** *3 1/2* **On The Waterline (IRE)**[19] [4231] 2-8-12 **75** SDrowne 10 74
(PDEvans) *trckd ldrs: swtchd lft and hdwy over 1f out: sn rdn and ev ch ent last: sn drvn and nt qckn* **14/1**

3223 **3** *1/2* **Dane's Castle (IRE)**[7] [4598] 2-8-12 **75** (b[1]) LDettori 8 72
(BJMeehan) *led: rdn along 2f out: hdd ent last: kpt on un der press* **10/1**

3212 **4** *shd* **Bold Minstrel (IRE)**[25] [4041] 2-9-7 **84** FNorton 2 81
(MQuinn) *cl up: effrt 2f out: rdn to ld briefly ent last: sn hdd & wknd* **14/1**

0100 **5** *1 1/4* **Rancho Cucamonga (IRE)**[16] [4325] 2-8-7 **70** KDarley 7 63
(TDBarron) *dwlt and sn pushed along in rr: hdwy and in tch 2f out: rdn and wknd over 1f out* **11/1**

416 **6** *hd* **Pro Tempore**[16] [4348] 2-8-4 **67** PHanagan 11 66+
(MrsJRRamsden) *dwlt and bhd: hdwy whn nt clr run and swtchd lft over 1f out: sn rdn and kpt on ins last: nrst fin* **11/1**

341 **7** *1* **Louphole**[28] [3986] 2-9-5 **82** SSanders 3 70
(PJMakin) *cl up: rdn along over 2f out: sn wknd* **7/1**[3]

040 **8** *3/4* **Tartatartufata**[10] [4514] 2-7-12 **61** oh1 JoannaBadger 1 47
(DShaw) *wnt lft s: racd alone centre: in tch tl wknd fnl 2f* **50/1**

0364 **9** *2* **Chilali (IRE)**[16] [4347] 2-7-12 **61** oh1 DaleGibson 4 40
(ABerry) *chsd ldrs: rdn along and wkng whn n.m.r over 1f out: sn bhd* **50/1**

100 **10** *2 1/2* **Tara Tara (IRE)**[61] [2970] 2-9-3 **80** RWinston 5 50
(JJQuinn) *in tch: pushed along 1/2-way: rdn and hld whn sltly hmpd over 1f out: bhd after* **6/1**[2]

4246 **11** *1 3/4* **Mauro (IRE)**[39] [3659] 2-8-2 **65** JQuinn 6 29
(PMPhelan) *s.i.s: a rr* **25/1**

60.71 secs (-1.09) **Going Correction** -0.20s/f (Firm) **11** Ran SP% **118.1**

Speed ratings: **100,94,93,93,91 91,89,88,85,81 78**CSF £21.18 CT £128.26 TOTE £1.80: £1.10, £3.40, £2.30; EX 21.50.

**Owner** Coleorton Moor Racing **Bred** A Holmes **Trained** Hambleton, N Yorks

**FOCUS**

A fair nursery and a smart winning time for the grade, just over a second faster than the following maiden, which makes the form look solid.

**NOTEBOOK**

**Coleorton Dancer**, turned out quickly under a penalty, ran out a decisive winner. The gelding operation certainly looks to have had a positive effect, and the Handicapper clearly has some catching up to do.

**On The Waterline(IRE)**, dropping back in trip on her handicap debut, could not cope with the well-handicapped winner, but she ran a solid race otherwise.

**Dane's Castle(IRE)**, blinkered for the first time, once again showed good early speed. He looks equally effective over five as six furlongs.

**Bold Minstrel(IRE)**, another making his handicap debut, also ran well, despite the ground being softer than ideal.

**Rancho Cucamonga(IRE)** had run poorly on her last two starts, but her handicap mark had dropped 6lb as a result. This was more encouraging, although six furlongs probably suits her better.

**Pro Tempore** is likely to do better when stepped up in trip.

**Mauro(IRE)** *Official explanation: jockey said filly was slowly into her stride*

## 4804 WRIGHT BROTHERS MAIDEN AUCTION STKS 5f 13y

**2:45** (2:48) (E) 2-Y-O **£3,916** (£1,205; £602; £301) **Stalls** High

Form RPR

0 **1** **Exponential (IRE)**[45] [3469] 2-8-11 (be) DAllan 10 80
(SCWilliams) *cl up: effrt 2f out: rdn to ld over 1f out: kpt on* **8/1**

0 **2** *1* **Starduster**[11] [4474] 2-8-2 SRighton 11 67
(BRMillman) *trckd ldrs: swtchd lft and hdwy 2f out: sn rdn and chsd wnr ins: kpt on* **66/1**

23 **3** *shd* **Breaking Shadow (IRE)**[14] [4388] 2-8-9 PHanagan 7 74
(RAFahey) *chsd ldrs: rdn along and outpcd wl over 2f out: styd on u.p ins last* **3/1**[1]

44 **4** 1/2 **Dispol Isle (IRE)**[44] 3514 2-8-2 JFanning 8 65
(TDBarron) *bmpd s: sn in tch: hdwy on outer 2f out: rdn and edgd lft ins last: no ex last 100 yds* **5/1**[3]

4 **5** 1 3/4 **Wigwam Willie (IRE)**[23] 4149 2-8-11 KDarley 15 68
(MJWallace) *bhd and pushed along after 1f: hdwy and rn green over 2f out: sn rdn and kpt on ins last: nt rch ldrs* **7/2**[2]

0 **6** 3/4 **Ben Casey**[66] 2860 2-8-9 FLynch 2 63
(BSmart) *racd far side tl swtchd rt after 1f: sn in tch: rdn along wl over 1f out and kpt on same pce* **50/1**

**7** nk **Ingleton** 2-8-9 GGibbons 6 62
(BAMcmahon) *towards rr and pushed along 1/2-way: hdwy over 1f out: kpt on ins last* **18/1**

0 **8** 1/2 **Doitforreel (IRE)**[15] 4364 2-8-2 FNorton 1 53
(IAWood) *racd far side: swtchd rt to join stands gp and bhd 1/2-way: styd on wl fnl f: nrst fin* **16/1**

0 **9** 1 1/2 **Blushing Russian (IRE)**[23] 4149 2-8-7 GFaulkner 12 53
(PCHaslam) *cl up: led over 2f out: sn rdn and hdd over 1f out: wknd* **7/1**

6304 **10** nk **Wizzskilad**[56] 3140 2-8-7 61 RHavlin 14 52
(MrsPNDutfield) *midfield: pushed along 2f out: sn rdn and no imp* **33/1**

06 **11** 1 1/4 **Kerny (IRE)**[16] 4347 2-8-11 GHind 5 52
(JJQuinn) *bhd tl sme late hdwy* **66/1**

065 **12** 4 **Sahara Mist (IRE)**[108] 1751 2-8-2 (v[1]) JoannaBadger 3 29
(DShaw) *racd far side tl swtchd rt 1/2-way: sn rdn along and bhd* **100/1**

30 **13** 1/2 **Lovelorn**[11] 4256 2-8-7 TLucas 9 32
(MWEasterby) *chsd ldrs: rdn along over 2f out and sn wknd* **20/1**

4 **14** 3/4 **Heartsonfire (IRE)**[19] 4243 2-8-2 AMcCarthy 13 24
(PWD'Arcy) *led: rdn along 1/2-way: sn hdd & wknd* **8/1**

**15** 3/4 **Season Ticket (GER)** 2-8-2 JQuinn 4 22
(WJHaggas) *racd far side: a rr* **16/1**

61.72 secs (-0.08) **Going Correction** -0.20s/f (Firm) **15** Ran SP% **129.3**
Speed ratings: **92,90,90,89,86 85,84,84,81,81 79,72,72,70,69**CSF £496.47 TOTE £5.80: £1.70, £14.00, £1.40; EX 361.80.
**Owner** The Exponential Partnership **Bred** Rossenarra Stud **Trained** Newmarket, Suffolk

**FOCUS**
A modest maiden, notable for the successful gamble on the winner. It was an advantage to race near the stands'-side rail, but the form is solid enough.

**NOTEBOOK**
**Exponential(IRE)**, backed in from 100-1 on course and from almost 280-1 on the exchanges, landed quite a touch for connections. He stepped up considerably on his debut effort at Beverley and the easier ground probably helped. He is not straightforward - he was equipped with both blinkers and an eyeshield as on his debut - but did all that was asked of him, and clearly this was a case of job done. *Official explanation: trainer said, regarding the improved form shown, gelding benefited from the experience of its first run and had also strengthened up between its two races*
**Starduster** was another to leave her debut form well behind. She hails from a stable with a good record (19% over the past five years) at this track with its juveniles.
**Breaking Shadow(IRE)** appreciated the easier conditions and ran a solid race in defeat. He is now eligible for nurseries and will not mind another furlong.
**Dispol Isle(IRE)**, bumped by the winner at the start, was brought with her challenge up the middle of the track, which was probably not the place to be. She too is now eligible for handicaps.
**Wigwam Willie(IRE)** had shaped with promise on his debut over six, but he found the drop back to the minimum trip all against him. Sure enough he was staying on at the finish, and he should appreciate a return to a longer trip.
**Ben Casey** improved on his debut effort and did not run badly, given that he was poorly drawn and had to be switched to race with the stands'-side group.

## 4805 WEATHERBYS BANK CONDITIONS STKS 5f 13y
3:15 (3:16) (C) 3-Y-O+ £8,694 (£3,297; £1,648; £749) Stalls High

Form RPR

0-30 **1** **Continent**[39] 3674 7-8-11 108 DHolland 7 110+
(DNicholls) *trckd ldrs: hdwy over 2f out: rdn and qcknd to ld ins last: sn clr* **11/4**[1]

3300 **2** 2 **Bishops Court**[18] 4269 10-8-11 105 LDettori 8 103+
(MrsJRRamsden) *trckd leaders: hdwy 2f out: rdn to ld over 1f out: hdd and nt qckn ins last* **7/2**[3]

0230 **3** 1 **Forever Phoenix**[9] 4526 4-8-6 93 KDarley 4 94+
(RMHCowell) *rrd bdly s: sn in tch: hdwy 2f out: sn rdn and kpt on fnl f: nrst fin* **3/1**[2]

3430 **4** 1 **Dragon Flyer (IRE)**[18] 4269 5-8-6 95 FNorton 5 91+
(MQuinn) *led: rdn along and edgd lft wl over 1f out: sn hdd and one pce* **9/2**

4050 **5** 3 **Strensall**[23] 4133 7-8-11 76 PHanagan 3 85?
(REBarr) *cl up: rdn along 2f out: sn drvn and wknd over 1f out* **66/1**

3-20 **6** 5 **First Order**[22] 4165 3-8-9 101 SSanders 1 67+
(SirMarkPrescott) *cl up on outer: pushed along over 2f out: sn rdn and btn wl over 1f out: eased* **9/2**

5006 **7** 3 **Percy Douglas**[5] 4635 4-8-11 40 (t) AnnStokell 2 56?
(MissAStokell) *prom: rdn along 1/2-way: sn wknd* **200/1**

59.77 secs (-2.03) **Going Correction** -0.20s/f (Firm)
**WFA** 3 from 4yo+ 2lb **7** Ran SP% **112.2**
Speed ratings: **108,104,103,101,96 88,84**CSF £12.26 TOTE £3.40: £2.00, £2.20; EX 11.70.
**Owner** Lucayan Stud **Bred** Juddmonte Farms **Trained** Sessay, N Yorks

**FOCUS**
A race for twilight horses and nice confidence booster for Continent. The form is just fair but not that strong for the grade.

**NOTEBOOK**
**Continent** was best in at the weights according to adjusted official ratings, and he ran out a comfortable winner in a race which was not run at a mad gallop. This was his first win since the Abbaye in 2002, and hopefully it will have done his confidence some good.
**Bishops Court** ran well in defeat but just lacked the toe of the winner in the closing stages. He is a difficult horse to place these days but usually runs his race.
**Forever Phoenix** reportedly cracked her head when rearing up and hitting the top of the stalls as the gates opened, so in the circumstances she ran well. She is another who is beginnning to look difficult to place, though.
**Dragon Flyer(IRE)** is a difficult horse to win with and yet another who is tricky to place, despite a slight drop in the handicap recently. *Official explanation: jockey said mare hung left-handed during the latter half of the race*
**First Order** was once again disappointing and has it all to prove now.

## 4806 NOTTINGHAMSHIRE COUNTY CRICKET CLUB H'CAP 1m 1f 213y
3:45 (3:45) (D) (0-80,80) 3-Y-O £5,785 (£1,780; £890; £445) Stalls Low

Form RPR

6104 **1** **Dance To My Tune**[31] 3897 3-8-1 60 DaleGibson 6 64
(MWEasterby) *hld up in rr: hdwy on outer 3f out: rdn over 1f out: styd on to ld ent last: drvn out* **15/2**[3]

0060 **2** 3/4 **In Deep**[31] 3908 3-8-5 64 ow2 RHavlin 4 67
(MrsPNDutfield) *a.p: led 3f out: rdn and hdd 2f out: drvn and ev ch ent last: no ex last 100 yds* **14/1**

2-65 **3** 3/4 **Serramanna**[25] 4049 3-9-0 73 JQuinn 5 75
(HRACecil) *hld up in rr: swtchd rght and hdwy over 2f out: rdn over 1f out: styd on ins last: nrst fin* **12/1**

0250 **4** shd **Spectested (IRE)**[35] 3806 3-7-5 57 oh11 (p) MHalford[(7)] 3 58
(AWCarroll) *hld up in rr: hdwy on inner and n.m.r over 2f out and switchd rt:sn rdn and kpt on ent last: no ex last 100 yds* **33/1**

2211 **5** nk **Dami (USA)**[18] 4264 3-9-4 77 (p) DHolland 11 78
(CEBrittain) *trckd ldrs: n.m.r and lost pl over 4f out: swtchd rt and rdn 2f out: styd on ent last: no ex last 100 yds* **9/2**[2]

3614 **6** hd **Rock Lobster**[12] 4449 3-8-5 64 MFenton 2 64
(JGGiven) *hld up: hdwy 3f out: rdn and edgd lft ent last: sn drvn and one pce* **4/1**[1]

3435 **7** 1 3/4 **Charlie Tango (IRE)**[9] 4536 3-8-8 67 KDarley 9 64
(NTinkler) *hld up: hdwy on outer 1/2-way: led 2f out: sn rdn: hdd ent last and wknd* **4/1**[1]

1306 **8** 1/2 **Doctored**[5] 4648 3-9-4 77 (b) SDrowne 7 73
(PDEvans) *trckd ldrs: effrt and rdn along 3f out: drvn 2f out and sn btn* **8/1**

000 **9** 13 **Live Wire Lucy (USA)**[15] 4368 3-9-7 80 PHanagan 1 51
(CTinkler) *led: rdn along 4f out: hdd 3f out and sn wknd* **50/1**

-005 **10** 3 1/2 **Mountcharge (IRE)**[47] 3426 3-9-1 74 SSanders 10 39
(GAHuffer) *cl up: rdn along 4f out: sn wknd* **15/2**[3]

2m 10.04s (0.54) **Going Correction** -0.20s/f (Firm) **10** Ran SP% **112.1**
Speed ratings: **89,88,87,87,87 87,85,85,75,72**CSF £102.37 CT £1233.00 TOTE £9.10: £2.60, £3.20, £2.90; EX 82.50 Trifecta £298.20 Pool: £840.17. 2.00 winning units..
**Owner** R S Cockerill (Farms) Ltd **Bred** R S Cockerill (farms) Ltd **Trained** Sheriff Hutton, N Yorks

**FOCUS**
A very moderate time for the grade, 1.84 seconds slower than the concluding apprentice handicap, and the form could be unreliable.

**NOTEBOOK**
**Dance To My Tune**, a heavy-ground winner in the spring, appreciated the easy surface and ground out a gutsy victory. This form is nothing special, but she should continue to run well when getting her conditions in the latter part of the season.
**In Deep**, 13lb lower than at the beginning of the season, looks to have dropped to a more realistic mark now. This was her best effort this season.
**Serramanna** ran poorly on easy ground last time but coped well enough with conditions on this occasion. She was staying on well at the finish and this should give connections some hope.
**Spectested(IRE)** ran a blinder from 11lb out of the handicap, but his performance also adds to the question marks regarding the value of the form.
**Dami(USA)**, chasing the hat-trick, has been doing her winning on quicker ground. Having been shuffled back on the turn into the straight, she could find only the one pace afterwards. *Official explanation: jockey said filly lost her action around the bend into the straight*
**Charlie Tango(IRE)** hit the front a quarter mile out, but looked a non-stayer in the ground as he dropped away inside the last.

## 4807 EUROPEAN BREEDERS FUND COLWICK PARK NOVICE STKS 1m 54y
4:15 (4:16) (D) 2-Y-O £4,907 (£1,510; £755; £377) Stalls Centre

Form RPR

31 **1** **Northern Splendour (USA)**[43] 3560 2-9-4 LDettori 1 98+
(SaeedBinSuroor) *mde all: qcknd over 3f out: rdn over 1f out: styd on strly* **7/2**[3]

213 **2** 2 **In The Fan (USA)**[17] 4295 2-9-2 93 SSanders 2 92
(JLDunlop) *trckd ldrs: hdwy over 2f out: rdn to chse wnr over 1f out: drvn ins last and kpt on same pce* **13/8**[1]

1 **3** 1 3/4 **Le Corvee (IRE)**[16] 4315 2-9-4 JDSmith 6 90
(AKing) *trckd ldrs: hdwy over 3f out: rdn over 2f out: kpt on same pce appr last* **2/1**[2]

6 **4** 7 **Hill Fairy**[74] 2617 2-8-7 JFanning 7 64
(TPTate) *wnt rt s: towards rr: hdwy 4f out: sn rdn along and kpt on same pce* **33/1**

051 **5** 1 3/4 **Blaise Hollow (USA)**[8] 4579 2-9-2 SDrowne 5 69
(RCharlton) *chsd wnr: rdn along over 3f out: sn drvn and wknd over 2f out* **15/2**

0 **6** 22 **Mytori**[8] 4567 2-8-7 DarrenWilliams 3 12
(DShaw) *outpcd and bhd fr 1/2-way* **150/1**

**7** 3/4 **Asharon** 2-8-9 J-PGuillambert[(3)] 4 15
(CEBrittain) *s.i.s: a bhd* **33/1**

1m 44.7s (-1.70) **Going Correction** -0.20s/f (Firm) **7** Ran SP% **112.0**
Speed ratings: **100,98,96,89,87 65,64**CSF £9.20 TOTE £4.20: £2.20, £1.30; EX 8.80.
**Owner** Godolphin **Bred** Darley **Trained** Newmarket, Suffolk

**FOCUS**
A decent little event for the track with a much-improved effort from the winner beating horses with previous solid form.

**NOTEBOOK**
**Northern Splendour(USA)** was given a good ride from the front by Dettori, who steadily increased the tempo early in the straight. He was always holding the favourite and gave the impression that he won with a bit up his sleeve. He has shown he is perfectly happy racing with give in the ground, and he looks the type who will appreciate middle distances in time.
**In The Fan(USA)** was expected to appreciate the extra furlong, and he certainly saw the trip out well enough, but the winner always looked to have his measure and he clearly has his limitations.
**Le Corvee(IRE)** may have been a shock winner on his debut, but there was no fluke about the result, and he confirmed the promise of that run, finishing well clear of the rest under his penalty. He may have preferred faster ground, however.
**Hill Fairy** was stepping up in trip, as demanded by her pedigree, and was not disgraced in this tough company.
**Blaise Hollow(USA)** looked to be found out by the easier ground.

## 4808 SCHOOLS OUT FOR SUMMER APPRENTICE H'CAP 1m 1f 213y
4:45 (4:46) (E) (0-75,74) 4-Y-O+ £3,835 (£1,180; £590; £295) Stalls Low

Form RPR

0013 **1** **Artistic Style**[16] 4327 4-9-3 63 MLawson 1 81+
(BEllison) *hld up in tch: hdwy 4f out: chsd ldr over 2f out: rdn to ld over 1f out: kpt on* **3/1**[1]

0060 **2** 1 1/4 **Mcqueen (IRE)**[41] 3614 4-8-1 50 AMullen[(3)] 13 64
(MrsHDalton) *mde most: rdn clr 3f out: drvn and hdd 1f out: kpt on* **9/1**

106 **3** 6 **First Dynasty (USA)**[20] 4209 4-9-11 74 HPoulton[(3)] 4 77
(MissSJWilton) *in tch: hdwy to chse ldrs 4f out: rdn wl over 2f out and kpt on same pce* **14/1**

3001 **4** 5 **Got To Be Cash**[4] 4669 5-8-10 56 6ex PPMathers 8 50
(WMBrisbourne) *hld up towards rr: hdwy over 3f out: sn rdn and kpt on: nt rch ldrs* **11/2**[3]

0300 **5** 3 **Dance World**[41] 3614 4-9-10 70 LTreadwell 5 58
(MissJFeilden) *in tch: hdwy to ldrs 4f out: rdn along 3f out and sn no imp* **9/1**

1324 **6** 1/2 **Pure Mischief (IRE)**[4] 4678 5-9-12 72 RoryMoore 2 59
(CRDore) *nvr nr ldrs* **7/2**[2]

-000 **7** 9 **Nopekan (IRE)**[15] 4363 4-9-13 73 (p) PGallagher 10 43
(MissKMarks) *chsd ldng pair: rdn along over 4f out and sn wknd* **16/1**

6-06 **8** *2 ½* **Legality**[21] [4201] 4-8-1 **50**............................................ MHalford(3) 11 15
(JulianPoulton) *in tch: hung rt 1/2-way: rn v wd home turn and sn bhd* **16/1**

0466 **9** *shd* **Derwent (USA)**[12] [4450] 5-8-11 **64**..................................(b) SShaw(7) 7 29
(JDBethell) *a rr* **14/1**

0000 **10** *3 ½* **Luxor**[27] [4005] 7-8-2 **55** oh1 ow11.............................. DJCavanagh(7) 6 13
(MrsGSRees) *cl up: rdn along 4f out: wknd qckly over 3f out* **20/1**

00-0 **11** *½* **Curragh Gold (IRE)**[28] [3997] 4-7-13 **50**........................ AmyBaker(5) 3 7
(MrsPNDutfield) *a bhd* **33/1**

-000 **12** *10* **Humdinger (IRE)**[155] [1016] 4-7-7 **44** oh4................ DonnaCaldwell(5) 9 —
(DShaw) *a bhd* **50/1**

0640 **13** *3 ½* **Marengo**[102] [1918] 10-7-5 **44** oh19........................................ MNem(7) 12 —
(MJPolglase) *s.i.s: a bhd* **80/1**

2m 8.20s (-1.30) **Going Correction** -0.20s/f (Firm) **13** Ran SP% **118.6**
Speed ratings: **97,96,91,87,84 84,77,75,75,72 71,63,61**CSF £29.41 CT £333.36 TOTE £5.80: £1.90, £3.70, £5.90; EX 64.50 Place 6 £154.72, Place 5 £90.83.
**Owner** Mr & Mrs D A Gamble **Bred** Juddmonte Farms **Trained** Norton, N Yorks

**FOCUS**
An ordinary handicap run in a time 1.84 seconds faster than the earlier three-year-old handicap, but still modest for the grade, but the first two were clearl and may possibly rate higher.

**NOTEBOOK**
**Artistic Style**, proven with cut in the ground, saw out the longer trip with no problem. He is in good form at present and should continue to run well even after being reassessed.
**Mcqueen(IRE)** set a decent pace in the conditions and it is to his credit that he kept on so well to finish a clear second. He looks well handicapped on turf and clearly goes well with a bit of give in the ground, so a little race could come his way in the not-too-distant future.
**First Dynasty(USA)** ran a bit better under top weight, but he was never really able to land a blow. He might need some more leniency from the Handicapper.
**Got To Be Cash** could never make up the ground from the rear on this occasion. Life is likely to be tough off her new mark but she is in good form.
**Dance World** has dropped 10lb during the course of this season, but she continues to struggle.
**Pure Mischief(IRE)** is generally consistent and the ground had come in her favour, but she never got close to the leaders on this occasion.
**Legality** *Official explanation: jockey said filly hung right-handed turning into the straight*
T/Jkpt: Not won. T/Plt: £260.80 to a £1 stake. Pool: £42,836.75. 119.90 winning tickets. T/Qpdt: £88.20 to a £1 stake. Pool: £2,826.30. 23.70 winning tickets. JR

## 4611 WINDSOR (R-H)
### Monday, August 16

**OFFICIAL GOING: Good (good to firm in places)**

## 4809 EUROPEAN BREEDERS FUND MAIDEN STKS 6f
**5:40** (5:40) (D) 2-Y-O **£5,239** (£1,612; £806; £403) **Stalls** High

Form RPR

3 **1** **Sant Jordi**[33] [3847] 2-9-0 .............................................. JFortune 12 86
(BJMeehan) *mde virtually all: rdn over 1f out: hld on wl whn strly chal thrght fnl f* **3/1**[1]

**2** *hd* **Something (IRE)** 2-9-0 .............................................. GCarter 17 85
(TGMills) *chsd ldrs: drvn to chal 1f out: pressed wnr ins last tl no ex last strides* **3/1**[1]

6 **3** *3* **Fasylitator (IRE)**[13] [4420] 2-9-0 .............................................. DHolland 1 76
(JAOsborne) *racd far side: and led two other runners that side: upsides wnr stands side fr 2f out: outpcd ins last* **12/1**[2]

6 **4** *1* **Brooklime (IRE)**[7] [4599] 2-9-0 .............................................. SWKelly 2 73
(JAOsborne) *one of three racing far side: pressed ldr and unpsides w stands side to 2f out: wknd ins fnl f* **50/1**

02 **5** *½* **Cool Panic (IRE)**[21] [4193] 2-9-0 .............................................. JPMurtagh 7 72
(MLWBell) *chsd wnr: rdn 2f out: wknd ins fnl f* **3/1**[1]

**6** *6* **Squaw Dance** 2-8-9 .............................................. MHills 11 49
(WJHaggas) *bhd: hdwy fr 2f out: kpt on fr over 1f out: nt pce to trble ldrs* **12/1**[2]

**7** *3 ½* **Benedict** 2-9-0 .............................................. RWinston 3 43
(SirMichaelStoute) *s.i.s: bhd: hdwy 2f out: styd on fnl f: nt trble ldrs* **12/1**[2]

0 **8** *1 ¾* **Killena Boy (IRE)**[7] [4599] 2-9-0 .............................................. MartinDwyer 5 38
(WJarvis) *one of three to r far side: wknd fr 2f out* **20/1**[3]

0 **9** *nk* **Young Boldric**[35] [3808] 2-8-11 .............................................. LPKeniry(3) 8 37
(KBell) *chsd ldrs tl wknd fr 2f out* **66/1**

**10** *nk* **Perez (IRE)** 2-9-0 .............................................. RHughes 4 36
(RHannon) *s.i.s: sn rcvrd in mid-div: styd on same pce fnl 2f* **12/1**[2]

**11** *nk* **Red Marteeney** 2-9-0 .............................................. DaneO'Neill 13 35
(DRCElsworth) *s.i.s: outpcd tl sme hdwy fnl 2f* **25/1**

04 **12** *3* **Heart Of Eternity (IRE)**[101] [1936] 2-8-9 .............................................. VVenkaya 6 21
(JRBoyle) *chsd ldrs 4f* **50/1**

00 **13** *2 ½* **Lighthorne Lad**[63] [2947] 2-8-7 .............................................. JJeffrey(7) 14 19
(JRJenkins) *in tch 4f* **66/1**

00 **14** *3 ½* **Worth Abbey**[42] [3588] 2-9-0 .............................................. PDobbs 9 —
(RHannon) *outpcd fr 1/2-way* **40/1**

P **15** *5* **Cavaradossi**[42] [3588] 2-8-11 .............................................. JFMcDonald(3) 16 —
(BJMeehan) *sn outpcd* **50/1**

**16** *5* **Touch Of Spice** 2-9-0 .............................................. TEDurcan 15 —
(JRJenkins) *n.d* **50/1**

60 **17** *9* **Just Bonnie**[21] [4191] 2-9-0 .............................................. ANicholls 10 —
(JMBradley) *spd over 3f* **50/1**

1m 13.0s (-0.87) **Going Correction** -0.25s/f (Firm) **17** Ran SP% **129.6**
Speed ratings: **95,94,90,89,88 80,76,73,73,72 72,68,65,60,53 47,35**CSF £10.55 TOTE £4.70: £2.00, £1.60, £3.10; EX 21.10.
**Owner** J S Threadwell **Bred** J A Porteous **Trained** Upper Lambourn, Berks

**FOCUS**
An ordinary maiden, which appeared to concern just three in the market. The field split into two groups, with two of the trio to race up the far side finishing third and fourth, so any draw advantage was inconclusive, and the form is hard to gauge.

**NOTEBOOK**
**Sant Jordi** was withdrawn on his latest appearance after bursting out of the stalls. Smartly away to grab the advantage of the stands' fence, he was involved in a lively tussle with one of his co-favourites and showed a good attitude to keep his head in front.
**Something(IRE)** is a half-brother to eight winners including July Cup victor Lake Coniston, himself sire of a couple of also-rans in this race. Well backed in the morning, he just failed to make a winning debut, only conceding defeat to a more experienced opponent close home. He holds a Middle Park entry and should go one better before long.
**Fasylitator(IRE)** stepped up on his debut effort. He was one of just three to race on the far side, and this was a decent effort considering he had so little to race with, although there seemed no disadvantage to racing up that flank.
**Brooklime(IRE)**, improving from his debut on Polytrack a week earlier, was always chasing his stablemate up the far side.
**Cool Panic(IRE)** was right there with a quarter of a mile to run, but was left behind by the first two on his side in the final furlong. He seemed not to fully see out the trip on this ground.
**Squaw Dance** is half-sister to two winners out of a mare who was a Listed winner at six furlongs. She kept on from out of the pack but was some way behind the principals on her side.
**Benedict** is a half-brother to Right Approach, who dead-heated for the Group One Dubai Duty Free after leaving the Stoute yard. He was drawn three, but his rider opted to cross over and race with the near-side bunch. Keeping on in his own time, he can improve on this.

## 4810 FIREWORKS EXTRAVAGANZA SATURDAY 6TH NOVEMBER H'CAP 5f 10y
**6:10** (6:10) (D) (0-85,83) 3-Y-O **£5,508** (£1,695; £847; £423) **Stalls** High

Form RPR

4513 **1** **Wunderbra (IRE)**[8] [4585] 3-7-7 **60**..................................(t) HayleyTurner(5) 3 69
(MLWBell) *trckd ldrs: slt ld ins fnl 2f: pushed out and r.o strly fnl f: hld on wl* **11/2**[3]

0505 **2** *hd* **Skyharbor**[17] [4289] 3-8-11 **73**.............................................. MartinDwyer 10 81
(AMBalding) *chsd ldrs: outpcd after 2f: hrd drvn 2f out: str run over 1f out to chse wnr last half f: no imp nr fin* **4/1**[1]

-050 **3** *1 ¼* **Marysienka**[7] [4608] 3-8-6 **68**.............................................. JEdmunds 1 72
(JBalding) *bhd: hdwy on outside whn n.m.r ins fnl 2f: swtchd rt 1f out: kpt on ins last but nt pce of ldrs* **20/1**

1200 **4** *nk* **Snow Wolf**[33] [3845] 3-9-3 **79**.............................................. RLMoore 2 82
(JMBradley) *sn pressing ldrs: ev ch fr 2f out tl wknd last half f* **12/1**

0440 **5** *1* **Incise**[17] [4289] 3-9-5 **81**.............................................. JFortune 5 80+
(BJMeehan) *bhd: hdwy and nt clr run ins fnl 2f: swtchd rt 1f out: kpt on u.p ins last but nt rch ldrs* **6/1**

3050 **6** *1 ¼* **Borzoi Maestro**[3] [4717] 3-8-10 **75**.............................................. LPKeniry(3) 7 70
(JLSpearing) *chsd ldrs: rdn to chal ins fnl 2f: wknd last half f* **16/1**

00-4 **7** *1* **King Egbert (FR)**[8] [4585] 3-7-5 **60**.............................................. TDean(7) 9 51+
(AWCarroll) *in tch: wkng whn hmpd and swtchd lft jst ins fnl f* **10/1**

0602 **8** *nk* **After The Show**[11] [4489] 3-8-7 **69**.............................................. TEDurcan 8 59+
(JRJenkins) *slt ld tl narrowly hdd over 2f out: wkng whn hmpd jst ins fnl f* **11/2**[3]

3100 **9** *2* **Silver Prelude**[17] [4289] 3-9-7 **83**.............................................. DHolland 4 66
(DKIvory) *w ldrs: led over 2f out: ins fnl quarter m: wknd appr fnl f* **9/2**[2]

60.14 secs (-1.06) **Going Correction** -0.25s/f (Firm) **9** Ran SP% **110.7**
Speed ratings: **98,97,95,95,93 91,90,89,86**CSF £25.95 CT £387.55 TOTE £4.20: £1.40, £1.80, £4.30; EX 23.90.
**Owner** Fitzroy Thoroughbreds **Bred** J F Tuthill And Mrs A Whitehead **Trained** Newmarket, Suffolk

**FOCUS**
Quite a well-contested handicap but ordinary form for the grade, and there were plenty in with a chance in the latter stages.

**NOTEBOOK**
**Wunderbra(IRE)** travelled sweetly and managed to avoid the traffic problems in a closely-bunched field. She likes it here and the drop to five furlongs was no problem.
**Skyharbor** has left David Nicholls since his last run and has been dropped a further 2lb. After coming under pressure by halfway, he stayed on well against the near rail. Five furlongs is a bit sharp for him on this evidence.
**Marysienka**, from a 5lb lower mark, ran her best race of the campaign so far but remains a maiden. This looks the way to ride her.
**Snow Wolf**, who raced on the outer, ran well on this drop back to five furlongs but could not quite get his head in front.
**Incise** found herself in rear after taking time to find her stride. A gap was slow to open up for her, but that cannot really be used as an excuse. She is certainly well handicapped at present.
**Borzoi Maestro**, as at Newbury over the weekend, was without the cheekpieces again.
**Silver Prelude** *Official explanation: jockey said colt was unsuited by the dead ground*

## 4811 FINSPREADS PREMIER CLAIMING STKS 6f
**6:40** (6:41) (D) 3-Y-O+ **£5,671** (£1,745; £872; £436) **Stalls** High

Form RPR

5420 **1** **Onlytime Will Tell**[16] [4349] 6-9-5 91.............................................. RWinston 8 79+
(DNicholls) *s.i.s: bhd: gd hdwy over 2f out: led over 1f out: shkn up ins last: comf* **9/4**[1]

0550 **2** *½* **Loyal Tycoon (IRE)**[17] [4291] 6-9-3 87.............................................. ANicholls 9 76+
(DNicholls) *mid-div: nt clr run and swtchd lft 2f out: hdwy over 1f out: chsd wnr ins last: kpt on but a hld* **7/2**[3]

0430 **3** *3* **Rocket (IRE)**[95] [2061] 3-8-4 57.............................................. RSmith 5 57
(RHannon) *bhd: rdn 3f out: hdwy fr 2f out: styd on to take 3rd ins fnl f but nvr gng pce to rch ldrs* **25/1**

4001 **4** *1 ¼* **Atlantic Viking (IRE)**[6] [4617] 9-9-2 91.............................................. JPMurtagh 7 62
(DNicholls) *chsd ldrs: rdn over 2f out: wknd fnl f* **11/4**[2]

5100 **5** *1 ¼* **Willheconquertoo**[7] [4614] 4-9-3 69..................................(t) JFEgan 4 59
(AndrewReid) *sn led: rdn over 2f out: hdd over 1f out: wknd ins last* **8/1**

0003 **6** *1* **Dexileos (IRE)**[28] [3991] 5-8-6 40..................................(t) SHitchcott(3) 2 48?
(ADWPinder) *bhd: hdwy on outside 3f out: nvr rchd ldrs and wknd appr fnl f* **66/1**

00 **7** *5* **Appolonious**[136] [1226] 3-8-6 .............................................. DaneO'Neill 3 33
(DRCElsworth) *s.i.s: a bhd* **33/1**

0036 **8** *1 ½* **Piccleyes**[8] [4585] 3-8-6 ..................................(b) RLMoore 10 29
(RHannon) *chsd ldrs tl wknd qukcly 2f out* **9/1**

0100 **9** *15* **Packin Em In**[98] [1986] 6-8-7 45..................................(b) VVenkaya 1 —
(JRBoyle) *s.i.s: hung lft 3f out: a in rr* **50/1**

0000 **10** *5* **Catchthebatch**[14] [4400] 8-8-7 39..................................(b) SCarson 6 —
(EAWheeler) *w ldr early: styd prom tl wknd rapidly ins fnl 3f* **66/1**

1m 12.51s (-1.36) **Going Correction** -0.25s/f (Firm)
**WFA** 3 from 4yo+ 3lb **10** Ran SP% **112.5**
Speed ratings: **99,98,94,92,91 89,83,81,61,54**CSF £9.53 TOTE £3.20: £1.50, £1.50, £4.90; EX 13.00.Loyal Tycoon was claimed by Anthony Parsons for £26,000. Rocket was claimed by H. J. Manners for £6,000.
**Owner** J Hair & D Faulkner **Bred** L C And Mrs A E Sigsworth **Trained** Sessay, N Yorks
■ David Nicholls sent out the first three in the market and they finished 1st, 2nd and 4th.

**FOCUS**
A modest time for the class of race, less than half a second faster than the two-year-old maiden, and the form has a mixed look.

**NOTEBOOK**
**Onlytime Will Tell**, dropped into a claimer, gained his first win since landing a valuable Epsom handicap on Derby day 2002. He was awkward from the stalls and had plenty on at halfway, but came through to win cosily in the end. He liked the easier underfoot conditions.
**Loyal Tycoon(IRE)**, like Onlytime Will Tell, is a former winner of the six-furlong handicap at Epsom on Derby Day. Down in grade, he was always being held by his stablemate who had taken first run, and would have preferred quicker ground. He was claimed after the race.
**Rocket(IRE)** put in an improved effort on this first run for three months, staying on nicely to foil a Nicholls clean sweep. He was claimed afterwards by John Manners.
**Atlantic Viking(IRE)** was best in on official adjusted ratings, but he found the six furlongs too far on what was easy ground. *Official explanation: jockey said gelding lost its action in the last half furlong*
**Willheconquertoo** showed his usual bright pace but had no answers once headed. He had plenty on at the weights.

## 4812 ROYAL WINDSOR FILLIES' RATED STKS (H'CAP) 1m 67y
7:10 (7:10) (C) (0-90,87) 3-Y-O+ £8,481 (£3,217; £1,608; £731) Stalls High

Form RPR
3120 **1** **Munaawashat (IRE)**[22] 4170 3-8-5 **71** .................... FNorton 4 77
(KRBurke) *in tch: hdwy over 2f out: hrd drvn to chal 1f out: slt ld fnl 100yds: jst hld on* **7/1**
1-02 **2** *shd* **Ultimata**[56] 3159 4-9-6 **80** .................... OUrbina 2 86
(JRFanshawe) *chsd ldrs: chal fr over 2f out tl slt ld wl over 1f out: hdd fnl 100yds: kpt on wl: jst failed* **3/1**[1]
2631 **3** *½* **Desert Cristal (IRE)**[23] 4125 3-8-12 **78** .................... MartinDwyer 5 83+
(JRBoyle) *rn wd and led bnd 6f out:v wd bnd 5f out but hld ld:hdd over 2f out: rallied gamely u.p fnl f: fin wl* **4/1**[2]
3003 **4** *1 ¾* **Surf The Net**[25] 4068 3-9-7 **87** .................... RHughes 6 88
(RHannon) *led tl hdd after 2f: styd chsng ldr tl slt ld over 2f out: hdd wl over 1f out: wknd last half f* **10/1**
5612 **5** *¾* **Summer Shades**[9] 4551 6-8-7 **72** .................... BSwarbrick(5) 3 71
(WMBrisbourne) *bhd: hdwy to chse ldrs over 2f out: hung rt and one pce u.p over 1f out* **3/1**[1]
5164 **6** *2 ½* **Madamoiselle Jones**[39] 3660 4-8-7 **67** .................... SDrowne 1 60
(HSHowe) *bhd: hdwy fr 4f out: chal over 2f out: wknd over 1f out* **5/1**[3]

1m 46.19s (0.59) **Going Correction** +0.15s/f (Good)
**WFA** 3 from 4yo+ 6lb **6** Ran SP% **108.3**
Speed ratings: **103,102,102,100,99 97**CSF £26.06 TOTE £9.00: £2.90, £1.70; EX 19.30.
**Owner** John A Duffy **Bred** Shadwell Estate Company Limited **Trained** Middleham Moor, N Yorks

**FOCUS**
Something of a muddling pace to this fairly decent fillies' handicap, resulting in a good finish but the form is nothing out of the ordinary.

**NOTEBOOK**
**Munaawashat(IRE)** was having her second run since leaving the Mark Johnston yard. A keen filly, she was saddled in the stable yard and brought into the paddock late, and settled better in the race. After missing the kick the plan to adopt her usual front-running tactics went out of the window, but she nosed ahead inside the last and just got there. She was suited by this drop back in trip. *Official explanation: trainer said, regarding the improved form shown, filly was better suited by today's shorter trip*
**Ultimata** liked the easy ground and went down fighting. This was only her fourth career run and there could be further improvement in her.
**Desert Cristal(IRE)**, making her handicap debut, gave her rider steering problems by running very wide on the bend into the straight, but retained the lead and managed to cross over and claim the stands' rail. Once back on an even keel, she stuck on well and, after being headed, she rallied in good style and might have got back up with a little further to run. She can be counted as unlucky.
**Surf The Net**, who has been dropped 5lb, ran her best race since her seasonal debut back in June.
**Summer Shades** found the ground slower than ideal and was racing off a career-high mark.
**Madamoiselle Jones** adopted different tactics in this small field, and the ground had gone against her too.

## 4813 VCCP/O2 MAIDEN STKS 1m 67y
7:40 (7:41) (D) 3-Y-O £4,199 (£1,292; £646; £323) Stalls High

Form RPR
43-5 **1** **Day To Remember**[126] 1352 3-9-0 80 .................... DHolland 8 83+
(EFVaughan) *mid-div: pushed along and gd hdwy fr 3f out: chsd ldr over 2f out: led jst ins fnl quarter m: sn clr: v easily* **6/4**[1]
**2** *3 ½* **Simonda** 3-8-9 .................... RLMoore 10 70
(MrsAJPerrett) *bhd: hdwy over 2f out: rn green: edgd lft and r.o fr over 1f out: chsd wnr ins last: kpt on but no ch* **13/2**[3]
0 **3** *5* **Dream Alive**[11] 4492 3-9-0 ....................(t) FNorton 6 64
(MBlanshard) *chsd ldrs: rdn over 2f out: styd on same pce to hold 3rd fnl f* **16/1**
0240 **4** *2* **Hunter's Valley**[51] 3320 3-8-9 66 .................... PDobbs 7 54
(RHannon) *chsd ldr to 5f out and again 3rd out tl over 2f out: sn rdn: wknd over 1f out* **9/1**
00 **5** *2* **Danze Romance**[15] 4369 3-8-9 .................... SDrowne 2 49
(JLDunlop) *bhd: stl plenty to do over 2f out: kpt on* **14/1**
-365 **6** *1* **Moors Myth**[45] 3487 3-9-0 76 .................... RHughes 4 52
(BWHills) *led tl hdd jst ins fnl 2f: sn wknd* **5/2**[2]
0 **7** *shd* **Count Boris**[93] 2114 3-9-0 .................... SCarson 1 52
(GBBalding) *bhd: rn wd bnd over 3f out: stl plenty to do 2f out: r.o wl: fnl f but nvr a danger* **33/1**
0- **8** *1 ¼* **Diequest (USA)**[385] 3646 3-9-0 .................... JFEgan 5 49
(JamiePoulton) *mid-div: hdwy to chse ldrs 3f out: wknd qckly 2f out* **20/1**
00 **9** *10* **Explicit (IRE)**[31] 3922 3-9-0 .................... MartinDwyer 9 26
(GCBravery) *chsd ldrs: wnt 2nd 5f out to 4f out: sn rdn: wknd 3f out* **25/1**

1m 46.38s (0.78) **Going Correction** +0.15s/f (Good) **9** Ran SP% **116.0**
Speed ratings: **102,98,93,91,89 88,88,87,77**CSF £11.69 TOTE £2.20: £1.20, £1.90, £2.70; EX 8.80.
**Owner** Racing For Gold **Bred** Stratford Place Stud **Trained** Newmarket, Suffolk
■ She's A Fox (20/1) was withdrawn after refusing to enter the stalls.

**FOCUS**
A weak maiden with no strength in depth, although the winner could be better than the bare form.

**NOTEBOOK**
**Day To Remember**, off the track since his seasonal return in April, ultimately ran out a facile winner, although in truth he had little to beat. It will be handicaps for him now from a mark in the 80s.
**Simonda** is half-sister to two winners out of a dam who won at a mile. This was a promising debut and she will come on for the experience, although she was flattered by the margin of defeat.
**Dream Alive** held the same position virtually throughout. He had been a 100/1 chance on his recent debut and in all probability is a pretty ordinary performer.
**Hunter's Valley**, who has not progressed and whose handicap mark has plunged in consequence, has had plenty of chances.
**Danze Romance**, having her third run, raced in the last pair until staying on past beaten rivals late in the day.
**Moors Myth** made the running, initially at a fast pace, before slowing things up. Once headed by the winner he offered very little resistance, and this run did not tell us whether he stayed the mile.

## 4814 SANDRA COLTMAN SURPRISE 60TH BIRTHDAY CLASSIFIED STKS 1m 2f 7y
8:10 (8:10) (E) 3-Y-O+ £3,474 (£1,069; £534; £267) Stalls Low

Form RPR
2020 **1** **El Chaparral (IRE)**[7] 4615 4-9-1 68 .................... DaneO'Neill 6 80
(DKIvory) *bhd: hdwy over 3f out: chsng ldrwhn carried lft to centre crse over 2f out: led 1f out: hrd rdn and hld on all out* **14/1**
003 **2** *nk* **Dream Magic**[2] 4737 6-9-4 73 .................... MartinDwyer 9 82
(MJRyan) *hld up in tch: hdwy 3f out: led 2f out: hdd 1f out: hrd drvn ins last: no ex nr fin* **4/1**[3]
6010 **3** *3 ½* **Ridge Boy (IRE)**[33] 3844 3-8-7 70 .................... PDobbs 2 72
(RHannon) *chsd ldrs: chal over 2f out and edgd lft u.p: edgd rt and one pce u.p 1f out* **12/1**
3113 **4** *4* **Dickie Deadeye**[11] 4486 7-8-10 70 .................... RThomas(5) 7 65
(GBBalding) *chsd ldrs: drvn to chal over 2f out: wknd fnl f* **11/4**[1]
660- **5** *2* **Serbelloni**[327] 5150 4-9-1 70 .................... DHolland 8 61
(PWHarris) *bhd: hdwy over 2f out: styd on same pce u.p fr over 1f out* **16/1**
3156 **6** *1 ½* **Ragged Jack (IRE)**[10] 4515 3-8-7 70 .................... SWKelly 5 58
(GAButler) *hld up in rr: drvn along 4f out and effrt: wknd 2f out* **25/1**
2002 **7** *¾* **Brave Dane (IRE)**[12] 4437 6-9-5 74 .................... JFortune 10 61
(AWCarroll) *s.i.s: bhd: rdn and effrt fr 3f out: nvr nr ldrs and wknd fnl 2f* **5/1**
0306 **8** *1 ¾* **Hail The Chief**[16] 4327 7-9-4 73 .................... RSmith 3 56
(JAkehurst) *in tch: rdn over 3f out: sn btn* **12/1**
0-20 **9** *nk* **Zariano**[9] 4549 4-9-0 72 .................... LPKeniry(3) 4 55
(RMStronge) *led after 2f: hdd over 3f out: wknd over 2f out* **20/1**
0213 **10** *1* **Du Pre**[15] 4368 3-8-8 74 .................... SDrowne 1 52
(MrsAJPerrett) *led 2f: styd chsng ldr tl led again over 3f out: hdd 2f out: wknd qckly over 1f out* **7/2**[2]

2m 8.74s (0.44) **Going Correction** +0.15s/f (Good)
**WFA** 3 from 4yo+ 8lb **10** Ran SP% **122.1**
Speed ratings: **104,103,100,97,96 94,94,92,92,91**CSF £72.68 TOTE £21.70: £3.40, £2.00, £3.00; EX 105.70 Place 6 £59.47, Place 5 £38.65.
**Owner** K T Ivory **Bred** Mrs E Roberts **Trained** Radlett, Herts

**FOCUS**
A typically tight classified event on official figures, run at a moderate pace, but the form looks sound

**NOTEBOOK**
**El Chaparral(IRE)**, 2lb badly in with the rest of the field on official adjusted ratings, would not have run had the rain not arrived in time. Settling better than of late, he appreciated the return to ten furlongs and just got the better of a duel with a rival racing some way apart from him.
**Dream Magic** had run well from the front at Goodwood over the weekend but adopted different tactics. Drifting over to the stands' rail under pressure, he went down fighting.
**Ridge Boy(IRE)**, who likes it here, stayed the ten furlongs and the easier ground was not a problem either.
**Dickie Deadeye** is not at his best over ten furlongs, but the reality is that the Handicapper is in charge now.
**Serbelloni**, having his first run for nearly 11 months, not for the first time shaped as if the step up to a mile and a half will bring about improvement.
**Brave Dane(IRE)** was unsuited by the lack of a true gallop.
**Du Pre** was well backed, but having got to the front she dropped away tamely. *Official explanation: trainer had no explanation for the poor form shown*
T/Plt: £113.80 to a £1 stake. Pool: £41,199.80. 264.10 winning tickets. T/Qpdt: £17.40 to a £1 stake. Pool: £4,225.30. 179.30 winning tickets. ST

# 4649 YARMOUTH (L-H)
Monday, August 16

**OFFICIAL GOING: Good to firm (good in places)**
Race times suggested the ground was a bit easier than the official description, possibly just on the soft side of Good.
Wind: slt across Weather: sunny, becoming cloudy

## 4815 BETFRED "THE BONUS KING" EBF MAIDEN STKS 5f 43y
5:25 (5:25) (D) 2-Y-O £3,682 (£1,133; £566; £283) Stalls High

Form RPR
3 **1** **Regina**[17] 4298 2-8-9 .................... KFallon 4 85+
(SirMichaelStoute) *chsd ldr: led ins fnl f: pushed out: readily* **11/10**[1]
2 **2** *1 ¼* **Honey Ryder**[24] 4099 2-8-9 .................... TPQueally 2 81+
(DRLoder) *led: rdn and rather ungainly over 1f out: hdd ins fnl f: wl hld after* **7/4**[2]
**3** *7* **Emerald Lodge** 2-9-0 .................... EAhern 3 62
(JNoseda) *chsd ldrs: rdn over 2f out: rn green: btn wl over 1f out* **16/1**
034 **4** *1 ¾* **Stephanie's Mind**[68] 2786 2-8-9 78 .................... RMullen 5 50
(GAHuffer) *keen early: hld up last: rdn over 2f out: sn btn* **7/2**[3]
**5** *1 ½* **William James** 2-9-0 .................... ACulhane 1 50
(MJWallace) *chsd ldrs: rdn over 2f out: sn wknd* **80/1**

64.25 secs (1.55) **Going Correction** +0.20s/f (Good) **5** Ran SP% **113.3**
Speed ratings: **95,93,81,79,76**CSF £3.46 TOTE £2.20: £1.10, £1.50; EX 3.40.
**Owner** Cheveley Park Stud **Bred** Cheveley Park Stud Ltd **Trained** Newmarket, Suffolk

**FOCUS**
A race run at only a fair pace, but the two market principals still pulled miles clear of the others, suggesting they are fairly useful.

**NOTEBOOK**
**Regina** took quite a hold, but was content to get a lead from the runner-up before quickening up nicely when asked. This trip looks plenty sharp enough for her now and better should follow when put up a furlong.
**Honey Ryder** took the field a long at only an ordinary pace and, though she pulled well clear of the others, found the winner too classy. The furlong-shorter trip compared with her debut was probably not ideal.
**Emerald Lodge**, a 90,000gns yearling, found the more experienced pair far too good in the second half of the contest. There is plenty of speed in his pedigree and he should be capable of much better.
**Stephanie's Mind**, well backed, was held up this time and the tactic did not suit as she pulled hard early and then found little off the bridle. She is much more exposed than her rivals and would surely be better off in nurseries.
**William James**, a 50,000gns half-brother to Sister Bluebird, showed little on this debut but should come on for it and will be suited by further.

## 4816 BETFRED.COM IN-RUNNING CLAIMING STKS 6f 3y
5:55 (5:55) (F) 2-Y-O £2,926 (£836; £418) Stalls High

Form RPR
6205 **1** **Megell (IRE)**[11] 4482 2-8-7 67 .................... TPQueally 6 56
(MGQuinlan) *stdd s and plld hrd: sn cl up: led 1f out: drvn and kpt on: all out* **10/3**[2]
2435 **2** *¾* **Campeon (IRE)**[10] 4508 2-9-2 74 .................... KFallon 1 63
(MJWallace) *slt ld: rdn over 2f out: hdd 1f out: hrd rdn and no imp after* **7/4**[1]
1365 **3** *shd* **Goldhill Prince**[17] 4304 2-8-3 65 ....................(p) CHaddon(7) 5 56
(WGMTurner) *w ldr: rdn and ev ch ins fnl f: one pced* **9/1**
0141 **4** *¾* **Tipsy Lillie**[21] 4200 2-8-8 59 .................... ACulhane 4 52
(JulianPoulton) *trckd ldrs: rdn over 2f out: one pce after: a hld fnl f* **5/1**[3]
0000 **5** *hd* **Fantasy Defender (IRE)**[12] 4446 2-8-11 .................... EAhern 2 55
(JJQuinn) *stdd s: rdn and outpcd 2f out: plugged on ins fnl f* **12/1**
030 **6** *½* **Alzarma**[34] 3818 2-8-5 63 .................... DTudhope(7) 3 54
(ABailey) *cl up: rdn and effrt 2f out: ev ch over 1f out: no ex* **11/2**

5615 **7** 5 **Sapphire Princess**[6] 4620 2-8-3 54 ........ PDoe 7 30
(IAWood) *bhd: rdn over 3f out: btn 2f out* **20/1**

1m 16.4s (2.80) **Going Correction** +0.20s/f (Good) **7** Ran **SP% 113.9**
Speed ratings: **89,88,87,86,86 85,79**CSF £9.53 TOTE £4.40: £2.00, £1.50; EX 11.50.
**Owner** Mrs J Quinlan **Bred** Francis Quinn And Tom Ryan **Trained** Newmarket, Suffolk

**FOCUS**
A poor claimer run at a modest pace and five in a line across the track over a furlong from home. The form is moderate but solid enough for the grade.

**NOTEBOOK**
**Megell(IRE)**, who had put up her best previous effort under identical conditions, was running over this trip for the first time since and appreciated the drop in class. She had to fight hard to score and this looks to be her level now.
**Campeon(IRE)** did not appear to appreciate being restrained in front and, though he hung in there until close to the line, he lacked toe where it mattered. He might have been better off being allowed to stride on, but has become very frustrating.
**Goldhill Prince** raced away from the others closer to the stands' rail and kept battling right to the line. This was a better effort, but the form is modest and he will remain hard to place.
**Tipsy Lillie** was very well backed, but could never land a blow and this effort shows just what poor races her two recent selling victories were.
**Fantasy Defender(IRE)** has shown nothing to date and even this drop in class did not bring about any improvement.
**Alzarma** raced furthest from the stands' rail, but again suggested he does not quite see out this trip.

## 4817 BETFRED.COM NOW ON-LINE H'CAP — 7f 3y
**6:25** (6:25) (E) (0-75,73) 3-Y-O — **£3,877** (£1,193; £596; £298) **Stalls** High

Form — RPR

0504 **1** **Glencalvie (IRE)**[16] 4338 3-8-7 **59** ........ (v[1]) EAhern 4 79+
(JNoseda) *handy: led 1/2-way: rdn clr 2f out: eased cl home: unchal* **11/2**[1]

0066 **2** 4 **Morag**[25] 4066 3-8-9 **61** ........ SSanders 3 62
(IAWood) *trckd ldrs: effrt to chse wnr fnl 2f: drvn and nvr able to chal* **6/1**[2]

4040 **3** 1 1/2 **Molinia**[16] 4338 3-7-12 **53** ........ (t) NMackay[(3)] 9 50
(RMBeckett) *s.i.s: rdn and hdwy to go 3rd over 1f out: no further prog* **11/2**[1]

6440 **4** 1/2 **Alchera**[40] 3628 3-8-10 **62** ........ RMullen 12 58
(RFJohnsonHoughton) *racd stands' pair: bhd and hanging lft: drvn and kpt on over 1f out: nvr able to chal* **14/1**

0640 **5** 1 1/2 **Violet Avenue**[23] 4127 3-8-5 **57** ........ JBramhill 11 49
(JGGiven) *hld up in rr: drvn and sme hdwy over 2f out: one pced and sn no imp* **20/1**

-304 **6** 3/4 **Soviet Sceptre (IRE)**[11] 4491 3-9-2 **68** ........ (t) ACulhane 2 58
(MissDMountain) *bhd: rdn 1/2-way: mod late prog: nvr nr ldrs* **12/1**

0005 **7** 1/2 **Get To The Point**[50] 3344 3-8-5 **60** ........ (b) BReilly[(3)] 7 48
(MissJFeilden) *chsd ldrs: drvn along fnl 2f: wknd ins fnl f* **16/1**

0-10 **8** 2 1/2 **Listen To Reason (IRE)**[12] 4438 3-8-13 **65** ........ MFenton 6 46
(JGGiven) *chsd ldrs to 1/2-way: rdn and btn over 2f out* **14/1**

1060 **9** 1 3/4 **Shifty Night (IRE)**[5] 4650 3-7-12 **50** oh3 ........ LisaJones 8 27
(MrsCADunnett) *handy 4f: sn btn* **18/1**

-500 **10** 1 1/4 **Tyzack (IRE)**[25] 4050 3-8-8 **60** ........ DeanMcKeown 10 33
(JBalding) *midfield: rdn 1/2-way: struggling after* **40/1**

0350 **11** 1/2 **Queenstown (IRE)**[12] 4451 3-8-9 **64** ........ (b) DCorby[(3)] 1 36
(BJMeehan) *led main gp in centre: hdd 1/2-way: hrd drvn and sn lost pl* **11/1**

1306 **12** 6 **Ali Deo**[24] 4079 3-9-7 **73** ........ TPQueally 14 29
(WJHaggas) *swtchd lft to join centre gp after 1f: bhd and sn struggling: eased fnl f* **7/1**[3]

0460 **13** 12 **Cazenove**[11] 4478 3-8-10 **62** ........ (p) KFallon 5 —
(MGQuinlan) *spd to 1/2-way: sn lost pl: eased and t.o* **9/1**

4001 **14** 1 **Dellagio (IRE)**[14] 4391 3-8-4 **56** ........ JQuinn 13 —
(CADwyer) *led stands' pair: rdn and wknd over 2f out: eased fnl f: t.o* **7/1**[3]

1m 26.3s (-0.20) **Going Correction** +0.20s/f (Good) **14** Ran **SP% 127.8**
Speed ratings: **109,104,102,102,100 99,99,96,94,92 92,85,71,70**CSF £39.99 CT £204.25 TOTE £7.30: £2.60, £2.70, £2.20; EX 54.90.
**Owner** Mrs Susan Roy **Bred** Top Of The Form Syndicate **Trained** Newmarket, Suffolk

**FOCUS**
What had looked a competitive, if modest, handicap on paper beforehand was turned into a procession and the winning time was very smart for the class of contest. Three horses raced away from the others close to the stands' rail early, though one crossed to join the main body after two furlongs.

**NOTEBOOK**
**Glencalvie(IRE)**, responding very well to the first-time visor, was always cantering over his rivals and fairly bolted up. He would be hard to beat under a penalty if the headgear works again.
**Morag** ◆, who has dropped to a very tasty mark, ran her best race for some time under conditions that suit and was unfortunate to come up against such a progressive rival. She hit form at around this time last year and looks to have done so again.
**Molinia** is yet to win, but again showed ability and should be capable of finding a race off this sort of mark.
**Alchera** was one of those that raced close to the stands' rail and it is debatable whether that helped or hindered his chances. However, this was only his second try at the trip and he seemed to see it out well enough. He is on an interesting mark now, being a stone lower than when winning a nursery last September.
**Violet Avenue**, another maiden, is probably better over a mile and lacked pace over this trip.
**Soviet Sceptre(IRE)** ran with a little credit as the trip may have been too sharp and the ground too quick.
**Cazenove** *Official explanation: trainer had no explanation for the poor form shown*
**Dellagio(IRE)** *Official explanation: trainer said was unsuited by the ground - needs it firmer*

## 4818 BETFRED.COM EARLY PRICES FROM 9 A.M. H'CAP — 1m 3y
**6:55** (6:57) (F) (0-55,55) 3-Y-O+ — **£3,423** (£978; £489) **Stalls** High

Form — RPR

0405 **1** **Band**[11] 4493 4-9-9 **54** ........ SSanders 12 62
(BAMcmahon) *midfield: rdn and outpcd over 2f out: str run fnl f: edgd lft: led on line* **5/1**[1]

3442 **2** shd **Kelseas Kolby (IRE)**[8] 4568 4-9-3 **55** ........ (v) RLucey-Butler[(7)] 11 63
(PButler) *chsd ldrs: rdn to chal over 1f out: led wl ins fnl f: edgd rt: jst ct* **12/1**

0031 **3** 3/4 **Fantasy Crusader**[10] 4519 5-9-7 **52** ........ (p) JQuinn 10 58
(JAGilbert) *chsd ldrs and plld hrd: rdn to chal over 1f out: nt qckn fnl 50 yds* **11/1**

0100 **4** hd **Oh So Rosie (IRE)**[11] 4479 4-9-3 **55** ........ (p) DerekNolan[(7)] 20 61
(JSMoore) *bhd: rdn and hdwy over 1f out: kpt on ins fnl f tl no ex cl home* **12/1**

0P01 **5** nk **Taiyo**[12] 4460 4-9-1 **46** ........ EAhern 7 51
(JWPayne) *prom: rdn to ld over 1f out: hdd and no ex wl ins fnl f* **20/1**

0400 **6** 1 1/2 **Expected Bonus (USA)**[19] 4246 5-8-13 **44** ........ WRyan 17 46
(SCWilliams) *settled towards rr: effrt 2f out: rdn and no imp fnl f* **6/1**[2]

3000 **7** 1/2 **Wodhill Be**[8] 4568 4-8-9 **40** ........ MTebbutt 16 41
(DMorris) *bmpd s: bhd: stl last over 3f out: str run over 1f out: drvn and no ex fnl 100 yds* **66/1**

6600 **8** 1 3/4 **Peartree House (IRE)**[66] 2854 10-8-9 **40** ........ ACulhane 9 37
(DWChapman) *cl up: rdn 2f out: no ex over 1f out* **40/1**

6611 **9** 2 1/2 **Sennen Cove**[56] 3148 5-8-13 **44** ........ (t) RFfrench 15 35
(RBastiman) *dwlt: hdwy to chse ldr after 2f: led over 2f out tl over 1f out: lost pl qckly* **12/1**

3412 **10** nk **Zonnebeke**[12] 4460 3-8-8 **48** ........ BReilly[(3)] 19 38
(MrsCADunnett) *midfield: rdn 1/2-way: effrt over 1f out: btn whn checked ins fnl f* **12/1**

3000 **11** 2 **Green Falcon**[66] 2847 3-9-4 **55** ........ (t) RMullen 1 40
(JWHills) *bhd early: nvr trbld ldrs* **20/1**

-550 **12** 3/4 **Midnight Mambo (USA)**[147] 1079 4-8-2 **40** ........ RMills[(7)] 3 24
(RGuest) *chsd ldrs tl drvn and wknd over 2f out* **33/1**

0060 **13** 1/2 **Daimajin (IRE)**[9] 4556 5-8-6 **39** ow1 ........ (p) ABeech[(3)] 13 23
(MrsLucindaFeatherstone) *dwlt: a bhd* **40/1**

0315 **14** 1/2 **Scarrottoo**[9] 4546 6-9-10 **55** ........ TPQueally 14 36
(SCWilliams) *chsd ldrs: rdn 1/2-way: btn over 2f out* **5/1**[1]

0030 **15** nk **Pagan Storm (USA)**[40] 3626 4-9-3 **55** ........ (t) KristinStubbs[(7)] 18 36
(MrsLStubbs) *bhd: rdn 1/2-way: nvr gng wl after* **14/1**

-000 **16** hd **Bowlegs Billy**[13] 4425 4-8-11 **42** ........ (p) DeanMcKeown 2 22
(JBalding) *plld hrd: midfield 5f: sn btn* **33/1**

1110 **17** 2 1/2 **Dial Square**[40] 3636 3-9-1 **52** ........ KFallon 8 27
(PHowling) *bhd: drvn and btn 3f out* **10/1**[3]

00P4 **18** 1 1/2 **Puri**[9] 4535 5-9-3 **48** ........ (b) MFenton 4 19
(JGGiven) *sn led: hdd & wknd rapidly over 2f out* **50/1**

0000 **19** 1/2 **Mutared (IRE)**[14] 4386 6-8-8 **39** ........ (p) LisaJones 6 9
(NPLittmoden) *chsd ldrs: rdn and btn over 2f out* **20/1**

00-0 **20** 2 **Vertedanz (IRE)**[24] 4083 4-8-10 **44** ........ NMackay[(3)] 5 9
(MissIECraig) *cl up to 1/2-way: sn btn* **66/1**

1m 40.6s (0.90) **Going Correction** +0.20s/f (Good)
**WFA** 3 from 4yo+ 6lb **20** Ran **SP% 132.5**
Speed ratings: **103,102,102,101,101 100,99,97,95,95 93,92,91,91,91 90,88,86,86,84**CSF £62.23 CT £662.81 TOTE £6.60: £1.70, £3.60, £4.40, £3.10; EX 92.30.
**Owner** D J Allen **Bred** Mrs J McMahon **Trained** Hopwas, Staffs

**FOCUS**
The whole field bunched mid-track. This was a moderate handicap, but very competitive nonetheless and the pace was sound and the placed horses indicate the level of the form. How tight things were can be seen by the fact that the horse in front half a furlong from home did not even make the first four.

**NOTEBOOK**
**Band** was a maiden after 15 attempts coming into this, but had slipped to a very winnable mark and was given a fine ride. Switched off in the ruck, he was switched right over to the stands' side to make his effort and maintained the momentum to get up right on the line. A strongly-run mile seems to suit him.
**Kelseas Kolby(IRE)** was beaten a short-head for the second race in a row over this extra furlong, having been produced with his effort at what seemed to be just the right time. Both his wins have been in selling company, but he is running well enough to win a race like this and deserves a change of luck.
**Fantasy Crusader** has shown his best recent form over further, so the strong pace was helpful to him and he had every chance, but he just lacked a telling turn of foot where it mattered.
**Oh So Rosie(IRE)** seems to like it here and stayed on all the way to the line, despite not appearing to have much room in which to manoeuvre inside the last furlong.
**Taiyo**, raised 4lb for his course-and-distance victory 12 days earlier, hit the front a furlong out but he could never get clear of his field and was completely swamped in the last 100 yards. This was still another solid effort.
**Expected Bonus(USA)** ◆, not unbacked, was given a much more patient ride this time and managed to get into a challenging position a furlong out, but could not quite maintain the effort. This was encouraging though, especially as he is now 35lb lower than the mark he started off last season on turf, and is one to watch out for especially if there is significant market support for him.
**Wodhill Be** made up a lot of ground from the back of the field, but was making no impression inside the last furlong. Seven furlongs probably suits her better.
**Sennen Cove** could never get away from his field after hitting the front and possibly found this too competitive.
**Zonnebeke** is not an easy ride, but would have been a couple of lengths closer had she not run out of room inside the last furlong.
**Scarrottoo** never looked like winning and the ground may not have been fast enough, despite the official description.
**Dial Square** *Official explanation: jockey said gelding lost its action*

## 4819 BETFRED "WE PAY DOUBLE RESULT" MAIDEN STKS — 1m 3f 101y
**7:25** (7:25) (D) 3-Y-0+ — **£3,425** (£1,054; £527; £263) **Stalls** Low

Form — RPR

0302 **1** **Gift Voucher (IRE)**[17] 4297 3-9-0 80 ........ (t) KFallon 8 80
(SirMichaelStoute) *led after 2f: sent 12 l clr 1/2-way: rdn 3f out: pressed over 1f out: styd on: all out* **1/2**[1]

04 **2** 1 1/2 **Samaria (GER)**[8] 4583 3-8-9 ........ RMullen 6 73
(CFWall) *hld up in rr: hdwy 5f out: wnt 2nd 3f out: rdn and tried to chal over 1f out: no imp* **8/1**[2]

00 **3** 1 1/2 **Enhancer**[26] 4028 6-9-9 ........ JQuinn 1 76
(MrsLCJewell) *prom in chsng gp: pushed along 3f out: kpt on gamely fnl f: no ex last 100 yds* **33/1**

00 **4** 6 **Onward To Glory (USA)**[26] 4033 4-9-9 68 ........ EAhern 7 66
(JLDunlop) *midfield: rdn and effrt over 3f out: v one-pced: btn 2f out* **22/1**

43-0 **5** shd **Timber Ice (USA)**[23] 4155 4-9-4 72 ........ WRyan 4 61
(HRACecil) *chsd ldr after 3f: rdn and demoted 3f out: fnd nil after* **8/1**[2]

**6** 9 **Menelaus** 3-9-0 ........ TPQueally 10 51
(DRLoder) *midfield: rdn 1/2-way: sn wl outpcd* **8/1**[2]

04 **7** 5 **West End Wonder (IRE)**[13] 4417 5-9-6 ........ DCorby[(3)] 3 43
(MJWallace) *nvr trbld ldrs: rdn and struggling 1/2-way: t.o* **100/1**

40/ **8** 1 3/4 **Repent At Leisure**[767] 2891 4-9-9 ........ ACulhane 2 41
(JulianPoulton) *led 2f: lost pl 4f out: t.o* **50/1**

**9** 1 1/4 **Hanazakari** 3-9-0 ........ SSanders 9 39
(JARToller) *drvn along and nvr gng wl in last: t.o fnl 3f* **12/1**[3]

000 **10** 1/2 **Trinity Fair**[17] 4306 3-8-9 ........ MFenton 5 33
(JGGiven) *bhd: rdn and btn 4f out: t.o* **80/1**

2m 28.49s (1.09) **Going Correction** +0.20s/f (Good)
**WFA** 3 from 4yo+ 9lb **10** Ran **SP% 119.2**
Speed ratings: **104,102,101,97,97 90,87,85,85,84**CSF £5.21 TOTE £1.40: £1.02, £1.90, £6.60; EX 4.50.
**Owner** Ballymacoll Stud **Bred** Ballymacoll Stud Farm Ltd **Trained** Newmarket, Suffolk

**FOCUS**
An uncompetitive maiden, but a strong pace thanks to the favourite and the front three finished a long way clear, suggesting the form is solid.

**NOTEBOOK**

**Gift Voucher(IRE)** did not want a dawdle, so was forced to set his own pace and was a long way clear by halfway. Things started to get desperate as the pack closed down the home straight, but he dourly stayed on to score. He may not have been impressive considering his price, but this was a funny race and he is probably better when getting a lead in a strongly-run race.

**Samaria(GER)** ◆ is improving with racing and looked a threat to the favourite when coming from off the pace to challenge over a furlong from home, but could not find anything more. There may still be more to come and it will be interesting to see what handicap mark she gets.

**Enhancer** ◆, a winner of three bumpers, ran a fine race and came right away from the fourth. He could be interesting in handicaps, or over hurdles.

**Onward To Glory(USA)** is still to make any impact in this country despite being tried over a variety of trips.

**Timber Ice(USA)** dropped away very tamely and has become very disappointing.

## 4820 BETFRED IN SHOPS, ON PHONE AND ON-LINE MAIDEN H'CAP 1m 6f 17y

7:55 (7:55) (E) (0-70,69) 3-Y-O+ £3,906 (£1,202; £601; £300) Stalls High

Form RPR

0060 **1** **Masterman Ready**[23] 4146 3-9-1 **64**.......................................... EAhern 2 71
(PWHarris) *plld hrd and prom: drvn along fnl 2f: sustained chal on rails fnl f: led nr fin* **7/1**[3]

2042 **2** *hd* **Munaawesh (USA)**[9] 4562 3-8-6 **55**..................................(b) ACulhane 8 62
(DWChapman) *hld up and bhd: given plenty of cover tl swtchd outside and hdwy over 1f out: rdn and ev ch ins fnl f: kpt on* **10/1**

056 **3** *hd* **Welkino's Boy**[32] 3882 3-8-13 **62**.............................. DaleGibson 6 69
(JMackie) *plld hrd and prom: led over 2f out: hrd drvn after: ct cl home* **33/1**

450 **4** *1* **Rossall Point**[28] 3994 3-8-13 **62**.......................................... KFallon 5 67
(JLDunlop) *towards rr: rdn to improve over 3f out: ev ch ins fnl f: one pce* **3/1**[2]

335 **5** *½* **Sunday City (JPN)**[42] 3574 3-9-6 **69**.................................. TPQueally 11 74
(DRLoder) *hld up: towards rr tl drvn and hdwy 3f out: kpt on one pce ins fnl f* **9/1**

4/06 **6** *1 ¼* **Lawrence Of Arabia (IRE)**[23] 4155 4-9-7 **58**...................... SSanders 4 61
(SirMarkPrescott) *hld up midfield: rdn 3f out: sn making no imp: edgd rt fnl f* **11/8**[1]

0006 **7** *shd* **Larking About (USA)**[26] 4033 4-9-1 **52**..............................(b[1]) RMullen 1 55
(WJMusson) *bhd: drvn over 4f out: kpt on fnl f but n.d* **16/1**

6660 **8** *3* **Lebenstanz**[12] 4448 4-9-7 **61**.......................................... NMackay[(3)] 7 60
(LMCumani) *towards rr: rdn 4f out: sn btn* **14/1**

5604 **9** *2 ½* **Morning Hawk (USA)**[17] 4302 3-7-12 **47** oh9.........................(b) JQuinn 9 42
(JSMoore) *prom: rdn to ld over 3f out: hdd over 2f out: dropped out qckly* **33/1**

-060 **10** *10* **Lahob**[9] 4554 4-9-4 **55**................................................ MFenton 10 36
(PHowling) *sn drvn into ld: hdd over 3f out: lost pl rapidly and eased* **33/1**

430 **11** *2* **Wodhill Hope**[9] 4554 4-8-11 **48**.......................................... MTebbutt 3 26
(DMorris) *bhd: effrt to midfield 5f out: sn btn: t.o* **66/1**

3m 9.78s (4.58) **Going Correction** +0.20s/f (Good)

**WFA** 3 from 4yo 12lb **11** Ran SP% **121.6**

Speed ratings: **94,93,93,93,92 92,92,90,89,83 82**CSF £75.10 CT £2184.17 TOTE £9.80: £1.70, £2.60, £8.10; EX 98.40 Place 6 £35.66, Place 5 £30.81.

**Owner** The Mastermen **Bred** Miss G J Abbey **Trained** Ringshall, Bucks

**FOCUS**

A messy race and not at all a test of stamina. The early pace was very moderate and it basically became a sprint down the home straight. The winning time was very modest for the class and several would not have been suited by the way the race was run, suggesting the form may prove unreliable.

**NOTEBOOK**

**Masterman Ready**, unplaced in all five of his previous starts, had a good position just behind the leaders in a steadily-run race, and showed real determination to come with his effort against the inside rail and win the race on the nod. The form may not be reliable though. *Official explanation: trainer said, regarding the improved form shown, gelding was struck into last time*

**Munaawesh(USA)** came from well off the pace and challenged strongly down the wide outside, only failing to get there by the minimum margin. This was the closest he has ever got to winning a race on his 17th start, but whether he truly stays this trip given the race was run is debatable.

**Welkino's Boy**, making his handicap debut and stepping up in trip, was always close to the pace and led coming to the quarter-mile pole, but was just run out of it. This is not great form, but he obviously has some ability.

**Rossall Point**, another making his handicap debut on this step up in trip, was off the bridle some way out. He made some progress without offering a threat, but looks a stayer and was almost certainly not suited by the way the race was run.

**Sunday City(JPN)**, yet another up in trip for his handicap debut, looks very one paced and does not have many options left on the level.

**Lawrence Of Arabia(IRE)**, not for the first time, was totally unsuited by the way the race was run and should not be condemned just yet.

T/Plt: £178.10 to a £1 stake. Pool: £31,133.70. 127.55 winning tickets. T/Qpdt: £141.80 to a £1 stake. Pool: £3,029.10. 15.80 winning tickets. IM

4821 - 4823a (Foreign Racing) - See Raceform Interactive

# 4631 HAMILTON (R-H)

Tuesday, August 17

**OFFICIAL GOING: Good to soft, changing to soft after race 5 (4.25)**

## 4824 KNOCKHILL RACING CIRCUIT MEDIAN AUCTION MAIDEN STKS (QUALIFIER HAMILTON PARK 2-Y-O SERIES) 6f 5y

2:05 (2:08) (E) 2-Y-O £4,322 (£1,330; £665; £332) Stalls High

Form RPR

532 **1** **Merchant (IRE)**[19] 4256 2-9-0 78.......................................... RMullen 4 91+
(MLWBell) *prom: rdn to ld over 1f out: r.o strly* **13/8**[2]

**2** *3 ½* **Lord Mayfair (USA)** 2-9-0.............................................. RWinston 11 81
(TDBarron) *led to over 1f out: kpt on: no ch w wnr* **6/1**[3]

0554 **3** *2 ½* **Profit's Reality (IRE)**[6] 4632 2-9-0.......................... DeanMcKeown 3 73
(PABlockley) *prom: rdn over 2f out: sn outpcd: rallied over 1f out: no imp fnl f* **6/4**[1]

0 **4** *4* **Lake Wakatipu**[20] 4243 2-8-9.............................................. SRighton 9 56
(MMullineaux) *outpcd tl hdwy over 1f out: n.d* **25/1**

4 **5** *½* **Rainbow Iris**[21] 4212 2-8-9.............................................. FLynch 7 55
(BSmart) *chsd ldrs: outpcd 1/2-way: n.d after* **14/1**

05 **6** *nk* **Kerry's Blade (IRE)**[47] 3444 2-9-0.................................. GFaulkner 10 59
(PCHaslam) *in tch to 1/2-way: sn outpcd* **25/1**

06 **7** *nk* **Balthasar**[6] 4633 2-8-9.............................................. MLawson[(5)] 6 58
(PABlockley) *cl up to over 1f out: wknd* **16/1**

**8** *2 ½* **Lady Vee (IRE)** 2-8-6.............................................. THamilton[(3)] 8 45
(PDNiven) *sn rdn in rr: n.d* **66/1**

**9** *5* **Percheron (IRE)** 2-9-0.............................................. JBramhill 1 35
(PABlockley) *sn wl bhd: nvr on terms* **40/1**

**10** *7* **Owed** 2-9-0..........................................................(t) WSupple 2 14
(MrsGSRees) *in tch: rn green over 2f out: sn wknd* **20/1**

00 **11** *21* **Benny The Bus**[11] 4507 2-9-0.......................................... ACulhane 5 —
(MrsGSRees) *sn wl bhd: no ch fr 1/2-way* **66/1**

1m 12.85s (-0.25) **Going Correction** -0.175s/f (Firm) **11** Ran SP% **118.2**

Speed ratings: **94,89,86,80,80 79,79,75,69,59 31**CSF £11.14 TOTE £1.90: £1.10, £1.60, £1.30; EX 13.40.

**Owner** H E Sheikh Rashid Bin Mohammed **Bred** John Foley **Trained** Newmarket, Suffolk

**FOCUS**

A weak maiden in which they finished well strung out. The winner recorded an improved effort and the form in behind looks solid.

**NOTEBOOK**

**Merchant(IRE)** confirmed the promise he showed on his three previous outings to get off the mark with a clear-cut success. He should prove just as effective back over another furlong, but his current rating means things will be a lot harder in handicaps.

**Lord Mayfair(USA)**, $17,000 yearling, dam unraced out of a half-sister to Running Stag, was quite well supported and made a pleasing debut. He showed plenty of pace and, although no match for the winner in the closing stages, he kept on well to finish clear of the remainder. Given normal improvement, he should be able to pick up a similar race.

**Profit's Reality(IRE)** was very strong in the market but he looked very one paced, again shaping as though in need of further.

**Lake Wakatipu** was well held but only needs one more run for a nursery mark and promises to improve when stepped up in trip.

**Rainbow Iris**, up a furlong in trip, did not really improve on her first run and is probably more of a nursery type.

**Balthasar** *Official explanation: jockey said colt had a breathing problem*

**Owed** *Official explanation: jockey said colt had a breathing problem and hung left-handed from halfway*

**Benny The Bus** *Official explanation: jockey said gelding didn't come down the hill*

## 4825 HORSEPOWER (S) STKS 1m 65y

2:40 (2:40) (E) 3-Y-O+ £3,607 (£1,110; £555; £277) Stalls High

Form RPR

-000 **1** **Lord Of Methley**[83] 2408 5-9-3 46..........................................(b) VHalliday 5 53
(RMWhitaker) *chsd ldrs: effrt over 3f out: rdn and wandered fr 2f out: jst hld on* **10/1**

0000 **2** *shd* **Tatweer (IRE)**[12] 4473 4-9-8 48..................................(v) DarrenWilliams 7 58
(DShaw) *hld up: hdwy over 2f out: effrt whn n.m.r briefly over 1f out: kpt on wl: jst hld* **14/1**

5303 **3** *2 ½* **Sophrano (IRE)**[6] 4635 4-9-3 56.................................. DeanMcKeown 11 48
(PABlockley) *mde most to over 1f out: sn outpcd* **3/1**[1]

0300 **4** *5* **Erupt**[6] 4624 11-9-3 40.......................................................... GParkin 3 37
(REBarr) *bhd tl styd on fr 2f out: nrst fin* **20/1**

0100 **5** *2* **Mehmaas**[9] 4577 8-9-3 56..........................................................(v) DAllan 6 33
(REBarr) *sn rdn towards rr: hdwy 2f out: nvr rchd ldrs* **11/2**[2]

0000 **6** *1 ¾* **Wood Fern (UAE)**[10] 4546 4-9-3 48.......................................... CCatlin 9 29
(MRChannon) *trckd ldrs: disp ld over 3f to over 1f out: sn btn* **11/1**

0500 **7** *1 ½* **Mount Pekan (IRE)**[13] 4447 4-9-3 39.................................. WSupple 12 26
(JSGoldie) *chsd ldrs: rdn over 3f out: wknd over 2f out* **9/1**

0305 **8** *½* **Bonjour Bond (IRE)**[21] 4207 3-8-11 44..............................(v) DMcGaffin 10 25
(BSmart) *in tch: rdn and hung rt over 3f out: sn outpcd* **10/1**

000 **9** *3 ½* **Wild Tide**[11] 4509 5-8-12.......................................................... RFfrench 4 13
(DWThompson) *midfield on outside: hmpd over 4f out: sn btn* **66/1**

4005 **10** *nk* **Abuelos**[14] 4421 5-9-3 43.......................................................... TWilliams 8 17
(DWThompson) *missed break: nvr on terms* **33/1**

5420 **U** **Merlins Profit**[60] 3041 4-9-0 43.......................................... LEnstone[(3)] 2 —
(MDods) *midfield: hmpd and uns rdr over 4f out* **7/1**[3]

3603 **F** **Compassion (IRE)**[10] 4535 3-8-6 43..........................................(p) RWinston 1 —
(MissLAPerratt) *w ldr: broke leg and fell over 4f out: dead* **8/1**

1m 51.28s (1.98) **Going Correction** +0.325s/f (Good)

**WFA** 3 from 4yo+ 6lb **12** Ran SP% **116.4**

Speed ratings: **103,102,100,95,93 91,90,89,86,85** —,—CSF £136.60 TOTE £13.40: £4.00, £6.60, £2.60; EX 143.90.There was no bid for the winner.

**Owner** R M Whitaker **Bred** A Lyons Bloodstock **Trained** Scarcroft, W Yorks

■ Stewards Enquiry : V Halliday caution: careless riding

**FOCUS**

A very moderate seller with the second providing the key to the form.

**NOTEBOOK**

**Lord Of Methley** appreciated the re-fitting of headgear and drop back from a mile and a half, and was just good enough to gain his first success of the season. However, he has never won outside of this grade and could well be one to take on if stepping up in class.

**Tatweer(IRE)** gained his only win to date over five furlongs but had been tried over a mile and a half on his previous start. Dropped back to a more suitable trip and with the ground in his favour, he was just held and can be considered unlucky, as he had to be switched for a run in the closing stages. However, he does not appeal as one to take too short a price about going one better.

**Sophrano(IRE)**, dropped in grade, had 10lb in hand of the winner at the weights but proved most disappointing. He has been placed over a mile and this trip should not have been a problem.

**Erupt** was again doing his best work late on and is surely worth another try over further.

**Mehmaas** was never really going and may not have appreciated the easy surface - he has never won on ground softer than good.

**Merlins Profit** still had quite a bit to do when badly hampered and parting company with Enstone.

**Compassion(IRE)** was still in contention when sadly breaking a leg half a mile out.

## 4826 TOTEPOOL SERIES FINAL (H'CAP) 1m 1f 36y

3:15 (3:17) (C) 3-Y-O+ £10,159 (£3,126; £1,563; £781) Stalls High

Form RPR

0000 **1** **Creskeld (IRE)**[37] 3779 5-9-5 **64**.......................................... FLynch 17 74
(BSmart) *cl up: led gng wl 2f out: sn rdn: kpt on wl fnl f: all out* **25/1**

1224 **2** *shd* **Yenaled**[21] 4213 7-9-10 **69**.......................................... ACulhane 10 79
(KARyan) *hld up: hdwy 2f out: rdn and kpt on wl fnl f: jst failed* **10/1**

4405 **3** *1* **Cherished Number**[9] 4569 5-9-11 **70**.................................. RWinston 8 78
(ISemple) *midfield: effrt whn n.m.r over 2f out: swtchd lft: hdwy over 1f out: kpt on fnl f* **12/1**

6343 **4** *¾* **Donna's Double**[17] 4328 9-8-5 **50**..........................................(v[1]) DAllan 5 57
(DEddy) *hld up: hdwy over 3f out: one pce fnl f* **16/1**

5235 **5** *½* **Apache Point (IRE)**[11] 4511 7-8-9 **54**.................................. KimTinkler 7 60
(NTinkler) *in tch: effrt 2f out: kpt on same pce ins fnl f* **8/1**[3]

1621 **6** *hd* **Double Ransom**[11] 4511 5-9-6 **65**..........................................(b) CCatlin 15 70
(MrsLStubbs) *hld up midfield: effrt 2f out: kpt on same pce ins fnl f* **11/2**[2]

4366 **7** *4* **No Chance To Dance (IRE)**[12] 4485 4-7-7 **45**.............(t) MHalford[(7)] 16 42
(HJCollingridge) *prom tl rdn and nt qckn fr 2f out* **8/1**[3]

0250 **8** *shd* **Encounter**[11] 4511 8-7-9 **45**.......................................... BSwarbrick[(5)] 4 42
(JHetherton) *hld up: effrt over 3f out: edgd rt: no imp over 1f out* **16/1**

5052 **9** *2 ½* **Sarraaf (IRE)**[10] 4535 8-9-5 **64**.......................................... VHalliday 1 56
(JSGoldie) *midfield: rdn over 3f out: outpcd fr 2f out* **25/1**

-064 **10** *½* **Kristiansand**[17] 4333 4-9-2 **64**.......................................... PMulrennan[(3)] 13 55
(PMonteith) *midfield: effrt 3f out: no imp fr wl over 1f out* **16/1**

1012 **11** 3½ **Wahoo Sam (USA)**[6] 4634 4-9-6 **70** ........ PMakin(5) 14 54
(TDBarron) *sn led: hdd 2f out: btn and eased fnl f* **9/2**[1]
4033 **12** ½ **Regent's Secret (USA)**[11] 4511 4-9-0 **59** ........ WSupple 6 42
(JSGoldie) *rdn in rr 1/2-way: nvr on terms* **12/1**
1066 **13** 2½ **Millennium Hall**[38] 3740 5-9-0 **62** ........ LEnstone(3) 11 40
(PMonteith) *trckd ldrs tl wknd fr 2f out* **25/1**
6000 **14** 1½ **Lucky Largo (IRE)**[19] 4276 4-8-7 **52** ........ (b) RFfrench 12 27
(MissLAPerratt) *cl up tl wknd over 2f out* **33/1**
3132 **15** 1¾ **Anthemion (IRE)**[17] 4333 7-9-1 **60** ........ DMcGaffin 3 31
(MrsJCMcgregor) *a bhd* **25/1**
1000 **16** 12 **Ace Coming**[12] 4490 3-9-0 **66** ........ (b) PFessey 2 13
(DEddy) *in tch to 1/2-way: sn rdn and btn* **33/1**
0400 **17** 5 **Pharoah's Gold (IRE)**[4] 4702 6-8-6 **51** ........ (v) DarrenWilliams 9 —
(DShaw) *missed break: nvr on terms* **33/1**

2m 1.05s (1.45) **Going Correction** +0.325s/f (Good)
**WFA** 3 from 4yo+ 7lb **17** Ran SP% **122.1**
Speed ratings: **106,105,105,104,103 103,100,100,97,97 94,93,91,90,88 78,73**CSF £242.16 CT £3146.80 TOTE £25.80: £3.40, £2.30, £3.40, £2.40; EX 244.80.
**Owner** Creskeld Racing **Bred** Broguestown Stud **Trained** Hambleton, N Yorks

**FOCUS**
By no means a great race for the class or money, but competitive enough and they went a good pace, indicating the form is fair and sound.

**NOTEBOOK**
**Creskeld(IRE)** had been out of sorts of far this season and has tumbled in the weights as a result. Racing off a mark 1lb lower than when last successful, he probably hit the front soon enough and was not helped when the long-time leader dropped away earlier than one might have expected, but he stuck on well. He should not go up too much for this and, now he is back to form, he could well add to this.
**Yenaled** was racing off a mark 13lb higher than when last winning on turf, but he is in the form of his life and was just denied. He remains one to keep on the right side of.
**Cherished Number ◆** has dropped to a very reasonable mark and again offered some promise. He has not won for well over a year, but could end that losing run sooner rather than later if maintaining this sort of form.
**Donna's Double**, 29lb lower than when last winning in 2002, had a visor replacing cheekpieces and, with conditions in his favour, ran well. Given his losing run, however, he is not one to be taking too short a price about to build on this.
**Apache Point(IRE)** continues in reasonable form without suggesting he is about to strike.
**Double Ransom**, 4lb higher than when successful at Haydock on his previous start, was a shade disappointing.
**Wahoo Sam(USA)** has been in great form lately but dropped out very tamely. The last time he was significantly below form, he bounced back with a win.
**Pharoah's Gold(IRE)** *Official explanation: jockey said gelding was unsuited by the good to soft ground*

## 4827 BILL MCHARG H'CAP 6f 5y
**3:50** (3:50) (E) (0-70,70) 3-Y-O+ **£4,485** (£1,380; £690; £345) **Stalls** High

Form RPR
0003 **1** **Bond Playboy**[13] 4447 4-9-6 **60** ........ FLynch 16 73
(BSmart) *chsd far side ldrs: rdn over 2f out: rallied to ld ins fnl f: kpt on wl* **9/2**[1]
-056 **2** 1 **Misaro (GER)**[52] 3295 3-9-13 **70** ........ DeanMcKeown 7 80
(PABlockley) *sn swtchd to far side: mde most to ins fnl f: kpt on* **20/1**
0430 **3** 1¾ **My Bayard**[32] 3894 5-9-5 **59** ........ DAllan 5 64
(JO'Reilly) *cl up stands side: swtchd to far side gp over 3f out: ev ch over 1f out: one pce ins fnl f* **14/1**[3]
4105 **4** 2 **Thornaby Green**[12] 4489 3-9-2 **64** ........ PMakin(5) 3 63
(TDBarron) *chsd stands side ldrs: led that gp 2f out: kpt on fnl f: nt rch first three* **16/1**
0664 **5** nk **Calculaite**[12] 4489 3-8-3 **46** ........ WSupple 1 44
(MrsGSRees) *cl up stands side: effrt over 2f out: no imp over 1f out* **25/1**
5031 **6** 2 **Frimley's Matterry**[10] 4557 4-8-10 **53** ........ PMulrennan(3) 4 45
(REBarr) *led stands side to 2f out: sn one pce* **25/1**
2060 **7** ¾ **Silver Seeker (USA)**[19] 4280 4-8-11 **51** ........ CCatlin 10 41
(ARDicken) *outpcd far side tl hdwy over 1f out: nrst fin* **50/1**
-000 **8** nk **The Wizard Mul**[13] 4447 4-9-3 **57** ........ JBramhill 14 46
(WStorey) *in tch far side: rdn over 2f out: sn no ex* **16/1**
0050 **9** nk **Carlton (IRE)**[13] 4447 10-8-11 **56** ........ BSwarbrick(5) 9 44
(CRDore) *in tch far side tl rdn and outpcd fr 2f out* **11/1**[2]
3354 **10** nk **Roman Empire**[4] 4702 4-8-11 **51** ........ (b) GParkin 8 38
(KARyan) *in tch far side: effrt and hung rt over 1f out: sn btn* **9/2**[1]
6040 **11** nk **Redoubtable (USA)**[14] 4425 13-8-11 **51** ........ ACulhane 15 37
(DWChapman) *hld up far side: shkn up over 2f out: n.d* **14/1**[3]
3240 **12** 2 **Mallia**[11] 4509 11-8-2 **42** ........ PFessey 2 22
(TDBarron) *prom stands side: rdn and hung rt over 2f out: sn btn* **20/1**
-300 **13** 4 **Fenwicks Pride (IRE)**[2] 4782 6-8-12 **55** ........ THamilton(3) 13 23
(RAFahey) *in tch far side: lost pl over 2f out: n.d after* **9/2**[1]
0300 **14** ¾ **Formeric**[53] 3269 8-7-13 **39** ........ RFfrench 12 5
(MissLCSiddall) *a bhd far side* **50/1**
3020 **15** 2½ **Orangino**[18] 4309 6-7-12 **43** ow2 ........ RKennemore(7) 11 3
(JSHaldane) *chsd far side ldrs to 1/2-way: sn lost pl* **20/1**
0650 **16** 13 **Pirlie Hill**[10] 4542 4-8-7 **47** ........ RWinston 6 —
(MissLAPerratt) *dwlt: swtchd to far side after 1f: hdwy 1/2-way: hung rt and wknd wl over 1f out: eased whn no ch fnl f* **16/1**

1m 13.62s (0.52) **Going Correction** +0.15s/f (Good)
**WFA** 3 from 4yo+ 3lb **16** Ran SP% **119.8**
Speed ratings: **102,100,98,95,95 92,91,91,90,90 90,87,82,81,77 60**CSF £102.27 CT £1220.74 TOTE £3.40: £1.40, £5.40, £5.00, £5.40; EX 76.80.
**Owner** R C Bond **Bred** P A Mason **Trained** Hambleton, N Yorks

**FOCUS**
Just a modest handicap in which My Bayard, Thornaby Green, Calculate, Frimley's Matterry and Mallia all opted to race stands' side in the early stages before eventually joining the main group towards the middle-to-far side.

**NOTEBOOK**
**Bond Playboy** returned to form with a good third over seven furlongs on his previous start and was able to confirm that over this furlong shorter trip. Rated 89 at his peak, he could well defy a rise in the weights for his in-form yard, especially on similar ground.
**Misaro(GER)** promised to be suited by a return to this sort of trip on easy ground and, granted such conditions, he ran a cracker. There is a similar race in him.
**My Bayard**, with the blinkers left off, is unlikely to have helped his chance by racing towards the stands' side in the early stages, but it would be hard to call him an unlucky loser.
**Thornaby Green** had never previously raced on ground with soft in the description, but this was a fair effort, especially considering he raced towards the stands' side in the early stages.
**Calculaite**, racing on easy ground for the first time, did not run a bad race and has a rating that allows him to run in an even lower grade.
**Roman Empire** was unable to build on the promise he showed at Catterick on his previous start and is still looking for his first win on turf.
**Fenwicks Pride(IRE)** shaped well on his previous start at Pontefract and promised to be suited by these conditions, so this was disappointing.

## 4828 PARKS OF HAMILTON CLASSIFIED STKS 5f 4y
**4:25** (4:28) (F) 3-Y-O+ **£3,066** (£876; £438) **Stalls** High

Form RPR
0621 **1** **Red Monarch (IRE)**[31] 3954 3-9-7 61 ........ FLynch 9 71
(PABlockley) *cl up: rdn over 2f out: led ent fnl f: kpt on strly* **7/1**[3]
0000 **2** ½ **Online Investor**[18] 4291 5-9-10 62 ........ RWinston 4 70+
(DNicholls) *missed break: hld up: nt clr run and swtchd lft over 1f out: kpt on wl: no ch w wnr* **8/1**
0334 **3** 1 **Tantric**[6] 4626 5-9-8 58 ........ DAllan 8 64
(JO'Reilly) *trckd ldrs: effrt 2f out: kpt on ins fnl f* **11/1**
0302 **4** shd **Sharp Hat**[27] 4011 10-9-11 63 ........ ACulhane 1 67
(DWChapman) *trckd ldrs: rdn and edgd rt 2f out: kpt on ins fnl f* **12/1**
2150 **5** nk **Aahgowangowan (IRE)**[24] 4133 5-9-7 62 ........ (t) RFfrench 7 62
(MDods) *led to ent fnl f: kpt on same pce* **7/2**[1]
0640 **5** dht **Mynd**[45] 3524 4-9-10 62 ........ DeanMcKeown 5 65
(RMWhitaker) *trckd ldrs: rdn 1/2-way: one pce fnl f* **8/1**
0602 **7** shd **He's A Rocket (IRE)**[4] 4701 3-9-1 58 ........ (p) BSwarbrick(5) 6 63
(KRBurke) *prom: effrt and rdn over 2f out: one pce fnl f* **14/1**
0000 **8** 1 **Karminskey Park**[13] 4452 5-9-7 62 ........ DMcGaffin 2 58
(TJEtherington) *hld up in tch: drvn over 2f out: no imp fnl f* **9/1**
0303 **9** 1 **Kings College Boy**[13] 4452 4-9-6 61 ........ (b) THamilton(3) 3 56
(RAFahey) *sn swtchd to far rail: prom tl outpcd fr 2f out* **5/1**[2]
0302 **10** 13 **Pays D'Amour (IRE)**[11] 4509 7-9-3 57 ........ (t) PMakin(5) 10 9
(MissLAPerratt) *sn outpcd: nvr on terms* **8/1**

61.84 secs (0.58) **Going Correction** +0.15s/f (Good)
**WFA** 3 from 4yo+ 2lb **10** Ran SP% **117.4**
Speed ratings: **101,100,98,98,97 97,97,96,94,73**CSF £62.31 TOTE £9.50: £2.70, £2.70, £2.40; EX 89.70.
**Owner** Bigwigs Bloodstock III **Bred** Michael Dalton **Trained** Southwell, Notts

**FOCUS**
A very tight race on the figures with just 6lb separating the field, and they finished pretty well bunched and the overall form is modest.

**NOTEBOOK**
**Red Monarch(IRE)**, off the mark in a maiden handicap over six furlongs at Ripon on his previous start, was not inconvenienced by this drop in trip and ran out a narrow winner. He is clearly progressing and the hat-trick cannot be ruled out, especially if kept to easy ground.
**Online Investor** was taking a significant drop in grade and was just denied. However, he has not won since scoring on his second start at two and is not one to take a short price about.
**Tantric** has never won over shorter than seven furlongs, but he is proving effective over this trip and ran another solid race.
**Sharp Hat** was always just being held and is still looking for his first win of the year.
**Mynd** did not look to have any excuses.
**Aahgowangowan(IRE)** had conditions to suit but was slightly disappointing.
**Kings College Boy** has handled similar ground well enough in the past, but he was below form and is probably just a better horse on a faster surface.

## 4829 FRIENDS OF SCOTTISH RACING RATING RELATED MAIDEN STKS 1m 3f 16y
**5:00** (5:00) (E) 3-Y-O **£3,786** (£1,165; £582; £291) **Stalls** High

Form RPR
2003 **1** **Late Opposition**[38] 3746 3-9-0 68 ........ (v) WSupple 1 49+
(EALDunlop) *keen: led after 3f: mde rest: clr whn rdn over 1f out: flashed tail ins last: r.o* **5/4**[1]
0402 **2** 5 **Mambina (USA)**[6] 4629 3-8-11 60 ........ CCatlin 5 39+
(MRChannon) *plld hrd: cl up: effrt and hung rt fr over 2f out: no imp fr over 1f out* **10/3**[3]
005 **3** 1¾ **Hollywood Critic (USA)**[32] 3899 3-8-11 47 ........ LEnstone(3) 3 40
(PMonteith) *rrd s: in tch: effrt over 3f out: one pce fr 2f out* **7/1**
5500 **4** ½ **Knight Of Hearts (IRE)**[36] 3804 3-9-0 42 ........ DeanMcKeown 2 39
(PABlockley) *in tch: rdn over 3f out: no imp fr 2f out* **66/1**
2260 **5** 9 **Awesome Love (USA)**[28] 4008 3-9-0 70 ........ RFfrench 4 26
(MJohnston) *cl up tl rdn and wknd fr over 2f out* **3/1**[2]
500 **6** 12 **Jordans Spark**[12] 4492 3-9-0 49 ........ PFessey 6 9
(ISemple) *in tch tl wknd over 3f out* **25/1**

2m 31.64s (5.14) **Going Correction** +0.45s/f (Yiel) **6** Ran SP% **110.4**
Speed ratings: **99,95,94,93,87 78**CSF £5.50 TOTE £2.00: £1.30, £1.70; EX 4.90.
**Owner** Saeed Maktoum Al Maktoum **Bred** Sheikh Saeed Bin Maktoum Al Maktoum **Trained** Newmarket, Suffolk

**FOCUS**
An uncompetitive maiden in which the field raced just off the far rail in the straight. The first two were below their best with the third and fourth holding the form down.

**NOTEBOOK**
**Late Opposition** had been proving quite frustrating, including in first-time headgear on his previous start, but the visor was persevered with and he proved far too good for these to gain his first success to date at the 11th attempt. Things are almost sure to be tougher back in handicaps, but this was a nice confidence booster.
**Mambina(USA)** was no match whatsoever for the winner, having raced very keenly early on.
**Hollywood Critic(USA)** was well held and would be better off in handicaps given his current rating.
**Knight Of Hearts(IRE)** is another who will finds things easier in handicaps.
**Awesome Love(USA)**, with the blinkers left off, had a cracking chance at the weights but ran a shocker.

## 4830 TELETEXT "HANDS AND HEELS" APPRENTICE H'CAP (ROUND 4 OF HAMILTON PARK APPRENTICE SERIES) 1m 4f 17y
**5:30** (5:30) (E) (0-70,69) 3-Y-O+ **£3,867** (£1,190; £595; £297) **Stalls** High

Form RPR
6305 **1** **Faraway Echo**[25] 4102 3-7-12 **50** oh3 ........ MHalford 4 60
(JamesMoffatt) *hld up in tch: effrt 3f out: rallied to ld ins fnl f: styd on* **25/1**
6042 **2** 1 **Alpine Special (IRE)**[5] 4678 3-8-8 **67** ........ GBartley(7) 1 76
(PCHaslam) *keen early: chsd ldrs: led over 2f out to ins fnl f: kpt on same pce* **7/2**
0531 **3** 17 **Easibet Dot Net**[17] 4328 4-9-11 **67** ........ (p) WHogg 2 52
(ISemple) *led to over 2f out: sn btn* **2/1**[1]
153 **4** 8 **Kid'Z'Play (IRE)**[36] 3796 8-9-13 **69** ........ HPoulton 5 43
(JSGoldie) *chsd ldr tl wknd fr over 3f out* **10/3**[3]
4224 **5** 11 **Spree Vision**[17] 4328 8-8-7 **49** ........ (v) AMullen 3 8
(PMonteith) *prom: rdn over 3f out: sn btn* **11/4**[2]

2m 43.35s (4.15) **Going Correction** +0.45s/f (Yiel)
**WFA** 3 from 4yo+ 10lb **5** Ran SP% **109.1**
Speed ratings: **104,103,92,86,79**CSF £103.72 TOTE £27.10: £7.60, £2.60; EX 55.40 Place 6 £160.18, Place 5 £148.51.
**Owner** Alf Chadwick **Bred** R P Williams **Trained** Cartmel, Cumbria



The Form Book, Raceform Ltd, Compton, RG20 6NL

**FOCUS**
A moderate apprentice handicap in which they finished incredibly well strung out and all across the track in the straight, with the first two home finishing up the stands' rail. As a result, the form wants treating with caution.
**NOTEBOOK**
**Faraway Echo** improved for the switch to soft ground and step up to a mile and a half, and was able to get off the mark despite drifting right the way across the track. It is hard to know what the form is worth, but at least connections now know her optimum conditions.
**Alpine Special(IRE)** had gained his only previous win over a mile on fast ground, but he handles soft conditions and this trip was not a problem either.
**Easibet Dot Net** gained his only previous turf win on fast ground and was a long way below form on this much easier surface.
**Kid'Z'Play(IRE)** should have been suited by the conditions but he was a long way below form.
**Spree Vision** was another that should have been suited by the ground, but was a long way below his best.
T/Plt: £161.90 to a £1 stake. Pool: £38,510.75. 173.55 winning tickets. T/Qpdt: £86.40 to a £1 stake. Pool: £2,769.80. 23.70 winning tickets. RY

## 4149 YORK (L-H)
### Tuesday, August 17

**OFFICIAL GOING: Good (good to soft in places)**
After the recent heavy rains the going was described by the jockeys as 'dead, hard work and a bit sticky'. They tended to avoid the running rail.
Wind: Moderate 1/2 behind. Weather: Fine and sunny.

### 4831 LADBROKE KNAVESMIRE STKS (H'CAP) — 1m 3f 198y
1:20 (1:23) (C) (0-95,94) 3-Y-O+ — £15,925 (£4,900; £2,450; £1,225) Stalls Low

Form | RPR
2314 **1** **Sualda (IRE)**[10] 4550 5-8-9 **74** ... SSanders 19 — 85
(RAFahey) *stdd s and bhd: hdwy over 4f out: str run to chal over 1f out: sn rdn: styd on u.p to ld nr fin* **33/1**
1320 **2** *nk* **Court Of Appeal**[24] 4123 7-9-5 **87** ... (t) TEaves(3) 3 — 98
(BEllison) *a.p: hdwy to ld 3f out: jnd and rdn over 1f out: drvn ins last: hdd and no ex nr line* **16/1**
2500 **3** *3* **Kristensen**[20] 4226 5-8-9 **77** ... (p) JFMcDonald(3) 1 — 83
(DEddy) *chsd ldrs: pushed along and outpcd over 3f out: rdn 2f out: kpt on wl u.p fnl f* **25/1**
1105 **4** *nk* **Millville**[17] 4345 4-9-6 **85** ... PRobinson 17 — 91
(MAJarvis) *hld up: hdwy on wd outside over 3f out: rdn wl over 1f out: kpt on same pce* **16/1**
-533 **5** *3/4* **Torinmoor (USA)**[41] 3641 3-9-2 **91** ... MJKinane 4 — 96
(MrsAJPerrett) *hld up towards rr: gd hdwy on wd outside 3f out: rdn to chse ldrs and hung bdly lft wl over 1f out: sn drvn and one pce* **12/1**
-160 **6** *1 1/4* **Ski Jump (USA)**[10] 4540 4-9-4 **83** ... (v) PHanagan 8 — 86
(RAFahey) *midfield: hdwy over 3f out: rdn 2f out: kpt on appr last: nrst fin* **25/1**
2-06 **7** *1 3/4* **Laggan Bay (IRE)**[94] 2110 4-8-7 **75** ... LPKeniry(3) 10 — 75
(JCFox) *swtg: bhd: hdwy 3f out: styd on wl fnl 2f: nrst fin* **50/1**
-252 **8** *1* **Genghis (IRE)**[32] 3909 5-9-2 **81** ... JFortune 2 — 79
(HMorrison) *cl up: led 7f out tl rdn along and hdd 3f out: grad wknd fnl 2f* **16/1**
2345 **9** *1 1/4* **Prins Willem (IRE)**[38] 3757 5-9-10 **89** ... JPMurtagh 7 — 85
(JRFanshawe) *midfield: hdwy 4f out: in tch and rdn along 3f out: wknd 2f out* **10/1**[2]
5625 **10** *4* **Jabaar (USA)**[38] 3756 6-9-6 **85** ... JPSpencer 16 — 75
(MWEasterby) *in rr and hmpd over 6f out: hdwy on inner over 2f out: sn rdn and kpt on: nt rch ldrs* **14/1**
4340 **11** *1 3/4* **Crathorne (IRE)**[40] 3678 4-8-12 **77** ... (p) LDettori 22 — 64
(JDBethell) *a rr* **20/1**
0040 **12** *3* **Turbo (IRE)**[45] 3521 5-10-0 **93** ... (p) SDrowne 18 — 75
(GBBalding) *hld up: a rr* **28/1**
**13** *nk* **Wet Lips (AUS)**[16] 6-8-6 **76** ... (bt) RoryMoore(5) 12 — 58
(RCGuest) *stmbld s: sn cl up: rdn along over 4f out and sn wknd* **50/1**
0054 **14** *nk* **Best Be Going (IRE)**[27] 4019 4-8-11 **76** ... EAhern 6 — 57
(PWHarris) *midfield: hdwy 1/2-way: effrt to chse ldrs 3f out: sn rdn and wknd fnl 2f* **20/1**
0-2 **15** *1/2* **Pretty Star (GER)**[2] 4777 4-9-9 **88** ... JFanning 15 — 68
(MJohnston) *chsd ldrs: rdn along 1/2-way: wknd over 4f out* **16/1**
2136 **16** *hd* **Les Arcs (USA)**[17] 4319 4-8-12 **77** ... KFallon 14 — 57
(RCGuest) *a rr* **16/1**
2130 **17** *6* **Etmaam**[20] 4229 3-9-5 **94** ... RHills 9 — 64
(MJohnston) *a rr* **15/2**[1]
-444 **18** *5* **Bagan (FR)**[96] 2066 5-9-9 **88** ... TGillet 13 — 50
(HRACecil) *chsd ldrs: rdn along over 4f out: sn drvn and wknd* **11/1**[3]
0-00 **19** *3 1/2* **Spectrometer**[31] 3310 7-9-1 **80** ... DHolland 11 — 37
(RCGuest) *s.i.s: sltly hmpd over 6f out: a bhd* **25/1**
1015 **F** **King Of Dreams (IRE)**[10] 4540 3-9-5 **94** ... SChin 21 — —
(MJohnston) *prom tl broke leg and fell over 6f out: dead* **12/1**
4436 **U** **Sporting Gesture**[16] 4363 7-8-10 **75** ... TLucas 20 — —
(MWEasterby) *hld up in rr whn bdly hmpd and uns rdr over 6f out* **33/1**

2m 32.89s (4.03) **Going Correction** +0.60s/f (Yiel)
**WFA** 3 from 4yo+ 10lb — **21 Ran SP% 115.0**
Speed ratings: **110,109,107,107,107 106,105,104,103,100 99,97,97,97,97 96,92,89,87,—,—**CSF £372.34 CT £9452.05 TOTE £35.70: £6.70, £4.00, £5.60, £3.60; EX 1033.80 TRIFECTA Not won..
**Owner** J H Tattersall **Bred** St Simon Foundation **Trained** Musley Bank, N Yorks
**FOCUS**
A typically competitive handicap for the track run at a decent pace, though not that many got into it. The time was creditable for the class given the easy conditions, although a few didn't show their form as a result, making the strength of the form debatable.
**NOTEBOOK**
**Sualda(IRE)** ◆, who ran over two miles last time, proved well suited by this fast-run 12 furlongs on a galloping track. He was very brave in a driving finish and, given that it seemed difficult for many to make ground from off the pace in this contest, his style of victory is all the more creditable. He is very consistent and, as this was the highest mark he has ever won off, he still seems to be improving even at the age of five.
**Court Of Appeal**, never far away, took it up passing the three-furlong pole and gave nothing away in the prolonged battle to the line with the winner. The easy ground was in his favour, but this was still a cracking effort off a 9lb higher mark than for his last win.
**Kristensen** usually races over trips of at least two miles these days, but was suited by the decent gallop and ran a fine race to make the frame. The problem is that it is well over two years since he won on turf, off a 10lb lower mark than this, and this effort is unlikely to see him drop.
**Millville**, unplaced in his only two previous outings on turf, looked a danger to all when moving up strongly down the middle of the track in the home straight, but was unable to maintain it. This was his first attempt on an easy surface and, given his liking for Polytrack, perhaps he needs it faster.
**Torinmoor(USA)**, stepping up two furlongs in trip, made up ground quickly on the wide outside starting up the home straight, but then faltered and started to hang as he got tired. This trip in the conditions appeared to stretch him.
**Ski Jump(USA)** ◆ has gained all three of his previous wins from the front, but ran well under a more patient ride this time without ever offering a threat. He is not the easiest of rides, but has the ability to win again when things go his way.
**Laggan Bay(IRE)** ◆, off since May, faced a stiff task in trying to come from off the pace, but did well to reach his final position on ground that was probably softer than ideal.
**Prins Willem(IRE)** would have preferred faster ground and did not get home in the conditions.
**Jabaar(USA)** ◆ was probably one of the chief sufferers in the melee at halfway, so should be rated a few lengths better than his final position.
**Crathorne(IRE)** more or less lost his chance with a tardy start.
**Etmaam** got slightly hampered in the incident involving King Of Dreams at halfway, but never looked like picking up and was very disappointing.
**Bagan(FR)**, never looked like reproducing his victory in this race last year on this much easier ground.
**Spectrometer**, winner of this race two years ago, is better known as a chaser these days. The ground would not have suited, but a slow start more or less sealed his fate and he never figured.
**Sporting Gesture** was right at the back of the field when running into the stricken King Of Dreams at halfway and his rider had no chance of staying aboard.
**King Of Dreams(IRE)** broke quickly from his wide draw and was disputing the lead when tragically breaking a leg at halfway.

### 4832 WEATHERBYS INSURANCE LONSDALE CUP (GROUP 2) — 1m 7f 198y
1:50 (1:54) (A) 3-Y-O+ — £58,000 (£22,000; £11,000; £5,000) Stalls Low

Form | RPR
-012 **1** **First Charter**[18] 4285 5-9-1 112 ... KFallon 2 — 118
(SirMichaelStoute) *hld up in tch: gd hdwy on outer 3f out: rdn and hung lft 1f out drvn and styd on wl to ld ins last* **7/1**[3]
1/12 **2** *nk* **Dancing Bay**[31] 3076 7-9-1 104 ... WRyan 5 — 118
(NJHenderson) *hld up in tch: hdwy 3f out: rdn to ld over 1f out: sn drvn and hdd ins last: kpt on gamely u.p* **25/1**
2-31 **3** *3* **Millenary**[96] 2067 7-9-4 118 ... (b) MJKinane 10 — 117
(JLDunlop) *lw: hld up: smooth hdwy on outer 3f out: chal over 1f out and ev ch tl rdn and one pce ins last* **11/8**[1]
5012 **4** *2 1/2* **Swing Wing**[52] 3310 5-9-1 110 ... JFortune 8 — 111
(PFICole) *cl up: led over 3f out: sn rdn along: drvn and hdd over 1f out: grad wknd* **7/1**[3]
3315 **5** *1 1/2* **Romany Prince**[19] 4270 5-9-1 109 ... RHughes 7 — 109
(DRCElsworth) *hld up in rr: hdwy 4f out: rdn along over 2f out: kpt on: nvr rch ldrs* **16/1**
16 **6** *1 3/4* **Corrib Eclipse**[45] 3538 5-9-1 104 ... JFEgan 6 — 107
(JamiePoulton) *hld up in rr: rdn along 4f out: kpt on u.p fnl 3f: nvr a factor* **50/1**
0442 **7** *1 1/2* **Royal Rebel**[19] 4270 8-9-1 110 ... (v) JPMurtagh 4 — 105
(MJohnston) *chsd ldrs and rn in snatches: chsd laong over 5f out: rdn along over 3f out and grad wknd* **14/1**
-532 **8** *1 3/4* **Bailamos (GER)**[16] 4-9-1 ... SSanders 1 — 103
(PSchiergen, Germany) *trckd ldrs: smooth hdwy over 3f out: ev ch over 2f out: sn rdn and wknd* **14/1**
3326 **9** *6* **Silver Gilt**[19] 4270 4-9-1 109 ... LDettori 3 — 96
(JHMGosden) *led: rdn along and hdd over 3f out: sn wknd* **12/1**
1215 **10** *5* **Duke Of Venice (USA)**[21] 4215 3-8-1 114 ... (t) KMcEvoy 9 — 90
(SaeedBinSuroor) *cl up: rdn along over 4f out and sn wknd* **13/2**[2]

3m 25.94s (2.69) **Going Correction** +0.60s/f (Yiel)
**WFA** 3 from 4yo+ 14lb — **10 Ran SP% 113.2**
Speed ratings: **117,116,115,114,113 112,111,110,107,105**CSF £158.58 TOTE £5.50: £2.10, £3.40, £1.30; EX 93.30 Trifecta £376.10 Pool £1,377.31, 2.60 w/u.
**Owner** Saeed Suhail **Bred** W And R Barnett Ltd **Trained** Newmarket, Suffolk
■ This race, previously known as the Lonsdale Stakes, has been upgraded to Group Two status.
**FOCUS**
A solid renewal for this staying contest and creditable winning time for a Group Two given the conditions, making the form looks solid.
**NOTEBOOK**
**First Charter**, a big drifter because of the ground, made very hard work of it. However, the champion was at his most determined and used all his body strength to put his head in front where it matters most. He is a tough individual, a typical improver late in life, the hallmark of his trainer.
**Dancing Bay**, out of sorts over hurdles a month earlier, had 8lb to find with the winner on official ratings. With the ground to suit, he ran the race of his life and in the end was just denied. After this handicaps will be out of the question.
**Millenary**, who had to give the Ascot Gold Cup a miss, returned to the scene of his Yorkshire Cup triumph. He travelled supremely well but was left toiling by the first two in the final furlong. He seems best at distances short of two miles.
**Swing Wing**, warm beforehand, showed a moderate action. He has failed to make his mark now in ten tries at Group level, and Listed races abroad offer his best winning opportunity.
**Romany Prince**, settled towards the rear, never got competitive.
**Corrib Eclipse** found this much too tough. He basically just stays.
**Royal Rebel**, who prefers quicker ground, was on and off the bridle and these days really needs the full two and a half miles.
**Duke Of Venice(USA)**, taking on his elders, was in an exuberant mood beforehand but was on the retreat once in line for home, his second successive below-par performance.

### 4833 DAILY TELEGRAPH GREAT VOLTIGEUR STKS (GROUP 2) (C&G) — 1m 3f 198y
2:25 (2:25) (A) 3-Y-O — £78,300 (£29,700; £14,850; £6,750) Stalls Low

Form | RPR
-224 **1** **Rule Of Law (USA)**[51] 3353 3-8-9 118 ... (t) LDettori 2 — 121
(SaeedBinSuroor) *lw: set stdy pce: qcknd 4f out: pushed along and qcknd again 2f out: rdn over 1f out and styd on wl* **11/8**[1]
1335 **2** *2 1/2* **Let The Lion Roar**[51] 3353 3-8-9 118 ... (v) MJKinane 1 — 117
(JLDunlop) *trckd ldrs: hdwy over 2f out: effrt to chse wnr wl over 1f out: sn rdn and one pce* **11/4**[2]
-32 **3** *1 1/2* **Go For Gold (IRE)**[21] 4215 3-8-9 ... JPSpencer 8 — 115
(APO'Brien, Ire) *hld up towards rr: gd hdwy 3f out: rdn to chse ldng pair wl over 1f out: sn drvn and one pce* **7/1**[3]
-023 **4** *1 1/4* **Always First**[20] 4229 3-8-9 95 ... KFallon 4 — 113
(SirMichaelStoute) *trac ked ldrs: hdwy to chse wnr after 5f: rdn along and outpcd 3f out: kpt on same pce u.p fnl 2f* **8/1**
-102 **5** *2 1/2* **Pukka (IRE)**[31] 3927 3-8-9 105 ... DHolland 5 — 109
(LMCumani) *hld up and bhd: hdwy over 3f out: sn rdn along and no imp* **8/1**
6060 **6** *2 1/2* **Red Lancer**[20] 4229 3-8-9 105 ... MFenton 6 — 105
(RJPrice) *hld up: hdwy to chse ldrs 3f out: rdn and wknd 2f out* **33/1**

7 12 **Rio De Janeiro (IRE)**[25] 4115 3-8-9 ............................(v[1]) JPMurtagh 7 85
(APO'Brien, Ire) *in tch: rdn along 1/2-way: wknd wl over 3f out* **40/1**

2m 37.1s (8.24) **Going Correction** +0.60s/f (Yiel) 7 Ran SP% **108.9**
Speed ratings: **96,94,93,92,90 89,81**CSF £4.65 TOTE £2.40: £1.50, £2.20; EX 4.40 Trifecta £20.40 Pool £940.16, 32.60 w/u.
**Owner** Godolphin **Bred** R E Sangster And Ben Sangster **Trained** Newmarket, Suffolk

**FOCUS**
A falsely-run race with Dettori dictating things from the front, but the best horse won and he is now favourite for the St Leger. The winning time was 4.21 seconds slower than Sualda took to win the opener, but the form still appears fairly sound.

**NOTEBOOK**
**Rule Of Law(USA)** ◆, who looked at his very best, set his own pace. Stepping up the gallop once in line for home, in the end he came clear to score in most decisive fashion. Though his breeding suggests otherwise, the extended trip in the St Leger should not be a problem and he must be the colt they all have to overcome.
**Let The Lion Roar** went in pursuit of the winner but for the fourth time this season he finished behind him. A half-brother to Millenary, the 2000 St Leger winner, connections will be hoping for a much stronger pace on the Town Moor.
**Go For Gold(IRE)**, a half-brother to the 2001 St Leger winner Milan, looked very fit indeed but the way he was ridden, in a race run at a crawl until the final turn, meant he had little chance of showing his true worth.
**Always First**, keeping tabs on the winner, stayed on after being tapped for toe halfway up the home straight. He might well come good in the Cup races at four.
**Pukka(IRE)**, on ground softer than he prefers, never got competitive and is another who will be seen in better light with another year over his head.
**Red Lancer**, very keen to post, has been one of the surprise packets this year but this was just too tough.
**Rio De Janeiro(IRE)**, tried in a visor this time, showed a very scratchy action. If he was not in as a pacemaker for Go For Gold, what was the point in bringing him for this?

## 4834 JUDDMONTE INTERNATIONAL STKS (GROUP 1) 1m 2f 88y
**3:00** (3:00) (A) 3-Y-0+ **£266,800** (£101,200; £50,600; £23,000) **Stalls** Low

Form RPR

-423 **1** **Sulamani (IRE)**[24] 4121 5-9-5 124 ............................(t) LDettori 9 126+
(SaeedBinSuroor) *hld up: stdy hdwy 4f out: styd on fnl 2f: led last 50 yds* **3/1**[2]

0441 **2** ¾ **Norse Dancer (IRE)**[5] 4685 4-9-5 116 ............................ JFEgan 1 125
(DRCElsworth) *trckd ldrs: led 2f out: hdd and no ex towards fin* **16/1**

1-11 **3** ¾ **Bago (FR)**[51] 3360 3-8-11 ............................ TGillet 6 123+
(JEPease, France) *trckd ldrs: drvn along over 4f out: kpt on same pce ins fnl f* **13/8**[1]

221 **4** 5 **Cacique (IRE)**[19] 4284 3-8-11 ............................ GaryStevens 10 114
(AFabre, France) *lw: hld up: effrt 4f out: edgd lft 2f out: nvr rchd ldrs* **10/1**

50-0 **5** ¾ **Millstreet**[18] 4285 5-9-5 110 ............................(t) KMcEvoy 4 113
(SaeedBinSuroor) *led: qcknd 7f out: sn clr: hdd 2f out: fdd* **100/1**

2131 **6** ½ **Kalaman (IRE)**[29] 3978 4-9-5 116 ............................ KFallon 2 112
(SirMichaelStoute) *lw: trckd ldrs: effrt over 3f out: fdd fnl f* **6/1**[3]

6003 **7** ½ **Imperial Dancer**[16] 4385 6-9-5 114 ............................ TEDurcan 8 111
(MRChannon) *hld up in last pl: kpt on fnl 3f: nvr a factor* **33/1**

-221 **8** 6 **Solskjaer (IRE)**[9] 4587 4-9-5 ............................ JPMurtagh 5 100
(APO'Brien, Ire) *chsd ldr: rdn and hung lft 3f out: lost pl over 1f out* **33/1**

4-36 **9** *dist* **Tycoon**[24] 4121 3-8-11 ............................ JPSpencer 7 —
(APO'Brien, Ire) *swtg: dwlt: a bhd: drvn along over 4f out: no rspnse: eased and t.o* **7/1**

2m 11.82s (2.38) **Going Correction** +0.60s/f (Yiel)
**WFA** 3 from 4yo+ 8lb 9 Ran SP% **111.7**
Speed ratings: **114,113,112,108,108 107,107,102,—**CSF £46.05 TOTE £3.30: £1.40, £3.40, £1.30; EX 46.60 Trifecta £180.20 Pool £3,045.99, 12.00 w/u.
**Owner** Godolphin **Bred** The Niarchos Family **Trained** Newmarket, Suffolk
■ Stewards Enquiry : L Dettori one-day ban: used whip with excessive frequency and without allowing horse time to respond (Aug 28)

**FOCUS**
Hardly a vintage renewal of this Group One, particularly with Azamour a late withdrawal, but a sound pace and the first three were clear. Sulamani picked up another £100,000 for winning the BHB Middle Distance Championship. The winning time was only fair for a Group One.

**NOTEBOOK**
**Sulamani(IRE)**, unimpressive as ever beforehand, never flinched, nailing the runner-up near the line. Suited by the give underfoot, he is a real battler in this sort of mood, but Godolphin have a much better candidate for the Arc in his Ascot conqueror Doyen.
**Norse Dancer(IRE)**, in the frame now in seven Group One events, really took the eye going to post. Sent on two furlongs out, he looked like holding on but in the end the winner was just too determined. His trainer, who defends him to the hilt, has the Cox Plate in mind.
**Bago(FR)**, unbeaten in six previous starts, is not that big and lacks scope. In trouble once in line for home, to his credit he stayed on all the way to the line. This was have taught him something and a much sharper track will suit him better.
**Cacique(IRE)**, whose two defeats in five starts were at the hands of Bago, is a grand type. He looked in real trouble early in the straight and then tended to go left-handed under a right-hand drive. He is not bred to handle easy ground and is a fair bit better than he was able to show on this occasion.
**Millstreet**, reportedly cast in his box, was carrying plenty of cuts and bruises. He was given a copybook pacemaking ride, and only really tired in the final furlong. He deserves a pat on the back for his vital part in Godolphin eventually taking this Group One prize.
**Kalaman(IRE)**, who disappointed in this a year ago, looked at his very best but was again below par. Perhaps this track does not suit him and he really prefers much quicker ground.
**Imperial Dancer** was far from disgraced but in truth was never a factor, and his Group One success last term was in Italy.
**Solskjaer(IRE)**, who has done well to come back from two serious injuries, was unable to dominate this time and the ground was much more testing.
**Tycoon**, edgy in the paddock, had two handlers and was very warm behind the stalls. He found nothing at all and eventually struggled to reach the winning line. His trainer explained he was unsuited by the ground, but that was surely only part of the story. *Official explanation: trainer said colt was unsuited by the ground*

## 4835 NATIONAL STUD NEVER SAY DIE CLUB ACOMB STKS (LISTED RACE) 6f 217y
**3:35** (3:35) (A) 2-Y-0 **£16,250** (£5,000; £2,500; £1,250) **Stalls** Low

Form RPR

1 **1** **Elliots World (IRE)**[39] 3718 2-8-13 ............................ JFanning 5 99
(MJohnston) *trckd ldrs: led 2f out: edgd lft: hld on wl towards fin* **5/2**[2]

1 **2** *nk* **Oude (USA)**[23] 4169 2-8-13 ............................ LDettori 1 98+
(SaeedBinSuroor) *t.k.h towards rr: stdy hdwy over 2f out: sn nt clr run: edgd lft over 1f out: nt qckn wl ins last* **9/4**[1]

2 **3** ½ **Shannon Springs (IRE)**[23] 4169 2-8-10 ............................ MHills 2 94
(BWHills) *lw: hld up: effrt 3f out: sn chsng ldrs: nt qckn ins last* **7/1**

3321 **4** 2 **Capable Guest (IRE)**[9] 4567 2-8-13 100 ............................ TEDurcan 7 92
(MRChannon) *dwlt: hdwy over 4f out: one pce fnl 2f* **7/2**[3]

2211 **5** 1½ **Jane Jubilee (IRE)**[19] 4278 2-8-5 95 ............................ SChin 3 80
(MJohnston) *w ldrs wknd over 1f out* **12/1**

31 **6** *shd* **Raza Cab (IRE)**[27] 4022 2-8-10 90 ............................ KFallon 6 85
(GAHuffer) *trckd ldrs: effrt over 3f out: lost pl 2f out* **11/1**

02 **7** 1½ **Shrine Mountain (USA)**[13] 4461 2-8-10 ............................ SSanders 4 81
(CEBrittain) *led tl 2f out: wkng whn hmpd over 1f out* **50/1**

1m 25.06s (1.75) **Going Correction** +0.30s/f (Good) 7 Ran SP% **112.0**
Speed ratings: **102,101,101,98,97 96,95**CSF £8.19 TOTE £2.90: £1.60, £1.80; EX 6.60.
**Owner** Atlantic Racing Limited **Bred** K And Mrs Cullen **Trained** Middleham Moor, N Yorks

**FOCUS**
A fairly good renewal of this contest but just a steady pace to halfway. Of the first two, the winner has more substance and scope, all the first three came into this with just once previous outing and are open to improvement.

**NOTEBOOK**
**Elliots World(IRE)** ◆, taken quietly to post, dived left towards the far rail in front but in the end did just enough. Quite a late foal, he still has a bit to learn and looks a smart prospect.
**Oude(USA)**, quite a tall, finely-made individual, travelled supremely well. Left short of room for a few strides at a vital stage, he quickened up in pursuit of the winner but on this ground was never quite going to close the gap. He looked the best horse on the day but may not be the better long-term prospect.
**Shannon Springs(IRE)** ◆, beaten a neck by Oude at Newmarket, was meeting him on 3lb better terms. He took a while to pick up but was staying on in willing fashion at the line. He is surely a ready-made winner in lesser company.
**Capable Guest(IRE)**, having his sixth start, is the benchmark for the value of the form.
**Jane Jubilee(IRE)**, winner of two nurseries, found this much too tough and much quicker ground seems to suit her a lot better.
**Raza Cab(IRE)** found this a big step up in class but was far from disgraced. However this will not have done his nursery mark much good.
**Shrine Mountain(USA)** led on sufferance and was on the retreat when the winner left him short of room. *Official explanation: jockey said colt was unsuited by the ground*

## 4836 IRWIN MITCHELL SOLICITORS STKS (NURSERY H'CAP) 6f
**4:10** (4:10) (C) 2-Y-0 **£11,797** (£3,630; £1,815; £907) **Stalls** Centre

Form RPR

1333 **1** **Space Shuttle**[9] 4575 2-8-13 **86** ............................ KFallon 9 97
(TDEasterby) *lw: hld up: hdwy 3f out: styd on wl to ld towards fin* **13/2**[3]

2214 **2** ½ **Distinctly Game**[11] 4508 2-8-7 **80** ............................ NCallan 15 89
(KARyan) *lw: trckd ldrs on outer: led over 1f out: hdd and no ex nr fin* **10/1**

4112 **3** 1 **The Crooked Ring**[13] 4439 2-8-11 **91** ............................ SJDonohoe[(7)] 13 97
(PDEvans) *hld up: hdwy 2f out: nt qckn fnl f* **16/1**

1320 **4** 5 **Piddies Pride (IRE)**[10] 4552 2-7-12 **74** ............................ FPFerris[(3)] 8 65
(PSMcentee) *chsd ldrs: outpcd appr fnl f* **25/1**

16 **5** 1¾ **Bolton Hall (IRE)**[59] 3071 2-9-0 **87** ............................ PHanagan 14 73
(RAFahey) *hld up and bhd: kpt on fnl 2f: nvr nr ldrs* **7/1**

3211 **6** ½ **Transaction (IRE)**[17] 4342 2-9-3 **90** ............................ SDrowne 12 74
(JMPEustace) *in tch on outer: effrt 2f out: nvr able chal* **6/1**[2]

3531 **7** *nk* **My Princess (IRE)**[13] 4432 2-8-5 **78** ............................ EAhern 6 61
(NACallaghan) *sltly hmpd s: sn chsng ldrs: wknd 1f out* **16/1**

01 **8** 2 **Toby's Dream (IRE)**[19] 4256 2-8-9 **82** ............................ JFanning 1 59
(MJohnston) *led tl over 1f out: sn wknd* **20/1**

51 **9** ½ **Lubeck**[23] 4172 2-8-11 **84** ............................ TPQueally 7 60
(DRLoder) *dwlt: sn trcking ldrs: wknd over 1f out* **13/2**[3]

2213 **10** ¾ **Melalchrist**[17] 4329 2-9-7 **94** ............................ DHolland 2 68
(JJQuinn) *sn in rr: nvr a factor* **16/1**

1250 **11** *nk* **Selkirk Storm (IRE)**[24] 4150 2-8-8 **81** ............................ DaleGibson 5 54
(MWEasterby) *hmpd s: sn chsng ldrs: hung lft and lost pl over 1f out* **33/1**

604 **12** 6 **Rich Albi**[54] 3248 2-8-0 **73** ............................(b[1]) FNorton 3 28
(TDEasterby) *sn drvn along in mid-field: lost pl 3f out: sn bhd and eased* **33/1**

321 **13** 2½ **Turnaround (GER)**[17] 4347 2-8-8 **81** ............................ IMongan 4 28
(MrsJRRamsden) *swvd rt s: sn chsng ldrs: edgd lft and lost pl over 1f out: eased* **3/1**[1]

1m 12.23s (-0.34) **Going Correction** -0.10s/f (Good) 13 Ran SP% **119.7**
Speed ratings: **98,97,96,89,87 86,85,83,82,81 81,73,69**CSF £66.91 CT £695.22 TOTE £7.40: £2.00, £4.90, £5.50; EX 156.90 Trifecta £1607.70 Pool £2,490.93, 1.10 w/u.
**Owner** Jennifer Pallister & Jonathan Gill **Bred** Miss S E Hall **Trained** Great Habton, N Yorks

**FOCUS**
A competitive nursery on paper run at a decent pace and those drawn high appeared to hold an advantage. The first three finished a long way clear of the others and the form looks very solid.

**NOTEBOOK**
**Space Shuttle**, who had shown ability on easy ground on his debut, was suited by the decent gallop and utilised his stamina to come from off the pace and get up near the line. Another furlong will be no problem and there are more races to be won with him.
**Distinctly Game**, given a positive ride from his stands'-side draw, looked the likely winner for a long way and did nothing wrong, but the winner had the legs of him near the line. He probably prefers faster ground and he should be found another opportunity.
**The Crooked Ring**, 8lb higher than his most recent winning mark, made his effort from the back of the field after halfway and looked a big danger to all, but had nothing left in the closing stages. He pulled a long way clear of the others and should be able to win again, considering his consistency and that he seems oblivious to ground conditions.
**Piddies Pride(IRE)** showed for a while, but could not stop the front three scampering clear. Both her wins have been in sellers and her best form has been on fast ground, so perhaps this was not so bad and she should win again at her own level.
**Bolton Hall(IRE)**, down in class but racing on the easiest ground he has encountered, was never going the early pace and his final placing was as close as he got. He needs to return to seven.
**Transaction(IRE)**, who had both Space Shuttle and Piddies Pride behind him when winning at Newmarket last time, probably found these different conditions a bigger problem than the 3lb higher mark.
**Turnaround(GER)**, well backed, was errant at the start but was still close enough if good enough for much of the way. He started to hang over to the far side over the last couple of furlongs and was allowed to coast home in his own time. He subsequently tested positive for ACP (tranquiliser). *Official explanation: jockey said colt hung left throughout*

## 4837 PATRINGTON HAVEN LEISURE PARK H'CAP 6f
**4:45** (4:46) (C) (0-100,97) 3-Y-0+ **£11,895** (£3,660; £1,830; £915) **Stalls** Centre

Form RPR

322 **1** **Fonthill Road (IRE)**[5] 4677 4-8-3 **73** ............................ PHanagan 8 85+
(RAFahey) *rr-div: hdwy over 2f out: r.o to ld post* **11/2**[2]

0000 **2** *shd* **Watching**[10] 4553 7-8-5 **78** ............................ TEaves[(3)] 7 90
(RAFahey) *mid-div: hdwy over 2f out: led last 75yds: hdd post* **16/1**

420 **3** 1 **Tom Tun**[3] 4759 9-9-13 **97** ............................(b) TLucas 10 106
(JBalding) *trckd ldrs: led 1f out: hdd and no ex wl ins last* **20/1**

1350 **4** 2 **Cloud Dancer**[24] 4122 5-8-6 **76** ............................ NCallan 9 79
(KARyan) *chsd ldrs: outpcd over 2f out: kpt on wl fnl f* **16/1**

-025 **5** *nk* **Golden Dixie (USA)**$^{25}$ [4090] 5-8-12 **82** MartinDwyer 6 84
(AMBalding) *chsd ldrs: hung rt and led over 1f out: sn hdd: fdd ins last* **12/1**

3502 **6** *nk* **Fair Shake (IRE)**$^{24}$ [4130] 4-7-12 **68** (v) DKinsella 14 69
(DEddy) *sn outpcd and bhd: styd on wl fnl 2f: nt rch ldrs* **12/1**

5210 **7** *1 1/4* **Tony The Tap**$^{18}$ [4294] 3-8-10 **83** LDettori 18 80
(NACallaghan) *swvd lft s: bhd: hdwy and wandered over 1f out: nvr nr ldrs* **9/1**$^{3}$

0006 **8** *nk* **Indian Spark**$^{15}$ [4394] 10-8-8 **78** TEDurcan 11 75
(JSGoldie) *hmpd s: bhd tl kpt on fnl 2f: nvr on terms* **10/1**

0216 **9** *shd* **Full Spate**$^{4}$ [4707] 9-8-1 **71** FNorton 17 67
(JMBradley) *hmpd s: bhd: wnt lft over 2f out: nvr on terms* **25/1**

1012 **10** *shd* **Fantasy Believer**$^{17}$ [4324] 6-9-11 **95** DHolland 3 91
(JJQuinn) *chsd ldrs on outer: ev ch 1f out: wknd last 150yds* **5/1**$^{1}$

0140 **11** *1* **Tally (IRE)**$^{8}$ [4614] 4-7-12 **68** oh1 JQuinn 15 61
(MJPolglase) *rr-div: sme hdwy 2f out: nvr on terms* **33/1**

0150 **12** *nk* **Mister Sweets**$^{24}$ [4152] 5-7-13 **72** FPFerris$^{(3)}$ 5 64
(DCarroll) *sn in rr* **50/1**

6600 **13** *nk* **Mr Wolf**$^{39}$ [3702] 3-8-1 **74** JFanning 4 65
(DWBarker) *led tl hdd & wknd over 1f out* **66/1**

1000 **14** *nk* **Artie**$^{3}$ [4759] 5-9-2 **86** JFortune 19 76
(TDEasterby) *swvd lft s: sn chsng ldrs: lost pl over 1f out* **10/1**

3601 **15** *1 1/4* **Semenovskii**$^{11}$ [4522] 4-8-3 **73** (v$^{1}$) TPQueally 1 60
(PWD'Arcy) *chsd ldrs: lost pl 2f out* **20/1**

5520 **16** *3/4* **Law Breaker (IRE)**$^{143}$ [1126] 6-9-2 **89** BReilly$^{(3)}$ 13 73
(JAGilbert) *chsd ldrs: hung rt and lost pl over 2f out* **28/1**

0002 **17** *3/4* **Brave Burt (IRE)**$^{3}$ [4748] 7-8-10 **80** KFallon 16 62
(DNicholls) *w ldrs: wknd and heavily eased fnl f* **9/1**$^{3}$

2000 **18** *hd* **Johnston's Diamond (IRE)**$^{32}$ [3901] 6-9-3 **87** SSanders 12 68
(EJAlston) *w ldrs: lost pl over 1f out* **20/1**

5150 **19** *15* **Chappel Cresent (IRE)**$^{54}$ [3235] 4-9-10 **94** ANicholls 2 30
(DNicholls) *sn bhd: eased and lost tch fnl 2f* **33/1**

1m 11.06s (-1.51) **Going Correction** -0.10s/f (Good)
**WFA** 3 from 4yo+ 3lb **19** Ran SP% **128.3**
Speed ratings: **106,105,104,101,101 101,99,99,98,98 97,97,96,96,94 93,92,92,72**CSF £81.87 CT £1689.00 TOTE £7.20: £2.00, £4.80, £4.40, £4.50; EX 129.80 Trifecta £2735.00 Pool £3,852.22, 0.70 w/u - part won. Place 6 £84.30, Place 5 £10.17.
**Owner** Mrs Una Towell **Bred** D N Wallace **Trained** Musley Bank, N Yorks

**FOCUS**
A typically competitive sprint handicap run at a decent pace and again it paid to be drawn middle to high. The form looks solid for the grade.

**NOTEBOOK**
**Fonthill Road(IRE)** had no Irish dark horse to worry about this time and, after being given a patient ride, stormed down the middle of the track to get up on the line. He is very consistent indeed, loves these conditions, and still seems to be improving.
**Watching**, on ground he likes, did everything right and looked to have timed his effort to perfection, only to have the prize snatched from him on the line. He has dropped to a mark he can win off and end a losing run stretching back more than four years.
**Tom Tun** appreciated being able to get his toe in and ran a fine race under a positive ride, but is creeping back up the handicap despite not winning.
**Cloud Dancer ◆** was staying on nicely at the end and deserves credit as all her best turf form has been on fast ground. She is one to watch back on a quicker surface.
**Golden Dixie(USA)** again ran well on ground that would have been easier than ideal, and got tired inside the last furlong. *Official explanation: jockey said gelding hung right-handed throughout*
**Fair Shake(IRE)** had conditions to suit, but did not get going until it was too late and does not look an easy ride.
**Tony The Tap** has shown all his best form on fast ground, so this was not a bad effort against his elders and another opportunity can be found.
**Fantasy Believer** is now on a very stiff mark after his cracking effort in the Stewards' Cup, and a brief effort right over on the far side of the track came to nothing. To be fair, all those drawn very low struggled to get into it.
**Mister Sweets** *Official explanation: jockey said gelding was unsuited by the ground*
**Mr Wolf ◆** is starting to drop back down the handicap and showed good speed for a long way before fading. This was not a bad effort considering his price, and he can win again at his own level when able to get his toe in.
**Law Breaker(IRE)** *Official explanation: jockey said gelding hung right-handed throughout*
**Brave Burt(IRE)** showed up for a while, but faded rather tamely and does not seem to run two races alike these days. *Official explanation: jockey said gelding lost its action*
**Chappel Cresent(IRE)** *Official explanation: jockey said gelding was moving badly throughout*
T/Jkpt: Not won. T/Plt: £211.80 to a £1 stake. Pool: £152,871.05. 526.65 winning tickets. T/Qpdt: £12.60 to a £1 stake. Pool: £10,468.20. 611.40 winning tickets. JR

## 4386 CARLISLE (R-H)
Wednesday, August 18
**4838 Meeting Abandoned** - Waterlogged

## 4438 KEMPTON (R-H)
Wednesday, August 18

**OFFICIAL GOING: Soft (good to soft in places)**
On the straight course they raced towards the far side, and on the round courses they came stands' side in the straight.
Wind: almost nil Weather: torrential downpour before racing; bright races 1-5; heavy rain race 6

### 4844 EVENING STANDARD MAIDEN STKS 6f
5:25 (5:28) (D) 2-Y-O £4,959 (£1,526; £763; £381) Stalls High

Form RPR

2 **1** **Rebuttal (USA)**$^{9}$ [4611] 2-9-0 JFortune 4 92
(BJMeehan) *lw: mde virtually all: shkn up over 1f out: hrd pressed and hung lft ins fnl f: drvn out* **5/6**$^{1}$

43 **2** *nk* **Tremar**$^{135}$ [1269] 2-9-0 GCarter 3 91
(TGMills) *pressed wnr thrght: rdn over 1f out: chalng whn carried lft ins fnl f: jst hld* **20/1**

22 **3** *1 3/4* **Daniel Thomas (IRE)**$^{19}$ [4296] 2-9-0 KDarley 8 86
(MrsAJPerrett) *lw: trckd ldrs: rdn over 1f out: kpt on same pce fnl f* **2/1**$^{2}$

**4** *3/4* **Bahia Breeze** 2-8-9 SDrowne 5 79
(RGuest) *cmpt: bit bkwd: trckd ldrs: rdn and outpcd over 1f out: styd on again ins fnl f* **66/1**

40 **5** *3* **Prince Samos (IRE)**$^{9}$ [4611] 2-9-0 RHughes 6 75
(RHannon) *hld up in last pair: outpcd wl over 1f out: nudged along and nvr on terms after* **20/1**

**6** *2 1/2* **Miss Trial** 2-8-9 MHenry 2 62
(MAJarvis) *neat: bit bkwd: t.k.h: hld up in tch: rdn over 2f out: wknd over 1f out* **50/1**

**7** *hd* **Aviation** 2-9-0 DaneO'Neill 7 67
(RHannon) *compt: pushed along in last and rn green: effrt over 2f out: sn wknd* **25/1**

2 **8** *1 3/4* **Middle Earth (USA)**$^{23}$ [4191] 2-8-11 LPKeniry$^{(3)}$ 1 61
(AMBalding) *lw: trckd ldrs tl rdn and wknd wl over 1f out* **8/1**$^{3}$

1m 16.61s (3.54) **Going Correction** +0.25s/f (Good) **8** Ran SP% **115.8**
Speed ratings: **86,85,83,82,78 74,74,72**CSF £23.85 TOTE £2.10: £1.10, £2.90, £1.10; EX 14.50.
**Owner** P Minikes **Bred** Cho Llc, & J P R Stables Llc **Trained** Upper Lambourn, Berks
■ Stewards Enquiry : G Carter caution: used whip with excessive frequency

**FOCUS**
A reasonably competitive maiden, but the pace was just modest in the early stages and the time was very slow time indeed for the grade, even allowing for the conditions. All the field raced towards the far rail. The winner ran to his debut form.

**NOTEBOOK**
**Rebuttal(USA)**, a good second on his debut at Windsor, built on that promise to get off the mark. He had to work quite hard to see off the eventual runner-up, but connections feel he was in front long enough, would not have appreciated the ease in the ground, and could be capable of better over another furlong. Quite highly regarded, he is in the Champagne Stakes, the Mill Reef and the Middle Park, and should be competitive in higher grades.
**Tremar** showed plenty of ability on both his previous starts, but had lost any chance of winning with slow starts both times. However, racing for the first time in 135 days, there were no such problems and he gave the well-fancied winner a good race. Providing he goes the right way from this, he should soon be winning.
**Daniel Thomas(IRE)**, runner-up in Newmarket maidens on both his previous starts, may not have been suited by the modest gallop and just lacked the pace of the front two. He was by no means knocked about when out of winning contention.
**Bahia Breeze**, a 5,000gns purchase out of a five-furlong juvenile winner, made a pleasing debut and looks capable of improvement.
**Prince Samos(IRE)**, behind today's winner when a beaten favourite at Windsor on his previous start, did not get the clearest of runs but was by no means unlucky and has so far failed to build on his debut. He is, though, now qualified for a handicap mark.
**Middle Earth(USA)** shaped really well when second on his debut at Windsor, but proved unable to go on from that despite appearing to have every chance and was disappointing.

### 4845 RETAIL TRUST MAIDEN STKS 6f
5:55 (5:58) (D) 3-Y-O £5,486 (£1,688; £844; £422) Stalls High

Form RPR

2333 **1** **Farewell Gift**$^{11}$ [4555] 3-9-0 **80** (v$^{1}$) RHughes 10 73
(RHannon) *lw: dwlt: sn chsd ldrs: rdn and prog 2f out: led jst over 1f out: drvn out* **11/4**$^{1}$

3650 **2** *1 1/4* **Dr Synn**$^{32}$ [3949] 3-9-0 **66** MTebbutt 1 69
(JAkehurst) *b: racd on outer: wl in rr and pushed along: prog u.p over 1f out: styd on to take 2nd nr fin* **7/1**

32-6 **3** *nk* **Thomas Lawrence (USA)**$^{18}$ [4337] 3-9-0 **88** JQuinn 12 68
(PFICole) *b.bhnd: trckd ldrs: nt clr run 2f out to over 1f out: rdn to chse wnr ins fnl f: unable qck: lost 2nd nr fin* **14/1**

6 **4** *2 1/2* **Victoriana**$^{103}$ [1942] 3-8-9 KDarley 9 56
(HJCollingridge) *disp ld: def advantage 2f out: hdd jst over 1f out: wknd wl ins fnl f* **20/1**

00 **5** *1 1/4* **Iltravitore (IRE)**$^{71}$ [2765] 3-9-0 JFEgan 11 57
(DRCElsworth) *b.bhnd: racd on inner: chsd ldrs: effrt and cl up over 1f out: pushed along and wknd ins fnl f* **50/1**

63 **6** *2 1/2* **Polar Sun**$^{32}$ [3948] 3-9-0 OUrbina 4 49
(JRFanshawe) *lw: racd towards outer: in tch: prog 1/2-way: chsd ldrs 2f out: pushed along and no hdwy after: fdd* **5/1**$^{3}$

33 **7** *1 1/4* **Bold Bunny**$^{18}$ [4337] 3-8-9 GCarter 5 41
(SCWilliams) *racd towards outer: in rr: pushed along over 2f out: sme prog wl over 1f out: no imp after* **11/1**

5 **8** *9* **Heavens Walk**$^{14}$ [4440] 3-9-0 DSweeney 7 19
(PJMakin) *lw: t.k.h: disp ld to 2f out: wknd rapidly fnl f* **12/1**

**9** *1 1/2* **Pearl Farm** 3-8-9 JFortune 2 9
(CAHorgan) *w'like: racd on outer: a in rr: struggling fnl 2f* **25/1**

00 **10** *shd* **Imperial Wizard**$^{14}$ [4440] 3-9-0 ADaly 8 14
(MDIUsher) *b: prom to 1/2-way: wknd* **100/1**

0502 **11** *6* **Imtalkinggibberish**$^{11}$ [4555] 3-9-0 **81** EAhern 6 —
(JRJenkins) *pressed ldrs tl wknd rapidly 2f out* **10/3**$^{2}$

00 **12** *dist* **Shannkara's Quest (USA)**$^{179}$ [845] 3-9-0 JBramhill 3 —
(CNKellett) *a in rr: wknd and eased over 2f out: t.o whn virtually p.u ins fnl f* **66/1**

1m 17.72s (4.65) **Going Correction** +0.25s/f (Good) **12** Ran SP% **114.7**
Speed ratings: **79,77,76,73,71 68,66,54,52,52 44,—**CSF £20.53 TOTE £3.30: £1.40, £2.20, £3.30; EX 19.00.
**Owner** Lady Whent And Friends **Bred** Lady Whent **Trained** East Everleigh, Wilts

**FOCUS**
With a 66-rated performer in second, the form of this maiden is clearly just modest, but they did go a real good pace, possibly too fast. Despite that, the time was even slower than the two-year-old maiden. The whole field raced towards the far rail.

**NOTEBOOK**
**Farewell Gift** was becoming very frustrating, running well but continually finding a couple too good. However, fitted with a visor for the first time, he showed a good attitude under pressure, picking up well having looked in a bit of trouble at halfway. Providing the headgear continues to have a positive effect, he should be competitive back in handicaps.
**Dr Synn**, quite well backed, came from a very unpromising position to grab second, but the winner was just too strong. This was a good effort considering he had 14lb to find with Farewell Gift at the weights and he clearly has a similar race in him, but he just finds this trip on the short side and has still to prove his stamina for seven furlongs.
**Thomas Lawrence(USA)**, disappointing when a beaten favourite on his reappearance, ran a little better but was stick a long way below is official mark of 88.
**Victoriana** was unable to sustain the decent gallop he helped set, but this was still a respectable effort and he could make his mark when handicapped.
**Iltravitore(IRE)** never really posed a serious threat, but is now qualified to run in handicaps and improvement cannot be ruled out in that sphere.
**Polar Sun** was pretty disappointing, especially considering he is bred to handle this sort of ground.
**Bold Bunny** *Official explanation: jockey said filly was unsuited by the good to soft ground*
**Imtalkinggibberish** had shown plenty of ability on his four previous starts, including one easy ground, but this was very disappointing. *Official explanation: jockey said gelding hung badly right in the final furlong*
**Shannkara's Quest(USA)** *Official explanation: jockey said colt had a breathing problem*

## 4846 BETFRED.COM "THE BONUS KING" H'CAP 7f (J)

6:25 (6:27) (D) (0-85,85) 3-Y-0+ £7,133 (£2,195; £1,097; £548) Stalls High

Form RPR

1044 **1** **King's Caprice**[12] 4510 3-9-12 **85** ... SCarson 7 97
(GBBalding) *lw: pressed ldr: pushed into ld over 1f out: hrd pressed ins fnl f: styd on gamely* **7/1**[3]

5430 **2** ½ **Azreme**[33] 3910 4-9-2 **70** ... DaneO'Neill 15 81
(DKIvory) *trckd ldng pair: rdn over 1f out: drvn to join wnr ins fnl f: nt qckn nr fin* **7/1**[3]

0220 **3** 1½ **Bi Polar**[33] 3910 4-9-3 **74** ... LPKeniry(3) 13 81
(DRCElsworth) *chsd ldrs: rdn over 2f out: sn outpcd: kpt on fnl f to take 3rd nr fin* **8/1**

2414 **4** ¾ **Fen Gypsy**[14] 4438 6-8-9 **70** ... SJDonohoe(7) 5 75
(PDEvans) *lw: led to over 1f out: one pce fnl f* **6/1**[1]

0206 **5** 3 **Blue Patrick**[48] 3455 4-9-3 **74** ... LFletcher(3) 14 72
(JMPEustace) *trckd ldng trio: rdn 2f out: fdd over 1f out* **16/1**

4060 **6** 1 **Kareeb (FR)**[11] 4553 7-9-3 **71** ... GCarter 11 66
(WJMusson) *hld up towards rr: shkn up over 2f out: sn outpcd: n.d after* **14/1**

4010 **7** 1 **Molcon (IRE)**[11] 4553 3-9-11 **84** ... JFEgan 6 77
(NACallaghan) *hld up in midfield: pushed along and outpcd 2f out: nvr on terms after* **7/1**[3]

0600 **8** 2 **Oakley Rambo**[6] 4672 5-9-8 **76** ... PDobbs 4 64
(RHannon) *lw: dwlt: racd wd and hld up in rr: outpcd over 2f out: pushed along and no prog after* **25/1**

-003 **9** shd **Ben Lomand**[5] 4727 4-9-3 **71** ... ADaly 16 59
(BWDuke) *settled towards rr: rdn over 2f out: no prog and btn wl over 1f out* **25/1**

1100 **10** 7 **Oh Boy (IRE)**[33] 3910 4-9-3 **71** ... RHughes 10 41
(RHannon) *trckd ldrs: lost pl 3f out: pushed along and steadily wknd* **16/1**

2125 **11** 1¼ **Balerno**[14] 4438 5-8-8 **62** ... NDay 2 29
(RIngram) *racd wd in rr: wknd over 2f out* **13/2**[2]

3000 **12** 12 **Just Fly**[33] 3910 4-9-7 **75** ... JQuinn 1 12
(SKirk) *swtg: s.s: hld up in last and swtchd to ins: pushed along and no prog over 2f out: eased over 1f out: t.o* **14/1**

5610 **13** 3½ **Hey Presto**[11] 4553 4-9-5 **73** ... KDarley 9 —
(CGCox) *a wl in rr: rdn and struggling 3f out: t.o* **9/1**

1m 31.18s (3.91) **Going Correction** +0.675s/f (Yiel)
**WFA** 3 from 4yo+ 5lb **13** Ran SP% **119.0**
Speed ratings: **104,103,101,100,97 96,95,92,92,84 83,69,65**CSF £55.17 CT £414.29 TOTE £7.40: £2.20, £2.50, £2.70; EX 34.20.
**Owner** Miss B Swire **Bred** Miss B Swire **Trained** Kimpton,Hants

**FOCUS**
A fair handicap, although the pace was just ordinary and it proved hard to come from a long way off it. The whole field raced towards the stands'-side rail in the straight. This is ordinary form, but sound.

**NOTEBOOK**
**King's Caprice** had gained his only previous win on fast ground, but is bred to be suited by an easy surface and handled conditions well. Having travelled better than anything for most of the way, he did not find as much as one might have expected but still did just enough. This was a good effort under a big weight.
**Azreme** relishes this sort of ground and pushed the winner all the way to the line. He is obviously one to keep in mind given similar conditions.
**Bi Polar** clearly handled this sort of ground, but he needed plenty of pressure from the saddle to get competitive and was never going as well as some of these.
**Fen Gypsy** has won on good to soft three times so the ground was not a problem, and he did not appear to have any excuses. He has now finished in the first four on his last six starts.
**Blue Patrick ◆** ran a good race considering he is much better suited to a faster surface and could just be about to hit form.
**Molcon(IRE)** could never get on terms with the principals under a sympathetic ride.
**Balerno** looks better a horse on decent ground. *Official explanation: jockey said gelding was unsuited by the good to soft ground*

## 4847 LA SENZA LINGERIE CLASSIFIED STKS 5f

6:55 (6:56) (D) 3-Y-0+ £6,841 (£2,105; £1,052; £526) Stalls High

Form RPR

0065 **1** **Further Outlook (USA)**[4] 4748 10-8-10 83 ... MHoward(7) 11 92
(DKIvory) *b.bhnd: mde all: shkn up over 1f out: styd on wl: unchal* **6/1**

5000 **2** 2½ **Dancing Mystery**[4] 4748 10-9-0 80 ...(b) SCarson 12 81
(EAWheeler) *t.k.h: hld up bhd ldrs: rdn to chse wnr wl over 1f out: no imp* **10/1**

0030 **3** 2 **Miss George**[9] 4614 6-8-12 81 ... DaneO'Neill 5 72
(DKIvory) *s.i.s: hld up in last pair: rdn and styd on fr 2f out to take 3rd nr fin* **8/1**

0550 **4** 1 **Spanish Ace**[19] 4289 3-9-3 85 ...(v) JFortune 8 76
(AMBalding) *lw: b: chsd wnr to wl over 1f out: fdd u.p* **4/1**[2]

1522 **5** 2½ **Jayanjay**[9] 4614 5-9-2 82 ... JQuinn 6 65
(MissBSanders) *lw: trckd ldrs: rdn 2f out: sn struggling and btn* **3/1**[1]

0005 **6** 3 **Little Edward**[9] 4614 6-9-0 83 ... LPKeniry(3) 7 56
(BGPowell) *t.k.h: hld up bhd ldrs: rdn and no prog 2f out: sn btn* **8/1**

3061 **7** 7 **Mr Malarkey (IRE)**[14] 4459 4-8-11 82 ...(bt) HayleyTurner(5) 2 32
(MrsCADunnett) *s.i.s: racd on outer: nvr gng wl: bhd fnl 2f* **11/2**[3]

1650 **8** 2½ **Zarzu**[4] 4748 5-8-9 78 ... RThomas(5) 1 21
(CRDore) *b: chsd ldrs tl wknd 2f out* **9/1**

61.36 secs (0.15) **Going Correction** +0.25s/f (Good)
**WFA** 3 from 4yo+ 2lb **8** Ran SP% **116.0**
Speed ratings: **108,104,100,99,95 90,79,75**CSF £64.05 TOTE £6.80: £1.70, £2.30, £3.50; EX 26.70.
**Owner** K T Ivory **Bred** Gainsborough Farm Inc **Trained** Radlett, Herts

**FOCUS**
A reasonable field despite the non-runners and just 4lb separated the entire field on official ratings, but Further Outlook got his own way in front and nothing could get into this. Therefore several of these can be forgiven below-par runs and the bare form is probably not worth a great deal. All bar the wayward Mr Malarkey raced towards the far side. High draws were favoured.

**NOTEBOOK**
**Further Outlook(USA)** loves to dominate on this sort of ground and, granted an uncontested lead, he made no mistake, showing tremendous enthusiasm for a horse of his age. The form cannot be taken too literally, but he is always one to have on your side on a soft surface.
**Dancing Mystery** has made all in the past so it was a surprise to see Carson so reluctant to go on. As a result, he pulled quite hard through the first furlong and was unable to peg back eventual leader Further Outlook.
**Miss George** has gained all of her turf wins on fast ground, but she seemed to handle these conditions well and was simply found out by the modest pace.
**Spanish Ace** was never really a danger and continues to struggle.
**Jayanjay** would surely have preferred a stronger pace. *Official explanation: trainer's representative had no explanation for the poor form shown*
**Mr Malarkey(IRE)** was very awkward out of stalls and never going thereafter.
**Zarzu** *Official explanation: jockey said gelding was unsuited by the good to soft ground*

## 4848 COLLINGWOOD TEAM SERVICES FILLIES' H'CAP 1m 1f (R)

7:25 (7:28) (E) (0-75,71) 3-Y-0 £4,319 (£1,329; £664; £332) Stalls High

Form RPR

-100 **1** **Farriers Charm**[10] 4580 3-8-13 **63** ... JFortune 3 69
(DJCoakley) *lw: racd v wd 1st 5f: in 4th pl whn jnd main gp: rdn over 3f out: narrow ld against nr rail ins fnl f: jst hld on* **5/1**[2]

4540 **2** hd **Queen Lucia (IRE)**[25] 4128 3-8-3 **53** ... JBramhill 5 59
(JGGiven) *prom: led over 2f out: drvn and hdd ins fnl f: rallied nr fin: jst failed* **14/1**

6005 **3** 1¾ **La Professoressa (IRE)**[14] 4443 3-8-8 **58** ... RHavlin 12 61
(MrsPNDutfield) *trckd ldrs: rdn and effrt 2f out: styd on same pce fr over 1f out* **5/1**[2]

0530 **4** ½ **Carriacou**[7] 4655 3-8-11 **64** ... LPKeniry(3) 8 66
(PWD'Arcy) *hld up in rr: prog on outer over 2f out: rdn and nt qckn over 1f out: one pce after* **6/1**[3]

1032 **5** 1 **Deign To Dance (IRE)**[10] 4580 3-8-10 **60** ... EAhern 13 60
(JGPortman) *trckd ldrs: rdn over 2f out: cl up over 1f out: fdd ins fnl f* **4/1**[1]

6000 **6** 1½ **Sonderborg**[10] 4580 3-7-11 **52** ...(b) HayleyTurner(5) 10 49
(MissAMNewton-Smith) *t.k.h: hld up in rr: effrt on outer over 2f out: one pce and no imp over 1f out* **33/1**

5550 **7** 3 **Blue Daze**[28] 4020 3-8-11 **61** ... RHughes 11 52
(RHannon) *racd in midfield: rdn and no prog over 2f out: btn after* **8/1**

0-00 **8** ¾ **Abington Angel**[77] 2587 3-9-3 **70** ...(b[1]) JFMcDonald(3) 7 59
(BJMeehan) *hld up in last pair: pushed along and nt qckn 3f out: struggling after : kpt on ins fnl f* **25/1**

0405 **9** ½ **Lady Blade (IRE)**[17] 4368 3-8-9 **59** ...(b[1]) LisaJones 2 47
(BHanbury) *hld up in rr: rdn and struggling 3f out: wknd* **11/1**

0-56 **10** 11 **Fabuloso**[13] 4496 3-7-12 **48** oh7 ... JQuinn 6 14
(VSmith) *led to over 2f out: wknd and eased* **9/1**

60 **11** 3½ **Kalimenta (USA)**[27] 4045 3-9-1 **65** ... ADaly 9 24
(SKirk) *lw: taken down early: racd in last pair: rdn and no rspnse over 3f out: sn bhd* **14/1**

-P00 **12** 1 **Grande Terre (IRE)**[89] 2259 3-8-10 **60** ... KDarley 4 17
(JGGiven) *lw: trckd ldrs tl wknd 3f out* **20/1**

2m 0.33s (6.00) **Going Correction** +0.675s/f (Yiel) **12** Ran SP% **121.9**
Speed ratings: **100,99,98,97,96 95,92,92,91,82 78,78**CSF £73.39 CT £381.02 TOTE £7.30: £2.40, £4.30, £2.60; EX 133.10.
**Owner** Alf Hall **Bred** Giles W Pritchard-Gordon (farming) Ltd **Trained** West Ilsley, Berks

**FOCUS**
A moderate handicap in which the winner raced away from the main group in the early stages in search of better ground, and it worked. In the straight, the entire field raced stands' side. This is pretty modest form.

**NOTEBOOK**
**Farriers Charm**, off the mark in a Fibresand handicap earlier in the season, had not gone on from that in two subsequent runs but, stepped up in trip and switched to easy ground, she returned to form. Given a fine tactical ride by Jimmy Fortune, who kept her away from the others soon after the start in search of better ground before grabbing the stands' rail in the straight, she could well be flattered, but will have to be worthy of respect if bidding to follow up on a similarly easy surface.
**Queen Lucia(IRE)**, racing on soft ground for the first time, ran her best race to date and only just failed to get off the mark. There is clearly a similar race in her, but she is just moderate is not one to take too short a price about.
**La Professoressa(IRE)** ran respectably and seemed to handle the ground, but it will be a very moderate contest she wins.
**Carriacou** is becoming disappointing and the soft ground cannot be used as an excuse.
**Deign To Dance(IRE)** failed to justify favouritism and did little to suggest the ground suited.
**Fabuloso** *Official explanation: jockey said filly ran too free early on*

## 4849 WILLIAMHILL.CO.UK H'CAP 1m 4f

7:55 (7:56) (E) (0-70,70) 3-Y-0+ £4,270 (£1,314; £657; £328) Stalls High

Form RPR

5500 **1** **Silver Prophet (IRE)**[26] 4080 5-9-4 **65** ... HayleyTurner(5) 2 74
(MRBosley) *racd in midfield: rdn and prog over 2f out: styd on wl fnl f to ld last strides* **20/1**

6062 **2** hd **Traveller's Tale**[4] 4736 5-8-6 **55** ... DerekNolan(7) 7 64
(PGMurphy) *trckd ldrs gng easily: effrt 2f out: rdn to ld ins fnl f: hdd last strides* **16/1**

1650 **3** nk **Sudden Flight (IRE)**[14] 4441 7-9-4 **67** ... SJDonohoe(7) 5 76
(PDEvans) *settled towards rr: stdy prog over 2f out: swtchd lft over 1f out: pushed along and styd on ins fnl f: nrst fin* **12/1**

5340 **4** nk **Saxe-Coburg (IRE)**[7] 4630 7-8-11 **56** ... JFMcDonald(3) 18 64
(GAHam) *racd in rr: rdn over 3f out: prog over 2f out: styd on fnl f: nvr quite able to chal* **25/1**

3424 **5** ½ **Head To Kerry (IRE)**[14] 4441 4-8-12 **54** ... EAhern 12 61
(DJSFfrenchDavis) *cl up: rdn to ld 2f out: hdd and no ex ins fnl f* **9/2**[2]

0262 **6** ½ **Aoninch**[7] 4642 4-9-4 **60** ... RHughes 16 67+
(MrsPNDutfield) *lw: hld up in last: smooth prog over 3f out: cl up whn nt clr run over 1f out: fnd nil whn in the clr ins fnl f* **6/1**[3]

0000 **7** 1¼ **Swift Alchemist**[9] 4616 4-8-13 **55** ...(p) GBaker 3 60
(MrsHSweeting) *trckd ldr: led over 3f out: rdn and hdd 2f out: stl upsides ent fnl f: wknd nr fin* **33/1**

2253 **8** nk **Ellway Heights**[21] 4250 7-8-11 **53** ... JFortune 20 58
(WMBrisbourne) *lw: racd towards rr: rdn over 3f out: prog u.p to press ldrs 1f out: no ex* **10/1**

6041 **9** 1¼ **Mount Benger**[32] 3929 4-9-8 **64** ...(p) KDarley 13 67
(RMBeckett) *racd in midfield: rdn over 3f out: effrt u.p and cl up jst over 1f out: fdd ins fnl f* **7/1**

-003 **10** 2½ **Efrhina (IRE)**[7] 4641 4-9-7 **63** ... RHavlin 11 62
(MrsStefLiddiard) *prom: rdn wl over 3f out: stl cl up wl over 1f out: wknd sn after* **16/1**

0000 **11** 2 **Persian Genie (IRE)**[17] 4368 3-8-10 **62** ... SCarson 8 59
(GBBalding) *racd in last quartet: rdn and struggling over 3f out: plugged on fnl 2f* **20/1**

0000 **12** 6 **Western (IRE)**[14] 4441 4-10-0 **70** ... DaneO'Neill 10 58
(JAkehurst) *lw: racd towards rr: shkn up and no prog over 3f out: btn over 2f out* **50/1**

40-1 **13** 1¾ **Worcester Lodge**[18] 4346 3-9-2 **68** ... SDrowne 1 54
(RCharlton) *b.bhnd: trckd ldrs: rdn 4f out: wknd over 2f out* **7/2**[1]

**14** 6 **Future To Future (IRE)**[266] 4-8-12 **54** ... ADaly 15 31
(LADace) *b: a wl in rr: struggling 4f out* **50/1**

10/0 **15** 2½ **Dr Cool**[16] 4398 7-9-10 **66** ... GCarter 14 40
(JAkehurst) *s.s: hld up in last: lost tch over 4f out: bhd after* **25/1**

0000 **16** 3 **Must Be Magic**[42] 3631 7-8-11 **56** ...(v) RMiles(3) 17 26
(HJCollingridge) *led to over 3f out: wknd rapidly over 2f out* **20/1**



The Form Book, Raceform Ltd, Compton, RG20 6NL

-605 **17** *8* **Secret Jewel (FR)**[34] [3866] 4-9-13 **69** JQuinn 19 27
(LadyHerries) *dwlt: hld up wl in rr: lost tch over 3f out: eased over 2f out* **25/1**

2m 46.08s (11.08) **Going Correction** +1.00s/f (Soft)
**WFA** 3 from 4yo+ 10lb **17** Ran SP% **128.4**
Speed ratings: **103,102,102,102,102 101,100,100,99,98 96,92,91,87,86 84,78**CSF £292.85 CT £4001.83 TOTE £31.20: £5.30, £4.10, £3.00, £3.60; EX 328.00 Place 6 £ 381.26, Place 5 £329.35.
**Owner** Mrs Jean M O'Connor **Bred** St Simon Foundation **Trained** Kingston Lisle, Oxon

**FOCUS**
A really competitive handicap, but a moderate early pace meant they finished pretty well bunched. However, the form appears reliable enough, if only ordinary.

**NOTEBOOK**
**Silver Prophet(IRE)**, with the cheekpieces left off, appreciated the return to an easy surface and, getting a clearer passage than some of these, just did enough. He started the season off a mark of 79 so will not look badly treated when he has been reassessed.
**Traveller's Tale**, carrying 3lb more than in future but still 10lb lower than when gaining his only previous success, confirmed he has hit form with another decent effort and should be winning soon enough.
**Sudden Flight(IRE)** ◆ was back on a winning mark, had conditions to suit and quite simply should have won. His rider continually found trouble and, when finally in the clear well inside the final furlong, he was not hard on him at all.
**Saxe-Coburg(IRE)**, 3lb higher than in future, made his challenge further away from the stands' rail that most of these, and for that reason emerges with credit.
**Head To Kerry(IRE)** appeared to run his usual race, keeping on but not doing enough to win and he continues to frustrate.
**Aoninch**, 3lb lower than in future, was given a lovely waiting ride and came to win her race, but the gaps did not appear when she most needed them.
**Worcester Lodge** failed to prove himself on the ground. *Official explanation: trainer's representative had no explanation for the poor form shown*
T/Plt: £947.90 to a £1 stake. Pool: £43,762.80. 33.70 winning tickets. T/Qpdt: £807.30 to a £1 stake. Pool: £3,382.00. 3.10 winning tickets. JN

## 4803 NOTTINGHAM (L-H)
### Wednesday, August 18

**OFFICIAL GOING: Good to soft (good in places)**
Heavy rain prior to racing eased the ground.
Wind: Moderate against Weather: Rain prior to racing clearing away leaving a fine evening

## 4850 RACING UK MEDIAN AUCTION MAIDEN STKS 1m 1f 213y
**5:40** (5:40) (F) 3-Y-O **£3,192** (£912; £456) **Stalls** Low

Form RPR
**1** **Look Again** 3-9-0 SSanders 5 88
(MrsAJPerrett) *dwlt: hld up: hdwy 1/2-way: chsd ldr over 3f out: led over 2f out: edgd lft over 1f out: pushed out* **15/2**
0-33 **2** *4* **Dundry**[35] [3843] 3-9-0 78 IMongan 2 81
(GLMoore) *chsd ldrs: rdn over 3f out: styd on same pce fnl 2f: wnt 2nd ins fnl f* **9/2**[3]
2-33 **3** *nk* **Flamboyant Lad**[43] [3603] 3-9-0 80 RHills 9 80
(BWHills) *sn chsng ldr: led 7f out: rdn and hdd over 2f out: wknd ins fnl f* **6/4**[1]
45 **4** *8* **Port 'n Starboard**[49] [3422] 3-9-0 NCallan 6 67
(CACyzer) *prom over 7f* **50/1**
-004 **5** *2* **My Michelle**[19] [4303] 3-8-9 64 ACulhane 1 58
(BPalling) *chsd ldrs 7f* **20/1**
-505 **6** *2 1/2* **Second Warning**[9] [4615] 3-9-0 60 JPMurtagh 4 59
(DJDaly) *prom over 6f* **20/1**
**7** *1 3/4* **Kipsigis (IRE)** 3-9-0 MFenton 7 56
(LadyHerries) *s.i.s: bhd: lost tch fnl 4f* **25/1**
**8** *18* **New York City (IRE)** 3-8-7 AHamblett(7) 3 26
(LMCumani) *s.s: outpcd* **33/1**
0 **9** *dist* **One So Marvellous**[33] [3916] 3-8-9 DHolland 8 —
(LMCumani) *led 3f: sn pushed along: wknd 1/2-way: eased* **5/2**[2]

2m 10.22s (0.72) **Going Correction** -0.025s/f (Good) **9** Ran SP% **116.8**
Speed ratings: **96,92,92,86,84 82,81,66,—**CSF £38.27 TOTE £8.10: £3.80, £1.80, £1.02; EX 95.40.
**Owner** J H Richmond-Watson **Bred** Lawn Stud **Trained** Pulborough, W Sussex

**FOCUS**
This was run at a steady pace, but the 2nd and 3rd had shown fair form in maidens and they finished well clear of the 4th, so the form may not be too bad.

**NOTEBOOK**
**Look Again**, a half-brother to Littlemissattitude and Ultimata, both winners between eight and 11 furlongs, was very green but still proved too good for his rivals. His trainer thought he may be better suited to a faster surface.
**Dundry** is a consistent colt, but he does lack a change of gear. He may have better luck when going handicapping.
**Flamboyant Lad** was ridden as though there were no doubts about his stamina, but he failed to get home on the rain-softened ground. Already proven on a soft surface, it could be that a mile is as far as he wants to go.
**Port 'n Starboard**, who gave trouble leaving the paddock, did not exactly shape like a winner waiting to happen, but he should face easier tasks when going handicapping.
**One So Marvellous** was soon struggling but was found to have a problem. *Official explanation: jockey said filly lost her action*

## 4851 BBAG BADEN-BADENER YEARLING SALES MAIDEN FILLIES' STKS 1m 54y
**6:10** (6:12) (D) 2-Y-O **£5,083** (£1,564; £782; £391) **Stalls** Centre

Form RPR
44 **1** **Night Of Joy (IRE)**[48] [3456] 2-8-11 NCallan 10 80
(MAJarvis) *chsd ldrs: led over 2f out: rdn over 1f out: styd on* **15/2**
**2** *1* **Dash To The Top** 2-8-11 DHolland 16 77+
(LMCumani) *s.i.s: bhd: swced rt over 2f out: hdwy and hung lft over 1f out: r.o wl* **14/1**
4 **3** *shd* **Singhalese**[18] [4315] 2-8-11 SWKelly 5 77
(JAOsborne) *hld up: swtchd rt and hdwy over 1f out: rdn to chse wnr over 1f out: kpt on* **11/2**[1]
4 **4** *1* **Mokaraba**[18] [4344] 2-8-11 RHills 4 75
(JLDunlop) *prom: outpcd over 3f out: rallied over 1f out: styd on* **6/1**[2]
0 **5** *2 1/2* **Pearl's A Singer (IRE)**[18] [4335] 2-8-11 RMullen 2 70
(MLWBell) *prom: rdn over 4f out: styd on same pce fnl f* **50/1**
4 **6** *3/4* **Authenticate**[39] [3741] 2-8-11 GGibbons 18 68
(BAMcmahon) *hld up: hdwy over 3f out: sn rdn: styd on same pce fnl f* **11/2**[1]
3 **7** *hd* **Elrafa Mujahid**[11] [4544] 2-8-11 IMongan 8 67
(JulianPoulton) *chsd ldrs: rdn and ev ch over 2f out: edgd lft over 1f out: no ex* **20/1**
**8** *2* **Creme De La Creme (IRE)** 2-8-11 TPQueally 3 63
(DRLoder) *chsd ldrs over 6f* **14/1**
0 **9** *1 1/2* **Kristalchen**[17] [4359] 2-8-11 ACulhane 11 60
(JGGiven) *mid-div: lost pl over 5f out: styd on ins fnl f* **28/1**
**10** *1/2* **Twyla Tharp (IRE)** 2-8-11 TEDurcan 14 59
(JHMGosden) *s.i.s: bhd: styd on ins fnl f: nvr nrr* **7/1**[3]
**11** *nk* **Sideshow** 2-8-11 SSanders 7 58
(DRLoder) *hld up in tch: rdn over 3f out: hung lft and wknd 2f out* **12/1**
0 **12** *2 1/2* **Ushindi (IRE)**[33] [3905] 2-8-11 JMackay 13 52
(MLWBell) *led over 5f: wknd over 1f out* **40/1**
**13** *5* **Bayreuth** 2-8-11 MFenton 17 41
(JGGiven) *sn lost pl and bhd* **40/1**
**14** *3/4* **Katana** 2-8-11 JPMurtagh 9 40
(IAWood) *s.i.s: sn bhd* **15/2**
04 **15** *1 1/2* **Gibraltar Bay (IRE)**[10] [4579] 2-8-11 AMcCarthy 6 37
(GGMargarson) *chsd ldrs 5f* **66/1**
**16** *1 1/2* **Line Ahead (IRE)** 2-8-11 RWinston 12 33
(SirMichaelStoute) *s.i.s: a in rr: bhd fr 1/2-way* **12/1**
0 **17** *24* **Welsh Galaxy (IRE)**[28] [4023] 2-8-11 RPrice 15 —
(PLGilligan) *dwlt: outpcd* **100/1**
**18** *6* **Magdelaine** 2-8-11 CCatlin 1 —
(PMPhelan) *s.i.s: outpcd* **66/1**

1m 46.6s (0.20) **Going Correction** -0.025s/f (Good) **18** Ran SP% **128.8**
Speed ratings: **98,97,96,95,93 92,92,90,88,88 88,85,80,79,78 76,52,46**CSF £107.12 TOTE £9.20: £2.70, £6.00, £3.50; EX 266.10.
**Owner** Saif Ali **Bred** Roundhill Stud And A Stroud **Trained** Newmarket, Suffolk

**FOCUS**
Probably a fair maiden for the track and it produced a decent wining time for the type of race. The form looks very solid.

**NOTEBOOK**
**Night Of Joy(IRE)** proved well suited to this step up in trip and the easier surface, but did have to battle quite hard for her victory. Her immediate prospects depend on the Handicapper's assesment of her.
**Dash To The Top**, from the same family as the high-class One In A Million, took age to grasp what was required, but she finished to such effect that she would have got there in another 50 yards. She will have learnt plenty from this and will be hard to beat in a similar race next time. *Official explanation: jockey said filly ran green*
**Singhalese** appeared to stay this trip well enough and will certainly find easier openings than she faced here.
**Mokaraba** still looked a little green and got caught out as the pace lifted. She is still learning.
**Pearl's A Singer(IRE)** comes from a high-class family including French 1000gns winner Culture Vulture, as well as Polish Precedent and Zilzal. She shaped a bit better than on her debut, and similar improvement should see her going close in an ordinary maiden.
**Authenticate** looked a big threat with a quarter of a mile to run, but her effort petered out in the closing stages. She may be better suited by seven furlongs at present.
**Kristalchen**, who is out of a mare that won over 12 furlongs, should do better in middle-distance handicaps next term.
**Welsh Galaxy(IRE)** *Official explanation: trainer said filly had hung throughout*

## 4852 MIDLANDS RACING H'CAP 1m 54y
**6:40** (6:40) (D) (0-80,80) 3-Y-O+ **£7,800** (£2,400; £1,200; £600) **Stalls** Centre

Form RPR
1006 **1** **Balearic Star (IRE)**[25] [4147] 3-8-8 **66** RWinston 14 78
(BRMillman) *chsd ldr tl led over 1f out: rdn out* **25/1**
-100 **2** *1 1/2* **Mount Hillaby (IRE)**[12] [4511] 4-8-5 **57** DaleGibson 7 66
(MWEasterby) *trckd ldrs: rdn over 2f out: r.o* **11/2**[2]
0101 **3** *1* **Threezedzz**[6] [4672] 6-9-7 **76** 6ex (t) FPFerris(3) 11 83
(PDEvans) *led over 6f: no ex ins fnl f* **5/1**[1]
352R **4** *1* **Kentucky King (USA)**[3] [4772] 4-10-0 **80** ACulhane 4 85
(PWHiatt) *s.i.s: hld up: hdwy over 1f out: r.o* **20/1**
0210 **5** *hd* **Arran**[9] [4602] 4-8-1 **53** JoannaBadger 3 57
(VSmith) *s.i.s: hld up: nt clr run over 2f out: hdwy over 1f out : r.o* **12/1**
0012 **6** *2 1/2* **Splodger Mac (IRE)**[10] [4577] 5-8-1 **53** FNorton 13 52
(NBycroft) *chsd ldrs: rdn over 3f out: wknd fnl f* **11/1**
4351 **7** *3/4* **Habshan (USA)**[19] [4293] 4-9-3 **69** DHolland 12 66
(CFWall) *chsd ldrs: rdn over 2f out: wknd fnl f* **11/2**[2]
5025 **8** *1 3/4* **Sahaat**[9] [4616] 6-9-4 **70** JPMurtagh 17 64
(MJPolglase) *chsd ldrs: rdn over 2f out: wknd over 1f out* **20/1**
6453 **9** *shd* **Tedstale (USA)**[11] [4558] 6-9-12 **78** (b) TEDurcan 8 72
(TDEasterby) *s.s: bhd: nvr nrr* **14/1**
-000 **10** *shd* **Out For A Stroll**[25] [4134] 5-9-7 **73** RLMoore 2 66
(SCWilliams) *hld up in tch: effrt over 3f out: wknd fnl f* **7/1**[3]
3000 **11** *1 1/4* **Uno Mente**[22] [4213] 5-7-13 **51** (v[1]) KimTinkler 9 42
(DonEnricoIncisa) *dwlt: outpcd* **50/1**
0350 **12** *1* **Skibereen (IRE)**[71] [2752] 4-8-8 **67** NataliaGemelova(7) 5 56
(IWMcinnes) *prom over 6f* **33/1**
01 **13** *2 1/2* **Nimello (USA)**[41] [3660] 8-9-12 **78** LDettori 10 61
(AGNewcombe) *hld up: hdwy over 3f out: wknd 2f out* **11/2**[2]
0600 **14** *nk* **Sinjaree**[13] [4493] 6-7-5 **50** oh11 DFentiman(7) 6 33
(MrsSLamyman) *s.i.s: hld up: rdn over 4f out: wknd over 2f out* **66/1**
4625 **15** *7* **Sewmore Character**[138] [1226] 4-9-2 **68** NCallan 1 36
(MBlanshard) *s.i.s: hld up: wknd over 2f out* **33/1**
463 **16** *4* **Warningcamp (GER)**[34] [3882] 3-9-8 **80** SSanders 16 40
(LadyHerries) *hld up: hdwy over 4f out: wknd over 2f out* **14/1**

1m 44.42s (-1.98) **Going Correction** -0.025s/f (Good)
**WFA** 3 from 4yo+ 6lb **16** Ran SP% **127.4**
Speed ratings: **108,106,105,104,104 101,101,99,99,99 97,96,94,94,87 83**CSF £155.80 CT £864.82 TOTE £28.50: £5.00, £2.30, £2.30, £3.80; EX 540.40.
**Owner** G W Dormer **Bred** William Shaughnessy **Trained** Kentisbeare, Devon

**FOCUS**
Despite the numbers this wasn't that competitive, but it was run at a fair clip and it suited those racing up with the pace.

**NOTEBOOK**
**Balearic Star(IRE)**, back down to a mark he has won off, had a nice tow off the free-running Threezedzz and never looked likely to be reeled in once he had struck for home.
**Mount Hillaby(IRE)** stuck to her task well enough and proved beyond doubt that she stays this far. She is one to keep in mind for a similar contest.
**Threezedzz** again had his own way in front, but he only succeeded in setting things up for the late finishers.
**Kentucky King(USA)** was on his best behaviour, even though he did not break as well as he might have.
**Arran** did not have much luck in running for, had he a clear passage, he might well have run into a place. Just 1lb higher than when successful on the Fibresand, he should be capable of scoring on turf.

**Splodger Mac(IRE)** had no chance of dominating in this with Threezedzz in opposition, so in the circumstances turned in a sound effort.

## 4853 SIMON IS ROUGHLEY 40 TODAY H'CAP — 1m 1f 213y

**7:10** (7:10) (F) (0-55,55) 3-Y-O — **£3,556** (£1,016; £508) **Stalls** Low

Form — RPR

0-05 **1** **Argentum**[41] [3666] 3-9-3 **52** SSanders 1 — 63
(LadyHerries) *s.s: bhd: hdwy over 3f out: led over 1f out: rdn clr: eased nr fin* **7/1**[2]

-546 **2** *1 1/2* **Bright Fire (IRE)**[14] [4443] 3-9-1 **50** RMullen 4 — 58
(WJMusson) *hld up: hdwy over 3f out: rdn and ev ch over 1f out: styd on same pce* **8/1**

0214 **3** *hd* **Go Green**[2] [4798] 3-9-2 **54** (t) FPFerris(3) 9 — 62
(PDEvans) *s.i.s: hdwy u.p over 3f out: ev ch over 1f out: styd on same pce* **8/1**

0014 **4** *6* **Music Mix (IRE)**[5] [4710] 3-9-6 **55** LDettori 7 — 52
(EALDunlop) *hld up: hmpd over 3f out: hdwy over 1f out: nvr trbld ldrs* **15/8**[1]

0246 **5** *nk* **The King Of Rock**[27] [4055] 3-9-5 **54** JPMurtagh 10 — 51
(AGNewcombe) *hld up: hdwy over 3f out: sn rdn: edgd lft over 1f out: no ex* **15/2**[3]

-600 **6** *1* **Armentieres**[7] [4628] 3-9-6 **55** (b) GHind 8 — 50
(JLSpearing) *hld up: hdwy 3f out: sn rdn: wknd fnl f* **33/1**

0600 **7** *2* **Cotton Easter**[26] [4083] 3-9-2 **51** PaulEddery 3 — 42
(MrsAJBowlby) *s.s: bhd tl styd on appr fnl f: nvr nrr* **33/1**

0040 **8** *2 1/2* **Mystic Moon**[7] [4654] 3-8-13 **48** TEDurcan 2 — 35
(JRJenkins) *chsd ldrs 7f* **50/1**

2201 **9** *hd* **Biscar Two (IRE)**[44] [3582] 3-9-3 **52** (b) VHalliday 13 — 38
(RMWhitaker) *s.s: sme hdwy over 1f out: n.d* **10/1**

4543 **10** *12* **Stanley Crane (USA)**[11] [4562] 3-9-6 **55** (t) DHolland 6 — 20
(BHanbury) *led and sn clr: hdd over 2f out: wknd over 1f out* **10/1**

5104 **11** *2* **Oktis Morilious (IRE)**[8] [4618] 3-9-5 **54** ACulhane 14 — 15
(AWCarroll) *chsd ldrs over 7f* **14/1**

5605 **12** *1 1/2* **Compton Micky**[9] [4610] 3-9-6 **55** (p) JEdmunds 11 — 13
(JBalding) *pild hrd and prom: wknd over 3f out* **66/1**

2606 **13** *10* **Russalka**[7] [4654] 3-9-2 **51** (v[1]) NCallan 12 — —
(JulianPoulton) *chsd ldrs: rdn whn hmpd over 3f out: sn wknd* **25/1**

3503 **14** *11* **Stylish Sunrise (IRE)**[32] [3934] 3-9-4 **53** (t) PDoe 16 — —
(IAWood) *chsd ldrs over 7f* **28/1**

065 **15** *nk* **Breaking The Rule (IRE)**[25] [4141] 3-9-1 **50** RLMoore 5 — —
(PRWebber) *chsd ldrs 7f* **40/1**

2m 10.67s (1.17) **Going Correction** -0.025s/f (Good) — **15** Ran SP% **125.2**
Speed ratings: **94,92,92,87,87 86,85,83,83,73 71,70,62,53,53**CSF £60.70 CT £472.27 TOTE £9.30: £2.50, £3.70, £2.30; EX 66.00.
**Owner** Lady Herries and Friends **Bred** Angmering Park Stud **Trained** Angmering, W Sussex

**FOCUS**
A poor contest run at an ordinary pace, but the winner was unexposed and may be capable of better.

**NOTEBOOK**
**Argentum**, tackling handicappers for the first time, appreciated this step up in trip and won with a shade more in hand than the verdict suggested. It would be no surprise to see him step up on this in due course.
**Bright Fire(IRE)** looks to be going the right way and may have been a shade unlucky to come up against another unexposed rival.
**Go Green** appeared to run her race, but may not have been suited by the rain-softened ground.
**Music Mix(IRE)**, although not having the best of runs, never looked likely to take a hand in the finish.
**The King Of Rock** has struggled over a variety of trips and it was no different this time.

## 4854 ED LEE 21ST BIRTHDAY CELEBRATION FILLIES' H'CAP — 5f 13y

**7:40** (7:40) (E) (0-75,68) 3-Y-O+ — **£3,770** (£1,160; £580; £290) **Stalls** High

Form — RPR

0504 **1** **Roman Mistress (IRE)**[18] [4331] 4-9-3 **61** (b) DAllan 2 — 76
(TDEasterby) *mde all: clr fnl f: eased nr fin* **8/1**[3]

2030 **2** *1 1/4* **Cerulean Rose**[21] [4232] 5-9-10 **68** RLMoore 8 — 78
(AWCarroll) *bhd: hdwy fnl f: nt rch wnr* **4/1**[2]

4100 **3** *nk* **Tender (IRE)**[8] [4622] 4-8-4 **48** (p) FNorton 4 — 57
(MrsStefLiddiard) *s.i.s: bhd: r.o ins fnl f: nrst fin* **12/1**

0362 **4** *1 1/2* **Diamond Ring**[11] [4557] 5-8-5 **49** ow2 GHind 10 — 53
(MrsJACandlish) *chsd wnr: rdn over 1f out: styd on same pce* **16/1**

001 **5** *1/2* **Mimic**[6] [4687] 4-8-7 **58** RMills(7) 7 — 60
(RGuest) *hld up: hdwy over 1f out: no ex ins fnl f* **7/2**[1]

1205 **6** *3 1/2* **Queen Of Night**[14] [4452] 4-8-12 **56** ACulhane 6 — 45
(DWChapman) *chsd ldrs over 3f* **9/1**

2040 **7** *shd* **White O' Morn**[70] [2778] 5-7-7 **42** (p) DFox(5) 9 — 31
(JWUnett) *s.s: outpcd* **33/1**

333 **8** *1/2* **Lady Protector**[8] [4622] 5-8-13 **57** DHolland 11 — 44
(JBalding) *chsd ldrs: lost pl and nt clr run over 1f out: n.d after* **7/2**[1]

5160 **9** *1 1/4* **Lydia's Look (IRE)**[36] [3820] 7-7-11 **48** KristinStubbs(7) 3 — 30
(TJEtherington) *dwlt: outpcd* **33/1**

6050 **10** *2* **Red Leicester**[34] [3864] 4-8-3 **47** (v) PHanagan 5 — 22
(JAGlover) *chsd ldrs over 3f* **14/1**

1424 **11** *3* **Jinksonthehouse**[8] [4622] 3-8-10 **56** SSanders 1 — 20
(MDIUsher) *prom: rdn 1/2-way: wknd over 1f out* **12/1**

60.45 secs (-1.35) **Going Correction** -0.20s/f (Firm)
**WFA** 3 from 4yo+ 2lb — **11** Ran SP% **119.4**
Speed ratings: **102,100,99,97,96 90,90,89,87,84 79**CSF £40.65 CT £394.33 TOTE £10.00: £3.50, £2.30, £4.80; EX 70.40.
**Owner** W H Ponsonby **Bred** Mrs Anne Marie Burns **Trained** Great Habton, N Yorks

**FOCUS**
A 0-68 in effect, and the winner had the advantage of the rails to race against.

**NOTEBOOK**
**Roman Mistress(IRE)**, who has run well in the face of some stiff tasks of late, took advantage of this easier task to gain her first success in two years. She should be capable of winning again at this level.
**Cerulean Rose** turned in a solid effort under her big weight, and proved she is just as effective with give underfoot as she is on a fast surface.
**Tender(IRE)** did not have things fall right for her, but she is clearly on good terms with herself at present.
**Diamond Ring** is running well enough at present, and is one to keep an eye on if dropped back into selling company.
**Mimic** ran well enough over a trip short of her best.
**Lady Protector** had no luck in running and is well worth another chance. *Official explanation: trainer said mare was unsuited by the soft ground*

## 4855 WATCH RACING UK ON SKY 425 CLASSIFIED STKS — 5f 13y

**8:10** (8:10) (E) 3-Y-O+ — **£3,640** (£1,120; £560; £280) **Stalls** High

Form — RPR

5642 **1** **Maddie's A Jem**[4] [4740] 4-9-0 73 LDettori 6 — 80+
(JRJenkins) *s.s: hld up: hdwy over 1f out: swtchd lft 1f out: r.o to ld wl ins fnl f: comf* **13/8**[1]

0214 **2** *1/2* **Foley Millennium (IRE)**[11] [4547] 6-9-3 73 SSanders 5 — 81
(MQuinn) *chsd ldr tl led over 1f out: hdd wl ins fnl f* **7/1**[3]

0363 **3** *1* **Paddywack (IRE)**[7] [4626] 7-9-3 73 (b) ACulhane 3 — 78
(DWChapman) *chsd ldrs: rdn and n.m.r 1f out: styd on same pce* **3/1**[2]

2402 **4** *3/4* **Flying Bantam (IRE)**[14] [4456] 3-8-12 70 PHanagan 2 — 72
(RAFahey) *chsd ldrs: pushed along 1/2-way: styng on same pce whn n.m.r ins fnl f* **8/1**

4250 **5** *3/4* **Soba Jones**[7] [4626] 7-9-2 72 JEdmunds 4 — 71
(JBalding) *chsd ldrs: rdn over 1f out: styd on same pce* **9/1**

0060 **6** *2* **Ok Pal**[55] [3243] 4-9-5 75 (b) DHolland 8 — 67
(TGMills) *sn outpcd: swtchd lft 1/2-way: nvr trbld ldrs* **8/1**

-000 **7** *3/4* **Strathclyde (IRE)**[12] [4522] 5-9-0 69 CCatlin 7 — 59
(AMHales) *led over 3f: wknd ins fnl f* **33/1**

0010 **8** *2* **Catch The Cat (IRE)**[14] [4452] 5-9-4 74 (v) GParkin 1 — 56
(JSWainwright) *sn outpcd* **16/1**

60.25 secs (-1.55) **Going Correction** -0.20s/f (Firm)
**WFA** 3 from 4yo+ 2lb — **8** Ran SP% **116.6**
Speed ratings: **104,103,101,100,99 96,94,91**CSF £14.20 TOTE £2.60: £1.30, £1.10, £1.70; EX 13.40 Place 6 £133.84, Place 5 £89.17.
**Owner** Mrs Wendy Jenkins **Bred** The Peel Stud **Trained** Royston, Herts
■ Stewards Enquiry : L Dettori caution: careless riding

**FOCUS**
Another ordinary contest in which the time was comparable with the earlier sprint.

**NOTEBOOK**
**Maddie's A Jem**, given a confident ride, came through to win with more in hand than the offical verdict suggested.
**Foley Millennium(IRE)** has enjoyed a good spell this year and did his best to make a fight of it. Although beaten, he was far from disgraced.
**Paddywack(IRE)** ran his race, and although beaten his trainer can be relied upon to find him another opening.
**Flying Bantam(IRE)** found things happening a shade too quickly for him over this trip.
**Soba Jones** found this easy five an insufficient test.
**Ok Pal** looks out of sorts. *Official explanation: jockey said gelding was reluctant to race*
**Strathclyde(IRE)** has plenty of pace, but is probably better on a faster surface.
T/Plt: £234.50 to a £1 stake. Pool: £32,187.60. 100.20 winning tickets. T/Qpdt: £36.10 to a £1 stake. Pool: £2,955.90. 60.50 winning tickets. CR

# 4831 YORK (L-H)

### Wednesday, August 18

**OFFICIAL GOING: Soft**
After overnight rain the ground on the round course was described as 'very soft'. The straight course was not as testing.
Wind: Moderate 1/2 behind. Weather: Humid and showery.

## 4856 MOTABILITY SUPPORTED BY ROYAL & SUNALLIANCE RATED STKS (H'CAP) — 1m 2f 88y

**1:20** (1:20) (B) (0-105,103) 3-Y-O+ — **£13,305** (£5,046; £2,523; £1,147) **Stalls** Low

Form — RPR

6311 **1** **Dunaskin (IRE)**[11] [4540] 4-8-7 **89** oh1 KDarley 8 — 105
(DEddy) *mde all: qcknd c lear over 3f out: rdn 2f out and styd on strly* **8/1**[2]

4000 **2** *7* **Zero Tolerance (IRE)**[24] [4173] 4-8-8 **90** DHolland 10 — 94
(TDBarron) *hld up and bhd: hdwy over 3f out: chsd wnr wl over 1f out: sn rdn and no imp fnl f* **9/2**[1]

2333 **3** *1 3/4* **Shahzan House (IRE)**[11] [4540] 5-9-1 **97** (p) PRobinson 1 — 98
(MAJarvis) *a.p: effrt 3f out: sn rdn and kpt on same pce fnl 2f* **9/2**[1]

1410 **4** *3/4* **Blue Spinnaker (IRE)**[39] [3756] 5-9-3 **102** PMulrennan(3) 2 — 102
(MWEasterby) *lw: hld up towards rr: pushed along and sltly outpcd 4f out: rdn and hdwy over 2f out: kpt on u.p fnl f: nvr a factor* **9/1**[3]

0100 **5** *4* **Ionian Spring (IRE)**[11] [4540] 9-8-11 **93** RSmith 6 — 86
(CGCox) *hld up in tch: smooth hdwy 1/2-way: trckd ldrs over 3f out: rdn and btn 2f out* **12/1**

3500 **6** *3* **Gold History (USA)**[20] [4271] 3-8-7 **97** JFanning 5 — 85
(MJohnston) *in tch: effrt 4f out: sn rdn along and wknd over 2f out* **25/1**

0103 **7** *hd* **Wing Commander**[11] [4528] 5-8-13 **95** PHanagan 4 — 83
(RAFahey) *chsd ldrs: rdn along over 3f out: sn wknd* **8/1**[2]

6300 **8** *nk* **Blythe Knight (IRE)**[22] [4214] 4-9-7 **103** LDettori 12 — 90
(EALDunlop) *lw: hld up and bhd: hdwy on outer 3f out: rdn 2f out: wknd over 1f out* **8/1**[2]

3100 **9** *14* **Bourgeois**[39] [3757] 7-9-2 **98** WSupple 3 — 61
(TDEasterby) *chsd wnr: rdn along over 4f out: sn wknd* **11/1**

-010 **10** *21* **Bishopric**[47] [3477] 4-8-12 **94** DaneO'Neill 11 — 22
(HCandy) *midfield: hdwy to chse ldrs 1/2-way: rdn along over 3f out and sn wknd* **16/1**

10/3 **11** *dist* **Rainbow Queen**[25] [4153] 4-8-10 **92** KFallon 9 — —
(SirMichaelStoute) *midfield: pushed along and lost pl over 4f out: sn bhd and virtually p.u 2f out* **10/1**

2m 14.62s (5.18) **Going Correction** +0.925s/f (Soft)
**WFA** 3 from 4yo+ 8lb — **11** Ran SP% **114.5**
Speed ratings: **116,110,109,108,105 102,102,102,91,74** —CSF £42.68 CT £182.86 TOTE £8.50: £2.60, £2.20, £2.00; EX 53.00 Trifecta £157.10 Pool £1,858.82. 8.40 winning units.
**Owner** Mrs I Battla **Bred** J P And Miss M Mangan **Trained** Ingoe, Northumberland

**FOCUS**
A decent handicap and a very smart winning time indeed for the grade given the conditions, but the winner did get his own way in front and picked up really well in the straight. There appeared no fluke about his effort but several other runners failed to show their form.

**NOTEBOOK**
**Dunaskin(IRE)** has been in top form of late, appears to go on any ground and, most importantly for him, was allowed an uncontested lead. He set a steady pace before powering clear in the straight for an authoritative win. He will take a hammering from the Handicapper for this performance, and connections may have to try and find a race in the coming days in which he can run under a penalty.
**Zero Tolerance(IRE)** could have done with a stronger pace as, although he stayed on well from the rear, he was never able to get in a blow at the winner, who had the run of the race. He loves soft ground though, and this effort confirmed that he is capable of winning off this sort of mark given a stronger end-to-end gallop.



The Form Book, Raceform Ltd, Compton, RG20 6NL

**Shahzan House(IRE)** was close enough to have his chance but was unable to match the winner when that rival kicked on. He is terribly consistent, but that is reflected in his rating.
**Blue Spinnaker(IRE)**, best suited by quicker ground than this, was another who was not helped by being held up towards the rear in a race not run at a fast pace early on. He remains in good form.
**Ionian Spring(IRE)**, who raced closer to the pace than usual, looked a strong candidate for second place entering the final two furlongs, but he failed to pick up and weakened out of the places in the latter stages.
**Gold History(USA)** has three wins to his name and made all the running for each of those successes. He has not looked as good held up.
**Wing Commander** has shown his best form on a quicker surface.
**Blythe Knight(IRE)** handles this sort of ground, but he looks a shade high in the weights at the moment, and he was another unsuited by the way the race was run.
**Rainbow Queen** *Official explanation: jockey said filly was unsuited by the soft ground*

## 4857 SCOTTISH EQUITABLE GIMCRACK STKS (GROUP 2) (C&G) 6f

1:50 (1:51) (A) 2-Y-O £75,000 (£28,750; £14,375; £6,875) Stalls Centre

Form RPR
145 **1** **Tony James (IRE)**[42] 3640 2-8-11 100 SSanders 2 107
(CEBrittain) *trckd ldrs: hdwy 2f out: rdn to ld appr last: styd on wl* **16/1**
1 **2** 1 1/4 **Andronikos**[33] 3900 2-8-11 KFallon 4 104
(PFICole) *chsd ldrs: rdn along over 2f out: styd on wl u.p fnl f* **10/1**
11 **3** 1/2 **Abraxas Antelope (IRE)**[34] 3865 2-8-11 RWinston 3 102
(JHowardJohnson) *led: pushed along over 2f out: sn rdn: hdd over 1f out: sn drvn and one pce ins last* **10/3[1]**
1135 **4** 3/4 **Sacred Nuts (IRE)**[18] 4342 2-8-11 93 RMullen 6 100
(MLWBell) *in tch: hdwy 2f out: sn rdn: kpt on u.p fnl f* **40/1**
41 **5** shd **Galeota (IRE)**[37] 3808 2-8-11 85 RHughes 1 100
(RHannon) *cl up: rdn along over 2f out: drvn and one pce appr last* **20/1**
14 **6** 6 **Stetchworth Prince**[19] 4288 2-8-11 TPQueally 10 83
(DRLoder) *in tch: hdwy to chse ldrs 1/2-way: rdn along 2f out and sn wknd* **16/1**
2154 **7** 1 1/4 **Turnkey**[31] 3965 2-8-11 100 TEDurcan 7 80
(MRChannon) *midfield: rdn along 1/2-way: sn wknd* **7/2[2]**
211 **8** 1 1/4 **Crimson Sun (USA)**[26] 4088 2-8-11 97 KMcEvoy 5 76
(SaeedBinSuroor) *chsd ldrs: rdn along over 2f out: sn wknd* **8/1**
521 **9** 10 **Big Hassle (IRE)**[36] 3818 2-8-11 89 WSupple 8 49
(TDEasterby) *bhd fr 1/2-way* **22/1**
1200 **10** 13 **Royal Island (IRE)**[22] 4217 2-8-11 100 JFanning 11 13
(MJohnston) *a rr* **20/1**
122 **11** 22 **Council Member (USA)**[42] 3640 2-8-11 100 LDettori 9 —
(SaeedBinSuroor) *sn outpcd and bhd: t.o and eased over 2f out* **4/1[3]**

1m 14.3s (1.73) **Going Correction** +0.35s/f (Good) **11** Ran SP% **113.6**
Speed ratings: **102,100,99,98,98 90,88,87,73,56 27**CSF £151.55 TOTE £24.90: £5.20, £2.90, £1.90; EX 192.50 Trifecta £957.30 Part won. Pool £1,348.37. 0.30 winning units..
**Owner** A J Richards **Bred** Ewar Stud Farms **Trained** Newmarket, Suffolk
■ Stewards Enquiry : S Sanders one-day ban: used whip with excessive frequency (Aug 29)

**FOCUS**
With less than three lengths covering the first five home it was hardly a vintage renewal of this contest and the time was modest for a Group Two. The worth of the form is limited by the ground conditions.

**NOTEBOOK**
**Tony James(IRE)**, who looked to have run up a bit light, found the ground no problem and never flinched in a modest renewal of this Group Two. His ambitious long-term target is next year's Kentucky Derby.
**Andronikos**, who looked very fit, was inclined to get a bit warm behind the stalls. He collected a bump at the start and kept on in game fashion.
**Abraxas Antelope(IRE)**, who took a bump at the start, took them along but did not see it out quite as well as the first two.
**Sacred Nuts(IRE)**, having his sixth start, moved well to post. He has already been beaten in nursery company, and his proximity rather holds down the overall value of the form.
**Galeota(IRE)**, whose trainer has farmed this race in the past, was taking a big step up in class and was racing on the wide outside. He has a lenient nursery mark but it will be revised sharply upwards after this.
**Stetchworth Prince**, a very lightly-made individual, probably failed to handle the ground.
**Turnkey**, who lacks size and scope, is proven on testing ground and, a positive on the exchanges, was very disappointing.
**Crimson Sun(USA)**, who has a soft-ground action, became very warm behind the stalls and was well below par.
**Council Member(USA)**, a good walker and fluent mover, never went a yard in the ground and in the end was simply asked to complete in his own time. This can safely be despatched to the recycle bin. *Official explanation: jockey said colt was unsuited by the soft ground*

## 4858 TOTESPORT EBOR (HERITAGE H'CAP) 1m 5f 197y

2:25 (2:26) (B) 3-Y-O+ £130,000 (£40,000; £20,000; £10,000) Stalls Low

Form RPR
5111 **1** **Mephisto (IRE)**[22] 4218 5-9-4 99 7ex DHolland 3 110
(LMCumani) *hld up towards rr: hdwy on outer 3f out: rdn wl over 1f out: hung bdly lft ins last: hdd nr fin: rallied to ld on line* **6/1[2]**
5316 **2** shd **Gold Ring**[18] 4345 4-8-10 91 SCarson 15 102
(GBBalding) *cl up: led 4f out: rdn along 2f out: edgd rt ent last:sn drvn: bmpd and hdd nr fin: rallied to ld again and ct line* **12/1**
1-44 **3** 2 1/2 **Mikado**[22] 4215 3-8-13 106 JPSpencer 13 114
(APO'Brien, Ire) *hld up and bhd: hdwy wl over 2f out: rdn wl over 1f out: drvn and styd on ins last: nrst fin* **9/1**
-030 **4** nk **Defining**[53] 3310 5-9-0 95 JPMurtagh 1 102
(JRFanshawe) *in tch: hdwy to chse ldrs 4f out: rdn along over 2f out: drvn over 1f out and kpt on* **16/1**
/065 **5** 3/4 **Self Defense**[22] 4218 7-9-5 100 PRobinson 18 106
(PRChamings) *midfield: hdwy on outer 4f out: rdn along to chade ldrs 2f out: drvn and kpt on fnl f* **10/1**
1412 **6** 3 1/2 **Star Member (IRE)**[39] 3757 5-9-2 97 KFallon 22 99
(APJarvis) *in tch: hdwy to chse ldrs 4f out: sn rdn along: drvn and grad wknd fnl 2f* **7/1[3]**
21-0 **7** hd **Fantastic Love (USA)**[22] 4214 4-9-7 102 (t) LDettori 6 103
(SaeedBinSuroor) *in tch: hdwy to chse ldr over 3f out: rdn along 2f out: grad wknd* **16/1**
1-03 **8** 1 1/4 **Jagger**[22] 4218 4-9-2 97 SSanders 7 97
(GABulter) *unruly going to start: hld up in midfield: gd hdwy on inner 6f out: chsd ldrs over 3f out: sn drvn and wknd fnl 2f* **11/2[1]**
0143 **9** 4 **Collier Hill**[39] 3757 6-9-8 103 DeanMcKeown 16 98
(GASwinbank) *hld up: hdwy on outer 4f out: rdn along and in tch over 2f out: sn drvn and no imp* **14/1**
1101 **10** 1 **Dorothy's Friend**[11] 4529 4-9-0 95 7ex SDrowne 19 88
(RCharlton) *midfield: pushed along and outpcd 1/2-way: styd on fnl 3f: nvr a factor* **14/1**
2260 **11** 3/4 **Pagan Dance (IRE)**[39] 3725 5-8-13 94 (p) MJKinane 11 86
(MrsAJPerrett) *lw: chsd ldrs on inner: rdn along 3f out. drvn and wknd fnl 2f* **25/1**
0040 **12** 1 1/4 **Santando**[11] 4529 4-8-6 90 (v) J-PGuillambert(3) 2 81
(CEBrittain) *bhd tl sme late hdwy* **28/1**
3352 **13** 2 1/2 **Crow Wood**[46] 3521 5-9-0 95 ACulhane 8 82
(JGGiven) *chsd ldrs: rdn along over 6f out: sn wknd* **33/1**
6500 **14** 8 **Trust Rule**[46] 3521 4-8-10 91 MHills 20 68
(BWHills) *lw: a rr* **25/1**
-600 **15** 1/2 **Salsalino**[91] 2220 4-9-8 103 JDSmith 14 79
(AKing) *a rr* **33/1**
4032 **16** 8 **Top Seed (IRE)**[42] 3639 3-8-12 105 TEDurcan 21 71
(MRChannon) *chsd ldrs: rdn along over 3f out: sn wknd* **25/1**
1450 **17** 2 1/2 **Royal Cavalier**[39] 3757 7-9-2 97 WSupple 4 60
(RHollinshead) *led: rdn along over 4f out: sn hdd & wknd* **40/1**
2623 **18** 9 **Grampian**[46] 3521 5-9-7 102 KDarley 12 53
(JGGiven) *a rr* **22/1**
-000 **19** 8 **Rayshan (IRE)**[53] 3310 4-8-9 90 RWinston 17 31
(JHowardJohnson) *chsd ldrs: pushed along and lost pl after 5f: bhd fnl 5f* **50/1**

3m 6.10s (9.70) **Going Correction** +0.925s/f (Soft)
**WFA** 3 from 4yo+ 12lb **19** Ran SP% **123.7**
Speed ratings: **109,108,107,107,106 104,104,104,101,101 100,100,98,94,93 89,87,82,78**CSF £66.33 CT £659.84 TOTE £7.80: £2.60, £5.60, £2.50, £4.30; EX 221.70 Trifecta £3499.50 Pool £10,350.66. 2.10 winning units.
**Owner** Mrs Angie Silver **Bred** Shadwell Estate Company Limited **Trained** Newmarket, Suffolk
■ The winner survived a lengthy enquiry on the day as well as a subsequent appeal by the connections of Gold Ring.
■ Stewards Enquiry : D Holland one-day ban: careless riding (Aug 29)

**FOCUS**
Probably not a great Ebor - only eight of the 19 runners had won a race in their last three starts, and three of them made the first three. The winning time was only fair considering the grade of contest, but the form is fairly solid considering the ground.

**NOTEBOOK**
**Mephisto(IRE)** ◆, who was 3lb well in despite a 7lb penalty, is probably not ideally suited by soft ground, but he handled conditions well enough and may have won despite the ground. He had to survive a pretty lengthy Stewards' enquiry as he hung into the runner-up near the finish, but he never really looked likely to lose the race. He looks up to Listed class and the Melbourne Cup is still an end-of-season possibility.
**Gold Ring** has performed consistently throughout the season and the easier ground was in his favour. He looked sure to score before the winner rallied and, although given a bump and only beaten narrowly, he did not look an unlucky loser. He is equally effective over a mile and a half and the November Handicap looks a suitable target.
**Mikado** was given a lot to do having been held up at the back of the field. He stayed on well to be nearest at the finish, and both the easier ground and return to this trip suited him well. Indeed, on this evidence he looks sure to get two miles, and as a lightly-raced colt there should be better to come.
**Defining** appreciated the drop back in distance and ran well off what remains a pretty high mark.
**Self Defense** continues to run with plenty of credit in these big-field handicaps. Enough, indeed, to keep his rating at a level that makes it difficult to win.
**Star Member(IRE)** handles this sort of ground but he was yet another who looked to have a tough task on his hands at the weights, being 5lb higher than when beaten over the course and distance last time.
**Fantastic Love(USA)** had both his stamina and ability to handle soft ground to prove. It looked like he failed to stay, although the ground may have accentuated that impression.
**Jagger** had done his winning on fast ground and had run poorly on his only previous start on soft ground, so it was something of a surprise to see him backed into favouritism for a competitive handicap such as this.
**Collier Hill** ran as well as could be expected under his big weight. He has paid with the Handicapper for some decent efforts this term.
**Dorothy's Friend**, like the winner shouldering a 7lb penalty, found the drop back from two miles against him.

## 4859 ASTON UPTHORPE YORKSHIRE OAKS (GROUP 1) (F&M) 1m 3f 198y

3:00 (3:00) (A) 3-Y-O+ £145,000 (£55,000; £27,500; £12,500) Stalls Low

Form RPR
5-13 **1** **Quiff**[62] 2997 3-8-8 105 KFallon 3 122
(SirMichaelStoute) *lw: hld up: hdwy 7f out: led over 3f out: edgd rt and styd on strly to forge clr fnl f* **7/2[2]**
3112 **2** 11 **Pongee**[18] 4321 4-9-4 107 JFortune 8 107
(LMCumani) *lw: chsd ldrs: lost pl over 4f out: rallied 3f out: styd on to go 2nd ins last: no ch w wnr* **10/1**
0-13 **3** 1 1/2 **Hazarista (IRE)**[31] 3968 3-8-8 MJKinane 9 105
(JohnMOxx, Ire) *hld up: hdwy to chse ldrs 6f out: wnt 2nd over 2f out: wknd ins fnl f* **9/2[3]**
1312 **4** 9 **Punctilious**[31] 3968 3-8-8 110 (t) LDettori 10 92
(SaeedBinSuroor) *led tl 6f out: chsd wnr tl wknd over 2f out: eased ins fnl f* **6/4[1]**
2221 **5** 8 **Sahool**[17] 4367 3-8-8 107 RHills 7 81
(MPTregoning) *trckd ldrs: lost pl over 2f out* **7/1**
4136 **6** 4 **Danelissima (IRE)**[31] 3968 3-8-8 (v[1]) WSupple 1 76
(JSBolger, Ire) *trckd ldr: styd on ins and led 6f out: hddover 3f out: edgd rt and lost pl over 2f out* **33/1**
0050 **7** 21 **Royal Tigress (USA)**[31] 3968 3-8-8 (v[1]) JPSpencer 2 46
(APO'Brien, Ire) *hld up in last: reminders over 4f out: no reponse and sn bhd* **33/1**
2106 **8** 5 **Menhoubah (USA)**[18] 4323 3-8-8 106 (p) SSanders 4 39
(CEBrittain) *chsd ldrs: drvn along 4f out: lost pl 3f out* **33/1**

2m 38.03s (9.17) **Going Correction** +0.925s/f (Soft)
**WFA** 3 from 4yo 10lb **8** Ran SP% **110.8**
Speed ratings: **106,98,97,91,86 83,69,66**CSF £34.45 TOTE £3.90: £1.50, £2.40, £1.70; EX 45.40 Trifecta £90.90 Pool £1,486.48. 11.60 winning units.
**Owner** K Abdulla **Bred** Juddmonte Farms **Trained** Newmarket, Suffolk

**FOCUS**
No Ouija Board, taken out at the eleventh hour because of the underfoot conditions, but a strong early pace and a highly impressive winner who looks bound for more success. Rated through Pongee, she comes out only a pound or two behind Ouija Board, although the Epsom form is more solid. The conditions must have eventually taken their toll though, because the winning time was moderate for a Group One.

**NOTEBOOK**
**Quiff** ◆, having just her fourth start, is a grand, big type. Revelling in the ground, she came right away and the St Leger - which her trainer has yet to win - must be a big temptation, but the ground will be a factor with the Vermeille one alternative.
**Pongee** is all heart and ran out of her skin, staying on in game fashion to secure a valuable second spot. This will be her final season before she retires to stud, where she will be a big asset.
**Hazarista(IRE)**, third behind Ouija Board in the Irish Oaks, went in pursuit of the winner but on this ground she became very leg-weary inside the last.

**Punctilious**, who looked very fit indeed, tried to repeat her all-the-way win in the Musidora here in May. However, she seemed to go too quick for her own good and, left toiling by the winner, was very tired when eased inside the last.
**Sahool**, runner-up to Punctilious at Royal Ascot and Pongee at Haydock, found this much too tough.
**Danelissima(IRE)**, who has failed at this level before, stuck to the inner when taking charge turning in and the winner, up the centre, left her for dead.

## 4860 COSTCUTTER ROSES STKS (LISTED RACE) (C&G) 5f

**3:35** (3:35) (A ) 2-Y-O **£16,250** (£5,000; £2,500; £1,250) **Stalls** Centre

Form RPR

1606 **1** **Dance Night (IRE)**[22] 4217 2-9-0 94 GGibbons 2 102
(BAMcmahon) *lw: w ldrs: led over 1f out: r.o wl* **7/1**

2126 **2** *1 1/2* **Moscow Music**[42] 3640 2-8-11 100 RLMoore 3 95
(MGQuinlan) *hld up: effrt over 2f out: sn outpcd: styd on to take 2nd nr line* **9/2**[3]

2404 **3** *hd* **Bigalos Bandit**[22] 4217 2-8-11 99 RWinston 6 94
(JJQuinn) *led tl over 1f out: kpt on same pce* **7/1**

2110 **4** *1 1/2* **Beckermet (IRE)**[22] 4217 2-9-0 100 RFfrench 7 93
(RFFisher) *lw: swvd rt s: sn trcking ldrs: effrt 2f out: sn rdn and no ex* **5/4**[1]

0133 **5** *3* **Bond City (IRE)**[32] 3938 2-8-11 95 FLynch 4 81
(BSmart) *hld up: effrt over 2f out: edgd lft and no imp* **4/1**[2]

62.13 secs (2.85) **Going Correction** +0.35s/f (Good) **5** Ran SP% **107.6**
Speed ratings: **91,88,88,85,81**CSF £34.59 TOTE £8.40: £3.70, £2.10; EX 38.70.
**Owner** J C Fretwell **Bred** Peter McClutcheon **Trained** Hopwas, Staffs

**FOCUS**
A weak Listed race run at no great pace to halfway and the winning time was very moderate for the grade, and the form is not strong for the level. A much improved run by the winner.

**NOTEBOOK**
**Dance Night(IRE)** looked at his very best beforehand and seemed to really appreciate getting his toe in. In the end he ran out a decisive winner. The Flying Childers at Doncaster may be aiming a little high, and a race such as the Cornwallis Stakes may prove more suitable.
**Moscow Music** stayed on after getting tapped for toe and will be suited by a return to six.
**Bigalos Bandit**, who finished two places ahead of the winner at Goodwood, enjoyed a soft lead but in the end was simply not good enough.
**Beckermet(IRE)**, out of luck at Goodwood, was a positive on the exchanges but, after travelling strongly, simply failed to quicken off the bridle on this ground.
**Bond City(IRE)**, happy to bide his time in last place, never entered the argument.

## 4861 NEWITTS.COM CONVIVIAL MAIDEN STKS 6f

**4:10** (4:11) (D) 2-Y-O **£10,773** (£3,315; £1,657; £828) **Stalls** Centre

Form RPR

4 **1** **Haunting Memories (IRE)**[19] 4296 2-9-0 PRobinson 10 94
(MAJarvis) *led: qcknd 1/2-way: hdd over 1f out: kpt on wl to ld nr fin* **5/2**[2]

2 **2** *1/2* **Rajwa (USA)**[22] 4219 2-9-0 (t) LDettori 6 93
(SaeedBinSuroor) *lw: w ldrs: led over 1f out: edgd rt: shkn up and hdd nr fin* **6/4**[1]

**3** *5* **My Putra (USA)** 2-9-0 JFanning 9 79
(PFICole) *wl grwn: chsd ldrs: outpcd fnl 2f* **8/1**[3]

**4** *2* **World Report (USA)** 2-9-0 RLMoore 3 73
(RHannon) *lengthy: wnt rt and hmpd s: bhd: sme hdwy over 1f out: nvr nr ldrs* **10/1**

**5** *4* **Burnley Al (IRE)** 2-9-0 PHanagan 4 62
(RAFahey) *cmpt: hmpd s: outpcd and hung lft over 2f out: nvr on terms* **11/1**

4 **6** *shd* **Tartan Special**[37] 3793 2-9-0 DarrenWilliams 5 62
(KRBurke) *hmpd s: sn chsng ldrs: rdn over 2f out: sn lost pl* **33/1**

04 **7** *1* **Jeune Loup**[25] 4131 2-8-9 RoryMoore(5) 1 59
(PCHaslam) *hld up: hdwy over 2f out: rdn and lost pl over 1f out* **33/1**

0 **8** *3/4* **Royal Wedding**[13] 4494 2-9-0 TPQueally 8 57
(DRLoder) *trckd ldrs: outpcd over 2f out: sn lost pl* **11/1**

60 **9** *16* **Midnight In Moscow (IRE)**[4] 4761 2-9-0 GFaulkner 2 13
(PCHaslam) *in tch on outer: rdn over 2f out: sn lost pl and bhd: eased* **50/1**

1m 14.67s (2.10) **Going Correction** +0.35s/f (Good) **9** Ran SP% **113.3**
Speed ratings: **100,99,92,90,84 84,83,82,60**CSF £6.35 TOTE £3.70: £1.40, £1.40, £2.10; EX 8.50 Trifecta £33.30 Pool £1,568.76. 33.36 winning units.
**Owner** Lawrence Wosskow **Bred** Hugo Merry **Trained** Newmarket, Suffolk

**FOCUS**
They bet 8/1 bar two which proved correct with the first two clear, in what may be an ordinary renewal of a race with a history of throwing up smart performers. However, it was a creditable winning time for the grade, just 0.37 seconds slower than the Gimcrack, and the form looks solid enough.

**NOTEBOOK**
**Haunting Memories(IRE)**, a solid type who has a round action, proved most determined and in the end worried the favourite out of it. A step up to seven will be very much in his favour.
**Rajwa(USA)** ◆, who looked in tip-top condition, showed a fluent action. He looked to be travelling the better but, drifting right carrying the winner across the track, he was edged out near the line without Dettori ever using his whip with any menace. Better ground will see him in a more favourable light and he will surely go one better.
**My Putra(USA)**, a well-made Silver Hawk colt, is out of speedy mare, but judged on this needs seven furlongs already. The first two ran clear away from him.
**World Report(USA)**, a March foal, is rather lightly-made but is an athletic type. After an unhappy start he stayed on in his own time and this will have taught him plenty.
**Burnley Al(IRE)**, an April foal, lacks scope and was never racing in a straight line. It will have at least taught him something.
**Tartan Special**, still carrying condition, looks to need more time and another furlong at least.

## 4862 EVENTMASTERS FALMOUTH H'CAP 5f

**4:45** (4:46) (C) (0-100,99) 3-Y-O **£11,017** (£3,390; £1,695; £847) **Stalls** Centre

Form RPR

1124 **1** **Enchantment**[40] 3702 3-9-0 92 RLMoore 5 109
(JMBradley) *mde all: shkn up over 1f out: sn rdn clr* **14/1**

6350 **2** *3 1/2* **Dispol Katie**[7] 4626 3-8-2 80 MartinDwyer 2 85
(TDBarron) *w wnr: nt qckn appr fnl f* **25/1**

3451 **3** *1* **Bygone Days**[16] 4394 3-8-11 89 MHills 8 91
(WJHaggas) *chsd ldrs: styd on same pce fnl 2f* **7/2**[1]

2203 **4** *2* **Imperial Echo (USA)**[10] 4576 3-8-2 80 PFessey 7 75
(TDBarron) *bhd: hdwy over 2f out: kpt on fnl f* **20/1**

-500 **5** *1* **Partners In Jazz (USA)**[4] 4759 3-8-3 86 PMakin(5) 13 78
(TDBarron) *racd stands' side: chsd ldrs: edgd lft 2f out: kpt on* **10/1**

0510 **6** *1/2* **Distant Times**[7] 4626 3-7-12 76 PHanagan 1 66
(TDEasterby) *chsd ldrs: rdn over 2f out: sn outpcd* **11/1**

1005 **7** *2* **Bonne De Fleur**[16] 4394 3-8-7 85 FLynch 9 69
(BSmart) *chsd ldrs: outpcd fnl 2f* **25/1**

0333 **8** *1* **Nights Cross (IRE)**[4] 4750 3-9-4 99 (v) SHitchcott(3) 6 79
(MRChannon) *s.i.s: bhd tl sme hdwy fnl 2f* **13/2**[3]

104 **9** *1/2* **Icenaslice (IRE)**[19] 4289 3-7-13 82 oh6 ow6 RoryMoore(5) 12 61
(JJQuinn) *racd stands' side: chsd ldrs: outpcd fnl 2f* **12/1**

0000 **10** *1/2* **Blue Crush (IRE)**[30] 3976 3-8-12 90 DarrenWilliams 14 67
(KRBurke) *racd stands' side: chsd ldrs: outpcd fnl 2f* **33/1**

6300 **11** *2* **Four Amigos (USA)**[32] 3926 3-8-2 80 JFanning 11 50
(JGGiven) *swtchd lft and racd far side: nvr on terms* **14/1**

4050 **12** *1/2* **Needles And Pins (IRE)**[30] 3976 3-8-12 90 KFallon 3 59
(MLWBell) *sn outpcd: nvr a factor* **4/1**[2]

0513 **13** *2* **Baron Rhodes**[9] 4608 3-8-2 80 RFfrench 15 42
(JSWainwright) *racd stands' side: outpcd fnl 2f* **12/1**

0420 **14** *11* **Sir Ernest (IRE)**[33] 3920 3-7-12 76 DKinsella 10 —
(MJPolglase) *swtchd rt s: led stands' side: wknd 2f out: sn bhd and eased* **33/1**

59.61 secs (0.33) **Going Correction** +0.35s/f (Good) **14** Ran SP% **120.0**
Speed ratings: **111,105,103,100,99 98,95,93,92,91 88,87,84,67**CSF £333.78 CT £1496.97 TOTE £11.50: £3.40, £6.00, £2.10; EX 301.80 Trifecta £1752.50 Part won. Pool £2,468.43. 0.30 winning units. Place 6 £157.44, Place 5 £91.75.
**Owner** Ms A M Williams **Bred** Downclose Stud **Trained** Sedbury, Gloucs

**FOCUS**
A decent sprint handicap and a creditable winning time for the grade, and a race that could rate higher. It proved a big advantage to race up with the pace.

**NOTEBOOK**
**Enchantment** had it to prove on the ground, but she has been in terrific form all season and, gaining a valuable uncontested lead, made every yard for a clear-cut success. On a day when it proved difficult to challenge from off the pace, she may well be flattered by the winning margin, but there was no denying the authority of her victory, and she looks worth trying in Pattern company.
**Dispol Katie** was another for whom the ground was a concern. She was quickly away though, which was an advantage in these conditions, and held second position throughout. She may be flattered by the bare result.
**Bygone Days** likes this sort of ground, but he was dropping back in trip and it proved very difficult in this race to challenge from off the pace. This was a creditable effort in the circumstances.
**Imperial Echo(USA)**, who had the visor left off this time, did best of those that were held up a fair way off the pace. Conditions were against his style of running, and in the circumstances he ran a decent race. He should be kept in mind for a similar contest.
**Partners In Jazz(USA)** came out best of those who raced nearer the stands'-side rail in the early part of the race. He is probably a bit better than his recent efforts suggest.
**Distant Times** needs a stiffer five furlongs or six to show his best.
**Icenaslice(IRE)**, who ran well from out of the handicap at Goodwood last time, was given an impossible task, being 6lb out of the handicap this time and having her rider carry 6lb overweight. She was also disadvantaged by racing with the stands'-side group in the early stages.
T/Jkpt: Not won. T/Plt: £255.00 to a £1 stake. Pool: £165,257.65. 472.95 winning tickets. T/Qpdt: £46.50 to a £1 stake. Pool: £8,052.80. 128.05 winning tickets. JR

4863 - 4865a (Foreign Racing) - See Raceform Interactive

# [4669] CHEPSTOW (L-H)

Thursday, August 19

**OFFICIAL GOING: Good to soft (soft in places)**
A dire card, with four maidens and a seller with no previous winners. There appeared no real draw advantage with winners coming from both flanks.
Wind: str across Weather: fine

## 4866 RACECOURSE GARAGE HONDA MEDIAN AUCTION MAIDEN STKS 6f 16y

**5:40** (5:41) (F) 2-Y-O **£3,283** (£938; £469) **Stalls** High

Form RPR

64 **1** **Brooklime (IRE)**[3] 4809 2-9-0 RWinston 6 76
(JAOsborne) *racd far side: chsd ldr: rdn to ld 1f out: r.o* **6/1**

02 **2** *1* **Viking Spirit**[26] 4149 2-8-7 MCoumbe(7) 12 73
(PWHarris) *hld up: hdwy over 2f out: r.o to take 2nd wl ins fnl f* **4/1**[2]

0 **3** *hd* **Duroob**[10] 4598 2-9-0 JFortune 1 72
(EALDunlop) *racd far side: chsd ldrs: rdn and kpt on one pce fnl f* **9/2**[3]

64 **4** *hd* **Watchmyeyes (IRE)**[18] 4359 2-9-0 JBramhill 9 72
(NPLittmoden) *trckd ldrs: rdn over 2f out: styd on ins fnl f* **14/1**

2653 **5** *shd* **Arabian Dancer**[14] 4498 2-8-9 88 CCatlin 2 67
(MRChannon) *racd far side: led tl rdn and hdd 1f out: no ex* **10/3**[1]

0 **6** *1 3/4* **Lighted Way**[17] 4399 2-8-6 LPKeniry(3) 13 61
(AMBalding) *led stands' side gp tl rdn and wknd fnl f* **50/1**

**7** *3/4* **Bathwick Finesse (IRE)** 2-8-9 SRighton 17 59
(BRMillman) *towards rr: styd on fnl f: nvr nr to chal* **25/1**

05 **8** *5* **Asteem**[42] 3659 2-9-0 SCarson 5 49
(RFJohnsonHoughton) *pushed along far side: nvr nr to chal* **50/1**

**9** *3* **Over Tipsy** 2-9-0 RSmith 4 40
(RHannon) *racd far side: chsd ldrs: no hdwy fnl 2f* **33/1**

000 **10** *3/4* **Aspen Ridge (IRE)**[10] 4599 2-8-6 FPFerris(3) 15 33
(CTinkler) *prom: rdn over 2f out: sn hung lft: wknd appr fnl f* **12/1**

**11** *1 1/4* **Lyric Dances (FR)** 2-8-9 NDay 7 29
(JJay) *slowly away: nvr on terms* **33/1**

00 **12** *1/2* **Inchcape Rock**[29] 4023 2-9-0 ADaly 11 33
(LGCottrell) *slowly aways: a in rr* **100/1**

03 **13** *hd* **San Deng**[14] 4481 2-9-0 SChin 14 32
(WRMuir) *chsd ldrs 4f* **25/1**

0 **14** *3 1/2* **Blade Runner (IRE)**[129] 1364 2-8-9 PaulEddery 16 16
(DHaydnJones) *a towards rr* **25/1**

**15** *1 1/4* **Hillabilla (IRE)** 2-8-9 DSweeney 8 13
(MBlanshard) *slowly away: a bhd* **40/1**

6 **16** *shd* **Penang Sapphire**[10] 4598 2-9-0 JoannaBadger 18 17
(GABulter) *slowly away: a bhd* **16/1**

0 **17** *22* **Mambazo**[25] 4172 2-9-0 OUrbina 3 —
(SCWilliams) *racd far side: lost tch half way: t.o* **14/1**

1m 15.95s (3.75) **Going Correction** +0.525s/f (Yiel) **17** Ran SP% **127.2**
Speed ratings: **96,94,94,94,94 91,90,84,80,79 77,76,76,71,70 69,40**CSF £28.63 TOTE £7.50: £4.00, £2.30, £2.10; EX 36.90.
**Owner** Mr & Mrs I H Bendelow **Bred** Rathbarry Stud **Trained** Upper Lambourn, Berks

**FOCUS**
An ordinary maiden in which the field split into two, with six, including the winner, racing on the far side. The form looks reliable.

**NOTEBOOK**
**Brooklime(IRE)**, making a quick reappearance, knuckled down well to score. Suited by cut in the ground, he should get seven furlongs, a trip his dam won over.
**Viking Spirit** did not get the best of breaks and was keeping on well at the end, finishing ahead of the other 11 runners in the stands'-side group. He obviously handles easy ground.
**Duroob**, a half-brother to two winners out of a mare who won at five and six furlongs, was well backed. He had been eased as though something was amiss on his debut on the Polytrack, and this run confirmed that he has the ability to win a maiden.
**Watchmyeyes(IRE)** was a little outpaced as the race hotted up, but kept on well inside the last as if in need of a return to seven furlongs.

**Arabian Dancer** has failed to live up to the promise of her Cherry Hinton fifth twice now, but the mile stretched her at Yarmouth and the soft ground could have been a factor here. She was only run out of the places near the finish but cannot afford any more excuses.
**Lighted Way** showed plenty of pace to lead overall but did not get home in the softish conditions.
**Bathwick Finesse(IRE)** was withdrawn on vet's advice from her intended debut a week earlier. Doing her best work at the finish, she is by a sprinter but her dam did all her winning at middle distances.

## 4867 SKYBET PRESS RED TO BET NOW (S) H'CAP 1m 4f 23y
6:10 (6:10) (G) (0-55,49) 3-Y-O £2,541 (£726; £363) Stalls Low

Form RPR
0050 1 **Trysting Grove (IRE)**[21] 4259 3-8-11 **40**.......... RWinston 7 51+
(KARyan) *hld up: hdwy on outside 5f out: wnt 2nd 3f out: sn led and wnt clr over 1f out* **5/1**[3]
-006 2 6 **Zuleta**[6] 4710 3-9-6 **49**.......... DSweeney 2 48
(MBlanshard) *trckd ldrs: rdn to chse wnr fnl 2f* **12/1**
4443 3 1 3/4 **Frambo (IRE)**[20] 4302 3-8-4 **36**..........(bt) FPFerris(3) 1 32
(JGPortman) *slowly away: hdwy 5f out: swtchd rt 2f out: r.o one pce* **9/2**[3]
4600 4 9 **Keltic Rainbow (IRE)**[31] 3996 3-8-11 **45**.......... RThomas(5) 4 28
(DHaydnJones) *led tl hdd wl over 2f out: sn wknd* **12/1**
-000 5 7 **Introduction**[31] 3984 3-8-6 **35**.......... PDoe 3 7
(RJPrice) *trckd ldr after 3f: rdn over 3f out: wknd over 2f out* **7/2**[2]
3456 6 16 **Regal Performer (IRE)**[15] 4433 3-9-6 **49**..........(b[1]) JFortune 6 —
(SKirk) *slowly away: a in rr: lost tch fnl 3f* **3/1**[1]
6625 7 19 **Buchanan Street (IRE)**[27] 4082 3-9-1 **44**.......... DKinsella 5 —
(JGMO'Shea) *trckd ldr for 3f: rdn 6f out: sn wknd: t.o* **11/2**

2m 46.15s (7.65) **Going Correction** +0.725s/f (Yiel) 7 Ran SP% **112.8**
Speed ratings: **103,99,97,91,87 76,63**CSF £58.21 TOTE £7.60: £3.80, £11.50; EX 104.90.The winner was sold to Mr E. Bevan for 8,000 gns.
**Owner** Mrs B Hayes & Mrs J Ryan **Bred** Knocktoran Stud **Trained** Hambleton, N Yorks

**FOCUS**
A desperate seller, but the winner scored easily and the time was decent for the grade.

**NOTEBOOK**
**Trysting Grove(IRE)**, taking a considerable step up in trip and in selling company for the first time, was the least exposed in the field and did it easily. She was sold at the auction and looks to have the scope to make a hurdler. *Official explanation: trainer's representative said filly had benefited from the step up in trip*
**Zuleta** again sweated up markedly beforehand. Dropped in grade, she stayed on in the last quarter-mile but had no chance with the facile winner.
**Frambo(IRE)**, from a 4lb lower mark, had the tongue-strap back on. A return to greater test of stamina may be required.
**Keltic Rainbow(IRE)**, without the headgear she has worn on her last two starts, had no answers when collared. She has shown very little on turf.
**Introduction**, having his second run for this yard, has yet to show that he stays this sort of trip.
**Regal Performer(IRE)** has become expensive to follow and the blinkers did not have the desired effect. He probably failed to handle the softish ground.

## 4868 SKYBET WATCH AND BET PRESS RED MAIDEN H'CAP 6f 16y
6:40 (6:43) (E) (0-70,66) 3-Y-O £4,615 (£1,420; £710; £355) Stalls High

Form RPR
2206 1 **Sabrina Brown**[7] 4680 3-8-13 **63**..........(t) RThomas(5) 13 77
(GBBalding) *racd stands' side: clr wl over 1f out: comf* **5/1**[2]
0033 2 2 **Instinct**[14] 4470 3-8-11 **56**.......... RSmith 9 64
(RHannon) *s.i.s: hdwy far side to chse wnr fnl f* **5/1**[2]
0035 3 1 1/2 **Indiana Blues**[26] 4148 3-9-4 **66**.......... LPKeniry(3) 6 69
(AMBalding) *chsd far side ldrs: kpt on fnl f* **14/1**
3060 4 1/2 **Pure Imagination (IRE)**[20] 4309 3-9-3 **62**.......... SCarson 2 64
(JMBradley) *prom far side: rdn over 1f out: kpt on* **12/1**
0002 5 1 1/4 **Fleet Anchor**[7] 4674 3-8-9 **54**.......... OUrbina 15 52
(JMBradley) *chsd wnr stands side over 4f: r.o to go 2nd again in gp ins fnl f* **9/2**[1]
0300 6 1/2 **Danish Monarch**[27] 4083 3-9-1 **60**.......... DSweeney 10 56
(ADWPinder) *led far side tl wknd appr fnl f* **25/1**
6044 7 1 **Nikiforos**[14] 4478 3-9-5 **64**..........(t) NDay 12 57
(JWHills) *prom stands side: rdn to chase wnr over 1f out tl ins fnl f* **16/1**
030 8 1/2 **Festive Chimes (IRE)**[27] 4097 3-8-10 **55**.......... RWinston 4 47
(JJQuinn) *prom far side tl rdn and wknd wl over 1f out* **14/1**
5200 9 3 **Indian Edge**[54] 3322 3-9-0 **62**.......... FPFerris(3) 16 45
(BPalling) *slowly away: sn mid-div: rdn over 2f out: no hdwy after* **10/1**[3]
0400 10 shd **Cellino**[20] 4309 3-7-12 **43** oh2.......... JMcAuley 17 25
(AndrewTurnell) *towards rr: rdn over 2f out: nvr nr to chal* **25/1**
5366 11 2 **Ligne D'Eau**[14] 4478 3-8-12 **57**..........(v[1]) RPrice 14 33
(PDEvans) *chsd ldrs stands side: rdn over 2f out: wknd over 1f out* **12/1**
5045 12 1/2 **Barabella (IRE)**[15] 4434 3-8-9 **54**..........(p) RHavlin 5 29
(RJHodges) *prom far side to 1/2-way* **16/1**
0330 13 1 **Blue Moon Hitman (IRE)**[11] 4585 3-8-12 **60**.......... DNolan(3) 1 32
(RBrotherton) *chsd ldrs far side: rdn 2f out: wknd fnl f* **20/1**
0-00 14 nk **Webbington Lass (IRE)**[7] 4674 3-7-7 **43** oh3..........(v) DFox(5) 18 14
(DrJRJNaylor) *a bhd* **100/1**
0-00 15 3/4 **Saintly Place**[6] 4717 3-9-1 **60**.......... CCatlin 19 29
(MRChannon) *a bhd* **33/1**
006- 16 shd **Chain Of Hope (IRE)**[344] 4820 3-9-0 **59**.......... PDoe 3 28
(DECantillon) *a bhd* **14/1**
-350 17 3 1/2 **Power To Burn**[134] 1293 3-8-7 **52**..........(v) DKinsella 8 10
(KBell) *prom far side to 1/2-way* **33/1**
0460 18 2 **Eight Ellington (IRE)**[48] 3486 3-8-13 **58**.......... JFortune 11 10
(MissGayKelleway) *a bhd* **16/1**
000- 19 1 **Katz Pyjamas (IRE)**[260] 6122 3-8-2 **47**.......... JoannaBadger 7 —
(GFHCharles-Jones) *bhd fr 1/2-way* **50/1**

1m 14.66s (2.46) **Going Correction** +0.525s/f (Yiel) 19 Ran SP% **134.9**
Speed ratings: **104,101,99,98,97 96,95,94,90,90 87,86,85,85,84 84,79,76,75**CSF £30.78 CT £363.71 TOTE £4.80: £1.70, £1.70, £4.10, £3.70; EX 35.00.
**Owner** Miss B Swire **Bred** Miss B Swire **Trained** Kimpton,Hants

**FOCUS**
Again they split into two groups, ten opting to go far side, but this time the winner came up the stands' rail. This is fair form for the grade.

**NOTEBOOK**
**Sabrina Brown**, equipped with a tongue tie, was smartly away and had managed to secure the berth next to the rail by halfway. Staying on strongly, she obviously relished the easy ground and looks to be on the upgrade.
**Instinct** did best of the ten to go the far-side route, but the drop back in trip did not really help his cause. He seems versatile as regards the ground and is running creditably at present.
**Indiana Blues**, who began the season rated 93, was encountering easy ground for the first time and obviously acts on it.
**Pure Imagination(IRE)** ran his best race to date in conditions that seem to suit him.
**Fleet Anchor** chased the eventual winner on the stands' side for much of the way and finished quite strongly to be second on that flank.
**Danish Monarch**, a stone lower than at the start of the season, had been well beaten on his only previous start on easy ground.
**Nikiforos** had his tongue tied for the first time. Racing on the outside of the stands'-side bunch, he moved into second place on that wing at one stage but faded inside the last.
**Indian Edge** *Official explanation: trainer said gelding had lost a front shoe*
**Ligne D'Eau**
**Power To Burn** *Official explanation: jockey said gelding lost its action*

## 4869 RACECOURSE GARAGE MITSUBISHI MAIDEN STKS 7f 16y
7:10 (7:11) (D) 3-Y-O+ £3,484 (£1,072; £536; £268) Stalls High

Form RPR
4 1 **Gentleman's Deal (IRE)**[34] 3916 3-9-0.......... JFortune 3 69+
(EALDunlop) *a in tch: hdwy and gng easily to ld 2f out: pushed clr appr fnl f* **1/3**[1]
0502 2 5 **Cafe Americano**[3] 4801 4-9-5 42..........(e) DSweeney 7 56
(DWPArbuthnot) *hld up: hdwy over 2f out: chsd easy wnr fnl f* **4/1**[2]
000 3 1 1/2 **Arian's Lad**[70] 2815 3-8-11.......... FPFerris(3) 5 52
(BPalling) *t.k.h: led tl hdd 2f out: lost 2nd 1f out: one pce* **20/1**[3]
06 4 3 1/2 **Dual Purpose (IRE)**[13] 4513 9-9-5.......... DKinsella 9 43
(CRoberts) *chsd ldr: rdn and short of room 2f out: sn wknd* **25/1**
0-0 5 4 **Mac's Elan**[108] 1820 4-9-5.......... JMcAuley 2 33
(ABCoogan) *bhd: sme hdwy 2f out: nvr on terms* **66/1**
6 6 19 **Ollijay**[19] 4316 3-9-0.......... RWinston 6 —
(MrsHDalton) *hld up in rr: lost tch over 2f out* **33/1**
000/ 7 shd **Velvet Jones**[438] 4181 11-9-5.......... JoannaBadger 4 —
(GFHCharles-Jones) *a wl in rr* **100/1**
0060 8 13 **Zambezi River**[69] 2836 5-9-5 45.......... OUrbina 8 —
(JMBradley) *trckd ldrs: rdn 3f out: wknd qckly: t.o* **40/1**

1m 28.19s (4.99) **Going Correction** +0.525s/f (Yiel)
**WFA** 3 from 4yo+ 5lb 8 Ran SP% **111.5**
Speed ratings: **92,86,84,80,76 54,54,39**CSF £1.54 TOTE £1.30: £1.02, £1.10, £2.70; EX 1.70.
**Owner** khalifa Sultan and Mohammed Jaber **Bred** C H Wacker Iii **Trained** Newmarket, Suffolk

**FOCUS**
Winner apart this was a desperately poor maiden, with the runner-up officially rated just 42, and the winning time was slow for the grade.

**NOTEBOOK**
**Gentleman's Deal(IRE)**, a son of 1000 Guineas winner Sleepytime, had nothing to beat in this poor event and he won easily once getting his full stride. A very big individual, standing 17.1 hands, he will only really come into his own next year.
**Cafe Americano**, who was taken early to post, had to wait for a run and then briefly hung fire when asked to go after the winner. He is not going to be easy to place, but at least proved that he handles softish ground.
**Arian's Lad** does possess a modicum of ability and might benefit from a return to shorter.
**Dual Purpose(IRE)**, who has come to racing very late in life, will be able to run in handicaps now off a pretty lowly mark.
**Velvet Jones** had not run on the Flat for three years but was in action in point-to-points in the spring of last year.
**Zambezi River** has no off eye. *Official explanation: jockey said gelding was unsuited by the good to soft (good in places) ground*

## 4870 SKYBET - RED BUTTON IN VISION BETTING MAIDEN STKS (H'CAP) 2m 2f
7:40 (7:40) (E) (0-70,70) 3-Y-O+ £4,182 (£1,287; £643; £321) Stalls Low

Form RPR
0040 1 **Indian Chase**[10] 4603 7-7-12 **40**.......... RThomas(5) 13 47
(DrJRJNaylor) *hld up: hdwy over 4f out: swtchd rt and rdn 2f out: styd on to ld ins fnl f: readily* **20/1**
0045 2 3/4 **Heart Springs**[10] 4603 4-8-3 **40**.......... ADaly 3 46
(DrJRJNaylor) *mid-div: hdwy 6f out: pressed ldrs over 2f out: led briefly 1f out: kpt on* **12/1**
23-0 3 1 1/2 **Assoon**[26] 4125 5-9-7 **58**..........(p) JFortune 11 63
(GLMoore) *a.p: led over 2f out: hdd 1f out: styd on one pce* **5/1**[1]
0045 4 3/4 **Bakhtyar**[26] 4129 3-8-2 **55**..........(b) RSmith 2 59
(RCharlton) *a.p: rdn 2f out: styd on one pce* **11/2**[2]
400 5 1/2 **Lord Nellsson**[29] 4028 8-9-5 **59**.......... LPKeniry(3) 9 62
(JSKing) *towards rr: hdwy over 5f out: kpt on at one pce fnl 3f* **20/1**
-300 6 6 **Hoh Nelson**[56] 3232 3-8-12 **65**.......... RHavlin 4 62
(HMorrison) *a in tch: rdn and wknd over 1f out* **20/1**
4030 7 1/2 **Calomeria**[15] 4448 3-8-4 **57**..........(b) SCarson 8 53
(RMBeckett) *trckd ldr: led 1m out: hdd 4f out: wknd over 2f out* **7/1**[3]
0-05 8 11 **Black Swan (IRE)**[13] 4513 4-8-0 **40**.......... BReilly(3) 12 24
(GAHam) *prom: led 4f out: hdd over 2f out: wknd* **33/1**
6/06 9 4 **Devote**[31] 3996 6-7-13 **39**.......... FPFerris(3) 7 19
(JDFrost) *hld up in mid-div: nvr nr to chal* **16/1**
0/00 10 1 1/2 **Stafford King (IRE)**[7] 4669 7-7-13 **36**.......... DKinsella 6 14
(JGMO'Shea) *slowly away: effrt over 5f out: nvr on terms* **20/1**
0543 11 2 1/2 **Fu Fighter**[53] 3341 3-9-3 **70**.......... SWKelly 1 45
(JAOsborne) *t.k.h: led tl hdd 1m out: wknd 4f out* **5/1**[1]
0000 12 29 **Hoops And Blades**[14] 4492 3-7-12 **51** oh2..........(t) JBramhill 15 —
(NPLittmoden) *a in rr* **25/1**
0040 13 20 **Song Of The Sea**[8] 4647 3-8-9 **62**.......... NDay 5 —
(JWHills) *a bhd: t.o* **33/1**
0064 14 2 **Olympias (IRE)**[34] 3919 3-8-3 **56**.......... CCatlin 14 —
(HMorrison) *racd wd in mid-div: hdwy 1/2-way: wknd over 4f out: eased ins fnl 2f: t.o* **12/1**
2240 15 dist **Sadler's Pride (IRE)**[23] 4210 4-10-0 **65**.......... DSweeney 10 —
(AndrewTurnell) *a towards rr: virtually p.u over 2f out and walked over line* **10/1**

4m 15.39s (15.19) **Going Correction** +0.725s/f (Yiel)
**WFA** 3 from 4yo+ 16lb 15 Ran SP% **120.4**
Speed ratings: **95,94,94,93,93 90,90,85,83,83 82,69,60,59,—**CSF £222.61 CT £1396.21 TOTE £20.70: £6.20, £4.00, £2.50; EX 300.90.
**Owner** The Indian Chase Partnership **Bred** R T Crellin **Trained** Shrewton, Wilts
■ Jeremy Naylor saddled the first and second.

**FOCUS**
Another poor event. The pace was pretty quick through the first couple of furlongs before steadying, and then picked up again in the final three-quarters of a mile. The winner only had to run up to the level of his claimer fourth here to score.

**NOTEBOOK**
**Indian Chase** came from off the pace to beat his stablemate, who had finished in front of him at Lingfield, a shade cosily in the end. A failed jumper, he stays very well.
**Heart Springs** had to work hard to force her head in front but was eventually denied by her stable companion. She has plenty of stamina and acts on an easy surface.
**Assoon**, a fast-ground bumper winner, wore cheekpieces for the first time on this handicap debut. He showed narrowly in front with two to run but was soon worn down.

**Bakhtyar** finished a little further behind Heart Springs than he had on the Lingfield Polytrack last time.
**Lord Nellsson**, making his handicap debut, could only plug on at the one pace in the last three furlongs.
**Hoh Nelson** *Official explanation: jockey said colt hung left*
**Calomeria**, not for the first time, swished her tail when pressure was applied.
**Black Swan(IRE)** struck for home early in the home straight, but was swallowed up approaching the two pole and weakened as if failing to stay.
**Fu Fighter** again failed to settle properly. *Official explanation: jockey said gelding hung right*
**Sadler's Pride(IRE)** *Official explanation: jockey said colt had a breathing problem*

## 4871 SKYBET PRESS RED TO BET NOW H'CAP — 1m 14y

**8:10** (8:13) (E) (0-70,76) 3-Y-O+ — **£4,615** (£1,420; £710; £355) **Stalls** High

Form — RPR

1-02 **1** — **Compton Drake**[8] 4641 5-9-10 **66** ... JFortune 4 — 82
(GAButler) *hld up: hdwy over 3f out: hrd rdn to ld ins fnl f: all out* **3/1**[1]

-050 **2** *nk* **Elidore**[12] 4542 4-9-5 **64** ... FPFerris(3) 1 — 79+
(BPalling) *racd far side tl swtchd over to stands' side over 3f out: hrd rdn to ld appr fnl f: hdd ins: kpt on gamely* **25/1**

1013 **3** *3 1/2* **Threezedzz**[1] 4852 6-9-13 **76** 6ex ... (t) SJDonohoe(7) 8 — 84
(PDEvans) *a.p: led 3f out: rdn and hdd appr fnl f: wknd ins last* **3/1**[1]

0406 **4** *3/4* **Basinet**[13] 4333 6-8-11 **53** ... (p) RWinston 15 — 59+
(JJQuinn) *in tch: rdn over 1f out: one pce after* **7/1**[3]

4060 **5** *4* **Petite Colleen (IRE)**[24] 4196 3-8-12 **60** ... DKinsella 14 — 58
(DHaydnJones) *hld up: hdwy to pass btn horses ins fnl 2f* **33/1**

0420 **6** *1/2* **Enna (POL)**[4] 4771 5-8-3 **45** ... SCarson 2 — 42
(MrsStefLiddiard) *racd promly far side: no imp fnl 2f* **9/2**[2]

-006 **7** *1 1/2* **Kama's Wheel**[17] 4386 5-7-6 **41** oh9 ow1 ... NataliaGemelova(7) 6 — 34
(JohnAHarris) *nvr bttr than mid-div* **50/1**

400- **8** *3/4* **Seven Shirt**[296] 5816 3-8-7 **60** ... DFox(5) 3 — 52
(EGBevan) *racd far side: no ch fnl 2f* **50/1**

40-0 **9** *1 1/2* **Another Deal (FR)**[31] 3988 5-9-4 **60** ... RHavlin 10 — 49
(RJHodges) *a towards rr* **66/1**

006 **10** *3 1/2* **Just One Look**[41] 3700 3-8-10 **58** ... DSweeney 7 — 39
(MBlanshard) *in tch: rdn over 3f out: wknd 2f out* **16/1**

2014 **11** *2 1/2* **Lord Chamberlain**[12] 4546 11-8-13 **55** ... (b) SWKelly 9 — 31
(JMBradley) *slowly away: a bhd* **10/1**

040/ **12** *5* **Ca'D'Oro**[1385] 5316 11-8-8 **55** ... RThomas(5) 13 — 21
(GBBalding) *in tch: rdn whn bmpd wl over 1f out: sn btn and eased* **20/1**

0100 **13** *2 1/2* **Mister Trickster (IRE)**[22] 4242 3-8-13 **61** ... LisaJones 5 — 21
(RDickin) *led tl hdd 3f out: wknd 2f out* **14/1**

00-0 **14** *2* **Stars At Midnight**[78] 2594 4-8-6 **48** ... CCatlin 11 — 4
(JMBradley) *a struggling in rr* **50/1**

/000 **15** *23* **Frederick James**[72] 2762 10-7-12 **40** oh9 ... JMcAuley 12 — —
(HEHaynes) *a bhd: t.o* **100/1**

1m 40.35s (4.45) **Going Correction** +0.525s/f (Yiel)
**WFA** 3 from 4yo+ 6lb — **15** Ran SP% **122.2**
Speed ratings: **98,97,94,93,89 88,87,86,85,81 79,74,71,69,46**CSF £90.18 CT £257.93 TOTE £4.10: £1.70, £9.70, £1.90; EX 128.30 Place 6 £160.71, Place 5 £86.44.
**Owner** Erik Penser **Bred** Meon Valley Stud **Trained** Blewbury, Oxon

**FOCUS**
At first those in the three lowest stalls took the far-side route, but eventual runner-up Elidore soon abandoned that course and tacked over.

**NOTEBOOK**
**Compton Drake** gained his last turf win in November off a 17lb lower mark. He had to work hard to get his head in front in the last half-furlong and would not mind a step back up in trip, but should continue to progress.
**Elidore**, minus the visor, can be counted unlucky. Initially leading the trio which raced up the far side, she started to tack over before the five pole and after racing down the centre of the track for a time, had joined the main bunch with three furlongs to run. Responding to pressure to get her head in front, she battled on willingly but found the bigger gelding just too strong. She has dropped considerably in the weights and, proven on softish ground, is capable of gaining compensation.
**Threezedzz**, who had finished third the previous night, was able to squeeze in another run under his penalty before his 4lb higher mark comes into effect at the weekend. Taken to post early, he had conditions to suit and ran another good race, but is going to be vulnerable now.
**Basinet** was a little short of room when attempting to improve, but did not look over-keen to run on when in the clear. He is the sort who needs everything to fall just right.
**Petite Colleen(IRE)**, who has shown her best form on faster ground, was without the cheekpieces she has worn on her last two runs.
**Enna(POL)** was left in front on the far side after two and a half furlongs, but for the rest of the way had only one horse to race with and the main action took place on the other side of the track.
**Kama's Wheel** *Official explanation: jockey said mare lost her action*
**Lord Chamberlain** *Official explanation: jockey said gelding was unsuited by the good to soft (soft in places) ground*
T/Plt: £218.40 to a £1 stake. Pool: £33,608.40. 112.30 winning tickets. T/Qpdt: £9.10 to a £1 stake. Pool: £3,666.60. 296.70 winning tickets. JS

# 4358 CHESTER (L-H)

Thursday, August 19

**OFFICIAL GOING: Good (good to soft in places)**
Wind: mod across Weather: fine

## 4872 SURRENDA-LINK NOVICE STKS — 7f 122y

**2:20** (2:21) (D) 2-Y-O — **£5,499** (£1,692; £846; £423) **Stalls** Low

Form — RPR

254 **1** — **Mastman (IRE)**[21] 4263 2-8-9 80 ... (t) JFMcDonald(3) 5 — 83
(BJMeehan) *prom: led over 3f out: rdn over 2f out: jst hld on* **8/1**

01 **2** *shd* **Skidrow**[26] 4131 2-9-0 88 ... MFenton 4 — 85
(MLWBell) *trckd ldrs: rdn 2f out: r.o ins fnl f: jst failed* **7/2**[3]

16 **3** *1 1/4* **Stagbury Hill (USA)**[22] 4227 2-9-5 ... RHills 3 — 87
(JWHills) *t.k.h: hld up: nt clr run and hdwy over 1f out: nt qckn ins fnl f* **11/8**[1]

6065 **4** *4* **Mirage Prince (IRE)**[23] 4208 2-8-12 ... SWKelly 2 — 71
(WMBrisbourne) *led: hdd over 3f out: rdn over 2f out: stl ev ch over 1f out: sn wknd* **25/1**

3 **5** *3/4* **L'Escapade (IRE)**[44] 3601 2-8-12 ... NCallan 6 — 69
(AMBalding) *stmbld s: t.k.h: trckd ldrs: effrt 2f out: wknd 1f out* **9/4**[2]

1m 36.07s (1.32) **Going Correction** -0.075s/f (Good) — **5** Ran SP% **110.1**
Speed ratings: **90,89,88,84,83**CSF £34.69 TOTE £11.20: £4.40, £1.50; EX 40.70.
**Owner** Kennet Valley Thoroughbreds Iii **Bred** Catridge Farm Stud And Burgage Stud **Trained** Upper Lambourn, Berks

**FOCUS**
An interesting little race which produced a tight finish, though the time was modest. The form is not all that solid but makes sense all the same.

**NOTEBOOK**
**Mastman(IRE)** had disappointed slightly since his promising debut effort, but he could be excused his run at Epsom and, on this easier ground, found just enough under pressure to hold on in a photo. Connections will surely be hoping the Handicapper does not raise him too much from his current rating of 80.
**Skidrow** appreciated the step up in trip and only just failed to grab the spoils on the line. He will be suited by a mile on this evidence.
**Stagbury Hill(USA)** was dropping in grade but he had to give weight all round. Short of room early in the straight, he kept on well once in the clear but was just unable to reel in the first two. Once again his chance was compromised by the fact that he raced keenly in the early stages.
**Mirage Prince(IRE)** looked to be up against it in this class and in the circumstances he ran a creditable race from the front.
**L'Escapade(IRE)** was well supported in the market but he was done no favours by being raced three wide for most of the way, and had no extra in the straight.

## 4873 BENTLEY MOTORS 40TH SERVICE CONDITIONS STKS — 7f 122y

**2:55** (2:55) (B) 3-Y-O — **£12,316** (£4,554; £2,277; £1,035) **Stalls** Low

Form — RPR

1511 **1** — **Peter Paul Rubens (USA)**[21] 4268 3-9-1 105 ... PHanagan 4 — 111+
(PFICole) *racd keenly: mde all: rdn out* **11/10**[1]

3320 **2** *1* **Jedburgh**[21] 4268 3-8-12 96 ... NCallan 5 — 105
(JLDunlop) *chsd wnr: rdn 2f out: nt qckn ins fnl f* **7/1**[3]

2503 **3** *2 1/2* **Milk It Mick**[19] 4317 3-8-12 107 ... SWKelly 1 — 99
(JAOsborne) *chsd ldrs: rdn over 2f out: kpt on same pce fnl f: b.b.v* **2/1**[2]

0044 **4** *hd* **Glaramara**[12] 4531 3-8-12 97 ... MFenton 2 — 98
(ABailey) *in tch: rdn over 1f out: kpt on one pce* **8/1**

21- **5** *20* **Oman Sea (USA)**[464] 1576 3-8-7 ... RHills 3 — 43
(BWHills) *a bhd* **10/1**

1m 33.01s (-1.74) **Going Correction** -0.075s/f (Good) — **5** Ran SP% **113.7**
Speed ratings: **105,104,101,101,81**CSF £9.77 TOTE £2.20: £1.40, £2.80; EX 11.90.
**Owner** Richard Green (fine Paintings) **Bred** Mueller Farm **Trained** Whatcombe, Oxon

**FOCUS**
An interesting conditions event, but not that competitive. Fair form, with the winner not needing to be at his best.

**NOTEBOOK**
**Peter Paul Rubens(USA)** had been doing his recent winning on fast ground so this slower surface was a worry. Being a front-runner though, the track was in his favour. He made every yard and, although getting tired at the finish, still had a length to spare at the line. He won despite the ground and will remain of interest when stepped up again in grade on fast ground.
**Jedburgh** has done his winning on fast ground but he also handles cut. He went in pursuit of the winner and ran right up to his best, but looks likely to continue to struggle back in handicap company off his current mark.
**Milk It Mick** has done his winning on fast ground, but he finished runner-up in the Solario Stakes on good to soft. He has been below form all season and could not take advantage of the favourable conditions of this race. *Official explanation: vet said colt was found to have bled internally*
**Glaramara** had a difficult task judged on official ratings and did well to finish so close.
**Oman Sea(USA)** had some good from last term but she was having her first start since splitting a pastern.

## 4874 BET@BLUESQ.COM H'CAP — 6f 18y

**3:30** (3:30) (C) (0-95,92) 3-Y-O — **£13,975** (£4,300; £2,150; £1,075) **Stalls** Low

Form — RPR

6000 **1** — **High Voltage**[12] 4531 3-9-7 92 ... (t) NCallan 2 — 103
(KRBurke) *mde all: rdn over 1f out: all out* **9/2**[1]

2122 **2** *shd* **Compton's Eleven**[13] 4510 3-9-2 90 ... SHitchcott(3) 8 — 101
(MRChannon) *a.p: rdn and ev ch fr over 1f out: r.o u.p* **5/1**[2]

4 **3** *1* **Mister Marmaduke**[21] 4280 3-8-4 78 ... THamilton(3) 4 — 86
(ISemple) *midfield: hdwy 2f out: sn rdn: r.o ins fnl f* **10/1**

0000 **4** *3/4* **Danzig River (IRE)**[12] 4531 3-9-5 90 ... RHills 5 — 96
(BWHills) *hld up: hdwy over 1f out: edgd lft ins fnl f: r.o* **10/1**

0055 **5** *1* **Tribute (IRE)**[55] 3273 3-8-4 75 ... PFessey 1 — 78
(KARyan) *chsd ldrs: rdn and edgd rt over 1f out: kpt on same pce* **12/1**

65U0 **6** *1 1/2* **Melody King**[9] 4617 3-7-7 69 oh4 ... (b) HayleyTurner(5) 3 — 67
(PDEvans) *s.i.s: bhd: rdn and hdwy over 2f out: one pce fnl f* **25/1**

4301 **7** *1/2* **Obe Bold (IRE)**[11] 4576 3-7-5 66 7ex oh3 ... CHaddon(7) 6 — 66
(ABerry) *chsd ldrs: rdn 2f out: no ex fnl f* **20/1**

6115 **8** *3 1/2* **Commando Scott (IRE)**[12] 4531 3-9-2 92 ... PPMathers(5) 7 — 78
(ABerry) *in tch: hdwy over 2f out: wknd 1f out* **13/2**[3]

6150 **9** *3 1/2* **Jadan (IRE)**[10] 4608 3-8-4 75 ... MFenton 12 — 51
(EJAlston) *prom: rdn and hung lft over 2f out: wknd over 1f out* **25/1**

6246 **10** *2 1/2* **Rising Shadow (IRE)**[11] 4570 3-8-13 84 ... PHanagan 14 — 52
(RAFahey) *s.i.s: a bhd* **12/1**

1000 **11** *6* **Times Review (USA)**[17] 4394 3-8-10 81 ... DAllan 16 — 31
(TDEasterby) *s.i.s: a bhd* **50/1**

020 **12** *shd* **Buy On The Red**[20] 4289 3-8-12 86 ... RMiles(3) 9 — 36
(WRMuir) *sn towards rr* **14/1**

0060 **13** *1* **Morse (IRE)**[33] 3941 3-9-2 87 ... SWKelly 11 — 34
(JAOsborne) *a outpcd* **16/1**

0622 **14** *1 3/4* **The Jobber (IRE)**[6] 4717 3-8-7 78 ... FNorton 13 — 20
(MBlanshard) *in tch: rdn and wknd over 2f out* **9/1**

1m 14.37s (-1.51) **Going Correction** -0.075s/f (Good) — **14** Ran SP% **118.7**
Speed ratings: **107,106,105,104,103 101,100,95,91,87 79,79,78,76**CSF £24.47 CT £222.92 TOTE £4.40: £2.00, £2.10, £2.70; EX 21.30.
**Owner** Mrs K Halsall **Bred** D P Martin **Trained** Middleham Moor, N Yorks

**FOCUS**
A race determined by the draw more than anything, but the form looks strong and should prove reliable.

**NOTEBOOK**
**High Voltage**, who had dropped down to rating just 1lb higher than his last winning mark, had the ground in his favour and likes to make the running, so he was well drawn in two. He made every yard, responding well to pressure when challenged.
**Compton's Eleven** has been running well of late and, although now 10lb higher than his last winning mark and racing on softer ground than probably ideal, once again ran a creditable race in defeat. The Handicapper will have no option than to raise him again for this, though.
**Mister Marmaduke** had shaped as though he could be placed to advantage off his current mark last time, and the shorter trip looked likely to suit. He ran well from his low draw and looks ready to strike.
**Danzig River(IRE)** found the easier surface bringing about an improved display, although he still looks high in the weights.
**Tribute(IRE)** had the headgear left off this time and ran a respectable race from the box draw.
**Commando Scott(IRE)** goes well with give in the ground but he was racing off an 8lb higher mark than when last successful.
**Buy On The Red** *Official explanation: jockey said colt was unsuited by the slow ground*
**Morse(IRE)** *Official explanation: jockey said colt did not handle the ground*
**The Jobber(IRE)** *Official explanation: jockey said gelding ran flat and had no more to give*

## 4875 GERRARD WEALTH MANAGEMENT NURSERY 5f 16y
4:05 (4:05) (D) 2-Y-O £6,873 (£2,115; £1,057; £528) Stalls Low

| Form | | | | RPR |
|---|---|---|---|---|
| 4011 | 1 | | **Coleorton Dancer**[3] 4803 2-8-2 71 6ex AMullen(7) 1 (KARyan) *in tch: hdwy 3f out: led wl ins fnl f: r.o wl* **1/1**[1] | 82+ |
| 3312 | 2 | 2 | **Wise Wager (IRE)**[5] 4752 2-8-11 73 PHanagan 3 (RAFahey) *w ldrs: rdn over 1f out: ev ch ins fnl f: nt qckn cl home* **9/4**[2] | 75 |
| 2156 | 3 | nk | **Wonderful Mind**[26] 4150 2-8-10 72 (b[1]) DAllan 2 (TDEasterby) *led after 1f: rdn over 1f out: hdd wl ins fnl f: no ex cl home* **14/1**[3] | 73 |
| 1604 | 4 | 2 | **Sapphire Dream**[12] 4541 2-9-2 83 HayleyTurner(5) 5 (ABailey) *towards rr: hdwy 2f out: kpt on: nt pce of ldrs* **20/1** | 77 |
| 2024 | 5 | 1 | **Hillside Heather (IRE)**[11] 4575 2-8-7 69 FNorton 9 (ABerry) *outpcd: hdwy 2f out: one pce ins fnl f* **25/1** | 59 |
| 3134 | 6 | shd | **Westbrook Blue**[13] 4514 2-8-11 80 CHaddon(7) 6 (WGMTurner) *in tch: rdn and lost pl 2f out: n.m.r over 1f out: kpt on ins fnl f* **25/1** | 70 |
| 2223 | 7 | 3 | **I'm Aimee**[7] 4676 2-8-12 77 SHitchcott(3) 10 (PDEvans) *led 1f: rdn 3f out: sn wknd* **14/1**[3] | 57 |
| 0044 | 8 | 4 | **Next Time (IRE)**[29] 4017 2-7-9 60 oh1 JFMcDonald(3) 7 (MJPolglase) *prom: rdn 1/2-way: sn wknd* **40/1** | 26 |
| 5000 | 9 | 8 | **Iam Foreverblowing**[8] 4637 2-7-6 61 oh15 ow1 DonnaCaldwell(7) 4 (SCBurrough) *a outpcd: rdr lost irons over 1f out* **100/1** | — |
| 4333 | 10 | 3/4 | **Angelofthenorth**[6] 4700 2-8-3 68 NMackay(3) 8 (JDBethell) *in tch: rdn and wknd 1/2-way* **25/1** | 3 |

61.67 secs (-0.31) **Going Correction** -0.075s/f (Good) 10 Ran SP% **113.8**
Speed ratings: **99,95,95,92,90 90,85,79,66,65**CSF £2.76 CT £15.88 TOTE £1.90: £1.10, £1.40, £1.90; EX 3.10.
**Owner** Coleorton Moor Racing **Bred** A Holmes **Trained** Hambleton, N Yorks

**FOCUS**
Once again the draw played its part, although the winner is clearly ahead of the Handicapper. The form looks very solid.

**NOTEBOOK**
**Coleorton Dancer** had run out a clear winner off this mark at Nottingham last time and was strongly fancied to follow up from the plum draw. He shaped as though he will get six, and he is clearly well suited by an easy surface. This success means that he has notched up a hat-trick since being gelded.
**Wise Wager(IRE)**, who continues to run well, has performed with credit on fast ground and an easy surface. She was unfortunate to run into a well-handicapped rival on this occasion.
**Wonderful Mind** showed speed from his good draw but, while the Handicapper looks to have his measure for the time being, the winner is undoubtedly ahead of the assessor.
**Sapphire Dream** confirmed the impression of her previous run, that she is not well handicapped at present.
**Hillside Heather(IRE)** was always going to struggle from her wide draw.
**Westbrook Blue** *Official explanation: jockey said colt had been struck into*
**I'm Aimee**, far more exposed than most of her rivals, used up too much energy trying to get to the front from the widest draw.
**Iam Foreverblowing** *Official explanation: jockey said filly suffered interference leaving the stalls and lost her irons in the straight on the final bend*
**Angelofthenorth** *Official explanation: jockey said filly lost her action*

## 4876 EUROPEAN BREEDERS FUND COMBERMERE FILLIES' CONDITIONS STKS 6f 18y
4:40 (4:40) (B) 2-Y-O £10,205 (£3,870; £1,935; £879) Stalls Low

| Form | | | | RPR |
|---|---|---|---|---|
| 3522 | 1 | | **Katie Boo (IRE)**[19] 4348 2-8-8 81 FNorton 5 (ABerry) *mde all: rdn over 1f out: r.o* **7/1**[3] | 85 |
| 3010 | 2 | 3/4 | **Vondova**[28] 4060 2-8-11 83 PDobbs 1 (RHannon) *trckd ldrs: rdn and swtchd rt over 1f out: bmpd and wnt 2nd ins fnl f: sn struck by rival's whip: nt qckn cl* **11/2**[2] | 86 |
| 2011 | 3 | nk | **Golden Legacy (IRE)**[18] 4358 2-8-11 96 PHanagan 7 (RAFahey) *trckd ldrs: wnt 2nd over 2f out: edgd lft and lost 2nd ins fnl f: nt qckn cl home* **4/6**[1] | 85 |
| 452 | 4 | 2 1/2 | **Indiena**[12] 4541 2-8-8 79 JFMcDonald 2 (BJMeehan) *racd keenly: in tch: rdn 2f out: one pce* **9/1** | 74 |
| 05 | 5 | 1/2 | **Flying Ridge (IRE)**[14] 4488 2-8-8 RHills 6 (AMBalding) *hld up: rdn and flashed tail over 1f out: nvr able to chal* **20/1** | 73 |
| 0161 | 6 | 6 | **Tequila Sheila (IRE)**[10] 4612 2-8-11 78 NCallan 4 (KRBurke) *in tch: rdn 3f out: wknd 2f out* **8/1** | 58 |
| 0 | 7 | 5 | **Bella Plunkett (IRE)**[14] 4487 2-8-8 SHitchcott 3 (WMBrisbourne) *w wnr: rdn over 2f out: sn wknd* **66/1** | 40 |

1m 15.59s (-0.29) **Going Correction** -0.075s/f (Good) 7 Ran SP% **115.2**
Speed ratings: **98,97,96,93,92 84,77**CSF £45.17 TOTE £7.20: £2.80, £2.90; EX 59.70.
**Owner** The Early Doors Partnership **Bred** Michael McGlynn **Trained** Cockerham, Lancs

**FOCUS**
The favourite was below-par due to the softish ground but the form looks reliable enough.

**NOTEBOOK**
**Katie Boo(IRE)**, quickly away, made every yard and saw the sixth furlong out well. The easy ground appeared to suit this daughter of Namid, and she may now head for a Listed race at Ayr in an attempt to collect some black type.
**Vondova** travelled well in behind the leader but she did not find as much as had looked likely, although the fact that she was hit over the head by the winning rider's whip may have contributed to that. She was clearly at home in the ground.
**Golden Legacy(IRE)** had won her two previous races, including her last over this course and distance, and looked to have a good deal in hand over her rivals on that evidence. However, those wins both came on fast ground and conditions were very different on this occasion. She still looks one to be interested in when she gets her preferred surface again.
**Indiena** was not disgraced on this step up in grade but her place is in nurseries.
**Flying Ridge(IRE)**, who once again flashed her tail when put under pressure, had a tough task on in this grade.

## 4877 BLUE SQUARE 0800 587 0200 APPRENTICE H'CAP 7f 2y
5:10 (5:20) (E) (0-75,75) 3-Y-O+ £6,971 (£2,145; £1,072; £536) Stalls Far side

| Form | | | | RPR |
|---|---|---|---|---|
| 0322 | 1 | | **Hills Of Gold**[31] 3985 5-9-13 74 PMulrennan 15 (MWEasterby) *in tch: rdn and hdwy over 2f out: led ins fnl f: r.o* **10/1** | 86 |
| 1204 | 2 | 1 | **Merdiff**[10] 4602 5-8-7 59 PPMathers(5) 3 (WMBrisbourne) *chsd ldrs: rdn to ld over 1f out: hdd ins fnl f: nt qckn* **9/2**[1] | 68 |
| 1051 | 3 | hd | **Tuscarora (IRE)**[14] 4477 5-8-12 59 RMiles 12 (AWCarroll) *s.s: bhd: hdwy over 1f out: edgd lft and r.o ins fnl f* **12/1** | 67+ |
| 2000 | 4 | 1 1/2 | **Whippasnapper**[10] 4602 4-9-2 66 MSavage(3) 1 (JRBest) *n.m.r sn after s: in tch: rdn over 2f out: styd on same pce fnl f* **10/1** | 71 |
| 1041 | 5 | 1 | **Showtime Annie**[90] 2259 3-8-11 63 NMackay 9 (ABailey) *midfield: rdn and hdwy over 1f out: kpt on: nt rch ldrs* **16/1** | 65 |
| 3331 | 6 | 2 1/2 | **Neon Blue**[26] 4151 3-9-3 72 HayleyTurner(3) 4 (RMWhitaker) *towards rr: hdwy whn swtchd rt over 1f out: kpt on* **5/1**[2] | 67 |
| 0044 | 7 | hd | **Iced Diamond (IRE)**[18] 4360 5-8-5 52 JFMcDonald 13 (WMBrisbourne) *towards rr: hdwy over 1f out: one pce fnl f* **12/1** | 47 |
| 3424 | 8 | 3/4 | **Sharoura**[21] 4260 8-9-5 66 THamilton 5 (RAFahey) *chsd ldr tl rdn 2f out: wknd over 1f out* **6/1**[3] | 59 |
| 1001 | 9 | nk | **Dara Mac**[10] 4605 5-8-7 59 6ex SuzanneFrance(5) 14 (NBycroft) *s.s: hdwy on wd outside over 1f out: kpt on: nvr trbld ldrs* **14/1** | 51 |
| 3412 | 10 | 1/2 | **Concer Eto**[11] 4569 5-9-12 73 (p) LFletcher 6 (SCWilliams) *midfield: hmpd after 1f: rdn over 2f out: one pce over 1f out* **9/2**[1] | 64 |
| 2030 | 11 | 1 1/4 | **Semper Paratus (USA)**[17] 4403 5-8-0 52 (b) CHaddon(5) 11 (VSmith) *midfield: rdn over 2f out: no hdwy* **16/1** | 40 |
| 00-0 | 12 | shd | **Perfect Love**[21] 4260 4-10-0 75 DAllan 10 (EJAlston) *led: rdn and hdd over 1f out: sn wknd* **33/1** | 62 |
| 0600 | 13 | 3 1/2 | **Risk Free**[6] 4702 7-8-9 56 (v) SHitchcott 8 (PDEvans) *midfield: rdn over 3f out: wknd over 1f out* **33/1** | 34 |
| 0005 | 14 | 5 | **Night Wolf (IRE)**[14] 4495 4-8-3 57 BO'Neill(7) 16 (MRChannon) *midfield: hdwy 4f out: rdn over 2f out: wknd over 1f out* **50/1** | 22 |
| 040- | 15 | 16 | **Miss Mytton (USA)**[336] 5011 3-8-8 67 NatalieHassall(7) 2 (ABailey) *s.s: a bhd* **33/1** | — |
| -004 | 16 | 2 1/2 | **Key Of Gold (IRE)**[15] 4456 3-8-8 65 DTudhope(5) 7 (DCarroll) *midfield: n.m.r after 1f: rdn over 2f out: sn wknd: eased ins fnl f* **16/1** | — |

1m 27.4s (-0.89) **Going Correction** -0.075s/f (Good)
**WFA** 3 from 4yo+ 5lb 16 Ran SP% **136.0**
Speed ratings: **102,100,100,98,97 94,94,93,93,92 91,91,87,81,63 60**CSF £59.51 CT £603.60 TOTE £10.40: £2.00, £1.60, £3.70, £2.70; EX 94.70 Place 6 £187.21, Place 5 £24.02.
**Owner** G Hart, D Scott & G Sparkes **Bred** Gainsborough Stud Management Ltd **Trained** Sheriff Hutton, N Yorks

**FOCUS**
There was a flip start to this ordinary handicap. This is fair form which looks very sound.

**NOTEBOOK**
**Hills Of Gold** won over this course and distance around this time last year off a 13lb lower mark and appreciated the drop back to seven furlongs. Having bagged a good early position, he got the split early in the straight and ran on well, but everything went right this time in a race which began with a flip start, and he may struggle once reassessed.
**Merdiff** came in for some support in the market and this previous course winner was another to gain a good early position from the flip start. He ran well but is a better horse on sand.
**Tuscarora(IRE)** ran a blinder given that she was slowly away from the flip start and was running over a trip short of her optimum. She came home well and once again proved that she is in the form of her life.
**Whippasnapper** was squeezed up and shuffled back on the approach to the first bend and in the circumstances he did well to stay on for fourth.
**Showtime Annie**, returning from a three-month absence, seems to go on any ground and shaped encouragingly.
**Neon Blue** is a consistent performer, but he was given a lot to do after dropping back towards the rear approaching the first bend.
**Concer Eto** has shown his best form on a quicker surface.
T/Plt: £215.00 to a £1 stake. Pool: £36,781.25. 124.85 winning tickets. T/Qpdt: £36.80 to a £1 stake. Pool: £2,441.80. 49.10 winning tickets. DO

# 4185 SOUTHWELL (L-H)
## Thursday, August 19

**OFFICIAL GOING: Standard**
Wind: Fresh half-behind Weather: Overcast

## 4878 AT THE RACES FROM 9 A.M. NURSERY 7f (F)
2:00 (2:01) (E) 2-Y-O £3,857 (£1,187; £593; £296) Stalls Low

| Form | | | | RPR |
|---|---|---|---|---|
| 0322 | 1 | | **Windy Prospect**[11] 4575 2-9-8 84 IMongan 9 (PABlockley) *w ldr tl led over 2f out: rdn over 1f out: edgd lft ins fnl f: r.o* **3/1**[1] | 89 |
| 5115 | 2 | 1 1/4 | **Diction (IRE)**[21] 4278 2-8-5 70 ow3 LEnstone(3) 10 (KRBurke) *s.i.s: hld up: hdwy over 2f out: rdn to chse wnr over 1f out: sn ev ch: styd on same pce ins fnl f* **8/1** | 72 |
| 6241 | 3 | 1/2 | **Caitlin (IRE)**[24] 4186 2-8-8 70 ow2 FLynch 7 (BSmart) *s.i.s: sn prom: rdn over 2f out: sn hung lft: no imp ins fnl f* **5/1**[2] | 71 |
| 0002 | 4 | 1 3/4 | **Countrywide Sun**[20] 4304 2-7-13 61 (p) JBramhill 8 (NPLittmoden) *led: rdn and hdd over 2f out: no ex fnl f* **14/1** | 57 |
| 0366 | 5 | 1 | **Guinea A Minute (IRE)**[13] 4524 2-8-1 63 JMackay 5 (MLWBell) *in rr: hdwy u.p and hung lft over 1f out: nt rch ldrs* **14/1** | 57 |
| 400 | 6 | 1 1/4 | **Union Jack Jackson (IRE)**[15] 4446 2-8-9 71 GBaker 12 (JGGiven) *hld up in tch: rdn over 2f out: hung lft over 1f out: styd on same pce* **20/1** | 62 |
| 3606 | 7 | 1/2 | **Lorna Dune**[34] 3893 2-8-0 62 DKinsella 1 (MrsJRRamsden) *prom: rdn over 2f out: wknd fnl f* **16/1** | 51 |
| 0324 | 8 | 2 1/2 | **Spinnakers Girl**[15] 4445 2-8-3 70 PMakin(5) 4 (JRWeymes) *chsd ldrs over 4f* **16/1** | 53 |
| 0202 | 9 | 2 1/2 | **Dan's Heir**[29] 4012 2-7-5 60 oh2 (p) DFentiman(7) 3 (PCHaslam) *sn outpcd* **9/1** | 37 |
| 0003 | 10 | hd | **Gryskirk**[16] 4601 2-8-2 64 (e[1]) TPQueally 13 (PWD'Arcy) *s.i.s: sn prom: rdn and wknd over 1f out* **6/1**[3] | 40 |
| 3033 | 11 | 4 | **Amphitheatre (IRE)**[13] 4521 2-8-2 64 SCarson 11 (RFJohnsonHoughton) *chsd ldrs over 4f* **10/1** | 30 |
| 6200 | 12 | 1 | **Itsa Monkey (IRE)**[20] 4304 2-7-12 67 oh11 ow7 KGhunowa(7) 2 (MJPolglase) *dwlt: outpcd* **50/1** | 31 |
| 0664 | 13 | 1 1/2 | **Serene Pearl (IRE)**[24] 4187 2-7-12 60 oh3 (t) LisaJones 6 (GMMoore) *mid-div: rdn 4f out: sn wknd* **40/1** | 20 |

1m 32.03s (1.23) **Going Correction** 0.0s/f (Stan) 13 Ran SP% **120.4**
Speed ratings: **92,90,90,88,86 85,84,82,79,78 74,73,71**CSF £26.65 CT £119.78 TOTE £3.20: £1.30, £2.00, £1.70; EX 25.30.
**Owner** bellhouseracing.com **Bred** T J Cooper **Trained** Southwell, Notts

**FOCUS**
A weak nursery but a decent enough performance from the top-weight Windy Prospect. The winner ran in a strong Redcar race last time and this form looks solid.

**NOTEBOOK**
**Windy Prospect**, successful on his only previous try on Fibresand, was suited by the return to this surface and step back up in trip. This was a game effort under a big weight, but the opposition was pretty moderate and a rise in the weights will make things tougher, although his turf mark of 86 may not be changed.

**Diction(IRE)**, successful on both her previous tries on Fibresand, including over this course and distance, was an estimated 9lb higher than when winning in this grade two starts back and ran respectably. She could go up again for this and the Handicapper could soon get her measure, but her ability to handle this surface so well is a big advantage and she will remain worthy of respect round here.
**Caitlin(IRE)**, off the mark in this grade over course and distance on his previous start, found this tougher off an estimated 6lb higher mark.
**Countrywide Sun**, beaten in a claimer at Thirsk on his previous start, ran respectably switched to nursery company on what was his Fibresand debut.
**Guinea A Minute(IRE)** got behind early on and was never really a threat.
**Gryskirk**, tried in an eyeshield for the first time on this Fibresand debut, was most disappointing and failed to prove his effectiveness on the surface.
**Amphitheatre(IRE)** *Official explanation: jockey said gelding had breathing problems*

## 4879 MIDLANDS RACING - 9 GREAT VENUES (S) STKS — 6f (F)
2:35 (2:35) (G) 3-Y-O+ — £2,618 (£748; £374) Stalls Low

Form — RPR
25-0 **1** **Siraj**[118] 1595 5-9-2 62 ... GHind 3 — 63
(MrsJCandlish) *w ldr tl led over 1f out: sn rdn: all out* — **13/2**
4060 **2** *hd* **Port St Charles (IRE)**[8] 4626 7-8-11 60 ... RThomas(5) 7 — 62
(CRDore) *hld up in tch: outpcd over 2f out: rallied over 1f out: r.o* — **3/1**[1]
2660 **3** *1 1/2* **Emaradia**[9] 4622 3-8-10 60 ... LEnstone(3) 9 — 58
(AWCarroll) *chsd ldrs: outpcd over 2f out: rallied over 1f out: r.o* — **11/2**[3]
3003 **4** *shd* **Wings Of Morning (IRE)**[8] 4631 3-9-4 65 ... (v) IMongan 2 — 63
(PABlockley) *sn pushed along to ld: rdn and hdd over 1f out: no ex ins fnl f* — **5/1**[2]
-250 **5** *1/2* **Go Free**[29] 4018 3-8-8 54 ... PMakin(5) 5 — 56
(AMHales) *chsd ldrs: outpcd over 2f out: styd on ins fnl f* — **33/1**
6200 **6** *hd* **Indian Music**[36] 3836 7-9-7 45 ... FLynch 6 — 61?
(ABerry) *hld up: hmpd over 3f: hdwy over 1f out: nt rch ldrs* — **12/1**
1500 **7** *1* **Bells Beach (IRE)**[13] 4517 6-9-2 51 ... TPQueally 8 — 53
(PHowling) *prom: outpcd over 2f out: styd on same pce fnl f* — **12/1**
4106 **8** *nk* **King Nicholas (USA)**[13] 4509 5-9-2 57 ... (tp) MLawson(5) 1 — 57
(JParkes) *s.i.s: hmpd wl over 3f out: n.d* — **7/1**
0001 **9** *6* **Fizzy Lizzy**[21] 4257 4-8-9 33 ... (p) WHogg(7) 10 — 34
(GAHam) *s.s: a in rr* — **16/1**
0504 **10** *3* **Polar Galaxy**[13] 4509 3-8-8 41 ... (p) VHalliday 4 — 20
(CWFairhurst) *s.s: hdwy 1/2-way: wknd over 2f out* — **12/1**
000 **11** *13* **Casey's House**[61] 3096 4-8-8 ... TEaves(3) 11 — —
(FWatson) *dwlt: hld up: bhd fr 1/2-way* — **50/1**

1m 17.92s (1.02) **Going Correction** 0.0s/f (Stan)
**WFA** 3 from 4yo+ 3lb — **11** Ran SP% **116.7**
Speed ratings: **93,92,90,90,89 89,88,87,79,75 58** CT £6.70 TOTE £2.60: £1.10, £1.50, £; EX35.40 1.The winner was sold to Mr P. McEntee for 9,000 gns.Port St Charles was claimed by Mr K. Tyrrell for £6,000. Wings of Morning was cl
**Owner** Racing For You Limited **Bred** Mrs S J Etches **Trained** Basford, Staffs

**FOCUS**
A competitive seller with just 2lb separating the first four home at the weights, but the winning time was modest for the grade and the form looks doubtful.

**NOTEBOOK**
**Siraj**, dropped into selling company for the first time, making his debut for a new stable and racing for the first time in 118 days, was best off at the weights and made no mistake. This was a good effort considering the only other horse to go with him early on, Wings Of Morning, dropped away in the closing stages. He will now join Phil McEntee who paid £9,000 for him.
**Port St Charles(IRE)**, whose last success came in a handicap off a mark of 74, is not in that sort of form at the moment but very nearly took advantage of this drop in grade.
**Emaradia** was suited by the return to Fibresand and drop in class, but was very one paced in the closing stages.
**Wings Of Morning(IRE)** failed to stay nine furlongs in a claimer on his previous start and, although he showed pace on this drop in trip, he was unable to sustain his challenge and is better suited by another furlong.
**Go Free**, racing over a trip this short for the first time since making his debut, stayed on at the one pace and looks in need of a little further.
**Indian Music** *Official explanation: jockey said gelding was hampered coming into the straight*

## 4880 AT THE RACES DEDICATED RACING CHANNEL MAIDEN STKS — 1m (F)
3:10 (3:11) (D) 3-Y-O — £3,360 (£1,034; £517; £258) Stalls Low

Form — RPR
2302 **1** **Adorata (GER)**[6] 4726 3-8-9 63 ... MTebbutt 2 — 64
(JJay) *trckd ldrs: rdn and ev ch fr over 1f out: styd on u.p to ld post* — **6/4**[1]
0-00 **2** *shd* **Native Turk (USA)**[42] 3666 3-9-0 ... TPQueally 5 — 69
(JARToller) *chsd ldr: led over 4f out: hung rt over 1f out: hrd rdn ins fnl f: hdd post* — **20/1**
200 **3** *10* **Noble Mind**[31] 3994 3-9-0 68 ... DKinsella 7 — 49
(PGMurphy) *chsd ldrs: rdn over 2f out: wknd over 1f out* — **7/2**[2]
4064 **4** *3 1/2* **Beamsley Beacon**[64] 2986 3-9-0 47 ... VHalliday 1 — 42
(IanEmmerson) *led over 3f: rdn over 2f out: wknd over 1f out* — **66/1**
0003 **5** *3 1/2* **Ragazzi (IRE)**[27] 4097 3-8-9 65 ... PMakin(5) 4 — 35
(TDBarron) *hld up: rdn 1/2-way: wknd over 3f out* — **10/1**
06 **6** *1/2* **Java Dancer**[20] 4306 3-9-0 ... PMQuinn 9 — 34
(TDEasterby) *s.i.s: hdwy 6f out: rdn and wknd over 3f out* — **25/1**
60 **7** *1 1/2* **Classic Expression**[12] 4555 3-8-9 ... GCarter 10 — 26
(BAMcmahon) *hld up: a bhd* — **20/1**
**8** *2* **Tarkeez (USA)**[55] 3287 3-9-0 70 ... FLynch 8 — 27
(RMHCowell) *chsd ldrs tl lost pl over 5f out: sn bhd* — **9/2**[3]
**9** *3* **Bonus Points (IRE)** 3-8-11 ... DCorby(3) 6 — 21
(BJMeehan) *s.s: hld up: rdn and wknd over 3f out* — **14/1**
0-00 **10** *9* **Almanac (IRE)**[175] 890 3-9-0 ... GHind 3 — —
(BPJBaugh) *sn outpcd* — **66/1**

1m 44.15s (-0.45) **Going Correction** 0.0s/f (Stan) — **10** Ran SP% **112.5**
Speed ratings: **102,101,91,88,84 84,82,80,77,68**CSF £39.01 TOTE £2.40: £1.10, £6.70, £1.20; EX 35.90.
**Owner** Fremel and Friends **Bred** K Laakmann **Trained** Newmarket, Suffolk

**FOCUS**
A very moderate maiden, with the first two finishing well clear.

**NOTEBOOK**
**Adorata(GER)** coped well with the switch to Fibresand to confirm the promise she showed in a classified event at Newmarket on her previous start. The Handicapper should not put her up much for this, if at all, and she should be competitive in handicaps.
**Native Turk(USA)** shaped with promise in a Newmarket maiden on his only start last season, but had failed to build on that in two runs this term, including when tailed-off in first-time blinkers on his previous outing. However, with the headgear left off on this switch to Fibresand, he ran his best race to date and showed there is a similarly moderate race in him.
**Noble Mind** has not gone on from his promising debut.
**Beamsley Beacon**, beaten in claimers over six furlongs on his last two starts, failed to improve for the step back up in trip.
**Ragazzi(IRE)** shaped well in a maiden here over six furlongs on his previous start, but was a long way below that form stepped up to a mile.
**Tarkeez(USA)** showed plenty of ability at up to ten furlongs when trained in Ireland by Dermot Weld, but offered very little promise on his debut in this country. *Official explanation: jockey said colt appeared to be jarred up*

## 4881 SKY 415, NTL 908, TELEWEST 534 H'CAP — 5f (F)
3:45 (3:48) (F) (0-55,55) 3-Y-O+ — £3,010 (£860; £430) Stalls High

Form — RPR
2363 **1** **Jagged (IRE)**[17] 4403 4-9-8 55 ... (v) TPQueally 8 — 68
(JRJenkins) *chsd ldr: rdn to ld ins fnl f: r.o* — **5/1**[1]
0040 **2** *3/4* **Kennington**[27] 4105 4-9-4 51 ... (v) LisaJones 6 — 61
(MrsCADunnett) *chsd ldr: rdn 1/2-way: n.m.r ins fnl f: r.o* — **11/2**[2]
2550 **3** *1 1/4* **The Leather Wedge (IRE)**[29] 4014 5-8-12 45 ... (p) PBradley 3 — 51
(ABerry) *led: hdd and unable qck ins fnl f* — **20/1**
0002 **4** *2 1/2* **Back In Spirit**[40] 3742 4-8-5 38 ... (t) GCarter 12 — 35
(BAMcmahon) *dwlt: hld up: hdwy over 1f out: nt rch ldrs* — **13/2**[3]
0000 **5** *1/2* **Leopard Creek**[17] 4391 3-8-12 47 ... IMongan 1 — 43
(MrsJRRamsden) *dwlt: hdwy over 3f out: rdn over 1f out: styd on same pce* — **12/1**
0005 **6** *nk* **So Sober (IRE)**[6] 4701 6-8-7 40 ... FLynch 11 — 34
(DShaw) *chsd ldrs over 3f* — **8/1**
0400 **7** *nk* **Savernake Brave (IRE)**[31] 3991 3-8-12 47 ... GBaker 4 — 40
(MrsHSweeting) *s.s: outpcd: hdwy u.p over 1f out: trbld ldrs* — **20/1**
0604 **8** *3/4* **Donegal Shore (IRE)**[10] 4605 5-8-10 43 ... (vt) GHind 9 — 34
(MrsJCandlish) *s.s: outpcd: nvr nrr* — **16/1**
45-0 **9** *hd* **The Baroness (IRE)**[29] 4026 4-9-5 55 ... DCorby(3) 10 — 45
(EROertel) *chsd ldrs: rdn 1/2-way: wknd fnl f: eased* — **25/1**
6020 **10** *1 1/2* **Scary Night (IRE)**[35] 3864 4-9-4 51 ... (p) JEdmunds 15 — 36
(JBalding) *chsd ldrs over 3f* — **8/1**
0504 **11** *1/2* **Scarlett Breeze**[15] 4440 3-8-11 46 ... MTebbutt 5 — 29
(JWHills) *s.s: n.d* — **25/1**
0000 **12** *1/2* **John O'Groats (IRE)**[37] 3820 6-8-13 51 ... (be[1]) PMakin(5) 2 — 32
(DWChapman) *outpcd fr 1/2-way* — **14/1**
0000 **13** *1/2* **Diaphanous**[15] 4440 6-7-11 37 ... (b) LiamJones(7) 7 — 17
(EAWheeler) *s.s: outpcd: rdn and hung rt 1/2-way: hung lft over 1f out: n.d* — **50/1**
5064 **14** *1* **Levelled**[12] 4557 10-8-9 42 ... JMackay 16 — 18
(DWChapman) *s.s: sn prom: wknd wl over 1f out* — **12/1**
0600 **15** *5* **Attorney**[20] 4291 6-8-10 50 ... (v) DerekNolan(7) 14 — 9
(DShaw) *s.s: outpcd* — **14/1**

59.23 secs (-1.17) **Going Correction** -0.20s/f (Stan)
**WFA** 3 from 4yo+ 2lb — **15** Ran SP% **121.4**
Speed ratings: **101,99,97,93,93 92,92,90,90,88 87,86,85,84,76**CSF £29.11 CT £518.84 TOTE £4.50: £1.70, £2.00, £5.90; EX 35.40.
**Owner** The Jagged Partnership **Bred** Ellesmere Bloodstock Ltd **Trained** Royston, Herts

**FOCUS**
A very moderate sprint but the form looks particularly sound for the grade. The winner is the one to take from the race.

**NOTEBOOK**
**Jagged(IRE)**, still a maiden after 22 starts going into this, was amazingly racing over a bare five furlongs for just the second time, despite being beaten just a neck on his only previous try over it. Always showing plenty of speed, he idled inside the final furlong but pulled out more when challenged by the eventual runner-up and is probably value for a little more than the winning margin. Now connections know his trip, he could well follow up.
**Kennington** gained his only previous win over seven furlongs, but has more than enough pace for this trip. He is flattered to get so close to the winner as that one was idling in front, but this was still a good effort.
**The Leather Wedge(IRE)** struggles to see out five furlongs on this deep track and has just one win to his name from 38 starts.
**Back In Spirit** ran well over a trip short of his best and better can be expected over another furlong.
**Leopard Creek** did not do enough to suggest she is about to strike, but it is interesting her connections are persevering with her.

## 4882 ARENA LEISURE H'CAP — 1m (F)
4:20 (4:21) (E) (0-75,74) 3-Y-O — £4,264 (£1,312; £656; £328) Stalls Low

Form — RPR
0002 **1** **Dont Call Me Derek**[7] 4680 3-8-5 58 ... GCarter 10 — 69+
(SCWilliams) *a.p: rdn to ld and hung lft over 1f out: styd on wl: eased nr fin* — **9/4**[1]
0405 **2** *3* **Mission Affirmed (USA)**[22] 4249 3-8-12 65 ... JEdmunds 9 — 70+
(TPTate) *s.s: hdwy over 4f out: rdn over 2f out: styd on* — **8/1**
0601 **3** *3/4* **Book Matched**[27] 4093 3-9-4 71 ... FLynch 1 — 74
(BSmart) *led 2f: remained handy: led 3f out: rdn and hdd over 1f out: wknd ins fnl f* — **15/2**
0246 **4** *1 3/4* **Multiple Choice (IRE)**[17] 4387 3-8-8 64 ... (t) J-PGuillambert(3) 8 — 64
(NPLittmoden) *chsd ldr tl led 6f out: hdd 3f out: wknd fnl f* — **16/1**
0002 **5** *nk* **Blue Java**[22] 4241 3-8-6 59 ... TPQueally 4 — 58
(HMorrison) *prom: rdn 1/2-way: outpcd 3f out: n.d after* — **7/2**[2]
0004 **6** *1* **Mr Midasman (IRE)**[15] 4451 3-8-4 57 ... JMackay 6 — 54
(RHollinshead) *chsd ldrs tl lost pl 1/2-way: n.d after* — **12/1**
1036 **7** *1 1/4* **Come What July (IRE)**[8] 4628 3-9-3 70 ... (v) LisaJones 11 — 64
(MrsNMacauley) *sn outpcd and bhd: styd on ins fnl f: nvr nrr* — **14/1**
6050 **8** *1 3/4* **Fit To Fly (IRE)**[14] 4493 3-8-13 66 ... GHind 2 — 57
(MrsJCandlish) *sn outpcd and bhd: mod late prog* — **14/1**
5304 **9** *1 1/4* **Turf Princess**[37] 3817 3-7-11 57 ... DFentiman(7) 5 — 45
(IanEmmerson) *chsd ldrs 6f* — **33/1**
00-0 **10** *5* **Iron Temptress (IRE)**[20] 4305 3-8-2 60 ... BSwarbrick(5) 3 — 38
(GMMoore) *sn outpcd and bhd* — **33/1**
0100 **11** *2* **Dispol Veleta**[39] 3780 3-9-2 74 ... PMakin(5) 7 — 48
(TDBarron) *prom 3f* — **9/2**[3]

1m 44.4s (-0.20) **Going Correction** 0.0s/f (Stan) — **11** Ran SP% **126.8**
Speed ratings: **101,98,97,95,95 94,92,91,89,84 82**CSF £23.36 CT £125.43 TOTE £3.00: £1.30, £2.30, £3.00; EX 27.10.
**Owner** J Lloyd and E Warder **Bred** Whitsbury Manor Stud **Trained** Newmarket, Suffolk

**FOCUS**
Just a moderate handicap, but the pace was good. The winner is on the upgrade.

**NOTEBOOK**
**Dont Call Me Derek**, well supported and a good second to a progressive rival on heavy ground at Haydock on his previous start, was able to race off a 3lb lower mark and handled the Fibresand well to confirm that promise and get off the mark. Kept wide in the straight to avoid the kick-back, he had the race won a furlong out and will be very hard to beat if turned out under a penalty.
**Mission Affirmed(USA)**, successful on two of his previous five starts on Fibresand, would surely have finished a lot closer had he not been so slowly away.
**Book Matched** found this tougher than the claimer he landed over course and distance on his previous start, but ran respectably and acts very well on Fibresand.

**Multiple Choice(IRE)**, back up on trip on this return to Fibresand, keeps finding a few too good and is proving hard to win with.
**Blue Java** was unable to build on the promise he showed when runner-up in a turf claimer on his previous start and has to be considered disappointing.
**Dispol Veleta**, successful over course and distance off a mark of 67 when last seen on Fibresand three starts back, has since beaten just two horses home on turf. This was another poor display and she looks one to avoid for the time being.

## 4883 COME RACING TOMORROW APPRENTICE H'CAP 1m 6f (F)
**4:50** (4:52) (G ) (0-55,54) 3-Y-0+ **£2,996** (£856; £428) **Stalls** Low

Form RPR
1333 **1** **Salut Saint Cloud**[14] [4467] 3-9-1 **53**........................(p) AQuinn 12 67
(GLMoore) *s.s: hld up: hdwy over 5f out: c centre ent st: led 2f out: pushed out* **7/2**[2]
-114 **2** *2 ½* **Magic Red**[10] [4603] 4-9-8 **53**........................ MHalford(5) 11 63
(MJRyan) *sn pushed along and prom: outpcd over 6f out: rallied over 4f out: n.m.r over 1f out: styd on* **2/1**[1]
0405 **3** *1 ¾* **Staff Nurse (IRE)**[34] [3919] 4-8-1 **34** oh2........ JaniceWebster(7) 14 42
(DonEnricoIncisa) *hld up: hdwy 6f out: rdn over 1f out: styd on same pce* **20/1**
0-2 **4** *5* **Black Legend (IRE)**[7] [4669] 5-9-2 **42**........................(t) BSwarbrick 13 43
(RLee) *s.i.s: hld up: hdwy 6f out: led over 3f out: hdd 2f out : wknd fnl f* **8/1**[3]
4212 **5** *14* **Mercurious (IRE)**[10] [4609] 4-9-6 **51**........................ DerekNolan(5) 3 32
(JMackie) *chsd ldrs over 10f* **7/2**[2]
0060 **6** *1 ¼* **Salford Rocket**[64] [2978] 4-8-3 **34** oh4........................ LauraPike(5) 6 13
(WJMusson) *hld up: mod late prog: nvr nrr* **50/1**
2100 **7** *1* **The Last Mohican**[69] [2851] 5-8-4 **35**........................ KristinStubbs(5) 9 13
(PHowling) *led over 10f: sn wknd* **20/1**
5000 **8** *1 ¾* **Macchiato**[14] [4499] 3-8-1 **44**........................(b[1]) LiamJones(5) 15 19
(RFJohnsonHoughton) *chsd ldrs: rdn over 3f out: wknd over 2f out* **33/1**
-260 **9** *12* **That's Racing**[122] [1501] 4-8-3 **34** oh1........................ KGhunowa(5) 1 —
(JHetherton) *hld up: hdwy 5f out: wknd over 3f out* **12/1**
0-50 **10** *9* **Tioga Gold (IRE)**[80] [2531] 5-8-3 **34** oh4........................ AReilly(5) 5 —
(LRJames) *hld up: n.d* **50/1**
4000 **11** *4* **Munfarid (IRE)**[134] [1302] 4-9-11 **54**........................(t) MLawson(3) 10 —
(PGMurphy) *chsd ldrs over 10f* **28/1**
6204 **12** *7* **Think Quick (IRE)**[16] [4423] 4-8-6 **35**........ StephanieHollinshead(3) 4 —
(RHollinshead) *bhd fr 1/2-way* **14/1**
003 **13** *1 ¾* **Pointed (IRE)**[79] [2555] 3-8-7 **45**........................ PMakin 7 —
(MrsJCandlish) *bhd fr 1/2-way* **50/1**
4000 **14** *9* **Sninfia (IRE)**[21] [4261] 4-9-1 **46**........................ WHogg(5) 8 —
(GAHam) *chsd ldr over 7f: wknd over 3f out* **25/1**
60-0 **15** *2 ½* **Caper**[21] [4261] 4-8-8 **41**........................ HFellows(7) 2 —
(RHollinshead) *a bhd* **50/1**
0-0P **16** *12* **Pattern Man**[31] [3984] 3-8-7 **50**........................ DFentiman(5) 16 —
(JRNorton) *sn wl bhd* **50/1**

3m 9.13s (-0.57) **Going Correction** 0.0s/f (Stan)
**WFA** 3 from 4yo+ 12lb **16** Ran SP% **132.8**
Speed ratings: **101,99,98,95,87 87,86,85,78,73 71,67,66,61,59 52**CSF £10.82 CT £129.41 TOTE £4.90: £2.00, £1.30, £6.60, £2.40; EX 18.60 Place 6 £12.31, Place 5 £7.13.
**Owner** A Grinter **Bred** Mill House Stud **Trained** Woodingdean, E Sussex

**FOCUS**
A moderate staying handicap run at a strong pace. The form looks sound enough for the grade.

**NOTEBOOK**
**Salut Saint Cloud**, with the cheekpieces back on and trying his furthest trip to date, needed a reminder down the back straight but ultimately stuck on gamely for pressure. This mile and six took some getting, so he should have little trouble in staying two miles, but in the meantime could bid to follow up back at Southwell over a mile and a half.
**Magic Red**, successful on both his previous runs over this course and distance, struggled to hold his position down the back straight and was very one paced close home. He looks in need of two miles.
**Staff Nurse(IRE)**, 2lb out of the handicap, ran an encouraging race and is another who should be effective over two miles.
**Black Legend(IRE)** shaped well on his return to the Flat over ten furlongs at Chepstow on his previous start, but was unable to confirm that on this step up in trip.
**Mercurious(IRE)** goes well on Fibresand and has been in good form lately, but this was most disappointing and there did not appear to be an obvious excuse.
T/Plt: £9.80 to a £1 stake. Pool: £22,387.10. 1,651.90 winning tickets. T/Qpdt: £4.60 to a £1 stake. Pool: £1,470.50. 233.70 winning tickets. CR

# 4856 YORK (L-H)
Thursday, August 19

**OFFICIAL GOING: Soft**
After a dry night the going was described as 'soft, very sticky and hard work' and it was again more testing on the round course than the straight track.
Wind: Fresh 1/2 behind. Weather: Overcast with showers.

## 4884 EBF GALTRES STKS (LISTED RACE) (F&M) 1m 3f 198y
**2:10** (2:10) (A ) 3-Y-0+ **£22,100** (£6,800; £3,400; £1,700) **Stalls** Low

Form RPR
-232 **1** **Tarakala (IRE)**[17] [4406] 3-8-8........................(b) MJKinane 6 105
(JohnMOxx, Ire) *lw: hld up: smooth hdwy to trck ldrs over 4f out: led 2f out: sn idled and rdn along: clr ent last* **7/2**[2]
1223 **2** *4* **Selebela**[18] [4367] 3-8-8 95........................ LDettori 2 99
(LMCumani) *a.p: hdwy to ld over 3f out: sn rdn and hdd 2f out: drvn and one pce appr last* **10/3**[1]
4400 **3** *nk* **Desert Royalty (IRE)**[12] [4530] 4-9-4 90........................ KFallon 4 99
(EALDunlop) *hld up in rr: hdwy over 4f out: rdn along over 2f out: styd on u.p fnl f* **7/1**[3]
314 **4** *1 ½* **Goslar**[33] [3944] 3-8-8 90........................ DaneO'Neill 1 96
(HCandy) *trckd ldrs tl lost pl over 4f out: hdwy 3f out: rdn along and kpt on fnl 2f* **9/1**
631 **5** *5* **Silver Sash (GER)**[43] [3625] 3-8-8 79........................ RMullen 10 89
(MLWBell) *hmpd s and t.k.h: in tch: hdwy 4f out: rdn along wl over 2f out and sn btn* **16/1**
0-1 **6** *5* **Payola (USA)**[17] [4396] 3-8-8 66........................ SSanders 8 82
(CEBrittain) *chsd ldrs: rdn along 4f out: sn wknd* **25/1**
0-41 **7** *5* **Castagna (USA)**[26] [4141] 3-8-8 87........................ WRyan 7 75
(HRACecil) *chsd ldrs: rdn along and lost pl 5f out: sn bhd* **11/1**
0033 **8** *5* **Kisses For Me (IRE)**[17] [4406] 3-8-8........................ JPSpencer 3 68
(APO'Brien, Ire) *hld up in tch: hdwy 4f out: sn rdn along and btn wl over 2f out* **7/2**[2]
0032 **9** *3* **Uig**[11] [4583] 3-8-8 77........................ SDrowne 9 64
(HSHowe) *wnt rt s: plld hrd and sn clr: hdd over 3f out and sn wknd* **80/1**

2m 37.68s (8.82) **Going Correction** +0.65s/f (Yiel)
**WFA** 3 from 4yo 10lb **9** Ran SP% **109.3**
Speed ratings: **96,93,93,92,88 85,82,78,76**CSF £14.14 TOTE £3.70: £1.50, £1.70, £2.30; EX 9.10 Trifecta £71.80 Pool: £1,387.13. 13.70 winning units..
**Owner** H H Aga Khan **Bred** H H Aga Khan's Stud S C **Trained** Currabeg, Co Kildare

**FOCUS**
A sub-standard renewal, although the form looks reliable enough. A strong pace early, but things got tough towards the end and they came home well strung out in the ground. The winning time was therefore modest for a race of this class, even allowing for the conditions.

**NOTEBOOK**
**Tarakala(IRE)**, put to sleep at the back, hit the front plenty soon enough but in the end drew away.
**Selebela**, whose trainer had won this eight times with 17 previous runners, continually swished her tail in the paddock. She is much improved since being stepped up in trip and she is to stay in training at four.
**Desert Royalty(IRE)**, sharper as a result of her Ascot outing, ran out of her skin and just failed to snatch second spot.
**Goslar**, a leggy, immature type, finished a fraction closer to Selebela than she had done at Newmarket. There may be even better to come with another year over her head.
**Silver Sash(GER)**, an exciteable type, was taking a huge step up in class and did as well as could be expected.
**Payola(USA)** was biting off a lot more than she could chew.
**Castagna(USA)**, a sparely-made filly and a good walker, was very keen to post. She was in trouble turning in.
**Kisses For Me(IRE)**, who looked as fit as a flea, dropped right away in the final quarter mile and her rider searching for the book of excuses blamed the ground. *Official explanation: jockey said filly was unsuited by the soft ground*
**Uig**, who pulled hard to post, poached a clear lead but, doing far too much in front, in the end predictably finished well beaten.

## 4885 JAGUAR LOWTHER STKS (GROUP 2) (FILLIES) 6f
**2:45** (2:45) (A ) 2-Y-0 **£51,000** (£19,550; £9,775; £4,675) **Stalls** Centre

Form RPR
121 **1** **Soar**[26] [4119] 2-9-0 100........................ JPMurtagh 8 108+
(JRFanshawe) *hld up towards rr: smooth hdwy over 2f out: swtchd lft and qcknd to ld over 1f out: edgd rt and kpt on wl fnl f* **2/1**[1]
132 **2** *1 ½* **Salsa Brava (IRE)**[44] [3599] 2-8-11 100........................ KFallon 4 101
(NPLittmoden) *chsd ldrs: pushed along 1/2-way: rdn to ld 2f out: drvn and hdd over 1f out: kpt on same pce ins last* **9/4**[2]
420 **3** *1 ½* **Spirit Of Chester (IRE)**[55] [3286] 2-8-11........................ RHavlin 2 96
(MrsPNDutfield) *sn led: rdn along and hdd 2f out: drvn and edgd rt ent last: one pce* **16/1**
14 **4** *1* **Notjustaprettyface (USA)**[5] [4744] 2-8-11........................ SDrowne 5 93
(HMorrison) *cl up: effrt and ev ch 2f out: sn rdn and wknd appr last* **8/1**[3]
0212 **5** *3 ½* **Castelletto**[5] [4744] 2-8-11 85........................ GGibbons 10 83
(BAMcmahon) *cl up: effrt and ch 2f out: sn rdn and hld in 4th whn n.m.r ent last* **10/1**
3345 **6** *1 ¾* **Umniya (IRE)**[54] [3316] 2-8-11 91........................ ACulhane 3 77
(MRChannon) *sn rdn along and a rr* **14/1**
62 **7** *nk* **Ghasiba (IRE)**[6] [4705] 2-8-11........................ SSanders 9 76
(CEBrittain) *chsd ldrs: rdn along 1/2-way: sn wknd* **20/1**
5163 **8** *7* **Kissing Lights (IRE)**[26] [4119] 2-8-11 100........................ DHolland 6 55
(MLWBell) *prom: rdn along 1/2-way and sn wknd* **14/1**

1m 15.9s (3.33) **Going Correction** +0.55s/f (Yiel) **8** Ran SP% **108.3**
Speed ratings: **99,97,95,93,89 86,86,76**CSF £5.85 TOTE £3.00: £1.30, £1.30, £3.10; EX 4.60 Trifecta £48.20 Pool: £1,751.41. 25.78 winning units..
**Owner** Cheveley Park Stud **Bred** Cheveley Park Stud Ltd **Trained** Newmarket, Suffolk

**FOCUS**
A much slower time than the Gimcrack the previous day but the winner looks a smart filly and the form appears solid.

**NOTEBOOK**
**Soar ◆**, whose action suggested the soft ground would not be a problem, was happy to sit off the pace. Pulled wide, she swept to the front in imperious fashion and this sets her up for a possible rematch with her Queen Mary conqueror Damson in the Cheveley Park.
**Salsa Brava(IRE)**, with the champion aboard this time, made hard work of it and had no answer when the winner swept by. She is now ready for the step up to seven.
**Spirit Of Chester(IRE)** put her Curragh flop behind her, but this quite tall filly was found to have bled from the nose. She is a very useful filly to still claim the maiden allowance. *Official explanation: trainer's representative said filly had bled from the nose*
**Notjustaprettyface(USA)**, making a quick reappearance, turned the tables on Castelletto but, in this better company, did not seem to truly see out the extra furlong.
**Castelletto**, another making a quick return to action, was taken to post very quietly but her stamina seemed at a low ebb when she ran out of racing room.
**Umniya(IRE)**, proven on soft ground, was never going the pace.
**Kissing Lights(IRE)** *Official explanation: jockey said filly was unsuited by the soft ground*

## 4886 VICTOR CHANDLER NUNTHORPE STKS (GROUP 1) 5f
**3:20** (3:21) (A ) 2-Y-0+ **£116,000** (£44,000; £22,000; £10,000) **Stalls** Centre

Form RPR
0016 **1** **Bahamian Pirate (USA)**[21] [4269] 9-9-11 110........................ SSanders 5 118
(DNicholls) *chsd ldrs: pushed along 1/2-way: rdn over 1f out: styd on wl to ld ins last: drvn out* **16/1**
4103 **2** *nk* **The Tatling (IRE)**[21] [4269] 7-9-11 115........................ RLMoore 11 117
(JMBradley) *trckd ldrs gng wl: hdwy 2f out: effrt over 1f out: sn rdn and kpt on wl fnl f* **13/2**
-051 **3** *1* **One Cool Cat (USA)**[11] [4590] 3-9-9........................ JPSpencer 15 114+
(APO'Brien, Ire) *hld up and bhd: swtchd lft and hdwy 2f out: swtchd rt and rdn whn n.m.r ent last: drvn and fin wl* **3/1**[1]
2154 **4** *hd* **Avonbridge**[21] [4269] 4-9-11 114........................(b[1]) SDrowne 9 113
(RCharlton) *lw: dwlt: sn c lose up: rdn and ev ch over 1f out tl drvn and no ex ins last* **8/1**
0531 **5** *hd* **Orientor**[47] [3537] 6-9-11 115........................ KFallon 14 118+
(JSGoldie) *lw: towards rr: pushed along 1/2-way: swtchd lft 2f out: swtchd rtand rdn ent last: styng on whn n.m.r last 75 yds* **9/2**[2]
6601 **6** *½* **Airwave**[31] [3976] 4-9-8 110........................ DHolland 3 108
(HCandy) *lw: cl up: led after 2f: rdn wl over 1f out: hdd ins last and one pce* **6/1**[3]
0-32 **7** *½* **Balmont (USA)**[27] [4091] 3-9-9 113........................ EAhern 7 109
(JNoseda) *chsd ldrs: rdn wl over 1f out: drvn and kpt on same pce fnl f* **13/2**
2202 **8** *½* **Talbot Avenue**[18] [4362] 6-9-11 90........................ KMcEvoy 12 107?
(MMullineaux) *racd wdm prom: rdn along 2f out: drvn and kpt on same pce appr last* **100/1**
1110 **9** *½* **Moss Vale (IRE)**[42] [3674] 3-9-9 112........................ MHills 10 106
(BWHills) *in tch: effrt 2f out: sn rdn along and no imp* **14/1**

-010 **10** *2* **Fayr Jag (IRE)**[42] 3674 5-9-11 113 ........ WSupple 2 99
(TDEasterby) *lw: cl up: rdn and ev ch wl over 1f out: sn drvn: wknd and eased ins last* **25/1**

4010 **11** *2* **Fire Up The Band**[21] 4269 5-9-11 99 ........ ANicholls 8 93
(DNicholls) *led 2f: cl up tl rdn along and wknd wl over 1f out* **33/1**

-010 **12** *14* **Night Prospector**[47] 3537 4-9-11 105 ........ JPMurtagh 6 46
(JWPayne) *sn outpcd and bhd fr 1/2-way* **66/1**

59.89 secs (0.61) **Going Correction** +0.55s/f (Yiel)
**WFA** 3 from 4yo+ 2lb **12** Ran SP% **117.1**
Speed ratings: **117,116,114,114,114 113,112,111,111,107 104,82**CSF £112.90 TOTE £18.00: £3.40, £2.20, £1.90; EX 90.30 Trifecta £2139.60 Pool: £8,136.56. 2.70 winning units..
**Owner** Lucayan Stud **Bred** Trackside Farm & Liberation Farm & G A Seelbinder **Trained** Sessay, N Yorks

**FOCUS**
The winner became the first 9-year-old to win a Group 1 in this country since the Pattern series was created in 1971, underlining the dearth of top-class sprinters this year. The time was as you would expect for a Group One in the conditions however.

**NOTEBOOK**
**Bahamian Pirate(USA)**, having his 68th start and never previously successful in anything better than a Group Three, looked at his very best beforehand and proved ideally suited by the give underfoot. Sticking to his task in willing fashion, he forced his head in front inside the last and would not be denied.
**The Tatling(IRE)**, no match for Oasis Dream a year ago, was having his 54th start. He travelled supremely well but, hard as he tried, he could not force his head in front. He remains in peak form and his trainer, who is adamant that he much prefers better ground, has one eye on a trip to Hong Kong with him.
**One Cool Cat(USA)**, who only took his chance after much debate, looked very fit and was warm and on edge. Dropped in, his rider elected to take him towards the far side, but he then had a change of mind only to run out of racing room for a few strides. He really took off inside the last and would have made it with a bit further to go. He has undoubted ability but his overall demeanour and his head carriage do not totally impress. His trainer however is totally confident that, given better ground, he will swamp his rivals in the Stanley Leisure Sprint Cup at Haydock.
**Avonbridge**, tried in blinkers, missed a beat at the start and, though in the end just found wanting, his trainer is confident he is capable of even better on a sounder surface.
**Orientor**, who has failed to make any impression in this for the last two years, had the ground in his favour this time but, after changing course twice, he was only keeping on in his own time when running out of racing room near the line. At this level an uphill track suits him a lot better.
**Airwave**, her confidence high after Ayr, looked at her very best but, in front before halfway, always looked to be doing too much in the conditions. Only worn down inside the last, there is still time for her to take a championship prize.
**Balmont(USA)**, last year's Gimcrack winner, was overturned by the winner at Newmarket and, put in his place here, seems marginally better suited by six.
**Talbot Avenue** had a mountain to climb and on paper at least, ran the race of his life.

## 4887 PERSIMMON HOMES RATED STKS (H'CAP) 7f 205y
**3:55** (3:55) (B ) (0-105,102) 3-Y-O+ **£14,788** (£5,609; £2,804; £1,274) **Stalls** Low

Form RPR

0246 **1** **Audience**[20] 4287 4-8-11 **92** ........ (p) DHolland 4 103
(JAkehurst) *mid-div: sn drvn along: hdwy over 2f out: styd on to ld nr fin* **11/1**

1141 **2** *½* **Take A Bow**[8] 4646 3-8-6 **93** 3ex ........ JQuinn 12 103+
(PRChamings) *trckd ldrs: effrt over 2f out: ev ch ins last: nt qckn* **10/3**[1]

1021 **3** *nk* **St Petersburg**[41] 3717 4-9-2 **97** ........ PRobinson 3 106
(MHTompkins) *trckd ldrs: t.k.h: styd on to ld jst ins last: hdd and no ex nr fin* **13/2**[2]

1305 **4** *2* **Unshakable (IRE)**[12] 4528 5-8-12 **93** ........ KFallon 7 98
(BobJones) *in tch: effrt 3f out: styd on same pce appr fnl f* **15/2**[3]

0000 **5** *hd* **Vicious Knight**[21] 4273 6-8-9 **90** ........ ANicholls 10 94
(DNicholls) *led tl jst ins last: no ex* **66/1**

034 **6** *7* **Blue Sky Thinking (IRE)**[41] 3717 5-8-11 **92** ........ DarrenWilliams 9 83
(KRBurke) *hld up: hdwy over 2f out: kpt on: nvr nr ldrs* **33/1**

0230 **7** *3* **Consonant (IRE)**[40] 3756 7-8-9 **90** ........ ACulhane 2 75
(DGBridgwater) *chsd ldrs: wknd over 1f out* **25/1**

0404 **8** *2* **El Coto**[20] 4287 4-9-5 **100** ........ SSanders 14 81
(BAMcmahon) *rr div: drvn along 4f out: nvr nr ldrs* **13/2**[2]

0235 **9** *1¼* **Dumaran (IRE)**[76] 2637 6-8-11 **92** ........ RMullen 6 71
(WJMusson) *dwlt: bhd: sme hdwy over 2f out: nvr a factor* **16/1**

-600 **10** *1½* **Jazz Messenger (FR)**[5] 4742 4-9-0 **95** ........ MJKinane 11 71
(GAButler) *bhd: hdwy and n.m.r 3f out: hung lft and wknd over 1f out* **8/1**

-030 **11** *2* **Excelsius (IRE)**[54] 3323 4-9-4 **99** ........ RLMoore 16 71
(JLDunlop) *mid-div: drvn along 3f out: no imp* **16/1**

00-3 **12** *2½* **Dark Charm (FR)**[145] 1125 5-8-10 **91** ........ RFfrench 5 58
(RAFahey) *dwlt: a in rr* **10/1**

0414 **13** *1½* **Always Esteemed (IRE)**[19] 4341 4-9-5 **100** ........ SDrowne 8 64
(GWragg) *chsd ldrs: wknd 2f out* **28/1**

5100 **14** *2* **State Dilemma (IRE)**[42] 3671 3-8-6 **93** ........ MHills 13 53
(BWHills) *sn bhd and drvn along* **50/1**

0604 **15** *2* **Anani (USA)**[23] 4214 4-9-7 **102** ........ LDettori 15 58
(EALDunlop) *chsd ldrs: hung lft and lost pl over 2f out* **16/1**

1m 40.12s (2.38) **Going Correction** +0.65s/f (Yiel)
**WFA** 3 from 4yo+ 6lb **15** Ran SP% **121.4**
Speed ratings: **114,113,113,111,111 104,101,99,97,96 94,91,90,88,86**CSF £45.61 CT £274.07 TOTE £15.00: £4.80, £2.10, £2.00; EX 76.30 Trifecta £354.10 Pool: £3,920.27. 7.86 winning units..
**Owner** Canisbay Bloodstock **Bred** Whitsbury Manor Stud And Gerald W Leigh **Trained** Epsom, Surrey

**FOCUS**
A high-class, competitive handicap run at a strong pace in the conditions and the time was decent for the grade. This is solid form. Only the winner got into contention from off the pace.

**NOTEBOOK**
**Audience**, who has been knocking on the door in similar handicaps all summer, seemed to benefit from the easy ground and a clear passage and made up a good deal of ground to hit the front inside the last. He was the only one to come from off the pace and deserves credit for that. He looks likely to take his chance in the Cambridgeshire, with a race such as the Ayrshire Handicap likely to offer suitable conditions.
**Take A Bow**, an improving three-year-old with form on easy ground, put up a brave effort under a 3lb penalty. He was just about to take the advantage off the third when the winner arrived on the scene. Due to go up to 98 from the weekend, he still looks to be on the upgrade, and connections may be tempted to go for the Tote Trifecta Handicap back over seven at Ascot at the end of next month.
**St Petersburg** ◆ loves soft ground and made a bold bid to follow up his course and distance win last month off a 4lb higher mark. He took a good hold in the early stages and that may have cost him at the end, but it would be no surprise to see him taking his chance in the Cambridgeshire, where the strong gallop will suit him.
**Unshakable(IRE)** handles cut in the ground, but has looked held since raised in the handicap for his win at Sandown early in the season. If the Handicapper relents a little he will be interesting in similar contests, especially at Sandown, which seems to suit him.
**Vicious Knight** ◆ adopted totally different tactics on this much softer ground and ran a lot better than of late. He is now 12lb lower than when gaining his last win at the start of 2003 and, if repeating these tactics in a lower grade, could well return to winning form.
**Blue Sky Thinking(IRE)** finished much further behind St Petersburg than he did over course and distance in July, despite being 5lb better off. His turf wins have all been on a sounder surface.
**Consonant(IRE)** did not run too badly, but will be of more interest back on the All-Weather.
**El Coto** has shown in the past that soft ground suits, but never got into contention on ths occasion. He looks held by the Handicapper at present.
**Jazz Messenger(FR)** well fancied after a promising return to action at the weekend, produced a lacklustre effort and possibly this came too soon. He can be given a chance to atone, and the Courage Handicap at Newbury appeals as a likely target.
**Always Esteemed(IRE)** *Official explanation: jockey said gelding tired in the closing stages in the soft ground*
**Anani(USA)** *Official explanation: jockey said colt was never travelling*

## 4888 KONE PLC MELROSE RATED STKS (H'CAP) 1m 5f 197y
**4:30** (4:30) (B ) (0-100,97) 3-Y-O **£12,945** (£4,910; £2,455; £1,116) **Stalls** Low

Form RPR

1542 **1** **Lost Soldier Three (IRE)**[6] 4715 3-8-11 **87** ........ KFallon 2 107
(LMCumani) *racd on inner to 7f out: hdwy over 4f out: styd on to ld 1f out: drvn clr* **3/1**[1]

5111 **2** *3½* **Peak Of Perfection (IRE)**[28] 4062 3-8-9 **85** ........ PRobinson 3 100
(MAJarvis) *led ins gp: led overall 4f out: hdd 1f out: no ex* **10/1**

1111 **3** *1¼* **Elusive Dream**[34] 3902 3-8-5 **81** ........ SSanders 12 95
(SirMarkPrescott) *t.k.h: hdwy over 3f out: ev ch over 1f out: nt qckn* **7/1**[3]

1131 **4** *5* **Lochbuie (IRE)**[21] 4274 3-9-7 **97** ........ JFEgan 13 104
(GWragg) *stdd s: hdwy 6f out: sn chsng ldrs: wknd over 1f out* **7/1**[3]

2311 **5** *5* **Lets Roll**[33] 3953 3-8-7 **83** ........ DeanMcKeown 4 84
(CWThornton) *racd on inner to 7f out: outpcd and lost pl over 4f out: hdwy over 3f out: lost pl over 1f out* **9/2**[2]

4120 **6** *3½* **Modesta (IRE)**[63] 2997 3-8-12 **88** ........ RHughes 5 84
(HRACecil) *racd on inner tl 7f out: chsd ldrs: drvn along over 4f out: wknd fnl 2f* **12/1**

1-21 **7** *½* **Soulacroix**[6] 4715 3-8-12 **88** 3ex ........ JPMurtagh 8 83
(MrsAJPerrett) *racd on inner tl 7f out: effrt and nt clr run over 4f out: hung lft and lost pl over 2f out* **8/1**

5212 **8** *2½* **Sand And Stars (IRE)**[34] 3919 3-8-6 **82** ow1 ........ DHolland 6 74
(MHTompkins) *overall ldr tl 4f out: wknd over 1f out* **22/1**

5316 **9** *5* **Always Waining (IRE)**[22] 4229 3-9-6 **96** ........ JFanning 1 82
(MJohnston) *racd on inner tl 7f out: chsd ldrs: lost pl over 3f out* **12/1**

1502 **10** *22* **Sound Of Fleet (USA)**[34] 3902 3-8-9 **85** ........ RLMoore 11 42
(PFICole) *t.k.h in rr: lost pl 4f out: sn bhd: eased* **33/1**

2105 **11** *2* **Reservoir (IRE)**[6] 4729 3-8-4 **80** ........ MartinDwyer 10 34
(WJHaggas) *chsd ldrs: wknd over 3f out: sn bhd and eased* **33/1**

4450 **12** *28* **Si Si Amiga (IRE)**[47] 3519 3-9-2 **92** ........ MHills 9 10
(BWHills) *trckd ldrs: lost pl 6f out: sn bhd and eased: t.o* **100/1**

2140 **13** *dist* **Le Tiss (IRE)**[22] 4229 3-8-13 **89** ........ TEDurcan 7 —
(MRChannon) *chsd ldrs: lost pl over 2f out: virtually p.u: wl t.o* **25/1**

3m 4.67s (8.27) **Going Correction** +0.65s/f (Yiel) **13** Ran SP% **118.8**
Speed ratings: **102,100,99,96,93 91,91,89,87,74 73,57,—**CSF £31.94 CT £198.07 TOTE £4.20: £1.90, £2.70, £2.60; EX 38.40 Trifecta £267.40 Pool: £2,448.42. 6.50 winning units..
**Owner** Sheikh Mohammed Obaid Al Maktoum **Bred** Darley **Trained** Newmarket, Suffolk

**FOCUS**
As usual a decent, competitive handicap and, although the pace was unexceptional for the grade, the field finished well strung out and, with progressive horses filling the places, the form looks sound and should throw up plenty of winners.

**NOTEBOOK**
**Lost Soldier Three(IRE)** ◆, who did not get the best of runs when beaten narrowly at Newbury last time, had a clear passage this time and picked up well to win with authority. He is lightly raced and progressive, and taking on older horses in the Mallard Handicap at Doncaster looks on the cards now, with the possibility that he could be Pattern class come next year. *Official explanation: jockey said gelding was hanging right-handed*
**Peak Of Perfection(IRE)** ◆ has progressed really well this summer and, stepping up in grade and off his highest-ever mark, made a bold bid under a positive ride. He beat the rest comfortably enough, and looks capable of picking up more good handicaps this autumn providing he avoids the winner, with Newbury's Autumn Cup appealing as a suitable target.
**Elusive Dream**, who notched a four-timer in lower-grade races in July, ran a fine race off a stone higher mark and only faded in the last furlong. He looks to have found his level now, but connections are likely to find opportunities for him at a slightly lower level.
**Lochbuie(IRE)**, running off a mark 25lb higher than at the start of the season, did well in the circumstances and looks better than the official margins indicate. A return to a faster surface should be in his favour.
**Lets Roll**, bidding for a hat-trick off a 7lb higher mark, found the step up in grade too much, but is likely to find easier opportunities at a slightly lower level.
**Modesta(IRE)** ran well enough until a combination of the longer trip and softer ground found her out.
**Soulacroix**, who beat the winner at Newbury last time, should have handled the conditions, having gained both his wins on easy ground, but never looked likely to get into contention and was allowed to come home in his own time. He is clearly better than this, and it may be that the race came too soon for him.
**Le Tiss(IRE)** *Official explanation: jockey said colt was unsuited by the soft ground*

## 4889 LEN MCCORMICK CITY OF YORK STKS (LISTED RACE) 6f 217y
**5:00** (5:01) (A ) 3-Y-O+ **£19,500** (£6,000; £3,000; £1,500) **Stalls** Low

Form RPR

-301 **1** **Polar Bear**[56] 3235 4-9-0 103 ........ ACulhane 7 113+
(WJHaggas) *stdd s: hld up in mid-div: effoer over 2f out: edgd rt ins last: r.o to ld post* **2/1**[1]

1465 **2** *shd* **Welsh Emperor (IRE)**[47] 3552 5-9-0 107 ........ (b) DHolland 11 111
(TPTate) *racd wd: led after 1f: qcknd over 2f out: r.o: jst ct* **10/1**

5310 **3** *1½* **Vanderlin**[23] 4216 5-9-0 109 ........ MartinDwyer 6 107
(AMBalding) *hw: in tch: effrt over 2f out: styd on fnl f* **14/1**

1120 **4** *1* **Material Witness (IRE)**[19] 4324 7-9-0 100 ........ SSanders 4 105
(WRMuir) *led 1f: chsd ldrs: kpt on same pce appr fnl f* **20/1**

6310 **5** *3* **Look Here's Carol (IRE)**[12] 4553 4-8-9 91 ........ GGibbons 3 92
(BAMcmahon) *chsd ldrs: fdd fnl f* **28/1**

3554 **6** *nk* **Babodana**[5] 4745 4-9-5 108 ........ PRobinson 5 101
(MHTompkins) *lw: chsd ldrs: effrt over 2f out: wkng whn sltly checked ins last* **11/2**[3]

1152 **7** *2½* **Mine (IRE)**[19] 4341 6-9-0 108 ........ (v) LDettori 9 90
(JDBethell) *hld up in last: effrt on inner over 2f out: nvr nr ldrs* **3/1**[2]

1454 **8** *5* **Rockets 'n Rollers (IRE)**[71] 2793 4-9-5 104 ........ DaneO'Neill 12 83
(RHannon) *chsd ldrs on outer: lost pl over 4f out: n.d after* **25/1**

5433 **9** *2* **Play That Tune**[35] 3867 4-8-9 90 ........ WRyan 1 68
(HRACecil) *mid-div: drvn along 3f out: sn lost pl* **25/1**

-140 **10** *2½* **Heretic**[42] 3673 6-9-0 103 ........ (v[1]) JPMurtagh 8 66
(JRFanshawe) *hld up in rr: rdn over 2f out: no rspnse* **12/1**

# [4532] AYR (L-H)

Friday, August 20

**OFFICIAL GOING: Soft (heavy in places on bottom bend)**

Wind: fairly strong, across Weather: cloudy, bright

## 4900 RENAULT TRAFIC MEDIAN AUCTION MAIDEN STKS — 7f 50y

2:20 (2:23) (E) 2-Y-O — **£3,699** (£1,138; £569; £284) **Stalls** Low

| Form | | | | RPR |
|---|---|---|---|---|
| 0 | **1** | | **Fenrir**[24] 4208 2-9-0 ... GHind 5<br>(JRWeymes) *in tch: rdn 3f out: led ins fnl f: styd on wl* **100/1** | 83 |
| 2 | **2** | *nk* | **King's Account (USA)**[11] 4606 2-9-0 ... JFanning 6<br>(MJohnston) *set stdy pce: rdn over 2f out: hdd ins fnl f: r.o* **11/4**[2] | 82 |
| 2 | **3** | *7* | **Spear (IRE)**[21] 4292 2-9-0 ... TPQueally 3<br>(DRLoder) *chsd ldrs: outpcd over 2f out: rallied u.p over 1f out: nt rch first two* **13/8**[1] | 65 |
| 3 | **4** | *¾* | **Haatmey**[15] 4480 2-9-0 ... ACulhane 1<br>(MRChannon) *in tch: lost pl after 3f: hdwy whn nt clr run appr fnl f: kpt on: nrst fin* **8/1** | 63+ |
| 0 | **5** | *1* | **Sydneyroughdiamond**[34] 3925 2-8-11 ... LEnstone(3) 7<br>(MMullineaux) *pressed ldr tl rdn and outpcd fr 2f out* **150/1** | 61 |
| 3 | **6** | *½* | **Coconut Squeak**[27] 4131 2-8-9 ... DeanMcKeown 4<br>(JGGiven) *prom tl rdn and one pce fr over 2f out* **14/1** | 55 |
| | **7** | *¾* | **White Star Magic** 2-8-9 ... BSwarbrick(5) 10<br>(JRWeymes) *hld up: rdn over 3f out: sn no imp* **100/1** | 58 |
| | **8** | *2* | **Thorntoun Piccolo** 2-8-9 ... PHanagan 11<br>(JSGoldie) *s.i.s: effrt on ins rail over 2f out: no imp over 1f out* **66/1** | 48 |
| 35 | **9** | *½* | **Good Investment**[11] 4606 2-8-7 ... GBartley(7) 8<br>(PCHaslam) *prom tl rdn and outpcd over 2f out* **16/1** | 52 |
| 05 | **10** | *4* | **Imperial Dynasty (USA)**[16] 4454 2-8-9 ... PMakin(5) 2<br>(TDBarron) *hld up: rdn over 3f out: n.d* **25/1** | 42 |
| 06 | **11** | *10* | **Harbour Legend**[37] 3834 2-8-6 ... (b[1]) NMackay(3) 9<br>(JGGiven) *bhd: rdn 1/2-way: sn btn* **100/1** | — |
| 42 | **12** | *30* | **Invertiel (USA)**[20] 4329 2-9-0 ... RWinston 12<br>(ISemple) *chsd ldrs tl lost pl qckly 2f out: sn eased: t.o* **13/2**[3] | — |

1m 40.06s (7.59) **Going Correction** +0.75s/f (Yiel) **12** Ran SP% **110.7**

Speed ratings: **86,85,77,76,75 75,74,71,71,66 55,21**CSF £343.02 TOTE £113.70: £16.00, £1.20, £1.10; EX 352.70.

**Owner** E G Moorey **Bred** E A Moorey **Trained** Middleham Moor, N Yorks

**FOCUS**

An ordinary event in which the pace was on the steady side in the testing conditions and the time was modest for the grade and a cautious view has been taken ratings-wise. Although the favourite failed to confirm debut promise on this different ground, the front two did well to pull clear of the remainder.

**NOTEBOOK**

**Fenrir**, who hinted at ability on fast ground on his debut, turned in a much-improved display under very different conditions. He will stay further and is entitled to improve again, but will find things tougher in nursery company back on quicker ground.

**King's Account(USA)** had the run of the race but fully confirmed debut promise on this more testing ground, and again showed enough to suggest that he can win a similar race at least.

**Spear(IRE)** looked the one to beat on his debut run but had his limitations exposed on this very different ground. He will be suited by further but may be happiest on a sound surface.

**Haatmey** left the impression that a stiffer test of stamina would have been in his favour, but he may be the type that is not seen to best effect until sent into nursery company.

**Sydneyroughdiamond**, well beaten on soft on his debut, fared better this time but did have the run of things to a bigger degree than most and may well be flattered by his proximity. He is likely to continue to look vulnerable in this grade.

**Coconut Squeak** failed to build on her debut promise but she too may have been inconvenienced by these much easier conditions and she will be more of interest when handicapped and back on a sound surface.

**Harbour Legend** *Official explanation: jockey said filly was never travelling*

**Invertiel(USA)** *Official explanation: jockey said colt lost its action*

## 4901 ARNOLD CLARK RENAULT H'CAP — 1m 2f

2:55 (2:55) (E) (0-75,74) 3-Y-O+ — **£3,653** (£1,124; £562; £281) **Stalls** Low

| Form | | | | RPR |
|---|---|---|---|---|
| 6300 | **1** | | **Maritime Blues**[13] 4556 4-8-13 **60** ... ACulhane 4<br>(JGGiven) *chsd ldrs: outpcd over 2f out: rallied to ld ins fnl f: hld on wl* **6/1** | 69 |
| 00-0 | **2** | *nk* | **Loaded Gun**[211] 585 4-8-0 **52** ... BSwarbrick(5) 1<br>(WMBrisbourne) *hld up in tch: hdwy over 1f out: disp ld ins fnl f: jst hld* **16/1** | 60 |
| 4-40 | **3** | *1 ¼* | **Young Rooney**[15] 4486 4-9-7 **68** ... TPQueally 3<br>(MMullineaux) *led: clr over 2f out: hdd and no ex ins fnl f* **8/1** | 74 |
| 2060 | **4** | *3* | **Compton Dragon (USA)**[20] 4319 5-9-13 **74** ... (v) ANicholls 2<br>(DNicholls) *hld up: effrt over 2f out: kpt on fnl f: no imp* **7/2**[1] | 75 |
| 1246 | **5** | *2 ½* | **Scurra**[15] 4493 5-8-4 **54** ... TEaves(3) 5<br>(ACWhillans) *prom: outpcd over 2f out: kpt on fnl f: no imp* **4/1**[2] | 51 |
| 5062 | **6** | *¾* | **Skiddaw Jones**[13] 4537 4-8-0 **47** ... PHanagan 8<br>(MissLAPerratt) *hld up: effrt outside over 2f out: sn n.d* **13/2** | 42 |
| 0000 | **7** | *nk* | **Repulse Bay (IRE)**[22] 4275 6-7-10 **46** ... NMackay(3) 6<br>(JSGoldie) *hld up: rdn over 3f out: sn n.d* **5/1**[3] | 41 |
| 0000 | **8** | *3* | **Lucky Largo (IRE)**[3] 4826 4-8-5 **52** ... (b) JFanning 7<br>(MissLAPerratt) *chsd ldr: rdn over 2f out: wknd over 1f out* **9/1** | 42 |

2m 17.06s (4.87) **Going Correction** +0.75s/f (Yiel) **8** Ran SP% **113.5**

Speed ratings: **110,109,108,106,104 103,103,101**CSF £91.50 CT £767.42 TOTE £8.30: £4.00, £1.90, £2.50; EX 78.10.

**Owner** Downlands Racing **Bred** Downlands Racing **Trained** Willoughton, Lincs

**FOCUS**

A modest race featuring several disappointing types, but a decent test of stamina in the conditions and the time was good for the grade, with the winner running to this year's best.

**NOTEBOOK**

**Maritime Blues** has not proved entirely reliable, but looked in good shape and put his best foot forward to notch his second win of the year and to confirm himself fully effective on soft. The return to a mile and a half will suit, but his record suggests he is not certain to put it all in next time.

**Loaded Gun** turned in an improved display on this first run since January and on this first start for his shrewd stable. He showed enough to suggest he can be placed to best advantage on a similar surface.

**Young Rooney** made this a decent test of stamina but, while he confirmed himself effective on soft and put a poor run behind him, again left the impression that he is likely to continue to look vulnerable in handicaps from this mark.

**Compton Dragon(USA)**, who is on a lengthy losing run, has form on soft ground and had the race run to suit but once again left the impression that he was not giving it his best shot and he remains one to tread carefully with.

**Scurra**, proven in the conditions and in decent heart for much of the year, looked to have more going for him than most in this company, so this tame effort has to go down as a bit of a disappointment.

**Skiddaw Jones**, back on softer ground, failed to reproduce his recent second placing at this track and, although faster ground may help, this inconsistent type remains one to tread carefully with.

## 4902 PARKS RENAULT H'CAP — 1m

3:25 (3:26) (D) (0-80,80) 3-Y-O — **£5,480** (£1,686; £843; £421) **Stalls** Low

| Form | | | | RPR |
|---|---|---|---|---|
| -121 | **1** | | **Boppys Princess**[8] 4680 3-7-12 **51** 6ex ... PHanagan 4<br>(RAFahey) *led after 2f: hdd over 2f out: rallied to ld ins fnl f: kpt on wl* **4/6**[1] | 58 |
| 1111 | **2** | *¾* | **She's Our Lass (IRE)**[11] 4610 3-9-6 **80** 6ex ... DTudhope(7) 1<br>(DCarroll) *chsd ldrs: shkn up over 2f out: kpt on ins fnl f* **5/2**[2] | 85 |
| 56-3 | **3** | *shd* | **The Number**[21] 4306 3-8-12 **65** ... RWinston 2<br>(ISemple) *keen: led 2f: chsd ldr: led over 2f out to ins fnl f: no ex towards fin* **20/1** | 70 |
| 0210 | **4** | *1 ¾* | **Musiotal**[15] 4489 3-7-13 **55** ... NMackay(3) 5<br>(JSGoldie) *prom: rdn over 2f out: kpt on ins fnl f: no imp* **12/1**[3] | 57 |
| 0301 | **5** | *15* | **Miskina**[84] 2451 3-8-0 **58** ... (t) BSwarbrick(5) 3<br>(WMBrisbourne) *in tch: rdn over 2f out: sn wknd* **20/1** | 30 |

1m 51.4s (8.28) **Going Correction** +0.75s/f (Yiel) **5** Ran SP% **105.8**

Speed ratings: **88,87,87,85,70**CSF £2.23 TOTE £1.70: £1.20, £1.10; EX 2.10.

**Owner** Mrs S Bond **Bred** Mrs Sylvia Bond **Trained** Musley Bank, N Yorks

**FOCUS**

An uncompetitive event run at a false pace in a slow time, but one in which the form horses came to the fore. This bare form may not be a reliable guide, though.

**NOTEBOOK**

**Boppys Princess**, who had conditions to suit, notched her third win from only four starts for her current stable and may well be capable of better, as she would have been suited by a much stiffer test. She remains one to keep on the right side, even after reassessment, and will be interesting upped to a mile and a quarter.

**She's Our Lass(IRE)** has been thriving of late and lost little in defeat against a bang in-form rival under her penalty. A stiffer test of stamina would have suited but, although she should continue to give it her best shot, may look vulnerable to progressive performers in handicap company.

**The Number** had the run of the race and seemed to show improved form on this handicap debut from a stiff-looking mark. However, her proximity to a couple of in-form fillies means she is going to continue to look vulnerable in handicaps for a while yet from this mark.

**Musiotal** did not fail through lack of stamina in a race that placed more of an emphasis on speed than stamina, but he may be better suited by a more strongly-run race back over seven furlongs.

**Miskina**, having her first run since winning at Wolverhampton in May, was well beaten on this first run on soft ground in the first-time tongue strap. Her form on turf has been very patchy. *Official explanation: jockey said filly may have resented the first-time fitted tongue strap*

## 4903 RENAULT MASTER CLASSIFIED STKS — 1m

4:00 (4:00) (E) 3-Y-O+ — **£3,516** (£1,082; £541; £270) **Stalls** Low

| Form | | | | RPR |
|---|---|---|---|---|
| 4633 | **1** | | **Millagros (IRE)**[22] 4258 4-9-0 70 ... (p) PHanagan 1<br>(ISemple) *prom: rdn to ld appr fnl f: kpt on wl* **6/1** | 79 |
| 0414 | **2** | *1 ¾* | **Scotland The Brave**[13] 4551 4-9-0 70 ... (p) TPQueally 5<br>(JDBethell) *cl up: led briefly appr fnl f: kpt on ins last* **7/2**[2] | 76 |
| 6062 | **3** | *½* | **Arry Dash**[7] 4719 4-9-5 72 ... ACulhane 2<br>(MRChannon) *in tch: drvn and edgd lft fr 1/2-way: hdwy over 1f out: kpt on: no imp fnl f* **5/2**[1] | 80 |
| -200 | **4** | *2 ½* | **Soller Bay**[13] 4543 7-9-3 73 ... LEnstone(3) 3<br>(KRBurke) *led to over 1f out: sn outpcd* **4/1**[3] | 76 |
| 6310 | **5** | *7* | **Zanjeer**[19] 4360 4-8-12 70 ... MLawson(5) 4<br>(NWilson) *keen: chsd ldrs: effrt and ch over 1f out: outpcd ins last* **4/1**[3] | 59 |

1m 48.3s (5.18) **Going Correction** +0.75s/f (Yiel) **5** Ran SP% **105.1**

Speed ratings: **104,102,101,99,92**CSF £23.95 TOTE £8.50: £2.80, £2.60; EX 26.00.

**Owner** James A Cringan **Bred** Elsdon Farms **Trained** Carluke, S Lanarks

**FOCUS**

An open race on paper but a clear-cut winner in Millagros, who proved her effectiveness on a testing surface with a decisive success. This looks a reliable-enough guide to the current ability of the first two.

**NOTEBOOK**

**Millagros(IRE)**, edgy in the preliminaries, settled better in the race with the first-time cheekpieces replacing the visor, and turned in her best effort of the year to prove her effectiveness on soft. She is capable of winning again in ordinary company, but her record suggests she is not one to place maximum faith in.

**Scotland The Brave**, who is proven on easy ground, had the run of the race and looks the best guide to the level of this form. She has been running creditably since being fitted with cheekpieces and should continue to give a good account.

**Arry Dash**, who has not won for over a year, came into this race in decent heart and ran creditably in terms of form, but he did not look entirely straightforward and he seems one to have reservations about.

**Soller Bay**, who handles testing ground, had the run of the race and performed better than he had on his last two starts, but does not really appeal as a winner waiting to happen on this evidence.

**Zanjeer** was the disappointment of the race but, as he failed to settle in the conditions, looks worth another chance for his capable trainer. He may be best when allowed an uncontested lead.

## 4904 17TH SEPTEMBER IS LADIES DAY H'CAP — 6f

4:35 (4:36) (D) (0-80,78) 3-Y-O+ — **£5,553** (£1,708; £854; £427) **Stalls** Low

| Form | | | | RPR |
|---|---|---|---|---|
| 0005 | **1** | | **Balakiref**[8] 4677 5-9-4 **68** ... RWinston 4<br>(MDods) *prom gng wl: shkn up to ld ins fnl f: comf* **5/2**[1] | 81 |
| 6630 | **2** | *1 ½* | **Highland Warrior**[27] 4130 5-9-4 **71** ... NMackay(3) 8<br>(JSGoldie) *keen in tch: effrt on ins over 1f out: kpt on fnl f: nt rch wnr* **5/2**[1] | 79 |
| 6665 | **3** | *nk* | **College Maid (IRE)**[13] 4534 7-8-7 **57** ... (v) PHanagan 3<br>(JSGoldie) *led to ins fnl f: kpt on same pce* **5/1**[2] | 64 |
| 0500 | **4** | *1 ½* | **Ulysees (IRE)**[9] 4635 5-9-6 **73** ... (p) TEaves(3) 9<br>(ISemple) *hld up in tch: effrt and edgd lft over 2f out: r.o fnl f: no imp* **7/1**[3] | 76 |
| 0204 | **5** | *1* | **Legal Set (IRE)**[9] 4635 8-8-13 **63** ... (t) AnnStokell 2<br>(MissAStokell) *cl up: effrt and ev ch over 1f out: sn one pce* **14/1** | 63 |
| 1500 | **6** | *11* | **Champagne Cracker**[22] 4279 3-8-11 **64** ... ACulhane 5<br>(MissLAPerratt) *trckd ldrs tl wknd fr 2f out* **16/1** | 31 |
| 3020 | **7** | *8* | **Pays D'Amour (IRE)**[3] 4828 7-8-7 **57** ... JFanning 1<br>(MissLAPerratt) *cl up to 2f out: sn lost pl* **8/1** | — |

1m 17.06s (3.34) **Going Correction** +0.75s/f (Yiel)

**WFA** 3 from 5yo+ 3lb **7** Ran SP% **110.0**

Speed ratings: **107,105,104,102,101 86,75**CSF £7.83 CT £24.74 TOTE £3.30: £1.80, £1.80; EX 8.90.

**Owner** Septimus Racing Group **Bred** S R Hope And D Erwin **Trained** Piercebridge, Co Durham

**FOCUS**

A very ordinary sprint handicap featuring several unreliable types and, although stalls 2 and 3 opened fractionally ahead of the rest, the Stewards deemed it made no difference to the result. The pace was sound in the conditions and the form looks solid enough for the grade.

0400 **11** *2* **Capricho (IRE)**[12] 4553 7-9-0 100 JQuinn 2 61
(JAkehurst) *mid-div: effrt 3f out: sn chsng ldrs: lost pl over 1f out* **16/1**
1m 26.17s (2.86) **Going Correction** +0.60s/f (Yiel) **11** Ran SP% **119.0**
Speed ratings: **107,106,105,104,100 100,97,91,89,86 84**CSF £22.31 TOTE £3.20: £1.40, £3.20, £3.20; EX 35.00 Trifecta £254.50 Pool: £1,721.21. 4.50 winning units..

**Owner** B Haggas **Bred** Cheveley Park Stud Ltd **Trained** Newmarket, Suffolk

■ Stewards Enquiry : A Culhane one-day ban: used whip without allowing gelding time to respond (Aug 30)

**FOCUS**
An ordinary time for a Listed event and the form is only fair for the grade, but should prove sound.

**NOTEBOOK**
**Polar Bear**, who looked very fit indeed, never flinched and, under pressure, put his head in front right on the line. Handicaps look out of the question for him now, but there should be plenty of opportunities in Listed company this autumn.

**Welsh Emperor(IRE)**, drawn one from the outside, enjoyed himself in front and, after looking in command, was nailed right on the line. A proven mudlark, he confirmed his stamina, thereby opening up another door.

**Vanderlin**, a 33/1 shot when taking this a year ago, looked right at his best and found the totally different ground no problem.

**Material Witness(IRE)**, who soon lost out to Welsh Emperor in the dash to lead, had something to find with the first three on official ratings.

**Look Here's Carol(IRE)** keeps running well but she had plenty to find and is possibly better suited by six than seven.

**Babodana**, making a quick return to action, had a 5lb penalty to shoulder and he had come to the end of his tether when nudged by the winner inside the last.

**Mine(IRE)**, happy to sit last, never got competitive. With him it seems the bigger the field the better, and this is not really his ground.

## 4890 MALTON NURSERY 6f 217y
5:30 (5:30) (C) 2-Y-O £11,943 (£3,675; £1,837; £918) Stalls Low

Form RPR
5321 **1** **Merchant (IRE)**[2] 4824 2-9-1 **84** 6ex RMullen 2 101+
(MLWBell) *hld up in last pl: hdwy: n.m.r and hit over hd over 2f out: led over 1f out: sn drew wl clr: eased towards fin* **7/2**[1]

6531 **2** *7* **Dove Cottage (IRE)**[14] 4475 2-7-12 **67** oh2 AMcCarthy 9 66
(WSKittow) *w ldrs: kpt on fnl 2f: no ch w wnr* **16/1**

061 **3** *hd* **Spaced (IRE)**[42] 3665 2-8-12 **81** RLMoore 4 80
(RHannon) *lw: mid-div: rdn over 3f out: hdwy on inner to join ldrs 2f out: styd on same pce* **13/2**[3]

0423 **4** *½* **Hallucinate**[14] 4482 2-8-2 **71** MartinDwyer 8 68
(RHannon) *chsd ldrs: kpt on same pce fnl 2f* **11/1**

1423 **5** *3 ½* **Sea Hunter**[27] 4089 2-9-4 **87** TEDurcan 3 76
(MRChannon) *bhd and drvn along: sme hdwy 2f out: nvr nr ldrs* **11/2**[2]

132 **6** *nk* **Sir Anthony (IRE)**[15] 4445 2-9-7 **90** DMcGaffin 5 78
(BSmart) *s.i.s: hdwy to chse ldrs 4f out: wknd fnl 2f* **9/1**

2462 **7** *nk* **Molly Marie (IRE)**[14] 4488 2-8-8 **77** WSupple 11 64
(TDEasterby) *sn trcking ldrs: rdn and wnt lft over 2f out: wknd 1f out* **13/2**[3]

5213 **8** *8* **Rockburst**[49] 3445 2-8-9 **78** ANicholls 7 45
(KRBurke) *led tl over 1f out: wknd* **16/1**

5344 **9** *¾* **Blackcomb Mountain (USA)**[10] 4601 2-8-1 **70** JFEgan 6 35
(MFHarris) *chsd ldrs: wknd over 2f out* **33/1**

5103 **10** *1 ½* **Snookered Again**[24] 4186 2-7-13 **68** DaleGibson 12 29
(MWEasterby) *chsd ldrs on outer: lost pl over 2f out* **14/1**

6225 **11** *½* **Tom Forest**[31] 3974 2-8-13 **82** EAhern 1 42
(ACrook) *lost pl 4f out: sn bhd* **25/1**

314 **12** *3* **Ariodante**[25] 4166 2-8-11 **80** SSanders 10 33
(JMPEustace) *swtchd lft after s: hdwy over 3f out: sn lost pl* **11/1**

1m 27.3s (3.99) **Going Correction** +0.60s/f (Yiel) **12** Ran SP% **116.2**
Speed ratings: **101,93,92,92,88 87,87,78,77,75 75,71**CSF £61.77 CT £355.45 TOTE £4.40: £1.80, £7.40, £2.30; EX 88.80 Trifecta £215.30 Pool: £1,364.93. 4.50 winning units. Place 6 £18.93, Place 5 £11.77.

**Owner** H E Sheikh Rashid Bin Mohammed **Bred** John Foley **Trained** Newmarket, Suffolk

■ Stewards Enquiry : W Supple two-day ban: improper riding (Aug 30-31)

**FOCUS**
A decent nursery but an impressive winner in a respectable time for the grade in the ground. The form looks solid.

**NOTEBOOK**
**Merchant(IRE)**, an easy winner of his maiden at Hamilton just two days before, took this in impressive style. Given a confident ride, he sliced through his field on the bridle and came right away in the closing stages. Likely to go up a fair amount after this, connections plan to run him at Newmarket before his new mark comes into effect. He looks capable of making his mark at a higher level given soft ground, and a proposed crack at an Italian Listed race before the end of the season looks reasonable.

**Dove Cottage(IRE)**, stepping up in grade and 2lb out of the handicap, as expected handled the softer ground but, despite running well, was no match for the winner. There will be plenty more opportunities for him, as he starts from a modest mark.

**Spaced(IRE)**, making his nursery debut, is another progressive sort but, like the runner-up, he had no chance with the winner despite keeping on. He does not appeal as being quite so well handicapped though.

**Hallucinate**, who had only previously raced on fast ground, is by a stallion whose progeny often prefer cut in the ground. This was a decent effort on this step up in class, and he should be able to get off the mark in similar conditions at a slightly lower level.

**Sea Hunter**, who ran his best race with cut in the ground, was 9lb higher and found this a bit too hot.

**Sir Anthony(IRE)**, all of whose runs have been with cut in the ground, missed the break but, after getting into contention, faded in the closing stages. He looks high in the handicap for what he has achieved.

**Molly Marie(IRE)** was quite keen early, but moved up looking likely to take a hand before tiring. Her best form has been on good ground, and she looks capable of picking up a small race off her current mark.

**Rockburst** *Official explanation: jockey said filly was unsuited by the soft ground*

T/Jkpt: Not won. T/Plt: £25.40 to a £1 stake. Pool: £177,600.41. 5,090.65 winning tickets. T/Qpdt: £15.90 to a £1 stake. Pool: £5,960.90. 276.45 winning tickets. JR

4891 - 4892a (Foreign Racing) - See Raceform Interactive

# 4503 TIPPERARY
Thursday, August 19

**OFFICIAL GOING: Soft changing to heavy after 6.45 (race 5)**

## 4893a IRISH STALLION FARMS EUROPEAN BREEDERS FUND FAIRY BRIDGE STKS (LISTED RACE) (F&M) 7f 100y
5:45 (5:46) 3-Y-O+ £32,091 (£9,415; £4,485; £1,528)

RPR
**1** **Queen Of Palms (IRE)**[88] 2330 3-8-11 88 PShanahan 11 102
(KevinPrendergast, Ire) *towards rr: prog into 6th and rdn fr early st: led fr under 1 1/2f out: clr ins fnl f: styd on wl* **8/1**

**2** *1* **Fearn Royal (IRE)**[23] 4222 5-9-2 98 (b) JAHeffernan 5 100
(PeterCasey, Ire) *towards rr: prog into 5th appr st: rdn fr over 2f out: kpt on wl into 2nd fnl f wout troubling wnr* **5/1**[2]

**3** *nk* **Amourallis (IRE)**[18] 4371 3-8-11 94 PCosgrave 7 99
(GMLyons, Ire) *s.i.s: impr into 7th and rdn fr early st: kpt on wl wout threatening to go 3rd ins fnl f* **6/1**[3]

**4** *3 ½* **Blue Dream (IRE)**[14] 4506 4-9-2 93 CO'Donoghue 4 92
(DJSelvaratnam, Ire) *sn settled 2nd: rdn fr early st: no imp and dropped to 4th ins fnl f* **16/1**

**5** *2* **Viva La Diva (IRE)**[26] 4157 4-9-2 83 CatherineGannon 1 88
(CCollins, Ire) *sn led: strly pressed and hdd under 1 1/2f out: sn no ex u.p* **14/1**

**6** *nk* **Sudden Silence (IRE)**[26] 4162 3-8-11 91 FMBerry 8 87
(DeclanGillespie, Ire) *trckd ldrs in 3rd: no imp u.p and kpt on same pce fr under 2f out* **8/1**

**7** *4* **Takrice**[88] 2330 3-8-11 103 DPMcDonogh 6 78
(KevinPrendergast, Ire) *chsd ldrs: 4th appr st: rdn and no imp fr 2f out: kpt on one pce* **11/4**[1]

**8** *20* **Blue Banner (IRE)**[109] 1809 3-8-11 79 (p) DMGrant 3 32
(MrsValerieKeatley, Ire) *chsd ldrs: rdn and dropped to rr 1/2-way: sn bhd: eased fr over 1f out* **20/1**

**9** *½* **Summer Sunset (IRE)**[47] 3547 3-8-11 93 PJSmullen 10 31
(DKWeld, Ire) *chsd ldrs: dropped to 8th and rdn appr st: sn n.d: bhd and eased fr over 1f out* **10/1**

**10** *1 ½* **Alexander Duchess (IRE)**[23] 4222 3-8-11 98 (p) DJCondon 9 27
(JGBurns, Ire) *chsd ldrs: dropped to 7th and rdn appr st: sn n.d: bhd and eased fr over 1f out* **7/1**

**11** *5* **Soviet Belle (IRE)**[354] 4601 3-8-11 NGMcCullagh 2 16
(JSBolger, Ire) *chsd ldrs: rdn and lost pl over 3f out: sn bhd: eased over 1f out* **13/2**

1m 40.5s
**WFA** 3 from 4yo+ 5lb **11** Ran SP% **132.1**
Speed ratings: CSF £53.98 TOTE £17.20: £4.90, £3.20, £2.30; DF 121.60.
**Owner** Mrs Anne Coughlan **Bred** S Coughlan **Trained** Friarstown, Co Kildare

**NOTEBOOK**
**Queen Of Palms(IRE)**, absent since beating only one home in the Irish 1,000 Guineas, handled this heavy ground well and was in total control from over a furlong out.
**Fearn Royal(IRE)** finds it hard to win but kept on well without ever seriously troubling the winner.
**Amourallis(IRE)** was an 80-rated handicapper two runs ago and continued her progress here.
**Blue Dream(IRE)** ran her best race of the season to date but this was stretching her a bit.
**Viva La Diva(IRE)** is only a handicapper.
**Takrice**, the better fancied stable companion of the winner, failed totally to run anywhere near her 103 rating. *Official explanation: vet said filly coughed post race*
**Alexander Duchess(IRE)** *Official explanation: jockey said filly was checked entering the straight*

# 4795 DEAUVILLE (R-H)
Thursday, August 19

**OFFICIAL GOING: Turf: very soft; aw: standard**

## 4899a PRIX DE LIEUREY HARAS DES CAPUCINES (LISTED) (FILLIES) 1m
2:55 (2:56) 3-Y-O £15,845 (£6,338; £4,754; £3,169)

RPR
**1** **Mamela (GER)**[312] 5531 3-8-12 DBoeuf 6 103
(AndreasLowe, Germany)

**2** *snk* **Belle Ange (FR)**[74] 3-8-12 CSoumillon 7 103
(MlleFGuedj, France)

**3** *2* **Tulipe Royale (FR)**[19] 4356 3-8-12 ELegrix 8 99
(J-MBeguigne, France)

**4** *nk* **Secret Melody (FR)**[19] 4356 3-8-12 C-PLemaire 2 98
(H-APantall, France)

**5** *nse* **Bright Abundance (USA)**[19] 4356 3-8-12 MBlancpain 5 98
(CLaffon-Parias, France)

**6** *¾* **Celtic Heroine (IRE)**[27] 4077 3-9-2 KDarley 9 100
(MAJarvis) *raced well in touch, 4th straight, ridden & outpaced 2f out, kept on final f but never in challenging position*

**7** *2* **Dalna (FR)**[42] 3688 3-8-12 ODoleuze 4 92
(MmeCHead-Maarek, France)

**8** *1* **Amie De Mix (FR)**[33] 3-8-12 GaryStevens 11 90
(AFabre, France)

**9** *2* **I Had A Dream**[78] 3-8-12 SPasquier 1 86
(MmeCHead-Maarek, France)

**10** *nk* **Sogna Di Me**[19] 4356 3-8-12 MDemuro 3 86
(BGrizzetti, Italy)

**11** **Lost Icon (IRE)**[74] 3-8-12 (b) OPeslier 10 86
(CLerner, France)

1m 46.5s **11** Ran
Speed ratings: .
**Owner** Stall Tessie **Bred** Werner Meyer **Trained** Germany

**NOTEBOOK**
**Celtic Heroine(IRE)** ran respectably, but could never really land a blow and the gound would have been soft enough.

**NOTEBOOK**

**Balakiref** is not entirely reliable but travelled strongly and won with more in hand than the official margin suggests. He will reportedly be aimed at the Silver Cup back here next month - a race his trainer won in 2002 - and, although he will have to improve to win that, he seems to like it here and would have each-way claims if putting it all in.

**Highland Warrior**, much better than the bare form of several of his runs this year suggests, jumped off on terms back at his favourite course and showed he can win another race from his current mark. However he is not certain to be as co-operative next time and, as such, remains one to be wary of at short odds.

**College Maid(IRE)**, who acts on any ground, had the run of the race and returned to something like her best. She is vulnerable to progressive or well handicapped sorts but is capable of winning another race in this grade before the season is out.

**Ulysees(IRE)**, bitterly disappointing on his last couple of starts, returned to something like his best but once again looked a less than easy ride and he is the type that needs things to fall just right. He is another to be wary of at short prices.

**Legal Set(IRE)** had the run of the race and was not disgraced in an ordinary event. He may be better suited by a sound surface these days but is another in this field not to trust implicitly.

**Champagne Cracker** has not been at her best of late and, while still to prove that six furlongs on soft ground are her optimum conditions, she was beaten well before the extra yardage became an issue. She is best watched for now.

**Pays D'Amour(IRE)** was again soundly beaten for his new stable.

## 4905 STEWARTS TURF H'CAP — 7f 50y

**5:10** (5:12) (E ) (0-70,68) 3-Y-O+ — **£3,715** (£1,143; £571; £285) **Stalls** Low

Form — RPR

0440 **1** **Locombe Hill (IRE)**[35] [3895] 8-8-11 **59**.......................... DTudhope(7) 13 — 74
(NWilson) *keen in tch: rdn and effrt over 1f out: led ins fnl f: r.o wl* **12/1**

0226 **2** *1* **Quicks The Word**[14] [4511] 4-8-13 **54**.......................... DeanMcKeown 11 — 66
(CWThornton) *cl up: led over 2f out: hdd ins fnl f: no ex towards fin* **10/1**[3]

00/0 **3** *1 1/2* **Zandeed (IRE)**[13] [4537] 6-9-2 **57**.......................... JFanning 16 — 66
(MissLAPerratt) *towards rr: rdn and hdwy over 2f out: kpt on fnl f: nt rch first two* **33/1**

6616 **4** *1 3/4* **Zhitomir**[7] [4702] 6-8-8 **52**.......................... LEnstone(3) 12 — 56
(MDods) *in tch: effrt 3f out: kpt on fnl f: no imp* **12/1**

1600 **5** *1 1/4* **Sandorra**[39] [3800] 6-8-5 **46**.......................... TWilliams 6 — 47
(MBrittain) *cl up: effrt and ev ch over 2f out: no ex over 1f out* **33/1**

0-31 **6** *1* **Pertemps Magus**[7] [4702] 4-9-8 **63** 6ex.......................... PHanagan 7 — 62
(RAFahey) *prom: effrt and ev ch 2f out: outpcd appr fnl f* **1/1**[1]

0100 **7** *2* **Stellite**[16] [4447] 4-8-2 **46**.......................... NMackay(3) 10 — 40
(JSGoldie) *towards rr: hdwy 2f out: no imp fnl f* **9/1**[2]

0465 **8** *7* **Irusan (IRE)**[25] [4188] 4-9-3 **58**.......................... ACulhane 9 — 34
(JeddO'Keeffe) *bhd and outpcd tl styd on fr over 1f out: nvr on terms* **33/1**

-002 **9** *1/2* **Stormville (IRE)**[16] [4447] 7-8-8 **54**.......................... MLawson(5) 5 — 29
(MBrittain) *cl up tl wknd fr 2f out* **9/1**[2]

6166 **10** *2* **Wood Dalling (USA)**[13] [4537] 6-9-1 **56**.......................... RWinston 14 — 26
(ISemple) *bhd: effrt over 2f out: n.d* **9/1**[2]

0060 **11** *3* **Howards Rocket**[13] [4537] 3-7-13 **45**.......................... PFessey 2 — 7
(JSGoldie) *hld up on ins: effrt over 2f out: btn over 1f out* **33/1**

1000 **12** *1/2* **Massey**[17] [4425] 8-8-4 **50**.......................... PMakin(5) 1 — 11
(TDBarron) *led to over 2f out: wknd* **25/1**

0000 **13** *1 3/4* **Capetown Girl**[28] [4104] 3-8-11 **57**.......................... ANicholls 4 — 14
(KRBurke) *bhd: rdn 1/2-way: n.d* **25/1**

0245 **14** *5* **Zahunda (IRE)**[13] [4535] 5-7-8 **40** oh1 ow1.......................... BSwarbrick(5) 15 — —
(WMBrisbourne) *prom on outside: rdn over 2f out: hung lft and sn btn* **33/1**

4/60 **15** *12* **Axford Lord**[9] [4635] 4-9-0 **55**.......................... JCarroll 8 — —
(ACWhillans) *s.i.s: sn wl bhd* **150/1**

1m 36.75s (4.28) **Going Correction** +0.75s/f (Yiel)
**WFA** 3 from 4yo+ 5lb — **15** Ran SP% **127.5**
Speed ratings: **105,103,102,100,98 97,95,87,86,84 81,80,78,72,59**CSF £123.62 CT £3884.44 TOTE £16.20: £3.50, £2.90, £8.20; EX 192.60 Place 6 £351.13, Place 5 £249.99.
**Owner** Ian W Glenton **Bred** Rathbarry Stud **Trained** Malton, N Yorks

**FOCUS**

Another ordinary handicap which did not take as much winning as seemed likely with the favourite failing to confirm his recent soft-ground promise. The pace was sound in the conditions and the form looks reasonably reliable.

**NOTEBOOK**

**Locombe Hill(IRE)** ◆ was always travelling strongly and ran up to his best on this first start for new connections, who do well with this type. He goes on most ground and, on this evidence, he is certainly capable of winning again in this company.

**Quicks The Word** ◆ extended his run of creditable efforts and may be a bit better than the bare form, as he fared the best of those that raced right up with the decent pace throughout. He has not always proved consistent but this showed he is capable of winning again from this mark.

**Zandeed(IRE)**, poorly drawn, showed he retains plenty of ability on only this second start since October 2002 and shaped as though the return to further would suit. He is one to keep an eye on.

**Zhitomir** reversed recent placings with Pertemps Magus and ran creditably back at a course where he has already won this year. He is not the most reliable though, so would not be certain to put it all in next time.

**Sandorra**, a dual banded-class All-Weather winner this year, was not disgraced on this first start after a short break, but may need to drop in grade before picking up the winning thread.

**Pertemps Magus**, from a stable in tremendous form, looked the one to beat after last week's polished Catterick win but, despite her penalty, proved a disappointment having attracted plenty of support. She is due to go up a further 2lb from tomorrow so will find things tougher from now on.

T/Plt: £241.50 to a £1 stake. Pool: £31,065.20. 93.90 winning tickets. T/Qpdt: £30.20 to a £1 stake. Pool: £2,102.60. 51.50 winning tickets. RY

# 4872 CHESTER (L-H)

## Friday, August 20

**OFFICIAL GOING: Soft**

With nearly half-an-inch of rain having fallen on the track in the morning, all of the races were run on very testing going.

Wind: mod across Weather: wet

## 4906 BLUE SQUARE 0800 587 0200 RATED STKS (H'CAP) — 1m 2f 75y

**2:10** (2:10) (C ) (0-90,89) 3-Y-O — **£12,481** (£4,734; £2,367; £1,076) **Stalls** High

Form — RPR

3646 **1** **Maclean**[18] [4401] 3-8-8 **76**..........................(p) KFallon 9 — 85
(SirMichaelStoute) *mde all: reminder over 4f out: drvn out* **10/1**

11 **2** *2 1/2* **Tarfah (USA)**[11] [4613] 3-9-3 **85** 3ex.......................... MJKinane 4 — 90
(GABulter) *racd keenly: chsd wnr: rdn over 2f out: ev ch over 1f out: one pce ins fnl f* **4/5**[1]

4-21 **3** *shd* **Triple Jump**[21] [4306] 3-8-7 **75**.......................... WSupple 10 — 80
(TDEasterby) *hld up: rdn over 3f out: hdwy over 1f out: styd on ins fnl f* **16/1**

5361 **4** *hd* **Bessemer (JPN)**[13] [4533] 3-9-2 **84**.......................... FLynch 8 — 89
(ISemple) *chsd ldrs: rdn and ev ch over 2f out: edgd lft 1f out: kpt on same pce* **20/1**

0103 **5** *1* **Keeper's Lodge (IRE)**[20] [4318] 3-8-4 **72** oh2.......................... JQuinn 6 — 75
(BAMcmahon) *racd keenly: hld up: rdn over 5f out: hdwy over 1f out: styd on ins fnl f* **33/1**

1600 **6** *1 3/4* **Swagger Stick (USA)**[35] [3915] 3-9-7 **89**.......................... SWKelly 1 — 89
(JLDunlop) *hld up: rdn over 3f out: hdwy over 1f out: kpt on: nvr rchd ldrs* **9/1**[3]

0534 **7** *2* **Great Scott**[18] [4395] 3-9-0 **82**.......................... SChin 5 — 79
(MJohnston) *hld up: rdn and outpcd over 3f out: kpt on again fnl f* **20/1**

2312 **8** *21* **Anna Pallida**[26] [4173] 3-9-0 **82**.......................... NCallan 7 — 43
(PWHarris) *chsd ldrs tl rdn and wknd over 2f out* **7/1**[2]

-311 **9** *19* **Tableau (USA)**[26] [4171] 3-9-4 **86**.......................... RHughes 3 — 15
(BWHills) *in tch tl rdn and wknd over 2f out* **10/1**

-000 **10** *shd* **Seneschal**[22] [4271] 3-8-12 **80**.......................... CCatlin 11 — 8
(MRChannon) *a bhd* **50/1**

2m 22.72s (10.17) **Going Correction** +1.025s/f (Soft) — **10** Ran SP% **116.5**
Speed ratings: **100,98,97,97,96 95,93,77,61,61**CSF £17.73 CT £138.16 TOTE £11.00: £2.50, £1.10, £2.80; EX 44.70.
**Owner** The Queen **Bred** The Queen **Trained** Newmarket, Suffolk

**FOCUS**

The field went off at an ordinary pace, but in the end they finished very tired and the form has a dubious look.

**NOTEBOOK**

**Maclean** made all the running and, under a persuasive ride from Fallon, repelled all challengers in the final quarter-mile and actually won with a bit to spare. He was racing in first-time cheekpieces and is clearly a bit quirky. It remains to be seen whether he can follow up from a revised mark.

**Tarfah(USA)**, who raced keenly early on, travelled well for much of the race, but in the end the going found her out for she bottomed out inside the final furlong. On better going she should stay ten furlongs.

**Triple Jump**appreciated the step up in trip and ran a solid race.

**Bessemer(JPN)** was up with the pace but failed to quicken.

**Swagger Stick(USA)** never really got into the race but made some late headway.

**Anna Pallida** was among those to be found out by the going in the final three furlongs. *Official explanation: jockey said filly was unsuited by the soft ground*

**Tableau(USA)** is a strong colt who was not given a hard time by his rider once his chance had gone, and he should be seen in better light on better going. *Official explanation: jockey said colt was unsuited by the soft ground*

## 4907 SHELL CHEMICALS PREMIER CLAIMING STKS — 7f 2y

**2:45** (2:45) (D ) 2-Y-O — **£4,901** (£1,508; £754; £377) **Stalls** Low

Form — RPR

0215 **1** **Good Wee Girl (IRE)**[15] [4475] 2-8-2 74 ow1.......................... JFEgan 4 — 71
(SKirk) *chsd ldrs: rdn to ld 1f out: edgd lft ins fnl f: all out* **10/3**[1]

0 **2** *shd* **River Liffey**[16] [4446] 2-9-0 .......................... MFenton 11 — 83
(MLWBell) *dwlt: towards rr: hdwy over 4f out: rdn over 2f out: edgd lft and ev ch ins fnl f: r.o u.p* **8/1**

1440 **3** *2* **Indibraun (IRE)**[25] [4186] 2-8-10 77.......................... GFaulkner 2 — 74
(PCHaslam) *led: rdn: edgd lft and hdd 1f out: no ex towards fin* **11/2**

61 **4** *5* **Arabian Ana (IRE)**[27] [4135] 2-8-12 83.......................... FLynch 6 — 63
(BSmart) *hld up: rdn and hdwy over 1f out: one pce fnl f* **4/1**[2]

1665 **5** *2* **King After**[16] [4439] 2-9-2 80.......................... KFallon 7 — 62
(JRBest) *chsd ldr: rdn and ev ch wl over 2f out: wknd 1f out* **5/1**[3]

6530 **6** *3* **Dusty Dane (IRE)**[25] [4186] 2-8-8 71.......................... ADaly 5 — 47
(WGMTurner) *in tch: pushed along over 5f out: wknd over 2f out* **14/1**

5004 **7** *1/2* **Northern Revoque (IRE)**[7] [4699] 2-7-13 ..........................(p) JQuinn 8 — 37
(ABerry) *chsd ldrs tl rdn and wknd over 2f out* **50/1**

000 **8** *2* **Mickey Pearce (IRE)**[8] [4681] 2-8-6 .......................... FNorton 9 — 39
(JGMO'Shea) *a bhd* **40/1**

00 **9** *hd* **Miss Cuisina**[53] [3377] 2-7-13 .......................... PMQuinn 1 — 31
(PDEvans) *a bhd* **66/1**

5 **10** *1 1/4* **Polesworth**[28] [4095] 2-7-6 .......................... MHalford(7) 3 — 28
(CNKellett) *dwlt: midfield: rdn and wknd over 2f out* **25/1**

5630 **11** *6* **Shujune Al Hawaa (IRE)**[19] [4365] 2-8-3 68.......................... CCatlin 10 — 17
(MRChannon) *midfield: rdn over 3f out: wknd over 2f out* **9/1**

1m 35.5s (7.21) **Going Correction** +1.025s/f (Soft) — **11** Ran SP% **112.6**
Speed ratings: **99,98,96,90,88 85,84,82,82,80 73**CSF £28.25 TOTE £3.50: £1.60, £2.50, £2.50; EX 27.00.The winner was claimed by Mr P. McEntee for £15,000.
**Owner** E Power & M Kavanagh **Bred** Auriga Partnership **Trained** Upper Lambourn, Berks

**FOCUS**

This was an interesting claimer and it produced a very good finish. The first four home all look better than average claiming performers, giving the form a strong look for the grade.

**NOTEBOOK**

**Good Wee Girl(IRE)**, who had tracked the leaders, got the split on the rail that she needed as they hit the home straight, led a furlong from home and kept on well in the final furlong. She handled both the step up in trip and going well.

**River Liffey** mounted a strong challenge and displayed his inexperience by occasionally shouting in the paddock, but he did very little wrong in the race and this was a fair effort on only his second run. The form of his debut is beginning to work out and, a likeable colt, he can improve again on this effort.

**Indibraun(IRE)** made the running and only gave way in the final furlong, but recorded his best effort since May.

**Arabian Ana(IRE)** kept on to be never nearer than at the finish without ever looking likely to play a leading part.

**King After** was given every chance but failed to get home in the conditions.

**Shujune Al Hawaa(IRE)** was never able to get competitive.

## 4908 CHESTER CHRONICLE RATED STKS (H'CAP) — 7f 2y

**3:15** (3:15) (B ) (0-100,98) 3-Y-O+ — **£12,232** (£4,639; £2,319; £1,054) **Stalls** Low

Form — RPR

0060 **1** **King Harson**[27] [4134] 5-8-7 **82** oh5..........................(v) KMcEvoy 3 — 90
(JDBethell) *mde all: rdn and r.o ins fnl f* **11/1**

2000 **2** *3* **Digital**[6] [4742] 7-9-1 **90**.......................... CCatlin 5 — 91
(MRChannon) *racd keenly: hld up: rdn and hdwy over 1f out: styd on to take 2nd ins fnl f: no imp on wnr* **4/1**[2]

0000 **3** *3/4* **Marshman (IRE)**[6] [4742] 5-8-9 **84**.......................... KFallon 4 — 83
(MHTompkins) *chsd ldrs: rdn over 2f out: styd on same pce fnl f* **2/1**[1]

1050 **4** *3/4* **Circuit Dancer (IRE)**[20] [4324] 4-9-5 **94**.......................... FLynch 8 — 91
(ABerry) *racd keenly: chsd wnr: rdn over 2f out: lost 2nd and no ex ins fnl f* **16/1**

0231 **5** *1 1/2* **Nashaab (USA)**[19] [4360] 7-9-1 **90**.......................... NCallan 7 — 83
(PDEvans) *dwlt: towards rr: niggled along thrght: hdwy over 3f out: one pce fnl f* **9/2**[3]

6525 **6** *nk* **Stoic Leader (IRE)**[32] [3977] 4-8-7 **82** oh1.......................... FNorton 1 — 74
(RFFisher) *chsd ldrs: rdn over 2f out: wknd ins fnl f* **11/2**

0-05 **7** *1* **Tashkil (IRE)**[20] 4317 3-9-4 **98** ........................ (t) WSupple 9 88
(JHMGosden) *s.i.s: in rr: effrt 3f out: no imp* **10/1**

130- **8** *dist* **Humid Climate**[141] 4819 4-8-4 **82** ........................ THamilton(3) 6 —
(RAFahey) *hld up: lost tch 3f out: t.o* **16/1**

1m 33.58s (5.29) **Going Correction** +1.025s/f (Soft)
**WFA** 3 from 4yo+ 5lb **8** Ran SP% **116.1**
Speed ratings: **110,106,105,104,103 102,101,**—CSF £55.44 CT £126.26 TOTE £15.70: £3.00, £1.50, £1.40; EX 48.50 Trifecta £173.80 Pool: £1,101.68. 4.50 winning units..
**Owner** C J Burley **Bred** Mrs Anne Bell **Trained** Middleham Moor, N Yorks

**FOCUS**
This was not a strong race and it saw Kerrin McEvoy win on his first ride at the track. The form looks weak for the grade and cannot be taken at face value.

**NOTEBOOK**
**King Harson** proved far too strong for his rivals in the final quarter-mile in the prevailing conditions but had the run of the race and may struggle to follow up. *Official explanation: trainer said, regarding the improved form shown, gelding was much better suited by today's soft ground*
**Digital** came from off the pace to finish second, which was a fair effort on the going, but he continues to find it difficult to make the winner's enclosure.
**Marshman(IRE)**, despite winning form on softish ground, seemed to labour when asked to challenge.
**Circuit Dancer(IRE)**, who looked a picture in the paddock, failed to last home after being given every chance. This was not surprising considering his best form is over no more than six furlongs on good or quicker ground.
**Tashkil(IRE)** showed a little more than on his two previous runs this season without ever looking threatening.

## 4909 LINPAC GROUP NURSERY **7f 2y**
**3:50** (3:51) (C) 2-Y-O **£8,443** (£2,598; £1,299; £649) **Stalls** Low

Form RPR

3551 **1** **Claret And Amber**[12] 4575 2-9-1 77 6ex ........................ THamilton(3) 4 89+
(RAFahey) *s.i.s: in tch: led over 2f out: r.o wl to draw clr fnl f* **11/4**[1]

031 **2** *6* **Following Flow (USA)**[17] 4420 2-9-7 **80** ........................ KFallon 9 79
(WJarvis) *bhd: hdwy over 3f out: rdn to take 2nd over 1f out: no imp on wnr* **9/2**[2]

044 **3** *5* **Young Thomas (IRE)**[43] 3679 2-8-13 **72** ........................ MFenton 7 60
(MLWBell) *towards rr: sn niggled along: kpt on fr over 1f out: nvr trbld ldrs* **9/1**

3160 **4** *4* **Earl Of Links (IRE)**[34] 3938 2-9-1 **74** ........................ RHughes 2 53
(RHannon) *led 1f: remained prom: led 3f out: rdn and hdd over 2f out: wknd over 1f out* **9/2**[2]

0210 **5** *1* **No Commission (IRE)**[30] 4012 2-9-2 **75** ........................ JFEgan 8 52
(RFFisher) *hld up: rdn and hdwy over 2f out: wknd over 1f out* **14/1**

2320 **6** *½* **Wasalat (USA)**[22] 4263 2-9-6 **79** ........................ CCatlin 3 55
(MRChannon) *in tch: rdn and wknd over 3f out* **12/1**

6301 **7** *¾* **Dartanian**[7] 4699 2-8-6 **65** 6ex ow2 ........................ NCallan 1 39
(PDEvans) *led after 1f: rdn and hdd 3f out: wknd over 1f out* **9/2**[2]

1041 **8** *21* **Lisa Mona Lisa (IRE)**[15] 4482 2-9-1 **74** ........................ JQuinn 5 —
(VSmith) *trckd ldrs: rdn over 2f out: sn wknd* **17/2**[3]

0420 **9** *shd* **Canary Dancer**[30] 4012 2-7-11 **63** ........................ MHalford(7) 6 —
(PCHaslam) *trckd ldrs tl rdn and wknd over 2f out* **25/1**

1m 35.95s (7.66) **Going Correction** +1.025s/f (Soft) **9** Ran SP% **119.9**
Speed ratings: **97,90,84,79,78 78,77,53,53**CSF £15.78 CT £100.95 TOTE £4.00: £1.80, £2.10, £3.20; EX 16.70.
**Owner** The Matthewman Partnership **Bred** D R Tucker **Trained** Musley Bank, N Yorks

**FOCUS**
Take out the winner and runner-up, who produced decent performances, and this was not the strongest of nurseries. Although it could be rated higher, it may be dangerous to take it at face value.

**NOTEBOOK**
**Claret And Amber** was slightly impeded at the start and probably found himself a little further back than ideal in the early stages. However, he showed good qualities in making up ground and, leading over two furlongs from home, ran out a very good winner. He clearly appreciated the step up in trip and is progressing.
**Following Flow(USA)** came from off the pace and around the field to mount his challenge, but found the winner far too strong in the final furlong and a half. He could well prove up to winning from his current mark on better ground.
**Young Thomas(IRE)** failed to trouble the leaders but may have a race in him.
**Earl Of Links(IRE)** failed to get home in the ground.

## 4910 DAVID MCLEAN MAIDEN FILLIES' STKS **1m 4f 66y**
**4:25** (4:25) (D) 3-Y-O **£5,330** (£1,640; £820; £410) **Stalls** Low

Form RPR

3 **1** **Daze**[91] 2280 3-8-11 ........................ KFallon 5 58+
(SirMichaelStoute) *s.i.s: in rr: hdwy over 4f out: led wl over 1f out: styd on wl to draw clr fnl f* **1/1**[1]

63 **2** *8* **Reem Two**[20] 4332 3-8-11 ........................ WSupple 1 47
(DMccain) *hld up: rdn over 6f out: hdwy over 2f out: styd on to take 2nd fnl strides: no ch w wnr* **20/1**

2300 **3** *hd* **Stocking Island**[41] 3743 3-8-11 71 ........................ KMcEvoy 4 47
(BHanbury) *chsd ldrs: wnt 2nd over 5f out: led over 2f out: rdn and hdd wl over 1f out: no ex fnl f: lost 2nd fnl strides* **7/2**[3]

2202 **4** *4* **Principessa**[10] 4618 3-8-11 68 ........................ NCallan 2 41
(BPalling) *chsd ldr: led over 5f out: rdn and hdd over 2f out: wknd over 1f out* **5/2**[2]

054 **5** *dist* **Danettie**[11] 4615 3-8-11 ........................ SWKelly 6 —
(WMBrisbourne) *led: hdd over 5f out: wknd qckly: t.o* **20/1**

2m 57.68s (17.16) **Going Correction** +1.625s/f (Heav) **5** Ran SP% **110.3**
Speed ratings: **107,101,101,98,**—CSF £20.48 TOTE £1.80: £1.30, £3.80; EX 13.80.
**Owner** Duke Of Devonshire **Bred** Side Hill Stud **Trained** Newmarket, Suffolk

**FOCUS**
Just an ordinary maiden, but a fair time in the conditions. The winner can be rated better than this, but the rest look mediocre.

**NOTEBOOK**
**Daze** put in a fine staying performance to pull clear of the field in the straight. She was on and off the bridle at various stages in the contest but, to be fair, stuck well to the task. She is still learning her trade but showed a willing attitude and can progress. On this run the Handicapper should not hit her too hard.
**Reem Two** stayed on without troubling the winner.
**Stocking Island** was given every chance in the race but disappointed.
**Principessa** was beaten turning for home.

## 4911 BOLLINGER CHAMPAGNE CHALLENGE SERIES H'CAP (FOR GENTLEMAN AMATEUR RIDERS) **1m 4f 66y**
**5:00** (5:00) (E) (0-80,79) 3-Y-O+ **£3,493** (£1,075; £537; £268) **Stalls** Low

Form RPR

3604 **1** **Giunchiglio**[12] 4571 5-10-8 **64** ........................ MrCDavies(5) 4 73
(WMBrisbourne) *s.i.s: in tch: rdn 4f out: hdwy over 2f out: led over 1f out: styd on* **6/1**[3]

0/60 **2** *2 ½* **Cyber Santa**[49] 3472 6-9-7 **47** oh2 ........................ MrLNewnes(3) 6 53
(JHetherton) *led: rdn and hdd over 1f out: no ex towards fin* **16/1**

1323 **3** *1 ¾* **Lennel**[15] 4493 6-11-6 **71** ........................ (b) MrSWalker 8 74
(ABailey) *in tch: hdwy over 6f out: rdn over 3f out: outpaaced over 2f out: styd on ins fnl f* **5/2**[1]

0202 **4** *¾* **Milk And Sultana**[25] 4196 4-9-13 **53** ........................ MrEDehdashti(3) 5 55
(GAHam) *trckd ldrs: wnt 2nd over 3f out tl over 2f out: rdn over 1f out: kpt on same pce* **7/1**

5022 **5** *hd* **Bucks**[5] 4772 7-11-9 **79** ........................ MrMichaelMurphy(5) 3 81
(DKIvory) *hld up: hdwy 4f out: rdn over 1f out: kpt on ins fnl f* **11/4**[2]

210/ **6** *6* **Revelino (IRE)**[14] 5243 5-11-3 **75** ........................ MrASwinswood(7) 1 68
(MissSJWilton) *w ldr tl over 3f out: sn wknd* **16/1**

6004 **7** *10* **Big Bad Burt**[16] 4458 3-9-5 **59** ........................ MrSWarren(7) 7 38
(GCHChung) *a bhd* **14/1**

0-00 **8** *hd* **Saddler's Quest**[18] 4398 7-10-1 **55** ........................ (p) MrSDobson(3) 9 34
(BPJBaugh) *a bhd* **14/1**

-400 **9** *dist* **Grand Wizard**[79] 2595 4-10-11 **65** ........................ MrJJBest(3) 2 —
(WJarvis) *prom tl lost pl 6f out: t.o* **10/1**

3m 0.64s (20.12) **Going Correction** +1.625s/f (Heav)
**WFA** 3 from 4yo+ 10lb **9** Ran SP% **116.2**
Speed ratings: **97,95,94,93,93 89,82,82,**—CSF £95.78 CT £301.60 TOTE £9.40: £2.90, £5.50, £1.60; EX 186.00 Place 6 £13.97, Place 5 £9.60.
**Owner** Nev Jones **Bred** Red House Stud **Trained** Great Ness, Shropshire

**FOCUS**
This modest handicap for amateur riders was run in a time more than 20 seconds slower than standard and the form is possibly misleading.

**NOTEBOOK**
**Giunchiglio** recorded his first success in testing conditions and over this trip.
**Cyber Santa** put in his best run of the season when making a bold bid to lead all the way before being outstayed.
**Lennel** has risen in the weights due to his consistancy this summer.
**Milk And Sultana** put in a fair run, offering a glimmer of hope.
**Bucks** raced wide and it was noted his near-fore bandage came loose around two furlongs from home. *Official explanation: jockey said gelding was unsuited by the soft ground*
**Big Bad Burt** *Official explanation: jockey said gelding was unsuited by the soft ground*
T/Jkpt: Part won. £270,454.90 to a £1 stake. Pool: £380,922.50. 0.50 winning tickets. T/Plt: £14.80 to a £1 stake. Pool: £69,739.05. 3434.40 winning tickets. T/Qpdt: £6.40 to a £1 stake. Pool: £2,988.10. 342.50 winning tickets. DO

# 4681 SALISBURY (R-H)
Friday, August 20

**OFFICIAL GOING: Good to soft**
Riders throughout the evening were unsure as to where the best place to race was as a result of the cut in the ground, and races were run all over the place.

## 4912 AXMINSTER CARPETS APPRENTICE H'CAP **1m**
**5:35** (5:35) (E) (0-70,70) 3-Y-O+ **£3,835** (£1,180; £590; £295) **Stalls** High

Form RPR

-304 **1** **Crail**[59] 3177 4-10-0 **70** ........................ LisaJones 9 82
(CFWall) *trckd ldrs: led appr fnl 2f: hrd drvn and hld on wl thrght fnl f* **4/1**[2]

1004 **2** *¾* **Oh So Rosie (IRE)**[4] 4818 4-8-5 **55** ........................ (p) DerekNolan(8) 3 65
(JSMoore) *bhd: hdwy and swtchd rt over 2f out: styd on wl to chse wnr ins last: sn str chal: no ex nr fin* **7/1**

0431 **3** *2 ½* **Didnt Tell My Wife**[7] 4719 5-9-3 **69** 6ex ........................ SO'Hara(10) 2 74
(CFWall) *hld up in rr: hdwy 3f out: chsd wnr appr fnl f: no mimp ins last and sn one pce* **7/2**[1]

5005 **4** *½* **Loch Laird**[38] 3828 9-8-3 **48** ........................ CHaddon(3) 6 52
(MMadgwick) *in tch: pushed along and outpcd 3f out: styd on fr over 1f out: kpt on ins last but nt pce of ldrs* **16/1**

0560 **5** *1 ¾* **Dash For Cover (IRE)**[79] 2573 4-8-9 **59** ........................ PGallagher(8) 5 59
(RHannon) *chsd ldrs: rdn 2f out: wknd fnl f* **14/1**

4323 **6** *1* **The Gaikwar (IRE)**[8] 4672 5-9-0 **62** ........................ (b) MSavage(6) 8 60
(NEBerry) *chsd ldrs: rdn over 2f out: wknd fnl f* **13/2**

6026 **7** *1 ¼* **Fleetwood Bay**[16] 4438 4-9-10 **66** ........................ (t) BReilly 12 62
(BRMillman) *broke wl: sn led on stands rail: rdn and hdd appr fnl 2f: wknd over 1f out* **11/2**[3]

6340 **8** *nk* **Due To Me**[38] 3828 4-7-6 **44** ........................ (p) JJones(10) 4 39
(GLMoore) *n.m.r on rails whn crowded after 1f: pushed along: hdwy and hung rt over 2f out: sn btn* **12/1**

5000 **9** *7* **Terraquin (IRE)**[24] 4220 4-9-9 **65** ........................ ABeech 10 45
(JJBridger) *sn pressing ldr: rdn and ev ch over 2f out: sn wknd* **12/1**

6366 **10** *½* **Cumbrian Princess**[7] 4719 7-7-10 **45** ........................ APutland(7) 11 24
(MBlanshard) *chsd ldrs: ev ch 3f out: wknd qckly 2f out* **25/1**

0000 **11** *9* **Harry Came Home**[11] 4600 3-7-10 **54** oh16 ow8 ......(b[1]) VictoriaHill(10) 7 14
(JCFox) *a in rr* **100/1**

00-0 **12** *¾* **Breezer**[115] 1687 4-8-0 **52** ........................ FrancesHarper(10) 1 11
(GBBalding) *a in rr* **20/1**

1m 48.27s (5.30) **Going Correction** +0.50s/f (Yiel)
**WFA** 3 from 4yo+ 6lb **12** Ran SP% **121.0**
Speed ratings: **93,92,89,89,87 86,85,84,77,77 68,67**CSF £32.40 CT £111.05 TOTE £6.70: £1.80, £2.50, £2.10; EX 41.00.
**Owner** The Crail Partnership **Bred** Mrs Mary E Chapman **Trained** Newmarket, Suffolk
■ Stewards Enquiry : Lisa Jones one-day ban: excessive use of the whip (Aug 31)

**FOCUS**
They all came stands' side - as is the norm when there is cut in the ground. The time was moderate for the grade though and the form is ordinary but sound.

**NOTEBOOK**
**Crail** has been hinting at a return to winning form and appreciated the ease in the going - he looked uncomfortable on the fast ground when fourth at Newbury latest. He had just about the best apprentice in the race on board to enhance his claims and, having raced just off the pace throughout, dug deep under pressure to hold the challenge of the second. Although likely to go up for this, he will still be on a decent mark and can win again with conditions in his favour.
**Oh So Rosie(IRE)** returned to form with a close-up fourth at Yarmouth earlier in the week, and built on that in second. She momentarily looked as though she would run the winner close, but Crail had enough to spare. If continuing to go the right way she should be back winning.

**Didnt Tell My Wife** won stylishly at Newbury the previous weekend but found the 6lb penalty too much. He still ran well though and a return to a stiffer test may suit.
**Loch Laird** was going on at the end but never looked like winning. He has never won beyond seven furlongs, but shapes as though this is his trip.
**Dash For Cover(IRE)** had his chance and ran one of his better races.
**Fleetwood Bay** took them along early but never looked like keeping up the gallop.

## 4913 EBF MAIDEN STKS 1m
6:05 (6:06) (D) 2-Y-O £6,077 (£1,870; £935; £467) Stalls High

Form RPR
4 **1** **Bayeux De Moi (IRE)**[28] 4078 2-9-0 JPMurtagh 6 78+
(MrsAJPerrett) *racd stands side: trckd ldrs: drvn to ld that gp and overall advantage 1f out: rdn and styd on strly ins last* **13/8**[1]
6 **2** *3* **Just Do It (UAE)**[13] 4544 2-9-0 TEDurcan 11 71+
(MRChannon) *racd far side: trckd ldrs: led that gp ins fnl 2f and ev ch overall: kpt on wl but nt pce of wnr stands side ins last* **40/1**
5 **3** *nk* **Almanshood (USA)**[49] 3483 2-9-0 RHills 1 71
(JHMGosden) *racd stands side: chsd ldrs: rdn and styd on same pce fr over 1f out* **11/2**[2]
**4** *3/4* **My Portfolio (IRE)** 2-9-0 SDrowne 14 69
(RCharlton) *racd far side: bhd and rdn 4f out: styd on fr over 2f out: fin wl but nt rch ldrs* **16/1**
5 **5** *1* **Mobarhen (USA)**[20] 4315 2-9-0 DHolland 8 67
(SirMichaelStoute) *racd stands side: chsd ldrs: led that gp over 2f out: sn rdn: hdd by wnr 1f out: sn one pce* **11/2**[2]
5 **6** *hd* **Knightsbridge Hill (IRE)**[15] 4480 2-9-0 DKinsella 12 66
(AKing) *racd far side: led that gp and up w stands side tl hdd ins fnl 2f: one pce fnl f* **33/1**
4 **7** *1 1/2* **Zamboozle (IRE)**[21] 4290 2-9-0 SCarson 13 63
(DRCElsworth) *racd far side: chsd ldrs: rdn 2f out: wknd ins fnl f* **11/2**[2]
00 **8** *2* **Voir Dire**[34] 3939 2-9-0 RHavlin 2 59
(MrsPNDutfield) *racd stands side: rdn 3f out: styd on same pce fnl 2f and n.d* **50/1**
0 **9** *hd* **Casual Glance**[22] 4272 2-8-9 MartinDwyer 7 53
(AMBalding) *racd stands side: s.i.s: pushed along to chse ldrs 4f out: wknd fnl f* **20/1**
00 **10** *2 1/2* **Sarah Brown (IRE)**[56] 3259 2-8-9 (p) PDoe 10 48
(IAWood) *racd far side: pushed along over 3f out: sme hdwy fr over 1f out* **100/1**
0 **11** *5* **Moshkil (IRE)**[69] 2890 2-9-0 WRyan 5 42
(MPTregoning) *racd stands side: bhd: sme hdwy fnl 2f: n.d* **33/1**
0 **12** *nk* **Shahama (IRE)**[30] 4030 2-9-0 LisaJones 3 41
(MPTregoning) *racd stands side: n.d* **50/1**
462 **13** *nk* **Ragged Glory (IRE)**[34] 3931 2-9-0 77 RLMoore 9 40
(RHannon) *racd far side: chsd ldrs tl swtchd lft to stands side over 2f out and sn wknd* **9/1**[3]
05 **14** *8* **River Biscuit (USA)**[28] 4078 2-9-0 JFortune 4 23
(RHannon) *racd stands side and led that gp tl hdd over 2f out and sn wknd* **20/1**

1m 47.46s (4.49) **Going Correction** +0.50s/f (Yiel) **14** Ran SP% **122.9**
Speed ratings: **97,94,93,92,91 91,90,88,88,85 80,80,79,71**CSF £100.01 TOTE £3.00: £1.20, £3.70, £2.80; EX 98.10.
**Owner** Lady Clague **Bred** Newberry Stud Company **Trained** Pulborough, W Sussex

**FOCUS**
A decent maiden where the field split into two groups and the stands' side had the advantage. The form looks reliable and the winner looks capable of better.

**NOTEBOOK**
**Bayeux De Moi(IRE)** set a decent standard on his debut fourth - Kamikiri and Capable Guest boosting the form - and with this step up to a mile sure to suit and easy going expected to be of no hindrance, he duly obliged in good fashion. He chose to race on the stands' side, but he would have won regardless of where he raced and with better to come he looks worthy of a step into Pattern company, with connections suggesting the Zetland Stakes over a mile two later in the year as a likely target.
**Just Do It(UAE)** improved dramatically on his debut sixth at Lingfield and is evidently going the right way. He raced far side, but did not seem at any real disadvantage and can win his maiden over this trip.
**Almanshood(USA)** came through with a good looking challenge but the winner was always going away from him and he could only plug on. Clearly not blessed with a tremendous amount of speed, he will stay farther now and can also win his maiden.
**My Portfolio(IRE)** ◆, the only debutant in the line-up, has already been gelded but that should not count against him and he shaped with plenty of promise, staying on nicely having taken time to get going. There is more to come from him and he should win his maiden.
**Mobarhen(USA)** made his debut in a fair race at Newcastle and showed only a little improvement for the step up to a mile. He may be more the type for nurseries.
**Knightsbridge Hill(IRE)** ◆ travelled strongly far side, taking them along for most of the way, and improved greatly on his debut fifth. His trainer tends to run some of his better juveniles here and this one will have no trouble winning races.
**Zamboozle(IRE)** showed ability in only a fair Goodwood maiden on his debut but did not build on that. He is better than this and will appreciate a return to a faster surface.
**Voir Dire** is now qualified for a handicap mark and has undoubtedly shown enough promise to win in that sphere.
**Casual Glance** still looks in needs of more time and experience and will do better once qualified for handicaps.
**Ragged Glory(IRE)** *Official explanation: jockey said colt had hung left*

## 4914 GAMEBOOKERS.COM NURSERY 6f
6:35 (6:36) (E) 2-Y-O £3,757 (£1,156; £578; £289) Stalls Centre

Form RPR
5333 **1** **Caly Dancer (IRE)**[19] 4365 2-9-0 77 JFortune 9 90
(DRCElsworth) *bmpd s: bhd: hdwy on ins 3f out: n.m.r fr 2f out: swtchd lft and chal over 1f out: led ins last: drvn out* **6/1**[1]
4502 **2** *1* **Ridder**[23] 4235 2-8-13 76 EAhern 10 86
(DJCoakley) *hld up in tch: smooth hdwy to ld ins fnl 2f: rdn appr fnl f: hdd ins last: kpt on: nt pce of wnr* **7/1**[2]
5305 **3** *5* **Fortnum**[19] 4365 2-8-0 63 RSmith 13 58
(RHannon) *chsd ldrs: rdn 2f out: styd on fr over 1f out but nvr gng pce of ldrs* **10/1**
1651 **4** *shd* **Treat Me Wild (IRE)**[16] 4439 2-8-10 73 RLMoore 3 68
(RHannon) *racd towards stands side 1f: sn veered to far side: bhd: rdn over 2f out: styd on fr over 1f out but nvr gng pce to rch ldr* **6/1**[1]
2252 **5** *nk* **Chutney Mary (IRE)**[15] 4468 2-8-8 71 DaneO'Neill 8 65
(JGPortman) *wnt rt s: sn led: hdd ins fnl 2f: wknd fnl f* **14/1**
0225 **6** *hd* **Flying Pass**[14] 4524 2-8-11 74 (v[1]) DHolland 2 67
(DJSFfrenchDavis) *racd towards stands side 1f: sn veered to join far side and pressed ldrs: ev ch 2f out: wknd fnl f* **6/1**[1]
6120 **7** *3/4* **Bibury Flyer**[12] 4575 2-9-7 84 TEDurcan 4 81+
(MRChannon) *racd towards stands side 1f: sn veered to join far side:bhd: hdwy on rails and n.m.r whn chsng ldrs over 1f out: nt rcvr* **6/1**[1]
645 **8** *10* **Mulberry Wine**[23] 4234 2-9-0 77 DSweeney 1 38
(MBlanshard) *racd towards stands side 1f: sn veered to join far side: nvr nr ldrs* **16/1**
040 **9** *shd* **Sastre (IRE)**[30] 4023 2-7-13 65 (p) JFMcDonald(3) 6 26
(PMPhelan) *chsd ldr: rdn over 2f out: weakning whn hmpd appr fnl f* **33/1**
041 **10** *3 1/2* **Apple Of My Eye**[18] 4399 2-9-2 79 WRyan 12 29
(JRJenkins) *t.k.h: chsd ldrs: rdn over 2f out and sn btn* **9/1**[3]
532 **11** *1* **Avertigo**[23] 4239 2-8-11 74 SDrowne 5 21
(WRMuir) *chsd ldrs over 3f* **14/1**
100 **12** *8* **Street Cred**[13] 4527 2-9-6 83 MartinDwyer 11 6
(AMBalding) *chsd ldrs over 3f* **14/1**

1m 17.57s (2.63) **Going Correction** +0.50s/f (Yiel) **12** Ran SP% **117.6**
Speed ratings: **102,100,94,93,93 93,92,78,78,74 72,62**CSF £46.51 CT £417.13 TOTE £8.30: £2.40, £2.30, £4.80; EX 60.60.
**Owner** The Caledonian Racing Society **Bred** Bryan Ryan **Trained** Whitsbury, Hants

**FOCUS**
A decent peformance frrom Caly Dancer who ran right away from the main pack and had plenty to hold off Ridder. The winning time was very smart for the type of contest.

**NOTEBOOK**
**Caly Dancer(IRE)** has been threatening to win and was well suited by this stiff six furlongs in the ground. He did not get the cleanest of runs, he was bumped at the start and short of room when trying to make ground, but he had raced over seven furlongs latest and that extra stamina saw him through in the final furlong. He does stay seven and should continue to prosper.
**Ridder** has shown improved form since running in nurseries but again finished second - frustrating as he pulled five lengths clear of the third. He will go up for this and it will not make life easy in future.
**Fortnum** ◆ was tracking the leaders throughout but did not have much room to manoeuvre in when he wanted to make his run. He stayed on to just get third on the line and has a race of this nature in him, as he is reportedly a lazy sort who needs plenty of stoking and the likelihood is we have yet to see the best of him.
**Treat Me Wild(IRE)** has recorded both wins on a sound surface and looked far from happy on this ground. Despite that she ran well enough, just losing out on third place, and can be seen to better effect back under faster conditions.
**Chutney Mary(IRE)** had her chance and ran well, just being run out on the places in the final strides.
**Flying Pass** is becoming frustrating and the visor failed to spark any improvement.
**Bibury Flyer** was unlucky not to get closer as she went across to join the far-side group after a furlong - costing her ground - and failed to get much of a run when trying to make headway.
**Street Cred** has not gone on from his debut and is one to leave alone until showing more. *Official explanation: jockey said mount lost its action*

## 4915 WILTON GRAPHICS H'CAP 1m 4f
7:05 (7:05) (D) (0-85,85) 3-Y-O £7,488 (£2,304; £1,152; £576) Stalls High

Form RPR
025 **1** **Topkat (IRE)**[19] 4369 3-8-6 70 DaneO'Neill 1 84+
(DRCElsworth) *t.k.h: stdd rr after 1f: hdwy on outside over 3f out: led ins fnl 2f: sn hrd drvn: hld on wl cl home* **11/1**
00-0 **2** *3/4* **Circassian (IRE)**[16] 4443 3-7-12 62 oh1 JMackay 9 74+
(SirMarkPrescott) *chsd ldrs: rdn and outpcd over 3f out: styd on u.p fr 2f out: kpt on wl fnl f: gng on cl home* **7/2**[2]
1221 **3** *1 3/4* **Velvet Waters**[10] 4618 3-8-3 67 6ex SCarson 4 77
(RFJohnsonHoughton) *chsd ldrs: rdn to ld over 2f out: hdd ins fnl quarter m: outpcd and lost 2nd fnl f* **13/2**[3]
3050 **4** *2 1/2* **Pangloss (IRE)**[20] 4346 3-8-1 65 (p) RLMoore 11 71
(GLMoore) *bhd: hrd drvn fr over 3f out: r.o fr over 1f out: fin wl but nt rch ldrs* **16/1**
3010 **5** *1/2* **Pagan Magic (USA)**[48] 3543 3-8-12 76 LisaJones 8 81
(JARToller) *mid-div: rdn and one pce over 3f out: styd on fr over 1f out but n.d* **12/1**
6154 **6** *1 1/4* **Stage Right**[7] 4715 3-9-7 85 MartinDwyer 3 88
(DRCElsworth) *sn led: hdd after 3f: styd trcking ldr: chal 5f out tl led over 3f out: hdd over 2f out: wknd over 1f out* **5/2**[1]
1030 **7** *3 1/2* **Incursion**[39] 3806 3-9-5 83 EAhern 5 81
(AKing) *remiders after s to chse ldrs: rdn 3f out: wknd over 1f out* **16/1**
032 **8** *4* **Turnstile**[13] 4554 3-8-13 77 RHughes 7 69
(RHannon) *bhd: sme hdwy 5f out: hung lft to outside and rdn 3f out: sn btn* **8/1**
21-0 **9** *5* **Quartino**[44] 3641 3-9-7 85 JFortune 10 70
(JHMGosden) *led after 3f: hdd over 3f out: sn wknd* **20/1**
1224 **10** *5* **Hatch A Plan (IRE)**[12] 4572 3-8-10 74 DHolland 2 51
(RMBeckett) *pressed ldrs tl wknd fr 3f out* **10/1**
-315 **11** *18* **Karamea (SWI)**[48] 3528 3-9-2 80 JPMurtagh 6 30
(JLDunlop) *hld up in rr: sme hdwy 5f out: wknd 3f out* **16/1**

2m 38.26s (1.91) **Going Correction** +0.225s/f (Good) **11** Ran SP% **122.8**
Speed ratings: **102,101,100,98,98 97,95,92,89,85 73**CSF £51.61 CT £283.23 TOTE £10.00: £2.80, £2.60, £2.60; EX 89.10.
**Owner** R Standring **Bred** Kitty's Sister Syndicate **Trained** Whitsbury, Hants

**FOCUS**
A competitive three-year-old handicap in which the form looks decent and the front two look well worth following.

**NOTEBOOK**
**Topkat(IRE)** came into this as one of the less exposed having had only three runs - all over shorter, each time staying on as though this trip was required - and won with a little to spare. Connections, who also owned the 2003 Ebor winner Saint Alebe, are keen to aim him at that race next season, where the extra distance will prove no problem and for the time being he should win again under similar conditions off a mark that will be in the mid-70s, as that would still look very fair indeed.
**Circassian(IRE)** ran well over too short a trip on his seasonal debut and was well served by the extra two furlongs. He will improve again for a mile six and, off a mark in the 60s, should be capable of stringing at least a couple of wins together before the season is out.
**Velvet Waters** has been in great form under much faster conditions and ran well despite of the easy surface. Although set to race off a 4lb higher mark in future, a return to a faster surface will help.
**Pangloss(IRE)** kept grinding away at his own pace to come through for fourth but was never getting to the principals. He is still a maiden after nine starts, but this was better and he is well served by soft ground.
**Pagan Magic(USA)**, disappointing when reportedly struck into at Sandown, ran better, albeit on ground he may have found a little too soft. He is entitled to improve for the run.
**Stage Right** has not looked the same horse of late under softer conditions - he shaped earlier in the season as though they would suit - and again ran below form as he had at Newbury. Given a break and back on faster ground, he should return to something like his best.
**Incursion** received early reminders to get him interested, but he was always toiling towards the rear and never made a move. He has now twice shaped as though this trip stretches him.
**Karamea(SWI)** was nibbled at in the market but again ran way below early-season form - her stable is still struggling to find form.

## 4916 SOVEREIGN WINDOWS & CONSERVATORIES MAIDEN FILLIES' STKS 6f

**7:35** (7:37) (D) 3-Y-O+ **£5,570** (£1,714; £857; £428) **Stalls** Centre

Form RPR

45 **1** **Rachel's Verdict**[13] 4555 3-8-11 ........ JPMurtagh 9 75+
(JRFanshawe) *hld up in rr: hdwy and green over 2f out: rdn and hung rt over 1f out: swtchd lft and rapid hdwy ins last: led last strides* **11/2**

0503 **2** *hd* **Zwadi (IRE)**[15] 4496 3-8-11 72 ........ DaneO'Neill 6 74
(HCandy) *trckd ldr: led ins fnl 3f: rdn and kpt on wl fr over 1f out: ct last strides* **9/2**[3]

00 **3** *1 ¾* **Miss Monza**[7] 4718 3-8-11 ........ TEDurcan 3 69
(BRMillman) *chsd ldrs: drvn along fr 3f out: styd on fr over 1f out but nt pce to chal ins last* **33/1**

53 **4** *shd* **Tetcott (IRE)**[7] 4718 3-8-11 ........ DHolland 1 68+
(MPTregoning) *in tch: hdwy on outside fr 3f out: rdn over 2f out: styd on ins fnl f but nt pce of ldrs* **7/4**[1]

3235 **5** *1 ½* **All Quiet**[71] 2808 3-8-11 75 ........ RHughes 11 64
(RHannon) *led tl hdd ins fnl 3f: styd chsng ldrs tl wknd ins fnl f* **4/1**[2]

**6** *nk* **Magic Spin** 4-9-0 ........ SCarson 7 63
(RFJohnsonHoughton) *bhd: rdn and hdwy 1/2-way: styd on ins fnl f but nvr gng pce to rch ldrs* **14/1**

5000 **7** *nk* **Gentle Raindrop (IRE)**[12] 4580 3-8-11 62 ........ (b[1]) JFortune 4 62
(SKirk) *bmpd s: bhd: rdn 3f out: styd on fnl f but nvr gng pce to rch ldrs* **20/1**

**8** *2 ½* **Sabander Bay (USA)** 3-8-11 ........ RHavlin 5 55
(JHMGosden) *s.i.s and wnt lft s: bhd: pushed along 1/2-way: mod prog fnl f* **8/1**

0/0- **9** *5* **Society Pet**[567] 430 5-8-7 40 ........ DerekNolan(7) 8 40
(DGBridgwater) *chsd ldrs: rdn 3f out: wknd 2f out* **100/1**

**10** *10* **Fiery Angel (IRE)** 3-8-8 ........ LPKeniry(3) 10 10
(AGNewcombe) *t.k.h: chsd ldrs over 3f* **20/1**

1m 18.32s (3.38) **Going Correction** +0.50s/f (Yiel)
**WFA** 3 from 4yo+ 3lb **10** Ran SP% **121.2**
Speed ratings: **97,96,94,94,92 91,91,88,81,68**CSF £30.53 TOTE £6.50: £1.90, £1.80, £8.10; EX 30.00.

**Owner** M Fisch **Bred** P And Mrs Venner **Trained** Newmarket, Suffolk

**FOCUS**

Rachel's Verdict beat a moderate bunch and will improve again for the experience, but the form looks sound enough if limited.

**NOTEBOOK**

**Rachel's Verdict** has looked in experienced in two previous runs and again showed signs of greeness when asked to go about her effort. It did not look as though she was going to get there until picking up strongly in the final strides and edging out Zwadi. There will be better to come from her in handicaps as she continues to improve with experience, and she should stay an extra furlong.

**Zwadi(IRE)** remains a maiden after 11 starts and connections will be disappointed as she looked to have done enough. Her turn will come one day.

**Miss Monza** is now qualified for a handicap mark and improved dramatically on recent form.

**Tetcott(IRE)** is evidently one of her stable's lesser lights, but has enough ability to pick up a small race when returned to farther.

**All Quiet** is another who continues to frustrate.

**Sabander Bay(USA)**, whilst entitled to improve for the experience, and boasting top connections, showed little and is nothing special.

## 4917 EUROPEAN BREEDERS' FUND CLASSIFIED STKS 6f 212y

**8:05** (8:06) (D) 3-Y-O+ **£8,209** (£2,526; £1,263; £631) **Stalls** Centre

Form RPR

1331 **1** **Eisteddfod**[32] 3995 3-8-11 84 ........ NDeSouza(5) 6 96+
(PFICole) *trckd ldrs: n.m.r and swtchd lft 2f out: led appr fnl f: styd on wl whn strly chal fnl f* **7/4**[1]

0153 **2** *hd* **St Pancras (IRE)**[36] 3884 4-9-3 80 ........ DHolland 7 91
(NACallaghan) *s.i.s: bhd: hdwy on outside fr 2f out: drvn to chal 1f out: pressed wnr thrght fnl f but a hld* **7/2**[2]

2460 **3** *4* **Waterside (IRE)**[13] 4553 5-9-3 80 ........ RLMoore 5 81
(GLMoore) *led: rdn over 2f out: hdd appr fnl f: wknd ins last* **11/2**

5254 **4** *nk* **Vienna's Boy (IRE)**[23] 4237 3-9-0 82 ........ DaneO'Neill 1 82
(RHannon) *trckds ldrs: rdn to chal ins fnl 2f: wknd ins fnl f* **14/1**

2005 **5** *1 ¾* **Star Pupil**[54] 3347 3-8-12 79 ........ MartinDwyer 4 75
(AMBalding) *rr but in tch: rdn over 2f out: wknd over 1f out* **9/1**

0353 **6** *2 ½* **Ammenayr (IRE)**[9] 4652 4-9-3 78 ........ (v[1]) JFortune 3 69
(TGMills) *s.i.s: rr but in tch: effrt and rdn over 2f out: sn btn* **12/1**

1152 **7** *2 ½* **Goodenough Mover**[28] 4084 8-9-5 82 ........ SDrowne 2 64
(JSKing) *pressed ldr over 3f: wknd over 1f out* **9/2**[3]

1m 30.45s (1.45) **Going Correction** +0.50s/f (Yiel)
**WFA** 3 from 4yo+ 5lb **7** Ran SP% **116.5**
Speed ratings: **111,110,106,105,103 101,98**CSF £8.33 TOTE £2.90: £1.60, £2.70; EX 8.50 Place 6 £75.63, Place 5 £49.02.

**Owner** Elite Racing Club **Bred** Elite Racing Club **Trained** Whatcombe, Oxon

**FOCUS**

This looked a tight heat on paper and the front two pulled clear of the third, with the progressive Eisteddfod coming out on top. The winning time was decent for the grade, but the form is only fair.

**NOTEBOOK**

**Eisteddfod** had the most progressive profile of these, having filled the placings in all fourth starts and added to his win tally, making it three, with a gutsy display. He looked set to be passed at one stage by St Pancras, but he showed a good attitude and dug deep to hold that one off. There is more to come from him and should continue to prosper.

**St Pancras(IRE)** was waited with in rear and it looked sure to pay dividends when he drew alongside Eisteddfod, but he was outbattled in the finish. This was a decent performance as he pulled four lengths clear of the third on ground he would probably have found too soft, and he should continue to run well.

**Waterside(IRE)** has lost his form the last twice, but this was better effort and he seemed suited by the return to a smaller field.

**Vienna's Boy(IRE)** seems to be struggling to find his best trip at present, and did nothing to suggest this was it.

**Star Pupil** travelled nicely but, whilst not having much room when angling to manoeuvre, he found little once getting into the clear and continues to frustrate.

**Goodenough Mover** has been in the form of his life this season but ran a rare bad race, with the ground the only possible excuse.

T/Plt: £77.00 to a £1 stake. Pool: £36,918.30. 349.75 winning tickets. T/Qpdt: £44.60 to a £1 stake. Pool: £2,934.50. 48.60 winning tickets. ST

# 4688 SANDOWN (R-H)

Friday, August 20

**OFFICIAL GOING: Good to soft (soft in places) on round course, soft on sprint course**

In races run on the round course, the runners raced up the centre of the track in the straight.

Wind: almost nil Weather: fine but cloudy

## 4918 BETFRED "THE BONUS KING" NURSERY 5f 6y

**2:00** (2:01) (D) 2-Y-O **£6,841** (£2,105; £1,052; £526) **Stalls** High

Form RPR

321 **1** **Countdown**[14] 4507 2-9-7 81 ........ SSanders 2 90+
(SirMarkPrescott) *hld up in last pair: gd prog on outer to ld wl over 1f out: shkn up to draw clr ins fnl f: readily* **2/1**[1]

2120 **2** *1 ½* **Kwame**[24] 4217 2-9-1 75 ........ SDrowne 3 79
(MissECLavelle) *sn chsd ldrs: rdn and unable qck wl over 1f out: kpt on to take 2nd nr fin* **16/1**

5401 **3** *nk* **Nova Tor (IRE)**[6] 4752 2-9-11 85 6ex ........ IMongan 7 88
(NPLittmoden) *sn w ldr: led 1/2-way to wl over 1f out: pressed wnr tl fdd wl ins fnl f* **7/2**[3]

4002 **4** *1 ¾* **Favouring (IRE)**[7] 4700 2-8-4 64 ........ AMcCarthy 1 61
(RAFahey) *hld up in last pair: outpcd 2f out: kpt on one pce fnl f* **11/4**[2]

0325 **5** *1 ¾* **Rusky Dusky (USA)**[9] 4637 2-9-5 79 ........ PDobbs 5 70
(RHannon) *t.k.h: hld up bhd ldrs: lost pl and nt clr run 2f out : n.d after* **25/1**

0633 **6** *¾* **Alsu (IRE)**[14] 4508 2-8-12 72 ........ MartinDwyer 4 60
(AMBalding) *led for 100yds: chsd ldrs after: rdn 2f out: fdd over 1f out* **10/1**

456 **7** *1* **Ninja Storm (IRE)**[14] 4514 2-9-1 75 ........ RLMoore 6 60
(GLMoore) *racd freely: led after 100yds to 1/2-way: sn lost pl u.p* **7/1**

65.21 secs (3.02) **Going Correction** +0.45s/f (Yiel) **7** Ran SP% **113.5**
Speed ratings: **93,90,90,87,84 83,81**CSF £34.20 TOTE £2.80: £1.90, £4.60; EX 27.40.

**Owner** Cheveley Park Stud **Bred** Lady Fairhaven **Trained** Newmarket, Suffolk

**FOCUS**

A decent nursery run at a strong early pace and the form looks solid.

**NOTEBOOK**

**Countdown** ◆ is improving with every run and followed up his Haydock maiden success in good style. With further progression likely, he should complete the hat-trick in this sphere.

**Kwame**, out of her depth in the Molecomb on her previous outing, was suited by the drop in grade and ran well. However, she took a while to pick up and was never a threat to the winner, suggesting she will be suited by a step up to six furlongs.

**Nova Tor(IRE)**, 3lb well-in under her 6lb penalty for a success in a competitive Newmarket nursery, recovered well from a slow start and ran well under a positive ride, sticking on gamely when headed. Things will be even tougher off her new mark and she appeals as one to oppose in the near future, although she is noticeably tough.

**Favouring(IRE)**, runner-up on his nursery debut over a furlong further at Catterick on his previous start, was 4lb lower than in future but just got going too late on this drop back in trip and looks better suited by six furlongs.

**Rusky Dusky(USA)**, making his nursery debut off a mark 2lb higher than in future, had shaped as though this trip would suit at Salisbury on his previous start, but he got stuck in behind horses and did not get a clear run. He is better than he showed and clearly has the ability to win a race, but would help his chances if settling better.

**Ninja Storm(IRE)** had shown real promise on all three of his previous starts, most noticeably when an unlucky sixth on the Polytrack on his previous outing but, making his handicap debut, he was disappointing. He had much more use made of him than had been the case in his previous runs and it did not appear to suit.

## 4919 COMBI UK CONDITIONS STKS 1m 14y

**2:30** (2:33) (C) 2-Y-O **£8,401** (£2,758; £1,379) **Stalls** High

Form RPR

2 **1** **Brahminy Kite (USA)**[9] 4625 2-8-12 ........ DHolland 1 92+
(MJohnston) *rn green: trckd ldr: shkn up to chal 3f out: narrow ld jst over 1f out: edgd rt but styd on wl* **2/1**[2]

1044 **2** *2* **Destinate (IRE)**[13] 4527 2-9-1 100 ........ PDobbs 3 91
(RHannon) *led: pressed 3f out: rdn and hdd jst over 1f out: unable qck ins fnl f* **8/13**[1]

1 **3** *6* **Simply St Lucia**[65] 2985 2-8-7 ........ SSanders 2 70
(JRWeymes) *s.i.s: a last: rdn 3f out: wknd 2f out* **10/1**[3]

1m 46.54s (2.62) **Going Correction** +0.25s/f (Good) **3** Ran SP% **104.3**
Speed ratings: **96,94,88**CSF £3.59 TOTE £3.00; EX 6.10.

**Owner** Abdulla Buhaleeba **Bred** Brereton C Jones **Trained** Middleham Moor, N Yorks

**FOCUS**

A disappointing turnout and they went pretty steady early on, but a decent enough enough performance from Brahminy Kite, who won despite running green, although the form is difficult to assess. All three runners made there way over to the stands' side in the straight, but the first two home drifted under pressure and ended up on the other side of the track.

**NOTEBOOK**

**Brahminy Kite(USA)** ran green when a well-beaten second on his debut in a Beverley maiden and again showed signs of inexperience. He needed to be cajoled along to go down to the start and in the race itself he drifted under pressure and took an age to get on top, but his ability and stamina saw him through. He does not hold any big-race entries, but is open to significant improvement and is one to have on your side.

**Destinate(IRE)**, slightly below his best in the Shergar Cup Juvenile at Ascot on his previous outing, was stepping up to a mile but was again below the form he showed to finish fourth in the Group Two Vintage Stakes. Happy enough to make the running, as he did when winning his maiden, he travelled strongly for Dobbs but did not find as much as had looked likely and was ultimately outstayed. He was carried right in the closing stages but it did not effect the result and he still has to prove his Goodwood run was not a fluke.

**Simply St Lucia**, off the mark in a very weak Southwell maiden over seven furlongs on her debut, found this much tougher and never landed a blow.

## 4920 COMBI UK H'CAP 1m 14y

**3:05** (3:05) (C) (0-90,90) 3-Y-O+ **£12,934** (£4,906; £2,453; £1,115) **Stalls** High

Form RPR

4003 **1** **Norton (IRE)**[8] 4690 7-10-0 90 ........ JFortune 4 101
(TGMills) *mde all: rdn 2f out: drvn 2l clr ent fnl f: hld on wl* **6/1**[2]

41 **2** *¾* **Literatim**[20] 4316 4-9-8 84 ........ DHolland 2 93+
(LMCumani) *trckd ldrs: rdn and unable qck over 1f out: styd on to chse wnr jst ins fnl f: clsd nr fin: a hld* **9/1**[3]

1154 **3** *1 ½* **Parnassian**[12] 4569 4-8-4 71 ........ RThomas(5) 9 77
(GBBalding) *trckd ldrs: drvn 2f out: prog 1f out: styd on same pce fnl f* **5/1**[1]

3431 **4** *nk* **African Sahara (USA)**[13] 4558 5-9-6 **82**..............................(t) OUrbina 1 88
(MissDMountain) *hld up in rr: gng easily over 2f out: shkn up and nt qckn over 1f out: rdn and styd on fnl f: nt rch ldrs* **6/1**[2]
0645 **5** *1 1/4* **Linning Wine (IRE)**[11] 4613 8-9-5 **81**.................................... SCarson 8 84
(BGPowell) *hld up in last: effrt 2f out: styd on fnl f: nvr rchd ldrs* **33/1**
3242 **6** *1 1/2* **Spirit's Awakening**[8] 4690 5-7-12 **60** oh2.............................. JMackay 3 60
(JAkehurst) *t.k.h: pressed wnr: ev ch over 1f out: wknd fnl f* **5/1**[1]
1300 **7** *hd* **Retirement**[42] 3714 5-9-4 **80**........................................ PRobinson 5 79
(MHTompkins) *racd in midfield: rdn and effrt 2f out: cl up over 1f out: wknd fnl f* **10/1**
110- **8** *nk* **Pagan Prince**[308] 5618 7-8-11 **73**.......................................... LisaJones 10 72
(JARToller) *hld up towards rr: rdn 2f out: one pce and no ch whn squeezed out ins fnl f* **25/1**
3000 **9** *1 1/4* **Finished Article (IRE)**[21] 4287 7-9-11 **87**.......................... DaneO'Neill 7 83
(DRCElsworth) *hld up towards rr: rdn over 2f out: struggling and btn over 1f out* **11/1**
0654 **10** *3/4* **Lifted Way**[8] 4690 5-9-2 **78**........................................................ SDrowne 6 73
(PRChamings) *prom: rdn over 2f out: wknd jst over 1f out* **5/1**[1]

1m 44.27s (0.35) **Going Correction** +0.25s/f (Good) **10** Ran SP% **112.8**
Speed ratings: **108,107,105,105,104 102,102,102,100,100**CSF £56.84 CT £294.60 TOTE £5.30: £2.60, £2.80, £1.50; EX 61.50.
**Owner** T G Mills **Bred** Kilfrush Stud Ltd **Trained** Headley, Surrey

**FOCUS**
A competitive handicap and, although they did not go flat to the boards, the pace was reasonable the form looks reliable. They raced up the centre of the track in the straight.

**NOTEBOOK**
**Norton(IRE)** had not been successful since landing the 2002 Royal Hunt Cup, yet had run several creditable races in defeat and was just 1lb lower. He got his own way out in front and was very much there to be shot at when the pace quickened, but he found plenty in front to gain a much-deserved success. Given that he has never won off a mark higher than 91, he must be opposed in this sphere if going up 2lb or more.
**Literatim**, a slightly fortunate winner at Doncaster on his previous outing, looked to better that form on this first venture into handicap company, finding only the battled-hardened winner too good. Very lightly raced, there should be more to come and he appeals as one to have on your side.
**Parnassian** would have appreciated the return to an easy surface, but he had no easy task off a mark 10lb higher than when last successful and, for the time being, is vulnerable to better-handicapped rivals.
**African Sahara(USA)** goes well here and also handles easy ground, so everything seemed prime for a big run. Indeed he did run well, but did not find as much as had looked likely and has never won a handicap off a mark higher than 78.
**Linning Wine(IRE)**, well held on his return from a two-month break at Windsor on his previous start, stepped up on that effort despite proving unable to pose a serious threat to the principals. He has never won on turf, but is running into form and should do even better over a little further.
**Spirit's Awakening** was 9lb higher than when gaining his only previous success but 2lb lower than in future. After racing keenly, he did not last home.
**Lifted Way** was a course and distance winner in similar conditions earlier in the season, but that was off a 4lb lower mark in Class E company. He had been running well in similar events recently, but this was disappointing. *Official explanation: jockey said horse was unsuited by the good to soft, soft in places going*

## 4921 COMBI UK PREMIER CLAIMING STKS 1m 2f 7y
**3:35** (3:36) (D) 3-Y-O **£6,711** (£2,065; £1,032; £516) **Stalls** High

Form RPR
5020 **1** **Top Spec (IRE)**[6] 4749 3-8-7 76.............................................. RLMoore 3 81
(RHannon) *racd in 3rd tl chsd ldr 5f out: clsd to ld wl over 1f out: lugged rt but clr fnl f* **6/4**[1]
2556 **2** *6* **Rabitatit (IRE)**[27] 4145 3-7-6 62............................... NataliaGemelova(7) 4 63
(JGMO'Shea) *t.k.h: led after 2f: clr 4f out: hdd wl over 1f out: no ch w wnr* **10/1**
6431 **3** *5* **Treason Trial**[9] 4654 3-8-6 57 ow2.......................................... SDrowne 2 62
(MrsStefLiddiard) *hld up in last: outpcd 4f out: rdn 3f out: no prog* **7/2**[3]
1000 **4** *1* **Another Choice (IRE)**[35] 3915 3-9-0 73.................................(t) EAhern 1 68
(NPLittmoden) *led for 2f: trckd ldr tl taken v wd bnd 5f out: rdn 3f out : no prog and btn 2f out: wknd* **7/4**[2]

2m 14.03s (3.85) **Going Correction** +0.25s/f (Good) **4** Ran SP% **107.7**
Speed ratings: **94,89,85,84**CSF £13.57 TOTE £2.10; EX 13.80.
**Owner** The Hill Top Partnership **Bred** Mrs Jacqueline Donnelly **Trained** East Everleigh, Wilts

**FOCUS**
A very uncompetitive claimer, run in a modest time, and not a race to dwell on. They raced down the centre of the track, although Another Choice came very wide into the straight in search of better ground and finished well beaten.

**NOTEBOOK**
**Top Spec(IRE)** had an obvious chance at the weights but had to prove himself on both the ground and at the trip. The conditions were not a problem against this calibre of opposition, although he did carry his head quite high, and it would have been interesting had he had a serious challenger.
**Rabitatit(IRE)** did not appear suited by easy ground on her only previous try on it, but she seemed to go through it well enough on this occasion. However, she was far too keen early on and was readily held by the winner.
**Treason Trial** was well beaten on his previous run on soft ground and again failed to run to his best on an easy surface. A disappointing debut for his new trainer, but he did have it all to do at the weights and better can be expected back on a faster surface.
**Another Choice(IRE)**, dropped in grade, came very wide into the straight, presumably in search of better ground, but he found little under pressure and has now finished last on three of his last four starts.

## 4922 EUROPEAN BREEDERS FUND COMBI UK MAIDEN STKS 7f 16y
**4:10** (4:11) (D) 2-Y-O **£7,263** (£2,235; £1,117; £558) **Stalls** High

Form RPR
0 **1** **Diktatorial**[21] 4295 2-9-0 ................................................ MartinDwyer 4 97+
(AMBalding) *mde all: hung bdly lft wl over 2f out: drew clr over 1f out: hung lft again ins fnl f: unchal* **7/1**
3 **2** *5* **Surwaki (USA)**[30] 4030 2-9-0 .............................................. PRobinson 9 84
(CGCox) *chsd ldrs: rdn to chse wnr 2f out: no imp* **13/2**[3]
**3** *shd* **Glen Ida** 2-9-0 ................................................................... RMullen 7 84+
(MLWBell) *bustled along in rr early: prog over 2f out: rdn and kpt on fnl f* **8/1**
**4** *4* **Torrens (IRE)** 2-9-0 .......................................................... DHolland 6 74+
(MJohnston) *racd in midfield: pushed along over 2f out: outpcd wl over 1f out: one pce after* **10/1**
65 **5** *2* **Silverleaf**[21] 4290 2-9-0 ........................................................ IMongan 3 69
(MRChannon) *prom: chsd wnr over 3f out to 2f out: wknd fnl f* **25/1**
0 **6** *1* **Penalty Kick (IRE)**[35] 3913 2-9-0 .............................................. OUrbina 1 66
(NACallaghan) *s.i.s: settled wl in rr: sme prog over 2f out: nudged along and no imp over 1f out: fdd* **33/1**
**7** *1/2* **Speightstown** 2-9-0 .............................................................. EAhern 12 65
(PFICole) *prom: pushed along bef 1/2-way: rdn and struggling 2f out: fdd* **3/1**[2]
**8** *1/2* **Night Guest (IRE)** 2-9-0 ................................................... DaneO'Neill 13 64
(RHannon) *mostly chsd wnr to over 3f out: sn outpcd and btn* **20/1**
**9** *2* **Oneiro Way (IRE)** 2-9-0 ....................................................... DSweeney 5 59
(PRChamings) *dwlt: hld up in rr: shkn up over 2f out: no prog* **33/1**
00 **10** *3 1/2* **South O'The Border**[14] 4523 2-9-0 ........................................ GCarter 8 50
(TGMills) *hld up in last: pushed along over 3f out: no ch fnl 2f* **33/1**
**11** *1 1/2* **Sovereign Spirit (IRE)** 2-9-0 ............................................. SDrowne 14 46
(PWHarris) *dwlt: sn in midfield: shkn up 3f out: wknd 2f out* **20/1**
**12** *nk* **Wiltshire (IRE)** 2-9-0 ......................................................... RLappin 10 46
(MRChannon) *reminder after 1f: a in rr: rdn and wknd 2f out* **33/1**
**13** *1 1/4* **Strike Gold** 2-9-0 ................................................................ PDobbs 2 42
(SKirk) *racd wd and rn green: a towards rr: struggling over 2f out* **20/1**
**14** *6* **Red Admiral (USA)** 2-9-0 ..................................................... LDettori 11 27
(SaeedBinSuroor) *taken down early and walked to post: prom tl wknd 3f out* **11/4**[1]

1m 31.24s (0.15) **Going Correction** +0.25s/f (Good) **14** Ran SP% **127.6**
Speed ratings: **109,103,103,98,96 95,94,94,91,87 86,85,84,77**CSF £49.14 TOTE £9.10: £2.70, £1.90, £2.60; EX 44.10.
**Owner** Tweenhills Thurloe **Bred** Mrs D O Joly **Trained** Kingsclere, Hants

**FOCUS**
A maiden capable of producing some very smart sorts; subsequent dual Listed winner Rimrod beat Oasis Dream in this two years previously and Derby winner North Light could manage only second in last year's renewal. This year's running looked of a decent standard especially as the time was very smart indeed for the grade, and the winner is potentially very useful. The field once again raced up the centre of the track in the straight, although Diktatorial did hang towards the stands' side.

**NOTEBOOK**
**Diktatorial ♦**, made to wait in the stalls for around seven minutes before offering some promise in a competitive conditions race at Newmarket on his debut, improved on that form to run out a decisive winner. Out in front on his own for a long time, he showed inexperience rather than waywardness by twice lugging to his left in the straight, but he did not lose much momentum in doing so and was simply too good for these lot. He handled the conditions better than some of these, but should be effective back on decent ground and looks a smart prospect. He does not hold any Group-race entries at the moment, but looks worth stepping up in grade - his stable won this two years previously with subsequent dual Listed-winner Rimrod.
**Surwaki(USA)**, an encouraging third in a reasonable fast-ground course and distance maiden on his debut, handled these much slower conditions well enough, but was simply no match for the winner having raced a touch keenly early on. He should find a similar race before too much longer.
**Glen Ida**, a 62,000gns half-brother to a winner in the USA, has been given a Derby entry. He never really looked like getting to the winner, but kept on well to make an encouraging debut and should improve considerably for the outing.
**Torrens(IRE)**, a 100,000euros first foal, out of a winner in the USA, made a pleasing introduction on a surface his breeding suggests would have been soft enough. He is another who can be expected to improve.
**Silverleaf** ran respectably but was ultimately well held and is now qualified for a nursery mark.
**Speightstown**, out of a useful 12-furlong winner in France, sister to the top-class middle-distance performer Fragrant Mix, was quite well-backed on course but could manage no better than mid-division. However, both his starting price and Group-race entries (Royal Lodge and Dewhurst) suggest he is thought capable of better and is not one to give up on just yet.
**Red Admiral(USA)**, a half-brother to the smart stayer Yorkshire, is entered in the Royal Lodge and next year's Derby. Sent off favourite to make a winning debut, he ran a shocker but is another who is evidently thought capable of better. *Official explanation: trainer had no explanation for the poor form shown*

## 4923 BETFRED 430 BRANCHES NATIONWIDE H'CAP 5f 6y
**4:45** (4:45) (E) (0-75,75) 3-Y-O+ **£5,642** (£1,736; £868; £434) **Stalls** High

Form RPR
0031 **1** **White Ledger (IRE)**[7] 4701 5-8-7 **54** 6ex..............................(v) PDobbs 5 63+
(RAFahey) *settled towards rr: swtchd to outer 2f out: rdn and prog over 1f out: r.o to ld last 100yds* **7/4**[1]
6035 **2** *nk* **Prince Cyrano**[14] 4522 5-9-10 **71**............................................ RMullen 9 79
(WJMusson) *trckd ldrs: nt clr run over 1f out: prog ent fnl f : chal last 100yds: jst outpcd by wnr* **7/2**[2]
0000 **3** *1/2* **Mayzin (IRE)**[13] 4546 4-7-13 **46**.......................................... AMcCarthy 12 52
(RMFlower) *led to 1/2-way: styd cl up: effrt to chal again 1f out: ev ch last 100yds: one pce* **14/1**
0055 **4** *nk* **Pulse**[5] 4774 6-8-11 **58**..........................................................(p) PFitzsimons 7 63
(JMBradley) *t.k.h: prom: led 2f out: hdd and one pce last 100yds* **13/2**[3]
5000 **5** *1 1/2* **Ela Figura**[23] 4232 4-7-6 **46**...................................(p) NataliaGemelova(7) 8 46
(AWCarroll) *t.k.h: prom: n.m.r and lost pl 2f out: one pce after* **20/1**
0005 **6** *1/2* **A Teen**[7] 4727 6-8-0 **54**................................................. KristinStubbs(7) 10 53
(PHowling) *towards rr: effrt over 1f out: bmpd along and kpt on one pce* **14/1**
00 **7** *1 1/2* **Free Wheelin (IRE)**[64] 3025 4-9-2 **63**.................................. MTebbutt 6 57
(WJarvis) *dwlt: racd in last pair: rdn over 1f out: kpt on ins fnl f : no ch* **9/1**
0005 **8** *nk* **Crewes Miss Isle**[29] 4052 3-8-8 **60**..................................... LPKeniry(3) 4 53
(AGNewcombe) *hld up in last pair: rdn wl over 1f out: no imp on ldrs* **25/1**
0000 **9** *3/4* **Multahab**[4] 4800 5-7-10 **50** ow5.......................................(t) LiamJones(7) 2 40
(PSMcentee) *racd in midfield: cl enough over 1f out: wknd fnl f* **14/1**
0000 **10** *1 1/2* **Boanerges (IRE)**[4] 4800 7-7-10 **48**.......................................... RThomas(5) 1 33
(JMBradley) *prom: led 1/2-way to 2f out: wknd fnl f* **20/1**
0106 **11** *3/4* **Kallista's Pride**[21] 4299 4-8-13 **60**.........................................(v[1]) IMongan 3 43
(JRBest) *dwlt and stmbld sn after s: effrt and rdn on outer 2f out: no prog whn n.m.r over 1f out: fdd* **16/1**

63.69 secs (1.50) **Going Correction** +0.45s/f (Yiel)
**WFA** 3 from 4yo+ 2lb **11** Ran SP% **121.2**
Speed ratings: **106,105,104,104,101 101,98,98,96,94 93**CSF £7.47 CT £68.62 TOTE £2.50: £1.20, £1.80, £4.20; EX 13.60 Place 6 £177.41, Place 5 £71.75.
**Owner** Castlemead Developments Limited **Bred** E Tynan **Trained** Musley Bank, N Yorks

**FOCUS**
Just a moderate sprint handicap, but ordinary form but sound.

**NOTEBOOK**
**White Ledger(IRE)**, 7lb lower than when last successful in a handicap, confirmed he is back in good heart by following up his recent success in a Catterick claimer. He should not go up much for this and could well complete the hat-trick in similar company.
**Prince Cyrano** gained both his previous wins over six furlongs, but he is fully effective over this trip and has to be considered a little unlucky, as he had to wait for gap while the eventual winner got a good run on the outside.
**Mayzin(IRE)** was racing over a bare five furlongs for just the second time, but showed plenty of pace to recover having stumbled at the start. He is a very reasonable mark and could find a similarly moderate affair whilst in this sort of form. *Official explanation: jockey said gelding had stumbled on leaving the stalls*
**Pulse** has gained both his previous wins on fast ground, but he handles an easy surface and ran respectably.
**Ela Figura**, with the cheekpieces back on, may have been closer with better luck but remains winless from 33 starts.

**Boanerges(IRE)** *Official explanation: jockey said gelding hung right immediately after leaving the stalls*
**Kallista's Pride** *Official explanation: jockey said filly clipped heels on leaving the stalls*
T/Plt: £47.80 to a £1 stake. Pool: £38,594.60. 588.55 winning tickets. T/Qpdt: £9.60 to a £1 stake. Pool: £2,422.50. 185.30 winning tickets. JN

# 4878 SOUTHWELL (L-H)

Friday, August 20

**OFFICIAL GOING: Standard changing to standard to fast after 6.50 (race 4)**

## 4924 AT THE RACES ON NTL, IRELAND MEDIAN AUCTION MAIDEN STKS — 5f (F)

**5:20** (5:25) (E) 2-Y-O — **£3,867** (£1,190; £595; £297) **Stalls** High

Form — RPR

6246 **1** **Komac**[48] 3531 2-9-0 69 .... SSanders 1 — 65
(BAMcmahon) *in tch far side: hdwy 1/2-way: rdn to ld over 1f out: styd on* **2/1**[1]

0400 **2** 3/4 **Tartatartufata**[4] 4803 2-8-9 60 .... JoannaBadger 3 — 57
(DShaw) *a cl up: led 2f out: sn rdn and hdd over 1f out: kpt on u.p fnl f* **14/1**

**3** 1 1/2 **Second Reef** 2-9-0 .... GParkin 6 — 57
(RAFahey) *a.p: effrt and ev ch 2f out: sn rdn and one pce appr last* **14/1**

46 **4** 5 **Zantero**[19] 4359 2-8-11 .... PMulrennan(3) 5 — 40
(RPElliott) *midfield far side: hdwy 2f out: sn rdn and kpt on: nrst fin* **10/1**

60 **5** *shd* **Eukleia (USA)**[27] 4137 2-8-9 .... DAllan 7 — 34
(TDBarron) *led: rdn along 1/2-way: hdd 2f out and grad wknd* **6/1**[3]

02 **6** *hd* **Ducal Diva**[23] 4245 2-8-2 .... DFentiman(7) 11 — 34
(JRWeymes) *cl up towards stands side: rdn and ch 2f out: drvn and wknd appr last* **7/1**

0 **7** *hd* **Jessica's Style (IRE)**[73] 2758 2-8-9 .... JBramhill 9 — 33
(JGGiven) *in tch: rdn along 1/2-way: kpt on appr last* **33/1**

**8** 1 1/4 **Desperation (IRE)** 2-9-0 .... DarrenWilliams 13 — 34
(KRBurke) *s.i.s: bhd and sn rdn along: hdwy wl over 1f out: kpt on ins last: nrst fin* **22/1**

**9** 3/4 **Russian Rio (IRE)** 2-8-9 .... RoryMoore(5) 15 — 31
(PCHaslam) *chsd ldrs stands side: rdn along 2f out: drvn and wknd over 1f out* **4/1**[2]

6 **10** 2 1/2 **All A Dream**[25] 4187 2-8-6 .... DCorby(3) 12 — 17
(RGuest) *bhd stands side tl sme late hdwy* **25/1**

55 **11** 3/4 **One Of Each (IRE)**[11] 4607 2-8-9 .... DaleGibson 14 — 15
(DCarroll) *prom stands side: rdn along over 2f out: grad wknd* **16/1**

0 **12** 1 3/4 **Preskani**[12] 4567 2-9-0 .... RFitzpatrick 2 — 13
(MrsNMacauley) *a rr far side* **66/1**

0400 **13** 3/4 **Make It Happen Now**[9] 4637 2-8-2 50 .... BO'Neill(7) 4 — 6
(SCBurrough) *a rr far side* **50/1**

**14** 3 **Mochaccino (IRE)** 2-8-4 .... HayleyTurner(5) 8 — —
(DShaw) *bhd fr 1/2-way* **28/1**

**15** 2 **Imperatrice** 2-8-9 .... MHenry 16 — —
(RMHCowell) *s.i.s: a bhd* **20/1**

60.11 secs (-0.29) **Going Correction** -0.20s/f (Stan) — **15** Ran SP% **131.2**
Speed ratings: **94,92,90,82,82 81,81,79,78,74 73,70,69,64,61**CSF £34.29 TOTE £2.60: £1.10, £7.60, £10.10; EX 36.40.
**Owner** Mrs J McMahon **Bred** D Lowe **Trained** Hopwas, Staffs

**FOCUS**
An ordinary maiden in which those drawn low appeared to have the advantage, but the form is nothing special.

**NOTEBOOK**
**Komac** took advantage of this easier task to finally get off the mark. He should be capable of picking up a nursery off his current rating.
**Tartatartufata** is rated 9lb behind the winning on official ratings, so in the circumstances this was a sound effort.
**Second Reef**, out of a mare that won over this trip as a juvenile, can be expected to improve for the experience.
**Zantero** found this trip too sharp for him.

## 4925 ST BERNARD OF CLAIRVAUX'S (S) STKS — 1m (F)

**5:50** (5:53) (G) 3-Y-0+ — **£2,611** (£746; £373) **Stalls** Low

Form — RPR

0062 **1** **Zarin (IRE)**[11] 4605 6-9-4 55 .... SSanders 8 — 67
(DWChapman) *mde all: rdn along over 1f out: styd on wl fnl f* **7/4**[1]

4060 **2** 1 1/2 **Kingston Town (USA)**[16] 4458 4-9-1 63 ....(p) J-PGuillambert(3) 3 — 64
(NPLittmoden) *a.p: hdwy 2f out: rdn and ch over 1f out tl drvn and one pce ins last* **4/1**[3]

0550 **3** 6 **Old Bailey (USA)**[20] 4350 4-9-6 58 ....(v) PMulrennan(3) 11 — 57
(TDBarron) *hdwy to trck ldrs after 3f: rdn along 2f out: drvn and wknd over 1f out* **11/1**

2104 **4** 1 3/4 **Bulawayo**[25] 4190 7-9-6 51 ....(b) DCorby(3) 9 — 54
(AndrewReid) *a.p: effrt to chal over 2f out: sn rdn along and wknd wl over 1f out* **9/2**

1000 **5** 1 1/4 **Super Dominion**[11] 4605 7-9-4 46 ....(p) StephanieHollinshead(5) 4 — 51
(RHollinshead) *in tch: hdwy over 2f out: sn rdn along and kpt on same pce* **20/1**

0006 **6** 1 **Wilson Bluebottle (IRE)**[25] 4185 5-9-9 48 ....(b) DaleGibson 6 — 49
(MWEasterby) *in tch and sn rdn along: outpcd 1/2-way: wd st and drvn along: no imp* **7/2**[2]

5-50 **7** 3/4 **Aggi Mac**[21] 4309 3-8-2 40 ow2 ....(e[1]) SuzanneFrance(7) 7 — 40
(AndrewTurnell) *s.i.s: a rr* **33/1**

0404 **8** 6 **Jamestown**[36] 3880 7-9-1 38 .... LFletcher(3) 1 — 31
(MJPolglase) *a rr* **16/1**

6400 **9** 1 1/4 **Marengo**[4] 4808 10-8-11 20 .... KGhunowa(7) 2 — 28
(MJPolglase) *s.i.s: hdwy and in tch 1/2-way: rdn along 3f out and sn wknd* **66/1**

2400 **10** 8 **Kustom Kit For Her**[28] 4093 4-8-13 42 ....(t) JBramhill 10 — 7
(SRBowring) *s.i.s: a rr* **33/1**

4000 **11** 6 **Miss Celerity**[127] 1403 4-8-13 30 .... JoannaBadger 5 — —
(MJHaynes) *chsd ldrs: rdn along 1/2-way: sn wknd* **66/1**

1m 43.13s (-1.47) **Going Correction** -0.325s/f (Stan)
**WFA** 3 from 4yo+ 6lb — **11** Ran SP% **124.6**
Speed ratings: **94,92,86,84,83 82,81,75,74,66 60**CSF £9.18 TOTE £3.00: £1.20, £1.70, £4.60; EX 10.50.There was no bid for the winner.
**Owner** J M Chapman **Bred** Mrs John McEnery **Trained** Stillington, N Yorks

**FOCUS**
A typical low-grade seller run in a modest time and the form is weak.

**NOTEBOOK**
**Zarin(IRE)** outstayed his rivals to gain only his second victory in 28 starts.
**Kingston Town(USA)** has been disappointing since getting off the mark here last year, but this drop in class was what he needed, and he looks capable of picking up one of these.
**Old Bailey(USA)** has yet to convince over this trip.
**Bulawayo** lacks consistency and is probably better around the bends at Wolverhampton.

## 4926 JOHN SALVIN RETIREMENT H'CAP — 6f (F)

**6:20** (6:21) (E) (0-70,70) 3-Y-0+ — **£3,432** (£1,056; £528; £264) **Stalls** Low

Form — RPR

1003 **1** **Mister Mal (IRE)**[5] 4782 8-8-13 55 .... PMulrennan(3) 4 — 65
(BEllison) *mde all: wd st: rdn and edgd rt wl over 1f out: drvn out* **5/1**[3]

3300 **2** 1/2 **Silent Storm**[11] 4602 4-9-8 64 .... J-PGuillambert(3) 2 — 72
(HJCyzer) *chsd ldrs: hdwy over 2f out: rdn and styd on to chal over 1f out: drvn and nt qckn wl ins last* **12/1**

0000 **3** 1 3/4 **Fools Entire**[14] 4515 3-9-0 56 ....(e[1]) GBaker 1 — 59
(JAGilbert) *dwlt: sn in tch on inner: hdwy 2f out: rdn over 1f out: kpt on same pce* **14/1**

0600 **4** 1 1/4 **Shifty Night (IRE)**[4] 4817 3-8-2 49 ....(p) HayleyTurner(5) 7 — 48
(MrsCADunnett) *chsd ldrs: rdn along 2f out: drvn and one pce over 1f out* **10/1**

2215 **5** 1/2 **Headland (USA)**[7] 4702 6-9-2 55 ....(be) SSanders 12 — 53
(DWChapman) *towards rr: hdwy on outer and wd st: rdn 2f out: styd on appr last: nrst fin* **11/4**[1]

1400 **6** *nk* **Tally (IRE)**[3] 4837 4-9-8 64 .... LFletcher(3) 10 — 61
(MJPolglase) *prom:rdn along 2f out: drvn and wknd appr last* **3/1**[2]

0-05 **7** 1/2 **Rue De Paris**[12] 4568 4-8-1 40 .... DaleGibson 8 — 35
(JohnAHarris) *cl up: rdn 2f out: grad wknd* **33/1**

043 **8** 2 **Set Alight**[56] 3261 3-8-11 53 .... JoannaBadger 13 — 42
(MrsCADunnett) *s.i.s: a rr* **20/1**

1035 **9** *nk* **Cherokee Nation**[23] 4244 3-10-0 70 ....(e) DAllan 9 — 58
(PWD'Arcy) *midfield and rdn along 1/2-way: nvr a factor* **10/1**

3060 **10** *shd* **Senor Bond (USA)**[45] 3615 3-9-4 60 .... DMcGaffin 6 — 48
(BSmart) *a rr* **12/1**

4030 **11** 3 1/2 **Xpres Digital**[46] 3585 3-9-13 69 ....(t) JBramhill 5 — 46
(SRBowring) *a rr* **12/1**

500 **12** 3 **Plattocrat**[63] 3040 4-7-5 37 oh2 .... DFentiman(7) 3 — 5
(RPElliott) *a rr* **66/1**

-000 **13** 14 **Lady Franpalm (IRE)**[27] 4125 4-8-8 47 .... DarrenWilliams 11 — —
(MJHaynes) *chsd ldrs on outer: rdn along 1/2-way: sn wknd* **25/1**

1m 14.69s (-2.21) **Going Correction** -0.325s/f (Stan)
**WFA** 3 from 4yo+ 3lb — **13** Ran SP% **129.3**
Speed ratings: **101,100,98,96,95 95,94,91,91,91 86,82,64**CSF £67.02 CT £594.68 TOTE £5.30: £1.10, £6.20, £6.40; EX 99.70.
**Owner** Mrs Andrea M Mallinson **Bred** Denis Cleary **Trained** Norton, N Yorks

**FOCUS**
This handicap was not that competitive with most of the runners having plenty to prove and the form is ordinary.

**NOTEBOOK**
**Mister Mal(IRE)**, at his best when he can dominate, stuck to his task well enough, despite hanging over to the stands' side in the latter stages.
**Silent Storm** has run well enough in both starts here over this trip, and should be capable of finding a small race.
**Fools Entire**, tackling the Fibresand for the first time, showed a bit more sparkle in the eyeshield.
**Shifty Night(IRE)**, back on her favoured surface, had no excuses.
**Headland(USA)** could never get competitive from his wide draw.

## 4927 KEVIN VOCE - 25 YEARS AT SOUTHWELL H'CAP — 1m 4f (F)

**6:50** (6:51) (F) (0-55,55) 3-Y-O — **£2,989** (£854; £427) **Stalls** Low

Form — RPR

0603 **1** **Scott**[15] 4499 3-9-1 50 .... GBaker 1 — 69
(JJay) *hld up in tch: smooth hdwy over 4f out: led 2f out: comf* **12/1**

-000 **2** 2 **Rawalpindi**[62] 3094 3-9-3 52 .... DaleGibson 2 — 68
(JARToller) *chsd ldrs: hdwy over 3f out: ev ch 2f out: sn rdn and kpt on* **25/1**

4320 **3** 17 **Holly Walk**[37] 3837 3-9-1 50 ....(p) DarrenWilliams 6 — 41
(MDods) *sn led: rdn along 4f out: hdd 2f out: sn drvn and wknd* **8/1**[3]

3331 **4** 9 **Salut Saint Cloud**[1] 4883 3-9-4 53 ....(p) SSanders 4 — 30
(GLMoore) *rn in snatches: in tch: chsd along after 3f: hdwy to trck ldrs 1/2-way: rdn along 3f out: sn btn* **8/13**[1]

6620 **5** 7 **Middleham Rose**[21] 2760 3-7-7 35 oh2 .... DFentiman(7) 3 — 2
(PCHaslam) *cl up: rdn along over 4f out: sn wknd* **25/1**

2051 **6** 1/2 **Garston Star**[6] 4736 3-8-13 55 .... LauraReynolds(7) 8 — 21
(JSMoore) *chsd ldrs: rdn along over 4f out: sn wknd* **10/3**[2]

3500 **7** 1 **Silver Rhythm**[21] 4307 3-9-0 49 .... VHalliday 7 — 13
(KRBurke) *chsd ldrs: pushed along 1/2-way: rdn and wknd over 4f out* **33/1**

0140 **8** 10 **Pepe (IRE)**[64] 3026 3-9-5 54 ....(p) JBramhill 5 — 3
(RHollinshead) *a rr* **25/1**

2m 37.56s (-4.54) **Going Correction** -0.325s/f (Stan) — **8** Ran SP% **118.3**
Speed ratings: **102,100,89,83,78 78,77,71**CSF £248.80 CT £2535.54 TOTE £12.70: £1.90, £5.40, £2.60; EX 215.10.
**Owner** Keith Wills **Bred** Keith Wills **Trained** Newmarket, Suffolk

**FOCUS**
A poor handicap in which the race unfolded up the centre of the track and the front pair pulled a long way clear in a fair time and the form is therefore rated positively.

**NOTEBOOK**
**Scott** looked to find plenty of improvement for tackling this surface and won with a ton in hand. Connections will be keen to get him out again as soon as possible before the Handicapper has time to react.
**Rawalpindi** improved for the step up in trip but, as he finished a mile clear of the third, he can expect no favours from the Handicapper.
**Holly Walk** already proven around here, was left standing when the front pair changed gear.
**Salut Saint Cloud** never looked that happy over this shorter trip.
**Middleham Rose** *Official explanation: jockey said filly lost her action*
**Pepe(IRE)** *Official explanation: trainer's representative said filly was found to be in season*

## 4928 AT THE RACES DEDICATED RACING CHANNEL CLASSIFIED STKS — 7f (F)

**7:20** (7:21) (E) 3-Y-0+ — **£3,360** (£1,034; £517; £258) **Stalls** Low

Form — RPR

-240 **1** **Khanjar (USA)**[94] 2210 4-9-1 70 .... DarrenWilliams 4 — 81
(KRBurke) *a.p: effrt 2f out: rdn to ld ent last: wandered and hdd last 50 yds: rallied to ld on line* **10/1**

1130 **2** *shd* **Downland (IRE)**[12] 4577 8-9-1 69 .... KimTinkler 8 — 81
(NTinkler) *hld up in tch: hdwy over 2f out: rdn to ld over 1f out: hdd ent last: rallied to ld last 50 yds: hdd on line* **3/1**[3]

4051 **3** *4* **Kingsmaite**[63] 3059 3-9-1 75..........(b) JBramhill 5 76
(SRBowring) *cl up: effrt and ev ch 2f out: sn rdn and one pce appr last* **2/1**[1]

4606 **4** *2* **Air Mail**[28] 4096 7-9-1 64.......... RFitzpatrick 2 65
(MrsNMacauley) *chsd ldrs: rdn along over 3f out: drvn and kpt on same pce fnl 2f* **33/1**

2400 **5** *1 1/4* **The Bonus King**[36] 3884 4-9-5 74.......... GBaker 7 66
(JJay) *outpcd and bhd: swtchd lft and hdwy 2f out: sn rdn and no imp* **9/1**

1500 **6** *1 1/4* **Mister Sweets**[3] 4837 5-9-0 72.......... DNolan(3) 1 61
(DCarroll) *led 2f: cl up: ev ch 2f out: sn rdn and wknd wl over 1f out* **5/2**[2]

1000 **7** *5* **Commander Bond**[16] 4456 3-8-10 70.......... DMcGaffin 3 46
(BSmart) *slwly into stride: sn chsng ldrs on inner: led after 2f: rdn along and hdd 2f out: sn drvn and wknd* **20/1**

-003 **8** *24* **Gem Bien (USA)**[9] 4624 6-9-4 73.......... SSanders 6 —
(DWChapman) *cl up 2f: sn lost pl and bhd fnl 3f* **12/1**

1m 27.8s (-3.00) **Going Correction** -0.325s/f (Stan)
**WFA** 3 from 4yo+ 5lb **8** Ran SP% **121.4**
Speed ratings: **104,103,99,97,95 94,88,61**CSF £42.75 TOTE £15.10: £5.10, £1.02, £2.20; EX 51.50.
**Owner** Spigot Lodge Partnership **Bred** Alexander-Groves Thoroughbreds **Trained** Middleham Moor, N Yorks

**FOCUS**
A fair contest and as in the previous race the action unfolded up the centre.

**NOTEBOOK**
**Khanjar(USA)**, having his first outing for current connections, was facing his easiest task to date. Without the headgear this time, he did little wrong, and this effort should have given his confidence a boost.
**Downland(IRE)** has really taken to this surface, but he was done no favours here by his wide draw. Struggling for cover through the first couple of furlongs, where he was quite free, he came through to have every chance before being denied in the photo. There will be other days for him.
**Kingsmaite**, who bounced back to form in the first-time blinkers at Redcar in June, has yet to finish out of the frame here.
**Air Mail** has gone a long time without winning and, although he is tumbling down the weights, does not exactly look as though he is about to put that right.
**The Bonus King**, who bled last time, is a long way below the form he showed as a juvenile.
**Mister Sweets** was most disappointing, for having had every chance dropped away tamely.
**Gem Bien(USA)** *Official explanation: jockey said gelding was never travelling*

## 4929 MIDLANDS RACING - 9 GREAT VENUES H'CAP 5f (F)
**7:50** (7:55) (E) (0-70,69) 3-Y-O **£3,425** (£1,054; £527; £263) **Stalls** High

Form RPR

5131 **1** **Wunderbra (IRE)**[4] 4810 3-8-8 **61** 6ex..........(t) HayleyTurner(5) 6 68
(MLWBell) *trckd ldrs: hdwy 2f out: rdn over 1f out: styd on wl to ld last 100 yds* **7/4**[1]

1020 **2** *1* **Blue Power (IRE)**[7] 4701 3-9-3 **65**.......... DarrenWilliams 1 69
(KRBurke) *chsd ldrs far side: hdwy and edgd rt 2f out: rdn to ld over 1f out: drvn ins last: hdd and nt qckn last 100 yds* **9/4**[2]

1655 **3** *1* **Wendy's Girl (IRE)**[11] 4608 3-8-11 **62**..........(b) PMulrennan(3) 13 63
(RPElliott) *led: rdn 2f out: hdd over 1f out: kpt on same pce ins last* **14/1**

1000 **4** *1/2* **Hello Roberto**[14] 4515 3-9-0 **69**.......... KGhunowa(7) 3 69+
(MJPolglase) *chsd ldrs far side: n.m.r and swtchd lft over 2f out:sn rdn and kpt on fnl f* **14/1**

**5** *3/4* **Dutch Key Card (IRE)**[19] 4370 3-9-1 **63**.......... RFitzpatrick 12 60
(GAButler) *sn outpcd and bhd: rdn along and hdwy whn hung lft over 1f out: styd on strly ins last: nrst fin* **25/1**

0000 **6** *nk* **Estoille**[20] 4351 3-7-13 **47** oh16 ow1..........(t) JBramhill 5 43
(MrsSLamyman) *cl up centre: rdn along 2f out: sn hung lft and wknd over 1f out* **100/1**

3440 **7** *1 1/2* **Pure Folly (IRE)**[18] 4390 3-8-9 **57**.......... SSanders 2 49
(SirMarkPrescott) *prom far side: rdn along and edgd rt over 2f out: sn btn* **7/2**[3]

0520 **8** *1/2* **Westborough (IRE)**[30] 4021 3-8-0 **48**.......... KimTinkler 4 38
(NTinkler) *dwlt: sn chsng ldrs: rdn along and edgd lft over 2f out: sn wknd* **16/1**

2532 **9** *3/4* **Park Ave Princess (IRE)**[150] 1086 3-8-11 **62**.......... LFletcher(3) 8 50
(MJPolglase) *sn outpcd and bhd fr 1/2-way* **9/1**

0202 **10** *1 3/4* **Burkees Graw (IRE)**[18] 4393 3-7-5 **46** oh14.......... DFentiman(7) 11 29
(MrsSLamyman) *in tch: rdn along 1/2-way: wkng whn hmpd over 1f out* **25/1**

04-0 **11** *12* **Big Tom (IRE)**[15] 4491 3-8-11 **59**.......... DaleGibson 10 6
(DCarroll) *sn outpcd and bhd* **25/1**

59.38 secs (-1.02) **Going Correction** -0.20s/f (Stan) **11** Ran SP% **131.1**
Speed ratings: **100,98,96,96,94 94,91,91,89,87 67**CSF £6.44 CT £48.10 TOTE £3.00: £1.80, £1.10, £4.70; EX 7.50 Place 6 £173.84, Place 5 £73.89.
**Owner** Fitzroy Thoroughbreds **Bred** J F Tuthill And Mrs A Whitehead **Trained** Newmarket, Suffolk

**FOCUS**
An ordinary contest and modest form, but won by an improving filly.

**NOTEBOOK**
**Wunderbra(IRE)** continues on the upgrade and, with her ability to handle a faster surface on turf, should find other openings.
**Blue Power(IRE)** looked to run as well as ever and was just unlucky to encounter an improving filly.
**Wendy's Girl(IRE)**, who stays further than this, had plenty of use made of her, but was easily picked off in the latter stages.
**Hello Roberto** has slipped to her last winning mark, but she lacks consistency and is not one to trust.
**Dutch Key Card(IRE)** found things happening too quickly for him and looks in need of a stiffer test.
T/Plt: £323.10 to a £1 stake. Pool: £25,630.25. 57.90 winning tickets. T/Qpdt: £67.50 to a £1 stake. Pool: £2,720.90. 29.80 winning tickets. JR

# 4906 CHESTER (L-H)
Saturday, August 21

**OFFICIAL GOING: Soft**
Wind: almost nil Weather: fine

## 4930 BLUE SQUARE 0800 587 0200 EBF MAIDEN STKS 7f 2y
**2:05** (2:06) (D) 2-Y-O **£7,280** (£2,240; £1,120; £560) **Stalls** Low

Form RPR

0 **1** **Ceiriog Valley**[23] 4272 2-8-9.......... MHills 2 83+
(BWHills) *in tch: rdn over 3f out: hdwy whn nt clr run over 2f out: led over 1f out: clr fnl f: comf* **5/1**[2]

4 **2** *8* **Haiban**[10] 4633 2-9-0.......... SWKelly 3 70
(GAButler) *chsd ldrs: rdn over 3f out: wnt 2nd 1f out: no ch w wnr* **8/1**

00 **3** *2 1/2* **Eskdale (IRE)**[27] 4175 2-8-11.......... DNolan(3) 15 65
(RFFisher) *midfield: rdn over 3f out: hdwy 2f out: styd on ins fnl f* **66/1**

5 **4** *3/4* **Ignition**[29] 4099 2-8-4.......... BSwarbrick(5) 9 58
(WMBrisbourne) *midfield: bmpd after 1f: rdn over 3f out: styd on ins fnl f: nt rch ldrs* **33/1**

0 **5** *1/2* **Grandos (IRE)**[16] 4487 2-9-0.......... WSupple 8 62
(TDEasterby) *chsd ldrs: rdn over 3f out: wknd fnl f* **25/1**

0 **6** *1 1/4* **Nasseem Dubai (USA)**[23] 4256 2-8-11.......... PMulrennan(3) 16 59
(MrsADuffield) *towards rr: rdn and hdwy whn nt clr run over 1f out: kpt on fnl f* **25/1**

04 **7** *2 1/2* **Makepeace (IRE)**[63] 3081 2-9-0.......... ACulhane 12 54
(MRChannon) *towards rr: bmpd after 1f: rdn over 3f out: kpt on fnl f: nvr nrr* **20/1**

0 **8** *1/2* **Toshi (USA)**[25] 4219 2-9-0.......... SChin 1 53
(MJohnston) *w ldr: led 3f out: rdn and hdd over 1f out: wknd fnl f* **7/1**[3]

6 **9** *nk* **Layed Back Rocky**[24] 4239 2-9-0.......... SRighton 14 52
(MMullineaux) *a bhd* **66/1**

5 **10** *2 1/2* **Majestic Movement (USA)**[9] 4689 2-9-0.......... KMcEvoy 10 47
(JHMGosden) *in tch: rdn over 3f out: wknd over 2f out* **5/1**[2]

**11** *6* **Egyptian Lady** 2-8-6.......... THamilton(3) 11 28
(RPElliott) *s.i.s: sn niggled along: a bhd* **66/1**

0 **12** *3* **Ansells Legacy (IRE)**[55] 3336 2-9-0.......... FNorton 6 27
(ABerry) *s.i.s: sn midfield: rdn and wknd over 3f out* **50/1**

3 **13** *10* **Oxford Street Pete (IRE)**[20] 4359 2-9-0.......... RWinston 7 5
(ABailey) *led: rdn and hdd 3f out: sn wknd: eased over 1f out* **10/1**

2 **P** **Aldente**[14] 4560 2-8-9.......... SSanders 4 —
(SirMarkPrescott) *midfield: edgd rt after 1f: pushed along over 4f out: hdwy 2f out: 4th whn broke leg over 1f out: sn p.u: dead* **5/2**[1]

1m 33.6s (5.31) **Going Correction** +0.775s/f (Yiel) **14** Ran SP% **116.4**
Speed ratings: **100,90,88,87,86 85,82,81,81,78 71,68,56,**—CSF £39.49 TOTE £6.20: £1.90, £2.80, £13.10; EX 35.00.
**Owner** R J McAlpine **Bred** Tilstone Lodge Stud **Trained** Lambourn, Berks

**FOCUS**
An ordinary maiden but the winner looks above average. A creditable winning time for the class.

**NOTEBOOK**
**Ceiriog Valley** is bred for middle distances and conditions clearly suited here. Closely related to Inglis Drever another furlong will not be a problem.
**Haiban** ran a solid race and will be well suited by a return to a mile.
**Eskdale(IRE)** has a speedy pedigree so it was surprising to see him staying on in the closing stages. He should win a small nursery over this trip.
**Ignition** showed promise on her debut and again ran a solid race here considering she found trouble early on in the race and then raced widest of all into the straight.
**Grandos(IRE)** is still week and will be better next year.
**Nasseem Dubai(USA)** was settled at the rear and was a long way behind turning in. He was staying on strongly when hampered at the furlong pole. With a more positive ride he would have finished much closer.
**Toshi(USA)** weakened very quickly and will appreciate quicker ground.
**Oxford Street Pete(IRE)** *Official explanation: jockey said gelding was unsuited by the soft ground*

## 4931 BET@BLUESQ.COM H'CAP 7f 122y
**2:40** (2:42) (C) (0-100,97) 3-Y-O+ **£14,430** (£4,440; £2,220; £1,110) **Stalls** Low

Form RPR

3030 **1** **Zonus**[35] 3943 3-9-2 90..........(b1) MHills 14 107
(BWHills) *hld up: hdwy 3f out: nt clr run over 2f out: swtchd rt over 1f out: sn led: r.o to draw clr ins fnl f* **8/1**[3]

2111 **2** *5* **Pango**[25] 4220 5-9-0 85.......... LFletcher(3) 10 91
(HMorrison) *in tch: rdn and hdwy 2f out: led over 1f out: sn hdd: no ch w wnr ins fnl f* **6/1**[2]

6564 **3** *2* **Sea Storm (IRE)**[13] 4577 6-8-10 78..........(p) SSanders 16 79
(DRMacleod) *midfield: hdwy 4f out: rdn over 2f out: kpt on same pce fnl f* **16/1**

0000 **4** *2* **Namroud (USA)**[14] 4543 5-8-9 77.......... PHanagan 8 73
(RAFahey) *prom: led 2f out: rdn and hdd over 1f out: no ex fnl f* **10/1**

1200 **5** *2* **Hawkit (USA)**[7] 4749 3-8-4 78..........(t) MartinDwyer 11 70
(PDEvans) *in tch: hdwy 4f out: rdn over 2f out: wknd over 1f out* **33/1**

2022 **6** *1* **Kirkby's Treasure**[7] 4751 6-8-8 76.......... FLynch 15 66
(ABerry) *stdd s: hld up bhd: nt clr run over 1f out: styd on fnl f: nvr rchd ldrs* **12/1**

0320 **7** *1/2* **Winning Venture**[25] 4220 7-8-13 81.......... PDoe 1 69
(AWCarroll) *led: rdn and hdd 2f out: wknd 1f out* **11/2**[1]

0444 **8** *1 1/2* **Glaramara**[2] 4873 3-9-9 97.......... PRobinson 5 82
(ABailey) *trckd ldrs: rdn over 1f out: sn wknd* **9/1**

-630 **9** *3/4* **Strong Hand**[37] 3867 4-8-5 76.......... PMulrennan(3) 2 59
(MWEasterby) *trckd ldrs: rdn over 1f out: wknd over 1f out: eased ins fnl f* **6/1**[2]

0005 **10** *1 1/4* **Tough Love**[14] 4543 5-8-13 81.......... DAllan 9 61
(TDEasterby) *towards rr: hdwy over 3f out: rdn and wknd over 2f out* **16/1**

0350 **11** *5* **H Harrison (IRE)**[20] 4360 4-8-6 79.......... PPMathers(5) 3 48
(IWMcinnes) *s.i.s: midfield: rdn over 3f out: wknd over 2f out* **14/1**

1130 **12** *1 1/4* **True Night**[14] 4558 7-9-1 83.......... RWinston 12 49
(DNicholls) *a in rr* **8/1**[3]

3021 **13** *dist* **Sawwaah (IRE)**[7] 4742 7-9-2 84.......... ANicholls 17 —
(DNicholls) *towards rr: sn niggled along: hdwy over 3f out: wknd over 2f out: eased fnl f: t.o* **18/1**

1m 39.14s (4.39) **Going Correction** +0.775s/f (Yiel)
**WFA** 3 from 4yo+ 6lb **13** Ran SP% **119.6**
Speed ratings: **109,104,102,100,98 97,96,95,94,93 88,86,**—CSF £55.46 CT £762.62 TOTE £10.40: £3.70, £2.50, £4.80; EX 81.90.
**Owner** Concord Racing,Bonnycastle,Grant,Morton **Bred** T H Bletsoe And Son **Trained** Lambourn, Berks

**FOCUS**
A fair handicap for the track run at a good pace. The finish was dominated by those drawn high and so the form may be best not taken at face value.

**NOTEBOOK**
**Zonus**, wearing the first time blinkers got very warm beforehand but he came from of the pace to score easily. The blinkers clearly had the desired effect and with this confidence booster under his belt he could do better still.
**Pango** was never far away but was made to look very pedestrian by the winner.
**Sea Storm(IRE)** ran respectably over a trip probably just short of his best on ground softer than ideal.
**Namroud(USA)**, from a trainer in form did best of those that set the pace and showed enough to suggest that his turn is not far away.
**Hawkit(USA)** is better than he showed here. He was on the wrong leg turning into the straight and couldn't organise himself on the ground. He should leave this form behind on a return to a quicker surface.
**Winning Venture**, set a strong pace but in testing conditions didn't get home.
**True Night** *Official explanation: jockey said gelding was unsuited by the soft ground*

**Sawwaah(IRE)** *Official explanation: jockey said gelding was never travelling*

## 4932 BLUE SQUARE CHESTER RATED STKS (H'CAP) (LISTED RACE) 1m 5f 89y
**3:15** (3:15) (A ) (0-110,109) 3-Y-0+ **£23,200** (£8,800; £4,400; £2,000) **Stalls** Low

Form RPR

3643 **1** **Swift Tango (IRE)**[14] 4530 4-9-0 **100** PHanagan 3 107+
(EALDunlop) *hld up: nt clr run over 1f out: sn swtchd rt: qcknd to ld ins fnl f: r.o* **5/1**[2]

420- **2** *1 ½* **Midas Way**[344] 4862 4-8-9 **95** SSanders 4 100
(PRChamings) *led: rdn over 2f out: hdd ins fnl f: nt qckn* **8/1**[3]

4406 **3** *½* **Hambleden**[14] 4530 7-8-10 **96** PRobinson 7 100
(MAJarvis) *hld up: pushed along over 2f out: styd on ins fnl f* **4/1**[1]

2-00 **4** *nk* **Albanov (IRE)**[14] 4529 4-8-9 **95** oh1 SChin 9 99
(MJohnston) *in tch: tk clsr order over 7f out: pushed along over 5f out: ev ch ins fnl f: nt qckn cl home* **4/1**[1]

2401 **5** *½* **Desert Quest (IRE)**[14] 4530 4-8-9 **95** oh1 (b) MartinDwyer 5 98
(AMBalding) *trckd ldrs: rdn over 2f out: ev ch ins fnl f: no ex cl home* **4/1**[1]

-025 **6** *¾* **Delsarte (USA)**[36] 3912 4-9-7 **107** (t) KMcEvoy 2 109
(SaeedBinSuroor) *trckd ldr: rdn over 3f out: ev ch 2f out: no ex ins fnl f* **4/1**[1]

3m 9.33s (13.94) **Going Correction** +0.775s/f (Yiel) 6 Ran SP% **107.8**
Speed ratings: **88,87,86,86,86 85**CSF £38.51 CT £150.90 TOTE £4.80: £2.00, £2.90; EX 55.90 Trifecta £196.20 Pool: £746.29. 2.70 winning tickets.
**Owner** Khalifa Sultan **Bred** Killeen Castle Stud **Trained** Newmarket, Suffolk

**FOCUS**
No pace on early and this race turned into a sprint. A very moderate time indeed for the class of contest and the form may not be that solid.

**NOTEBOOK**
**Swift Tango(IRE)**, trying the trip for the first time was suited by the slow early pace and came from last to first to score.
**Midas Way**, having his first run for almost a year dictated matters at a pedestrian pace, looked in need of the run and will certainly be sharper next time.
**Hambleden** generally front runs but was held up here. He certainly wasn't disgraced considering the slow early pace was against him. There are still some good prizes to be won with him.
**Albanov(IRE)** still only has a maiden win to his name and is very one paced.
**Desert Quest(IRE)** was very fractious coming out on to the course, he is a quirky sort. *Official explanation: jockey said gelding had hung left-handed*
**Delsarte(USA)**, from a trainer in form, had no excuses and is one to watch at present.

## 4933 BLUE SQUARE PAYS DOUBLE RESULTS CONDITIONS STKS (C&G) 6f 18y
**3:50** (3:51) (C ) 2-Y-O **£9,353** (£3,458; £1,729; £786) **Stalls** Low

Form RPR

61 **1** **Cupid's Glory**[12] 4598 2-8-10 SSanders 2 97+
(SirMarkPrescott) *trckd ldrs: rdn to ld ins fnl f: sn qcknd clr* **5/2**[2]

1160 **2** *3 ½* **Dahteer (IRE)**[24] 4227 2-8-13 90 ACulhane 5 91
(MRChannon) *w ldr: rdn to ld briefly over 1f out: styd on: nt pce of wnr ins fnl f* **9/1**[3]

51 **3** *½* **One Putra (IRE)**[12] 4611 2-8-13 PRobinson 6 90
(MAJarvis) *trckd ldrs: rdn to ld over 1f out: hdd ins fnl f: no ex* **4/6**[1]

022 **4** *11* **Wizardmicktee (IRE)**[7] 4761 2-8-10 RWinston 3 59
(ABailey) *led: rdn and hdd over 1f out: sn wknd* **12/1**

0000 **5** *20* **Den Perry**[7] 4757 2-8-5 (p) PPMathers[(5)] 1 9
(ABerry) *bdly outpcd fr 1/2-way: a bhd* **40/1**

1m 19.89s (4.01) **Going Correction** +0.775s/f (Yiel) 5 Ran SP% **108.7**
Speed ratings: **104,99,98,84,57**CSF £21.77 TOTE £3.60: £1.60, £3.70; EX 22.90.
**Owner** Hesmonds Stud **Bred** Cheveley Park Stud Ltd **Trained** Newmarket, Suffolk

**FOCUS**
An interesting contest on paper, the winner always had matters under control. A decent winning time for the grade in the conditions and the form looks reasonable.

**NOTEBOOK**
**Cupid's Glory** ◆ had only ever run on the polytrack before this but the switch to turf proved to be no problem for this impressive winner. Despite running green during the first furlong the winner got the hang of things and travelled strongly from halfway before easing clear. He will improve again for the experience and has plenty of gears.
**Dahteer(IRE)**, whose both previous wins had come on fast ground, ran to form here and will be better on a quicker surface.
**One Putra(IRE)** had no excuses leading over a furlong out but found little for pressure. His previous victory has worked out well and he should be capable of winning a similar race.
**Wizardmicktee(IRE)** set a good pace but faded tamely, he looks in need of a break.
**Den Perry** unseated his rider when leaving the parade ring and was always well behind in a race in which he was completely outclassed in.

## 4934 BLUE SQUARE GAMES H'CAP 1m 7f 195y
**4:25** (4:25) (D ) (0-85,84) 3-Y-O+ **£7,020** (£2,160; £1,080; £540) **Stalls** Low

Form RPR

2106 **1** **Dr Sharp (IRE)**[15] 4512 4-9-8 **79** RWinston 5 92+
(TPTate) *hld up: hdwy over 5f out: led over 3f out: pushed out* **9/2**[2]

0200 **2** *1 ¼* **Master Wells (IRE)**[30] 4062 3-8-4 **75** PHanagan 10 84
(JDBethell) *hld up: rdn and hdwy over 4f out: styd on fnl f* **10/1**

0404 **3** *hd* **Almizan (IRE)**[24] 4226 4-9-11 **82** (v) ACulhane 13 91
(MRChannon) *hld up: rdn and hdwy over 3f out: styd on fnl f* **8/1**[3]

56-6 **4** *½* **Contact Dancer (IRE)**[39] 3821 5-9-13 **84** SChin 14 92
(MJohnston) *hld up: hdwy 6f out: rdn over 2f out: kpt on fnl f* **10/1**

5115 **5** *15* **Toni Alcala**[13] 4578 5-9-3 **77** PMulrennan[(3)] 15 69
(RFFisher) *hld up: rdn and hdwy over 3f out: wknd over 2f out* **14/1**

1511 **6** *1 ¾* **Lucky Judge**[48] 3564 7-9-2 **73** KMcEvoy 6 63
(GASwinbank) *hld up: hdwy 6f out: rdn over 4f out: wknd over 1f out* **3/1**[1]

6600 **7** *1 ¾* **Teresa**[24] 4226 4-9-2 **73** PRobinson 7 61
(JLDunlop) *cl up tl rdn and wknd over 2f out* **8/1**[3]

0501 **8** *12* **Astyanax (IRE)**[17] 4457 4-9-5 **76** SSanders 4 51
(SirMarkPrescott) *midfield: pushed along 7f out: hdwy over 4f out: wknd 2f out* **8/1**[3]

2240 **9** *8* **Rajam**[6] 4772 6-9-6 **77** ANicholls 12 43
(DNicholls) *midfield: n.m.r and lost pl over 5f out: n.d* **25/1**

45-0 **10** *30* **Gondolin (IRE)**[8] 4715 4-9-11 **82** (v[1]) SWKelly 9 15
(GAButler) *led: rdn and hdd over 3f out: wknd qckly* **25/1**

3141 **11** *20* **Rolex Free (ARG)**[12] 4600 6-7-5 **55** oh4 (v) DFentiman[(7)] 2 —
(DFlood) *chsd ldr: rdn 7f out: wknd over 5f out* **14/1**

0062 **12** *dist* **Bravely Does It (USA)**[23] 4261 4-8-1 **58** ow2 MartinDwyer 11 —
(WMBrisbourne) *trckd ldrs: pushed along 7f out: wknd over 5f out: t.o* **25/1**

3m 44.8s (11.02) **Going Correction** +0.775s/f (Yiel)
**WFA** 3 from 4yo+ 14lb 12 Ran SP% **119.6**
Speed ratings: **103,102,102,102,94 93,92,86,82,67 57,**—CSF £48.33 CT £344.60 TOTE £5.70: £1.90, £3.90, £3.50; EX 64.80.
**Owner** The Ivy Syndicate **Bred** Mrs Ann Fortune **Trained** Tadcaster, N Yorks

**FOCUS**
A competitive handicap run at a good pace and the form appears sound.

**NOTEBOOK**
**Dr Sharp(IRE)** has progressed well this season and thrives on soft ground, recorded his third win of the season. Although not over big he has a great attitude and connections are hopeful of him making up into a high class hurdler.
**Master Wells(IRE)** appreciated this easier surface and this son of Saddlers Well put a couple of disappointing performances behind him with a return to form here despite getting very warm in the prelimaries.
**Almizan(IRE)** stayed on but is generally most effective over further.
**Contact Dancer(IRE)** will come on for the run and showed enough here to suggest that if he stays sound he will pick up a similar race.
**Teresa** *Official explanation: jockey said filly hung right-handed throughout*
**Gondolin(IRE)**, was lit up by the first time visor and went off far too fast, he has always been quirky and is one to avoid for the time being.
**Rolex Free(ARG)** didn't stay.

## 4935 BLUE SQUARE CASINO H'CAP 5f 16y
**4:55** (4:55) (D ) (0-85,83) 3-Y-0+ **£6,890** (£2,120; £1,060; £530) **Stalls** Low

Form RPR

3030 **1** **Kings College Boy**[4] 4828 4-8-6 **61** (b) DaleGibson 10 74
(RAFahey) *bhd: rdn and hdwy over 1f out: led ins fnl f: r.o* **16/1**

0460 **2** *1 ½* **Endless Summer**[35] 3945 7-9-4 **73** PDoe 1 81
(AWCarroll) *bhd: nt clr run over 2f out: swtchd rt and hdwy over 1f out: styd on to chse wnr ins fnl f: nt qckn cl home* **10/1**

303 **3** *3 ½* **Prince Of Blues (IRE)**[9] 4677 6-8-2 **57** (b) AMcCarthy 8 53
(MMullineaux) *in tch: rdn to chse ldrs 2f out: styd on same pce* **14/1**

1362 **4** *hd* **Hout Bay**[10] 4626 7-8-1 **56** PHanagan 5 52
(RAFahey) *in tch: rdn and hdwy 2f out: kpt on same pce fnl f* **4/1**[2]

0505 **5** *hd* **Strensall**[5] 4805 7-9-4 **76** TEaves[(3)] 3 71
(REBarr) *in tch: hdwy over 2f out: rdn over 1f out: no ex wl ins fnl f* **11/1**

3060 **6** *1 ½* **The Lord**[7] 4748 4-9-7 **81** LTreadwell[(5)] 4 71
(WGMTurner) *led early: remained prom: led again over 2f out: rdn over 1f out: hdd and edgd lft ins fnl f: sn wknd* **8/1**[3]

1120 **7** *4* **Frascati**[42] 3744 4-9-3 **77** PPMathers[(5)] 2 54
(ABerry) *bhd: effrt over 2f out: wknd fnl f* **7/2**[1]

6000 **8** *nk* **Laurel Dawn**[7] 4751 6-7-10 **58** NataliaGemelova[(7)] 12 34
(IWMcinnes) *in tch: rdn and outpcd over 2f out* **28/1**

0200 **9** *3* **The Fisio**[25] 4211 4-9-5 **74** (v) MartinDwyer 7 40
(SGollings) *prom: losing pl whn n.m.r over 2f out: n.d after* **14/1**

0010 **10** *6* **Izmail (IRE)**[27] 4181 5-8-12 **70** FPFerris[(3)] 13 16
(PDEvans) *prom: rdn over 2f out: wknd over 1f out* **33/1**

0020 **11** *13* **Brave Burt (IRE)**[4] 4837 7-10-0 **83** SSanders 6 —
(DNicholls) *sn led: hdd over 2f out: sn wknd* **4/1**[2]

4215 **12** *½* **Blue Maeve**[10] 4626 4-8-6 **61** SRighton 11 —
(JHetherton) *in tch: rdn and wknd over 2f out* **14/1**

65.94 secs (3.96) **Going Correction** +0.775s/f (Yiel) 12 Ran SP% **123.0**
Speed ratings: **99,96,91,90,90 87,81,81,76,66 45,45**CSF £173.34 CT £2353.40 TOTE £24.30: £6.40, £3.20, £5.50; EX 285.00 Place 6 £8,576.73, Place 5 £2,384.98.
**Owner** The Dandy Dons Partnership **Bred** Lady Jennifer Green **Trained** Musley Bank, N Yorks

**FOCUS**
A run-of-the-mill handicap run at a strong pace with the first two coming from way off the gallop. A modest time for the grade and probably best not to take the form at face value.

**NOTEBOOK**
**Kings College Boy**, from a stable in form came from a long way back to score here. After a tardy start he had just one behind turning for home but finished strongly to win despite being out wide.
**Endless Summer** came right back to form here and has to be considered a shade unlucky, constantly being checked when making good progress through the field.
**Prince Of Blues(IRE)** is on a long losing run but is slowly coming down the handicap.
**Hout Bay** had every chance.
**Frascati** was strongly supported in the betting exchanges but couldn't make the most of her good draw. *Official explanation: jockey said filly was in season*
**Brave Burt(IRE)** *Official explanation: jockey said gelding was never travelling*
**Blue Maeve** *Official explanation: jockey said gelding lost its action*
T/Plt: £3,793.30 to a £1 stake. Pool: £75,867.95. 14.60 winning tickets. T/Qpdt: £353.60 to a £1 stake. Pool: £4,349.20. 9.10 winning tickets. DO

# 4598 LINGFIELD (L-H)
## Saturday, August 21

**OFFICIAL GOING: Turf: good to soft aw: standard**
Wind: almost nil Weather: bright

## 4936 KGN PILLINGER MAIDEN AUCTION STKS 6f
**5:20** (5:22) (E ) 2-Y-O **£3,805** (£1,171; £585; £292) **Stalls** High

Form RPR

4 **1** **Sudden Dismissal (IRE)**[12] 4611 2-8-11 JPMurtagh 16 86+
(GAButler) *pressed ldr: rdn to ld wl over 1f out: clr fnl f: readily* **11/8**[1]

45 **2** *2 ½* **Enforcer**[12] 4611 2-8-9 SDrowne 17 76
(WRMuir) *racd in midfield: prog over 2f out: drvn to chse wnr 1f out: no imp* **9/2**[2]

**3** *2 ½* **Pinafore** 2-8-2 DKinsella 11 62
(HMorrison) *racd in midfield: pushed along 1/2-way: prog 2f out: rdn and styd on fnl f: nrst fin* **25/1**

64 **4** *1* **General Haigh**[8] 4704 2-8-11 NPollard 20 68
(JRBest) *mde most to wl over 1f out: fdd fnl f* **20/1**

4 **5** *1* **Bamzooki**[45] 3632 2-8-4 OUrbina 12 58
(JRFanshawe) *trckd ldrs gng wl: shkn up 2f out: one pce and no imp over 1f out* **5/1**[3]

5 **6** *hd* **Luciferous (USA)**[28] 4143 2-8-1 RMiles[(3)] 15 57
(JaneSouthcombe) *dwlt and veered rt s: rcvrd into midfield after 2f: gng wl 2f out: shkn up and one pce over 1f out* **16/1**

05 **7** *2 ½* **Cabin Fever**[11] 4621 2-7-11 RThomas[(5)] 18 47
(JCFox) *chsd ldrs: rdn whn hmpd and lost pl 2f out: one pce after* **25/1**

0 **8** *½* **Season Ticket (GER)**[5] 4804 2-8-2 MHenry 14 46
(WJHaggas) *towards rr of main gp: effrt over 2f out: no prog and btn over 1f out* **66/1**

4 **9** *1* **Methodical**[30] 4048 2-8-3 ow1 RMullen 7 44
(IAWood) *racd on outer: chsd ldrs: wknd over 1f out* **8/1**

55 **10** *2* **Crocodile Kiss (IRE)**[23] 4256 2-8-9 TPQueally 2 44
(JAOsborne) *sn detached in last quintet: rdn and kpt on fnl 2f: nvr nrr* **12/1**

**11** *shd* **Summer Charm** 2-7-11 HayleyTurner[(5)] 6 37
(WJarvis) *dwlt: sn detached in last quintet: kpt on fnl 2f: nrst fin* **66/1**


The Form Book, Raceform Ltd, Compton, RG20 6NL

00 **12** 3/4 **Before The Dawn**[29] 4081 2-8-2 ............ CCatlin 10 34
(AGNewcombe) *towards rr of main gp: rdn and struggling over 2f out* **33/1**

50 **13** 1 1/2 **Beau Marche**[6] 4770 2-8-8 ow1............ IMongan 4 36
(IAWood) *towards rr of main gp: hung rt and wknd 2f out* **66/1**

**14** *nk* **Slip Catch (IRE)** 2-8-2 ............ LisaJones 19 29
(WJarvis) *s.s: detached in last quintet: nvr a factor* **50/1**

**15** *hd* **Bob's Flyer** 2-8-4 ............ JMackay 13 30
(JGGiven) *pressed ldng pair tl wknd rapidly 2f out* **20/1**

**16** *shd* **Amigra (IRE)** 2-7-13 ............ JFMcDonald(3) 1 28
(MissJacquelineSDoyle) *detached in last quintet: a wl bhd* **33/1**

**17** 6 **Sergeant Small (IRE)** 2-8-9 ............ GCarter 9 17
(JohnBerry) *detached in last quintet: a wl bhd* **66/1**

00 **18** 28 **Aleshanee**[8] 4704 2-8-6 ............ DSweeney 8 —
(JRBest) *prom to 1/2-way: wknd v rapidly: t.o* **66/1**

1m 11.82s (0.17) **Going Correction** +0.025s/f (Good) **18** Ran SP% **134.2**
Speed ratings: **99,95,92,91,89 89,86,85,84,81 81,80,78,77,77 77,69,32**CSF £6.97 TOTE £2.60: £1.30, £1.90, £9.00; EX 15.60.
**Owner** The Schtum Partnership **Bred** Skymarc Farm And Castlemartin Stud **Trained** Blewbury, Oxon

**FOCUS**
A maiden containing horses of a wide range of ability and the winning time was fair for the grade. The winner looks promising and the form is solid behind him. High draws dominated but that was where the two market leaders were.

**NOTEBOOK**
**Sudden Dismissal(IRE)** confirmed the promise of his debut with a tidy win. He looks sure to go on from here.
**Enforcer** had finished a similar distance behind the winner last time at Windsor. Though obviously inferior to his conqueror, he is capable of finding a maiden, or nursery now he is qualified.
**Pinafore** a cheap purchase but a sturdy, decent-looking sort, looks a fair buy on the evidence of this debut. She did well to chase home two decent types, admittedly with a handy weight advantage, and should stay at least another furlong.
**General Haigh** is looking a bit exposed in maiden company but has some ability and should be at home in nurseries.
**Bamzooki** is proving a bit disappointing but should be placed to advantage when qualified for nurseries. Furthermore, faster ground may be in her favour.
**Luciferous(USA)** is showing a fair level of form but needs to be aimed at run-of-the-mill company to have a live chance of success. *Official explanation: trainer said filly missed the break*

## 4937 DREAMS OF EASTWELL MANOR FILLIES' H'CAP — 6f
**5:50** (5:50) (E) (0-70,65) 3-Y-0+ **£3,581** (£1,102; £551; £275) **Stalls** High

Form RPR

5455 **1** **Fair Compton**[14] 4547 3-9-2 57 ............ RLMoore 6 64
(RHannon) *w ldr: rdn 2f out: narrow ld ins fnl f: all out* **10/1**

5302 **2** *hd* **I Wish**[18] 4414 6-9-5 57 ............ GBaker 2 63
(MMadgwick) *hld up in rr: stdy prog over 2f out: drvn over 1f out: styd on fnl f: jst failed* **9/2**[3]

4063 **3** *hd* **Stokesies Wish**[14] 4547 4-9-3 60 ............ HayleyTurner(5) 8 65
(JLSpearing) *t.k.h: mde most: hrd rdn 2f out: narrowly hdd ins fnl f: jst hld* **7/2**[2]

10- **4** *shd* **Riquewihr**[294] 5872 4-9-8 60 ............ TPQueally 10 65
(DRLoder) *wl in tch: chsd ldng pair over 2f out: hrd rdn over 1f out: styd on ins fnl f: jst hld* **7/1**

3212 **5** 1 3/4 **Cut Ridge (IRE)**[8] 4708 5-9-3 55 ............ EAhern 9 55
(JSWainwright) *trckd ldrs: rdn and nt qckn wl over 1f out: kpt on same pce after* **13/8**[1]

0400 **6** 5 **La Vie Est Belle**[13] 4580 3-9-10 65 ............ GCarter 5 50
(BRMillman) *t.k.h: pressed ldng pair tl wknd over 2f out* **12/1**

1000 **7** 1 3/4 **Alizar (IRE)**[23] 4267 3-9-2 57 ............ LisaJones 7 37
(SDow) *hld up in rr: shkn up over 2f out: no prog and btn fnl 2f* **25/1**

00-0 **8** 3 **Bayonet**[28] 4148 8-7-13 40 ............ JFMcDonald(3) 3 11
(JaneSouthcombe) *chsd ldrs to 1/2-way: sn u.p and btn* **40/1**

5000 **9** 2 **Bells Beach (IRE)**[2] 4879 6-8-7 45 ............ RMullen 1 10
(PHowling) *a towards rr: rdn and struggling after 2f* **12/1**

-000 **10** 5 **Averlline**[18] 4414 3-9-5 60 ............(t) DKinsella 4 10
(BDeHaan) *s.s: a detached in last: pushed along and no prog 1/2-way* **20/1**

1m 11.23s (-0.42) **Going Correction** +0.025s/f (Good)
**WFA** 3 from 4yo+ 3lb **10** Ran SP% **126.5**
Speed ratings: **103,102,102,102,100 93,91,87,84,77**CSF £58.28 CT £201.81 TOTE £14.70: £3.70, £1.20, £1.90; EX 88.70.
**Owner** Jubert Family **Bred** Mrs B Skinner And D F Powell **Trained** East Everleigh, Wilts

**FOCUS**
A typical race of its type for the course, and the form is modest but ordinary.

**NOTEBOOK**
**Fair Compton** had looked well exposed but she had been running with credit for the most part and she found just enough in a desperate four-way finish.
**I Wish** stays a bit farther than this and could have done with an extra few yards.
**Stokesies Wish** again ran her race, only to go under narrowly in a close finish. She is only moderate but looks in good shape at present.
**Riquewihr**, lightly raced, looks to be on the right sort of handicap mark and cannot be ruled out in similar company if coming out of this race well.
**Cut Ridge(IRE)** has been in smart form of late and again ran well, though not quite good enough at the weights.
**La Vie Est Belle** could do with some mercy from the Handicapper.
**Bayonet** *Official explanation: trainer said mare hung left throughout*

## 4938 KMFM: WEST KENT'S WINNING MUSIC STATION H'CAP — 7f
**6:20** (6:21) (D) (0-80,77) 3-Y-0 **£5,681** (£1,748; £874; £437) **Stalls** High

Form RPR

0415 **1** **Stevedore (IRE)**[11] 4619 3-8-13 69 ............ GCarter 2 80
(BRMillman) *pressed ldr: led wl over 1f out: hrd rdn fnl f: hld on wl* **20/1**

1 **2** *hd* **Polar Magic**[58] 3251 3-9-0 70 ............ JPMurtagh 3 81+
(JRFanshawe) *t.k.h: trckd ldrs: rdn to chse wnr over 1f out: str chal fnl f: jst hld* **1/1**[1]

4310 **3** 1 3/4 **Corky (IRE)**[10] 4646 3-9-7 77 ............ RLMoore 9 83
(RHannon) *trckd ldrs: swtchd lft wl over 2f out: effrt to chse ldng pair fnl f: kpt on but no imp* **8/1**

6311 **4** 1 1/4 **United Spirit (IRE)**[15] 4517 3-8-9 65 ............(b) EAhern 5 68
(MAMagnusson) *racd freely: led to wl over 1f out: nt qckn* **7/1**[3]

5100 **5** 1 1/4 **Sweet Reply**[39] 3819 3-9-3 73 ............ TPQueally 8 73
(IAWood) *chsd ldng pair to 2f out: hrd rdn and fdd* **25/1**

2063 **6** 3/4 **Princess Galadriel**[16] 4483 3-8-2 58 ............ DKinsella 1 56
(JRBest) *racd awkwardly: hld up in last: taken to outside over 2f out: hrd rdn and hanging lft: no real prog* **16/1**

0203 **7** 1/2 **Lorien Hill (IRE)**[10] 4646 3-9-3 73 ............ DHolland 4 69
(BWHills) *racd in last pair: pushed along 1/2-way: struggling after: one pce fnl 2f* **4/1**[2]

6502 **8** 3 1/2 **Dr Synn**[3] 4845 3-8-10 66 ............ MTebbutt 6 53
(JAkehurst) *a towards rr: jockey dropped whip over 2f out: n.d after* **8/1**

0000 **9** 8 **Mutassem (FR)**[8] 4726 3-8-9 65 ............ MHenry 7 31
(TKeddy) *t.k.h: chsd ldrs: bmpd wl over 2f out: wknd* **100/1**

1m 24.0s (-0.21) **Going Correction** +0.025s/f (Good) **9** Ran SP% **120.2**
Speed ratings: **102,101,99,98,96 96,95,91,82**CSF £41.75 CT £198.71 TOTE £18.60: £3.40, £1.20, £2.20; EX 86.00.
**Owner** Mrs S Clifford **Bred** C J Foy **Trained** Kentisbeare, Devon
■ Stewards Enquiry : R L Moore one-day ban: careless riding (Sep 1)

**FOCUS**
A confusing result, with the winner stepping up on recent performances. The form is fair, but the second is progressive and on a fair mark.

**NOTEBOOK**
**Stevedore(IRE)** was given a positive ride and proved he is effective on ground with cut in it. The change of stable appears to have done him good.
**Polar Magic** disappointed his supporters but he only just went under and his handicap mark looks right. It will be interesting to see if he is tried on fast ground, and how he performs on it, but he looks one to keep in mind when there is some cut..
**Corky(IRE)**, whose victory came on similar ground, put up a fair effort off top-weight.
**United Spirit(IRE)** was readily beaten on her hat-trick bid, thus exposing her limitations.
**Sweet Reply** has become inconsistent but may be better on faster ground.
**Princess Galadriel** did not look comfortable and may be most effective on fast ground.

## 4939 MERCEDES-BENZ DIRECT MAIDEN STKS — 1m 4f (P)
**6:50** (6:52) (D) 3-Y-0+ **£3,640** (£1,120; £560; £280) **Stalls** Low

Form RPR

22-2 **1** **Red Damson (IRE)**[15] 4513 3-8-12 80 ............ JMackay 12 83
(SirMarkPrescott) *led for 2f: chsd ldr: rdn to ld again 4f out: drvn clr fnl f* **7/2**[3]

0-33 **2** 2 1/2 **Dalisay (IRE)**[54] 3374 3-8-7 74 ............ KFallon 7 74
(SirMichaelStoute) *trckd ldng pair: chsd wnr over 3f out: hrd rdn and nt qckn over 1f out* **5/2**[1]

5452 **3** 3 1/2 **Mouftari (USA)**[47] 3574 3-8-12 80 ............ DHolland 13 73
(BWHills) *led after 2f to 4f out: drvn and one pce fnl 3f* **3/1**[2]

**4** *nk* **Alph**[98] 7-9-8 ............ RHavlin 6 73
(RIngram) *racd in midfield: pushed along and prog to chse clr ldng trio 2f out: kpt on* **100/1**

-0 **5** 7 **Sunshine On Me**[20] 4369 3-8-7 ............ RMullen 10 57
(CFWall) *taken down early and mounted on crse: dwlt: wl in rr: sme prog into midfield 3f out: n.d* **20/1**

56 **6** *nk* **Rollswood (USA)**[16] 4492 4-9-8 ............(p) GCarter 8 61
(PRHedger) *t.k.h: trckd ldrs: outpcd 4f out: fdd over 2f out* **25/1**

0 **7** *shd* **Constructor**[26] 4195 3-8-12 ............ DSweeney 1 61
(CACyzer) *trckd ldrs: outpcd 4f out: wknd 2f out* **50/1**

0600 **8** 3/4 **Madame Marie (IRE)**[21] 4339 4-9-3 48 ............ LisaJones 9 55
(SDow) *s.s: nvr beyond midfield: outpcd and btn over 3f out* **33/1**

**9** 1 **Sadler's Rock (IRE)**[35] 6-9-8 ............ RLMoore 5 58
(GLMoore) *s.v.s: wl in rr: outpcd over 4f out but stl gng wl enough: nvr nr ldrs after* **7/1**

6-00 **10** *hd* **Abbeygate**[10] 4628 3-8-12 64 ............ MHenry 15 58
(TKeddy) *wl in rr: rdn and struggling 5f out: kpt on over 1f out* **33/1**

0-02 **11** 3 **So Determined (IRE)**[18] 4417 3-8-12 60 ............ EAhern 3 53
(GAButler) *racd in midfield: outpcd 4f out: no ch after* **10/1**

0 **12** 10 **Patterson (IRE)**[13] 4583 3-8-7 ............ ADaly 4 32
(MMadgwick) *chsd ldrs tl wknd over 3f out* **66/1**

**13** 1 **Charing Cross (IRE)**[86] 3-8-12 ............ RBrisland 11 36
(GLMoore) *dwlt: a in rr: lost tch 5f out* **25/1**

00 **14** *dist* **Peters Ploy**[37] 3882 4-9-5 ............ J-PGuillambert(3) 2 —
(TKeddy) *restrained s: hld up in rr: lost tch 5f out: sn t.o* **100/1**

0506 **15** 6 **Stylish Dancer**[28] 4128 3-8-8 47 ow1 ............ IMongan 14 —
(MBlanshard) *a towards rr: wknd and eased 3f out: t.o* **50/1**

2m 33.78s (-0.46) **Going Correction** +0.10s/f (Slow)
**WFA** 3 from 4yo+ 10lb **15** Ran SP% **123.1**
Speed ratings: **105,103,101,100,96 95,95,95,94,94 92,85,85,—,—**CSF £11.78 TOTE £3.80: £1.30, £2.00, £1.70; EX 12.10.
**Owner** W E Sturt-Osborne House V **Bred** Eyrefield Lodge Stud **Trained** Newmarket, Suffolk

**FOCUS**
A decent race of its type, with the first four home looking relatively useful. The runner-up should win a similar contest, but the overall form looks muddling despite the fair time.

**NOTEBOOK**
**Red Damson(IRE)** had been runner-up on his four previous starts but made no mistake this time. The real test will come when he is back in handicap company, but this was a step in the right direction..
**Dalisay(IRE)**, a late-maturing type, is short on finishing speed but has been showing enough to hold fair prospects. She should be placed to get off the mark at this trip and maybe beyond, with All-Weather surfaces now an option.
**Mouftari(USA)** just about got the trip but did it rather slowly and it remains to be seen whether this distance, or ten furlongs, is his best.
**Alph**, unplaced in two races over hurdles, made a most respectable Flat debut at the age of seven. A well-built sort, he could be interesting around the gaffs if his trainer can find the right race.
**Sunshine On Me** looks like a handicapper and she will be qualified after one more run.
**Rollswood(USA)** is now qualified for handicaps and will be more at home in that company.
**Constructor** looks like he is heading for handicaps, but he needs another run to qualify.
**Sadler's Rock(IRE)** was never competitive after walking out of the stalls, but looks capable of a bit better.

## 4940 MERCEDES-BENZ DIRECT CLAIMING STKS — 1m 2f (P)
**7:20** (7:20) (E) 3-4-Y-0 **£4,225** (£1,300; £650; £325) **Stalls** Low

Form RPR

-006 **1** **Belisco (USA)**[7] 4738 3-9-2 69 ............(bt[1]) JPMurtagh 1 67+
(MrsAJPerrett) *trckd ldrs and a gng easily: effrt to ld over 1f out: hung lft but sn rdn clr* **7/1**[3]

3261 **2** 2 **One Upmanship**[16] 4491 3-9-2 65 ............ RLMoore 4 64+
(JGPortman) *trckd ldrs: effrt 2f out: chsd wnr ins fnl f: kpt on but no ch* **5/1**[2]

0040 **3** 1 1/4 **Canni Thinkaar (IRE)**[28] 4138 3-8-6 59 ............ EAhern 6 51
(PWHarris) *prom: rdn over 4f out: kpt on u.p fnl 3f* **11/1**

4040 **4** *shd* **Maria Bonita (IRE)**[29] 4086 3-8-7 63 ............(b) DHolland 11 52
(RMBeckett) *hld up in rr: prog over 2f out: clsng whn hmpd jst over 1f out: styd on ins fnl f* **8/1**

5505 **5** 1/2 **Esperance (IRE)**[17] 4460 4-8-13 48 ............ SHitchcott(3) 8 52
(JAkehurst) *hld up towards rr: gng wl enough over 2f out: effrt over 1f out: hrd rdn and kpt on one pce* **20/1**

00-4 **6** *3 ½* **French Gigolo**[38] [3846] 4-9-4 59 GCarter 10 47
(CNAllen) *prom: trckd ldr 6f out: led 3f out: hdd over 1f out: wknd fnl f* **20/1**

3654 **7** *½* **Platinum Pirate**[73] [2783] 3-9-6 61 (v) DarrenWilliams 5 56
(KRBurke) *racd in midfield: cl enough over 3f out: wknd wl over 1f out* **7/1**[3]

0205 **8** *1 ½* **Another Con (IRE)**[12] [4600] 3-8-6 60 ow1 KFallon 2 40
(PHowling) *led: drvn 4f out: hdd 3f out: btn whn hmpd jst over 1f out: eased* **7/4**[1]

3025 **9** *nk* **Bretton**[33] [3990] 3-9-3 44 BReilly(3) 12 53?
(BAPearce) *wl in rr: outpcd fr 3f out: n.d after* **33/1**

0-06 **10** *shd* **Richie Boy**[26] [4195] 3-9-6 64 MHenry 9 53
(MAJarvis) *dwlt: wl in rr: prog on outer over 2f out to chse ldrs: wknd over 1f out* **14/1**

5004 **11** *nk* **Zalkani (IRE)**[9] [4669] 4-8-9 61 AHindley(7) 3 40
(BGPowell) *hld up in rr: prog on inner 3f out: clsng whn hmpd against rail jst over 1f out: nt rcvr* **25/1**

6000 **12** *6* **Estrella Levante**[15] [4519] 4-8-13 38 (p) LisaJones 7 26
(RMFlower) *pressed ldrs tl wknd 3f out* **66/1**

0062 **P** **Auroville**[10] [4654] 3-9-2 57 RMullen 13 —
(MLWBell) *racd in midfield: wknd 3f out: t.o whn p.u and dismntd nr fin* **8/1**

2m 7.89s (0.04) **Going Correction** +0.10s/f (Slow)
**WFA** 3 from 4yo 8lb **13** Ran SP% **133.1**
Speed ratings: **103,101,100,100,99 97,96,95,95,95 94,90,—** CT £10.00 TOTE £3.30: £1.90, £3.60, £; EX72.00 1.Belisco was claimed by C. A. Dwyer for £10,000. Canni Thinkaar was claimed by P. Butler for £5,000. Richie Boy was cla
**Owner** Michael H Watt **Bred** Tall Oaks Farm **Trained** Pulborough, W Sussex
■ Stewards Enquiry : G Carter caution: careless riding

**FOCUS**
Run at a steady pace, but not a bad claimer of its type. The first two home set a reasonable level of performance, but overall the form is modest.

**NOTEBOOK**
**Belisco(USA)**, less exposed than most of these, was helped by the first-time blinkers, though his tendency to hang was an indication that he is not entirely straightforward. However, he seemed at home on the surface and got the trip well.
**One Upmanship** has been in pretty good form in recent races and this was another decent effort. He can now be said to stay ten furlongs.
**Canni Thinkaar(IRE)** is well exposed but this was one of his better performances.
**Maria Bonita(IRE)** ran reasonably well and looks worth another try on sand.
**Esperance(IRE)** is essentially a plater and ran as well as could be expected.
**French Gigolo** has been lightly raced but showed a bit of form. He would be interesting in a seller.
**Another Con(IRE)**, plenty short enough in the betting, was in trouble a long way out.
**Auroville** was eased after losing his action. *Official explanation: jockey said colt lost its action*

## 4941 BURDEN GROUP H'CAP — 1m 2f (P)
**7:50** (7:52) (F) (0-55,55) 3-Y-O — **£3,066** (£876; £438) **Stalls** Low

Form RPR

0160 **1** **Mister Completely (IRE)**[22] [4302] 3-9-0 **49** TPQueally 11 52
(JRBest) *chsd ldrs: rdn over 2f out: styd on u.p to ld last 100yds: hld on* **16/1**

0054 **2** *nk* **Nina Fontenail (FR)**[6] [4775] 3-8-5 **40** RHavlin 10 42
(BRMillman) *settled in rr: rdn over 2f out: styd on wl fr over 1f out: clsd on wnr nr fin: jst hld* **12/1**

0-00 **3** *¾* **Sixtilsix (IRE)**[33] [3994] 3-8-6 **41** ow1 RLappin 3 42
(WJarvis) *trckd ldrs: gng easily over 2f out: effrt over 1f out: drvn to ld ins fnl f: sn hdd and one pce* **33/1**

0320 **4** *½* **Mr Belvedere**[24] [4242] 3-9-2 **51** EAhern 6 51
(AJLidderdale) *racd in midfield: effrt whn nt clr run briefly 2f out: drvn and styd on fnl f: one pce nr fin* **10/1**

0432 **5** *¾* **Rubaiyat (IRE)**[28] [4128] 3-9-4 **53** JFEgan 13 52+
(GWragg) *racd wd: hld up: rapid prog 4f out: led 2f out: hanging lft over 1f out: hdd & wknd ins fnl f* **5/4**[1]

0006 **6** *1* **Sonderborg**[3] [4848] 3-9-1 **50** (b) LisaJones 7 47
(MissAMNewton-Smith) *settled in rr: rdn and outpcd over 2f out: styd on fnl f: nvr nrr* **10/1**

4565 **7** *3* **Fiddles Music**[16] [4467] 3-8-5 **40** CCatlin 1 31
(MissSheenaWest) *trckd ldr: led over 3f out to 2f out: wknd fnl f* **14/1**

4200 **8** *7* **Forge Lane (IRE)**[5] [4798] 3-9-3 **52** (b) RLMoore 12 30
(GLMoore) *hld up in rr: jst in tch whn nt clr run 2f out: no ch after* **4/1**[2]

5404 **9** *nk* **Prince Valentine**[33] [3990] 3-9-3 **52** MTebbutt 9 29
(DBFeek) *trckd ldrs: cl enough over 2f out: rdn and wknd rapidly over 1f out* **20/1**

3500 **10** *1 ¾* **Almost Welcome**[47] [3572] 3-9-0 **49** IMongan 2 23
(SDow) *sn last: hanging and lost tch bef 1/2-way: wl bhd 3f out* **25/1**

0003 **11** *8* **Tshukudu**[10] [4654] 3-8-1 **36** DKinsella 8 —
(MBlanshard) *prom tl wknd over 4f out* **20/1**

0000 **12** *2 ½* **Dream Of Dubai (IRE)**[15] [4517] 3-9-1 **50** (p) KFallon 4 4
(PMitchell) *led to over 3f out: wkng whn hmpd over 2f out* **7/1**[3]

2m 8.98s (1.13) **Going Correction** +0.10s/f (Slow) **12** Ran SP% **131.7**
Speed ratings: **99,98,98,97,97 96,93,88,88,86 80,78** CSF £204.71 CT £6208.17 TOTE £20.80: £4.40, £3.20, £6.90; EX 139.10 Place 6 £267.52, Place 5 £174.35.
**Owner** G G Racing **Bred** Eamonn Griffin **Trained** Hucking, Kent
■ Stewards Enquiry : R Lappin one-day ban: careless riding (Sep 1)

**FOCUS**
A poor race little better than a seller, with a disappointing favourite and so rated negatively for the present.

**NOTEBOOK**
**Mister Completely(IRE)** was more at home over this trip, but this was a weak race.
**Nina Fontenail(FR)** put in a sound effort, albeit in a low-grade field. She looked well at home on the surface.
**Sixtilsix(IRE)** found this company more like it and is worth trying again in a similar event.
**Mr Belvedere** got the trip well and looks sure to turn up in similar races following this effort.
**Rubaiyat(IRE)** is becoming frustrating. He cannot drop much more in grade without going to claiming or selling company.
**Sonderborg** occasionally shows flashes of ability, but there was nothing to get excited about here.
**Almost Welcome** *Official explanation: jockey said colt hung right in the early stages*
T/Plt: £241.50 to a £1 stake. Pool: £31,531.25. 95.30 winning tickets. T/Qpdt: £45.90 to a £1 stake. Pool: £2,946.90. 47.50 winning tickets. JN

# 4757 RIPON (R-H)
Saturday, August 21
**4942 Meeting Abandoned** - Waterlogged

# 4918 SANDOWN (R-H)
Saturday, August 21

**OFFICIAL GOING: Soft**

## 4948 VARIETY CLUB ATALANTA STKS (LISTED RACE) (F&M) — 1m 14y
**1:40** (1:40) (A) 3-Y-O+ — **£17,850** (£6,600; £3,300; £1,500) **Stalls** High

Form RPR

-503 **1** **Zietory**[6] [4773] 4-9-0 99 LDettori 2 98
(PFICole) *lw: trckd ldr: drvn to ld ins fnl 2f: edgd lft jst ins last: drvn out* **4/1**[3]

5 **2** *nk* **Bayberry (UAE)**[10] [4640] 4-9-0 90 WRyan 3 97
(HRACecil) *b.hind: chsd ldrs: drvn and styd on fr over 1f out: chsd wnr ins last but no ex nr fin* **8/1**

-012 **3** *½* **Three Secrets (IRE)**[30] [4068] 3-8-8 85 RHughes 1 97+
(PWChapple-Hyam) *lw: sn set modest pce: rdn over 2f out: hdd ins fnl quarter m: styng on whn hmpd jst ins last: swtchd rt:nt rcvr* **10/1**

1-16 **4** *¾* **Silk Fan (IRE)**[22] [4286] 3-8-8 95 DHolland 5 95
(PWHarris) *lw: hld up in rr: rdn and hdwy 2f out: styd on to chse ldrs ins fnl f: sn one pce* **5/4**[1]

4110 **5** *3* **Imperialistic (IRE)**[78] [2641] 3-8-8 94 (p) DarrenWilliams 4 89
(KRBurke) *sn in tch: hdwy to chse ldrs 5f out: effrt and rdn over 2f out: wknd last half f* **7/2**[2]

1m 47.57s (3.65) **Going Correction** +0.475s/f (Yiel)
**WFA** 3 from 4yo 6lb **5** Ran SP% **106.9**
Speed ratings: **100,99,99,98,95** CSF £29.83 TOTE £3.70: £2.10, £3.10; EX 25.70.
**Owner** The Fairy Story Partnership **Bred** Deepwood Farm Stud **Trained** Whatcombe, Oxon

**FOCUS**
Not the strongest of Listed races and it was run at a moderate gallop resulting in a modest time.

**NOTEBOOK**
**Zietory** is a proven performer in this grade under the conditions - unlike many of her rivals - and had 4lb plus in hand on her rivals on adjusted official figures. She was never far off the pace and came through with a winning challenge over a furlong and a half out. Always holding the runner-up, she is in good heart at present and, as she is at her best with cut in the ground, should continue to pay her way.
**Bayberry(UAE)** made a pleasing start to her British career when fifth over a mile two at Salisbury behind New Morning, and improved on that to run a good second. This easier going would have suited and she can win a Listed race, although her stable's runners seem to find it mighty hard to hold their form these days.
**Three Secrets(IRE)** had the run of things from the front and was out of contention for winning when impeded in the final furlong. She is not up to this level in this country but may sneak a poor Listed race abroad.
**Silk Fan(IRE)** has struggled the last twice now in Group and Listed company. She was not beaten far but needs to find improvement from somewhere if she is to win at this level.
**Imperialistic(IRE)** is another who has fallen short at this sort of level the last twice and she never looked like getting involved.

## 4949 IVECO DAILY SOLARIO STKS (GROUP 3) — 7f 16y
**2:15** (2:18) (A) 2-Y-O — **£26,100** (£9,900; £4,950; £2,250) **Stalls** High

Form RPR

41 **1** **Windsor Knot (IRE)**[15] [4523] 2-8-11 LDettori 2 108
(JHMGosden) *lw: mde virtually all: shkn up 2f out: styd on strly fnl f and forged clr nr fin* **9/2**[2]

616 **2** *2 ½* **Embossed (IRE)**[14] [4527] 2-8-11 98 RLMoore 4 102
(RHannon) *lw: chsd ldrs: pushed wd bnd 5f out: rdn over 2f out: swtchd rt and chsd wnr ins fnl f but no imp* **14/1**

13 **3** *nk* **Propinquity**[42] [3726] 2-8-11 DHolland 8 101
(PWHarris) *lw: hld up in rr: drvn and hdwy over 2f out: chsd ldrs over 1f out and disp 2nd tl ins last: kpt on same pce* **12/1**

15 **4** *2 ½* **Pivotal Flame**[44] [3672] 2-8-11 RHughes 7 95
(BAMcmahon) *hld up in rr: hdwy fr over 2f out to chse wnr over 1f out: sn rdn: wknd ins last* **8/1**

1313 **5** *2* **Silver Wraith (IRE)**[22] [4288] 2-8-11 100 TPQueally 3 90
(NACallaghan) *chsd ldrs: c wd bnd 5f out: hrd rdn over 2f out: wknd over 1f out* **9/1**

2143 **6** *1 ¼* **Fox**[24] [4227] 2-8-11 100 KFallon 5 87
(CEBrittain) *chsd ldrs: rdn over 2f out: sn btn* **11/2**

11 **7** *hd* **Johnny Jumpup (IRE)**[42] [3748] 2-8-11 EAhern 1 87
(RMBeckett) *chsng ldrs: rn wd bnd 5f out: styd pressing ldrs tl rdn 3f out: sn lost pl: mod hdwy u.p ins last* **5/1**[3]

11 **8** *2* **Leo's Lucky Star (USA)**[54] [3373] 2-8-11 RHills 6 82
(MJohnston) *lw: chsd ldrs: rdn 3f out: styd in tch tl wknd rapidly fnl f* **5/2**[1]

1m 32.12s (1.03) **Going Correction** +0.475s/f (Yiel) **8** Ran SP% **114.3**
Speed ratings: **113,110,109,106,104 103,103,100** CSF £63.33 TOTE £5.80: £1.90, £3.30, £3.20; EX 58.20.
**Owner** Sheikh Mohammed **Bred** Tally-Ho Stud **Trained** Manton, Wilts

**FOCUS**
A modest Group Three with the form horses running below par as a result of the soft ground and Dettori being allowed to lead throughout on Windsor Knot. Despite that, the winning time was smart given the conditions, but the majority are no better than Listed level.

**NOTEBOOK**
**Windsor Knot(IRE)** came into this on the back of a maiden win at Newmarket and had a bit to find with the proven performers. However, the necessary improvement was forthcoming - reversing debut form with Embossed in the process, and under a good front-running ride from Dettori, was able to take a decisive advantage before staying on well to win comfortably. Undoubtedly flattered by the winning margin, he will need to raise his game significantly to take a hand in the better juvenile races, the Royal Lodge given as a possible target, as this was only modest Group Three form. However, he does have the scope to improve on this and will stay a mile.
**Embossed(IRE)** was a little unlucky not to get closer in the Shergar Cup Juvenile and showed his true form, running on to claim second late on. This is about his level and he will stay a mile.
**Propinquity** improved on previous form to take third, but in all honesty is a Listed performer at best. He still has some improving to do though and will get farther.
**Pivotal Flame** looks to have inherited his sire's speed, as he travelled well before finding conditions taxing his stamina and he ultimately weakened. Back over six furlongs on this sort of ground will see him in a better light.
**Silver Wraith(IRE)** has done all his racing on a fast surface and struggled to raise his game in the conditions. He should have the run ignored.

**Fox** ran a long way below form and is another for whom ground conditions would not have suited. He is another to disappoint from the Vintage Stakes, and that form is now beginning to look a little suspect.
**Johnny Jumpup(IRE)** had a bit to prove and it was only his liking for this ground that made him third favourite. He raced lazily when winning at Salisbury, but simply seemed not good enough and began to struggle once the pace quickened.
**Leo's Lucky Star(USA)** came into this on the back of two easy wins over six furlongs on fast ground and was made favourite on the strength of reputation - trainer Mark Johnston putting him up along with Shamardal and Elliots World as one of his better juveniles - but he simply could not go on the ground and was always struggling. This was evidently not his running, and one can expect to see a totally different horse back on a faster surface. *Official explanation: trainer's representative had no explanation for the poor form shown*

## 4950 WILLIAM HILL H'CAP — 1m 2f 7y
**2:50** (2:52) (C) (0-90,87) 3-Y-O+ **£12,644** (£4,796; £2,398; £1,090) **Stalls** High

Form — RPR
0000 **1** **Telemachus**[14] [4540] 4-9-7 **80**....(b) MFenton 12 — 91
(JGGiven) *trckd ldrs: rdn over 2f out: led 1f out: drvn and styd on wl fnl f* **16/1**
1030 **2** 1 1/2 **Silvaline**[14] [4540] 5-9-7 **80**.... JPMurtagh 6 — 88
(TKeddy) *trckd ldr: narrow ld ins fnl 3f: sn drvn along: hdd 1f out: kpt on fnl f but no imp on wnr* **10/1**
032 **3** 1 3/4 **Dream Magic**[5] [4814] 6-9-2 **75**.... DHolland 4 — 80
(MJRyan) *chsd ldrs: pushed along fr 4f out: hrd drvn fr over 2f out: styd on fnl f but nt pce to chal* **15/2**[3]
1 **4** 1/2 **Deep Purple**[38] [3843] 3-9-4 **85**.... ADaly 10 — 89+
(MPTregoning) *h.d.w: lw: bhd: pushed along on outside and green over 2f out: styd on fr over 1f out: fin wl but nt rch ldrs* **12/1**
1-14 **5** 1/2 **Faayej (IRE)**[71] [2845] 4-9-10 **83**.... RHills 2 — 86+
(SirMichaelStoute) *lw: bhd: rdn 3f out: hung rt 2f out: styd on fr over 1f out and r.o ins last but nvr gng pce to rch ldrs* **11/2**[1]
1511 **6** nk **Desert Island Disc**[18] [4416] 7-9-2 **75**.... TPQueally 5 — 78
(JJBridger) *led: hdd jst ins fnl 3f: styd chsng ldr: wknd ins fnl f* **9/1**
0052 **7** 3/4 **Ryan's Future (IRE)**[9] [4691] 4-8-13 **75**.... SHitchcott(3) 11 — 77
(JAkehurst) *in tch 5f out: rdn to chse ldrs 3f out: one pce over 1f out: wknd ins last* **8/1**
0-20 **8** 3 1/2 **Golano**[56] [3325] 4-9-7 **80**.... RHughes 8 — 76
(PRWebber) *mid-div: pushed along over 3f out: rdn and one pce fnl 2f* **20/1**
-006 **9** 4 **Travelling Band (IRE)**[37] [3872] 6-8-13 **75**.... LPKeniry(3) 13 — 64
(AMBalding) *bhd: impr 5f out: nvr rchd ldrs: rdn 3f out: wknd fr 2f out* **14/1**
4104 **10** 3/4 **Silent Hawk (IRE)**[45] [3641] 3-9-6 **87**....(t) LDettori 1 — 74
(SaeedBinSuroor) *in tch: pushed along 3f out: no ch whn hung rt over 1f out* **8/1**
0530 **11** nk **Sir Haydn**[26] [4196] 4-8-5 **64**....(b) RLMoore 14 — 51
(JRJenkins) *rdn over 3f out: a bhd* **28/1**
0003 **12** 3 1/2 **Breathing Sun (IRE)**[13] [4582] 3-8-8 **75**....(t) RMullen 7 — 56
(WJMusson) *a in rr* **9/1**
5125 **13** 4 **Miss Pebbles (IRE)**[7] [4760] 4-9-1 **74**....(v) NPollard 3 — 48
(SCWilliams) *hung rt 3f out: a in rr* **14/1**
0641 **14** 6 **Barry Island**[21] [4343] 5-9-4 **77**.... KFallon 9 — 41
(DRCElsworth) *rdn 3f out: a in rr* **7/1**[2]

2m 13.96s (3.78) **Going Correction** +0.475s/f (Yiel) **14** Ran SP% **126.1**
**WFA** 3 from 4yo+ 8lb
Speed ratings: **103,101,100,100,99 99,98,95,92,92 91,89,85,81**CSF £175.41 CT £1326.58 TOTE £22.40: £4.20, £3.50, £3.30; EX 172.50 Trifecta £1660.10 Part won. Pool £2,338.30. 0.40 winning units..
**Owner** The Travellers **Bred** Cheveley Park Stud Ltd **Trained** Willoughton, Lincs

**FOCUS**
They went a decent pace in the ground and this appears strong form for the grade.

**NOTEBOOK**
**Telemachus**, running off a 6lb lower mark than when last successful, has been badly out of form. However, these were the softest conditions he has had for a while, and he was able to reverse recent Haydock form with Silvaline. He showed a willing attitude in grinding up the stiff finish and was never going to be caught. He is always a danger when the ground is soft, and there is no reason why he should not continue to run well with the going now set to be in his favour for a while.
**Silvaline**, last year's winner of the race, has been finding things tougher off this sort of mark recently. However, he too was well favoured by the going and he kept plugging away to hold second. His best form is when coming from off the pace and he will do better under more restrained tactics.
**Dream Magic** has returned to form of late with some solid placed efforts and this represented another sound run. Although not getting any better, he is still capable and will be suited by a return to a faster surface.
**Deep Purple** is probably the one to take from the race as he came into this on the back of a sole run - narrow winner of a fast-ground Kempton maiden - and found himself a bit behind and running green under pressure. He stayed on nicely in the final furlong towards the centre of the track and was gaining with every stride at the line. His stable remain a little out of form but, when they find their feet again, there is a decent race in this one.
**Faayej(IRE)** has now run well on all three starts here this season - winning first time up before finishing fourth under a penalty - and he again ran a sound race. He looked in trouble at one stage, but got going once hitting the rising ground and kept on well enough. A mile and a half back on faster ground will see him in a better light.
**Desert Island Disc** took them along at a decent clip but could not respond when asked to go again in the ground. This trip in this ground would not have been ideal and he can do better back on faster going.
**Ryan's Future(IRE)** failed to run up to form and may have found this ground too soft.
**Silent Hawk(IRE)** *Official explanation: jockey said colt was unsuited by the soft ground*
**Breathing Sun(IRE)** *Official explanation: jockey said colt finished distressed*
**Barry Island** *Official explanation: jockey said gelding lost its action*

## 4951 MICHAEL SHANLY RATED STKS (H'CAP) — 5f 6y
**3:25** (3:29) (B) (0-100,108) 3-Y-O+ **£15,314** (£5,808; £2,904; £1,320) **Stalls** High

Form — RPR
0011 **1** **Smokin Beau**[7] [4759] 7-10-1 **108**.... KFallon 1 — 116
(NPLittmoden) *lw: trckd ldrs: drvn and styd on str fnl f to ld last strides* **2/1**[1]
010 **2** hd **Mutawaqed (IRE)**[21] [4324] 6-8-10 **89**....(t) RLMoore 5 — 96
(MAMagnusson) *b: b.hind: s.i.s: sn in tch: gd hdwy on rails and rdn fnl f: slt ld cl home: hdd last strides* **7/2**[2]
5402 **3** shd **Devise (IRE)**[14] [4538] 5-8-4 **86** oh4.... RMiles(3) 7 — 93
(MSSaunders) *pressed ldr tl led 2f out: rdn and edgd lft ins last: hdd and no ex cl home* **11/2**
2200 **4** 3/4 **Caustic Wit (IRE)**[12] [4614] 6-8-7 **86** oh1....(p) DHolland 2 — 90
(MSSaunders) *rr but in tch: rdn and hung lft 1f out: c rt and r.o wl fnl f: nt rch ldrs* **11/2**
1422 **5** 3/4 **Fruit Of Glory**[6] [4779] 5-9-2 **95**.... LDettori 3 — 97
(JRJenkins) *pressed ldrs over 3f: rdn fnl f: kpt on same pce* **9/2**[3]
3004 **6** 1 **Speed Cop**[14] [4526] 4-8-9 **95**.... TBlock(7) 4 — 94
(AMBalding) *b.hind: slt ld 3f: styd chsng ldrs tl wknd wl ins fnl f* **11/1**

63.70 secs (1.51) **Going Correction** +0.475s/f (Yiel) **6** Ran SP% **112.8**
Speed ratings: **106,105,105,104,103 101**CSF £9.30 TOTE £2.60: £1.70, £2.10; EX 13.00.
**Owner** Turf 2000 Limited **Bred** Alan Spargo **Trained** Newmarket, Suffolk

**FOCUS**
Another excellent performance from Smokin Beau who was winning for the third consecutive Saturday, and the form is solid.

**NOTEBOOK**
**Smokin Beau** continued his rich vein of form with a battling display under Fallon who only got him up in the dying strides. He had bolted up in the Great St Wilfred the previous Saturday, and was winning off a 10lb higher mark over a trip probably a furlong short of his best. There is no reason to believe his winning run stops here, and a return to Group company must surely be on the cards with something like the Haydock Sprint Cup seeming an ideal target, although connections had spoken of the Abbaye, where he is likely to finds things happening a bit too quickly.
**Mutawaqed(IRE)** looked to have done enough until collared close home. He went some way to reversing Goodwood form with Smokin Beau, and this was a better effort considering he was tardy at the gate.
**Devise(IRE)** was another who could easily have been called the winner at one stage, and he simply could offer no more late on.
**Caustic Wit(IRE)** ran a much better race than he has the last twice and was gaining on them with every stride.
**Fruit Of Glory** would have found this too sharp a test against some speedsters and could only muster the one pace.
**Speed Cop** would have been inconvenienced by the ground and deserves another chance to build on his Shergar Cup run.

## 4952 CURRENCIES DIRECT H'CAP — 5f 6y
**4:00** (4:01) (D) (0-85,87) 3-Y-O **£6,873** (£2,115; £1,057; £528) **Stalls** High

Form — RPR
2-51 **1** **Out After Dark**[17] [4456] 3-8-12 **76**.... LDettori 5 — 91+
(CGCox) *lw: mde virtually all: drvn and styd on strly fnl f: readily* **9/2**
-013 **2** 1 1/4 **Morgan Lewis (IRE)**[8] [4717] 3-8-4 **68**.... SCarson 2 — 79+
(GBBalding) *lw: trckd ldrs: wnt 2nd over 2f out: rdn fnl f: hung rt u.p and no imp ins last* **3/1**[2]
5052 **3** 1 **Skyharbor**[5] [4810] 3-8-9 **73**.... DHolland 7 — 81
(AMBalding) *chsd ldrs: rdn over 1f out: edgd rt u.p and one pce ins last* **4/1**[3]
2401 **4** 2 **Rydal (USA)**[9] [4688] 3-9-9 **87**....(v) KFallon 3 — 89+
(GAButler) *b.hind: chsd ldrs: rdn 2f out: wknd ins fnl f* **5/2**[1]
0213 **5** 1/2 **Trick Cyclist**[11] [4617] 3-8-2 **73**.... TBlock(7) 1 — 74
(AMBalding) *rr but in tch: hdwy on rails whn nt clr run over 1f out: swtchd lft: rdn and sn btn* **14/1**
1000 **6** 1 **Extremely Rare (IRE)**[47] [3585] 3-8-2 **66**.... JQuinn 4 — 64
(MSSaunders) *bhd: rdn fr 2f out: a outpcd* **25/1**
142 **7** 1 3/4 **Tregarron**[23] [4267] 3-8-8 **72**.... RLMoore 6 — 64
(RHannon) *chsd wnr tl appr fnl 2f: wknd qckly over 1f out* **7/1**

63.70 secs (1.51) **Going Correction** +0.475s/f (Yiel) **7** Ran SP% **114.8**
Speed ratings: **106,104,102,99,98 96,94**CSF £18.54 TOTE £4.20: £2.00, £2.40; EX 17.50.
**Owner** The Night Owls **Bred** C J Mills **Trained** Lambourn, Berks

**FOCUS**
A smart effort from Out After Dark, who has the profile of a really progressive sprinter, winning with a bit to spare and the form is strong.

**NOTEBOOK**
**Out After Dark** ◆ had been given a break since running well on soft ground at Ascot in April, and returned with a narrow maiden win at Pontefract - not achieving much on form. This however represented a step up and having bounced out well and got the rail, he was given a perfect ride by Dettori, who did not commit too soon, and he responded well when asked to bound away to win comfortably. Effective on both soft and fast ground, over five and six furlongs, he is one to follow and looks to have much more to offer.
**Morgan Lewis(IRE)** was inconvenienced by this drop in trip - shaping over six furlongs as though a seventh was the answer - and he simply did not have the legs of the winner. Undoubtedly progressive, he too acts on any ground and has a decent race in him back over a stiffer trip.
**Skyharbor** was a little unlucky when just touched off at Windsor last week and again ran well. He is proven on this ground and should continue to run well, but has nothing in hand of the Handicapper.
**Rydal(USA)** was a narrow winner under similar conditions at the last meeting, but the visor which he had on for the first time that day did not have the same effect and the 4lb higher mark would also have made things a little tougher.
**Trick Cyclist** was a little unlucky not to get closer - being denied a clear run when trying to make headway - but he would not have won anyhow.

## 4953 CROWN PERSONNEL NURSERY — 7f 16y
**4:35** (4:38) (D) 2-Y-O **£7,280** (£2,240; £1,120; £560) **Stalls** High

Form — RPR
0654 **1** **Im Spartacus**[16] [4482] 2-8-8 **69**.... MFenton 2 — 73
(IAWood) *lw: chsd ldrs: rdn over 2f out: str run to ld ins fnl f: r.o wl* **20/1**
6243 **2** 1 1/4 **Mozafin**[18] [4420] 2-9-3 **78**.... LDettori 6 — 79
(MRChannon) *led 1f: styd chsng ldrs: rdn over 2f out: led 1f out: hdd and no ex ins fnl f* **9/2**[2]
0403 **3** 1 3/4 **Ivana Illyich (IRE)**[12] [4612] 2-8-12 **73**.... JFEgan 4 — 70
(SKirk) *rn wd bnd 5f out: rr: rdn over 2f out: r.o u.p fnl f: nt rch ldrs* **9/1**[3]
6000 **4** 1 1/2 **Norcroft**[21] [4342] 2-9-2 **77**....(b[1]) DHolland 7 — 70
(NACallaghan) *awkward stalls: led after 1f: clr 3f out: hung lft over 1f out: sn hdd: no ex ins fnl f* **12/1**
3031 **5** 3 **Keep Bacckinhit (IRE)**[21] [4326] 2-9-5 **80**.... RLMoore 9 — 66
(GLMoore) *b.hind: rn wd bnd 5f out: sn trcking ldrs: rdn over 2f out: wknd fnl f* **10/1**
421 **6** 1 **Little Dalham**[28] [4149] 2-9-7 **82**.... KFallon 5 — 66
(PWChapple-Hyam) *in tch: rdn and effrt over 2f out: chsd ldrs u.p 1f out: wknd ins last* **13/8**[1]
0041 **7** 9 **King Of Blues (IRE)**[20] [4365] 2-9-0 **75**....(t) EAhern 3 — 37
(MAMagnusson) *lw: bhd: rdn and effrt over 2f out: nvr rch ldrs and wknd fnl f* **9/2**[2]
305 **8** 5 **Homme Dangereux**[26] [4187] 2-7-13 **60**.... JQuinn 8 — 10
(CREgerton) *plld hrd. chsd ldrs: lost pl over 3f out: rdn and effrt 2f out: n.d and wknd qckly over 1f out* **14/1**

1m 34.3s (3.21) **Going Correction** +0.475s/f (Yiel) **8** Ran SP% **112.7**
Speed ratings: **100,98,96,94,91 90,80,74**CSF £104.19 CT £889.85 TOTE £19.30: £3.40, £1.70, £2.10; EX 83.90.
**Owner** John Purcell **Bred** John Purcell **Trained** Upper Lambourn, Berks

**FOCUS**
With many of the principals running below form as a result of the ground, the form is nothing special. It was an improved effort from the winner however and an even stiffer test will suit.

**NOTEBOOK**

**Im Spartacus** has struggled since winning his maiden at Bath, but he ran better against lesser opposition at Folkestone recently and he was able to build on that, being well suited by the stiff finish. It is surprising he managed to win over five and a half furlongs on fast ground earlier in the season, as he is bred and shapes as though a mile is required, and there should be more to come from him when stepping up.

**Mozafin** was up there throughout and looked the likely winner when going on. However, he struggled with the stiff finish and was outstayed by the winner. Faster ground is the key to him and he will stay a mile.

**Ivana Illyich(IRE)** had been racing over six furlongs and looked in need of every yard of this seven furlong trip on what was her handicap debut - staying on when the race was all over. There is more to come from her and, although very speedily bred, shapes as though a mile will suit.

**Norcroft** was rushed up to lead after about a furlong having been awkward at the gates, and probably did a bit too much too early. He hung under pressure and was running on empty in the closing stages.

**Keep Bacckinhit(IRE)** came into this on the back of a nursery win at Goodwood, but was not suited by the ground and did not quite see out the trip in the going.

**Little Dalham** proved a big disappointment, running a long way below previous form over this seventh furlong on the softest ground he has encountered to date. He had stayed the trip well enough earlier in the year, so the run can primarily be put down to the ground.

**King Of Blues(IRE)** was another to run below form on this ground and he can given another chance. *Official explanation: jockey said was unsuited by the soft ground*

**Homme Dangereux** raced far too keenly and stopped sharply as a result. *Official explanation: jockey said colt failed to handle the bend*

## 4954 CAPITAL AVIATION MAIDEN FILLIES' STKS — 1m 14y

5:05 (5:13) (D) 3-Y-O — £5,486 (£1,688; £844; £422) Stalls High

Form — RPR

0- **1** **Porthcawl**[322] 5367 3-8-11 ........ LDettori 5 — 76
(MrsAJPerrett) *trckd ldr 1f and again 3f out: led appr fnl 2f: pushed out fnl f: readily* — **9/1**[3]

6255 **2** 1 1/4 **Anna Panna**[13] 4580 3-8-11 69 ........ DaneO'Neill 2 — 73
(HCandy) *bhd: hdwy 3f out: drvn to chse ldrs over 1f out: edgd rt ins last and styd on to go 2nd cl home: but no ch w wnr* — **9/1**[3]

2024 **3** 1 1/2 **Noora (IRE)**[9] 4683 3-8-11 72 ........ RHills 6 — 70
(MPTregoning) *in tch: rdn to chse wnr ins fnl 2f: kpt on tl outpcd ins last: lost 2nd nr fin* — **9/2**[2]

**4** 2 **Go Supersonic** 3-8-11 ........ KFallon 9 — 73+
(SirMichaelStoute) *lengthy: unf: chsd ldr after 2f tl 3f out: sn rdn: styng on one pce and hld whn hmpd ins fnl f* — **1/1**[1]

0005 **5** 3 1/2 **Tipsy Lady**[10] 4644 3-8-8 62 ........ LPKeniry(3) 3 — 59
(DRCElsworth) *b: led tl hdd appr fnl 2f: wknd over 1f out* — **16/1**

5036 **6** 1 3/4 **Halabaloo (IRE)**[8] 4726 3-8-11 73 ........(b[1]) JFEgan 1 — 56
(GWragg) *led to s: plld hrd and chsd ldrs: rdn 3f out: wknd 2f out* — **12/1**

**7** 6 **Poetry 'n Passion** 3-8-11 ........ WRyan 8 — 44
(CACyzer) *wl-grwn: str: bkwd: slowly away: a in rr* — **20/1**

**8** 3/4 **Abigail Adams** 3-8-11 ........ DHolland 10 — 42
(PWHarris) *str: bkwd: s.i.s: a in rr* — **10/1**

1m 47.54s (3.62) **Going Correction** +0.475s/f (Yiel) — **8** Ran SP% **115.6**

Speed ratings: **100,98,97,95,91 90,84,83**CSF £86.41 TOTE £8.10: £1.60, £2.00, £1.70; EX 81.70 Place 6 £1,053.75, Place 5 £182.12.

**Owner** Usk Valley Stud **Bred** K J Mercer **Trained** Pulborough, W Sussex

**FOCUS**

Not a strong maiden by any means with both second and third giving the form a moderate look.

**NOTEBOOK**

**Porthcawl** finished last of ten on her sole start last season over six furlongs at Newmarket and has clearly developed into a better three-year-old. The extra distance suited and, although beating a modest bunch, should improve and can probably make her mark in handicaps.

**Anna Panna** is exposed and her proximity does little for the form. She stayed on well but was never going to get there and remains frustrating.

**Noora(IRE)** is another exposed sort and she did not see her race out.

**Go Supersonic** will improve for this as she looked inexperienced, and much better can be expected over an extra couple of furlongs. She will have little trouble winning her maiden.

**Tipsy Lady** ran another honest race from the front without proving good enough to hold off the challengers.

**Halabaloo(IRE)** proved difficult before the start and pulled hard in the race. As a result he had little left at the business end.

**Poetry 'n Passion**, althougn beaten a long way, can be expected to show improvement on this.

**Abigail Adams** is another who will leave this running behind in time.

T/Plt: £836.10 to a £1 stake. Pool: £86,302.00. 75.35 winning tickets. T/Qpdt: £29.10 to a £1 stake. Pool: £6,479.10. 164.70 winning tickets. ST

4955 - (Foreign Racing) - See Raceform Interactive

# 4586 CURRAGH (R-H)

Saturday, August 21

**OFFICIAL GOING: Good to firm**

## 4956a EMERALD BLOODSTOCK BELGRAVE STKS (LISTED) — 6f

2:45 (2:45) 3-Y-O+ — £25,214 (£7,397; £3,524; £1,200)

RPR

**1** **Ulfah (USA)**[13] 4590 3-9-0 99 ........ DPMcDonogh 10 — 107
(KevinPrendergast, Ire) *cl up: led bef 1/2-way: strly pressed fnl f: kpt on wl: all out* — **7/1**[3]

**2** hd **Desert Fantasy (IRE)**[13] 4590 5-9-6 108 ........(bt) FMBerry 9 — 109
(CRoche, Ire) *s.i.s: prog 1/2-way: 4th and rdn over 2f out: styd on wl ins fnl f: jst failed* — **9/2**[1]

**3** 1 **Grand Reward (USA)**[13] 4590 3-9-0 106 ........ JPSpencer 7 — 103
(APO'Brien, Ire) *towards rr: hdwy 2f out: 5th over 1f out: kpt on wl* — **11/2**[2]

**4** 3/4 **Wathab (IRE)**[35] 3959 3-9-3 108 ........(t) PJSmullen 6 — 104
(DKWeld, Ire) *cl up: 3rd 2f out: 2nd and chal 1f out: no imp: kpt on same pce* — **7/1**[3]

**5** 1/2 **Hanabad (IRE)**[13] 4590 4-9-6 103 ........(b) MJKinane 4 — 103
(JohnMOxx, Ire) *hld up: hdwy 2f out: 4th under 1f out: sn no ex: eased cl home* — **9/1**

**6** nk **Shersha (IRE)**[19] 4405 5-9-0 98 ........ NGMcCullagh 8 — 96
(SJTreacy, Ire) *chsd ldrs: rdn over 2f out: kpt on ins fnl f* — **14/1**

**7** 1/2 **Glocca Morra (IRE)**[55] 3351 6-9-3 100 ........ JMO'Dwyer 5 — 97
(WTFarrell, Ire) *hld up: swtchd to outer 2f out: kpt on one pced fnl f* — **8/1**

**8** nk **Lupine (IRE)**[35] 3961 5-9-0 85 ........ RMBurke 3 — 93
(GWRobinson, Ire) *led early: hdd bef 1/2-way: wknd fr 2f out* — **25/1**

**9** 1/2 **Dangle (IRE)**[49] 3547 3-8-11 100 ........ JAHeffernan 2 — 92
(EdwardLynam, Ire) *hld up on stand's rail: no imp fr 2f out* — **12/1**

**10** 1/2 **New Seeker**[28] 4120 4-9-3 ........ RSmith 12 — 93
(CGCox) *sn prom: 2nd appr 1/2-way: rdn 2f out: wknd fr over 1f out* — **9/2**[1]

**11** 1 **Libras Child (IRE)**[16] 4506 5-9-3 82 ........ PaulEddery 1 — 90
(PDelaney, Ire) *hld up in rr: rdn and no imp fr 2f out* — **25/1**

**12** 3 **Raining**[35] 3961 6-9-0 82 ........ PCosgrave 11 — 78
(TGMccourt, Ire) *chsd ldrs: 4th appr 1/2-way: sn rdn and wknd* — **25/1**

1m 11.6s **Going Correction** -0.15s/f (Firm)

**WFA** 3 from 4yo+ 3lb — **12** Ran SP% **123.8**

Speed ratings: **114,113,112,111,110 110,109,109,108,107 106,102**CSF £39.42 TOTE £7.60: £2.30, £2.30, £2.40; DF 62.80.

**Owner** Hamdan Al Maktoum **Bred** Shadwell Farm Llc **Trained** Friarstown, Co Kildare

**NOTEBOOK**

**Ulfah(USA)** overcame her poor draw and was in front before halfway on the stands rail. She held on gamely in the style of a still improving filly.

**Desert Fantasy(IRE)** missed the break. He wasn't making much headway with two furlongs to run but was the only threat to the winner inside the last where his tendency to edge right under pressure might have cost him the race.

**Grand Reward(USA)** just couldn't quicken inside the last.

**Wathab(IRE)** had his chance over a furlong out but, bluntly, doesn't find much under pressure.

**Hanabad(IRE)** has had plenty of chances in varied company. He was eased inside the last here as though something might have been wrong.

**Lupine(IRE)** *Official explanation: trainer said mare broke a blood vessel*

**New Seeker** ran with them until after halfway but dropped behind over a furlong down.

## 4958a TATTERSALLS IRELAND SALE STKS — 6f

3:50 (3:51) 2-Y-O — £103,521 (£40,140; £24,295; £13,732)

RPR

**1** **Beaver Patrol (IRE)**[14] 4527 2-8-12 ........ MJKinane 15 — 105
(RFJohnsonHoughton) *a.p: 3rd 1/2-way: led under 2f out: hdd 1 1/2f out: regained ld ins fnl f: styd on wl* — **9/2**[2]

**2** 1 **Indesatchel (IRE)**[34] 3965 2-8-12 ........ JPSpencer 8 — 102+
(DavidWachman, Ire) *hld up towards rr: hdwy on outer over 2f out: led 1 1/2f out: hdd ins fnl f: kpt on wl u.p* — **6/4**[1]

**3** 1 **Visionist (IRE)**[22] 4295 2-8-12 ........ PJSmullen 5 — 98
(JAOsborne) *mid-div: 6th over 1f out: r.o wl ins fnl f* — **11/2**[3]

**4** 3 **Celtic Spa (IRE)**[35] 3938 2-8-7 ........ NGMcCullagh 3 — 83
(MrsPNDutfield) *chsd ldrs: 4th 1/2-way: 3rd 1 1/2f out: sn no ex* — **16/1**

**5** 2 **Easy Feeling (IRE)**[21] 4325 2-8-7 ........ JAHeffernan 7 — 76
(RHannon) *led: hdd under 2f out: no ex fr over 1f out* — **6/1**

**6** nk **Malinsa Blue (IRE)**[50] 3476 2-8-8 ow1 ........ FMBerry 14 — 75
(JAGlover) *hld up: hdwy on outer 2f out: 5th over 1f out: sn no ex* — **16/1**

**7** 1 **Starling (IRE)**[21] 4353 2-8-7 ........(b[1]) DPMcDonogh 2 — 71?
(KevinPrendergast, Ire) *hld up: kpt on one pced fr 2f out* — **33/1**

**8** shd **Don't Tell Trigger (IRE)**[15] 4521 2-8-7 ........ JDSmith 12 — 71?
(JSMoore) *hld up in tch: rdn and one pced fr 2f out* — **25/1**

**9** 2 **Tiviski (IRE)**[20] 4358 2-8-7 ........ PShanahan 4 — 64
(EJAlston) *prom: 4th bef 1/2-way: no ex fr 2f out* — **20/1**

**10** nk **Demesne Man (IRE)**[86] 2431 2-8-12 ........ TPO'Shea 6 — 68?
(JEMulhern, Ire) *nvr a factor* — **66/1**

**11** nk **Imperial Rose (IRE)**[21] 4353 2-8-7 ........ DMGrant 1 — 62
(HRogers, Ire) *nvr a factor* — **25/1**

**12** nk **Ethon (IRE)** 2-8-12 ........ PCosgrave 17 — 65
(PatrickJFlynn, Ire) *mid-div: 7th and rdn after 1/2-way: no ex fr 2f out* — **66/1**

**13** nk **Omachaun (IRE)**[76] 2708 2-8-12 ........(b[1]) MJFlynn 13 — 64
(GMLyons, Ire) *a bhd: rdn and no imp fr 1/2-way* — **33/1**

**14** 3/4 **Look At The Stars (IRE)**[16] 4488 2-8-12 ........ RSmith 11 — 62
(CGCox) *a bhd* — **12/1**

**15** 1 **Take A Tangle (IRE)**[19] 4409 2-8-12 ........ WJO'Connor 16 — 58
(HRogers, Ire) *chsd ldrs on outer: wknd after 1/2-way* — **33/1**

**16** 3 **Rince Donn (IRE)**[16] 4505 2-8-12 ........ CatherineGannon 9 — 48
(TGMccourt, Ire) *sn cl up: 2nd bef 1/2-way: wknd over 2f out* — **66/1**

1m 12.8s **Going Correction** -0.15s/f (Firm) — **16** Ran SP% **133.1**

Speed ratings: **106,104,103,99,96 96,94,94,92,91 91,90,90,89,88 84**CSF £11.58 TOTE £5.30: £1.40, £1.20, £1.80, £3.50; DF 9.50.

**Owner** G C Stevens **Bred** Kevin B Lynch **Trained** Blewbury, Oxon

**NOTEBOOK**

**Beaver Patrol(IRE)**, always with the leaders, had a narrow lead two furlongs out but came back with real gusto to lead again inside the last and stayed on bravely.

**Indesatchel(IRE)** was duelling with the winner from the two marker. He gained the initiative a furlong and a half out but couldn't shake off the winner's final effort An extra furlong is needed.

**Visionist(IRE)** was in fifth place from two furlongs down but stayed on well in third inside the last without appearing to quicken.

**Celtic Spa(IRE)** chased the leaders in fourth place with two furlongs to race but was struggling inside the last.

**Easy Feeling(IRE)** took them along but was a beaten third inside the last quarter mile.

**Malinsa Blue(IRE)** made headway on the outer with a furlong and a half to race but was a one-paced sixth inside the last.

**Don't Tell Trigger(IRE)** was just staying on at the one pace.

**Tiviski(IRE)** chased the leaders until after halfway.

**Look At The Stars(IRE)** was never involved.

## 4959a GALILEO EUROPEAN BREEDERS FUND FUTURITY STKS (GROUP 2) — 7f

4:25 (4:25) 2-Y-O — £56,760 (£17,394; £8,239; £2,746)

RPR

**1** **Oratorio (IRE)**[13] 4589 2-9-0 ........ JPSpencer 2 — 114+
(APO'Brien, Ire) *cl up on 2nd: sltly hmpd 1/2-way: led travelling easily 2 1/2f out: qcknd clr under 2f out: eased cl home: impressive* — **5/4**[1]

**2** 2 **Democratic Deficit (IRE)**[55] 3352 2-9-4 ........ MJKinane 1 — 110
(JSBolger, Ire) *trckd ldrs: impr into 2nd under 2 1/2f out: rdn and no imp fr over 1 1/2f out: kpt on wl wout troubling wnr ins fnl f* — **7/2**[2]

**3** 1 **Elusive Double (IRE)**[28] 4158 2-9-0 ........ PJSmullen 4 — 103
(DKWeld, Ire) *hld up in rr: 4th and rdn over 2f out: kpt on u.p fnl f* — **13/2**

**4** nk **Carnegie Hall (IRE)**[34] 3966 2-9-0 ........ JAHeffernan 3 — 102
(APO'Brien, Ire) *trckd ldrs: 2nd briefly 2 1/2f out: sn rdn: kpt on u.p fr over 1f out* — **6/1**

**5** 6 **Melrose Avenue (USA)**[50] 3483 2-9-0 ........ RFfrench 5 — 87
(MJohnston) *led: hung thrght: jinked lft 1/2-way: sn rdn: hdd & wknd fr 2 1/2f out* — **9/2**[3]

1m 25.7s **Going Correction** -0.15s/f (Firm) — **5** Ran SP% **112.5**

Speed ratings: **106,103,102,102,95**CSF £6.06 TOTE £2.40: £1.60, £1.50; DF 4.90.

**Owner** Mrs John Magnier **Bred** Barronstown Stud & Orpendale **Trained** Ballydoyle, Co Tipperary

**NOTEBOOK**
**Oratorio(IRE)** quickened nicely off an uneven pace after being slightly hampered by Melrose Avenue at halfway and was calling all the shots from the front over the last furlong and a half. The Group 1 National Stakes here on September 19th, over the same trip, is the next step. He's maturing nicely but still has plenty to prove.
**Democratic Deficit(IRE)** had a stiff task with a 4lb penalty and would appreciate another furlong but he was the only one to put up a challenge.
**Elusive Double(IRE)** lost his unbeaten record, being made look very one paced when coming under pressure two furlongs down.
**Carnegie Hall(IRE)**, stable companion of the winner, failed to build on the promise of his maiden win here but still ran tidy race although unable to quicken when the pace was turned on.
**Melrose Avenue(USA)** went off in front but showed a pronounced tendency to hang and jinked left at halfway. Soon under pressure, he dropped right out with two and a half furlongs to run. *Official explanation: jockey said colt was hanging throughout*

4960 - 4961a (Foreign Racing) - See Raceform Interactive

## 4899 DEAUVILLE (R-H)
Saturday, August 21

**OFFICIAL GOING: Heavy**

### 4962a PRIX DE LA VALLEE D'AUGE (LISTED) 5f
**1:05** (1:04) 2-Y-O **£15,845** (£5,546; £5,546; £3,169)

RPR
1 **Beautifix (GER)**[20] [4382] 2-8-9 ow1 ... OPeslier 3 94
(CLaffon-Parias, France)
2 ½ **Madame Topflight**[20] [4358] 2-8-8 ... DBonilla 5 91
(MrsGSRees) *chased leaders, headway towards outside from over 1f out, ran on final f to share 2nd on line*
2 dht **Cammies Future**[30] [4048] 2-8-11 ... ODoleuze 7 94
(PWChapple-Hyam) *pressed ldr, rdn & edged lft - bumping Siena Gold - over 1f out, disp ld ins fnl f, hdd 100y out, ran on*
4 shd **Siena Gold**[25] [4217] 2-8-8 ... TEDurcan 4 91
(BJMeehan) *led narrowly til hdd 1 1/2f out, sn rdn & edged rt - bumping Cammies Future, disp ld ins fnl f, hdd 100y out, ran on*
5 ¾ **Toupie**[13] [4597] 2-8-8 ... J-BEyquem 8 89
(FRohaut, France) 1
6 snk **Prince Charming**[82] [2532] 2-8-11 ... JFanning 2 91
(JHMGosden) *prominent on inside til led narrowly 1 1/2f out, headed inside final f, weakened*
7 4 **Nipping (IRE)**[20] [4381] 2-8-8 ... CSoumillon 9 76
(RobertCollet, France)
8 snk **Dilag (IRE)** 2-8-8 ... GaryStevens 1 76
(AFabre, France)
9 1 ½ **Reine D'Opale (FR)** 2-8-8 ... FBlondel 6 71
(MPimbonnet, France)

62.80 secs **9 Ran SP% 9.7**
Speed ratings: .
**Owner** Wertheimer Et Frere **Bred** *unknown **Trained** France

**NOTEBOOK**
**Madame Topflight** finished well to dead heat for second place.
**Cammies Future** was unable to hold the late burst of the winner and was then forced to share second place in the final few strides.
**Siena Gold** made most of the early running and was only beaten inches for second place.
**Prince Charming** was always in the leading group before just fading as the race came to an end.

### 4963a CRITERIUM DU FONDS EUROPEEN DE L'ELEVAGE (LISTED) 1m
**1:35** (1:35) 2-Y-O **£42,958** (£17,183; £12,887; £8,592)

RPR
1 **Berkhamsted (IRE)**[24] [4227] 2-8-11 ... GaryStevens 6 95+
(JAOsborne) *always close up, 3rd straight on outside, led over 1f out, pushed out & just held on, cleverly*
2 hd **Glazed Frost (FR)**[72] [2828] 2-8-8 ... TThulliez 2 92
(PBary, France)
3 1 **Doctor Dino (FR)**[21] 2-8-11 ... TJarnet 1 93
(RGibson, France)
4 1 ½ **Little Miss Gracie**[13] [4584] 2-8-8 ... TEDurcan 4 87
(ABHaynes) *tracked leaders, close 5th straight, kept on under pressure*
5 2 **Seulement (USA)**[42] 2-8-11 ... OPeslier 3 86
(CLaffon-Parias, France)
6 3 **Bedamix (FR)**[18] 2-8-11 ... SPasquier 5 80
(ELellouche, France)
7 5 **Kappelmann (FR)**[41] [3790] 2-8-11 ... CSoumillon 7 70
(RobertCollet, France)

1m 52.3s **Going Correction** +0.70s/f (Yiel) **7 Ran**
Speed ratings: **82,81,80,79,77 74,69.**
**Owner** Richard Leslie **Bred** E Lonergan **Trained** Upper Lambourn, Berks

**NOTEBOOK**
**Berkhamsted(IRE)** soon took a two length advantage but hung to the right inside the final furlong and had to pull out all the stops to hold the runner-up. He could return to France for a Group race like the Prix des Chenes.
**Little Miss Gracie** appeared to get outpaced early in the straight before running on again near the finish.

### 4964a PRIX DU CALVADOS - HARAS DU LOGIS (GROUP 3) (FILLIES) 7f (S)
**2:05** (2:06) 2-Y-O **£25,704** (£10,282; £7,711; £5,141)

RPR
1 **Cours De La Reine (IRE)**[64] [3031] 2-8-9 ... CSoumillon 5 105
(PWChapple-Hyam) *tracked leader on outside, led 2f out til approaching final f, ran on under pressure to lead again last strides*
2 snk **Royal Copenhagen (FR)**[61] 2-8-9 ... TJarnet 4 104
(RGibson, France) *a in tch, hdwy under pressure on stands rail fr over 1f out, ev ch wl ins fnl f, no ex last strides* 1
3 snk **Gorella (FR)**[43] 2-8-9 ... ELegrix 8 104
(JDeRoualle, France) *hld up in rr, hdwy on outside 2f out, led appr fnl f, driven ¾l up, unable to qckn & caught last strides*
4 5 **Portrayal (USA)**[27] [4184] 2-8-9 ... GaryStevens 3 92
(AFabre, France) *tracked leader on rail, ridden over 2f out, soon beaten* 2
5 nk **Sur Ma Vie (USA)**[40] 2-8-9 ... OPeslier 6 91
(DSmaga, France) *mid-division, closed up 2f out, every chance over 1f out, soon ridden & outpaced*
6 6 **Ascot Dream (IRE)**[41] [3790] 2-8-9 ... (b) YBarberot 7 76
(SWattel, France) *held up in rear, lost touch from 1 1/2f out*
7 nk **Love Money (IRE)** 2-8-9 ... MDemuro 2 75
(BGrizzetti, Italy) *held up on rails, ridden well over 1f out, never a factor & eased inside final f* 3
8 6 **Glorious Step (USA)**[13] [4584] 2-8-9 ... JFortune 9 60
(JHMGosden) *led to 2f out, soon weakened, eased final f*

1m 32.3s **Going Correction** +0.75s/f (Yiel) **8 Ran SP% 122.8**
Speed ratings: **101,100,100,94,94 87,87,80.**
**Owner** Classic St Gatien Partnership **Bred** Barry Noone **Trained** Newmarket, Suffolk

**NOTEBOOK**
**Cours De La Reine(IRE)** looked beaten when challenged by the third inside the final furlong, but she rallied gamely in the final stages. An excellent effort from a filly who went into the race as a maiden and she could now go for the Prix Marcel Boussac.
**Royal Copenhagen(FR)** did not seem totally at ease during the early part of the race but she quickened well from one out and finished best of all.
**Gorella(FR)** came with a sweeping late run up the centre of the track and, after hitting the front inside the final furlong, was just run out of things late on.
**Portrayal(USA)** did not appear to enjoy the ground.
**Glorious Step(USA)**, soon at the head of affairs, she kept up the good work until one and a half out before dropping back to last place.

### 4965a PRIX GUILLAUME D'ORNANO (GROUP 2) 1m 2f
**2:35** (2:36) 3-Y-O **£42,148** (£16,268; £7,764; £5,176)

RPR
1 **Mister Monet (IRE)**[14] [4539] 3-8-11 ... JFanning 8 121+
(MJohnston) *made all, pushed clear well over 1f out, pushed out & ran on strongly* 1
2 4 **Delfos (IRE)**[38] [3863] 3-8-11 ... MBlancpain 2 113
(CLaffon-Parias, France) *always in touch, close 3rd on inside straight, chased winner final 2f, no impression* 2
3 1 ½ **Islero Noir (FR)**[20] [4384] 3-8-11 ... SPasquier 1 110
(YDeNicolay, France) *always in touch, 5th straight, went 3rd 2f out, beaten approaching final f*
4 nk **Apeiron (GER)**[23] [4284] 3-8-11 ... TThulliez 5 109
(MarioHofer, Germany) *held up in rear, last straight, stayed on final 2f, never nearer*
5 3 **Gatwick (IRE)**[23] [4271] 3-8-11 ... TEDurcan 6 104
(MRChannon) *mid-division, pushed along 3f out, 6th straight, hard ridden well over 1f out, never a factor*
6 5 **Lord Mayor**[35] [3927] 3-8-11 ... GaryStevens 4 96
(SirMichaelStoute) *tracked winner, 2nd straight, beaten 2f out*
7 1 **Kaypen (IRE)**[20] [4384] 3-8-11 ... MDemuro 9 94
(BGrizzetti, Italy) *prominent, 4th straight, soon beaten*
8 2 **Artiste Royal (IRE)**[20] [4384] 3-8-11 ... (b) OPeslier 10 91
(ELellouche, France) *held up, 7th straight, soon beaten* 3
9 4 **Antananarivo (FR)**[14] 3-8-12 ow1 ... YLerner 7 85
(CLerner, France) *held up, 8th straight, ridden & beaten 2f out*

2m 14.4s **Going Correction** +0.70s/f (Yiel) **9 Ran SP% 122.7**
Speed ratings: **115,111,110,110,107 103,103,101,98.**
**Owner** Syndicate 2002 **Bred** Barronstown Stud, Orpendale And Mrs T Stack **Trained** Middleham Moor, N Yorks

**NOTEBOOK**
**Mister Monet(IRE)** was given a positive ride to ensure this did not turn into a sprint and ran out a most impressive winner, quickening well from two out. He should go on to even better things and the Champion Stakes at Newmarket in October, although he could well go for the Irish version in the meantime. Looking ahead to next year, the Dubai World Cup had been mentioned a possible target.
**Delfos(IRE)** made a forward move early in the straight but never looked like getting on terms with the winner and should be suited by a little further.
**Islero Noir(FR)** lacked a change of pace.
**Apeiron(GER)** was given an awful lot to do rounding the final turn and, although he made up some ground, he was never a threat.
**Gatwick(IRE)** could never really land a serious blow.
**Lord Mayor** dropped right out in the closing stages.

## 4704 FOLKESTONE (R-H)
Sunday, August 22

**OFFICIAL GOING: Good**
Wind: It across Weather: fine

### 4966 GARDEN OF ENGLAND MAIDEN AUCTION STKS (DIV I) 7f (S)
**1:50** (1:54) (E) 2-Y-O **£3,571** (£1,099; £549; £274) **Stalls** Low

Form RPR
2 1 **Innocent Splendour**[25] [4234] 2-8-6 ... EAhern 12 78+
(EALDunlop) *dwlt: trckd far side ldrs gng easily: effrt 2f out: shkn up to ld jst ins fnl f: sn in command* **1/1**[1]
65 2 2 ½ **Briannsta (IRE)**[14] [4584] 2-8-6 ... SHitchcott[(3)] 16 75
(MRChannon) *w far side ldr: led 3f out: kicked on over 2f out: hdd and fdd jst ins fnl f* **7/1**[3]
05 3 nk **Kapaje**[30] [4081] 2-8-2 ... JoannaBadger 10 67
(PDEvans) *prom far side: rdn over 2f out: kpt on same pce fr over 1f out* **25/1**
50 4 ½ **Ringarooma**[27] [4198] 2-8-4 ... PRobinson 8 68
(MHTompkins) *pressed far side ldrs: rdn over 2f out: kpt on one pce fr over 1f out* **12/1**
5 hd **Oasis Way (GR)** 2-8-4 ... RLMoore 13 68
(PRChamings) *dwlt: towards rr far side and off the pce: shkn up over 2f out: styd on fnl f: nrst fin* **33/1**
6 4 **Star Side (IRE)** 2-8-9 ... SDrowne 15 63
(CTinkler) *racd far side: a towards rr and off the pce: no imp ldrs fnl 2f* **33/1**
2 7 ½ **Double Kudos (FR)**[27] [4198] 2-9-0 ... IMongan 14 66
(JGGiven) *cl up far side: drvn over 2f out: wknd over 1f out* **7/2**[2]
8 shd **Mangrove Cay (IRE)** 2-8-11 ... TPQueally 3 63
(DRLoder) *mde most on nr side: clr of rest fnl 2f but no ch w far side ldrs* **14/1**
25 9 1 ½ **Kumala Ocean (IRE)**[24] [4277] 2-8-2 ... JBramhill 11 50
(PABlockley) *mde most far side to 3f out: wknd rapidly 2f out* **33/1**
00 10 1 **Rhoslan (IRE)**[22] [4335] 2-8-11 ... JDSmith 6 57
(CADwyer) *swtchd to r far side after 1f: a wl in rr* **100/1**
11 1 ½ **Bonnabee (IRE)** 2-8-2 ... RMullen 2 44
(CFWall) *uns rdr on way to s: dwlt: pressed nr side ldr to 1/2-way: sn outpcd u.p: swtchd rt and kpt on fnl f* **50/1**

0 **12** *1 1/4* **Silver Creek**[7] 4770 2-8-7 PDoe 4 46
(IAWood) *racd nr side: chsd ldrs: wknd over 2f out: no ch* **100/1**
000 **13** *2* **Play Up Pompey**[32] 4022 2-8-4 JFMcDonald(3) 7 41
(JJBridger) *racd nr side: prom tl wknd 2f out: no ch* **100/1**
**14** *7* **Luna Blu (IRE)** 2-7-11 HayleyTurner(5) 9 18
(MWigham) *s.s: racd far side: sn u.p and bhd* **100/1**
000 **15** *12* **Gurrun**[9] 4730 2-9-0 KFallon 1 —
(NACallaghan) *racd nr side: in tch 4f: sn wl bhd* **16/1**

1m 27.7s (-0.10) **Going Correction** -0.10s/f (Good) **15** Ran SP% **123.6**
Speed ratings: **96,93,92,92,92 87,86,86,85,83 82,80,78,70,56**CSF £8.24 TOTE £1.90: £1.10, £2.70, £5.20; EX 11.20.
**Owner** The Granite Partnership **Bred** Usk Valley Stud **Trained** Newmarket, Suffolk

**FOCUS**
Just an ordinary maiden in which the majority of runners raced far side and had a distinct advantage. The form, rated through thesecond and fourth, looks pretty reliable.

**NOTEBOOK**
**Innocent Splendour**, a promising second on her debut at Kempton, found this easier and did what was required. She should not be too harshly treated and can get competitive in nurseries.
**Briannsta(IRE)**, dropped back from a mile, again did enough to suggest he can win a race this season and is now qualified for a nursery mark.
**Kapaje** is improving with racing and ran her best race to date. She is now qualified for a nursery mark and is one to keep on the right side.
**Ringarooma**, too keen when a beaten favourite at Yarmouth on her previous start, left that form behind, but she was still well held and may be more of a nursery type.
**Oasis Way(GR)**, a 12,000gns yearling out of a juvenile winner, made a pleasing debut and should be capable of significant improvement.
**Double Kudos(FR)** shaped well when runner-up on his debut at Yarmouth, but this represented a step back.
**Mangrove Cay(IRE)**, a 17,000gns half-brother to several winners, including a couple of juveniles, won the race on the near side but had no chance with the others.
**Kumala Ocean(IRE)** *Official explanation: jockey said filly had been struck into*

## 4967 GARDEN OF ENGLAND MAIDEN AUCTION STKS (DIV II) 7f (S)
**2:20** (2:23) (E) 2-Y-O **£3,571** (£1,099; £549; £274) **Stalls** Low

Form RPR
40 **1** **Fong Shui**[32] 4022 2-8-9 DSweeney 10 81
(PJMakin) *trckd ldrs gng wl: prog to ld wl over 1f out: drvn 2l clr ins fnl f: jst hld on* **9/2**[3]
4220 **2** *nk* **Group Captain**[15] 4527 2-8-9 88 RLMoore 11 80
(SKirk) *chsd ldrs: effrt and nt clr run briefly 2f out: rdn and hanging over 1f out: styd on strly fnl f: jst failed* **11/4**[1]
**3** *1/2* **Red River Rock (IRE)** 2-8-11 SHitchcott(3) 1 84
(CTinkler) *chsd ldrs: pushed along 1/2-way: effrt to chse ldng pair over 1f out: styd on ins fnl f: nrst fin* **66/1**
43 **4** *hd* **Diamonds And Dust**[17] 4488 2-8-7 PRobinson 6 76
(MHTompkins) *sn led: rdn and hdd wl over 1f out: kpt on again ins fnl f* **4/1**[2]
43 **5** *1* **Call Me Max**[14] 4584 2-9-0 EAhern 8 81
(EALDunlop) *t.k.h: cl up: n.m.r 5f out: rdn and unable qck 2f out: one pce and btn whn n.m.r nr fin* **8/1**
**6** *2 1/2* **Princelywallywogan** 2-8-7 TPQueally 15 68
(IAWood) *dwlt: racd in last and sn rdn: sme prog 2f out: styd on wl fnl f: nvr nrr* **25/1**
3 **7** *1* **Uncle Bulgaria (IRE)**[47] 3611 2-8-6 LPKeniry(3) 14 67
(GCBravery) *racd in midfield: rdn and outpcd over 2f out: kpt on same pce after* **25/1**
**8** *3/4* **Water Pistol** 2-9-0 SDrowne 13 70
(MrsAJPerrett) *wl in rr: pushed along 4f out: struggling 3f out: sme late prog* **12/1**
30 **9** *3/4* **Flag Point (IRE)**[22] 4335 2-8-11 KFallon 16 65
(JLDunlop) *pressed ldrs: drvn 3f out: btn 2f out: wknd* **4/1**[2]
000 **10** *2 1/2* **Hows That**[8] 4761 2-8-2 RMullen 5 50
(PJMcbride) *prom: rdn over 2f out: wknd wl over 1f out* **66/1**
00 **11** *8* **Coombe Centenary**[27] 4193 2-8-2 PDoe 3 30
(SDow) *pressed ldr to over 2f out: wknd rapidly* **100/1**
0 **12** *1* **Laurollie**[21] 4359 2-8-2 ADaly 12 28
(DrJRJNaylor) *dwlt: lost pl and in rr after 2f: sn struggling* **100/1**
0 **13** *hd* **Volitio**[10] 4681 2-8-11 PDobbs 9 36
(SKirk) *dwlt: a in rr: struggling 3f out* **66/1**
00 **14** *1 1/2* **Speedie Rossini (IRE)**[17] 4480 2-8-9 JBramhill 4 30
(SCWilliams) *sn pushed along in rr: no ch over 2f out* **50/1**

1m 27.96s (0.16) **Going Correction** -0.10s/f (Good) **14** Ran SP% **119.8**
Speed ratings: **95,94,94,93,92 89,88,87,87,84 75,73,73,71**CSF £16.47 TOTE £5.70: £1.90, £1.70, £8.70; EX 27.70.
**Owner** Camamile Hessert Scott Partnership **Bred** Charlock Farm Stud **Trained** Ogbourne Maisey, Wilts

**FOCUS**
Like the first division, an ordinary maiden, although this time the whole field raced far side, and the form looks reliable.

**NOTEBOOK**
**Fong Shui** really caught the eye at Lingfield on his previous start when getting no luck in running and, backed to confirm that promise, he duly obliged. His future would appear in the hands of the Handicapper.
**Group Captain**, disappointing in the Shergar Cup Juvenile on his previous start, was a touch unlucky as he got squeezed up two furlongs from home. A fair effort, but he was still below his best.
**Red River Rock(IRE)**, a 24,000gns yearling first foal out of a six-furlong two-year-old winner, was friendless in the market but made a very pleasing debut, showing enough to suggest she will soon be winning in similar company.
**Diamonds And Dust** ran well enough, but would not appear to be progressing and is worth opposing in similar company.
**Call Me Max** did not get the clearest of runs but was not unlucky. He is now qualified for a handicap mark.
**Princelywallywogan**, a half-brother to a seven-furlong three-year-old winner, stayed on from an unpromising position to make a pleasing debut. He looks capable of improvement.
**Flag Point(IRE)** again failed to confirm his debut promise.

## 4968 COME RACING IN KENT H'CAP 6f
**2:50** (2:50) (F) (0-55,56) 3-Y-0 **£3,052** (£872; £436) **Stalls** Low

Form RPR
4461 **1** **Danifah (IRE)**[10] 4674 3-9-5 56 KFallon 14 66
(PDEvans) *led main gp on far side: edgd lft over 2f out: drvn and edgd lft again over 1f out: edgd rt but in command ins fnl f* **11/8**[1]
0000 **2** *1 1/4* **Rockley Bay (IRE)**[45] 3684 3-9-4 55 (t) DSweeney 13 61
(PJMakin) *racd against far side rail: trckd ldrs: rdn to chse wnr over 1f out: no imp fnl f* **25/1**
0000 **3** *1 3/4* **Crimson Star (IRE)**[27] 4195 3-8-1 38 DKinsella 11 39
(CTinkler) *dwlt: sn prom: chsd wnr 3f out to over 1f out: one pce* **25/1**
5040 **4** *1* **Scarlett Breeze**[3] 4881 3-8-5 49 ow3 DerekNolan(7) 1 47+
(JWHills) *racd alone nr side: wl on terms: looked overall ldr 2f out: wknd fnl f* **20/1**
-033 **5** *nk* **Essex Star (IRE)**[44] 3710 3-8-8 48 BReilly(3) 12 45
(MissJFeilden) *chsd wnr to 3f out: fdd u.p over 1f out* **10/1**
0006 **6** *hd* **Emperor Cat (IRE)**[41] 3800 3-8-8 45 JBramhill 9 42
(PABlockley) *dwlt: racd towards rr: prog over 2f out: no imp over 1f out* **28/1**
4046 **7** *1 3/4* **Lord Wishingwell (IRE)**[18] 4440 3-8-0 37 CCatlin 10 28
(JSWainwright) *racd towards rr: drvn over 2f out: one pce and nvr rchd ldrs* **20/1**
0060 **8** *nk* **Costa Del Sol (IRE)**[19] 4419 3-7-9 35 oh3 JFMcDonald(3) 2 25
(JJBridger) *wl in rr and sn rdn: u.str.p 1/2-way: sme prog 2f out: fdd fnl f* **50/1**
0604 **9** *3* **Pink Supreme**[9] 4708 3-8-12 49 TPQueally 6 30
(IAWood) *chsd ldrs: hrd rdn and wknd 2f out* **7/1**[3]
0060 **10** *3/4* **Pardon Moi**[11] 4650 3-8-1 43 HayleyTurner(5) 8 22
(MrsCADunnett) *a towards rr: rdn and struggling over 2f out* **12/1**
3562 **11** *nk* **Lakeside Guy (IRE)**[17] 4484 3-9-4 55 RLMoore 4 33
(PSMcentee) *dwlt: racd in midfield: rdn and fdd over 2f out* **10/1**
5233 **12** *shd* **Tsarbuck**[27] 4188 3-8-12 49 (v) EAhern 5 27
(RMHCowell) *racd towards outer: in tch tl wknd 2f out* **6/1**[2]
2566 **13** *1* **Jasmine Pearl (IRE)**[19] 4419 3-8-0 44 MHalford(7) 3 19
(TMJones) *racd on outer: a towards rr: wknd 2f out* **20/1**
5600 **14** *6* **Joans Jewel**[89] 2380 3-8-11 48 AMcCarthy 7 5
(GGMargarson) *racd on outer: chsd ldrs to 1/2-way: sn wknd* **33/1**

1m 13.55s (-0.05) **Going Correction** -0.10s/f (Good) **14** Ran SP% **125.1**
Speed ratings: **96,94,92,90,90 90,87,87,83,82 81,81,80,72**CSF £51.00 CT £604.94 TOTE £2.20: £1.10, £11.10, £9.10; EX 32.80.
**Owner** E A R Morgans **Bred** Rocklow Stud **Trained** Pandy, Gwent

**FOCUS**
A moderate handicap in which the field split into two groups and the far side once again looked at an advantage - the first three home were drawn in double figure stalls and raced on that side of the track. The form looks modest and is likely to have limited bearing on future events.

**NOTEBOOK**
**Danifah(IRE)**, back to form with an eight-length success over seven furlongs at Chepstow on her previous start, coped with both the drop in trip and 14lb rise in the weights to follow up. She will be forced to step up in grade when reassessed and could well complete the hat-trick.
**Rockley Bay(IRE)**, with the blinkers left off and the tongue-tie on, ran well dropped back two furlongs in trip and is up to winning a similarly moderate affair.
**Crimson Star(IRE)** ◆ showed little in four runs in maiden company, but was sent off at just 4/1 first time up and was possibly thought capable of better than she showed. Making her handicap debut off a feather weight, she showed enough to suggest he current rating can be exploited.
**Scarlett Breeze** did well to come home best of those on the stands' side.
**Essex Star(IRE)**, dropped back from a mile, was racing off a mark 12lb lower than when first running in a handicap but was well held.
**Pink Supreme** was unable to build on the promise she showed on her previous start.
**Tsarbuck** has never really shown his best on turf and was well beaten.

## 4969 HELEN SANTER 12TH BIRTHDAY CLASSIFIED STKS 7f (S)
**3:20** (3:21) (E) 3-Y-0+ **£4,251** (£1,308; £654; £327) **Stalls** Low

Form RPR
0006 **1** **Arctic Desert**[13] 4602 4-9-7 72 KFallon 4 85+
(AMBalding) *hld up bhd ldrs: effrt to ld wl over 1f out: sn kicked 4l clr: eased nr fin* **4/1**[2]
6140 **2** *2 1/2* **Go Yellow**[11] 4646 3-9-0 67 NCallan 7 72
(PDEvans) *hld up bhd ldrs: effrt to chse wnr over 1f out: no ch but kpt on wl to hold on for 2nd* **14/1**
0000 **3** *hd* **Terraquin (IRE)**[2] 4912 4-9-5 65 TPQueally 9 71
(JJBridger) *settled in rr: rdn and prog over 2f out: kpt on fnl f* **25/1**
0005 **4** *shd* **Cheese 'n Biscuits**[9] 4731 4-9-2 68 (p) RLMoore 2 68
(GLMoore) *hld up in last pair: prog 2f out: rdn to dispute 2nd pl fnl f: kpt on* **7/1**[3]
1340 **5** *3 1/2* **Nearly A Fool**[13] 4602 6-9-6 71 (v) AMcCarthy 3 63
(GGMargarson) *pressed ldr: pushed along 1/2-way: outpcd 2f out* **8/1**
5312 **6** *2 1/2* **Iphigenia (IRE)**[9] 4702 3-9-0 73 LisaJones 5 56
(PWHiatt) *led to wl over 1f out: hanging rt and wknd* **4/1**[2]
4302 **7** *1* **Azreme**[4] 4846 4-8-12 70 MHoward(7) 6 53
(DKIvory) *prom gng wl: rdn 2f out: fnd nil and sn btn* **9/4**[1]
0656 **8** *1* **Generous Gesture (IRE)**[25] 4244 3-8-11 70 RMullen 8 47
(MLWBell) *t.k.h: in tch: rdn 1/2-way: sn btn* **16/1**

1m 26.61s (-1.19) **Going Correction** -0.10s/f (Good)
**WFA** 3 from 4yo+ 5lb **8** Ran SP% **110.8**
Speed ratings: **102,99,98,98,94 91,90,89**CSF £53.14 TOTE £5.50: £1.80, £3.00, £9.30; EX 76.20.
**Owner** Holistic Racing Ltd **Bred** Whatton Manor Stud **Trained** Kingsclere, Hants

**FOCUS**
A modest classified stakes with just 8lb between the field on the figures, but Arctic Desert was too good and ran out a comfortable winner. The form is not easy to rate and is not that solid.

**NOTEBOOK**
**Arctic Desert**, with the visor left off and switched back to the turf, gained his first win since taking a Polytrack maiden back in April 2003 in good style. He could well follow up under a penalty.
**Go Yellow** appreciated the drop in grade and had conditions to suit, but he was no match for the winner.
**Terraquin(IRE)** ran better than he had been, especially considering he had 5lb to find with the eventual winner at the weights.
**Cheese 'n Biscuits**, a shade unlucky at Newmarket on her previous start, ran well enough and was clear of the remainder.
**Nearly A Fool** was not at his best despite appearing to have conditions to suit.
**Iphigenia(IRE)**, joint best in at the weights, was not at her best and has to be considered disappointing.
**Azreme** was unable to confirm the promise he showed on soft ground on his previous outing.

## 4970 WESTENHANGER FILLIES' H'CAP 5f
**3:50** (3:51) (E) (0-75,73) 3-Y-0+ **£4,143** (£1,275; £637; £318) **Stalls** Low

Form RPR
4500 **1** **Tizzy's Law**[13] 4608 3-8-11 60 SDrowne 5 69
(MABuckley) *hld up last of nr side gp: prog 2f out: led gp entetring fnl f: r.o to take overall ld last 100yds* **13/2**
6120 **2** *1 1/2* **Roxanne Mill**[9] 4701 6-9-12 73 (p) NCallan 6 77
(PABlockley) *pressed far side ldr: led gp and overall ldr 2f out: wknd and hdd last 100yds* **11/2**
5000 **3** *nk* **Flapdoodle**[20] 4400 6-7-12 45 oh2 (v1) LisaJones 1 48
(AWCarroll) *led nr side gp: hdd and one pce ent fnl f* **7/1**

0000 **4** *hd* **Tripti (IRE)**[20] 4400 4-7-9 **45** oh1 ............ JFMcDonald(3) 7 47
(JJBridger) *chsd ldng pair far side: outpcd 1/2-way: styd on ins fnl f* **33/1**
1060 **5** *½* **Kallista's Pride**[2] 4923 4-8-13 **60** ............ (v[1]) KFallon 2 60
(JRBest) *dwlt: swtchd to far side after 1f and wl in rr: drvn and styd on over 1f out: nt qckn last 100yds* **11/2**
1003 **6** *1½* **Tender (IRE)**[4] 4854 4-8-1 **48** ............ (p) CCatlin 4 43
(MrsStefLiddiard) *chsd nr side ldr to over 1f out: fdd* **4/1**[1]
4520 **7** *½* **College Queen**[30] 4104 6-9-2 **63** ............ (b) IMongan 8 56
(SGollings) *overall ldr far side to 2f out: wknd fnl f* **5/1**[3]
031 **8** *½* **Dance To The Blues (IRE)**[17] 4484 3-8-8 **57** ............ PDobbs 3 48
(BDeHaan) *chsd ldng pair nr side: wknd over 1f out* **9/2**[2]

59.70 secs (-1.00) **Going Correction** -0.10s/f (Good)
**WFA** 3 from 4yo+ 2lb **8** Ran SP% **114.4**
Speed ratings: **104,101,101,100,100 97,96,96**CSF £41.89 CT £259.96 TOTE £7.70: £2.30, £2.10, £1.90; EX 64.00.
**Owner** North Cheshire Trading & Storage Ltd **Bred** North Cheshire Trading And Storage Ltd **Trained** Castle Bytham, Lincs
■ Stewards Enquiry : I Mongan one-day ban: failed to keep straight from stalls (Sep 2)

**FOCUS**
A modest sprint handicap and ordianry form that could possibly rate a little higher. The field split into two groups and, although the winner stayed nearside, there did not appear to be any great bias.

**NOTEBOOK**
**Tizzy's Law**, not really at her best since winning a Thirsk maiden on her reappearance, was 9lb lower than when first running in a handicap and ran out a clear-cut winner.
**Roxanne Mill**, very disappointing in claiming company on her previous start, returned to form to win her race on the far side of the track.
**Flapdoodle**, with a visor on for the first time, ran better than she had been lately, although the headgear is not sure to work as well next time.
**Tripti(IRE)** fared second best of those on the far side of the track, but has just one win to her name from 31-career starts.
**Kallista's Pride**, fitted with a visor for the first time, did not help her chance with a slow start over a trip short enough.
**Tender(IRE)** was very disappointing with no obvious excuse.
**College Queen**, just 1lb higher than when last successful, was not at her best and remains winless this term.
**Dance To The Blues(IRE)** would have found this tougher than the maiden she won over course and distance on her previous start, but was below form in any case.

## 4971 NIGEL COLLISON FUELS H'CAP 1m 4f
4:20 (4:20) (E) (0-70,70) 3-Y-O+ **£4,576** (£1,408; £704; £352) **Stalls** Low

Form RPR
3005 **1** **Dance World**[6] 4808 4-9-11 **70** ............ BReilly(3) 9 79
(MissJFeilden) *led for 2f: led again 7f out: clr w runner-up 5f out: rdn and hdd wl over 1f out: rallied to ld ins fnl f* **16/1**
0004 **2** *hd* **Turtle Patriarch (IRE)**[9] 4711 3-8-6 **58** ............ RLMoore 13 67
(MrsAJPerrett) *prom: trckd wnr 6f out and sn clr of rest: rdn to ld wl over 1f out: hdd ins fnl f: jst hld* **8/1**
3000 **3** *1½* **Wyoming**[45] 3669 3-8-4 **56** ............ EAhern 10 62
(JARToller) *prom: outpcd 5f out: styd on to chse clr ldng pair over 1f out: clsng nr fin* **20/1**
5444 **4** *¾* **Gallant Boy (IRE)**[7] 4772 5-9-9 **65** ............ (vt) NCallan 11 70
(PDEvans) *hld up: outpcd 5f out: prog to chse clr ldng pair 2f out: hanging and looked reluctant: kpt on fnl f* **15/2**
5001 **5** *1* **Nounou**[9] 4711 3-8-4 **63** ............ MHalford(7) 12 66
(DJDaly) *hld up in rr: outpcd 5f out: drvn and styd on fnl 2f: nrst fin* **7/1**[3]
2555 **6** *¾* **Make My Hay**[36] 3942 5-8-5 **47** ............ TPQueally 1 49
(JGallagher) *hld up wl in rr: outpcd 5f out: sme prog over 2f out: shkn up and styd on wl fnl f: hopeless task* **10/1**
1500 **7** *8* **Man The Gate**[6] 4736 5-9-0 **56** ............ SDrowne 4 45
(PDCundell) *in rr whn rn wd bnd after 2f: outpcd 5f out: effrt u.p 3f out: no prog 2f out: eased fnl f* **4/1**[1]
002 **8** *4* **Jidiya (IRE)**[20] 4396 5-10-0 **70** ............ IMongan 6 53
(SGollings) *led after 2f to 7f out: drvn and outpcd by ldng pair 5f out: wknd 2f out* **8/1**
0040 **9** *3* **Best Flight**[30] 4075 4-9-3 **66** ............ KMay(7) 3 44
(BWHills) *s.s: in rr whn rn wd bnd after 2f: outpcd 5f out: n.d after* **17/2**
-000 **10** *4* **Vin Du Pays**[10] 4686 4-8-3 **45** ............ AMcCarthy 14 17
(MBlanshard) *a towards rr: outpcd 5f out: struggling after* **33/1**
0450 **11** *2½* **Cracow (IRE)**[18] 4433 7-8-0 **42** ............ (p) LisaJones 7 10
(AMHales) *prom: outpcd 5f out: hanging and wknd 2f out* **33/1**
0-00 **12** *10* **Outside Investor (IRE)**[27] 4192 4-10-0 **70** ............ TWilliams 5 22
(NJGifford) *chsd ldrs: outpcd 5f out: effrt u.p and sme prog 3f out: wknd 2f out: eased* **25/1**
4-06 **13** *2½* **Smoothie (IRE)**[17] 4486 6-9-2 **58** ............ KFallon 2 6
(IanWilliams) *rn wd bnd after 2f: prog 7f out: sn lost pl and outpcd: wknd and eased over 2f out* **9/2**[2]

2m 38.3s (-2.10) **Going Correction** -0.10s/f (Good)
**WFA** 3 from 4yo+ 10lb **13** Ran SP% **124.7**
Speed ratings: **103,102,101,101,100 100,94,92,90,87 85,79,77**CSF £138.85 CT £2596.68 TOTE £23.60: £6.10, £3.20, £7.30; EX 178.80.
**Owner** Stowstowquickquickstow Partnership **Bred** Juddmonte Farms **Trained** Exning, Suffolk

**FOCUS**
A modest handicap and the form looks ordinary but seems sound.

**NOTEBOOK**
**Dance World** had been held since landing a Southwell maiden earlier in the season, but has dropped 10lb since making his handicap debut and came right back to form with a narrow success. However, he is not that consistent and appeals as one to take on next time.
**Turtle Patriarch(IRE)** appreciated the step up in trip and ran one of his bet races to date. He looks capable of taking a similar event.
**Wyoming** ran respectably but needed every yard of this mile and a half and should get further.
**Gallant Boy(IRE)** probably would have preferred faster ground and continues on a losing run.
**Nounou**, 3lb higher than when successful over an extended nine furlongs on his previous start, was probably ridden to get the trip and was never a serious threat.
**Make My Hay** was given plenty to do and could never get on terms.
**Man The Gate** was again below his best and has now been a beaten favourite on three of his last four starts.
**Smoothie(IRE)** has dropped to a reasonable mark but was beaten a mile. *Official explanation: trainer said gelding received a bump on the first bend and lost interest afterwards*

## 4972 FAMILY FUN MAIDEN STKS 1m 1f 149y
4:50 (4:51) (D) 3-Y-O+ **£3,896** (£1,199; £599; £299) **Stalls** Low

Form RPR
3 **1** **Play The Melody (IRE)**[108] 1911 3-8-13 ............ RMullen 4 66+
(CTinkler) *led after 1f: mde most tl rdn and hdd wl over 1f out: rallied to ld ent fnl f: hld on wl* **8/1**[2]
0030 **2** *nk* **Efrhina (IRE)**[4] 4849 4-9-2 64 ............ RHavlin 7 60
(MrsStefLiddiard) *trckd ldrs: prog to chal 3f out: rdn to ld wl over 1f out: hdd ent fnl f: hld nr fin* **8/1**[2]
-04 **3** *5* **Innocent Rebel (USA)**[85] 2486 3-8-13 ............ EAhern 10 56
(EALDunlop) *settled in midfield: outpcd 4f out: shkn up and prog 2f out: styd on to take 3rd ins fnl f* **10/1**[3]
3050 **4** *1¼* **Bailaora (IRE)**[12] 4618 3-8-13 66 ............ (t) ADaly 6 53
(BWDuke) *led for 1f: styd prom: drvn to chal over 2f out: wknd over 1f out* **16/1**
64 **5** *hd* **Coppice (IRE)**[21] 4369 3-8-13 ............ KFallon 8 53
(LMCumani) *dwlt: t.k.h: sn trckd ldrs: chal 3f out: rdn and nt qckn over 2f out: wknd over 1f out* **4/7**[1]
0005 **6** *shd* **Ryan's Bliss (IRE)**[16] 4519 4-8-13 40 ............ RMiles(3) 5 48?
(TDMccarthy) *settled in last pair: outpcd 4f out: stdy prog over 2f out: shkn up and kpt on fnl f: nvr nr ldrs* **28/1**
**7** *8* **Sandokan (GER)** 3-8-13 ............ TPQueally 9 37
(BJCurley) *dwlt: hld up in rr: rn green and detached in last 3f out: shuffled along and kpt on steadily fnl 2f: bttr for experience* **10/1**[3]
0600 **8** *shd* **Purr**[7] 4778 3-8-6 49 ............ AHamblett(7) 1 37
(TTClement) *hld up in rr: outpcd 4f out: n.d after* **66/1**
0-00 **9** *1½* **Whispering Valley**[16] 4513 4-9-2 ............ RLMoore 11 29
(MrsAJPerrett) *hld up in rr: outpcd over 3f out: effrt and hanging lft over 2f out: sn wknd* **33/1**
000 **10** *10* **Coco Point Breeze**[11] 4644 3-8-8 ............ IMongan 3 10
(JGGiven) *chsd ldrs: wknd rapidly over 2f out* **50/1**
0 **11** *22* **Russian Applause**[13] 4615 4-9-7 ............ SDrowne 2 —
(PRChamings) *dwlt: w ldr whn hung bdly lft bnd 7f out: wknd 4f out: t.o* **33/1**

2m 4.01s (-1.15) **Going Correction** -0.10s/f (Good)
**WFA** 3 from 4yo 8lb **11** Ran SP% **122.7**
Speed ratings: **100,99,95,94,94 94,88,88,86,78 61**CSF £70.20 TOTE £12.40: £2.50, £2.70, £2.40; EX 63.10 Place 6 £747.42, Place 5 £490.57..
**Owner** Doubleprint **Bred** Gatebest Ltd **Trained** Compton, Berks

**FOCUS**
A very modest maiden and an ordinary time for the grade, with the runner-up providing the level of the form.

**NOTEBOOK**
**Play The Melody(IRE)**, a promising third in a soft-ground course and distance maiden on his debut, handled this faster surface well and got off the mark in game fashion. His future now lies in the hands of the Handicapper.
**Efrhina(IRE)**, disappointing on soft ground at Kempton on her previous starts, returned to form and was just held. Clear of the remainder, she should find a similarly modest event.
**Innocent Rebel(USA)** is going the right way, but he was no match for the first two and should find things easier now he is qualified for a mark.
**Bailaora(IRE)**, with the blinkers left off but the tongue-tie on, should have been much closer judged on official ratings.
**Coppice(IRE)** had shown promise in much better races than this one on his first two starts but, having raced keenly, he was well held. This was disappointing, but he is now qualified for a handicap mark. *Official explanation: trainer had no explanation for the poor form shown*
**Coco Point Breeze** *Official explanation: jockey said filly did not handle the track*
T/Jkpt: £38,947.30 to a £1 stake. Pool: £356,560.25. 6.50 winning tickets. T/Plt: £1,140.50 to a £1 stake. Pool: £56,482.10. 36.15 winning tickets. T/Qpdt: £207.70 to a £1 stake. Pool: £2,357.70. 8.40 winning tickets. JN

4973 - 4976a (Foreign Racing) - See Raceform Interactive

# 4110 FAIRYHOUSE (R-H)
Sunday, August 22

**OFFICIAL GOING: Good changing to good to yielding after 2.35 (race 1)**

## 4977a BALLYCULLEN STKS (LISTED) 1m 6f
4:35 (4:37) 3-Y-O+ **£22,922** (£6,725; £3,204; £1,091)

RPR
**1** **Holy Orders (IRE)**[23] 4311 7-9-7 102 ............ (b) DJCondon 8 113
(WPMullins, Ire) *hld up towards rr: smooth hdwy ent st: led 1 1/2f out: sn drew clr: easily* **8/1**
**2** *3½* **Mkuzi**[7] 4784 5-9-12 110 ............ MJKinane 10 113
(JohnMOxx, Ire) *settled 4th: 5th and pushed along 1/2-way: impr into 3rd appr st: kpt on one pce u.p fr 2f out* **13/8**[1]
**3** *¾* **Maharib (IRE)**[57] 3333 4-9-7 108 ............ PShanahan 4 107
(DKWeld, Ire) *hld up in rr: prog appr st: 4th over 1f out: kpt on* **10/1**
**4** *nk* **High Priestess (IRE)**[23] 4311 5-9-4 86 ............ JAHeffernan 2 104?
(MJPO'Brien, Ire) *trckd ldrs in 5th: 4th into st: sn rdn: kpt on u.p fr over 1f out* **8/1**
**5** *1* **Ivowen (USA)**[39] 3862 4-9-4 103 ............ PJSmullen 11 102
(DKWeld, Ire) *trckd ldrs in 3rd: 2nd travelling wl 3f out: rdn to chal ent st: no ex over 1f out* **6/1**[3]
**6** *7* **Jade Quest (IRE)**[39] 3862 4-9-10 100 ............ FMBerry 6 98
(CharlesO'Brien, Ire) *hld up in tch: 6th 4f out: 5th into st: no ex fr 2f out* **14/1**
**7** *1* **One Off**[339] 5023 4-9-7 ............ SSanders 7 94
(SirMarkPrescott) *led: rdn and strly pressed st: hdd & wknd 1 1/2f out* **6/1**[3]
**8** *8* **Royal Devotion (IRE)**[67] 2993 4-9-4 94 ............ TPO'Shea 1 80
(MHalford, Ire) *s.i.s and hld up: rdn 5f out: no imp st* **16/1**
**9** *25* **Cobra (IRE)**[39] 3857 3-8-9 103 ............ (b[1]) PCosgrave 5 48
(APO'Brien, Ire) *settled 2nd: rdn 4f out: wknd over 3f out* **4/1**[2]
**10** *9* **Blue Corrig (IRE)**[39] 4425 4-9-7 101 ............ CO'Donoghue 9 35
(JosephCrowley, Ire) *s.i.s: sn trckd ldrs in 6th: rdn 4f out: wknd appr st* **20/1**
**11** *20* **Liss Ard (IRE)**[39] 3862 3-8-9 97 ............ DMGrant 3 7
(JohnJosephMurphy, Ire) *upset in stalls. hld up: 8th and pushed along 1/2-way: wknd over 4f out: t.o st* **14/1**

3m 1.00s
**WFA** 3 from 4yo+ 12lb **11** Ran SP% **142.0**
Speed ratings: CSF £26.00 TOTE £9.40: £2.50, £1.10, £5.70; DF 39.10.
**Owner** A McLuckie **Bred** Dunderry Stud **Trained** Bagenalstown, Co Carlow

**NOTEBOOK**
**Holy Orders(IRE)** has his own ideas about the game but with ground conditions to suit (much more testing than the official "good to yielding") he ran away with this after leading over a furlong and a half out. The Doncaster Cup is a possibility
**Mkuzi** was been niggled along well before the turn for home and was left flat-footed when the winner quickened clear.
**Maharib(IRE)**carried through with a sustained effort over the last furlong and a half that augers well.

**High Priestess(IRE)** had no chance at these weights but stuck to it well.
**Ivowen(USA)** flattered early in the straight.
**One Off** wasn't well treated by the weight conditions and his front running tactics were doomed early in the straight.
**Cobra(IRE)** gave trouble in the stalls and was found to be lame afterwards. *Official explanation: vet said colt finished slightly lame*

4978 - 4979a (Foreign Racing) - See Raceform Interactive

## 1259 BREMEN
Sunday, August 22

**OFFICIAL GOING: Good**

### 4980a GROSSER SWB STUTENPREIS VON BREMEN (GROUP 3) (F&M) 1m 3f
**3:55** (4:04) 3-Y-0+ **£26,761** (£10,563; £5,282; £3,169)

RPR

1 **Vallera (GER)**$^{51}$ [3504] 3-8-8 .................... IFerguson 6 100
(UOstmann, Germany) *mid division, 5th straight, switched to outside 2f out, led approaching final f, ran on strongly* 3

2 2 1/2 **Daytona (GER)**$^{51}$ [3504] 3-8-8 .................... ABoschert 7 96
(FrauABertram, Germany) *always close up, 3rd straight, disputed lead 2f out til headed approaching final f, one pace*

3 1 **Mity Dancer (GER)**$^{21}$ [4380] 4-9-5 .................... THellier 2 96
(DKRichardson, Germany) *close up, 4th straight, disputed lead 2f out, headed and no extra approaching final f*

4 1/2 **Kastoria (GER)**$^{35}$ [3973] 5-9-5 .................... EPedroza 12 95
(AWohler, Germany) *chased leader, 2nd straight, disputed lead over 2f out to over 1f out, no extra*

5 1 1/2 **Deva (GER)**$^{21}$ [4385] 5-9-5 .................... J-PCarvalho 11 93
(DRonge, Germany) *held up in rear, stayed in final 2f, never nearer* 2

6 nse **Summitville**$^{22}$ [4321] 4-9-5 .................... JQuinn 10 93
(JGGiven) *held up on inside, 7th straight, one pace final 1 1/2f* 1

7 4 **Quetena (GER)**$^{35}$ [3973] 4-9-5 .................... MTimpelan 9 86
(PRau, Germany) *towards rear, kept on past beaten horses final 1 1/2f*

8 shd **Wild Angel (IRE)** 3-8-8 .................... GHind 8 84
(AndreasLowe, Germany) *last to staraight, some late headway*

9 nse **Wurfklinge (GER)**$^{322}$ [5400] 4-9-5 .................... WPanov 1 86
(PRau, Germany) *always in rear*

10 2 1/2 **Antique Rose (GER)**$^{19}$ [4431] 4-9-5 .................... JBojko 3 82
(HSteinmetz, Germany) *midfield, 6th straight, soon beaten*

11 1 1/4 **Anna Victoria (GER)**$^{51}$ [3504] 4-9-5 .................... DSmith 4 80
(GSybrecht, Germany) *midfield, 8th straight, soon weakened*

12 1 1/2 **Mariella (GER)**$^{35}$ [3973] 3-8-8 .................... PRoberts 5 76
(CVonDerRecke, Germany) *led to 2f out, weakened quickly*

2m 21.88s
**WFA** 3 from 4yo+ 9lb **12** Ran SP% **130.7**
Speed ratings: .
**Owner** Gestut Auenquelle **Bred** Gestut Auenquelle **Trained** Germany

**NOTEBOOK**
**Vallera(GER)** came with a strong run down the outside to notched her second successive Group Three win. She may drop back to a mile and a quarter to contest a Group 2 event at Frankfurt on September 19.
**Summitville** held a reasonable position behind the leaders turning for home but was unable to raise her game in the closing stages.

## 4962 DEAUVILLE (R-H)
Sunday, August 22

**OFFICIAL GOING: Turf: very soft; aw: standard**

### 4981a PRIX MORNY CASINOS BARRIERE (GROUP 1) (C&F) 6f
**2:20** (2:31) 2-Y-0 **£100,599** (£40,246; £20,123; £10,053)

RPR

1 **Divine Proportions (USA)**$^{28}$ [4184] 2-8-11 .................... C-PLemaire 9 117+
(PBary, France) *always in touch, led inside final f, ridden out* **15/8**$^{2}$

2 1 1/2 **Layman (USA)**$^{21}$ [4382] 2-9-0 .................... GaryStevens 8 116+
(AFabre, France) *led, ridden & hung right approaching final f, hung right & headed inside final f, no extra last 100y* **6/4**$^{1}$

3 1 1/2 **Russian Blue (IRE)**$^{14}$ [4589] 2-9-0 .................... JPSpencer 6 113
(APO'Brien, Ire) *disputed 2nd, hard ridden & every chance 1f out, one pace* **5/1**$^{3}$

4 3 **Captain Hurricane**$^{46}$ [3640] 2-9-0 .................... JFortune 7 105
(PWChapple-Hyam) *dwelt, settled in rear, headway on outside over 2f out, hard ridden & one pace final 1 1/2f* **8/1**

5 5 **Mystical Land (IRE)**$^{23}$ [4288] 2-9-0 .................... LDettori 4 93
(JHMGosden) *in touch, 4th at half-way, beaten 2f out* **11/1**

6 1 1/2 **Salut Thomas (FR)**$^{21}$ [4382] 2-9-0 ....................(b) CSoumillon 3 89
(RobertCollet, France) *held up in rear, never near to challenge* **50/1**

7 3 **Tournedos (IRE)**$^{26}$ [4217] 2-9-0 .................... TEDurcan 2 81
(MRChannon) *last to over 2f out, never a factor* **25/1**

8 2 1/2 **Doctor's Cave**$^{26}$ [4219] 2-9-0 .................... OPeslier 5 75
(CEBrittain) *mid-division til weakening quickly over 2f out* **50/1**

9 5 **Shifting Place**$^{28}$ [4184] 2-8-11 .................... DVargiu 1 60
(RMenichetti, Italy) *disputed 2nd to half-way, beaten 2f out* **16/1**

1m 12.8s **Going Correction** +0.175s/f (Good) **9** Ran SP% **124.5**
Speed ratings: **108,106,104,100,93 91,87,84,77.**
**Owner** Niarchos Family **Bred** Flaxman Holding Ltd **Trained** France

**NOTEBOOK**
**Divine Proportions(USA)** looked extremely well in the paddock and posted a top-class performance in the race itself. Having settled well in mid-division, she cruised into the lead inside the final furlong and really dominated a good field in the latter stages. Now unbeaten in four races, three of them Group, she heads for the Prix Marcel Boussac and has already been made second favourite for the 1,000 Guineas.
**Layman(USA)**, a really powerful colt, set a reasonable pace but was no match for the winner in the closing stages. He did not appear to handle the ground very well and is worth another chance on a better surface.
**Russian Blue(IRE)** tried to tackle the leader two out but was unable to quicken and is another who found it extremely difficult to handle the ground.
**Captain Hurricane** kept on gamely but was never a threatened to the front three.
**Mystical Land(IRE)** was well held and Dettori felt the ground was against him.
**Tournedos(IRE)** was a spent force some way from the post.
**Doctor's Cave** ran out of steam from one and a half out and finished a tired horse.



### 4982a PRIX JEAN ROMANET (GROUP 2) (F&M) 1m 2f
**2:50** (3:02) 4-Y-0+ **£42,148** (£16,268; £7,764; £5,176)

RPR

1 **Whortleberry (FR)**$^{15}$ [4566] 4-8-12 ....................(b) TGillet 5 116
(FRohaut, France) *always close up, 4th straight, led well over 1f out, ran on well*

2 2 **Pride (FR)**$^{49}$ [3567] 4-8-12 .................... DBonilla 9 113
(ADeRoyer-Dupre, France) *mid-division, close 6th straight, kept on steadily final f, never reached winner* 2

3 nk **Chorist**$^{22}$ [4323] 5-9-2 .................... DHolland 4 116
(WJHaggas) *led to 3f out, 2nd straight, soon led again, headed well over 1f out, kept on same pace* 1

4 2 **Sasanuma (USA)**$^{70}$ 4-8-12 .................... CSoumillon 10 109
(ADeRoyer-Dupre, France) *mid-division, close 7th straight, stayed on same pace final 2f*

5 1 1/2 **Monturani (IRE)**$^{21}$ [4383] 5-8-12 .................... TEDurcan 7 106
(GWragg) *prominent, 5th straight, one pace from over 1f out* 3

6 hd **Samando (FR)**$^{32}$ [4039] 4-8-12 .................... TThulliez 13 106
(FDoumen, France) *held up in rear to straight, headway final 2f, nearest at finish*

7 1 1/2 **Russian Hill**$^{83}$ [2543] 4-8-12 .................... GaryStevens 3 103
(AFabre, France) *mid-division, close 8th on inside straight, one pace final 2f*

8 shd **Petite Speciale (USA)**$^{28}$ 5-8-12 .................... DBoeuf 2 103
(ELecoiffier, France) *held up, some progress on inside entering straight, soon one pace*

9 2 **Soldera (USA)**$^{57}$ [3331] 4-8-12 .................... JPMurtagh 8 99
(JRFanshawe) *prominent, 3rd straight, weakened over 1f out*

10 2 **Silver Rain (FR)**$^{300}$ [5809] 4-8-12 .................... OPeslier 12 96
(MmeCHead-Maarek, France) *held up in rear, never a factor*

11 **Felicity (IRE)**$^{44}$ [3699] 4-8-12 .................... JFortune 6 96
(JHMGosden) *tracked leader, led 3f out to over 2f out, soon weakened*

12 **Hanami**$^{57}$ [3331] 4-8-12 .................... LDettori 1 96
(JARToller) *last straight, always in rear*

13 **Maredsous (FR)**$^{83}$ [2543] 4-8-12 .................... ELegrix 14 96
(DSepulchre, France) *mid-division, headway on outside over 3f out, came wide & close 9th straight, soon weakened*

2m 12.9s **Going Correction** +0.475s/f (Yiel) **13** Ran SP% **124.0**
Speed ratings: **112,110,110,108,107 107,106,105,104,102 102,102,102.**
**Owner** J Beres **Bred** Mme Gilles Forien & Gilles Forien **Trained** France

**NOTEBOOK**
**Whortleberry(FR)**, fitted with blinkers for the first time, quickened really well on the ground that suits so well and won with plenty in hand. If it remains soft for the Prix Vermeille she may well be a force to be reckoned with.
**Pride(FR)** burst on the scene from the furlong marker to take second place close home. Connections may well look at the Prix de l'Opera now for this Group winner.
**Chorist** put up a magnificent performance considering she was giving 5lb to the rest of the field. She is another possible for the Opera.
**Sasanuma(USA)** may been suited by a better surface.
**Monturani(IRE)** was unable to quicken in the straight. She may well come back to France for the Prix de Royallieu during the Arc meeting.
**Soldera(USA)** was well up early on and still there at the entrance to the straight, but she could offer little close home.
**Felicity(IRE)** dropped out tamely.
**Hanami** was never dangerous.

### 4983a PRIX KERGORLAY (GROUP 2) 1m 7f
**3:20** (3:36) 3-Y-0+ **£42,148** (£16,268; £7,764; £5,176)

RPR

1 **Gold Medallist**$^{15}$ [4529] 4-9-4 .................... RHughes 9 109
(DRCElsworth) *led after 1 1/2f, made rest, driven out final 2f*

2 1 1/2 **Brian Boru**$^{28}$ [4183] 4-9-8 .................... JPSpencer 5 111
(APO'Brien, Ire) *hld up towards rr, 7th str, hdwy on ins to 4th over 1f out, rdn & ran on but pinned on rail bhd wnr fnl 150y, just got 2nd* 3

3 nse **Cut Quartz (FR)**$^{56}$ [3358] 7-9-4 .................... TJarnet 3 107
(RGibson, France) *disputed 4th, 5th & ridden straight, went 2nd approaching final f, hard ridden & ran on one pace, lost 2nd on line* 2

4 2 **Double Obsession**$^{15}$ [4529] 4-9-4 ....................(v) JFEgan 2 105
(MJohnston) *always prominent, 2nd & pushed along straight, no extra from distance*

5 2 1/2 **Clety (FR)**$^{56}$ [3358] 8-9-4 ....................(b) TThulliez 1 103
(FDoumen, France) *led 1 1/2f, 3rd straight, one pace final 2f*

6 2 **Behkara (IRE)**$^{301}$ [5782] 4-9-3 .................... CSoumillon 6 100
(ADeRoyer-Dupre, France) *held up, 8th straight, kept on but never near to challenge* 1

7 8 **Clear Thinking**$^{36}$ [3963] 4-9-4 .................... GaryStevens 8 93
(AFabre, France) *held up in last til some progress to 6th 6f out, pushed along over 4f out, 6th straight, soon beaten*

8 2 **The Great Gatsby (IRE)**$^{8}$ [4746] 4-9-4 ....................(b) LDettori 7 91
(JHMGosden) *in touch, 4th straight, beaten well over 1f out*

9 4 **Coroner (IRE)**$^{22}$ 4-9-4 .................... ELegrix 4 87
(J-CRouget, France) *always in rear, last final 7f*

3m 20.9s **Going Correction** +0.475s/f (Yiel) **9** Ran SP% **122.8**
Speed ratings: **117,116,116,115,113 112,108,107,105.**
**Owner** J C Smith **Bred** Littleton Stud **Trained** Whitsbury, Hants

**NOTEBOOK**
**Gold Medallist** was allowed his own way in front and made virtually every yard of the running. Quickening things up rounding the final furlong, he kept on resolutely to the line and hold off all challenges. He is back to his very best and could for the Doncaster Cup or the Cadran, while the Melbourne Cup has also been mentioned.
**Brian Boru** has to be considered unlucky as his jockey took a decision to make a run up the rail but he was completely hemmed in throughout the final furlong. This was a good effort and he could now go for the Irish St Leger.
**Cut Quartz(FR)** was beautifully placed rounding the final turn before battling all the way up the straight. A tilt at the Prix Gladiateur is now on the cards.
**Double Obsession** just lacked a change of pace and this ground was probably soft enough.
**The Great Gatsby(IRE)** had every chance but was well beaten soon after entering the straight.

# OVREVOLL (R-H)

Sunday, August 22

**OFFICIAL GOING: Soft**

## 4984a MARIT SVEAS MINNELOP (GROUP 3) 1m 1f

2:20 (12:00) 3-Y-O+ **£60,453** (£20,151; £10,076; £6,045)

RPR

1 **Mandrake El Mago (CHI)**[108] [1954] 5-9-2 .......................... MSantos 6 106
(FCastro, Sweden) *raced in 7th, 5th straight, headway 2f out, led 50 yards out, ran on well* 1

2 1 **Hovman (DEN)**[24] 5-9-2 .......................... MLarsen 2 104
(MsCErichsen, Norway) *led, 2 lengths clear 1f out, headed 50 yards out, no extra*

3 1 **Binary File (USA)**[21] [4380] 6-9-2 .......................... NCordrey 4 102
(SJensen, Denmark) *raced in 6th, 4th straight, stayed on under pressure final 2f*

4 2 **Alpino Chileno (ARG)**[21] [4380] 5-9-2 ..........................(b) MMartinez 5 98
(RuneHaugen, Norway) *prominent early, dropped back to 6th over 2f out, stayed on steadily from over 1f out*

5 ½ **Killaden (IRE)**[499] 4-9-2 .......................... YvonneDurant 13 97
(WidoNeuroth, Norway) *always mid division* 3

6 1 **Checkit (IRE)**[15] [4539] 4-9-2 .......................... ACulhane 10 95
(MRChannon) *tracked winner, 6th straight, one pace final 2f* 2

7 1 **Royal Experiment (USA)**[21] [4380] 5-9-2 .......................... FJohansson 7 93
(WidoNeuroth, Norway) *held up in 13th, ran on well from over 1f out, nearest finish*

8 7 **Tesorero (SWE)**[364] [4431] 8-9-2 .......................... KAnderson 14 80
(AreHyldmo, Norway) *raced in 3rd, weakened 2f out*

9 1 **Arlecchina (GER)**[21] [4378] 4-8-12 .......................... FNorton 11 74
(UStoltefuss, Germany) *raced in 12th, never a factor*

10 hd **Ecology (IRE)**[24] 6-9-2 .......................... FDiaz 8 78
(RuneHaugen, Norway) *raxced in 9th, always towards rear*

11 1 **Year Two Thousand**[364] [4431] 6-9-2 .......................... JohnFortune 15 76
(ALund, Norway) *held up in last, always behind*

12 1½ **Bellamont Forest (USA)**[24] 8-9-2 .......................... JJohansen 1 73
(OLarsen, Sweden) *raced in 4th, 2nd straight, soon weakened*

13 hd **Honeysuckle Player (SWE)**[108] [1954] 6-9-2 .....(b) LHammer-Hansen 9 73
(FReuterskiold, Sweden) *raced in 10th, always in rear*

14 hd **Corriolanus (GER)**[16] [4525] 4-9-2 .......................... MartinDwyer 3 72
(PMitchell) *always in rear*

1m 48.1s **14 Ran SP% 125.2**
Speed ratings: .
**Owner** Mac Racing & Stall Chicken & Bernerup **Bred** Haras Matancilla **Trained** Sweden

**NOTEBOOK**
**Checkit(IRE)** was all at sea on the soft ground and struggled to negotiate the sharp home turn. Given the conditions, he performed creditably against some of Scandinavia's best horses.
**Corriolanus(GER)** failed to get into the race on ground that was softer than he prefers.

# [4824] HAMILTON (R-H)

Monday, August 23

**OFFICIAL GOING: Good to soft (good in places)**

## 4985 PERFECT DAY CLAIMING STKS 1m 1f 36y

2:15 (2:15) (E) 3-Y-O+ **£3,493** (£1,075; £537; £268) **Stalls High**

Form RPR

5006 1 **Jordans Spark**[6] [4829] 3-8-10 49..........................(p) RWinston 9 63
(ISemple) *in tch: effrt over 2f out: led wl ins fnl f: styd on* **25/1**

3516 2 1¼ **Senor Eduardo**[19] [4458] 7-9-3 54.......................... KDarley 5 60
(SGollings) *hld up in tch: rdn to ld over 1f out: hdd wl ins fnl f: no ex* **11/4**[2]

6511 3 3½ **Bailieborough (IRE)**[16] [4535] 5-9-13 68..........................(v) AlexGreaves 2 63
(DNicholls) *trckd ldrs: hung rt and led over 2f out: hdd over 1f out: sn btn* **11/8**[1]

420U 4 2½ **Merlins Profit**[6] [4825] 4-8-11 43.......................... PHanagan 6 42
(MDods) *hld up: effrt over 2f out: no imp over 1f out* **9/1**

6000 5 4 **Chisel**[16] [4562] 3-8-3 50.......................... RFfrench 8 33
(MJohnston) *chsd ldrs tl wknd over 2f out* **11/2**[3]

0050 6 3½ **Abuelos**[6] [4825] 5-8-10 43.......................... TWilliams 4 26
(DWThompson) *missed break: rdn 3f out: n.d* **33/1**

0/00 7 shd **Society Times (USA)**[16] [4537] 11-8-4 24..........................(t) DFentiman[(7)] 7 27
(DANolan) *led to over 2f out: sn btn* **25/1**

404/ 8 29 **Never Forget Bowie**[678] [5275] 8-8-5 40.......................... PPMathers[(5)] 1 —
(RAllan) *prom: rdn over 3f out: sn wknd* **20/1**

2m 1.30s (1.70) **Going Correction** +0.05s/f (Good)
**WFA** 3 from 4yo+ 7lb **8 Ran SP% 109.6**
Speed ratings: **94,92,89,87,84 80,80,55**CSF £85.83 TOTE £14.10: £3.90, £1.30, £1.10; EX 64.30.
**Owner** Ian Crawford & Brian Jordan Jnr **Bred** Egerton Stud Farms **Trained** Carluke, S Lanarks

**FOCUS**
A modest claimer and a surprise result, with Jordans Spark finding improvement from somewhere, but several were below form and the runner-up offers the best guide to the level.

**NOTEBOOK**
**Jordans Spark**, racing off a mark of 49, had a bit to find at the weights with a few of his rivals, but he handled conditions best on the day and ran on strongly to deny his elders. This represented a big improvement on previous form and if able to build on this is worth his place in handicaps.
*Official explanation: trainer said, regarding the improved form shown, gelding appeared to be suited by the drop in trip and class together with the fitting of sheepskin cheekpieces for the first time*
**Senor Eduardo** was well held in this grade earlier in the month, and ran much better with a little cut in the ground. Under similar conditions he can probably pick up a claimer.
**Bailieborough(IRE)** has been on a roll over shorter on faster going and found the combination of the extra distance on softish ground too much of a test. Back under ideal conditions, he will continue to be a force to be reckoned with in this sort of grade.
**Merlins Profit** finished riderless at the course last week and managed to complete with jockey intact. He was beaten far enough and remains a maiden.
**Chisel** is evidently one of his stable's lesser performers and he never looked like it. It is going to be a struggle to win a race with him unless he improves.

## 4986 ROYAL BANK OF SCOTLAND MAIDEN STKS 5f 4y

2:45 (2:46) (D) 2-Y-O **£4,803** (£1,478; £739; £369) **Stalls High**

Form RPR

1 **Cyclical** 2-9-0 .......................... PHanagan 3 78
(GAButler) *dwlt: sn chsng ldrs: rdn to ld appr fnl f: edgd lft ins last: kpt on wl* **5/6**[1]

52 2 1¼ **Howards Princess**[37] [3950] 2-8-9 .......................... KDarley 4 69
(JSGoldie) *trckd ldrs: effrt and ev ch over 1f out: no ex ins fnl furlong* **9/4**[2]

42 3 1½ **Bond Babe**[21] [4388] 2-8-9 .......................... FLynch 1 67+
(BSmart) *led tl hdd and nt qckn appr fnl f* **9/2**[3]

6306 4 12 **Nee Lemon Left**[49] [3577] 2-8-4 63.......................... PPMathers[(5)] 2 22
(ABerry) *cl up tl hung lft and wknd fr 2f out* **25/1**

61.52 secs (0.26) **Going Correction** +0.05s/f (Good) **4 Ran SP% 107.4**
Speed ratings: **99,97,94,75**CSF £2.92 TOTE £1.80; EX 2.70.
**Owner** Cheveley Park Stud **Bred** Cheveley Park Stud Ltd **Trained** Blewbury, Oxon

**FOCUS**
An ordinary maiden and the only colt in the line-up Cyclical proved good enough to score on his debut.

**NOTEBOOK**
**Cyclical** is bred to be speedy and was clearly expected to make a winning debut - backed into odds-on on the betting exchanges. Despite being slowly away he was soon on terms and although taking time to get going, he ran on strongly and ultimately won with something to spare. There should be more to come but he is unlikely to prove up to Pattern level.
**Howards Princess** has shown plenty on all three starts, and it is just a matter of time before she wins, whether it be in maiden of nursery company. A return to six furlongs will also help.
**Bond Babe** is now qualified for a handicap mark and over six furlongs should be capable of improvement.
**Nee Lemon Left** never featured and will be better in nurseries.

## 4987 FRIENDS OF SCOTTISH RACING MAIDEN STKS 1m 1f 36y

3:15 (3:18) (D) 3-Y-O+ **£5,551** (£1,708; £854; £427) **Stalls High**

Form RPR

3002 1 **Templet (USA)**[12] [4631] 4-9-0 60..........................(b) RWinston 9 73
(ISemple) *trckd ldrs: effrt over 2f out: disp ld fnl f: led last stride* **3/1**[2]

2305 2 shd **Just A Fluke (IRE)**[25] [4258] 3-8-7 74.......................... RFfrench 4 73
(MJohnston) *cl up: rdn to ld over 2f out: kpt on: hdd last stride* **2/1**[1]

-6L3 3 3½ **Elusive Kitty (USA)**[15] [4580] 3-8-2 69..........................(t) PHanagan 10 61
(GAButler) *in tch: effrt over 2f out: r.o same pce fnl f* **4/1**[3]

0040 4 4 **Moonshaft (USA)**[82] [2567] 3-8-7 67.......................... KDarley 1 58
(EALDunlop) *led to over 2f out: sn one pce* **9/1**

55- 5 ¾ **Flight Commander (IRE)**[412] [3083] 4-9-0 .......................... DAllan 6 56
(ISemple) *in tch: outpcd 3f out: n.d after* **16/1**

6 3 **Sarenne** 3-8-2 .......................... JFanning 7 45
(MJohnston) *hld up: effrt centre 3f out: no imp fr 2f out* **10/1**

0 7 3 **Stravonian**[134] [1344] 4-8-9 .......................... PPMathers[(5)] 2 44
(DANolan) *s.i.s: keen and hld up: rdn over 2f out: sn outpcd* **100/1**

6 8 26 **Fizzy Pop**[23] [4351] 5-8-2 .......................... DFentiman[(7)] 8 —
(WSCunningham) *a bhd* **66/1**

04 9 nk **Dalkeys Lass**[23] [4332] 3-8-6 ow4.......................... VHalliday 3 —
(MrsLBNormile) *chsd ldrs tl wknd fr 3f out* **100/1**

10 dist **Swords At Dawn (IRE)** 3-8-5 ow6.......................... PMulrennan[(3)] 5 —
(JBarclay) *bhd: rdn over 4f out: sn lost tch* **33/1**

2m 0.90s (1.30) **Going Correction** +0.05s/f (Good)
**WFA** 3 from 4yo+ 7lb **10 Ran SP% 109.7**
Speed ratings: **96,95,92,89,88 85,83,60,59,—**CSF £8.52 TOTE £3.80: £1.30, £1.10, £1.70; EX 11.20.
**Owner** J And J Hunter **Bred** Warren W Rosenthal **Trained** Carluke, S Lanarks

**FOCUS**
A modest winning time for the grade, but a basically disappointing field and the form is not expected to work out.

**NOTEBOOK**
**Templet(USA)** ran a better race in claiming company most recently and narrowly proved good enough to get his head in front in what was a poor maiden. He could win a handicap but claiming level is about right for him.
**Just A Fluke(IRE)**, thought of as one of his trainer's better prospects last season, is still a maiden and again found one too good. This was his ninth attempt at winning a race, but it will no doubt all fall right one day.
**Elusive Kitty(USA)** probably ran a little below form and was comfortably held.
**Moonshaft(USA)** led early but was readily beaten. He will be best of dropped into a claimer.
**Flight Commander(IRE)** ran well enough on this seasonal debut and wants a return to farther.
**Sarenne** looked in need of the outing and should come on for the outing.

## 4988 ALEX SALMOND PICK A WINNER SCOTTISH TROPHY STKS (H'CAP) 1m 65y

3:45 (3:45) (C) (0-90,86) 3-Y-O+ **£10,409** (£3,203; £1,601; £800) **Stalls High**

Form RPR

4520 1 **Nevada Desert (IRE)**[30] [4155] 4-8-13 **71**..........................(p) SChin 4 79
(RMWhitaker) *cl up: rdn over 2f out: led ins fnl f: kpt on wl* **10/1**

0350 2 ½ **Penrith (FR)**[16] [4540] 3-9-8 **86**.......................... JFanning 8 93
(MJohnston) *sn prom: effrt over 2f out: kpt on fnl f: nt rch wnr* **11/1**

1621 3 shd **Young Mr Grace (IRE)**[16] [4543] 4-9-8 **80**.......................... DAllan 10 87
(TDEasterby) *led: rdn over 2f out: hdd ins fnl f: kpt on* **8/1**

3221 4 shd **Hills Of Gold**[4] [4877] 5-8-13 **74**.......................... PMulrennan[(3)] 1 81
(MWEasterby) *hld up: rdn over 3f out: r.o fnl f: nrst fin* **13/2**

1-23 5 1½ **Straw Bear (USA)**[11] [4691] 3-8-13 **77**.......................... JMackay 9 80
(SirMarkPrescott) *cl up: rdn over 3f out: one pce over 1f out* **4/1**[2]

2020 6 2½ **Qualitair Wings**[16] [4558] 5-9-0 **72**.......................... KDarley 6 70
(JHetherton) *hld up in tch: rdn over 3f out: no imp fr 2f out* **20/1**

4053 7 nk **Cherished Number**[6] [4826] 5-8-11 **69**.......................... RWinston 3 67
(ISemple) *hld up: rdn over 3f out: nvr rchd ldrs* **7/2**[1]

0501 8 hd **Danelor (IRE)**[12] [4634] 6-10-0 **86**.......................... PHanagan 7 83
(RAFahey) *keen: cl up tl wknd over 1f out* **9/2**[3]

6106 9 3½ **Tony Tie**[12] [4634] 8-9-9 **84**.......................... NMackay[(3)] 2 74
(JSGoldie) *in tch: rdn and outpcd 3f out: n.d after* **22/1**

4540 10 5 **Low Cloud**[23] [4327] 4-9-3 **75**..........................(v) AlexGreaves 5 54
(DNicholls) *s.i.s: nvr on terms* **33/1**

1m 48.49s (-0.81) **Going Correction** +0.05s/f (Good)
**WFA** 3 from 4yo+ 6lb **10 Ran SP% 114.3**
Speed ratings: **106,105,105,105,103 101,101,100,97,92**CSF £108.44 CT £939.83 TOTE £13.30: £4.00, £2.90, £3.70; EX 128.80 Trifecta £905.50 Part won. Pool: £1,275.46. 0.80 winning tickets..
**Owner** J Barry Pemberton **Bred** Bryan Ryan **Trained** Scarcroft, W Yorks

**FOCUS**
Not a bad little race and it paid to race up with the pace as they did not go that quick. Despite that, the form looks solid.

**NOTEBOOK**
**Nevada Desert(IRE)** was always travelling nicely and found plenty for pressure, pulling out more close home to hold the late challengers. This was his first win for over a year, but he is proven on this ground and appreciated the drop back in trip.
**Penrith(FR)** was never too far away but could not pick up in time. He seems to have lost many races this season as a result of being too far off the pace, and it is interesting to know why he does not make the running - he did so when winning on his debut which is typical for his trainer's horses.
**Young Mr Grace(IRE)** was always up there and kept grinding away, just being run out of things in the closing stages.
**Hills Of Gold** won well last week and was not disgraced off the same mark, finishing well having been a bit behind. He is due to go up in the weights in future and will need to improve to defy a new mark.
**Straw Bear(USA)** had every chance but simply lacked the pace to make a race winning challenge.
**Cherished Number** got a bit behind and could not make up the ground in time.

## 4989 GEORGE WIMPEY H'CAP — 1m 1f 36y
**4:15** (4:16) (E) (0-75,71) 3-Y-O — **£4,208** (£1,295; £647; £323) **Stalls** High

Form — RPR
2204 **1** **Eboracum (IRE)**[16] [4562] 3-8-12 **62**........(b) DAllan 1 70
(TDEasterby) *cl up: led 1/2-way: mde rest: pushed out* **10/3**[2]
0423 **2** 1 ½ **Sunset Mirage (USA)**[10] [4711] 3-9-4 **68**........(b[1]) KDarley 4 73
(EALDunlop) *hld up in tch: hdwy to press wnr over 2f out: one pce ins fnl f* **5/2**[1]
0002 **3** 3 ½ **Argent**[23] [4332] 3-7-12 **48**........(p) RFfrench 2 46
(MissLAPerratt) *chsd ldrs: outpcd over 2f out: n.d after* **5/1**[3]
30P1 **4** nk **Banana Grove (IRE)**[15] [4573] 3-9-2 **71**........ PPMathers[(5)] 5 68
(ABerry) *dwlt: chsd ldrs after 2f: rdn and wknd over 2f out* **14/1**
6000 **5** 2 ½ **Koodoo**[25] [4259] 3-7-5 **48** oh5........ DFentiman[(7)] 3 40
(ACrook) *led to 1/2-way: wknd over 2f out* **20/1**
-400 **6** 6 **Devious Ayers (IRE)**[23] [4346] 3-8-11 **61**........ PHanagan 6 41
(GABulter) *hld up in tch: rdn and hung rt over 3f out: sn btn* **5/2**[1]

2m 1.94s (2.34) **Going Correction** +0.05s/f (Good) **6** Ran SP% **108.3**
Speed ratings: **91,89,86,86,84 78**CSF £11.18 TOTE £4.60: £2.70, £1.10; EX 10.40.
**Owner** T D Easterby **Bred** Tullamaine Castle Stud **Trained** Great Habton, N Yorks

**FOCUS**
A weak handicap and a moderate time for the class, slower than both the claimer and the maiden run over the same trip earlier in the afternoon.

**NOTEBOOK**
**Eboracum(IRE)** ran one of her best races to date on this sort of ground and, with the blinkers seemingly working better second time around, proved too strong for Sunset Mirage. She shaped as though a mile and a half will be fine and this ground is all important.
**Sunset Mirage(USA)** continues to run well but does not find winning easy. She stayed on well enough and was clear of the third.
**Argent** is well exposed and does little for the form. He had no change of gear.
**Banana Grove(IRE)** won a weak race last time and struggled in this better grade of race.
**Koodoo** showed up early but was readily brushed aside.
**Devious Ayers(IRE)** is an awkward ride and looked far from enthusiastic.

## 4990 TOTEPOOL H'CAP — 1m 5f 9y
**4:45** (4:45) (D) (0-85,78) 3-Y-O+ — **£8,248** (£2,538; £1,269; £634) **Stalls** High

Form — RPR
2033 **1** **Sahem (IRE)**[8] [4777] 7-9-10 **78**........ DAllan 6 89
(CJTeague) *hld up in tch: effrt over 1f out: qcknd to ld ins fnl f: r.o wl* **7/1**
3232 **2** 1 ½ **Yankeedoodledandy (IRE)**[9] [4762] 3-8-12 **77**........(p) KDarley 5 86
(PCHaslam) *led: rdn over 2f out: hdd and nt qckn ins fnl f* **7/2**[2]
5404 **3** 3 **Colorado Falls (IRE)**[19] [4448] 6-9-5 **73**........ PHanagan 7 78
(PMonteith) *prom: effrt over 2f out: one pce over 1f out* **3/1**[1]
4-05 **4** hd **Minivet**[8] [3149] 9-7-6 **53** ow1........ DFentiman[(7)] 8 57
(RAllan) *trckd ldrs tl rdn and nt qckn fr over 1f out* **8/1**
1534 **5** 1 ½ **Kid'Z'Play (IRE)**[6] [4830] 8-8-12 **69**........ NMackay[(3)] 4 71
(JSGoldie) *cl up tl rdn and outpcd fr wl over 1f out* **12/1**
0660 **6** 5 **Millennium Hall**[6] [4826] 5-8-5 **62**........ PMulrennan[(3)] 2 57
(PMonteith) *hld up in tch: effrt whn n.m.r over 2f out: rdn and btn over 1f out* **12/1**
0/00 **7** 6 **Leopard Spot (IRE)**[8] [4778] 6-7-12 **52** oh4........(tp) RFfrench 1 39
(ISemple) *missed break: hld up: rdn over 3f out: sn btn* **6/1**[3]
4 **8** 1 ½ **Pilgrims Progress (IRE)**[17] [4512] 4-9-5 **73**........ RWinston 3 58
(DWThompson) *prom: effrt over 3f out: wknd 2f out* **6/1**[3]

2m 54.18s (0.78) **Going Correction** +0.05s/f (Good)
**WFA** 3 from 4yo+ 11lb **8** Ran SP% **114.8**
Speed ratings: **99,98,96,96,95 92,88,87**CSF £31.86 CT £89.48 TOTE £9.40: £2.40, £1.30, £1.40; EX 31.60 Place 6 £33.26, Place 5 £24.59.
**Owner** Robert Gray **Bred** Barronstown Stud And Orpendale **Trained** Wingate, Co Durham

**FOCUS**
A modest time for the grade, but a decent performance from Sahem and the form looks sound.

**NOTEBOOK**
**Sahem(IRE)** is proven under these conditions and, having been off the pace, came with a strong late run to cut down Yankeedoodledandy and win going away. This was the worst race he has run in for a while and he seemed suited to giving weight to inferior rivals.
**Yankeedoodledandy(IRE)** was clear of the third and continues to run consistently well, again giving his all.
**Colorado Falls(IRE)** goes well here, but found the trip too short and was doing his best work towards the end of the race.
**Minivet** is another for whom this would have been an inadequate test. He is getting on but remains in good form.
T/Jkpt: Not won. T/Plt: £57.40 to a £1 stake. Pool: £57,827.50. 734.65 winning tickets. T/Qpdt: £11.60 to a £1 stake. Pool: £3,918.30. 248.90 winning tickets. RY

# [4567] LEICESTER (R-H)
Monday, August 23
**4991 Meeting Abandoned** - waterlogged

# [4924] SOUTHWELL (L-H)
Monday, August 23

**OFFICIAL GOING: Slow**
After 6" rain over the previous two weeks the ground was riding very slow and due to a problem on the inner the stalls over 6 furlongs were outside.
Wind: Almost nil. Weather: Persistent rain.

## 4997 NATIONAL PLUMBERS DAY CLAIMING STKS — 6f (F)
**5:10** (5:13) (E) 2-Y-O — **£4,114** (£1,266; £633; £316) **Stalls** High

Form — RPR
0433 **1** **Roko**[11] [4675] 2-8-10 59........(b) TLucas 11 51
(MWEasterby) *mid-div: hdwy on outer over 2f out: hrd rdn and styd on to ld nr fin* **10/1**
05 **2** ½ **Hiamovi (IRE)**[56] [3377] 2-9-3........ MHenry 3 57
(RMHCowell) *led: no ex and hdd nr fin* **20/1**
4U05 **3** nk **Fold Walk**[35] [3980] 2-8-7 46........ DaleGibson 4 46
(MWEasterby) *mid-div: hdwy over 2f out: ev ch ins last: nt qckn nr fin* **33/1**
4352 **4** 1 ½ **Campeon (IRE)**[7] [4816] 2-9-0 74........(v[1]) DCorby[(3)] 1 51
(MJWallace) *hmpd s: hdwy to trck ldrs over 4f out: ev ch fnl 2f: nt qckn ins last* **11/4**[1]
5 **5** nk **Weet N Measures**[11] [4675] 2-9-3........ ACulhane 5 50
(RHollinshead) *chsd ldrs: ev ch 2f out: nt qckn ins last* **6/1**[3]
05 **6** 1 **Champagne Rossini (IRE)**[18] [4498] 2-9-7........ LVickers 2 51
(MCChapman) *swvd bdly lft s: sn chsng ldrs: one pce appr fnl f* **40/1**
6600 **7** nk **Skippit John**[10] [4700] 2-9-6 65........ DeanMcKeown 12 49
(RonaldThompson) *chsd ldrs: one pce fnl 2f* **16/1**
5 **8** ½ **Danescourt (IRE)**[14] [4599] 2-9-3........ CCatlin 6 45
(JAOsborne) *trckd ldrs: rdn over 2f out: outpcd over 1f out: kpt on ins last* **10/3**[2]
0 **9** nk **Ferrara Flame (IRE)**[13] [4621] 2-8-9........ LFletcher[(3)] 14 39
(JAOsborne) *lost pl over 4f out: hdwy over 1f out: nt rch ldrs* **33/1**
061 **10** 1 ½ **Hopelessly Devoted**[11] [4675] 2-8-4 58........ RoryMoore[(5)] 10 31
(PCHaslam) *chsd ldrs: wknd over 1f out* **13/2**
0065 **11** 4 **Lane Marshal**[10] [4699] 2-8-8........(b) TEaves[(3)] 13 21
(MESowersby) *chsd ldrs: hung lft and lost pl over 1f out* **40/1**
0 **12** 1 **Smiling Starduster (IRE)**[14] [4606] 2-8-6........ DTudhope[(7)] 7 20
(DCarroll) *sn bhd* **40/1**
**13** 25 **Nibbles (IRE)** 2-9-4........ THamilton[(3)] 8 —
(RPElliott) *rrd s: a bhd: t.o* **33/1**
0050 **14** dist **Timmy**[16] [4559] 2-8-8........ GParkin 9 —
(MESowersby) *bhd: virtually p.u over 2f out: wl t.o* **66/1**

1m 20.63s (3.73) **Going Correction** +0.20s/f (Slow) **14** Ran SP% **114.7**
Speed ratings: **83,82,81,79,79 78,77,77,76,74 69,68,34,—**CSF £192.37 TOTE £10.30: £3.70, £7.50, £10.40; EX 115.50.Roko was claimed by Keith Nicholls for £5,000.
**Owner** John Southway & John Walsh **Bred** Peter Holmes **Trained** Sheriff Hutton, N Yorks

**FOCUS**
The surface could only be worked with discs and could not be rolled as a result of the rain, resulting in a very slow time, 2.84 seconds slower than the 0 to 55 handicap later on the card, and the form looks weak.

**NOTEBOOK**
**Roko**, improved since being fitted with blinkers, made hard work of it after having difficulty making the bend. Making his effort on the wide outside, his stamina carried the day. He was claimed and joins Derek Shaw's yard.
**Hiamovi(IRE)** settled much better in front over this shorter trip and was only just worn down.
**Fold Walk**, making her All-Weather bow, had plenty to find with the winner, her stablemate, on Beverley running, and this was her best effort to date.
**Campeon(IRE)**, in a first-time visor, was taken to post early. Knocked sideways at the start, he could find no more inside the last and is now looking fully exposed.
**Weet N Measures**, who looked very fit, raced on an even keel this time and was only found lacking late on.
**Champagne Rossini(IRE)**, a handful beforehand, was mounted on the track. He dived left leaving the stalls but showed a lot more than he had done on two previous outings on turf.
**Skippit John**, making his All-Weather debut, was nibbled at in the market. Rated 65, he looks the measure of the form.
**Danescourt(IRE)**, easily the paddock pick, ran as if in need of a seventh furlong.
**Timmy** *Official explanation: jockey said colt hung right-handed throughout*

## 4998 KING RICHARD III FILLIES' H'CAP — 1m 4f (F)
**5:40** (5:42) (E) (0-70,62) 3-Y-O+ — **£3,341** (£1,028; £514; £257) **Stalls** Low

Form — RPR
5241 **1** **Crocolat**[42] [3799] 3-9-4 **56**........ FNorton 6 79+
(MrsStefLiddiard) *sn chsng ldrs: pushed along 6f out: rdn 3f out: styd on strly to ld over 1f out: sn drew clr: eased towards fin* **5/4**[1]
4224 **2** 8 **Heathers Girl**[59] [3281] 5-9-10 **52**........ GGibbons 7 57
(DHaydnJones) *trckd ldrs: led on bit over 2f out: hdd over 1f out: no ch w wnr* **8/1**
4053 **3** 2 **Staff Nurse (IRE)**[4] [4883] 4-8-4 **32**........ KimTinkler 4 34
(DonEnricoIncisa) *chsd ldrs: wl outpcd 5f out: kpt on fnl 2f* **7/1**[3]
5200 **4** 4 **Dalriath**[21] [4397] 5-7-13 **32**........ StephanieHollinshead[(5)] 5 28
(MCChapman) *trckd ldrs: led on bit over 3f out: hdd over 2f out: hung lft: wknd over 1f out* **14/1**
3051 **5** 2 ½ **Faraway Echo**[6] [4830] 3-8-2 **47**........ MHalford[(7)] 3 39
(JamesMoffatt) *chsd ldrs: outpcd 4f out: n.d after* **10/1**
-245 **6** 13 **Our Emmy Lou**[12] [4630] 3-9-9 **61**........(b[1]) TPQueally 8 34
(SirMarkPrescott) *led and sn clr: hdd over 3f out: sn wknd* **9/2**[2]
3150 **7** 6 **Dash Of Magic**[10] [4698] 6-9-3 **45**........ MTebbutt 1 9
(JHetherton) *v unruly in stalls: s.s: a bhd* **7/1**[3]
5036 **8** 9 **Opera Star (IRE)**[57] [3341] 3-9-10 **62**........ ACulhane 2 12
(BWHills) *chsd ldrs: rdn over 7f out: sn lost pl and bhd* **14/1**

2m 44.72s (2.62) **Going Correction** +0.20s/f (Slow)
**WFA** 3 from 4yo+ 10lb **8** Ran SP% **121.2**
Speed ratings: **99,93,92,89,88 79,75,69**CSF £13.33 CT £55.53 TOTE £1.60: £1.10, £3.30, £4.60; EX 16.00.
**Owner** Mrs S Clifford **Bred** Addison Racing Ltd Inc **Trained** Great Shefford, Berks



The Form Book, Raceform Ltd, Compton, RG20 6NL

**FOCUS**
In moderate handicap run at a very strong pace early in the ground, but the overall time was very modest and they came home in single file.

**NOTEBOOK**
**Crocolat**, having her first outing for her new trainer, made hard work of it but, really warming to her task, shot clear and in the end won easing right down. Unfortunately the track is now closed down and she will not be able to return under a penalty.
**Heathers Girl**, bang in form, took it up on the bridle but, when the winner challenged, she found little and proved no match.
**Staff Nurse(IRE)** again proved well suited by the furious pace but this trip is her bare minimum.
**Dalriath**, whose only previous win was here, let the leader cut her own throat. She took it up running away but soon challenged, found little.
**Faraway Echo**, 3lb lower, was having only her second outing on the All-Weather and she was in trouble leaving the back stretch.
**Our Emmy Lou**, fitted with blinkers on her All-Weather debut, set off as if her rider had a train to catch. She fell in a heap when headed.
**Dash Of Magic** became very upset in the stalls. She lost many lengths, and also as as it turned out, a front shoe. *Official explanation: jockey said mare missed the break and lost a front shoe*
**Opera Star(IRE)** *Official explanation: jockey said filly had a breathing problem*

## 4999 FESTIVAL OF FIRE FILLIES' (S) STKS 5f (F)
**6:10** (6:12) (G ) 2-Y-O **£2,541** (£726; £363) **Stalls** High

Form RPR
0422 **1** **Paris Tapis**[11] [4675] 2-8-9 58 PFessey 7 55
(KARyan) *chsd ldrs: rdn to ld over 1f out: styd on wl* **1/1**[1]
3640 **2** *2 ½* **Chilali (IRE)**[7] [4803] 2-8-9 60 FNorton 6 46
(ABerry) *trckd ldrs: led 2f out: sn hdd and nt qckn* **9/4**[2]
000 **3** *5* **Bregaglia**[9] [4753] 2-8-9 (v[1]) MHenry 4 29
(RMHCowell) *sn outpcd and bhd: hdwy 2f out: styd on wl ins last* **28/1**
2640 **4** *shd* **Emma's Venture**[91] [2364] 2-8-9 49 DaleGibson 1 28
(MWEasterby) *led over 1f: chsd ldrs: wknd over 1f out* **15/2**[3]
356 **5** *shd* **Artadi**[18] [4482] 2-8-9 50 (b[1]) CCatlin 9 28
(PMPhelan) *sn outpcd and bhd: styd on appr fnl f* **14/1**
0 **6** *5* **Ms Three**[18] [4488] 2-8-9 JoannaBadger 5 11
(RFord) *dwlt: t.k.h: led over 3f out: hdd 2f out: wknd over 1f out* **66/1**
0000 **7** *½* **Star Of Kildare (IRE)**[14] [4607] 2-8-9 KimTinkler 10 9
(NTinkler) *s.i.s: nvr a factor* **20/1**
0 **8** *1 ¾* **Isle Of Light (IRE)**[26] [4243] 2-8-9 LisaJones 8 3
(WRMuir) *chsd ldrs: drvn along over 2f out: edgd lft and lost pl over 1f out* **16/1**
**9** *15* **La Providence** 2-8-9 (be[1]) PMQuinn 2 —
(DWChapman) *s.s: rn green and a wl bhd* **40/1**
0003 **10** *1* **Eternal Sunshine (IRE)**[45] [3709] 2-8-6 39 (b[1]) THamilton[(3)] 3 —
(RPElliott) *lost pl over 3f out: sn bhd* **20/1**

63.17 secs (2.77) **Going Correction** +0.325s/f (Slow) **10** Ran SP% **122.0**
Speed ratings: **90,86,78,77,77 69,68,66,42,40**CSF £3.24 TOTE £2.00: £1.10, £1.10, £10.50; EX 4.70.The winner was sold to by Phil McEntee for 9,000gns.
**Owner** Calverts Carpets **Bred** Calvert Carpets Ltd **Trained** Hambleton, N Yorks

**FOCUS**
A very ordinary seller in which they finished well strung out.

**NOTEBOOK**
**Paris Tapis** never left the stands' side rail and in the end was right on top. Connections let her go, and it remains to be seen if she proves worth the money she cost.
**Chilali(IRE)**, having her second outing on Fibresand, travelled better than the winner but in the end was very much second best.
**Bregaglia**, dropped in class and fitted with a first-time visor on her All-Weather bow, needs at least a sixth furlong.
**Emma's Venture**, absent for three months, was making her All-Weather debut. Her stride shortened in the closing stages and in the end she just missed out on third spot. *Official explanation: jockey said filly moved badly throughout and tired rapidly in the final furlong*
**Artadi**, with blinkers fitted on her All-Weather debut, only got going too late and needs at least another furlong.
**Ms Three**, far too keen to post, did too much in front on the way back and failed hopelessly to see it out.

## 5000 ST ROSE OF LIMA H'CAP 6f (F)
**6:40** (6:44) (F ) (0-55,61) 3-Y-O+ **£3,073** (£878; £439) **Stalls** High

Form RPR
2155 **1** **Headland (USA)**[3] [4926] 6-9-9 **55** (be) ACulhane 3 64
(DWChapman) *hdwy over 4f out: sn trcking ldrs: styd on to ld nr fin* **5/1**[2]
3631 **2** *nk* **Jagged (IRE)**[4] [4881] 4-10-1 **61** 6ex (v) LDettori 4 69
(JRJenkins) *led: edgd rt over 1f out: no ex and hdd nr fin* **2/1**[1]
0560 **3** *½* **Lucius Verrus (USA)**[16] [4542] 4-9-3 **49** (be[1]) DarrenWilliams 7 56
(DShaw) *hld up: hdwy over 4f out: sn chsng ldrs: ev ch 1f out: nt qckn* **14/1**
0000 **4** *1 ¼* **Bold Wolf**[16] [4548] 3-9-0 **49** GHind 16 52
(JLSpearing) *chsd ldrs: nt qckn appr fnl f* **50/1**
3350 **5** *3 ½* **Ace-Ma-Vahra**[14] [4605] 6-8-13 **45** (b) JBramhill 9 37
(SRBowring) *chsd ldrs: outpcd over 2f out: kpt on fnl f* **16/1**
0402 **6** *1 ¼* **Travelling Times**[28] [4185] 5-8-12 **47** (v) TEaves[(3)] 11 36
(JSWainwright) *chsd ldrs: rdn 3f out: sn outpcd: kpt on fnl f* **11/2**[3]
6645 **7** *1 ¼* **Calculaite**[6] [4827] 3-8-11 **46** FNorton 6 31
(MrsGSRees) *in tch: lost pl over 3f out: kpt on fnl f* **10/1**
4-54 **8** *shd* **Otylia**[178] [906] 4-9-1 **47** MHenry 5 31
(RMHCowell) *chsd ldrs: wknd over 1f out* **33/1**
446 **9** *¾* **Sylva Royal (IRE)**[12] [4653] 3-9-0 **52** J-PGuillambert[(3)] 15 34
(CEBrittain) *swvd lft s: bhd and hung bdly lft 2f out: nvr a factor* **14/1**
0-05 **10** *2 ½* **Noble Desert (FR)**[12] [4653] 3-9-0 **49** TPQueally 2 24
(RGuest) *chsd ldrs: rdn over 2f out: sn btn* **14/1**
0050 **11** *1 ¾* **Extinguisher**[54] [3409] 5-9-9 **55** MFenton 13 24
(TJFitzgerald) *sn bhd and drvn along* **25/1**
0506 **12** *5* **Game Flora**[21] [4391] 3-8-11 **49** THamilton[(3)] 8 3
(MESowersby) *sn bhd* **33/1**
5100 **13** *2* **Miss Wizz**[16] [4557] 4-8-6 **43** (p) RoryMoore[(5)] 12 —
(WStorey) *mid-div: lost pl over 2f out* **12/1**
-400 **14** *½* **Key Factor**[69] [2962] 3-9-6 **55** DaleGibson 14 2
(MWEasterby) *hmpd s: a bhd* **40/1**

1m 17.79s (0.89) **Going Correction** +0.20s/f (Slow)
**WFA** 3 from 4yo+ 3lb **14** Ran SP% **122.2**
Speed ratings: **102,101,100,99,94 92,91,91,90,86 84,77,75,74**CSF £14.82 CT £137.69 TOTE £5.40: £2.20, £1.30, £4.40; EX 14.70.
**Owner** Harold D White **Bred** O J Martinez **Trained** Stillington, N Yorks
■ Stewards Enquiry : T Eaves two-day ban: used whip with excessive force (Sep 3,5)

**FOCUS**
In effect a 0-61 handicap, a seller in all but name, but run at a strong pace in deteriorating conditions, and the form loks ordinary but sound.

**NOTEBOOK**
**Headland(USA)**, ideally suited by the strong pace, saw it out just the better.
**Jagged(IRE)**, attempting to make it two wins on his 24th start, attracted Dettori here on a very wet night. He seemed to do too much in front and in the end the winner saw out the extra furlong just the better.
**Lucius Verrus(USA)**, with a different headgear tried, ran easily his best race for some time.
**Bold Wolf**, a maiden after 13 previous starts, ran a lot better than of late.
**Ace-Ma-Vahra**, whose sole win was here over a mile, found this trip on the sharp side.
**Travelling Times**, who has not tasted success for over two years, looks worth a try over seven furlongs or even a mile.

## 5001 GENE KELLY MEDIAN AUCTION MAIDEN STKS 7f (F)
**7:10** (7:12) (F ) 3-Y-O **£2,919** (£834; £417) **Stalls** Low

Form RPR
2053 **1** **Oh Golly Gosh**[15] [4573] 3-9-0 66 (v) TPQueally 2 67
(NPLittmoden) *w ldrs: led over 4f out: qckned clr 3f out: c stands' side: rdn over 1f out: all out* **9/2**[3]
-400 **2** *¾* **Aliba (IRE)**[74] [2815] 3-9-0 60 DMcGaffin 4 65
(BSmart) *chsd ldrs: hrd rdn and styd on fnl f: jst hld* **25/1**
00 **3** *5* **Through The Slips (USA)**[24] [4303] 3-8-9 MFenton 5 47
(JGGiven) *outpcd and lost pl over 4f out: sn bhd: gd hdwy over 1f out: styd on ins last* **33/1**
**4** *3 ½* **Roman Love (IRE)** 3-8-9 OUrbina 6 38
(JRFanshawe) *s.i.s: hdwy over 2f out: nvr a threat* **11/4**[2]
5056 **5** *1* **Chertsey (IRE)**[12] [4650] 3-8-6 56 J-PGuillambert[(3)] 3 35
(CEBrittain) *chsd ldrs: styd on inner 3f out: edgd rt 2f out: wknd fnl f* **11/2**
002 **6** *nk* **Antigua Bay (IRE)**[12] [4653] 3-8-9 74 LisaJones 1 35
(JARToller) *chsd ldrs: lost pl 3f out: n.d after* **11/8**[1]
-036 **7** *6* **Saccharine**[7] [4801] 3-8-2 44 KGhunowa[(7)] 7 19
(MJPolglase) *led tl over 4f out: lost pl over 2f out* **40/1**
000 **8** *16* **Explicit (IRE)**[7] [4813] 3-9-0 CCatlin 8 —
(GCBravery) *sn outpcd: bhd after 2f: soo lost tch* **50/1**
00-0 **9** *13* **Skelthwaite**[41] [3817] 3-9-0 35 DarrenWilliams 9 —
(MissDAMchale) *swvd rt s: sn w ldrs: lost pl 4f out: sn bhd* **100/1**

1m 32.17s (1.37) **Going Correction** +0.20s/f (Slow) **9** Ran SP% **114.5**
Speed ratings: **100,99,93,89,88 87,81,62,47**CSF £100.78 TOTE £4.70: £1.70, £4.50, £6.90; EX 68.70.
**Owner** Mrs Gillian Curley **Bred** G Rollain **Trained** Newmarket, Suffolk

**FOCUS**
A poor maiden run at no great pace with the winner seizing the initiative and the favourite well below a decent recent turf effort.

**NOTEBOOK**
**Oh Golly Gosh** made it tenth time lucky under an enterprising ride. In the end there was not an ounce to spare.
**Aliba(IRE)**, back after a ten-week break, had 6lb to find with the winner on official ratings but, sticking to his task, was in the end only just held at bay.
**Through The Slips(USA)**, beaten out of sight in two previous starts on turf, stayed on after getting a long way behind. Now qualified for a handicap mark, she will presumably take a big step up in trip.
**Roman Love(IRE)**, a half-sister to the top-class Grandera, is nothing at all to look at but she did show a glimmer of ability on her debut and, if her trainer can find an opportunity for her, it will do wonders for her stud value.
**Chertsey(IRE)** made the fatal mistake of sticking to the inner, and the slower surface, coming off the home turn.
**Antigua Bay(IRE)**, fitted with a Monty Roberts rope halter, was drawn bang on the inside and looked to resent the kick-back.
**Skelthwaite** *Official explanation: jockey said gelding became tired and had no more to give*

## 5002 SEE YOU ON 7TH NOVEMBER H'CAP 1m (F)
**7:40** (7:41) (F ) (0-55,61) 3-Y-O+ **£3,052** (£872; £436) **Stalls** Low

Form RPR
0300 **1** **Dubonai (IRE)**[28] [4190] 4-9-2 **50** DCorby[(3)] 9 59
(AndrewTurnell) *chsd ldrs: led over 1f out: hld on towards fin* **33/1**
0000 **2** *½* **Gustavo**[53] [3448] 3-9-3 **54** (b[1]) DeanMcKeown 8 62
(BWHills) *chsd ldrs: ev ch 2f out: nt qckn wl ins last* **20/1**
3600 **3** *1 ½* **Pacific Ocean (ARG)**[12] [4641] 5-9-10 **55** (t) FNorton 2 60
(MrsStefLiddiard) *sn bhd: hdwy on wd outside 2f out: styd on ins last* **12/1**
1643 **4** *1 ¼* **Cryfield**[16] [4537] 7-9-10 **55** KimTinkler 4 58
(NTinkler) *s.i.s: hdwy over 4f out: sn chsng ldrs: kpt on same pce fnl 2f* **7/2**[1]
0002 **5** *1 ½* **Tatweer (IRE)**[6] [4825] 4-9-3 **48** (be[1]) DarrenWilliams 1 48
(DShaw) *hld up: hdwy over 4f out: sn chsng ldrs: nt qckn appr fnl f* **16/1**
5000 **6** *2* **Dubai Dreams**[38] [3921] 4-9-3 **53** (b) BSwarbrick[(5)] 5 49
(SRBowring) *mde most hdd over 1f out: fdd ins last* **18/1**
5233 **7** *1* **Miss Glory Be**[14] [4604] 6-9-4 **52** (p) SHitchcott[(3)] 14 46
(EROertel) *racd wd: chsd ldrs: chal 3f out: sn rdn: wknd fnl f* **8/1**
1405 **8** *1 ¾* **Sorbiesharry (IRE)**[100] [2128] 5-9-4 **49** (p) RFitzpatrick 15 39
(MrsNMacauley) *slwoly into stride: racd wd: bhd tl kpt on fnl 2f* **25/1**
3143 **9** *½* **Sudra**[56] [3380] 7-9-8 **53** (b) CCatlin 16 42
(DJDaly) *racd wd: sn outpcd and drvn along: kpt on fnl 2f: nvr a danger* **11/1**
-000 **10** *8* **Midmaar (IRE)**[14] [4604] 3-9-1 **52** MTebbutt 7 25
(MWigham) *mid-div: styd far side 3f out: sn wknd* **100/1**
0025 **11** *5* **Islands Farewell**[26] [4246] 4-9-6 **51** LDettori 11 14
(DNicholls) *racd wd: chsd ldrs: drvn along over 3f out: lost pl over 2f out* **9/2**[2]
3-40 **12** *2 ½* **Magari**[14] [4615] 3-9-2 **53** MFenton 13 11
(JGGiven) *swtchd lft after 1f: a bhd* **12/1**
5450 **13** *3* **Disabuse**[28] [4189] 4-9-7 **52** (b) DaleGibson 6 4
(MWEasterby) *s.i.s: a in rr* **6/1**[3]
2100 **14** *18* **Mitzi Caspar**[12] [4650] 3-9-1 **52** RPrice 12 —
(PLGilligan) *swtchd lft after 1f: sn bhd: t.o* **66/1**
004 **15** *2 ½* **Private Jessica**[32] [4069] 3-9-4 **55** OUrbina 10 —
(JRFanshawe) *w ldrs: lost pl over 3f out: sn bhd: t.o* **15/2**

1m 45.58s (0.98) **Going Correction** +0.20s/f (Slow)
**WFA** 3 from 4yo+ 6lb **15** Ran SP% **126.5**
Speed ratings: **103,102,101,99,98 96,95,93,93,85 80,77,74,56,54**CSF £589.33 CT £8288.12 TOTE £64.70: £17.90, £7.50, £3.80; EX 1414.00 Place 6 £3,201.09, Place 5 £192.34.
**Owner** Geoff Jewson **Bred** Paradime Ltd **Trained** Malton, N Yorks
■ Stewards Enquiry : Dean McKeown four-day ban: used whip with excessive frequency Sep (19-22)

**FOCUS**
A 0-55 handicap run at just a steady pace early on with water lying on the rain-sodden surface and the form does not look all that reliable.

**NOTEBOOK**
**Dubonai(IRE)**, having his second try on Fibresand, did just enough to open his account at the 16th attempt.
**Gustavo**, sporting first-time blinkers on his handicap bow, responded to strong pressure and in the end was just held at bay.
**Pacific Ocean(ARG)**, a maiden after 18 starts, was fitted with a tongue tie rather than cheekpieces. Soon struggling badly, he picked up in good style late on down the wide outside.
**Cryfield** does not pick up in a hurry and could have done with a much stronger early pace.
**Tatweer(IRE)**, in blinkers rather an a visor, finds it tough going outside selling or claiming company.
**Dubai Dreams**, happy to be back on this surface, ran his best race for his present trainer.
**Islands Farewell**, one of four to take the by-pass route in the back stretch, was flat out and getting nowhere turning in, and Dettori would surely have been happier at home watching Kelly Holmes take the gold medal at the Olympic Games. *Official explanation: jockey said gelding lost its action*
**Private Jessica** *Official explanation: jockey said filly lost her action*
T/Plt: £2,528.80 to a £1 stake. Pool: £31,351.05. 9.05 winning tickets. T/Qpdt: £151.30 to a £1 stake. Pool: £3,455.50. 16.90 winning tickets. WG

## 4809 WINDSOR (R-H)
Monday, August 23

**OFFICIAL GOING: Good to soft**
Although the ground was officially on the soft side of good, the stands' rail in the straight was the place to be.

## 5003 SHARP MINDS WINNERS WELCOME MAIDEN STKS — 5f 10y
5:25 (5:28) (D) 2-Y-0 — **£4,966** (£1,528; £764; £382) **Stalls** High

Form — RPR
**1** **Woodcote (IRE)** 2-9-0 ... PRobinson 11 — 82+
(CGCox) *racd stands side: trckd ldr: drvn to ld 1f out: r.o strly* **12/1**
**2** 1½ **Dixieanna** 2-8-9 ... MHills 12 — 72
(BWHills) *racd stands side and led overall: rdn and hdd 1f out: nt pce of wnr ins fnl f* **9/1**[3]
4 **3** 2½ **Park Approach (IRE)**[10] [4712] 2-8-9 ... EAhern 5 — 70+
(JNoseda) *racd far side and led that gp but nt pce of stands side: hdd far side 1f out: kpt on wl to retake ld that side last strides* **3/1**[2]
2243 **4** shd **Juantorena**[12] [4649] 2-9-0 92 ... RMullen 3 — 75+
(MLWBell) *racd far side: chsd ldr that side and led 1f out: nvr gng pce of stands side and lost ld far side gp last strides* **6/4**[1]
**5** ½ **Three Deuces (USA)** 2-8-9 ... JFortune 10 — 61
(BJMeehan) *racd stands side and s.i.s: sn rcvrd: chsd ldrs: rdn and kpt on same pce ins last* **14/1**
560 **6** 1½ **Limonia (GER)**[82] [2585] 2-8-9 ... DSweeney 9 — 56
(DKIvory) *racd stands side: chsd ldrs: hung lft to centre crse 2f out: styd on same pce* **50/1**
**7** 1¼ **Forest Delight (IRE)** 2-8-9 ... JFEgan 8 — 52
(CTinkler) *racd stands side: in tch: pushed along over 2f out: kpt on same pce fr over 1f out* **25/1**
**8** 5 **Attishoe** 2-8-9 ... SDrowne 2 — 48
(MissBSanders) *racd far side: nvr gng pce to rch ldrs* **16/1**
**9** 1½ **Cesar Manrique (IRE)** 2-9-0 ... SSanders 4 — 41
(BWHills) *racd far side: in tch: rdn over 2f out: sn wknd* **20/1**
63 **10** ¾ **Edge Of Blue**[12] [4643] 2-9-0 ... RHughes 14 — 31
(RHannon) *racd stands side: chsd ldrs 3f* **11/1**
**11** nk **Sir Bluebird (IRE)** 2-9-0 ... PDobbs 6 — 37
(RHannon) *racd far side: bmpd s: outpcd* **33/1**
**12** ½ **Tractor Boy** 2-9-0 ... DHolland 7 — 28
(WJHaggas) *wnt lft s: racd stands side: a bhd* **11/1**
606 **13** 1¾ **Jonny Fox'S (IRE)**[51] [3526] 2-9-0 ... DKinsella 13 — 22
(JGallagher) *racd stands sid: a bhd* **100/1**
**14** 5 **Aramat** 2-8-9 ... VWenkaya 1 — —
(JRBoyle) *racd far side: s.i.s: bhd: no ch whn hung rt to stands side fr 2f out* **66/1**

61.13 secs (-0.07) **Going Correction** -0.15s/f (Firm) — **14 Ran SP% 127.9**
Speed ratings: **94,91,87,87,86 84,82,74,71,70 70,69,66,58**CSF £116.94 TOTE £17.20: £3.80, £4.20, £1.90; EX 146.10.
**Owner** Dennis Shaw **Bred** Liscannor Stud Ltd **Trained** Lambourn, Berks

**FOCUS**
Hard to know exactly what to make of the from as the field split into two groups and those on the stands' side were at a significant advantage. As a result, the bare form must be treated with caution.

**NOTEBOOK**
**Woodcote(IRE)**, a 15,000gns half-brother to three juvenile winners, out of a winner in France, attracted some support on the betting exchanges and made a successful debut. This was a pleasing performance and, with normal improvement, he should be competitive in better company.
**Dixieanna**, the first foal of a mile three-year-old winner, was soon able to grab the favoured stands'-side rail and seemed to know her job. She has a maiden in her, but may not improve as much as some of these.
**Park Approach(IRE)**, a Cheveley Park entry who shaped well on her debut in a six-furlong Newbury maiden, narrowly got the better of the 92-rated Juantorena on the far side of the track, but had no chance with those on the stands' side.
**Juantorena** again failed to confirm the ability he showed to finish fourth in the Windsor Castle, only managing to come out second best of those who raced far side. However, this was his first run on easy ground, and he may be capable of better back on a faster surface.
**Three Deuces(USA)**, $110,000 half-sister to a smart sprinter in the USA, out of a triple juvenile winner, made a respectable debut on ground that may have been soft enough. She should improve enough to take a similar race.
**Limonia(GER)** *Official explanation: jockey said filly hung left*
**Jonny Fox'S(IRE)** *Official explanation: jockey said gelding hung left throughout*

## 5004 SHARP MINDS BETFAIR CLASSIFIED STKS — 1m 67y
5:55 (5:57) (D) 3-Y-0+ — **£5,525** (£1,700; £850; £425) **Stalls** High

Form — RPR
3605 **1** **Krugerrand (USA)**[23] [4319] 5-9-7 85 ... GCarter 13 — 94
(WJMusson) *hld up in rr: stl plenty to do over 2f out: rapid hdwy over 1f out: qcknd to ld last half f: pushed out: readily* **14/1**
1220 **2** ½ **Evaluator (IRE)**[27] [4220] 3-8-13 83 ... JFortune 11 — 91
(TGMills) *bhd: hdwy over 3f out: pressed wnr ins fnl 2f: slt ld 1f out: hdd last half f and outpcd but hld on wl for 2nd* **9/4**[1]
2120 **3** 1½ **Arkholme**[12] [4648] 3-8-10 80 ... (b) PDoe 14 — 85
(PWinkworth) *chsd ldr: chal 4f out tl slt ld over 3f out: rdn 2f out: hdd 1f out: outpcd ins last* **20/1**
-535 **4** shd **Leoballero**[39] [3884] 4-9-2 79 ... (t) DHolland 5 — 88+
(DJDaly) *s.i.s: hld up in rr: hmpd 3f out: stl plenty to do over 2f out: str run over 1f out: fin wl: nt rch ldrs* **20/1**
0014 **5** 1¼ **Giocoso (USA)**[11] [4672] 4-9-2 83 ... FPFerris[(3)] 2 — 85
(BPalling) *led: rdn and narrowly hdd 3f out: styd pressing ldrs tl wknd fnl f* **25/1**
4630 **6** 3 **Freak Occurence (IRE)**[79] [2676] 3-8-11 81 ... SDrowne 7 — 77
(MissECLavelle) *chsd ldrs: rdn over 2f out: wknd over 1f out* **6/1**[2]
3100 **7** shd **Little Venice (IRE)**[29] [4178] 4-9-3 84 ... RHughes 1 — 76
(CFWall) *t.k.h: mid-div: hdwy 3f out: pushed along and no imp on ldrs 2f out out: wknd appr fnl f* **16/1**
4200 **8** 1½ **Blue Trojan (IRE)**[11] [4690] 4-9-7 85 ... JFEgan 3 — 77
(SKirk) *bhd: rdn and hdwy on outside fr 3f out: pressed ldrs 2f out: wknd over 1f out* **10/1**
3316 **9** 1 **Best Before (IRE)**[29] [4164] 4-9-2 80 ... EAhern 12 — 70
(PDEvans) *hmpd bnd 5f out: a in rr* **8/1**[3]
0-00 **10** 1 **Border Edge**[191] [770] 6-9-4 85 ... (v) JFMcDonald[(3)] 8 — 73
(JJBridger) *awkward bnd 5f out: sn chsng ldrs: wknd 2f out* **50/1**
0141 **11** 2 **Supreme Salutation**[100] [2120] 8-8-12 83 ... MHoward[(7)] 9 — 67
(DKIvory) *hld up in tch: pressed ldrs and shkn up over 2f out and sn wknd* **16/1**
2000 **12** 2 **Serieux**[19] [4442] 5-9-6 84 ... (p) PRobinson 4 — 64
(MrsAJPerrett) *chsd ldrs tl wknd ins fnl 3f* **14/1**
3115 **13** 2 **Harry Potter (GER)**[23] [4349] 5-9-2 80 ... (v) DSweeney 10 — 56
(KRBurke) *bhd most of way* **10/1**
/32- **14** 1¼ **Lasanga**[378] [4053] 5-9-2 80 ... SSanders 6 — 53
(LadyHerries) *bhd: sme hdwy 4f out: sn wknd* **14/1**

1m 45.29s (-0.31) **Going Correction** +0.10s/f (Good)
**WFA** 3 from 4yo+ 6lb — **14 Ran SP% 121.4**
Speed ratings: **105,104,103,102,101 98,98,97,96,95 93,91,89,87**CSF £43.83 TOTE £15.40: £4.00, £1.50, £6.70; EX 55.70.
**Owner** The Square Table II **Bred** T Farmer **Trained** Newmarket, Suffolk

**FOCUS**
A decent classified event with just 4lb between these on the figures and obviously a very competitive heat and the form looks sound. The entire field stayed stands' side in the straight.

**NOTEBOOK**
**Krugerrand(USA)** had gained all of his previous wins on good to firm ground, but had shown the ability to handle an easy surface and coped with these conditions. Given a well-judged ride by Gary Carter, he picked nicely and always looked like getting on top, but he has never previously followed up and a rise in the weights could be enough to stop him next time.
**Evaluator(IRE)**, who ran respectably from an unfavourably low draw at Goodwood on his previous start, continued his good run of form with another solid effort, but was simply beaten by a better horse.
**Arkholme**, with the blinkers re-fitted, looked keen to get to the front in the early stages but was unable to do so and ran well in the circumstances.
**Leoballero**, proving a little frustrating in recent runs, came from a very unpromising position to take fourth and would have gone close with better luck in running. *Official explanation: jockey said gelding had missed the break*
**Giocoso(USA)** had to work quite hard to lead and could offer little close home.
**Freak Occurence(IRE)**, below form when upped to ten furlongs at Epsom on his previous start, was again below his best dropped back in trip.
**Best Before(IRE)** can be rated a little better than the bare form, as he got hampered turning in.

## 5005 SHARP MINDS BETFAIR: BEST ODDS NURSERY — 5f 10y
6:25 (6:25) (E) 2-Y-0 — **£3,552** (£1,093; £546; £273) **Stalls** High

Form — RPR
1144 **1** **Key Secret**[9] [4752] 2-9-1 80 ... HayleyTurner[(5)] 5 — 88+
(MLWBell) *trckd ldr tl led wl over 1f out: drvn and styd on wl fnl f* **4/1**[2]
3211 **2** 5 **Countdown**[3] [4918] 2-9-13 87 6ex ... SSanders 4 — 82+
(SirMarkPrescott) *sn pushed along to chse ldrs: styd on to chse wnr and edgd lft fnl f: a hld* **4/7**[1]
6644 **3** ½ **Pennestamp (IRE)**[19] [4439] 2-8-6 66 ... RHavlin 2 — 55
(MrsPNDutfield) *pressed ldrs: rdn 2f out: readily outpcd ins fnl f* **12/1**
0406 **4** shd **Waterline Lover**[18] [4475] 2-7-9 58 oh2 ... JFMcDonald[(3)] 3 — 46
(PDEvans) *rdn along in rr: styd on fnl f: pressing for 3rd whn rn out of room last strides* **20/1**
0052 **5** nk **Cree**[10] [4704] 2-7-13 59 ... (b) DKinsella 7 — 46
(WRMuir) *sn led: rdn: hung lft and hdd wl over 1f out: styd on one pce* **11/1**[3]
653 **6** 9 **Robmantra**[45] [3696] 2-8-10 73 ... FPFerris[(3)] 1 — 29
(BJLlewellyn) *sn rdn: a in rr* **16/1**

60.95 secs (-0.25) **Going Correction** -0.15s/f (Firm) — **6 Ran SP% 110.3**
Speed ratings: **96,88,87,87,86 72**CSF £6.44 TOTE £5.70: £2.10, £1.20; EX 10.50.
**Owner** Joy And Valentine Feerick **Bred** Barry Minty **Trained** Newmarket, Suffolk

**FOCUS**
A small field and no doubt several trainers were scared off by the presence of Countdown, but that one was below his best and as a result, the form is probably not worth a great deal. They all stayed stands' side.

**NOTEBOOK**
**Key Secret**, dropped two classes, took advantage of the favourite running below par to gain her fourth win from six starts. Although the form may not amount to much, she is likely to take a significant rise in the weights and would therefore be of interest if turned out under a penalty.
**Countdown**, racing under a 6lb penalty for his success in arguably better company at Sandown just three days previously, was always having to be niggled along by Sanders and never really looked like getting to the eventual winner. Prior to this he had been progressing well, and can be given another chance.
**Pennestamp(IRE)**, dropped back a furlong in trip and racing on easy ground for the first time, did not do enough to suggest he will be winning in similar company next time.
**Waterline Lover**, back to five furlongs, was unable go the pace and would have stayed on for third with a clearer run. A step back up in trip should suit.
**Cree** could offer little close home and maybe faster ground will suit.

## 5006 SHARP MINDS BETFAIR: BACK AND LAY PREMIER CLAIMING STKS — 1m 2f 7y
6:55 (6:56) (D) 3-Y-0+ — **£5,655** (£1,740; £870; £435) **Stalls** Low

Form — RPR
1626 **1** **Barking Mad (USA)**[9] [4754] 6-9-9 84 ... KFallon 3 — 89
(MLWBell) *mde all: shkn up 2f out: clr over 1f out: eased cl home* **9/2**[2]
512- **2** 1½ **Whaleef**[25] [3340] 6-9-3 82 ... (tp) FPFerris[(3)] 1 — 83
(BJLlewellyn) *disp 2nd tl chsd wnr fr 4f out: rdn and styd on wl fr over 2f out but a readily hld* **20/1**
5456 **3** 1½ **Ben Hur**[11] [4691] 5-9-5 74 ... EAhern 7 — 80
(WMBrisbourne) *chsd ldrs: rdn over 3f out: styd on one pce u.p fnl 2f* **8/1**
0250 **4** 3 **Sahaat**[5] [4852] 6-9-2 69 ... DHolland 10 — 71
(MJPolglase) *mid-div: rdn and styd on fr 3f out: chsd ldrs over 2f out but no imp and wknd ins last* **10/1**
0050 **5** 6 **Mamore Gap (IRE)**[12] [4641] 6-9-3 67 ... RHughes 5 — 61
(RHannon) *bhd: pushed along 3f out: sme hdwy fr over 2f out but nvr in contention* **20/1**

1010 **6** *2 ½* **Scotty's Future (IRE)**[153] 1088 6-9-8 72 .................. SSanders 6 62
(DNicholls) *hld up in rr: hdwy over 3f out: effrt over 2f out but nvr gng pce to rch ldrs: sn wknd* **11/2**[3]

0204 **7** *7* **Epaminondas (USA)**[31] 4079 3-8-12 65 .................. JFortune 4 47
(RHannon) *chsd ldrs: rdn 4f out: styd in tch tl wknd qckly ins fnl 2f* **20/1**

0 **8** *22* **Miss De Bois**[20] 4423 7-8-4 .................. HayleyTurner(5) 8 —
(WMBrisbourne) *in tch to 1/2-way: sn wknd* **66/1**

2352 **9** *nk* **Eton (GER)**[20] 4423 8-9-8 69 .................. ANicholls 11 9
(DNicholls) *chsd wnr 6f: sn rdn: wknd 3f out* **9/1**

15-2 **10** *20* **Morahib**[19] 4458 6-9-10 80 .................. GCarter 2 —
(WJMusson) *sn bhd: no ch fnl 5f* **10/1**

52R4 **R** **Kentucky King (USA)**[5] 4852 4-9-5 83 .................. RMiles(3) 9 —
(PWHiatt) *ref to r* **5/2**[1]

2m 10.42s (2.12) **Going Correction** +0.375s/f (Good)
**WFA** 3 from 4yo+ 8lb **11** Ran SP% **117.2**
Speed ratings: **106,104,103,101,96 94,88,71,70,54** —CSF £94.93 TOTE £3.60: £1.80, £6.50, £2.40; EX 190.50.
**Owner** Christopher Wright **Bred** Andrade Farm **Trained** Newmarket, Suffolk

**FOCUS**
This looked like a reasonably competitive claimer, but the well-backed favourite Kentucky King refused to race and, with Barking Mad able to dictate things from the front, very few got into this, which does not inspire confidence in the form. The field again stayed stands' side in the straight.

**NOTEBOOK**
**Barking Mad(USA)** is not always the easiest to predict (not many got it right this time as he was very easy to back) but, very much allowed his own way in front on this drop in class, he ran out a very comfortable winner.
**Whaleef**, returned to Flat for the first time in 403 days (he has been running over hurdles and fences) on his debut for a new trainer, had a tongue-tie and cheekpieces on for the first time. He was best off at the weights but was readily held by the winner.
**Ben Hur**, dropped back into a more suitable grade, may have done better had he been ridden more positively and put more pressure on the eventual winner.
**Sahaat**, quite well supported on this drop in grade, could never really get on terms.
**Mamore Gap(IRE)** may have preferred a stronger pace.
**Scotty's Future(IRE)**, who won a couple of sellers for David Loder earlier in the year, would have preferred a stronger pace on this first run back with his former trainer, but is quite simply not as good as he once was.
**Eton(GER)** ran a shocker in a grade he usually goes well in and is better than this.
**Kentucky King(USA)** was quite well backed but gave his supporters absolutely no chance of collecting. He has done this in the past and is not one to trust.

## 5007 SHARP MINDS BETFAIR MAIDEN STKS 1m 2f 7y
**7:25** (7:27) (D) 3-Y-0 **£3,523** (£1,084; £542; £271) **Stalls** Low

Form RPR

3 **1** **Day Of Reckoning**[35] 3994 3-8-9 .................. KFallon 4 77+
(SirMichaelStoute) *trckd ldrs: pushed along to chse ldr over 2f out: led ins last: reminder and flashed tail: sn clr: easily* **11/8**[1]

4 **2** *2* **Pleasant**[21] 4402 3-8-9 .................. IMongan 1 74
(LGCottrell) *sn trcking ldr: led jst ins fnl 3f: pushed along over 2f out: hdd ins fnl f: kpt on but no ch w wnr* **25/1**

243 **3** *1 ½* **Line Drawing**[64] 3129 3-9-0 74 .................. RHughes 9 76
(BWHills) *trckd ldrs: shkn up 2f out: kpt on fnl f but nt pce of ldrs* **7/1**[3]

2 **4** *4* **Newnham (IRE)**[14] 4615 3-9-0 .................. DHolland 2 69
(LMCumani) *prom: n.m.r and outpcd over 2f out tl drvn and kpt on fr over 1f out: nt pce to rch ldrs* **11/4**[2]

**5** *hd* **Neath** 3-8-9 .................. SDrowne 6 63
(MrsAJPerrett) *mid-div: n.m.r and outpcd over 2f out: kpt on again fnl f but nvr a danger* **14/1**

00- **6** *shd* **Dream Valley (IRE)**[289] 5948 3-8-9 .................. MHills 8 63
(BWHills) *bhd: hdwy 4f out: drvn to chse ldrs over 2f out: wknd over 1f out* **16/1**

00 **7** *2 ½* **Count Boris**[7] 4813 3-9-0 .................. SCarson 10 64
(GBBalding) *bhd: rdn over 3f out and mod hdwy over 2f out: nvr gng pce to trble ldrs* **50/1**

0-0 **8** *3 ½* **Diequest (USA)**[7] 4813 3-9-0 .................. JFEgan 5 57
(JamiePoulton) *bhd: rdn and effrt 4f out: chsd ldrs 3f out: wknd 2f out* **66/1**

03 **9** *nk* **Royal Lustre**[19] 4455 3-9-0 .................. JFortune 7 57
(JHMGosden) *sn led: hdd ins fnl 3f: wknd over 1f out* **12/1**

**10** *24* **Winslow Homer (FR)** 3-9-0 .................. RHavlin 11 14
(JHMGosden) *slowly away: a in rr* **33/1**

005 **11** *5* **Charmed By Fire (USA)**[11] 4693 3-9-0 68 .................. (t) SSanders 3 5
(MrsAJPerrett) *s.i.s: a in rr* **14/1**

2m 11.91s (3.61) **Going Correction** +0.375s/f (Good) **11** Ran SP% **118.4**
Speed ratings: **100,98,97,94,93 93,91,88,88,69 65**CSF £47.35 TOTE £2.40: £1.40, £6.50, £1.70; EX 58.90.
**Owner** The Queen **Bred** The Queen **Trained** Newmarket, Suffolk

**FOCUS**
A pretty ordinary maiden and the form is nothing special, although quite a few of these should improve. They all stayed stands' side in the straight.

**NOTEBOOK**
**Day Of Reckoning**, a pleasing third in a fast-ground course and distance maiden on her debut, handled conditions well enough and showed improved form to get off the mark. This was a good boost for her paddock value and that is where her long-term future lies.
**Pleasant**, a respectable fourth in a fast-ground course and distance maiden on her debut, improved on that form switched to an easier surface. She has got the ability to win a similar race, but her long-term future lies in the hands of the assessor.
**Line Drawing** travelled strongly, but was pretty one paced in the closing stages and keeps finding one or two too good.
**Newnham(IRE)**, runner-up on his debut here over a mile, ran better than his finishing position suggests, as he did not get a clear run and was not knocked about when chance had gone.
**Neath**, a sister to the very useful juvenile miler Rainwashed Gold, out of a smart eight to ten-furlong performer in France, did not get the best of luck in running and stayed on all too late.
**Diequest(USA)** *Official explanation: jockey said colt lost its action*

## 5008 SHARP MINDS PHONE 0870 90 80 121 H'CAP 6f
**7:55** (7:57) (E ) (0-75,75) 3-Y-0+ **£4,901** (£1,508; £754; £377) **Stalls** High

Form RPR

6063 **1** **Nivernais**[11] 4687 5-9-9 **70** .................. DaneO'Neill 16 81
(HCandy) *chsd ldrs: sn pushed along: styd on strly fnl f: qcknd to ld nr fin: readily* **7/1**[3]

1413 **2** *½* **Tancred Times**[19] 4459 9-8-9 **61** .................. HayleyTurner(5) 20 71
(CFWall) *led: tl narrowly hdd 3f out: led again wl over 2f out and hung lft u.p: kpt on wl tl ct nr fin* **7/1**[3]

0400 **3** *1 ½* **Charlottebutterfly**[40] 3841 4-8-3 **53** .................. JFMcDonald(3) 15 58
(TTClement) *mid-div: rdn and hdwy over 1f out: styd on wl fnl f: but nt rch ldrs* **25/1**

3040 **4** *½* **Val De Maal (IRE)**[76] 2750 4-9-8 **69** .................. SSanders 12 73
(GCHChung) *chsd ldrs: rdn over 2f out: nt qckn ins fnl f* **20/1**

14 **5** *1 ¼* **Polar Impact**[33] 4034 5-10-0 **75** .................. RLMoore 18 75
(GLMoore) *bhd: stl plenty to do 2f out: rdn and hdwy over 1f out: kpt on ins last but nvr gng pce to rch ldrs* **3/1**[1]

0635 **6** *hd* **Moritat (IRE)**[16] 4548 4-8-3 **53** .................. (t) FPFerris(3) 13 52
(PDEvans) *w ldr tl slt ld 3f out: hdd wl over 2f out: styd front rnk tl wknd ins fnl f* **16/1**

6120 **7** *½* **Double M**[9] 4748 7-9-0 **66** .................. (v) RThomas(5) 5 64
(MrsLRichards) *in tch: rdn: swtchd lft and effrt over 1f out: nvr gng pce of ldrs* **10/1**

-600 **8** *¾* **Emerald Fire**[44] 3747 5-8-13 **63** .................. LPKeniry(3) 19 58
(AMBalding) *bhd: hdwy over 1f out: r.o ins last but nvr a danger* **14/1**

0035 **9** *1* **Smirfys Party**[8] 4782 6-8-2 **49** .................. (v) PDoe 6 41
(DNicholls) *sn pressing ldrs: chal 1/2-way: styd front rnk tl wknd fnl f* **10/1**

006 **10** *hd* **Highland Lass**[10] 4718 3-8-8 **58** .................. EAhern 8 50
(MrsHSweeting) *bmpd s: bhd: swtchd lft to outside and sme hdwy ins fnl 2f: n.d* **33/1**

4-05 **11** *shd* **Flaran**[7] 4800 4-8-12 **59** .................. RHughes 17 51
(EFVaughan) *chsd ldrs on stands side: outpcd and btn whn hmpd over 1f out* **25/1**

2420 **12** *shd* **Treetops Hotel (IRE)**[9] 4736 5-8-6 **58** .................. (tp) NChalmers(5) 3 49
(BRJohnson) *bhd: swtchd lft to outside over 2f out: nvr gng pce of ldrs* **16/1**

00 **13** *2 ½* **Free Wheelin (IRE)**[3] 4923 4-9-2 **63** .................. JFortune 14 47
(WJarvis) *hld up in rr: sme hdwy but nt a danger whn nt clr run and wknd over 1f out* **14/1**

3500 **14** *2* **Sir Don (IRE)**[24] 4291 5-9-2 **63** .................. (v) ANicholls 2 41
(DNicholls) *nvr bttr than mid-div* **20/1**

1005 **15** *shd* **Antonio Canova**[12] 4652 8-9-13 **74** .................. (v[1]) JFEgan 4 51
(BobJones) *bhd: mod hdwy whn nt clr run and wknd over 1f out* **10/1**

0-1 **16** *5* **Dave (IRE)**[32] 4052 3-8-13 **63** .................. KFallon 9 25
(JRBest) *pressed ldrs: stl ev ch fr 2f out: wknd appr fnl f* **9/2**[2]

4201 **17** *nk* **Sewmuch Character**[10] 4707 5-9-8 **69** .................. DSweeney 10 31
(MBlanshard) *chsd ldrs: wkng whn bmpd over 1f out* **14/1**

1m 13.67s (-0.20) **Going Correction** +0.05s/f (Good)
**WFA** 3 from 4yo+ 3lb **17** Ran SP% **147.4**
Speed ratings: **103,102,100,99,98 97,97,96,94,94 94,94,90,88,88 81,81**CSF £62.99 CT £848.47 TOTE £9.10: £2.20, £2.00, £7.10, £5.00; EX 52.30 Place 6 £137.17, Place 5 £49.90.
**Owner** M J M Tricks **Bred** Mrs V M Tricks **Trained** Wantage, Oxon

**FOCUS**
A competitive enough sprint, although it appeared a big advantage to be drawn high, with the first six home all coming from a double-figure stall. The form is ordinary, but solid for the grade. Again, they all stayed stands' side.

**NOTEBOOK**
**Nivernais** had never previously won on ground softer than good but he does appreciate a bit of give, and the strong pace also suited. He had been proving quite frustrating this season but this was a nice confidence boost.
**Tancred Times**, racing from the highest stall of all, was just denied and continues in cracking form.
**Charlottebutterfly**, still a maiden, showed signs of a return to form and has a rating that allows her to run in a lower grade.
**Val De Maal(IRE)** ran respectably on ground possibly a touch easier than he would have liked.
**Polar Impact** would have appreciated the ground and had a good draw, but he got behind and just lacked the pace to get to the principals.
**Flaran** *Official explanation: jockey said gelding suffered interference in running*
**Dave(IRE)**, 8lb higher than when winning at Folkestone on his previous start, was a big disappointment on this first run on a soft surface. *Official explanation: jockey said gelding had a breathing problem*
T/Plt: £105.20 to a £1 stake. Pool: £50,519.80. 350.25 winning tickets. T/Qpdt: £16.40 to a £1 stake. Pool: £4,320.10. 194.80 winning tickets. ST

5012 - 5014a (Foreign Racing) - See Raceform Interactive

# 4797 BRIGHTON (L-H)
Tuesday, August 24

**OFFICIAL GOING: Race 1 - good (good to soft in places); races 2 to 5 - good to soft; remainder - soft**
Wind: Strong across Weather: Heavy showers

## 5015 EUROPEAN BREEDERS FUND MAIDEN STKS 5f 213y
**2:00** (2:00) (D ) 2-Y-0 **£4,774** (£1,469; £734; £367) **Stalls** Low

Form RPR

2322 **1** **Yajbill (IRE)**[10] 4739 2-9-0 81 .................. (v[1]) TEDurcan 2 85
(MRChannon) *mde all: rdn 2f out: hld on nr fin* **5/1**

**2** *nk* **Oligarch (IRE)** 2-9-0 .................. RMullen 10 84
(NACallaghan) *towards rr: rdn and hdwy 2f out: r.o fnl f: jst hld* **4/1**[2]

**3** *2 ½* **The Pheasant Flyer** 2-8-11 .................. JFMcDonald(3) 6 76
(BJMeehan) *prom: rdn and edgd lft over 1f out: one pce* **14/1**

5 **4** *hd* **Cordage (IRE)**[10] 4739 2-9-0 .................. EAhern 1 76
(GAButler) *rdn and lost tch over 4f out: styd on strly fr over 1f out* **10/1**

32 **5** *1 ¾* **Peeptoe (IRE)**[45] 3741 2-8-9 .................. RLMoore 8 66
(JLDunlop) *in tch: pushed along after 2f: rdn to chse ldrs 2f out: no ex fnl f* **11/4**[1]

63 **6** *3* **Fasylitator (IRE)**[8] 4809 2-9-0 .................. DaneO'Neill 4 61
(JAOsborne) *prom tl wknd over 1f out* **9/2**[3]

2632 **7** *1 ¼* **Come Good**[12] 4671 2-9-0 73 .................. RHughes 9 58
(RHannon) *prom over 4f* **8/1**

0 **8** *7* **Kirkhammerton (IRE)**[15] 4611 2-9-0 .................. VSlattery 5 36
(JAOsborne) *dwlt: rdn along: sn wl bhd* **66/1**

206 **9** *3 ½* **Dreamer's Lass**[44] 3770 2-8-9 60 .................. SDrowne 7 21
(JMBradley) *bhd fnl 4f* **50/1**

00 **10** *20* **Angela's Girl**[64] 3140 2-8-9 .................. CCatlin 3 —
(JMBradley) *dwlt: sn t.o* **100/1**

1m 12.57s (2.47) **Going Correction** +0.425s/f (Yiel) **10** Ran SP% **112.8**
Speed ratings: **100,99,96,96,93 89,88,78,74,47**CSF £24.36 TOTE £5.00: £1.70, £3.40, £1.80; EX 42.10.
**Owner** Sheikh Ahmed Al Maktoum **Bred** N Poole And A Franklin **Trained** West Ilsley, Berks

**FOCUS**
This was a reasonable maiden for the track, with a couple of reliable looking yardsticks with previous experience and two fairly interesting newcomers giving the form a solid appearance.

**NOTEBOOK**
**Yajbill(IRE)**, who had hit the frame in each of his four previous maiden outings, gained a deserved success and the visor clearly had the desired effect. However, he already has a rating of 81, does not look the easiest of rides, and will likely have to improve to justify that mark in a nursery.

**Oligarch(IRE)**, a half-brother to his stable's 2003 Solario Stakes winner Barbajuan, made a pleasing debut and was really motoring at the finish, but just failed. He was outpaced at halfway, then ran green under pressure, but picked up well and would probably have scored with a little further to go. He looks to have a future.

**The Pheasant Flyer** clearly knew his job ahead of this debut, and ran well for a long way until finding lack of a previous run against him when it mattered. This was a decent debut effort and, like many of his yard's debutants, should come on for the experience.

**Cordage(IRE)**, beaten around three lengths by the winner last time on his debut, got badly outpaced early on, but really picked up nicely in the final two furlongs, and only just missed out on third place. Bred to do better over further in time, he will be one to look out for when eligible for nurseries.

**Peeptoe(IRE)**, who had shown definite ability on her previous two starts, was slightly disappointing. She had every chance, but found little under pressure and was well held. Although having it all to prove now, she may improve when reverting to faster ground, and now has the option of nurseries.

**Fasylitator(IRE)** again showed good early pace but, racing wide of the pack in the straight, found nil when off the bridle and ran well below the form of his previous start at Windsor. His entry in the Middle Park is clearly tilting at windmills.

## 5016 MANMATTERS.CO.UK H'CAP — 5f 59y

**2:30** (2:30) (E ) (0-75,69) 3-Y-O+ — **£3,386** (£1,042; £521; £260) **Stalls** Low

Form — RPR

1004 **1** — **Molotov**[30] [4181] 4-7-7 **45** ........ NataliaGemelova(7) 12 — 57
(IWMcinnes) *mde all: clr over 1f out: drvn out* — **14/1**

1050 **2** 1 1/2 **Gone'N'Dunnett (IRE)**[8] [4800] 5-9-0 **59** ........(v) DaneO'Neill 8 — 66
(MrsCADunnett) *prom: rdn to chse wnr 1f out: nt qckn* — **10/1**

3042 **3** 1/2 **Redwood Star**[8] [4800] 4-8-4 **54** ........(e) DFox(5) 10 — 59
(PLGilligan) *in tch: outpcd 1/2-way: rallied over 1f out: styd on same pce* — **12/1**

0002 **4** nk **Online Investor**[7] [4828] 5-9-3 **62** ........ TEDurcan 6 — 66+
(DNicholls) *s.s: sn in midfield: effrt and nt clr run 2f out: styd on* — **5/1**[2]

0041 **5** nk **One Way Ticket**[8] [4800] 4-9-10 **69** ........(p) RLMoore 9 — 72
(JMBradley) *chsd wnr tl 1f out: one pce* — **7/2**[1]

0000 **6** 5 **Multahab**[4] [4923] 5-7-9 **45** ........(t) BSwarbrick(5) 1 — 30
(PSMcentee) *mid-div: effrt over 2f out: nt pce to chal* — **25/1**

0554 **7** shd **Pulse**[4] [4923] 6-8-13 **58** ........(p) PFitzsimons 2 — 43
(JMBradley) *mid-div: outpcd 1/2-way: n.d after* — **7/1**

2043 **8** hd **Yorkie**[8] [4800] 5-8-11 **56** ........ DeanMcKeown 11 — 40
(PABlockley) *prom over 3f* — **13/2**

6603 **9** 2 1/2 **Emaradia**[5] [4879] 3-7-7 **47** ........ CHaddon(7) 3 — 22
(AWCarroll) *rdn along: chsd ldrs 3f* — **20/1**

0600 **10** 6 **Banjo Bay (IRE)**[16] [4577] 6-9-9 **68** ........ ANicholls 5 — 21
(DNicholls) *rrd and s.s: bhd: mod effrt and hrd rdn 2f out: nvr trbld ldrs* — **6/1**[3]

0500 **11** 5 **Landing Strip (IRE)**[25] [4291] 4-9-4 **66** ........ LFletcher(3) 4 — 1
(JMPEustace) *sn outpcd* — **25/1**

0000 **12** 17 **Sweet Talking Girl**[11] [4708] 4-7-9 **43** oh18........(tp) FPFerris(3) 7 — —
(JMBradley) *awkward leaving stalls and s.s: sn wl bhd* — **100/1**

64.54 secs (2.27) **Going Correction** +0.60s/f (Yiel)
**WFA** 3 from 4yo+ 2lb — **12** Ran SP% **115.9**
Speed ratings: **105,102,101,101,100 92,92,92,88,78 70,43**CSF £137.58 CT £1732.78 TOTE £16.80: £5.10, £3.60, £4.30; EX 240.00.
**Owner** Ivy House Racing **Bred** Guy Reed And Mrs A H Daniels **Trained** Catwick, E Yorks

**FOCUS**

A typical sprint for the track, which saw those racing on the pace at a distinct advantage, and again the field made a bee-line for the near side on entering the straight. As a result the form is slightly dubious.

**NOTEBOOK**

**Molotov** won the early battle for the lead and, once bagging the rail in the straight, never saw another rival en-route to a ready success. He has been called some names in the past due to his headstrong nature, but had hinted at a definite return to form last time and is clearly in great heart at present, although a touch flattered by this.

**Gone'N'Dunnett(IRE)** again ran a sound race over a course and distance he has a distinct liking for but, try as he might, never looked like pegging back the winner. He should continue to pay his way at this level, but remains vulnerable to an improver.

**Redwood Star** deserves credit, as she did best of those to race from off the gallop and was finishing best of all. The ground was not ideal and she could well be about to strike again, when reverting to faster underfoot conditions.

**Online Investor** was yet again slow to break, but still recovered to have every chance, and was unable to make a serious impression. He definitely has a similar race within his compass, but is not one to place any real faith in.

**One Way Ticket**, who made all to win the recent controversial voided race at this track, was unable to dominate this time and did not look all that suited to the easy surface.

**Banjo Bay(IRE)** lost ground at the start and was never able to land a blow in the straight from off the pace. He is capable of better and has plummeted in the weights since joining his current connections this term, but is fast running out of excuses.

## 5017 TOTESPORT.COM H'CAP — 7f 214y

**3:00** (3:00) (D ) (0-80,78) 3-Y-O+ — **£5,525** (£1,700; £850; £425) **Stalls** Low

Form — RPR

4403 **1** — **Lucefer (IRE)**[8] [4802] 6-7-9 **50** oh6........ JFMcDonald(3) 7 — 57
(GCHChung) *hld up towards rr: rdn and hdwy over 1f out: led ins fnl f: spooked and swvd lft: jst hld on* — **13/2**

4002 **2** hd **Flint River**[20] [4435] 6-9-4 **73** ........ LFletcher(3) 11 — 80
(HMorrison) *trckd ldrs: led on bit over 2f out tl over 1f out: hrd rdn and ev ch fnl f: r.o* — **11/2**[2]

2046 **3** 3/4 **Johannian**[12] [4672] 6-9-3 **69** ........ RLMoore 9 — 74
(JMBradley) *hld up in tch: smooth hdwy to ld over 1f out: hdd ins fnl f: kpt on* — **7/1**

5600 **4** 1 **Star Sensation (IRE)**[33] [4067] 4-9-12 **78** ........ IMongan 2 — 81
(PWHarris) *dwlt: bhd: rdn and hdwy over 1f out: nrst fin* — **20/1**

4001 **5** 1/2 **Juste Pour L'Amour**[8] [4802] 4-8-10 **67** ........ DFox(5) 4 — 69
(PLGilligan) *towards rr: rdn and hdwy over 2f out: no ex fnl f* — **9/2**[1]

0555 **6** 4 **Tiber Tiger (IRE)**[16] [4577] 4-9-9 **75** ........ TEDurcan 12 — 68
(NPLittmoden) *dwlt: sn in midfield: rdn 4f out: no headway final 2f* — **6/1**[3]

3520 **7** 5 **Londoner (USA)**[20] [4435] 6-8-8 **60** ........ PDoe 8 — 43
(SDow) *w ldr 5f: hrd rdn and wknd 2f out* — **12/1**

0121 **8** 1 1/2 **Didoe**[9] [4771] 5-8-1 **53** 6ex........ JoannaBadger 10 — 33
(PWHiatt) *led: pushed along 4f out: hdd over 2f out: sn wknd* — **12/1**

-100 **9** 3 1/2 **Gallery Breeze**[17] [4549] 5-9-3 **69** ........ VSlattery 3 — 41
(JLSpearing) *in tch: rdn and n.m.r over 2f out: swtchd lft: sn wknd* — **25/1**

4044 **10** 1 1/4 **Alafzar (IRE)**[17] [4549] 6-8-2 **57** ........(bt) FPFerris(3) 5 — 27
(PDEvans) *plld hrd: w ldrs over 5f: wknd qckly* — **12/1**

0201 **11** 1 1/2 **El Chaparral (IRE)**[8] [4814] 4-9-8 **74** 6ex........ DaneO'Neill 1 — 41
(DKIvory) *dwlt: bhd: mod effrt over 2f out: n.d* — **11/1**

1m 39.32s (4.32) **Going Correction** +0.60s/f (Yiel)
**WFA** 3 from 4yo+ 6lb — **11** Ran SP% **113.7**
Speed ratings: **102,101,101,100,99 95,90,89,85,84 82**CSF £40.65 CT £257.08 TOTE £8.50: £2.00, £2.50, £2.40; EX 43.50.
**Owner** Ian Pattle **Bred** Michael O'Leary **Trained** Newmarket, Suffolk

**FOCUS**

A modest if fairly competitive handicap, which again saw those racing close to the nearside rail at a distinct advantage. It was run at just a modest gallop and the first five finished clear, and the form adds up if not that strong.

**NOTEBOOK**

**Lucefer(IRE)** , who was very well-backed throughout the day, and duly landed the odds. Hitting the front entering the final furlong looking all over the winner, he then proceeded to hang markedly both to his left and right, which very nearly cost him victory. Although in good heart, he will take a hike in the weights now and could struggle as a result.

**Flint River**, a decent second over course and distance latest, held every chance, but could find no more when challenged by the winner. He did hang towards the centre of the track late on, but it made little difference to the result. A similar race could come his way off this sort of mark.

**Johannian** ran a solid race on ground softer than ideal and deserves to find a race of this nature. He tends to have trouble finishing his races these days, but is genuine

**Star Sensation(IRE)** ◆ made good headway from the back of the pack from two out, but never seriously threatened the principals. He has slipped to a fair mark recently on account of his poor form, but could be about to capitalise and would be suited by a return to faster ground.

**Juste Pour L'Amour** , unpenalised for finally getting back to winning ways over course and distance last time, had to come down the centre of the track to challenge and can be rated slightly better than the bare form. He too would have been unsuited by the recent ease in the going and is not one to write off.

**Tiber Tiger(IRE)** was hard at it from some way out on this ground and ran well below par.

## 5018 IAN CARNABY (S) STKS — 1m 1f 209y

**3:30** (3:31) (G ) 3-Y-O — **£2,511** (£717; £358) **Stalls** High

Form — RPR

0050 **1** — **Ivory Coast (IRE)**[13] [4654] 3-8-13 57........(b[1]) SDrowne 3 — 58
(WRMuir) *chsd ldr after 3f: led over 3f out: drvn clr ins fnl f* — **3/1**[2]

0030 **2** 5 **Tshukudu**[3] [4941] 3-8-7 36........ DKinsella 5 — 43
(MBlanshard) *cl up: chsd wnr 3f out: no ex fnl f* — **7/1**

5045 **3** 3 **Miss Procurer (IRE)**[19] [4491] 3-8-7 57........ RLMoore 4 — 38
(PFICole) *hdwy 3f out: hrd rdn and hung lft 2f out: wknd over 1f out* **6/4**[1]

0040 **4** 12 **Big Bad Burt**[4] [4911] 3-8-5 59........ DeanWilliams(7) 6 — 23
(GCHChung) *s.s: bhd and nvr gng wl: passed btn horses fnl 3f* — **6/1**[3]

0005 **5** 2 **Tamarina (IRE)**[19] [4476] 3-8-4 38........(b) JFMcDonald(3) 7 — 14
(NEBerry) *led tl over 3f out: hung lft and wknd over 2f cut* — **33/1**

000 **6** 3 **Prince Renesis**[55] [3410] 3-8-12 ........ SRighton 2 — 14
(IWMcinnes) *in rr of main gp: hrd rdn and lost tch 3f out* — **12/1**

0-00 **7** 1 **Venerdi Tredici (IRE)**[57] [3368] 3-8-7 48........ DeanMcKeown 1 — 7
(PABlockley) *chsd ldrs 7f* — **8/1**

2m 12.76s (10.22) **Going Correction** +0.775s/f (Yiel) — **7** Ran SP% **113.5**
Speed ratings: **90,86,83,74,72 70,69**CSF £23.57 TOTE £4.90: £2.00, £3.00; EX 29.10.The winner was bought in for 6,500gns
**Owner** Mrs J M Muir **Bred** Ian Bryant **Trained** Lambourn, Berks

**FOCUS**

A dire contest and not one to dwell on. It was a modest time, even allowing for the conditions and class of race.

**NOTEBOOK**

**Ivory Coast(IRE)**, the only runner to have previously won a race, was always travelling best on the pace and, once hitting the front and bagging the near rail on turning for home, never seriously looked in danger. She handled the ground without fuss and the blinkers had the desired effect, but is not one to lump on for a follow-up bid.

**Tshukudu** , who would have been 15lb better off with Ivory Coast in a handicap, ran up to the form of her penultimate outing in a Yarmouth claimer and had no chance with the winner.

**Miss Procurer(IRE)** , best in at these weights, was hard at it from some way out and ran another disappointing race. She may not have got this trip too well, and could do better back over shorter, but remains one to have serious reservations about.

**Big Bad Burt** gave himself no chance at the start and was never going at any stage. *Official explanation: jockey said gelding had hung left*

## 5019 FARM FRESH SUPPLIES FILLIES' H'CAP — 1m 3f 196y

**4:00** (4:02) (E ) (0-70,67) 3-Y-O+ — **£3,413** (£1,050; £525; £262) **Stalls** High

Form — RPR

4400 **1** — **Papeete (GER)**[20] [4443] 3-8-9 **52** ........ SDrowne 4 — 59
(MissBSanders) *trckd ldrs: outpcd and hrd rdn 2f out: styd on to ld ins fnl f* — **20/1**

16-4 **2** 1/2 **Precious Mystery (IRE)**[22] [4398] 4-9-10 **57** ........ EAhern 2 — 63
(AKing) *w ldr: led over 2f out: hrd rdn and hdd ins fnl f: kpt on* — **6/1**[3]

0022 **3** 4 **Tata Naka**[19] [4499] 4-8-10 **43** ........ LisaJones 7 — 43
(MrsCADunnett) *hld up in rr: hdwy to press ldrs 3f out: hung lft over 1f out: no ex* — **7/1**

-400 **4** 2 1/2 **Spring Adieu**[20] [4443] 3-9-5 **62** ........ RLMoore 6 — 58
(MrsAJPerrett) *led tl over 2f out: hung lft and wknd 1f out* — **16/1**

0/23 **5** 3 **Serraval (FR)**[10] [4736] 6-9-5 **57** ........ RThomas(5) 8 — 49
(GBBalding) *hld up in rr: rdn and hdwy 2f out: wknd over 1f out* — **4/1**[2]

6211 **6** 6 **Science Academy (USA)**[11] [4710] 3-9-5 **67** ........ NDeSouza(5) 5 — 50
(PFICole) *prom tl wknd over 2f out: 6th and btn whn hung lft over 1f out* — **1/1**[1]

4010 **7** 5 **Ellovamul**[24] [4339] 4-9-1 **53** ........ PMakin(5) 9 — 28
(WMBrisbourne) *bhd fnl 3f* — **20/1**

0000 **8** dist **Spot In Time**[39] [3896] 4-9-1 **55** ........ NataliaGemelova(7) 10 — —
(IWMcinnes) *lost tch 4f out: sn t.o* — **25/1**

2m 41.07s (8.97) **Going Correction** +0.775s/f (Yiel)
**WFA** 3 from 4yo+ 10lb — **8** Ran SP% **116.0**
Speed ratings: **101,100,98,96,94 90,87,**—CSF £132.59 CT £938.88 TOTE £25.70: £4.90, £1.60, £1.90; EX 136.70.
**Owner** Mark L Champion **Bred** K Nercessian **Trained** Epsom, Surrey

**FOCUS**

A moderate handicap and modest form again, although the third and fourth give it a sound appearance.

**NOTEBOOK**

**Papeete(GER)**, who had yet to prove she had trained on as a three-year-old, finally put her best foot forward for her new connections and gamely held off the runner-up against the rail in the final strides. She relished the ground and could build on this, as she has fallen over two stone in the weights since the start of the year, and her confidence will have been done the world of good.

**Precious Mystery(IRE)** , a novice hurdle winner in January, went down fighting and clearly handled conditions better than most. She would have been better served by a stronger all-round gallop and was clear in second, so could be placed to go one better in this grade.

**Tata Naka** ran her race, but did not see it out as well as the front pair and finished tired. She seemed to handle this ground and is in good heart at present, but may need a drop back in grade.

**Spring Adieu**, previously unraced on ground this soft, set the moderate gallop for most of the way, but was readily brushed aside when the race got serious. It is hard to tell whether she truly got this trip, but was not disgraced in defeat and could be slowly going the right way.
**Serraval(FR)** looked to be going as well as any two out, but fell in a hole under pressure and failed to let herself down on this ground. She is capable of better on a fast surface.
**Science Academy(USA)** ◆, who came into this in great form and, bidding for the hat-trick, was beaten some way out and ran below her best. She has been raised 13lb for scoring the last twice, but it was the combination of a slow pace and testing ground on this unconventional track, rather than her new mark, that found her out. She is worth another chance. *Official explanation: trainer's representative said filly was unsuited by the soft going*
**Spot In Time** *Official explanation: jockey said filly had lost her action*

## 5020 ALEXANDER CATERING CLASSIFIED STKS — 6f 209y
**4:30** (4:31) (F) 3-Y-0+ — **£3,052** (£872; £436) **Stalls** Low

Form — RPR
-206 **1** **Landucci**92 [2371] 3-9-3 63 ....(t) SDrowne 1 72+
(JWHills) *racd alone on ins early: hdwy 3f out and jnd main gp on stands' side: led wl over 1f out: hld on wl* **25/1**
2154 **2** *shd* **Prime Offer**21 [4418] 8-9-9 64 .... GBaker 14 73+
(JJay) *hld up in tch: nt clr run and swtchd lft over 2f out: swtchd lft over 1f out: str chal fnl f: r.o* **8/1**3
0550 **3** *1 1/4* **Welcome Signal**17 [4556] 4-9-8 63 ....(p) JDSmith 16 69+
(JRFanshawe) *dwlt: outpcd and wl bhd: nt clr run over 2f out: hdwy whn nt clr run over 1f out: squeezed through: fin wl* **12/1**
0042 **4** *2* **Roman Maze**23 [4360] 4-9-6 61 .... RHughes 4 62
(WMBrisbourne) *chsd ldrs: one pce fnl 2f* **6/1**2
400 **5** *1 1/4* **Land Of Nod (IRE)**25 [4307] 3-8-11 60 ....(v1) EAhern 18 55
(GABulter) *mid-div: rdn over 3f out: styd on fnl f* **14/1**
1201 **6** *hd* **Mister Clinton (IRE)**21 [4418] 7-9-7 62 .... DaneO'Neill 3 59
(DKIvory) *stdd s: hdwy 4f out: no ex fnl 2f* **10/1**
0662 **7** *2 1/2* **Morag**8 [4817] 3-8-12 61 .... PDoe 11 49
(IAWood) *dwlt: hdwy 4f out: wknd over 1f out* **8/1**3
62-0 **8** *3/4* **Ice Dragon**83 [2596] 3-9-0 63 .... PRobinson 8 49
(MHTompkins) *prom 5f* **14/1**
5420 **9** *1 1/2* **Head Boy**17 [4546] 3-9-0 59 .... RLMoore 9 45
(SDow) *chsd ldrs 2f: lost pl: sme hdwy 2f out: no imp* **16/1**
0-10 **10** *1/2* **Dave (IRE)**1 [5008] 3-8-12 63 .... MSavage(5) 15 47
(JRBest) *chsd ldr 5f: wknd over 1f out* **12/1**
0633 **11** *hd* **Stokesies Wish**3 [4937] 4-9-2 60 .... LisaJones 5 41
(JLSpearing) *led: styd alone centre: hdd wl over 1f out: sn wknd* **10/1**
0053 **12** *1 1/2* **Beauty Of Dreams**9 [4771] 3-8-9 61 .... SHitchcott(3) 13 38
(MRChannon) *rrd s: in rr: drvn into midfield over 2f out: no further prog* **5/1**1
2520 **13** *1/2* **Nemo Fugat (IRE)**11 [4702] 5-9-7 62 ....(v) TEDurcan 17 41
(DNicholls) *dwlt: a in rr* **20/1**
5000 **14** *2* **Sir Don (IRE)**1 [5008] 5-9-8 63 ....(v) ANicholls 6 37
(DNicholls) *s.s: bhd: hdwy 4f out: wknd 2f out: wl btn whn bmpd and eased jst ins fnl f* **25/1**
0002 **15** *9* **Nine Red**60 [3280] 3-8-11 59 .... PFitzsimons 7 8
(JMBradley) *in tch: rdn 4f out: sn outpcd* **33/1**
3500 **16** *13* **Rowan Pursuit**14 [4619] 3-8-11 60 .... CCatlin 10 —
(JAkehurst) *mid-div: rdn and lost pl after 2f: sn wl bhd* **20/1**

1m 28.97s (6.37) **Going Correction** +0.95s/f (Soft)
**WFA** 3 from 4yo+ 5lb — **16** Ran SP% **126.1**
Speed ratings: **101,100,99,97,95 95,92,91,90,89 89,87,87,84,74 59**CSF £208.71 TOTE £42.40: £9.60, £3.20, £4.90; EX 461.00.
**Owner** R J Tufft **Bred** D J And Mrs Deer **Trained** Upper Lambourn, Berks

**FOCUS**
A modest handicap and fair form, but not as strong as it might have been, although it could rate higher.

**NOTEBOOK**
**Landucci** produced a remarkable performance to score all out and win his first race at the sixth time of asking. Digging deep to just hold off the runner-up in the final strides, he deserves all the plaudits, as he covered more ground than any other runner and looks to be coming right.
**Prime Offer** held every chance, but could not peg back the winner. He may well have won had he bagged the rail, but still turned in another solid effort and handled this ground well.
**Welcome Signal** ◆, dropping markedly in trip, ran his best race of the current campaign and seemed suited by the underfoot conditions. He was clear of the rest and could be placed to advantage now he has dropped to a fair mark.
**Roman Maze** seemed to handle this surface and ran his race with no obvious excuses.
**Land Of Nod(IRE)**, taking a big drop in trip, improved for the application of a visor and was staying on at the death.
**Mister Clinton(IRE)**, up 3lb for winning at this venue last time, kept on without ever threatening the principals, and would have ideally preferred faster ground. *Official explanation: trainer said gelding was unsuited by the soft going*
**Beauty Of Dreams** lost ground at the start and was up against it from then on.

## 5021 EXPRESS CHEF AMATEUR RIDERS H'CAP — 1m 1f 209y
**5:00** (5:03) (F) (0-55,55) 3-Y-0+ — **£3,038** (£868; £434) **Stalls** High

Form — RPR
6550 **1** **Lucayan Dancer**28 [4220] 4-11-4 55 .... MissKellyHarrison(3) 12 64
(DNicholls) *hld up in midfield: rdn over 2f out: hdwy over 1f out: r.o to ld fnl strides* **14/1**
2143 **2** *nk* **Go Green**6 [4853] 3-10-9 54 ....(t) MissEFolkes(3) 16 62
(PDEvans) *chsd ldrs: led 4f out: hrd rdn over 1f out: kpt on: hdd fnl strides* **12/1**
46-0 **3** *2 1/2* **Emperor's Well**28 [4213] 5-11-7 55 ....(b) MissSBrotherton 13 59
(MWEasterby) *prom: rdn and ev ch over 1f out: one pce* **16/1**
3263 **4** *1/2* **Private Seal**20 [4458] 9-10-4 45 ....(t) MrAChahal(7) 3 48
(JulianPoulton) *s.s: bhd: rdn and styd on wl fnl 2f: nrst fin* **25/1**
4265 **5** *nk* **Lazzaz**21 [4424] 6-10-6 45 .... MrsMarieKing(5) 1 47
(PWHiatt) *mid-div: rdn and styd on fnl 2f: nvr nrr* **7/1**2
0303 **6** *1 1/4* **Molly's Secret**19 [4473] 6-10-8 47 ....(b1) MissNadineForde(5) 2 47
(CGCox) *bhd: gd hdwy 3f out: ev ch over 1f out: no ex* **12/1**
2-00 **7** *3 1/2* **Healey (IRE)**39 [3921] 6-10-8 45 .... MrSDobson(3) 11 39
(IWMcinnes) *towards rr: hdwy over 2f out: hrd rdn: no ex over 1f out* **25/1**
3044 **8** *7* **Hirayna**9 [4771] 5-10-11 50 .... MrCDavies(5) 15 33
(WMBrisbourne) *chsd ldrs tl wknd wl over 1f out* **8/1**3
6300 **9** *1* **Coolfore Jade (IRE)**12 [4669] 4-10-0 41 .... MrJoshuaHarris(7) 9 22
(NEBerry) *mid-div: styd in far side pair st: hdwy over 2f out: wknd over 1f out* **50/1**
5506 **10** *1/2* **Duke's View (IRE)**19 [4467] 3-10-10 55 .... MissLJHarwood(3) 10 35
(MrsAJPerrett) *in tch: styd in far side pair st: effrt over 2f out: wknd over 1f out* **16/1**
3205 **11** *8* **Jessinca**33 [4045] 8-10-1 38 .... MrEDehdashti(3) 8 4
(APJones) *chsd ldrs: hrd rdn 2f out: sn wknd* **10/1**
1433 **12** *5* **Absinther**15 [4616] 7-11-1 49 .... MrsSBosley 17 7
(MRBosley) *rrd and s.s: lost 10 l: wl bhd tl passed btn horses fnl 2f* **5/1**1
4401 **13** *3/4* **Chubbes**22 [4387] 3-10-2 51 ....(b) MissAFrieze(7) 20 8
(BJLlewellyn) *in tch on outside: outpcd 1/2-way: sn lost pl* **20/1**
1601 **14** *1 1/2* **Mister Completely (IRE)**3 [4941] 3-10-4 51 6ex .... MissKManser(5) 14 5
(JRBest) *prom tl wknd over 2f out* **9/1**
4200 **15** *10* **Holly Rose**24 [4339] 5-11-5 53 ....(p) MsCWilliams 7 —
(DECantillon) *mid-div: bmpd after 1f: hdwy 5f out: wknd 2f out* **14/1**
4040 **16** *6* **Prince Valentine**3 [4941] 3-10-3 52 ....(p) MrNStorey(7) 4 —
(DBFeek) *mid-div: bmpd after 1f: sn bhd* **25/1**
-442 **17** *5* **Flaming Spirt**11 [4713] 5-10-13 50 .... MrsSMoore(3) 19 —
(JSMoore) *s.s: sn in midfield: wknd over 2f out* **7/1**2
0100 **18** *16* **Night Market**22 [4386] 6-11-0 51 ....(p) MrsNWilson(3) 5 —
(NWilson) *led tl 4f out: sn wknd: eased whn wl btn over 2f out* **16/1**
3005 **19** *dist* **Margery Daw (IRE)**71 [2928] 4-10-7 46 .... MissJCDuncan(5) 18 —
(PSMcentee) *in tch towards outside: wknd 1/2-way: t.o fnl 3f* **50/1**

2m 14.18s (11.64) **Going Correction** +0.95s/f (Soft)
**WFA** 3 from 4yo+ 8lb — **19** Ran SP% **138.5**
Speed ratings: **91,90,88,88,88 87,84,78,77,77 71,67,66,65,57 52,48,35,—**CSF £179.42 CT £2775.87 TOTE £18.30: £4.80, £2.80, £4.90, £6.60; EX 318.10 Place 6 £2,492.04, Place 5 £915.80.
**Owner** Lucayan Stud **Bred** The National Stud Owner Breeders Club Ltd **Trained** Sessay, N Yorks

**FOCUS**
A typically messy low-grade amateur riders' event, which saw the runners well strung out from an early stage and spread right across the track in the home straight. The form is modest although the winner could be on a good mark on his old form.

**NOTEBOOK**
**Lucayan Dancer** won his first race since taking his maiden as a juvenile in 2002. This drop in class proved ideal and was given a fine ride to get up. His rider had clearly worked out the place to be was on the nearside rail. He has dropped in the weights, and does look well-treated on his old form, so could build on this if able to maintain it..
**Go Green** gave her all in defeat and was only just denied. She was in front plenty soon enough on this occasion and tended to idle a bit in the lead, but deserves credit and may be able to gain compensation off this mark.
**Emperor's Well** had every chance, and showed the benefit of his recent comeback at Beverley, but could not quicken on this ground and will likely do better back on a quicker surface.
**Private Seal** lost ground at the start, but plugged on late and looked one paced on this surface.
**Lazzaz** was unable to get to the front as he prefers, but again gave his all and did well on ground softer than ideal.
**Absinther** lost a lot of ground at the start and was up against it from then on. Something may well have been amiss, as this was way below his best. *Official explanation: jockey said gelding reared in the stalls as the gates opened*
**Night Market** *Official explanation: jockey said gelding was hanging right*
T/Jkpt: Not won. T/Plt: £5,374.50 to a £1 stake. Pool: £49,696.55. 6.75 winning tickets. T/Qpdt: £221.90 to a £1 stake. Pool: £4,229.30. 14.10 winning tickets. LM

# 4815 YARMOUTH (L-H)
### Tuesday, August 24

**OFFICIAL GOING: Soft (good to soft in places) changing to soft after race 2 (2:45pm) and to heavy after race 3 (3:15pm)**
The first two home in the last raced close to the far rail in the straight, but the centre of the track did look to be riding quickest in the other five races.
Wind: Fresh across Weather: Heavy showers

## 5022 PETER HIGBY RACECOURSE PHOTOGRAPHER (S) NURSERY — 6f 3y
**2:15** (2:15) (G) 2-Y-0 — **£2,576** (£736; £368) **Stalls** High

Form — RPR
010 **1** **Marcela Zabala**18 [4516] 2-8-4 54 .... JFanning 8 55
(JGGiven) *a.p: chsd ldr over 1f out: rdn to ld ins fnl f: r.o* **10/1**
4005 **2** *hd* **Chicago Nights (IRE)**32 [4094] 2-7-6 49 .... DFentiman(7) 4 49
(PCHaslam) *led: rdn and hdd ins fnl f: r.o* **15/2**
0640 **3** *2 1/2* **Justenjoy Yourself**11 [4700] 2-7-7 48 oh6 .... HayleyTurner(5) 5 41
(CADwyer) *hld up: hdwy over 1f out: styd on* **16/1**
0300 **4** *1/2* **Joe Ninety (IRE)**13 [4638] 2-7-9 48 oh1 .... NMackay(3) 6 39
(JSMoore) *chsd ldrs: rdn over 1f out: styd on same pce* **12/1**
6046 **5** *shd* **Faithful Flash**25 [4304] 2-8-1 51 .... FNorton 3 42
(CADwyer) *sn pushed along in rr: hdwy u.p over 2f out: styd on same pce fnl f* **8/1**
032 **6** *2* **His Majesty**13 [4651] 2-8-5 62 .... StevenHarrison(7) 1 47
(NPLittmoden) *chsd ldr tl rdn over 2f out: wknd fnl f* **10/1**
002 **7** *1 1/4* **Yeldham Lady**18 [4516] 2-8-0 50 .... JQuinn 7 31
(JPearce) *dwlt: hld up: rdn over 1f out: n.d* **10/3**1
003 **8** *2* **Emeraude Du Cap**28 [4212] 2-8-1 51 .... JMackay 10 26
(MLWBell) *hld up: hdwy 1/2-way: wknd over 1f out* **4/1**2
2303 **9** *1/2* **General Nuisance (IRE)**13 [4651] 2-8-5 55 ....(p) SChin 9 28
(JSMoore) *chsd ldrs over 4f* **13/2**3

1m 17.86s (4.26) **Going Correction** +0.475s/f (Yiel) — **9** Ran SP% **111.0**
Speed ratings: **90,89,86,85,85 82,81,78,77**CSF £77.83 CT £1156.59 TOTE £12.40: £2.40, £3.40, £2.90; EX 117.50.The winner was bought in for 5,200gns
**Owner** Zaha Racing Syndicate **Bred** A Smith **Trained** Willoughton, Lincs

**FOCUS**
A moderate selling nursery in which they raced just off the stands' rail and the form is modest.

**NOTEBOOK**
**Marcela Zabala**, last but badly hampered in a Polytrack seller on her previous start, got a better run switched back to turf and returned to a straight track. This was a good effort to hold off the reasonably well-backed runner-up and pull clear of the remainder, and she is now two from two on turf. However, she can no longer run in sellers this year.
**Chicago Nights(IRE)**, dropped back into selling company and returned to turf, ran her best race to date and showed enough to suggest there is a similar race in her, pulling clear of all bar the winner.
**Justenjoy Yourself**, back down to a more realistic level, ran well from 6lb out of the handicap and has a very minor race in her.
**Joe Ninety(IRE)**, very disappointing in a seven-furlong claimer at Salisbury on his previous start, ran a little better dropped in grade and trip, but was still well held.
**Faithful Flash**, with the blinkers left off this time, did not appear to appreciate the drop back from seven furlongs. *Official explanation: jockey said filly hung right in the closing stages*
**Yeldham Lady**, a beaten favourite in a similar event on Polytrack on her previous start, lacked the pace to pose a threat and appears in need of seven furlongs.
**Emeraude Du Cap** offered some promise at Beverley on her previous start but was unable to build on that. However, this was her first run on easy ground and it may not have suited.

## 5023 HAVEN CAISTER HOLIDAY PARK MAIDEN STKS 1m 3y

2:45 (2:45) (D) 2-Y-O £3,828 (£1,178; £589; £294) Stalls High

Form RPR

0 **1** **Fantasy Ride**[25] 4292 2-9-0 ........................ JQuinn 5 89
(JPearce) *racd centre: s.i.s: sn chsng ldrs: led over 1f out: rdn clr* **16/1**

**2** 11 **Inca Wood (UAE)** 2-8-9 ........................ JFanning 4 64
(MJohnston) *racd stands' side: chsd ldrs: rdn over 2f out: wknd over 1f out* **11/1**[3]

0 **3** 2 **Sand Repeal (IRE)**[30] 4169 2-8-11 ........................ BReilly(3) 1 66
(MissJFeilden) *swtchd to r stands' side: led that gp 2f: remained handy: hung lft 1/2-way: rdn over 2f out: wknd over 1f out* **40/1**

62 **4** 1 **Pianoforte (USA)**[16] 4567 2-9-0 ........................ TPQueally 9 64
(DRLoder) *racd stands' side: led that gp 6f out: rdn and hdd over 1f out: hunt lft and wknd ins fnl f* **5/6**[1]

00 **5** ½ **Terminate (GER)**[17] 4544 2-9-0 ........................ SSanders 6 63
(SirMarkPrescott) *racd stands' side: chsd ldrs over 5f* **25/1**

0 **6** 10 **Asharon**[8] 4807 2-9-0 ........................ KFallon 3 45
(CEBrittain) *racd centre: s.i.s: rcvrd to ld that gp over 6f out: rdn and ev ch over 1f out: wknd qckly* **14/1**

0 **7** 7 **Wandering Act (IRE)**[20] 4432 2-9-0 ........................ JFortune 2 32
(MJWallace) *racd centre: prom to 1/2-way* **66/1**

**8** *dist* **Irish Ballad** 2-9-0 ........................ NCallan 7 —
(PWHarris) *racd stands' side: s.s: outpcd* **20/1**

62 **9** 16 **Zalaal (USA)**[17] 4544 2-9-0 ........................ LDettori 8 —
(SaeedBinSuroor) *racd stands' side: sn outpcd* **3/1**[2]

1m 45.51s (5.81) **Going Correction** +0.65s/f (Yiel) **9** Ran SP% **113.0**
Speed ratings: **96,85,83,82,81 71,64,—,—**CSF £161.99 TOTE £24.60: £3.80, £2.50, £6.80; EX 170.40.
**Owner** J P Hayes **Bred** A J Holder **Trained** Newmarket, Suffolk

**FOCUS**
With the front two in the betting not running to form, this was a pretty uncompetitive maiden and they finished well-strung out on ground that would have proved quite testing for any horse, let alone juveniles. The winner is flattered by the form and the third and fifth provide the best guide, although there are doubts over it. They split into two groups early on, but finished together up the centre of the track.

**NOTEBOOK**
**Fantasy Ride** offered plenty of promise in a good fast-ground seven-furlong Newmarket maiden, and was able to confirm that promise under these very different conditions. He was driven out right the way to the line to maximise a winning margin that surely flatters him given the conditions, but he is still clearly worthy of a step up in grade, and appeals as the sort to go well in something like the Zetland Stakes later in the year.
**Inca Wood(UAE)**, out of an unraced half-sister to the high-class three-year-old winners Hazaam and Sharman, came here in preference to a Newmarket maiden later in the week. Easy to back, he was no match whatsoever to the winner but was clear of the remainder and should progress.
**Sand Repeal(IRE)** seemed to run well on his debut in a Newmarket maiden behind Oude and again showed ability. However, he did not help his chance by hanging and was left behind when it mattered.
**Pianoforte(USA)** had offered promise on both his previous starts, but ran below form upped in trip and racing on easy ground for the first time.
**Terminate(GER)** offered some promise and is now qualified for an all-important handicap mark.
**Asharon** showed nothing on his debut at Nottingham, but Fallon was an interesting booking. Although ultimately well beaten, he showed real signs of ability and is one to keep in mind.
**Zalaal(USA)** was unable to build on the promise he showed on his two previous outings and probably hated the ground - he is not exactly bred to go on it. *Official explanation: jockey said colt was unsuited by today's very testing soft ground*

## 5024 BBC LOOK EAST CLASSIFIED STKS 7f 3y

3:15 (3:15) (D) 3-Y-O £6,734 (£2,072; £1,036; £518) Stalls High

Form RPR

0606 **1** **Jath**[13] 4646 3-8-9 80 ........................ NCallan 4 84
(JulianPoulton) *trckd ldr: rdn and ev ch fr over 1f out: r.o to ld post* **5/1**

6313 **2** *shd* **Desert Cristal (IRE)**[8] 4812 3-8-9 78 ........................ LDettori 2 84
(JRBoyle) *led over 5f: rallied to ld wl ins fnl f: hdd post* **7/4**[1]

31 **3** ½ **Majors Cast (IRE)**[10] 4741 3-9-3 85 ........................ JPMurtagh 3 91
(JNoseda) *trckd ldrs: rdn to ld over 1f out: sn hdd: rallied to ld ins fnl f: sn hdd and unable qck* **15/8**[2]

6114 **4** *nk* **Keyaki (IRE)**[24] 4318 3-8-9 80 ........................ SSanders 1 82
(CFWall) *hld up in tch: rdn to ld over 1f out: hdd and unable qck ins fnl f* **7/2**[3]

1m 31.46s (4.96) **Going Correction** +0.80s/f (Soft) **4** Ran SP% **110.0**
Speed ratings: **103,102,102,101**CSF £14.14 TOTE £6.20; EX 24.10.
**Owner** Meddler Bloodstock **Bred** John James **Trained** Kentford, Suffolk

**FOCUS**
A decent contest with just 3lb between these four on the ratings and clearly quite a tight affair. However, the early pace was very steady which resulted in a sprint finish and, with under a length separating the whole field at the line. They raced up the centre of the track.

**NOTEBOOK**
**Jath**, second last in the 1000 Guineas on her previous start, is now racing at a much more realistic level and built on the promise she showed at Sandown on her previous start. It is not easy to assess the value of the form, but she is clearly on good terms with herself and is one to keep in mind when there is a bit of give in the ground.
**Desert Cristal(IRE)** gained her only previous win on fast ground, but handles a soft surface and was just held.
**Majors Cast(IRE)** found this tougher than the Goodwood maiden he landed on his previous start, but can be given another chance in a more truly-run affair.
**Keyaki(IRE)** may not have been ideally suited by the soft ground but was still beaten less than a length.

## 5025 SALTWELL SIGNS VIRGINIA RATED STKS (H'CAP) (LISTED RACE) (F&M) 1m 2f 21y

3:45 (3:46) (A) (0-110,96) 3-Y-O+ £17,400 (£6,600; £3,300; £1,500) Stalls Low

Form RPR

3215 **1** **Posteritas (USA)**[39] 3915 3-7-13 82 ........................ JQuinn 9 93
(HRACecil) *hld up in tch: c centre over 3f out: led over 1f out: rdn out* **10/1**

2111 **2** 1 **La Persiana**[31] 4153 3-8-13 96 ........................ KDarley 10 105
(WJarvis) *a.p: rdn and ev ch over 1f out: unable qck ins fnl f* **9/1**[3]

-122 **3** 1 **Bowstring (IRE)**[108] 1963 3-8-12 95 ........................ JFortune 11 103
(JHMGosden) *led 3f: remained handy: c centre and led over 3f out: hung lft over 2f out: rdn and hdd over 1f out: styd on same pce* **10/1**

-321 **4** 1 **Ice Palace**[59] 3311 4-9-7 96 ........................ JPMurtagh 3 102
(JRFanshawe) *hld up in tch: rdn over 1f out: no ex ins fnl f* **15/8**[1]

3060 **5** 2 **Mystical Girl (USA)**[25] 4287 3-8-9 92 ........................ JFanning 5 95
(MJohnston) *chsd ldrs: rdn and ev ch over 1f out: no ex* **12/1**

2126 **6** 1 **Wee Dinns (IRE)**[10] 4737 3-8-2 85 ........................ FNorton 12 86
(SKirk) *hld up: hdwy over 2f out: wknd ins fnl f* **20/1**

4260 **7** 5 **Windy Britain**[17] 4540 5-8-13 88 ........................ DHolland 7 80
(LMCumani) *hld up: sme hdwy over 1f out: nvr trbld ldrs* **10/1**

-363 **8** 3½ **Carini**[18] 4525 3-8-11 94 ........................ DSweeney 6 80
(HCandy) *chsd ldr tl led 7f out: hdd over 3f out: wknd 2f out* **33/1**

-022 **9** 1¼ **Ultimata**[8] 4812 4-8-7 82 oh2 ........................ OUrbina 8 66
(JRFanshawe) *hld up: a in rr* **14/1**

4105 **10** 13 **Flowerdrum (USA)**[9] 4773 4-8-11 86 ........................ KFallon 1 48
(WJHaggas) *chsd ldrs over 7f* **10/1**

-215 **11** 1¼ **Crystal (IRE)**[81] 2640 3-8-10 93 ........................ LDettori 4 53
(BJMeehan) *hld up: wknd over 3f out* **11/2**[2]

5405 **12** *dist* **Qudrah (IRE)**[30] 4176 4-8-7 82 oh2 ........................ SSanders 2 —
(EJO'Neill) *s.s: a bhd* **66/1**

2m 14.29s (6.32) **Going Correction** +0.80s/f (Soft)
**WFA** 3 from 4yo+ 8lb **12** Ran SP% **120.1**
Speed ratings: **106,105,104,103,102 101,97,94,93,83 82,—**CSF £96.59 CT £936.55 TOTE £9.50: £2.40, £3.60, £2.60; EX 87.70 Trifecta £1183.20 Part won. Pool £1,666.53. 0.60 winning units..
**Owner** K Abdulla **Bred** Juddmonte Farms Inc **Trained** Newmarket, Suffolk

**FOCUS**
A reasonable Listed contest and competitive enough thanks to its handicap status. Two of the first three home raced up the centre of the track in the straight and that is where is the best ground looked to be.

**NOTEBOOK**
**Posteritas(USA)** won her maiden on fast ground and was unraced on anything softer than good. Although she clearly handled these conditions, Henry Cecil felt she was unsuited by the easy surface - she benefited from racing up the centre of the track. All-important black type was gained and, although there are no firm plans for her, she should continue to go well in similar company.
**La Persiana**, 9lb higher than when successful at York on her previous start, was unraced on ground easier than good to firm but handled the conditions and was just denied the four-timer. Although she raced off the far rail, the eventual winner raced more towards the centre of the track. She looks capable of making a winning mark in this grade.
**Bowstring(IRE)**, a well-beaten second in the Lingfield Oaks Trial when last seen 108-days previously, had not really convinced on this sort of ground previously, but she seemed to handle it and ran well, racing with the winner down the centre of the track. It would be no surprise to see her win in Pattern company abroad.
**Ice Palace**, successful on soft ground in this grade at Newcastle on her previous start, probably ran a little better than her finishing position suggests as she made her challenge close to the far rail, away from the winner.
**Mystical Girl(USA)**, 17lb higher than when gaining her only previous win in a handicap, can have no excuses.
**Wee Dinns(IRE)** did not run badly considering she made her challenge close to the far-side rail.
**Crystal(IRE)**, not seen since finishing a well-beaten fifth in the Oaks, is held in some regard but again failed to show her true capabilities. *Official explanation: jockey said filly lost her action*

## 5026 HAVEN SEASHORE HOLIDAY PARK CLAIMING STKS 6f 3y

4:15 (4:15) (E) 3-4-Y-O £4,026 (£1,239; £619; £309) Stalls High

Form RPR

0023 **1** **Beauvrai**[19] 4472 4-8-8 75 ........................ (p) KFallon 5 58+
(VSmith) *rdr removed blindfold late: s.s: racd centre: hld up: hdwy over 2f out: led ins fnl f: comf* **4/6**[1]

5000 **2** 1½ **Indrani**[11] 4708 3-7-7 38 ........................ (p) HayleyTurner(5) 3 40
(JohnAHarris) *led centre tl hdd and unable qck ins fnl f* **14/1**

00/3 **3** 1¼ **Hammer Of The Gods (IRE)**[20] 4462 4-9-0 45 ........................ (vt[1]) NCallan 1 49
(JulianPoulton) *racd centre: chsd ldr: rdn and ev ch whn hung lft and no ex ins fnl f* **7/1**[3]

0002 **4** 10 **Elliot's Choice (IRE)**[10] 4758 3-8-7 60 ........................ (b[1]) SSanders 4 15
(DCarroll) *racd alone stands' side: prom over 4f* **3/1**[2]

0000 **5** 8 **Trusted Instinct (IRE)**[71] 2928 4-8-3 57 ........................ BReilly(3) 2 —
(CADwyer) *racd centre: chsd ldrs: hung rt and wknd 1/2-way* **25/1**

1m 17.95s (4.35) **Going Correction** +0.80s/f (Soft)
**WFA** 3 from 4yo 3lb **5** Ran SP% **108.0**
Speed ratings: **103,101,99,86,75**CSF £10.58 TOTE £1.70: £1.10, £4.40; EX 8.30.Beauvrai was claimed by D J Flood for £8,000
**Owner** R J Baines **Bred** P Asquith **Trained** Exning, Suffolk

**FOCUS**
A very weak claimer in which Beauvrai had upwards of 16lb in hand of his rivals and did what was required. They raced towards the centre of the track, with the exception of Elliot's Choice who stayed stands' side.

**NOTEBOOK**
**Beauvrai** broke a blood-vessel when a beaten favourite at Brighton on his previous start, but there were no such problems this time around and he was too good for these - he had upwards of 16lb in hand of his rivals.
**Indrani** had no less than 30lb to find with the winner at the weights, and acquitted herself with credit in the circumstances.
**Hammer Of The Gods(IRE)**, having just his second start since 2002, ran respectably considering he had 36lb to find with the winner at the weights.
**Elliot's Choice(IRE)**, just held in a very weak five-furlong maiden on his previous start, ran a long way below that form with the blinkers replacing a visor. The ground should not have been a problem, but his stamina was unproven and he did not get home against the stands' rail.
**Trusted Instinct(IRE)** was the second best off at the weights, but has now failed to beat a rival on his last four starts. *Official explanation: jockey said colt hung right-handed throughout*

## 5027 AYLSHAM BATHROOM & KITCHEN CENTRE H'CAP 2m

4:45 (4:46) (E) (0-70,69) 3-Y-O+ £4,085 (£1,257; £628; £314) Stalls High

Form RPR

1113 **1** **Sendintank**[140] 1282 4-9-6 62 ........................ NCallan 5 82+
(SCWilliams) *hld up: hdwy 10f out: chsd ldr over 3f out: led on bit over 1f out: shkn up and styd on wl* **2/1**[1]

0060 **2** 5 **Larking About (USA)**[8] 4820 4-8-10 52 ........................ (b) KFallon 10 55
(WJMusson) *s.i.s: hld up: hdwy 11f out: chsd ldr over 5f out: led over 4f out: rdn and hdd over 1f out: sn outpcd* **11/1**

0020 **3** 17 **Peak Park (USA)**[47] 3667 4-8-4 46 ........................ (v) TPQueally 1 29
(JARToller) *chsd ldrs: led over 5f out: hdd over 4f out: hung rt and wknd over 2f out* **25/1**

0144 **4** 5 **Sonoma (IRE)**[24] 4352 4-9-1 62 ........................ HayleyTurner(5) 3 39
(MLWBell) *hld up: effrt over 5f out: sn wknd* **10/1**

000P **5** *dist* **Madiba**[41] 3851 5-9-0 56 ........................ JFanning 7 —
(PHowling) *chsd ldrs tl wknd 5f out* **20/1**

0202 **6** 7 **Riyadh**[20] 4448 6-9-13 69 ........................ KDarley 6 —
(MJohnston) *hld up: rdn over 5f out: sn wknd* **5/1**[3]

0000 **7** 28 **Vanbrugh (FR)**[29] 4202 4-7-12 40 oh3 ........................ (vt) JMcAuley 2 —
(MissDAMchale) *sn led: hdd over 5f out: wknd over 4f out* **33/1**

004- **8** 11 **Seattle Prince (USA)**[490] 1180 6-8-9 51 ........................ DHolland 4 —
(SGollings) *chsd ldrs: lost pl 11f out: sn bhd* **20/1**

/066 **9** 1½ **Lawrence Of Arabia (IRE)**[8] 4820 4-9-2 58 ........................ SSanders 9 —
(SirMarkPrescott) *prom: pushed along 1/2-way: wknd over 6f out* **9/4**[2]

-666 **10** *1 1/4* **Simon's Seat (USA)**[17] 4554 5-9-4 60................................. MFenton 8 —
(PHowling) *sn pushed along: a in rr: bhd fnl 7f* **33/1**

3m 45.02s (15.02) **Going Correction** +1.025s/f (Soft) **10** Ran SP% **117.4**
Speed ratings: **103,100,92,89,— —,—,—,—,—**CSF £22.72 CT £421.46 TOTE £2.80: £1.20, £2.80, £5.60; EX 27.10 Place 6 £5,045.99, Place 5 £762.80.
**Owner** Steve Jones And Phil McGovern **Bred** K G Powter **Trained** Newmarket, Suffolk

**FOCUS**
A moderate handicap in which they went off pretty quick considering the conditions and only two got home - they both raced close to the far rail in the straight. The form does not look that reliable, with several below form.

**NOTEBOOK**
**Sendintank** landed a four-timer over a mile and a half on Fibresand earlier in the year and ran a fair race switched to turf off the back of a break when last seen in April. Racing for the first time in 140 days and stepped up in trip, he justified strong market support with an easy victory, seeing out the distance really well. He should be able to follow up under a penalty, but he did carry his head awkwardly when asked to go on and things would have been interesting had he been seriously challenged.
**Larking About(USA)** ◆ had not been at her best so far this season, but appreciated the testing ground and was simply unlucky to bump into such a well-handicapped rival. She was 17 lengths clear of the remainder and looks up to winning a similar race when there is give underfoot.
**Peak Park(USA)** got home better than most, but the conditions still stretched her.
**Sonoma(IRE)** has only ever won on fast ground.
**Madiba** should not have minded the conditions but was beaten a mile.
**Riyadh** prefers decent ground.
**Lawrence Of Arabia(IRE)** ran an incredibly lacklustre race and, beaten before stamina became an issue, he may not have been suited by the ground. *Official explanation: jockey said gelding was unsuited by today's heavy ground*
T/Plt: £7,095.70 to a £1 stake. Pool: £40,338.80. 4.15 winning tickets. T/Qpdt: £147.60 to a £1 stake. Pool: £4,348.90. 21.80 winning tickets. CR

5028 - 5031a (Foreign Racing) - See Raceform Interactive

## 4981 DEAUVILLE (R-H)
### Tuesday, August 24

**OFFICIAL GOING: Turf course - very soft; all-weather - standard**

### 5032a PRIX DE LA NONETTE (GROUP 3) (FILLIES) 1m 2f
12:10 (12:13) 3-Y-O £28,274 (£10,282; £7,711; £5,141)

RPR
**1** **Grey Lilas (IRE)**[72] 2925 3-9-0 ........................................ GaryStevens 8 113
(AFabre, France) *set very slow pace, quickened 3f out, pushed clear 1 1/2f out, very easily*
**2** *5* **Trinity Joy**[114] 1803 3-9-0 ........................................(b) TJarnet 1 104
(RGibson, France) *held up in 3rd, ridden to dispute 2nd 1 1/2f out, took 2nd 100y out but no chance with winner*
**3** *3/4* **Polyfirst (FR)**[24] 4356 3-9-0 ........................................ OPeslier 5 103
(MmeCHead-Maarek, France) *held up in 4th, effort to dispute 2nd 1f out, lost 2nd 100y out*
**4** *hd* **Green Noon (FR)**[324] 5404 3-9-0 ........................................ YLerner 2 103
(CLerner, France) *raced in 2nd, ridden 1 1/2f out, lost 2nd 100y out*

2m 29.8s **Going Correction** +1.225s/f (Soft) **4** Ran
Speed ratings: **74,70,69,69.**
**Owner** Gestut Ammerland **Bred** Azienda Agricola Il Tiglio Di Amelia Prevedello **Trained** France

**FOCUS**
The race was originally run two days earlier, but there was a false start and three runners failed to see the recall flag, Shapira beating Polyfirst and Green Swallow.

**NOTEBOOK**
**Grey Lilas(IRE)** was allowed to bowl along at her own pace and caught the others out with a sudden change of pace before staying on strongly. The form is worth little but she at least proved she has plenty of tactical speed. Her future could now be in the States, but the Prix de l'Opera may also be looked at before her departure.
**Trinity Joy** won the battle for second place having been third early on. She had no chance with the winner.
**Polyfirst(FR)** dropped out last and then came with a late run. This was not a bad effort considering she had finished last of three in the first edition of the Nonette, which was later annulled by the officials.
**Green Noon(FR)** had not been out since third in the Prix Marcel Boussac last year. She failed to run up to her juvenile form but much better can be expected in time.

### 5033a PRIX MINERVE (GROUP 3) (FILLIES) 1m 4f 110y
1:50 (1:52) 3-Y-O £25,704 (£10,282; £7,711; £5,141)

RPR
**1** **Silverskaya (USA)**[51] 3566 3-9-0 ........................................ IMendizabal 7 102
(J-CRouget, France) *hld up, slightly hmpd 2 1/2f out, 8th str, hdwy between horses fr 2f out, rdn over 1f out, led 150 yds out, ran on well* 1
**2** *1* **Reverie Solitaire (IRE)**[51] 3566 3-8-10 ........................................ OPeslier 3 96
(CLaffon-Parias, France) *raced in 3rd, 4th straight, led narrowly over 1f out to 150 yards out, kept on*
**3** *nk* **Anabaa Republic (FR)**[31] 3-8-10 ........................................ ELegrix 8 96
(FDoumen, France) *raced in 2nd til led entering straight, headed over 1f out, kept on*
**4** *1/2* **Diamond Tango (FR)**[105] 2028 3-8-10 ........................................ GaryStevens 4 95
(AFabre, France) *towards rear early, headway around outside halfway, 3rd straight, ridden over 1f out, stayed on at one pace* 2
**5** *2* **Barancella (FR)**[72] 2925 3-8-10 ........................................ DBonilla 9 92
(FHead, France) *geld up in last, headway around outside to go 6th entering straight, effort and unable to quicken over 1f out* 3
**6** *3* **Briviesca**[42] 3833 3-8-10 ........................................ MBlancpain 2 88
(CLaffon-Parias, France) *held up, 7th straight, headway on inside to chase leaders over 1 1/2f out, one pace from over 1f out*
**7** *3/4* **Pink Palace (IRE)**[42] 3833 3-8-10 ........................................ C-PLemaire 6 87
(DSepulchre, France) *held up towards rear, last straight, never a factor*
**8** *6* **Kate Winslet (USA)**[42] 3833 3-8-10 ........................................ TThulliez 1 78
(MRolland, France) *led til headed over 2f out, steadily weakened*
**9** *2* **Chandi Dasa (IRE)**[75] 2830 3-8-10 ........................................ SPasquier 5 75
(ELellouche, France) *raxed in 4th, 5th straight, weakened over 1 1/2f out*

2m 55.9s **Going Correction** +0.90s/f (Soft) **9** Ran SP% **122.2**
Speed ratings: **107,106,106,105,104 102,102,98,97.**
**Owner** Earl Champ Gignoux **Bred** M3 Elevage, Pontchartrain Stud & Haras D'Etreham **Trained** France

**NOTEBOOK**
**Silverskaya(USA)** came from a long way back to win going away despite having been hampered early in the straight. This was a decent effort and she is ready for a step back up in grade. She was in season when disappointing in her previous outing, and will now be heading for either the Prix de Royallieu or the Prix Vermeille.
**Reverie Solitaire(IRE)**, always up with the pace, she joined battle with the winner early in the straight and stayed on gamely until the line to hold second place. She continues to run well at this level without proving good enough to score. Her turn will come.
**Anabaa Republic(FR)** was up there throughout and kept grinding away once passed. She will stay farther.
**Diamond Tango(FR)**, last early on, improved rounding the final turn and shortly after she challenged the leading group. She was probably given a bit too much too do and ran better than her finishing position suggests.

## 5015 BRIGHTON (L-H)
### Wednesday, August 25

**OFFICIAL GOING: Heavy**
Jockeys reported that the ground was riding very sticky, and was worst in the dip.
Due to the ground there were no fewer than 42 non-runners on the card.
Wind: Fresh across Weather: Fair, improving

### 5034 WELLINGTON MAIDEN AUCTION STKS 6f 209y
2:10 (2:11) (E) 2-Y-O £3,429 (£1,055; £527; £263) Stalls Low

Form RPR
03 **1** **Daisy Bucket**[30] 4198 2-8-2 ........................................ CCatlin 4 64
(DMSimcock) *took keen hold, hdwy 3f out: led wl over 1f out: drvn clr and swished tail fnl f* **9/4**[2]
000 **2** *3* **Grand Welcome (IRE)**[67] 3083 2-8-9 ..........................(b[1]) SDrowne 10 64
(CTinkler) *led: clr after 2f: hdd wl over 1f out: kpt on same pce* **5/1**[3]
403 **3** *5* **Phlaunt**[20] 4487 2-8-2 70........................................ SCarson 5 46
(RFJohnsonHoughton) *t.k.h in rr: rdn 3f out: hdwy to chse ldrs 2f out: wknd 1f out* **5/4**[1]
0 **4** *1 1/2* **Pralin Star (IRE)**[39] 3931 2-8-11 ........................................ GBaker 8 52
(MrsHSweeting) *hld up in 4th: hrd rdn and styd alone centre in st: hdwy and hung lft 2f out: wknd over 1f out* **33/1**
0 **5** *1/2* **Cross My Shadow (IRE)**[17] 4579 2-8-13 ......................(t) DaneO'Neill 7 53
(MFHarris) *stdd s: t.k.h and sn chsng ldr: outpcd 3f out: rallied 2f out: wknd over 1f out* **10/1**
00 **6** *2* **Ugly Sister (USA)**[58] 3377 2-8-3 ow1........................ LPKeniry[(3)] 3 41
(GCBravery) *plld hrd: prom: outpcd 3f out: swtchd lft and rallied 2f out: wknd over 1f out* **25/1**

1m 26.9s (4.30) **Going Correction** +0.525s/f (Yiel) **6** Ran SP% **107.8**
Speed ratings: **96,92,86,85,84** **82**CSF £12.54 TOTE £2.80: £1.60, £2.30; EX 13.60.
**Owner** Old Suffolk Stud **Bred** Old Suffolk Stud **Trained** Newmarket, Suffolk

**FOCUS**
A modest maiden, and a bit of a slog for these two-year-olds in the conditions and, even moderate rating could on the high side.

**NOTEBOOK**
**Daisy Bucket**, who has improved with each run, coped with the testing ground best of all. She flashed her tail under pressure, but kept on well enough, and on this evidence she will have no trouble getting a mile.
**Grand Welcome(IRE)**, blinkered for the first time, clearly appreciated the return to an easier surface. He was the first to grab the favoured stands'-side rail but, having cut out the running at a fair pace, had nothing more to offer when the winner came to challenge.
**Phlaunt** is not very big and, although her sister Pheisty won in heavy ground, she appeared to find the conditions all too much on her first attempt over seven furlongs.
**Pralin Star(IRE)** did himself few favours by racing mid-track in the straight while the action was next to the stands'-side rail.

### 5035 DEARLE & HENDERSON (S) STKS 6f 209y
2:40 (2:40) (G) 3-Y-O+ £2,584 (£738; £369) Stalls Low

Form RPR
0006 **1** **Wood Fern (UAE)**[8] 4825 4-9-1 48........................................(v) CCatlin 6 54
(MRChannon) *w ldr 2f: sn rdn in chsng gp: drvn to ld nr fin* **14/1**
0051 **2** *nk* **Rileys Dream**[20] 4469 5-8-12 48........................................(p) DCorby[(3)] 3 53
(BJLlewellyn) *chsd ldrs: hrd rdn over 1f out: slt ld ins fnl f: hdd and nt qckn nr fin* **5/1**[3]
0400 **3** *nk* **Confuzed**[15] 4617 4-8-12 40........................................(e) SHitchcott[(3)] 2 52
(DFlood) *t.k.h: stdd in rr: hdwy over 2f out: wandered and ev ch fnl f: nt qckn nr fin* **20/1**
6406 **4** *hd* **Young Love**[20] 4477 3-8-5 49........................................ RMullen 8 47
(MissECLavelle) *in tch: rdn and dropped to rr 3f out: rallied over 1f out: clsng wl at fin* **9/1**
0263 **5** *2 1/2* **Elsinora**[28] 4241 3-8-5 42........................................ DKinsella 14 41
(HMorrison) *hld up in rr: rdn and hdwy over 2f out: one pce appr fnl f* **9/1**
0005 **6** *nk* **Florian**[22] 4418 6-9-1 57........................................ KFallon 9 45
(TGMills) *led: clr 4f out: hdd & wknd ins fnl f* **7/2**[2]
4206 **7** *2 1/2* **Enna (POL)**[6] 4871 5-8-10 45........................................ SDrowne 16 34
(MrsStefLiddiard) *prom 3f* **5/2**[1]
0000 **8** *4* **Social Contract**[41] 3871 7-9-1 44........................................(v) TPQueally 17 29
(SDow) *sn towards rr: hrd rdn over 2f out: nt trble ldrs* **8/1**
0500 **9** *3* **Fulvio (USA)**[13] 4687 4-9-1 49........................................(v) PDoe 4 21
(JamiePoulton) *hrd rdn over 2f out: a bhd* **20/1**

1m 26.75s (4.15) **Going Correction** +0.525s/f (Yiel)
**WFA** 3 from 4yo+ 5lb **9** Ran SP% **114.8**
Speed ratings: **97,96,96,96,93 92,90,85,82**CSF £81.92 TOTE £18.20: £3.70, £2.00, £5.40; EX 113.20.There was no bid for the winner.
**Owner** Wooden Tops Partnership **Bred** Darley Dubai **Trained** West Ilsley, Berks
■ Stewards Enquiry : D Corby caution: used whip with excessive frequency
C Catlin one-day ban: excessive use of the whip (Sep 5)

**FOCUS**
A poor seller and half of those declared to run were taken out in the morning. The form looks reasonable rated through the first two, although the proximity of the third raises doubts.

**NOTEBOOK**
**Wood Fern(UAE)** proved just good enough in a tight finish. The visor was on again this time after being left off on his last two starts, and the drop back in trip suited after he failed to stay a mile at Hamilton.
**Rileys Dream** is something of a course specialist and ran a decent race on ground softer than ideal. She boasts a decent strike-rate for one so modest.
**Confuzed**, worst in at the weights, would have been getting plenty of weight from his rivals had this been a handicap, so this must go down as a creditable performance.
**Young Love** was the one finishing best of all. This was her first start in selling grade and a return to a mile will help her.
**Florian** was best in at the weights and, as is his style, set a decent gallop in front. He had no form in this sort of ground, though, and it was not a great shock to see him fall in a heap with a furlong to run.

## 5036 C. BREWER AND SONS FILLIES' H'CAP 7f 214y

3:10 (3:12) (F) (0-55,53) 3-Y-O £3,052 (£872; £436) Stalls Low

Form RPR

5650 **1** **Fiddles Music**[4] [4941] 3-8-5 **40** ........ CCatlin 2 46
(MissSheenaWest) *mde virtually all: drvn clr fnl f* **12/1**

6006 **2** *4* **Armentieres**[7] [4853] 3-9-4 **53** ........(b) SDrowne 3 51
(JLSpearing) *chsd ldrs: wnt 2nd over 2f out: nt qckn fnl f* **13/2**[3]

53 **3** *2 ½* **La Calera (GER)**[23] [4387] 3-9-0 **49** ........(v) OUrbina 12 42
(GCHChung) *hld up in midfield: hdwy to trck ldrs 4f out: hrd rdn and n.m.r over 2f out tl 1f out: no ex fnl f* **5/1**[2]

4445 **4** *2 ½* **Magic Verse**[20] [4471] 3-9-0 **49** ........ RLMoore 9 37
(RGuest) *in rr: pushed along whn hmpd over 3f out: sme hdwy 2f out: no imp* **10/3**[1]

6004 **5** *1 ½* **Keltic Rainbow (IRE)**[6] [4867] 3-8-7 **45** ........ JFMcDonald(3) 8 30
(DHaydnJones) *t.k.h: w ldrs over 4f: sn outpcd* **10/1**

4120 **6** *5* **Zonnebeke**[9] [4818] 3-8-13 **48** ........ DaneO'Neill 4 23
(MrsCADunnett) *sed fr stall 4: chsd ldrs: disp ld briefly over 3f out: wknd over 1f out* **7/1**

3504 **7** *13* **Soviet Spirit**[14] [4654] 3-8-13 **53** ........ RThomas(5) 10 2
(CADwyer) *towards rr: drvn along over 3f out: lost tch 2f out* **10/1**

0400 **8** *5* **Mystic Moon**[7] [4853] 3-8-10 **45** ........ RMullen 15 —
(JRJenkins) *prom to 1/2-way* **10/1**

04-0 **9** *13* **Great Blasket (IRE)**[37] [3993] 3-9-3 **52** ........ KFallon 6 —
(EJO'Neill) *sed fr stall 6: in rr: rdn 5f out: n.m.r over 3f out: lost tch 2f out: eased* **7/1**

1m 39.61s (4.61) **Going Correction** +0.525s/f (Yiel) **9** Ran SP% **113.0**
Speed ratings: **97,93,90,88,86 81,68,63,50**CSF £85.64 CT £446.14 TOTE £13.40: £2.70, £2.60, £2.30; EX 72.00.
**Owner** Michael Moriarty **Bred** F Rowland **Trained** Lewes, E Sussex
■ Stewards Enquiry : K Fallon £150 fine: started from wrong stall (6 instead of 4)
Dane O'Neill £150 fine: started from wrong stall (4 instead of 6)

**FOCUS**
A moderate heat, no better than a seller, and the form is not expected to work out.

**NOTEBOOK**
**Fiddles Music** is rated only 40 and has not been getting home over middle distances recently. The drop back to a mile proved just what was required and she ran out a clear-cut winner.
**Armentieres** ran well here last backend, but is another who has struggled this term over middle distances. She kept on well without ever being able to reach the winner.
**La Calera(GER)** did not show much of a liking for soft ground in Europe for her previous trainer, and in the circumstances this was a solid effort.
**Magic Verse** appeared to be suited by the drop back to a mile.
**Keltic Rainbow(IRE)** could not pick up in the ground.
**Zonnebeke** was another who looked to be found out by the testing conditions.
**Soviet Spirit** *Official explanation: trainer said filly could not handle the heavy ground*

## 5037 ARMY BENEVOLENT FUND JUBILEE H'CAP 1m 3f 196y

3:40 (3:41) (E) (0-70,68) 3-Y-O £3,818 (£1,175; £587; £293) Stalls High

Form RPR

0212 **1** **Quarrymount**[18] [4536] 3-9-2 **63** ........ JMackay 5 74+
(SirMarkPrescott) *mde all: set sedate pce: rdn and qcknd clr over 2f out: easily* **10/11**[1]

6-00 **2** *7* **Rumbling Bridge**[14] [4641] 3-8-9 **56** ........ PDoe 2 56
(JLDunlop) *in tch: pushed along 4f out: chsd wnr 2f out: hld whn hung lft over 1f out* **7/1**[3]

4313 **3** *5* **Treason Trial**[5] [4921] 3-8-10 **57** ........ SDrowne 4 50
(MrsStefLiddiard) *broke wl: plld hrd and stdd in rr: hdwy 1/2-way: rdn and btn over 2f out* **4/1**[2]

100 **4** *nk* **Komoto**[15] [4618] 3-9-2 **63** ........(v[1]) TPQueally 6 56
(GAButler) *cl up: outpcd over 2f out: 3rd and wkng whn hung lft fnl f* **8/1**

003 **5** *3 ½* **Hinode (IRE)**[47] [3707] 3-9-2 **63** ........ MTebbutt 3 51
(JARToller) *cl up tl wknd over 2f out* **8/1**

2m 42.76s (10.66) **Going Correction** +0.525s/f (Yiel) **5** Ran SP% **107.1**
Speed ratings: **85,80,77,76,74**CSF £7.21 TOTE £1.90: £1.10, £3.90; EX 8.70.
**Owner** Lady Fairhaven **Bred** Lord Fairhaven **Trained** Newmarket, Suffolk

**FOCUS**
A weak handicap and a very slow time for the grade, even allowing for the conditions, but the winner looks a progressive sort.

**NOTEBOOK**
**Quarrymount** had it to prove in these testing conditions but, given that he is by Polar Falcon, there was plenty to encourage his supporters. Given his own way in front, he dictated a steady pace before winding it up with half a mile to run. He went on to score with such ease that he will surely be out again on Bank Holiday Monday to take up one of his two engagements under a penalty.
**Rumbling Bridge** came home best of the rest. Having his first start on anything other than good to firm, his stable is still not firing on all cylinders and he is surely capable of better in time.
**Treason Trial**, whose connections had been worried about the gelding's ability to handle the easy ground at Sandown last time, unsurprisingly failed to deliver in these even more testing conditions.
**Komoto**, visored for the first time, has failed to progress from his maiden victory on the Polytrack last month.

## 5038 MONTPELIER RE H'CAP 1m 1f 209y

4:10 (4:10) (E) (0-70,70) 3-Y-O+ £3,507 (£1,079; £539; £269) Stalls High

Form RPR

-500 **1** **Secluded**[40] [3911] 4-9-8 **64** ........(b[1]) SDrowne 5 73
(EFVaughan) *dwlt: covered up: hdwy 4f out: eased out 2f out: led 1f out: drvn out* **11/4**[2]

66 **2** *4* **Miss Inkha**[62] [3246] 3-8-11 **61** ........ KFallon 10 63
(RGuest) *chsd ldrs: wnt 2nd 5f out: led 2f out tl 1f out: one pce* **7/2**[3]

3060 **3** *5* **Pending (IRE)**[12] [4726] 3-9-6 **70** ........(p) DaneO'Neill 9 64
(JRFanshawe) *led after 2f tl 2f out: sn btn* **7/2**[3]

1100 **4** *¾* **Kernel Dowery (IRE)**[21] [4436] 4-9-7 **63** ........(p) EAhern 2 55
(PWHarris) *hld up in rr: effrt over 2f out: no ex over 1f out* **5/2**[1]

0 **5** *17* **Richmond Lodge (IRE)**[14] [4641] 4-8-12 **54** ........ GBaker 6 18
(MMadgwick) *led 2f: wknd and hung lft 2f out* **12/1**

2m 8.00s (5.46) **Going Correction** +0.525s/f (Yiel)
**WFA** 3 from 4yo+ 8lb **5** Ran SP% **107.4**
Speed ratings: **99,95,91,91,77**CSF £11.84 TOTE £4.00: £1.90, £2.00; EX 14.30.
**Owner** Racing For Gold **Bred** Dr Anthony Nicholas Howard **Trained** Newmarket, Suffolk

**FOCUS**
An modest handicap in which the original field of 14 was reduced to five by non-runners. The form is weak.

**NOTEBOOK**
**Secluded**, wearing first-time blinkers, had shown enough to suggest a race of this nature was within his ability and, having been settled in behind, picked up well to win in good style. Although this race probably did not take a lot of winning, he could be capable of a bit of improvement.
**Miss Inkha** had shaped as though she might appreciate the step up to ten furlongs, and she duly improved on her previous form.
**Pending(IRE)**, who made most of the running, had been struggling to get home over a mile, so it was not a great surprise to see him dropping away in the closing stages of this race.
**Kernel Dowery(IRE)** has run all his best races on fast ground and also gives the impression that the Handicapper has his measure for the time being.

## 5039 BRIGHTON SQUARE SUPPORTS THE MARTLETS HOSPICE H'CAP 6f 209y

4:40 (4:41) (E) (0-70,69) 3-Y-O+ £3,523 (£1,084; £542; £271) Stalls Low

Form RPR

43- **1** **Plum**[406] [3312] 4-9-12 **67** ........ KFallon 9 77+
(EFVaughan) *dwlt: hld up towards rr: rdn and hdwy over 1f out: r.o to ld nr fin* **5/1**[2]

3041 **2** *hd* **Jazzy Millennium**[18] [4548] 7-9-1 **56** ........(v) SDrowne 11 65
(BRMillman) *chsd ldrs: led 2f out: hrd rdn and kpt on fnl f: hdd nr fin* **9/2**[1]

0054 **3** *2* **Loch Laird**[5] [4912] 9-8-0 **48** ........ CHaddon(7) 2 52
(MMadgwick) *hld up: hdwy 2f out: ev ch 1f out: edgd lft: no ex fnl 100 yds* **7/1**[3]

5600 **4** *shd* **Zinging**[39] [3932] 5-7-7 **39** oh3 ........ HayleyTurner(5) 10 43
(JJBridger) *hld up in rr: hdwy over 2f out: ev ch over 1f out: kpt on same pce* **25/1**

0266 **5** *2 ½* **Harbour House**[18] [4548] 5-8-4 **45** ........ ADaly 1 43
(JJBridger) *led after 1f tl over 3f out: ev ch 2f out: one pce* **14/1**

4054 **6** *½* **Temper Tantrum**[43] [3826] 6-9-2 **57** ........(p) NPollard 15 53
(JRBest) *dwlt: in tch in rr: outpcd 3f out: sltly hmpd 2f out: styd on fnl f* **7/1**[3]

2030 **7** *½* **Tojoneski**[18] [4546] 5-8-1 **45** ........(p) JFMcDonald(3) 18 40
(IWMcinnes) *w ldrs: led over 3f out tl 2f out: wknd over 1f out* **9/2**[1]

6406 **8** *3* **Hilarious (IRE)**[13] [4669] 4-7-11 **43** ........(b[1]) RThomas(5) 13 31
(DrJRJNaylor) *in tch: outpcd 1/2-way: sn btn* **25/1**

3 **9** *¾* **Musical Top (USA)**[23] [4390] 4-9-4 **59** ........ MFenton 12 45
(HMorrison) *led 1f: prom tl rdn and btn over 2f out: no ch whn hung lft over 1f out* **12/1**

0020 **10** *1* **Hand Chime**[13] [4687] 7-10-0 **69** ........ TPQueally 14 52
(WJHaggas) *chsd ldrs over 4f* **9/2**[1]

1m 25.52s (2.92) **Going Correction** +0.525s/f (Yiel) **10** Ran SP% **118.3**
Speed ratings: **104,103,101,101,98 97,97,93,93,91**CSF £28.25 CT £156.77 TOTE £5.80: £2.80, £1.40, £2.70; EX 17.50 Trifecta £168.60 Pool: £2,232.22. 9.40 winning units..
**Owner** Sir Robert Stewart **Bred** Mrs J D Railton And Miss R Dobson **Trained** Newmarket, Suffolk

**FOCUS**
An ordinary handicap, but the form is fair for the grade and sound.

**NOTEBOOK**
**Plum**, who was making a belated seasonal reappearance, looks capable of better. She had suffered niggly problems and connections had been waiting for this easier ground, and she certainly seemed to relish conditions. She only got on top close home and looks sure to appreciate a step up to a mile.
**Jazzy Millennium**, a course specialist, arrived here in top form and ran a fine race in defeat. Equally effective over six and seven furlongs, he seems to handle any ground.
**Loch Laird** is another who seems to go on anything and ran another solid race.
**Zinging** did not run too badly from 3lb out of the handicap, but he has only ever won one race on turf.
**Harbour House** looked to be found out by a lack of stamina over this extra furlong.
**Tojoneski** was disappointing, even allowing for the fact that he was racing in better grade than he normally contests.

## 5040 MANMATTERS CLASSIFIED STKS 5f 59y

5:10 (5:10) (F) 3-Y-O £2,940 (£840; £420) Stalls Low

Form RPR

1311 **1** **Wunderbra (IRE)**[5] [4929] 3-8-12 60 ........(t) HayleyTurner(5) 6 77+
(MLWBell) *trckd ldrs gng wl: shkn up and led over 1f out: sn qcknd clr: easily* **9/4**[2]

5004 **2** *3 ½* **Ace Club**[21] [4434] 3-9-4 64 ........ TPQueally 9 65
(WJHaggas) *chsd ldrs: rdn 3f out: kpt on to take 2nd fnl 75 yds: no ch w wnr* **2/1**[1]

6553 **3** *¾* **Wendy's Girl (IRE)**[5] [4929] 3-8-9 61 ........(b) THamilton(3) 7 56
(RPElliott) *led tl over 1f out: sn outpcd* **8/1**

0002 **4** *3* **Arfinnit (IRE)**[15] [4617] 3-8-11 58 ........(v) SHitchcott(3) 3 48
(MRChannon) *towards rr: sn rdn along: nvr rchd ldrs* **5/1**[3]

0024 **5** *nk* **Ardkeel Lass (IRE)**[45] [3772] 3-8-11 58 ........ PaulEddery 2 43
(DHaydnJones) *t.k.h: in tch: effrt over 2f out: wknd over 1f out* **12/1**

0000 **6** *12* **Cheeky Chi (IRE)**[94] [2326] 3-8-11 60 ........ RLMoore 11 —
(PSMcentee) *prom 3f* **13/2**

0060 **7** *6* **Easily Averted (IRE)**[18] [4546] 3-8-9 48 ........(t) RThomas(5) 10 —
(PButler) *s.s: a in rr* **33/1**

64.04 secs (1.77) **Going Correction** +0.525s/f (Yiel) **7** Ran SP% **115.8**
Speed ratings: **106,100,99,94,93 74,65**CSF £7.41 TOTE £3.50: £2.00, £1.80; EX 8.50 Place 6 £338.90, Place 5 £22.90.
**Owner** Fitzroy Thoroughbreds **Bred** J F Tuthill And Mrs A Whitehead **Trained** Newmarket, Suffolk

**FOCUS**
There were not many in-form runners lining up for this classified stakes, but the progressive winner recorded a decent time for the grade given the conditions and looks well treated at present.

**NOTEBOOK**
**Wunderbra(IRE)**, despite being weak in the market on account of this being her first start on ground as bad as this, hacked up. Since being fitted with a tongue tie she has improved with every run, on this occasion beating the more exposed Wendy's Girl, who finished two lengths behind her at Southwell last time, by over four lengths eased down. This performance may persuade connections to turn her out under a penalty at Goodwood on Saturday.
**Ace Club** was popular in the market as his effectiveness in testing ground was already proven. He ran well and was just unlucky to run into a progressive rival.
**Wendy's Girl(IRE)** was beaten further by the winner on this occasion than when they last met on the Southwell Fibresand, and while this was a solid effort, her performance only went to show that the winner is progressing fast.
**Arfinnit(IRE)**, beaten in a claimer last time, looks flattered by his current rating and once again found a few too good at the weights.
**Ardkeel Lass(IRE)** is a fast-ground performer and failed to cope with these more testing conditions.
**Cheeky Chi(IRE)**, for whom there was some support in the ring on her return from a three-month absence, handles soft ground but, having shown early dash, dropped away tamely.
T/Jkpt: Not won. T/Plt: £338.90 to a £1 stake. Pool: £83,502.95. 179.85 winning tickets. T/Qpdt: £22.90 to a £1 stake. Pool: £4,466.50. 144.20 winning tickets. LM

## 4698 CATTERICK (L-H)

Wednesday, August 25

**5041 Meeting Abandoned** - Waterlogged

5047 - 5050a (Foreign Racing) - See Raceform Interactive

## 4936 LINGFIELD (L-H)

Thursday, August 26

**OFFICIAL GOING: Turf course - good (good to soft in places); all-weather - standard**

Wind: almost nil Weather: bright

### 5051 HAYS MONTROSE NOVICE STKS — 7f (P)

2:20 (2:22) (D ) 2-Y-O — £3,562 (£1,096; £548; £274) Stalls Low

Form — RPR

3 **1** **Linngari (IRE)**[22] 4461 2-8-12 ... KFallon 5 — 90
(SirMichaelStoute) *lw: pressed ldr: pushed into ld wl over 1f out: shkn up ins fnl f: readily* — **3/1**[3]

316 **2** ½ **Raza Cab (IRE)**[9] 4835 2-9-2 90 ... DHolland 6 — 93
(GAHuffer) *cl up: chsd ldng pair over 2f out: drvn to press wnr ins fnl f: styd on but a hld* — **5/2**[2]

411 **3** 1¼ **Hypnotic**[17] 4601 2-9-6 96 ... JMackay 2 — 94
(SirMarkPrescott) *led: rdn and hdd wl over 1f out: one pce after* — **2/1**[1]

35 **4** 2 **Bunny Rabbit (USA)**[27] 4295 2-8-12 ... MHills 7 — 81
(BJMeehan) *racd wd: trckd ldng pair tl outpcd over 2f out: pushed along and one pce after* — **11/2**

**5** 2½ **Takhleed (USA)** 2-8-8 ... RHills 4 — 71
(MPTregoning) *lengthy: scope: bit bkwd: s.i.s: rn green in last trio: outpcd over 2f out: one pce after* — **16/1**

**6** 1 **Aberdeen (IRE)** 2-8-8 ... JFEgan 3 — 68
(PMitchell) *w'like: bit bkwd: trckd ldrs: n.m.r on inner over 2f out: lost pl and grad fdd* — **50/1**

0 **7** 2½ **Antonio Stradivari (IRE)**[33] 4117 2-8-12 ... MartinDwyer 1 — 66
(AMBalding) *s.i.s: in tch in last trio: pushed along and no prog over 2f out: wknd over 1f out* — **33/1**

**8** 5 **Turtle Bay** 2-8-3 ... EStack 8 — 45
(APJarvis) *w'like: leggy: a last: lost tch 3f out* — **66/1**

1m 25.5s (-0.44) **Going Correction** -0.125s/f (Stan) — **8** Ran SP% **114.6**

Speed ratings: **97,96,95,92,89 88,85,80**CSF £10.90 TOTE £4.00: £1.60, £1.20, £1.10; EX 14.70.

**Owner** H H Aga Khan **Bred** His Highness The Aga Khan's Studs S C **Trained** Newmarket, Suffolk

**FOCUS**

A decent-looking juvenile novice event, notable for a dynamic betting market as much as what happened on the track, although the form, rated through the third, looks solid. There seemed to be a bias towards those that raced up with the pace and that was true throughout the meeting.

**NOTEBOOK**

**Linngari(IRE)** ◆ stepped up considerably on his debut when third of four in a slowly-run novice event at Yarmouth. Never far away, he took over from the favourite turning for home and kept on strongly to repel the late effort of the runner-up. The way he won this, and his pedigree, suggests he will appreciate further and he should continue to progress.

**Raza Cab(IRE)**, sixth in the Acomb since his course-and-distance maiden victory which has worked out very well, was clawing the winner back all the way to the line and on this showing is another that will appreciate further.

**Hypnotic**, bidding for a course-and-distance hat-trick, had the run of the race out in front, but found the front pair too strong and there seemed no real excuse.

**Bunny Rabbit(USA)**, weak on the exchanges but backed on-course, was bred to appreciate the switch to sand but was comfortably shaken off over the last couple of furlongs. He has faced stiff tasks in all three of his starts to date and may need to drop into maiden company.

**Takhleed(USA)**, a half-brother to a winner in the US, is bred to appreciate the sand but faced a stiff task on this racecourse debut. He did best of the three newcomers, if never able to land a blow, but ought to improve for the experience.

**Aberdeen(IRE)** was another to face a stiff task on this debut, but showed enough to suggest a race can be found if his sights are lowered.

### 5052 CASTLEMAINE XXXX NURSERY — 7f (P)

2:50 (2:53) (E ) 2-Y-O — £3,601 (£1,108; £554; £277) Stalls Low

Form — RPR

611 **1** **Cupid's Glory**[5] 4933 2-10-0 97 7ex ... JMackay 5 — 103
(SirMarkPrescott) *w ldr: led over 2f out: drvn and pressed ent fnl f: styd on strly* — **7/4**[1]

4230 **2** 1½ **Langston Boy**[49] 3677 2-8-1 70 ... JQuinn 7 — 72
(MLWBell) *lw: trckd ldrs gng wl: prog to chse wnr over 1f out: rdn to chal ent fnl f: sn no imp* — **20/1**

003 **3** 1¼ **Wise Dennis**[21] 4494 2-8-9 78 ... EStack 1 — 77
(APJarvis) *s.s: hld up wl in rr: gng wl 3f out: prog 2f out: hrd rdn and r.o fnl f: nrst fin* — **20/1**

31 **4** 1¼ **Wedding Party**[17] 4599 2-8-11 80 ... KFallon 4 — 76
(MrsAJPerrett) *led after 2f: drvn and hdd over 2f out: wknd ins fnl f* — **15/8**[2]

356 **5** 1¾ **Hawridge King**[18] 4579 2-8-1 70 ... DKinsella 2 — 62
(WSKittow) *reluctant to enter stalls: racd midfield: prog on inner to chse clr ldrs 2f out: kpt on same pce after* — **33/1**

1052 **6** 4 **Lateral Thinker (IRE)**[17] 4601 2-8-2 71 ... MartinDwyer 6 — 53
(JAOsborne) *lw: led for 2f: styd prom tl wknd wl over 1f out* — **11/1**

2050 **7** nk **Clinet (IRE)**[34] 4089 2-8-0 69 oh2 ow2 ... CCatlin 11 — 50
(PMPhelan) *dwlt: racd on outer and wl in rr: pushed along 3f out: c wd bnd 2f out: kpt on: n.d* — **40/1**

4104 **8** nk **Time For You**[14] 4671 2-7-9 67 oh1 ... FPFerris(3) 8 — 47
(PJMcbride) *racd midfield: drvn to chse ldrs 1/2-way: sn no imp: wknd over 1f out* — **25/1**

030 **9** nk **Dreemon**[40] 3931 2-8-5 74 ... JFEgan 9 — 53
(BRMillman) *lw: plld hrd early: sn in last trio: rdn 4f out: struggling after* — **33/1**

15 **10** ½ **Bridge T'The Stars**[19] 4541 2-8-7 76 ... SCarson 3 — 54
(RFJohnsonHoughton) *s.i.s: wl in rr: last 3f out: kpt on fnl f: no ch* — **33/1**

16 **11** 1½ **Nightfall (USA)**[18] 4581 2-9-3 86 ... (t) LDettori 10 — 60
(SaeedBinSuroor) *drvn to go prom on outer: u.p 1/2-way: wknd 2f out* — **10/1**[3]

2024 **12** nk **Scrooby Baby**[10] 4797 2-8-6 75 ... DHolland 12 — 49
(JAOsborne) *a towards rr: no ch over 2f out* — **20/1**

223 **13** 2 **Connotation**[23] 4413 2-8-0 69 ... AMcCarthy 14 — 38
(PWD'Arcy) *racd midfield: drvn to chse ldrs 1/2-way: wknd over 2f out* — **16/1**

0340 **14** nk **Lady Ann Summers (USA)**[12] 4752 2-8-1 73 ... (p) JFMcDonald(3) 13 — 41
(BJMeehan) *racd midfield: u.p bef 1/2-way: sn btn* — **20/1**

1m 25.28s (-0.66) **Going Correction** -0.125s/f (Stan) — **14** Ran SP% **128.6**

Speed ratings: **98,96,94,93,91 86,86,86,85,85 83,83,80,80**CSF £46.40 CT £603.22 TOTE £2.50: £1.40, £4.20, £5.40; EX 72.00.

**Owner** Hesmonds Stud **Bred** Cheveley Park Stud Ltd **Trained** Newmarket, Suffolk

**FOCUS**

A competitive-looking nursery on paper, but just a two-horse race according to the betting. A strong pace resulted in a slightly faster time than in the opener and not that many managed to get into it.

**NOTEBOOK**

**Cupid's Glory** ◆, stepping up a furlong in trip and carrying a 7lb penalty, completed the hat-trick in good style, and the fact that he had such a big weight and was involved in a speed duel early makes this effort all the more commendable. He looks worth stepping up in class now.

**Langston Boy**, making his sand debut, had been gelded since his last outing and the operation seems to have done him no harm judged on this effort. He even looked like picking off the winner a furlong from home, but found his rival just too determined. There should be a race in him.

**Wise Dennis** ◆ completely fluffed the start, so did extremely well to finish so close and was really motoring at the end, just as he was at Yarmouth on his previous start. Another making his sand debut, he has the ability to win races and is one to keep a close eye on.

**Wedding Party** the only danger to the favourite according to the market, was involved in the early battle for the lead, but faded in the last furlong after appearing to have every chance.

**Hawridge King**, stepping down a furlong, made a more than satisfactory sand debut and could find a race on this surface, though he has looked a difficult ride on occasions.

**Lateral Thinker(IRE)** probably paid for trying to go with the early pace.

**Nightfall(USA)** appears to have gone backwards.

### 5053 CASTLEMAINE XXXX MEDIAN AUCTION MAIDEN STKS (DIV I) — 6f (P)

3:20 (3:21) (E ) 2-Y-O — £3,503 (£1,078; £539; £269) Stalls Low

Form — RPR

63 **1** **Toffee Vodka (IRE)**[29] 4231 2-8-9 ... RHills 1 — 69
(JWHills) *mde all: drvn and hrd pressed fnl f: hld on* — **3/1**[1]

000 **2** hd **Corniche Dancer**[18] 4579 2-8-9 ... TEDurcan 5 — 68
(MRChannon) *dwlt: settled in rr: prog 2f out: rdn and r.o wl fnl f: jst failed* — **66/1**

6 **3** shd **Chicken Soup**[21] 4487 2-9-0 ... DHolland 9 — 73
(JAOsborne) *hld up bhd ldrs gng wl: effrt over 1f out: drvn to press wnr ins fnl f: nt qckn nr fin* — **9/2**[2]

3 **4** nk **Flying Dancer**[24] 4399 2-8-9 ... JDSmith 7 — 67
(AKing) *prom: trckd wnr 1/2-way: drvn to chal 1f out: nt qckn ins fnl f* **5/1**[3]

**5** 2½ **Beauchamp Turbo** 2-9-0 ... LDettori 3 — 65
(GAButler) *lengthy: unf: bit bkwd: b.hind: settled in rr: shkn up 2f out: no prog tl styd on fnl f: nvr nrr* — **10/1**

06 **6** 1 **Go Mo (IRE)**[17] 4611 2-9-0 ... JFEgan 4 — 62
(SKirk) *lw: w ldrs to 2f out: fdd u.p fnl f* — **6/1**

**7** 3 **Depressed** 2-8-9 ... SDrowne 6 — 48
(AndrewReid) *b: b.hind: w'like: dwlt: sn trckd ldrs: cl up 2f out: wknd and eased fnl f* — **25/1**

55 **8** 1 **Insignia (IRE)**[21] 4481 2-9-0 ... JFortune 11 — 50
(JHMGosden) *settled in rr: outpcd 2f out: shuffled along and nvr nr ldrs after: do bttr* — **25/1**

2 **9** 3½ **Killington (IRE)**[15] 4643 2-9-0 ... (t) SWKelly 2 — 39
(GAButler) *dwlt: plld hrd and sn cl up: stl taking t.k.h over 2f out: shkn up and wknd wl over 1f out* — **12/1**

**10** ¾ **Foxy Gwynne** 2-8-9 ... MartinDwyer 10 — 32
(AMBalding) *leggy: scope: s.s: v green and sn t.o: styd on fr over 1f out* — **50/1**

00 **11** hd **Eden Star (IRE)**[17] 4611 2-8-9 ... DaneO'Neill 8 — 31
(DKIvory) *pressed wnr to 1/2-way: wknd 2f out* — **66/1**

**12** 5 **Storm Chase (USA)** 2-9-0 ... KFallon 12 — 21
(APJarvis) *w'like: bit bkwd: rn green and sn bdly outpcd: a bhd* — **6/1**

1m 13.84s (0.92) **Going Correction** -0.125s/f (Stan) — **12** Ran SP% **117.8**

Speed ratings: **88,87,87,87,83 82,78,77,72,71 71,64**CSF £246.18 TOTE £5.10: £1.80, £17.40, £2.00; EX 377.10.

**Owner** G And Mrs L Woodward **Bred** Mrs K Smyth **Trained** Upper Lambourn, Berks

**FOCUS**

An interesting-looking maiden with some big yards represented, but a blanket could have covered the first four home, so the form may not be that strong - but looks solid formnow - and the time was nearly a second slower than the second division.

**NOTEBOOK**

**Toffee Vodka(IRE)**, who had missed the break in both her previous starts, started well this time from her rails draw and made just about all the running before showing real determination to hold off her nearest challengers late on. This looked to be as far as she wants and she is now likely to head for the Sales race at the St Leger meeting.

**Corniche Dancer**, beaten out of sight in three starts on turf, improved beyond all recognition on this sand debut and very nearly got up to win. She looks well worth another try on the surface, though her proximity does not do much for the form.

**Chicken Soup**, highly regarded by his trainer, had every chance and was not beaten far, but does not look anything special on the evidence so far.

**Flying Dancer** ran another solid race on this sand debut and might do even better once handicapped.

**Beauchamp Turbo** ◆ stayed on without being by any means knocked about and did best of the newcomers. He should come on quite a bit for this.

**Go Mo(IRE)** did not necessarily improve for the switch to sand.

**Depressed** is a full-sister to two winners on Polytrack, and on this showing she has a good chance of joining them at some stage.

**Killington(IRE)** was very disappointing after taking a fierce hold early.

**Foxy Gwynne** *Official explanation: jockey said filly was slowly away and resented kickback*

### 5054 CASTLEMAINE XXXX MEDIAN AUCTION MAIDEN STKS (DIV II) — 6f (P)

3:50 (3:53) (E ) 2-Y-O — £3,503 (£1,078; £539; £269) Stalls Low

Form — RPR

432 **1** **Tremar**[8] 4844 2-9-0 ... GCarter 1 — 85
(TGMills) *lw: mde all: shkn up and drew clr over 1f out: in command fnl f* — **5/4**[1]

03 **2** 2 **Fantaisiste**[21] 4468 2-8-9 ... JMackay 2 — 74
(SirMarkPrescott) *w wnr to over 1f out: shkn up and unable qck: one pce after* — **12/1**

405 **3** ½ **Prince Samos (IRE)**[8] 4844 2-9-0 ... KFallon 9 — 78
(RHannon) *trckd ldrs: pushed along 1/2-way: rdn and one pce over 1f out* — **6/1**[3]

230 **4** hd **Beautiful Mover (USA)**[59] 3382 2-8-9 76 ... RHills 12 — 72
(JWHills) *lw: reluctant to enter stalls: racd midfield: prog 2f out: rdn and styd on same pce fnl f* — **10/1**

**5** 2½ **Optimus (USA)** 2-9-0 ... LDettori 6 — 69
(GAButler) *w'like: scope: bit bkwd: racd midfield: pushed along and outpcd 2f out: hanging over 1f out: styd on ins fnl f* — **7/2**[2]

4023 **6** 3/4 **Lakesdale (IRE)**[13] [4699] 2-8-9 59 ... OUrbina 10 62
(MissDMountain) *pressed ldrs: rdn over 2f out: wknd fnl f* **25/1**

**7** 1 1/2 **Beauchamp Trump** 2-9-0 ... SWKelly 7 63
(GAButler) *w'like: bit bkwd: dwlt: racd towards rr: rdn over 2f out: one pce and no imp on ldrs* **25/1**

**8** 3 1/2 **Secret Affair** 2-9-0 ... JDSmith 4 52
(AKing) *a in rr: outpcd in last pair and wl bhd 1/2-way: no ch after* **12/1**

**9** 1 1/4 **Savoy Chapel** 2-9-0 ... DHolland 8 48
(JAOsborne) *w'like: leggy: bit bkwd: dwlt: rn green and a in rr: struggling over 2f out* **20/1**

**10** nk **Edge Of Italy** 2-8-9 ... CCatlin 11 43
(KBell) *w'like: dwlt: hanging rt thrght: bhd fr 1/2-way: rn wd bnd 2f out* **50/1**

4046 **11** 1 1/4 **Gogetter Girl**[90] [2458] 2-8-9 68 ... NCallan 5 39
(JGallagher) *t.k.h early: chsd ldrs tl wknd rapidly 2f out* **25/1**

**12** 7 **Takemetoyourheart** 2-8-9 ... PDoe 3 18
(IAWood) *neat: bit bkwd: dwlt: rn v green and a bhd: t.o* **40/1**

1m 12.98s (0.06) **Going Correction** -0.125s/f (Stan) **12 Ran SP% 126.1**
Speed ratings: **94,91,90,90,87 86,84,79,77,77 75,66**CSF £18.54 TOTE £2.10: £1.10, £3.10, £1.40; EX 10.90.
**Owner** T Jacobs **Bred** Mrs Mary Taylor **Trained** Headley, Surrey

**FOCUS**
Almost certainly the stronger of the two divisions and the time was nearly a second quicker than the first and, although fairly reliable form, is still only average for the grade.

**NOTEBOOK**
**Tremar ◆**, who had shown decent form in three soft-ground maidens on turf, especially when bustling up a well-regarded sort at Kempton last time, bounced out of the stalls from his inside draw and made every yard to score with ease. He seems to be improving and can make his mark at a higher level.
**Fantaisiste**, stepping back a furlong, stalked the winner the whole way but in the final dash for home it proved no contest. She may need to go back up in trip.
**Prince Samos(IRE)**, below form in two soft-ground contests on turf after a promising debut on fast ground, seemed to appreciate this sounder surface. An extra furlong and nurseries may be his best option now.
**Beautiful Mover(USA)** threatened to get into it starting up the home straight, but her effort flattened out in the closing stages. She is beginning to look exposed.
**Optimus(USA) ◆** took a while to realise what was required, but was doing some decent work in the home straight and is sure to improve.
**Gogetter Girl** *Official explanation: jockey said filly had hung right throughout*

## 5055 LINGFIELD-RACECOURSE.CO.UK H'CAP 7f (P)
4:20 (4:23) (D ) (0-85,85) 3-Y-O+ **£6,922** (£2,130; £1,065; £532) **Stalls** Low

Form RPR

5320 **1** **Distant Connection (IRE)**[28] [4268] 3-9-9 **85** ... KFallon 13 103+
(APJarvis) *trckd ldr: led wl over 2f out: clr over 1f out: comf* **4/1**[1]

2010 **2** 2 1/2 **Obrigado (USA)**[19] [4558] 4-9-11 **82** ... SWKelly 8 89
(WJHaggas) *b.hind: swtg: led to wl over 2f out: no ch w wnr fr over 1f out: jst hld on for 2nd* **16/1**

0125 **3** hd **Doctorate**[56] [3452] 3-9-7 **83** ... EAhern 5 89
(EALDunlop) *lw: trckd ldrs: effrt 2f out: drvn to chal for 2nd pl fnl f: one pce* **6/1**[2]

-520 **4** 1 3/4 **Point Of Dispute**[14] [4690] 9-9-8 **79** ...(v) JFortune 4 80+
(PJMakin) *b.hind: dwlt: hld up wl in rr: effrt 2f out: nt clr run and swtchd lft over 1f out: r.o fnl f* **12/1**

6005 **5** 3/4 **Binanti**[14] [4690] 4-9-12 **83** ...(v) JQuinn 3 83
(PRChamings) *b: racd midfield: rdn over 2f out: hanging u.p over 1f out: kpt on* **12/1**

3500 **6** 1 1/4 **H Harrison (IRE)**[5] [4931] 4-9-5 **79** ... LFletcher(3) 6 75
(IWMcinnes) *prom: rdn over 3f out: outpcd u.p 2f out: fdd fnl f* **20/1**

3063 **7** shd **Hard To Catch (IRE)**[20] [4522] 6-9-1 **77** ... MSavage(5) 11 73
(DKIvory) *s.i.s: racd towards rr: rdn and sme prog 2f out: n.d* **20/1**

6106 **8** nk **Tre Colline**[19] [4549] 5-9-7 **78** ... RMullen 12 73
(NTinkler) *sn in midfield: rdn over 2f out: fdd over 1f out* **9/1**

2030 **9** nk **Flying Express**[25] [4360] 4-9-12 **83** ... MHills 2 77
(BWHills) *lw: settled towards rr: shuffled along on inner 2f out: nvr on terms* **14/1**

0303 **10** 3/4 **Miss George**[8] [4847] 6-10-0 **85** ... DaneO'Neill 9 77
(DKIvory) *sn pressed ldrs: cl up over 2f out: wknd wl over 1f out* **9/1**

2600 **11** 1/2 **Mallard (IRE)**[22] [4447] 6-9-6 **77** ... MFenton 14 68
(JGGiven) *racd wd: hld up wl in rr: nvr a factor* **10/1**

0054 **12** 3 1/2 **Cheese 'n Biscuits**[4] [4969] 4-9-7 **78** ...(p) RLMoore 1 60
(GLMoore) *dwlt: a in rr: no ch fnl 2f* **11/1**

-503 **13** 1/2 **Last Appointment (USA)**[19] [4549] 4-9-8 **79** ... DHolland 7 60
(JMPEustace) *lw: prom: rdn and wknd over 2f out* **13/2**[3]

5-56 **14** 2 **High Finance (IRE)**[96] [2282] 4-9-6 **77** ... RHills 10 53
(JWHills) *a towards rr: struggling over 2f out* **33/1**

1m 24.37s (-1.57) **Going Correction** -0.125s/f (Stan)
**WFA** 3 from 4yo+ 5lb **14 Ran SP% 125.4**
Speed ratings: **103,100,99,97,97 95,95,95,94,93 93,89,88,86**CSF £72.89 CT £405.85 TOTE £5.40: £2.50, £5.60, £2.10; EX 128.20.
**Owner** Mrs Ann Jarvis **Bred** Mrs C F Van Straubenzee And Partners **Trained** Twyford, Bucks

**FOCUS**
A competitive handicap and the form looks fair but sound. However, at this meeting it was proving crucial to be up with the pace and again very few managed to get into it. The first two home were the front pair throughout.

**NOTEBOOK**
**Distant Connection(IRE) ◆**, making his sand debut, managed to get across from his high draw to hold a handy position and, when asked to go and win his race, quickly put plenty of daylight between himself and his rivals. He was value for a lot more than the official margin and can win again.
**Obrigado(USA)**, also making his sand debut and with the visor left off this time, tried to make all the running and, even though the winner proved far too good, he managed to hold on for second. The way the track was riding was a help to him though, and he has not always looked straightforward in the past.
**Doctorate**, the least-exposed in the field, was yet another making his sand debut and ran with plenty of credit. There should be a race for him on this surface.
**Point Of Dispute** was the only one to make up any significant ground from off the pace and finished in fine style. Under normal circumstances this would have been an eye-catching effort, but he is a notoriously awkward ride so it would be unwise to get too carried away by this.
**Binanti** is a winner on Fibresand, but this was his best effort on Polytrack on his third attempt. He is well handicapped at present, but does look a better horse on turf.
**Last Appointment(USA)** had every chance coming to the final bend, but already looked to be struggling when appearing to get a bump and briefly lose his footing about two furlongs from home.

## 5056 CASTLEMAINE XXXX (S) STKS 1m 3f 106y
4:50 (4:52) (G ) 3-Y-O+ **£2,933** (£838; £419) **Stalls** High

Form RPR

610- **1** **Perelandra (USA)**[304] [5795] 4-9-0 75 ... KFallon 6 63+
(MJWallace) *trckd ldng pair: led over 2f out: shkn up wl over 1f out: sn drew clr* **9/4**[1]

0-11 **2** 7 **Barton Sands (IRE)**[15] [4655] 7-9-11 69 ... DHolland 2 66+
(JJay) *lw: hld up in last: prog 5f out: effrt to join wnr 2f out: sn shkn up and btn: wknd fnl f* **9/4**[1]

3014 **3** 2 1/2 **Ambersong**[21] [4476] 6-9-11 51 ... JFortune 3 59
(AWCarroll) *s.s: sn in midfield: outpcd over 3f out: kpt on to take modest 3rd over 1f out* **7/1**[3]

1410 **4** 5 **Rolex Free (ARG)**[5] [4934] 6-9-11 51 ...(v) EAhern 5 51
(DFlood) *mde most to over 2f out: steadily wknd* **4/1**[2]

0-05 **5** 3/4 **Blue Streak (IRE)**[22] [4433] 7-9-5 45 ...(b) RLMoore 7 44
(GLMoore) *rousted along early to join ldr: ev ch 3f out: wknd over 2f out* **14/1**

-520 **6** 9 **White Park Bay (IRE)**[31] [4189] 4-8-7 54 ... MHalford(7) 8 24
(MissSuzySmith) *in tch: outpcd 4f out: wknd 3f out* **12/1**

000 **7** 3 1/2 **Environment Audit**[17] [3387] 5-8-12 60 ...(v) JJeffrey(7) 1 24
(JRJenkins) *t.k.h: hld up in rr: outpcd 4f out: sn wknd* **20/1**

0-0 **8** dist **Splendid Touch**[227] [500] 4-9-0 35 ... RMullen 4 —
(JRJenkins) *b: rrd s: plld hrd: chsd ldrs tl wknd rapidly over 5f out: t.o* **50/1**

2m 33.97s (4.45) **Going Correction** +0.35s/f (Good) **8 Ran SP% 115.1**
Speed ratings: **97,91,90,86,85 79,76,—**CSF £7.24 TOTE £3.60: £1.20, £1.10, £2.30; EX 5.00.The winner was bought in for 17,000gns. Barton Sands was claimed by Mr A. S. Reid for £6,000.
**Owner** Lucayan Stud **Bred** Heatherwold Stud **Trained** Newmarket, Suffolk

**FOCUS**
An ordinary turf seller and few in the field had a realistic chance at the weights. The third provides the line to the form.

**NOTEBOOK**
**Perelandra(USA)** would have been conceding upwards of 8lb to her rivals had this been a handicap. Making her debut for the yard and racing for the first time in ten months, the only question was whether she retained enough ability. However, she looked fit and the market-confidence was proved right as she absolutely bolted up. Connections had to go to 17,000gns to buy her back, so they must believe she can win again in better company.
**Barton Sands(IRE)**, bidding for a hat-trick, would probably have preferred faster ground but still ran with credit. He can be counted unlucky to have run into one such as the winner, but beat the others well enough and should be able to find another modest contest.
**Ambersong** at least had some recent winning form to his name and did about as well as could be expected considering he would have been 35lb better off with the winner in a handicap.
**Rolex Free(ARG)** set the pace as usual, but was very easily picked off. His best recent efforts have been on sand and he has run poorly every time he has encountered soft ground under both codes.
**Blue Streak(IRE)** remains out of form both on the Flat and over hurdles.
**Splendid Touch** *Official explanation: jockey said filly had a breathing problem*

## 5057 CASTLEMAINE XXXX H'CAP 1m 2f
5:20 (5:21) (E ) (0-75,74) 3-Y-O **£3,610** (£1,111; £555; £277) **Stalls** Low

Form RPR

0023 **1** **Willhego**[33] [4128] 3-8-4 **57** ... MartinDwyer 3 67
(JRBest) *mde all: hrd pressed fnl 2f: drvn and hld on* **8/1**

1033 **2** 3/4 **Magic Sting**[15] [4628] 3-8-10 **68** ... HayleyTurner(5) 1 77
(MLWBell) *lw: hld up in tch: prog on inner to trck ldng pair over 2f out: nt qckn over 1f out: swtchd rt and kpt on to take 2nd nr fi* **11/2**[2]

1000 **3** hd **Planters Punch (IRE)**[41] [3917] 3-9-0 **67** ... KFallon 13 76
(RHannon) *trckd wnr: drvn to chal over 2f out: nt qckn over 1f out: lost 2nd nr fin* **12/1**

5263 **4** 3 **General Flumpa**[15] [4655] 3-8-11 **64** ... RMullen 4 67
(CFWall) *hld up in rr: prog on inner 3f out: rdn and kpt on same pce fnl 2f* **8/1**

3013 **5** 1 1/4 **Fuel Cell (IRE)**[15] [4648] 3-9-3 **70** ...(b) RLMoore 8 71+
(RHannon) *hld up in rr: effrt on outer 3f out: hanging and reluctant but kpt on u.p: n.d* **5/1**[1]

5000 **6** 2 **Amwell Brave**[83] [2665] 3-8-0 **56** ... JFMcDonald(3) 5 53
(JRJenkins) *hld up in last pair: sme prog on inner 3f out: one pce and nvr rchd ldrs last 2f* **25/1**

5304 **7** 1 1/2 **Carriacou**[8] [4848] 3-8-7 **63** ... LPKeniry(3) 6 57
(PWD'Arcy) *s.i.s: t.k.h and hld up in last pair: one pce and no imp ldrs fnl 3f* **10/1**

4004 **8** 1 **Anduril**[14] [4680] 3-8-10 **63** ... JFEgan 11 55
(JMPEustace) *s.i.s: sn in midfield: rdn 3f out: no prog and btn sn after* **16/1**

0424 **9** 3 **Uncle John**[32] [4167] 3-8-7 **60** ... PDobbs 2 46
(SKirk) *trckd ldng pair: hrd rdn over 3f out: sn wknd* **14/1**

1003 **10** 6 **Waziri (IRE)**[13] [4719] 3-9-7 **74** ... SDrowne 7 49
(HMorrison) *trckd ldrs: rdn over 3f out: wknd over 2f out* **8/1**

0341 **11** 3/4 **Thirteen Tricks (USA)**[23] [4417] 3-9-7 **74** ... EAhern 12 47
(MrsAJPerrett) *racd in midfield: lost pl and pushed along 5f out: struggling fnl 3f* **13/2**[3]

00-5 **12** shd **Rhetorical**[19] [4562] 3-8-4 **57** ...(b[1]) JMackay 9 30
(SirMarkPrescott) *pushed up to go prom: rdn 4f out: wknd 3f out* **12/1**

-204 **13** 1 3/4 **Al Shuua**[58] [3392] 3-9-7 **74** ... DHolland 10 44
(CEBrittain) *settled in rr: wknd 3f out* **16/1**

2m 12.78s (3.18) **Going Correction** +0.35s/f (Good) **13 Ran SP% 125.5**
Speed ratings: **101,100,100,97,96 95,94,93,90,86 85,85,83**CSF £54.29 CT £545.42 TOTE £7.60: £2.60, £2.70, £3.40; EX 65.10 Place 6 £10.30, Place 5 £8.98.
**Owner** G G Racing **Bred** J R Wills **Trained** Hucking, Kent

**FOCUS**
A modest three-year-old handicap and, as was the case on the Polytrack, it was important to race up with the pace. Despite that, the form looks sound.

**NOTEBOOK**
**Willhego** made every yard of the running to get off the mark at the eighth attempt and transfer his recent improvement on Polytrack back on to turf. He seems to have progressed since being stepped up to this sort of trip and there may be a bit more to come.
**Magic Sting**, a winner over this trip in soft ground, may have been a bit unlucky as he did not have much room against the inside rail in the home straight, especially in the last 50 yards. He has the ability to win off this mark.
**Planters Punch(IRE)**, who was always up with the pace, had every chance and certainly ran better with the visor left off. He had previously shown very little with cut in the ground.
**General Flumpa** ran with credit, but remains a maiden after nine attempts.
**Fuel Cell(IRE)**, racing on a softish surface for the first time, tried to make ground from off the pace but, under these conditions, that was proving very difficult.
**Waziri(IRE)**, back on a winning mark and racing over his best trip, was disappointing even allowing for the ground being softer than ideal.

**Thirteen Tricks(USA)** was disappointing, but reportedly spread a plate during the race. *Official explanation: trainer said filly spread a plate*
T/Plt: £23.10 to a £1 stake. Pool: £38,366.25. 1,207.65 winning tickets. T/Qpdt: £9.60 to a £1 stake. Pool: £2,873.50. 220.50 winning tickets. JN

# 4275 MUSSELBURGH (R-H)

Thursday, August 26

**OFFICIAL GOING: Good to firm (straight course - good in places; round course - firm in places)**

## 5058 RACING UK APPRENTICE H'CAP — 1m 6f

**2:30** (2:30) (E) (0-70,67) 3-Y-O+ — **£3,393** (£1,044; £522; £261) **Stalls** High

| Form | Pos | Dist | Horse / Trainer / Comment | Jockey | SP | RPR |
|---|---|---|---|---|---|---|
| 0333 | **1** | | **Red Forest (IRE)**[23] 4424 5-9-8 **61** (JMackie) *trckd ldrs: led over 2f out: drvn out* | (t) DNolan 3 | **5/1**[1] | 74 |
| 3-00 | **2** | *1¾* | **Turn Of Phrase (IRE)**[30] 4210 5-9-1 **54** (RAFahey) *hld up: hdwy to chse wnr over 1f out: kpt on ins last* | (v1) THamilton 7 | **15/2**[3] | 65 |
| 4000 | **3** | *3* | **Redspin (IRE)**[22] 4457 4-9-4 **60** (JSMoore) *hld up: hdwy centre 2f outt: no imp fnl f* | DerekNolan(3) 8 | **20/1** | 66 |
| 0000 | **4** | *1¾* | **Zan Lo (IRE)**[24] 4397 4-8-5 **44** (BSRothwell) *hld up midfield: drvn over 2f out: kpt on fnl f: nrst fin* | TEaves 1 | **25/1** | 48 |
| 0312 | **5** | *shd* | **Cosmic Case**[26] 4328 9-8-10 **49** (JSGoldie) *hld up midfield: effrt over 2f out: no imp over 1f out* | NMackay 11 | **8/1** | 53 |
| 052 | **6** | *nk* | **Sherwood Forest**[28] 4275 4-8-2 **44** (MissLAPerratt) *cl up tl rdn and no ex fr 2f out* | (v) LeanneKershaw(3) 2 | **14/1** | 47 |
| 6606 | **7** | *1* | **Millennium Hall**[3] 4990 5-9-9 **62** (PMonteith) *hld up: rdn over 2f out: nvr rchd ldrs* | PMulrennan 9 | **11/1** | 64 |
| 0000 | **8** | *¾* | **Repulse Bay (IRE)**[6] 4901 6-8-7 **46** (JSGoldie) *keen: trckd ldrs: effrt and edgd rt 2f out: sn btn* | LisaJones 6 | **12/1** | 47 |
| 0024 | **9** | *2* | **Bold Blade**[15] 4636 3-8-4 **60** (MJPolglase) *keen and sddle slipped sn after s: led to over 2f out: sn btn* | KGhunowa(5) 10 | **16/1** | 58 |
| 3032 | **10** | *¾* | **Claradotnet**[18] 4578 4-9-10 **63** (MRChannon) *hld up midfield: rdn over 2f out: btn over 1f out* | SHitchcott 5 | **7/1**[2] | 60 |
| 3521 | **11** | *3* | **Romil Star (GER)**[13] 4698 7-8-8 **54** (KRBurke) *in tch: rdn over 2f out: sn btn* | (v) SBushby(7) 12 | **11/1** | 47 |
| 0422 | **12** | *dist* | **Alpine Special (IRE)**[9] 4830 3-8-9 **67** (PCHaslam) *keen and sddle slipped sn after s: pressed ldr to over 3f out: sn btn and eased* | GBartley(7) 4 | **15/2**[3] | — |

3m 5.75s (0.15) **Going Correction** +0.025s/f (Good)
**WFA** 3 from 4yo+ 12lb — **12** Ran SP% **109.3**
Speed ratings: **100,99,97,96,96 96,95,95,93,93 91,**—CSF £37.43 CT £623.12 TOTE £5.40: £2.30, £3.00, £4.30; EX 62.70.
**Owner** P Riley **Bred** Olympic B'Stock Ltd, Freynestown B'Stock And B Hi **Trained** Church Broughton, Derbys

**FOCUS**
An moderate handicap and the form is ordinary for the grade.

**NOTEBOOK**
**Red Forest(IRE)** looked high enough in the weights beforehand, but he had proven his stamina over this trip on his last start and has a respectable strike-rate for a modest performer. Fast ground suits him well, although he has shown he acts on soft going in the past.
**Turn Of Phrase(IRE)** turned in a respectable effort in the first-time visor. His stable is in cracking form at present.
**Redspin(IRE)** ran well enough but he continues to find winning difficult, despite having dropped 15lb in the handicap since the start of the turf season.
**Zan Lo(IRE)** is another who has dropped a long way in the handicap during the course of this season, 21lb to be exact, and she appeared suited by the step up in trip.
**Cosmic Case**, five times a previous course winner, would have been suited by a stronger all-round gallop.
**Bold Blade** *Official explanation: jockey said saddle slipped*
**Alpine Special(IRE)** *Official explanation: jockey said saddle slipped*

## 5059 DM HALL (S) STKS — 7f 30y

**3:00** (3:00) (E) 2-Y-O — **£6,903** (£2,124; £1,062; £531) **Stalls** Low

| Form | Pos | Dist | Horse / Trainer / Comment | Jockey | SP | RPR |
|---|---|---|---|---|---|---|
| 0402 | **1** | | **Toldo (IRE)**[13] 4699 2-8-11 53 (ABerry) *stmbld s: hdwy into midfield 1/2-way: nt clr run and swtchd over 1f out: hung lft and led wl ins fnl f: r.o* | FLynch 7 | **33/1** | 66 |
| 003 | **2** | *¾* | **Eskdale (IRE)**[5] 4930 2-8-11 (RFFisher) *chsd ldrs: drvn along 1/2-way: no imp tl rallied appr fnl f: kpt on* | RFfrench 6 | **8/1** | 64 |
| 6044 | **3** | *1¾* | **Zolash (IRE)**[15] 4638 2-8-4 65 (JSMoore) *midfield: effrt over 2f out: kpt on fnl f: no imp* | DerekNolan(7) 4 | **14/1** | 60 |
| 4403 | **4** | *¾* | **Indibraun (IRE)**[6] 4907 2-9-2 77 (PCHaslam) *w ldr: led 1/2-way to wl ins fnl f: no ex* | GFaulkner 3 | **5/1**[2] | 63 |
| 3030 | **5** | *1* | **Mytton's Bell (IRE)**[21] 4488 2-8-6 69 (ABailey) *chsd ldrs: effrt over 2f out: no ex ins fnl f* | DAllan 11 | **9/2**[1] | 50 |
| 640 | **6** | *hd* | **Royal Flynn**[41] 3918 2-8-6 70 (MDods) *hld up: rdn over 2f out: rallied over 1f out: styng on whn n.m.r wl ins last* | PMakin(5) 8 | **20/1** | 55 |
| 3650 | **7** | *shd* | **Twice Nightly**[22] 4445 2-8-11 66 (JDBethell) *led to 1/2-way: rallied and ev ch tl outpcd fnl f* | JFanning 10 | **6/1**[3] | 55 |
| 3056 | **8** | *½* | **Strathtay**[13] 4700 2-8-6 66 (PCHaslam) *hld up: effrt outside over 2f out: no imp over 1f out* | (p) KDarley 1 | **14/1** | 48 |
| 050 | **9** | *2* | **Mr Maxim**[53] 3560 2-8-11 (RMWhitaker) *in tch: rdn and edgd rt over 2f out: sn btn* | DeanMcKeown 12 | **16/1** | 48 |
| 6 | **10** | *2½* | **Purple Door**[16] 4621 2-8-6 (RMBeckett) *midfield: rdn over 2f out: sn outpcd* | FNorton 9 | **8/1** | 37 |
| 06 | **11** | *6* | **Blissphilly**[19] 4559 2-8-6 (RAFahey) *in tch tl rdn and wknd fr over 2f out* | PHanagan 14 | **16/1** | 22 |
| | **12** | *shd* | **Bronze Dancer (IRE)** 2-8-8 (GASwinbank) *bhd: rdn 1/2-way: n.d* | PMulrennan(3) 2 | **33/1** | 27 |
| 0 | **13** | *7* | **Wiltshire (IRE)**[6] 4922 2-8-11 (MRChannon) *hld up: rdn over 3f out: sn btn* | ACulhane 5 | **10/1** | 9 |
| 0 | **14** | *dist* | **La Providence**[3] 4999 2-8-6 (DWChapman) *keen: hld up ins: wknd fr 1/2-way* | (be) JBramhill 13 | **100/1** | — |

1m 30.18s (0.65) **Going Correction** +0.025s/f (Good) — **14** Ran SP% **117.2**
Speed ratings: **97,96,94,93,92 91,91,91,88,86 79,79,71,**—CSF £267.08 TOTE £22.30: £7.00, £3.40, £5.40; EX 324.00.The winner was bought in for 7,000gns.
**Owner** Anthony White **Bred** Mrs C A Moore **Trained** Cockerham, Lancs

**FOCUS**
There was a strong pace on here and the leaders fell in a hole. Despite this the form looks good for the grade.

**NOTEBOOK**
**Toldo(IRE)**, runner-up in a similar race last time out, had the race run to suit. He picked up well from mid-division as the leaders hit the wall, and went on to score with a bit in hand.
**Eskdale(IRE)**, dropping in grade from maiden company, clearly gets this trip well and was another suited by the way the race was run. He appeared to handle these quicker conditions perfectly well.
**Zolash(IRE)** looked a bit more exposed than some of the others coming into this, but he ran another sound race.
**Indibraun(IRE)** would have preferred an uncontested lead. As it was he was taken on for the lead and went too quick early on.
**Mytton's Bell(IRE)** had her chance but appeared to fail through lack of stamina.
**Twice Nightly**, dropping into a seller for the first time, was ridden differently this time. In the event he did too much too soon in front, being taken on for the lead, and he fell in a heap inside the final furlong.

## 5060 WATCH LIVE ON RACING UK NURSERY (H'CAP) — 5f

**3:30** (3:30) (D) 2-Y-O — **£6,890** (£2,120; £1,060; £530) **Stalls** Low

| Form | Pos | Dist | Horse / Trainer / Comment | Jockey | SP | RPR |
|---|---|---|---|---|---|---|
| 01 | **1** | | **Monashee Rose (IRE)**[24] 4388 2-8-2 **72** (JSMoore) *dwlt: hld up: hdwy 2f out: led ins fnl f: r.o wl* | NMackay(3) 7 | **9/2**[3] | 74 |
| 1563 | **2** | *nk* | **Wonderful Mind**[7] 4875 2-8-4 **71** (TDEasterby) *cl up: led over 2f out to ins fnl f: kpt on* | DAllan 4 | **7/2**[2] | 72 |
| 0340 | **3** | *hd* | **Llamadas**[33] 4131 2-7-12 **65** oh1 (MDods) *s.i.s and swtchd lft s: bhd: hdwy and hung rt fr over 1f out: fin strly* | (b1) PFessey 12 | **25/1** | 65 |
| 6056 | **4** | *nk* | **Handsome Lady**[20] 4508 2-8-7 **74** (ISemple) *chsd ldrs: effrt over 2f out: kpt on same pce fnl f* | PHanagan 11 | **12/1** | 73 |
| 130 | **5** | *2* | **Oh Dara (USA)**[12] 4744 2-9-7 **88** (PABlockley) *led to over 2f out: kpt on same pce over 1f out* | DeanMcKeown 9 | **7/1** | 80 |
| 5045 | **6** | *nk* | **Ochil Hills Dancer (IRE)**[26] 4330 2-7-5 **65** oh3 (ACrook) *sn outpcd: hdwy over 1f out: nrst fin* | (t) DFentiman(7) 10 | **50/1** | 56 |
| 306 | **7** | *nk* | **African Gift**[19] 4560 2-8-1 **68** (JGGiven) *bhd tl sme late hdwy: nvr rchd ldrs* | JBramhill 8 | **25/1** | 58 |
| 0224 | **8** | *1¼* | **Wizardmicktee (IRE)**[5] 4933 2-8-10 **77** (ABailey) *prom tl rdn and wknd over 1f out* | KDarley 6 | **14/1** | 63 |
| 1451 | **9** | *hd* | **Smiddy Hill**[31] 4197 2-9-1 **82** (RBastiman) *w ldrs: rdn and hung rt fr 2f out: btn ins fnl f* | RFfrench 3 | **11/4**[1] | 67 |
| 643 | **10** | *2* | **Ne Oublie**[17] 4607 2-8-0 **67** (JMackie) *sn outpcd: n.d* | DaleGibson 1 | **10/1** | 45 |
| P634 | **11** | *3* | **Shatin Leader**[24] 4388 2-8-0 **67** oh4 ow2 (MissLAPerratt) *in tch to 1/2-way: sn rdn and btn* | FNorton 2 | **25/1** | 35 |
| 3064 | **12** | *11* | **Nee Lemon Left**[3] 4986 2-7-12 **65** oh2 (ABerry) *sn outpcd: no ch fr 1/2-way* | (b1) LisaJones 5 | **33/1** | — |

60.97 secs (0.57) **Going Correction** -0.025s/f (Good) — **12** Ran SP% **119.5**
Speed ratings: **94,93,93,92,89 89,88,86,86,83 78,60**CSF £19.55 CT £364.92 TOTE £6.10: £2.70, £2.80, £8.80; EX 24.40.
**Owner** The Fairway Connection **Bred** Mrs Eithne Thompson **Trained** East Garston, Berks

**FOCUS**
There was a strong early pace on for this competitive nursery and the form looks solid.

**NOTEBOOK**
**Monashee Rose(IRE)**, withdrawn on account of good to soft ground on her latest intended outing, clearly relishes firm conditions. She stayed on strongly to lead inside the last and win narrowly, and looks progressive.
**Wonderful Mind** ran well in face of a stiff task last time and once again put up a sound performance. Things are not going to get any easier in the short term though, as he is due to go up 4lb from Saturday.
**Llamadas**, blinkered for the first time for this handicap debut, was found out slightly by the drop back to five furlongs from seven. He was staying on particularly well at the finish and will appreciate a return to six.
**Handsome Lady** ran well off what looked a stiff enough mark, but in the short term she is likely to continue to meet one or two too good at the weights.
**Oh Dara(USA)**, withdrawn from the Lowther Stakes on account of soft ground, was dropping from Listed grade and showed plenty of pace. In fact, she probably did too much too soon in a race run at a strong gallop.
**Smiddy Hill**, denied an uncontested lead, paid for helping to set a strong early gallop. *Official explanation: jockey said filly hung right handed throughout*
**Shatin Leader** *Official explanation: jockey said filly hung right handed from half way*
**Nee Lemon Left** *Official explanation: jockey said saddle slipped*

## 5061 GEBALS PREMIER CLAIMING STKS — 1m 1f

**4:00** (4:01) (D) 3-Y-O+ — **£5,538** (£1,704; £852; £426) **Stalls** High

| Form | Pos | Dist | Horse / Trainer / Comment | Jockey | SP | RPR |
|---|---|---|---|---|---|---|
| 2242 | **1** | | **Yenaled**[9] 4826 7-8-12 69 (KARyan) *hld up: hdwy to ld 2f out: pushed out* | DonnaCaldwell(7) 2 | **3/1**[2] | 64+ |
| 5113 | **2** | *1¼* | **Bailieborough (IRE)**[3] 4985 5-9-5 68 (DNicholls) *keen: prom: effrt and chal 2f out: hung rt: one pce fnl f* | (v) AlexGreaves 6 | **10/3**[3] | 61+ |
| 0520 | **3** | *hd* | **Sarraaf (IRE)**[9] 4826 8-8-13 64 (JSGoldie) *hld up in tch: nt clr run over 2f to over 1f out: no imp fnl f* | NMackay(3) 3 | **5/1** | 58+ |
| 064 | **4** | *6* | **Phoenix Nights (IRE)**[12] 4755 4-8-11 52 (ABerry) *hld up: effrt over 2f out: sn no imp* | PPMathers(5) 1 | **25/1** | 46 |
| 2003 | **5** | *1½* | **Takes Tutu (USA)**[22] 4435 5-9-10 76 (KRBurke) *keen: prom: chal 2f out: rdn and hung rt: sn btn* | (v) DarrenWilliams 8 | **9/4**[1] | 51 |
| 000- | **6** | *1½* | **Quintoto**[43] 5821 4-9-10 69 (RAFahey) *led to 2f out: sn btn* | PHanagan 7 | **14/1** | 48 |
| 0500 | **7** | *¾* | **Myannabanana (IRE)**[131] 1465 3-8-7 46 (JRWeymes) *cl up tl rdn and wknd over 2f out* | (v) KDarley 4 | **25/1** | 36 |
| /000 | **8** | *½* | **Society Times (USA)**[3] 4985 11-8-3 24 (DANolan) *chsd ldrs tl wknd over 2f out* | (t) DFentiman(7) 9 | **100/1** | 31? |

1m 53.52s (0.32) **Going Correction** +0.025s/f (Good)
**WFA** 3 from 4yo+ 7lb — **8** Ran SP% **110.9**
Speed ratings: **99,97,97,92,91 89,89,88**CSF £12.48 TOTE £3.90: £1.40, £1.20, £2.10; EX 9.70.
**Owner** The Fishermen **Bred** R S A Urquhart **Trained** Hambleton, N Yorks

**FOCUS**
An ordinary claimer and a modest time for the grade.

**NOTEBOOK**
**Yenaled**, held up off the pace as usual, picked up well when asked to take the leaders and won comfortably. He is useful in this sort of grade and showed that he does not necessarily need a strong pace to show his best.
**Bailieborough(IRE)** has been running well in claimers this season and the ground suited him much better than at Hamilton last time. He had his chance but just met one too good.
**Sarraaf(IRE)** did not get the best of runs inside the final two furlongs but it would be stretching it to say he was unlucky.
**Phoenix Nights(IRE)** had a tough task at these weights and was not disgraced in the circumstances.
**Takes Tutu(USA)**, backed into favouritism, had his chance but did not fancy it much. He hung under pressure and looks to have his own ideas about the game. *Official explanation: jockey said gelding had ran too free*

## 5062 QUALITY RACING ON RACING UK H'CAP 5f

**4:30** (4:31) (C ) (0-90,90) 3-Y-O+ **£10,276** (£3,162; £1,581; £790) **Stalls** Low

Form RPR

0610 **1** **Justalord**[27] 4299 6-8-10 **72**....(b) JEdmunds 11 89
(JBalding) *cl up: led over 1f out: r.o strly* **16/1**

5055 **2** *2* **Strensall**[5] 4935 7-8-9 **76**.... PPMathers(5) 7 85
(REBarr) *prom: rdn 1/2-way: effrt over 1f out: kpt on fnl f* **14/1**

600 **3** *3/4* **Musical Fair**[15] 4626 4-8-13 **75**.... ACulhane 3 81
(JAGlover) *hld up: hdwy over 1f out: kpt on fnl f: no imp* **20/1**

6040 **4** *hd* **Obe One**[27] 4291 4-8-4 **66**.... DaleGibson 15 71
(ABerry) *bhd and outpcd: hdwy over 1f out: r.o fnl f* **10/1**

43 **5** *1/2* **Mister Marmaduke**[7] 4874 3-9-0 **78**.... DAllan 14 81
(ISemple) *hld up: hdwy and in tch 2f out: rdn and no imp fnl f* **11/1**

0400 **6** *1 1/4* **Twice Upon A Time**[27] 4299 5-8-1 **63**.... FNorton 10 61
(BSmart) *bhd tl sme late hdwy: n.d* **33/1**

0530 **7** *hd* **Dame De Noche**[24] 4394 4-9-11 **87**.... DeanMcKeown 5 84
(JGGiven) *prom tl rdn and nt qckn over 1f out* **10/1**

2211 **8** *shd* **True Magic**[17] 4608 3-8-10 **74**.... JFanning 12 71
(JDBethell) *prom tl rdn and no ex over 1f out* **9/1**

0633 **9** *hd* **Hiccups**[12] 4759 4-9-2 **78**.... AlexGreaves 13 74
(DNicholls) *hld up midfield: effrt over 2f out: n.d* **11/2**[1]

0000 **10** *1* **Blue Crush (IRE)**[8] 4862 3-9-12 **90**.... DarrenWilliams 4 82
(KRBurke) *prom tl rdn and wknd fr over 1f out* **50/1**

6-00 **11** *3/4* **Impressive Flight (IRE)**[12] 4759 5-9-11 **87**.... KDarley 16 76
(TDBarron) *racd on outside of main stands side gp: no imp fr 1/2-way* **25/1**

0046 **12** *shd* **Maktavish**[19] 4538 5-9-4 **80**....(p) PHanagan 17 69
(ISemple) *racd alone stands side: n.d fr 1/2-way* **13/2**[2]

0000 **13** *nk* **Chico Guapo (IRE)**[15] 4626 4-8-4 **69**....(p) PMulrennan(3) 6 57
(JAGlover) *led to over 1f out: sn btn* **25/1**

0100 **14** *1/2* **Catch The Cat (IRE)**[8] 4855 5-8-12 **74**....(v) GParkin 9 60
(JSWainwright) *bhd and outpcd: nvr on terms* **14/1**

0030 **15** *3/4* **Beyond The Clouds (IRE)**[15] 4626 8-8-10 **75**.... TEaves(3) 2 58
(JSWainwright) *in tch to 1/2-way: sn lost pl* **10/1**

1202 **16** *3/4* **Roxanne Mill**[4] 4970 6-8-11 **73**....(p) FLynch 1 53
(PABlockley) *w ldrs to 1/2-way: wknd 2f out* **8/1**[3]

59.16 secs (-1.24) **Going Correction** -0.025s/f (Good)
**WFA** 3 from 4yo+ 2lb **16** Ran SP% **122.0**
Speed ratings: **108,104,103,103,102 100,100,100,99,98 96,96,96,95,94 93**CSF £210.82 CT £4629.38 TOTE £20.00: £3.10, £3.30, £5.50, £2.20; EX 323.20 Trifecta £848.50 Part won. Pool £1,195.12 - 0.10 winning units..
**Owner** T H Heckingbottom **Bred** Mrs M S Teversham **Trained** Scrooby, Notts

**FOCUS**
A competitive handicap run at a good pace and, although not easy to rate, the form looks fair.

**NOTEBOOK**
**Justalord** was running off a career-high turf mark but he made light of that, running out a clear-cut winner. Successful twice from three starts at this venue, he is at his best on a sharp track.
**Strensall** continues to look high in the handicap, but he too is well suited by a sharp track and this was a solid effort.
**Musical Fair** could be forgiven her last two efforts as they were on easy ground and she is a confirmed fast-ground performer. She is yet another who reserves her best for sharp tracks. *Official explanation: jockey said filly hung left handed in the final furlong and a half*
**Obe One** does not win very often but he has run well here on more than one occasion. He stayed on well from off the pace and is certainly fairly handicapped at present. *Official explanation: jockey said gelding hung right handed in final stages*
**Mister Marmaduke** came out best of the three-year-olds and continues to threaten to enter the winner's enclosure.
**Twice Upon A Time** stayed on without ever really posing a threat. She is the type for whom everything has to fall right.
**Hiccups** got upset and reared up in the stalls, and failed to run to his best. *Official explanation: jockey said gelding became upset in stalls*
**Impressive Flight(IRE)** *Official explanation: jockey said mare lost its action from half way through*
**Chico Guapo(IRE)** *Official explanation: jockey said gelding hung right handed throughout*

## 5063 RECTANGLE GROUP H'CAP 7f 30y

**5:00** (5:00) (E ) (0-70,65) 3-Y-O **£4,192** (£1,290; £645; £322) **Stalls** Low

Form RPR

2030 **1** **Saros (IRE)**[24] 4390 3-9-0 **58**.... FLynch 10 68
(BSmart) *cl up: led over 2f out: drifted lft to stands rail: kpt on wl fnl f* **10/1**

0014 **2** *1 1/4* **Joshua's Gold (IRE)**[23] 4425 3-8-4 **55**....(v) DTudhope(7) 11 62
(DCarroll) *keen early: chsd ldrs: effrt over 2f out: r.o fnl f: kpt on same pce* **9/2**[1]

2616 **3** *3* **Flash Ram**[21] 4489 3-9-7 **65**.... DAllan 6 64
(TDEasterby) *prom: rdn over 2f out: kpt on same pce over 1f out* **10/1**

4003 **4** *1/2* **Rare Coincidence**[14] 4680 3-9-4 **65**....(p) DNolan(3) 3 63
(RFFisher) *led to over 2f out: nt qckn* **20/1**

6-33 **5** *1/2* **The Number**[6] 4902 3-9-4 **65**.... TEaves(3) 7 61
(ISemple) *in tch: rdn 3f out: sn one pce* **6/1**[2]

0600 **6** *nk* **Pure Vintage (IRE)**[22] 4449 3-9-0 **58**.... PHanagan 8 53
(RAFahey) *hld up: rdn 2f out: kpt on fnl f: n.d* **10/1**

1054 **7** *nk* **Thornaby Green**[9] 4827 3-9-1 **64**.... PMakin(5) 5 59
(TDBarron) *midfield: effrt over 2f out: sn no imp* **10/1**

0415 **8** *nk* **Showtime Annie**[7] 4877 3-9-2 **63**.... NMackay(3) 4 57
(ABailey) *in tch tl rdn and outpcd fr 2f out* **10/1**

6201 **9** *1 1/4* **Son Of Thunder (IRE)**[29] 4246 3-9-0 **61**.... LEnstone(3) 1 51
(MDods) *hld up: rdn 3f out: edgd rt: nvr rchd ldrs* **7/1**[3]

4320 **10** *nk* **Bowling Along**[19] 4557 3-8-11 **58**.... THamilton(3) 2 48
(MESowersby) *hld up: rdn over 2f out: n.d* **16/1**

5445 **11** *1/2* **Graceful Air (IRE)**[29] 4248 3-8-11 **55**....(v[1]) KDarley 9 43
(JRWeymes) *hld up: rdn 3f out: n.d* **16/1**

-100 **12** *2* **Listen To Reason (IRE)**[10] 4817 3-9-7 **65**.... ACulhane 14 48
(JGGiven) *hld up: pushed along over 2f out: nvr on terms* **20/1**

0655 **13** *3 1/2* **Dark Day Blues (IRE)**[22] 4451 3-9-6 **64**.... DarrenWilliams 13 37
(MDHammond) *prom: rdn and edgd rt wl over 1f out: sn btn* **12/1**

3000 **14** *5* **Mister Regent**[50] 3622 3-9-2 **60**....(b) GParkin 12 20
(KARyan) *in tch: rdn and no imp whn bdly hmpd wl over 1f out: sn btn* **50/1**

1m 28.56s (-0.97) **Going Correction** +0.025s/f (Good) **14** Ran SP% **121.4**
Speed ratings: **106,104,101,100,100 99,99,98,97,97 96,94,90,84**CSF £53.69 CT £476.34 TOTE £11.20: £4.40, £1.90, £3.30; EX 66.70 Place 6 £560.00, Place 5 £217.35..
**Owner** Pinnacle Desert Sun Partnership **Bred** Patrick K Stephens **Trained** Hambleton, N Yorks
■ Stewards Enquiry : P Makin caution: careless riding

**FOCUS**
A modest race run at a good pace, and a decent winning time for a race of its type which gives the form a solid look.

**NOTEBOOK**
**Saros(IRE)** proved suited by the good pace and probably gained an advantage by coming towards the stands' side in the straight. Twice a winner on the Southwell Fibresand, this was his first victory on turf. *Official explanation: trainer had no explanation for the improved form shown*
**Joshua's Gold(IRE)** came out well on top of those who stayed towards the far side. He clearly remains in good form.
**Flash Ram** won a poor maiden at Carlisle last month and continues to look held off her current mark.
**Rare Coincidence** attempted to make all over a trip short of his best but could not match the pace of the principals in the closing stages.
**The Number** ran well enough without suggesting that he is particularly well treated.
T/Jkpt: Not won. T/Plt: £1,304.60 to a £1 stake. Pool: £53,169.75. 29.75 winning tickets. T/Qpdt: £67.40 to a £1 stake. Pool: £4,493.60. 49.30 winning tickets. RY

5064 - 5067a (Foreign Racing) - See Raceform Interactive

# 4770 BATH (L-H)

Friday, August 27

**OFFICIAL GOING: Good to soft (good in places)**
Wind: moderate against Weather: fine

## 5068 CANTOR ODDS NOVICE AUCTION STKS 5f 161y

**5:10** (5:12) (E ) 2-Y-O **£3,682** (£1,133; £566; £283) **Stalls** Low

Form RPR

100 **1** **Happy Event**[41] 3938 2-8-13 83.... GBaker 3 84
(BRMillman) *s.i.s: hld up in tch: rdn over 1f out: styd on to ld fnl 50yds* **10/1**

2124 **2** *1* **Bold Minstrel (IRE)**[11] 4803 2-8-13 84.... CCatlin 4 81
(MQuinn) *led: strly rdn over 1f out: nt qckn and hdd fnl 50yds* **4/1**[2]

051 **3** *2* **Rosiella**[17] 4621 2-8-8 71.... FNorton 7 69
(MBlanshard) *s.i.s and hld up: hdwy to go 2nd 2f out: no ex fnl f* **5/1**

31 **4** *1 1/4* **Cusoon**[24] 4413 2-8-13 83.... IMongan 5 70
(GLMoore) *sn outpcd and rdn: styd on fnl f: nvr nr to chal* **2/1**[1]

2010 **5** *1 1/4* **Withering Lady (IRE)**[18] 4612 2-8-6 77.... RHavlin 9 59
(MrsPNDutfield) *in tch: rdn over 1f out: sn wknd* **7/1**

114 **6** *5* **Aastral Magic**[19] 4581 2-9-0 87.... PDobbs 2 50
(RHannon) *trckd ldr: rdn and wknd over 2f out* **9/2**[3]

**7** *1 3/4* **In The Shadows** 2-8-4.... DKinsella 6 34
(WSKittow) *outpcd and a bhd* **40/1**

0 **8** *3 1/2* **Nip Nip (IRE)**[15] 4682 2-7-9.... CHaddon(7) 1 21
(ADSmith) *slowly away: a bhd* **66/1**

1m 14.43s (3.29) **Going Correction** +0.375s/f (Good) **8** Ran SP% **113.7**
Speed ratings: **93,91,89,87,85 79,76,72**CSF £49.14 TOTE £11.10: £2.20, £1.40, £2.00; EX 32.80.
**Owner** Robin Lawson **Bred** R Lawson **Trained** Kentisbeare, Devon

**FOCUS**
A fair novice event, and the form looks solid.

**NOTEBOOK**
**Happy Event**, stepping down in grade, stayed on the inner in the straight and came through a narrow gap to nail the leader near the finish. He handled the easy ground well.
**Bold Minstrel(IRE)** tried to make all but was unable to fend off the winner's challenge. He is holding his form well but is probably best over the bare five furlongs.
**Rosiella**, who was a bit free in the early stages, improved to chase the leader with a quarter of a mile to run but lost second spot inside the last. All her previous outings have been on fast ground.
**Cusoon** was being driven along from an early stage, and the drop back in trip clearly did not suit him.
**Withering Lady(IRE)**, who finished in front of today's winner in the Weatherbys Super Sprint, has shown her best form over five furlongs on fast ground.
**Aastral Magic**, conceding weight all round, had not previously run over less than six furlongs or on easy ground.

## 5069 CANTORODDS.COM (S) STKS 1m 3f 144y

**5:40** (5:44) (G ) 3-4-Y-O **£2,548** (£728; £364) **Stalls** Low

Form RPR

1040 **1** **Oktis Morilious (IRE)**[9] 4853 3-9-2 53.... LDettori 8 65
(AWCarroll) *hld up: hdwy over 4f out: rdn over 3f out: rdn to ld 1f out: sn clr* **7/2**[1]

0062 **2** *6* **Zuleta**[8] 4867 3-8-6 49.... DKinsella 10 45
(MBlanshard) *a.p: led 3f out: hdd 1f out: outpcd* **4/1**[2]

0-00 **3** *5* **Breezer**[7] 4912 4-9-7 52.... RHavlin 7 42
(GBBalding) *hld up: rdn over 3f out: styd on past btn horses ins fnl 2f* **12/1**

0236 **4** *5* **Relative Hero (IRE)**[16] 4630 4-9-2 50....(v) AQuinn(5) 2 34
(MissSJWilton) *trckd ldrs: wnt 2nd 3f out: wknd over 1f out* **4/1**[2]

0000 **5** *7* **Romeo's Day**[14] 4710 3-8-11 42....(v) CCatlin 1 23
(MRChannon) *trckd ldr to 3f out: rdn and wknd wl over 1f out* **11/2**[3]

64 **6** *1/2* **Ffizzamo Go**[20] 4561 3-8-11....(b) FNorton 6 22
(RMBeckett) *slowly away: nvr on terms* **16/1**

6050 **7** *dist* **Regulated (IRE)**[8] 4600 3-8-13 62....(b[1]) J-PGuillambert(3) 9 —
(DBFeek) *led for 1f: behin fnl 4f: t.o* **16/1**

000 **8** *2* **Pearnickity**[19] 4583 3-8-6.... RSmith 4 —
(AWCarroll) *v.s.a: a bhd: t.o* **33/1**

0005 **9** *nk* **Introduction**[8] 4867 3-8-8 35....(v[1]) RMiles(3) 5 —
(RJPrice) *in tch for 3f: wl bhd fnl 4f: t.o* **16/1**

0000 **10** *2 1/2* **Sninfia (IRE)**[8] 4883 4-9-2 46....(p) IMongan 3 —
(GAHam) *prom: led over 5f out: hdd 3f out: wknd rapidly: t.o* **12/1**

2m 35.14s (4.84) **Going Correction** +0.375s/f (Good)
**WFA** 3 from 4yo 10lb **10** Ran SP% **113.6**
Speed ratings: **98,94,90,87,82 82,—,—,—,—**CSF £16.86 TOTE £4.50: £1.70, £1.20, £4.00; EX 10.40.There was no bid for the winner. Zuleta was claimed by Mr C B Beck for £6,000.
**Owner** Dennis Deacon **Bred** Lord Vestey **Trained** Wixford, Warwicks

**FOCUS**
A poor seller, but the pace was fair and they finished well strung out.

**NOTEBOOK**
**Oktis Morilious(IRE)** has been held in handicaps since winning in this grade at Warwick. Coming from off the pace to score comfortably, he looks to be improving but would not want the ground much softer than this.
**Zuleta** was up with the pace throughout and this was a decent effort in the circumstances. Claimed afterwards, she is capable of winning a little race.
**Breezer**, back in selling company, improved for the step up in trip and passed a number of rivals in the latter stages, but was never going to reach the front two.
**Relative Hero(IRE)** ran his race, but is best suited by ten furlongs and fast ground.
**Romeo's Day**, with the visor back on, failed to get home after racing prominently.
**Sninfia(IRE)** *Official explanation: jockey said filly refused to face cheek pieces*



The Form Book, Raceform Ltd, Compton, RG20 6NL

## 5070 CANTOR ODDS/E.B.F. MAIDEN FILLIES' STKS 5f 11y

6:10 (6:14) (D) 2-Y-O £4,163 (£1,281; £640; £320) Stalls Low

Form RPR

23 **1** **Dancing Rose (IRE)**[22] 4474 2-8-11 ........................ RSmith 9 75
(CGCox) *trckd ldrs: led 2f out: drvn out fnl f* **6/1**[3]

**2** ¾ **Rubies** 2-8-11 ........................ SCarson 10 72
(RFJohnsonHoughton) *hld up: short of room over 2f out: rdn tover 1f out and kpt on strly to chse wnr ins fnl f* **6/1**[3]

**3** 1 ½ **World Music (USA)** 2-8-11 ........................ SDrowne 8 67+
(SaeedBinSuroor) *slowly away: hdwy on outside over 2f out: styd on fnl f: nvr nrr* **14/1**

**4** nk **May Morning (IRE)** 2-8-4 ........................ KMay(7) 7 66+
(BWHills) *towards rr: styd on ins fnl 2f: nvr nr to chal* **14/1**

5 **5** 1 ¼ **Auwitesweetheart**[77] 2837 2-8-11 ........................(t) FNorton 12 62
(BRMillman) *racd wd: hdwy over 2f out: rdn over 1f out: wknd ins fnl f* **33/1**

06 **6** 1 ¼ **Lighted Way**[8] 4866 2-8-8 ........................ LPKeniry(3) 3 57
(AMBalding) *led tl hdd 2f out: wknd appr fnl f* **25/1**

2 **7** hd **Rasseem (IRE)**[28] 4298 2-8-11 ........................ LDettori 4 64+
(SaeedBinSuroor) *hld up: prog on ins whn short of room over 1f out: swtchd rt: sn btn* **7/4**[1]

0344 **8** 6 **Stephanie's Mind**[11] 4815 2-8-4 78........................(p) DerekNolan(7) 6 36
(GAHuffer) *in tch: tl rdn and wknd wl over 1f out* **12/1**

6 **9** nk **Edged In Gold**[15] 4670 2-8-11 ........................ DSweeney 2 35
(PJMakin) *in tch on ins: rdn 2f out: sn btn* **40/1**

03 **10** hd **Encouragement**[26] 4364 2-8-11 ........................ PDobbs 1 34
(RHannon) *trckd ldr tl wknd wl over 1f out* **7/2**[2]

5 **11** 4 **Some Night (IRE)**[99] 2245 2-8-11 ........................ RHavlin 11 20
(JHMGosden) *in tch tl rdn and wknd 2f out* **20/1**

64.74 secs (2.24) **Going Correction** +0.375s/f (Good) **11 Ran SP% 122.2**
Speed ratings: **97,95,93,92,90 88,88,79,78,78 71**CSF £41.81 TOTE £7.20: £1.70, £1.90, £4.80; EX 54.50.
**Owner** The Eighteen Dreamers **Bred** Mark Commins **Trained** Lambourn, Berks

**FOCUS**
A fair fillies' maiden, with the sixth home setting the standard.

**NOTEBOOK**
**Dancing Rose(IRE)**, who has an action suited to this sort of ground, scored with a little in hand. She should get another furlong.
**Rubies ◆**, a sister to Listed winner So Will I, was a little short of racing room for a time but ran on well once in the clear. She should certainly win a maiden.
**World Music(USA)**, the Godolphin second string, is a half-sister to the yard's Group Three winner Ancient World. After a tardy start, she was obliged to race on the outside, but was doing some nice work at the end.
**May Morning(IRE)**, a half-sister to the weekend's Listed winner Naheef, holds some decent entries. After going out to her right leaving the stalls, she was at the back of the field until picking up well inside the last quarter-mile. Sure to know more next time, she will improve for an extra furlong.
**Auwitesweetheart**, down in trip from her debut, ran a decent race in the first-time tongue tie. *Official explanation: jockey said filly hung left handed*
**Lighted Way**, dropped in trip, confirmed that she possesses pace but faded once headed.
**Rasseem(IRE)** never really looked like picking up the leaders, and was not given a hard time when it was obvious that she was not going to be involved. The ground might have been to blame and she is probably worth another chance.
**Encouragement** did not appear to handle the underfoot conditions.

## 5071 CANTORODDS.COM CLASSIFIED STKS 5f 11y

6:40 (6:40) (D) 3-Y-O+ £5,811 (£1,788; £894; £447) Stalls Low

Form RPR

5504 **1** **Spanish Ace**[9] 4847 3-9-5 85........................(b[1]) SDrowne 10 99
(AMBalding) *sn pushed along fr wd draw: rdn and hdwy over 1f out: r.o u.p to ld last strides* **11/1**

4023 **2** hd **Devise (IRE)**[6] 4951 5-9-1 82........................ RMiles(3) 3 95
(MSSaunders) *slways in tch on ins: led wl over 1f out: rdn and hdd last strides* **10/3**[2]

2116 **3** 2 ½ **Royal Challenge**[28] 4289 3-9-0 80........................ LDettori 11 84
(GAButler) *outpcd in rr earlys: swtchd to centre fr wd draw: styd on fnl f: nvr nrr* **2/1**[1]

0000 **4** 1 **Willhewiz**[13] 4742 4-8-13 77........................ JFMcDonald(3) 9 80
(RMStronge) *a.p: rdn and ev ch 2f out tl wknd ins fnl f* **25/1**

0651 **5** ¾ **Further Outlook (USA)**[9] 4847 10-9-2 81........................ MHoward(7) 8 85
(DKIvory) *led for 1f: rdn and wknd ins fnl f* **10/1**

0406 **6** shd **Malapropism**[13] 4748 4-9-2 80........................ CCatlin 6 77
(MRChannon) *in tch: rdn 2f out: one pce after* **7/1**[3]

2004 **7** 2 ½ **Seven No Trumps**[13] 4748 7-9-2 75........................(p) FNorton 5 68
(JMBradley) *mid-div: rdn 1/2-way: fdd over 1f out* **11/1**

030- **8** 2 **Lord Kintyre**[346] 4972 9-9-5 83........................ GBaker 1 64
(BRMillman) *s.i.s: a bhd* **25/1**

0002 **9** 1 ¾ **Dancing Mystery**[9] 4847 10-9-2 78........................(b) SCarson 7 55
(EAWheeler) *led after 1f: rdn and hdd wl over 1f out: sn wknd* **10/1**

5100 **10** 3 ½ **Salviati (USA)**[13] 4748 7-9-4 82........................(p) PFitzsimons 4 44
(JMBradley) *slowly away: a bhd* **14/1**

0000 **11** 3 **Palawan**[83] 2679 8-8-9 74........................ RJKilloran(7) 2 31
(AMBalding) *a struggling in rr* **25/1**

63.00 secs (0.50) **Going Correction** +0.375s/f (Good)
**WFA** 3 from 4yo+ 2lb **11 Ran SP% 122.0**
Speed ratings: **111,110,106,105,103 103,99,96,93,88 83**CSF £48.40 TOTE £11.50: £2.80, £1.50, £2.00; EX 73.80.
**Owner** The Farleigh Court Racing Partnership **Bred** Farleigh Court Racing Partnership **Trained** Kingsclere, Hants

**FOCUS**
A very decent winning time for the class. This is fair form for the grade.

**NOTEBOOK**
**Spanish Ace** , who had not been firing this season, wore blinkers and ear plugs rather than a visor. After going right on leaving the stalls, he ran on to put his head in front near the line. This was a return to the form he showed at two, but it remains to be seen if the headgear combination works as well again. *Official explanation: trainer said, regarding the improved form shown, gelding was better suited by wearing first-time blinkers and hood today*
**Devise(IRE)**, who keeps improving, edged right inside the last and was just pipped. He likes it here and has no problem with softish ground.
**Royal Challenge** was carried right leaving the stalls by the eventual winner. Never within striking distance of the principals, he should not be written off back on a stiff track.
**Willhewiz** has found things a struggle since back-to-back wins in June, but put in a more encouraging run back over the minimum trip. He has gained his last four victories in a visor.
**Further Outlook(USA)** was unable to have things his own way in front this time.

## 5072 CANTOR ODDS H'CAP 1m 5y

7:10 (7:10) (F) (0-55,55) 3-Y-O £3,416 (£976; £488) Stalls Low

Form RPR

6004 **1** **Grand Rapide**[15] 4674 3-8-11 48........................ SDrowne 13 60
(JLSpearing) *mid-div: hdwy over 2f out: rdn and r.o wl to ld last strides* **8/1**

4504 **2** nk **Otago (IRE)**[30] 4246 3-9-2 53........................ IMongan 4 64
(JRBest) *a in tch: rdn over 3f out: led wl over 1f out: kpt on: hdd last strides* **7/1**[3]

5402 **3** 5 **Queen Lucia (IRE)**[9] 4848 3-9-2 53........................ LDettori 15 54+
(JGGiven) *a.p: rdn over 1f out: one pce after* **9/4**[1]

0000 **4** 2 **Farnborough (USA)**[29] 4259 3-8-10 50........................ RMiles(3) 6 46
(RJPrice) *towards rr: hdwy 2f out: kpt on: n.d* **40/1**

-400 **5** ½ **Maid The Cut**[15] 4674 3-8-8 45........................ ADaly 12 40
(ADSmith) *mid-div: kpt on one pce fnl 2f* **50/1**

5105 **6** 2 ½ **City General (IRE)**[11] 4798 3-8-8 52........................(p) DerekNolan(7) 10 42
(JSMoore) *led tl hdd wl over 1f out: sn btn* **12/1**

1000 **7** 1 **Fizzy Lady**[30] 4241 3-8-13 55........................(t) MSavage(5) 1 43
(NEBerry) *mid-div: rdn over 2f out: no hdwy after* **25/1**

4-00 **8** ½ **Great Blasket (IRE)**[2] 5036 3-8-12 52........................ J-PGuillambert(3) 8 39
(EJO'Neill) *mid-div: rdn over 2f out: sn btn* **33/1**

6500 **9** hd **Night Worker**[15] 4674 3-8-9 46........................ PDobbs 9 32
(RHannon) *a mid-div: n.d* **16/1**

-030 **10** 1 ¼ **Welsh Empress**[78] 2820 3-8-13 50........................ SCarson 14 34
(PLGilligan) *prom on outside: rdn 2f out: sn wknd* **33/1**

5503 **11** 5 **Cobalt Blue (IRE)**[11] 4798 3-9-0 51........................(v) DSweeney 3 24
(WJHaggas) *chsd ldrs: rdn 3f out: wknd over 1f out* **7/2**[2]

530 **12** 1 ¾ **Hana Dee**[17] 4619 3-9-1 52........................ CCatlin 5 22
(MRChannon) *prom: rdn over 3f out: wknd 2f out* **10/1**

6006 **13** 3 ½ **Whiplash (IRE)**[15] 4674 3-8-8 48........................(b) DCorby(3) 16 10
(KOCunningham-Brown) *prom tl rdn and wknd over 2f out* **20/1**

1050 **14** 1 ¾ **Lady Predominant**[65] 3193 3-8-1 45........................ FrancesPickard(7) 11 4
(GFBridgwater) *s.i.s: a in rr* **66/1**

0-63 **15** 24 **Mr Strowger**[93] 2395 3-8-8 45........................ RSmith 7 —
(ACharlton) *a outpcd in rr: wl bhd fnl fr 1/2-way* **16/1**

1m 44.06s (3.06) **Going Correction** +0.375s/f (Good) **15 Ran SP% 125.5**
Speed ratings: **99,98,93,91,91 88,87,87,87,85 80,79,75,73,49**CSF £61.51 CT £176.03 TOTE £10.20: £2.40, £2.60, £1.80; EX 100.30.
**Owner** A J & Mrs L Brazier **Bred** A J And Mrs L Brazier **Trained** Kinnersley, Worcs

**FOCUS**
A modest handicap in which the first two finished clear.

**NOTEBOOK**
**Grand Rapide**, who had been dropped 3lb, was carried towards the centre of the track by the eventual third when delivering her challenge but just got there. She appreciated the extra furlong and appears to be improving.
**Otago(IRE)** got to the front against the rail, but was just pipped by a rival in the centre of the track. He seems to be on the upgrade.
**Queen Lucia(IRE)** had her chance but, after drifting to her left, had no more to offer inside the final furlong. She is running well at present. *Official explanation: jockey said filly ran flat*
**Farnborough(USA)** began the season on a 9lb higher mark. He had only one behind him turning into the straight, but made late headway and will benefit from a return to farther.
**Maid The Cut**, who was behind tonight's winner at Chepstow last time, was never in the hunt.
**City General(IRE)** won the early tussle for the lead but had no answers when headed. He has not always been the most consistent but is running reasonably well of late.
**Cobalt Blue(IRE)**, down in trip and tackling easier ground, was unable to secure the lead on this occasion.

## 5073 CANTORODDS.COM H'CAP 1m 5f 22y

7:40 (7:40) (E) (0-70,70) 3-Y-O+ £4,173 (£1,284; £642; £321) Stalls Low

Form RPR

212 **1** **Belle Rouge**[16] 4647 6-9-10 66........................ LDettori 2 77
(CAHorgan) *a in tch on ins: shkn up to ld over 1f out: sn clr* **7/2**[1]

6403 **2** 2 ½ **Typhoon Tilly**[15] 4686 7-9-12 68........................ SDrowne 5 75
(CREgerton) *hld up in mid-div: rdn 2f out: r.o wl fnl f to go 2nd post* **7/2**[1]

0512 **3** hd **Danebank (IRE)**[22] 4473 4-8-12 54........................(p) SCarson 8 61
(JMackie) *trckd ldrs: led 3f out: hdd over 1f out: rdn and lost 2nd post* **7/1**[3]

000- **4** ½ **Spring Pursuit**[108] 6043 8-8-1 46........................ RMiles(3) 13 52
(EGBevan) *in tch: styd on one pce fnl 2f: nvr nrr* **14/1**

3006 **5** nk **Hashid (IRE)**[35] 4080 4-9-6 62........................ IMongan 7 68
(PCRitchens) *prom: pushed along 4f out: kpt on one pce ins fnl 2f* **33/1**

3404 **6** 1 ½ **Saxe-Coburg (IRE)**[9] 4849 7-8-8 53........................ JFMcDonald(3) 12 57
(GAHam) *in rr: styd on one pce fnl 2f: nvr nr to chal* **7/1**[3]

5006 **7** ¾ **Jasmick (IRE)**[12] 4777 6-9-11 70........................ LFletcher(3) 9 73
(HMorrison) *mid-div: rdn 3f out: one pce after* **14/1**

0615 **8** 3 ½ **Top Trees**[16] 4647 6-8-10 52........................ FNorton 15 50
(WSKittow) *towards rr: nvr rchd chalng position* **12/1**

5-65 **9** ½ **Javelin**[15] 4686 8-7-10 45........................(b[1]) CHaddon(7) 14 42
(IanWilliams) *a towards rr* **20/1**

00-6 **10** 1 ½ **Dingley Lass**[20] 4545 4-8-7 49 ow1........................ PDobbs 4 44
(HMorrison) *led for 1f: rdn 1/2-way: wknd over 2f out* **33/1**

0622 **11** 1 ½ **Traveller's Tale**[9] 4849 5-8-3 52........................ DerekNolan(7) 11 45
(PGMurphy) *t.k.h: led over 5f out: hdd 3f out: sn wknd* **5/1**[2]

0000 **12** 5 **Enchanted Ocean (USA)**[16] 4642 5-8-2 49........................ RThomas(5) 6 35
(GBBalding) *a bhd* **50/1**

3610 **13** 24 **The Varlet**[20] 4550 4-9-10 69........................(p) DCorby(3) 3 21
(BICase) *v.s.a: a bhd* **25/1**

0000 **14** 1 ½ **Royal Trigger**[22] 4473 4-8-7 49........................(bt) CCatlin 10 —
(IanWilliams) *led after 1f: hdd over 5f out: wknd over 3f out* **50/1**

2m 56.53s (5.23) **Going Correction** +0.375s/f (Good) **14 Ran SP% 125.5**
Speed ratings: **98,96,96,96,95 94,94,92,92,91 90,87,72,71**CSF £14.51 CT £85.06 TOTE £3.40: £1.70, £2.40, £2.50; EX 9.60 Place 6 £59.60, Place 5 £14.76.
**Owner** Mrs B Woodford **Bred** Whitsbury Manor Stud **Trained** Ogbourne Maisey, Wilts

**FOCUS**
An ordinary handicap run in modest time for the class. The main action took place up the centre of the track in the home straight.

**NOTEBOOK**
**Belle Rouge** is admirably consistent and has not been worse than second in her last nine runs. Runner-up to the progressive Strangely Brown at Sandown last time in a race that is paying to follow, she took this comfortably and is still on the upgrade. She loves cut in the ground.
**Typhoon Tilly** gained his last win in this event 12 months ago, but was 2lb lower and is certainly on a fair mark. He does act on this ground but is better in fast conditions.
**Danebank(IRE)**, 3lb higher, is an improved performer since joining this yard and this was another decent effort.
**Spring Pursuit** stayed on nicely on this first start since May. This should have sharpened him up for another hurdles campaign, but there could still be a race to be won on the Flat with him first.

**Hashid(IRE)** is still a maiden but he has certainly been handed a chance by the Handicapper.
**Saxe-Coburg(IRE)** had conditions to suit but could never get in a blow at the leaders.
**The Varlet** *Official explanation: jockey said gelding reared as stalls opened*
T/Plt: £139.10 to a £1 stake. Pool: £32,827.10. 172.20 winning tickets. T/Qpdt: £29.60 to a £1 stake. Pool: £3,631.40. 90.70 winning tickets. JS

## 4736 GOODWOOD (R-H)

Friday, August 27

**OFFICIAL GOING: Straight course - soft (heavy in places); round course - good to soft**

Wind: lt across Weather: murky; heavy showers race 4 onwards

### 5074 COORS FINE LIGHT BEER STKS (H'CAP) 1m 4f

**2:05** (2:05) (D ) (0-85,83) 3-Y-0+ **£7,020** (£2,160; £1,080; £540) **Stalls** Low

Form RPR

0411 **1** **Jack Of Trumps (IRE)**[34] 4155 4-9-3 **73**........ FNorton 8 82
(GWragg) *settled midfield: gng wl 4f out: prog to chse ldr over 2f out: rdn to ld over 1f out: jst hld on* **7/2**[2]

5011 **2** *hd* **Hezaam (USA)**[13] 4762 3-9-0 **80**........ WSupple 3 89
(JLDunlop) *settled midfield: effrt and cl up 3f out: swtchd rt over 1f out: r.o to press wnr ins fnl f: jst failed* **5/2**[1]

2621 **3** *3/4* **Michabo (IRE)**[15] 4693 3-8-11 **77**........ JFEgan 6 85
(DRCElsworth) *led: rdn and hdd over 1f out: kpt on wl tl no ex wl ins fnl f* **10/1**

6-33 **4** *4* **Royal Bathwick (IRE)**[16] 4642 4-9-5 **75**........ GBaker 7 77
(BRMillman) *dwlt: hld up in last: prog to chse ldrs over 2f out: wandering and nt qckn wl over 1f out* **12/1**

0203 **5** *3* **Devant (NZ)**[15] 4678 4-9-7 **77**........ JPMurtagh 5 74
(MAJarvis) *hld up towards rr: rdn 3f out: outpcd by ldrs 2f out: one pce after* **13/2**

6321 **6** *10* **Night Spot**[13] 4749 3-9-3 **83**........ SDrowne 4 65
(RCharlton) *trckd ldr to 8f out: rdn 3f out: sn wknd* **5/1**[3]

0000 **7** *hd* **Gallery God (FR)**[34] 4123 8-9-6 **83**........ LSmith(7) 9 65
(SDow) *t.k.h: prom: chsd ldr 8f out to 6f out: wknd 3f out* **16/1**

60-1 **8** *9* **Arabian Moon (IRE)**[11] 4799 8-9-3 **76** 5ex........ DNolan(3) 1 45
(RBrotherton) *hld up in last pair: rdn over 3f out: sn btn* **20/1**

100 **9** *dist* **Littleton Telchar (USA)**[19] 4588 4-9-6 **76**........ MHenry 2 —
(MJRyan) *prom: chsd ldr 6f out to over 3f out: wknd rapidly: eased and t.o* **33/1**

2m 47.87s (8.94) **Going Correction** +0.925s/f (Soft)
**WFA** 3 from 4yo+ 10lb **9** Ran SP% **111.2**
Speed ratings: **107,106,106,103,101 95,94,88,**—CSF £11.91 CT £73.59 TOTE £4.10: £1.60, £1.20, £3.10; EX 9.50.
**Owner** Mollers Racing **Bred** Miss Susan Bates **Trained** Newmarket, Suffolk

**FOCUS**
A fair race dominated by progressive types towards the bottom of the weights. The form appears sound.

**NOTEBOOK**
**Jack Of Trumps(IRE)**, a progressive type, notched up the hat-trick in game fashion and confirmed himself one step ahead of the Handicapper. The fact that he handled these testing conditions means that he should remain competitive in the latter part of the season.
**Hezaam(USA)**, also chasing a hat-trick, was not done any favours when Michabo crossed in front of him as they reached the stands'-side rail. It meant he had to be switched out wide to make his move, and the narrowness of his defeat suggests this cost him the win. He clearly stays well.
**Michabo(IRE)**, who made the running, coped with these conditions well and finished nicely clear of the fourth, proving his stamina over this trip in the process.
**Royal Bathwick(IRE)** had never run on ground as soft as this before but once again ran a solid race in defeat. She continues to look vulnerable to more progressive types, though.
**Devant(NZ)** still has her stamina to prove over this trip.
**Night Spot** did not get home in the ground. A faster surface is probably required. *Official explanation: jockey said gelding was unsuited by good to soft ground*

### 5075 LADBROKES.COM H'CAP 6f

**2:40** (2:40) (C ) (0-95,88) 3-Y-0+ **£18,966** (£7,194; £3,597; £1,635) **Stalls** Low

Form RPR

4004 **1** **Marker**[15] 4677 4-8-4 **73**........ RThomas(5) 7 89
(GBBalding) *cl up gng wl: pushed into ld over 1f out: rdn and hrd pressed fnl f: styd on wl* **9/1**

50 **2** *1/2* **Kingscross**[13] 4759 6-8-11 **75**........ DSweeney 11 89
(MBlanshard) *hld up in last pair: stdy prog whn nt clr run 2f out: effrt to chal ins fnl f: fnd little and hld nr fin* **16/1**

0002 **3** *3/4* **Watching**[10] 4837 7-9-0 **78**........ PHanagan 3 90
(RAFahey) *pressed ldr for 2f: lost pl and sn rdn: rallied on inner to press wnr 1f out: unable qck* **5/2**[1]

0356 **4** *3/4* **Sir Desmond**[13] 4751 6-8-13 **77**........(p) JPMurtagh 6 87
(RGuest) *settled in midfield: effrt and n.m.r 2f out: drvn and styd on fnl f: nvr quite able to chal* **11/1**

0124 **5** *1 1/4* **Machinist (IRE)**[13] 4759 4-9-4 **82**........ AlexGreaves 9 88+
(DNicholls) *settled towards rr: effrt whn squeezed out wl over 1f out: drvn and r.o fnl f* **6/1**[2]

0435 **6** *1/2* **Cd Flyer (IRE)**[13] 4759 7-9-5 **86**........ SHitchcott(3) 1 91+
(BEllison) *hld up in tch: n.m.r over 2f out and again wl over 1f out whn stmbld bdly: swtchd rt and lft fnl f: r.o: nt rcvr* **8/1**

0006 **7** *1 3/4* **Madrasee**[13] 4740 6-7-12 **65**........ JFMcDonald(3) 2 64
(LMontagueHall) *led to over 1f out: hanging rt and wknd* **25/1**

001 **8** *2 1/2* **Canterloupe (IRE)**[13] 4740 6-8-12 **76**........ DHolland 5 68
(PJMakin) *stdd s and hld up in last pair: t.k.h and hanging: shkn up and no rspnse over 1f out: one pce after* **9/1**

45 **9** *1 3/4* **Polar Impact**[4] 5008 5-8-11 **75**........ RLMoore 12 62
(GLMoore) *racd on outer: trckd ldrs: rdn over 2f out: wknd jst over 1f out* **7/1**[3]

300 **10** *shd* **Bond Boy**[13] 4759 7-9-10 **88**........ WSupple 8 74
(BSmart) *trckd ldrs: rdn 2f out: wknd fnl f* **14/1**

4002 **11** *3 1/2* **Devon Flame**[12] 4774 5-8-9 **73**........ SDrowne 10 49
(RJHodges) *racd towards outer: in tch in rr: effrt 1/2-way: wknd over 1f out* **16/1**

0010 **12** *3 1/2* **Michelle Ma Belle (IRE)**[18] 4614 4-8-11 **75**........(b) JFEgan 4 40+
(SKirk) *t.k.h: pressed ldr after 2f to over 2f out: wknd and eased* **25/1**

1m 16.51s (3.67) **Going Correction** +0.825s/f (Soft) **12** Ran SP% **120.9**
Speed ratings: **108,107,106,105,103 103,100,97,95,94 90,85**CSF £147.15 CT £475.40 TOTE £9.80: £2.60, £5.00, £1.50; EX 159.20 Trifecta £985.30 Pool: £4,995.96. 3.60 winning units..
**Owner** Miss B Swire **Bred** Miss B Swire **Trained** Kimpton,Hants
■ Stewards Enquiry : P Hanagan two-day ban: careless riding (Sep 7-8)

**FOCUS**
A decent sprint, and solid form even though it had its full compliment of hard-luck stories.

**NOTEBOOK**
**Marker**, undeniably well handicapped, having dropped 19lb in the ratings this season, relished the underfoot conditions and kept finding when his rivals came to challenge. His stable is in much better form now than it was earlier in the season, and he will still be on a fair mark when reassessed.
**Kingscross**, disappointing in the Great St Wilfrid even allowing for the fact that he was drawn on the wrong side, usually runs well at this track, and bounced back to his best. He is certainly suited by soft ground.
**Watching** is on a long losing run but has shown much improved form since switching stables and is certainly on a winning mark.
**Sir Desmond**, sent off favourite for the greys' race last time out, put up a better show this time. He had nowhere to go inside the last and would have finished even closer with a clear run.
**Machinist(IRE)**, 1lb lower than when fourth in the Great St Wilfrid, could have enjoyed a smoother passage. He was staying on at the finish and looks one to bear in mind for the Ayr Silver Cup, over a course and distance on which he has been successful in the past.
**Cd Flyer(IRE)**, another who ran well at Ripon last time, was denied a clear run next to the rail by Watching, and he all but fell with a quarter mile to run. He rallied gamely from a hopeless position though, and must be considered very unlucky to finish only sixth.
**Madrasee** enjoyed the run of the race next to the stands'-side rail.
**Canterloupe(IRE)**, who won over this course and distance last time, raced keenly and hung once again. She has form on this sort of ground but never looked likely to land a blow on this occasion.
**Bond Boy** *Official explanation: jockey said gelding had lost a shoe*
**Michelle Ma Belle(IRE)** *Official explanation: jockey said filly was never travelling*

### 5076 RACING POST RATED STKS (H'CAP) 1m 1f

**3:15** (3:15) (C ) (0-100,90) 3-Y-0 **£10,569** (£3,252; £1,626; £813) **Stalls** Low

Form RPR

3-1 **1** **Exterior (USA)**[20] 4545 3-9-0 **83**........ SDrowne 1 103+
(MrsAJPerrett) *racd in 3rd tl trckd ldr 4f out: led over 2f out: rdn over 1f out: sn clr* **11/1**

6004 **2** *6* **Cello**[15] 4691 3-8-9 **78**........(t) RLMoore 2 86
(RHannon) *hld up in last: prog 3f out: chsd wnr over 1f out: sn no imp and btn* **7/2**[2]

-435 **3** *1/2* **Warrad (USA)**[29] 4271 3-9-5 **88**........ PHanagan 5 95
(GAButler) *racd in 4th: rdn 3f out: sn struggling: plugged on fr over 1f out* **9/2**[3]

1450 **4** *3* **Vantage (IRE)**[83] 2676 3-8-9 **78**........(p) DHolland 4 79
(NPLittmoden) *led to over 2f out: wknd over 1f out* **11/1**

03-1 **5** *15* **Cape Vincent**[15] 4683 3-9-7 **90**........ JPMurtagh 3 61
(JHMGosden) *t.k.h: trckd ldr to 4f out: shkn up over 2f out: carried hd high and fnd nil: wknd* **1/1**[1]

2m 2.64s (5.78) **Going Correction** +0.925s/f (Soft) **5** Ran SP% **107.1**
Speed ratings: **111,105,105,102,89**CSF £44.85 TOTE £6.50: £3.60, £2.00; EX 21.70.
**Owner** K Abdulla **Bred** Juddmonte Farms Inc **Trained** Pulborough, W Sussex

**FOCUS**
A 0-100 handicap, but the top weight was rated just 90. The form does not look that solid, although the winner recorded a decent time considering the type of race and the conditions.

**NOTEBOOK**
**Exterior(USA)** ◆ did not beat a lot at Lingfield last time but there was no denying he was impressive there. The softer ground and shorter trip were worries here, but the betting completely underestimated his chance - he was put in as 11-4 second favourite in the paper - and he belied his eventual market position in no uncertain manner. There is a chance he was flattered, but this was only his third run and there could be plenty more to come. He could well run over a mile and a half under a penalty at Kempton on Friday and would take all the beating if showing up there, especially as the step up in trip should suit.
**Cello** did not see the trip out as well as the unexposed winner but ran a solid race. He likes these sort of conditions and a drop back to a mile will suit.
**Warrad(USA)** ran well here at the end of last month but the ground was faster on that occasion. He has now disappointed twice on easier going.
**Vantage(IRE)**, wearing cheekpieces for the first time, looked more exposed than most of his rivals here and was running over a trip short of his best as well.
**Cape Vincent** was disappointing, although he had his excuses and was dismounted after the line. *Official explanation: vet said colt was lame*

### 5077 P.P.S. (SOFTWOODS) CLASSIFIED STKS 7f

**3:50** (3:50) (D ) 3-Y-0+ **£5,642** (£1,736; £868; £434) **Stalls** High

Form RPR

4603 **1** **Waterside (IRE)**[7] 4917 5-9-8 80........ RLMoore 2 92
(GLMoore) *cl up: led jst over 2f out: drew clr over 1f out: rdn out* **7/2**[3]

2300 **2** *7* **Idle Power (IRE)**[28] 4291 6-9-6 78........(p) JPMurtagh 1 73
(JRBoyle) *hld up: cl up over 2f out: sn rdn and nt qckn: wandered but plugged on to take 2nd ins fnl f* **7/2**[3]

0114 **3** *4* **Savile's Delight (IRE)**[35] 4084 5-9-2 77........ DNolan(3) 3 62
(RBrotherton) *trckd ldr: led briefly over 2f out: rdn and hung rt over 1f out: wknd* **2/1**[1]

0003 **4** *3 1/2* **Fools Entire**[7] 4926 3-8-12 59........(e) DHolland 4 51
(JAGilbert) *plld hrd early: hld up in last: lost tch and struggling 1/2-way: no ch after* **20/1**

0601 **5** *5* **King Harson**[7] 4908 5-9-11 77........(v) WSupple 5 46
(JDBethell) *led to over 2f out: immediately wknd: eased fnl f* **10/3**[2]

1m 32.31s (4.28) **Going Correction** +0.925s/f (Soft)
**WFA** 3 from 5yo+ 5lb **5** Ran SP% **105.6**
Speed ratings: **112,104,99,95,89**CSF £14.38 TOTE £4.40: £1.90, £2.00; EX 14.60.
**Owner** Nigel Shields **Bred** Yeomanstown Stud **Trained** Woodingdean, E Sussex

**FOCUS**
There was a decent pace on here and the winner clocked a very smart time for the grade in the conditions. However, there is a strong suspicion he was the only one to show his form.

**NOTEBOOK**
**Waterside(IRE)** could not make the running with King Harson in the field, but it did not seem to bother him. He grabbed the valuable stands'-side rail in the straight and went on to win convincingly, coping with the ground far better than his rivals. His connections will be hoping the Handicapper does not take this form literally.
**Idle Power(IRE)** has won over seven furlongs in the past but those successes came on fast ground. He kept on well for second, but was not a threat to the runaway winner.
**Savile's Delight(IRE)**, who had conditions to suit, was slightly disappointing, hanging noticeably under pressure.
**Fools Entire** had plenty on at the weights and pulled too hard in the early stages. He is difficult to win with.
**King Harson**, who enjoyed the run of the race when successful from out of the handicap at Chester last time, went too quick in front on this occasion and was treading water with two furlongs to run. *Official explanation: trainer was unable to offer any explanation for poor form shown*

## 5078 ROYAL SUSSEX REGIMENT NURSERY 5f
4:25 (4:25) (D) 2-Y-O £4,810 (£1,480; £740; £370) Stalls Low

Form RPR
32S3 1 **Miss Cassia**[39] 3986 2-8-8 **70** RLMoore 5 71
(RHannon) *cl up: led wl over 1f out: drvn and kpt on fnl f: all out* **5/1**[3]
0525 2 ¾ **Cree**[4] 5005 2-7-12 **60** oh1 PHanagan 1 59
(WRMuir) *cl up: nt clr run 2f out and lost pl: drvn and kpt on fnl f to take 2nd last strides* **6/1**
1200 3 nk **Bibury Flyer**[7] 4914 2-9-4 **83** SHitchcott(3) 3 81
(MRChannon) *s.i.s: outpcd and wl bhd: gd prog over 2f out: pressed wnr fnl f: nt qckn and hld nr fin* **4/1**[2]
0644 4 1 **Kempsey**[41] 3930 2-8-5 **67** (p) ADaly 2 62
(JJBridger) *prom: lost pl after 2f and swtchd to outer: drvn and nt qckn over 1f out: kpt on* **5/1**[3]
1404 5 1¼ **Talcen Gwyn (IRE)**[27] 4325 2-9-3 **79** DHolland 6 70
(MFHarris) *sn pressed ldr: led over 2f out to wl over 1f out: one pce after* **7/2**[1]
5220 6 6 **African Storm (IRE)**[16] 4637 2-8-12 **74** JFEgan 4 47
(SKirk) *taken v steadily to post: led to over 2f out: wknd over 1f out* **4/1**[2]

63.87 secs (4.82) **Going Correction** +0.825s/f (Soft) 6 Ran SP% **109.8**
Speed ratings: **94,92,92,90,88 79**CSF £32.15 TOTE £5.50: £1.80, £3.50; EX 25.70.
**Owner** William Durkan **Bred** Whitsbury Manor Stud **Trained** East Everleigh, Wilts

**FOCUS**
An ordinary nursery and the form is unexceptional.

**NOTEBOOK**
**Miss Cassia**, who was making her debut in handicap company, coped well with the softer conditions and hung on well when challenged late on. She looks to have recovered well from her unfortunate experience at Bath last month.
**Cree** had the blinkers left off this time and, although running from out of the handicap, could be expected to appreciate the conditions given that he is a son of Indian Ridge. He stayed on well for second and shapes as though he will appreciate six furlongs.
**Bibury Flyer** missed the break badly and, although she came through to hold every chance inside the last, she may have used up too much energy getting there. Her poor strike-rate tempers enthusiasm regarding her ability to go two better soon, though.
**Kempsey**, in first-time cheekpieces, was not helped by having to race furthest off the fence.
**Talcen Gwyn(IRE)** did not get home in the ground.
**African Storm(IRE)** *Official explanation: jockey said colt lost his action*

## 5079 AUGUST MEDIAN AUCTION MAIDEN STKS 1m 3f
5:00 (5:00) (E) 3-4-Y-O £4,075 (£1,254; £627; £313) Stalls Low

Form RPR
-35P 1 **Trullitti (IRE)**[22] 4486 3-8-7 73 (b[1]) WSupple 3 78
(JLDunlop) *hld up in last and a gng wl: prog to ld over 2f out: rdn clr over 1f out* **11/2**[3]
-332 2 3½ **Dundry**[9] 4850 3-8-12 77 (p) RLMoore 5 78
(GLMoore) *cl up: effrt to chal and ev ch over 2f out: one pce and btn over 1f out* **11/8**[1]
030- 3 nk **Lomapamar**[307] 5757 3-8-7 78 PHanagan 1 73
(MrsAJPerrett) *racd in 4th pl: rdn and effrt over 3f out: one pce fnl 2f* **9/4**[2]
454 4 16 **Port 'n Starboard**[9] 4850 3-8-12 JFEgan 4 56
(CACyzer) *led to over 2f out: wknd* **7/1**
0-00 5 2 **Lasser Light (IRE)**[18] 4615 4-9-7 SRighton 2 53
(DGBridgwater) *chsd ldr: rdn 5f out: wknd over 3f out* **16/1**

2m 38.26s (12.15) **Going Correction** +0.925s/f (Soft)
**WFA** 3 from 4yo 9lb 5 Ran SP% **106.6**
Speed ratings: **92,89,89,77,76**CSF £12.76 TOTE £4.80: £1.90, £1.30; EX 9.90.
**Owner** Mrs Sonia Rogers **Bred** Airlie Stud **Trained** Arundel, W Sussex

**FOCUS**
A moderate time for the grade, even allowing for the conditions. Questionable form, with the ground clearly playing its part.

**NOTEBOOK**
**Trullitti(IRE)** was in there with a solid chance on official ratings and coped best with the worsening conditions. The first-time blinkers may also have helped, and although she won in clear-cut style the form does not look that strong.
**Dundry**, stepping up in trip, was another wearing headgear for the first time. He kept on for second but never really looked happy on the ground.
**Lomapamar**, racing over a trip which should suit this season, found the conditions a bit too testing on her belated reappearance. She is entitled to improve for the outing.
**Port 'n Starboard** had a bit to find with the principals on previous form and was soon beaten off when the pace hotted up early in the straight.

## 5080 BOLLINGER CHAMPAGNE CHALLENGE SERIES STKS (H'CAP) (FOR GENTLEMAN AMATEUR RIDERS) 1m
5:35 (5:35) (F) (0-55,54) 3-Y-0+ £3,591 (£1,105; £552; £276) Stalls High

Form RPR
0602 1 **Mcqueen (IRE)**[11] 4808 4-11-10 **50** MrSWalker 14 75+
(MrsHDalton) *led after 2f: clr 3f out: drvn but in n.d fnl 2f* **7/4**[1]
3500 2 6 **Mythical Charm**[13] 4740 5-11-8 **48** (t) MrDHDunsdon 2 55
(JJBridger) *hld up in rr: prog on outer over 2f out: chsd wnr over 1f out: no imp* **14/1**
0250 3 3½ **Islands Farewell**[4] 5002 4-11-6 **51** MrMWalford(5) 1 51
(DNicholls) *settled towards rr: effrt on outer over 2f out: kpt on to take modest 3rd ins fnl f* **14/1**
4000 4 5 **Catch The Fox**[14] 4713 4-10-11 **40** MrJMorgan(3) 4 30
(JJBridger) *hld up in rr: prog on outer 3f out: chsd wnr briefly 2f out: fdd fnl f* **14/1**
0306 5 ½ **Somayda (IRE)**[25] 4398 9-10-6 **39** (p) JDoyle(7) 12 27
(MissJacquelineSDoyle) *led for 2f: mostly chsd wnr to 2f out: no ch after* **15/2**[3]
0063 6 3 **Anisette**[23] 4460 3-10-2 **41** MrAChahal(7) 13 23
(JulianPoulton) *s.v.s: wl in rr: sme prog on outer over 2f out: wknd over 1f out* **14/1**
0-00 7 4 **Cote Soleil**[14] 4713 7-11-10 **50** MrTGreenall 9 24
(CREgerton) *trckd ldrs: outpcd over 3f out: hanging bdly rt and wknd over 1f out* **12/1**
0550 8 1½ **Open Handed (IRE)**[43] 3869 4-11-6 **49** (t) MrSDobson(3) 10 20
(BEllison) *racd in midfield: outpcd and rdn over 3f out: struggling over 2f out* **4/1**[2]
1506 9 ½ **Mobo-Baco**[20] 4546 7-11-11 **54** MrJJBest(3) 8 24
(RJHodges) *racd midfield: rdn and struggling 3f out: steadily wknd* **12/1**
0000 10 ½ **Rumour Mill (IRE)**[22] 4476 3-10-2 **41** ow1 MrJoshuaHarris(7) 5 10
(NEBerry) *nvr on terms w ldrs: c wd bnd over 3f out: sn struggling* **33/1**
0000 11 1 **High View (USA)**[50] 3669 3-11-5 **54** MrJOwen(3) 11 20
(FJordan) *prom: disp 2nd pl over 3f out: sn wknd* **33/1**
4505 12 10 **Even Easier**[22] 4470 3-11-1 **50** (b) MrEDehdashti(3) 3 —
(GLMoore) *dwlt: rcvrd into midfield after 3f: wknd 3f out* **12/1**
6-03 13 dist **Chorus**[214] 608 7-11-1 **48** MrJMillman(7) 7 —
(BRMillman) *racd wd: prom tl wknd over 3f out: eased: t.o* **16/1**
0000 P **Mutabari (USA)**[29] 4265 10-10-1 **34** oh8 MrJohnEvans(7) 6 —
(JLSpearing) *lost action and p.u after 3f: dismntd* **33/1**

1m 49.37s (9.10) **Going Correction** +0.925s/f (Soft)
**WFA** 3 from 4yo+ 6lb 14 Ran SP% **132.6**
Speed ratings: **91,85,81,76,76 73,69,67,67,66 65,55,—,—**CSF £33.06 CT £297.06 TOTE £2.80: £1.60, £3.90, £4.90; EX 52.40 Place 6 £451.73, Place 5 £293.40.
**Owner** R Edwards And W J Swinnerton **Bred** Philip Newton **Trained** Shifnal, Shropshire

**FOCUS**
Moderate fare and ordinary form.

**NOTEBOOK**
**Mcqueen(IRE)** hinted that he was about to return to the winner's enclosure last time out, and finally recaptured the form of his runaway victory on the Fibresand at Southwell in November. He was running off an 11lb lower mark than on that occasion and connections will be keen to turn him out under a penalty while in this form.
**Mythical Charm** coped with conditions well but found the well-handicapped winner too strong in the latter stages.
**Islands Farewell** had not shown much on soft ground in the past, but he handled the conditions well enough on this occasion. This was probably his best run to date.
**Catch The Fox**, whose form looks regressive, remains a maiden after 23 starts.
**Somayda(IRE)** showed decent form on soft ground for John Dunlop in the dim and distant past, but he is nowhere near the horse he once was.
**Open Handed(IRE)** was disappointing, but he had his excuses. *Official explanation: jockey said gelding had a breathing problem*
T/Plt: £275.70 to a £1 stake. Pool: £52,401.90. 138.70 winning tickets. T/Qpdt: £31.70 to a £1 stake. Pool: £3,102.70. 72.40 winning tickets. JN

# 4444 NEWCASTLE (L-H)
Friday, August 27

**OFFICIAL GOING: Heavy**
Wind: breezy, hlf against Weather: cloudy

## 5081 CANTORSPORT.CO.UK APPRENTICE H'CAP 6f
5:25 (5:25) (F) (0-55,54) 3-Y-0+ £3,171 (£906; £453) Stalls High

Form RPR
5503 1 **Old Bailey (USA)**[7] 4925 4-8-8 **41** (v) PMakin 2 52
(TDBarron) *cl up far side: led over 2f out: pushed out* **9/2**[1]
45-5 2 1½ **M For Magic**[28] 4309 5-8-2 **40** KPierrepont(5) 6 48+
(CWFairhurst) *prom far side: effrt over 2f out: kpt on fnl f: nt rch wnr* **9/1**[3]
1100 3 1¼ **Mickledor (FR)**[20] 4557 4-9-3 **53** (p) DTudhope(3) 8 56
(MDods) *prom far side: outpcd over 2f out: r.o fnl f* **10/1**
0400 4 shd **Redoubtable (USA)**[10] 4827 13-8-13 **51** MHalford(5) 5 53
(DWChapman) *hld up far side: hdwy over 2f out: one pce wl ins fnl f* **12/1**
2006 5 ½ **Indian Music**[8] 4879 7-8-2 **42** CEly(7) 4 43
(ABerry) *hld up far side: swtchd to far rail whn hmpd 3f out: sn rdn: kpt on fnl f: no imp* **14/1**
0000 6 hd **The Gambler**[27] 4350 4-8-9 **45** (p) StephanieHollinshead(3) 9 45
(PaulJohnson) *led far side to over 2f out: nt qckn ins fnl f* **50/1**
303 7 2 **Wares Home (IRE)**[22] 4495 3-8-3 **46** SBushby(7) 14 46+
(KRBurke) *cl up centre: led that gp 1/2-way: hung lft over 1f out: no imp fnl f* **14/1**
0500 8 1 **Bennanabaa**[15] 4687 5-8-4 **42** (t) BO'Neill(5) 15 33+
(SCBurrough) *prom centre: rdn 1/2-way: hung lft and no imp over 1f out* **33/1**
-040 9 ½ **Lord Arthur**[32] 4188 3-8-12 **53** TBlock(5) 3 43
(MWEasterby) *midfield far side: rdn 1/2-way: sn outpcd* **25/1**
5000 10 1¼ **Dark Champion**[12] 4782 4-9-2 **54** HPoulton(5) 11 40+
(REBarr) *cl up centre tl wknd over 1f out* **40/1**
0103 11 1¼ **Sam The Sorcerer**[64] 3234 3-8-6 **45** MLawson(3) 12 27+
(JRNorton) *sn outpcd centre: hdwy over 1f out: n.d* **9/1**[3]
0065 12 6 **Desert Fury**[32] 4190 7-8-8 **41** BSwarbrick 7 5
(RBastiman) *racd far side: rdn 1/2-way: n.d* **6/1**[2]
1006 13 11 **Rosie's Result**[12] 4782 4-8-12 **50** JemmaMarshall(5) 1 —
(MTodhunter) *trckd far side ldrs to 2f out: sn btn* **10/1**
3040 14 ½ **Turf Princess**[8] 4882 3-9-0 **53** DFentiman(3) 10 —
(IanEmmerson) *chsd centre ldrs to 1/2-way: sn struggling* **12/1**
0004 15 6 **Kew The Music**[11] 4800 4-8-12 **52** (v) TO'Brien(7) 13 —
(MRChannon) *led centre to 1/2-way: rdn and wknd 2f out* **16/1**

1m 21.86s (6.82) **Going Correction** +1.075s/f (Soft)
**WFA** 3 from 4yo+ 3lb 15 Ran SP% **116.4**
Speed ratings: **97,95,93,93,92 92,89,88,87,85 84,76,61,60,52**CSF £40.56 CT £394.88 TOTE £6.30: £2.20, £4.60, £3.40; EX 69.90.
**Owner** J Baggott **Bred** Barbara Hunter **Trained** Maunby, N Yorks
■ Stewards' Enquiry : M Halford 10-day ban: failed to ride out for third place (Sep 7-16)
K Pierrepont one-day ban: failed to keep straight from stalls (Sep 7)
Stephanie Hollinshead one-day ban: failed to keep straight from stalls (Sep 7)

**FOCUS**
A very ordinary handicap featuring exposed and unreliable sorts but one in which the pace was sound in the conditions. The far side group held the edge over those that raced in the centre.

**NOTEBOOK**
**Old Bailey(USA)** has not been the most consistent but notched his second turf win (both at this course) from his favourable draw. He goes on any ground but, given his record and the fact this was a weak event, would not be one to lump on at short odds next time.
**M For Magic** has yet to win a race in 20 starts but left the impression that a return to seven furlongs would be in his favour. He goes on most ground but that record means he remains one to tread carefully with.
**Mickledor(FR)** proved her effectiveness in very testing conditions with a fair effort, but she is likely to continue to look vulnerable from her current mark against well handicapped or unexposed sorts.
**Redoubtable(USA)**, a grand veteran, ran right up to his recent best and fared the best of those that were held up. His rider was banned for easing him off and getting caught for third spot close home but he should continue to go well in this grade.
**Indian Music** may be a bit better than the bare form as he was hampered when initially asked for his effort. However, his inconsistency and the fact he has not won on grass for over three years has to be a concern.
**The Gambler** had the run of the race on the favoured far side but was beaten on merit. His losing run of over a year is a concern.
**Wares Home(IRE)** fared the best of those that raced in the centre of the track so may be a bit better than the bare form, but once again he looked anything but an easy ride and he may always be best with strong handling.
**Sam The Sorcerer** *Official explanation: trainer said gelding was unsuited by the heavy ground*
**Desert Fury** *Official explanation: jockey said gelding was unsuited by heavy ground*

## 5082 CANTORINDEX.CO.UK NOVICE AUCTION STKS 1m 3y(S)
5:55 (5:55) (F) 2-Y-O £2,933 (£838; £419) Stalls High

Form RPR

31 **1** **Thunderwing (IRE)**$^{18}$ [4606] 2-9-1 .............................. DarrenWilliams 1 90+
(KRBurke) *keen: trckd ldrs: nt clr run and swtchd over 2f out: led ins fnl f: edgd rt: kpt on wl* **11/8**$^{2}$

012 **2** *2* **Skidrow**$^{8}$ [4872] 2-8-13 88 .............................. MFenton 2 85+
(MLWBell) *trckd ldrs: led over 2f out: hdd ins fnl f: one pce whn n.m.r last 75yds* **5/4**$^{1}$

13 **3** *13* **Simply St Lucia**$^{7}$ [4919] 2-8-6 .............................. GHind 4 61+
(JRWeymes) *cl up: ev ch over 2f out: rdn and wknd over 1f out* **8/1**$^{3}$

00 **4** *27* **Saint Clements (USA)**$^{83}$ [2674] 2-8-12 .............................. SChin 3 3
(MJohnston) *led to over 2f out: sn btn* **12/1**

1m 52.28s (11.08) **Going Correction** +1.075s/f (Soft) 4 Ran SP% **105.4**
Speed ratings: **87,85,72,45**CSF £3.26 TOTE £2.30; EX 2.60.
**Owner** Market Avenue Racing Club Ltd **Bred** Agricola Del Parco **Trained** Middleham Moor, N Yorks

**FOCUS**
An uncompetitive event and the steady gallop in the conditions not surprisingly resulted in a modest time. The form has been rated through the second.

**NOTEBOOK**
**Thunderwing(IRE)** ◆ has improved with every outing and turned in easily his best effort yet, despite failing to settle in the first half of the contest. It will be no surprise to see him progress again on less testing ground, especially if he can settle better.
**Skidrow** ran creditably on the most testing conditions he has encountered to date but, although the inteference suffered late on made no difference to the result, he left the impression that a sounder surface would be in his favour.
**Simply St Lucia** was below her best on the most testing conditions she has encountered, but she was eased and ran better than the bare facts suggest. She may not be the easiest to place successfully.
**Saint Clements(USA)** was well below even the modest form he had showed on a sound surface and he will be seen to better effect in low-grade handicaps from now on.

## 5083 CANTORSPORT.CO.UK CLAIMING STKS 1m (R)
6:25 (6:27) (F) 2-Y-O £3,003 (£858; £429) Stalls Low

Form RPR

4021 **1** **Toldo (IRE)**$^{1}$ [5059] 2-8-13 53 .............................. FLynch 4 66+
(ABerry) *dwlt: hld up: smooth hdwy over 2f out: led ins fnl f: pushed out* **10/3**$^{2}$

45 **2** *1* **Bongoali**$^{22}$ [4468] 2-9-2 .............................. DAllan 1 67
(MRChannon) *in tch: rdn to ld over 1f out: hdd ins fnl f: kpt on* **11/4**$^{1}$

63 **3** *3 ½* **Dancing Shirl**$^{28}$ [4304] 2-8-9 .............................. LEnstone(3) 2 56
(CWFairhurst) *prom: rdn over 2f out: kpt on same pce fnl f* **11/1**

6200 **4** *1 ½* **Dane's Rock (IRE)**$^{14}$ [4699] 2-7-10 59 .............................. (b) DFentiman(7) 8 44+
(PCHaslam) *plld hrd: led and clr: hung to stands side ent st: hdd over 2f out: kpt on same pce* **9/1**

**5** *1 ¼* **Eastern Mandarin** 2-9-7 .............................. MFenton 9 60
(MrsLStubbs) *s.i.s: effrt over 2f out: no imp over 1f out* **16/1**

050 **6** *1 ¼* **Dramatic Review (IRE)**$^{91}$ [2453] 2-9-1 .............................. (vt$^{1}$) GFaulkner 3 51
(PCHaslam) *hld up: rdn and hung lft over 2f out: sn n.d* **10/1**

3436 **7** *½* **Tonight (IRE)**$^{37}$ [4010] 2-8-2 60 .............................. BSwarbrick(5) 10 42
(WMBrisbourne) *trckd ldrs: rdn over 2f out: sn btn* **7/1**$^{3}$

000 **8** *½* **Belton**$^{14}$ [4699] 2-9-7 .............................. DeanMcKeown 7 55?
(RonaldThompson) *chsd ldrs tl wknd over 2f out* **20/1**

0 **9** *1 ¼* **White Star Magic**$^{7}$ [4900] 2-9-3 .............................. GHind 6 49
(JRWeymes) *cl up: led over 2f to over 1f out: sn btn* **9/1**

006 **10** *1 ¾* **Fransiscan**$^{69}$ [3100] 2-8-6 .............................. (v) GBartley(7) 5 41
(PCHaslam) *in tch to 1/2-way: sn struggling* **50/1**

1m 53.75s (10.27) **Going Correction** +0.70s/f (Yiel) 10 Ran SP% **112.3**
Speed ratings: **76,75,71,70,68 67,67,66,65,63** CT £4.00 TOTE £1.80: £1.20, £1.70, £; EX9.80
1.The winner was claimed by Mr J W Armstrong for £8,000. Dane's Rock was claimed by Mrs H Sweeting for £3,000. Eastern Mandarin was claimed by Mr Don
**Owner** Anthony White **Bred** Mrs C A Moore **Trained** Cockerham, Lancs

**FOCUS**
A gallop that was soon on the decent side but a very pedestian time, even for the conditions. The form is modest at best.

**NOTEBOOK**
**Toldo(IRE)** turned out quickly after winning at Musselburgh the previous day, proved himself equally at home under these much more testing conditions. He travelled strongly for a long way and should continue to go well for new connections, who purchased him for £8,000.
**Bongoali** is now proven on both extremes of going and again showed enough to suggest he can win a similar event in the near future.
**Dancing Shirl** ran creditably but left the impression that the step into ordinary nursery company and an even stiffer test of stamina would see her in a better light.
**Dane's Rock(IRE)** ran well considering that he failed to settle and hung to the stands side turning for home. He is probably a fair bit better than the bare form but would not be one to lump on. *Official explanation: jockey said gelding hung right handed in straight*
**Eastern Mandarin**, who is related to winners up to middle distances, hinted at ability on this racecourse debut and is entitled to come on for the experience. He was claimed by Don Eddy for £12,000.
**Dramatic Review(IRE)**, tried in the first time visor and tongue-tie, was below his best on this first run on very testing ground and did not look the easiest of rides. He will have to improve to win a similar contest.

## 5084 CANTORINDEX.CO.UK NOVICE STKS 5f
6:55 (6:55) (D) 2-Y-O £3,415 (£1,051; £525; £262) Stalls High

Form RPR

42 **1** **Sentiero Rosso (USA)**$^{12}$ [4776] 2-8-9 .............................. TEaves(3) 3 79+
(BEllison) *cl up gng wl: led ins fnl f: pushed out* **4/6**$^{1}$

02 **2** *1 ¼* **Wolf Hammer (USA)**$^{25}$ [4392] 2-8-9 .............................. PMulrennan(3) 1 75
(JHowardJohnson) *led to ins fnl f: kpt on same pce* **6/1**$^{3}$

03 **3** *1 ¾* **Peters Delite**$^{27}$ [4347] 2-8-9 .............................. THamilton(3) 2 69
(RAFahey) *trckd ldrs: effrt over 2f out: one pce over 1f out* **10/3**$^{2}$

**4** *11* **Parchment (IRE)** 2-8-8 .............................. RFfrench 4 30
(JHowardJohnson) *chsd ldrs tl wknd over 2f out* **9/1**

66.50 secs (4.97) **Going Correction** +1.075s/f (Soft) 4 Ran SP% **107.4**
Speed ratings: **103,101,98,80**CSF £4.94 TOTE £1.50; EX 3.50.
**Owner** Graeme Redpath **Bred** Thomas And Lakin **Trained** Norton, N Yorks

**FOCUS**
A very decent time for the grade given the conditions and the winner, who travelled strongly for much of the way, may be the type to improve again.

**NOTEBOOK**
**Sentiero Rosso(USA)** has improved with every outing and looks a bit better than the bare form, as he travelled strongly and merely had to be pushed out. He should prove equally effective over six furlongs and may be capable of further success.
**Wolf Hammer(USA)**, back in trip and on heavy ground for the first time, showed much improved form but looks sure to appreciate the return to six furlongs. He looks capable of picking up a small event over that distance.
**Peters Delite** has plenty of speed in his pedigree and again ran creditably, although he left the impression that switching into ordinary nursery company, ideally on a sounder surface, will suit him better.
**Parchment(IRE)**, related to a modest performer, offered little immediate promise on this racecourse debut but may be capable of better in due course.

## 5085 CANTORSPORT.CO.UK H'CAP 1m 1f 9y
7:25 (7:26) (E) (0-70,67) 3-Y-O+ £3,688 (£1,135; £567; £283) Stalls Low

Form RPR

0131 **1** **Artistic Style**$^{11}$ [4808] 4-9-4 **63** .............................. TEaves(3) 13 78+
(BEllison) *hld up in tch: effrt over 2f out: led ins fnl f: rdn out* **7/2**$^{1}$

0053 **2** *1 ¾* **General**$^{35}$ [4093] 7-9-9 **65** .............................. MFenton 3 77
(CRDore) *trckd ldrs: effrt and ev ch over 1f out: edgd rt and led briefly ins last: kpt on* **12/1**

006 **3** *1* **Mobane Flyer**$^{16}$ [4624] 4-9-1 **60** .............................. THamilton(3) 10 70
(RAFahey) *trckd ldrs: led over 2f out to ins fnl f: nt qckn wl ins last* **20/1**

L365 **4** *3* **Tagula Blue (IRE)**$^{34}$ [4142] 4-9-11 **67** .............................. DeanMcKeown 7 72
(JAGlover) *missed break: hdwy 2f out: hung lft: no imp fnl f* **12/1**

2355 **5** *1 ½* **Apache Point (IRE)**$^{10}$ [4826] 7-8-12 **54** .............................. KimTinkler 15 56
(NTinkler) *in tch: effrt 2f out: one pce fnl f* **6/1**

2321 **6** *3 ½* **Melodian**$^{22}$ [4493] 9-9-4 **65** .............................. (b) MLawson(5) 9 61
(MBrittain) *dwlt: rdn in rr over 3f out: sme late hdwy: n.d* **4/1**$^{2}$

0000 **7** *¾* **Hoh's Back**$^{30}$ [4246] 5-8-4 **51** .............................. (p) StephanieHollinshead(5) 14 45
(PaulJohnson) *hld up: rdn and effrt 2f out: nvr able to chal* **25/1**

0524 **8** *9* **Third Empire**$^{33}$ [4177] 3-9-1 **64** .............................. PFessey 6 42
(CGrant) *led to over 2f out: wknd over 1f out* **16/1**

1002 **9** *hd* **Mount Hillaby (IRE)**$^{9}$ [4852] 4-9-1 **57** .............................. DaleGibson 4 35
(MWEasterby) *keen: cl up tl rdn and wknd over 1f out* **5/1**$^{3}$

4350 **10** *1 ½* **King's Envoy (USA)**$^{86}$ [2583] 5-9-4 **60** .............................. DMcGaffin 8 35
(MrsJCMcgregor) *prom: rdn over 2f out: sn wknd* **66/1**

0014 **11** *2 ½* **Got To Be Cash**$^{11}$ [4808] 5-8-7 **54** .............................. BSwarbrick(5) 1 25
(WMBrisbourne) *hld up midfield: effrt over 2f out: wknd wl over 1f out* **15/2**

0-30 **12** *12* **Shardda**$^{112}$ [1931] 4-9-4 **63** .............................. PMulrennan(3) 12 12
(FWatson) *hld up: rdn and wknd fr 4f out* **50/1**

2m 3.06s (5.26) **Going Correction** +0.70s/f (Yiel)
**WFA** 3 from 4yo+ 7lb 12 Ran SP% **118.3**
Speed ratings: **104,102,101,98,97 94,93,85,85,84 82,71**CSF £44.77 CT £743.00 TOTE £4.80: £1.90, £3.20, £5.20; EX 90.10.
**Owner** Mr & Mrs D A Gamble **Bred** Juddmonte Farms **Trained** Norton, N Yorks

**FOCUS**
The gallop was only fair given the conditions but the form has been rated positively, since the second and third looked potentially well treated. Artistic Style continues to progress and remains one to keep on the right side.

**NOTEBOOK**
**Artistic Style** ◆ is in tremendous form and notched his third win from his last four starts and, in doing so, proved himself fully effective in testing ground. He was 5lb well in here, but his previous win had already been boosted and he will not be badly treated off his new mark.
**General** had the run of the race on this first run for his new yard and returned to form on his favoured testing ground. He is capable of winning from this mark but his lack of consistency means he is not one to place maximum faith in.
**Mobane Flyer** ◆, from a stable in tremendous form, showed more than enough on his first start over this trip to suggest that he will be placed to good advantage in due course. He has slipped to a decent mark and looked back to somewhere near his Irish form.
**Tagula Blue(IRE)** ran creditably and fared the best of those held up, but his tendency to lose ground at the start is a concern and he did not look the most straightforward when asked for his effort. He remains one to tread carefully with. *Official explanation: jockey said he missed the break*
**Apache Point(IRE)** is mainly consistent and was not disgraced from his wide draw, but the fact that he has not won a race for over a year is becoming a concern.
**Melodian** relishes these conditions but lost his chance at the start and looks worth another chance. *Official explanation: jockey said he missed the break*
**Mount Hillaby(IRE)** was too keen in the conditions but is worth another chance over this trip back on a less testing surface.
**King's Envoy(USA)** *Official explanation: jockey said gelding was unsuited by heavy going*

## 5086 CANTORINDEX.CO.UK MAIDEN STKS 7f
7:55 (7:55) (D) 3-Y-O+ £3,474 (£1,069; £534; £267) Stalls High

Form RPR

3042 **1** **Tropical Storm (IRE)**$^{14}$ [4707] 3-9-0 73 .............................. KDarley 4 63
(JNoseda) *cl up: led over 2f out: drvn and kpt on fnl f* **4/11**$^{1}$

5- **2** *hd* **Queen's Echo**$^{336}$ [5190] 3-8-6 .............................. LEnstone(3) 3 57
(MDods) *prom: rdn over 2f out: kpt on wl fnl f: jst hld* **9/1**$^{2}$

2050 **3** *5* **La Fonteyne**$^{22}$ [4489] 3-8-6 44 .............................. THamilton(3) 8 45
(CBBBooth) *dwlt: hld up in tch: effrt over 2f out: kpt on fnl f: no imp* **33/1**

0 **4** *3 ½* **Grey Fortune**$^{111}$ [1972] 5-8-9 .............................. MLawson(5) 5 36
(MBrittain) *in tch: hdwy to chal over 2f out: sn rdn and outpcd* **28/1**

0 **5** *½* **Ink In Gold (IRE)**$^{88}$ [2517] 3-9-0 .............................. PBradley 2 40
(PABlockley) *dwlt: hld up in tch: effrt over 2f out: sn no imp* **16/1**

0503 **6** *2* **Speed Racer**$^{33}$ [4180] 3-8-9 51 .............................. KimTinkler 10 30
(DonEnricoIncisa) *disp ld after 2f to over 2f out: sn btn* **14/1**

**7** *shd* **Swinton** 3-9-0 .............................. TWilliams 9 34
(MBrittain) *s.i.s: drvn along 1/2-way: nvr rchd ldrs* **25/1**

4024 **8** *¾* **Borodinsky**$^{19}$ [4573] 3-8-11 47 .............................. TEaves(3) 7 32
(REBarr) *mde most to over 2f out: sn wknd* **12/1**$^{3}$

06 **9** *11* **After Lent (IRE)**$^{27}$ [4332] 3-9-0 .............................. DeanMcKeown 6 5
(PABlockley) *hld up: pushed along over 3f out: sn btn* **28/1**

40 **10** *28* **Perrywinkle Boy**$^{12}$ [4781] 3-9-0 .............................. DarrenWilliams 1 —
(MDHammond) *in tch to 3f out: sn btn* **50/1**

1m 35.87s (7.85) **Going Correction** +1.075s/f (Soft)
**WFA** 3 from 5yo 5lb 10 Ran SP% **119.2**
Speed ratings: **98,97,92,88,87 85,85,84,71,39**CSF £4.05 TOTE £1.30: £1.10, £2.20, £7.70; EX 6.10 Place 6 £32.74, Place 5 £14.82 .
**Owner** Lucayan Stud **Bred** Michael Dalton **Trained** Newmarket, Suffolk

**FOCUS**
A race lacking strength, but what looked a straightforward task for the favourite proved anything but that in the conditions. Third-placed La Fonteyne, with a BHB mark of just 44, is probably the best guide to the form.

**NOTEBOOK**
**Tropical Storm(IRE)** looked to have strong claims in a weak race but was below form and had to work very hard to land the odds. Faster ground may suit but he will be one to take on in handicaps from his current mark on this evidence.
**Queen's Echo** not seen since hinting at ability on her debut last September, bettered that effort over this longer trip. She has only raced on testing ground to date and looks capable of picking up a small race if staying sound.



The Form Book, Raceform Ltd, Compton, RG20 6NL

**La Fonteyne** was not disgraced back over this longer trip and on this first run on heavy. She is worth another try over a mile but is not very consistent and will continue to look vulnerable in this grade.
**Grey Fortune** hinted at ability in this modest event but will be seen to better effect in weak handicap company in due course.
**Ink In Gold(IRE)** did not do enough to suggest he was about to win a race in this grade in the near future.
**Speed Racer**, a modest and unreliable sort up to a mile, offered little immediate promise.
**Perrywinkle Boy** *Official explanation: jockey said gelding had a breathing problem*
T/Plt: £53.60 to a £1 stake. Pool: £31,072.25. 422.90 winning tickets. T/Qpdt: £4.20 to a £1 stake. Pool: £2,025.60. 353.90 winning tickets. RY

# 4750 NEWMARKET (JULY) (R-H)

Friday, August 27

**OFFICIAL GOING: Soft**

The ground was as soft as it had been here all year and favoured those to race close to the stands' side rail in the early races..
Wind: Slight behind first four races, but becoming fresher Weather: Overcast

## 5087 SANDALS EBF MAIDEN STKS (DIV I) 7f

1:15 (1:17) (D) 2-Y-O £5,512 (£1,696; £848; £424) Stalls High

| Form | | | Horse | Jockey | RPR |
|---|---|---|---|---|---|
| 04 | 1 | | **Chief Scout**[14] 4730 2-8-11 (BJMeehan) *mde all: rdn over 1f out: styd on* **4/1**[2] | KFallon 11 | 84 |
| 3 | 2 | 3/4 | **Red Affleck (USA)**[137] 1374 2-8-11 (PWChapple-Hyam) *lw: chsd ldrs: rdn 1/2-way: ev ch fr over 1f out: edgd lft ins fnl f: styd on* **12/1** | AMcCarthy 8 | 82 |
| 4 | 3 | 1 1/2 | **Palatinate (FR)**[34] 4143 2-8-11 (HCandy) *lw: chsd ldrs: rdn and ev ch over 1f out: no ex ins fnl f* **5/1**[3] | DaneO'Neill 2 | 78 |
| | 4 | 1 | **Top The Charts** 2-8-11 (RHannon) *gd sort: leggy: s.s: sn pushed along in rr: hdwy and edgd lft over 1f out: hung rt ins fnl f: styd on same pce* **14/1** | RHughes 5 | 76 |
| | 5 | 1 1/2 | **War At Sea (IRE)** 2-8-11 (MPTregoning) *w'like: scope: bkwd: dwlt: outpcd: styd on ins fnl f: nvr nrr* **7/1** | MartinDwyer 12 | 72 |
| | 6 | 3/4 | **Boxhall (IRE)** 2-8-11 (PWHarris) *w'like: sn pushed along in rr: styd on ins fnl f: nt trble ldrs* **33/1** | NCallan 4 | 70 |
| 0 | 7 | 1 3/4 | **Stancomb Wills (IRE)**[14] 4730 2-8-11 (MHTompkins) *chsd ldrs: rdn over 1f out: wknd ins fnl f* **100/1** | PRobinson 10 | 66 |
| | 8 | 1 1/2 | **Ustad (IRE)** 2-8-11 (JLDunlop) *w'like: unf: bit bkwd: s.s: outpcd: nvr nrr* **20/1** | RHills 7 | 62 |
| 0 | 9 | shd | **Jack The Giant (IRE)**[53] 3588 2-8-11 (BWHills) *chsd wnr 5f: sn wknd* **3/1**[1] | MHills 1 | 62 |
| | 10 | hd | **Rossbeigh (IRE)** 2-8-11 (DRLoder) *gd sort: chsd ldrs: lost pl 1/2-way: wknd over 1f out* **8/1** | JFortune 3 | 61 |
| 3 | 11 | 8 | **Gitche Manito (IRE)**[15] 4682 2-8-11 (AKing) *chsd ldrs: rdn over 2f out: wknd over 1f out* **16/1** | JDSmith 9 | 41 |

1m 29.82s (3.05) **Going Correction** +0.30s/f (Good) **11** Ran SP% **114.2**
Speed ratings: **94,93,91,90,88 87,85,84,83,83 74**CSF £48.70 TOTE £4.70: £2.10, £2.70, £1.80; EX 41.90.
**Owner** J R Good **Bred** J R And Mrs P Good **Trained** Upper Lambourn, Berks

**FOCUS**
All the maidens run over this trip were run in a similar time. This could be a decent maiden, but the ordinary time and the limited previous form restricts confidence.

**NOTEBOOK**
**Chief Scout** had the edge in experience over his rivals and, on ground as soft as this, that made all the difference.
**Red Affleck(USA)**, one of the first off the bridle, stuck to his task well enough although he did tend to edge towards the centre of the track in the latter stages.
**Palatinate(FR)** is going the right way, but may appreciate better ground than he faced here.
**Top The Charts**, a half-brother to the useful ten-furlong performers Mingling and Tier Worker, was very green and can be expected to have learnt plenty from this.
**War At Sea(IRE)**, who is out of a mare that won over this trip as a juvenile, was very green and can be expected to leave this behind in due course.
**Jack The Giant(IRE)** is a fine individual, but the best of him may not be seen until next year. He was reported by his jockey not to have handled the ground. *Official explanation: jockey said colt was unsuited by Soft ground*

## 5088 BEACHES RESORTS EBF MAIDEN FILLIES' STKS (DIV I) 7f

1:45 (1:46) (D) 2-Y-O £5,499 (£1,692; £846; £423) Stalls High

| Form | | | Horse | Jockey | RPR |
|---|---|---|---|---|---|
| 5 | 1 | | **Thakafaat (IRE)**[27] 4344 2-8-11 (JLDunlop) *chsd ldrs: rdn to ld and hung lft ins fnl f: r.o* **9/2**[2] | RHills 8 | 84 |
| | 2 | 1 | **Celtique** 2-8-11 (SirMichaelStoute) *w'like: leggy: dwlt: sn chsng ldrs: pushed along 1/2-way: rdn to ld over 1f out: hung lft and hdd ins fnl f: no ex nr fin* **5/1**[3] | KFallon 3 | 81 |
| 43 | 3 | 1 3/4 | **Singhalese**[9] 4851 2-8-11 (JAOsborne) *lw: hld up in tch: rdn over 2f out: styd on* **3/1**[1] | LDettori 6 | 77 |
| 5 | 4 | nk | **Blueberry Tart (IRE)**[14] 4714 2-8-11 (BJMeehan) *led: hung lft and hdd over 1f out: no ex ins fnl f* **9/2**[2] | JFortune 11 | 76 |
| 0 | 5 | 2 1/2 | **Love Me Tender**[20] 4560 2-8-11 (HRACecil) *lw: chsd ldrs: rdn over 1f out: wknd ins fnl f* **8/1** | WRyan 2 | 70 |
| | 6 | nk | **Zayn Zen** 2-8-11 (MAJarvis) *w'like: scope: hld up: swtchd lft over 1f out: nvr trbld ldrs* **8/1** | PRobinson 7 | 69 |
| | 7 | 4 | **Hoh My Darling** 2-8-11 (MLWBell) *neat: s.i.s: sn prom: rdn and wknd over 1f out* **20/1** | RMullen 10 | 59 |
| | 8 | 1/2 | **Make It Snappy** 2-8-11 (PWHarris) *lt-f: unf: s.s: outpcd* **20/1** | DaneO'Neill 1 | 58 |
| 0 | 9 | hd | **Hallowed Dream (IRE)**[22] 4498 2-8-11 (CEBrittain) *chsd ldr tl wknd wl over 1f out* **33/1** | RHughes 4 | 58 |
| 0060 | 10 | 13 | **Sherbourne**[21] 4523 2-8-11 (MGQuinlan) *plld hrd and prom: wknd over 2f out* **100/1** | PaulEddery 9 | 25 |

1m 29.8s (3.03) **Going Correction** +0.30s/f (Good) **10** Ran SP% **113.7**
Speed ratings: **94,92,90,90,87 87,82,82,81,67**CSF £25.31 TOTE £4.90: £1.40, £1.90, £1.70; EX 34.00.
**Owner** Hamdan Al Maktoum **Bred** Norelands Bloodstock **Trained** Arundel, W Sussex

**FOCUS**
Probably a fair fillies' maiden and, as in the first race, the winner had the edge in experience. The race should work out.

**NOTEBOOK**
**Thakafaat(IRE)**, with the benefit of an outing just knew too much for the runner-up. By Unfuwain, she really appreciated the give in the ground.
**Celtique** ◆, a half-sister to the useful National Anthem, was very green and is sure to have learnt plenty from the experience. She should have no trouble paying her way, especially when stepping up in trip.
**Singhalese** had shown fair form coming into this and appeared to run her race again. She may have more luck in nurseries.
**Blueberry Tart(IRE)** had the run of the race and had no excuses. Her future looks to lie in handicaps.
**Love Me Tender** showed a bit more than on her debut until getting tired in the ground.
**Zayn Zen**, who is out of a mare that won over ten furlongs, was not knocked around on this ground and should repay the kindness shown in due course.

## 5089 BEACHES RESORTS EBF MAIDEN FILLIES' STKS (DIV II) 7f

2:15 (2:17) (D) 2-Y-O £5,499 (£1,692; £846; £423) Stalls High

| Form | | | Horse | Jockey | RPR |
|---|---|---|---|---|---|
| 2 | 1 | | **Playful Act (IRE)**[13] 4753 2-8-11 (JHMGosden) *mde all: pushed out* **8/15**[1] | JFortune 8 | 82+ |
| | 2 | 1 3/4 | **Naivety** 2-8-11 (CEBrittain) *cmpt: prom: racd keenly: chsd wnr fnl f: no imp* **33/1** | RHills 5 | 77 |
| 0 | 3 | 1 3/4 | **This Is My Song**[14] 4712 2-8-11 (MrsAJPerrett) *prom: chsd wnr 2f out to 1f out: styd on same pce* **16/1** | LDettori 2 | 73 |
| | 4 | 5 | **Bowled Out (GER)** 2-8-11 (PJMcbride) *cmpt: bkwd: trckd ldrs: outpcd 2f out: styd on ins fnl f* **100/1** | GCarter 9 | 61 |
| | 5 | 1 | **Napapijri (FR)** 2-8-11 (DPKeane) *w'like: bkwd: slowly into stride: sn prom: lost pl 5f out: hdwy 1/2-way: hung lft over 1f out: hung lft and wknd fnl f* **33/1** | DaneO'Neill 3 | 58 |
| | 6 | 1 1/4 | **Bronwen (IRE)** 2-8-11 (JNoseda) *gd sort: hld up: n.d* **20/1** | EAhern 6 | 55 |
| 2 | 7 | 1/2 | **Love Affair (IRE)**[29] 4272 2-8-11 (RHannon) *chsd wnr 5f: sn wknd* **11/2**[3] | RHughes 1 | 54 |
| | 8 | hd | **Raze** 2-8-11 (SirMichaelStoute) *leggy: scope: dwlt: sn pushed along and prom: rdn 1/2-way: wknd wl over 1f out* **5/1**[2] | KFallon 7 | 53 |
| 00 | 9 | 2 | **Lola Sapola (IRE)**[13] 4753 2-8-11 (NACallaghan) *outpcd* **66/1** | AMackay 4 | 48 |

1m 29.75s (2.98) **Going Correction** +0.30s/f (Good) **9** Ran SP% **116.3**
Speed ratings: **94,92,90,84,83 81,81,80,78**CSF £33.10 TOTE £1.60: £1.02, £8.00, £3.20; EX 33.40.
**Owner** Sangster Family **Bred** Swettenham Stud **Trained** Manton, Wilts

**FOCUS**
There did not look much strength in depth, but the winner impressed and is clearly a smart performer in the making.

**NOTEBOOK**
**Playful Act(IRE)** comfirmed the promise of her debut and did not have to work too hard to see off her rivals. With improvement to come over further, she looks a filly of some promise and would be of interest in the Fillies' Mile, if allowed to take her chance.
**Naivety**, a half-sister to six-furlong winner Najeyba, is quite a late foal, but shaped with plenty of promise.
**This Is My Song** appears to be going the right way, but may have done better still on a less testing surface.
**Bowled Out(GER)**, a late foal, did not shape too badly and can be found an opening at a lower level.
**Napapijri(FR)** was very green and can only have learnt from the experience.
**Bronwen(IRE)**, a half-sister to Group One winner Teggiano, is quite a late foal and looks the sort to do better next year.
**Raze**, who is related to several winners, was too green to do herself justice and better will be seen of her next year when tackling middle distances.

## 5090 COCO REEF RESORT AND GOLDEN CARIBBEAN NURSERY 1m

2:50 (2:50) (C) 2-Y-O £8,521 (£2,622; £1,311; £655) Stalls High

| Form | | | Horse | Jockey | RPR |
|---|---|---|---|---|---|
| 3211 | 1 | | **Merchant (IRE)**[8] 4890 2-9-8 **84** 6ex (MLWBell) *hld up: racd keenly: hdwy over 2f out: hung rt and led over 1f out: r.o wl* **8/11**[1] | HayleyTurner(5) 6 | 95+ |
| 4000 | 2 | 2 1/2 | **Master Joseph**[23] 4445 2-8-3 **60** (MRChannon) *chsd ldr tl led over 2f out: hdd over 1f out: styd on same pce* **50/1** | JFanning 11 | 62 |
| 51 | 3 | 1 1/4 | **Vale De Lobo**[35] 4095 2-9-1 **72** (AWCarroll) *chsd ldrs: rdn over 1f out: styd on* **20/1** | NCallan 13 | 71 |
| 2452 | 4 | shd | **Alright My Son (IRE)**[21] 4524 2-9-6 **77** (RHannon) *lw: hld up: hdwy over 1f out: sn rdn: styd on same pce fnl f* **14/1** | DaneO'Neill 4 | 76 |
| 5310 | 5 | 1 3/4 | **My Princess (IRE)**[10] 4836 2-9-7 **78** (NACallaghan) *hld up: hdwy 2f out: no imp fnl f* **16/1** | EAhern 10 | 74 |
| 0333 | 6 | 2 | **Tumbleweed Galore (IRE)**[14] 4728 2-9-7 **78** (BJMeehan) *lw: s.i.s: hld up: nvr trbld ldrs* **14/1** | JFortune 8 | 70 |
| 0406 | 7 | shd | **Our Choice (IRE)**[18] 4601 2-8-5 **62** (NPLittmoden) *led over 5f: wknd over 1f out* **50/1** | JBramhill 2 | 53 |
| 2151 | 8 | 3 | **Good Wee Girl (IRE)**[7] 4907 2-9-9 **80** 6ex (PSMcentee) *lw: hld up: hdwy over 2f out: nt clr run wl over 1f out: sn wknd* **16/1** | LDettori 9 | 65 |
| 0004 | 9 | 1 3/4 | **Fair Along (GER)**[19] 4584 2-9-1 **72** (WJarvis) *racd alone far side: prom over 5f* **16/1** | PRobinson 1 | 54+ |
| 5410 | 10 | 1 1/4 | **Emerald Penang (IRE)**[27] 4326 2-9-6 **77** (PWChapple-Hyam) *hld up: pushed along over 3f out: wknd over 1f out* **10/1**[3] | KFallon 12 | 56 |
| 01 | 11 | 3/4 | **Hidden Chance**[36] 4053 2-9-1 **72** (RHannon) *s.s: hdwy 6f out: wknd wl over 1f out* **20/1** | MartinDwyer 7 | 50 |
| 046 | 12 | 1 1/4 | **Discomania**[29] 4263 2-9-4 **75** (RCharlton) *chsd ldrs: rdn over 2f out: wknd wl over 1f out* **9/1**[2] | RHughes 5 | 50 |
| 004 | 13 | 1/2 | **Lord Normacote**[22] 4480 2-8-11 **68** (CADwyer) *prom 6f* **66/1** | TEDurcan 3 | 42 |

1m 43.26s (2.78) **Going Correction** +0.30s/f (Good) **13** Ran SP% **122.9**
Speed ratings: **98,95,94,94,92 90,90,87,85,84 83,82,81**CSF £74.14 CT £522.79 TOTE £1.90: £1.30, £8.70, £5.30; EX 33.50.
**Owner** H E Sheikh Rashid Bin Mohammed **Bred** John Foley **Trained** Newmarket, Suffolk

**FOCUS**
A fair nursery and a smart peformance from the winner, who could turn out to be better than a handicapper, although the form behind is unexceptional.

**NOTEBOOK**
**Merchant(IRE)** was ridden with plenty of confidence and won with something in hand to complete a ten-day hat-trick. This step up in trip clearly suited well, and connections now intend taking him to Italy for the Group One Gran Criterium.
**Master Joseph** found improvement for the step up in trip and, if reproducing this effort, should have no trouble getting off the mark.
**Vale De Lobo**, a costly purchase out of a Southwell seller, left that form behind and could well turn out to be something of a bargain.

**Alright My Son(IRE)** appeared to stay this trip well enough, but he will need his sights lowering if he is to get off the mark.
**My Princess(IRE)** was not knocked around on ground which may have been too soft for her.
**Discomania** *Official explanation: jockey said colt was unsuited by Soft ground*

## 5091 SANDALS EBF MAIDEN STKS (DIV II) 7f
3:25 (3:27) (D ) 2-Y-O **£5,499** (£1,692; £846; £423) **Stalls** High

Form RPR
00 **1** **The Coires (IRE)**[21] 4523 2-8-11 ........ RHughes 3 87
(RHannon) *w ldrs tl led 2f out: hung rt over 1f out: rdn out* **8/1**[3]
**2** 1 1/2 **Dhaular Dhar (IRE)** 2-8-11 ........ MHills 8 83
(BWHills) *w'like: scope: trckd ldrs: nt clr run over 1f out: unable qck ins fnl f* **12/1**
3 **3** 1 1/2 **The Duke Of Dixie (USA)**[76] 2898 2-8-11 ........ KFallon 4 79
(PFICole) *w ldr: rdn 1/2-way: ev ch 2f out: n.m.r over 1f out : styd on same pce* **5/4**[1]
**4** *nk* **Mutajammel (FR)** 2-8-11 ........ RHills 5 79+
(SirMichaelStoute) *gd sort: bit bkwd: prom: outpcd 4f out: nt clr run over 1f out: styd on ins fnl f* **7/1**[2]
0 **5** *shd* **Eva Soneva So Fast (IRE)**[15] 4681 2-8-11 ........ JQuinn 1 78
(JLDunlop) *s.i.s: hld up: hdwy 2f out: styd on same pce ins fnl f* **50/1**
0 **6** *hd* **Press Express (IRE)**[14] 4730 2-8-11 ........ TEDurcan 2 78
(MRChannon) *lw: chsd ldrs: rdn over 1f out: wknd ins fnl f* **14/1**
**7** *4* **Billy One Punch** 2-8-11 ........ AMcCarthy 12 68
(PWChapple-Hyam) *w'like: scope: trckd ldrs: rdn over 1f out: sn wknd* **10/1**
**8** *nk* **Battledress (IRE)** 2-8-11 ........ MartinDwyer 7 67
(MPTregoning) *neat: bkwd: s.s: hdwy 1/2-way: wknd over 1f out* **20/1**
20 **9** *1* **Danehill Willy (IRE)**[28] 4292 2-8-11 ........ RMullen 9 65
(NACallaghan) *prom: lost pl over 4f out: n.d after* **10/1**
**10** 1 1/4 **Cost Analysis (IRE)** 2-8-11 ........ PRobinson 10 61
(MAJarvis) *cmpt: scope: bit bkwd: led 5f: wknd fnl f* **14/1**
0 **11** 3 1/2 **Scarp (USA)**[14] 4730 2-8-11 ........ EAhern 6 53
(JNoseda) *lw: hld up: shkn up over 1f out: nvr nr to chal* **20/1**
**12** *dist* **Bahamian Spring (IRE)** 2-8-11 ........ JFortune 11 —
(DRLoder) *str: cmpt: bit bkwd: s.s: hdwy 1/2-way: wknd and eased over 1f out* **14/1**

1m 29.24s (2.47) **Going Correction** +0.30s/f (Good) **12 Ran SP% 125.4**
Speed ratings: **97,95,93,93,93 92,88,87,86,85 81**,—CSF £103.62 TOTE £11.10: £2.60, £2.50, £1.20; EX 134.10.
**Owner** The Queen **Bred** The Queen **Trained** East Everleigh, Wilts

**FOCUS**
Hard to know what to make of this, but the time compared favourably with the other maidens run over this trip and the form may prove to be decent.

**NOTEBOOK**
**The Coires(IRE)** seemed to find improvement for getting his toe in and, as he had already had the benefit of a couple of races, he just knew too much for the runner-up.
**Dhaular Dhar(IRE)**, out of a mare that won over five furlongs as a juvenile, is quite a late foal. He shaped with plenty of promise and looks a ready-made winner.
**The Duke Of Dixie(USA)** off the bridle some way out, looked to be hating the ground.
**Mutajammel(FR)**, a 520,000 gns yearling, looked very green and can only improve for the experience.
**Eva Soneva So Fast(IRE)** is still learning and looks the sort to do better next term in staying handicaps.
**Press Express(IRE)** showed a bit more sparkle before getting tired on the ground.
**Billy One Punch**, a half-brother to a couple of winners, travelled well for a long way until lack of a previous outing caught him out.
**Cost Analysis(IRE)** *Official explanation: jockey said colt hung left throughout*
**Bahamian Spring(IRE)** *Official explanation: jockey said colt lost his action*

## 5092 HALF MOON CLAIMING STKS 7f
4:00 (4:00) (E ) 3-Y-O **£4,163** (£1,281; £640; £320) **Stalls** High

Form RPR
2544 **1** **Vienna's Boy (IRE)**[7] 4917 3-9-7 82 ........ DaneO'Neill 14 81
(RHannon) *lw: racd centre: hld up: hdwy 3f out: led over 1f out: hung lft fnl f: rdn out* **4/1**[2]
0545 **2** 1 1/2 **Honest Injun**[12] 4780 3-9-7 74 ........ MHills 11 77
(BWHills) *racd centre: hld up: hdwy 1/2-way: led 2f out: sn rdn and hdd: styd on same pce ins fnl f* **7/2**[1]
4002 **3** 2 1/2 **Jarvo**[17] 4619 3-9-2 62 ........ KFallon 13 66
(NPLittmoden) *s.i.s: racd centre: sn chsng ldrs: led 1/2-way: rdn and hdd 2f out: no ex fnl f* **15/2**
0210 **4** 3 1/2 **Hoh Bleu Dee**[23] 4435 3-9-3 75 ........(b) JFortune 5 58
(SKirk) *swtg: racd centre: hld up: hdwy and bmpd 1/2-way: rdn over 2f out: no ex over 1f out* **6/1**
00 **5** *4* **Blake Hall Lad (IRE)**[112] 1939 3-8-8 ........ BReilly(3) 7 42
(MissJFeilden) *racd centre: prom over 4f* **50/1**
6500 **6** *nk* **David's Girl**[22] 4497 3-8-1 38 ........ JMackay 2 32
(DMorris) *lw: racd centre: chsd ldrs over 5f* **50/1**
0500 **7** *1/2* **Soul Provider (IRE)**[21] 4517 3-8-4 44 ........(p) JFanning 10 33
(MJAttwater) *led centre to 1/2-way: wknd over 1f out* **40/1**
3046 **8** 2 1/2 **Soviet Sceptre (IRE)**[11] 4817 3-8-12 68 ........(t) OUrbina 12 35
(MissDMountain) *b: racd centre: sn pushed along in rr: hung rt over 2f out: n.d* **14/1**
0040 **9** *2* **Petrolina (IRE)**[32] 4190 3-8-6 53 ........(t) MartinDwyer 15 24
(HMorrison) *racd centre: prom 5f* **50/1**
-000 **10** *nk* **Pleasure Seeker**[78] 2820 3-7-11 57 ........ AshleighHorton(7) 1 21
(MDIUsher) *lw: s.s: racd centre: a bhd* **40/1**
0000 **11** 1 1/2 **Shebaan**[22] 4496 3-8-1 42 ........ AMcCarthy 6 15
(PSMcentee) *racd centre: chsd ldrs: edgd lft 1/2-way: sn wknd* **66/1**
1566 **12** 1 1/4 **Ragged Jack (IRE)**[11] 4814 3-9-2 70 ........(p) SWKelly 4 26
(GABufler) *racd centre: chsd ldrs over 4f* **14/1**
3406 **13** 1 1/2 **Spin King (IRE)**[27] 4340 3-8-13 72 ........ RMullen 8 20
(MLWBell) *racd centre: hld up: rdn 1/2-way: a bhd* **9/2**[3]
3204 **14** *27* **Yashin (IRE)**[22] 4483 3-8-13 59 ........ NCallan 16 —
(MHTompkins) *lw: bolted to post: racd alone stands' side: prom 4f: eased* **25/1**

1m 27.95s (1.18) **Going Correction** +0.30s/f (Good) **14 Ran SP% 115.9**
Speed ratings: **105,103,100,96,91 91,90,88,85,85 83,82,80,49**CSF £16.73 TOTE £5.50: £2.20, £1.70, £2.30; EX 22.60.The winner was claimed by Mr W J Musson for £20,000. Honest Injun was claimed by Mr J G M O'Shea for £20,000.
**Owner** M Sines **Bred** Mark Commins **Trained** East Everleigh, Wilts

**FOCUS**
A fair time for the grade, but the field had the benefit of a strengthening wind behind them and all but one of them raced on the fresher ground up the centre of the track. The first three set the standard and the form should prove sound.

**NOTEBOOK**
**Vienna's Boy(IRE)** has been somewhat disappointing this term, but this drop in class did the trick and he will now join Willie Musson, who paid £20,000 for him.
**Honest Injun** had his ideal conditions and ran as well as could be expected. Now there is plenty of soft ground about he can be found an opening.
**Jarvo**, tackling his softest surface to date, ran his race and had no excuses.
**Hoh Bleu Dee** has done his winning on a faster surface and may not have been entirely suited by this ground.
**Blake Hall Lad(IRE)** has shown little in three starts to date, but this effort should ensure he starts life in handicaps off a favourable mark.
**Spin King(IRE)** *Official explanation: trainer said colt was unsuited by Soft ground*
**Yashin(IRE)** *Official explanation: jockey said gelding ran too freely to post*

## 5093 BREHENY H'CAP 1m 6f 175y
4:35 (4:37) (C ) (0-95,95) 3-Y-O+ **£9,763** (£3,004; £1,502; £751) **Stalls** High

Form RPR
1131 **1** **Sendintank**[3] 5027 4-8-0 67 5ex ........ MartinDwyer 11 81+
(SCWilliams) *hld up: hdwy over 2f out: rdn to ld over 1f out: hung rt ins fnl f: eased nr fin* **7/4**[1]
2040 **2** 3 1/2 **Promoter**[30] 4226 4-9-8 89 ........ EAhern 14 98
(JNoseda) *hld up: hdwy over 2f out: nt rch wnr* **18/1**
4126 **3** *1* **Act Of The Pace (IRE)**[42] 3902 4-8-11 78 ........ JFanning 4 86
(MJohnston) *sn led: rdn and hdd over 1f out: no ex* **28/1**
-630 **4** *3/4* **Argonaut**[27] 4345 4-9-8 89 ........ KFallon 2 96
(SirMichaelStoute) *hld up: hdwy 1/2-way: jnd ldr over 3f out: styd on same pce appr fnl f* **16/1**
3360 **5** *3* **High Point (IRE)**[35] 4075 6-8-10 77 ........ DaneO'Neill 1 80
(GPEnright) *lw: chsd ldrs: ev ch over 3f out: wknd fnl f* **33/1**
6022 **6** *1* **Tilla**[15] 4686 4-8-3 70 ........ JQuinn 8 72
(HMorrison) *hld up: hdwy over 3f out: rdn and wknd over 1f out* **10/1**
060 **7** *5* **Laggan Bay (IRE)**[10] 4831 4-8-5 75 ........ BReilly(3) 3 70
(JCFox) *b: mid-div: hdwy over 4f out: wknd over 2f out* **25/1**
/005 **8** *1/2* **Ranville**[12] 4777 6-9-5 86 ........ PRobinson 6 80
(MAJarvis) *b: prom: outpcd over 3f out: n.d after* **9/2**[2]
0-30 **9** 1 1/2 **Ten Carat**[30] 4226 4-10-0 95 ........ RHughes 16 87
(MrsAJPerrett) *lw: w ldr 10f: wknd over 2f out* **12/1**
0005 **10** *5* **Bukit Fraser (IRE)**[23] 4441 3-7-12 78 oh1 ........(t) JMackay 13 64
(PFICole) *hld up: hdwy over 3f out: wknd over 2f out* **25/1**
0400 **11** *1* **Mamcazma**[20] 4550 6-9-5 86 ........ MTebbutt 15 71
(DMorris) *chsd ldrs: rdn over 4f out: sn wknd* **28/1**
3060 **12** *3* **Domenico (IRE)**[12] 4778 6-7-7 65 oh2 ........ HayleyTurner(5) 9 46
(JRJenkins) *lw: hld up: hdwy over 5f out: wknd 2f out* **100/1**
2230 **13** 1 1/2 **Theatre (USA)**[48] 3725 5-8-13 80 ........ RMullen 5 59
(JamiePoulton) *dwlt: hdwy 7f out: wknd 3f out* **33/1**
1443 **14** *3* **Bumptious**[51] 3639 3-8-10 90 ........(b) RHills 7 65
(MHTompkins) *hld up in tch: rdn and wknd over 2f out* **33/1**
0/22 **15** *17* **Captain Miller**[97] 2305 8-8-5 72 ........(t) WRyan 10 25
(NJHenderson) *hld up: hdwy over 5f out: wknd over 2f out* **15/2**[3]
1600 **16** *22* **Grooms Affection**[14] 4715 4-9-1 82 ........(t) NCallan 12 6
(PWHarris) *hld up: plld hrd: hdwy over 5f out: wknd over 3f out* **16/1**
3104 **17** *shd* **Anousa (IRE)**[29] 4274 3-8-13 93 ........ JFortune 17 17
(PHowling) *prom 10f* **20/1**

3m 11.35s (0.59) **Going Correction** +0.30s/f (Good)
**WFA** 3 from 4yo+ 13lb **17 Ran SP% 129.3**
Speed ratings: **110,108,107,107,105 105,102,102,101,98 98,96,95,94,85 73,73**CSF £35.89 CT £736.12 TOTE £2.80: £1.20, £4.80, £4.90, £3.50; EX 80.10.
**Owner** Steve Jones And Phil McGovern **Bred** K G Powter **Trained** Newmarket, Suffolk

**FOCUS**
A fair staying contest run at what appeared a decent clip and the form could work out well. The winner is still progressing and has not stopped winning yet.

**NOTEBOOK**
**Sendintank ◆** continues up the ladder, and the way he won here suggested there is still plenty more to come.
**Promoter** got going far too late, but at least confirmed he does handle give underfoot. Although he only has a maiden win to his name, there is no doubt he does have his fair share of ability.
**Act Of The Pace(IRE)** proved well suited by this step up in trip and, as she is from the same family as the high-class stayer Yavana's Pace, she can be expected to get better as she gets older.
**Argonaut** appeared to stay this longer trip well enough, but he may be better served by a sounder surface.
**High Point(IRE)** has struggled off slightly higher marks this term and, even though he is beginning to get some respite now, still looks to need to come down further still before he gets back to winning ways.
**Tilla**, who is not an easy ride, was 4lb higher than when beaten at Haydock.
**Ten Carat**
**Captain Miller** *Official explanation: vet said gelding was distressed*
**Grooms Affection** *Official explanation: jockey said colt finished distressed*
**Anousa(IRE)** *Official explanation: trainer said colt was unsuited by Soft ground*

## 5094 AIR JAMAICA H'CAP 5f
5:05 (5:07) (D ) (0-85,75) 3-Y-O+ **£6,864** (£2,112; £1,056; £528) **Stalls** High

Form RPR
3624 **1** **Hout Bay**[6] 4935 7-8-5 56 ........ JQuinn 9 67
(RAFahey) *lw: trckd ldrs: rdn to ld ins fnl f: r.o* **11/2**[3]
6010 **2** *1/2* **Taboor (IRE)**[11] 4800 6-8-5 56 ........(bt) MartinDwyer 5 65
(JWPayne) *hld up: rdn over 1f out: r.o ins fnl f: nt rch wnr* **16/1**
0500 **3** *3/4* **Sweet Cando (IRE)**[13] 4748 3-8-5 58 ........(p) TEDurcan 8 65
(MissLAPerratt) *b.hind: sn pushed along in rr: r.o wl ins fnl f: nrst fin* **33/1**
0302 **4** *1/2* **Cerulean Rose**[9] 4854 5-9-3 68 ........ JFortune 2 73
(AWCarroll) *mid-div: sn pushed along: hdwy u.p over 1f out: ev ch ins fnl f: no ex towards fin* **4/1**[1]
6000 **5** *hd* **Mr Wolf**[10] 4837 3-9-7 74 ........ JFanning 7 78
(DWBarker) *lw: led: hdd and no ex ins fnl f* **16/1**
1000 **6** *nk* **Polish Emperor (USA)**[30] 4232 4-9-10 75 ........(e) NCallan 12 78
(PWHarris) *lw: jnd ldr 4f out: rdn over 1f out: no ex ins fnl f* **7/1**
5021 **7** *nk* **Strawberry Patch (IRE)**[13] 4748 5-8-7 58 ........(p) JMackay 10 60
(MissLAPerratt) *b: chsd ldrs: rdn over 1f out: styd on same pce ins fnl f* **7/1**
2142 **8** *5* **Foley Millennium (IRE)**[9] 4855 6-9-8 73 ........ NPollard 4 59
(MQuinn) *chsd ldrs: rdn over 1f out: wknd ins fnl f* **10/1**
0352 **9** *3/4* **Prince Cyrano**[7] 4923 5-9-6 71 ........ RMullen 6 54
(WJMusson) *b.hind: s.s: hdwy and hung lft over 1f out: wknd fnl f* **5/1**[2]
5-01 **10** *6* **Siraj**[8] 4879 5-8-12 68 6ex ........ HayleyTurner(5) 11 31
(PSMcentee) *chsd ldrs to 1/2-way* **16/1**
21-0 **11** *hd* **St Austell**[14] 4727 4-9-5 70 ........ EAhern 3 33
(JARToller) *trckds ldrs: hung lft and wknd 2f out* **25/1**

0040 **12** 2 ½ **Prime Recreation**[28] 4299 7-9-0 **65** ........................ LisaJones 1 20
(PSFelgate) *b: s.i.s: sn chsng ldrs: wknd over 1f out* **16/1**

60.60 secs (0.95) **Going Correction** +0.30s/f (Good)
**WFA** 3 from 4yo+ 2lb **12** Ran SP% **116.5**
Speed ratings: **104,103,102,101,100 100,99,91,90,81 80,76**CSF £88.56 CT £2632.87 TOTE £7.10: £2.30, £4.40, £7.50; EX 138.90 Place 6 £13.34, Place 5 £4.59.
**Owner** Northumbria Leisure Ltd **Bred** Mrs Mary Taylor **Trained** Musley Bank, N Yorks

**FOCUS**
A weak sprint for the grade, but it was run at a decent clip and the form is solid for the level.

**NOTEBOOK**
**Hout Bay** is well suited by plenty of give and, with conditions to suit, made no mistake.
**Taboor(IRE)** has not looked back since being fitted with the tongue-tie, and confirmed himself in good form when running on into second, despite the ground being softer than ideal.
**Sweet Cando(IRE)** is none too reliable and looked more likely to finish out the back. However, on meeting the rising ground she finished best of all and clearly has the ability, if she can be persuaded to use it.
**Cerulean Rose** has found life tough since winning this last year, but was far from disgraced off a 5lb higher mark.
**Mr Wolf** is a pacey fellow and did not give way until late on. While he is getting some respite now, he still looks to need a bit more help.
**Foley Millennium(IRE)** *Official explanation: jockey said gelding was unsuited by Soft ground*
T/Jkpt: £5,792.30 to a £1 stake. Pool: £65,266.00. 8.00 winning tickets. T/Plt: £16.20 to a £1 stake. Pool: £42,745.95. 1,917.40 winning tickets. T/Qpdt: £4.40 to a £1 stake. Pool: £2,512.60. 414.00 winning tickets. CR

## 4605 THIRSK (L-H)

Friday, August 27

**OFFICIAL GOING: Good to soft (soft in places)**

## 5095 FARMERS INN - HELPERBY MAIDEN AUCTION STKS (DIV I) 7f

**1:55** (1:56) (E) 2-Y-O **£3,653** (£1,124; £562; £281) **Stalls** Low

Form RPR

**1** **Desert Move (IRE)** 2-8-9 ........................ ACulhane 9 75
(MRChannon) *trckd ldrs: hdwy to ld over 2f out: rdn appr last and styd on wel* **9/2**[3]

06 **2** 1 ¼ **Nasseem Dubai (USA)**[6] 4930 2-9-0 ........................ GHind 10 77
(MrsADuffield) *in tch: hdwy on outer over 2f out: chal and ev ch over 1f out: sn rdn and edgd lft: nt qckn* **8/1**

6 **3** 3 **Red Rudy**[32] 4193 2-8-9 ........................ KMcEvoy 3 64
(RMBeckett) *trckd ldrs: effrt over 2f out: sn rdn and one pce appr last* **4/1**[2]

05 **4** 1 ½ **Tit For Tat**[73] 2961 2-8-6 ........................ MFenton 2 57
(JGGiven) *cl up: rdn along over 2f out: sn drvn and one pce* **14/1**

04 **5** 3 ½ **Comical Errors (USA)**[18] 4606 2-8-9 ........................ GFaulkner 5 51
(PCHaslam) *hmpd s: sn midfield: hdwy over 2f out: sn rdn along and kpt on: nrst fin* **12/1**

0 **6** shd **Andy Mal**[18] 4606 2-8-2 ow3 ........................ THamilton(3) 8 47
(RAFahey) *midfield: pushed along and hdwy over 2f out: sn rdn and no imp* **20/1**

03 **7** 1 ½ **Northern Secret**[14] 4705 2-8-4 ........................ KDarley 1 42
(AMBalding) *led: rdn along and hdd over 2f out: sn drvn and wknd* **9/4**[1]

**8** ¾ **Shankly Bond (IRE)** 2-8-11 ........................ FLynch 11 52+
(BSmart) *s.i.s and bhd: hdwy over 2f out: nvr nr ldrs* **16/1**

0 **9** nk **Last Pioneer (IRE)**[48] 3760 2-8-7 ........................ JEdmunds 13 42
(TPTate) *bhd tl sme late hdwy* **25/1**

00 **10** 1 ¼ **Morning Major (USA)**[34] 4131 2-8-7 ........................ PFessey 4 39
(TDBarron) *wnt rt s: sn in tch on inner: rdn along 3f out and sn btn* **50/1**

000 **11** nk **Admittance (USA)**[13] 4761 2-8-4 ........................ LGoncalves 14 35
(MrsJRRamsden) *a rr* **20/1**

0 **12** nk **Trigony (IRE)**[34] 4131 2-8-9 ........................ GGibbons 6 39
(TDEasterby) *hmpd s: a rr* **66/1**

0 **13** 11 **Mark Your Card**[13] 4761 2-8-2 ........................ DAllan 7 4
(TDEasterby) *prom: rdn along 1/2-way: wknd wl over 2f out* **25/1**

**14** 12 **Brave Tara (IRE)** 2-8-2 ........................ PMQuinn 12 —
(TDEasterby) *a bhd* **33/1**

1m 30.71s (3.61) **Going Correction** +0.50s/f (Yiel) **14** Ran SP% **123.9**
Speed ratings: **99,97,94,92,88 88,86,85,85,83 83,83,70,57**CSF £38.28 TOTE £5.40: £2.00, £2.60, £2.10; EX 48.70.
**Owner** Jaber Abdullah **Bred** Rathasker Stud **Trained** West Ilsley, Berks

**FOCUS**
An ordinary-looking first division of the auction maiden, which was run at a fair gallop and the field were strung out early as a result. Very few managed to get into the argument and the first four came clear, but the form is unlikely to prove any better than initially rated.

**NOTEBOOK**
**Desert Move(IRE)** , well-backed in the betting ring, clearly knew her job for this debut as she attained a good early position, and responded well to pressure in the straight to go and win her race. She has no fancy entries at this stage, and is bred to be better over farther in time, but there was a fair bit to like about this debut success and she looks to have a future.
**Nasseem Dubai(USA)** showed his best form to date and was a clear second best, but had no chance with the winner. He now qualifies for nurseries, enjoyed the underfoot conditions and is clearly going the right way.
**Red Rudy** , who showed definite promise on her Windsor debut, turned in another sound effort but did look a little one paced on this different ground, and was never a serious threat over this extra furlong.
**Tit For Tat** , previously unraced on ground this soft, stayed on well enough on this debut for new connections and will fare better now she is eligible for nurseries.
**Northern Secret** found little for pressure when challenged by the winner at the top of the straight, and was disappointing. She now qualifies for nurseries however, and should be better back on a quicker surface, so it may be a bit too soon to write her off.
**Shankly Bond(IRE)** was slowly away on this debut, but still shaped with a degree of promise late on and should be wiser next time.

## 5096 EUROPEAN BREEDERS FUND MAIDEN STKS 6f

**2:25** (2:27) (D) 2-Y-O **£7,319** (£2,252; £1,126; £563) **Stalls** High

Form RPR

0 **1** **Entailment**[12] 4776 2-9-0 ........................ LGoncalves 12 72
(MrsJRRamsden) *trckd ldrs stands side: effrt 2f out: rdn to chal over 1f out styd on to ld ins last* **33/1**

45 **2** nk **Rainbow Iris**[10] 4824 2-8-9 ........................ DMcGaffin 6 66
(BSmart) *overall ldr stands side: rdn along over 1f out: drvn and hdd ins last: nt qckn* **33/1**

0 **3** 1 ¼ **Come On Jonny (IRE)**[18] 4611 2-9-0 ........................ MFenton 14 67
(RMBeckett) *in tch stands side: hdwy to chse ldesr wl over 1f out: sn rdn and kpt on fnl f* **33/1**

F2 **4** shd **Stretford End (IRE)**[23] 4446 2-9-0 ........................ FLynch 5 86+
(BSmart) *a led far side gp: rdn along and v ch over 1f out: drvn ins last: no ex towards fin* **4/6**[1]

00 **5** 1 **Halla San**[12] 4776 2-8-11 ........................ ABeech(3) 16 67+
(MrsJRRamsden) *towds rr stands side and pushed along 1/2-way: swtchd lft wl over 1f out and styd ons trongly ins last: nrst fin* **50/1**

**6** 1 ¾ **Premier Fantasy** 2-9-0 ........................ DarrenWilliams 3 78+
(TDBarron) *trckd ldrs far side: hdwy to chal over 1f out: sn rdn and ev ch tl no ex wl ins last* **11/2**[2]

**7** nk **Ecologically Right** 2-8-9 ........................ ACulhane 8 53
(MrsJRRamsden) *in tch stands side: pushed along and edgd rt over 2f out: sn rdn and kpt on same pce* **33/1**

05 **8** 1 ¼ **Grandos (IRE)**[6] 4930 2-9-0 ........................ GGibbons 15 54
(TDEasterby) *chsd ldrs stands side: rdn along over 2f out: drvna nd one pce over 1f out* **20/1**

34 **9** hd **Game Lad**[23] 4446 2-9-0 ........................ DAllan 7 53
(TDEasterby) *bhd stands side tl sme late hdwy* **12/1**

4 **10** 2 ½ **Jaamid**[24] 4420 2-9-0 ........................ KDarley 1 65+
(MJohnston) *cl up far side: rdn along over 2f out: grad wknd* **13/2**[3]

5 **11** 1 ½ **Tahlal (IRE)**[42] 3893 2-9-0 ........................ GHind 13 41
(MrsADuffield) *chsd ldr stands side: rdn along 1/2-way: sn wknd* **33/1**

**12** 1 ¾ **Daisy Pooter (IRE)** 2-8-4 ........................ PMakin(5) 2 50+
(TDBarron) *trckd ldrs far side: rdn along 2f out: sn wknd* **33/1**

0 **13** 3 ½ **Falcon Goer (USA)**[101] 2213 2-8-9 ........................ JoannaBadger 4 21
(NTinkler) *dwlt and swtchd rt s to r stands side: a rr* **100/1**

**14** 3 **Cut To The Chase** 2-9-0 ........................ (t) KimTinkler 11 17
(NTinkler) *chsd ldrs stand side: rdn along after 2f: wknd 1/2-way* **66/1**

**15** nk **Love From Russia** 2-9-0 ........................ RFfrench 10 16
(ABerry) *s.i.s: a bhd stands side* **50/1**

**16** 3 **Graceful Flight** 2-8-9 ........................ RFitzpatrick 9 2
(PTMidgley) *a rr stands side* **80/1**

1m 14.91s (2.41) **Going Correction** +0.225s/f (Good) **16** Ran SP% **126.4**
Speed ratings: **92,91,89,89,88 86,85,84,83,80 78,76,71,67,67 63**CSF £838.39 TOTE £108.30: £12.90, £10.30, £4.50; EX 2283.60.
**Owner** Nigel Munton **Bred** Plantation Stud **Trained** Sandhutton, N Yorks

**FOCUS**
This looked to lack any real strength in depth and is not easy to rate with little to go on. The field came home well strung out and the high numbers were at a definite advantage, with the four runners to go low losing out.

**NOTEBOOK**
**Entailment** showed the benefit of his recent debut and produced a much-improved display to score over this more suitable distance. He will do better over farther next year, but could well find further success this year in nurseries, as he won with a bit up his sleeve.
**Rainbow Iris** took the field along on the near side at a reasonable gallop and duly improved on her two previous efforts, but had no answer to the winner when challenged. She appreciated this extra furlong, is now eligible for nurseries, and could be capable of better.
**Come On Jonny(IRE)** , as on his recent Windsor debut, ran green early, but gradually got the hang of things from two out, and was staying on with promise in the closing stages. He will do better with further experience.
**Stretford End(IRE)** was soon leading the small group who tracked over to the far side, but was up against it from halfway. He has endured a luckless start to his career and is almost certainly capable of winning races, but his big-race entries are beginning to look ambitious now.
**Premier Fantasy** , an expensive purchase, was popular in the ring for this debut, but held little chance when electing to race far side. He shaped with definite promise however, and should improve plenty for the experience.
**Grandos(IRE)** *Official explanation: jockey said colt lost its action*

## 5097 HELMSLEY (S) STKS 7f

**3:00** (3:02) (F) 2-Y-O **£3,255** (£930; £465) **Stalls** Low

Form RPR

0 **1** **Beaumont Girl (IRE)**[15] 4675 2-8-6 ........................ DeanMcKeown 6 53
(GASwinbank) *in tch: hdwy to chse ldrs wl over 2f out: rdn to ld 1f out: sn drvn and styd on wl* **9/1**

000 **2** nk **Apetite**[12] 4776 2-8-4 ........................ AReilly(7) 12 57
(NBycroft) *stdd s and swtchd outside and hdwy 2f out: rdn to chal isnide last and ev ch tl drvn and no ex nr fin* **25/1**

4003 **3** 2 **Lara's Girl**[16] 4638 2-8-6 **51** ........................ PDoe 3 47
(IAWood) *in tch: hdwy to chse ldrs over 2f out: sn rdn and kpt on same pce fnl f* **9/1**

000 **4** 2 ½ **Herencia (IRE)**[18] 4607 2-8-11 ........................ FLynch 13 45
(PABlockley) *in tch on outer tl lost pl and bhd 3f out: sn rdn and kpt on u.p appr last: nrst fin* **11/1**

4410 **5** 2 **Maureen's Lough (IRE)**[21] 4521 2-8-9 **55** ........................ NMackay(3) 5 41
(JHetherton) *trckd ldrs: hdwy to ld 2f out: sn rdn: drvn and hdd ent appr last: grad wknd* **4/1**[1]

5004 **6** 1 ¼ **Lanas Turn**[28] 4304 2-8-6 **52** ........................ (b[1]) DAllan 4 32
(TDEasterby) *dwlt and stmbld s: sn chsng ldrs on inner: rdn 2f out and ev ch tl drvn and wknd appr last* **15/2**

4200 **7** hd **Canary Dancer**[7] 4909 2-8-6 **63** ........................ GFaulkner 1 31
(PCHaslam) *led: rdn along over 2f out: sn hdd and drvn: wknd appr last* **6/1**[3]

0500 **8** shd **Desert Buzz (IRE)**[18] 4607 2-8-11 ........................ KDarley 10 36
(JHetherton) *b ehind: hdwy and in tch 2f out: sn rdn and wknd* **5/1**[2]

0530 **9** 1 ½ **Singhalongtasveer**[28] 4304 2-8-11 **51** ........................ DarrenWilliams 14 32
(WStorey) *in tch on outer: rdn along 1/2-way: sn wknd* **12/1**

000 **10** ½ **Xeight Express (IRE)**[48] 3729 2-8-6 ........................ RFfrench 2 26
(MABuckley) *chsd ldr: rdn along over 2f out: wknd over 1f out* **33/1**

U053 **11** 3 ½ **Fold Walk**[4] 4997 2-8-6 **46** ........................ TLucas 11 17
(MWEasterby) *chsd ldrs: rdn along over 2f out: sn wknd* **12/1**

000 **12** 3 **Mist Opportunity (IRE)**[34] 4135 2-8-4 ........................ GBartley(7) 8 14
(PCHaslam) *a bhd* **50/1**

00 **13** 6 **Filey Buoy**[44] 3834 2-8-11 ........................ VHalliday 7 —
(RMWhitaker) *bhd fr 1/2-way* **33/1**

**14** 24 **Liseberg (IRE)** 2-8-6 ........................ BSwarbrick(5) 9 —
(IAWood) *s.i.s: a wl bhd* **28/1**

1m 32.37s (5.27) **Going Correction** +0.50s/f (Yiel) **14** Ran SP% **121.6**
Speed ratings: **89,88,86,83,81 79,79,79,77,77 73,69,62,35**CSF £226.44 TOTE £13.20: £3.60, £6.80, £2.20; EX 297.00.There was no bid for the winner.
**Owner** G Stephenson **Bred** Brian Killeen **Trained** Melsonby, N Yorks

**FOCUS**
A weak, but wide-open looking juvenile seller, which was run at a decent early pace, although the overall time was moderate. The first three were clear of the remainder and the field again finished well strung out, but the form looks poor.

**NOTEBOOK**
**Beaumont Girl(IRE)** responded gamely to her rider's urgings and did well to hold off the runner-up in the dying strides to score. She clearly appreciated the underfoot conditions, was suited by this longer trip, and is open to further improvement at this sort of level.

**Apetite** was slow to break, but enjoyed racing off the decent early gallop and went down fighting in defeat. This was by far his best effort to date and the longer trip suited, so he could gain compensation before long in a similar race.
**Lara's Girl** took time to hit her full stride, and was under pressure some way out, but kept on gamely from over one out and deserves to win a race at this level.
**Herencia(IRE)** was doing all of his best work late on, having had to come wide to challenge, and showed his best form to date over this longer trip.
**Maureen's Lough(IRE)** went for home two out and looked to be hold every chance, but could not sustain her gallop on this ground and finished well held. She was not helped by chasing the early pace and is a brave performer, but will always look vulnerable to an improver.
**Lanas Turn** lost ground at the start in the first-time blinkers, but soon recovered to hold every chance at the top of the straight, and was a little disappointing.

## 5098 FARMERS INN - HELPERBY MAIDEN AUCTION STKS (DIV II) 7f
**3:35** (3:36) (E) 2-Y-O **£3,653** (£1,124; £562; £281) **Stalls** Low

Form RPR
235 **1** **Secret History (USA)**[35] [4074] 2-8-6 76 KDarley 6 72
(MJohnston) *cl up: led 3f out: rdn wl over 1f out: styd on strly fnl f* **2/1**[1]
03 **2** 2 1/2 **Robinzal**[18] [4606] 2-8-9 DAllan 8 69
(TDEasterby) *cl up: effrt 3f out and ev ch tl rdn wl over 1f out and one pce ent last* **6/1**[3]
5 **3** 1 **Askwith (IRE)**[34] [4135] 2-8-9 KMcEvoy 3 66
(JDBethell) *chsd ldrs: swtchd rt and rdn wl over 1f out: kpt on u.p fnl f* **3/1**[2]
0 **4** 3/4 **Tidal Fury (IRE)**[42] [3918] 2-8-11 ACulhane 5 66
(JJay) *chsd ldrs: rdn along over 2f out: drvn and kpt on same pce appr last* **14/1**
**5** 2 **Mr Marucci (USA)** 2-8-6 TEaves(3) 9 59
(BEllison) *dwlt: smooth hdwy to trck ldrs 1/2-way: pushed along 2f out: rdn over 1f out and kpt on same pce appr last* **25/1**
0 **6** 4 **Kashtanka (IRE)**[23] [4446] 2-8-7 MFenton 14 46
(JJQuinn) *chsd ldrs on outer: rdn along 1/2-way: drvn and one pce fnl 2f* **66/1**
36 **7** nk **Coconut Squeak**[7] [4900] 2-8-2 DaleGibson 2 41
(JGGiven) *led: rdn along and hdd 3f out: sn drvn and grad wknd* **13/2**
066 **8** shd **Nowaday (GER)**[16] [4625] 2-8-9 RFfrench 4 47
(TPTate) *in tch: pushed along 1/2-way: sn rdn and wknd* **18/1**
0 **9** 3/4 **Percheron (IRE)**[10] [4824] 2-8-9 DeanMcKeown 11 45
(PABlockley) *midfield: n.m.r bnd after 2f: sn rdn along and no hdwy* **40/1**
0 **10** 1 **Cala Fons (IRE)**[36] [4048] 2-8-4 KimTinkler 12 38
(NTinkler) *a rr* **66/1**
**11** 1 1/4 **Jeffslottery** 2-8-7 GHind 10 38
(JRWeymes) *sn pushed along: a rr* **33/1**
000 **12** shd **Allstar Princess**[34] [4131] 2-8-2 ow3 THamilton(3) 13 35
(RAFahey) *bhd fr 1/2-way* **25/1**
56 **13** 3 **Satin Rose**[72] [2985] 2-8-4 GGibbons 7 27
(TDEasterby) *s.i.s: a bhd* **12/1**
60 **14** hd **Golden Squaw**[36] [4048] 2-8-2 PMQuinn 1 24
(TDEasterby) *s.i.s: a rr* **25/1**

1m 31.28s (4.18) **Going Correction** +0.50s/f (Yiel) **14** Ran **SP%** **125.5**
Speed ratings: **96,93,92,91,88 84,83,83,82,81 80,80,76,76**CSF £14.08 TOTE £2.90: £1.70, £1.90, £2.00; EX 17.50.
**Owner** J Shack **Bred** R D Randal **Trained** Middleham Moor, N Yorks

**FOCUS**
This maiden looked the stronger of the two divisions, but the time was slower, and it is still probably just ordinary form.

**NOTEBOOK**
**Secret History(USA)** had shown ability in three previous maidens and scored with a tenacious display. She was on the pace throughout and gamely found an extra gear when challenged, and the extra furlong proved right up her street. She looks like improving further once handicapped.
**Robinzal**, who improved to finish third over course and distance last time, looked a live danger to the eventual winner two out, but could not quicken when it mattered. He kept on gamely however, has now improved with each of his three runs, and should fare better now he qualifies for nurseries.
**Askwith(IRE)**, well backed to improve on his debut, hit a flat spot two out and looked like going backwards, but stuck to his task and was closing at the finish. He is another who looks the type to fare better when handicapped, possibly over another furlong.
**Tidal Fury(IRE)** played up at the start, but turned in an improved display and is going the right way. He may prefer a quicker surface.
**Mr Marucci(USA)** was travelling as well as any turning for home, but ran green when asked to close on the principals. He will have learnt plenty for this debut experience and shaped with definite promise.
**Golden Squaw** *Official explanation: jockey said filly hung right throughout*

## 5099 BRIDLINGTON CLASSIFIED STKS 1m
**4:10** (4:10) (C) 3-Y-O+ **£8,566** (£3,249; £1,624; £738) **Stalls** Low

Form RPR
2151 **1** **Dawn Surprise (USA)**[23] [4442] 3-8-9 91 (t) KMcEvoy 5 99+
(SaeedBinSuroor) *trckd ldr: led wl over 2f out: comf* **2/1**[1]
346 **2** 1 1/4 **Blue Sky Thinking (IRE)**[8] [4887] 5-9-5 92 DarrenWilliams 3 100
(KRBurke) *trckd ldrs: hdwy over 2f out: rdn to chse wnr over 1f out: sn drvn and no imp* **4/1**[3]
0005 **3** 5 **Vicious Knight**[8] [4887] 6-9-3 90 ANicholls 1 88
(DNicholls) *led: rdn along 3f out: sn hdd and kpt on same pce fnl 2f* **3/1**[2]
2000 **4** 1 1/4 **Mysterinch**[20] [4553] 4-9-0 87 NMackay(3) 4 85
(JeddO'Keeffe) *chsd ldrs: rdn along over 3f out: drvn along over 2f out and sn outpcd* **10/1**
0555 **5** nk **Wizard Of Noz**[20] [4553] 4-9-8 95 (v) KDarley 7 89
(JNoseda) *chsd ldrs: rdn along 3f out: sn btn* **4/1**[3]
644 **6** 24 **Phoenix Nights (IRE)**[1] [5061] 4-8-12 52 PPMathers(5) 6 34
(ABerry) *a rr* **125/1**

1m 43.6s (3.90) **Going Correction** +0.50s/f (Yiel)
**WFA** 3 from 4yo+ 6lb **6** Ran **SP%** **108.2**
Speed ratings: **100,98,93,92,92 68**CSF £9.53 TOTE £2.20: £1.20, £2.40; EX 7.20.
**Owner** Godolphin **Bred** Gainsborough Stud Management Llc **Trained** Newmarket, Suffolk

**FOCUS**
An interesting affair which featured some useful performers. It was a modest time for the grade of contest and the form is just fair for the grade.

**NOTEBOOK**
**Dawn Surprise(USA)** readily followed up her recent Kempton success. Despite being far from certain to act on this softer ground, she duly did so with the minimum amount of fuss, and showed a neat turn of foot when hitting the front to settle the issue. She does look progressive and deserves to take her chance at a higher level now.
**Blue Sky Thinking(IRE)**, winner of the corresponding event last year, ran a solid race in defeat, but was always being held by the winner. He is ideally suited by farther these days, and did more than enough to suggest he can get back to winning ways when reverting to around ten furlongs.
**Vicious Knight**, who showed improved form last time at York, was the subject of strong support in the market. However, despite having his own way out in front, he never seriously threatened to land the gamble. He is inconsistent, but should find easier opportunities.
**Mysterinch** rallied to get back up for fourth close home, having looked like folding over a furlong out, but is regressive and needs respite in the weights.
**Wizard Of Noz** found nothing over this extra furlong and never seriously threatened. He is on a fair mark at present, but remains a tricky customer and has not won since his debut in 2002.

## 5100 WISKE H'CAP 2m
**4:45** (4:45) (D) (0-85,76) 3-Y-O+ **£5,616** (£1,728; £864; £432) **Stalls** Low

Form RPR
2002 **1** **Master Wells (IRE)**[6] [4934] 3-8-12 75 KMcEvoy 5 85
(JDBethell) *hld up in tch: hdwy 4f out: rdn to ld wl over 1f out: drvn out* **3/1**[1]
6433 **2** 1/2 **Vicars Destiny**[12] [4778] 6-8-5 61 AndrewWebb(7) 1 70
(MrsSLamyman) *hld up: stdy hdwy to trck ldrs 6f out: effrt on outer over 2f 2f out and sn evc hance: rdn and edgd lft over 1f out: kpt on* **7/1**
6010 **3** 2 1/2 **Tomasino**[34] [4155] 6-9-7 70 (t) KDarley 6 76
(KGReveley) *cl up: led over 3f out: rdn over 2f out: drvn and hdd wl over 1f out: sn one pce* **16/1**
4634 **4** 2 **Pope's Hill (IRE)**[16] [4647] 3-8-6 72 NMackay(3) 4 76
(LMCumani) *trckd ldrs: effrt over 3f out: sn rdn along and one pce fnl 2f* **3/1**[1]
5116 **5** 2 **Lucky Judge**[6] [4934] 7-9-10 73 DaleGibson 3 74
(GASwinbank) *hld up in tch: effrt 4f out: sn rdn along and beatren wl over 2f out* **4/1**[2]
5615 **6** 11 **Hathlen (IRE)**[36] [4062] 3-8-13 76 ACulhane 2 64
(MRChannon) *a rr: rdn along over 3f out and sn outpcd* **6/1**[3]
0056 **7** 10 **Greenwich Meantime**[16] [4627] 4-9-2 65 LGoncalves 7 41
(MrsJRRamsden) *led: rdn along over 4f out: hdd over 3f out and son wknd* **9/1**

3m 37.6s (6.40) **Going Correction** +0.50s/f (Yiel)
**WFA** 3 from 4yo+ 14lb **7** Ran **SP%** **112.7**
Speed ratings: **104,103,102,101,100 95,90**CSF £23.62 TOTE £3.70: £2.60, £4.00; EX 22.20.
**Owner** Jordan Ellison Lund **Bred** Barronstown Stud And Orpendale **Trained** Middleham Moor, N Yorks
■ Tomasino was Keith Reveley's first runner since taking over the licence from his mother Mary.

**FOCUS**
This was a decent test of stamina in the conditions, yet the steady early gallop meant it developed into a tactical affair, and there were plenty in with a chance turning for home. However, the form is ordinary but sound.

**NOTEBOOK**
**Master Wells(IRE)**, who went close at Chester last time, duly went one better in determined fashion and continued the recent domination of the three-year-olds in this event. He was proven on the ground and this does look to be his trip, so he will be hard to beat if turned out under a penalty, and could have more to offer still.
**Vicars Destiny** gave her all in defeat and turned in another solid display. She would have preferred a stronger gallop, as she stays all day long.
**Tomasino** put a poor run last time behind him with an improved effort, but had no excuses and seemed to get this trip.
**Pope's Hill(IRE)**, who suggested a race like this was well within his compass at Sandown last time, was slightly disappointing. He was not suited by the lack of early pace however and, despite being a son of Sadler's Wells, he has not looked totally suited by soft ground now in two attempts.
**Lucky Judge** may have found this coming a bit too soon. However, on a course and distance he has won twice over, he never looked like reversing his recent form with the winner and may be high enough in the weights now. *Official explanation: may have found this coming a bit too soon. However, on a course and distance he has won twice over, he never looked like reversing his recent form with the winner and may be high enough in the weights now.*

## 5101 GRETA APPRENTICE FILLIES' STKS (H'CAP) 5f
**5:20** (5:23) (E) (0-70,67) 3-Y-O+ **£3,623** (£1,115; £557; £278) **Stalls** High

Form RPR
-565 **1** **Mecca's Mate**[13] [4751] 3-8-8 55 AMullen(5) 2 64
(DWBarker) *hld up: hdwy on outer 2f out: rdn over 1f out: styd on ins last to ld nr fin* **6/1**[2]
1505 **2** shd **Aahgowangowan (IRE)**[10] [4828] 5-9-3 62 (t) WHogg(5) 8 71
(MDods) *led: rdn over 1f out: drvn ins last: hdd and no ex nr fin* **13/8**[1]
0005 **3** 1/2 **Ela Figura**[7] [4923] 4-8-3 46 (p) NataliaGemelova(3) 3 53
(AWCarroll) *cl up: effrt 2f out: sn rdn and ev ch tl drvn and nt qckn nr fin* **8/1**[3]
2660 **4** nk **Marabar**[60] [3372] 6-8-11 56 DeanWilliams(5) 4 62
(DWChapman) *in tch: hdwy wl over 1f out:sn rdn and kpt on ins last* **10/1**
3066 **5** 3/4 **Shielaligh**[14] [4701] 3-9-8 67 (p) LTreadwell(3) 6 70
(MissGayKelleway) *chsd ldrs: rdn over 1f out: kpt on same pce ins last* **16/1**
2056 **6** 2 1/2 **Queen Of Night**[9] [4854] 4-8-13 56 PPMathers(3) 1 50
(DWChapman) *in tch on outer: rdn wl over 1f out: sn one pce* **8/1**[3]
00-0 **7** 2 1/2 **Petite Mac**[12] [4782] 4-8-8 53 AReilly(5) 5 38
(NBycroft) *a rr* **25/1**
0006 **8** shd **Estoille**[7] [4929] 3-7-9 40 oh10 (t) LeanneKershaw(3) 9 25
(MrsSLamyman) *dwlt: chsd ldrs: swtchd lft and rdn wl over 1f out: sn btn* **20/1**
-050 **9** 1 **Mitsuki**[28] [4308] 5-9-0 61 JCavanagh(7) 7 42
(JDBethell) *s.i.s: a rr* **6/1**[2]

60.03 secs (0.13) **Going Correction** +0.225s/f (Good)
**WFA** 3 from 4yo+ 2lb **9** Ran **SP%** **112.5**
Speed ratings: **107,106,106,105,104 100,96,96,94**CSF £15.59 CT £77.39 TOTE £4.00: £2.20, £1.30, £2.50; EX 13.20 Place 6 £1,816.81, Place 5 £883.67.
**Owner** David T J Metcalfe **Bred** Miss C Tagart **Trained** Scorton, N Yorks

**FOCUS**
A modest sprint that was run at a decent gallop and the form looks solid for the grade.

**NOTEBOOK**
**Mecca's Mate** used her stamina to great effect on this drop back to the minimum trip, and produced a tenacious display to get off the mark at the fifth time of asking. This looks to be her ideal trip and she can be rated slightly better than the bare form, as she had to come down the centre of the track to win her race. *Official explanation: trainer said, regarding the improved form shown, filly had benefited from the drop in trip*
**Aahgowangowan(IRE)** quickly bagged the favoured stands'-side rail, showing her customary early pace, but could find no more in the closing stages when pressed by the winner. This was another sound effort and she remains in good form.
**Ela Figura** held every chance if good enough, but lacked a change of gear when it mattered. She always gives her all, but remains winless after 34 outings now.
**Marabar** appreciated this drop in trip and turned in an improved effort. He looks worth another chance off this mark, when facing a stiffer test at this distance.
**Shielaligh**, beaten in a claimer last time, ran slightly better, but never seriously threatened the principals. She would have preferred a faster surface.
**Mitsuki** was popular in the betting, but lost all chance with a slow start.


The Form Book, Raceform Ltd, Compton, RG20 6NL

T/Plt: £1,917.90 to a £1 stake. Pool: £26,929.45. 10.25 winning tickets. T/Qpdt: £12.70 to a £1 stake. Pool: £2,975.10. 172.40 winning tickets. JR

5102 - (Foreign Racing) - See Raceform Interactive

## 5032 DEAUVILLE (R-H)

Friday, August 27

**OFFICIAL GOING: Turf course - very soft; all-weather - standard**

### 5103a PRIX DE SAINT-VAAST EN AUGE (CLAIMER) (ALL-WEATHER) 7f 110y

**4:00** (4:05) 4-Y-0+ **£5,634** (£2,254; £1,690; £1,127)

RPR

1 **Mosaahim (IRE)**[16] 6-9-5 ........ SPasquier —
(MarioHofer, Germany)

2 2 **The Prince**[16] 4631 10-9-1 ........ TJarnet —
(IanWilliams) *hld up towards rr, prog on ins ent str, ran on wl to get 2nd ins fnl f, nvr reached wnr*

3 3 **Johanino (FR)**[8] 5-9-0 ........(b) JGrosjean(5) —
(VSartori, France)

4 snk **Rio Real (FR)**[50] 7-8-11 ........ —
(AFracas, France)

5 3/4 **Leiden (FR)**[16] 4-9-4 ........ —
(XGuigand, France)

6 snk **North's Law (FR)**[24] 4-8-8 ........ —
(PTual, France)

7 1/2 **Grand Desert (FR)**[16] 4-9-5 ........ —
(GCollet, France)

8 1 **Try And Fly (FR)**[48] 7-9-5 ........ —
(LFerard, France)

9 3/4 **Salsaneyev (FR)**[32] 4-8-8 ........ —
(MmeLAudon, France)

10 3/4 **Vahana (FR)**[48] 7-8-12 ........ —
(PVanDePoele, France)

0 **Torbato**[48] 4-9-8 ........(b) —
(JRossi, France)

0 **Ziyar (FR)**[24] 4-9-1 ........ —
(MNigge, France)

0 **Nord (FR)**[16] 4-9-2 ........ —
(Y-MPorzier, France)

0 **Rodin (IRE)**[16] 8-8-11 ........(b) —
(DLenfant, France)

0 **Baccino (USA)**[50] 6-8-11 ........ —
(PVanDePoele, France)

0 **Jeune Vigne (FR)**[19] 5-8-8 ........ —
(FXDeChevigny, France)

1m 29.8s **16** Ran

Speed ratings: .

**Owner** Stall White Star **Bred** Shadwell Estate Company Limited **Trained** Germany

**NOTEBOOK**

**The Prince** lost his chance at the start when slowly away. He then had to wait for a gap before making up a lot of late ground. This was a decent effort and he should win next time in this grade.

## 4624 BEVERLEY (R-H)

Saturday, August 28

**OFFICIAL GOING: Good to soft**

### 5104 PRIORY PARK VOLKSWAGEN MAIDEN STKS 5f

**2:05** (2:06) (D) 3-Y-0+ **£3,542** (£1,090; £545; £272) **Stalls** High

Form RPR

323 **1** **Lake Charlotte (USA)**[17] 4653 3-8-9 70 ........ NPollard 10 62
(DRLoder) *mde all: rdn over 1f out: kpt on wl fnl f* **13/8**[1]

5260 **2** 1 **Sir Loin**[19] 4608 3-9-0 55 ........ WRyan 5 63
(NTinkler) *sn chsng wnr: effrt to chal over 1f out: sn rdn and edgd rt ins last: drien and nt qckn towards fin* **9/1**

0425 **3** 1/2 **Brain Washed**[45] 3839 3-8-9 70 ........ RWinston 11 56
(TDEasterby) *dwlt: sn chsng ldrs: effrt and n.m.r on inner over 1f out: switrchd rt and rdn ins last: kpt on* **9/2**[2]

0434 **4** 2 1/2 **Nicholas Nickelby**[14] 4751 4-9-2 53 ........ SSanders 9 52
(MJPolglase) *chsd ldrs: rdn along 2f out: sn one pce* **6/1**

64 **5** 1/2 **Victoriana**[10] 4845 3-8-9 ........ JQuinn 4 45
(HJCollingridge) *midfield: pushed along 1/2-way: styd on appr last: nrst fin* **14/1**

5200 **6** 1 1/2 **Westborough (IRE)**[8] 4929 3-9-0 54 ........ ACulhane 3 45
(NTinkler) *towards rr: hdwy 2f out: sn rdn and edgd rt: drvn and no imp over 1f out* **20/1**

3 **7** 2 1/2 **Ariesanne (IRE)**[14] 4758 3-8-6 ........ THamilton(3) 8 31
(RAFahey) *chsd ldrs: rdn along 1/2-way: sn wknd* **5/1**[3]

0-00 **8** nk **Warren Place**[21] 4557 4-9-2 35 ........ WSupple 6 35
(JHetherton) *towards rr: hdwy on inner 2f out: sn rdn and n.m.r wl over 1f out: sn wknd* **66/1**

0004 **9** 6 **Designer City (IRE)**[26] 4393 3-8-9 35 ........ FNorton 2 8
(ABerry) *a rr* **50/1**

4-00 **10** 2 **Big Tom (IRE)**[8] 4929 3-8-7 54 ........ DTudhope(7) 7 6
(DCarroll) *a rr* **25/1**

**11** 6 **Home Front (IRE)** 3-9-0 ........ GGibbons 1 —
(MsDeborahJEvans) *a rr* **66/1**

65.16 secs (1.16) **Going Correction** +0.325s/f (Good)

**WFA** 3 from 4yo 2lb **11** Ran SP% **117.5**

Speed ratings: **103,101,100,96,95 93,89,88,79,76 66**CSF £16.78 TOTE £2.60: £1.20, £3.50, £1.30; EX 26.00.

**Owner** Sheikh Mohammed **Bred** Darley **Trained** Newmarket, Suffolk

**FOCUS**

A weak maiden, with the fully exposed 55-rated Sir Loin finishing second.

**NOTEBOOK**

**Lake Charlotte(USA)** was lucky to find a weak maiden and made the most of it, leading throughout. She handled the ground well enough, despite her breeding suggesting that might be a problem, but she makes little appeal if moving into nursery company.

**Sir Loin** is fully exposed and his performance only goes to underline the weakness of the form.

**Brain Washed** had the best of the draw but missed the break slightly and was always playing catch-up thereafter. This trip was probably on the short side for her.

**Nicholas Nickelby** has been beaten in sellers this year and is another whose performance underlines the modest quality of the race.

**Victoriana**, fourth in a stronger maiden at Kempton last time, looked likely to appreciate the drop back in trip but, in the event, was staying on all too late. She now qualifies for a handicap mark.

**Ariesanne(IRE)**, who lost her chance with a slow start on her debut, came in for significant support in the market, and presumably she is thought capable of much better than was seen on this occasion. She might be one to bear in mind once she goes handicapping. *Official explanation: jockey said filly bled from nose*

### 5105 TOTEPOOL BEVERLEY BULLET SPRINT STKS (LISTED RACE) 5f

**2:40** (2:40) (A) 3-Y-0+ **£17,400** (£6,600; £3,300; £1,500) **Stalls** High

Form RPR

500 **1** **Chookie Heiton (IRE)**[43] 3901 6-8-12 98 ........ TEaves 6 109
(ISemple) *trckd ldrs: swtchd ins and hdwy 2f out: squeezed through on far rail and qcknd to ld ins last: rdn and styd on wl* **40/1**

6503 **2** 1 1/4 **Simianna**[13] 4779 5-8-7 94 ........(p) WSupple 3 100
(ABerry) *hld up and bhd: swtchd outside and gd hdwy over 1f out: str run ins last: fin wl* **16/1**

-601 **3** shd **Baltic King**[34] 4165 4-8-12 106 ........(t) SSanders 10 104
(HMorrison) *n.m.r and shuffled to rr after 1f: hdwy 2f out: effrt whnn.m.r and hmpd over 1f: styd on wl u.p fnl f* **11/4**[1]

1241 **4** hd **Enchantment**[10] 4862 3-8-5 92 ........ FNorton 7 98
(JMBradley) *led: rdn ent fnl f: sn hdd and nt qckn* **3/1**[2]

3002 **5** 1 1/4 **Bishops Court**[12] 4805 10-8-12 105 ........ ACulhane 9 99
(MrsJRRamsden) *trckd ldrs: rdn and edgd lft ent last: sn drvn and one pce* **13/2**

2303 **6** 1 **Forever Phoenix**[12] 4805 4-8-7 93 ........ JQuinn 2 90
(RMHCowell) *chsd ldrs on outer: rdn and hung rt over 1f out: sn drvn and one pce* **12/1**

-301 **7** 2 **Continent**[12] 4805 7-8-12 108 ........ ANicholls 4 88
(DNicholls) *midfield: swtchd rt after 1f: effrt and nt clr run 2f out: switchd lft and hdwy over 1f out: sn rdn and no imp* **6/1**[3]

5130 **8** 1 3/4 **Baron Rhodes**[10] 4862 3-8-5 80 ........ DAllan 8 77
(JSWainwright) *chsd ldrs: rdn along 2f out: wkng whn hmpd over 1f out* **100/1**

0556 **9** 1 1/4 **Vita Spericolata (IRE)**[13] 4779 7-8-7 81 ........(v) GParkin 11 72
(JSWainwright) *prom: rdn along 2f out: wkng whn hmpd over 1f out* **25/1**

6060 **10** nk **Absent Friends**[50] 3713 7-8-12 89 ........ JEdmunds 5 76
(JBalding) *cl up: rdn along 2f out: sn wknd* **50/1**

2110 **11** 1 1/2 **Caribbean Coral**[28] 4324 5-8-12 102 ........ RWinston 1 71
(JJQuinn) *a rr* **7/1**

63.99 secs (-0.01) **Going Correction** +0.325s/f (Good)

**WFA** 3 from 4yo+ 2lb **11** Ran SP% **114.6**

Speed ratings: **113,111,110,110,108 106,103,100,98,98 96**CSF £552.63 TOTE £45.80: £9.10, £3.80, £1.40; EX 267.40.

**Owner** Hamilton Park Members Syndicate **Bred** Michael Collins **Trained** Carluke, S Lanarks

■ Stewards Enquiry : J Quinn caution: careless riding

**FOCUS**

A decent event but a shock result. It was run in a fair time for a Listed contest, but with several below par the form is not that strong overall.

**NOTEBOOK**

**Chookie Heiton(IRE)** ran really well from a poor draw in the Cammidge Trophy on his seasonal reappearance but he had failed to reproduce that form since. Five times a winner over six furlongs, he found this stiff five ideal, and returned from a six-week break to record a shock victory. He is now on course for the Ayr Gold Cup.

**Simianna** has been running well for most of the season and once again ran a terrific race, this time from a poor draw. She finds winning difficult but is very consistent.

**Baltic King** could have done with a sounder surface and did not get the best of runs. In the circumstances this was a sound effort, and he certainly has the ability to win in Listed grade.

**Enchantment**, stepping out of handicap company, showed her customary early pace to take the lead and looked set for success until faltering inside the last. An easier five furlongs would surely be ideal for her.

**Bishops Court** had a perfect pitch for much of the race but just could not find the change of gear required at the end of the race. *Official explanation: vet said gelding bled from nose*

**Forever Phoenix** had it to do from her draw and was forced to challenge wide.

**Continent** has a poor strike-rate and is the type who needs everything to fall right. He has never won two races in a row.

### 5106 TOTESPORT STKS (HERITAGE H'CAP) 1m 1f 207y

**3:15** (3:15) (B) (0-105,103) 3-Y-0 **£29,000** (£11,000; £5,500; £2,500) **Stalls** High

Form RPR

0605 **1** **Gatwick (IRE)**[7] 4965 3-9-3 **102** ........ SHitchcott(3) 10 112+
(MRChannon) *hld up: hdwy 3f out: rdn along 2f out: styng on whn nt clr run over 1f out: swtchd lft and styd on strly to ld last 50 yds* **7/1**[3]

2001 **2** 1 **Invasion (IRE)**[15] 4709 3-8-13 **95** ........ WRyan 1 103+
(HRACecil) *led: rdn along and jnd 3f out: drvn over 1f out: hdd and no ex last 50 yds* **11/2**[2]

0254 **3** 1/2 **Hello It's Me**[28] 4343 3-8-3 **85** ........ JQuinn 9 90+
(HJCollingridge) *chsd ldrs: hdwy 3f out: rdn and nt clr run on inner over 1f out: swtchd lft and styd on wl fnl f* **11/1**

6122 **4** 1 **Inchloss (IRE)**[23] 4490 3-8-2 **84** ow3 ........ GGibbons 11 88
(BAMcmahon) *chsd ldng pair: hdwy 3f out: rdn and ch over 1f out: drvn and one pce ins last* **7/1**[3]

5006 **5** 1 1/2 **Gold History (USA)**[10] 4856 3-8-12 **94** ........ RFfrench 4 95
(MJohnston) *chsd ldr: hdwy to chal 3f out and ev ch tl rdn and edgd rt over 1f out: one pce* **20/1**

4404 **6** 3/4 **Sew'N'So Character (IRE)**[15] 4709 3-8-8 **90** ........ SSanders 5 89
(MBlanshard) *hld up towards rr: hdwy over 2f out: sn rdn and kpt on ins last: nrst fin* **8/1**

0534 **7** 1 1/4 **Sweet Indulgence (IRE)**[14] 4756 3-7-13 **81** oh1 ow1 ........ FNorton 7 78
(DrJDScargill) *chsd ldrs: hdwy 3f out: rdn 2f out and ch tl drvn and wknd appr last* **25/1**

4100 **8** 3/4 **Gavroche (IRE)**[15] 4709 3-8-4 **89** ........ J-PGuillambert(3) 6 85
(CADwyer) *s.i.s and bhd tl sme late hdwy* **25/1**

0021 **9** nk **Ringsider (IRE)**[28] 4327 3-8-2 **84** ........ LisaJones 2 79
(GAButler) *s.i.s and awkward s: a rr* **8/1**

3044 **10** 1 1/2 **Mutafanen**[21] 4540 3-9-7 **103** ........(v) WSupple 3 96
(EALDunlop) *in tch: effrt 3f out and sn pushed along: rdn 2f out and sn btn* **4/1**[1]

-510 **11** 1 1/4 **Burning Moon**[51] 3678 3-8-4 **86** ........ DaleGibson 8 76
(JNoseda) *midfield: hdwy and in tch 3f out: sn rdn and wknd* **11/1**

2m 7.13s (-0.07) **Going Correction** +0.225s/f (Good) **11** Ran SP% **111.7**

Speed ratings: **109,108,107,107,105 105,104,103,103,102 101**CSF £41.62 CT £412.21 TOTE £5.90: £2.10, £2.00, £4.00; EX 32.90 Trifecta £285.20 Pool of £923.91 - 2.30 winning units.

**Owner** W H Ponsonby **Bred** M J Dargan **Trained** West Ilsley, Berks

**FOCUS**

A valuable handicap and a welcome return to form for Gatwick. The form appears solid and should prove reliable.

**NOTEBOOK**

**Gatwick(IRE)**, highly tried since his run of success in the spring, appreciated the drop back to handicap company, and the decent gallop meant the race was run to suit. He won going away and he clearly has the ability to win in Listed grade, although a sound pace seems essential.
**Invasian(IRE)**, who has made all for both his wins, adopted front-running tactics once again and almost pulled it off. He is progressive and is well served by a little cut in the ground.
**Hello It's Me** continues to find one or two too good off this sort of mark, and this effort will not encourage any leniency from the Handicapper.
**Inchloss(IRE)** could not be said to have failed through lack of stamina.
**Gold History(USA)** has yet to run to the best of his spring form when not making the running.
**Sew'N'So Character(IRE)** has a poor strike-rate and continues to look held by the Handicapper.
**Mutafanen**, who does not look the most straightforward, was disappointing and is the type who is always likely to be seen at his best in a big field. *Official explanation: trainer was unable to offer any explanation for poor form shown*

## 5107 WILL IT BE A WINSTON WINNER H'CAP — 5f

**3:45** (3:47) (E ) (0-75,75) 3-Y-O+ — **£6,019** (£1,852; £926; £463) **Stalls** High

Form — RPR

6241 **1** **Hout Bay**[1] [5094] 7-9-1 **62** 6ex ... RFfrench 13 — 72
(RAFahey) *in tch: edgd rt after 2f: hdwy 2f out: swtchd lft and rdn over 1f out: styd on strly to ld last 100 yds:jst hld on* **9/2**[1]

0031 **2** *shd* **Mister Mal (IRE)**[8] [4926] 8-8-7 **54** ... SSanders 14 — 64
(BEllison) *bhd and hmpd after 2f: hdwy 2f out: swtchd lft over 1f out: styd on strly fnl f: jst failed* **11/2**[2]

2550 **3** *1 3/4* **Brigadier Monty (IRE)**[34] [4181] 6-8-5 **52** ... JQuinn 7 — 55+
(MrsSLamyman) *bhd: hdwy 2f out: nt clr run ent last: swtchd lft wl ins last: fin ished strly* **33/1**

3311 **4** *3/4* **On The Trail**[13] [4782] 7-8-7 **54** ... ACulhane 15 — 55
(DWChapman) *chsd ldr: hdwy to ld 2f out: sn rdn: drvn ent last: hdd and no ex last 100 yds* **7/1**

3060 **5** *nk* **Brantwood (IRE)**[21] [4542] 4-8-9 **56** ... (t) GGibbons 12 — 56+
(BAMcmahon) *chsd ldrs: hung rt after 2f: n.m.r 2f out and again over 1f out: styd on u.p fnl f* **16/1**

0300 **6** *nk* **Beyond The Clouds (IRE)**[2] [5062] 8-10-0 **75** ... (p) RWinston 3 — 73+
(JSWainwright) *prom: rdn along 2f out: drvn and wknd appr last* **20/1**

2100 **7** *1/2* **Compton Plume**[24] [4452] 4-9-4 **65** ... DaleGibson 10 — 62
(WHTinning) *bhd: hdwy wl over 1f out: styd on ins last: nrst fin* **50/1**

0000 **8** *3/4* **Laurel Dawn**[7] [4935] 6-8-2 **56** ... NataliaGemelova(7) 18 — 50+
(IWMcinnes) *in tch whn bdly hmpd on inner and lost pl after 2f: hdwy on inner over 1f out: kpt on ins last: nrst fin* **7/1**

0301 **9** *1/2* **Kings College Boy**[7] [4935] 4-9-4 **68** ... (b) THamilton(3) 16 — 60
(RAFahey) *s.i.s and bhd tl styd on appr last: nrst fin* **6/1**[3]

5041 **10** *3/4* **Roman Mistress (IRE)**[10] [4854] 4-9-6 **67** ... (b) DAllan 6 — 56
(TDEasterby) *chsd ldrs: rdn wl over 1f out: wknd ent last* **16/1**

0004 **11** *1/2* **Tomthevic**[38] [4014] 6-8-2 **49** ... FNorton 4 — 37
(JMBradley) *prom: rdn 2f out: drvn over 1f out and grad wknd* **50/1**

6405 **12** *1 1/4* **Mynd**[11] [4828] 4-9-0 **61** ... DeanMcKeown 9 — 44
(RMWhitaker) *midfield whn hmpd after 2f and bhd: hdwy over 1f out: kpt on: nvr a factor* **16/1**

00-0 **13** *1 3/4* **Fly More**[16] [4687] 7-9-6 **74** ... CJDavies(7) 8 — 51
(JMBradley) *a towards rr* **40/1**

0024 **14** *nk* **Elliot's Choice (IRE)**[4] [5026] 3-8-11 **60** ... (b) LisaJones 11 — 36
(DCarroll) *n.d* **50/1**

000 **15** *1 3/4* **Tommy Smith**[32] [4211] 6-9-7 **71** ... (b) TEaves(3) 19 — 41
(JSWainwright) *led: rdn along and hdd 2f out: sn drvn and grad wknd* **12/1**

0046 **16** *1/2* **Consensus (IRE)**[17] [4626] 5-9-11 **72** ... TWilliams 1 — 40
(MBrittain) *a rr* **33/1**

5000 **17** *1/2* **Chairman Bobby**[38] [4011] 6-9-6 **67** ... FLynch 2 — 33
(DWBarker) *midfield: rdn along 1/2-way: sn wknd* **33/1**

2303 **18** *hd* **Soaked**[15] [4701] 11-9-0 **61** ... (b) ANicholls 5 — 26
(DWChapman) *midfield: rdn along 1/2-way: sn wknd* **25/1**

0000 **19** *2 1/2* **Regal Song (IRE)**[106] [2079] 8-9-3 **64** ... (b) DMcGaffin 17 — 20
(TJEtherington) *a rr* **16/1**

65.14 secs (1.14) **Going Correction** +0.325s/f (Good)
**WFA** 3 from 4yo+ 2lb — **19** Ran SP% **129.8**
Speed ratings: **103,102,100,98,98 97,97,95,95,93 93,91,88,87,85 84,83,83,79**CSF £26.50 CT £776.09 TOTE £5.20: £2.00, £2.20, £8.40, £1.90; EX 46.40.
**Owner** Northumbria Leisure Ltd **Bred** Mrs Mary Taylor **Trained** Musley Bank, N Yorks
■ Stewards Enquiry : G Gibbons three-day ban: careless riding (Sep 8-10)

**FOCUS**

A moderate sprint in which high draws dominated as usual. The form looks solid for the grade.

**NOTEBOOK**

**Hout Bay**, successful 24 hours earlier at Newmarket, followed up under a 6lb penalty. His stable is in good form at present and his current trainer has now got three wins out of him from seven starts, compared with his previous trainers who, between them, managed to get just three wins out of him from 60 starts.
**Mister Mal(IRE)** is happier over six furlongs but he ran well over this stiff five. He did not enjoy the best of runs but finished with real purpose and would have got there in another yard or two.
**Brigadier Monty(IRE)**, having looked likely to figure among the backmarkers two furlongs out, finished with some purpose to claim third spot. On face value this effort from a poor draw looks promising for the future, but he has an awful strike-rate and is likely to remain difficult to win with.
**On The Trail** is running consistently well at present, had a decent draw and made the most of it. He put up a decent effort in search of the hat-trick.
**Brantwood(IRE)** has not won since his maiden victory on his debut and, despite dropping a stone in the handicap this term, still looks difficult to win with.
**Beyond The Clouds(IRE)** had an impossible task from his low draw and did not shape too badly in the circumstances.
**Compton Plume** has suffered badly for beating a 75-rated horse in a Catterick maiden in June, and now looks handicapped to the hilt.
**Laurel Dawn**, who is slowly dropping down to a more realistic mark, was not done any favours when hampered on the turn into the straight.
**Kings College Boy** *Official explanation: jockey said gelding was denied a clear run*
**Mynd** *Official explanation: jockey said gelding suffered interference*

## 5108 JOHN JENKINS MEMORIAL H'CAP — 7f 100y

**4:20** (4:20) (E ) (0-70,67) 3-Y-O+ — **£4,082** (£1,256; £628; £314) **Stalls** High

Form — RPR

4336 **1** **Riska King**[40] [3982] 4-9-8 **67** ... THamilton(3) 11 — 77
(RAFahey) *in tch: smooth hdwy on inner 3f out: led wl over 1f out: rdn and kpt on wl fnl f* **7/1**[2]

0061 **2** *1 1/2* **Jubilee Street (IRE)**[25] [4425] 5-9-1 **57** ... GHind 14 — 63
(MrsADuffield) *trckd ldrs: hdwy over 2f out: rdn over 1f out: kpt on ins last* **8/1**[3]

0314 **3** *1/2* **Gifted Flame**[21] [4537] 5-9-6 **67** ... PMakin(5) 4 — 72
(TDBarron) *hld up towards rr: hdwy over 2f out: rdn and kpt on appr last: nrst fin* **7/1**[2]

3560 **4** *3/4* **Oases**[15] [4702] 5-8-10 **52** ... (p) LisaJones 5 — 55
(DShaw) *bhd: hdwy on outer over 2f out: sn rdn and kpt on wl fnl f: nrst fin* **16/1**

4401 **5** *nk* **Locombe Hill (IRE)**[8] [4905] 8-9-1 **64** ... DTudhope(7) 8 — 66
(NWilson) *a.p: effrt and ev ch 2f out: rdn over 1f out and grad wknd* **6/1**[1]

1060 **6** *1/2* **King Nicholas (USA)**[9] [4879] 5-8-5 **52** ... (tp) RoryMoore(5) 13 — 53
(JParkes) *cl up: led over 2f out: rdn and hdd wl over 1f out: grad wknd* **16/1**

0000 **7** *1/2* **Colemanstown**[35] [4122] 4-8-11 **56** ... TEaves(3) 1 — 56
(BEllison) *bhd tl styd on fnl 2f: nrst fin* **20/1**

3406 **8** *1/2* **True (IRE)**[13] [4781] 3-9-0 **61** ... RWinston 6 — 59
(MrsSLamyman) *bhd: hdwy over 2f out: rdn over 1f out: kpt on ins last: nrst fin* **14/1**

0000 **9** *5* **Motu (IRE)**[49] [3745] 3-9-6 **67** ... SSanders 2 — 53
(JLDunlop) *a towards rr* **7/1**[2]

0500 **10** *3/4* **Carlton (IRE)**[11] [4827] 10-8-12 **54** ... RFfrench 9 — 38
(CRDore) *in tch: hdwy on inner to chse ldrs 2f out: sn rdn and wknd over 1f out* **16/1**

-115 **11** *2* **Tap**[52] [3623] 7-8-9 **58** ... (p) DFentiman(7) 10 — 37
(IanEmmerson) *led: rdn along and hdd over 2f out: sn wknd* **9/1**

0036 **12** *1* **Yorker (USA)**[73] [2989] 6-9-1 **60** ... SHitchcott(3) 12 — 37
(MsDeborahJEvans) *chsd ldrs: rdn along 3f out: sn wknd* **16/1**

0000 **13** *1/2* **Prince Of Gold**[20] [4569] 4-9-8 **64** ... (p) WSupple 7 — 39
(RHollinshead) *chsd ldrs: rdn along over 2f out: sn wknd* **10/1**

6250 **14** *10* **Sewmore Character**[10] [4852] 4-9-8 **64** ... FNorton 3 — 14
(MBlanshard) *a towards rr* **16/1**

1m 35.72s (1.42) **Going Correction** +0.30s/f (Good)
**WFA** 3 from 4yo+ 5lb — **14** Ran SP% **122.8**
Speed ratings: **103,101,100,99,99 98,98,97,92,91 88,87,87,75**CSF £63.43 CT £427.68 TOTE £7.70: £2.60, £3.00, £2.70; EX 93.30.
**Owner** Market Avenue Racing Club Ltd **Bred** D R Tucker **Trained** Musley Bank, N Yorks

**FOCUS**

A very average handicap but solid enough form for the grade.

**NOTEBOOK**

**Riska King**, successful over this course and distance last summer off a 6lb higher mark, was well drawn and representing a trainer in fine form. He looks the type who could go in again while still fairly handicapped.
**Jubilee Street(IRE)** has done his winning on good to firm ground, so this was a very respectable effort on what was surely a slower surface than ideal.
**Gifted Flame**, another fast-ground performer, was not well drawn, but he gets farther than this and was staying on well at the finish.
**Oases**, who had cheekpieces on for a change, was as usual doing his best work in the latter part of the race.
**Locombe Hill(IRE)** may have won over a mile in the past, but he has shown more speed of late. He has shown himself able to compete over six furlongs this summer and did not get home over this extended seven furlongs.
**King Nicholas(USA)** has done his winning over shorter distances.
**Yorker(USA)** *Official explanation: trainer said gelding had broken a blood vessel*
**Sewmore Character** *Official explanation: jockey said colt swallowed her tongue*

## 5109 EBF BP SALTEND MAIDEN FILLIES' STKS — 7f 100y

**4:55** (4:56) (D ) 2-Y-O — **£5,622** (£1,730; £865; £432) **Stalls** High

Form — RPR

3 **1** **Gold Queen**[15] [4712] 2-8-11 ... ACulhane 12 — 73+
(MRChannon) *trckd ldrs: hdwy 2f out: rdn over 1f out: drvn ins last: led on line* **4/1**[2]

000 **2** *shd* **Musical Day**[15] [4706] 2-8-11 ... FNorton 11 — 73
(BJMeehan) *cl up: led 1/2-way: rdn wl over 1f out: drvn enteringt last: ct on line* **33/1**

**3** *1/2* **Intrigued** 2-8-11 ... SSanders 10 — 72+
(SirMarkPrescott) *dwlt: sn in tch: hdwy on inner over 2f out: effrt and n.m.r over 1f out: swtchd lft ins last: styd on wl* **10/11**[1]

0 **4** *5* **Calamari (IRE)**[36] [4099] 2-8-11 ... JCarroll 5 — 59
(MrsADuffield) *towards rr: hdwy on inner 2f out: sn rdn and kpt on fnl f: nrst fin* **66/1**

056 **5** *1/2* **Scorpio Sally (IRE)**[35] [4131] 2-8-11 ... PMQuinn 6 — 58
(MDHammond) *led: pushed along and hdd 1/2-way: rdn over 2f out and grad wknd* **66/1**

**6** *1/2* **Melody Que (IRE)** 2-8-11 ... RWinston 8 — 57
(JHowardJohnson) *chsd ldrs: rdn along over 2f out: grad wknd* **12/1**

4 **7** *nk* **Street Ballad (IRE)**[24] [4454] 2-8-11 ... JQuinn 2 — 56
(MrsJRRamsden) *hld up in rr: hdwy over 2f out: styd on appr last: nvr a factor* **18/1**

6 **8** *shd* **Tohama**[28] [4344] 2-8-11 ... WRyan 1 — 56
(JLDunlop) *bhd tl sme late hdwy* **14/1**

0 **9** *3/4* **Riyma (IRE)**[58] [3456] 2-8-11 ... FLynch 4 — 54
(SirMichaelStoute) *chsd ldrs: rdn along over 2f out and sn wknd* **14/1**

**10** *3* **Caribbean Dancer (USA)** 2-8-11 ... RFfrench 7 — 46
(MJohnston) *towards rr: rdn along 1/2-way: nvr a factor* **16/1**

30 **11** *2* **Sharaby (IRE)**[30] [4272] 2-8-11 ... WSupple 9 — 41
(EALDunlop) *in tch: pushed along over 2f out: sn rdn and wknd wl over 1f out* **7/1**[3]

**12** *30* **Mountain Breeze** 2-8-11 ... LisaJones 3 — —
(DShaw) *s.i.s: a outpcd and wl bhd* **66/1**

1m 38.91s (4.61) **Going Correction** +0.575s/f (Yiel) — **12** Ran SP% **124.5**
Speed ratings: **96,95,95,89,89 88,88,88,87,83 81,47**CSF £139.08 TOTE £4.10: £1.70, £8.70, £1.20; EX 136.50.
**Owner** Jaber Abdullah **Bred** Stratford Place Stud **Trained** West Ilsley, Berks

**FOCUS**

Possibly a decent maiden for the track, with three of these holding entries in the Fillies' Mile, including the winner and third. However, the runner-up is exposed and the top three stalls finished one-two-three.

**NOTEBOOK**

**Gold Queen**, third to Guineas fancy Shanghai Lily on her debut, drifted in the market in the face of support for the Prescott newcomer. Always well placed from her good draw, her rider cleverly kept the favourite hemmed in next to the rail, and in the end that tactic secured the win. She holds a Fillies' Mile entry, but realistically it looks like nurseries for her.
**Musical Day** enjoyed the run of the race but this was still a big step up on her previous form. This will not have done her handicap mark any good, though.
**Intrigued**, a sister to Approach, winner of this race in 2002 and subsequently successful in Listed grade, is a daughter of Last Second, winner of the Nassau and Sun Chariot Stakes. All the rage in the market beforehand, she did not get the gap next to the rail when she needed it and took a while to get into top gear once switched. With a clear run she would have probably won, and she looks likely to appreciate a mile on a more galloping track.
**Calamari(IRE)** appreciated the longer trip and easier ground to step up considerably on his debut effort.
**Scorpio Sally(IRE)** ran as well as could be expected and needs dropping in grade.



The Form Book, Raceform Ltd, Compton, RG20 6NL

**Sharaby(IRE)**, the third Fillies' Mile entry in the race, may not have coped with conditions underfoot, but this was still a disappointing effort.

## 5110 TELETEXT RACING "HANDS AND HEELS" APPRENTICE MAIDEN H'CAP — 1m 1f 207y

**5:30** (5:33) (F) (0-55,55) 3-Y-O+ — **£3,412** (£975; £487) **Stalls** High

Form — RPR

5500 **1** **Snowed Under**[35] [4138] 3-9-2 **55**.................................... JCavanagh(6) 1 — 65
(JDBethell) *sn prom: hdwy to ld wl over 1f out: styd on wl* **12/1**

6040 **2** *2 1/2* **Danefonique (IRE)**[17] [4628] 3-9-0 **50**.......................... NeilBrown(3) 16 — 55
(DCarroll) *chsd ldrs: hdwy 3f out: rdn to chse wnr ent last: kpt on* **11/1**

0200 **3** *1 1/4* **Plausabelle**[29] [4307] 3-9-1 **48**...........................................(b) WHogg 15 — 51
(TDEasterby) *trckd ldrs: hdwy to ld wl over 2f out: rdn and hdd wl over 1f out: grad wknd* **8/1**

00-0 **4** *2 1/2* **Mandinka**[71] [3060] 4-8-4 **32**........................................ SYourston(3) 8 — 30
(JFCoupland) *s.i.s and bhd: hdwy on outer over 2f out: styd on wl fnl f* **40/1**

0060 **5** *4* **Mr Moon**[26] [4387] 3-7-9 **31** oh2.................................. DonnaCaldwell(3) 5 — 22
(JParkes) *midfield: hdwy 2f out: kpt on ins last* **25/1**

5450 **6** *hd* **Eddies Jewel**[17] [4630] 4-8-9 **37**....................................... RKeogh(3) 3 — 28
(JSWainwright) *led: rdn along and hedaed wl over 2f out: grad wknd* **6/1**[1]

5003 **7** *3* **Dancer King (USA)**[19] [4610] 3-9-4 **51**.................................. HPoulton 4 — 36
(TPTate) *midfield: hdwy 3f out: rdn 2f out: sn no imp* **13/2**[2]

40U- **8** *1 1/4* **Amalfi Coast**[311] [5705] 5-9-7 **49**................................ KPierrepont(3) 6 — 32
(WSCunningham) *chsd ldrs: rdn along over 3f out: sn wknd* **50/1**

/030 **9** *1/2* **Awwal Marra (USA)**[32] [4213] 4-9-5 **44**......................... DeanWilliams 17 — 26
(EWTuer) *towards rr tl styd on fnl 2f* **12/1**

0605 **10** *1 1/4* **Beneking**[32] [4213] 4-9-6 **51**............................................... HFellows(6) 9 — 31
(RHollinshead) *bhd tl sme late hdwy* **10/1**

000- **11** *2 1/2* **Boppys Babe**[332] [5296] 3-7-9 **31** oh1.............................. KJackson(3) 10 — 6
(RAFahey) *a towards rr* **12/1**

2334 **12** *nk* **Monkey Or Me (IRE)**[96] [2349] 3-8-0 **33**.............................. MHalford 14 — 8
(PTMidgley) *chsd ldrs tl wknd fnl 2f* **7/1**[3]

060 **13** *1 1/4* **Sonearsofar (IRE)**[13] [4781] 4-9-2 **44**.......................... KGhunowa(3) 11 — 17
(JParkes) *nvr nr ldrs* **25/1**

0053 **14** *5* **Campbells Lad**[32] [4207] 3-8-0 **39**........................................ CEly(6) 13 — 3
(ABerry) *hld up and bhd: wd st: nvr a factor* **9/1**

500 **15** *2* **Lucky Piscean**[117] [1820] 3-9-4 **54**............................ AndrewWebb(3) 2 — 14
(CWFairhurst) *a rr* **25/1**

0600 **16** *1 3/4* **Grey Orchid**[61] [3368] 3-8-4 **40**.................................... LiamJones(3) 18 — —
(TJEtherington) *in tch: pushed along over 3f out: sn wknd* **50/1**

0000 **17** *3/4* **Quay Walloper**[38] [4015] 3-7-7 **32** oh5 ow1.............................. TDean(6) 12 — —
(JRNorton) *chsd ldrs on inner: pushed along over 3f out: sn wknd* **40/1**

4660 **18** *4* **Inmom (IRE)**[33] [4190] 3-9-4 **54**............................................ AReilly(3) 7 — 2
(SRBowring) *s.i.s: a bhd* **14/1**

2m 12.53s (5.33) **Going Correction** +0.575s/f (Yiel)
**WFA** 3 from 4yo+ 8lb — **18** Ran SP% **128.7**
Speed ratings: **101,99,98,96,92 92,90,89,88,87 85,85,84,80,79 77,77,73**CSF £135.52 CT £1145.52 TOTE £20.00: £5.00, £2.20, £3.20, £14.30; EX 482.70 Place 6 £77.35, Place 5 £52.60.

**Owner** Mrs G Fane **Bred** Mrs G Fane **Trained** Middleham Moor, N Yorks

**FOCUS**
A weak handicap, and the form is sound but very modest.

**NOTEBOOK**
**Snowed Under**, who shaped with more promise over this trip last time out, was effectively taking a drop in grade. He did well to defy the worst of the draw, but this was not a strong contest. *Official explanation: trainer's representative said, regarding the improved form shown, gelding had benefited from the drop in class*
**Danefonique(IRE)** has finished well in his races in the past, over a variety of distances, and did so again. He looks a difficult horse to win with.
**Plausabelle**, who was well drawn, had the blinkers back on and appeared to appreciate the drop back in trip.
**Mandinka**, returning from a ten-week absence, is only of moderate ability but he was staying on well at the end.
**Mr Moon** appears tripless.
**Eddies Jewel** did well to get to the front from his low draw. He is, however, another whose ideal trip remains a mystery.
**Monkey Or Me(IRE)** *Official explanation: trainer said gelding failed to stay*
T/Plt: £71.00 to a £1 stake. Pool: £52,426.80. 538.80 winning tickets. T/Qpdt: £13.50 to a £1 stake. Pool: £3,102.60. 169.00 winning tickets. JR

# 5074 GOODWOOD (R-H)

## Saturday, August 28

**OFFICIAL GOING: Round course - good to soft; straight course - soft (heavy in places)**
As on the previous day, the runners came stands' side in the straight and there seemed to be a bias towards those that managed to get tight against the rail.
Wind: lt against Weather: fine but cloudy

## 5111 TRAVELSPHERE HOLIDAYS MARCH STKS (LISTED RACE) — 1m 6f

**2:00** (2:02) (A) 3-Y-O+ — **£17,850** (£6,600; £3,300; £1,500) **Stalls** High

Form — RPR

4-61 **1** **Orange Touch (GER)**[14] [4755] 4-9-7 112............................. JPMurtagh 3 — 112+
(MrsAJPerrett) *lw: sn trckd ldr: led jst over 3f out: drew rt away fr 2f out: easily* **5/4**[1]

6431 **2** *11* **Swift Tango (IRE)**[7] [4932] 4-9-10 100............................... JFortune 5 — 100
(EALDunlop) *hld up: effrt to chse wnr 3f out: sn outpcd and btn* **5/2**[2]

1546 **3** *4* **Stage Right**[8] [4915] 3-8-7 85......................................... MartinDwyer 4 — 90
(DRCElsworth) *lw: trckd ldrs: rdn 4f out: outpcd and btn 3f out* **7/1**

-040 **4** *1 1/2* **Supremacy**[30] [4270] 5-9-10 105........................................... KFallon 2 — 93
(SirMichaelStoute) *sn led and set decent pce: rdn and hdd jst over 3f out: wknd u.p* **6/1**[3]

112 **5** *3* **Wait For The Will (USA)**[28] [4345] 8-9-7 90.........................(b) RLMoore 1 — 86
(GLMoore) *hld up in last: shkn up 4f out: no rspnse and sn lost tch* **14/1**

3m 9.47s (5.72) **Going Correction** +0.725s/f (Yiel)
**WFA** 3 from 4yo+ 12lb — **5** Ran SP% **106.5**
Speed ratings: **112,105,103,102,100**CSF £4.20 TOTE £2.30: £1.30, £1.60; EX 4.70.
**Owner** Cheveley Park Stud **Bred** Gestut Auenquelle **Trained** Pulborough, W Sussex

**FOCUS**
Despite there only being five runners, the pace was decent thanks to Supremacy and the time was as you would expect for a Listed race, but the extended distances make the form difficult to rate. As was the case the previous day, the field made for the stands' rail in the home straight.

**NOTEBOOK**
**Orange Touch(GER)** ◆, who loves this ground and was best in at the weights, had no problem with the longer trip and always had the leader in his sights. Once he managed to bag the stands' rail in the home straight, despite looking at the crowd he pulled right away as though his rivals were walking. Given these conditions, there should be plenty more decent prizes in him and the Irish St Leger is a possibility.
**Swift Tango(IRE)**, effective in these conditions, was given a patient ride until moving up turning for home and looked like he might make a race of it, but he was then very quickly put in his place. He was 15lb badly in with the winner on official ratings, so connections should not be too disappointed.
**Stage Right**, the only three-year-old in the field, had no chance at the weights and is a better horse on faster ground so he can be said to have emerged with a bit of credit, despite being well beaten.
**Supremacy**, withdrawn at Chester seven days previously due to soft ground, was sent into a clear early lead, but probably did too much too soon in the conditions and the writing was on the wall for him some way out.
**Wait For The Will(USA)** was outclassed and prefers fast ground.

## 5112 TOTEPOOL RATED STKS (H'CAP) — 7f

**2:30** (2:31) (B) (0-105,100) 3-Y-O+ — **£12,841** (£4,870; £2,435; £1,107) **Stalls** High

Form — RPR

1204 **1** **Material Witness (IRE)**[9] [4889] 7-9-7 **100**...................... MartinDwyer 8 — 110
(WRMuir) *lw: mde all: rdn 3l clr ent fnl f: tired and drvn out nr fin* **11/2**[2]

0002 **2** *3/4* **Digital**[8] [4908] 7-8-9 **88**............................................................ CCatlin 1 — 96
(MRChannon) *lw: settled in last: drvn over 2f out: prog over 1f out: chsd wnr ins fnl f: gaining at fin* **6/1**[3]

5402 **3** *2 1/2* **Kool (IRE)**[14] [4742] 5-8-11 **90**................................................ DHolland 2 — 92
(PFICole) *lw: settled in tch: pushed along over 3f out: chsd wnr jst over 2f out: no imp over 1f out: one pce after* **7/2**[1]

0040 **4** *6* **Selective**[21] [4528] 5-8-12 **91**................................................ SDrowne 5 — 78
(EFVaughan) *hld up in tch: effrt on wd outside 3f out: floundering u.p wl over 1f out: wknd* **10/1**

0441 **5** *2 1/2* **King's Caprice**[10] [4846] 3-8-5 **89**........................................ SCarson 7 — 70
(GBBalding) *lw: mostly trckd wnr to jst over 2f out: shkn up and sn wknd* **7/2**[1]

0003 **6** *1/2* **Taranaki**[14] [4742] 6-8-5 **87**.............................................. LPKeniry(3) 6 — 66
(PDCundell) *settled in tch: effrt and wl on terms on outer over 2f out: wknd rapidly wl over 1f out* **12/1**

5000 **7** *21* **Camp Commander (IRE)**[21] [4528] 5-8-13 **92**...................... JFortune 4 — 19
(CEBrittain) *in tch: lost pl and btn 3f out: eased over 1f out: t.o* **12/1**

0-50 **8** *7* **Grizedale (IRE)**[35] [4120] 5-9-0 **93**........................................(t) KFallon 3 — 2
(JAkehurst) *prom: disp 2nd pl over 3f out: drvn and hanging over 2f out: wknd wl over 1f out: virtually p.u fnl f* **11/2**[2]

1m 31.45s (3.42) **Going Correction** +0.725s/f (Yiel)
**WFA** 3 from 5yo+ 5lb — **8** Ran SP% **114.0**
Speed ratings: **109,108,105,98,95 95,71,63**CSF £37.92 CT £131.59 TOTE £6.30: £2.10, £1.70, £1.70; EX 33.70 Trifecta £47.10 Pool of £1,227.80 - 18.50 winning units.
**Owner** M J Caddy **Bred** M Henochsberg **Trained** Lambourn, Berks

**FOCUS**
A decent, competitive handicap and a sound pace, but the outcome was very much influenced by the track as both the front two came right up the stands' rail.

**NOTEBOOK**
**Material Witness(IRE)** continues in great form despite edging up the handicap. Soon in front, his rider made sure he bagged the stands' rail at the earliest opportunity after turning for home and that is probably where the best ground was. None of his rivals could get to him and, though he did get tired late on, hanging away from the rail which allowed the runner-up to get close, he was never going to be caught.
**Digital**, who goes in the ground, appeared to be struggling some way out but, following the winner up the stands' rail, found a rare turn of foot and closed that rival down though he never quite looked like getting there. He is talented, but very hard to win with these days.
**Kool(IRE)** ran another decent race under conditions that suit but continues to just miss out.
**Selective** ◆ ran well enough but deserves extra credit as he made his effort furthest from the stands' rail and appeared to get bogged down in the ground. He is becoming well handicapped and is one to note.
**King's Caprice**, raised 4lb for his Kempton win, was free to post. He was a bit disappointing as, even though this was a better race, the ground should have been in his favour.
**Camp Commander(IRE)** *Official explanation: jockey said horse hung right throughout*
**Grizedale(IRE)** may have done too much too soon and eventually floundered in the ground.

## 5113 TOTESPORT CELEBRATION MILE (GROUP 2) — 1m

**3:05** (3:05) (A) 3-Y-O+ — **£58,000** (£22,000; £11,000; £5,000) **Stalls** High

Form — RPR

6031 **1** **Chic**[14] [4745] 4-8-12 101.......................................................... KFallon 5 — 123
(SirMichaelStoute) *lw: racd in last: pushed along fr 5f out: prog wl over 1f out: weaved through to chse ldr ins fnl f: drvn to ld last 75yds* **4/1**[2]

-302 **2** *1 1/4* **Nayyir**[31] [4228] 6-9-1 120.................................................... MJKinane 2 — 124
(GAButler) *lw: hld up: clsd on ldrs over 2f out: plld out and led wl over 1f out : hanging but sn rdn clr: hdd last 75yds* **5/4**[1]

0303 **3** *5* **Hurricane Alan (IRE)**[16] [4685] 4-9-4 114................................ PDobbs 3 — 117
(RHannon) *lw: settled w main gp: effrt 3f out: rdn to chse ldr over 1f out: no imp* **11/2**[3]

5421 **4** *nk* **Court Masterpiece**[35] [4120] 4-9-1 110................................... JFortune 4 — 113
(EALDunlop) *hld up: gng wl 3f out: effrt 2f out: rdn to dispute 2nd plcd over 1f out: nt qckn and btn after* **8/1**

-104 **5** *5* **Passing Glance**[16] [4685] 5-9-4 118.............................. MartinDwyer 6 — 106
(AMBalding) *pressed ldr: clr w him 1/2-way: led 3f out: hdd & wknd wl over 1f out* **12/1**

1150 **6** *2 1/2* **Brunel (IRE)**[20] [4595] 3-8-12 113........................................ DHolland 7 — 101
(WJHaggas) *t.k.h: hld up: rdn over 2f out: wknd rapidly over 1f out* **12/1**

0446 **7** *25* **Naahy**[20] [4596] 4-9-1 109.................................................... JPMurtagh 1 — 48
(MRChannon) *led: kicked on and clr w one rival 1/2-way: hdd 3f out: wknd rapidly sn after: eased: t.o* **25/1**

1m 43.22s (2.95) **Going Correction** +0.725s/f (Yiel)
**WFA** 3 from 4yo+ 6lb — **7** Ran SP% **110.2**
Speed ratings: **114,112,107,107,102 99,74**CSF £8.68 TOTE £4.00: £2.40, £1.50; EX 10.40.
**Owner** Cheveley Park Stud **Bred** Cheveley Park Stud Ltd **Trained** Newmarket, Suffolk

**FOCUS**
A rapid pace given the ground, with two established front-runners taking each other on and setting the race up for others. The winning time was as you would expect for a Group Two in the conditions, although the form cannot be described as solid given the circumstances.

**NOTEBOOK**
**Chic**, who had never raced on soft ground before, was held up out the back but looked more likely to finish last rather than first two furlongs out. However, after she was switched and went past a few weakening rivals, she suddenly took off and caught the flagging favourite in the dying strides. She looks ready for a crack at the highest class now.

**Nayyir**, given a patient ride, rather got tangled up as the two pace-setters fell in his lap and had to take evasive action. As a result he may have found himself in front sooner than ideal and, even though he established a sizeable advantage, he never looked that convincing and managed to get mugged inside the last half-furlong. He has the talent, but his effort needs timing to perfection and he never seems to get the rub of the green.
**Hurricane Alan(IRE)** is not being helped by his penalty, but ran another solid race at this level if finding the front pair far too classy.
**Court Masterpiece**, stepping up from handicap company, had a bit to find with some of these on official ratings but acquitted himself well. He handles cut, but may be best suited by genuinely good ground.
**Passing Glance** could not get to the front on his own with Naahy in the field and they conspired to cut each other's throats.
**Brunel(IRE)** took too keen a hold early in the conditions and ran his second consecutive moderate race on soft ground.
**Naahy**, edgy beforehand, needs faster ground, but even so he went off far too fast in the conditions, probably due to Passing Glance lighting him up, and eventually fell in a complete heap.

## 5114 CHAPEL DOWN ENGLISH WINES MAIDEN AUCTION STKS 1m
**3:40** (3:42) (D ) 2-Y-O **£4,969** (£1,529; £764; £382) **Stalls High**

Form RPR
30 **1** **Jamaaron**[23] [4480] 2-8-13 .......... RLMoore 9 76
(RHannon) *trckd ldrs: rdn to ld on inner jst over 2f out: drvn and kpt on wl fnl f* **6/1**[3]
0 **2** *1 ¼* **Krasivi's Boy (USA)**[21] [4544] 2-8-10 .......... DHolland 6 70
(GLMoore) *w ldrs: rdn over 2f out: chsd wnr over 1f out: chal ins fnl f: hld last 100yds* **33/1**
06 **3** *½* **Penny Island (IRE)**[20] [4567] 2-8-12 .......... JDSmith 15 71
(AKing) *t.k.h: hld up in midfield: rdn and effrt over 2f out: styd on same pce fr over 1f out* **6/1**[3]
56 **4** *2* **Sir Monty (USA)**[16] [4682] 2-8-13 .......... MJKinane 2 68
(MrsAJPerrett) *swtg: hld up midfield: n.m.r on inner over 2f out: nudged along and styng on whn nt clr run over 1f out: nvr nrr: do bttr* **11/2**[2]
0 **5** *¾* **Lord Of Dreams (IRE)**[36] [4081] 2-8-13 .......... MartinDwyer 10 67
(DWPArbuthnot) *settled towards rr: effrt and n.m.r over 2f out: kpt on same pce fnl 2f* **33/1**
2 **6** *1 ¾* **Lithos**[20] [4579] 2-8-11 .......... JPMurtagh 3 61
(JAOsborne) *mde most to jst over 2f out: hanging and grad fdd* **9/2**[1]
000 **7** *2 ½* **Sabbiosa (IRE)**[15] [4705] 2-8-7 .......... DaneO'Neill 5 52
(JLDunlop) *w ldrs: losing pl whn nt clr run over 2f out and swtchd: no prog after* **14/1**
060 **8** *1 ½* **Spinning Coin**[31] [4234] 2-8-1 .......... RMiles(3) 7 46
(JGPortman) *rr of main gp: hmpd on inner 3f out and swtchd rt: shuffled along and nvr nr ldrs after* **6/1**[3]
00 **9** *1* **Election Seeker (IRE)**[15] [4730] 2-8-8 .......... AQuinn(5) 11 53
(GLMoore) *racd midfield: drvn over 2f out: no prog and sn btn* **25/1**
0000 **10** *1 ¼* **Play Up Pompey**[6] [4966] 2-8-5 .......... JFMcDonald(3) 1 46
(JJBridger) *towards rr: drvn on outer and sme prog over 2f out: wknd over 1f out* **33/1**
**11** *2* **Proprioception (IRE)** 2-8-5 .......... CCatlin 4 39
(MRChannon) *w'like: outpcd in last trio whn hmpd after 2f: nvr on terms* **14/1**
0 **12** *3 ½* **Katana**[10] [4851] 2-8-6 ow2.......... SDrowne 8 33
(IAWood) *prom tl wknd wl over 2f out* **14/1**
000 **13** *nk* **Looking Great (USA)**[20] [4584] 2-8-11 .......... SCarson 13 37
(RFJohnsonHoughton) *sn outpcd in last pair: nvr a factor* **33/1**
**14** *12* **Yankey** 2-8-8 .......... JFortune 14 10
(CEBrittain) *w'like: bit bkwd: s.s: a last: pushed along and no prog 3f out: t.o* **25/1**
6 **U** **Tranquilizer**[20] [4584] 2-7-12 ..........(t) HayleyTurner(5) 12 —
(DJCoakley) *in tch whn stmbld and uns rdr after 2f* **14/1**

1m 47.54s (7.27) **Going Correction** +0.725s/f (Yiel) **15** Ran SP% **122.5**
Speed ratings: **92,90,90,88,87 85,83,81,80,79 77,74,73,61,—**CSF £206.31 TOTE £6.70: £2.60, £11.40, £2.60; EX 321.60.
**Owner** N A Woodcock **Bred** M Doyle **Trained** East Everleigh, Wilts

**FOCUS**
Not a strong maiden and the time was ordinary, making the form appear messy. A big field congregating on the stands' rail inevitably caused a few traffic problems.
**NOTEBOOK**
**Jamaaron** appreciated the return to easier conditions and the extra furlong, but being able to bag that vital position against the stands' rail turning for home was another major factor. The form does not look anything special though, and nurseries may be his best option.
**Krasivi's Boy(USA)** improved no end from his Polytrack debut and had no problem with the ground. He should get further and looks capable of picking up a small maiden.
**Penny Island(IRE)** ran his best race yet on this first encounter with soft ground. The form may not be great, but he now qualifies for nurseries and will appreciate even further.
**Sir Monty(USA)** ◆ again did not have much luck on his side, this time running into a dead end against the stands' rail on more than one occasion. He would have finished a good deal closer otherwise and is worth looking out for in nurseries.
**Lord Of Dreams(IRE)**, stepping up two furlongs from his debut and racing on much softer ground, did not have the clearest of passages in the home straight but stayed on pleasingly enough. A modest maiden should be within his capabilities.
**Lithos** was given a positive ride, but did not get home in the ground. He should be given another chance back on a sounder surface. *Official explanation: jockey said colt was unsuited by good to soft ground*
**Spinning Coin** got into a bit of trouble when the field converged against the stands' rail and was never a threat thereafter. Her form figures show four duck eggs, but she is better than that.
**Proprioception(IRE)** *Official explanation: vet said filly was lame behind*

## 5115 EBF PROGRESSIVE MAIDEN FILLIES' STKS 6f
**4:15** (4:15) (D ) 2-Y-O **£4,979** (£1,532; £766; £383) **Stalls Low**

Form RPR
**1** **Annals** 2-8-11 .......... DaneO'Neill 5 80+
(HCandy) *leggy: racd in 4th: prog on outer 2f out: pushed into ld jst ins fnl f: sn in command: comf* **7/2**[2]
03 **2** *1 ½* **Je Suis Belle**[13] [4776] 2-8-11 .......... DHolland 1 70
(BWHills) *swtg: trckd ldng pair: nt clr run 2f out: swtchd rt and rdn: kpt on to take 2nd wl ins fnl f: no ch w wnr* **11/10**[1]
50 **3** *1 ½* **Theas Dance**[50] [3693] 2-8-11 .......... MJKinane 3 65
(DRLoder) *lw: led at stdy pce: shkn up 2f out: hdd and outpcd jst ins fnl f* **6/1**
50 **4** *6* **Flaunting It (IRE)**[16] [4682] 2-8-11 .......... SDrowne 2 47
(JAOsborne) *dwlt: racd in last: pushed along over 2f out: wknd over 1f out* **14/1**
**5** *hd* **Zeena** 2-8-11 .......... MartinDwyer 4 46
(MPTregoning) *neat: w ldr to 2f out: wknd* **4/1**[3]

1m 18.78s (5.94) **Going Correction** +0.90s/f (Soft) **5** Ran SP% **110.8**
Speed ratings: **96,94,92,84,83**CSF £7.90 TOTE £5.10: £2.00, £1.50; EX 9.50.
**Owner** Major M G Wyatt **Bred** Dunchurch Lodge Stud Co **Trained** Wantage, Oxon

**FOCUS**
An uncompetitive fillies' maiden, but the time was fair and the winner could be useful.
**NOTEBOOK**
**Annals** ◆, a half-sister to Goslar and a multiple winner in Germany, was brought with her effort widest of all and showed a decent turn of foot in the conditions. An athletic type, she looks a nice prospect and her pedigree suggests she will stay further.
**Je Suis Belle**, slightly awkward leaving the stalls, did not make full use of her rails draw, preferring instead to sit in behind. As things turned out the tactic did not help her, as while she was meeting traffic problems the winner was being produced with her effort on the outside, and by the time she saw daylight she had too much ground to make up. She cannot be said to have been unlucky though, considering the winner's authority.
**Theas Dance** had the run of the race out in front against the stands' rail but was swamped for speed in the closing stages. She does not seem to be progressing.
**Flaunting It(IRE)** did not improve for dropping down a furlong, but may need faster ground and should do better in nurseries.
**Zeena**, first foal of the dual winner Forest Fire, did not get home in these testing conditions and is worth another chance on better ground.

## 5116 HORIZON MAIDEN STKS (H'CAP) 2m
**4:50** (4:51) (E ) (0-70,70) 3-Y-O **£3,874** (£1,192; £596; £298) **Stalls High**

Form RPR
5233 **1** **Race The Ace**[17] [4647] 3-9-7 **70**.......... JPMurtagh 4 83+
(JLDunlop) *t.k.h early: cl up: chsd ldr over 4f out: drvn to ld wl over 1f out: steadily drew clr* **5/2**[1]
0002 **2** *4* **Sharadi (IRE)**[16] [4692] 3-9-2 **65**.......... JoannaBadger 2 73
(VSmith) *lw: led after 4f: kicked on over 4f out: hdd wl over 1f out: one pce* **11/2**[3]
3000 **3** *1 ¼* **Irish Blade (IRE)**[14] [4749] 3-9-5 **68**.......... DaneO'Neill 10 75
(HCandy) *b.hind: plld hrd early: hld up: prog 5f out: rdn to chse ldng pair wl over 2f out: kpt on same pce* **8/1**
3006 **4** *2* **Hoh Nelson**[9] [4870] 3-8-13 **62**.......... SDrowne 9 66
(HMorrison) *hld up towards rr: rdn over 3f out: sme prog fr over 2f out: no ch w ldrs* **14/1**
0504 **5** *3* **Pangloss (IRE)**[8] [4915] 3-9-1 **64**..........(b) RLMoore 12 65
(GLMoore) *hld up in rr: swtchd rt and drvn 3f out: plugged on: nvr a danger* **5/1**[2]
0053 **6** *4* **Bayou Princess**[16] [4673] 3-8-6 **58**.......... LPKeniry(3) 7 54
(BDeHaan) *racd in midfield: pushed along 6f out: effrt over 4f out: struggling wl over 2f out* **50/1**
0003 **7** *nk* **Wyoming**[6] [4971] 3-8-7 **56**.......... MartinDwyer 11 51
(JARToller) *hld up last: prog 4f out: rdn to dispute 3rd pl over 2f out: wknd over 1f out: eased* **7/1**
0540 **8** *1* **Molehill**[13] [4778] 3-8-7 **56**.......... IMongan 1 50
(JGGiven) *prom tl wknd 3f out* **10/1**
5430 **9** *10* **Fu Fighter**[9] [4870] 3-9-5 **68**.......... DHolland 5 50
(JAOsborne) *led for 4f: chsd ldr to over 4f out: wknd wl over 2f out: eased* **8/1**
00 **10** *7* **Icarus Dream (IRE)**[14] [4736] 3-9-2 **65**.......... SCarson 6 39
(PRHedger) *prom tl wknd over 3f out* **50/1**
-050 **11** *14* **Blue Hills**[88] [2561] 3-8-13 **65**.......... RMiles(3) 3 22
(PWHiatt) *in tch tl wknd 4f out: wl bhd fnl 2f* **33/1**
0450 **12** *23* **Royal Starlet**[12] [4798] 3-7-12 **47** oh2.......... CCatlin 8 —
(MrsAJPerrett) *racd midfield: drvn and wknd over 4f out: t.o 3f out* **20/1**

3m 40.84s (10.18) **Going Correction** +0.725s/f (Yiel) **12** Ran SP% **122.7**
Speed ratings: **103,101,100,99,97 95,95,95,90,86 79,68**CSF £16.04 CT £99.38 TOTE £3.00: £1.40, £2.40, £3.90; EX 21.20.
**Owner** I H Stewart-Brown & M J Meacock **Bred** I Stewart-Brown And M Meacock **Trained** Arundel, W Sussex

**FOCUS**
A very moderate event and several of these are likely to end up over hurdles this coming autumn, but at least it was run at a fair pace. The form is fair for the grade and seems sound enough.
**NOTEBOOK**
**Race The Ace** was never far away and the further they went the better he was going. At least his form had a progressive look to it and he seemed to relish the trip in the conditions, so there seems no reason why he should not continue to progress.
**Sharadi(IRE)**, proven on soft ground, did everything right under a positive ride and bagged the stands' rail in the home straight, but he just ran into a more progressive rival.
**Irish Blade(IRE)**, stepping up half a mile in trip, is proven in soft ground but the surface did mean that this was going to be an even greater test of his stamina. Taking a good hold early added to the doubts, but he travelled well and certainly did not fail because he did not stay. He is worth another go over this sort of trip.
**Hoh Nelson** was made to look very one-paced over the last couple of furlongs and may do better over hurdles.
**Pangloss(IRE)** goes on the ground, but did not improve for the extra half-mile.
**Bayou Princess** was another that did not improve for the longer trip.
**Fu Fighter** probably did too much too soon in the conditions and his stable will do well to get a race out of him on the level. *Official explanation: jockey said gelding was unsuited by good to soft going*
**Blue Hills** *Official explanation: jockey said gelding was unsuited by good to soft going*

## 5117 STAYIN ALIVE STKS (H'CAP) 5f
**5:25** (5:25) (D ) (0-80,78) 3-Y-O **£5,473** (£1,684; £842; £421) **Stalls Low**

Form RPR
4006 **1** **La Vie Est Belle**[7] [4937] 3-8-3 **60**.......... MartinDwyer 5 69
(BRMillman) *lw: led: rdn and hdd wl over 1f out: rallied u.p to ld nr fin* **16/1**
3111 **2** *¾* **Wunderbra (IRE)**[3] [5040] 3-8-11 **73** 7ex..........(t) HayleyTurner(5) 4 80+
(MLWBell) *b: t.k.h: trckd ldrs: led gng easily wl over 1f out: shkn up fnl f: hdd nr fin* **11/8**[1]
6020 **3** *1 ¼* **Imperium**[12] [4800] 3-8-11 **68**.......... DHolland 3 71
(MrsStefLiddiard) *trckd ldr to 2f out: sn rdn and unable qck: kpt on same pce after* **12/1**
3000 **4** *1 ¾* **Four Amigos (USA)**[10] [4862] 3-9-7 **78**.......... IMongan 7 76
(JGGiven) *lw: hld up in last pair: rdn and struggling 2f out: kpt on ins fnl f* **6/1**[3]
5001 **5** *hd* **Tizzy's Law**[6] [4970] 3-8-10 **67** 7ex.......... SDrowne 6 64
(MABuckley) *t.k.h: hld up: effrt 2f out: sn rdn: wknd fnl f* **9/2**[2]
0024 **6** *3 ½* **Arfinnit (IRE)**[3] [5040] 3-8-1 **58**..........(v) CCatlin 2 45
(MRChannon) *pressed ldrs early: last and struggling 1/2-way: no ch after* **8/1**
6401 **7** *1* **Mirasol Princess**[20] [4585] 3-9-2 **73**.......... DaneO'Neill 1 57
(DKIvory) *sed v awkwardly: racd in rr: drvn and btn wl over 1f out* **9/1**

63.18 secs (4.13) **Going Correction** +0.90s/f (Soft) **7** Ran SP% **109.3**
Speed ratings: **102,100,98,96,95 90,88**CSF £35.33 TOTE £21.20: £6.70, £1.40; EX 47.30 Place 6 £11.26, Place 5 £9.62.
**Owner** Robin Lawson **Bred** V Robin Lawson **Trained** Kentisbeare, Devon


The Form Book, Raceform Ltd, Compton, RG20 6NL

■ Stewards Enquiry : Martin Dwyer caution: used whip with arm above shoulder height

**FOCUS**

An ordinary handicap of its type and yet again position on the track probably played its part, but the form looks reasonable with the runner-up slightly better than the bare form.

**NOTEBOOK**

**La Vie Est Belle**, who had shown very little on soft ground before, has dropped 16lb since the start of the season. Given a positive ride, she looked beaten when the favourite went past, but she was racing next to the stands' rail and that enabled her to rally and snatch the race back.

**Wunderbra(IRE)**, racing off a 13lb higher mark than for her last handicap on turf, looked all over the winner when sent to the front a furlong from home. However, she had taken a good hold early and was racing further away from the stands' rail than the eventual winner, which may help explain her eventual capitulation.

**Imperium** ran with some credit, but needs faster ground and seems to reserve his best for Brighton these days.

**Four Amigos(USA)** goes in the ground and is getting some help from the Handicapper, but this sharp five looks an inadequate test for him now.

**Tizzy's Law** took a good hold early and raced wide of the field, which probably explains why she did not get home.

**Mirasol Princess** effectively lost all chance at the start. *Official explanation: jockey said filly reared as stalls opened*

T/Plt: £20.60 to a £1 stake. Pool: £62,655.80. 2,219.25 winning tickets. T/Qpdt: £10.90 to a £1 stake. Pool: £2,265.60. 153.20 winning tickets. JN

# [5087] NEWMARKET (JULY) (R-H)

## Saturday, August 28

**OFFICIAL GOING: Good to soft**

After a dry night the ground had dried out a little and the centre of the track appeared to be the best place to be.

Wind: Slight behind Weather: Overcast

## 5118 MCKEEVER ST LAWRENCE EBF MAIDEN STKS — 6f

1:55 (1:56) (D) 2-Y-O — **£4,891** (£1,505; £752; £376) Stalls High

Form — RPR

1 **Echelon** 2-8-6 .......... NMackay(3) 4 — 93
(SirMichaelStoute) *gd sort: lw: hld up in tch: led ins fnl f: r.o wl* **7/1**

2 2 **Newsround** 2-9-0 .......... PRobinson 8 — 92
(MAJarvis) *gd sort: leggy: led: rdn and edgd lft over 1f out: hdd and unable qck ins fnl f* **6/1**

3 5 **River Royale** 2-9-0 .......... AMcCarthy 1 — 77
(PWChapple-Hyam) *w'like: scope: chsd ldrs: rdn and ev ch over 1f out: wknd ins fnl f* **11/2**[3]

2 — 4 nk **Wise Owl**[77] [2898] 2-9-0 .......... JFanning 2 — 76
(MJohnston) *w ldrs over 4f: wknd ins fnl f* **3/1**[1]

5 2 **Breathing Fire** 2-9-0 .......... RMullen 3 — 70
(WJMusson) *str: scope: s.s: hld up: hdwy over 1f out: nt trble ldrs* **33/1**

6 nk **Victory Design (IRE)** 2-9-0 .......... EAhern 5 — 69
(JNoseda) *gd sort: chsd ldrs over 4f* **4/1**[2]

7 shd **Musahim (USA)** 2-9-0 .......... RHills 11 — 69
(BWHills) *w'like: hld up: swtchd lft and hdwy over 1f out: nvr nr to chal* **17/2**

0 — 8 ¾ **Rapid Flow**[14] [4747] 2-9-0 .......... RHughes 10 — 67
(MrsAJPerrett) *lw: chsd ldrs over 4f* **25/1**

0 — 9 1 **Sir Bluebird (IRE)**[5] [5003] 2-9-0 .......... JFEgan 7 — 64
(RHannon) *lw: mid-div: sn pushed along: wknd over 1f out* **50/1**

10 nk **Pacific Pirate (IRE)** 2-9-0 .......... SWKelly 9 — 63
(MGQuinlan) *neat: unf: mid-div: rdn 1/2-way: wknd over 1f out* **50/1**

11 ¾ **Padrao (IRE)** 2-9-0 .......... KDarley 6 — 60
(DRLoder) *leggy: scope: w ldrs over 4f: wknd qckly* **20/1**

12 7 **Selika (IRE)** 2-9-0 .......... NCallan 13 — 39
(MHTompkins) *w'like: scope: bkwd: s.s: a bhd* **100/1**

0 — 13 hd **Perez (IRE)**[12] [4809] 2-9-0 .......... PaulEddery 12 — 39
(RHannon) *prom: rdn over 2f out: sn hung lft and wknd* **50/1**

1m 14.14s (0.82) **Going Correction** +0.20s/f (Good) **13 Ran SP% 116.1**

Speed ratings: **102,99,92,92,89 89,89,88,86,86 85,76,75**CSF £44.49 TOTE £8.60: £2.90, £2.40, £2.60; EX 69.70.

**Owner** Cheveley Park Stud **Bred** Cheveley Park Stud Ltd **Trained** Newmarket, Suffolk

**FOCUS**

Several nice types on show and a decent winning time for the type of race, 0.32 seconds faster than the the valuable nursery over the same trip.

**NOTEBOOK**

**Echelon**, a half-sister to Group Two winner Chic, was the only filly in the race. She clearly has plenty of ability and looks to have a bright future.

**Newsround ◆**, a 220,000 gns yearling, clearly knew his job and only gave best on the final climb. He pulled well clear of third and should have no trouble going one better.

**River Royale ◆**, who is out of a mare that won over seven furlongs as a juvenile, showed enough to suggest he can win his maiden, especially when stepping up in trip.

**Wise Owl** matched strides with the leaders for much of the trip before fading up the hill. He will be suited by a stiffer test in time.

**Breathing Fire**, who is out of a mare that was sharp enough to win over the minimum as a juvenile, but stayed well enough to win over two miles as a four-year-old, came from a long way back and can be expected to have learnt plenty from this.

**Victory Design(IRE)**, a 250,000 gns yearling, ran well for much of the way until getting tired going into the dip. He can be expected to improve on this, especially on a less-testing surface.

**Perez(IRE)** *Official explanation: jockey said colt was hanging left from 3f out*

## 5119 SIEMENS SMART HOME TECHNOLOGY NURSERY — 6f

2:25 (2:26) (B) 2-Y-O — **£14,040** (£4,320; £2,160; £1,080) Stalls High

Form — RPR

0111 — 1 **Coleorton Dancer**[9] [4875] 2-8-13 **82** .......... NCallan 3 — 91
(KARyan) *lw: racd centre: hld up: hdwy over 2f out: edgd rt and led ins fnl f: rdn out* **5/1**[2]

2421 — 2 ½ **Marching Song**[23] [4481] 2-9-3 **86** .......... RHughes 11 — 93
(RHannon) *s.s: racd centre: hld up: hdwy to ld 1f out: sn hdd: r.o* **8/1**[3]

211 — 3 2 **Spy King (USA)**[17] [4632] 2-9-7 **90** .......... KDarley 6 — 91
(MJohnston) *racd centre: chsd ldrs: rdn and ev ch over 1f out: styd on same pce* **4/1**[1]

256 — 4 ½ **Alexander Capetown (IRE)**[43] [3904] 2-8-2 **71** ow1 .......... RMullen 8 — 71
(BWHills) *lw: racd centre: chsd ldrs: led 4f out: rdn and hdd 1f out: styd on same pce* **14/1**

1202 — 5 1 ¼ **Kwame**[8] [4918] 2-8-9 **78** .......... TEDurcan 1 — 74
(MissECLavelle) *lw: s.s: racd centre: hld up: swtchd lft and hdwy over 1f out: no ex ins fnl f* **16/1**

165 — 6 shd **Bolton Hall (IRE)**[11] [4836] 2-9-2 **85** .......... PHanagan 7 — 80
(RAFahey) *racd centre: chsd ldrs: rdn over 2f out: styd on same pce appr fnl f* **8/1**[3]

3136 — 7 nk **Society Music (IRE)**[24] [4445] 2-8-9 **78** .......... EAhern 9 — 73
(MDods) *b. nr hind: racd centre: chsd ldrs: rdn and hung rt over 1f out: styd on same pce* **50/1**

6655 — 8 1 ½ **King After**[8] [4907] 2-7-13 **75** .......... CHaddon(7) 4 — 65
(JRBest) *racd centre: sn pushed along in rr: n.d* **33/1**

3121 — 9 nk **Rowan Lodge (IRE)**[15] [4700] 2-8-12 **81** .......... PRobinson 16 — 70
(MHTompkins) *mde most stands' side: no ch w centre gp* **14/1**

641 — 10 nk **Brooklime (IRE)**[9] [4866] 2-8-9 **78** .......... SWKelly 15 — 66
(JAOsborne) *lw: racd stands' side: chsd ldrs: btn whn hung lft ins fnl f* **14/1**

3042 — 11 1 ¾ **On The Waterline (IRE)**[12] [4803] 2-8-2 **76** .......... NChalmers(5) 12 — 59
(PDEvans) *chsd ldrs stands' side: no ex fnl f* **12/1**

3010 — 12 2 ½ **Prospect Court**[28] [4342] 2-8-13 **82** .......... KMcEvoy 13 — 58
(JDBethell) *racd stands' side: hld up in tch: no ch whn hmpd ins fnl f* **25/1**

5340 — 13 hd **Monashee Prince (IRE)**[14] [4752] 2-8-12 **81** .......... DKinsella 14 — 56
(JRBest) *w ldrs stands' side 5f* **33/1**

3012 — 14 ½ **Whatatodo**[36] [4089] 2-8-3 **72** .......... JMackay 2 — 45
(MLWBell) *b.hind: racd centre: chsd ldrs over 4f* **16/1**

0401 — 15 1 ¾ **Grand Place**[15] [4704] 2-8-4 **73** .......... JFEgan 5 — 41
(RHannon) *racd centre: plld hrd and prom: wknd over 1f out* **14/1**

043 — 16 1 ¼ **Naval Force**[30] [4256] 2-8-10 **79** .......... (t) MFenton 10 — 43
(HMorrison) *led centre 2f: wknd 2f out* **14/1**

1m 14.46s (1.14) **Going Correction** +0.20s/f (Good) **16 Ran SP% 123.4**

Speed ratings: **100,99,96,96,94 94,93,91,91,91 88,85,85,84,82 80**CSF £43.86 CT £187.58 TOTE £6.90: £2.40, £2.30, £1.70, £2.90; EX 76.10 Trifecta £127.40 Pool of £987.10 - 5.50 winning units.

**Owner** Coleorton Moor Racing **Bred** A Holmes **Trained** Hambleton, N Yorks

**FOCUS**

A competitive contest with 13 of the runners winners, and it was run at a fair pace. Those who raced up the centre of the track had the edge.

**NOTEBOOK**

**Coleorton Dancer** confirmed himself an improved performer and had no difficulty staying this extra furlong. While he is sure to take a further hike up the ratings, there is no doubt that there is still more to come from him.

**Marching Song** took a while to get his act together, but he confirmed himself a progressive performer and, had he not given ground away at the start, may well have scored.

**Spy King(USA)**, facing his stiffest task to date, was far from disgraced giving weight away all round.

**Alexander Capetown(IRE)** tackling handicappers for the first time, had plenty of use made of her and, although beaten, was not disgraced. She can be placed to advantage off her current mark.

**Kwame** is a consistent filly and appeared to run her race, despite giving the impression that this trip looked to stretch her.

**Bolton Hall(IRE)** has not really progressed from his debut, where he had quite a hard introduction.

**Grand Place** *Official explanation: jockey said gelding lost his action*

## 5120 CHRIS BLACKWELL MEMORIAL H'CAP — 7f

2:55 (2:56) (C) (0-90,89) 3-Y-O — **£14,170** (£4,360; £2,180; £1,090) Stalls High

Form — RPR

2211 — 1 **My Paris**[20] [4570] 3-8-12 **87** .......... AMullen(7) 5 — 99
(KARyan) *s.i.s: sn prom: rdn to ld over 1f out: hung lft ins fnl f: jst hld on* **13/2**[3]

-100 — 2 shd **Alfonso**[118] [1795] 3-8-5 **73** .......... MHills 2 — 85+
(BWHills) *a.p: rdn over 1f out: n.m.r ins fnl f: r.o* **8/1**

2215 — 3 1 ¾ **Flipando (IRE)**[14] [4750] 3-9-4 **86** .......... KDarley 4 — 93
(TDBarron) *lw: chsd ldrs: rdn and hung rt over 1f out: r.o* **4/1**[1]

5116 — 4 nk **Hazewind**[34] [4171] 3-7-9 **66** oh1 .......... (vt) NMackay(3) 12 — 72
(PDEvans) *led over 5f out: rdn and hdd over 1f out: edgd lft ins fnl f: styd on same pce* **12/1**

6602 — 5 ¾ **Granston (IRE)**[28] [4340] 3-8-7 **75** .......... PRobinson 6 — 82+
(JDBethell) *chsd ldrs: rdn and ev ch over 1f out: looked hld whn hmpd wl ins fnl f* **9/1**

1226 — 6 ½ **Doitnow (IRE)**[21] [4531] 3-9-7 **89** .......... PHanagan 8 — 92
(RAFahey) *hld up: hdwy over 1f out: styd on same pce ins fnl f* **8/1**

3160 — 7 shd **Burley Flame**[17] [4646] 3-8-11 **79** .......... MFenton 9 — 82
(JGGiven) *hld up: hdwy over 1f out: nt rch ldrs* **16/1**

0341 — 8 1 ¼ **Bright Sun (IRE)**[15] [4726] 3-8-7 **75** .......... KimTinkler 1 — 74
(NTinkler) *lw: chsd ldrs: rdn over 2f out: styd ons ame pce appr fnl f* **11/1**

0000 — 9 ¾ **Seneschal**[8] [4906] 3-8-7 **75** .......... TEDurcan 7 — 73
(MRChannon) *hld up: sme hdwy fnl f: n.d* **50/1**

2001 — 10 3 ½ **King Of Diamonds**[14] [4756] 3-8-9 **77** .......... NCallan 10 — 65
(JRBest) *lw: hld up: plld hrd: hdwy over 2f out: wknd fnl f* **6/1**[2]

0450 — 11 2 ½ **Mission Man**[13] [4780] 3-8-10 **78** .......... RHughes 11 — 60
(RHannon) *hdd over 5f out: wknd over 1f out* **11/1**

-200 — 12 1 ¾ **Big Bradford**[53] [3598] 3-9-6 **88** .......... (v) DKinsella 3 — 65
(PGMurphy) *dwlt: hld up: wknd over 2f out* **20/1**

1m 27.42s (0.65) **Going Correction** +0.20s/f (Good) **12 Ran SP% 116.8**

Speed ratings: **104,103,101,101,100 100,100,98,97,93 90,88**CSF £56.87 CT £236.20 TOTE £5.40: £1.60, £2.90, £2.00; EX 69.60 Trifecta £379.50 Pool of £748.40 - 1.40 winning tickets.

**Owner** J And A Spensley **Bred** J And A Spensley **Trained** Hambleton, N Yorks

■ Stewards Enquiry : A Mullen three-day ban: careless riding (Sep 8-10)

**FOCUS**

Another competitive handicap and although the stalls were on the stands' side, the field ended up racing over the far side. The form is fair and sound for the grade.

**NOTEBOOK**

**My Paris** goes from strength to strength and never really looked like getting beaten, despite coming off a true line in the latter stages.

**Alfonso**, who had been gelded since last seen on a racecourse, proved well suited to the easy surface. Granted a similar surface he should not find it too difficult to add to his All-Weather win.

**Flipando(IRE)** is a consistent sort but, just as he had here earlier in the month, did not come down the hill as well as he might have. A flatter track may suit better.

**Hazewind** was again far from disgraced in this company, but he does need his sights lowering if he is to get back to winning ways.

**Granston(IRE)** may well have finished third had he not been all but mugged by the winner in the closing stages.

**Doitnow(IRE)** is finding life difficult at present and will need placing with care.

## 5121 SHARP MINDS BETFAIR BE HOPEFUL STKS (LISTED RACE) — 6f

3:30 (3:30) (A) 3-Y-O+ — **£17,400** (£6,600; £3,300; £1,500) Stalls High

Form — RPR

3151 — 1 **Prince Aaron (IRE)**[50] [3691] 4-9-0 89 .......... GCarter 6 — 99+
(CNAllen) *hld up: hdwy over 1f out: rdn to ld and hung lft ins fnl f: r.o* **3/1**[1]

0500 — 2 ½ **Atavus**[21] [4553] 7-9-0 85 .......... JMackay 3 — 98
(GGMargarson) *chsd ldr: rdn over 2f out: led 1f out: sn hdd: r.o* **16/1**

112 **3** *hd* **Red Romeo**[37] 4051 3-8-11 92 .......... PHanagan 1 97
(GASwinbank) *lw: b.hind: chsd ldrs: rdn and hung lft over 1f out: r.o* **6/1**[3]
2400 **4** *¾* **Millybaa (USA)**[13] 4779 4-8-9 97 .......... KDarley 7 90
(RGuest) *dwlt: sn prom: rdn over 1f out: ev ch ins fnl f: no ex* **9/1**
0200 **5** *hd* **Coconut Penang (IRE)**[28] 4324 4-9-0 95 .......... EAhern 2 94
(PWChapple-Hyam) *chsd ldrs: effrt over 1f out: styd on same pce* **7/2**[2]
1100 **6** *1* **Celtic Mill**[30] 4269 6-9-4 106 .......... LEnstone 8 95
(DWBarker) *lw: led: rdn over 1f out: sn edgd lft and hdd: no ex* **6/1**[3]
000 **7** *hd* **Enchanted**[29] 4286 5-8-9 94 .......... JFEgan 4 86
(NACallaghan) *lw: hld up: rdn over 2f out: nt trble ldrs* **13/2**
6300 **8** *2½* **Dowager**[13] 4779 3-8-6 100 .......... RHughes 5 78
(RHannon) *hld up: rdn over 2f out: wknd fnl f* **15/2**

1m 14.02s (0.70) **Going Correction** +0.20s/f (Good)
**WFA** 3 from 4yo+ 3lb **8** Ran SP% **116.8**
Speed ratings: **103,102,102,101,100 99,99,95**CSF £52.06 TOTE £4.20: £1.70, £4.00, £1.30; EX 56.00.
**Owner** Black Star Racing **Bred** Peter Charles And J R Bamforth **Trained** Newmarket, Suffolk

**FOCUS**

A modest time for a Listed contest, just 0.12 seconds faster than the opening two-year-old maiden, and not great form for the grade..

**NOTEBOOK**

**Prince Aaron(IRE)** continued his climb up the ladder with an impressive display, although it has to be said this was not the strongest of Listed contests. The Ayr Gold Cup is his next target.
**Atavus** is not the force he was, but showed he still retains a little ability.
**Red Romeo** was not disgraced on his first run at this level, but he will need to find more if he is to add to his tally.
**Millybaa(USA)** had no excuses and remains difficult to place.
**Coconut Penang(IRE)** was something of a disappointment for, having travelled well, he found little when push came to shove.
**Celtic Mill** would have preferred a sounder surface.

## 5122 DETTORI'S ITALIAN ICE CREAM CHALLENGE RATED STKS (H'CAP) 1m 2f

**4:00** (4:04) (C) (0-95,90) 3-Y-0+ **£15,428** (£5,852; £2,926; £1,330) **Stalls** High

Form RPR
441- **1** **Border Castle**[305] 5810 3-8-1 81 .......... NMackay(3) 9 95+
(SirMichaelStoute) *h.d.w: hld up: swtchd centre 7f out: hdwy 3f out: rdn to ld ins fnl f: r.o* **4/1**[2]
0002 **2** *2* **Zero Tolerance (IRE)**[10] 4856 4-9-7 90 .......... MFenton 5 100
(TDBarron) *plld hrd: prom: swtchd centre 7f out: chsd ldr 4f out: ridde n to ld over 1f out: hdd and unable qck ins fnl f* **9/2**[3]
4250 **3** *1¾* **Ofaraby**[21] 4540 4-9-5 88 .......... PRobinson 2 95
(MAJarvis) *lw: hld up: swtchd centre 7f out: hdwy over 1f out: nt rch ldrs* **9/1**
5335 **4** *½* **Torinmoor (USA)**[11] 4831 3-8-13 90 .......... KDarley 3 96+
(MrsAJPerrett) *chsd ldr tl swtchd centre and led that gp 7f out: rdn over 2f out: edgd rt and hdd over 1f out: styd on same pce* **10/3**[1]
5010 **5** *2* **Danelor (IRE)**[5] 4988 6-9-3 86 .......... PHanagan 1 88
(RAFahey) *led: remained stands' ent st: rdn and hdd over 1f out: sn wknd* **16/1**
0302 **6** *½* **Silvaline**[7] 4950 5-8-13 82 .......... TEDurcan 8 83
(TKeddy) *prom: lft chsng ldr on stands' side 7f out: hung lft over 1f out: nvr trbld ldrs* **5/1**
2560 **7** *3½* **Cripsey Brook**[21] 4540 6-9-1 84 .......... KimTinkler 6 79
(DonEnricoIncisa) *plld hrd and prom: swtchd centre and chsd ldr 7f out: rdn 4f out: wknd over 2f out* **22/1**
1532 **8** *5* **St Pancras (IRE)**[8] 4917 4-8-13 82 .......... NCallan 7 68
(NACallaghan) *s.s: hld up: swtchd centre 7f out: rdn and wknd over 2f out* **10/1**
2602 **9** *1¼* **Solo Flight**[14] 4754 7-9-2 85 .......... RHughes 4 69
(HMorrison) *dwlt: hld up: swtchd centre 7f out: hdwy over 2f out: wknd over 1f out* **16/1**

2m 6.11s (-0.35) **Going Correction** +0.20s/f (Good)
**WFA** 3 from 4yo+ 8lb **9** Ran SP% **113.1**
Speed ratings: **109,107,106,105,104 103,100,96,95**CSF £21.86 CT £149.90 TOTE £4.60: £2.20, £1.90, £3.10; EX 19.70 Trifecta £618.70 Pool of £958.70 - 1.10 winning units.
**Owner** The Queen **Bred** The Queen **Trained** Newmarket, Suffolk

**FOCUS**

A decent contest run at a good clip, and those who raced down the centre once in line for home held the call. The form has a solid appearance.

**NOTEBOOK**

**Border Castle** made an impressive return to action when staying on far too well for his rivals. With improvement to come over an extra furlong or two, he should have no trouble adding to this.
**Zero Tolerance(IRE)**, who has not looked the easiest of rides of late, did nothing wrong and was just unlucky to come up against an unexposed rival.
**Ofaraby** was doing his best work in the closing stages and may be returning to form.
**Torinmoor(USA)**, left clear when switching to the centre once in line for home, may have done too much too soon.
**Danelor(IRE)** was one of two that elected to stay stands' side once in line for home, and was still there until weakening in the dip.
**Silvaline** did not have things go his way, although he does look in the grip of the Handicapper now.
**Solo Flight** *Official explanation: jockey said gelding was unsuited by Good to Soft ground*

## 5123 NEW TIGRA ARRIVES AT MARSHALL ELY MAIDEN STKS 1m

**4:35** (4:36) (D) 3-Y-0+ **£5,616** (£1,728; £864; £432) **Stalls** High

Form RPR
**1** **Eyes Only (USA)** 3-8-6 .......... RHughes 10 82
(HRACecil) *gd sort: scope: a.p: led over 1f out: rdn clr* **7/4**[1]
0 **2** *6* **Thistle**[13] 4781 3-8-11 .......... RHills 15 75
(JHMGosden) *lw: led over 6f: sn outpcd* **25/1**
35- **3** *½* **High Reserve**[320] 5539 3-8-6 .......... OUrbina 4 69
(JRFanshawe) *hld up: hdwy 1/2-way: rdn over 2f out: styd on ins fnl f* **8/1**[3]
3 **4** *¾* **Play Bouzouki**[29] 4303 3-8-3 .......... NMackay(3) 16 67
(LMCumani) *chsd ldrs: rdn over 2f out: styd on same pce appr fnl f* **5/1**[2]
0-26 **5** *shd* **River Of Babylon**[106] 2097 3-8-6 64 .......... JMackay 5 67
(MLWBell) *lw: plld hrd and prom: rdn over 2f out: no ex fnl f* **11/1**
5-4 **6** *3* **Residential**[35] 4125 3-8-11 .......... PHanagan 14 66
(MrsAJPerrett) *lw: hld up in tch: hung lft and wknd over 1f out* **9/1**
**7** *1* **Harrycat (IRE)** 3-8-11 .......... GCarter 17 64
(VSmith) *w'like: hld up: styd on ins fnl f: nvr nrr* **50/1**
**8** *nk* **River Of Diamonds** 3-8-11 .......... JFEgan 8 63
(RGuest) *cmpt: hld up: rdn over 2f out: nvr trbld ldrs* **50/1**
3- **9** *1¼* **Nadir**[295] 5939 3-8-11 .......... MHills 3 60
(PHowling) *hld up: nvr nr to chal* **11/1**
000 **10** *1* **Bonnetts (IRE)**[15] 4718 3-8-6 .......... MFenton 13 53
(HCandy) *hld up: bhd 1/2-way: hung lft over 1f out: n.d* **66/1**
3/3- **11** *6* **Corbel (USA)**[443] 2310 4-8-12 72 .......... TEDurcan 9 41
(MissGayKelleway) *hld up: wknd over 2f out* **40/1**
05 **12** *shd* **Celebre Citation (IRE)**[26] 4402 3-8-11 .......... (t) RMullen 6 45
(JRFanshawe) *lw: chsd ldrs: rdn over 2f out: wknd over 1f out* **33/1**
0-5 **13** *½* **Homeward (IRE)**[23] 4478 3-8-6 .......... DKinsella 11 39
(AMBalding) *b: prom 5f* **50/1**
45 **14** *hd* **Tregenna**[28] 4316 3-8-6 .......... MHenry 2 39
(RMHCowell) *prom over 5f* **66/1**
U000 **15** *2½* **Aljafliyah**[15] 4718 3-7-13 .......... AHamblett(7) 12 34
(LMCumani) *hld up: rdn and wknd over 2f out* **50/1**
52 **16** *1½* **Wait For Spring (USA)**[16] 4693 3-8-6 .......... KDarley 1 31
(JHMGosden) *prom: chsd ldr over 4f out: rdn and wknd over 1f out: eased fnl f* **5/1**[2]
**17** *dist* **Arctic Cove** 3-8-11 .......... NCallan 7 —
(JNicol) *w'like: bkwd: s.s: hld up rdn and wknd 1/2-way* **50/1**

1m 41.21s (0.73) **Going Correction** +0.20s/f (Good)
**WFA** 3 from 4yo 6lb **17** Ran SP% **129.5**
Speed ratings: **104,98,97,96,96 93,92,92,91,90 84,84,83,83,80 79,—**CSF £59.85 TOTE £2.80: £1.40, £4.50, £3.20; EX 67.40.
**Owner** K Abdulla **Bred** Juddmonte Farms Inc **Trained** Newmarket, Suffolk
■ Stewards Enquiry : N Callan £110 fine: passport irregularity

**FOCUS**

This did not look a great race, especially as the fifth home was rated just 64, but the winner is clearly smart and open to plenty of improvement.

**NOTEBOOK**

**Eyes Only(USA)**, who is from the same family as the high-class pair Commander In Chief and Warning, made an impressive start to her career when quickening right away from her field. While this may not have taken much winning, she could hardly have been more impressive.
**Thistle** had clearly learnt from his debut, but was easily brushed aside when the winner changed gear.
**High Reserve** did not shape too badly on this return to action, and should not be too difficult to place in handicaps.
**Play Bouzouki** does not do anything quickly and may appreciate a step up in trip.
**River Of Babylon** did herself no favours by taking a fierce grip early.
**Residential** will at least have more options open to him now in handicaps.
**Wait For Spring(USA)** *Official explanation: jockey said filly finished stiff behind.*
**Arctic Cove** *Official explanation: jockey said gelding dropped himself out of contest*

## 5124 BRETTENHAM H'CAP 6f

**5:10** (5:10) (D) (0-85,82) 3-Y-0+ **£5,811** (£1,788; £894; £447) **Stalls** High

Form RPR
3221 **1** **Fonthill Road (IRE)**[11] 4837 4-9-9 78 .......... PHanagan 4 88+
(RAFahey) *lw: trckd ldrs: plld hrd: lost pl over 3f out: hdwy over 1f out: r.o to ld post* **6/4**[1]
530/ **2** *hd* **Nisr**[898] 572 7-9-4 73 .......... JFEgan 6 82
(JWPayne) *b: chsd ldrs: rdn and edgd lft over 1f out: led ins fnl f: ct post* **33/1**
0051 **3** *nk* **Balakiref**[8] 4904 5-9-4 73 .......... NCallan 11 81+
(MDods) *b: b.hind: hld up in tch: lost pl 1/2-way: hdwy over 1f out: r.o* **9/2**[2]
5001 **4** *nk* **Branston Tiger**[33] 4185 5-8-2 62 .......... (v[1]) NChalmers(5) 8 69
(PDEvans) *chsd ldrs: rdn over 1f out: r.o* **6/1**[3]
2100 **5** *nk* **Tony The Tap**[11] 4837 3-9-7 82 .......... NMackay(3) 2 88
(NACallaghan) *w ldr tl led over 3f out: hdd and unable qck ins fnl f* **9/1**
0054 **6** *hd* **Fearby Cross (IRE)**[15] 4727 8-8-6 61 .......... RMullen 1 67
(WJMusson) *chsd ldrs: rdn and edgd lft over 1f out: no ex wl ins fnl f* **10/1**
-010 **7** *¾* **Wyatt Earp (IRE)**[48] 3775 3-9-4 76 .......... KDarley 10 79
(JARToller) *lw: hld up: hdwy 1/2-way: styd on same pce fnl f* **20/1**
-300 **8** *3* **Stormy Nature (IRE)**[99] 2269 3-9-1 73 .......... MFenton 13 67
(PWHarris) *s.i.s: hld up: effrt and edgd lft over 1f out: sn wknd* **25/1**
6300 **9** *2* **Najeebon (FR)**[42] 3941 5-9-9 78 .......... TEDurcan 7 66
(MRChannon) *dwlt: hld up: rdn over 2f out: wknd over 1f out* **10/1**
-055 **10** *1½* **Mandarin Spirit (IRE)**[82] 2727 4-9-0 69 .......... MHenry 3 53
(GCHChung) *led: hdd over 3f out: wknd fnl f* **33/1**
0050 **11** *shd* **Antonio Canova**[5] 5008 8-9-5 74 .......... DKinsella 9 58
(BobJones) *hld up: rdn over 2f out: a in rr* **14/1**
1000 **12** *nk* **Toronto Heights (USA)**[22] 4515 3-9-3 75 .......... AMcCarthy 5 58
(PWChapple-Hyam) *chsd ldrs 4f* **20/1**

1m 13.95s (0.63) **Going Correction** +0.20s/f (Good)
**WFA** 3 from 4yo+ 3lb **12** Ran SP% **126.6**
Speed ratings: **103,102,102,101,101 101,100,96,93,91 91,91**CSF £78.98 CT £208.50 TOTE £2.60: £1.30, £10.40, £2.00; EX 111.30 Place 6 £69.67, Place 5 £20.00.
**Owner** Mrs Una Towell **Bred** D N Wallace **Trained** Mulsey Bank, N Yorks

**FOCUS**

An ordinary handicap but solid form despite the blanket finish.

**NOTEBOOK**

**Fonthill Road(IRE)**, a much improved sprinter, again left the impression there may be more in the locker.
**Nisr** turned in a solid performance on this return to action and clearly retains his ability.
**Balakiref** came into this in good form, and there is no reason to believe he did not run his race. At his best with give underfoot he should continue to give a good account when conditions are in his favour.
**Branston Tiger**, followed up his All-Weather victory with another solid effort in the first-time visor.
**Tony The Tap** turned in a sound effort under his big weight, but is probably better on a faster surface.
**Fearby Cross(IRE)** is beginning to look well treated, but he is a funny customer who is difficult to catch right.

T/Plt: £116.50 to a £1 stake. Pool: £69,235.15. 433.65 winning tickets. T/Qpdt: £17.80 to a £1 stake. Pool: £4,018.50. 166.30 winning tickets. CR

# 4573 REDCAR (L-H)

### Saturday, August 28

**OFFICIAL GOING: Good to soft**

## 5125 LADIES EVENING MEDIAN AUCTION MAIDEN STKS 6f

**5:20** (5:21) (F) 2-Y-0 **£3,679** (£1,051; £525) **Stalls** Centre

Form RPR
33 **1** **Tsaroxy (IRE)**[47] 3793 2-8-11 .......... PMulrennan(3) 9 77
(JHowardJohnson) *mde all: 2 l clr ent fnl f: drvn out* **9/4**[1]
45 **2** *½* **Wigwam Willie (IRE)**[12] 4804 2-8-11 .......... DCorby(3) 6 75
(MJWallace) *chsd wnr: rdn 2f out: no imp tl styd on ins fnl f: clsng on wnr fin* **5/2**[2]
5 **3** *1¾* **Leslingtaylor (IRE)**[13] 4776 2-8-9 .......... BSwarbrick(5) 2 70
(JJQuinn) *prom: drvn along 2f out: styd on: no imp on first 2 fnl f* **5/1**[3]

0004 **4** 5 **Mister Buzz**[38] 4009 2-9-0 60 ........ DarrenWilliams 8 55
(MDHammond) *in tch: rdn 2f out: kpt on same pce* **25/1**

**5** shd **Sweet Potato (IRE)** 2-8-9 ........ PFessey 4 49
(TDBarron) *prom: rdn and outpcd 2f out: n.d after* **25/1**

0 **6** 3/4 **Dancing Deano (IRE)**[104] 2141 2-9-0 ........ VHalliday 5 52
(RMWhitaker) *s.i.s: towards rr: sme hdwy u.p over 1f out: no further prog fnl f* **22/1**

**7** nk **Enborne Again (IRE)** 2-9-0 ........ GFaulkner 7 51
(RAFahey) *slowly away: wl bhd: styd on u.p fr over 1f out: n.d* **20/1**

**8** 2 1/2 **Blades Boy** 2-9-0 ........ GParkin 3 44
(KARyan) *s.i.s: in rr most of way* **14/1**

00 **9** 3 1/2 **Jessica's Style (IRE)**[8] 4924 2-8-9 ........ JBramhill 1 28
(JGGiven) *sn in rr* **50/1**

**10** 3 **Interwoven (IRE)** 2-9-0 ........ SChin 10 24
(MJohnston) *slowly away: wl bhd most of way* **7/1**

1m 13.21s (1.51) **Going Correction** +0.05s/f (Good) **10 Ran SP% 113.9**
Speed ratings: **91,90,88,81,81 80,79,76,71,67**CSF £7.11 TOTE £3.30: £1.10, £1.40, £2.10; EX 6.60.
**Owner** Andrea & Graham Wylie **Bred** E O'Leary **Trained** Crook, Co Durham

**FOCUS**
A fair maiden for the track and the first three appear to be improving.

**NOTEBOOK**
**Tsaroxy(IRE)** idled in front, maybe through greenness, and is value for a slightly wider margin of victory. He was suited by the return to soft ground.
**Wigwam Willie(IRE)** chased the favourite all the way and stuck on despite showing a slightly high head carriage. Now eligible for nurseries, he appreciated the return to this trip and had no problem with the ground.
**Leslingtaylor(IRE)** , whose knee action is well suited to this sort of ground, ran a decent race over the extra furlong.
**Mister Buzz**, who has started at 25/1 or bigger on each of his starts, was outpaced at the business end. He is probably better on fast ground.
**Sweet Potato(IRE)**, out of a middle-distance winner in France, was staying on over what is likely to prove an inadequate trip.
**Dancing Deano(IRE)** has been gelded since his debut back in May.
**Enborne Again(IRE)**, a cheap buy, made a bit of late progress after missing the break.
**Interwoven(IRE)**, out of a seven-furlong Listed winner, was always trailing after missing the break badly.

## 5126 BETTER HALF CLASSIFIED STKS 6f
**5:50** (5:50) (F) 3-Y-0+ **£3,435** (£981; £490) **Stalls Centre**

Form RPR

0031 **1** **Bond Playboy**[11] 4827 4-9-7 66 ........ FLynch 3 74
(BSmart) *mde all: wandered over 1f out: kpt on u.p fnl f: jst hld on* **7/2**[2]

2020 **2** shd **Bollin Edward**[20] 4577 5-9-5 64 ........(v) DAllan 5 71
(TDEasterby) *sn towards rr and pushed along: hdwy over 1f out: wnt 2nd ins fnl f: edgd lft u.p: jst failed* **5/1**[3]

0506 **3** 1 3/4 **William's Well**[21] 4542 10-8-12 55 ........(b) PMulrennan(3) 6 62
(MWEasterby) *rr: rdn 2f out: hdwy appr fnl f: r.o wl ins last: nrst fin* **12/1**

40-0 **4** nk **Jilly Why (IRE)**[183] 906 3-8-9 60 ........ ANicholls 8 58
(MsDeborahJEvans) *prom: chsd wnr and rdn over 1f out: no ex fnl f* **100/1**

0000 **5** 1/2 **Karminskey Park**[11] 4828 5-8-5 60 ........ KristinStubbs(7) 12 57
(TJEtherington) *in tch: sme hdwy 2f out: rdn and no ex fnl f* **12/1**

0316 **6** 1 **Frimley's Mattery**[11] 4827 4-8-10 53 ........ PPMathers(5) 4 57
(REBarr) *midfield: rdn over 2f out: kpt on same pce* **33/1**

2045 **7** hd **Legal Set (IRE)**[8] 4904 8-8-8 60 ........(t) LeanneKershaw(7) 7 56
(MissAStokell) *midfield: rdn over 2f out: kpt on same pce* **14/1**

0000 **8** 1 1/4 **Viewforth**[21] 4542 6-9-3 62 ........(v[1]) VHalliday 9 54
(JSGoldie) *towards rr: sme hdwy u.p 2f out: no further prog* **7/1**

0060 **9** 7 **Percy Douglas**[12] 4805 4-8-8 40 ........(t) MStainton(7) 2 31
(MissAStokell) *sn towards rr: hdwy into midfield over 2f out: sn rdn and btn* **66/1**

6211 **10** 2 **Red Monarch (IRE)**[11] 4828 3-8-12 63 ........ LFletcher(3) 1 28
(PABlockley) *prom: rdn 1/2-way: sn btn* **9/4**[1]

0040 **11** 6 **Key Of Gold (IRE)**[9] 4877 3-8-12 60 ........ DarrenWilliams 11 7
(DCarroll) *in tch: rdn 1/2-way: sn wknd* **20/1**

4441 **12** shd **Troodos Jet**[14] 4758 3-9-2 64 ........ ACulhane 10 11
(ABerry) *trckd ldrs to 1/2-way: sn rdn and wknd* **12/1**

1m 11.65s (-0.05) **Going Correction** +0.05s/f (Good)
**WFA** 3 from 4yo+ 3lb **12 Ran SP% 122.1**
Speed ratings: **102,101,99,99,98 97,96,95,85,83 75,75**CSF £21.64 TOTE £4.50: £2.40, £2.20, £3.10; EX 23.70.
**Owner** R C Bond **Bred** P A Mason **Trained** Hambleton, N Yorks

**FOCUS**
A tightly matched classified sprint run at a fair pace for the grade in the conditions, but ordinary form.

**NOTEBOOK**
**Bond Playboy** , who likes this ground and enjoys being able to dominate, edged left under pressure but stuck out his neck willingly to hold on. He is in good heart at present and there could be more to come judged on last season's form.
**Bollin Edward** went down narrowly on this drop in trip. He deserves to end his long losing run.
**William's Well** ran another sound race and is in good heart at present. He handles this ground but a faster surface is ideal.
**Jilly Why(IRE)** ran a good race on her first start for six months. This was her first run on soft ground.
**Karminskey Park** is best at the minimum trip.
**Red Monarch(IRE)** came here at the top of his game and had ground conditions to suit, so this has to go down as disappointing. *Official explanation: trainer was unable to offer any explanation for poor form shown other than that race possibly had come too soon after the previous run*
**Key Of Gold(IRE)** *Official explanation: jockey said gelding lost its action behind*
**Troodos Jet** *Official explanation: jockey said gelding lost its action*

## 5127 LADIES NIGHT OUT H'CAP 1m
**6:20** (6:21) (D) (0-80,79) 3-Y-0+ **£11,241** (£3,459; £1,729; £864) **Stalls Centre**

Form RPR

0/03 **1** **Zandeed (IRE)**[8] 4905 6-8-5 57 ........ PFessey 12 66
(MissLAPerratt) *s.i.s: sn midfield: clsd on ldrs over 1f out: styd on wl u.p to ld wl ins fnl f* **14/1**

0340 **2** 3/4 **Cat's Whiskers**[49] 3731 5-9-13 79 ........ DaleGibson 3 86
(MWEasterby) *cl up: led 1/2-way: styd on u.p: hdd wl ins fnl f: no ex* **11/1**

0206 **3** shd **Qualitair Wings**[5] 4988 5-9-6 72 ........ DMcGaffin 6 79
(JHetherton) *dwlt: rr div: rdn over 2f out: hdwy over 1f out: styd on wl to chal wl ins fnl f: no ex clsng stages* **16/1**

0001 **4** 3/4 **Creskeld (IRE)**[11] 4826 5-9-2 68 ........ FLynch 4 74
(BSmart) *prom: rdn to chal over 1f out: ev ch tl no ex wl ins fnl f* **4/1**[1]

621 **5** 1 1/2 **Zarin (IRE)**[8] 4925 6-8-1 53 ........ ANicholls 2 55
(DWChapman) *prom: ev ch and rdn 2f out: kpt on same pce* **6/1**[3]

0010 **6** shd **Dara Mac**[9] 4877 5-8-10 62 ........ DeanMcKeown 5 64
(NBycroft) *dwlt: hld up in rr: hdwy 3f out: in tch and rdn appr fnl f: no further prog* **16/1**

1000 **7** 1 1/4 **Rarefied (IRE)**[13] 4780 3-9-4 76 ........ DAllan 7 76
(TDEasterby) *midfield: rdn 1/2-way: kpt on fnl 2f: n.d* **33/1**

4000 **8** 2 **Pharoah's Gold (IRE)**[11] 4826 6-7-8 51 oh1 ow1 ....(v) BSwarbrick(5) 10 46
(DShaw) *dwlt: rr div: sme hdwy 3f out: wknd over 1f out* **50/1**

-030 **9** nk **Fair Spin**[43] 3921 4-8-10 62 ........ ACulhane 8 57
(MDHammond) *reminders after 2f: nvr bttr than mid-div* **4/1**[1]

0126 **10** 1 **Splodger Mac (IRE)**[10] 4852 5-8-3 55 ........ JBramhill 11 48
(NBycroft) *prom tl rdn and wknd 2f out* **10/1**

1210 **11** 3 **Parisian Playboy**[22] 4511 4-7-5 50 oh1 ........ LeanneKershaw(7) 9 36
(JeddO'Keeffe) *towards rr: hdwy u.p into midfield 2f out: wknd appr fnl f* **9/2**[2]

2004 **12** 2 **Soller Bay**[8] 4903 7-9-6 72 ........ DarrenWilliams 1 54
(KRBurke) *led tl rdn and hdd 1/2-way: fdd* **14/1**

1m 38.88s (1.18) **Going Correction** +0.05s/f (Good)
**WFA** 3 from 4yo+ 6lb **12 Ran SP% 119.9**
Speed ratings: **96,95,95,94,92 92,91,89,89,88 85,83**CSF £161.21 CT £2528.39 TOTE £13.60: £2.90, £3.10, £3.70; EX 112.80.
**Owner** Miss L A Perratt **Bred** Mrs R D Peacock **Trained** Ayr, Strathclyde
■ Stewards Enquiry : P Fessey five-day ban: used whip with excessive frequency and without allowing gelding time to respond (Sep 8-12)

**FOCUS**
A fair handicap but a moderate winning time for the grade.

**NOTEBOOK**
**Zandeed(IRE)** had been withdrawn from a race on heavy ground the previous night. Racing towards the near rail, he responded to a hard ride to get on top near the finish. Back in action this term after suffering a career-threatening injury, he is well handicapped on his old form for Ed Dunlop.
**Cat's Whiskers** could never shake off his pursuers and was eventually run out of it close home. He is without a win for two years but is weighted to score again.
**Qualitair Wings** likes this ground and this is his time of year, but remains 9lb above his last winning mark.
**Creskeld(IRE)** went up 4lb after winning at Hamilton but remains on a fair mark. He was driven up to have his chance but could not muster a change of gear.
**Zarin(IRE)** found this tougher than the All-Weather seller that he won last time, but this was still a fair effort.
**Fair Spin** had his ground, but did not look happy from an early stage.
**Parisian Playboy** *Official explanation: jockey said gelding lost its action*

## 5128 THE FAIRER SEX NOVICE MEDIAN AUCTION STKS 7f
**6:50** (6:51) (E) 2-Y-0 **£5,070** (£1,560; £780; £390) **Stalls Centre**

Form RPR

025 **1** **Cool Panic (IRE)**[12] 4809 2-8-12 78 ........ RWinston 6 84
(MLWBell) *trckd ldrs: drvn to ld ent fnl f: styd on* **5/2**[2]

1326 **2** 2 1/2 **Sir Anthony (IRE)**[9] 4890 2-9-4 90 ........ FLynch 7 84
(BSmart) *slowly away: hld up in rr: hdwy to chse ldrs over 1f out: styd on u.p ins last: wnt 2nd on line* **10/11**[1]

**3** shd **Il Colosseo (IRE)** 2-8-12 ........ DAllan 8 78
(MrsLStubbs) *dwlt: sn prom: led 3f out: rdn and hdd ent fnl f: no ex* **33/1**

06 **4** 6 **Paris Heights**[55] 3560 2-8-12 ........ DeanMcKeown 4 63
(RMWhitaker) *trckd ldrs: rdn 3f out: sn btn* **25/1**

01 **5** 1 1/4 **Fenrir**[8] 4900 2-9-1 86 ........ PMulrennan(3) 2 66
(JRWeymes) *prom: rdn over 2f out: wknd over 1f out* **4/1**[3]

0660 **6** 4 **Forpetesake**[32] 4208 2-8-12 ........ ANicholls 3 50
(MsDeborahJEvans) *led tl hdd 3f out: wknd 2f out* **50/1**

0 **7** 4 **Azahara**[24] 4446 2-8-7 ........ ACulhane 5 35
(KGReveley) *a rr div* **50/1**

**8** dist **Cool Sands (IRE)** 2-8-12 ........ DarrenWilliams 1 —
(DShaw) *slowly away: rr div: lost tch fnl 2f: t.o* **20/1**

1m 26.05s (1.15) **Going Correction** +0.05s/f (Good) **8 Ran SP% 116.4**
Speed ratings: **95,92,92,85,83 79,74,—**CSF £5.03 TOTE £3.70: £1.30, £1.10, £4.40; EX 6.80.
**Owner** D W & L Y Payne **Bred** Roger And Henry O'Callaghan **Trained** Newmarket, Suffolk
■ Stewards Enquiry : D Allan ten-day ban: failed to ride out for second place (Sep 8-17)

**FOCUS**
Fair form for the track, probably best judged through the fourth.

**NOTEBOOK**
**Cool Panic(IRE)** had appeared not to get home over six at Windsor, but had no problem with seven furlongs in softish ground and came clear to score decisively.
**Sir Anthony(IRE)**, slowly away again, hung left under pressure and found his stride too late. Perhaps not a straightforward ride, he should get a mile.
**Il Colosseo(IRE)**, a half-brother to two winners at up to 12 furlongs, notably Mumbling, played up in the stalls and missed the break. He ran a promising race and, after wandering in front and being headed, he lost second spot when his rider dropped his hands.
**Paris Heights** was well beaten in the end, but this run qualifies him for nurseries.
**Fenrir** was held under the penalty for his 100/1 success at Ayr.

## 5129 DON'T BE LATE STKS (H'CAP) 1m 2f
**7:20** (7:20) (E) (0-70,63) 3-Y-0+ **£5,343** (£1,644; £822; £411) **Stalls Low**

Form RPR

0000 **1** **Swift Alchemist**[10] 4849 4-8-13 52 ........(p) DarrenWilliams 4 61
(MrsHSweeting) *in tch: hdwy over 2f out: rdn to chal over 1f out: styd on wl u.p to ld cl home* **7/1**

1041 **2** shd **Dance To My Tune**[12] 4806 3-9-1 62 ........ DaleGibson 9 71
(MWEasterby) *hld up: keen: hdwy over 2f out: led over 1f out:l styd on wl u.p fnl f: hdd cl home* **7/2**[2]

0410 **3** 3 1/2 **Mount Benger**[10] 4849 4-9-9 62 ........(p) FLynch 7 65
(RMBeckett) *hld up in rr: hdwy over 2f out: in tch and rdn over 1f out: kpt on ins fnl f: no imp on first 2* **3/1**[1]

1504 **4** 3/4 **Jake Black (IRE)**[87] 2584 4-9-5 58 ........ RWinston 6 60
(JJQuinn) *cl up: led 3f out: hdd over 1f out: no ex* **9/2**[3]

2500 **5** 1 1/2 **Encounter**[11] 4826 8-8-6 45 ........ DAllan 2 44
(JHetherton) *hld up: hdwy over 2f out: rdn over 1f out: no further prog* **9/1**

500- **6** 4 **Beady (IRE)**[297] 5928 5-9-5 58 ........ DMcGaffin 3 50
(BSmart) *in tch: effrt 3f out: sn rdn and btn* **25/1**

3001 **7** 1 1/2 **Maritime Blues**[8] 4901 4-9-10 63 ........ ACulhane 5 52
(JGGiven) *trckd ldrs: drvn along 4f out: sn btn* **5/1**

0500 **8** 1 **Stepastray**[17] 4624 7-7-12 42 ow2 ........ PPMathers(5) 8 29
(REBarr) *prom: ch 3f out: hung lft and wknd over 1f out* **22/1**

2600 **9** 3 1/2 **That's Racing**[9] 4883 4-7-5 37 oh6 ........ DFentiman(7) 1 18
(JHetherton) *led tl rdn and hdd 3f out: sn wknd* **33/1**

2m 9.01s (2.21) **Going Correction** +0.275s/f (Good)
**WFA** 3 from 4yo+ 8lb **9 Ran SP% 115.7**
Speed ratings: **102,101,99,98,97 94,92,92,89**CSF £31.09 CT £89.88 TOTE £8.30: £1.90, £1.40, £2.30; EX 55.90.
**Owner** The Kennet Connection **Bred** B Minty **Trained** Marlborough, Wilts

**FOCUS**
The pace was ordinary and this is modest form.

**NOTEBOOK**
**Swift Alchemist** just prevailed in a good duel despite carrying her head a little high. No less than 18lb lower than at the start of the season, she was suited by the drop in trip.
**Dance To My Tune**, who went up only 2lb after Nottingham, took it up going well but was just worried out of it. Well at home in easy ground, she improved again on her Nottingham run but is not particularly progressive.
**Mount Benger**, only 2lb higher than when winning at Haydock last month, hung right and could never get in a blow at the first two. *Official explanation: jockey said gelding hung right handed throughout*
**Jake Black(IRE)** appreciated the easy ground but looks held by the Handicapper.
**Encounter**, without a win since May 2003, is most effective at a mile.
**Beady(IRE)**, having his first run since the end of the last turf season, is effective on Fibresand and is likely to be seen in action through the winter.

## 5130 BEST DRESSED LADY H'CAP — 1m 6f 19y
**7:50** (7:50) (F) (0-55,55) 3-Y-O — **£3,848** (£1,184; £592; £296) **Stalls** Low

Form — RPR
0-00 **1** **Restart (IRE)**[57] 3479 3-9-4 **55** ... GFaulkner 9 — 62
(PCHaslam) *in tch: hdwy over 3f out: led over 2f out: styd on u.p* **16/1**
5115 **2** *1 3/4* **Let It Be**[29] 4307 3-9-0 **51** ... ACulhane 11 — 56
(KGReveley) *hld up in rr: hdwy 3f out: rdn 2f out: styd on u.p to go 2nd clsng stages: nt trble wnr* **11/4**[2]
0000 **3** *nk* **Nod's Star**[57] 3473 3-8-6 **43** ow1 ... RWinston 5 — 47
(MissJACamacho) *hld up: hdwy over 3f out: ev ch over 2f out: sn chsng wnr: kpt on: no imp* **25/1**
4360 **4** *3 1/2* **Savannah River (IRE)**[28] 4346 3-8-3 **43** ... (t) PMulrennan(3) 12 — 43
(CWThornton) *chsd ldrs: ev ch and rdn over 2f out: kpt on same pce* **14/1**
0232 **5** *1 3/4* **Spring Breeze**[29] 4302 3-8-12 **52** ... (b) LEnstone(3) 2 — 50
(MDods) *mde most tl rdn and hdd over 2f out: no ex* **9/4**[1]
5330 **6** *2 1/2* **Defana**[38] 4018 3-8-6 **50** ... DTudhope(7) 7 — 44
(MDods) *hld up in rr: hdwy 3f out: rdn 2f out: no further prog* **20/1**
0000 **7** *hd* **Barton Flower**[40] 3984 3-8-5 **42** ... (b[1]) DaleGibson 4 — 36
(MWEasterby) *prom: rdn 3f out: fdd fnl 2f* **50/1**
6625 **8** *3* **Aston Lad**[17] 4628 3-8-13 **50** ... DarrenWilliams 3 — 40
(MDHammond) *hld up: effrt 3f out: sn rdn: no hdwy* **11/2**[3]
0-60 **9** *nk* **Bay Solitaire**[45] 3837 3-8-8 **45** ... SSanders 14 — 35
(TDEasterby) *in tch: hdwy and prom 1/2-way: rdn 3f out: sn btn* **14/1**
0046 **10** *3* **Twilight Years**[29] 4302 3-8-6 **43** ... DAllan 8 — 29
(TDEasterby) *a rr div* **14/1**
-540 **11** *1/2* **Over The Years (USA)**[40] 3984 3-7-13 **36** ow1 ... (b[1]) JQuinn 1 — 21
(TPTate) *chsd ldrs tl wknd over 3f out* **16/1**
0003 **12** *3 1/2* **Venetian Romance (IRE)**[15] 4710 3-7-9 **37** ... BSwarbrick(5) 10 — 18
(APJones) *midfield: rdn over 3f out: sn btn* **12/1**
450 **13** *21* **Ses Seline**[96] 2357 3-8-5 **42** ow2 ... (p) DeanMcKeown 13 — —
(JohnAHarris) *cl up tl wknd 4f out: t.o* **50/1**

3m 8.99s (3.99) **Going Correction** +0.275s/f (Good) — **13** Ran SP% **124.8**
Speed ratings: **99,98,97,95,94 93,93,91,91,89 89,87,75**CSF £60.67 CT £1154.21 TOTE £21.50: £6.90, £1.80, £9.50; EX 146.60 Place 6 £138.62, Place 5 £116.95.
**Owner** J Roundtree **Bred** Acacia Holdings **Trained** Middleham Moor, N Yorks

**FOCUS**
A very moderate handicap in which they went no pace and this is modest form.

**NOTEBOOK**
**Restart(IRE)**, back to the form he showed as a two-year-old on Fibresand, won this modest event a shade comfortably. Lightly raced, this big individual will get two miles and there could be a bit more to come.
**Let It Be** had no problem with the different ground or the longer trip and this was a decent effort from a 5lb higher mark.
**Nod's Star** acted in the ground, but was just found out by the trip in the end and was caught for second inside the last.
**Savannah River(IRE)** was a market drifter. She probably stayed but lacks a change of gear at any trip.
**Spring Breeze** set a steady pace before fading under pressure. He is well treated on his second to Strangely Brown at Nottingham and is worth another chance on better ground.
**Defana** may prove best at 12 furlongs.
T/Plt: £142.60 to a £1 stake. Pool: £27,146.10. 138.95 winning tickets. T/Qpdt: £65.00 to a £1 stake. Pool: £2,434.50. 27.70 winning tickets. JF

# 5003 WINDSOR (R-H)
Saturday, August 28

**OFFICIAL GOING: Good to soft (good in places)**
The bend was 10 yards out from the tightest configuration.
Wind: nil Weather: mainly cloudy

## 5131 EUROPEAN BREEDERS FUND NOVICE MEDIAN AUCTION STKS — 6f
**5:05** (5:06) (D) 2-Y-O — **£5,265** (£1,620; £810; £405) **Stalls** High

Form — RPR
3361 **1** **Angel Sprints**[40] 3992 2-9-1 86 ... ADaly 5 — 85
(LGCottrell) *lw: mde all: rdn fnl f: r.o wl* **9/2**[3]
14 **2** *1 3/4* **Deeday Bay (IRE)**[49] 3748 2-9-1 87 ... GBaker 6 — 80
(CFWall) *lw: a.p: chsd wnr over 2f out: rdn over 1f out: nt qckn ins fnl f* **7/2**[2]
4533 **3** *1 1/4* **Canton (IRE)**[14] 4752 2-9-4 89 ... KFallon 2 — 79
(RHannon) *hung rt thrght: hld up in tch: rdn and effrt whn nt clr over 2f out: nt qckn fnl f: fin lame* **4/7**[1]
**4** *5* **Ten-Cents** 2-8-3 ... PDoe 4 — 49
(CACyzer) *leggy: unf: s.i.s: sn outpcd: rdn and hdwy over 2f out: wknd over 1f out* **16/1**
0 **5** *3 1/2* **Come To Daddy (IRE)**[24] 4454 2-8-12 ... RHavlin 1 — 48
(FJordan) *s.i.s: sn hung lft: effrt on outside over 2f out: hung lft and wknd over 1f out* **66/1**
0 **6** *8* **Pussy Cat**[17] 4637 2-8-7 ... JFanning 3 — 19
(KOCunningham-Brown) *chsd wnr over 3f out: wknd 2f out* **33/1**

1m 14.95s (1.08) **Going Correction** +0.15s/f (Good) — **6** Ran SP% **114.4**
Speed ratings: **98,95,94,87,82 72**CSF £20.95 TOTE £5.70: £2.40, £2.30; EX 18.00.
**Owner** Mrs Lucy Halloran **Bred** Bishopswood Bloodstock And Trickledown Stud **Trained** Dulford, Devon

**FOCUS**
A fair juvenile event but the value of the form is in doubt as the odds-on favourite was found to be lame after finishing third.

**NOTEBOOK**
**Angel Sprints** again dominated from the front to supplement last month's course and distance victory; a race in which the form has worked out well.
**Deeday Bay(IRE)** had no excuses on this occassion and simply met one too good.
**Canton(IRE)** was found to be lame on his off fore after Fallon reported his mount had hung right from the word go. *Official explanation: trainer's representative's said colt was hanging throughout; vet said colt was lame in right fore*
**Ten-Cents**, a half-sister to a mile winner, should be better for the experience.
**Come To Daddy(IRE)** may not have been helped by being drawn on the outside.

## 5132 RECTANGLE GROUP (S) STKS — 5f 10y
**5:35** (5:35) (E) 2-Y-O — **£3,376** (£1,039; £519; £259) **Stalls** High

Form — RPR
003 **1** **Ruby Muja**[18] 4620 2-8-6 55 ... RSmith 2 — 58
(RHannon) *lw: plld hrd: sn chsng ldr: rdn to ld jst over 1f out: pushed out* **11/2**[3]
3524 **2** *2* **Campeon (IRE)**[5] 4997 2-8-11 71 ... (v) KFallon 6 — 56
(MJWallace) *swtg: b.hind: hld up and plld hrd: hdwy over 1f out: rdn and wnt 2nd ins fnl f: nt trble wnr* **1/1**[1]
3040 **3** *1 1/4* **Wizzskilad**[12] 4804 2-8-11 60 ... RHavlin 4 — 51
(MrsPNDutfield) *led: rdn and hdd jst over 1f out: no ex ins fnl f* **10/1**
0346 **4** *1 3/4* **Turtle Magic (IRE)**[13] 4770 2-8-6 53 ... (p) ADaly 3 — 40
(WGMTurner) *s.i.s: t.k.h: hdwy 2f out: sn rdn: wknd ins fnl f* **10/1**
02 **5** *5* **Slite**[17] 4638 2-8-6 ... EAhern 7 — 22
(RJHodges) *bhd: hdwy 2f out: sn rdn: eased whn btn ins fnl f* **10/3**[2]
3146 **6** *3* **Von Wessex**[16] 4675 2-8-9 61 ... CHaddon(7) 5 — 21
(WGMTurner) *plld hrd: prom over 2f* **12/1**
00 **7** *1/2* **Our Nigel (IRE)**[54] 3570 2-8-11 ... JFanning 1 — 14
(MrsPNDutfield) *hld up: sn in tch: wknd wl over 1f out* **20/1**
00 **8** *3/4* **Fire At Will**[54] 3571 2-8-11 ... (v[1]) PDoe 8 — 11
(AWCarroll) *lw: s.i.s: outpcd* **25/1**

62.83 secs (1.63) **Going Correction** +0.15s/f (Good) — **8** Ran SP% **122.9**
Speed ratings: **92,88,86,84,76 71,70,69**CSF £12.36 TOTE £6.30: £1.80, £1.30, £2.60; EX 16.80.The winner was sold to Emma Lavelle for 8,400gns. Campeon (IRE) was claimed by J. M. Bradley for £6,000.
**Owner** William J Kelly **Bred** Mrs J Mitchell **Trained** East Everleigh, Wilts

**FOCUS**
Some of these had already had plenty of chances in this ordinary seller, and the placed horses have been below their best of late, which holds down the form.

**NOTEBOOK**
**Ruby Muja** proved much too good for this opposition despite taking a real tug early on. She subsequently changed hands for 8,400 gns.
**Campeon(IRE)** was another who proved a real handful and did not seem to appreciate the drop back to five.
**Wizzskilad** again had his limitations exposed.
**Turtle Magic(IRE)** did not find a return to selling company the answer.

## 5133 STANJAMESUK.COM AUGUST STKS (LISTED RACE) — 1m 3f 135y
**6:05** (6:07) (A) 3-Y-O+ — **£17,400** (£6,600; £3,300; £1,500) **Stalls** Low

Form — RPR
-350 **1** **Naheef (IRE)**[52] 3642 5-9-2 109 ... (vt) KMcEvoy 3 — 114
(SaeedBinSuroor) *lw: w ldr: led over 2f out: rdn out* **10/3**[3]
1124 **2** *1 1/2* **Hawridge Prince**[21] 4530 4-9-2 95 ... KFallon 2 — 112
(LGCottrell) *hld up: hdwy 2f out: rdn and wnt 2nd 1f out: sn edgd lft: nt qckn* **9/4**[2]
0653 **3** *1 1/4* **Compton Bolter (IRE)**[14] 4746 7-9-2 109 ... JFortune 6 — 110
(GAButler) *lw: mde most: rdn and hdd over 2f out: one pce fnl f* **15/8**[1]
243/ **4** *6* **Ovambo (IRE)**[658] 5667 6-9-2 ... DSweeney 7 — 100
(PJMakin) *prom: rdn and wkng whn edgd rt jst over 1f out* **12/1**
4005 **5** *6* **Tizzy May (FR)**[22] 4525 4-9-2 97 ... PDobbs 5 — 90
(RHannon) *prom: rdn over 3f out: wknd 2f out* **12/1**
0660 **6** *6* **Foodbroker Founder**[32] 4214 4-9-2 94 ... EAhern 1 — 81
(DRCElsworth) *t.k.h in tch: rdn over 3f out: sn wknd* **16/1**
0 **7** *7* **Sadler's Rock (IRE)**[7] 4939 6-9-2 ... RBrisland 4 — 70
(GLMoore) *a bhd* **100/1**

2m 33.27s (3.17) **Going Correction** +0.425s/f (Yiel) — **7** Ran SP% **110.9**
Speed ratings: **106,105,104,100,96 92,87**CSF £10.54 TOTE £3.80: £2.50, £2.00; EX 11.90.
**Owner** Godolphin **Bred** Gainsborough Stud Management Ltd **Trained** Newmarket, Suffolk

**FOCUS**
A modest time for a race which had been upgraded to Listed status, despite which the form looks decent for the level.

**NOTEBOOK**
**Naheef(IRE)**, who landed the Winter Hill on this card two years ago, showed he is still useful, having been used as a pacemaker for Sulamani last time.
**Hawridge Prince**, stepping up from handicap company, did not help Fallon by edging away from the whip.
**Compton Bolter(IRE)** always had the winner for company and the game was up in the final 200 yards.
**Ovambo(IRE)** had not been seen since the very end of the 2002 turf season and had run his race when drifting over to the stands' rail.
**Tizzy May(FR)** still seems to be struggling to find the right trip. *Official explanation: jockey said colt ran flat*

## 5134 STAN JAMES WINTER HILL STKS (GROUP 3) — 1m 2f 7y
**6:35** (6:37) (A) 3-Y-O+ — **£29,000** (£11,000; £5,500; £2,500) **Stalls** Low

Form — RPR
2210 **1** **Ancient World (USA)**[16] 4685 4-9-0 110 ... KMcEvoy 1 — 116
(SaeedBinSuroor) *hld up in tch: led over 2f out: rdn out* **5/1**[3]
3122 **2** *1 1/4* **Gateman**[40] 3978 7-9-4 114 ... JFanning 3 — 117
(MJohnston) *lw: b.hind: led early: a.p: led 3f out: sn rdn and hdd: nt qckn fnl f* **15/8**[1]
-510 **3** *4* **Fruhlingssturm**[40] 3978 4-9-8 112 ... PRobinson 6 — 114
(MAJarvis) *a.p: rdn over 2f out: wknd ins fnl f* **10/1**
5-01 **4** *3 1/2* **Pawn Broker**[28] 4341 7-9-0 109 ... KFallon 5 — 100
(DRCElsworth) *lw: hld up: hdwy 3f out: sn rdn: wknd 1f out* **11/2**
2134 **5** *2* **Nysaean (IRE)**[88] 2559 5-9-4 114 ... PDobbs 4 — 100
(RHannon) *lw: hld up in rr: rdn 3f out: nvr trbld ldrs* **5/2**[2]
2050 **6** *nk* **Duck Row (USA)**[14] 4745 9-9-0 104 ... EAhern 2 — 95
(JARToller) *hld up: hdwy over 3f out: rdn over 2f out: wknd qckly over 1f out* **20/1**
1150 **7** *5* **A One (IRE)**[13] 4772 5-9-0 83 ... DSweeney 8 — 86
(HJManners) *sn led: hdd 3f out: sn wknd* **50/1**
0030 **8** *dist* **Tuning Fork**[14] 4742 4-9-0 89 ... MTebbutt 9 — —
(JAkehurst) *hld up: dropped rr 4f out: eased whn no ch over 1f out* **50/1**

2m 8.97s (0.67) **Going Correction** +0.425s/f (Yiel) — **8** Ran SP% **113.2**
Speed ratings: **114,113,109,107,105 105,101,—**CSF £14.46 TOTE £6.40: £2.10, £1.60, £2.60; EX 16.30.
**Owner** Godolphin **Bred** Darley Stud Management, L L C **Trained** Newmarket, Suffolk

**FOCUS**
A One made sure this was the sort of time you would expect for a Group Three event. The form is fair and solid for the grade.

**NOTEBOOK**

**Ancient World(USA)** was back on song over this longer distance and put his disappointing effort at Salisbury behind him.

**Gateman** was content to let A One set a good pace. Despite his renowned battling qualities he was always being held in the final furlong.

**Fruhlingssturm** would not have been helped by the fact that the ground had dried out during the day.

**Pawn Broker** should have been suited by the return to a longer distance.

**Nysaean(IRE)** could never get competitive after a three-month break.

**Duck Row(USA)** had yet to score beyond a mile.

## 5135 STANJAMESUK.COM RATED STKS (H'CAP) 1m 67y

**7:05** (7:07) (D) (0-85,83) 3-Y-0+ **£5,493** (£2,083; £1,041; £473) **Stalls** High

Form RPR

10-0 **1** **Pagan Prince**[8] 4920 7-8-10 **72** EAhern 10 85
(JARToller) *lw: hld up and bhd: hdwy over 1f out: sn swtchd lft: led ins fnl f: r.o wl* **14/1**

4314 **2** 1 3/4 **African Sahara (USA)**[8] 4920 5-9-6 **82** (t) OUrbina 8 91
(MissDMountain) *lw: hld up in mid-div: hdwy over 3f out: led briefly ins fnl f: nt qckn* **5/1**[2]

-043 **3** 1/2 **Impersonator**[21] 4543 4-9-0 **76** PDoe 6 84
(JLDunlop) *led 2f: remained prom: led again over 2f out: hdd ins fnl f: nt qckn* **6/1**

1410 **4** nk **Supreme Salutation**[5] 5004 8-9-0 **83** MHoward(7) 13 90
(DKIvory) *s.i.s: sn mid-div: hdwy over 1f out: kpt on ins fnl f* **25/1**

3014 **5** 1 **Freeloader (IRE)**[32] 4220 4-9-2 **78** RLMoore 1 83
(JWHills) *lw: hld up and bhd: hdwy over 2f out: ev ch 1f out: no ex* **11/2**[3]

0061 **6** 1/2 **Arctic Desert**[6] 4969 4-8-13 **75** 3ex KFallon 5 79+
(AMBalding) *lw: b.hind: hld up: hdwy whn n.m.r 2f out: one pce fnl f* **9/4**[1]

4404 **7** 2 1/2 **Alchera**[12] 4817 3-7-8 **69** oh9 CHaddon(7) 2 68
(RFJohnsonHoughton) *hld up and bhd: hdwy on outside over 2f out: wknd fnl f* **33/1**

6306 **8** 1 **Freak Occurence (IRE)**[5] 5004 3-8-13 **81** (v) SDrowne 3 78
(MissECLavelle) *prom: hrd rdn over 1f out: wknd fnl f* **8/1**

2010 **9** 1/2 **El Chaparral (IRE)**[4] 5017 4-8-11 **73** DSweeney 11 69
(DKIvory) *hld up and bhd: rdn over 2f out: n.d* **12/1**

01 **10** 1/2 **Submissive**[124] 1679 3-8-0 **75** KMay(7) 4 70
(BWHills) *prom: rdn over 3f out: wknd over 1f out* **16/1**

1646 **11** 5 **Madamoiselle Jones**[12] 4812 4-8-4 **69** oh3 JFMcDonald(3) 12 53
(HSHowe) *hld up in tch: rdn over 3f out: wknd over 2f out* **20/1**

/000 **12** 3 **Lizarazu (GER)**[20] 4569 5-8-4 **69** RMiles(3) 7 47
(FJordan) *hld up: hdwy 4f out: wknd over 2f out* **20/1**

0203 **13** 1 1/4 **Mbosi (USA)**[21] 4533 3-9-0 **82** (b[1]) JFanning 9 57
(MJohnston) *led after 2f tl over 2f out: sn wknd* **16/1**

1m 47.42s (1.82) **Going Correction** +0.425s/f (Yiel)
**WFA** 3 from 4yo+ 6lb **13** Ran **SP%** **130.7**
Speed ratings: **107,105,104,104,103 102,100,99,98,98 93,90,89**CSF £86.49 CT £489.96 TOTE £20.00: £4.50, £2.10, £2.00; EX 98.30.
**Owner** Gap Partnership & Mrs J Toller **Bred** M E Wates **Trained** Newmarket, Suffolk

**FOCUS**

This turned out to be a very competitive handicap, and the form is decent for the grade.

**NOTEBOOK**

**Pagan Prince**, all the better for his recent run at Sandown, came from last to first to win going away.

**African Sahara(USA)** had finished over three lengths in front of the winner on a pound better terms at Sandown last week. However, Pagan Prince met with interference late on that day and was cherry ripe this time.

**Impersonator** again found the drying ground against him.

**Supreme Salutation** found this trip on the short side with the ground not really putting the emphasis on stamina.

**Freeloader(IRE)**, raised another pound, was again chopped for finishing speed over this trip.

**Arctic Desert**, attempting a quick follow-up, was having only his second race at beyond seven furlongs.

**Alchera**, attempting a mile for the first time, may have failed to stay but was 9lb out of the handicap.

## 5136 MARK & JULIE LANCASTER FILLIES' H'CAP 1m 67y

**7:35** (7:36) (D) (0-85,83) 3-Y-0+ **£5,801** (£1,785; £892; £446) **Stalls** High

Form RPR

1201 **1** **Munaawashat (IRE)**[12] 4812 3-8-11 **73** JFanning 8 84
(KRBurke) *swtg: chsd ldr: led 5f out: rdn over 1f out: r.o wl* **10/1**

521 **2** 2 **Sea Nymph (IRE)**[19] 4615 3-9-0 **76** KFallon 4 83
(SirMichaelStoute) *lw: hld up in tch: rdn 2f out: chsd wnr fnl f: no imp* **15/8**[1]

0513 **3** 1 1/2 **Tuscarora (IRE)**[9] 4877 5-8-2 **61** RMiles(3) 7 65
(AWCarroll) *hld up and bhd: hdwy on outside over 2f out: one pce fnl f* **9/2**[2]

0320 **4** 1/2 **Uig**[9] 4884 3-8-13 **75** PDoe 2 78
(HSHowe) *led: hdd 5f out: rdn over 2f out: one pce* **25/1**

1001 **5** nk **Farriers Charm**[10] 4848 3-8-5 **67** ow1 EAhern 10 69
(DJCoakley) *lw: hld up in tch: rdn and one pce fnl 2f* **14/1**

-206 **6** 1 1/4 **Czarina Waltz**[42] 3933 5-9-13 **83** RMullen 6 83
(CFWall) *a.p: rdn over 1f out: wknd ins fnl f* **16/1**

5300 **7** nk **Cuddles (FR)**[17] 4640 5-7-12 **57** JFMcDonald(3) 1 56
(KOCunningham-Brown) *hld up and bhd: hdwy on outside over 2f out: no ex ins fnl f* **16/1**

2552 **8** 1 1/4 **Anna Panna**[7] 4954 3-8-10 **72** DaneO'Neill 5 68
(HCandy) *s.i.s: hld up: stdy hdwy 5f out: no imp fnl 2f* **12/1**

3022 **9** 14 **Brazilian Terrace**[13] 4771 4-9-5 **75** SDrowne 11 42
(MLWBell) *hld up in mid-div: rdn over 2f out: sn bhd* **8/1**

5140 **10** 2 1/2 **Hot Lips Page (FR)**[21] 4551 3-8-11 **73** RLMoore 13 35
(RHannon) *hld up in mid-divison: rdn over 4f out: sn struggling* **25/1**

6624 **11** 1 3/4 **Red Sahara (IRE)**[16] 4684 3-9-2 **78** PRobinson 12 36
(WJHaggas) *lw: hld up: sn bhd: rdn over 2f out: no rspnse* **6/1**[3]

1m 48.24s (2.64) **Going Correction** +0.425s/f (Yiel)
**WFA** 3 from 4yo+ 6lb **11** Ran **SP%** **120.1**
Speed ratings: **103,101,99,99,98 97,97,95,81,79 77**CSF £28.97 CT £99.83 TOTE £9.50: £2.40, £1.60, £2.20; EX 21.70 Place 6 £58.74, Place 5 £19.47.
**Owner** John A Duffy **Bred** Shadwell Estate Company Limited **Trained** Middleham Moor, N Yorks

**FOCUS**

A fair handicap and reasonable form for the grade, but this was won in a time the best part of a second slower than the previous race.

**NOTEBOOK**

**Munaawashat(IRE)** was only 2lb higher than when successful over course and distance earlier in the month. Reverting to front-running tactics, she had matters well under control in the closing stages.

**Sea Nymph(IRE)** ◆ looked reasonably treated on this switch to handicaps and may now be ready to tackle further.

**Tuscarora(IRE)** could not sustain her effort off a mark 7lb higher than when winning at Chepstow earlier in the month.

**Uig**, highly tried last time, was having her first run over a distance short of a mile and a quarter.

**Farriers Charm** was 3lb higher than when successful over slightly further on softer ground at Kempton.

**Czarina Waltz** did tie up in the closing stages but probably really wants further.

**Brazilian Terrace** *Official explanation: jockey said filly was unsuited by good to soft ground*

**Hot Lips Page(FR)** *Official explanation: jockey said filly was unsuited by good to soft ground*

**Red Sahara(IRE)** *Official explanation: jockey said filly lost her action*

T/Plt: £45.20 to a £1 stake. Pool: £29,524.30. 476.60 winning tickets. T/Qpdt: £12.80 to a £1 stake. Pool: £3,827.10. 220.75 winning tickets. KH

# 5104 BEVERLEY (R-H)

Sunday, August 29

**OFFICIAL GOING: Good to soft changing to soft after race 3 (3.40)**

## 5141 JOHNSON WEDDING ANNIVERSARY CLAIMING STKS 7f 100y

**2:30** (2:31) (E) 3-Y-0 **£3,549** (£1,092; £546; £273) **Stalls** High

Form RPR

3012 **1** **Kings Rock**[24] 4497 3-8-11 55 (b) NCallan 13 66
(KARyan) *mde virtually all: rdn clr 2f out: styd on* **7/2**[1]

5060 **2** 4 **Game Flora**[6] 5000 3-8-4 53 ow2 TEaves(3) 11 52
(MESowersby) *chsd ldrs: hdwy over 2f out: sn rdn: kpt on chse wnr appr last: no imp* **16/1**

1001 **3** 2 1/2 **Shinko Femme (IRE)**[21] 4568 3-8-4 53 DAllan 12 43
(NTinkler) *bhd: hdwy 3f out: rdn and styd on appr last: nrst fin* **13/2**

2240 **4** 1 1/4 **Lord Baskerville**[31] 4259 3-8-11 53 JBramhill 5 47
(WStorey) *a.p: rdn along to chse wnr over 2f out: sn drvn and one pce* **14/1**

-331 **5** 4 **Two Of Clubs**[15] 942 3-8-8 68 (p) GFaulkner 10 34
(PCHaslam) *midfield: rdn along 1/2-way: styd on u.p fnl 2f: nvr a factor* **5/1**[2]

0530 **6** 1 1/4 **Beauty Of Dreams**[5] 5020 3-8-6 60 ACulhane 8 29
(MRChannon) *s.i.s and wl bhd: hdwy 3f out: styd on u.p fnl 2f: nvr a factor* **7/2**[1]

6040 **7** 4 **Firebird Rising (USA)**[16] 4702 3-8-6 53 DMernagh 3 19
(TDBarron) *chsd ldrs on outerm rdn along over 2f out: drvn and wknd well over 1f out* **6/1**[3]

0644 **8** 2 **Beamsley Beacon**[10] 4880 3-8-9 47 VHalliday 14 17
(IanEmmerson) *midfield: rdn along and sme hdwy over 2f out: sn drvn and no imp* **50/1**

0050 **9** 3 **Blue Nun**[25] 4444 3-8-1 40 JMackay 2 1
(MrsADuffield) *outpcd and wl bhd tl a lttle late hdwy* **50/1**

-020 **10** nk **Tiz Wiz**[27] 4391 3-7-10 41 RoryMoore(5) 4 —
(WStorey) *chsd ldrs on outer: rdn along over 2f out: grad wknd* **33/1**

0065 **11** 2 **Bank Games**[27] 4393 3-8-6 43 TLucas 1 —
(MWEasterby) *prom: rdn along over 2f out: grad wknd* **33/1**

0055 **12** 5 **Garnock Venture (IRE)**[27] 4387 3-8-12 49 (b) FLynch 7 —
(ABerry) *midfield: rapid hdwy on outer to chse wnr 1/2-way: sn rdn and wknd over 2f out* **16/1**

430- **13** 2 1/2 **Faites Vos Jeux**[286] 6011 3-8-2 50 TWilliams 6 —
(CNKellett) *in tch: rdn along 3f out: sn wknd* **50/1**

00 **14** 5 **Zoomiezando**[21] 4573 3-8-6 PMakin(5) 9 —
(MrsLucindaFeatherstone) *a rr* **100/1**

1m 40.58s (6.28) **Going Correction** +0.95s/f (Soft) **14** Ran **SP%** **119.9**
Speed ratings: **102,97,94,93,88 87,82,80,76,76 74,68,65,59**CSF £61.70 TOTE £5.00: £2.40, £3.50, £2.20; EX 87.00.The winner was claimed by J. T. Billson for £10,000.
**Owner** Miss Claire King and Peter McBride **Bred** M S Anderson **Trained** Hambleton, N Yorks

**FOCUS**

An ordinary claimer in which some of the better fancied horses ran below form and, as a result, this was not very competitive and the form is moderate.

**NOTEBOOK**

**Kings Rock** had gained his only previous win on fast ground, but this soft surface was not a problem and he continued the good recent run of his stable with a clear-cut success. Claimed for £10,000, he should be competitive back in handicaps.

**Game Flora**, racing beyond six furlongs for the first time, would have appreciated the conditions and appeared to get the trip. The winner was too good, but she was clear of the remainder.

**Shinko Femme(IRE)** did not run to the form she showed to win a fast-ground seller at Leicester on her previous start.

**Lord Baskerville** did not stay and remains a maiden.

**Two Of Clubs**, pulled up on two starts over hurdles, offered little encouragement returned to the Flat despite being best off at the weights.

**Beauty Of Dreams** had the ground in her favour and had a sound chance at the weights, but she ran below form.

**Firebird Rising(USA)** did not improve for the drop in class and was a little disappointing.

## 5142 EBF JOAN GRAVES BIRTHDAY CELEBRATION MEDIAN AUCTION MAIDEN STKS 1m 100y

**3:05** (3:06) (E) 2-Y-0 **£4,485** (£1,380; £690; £345) **Stalls** High

Form RPR

5 **1** **Rocamadour**[16] 4716 2-9-0 ACulhane 8 85
(MRChannon) *trckd ldrs: hdwy to ld 3f out: rdn 2f out: drvn ins last and kpt on wl* **13/8**[1]

02 **2** 1 **River Liffey**[9] 4907 2-9-0 RMullen 4 83
(MLWBell) *in tch: hdwy to trck ldrs 1/2-way: effrt 2f out and sn rdn: ever ch: drvn: put hd in air: wandered and nt qckn ins last* **15/8**[2]

002 **3** 2 **Tcherina (IRE)**[26] 4420 2-8-9 73 DAllan 11 74
(TDEasterby) *in tch: hdwy 3f out: rdn to chse ldng pair 1f out: edgd rt and one pce ins last* **10/1**[3]

03 **4** 5 **Young Mick**[29] 4335 2-9-0 NCallan 10 69
(GGMargarson) *a.p: effiort whn n.m.r and stmbld 2f out: sn rdn and wknd appr last* **11/1**

00 **5** 1 3/4 **Akraan**[16] 4706 2-8-9 RHills 6 61
(EALDunlop) *cl up: effrt over 2f out and sn rdn: ev ch tl drvn and wknd over 1f out* **11/1**

000 **6** 5 **Succession**[16] 4730 2-8-9 JMackay 12 51
(SirMarkPrescott) *s.i.s and bhd tl styd on fnl 2f: nrets fin* **14/1**

2000 **7** 2 1/2 **Itsa Monkey (IRE)**[10] 4878 2-8-11 43 (b[1]) DNolan(3) 2 51?
(MJPolglase) *led: rdn along and hdd 3f out: sn wknd* **100/1**

**8** 15 **Indonesia** 2-9-0 RFfrench 3 21
(MJohnston) *s.i.s and bmpd s: sn wl bhd* **12/1**

0000 **9** 5 **Lord Chalfont (IRE)**[21] 4579 2-8-7 ............................(b) KGhunowa(7) 1 11
(MJPolglase) *prom: rdn along and wknd 1/2-way: hung bdly lft over 2f out and sn wl bhd* **100/1**

00 **10** 4 **French Kisses**[38] 4048 2-8-9 ........................ DeanMcKeown 5 —
(RonaldThompson) *midfield: rdn along 3f out: sn wknd* **100/1**

000 **11** 5 **Lady Indiana (IRE)**[71] 3100 2-8-9 ........................ PMQuinn 7 —
(JSWainwright) *dwlt: a bhd* **100/1**

**12** 16 **Time To Succeed** 2-9-0 ........................ GParkin 9 —
(JSWainwright) *s.i.s: a wl bhd* **50/1**

1m 55.5s (8.20) **Going Correction** +0.95s/f (Soft) **12** Ran SP% **118.9**
Speed ratings: **97,96,94,89,87 82,79,64,59,55 50,34**CSF £4.79 TOTE £2.50: £1.10, £1.20, £2.60; EX 7.50.
**Owner** Salem Suhail **Bred** Gainsborough Stud Management Ltd **Trained** West Ilsley, Berks

**FOCUS**
Just an ordinary maiden, although the form looks fairly sound and it should produce some winners.

**NOTEBOOK**
**Rocamadour** finished last but offered plenty of promise in a five-runner Listed event at Newbury on his debut, but did not really impress in this much lower contest despite doing enough to get off the mark. Had the runner-up not carried his head high in the closing stages the result may well have been different, but he is held in quite regard and should not be underestimated when stepping back up in grade, as a stronger pace should see him in a better light.
**River Liffey**, an unlucky loser when going down by just a short head on his debut in a good Chester claimer on his previous start, may well have won had he not carried his head high. He can be given another chance to prove he is not ungenuine, however, as he simply appeared to resent having the eventual winning rider's whip waved in his face.
**Tcherina(IRE)** ran his best race to date when runner-up at 100/1 at Catterick on his previous start, and was able to confirm the promise with another respectable effort. However, his current rating of 73 gives him no easy task in nurseries.
**Young Mick** would have finished closer had he got a run against the rail two out, as he stumbled and gradually dropped out of contention.
**Akraan**, stepping up in trip and racing on easy ground for the first time, travelled well but did not get home.
**Succession** was well held but improvement cannot be ruled out when she goes handicapping.
**Indonesia** stayed on past beaten horses and offered little promise, but he should improve a bundle for the outing.

## 5143 BRITANNIA RESCUE NURSERY 5f
3:40 (3:41) (C) 2-Y-O £10,757 (£3,310; £1,655; £827) Stalls High

Form RPR

3100 **1** **Nufoos**[54] 3599 2-9-2 **85** ........................ RHills 4 95+
(MJohnston) *chsd ldrs on outer: gd hdwy to ld over 1f out: sn rdn and clr ins last: styd on wl* **11/4**[1]

21 **2** 3 **Graze On**[14] 4776 2-8-13 **82** ........................ RWinston 3 81
(JJQuinn) *hld up: hdwy 2f out: sn rdn: kpt on wl fnl f* **4/1**[2]

4060 **3** shd **Apologies**[23] 4508 2-8-2 **71** ........................(b[1]) GGibbons 1 70
(BAMcmahon) *in tch: rdn along 2f out: kpt on u.p appr last* **22/1**

5102 **4** 2 **Monsieur Mirasol**[17] 4676 2-8-10 **79** ........................ NCallan 5 70
(KARyan) *towards rr: hdwy 2f out: sn rdn and kpt on appr last* **4/1**[2]

1106 **5** 1 **Miss Meggy**[54] 3599 2-9-7 **90** ........................ DAllan 2 78
(TDEasterby) *stdd and swtchd rt s: bhd tl hdwy wl over 1f out: swtchd lft and kpt on ins last: nrst fin* **6/1**[3]

6141 **6** 2 **Baymist**[23] 4508 2-7-12 **67** ........................ DaleGibson 7 48
(MWEasterby) *trckd ldrs: hdwy on inner to ld 1/2-way: rdn and hdd over 1f out: sn wknd* **7/1**

0245 **7** 5 **Hillside Heather (IRE)**[10] 4875 2-7-12 **67** ........................(p) JBramhill 6 30
(ABerry) *chsd ldrs: rdn along 2f out: grad wknd* **12/1**

4002 **8** 6 **Tartatartufata**[9] 4924 2-7-12 **67** oh2 ........................ JoannaBadger 9 8
(DShaw) *chsd ldr: rdn along over 2f out: sn wknd* **16/1**

0640 **9** 3 ½ **Sowerby**[50] 3753 2-7-12 **67** oh3 ........................ DMernagh 8 —
(MBrittain) *chsd ldrs to 1/2-way: sn lost pl and bhd* **25/1**

1500 **10** 1 **Our Louis**[29] 4348 2-7-12 **67** oh13 ........................ PMQuinn 10 —
(JSWainwright) *led: rdn along: hung lft and hdd 1/2-way: sn wknd* **50/1**

67.15 secs (3.15) **Going Correction** +0.60s/f (Yiel) **10** Ran SP% **117.2**
Speed ratings: **98,93,93,89,88 85,77,67,61,60**CSF £13.40 CT £184.12 TOTE £3.60: £1.80, £2.10, £4.60; EX 23.10.
**Owner** Hamdan Al Maktoum **Bred** R And Mrs Watson And Mrs A J Ralli **Trained** Middleham Moor, N Yorks

**FOCUS**
A reasonable-looking nursery, but a clear-cut winner in Nufoos, who was dropping from Group company. The form, rated through the runner-up, looks solid.

**NOTEBOOK**
**Nufoos**, thought good enough to contest the Albany at Ascot and the Cherry Hinton at Newmarket, was simply too good for these on this drop in class. Entered in Group Three company, she will be worthy of respect if stepped back up in grade, but would take all the beating in a nursery under a penalty.
**Graze On**, off the mark at Pontefract on his previous start, had no easy task on this handicap debut off a mark of 82 and was no match for the winner.
**Apologies** showed signs of a return to form fitted with blinkers for the first time.
**Monsieur Mirasol** was unsuited by this drop back from six furlongs despite having the ground in his favour.
**Miss Meggy**, in front of today's winner in both the Albany and the Cherry Hinton on her previous starts, is better than she showed as she got no run when looking to make her move against the rail.
**Tartatartufata** *Official explanation: jockey said filly hung left throughout*
**Sowerby** *Official explanation: jockey said colt had no more to give*

## 5144 NIGEL BRIGGS 50TH BIRTHDAY H'CAP 1m 4f 16y
4:15 (4:16) (E) (0-75,72) 3-Y-O+ £5,086 (£1,565; £782; £391) Stalls High

Form RPR

5055 **1** **Bramantino (IRE)**[16] 4698 4-8-3 **52** ........................(b) THamilton(3) 4 65
(RAFahey) *trckd ldrs: hdwy 3f out: rdn to chal 2f out: led ent last: sn drvn and hld on wl* **7/1**

06-1 **2** shd **Can Can Flyer (IRE)**[18] 4628 3-8-7 **63** ........................ RFfrench 1 76
(MJohnston) *in tch: hdwy 3f out: effrt 2f out: rdn to chal wl over 1f out: drvn and kpt on wl fnl f: jst hld* **4/1**[2]

2100 **3** hd **Merrymaker**[24] 4486 4-9-0 **65** ........................ PPMathers(5) 12 78
(WMBrisbourne) *s.i.s and bhd: hdwy on wd outside over 2f out: rdn and ev ch over 1f out: drvn and edgd rt ins last: styd on* **20/1**

6352 **4** 5 **East Cape**[33] 4210 7-7-12 **44** oh2 ........................ KimTinkler 14 50
(DonEnricoIncisa) *hld up and bhd: hdwy on inner 2f out: nt clr run and swtchd lft ent last: styd on wl: nrst fin* **16/1**

2322 **5** 1 **Tedsdale Mac**[29] 4319 5-8-13 **59** ........................ NCallan 9 63
(NBycroft) *hld up towards rr: hdwy 2f out: rdn over 1f out: kpt on ins last: nrst fin* **9/2**[3]

3331 **6** hd **Red Forest (IRE)**[3] 5058 5-9-1 **61** ........................(t) DaleGibson 10 65
(JMackie) *keen: trckd ldr: effrort to chal over 3f out: sn rdn and wknd fnl 2f* **3/1**[1]

0203 **7** 1 ¾ **Allied Victory (USA)**[18] 4634 4-9-12 **72** ........................(t) DeanMcKeown 2 73
(EJAlston) *sn led: stdd pce after 3f: rdn along and hdd 2f out: sn wknd* **25/1**

/602 **8** ½ **Cyber Santa**[9] 4911 6-8-4 **50** ow1 ........................ DAllan 11 51
(JHetherton) *trckd ldr: hdwy to ld 2f out and sn rdn: drvn and hdd ent last: wknd* **14/1**

3216 **9** hd **Melodian**[2] 5085 9-9-0 **65** ........................(b) MLawson(5) 6 65
(MBrittain) *trckd ldrs: effrt 2f out: sn rdn and n.m.r on inner over 1f out: sn drvn and wknd* **15/2**

3040 **10** 1 ¼ **Michaels Dream (IRE)**[45] 3018 5-7-12 **44** oh2 ........................ SRighton 13 43
(JHetherton) *chsd ldrs: rdn along over 3f out: sn wknd* **25/1**

422- **11** hd **Colway Ritz**[289] 5823 10-9-1 **61** ........................ JBramhill 3 59
(WStorey) *trckd ldrs gng wl: effrt 3f out: sn rdn and btn* **50/1**

2302 **12** 14 **Field Spark**[45] 3866 4-8-12 **58** ........................(p) RWinston 5 37
(JAGlover) *hld up: a rr* **10/1**

2m 50.0s (10.70) **Going Correction** +0.95s/f (Soft)
**WFA** 3 from 4yo+ 10lb **12** Ran SP% **123.5**
Speed ratings: **102,101,101,98,97 97,96,96,96,95 95,85**CSF £35.19 CT £554.97 TOTE £11.10: £2.90, £2.30, £5.80; EX 42.90.
**Owner** Mrs Kenyon, A Rhodes Haulage, P Timmins **Bred** Mrs Brid Cosgrove **Trained** Musley Bank, N Yorks

**FOCUS**
A moderate handicap but above average form for the grade and, with the early pace just steady, there was something of a dash to the line resulting in the first three home finishing pretty well bunched.

**NOTEBOOK**
**Bramantino(IRE)**, 1lb lower than when gaining his only previous win (Fibresand), had a good apprentice taking over from an amateur and narrowly gained his first success on the turf.
**Can Can Flyer(IRE)**, off the mark on his handicap debut over ten furlongs here on his previous start, ran well from a 4lb higher mark on this step up in trip and was just held. He still looks reasonably weighted and there should be more to come.
**Merrymaker**, racing on soft ground for the first time, handled conditions well and was just denied. He goes really well for Mathers.
**East Cape** looks ideally suited by further these days.
**Tedsdale Mac**, apparently ridden to get the trip on this first run beyond ten furlongs, could never get competitive.
**Red Forest(IRE)**, able to race off the same mark as when successful over a mile six at Musselburgh on his previous start, did not help his chances by racing keenly on ground that was probably softer than ideal.

## 5145 JIM AND MARY RICHARDSON RUBY ANNIVERSARY FILLIES' H'CAP 1m 1f 207y
4:50 (4:50) (E) (0-75,70) 3-Y-O+ £4,303 (£1,324; £662; £331) Stalls High

Form RPR

3142 **1** **Shotley Dancer**[18] 4627 5-8-2 **46** ........................ RFfrench 6 53
(NBycroft) *cl up: led over 2f out: sn rdn: drvn ent last: styd on gamely* **6/1**

1035 **2** nk **Keeper's Lodge (IRE)**[9] 4906 3-9-4 **70** ........................ GGibbons 10 78+
(BAMcmahon) *trckd ldrs: hdwy 3f out: rdn and nt clr run on inner over 1f out: swtchd lft ent last and styd on wl* **7/1**

6241 **3** 2 **Sienna Sunset (IRE)**[15] 4760 5-8-9 **58** ........................ BSwarbrick(5) 9 61
(WMBrisbourne) *midfield: hdwy and in tch 1/2-way: effrt 2f out: rdn wl over 1f out and ev ch tl drvn: edgd rt and one pce ins last* **11/2**[3]

0364 **4** 6 **Megan's Magic**[40] 4005 4-9-10 **68** ........................(e[1]) JBramhill 1 61
(WStorey) *dwlt and bhd: gd hdwy 1/2-way: chsd ldrs 3f out: rdn 2f out: drvn and one pce over 1f out* **5/1**[2]

0214 **5** 8 **Pay Attention**[18] 4630 3-8-11 **63** ........................ DAllan 7 42
(TDEasterby) *chsd ldrs: rdn along 4f out: drvn wl over 2f out and sn wknd* **4/1**[1]

64-6 **6** 1 ¼ **Maid For Life (IRE)**[24] 4471 4-8-12 **56** ........................ RWinston 3 33
(MJWallace) *chsd ldrs on outer: rdn along over 4f out: sn wknd* **12/1**

545 **7** hd **Charmatic (IRE)**[66] 3231 3-8-13 **65** ........................ DeanMcKeown 11 42
(JAGlover) *led: rdn along 3f out: sn hdd & wknd fnl 2f* **4/1**[1]

2204 **8** 13 **Estimate**[16] 4713 4-8-9 **53** ........................(v) NCallan 8 8
(JohnAHarris) *chsd ldrs: rdn along 1/2-way: sn wknd* **20/1**

546R **9** 2 ½ **Princess Ismene**[21] 4568 3-7-12 **50** oh5 ........................ SRighton 4 —
(MAppleby) *a rr* **66/1**

00/0 **10** 24 **Artists Retreat**[24] 4476 5-7-12 **42** oh5 ........................ PMQuinn 2 —
(BDLeavy) *a bhd* **66/1**

2m 16.49s (9.29) **Going Correction** +0.95s/f (Soft)
**WFA** 3 from 4yo+ 8lb **10** Ran SP% **114.3**
Speed ratings: **100,99,98,93,86 85,85,75,73,54**CSF £45.85 CT £242.19 TOTE £7.40: £1.40, £2.40, £2.20; EX 64.70.
**Owner** J A Swinburne **Bred** J A And Mrs Duffy **Trained** Brandsby, N Yorks
■ Stewards Enquiry : R Ffrench one-day ban: used whip without giving mare time to respond (Sep 9)

**FOCUS**
Just a modest handicap run at ordinary pace and the form is moderate.

**NOTEBOOK**
**Shotley Dancer**, runner-up over two miles here on her previous start, was not inconvenienced by this drop in trip and ran out a determined winner. Versatile with regards to trip and ground, and likely to still be on a reasonable mark when reassessed, she should continue to go well.
**Keeper's Lodge(IRE)**, dropping from Class C company, ran well off a mark 4lb higher than when gaining her only previous win - keeping on after getting hampered - and looks up to winning a similar event.
**Sienna Sunset(IRE)**, 3lb higher than when winning a slightly-better class race at Ripon on her previous start, was slightly below that form despite having conditions to suit.
**Megan's Magic** did not improve for the fitting of a visor and was in fact a little disappointing. This ground may have been soft enough.
**Pay Attention** had conditions to suit but was below form for the second race running. *Official explanation: jockey said filly made a noise*
**Charmatic(IRE)** did not get home and should do better back over slightly shorter.
**Estimate** *Official explanation: jockey said filly was unsuited by the ground*

## 5146 BEVERLEY LIONS MAIDEN STKS 1m 1f 207y
5:25 (5:26) (D) 3-Y-O+ £3,828 (£1,178; £589; £294) Stalls High

Form RPR

22 **1** **Autumn Wealth (IRE)**[36] 4141 3-8-8 ........................ ACulhane 6 71
(MrsAJPerrett) *chsd ldrs on outer: rn wd bnd at 1/2-way and on home turn: rdn and hung bdly lft 2f out: styd on to ld over 1f out: drvn ou* **1/1**[1]

452- **2** 4 **Tricky Venture**[371] 4403 4-9-2 **65** ........................ PMakin(5) 7 69
(PWHiatt) *hld up towards rr: gd hdwy over 3f out: rdn to chal wl over 1f out and ev ch tl drvn and one pce ent last* **18/1**

42 **3** 1 ½ **St Barchan (IRE)**[25] 4444 3-8-10 ........................ DNolan(3) 9 66
(WJarvis) *trckd ldrs: hdwy on inner to ld 3f out: rdn and hung bdly lft 2f out: sn drvn: hdd over 1f out and kpt on same pce* **4/1**[2]

03 **4** *1 1/4* **Dream Alive**[13] 4813 3-8-13 ....(t) NCallan 11 64
(MBlanshard) *chsd ldrs: gd hdwy on inner over 2f out: sn rdn and edgd lft wl over 1f out: sn drvn and one pce* **6/1**[3]

3 **5** *13* **Medalla (FR)**[14] 4781 4-9-2 .... MLawson(5) 2 42
(MBrittain) *prom: effrt 3f out: rdn and wknd 2f out* **6/1**[3]

64 **6** *8* **Mount Cottage**[17] 4679 3-8-8 .... JBramhill 13 24
(JGGiven) *in tch: hdwy 4f out: rdn to chse ldrs 3f out: sn drvn and btn* **14/1**

00-0 **7** *6* **St Jude**[30] 4306 4-9-7 .... DAllan 12 18
(JBalding) *led: rdn along and hdd 3f out: sn wknd* **50/1**

0 **8** *1 3/4* **Shameless**[45] 2851 7-9-0 ....(t) RKeogh(7) 10 15
(HAlexander) *s.i.s: a rr* **100/1**

**9** *13* **Parisi Princess** 3-8-5 .... PMulrennan(3) 8 —
(GPKelly) *s.i.s: a rr* **50/1**

0- **10** *7* **Lady Lucinda**[296] 5940 3-8-8 .... DeanMcKeown 5 —
(JohnAHarris) *in tch: rdn along 1/2-way: sn wknd* **50/1**

0 **11** *dist* **Gentle Warning**[18] 4644 4-8-9 .... DFentiman(7) 1 —
(MAppleby) *a rr: wl bhd and eased over 3f out* **50/1**

2m 16.04s (8.84) **Going Correction** +0.95s/f (Soft) **11** Ran SP% **119.3**
**WFA** 3 from 4yo+ 8lb
Speed ratings: **102,98,97,96,86 79,75,73,63,57** —CSF £23.94 TOTE £2.00: £1.10, £3.60, £1.40; EX 33.90 Place 6 £67.45, Place 5 £29.23.
**Owner** D J Burke **Bred** Ennistown Stud **Trained** Pulborough, W Sussex

**FOCUS**
A very weak maiden in which Autumn Wealth hung so badly in the straight that he ended up racing against the stands'-side rail. The runner-up provides the line to the value of the form.

**NOTEBOOK**
**Autumn Wealth(IRE)**, well beaten into second at Nottingham on her previous start, stepped up on that form to get off the mark despite hanging to her left and eventually ending up against the stands'-side rail.
**Tricky Venture**, not seen since running into second at 100/1 in this very race last year, ran a cracker to fill the same position once again. The long absence would suggest he has had his problems, but there is a minor race in him providing he can be kept sound.
**St Barchan(IRE)** had shown promise on both his previous starts, but ran below form and was disappointing.
**Dream Alive** is now qualified for a handicap mark and should find things easier in that sphere.
**Medalla(FR)** did not get home and to be beaten so far was disappointing.
**Mount Cottage** *Official explanation: jockey said filly was unsuited by the ground*
T/Plt: £52.00 to a £1 stake. Pool: £42,126.15. 590.55 winning tickets. T/Qpdt: £24.10 to a £1 stake. Pool: £2,324.80. 71.10 winning tickets. JR

## 5111 GOODWOOD (R-H)

### Sunday, August 29

**OFFICIAL GOING: Round course - good to soft; straight course - soft (heavy in places)**
Middle to stands' side was the place they chose to race all afternoon and if anything it was those neare the centre of the track that benefited.
Wind: brisk hlf against Weather: overcast

## 5147 BRITANNIA RESCUE MEDIAN AUCTION MAIDEN STKS 6f
**2:10** (2:13) (E) 3-4-Y-O **£5,408** (£1,664; £832; £416) **Stalls** Low

Form RPR

0302 **1** **Growler**[26] 4419 3-9-0 56....(v) RHughes 5 73
(JLDunlop) *lw: prom: pressed ldr over 2f out: shkn up to ld over 1f out: styd on wl* **5/1**[3]

-220 **2** *2 1/2* **Stargem**[25] 4459 3-8-9 66.... KFallon 1 60
(JPearce) *mde most: rdn and hdd over 1f out: one pce fnl f* **7/2**[1]

0-54 **3** *1 3/4* **Asbo**[25] 4459 4-8-12 59.... KDarley 6 55
(DrJDScargill) *wl in tch: rdn and cl up 2f out: one pce fr over 1f out* **4/1**[2]

50 **4** *5* **Heavens Walk**[11] 4845 3-9-0 .... DSweeney 9 45
(PJMakin) *lw: hld up in last pair: prog over 2f out: rdn and no imp on ldrs fr over 1f out* **12/1**

-023 **5** *2 1/2* **Text**[15] 4741 3-9-0 65.... JFEgan 3 37
(MrsStefLiddiard) *cl up: lost pl and pushed along bef 1/2-way: struggling whn n.m.r briefly over 1f out* **7/1**

0 **6** *3 1/2* **Dine 'N' Dash**[17] 4683 3-8-11 .... LPKeniry(3) 8 27
(AGNewcombe) *racd in last pair: rdn and struggling 1/2-way: n.d after* **66/1**

5022 **7** *2 1/2* **Cafe Americano**[10] 4869 4-9-3 48....(e) JFortune 10 19
(DWPArbuthnot) *settled in rr: effrt on outer 1/2-way: wknd 2f out* **8/1**

23 **8** *13* **Sokoke**[39] 4021 3-9-0 .... RLMoore 4 —
(RMBeckett) *w ldr to over 2f out: wknd rapidly: t.o* **11/2**

56 **9** *4* **Silver Reign**[144] 1293 3-8-9 .... RThomas(5) 2 —
(GBBalding) *trckd ldrs: n.m.r over 2f out: wknd rapidly: t.o* **25/1**

1m 16.56s (3.72) **Going Correction** +0.70s/f (Yiel) **9** Ran SP% **110.9**
**WFA** 3 from 4yo 3lb
Speed ratings: **103,99,97,90,87 82,79,62,56**CSF £21.45 TOTE £5.10: £1.90, £1.60, £1.90; EX 20.00.
**Owner** P D Player **Bred** Peter D Player And John L Dunlop **Trained** Arundel, W Sussex

**FOCUS**
A poor race that went to 56-rated performer Growler, and despite the reasonable time the overall form looks modest.

**NOTEBOOK**
**Growler** has been racing over farther on faster ground and seemed to find the drop in trip and soft going playing to his strengths. He was always going well and powered away in the closing stages. There may be a small handicap in him.
**Stargem** had plenty in hand on Growler at the weights, but on the day the winner handled conditions best and she was comfortably held.
**Asbo** was a bit disappointing as her last run entitled her to go close. The return to a faster surface may suit.
**Heavens Walk** is bred to appreciate a sound surface and was noted making some late headway, so may have a small handicap in him in decent going.
**Text** had his chance and remains a frustrating maiden.
**Sokoke** found the ground too soft and deserves another chance. *Official explanation: jockey said gelding was unsuited by the ground (heavy, soft in places)*
**Silver Reign** *Official explanation: trainer said gelding was unsuited by the ground (heavy, soft in places)*

## 5148 SEAFRANCE FILLIES' STKS (H'CAP) 7f
**2:45** (2:45) (D) (0-85,84) 3-Y-O **£7,036** (£2,165; £1,082; £541) **Stalls** High

Form RPR

31 **1** **New Order**[59] 3448 3-8-8 71.... RHughes 2 83+
(BWHills) *trckd ldr: rdn to ld wl over 1f out: hanging rt but in command fnl f* **9/2**[2]

2061 **2** *1 3/4* **Sabrina Brown**[10] 4868 3-8-3 71....(t) RThomas(5) 4 77
(GBBalding) *led: rdn and hdd wl over 1f out: styd on same pce fnl f* **13/2**[3]

5-1 **3** *1 1/4* **Enrapture (USA)**[16] 4718 3-9-2 79.... KFallon 6 82
(MrsAJPerrett) *lw: racd midfield: effrt over 2f out: drvn and unable qck over 1f out: one pce after* **13/8**[1]

-403 **4** *nk* **Enford Princess**[17] 4684 3-9-7 84.... RLMoore 5 86
(RHannon) *settled last pair: effrt on outer over 2f out: drvn and kpt on same pce* **14/1**

-100 **5** *1* **Saristar**[36] 4126 3-9-6 83.... JFanning 7 83
(PFICole) *hld up in last pair: prog over 2f out: chsd ldrs over 1f out: fdd ins fnl f* **10/1**

2135 **6** *1/2* **Here To Me**[23] 4515 3-8-9 72.... JFortune 3 70
(RHannon) *racd midfield: rdn 2f out: sn outpcd: one pce fnl f* **16/1**

6033 **7** *3 1/2* **Scarlett Rose**[29] 4340 3-8-2 65.... MartinDwyer 8 55
(DrJDScargill) *trckd ldng pair: rdn and lost pl wl over 1f out: eased whn no ch ins fnl f* **11/1**

13 **8** *6* **Surreptitious**[16] 4726 3-8-5 68.... KDarley 1 43
(DRLoder) *dwlt: in tch: rdn over 2f out: sn wknd* **13/2**[3]

1m 31.51s (3.48) **Going Correction** +0.70s/f (Yiel) **8** Ran SP% **112.9**
Speed ratings: **108,106,104,104,103 102,98,91**CSF £32.70 CT £65.86 TOTE £5.40: £2.20, £1.80, £1.10; EX 39.80.
**Owner** K Abdulla **Bred** Juddmonte Farms **Trained** Lambourn, Berks

**FOCUS**
A fair handicap and a decent time for the grade of contest. The winner is likely to prove better than the bare form indicates.

**NOTEBOOK**
**New Order** came into this as one of the least exposed and, given her stable have emerged from the doldrums in recent weeks, could be given a major chance. Always well placed, she came through with her winning challenge approaching the final furlong and won nicely despite hanging a little. There is more to come from this filly and she may be up to Listed class in time if continuing to go the right way.
**Sabrina Brown** comes from a family who traditionally relish this sort of ground and she looks no exception. Having led for most of the race, she was passed by New Order but stuck on gamely suggesting the return to a mile may suit.
**Enrapture(USA)** was starting out her handicap career on a high enough mark and was surprisingly made a short-price favourite. She had every chance and was not good enough. The step up to a mile is the only thing that could see some improvement.
**Enford Princess** kept on steadily from the rear without ever looking like it.
**Saristar** did not stay the trip, fading disappointingly having looked to hold every chance two out.
**Surreptitious** ran a shocker without any apparent excuse.

## 5149 CITROEN C5 PRESTIGE STKS (GROUP 3) (FILLIES) 7f
**3:20** (3:23) (A) 2-Y-O **£23,200** (£8,800; £4,400; £2,000) **Stalls** High

Form RPR

31 **1** **Dubai Surprise (IRE)**[22] 4560 2-8-9 84.... RLMoore 10 104
(DRLoder) *towards rr: pushed along 1/2-way: n.m.r on inner 2f out: squeezed through over 1f out: drvn and styd on wl to ld last 75yds* **16/1**

**2** *1/2* **Nanabanana (IRE)**[19] 2-8-9 .... KDarley 11 103+
(MmeCHead-Maarek, France) *w'like: lengthy: scope: prom: led gng easily over 2f out: rdn over 1f out: worn down last 75yds* **9/2**[2]

1 **3** *3* **Red Peony**[31] 4263 2-8-9 .... JPMurtagh 9 95
(SirMarkPrescott) *str: scope: lw: trckd ldrs: lost pl on inner over 2f out: drvn and styd on again fnl f* **3/1**[1]

1 **4** *shd* **Favourita**[24] 4468 2-8-9 .... J-PGuillambert 1 95
(CEBrittain) *reluctant to go to post: racd midfield: hmpd on inner and lost pl 3f out: swtchd wd: carried hd high but styd on wl fnl 2f* **50/1**

0321 **5** *1* **Justaquestion**[22] 4527 2-8-9 93.... PDoe 2 93
(IAWood) *hld up in last pair: prog over 2f out: chsd ldr wl over 1f out: no imp: wknd ins fnl f* **12/1**

3456 **6** *1/2* **Umniya (IRE)**[10] 4885 2-8-9 91....(v[1]) CCatlin 6 91
(MRChannon) *settled in rr: effrt and nt clr run over 2f out and again 2f out: drvn and kpt on fnl f* **50/1**

02 **7** *2 1/2* **Luas Line (IRE)**[21] 4592 2-8-9 .... KFallon 4 85
(DavidWachman, Ire) *w'like: str: prog to join ldrs over 4f out: outpcd wl over 2f out: swtchd rt & rallied over 1f out: btn and eased last 150y* **3/1**[1]

120 **8** *2* **Royal Alchemist**[22] 4552 2-8-9 94.... ADaly 13 80
(MDIUsher) *dwlt: racd in rr: rdn wl over 2f out: no imp on ldrs over 1f out: fdd* **10/1**[3]

533 **9** *3* **Subyan Dreams**[16] 4716 2-8-9 95.... RHughes 7 73
(PWChapple-Hyam) *lw: mde most to over 2f out: wknd wl over 1f out* **14/1**

2115 **10** *5* **Jane Jubilee (IRE)**[12] 4835 2-8-9 95.... JFanning 12 60
(MJohnston) *nvr beyond midfield: rdn whn n.m.r 2f out: wknd* **12/1**

41 **11** *2* **Miss L'Augeval**[31] 4272 2-8-9 82.... MartinDwyer 8 55
(GWragg) *racd midfield: n.m.r 4f out: rdn and wknd wl over 2f out* **20/1**

021 **12** *9* **Sharp As A Tack (IRE)**[17] 4681 2-8-9 83.... JFortune 5 33
(BJMeehan) *pressed ldrs tl wknd over 2f out: hanging bdly rt after* **20/1**

1m 32.3s (4.27) **Going Correction** +0.70s/f (Yiel) **12** Ran SP% **118.7**
Speed ratings: **103,102,99,98,97 97,94,92,88,82 80,70**CSF £83.66 TOTE £18.40: £5.00, £1.80, £1.90; EX 95.90.
**Owner** Dr Ali Ridha **Bred** James F Hanly **Trained** Newmarket, Suffolk

**FOCUS**
An average-looking renewal of this Group Three, but a fair time for the grade given the conditions and two smart performances from Dubai Surprise and Nanabanana.

**NOTEBOOK**
**Dubai Surprise(IRE)** had shown the benefit of experience when getting off the mark at Redcar earlier in the month and, by a sire whose juveniles are proving most effective with some give in the ground, was able to step up again. She sat in rear for most of the race - it proved the place to be - and came with a strong winning challenge having been short of room and forced to switch. Held in high regard, she is going the right way and, with a mile set to prove no problem, has earned her place in the Fillies' Mile line-up.
**Nanabanana(IRE)** was the only one of the first six home to have raced up with the pace, and deserves plenty of credit for the effort as they went a bit too fast. She stuck to the centre of the course and kept galloping away but the winner had a finishing kick. Fully effective on this ground, she is solid at this level and can win one back in her homeland, possibly back over six furlongs.
**Red Peony** had not been seen since making an impressive winning debut at Epsom and did not look out of place in this grade. She stayed on again having got outpaced and was closing with every stride at the line. There is more to come from this daughter of Montjeu and a mile will suit.
**Favourita** stepped up massively on her Brighton maiden win and proved just as effective on this softer surface. She stayed on nicely having got behind and, despite looking awkward under pressure, hinted at better to come.
**Justaquestion** came into this on the back of her Shergar Cup win - a race that has worked out well - and held solid place claims. She was always at the back of the field and may have made her ground up too quickly as she emptied out in the final furlong. She ran better than her finishing position suggests and is up to winning at Listed level.
**Umniya(IRE)** has been well exposed at this sort of level of late and again ran well enough without threatening to win.

**Luas Line(IRE)** cut little ice on this British debut and failed to see her race out having been up there early. The return to a faster surface may suit.
**Royal Alchemist** ran a little below form and deserves another chance back on faster ground.
**Subyan Dreams** did a little too much too early and was ultimately disappointing. Despite still being a maiden her form prior to today had shown her to be Listed standard, and she should at least win her maiden if asked to.
**Jane Jubilee(IRE)** has found easy going against her the last twice, and on a faster surface back in a more suitable grade, she can be expected to return to form.

## 5150 MOTORING & LEISURE STKS (H'CAP) 1m
3:55 (3:57) (D) (0-85,85) 3-Y-O **£7,133** (£2,195; £1,097; £548) **Stalls** High

Form RPR
-301 **1** **Flying Adored**[15] 4738 3-8-10 **74** ... KFallon 7 83+
(JLDunlop) *racd midfield: prog in centre 3f out: drvn to ld over 1f out: kpt on wl u.p* **5/2**[1]
4104 **2** *2* **Dr Thong**[18] 4646 3-9-4 **82** ... KDarley 8 87
(PFICole) *pressed ldr: led 1/2-way: rdn and hdd in centre over 1f out: one pce fnl f* **3/1**[2]
3-51 **3** *1¾* **Day To Remember**[13] 4813 3-9-7 **85** ... JFortune 2 87
(EFVaughan) *trckd ldrs: rdn and cl up in centre 2f out: sn unable qck: kpt on again fnl f* **5/1**[3]
0411 **4** *5* **General Feeling (IRE)**[24] 4470 3-8-12 **76** ... JFEgan 5 68
(SKirk) *lw: settled last of main gp: prog in centre 3f out: rdn to chal 2f out: wknd over 1f out* **13/2**
4151 **5** *1* **Stevedore (IRE)**[8] 4938 3-8-9 **73** ... GCarter 1 63
(BRMillman) *mde most to 1/2-way: c towards nr side st: outpcd over 2f out : plugged on* **8/1**
0040 **6** *3* **Lord Of The Sea (IRE)**[71] 3089 3-7-12 **62** oh1 ... DKinsella 4 46
(JamiePoulton) *cl up tl wknd 2f out* **28/1**
11-0 **7** *11* **Taminoula (IRE)**[32] 4230 3-9-2 **80** ... JPMurtagh 3 42
(MrsAJPerrett) *wl in tch: c to nr side in st: floundering over 2f out: wl bhd and eased fnl f* **7/1**
352- **P** **Little London**[317] 5607 3-9-1 **79** ... RLMoore 6 —
(JLDunlop) *s.s: lost tch rapidly after 3f: p.u 1/2-way: dismntd* **14/1**

1m 45.09s (4.82) **Going Correction** +0.70s/f (Yiel) **8** Ran SP% **117.3**
Speed ratings: **103,101,99,94,93 90,79,**—CSF £10.47 CT £34.66 TOTE £3.00: £1.50, £1.40, £2.20; EX 13.20.
**Owner** Mrs Mark Burrell **Bred** Mrs M Burrell **Trained** Arundel, W Sussex

**FOCUS**
A fair handicap but a good display from the progressive Flying Adored and the form of those immediately behind is solid.

**NOTEBOOK**
**Flying Adored**, off the mark over course and distance earlier in the month, had no trouble with this softer surface and surged ahead before staying on strongly. She is going the right way and, as her stable has returned to a bit of form in recent weeks, the completion of a hat-trick cannot be ruled out.
**Dr Thong** was 6lb worse off with the winner on Leicester form from July, but that should not have been enough to reverse the form and it is more a case of the winner having improved since. This was still a fair effort.
**Day To Remember**, an easy winner of his maiden at Windsor, was slightly disappointing, although in all honesty he did start out his handicap career off a high-enough mark. A mile and a quarter may bring about some improvement.
**General Feeling(IRE)** had won his last two on fast ground and struggled on this softer surface. He deserves another chance to confirm his progressive profile.
**Stevedore(IRE)** was outpaced having led early and did not seem inconvenienced by the trip.
**Taminoula(IRE)** *Official explanation: jockey said filly was unsuited by the ground (heavy, soft in places)*

## 5151 TRUNDLE PREMIER CLAIMING STKS 1m 1f
4:30 (4:31) (D) 3-Y-O+ **£5,616** (£1,728; £864; £432) **Stalls** Low

Form RPR
-112 **1** **The Prince**[2] 5103 10-9-2 84 ... CCatlin 5 75
(IanWilliams) *lw: racd midfield: clsd 3f out: rdn to chse ldr 2f out: styd on wl to ld last 100yds* **9/2**[2]
0060 **2** *2* **Travelling Band (IRE)**[8] 4950 6-9-2 72 ... (v[1]) LPKeniry[(3)] 2 74
(AMBalding) *lw: trckd ldng pair: led gng easily wl over 2f out: rdn over 1f out: c to nr rail: wknd and hdd last 100yds* **10/1**
2612 **3** *2½* **One Upmanship**[8] 4940 3-8-12 65 ... RLMoore 8 69
(JGPortman) *trckd ldrs: rdn to chse ldng pair wl over 1f out: tried to cl ent fnl f: sn nt qckn* **14/1**
4034 **4** *6* **Highland Reel**[25] 4442 7-9-7 87 ... RHughes 1 59
(DRCElsworth) *hld up in rr and wl off the pce: tried to cl over 2f out: sn rdn and no rspnse: no ch after* **2/1**[1]
6455 **5** *1¼* **Linning Wine (IRE)**[9] 4920 8-9-7 80 ... SCarson 3 57
(BGPowell) *hld up midfield: effrt 3f out: rdn and fnd nil 2f out: wknd rapidly ent fnl f* **9/2**[2]
6 **6** *1* **Montgomery**[14] 4775 3-8-2 ... NChalmers[(5)] 9 48
(AGNewcombe) *wl in rr: nrly t.o 3f out: r.o wl fnl f* **50/1**
50/0 **7** *1½* **Knocktopher Abbey**[167] 740 7-8-11 60 ... (b) SHitchcott[(3)] 4 45
(AGNewcombe) *dwlt: last and wl bhd: t.o 3f out: kpt on u.p fnl 2f* **50/1**
4540 **8** *1* **Cartronageeraghlad (IRE)**[25] 4443 3-9-5 75 ... (b) MartinDwyer 6 55
(JAOsborne) *led: c to nr side rail in st: hdd & wknd wl over 2f out* **10/1**
4563 **9** *1½* **Ben Hur**[6] 5006 5-9-5 74 ... KDarley 10 45
(WMBrisbourne) *chsd ldr: rdn and fnd nil 3f out: wknd rapidly* **5/1**[3]

2m 3.01s (6.15) **Going Correction** +0.70s/f (Yiel)
**WFA** 3 from 5yo+ 7lb **9** Ran SP% **115.1**
Speed ratings: **100,98,96,90,89 88,87,86,85**CSF £48.40 TOTE £4.60: £2.00, £3.50, £2.20; EX 43.90.
**Owner** Patrick Kelly **Bred** Bottisham Heath Stud **Trained** Portway, Warwicks

**FOCUS**
A fair claimer run in a modest time for the class and the form is not particularly strong.

**NOTEBOOK**
**The Prince** was taken to Deauville for a claimer only two days previously and ran well to finish second - on an All-Weather surface - and showed no ill-effects of the quick reappearance. Although now ten, he seems to be nearly as good as ever.
**Travelling Band(IRE)** had quite a bit to find with the winner at the weights and ran well. He looked the likely winner at one stage - came there travelling strongly and was going best of all - but he found little and ultimately faded.
**One Upmanship** has been running consistently well in this sort of grade and again gave his all in defeat. He will find less competitive claimers.
**Highland Reel** had the highest official rating of these but found the ground too tacky and failed to run his race. He is better than this. *Official explanation: jockey said gelding was never travelling*
**Linning Wine(IRE)** stopped quickly under pressure and does not always produce when the chips are down.
**Cartronageeraghlad(IRE)** went off too fast and faded tamely under pressure. *Official explanation: jockey said gelding was too keen early on*
**Ben Hur** ran way below form and paid for chasing the fast early pace.

## 5152 PICNIC H'CAP 1m 6f
5:05 (5:05) (E ) (0-75,75) 3-Y-O+ **£4,309** (£1,326; £663; £331) **Stalls** High

Form RPR
0014 **1** **Stoop To Conquer**[70] 3120 4-9-11 **72** ... JPMurtagh 5 82+
(JLDunlop) *led for 4f: pressed ldr to 3f out: looked btn u.p in centre 2f out: rallied over 1f out: urged along and led last 75yds* **11/4**[1]
0060 **2** *nk* **Jasmick (IRE)**[2] 5073 6-9-3 **67** ... LFletcher[(3)] 2 74
(HMorrison) *sn trckd ldng pair: effrt to ld over 2f out and c to nr side rail: looked in command over 1f out: worn down last 75yds* **6/1**
02-3 **3** *7* **Market Leader**[37] 4103 3-8-12 **71** ... RHughes 3 69
(MrsAJPerrett) *trckd ldrs: rdn over 2f out: no imp and btn wl over 1f out: tk 3rd nr fin* **7/2**[2]
0000 **4** *½* **Establishment**[37] 4075 7-9-4 **65** ... DSweeney 1 62
(CACyzer) *led after 4f: rdn and hdd over 2f out: wknd jst over 1f out* **13/2**
3-0 **5** *3½* **High Hope (FR)**[239] 418 6-9-10 **71** ... (p) RLMoore 4 64
(GLMoore) *b: lw: hld up in tch: rdn over 3f out: wknd 2f out* **4/1**[3]
5-15 **6** *½* **Goodwood Finesse (IRE)**[44] 3908 3-9-2 **75** ... GCarter 7 67
(JLDunlop) *lw: hld up in last pair: rdn 3f out: wknd 2f out* **7/1**
0/00 **7** *21* **Dr Cool**[11] 4849 7-8-13 **60** ... PDoe 6 25
(JAkehurst) *s.s: a in last pair: wknd over 2f out: t.o* **20/1**

3m 13.55s (9.80) **Going Correction** +0.70s/f (Yiel)
**WFA** 3 from 4yo+ 12lb **7** Ran SP% **113.8**
Speed ratings: **100,99,95,95,93 93,81**CSF £19.41 TOTE £3.30: £2.00, £3.30; EX 21.90.
**Owner** I H Stewart-Brown & M J Meacock **Bred** I Stewart-Brown And M Meacock **Trained** Arundel, W Sussex
■ Stewards Enquiry : L Fletcher one-day ban: used whip with excessive frequency (Sep 9)

**FOCUS**
A modest handicap in which they went no real pace and is difficult to rate positively, although Stoop To Conquer did well to win.

**NOTEBOOK**
**Stoop To Conquer** appeared to not quite get the trip of two miles' two at Pontefract and just about found this trip far enough getting up in the closing stages to win a shade comfortably. The way the race was run would not have played to his strengths and two miles looks to be his ideal trip. There is more to come from him at that distance.
**Jasmick(IRE)** went close to winning her first race in over two years, just getting run out of it late on. She was clear of the third and deserves plenty of credit for the effort.
**Market Leader** was well held on this handicap debut and may not have been suited by the ground. She deserves another chance.
**Establishment** remains some way below his best.
**Goodwood Finesse(IRE)** did not get home over this extra distance.

## 5153 HARVEST STKS (H'CAP) 1m 1f 192y
5:40 (5:40) (E ) (0-75,73) 3-Y-O+ **£4,358** (£1,341; £670; £335) **Stalls** High

Form RPR
-006 **1** **Polish Spirit**[18] 4641 9-8-13 **60** ... JFortune 10 70
(BRMillman) *hld up bhd ldrs: effrt to ld 2f out: jnd on all sides fnl f: battled on gamely* **5/1**[3]
0623 **2** *hd* **Arry Dash**[9] 4903 4-9-9 **73** ... SHitchcott[(3)] 12 83
(MRChannon) *lw: hld up in rr: prog to trck ldrs 2f out: swtchd lft ent fnl f: r.o nr fin: jst failed* **9/2**[2]
/235 **3** *nk* **Serraval (FR)**[5] 5019 6-8-5 **57** ... RThomas[(5)] 2 66
(GBBalding) *lw: hld up in rr: stdy prog over 2f out: rdn to chal over 1f out: w wnr ins fnl f: nt qckn nr fin* **8/1**
4245 **4** *½* **Head To Kerry (IRE)**[11] 4849 4-8-7 **54** ... KFallon 1 62
(DJSFfrenchDavis) *sn midfield: prog to trck ldrs gng wl 3f out: got through to chal over 1f out: ev ch ins fnl f: nt qckn* **9/4**[1]
-200 **5** *6* **Competitor**[62] 3387 3-8-10 **65** ... GCarter 4 62
(JAkehurst) *sn last: lost tch 1/2-way: t.o over 3f out: rdn and r.o fnl 2f: nvr nrr* **22/1**
5400 **6** *1½* **Desert Hawk**[16] 4719 3-8-13 **68** ... RLMoore 9 63
(RHannon) *mde most to 2f out: wknd jst over 1f out* **16/1**
0000 **7** *½* **Green Falcon**[13] 4818 3-7-12 **53** ... DKinsella 8 47
(JWHills) *rn in snatches: rdn in rr 1/2-way: effrt to chse ldrs 3f out: wknd over 1f out* **28/1**
0302 **8** *1* **Efrhina (IRE)**[7] 4972 4-9-2 **63** ... RHavlin 13 55
(MrsStefLiddiard) *lw: t.k.h: hld up bhd ldrs: effrt to chal over 2f out: wknd over 1f out* **9/1**
6000 **9** *8* **Purr**[7] 4972 3-7-7 **55** oh8 ow2 ... AHamblett[(7)] 7 33
(TTClement) *prom tl bmpd along and wknd 3f out* **50/1**
0006 **10** *½* **Kirov King (IRE)**[47] 3825 4-8-8 **62** ... AHindley[(7)] 5 39
(BGPowell) *cl up: styd against far side rail st: sn struggling* **33/1**
6564 **11** *11* **African Star**[36] 4128 3-7-13 **54** oh1 ow1 ... (p) CCatlin 6 11
(MrsAJPerrett) *w ldr to 3f out: wknd rapidly* **12/1**
3-60 **12** *dist* **Rozanee**[139] 1369 4-8-13 **60** ... JPMurtagh 3 —
(JWPayne) *midfield: wknd 4f out: t.o whn eased over 1f out* **16/1**

2m 13.99s (6.31) **Going Correction** +0.70s/f (Yiel)
**WFA** 3 from 4yo+ 8lb **12** Ran SP% **118.9**
Speed ratings: **102,101,101,101,96 95,94,94,87,87 78,**—CSF £26.81 CT £180.39 TOTE £6.00: £1.90, £1.80, £3.20; EX 30.30 Place 6 £25.26, Place 5 £18.05.
**Owner** Mrs Izabel Palmer **Bred** Victor G And Mrs Izabel Palmer **Trained** Kentisbeare, Devon

**FOCUS**
A good finish to this modest handicap with the first three home being seperated by a head and a neck. The form is sound but ordinary for the grade.

**NOTEBOOK**
**Polish Spirit** ran a better race at Salisbury when last seen and confirmed that promise in winning here, digging deep to hold the last-gasp effort of Arry Dash, having already seen off several other challenges. This was a brave performance and when ground conditions are in his favour -he loves soft ground - he will remain a threat in his races.
**Arry Dash** has proved disappointing this season as he had shaped at three as though he was the type to win a decent race. He has however, been running consistently of late, and was finishing best of all here and would have got there in a few more strides. Soft ground is the key to him.
**Serraval(FR)** comes from a stable whose horses are in top form at the minute and she ran a good race in third, but remains winless for well over two years.
**Head To Kerry(IRE)** continues to fail to see his races out having held every chance until a furlong out.
**Competitor** stayed on for sixth having been detatched in last for most of the way. This was at least an improvement on his recent efforts.
**Desert Hawk** is going the wrong way.
**Green Falcon** does not have a suitable trip.
**Rozanee** *Official explanation: jockey said filly had a breathing problem*
T/Jkpt: £4,733.30 to a £1 stake. Pool: £10,000.00. 1.50 winning tickets. T/Plt: £28.60 to a £1 stake. Pool: £57,976.80. 1,476.15 winning tickets. T/Qpdt: £12.70 to a £1 stake. Pool: £2,555.75. 148.60 winning tickets. JN

5022 **YARMOUTH (L-H)**

Sunday, August 29

**OFFICIAL GOING: Soft (heavy in places)**

Wind: Fresh across Weather: Showery

## 5154 GREAT YARMOUTH RACECOURSE BOOKMAKERS/E.B.F. MAIDEN STKS — 6f 3y

2:20 (2:21) (D ) 2-Y-0 — **£4,832** (£1,487; £743; £371) **Stalls** High

Form — RPR

06 **1** **Fighting Tom Cat (USA)**[18] 4649 2-9-0 .....(t) LDettori 8 — 78
(SaeedBinSuroor) *mde virtually all: jst hld on* — **3/1**[3]

6 **2** *shd* **Love Thirty**[24] 4494 2-8-9 ..... TEDurcan 2 — 73
(MRChannon) *chsd ldrs: rdn and ev ch whn hung lft over 1f out: r.o* **11/4**[2]

624 **3** *3 ½* **Sign Writer (USA)**[29] 4334 2-9-0 83 ..... EAhern 3 — 67
(JNoseda) *hld up in tch: rdn over 1f out: styd on same pce* — **15/8**[1]

0 **4** *2 ½* **Rudaki**[64] 3319 2-9-0 ..... MTebbutt 4 — 60
(MGQuinlan) *s.i.s: outpcd: r.o ins fnl f: nvr nrr* — **9/1**

**5** *1* **Muddy (IRE)** 2-9-0 ..... JQuinn 1 — 57
(GAHuffer) *prom over 4f* — **11/1**

0 **6** *5* **Fly Me To Dunoon (IRE)**[31] 4277 2-8-9 .....(v[1]) DarrenWilliams 5 — 37
(KRBurke) *dwlt: jnd wnr 5f out: rdn and wknd wl over 1f out* — **20/1**

**7** *8* **Great General (IRE)** 2-9-0 ..... MFenton 7 — 18
(SLKeightley) *sn outpcd* — **40/1**

00 **8** *dist* **Little Waltham**[22] 4544 2-8-9 ..... PHanagan 6 — —
(KAMorgan) *chsd ldrs: lost pl 5f out: wknd 1/2-way* — **100/1**

1m 17.1s (3.50) **Going Correction** +0.425s/f (Yiel) — **8** Ran SP% **113.0**

Speed ratings: **93,92,88,84,83 76,66,**—CSF £11.34 TOTE £3.60: £1.40, £1.30, £1.10; EX 10.00.

**Owner** Godolphin **Bred** Darley **Trained** Newmarket, Suffolk

**FOCUS**

A weak maiden by Yarmouth standards and the time was not great either. The future does not look too bright for those outside the front pair.

**NOTEBOOK**

**Fighting Tom Cat(USA)**, whose performances so far have been moderate, improved quite a bit on this softer ground and just managed to prevail following a positive ride. His stable's juveniles do not normally take three attempts before clicking though, so the conclusion must be that he is very ordinary.

**Love Thirty**, who beat just one home on her debut here, improved from that and only just failed in a driving finish. However this was a moderate contest and she will need to improve again in order to find a race.

**Sign Writer(USA)** had the form to win this, but was comfortably put in his place by the front two. The softer ground may have been to blame, but it does seem as though he is not progressing.

**Rudaki** performed as though he needs further. He is a half-brother to four winners so may well be capable of a bit better.

**Muddy(IRE)**, a half-brother to three winners including Football Crazy, showed up for a while and is another that may improve for a longer trip.

## 5155 LET'S TALK FILLIES' H'CAP — 7f 3y

2:55 (2:57) (D ) (0-80,74) 3-Y-0+ — **£6,682** (£2,056; £1,028; £514) **Stalls** High

Form — RPR

0636 **1** **Princess Galadriel**[8] 4938 3-8-3 **56** ..... WSupple 6 — 67
(JRBest) *racd stands' side: hld up: hdwy 2f out: rdn to ld 1f out: edgd lft ins fnl f: r.o* — **16/1**

6001 **2** *nk* **Glebe Garden**[24] 4496 3-9-7 **74** ..... LDettori 9 — 84
(MLWBell) *led stands' side: rdn and hdd 1f out: bmpd ins fnl f: r.o* — **9/2**[3]

-316 **3** *4* **Pertemps Magus**[9] 4905 4-9-2 **64** ..... PHanagan 5 — 64
(RAFahey) *racd stands' side: chsd ldrs: rdn and hung lft over 2f out: no ex fnl f* — **9/4**[1]

2020 **4** *1 ¼* **In The Pink (IRE)**[22] 4551 4-9-10 **72** ..... TEDurcan 4 — 69
(MRChannon) *dwlt: racd stands' side: hld up: hdwy over 1f out: no ex fnl f* — **8/1**

1223 **5** *2* **Lady Mo**[26] 4414 3-8-13 **66** ..... AMcCarthy 8 — 58
(GGMargarson) *racd stands' side: chsd ldrs: rdn over 1f out: sn wknd* — **10/1**

645 **6** *½* **Double Dagger Lady (USA)**[55] 3592 3-8-9 **62** ..... EAhern 3 — 53
(JNoseda) *led centre duo: wknd fnl f* — **7/2**[2]

0036 **7** *7* **Sister Sophia (USA)**[22] 4551 4-8-13 **61** ..... MFenton 7 — 34
(WJMusson) *s.i.s: racd stands' side: hld up: wknd over 2f out* — **10/1**

0430 **8** *½* **Set Alight**[9] 4926 3-7-12 **51** oh1 ..... LisaJones 2 — 23
(MrsCADunnett) *racd stands' side: chsd ldrs: hung lft and wknd over 2f out* — **14/1**

333 **9** *2* **Emsam Ballou (IRE)**[155] 1133 3-8-13 **66** ..... MTebbutt 10 — 33
(VSmith) *racd stands' side: prom: plld hrd: wknd over 2f out* — **20/1**

6006 **10** *5* **Bad Intentions (IRE)**[31] 4265 4-8-12 **60** ..... OUrbina 1 — 14
(MissDMountain) *racd centre: chsd ldr: rdn 1/2-way: wknd over 2f out* — **50/1**

1m 29.32s (2.82) **Going Correction** +0.425s/f (Yiel)

**WFA** 3 from 4yo 5lb — **10** Ran SP% **119.7**

Speed ratings: **100,99,95,93,91 90,82,82,79,74**CSF £89.00 CT £230.70 TOTE £21.10: £4.70, £2.50, £1.40; EX 163.00.

**Owner** Mrs Pam Akhurst **Bred** N J And Mrs Hubbard **Trained** Hucking, Kent

**FOCUS**

A modest fillies' handicap run at an ordinary pace. Most of the field raced towards the stands' side, but two raced down the middle of track and the tactic did not seem to do them any favours. The front pair finished clear and their form looks sound if ordinary.

**NOTEBOOK**

**Princess Galadriel** has some form on soft ground, but it may be that getting a position next to the stands' rail was her biggest advantage and she just managed to prevail in a driving finish. This looks her best trip.

**Glebe Garden**, raised 4lb for her course-and-distance victory earlier in the month, was on very different ground this time and ran well under a positive ride. She looks capable of winning off this mark.

**Pertemps Magus** goes on the ground and had every chance, but was completely left behind by the front pair in the closing stages. She looks held off this sort of mark. *Official explanation: jockey said filly was hanging*

**In The Pink(IRE)** is 10lb higher than for her last win, but has run very well off this mark lately and it is more likely the softer ground held her back.

**Lady Mo** is consistent, but she does look better on faster ground and had nothing more to offer over the last couple of furlongs.

**Double Dagger Lady(USA)** ◆, making her handicap debut and on soft ground for the first time, raced away from the bulk of the field towards the far side, and the fact that she lasted a good deal longer than the only other one who raced over there suggests the tactic backfired and she could be a lot better than her finishing position.

**Bad Intentions(IRE)** *Official explanation: jockey said filly was unsuited by soft (heavy in places) ground*

## 5156 LOWESTOFT JOURNAL CLASSIFIED STKS — 1m 3y

3:30 (3:31) (F ) 3-Y-0 — **£3,529** (£1,086; £543; £271) **Stalls** High

Form — RPR

3230 **1** **Pella**[21] 4580 3-8-10 61 ..... LDettori 7 — 70
(MBlanshard) *hld up: swtchd lft and hdwy wl over 1f out: rdn to ld and edgd rt 1f out: r.o* — **5/1**[3]

443 **2** *1 ¼* **Premier Rouge**[18] 4629 3-9-3 65 ..... PRobinson 4 — 75
(EFVaughan) *hld yp: swtchd lft and hdwy over 2f out: edgd rt over 1f out: sn rdn: ev ch whn hmpd 1f out: styd on same pce* — **8/1**

0021 **3** *2* **Dont Call Me Derek**[10] 4882 3-9-4 66 ..... SWKelly 15 — 72
(SCWilliams) *chsd ldrs: rdn and ev ch 1f out: no ex* — **13/8**[1]

5000 **4** *shd* **King Of Knight (IRE)**[18] 4655 3-8-12 60 ..... JQuinn 1 — 65
(GProdromou) *s.s: bhd: hdwy over 1f out: r.o* — **25/1**

0034 **5** *2* **Fools Entire**[2] 5077 3-8-9 58 .....(e) BReilly[(3)] 6 — 61
(JAGilbert) *w ldrs tl led over 4f out: rdn and hdd 1f out: wkng whn hmpd ins fnl f* — **25/1**

0-00 **6** *1* **King Of Music (USA)**[18] 4652 3-8-12 60 ..... OUrbina 5 — 59
(GProdromou) *dwlt: hld up: hdwy over 2f out: styd on same pce appr fnl f* — **40/1**

6405 **7** *6* **Violet Avenue**[13] 4817 3-8-9 55 ..... MFenton 3 — 44
(JGGiven) *hld up: sme hdwy 2f out: sn wknd* — **22/1**

0004 **8** *2* **Flame Queen**[24] 4496 3-8-13 64 ..... LisaJones 2 — 44
(MrsCADunnett) *hld up: hdwy 1/2-way: rdn and wknd over 1f out* — **20/1**

3066 **9** *4* **Night Frolic**[21] 4580 3-8-10 61 ..... MHills 14 — 33
(JWHills) *prom: hmpd and dropped rr over 3f out: n.d after* — **9/2**[2]

5440 **10** *½* **Appetina**[16] 4698 3-8-9 60 ..... SChin 12 — 31
(JGGiven) *led over 3f: rdn and wknd wl over 1f out* — **25/1**

0430 **11** *¾* **My Pension (IRE)**[85] 2688 3-9-3 65 ..... TEDurcan 9 — 38
(PHowling) *hld up: n.d* — **16/1**

0515 **12** *shd* **Best Desert (IRE)**[15] 4756 3-9-3 65 ..... NPollard 11 — 38
(JRBest) *chsd ldrs: rdn and lost pl 3f out: wknd 2f out* — **16/1**

3660 **13** *13* **La Landonne**[29] 4338 3-8-5 63 .....(v[1]) MHoward[(7)] 13 — 7
(PMPhelan) *chsd ldrs over 4f* — **25/1**

5060 **14** *11* **Haydn (USA)**[22] 4556 3-8-7 62 .....(v[1]) DerekNolan[(7)] 10 — —
(GAHuffer) *chsd ldrs over 4f: eased fnl 2f* — **33/1**

1m 43.1s (3.40) **Going Correction** +0.425s/f (Yiel) — **14** Ran SP% **125.7**

Speed ratings: **100,98,96,96,94 93,87,85,81,81 80,80,67,56**CSF £41.25 TOTE £7.00: £2.20, £2.20, £1.50; EX 37.10.

**Owner** The Pella Partnership **Bred** Whitsbury Manor Stud **Trained** Upper Lambourn, Berks

**FOCUS**

A low-grade contest, but a fair pace which suited those held up for a late run and the whole field raced stands' side. The front six finished well clear of the rest and the form appears fairly sound.

**NOTEBOOK**

**Pella**, held up out the back, may have appreciated further, but the solid pace was a help to her and she showed a decent turn of foot to pick off the pacemaker and go on to break her duck at the tenth attempt.

**Premier Rouge** ◆ was another that probably needs further and was able to get so close thanks to the solid pace. He was short of room a furlong from home, but the result was not affected. He will be very interesting over ten furlongs.

**Dont Call Me Derek**, very well backed, goes on the ground and did best of those that raced close to the pace, but could do nothing to stop the front pair pulling away from him.

**King Of Knight(IRE)**, stepping down again in trip, stayed on from well off the pace but was never a threat to the principals. He would appear to need further judged on this effort, but looked a non-stayer over an extra quarter mile on faster ground last time, so connections can be forgiven for scratching their heads.

**Fools Entire** was allowed to stride on this time and tried to nick the race from the front just after halfway. However, he found this trip in the conditions too much and had already been swept aside when running out of room inside the last furlong.

**King Of Music(USA)**, on a soft surface for the first time, made up some late ground and this was his best performance since his belated reappearance. He looks worth a try over further and is not totally without hope.

**Night Frolic**, whose best previous effort by far came on heavy ground, held a good position when meeting traffic problems just after halfway and there was no way back from there.

## 5157 JOHN SMITH'S EXTRA SMOOTH H'CAP — 5f 43y

4:05 (4:06) (D ) (0-80,80) 3-Y-0+ — **£6,968** (£2,144; £1,072; £536) **Stalls** High

Form — RPR

0400 **1** **Prime Recreation**[2] 5094 7-8-13 **65** ..... LisaJones 9 — 77
(PSFelgate) *mde all: rdn out* — **22/1**

1242 **2** *1* **Never Without Me**[25] 4452 4-8-10 **62** ..... WSupple 6 — 71
(JFCoupland) *chsd ldrs: rdn over 1f out: sn ev ch unable qck ins fnl f* — **13/2**[3]

0520 **3** *3* **Valiant Romeo**[25] 4452 4-8-0 **55** .....(p) FPFerris[(3)] 1 — 55
(RBastiman) *hdwy 1/2-way: styd on same pce appr fnl f* — **16/1**

0402 **4** *1 ½* **Kennington**[10] 4881 4-7-13 **51** .....(v) AMcCarthy 2 — 47
(MrsCADunnett) *chsd ldrs: rdn over 1f out: wknd fnl f* — **12/1**

0103 **5** *nk* **Boisdale (IRE)**[16] 4702 6-7-12 **50** oh2 ..... JQuinn 10 — 45
(SLKeightley) *hld up: r.o ins fnl f: nvr nr to chal* — **8/1**

6421 **6** *shd* **Maddie's A Jem**[11] 4855 4-9-9 **75** ..... LDettori 5 — 69
(JRJenkins) *hld up: edgd rt 3f out: rdn over 1f out: nvr trbld ldrs* — **2/1**[1]

4040 **7** *1 ¼* **Tuscan Flyer**[22] 4534 6-8-8 **60** .....(b) DarrenWilliams 8 — 51
(RBastiman) *prom: chsd wnr over 3f out: wknd over 1f out* — **28/1**

0311 **8** *1 ¼* **White Ledger (IRE)**[9] 4923 5-8-6 **58** ..... PHanagan 7 — 45
(RAFahey) *sn pushed along in rr: hmpd 3f out: n.d* — **9/4**[2]

0060 **9** *½* **Trinculo (IRE)**[109] 2041 7-9-9 **80** .....(p) MSavage[(5)] 3 — 65
(NPLittmoden) *chsd ldrs over 3f* — **11/1**

63.90 secs (1.20) **Going Correction** +0.425s/f (Yiel) — **9** Ran SP% **118.3**

Speed ratings: **107,105,100,98,97 97,95,93,92**CSF £161.35 CT £2400.77 TOTE £22.00: £4.40, £1.80, £4.50; EX 74.30 Trifecta £752.00 Part won. Pool of £1,059.20 - 0.10 winning tickets..

**Owner** Michael Heywood **Bred** Alan Gibson **Trained** Grimston, Leics

**FOCUS**

A modest handicap in which the stands' rail was again the place to be. The form looks solid enough.

**NOTEBOOK**

**Prime Recreation**, well beaten two days earlier, grabbed the advantage of the stands' rail and was always in control. He wins only infrequently, but easy ground and a rail to his right side are his conditions. *Official explanation: trainer said, regarding the improved form shown, gelding was badly drawn at Newmarket and was better suited by racing on the rail today*

**Never Without Me** is a consistent individual and this was another decent effort. The Handicapper is taking no chances, but he is capable of picking up a race either on turf or Fibresand.

**Valiant Romeo** was back in headgear but this time it was cheekpieces rather than the familiar visor. He does act on this sort of ground but prefers faster conditions.

**Kennington** handled the ground but was not helped by having to race on the outside of the field. This was a creditable effort in the circumstances.

**Boisdale(IRE)** was ridden differently on this drop down in trip and made late progress when it was all over. *Official explanation: jockey said gelding stumbled leaving stalls*

**Maddie's A Jem** had conditions to suit, but was never able to land a blow. *Official explanation: jockey said filly ran flat*

## 5158 GREAT YARMOUTH MERCURY CLASSIFIED STKS 1m 2f 21y

**4:40** (4:40) (E) 3-Y-O+ **£4,556** (£1,402; £701; £350) **Stalls** Low

| Form | | | | RPR |
|---|---|---|---|---|
| 0004 | **1** | | **Another Choice (IRE)**[9] 4921 3-8-12 73.......................(t) TEDurcan 9 (NPLittmoden) *s.s: hld up: remained far side ent st: hdwy over 3f out: rdn to ld over 1f out: r.o* **12/1** | 83 |
| 1515 | **2** | *1 ½* | **Opening Ceremony (USA)**[21] 4571 5-9-5 75.................. PHanagan 2 (RAFahey) *trckd ldrs: racd keenly: styd far side ent st: led over 4f out: rdn and hdd over 1f out: no ex wl ins fnl f* **7/2**[1] | 79 |
| 0234 | **3** | *5* | **Recount (FR)**[32] 4233 4-9-3 75.................................... MSavage(5) 6 (JRBest) *hld up: styd far side ent st: hdwy over 2f out: nvr trbld ldrs* **12/1** | 74 |
| 1210 | **4** | *¾* | **Party Ploy**[26] 4416 6-9-3 70.......................................... DarrenWilliams 7 (KRBurke) *trckd ldr: carried over to stands' side ent st: led that duo over 2f out: wknd fnl f* **4/1**[2] | 67+ |
| 3246 | **5** | *½* | **Pure Mischief (IRE)**[13] 4808 5-9-5 72........................... MFenton 5 (CRDore) *hld up: styd far side ent st: hdwy over 2f out: wknd over 1f out* **13/2** | 68 |
| 4362 | **6** | *nk* | **Magic Amigo**[16] 4711 3-9-0 75...................................... LDettori 8 (JRJenkins) *prom: styd far side ent st: chsd ldr over 3f out: rdn and wknd over 1f out* **9/2**[3] | 71 |
| 0-04 | **7** | *½* | **Kind Emperor**[18] 4655 7-9-3 62...................................... AMackay 10 (PLGilligan) *led: c stands' side ent st: hdd over 2f out: wknd over 1f out* **12/1** | 65 |
| 5550 | **8** | *7* | **Internationalguest (IRE)**[20] 4616 5-9-3 67...............(b) AMcCarthy 3 (GGMargarson) *hld up: styd far side ent s: rdn and wknd over 2f out* **11/1** | 53 |
| 522 | **9** | *22* | **Marsh Orchid**[21] 4573 3-9-0 75....................................... MTebbutt 1 (WJarvis) *chsd ldrs tl lft in ld far side wl over 4f out: sn hdd: wknd over 2f out* **6/1** | 21 |

2m 11.84s (3.87) **Going Correction** +0.425s/f (Yiel)
**WFA** 3 from 4yo+ 8lb **9** Ran SP% **119.4**
Speed ratings: **101,99,95,95,94 94,94,88,70**CSF £55.73 TOTE £17.40: £3.80, £2.00, £3.70; EX 76.40.
**Owner** A A Goodman **Bred** Lloyd Farm Stud **Trained** Newmarket, Suffolk

**FOCUS**
A fair handicap in which they went a decent pace and the form is ordinary but seems sound. The leading pair crossed over to the stands' side on entering the straight, although in Party Ploy's case it seemed unintentional.

**NOTEBOOK**
**Another Choice(IRE)** bounced back to form after some very modest efforts. Staying on the far side in the straight, although momentarily it looked like he would tack over, he came from off the pace to assert. He was suited by the strong gallop and soft ground.
**Opening Ceremony(USA)** was left in front of the main bulk of the field when the two leaders crossed to the stands' side in the straight. Headed going to the furlong pole, she only conceded defeat in the last 50 yards. She remains in good form.
**Recount(FR)**, 7lb higher, was last turning for home but stayed on steadily in the final quarter mile. He does most of his racing on fast ground.
**Party Ploy** was left with no option but to head for the stands' rail when the leader, who was just ahead of him, took that route at the entrance to the home straight. He got the better of a sustained tussle with that opponent but the far side eventually prevailed. He can be counted as somewhat unlucky.
**Pure Mischief(IRE)** has been running respectably since joining this yard but looks held off this mark.
**Magic Amigo** stayed with the main body of the field in the straight although it briefly seemed that Dettori was going to tack across. He is not getting any respite from the Handicapper.
**Kind Emperor**
**Marsh Orchid** *Official explanation: trainer said gelding was later found to be lame*

## 5159 DFDS H'CAP 1m 6f 17y

**5:15** (5:15) (E) (0-75,74) 3-Y-O+ **£4,605** (£1,417; £708; £354) **Stalls** High

| Form | | | | RPR |
|---|---|---|---|---|
| 0-55 | **1** | | **Patrixprial**[37] 4087 3-9-2 **70**.................................... PRobinson 2 (MHTompkins) *chsd ldrs: rdn to ld over 1f out: styd on wl* **12/1** | 81 |
| 0041 | **2** | *2 ½* | **Annakita**[34] 4202 4-7-12 **40**.......................................... LisaJones 10 (WJMusson) *hld up: hdwy over 3f out: styd on same pce ins fnl f* **10/1** | 47 |
| 0601 | **3** | *2 ½* | **Masterman Ready**[13] 4820 3-8-12 **66**.............................. MFenton 8 (PWHarris) *hld up: hdwy over 2f out: rdn over 1f out: styd on same pce* **7/1** | 70 |
| 2201 | **4** | *1* | **Levitator**[17] 4692 3-9-6 **74**............................................ LDettori 1 (SirMichaelStoute) *trckd ldrs: chal 3f out: sn rdn: wknd ins fnl f* **6/4**[1] | 77 |
| 4032 | **5** | *¾* | **Jolizero**[18] 4630 3-8-8 **62**............................................. AMcCarthy 3 (PWChapple-Hyam) *led: hung rt and bit slipped through mouth 8f out: rdn and hdd over 1f out: wknd ins fnl f* **7/2**[2] | 64 |
| 1263 | **6** | *¾* | **Winslow Boy (USA)**[17] 4692 3-8-5 **59**.............................. JQuinn 7 (CFWall) *hld up: hdwy over 3f out: rdn and ev ch over 1f out: wknd ins fnl f* **13/2**[3] | 60 |
| 0000 | **7** | *2 ½* | **Vanbrugh (FR)**[5] 5027 4-7-12 **40** oh3................................(vt) JMcAuley 9 (MissDAMchale) *dwlt: hld up: n.d* **40/1** | 38 |
| 40/0 | **8** | *18* | **Repent At Leisure**[13] 4819 4-7-13 **48**............................. MHalford(7) 5 (JulianPoulton) *trckd ldr: racd keenly: wknd over 2f out* **66/1** | 22 |
| 0606 | **9** | *shd* | **Salford Rocket**[10] 4883 4-7-9 **40** oh11............................. FPFerris(3) 6 (WJMusson) *plld hrd and prom: wknd over 2f out* **66/1** | 14 |
| -000 | **10** | *13* | **Muskatsturm (GER)**[43] 3947 5-9-10 **66**............................. SWKelly 4 (BJCurley) *prom over 10f* **16/1** | 23 |

3m 9.61s (4.41) **Going Correction** +0.425s/f (Yiel)
**WFA** 3 from 4yo+ 12lb **10** Ran SP% **116.1**
Speed ratings: **104,102,101,100,100 99,98,88,87,80**CSF £123.79 CT £907.49 TOTE £12.80: £3.50, £2.80, £2.30; EX 144.40 Place 6 £244.12, Place 5 £213.75.
**Owner** P H Betts **Bred** Belgrave Bloodstock Ltd **Trained** Newmarket, Suffolk

**FOCUS**
A moderate handicap run at a fair pace, but there were six with a chance going to the furlong pole. The form should prove reliable at this level.

**NOTEBOOK**
**Patrixprial ◆**, upped in trip for his handicap bow, scored readily in the end. Well suited by easy ground, he looks a young stayer on the upgrade and can score again this autumn. *Official explanation: trainer's representative said, regarding the improved form shown, colt had benefited from the step up in trip and soft ground*
**Annakita**, raised 3lb for her win at this track last month but still 6lb lower than at the start of the season, coped with the shorter trip and different ground but found one too good.
**Masterman Ready**, successful in a falsely-run race over course and distance, went up only 2lb for that and ran a sound race.
**Levitator** had trip and ground to suit, but he was ultimately found wanting from a 6lb higher mark.
**Jolizero** was tackling this trip for the first time. He was in front when the bit slipped right through his mouth at halfway, and it is to his and his rider's credit that he only gave best going to the final furlong. *Official explanation: jockey said bit came out of the horse's mouth on final bend*
**Winslow Boy(USA)**, 7lb better of with Levitator on Sandown running, ran a fair race on ground that does not really suit him.
**Vanbrugh(FR)** has never been placed in 15 tries on turf, but is capable of paying his way on Fibresand through the winter.
**Muskatsturm(GER)** *Official explanation: jockey said gelding made a noise; trainer said gelding had bled from the nose*

T/Plt: £353.40 to a £1 stake. Pool: £41,739.35. 86.20 winning tickets. T/Qpdt: £141.20 to a £1 stake. Pool: £2,099.00. 11.00 winning tickets. CR

5160 - 5161a (Foreign Racing) - See Raceform Interactive

# 4656 GOWRAN PARK (R-H)

Sunday, August 29

**OFFICIAL GOING: Good to soft**

## 5162a DENNY CORDELL LAVARACK MEMORIAL EUROPEAN BREEDERS FUND FILLIES STKS (LISTED RACE) 1m 1f 100y

**3:20** (3:20) 3-Y-O+ **£34,383** (£10,088; £4,806; £1,637)

| | | | RPR |
|---|---|---|---|
| **1** | | **Cache Creek (IRE)**[5] 5029 6-9-3 107........................ FMBerry 8 (PHughes, Ire) *mid-div: 7th and smooth hdwy early st: led over 1f out: r.o wl* **4/1**[1] | 96 |
| **2** | *1 ½* | **Queen Astrid (IRE)**[127] 1634 4-9-3 102............................ PShanahan 15 (DKWeld, Ire) *led: strly pressed st: hdd over 1f out: kpt on wl* **14/1** | 93 |
| **3** | *½* | **Kisses For Me (IRE)**[10] 4884 3-8-10 99...........................(t) JPSpencer 11 (APO'Brien, Ire) *trckd ldrs: racd wd: 3rd 1/2-way: 4th early st: kpt on fr 1 1/2f out* **10/1** | 92 |
| **4** | *1 ½* | **Treasure The Lady (IRE)**[42] 3969 3-8-10 96..................... MJKinane 13 (JohnMOxx, Ire) *settled 4th: 3rd and chal early st: no imp fr 1 1/2f out: kpt on same pce* **6/1**[2] | 89 |
| **5** | *shd* | **Leonor Fini (IRE)**[27] 4406 3-8-10 97............................ DPMcDonogh 10 (KevinPrendergast, Ire) *trckd ldrs in 5th: rn wd and lost pl ent st: 6th 1f out: kpt on* **10/1** | 89 |
| **6** | *hd* | **Mount Grace (IRE)**[13] 4823 3-8-10 74.....................(b[1]) CO'Donoghue 12 (JosephCrowley, Ire) *cl up in 2nd: rdn to chal st: no ex ins fnl f* **25/1** | 89 |
| **7** | *½* | **Sudden Silence (IRE)**[10] 4893 3-8-10 90.......................(p) MCHussey 4 (DeclanGillespie, Ire) *towards rr: kpt on fr 2f out* **20/1** | 88 |
| **8** | *½* | **Miss Childrey (IRE)**[78] 2903 3-8-10 104.......................... DMGrant 2 (FrancisEnnis, Ire) *s.i.s and hld up towards rr: kpt on on inner fr 1 1/2f out* **14/1** | 87 |
| **9** | *nk* | **Amourallis (IRE)**[10] 4893 3-8-10 96............................... PCosgrave 16 (GMLyons, Ire) *s.i.s and hld up: kpt on one pce st: no imp whn checked ins fnl f* **8/1** | 87 |
| **10** | *nk* | **Misty Heights**[57] 3-9-1 105........................................... PJSmullen 5 (DKWeld, Ire) *mid-div: 7th 1/2-way: one pce st* **6/1**[2] | 91 |
| **11** | *¾* | **Livadiya (IRE)**[33] 4222 8-9-8 105.................................. JAHeffernan 3 (HRogers, Ire) *hld up in rr: effrt and no imp st* **7/1**[3] | 90 |
| **12** | *nk* | **Sand N Sea (IRE)**[5] 5029 3-8-10 90................................ RMBurke 14 (THogan, Ire) *chsd ldrs in mid-div: wknd st* **20/1** | 84 |
| **13** | *½* | **Blue Oasis (IRE)**[64] 3311 3-8-10....................................... DJCondon 7 (RGuest) *hld up: effrt early st: no ex fr 1 1/2f out* **10/1** | 83 |
| **14** | *1* | **Humilis (IRE)**[154] 1156 4-9-3 94...................................... NGMcCullagh 9 (DKWeld, Ire) *rr of mid-div: wknd st* **20/1** | 81 |
| **15** | *¾* | **Beautifulballerina (USA)**[71] 3114 4-9-3 81........................ KJManning 1 (JSBolger, Ire) *a bhd* **20/1** | 80 |
| **16** | *4 ½* | **Blue Reema (IRE)**[42] 3969 4-9-3 96...............................(tp) TPO'Shea 6 (MHalford, Ire) *mid-div: rdn 1/2-way: wknd st: eased over 1f out* **16/1** | 72 |

2m 5.30s
**WFA** 3 from 4yo+ 7lb **16** Ran SP% **141.6**
Speed ratings: CSF £68.18 TOTE £4.60: £1.50, £3.10, £2.90, £2.20; DF 123.20.
**Owner** Sean Hughes **Bred** W Lazy T Ranch **Trained** Bagenalstown, Co Carlow

**NOTEBOOK**
**Cache Creek(IRE)** has been the model of consistency but has aborted her foal. She found the mile last time too short for her and there is a ten-furlong Group Two opportunity for her now in the Blandford Stakes at the Curragh on September 19th.
**Queen Astrid(IRE)**, absent since April, tried to make all but the winner was too strong throughout the last furlong.
**Kisses For Me(IRE)** showed her York form to be all wrong and will get a turn soon.
**Treasure The Lady(IRE)** could only keep on at the one pace.
**Leonor Fini(IRE)** ran to her mark.
**Amourallis(IRE)** had no luck at all in running but this class is just above her capabilities.
**Misty Heights** might not have recovered from her American exertions.
**Livadiya(IRE)** appears to have lost the plot at the moment.
**Blue Oasis(IRE)** ran well enough until halfway up the straight when unable to raise her effort.
**Blue Reema(IRE)** *Official explanation: trainer said filly inhaled kickback during the race*

5163 - 5167a (Foreign Racing) - See Raceform Interactive

# 2508 BADEN-BADEN (L-H)

Sunday, August 29

**OFFICIAL GOING: Good**

## 5168a FURSTENBERG-RENNEN (GROUP 3) 1m 2f

**3:25** (3:43) 3-Y-O **£26,761** (£10,563; £5,634; £3,169)

| | | | RPR |
|---|---|---|---|
| **1** | | **Lyonels Glory**[33] 4215 3-8-9 ............................................ ASuborics 4 (USuter, Germany) *held up, 7th straight, headway 2f out, ridden to lead 1f out, driven out* | 108 |
| **2** | *½* | **Saldentigerin (GER)**[56] 3565 3-8-8 ow1............................. WMongil 1 (PSchiergen, Germany) *sn trckng ldrs, led ent str (2 1/2f out), hung rt fr wl over 1f out, hdd 1f out, ran on under pressure* 1 | 106 |
| **3** | *2 ½* | **Quilanga (GER)**[26] 4430 3-8-9 .......................................... EPedroza 6 (AWohler, Germany) *always in touch, 3rd straight, every chance 1f out, carried right & slightly hampered inside final f, kept on* 2 | 103 |
| **4** | *½* | **Sweet Wake (GER)**[56] 3565 3-8-11 ...................................... AStarke 3 (MarioHofer, Germany) *mid-division, 6th straight, kept on under pressure to take 4th close home* 3 | 104 |
| **5** | *2* | **Salonhonor (GER)**[56] 3565 3-8-11 ....................................... JPalik 8 (AndreasLowe, Germany) *sn led, hdd ent str, rdn & ev ch wl over 1f out, n.m.r appr fnl f, kpt on one pace* | 100 |
| **6** | *8* | **Golden Millenium (GER)**[56] 3565 3-8-9 ............................. NRichter 7 (THHansen, Germany) *prominent, 5th on inside straight, one pace final 2f* | 84 |
| **7** | *¾* | **Oublies Ca (FR)**[28] 4384 3-8-11 .......................................(b) FilipMinarik 2 (WHefter, Germany) *always towards rear* | 85 |



The Form Book, Raceform Ltd, Compton, RG20 6NL

**8** 1 1/4 **Genios (GER)**[90] 2541 3-8-11 ................................ LHammer-Hansen 9 83
(DrABolte, Germany) *started slowly, always behind*
**9** 6 **Art Affair (GER)** 3-8-5 ................................ J-PCarvalho 10 66
(WHimmel, Germany) *always behind*
**10** 2 1/2 **Brahy (USA)** 3-8-9 ................................ ZVarga 5 66
(AFriebert, Hungary) *4th on outside straight, soon weakened*

2m 6.25s **10** Ran SP% **132.1**
Speed ratings: .
**Owner** Mrs R J Jacobs **Bred** Gestut Fahrhof **Trained** Germany

## 5102 DEAUVILLE (R-H)

Sunday, August 29

**OFFICIAL GOING: Heavy**

### 5169a PRIX QUINCEY FOUQUET'S BARRIERE (GROUP 3) (STRAIGHT COURSE) 1m

**2:15** (2:22) 3-Y-0+ **£25,704** (£10,282; £7,711; £5,141)

RPR
**1** **Autumn Glory (IRE)**[17] 4685 4-9-0 ................................ SDrowne 7 111
(GWragg) *pressed leader on outside til led well over 1f out, hard ridden approaching final f, driven out*
**2** snk **Keltos (FR)**[38] 6-9-0 ................................ MBlancpain 9 111
(CLaffon-Parias, France) *a in tch on outside, clsd up wl over 1f out, hard rdn & ev ch wl ins fnl f, unable to qckn cl home* 3
**3** 3/4 **Mister Sacha (FR)**[84] 2721 3-9-1 ................................ IMendizabal 10 116
(J-CRouget, France) *tracked leader on outside, challenged over 1f out, every chance inside final f, no extra last 100yds* 2
**4** 4 **Open Offer**[68] 4-8-10 ................................ TThulliez 4 97
(MmeCBoqueho-Vergne, France) *tracked leaders til one pace from over 1f out*
**5** 3/4 **Ryono (USA)**[49] 3791 5-9-6 ................................ TCastanheira 11 106
(PLautner, Germany) *mid-division on outside, never near to challenge* 1
**6** 1 **Joursanvault (FR)**[49] 3791 3-8-10 ................................ CSoumillon 3 100
(ADeRoyer-Dupre, France) *led to well over 1f out, one pace*
**7** 1/2 **Almond Mousse (FR)**[21] 4594 5-8-13 ................................ C-PLemaire 5 96
(RobertCollet, France) *mid-division, beaten approaching final f*
**8** 2 1/2 **Ershaad (USA)**[31] 4284 3-8-10 ................................ TGillet 6 94
(JEHammond, France) *held up in rear, effort 2f out, soon beaten*
**9** shd **Grandes Illusions (FR)**[105] 2160 3-8-5 ................................ DBoeuf 8 89
(DSmaga, France) *always in rear*
**10** 3 **Matin De Tempete (FR)**[21] 4594 4-8-10 ................................ TJarnet 2 82
(SMorineau, France) *tracked leader on rails til weakened well over 1f out*
**11** **Tiganello (GER)**[19] 4623 3-8-8 ................................ OPeslier 1 86
(FHead, France) *in touch on rails til weakened 2f out*

1m 43.2s **Going Correction** +0.325s/f (Good)
**WFA** 3 from 4yo+ 6lb **11** Ran SP% **123.3**
Speed ratings: **113,112,112,108,107 106,105,103,103,100 100**.
**Owner** Mollers Racing **Bred** Margaret Conlon **Trained** Newmarket, Suffolk

**NOTEBOOK**
**Autumn Glory(IRE)** acted well on the testing ground. Quickly into his stride, he took the advantage one out and then fended off all challenges in the gamest manner. He will now race only on soft ground, and could come back to France for the Prix du Rond-Point during the Arc weekend. He appears to be improving with age.
**Keltos(FR)** this was a terrific effort from this ex-Group One winner, who was put back in training after failing at stud. Held up early on, he came with a well-timed late challenge but could not quite peg back the winner. He looks sure to win a Group race before the end of the season.
**Mister Sacha(FR)**, off the track for nearly three months and giving weight to older horses in front of him, this was a fine effort. Never far from the leaders, he looked dangerous one out but his stride just shortened in the closing stages. He will strip much fitter next time and could also go for the Rond-Point.
**Open Offer** was always thereabouts but never looked like catching the first three inside the final furlong. He stayed on like a horse who might need a longer trip.

### 5170a GRAND PRIX DE DEAUVILLE LUCIEN BARRIERE (GROUP 2) 1m 4f 110y

**2:45** (2:51) 3-Y-0+ **£52,183** (£20,141; £9,613; £6,408)

RPR
**1** **Cherry Mix (FR)**[36] 3-8-8 ow2................................ TGillet 7 118+
(AFabre, France) *held up in rear, 6th straight, good headway 2f out, led 1f out, pushed clear, ran on strongly*
**2** 4 **Martaline**[26] 4431 5-9-3 ................................ GaryStevens 5 110
(AFabre, France) *led to 2f out, every chance over 1f out, one pace* 2
**3** shd **Bailador (IRE)**[39] 4039 4-9-3 ................................ CSoumillon 2 110
(AFabre, France) *held up in rear, last 2 1/2f out, slipped through on inside & 3rd straight, led 2f out to 1f out, one pace* 3
**4** 3 **Swing Wing**[12] 4832 5-9-3 ................................ SDrowne 4 106
(PFICole) *tracked leader on inside, 2nd straight, every chance 2f out, soon beaten*
**5** 2 1/2 **Kindjhal (FR)**[26] 4431 4-9-3 ................................ SPasquier 3 103
(ELellouche, France) *tracked leader, 4th straight, ridden 2f out, never able to challenge*
**6** 6 **Fair Mix (IRE)**[77] 2924 6-9-3 ................................ OPeslier 1 94
(MRolland, France) *held up in touch, 5th straight, ridden & beaten 2f out* 1
**7** 3 **Franklins Gardens**[22] 4539 4-9-3 ................................ DBoeuf 6 90
(MHTompkins) *pressed leader on outside til weakening well over 2f out, last & beaten straight*

2m 55.1s **Going Correction** +1.00s/f (Soft)
**WFA** 3 from 4yo+ 10lb **7** Ran SP% **115.6**
Speed ratings: **113,110,110,108,107 103,101**.
**Owner** Lagardere Family **Bred** Snc Lagardere Elevage **Trained** France

**NOTEBOOK**
**Cherry Mix(FR)** settled towards the tail of the field in the early stages and was always moving well within himself. He made a forward move early in the straight and then totally outclassed the field. This was an impressive performance by an individual who thrived on the ground. If it prevails at Longchamp in October he may well be in at the kill at the end of the Arc de Triomphe.
**Martaline** tried to make all the running. He could not quicken like the winner, but hung on bravely to take second place. The jockey felt that he was unsuited by the sticky ground. He is also engaged in the Arc and the long-distance Prix du Cadran on the same day.
**Bailador(IRE)** was last for the first part of this race, then began to make progress up the far rail in the straight. He looked sure to take second place but was run out of it in the final few strides. He possibly did not quite get home on the testing surface.
**Swing Wing** ran his usual game race. Always close to the leader, he came under pressure early in the straight and then stayed on at the same pace. He was racing over a distance short of his best, but still put up a respectable performance.
**Franklins Gardens** was settled behind the leaders until the straight where he dropped completely out of contention to finish a remote last.

### 5171a PRIX DE MEAUTRY ROYAL BARRIERE (GROUP 3) 6f

**3:20** (3:21) 3-Y-0+ **£25,704** (£10,282; £7,711; £5,141)

RPR
**1** **Star Valley (FR)**[38] 4-9-0 ................................ IMendizabal 7 114
(J-CRouget, France) *held up towards rear, switched to rails well over 1f out, driven to lead 120yds out, ran on well* 2
**2** 2 **Swedish Shave (FR)**[29] 4357 6-9-0 ................................ TJarnet 6 108
(RGibson, France) *always close up, led just inside final f to 120yds out, no extra* 3
**3** 2 1/2 **Striking Ambition**[155] 1126 4-9-0 ................................ SDrowne 2 101
(RCharlton) *led to 2f out, led again briefly approaching final f to just inside, one pace*
**4** 3/4 **Puppeteer**[77] 2923 4-9-5 ................................ CSoumillon 1 103
(ADeRoyer-Dupre, France) *raced in rear, headway on outside well over 1f out, stayed on to take 4th well inside final f* 1
**5** hd **Blanche (FR)**[29] 4357 5-8-11 ................................ DBonilla 4 95
(JRossi, France) *in rear til closing up on outside 2f out, one pace from approaching final f lost 4th close home*
**6** 4 **Rum Shot**[15] 4745 3-8-11 ................................ DaneO'Neill 8 86
(HCandy) *slowly into stride, soon recovered to press leaders on outside, led 2f out to approaching final f, soon weakened*
**7** 1/2 **The Kiddykid (IRE)**[21] 4590 4-9-5 ................................ GaryStevens 9 89
(PDEvans) *with leaders 4f, soon weakened*
**8** 3/4 **Night Chapter**[26] 3-8-11 ................................ OPeslier 3 82
(MmeCHead-Maarek, France) *always outpaced*
**9** 3 **Together (FR)**[29] 4357 4-8-11 ................................(b) DSicaud 5 70
(MmeCBoqueho-Vergne, France) *always outpaced*
**10** 5 **Nights Cross (IRE)**[11] 4862 3-8-11 ................................(v) TThulliez 10 58
(MRChannon) *with leaders til weakened quickly well over 1f out, eased*

1m 13.0s **Going Correction** +0.325s/f (Good)
**WFA** 3 from 4yo+ 3lb **10** Ran SP% **123.0**
Speed ratings: **113,110,107,106,105 100,99,98,94,88**.
**Owner** A Caro **Bred** R Huggins **Trained** France

**NOTEBOOK**
**Star Valley(FR)** settled well on this occasion and finally won with plenty in hand. He arrived late on the scene and took the lead inside the final furlong before dominating the final 100 yards. The experiment to bring him back in distance paid off, and connections will now be looking at the Prix de la Foret as a long-term target.
**Swedish Shave(FR)** ran his usual sound race and greatly appreciated the distance and the testing ground. Fifth early on, he took over the lead for a short time before being passed by the winner. No doubt he will now go for the Prix de Seine-et-Oise at Maisons-Laffitte.
**Striking Ambition** ran a terrific race considering he had been off the track for five months. He was always up with the pace and took the lead at the halfway stage. He stayed there until the furlong marker and this effort augers well for the future, as this outing will have put him spot on for his next race which will also be on soft ground.
**Puppeteer** was towards the tail of the field early on. He made some late progress up the centre of the track and was putting in his best work at the finish. This trip was probably a little on the sharp side for him.
**Rum Shot** quickly recovered from a slow start, and was one of the leaders for the first four furlongs before dropping away as the race warmed up.
**The Kiddykid(IRE)**, always in the leading group, he was under pressure two and a half out and was not given a hard time by his jockey. He reported the horse was totally unsuited by the state of the ground.
**Nights Cross(IRE)**, well placed early on, he was a spent force two out and finished a remote last.

## 4866 CHEPSTOW (L-H)

Monday, August 30

**OFFICIAL GOING: Soft**

### 5172 EUROPEAN BREEDERS FUND MAIDEN FILLIES' STKS 1m 14y

**2:25** (2:25) (D) 2-Y-0 **£3,571** (£1,099; £549; £274) **Stalls** High

Form RPR
00 **1** **Alpine Gold (IRE)**[16] 4753 2-8-11 ................................ IMongan 3 72
(JLDunlop) *trckd ldrs: wnt 2nd ins fnl 2f: led jst ins last: pushed out: comf* **7/1**
3446 **2** 2 **Madam Caversfield**[25] 4468 2-8-11 71................................ RSmith 11 68
(RHannon) *slt ld tl hdd over 4f out: led again over 2f out: rdn and hdd jst ins last: kpt on same pce* **7/1**
06 **3** 1 1/2 **You Found Me**[66] 3259 2-8-11 ................................ DKinsella 9 65
(CTinkler) *rr but in tch: pushed along and hung lft fr 3f out: hdwy 2f out: styd on to take 3rd ins fnl f: nt pce to rch ldrs* **20/1**
06 **4** 1 **Big Hoo Hah**[17] 4705 2-8-11 ................................ DSweeney 5 63
(CACyzer) *pressed ldrs: rdn over 2f out: outpcd over 1f out: no ex and lost 3rd ins last* **25/1**
0 **5** 7 **Moonmaiden**[16] 4753 2-8-11 ................................ TEDurcan 6 49
(MRChannon) *sn in tch: pushed along and outpcd 3f out: n.d after* **4/1**[3]
**6** 3/4 **Fine Lady** 2-8-11 ................................ DHolland 10 48
(MJohnston) *w ldr tl led over 4f out: hdd over 2f out: wknd ins fnl 2f* **7/2**[2]
003 **7** 6 **Resistance Heroine**[23] 4560 2-8-11 78................................ JFEgan 8 36
(EALDunlop) *chsd ldrs: rdn 3f out: sn wknd* **11/4**[1]
00 **8** 1/2 **Garance**[30] 4344 2-8-11 ................................ PDobbs 1 35
(RHannon) *pressed ldrs: rdn 4f out: wknd fr 3f out* **14/1**
05 **9** 20 **Dizzy Lizzy**[52] 3696 2-8-11 ................................ JMackay 7 —
(NickWilliams) *s.i.s: a outpcd* **25/1**
000 **10** dist **Sarah Brown (IRE)**[10] 4913 2-8-8 ................................(p) FPFerris[(3)] 2 —
(IAWood) *early spd: bhd fnl 5f: t.o* **50/1**
**11** dist **Silver Dreamer (IRE)** 2-8-8 ................................ ABeech[(3)] 4 —
(HSHowe) *veered bdly lft s and a wl bhd: t.o* **33/1**

1m 41.11s (5.21) **Going Correction** +0.55s/f (Yiel) **11** Ran SP% **117.9**
Speed ratings: **95,93,91,90,83 82,76,76,56,— —**CSF £51.54 TOTE £7.40: £2.50, £3.00, £5.60; EX 49.90.
**Owner** Windflower Overseas Holdings Inc **Bred** Windflower Overseas Holdings Inc **Trained** Arundel, W Sussex

**FOCUS**
Not a strong maiden and ordinary form.

**NOTEBOOK**

**Alpine Gold(IRE)**, who was switched to the outside after three furlongs, was well on top inside the last. She got the mile well and will stay middle distances next term.

**Madam Caversfield**, tackling a mile for the first time, had the advantage of the stands' rail to race against but, after a decent tussle, was second best inside the final furlong. She has had plenty of chances and, officially rated 71, is a decent yardstick.

**You Found Me**, returning from a break, was encountering soft ground for the first time. Doing good late work on this first run at a mile, she looks a likely type for nurseries.

**Big Hoo Hah** was outpaced by the first two when the race hotted up. She is now eligible for nurseries.

**Moonmaiden**, who finished further behind Alpine Gold than she had at Newmarket, was keen in the early stages on this first try at a mile.

**Fine Lady**, a half-sister to three winners including Gypsy Passion, showed up well for a long way and should be capable of a bit better next time.

**Resistance Heroine** was held when her rider took a look down at her over a furlong out. *Official explanation: jockey said filly lost her action*

**Silver Dreamer(IRE)** *Official explanation: jockey said filly hung left throughout*

## 5173 EUROPEAN BREEDERS FUND MAIDEN STKS (C&G) 1m 14y

**2:55** (2:55) (D) 2-Y-O **£3,542** (£1,090; £545; £272) **Stalls** High

Form RPR

4 **1** **Torrens (IRE)**$^{10}$ [4922] 2-8-11 DHolland 5 74
(MJohnston) *front rnk: pressed ldr fr 5f out: drvn to ld over 2f out:rdn and styd on u.p whn chal thrght fnl f* **4/6**$^{1}$

000 **2** ½ **Inchcape Rock**$^{11}$ [4866] 2-8-11 DKinsella 6 73
(LGCottrell) *sn led: narrowly hdd over 2f out: styd pressing wnr and str chal thrght fnl f tl no ex nr fin* **66/1**

5 **3** 1½ **Maktu**$^{22}$ [4579] 2-8-6 NDeSouza$^{(5)}$ 4 70
(PFICole) *bhd: rdn hung lft and no rspnse 3f out: edgd lft again 2f out: hdwy over 1f out: r.o strly ins last: gng on nr fin* **16/1**

00 **4** 2½ **Asaateel (IRE)**$^{18}$ [4689] 2-8-11 IMongan 1 65
(JLDunlop) *stdd s: t.k.h and sn in tch: hdwy fr 2f out: rdn to press ldrs over 1f out: no imp: wknd ins last* **8/1**$^{3}$

62 **5** 5 **Just Do It (UAE)**$^{10}$ [4913] 2-8-11 TEDurcan 8 55
(MRChannon) *chsd ldrs: rdn and hung lft over 2f out: sn btn* **7/2**$^{2}$

00 **6** 3 **Golden Dynasty**$^{16}$ [4747] 2-8-11 PDobbs 7 49
(RHannon) *chsd ldrs: rdn 3f out: wknd qckly over 2f out* **33/1**

00 **7** 2 **Scale The Heights (IRE)**$^{53}$ [3679] 2-8-11 JMackay 3 45
(BWHills) *sn drvn along: a bhd* **16/1**

0566 **8** 22 **Merrymadcap (IRE)**$^{25}$ [4480] 2-8-11 JFEgan 2 1
(MBlanshard) *pressed ldrs tl wknd qckly over 3f out* **20/1**

**9** 7 **Mount Arafat** 2-8-11 DSweeney 9 —
(MSalaman) *a in rr: lost tch fnl 3f* **40/1**

1m 41.82s (5.92) **Going Correction** +0.55s/f (Yiel) **9** Ran SP% **116.7**

Speed ratings: **92,91,90,87,82 79,77,55,48**CSF £83.73 TOTE £1.70: £1.10, £10.50, £2.40; EX 91.00.

**Owner** Sheikh Mohammed **Bred** Dermot Cantillon And Forenaghts Stud **Trained** Middleham Moor, N Yorks

**FOCUS**

A weak maiden, run in a time fractionally slower than the fillies' equivalent half an hour earlier. The presence of the second and third make the form misleading.

**NOTEBOOK**

**Torrens(IRE)** made hard work of what on paper looked a straightforward task, but stuck his neck out bravely to score and should improve on faster ground.

**Inchcape Rock** had failed to get away on terms in three previous tries. Soon in front against the stands' rail, he rallied when headed by the favourite and lost nothing in defeat. This was a big improvement on his previous runs.

**Maktu**, keen in rear, showed a tendency to go out to his left but was finishing nicely. Obviously not an easy ride, he still needs experience.

**Asaateel(IRE)** has ability but nothing like enough to warrant his Royal Lodge and Derby entries. He could need a flatter track.

**Just Do It(UAE)**, who carried Sheikh Mohammed's first colours, was well placed against the rail, but hung to his left when the pressure was on. The ground and the undulating track seemed against him. *Official explanation: jockey said colt was unsuited by the soft ground*

**Golden Dynasty** is not getting home in his races.

**Merrymadcap(IRE)** *Official explanation: jockey said colt was unsuited by the trip*

## 5174 ETHEL GOLD MEMORIAL SPONSORED BY PICKWICKS NURSERY STKS (H'CAP) 5f 16y

**3:30** (3:30) (D) 2-Y-O **£4,803** (£1,478; £739; £369) **Stalls** High

Form RPR

4032 **1** **Our Fugitive (IRE)**$^{25}$ [4474] 2-9-0 **75** DHolland 5 86+
(AWCarroll) *led tl narrowly hdd jst ins fnl 2f: pushed along to ld again jst ins last: kpt on wl* **11/4**$^{1}$

1345 **2** 1¾ **Princely Vale (IRE)**$^{18}$ [4676] 2-8-1 **69** (p) CHaddon$^{(7)}$ 1 70
(WGMTurner) *sn rdn to chse ldrs: wnt 2nd 3f out: drvn to ld jst ins fnl 2f: hdd jst ins last: sn outpcd* **9/1**

2003 **3** 1¾ **Bibury Flyer**$^{3}$ [5078] 2-9-0 **82** BO'Neill$^{(7)}$ 3 78
(MRChannon) *outpcd in rr: hdwy fr 2f out: edgd rt and styd on ins last: nt trble ldrs* **7/2**$^{2}$

2230 **4** 2 **I'm Aimee**$^{11}$ [4875] 2-8-12 **76** FPFerris$^{(3)}$ 2 66
(PDEvans) *chsd wnr 2f: wknd fr 2f out: no ch whn crossed and swtchd lft ins last* **4/1**$^{3}$

003 **5** 4 **Molly Dancer**$^{14}$ [4797] 2-8-10 **71** TEDurcan 4 49
(MRChannon) *chsd ldrs: rdn and hung lft over 2f out: sn btn* **7/1**

1604 **6** 5 **Earl Of Links (IRE)**$^{10}$ [4909] 2-8-10 **71** PDobbs 6 34
(RHannon) *rdn over 3f out: sn bhd* **4/1**$^{3}$

63.02 secs (3.52) **Going Correction** +0.55s/f (Yiel) **6** Ran SP% **111.4**

Speed ratings: **93,90,87,84,77 69**CSF £26.50 TOTE £3.20: £2.30, £4.20; EX 32.90.

**Owner** Serafino Agodino **Bred** Dr Paschal Carmody **Trained** Wixford, Warwicks

**FOCUS**

An ordinary nursery which quickly became a two-horse race. The winner is likely to prove better than the bare form.

**NOTEBOOK**

**Our Fugitive(IRE)** was just headed by the eventual runner-up passing the two pole, but Holland had kept something up his sleeve. Speedy, but maybe not straightforward, he is more at home on faster ground.

**Princely Vale(IRE)**, who has been held in nurseries since winning two sellers and a claimer in June, was having his first run over the minimum trip since his debut in April. Racing on the outside of the field from his low draw, he gave the favourite a race but was second best in the final furlong.

**Bibury Flyer**, making a quick reappearance, ran a respectable race, but she is hard to win with and might need a return to six furlongs.

**I'm Aimee** was held when the third went across her inside the final furlong. She looks high enough in the weights and will remain vulnerable.

**Molly Dancer**, the Channon second string, was tackling soft ground for the first time. It was also her first run over the minimum trip and she found it too sharp.

**Earl Of Links(IRE)** is not going the right way.

## 5175 RACECOURSE GARAGE HONDA H'CAP 1m 2f 36y

**4:05** (4:07) (F) (0-55,58) 3-Y-O+ **£3,507** (£1,002; £501) **Stalls** Low

Form RPR

6021 **1** **Mcqueen (IRE)**$^{3}$ [5080] 4-10-1 **58** 6ex JFEgan 5 75+
(MrsHDalton) *mde all: shkn up whn chal over 3f out: pushed clr over 2f out: readily* **11/4**$^{1}$

5341 **2** 5 **Bojangles (IRE)**$^{17}$ [4713] 5-9-7 **53** DNolan$^{(3)}$ 13 61
(RBrotherton) *chsd ldrs: rdn 3f out: styd on to chse wnr ins fnl 2f: no ch but kpt on wl for 2nd* **7/2**$^{2}$

6000 **3** 2 **Cotton Easter**$^{12}$ [4853] 3-8-5 **49** TBlock$^{(7)}$ 3 54
(MrsAJBowlby) *bhd: hdwy on outside fr 2f out: r.o wl fnl f but nt trble ldrs* **33/1**

0400 **4** ¾ **Ribbons And Bows (IRE)**$^{21}$ [4603] 4-9-8 **51** DSweeney 9 58+
(CACyzer) *bhd: hdwy fr 3f out: styd on fr over 1f out but nvr gng pce to be dangerous* **33/1**

01-0 **5** 5 **Denise Best (IRE)**$^{53}$ [3682] 6-9-7 **50** (p) IMongan 15 45
(MissKMGeorge) *chsd ldrs: rdn to chal 3f out: outpcd 2f out: wknd fnl f* **25/1**

1432 **6** 3 **Go Green**$^{6}$ [5021] 3-9-0 **54** (t) FPFerris$^{(3)}$ 10 44
(PDEvans) *in tch: rdn over 3f out: sn btn* **4/1**$^{3}$

0005 **7** shd **Lord Lahar**$^{19}$ [4624] 5-9-2 **45** TEDurcan 11 35
(MRChannon) *pushed along 4f out: nt pce to get out of mid-div* **20/1**

0040 **8** ½ **Zalkani (IRE)**$^{9}$ [4940] 4-8-9 **45** AHindley$^{(7)}$ 7 34
(BGPowell) *bhd: gd hdwy on outside over 4f out: chsd ldrs and rdn 3f out: wknd over 2f out* **33/1**

0-24 **9** 3 **Black Legend (IRE)**$^{11}$ [4883] 5-9-2 **45** (t) JMackay 2 29
(RLee) *bhd: hdwy over 4f out: rdn to chse ldrs over 3f out: wknd qckly over 2f out* **10/1**

2224 **10** 5 **Midshipman**$^{38}$ [4096] 6-9-12 **55** (vt) DHolland 16 31
(AWCarroll) *sn chsng wnr: rdn to chal over 3f out: sn no ch: lost 2nd ins fnl 2f: wknd rapidly over 1f out* **6/1**

0-00 **11** 5 **Another Deal (FR)**$^{11}$ [4871] 5-9-12 **55** DKinsella 4 22
(RJHodges) *chsd ldrs tl wknd qckly 3f out* **14/1**

2040 **12** 7 **Bevier**$^{117}$ [1888] 10-8-11 **40** RSmith 8 —
(TWall) *chsd ldrs over 6f* **25/1**

00-0 **13** ½ **Mark Your Way**$^{19}$ [4641] 4-9-2 **52** CHaddon$^{(7)}$ 6 6
(PRChamings) *a in rr* **33/1**

5500 **14** 3 **Midnight Mambo (USA)**$^{14}$ [4818] 4-8-11 **40** PDobbs 1 —
(RGuest) *a in rr* **50/1**

-620 **15** 8 **Blue Quiver (IRE)**$^{88}$ [2614] 4-9-11 **54** GBaker 14 —
(CAHorgan) *t.k.h: in tch: rdn: hung lft and wknd 3f out* **25/1**

2m 16.29s (6.69) **Going Correction** +0.55s/f (Yiel)

**WFA** 3 from 4yo+ 8lb **15** Ran SP% **129.0**

Speed ratings: **95,91,89,88,84 82,82,81,79,75 71,65,65,63,56**CSF £11.42 CT £282.27 TOTE £4.10: £1.60, £2.20, £7.20; EX 15.50.

**Owner** R Edwards And W J Swinnerton **Bred** Philip Newton **Trained** Shifnal, Shropshire

**FOCUS**

A fairly weak handicap in which the winner set a moderate gallop and few got into it from off the pace. The time was modest for the grade, but the winner is in cracking form and may prove hard to beat at this sort of level.

**NOTEBOOK**

**Mcqueen(IRE)** followed up his Goodwood win under a penalty. Stretching clear to score comfortably after dictating the pace, he loves soft ground and will remain well handicapped compared with his All-Weather rating. His yard appears to have turned the corner.

**Bojangles(IRE)** looked likely to drop away when coming under pressure but stayed on quite strongly. He went up 4lb after Newbury but is still well treated on his old form.

**Cotton Easter**, who has started at 33/1 or bigger every time, stayed on late in the day to record her first placed effort. This was the softest ground she has encountered and she appears to be improving.

**Ribbons And Bows(IRE)** stayed on all too late over this shorter trip. She started the season on a 29lb higher mark.

**Denise Best(IRE)**, in re-applied cheekpieces, ran a better race than on her reappearance.

**Go Green** has been found wanting from this mark, albeit narrowly on one occasion, since winning over course and distance earlier in the month.

**Another Deal(FR)** *Official explanation: jockey said gelding had hung right*

**Blue Quiver(IRE)** *Official explanation: jockey said colt was unsuited by the soft ground*

## 5176 HAYES ELECTRICAL CONTRACTORS H'CAP 1m 14y

**4:40** (4:40) (E) (0-70,70) 3-Y-O+ **£4,052** (£1,247; £623; £311) **Stalls** High

Form RPR

6040 **1** **Smoothly Does It**$^{14}$ [4802] 3-9-0 **62** JFEgan 12 73
(MrsAJBowlby) *hld up in tch: hdwy 1/2-way: rdn to 1f out: kpt on strly cl home* **8/1**

0463 **2** 1¾ **Johannian**$^{6}$ [5017] 6-9-13 **69** RSmith 3 77
(JMBradley) *hld up in rr: stdy hdwy fr 3f out: rdn to chse ldrs over 1f out: styd on to take 2nd cl home but no imp on wnr* **11/1**

4144 **3** nk **Fen Gypsy**$^{12}$ [4846] 6-9-11 **70** DNolan$^{(3)}$ 14 77
(PDEvans) *w ldr tl led 5f out: rdn over 2f out: hdd 1f out: outpcd ins last and lost 2nd cl home* **11/2**$^{2}$

0502 **4** 3 **Elidore**$^{11}$ [4871] 4-9-10 **69** FPFerris$^{(3)}$ 15 70
(BPalling) *led 3f: styd pressing ldrs: rdn over 2f out: styd on same pce fr over 1f out* **9/2**$^{1}$

0505 **5** ½ **Mamore Gap (IRE)**$^{7}$ [5006] 6-9-11 **67** PDobbs 4 67
(RHannon) *bhd: pushed along over 2f out: styd on fr over 1f out and kpt on ins last: nvr gng pce to rch ldrs* **25/1**

1600 **6** nk **Chandelier**$^{18}$ [4672] 4-8-7 **49** TEDurcan 2 48
(MSSaunders) *s.i.s: bhd: pushed along 3f out: kpt on fr over 1f out but nvr gng pce to rch ldrs* **20/1**

004- **7** 3½ **Bathwick Bruce (IRE)**$^{308}$ [5796] 6-9-9 **65** GBaker 1 57
(BRMillman) *pressed ldrs over 4f: wknd over 1f out* **16/1**

4031 **8** 1¼ **Lucefer (IRE)**$^{6}$ [5017] 6-8-2 **51** 6ex DeanWilliams$^{(7)}$ 8 41
(GCHChung) *in tch: rdn and effrt 3f out: nvr gng pce to trble ldrs and wknd over 1f out* **6/1**$^{3}$

064 **9** 1 **Dual Purpose (IRE)**$^{11}$ [4869] 9-9-3 **59** DKinsella 7 47
(CRoberts) *chsd ldrs: rdn 3f out: wknd ins fnl 2f* **14/1**

-600 **10** 2½ **How's Things**$^{17}$ [4719] 4-8-12 **57** ABeech$^{(3)}$ 10 40
(DHaydnJones) *sn chsng ldrs: rdn over 3f out: wknd qckly 2f out* **25/1**

0000 **11** 3½ **Dusty Carpet**$^{19}$ [4641] 6-8-13 **55** IMongan 11 31
(MJWeeden) *chsd ldrs: rdn 3f out: sn btn* **25/1**

060 **12** 1½ **Richie Boy**$^{9}$ [4940] 3-8-10 **63** (p) AQuinn$^{(5)}$ 9 36
(GLMoore) *s.i.s: sn rcvrd: rdn to chse ldrs 1/2-way: wknd 3f out* **25/1**

0002 **13** 6 **Cool Temper**$^{18}$ [4672] 8-9-6 **62** DHolland 5 23
(PFICole) *nvr gng wl: sn rdn: a bhd* **9/2**$^{1}$

00-0 **14** 6 **Seven Shirt**$^{11}$ [4871] 3-8-12 **60** JMackay 13 9
(EGBevan) *s.i.s: sn in tch: wknd 1/2-way* **50/1**

0040 **15** 1 ½ **Logger Rhythm (USA)**[104] 2212 4-9-0 **56**.......................... DSweeney 6 2
(RDickin) *a in rr* **50/1**

1m 38.78s (2.88) **Going Correction** +0.55s/f (Yiel)
**WFA** 3 from 4yo+ 6lb **15** Ran SP% **122.1**
Speed ratings: **107,105,104,101,101 101,97,96,95,92 89,87,81,75,74**CSF £85.90 CT £542.80 TOTE £9.70: £2.40, £5.00, £2.30; EX 155.70.
**Owner** Michael Bowlby Racing **Bred** Mrs R Pease **Trained** Kingston Lisle, Oxon

**FOCUS**
A modest handicap but fair form for the grade and it looks solid. The action took place down the centre of the track.

**NOTEBOOK**
**Smoothly Does It**, who has run well here before, broke his maiden in decisive fashion. The soft ground would seem to be the key to him.
**Johannian** stayed on well but the leaders had taken first run. He is performing creditably at present since the Handicapper dropped him a couple of pounds.
**Fen Gypsy**, who was one of three to race towards the stands' side before moving out to join the main bulk of the field, is high enough in the weights but is running well enough to add to his tally.
**Elidore** was unlucky here last time and things did not really go her way again, as she was one of three who initially raced apart from the main body of the field before moving over to join them in racing down the centre. The 5lb she was raised after finishing second no doubt contributed to this defeat.
**Mamore Gap(IRE)**, who made late progress, is creeping down the weights.
**Chandelier**, done no favours by his draw, has been found wanting in open handicaps since taking a seller here from a 7lb lower mark.
**Dual Purpose(IRE)** *Official explanation: jockey said gelding was unsuited by the soft, holding ground*
**Cool Temper** *Official explanation: jockey said gelding was reluctant to race in holding ground*
**Seven Shirt** *Official explanation: jockey said gelding was hanging badly left*

## 5177 RACECOURSE GARAGE MITSUBISHI CLASSIFIED STKS 7f 16y
**5:10** (5:10) (D ) 3-Y-0+ **£5,785** (£1,780; £890; £445) **Stalls** High

Form RPR
0133 **1** **Threezedzz**[11] 4871 6-8-13 78..........................................(t) FPFerris(3) 4 90
(PDEvans) *mde virtually all: hrd drvn and kpt on wl whn strly chal and carried rt thrght fnl f* **9/2**[2]
3200 **2** *nk* **Winning Venture**[9] 4931 7-9-3 81.......................................... GBaker 7 90
(AWCarroll) *stdd s:t.k.h rr:stdy hdwy 3f out: chsd wnr 2f out: str chal and hung rt ins fnl f: no ex cl home* **13/2**
0003 **3** 3 ½ **Marshman (IRE)**[10] 4908 5-9-4 82..........................................(b[1]) DHolland 5 83
(MHTompkins) *bhd: drvn along 4f out: edgd lft and hdwy over 2f out: nvr gng pce to rch ldrs and styd on same pce* **2/1**[1]
0145 **4** *5* **Giocoso (USA)**[7] 5004 4-9-4 82.......................................... JFEgan 8 70
(BPalling) *sn chsng wnr: rdn 3f out: wknd qckly 2f out* **11/2**[3]
0055 **5** 1 ½ **Star Pupil**[10] 4917 3-8-11 76.......................................... DSweeney 9 64
(AMBalding) *chsd ldrs tl wknd appr fnl 2f* **10/1**
0404 **6** *10* **Jay Gee's Choice**[16] 4742 4-9-5 83.......................................... TEDurcan 3 42
(MRChannon) *rdn 1/2-way: a outpcd* **9/2**[2]
3033 **7** *5* **Sophrano (IRE)**[13] 4825 4-9-2 55.......................................... PBradley 2 27
(PABlockley) *chsd ldrs 4f* **50/1**
0004 **8** 1 ½ **Crafty Calling (USA)**[66] 3260 4-8-11 80.......................... NDeSouza(5) 6 23
(PFICole) *early spd: bhd fr 1/2-way* **16/1**

1m 25.59s (2.39) **Going Correction** +0.55s/f (Yiel)
**WFA** 3 from 4yo+ 5lb **8** Ran SP% **115.3**
Speed ratings: **108,107,103,97,96 84,79,77**CSF £33.93 TOTE £3.50: £1.30, £2.90, £1.40; EX 49.20.
**Owner** Barry McCabe **Bred** Mrs R Pease **Trained** Pandy, Gwent

**FOCUS**
Fair form although only two ran to their best, although the winner could rate higher. The field came down the centre.

**NOTEBOOK**
**Threezedzz**, who keeps improving, rallied well to beat the reluctant runner-up. Just as happy over this trip as a mile, he loves soft ground.
**Winning Venture** closed going well and looked sure to win, but hung right and, despite briefly getting his head in front, allowed Threezedzz to get back at him. It is no coincidence that he is on a long losing run. *Official explanation: jockey said gelding hung right under pressure*
**Marshman(IRE)** ended up racing on the outside and could never mount an effective challenge. Blinkered for the first time, he does not look an easy ride.
**Giocoso(USA)** enjoyed an easy lead when successful at Leicester but has been unable to dominate since and has been found wanting.
**Star Pupil** was slow to find his stride but soon recovered. He remains a maiden and is not going to be easy to place.

## 5178 COUNTY OF MONMOUTHSHIRE RACEDAY H'CAP 2m 49y
**5:40** (5:40) (F ) (0-55,55) 3-Y-0 **£3,241** (£926; £463) **Stalls** Low

Form RPR
3314 **1** **Salut Saint Cloud**[10] 4927 3-8-11 **53**..........................................(p) AQuinn(5) 2 72+
(GLMoore) *hld up in tch: led on bit 4f out and sn wl clr: eased thrght fnl f and trotted over line* **3/1**[1]
2504 **2** *16* **Spectested (IRE)**[14] 4806 3-9-4 **55**..........................................(p) DHolland 4 46+
(AWCarroll) *bhd: rdn: carried hd high and hdwy 3f out: wnt mod 2nd 2f out: eased whn nt the remotest ch fnl f* **7/1**
0630 **3** *8* **Genuinely (IRE)**[31] 4302 3-8-6 **43** ow3..........................................(v) TEDurcan 7 26
(WJMusson) *bhd: sme hdwy 5f out: nvr a ch: styd on as wnr and 2nd eased thrght fnl f* **10/1**
6040 **4** *4* **Morning Hawk (USA)**[14] 4820 3-8-3 **40**..........................................(b) JFEgan 6 19
(JSMoore) *sn led: hdd 4f out: sn no ch w wnr and wknd* **12/1**
0534 **5** 1 ½ **Rinneen (IRE)**[39] 4055 3-8-9 **46**..........................................(v) PDobbs 3 24
(RHannon) *chsd ldrs tl wknd 5f out* **9/2**[3]
4433 **6** ¾ **Frambo (IRE)**[11] 4867 3-7-9 **35**..........................................(bt) FPFerris(3) 8 12
(JGPortman) *chsd ldrs: wnt 2nd 7f out to 5f out: wknd fr 4f out* **5/1**
0-00 **7** *dist* **Ballet Ruse**[31] 4306 3-8-11 **48**.......................................... JMackay 5 —
(SirMarkPrescott) *sn rdn in rr: sme hdwy 10f: sn rdn and bhd: t.o fnl 6f* **7/2**[2]
5004 **8** *11* **Knight Of Hearts (IRE)**[13] 4829 3-8-9 **46**.......................................... IMongan 1 —
(PABlockley) *chsd ldrs 9f: sn t.o* **14/1**

3m 47.95s (8.85) **Going Correction** +0.55s/f (Yiel) **8** Ran SP% **118.0**
Speed ratings: **99,91,87,85,84 83,—,—**CSF £25.41 CT £189.16 TOTE £3.10: £1.20, £2.40, £2.90; EX 27.80 Place 6 £154.49, Place 5 £21.59..
**Owner** A Grinter **Bred** Mill House Stud **Trained** Woodingdean, E Sussex

**FOCUS**
A poor handicap but an exceptionally easy winner who could rate higher and may need to turn out before being re-assessed.

**NOTEBOOK**
**Salut Saint Cloud** had won off this mark on Fibresand earlier in the month but was beaten back at Southwell the next day. With his rider looking over his shoulder at trailing rivals in the last quarter mile before easing him up in the final furlong, he ran out a ridiculously easy winner of a poor race. He stays well and looks to be on the upgrade, but the Handicapper is going to take no chances with him.
**Spectested(IRE)**, taking a big step up in trip, chased the winner at a respectful distance in the final quarter mile. The way he carried his head suggests that he is not straightforward.
**Genuinely(IRE)** probably found this trip in the ground too far, although she did plug on.
**Morning Hawk(USA)** set an ordinary pace until the winner eased by at the head of the straight. She is a very limited performer.
**Frambo(IRE)**
**Ballet Ruse**, who has never run at beyond a mile before, was being scrubbed along from an early stage and looked most reluctant to exert herself. She is one to be very wary of. *Official explanation: jockey said filly was never travelling*
**Knight Of Hearts(IRE)** *Official explanation: trainer said gelding did not handle the track*
T/Plt: £182.40 to a £1 stake. Pool: £29,284.20. 117.20 winning tickets. T/Qpdt: £21.40 to a £1 stake. Pool: £1,782.00. 61.60 winning tickets. ST

# 4262 EPSOM (L-H)
### Monday, August 30
**OFFICIAL GOING: Good (good to soft in places on round course)**

## 5179 EUROPEAN BREEDERS FUND ROGER WHITE MEDIAN AUCTION MAIDEN STKS 7f
**2:10** (2:10) (D ) 2-Y-0 **£5,668** (£1,744; £872; £436) **Stalls** Low

Form RPR
0 **1** **Atlantic Story (USA)**[17] 4730 2-9-0 .......................................... LDettori 6 88
(SaeedBinSuroor) *hdw: lw: mde all: drew 3l clr wl over 1f out: shkn up fnl f: a holding on* **8/1**
0 **2** ½ **Rumbalara**[32] 4272 2-8-9 .......................................... JFortune 7 82
(JHMGosden) *lw: wnt rt s: chsd wnr: rdn and nt qckn 2f out: flashed tail but clsd ins fnl f: a hld* **9/2**[3]
522 **3** *2* **Mister Genepi**[17] 4730 2-9-0 86.......................................... MartinDwyer 3 82
(WRMuir) *lw: t.k.h: hld up: 10th st: prog over 2f out: styd on to take 3rd ent fnl f: nrst fin* **11/4**[1]
56 **4** 2 ½ **Pollito (IRE)**[14] 4797 2-8-11 .......................................... JFMcDonald(3) 11 75+
(BJMeehan) *prom: 3rd st: c to nr side rail fr 3f out: nvr on terms w ldrs after: kpt on* **50/1**
5 **5** *nk* **Patronage**[17] 4730 2-9-0 .......................................... JPMurtagh 8 74
(MLWBell) *dwlt and bmpd s: racd midfield: bmpd and awkward downhill 4f out: 9th st: prog 2f out: styd on fnl f* **4/1**[2]
65 **6** *nk* **Eltizaam (USA)**[23] 4544 2-9-0 .......................................... DaneO'Neill 9 73+
(EALDunlop) *dwlt and bmpd s: racd wd towards rr: 7th st: c nr side fr 3f out: nt on terms after: kpt on* **33/1**
63 **7** *3* **Chicken Soup**[4] 5053 2-9-0 .......................................... RLMoore 1 66+
(JAOsborne) *swtg: prom: 4th st: rdn to dispute 2nd pl over 2f out: wknd jst over 1f out* **8/1**
0 **8** 3 ½ **Benedict**[14] 4809 2-9-0 .......................................... KFallon 4 57
(SirMichaelStoute) *racd midfield: 6th st: shkn up and no prog 3f out: wknd 2f out* **9/2**[3]
00 **9** *shd* **Ifit (IRE)**[29] 4364 2-8-2 .......................................... TDean(7) 2 51
(MRChannon) *dwlt: hmpd on inner after 1f: last st: nvr a factor* **66/1**
0 **10** 1 ¼ **Beauchamp Trump**[4] 5054 2-9-0 .......................................... LisaJones 5 53
(GAButler) *bit bkwd: chsd ldrs: 5th st: steadily wknd fr 3f out* **50/1**
5 **11** *11* **William James**[14] 4815 2-9-0 ..........................................(v[1]) PDoe 10 24
(MJWallace) *lw: trckd ldrs: nt handle downhill and lost pl 4f out: 8th st: sn wknd* **66/1**

1m 25.7s (1.75) **Going Correction** +0.225s/f (Good) **11** Ran SP% **115.1**
Speed ratings: **99,98,96,93,92 92,89,85,85,83 71**CSF £42.01 TOTE £9.20: £2.50, £2.00, £1.80; EX 57.70.
**Owner** Godolphin **Bred** A I Appleton **Trained** Newmarket, Suffolk

**FOCUS**
A fair maiden run at a sound gallop and the field came home strung out. The form looks sound.

**NOTEBOOK**
**Atlantic Story(USA)** cleverly made all to lose his maiden tag at the second time of asking. He showed the benefit of his recent Newmarket debut and appreciated this better ground, reversing form with a few of these in the process. A mile will be well within his compass next year, but he is no star on this evidence.
**Rumbalara** was closing on the winner at the finish and improved markedly on her debut display. She again flashed her tail under pressure, but looks like improving once more for this experience, and should have little trouble in winning her maiden.
**Mister Genepi** ran too keenly through the early parts and was staying on all too late in the day. He failed to confirm his recent form with the winner and may now benefit from a switch to nurseries.
**Pollito(IRE)** made his move to the stands' side over two out, but did not look to pose any real advantage and was never a serious threat. He should fare better now he is eligible for nurseries and seemed to get this trip.
**Patronage** was done no favours at the start and did not look to be enjoying this undulating track. He again showed ability however, so could leave this form behind in due course when racing on a more conventional track and on faster ground.
**Eltizaam(USA)** would have fared a deal better but for being hampered at the start. He looks to be slowly going the right way and now qualifies for nurseries, in which he should not be harshly treated.
**Benedict** failed to improve on his fair debut effort and looks the type to do better next year.

## 5180 JRA GOLDEN JUBILEE CONDITIONS STKS 1m 2f 18y
**2:40** (2:43) (B ) 3-Y-0+ **£12,122** (£4,598; £2,299; £1,045) **Stalls** Low

Form RPR
612- **1** **Sights On Gold (IRE)**[406] 3454 5-8-13 114..........................(t) LDettori 2 105
(SaeedBinSuroor) *lw: trckd ldng pair: effrt 2f out: shkn up to ld jst over 1f out: pushed out fnl f* **1/1**[1]
0-30 **2** ¾ **Battle Chant (USA)**[31] 4287 4-8-13 103.......................................... JPMurtagh 3 104
(MrsAJPerrett) *lw: hld up in last: prog over 2f out: hanging over 1f out: drvn and r.o fnl f to take 2nd nr fin* **11/2**[3]
46-6 **3** *hd* **Island Sound**[24] 4525 7-8-13 98.......................................... JFortune 4 104
(DRCElsworth) *lw: pushed up to ld: rdn and hdd ent st: outpcd 2f out: rallied fnl f: clsng at fin* **14/1**
20-0 **4** *nk* **Famous Grouse**[121] 1762 4-8-13 98.......................................... RKingscote 6 103
(RCharlton) *trckd ldng trio: shkn up and unable qck 3f out: styd on fr over 1f out: nrst fin* **33/1**
3305 **5** *shd* **Crystal Curling (IRE)**[65] 3311 3-8-0 99.......................................... MartinDwyer 5 98
(BWHills) *pressed ldr: led ent st: rdn and hdd jst over 1f out: hld whn n.m.r nr fin and lost 3 pls* **11/1**

0-13 **6** *4* **Alphecca (USA)**$^{36}$ 4163 3-8-6 **95** ow1 KFallon 1 96+
(SirMichaelStoute) *racd in 5th: rdn 3f out: no prog and sn btn* **11/4**$^{2}$

2m 9.30s (0.60) **Going Correction** +0.225s/f (Good)
**WFA** 3 from 4yo+ 8lb **6** Ran SP% **110.0**
Speed ratings: **106,105,105,105,104 101**CSF £6.73 TOTE £2.00: £1.40, £2.40; EX 8.40.
**Owner** Godolphin **Bred** Moyglare Stud Farm Ltd **Trained** Newmarket, Suffolk

**FOCUS**
A decent event run at a fair pace, but the first five were covered by a length at the finish and the form may be unreliable.

**NOTEBOOK**
**Sights On Gold(IRE)**, absent since finishing a close second in the Scottish Derby 406 days previously, returned successful with a workmanlike display. He was always holding his rivals inside the last furlong, and, despite the fact he should have won with more in hand according to official ratings, deserves credit for defying his lengthy absence. He is entitled to improve plenty for this and looks worth another crack at Pattern company.
**Battle Chant(USA)** was held up to get the trip and was doing all of his best work in the closing stages, but was always being held by the winner. This was a sound effort, but he again played up going to the start, and is beginning to look tricky.
**Island Sound** led as he prefers, but was readily passed on entering the straight, and did well to battle back close home to finish a fine third. This was an improvement on his recent comeback at Newmarket, and he may have a race in him off this mark before resuming his jumping career.
**Famous Grouse**, who had gone the wrong way last year after showing definite promise, was fighting back at the death and ran his best race for some time. This lightly-raced performer looks to be coming back to himself and may be capable of better.
**Crystal Curling(IRE)** turned in an improved effort against the colts and can be rated slightly better then the bare form, as she was hampered late on. This looks to be her trip.
**Alphecca(USA)** was disappointing. He has' looked a most promising colt when second to Wunderwood at Ascot last time, but failed to run up to that form and looked all at sea on this undulating circuit. He is worthy of another chance, and may have been unsuited by this ground, but has something to prove now.

## 5181 TOTEEXACTA SPRINT STKS (H'CAP) 5f
**3:15** (3:16) (B) (0-105,103) 3-Y-O+ **£23,200** (£8,800; £4,400; £2,000) **Stalls** High

Form RPR
0014 **1** **Atlantic Viking (IRE)**$^{14}$ 4811 9-8-10 **88** LPKeniry$^{(3)}$ 9 100
(DNicholls) *lw: trckd ldrs on inner: effrt against rail over 1f out: led ent fnl f: r.o wl* **10/1**
0660 **2** *½* **Texas Gold**$^{30}$ 4324 6-8-12 **87** JDSmith 7 97+
(WRMuir) *lw: hld up in last trio: plenty to do 2f out: prog and swtchd to wd outside ent fnl f: r.o wl to take 2nd nr fin* **8/1**$^{3}$
0200 **3** *nk* **Plateau**$^{31}$ 4291 5-8-7 **82** PDoe 10 91
(DNicholls) *pushed along in midfield: effrt 2f out: r.o against nr side rail fnl f: nrst fin* **7/1**$^{2}$
0510 **4** *¾* **Tychy**$^{15}$ 4779 5-9-8 **97** JPMurtagh 2 103
(SCWilliams) *lw: trckd ldrs: gng wl 2f out: rdn and nt qckn 1f out: styd on same pce* **8/1**$^{3}$
3603 **5** *hd* **Corridor Creeper (FR)**$^{23}$ 4538 7-9-6 **95** (p) RLMoore 1 101
(JMBradley) *racd on outer: prom: rdn to chal and ev ch 1f out: one pce* **11/1**
0025 **6** *½* **Bishops Court**$^{2}$ 5105 10-10-0 **103** LDettori 8 107
(MrsJRRamsden) *b: hld up wl in rr: plenty to do whn nt clr run over 1f out: swtchd lft and r.o fnl f: no ch* **5/1**$^{1}$
000 **7** *nk* **Henry Hall (IRE)**$^{23}$ 4538 8-9-2 **91** KimTinkler 4 94
(NTinkler) *racd in midfield: bmpd along over 1f out: kpt on same pce: nvr able to chal* **25/1**
5225 **8** *shd* **Jayanjay**$^{12}$ 4847 5-8-7 **82** LisaJones 3 84
(MissBSanders) *racd on outer: cl up: rdn and effrt over 1f out: fdd ins fnl f* **14/1**
0046 **9** *shd* **Speed Cop**$^{9}$ 4951 4-9-5 **94** (v$^{1}$) MartinDwyer 6 96
(AMBalding) *b.hind: w ldr: ev ch ent fnl f: wknd last 100yds* **16/1**
5500 **10** *½* **Green Manalishi**$^{31}$ 4289 3-8-12 **89** JFortune 5 89
(DWPArbuthnot) *lw: racd in midfield: rdn and hanging lft fr over 1f out: nt qckn and nvr rchd ldrs* **20/1**
0200 **11** *1 ¼* **Brave Burt (IRE)**$^{9}$ 4935 7-8-7 **82** KFallon 12 85+
(DNicholls) *b: mde most against nr side rail: edgd lft over 1f out: hdd ent fnl f: wkng whn hmpd nr fin* **7/1**$^{2}$
6515 **12** *¾* **Further Outlook (USA)**$^{3}$ 5071 10-9-1 **90** DaneO'Neill 11 90+
(DKIvory) *b: b.hind: w ldr tl wknd over 1f out* **12/1**
0000 **13** *2 ½* **Whitbarrow (IRE)**$^{30}$ 4324 5-8-12 **92** (b) RThomas$^{(5)}$ 14 76
(JMBradley) *lw: s.s: bmpd and hmpd wl over 3f out: nvr able to rcvr* **12/1**
4200 **14** *3* **Sir Ernest (IRE)**$^{12}$ 4862 3-7-9 **75** oh1 (p) JFMcDonald$^{(3)}$ 13 48
(MJPolglase) *dwlt: bmpd and hmpd wl over 3f out: a bhd* **50/1**

55.52 secs (-0.16) **Going Correction** +0.225s/f (Good)
**WFA** 3 from 4yo+ 2lb **14** Ran SP% **119.8**
Speed ratings: **110,109,108,107,107 106,105,105,105,104 102,101,97,92**CSF £85.58 CT £606.89 TOTE £11.80: £3.20, £3.20, £2.80; EX 136.90 Trifecta £1569.00 Pool: £3,756.88. 1.70 winning units..
**Owner** David Faulkner **Bred** Kilcarn Stud **Trained** Sessay, N Yorks
■ Stewards Enquiry : P Doe three-day ban: careless riding (Sep 10-12)
Martin Dwyer two-day ban: careless riding (Sep 10,12)

**FOCUS**
A competitive sprint, featuring plenty of previous course winners, and a high draw again proved to be an advantage. The form looks rock solid for the grade.

**NOTEBOOK**
**Atlantic Viking(IRE)**, winner of this race in 2002 and the Dash at this track off an 8lb higher mark last year, posted another ready success at a track he clearly loves. He did not need a second invitation when the gap came entering the final furlong and showed a neat turn of foot to score. Although he is clearly in good heart, he would be no certainty to reproduce this at another track next time, and could struggle off an inevitably higher mark.
**Texas Gold** was given a fair bit to do and had to be switched down the centre of the track to challenge, so can be considered unlucky. He has yet to score this season, but was far from disgraced in the Stewards' Cup last time and appeals as the type to go well in the Ayr Gold Cup, should he get in.
**Plateau**, a fast finishing runner-up in the Dash at this track in June, improved for this drop back to five furlongs on a track he clearly enjoys. He is the sort who could run a big race in something like the Silver Cup at Ayr in September, granted a favourable draw.
**Tychy** had every chance when in the clear late on, but failed to find as much as looked likely under maximum pressure. This was still a solid effort under her big weight and should continue to pay her way at this level.
**Corridor Creeper(FR)**, winner of the corresponding event last year off a 10lb lower mark, ran a sound race from his wide draw and remains in good form, but still looks in the Handicapper's grip at present.
**Bishops Court** did not have the best of runs when challenging late on and can be rated slightly better than the bare form. However, although he goes well at this track, he needs all to fall right in his races and remains vulnerable in handicaps off this mark.

## 5182 BURTON & SMITH AMATEUR DERBY (HANDICAP FOR GENTLEMAN AMATEUR RIDERS) 1m 4f 10y
**3:50** (3:51) (C) (0-90,83) 3-Y-O+ **£12,180** (£4,620; £2,310; £1,050) **Stalls** Centre

Form RPR
1021 **1** **Tender Falcon**$^{15}$ 4772 4-11-7 **76** MrAELynch 8 89
(RJHodges) *lw: racd wd: in tch: prog and 2nd st: rdn to ld wl over 2f out: styd on u.p* **9/2**$^{1}$
1110 **2** *1 ¼* **Flying Spirit (IRE)**$^{15}$ 4772 5-11-7 **76** MrSWalker 6 87
(GLMoore) *lw: cl up: prog to ld ent st: rdn and hdd wl over 2f out: hanging lft after: kpt on but a hld* **5/1**$^{2}$
5116 **3** *2 ½* **Desert Island Disc**$^{9}$ 4950 7-11-6 **75** MrSDobson 5 82
(JJBridger) *racd midfield: 7th st: effrt over 2f out: chsd ldng pair over 1f out: no imp* **9/1**
1240 **4** *¾* **Scottish River (USA)**$^{23}$ 4540 5-11-12 **81** MrLNewnes 2 87
(MDIUsher) *s.s: wl in rr: 9th and sme prog st: effrt over 2f out: hanging lft but kpt on fnl 2f: n.d* **14/1**
4415 **5** *hd* **Skylarker (USA)**$^{28}$ 4398 6-11-5 **74** MrTCallejo 11 79
(WSKittow) *lw: disp ld tl hdd and 3rd ent st: styd pressing ldng pair tl wknd over 1f out* **11/1**
4301 **6** *1 ¼* **Flotta**$^{26}$ 4453 5-12-0 **83** MrEDehdashti 3 86
(MRChannon) *towards rr: 8th st: effrt on inner over 2f out: one pce and nvr rchd ldrs* **9/1**
3233 **7** *hd* **Lennel**$^{10}$ 4911 6-11-2 **71** (b) MrJJBest 10 74
(ABailey) *rn in snatches: in tch: 6th and wd st: no imp on ldrs fr over 2f out* **9/1**
0200 **8** *2 ½* **Anticipating**$^{17}$ 4729 4-12-0 **83** MrLJefford 1 82
(AMBalding) *lw: disp ld tl 4th st: steadily lost pl fnl 3f* **7/1**$^{3}$
2400 **9** *6* **Rajam**$^{9}$ 4934 6-11-6 **75** (v) MrHEngblom 4 65
(DNicholls) *towards rr: 10th st: sn rdn and struggling* **14/1**
-120 **10** *1 ½* **Wasted Talent (IRE)**$^{76}$ 2958 4-11-7 **76** (v) MrLoekVanDerHam 9 63
(JGPortman) *disp ld tl 5th and sing to struggle st: wknd 3f out* **12/1**
2246 **11** *3 ½* **Danakil**$^{17}$ 4729 9-11-6 **75** MrCGuimard 12 57
(SDow) *settled in rr: 11th st: sn no prog and btn* **14/1**
4565 **12** *10* **Dissident (GER)**$^{60}$ 3442 6-12-0 **83** (v) MrOSauer 7 49
(DFlood) *a towards rr: last and detached st: wl bhd after* **16/1**

2m 43.36s (4.64) **Going Correction** +0.225s/f (Good) **12** Ran SP% **119.3**
Speed ratings: **93,92,90,90,89 89,88,87,83,82 79,73**CSF £26.49 CT £197.81 TOTE £6.30: £2.40, £2.30, £2.50; EX 22.00.
**Owner** P E Axon **Bred** P E Axon **Trained** Charlton Adam, Somerset

**FOCUS**
A fair renewal of this event and it was run at a strong pace. The field came home strung out and the form looks solid, although it is worth treating with a degree of caution due to the nature of the race.

**NOTEBOOK**
**Tender Falcon** again relished the strong early gallop and readily followed-up his facile success at Bath last time off this 5lb higher mark. He handled the track and always looked like holding the runner-up, despite idling a touch in the lead late on. In the form of his life, he could have more to offer still, but does need a decent gallop to be seen at his best.
**Flying Spirit(IRE)** did his best to close again on the winner inside the final furlong, but was always being held. He loves this sort of undulating track and was a clear second best, yet this does look to be about as good as he is.
**Desert Island Disc** did her best to close on the principals in the straight, but could not find a change of gear when it mattered and finished well held. She appreciated the return to this trip and will be better when able to race more handily.
**Scottish River(USA)** looked to be travelling nicely off the pace about two out, but did not find as much as looked likely under pressure and was well held. He looks too high in the weights at present.
**Anticipating** went off a bit too quick this time and did well to stick to his task when beaten. He is hard to catch right and struggling to find an optimum trip.

## 5183 TOTEPLACEPOT H'CAP 1m 2f 18y
**4:25** (4:27) (C) (0-90,87) 3-Y-O+ **£10,426** (£3,208; £1,604; £802) **Stalls** Low

Form RPR
1-50 **1** **Wiggy Smith**$^{107}$ 2110 5-9-10 **80** DaneO'Neill 7 90
(HCandy) *trckd ldrs: 5th and gng easily st: rdn to ld over 1f out: styd on wl fnl f* **14/1**
4325 **2** *1 ½* **Camrose**$^{65}$ 3325 3-9-9 **87** JFortune 6 94
(JLDunlop) *mostly trckd ldr: rdn to ld 2f out: hdd over 1f out: kpt on same pce* **6/1**$^{3}$
323 **3** *hd* **Dream Magic**$^{9}$ 4950 6-9-5 **75** MartinDwyer 1 82
(MJRyan) *dwlt: hld up in rr: 9th st: rdn over 2f out: no prog tl r.o wl fnl f: tk 3rd nr fin* **8/1**
3210 **4** *1 ½* **Rondelet (IRE)**$^{30}$ 4319 3-9-3 **81** JPMurtagh 9 87+
(RMBeckett) *hld up in rr: 10th st: prog over 2f out: hanging lft fnl 2f : styng on whn n.m.r nr fin* **9/2**$^{2}$
1212 **5** *shd* **Burgundy**$^{22}$ 4571 7-8-8 **64** (b) PDoe 4 68
(PMitchell) *lw: s.s: wl in rr: last st: gd prog on outer over 2f out: jnd ldr over 1f out: hung lft and wknd ins fnl f* **7/1**
1000 **6** *1* **Over The Rainbow (IRE)**$^{58}$ 3543 3-8-11 **82** KMay$^{(7)}$ 10 84
(BWHills) *lw: trckd ldng pair: rdn over 2f out: steadily fdd fr over 1f out* **33/1**
0345 **7** *1* **Katiypour (IRE)**$^{18}$ 4691 7-9-5 **75** LisaJones 8 75
(MissBSanders) *lw: settled towards rr: 8th st: shuffled along and no prog 2f out* **14/1**
5502 **8** *¾* **Prime Powered (IRE)**$^{16}$ 4737 3-9-9 **87** (p) RLMoore 11 86
(GLMoore) *lw: chsd ldrs: rdn 5f out: 6th and u.p st: btn 2f out* **7/1**
0100 **9** *nk* **Factual Lad**$^{26}$ 4435 6-8-12 **71** LPKeniry$^{(3)}$ 5 69
(BRMillman) *sn chsd ldrs: 4th st: rdn and lost pl over 2f out: no ch after: kpt on nr fin* **50/1**
6544 **10** *¾* **Rani Two**$^{16}$ 4760 5-8-7 **68** NChalmers$^{(5)}$ 3 65
(WRMuir) *racd midfield: 7th st: rdn on inner over 2f out: sn btn* **20/1**
6461 **11** *5* **Maclean**$^{10}$ 4906 3-9-2 **80** (p) KFallon 2 67
(SirMichaelStoute) *pushed up to ld: rdn and hdd 2f out: fnd nil and btn after: wkng whn hmpd 1f out* **3/1**$^{1}$

2m 9.76s (1.06) **Going Correction** +0.225s/f (Good)
**WFA** 3 from 5yo+ 8lb **11** Ran SP% **116.6**
Speed ratings: **104,102,102,101,101 100,99,99,98,98 94**CSF £93.24 CT £728.57 TOTE £15.80: £3.50, £2.90, £2.50; EX 178.20 Trifecta £981.70 Part won. Pool: £1,382.68. 0.10 winning units..
**Owner** Mrs George Tricks **Bred** Mrs V M Tricks **Trained** Wantage, Oxon
■ Stewards Enquiry : J P Murtagh caution: careless riding

**FOCUS**
A useful field for this handicap; the form looks solid and the form should work out.

**NOTEBOOK**
**Wiggy Smith** produced a decent display under top weight to win his first race since scoring at Newbury in July 2003. He has had his problems this year, but looks to have come right and could have more to offer still, especially when faced with a step up in trip.
**Camrose** ran another solid race in defeat and appreciated this drop back to ten furlongs. He can be placed to advantage now his stable are emerging from a lean spell.
**Dream Magic** came home best of all from off the pace and turned in another sound effort. However, he is a hard horse to win with and has not scored since March 2003, despite easing in the weights.
**Rondelet(IRE)**, finally off the mark over course and distance in July, hung markedly to towards the rail under pressure and was short of room close home. He looks to be weighted to his best now.
**Burgundy** got to the front too soon in the straight and hung fire, costing him a place. He has been rejuvenated by his current connections of late and coped with this step up in grade well, so is not one to be writing off yet.
**Over The Rainbow(IRE)**
**Maclean** was hard at it from the turn for home and never looked like following-up his recent Chester success off this 4lb higher mark. He is a frustrating performer. *Official explanation: trainer was unable to offer any explanation for poor form shown*

## 5184 CHANTILLY CLAIMING STKS 6f
4:55 (5:01) (E ) 3-Y-0+ £4,836 (£1,488; £744; £372) Stalls High

Form RPR
0231 1 **Beauvrai**[6] [5026] 4-9-6 75 ....(b[1]) MartinDwyer 4 85
(DFlood) *lw: trckd ldrs gng easily: 4th st: led wl over 1f out: drew rt away* **10/3**[1]
0004 2 5 **Hurricane Floyd (IRE)**[61] [3426] 6-9-12 77 .... JFortune 3 76
(DNicholls) *lw: dwlt: wl off the pce in rr: 9th st: drvn and sme prog over 2f out: r.o fnl f to take 2nd nr fin* **10/3**[1]
-604 3 ¾ **Gameset'N'Match**[32] [4265] 3-7-12 57 ....(p) RThomas(5) 11 54
(WGMTurner) *pressed ldr: rdn and ev ch 2f out: vain pursuit of wnr after: lost 2nd nr fin* **15/2**
0100 4 ½ **Firework**[28] [4403] 6-8-10 59 .... KFallon 6 56
(JAkehurst) *trckd ldng pair: rdn over 2f out: styd on same pce* **4/1**[2]
0004 5 1¼ **Tripti (IRE)**[8] [4970] 4-8-0 45 .... JFMcDonald(3) 1 46
(JJBridger) *chsd ldrs: 5th st: rdn and no imp over 2f out: one pce after* **16/1**
0000 6 ½ **Social Contract**[5] [5035] 7-8-8 45 ....(v) DaneO'Neill 2 49
(SDow) *off the pce towards rr: 7th st: hrd rdn 3f out: nvr on terms* **40/1**
0506 7 nk **Borzoi Maestro**[14] [4810] 3-8-10 72 .... LPKeniry(3) 10 56
(JLSpearing) *led to wl over 1f out: wknd* **11/2**[3]
4450 8 3½ **Beyond Calculation (USA)**[30] [4350] 10-8-6 48 ....(b) LisaJones 5 36
(JMBradley) *settled wl in rr and off the pce: 8th st: shuffled along on outer and no prog over 2f out* **12/1**
0000 9 1¾ **Boanerges (IRE)**[10] [4923] 7-8-12 45 .... RLMoore 8 36
(JMBradley) *chsd ldrs: 6th and outpcd st: struggling 3f out: wknd* **20/1**
06-0 10 shd **Chain Of Hope (IRE)**[11] [4868] 3-8-11 54 .... JPMurtagh 9 38
(DECantillon) *lw: settled wl in rr and off the pce: 10th st: no ch* **33/1**
4000 11 ½ **Marengo**[10] [4925] 10-8-8 30 .... PDoe 7 31
(MJPolglase) *dwlt: a bhd: last and struggling st* **50/1**

1m 10.8s (0.17) **Going Correction** +0.225s/f (Good)
**WFA** 3 from 4yo+ 3lb **11** Ran SP% **119.0**
Speed ratings: **107,100,99,98,97 96,95,91,88,88 88**CSF £13.98 TOTE £4.10: £1.80, £1.70, £2.80; EX 12.00.The winner was claimed by G. Chung for £12,000. Hurricane Floyd was claimed by D. Flood for £15,000.
**Owner** Alan Smith (Edinburgh) **Bred** P Asquith **Trained** Upper Lambourn, Berks

**FOCUS**
A fair event for the class, and it was run at a solid gallop, but it lacked any strength in depth.

**NOTEBOOK**
**Beauvrai**, an easy winner at this level six days previously, followed-up in a similarly facile manner on this debut for new connections. He has bled in the past, but is clearly a force to be reckoned with at this level and his confidence will be sky high now. He was claimed by Greg Chung at the subsequent auction.
**Hurricane Floyd(IRE)**, down in trip and class, ran on all too late in the day and had no chance with the winner, but did enough to suggest he can get back to winning ways at this lowly level. He was claimed by David Flood (trainer of the winner) at the subsequent auction.
**Gameset'N'Match**, droppin back a furlong, did the best of those to race up with the pace. He dis a disappoitning sort, who has trouble finishing his races, but was not disgraced this time.
**Firework**, with the usual cheekpieces left off this time, improved for this easier grade, but was again one paced when push came to shove. This would now appear to be his level, but he may at least improve a touch for faster ground.
**Borzoi Maestro**, dropping in class, paid for setting the pace and had nothing left to give entering the final furlong. He was slightly the best in at the weights and has to be considered disappointing.

## 5185 MARK TRACEY 40TH BIRTHDAY H'CAP 1m 114y
5:30 (5:35) (D ) (0-80,78) 3-Y-0+ £10,660 (£3,280; £1,640; £820) Stalls Low

Form RPR
6153 1 **Carry On Doc**[26] [4437] 3-9-3 74 .... RLMoore 14 87
(JWHills) *lw: settled in rr: 11th st: rdn on outer over 2f out: gd prog to ld 1f out: drvn clr* **16/1**
-021 2 1¾ **Compton Drake**[11] [4871] 5-9-8 72 .... JFortune 2 81
(GAButler) *lw: trckd ldrs: 7th st: cl up 2f out: rdn to chal over 1f out: nt pce of wnr* **7/2**[1]
2106 3 ½ **Mr Velocity (IRE)**[22] [4569] 4-9-4 71 .... JFMcDonald(3) 3 86+
(EFVaughan) *hld up midfield: 9th st: nt clr run 3f out: prog whn nowhere to go over 1f out: swtchd and r.o fnl f* **6/1**[3]
0030 4 1½ **Jackie Kiely**[19] [4648] 3-8-1 65 ....(t) JBrennan(7) 5 70
(PSMcentee) *racd in last: wl off the pce st: styd on strly on outer fr over 1f out: no ch* **33/1**
4541 5 nk **Franksalot (IRE)**[21] [4602] 4-9-6 70 .... JPMurtagh 12 74
(MissBSanders) *trckd ldrs: 4th st: nt clr run briefly 2f out: shkn up and one pce after* **10/1**
-531 6 1 **Grandalea**[40] [4024] 3-9-7 78 .... KFallon 6 80
(SirMichaelStoute) *prom: 3rd st: sn rdn: effrt to ld briefly jst over 1f out: wknd ins fnl f* **6/1**[3]
1543 7 hd **Parnassian**[10] [4920] 4-9-1 70 .... RThomas(5) 1 72
(GBBalding) *settled in rr: 12th st: effrt on inner 2f out: nt clr run briefly sn after: kpt on one pce* **11/2**[2]
3060 8 ¾ **Hail The Chief**[14] [4814] 7-9-6 70 .... PDoe 9 70
(JAkehurst) *lw: sn led: hdd & wknd jst over 1f out* **20/1**
3353 9 1¼ **Go Solo**[32] [4266] 3-8-12 76 .... KMay(7) 8 74
(BWHills) *trckd ldedrs: 6th st: cl up on inner 2f out: wknd fnl f* **14/1**
0U60 10 ¾ **Jools**[21] [4613] 6-9-10 74 .... DaneO'Neill 10 70
(DKIvory) *b: b.hind: trckd ldrs: 5th st: effrt to chal 2f out: wknd jst over 1f out* **20/1**
0326 11 ½ **Island Rapture**[15] [4771] 4-9-7 71 .... LisaJones 11 66
(JARToller) *s.s: settled wl in rr: 13th st: shuffled along over 2f out: nvr nr ldrs* **20/1**
/41- 12 ½ **The Player**[339] [5199] 5-9-5 72 .... LPKeniry(3) 7 66
(AMBalding) *lw: t.k.h: hld up bhd ldrs: 8th st: sn lost pl and struggling* **11/1**
5556 13 ¾ **Tiber Tiger (IRE)**[6] [5017] 4-9-4 75 ....(b) StevenHarrison(7) 13 68
(NPLittmoden) *racd midfield: 10th and pushed along st: struggling over 2f out* **16/1**
650 14 7 **Dance On The Top**[26] [4435] 6-9-13 77 ....(t) MartinDwyer 15 55
(JRBoyle) *prom: 2nd st: wknd rapidly 2f out* **25/1**

1m 46.82s (1.08) **Going Correction** +0.225s/f (Good)
**WFA** 3 from 4yo+ 7lb **14** Ran SP% **123.1**
Speed ratings: **104,102,102,100,100 99,99,98,97,96 96,96,95,89**CSF £67.53 CT £401.75 TOTE £15.10: £3.00, £2.00, £3.10; EX 85.20 Place 6 £88.81, Place 5 £47.41.
**Owner** Stuart Whitehouse & Abbott Racing Partne **Bred** Bearstone Stud **Trained** Upper Lambourn, Berks

**FOCUS**
A fair handicap run at a reasonable pace and the first three are all open to improvement.

**NOTEBOOK**
**Carry On Doc** produced a fair turn of foot on the outside of the pack to hit the front a furlong out and settle the issue. Much suited by this return to a mile, he is slowly progressing and clearly enjoys this sort of track.
**Compton Drake** could not go with the winner late on, but still turned in another respectable effort. He had been raised 6lb for his previous success, but that is unlikely to stop him once he reverts to further.
**Mr Velocity(IRE)** ◆was unlucky. He twice had nowhere to go when full of running in the straight and would have gone close with a clearer run. He should gain compensation, granted similar conditions.
**Jackie Kiely** finished strongly over this shorter trip and would have been closer under stronger handling. He is one to keep an eye on.
**Grandalea**, 3lb higher than when winning on the Polytrack last time, dropped out quickly after hitting the front and did not stay this trip too well. She looks a real-seven furlong performer and is worth another chance.
**Parnassian** would have been a bit closer but for meeting trouble over one out, but it made no difference to the result. He ran as though he may just be feeling the effects of a busy season and is high enough in the weights now.
T/Jkpt: Not won. T/Plt: £74.50 to a £1 stake. Pool: £66,997.70. 655.65 winning tickets. T/Qpdt: £26.00 to a £1 stake. Pool: £2,903.60. 82.60 winning tickets. JN

# 5081 NEWCASTLE (L-H)
## Monday, August 30

**OFFICIAL GOING: Soft (heavy in places)**
Wind: fresh across Weather: cloudy & bright, race 6 rain

## 5186 UNISON FAMILY DAY EBF MAIDEN STKS 7f
2:15 (2:16) (D ) 2-Y-0 £4,527 (£1,393; £696; £348) Stalls High

Form RPR
0 1 **Just Waz (USA)**[19] [4625] 2-9-0 .... FLynch 7 68
(RMWhitaker) *s.i.s: hld up: swtchd lft 2f out: led ins fnl f: r.o wl* **25/1**
2 nk **Alani (IRE)** 2-8-9 .... MFenton 4 63
(JeddO'Keeffe) *w ldrs: rdn over 2f out: rallied and ev ch ins fnl f: kpt on* **33/1**
3 shd **Onyergo (IRE)** 2-8-11 .... PMulrennan(3) 5 67
(JRWeymes) *chsd ldrs: effrt over 2f out: kpt on wl towards fin* **33/1**
40 4 ½ **Harrys House**[15] [4776] 2-9-0 .... JFanning 8 66
(JJQuinn) *keen: mde most to ins fnl f: kpt on same pce* **11/1**[3]
0 5 ½ **Desperation (IRE)**[10] [4924] 2-8-11 .... LEnstone(3) 6 65
(KRBurke) *dwlt: hld up in tch: shkn up whn n.m.r over 2f out: kpt on fnl f: no imp* **16/1**
0032 6 shd **Eskdale (IRE)**[4] [5059] 2-9-0 73 .... PHanagan 2 65
(RFFisher) *trckd ldrs: effrt over 1f out: hung lft: one pce ins fnl f* **13/2**[2]
7 3½ **Tetra Sing (IRE)** 2-8-9 .... GFaulkner 3 51
(PCHaslam) *dwlt: in tch on outside: rdn over 2f out: wknd over 1f out* **25/1**
2432 8 ¾ **Mozafin**[9] [4953] 2-9-0 81 .... SSanders 1 54
(MRChannon) *cl up: rdn over 2f out: wknd ent fnl f* **4/11**[1]

1m 32.52s (4.50) **Going Correction** +0.675s/f (Yiel) **8** Ran SP% **114.4**
Speed ratings: **101,100,100,99,99 99,95,94** TOTE £24.90: £4.60, £7.30, £11.30.
**Owner** Mrs L Ziegler **Bred** Lochlow Farm **Trained** Scarcroft, W Yorks

**FOCUS**
With the favourite running poorly, a steady pace and just over a length covering the first six, this form has a distinctly ordinary look to it and may not prove that reliable

**NOTEBOOK**
**Just Waz(USA)** left his debut effort behind when winning this ordinary event, and may well be better than the bare form as he made up ground off a steady pace. He should stay a mile and his future lies in modest handicap company.
**Alani(IRE)**, related to a winner in Italy and out of a dam who won over a mile and six, showed enough on this racecourse debut to suggest she can win a small event when the emphasis is on stamina.
**Onyergo(IRE)**, related to several sprint winners and to a middle distance scorer, looks to have more stamina than speed and ran creditably on this racecourse debut. He is open to progress but may do better when handicapped.
**Harrys House** had the run of this steadily-run race and performed creditably, but left the impression that the drop back to six furlongs and the step into ordinary handicap company would suit.
**Desperation(IRE)** ◆, who took the eye in the preliminaries, bettered his debut effort and may be better than the bare form given the way this race panned out. He has physical scope and will be one to keep an eye on when handicapped. *Official explanation: jockey said gelding never got a run*
**Eskdale(IRE)**, back on a soft surface, probably ran to a similar level as at Musselburgh last week, but did not look an easy ride this time and is likely to continue to look vulnerable in this type of event. *Official explanation: jockey said gelding hung left in last two furlongs*
**Mozafin** looked the one to beat but, after enjoying the run of the race, dropped out in disappointing fashion and, although he may not have handled the sticky ground, he looks exposed and may be one to tread carefully with.

## 5187 UNISON FAMILY DAY CLAIMING STKS 1m 3y(S)
2:45 (2:46) (F ) 3-Y-0+ £2,954 (£844; £422) Stalls High

Form RPR
0030 1 **Eastern Hope (IRE)**[45] [3911] 5-9-4 59 .... KristinStubbs(7) 11 63
(MrsLStubbs) *slowly away: hld up: hdwy over 2f out: led appr fnl f: kpt on wl* **10/1**
00/4 2 nk **Ash Bold (IRE)**[19] [4624] 7-8-8 40 .... PMulrennan(3) 13 48
(BEllison) *cl up: led briefly over 1f out: r.o fnl f* **9/1**[3]
3004 3 nk **Erupt**[13] [4825] 11-8-7 40 ow1 .... MLawson(5) 8 48
(REBarr) *hld up: hdwy 2f out: kpt on wl fnl f* **14/1**
3000 4 ¾ **Summer Special**[21] [4605] 4-8-8 45 .... LEnstone(3) 5 46
(DWBarker) *cl up: ev ch over 1f out: no ex wl ins last* **14/1**

0602 **5** *hd* **Kingston Town (USA)**[10] 4925 4-9-4 57................(p) J-PGuillambert(3) 3 56
(NPLittmoden) *hld up: hdwy over 2f out: swtchd rt over 1f out: one pce wl ins last* **13/2**[2]

3434 **6** *shd* **Donna's Double**[13] 4826 9-9-3 50.......................................(p) PHanagan 4 51
(DEddy) *in tch: effrt 2f out: hung lft: kpt on same pce fnl f* **9/4**[1]

1005 **7** *2 ½* **Mehmaas**[13] 4825 8-8-10 53........................................(v) PPMathers(5) 12 44
(REBarr) *led to over 1f out: no ex* **11/1**

0300 **8** *5* **Noble Pursuit**[21] 4605 7-9-1 49............................................ SSanders 1 34
(REBarr) *in tch: rdn whn nt clr run and lost pl over 2f out: n.d after* **10/1**

1030 **9** *8* **Tancred Miss**[26] 4447 5-8-8 40............................................ TWilliams 2 11
(DWBarker) *in tch tl rdn and wknd fr over 2f out* **16/1**

0450 **10** *1* **Turftanzer (GER)**[28] 4397 5-8-6 30.........................(t) JaniceWebster(7) 9 14
(DonEnricoIncisa) *in tch to 1/2-way: sn lost pl* **66/1**

0005 **11** *¾* **Chisel**[7] 4985 3-8-5 50.............................................................. JFanning 7 11
(MJohnston) *bhd: rdn 1/2-way: btn over 1f out* **10/1**

0500 **12** *14* **Delta Lady**[38] 4102 3-7-12 40.............................................. DMernagh 10 —
(RBastiman) *cl up tl wknd over 2f out* **33/1**

1m 47.65s (6.45) **Going Correction** +0.675s/f (Yiel)
**WFA** 3 from 4yo+ 6lb **12** Ran SP% **113.4**
Speed ratings: **94,93,93,92,92 92,89,84,76,75 75,61**CSF £92.69 TOTE £12.40: £3.60, £3.60, £3.20; EX 78.80.Chisel was claimed by Miss D. A. McHale for £3,000.
**Owner** T C Chiang **Bred** R C Snaith **Trained** Malton, N. Yorks

**FOCUS**
A low-grade event run at just an ordinary pace in a moderate time and one in which the whole field raced on the far side.

**NOTEBOOK**
**Eastern Hope(IRE)** is not very reliable and once again lost ground at the start, but elected to put his best foot forward under suitable conditions to win a modest race. Whether this will be reproduced next time remains to be seen, though.
**Ash Bold(IRE)** once again shaped as though retaining plenty of ability. He travelled strongly for much of the way and looks capable of winning a similarly modest event.
**Erupt** ran creditably given the uncompromising position he was in passing halfway but, as is usually the case with him, he is anything but certain to put it all in next time.
**Summer Special** had the run of the race and ran creditably but a record of no wins from 33 starts confirms he is not one to place a great deal of faith in.
**Kingston Town(USA)**, tackling soft ground for the first time on turf, ran his best race to date away from artificial surfaces and may be capable of picking up a modest race this autumn.
**Donna's Double**'s recent Hamilton run in much better company gave him leading claims in this grade but, although not beaten far, he again looked anything but straightforward and is not one to take too short a price about.

## 5188 CHISHOLM BOOKMAKERS BLAYDON RACE (NURSERY H'CAP) 1m 3y(S)
**3:20** (3:21) (C) 2-Y-O **£10,322** (£3,176; £1,588; £794) **Stalls** High

Form RPR

441 **1** **Night Of Joy (IRE)**[12] 4851 2-9-0 **80**.......................................... PRobinson 6 89
(MAJarvis) *keen early: trckd ldrs: swtchd lft and led over 2f out: sn clr: r.o strly: eased cl home* **9/2**[2]

5031 **2** *1 ¼* **Lady Misha**[26] 4445 2-8-3 **69**.................................................. PHanagan 9 75
(JeddO'Keeffe) *in tch: effrt whn checked over 2f out: sn drvn: rallied over 1f out: styd on strly: nt rch wnr* **13/2**[3]

0443 **3** *5* **Young Thomas (IRE)**[10] 4909 2-8-6 **72**................................. MFenton 2 68
(MLWBell) *chsd ldrs: outpcd 2f out: rallied fnl f: no imp* **10/1**

614 **4** *½* **Arabian Ana (IRE)**[10] 4907 2-8-13 **79**.......................................... FLynch 7 74
(BSmart) *mde most to over 2f out: nt qckn* **16/1**

021 **5** *1* **Kalmini (USA)**[17] 4706 2-9-0 **80**.............................................. SSanders 1 73
(MRChannon) *bhd: drvn 1/2-way: kpt on fnl f: nvr rchd ldrs* **7/2**[1]

054 **6** *shd* **Patxaran (IRE)**[23] 4560 2-7-13 **70**.................................. RoryMoore(5) 3 63
(PCHaslam) *hld up in tch: effrt over 2f out: sn rdn and btn* **16/1**

001 **7** *1 ¾* **Velvet Heights (IRE)**[18] 4689 2-9-7 **87**.................................... GCarter 8 76
(JLDunlop) *hld up: hdwy over 2f out: rdn and wknd appr fnl f* **7/2**[1]

6256 **8** *1 ¾* **Ming Vase**[18] 4676 2-7-12 **64** oh2........................................ DaleGibson 5 50
(DCarroll) *w ldr to over 2f out: sn btn* **16/1**

4044 **U** **Sharp N Frosty**[40] 4012 2-7-5 **64** oh1................................. MHalford(7) 4 —
(WMBrisbourne) *hld up: uns rdr over 6f out* **14/1**

1m 47.0s (5.80) **Going Correction** +0.675s/f (Yiel) **9** Ran SP% **109.4**
Speed ratings: **98,96,91,91,90 90,88,86,—**CSF £30.76 CT £251.91 TOTE £4.60: £2.00, £1.80, £2.40; EX 29.20.
**Owner** Saif Ali **Bred** Roundhill Stud And A Stroud **Trained** Newmarket, Suffolk
■ Stewards Enquiry : M Fenton one-day ban: used whip with excessive frequency (Sep 10)

**FOCUS**
A fair nursery in which the pace was on the steady side and the field again raced on the far side. The first two did well to pull clear of the remainder and both appeal as likely to win more races, with the form behind appearing sound.

**NOTEBOOK**
**Night Of Joy(IRE)** ◆'s strong-travelling style ensured she had the run of the race and, although she got first run, looked good value for the winning margin. She is almost certainly capable of better and appeals as the type to win again this autumn.
**Lady Misha** ◆, upped to this trip for the first time, turned in an improved effort and would almost certainly have finished a bit closer but for being checked when asked to make her effort. She goes well on easy ground and is sure to win more races on this evidence.
**Young Thomas(IRE)**, upped to this trip for the first time, left the impression that a stiffer test of stamina would have been in his favour .However, he may continue to look vulnerable in nursery company from his current mark.
**Arabian Ana(IRE)** had the run of the race and was not disgraced on his first start over this trip. However he is still a bit on the leg at present and the best may not be seen of him until next year.
**Kalmini(USA)**, who did not really take the eye in the paddock, looked to face a stiff task from this mark on this nursery debut and turned in a laboured effort on her first start over this trip. While this ground may not have suited, she will have to improve to win from this mark.
**Patxaran(IRE)**, fourth to a subsequent Group three winner on her previous start, did not get home on this first run over this trip and on this first start away from fast ground. She is in good hands though, and is not one to write off yet.
**Velvet Heights(IRE)**, who may well have been flattered by racing wide at Sandown on his previous start, failed to build on that promise over a trip that should have suited. However the ground may not have suited and, given his physique, is not one to write off yet. *Official explanation: jockey said colt finished lame*
**Ming Vase** *Official explanation: jockey said colt hung right handed in final 3f*

## 5189 UNISON FAMILY DAY MEDIAN AUCTION MAIDEN STKS 1m 2f 32y
**3:55** (3:55) (E) 3-4-Y-O **£3,646** (£1,122; £561; £280) **Stalls** Low

Form RPR

3643 **1** **Tytheknot**[36] 4177 3-8-13 74.................................................. PHanagan 3 67
(JeddO'Keeffe) *trckd ldrs gng wl: led over 1f out: sn rdn: kpt on: all out* **11/10**[1]

30-2 **2** *shd* **Zakfree (IRE)**[198] 769 3-8-10 66...........................(b) J-PGuillambert(3) 1 67
(NPLittmoden) *dwlt: hld up in tch: effrt 2f out: edgd rt and r.o wl fnl f: jst hld* **11/2**[3]

0052 **3** *nk* **Super King**[19] 4628 3-8-13 61............................................... PRobinson 6 66
(NBycroft) *cl up: led briefly 2f out: rallied: hld towards fin* **5/2**[2]

606 **4** *9* **Cronkyvoddy**[60] 3448 3-8-13 58...........................................(t) SSanders 2 51
(MissGayKelleway) *led to 2f out: sn outpcd* **7/1**

P **5** *2 ½* **Rhum**[15] 4781 4-9-4 ........................................................ PMulrennan(3) 5 47
(ISemple) *prom: rdn whn n.m.r 3f out: sn btn* **20/1**

0 **6** *5* **Super Boston**[70] 3154 4-9-7 .................................................. JFanning 4 38
(MissLCSiddall) *hld up in tch: rdn over 3f out: sn btn* **40/1**

2m 19.06s (7.46) **Going Correction** +0.45s/f (Yiel)
**WFA** 3 from 4yo 8lb **6** Ran SP% **111.3**
Speed ratings: **88,87,87,80,78 74**CSF £7.63 TOTE £1.90: £1.30, £4.00; EX 8.30.
**Owner** Arthur Walker and Paul Chapman **Bred** Milton Park Stud **Trained** Middleham Moor, N Yorks

**FOCUS**
An uncompetitive maiden in which the pace was on the steady side and the time was moderate for the class, even in the conditions. This form, rated through the placed horses, may not prove a reliable guide.

**NOTEBOOK**
**Tytheknot**, who has been running consistently well, did not find as much as seemed likely off the bridle and did just enough to a rival he would have been conceding 8lb in a handicap. He will find things tougher back in handicaps from now on.
**Zakfree(IRE)** ran creditably on this first start since February and seems best with cut in the ground, but he has had plenty of chances and may not be entirely straightforward.
**Super King** had the run of the race and performed creditably in the face of a stiffish task.However, he will find life tougher back in handicaps if the assessor raises him for this seemingly improved effort.
**Cronkyvoddy** had the run of the race but was quickly dropped once headed and is likely to continue to look vulnerable in this type of event.
**Rhum** did not really get the run of the race but dropped out disappointingly and is likely to remain vulnerable in this type of event.
**Super Boston** again offered no immediate promise.

## 5190 CHISHOLM BOOKMAKERS H'CAP 1m 6f 97y
**4:30** (4:30) (D ) (0-80,75) 3-Y-O+ **£5,343** (£1,644; £822; £411)**Stalls** Far side

Form RPR

1311 **1** **Sendintank**[3] 5093 4-9-6 **68** 6ex............................................. SSanders 4 79+
(SCWilliams) *in tch: niggled briefly over 3f out: hdwy and hung lft over 2f out: led appr fnl f: styd on strly* **1/2**[1]

0031 **2** *1 ¼* **Late Opposition**[13] 4829 3-8-8 **68**......................................(v) PRobinson 5 77
(EALDunlop) *hld up: stdy hdwy to chse wnr ins fnl f: sn rdn and flashed tail: kpt on* **4/1**[2]

0563 **3** *3 ½* **Welkino's Boy**[14] 4820 3-8-3 **63**.......................................... DaleGibson 6 67
(JMackie) *cl up: led over 2f out to appr fnl f: sn outpcd* **20/1**

4043 **4** *4* **Colorado Falls (IRE)**[7] 4990 6-9-11 **73**................................ PHanagan 3 72
(PMonteith) *chsd ldrs: rdn over 2f out: sn outpcd* **9/1**[3]

0/00 **5** *2 ½* **Ebinzayd (IRE)**[57] 3564 8-9-11 **73**.......................................... JFanning 2 69
(LLungo) *led to over 2f out: sn btn* **25/1**

1155 **6** *hd* **Toni Alcala**[9] 4934 5-9-10 **75**...................................... PMulrennan(3) 1 71
(RFFisher) *in tch: rdn over 2f out: sn btn* **14/1**

3m 14.2s (4.30) **Going Correction** +0.45s/f (Yiel)
**WFA** 3 from 4yo+ 12lb **6** Ran SP% **111.9**
Speed ratings: **105,104,102,100,98 98**CSF £2.79 TOTE £1.50: £1.10, £2.00; EX 3.00.
**Owner** Steve Jones And Phil McGovern **Bred** K G Powter **Trained** Newmarket, Suffolk

**FOCUS**
A modest handicap in which a flip start was used, but the fair pace played to the strengths of Sendintank, the one progressive horse in the field.

**NOTEBOOK**
**Sendintank**, only 1lb higher than when successful at Newmarket last week, had conditions in his favour and the race run to suit. Life will be tougher from Saturday but he is open to further improvement and he will be hard to beat if turned out under the same penalty on Friday.
**Late Opposition** faced a much stiffer task than in uncompetitive maiden company at Hamilton, but ran with credit and had no problems with the longer trip. His tail-flashing tendency does not endear him to many, though.
**Welkino's Boy** was not disgraced but left the impression that the return to a quicker surface would be in his favour. He is in good hands and is sure to be placed to best advantage.
**Colorado Falls(IRE)** handles testing ground and had the run of the race, but did not find much when asked for his effort and is vulnerable to progressive sorts from his current mark.
**Ebinzayd(IRE)**, better than ever over hurdles in the spring but reappearing after a short break, was easy to back and was well beaten after making this a decent test in the conditions. He is high enough in the weights but is not one to write off yet.
**Toni Alcala** is probably better on a sound surface but there is also the possibility that a busy campaign is taking its toll and he again offered little resistance. He is best watched for now.

## 5191 NOTH EAST MOTOR SHOW H'CAP 1m 4f 93y
**5:00** (5:02) (E ) (0-75,74) 3-Y-O **£3,532** (£1,087; £543; £271) **Stalls** Low

Form RPR

0026 **1** **Killmorey**[16] 4749 3-8-9 **62**....................................................... GCarter 1 76
(SCWilliams) *chsd ldr: rdn to ld appr fnl f: kpt on wl* **4/1**[3]

2121 **2** *2 ½* **Quarrymount**[5] 5037 3-9-2 **69** 6ex.......................................... SSanders 4 79
(SirMarkPrescott) *led to appr fnl f: kpt on same pce* **1/1**[1]

-166 **3** *7* **Marine City (JPN)**[91] 2529 3-9-7 **74**.................................... PRobinson 2 74
(MAJarvis) *in tch: outpcd 1/2-way: sme late hdwy: no ch w first two* **7/1**

5131 **4** *3* **Richtee (IRE)**[19] 4636 3-9-5 **72**............................................ PHanagan 3 68
(RAFahey) *chsd ldrs: rdn and hung lft over 2f out: sn btn* **5/2**[2]

2m 45.6s (2.30) **Going Correction** +0.45s/f (Yiel) **4** Ran SP% **111.1**
Speed ratings: **110,108,103,101**CSF £8.79 TOTE £5.80; EX 9.40 Place 6 £3,142.02, Place 5 £101.58..
**Owner** Wood Farm Stud (Waresley) Partnership **Bred** Wood Farm Stud (waresley) **Trained** Newmarket, Suffolk

**FOCUS**
Only four runners but a fair test in the conditions and the time was decent. An improved effort from Killmorey, who may be capable of better.

**NOTEBOOK**
**Killmorey**, who fared the best of those held up on his handicap debut last time, turned in an improved effort on this first start over this trip and, although carrying his head awkwardly, has plenty of scope for improvement and may be capable of better.
**Quarrymount**, under a penalty for his recent Brighton win, was not disgraced against an unexposed sort under a penalty. He may be able to win again in ordinary company when allowed his own way in front.
**Marine City(JPN)** has form on soft ground but continues below her best and, in any case, she looks high enough in the weights at present.
**Richtee(IRE)**, closely matched with Quarrymount on a recent Ayr run, had winning form on soft but did not seem to handle these sticky conditions and was the disappointment of the race. Given her record of late she is worth another chance, though.
T/Plt: £7,968.10 to a £1 stake. Pool: £28,379.75. 2.60 winning tickets. T/Qpdt: £39.90 to a £1 stake. Pool: £1,982.60. 36.70 winning tickets. RY

# [4757]RIPON (R-H)

## Monday, August 30

**OFFICIAL GOING: Good to soft (soft in places)**

### 5192 BANK HOLIDAY IS FOR RACING (S) STKS 6f

**2:20** (2:21) (F ) 2-Y-O £3,269 (£934; £467) **Stalls High**

Form RPR

0002 **1** **Apetite**[3] [5097] 2-8-11 ........ CCatlin 8 64
(NBycroft) *dwlt: bhd: hdwy over 2f out: r.o wl u.p to ld ins fnl f* **5/1**[2]

0000 **2** *1/2* **Hows That**[8] [4967] 2-8-6 ........ RMullen 7 58
(PJMcbride) *towards rr: sn drvn along: hdwy 1/2-way: rdn to ld appr fnl f: hdd ins last: r.o* **5/1**[2]

000 **3** *6* **Outrageous Flirt (IRE)**[56] [3583] 2-8-6 ........ RWinston 4 40
(ADickman) *towards rr: sme hdwy 1/2-way: kpt on fnl f: nvr able to chal* **11/1**

0 **4** *nk* **Thornber Court (IRE)**[40] [4009] 2-8-6 ........ FNorton 1 39
(ABerry) *chsd ldrs: led 2f out: rdn and hdd appr fnl f: wknd ins last* **7/1**[3]

0650 **5** *3* **Lane Marshal**[7] [4997] 2-8-8 ........(b) TEaves[(3)] 9 35
(MESowersby) *led 2f: led again 1/2-way tl hdd 2f out: wknd appr fnl f* **33/1**

060 **6** *2 1/2* **Balthasar**[13] [4824] 2-8-11 ........ DeanMcKeown 3 27
(PABlockley) *cl up: led after 2f: hdd 1/2-way: sn rdn and btn* **2/1**[1]

300 **7** *nk* **Shuchbaa**[58] [3506] 2-8-6 40........ NCallan 2 21
(KARyan) *midfield: hdwy and in tch 2f out: wknd over 1f out* **20/1**

3204 **8** *8* **Danehill Fairy (IRE)**[18] [4675] 2-8-6 45........(b) JCarroll 5 —
(MrsADuffield) *prom to 1/2-way: sn wknd* **9/1**

00 **9** *3/4* **Elliebow**[60] [3444] 2-8-6 ........ DAllan 6 —
(TDEasterby) *a bhd* **9/1**

1m 16.09s (3.19) **Going Correction** +0.25s/f (Good) **9** Ran SP% **115.2**
Speed ratings: **88,87,79,78,74 71,71,60,59**CSF £30.12 TOTE £6.00: £2.00, £1.90, £3.00; EX 24.90.There was no bid for the winner. Hows That was claimed by K. R. Burke £6,000.
**Owner** N Bycroft **Bred** T Umpleby **Trained** Brandsby, N Yorks

**FOCUS**
Poor stuff and a modest time, but the form looks reasonable for the grade.

**NOTEBOOK**
**Apetite** ran well at Thirsk when second to an unexposed sort, and stumbled upon a lesser race in which he was able to get off the mark. He picked up strongly in the final third of the race having been off the pace and won with a little in hand, seeming well suited by the drop back in trip. Although not that big and pretty exposed, he should continue to pay his way in this sort of company.
**Hows That** had shown very little prior to this and is evidently more at home in this sort of grade. She was well clear of the third and can win at this level.
**Outrageous Flirt(IRE)** pluged on from the rear to claim a remote third and should be suited by a further step up in trip. *Official explanation: jockey said filly hung left throughout*
**Thornber Court(IRE)** showed good early speed and had every chance until finding the sixth furlong one too many. A drop to the minimum distance should see an improved performance.
**Balthasar** was reported to have a breathing problem when last seen and did nothing to suggest he will be winning anytime soon.
**Elliebow** *Official explanation: jockey said filly had a breathing problem*

### 5193 BILLY NEVETT MEMORIAL H'CAP 6f

**2:50** (2:51) (D ) (0-80,80) 3-Y-O £6,201 (£1,908; £954; £477) **Stalls High**

Form RPR

2034 **1** **Imperial Echo (USA)**[12] [4862] 3-9-7 **80**........ PFessey 20 88
(TDBarron) *racd far side: trckd ldr 2f out: hld on wl u.p fnl f* **12/1**[3]

4321 **2** *nk* **Trojan Flight**[19] [4626] 3-8-5 **64**........ RWinston 19 78+
(MrsJRRamsden) *racd far side: hld up: hdwy over 2f out: pressing ldrs whn nt clr run fnl f: r.o wl clsng stages: jst hld* **6/4**[1]

1420 **3** *1/2* **Tregarron**[9] [4952] 3-8-12 **71**........ RHills 18 77
(RHannon) *racd far side: in tch: hdwy over 2f out: ev ch and rdn fnl f: no ex clsng stages* **12/1**[3]

0562 **4** *3 1/2* **Misaro (GER)**[13] [4827] 3-9-0 **73**........ DeanMcKeown 2 68+
(PABlockley) *racd stands side: led gp thrght: r.o wl u.p fnl f* **10/1**[2]

0240 **5** *nk* **Elliot's Choice (IRE)**[2] [5107] 3-7-8 **60**........(b) DanielleMcCreery[(7)] 12 54
(DCarroll) *racd far side: s.i.s: towards rr: nt clr run over 2f out: hdwy over 1f out: r.o fnl f: nvr able to chal* **50/1**

4350 **6** *3/4* **Sessay**[31] [4289] 3-8-9 **68**........ ANicholls 6 60+
(DNicholls) *racd stands side: hld up: hdwy over 2f out: rdn to chse gp ldr appr fnl f: no ex ins last* **16/1**

4024 **7** *1 1/2* **Flying Bantam (IRE)**[12] [4855] 3-8-11 **70**........ RFfrench 9 57
(RAFahey) *in tch far side: rdn 2f out: kpt on same pce* **14/1**

2005 **8** *2* **Piccolo Prince**[30] [4320] 3-8-8 **67**........ FNorton 1 48+
(EJAlston) *chsd stands side ldrs: rdn 2f out: kpt on same pce* **20/1**

1215 **9** *1 1/4* **Bridgewater Boys**[51] [3737] 3-9-4 **80**........(b) TEaves[(3)] 14 58
(KARyan) *sn towards rr far side: kpt on fnl f: n.d* **14/1**

5040 **10** *nk* **Fox Covert (IRE)**[36] [4181] 3-7-12 **57** oh2........(v) JMcAuley 17 34
(DWBarker) *racd far side: led tl hdd 2f out: sn rdn and btn* **25/1**

5106 **11** *1 1/4* **Distant Times**[12] [4862] 3-9-2 **75**........ DAllan 15 48
(TDEasterby) *racd far side: stmbld s: sn midfield: drvn along over 2f out: no hdwy* **10/1**[2]

**12** *1* **Hallahoise Hydro (IRE)**[94] [2463] 3-7-12 **57**........ PMQuinn 8 27
(BSRothwell) *dwlt: towards rr far side most of way: n.d* **66/1**

4306 **13** *1 1/2* **Open Mind**[77] [2942] 3-7-5 **57** oh9........ NataliaGemelova[(7)] 3 23+
(EJAlston) *in tch stands side: sn pushed along: no imp on gp ldrs* **66/1**

3010 **14** *shd* **Obe Bold (IRE)**[11] [4874] 3-8-9 **68**........ JCarroll 13 33
(ABerry) *prom far side: drvn along 1/2-way: wknd 2f out* **33/1**

4006 **15** *hd* **Baylaw Star**[21] [4608] 3-8-8 **67**........(p) NCallan 7 32+
(KARyan) *cl up stands side: rdn 2f out: wknd appr fnl f* **20/1**

6000 **16** *nk* **Attacca**[22] [4574] 3-8-6 **65**........ CCatlin 16 29
(JRWeymes) *prom far side: drvn along 1/2-way: wknd 2f out* **50/1**

-444 **17** *2 1/2* **Kamenka**[21] [4608] 3-8-7 **69**........ THamilton[(3)] 5 25
(RAFahey) *in tch far side tl rdn and wknd 2f out* **16/1**

5606 **18** *2* **Scooby Dooby Do**[28] [4393] 3-7-9 **57** oh7........(p) HayleyTurner[(3)] 11 7
(RMWhitaker) *racd far side: sn bhd* **66/1**

4000 **19** *shd* **Party Princess (IRE)**[19] [4650] 3-7-8 **60**........ DFentiman[(7)] 4 10+
(JAGlover) *chsd stands side ldrs tl rdn and wknd 2f out* **50/1**

0600 **20** *4* **George The Best (IRE)**[44] [3926] 3-8-8 **67** ow3........ DarrenWilliams 10 5+
(MDHammond) *racd stands side: slowly away: a bhd* **40/1**

1m 14.64s (1.74) **Going Correction** +0.25s/f (Good) **20** Ran SP% **127.8**
Speed ratings: **98,97,96,92,91 90,88,86,84,84 82,81,79,79,78 78,75,72,72,66**CSF £27.93 CT £232.76 TOTE £16.20: £3.70, £1.50, £2.50, £2.20; EX 36.70.
**Owner** J Stephenson **Bred** Derby Lane Farm **Trained** Maunby, N Yorks

**FOCUS**
The first three home had the top three stalls - further underlining the advantages of racing against the far rail. The time was modest for the grade, despite which the form appears solid.

**NOTEBOOK**
**Imperial Echo(USA)** had the best of the draw and held a good early position, just off the pace-setters. His last run came over five furlongs and this return to six suited, as he stuck on stoutly to hold the fast finishing favourite. It is worth bearing in mind however that he was at a big advantage in stall 20 and it would be unwise to get carried away with the form.
**Trojan Flight** was up 5lb for his Beverley win and seemingly well fancied to follow up. He could be called an unlcuky loser as he was making ground when short of room and only just failed to get there.
**Tregarron** made it a one, two, three for the three highest stalls and pulled clear of the fourth. He left behind a poor run at Sandown and handled the ground well enough.
**Misaro(GER)** fared best of those stands' side and won his race by just under a length.
**Elliot's Choice(IRE)** was a little unlucky not to get closer and ran better than his finishing position suggests. He remains a maiden however and finds it hard to win in whatever type of contest he runs in.
**Sessay** did second best of the stands'-side runners, but he too is still awaiting his first win.

### 5194 BARRY PEMBERTON 60TH BIRTHDAY RIPON ROWELS STKS (H'CAP) 1m

**3:25** (3:25) (C ) (0-100,93) 3-Y-0+ £12,272 (£4,655; £2,327; £1,058) **Stalls High**

Form RPR

0113 **1** **Another Bottle (IRE)**[49] [3797] 3-8-10 **83**........ RWinston 13 92+
(TPTate) *trckd ldrs: led 2f out: hld on wl u.p fnl f* **8/1**

0136 **2** *nk* **Will He Wish**[18] [4690] 8-9-5 **89**........(b) TEaves[(3)] 12 97
(SGollings) *midfield: drvn along over 2f out: gd hdwy u.p appr fnl f: ev ch wl ins last: no ex* **33/1**

3022 **3** *shd* **Vicious Warrior**[36] [4178] 5-9-5 **86**........ DeanMcKeown 8 94
(RMWhitaker) *cl up: rdn to chal ent fnl f: ev ch ins last: no ex clsng stages* **13/2**[2]

4021 **4** *1/2* **Trouble Mountain (USA)**[18] [4678] 7-8-4 **71**........ RFfrench 4 78
(MWEasterby) *towards rr: pushed along 1/2-way: hdwy over 2f out: rdn and in tch over 1f out: styd on ins last: nvr able to chal* **16/1**

1105 **5** *1/2* **Imperialistic (IRE)**[9] [4948] 3-9-6 **93**........ DarrenWilliams 1 102+
(KRBurke) *hld up in rr: nt clr run over 1f out: r.o wl fnl f: nt rch ldrs* **12/1**

1132 **6** *hd* **Goodbye Mr Bond**[32] [4258] 4-8-4 **71**........ FNorton 7 76+
(EJAlston) *hld up: nt clr run over 1f out: r.o wl fnl f: nt rch ldrs* **6/1**[1]

3110 **7** *2* **Tableau (USA)**[10] [4906] 3-8-13 **86**........ MHills 11 87
(BWHills) *cl up: pushed along 3f out: outpcd over 1f out: kpt on ins last* **10/1**

5201 **8** *1 1/4* **Nevada Desert (IRE)**[7] [4988] 4-8-10 **77** 6ex........(p) SChin 3 75
(RMWhitaker) *midfield: rdn and in tch 2f out: wknd appr fnl f* **8/1**

6213 **9** *3/4* **Young Mr Grace (IRE)**[7] [4988] 4-8-13 **80**........ DAllan 6 77
(TDEasterby) *led tl rdn and hdd 2f out: wknd fnl f* **7/1**[3]

1463 **10** *shd* **Alchemist Master**[30] [4349] 5-8-2 **72**........(p) HayleyTurner[(3)] 9 69
(RMWhitaker) *hld up in rr: effrt over 1f out: sn rdn and btn* **14/1**

3000 **11** *1 1/4* **Retirement**[10] [4920] 5-8-11 **78**........ NCallan 10 72
(MHTompkins) *midfield: rdn over 2f out: btn whn hmpd ins fnl f* **15/2**

6300 **12** *1/2* **Strong Hand**[9] [4931] 4-8-7 **74**........ TLucas 5 67
(MWEasterby) *chsd ldrs: ch over 2f out: sn rdn and wknd* **12/1**

1110 **13** *8* **Ace Of Hearts**[58] [3539] 5-9-10 **91**........ RMullen 2 67
(CFWall) *hld up: sme hdwy u.p over 2f out: wknd over 1f out: lost tch and eased ins last* **14/1**

1m 40.96s (-0.14) **Going Correction** +0.15s/f (Good)
**WFA** 3 from 4yo+ 6lb **13** Ran SP% **120.7**
Speed ratings: **106,105,105,105,104 104,102,101,100,100 99,98,90**CSF £245.64 CT £1825.58 TOTE £8.10: £3.30, £7.70, £2.70; EX 189.40.
**Owner** J Hanson **Bred** Killeen Castle Stud **Trained** Tadcaster, N Yorks
■ Stewards Enquiry : Dean McKeown two-day ban: used whip without giving gelding time to respond (Sep 10-11)

**FOCUS**
A competitive handicap and solid form with only a neck and a short head separating the front three.

**NOTEBOOK**
**Another Bottle(IRE)** had been progressive - winning his maiden and following up in handicap company - prior to his defeat in a small field at Ayr last month (both races on fast ground), and this softer surface did him no harm at all. If anything it suited as it placed extra emphasis on stamina, and he continually shapes as though a mile two is within his compass. He dug deep under pressure when hard pressed and does not want for battling qualities, so off what is still a reasonable mark, can win again in the coming weeks.
**Will He Wish** responded well to pressure to throw down a challenge to the winner, but was always just being held on the run to the line. He has never won over this trip but does stay it well enough.
**Vicious Warrior** continues to run well without winning and it was only in the last 50 yards he cried enough. His turn will come again.
**Trouble Mountain(USA)** made some late headway but was never going to win. He had taken plenty of driving to get into a challenging position and could offer no more once there.
**Imperialistic(IRE)** was finishing best of all and was arguably unlucky not to get closer, as she was a little short of room a furlong out.
**Goodbye Mr Bond** was another who came home strongly having not had the clearest of passages, and he remains in good fettle.
**Tableau(USA)** comes from a stable whose horses are back to a little bit of form and he should be back winning before long.

### 5195 RIPON CHAMPION TWO YRS OLD TROPHY, 2004 (LISTED RACE) 6f

**4:00** (4:00) (A ) 2-Y-O £15,660 (£5,940; £2,970; £1,350) **Stalls High**

Form RPR

3331 **1** **Space Shuttle**[13] [4836] 2-8-11 93........ DAllan 2 100
(TDEasterby) *cl up: rdn to ld 2f out and qcknd: hld on wl u.p fnl f* **12/1**

113 **2** *1/2* **Abraxas Antelope (IRE)**[12] [4857] 2-8-11 100........ RWinston 4 99
(JHowardJohnson) *slt ld tl hdd 2f out: ev ch and rdn ins fnl f: no ex* **5/4**[1]

421 **3** *nk* **Sentiero Rosso (USA)**[3] [5084] 2-8-11 ........ TEaves 6 98
(BEllison) *hld up: hdwy over 1f out: chsd first 2 and rdn fnl f: r.o* **20/1**

61 **4** *1/2* **Reqqa**[26] [4454] 2-8-11 ........ RHills 5 96
(MJohnston) *in tch: effrt 2f out: kpt on wl u.p fnl f* **5/2**[2]

2021 **5** *3* **Dario Gee Gee (IRE)**[16] [4757] 2-8-11 95........ NCallan 1 87
(KARyan) *wnt lft s: sn in tch: effrt 2f out: outpcd and btn whn hmpd appr fnl f* **11/2**[3]

4140 **6** *5* **Satin Finish (IRE)**[16] [4744] 2-8-6 97........ CCatlin 3 67
(MRChannon) *w ldr tl rdn and wknd qckly 2f out* **12/1**

1m 14.63s (1.73) **Going Correction** +0.25s/f (Good) **6** Ran SP% **108.5**
Speed ratings: **98,97,96,96,92 85**CSF £25.96 TOTE £13.00: £3.70, £1.40; EX 32.60.
**Owner** Jennifer Pallister & Jonathan Gill **Bred** Miss S E Hall **Trained** Great Habton, N Yorks

**FOCUS**
A decent renewal but they did not go much of a gallop, the time was modest for the grade, and this counted against the likes of Abraxas Antelope and Reqqa, but the winner who is going the right way and can plunder another decent prize later in the season.

**NOTEBOOK**

**Space Shuttle** stepped up massively on his York nursery win, handling the ground well and quickening up best off the gallop to win a shade comfortably. Evidently progressive, he looks the ideal type for something like the Redcar Two-Year-Old Trophy or October Yearling Sales race at Doncaster.

**Abraxas Antelope(IRE)** failed to run up to York form and would have been better suited by a truer gallop. He is better than this but will need to raise his game if taking up his engagement in the Middle Park.

**Sentiero Rosso(USA)** stepped up on recent form and did well given he was one of those who raced right at the back of the field.

**Reqqa**, despite having won his maiden on soft, is bred to appreciate fast ground and this slowly-run race on the ground would not have been to his advantage. He simply failed to quicken once getting out in the open and, once getting a fast surface and bigger field, should show masses of improvement.

**Dario Gee Gee(IRE)** is exposed at this sort of level.

**Satin Finish(IRE)** stopped as though something was amiss and has failed to see her race out the last thrice now.

## 5196 FAMILY DAY MAIDEN STKS — 1m 4f 60y

4:35 (4:36) (D) 3-Y-O+ — £4,095 (£1,260; £630; £315) Stalls High

| Form | | | Horse | Jockey | RPR |
|---|---|---|---|---|---|
| 50 | 1 | | **Qudraat (IRE)**[61] 3417 3-8-13 | RHills 5 | 83 |
| | | | (EFVaughan) *prom: led over 2f out: styd on u.p* | 4/1[3] | |
| 2433 | 2 | ¾ | **Line Drawing**[7] 5007 3-8-13 74 | MHills 9 | 82 |
| | | | (BWHills) *led: qcknd over 3f out: hdd over 2f out: styd on u.p* | 5/2[1] | |
| -653 | 3 | 1 ¾ | **Serramanna**[14] 4806 3-8-8 73 | WRyan 1 | 74 |
| | | | (HRACecil) *in tch: hdwy to chse ldng pair 4f out: rdn 3f out: styd on: no imp* | 9/2 | |
| 042 | 4 | 5 | **Samaria (GER)**[14] 4819 3-8-8 74 | RMullen 3 | 67 |
| | | | (CFWall) *midfield: stmbld over 5f out: sn drvn along: styd on u.p fnl 3f: nvr able to chal* | 3/1[2] | |
| 6 | 5 | 12 | **Ismahaan**[22] 4583 5-9-4 | FNorton 8 | 49 |
| | | | (GWragg) *chsd ldrs tl outpcd over 3f out: sn no ch* | 12/1 | |
| 66 | 6 | 2 | **Alpha Juliet (IRE)**[22] 4573 3-8-8 | NPollard 7 | 46 |
| | | | (GMMoore) *hld up: hdwy into midfield 4f out: rdn over 2f out: no further prog* | 40/1 | |
| 0 | 7 | 10 | **Sweet At Heart (IRE)**[80] 2853 3-8-8 | DeanMcKeown 6 | 31 |
| | | | (PABlockley) *sn towards rr: n.d* | 100/1 | |
| 6- | 8 | 7 | **Mitrash**[452] 2144 4-9-9 | ANicholls 2 | 25 |
| | | | (DMccain) *sn bhd* | 66/1 | |
| 05 | 9 | 1 ½ | **Ink In Gold (IRE)**[3] 5086 3-8-13 | NCallan 11 | 23 |
| | | | (PABlockley) *in tch tl outpcd over 3f out* | 33/1 | |
| 5 | 10 | 3 | **Minstrel's Double**[45] 3896 3-8-10 | TEaves(3) 4 | 18 |
| | | | (FPMurtagh) *sn bhd* | 100/1 | |
| 0- | 11 | ½ | **Pagan Ceremony (USA)**[379] 4208 3-8-13 | RWinston 10 | 18 |
| | | | (MrsAJPerrett) *prom tl wknd 4f out* | 11/1 | |

2m 40.11s (0.21) **Going Correction** +0.15s/f (Good)
**WFA** 3 from 4yo+ 10lb — **11 Ran SP% 116.6**
Speed ratings: **105,104,103,100,92 90,84,79,78,76 76**CSF £14.08 TOTE £5.30: £1.60, £1.60, £1.60; EX 16.40.
**Owner** Hamdan Al Maktoum **Bred** Fieldspring Ltd **Trained** Newmarket, Suffolk

**FOCUS**

A fair maiden in which Qudraat clearly benefited from a break. He should rate higher and will pay his way in handicaps, with an extra couple of furlongs holding no fears.

**NOTEBOOK**

**Qudraat(IRE)**, a disappointment when last seen having previously shown plenty on his debut, had been given a break and, on ground that he clearly handled, was able to get off the mark. He stayed on well for pressure and further will be of no inconvenience in handicaps.

**Line Drawing** tried to nick it from the front and only found the one too good. He is pretty exposed and will need to raise his game if he is to be winning.

**Serramanna** plugged on at the one pace and will be better off back in handicaps.

**Samaria(GER)** was a bit disappointing given she had previously been progressive and this was not in keeping with her profile.

**Pagan Ceremony(USA)** is clearly one of his stable's lesser lights and will find life easier once handicapped. *Official explanation: jockey said gelding was unsuited by track*

## 5197 PATELEY BRIDGE H'CAP — 1m 2f

5:05 (5:06) (E) (0-70,68) 3-Y-O — £3,863 (£1,188; £594; £297) Stalls High

| Form | | | Horse | Jockey | RPR |
|---|---|---|---|---|---|
| 0666 | 1 | | **Prelude**[23] 4536 3-8-9 56 | DAllan 11 | 63 |
| | | | (WMBrisbourne) *trckd ldrs: effrt 3f out: rdn to chse ldr over 1f out: led ins fnl f: all out* | 10/1 | |
| 0134 | 2 | hd | **Futoo (IRE)**[19] 4628 3-9-5 66 | NPollard 9 | 73 |
| | | | (GMMoore) *led tl rdn and hdd ins fnl f: styd on* | 4/1[1] | |
| 5300 | 3 | 4 | **Tancred Imp**[34] 4207 3-7-5 45 oh5 | DFentiman(7) 12 | 44 |
| | | | (DWBarker) *in tch: drvn along 4f out: styd on u.p: wnt 3rd ins fnl f: no ch w first 2* | 33/1 | |
| 145 | 4 | ¾ | **Quickstyx**[138] 1392 3-9-7 68 | CCatlin 8 | 66 |
| | | | (MRChannon) *s.i.s: hld up: hdwy into midfield 3f out: kpt on u.p fnl 2f: nvr able to chal* | 4/1[1] | |
| 006 | 5 | 1 | **Gay Romance**[29] 4369 3-9-1 62 | MHills 2 | 58 |
| | | | (BWHills) *cl up: ev ch and rdn 2f out: wknd appr fnl f* | 10/1 | |
| 0554 | 6 | ¾ | **Boris The Spider**[48] 3822 3-8-0 50 | HayleyTurner(3) 10 | 45 |
| | | | (MDHammond) *hld up: hdwy into midfield over 3f out: rdn 2f out: no further prog* | 20/1 | |
| 4030 | 7 | 3 | **Lillianna (IRE)**[47] 3852 3-9-1 62 | WRyan 4 | 52 |
| | | | (HRACecil) *rr div: kpt on u.p fnl 3f: n.d* | 10/1 | |
| 0144 | 8 | nk | **Music Mix (IRE)**[12] 4853 3-9-3 64 | RMullen 5 | 53 |
| | | | (EALDunlop) *midfield: effrt over 3f out: sn rdn: no hdwy* | 11/2[2] | |
| 5000 | 9 | nk | **Myannabanana (IRE)**[4] 5061 3-7-13 46 | (v) RFfrench 7 | 34 |
| | | | (JRWeymes) *chsd ldrs: rdn 4f out: wknd over 2f out* | 20/1 | |
| 3604 | 10 | 19 | **Savannah River (IRE)**[2] 5130 3-7-13 46 ow1 | (t) FNorton 1 | — |
| | | | (CWThornton) *sn bhd: t.o* | 11/1 | |
| 5030 | 11 | 6 | **Smart Boy Prince (IRE)**[77] 2928 3-8-4 58 | GEdwards(7) 3 | 1 |
| | | | (MJAttwater) *prom on outer to 1/2-way: sn wknd: t.o* | 28/1 | |
| 0622 | 12 | 1 ¾ | **Cayman Calypso (IRE)**[19] 4624 3-9-3 64 | RWinston 6 | 4 |
| | | | (JMJefferson) *midfield: rdn over 3f out: sn btn: bhd whn eased ins fnl f: t.o* | 8/1[3] | |

2m 9.33s (1.33) **Going Correction** +0.15s/f (Good) — **12 Ran SP% 118.0**
Speed ratings: **100,99,96,96,95 94,92,92,91,76 71,70**CSF £47.13 CT £1293.27 TOTE £11.50: £2.50, £1.70, £9.50; EX 43.30 Place 6 £111.95, Place 5 £32.51.
**Owner** A P Burgoyne **Bred** Cheveley Park Stud Ltd **Trained** Great Ness, Shropshire

**FOCUS**

A moderate handicap that saw the first two finish clear, but the form is ordinary.

**NOTEBOOK**

**Prelude** got her head up on the line to win her first race at the seventh attempt, but made heavy weather of doing so. She has her quirks, but could be capable of scoring again while at the right end of the handicap, and headgear would not go amiss. *Official explanation: trainer's representative said, regarding the improved form shown, filly had benefited from the good to soft ground on this occasion*

**Futoo(IRE)** made a bold bid to make all and led everywhere but the line. He has been running respectably since scoring in June and deserves to gain compensation.

**Tancred Imp**, 5lb out of the handicap, ran on well enough without troubling the principals and deserves credit.

**Quickstyx**, returning from an absence of 138 days, ran as though this was needed and should go closer next time.

**Music Mix(IRE)** was well beaten and has now failed to cut the mustard in three outings on turf, since his decisive win on the Polytrack.

T/Plt: £93.80 to a £1 stake. Pool: £39,668.10. 308.50 winning tickets. T/Qpdt: £21.70 to a £1 stake. Pool: £1,753.90. 59.80 winning tickets. JF

# [3679] WARWICK (L-H)

Monday, August 30

**OFFICIAL GOING: Good to soft (good in places)**

The ground was drying out all the time and rode faster than the official description.
Wind: mod across Weather: fine

## 5198 SANDALL HOUSE MAIDEN AUCTION STKS (DIV I) — 7f 26y

2:00 (2:05) (E) 2-Y-O — £4,004 (£1,232; £616; £308) Stalls Low

| Form | | | Horse | Jockey | RPR |
|---|---|---|---|---|---|
| 652 | 1 | | **Briannsta (IRE)**[8] 4966 2-8-8 | SHitchcott(3) 10 | 72 |
| | | | (MRChannon) *hld up in tch: rdn over 2f out: wnt 2nd over 1f out: led wl ins fnl f: r.o* | 9/2[1] | |
| | 2 | nk | **Moon Forest (IRE)** 2-8-11 | AMcCarthy 1 | 71 |
| | | | (PWChapple-Hyam) *a.p: led over 4f out: rdn wl over 1f out: hdd wl ins fnl f* | 9/2[1] | |
| 54 | 3 | 2 ½ | **Ignition**[9] 4930 2-7-13 | BSwarbrick(5) 4 | 58 |
| | | | (WMBrisbourne) *a.p: chsd wnr over 2f out tl rdn over 1f out: edgd lft ins fnl f: one pce* | 7/1[2] | |
| 2500 | 4 | 3 ½ | **Grand Option**[33] 4235 2-8-9 71 | ADaly 14 | 54 |
| | | | (BWDuke) *a.p: rdn over 1f out: wknd ins fnl f* | 11/1 | |
| 00 | 5 | 1 | **Tomobel**[17] 4706 2-8-2 | MHenry 8 | 44 |
| | | | (MHTompkins) *dwlt: bhd tl hdwy on outside over 1f out: nvr nrr* | 25/1 | |
| 05 | 6 | shd | **Tuvalu (GER)**[60] 3438 2-8-12 | KDarley 17 | 54+ |
| | | | (AMBalding) *hld up: hdwy over 3f out: wknd ins fnl f* | 8/1[3] | |
| 0 | 7 | 1 ¼ | **Archie Wright**[17] 4730 2-8-9 | OUrbina 15 | 48+ |
| | | | (RHannon) *hld up: hdwy 3f out: edgd lft jst over 1f out: no imp* | 20/1 | |
| 05 | 8 | 1 ¾ | **Lady Luisa (IRE)**[36] 4166 2-7-13 | NMackay(3) 12 | 36 |
| | | | (JSMoore) *dwlt: nvr nrr* | 11/1 | |
| 05 | 9 | 1 | **Cross My Shadow (IRE)**[5] 5034 2-8-12 | (t) KMcEvoy 11 | 43 |
| | | | (MFHarris) *led over 2f out: wknd over 1f out* | 14/1 | |
| 4 | 10 | shd | **Bob Baileys**[21] 4599 2-8-7 | JQuinn 2 | 38 |
| | | | (PRChamings) *dwlt: nvr nr ldrs* | 10/1 | |
| 0 | 11 | 1 ½ | **Monad (IRE)**[18] 4682 2-8-8 ow4 | RHavlin 16 | 35 |
| | | | (MrsPNDutfield) *mid-div: pushed along 3f out: wknd 2f out* | 100/1 | |
| | 12 | 1 ¼ | **Stolen** 2-8-9 | SDrowne 9 | 33 |
| | | | (WRMuir) *dwlt: a bhd* | 66/1 | |
| | 13 | nk | **Saxon Lil (IRE)** 2-8-2 | JoannaBadger 13 | 25 |
| | | | (JLSpearing) *s.s: a bhd* | 33/1 | |
| | 14 | ¾ | **Dewin Coch** 2-8-7 | SWKelly 5 | 28 |
| | | | (WMBrisbourne) *dwlt: sn chsng ldrs: rdn and wknd over 1f out* | 66/1 | |
| 5 | 15 | nk | **Silsong (USA)**[18] 4682 2-8-6 | SRighton 3 | 26+ |
| | | | (BRMillman) *mid-div: rdn 3f out: sn bhd* | 20/1 | |
| | 16 | 2 | **Flower Seeker** 2-8-7 | EAhern 6 | 22 |
| | | | (CTinkler) *sn pushed along: a bhd* | 16/1 | |
| 000 | 17 | 2 ½ | **David's Symphony (IRE)**[22] 4579 2-8-13 | PaulEddery 7 | 22 |
| | | | (RHannon) *mid-div: lost pl 4f out: bhd fnl 3f* | 50/1 | |

1m 23.94s (-0.96) **Going Correction** -0.175s/f (Firm) — **17 Ran SP% 120.5**
Speed ratings: **98,97,94,90,89 89,88,86,84,84 83,81,81,80,80 77,75**CSF £20.19 TOTE £4.30: £2.10, £2.60, £2.30; EX 25.60.
**Owner** B Brooks **Bred** Anthony M Cahill **Trained** West Ilsley, Berks

**FOCUS**

a fair maiden in which the winning time was nearly one and a half seconds faster than the other division. The form is ordinary but the runner-up should be better for this debut.

**NOTEBOOK**

**Briannsta(IRE)** has improved with each start and a return to a mile will not bother him.

**Moon Forest(IRE)** ◆, a half-brother to dual five-furlong juvenile winner Woodsmoke, did more than enough to suggest that he can soon go one better.

**Ignition** is continuing to progress along the right lines.

**Grand Option** may be out of a mare who won over a mile and a quarter, but did not appear to stay the seven at this stage of his career.

**Tomobel** should be suited by a mile but does need to get her act together at the start.

**Tuvalu(GER)** was a bit disappointing given that the ground was probably not as slow as the official description.

**Lady Luisa(IRE)** *Official explanation: jockey said filly missed the break*

**Cross My Shadow(IRE)** *Official explanation: jockey said colt ran too freely early on*

**Bob Baileys** *Official explanation: jockey said gelding was hampered leaving stalls*

## 5199 LAW COMMISSION CONDITIONS STKS — 7f 26y

2:30 (2:31) (C) 3-Y-O+ — £9,951 (£3,679; £1,839; £836) Stalls Low

| Form | | | Horse | Jockey | RPR |
|---|---|---|---|---|---|
| 0320 | 1 | | **Polar Way**[16] 4745 5-9-0 114 | RHughes 1 | 109+ |
| | | | (MrsAJPerrett) *hld up in tch: qckn to ld jst over 1f out: drvn out* | 8/11[1] | |
| -025 | 2 | ½ | **Desert Destiny**[45] 3906 4-8-11 110 | (t) KMcEvoy 4 | 105+ |
| | | | (SaeedBinSuroor) *hld up: hdwy 2f out: sn rdn: edgd lft and wnt 2nd ins fnl f: kpt on* | 5/2[2] | |
| -064 | 3 | 2 | **Prince Tum Tum (USA)**[45] 3906 4-8-11 97 | KDarley 3 | 100 |
| | | | (JLDunlop) *chsd ldr: rdn over 2f out: led briefly over 1f out: no ex ins fnl f* | 9/2[3] | |
| 103- | 4 | 5 | **Romaric (USA)**[382] 4108 3-8-6 85 | JBramhill 2 | 87 |
| | | | (JRNorton) *hld up: rdn over 2f out: no rspnse* | 50/1 | |
| 6255 | 5 | 1 | **Dancing King (IRE)**[94] 2445 8-9-0 48 | JoannaBadger 5 | 87? |
| | | | (PWHiatt) *led: rdn over 2f out: hdd over 1f out: sn wknd* | 150/1 | |

1m 22.73s (-2.17) **Going Correction** -0.175s/f (Firm)
**WFA** 3 from 4yo+ 5lb — **5 Ran SP% 107.3**
Speed ratings: **105,104,102,96,95**CSF £2.61 TOTE £1.70: £1.10, £1.70; EX 2.90.
**Owner** K Abdulla **Bred** Juddmonte Farms **Trained** Pulborough, W Sussex



The Form Book, Raceform Ltd, Compton, RG20 6NL

**FOCUS**
A decent contest and fair form, bt only three mattered although the rank outsider did ensure a good pace.

**NOTEBOOK**
**Polar Way** showed his form in the Hungerford Stakes to be all wrong. He had to be kept up to his work after displaying a nice turn of foot to strike the front.
**Desert Destiny** had finished nearly three lengths behind the winner on identical terms at Newbury in July. He did little wrong despite being inclined to drift towards his rival.
**Prince Tum Tum(USA)** had split the first two at Newbury in July when he finished just in front of Desert Destiny.
**Romaric(USA)** made only 4,500 gns when sold by Sheikh Mohammed nearly three months ago.

## 5200 SANDALL HOUSE MAIDEN AUCTION STKS (DIV II) 7f 26y
**3:00** (3:05) (E) 2-Y-O **£4,017** (£1,236; £618; £309) **Stalls** Low

Form RPR
264 **1** **Polar Dawn**[18] 4681 2-8-2 70 SRighton 4 69+
(BRMillman) *hld up: hdwy on ins over 2f out: plld out over 1f out: edgd lft and r.o wl to ld nr fin* **7/2**[1]
6324 **2** ½ **Geisha Lady (IRE)**[25] 4475 2-8-2 74 SCarson 7 68
(RMBeckett) *a.p: rdn 3f out: led jst over 1f out: hdd nr fin* **5/1**[3]
0 **3** *hd* **My Gacho (IRE)**[21] 4611 2-8-11 RHavlin 9 76
(MrsPNDutfield) *led after 1f: rdn 3f out: hung lft 2f out: hdd jst over 1f out: r.o* **40/1**
0 **4** *nk* **Raffish**[25] 4480 2-8-12 ow4 LFletcher(3) 6 79
(JMPEustace) *hld up in tch: rdn 3f out: hdwy over 1f out: kpt on towards fin* **40/1**
056 **5** *1* **High Dyke**[40] 4016 2-8-9 GGibbons 13 71
(DHaydnJones) *hld up in mid-div: hdwy over 3f out: rdn and edgd lft jst over 1f out: nt qckn ins fnl f* **9/2**[2]
40 **6** *3* **Baddam**[22] 4567 2-8-12 SDrowne 1 66
(JLDunlop) *hld up and bhd: hdwy over 2f out: styd on ins fnl f* **7/1**
00 **7** ½ **Bella Plunkett (IRE)**[11] 4876 2-7-11 BSwarbrick(5) 16 55
(WMBrisbourne) *hld up and bhd: rdn over 2f out: hdwy over 1f out: n.d* **66/1**
50 **8** 1¼ **Tahlal (IRE)**[3] 5096 2-8-11 GHind 2 60+
(MrsADuffield) *hld up in mid-div: hdwy on ins whn nt clr run over 1f out: nvr trbld ldrs* **20/1**
00 **9** *shd* **The Keep**[29] 4364 2-8-4 PaulEddery 12 53
(RHannon) *prom: rdn over 2f out: wknd fnl f* **14/1**
05 **10** *shd* **Captain Margaret**[35] 4198 2-8-7 (t) AMcCarthy 14 56
(JPearce) *hld up in tch: rdn 2f out: wknd over 1f out* **8/1**
**11** 1¼ **Trappeto (IRE)** 2-8-13 RHughes 3 59
(WRMuir) *s.i.s: a bhd* **14/1**
0 **12** ½ **Summer Charm**[9] 4936 2-8-4 KMcEvoy 10 48+
(WJarvis) *a bhd* **20/1**
0654 **13** ¾ **Mirage Prince (IRE)**[11] 4872 2-8-11 73 SWKelly 8 53
(WMBrisbourne) *led 1f: w ldr: rdn over 2f out: wknd over 1f out* **16/1**
**14** ¾ **Indian Well (IRE)** 2-8-9 OUrbina 17 49
(SKirk) *s.i.s: a bhd* **20/1**
**15** *1* **Overtop Way (GR)** 2-8-11 JQuinn 11 49
(PRChamings) *s.i.s: a in rr* **33/1**
00 **16** 1½ **Silver Creek**[8] 4966 2-8-7 JBramhill 15 41
(IAWood) *bhd fnl 2f* **40/1**
**17** 3½ **Poppyfields** 2-8-2 ADaly 5 27
(MBlanshard) *s.i.s: a in rr* **40/1**

1m 25.39s (0.49) **Going Correction** -0.175s/f (Firm) **17** Ran **SP%** **128.4**
Speed ratings: **90,89,89,88,87 84,83,82,82,82 80,80,79,78,77 75,71**CSF £18.90 TOTE £3.90: £2.10, £2.20, £12.80; EX 12.30.
**Owner** T E Pocock **Bred** T E Pocock **Trained** Kentisbeare, Devon

**FOCUS**
A fair maiden which was won in a time nearly a second and a half slower than the first division. The form, rated through the runner-up, may not prove that straightforward.

**NOTEBOOK**
**Polar Dawn** appreciated more patient tactics and turned around the Chepstow form with the runner-up.
**Geisha Lady(IRE)**, trying a longer trip, had finished just over a length in front of the winner on a pound better terms at Chepstow last month. There was no disgrace in this effort.
**My Gacho(IRE)**, a half-brother to five winners, showed tremendous improvement on his Windsor debut despite hanging over to the far rail early in the straight.
**Raffish**, a half-brother to numerous winners, was another to step up considerably on his debut run and should be suited to a mile.
**High Dyke** was supported in the ring but had no excuses.
**Baddam** was not knocked about and shaped like a stayer in the making.
**Trappeto(IRE)** *Official explanation: trainer said colt was found to have been badly struck into behind*
**Silver Creek** *Official explanation: jockey said colt suffered interference at 2f marker*

## 5201 WARWICKRACECOURSE.CO.UK H'CAP 6f 21y
**3:35** (3:36) (E) (0-70,70) 3-Y-O+ **£4,095** (£1,260; £630; £315) **Stalls** Low

Form RPR
0400 **1** **Magic Amour**[22] 4577 6-8-11 53 (v[1]) KDarley 4 65
(IanWilliams) *sn led: hdd 4f out: rdn and swtchd rt 2f out: led ins fnl f: drvn out* **11/1**
0014 **2** ½ **Northern Games**[28] 4390 5-9-3 59 (b) GParkin 10 69
(KARyan) *led early: remained prom: led jst over 1f out: rdn and hdd jst ins fnl f: r.o: b.b.v* **12/1**
0014 **3** *hd* **Branston Tiger**[2] 5124 5-9-3 62 (v) SHitchcott(3) 1 71
(PDEvans) *a.p: led 4f out: hrd rdn 2f out: hdd jst over 1f out: r.o* **9/2**[1]
0353 **4** 1½ **Indiana Blues**[11] 4868 3-9-6 65 KMcEvoy 8 70
(AMBalding) *hld up: sltly outpcd 3f out: hdwy fnl f: nt rch ldrs* **13/2**[3]
1032 **5** ½ **Enjoy The Buzz**[23] 4548 5-8-10 52 SWKelly 12 55
(JMBradley) *towards rr: rdn over 2f out: hdwy on outside over 1f out: one pce fnl f* **5/1**[2]
0404 **6** *nk* **Val De Maal (IRE)**[7] 5008 4-9-13 69 OUrbina 13 72
(GCHChung) *a.p: rdn and one pce fnl 2f* **11/1**
0602 **7** 1¾ **Port St Charles (IRE)**[11] 4879 7-8-12 54 EAhern 7 51
(PRChamings) *prom: rdn 2f out: wknd ins fnl f* **7/1**
2160 **8** *nk* **Full Spate**[13] 4837 9-9-7 70 CJDavies(7) 5 66
(JMBradley) *s.i.s: hld up: hdwy 4f out: rdn 2f out: wknd fnl f* **12/1**
0030 **9** ¾ **Ben Lomand**[12] 4846 4-9-9 65 ADaly 11 59
(BWDuke) *hld up and bhd: rdn 2f out: n.d* **40/1**
0260 **10** *nk* **Fleetwood Bay**[10] 4912 4-9-10 66 RHughes 3 59
(BRMillman) *prom: rdn wl over 1f out: wknd fnl f* **13/2**[3]
0230 **11** *2* **Mac's Talisman (IRE)**[45] 3911 4-8-10 52 MTebbutt 6 39
(VSmith) *a bhd* **20/1**
1000 **12** 1½ **Full Pitch**[58] 3524 8-9-6 65 LFletcher(3) 14 48
(WJenks) *s.i.s: a bhd* **20/1**
460- **13** *19* **Romantic Drama (IRE)**[258] 6197 3-9-2 61 SDrowne 9 —
(MrsALMKing) *sn bhd: eased whn no ch ins fnl f* **40/1**

1m 10.78s (-1.52) **Going Correction** -0.175s/f (Firm)
**WFA** 3 from 4yo+ 3lb **13** Ran **SP%** **120.5**
Speed ratings: **103,102,102,100,99 99,96,96,95,94 92,90,64**CSF £131.38 CT £708.94 TOTE £12.90: £3.90, £3.20, £2.10; EX 215.40.
**Owner** Mrs Maggie Bull **Bred** Juddmonte Farms **Trained** Portway, Warwicks

**FOCUS**
A moderate handicap but solid form for the grade. The first three were always in the van in a solidly-run race.

**NOTEBOOK**
**Magic Amour**, visored for the first time, appreciated the fact that the ground had dried out and took advantage of having slipped back down the ratings.
**Northern Games** lost nothing in defeat and the fact he broke a blood-vessel makes this performance all the more praiseworthy. *Official explanation: jockey said gelding bled from nose*
**Branston Tiger**, making a quick reappearance, had a hard race and deserves full marks for not shirking the issue.
**Indiana Blues** seems worth another try at seven.
**Enjoy The Buzz** could not quite sustain his effort.
**Val De Maal(IRE)** would make no impression in the home straight.
**Fleetwood Bay** *Official explanation: jockey said gelding hung right-handed throughout*
**Romantic Drama(IRE)** *Official explanation: trainer said filly was found to be in season on returning to the yard*

## 5202 SALTISFORD NURSERY 6f 21y
**4:10** (4:11) (E) 2-Y-O **£3,978** (£1,224; £612; £306) **Stalls** Low

Form RPR
3250 **1** **Simplify**[29] 4365 2-8-6 73 (b) KDarley 2 79
(DRLoder) *s.i.s: rdn and hdwy over 1f out: led wl ins fnl f: r.o wl* **12/1**
626 **2** 1½ **Unreal**[33] 4231 2-8-13 80 RHughes 4 82
(BWHills) *a.p: rdn 2f out: led 1f out: hdd and no ex wl ins fnl f* **3/1**[2]
2143 **3** *hd* **Tesary**[44] 3930 2-8-8 75 EAhern 11 76
(EALDunlop) *prom: lost pl 4f out: rdn and hdwy on outside over 1f out: r.o wl towards fin* **7/1**[3]
4120 **4** *nk* **Catwalk Cleric (IRE)**[76] 2954 2-9-0 88 AMullen(7) 14 88
(MJWallace) *hld up: rdn and hdwy over 1f out: kpt on towards fin* **10/1**
2503 **5** ¾ **Unlimited**[28] 4392 2-8-5 72 GHind 3 70
(MrsADuffield) *led: rdn over 2f out: hdd 1f out: one pce* **33/1**
44 **6** *shd* **Casterossa**[28] 4399 2-8-5 72 GGibbons 5 70
(DHaydnJones) *hld up in tch: rdn and edgd rt over 1f out: one pce* **25/1**
231 **7** 1¼ **Moth Ball**[16] 4739 2-9-2 83 SWKelly 6 77
(JAOsborne) *s.i.s: sn rcvrd: hdwy on ins over 3f out: rdn over 1f out: wknd ins fnl f* **7/4**[1]
1140 **8** *shd* **Island Swing (IRE)**[21] 4612 2-9-0 81 SDrowne 8 75
(JLSpearing) *prom: rdn over 1f out: wknd ins fnl f* **33/1**
030 **9** ½ **Storm Fury (USA)**[16] 4743 2-8-3 70 AMcCarthy 7 62
(PWChapple-Hyam) *hld up: hdwy 3f out: rdn wl over 1f out: wknd fnl f* **25/1**
0504 **10** *shd* **Mabella (IRE)**[20] 4621 2-7-13 66 SRighton 12 58
(BRMillman) *s.i.s: nvr nrr* **25/1**
2255 **11** 1¾ **Dante's Diamond (IRE)**[91] 2522 2-8-12 79 JQuinn 10 65
(FJordan) *a bhd* **25/1**
3420 **12** 3½ **Safendonseabiscuit**[30] 4342 2-8-6 73 KMcEvoy 9 49
(SKirk) *prom: lost pl over 3f out: eased 2f out* **14/1**
1544 **13** 3½ **Alvarinho Lady**[21] 4612 2-8-7 74 PaulEddery 1 39
(DHaydnJones) *hld up: hdwy on ins 3f out: sn rdn: wknd wl over 1f out* **16/1**

1m 11.53s (-0.77) **Going Correction** -0.175s/f (Firm) **13** Ran **SP%** **124.5**
Speed ratings: **98,96,95,95,94 94,92,92,91,91 89,84,79**CSF £46.28 CT £294.45 TOTE £15.80: £3.80, £1.50, £2.70; EX 62.60.
**Owner** Jumeirah Racing **Bred** Mrs Barbara Facchino **Trained** Newmarket, Suffolk

**FOCUS**
A typically competitive nursery and the form is solid.

**NOTEBOOK**
**Simplify**, dropped 6lb, had to come from behind after missing the break and will not be inconvienced by a return to seven.
**Unreal** looks set to score when striking the front but had no answer to the winner's late run.
**Tesary** finished with a flourish and is now ready to tackle seven.
**Catwalk Cleric(IRE)**, not seen since outclassed in the Coventry at Royal Ascot, is another who shaped as if he now wants further.
**Unlimited** seemed to benefit from a change of tactics.
**Casterossa** only ran because the ground had dried out.
**Moth Ball** found disappointingly little when let down.
**Safendonseabiscuit** *Official explanation: jockey said colt had hung right-handed round the bend*
**Alvarinho Lady** *Official explanation: jockey said filly had suffered interference in running*

## 5203 HOYS.CO.UK H'CAP 1m 4f 134y
**4:45** (4:45) (E) (0-75,74) 3-Y-O+ **£4,046** (£1,245; £622; £311) **Stalls** Low

Form RPR
1354 **1** **Smart John**[17] 4729 4-9-4 69 BSwarbrick(5) 7 76
(WMBrisbourne) *hld up in mid-div: stdy hdwy over 4f out: rdr dropped whip over 1f out: led jst ins fnl f: sn hdd: led again post* **11/2**[2]
0230 **2** *shd* **Great View (IRE)**[33] 4233 5-9-4 64 (v) JQuinn 2 71
(MrsALMKing) *hld up in tch: hrd rdn over 1f out: led ins fnl f: hdd post* **14/1**
-101 **3** *nk* **Wellington Hall (GER)**[23] 4556 6-9-5 65 AMcCarthy 1 72
(PWChapple-Hyam) *a.p: led over 2f out: sn rdn: hdd jst ins fnl f: r.o* **3/1**[1]
3024 **4** 1½ **Dr Cerullo**[25] 4486 3-8-13 73 SHitchcott(3) 6 77
(CTinkler) *hld up and bhd: rdn over 3f out: hdwy and nt clr run briefly 2f out: nt qckn fnl f* **6/1**[3]
5001 **5** *3* **Silver Prophet (IRE)**[12] 4849 5-9-0 67 DerekNolan(7) 11 67
(MRBosley) *s.i.s: bhd: rdn over 6f out: swtchd lft and hdwy on ins over 1f out: one pce fnl f* **10/1**
4320 **6** ¾ **Kythia (IRE)**[42] 3989 3-9-1 72 SDrowne 8 71
(HMorrison) *hld up in tch: rdn and ev ch over 1f out: eased whn btn ins fnl f* **16/1**
5342 **7** 1¼ **Fort Churchill (IRE)**[17] 4698 3-9-1 72 (b) KDarley 4 69
(MHTompkins) *hld up and bhd: rdn over 3f out: hdwy and edgd lft jst over 1f out: sn no imp* **9/1**
4160 **8** 3½ **Isa'Af (IRE)**[17] 4698 5-9-3 68 PMakin(5) 13 60
(PWHiatt) *prom: rdn over 2f out: wknd wl over 1f out* **20/1**
0400 **9** 1¼ **Best Flight**[8] 4971 4-9-6 66 EAhern 12 56
(BWHills) *chsd ldr: rdn 3f out: wknd wl over 1f out* **33/1**
2626 **10** 1½ **Aoninch**[12] 4849 4-9-2 62 RHavlin 9 49
(MrsPNDutfield) *hld up and bhd: hdwy 6f out: wknd 2f out* **11/1**

0203 **11** 2½ **Leighton (IRE)**[22] 4572 4-10-0 **74** RHughes 5 58
(RMStronge) *hld up: hdwy on ins over 3f out: rdn wl over 1f out: sn wknd* **20/1**

0006 **12** ½ **Caroubier (IRE)**[55] 3614 4-9-9 **69** KMcEvoy 10 52
(JGallagher) *a bhd* **33/1**

0051 **13** 9 **Dance World**[8] 4971 4-9-11 **74** 6ex BReilly(3) 3 43
(MissJFeilden) *led: rdn and hdd over 2f out: sn wknd* **7/1**

2m 43.64s (0.34) **Going Correction** +0.15s/f (Good)
**WFA** 3 from 4yo+ 11lb **13** Ran SP% **122.5**
Speed ratings: **104,103,103,102,100 100,99,97,96,95 94,94,88**CSF £78.13 CT £276.90 TOTE £6.80: £2.30, £3.50, £1.70; EX 149.50.
**Owner** Mr & Mrs D J Smart **Bred** D J And Mrs K D Smart **Trained** Great Ness, Shropshire

**FOCUS**
This ordinary handicap produced a blanket finish. The pace was reasonable and the form looks sound, if ordinary.

**NOTEBOOK**
**Smart John**, who has been finding the ground softer than ideal, just got the better of an exciting finish despite his rider losing his whip.
**Great View(IRE)** seemed to have benefited from a short break and was only beaten on the nod.
**Wellington Hall(GER)**, reverting to a longer trip, could not quite overcome a 3lb rise in the weights.
**Dr Cerullo** was forced to check briefly when making ground early in the home straight but the lack of a turn of foot was the real problem.
**Silver Prophet(IRE)** did not appreciate the fact that the ground had dried out.
**Kythia(IRE)** was not unduly punished once her chance had gone.
**Aoninch** *Official explanation: jockey said filly hung throughout*
**Dance World** *Official explanation: jockey said gelding was unsuited by today's good ground*

## 5204 RAYMOND TOOTH RACING MAIDEN STKS 7f 26y
**5:15** (5:31) (D) 3-Y-O+ **£4,290** (£1,320; £660; £330) **Stalls** Low

Form RPR

344- **1** **Vonadaisy**[338] 5222 3-8-8 70 SWKelly 5 67
(WJHaggas) *s.i.s: sn prom: rdn to ld 1f out: r.o wl* **7/2**[1]

5- **2** 2 **Bluebok**[429] 2796 3-8-13 KDarley 8 67
(DRLoder) *a.p: rdn to ld wl over 1f out: hdd 1f out: nt qckn* **5/1**[2]

6 **3** nk **Encora Bay**[18] 4683 3-8-8 JQuinn 16 61
(PRChamings) *a.p: rdn and ev ch over 1f out: r.o one pce fnl f* **16/1**

00 **4** nk **Russian Applause**[8] 4972 4-9-1 SHitchcott(3) 11 65
(PRChamings) *hld up and bhd: rdn over 2f out: hdwy over 1f out: hung lft ent fnl f: kpt on same pce* **50/1**

6 **5** 2 **Magic Spin**[10] 4916 4-8-13 SCarson 9 55
(RFJohnsonHoughton) *dwlt: hld up: hdwy whn nt clr run and swtchd lft wl over 1f out: sn rdn: hung lft ins fnl f: one pce* **10/1**

0 **6** nk **Mister Muja (IRE)**[18] 4683 3-8-13 (t) EAhern 10 59
(PWHarris) *hld up in mid-div: hdwy 3f out: rdn wl over 1f out: no imp fnl f; bbv* **9/1**

0 **7** nk **Zalebe**[91] 2519 3-8-8 AMcCarthy 12 53
(JPearce) *hld up in mid-div: hdwy 3f out: rdn over 1f out: one pce* **100/1**

0- **8** nk **Mannyman (IRE)**[304] 5850 3-8-8 MTebbutt 6 53
(WJarvis) *prom: rdn over 2f out: ev ch over 1f out: wknd fnl f* **33/1**

0020 **9** 1¼ **Nine Red**[6] 5020 3-8-8 59 PFitzsimons 14 49
(JMBradley) *s.i.s: bhd: rdn and hung rt bnd over 3f out: nvr trbld ldrs* **20/1**

66 **10** 2½ **Ollijay**[11] 4869 3-8-13 GGibbons 7 48
(MrsHDalton) *s.i.s: a bhd* **100/1**

50 **11** 3 **Mujawer (USA)**[29] 4369 3-8-13 (b[1]) ADaly 13 40
(MPTregoning) *chsd ldrs tl lost pl over 2f: n.d after* **6/1**[3]

0 **12** 8 **Tanne Blixen**[38] 4097 3-8-8 GParkin 15 14
(PSFelgate) *led: rdn and hdd wl over 1f out: sn wknd* **100/1**

**13** 18 **Master Rat** 3-8-13 RHavlin 3 —
(RJHodges) *dwlt: sn wl bhd: t.o* **50/1**

1m 25.57s (0.67) **Going Correction** -0.175s/f (Firm)
**WFA** 3 from 4yo 5lb **13** Ran SP% **92.7**
Speed ratings: **89,86,86,86,83 83,83,82,81,78 75,65,45**CSF £11.20 TOTE £4.20: £1.40, £1.70, £5.10; EX 15.60.
**Owner** B Smith/A Duke/J Netherthorpe/J Guthrie **Bred** D J And Mrs Deer **Trained** Newmarket, Suffolk

**FOCUS**
They went no great pace in this ordinary maiden and the time was slow. The form is modest at best.

**NOTEBOOK**
**Vonadaisy** really got her act together on this belated reappearance. She looks set to make up for lost time.
**Bluebok**, who made his debut in June last year, could not cope with the winner but should soon find a suitable opening.
**Encora Bay** is out of a mare who won over a mile and should do better at that trip.
**Russian Applause** again showed a tendency to hang left but was racing that way this time and improved dramatically as a consequence.
**Magic Spin**, trying another furlong, has now shown signs of ability in both her starts.
**Mister Muja(IRE)** has made an inauspicious start to his career. *Official explanation: trainer said gelding had bled from the nose*
**Ollijay** *Official explanation: jockey said gelding was outpaced all the way*

## 5205 EMAIL WARWICK@RHT.NET H'CAP 2m 39y
**5:45** (6:01) (E) (0-70,69) 3-Y-O+ **£4,855** (£1,494; £747; £373) **Stalls** Low

Form RPR

1031 **1** **Moonshine Beach**[19] 4627 6-9-8 69 PMakin(5) 11 77
(PWHiatt) *a.p: rdn over 3f out: styd on to ld cl home* **4/1**[1]

0400 **2** ½ **Henry Island (IRE)**[19] 4647 11-9-1 57 EAhern 2 64
(MrsAJBowlby) *hld up in tch: c stands' side and led over 1f out: sn rdn: hdd cl home* **10/1**

0310 **3** nk **Astromancer (USA)**[61] 3429 4-8-7 49 KDarley 12 56
(MHTompkins) *hld up in tch: rdn and sltly outpcd 3f out: rallied over 1f out: ev ch ins fnl f: styd on* **16/1**

0006 **4** nk **Snow's Ride**[70] 3153 4-9-4 60 PaulEddery 4 67
(WRMuir) *hld up and bhd: hdwy over 3f out: rdn wl over 1f out: styd on ins fnl f* **11/1**

2613 **5** 1¼ **Calamintha**[70] 3153 4-9-8 64 KMcEvoy 13 69
(MCPipe) *a.p: led 4f out: rdn over 2f out: hdd over 1f out: wknd wl ins fnl f* **9/2**[2]

1206 **6** 8 **Darn Good**[19] 4647 3-8-12 68 (b) RHughes 7 64
(RHannon) *hld up towards rr: reminders over 7f out: hdwy over 6f out: wknd over 4f out* **8/1**[3]

-610 **7** 1 **Teorban (POL)**[19] 4647 5-9-1 57 JQuinn 5 51
(DJSFfrenchDavis) *hld up and bhd: hdwy 2f out: nvr nr ldrs* **20/1**

1100 **8** nk **Court One**[32] 4261 6-7-13 46 BSwarbrick(5) 15 40
(RJPrice) *hld up and bhd: hung lft wl over 1f out and ent fnl f: nvr nr ldrs* **25/1**

0240 **9** nk **Bold Blade**[4] 5058 3-8-4 60 GGibbons 10 54
(MJPolglase) *led: hdd 4f out: sn rdn: wknd over 1f out: eased whn btn fnl f* **33/1**

-003 **10** 7 **Caliban (IRE)**[72] 3108 6-8-5 47 RFitzpatrick 16 32
(IanWilliams) *t.k.h in rr: a bhd* **14/1**

2036 **11** 1½ **Sashay**[95] 2429 6-7-12 45 StephanieHollinshead(5) 1 28
(RHollinshead) *prom: lost pl over 6f out: rdn over 4f out: n.d after* **22/1**

4504 **12** 5 **Rossall Point**[14] 4820 3-8-7 63 ow1 SKelly 6 40
(JLDunlop) *hld up in mid-div: rdn and hdwy over 4f out: wknd 3f out* **8/1**[3]

0340 **13** 14 **Fleetfoot Mac**[34] 4210 3-8-8 67 ow1 (v[1]) SHitchcott(3) 3 28
(PDEvans) *w ldr tl rdn and wknd over 6f out: t.o* **14/1**

0000 **14** 11 **Vin Du Pays**[8] 4971 4-8-3 45 SCarson 9 —
(MBlanshard) *mid-div: rdn and hdwy over 6f out: wknd over 4f out: t.o* **33/1**

540- **15** 11 **Business Traveller (IRE)**[134] 3762 4-8-3 45 AMcCarthy 14 —
(RJPrice) *rdn over 6f out: a bhd: t.o* **8/1**[3]

00-R **16** 5 **Jawwala (USA)**[15] 4778 5-9-3 59 (p) RHavlin 8 —
(JRJenkins) *mid-div: rdn along after 3f: lost pl over 7f out: sn bhd: t.o* **100/1**

3m 33.63s (1.82) **Going Correction** +0.15s/f (Good)
**WFA** 3 from 4yo+ 14lb **16** Ran SP% **128.0**
Speed ratings: **101,100,100,100,99 95,95,95,95,91 90,88,81,75,70 67**CSF £42.92 CT £607.85 TOTE £4.80: £1.60, £2.30, £4.30, £2.80; EX 35.90 Place 6 £57.41, Place 5 £26.03.
**Owner** Ken Read **Bred** Lawrence Shepherd **Trained** Hook Norton, Oxon

**FOCUS**
A competitive staying handicap and the form looks sound enough.

**NOTEBOOK**
**Moonshine Beach** continues to go from strength to strength and registered his fourth win of the summer despite having gone up a total of 25lb.
**Henry Island(IRE)**, 7lb lower than when landing this race last year, made a brave attempt to follow up.
**Astromancer(USA)** put any doubts to rest that she does not stay two miles.
**Snow's Ride** bounced back to form after a couple of months off.
**Calamintha** found the drying ground against her.
T/Plt: £42.60 to a £1 stake. Pool: £27,603.85. 472.95 winning tickets. T/Qpdt: £32.00 to a £1 stake. Pool: £1,395.60. 32.20 winning tickets. KH

5206 - 5208a (Foreign Racing) - See Raceform Interactive

# 5192 RIPON (R-H)
### Tuesday, August 31

**OFFICIAL GOING: Good to soft (soft in places)**
The ground had dried out overnight and continued to do so throughout a warm and sunny afternoon but on the straight course the far rail was the place to be.
Wind: Almost nil. Weather: Fine and sunny.

## 5209 BLACK SHEEP BREWERY MAIDEN AUCTION STKS 5f
**2:15** (2:17) (E) 2-Y-O **£4,071** (£1,252; £626; £313) **Stalls** Low

Form RPR

002 **1** **Oceanico Dot Com (IRE)**[22] 4607 2-8-5 67 FNorton 11 72
(ABerry) *mde all far side: clr over 1f out: r.o wl* **11/4**[1]

0 **2** 4 **Bond Puccini**[57] 3577 2-8-10 DMcGaffin 13 63
(BSmart) *racd far side: chsd wnr: kpt on fnl f* **20/1**

423 **3** 1¼ **Bond Babe**[6] 4986 2-8-9 FLynch 3 67+
(BSmart) *led stands' side: clr over 1f out on that side: no ch w wnr far side* **9/2**[2]

0 **4** 2 **Bob's Flyer**[10] 4936 2-8-9 DeanMcKeown 7 51
(JGGiven) *swtchd rt after 150yds to r far side: chsd ldrs: hung lft over 1f out: one pce* **10/1**[3]

**5** 1¾ **Dispol Charm (IRE)** 2-8-2 PFessey 14 38
(TDBarron) *leggy: unf: swvd rt s: racd far side: chsd ldrs: fdd over 1f out* **10/1**[3]

**6** 1¼ **Danethorpe Lady (IRE)** 2-8-6 ow1 DarrenWilliams 10 37
(DShaw) *neat: dwlt: swtchd rt after 150 yds and racd far side: kpt on fnl 2f: nvr a threat* **25/1**

**7** 2½ **El Potro** 2-8-7 SSanders 4 38+
(BAMcmahon) *w'like: cmpt: dwlt: racd stands' side: hdwy over 2f out: kpt on fnl f* **11/4**[1]

0 **8** nk **Mochaccino (IRE)**[11] 4924 2-7-13 HayleyTurner(3) 6 32+
(DShaw) *racd stands' side: chsd ldr: wknd fnl f* **50/1**

0000 **9** 1 **The Terminator (IRE)**[24] 4532 2-8-10 PBradley 1 37+
(ABerry) *racd stands' side: chsd ldrs: outpcd fnl 2f* **100/1**

0 **10** ¾ **Kimberley Hall**[92] 2526 2-8-2 PHanagan 12 17
(JAGlover) *s.i.s: racd far side: nvr wnt pce* **20/1**

0 **11** 2½ **Agreat Dayoutwithu**[72] 3116 2-8-4 ow2 RFitzpatrick 8 19+
(PTMidgley) *racd stands' side: chsd ldrs: wknd 2f out* **100/1**

**12** 1 **Lightning Prospect** 2-8-5 GFaulkner 2 17+
(PCHaslam) *lengy: unf: dwlt: racd stands' side: sme hdwy and swtchd rt over 1f out: sn wknd* **10/1**[3]

060 **13** 2½ **Mindful**[82] 2812 2-8-3 KGhunowa(7) 9 13+
(MJPolglase) *racd stands' side: outpcd and bhd fnl 2f* **50/1**

60.84 secs (0.64) **Going Correction** -0.025s/f (Good) **13** Ran SP% **118.1**
Speed ratings: **93,86,84,81,78 76,72,72,70,69 65,63,59**CSF £65.06 TOTE £4.10: £1.60, £6.90, £1.20; EX 57.80.
**Owner** The Red And The Green **Bred** Mrs C Hartery **Trained** Cockerham, Lancs

**FOCUS**
A very moderate maiden auction race and fair form, with the first two possibly advantaged by racing on the far side.

**NOTEBOOK**
**Oceanico Dot Com(IRE)** had no Coleorton Dancer to cope with this time and ran out a wide-margin winner of a very modest event.
**Bond Puccini**, who burst out of the stalls on his intended second start, is a poor walker and moderate mover. He appreciated the ease in the ground and followed the winner home on the far side.
**Bond Babe** won hands down on the stands' side, but at the line was overall only third best.
**Bob's Flyer**, very keen to post, was switched early on to race on the far side. He hung under pressure and still has something to learn.
**Dispol Charm(IRE)**, an April foal, is a half-sister to Cardinal Venture. On the leg and weak, she went sideways leaving the stalls but shaped nicely until tiring late on.
**Danethorpe Lady(IRE)**, born on April Fool's Day, lacks size and scope but she made a satisfactory debut.
**El Potro**, a March foal, was noisy in the paddock and showed a modearate action going down. After missing a beat at the start he finished second best on the stands' side. Presumably he had been showing better at home.

## 5210 GREEN-TECH CLASSIC PREMIER CLAIMING STKS 1m
2:45 (2:45) (D ) 3-4-Y-0 £5,428 (£1,670; £835; £417) Stalls High

Form RPR
4-00 1 **Familiar Affair**[16] 4780 3-8-9 78 FLynch 7 81
(BSmart) *led: qcknd over 3f out: kpt on wl: eased nr fin: unchal* **9/1**
2401 2 *1* **Khanjar (USA)**[11] 4928 4-9-9 73 DarrenWilliams 4 87
(KRBurke) *hld up: effrt over 3f out: styd on to go 2nd over 1f out: no imp* **7/1**
2310 3 *nk* **Todlea (IRE)**[27] 4435 4-9-3 78 DHolland 5 80
(JAOsborne) *t.k.h: nt clr run over 2f out: styd on wl fnl f* **7/4**[1]
3644 4 *5* **Fossgate**[16] 4781 3-8-9 70 (p) PRobinson 3 68
(JDBethell) *chsd ldrs: effrt and hung rt 4f out: one pce* **13/2**[3]
0000 5 *6* **Commander Bond**[11] 4928 3-8-6 68 JFanning 2 52
(BSmart) *swvd lft s: hdwy over 5f out: sn chsng ldrs: wknd over 1f out* **25/1**
0003 6 *3/4* **Ephesus**[23] 4569 4-9-3 78 (v) IMongan 1 56
(MissGayKelleway) *chsd ldrs: lost pl over 1f out* **5/2**[2]
0P14 7 *1/2* **Banana Grove (IRE)**[8] 4989 3-8-11 71 FNorton 6 55
(ABerry) *in rr: effrt and sme hdwy over 3f out: lost pl 2f out* **20/1**

1m 39.77s (-1.33) **Going Correction** -0.025s/f (Good)
**WFA** 3 from 4yo 6lb **7** Ran SP% **109.4**
Speed ratings: **105,104,103,98,92 91,91**CSF £62.69 TOTE £9.10: £3.90, £3.10; EX 76.10.The winner was claimed by Mr Nigel Shields for £20,000.
**Owner** Pinnacle Intikhab Partnership **Bred** Silfield Bloodstock And Iona Stud **Trained** Hambleton, N Yorks

**FOCUS**
A fair claimer but ust a steady gallop with the winner allowed to dictate things from the front.

**NOTEBOOK**
**Familiar Affair**, best in on official figures, was given his own way in front and his rider deserves full marks. He was claimed, and is expected to join David Barron.
**Khanjar(USA)**, who had 13lb to find with the winner on official ratings, stayed on to follow him home but, the way the race was run, he was never going to land a blow.
**Todlea(IRE)**, who looked in peak condition, took a fierce grip in the rear. Still last when short of racing room over two out, he picked up in good style late on, but far too late to trouble the winner.
**Fossgate**, who had a bit to find, never seemed to be happy in his work and is now a maiden after nine starts. *Official explanation: jockey said gelding hung right*
**Commander Bond**, who went sideways leaving the stalls, tried to keep tabs on the winner but his one success on his tenth start was on the All-Weather.
**Ephesus**, rated just 2lb inferior to the winner on official figures, tried to keeb tabs on him but he has yet to show he can handle easy ground and in the end was well beaten. *Official explanation: jockey said gelding lost action under pressure*

## 5211 CITY OF RIPON STKS (H'CAP) 1m 2f
3:15 (3:15) (C ) (0-90,88) 3-Y-0+ £9,396 (£3,564; £1,782; £810) Stalls High

Form RPR
3440 1 **Stretton (IRE)**[31] 4343 6-9-1 75 PRobinson 9 86
(JDBethell) *hld up in mid-div: hdwy 2f out: styd on ins last: led post* **9/1**
2560 2 *shd* **La Sylphide**[76] 2982 7-9-4 78 SWKelly 2 89
(GMMoore) *swtchd lft after s: led: qcknd 3f out: kpt on wl: jst ct* **12/1**
-610 3 *1 3/4* **Galvanise (USA)**[55] 3641 3-9-3 85 RHughes 7 93
(BWHills) *swvd lft s: trckd ldrs: chal 3f out: nt qckn fnl f* **13/2**[2]
4530 4 *1 1/2* **Tedstale (USA)**[13] 4852 6-9-4 78 (b) DAllan 6 83
(TDEasterby) *sltly hmpd s: bhd: nt clr run over 2f out: kpt on: nvr rchd ldrs* **33/1**
0001 5 *shd* **Telemachus**[10] 4950 4-9-11 85 (b) MFenton 4 90
(JGGiven) *t.k.h in rr: racd on outer: hdwy over 3f out: kpt on fnl 2f* **7/1**[3]
6113 6 *1/2* **Jimmy Byrne (IRE)**[45] 3929 4-9-1 78 TEaves(3) 12 82
(BEllison) *chsd ldrs: sn drvn along: ev ch over 3f out: one pce fnl 2f* **14/1**
3402 7 *1/2* **Cat's Whiskers**[3] 5127 5-9-5 79 DaleGibson 14 82
(MWEasterby) *sn chsng ldrs: effrt over 3f out: hrd rdn and one pce fnl 2f* **11/1**
6250 8 *shd* **Jabaar (USA)**[14] 4831 6-9-6 83 (b1) PMulrennan(3) 10 86
(MWEasterby) *hld up in rr div: hung rt over 1f out: kpt on ins last: nvr nr ldrs* **7/1**[3]
1251 9 *2* **Rotuma (IRE)**[23] 4571 5-8-8 75 (b) DTudhope(7) 5 74
(MDods) *hmpd s: bhd whn hmpd 6f out: gd hdwy over 3f out: fdd fnl 2f* **20/1**
0604 10 *2* **Compton Dragon (USA)**[11] 4901 5-9-0 74 (v) SSanders 11 70
(DNicholls) *s.i.s: bhd whn hmpd 6f out: sme hdwy on outer over 3f out: nvr nr ldrs* **20/1**
1200 11 *5* **Akash (IRE)**[24] 4530 4-10-0 88 JFanning 8 75
(MJohnston) *chsd ldrs: wknd over 2f out* **14/1**
0531 12 *1 1/2* **Rasid (USA)**[59] 3534 6-9-4 78 DHolland 13 62
(CADwyer) *bhd: hit rail 6f out: nvr a factor* **12/1**
0-30 13 *10* **Kentucky Blue (IRE)**[112] 2022 4-9-8 82 RWinston 3 48
(TDEasterby) *bhd whn hmpd 6f out: nvr a factor: eased* **25/1**
2441 14 *6* **Strider**[19] 4691 3-8-10 78 (v1) KFallon 1 33
(SirMichaelStoute) *chsd ldrs: drvn along over 3f out: lost pl over 2f out: sn bhd and eased* **9/2**[1]

2m 6.30s (-1.70) **Going Correction** -0.025s/f (Good)
**WFA** 3 from 4yo+ 8lb **14** Ran SP% **119.9**
Speed ratings: **105,104,103,102,102 101,101,101,99,98 94,92,84,80**CSF £106.16 CT £759.20 TOTE £10.10: £3.00, £4.60, £2.80; EX 163.00 Trifecta £2212.10 Pool: £4,673.54. 1.50 winning units..
**Owner** M J Dawson **Bred** Burton Agnes Stud Co Ltd **Trained** Middleham Moor, N Yorks

**FOCUS**
A decent handicap run at a sound pace, and the form looks sound.

**NOTEBOOK**
**Stretton(IRE)**, who has dropped to his lowest mark for three years, was a winner waiting to happen and everything fell into place here. Suited by the strong pace he enjoyed an uninterrupted passage and put his head in front right on the line.
**La Sylphide**, in great shape after an 11-week break, did well to show in front from a draw just one off the outside. She went for home halfway up the straight but was nailed on the line. She loves getting her toe in.
**Galvanise(USA)**, found to have mucus in his throat after Newmarket, looked in tip-top shape. He travelled strongly but was found wanting in the final furlong and was later reported to have a breathing problem. *Official explanation: jockey said colt had a breathing problem*
**Tedstale(USA)**, on a lengthy losing run, was on the back foot after being left short of room at the start. He ran out of racing room, but the way he was staying on at the death suggested this extended trip might be what he needs now.
**Telemachus**, pushed wide from his low draw, saw too much day light and was always tending to do too much.
**Jimmy Byrne(IRE)**, 8lb higher than his win two outings ago, was up in grade and was soon hard at work.
**Cat's Whiskers**, having his second outing in four days, did not look at anything like his best beforehand.
**Strider**, hoisted 2lb after Sandown, was most disappointing and the champion reported that he resented the first-time visor. *Official explanation: jockey said colt resented the visor*

## 5212 STEVE NESBITT CHALLENGE TROPHY NURSERY 6f
3:45 (3:46) (D ) 2-Y-0 £4,886 (£1,503; £751; £375) Stalls Low

Form RPR
233 1 **Breaking Shadow (IRE)**[15] 4804 2-8-3 72 PHanagan 6 81+
(RAFahey) *racd far side: trckd ldrs: nt clr run and swtchd lft over 1f out: led ins last: r.o strly* **4/1**[2]
31 2 *2 1/2* **Zomerlust**[17] 4761 2-8-9 78 RWinston 2 79
(JJQuinn) *racd stands' side: chsd ldr: led that gp over 2f out: styd on wl fnl f* **10/1**
6321 3 *nk* **Coleorton Dane**[33] 4277 2-8-9 78 NCallan 9 78
(KARyan) *led far side tl ins last: no ex* **7/1**[3]
513 4 *nk* **Generous Option**[43] 3975 2-9-2 85 JFanning 10 84
(MJohnston) *racd far side: chsd ldrs: hmpd over 1f out: kpt on wl ins last* **3/1**[1]
6410 5 *1/2* **Brooklime (IRE)**[3] 5119 2-8-9 78 DHolland 8 75
(JAOsborne) *racd far side: chsd ldrs: styd on same pce fnl f* **9/1**
10 6 *3/4* **Rosein**[90] 2568 2-8-9 78 SSanders 7 73
(MrsGSRees) *racd far side chsd ldrs: hung bdly lft 1f out: kpt on wl towards fin* **11/1**
1021 7 *2 1/2* **Make Us Flush**[19] 4676 2-8-7 76 FNorton 1 63
(ABerry) *racd stands' side: outpcd fnl 2f* **10/1**
3115 8 *2 1/2* **Word Perfect**[17] 4757 2-9-7 90 KFallon 5 70
(MWEasterby) *rrd s: racd far side: outpcd fnl 2f* **7/1**[3]
036 9 *1/2* **Along The Nile**[17] 4761 2-8-6 75 LGoncalves 4 53
(MrsJRRamsden) *swvd rt s: racd stands's ide: hung rt and bhd fnl 2f* **20/1**
4034 10 *1 3/4* **Melvino**[46] 3898 2-8-7 76 (v) MFenton 3 49
(TDBarron) *led stands' side tl over 2f out: sn lost pl* **20/1**

1m 14.06s (1.16) **Going Correction** -0.025s/f (Good) **10** Ran SP% **116.0**
Speed ratings: **91,87,87,86,86 85,81,78,77,75**CSF £43.50 CT £274.20 TOTE £5.20: £1.80, £3.10, £2.70; EX 59.40.
**Owner** G Morrill **Bred** Christoph Amerian **Trained** Musley Bank, N Yorks
■ Stewards Enquiry : P Hanagan three-day ban: careless riding (Sep 11-13)

**FOCUS**
A fair nursery in which the first two raced on opposite wings. A modest winning time for the grade but the winner should rate higher.

**NOTEBOOK**
**Breaking Shadow(IRE)** ◆, who had shown ability on three previous outings in maidens, seemed to thoroughly appreciate getting his toe in. Trapped on the far-side rail, he burst through went the gaps appreared and went clear in good style. He can win again at this level.
**Zomerlust** ◆ is progressing nicely and won hands down on the stands' side. He deserves another success.
**Coleorton Dane**, dropping back in trip, led them a merry dance on the far side but six furlongs looks to be his bare minimum.
**Generous Option** was knocked out of her stride by the winner and looked second-best on merit on the far side.
**Brooklime(IRE)**, making a quick return to action, had no excuse and looks rated to the very limit.
**Rosein** seemed to lose her way lacking company racing on the outside of the far-side group. Picking up again at the finish, this should have taught her a fair bit.

## 5213 SAPPER CONDITIONS STKS 5f
4:15 (4:15) (C ) 2-Y-0 £7,252 (£2,750; £1,375; £625) Stalls Low

Form RPR
12 1 **Sundance (IRE)**[25] 4514 2-8-12 JQuinn 3 95
(HJCollingridge) *trckd ldrs: shkn up to ld over 1f out: r.o strly* **9/4**[2]
1335 2 *1* **Bond City (IRE)**[13] 4860 2-8-12 95 FLynch 1 92
(BSmart) *trckd ldrs on inner: swtchd rt appr fnl f: nt qckn ins last* **9/2**[3]
4043 3 *1 3/4* **Bigalos Bandit**[13] 4860 2-9-0 99 RWinston 2 87
(JJQuinn) *trckd ldrs: ev ch over 1f out: nt qckn* **2/1**[1]
2130 4 *shd* **World At My Feet**[52] 3753 2-8-9 85 FNorton 8 82
(NBycroft) *chsd ldrs: keeping on same pce whn sltly hmpd jst ins last* **10/1**
5 *5* **Malaika** 2-7-11 StephanieHollinshead(5) 7 57
(RHollinshead) *rangy: unf; scope: slowly away: hdwy to chse ldrs over 2f out: wknd over 1f out* **66/1**
5410 6 *1* **Theatre Of Dreams**[35] 4217 2-8-12 89 ANicholls 5 63
(DNicholls) *led tl over 1f out: wknd and eased ins last* **5/1**
5500 7 *6* **Steal The Thunder**[83] 2773 2-8-5 PPMathers(5) 6 40
(ABerry) *s.i.s: a outpcd and bhd* **200/1**
0005 8 *shd* **Den Perry**[10] 4933 2-8-3 CEly(7) 4 39
(ABerry) *s.i.s: a outpcd and bhd* **200/1**

60.10 secs (-0.10) **Going Correction** -0.025s/f (Good) **8** Ran SP% **110.5**
Speed ratings: **99,97,94,94,86 84,75,75**CSF £11.89 TOTE £3.40: £1.10, £2.20, £1.20; EX 18.20.
**Owner** Richard Farquhar **Bred** Mrs Noelle Walsh **Trained** Exning, Suffolk

**FOCUS**
A decent juvenile contest in which they all elected to stick to the stands'-side rail. The form looks solid for the grade.

**NOTEBOOK**
**Sundance(IRE)**, who continually swished his tail in the paddock, appreciated the return to turf and his action suggests he likes getting his toe in. He scored with something in hand and deserves a crack now in Listed company.
**Bond City(IRE)**, a sharp type, improved on his York effort but in the end was very much second best. This might be as good as he is.
**Bigalos Bandit**, who looked very fit indeed, was giving weight away all round. He may have reached the limit of his improvement.
**World At My Feet** had something to find and this bold showing will not have done her nursery mark any good.
**Malaika**, a half-sister to five winners including Goldeva, is an April foal who stands over a fair amount of ground. She made a pleasing bow but looks more of a long-term prospect.
**Theatre Of Dreams**, edgy beforehand, showed bags of toe but, on the easy ground, tired badly late on. *Official explanation: trainer said colt had lost its action*
**Steal The Thunder**, hopelessly outclassed, picked up £500 for just turning up under the misguided appearance money scheme.
**Den Perry**, another 200/1 shot, was handed £500 for simply making up the field.

## 5214 EAT SLEEP DRINK AT NAGS HEAD, PICKHILL H'CAP 2m
4:45 (4:45) (E ) (0-75,71) 3-Y-0+ £3,777 (£1,162; £581; £290) Stalls High

Form RPR
-006 1 **Trilemma**[31] 4346 3-8-10 61 SSanders 1 74
(SirMarkPrescott) *hld up: stdy hdwy 6f out: chal over 2f out: styd on to ld last 150yds* **9/2**[2]
1623 2 *3/4* **Oops (IRE)**[22] 4609 5-8-5 45 NMackay(3) 3 57
(JFCoupland) *trckd ldrs: led 3f out: rdn over 1f out: carried hd high: hdd and no ex ins last* **3/1**[1]

1213 **3** *5* **Hearthstead Dream**[17] [4762] 3-9-6 **71** ... JFanning 6 77
(JDBethell) *hld up: hdwy over 4f out: wnt 3rd 2f out: sn wl outpcd* **5/1**[3]

3265 **4** *7* **Vicario**[19] [4692] 3-8-10 **61** ... JMackay 7 59
(MLWBell) *mid-div: effrt over 4f out: kpt on same pce: nvr nr to chal* **11/1**

4060 **5** *nk* **Simple Ideals (USA)**[22] [4609] 10-7-12 **35** ... KimTinkler 8 32
(DonEnricoIncisa) *hld up towards rr: kpt on fnl 3f: nvr a factor* **16/1**

1231 **6** *5* **Spitting Image (IRE)**[23] [4578] 4-9-7 **61** ... TEaves(3) 4 52
(KGReveley) *led 1f: led and qcknd 9f out: clr 6f out: hdd 3f out: wknd 2f out* **5/1**[3]

0-30 **7** *3* **Celtic Blaze (IRE)**[31] [4352] 5-9-3 **54** ... (tp) RWinston 9 42
(BSRothwell) *dwlt: hld up and bhd: nvr a factor* **12/1**

2305 **8** *shd* **Habitual Dancer**[16] [4778] 3-8-7 **58** ... PHanagan 2 46
(JeddO'Keeffe) *led after 1f tl 9f out: lost pl over 2f out* **13/2**

000- **9** *dist* **Subadar Major**[368] [4547] 7-7-13 **36** oh5 ow1 ... JQuinn 5 —
(MrsGSRees) *trckd ldrs: lost pl over 4f out: bhd and eased 3f out: virtually p.u: t.o* **100/1**

3m 28.1s (-5.40) **Going Correction** -0.025s/f (Good)
**WFA** 3 from 4yo+ 14lb **9** Ran SP% **112.7**
Speed ratings: **112,111,109,105,105 102,101,101,—**CSF £17.87 CT £68.30 TOTE £5.10: £2.40, £1.30, £1.90; EX 21.60 Place 6 £220.55, Place 5 £120.99.
**Owner** Mrs Sonia Rogers **Bred** Hesmonds Stud Ltd **Trained** Newmarket, Suffolk

**FOCUS**
A modest handicap in which the sound pace picked up at the halfway mark, and the form is fair for the level. The winning time was decent for the grade and was just 0.3 seconds outside the 11-year-old course record.

**NOTEBOOK**
**Trilemma**, a daughter of Slip Anchor, looked in tip-top trim. Given a canny ride, she crowded the runner-up and gained the upper hand near the line. With her it seems a case of the further she goes the better and, rated just 61, her wily handler has plenty of room to manoeuvre. *Official explanation: trainer's representative said, regarding the improved form shown, filly had benefited from the step up in trip and good to soft ground*
**Oops(IRE)**, well backed, went on travelling best but, in front he carried his head high and the wily Sanders kept his mount hard upsides and his rider had trouble using his whip to full effect.
**Hearthstead Dream**, stepping up in trip, had the blinkers left off and he did not see it out anywhere near as well as the first two.
**Vicario**, still 11lb higher than his sole success in May, has not really improved for the step up in trip.
**Simple Ideals(USA)**, having his 105th start, has not won for over two years and in his 11th year, time is hardly on his side.
**Spitting Image(IRE)**, attempting to get her trainer off the mark, went on and stepped up the gallop. Soon half a dozen lengths clear, when collared she dropped right away. Her two wins were both at Redcar have been on firm ground.
**Habitual Dancer** *Official explanation: jockey said gelding hung left*
**Subadar Major** *Official explanation: jockey said gelding was never moving well*
T/Jkpt: Not won. T/Plt: £95.30 to a £1 stake. Pool: £70,009.95. 536.05 winning tickets. T/Qpdt: £11.30 to a £1 stake. Pool: £4,967.70. 323.25 winning tickets. WG

## [5168] BADEN-BADEN (L-H)
### Tuesday, August 31

**OFFICIAL GOING: Soft**

## 5215a DARLEY OETTINGEN-RENNEN (GROUP 2) 1m
**3:25** (3:27) 3-Y-O+ **£35,211** (£14,085; £7,042; £3,521)

RPR

**1** **Pepperstorm (GER)**[30] [4378] 3-8-7 ... ABoschert 4 115
(UOstmann, Germany) *held up in rear, last straight, smooth progress to lead 1f out, ran on strongly* 2

**2** *2* **Checkit (IRE)**[9] [4984] 4-9-0 ... ACulhane 1 112
(MRChannon) *always close up, 3rd & ridden straight, every chance 1f out, kept on same pace under pressure* 3

**3** *2 ½* **Assiun (GER)**[51] [3792] 3-8-7 ... ASuborics 9 106
(PSchiergen, Germany) *led 2f, 2nd straight, led 2f out to 1f out, one pace* 1

**4** *4 ½* **Bear King (GER)**[30] [4378] 7-9-0 ... AStarke 7 98
(CSprengel, Germany) *always in touch, 6th straight, soon ridden & kept on same pace*

**5** *4 ½* **Horeion Directa (GER)**[30] [4378] 5-9-0 ... WMongil 5 89
(AndreasLowe, Germany) *tracked leaders, 4th on inside straight, soon beaten*

**6** *1 ½* **Up And Away (GER)**[66] [3335] 10-9-0 ... LHammer-Hansen 8 86
(FrauEMader, Germany) *5th straight on outside, weakened well over 1f out*

**7** *1 ¾* **Peppershot (GER)**[122] 5-9-0 ... (b) ADeVries 6 83
(WHefter, Germany) *led after 2f, headed 2f out, soon weakened*

1m 41.77s
**WFA** 3 from 4yo+ 6lb **7** Ran SP% **130.5**
Speed ratings: .
**Owner** Gestut Hony-Hof **Bred** P A Battel Et Al **Trained** Germany

**NOTEBOOK**
**Checkit(IRE)** for the second time in nine days travelled abroad only to see the ground go against him in the hours before the race. He still ran an honest race, but Pepperstorm swept past just as he was getting the better of Assiun at the furlong pole. He deserves a Pattern win and one day everything will fall right for him.

## [5051] LINGFIELD (L-H)
### Wednesday, September 1

**OFFICIAL GOING: Turf course - good to firm; all-weather - standard**
Wind: almost nil Weather: sunny

## 5216 EAST GRINSTEAD MAIDEN STKS (DIV I) 1m 4f (P)
**1:50** (1:54) (D3) 3-Y-O+ **£3,789** (£1,166; £583; £291) **Stalls** Low

Form RPR

034 **1** **Wedding Cake (IRE)**[42] [4028] 3-8-5 **73** ... NMackay(3) 1 73+
(SirMichaelStoute) *lw: a in tch: rdn to ld 1f out: edgd lft: but r.o wl* **3/1**[1]

23 **2** *1 ½* **Champagne Shadow (IRE)**[67] [3304] 3-8-13 **69** ... (b) JFortune 8 76
(GLMoore) *hld up: in mid-div: rdn 4f out: styd on to chse wnr fnl f* **7/1**

0003 **3** *2 ½* **Nassiria**[27] [4471] 3-8-5 **64** ... (p) J-PGuillambert(3) 7 67
(CEBrittain) *lw: trckd ldrs: rn wd on bnd after 3f: chsd ldr 7f out: rdn and ev ch appr fnl f: one pce ins* **16/1**

-032 **4** *5* **Turn 'n Burn**[17] [4775] 3-8-13 **78** ... MartinDwyer 3 64
(CACyzer) *led tl rdn and hdd 1f out: wknd ins fnl f* **4/1**[3]

0 **5** *20* **Hanazakari**[16] [4819] 3-8-13 ... JQuinn 2 32
(JARToller) *a in rr* **33/1**

0-42 **6** *1* **Four Pence (IRE)**[62] [3454] 3-8-13 **68** ... SSanders 9 30
(BWHills) *slowly away: sn prom: rdn over 3f out: wknd qckly* **7/2**[2]

0400 **7** *1 ½* **Song Of The Sea**[13] [4870] 3-8-8 **58** ... EAhern 6 23
(JWHills) *prom to 1/2-way: sn bhd* **33/1**

000 **8** *dist* **Peters Ploy**[11] [4939] 4-9-8 ... MHenry 4 —
(TKeddy) *chsd ldr to 7f out: rdn and sn btn: t.o* **100/1**

**9** *12* **Aetheling (USA)** 3-8-8 ... RHughes 5 —
(MrsAJPerrett) *w'like: leggy: bit bkwd: v.s.a: a bhd: t.o* **10/1**

2m 32.55s (-1.69) **Going Correction** +0.025s/f (Slow)
**WFA** 3 from 4yo+ 9lb **9** Ran SP% **101.6**
Speed ratings: **106,105,103,100,86 86,85,—,—**CSF £18.70 TOTE £2.40: £1.10, £2.00, £4.10; EX 9.90.
**Owner** Ballymacoll Stud **Bred** Ballymacoll Stud Farm Ltd **Trained** Newmarket, Suffolk

**FOCUS**
A pretty modest maiden, but the pace was quite good and there were few excuses, so it looks the more solid of the two divisions.

**NOTEBOOK**
**Wedding Cake(IRE)** does not have the ability of her half-brothers Gamut and Multicoloured, but she is progressing and was good enough to gain a success that will have done wonders for her paddock value. Always going well, she had to be switched for a run in the straight and that handed the initiative to the eventual runner-up, but she was always doing enough.
**Champagne Shadow(IRE)**, fresh from a 67-day break, again showed enough to suggest there is a similar race in him, responding well to pressure to give the winner a race in the straight.
**Nassiria** again simply found a couple too good for her. She was carried wide on the first bend, but it did not affect the result and she may be better off in handicaps. *Official explanation: again simply found a couple too good for her. She was carried wide on the first bend, but it did not affect the result and she may be better off in handicaps.*
**Turn 'n Burn** raced a little freely early and, after running wide on first bend, he could offer little close home. He was not at his best, but does not look worthy of his current rating in any case.
**Four Pence(IRE)**, racing for the first time in 62 days, did not respond to some serious reminders and is becoming disappointing. *Official explanation: , racing for the first time in 62 days, did not respond to some serious reminders and is becoming disappointing.*
**Song Of The Sea** *Official explanation: jockey said filly hung left*
**Aetheling(USA)**, a half-sister to the top-class ten-furlong performer Flemenfirth, lost several lengths at the start and could never get into contention thereafter thanks to the good pace.

## 5217 EAST GRINSTEAD MAIDEN STKS (DIV II) 1m 4f (P)
**2:20** (2:20) (D3) 3-Y-O+ **£3,779** (£1,163; £581; £290) **Stalls** Low

Form RPR

-000 **1** **Abington Angel**[14] [4848] 3-8-8 **67** ... (b) JFortune 7 62+
(BJMeehan) *hld up in rr: rdn and rapid hdwy over 3f out: led 2f out: sn clr: v easily* **10/1**

5324 **2** *8* **Mikao (IRE)**[27] [4492] 3-8-13 **80** ... DHolland 1 55+
(MHTompkins) *lw: trckd ldrs: rdn and styd on to chse easy wnr over 1f out* **2/1**[1]

0634 **3** *1* **Scarrabus (IRE)**[32] [4346] 3-8-13 **66** ... DSweeney 8 54
(BGPowell) *a.p: rdn 4f out: short of room 2f out: styd on one pce after* **5/1**[3]

0554 **4** *nk* **Zuma (IRE)**[40] [4087] 3-8-13 **73** ... (p) RHughes 3 53
(RHannon) *lw: in tch: rdn over 3f out and outpcd: kpt on ins fnl 2f* **5/1**[3]

0-00 **5** *nk* **Lysander's Quest (IRE)**[26] [4513] 6-9-8 **40** ... NDay 6 53?
(RIngram) *in rr: hdwy on outside 2f out: kpt on one pce* **50/1**

00-6 **6** *3 ½* **Dream Valley (IRE)**[9] [5007] 3-8-8 ... SSanders 9 43
(BWHills) *chsd ldr: rdn and ev ch 2f out: wknd qckly appr fnl f* **4/1**[2]

0 **7** *5* **Charing Cross (IRE)**[11] [4939] 3-8-13 ... RBrisland 4 40
(GLMoore) *hld up: a bhd* **25/1**

**8** *nk* **Mad** 3-8-8 ... JFEgan 2 35
(AndrewReid) *w'like: str: bit bkwd: b: b.hind: s.i.s: sn in tch* **12/1**

00 **9** *3* **Constructor**[11] [4939] 3-8-13 ... MartinDwyer 5 35
(CACyzer) *t.k.h: led tl hdd jst over 2f out: wkng whn hmpd wl over 1f out* **14/1**

2m 34.01s (-0.23) **Going Correction** +0.025s/f (Slow)
**WFA** 3 from 6yo 9lb **9** Ran SP% **115.9**
Speed ratings: **101,95,95,94,94 92,88,88,86**CSF £30.50 TOTE £12.40: £3.30, £1.50, £1.10; EX 54.70.
**Owner** F C T Wilson **Bred** Watership Down Stud **Trained** Upper Lambourn, Berks
■ Stewards Enquiry : D Holland two-day ban: careless riding (Sep 12-13)

**FOCUS**
Probably the weaker of the two divisons and a slower time, but won in emphatic style by Abington Angel. The fifth holds down the form, and those in the frame do not look well treated.

**NOTEBOOK**
**Abington Angel** was slowly away from the stalls and remained detached for most of the race by at least two lengths, although always travelling comfortably. She made her move entering the final turn and swept past the entire field to win easily. This was a big step up in trip and it appeared to work the oracle for her.
**Mikao(IRE)** broke well and travelled nicely in the front rank. When the pace increased four furlongs out he came under pressure, but looked to be staying on well enough when he encountered a bit of trouble entering the home straight. The winner scored too easily to say he was unlucky not to win on this occasion.
**Scarrabus(IRE)** was always in the front rank but was under pressure four furlongs out. He stuck on well enough, and could be suited by a further step up in trip.
**Zuma(IRE)** looks to be a bit of a tricky character. He did not travel that well during the race and the jockey tried his best to keep him interested, but when hitting the straight he picked up again. He remains difficult to win with.
**Lysander's Quest(IRE)** is rated only 40 but ran on well at the end without ever looking likely to trouble the leaders.

## 5218 CRAWLEY (S) STKS 6f
**2:50** (2:53) (G4) 2-Y-O **£2,961** (£846; £423) **Stalls** High

Form RPR

0236 **1** **Lakesdale (IRE)**[6] [5054] 2-8-6 **59** ... OUrbina 11 57
(MissDMountain) *a.p: rdn to ld jst ins fnl f: drvn out* **7/2**[2]

500 **2** *½* **Beau Marche**[11] [4936] 2-8-11 ... IMongan 9 61
(IAWood) *a.p: rdn to chse wnr fnl f* **20/1**

50 **3** *shd* **Danescourt (IRE)**[6] [4997] 2-8-11 ... DHolland 12 61
(JAOsborne) *lw: led tl rdn and hdd jst ins fnl f: kpt on* **3/1**[1]

565 **4** *2 ½* **Artadi**[9] [4999] 2-8-6 **50** ... (b) CCatlin 18 48+
(PMPhelan) *s.i.s: swtchd lft and hdwy over 2f out: short of room over 1f out: kpt on ins fnl f* **20/1**

0000 **5** *1 ½* **Pips Pearl (IRE)**[24] [4584] 2-8-6 ... (vt[1]) NPollard 14 44
(MrsPNDutfield) *s.i.s: sn mid-div: styd on fnl f: styd on past btn horses fnl f* **50/1**

0 **6** *¾* **Imperatrice**[12] [4924] 2-8-6 ... EAhern 5 41
(RMHCowell) *chsd ldrs: rdn 2f out: one pce after* **20/1**

00 **7** 1 ½ **Ferrara Flame (IRE)**[9] 4997 2-8-6 .................................. MartinDwyer 6 37
(JAOsborne) *s.i.s: sn mid-div: kpt on fnl 2f but nvr a danger* **14/1**
050 **8** 1 ¾ **Cabin Fever**[11] 4936 2-8-6 .................................. RSmith 7 32
(JCFox) *hld up in mid-div: one pce fnl 2f* **11/2**[3]
0000 **9** nk **Secret Diva (IRE)**[21] 4638 2-8-3 .................................. JFMcDonald(3) 15 31
(MrsPNDutfield) *chsd ldrs tl dropped rr 1/2-way* **50/1**
0 **10** ½ **Tiger Hunter**[62] 3458 2-8-11 .................................. JFortune 8 34
(PHowling) *prom in cnter: wknd wl over 1f out* **50/1**
3004 **11** ½ **Joe Ninety (IRE)**[8] 5022 2-8-4 47.................................(p) DerekNolan(7) 2 33
(JSMoore) *in tch on outside tl rdn wknd wl over 1f out* **25/1**
3500 **12** ¾ **Trackattack**[31] 4365 2-8-11 70..................................(b[1]) SWKelly 3 30
(JAOsborne) *mid-div on outside: rdn over 2f out: sn btn* **7/1**
0003 **13** ½ **Bregaglia**[9] 4999 2-8-6 ..................................(v) MHenry 4 24
(RMHCowell) *chsd ldrs tl wknd over 2f out* **20/1**
505 **14** 1 ¾ **Listen To Me**[21] 4638 2-8-11 .................................. PaulEddery 17 24
(DHaydnJones) *a bhd* **14/1**
0 **15** 1 **Tinker's First**[22] 4620 2-7-13 .................................. CHaddon(7) 13 16
(WGMTurner) *a bhd* **50/1**
0546 **16** 5 **Ahaz**[21] 4638 2-8-11 55..................................(b) SSanders 1 6
(IAWood) *prom on outside to 1/2-way* **12/1**
0 **17** 14 **Time Traveller**[23] 4598 2-8-11 ..................................(b[1]) DaneO'Neill 10 —
(TMJones) *v.s.a: a bhd* **50/1**

1m 11.9s (0.25) **Going Correction** -0.20s/f (Firm) **17** Ran SP% **128.8**
Speed ratings: **90,89,89,85,83 82,80,78,78,77 76,75,75,72,71 64,46** CT £5.20 TOTE £1.90: £7.60, £2.20, £; EX203.30 1.There was no bid for the winner. Danescourt was claimed by Mr Alan Pirie for £6,000. Beau Marche was subject to a friendly cla
**Owner** A Cavanagh **Bred** Yeomanstown Stud **Trained** Newmarket, Suffolk

**FOCUS**
Just a moderate seller, but plenty of runners and the form should work out at a similar level. They raced towards the stands' side.

**NOTEBOOK**
**Lakesdale(IRE)**, on her fourth trainer already, had not run too badly in a Polytrack maiden on her debut for her latest connections on her previous outing and, dropped back into a more suitable grade, she came good at the tenth attempt. Exposed, she is one to take on in this grade under a penalty.
**Beau Marche**, dropped in grade, fared best of those in a single-figure stall to run his best race to date, showing enough to suggest he can make his mark at a similar level.
**Danescourt(IRE)**, dropped down from claiming company, ran his race and did not look to have any excuses. Clear of the remainder, there should be a similar race in him.
**Artadi** picked up all too late and is worth another chance in this grade over seven furlongs.
**Pips Pearl(IRE)**, fitted with a tongue-tie and a visor for the first time on this drop on grade, did not help her chance with a slow start and was well held. There was enough promise, however, to suggest there could be a similar event in her given some improvement.
**Cabin Fever** was below form on this drop in grade.
**Trackattack** should have run better on this drop in grade, but the blinkers clearly failed to work.
**Bregaglia** *Official explanation: jockey said filly had lost her action*

## 5219 REIGATE H'CAP 6f
**3:25** (3:25) (E3) (0-55,70) 3-Y-O **£3,610** (£1,111; £555; £277) **Stalls** High

Form RPR
-143 **1** **Chimali (IRE)**[42] 4026 3-9-4 **67**..................................(v[1]) EAhern 9 77+
(JNoseda) *a.p: led over 1f out: r.o wl* **10/1**
1201 **2** 1 ½ **Rise**[21] 4650 3-9-7 **70**..................................(b) JFEgan 12 75
(AndrewReid) *lw: b: b.hind: mid-div: hdwy over 2f out: chsd wnr fnl f* **10/1**
4611 **3** ½ **Danifah (IRE)**[10] 4968 3-8-10 **62** 6ex.................................. FPFerris(3) 5 66
(PDEvans) *led tl hdd over 1f out: kpt on one pce* **12/1**
3305 **4** ½ **Ask The Clerk (IRE)**[19] 4717 3-9-2 **70**.................................. RoryMoore(5) 17 72+
(VSmith) *mid-div: swtchd lft 1/2-way: nt clr run and swtchd lft again over 1f out: r.o fnl f* **12/1**
3114 **5** nk **United Spirit (IRE)**[11] 4938 3-9-2 **65**.................................. JFortune 16 66
(MAMagnusson) *lw: rrd s and bmpd: hld up: hdwy over 1f out: fin wl fnl f: nvr nrr* **5/1**[1]
-052 **6** 1 **Darla (IRE)**[21] 4650 3-9-6 **69**.................................. JPMurtagh 4 67
(JWPayne) *c rapidly over to stands' side s fr low draw: in rr tl hdwy over 1f out: r.o* **12/1**
0-60 **7** ¾ **Innstyle**[66] 3344 3-8-8 **60**.................................. SHitchcott(3) 10 56
(JLSpearing) *chsd ldrs: ev ch 2f out: wknd fnl f* **40/1**
0604 **8** hd **Pure Imagination (IRE)**[13] 4868 3-8-6 **60**.................................. RThomas(5) 7 55
(JMBradley) *hld up in tch: rdn and wknd appr fnl f* **25/1**
3006 **9** ½ **Danish Monarch**[13] 4868 3-8-8 **57**.................................. CCatlin 18 51
(ADWPinder) *a mid-div* **33/1**
0202 **10** hd **Minimum Bid**[42] 4025 3-8-8 **57**.................................. SSanders 20 50
(MissBSanders) *bhd and hung rt into stands' rail: hdwy past btn horses fnl f* **8/1**[3]
0042 **11** ¾ **Ace Club**[7] 5040 3-9-1 **64**.................................. DHolland 14 55
(WJHaggas) *bhd: effrt 2f out: wknd over 1f out* **11/2**[2]
0440 **12** 1 **Nikiforos**[13] 4868 3-8-12 **61**.................................. NDay 13 49
(JWHills) *hld up in mid-div: wknd wl over 1f out* **40/1**
0000 **13** shd **Mutassem (FR)**[11] 4938 3-8-9 **58**.................................. MHenry 2 46
(TKeddy) *racd centre: short of room over 2f out: sn btn* **66/1**
0000 **14** shd **Smokin Joe**[26] 4515 3-8-8 **57**..................................(v) NPollard 11 44
(JRBest) *prom tl rdn and wknd over 1f out* **20/1**
0300 **15** ½ **Turkish Delight**[21] 4650 3-8-8 **57**..................................(p) JEdmunds 19 43
(JBalding) *a bhd* **14/1**
036 **16** 1 ¼ **Witches Broom**[21] 4644 3-8-8 **57**.................................. MartinDwyer 15 39
(CACyzer) *a bhd: rdr reported lost action* **33/1**
3001 **17** 4 **Miss Judgement (IRE)**[25] 4547 3-8-12 **64**.................................. RMiles(3) 34
(WRMuir) *in tch on outside tl wknd over 2f out* **9/1**
0064 **18** shd **Black Sabbeth**[27] 4484 3-9-1 **64**.................................. DSweeney 1 34
(PJMakin) *in tch on outside rdn and wknd 2f out* **50/1**
0000 **19** 1 ½ **Alizar (IRE)**[11] 4937 3-8-7 **56** oh1.................................. LisaJones 6 21
(SDow) *in tch tl rdn and wknd 1/2-way* **50/1**
-246 **20** nk **Sweet Pickle**[25] 4547 3-9-3 **66**.................................. DaneO'Neill 8 30
(DJCoakley) *chsd ldrs: rdn over 2f out: wknd qckly wl over 1f out* **33/1**

1m 10.03s (-1.62) **Going Correction** -0.20s/f (Firm) **20** Ran SP% **128.8**
Speed ratings: **102,100,99,98,98 96,95,95,95,94 93,92,92,92,91 89,84,84,82,81**CSF £100.50 CT £1270.99 TOTE £11.30: £2.90, £2.90, £3.80, £3.10; EX 108.60.
**Owner** Mrs Susan Roy **Bred** Redpender Stud Ltd **Trained** Newmarket, Suffolk

**FOCUS**
A modest but competitive sprint in which they all raced towards the stands' side. The form is ordinary, with several fancied horses well beaten.

**NOTEBOOK**
**Chimali(IRE)**, fitted with a visor for the first time on this first run since July, showed improved form to gain his first win in a handicap. Further progression cannot be ruled out and he should continue to go well when reassessed.
**Rise**, 6lb higher than when successful in a similar event Yarmouth on her previous start, needed plenty of encouragement from the saddle and has clearly got blinkers on for a reason. This was a fair effort, but she may just be worth another try over seven furlongs.
**Danifah(IRE)**, chasing the hat-trick under a 6lb penalty for her success in a weak race at Folkestone on her previous start, ran well but just found this tougher.
**Ask The Clerk(IRE)**, 4lb higher than when gaining his only previous win, would have been much closer with better luck in running.
**United Spirit(IRE)**, with the blinkers left off this time, found this trip a bit short after starting slowly and getting bumped, and she looks better over seven furlongs.
**Minimum Bid** did not help her chances by hanging. *Official explanation: jockey said filly hung right throughout*
**Ace Club** had been in reasonable form lately, but this was disappointing.
**Witches Broom** *Official explanation: jockey said filly lost her action*
**Miss Judgement(IRE)** *Official explanation: trainer said rider was unable to drop the filly in from her draw of 3 of 20*

## 5220 HORSHAM H'CAP 7f (P)
**3:55** (3:55) (D2) (0-85,91) 3-Y-O **£7,155** (£2,201; £1,100; £550) **Stalls** Low

Form RPR
313 **1** **Majors Cast (IRE)**[8] 5024 3-9-7 **85**.................................. EAhern 3 102+
(JNoseda) *lw: a.p and gng wl: led ins fnl f: hld off late chal cl home* **8/1**[3]
4220 **2** nk **Eccentric**[34] 4268 3-9-2 **80**.................................. JFEgan 2 93
(AndrewReid) *b: b.hind: led tl hdd and hung rt ins fnl f: rallied cl home but a hld* **8/1**[3]
3201 **3** 2 ½ **Distant Connection (IRE)**[6] 5055 3-9-13 **91** 6ex.................................. DHolland 5 98
(APJarvis) *chsd ldr tl over 1f out: fdd ins fnl f* **6/4**[1]
-000 **4** shd **Zerlina (USA)**[19] 4731 3-9-3 **81**.................................. CCatlin 10 87
(WJMusson) *bhd tl rdn and hdwy 2f out: styd on: nvr nrr* **66/1**
4112 **5** 1 ½ **Our Jaffa (IRE)**[67] 3320 3-9-5 **83**.................................. JPMurtagh 9 85
(DJDaly) *lw: a mid-div: sme hdwy 2f out: wknd over 1f out* **9/2**[2]
6000 **6** ½ **Forthright**[17] 4780 3-9-4 **85**..................................(p) J-PGuillambert(3) 6 86
(CEBrittain) *chsd ldrs tl rdn and wknd wl over 1f out* **33/1**
0320 **7** 5 **Whitgift Rock**[48] 3872 3-8-11 **75**.................................. JQuinn 4 63
(SDow) *t.k.h: in tch tl 1/2-way* **12/1**
0004 **8** hd **I Won't Dance (IRE)**[39] 4126 3-8-9 **73**.................................. RHughes 7 61
(RHannon) *hld up in rr: a bhd* **20/1**
6-64 **9** 1 ¾ **Go Bananas**[24] 4570 3-9-6 **84**.................................. JFortune 1 67
(BJMeehan) *in tch tl wknd 2f out* **16/1**
16 **10** 1 ½ **Davorin (JPN)**[109] 2135 3-9-5 **83**..................................(v[1]) SSanders 8 62
(DRLoder) *lw: slowly away: sn given reminders: a bhd* **12/1**
3310 **11** 3 **St Savarin (FR)**[25] 4549 3-8-12 **76**.................................. NPollard 13 47
(JRBest) *in tch: rdn 3f out: dropped out qckly* **20/1**
0001 **12** 3 **Finders Keepers**[26] 4515 3-9-1 **79**.................................. DaneO'Neill 14 42
(EALDunlop) *t.k.h: hdwy on outside: 1/2-way: wknd 2f out* **16/1**
3166 **13** 3 ½ **Extra Cover (IRE)**[28] 4456 3-8-8 **72**.................................. RMullen 12 26
(NACallaghan) *slowly away: a bhd* **33/1**

1m 24.95s (-0.99) **Going Correction** +0.025s/f (Slow) **13** Ran SP% **124.5**
Speed ratings: **106,105,102,102,100 100,94,94,92,90 87,83,79**CSF £69.40 CT £151.42 TOTE £12.40: £2.50, £4.50, £1.30; EX 141.00.
**Owner** Mrs Susan Roy **Bred** Joe Fogarty **Trained** Newmarket, Suffolk

**FOCUS**
A decent handicap and a fair time for the class, giving the form a sound appearance.

**NOTEBOOK**
**Majors Cast(IRE)** was paying his first visit to the All-Weather, and won this competitive event quite nicely. Settled up with the pace, he made his move a furlong out and resisted the renewed challenge of the runner-up. This was in keeping with his progressive profile despite disappointing on soft last time, and he should keep on improving on this evidence.
**Eccentric** has a decent record here on the All-Weather and returned a fine effort after not having much of a chance from his draw last time in a tough Goodwood handicap. His racing style really suits the surface and he looks in fine heart at the moment, battling on bravely after headed. He stays seven furlongs well.
**Distant Connection(IRE)** raced prominently, as is his nature, and had every chance entering the straight. He faded quickly entering the final furlong and only just held on for third, but may have met two decent opponents. The way he weakened late on was worrying, and he may be high enough in the handicap at the moment.
**Zerlina(USA)** ◆ was the eye-catcher of the race. She had not returned to Lingfield since her win as a two-year-old, but made up lots of ground in the straight after being too far off the pace as this race turned out. If returning to the All-Weather soon, she will be of serious interest.
**Our Jaffa(IRE)** came to have a chance in the straight but never looked like troubling the principals by the end of the race.
**Forthright**, having his first run on the All-Wweather since returning from Dubai, likes this surface but probably needs a longer trip.
**Finders Keepers** *Official explanation: jockey said gelding ran too freely early on*

## 5221 ANDREW MACFARLANE H'CAP 2m (P)
**4:30** (4:30) (F4) (0-55,55) 3-Y-O+ **£2,945** (£841; £420) **Stalls** Low

Form RPR
4330 **1** **Most-Saucy**[29] 4416 8-9-4 **53**.................................. JPMurtagh 8 62
(IAWood) *hld up in rr: stdy hdwy fr 6f out: rdn and led wl ins fnl f: drvn out* **7/1**
0203 **2** ½ **Peak Park (USA)**[8] 5027 4-8-11 **46**..................................(v) EAhern 11 54
(JARToller) *hld up in rr: hdwy ½-wy: wnt 2nd 5f out: hmpd on bnd wl over 1f out: led briefly ins fnl f: kpt on* **9/2**[3]
3120 **3** nk **Montosari**[100] 2375 5-9-5 **54**.................................. DHolland 2 62
(PMitchell) *hld up in mid-div: str hdwy on outside to ld over 2f out: riddden and hdd ins fnl f: nt qckn cl home* **12/1**
6333 **4** 3 ½ **Vandenberghe**[23] 4603 5-9-4 **53**.................................. SWKelly 6 56
(JAOsborne) *lw: a in tch: kpt on one pce ins fnl 2f* **7/2**[1]
5030 **5** 1 **Stylish Sunrise (IRE)**[14] 4853 3-8-2 **50**..........................(vt[1]) DKinsella 10 52
(IAWood) *hld up in tch: racd wd thrght: rdn and hdwy whn hmpd 2f out: one pce after* **33/1**
0236 **6** nk **Waltzing Beau**[16] 4798 3-8-4 **55**.................................. RMiles(3) 7 57
(BGPowell) *in tch: led 7f out: hdd over 2f out: hmpd on bnd wl over 1f out: nt rcvr* **33/1**
2424 **7** ½ **Compton Eclaire (IRE)**[20] 4686 4-9-6 **55**..........................(b) JFortune 4 56
(GAButler) *s.i.s: in rr tl hdwy 2f out: kpt on one pce* **4/1**[2]
6000 **8** 8 **Madame Marie (IRE)**[11] 4939 4-9-2 **51**.................................. LisaJones 13 43
(SDow) *plld hrd: a in rr* **33/1**
4023 **9** 19 **Circus Maximus (USA)**[37] 4202 7-9-4 **53**..........................(p) SSanders 1 22
(IanWilliams) *in tch: rdn 1/2-way: sn bhd* **11/2**
0450 **10** 21 **Columbian Emerald (IRE)**[25] 4536 3-8-0 **48**.................. MartinDwyer 9 —
(TJEtherington) *lw: bhd: hmpd over 4f out: nvr on terms* **33/1**
30/0 **11** 1 ¾ **Ash Hab (USA)**[39] 4146 6-8-13 **55**..........................(p) DerekNolan(7) 12 —
(ABHaynes) *a bhd* **66/1**
025- **12** 3 **Finnforest (IRE)**[375] 4365 4-9-4 **53**.................................. JFEgan 5 —
(MrsAJBowlby) *t.k.h: led after 3f: hdd 7f out: wknd qckly* **20/1**

412- **13** *dist* **Queensberry**[159] [6198] 5-9-2 **51**........................................(b[1]) IMongan 14 —
(MrsLJMongan) *chsd ldrs tl wknd over 3f out: t.o* **20/1**

0 **14** *3 ½* **Future To Future (IRE)**[14] [4849] 4-9-0 **49**................................ CCatlin 3 —
(LADace) *led for 3f: bhd fr 1/2-way: t.o* **50/1**

3m 28.11s (-0.47) **Going Correction** +0.025s/f (Slow)
**WFA** 3 from 4yo+ 13lb **14** Ran SP% **120.7**
Speed ratings: **102,101,101,99,99 99,98,94,85,74 74,72,—,—**CSF £35.23 CT £381.85 TOTE £9.10: £2.40, £2.10, £4.20; EX 55.10.

**Owner** Mrs A M Riney **Bred** Wyck Hall Stud Ltd **Trained** Upper Lambourn, Berks

■ Stewards Enquiry : D Holland one-day ban: careless riding (Sep 14); caution:careless riding

**FOCUS**
A moderate but competitive staying handicap run at a decent enough pace and the form looks fairly solid for the grade.

**NOTEBOOK**
**Most-Saucy** gained a much-deserved first success of the season under a fine tactical ride from Murtagh. Now she has proven herself over this trip, there should be more options open to her.

**Peak Park(USA)** showed no ill-effects of his recent run at Yarmouth when he was beaten 22 lengths into third, recovering well from being hampered turning in to hold every chance in the straight. He is still a maiden, but is on a reasonable mark and should pick up a similar race.

**Montosari**, who made his mark at up to a mile five in banded company round here earlier in the year, ran a pleasing first race in 100 days, only just failing to last home having made a bold move down the false straight - he caused trouble to several in the process.

**Vandenberghe**, an unlucky third in a similar event over course and distance on his previous start, failed to gain compensation but did fare best of those to race near the pace.

**Stylish Sunrise(IRE)** had never previously raced beyond a mile and a half but, fitted with a visor for the first time, he seemed to just about get this trip, posting a respectable effort in the process.

**Waltzing Beau** lost any chance of battling out a place when badly hampered by the eventual third on the turn-in. His half-brother Rebelle won twice over this trip on Fibresand and he is surely worth another try on that surface.

**Compton Eclaire(IRE)**, four lengths clear of today's winner two starts back, was not at her best.

**Circus Maximus(USA)**, in good form on turf lately, was a long way below form switched back to Polytrack.

**Finnforest(IRE)** *Official explanation: jockey said gelding ran too free and tired*

## 5222 REDHILL APPRENTICE CLASSIFIED STKS — 1m (P)
**5:00** (5:00) (F3) 3-Y-0+ **£3,474** (£1,069; £534; £267) **Stalls** High

Form RPR

5200 **1** **Londoner (USA)**[8] [5017] 6-9-3 60........................................ LisaJones 10 70
(SDow) *mde all: pushed clr 2f out: r.o wl fnl f* **8/1**

0025 **2** *2 ½* **Blue Java**[13] [4882] 3-8-12 59.................................................. LFletcher 12 64
(HMorrison) *b.hind: in tch on outside: hdwy 2f out: chsd wnr fnl f* **6/1**[3]

1035 **3** *½* **Knickyknackienoo**[35] [4242] 3-8-12 59........................................ DNolan 4 63
(AGNewcombe) *hld up: rdn and hdwy over 1f out: r.o: nvr nrr* **4/1**[1]

4200 **4** *nk* **Treetops Hotel (IRE)**[9] [5008] 5-9-0 60......................(vt[1]) NChalmers(3) 1 62
(BRJohnson) *mid-div on ins: swtchd rt over 2f out: hung lft but r.o fnl f* **11/2**[2]

4422 **5** *¾* **Kelseas Kolby (IRE)**[16] [4818] 4-9-0 57..........................(v) RThomas(3) 8 61
(PButler) *t.k.h: a.p: chsd wnr over 2f out tl 1f out: wknd ins fnl f* **11/2**[2]

-041 **6** *2* **State Of Balance**[117] [1940] 6-9-0 60........................................ LPKeniry 6 53
(KBell) *in tch on outside: hld up in rr: hdwy over 1f out: kpt on one pce* **6/1**[3]

3000 **7** *3 ½* **Raheel (IRE)**[19] [4713] 4-9-3 60...........................................(t) SHitchcott 7 48
(PMitchell) *mid-div: rdn and wknd over 1f out* **10/1**

-000 **8** *1* **My Sunshine (IRE)**[22] [4619] 3-8-6 59.............................. AMedeiros(3) 9 43
(BWHills) *in tch on outside tl wknd over 2f out* **33/1**

4050 **9** *½* **Lady Blade (IRE)**[14] [4848] 3-8-4 60...................................(b) CHaddon(5) 11 42
(BHanbury) *chsd ldrs: wnt 2nd 4f out tl over 2f out: wknd over 1f out* **20/1**

0060 **10** *1 ¼* **Chica Roca (USA)**[77] [2984] 3-8-9 60......................................(t) JFMcDonald 5 39
(BJMeehan) *plld hrd in mid-div: bhd sn after 1/2-way* **50/1**

6-00 **11** *6* **Reign Of Fire (IRE)**[107] [2169] 3-8-4 60.......................... DerekNolan(5) 3 25
(JWHills) *hld up in mid-div: wknd over 3f out* **12/1**

-000 **12** *5* **Carlburg (IRE)**[32] [4338] 3-8-12 60................................ J-PGuillambert 2 16
(CEBrittain) *chsd wnr to 4f out: wknd qckly over 2f out* **25/1**

1m 40.12s (0.57) **Going Correction** +0.025s/f (Slow)
**WFA** 3 from 4yo+ 5lb **12** Ran SP% **120.7**
Speed ratings: **98,95,95,94,93 91,88,87,86,85 79,74**CSF £54.33 TOTE £6.40: £4.20, £3.40, £1.30; EX 37.40 Place 6 £105.17, Place 5 £44.18.

**Owner** P McCarthy **Bred** Newgate Stud Farm Inc **Trained** Epsom, Surrey

**FOCUS**
A moderate race full of questionable types won easily by Londoner but the form is ordinary.

**NOTEBOOK**
**Londoner(USA)** loves to have his own way out in front and took up the running from two furlongs out, a move which took him clear of the field. He won as he liked in the end, but has a history of being unpredictable so whether he repeats this form is open to debate.

**Blue Java** was disappointing on the slower surface of Southwell last time, but showed much more on this quicker surface. He is still fairly lightly raced and can improve a bit more, and maybe a step up in trip will aid his cause given the way he stayed on.

**Knickyknackienoo** finished best of all after being held up at the back of the field. He encountered a bit of trouble on the home turn and stayed on nicely up the straight. At recent meetings at Lingfield it has not been easy to come from so far off the pace, so it would be difficult if he were to return there and ridden the same way given the same course conditions. That aside, he ran a good race and looks in good heart.

**Treetops Hotel(IRE)** had the visor on for the first time and kept on well up the home straight. He has only won one race to date, from 27 attempts, and probably needs things to fall right for him to get his head in front.

**Kelseas Kolby(IRE)** was travelling really well entering the straight, but appeared to find nothing when let down. He has been a model of consistency in the last month so his weakening is probably due to being a bit high in the weights now as he stays this trip fine.

**State Of Balance** did not appear to find the step back in trip to her liking as she did not seem to have the pace to get competitive from her mid-field position.

T/Plt: £115.30 to a £1 stake. Pool: £33,745.30. 213.50 winning tickets. T/Qpdt: £37.10 to a £1 stake. Pool: £2,351.70. 46.80 winning tickets. JS

# [4884] YORK (L-H)
Wednesday, September 1

**OFFICIAL GOING: Good to soft changing to good after race 2 (2.40)**
The going was described as 'on the slow side of good and a bit dead' after the first race but it dried out on a late summer's day and was soon 'genuine good'.
Wind: Almost nil. Weather: Fine, sunny and warm.

## 5223 PATRINGTON HAVEN LEISURE PARK STKS (H'CAP) — 7f 205y
**2:10** (2:11) (E3) (0-70,69) 3-Y-0 **£5,660** (£1,741; £870; £435) **Stalls** Low

Form RPR

2041 **1** **Eboracum (IRE)**[9] [4989] 3-9-6 **68** 6ex....................................(b) DAllan 1 78
(TDEasterby) *in tch: hdwy over 2f out: led appr fnl f: styd on wl* **9/1**[3]

1000 **2** *2 ½* **Dispol Veleta**[13] [4882] 3-9-3 **65**............................................. NCallan 3 70
(TDBarron) *dwlt: rr div: hdwy over 3f out: styd on wl u.p to go 2nd ins fnl f: nt trble wnr* **16/1**

0600 **3** *1* **Chigorin**[40] [4092] 3-9-3 **65**............................................. TEDurcan 8 68
(JMPEustace) *in tch: hdwy over 2f out: nt clr run over 1f out: styd on u.p fnl f* **10/1**

2404 **4** *½* **Hunter's Valley**[16] [4813] 3-9-4 **66**........................................ LDettori 16 68
(RHannon) *led tl rdn and hdd appr fnl f: styd on* **14/1**

-566 **5** *1 ¾* **Sierra**[28] [4451] 3-9-0 **62**.......................................................... KMcEvoy 5 60
(CEBrittain) *chsd ldrs: rdn 2f out: kpt on same pce* **25/1**

-020 **6** *hd* **Almond Willow (IRE)**[20] [4680] 3-9-3 **65**.............................. TPQueally 4 63
(JNoseda) *midfield: rdn over 2f out: kpt on u.p fnl f* **10/1**

2500 **7** *½* **Heversham (IRE)**[28] [4447] 3-9-5 **67**...................................... MTebbutt 13 64
(JHetherton) *hld up in midfield: pushed along and hdwy 1/2-way: in tch and rdn over 2f out: kpt on u.p fnl f* **40/1**

6504 **8** *½* **Wrenlane**[23] [4610] 3-9-0 **62**................................................... PHanagan 9 58
(RAFahey) *dwlt: sn midfield: effrt whn nt clr run over 1f out: kpt on fnl f: n.d* **6/1**[1]

4350 **9** *1* **Charlie Tango (IRE)**[16] [4806] 3-9-4 **66**................................. KDarley 15 60
(NTinkler) *towards rr: sme hdwy whn nt clr run 2f out: n.d* **12/1**

3466 **10** *nk* **Rosie Mac**[30] [4395] 3-8-9 **57**................................................. FNorton 17 50
(NBycroft) *chsd ldrs: rdn over 2f out: fdd fr over 1f out* **40/1**

3303 **11** *½* **Mistress Twister**[34] [4260] 3-9-1 **68**.................................. PMakin(5) 19 60
(TDBarron) *s.i.s: rr div: effrt over 2f out: sn rdn: kpt on u.p fnl f: n.d* **16/1**

3021 **12** *½* **Adorata (GER)**[13] [4880] 3-9-7 **69**........................................ GBaker 20 60
(JJay) *hld up in midfield: effrt over 2f out: sn rdn and btn* **16/1**

6466 **13** *hd* **Orion Express**[11] [4449] 3-8-7 **58**.................................. PMulrennan(3) 18 48
(MWEasterby) *s.i.s: towards rr: rdn over 2f out: kpt on u.p fnl f: n.d* **22/1**

0020 **14** *nk* **Royal Distant (USA)**[33] [4307] 3-9-5 **67**............................... TLucas 2 57
(MWEasterby) *midfield: pushed along after 3f: outpcd 3f out: n.d* **7/1**[2]

6602 **15** *2* **Cottingham (IRE)**[23] [4610] 3-8-7 **60**.............. StephanieHollinshead(5) 14 46
(MCChapman) *cl up: ev ch and rdn 2f out: sn wknd* **16/1**

-000 **16** *¾* **Cheverak Forest (IRE)**[23] [4610] 3-8-12 **60**........................ KimTinkler 7 44
(DonEnricoIncisa) *dwlt: rr div: rdn 2f out: no hdwy* **100/1**

630- **17** *1* **Passion Fruit**[310] [5789] 3-8-9 **57**........................................... JFanning 6 39
(CWFairhurst) *midfield: rdn over 2f out: wknd over 1f out* **40/1**

5320 **18** *shd* **Park Ave Princess (IRE)**[12] [4929] 3-9-0 **62**........................ GGibbons 10 44
(MJPolglase) *chsd ldrs: wkng whn hmpd wl over 1f out* **33/1**

6013 **19** *½* **Book Matched**[13] [4882] 3-9-0 **62**....................................... DMcGaffin 12 43
(BSmart) *cl up: rdn and ev ch over 2f out: sn wknd* **12/1**

-000 **20** *5* **Named At Dinner**[96] [2457] 3-9-0 **62**.................................... JCarroll 11 32
(MrsADuffield) *bhd most of way* **100/1**

1m 39.03s (1.29) **Going Correction** +0.35s/f (Good) **20** Ran SP% **121.0**
Speed ratings: **107,104,103,103,101 101,100,100,99,98 98,97,97,97,95 94,93,93,92,87**CSF £131.23 CT £1504.93 TOTE £6.00: £2.00, £7.60, £3.90, £3.10; EX 260.50.

**Owner** T D Easterby **Bred** Tullamaine Castle Stud **Trained** Great Habton, N Yorks

■ A routine event, but notable as the first race to be run under the new handicap system.

**FOCUS**
A modest race for the track but a competitive handicap that looks sound form-wise and an appropriate winner. The field came down the centre of the track in the home straight.

**NOTEBOOK**
**Eboracum(IRE)** had the run of the race when breaking her duck at Hamilton, but did this wholly on merit. Over this shorter trip, she required some stoking up to find full stride but ran out a most decisive winner. She went up only 3lb for Hamilton so was theoretically badly in under the penalty, but she is a filly on the upgrade who may still be worth supporting when the handicapper has taken this win into account.

**Dispol Veleta**, who did not get away from the stalls well, was one of the few to become involved from off the pace. This was something of a return to form after some uninspiring efforts and she appeared to benefit from being ridden like this.

**Chigorin** had to wait for a run, but was unable to quicken up when in the clear. Still a maiden, he has the ability to rectify that but is perhaps not a straightforward ride.

**Hunter's Valley** was able to get to the front from her wide draw but could only stick on at the one pace when headed by the eventual winner. This was her first experience of soft ground and she got through it well.

**Sierra** was always prominent and had no excuses, but this was a better effort from a 3lb lower mark.

**Almond Willow(IRE)** stayed on quite well and might be worth another try over further.

**Wrenlane** met with trouble with running but stayed on quite nicely once free. This is his ground and he remains in good heart.

**Royal Distant(USA)**, who was to have been ridden by Kieren Fallon, was a market drifter. Outpaced at halfway, she could never get into the hunt.

## 5224 BASF H'CAP — 6f
**2:40** (2:41) (C1) (0-100,100) 3-Y-0+ **£12,783** (£4,848; £2,424; £1,102) **Stalls** Centre

Form RPR

5005 **1** **Partners In Jazz (USA)**[14] [4862] 3-8-5 **86** oh2........................ WSupple 11 94
(TDBarron) *led after 1f: hld on wl* **9/1**

2000 **2** *nk* **Marsad (IRE)**[23] [4614] 10-8-7 **86** oh1........................................ PDoe 10 93
(JAkehurst) *hld up in mid-div: hdwy 2f out: hrd rdn and edgd lft: styd on towards fin* **16/1**

1304 **3** *nk* **Mystic Man (FR)**[69] [3235] 6-8-9 **88** ow1.................................... NCallan 7 94
(KARyan) *hld up: effrt 2f out: swtchd rt: styd on strly fnl f* **12/1**

4201 **4** *hd* **Onlytime Will Tell**[16] [4811] 6-8-12 **91**.................................. JFanning 2 97
(DNicholls) *w ldrs: chal over 1f out: nt qckn ins last* **9/1**

4203 **5** *hd* **Tom Tun**[15] [4837] 9-9-6 **99**................................................(b) TLucas 13 104
(JBalding) *chsd ldrs: nt qckn ins last* **12/1**

2235 **6** *1* **Ellens Academy (IRE)**[26] [4510] 9-8-7 **86**.............................. FNorton 5 88
(EJAlston) *trckd ldrs: t.k.h: fdd towards fin* **8/1**[3]

0504 **7** *1 ½* **Circuit Dancer (IRE)**[12] [4908] 4-9-0 **93**............................... TEDurcan 9 90
(ABerry) *led 1f: w ldrs: wknd ins last* **20/1**

4136 **8** ½ **Khabfair**[18] 4750 3-9-0 **95** LDettori 8 100+
(MrsAJPerrett) *hld up in rr div: hdwy 2f out: bmpd over 1f out: hmpd and eased ins last* **10/3**[1]

11-0 **9** 2 **Smart Hostess**[159] 1113 5-9-0 **93** PHanagan 1 83
(JJQuinn) *chsd ldrs on outer: wknd fnl f* **25/1**

0146 **10** hd **Pinchbeck**[26] 4510 5-8-7 **86** (p) PRobinson 6 75
(MAJarvis) *bhd: sme hdwy over 1f out: nvr nr to chal* **9/1**

0321 **11** 2½ **Apex**[19] 4717 3-8-8 **89** SDrowne 3 71
(EALDunlop) *dwlt: sme hdwy 2f out: wknd fnl f* **5/1**[2]

5200 **12** 1 **Law Breaker (IRE)**[15] 4837 6-8-8 **87** KDarley 4 66
(JAGilbert) *chsd ldrs: wknd over 1f out* **20/1**

1160 **13** 1 **Aleutian**[130] 1610 4-9-7 **100** TPQueally 12 76
(DRLoder) *s.i.s: in rr: checked over 1f out: nvr a factor* **33/1**

1m 11.45s (-1.12) **Going Correction** 0.0s/f (Good)
**WFA** 3 from 4yo+ 2lb **13** Ran SP% **118.4**
Speed ratings: **107,106,106,105,105 104,102,101,99,98 95,94,92**CSF £135.07 CT £1737.61 TOTE £11.80: £4.30, £6.10, £5.30; EX 226.70 Trifecta £1030.50 Part won. Pool: £1,451.54. 0.10 winning units..
**Owner** Sporting Occasions Racing No 2 **Bred** Charles Nuckols Jr And Sons **Trained** Maunby, N Yorks
■ Stewards Enquiry : P Doe one-day ban: careless riding (Sep 12); further caution: careless riding

**FOCUS**
Quite a well-contested handicap in which the action took place down the centre of the track. Both the first two home were just out of the weights but the form looks solid.

**NOTEBOOK**
**Partners In Jazz(USA)** has taken time to find his form this year, but he appreciated the return to six furlongs and found plenty when challenged. He could go for the Portland now but may not get the easy ground he needs at Doncaster.
**Marsad(IRE)** likes it here and was cutting back the winner's advantage near the line despite edging to his left. This was a big run, but he is hard to catch right and is without a win since May 2002.
**Mystic Man(FR)** ran a fine race on his first ever try over a sprint trip, running on well on the slower ground towards the stands' side. He has returned from a break in good heart and will now go for a seven-furlong event at the big Ayr meeting later in the month.
**Onlytime Will Tell** had every chance and might even have put his head in front for a few strides over a furlong out. This ground seemed ideal and he is well treated on the pick of last season's efforts. *Official explanation: jockey said gelding hung left from two furlongs out*
**Tom Tun** was always chasing the pace but could not quite mount an effective challenge. He will continue to acquit himself well, particularly if the ground is riding softer, but is high enough in the handicap.
**Ellens Academy(IRE)** raced more prominently on this occasion. He is running well at present but it is not helping his handicap mark.
**Circuit Dancer(IRE)** showed plenty of dash before fading in the final furlong. His four career wins have all come on fast ground.
**Khabfair** became involved in a bit of a barging match with Marsad when attempting to deliver his challenge and was held when squeezed out inside the last. He can leave this running behind over seven furlongs on fast ground.
**Apex**, racing from a 9lb higher mark, could never get into the action after a tardy start.

## 5225 SPORTINGOPTIONS.CO.UK BETTING EXCHANGE STRENSALL STKS (GROUP 3) 1m 208y

**3:15** (3:15) (A1) 3-Y-0+ **£31,000** (£11,000; £5,500; £2,500) **Stalls** Low

Form RPR

1-43 **1** **Red Bloom**[75] 3033 3-8-8 **113** KDarley 4 118+
(SirMichaelStoute) *trckd ldr: drvn along 3f out: styd on u.p to ld ins fnl f: eased cl home* **1/1**[1]

2305 **2** ½ **Salselon**[17] 4795 5-9-3 **118** (v[1]) LDettori 3 117
(LMCumani) *hld up in rr: outpcd briefly over 3f out: hdwy 2f out: rdn and ch jst ins fnl f: no imp on wnr* **2/1**[2]

0030 **3** nk **Imperial Dancer**[15] 4834 6-9-3 **110** TEDurcan 2 117
(MRChannon) *in tch: rdn and outpcd briefly 2f out: styd on u.p f* **9/2**[3]

5546 **4** nk **Babodana**[13] 4889 4-9-3 **107** (b[1]) PRobinson 1 116?
(MHTompkins) *led: qckd 4f out: rdn and hdd ins fnl f: no ex* **12/1**

1m 54.74s (4.78) **Going Correction** +0.35s/f (Good)
**WFA** 3 from 4yo+ 6lb **4** Ran SP% **109.2**
Speed ratings: **92,91,91,91**CSF £3.31 TOTE £2.00; EX 3.90.
**Owner** Cheveley Park Stud **Bred** Cheveley Park Stud Ltd **Trained** Newmarket, Suffolk

**FOCUS**
An intriguing Group Three contest with no obvious front-runner, and there was a steady gallop until early in the straight. The winning time was very slow for a Group Three, but the winner is value for a little more.

**NOTEBOOK**
**Red Bloom**, already one of the best fillies of her generation, was having her first outing since Royal Ascot and connections believed the run was needed. Although the race was not run to suit, as she was quite keen early, she picked up well when asked and scored a shade cosily. She was not inconvenienced by the slower ground, and a step up to ten furlongs is likely with the Prix de L'Opera on the agenda, although the Sun Chariot is an alternative.
**Salselon**, equipped with a first-time visor, was held up as is often the case. He appeared to have every chance inside the final furlong but could not reach the winner, and looks to be saving a little for himself.
**Imperial Dancer** was dropping back to the shortest trip he has tried for two and a half years. As a result the steady early gallop was not in his favour and he was short of pace when the sprint for home began.
**Babodana** was given a sensible tactical ride but was just not good enough, and also looked as if the longer trip was stretching his stamina.

## 5226 ELITE HOMES GARROWBY H'CAP 1m 3f 198y

**3:45** (3:45) (C1) (0-100,100) 3-Y-0 **£12,481** (£4,734; £2,367; £1,076) **Stalls** Low

Form RPR

11 **1** **Into The Dark**[47] 3915 3-9-7 **100** (vt) LDettori 1 114+
(SaeedBinSuroor) *mde all: pushed 4 l clr fnl f: eased clsng stages* **1/1**[1]

5012 **2** 2½ **Secretary General (IRE)**[19] 4709 3-8-7 **91** NDeSouza[(5)] 6 99
(PFICole) *swtg: rrd leaving stalls: hld up: hdwy over 3f out: styd on u.p to go 2nd jst ins fnl f: no ch w wnr* **20/1**

0413 **3** 1¾ **Credit (IRE)**[18] 4749 3-8-11 **90** TPQueally 2 95
(RHannon) *lw: prom: drvn along 3f out: kpt on same pce* **16/1**

3160 **4** 1 **Always Waining (IRE)**[13] 4888 3-9-2 **95** JFanning 3 99
(MJohnston) *cl up: drvn along over 3f out: kpt on same pce* **16/1**

2312 **5** nk **Larkwing (IRE)**[35] 4229 3-8-9 **88** FNorton 8 91
(GWragg) *lw: in tch: drvn along over 3f out: kpt on same pce* **9/2**[2]

1300 **6** 3½ **Etmaam**[15] 4831 3-8-13 **92** (b[1]) RHills 7 90
(MJohnston) *hld up: sme hdwy 3f out: fdd fnl 2f* **16/1**

1320 **7** hd **Keelung (USA)**[76] 2999 3-8-9 **88** PRobinson 5 85
(MAJarvis) *lw: hld up: keen early: sme hdwy over 2f out: hung lft over 1f out: no further prog* **18/1**

2156 **8** 12 **Rehearsal**[55] 3671 3-9-2 **95** KDarley 9 73
(CGCox) *hld up: sme hdwy 1/2-way: drvn along 4f out: sn btn* **16/1**

0140 **9** ½ **Protective**[35] 4229 3-8-9 **88** WSupple 4 65
(JGGiven) *s.i.s: hld up: effrt 4f out: sn rdn and btn* **100/1**

-104 **10** ¾ **Odiham**[35] 4229 3-8-8 **87** SDrowne 10 63
(HMorrison) *in tch tl lost pl 5f out: sn in rr* **6/1**[3]

2m 31.4s (2.54) **Going Correction** +0.35s/f (Good) **10** Ran SP% **117.0**
Speed ratings: **105,103,102,101,101 98,98,90,90,90**CSF £26.26 CT £217.40 TOTE £2.00: £1.40, £3.60, £2.80; EX 33.20 Trifecta £131.90 Pool: £1,368.02. 7.36 winning units..
**Owner** Godolphin **Bred** Gainsborough Stud Management Ltd **Trained** Newmarket, Suffolk

**FOCUS**
A decent handicap which revolved around the unbeaten and potentially smart Into The Dark and the placed horses set a solid standard.

**NOTEBOOK**
**Into The Dark**, whose Newmarket form could not have worked out any better, had his stamina to prove over this mile and a half - his dam was all speed - but his style of racing and St Leger entry suggested it would not be a problem. Well backed beforehand, he was again allowed to dictate his own pace in front, with Dettori getting a breather into him rounding the home turn, before kicking on again in the straight. He was pulling further clear towards the finish and shapes as though he will stay a longer distance, although as Godolphin have Rule Of Law for the final Classic, he is apparently unlikely to take up his Doncaster engagement. He was, however, winning off a mark of 100 here, so fully deserves to take his chance in Group company next time.
**Secretary General(IRE)**, despite being by Fasliyev, appears to have improved for being stepped up to middle distances. Having been held up, he came through to secure second spot in the straight, and he looks capable of winning a similar race off this sort of mark.
**Credit(IRE)** had it to prove on this easier ground over this longer trip, and although he travelled well for much of the race, he could not find any extra when the gun was put to his head. He did not seem to see the trip out as well as some of his rivals.
**Always Waining(IRE)** looks to be in the grip of the Handicapper for the time being, and he has also shown his best form on top of the ground.
**Larkwing(IRE)** did little to boost the form of the Goodwood handicap he ran in last time. He looked sure to appreciate this more galloping track but failed to land a blow.
**Etmaam** remains way below his best and the frst-time blinkers failed to rekindle his enthusiasm.
**Keelung(USA)** *Official explanation: jockey said gelding hung badly left*
**Odiham** dropped out very tamely as though something was amiss. *Official explanation: jockey said gelding was never travelling*

## 5227 CHAMPIONS ARE SOLD IN IRELAND MAIDEN AUCTION STKS 7f 205y

**4:20** (4:21) (E2) 2-Y-0 **£9,542** (£2,936; £1,468; £734) **Stalls** Low

Form RPR

**1** **Xtra Torrential (USA)** 2-8-10 NCallan 9 81
(DMSimcock) *rangy: scope: slowly away: bhd: hdwy over 3f out: chsng first 2 whn hung lft ins fnl f: r.o strly clsng stages: led nr fin* **16/1**

22 **2** nk **Woodsley House (IRE)**[42] 4030 2-8-7 RHavlin 14 78
(MrsPNDutfield) *led: rdn over 1f out: styd on: hdd nr fin* **11/8**[1]

4234 **3** 1¼ **Hallucinate**[13] 4890 2-8-10 **70** LDettori 7 78
(RHannon) *prom: rdn over 3f out: ch ins fnl f: no ex u.p* **2/1**[2]

0 **4** 1¼ **Globe Trekker (USA)**[27] 4488 2-8-8 RFfrench 4 73
(JamesMoffatt) *chsd ldrs: rdn 3f out: styd on fnl f* **66/1**

**5** 8 **Boschette** 2-8-5 KMcEvoy 2 52
(JDBethell) *rangy: unf: towards rr: hdwy into midfield 1/2-way: rdn over 2f out: no further prog* **16/1**

0 **6** 2½ **Liability (IRE)**[23] 4606 2-8-2 JoannaBadger 1 43
(NTinkler) *prom tl outpcd 3f out: sn n.d* **125/1**

033 **7** hd **Cava Bien**[34] 4277 2-8-7 **70** MFenton 3 47
(JGGiven) *midfield: drvn along 1/2-way: no hdwy* **10/1**[3]

00 **8** 4 **Shingle Street (IRE)**[88] 2674 2-8-13 PRobinson 6 44
(MHTompkins) *sn wl bhd: rdn 2f out: styd on fnl f: n.d* **25/1**

500 **9** 6 **Artic Fox**[18] 4761 2-8-13 DAllan 5 30
(TDEasterby) *towards rr most of way* **25/1**

5003 **10** 2 **Dixie Queen (IRE)**[39] 4135 2-8-5 **65** PHanagan 13 18
(MDods) *sn wl bhd: rdn 2f out: styd on fnl f: n.d* **14/1**

00 **11** 3½ **Lauren Louise**[77] 2985 2-8-2 (t) KimTinkler 12 7
(NTinkler) *dwlt: a bhd* **125/1**

00 **12** 14 **Mark Your Card**[5] 5095 2-8-5 WSupple 8 —
(TDEasterby) *midfield tl wknd 3f out: t.o* **33/1**

00 **13** 25 **Welsh Galaxy (IRE)**[14] 4851 2-8-6 ow1 RPrice 10 —
(PLGilligan) *chsd ldrs tl hung bdly rt 4f out: sn bhd: t.o* **125/1**

1m 38.97s (1.23) **Going Correction** +0.35s/f (Good) **13** Ran SP% **117.5**
Speed ratings: **107,106,105,104,96 93,93,89,83,81 78,64,39**CSF £36.84 TOTE £36.10: £5.80, £1.30, £1.50; EX 86.30.
**Owner** The Wight Wons **Bred** Good Luck Farm **Trained** Newmarket, Suffolk

**FOCUS**
A modest maiden auction in which only a few had an obvious chance and the first four drew well clear. However, the winning time was very smart for the grade, just 0.06 seconds slower than the opening handicap, and the form looks good for the grade.

**NOTEBOOK**
**Xtra Torrential(USA)**, who was noisy in the paddock, overcame a slow start to make a winning debut. This half-brother to three winners in the USA gradually picked his way through his field and, despite running green, was able to collar the favourite in the dying strides. He will have learnt a lot from this, and can go on to further success. He may take his chance in the Haynes, Hanson and Clark at Newbury, but a lot depends on how he comes out of this.
**Woodsley House(IRE)** drifted from odds on and was edgy beforehand. He was able to get over from his outside stall to make the running, but was given no peace in front and, despite running on gamely, was run down near the finish. He has now been runner-up on all three appearances and deserves to get his head in front.
**Hallucinate** chased the favourite all the way up the straight, but he could never get past and was well held. His best chance of future success is likely to be in handicaps, but he showed a tendency to edge left and may need the help of some headgear.
**Globe Trekker(USA)** improved considerably on her debut, keeping on having been on the heels of the leaders throughout. She is another likely to find her best opportunities in handicaps.
**Boschette**, who was backed at long odds, showed some promise on this debut although well beaten by the principals.
**Cava Bien**, who has raced mainly on faster ground, never got into a challenging position.
**Mark Your Card** *Official explanation: jockey said filly lost her action*
**Welsh Galaxy(IRE)** *Official explanation: jockey said filly hung right*

## 5228 EBF PRINCE OF WALES'S OWN REGIMENT OF YORKSHIRE MAIDEN STKS 6f 217y

**4:50** (4:51) (D3) 2-Y-0 **£5,209** (£1,603; £801; £400) **Stalls** Low

Form RPR

**1** **Subpoena** 2-9-0 PRobinson 9 91
(MAJarvis) *rangy: scope: trckd ldrs: led ent fnl f: styd on wl* **10/1**

3 **2** 2 **Paper Talk (USA)**[56] 3643 2-9-0 MHills 4 86
(BWHills) *led tl rdn and hdd ent fnl f: styd on* **15/8**[2]

3 **3** 1½ **Banchieri**[24] 4567 2-9-0 LDettori 1 82
(SaeedBinSuroor) *in tch: hdwy over 2f out: ch and rdn appr fnl f: no ex ins last* **7/4**[1]

22 **4** ½ **Love Palace (IRE)**[21] 4633 2-9-0 .......... JFanning 2 81
(MJohnston) *w ldr: rdn 2f out: no ex fnl f* **5/1**[3]

0 **5** 2½ **Wingman (IRE)**[26] 4523 2-9-0 .......... RHills 5 74
(JWHills) *in tch: rdn 2f out: sn btn* **33/1**

**6** 4 **Gidam Gidam (IRE)** 2-9-0 .......... TEDurcan 7 64
(CEBrittain) *w'like: cmpt: s.i.s: hld up: effrt 3f out: sn rdn and btn* **50/1**

**7** 2½ **Rainbow Treasure (IRE)** 2-8-9 .......... WSupple 8 52
(JSGoldie) *leggy: unf: scope: hld up: sme hdwy over 2f out: outpcd over 1f out* **33/1**

**8** 3 **Sugitani (USA)** 2-9-0 .......... (t) KMcEvoy 3 50
(SaeedBinSuroor) *rangy: scope: hld up: effrt 3f out: sn rdn and btn* **16/1**

1m 25.75s (2.44) **Going Correction** +0.35s/f (Good) **8 Ran SP% 110.6**
Speed ratings: **100,97,96,95,92 88,85,81**CSF £27.33 TOTE £10.00: £2.10, £1.40, £1.30; EX 28.80.

**Owner** Sheikh Mohammed **Bred** Darley **Trained** Newmarket, Suffolk

**FOCUS**
This looked a decent maiden on paperand the form appears reasonably solid.

**NOTEBOOK**
**Subpoena**, a Middle Park entry, looks one to follow. He showed a nice turn of foot to settle matters in the closing stages, leaving the first three in the betting, who all had the benefit of previous experience, behind in the process. His stable won this race three years ago with the ill-fated Coshocton, and this half-brother to Three Graces looks another classy individual. His trainer will not be rushing him this year, however.

**Paper Talk(USA)**, who was somewhat unlucky to come up against potentially a very smart performer, looks fully capable of winning a similar maiden. He is another who will not be seen at his best until next year, though.

**Banchieri** appears to have his limitations. He ran well enough and was not knocked about in a lost cause inside the last, but on this evidence he would not be in the top division of the stable's juveniles.

**Love Palace(IRE)** was dropping back from an extended mile so it was rather surprising that he did not bag the outright lead and try and force the pace. He is now eligible for handicaps, and it will be interesting to see what sort of mark he gets.

**Wingman(IRE)**, whose Dewhurst and Royal Lodge entries look highly optimistic, looks sure to be going the nursery route before long. He was not given a hard race and will appreciate a mile in time.

## 5229 BOLLINGER CHAMPAGNE CHALLENGE SERIES H'CAP (FOR GENTLEMAN AMATEUR RIDERS) 1m 3f 198y

**5:20** (5:20) (E3) (0-70,70) 4-Y-O+ **£5,055** (£1,555; £777; £388) **Stalls** Low

Form RPR

0551 **1** **Bramantino (IRE)**[3] 5144 4-10-13 **58** 6ex.......... (b) MrRStephens(3) 9 67
(RAFahey) *hld up: hdwy into midfield 4f out: clsd on ldrs 2f out: rdn to ld jst ins fnl f: styd on* **5/1**[2]

3155 **2** ½ **Calatagan (IRE)**[109] 2121 5-11-4 **63**.......... MSeston(3) 11 71
(JMJefferson) *cl up: led 2f out: rdn and hdd jst ins fnl f: styd on* **11/1**

5162 **3** 5 **Senor Eduardo**[9] 4985 7-10-7 **56** oh2.......... MrTFWoodside(7) 8 56
(SGollings) *dwlt: hld up: hdwy and in tch 4f out: styd on u.p to chse first 2 appr fnl f: no imp ins last* **33/1**

0-02 **4** ½ **Loaded Gun**[12] 4901 4-10-9 **56** oh2.......... MrCDavies(5) 6 55
(WMBrisbourne) *midfield: rdn 3f out: kpt on u.p fnl 2f* **8/1**

3441 **5** 1¾ **Night Sight (USA)**[28] 4450 7-11-10 **69**.......... MrJMorgan(3) 5 65
(MrsSLamyman) *hld up in rr: hdwy over 3f out: ch and rdn 2f out: no further prog* **13/2**[3]

5210 **6** 2 **Romil Star (GER)**[6] 5058 7-10-11 **56** oh2.......... (v) MrSDobson(3) 4 49
(KRBurke) *in tch: tk clsr order 4f out: ch and rdn 2f out: no ex* **20/1**

-156 **7** nk **Middlethorpe**[144] 1326 7-11-9 **65**.......... (b) MrTGreenall 13 58
(MWEasterby) *midfield on outer: lost pl and dropped rr bnd over 4f out: kpt on u.p fnl 2f: n.d* **10/1**

2400 **8** 2½ **Sadler's Pride (IRE)**[13] 4870 4-11-7 **63**.......... (t) MrNickyTinkler 3 52
(AndrewTurnell) *in tch tl lost pl and dropped towards rr 5f out: n.d after* **33/1**

1134 **9** hd **Dickie Deadeye**[16] 4814 7-11-11 **70**.......... MrJJBest(3) 2 58
(GBBalding) *cl up: led 1/2-way: rdn and hdd 2f out: sn wknd* **4/1**[1]

4-00 **10** 1¼ **Dramatic Quest**[30] 4398 7-11-9 **70**.......... (p) MrMichaelMurphy(5) 1 56
(IanWilliams) *in tch: tk clsr order over 4f out: ev ch and rdn 2f out: sn wknd* **33/1**

0150 **11** 14 **Archie Babe (IRE)**[109] 2121 8-11-10 **66**.......... MrSWalker 10 30
(JJQuinn) *hld up: effrt 3f out: sn rdn and btn: t.o* **8/1**

000- **12** 3 **Kings Square**[167] 2265 4-10-7 **56** oh16.......... MrOGreenall(7) 7 15
(MWEasterby) *led tl hdd 1/2-way: wknd 4f out: t.o* **100/1**

526 **13** 1 **Sherwood Forest**[6] 5058 4-10-7 **56** oh11.......... (v) MrEWhillans(7) 12 14
(MissLAPerratt) *chsd ldrs tl rdn and wknd over 3f out: t.o* **40/1**

3444 **14** 5 **Kylkenny**[21] 4641 9-12-0 **70**.......... (t) MrJRees 14 20
(HMorrison) *midfield on outer tl lost pl and dropped rr bnd over 4f out: lost tch fnl 2f: t.o* **9/1**

2m 35.03s (6.17) **Going Correction** +0.35s/f (Good) **14 Ran SP% 116.7**
Speed ratings: **93,92,89,89,87 86,86,84,84,83 74,72,71,68**CSF £52.96 CT £1636.65 TOTE £5.80: £2.20, £3.60, £6.00; EX 93.20 Place 6 £94.85, Place 5 £20.99.

**Owner** Mrs Kenyon, A Rhodes Haulage, P Timmins **Bred** Mrs Brid Cosgrove **Trained** Musley Bank, N Yorks

**FOCUS**
An ordinary amateurs' handicap run at a moderate pace and the form does not look particularly strong.

**NOTEBOOK**
**Bramantino(IRE)** followed up his win at Beverley on Sunday under a 6lb penalty, taking it up entering the last under a well-timed ride. He is in top form at present and, with his stable enjoying a good time of it, may yet notch the hat-trick.

**Calatagan(IRE)** took up the running going well and did nothing wrong, but met one too good at the weights. This was a highly satisfactory return to action after a summer break and he is likely to attempt compensation in a race at the Ayr Western meeting.

**Senor Eduardo** stayed on under pressure to prove his stamina over this longer trip, but drifted across the course under pressure and ended up racing close to the far rail.

**Loaded Gun** was unable to build on the promise he showed at Ayr in this better race. He did not appear to be helping his rider as he hung to the left when the pressure was on.

**Night Sight(USA)**, only 2lb higher than when successful at Pontefract, picked up ground in the straight but could never quite get to grips with the leaders.

**Dickie Deadeye** raced at the head of affairs but was quickly on the retreat once collared. The return to this trip ought to have been in his favour but the handicapper seems to have his measure now.

T/Jkpt: Not won. T/Plt: £302.60 to a £1 stake. Pool: £76,048.00. 183.45 winning tickets. T/Qpdt: £5.20 to a £1 stake. Pool: £5,502.00. 779.05 winning tickets. JF

5230 - 5232a (Foreign Racing) - See Raceform Interactive

# 4386 CARLISLE (R-H)

Thursday, September 2

**OFFICIAL GOING: Good (good to soft in places)**

## 5233 SANDS MAIDEN AUCTION STKS 5f

**2:30** (2:30) (E4) 2-Y-O **£3,150** (£900; £450) **Stalls** High

Form RPR

055 **1** **Flying Ridge (IRE)**[14] 4876 2-8-6 .......... RMullen 3 76
(AMBalding) *cl up: led 2f out: rdn and flashed tail fnl f: kpt on wl* **5/1**[3]

2204 **2** ¾ **Chiselled (IRE)**[24] 4607 2-8-10 80.......... (t) DarrenWilliams 1 77
(KRBurke) *trckd ldrs: effrt over 1f out: kpt on fnl f: a hld* **3/1**[1]

2060 **3** 1¾ **Lady Dan (IRE)**[25] 4575 2-8-3 68.......... DaleGibson 4 64
(MWEasterby) *towards rr: drvn 1/2-way: kpt on fnl f: nt rch first two* **6/1**

444 **4** ¾ **Dispol Isle (IRE)**[17] 4804 2-8-2 65.......... PFessey 8 60
(TDBarron) *towards rr tl hdwy over 1f out: nrst fin* **4/1**[2]

0 **5** hd **Russian Rio (IRE)**[13] 4924 2-8-4 .......... RoryMoore(5) 9 66
(PCHaslam) *led to 2f out: kpt on same pce fnl f* **20/1**

3403 **6** ½ **Llamadas**[7] 5060 2-8-10 64.......... (b) SWKelly 7 65
(MDods) *towards rr on ins: outpcd 1/2-way: kpt on fnl f: no imp* **8/1**

500 **7** 1¾ **Waggledance (IRE)**[39] 4175 2-8-9 .......... GParkin 11 61+
(JSWainwright) *cl up tl rdn and outpcd fr 2f out* **40/1**

0 **8** nk **Egyptian Lady**[12] 4930 2-8-2 ow3.......... THamilton(3) 2 53
(RPElliott) *racd wd in rr: n.d* **80/1**

66 **9** 2½ **Joe Jo Star**[117] 1961 2-8-6 .......... HayleyTurner(3) 12 48
(PABlockley) *in tch to 2f out: sn btn* **20/1**

54 **10** shd **Middle Eastern**[28] 4487 2-8-9 .......... PBradley 10 48
(PABlockley) *chsd ldrs to 1/2-way: sn rdn and btn* **10/1**

**11** hd **Geordie Dancer (IRE)** 2-8-4 .......... PPMathers(5) 6 47
(ABerry) *s.i.s: nvr on terms* **20/1**

**12** ½ **Fern House (IRE)** 2-8-9 .......... RFfrench 5 45
(JamesMoffatt) *s.i.s: a bhd* **25/1**

61.50 secs **Going Correction** -0.125s/f (Firm) **12 Ran SP% 118.0**
Speed ratings: **95,93,91,89,89 88,85,85,81,81 80,80**CSF £18.34 TOTE £6.90: £2.20, £1.80, £1.30; EX 18.40.

**Owner** E N Kronfeld **Bred** Dr Karen Monica Sanderson **Trained** Kingsclere, Hants

**FOCUS**
A modest maiden auction and ordinary but sound form. Flying Ridge proved well suited by the minumum trip but will struggle in nurseries unless improving. Chiselled failed to run up to his mark of 80 in second and is probably flattered by that mark.

**NOTEBOOK**
**Flying Ridge(IRE)** had shaped with promise on all starts prior to this in better company and, having been up with the pace, went on just over two out before staying on strongly to deny the favourite. In beating the 80-rated Chiselled, she is likely to get a stiff mark, but that one seems to be going the wrong way. On the plus side though, this first crack at five furlongs suited and for the time being is clearly her best trip.

**Chiselled(IRE)** has not really gone on from his early season efforts - he was entitled to win this on form - but he did at least run a bit better back on this surface having been unsuited by the soft ground at Thirsk. He will find a race eventually but will always be vulnerable to something a bit less exposed.

**Lady Dan(IRE)** has been contesting nurseries and ran better back in this sphere. She is another who has not quite gone on as expected, but there is a low-grade nursery in her.

**Dispol Isle(IRE)** was filling this position for the fourth occasion and looks ready for a step up to six furlongs. Off a mark of 65 she is capable of winning a nursery.

**Russian Rio(IRE)** showed a lot of good early speed and went some way toward making up for a disappointing debut. With another run under his belt he will be interesting in nurseries.

**Llamadas** is exposed and may need a drop into claiming/selling company to score.

**Waggledance(IRE)** is not without ability and is another low-grade nursery type.

**Egyptian Lady** *Official explanation: jockey said filly hung left handed throughout*

## 5234 BORDER CONSTRUCTION NURSERY 5f 193y

**3:00** (3:04) (E3) (0-75,73) 2-Y-O **£5,505** (£1,694; £847; £423) **Stalls** High

Form RPR

055 **1** **Kingsgate Bay (IRE)**[22] 4643 2-9-0 **66**.......... NPollard 1 74
(JRBest) *cl up: led over 2f out: clr whn edgd rt u.p over 1f out: flashed tail: r.o wl* **12/1**

41 **2** 1½ **Hansomelle (IRE)**[33] 4329 2-9-6 **72**.......... RFfrench 9 76
(BMactaggart) *in tch: effrt over 2f out: kpt on fnl f: nt rch wnr* **12/1**

4166 **3** 1½ **Pro Tempore**[17] 4803 2-8-10 **65**.......... ABeech(3) 3 64+
(MrsJRRamsden) *hld up: hdwy and shkn up over 1f out: hung rt: kpt on fnl f: no imp* **5/1**[1]

004 **4** ½ **Royal Pardon**[28] 4481 2-8-6 **58**.......... RMullen 6 56
(MLWBell) *towards rr on outside: hdwy over 1f out: nvr rchd ldrs* **8/1**[3]

0610 **5** 2½ **Hopelessly Devoted**[10] 4997 2-8-1 **58**.......... RoryMoore(5) 13 48
(PCHaslam) *keen: trckd ldrs tl rdn and nt qckn over 1f out* **25/1**

464 **6** ¾ **Zantero**[13] 4924 2-8-13 **65**.......... JMackay 7 53
(RPElliott) *bhd: hdwy on outside over 1f out: nvr able to chal* **20/1**

0640 **7** hd **Chairman Rick (IRE)**[29] 4439 2-8-13 **65**.......... AlexGreaves 19 52
(DNicholls) *in tch: rdn over 2f out: sn one pce* **25/1**

030 **8** 1¼ **Choreographic (IRE)**[28] 4488 2-8-6 **61**.......... THamilton(3) 16 44
(RAFahey) *hmpd s: hld up: pushed along 1/2-way: no imp* **6/1**[2]

2105 **9** hd **No Commission (IRE)**[13] 4909 2-9-4 **73**.......... DNolan(3) 10 56
(RFFisher) *s.i.s: effrt over 3f out: no imp* **12/1**

4004 **10** shd **Lord John**[20] 4700 2-8-3 **55**.......... DaleGibson 5 38
(MWEasterby) *hld up: effrt over 1f out: nt pce to chal* **10/1**

5055 **11** 1¼ **Kilmovee**[64] 3408 2-9-3 **69**.......... KimTinkler 18 48
(NTinkler) *led to over 2f out: sn rdn and btn* **40/1**

0530 **12** shd **Ryedane (IRE)**[27] 4508 2-8-13 **65**.......... SWKelly 8 43
(TDEasterby) *hld up on outside: effrt over 2f out: wknd over 1f out* **14/1**

0044 **13** 1¾ **Mister Buzz**[5] 5125 2-8-8 **60**.......... LisaJones 17 33
(MDHammond) *midfield: outpcd over 3f out: n.d after* **16/1**

060 **14** hd **Zarova (IRE)**[48] 3918 2-8-4 **56**.......... TLucas 14 29
(MWEasterby) *hld up: n.d* **25/1**

540 **15** 4 **Kaggamagic**[56] 3679 2-9-3 **69**.......... DarrenWilliams 2 30
(JRNorton) *prom tl rdn and wknd wl over 1f out* **20/1**

4105 **16** 1 **Maureen's Lough (IRE)**[6] 5097 2-8-0 **55**.......... HayleyTurner(3) 12 13
(JHetherton) *cl up to 2f out: sn wknd* **25/1**

605 **17** shd **Eukleia (USA)**[13] 4924 2-8-13 **65**.......... PFessey 15 22
(TDBarron) *trckd ldrs: rdn over 2f out: sn wknd* **20/1**

460 **18** 2½ **Zendaro**[75] 3080 2-8-5 **60** ow3.......... SHitchcott(3) 11 10
(WMBrisbourne) *in tch to over 3f out: sn lost pl* **14/1**

0050 19 14 **Kristikhab (IRE)**[21] 4675 2-8-0 57 ow1... PPMathers(5) 4 —
(ABerry) *s.v.s: nvr on terms* **20/1**

1m 14.26s (0.06) **Going Correction** -0.125s/f (Firm) **19** Ran SP% **130.3**
Speed ratings: **94,92,90,89,86 85,84,83,82,82 81,80,78,78,72 71,71,68,49**CSF £133.07 CT £855.81 TOTE £17.80: £4.40, £2.70, £1.90, £2.60; EX 244.50.
**Owner** John Mayne **Bred** Mrs A Hughes **Trained** Hucking, Kent

**FOCUS**
A fair nursery that looks sound on paper and seems sure to produce future winners. This was a good effort from the winner given he had to do a bit of early running to get across from his draw and he won with something to spare.

**NOTEBOOK**
**Kingsgate Bay(IRE)** had found five furlongs an inadequate test since making a pleasing debut over six at Salisbury and appreciated the step back up for this nursery debut. He was quickly into his stride from the lowest draw of all and came across to sit just off the pace. Once taking it up he was always holding his pursuers and won with a little in hand. His stable is back in form and there may be more to come. *Official explanation: trainer said, regarding the improved form shown, gelding had benefited from the step up in trip on this occasion*
**Hansomelle(IRE)** showed improved form for the step up to this trip when winning at Hamilton and progressed again off what was a high-enough mark. She will get another furlong and is evidently improving.
**Pro Tempore** has been finding five furlongs too sharp and was suited by the extra distance. There is more to come and she should prove better than her mark of 65 in time.
**Royal Pardon** made some late headway and will improve for a more positive ride.
**Hopelessly Devoted** has been running in claiming company and stepped up on those efforts in fifth. There is more to come from her on turf and her current rating looks reasonable.
**Zantero** made some late headway and wants at least another furlong.
**Chairman Rick(IRE)** ran his best race to date but needs to build on it if he is going to win.
**Choreographic(IRE)** was never in the hunt having been interfered with at the start, and should have the run ignored.
**Kaggamagic** showed up well for most of the way but stopped rather sharply. He has the ability to win but it would have been nice to see him finish his race a bit better.

## 5235 WILLY HOLME H'CAP 6f 192y
**3:30** (3:34) (F4) (0-55,55) 3-Y-0+ **£3,295** (£941; £470) **Stalls** High

Form RPR
0606 1 **Mon Secret (IRE)**[36] 4246 6-8-12 **51**... DMcGaffin 4 61
(BSmart) *hld up: rn 1/2-way: hdwy far rail to ld ins fnl f: r.o wl* **14/1**
0440 2 nk **Iced Diamond (IRE)**[14] 4877 5-8-8 **50**...(t) SHitchcott(3) 9 59
(WMBrisbourne) *dwlt: hld up: effrt and swtchd over 1f out: hrd rdn and ev ch ins fnl f: jst hld* **8/1**[3]
0142 3 3/4 **Joshua's Gold (IRE)**[7] 5063 3-8-5 **55**...(v) DTudhope(7) 5 62
(DCarroll) *cl up: disp ld over 2f out to ins fnl f: no ex* **13/2**[2]
505 4 1 1/4 **Linden's Lady**[30] 4425 4-8-9 **51**... ABeech(3) 6 55
(JRWeymes) *keen: hld up: hdwy outside over 1f out: nrst fin* **16/1**
3555 5 nk **Apache Point (IRE)**[6] 5085 7-9-1 **54**... KimTinkler 10 57
(NTinkler) *keen towards rr: lost pl 1/2-way: hdwy over 1f out: kpt on: n.d* **8/1**[3]
1660 6 1 3/4 **Wood Dalling (USA)**[13] 4905 6-9-2 **55**... PFessey 15 53
(ISemple) *trckd ldrs: effrt over 2f out: edgd rt and nt qckn fnl f* **9/1**
2125 7 hd **Cut Ridge (IRE)**[12] 4937 5-9-2 **55**... RFfrench 13 53
(JSWainwright) *plld hrd: mde most to ins fnl f: wknd* **8/1**[3]
0000 8 hd **The Wizard Mul**[16] 4827 4-8-12 **54**... HayleyTurner(3) 11 51
(WStorey) *cl up tl rdn and one pce wl over 1f out* **50/1**
3001 9 nk **Dubonai (IRE)**[10] 5002 4-8-12 **54** 6ex... DCorby(3) 3 51
(AndrewTurnell) *racd wd in midfield: hdwy and prom 1/2-way: nt qckn over 1f out* **10/1**
6164 10 hd **Zhitomir**[13] 4905 6-8-11 **50**... SWKelly 12 46
(MDods) *midfield: rdn 2f out: sn btn* **6/1**[1]
3406 11 hd **Waltzing Wizard**[31] 4390 5-8-7 **51**... PPMathers(5) 1 47
(ABerry) *racd wd in rr: rdn and outpcd fr 3f out* **16/1**
0300 12 1 1/4 **Golden Spectrum (IRE)**[20] 4702 5-9-0 **53**...(v) AlexGreaves 8 45
(DNicholls) *hld up towards rr: rdn over 3f out: nvr on terms* **14/1**
0020 13 shd **Stormville (IRE)**[13] 4905 7-8-10 **54**... MLawson(5) 7 46
(MBrittain) *chsd ldrs to 3f out: sn rdn and btn* **25/1**
3000 14 2 **Fenwicks Pride (IRE)**[16] 4827 6-8-11 **53**... THamilton(3) 2 40
(RAFahey) *prom tl rdn and wknd fr 2f out* **20/1**

1m 28.29s (1.19) **Going Correction** +0.15s/f (Good)
**WFA** 3 from 4yo+ 4lb **14** Ran SP% **115.7**
Speed ratings: **99,98,97,96,96 94,93,93,93,93 92,91,91,88**CSF £114.68 CT £804.82 TOTE £15.10: £4.00, £2.40, £2.20; EX 222.70.
**Owner** Pinnacle Monash Partnership **Bred** John Hutchinson **Trained** Hambleton, N Yorks

**FOCUS**
A moderate handicap in which the whole field were pretty well packed together at the finish. The placed horses provide the key to the form.

**NOTEBOOK**
**Mon Secret(IRE)** hinted at a return to form when an unlucky in running sixth at Musselburgh when last seen, and the return to seven furlongs proved right up his street. In rear early, he responded well to pressure and came with a strong run against the far rail to edge ahead in the closing stages. He is not the most consistent and as a result would not be one to bank on to follow up.
**Iced Diamond(IRE)** does not win that often but ran one of his better races and was only just held. It is doubtful he can build on this next time, however.
**Joshua's Gold(IRE)** again ran well and remains in good form.
**Linden's Lady** was gaining with every stride at the line but remains without a win in nearly two years.
**Apache Point(IRE)** has a string of fives next to his name and continues to run well without winning.
**The Wizard Mul** ran better than his price entitled him to and may be coming back to form.
**Zhitomir** was disappointing without any obvious excuse.

## 5236 CARLISLE GLASS H'CAP 7f 200y
**4:00** (4:02) (E3) (0-70,73) 3-Y-0+ **£5,328** (£1,639; £819; £409) **Stalls** High

Form RPR
5042 1 **Otago (IRE)**[6] 5072 3-8-2 **53**... RFfrench 16 62
(JRBest) *chsd ldrs: rdn and led over 1f out: edgd lft ins last: hld on wl* **11/2**[2]
0155 2 1/2 **Hula Ballew**[38] 4201 4-8-13 **59**...(p) SWKelly 14 67+
(MDods) *hld up midfield: hdwy over 2f out: ev ch fnl f: jst hld* **9/1**
-006 3 1 1/2 **Able Mind**[53] 3779 4-8-11 **57**... PFessey 15 62
(ACWhillans) *in tch: rdn 1/2-way: rallied to chse ldrs over 1f out: hung rt u.p: one pce fnl f* **14/1**
0021 4 3/4 **Templet (USA)**[10] 4987 4-9-6 **66** 6ex... GParkin 5 69
(ISemple) *bhd and rdn along: hdwy over 1f out: kpt on: nrst fin* **14/1**
3361 5 nk **Riska King**[5] 5108 4-9-10 **73** 6ex... THamilton(3) 18 75
(RAFahey) *in tch: effrt over 2f out: one pce fnl f* **6/1**[3]
3143 6 shd **Gifted Flame**[5] 5108 5-9-2 **67**... PMakin(5) 13 69
(TDBarron) *bhd: hdwy and in tch whn nt clr run over 1f out: one pce fnl f* **5/1**[1]
4051 7 nk **Band**[17] 4818 4-8-8 **57**... SHitchcott(3) 12 58
(BAMcmahon) *hld up: hdwy on outside 2f out: no imp fnl f* **11/2**[2]
215 8 hd **Zarin (IRE)**[5] 5127 6-8-7 **53**... NPollard 4 54
(DWChapman) *keen: w ldr tl outpcd fnl f* **16/1**
6434 9 1 **Cryfield**[10] 5002 7-9-0 **60**... KimTinkler 8 58
(NTinkler) *towards rr: rdn 1/2-way: nt pce to chal* **14/1**
4450 10 nk **Graceful Air (IRE)**[7] 5063 3-8-4 **55**... JoannaBadger 3 53
(JRWeymes) *in tch to 2f out: sn outpcd* **50/1**
20 11 1 1/2 **Flying Spud**[22] 4624 3-8-2 **53** oh5... LisaJones 6 47
(JLSpearing) *cl up tl rdn and wknd over 2f out* **25/1**
0100 12 3/4 **Time To Regret**[36] 4246 4-8-2 **53** oh1... PPMathers(5) 2 46
(JSWainwright) *mde most to over 1f out: sn btn* **25/1**
0000 13 1 3/4 **Pharoah's Gold (IRE)**[5] 5127 6-8-7 **53** oh4...(p) DarrenWilliams 1 42
(DShaw) *keen: hld up: rdn 3f out: hung rt and sn btn* **50/1**
4424 14 nk **Newcorp Lad**[27] 4511 4-8-13 **59**...(v[1]) JMackay 7 47
(MrsGSRees) *keen in tch: rdn and hung rt 2f out: sn btn* **10/1**
0400 15 8 **Lord Arthur**[6] 5081 3-8-2 **53**...(b[1]) DaleGibson 10 22
(MWEasterby) *trckd ldrs tl hung rt and wknd over 2f out* **50/1**

1m 40.57s (0.57) **Going Correction** +0.15s/f (Good)
**WFA** 3 from 4yo+ 5lb **15** Ran SP% **120.3**
Speed ratings: **103,102,101,100,99 99,99,99,98,98 96,95,94,93,85**CSF £51.54 CT £475.28 TOTE £5.50: £2.10, £2.70, £2.70; EX 68.10.
**Owner** Mrs L M Askew **Bred** W J Hamilton **Trained** Hucking, Kent
■ Stewards Enquiry : Darren Williams caution: used whip when out of contention

**FOCUS**
A competitive handicap despite five horses racing from out of the handicap, but ordinary form for the grade, although the sound pace gives it a solid look. Just one of the first seven home was drawn in a single-figure stall.

**NOTEBOOK**
**Otago(IRE)**, due to be raised 5lb following his close second in a similar event at Bath on his previous start, proved good enough to take advantage of his current mark. Things will be tougher in future, but he is going the right way.
**Hula Ballew**, dropped back from ten furlongs, returned to somewhere near her best and, although she did not get the clearest of passages, she can have no excuses.
**Able Mind** is still a maiden, but he was racing off a career-low mark and ran well. He looks to have found his level.
**Templet(USA)**, 6lb lower than in future under his penalty, had the blinkers left off this time and did not appear suited by this drop back from nine furlongs, but still fared best of those in single-figure stalls.
**Riska King**, 1lb wrong under his penalty for his recent Beverley success, was below form with no obvious excuse.
**Gifted Flame** raced a little keenly, did not get the clearest of runs, and would have preferred faster ground.
**Band**, off the mark in a 20-runner handicap at Yarmouth on his previous start, found this tougher off a 3lb higher mark.

## 5237 DENTON HOLME MEDIAN AUCTION MAIDEN STKS 1m 1f 61y
**4:30** (4:32) (E4) 3-4-Y-0 **£3,136** (£896; £448) **Stalls** High

Form RPR
62 1 **Countrywide Luck**[28] 4492 3-8-9... J-PGuillambert(3) 8 73+
(NPLittmoden) *in tch: effrt over 2f out: led appr fnl f: hung rt u.p: kpt on wl* **4/9**[1]
-403 2 2 1/2 **Young Rooney**[13] 4901 4-9-4 68... RMullen 14 68
(MMullineaux) *racd wd: led tl wandered and hdd appr fnl f: no ex* **6/1**[2]
0545 3 6 **Dream Easy**[20] 4726 3-8-12 70... RPrice 13 56
(PLGilligan) *bhd: hdwy over 2f out: kpt on: no ch w first two* **11/1**[3]
-056 4 3/4 **Grele (USA)**[35] 4259 3-8-2 45... PMakin(5) 12 50?
(RHollinshead) *hld up: hdwy 3f out: one pce fr 2f out* **50/1**
-060 5 5 **Schinken Otto (IRE)**[51] 3822 3-8-9 45... THamilton(3) 9 45?
(JMJefferson) *s.s: hdwy over 3f out: no imp over 1f out* **66/1**
6 6 3/4 **Sarenne**[10] 4987 3-8-7... RFfrench 4 38
(MJohnston) *hld up: outpcd over 3f out: sme late hdwy: nvr on terms* **16/1**
632 7 2 1/2 **Reem Two**[13] 4910 3-8-7 55... JMackay 6 33
(DMccain) *prom: effrt 3f out: btn over 1f out* **16/1**
6400 8 nk **Royaltea**[97] 2456 3-8-7 47... JoannaBadger 1 32
(MsDeborahJEvans) *racd wd towards rr: rdn over 3f out: hung rt and sn no imp* **66/1**
0- 9 15 **Bobering**[360] 4780 4-8-13... PPMathers(5) 2 7
(BPJBaugh) *in tch tl wknd over 3f out* **100/1**
04 10 6 **Transkei**[20] 4703 3-8-7... SWKelly 7 —
(MrsLStubbs) *hld up: rdn over 3f out: n.d* **100/1**
030- 11 2 **Well Connected (IRE)**[318] 5672 4-9-4 45... DMcGaffin 5 —
(BSmart) *prom to over 3f out: sn rdn and btn* **16/1**
0- 12 7 **Starbright**[359] 4788 3-8-12... TLucas 11 —
(MissSEHall) *keen: cl up to over 3f out: sn btn* **80/1**
13 2 1/2 **Jonnyem** 3-8-12... DaleGibson 3 —
(GASwinbank) *sn wl bhd: no ch fr 1/2-way* **28/1**
14 18 **La Mago**[165] 4-8-13... DMernagh 10 —
(FPMurtagh) *s.i.s: sn wl bhd* **100/1**

1m 58.64s (0.61) **Going Correction** +0.15s/f (Good)
**WFA** 3 from 4yo 6lb **14** Ran SP% **122.1**
Speed ratings: **103,100,95,94,90 89,87,87,73,68 66,60,58,42**CSF £3.37 TOTE £1.50: £1.10, £1.50, £3.50; EX 5.40.
**Owner** Countrywide Steel & Tubes Ltd **Bred** Miss Nicola Kent **Trained** Newmarket, Suffolk
■ Stewards Enquiry : R Price seven-day ban: used whip with excessive frequency (Sep 13-19)

**FOCUS**
A weak maiden with the proximity of the fourth and fifth holding the form down, but at least the pace was good.

**NOTEBOOK**
**Countrywide Luck** had shown ability on both his previous starts in much better races than this, but had to work quite hard to see off the eventual runner-up and appeals as one to take on in handicaps.
**Young Rooney** gained an uncontested lead and set a decent pace, but was just beaten by a better horse. He is likely to continue to prove hard to win with unless dropped in grade. *Official explanation: jockey said gelding hung left handed throughout*
**Dream Easy** soon found himself in a very unpromising position and lacked the pace to get on terms and pose a threat. He will be suited by further but looks very harshly treated on a mark of 70.
**Grele(USA)** was way out of her depth but acquitted herself creditably.
**Well Connected(IRE)** *Official explanation: jockey said gelding bolted to start*

## 5238 BATTLE HOLME H'CAP 1m 3f 206y
**5:00** (5:03) (F4) (0-55,54) 3-Y-0+ **£3,242** (£926; £463) **Stalls** Low

Form RPR
-002 1 **Turn Of Phrase (IRE)**[7] 5058 5-9-1 **54**...(v) THamilton(3) 17 70
(RAFahey) *midfield: effrt and swtchd over 2f out: rdn and ev ch fnl f: led post* **15/8**[1]

2465 **2** *shd* **Scurra**[13] 4901 5-8-10 **53** .................................... DTudhope(7) 8 69
(ACWhillans) *hld up: hdwy on outside to ld 2f out: hrd pressed fnl f: kpt on: hdd post* **12/1**

00/0 **3** *11* **Dee Pee Tee Cee (IRE)**[22] 4624 10-8-10 **46** .................... TLucas 12 44
(MWEasterby) *set str pce: mde most to 2f out: nt qckn* **16/1**

5162 **4** *1 1/4* **Life Is Beautiful (IRE)**[26] 4561 5-9-0 **50** .................... DaleGibson 4 46
(WHTinning) *midfield: rdn over 3f out: no imp fr 2f out* **7/1**[2]

0/55 **5** *2 1/2* **Mr Midaz**[35] 4261 5-8-9 **45** .................................... RFfrench 2 37
(DWWhillans) *midfield: outpcd over 3f out: rallied over 1f out: no imp* **18/1**

0402 **6** *3/4* **Danefonique (IRE)**[5] 5110 3-8-5 **50** .................................... RMullen 1 41
(DCarroll) *disp ld tl wknd fr over 2f out* **10/1**[3]

0005 **7** *nk* **Canlis**[24] 4605 5-8-9 **45** .................................... (p) DMernagh 10 36
(DWThompson) *keen: in tch: effrt over 2f out: sn rdn and btn* **16/1**

260 **8** *nk* **Sherwood Forest**[1] 5229 4-8-6 **45** .................................... (v) DCorby(3) 15 35
(MissLAPerratt) *bhd: rdn over 4f out: nvr on terms* **20/1**

0060 **9** *hd* **Cantemerle (IRE)**[47] 3928 4-8-10 **46** .................................... (b) SWKelly 5 36
(WMBrisbourne) *hld up: reminders 1/2-way: drvn over 4f out: n.d* **12/1**

500 **10** *1/2* **Sharabad (FR)**[35] 4276 6-8-9 **45** .................................... DMcGaffin 16 34
(MrsLBNormile) *chsd ldrs tl wknd fr 2f out* **100/1**

0-00 **11** *2 1/2* **Caper**[14] 4883 4-8-9 **45** oh5 .................................... JMackay 9 30
(RHollinshead) *s.i.s: nvr on terms* **66/1**

044 **12** *1 1/4* **Border Terrier (IRE)**[40] 4139 6-8-6 **45** oh5 ........... (v[1]) HayleyTurner(3) 13 28
(MDHammond) *a bhd* **12/1**

-000 **13** *7* **Saddler's Quest**[13] 4911 7-9-0 **50** .................................... DarrenWilliams 7 22
(BPJBaugh) *in tch tl wknd over 3f out* **28/1**

0030 **14** *1* **Lady Stratagem**[30] 4424 5-8-9 **45** oh5 .................................... GParkin 14 15
(EWTuer) *prom tl edgd rt and wknd fr 3f out* **40/1**

004- **15** *5* **Needwood Spirit**[233] 1920 9-8-4 **45** oh10 .................... PPMathers(5) 11 7
(MrsAMNaughton) *hld up: rdn 5f out: sn btn* **40/1**

45-0 **16** *dist* **Special Branch**[18] 4778 4-8-9 **45** .................................... NPollard 6 —
(JeddO'Keeffe) *hld up: drvn 1/2-way: sn lost tch* **16/1**

2m 34.04s (1.64) **Going Correction** +0.15s/f (Good)
**WFA** 3 from 4yo+ 9lb **16** Ran SP% **117.9**
Speed ratings: **100,99,92,91,90 89,89,89,89,88 87,86,81,80,77** —CSF £21.45 CT £253.95 TOTE £2.40: £1.10, £2.80, £5.10, £1.70; EX 33.90 Place 6 £61.34, Place 5 £43.36.
**Owner** Jacksons Transport (West Riding) Ltd **Bred** Moyglare Stud Farm Ltd **Trained** Musley Bank, N Yorks

**FOCUS**
A very moderate handicap; dire stuff in behind the front two, who pulled clear and have been capable of better in te past.

**NOTEBOOK**
**Turn Of Phrase(IRE)**, runner-up over a mile six at Musselburgh on his previous start, was 4lb lower than in future and needed every yard of this shorter distance to get on top. His new mark will force him to step up in grade, but he promises to improve once stepped back up in trip.
**Scurra** did absolutely nothing wrong, as he pulled clear of the remainder and only lost out on the line.
**Dee Pee Tee Cee(IRE)** has not won on the Flat since 1999 and was left behind by the front two.
**Life Is Beautiful(IRE)**, disappointing in a claimer on her previous start, was again below form.
**Mr Midaz** was beaten a long way and offered little encouragement.
T/Plt: £52.10 to a £1 stake. Pool: £38,123.80. 533.15 winning tickets. T/Qpdt: £17.20 to a £1 stake. Pool: £2,837.50. 121.90 winning tickets. RY

## 5125 REDCAR (L-H)
### Thursday, September 2

**OFFICIAL GOING: Good to firm (firm in places)**
The riders described the going as 'just on the quick side of good'.
Wind: Almost nil. Weather: Fine and sunny.

## 5239 CRAB MAIDEN STKS — 1m 1f
**2:10** (2:14) (D3) 3-Y-0+ **£3,552** (£1,093; £546; £273) **Stalls** Low

Form RPR

**1** **Focus Group (USA)** 3-9-0 .................................... WRyan 1 77
(HRACecil) *rangy: hld up and bhd: hdwy over 3f out: styd on to ld jst ins last: r.o wl* **9/2**[3]

**2** *1* **Namat (IRE)** 3-8-9 .................................... WSupple 4 70
(MPTregoning) *lengthy: unf: dwely: smooth hdwy 6f out: led over 1f out: hdd jst ins last: nt qckn* **13/2**

4- **3** *hd* **Dream Scene (IRE)**[412] 3369 3-8-9 .................................... SSanders 7 70
(JHMGosden) *w ldr: led 3f out tl over 1f out: styd on same pce* **7/2**[2]

3304 **4** *1* **Ma Yahab**[28] 4493 3-8-11 72 .................................... NMackay(3) 5 76+
(LMCumani) *hld up towards rr: stdy hdwy 3f out: keeping on same pce whn n.m.r ins last* **10/3**[1]

-000 **5** *1/2* **Business Matters (IRE)**[10] 5010 4-8-10 45 .................... BSwarbrick(5) 9 67?
(MsRebeccaBowden, Ire) *chsd ldrs: kpt on same pce appr fnl f* **25/1**

2-62 **6** *8* **Heart's Desire (IRE)**[55] 3701 3-8-9 70 .................................... ACulhane 10 51
(BWHills) *led tl 3f out: wknd and eased over 1f out* **7/1**

**7** *1 1/4* **Lady Karr** 3-8-9 .................................... JFanning 11 49
(MJohnston) *lengthy: unf: sn chsng ldrs: drvn along 4f out: lost pl over 2f out* **7/1**

5 **8** *12* **Wizards Princess**[20] 4703 4-9-1 .................................... AMcCarthy 2 25
(DWThompson) *s.i.s: sme hdwy over 5f out: lost pl over 3f out: sn bhd* **150/1**

0 **9** *5* **Rosings**[59] 3592 3-8-9 .................................... MFenton 8 15
(PWHarris) *chsd ldrs: drvn along 4f out: sn lost pl and bhd* **33/1**

1m 51.48s (-1.92) **Going Correction** -0.20s/f (Firm)
**WFA** 3 from 4yo+ 6lb **9** Ran SP% **109.3**
Speed ratings: **100,99,98,98,97 90,89,78,74**CSF £30.39 TOTE £5.40: £2.60, £3.20, £1.90; EX 42.40.
**Owner** K Abdulla **Bred** Juddmonte Farms Inc **Trained** Newmarket, Suffolk

**FOCUS**
An average maiden for the track, with a number of big stables represented. The proximity of the fifth raises doubts, but the winner should improve on this debut.

**NOTEBOOK**
**Focus Group(USA)**, who stands over plenty of ground, looked fit and was loaded with a blanket. Settled in last place, he came with a sustained run down the wide outside and in the end scored in decisive fashion. He should go on from here.
**Namat(IRE)**, long in the back and weak, is a moderate walker. She went on but had no answer when the winner came by on her outside.
**Dream Scene(IRE)**, who showed ability in one outing at two, looked backward in her coat. After being sent for home she kept on in willing fashion when headed.
**Ma Yahab**, who continually swished his tail in the paddock, was humoured along but was not doing a lot when left short of racing room inside the last. Rated 72, he is the key to the overall value of the form.
**Business Matters(IRE)**, back to form last time at Tralee, is now a maiden after 18 attempts.
**Heart's Desire(IRE)**, very fit, was edgy in the paddock and over this extended trip her stamina seemed to give out completely.
**Rosings** *Official explanation: jockey said filly hung left handed in straight*

## 5240 CRAY FISH NURSERY — 7f
**2:40** (2:44) (E3) (0-75,72) 2-Y-0 **£4,329** (£1,332; £666; £333) **Stalls** Centre

Form RPR

2413 **1** **Caitlin (IRE)**[14] 4878 2-9-5 **70** .................................... FLynch 17 75
(BSmart) *mde all: edgd lft over 3f out: hung lft: jst hld on* **12/1**

01 **2** *hd* **The Pen**[26] 4559 2-8-5 **56** .................................... GFaulkner 16 60
(PCHaslam) *dwlt: sn chsng ldrs: effrt over 2f out: styd on wl fnl f: jst failed* **6/1**[2]

642 **3** *1/2* **Cerebus**[36] 4243 2-9-4 **72** .................................... LFletcher(3) 20 75
(NPLittmoden) *chsd ldrs: effrt over 2f out: styd on wl ins last* **10/1**[3]

300 **4** *hd* **Drax**[58] 3601 2-9-6 **71** .................................... KDarley 9 73
(DRLoder) *w ldrs: ev ch over 1f out: nt qckn ins last* **10/1**[3]

0002 **5** *1 1/2* **Master Joseph**[6] 5090 2-8-9 **60** .................................... ACulhane 13 59
(MRChannon) *chsd ldrs: effrt over 2f out: styd on fnl f* **5/1**[1]

065 **6** *hd* **Algorithm**[33] 4347 2-8-7 **58** .................................... WSupple 15 56
(TDEasterby) *rr-div: hdwy over 2f out: styd on wl ins last* **50/1**

200 **7** *1 1/4* **As Handsome Does**[29] 4446 2-9-0 **65** .................................... (t) WRyan 5 60
(NTinkler) *s.i.s: hdwy over 2f out: styd on fnl f* **25/1**

1030 **8** *1 1/2* **Snookered Again**[14] 4890 2-8-10 **64** .................... PMulrennan(3) 19 55
(MWEasterby) *chsd ldrs: nt qckn fnl 2f* **20/1**

0434 **9** *1/2* **Burton Ash**[27] 4524 2-9-7 **72** .................................... MFenton 11 62
(JGGiven) *swvd rt s: styd on fnl 2f: nt rch ldrs* **20/1**

006 **10** *nk* **Zando**[40] 4135 2-8-4 **62** .................................... DFentiman(7) 3 51
(PCHaslam) *w ldrs: wknd over 1f out* **66/1**

050 **11** *1 1/4* **Imperial Dynasty (USA)**[13] 4900 2-8-12 **63** .................... SSanders 8 49
(TDBarron) *chsd ldrs: rdn over 2f out: wknd appr fnl f* **10/1**[3]

250 **12** *3 1/2* **Tybalt**[29] 4454 2-9-1 **66** .................................... NCallan 4 42
(PWHarris) *mid-div: hrd rdn over 2f out: nvr nr ldrs* **10/1**[3]

0005 **13** *3* **Fantasy Defender (IRE)**[17] 4816 2-8-9 **60** .................... RWinston 2 29
(JJQuinn) *s.i.s: bhd tl sme hdwy fnl 2f* **40/1**

060 **14** *1 1/2* **Loyalty Lodge (IRE)**[60] 3560 2-8-8 **59** .................... JFanning 7 24
(JDBethell) *mid-div: drvn along over 3f out: nvr on terms* **40/1**

040 **15** *1/2* **Summer Silks**[24] 4606 2-8-11 **62** .................................... PHanagan 14 25
(RAFahey) *chsd ldrs: wkng whn hmpd over 3f out* **16/1**

566 **16** *3/4* **Town End Tom**[62] 3491 2-8-9 **60** .................................... CCatlin 6 22
(DMSimcock) *mid-div: effrt over 2f out: sn lost pl* **14/1**

0201 **17** *3/4* **Jay (IRE)**[22] 4651 2-8-7 **61** .................................... (p) NMackay(3) 1 21
(NACallaghan) *swvd bdlyrt s: a in rr* **20/1**

5446 **18** *3/4* **Sweet Marguerite**[61] 3532 2-8-12 **63** .................................... DAllan 10 21
(TDEasterby) *in rr: drvn along 3f out: nvr on terms* **25/1**

0051 **19** *1 1/4* **Ladruca**[22] 4638 2-8-9 **60** .................................... AMcCarthy 12 14
(GGMargarson) *chsd ldrs: effrt over 2f out: sn wknd* **14/1**

5405 **20** *1* **Tantien**[66] 3373 2-9-0 **65** .................................... DeanMcKeown 18 17
(JohnAHarris) *sn bhd* **50/1**

1m 24.14s (-0.76) **Going Correction** -0.20s/f (Firm) **20** Ran SP% **126.5**
Speed ratings: **96,95,95,94,93 93,91,89,89,88 87,83,80,78,77 76,76,75,73,72**CSF £74.10 CT £536.58 TOTE £14.70: £5.20, £1.90, £2.90, £3.40; EX 127.10.
**Owner** EKOS Pinnacle Partnership **Bred** Shadwell Estate Company Limited **Trained** Hambleton, N Yorks
■ Stewards Enquiry : F Lynch one-day ban: careless riding (Sep 13)

**FOCUS**
A fair nursery but the form looks solid for the grade.

**NOTEBOOK**
**Caitlin(IRE)** is in good form and really put her head down and battled. At the line there was not an ounce to spare.
**The Pen**, who accounted for a subsequent winner when taking a seller here over six, only really found her stride inside the last and would have made it with a bit further to go.
**Cerebus**, who looked at her best, throughly appreciated the step up to seven and in the end was just found lacking.
**Drax**, well supported in the morning, looks to have grown in his abscence and at lastseems to have learnt what the game is all about. He ran well, especially as he was rather isolated towards the far side.
**Master Joseph** seemed to find the drop back to seven on much faster ground against him. He was putting in all his best work at the finish.
**Algorithm** improved for the step up in trip and a mile will suit her even better.
**As Handsome Does**, a June foal, stayed on from a hopeless position and is the type to do better at three.
**Burton Ash**, who looks to have started life from a tough mark, did as well as could be expected after swerving leaving the stalls, resulting in her rider losing an iron. *Official explanation: jockey lost an iron leaving stalls*
**Ladruca** *Official explanation: jockey said filly was struck into*
**Tantien** *Official explanation: jockey said filly finished unsound*

## 5241 COCKLE MAIDEN AUCTION STKS — 5f
**3:10** (3:12) (E4) 2-Y-0 **£2,975** (£850; £425) **Stalls** Centre

Form RPR

44 **1** **Danzili Bay**[18] 4770 2-8-13 .................................... SSanders 2 81
(RMBeckett) *cl up: led wl over 1f out: r.o u.p: all out* **9/1**[2]

2203 **2** *nk* **Tagula Sunrise (IRE)**[29] 4446 2-8-8 82 .................................... PHanagan 1 75
(RAFahey) *dwlt: towards rr: hdwy 1/2-way: rdn to go 2nd ent fnl f: r.o u.p: clsng on wnr fin* **2/5**[1]

06 **3** *2 1/2* **Ben Casey**[17] 4804 2-8-7 .................................... RWinston 5 65
(BSmart) *led tl rdn and hdd wl over 1f out: kpt on* **25/1**

5 **4** *1 1/2* **High Petergate (IRE)**[100] 2388 2-8-3 .................... PMulrennan(3) 7 59
(MWEasterby) *chsd ldrs: rdn 2f out: kpt on fnl f* **14/1**

0 **5** *1 3/4* **Tiger Bond**[51] 3818 2-8-7 .................................... DAllan 3 53
(BSmart) *in tch: drvn along 1/2-way: no imp on ldrs: kpt on fnl f* **33/1**

**6** *1 1/2* **Sharp Diversion (USA)** 2-8-6 .................................... MFenton 11 47
(JGGiven) *rangy: unf: wnt rt s: sn prom: rdn 2f out: fdd* **28/1**

026 **7** *shd* **Ducal Diva**[13] 4924 2-8-2 66 .................................... JQuinn 10 43
(JRWeymes) *trckd ldrs: keen early: rdn 2f out: sn btn* **25/1**

060 **8** *5* **Jasmine Hill**[24] 4607 2-8-2 .................................... CCatlin 9 25
(NBycroft) *chsd ldrs to 1/2-way: sn wknd* **100/1**

0 **9** *3* **Tyrone Sam**[39] 4175 2-8-13 .................................... NCallan 8 25
(KARyan) *slowly away: a bhd* **10/1**[3]

**10** *8* **Isle Dream** 2-8-3 ow1 .................................... JEdmunds 4 —
(JBalding) *bkwd: wl bhd fr 1/2-way* **100/1**

58.02 secs (-0.68) **Going Correction** -0.20s/f (Firm) **10** Ran SP% **113.2**
Speed ratings: **97,96,92,90,87 84,84,76,71,59**CSF £12.23 TOTE £7.50: £1.70, £1.02, £4.40; EX 16.50.
**Owner** The Mid-Landers **Bred** T Lightbowne **Trained** Lambourn, Berks



The Form Book, Raceform Ltd, Compton, RG20 6NL

**FOCUS**
Probably an ordinary maiden, but the second appeared to run below his rating, and the third and fourt provide a better guide to the value of the form.

**NOTEBOOK**
**Danzili Bay**, hampered last time, really put his head down and battled but with the runner-up receiving 5lb and rated 82 he cannot expect a lenient nursery mark.
**Tagula Sunrise(IRE)**, dropping back to the minimum trip, does nothing wrong but had to settle for second spot for the fourth time.
**Ben Casey** is getting better with every outing and with three runs under his belt, he can now ply his trade in nurseries.
**High Petergate(IRE)**, absent for 100 days, stayed on in pleasing fashion and can do better over further in time.
**Tiger Bond**, who looked very fit, looks as though he needs at least a sixth furlong.
**Sharp Diversion(USA)**, an April foal, stands over a fair amount of ground but she looks as though she needs more time yet.

## 5242 ALBERT CLAMP MEMORIAL H'CAP — 6f
**3:40** (3:42) (E3) (0-70,70) 3-Y-0+ — **£4,329** (£1,332; £666; £333) **Stalls** Centre

Form — RPR
3212 **1** **Trojan Flight**[3] 5193 3-8-8 **64** ... RWinston 9 — 81+
(MrsJRRamsden) *midfield: nt clr run 2f out and over 1f out: gd hdwy appr fnl f: r.o strly to ld post* **7/4**[1]
5026 **2** *shd* **Fair Shake (IRE)**[16] 4837 4-8-13 **67** ... (v) KDarley 7 — 75
(DEddy) *in rr and sn drvn along: hdwy over 2f out: r.o wl u.p to ld cl home: hdd post* **10/1**[2]
1501 **3** *nk* **Playful Dane (IRE)**[41] 4105 7-8-6 **67** ... DFentiman(7) 11 — 74
(WSCunningham) *sn led: 4 l clr over 2f out: hung lft u.p ins fnl f: ct cl home* **10/1**[2]
0404 **4** *hd* **Obe One**[7] 5062 4-8-12 **66** ... FLynch 6 — 73
(ABerry) *midfield: rdn 2f out: r.o wl u.p fnl f* **14/1**
5200 **5** *1 1/4* **College Queen**[11] 4970 6-8-9 **63** ... WSupple 13 — 66
(SGollings) *sn prom: chsd ldr over 2f out: kpt on u.p: no ex ins fnl f* **33/1**
210 **6** *nk* **Strawberry Patch (IRE)**[6] 5094 5-8-4 **58** ... (p) JFanning 4 — 60
(MissLAPerratt) *in tch: drvn along over 2f out: kpt on fnl f* **12/1**[3]
5334 **7** *shd* **Snow Bunting**[27] 4522 6-8-8 **62** ... MFenton 12 — 64
(JeddO'Keeffe) *rr div: hdwy u.p over 1f out: r.o wl ins fnl f: nrst fin* **10/1**[2]
0450 **8** *3/4* **Legal Set (IRE)**[5] 5126 8-7-13 **60** ... (t) LeanneKershaw(7) 1 — 59
(MissAStokell) *prom: rdn 2f out: kpt on same pce* **33/1**
0310 **9** *1/2* **Midnight Parkes**[29] 4452 5-9-2 **70** ... (p) MHenry 2 — 68
(EJAlston) *cl up: rdn 2f out: kpt on same pce* **20/1**
0000 **10** *shd* **Chairman Bobby**[5] 5107 6-8-10 **67** ... LEnstone(3) 10 — 65
(DWBarker) *chsd ldrs: rdn 1/2-way: no hdwy* **20/1**
6600 **11** *shd* **Silver Chime**[19] 4751 4-8-11 **65** ... SSanders 3 — 62
(DMSimcock) *in tch: drvn along over 2f out: no hdwy* **16/1**
4240 **12** *hd* **Sharoura**[14] 4877 8-8-11 **65** ... PHanagan 14 — 62
(RAFahey) *towards rr: effrt whn nt clr run 2f out: n.d* **16/1**
6653 **13** *1/2* **College Maid (IRE)**[13] 4904 7-8-0 **57** ... (v) NMackay(3) 15 — 52
(JSGoldie) *hld up: nt clr run 2f out: n.d* **20/1**
5500 **14** *nk* **Ronnie From Donny (IRE)**[43] 4013 4-8-4 **61** ... TEaves(3) 19 — 55
(BEllison) *sn in rr: n.d* **28/1**
2150 **15** *shd* **Blue Maeve**[12] 4935 4-8-6 **60** ... SRighton 8 — 54
(JHetherton) *slowly away: rr div: sme hdwy over 2f out: rdn and wknd over 1f out* **12/1**[3]
0513 **16** *2* **Kingsmaite**[13] 4928 3-8-12 **68** ... (b) JBramhill 18 — 56
(SRBowring) *in tch: drvn along over 2f out: sn btn* **14/1**
0036 **17** *5* **Fitzwarren**[25] 4576 3-8-7 **63** ... (v) CCatlin 20 — 36
(NBycroft) *towards rr most of way* **33/1**
0000 **18** *7* **Feu Duty (IRE)**[35] 4279 3-8-7 **63** ... JMcAuley 5 — 15
(TJEtherington) *prom tl wknd qckly over 2f out* **100/1**

69.84 secs (-1.86) **Going Correction** -0.20s/f (Firm)
**WFA** 3 from 4yo+ 2lb — **18** Ran SP% **131.7**
Speed ratings: **104,103,103,103,101 101,101,100,99,99 99,98,98,97,97 94,88,78**CSF £18.13 CT £157.61 TOTE £2.40: £1.10, £3.30, £3.80, £2.50; EX 23.70.
**Owner** Timothy O'Gram **Bred** L C And Mrs A E Sigsworth **Trained** Sandhutton, N Yorks
■ Stewards Enquiry : D Fentiman caution:careless riding

**FOCUS**
A modest handicap in which the leader went off very fast and the first two home were amongst the backmarkers at halfway. The form, rated through the runner-up, appears solid.

**NOTEBOOK**
**Trojan Flight**, sent off a very short-priced favourite, was on offer at 1,000/1 on the exchanges and backed at that price when last with two furlongs left to run. Despite the ground being plenty quick enough, he overcame traffic problems to put his head in front right on the line.
**Fair Shake(IRE)**, who two wins were on easy ground, struggled to go the furious pace. He worked hard to show ahead on the far side near the line, only to be pipped on the post.
**Playful Dane(IRE)**, an enormous individual, was full of himself after a six-week break. He soon showed in a commanding lead but he came off a straight line and was edged out near the line. A drop back to the minimum trip will surely suit.
**Obe One**, whose two wins were over five, seemed to thoroughly appreciate the sixth furlong and, with a bit further to go, would have finished in second spot behind the winner.
**College Queen**, who looked at her very best, bounced back after two below-par efforts.
**Strawberry Patch(IRE)**, as usual taken to post early, ran much better than Newmarket but he is still 5lb higher than his Newbury win. All three of his career wins have been over five furlongs.
**Kingsmaite** *Official explanation: jockey said gelding was never travelling*

## 5243 CLAM H'CAP — 1m 6f 19y
**4:10** (4:10) (F4) (0-55,61) 3-Y-0+ — **£2,983** (£852; £426) **Stalls** Low

Form — RPR
0004 **1** **Zan Lo (IRE)**[7] 5058 4-8-9 **46** oh1 ... RWinston 11 — 54
(BSRothwell) *bhd: hdwy on outer 6f out: styd on wl to ld last 75yds* **18/1**
4520 **2** *1 1/2* **Sovereign State (IRE)**[24] 4609 7-8-9 **49** ... (p) LEnstone(3) 4 — 55
(DWThompson) *hld up: hdwy over 3f out: led 1f out: hdd and no ex wl ins last* **12/1**
004 **3** *nk* **Rouge Et Noir**[31] 4396 6-8-10 **50** ... (t) TEaves(3) 2 — 56
(KGReveley) *hld up: hdwy on ins 4f out: ev ch 1f out: nt qckn ins last* **7/1**[3]
100/ **4** *1* **Regency Red (IRE)**[670] 5383 6-8-4 **46** oh1 ... BSwarbrick(5) 12 — 50
(WMBrisbourne) *rr-div: hdwy 7f out: hung lft and led over 2f out: hdd 1f out: wknd towards fin* **25/1**
3002 **5** *1/2* **Muslin**[42] 4070 3-8-6 **54** ... OUrbina 14 — 57
(JRFanshawe) *trckd ldrs: nt clr run over 2f out and over 1f out: kpt on ins last* **7/1**[3]
0000 **6** *nk* **Narciso (GER)**[48] 3896 4-8-9 **49** ... PMulrennan(3) 5 — 52
(MWEasterby) *chsd ldrs: drvn along 4f out: kpt on fnl 2f* **50/1**
-501 **7** *1* **Chevin**[30] 4424 5-8-9 **46** ... PHanagan 3 — 48
(RAFahey) *trckd ldrs: hdwy to chal over 2f out: fdd appr fnl f* **5/2**[1]
-001 **8** *3/4* **Restart (IRE)**[5] 5130 3-8-13 **61** 6ex ... GFaulkner 6 — 62
(PCHaslam) *mid-div: effrt on inner 3f out: one pce fnl 2f* **8/1**
4000 **9** *5* **River Line (USA)**[29] 4448 3-8-0 **48** ow1 ... CCatlin 9 — 42
(CWFairhurst) *led: qckd 6f out: hdd over 2f out: lost pl over 1f out* **100/1**
3061 **10** *6* **Righty Ho**[26] 4561 10-8-6 **50** ... KristinStubbs(7) 10 — 35
(WHTinning) *trckd ldr: pushed along 6f out: lost pl 3f out* **16/1**
0065 **11** *7* **Theatre Belle**[66] 3371 3-8-2 **50** ow1 ... DAllan 15 — 25
(TDEasterby) *sn chsng ldrs: lost pl over 4f out* **40/1**
0400 **12** *8* **Banners Flying (IRE)**[24] 4609 4-8-9 **46** oh1 ... ACulhane 1 — 10
(DWChapman) *mid-div: lost pl over 3f out: sn bhd* **40/1**
0602 **13** *dist* **Larking About (USA)**[9] 5027 4-9-0 **51** ... (b) KDarley 8 — —
(WJMusson) *s.i.s: a last: t.o 4f out: virtually p.u* **3/1**[2]

3m 5.02s (0.02) **Going Correction** -0.20s/f (Firm)
**WFA** 3 from 4yo+ 11lb — **13** Ran SP% **120.2**
Speed ratings: **91,90,89,89,89 88,88,87,85,81 77,73,**—CSF £212.11 CT £1672.46 TOTE £14.20: £6.90, £4.60, £2.20; EX 190.90.
**Owner** D J Coles **Bred** K Molloy **Trained** Nawton, N Yorks

**FOCUS**
In effect a 0-51 handicap run at a very modest pace to past halfway and a very moderate winning time for the grade, although on paper the race appears sound.

**NOTEBOOK**
**Zan Lo(IRE)**, who has slipped to a lenient mark, came with a sustained run down the wide outside to give her trainer, who led her up, a welcome change of luck.
**Sovereign State(IRE)**, suited by the much quicker ground, travelled strongly but had no answer to the winner's late charge.
**Rouge Et Noir**, stepping up in trip on his handicap bow, stuck to the inner. Working his way upsides entering the final furlong, he would have appreciated a much stronger early pace.
**Regency Red(IRE)**, last seen in action over hurdles in November 2002, has changed stables since. He hung when hitting the front and his stride shortened noticeably near the line.
**Muslin**, on her toes beforehand, had no luck at all in the home straight on just her sixth start. She looks a real stayer and hopefully an opportunity can be found for her in a low-grade handicap.
**Narciso(GER)**, unplaced in four previous starts, showed a fair bit more taking up a big step up in trip on his handicap bow.
**Chevin**, 5lb higher, had every chance but she did not get home.
**Larking About(USA)**, racing on totally different ground, was in last place throughout. She seemed to lose her action on the home turn and was soon detached. *Official explanation: jockey said filly lost her action*

## 5244 LOBSTER CLASSIFIED STKS — 7f
**4:40** (4:40) (D2) 3-Y-0+ — **£6,987** (£2,150; £1,075; £537) **Stalls** Centre

Form — RPR
1141 **1** **Hartshead**[34] 4308 5-9-3 75 ... DeanMcKeown 6 — 84
(GASwinbank) *hld up: hdwy over 2f out: styd on wl u.p to ld cl home* **4/1**[1]
15 **2** *nk* **Night Air (IRE)**[107] 2207 3-8-13 74 ... KDarley 3 — 83
(DRLoder) *dwlt: sn in tch: hdwy 2f out: rdn to ld appr fnl f: hdd cl home* **9/2**[2]
0420 **3** *1 1/2* **Reidies Choice**[40] 4151 3-8-13 73 ... ACulhane 9 — 79
(JGGiven) *hld up in rr: effrt whn n.m.r over 1f out: r.o wl u.p fnl f: nrst fin* **12/1**
0600 **4** *nk* **Borrego (IRE)**[29] 4435 4-9-3 72 ... (b[1]) SSanders 1 — 79
(CEBrittain) *trckd ldrs: chal and rdn over 1f out: no ex fnl f* **20/1**
0020 **5** *hd* **Abbajabba**[19] 4759 8-9-3 74 ... JFanning 7 — 78
(CWFairhurst) *mid-field: hdwy u.p over 1f out: edgd rt ins last: kpt on* **14/1**
4201 **6** *shd* **Samuel Charles**[29] 4437 6-8-12 75 ... BSwarbrick(5) 2 — 78
(WMBrisbourne) *swtg: led: rdn over 2f out: hdd appr fnl f: kpt on* **12/1**
3316 **7** *2 1/2* **Neon Blue**[14] 4877 3-8-13 72 ... SChin 13 — 71
(RMWhitaker) *mid-field: rdn over 2f out: no hdwy* **10/1**
3333 **8** *1/2* **Master Theo (USA)**[19] 4738 3-8-13 74 ... JQuinn 4 — 70
(HJCollingridge) *chsd ldrs: rdn over 2f out: btn whn sltly hmpd ins last* **8/1**[3]
5412 **9** *1/2* **Efidium**[26] 4558 6-9-3 74 ... CCatlin 12 — 68
(NBycroft) *hld up: effrt over 2f out: sn rdn and btn* **9/2**[2]
-600 **10** *nk* **Vademecum**[40] 4151 3-8-13 73 ... FLynch 8 — 67
(BSmart) *hld up: effrt whn nt clr run over 1f out: n.d* **12/1**
2-00 **11** *1 1/4* **Sion Hill (IRE)**[42] 4059 3-8-13 75 ... PHanagan 5 — 64
(JO'Reilly) *chsd ldrs: rdn over 2f out: fdd* **33/1**
2203 **12** *3/4* **Marinaite**[92] 2587 3-8-10 73 ... JBramhill 14 — 59
(SRBowring) *cl up tl rdn and wknd 2f out* **20/1**
0-00 **13** *22* **Perfect Love**[14] 4877 4-9-0 70 ... DAllan 10 — —
(EJAlston) *towards rr: hung bdly rt 3f out: sn wl bhd: t.o* **50/1**

1m 22.31s (-2.59) **Going Correction** -0.20s/f (Firm)
**WFA** 3 from 4yo+ 4lb — **13** Ran SP% **120.7**
Speed ratings: **106,105,103,103,103 103,100,99,99,98 97,96,71**CSF £20.73 TOTE £4.90: £2.60, £2.10, £3.20; EX 30.50.
**Owner** B Valentine **Bred** Gainsborough Stud Management Ltd **Trained** Melsonby, N Yorks

**FOCUS**
A tight classified stakes with only 4lb separating the entire field on official figures. The fifith and sixth set the standard and the form looks solid.

**NOTEBOOK**
**Hartshead**, raised 3lb after Thirsk, was given a fair bit to do. He never flinched and put his head in front almost on the line. Highly progressive, he will make an even better performer next year.
**Night Air(IRE)**, absent since May, was having only his third-ever start and in the end was just edged out.
**Reidies Choice** was set a very stiff task and, after meeting traffic problems, finished with a real flourish down the stands' side. He has the ability but it is mind games with him.
**Borrego(IRE)**, badly out of form, staged a revival in first-time blinkers. His two career wins were over a mile.
**Abbajabba**, without a win for over two years, has shown a marked preference for give underfoot in the past.
**Samuel Charles**, awash with sweat, set a good pace but he missed out in the dash to the line.
**Efidium** seemed to lay out of his ground and never got competitive.
**Vademecum** *Official explanation: jockey said gelding was continually denied a run*
**Marinaite** *Official explanation: jockey said filly was unsuited by the good to firm, firm in places ground*
**Perfect Love** *Official explanation: jockey said filly hung right and lost her action from half way*

## 5245 MUSSEL H'CAP — 1m 2f
**5:10** (5:11) (E3) (0-70,70) 3-Y-0 — **£4,198** (£1,291; £645; £322) **Stalls** Low

Form — RPR
-050 **1** **Stephano**[21] 4680 3-8-10 **59** ... PHanagan 12 — 73+
(BWHills) *rr-div: drvn along over 4f out: styd on wl to ld 2f out: styd on strly* **25/1**
4041 **2** *2 1/2* **Havetoavit (USA)**[26] 4562 3-9-2 **65** ... JFanning 8 — 71
(JDBethell) *trckd ldrs: led 3f out tl 2f out: styd on same pce* **9/2**[2]
3204 **3** *nk* **Wing Collar**[22] 4627 3-9-2 **65** ... WSupple 4 — 70
(TDEasterby) *rr-div: drvn along 4f out: styd on fnl 2f* **11/1**
0412 **4** *1/2* **Dance To My Tune**[5] 5129 3-8-10 **62** ... PMulrennan(3) 9 — 66
(MWEasterby) *bhd: hdwy and nt clr run over 2f out: swtchd rt: kpt on wl* **6/1**[3]

0-40 **5** *nk* **Bluetoria**[73] 3154 3-9-5 **68** ........ DeanMcKeown 5 72
(JAGlover) *rr-div: hdwy over 3f out: wandered: hrd rdn over 1f out: edgd lft and kpt on* **50/1**

6020 **6** *hd* **Cottingham (IRE)**[1] 5223 3-8-6 **60** ........ StephanieHollinshead(5) 15 64
(MCChapman) *bhd: hdwy over 3f out: kpt on wl fnl 2f* **33/1**

0060 **7** *2 ½* **Bertocelli**[19] 4738 3-8-7 **56** ........ AMcCarthy 1 55
(GGMargarson) *chsd ldrs: effrt 3f out: wknd over 1f out* **50/1**

0-42 **8** *¾* **Edgehill (IRE)**[41] 4079 3-9-1 **64** ........ MFenton 7 61
(CREgerton) *chsd ldrs: drvn along 4f out: wknd over 1f out* **9/2**[2]

0422 **9** *2* **Munaawesh (USA)**[17] 4820 3-8-7 **56** ........ (b) ACulhane 11 50
(DWChapman) *bhd: sme hdwy 4f out: lost pl over 2f out* **14/1**

6330 **10** *hd* **Turner**[41] 4079 3-9-2 **70** ........ BSwarbrick(5) 13 63
(WMBrisbourne) *hld up and bhd: effrt on outer over 3f out: nvr a factor* **50/1**

5025 **11** *4* **Golden Drift**[22] 4655 3-8-11 **60** ........ KDarley 3 46
(GWragg) *chsd ldrs: pushed along 6f out: lost pl and eased over 1f out* **9/1**

5055 **12** *7* **Dan Di Canio (IRE)**[41] 4092 3-9-0 **63** ........ (t) NCallan 6 35
(PWHarris) *mid-div: drvn along over 3f out: sn btn* **16/1**

0061 **13** *7* **Belisco (USA)**[12] 4940 3-9-3 **69** ........ (vt[1]) BReilly(3) 14 28
(CADwyer) *chsd ldrs: hung lft and lost pl 3f out* **14/1**

-061 **14** *dist* **Optimal (IRE)**[28] 4471 3-9-1 **64** ........ (b) SSanders 2 —
(SirMarkPrescott) *led tl 3f out: fnd nil: bhd and eased over 1f out: virtually p.u: t.o* **4/1**[1]

2m 4.27s (-2.53) **Going Correction** -0.20s/f (Firm) **14** Ran SP% **120.9**
Speed ratings: **102,100,99,99,99 98,96,96,94,94 91,85,80,**—CSF £131.82 CT £1339.16 TOTE £26.70: £7.40, £2.20, £4.40; EX 340.70 Place 6 £98.07, Place 5 £49.55.
**Owner** Guy Reed **Bred** G Reed **Trained** Lambourn, Berks

**FOCUS**
A modest contest and ordinary form overall, the winner excepted.

**NOTEBOOK**
**Stephano**, dropped 3lb after his handicap bow on heavy ground, took some stoking up but in the end he ran out a most decisive winner. *Official explanation: trainer's representative said, regarding the improved form shown, gelding may have benefited from the step up in trip*
**Havetoavit(USA)**, raised 7lb, went on but was soon put firmly in his place by the winner.
**Wing Collar** has now been placed four times from 11 starts. He looks a potential juvenile hurdler.
**Dance To My Tune**, narrowly denied here six days ago, was racing on much quicker ground and she met traffic problems. She finished in good style and is clearly in very good heart.
**Bluetoria**, absent since June, was having just her fourth start and was making her handicap bow from what looked a stiffish mark. Her inexperience showed and her traffic problems seemed to be of her own making. She would not want the ground any quicker. *Official explanation: jockey said filly was continually denied a run*
**Cottingham(IRE)** did well considering it was his second outing on succesive days.
**Edgehill(IRE)** did not improve for the step up in trip.
**Turner** *Official explanation: jockey said gelding lost its action*
**Belisco(USA)** *Official explanation: jockey said colt hung left handed in home straight*
**Optimal(IRE)**, 3lb higher, made no appeal whatsoever in the paddock. After taking them along, she found nothing and in the end struggled to reach the finishing line. She was later found to be suffering from a nasal discharge. *Official explanation: vet said filly had nasal discharge*
T/Plt: £224.50 to a £1 stake. Pool: £40,060.15. 130.25 winning tickets. T/Qpdt: £63.20 to a £1 stake. Pool: £2,972.30. 34.80 winning tickets. WG

# 4912 SALISBURY (R-H)
## Thursday, September 2

**OFFICIAL GOING: Good (good to firm in places)**
Wind: Almost nil Weather: Warm and sunny

## 5246 WHITSBURY MANOR STUD EBF NOVICE STKS 1m
1:50 (1:50) (D2) 2-Y-O **£7,046** (£2,168; £1,084; £542) **Stalls** High

Form RPR

10 **1** **Liakoura (GER)**[34] 4295 2-9-5 ........ (p) JPMurtagh 4 96
(MrsAJPerrett) *hld up in rr: drvn and hung lft over 2f out: hdwy over 1f out: styd on to ld fnl 50 yds* **6/1**

1 **2** *1* **Sun Kissed (JPN)**[34] 4296 2-9-5 ........ LDettori 1 94
(SaeedBinSuroor) *hld up in rr: hdwy 3f out: led 2f out: hrd rdn fnl f: hdd and no ex fnl 50 yds* **7/4**[2]

10 **3** *hd* **Solent (IRE)**[36] 4227 2-9-5 ........ DaneO'Neill 2 93
(RHannon) *chsd ldr tl outpcd over 2f out: rallied and styd on ins fnl f* **16/1**

43 **4** *hd* **Golden Fury**[27] 4523 2-8-12 ........ KFallon 3 86
(JLDunlop) *led tl 2f out: kpt on same pce* **5/1**[3]

133 **5** *¾* **Propinquity**[12] 4949 2-9-5 100 ........ DHolland 5 91
(PWHarris) *plld hrd early: cl up: rdn over 2f out: kpt on same pce* **13/8**[1]

1m 42.75s (-0.22) **Going Correction** -0.10s/f (Good) **5** Ran SP% **111.3**
Speed ratings: **97,96,95,95,94**CSF £17.18 TOTE £8.50: £4.10, £1.20; EX 23.10.
**Owner** Mark Tracey **Bred** Dr Chr Berglar **Trained** Pulborough, W Sussex
■ Stewards Enquiry : L Dettori caution: used whip in an incorrect place

**FOCUS**
A decent novice event in which all of the runners had previously shown a fair level of ability. The pace was just modest, however, and the overall form may be suspect.

**NOTEBOOK**
**Liakoura(GER)**, who had boiled over at the start when last at Newmarket previously, responded well to his rider's urgings and picked up strongly to win going away in the end. The application of cheekpieces clearly helped, he appreciated this step up to a mile and was still green this time, so should be capable of further improvement.
**Sun Kissed(JPN)** , who did well to win over slowly-run six on his debut at Newmarket last time, seemed to get this trip well enough and would have been better suited by a stronger gallop, so should not be written off just yet, although he does not look one of his stable's leading lights at this stage.
**Solent(IRE)**, who got warm between his legs beforehand, ran freely early on due to the lack of pace and was one of the first under pressure when the tempo increased. However, he stuck to his task gamely and was fighting back at the finish, suggesting he appreciated this longer trip.
**Golden Fury** , who had shown ability in two previous maiden outings, set the steady gallop for most of the way, until he could only find the one pace from two out. He was staying on however, improved for this extra furlong and should have no trouble in winning races.
**Propinquity** , whose latest third in the Solario Stakes set the standard in this, was somewhat disappointing over this extra furlong. He was a little tight for room when trying to challenge a quarter mile out, but never really looked like getting to the front and has a bit to prove now. *Official explanation: jockey said colt was hanging right*

## 5247 EUROPEAN BREEDERS FUND QUIDHAMPTON MAIDEN FILLIES' STKS (DIV I) 6f 212y
2:20 (2:22) (D1) 2-Y-O **£10,725** (£3,300; £1,650; £825) **Stalls** Centre

Form RPR

5 **1** **Donyana**[19] 4753 2-8-11 ........ PRobinson 14 84
(MAJarvis) *mde all: drvn clr fnl f* **4/1**[1]

**2** *2* **Miss The Boat** 2-8-11 ........ DaneO'Neill 13 79
(JLDunlop) *leggy: chsd wnr over 4f: kpt on to regain 2nd ins fnl f* **50/1**

**3** *1* **Nice Tune** 2-8-11 ........ RHills 2 76+
(CEBrittain) *w'like: bkwd: str: hld up and bhd: shkn up and r.o wl fnl 2f: improve* **40/1**

**4** *hd* **Love Always** 2-8-11 ........ JPMurtagh 3 76
(MrsAJPerrett) *w'like: bit bkwd: mid-div: effrt over 2f out: styd on fnl f* **33/1**

**5** *2* **Classicism (USA)** 2-8-11 ........ LDettori 5 79+
(SaeedBinSuroor) *w'like: str: prom: ev ch 2f out: 3rd and btn whn went lame and heavily eased wl ins fnl f* **9/2**[2]

**6** *½* **Abide (FR)** 2-8-11 ........ RLMoore 4 69
(RHannon) *leggy: unf: bit bkwd: chsd ldrs: no ex fnl 2f* **25/1**

0 **7** *1* **Maggie Tulliver (IRE)**[59] 3588 2-8-11 ........ DHolland 7 67
(PWHarris) *in rr: rdn over 2f out: sme late hdwy* **40/1**

0 **8** *nk* **Jenna Stannis**[19] 4753 2-8-6 ........ NChalmers(5) 16 66
(RMBeckett) *prom 5f* **66/1**

**9** *nk* **Red Duchess** 2-8-11 ........ KFallon 9 65
(SirMichaelStoute) *w'like: scope: lengthy: dwlt: in rr: drvn along over 3f out: nvr rchd ldrs* **9/2**[2]

46 **10** *shd* **Authenticate**[15] 4851 2-8-11 ........ GGibbons 11 65
(BAMcmahon) *chsd ldrs 5f* **16/1**

**11** *shd* **Intended** 2-8-11 ........ MartinDwyer 12 65
(AMBalding) *w'like: leggy: bit bkwd: dwlt: sn in tch: wknd over 2f out* **50/1**

**12** *2 ½* **Ask For Rain** 2-8-11 ........ MHills 8 58
(BWHills) *w'like: bit bkwd: dwlt: rdn 1/2-way: a bhd* **20/1**

40 **13** *shd* **Something Exciting**[35] 4272 2-8-11 ........ JFEgan 10 58
(DRCElsworth) *t.k.h in midfield: rdn over 2f out: sn wknd* **10/1**[3]

0 **14** *6* **Montjeu Baby (IRE)**[54] 3741 2-8-11 ........ PDobbs 6 42
(RHannon) *a midfield to rr: no ch fnl 2f* **20/1**

46 **15** *4* **Classic Guest**[72] 3176 2-8-11 ........ TEDurcan 15 32
(MRChannon) *s.s: a towards rr: no ch fnl 2f* **20/1**

1m 28.72s (-0.28) **Going Correction** -0.10s/f (Good) **15** Ran SP% **102.7**
Speed ratings: **97,94,93,93,91 90,89,89,88,88 88,85,85,78,74**CSF £146.23 TOTE £4.30: £1.70, £9.30, £17.40; EX 170.10.
**Owner** Sheikh Ahmed Al Maktoum **Bred** Darley **Trained** Newmarket, Suffolk
■ Trick Of Light (4/1JF) withdrawn (upset at start). R4 applies, deduct 20p in the £.

**FOCUS**
A fair first division of the fillies' maiden, which was run at a reasonable gallop, and a high draw proved to be an advantage. The field came home strung out, but the time was 0.2 seconds slower than the second division.

**NOTEBOOK**
**Donyana** showed the benefit of her recent Newmarket debut and readily made all from her decent draw, appreciating this better ground. This half-sister to the stable's 1000 Guineas heroine Ameerat, holds no fancy entries at this stage, but is entitled to improve again and will be well suited by a mile in due course.
**Miss The Boat** , related to several winners over different trips, posted a pleasing debut. She was handy throughout from her decent draw, belying her odds of 50-1, suggesting she will be a lot sharper next time and is another who will do better over further in the future.
**Nice Tune ◆** , half-sister to the useful Play That Tune amongst others, shaped with promise and was doing all of her best work late in the day. She deserves extra credit having been drawn low and, like the majority of her yard's juveniles, will come on plenty for this run.
**Love Always** , a half-sister to her stable's useful handicapper Vengeance, was getting the hang of things late on and this experience should do her the world of good.
**Classicism(USA)**, half-sister to the stable's Breeders' Cup Juvenile Fillies heroine Tempera, and to high-class miler Equerry, looked fairly straight and was booked for a place before she broke down inside the final furlong, but would not have won. This was an unfortunate debut, but she showed definite promise. *Official explanation: jockey said filly was lame*
**Abide(FR)** stayed on nicely without being knocked about late on and will no doubt improve considerably for the experience.
**Red Duchess** , whose dam was unraced at two and won over 12 furlongs at three, was never able to go the pace and will not come into her own until racing over further next season.
**Intended** , bred to appreciate much further, was not given a hard time for this debut and is one to watch out for next year.

## 5248 EUROPEAN BREEDERS FUND QUIDHAMPTON MAIDEN FILLIES' STKS (DIV II) 6f 212y
2:50 (2:51) (D1) 2-Y-O **£10,692** (£3,290; £1,645; £822) **Stalls** Centre

Form RPR

2 **1** **Almansoora (USA)**[56] 3676 2-8-11 ........ LDettori 3 84
(SaeedBinSuroor) *lw: hld up in midfield: hdwy to join ldr over 1f out: hrd rdn fnl f: jst got up* **4/1**[2]

2 **2** *shd* **Elizabethan Age (FR)**[33] 4344 2-8-11 ........ TPQueally 8 84
(DRLoder) *w ldr: led over 2f out: jnd by wnr over 1f out: hrd rdn: jst shaded* **14/1**

4 **3** *½* **Bahja (USA)**[19] 4753 2-8-11 ........ RHills 5 82
(JHMGosden) *lw: prom: rdn and ev ch 1f out: kpt on wl* **5/1**[3]

**4** *3 ½* **Highland Diva (IRE)** 2-8-11 ........ KFallon 1 73+
(SirMichaelStoute) *w'like: scope: dwlt: hld up in midfield: rdn and styd on fnl 2f: nvr able to chal* **20/1**

**5** *¾* **Tamalain (USA)** 2-8-11 ........ JPMurtagh 7 71
(MrsAJPerrett) *w'like: leggy: bit bkwd: towards rr: rdn over 2f out: styd on* **40/1**

2 **6** *shd* **Proud Scholar (USA)**[48] 3905 2-8-11 ........ RHughes 15 71
(MrsAJPerrett) *trckd ldrs: rdn over 2f out: no ex over 1f out* **5/2**[1]

**7** *1* **Amalie (IRE)** 2-8-11 ........ TEDurcan 12 69
(CEBrittain) *w'like: scope: lengthy: bit bkwd: dwlt: in rr: rdn 1/2-way: nvr rchd ldrs* **66/1**

0 **8** *½* **Montecito**[20] 4714 2-8-11 ........ RLMoore 10 67
(RHannon) *lw: chsd ldrs over 5f* **66/1**

4 **9** *½* **Tiggers Touch**[22] 4637 2-8-11 ........ SDrowne 6 66
(BRMillman) *t.k.h in midfield: effrt over 2f out: no imp* **33/1**

4 **10** *½* **House Martin**[34] 4292 2-8-11 ........ MartinDwyer 11 65
(AMBalding) *led tl over 2f out: sn wknd* **8/1**[3]

**11** *1 ¾* **Brandexe (IRE)** 2-8-11 ........ MHills 2 60
(BWHills) *w'like: bit bkwd: dwlt: bhd: drvn over 2f out: n.d* **100/1**

5 **12** *4* **Scent**[20] 4712 2-8-11 ........ JFortune 9 50
(JLDunlop) *mid-div: rdn over 2f out: sn wknd* **16/1**

06 **13** *nk* **Pussy Cat**[5] 5131 2-8-8 ........ LPKeniry(3) 4 49
(KOCunningham-Brown) *hrd rdn over 2f out: a bhd* **150/1**

0 **14** *5* **Desert Classic**[27] 4523 2-8-11 ........ EAhern 13 36
(EALDunlop) *mid-div: wknd 3f out: sn bhd* **40/1**

**15** *1 ¼* **Swift Dame (IRE)** 2-8-11 ........ DaneO'Neill 16 33
(RHannon) *w'like: bit bkwd: str: plld hrd towards rr: rdn over 2f out: sn no ch* **66/1**

0 **16** ½ **Hillabilla (IRE)**[14] 4866 2-8-11 .......... DSweeney 14 31
(MBlanshard) *mid-div tl wknd over 2f out* **125/1**

1m 28.52s (-0.48) **Going Correction** -0.10s/f (Good) **16** Ran SP% **120.3**
Speed ratings: **98,97,97,93,92 92,91,90,90,89 87,82,82,76,75 74**CSF £54.82 TOTE £4.80: £2.10, £4.00, £1.60; EX 50.60.
**Owner** Godolphin **Bred** Shadwell Farm Inc **Trained** Newmarket, Suffolk

**FOCUS**
This second division of the fillies' maiden looked the stronger. The time was 0.2 seconds quicker, and the first three pulled nicely clear at the finish.

**NOTEBOOK**
**Almansoora(USA)** , a Derby entry who showed definite ability on her debut in July, relished this extra distance and stayed on gamely inside the final furlong to collar the runner-up on the line. She already looks in need of a mile, so could prove useful over further next year and will not be rushed this term.
**Elizabethan Age(FR)** ◆ , who narrowly failed to score on her debut at Newmarket, gave her all but again found one too good. She looks a relentless galloper, should have no trouble in deservedly going one better and is another who is unlikely to really come into her own until next season.
**Bahja(USA)** ◆ , well-backed to improve on her recent Newmarket debut, held every chance if good enough, but failed to see her race out quite as well as the front pair. This was indeed an improved effort, and this choicely-bred filly should have no trouble in losing her maiden tag en route to better things. *Official explanation: jockey said filly was hanging left*
**Highland Diva(IRE)**, whose dam won over ten furlongs as a three-year-old, caught the eye staying on under a sympathetic ride on this debut. She will stay middle-distances next year and has a future.
**Tamalain(USA)** , a 200,000gns half-sister to the sprinter CD Europe, was getting the hang of things late on, having run distinctly green at halfway. She will be a different proposition next time out.
**Proud Scholar(USA)** , whose debut second at Newbury has worked out very well, was disappointing. She held every chance from her decent draw, but failed to find a change of gear and was well held at the finish. She has it to prove next time.
**Amalie(IRE)** posted a fair debut effort and was staying nicely at the end.
**Montecito** looks in need of a mile and will no doubt fare best when handicapped.
**House Martin** *Official explanation: jockey said filly was hanging left*

## 5249 EBF LOCHSONG FILLIES' STKS (H'CAP) 6f 212y
**3:20** (3:21) (C1) (0-100,99) 3-Y-O+ **£15,239** (£5,780; £2,890; £1,313) **Stalls** Centre

Form RPR
001 **1** **Attune**[33] 4340 3-8-4 **85** oh2 .......... JFMcDonald(3) 13 97
(BJMeehan) *mde all: drvn clr fnl f* **9/1**
3105 **2** 1¾ **Look Here's Carol (IRE)**[14] 4889 4-9-3 **91** .......... KFallon 10 98
(BAMcmahon) *chsd wnr: hrd rdn over 1f out: kpt on: a hld* **6/1**[3]
1510 **3** ½ **Golden Island (IRE)**[18] 4773 3-8-7 **85** .......... RHills 9 91
(JWHills) *lw: in tch: hrd rdn over 1f out: styd on fnl f* **12/1**
-164 **4** nk **Silk Fan (IRE)**[12] 4948 3-9-3 **95** .......... DHolland 8 100
(PWHarris) *chsd ldrs: hrd rdn fnl 3f: styd on same pce* **4/1**[1]
0035 **5** 1½ **Fanny's Fancy**[26] 4526 4-9-0 **88** .......... (t) JFortune 14 89
(CFWall) *plld hrd: a.p: no ex over 1f out* **9/2**[2]
0000 **6** hd **Convent Girl (IRE)**[34] 4287 4-9-0 **88** .......... RHavlin 5 89
(MrsPNDutfield) *dwlt: towards rr: rdn 3f out: styd on fnl 2f: nvr nrr* **16/1**
4034 **7** nk **Enford Princess**[4] 5148 3-8-7 **85** oh1 .......... DaneO'Neill 6 85
(RHannon) *mid-div: effrt in centre over 2f out: one pce appr fnl f* **25/1**
0100 **8** 1¼ **Music Maid (IRE)**[40] 4148 6-8-11 **85** oh21 .......... DKinsella 7 81
(HSHowe) *plld hrd: sn stdd in rr: rdn over 2f out: nvr rchd ldrs* **50/1**
0202 **9** ½ **Cusco (IRE)**[20] 4731 3-8-12 **90** .......... RLMoore 12 85
(RHannon) *prom 5f* **14/1**
0103 **10** 1½ **Caveral**[26] 4526 3-9-3 **95** .......... RHughes 11 86
(RHannon) *b.hind: lw: plld hrd: in tch: rdn whn n.m.r ins fnl 2f: n.d after* **10/1**
5031 **11** 1½ **Zietory**[12] 4948 4-9-11 **99** .......... LDettori 4 86
(PFICole) *sn towards rr: sme hdwy whn hmpd ins fnl 2f: n.d after* **6/1**[3]
5-50 **12** 1 **Asia Winds (IRE)**[103] 2295 3-9-1 **93** .......... MHills 1 78
(BWHills) *a bhd* **12/1**
6610 **13** ¾ **Go Between**[20] 4731 3-8-7 **85** .......... EAhern 2 68
(EALDunlop) *dwlt: t.k.h in midfield: rdn and btn over 2f out* **33/1**
0-05 **14** 1 **Betty Stogs (IRE)**[21] 4684 3-8-7 **85** oh5 .......... MartinDwyer 3 65
(DRCElsworth) *rrd s: a bhd* **50/1**

1m 27.1s (-1.90) **Going Correction** -0.10s/f (Good)
**WFA** 3 from 4yo+ 4lb **14** Ran SP% **124.5**
Speed ratings: **106,104,103,103,101 101,100,99,98,97 95,94,93,92**CSF £62.81 CT £668.05 TOTE £7.70: £1.80, £3.20, £5.00; EX 71.50 Trifecta £2291.40 Pool of £3,227.45 - 0.80 winning tickets.
**Owner** Wyck Hall Stud **Bred** Wyck Hall Stud Ltd **Trained** Upper Lambourn, Berks

**FOCUS**
A valuable and competitive fillies' handicap, run considerably faster than the preceding divisions of the juvenile maiden. Very few got into contention from off the pace, which does suggest the form may not be that reliable.

**NOTEBOOK**
**Attune** , with the blinkers left off this time, was given a good ride from the front and responded really well to pressure. She was effectively 8lb higher than when scoring at Newmarket, having been raised 6lb and being 2lb out of the handicap. She looks progressive and will now go in search of some black type.
**Look Here's Carol(IRE)** was always close to the pace and had every chance, but may prefer a flatter track.
**Golden Island(IRE)** , who was dropping in trip, was tucked away behind the leaders and picked up well in the last furlong without ever landing a blow. She will appreciate a return to farther.
**Silk Fan(IRE)** was well-enough placed throughout, but failed to pick up as well as might have been expected. This was disappointing.
**Fanny's Fancy** pulled too hard in the early stages on this step up in trip and consequently gave herself little chance of lasting home. *Official explanation: jockey said filly was too keen early on*
**Convent Girl(IRE)** , dropped in trip, ran as if it was too short, doing her best work at the finish. She may be worth another try on soft ground.
**Enford Princess** , who was just out of the weights, put up a decent effort despite having to race wide. She is running well at present and is one to keep in mind back in a lower grade.
**Zietory** was settled in at the rear from her low draw, which was a disadvantage, and never figured. She was unsuited by the drying ground.

## 5250 E.B.F./IRISH THOROUGHBRED MARKETING DICK POOLE FILLIES' STKS (LISTED RACE) 6f
**3:50** (3:51) (A1) 2-Y-O **£18,850** (£7,150; £3,575; £1,625) **Stalls** High

Form RPR
1 **1** **Suez**[36] 4231 2-8-9 .......... PRobinson 3 105+
(MAJarvis) *mde all: drvn clr 1f out: readily* **8/11**[1]
2125 **2** 2½ **Castelletto**[14] 4885 2-8-9 99 .......... GGibbons 2 97
(BAMcmahon) *chsd wnr: hrd rdn over 1f out: nt qckn* **28/1**
2156 **3** 1 **Roodeye**[19] 4744 2-8-9 94 .......... MartinDwyer 5 94
(RFJohnsonHoughton) *chsd ldrs: one pce fnl 2f* **25/1**
101 **4** nk **Satin Kiss (USA)**[26] 4541 2-8-9 88 .......... LDettori 1 93
(SaeedBinSuroor) *wnt lft s: hld up in midfield: effrt over 2f out: styd on same pce* **12/1**
415 **5** nk **All For Laura**[19] 4744 2-8-9 95 .......... TPQueally 9 92
(DRLoder) *hld up midfield: rdn to chse ldrs whn hmpd on rail over 1f out: r.o again ins fnl f* **14/1**
31 **6** 3 **Regina**[17] 4815 2-8-9 .......... KFallon 10 83
(SirMichaelStoute) *chsd ldrs: rdn over 2f out: no ex over 1f out* **11/2**[2]
1 **7** ½ **Ghurra (USA)**[28] 4494 2-8-9 .......... RHills 7 82
(EALDunlop) *towards rr: rdn 1/2-way: nt pce to chal* **14/1**
120 **8** hd **Valentin (IRE)**[26] 4552 2-8-9 100 .......... RHughes 11 81
(RHannon) *in rr: rdn over 2f out: n.d* **12/1**
0102 **9** 2½ **Vondova**[14] 4876 2-8-9 84 .......... DaneO'Neill 8 74
(RHannon) *stdd s: t.k.h in rr: rdn 2f out: nvr trbld ldrs* **40/1**
1 **10** 3 **Free Lift**[48] 3904 2-8-9 .......... SDrowne 4 65
(RCharlton) *prom tl hrd rdn and wknd over 2f out* **10/1**[3]
00 **11** 6 **Saffa Garden (IRE)**[56] 3676 2-8-9 .......... DHolland 6 47
(CEBrittain) *midfield to rr: no ch fnl 2f* **100/1**

1m 13.46s (-1.48) **Going Correction** -0.10s/f (Good) **11** Ran SP% **121.8**
Speed ratings: **105,101,100,99,99 95,94,94,91,87 79**CSF £35.51 TOTE £4.10: £1.10, £7.30, £6.80; EX 43.70.
**Owner** Sheikh Mohammed **Bred** Meon Valley Stud **Trained** Newmarket, Suffolk

**FOCUS**
A decent renewal of a Listed race that has been won by some smart fillies in the past and it was run at a solid pace throughout. The winning time was useful for the type of race, and the form looks sound.

**NOTEBOOK**
**Suez**, who looked potentially very smart when winning impressively on her debut at Goodwood in July, confirmed that potential by scoring with authority and maintaining her unbeaten record. She again showed serious early pace to track across to the favoured rail from her wide draw, and soon had the majority of her rivals hard at work, setting a strong gallop. A sound surface is crucial to her, as she has a fast-ground action, and she will now deservedly take her place in the Group One Cheveley Park at the end of the month, where she should go close.
**Castelletto** ran her best race in defeat and did well to sustain her gallop all the way to the line. She appreciated this better ground and got the trip well, but is relatively exposed and vulnerable to an improver at this level.
**Roodeye** was never a serious threat, but showed her true colours over this extra furlong and ran her best race to date. She is entered in the Two-Year-Old Trophy at Redcar and, providing she gets a sound surface, would be entitled to go close.
**Satin Kiss(USA)** was unable to get to the front this time and never got into the argument. She now looks exposed.
**All For Laura** improved for this extra furlong and turned in a sound effort. She could find a small race at this level.
**Regina** threatened to get involved at halfway, but paid for running too freely in the early stages and dropped out tamely.
**Ghurra(USA)** was unable to go this pace and now looks worth a try over another furlong. She is not one to write off just yet.
**Free Lift** , who created a good impression when winning her debut at Newbury in July, never looked happy and dropped out as though something was amiss.

## 5251 ELY FUND MANAGERS CONDITIONS STKS 1m 6f 15y
**4:20** (4:21) (C2) 3-Y-O+ **£9,251** (£3,509; £1,754; £797) **Stalls** Far side

Form RPR
0101 **1** **Barolo**[50] 3862 5-9-10 106 .......... DHolland 2 118
(PWHarris) *chsd clr ldr: led wl over 1f out: drvn to hold on fnl f* **4/1**[2]
6230 **2** nk **Grampian**[15] 4858 5-9-1 102 .......... KFallon 3 109
(JGGiven) *chsd ldrs: str chal fnl f: jst hld* **7/1**
20-0 **3** 1½ **Fight Your Corner**[111] 2076 5-9-1 107 .......... (t) LDettori 7 107
(SaeedBinSuroor) *lw: led: clr after 4f tl 4f out: hdd wl over 1f out: one pce fnl f* **4/1**[2]
0-22 **4** hd **Westmoreland Road (USA)**[48] 3912 4-9-1 108 .......... JPMurtagh 1 107
(MrsAJPerrett) *hld up in tch: rdn and wandered over 1f out: swtchd rt ins fnl f: kpt on* **5/4**[1]
-035 **5** 6 **Gulf (IRE)**[61] 3538 5-9-1 105 .......... (t) RHughes 6 98
(DRCElsworth) *lw: hld up towards rr: effort 3f out: no impression* **13/2**[3]
**6** dist **Toile** 3-7-13 .......... DKinsella 4 —
(JGGiven) *leggy: angular: a bhd: no ch fnl 4f* **200/1**
-000 **7** dist **Herodotus**[54] 3752 6-9-1 55 .......... (t) DaneO'Neill 5 —
(KOCunningham-Brown) *rr 1/2-way: bhd whn eased over 5f out: sn t.o* **250/1**

3m 8.00s (3.48) **Going Correction** -0.10s/f (Good)
**WFA** 3 from 4yo+ 11lb **7** Ran SP% **111.2**
Speed ratings: **90,89,88,88,85** —,—CSF £29.62 TOTE £6.30: £4.20, £14.20; EX 25.70.
**Owner** Mrs P W Harris **Bred** Pendley Farm **Trained** Ringshall, Bucks

**FOCUS**
A small, but select group of stayers in this conditions stakes. It was run at a very steady gallop, and the race only really got serious on entering the straight, so the form looks suspect as a result. The time was inevitably very slow.

**NOTEBOOK**
**Barolo** , who produced a lifetime best when taking a Listed race in Ireland last time, defied his penalty for that success with a tenacious display. Perfectly placed to strike as the tempo quickened, it needed all of his rider's strength in the end to hold the runner-up at bay. He can be rated better than the bare form, and deserves to step back up in class in order to continue his progression, but his entry in the Melbourne Cup does look slightly ambitious.
**Grampian** went down fighting and proved his Ebor running to be all wrong. He is not the easiest horse to place, and was probably best suited to the lack of a true gallop over this trip, but gave his all and may not be far off going one better.
**Fight Your Corner** set the moderate pace for most of the contest, but was readily brushed aside when headed in the straight, and ran as though this race was needed. He should come on for the outing, but may be regressive.
**Westmoreland Road(USA)** looked to be travelling best of all two out, but found less than expected when asked for maximum effort and ultimately proved disappointing. Granted he would have preferred a stronger gallop, but he had a good chance at these weights and has a lot prove now.
**Herodotus** *Official explanation: jockey said gelding had a breathing problem*

## 5252 WILTSHIRE LIFE H'CAP 1m
**4:50** (4:51) (E3) (0-70,70) 3-Y-O+ **£3,731** (£1,148; £574; £287) **Stalls** High

Form RPR
3034 **1** **Liberty Royal**[17] 4802 5-8-11 **62** .......... (p) DSweeney 6 70
(PJMakin) *lw: bhd: gd hdwy over 2f out: jnd ldr over 1f out: drvn to ld fnl strides* **8/1**
0103 **2** hd **Ridge Boy (IRE)**[17] 4814 3-9-0 **70** .......... RLMoore 1 78
(RHannon) *chsd ldrs: led over 2f out: jnd by wnr over 1f out: hrd rdn and kpt on: hdd fnl strides* **14/1**
3510 **3** shd **Habshan (USA)**[15] 4852 4-9-4 **69** .......... DHolland 5 76+
(CFWall) *towards rr: swtchd outside over 2f out: rapid hdwy over 1f out: str run and veered rt ins fnl f: r.o* **5/1**[2]

5133 **4** 3 1/2 **Tuscarora (IRE)**[5] 5136 5-8-10 **61** .......... JFortune 11 60
(AWCarroll) *mid-div: effrt over 2f out: no imp appr fnl f* **9/2**[1]

343- **5** 1 1/4 **Young Alex (IRE)**[346] 5130 6-9-2 **67** .......... (p) MartinDwyer 2 63
(MCPipe) *lw: t.k.h towards rr: hdwy 3f out: edgd rt over 1f out: no ex* **11/1**

0003 **6** 1/2 **Terraquin (IRE)**[11] 4969 4-8-12 **63** .......... (p) TPQueally 4 58
(JJBridger) *b: mid-div: drvn and hdwy over 2f out: no imp appr fnl f* **20/1**

2301 **7** 2 **Pella**[4] 5156 3-8-11 **67** 6ex .......... LDettori 3 58
(MBlanshard) *dwlt: hdwy over 2f out: wknd over 1f out* **11/2**[3]

-200 **8** 2 **Zariano**[17] 4814 4-9-1 **69** .......... LPKeniry(3) 14 55
(RMStronge) *chsd ldrs over 5f* **33/1**

000 **9** 2 1/2 **Jahia (NZ)**[20] 4719 5-8-12 **63** .......... GBaker 15 43
(MMadgwick) *b.hind: bhd: rdn over 2f out: n.d* **100/1**

-550 **10** shd **Fisby**[20] 4717 3-8-8 **64** .......... JFEgan 9 44
(SKirk) *chsd ldrs 6f* **14/1**

-420 **11** nk **Malak Al Moulouk (USA)**[24] 4616 4-9-2 **67** .......... JTate 16 46
(JMPEustace) *bhd: drvn along over 2f out: nvr trbld ldrs* **16/1**

0000 **12** 1 1/4 **Off Beat (USA)**[72] 3180 3-8-9 **65** .......... SCarson 7 41
(RFJohnsonHoughton) *chsd ldrs 4f* **66/1**

5605 **13** 2 **Dash For Cover (IRE)**[13] 4912 4-8-6 **57** .......... PDobbs 8 29
(RHannon) *w ldrs over 5f* **14/1**

664 **14** 3 **Priors Dale**[106] 2226 4-9-1 **66** .......... DaneO'Neill 12 31
(KBell) *dwlt: sn in midfield: n.m.r 3f out: sn wknd* **16/1**

1000 **15** 7 **Oh Boy (IRE)**[15] 4846 4-9-5 **70** .......... RHughes 10 19
(RHannon) *w ldrs: led briefly 3f out: wknd qckly* **16/1**

2 **16** 10 **Hallings Overture (USA)**[143] 1352 5-9-5 **70** .......... RHills 13 —
(CAHorgan) *b: led 5f: wknd qckly* **12/1**

1m 41.96s (-1.01) **Going Correction** -0.10s/f (Good)
**WFA** 3 from 4yo+ 5lb **16** Ran SP% **125.2**
Speed ratings: **101,100,100,97,95 95,93,91,88,88 88,87,85,82,75 65**CSF £115.59 CT £466.89 TOTE £10.70: £2.30, £3.00, £2.20, £1.50; EX 146.00.
**Owner** T W Wellard & Partners **Bred** Ambersham Stud **Trained** Ogbourne Maisey, Wilts

**FOCUS**
A modest handicap. The pace was fair and the first three came clear at the finish, but the form is ordinary for the grade.

**NOTEBOOK**
**Liberty Royal** turned in a gritty display to register his first success since scoring on his debut as a juvenile in 2001. He looked like scoring readily when easing to the lead two out, but in the end he had to dig deep to repel the runner-up and this trip looks as far as he wants to go. Having found his form of late since the application of cheekpieces, he may be able to hold his own off a higher mark in the future, and is relatively lightly-raced for his age.
**Ridge Boy(IRE)** just failed and deserves extra credit, as he was drawn widest of all. He stuck to his task well in the closing stages and the drop back in trip suited. It will be a surprise was he not placed to gain compensation off this sort of mark.
**Habshan(USA)** was flying at the finish, but hung markedly to his right under pressure, giving his rider a hard time. He is capable of scoring off this sort of rating and appreciated this better ground, but is tricky and not one to place great faith in.
**Tuscarora(IRE)** ran her usual sound race, but never looked a serious threat.
**Young Alex(IRE)** ◆ , making his debut for a new stable, did particularly well on this return from his 346-day layoff, showing enough to suggest he can resume winning ways with this outing under his belt.
**Pella**, off the mark against his own age group last time, never looked like following up under his penalty.

## 5253 AXMINSTER CARPETS APPRENTICE H'CAP — 5f
**5:20** (5:20) (E3) (0-70,69) 3-Y-0+ **£5,025** (£1,546; £773; £386) **Stalls** High

Form RPR

0030 **1** **Maromito (IRE)**[30] 4422 7-8-2 **55** .......... AMullen(5) 3 68
(RBastiman) *swtg: prom: led 2f out: rdn clr fnl f* **12/1**

6021 **2** 2 **Who's Winning (IRE)**[29] 4434 3-8-13 **67** .......... AHindley(5) 15 73
(BGPowell) *chsd ldrs: wnt 2nd and hung lft fnl f: nt pce of wnr* **9/1**

632 **3** 1 **Millinsky (USA)**[29] 4440 3-8-2 **56** .......... RMills(5) 11 58+
(RGuest) *in rr: rdn and r.o fnl 2f: nrst fin* **11/4**[1]

0500 **4** shd **Formalise**[18] 4774 4-8-7 **55** oh3 .......... (p) RThomas 8 57+
(GBBalding) *led stands' side trio: kpt on fnl f: hld by far side gp* **12/1**

0040 **5** 1 **Tomthevic**[5] 5107 6-8-4 **55** oh6 .......... CHaddon(3) 7 53
(JMBradley) *b: b.hind: hld up in midfield: n.m.r 3f out: rdn to chse ldrs over 1f out: one pce* **20/1**

2100 **6** 1/2 **Stagnite**[30] 4415 4-8-10 **58** .......... (p) AQuinn 16 55
(MrsHSweeting) *led 3f: wknd over 1f out* **12/1**

**7** nk **Chantelle (IRE)**[41] 4113 4-8-1 **56** .......... JDWalsh(7) 1 52
(SKirk) *racd in stands' side trio: in tch: edgd rt and jnd far side gp 2f out: hrd rdn: no imp* **33/1**

0134 **8** nk **Byo (IRE)**[23] 4617 6-9-2 **69** .......... KMay(5) 9 63
(MQuinn) *chsd ldrs over 3f* **10/1**

1200 **9** nk **Double M**[10] 5008 7-8-13 **66** .......... (v) MHoward(5) 2 59+
(MrsLRichards) *chsd stands' side ldr: hrd rdn over 1f out: one pce* **7/1**[3]

5540 **10** hd **Pulse**[9] 5016 6-8-5 **58** .......... (p) DerekNolan(5) 6 51
(JMBradley) *hld up in midfield: no hdwy fnl 2f* **10/1**

0415 **11** 2 **One Way Ticket**[9] 5016 4-9-2 **69** .......... (p) CJDavies(5) 13 54
(JMBradley) *w ldrs 3f* **13/2**[2]

0605 **12** 3/4 **Kallista's Pride**[11] 4970 4-8-11 **59** .......... (v) MSavage 12 42
(JRBest) *chsd ldrs 3f* **12/1**

5000 **13** shd **Bennanabaa**[6] 5081 5-8-2 **55** oh10 .......... (bt[1]) BO'Neill(5) 5 37
(SCBurrough) *s.s: hrd rdn 1/2-way: a bhd* **66/1**

005 **14** 2 **Iltravitore (IRE)**[15] 4845 3-9-2 **65** .......... NChalmers 10 40
(DRCElsworth) *dwlt: a bhd* **25/1**

0000 **15** 2 **Catchthebatch**[17] 4811 8-8-2 **55** oh15 .......... (b) LiamJones(5) 4 23
(EAWheeler) *rrd s: sn in midfield on far rail: wknd 2f out* **66/1**

60.11 secs (-1.46) **Going Correction** -0.10s/f (Good)
**WFA** 3 from 4yo+ 1lb **15** Ran SP% **126.0**
Speed ratings: **107,103,102,102,100 99,99,98,98,97 94,93,93,90,86**CSF £115.41 CT £399.15 TOTE £16.40: £5.50, £3.90, £1.30; EX 304.30 Place 6 £258.28, Place 5 £121.23.
**Owner** Mrs C B Bastiman **Bred** Joseph Finnegan **Trained** Cowthorpe, N Yorks

**FOCUS**
This was run at a true pace, with the field spread right across the track at the finish. Although the form is ordinary, it produced a fair winning time for the grade.

**NOTEBOOK**
**Maromito(IRE)** was prominent throughout, produced a neat turn of foot to score readily and produced his best effort on turf for some time in the process. The manner of this success did enough to suggest he can win again, as he is undoubtedly well treated on the best of his previous form.
**Who's Winning(IRE)** ran another solid race from his good draw, but was never a serious threat to the winner. He remains in good form.
**Millinsky(USA)** , an unlucky loser at Kempton last time, again got going too late on this handicap debut. She has ability, and is on a fair mark, but her style of running means she will always need things to fall just right in her races.
**Formalise** was soon leading the few to track over to the stands'-side rail and improved on his recent efforts, but lost third late on by hanging and is a hard horse to catch right.
**Tomthevic**, having his second outing for his new yard, showed promise and is on a winning mark if recapturing his old form.
**Double M**
**One Way Ticket** had no obvious excuses and ran below his best.
T/Jkpt: £25,078.30 to a £1 stake. Pool: £52,982.50. 1.50 winning tickets. T/Plt: £192.20 to a £1 stake. Pool: £44,916.55. 170.55 winning tickets. T/Qpdt: £67.50 to a £1 stake. Pool: £2,771.80. 30.35 winning tickets. LM

# 5215 BADEN-BADEN (L-H)
### Wednesday, September 1

**OFFICIAL GOING: Soft**

## 5254a KABA BADENER-STEHER-CUP (LISTED) — 1m 6f
**1:35** (1:36) 3-Y-0+ **£13,380** (£5,282; £2,465; £1,408)

RPR

**1** **Soterio (GER)**[31] 4-9-3 .......... IFerguson 2 114
(WBaltromei, Germany)

**2** hd **Kasus (GER)**[284] 6-8-13 .......... (b) AStarke 4 110
(PVovcenko, Germany)

**3** 2 **No Refuge (IRE)**[338] 5274 4-9-0 ow1 .......... THellier 1 109
(SirMarkPrescott) *set slow pace, headed over 1f out, one pace (16/10)*

**4** 3 **Liquido (GER)**[64] 5-9-3 .......... ABoschert 3 109
(HSteinmetz, Germany)

3m 10.38s **4** Ran
Speed ratings: .
**Owner** Frau J Kumpernas **Bred** Stiftung Gestut Fahrhof **Trained** Germany

**NOTEBOOK**
**No Refuge(IRE)** was fancied to go well on his return from a long absence, but could find no extra when pressed approaching the final furlong after trying to make all.

## 5255a FAHRHOF GOLDENE PEITSCHE (GROUP 2) — 6f
**3:25** (3:32) 3-Y-0+ **£45,775** (£18,310; £9,155; £4,930)

RPR

**1** **Raffelberger (GER)**[32] 4357 3-8-13 .......... ASuborics 14 111
(MarioHofer, Germany) *always in touch, pushed along and 3rd straight, challenged over 1f out, led inside final f, ran on well*

**2** 1/2 **Key To Pleasure (GER)**[24] 4596 4-9-2 .......... J-PCarvalho 4 110
(MarioHofer, Germany) *prominent, effort entering straight, finished strongly to take 2nd 100 yards out*

**3** 3/4 **Lucky Strike**[24] 4595 6-9-2 .......... ADeVries 15 108
(ATrybuhl, Germany) *led on stands side, ridden entering straight, headed inside final f, no extra* 1

**4** 1 3/4 **Felicity (GER)**[24] 4596 3-8-8 .......... ABoschert 8 97
(PRau, Germany) *mid division, stayed on under pressure from 1 1/2f out, nearest finish*

**5** 1/2 **Golden Nun**[24] 4595 4-8-12 .......... (b) RWinston 7 97
(TDEasterby) *mid division, stayed on final stages, nearest finish*

**6** shd **Diable**[66] 5-9-2 .......... LHammer-Hansen 16 101
(HHesse, Germany) *mid division, stayed on final f, never dangerous*

**7** nk **Matrix (GER)**[24] 4596 3-8-13 .......... IFerguson 13 99
(WBaltromei, Germany) *prominent, 2nd straight, ran on under pressure til no extra from over 1f out*

**8** 2 **Sacho (GER)**[31] 6-9-2 .......... AHelfenbein 10 94
(WKujath, Germany) *always behind*

**9** 1 1/4 **Fayr Jag (IRE)**[13] 4886 5-9-2 .......... ACulhane 5 90
(TDEasterby) *behind and soon pushed along, never in contention* 2

**10** hd **Areias (GER)**[24] 4596 6-9-2 .......... AStarke 1 90
(ASchutz, Germany) *never dangerous*

**11** 1 1/4 **Landerneau (IRE)**[8] 3-8-8 .......... CSoumillon 6 80
(RobertCollet, France) *prominent 2f, soon weakened* 3

**12** 3 **Arc Royal (GER)**[364] 4674 7-9-2 .......... JBojko 12 77
(DFechner, Germany) *never dangerous*

**13** shd **Gold Type (IRE)**[24] 4596 5-9-2 .......... THellier 11 77
(KWoodburn) *never a factor*

**14** 1 **Fiepes Shuffle (GER)**[24] 4596 4-9-2 .......... EPedroza 9 74
(MarioHofer, Germany) *speed to halfway*

**15** 5 **Glad To Be Fast (IRE)**[53] 3769 4-9-2 .......... NRichter 2 59
(MarioHofer, Germany) *always in rear*

**16** 7 **Call Me Big (GER)**[96] 2466 6-9-2 .......... WMongil 3 38
(TDunkel, Germany) *towards rear, effort entering straight, no impression*

69.47 secs
**WFA** 3 from 4yo+ 2lb **16** Ran SP% **130.8**
Speed ratings: .
**Owner** Stall Jenny **Bred** Gestut Rheinberg **Trained** Germany

**NOTEBOOK**
**Raffelberger(GER)** gave a strong showing and showed a willing attitude. Reportedly helped by being gelded in mid-season, he heads to the Prix de l'Abbaye and while much more will be required there, he appears on the upgrade.
**Key To Pleasure(GER)** gave his trainer a 1-2 when running on well in the final furlong. His German sprint runs are respectable and helps give the form of this race a more solid look.
**Lucky Strike**, racing prominently as usual, he had to give best inside the final furlong. He still gave a creditable showing and can win another Group race before the end of the season.
**Golden Nun** was doing all her best work at the finish and her rider reported a stronger pace in the first half of the race would have been much more beneficial. Connections stated a step up to seven furlongs is likely for her next start.
**Fayr Jag(IRE)** was most disappointing and this run is probably best forgotten.

# 5172 CHEPSTOW (L-H)
### Friday, September 3

**OFFICIAL GOING: Good**
Wind: nil Weather: sunny

## 5256 RON ULLAH MAIDEN AUCTION STKS — 1m 14y
**2:20** (2:20) (F3) 2-Y-0 **£3,474** (£1,069; £534; £267) **Stalls** High

Form RPR

0 **1** **Bathwick Finesse (IRE)**[15] 4866 2-8-2 .......... SRighton 1 70
(BRMillman) *t.k.h: mde virtually all: clr over 3f out: shkn up over 1f out: rdn out* **12/1**



The Form Book, Raceform Ltd, Compton, RG20 6NL

22 **2** *1 ½* **King's Account (USA)**[14] 4900 2-8-9 .................................. JFanning 10 74
(MJohnston) *a.p: wnt 2nd over 4f out: rdn 3f out: edgd lft over 1f out: kpt on same pce* **6/4**[1]

2202 **3** *nk* **Group Captain**[12] 4967 2-8-7 88 .................................. JFEgan 7 71
(SKirk) *a.p: rdn 3f out: disp 2nd fnl 2f: kpt on one pce* **7/4**[2]

5306 **4** *1 ½* **Dusty Dane (IRE)**[14] 4907 2-8-0 67 .................................. CHaddon(7) 8 68
(WGMTurner) *hld up: hdwy 4f out: sn rdn: one pce fnl 2f* **50/1**

64 **5** *3* **William Tell (IRE)**[22] 4689 2-9-0 .................................. CCatlin 5 68
(MRChannon) *hld up in tch: rdn over 3f out: sn outpcd: styd on ins fnl f* **8/1**[3]

0 **6** *shd* **Arch Folly**[26] 4584 2-8-4 .................................. FPFerris(3) 9 61
(JGPortman) *bhd: rdn over 3f out: sme late hdwy* **66/1**

06 **7** *3* **Just A Try (USA)**[22] 4681 2-9-0 .................................. PDobbs 4 61
(RHannon) *hld up in rr: hdwy over 2f out: wknd ins fnl f* **20/1**

0 **8** *3* **Prince Vettori**[20] 4743 2-8-9 .................................. TPQueally 2 49
(DJCoakley) *hld up: rdn over 3f out: sn bhd* **50/1**

0 **9** *1 ¾* **Water Pistol**[12] 4967 2-8-9 .................................. JQuinn 11 45
(MrsAJPerrett) *hld up in tch: wknd over 3f out* **14/1**

00 **10** *½* **Laurollie**[12] 4967 2-7-11 .................................. RThomas(5) 3 37
(DrJRJNaylor) *prom 4f* **100/1**

050 **11** *6* **Lady Luisa (IRE)**[4] 5198 2-8-2 .................................. SCarson 6 23
(JSMoore) *dwlt: a bhd* **25/1**

1m 38.18s (2.28) **Going Correction** +0.10s/f (Good) **11** Ran SP% **116.8**
Speed ratings: **92,90,90,88,85 85,82,79,77,77 71**CSF £29.23 TOTE £17.20: £4.60, £1.10, £1.30; EX 36.60.
**Owner** Mrs S Clifford **Bred** J C Fagan **Trained** Kentisbeare, Devon

**FOCUS**
An ordinary maiden in which the winner was able to make virtually all off a slow pace and the market leaders were never able to land a telling blow at her. The form does not look particularly sound.

**NOTEBOOK**
**Bathwick Finesse(IRE)** had found things happening too quickly on her debut here over six furlongs, but she knew a lot more this time. Smartly away and soon able to tack over from the number one stall to claim the stands' rail, she was allowed too much rope by the principals freewheeling downhill passing halfway and was not hard pressed to hold on, although she was tying up inside the last and would not want to go any farther at this stage. Her in-form trainer Rod Millman reported that the filly has had her problems and that they have not been able to do much with her at home, and she is not yet the finished article physically.
**King's Account(USA)**, who has now finished second on each of his three starts, was tackling a mile for the first time and this was the fastest surface he has encountered so far. Although he got the better of a duel with market rival Group Captain, he never looked like overhauling the filly and the way he carried his head suggested he was ill at ease on the track's undulations.
**Group Captain** was perhaps intimidated a little by the eventual runner-up but that should not be used as an excuse. He is obviously capable of winning a maiden, but he is nowhere near as good as his BHB rating suggests and has become expensive to follow.
**Dusty Dane(IRE)** is exposed, but he did appear to stay this longer trip.
**William Tell(IRE)** did not build on his previous starts but is now eligible for a handicap mark.
**Arch Folly**, who still looked a shade green in the preliminaries, made modest late progress and is going to need farther next year.
**Just A Try(USA)** made progress from the rear at halfway but did not see out this longer trip.

## 5257 RUSSELL REYNOLDS CLAIMING STKS 1m 4f 23y
**2:50** (2:50) (F4) 3-Y-O+ **£2,604** (£744; £372) **Stalls** Low

Form RPR

0043 **1** **On Cloud Nine**[23] 4630 3-8-1 62 .................................. HayleyTurner(3) 2 54
(MLWBell) *hld up: hdwy on ins over 4f out: swtchd rt over 2f out: led wl over 1f out: rdn and hdd 1f out: led ins fnl f: r.o* **9/4**[1]

1322 **2** *1* **Banningham Blaze**[18] 4799 4-9-3 48 ..................................(v) TPQueally 5 56
(AWCarroll) *s.i.s: hld up: hdwy over 4f out: rdn and edgd lft over 2f out: led 1f out tl ins fnl f: nt qckn* **9/2**[2]

4104 **3** *4* **Rolex Free (ARG)**[8] 5056 6-9-6 51 ..................................(v) JFEgan 6 53
(DFlood) *led: rdn over 3f out: hdd wl over 1f out: wknd fnl f* **8/1**

0510 **4** *nk* **Mr Whizz**[19] 4778 7-9-0 40 ..................................(p) DNolan(3) 13 49
(APJones) *hld up: hdwy over 4f out: rdn and ev ch 2f out: wknd ins fnl f* **14/1**

-240 **5** *6* **Black Legend (IRE)**[4] 5175 5-8-9 45 .................................. BSwarbrick(5) 3 37
(RLee) *hld up: hdwy on outside over 3f out: rdn over 2f out: wknd over 1f out* **9/1**

2504 **6** *3 ½* **Sahaat**[11] 5006 6-8-11 68 .................................. KGhunowa(7) 7 35
(MJPolglase) *hld up: hdwy over 5f out: rdn over 3f out: wknd over 2f out* **5/1**[3]

-000 **7** *5* **Zarneeta**[27] 4562 3-8-4 45 .................................. PDoe 12 22
(WDeBest-Turner) *prom: wnt 2nd over 4f out: rdn over 3f out: sn wknd* **100/1**

3630 **8** *4* **Our Imperial Bay (USA)**[33] 4082 5-9-1 45 ..........(v) J-PGuillambert(3) 11 21
(MrsJCandlish) *hld up and bhd: hdwy over 5f out: rdn over 4f out: sn wknd* **20/1**

0045 **9** *1 ¾* **Keltic Rainbow (IRE)**[9] 5036 3-7-10 40 ow3 .................. RThomas(5) 1 10
(DHaydnJones) *sn chsng ldr: lost 2nd over 4f out: wknd over 3f out* **40/1**

002- **10** *6* **Tweed**[455] 2178 7-9-2 50 .................................. DKinsella 9 6
(CRoberts) *a bhd* **20/1**

0003 **11** *1 ¾* **Dash For Glory**[13] 4417 5-9-0 30 .................................. VSlattery 4 1
(JSKing) *prom tl rdn and wknd qckly over 5f out* **100/1**

5060 **12** *4* **Lyrical Girl (USA)**[29] 4479 3-8-1 54 .................................. FPFerris(3) 8 —
(HJManners) *bhd tl hdwy over 4f out: sn rdn: wknd 3f out: virtually p.u ins fnl f* **16/1**

2m 38.96s (0.46) **Going Correction** +0.10s/f (Good)
**WFA** 3 from 4yo+ 9lb **12** Ran SP% **113.2**
Speed ratings: **102,101,98,98,94 92,88,86,84,80 79,77**CSF £10.50 TOTE £2.90: £1.10, £1.70, £3.10; EX 8.80.The winner was claimed by Mr J. O'Shea for £8,000. Sahaat was claimed by Mr C. Dore for £8,000.
**Owner** Mrs Alison C Farrant **Bred** Mrs A C Farrant And F A Farrant **Trained** Newmarket, Suffolk

**FOCUS**
Just a routine claimer, run at a fair pace. The winner did not need to run anywhere near her handicap form.

**NOTEBOOK**
**On Cloud Nine**, dropped in class, held a clear chance on official adjusted ratings, with 8lb and more in hand of all bar Sahaat. She stays well and could have chances back in minor handicaps.
**Banningham Blaze** was well supported and, although momentarily hanging fire when brought with her challenge, she went down fighting. A consistent performer, she does lack a change of gear and faster ground would have helped her cause.
**Rolex Free(ARG)** made much of the running and boxed on to reclaim third place inside the last. All his winning has been done on artificial surfaces.
**Mr Whizz**, a versatile performer, had Banningham Blaze behind when scoring at Brighton a month ago but was considerably worse off with that filly here. He had his chance but faded in the final furlong.
**Black Legend(IRE)**, minus the tongue tie, briefly threatened to take a hand when closing down the centre of the track but could not sustain the run.
**Sahaat** had a chance on official figures, but is most frustrating and a return to Fibresand could represent his best opportunity.
**Tweed** *Official explanation: jockey said gelding had no more to give*
**Lyrical Girl(USA)** *Official explanation: jockey said filly lost her action and was hanging*

## 5258 ESCAPE DESIGN H'CAP 1m 2f 36y
**3:25** (3:26) (E3) (0-70,69) 3-Y-O+ **£3,675** (£1,130; £565; £282) **Stalls** Low

Form RPR

0332 **1** **Magic Sting**[8] 5057 3-8-10 **68** .................................. HayleyTurner(3) 2 80+
(MLWBell) *hld up and bhd: hdwy over 3f out: led 2f out: edgd lft over 1f out: drew clr fnl f: r.o wl* **3/1**[2]

56-0 **2** *3 ½* **Cornish Gold**[81] 2949 3-8-7 **62** .................................. JMackay 15 67
(NJHenderson) *hld up: hdwy 5f out: rdn to ld over 2f out: sn hdd: one pce* **33/1**

4022 **3** *½* **Mambina (USA)**[17] 4829 3-8-4 **59** .................................. CCatlin 9 63
(MRChannon) *hld up: hdwy over 3f out: rdn over 2f out: styd on one pce fnl f* **11/1**

**4** *½* **Wild Power (GER)**[28] 6-8-7 **55** .................................. RHavlin 13 58
(JGMO'Shea) *hld up: hdwy over 2f out: styd on fnl f* **25/1**

3310 **5** *nk* **Billy Bathwick (IRE)**[54] 3773 7-8-8 **59** .................................. FPFerris(3) 14 62
(JMBradley) *hld up: hdwy over 4f out: rdn over 2f out: one pce fnl f* **10/1**

3000 **6** *2 ½* **Cuddles (FR)**[6] 5136 5-8-9 **57** .................................. JFEgan 10 55
(KOCunningham-Brown) *s.i.s: hld up and bhd: rdn and hdwy over 3f out: no further prog fnl 2f* **12/1**

2313 **7** *½* **Stolen Hours (USA)**[21] 4729 4-9-3 **65** .................................. JQuinn 6 62
(JAkehurst) *hld up and bhd: hdwy on ins whn nt clr run and swtchd rt over 4f out: rdn over 3f out: n.d* **5/2**[1]

0566 **8** *1 ¾* **Our Destiny**[30] 4436 6-8-3 **56** .................................. RThomas(5) 7 50
(AWCarroll) *hld up and bhd: sme hdwy over 2f out: sn rdn: nvr trbld ldrs* **14/1**

4062 **9** *2 ½* **Fortune Point (IRE)**[30] 4436 6-8-11 **59** ..................................(v) TPQueally 5 48
(AWCarroll) *led: rdn and hdd over 2f out: wknd over 1f out* **8/1**[3]

2205 **10** *1* **Starry Mary**[16] 3153 6-8-2 **55** oh3 .................................. BSwarbrick(5) 16 42
(RJPrice) *a bhd* **20/1**

0605 **11** *4* **Petite Colleen (IRE)**[15] 4871 3-8-4 **59** .................................. AMcCarthy 12 38
(DHaydnJones) *prom: rdn over 3f out: wknd over 2f out* **25/1**

0640 **12** *nk* **Dual Purpose (IRE)**[4] 5176 9-8-11 **59** .................................. DKinsella 8 38
(CRoberts) *prom: rdn over 4f out: wknd 3f out* **50/1**

0053 **13** *6* **La Professoressa (IRE)**[16] 4848 3-8-3 **58** .................................. JFanning 4 25
(MrsPNDutfield) *prom: ev ch over 3f out: sn rdn: wknd over 2f out* **11/1**

0000 **14** *3* **Among Friends (IRE)**[62] 3536 4-8-7 **55** oh1 .................................. PDoe 1 17
(BPalling) *a bhd* **50/1**

600 **15** *8* **Kalimenta (USA)**[16] 4848 3-8-7 **62** .................................. SChin 3 8
(SKirk) *hld up in tch: wknd 4f out* **25/1**

6000 **16** *shd* **Glimmer Of Light (IRE)**[44] 4029 4-9-7 **69** ..................................(b[1]) SCarson 11 15
(PWHarris) *chsd ldr tl over 4f out: wknd qckly over 3f out* **25/1**

2m 10.6s (1.00) **Going Correction** +0.10s/f (Good)
**WFA** 3 from 4yo+ 7lb **16** Ran SP% **131.8**
Speed ratings: **100,97,96,96,96 94,93,92,90,89 86,86,81,78,72 72**CSF £116.33 CT £1029.24 TOTE £4.30: £1.20, £9.00, £2.40, £7.20; EX 167.70.
**Owner** Mrs P T Fenwick **Bred** Michael Watt And Exors Of The Late Miss Jemima Joh **Trained** Newmarket, Suffolk

**FOCUS**
They went a brisk pace in this handicap and the form ought to prove sound.

**NOTEBOOK**
**Magic Sting**, who has been knocking on the door of late from this mark, was a bit slow to break, but he made steady progress from the back of the field and scooted clear to score pretty comfortably. He handles most types of ground and can score again.
**Cornish Gold**, not seen since her debut for this yard in June, was 3lb lower here. She was keeping on in the latter stages and might benefit from a step up to 12 furlongs.
**Mambina(USA)** is perhaps not the easiest of rides, but she is running well at present and there could be a small race for her.
**Wild Power(GER)**, better known as a jumper, was a Flat winner in Germany in his younger days. He stayed on quite takingly but has never been one to find a great deal for pressure.
**Billy Bathwick(IRE)** is a rather hot and cold performer and this was a decent run on ground that was not as fast as he would have liked.
**Cuddles(FR)**, due to race off a 3lb lower mark from the weekend, is well treated on the best of last season's form but while she kept on through beaten rivals her lengthy losing run looks set to continue.
**Stolen Hours(USA)**, chased along from the stalls, made ground going nicely on the turn in. Short of room at the half-mile pole, he was soon under pressure and could never land a blow at the leaders despite keeping on. *Official explanation: jockey said colt was never travelling*

## 5259 MAKE-A-WISH CLASSIFIED STKS 1m 14y
**3:55** (3:58) (F3) 3-Y-O+ **£3,497** (£1,076; £538; £269) **Stalls** High

Form RPR

0040 **1** **Zafarshah (IRE)**[35] 4301 5-8-11 59 .................................. BSwarbrick(5) 10 70
(PDEvans) *hld up: hdwy 4f out: rdn 2f out: r.o to ld wl ins fnl f* **12/1**

300/ **2** *1 ¼* **Redswan**[625] 5930 9-8-13 59 ..................................(t) DNolan(3) 4 67
(AEJones) *uns rdr and bolted bef s: led: rdn and hung lft fr over 1f out: hdd and no ex wl ins fnl f* **14/1**

0040 **3** *3 ½* **Jomus**[36] 4266 3-8-11 58 .................................. PDobbs 1 59
(LMontagueHall) *hld up and bhd: rdn and hdwy over 2f out: r.o ins fnl f* **33/1**

2334 **4** *1* **Archerfield (IRE)**[36] 4264 3-8-8 60 ..................................(t) TPQueally 14 54
(JWHills) *hld up: hdwy 4f out: rdn 3f out: r.o one pce fnl f* **7/1**[3]

0040 **5** *hd* **Craic Sa Ceili (IRE)**[20] 4740 4-8-13 60 .................................. JFanning 3 53
(MSSaunders) *t.k.h: hdwy over 4f out: ev ch 2f out: sn rdn: wknd ins fnl f* **7/1**[3]

005 **6** *3 ½* **Land Of Nod (IRE)**[10] 5020 3-8-8 60 ..................................(v) SChin 5 45
(GAButler) *prom: rdn 3f out: wknd fnl f* **16/1**

0005 **7** *½* **Beltane**[26] 4574 6-9-2 46 .................................. RSmith 2 47
(WDeBest-Turner) *hld up and bhd: sme hdwy over 2f out: n.d* **100/1**

4200 **8** *hd* **Head Boy**[10] 5020 3-8-11 59 .................................. PDoe 11 47
(SDow) *hld up and bhd: rdn and hdwy over 2f out: wknd fnl f* **28/1**

4022 **9** *1* **Adalar (IRE)**[18] 4802 4-8-13 58 .................................. FPFerris(3) 12 44
(PDEvans) *chsd ldrs: rdn over 3f out: wknd 2f out* **9/2**[1]

4603 **10** *nk* **Master Mahogany**[24] 4619 3-8-8 60 .................................. LPKeniry(3) 19 44
(RJHodges) *prom under stands' rail: rdn and edgd lft jst over 2f out: sn wknd* **9/1**

2000 **11** *1* **Indian Edge**[15] 4868 3-8-11 58 .................................. DKinsella 6 41
(BPalling) *hld up and bhd: swtchd lft over 5f out: sme hdwy 3f out: rdn and wknd 2f out* **50/1**

0234 **12** *2* **Teehee (IRE)**[53] 3800 6-9-2 58 ..................................(b) JQuinn 8 37
(BPalling) *prom tl rdn and wknd over 2f out* **14/1**

0-00 **13** *5* **Lord Greystoke (IRE)**[116] 1997 3-8-11 55 ........ RHavlin 7 25
(CPMorlock) *rdn over 4f out: sn bhd* **80/1**

0000 **14** *hd* **Harry Came Home**[14] 4912 3-8-4 30 ........ (b) PGallagher(7) 9 25
(JCFox) *a bhd* **100/1**

0000 **15** *6* **Senior Minister**[37] 4238 6-8-11 60 ........ AQuinn(5) 13 11
(PWHiatt) *prom tl rdn and wknd over 2f out* **50/1**

-000 **16** *1 3/4* **First Dawn**[71] 3246 3-8-8 60 ........ CCatlin 18 4
(MRChannon) *hld up: pushed along over 3f out: sn bhd* **25/1**

0-40 **17** *8* **Dreams Forgotten (IRE)**[23] 4655 4-8-13 57 ........ AMcCarthy 16 —
(GGMargarson) *hld up: rdn over 3f out: sn bhd* **25/1**

0020 **18** *10* **Burlington Place**[31] 4418 3-8-11 60 ........ JFEgan 15 —
(SKirk) *hld up: rdn 5f out: bhd whn eased over 2f out* **16/1**

2005 **19** *17* **Phred**[21] 4719 4-9-2 58 ........ SCarson 17 —
(RFJohnsonHoughton) *s.i.s: sn wl bhd: t.o* **6/1**[2]

1m 36.56s (0.66) **Going Correction** +0.10s/f (Good)
**WFA** 3 from 4yo+ 5lb **19** Ran SP% **121.5**
Speed ratings: **100,98,95,94,94 90,90,89,88,88 87,85,80,80,74 72,64,54,37**CSF £155.34 TOTE £12.80: £4.20, £5.30, £13.00; EX 245.30.
**Owner** Waterline Racing Club **Bred** His Highness The Aga Khan's Studs S C **Trained** Pandy, Gwent

**FOCUS**
Modest form. The main action took place in the centre of the track, but Master Mahogany and First Dawn raced alone down the stands' side in the early stages before a number of the others came over to join them.

**NOTEBOOK**
**Zafarshah(IRE)**, with the visor left off, responded to presure to get on top in the last 75 yards. He was scoring for only the second time on turf, having finished last at Nottingham on his previous start, and trainer David Evans admitted that he is inconsistent. *Official explanation: trainer said, regarding the improved form shown, gelding is inconsistent*
**Redswan**was well backed on this first run since December 2002. After unseating his rider and running loose to the start, he looked set to land the gamble, but he hung badly to his left and his rider only pulled his whip through when it was too late. He obviously retains ability but is not straightforward.
**Jomus** was doing his best work in the latter stages. He recorded his sole win to date on Polytrack but is running well enough on turf at present.
**Archerfield(IRE)** made her move at the same time as the winner but lacked the pace to become involved. A step up to ten furlongs could pay off.
**Craic Sa Ceili(IRE)**, back up in trip and on more suitable ground, travelled quite well but did not find as much as she had promised.
**Burlington Place** *Official explanation: jockey said gelding was changing legs for much of the race*
**Phred** *Official explanation: jockey said gelding had breathing problems*

## 5260 BETFRED "THE BONUS KING" H'CAP 7f 16y
**4:30** (4:31) (F4) (0-55,55) 3-Y-0+ **£2,746** (£784; £392) **Stalls** High

Form RPR

3020 **1** **Nautical**[20] 4751 6-9-4 52 ........ PDobbs 11 62
(AWCarroll) *hld up: hdwy 2f out: rdn to ld ins fnl f: r.o wl* **6/1**[3]

0140 **2** *1 1/4* **Lord Chamberlain**[15] 4871 11-9-0 55 ........ (b) CJDavies(7) 10 62
(JMBradley) *hld up in tch: rdn to ld wl over 1f out: hdd and edgd rt ins fnl f: nt qckn* **16/1**

062 **3** *1/2* **Armentieres**[9] 5036 3-8-12 53 ........ (b) HayleyTurner(3) 14 58
(JLSpearing) *chsd ldrs: lost pl over 3f out: rallied u.p 2f out: edgd rt and kpt on ins fnl f* **12/1**

5060 **4** *1* **Mobo-Baco**[7] 5080 7-9-3 54 ........ LPKeniry(3) 2 57
(RJHodges) *hld up: hdwy jst over 2f out: rdn wl over 1f out: no ex ins fnl f* **25/1**

060 **5** *hd* **Just One Look**[15] 4871 3-8-12 55 ........ RThomas(5) 5 57
(MBlanshard) *bhd: hdwy wl over 1f out: kpt on wl towards fin: nvr nrr* **40/1**

0-00 **6** *4* **Stars At Midnight**[15] 4871 4-8-12 46 ........ RSmith 6 38
(JMBradley) *chsd ldrs: rdn 2f out: no imp fnl f* **66/1**

0531 **7** *shd* **Pretty Kool**[21] 4708 4-9-5 53 ........ TPQueally 12 45
(SCWilliams) *prom: ev ch 2f out: sn rdn: wknd jst over 1f out* **9/2**[2]

2000 **8** *hd* **Meelup (IRE)**[28] 4511 4-9-6 54 ........ (p) VSlattery 9 45
(JaneSouthcombe) *led: rdn over 2f out: hdd wl over 1f out: sn wknd* **33/1**

0500 **9** *2* **Logistical**[51] 3841 4-9-4 52 ........ JFanning 18 38
(ADWPinder) *racd stands' side: hld up: rdn over 2f out: n.d* **16/1**

0543 **10** *nk* **Loch Laird**[9] 5039 9-8-13 47 ........ (p) GBaker 8 32
(MMadgwick) *nvr nrr* **8/1**

0000 **11** *1 1/4* **Toppling**[27] 4546 6-9-0 48 ........ (b[1]) PFitzsimons 17 30
(JMBradley) *led stands' side: rdn 2f out: sn wknd* **33/1**

0300 **12** *3* **Welsh Empress**[7] 5072 3-8-12 50 ........ JFEgan 7 24
(PLGilligan) *a bhd* **33/1**

2105 **13** *shd* **Arran**[16] 4852 4-9-5 53 ........ JQuinn 13 27
(VSmith) *hld up: rdn and hdwy over 2f out: wknd over 1f out* **4/1**[1]

0000 **14** *1 1/4* **Fizzy Lady**[7] 5072 3-8-10 55 ........ (t) MHalford(7) 1 26
(NEBerry) *a bhd* **40/1**

-010 **15** *3/4* **Icecap**[19] 4771 4-9-0 53 ........ AQuinn(5) 15 22
(WGMTurner) *t.k.h: prom over 4f* **16/1**

0000 **16** *4* **Annijaz**[19] 4771 7-8-9 46 ........ (p) FPFerris(3) 3 4
(JMBradley) *prom: rdn over 2f out: sn wknd* **16/1**

0005 **17** *nk* **Snow Joke (IRE)**[22] 4683 3-9-1 53 ........ RHavlin 16 10
(MrsPNDutfield) *s.i.s: sn prom stands' side: rdn over 2f out: sn wknd* **33/1**

0-10 **18** *2 1/2* **Poker**[144] 1363 3-9-0 55 ........ J-PGuillambert(3) 19 6
(MrsJCandlish) *racd stands' side: bhd fnl 3f* **25/1**

004 **19** *1 1/4* **Inescapable (USA)**[20] 4741 3-9-1 53 ........ SChin 20 1
(WRMuir) *racd stands' side: bhd fnl 3f* **33/1**

0061 **20** *5* **Wood Fern (UAE)**[9] 5035 4-9-6 54 6ex ........ (v) CCatlin 4 —
(MRChannon) *prom tl rdn and wknd 2f out* **16/1**

1m 23.95s (13.36) **Going Correction** +0.10s/f (Good)
**WFA** 3 from 4yo+ 4lb **20** Ran SP% **129.5**
Speed ratings: **99,97,97,95,95 91,90,90,88,88 86,83,83,81,80 76,75,73,71,65**CSF £92.67 CT £1155.04 TOTE £9.10: £2.90, £3.70, £2.40, £6.60; EX 105.90.
**Owner** Gary J Roberts **Bred** Sheikh Mohammed Bin Rashid Al Maktoum **Trained** Wixford, Warwicks

**FOCUS**
A run-of-the-mill handicap, but the time was decent for the grade and the form looks solid. The five to race on the stands' side apart from the main body of the field were never seen with a chance.

**NOTEBOOK**
**Nautical** picked off the leader inside the last and did it well despite drifting to his left in front. Well suited by this sort of his trip, he probably has a few ideas of his own but can win again in this mood.
**Lord Chamberlain**, one of four runners from the Milton Bradley yard, was a couple of lengths to the good entering the final furlong but was cut down. He likes it here, but was perhaps in front too soon and is probably happiest at a mile.
**Armentieres** was keeping on despite edging over towards the stands' rail under pressure. She will be suited by a step back up to a mile.
**Mobo-Baco** ran a decent race but is ideally served by faster ground and an extra furlong.
**Just One Look**, who began the season on a 16lb higher mark, finished well and looks to be on the way back. She could be one to keep an eye on.
**Welsh Empress** *Official explanation: jockey said filly was unsuited by good ground*
**Snow Joke(IRE)** *Official explanation: jockey said filly did not come down the hill*

## 5261 RITA NAYLOR BIRTHDAY H'CAP 6f 16y
**5:00** (5:02) (F4) (0-55,55) 3-Y-0+ **£2,669** (£762; £381) **Stalls** High

Form RPR

0403 **1** **Yorkies Boy**[20] 4751 9-8-4 46 ........ (p) RThomas(5) 16 55
(NEBerry) *hld up: rdn and hdwy over 1f out: r.o wl to ld cl home* **10/1**

0026 **2** *3/4* **Salon Prive**[28] 4522 4-9-2 53 ........ JFEgan 5 60
(CACyzer) *led: rdn over 2f out: edgd rt over 1f out: hdd cl home* **12/1**

6356 **3** *1/2* **Moritat (IRE)**[11] 5008 4-8-13 53 ........ (t) FPFerris(3) 19 58
(PDEvans) *hld up: rdn and hdwy over 2f out: sn edgd lft: r.o ins fnl f* **8/1**[3]

0030 **4** *1* **Captain Cloudy**[18] 4802 4-8-13 53 ........ LPKeniry(3) 8 55
(MMadgwick) *hld up in tch: rdn wl over 1f out: kpt on wl towards fin* **33/1**

0325 **5** *nk* **Enjoy The Buzz**[4] 5201 5-9-1 52 ........ TPQueally 1 53
(JMBradley) *chsd ldrs: rdn over 1f out: nt qckn ins fnl f* **7/1**[2]

4103 **6** *nk* **My Girl Pearl (IRE)**[21] 4708 4-8-10 47 ........ VSlattery 10 47
(MSSaunders) *a.p: rdn over 1f out: no ex ins fnl f* **12/1**

0056 **7** *hd* **A Teen**[14] 4923 6-8-13 50 ........ DKinsella 14 50+
(PHowling) *hld up: nt clr run over 1f out: swtchd rt and hdwy ent fnl f: nrst fin* **11/1**

0040 **8** *nk* **Kew The Music**[7] 5081 4-9-1 52 ........ (v) CCatlin 18 51
(MRChannon) *bhd: rdn 3f out: hdwy fnl f: r.o* **33/1**

3624 **9** *nk* **Diamond Ring**[16] 4854 5-8-7 47 ........ BReilly(3) 20 45
(MrsJCandlish) *hld up: hdwy over 1f out: no ex ins fnl f* **16/1**

0006 **10** *shd* **Millfields Dreams**[24] 4617 5-9-1 55 ........ DNolan(3) 9 53
(RBrotherton) *prom: rdn over 2f out: wknd ins fnl f* **20/1**

1253 **11** *nk* **Yamato Pink**[81] 2942 3-8-13 52 ........ GBaker 6 49+
(MrsHSweeting) *hld up: hdwy over 1f out: nvr nr to chal* **14/1**

0300 **12** *shd* **Semper Paratus (USA)**[15] 4877 5-8-12 49 ........ (b) MTebbutt 7 46
(VSmith) *sn bhd: late hdwy: nvr nrr* **25/1**

2464 **13** *nk* **Multiple Choice (IRE)**[15] 4882 3-8-13 55 ........ (t) J-PGuillambert(3) 11 51
(NPLittmoden) *hld up: no hdwy fnl 2f* **14/1**

3125 **14** *hd* **Mr Pertemps**[207] 721 6-9-0 54 ........ (p) THamilton(3) 4 49
(JJQuinn) *prom: chsd ldr tl rdn 2f out: wknd ins fnl f* **11/2**[1]

0450 **15** *3/4* **Barabella (IRE)**[15] 4868 3-8-11 50 ........ SCarson 2 43
(RJHodges) *bhd: hdwy on far rail over 1f out: n.d* **33/1**

6060 **16** *1* **Regal Flight (IRE)**[34] 4338 3-8-11 50 ........ RSmith 15 40
(JMBradley) *chsd ldrs tl rdn and wknd over 2f out* **66/1**

0512 **17** *2* **Rileys Dream**[9] 5035 5-8-11 48 ........ (p) RHavlin 3 32
(BJLlewellyn) *chsd ldrs tl wknd 1f out* **16/1**

-403 **18** *1/2* **Pappy (IRE)**[22] 4674 3-8-7 46 ........ PDoe 13 28+
(AWCarroll) *hld up: rdn and hung lft whn nt clr run 2f out: n.d after* **12/1**

0002 **19** *2* **Rockley Bay (IRE)**[12] 4968 3-9-2 55 ........ (t) JMackay 12 31
(PJMakin) *lost pl and rdn over 3f out: sn bhd* **14/1**

-030 **20** *3* **Chorus**[7] 5080 7-8-11 48 ........ JQuinn 17 15
(BRMillman) *chsd ldrs tl wknd over 2f out* **33/1**

1m 12.34s (0.14) **Going Correction** +0.10s/f (Good)
**WFA** 3 from 4yo+ 2lb **20** Ran SP% **133.1**
Speed ratings: **103,102,101,100,99 99,98,98,98,98 97,97,97,96,95 94,91,91,88,84**CSF £124.43 CT £1061.07 TOTE £13.80: £2.70, £3.30, £2.70, £13.20; EX 257.00 Place 6 £394.38, Place 5 £329.47.
**Owner** Paul & Ann de Weck **Bred** J And Mrs M Beddis **Trained** Earlswood, Monmouths

**FOCUS**
Only a 9lb weight range in this cavalry charge and they finished in a heap. This is modest form.

**NOTEBOOK**
**Yorkies Boy**, a Group Three winner in his pomp, got on top close home to record his first win since May 2001, when rated no less than 54lb higher. Like Nautical, winner of the previous race on this card, he ran in the greys-only event at Newmarket on his latest start.
**Salon Prive**made a bold bid from the front, but edged markedly right when the pressure was on and was just caught. He is currently rated 11lb higher on the All-Weather and looks capable of breaking his duck under either code. *Official explanation: jockey said gelding hung right*
**Moritat(IRE)**, ridden differently, was keeping on well inside the last. Yet to get his head in front, this looks his optimum trip.
**Captain Cloudy** is an exasperating individual who has had plenty of chances, but he ran well on this drop in trip.
**Enjoy The Buzz**is a consistent sort and this was a decent effort off a career-high mark.
**My Girl Pearl(IRE)**has a poor strike rate but she is running creditably at present.
**A Teen**, who has become well handicapped, would have finished closer had the breaks come for him.
**Multiple Choice(IRE)** *Official explanation: jockey said colt hung violently right*
**Chorus** *Official explanation: jockey said mare lost her action*
T/Plt: £1,373.50 to a £1 stake. Pool: £41,771.60. 22.20 winning tickets. T/Qpdt: £1,018.20 to a £1 stake. Pool: £2,201.70. 1.60 winning tickets. KH

# 4675 HAYDOCK (L-H)
### Friday, September 3

**OFFICIAL GOING: Good (good to soft in places)**
Wind: slt against Weather: fine

## 5262 EUROPEAN BREEDERS FUND MAIDEN STKS 5f
**2:30** (2:31) (D3) 2-Y-O **£4,979** (£1,532; £766; £383) **Stalls** Centre

Form RPR

6 **1** **Premier Fantasy**[7] 5096 2-9-0 ........ PHanagan 9 90
(TDBarron) *dwlt: sn prom: rdn to ld ins fnl f: r.o* **4/1**[2]

2434 **2** *1 1/4* **Juantorena**[11] 5003 2-9-0 92 ........ RMullen 6 85
(MLWBell) *led: rdn over 1f out: hdd ins fnl f: nt qckn* **13/8**[1]

**3** *3* **Beaune** 2-9-0 ........ SWKelly 10 75
(WJHaggas) *midfield: hdwy over 1f out: edgd lft ins fnl f: styd on: nt pce of ldrs* **11/1**

**4** *3* **Aynsley** 2-8-9 ........ PRobinson 2 59
(MAJarvis) *racd alone far side: prom: rdn over 1f out: sn wknd* **14/1**

3 **5** *hd* **Emerald Lodge**[18] 4815 2-9-0 ........ DHolland 8 63
(JNoseda) *prom tl rdn and wknd over 1f out* **5/1**[3]

0 **6** *1* **Cilla's Smile**[142] 1399 2-8-9 ........ DAllan 7 54
(MABuckley) *s.i.s: chsd ldrs: rdn and edgd lft over 2f out: wknd over 1f out* **50/1**

**7** *nk* **Guadiaro (USA)** 2-9-0 ........ KDarley 4 58
(BWHills) *midfield: outpcd over 1f out* **14/1**

**8** *3* **Cavalarra** 2-9-0 ........ ACulhane 11 48
(BWHills) *s.s and wnt rt s: hld up: effrt over 2f out: wknd over 1f out* **12/1**

**9** *7* **Danzatrice** 2-8-9 ........ DeanMcKeown 5 17
(CWThornton) *s.s: a bhd* **66/1**

0 **10** *5* **Cool Cristal**[64] 3438 2-8-6 ........................ PMulrennan(3) 1 —
(MWEasterby) *s.i.s: a outpcd* **66/1**
**11** *9* **Randalls Touch** 2-9-0 ........................ DMernagh 3 —
(BDLeavy) *s.i.s: rn green: a bhd* **66/1**

61.18 secs (-0.89) **Going Correction** -0.175s/f (Firm) **11** Ran SP% **110.6**
Speed ratings: **100,98,93,88,88 86,86,81,70,62 47**CSF £10.00 TOTE £4.60: £1.60, £1.10, £3.10; EX 12.30.
**Owner** J Browne **Bred** P G Jacobs, J Osborne And A Briam **Trained** Maunby, N Yorks

**FOCUS**
Decent maiden form and a fair performance from Premier Fantasy, who confirmed the promise of his initial outing.

**NOTEBOOK**
**Premier Fantasy** shaped with plenty of promise on his debut at Thirsk and clearly learned a lot from the initial experience. He was always up with the pace and having got into a duel with favourite Juantorena, pulled out extra and drew away I in final 150 yards. This was a fair performance and he deserves a crack a something a bit better now.
**Juantorena** has become disappointing - running below early season form of late - and he again found one too good. There were no excuses here but his winning turn should come one day.
**Beaune**, whose dam won over a mile four, unsurprisingly found this an inadequate test but was making some good late headway and will learn a lot from the outing.
**Aynsley** drifted right out in the betting ring and was clearly expected to be in need of the run. She was taken to the far side of the course under Philip Robinson - feels obliged to try something different - and did not shape without promise.
**Emerald Lodge** probably failed to show any improvement on his debut form and looks more the type for handicaps next season.
**Cilla's Smile** will do better once handicapped.
**Guadiaro(USA)** did not know enough at this stage of his career over this trip to do himself justice.
**Cavalarra**, like his stable companion, did not know enough at this stage to get competitive. Much better can be expected in time.

## 5263 EUROPEAN BREEDERS FUND CLASSIFIED STKS 6f
**3:05** (3:06) (D2) 3-Y-0+ **£9,074** (£2,792; £1,396; £698) **Stalls** Centre

Form RPR
4443 **1** **Solar Power (IRE)**[21] 4731 3-8-11 83 ........................ JPMurtagh 8 93+
(JRFanshawe) *wnt rt s: in tch: n.m.r 2f out: rdn to ld jst over 1f out: r.o* **4/1**[2]
502 **2** *1* **Kingscross**[7] 5075 6-8-13 75 ........................ DSweeney 5 90
(MBlanshard) *bhd: hdwy 1f out: r.o ins fnl f: nt rch wnr* **13/2**
511 **3** *nk* **Out After Dark**[13] 4952 3-8-12 81 ........................ PRobinson 2 90
(CGCox) *a.p: rdn and ev ch 1f out: nt qckn ins fnl f* **2/1**[1]
-103 **4** *1 3/4* **Flur Na H Alba**[45] 4006 5-9-1 82 ........................ (p) RWinston 10 86
(ISemple) *prom: rdn to ld briefly over 1f out: no ex wl ins fnl f* **25/1**
1600 **5** *1 1/4* **Sierra Vista**[20] 4759 4-8-7 79 ........................ LEnstone(3) 9 77
(DWBarker) *squeezed out s: hld up: hdwy whn n.m.r 2f out: sn rdn and swtchd rt: one pce ins fnl f* **14/1**
2004 **6** *1 3/4* **Caustic Wit (IRE)**[13] 4951 6-9-4 85 ........................ (p) DHolland 7 80
(MSSaunders) *chsd ldrs: rdn 2f out: wknd ins fnl f* **11/2**[3]
0000 **7** *1/2* **Pax**[35] 4291 7-8-13 80 ........................ ANicholls 1 73
(DNicholls) *stmbld s: in tch: effrt whn nt clr run over 1f out: no imp fnl f: b.b.v* **16/1**
4050 **8** *hd* **Totally Yours (IRE)**[37] 4230 3-8-13 85 ........................ FNorton 11 75
(WRMuir) *hld up: pushed along 1/2-way: no imp* **20/1**
0050 **9** *2 1/2* **Bonne De Fleur**[16] 4862 3-8-8 80 ........................ FLynch 6 62
(BSmart) *prom: led 1/2-way: rdn and hdd over 1f out: wknd fnl f: fin lame* **12/1**
11-0 **10** *13* **Little Ridge (IRE)**[94] 2549 3-8-10 82 ........................ LFletcher(3) 3 28
(HMorrison) *led to 1/2-way: sn rdn and wknd* **50/1**
U1 **11** *5* **Conjuror**[27] 4555 3-8-7 83 ........................ RJKilloran(7) 4 14
(AMBalding) *a bhd: fin lame* **14/1**

1m 13.65s (-1.24) **Going Correction** -0.175s/f (Firm)
**WFA** 3 from 4yo+ 2lb **11** Ran SP% **119.5**
Speed ratings: **101,99,99,96,95 92,92,92,88,71 64**CSF £30.16 TOTE £5.50: £1.70, £1.80, £1.50; EX 34.80.
**Owner** Deln Ltd **Bred** Deln Ltd **Trained** Newmarket, Suffolk

**FOCUS**
An ordinary time, but solid form. Solar Power was well served by the drop in trip and stayed on strongly to record her first win of the season.

**NOTEBOOK**
**Solar Power(IRE)** has been running consistently well in defeat all season and deserved to get her head in front. She settled better over this shorter trip, and there may be more to come now.
**Kingscross** has run much better the last twice - finishing second on both occasions - and is not on a bad mark. His winning turn may not be far away.
**Out After Dark** is a progressive three-year-old and ran a solid race, just being unable to cope with his elders. Back in his own age group, he should be back winning.
**Flur Na H Alba** is used to running over farther and ran well for a long way before being outspeeded in the closing stages.
**Sierra Vista** could not obtain a good early position, having been squeezed out at the start, and then failed to get a run when trying to come through. By the time she got clear the principals had flown and she is one to watch out for when there is a bit more juice in the ground. *Official explanation: jockey said filly was short of room 2f out*
**Caustic Wit(IRE)** *Official explanation: jockey said gelding was fractious in the stalls*
**Pax** did not have much luck in running but had little left in the closing stages anyhow. *Official explanation: jockey said gelding bled from nose*
**Bonne De Fleur** *Official explanation: reported lame by vet after race*
**Conjuror** *Official explanation: reported lame by vet after race*

## 5264 NATIONAL STUD NEVER SAY DIE CLUB MEDIAN AUCTION MAIDEN STKS 1m 30y
**3:35** (3:37) (E3) 2-Y-0 **£3,610** (£1,111; £555; £277) **Stalls** Low

Form RPR
34 **1** **Saadigg (IRE)**[27] 4544 2-9-0 ........................ PRobinson 1 88
(MAJarvis) *mde all: rdn over 2f out: r.o* **8/1**[2]
3 **2** *1 1/2* **Glen Ida**[14] 4922 2-9-0 ........................ RMullen 8 84
(MLWBell) *s.i.s: hld up: hdwy 4f out: rdn over 3f out: ev ch 1f out: nt qckn ins fnl f* **6/5**[1]
435 **3** *1 1/2* **Call Me Max**[12] 4967 2-9-0 ........................ KDarley 6 81
(EALDunlop) *t.k.h: a.p: rdn over 2f out: ev ch 1f out: no ex ins fnl f* **10/1**[3]
**4** *1 1/2* **Kames Park (IRE)** 2-9-0 ........................ RWinston 2 78
(ISemple) *s.s: t.k.h: rn green: bhd: styd on fnl f: nvr nr to chal* **50/1**
26 **5** *1/2* **Lithos**[6] 5114 2-9-0 ........................ SWKelly 7 76
(JAOsborne) *trckd ldrs: rdn and outpcd over 2f out: one pce after* **14/1**
50 **6** *8* **Commendable Coup (USA)**[55] 3758 2-9-0 ........................ PHanagan 3 58
(TDBarron) *a towards rr* **22/1**
00 **7** *8* **Cala Fons (IRE)**[7] 5098 2-8-9 ........................ KimTinkler 5 35
(NTinkler) *t.k.h: trckd ldrs tl hung rt and lost pl 5f out: bhd after* **100/1**
**8** *14* **Grizebeck (IRE)** 2-8-11 ........................ LFletcher(3) 10 7
(RFFisher) *s.s: hld up: pushed along over 3f out: nvr on terms* **66/1**

1m 43.46s (-2.09) **Going Correction** -0.25s/f (Firm) **8** Ran SP% **81.1**
Speed ratings: **100,98,97,95,95 87,79,65**CSF £8.68 TOTE £6.70: £1.40, £1.10, £1.30; EX 8.20.
**Owner** Sheikh Ahmed Al Maktoum **Bred** M Coogan **Trained** Newmarket, Suffolk
■ Kristinor (9/4, ref to ent stalls) & Winter Mist (100/1, uns rdr gng to post) were withdrawn. R4 applies, deduct 30p in the £.

**FOCUS**
A good ride from Philip Robinson enabled Saadigg to get off the mark in what was an average affair, though the time was decent for the type of race. The form has initially been taken at face value, but it may have been rated too high.

**NOTEBOOK**
**Saadigg(IRE)** was given a good front-running ride by Phillip Robinson to hold off the challenge of Glen Ida in the final quarter mile. This looks a big step up on the form he showed on the Polytrack when third and fourth, and it looks as if he is going to make up into a better turf performer.
**Glen Ida**, a debut third to Diktatorial in what looked a good maiden at the time, looked very one paced and could only plug on. Evidently not the quickest, he already looks in need of a mile and a quarter.
**Call Me Max** does little for the form as he is pretty exposed and more of a nursery type.
**Kames Park(IRE)** shaped with promise but will not be seen at his best until contesting handicaps at three.
**Commendable Coup(USA)** is more of a nursery type. *Official explanation: jockey said colt hung right from halfway*
**Cala Fons(IRE)** *Official explanation: jockey said filly hung right round bend*

## 5265 KINGS REGIMENT CUP H'CAP 1m 30y
**4:10** (4:12) (D2) (0-85,85) 3-Y-O+ **£7,361** (£2,265; £1,132; £566) **Stalls** Low

Form RPR
1326 **1** **Goodbye Mr Bond**[4] 5194 4-8-13 71 ........................ FNorton 5 83
(EJAlston) *hld up: rdn and hdwy over 2f out: edgd lft and led ins fnl f: r.o* **4/1**[1]
3142 **2** *1 1/2* **African Sahara (USA)**[6] 5135 5-9-10 82 ........................ (t) OUrbina 2 91+
(MissDMountain) *midfield: hdwy whn nt clr run over 1f out: sn rdn and swtchd rt: r.o ins fnl f: nt rch wnr* **11/2**[2]
4140 **3** *3/4* **Mr Jack Daniells (IRE)**[20] 4749 3-8-12 75 ........................ JPMurtagh 6 82
(WRMuir) *led to 1/2-way: sn rdn: regained ld over 1f out: hdd ins fnl f: no ex towards fin* **10/1**
256 **4** *1 1/4* **Stoic Leader (IRE)**[14] 4908 4-9-5 80 ........................ LFletcher(3) 4 84
(RFFisher) *midfield: hdwy over 3f out: rdn over 2f out: styd on ins fnl f* **20/1**
1030 **5** *3/4* **Play Master (IRE)**[41] 4122 3-8-10 73 ........................ PaulEddery 15 76
(DHaydnJones) *bhd: rdn and swtchd rt 2f out: styd on fnl f: nvr nrr* **50/1**
2214 **6** *hd* **Hills Of Gold**[11] 4988 5-9-3 78 ........................ PMulrennan(3) 13 80
(MWEasterby) *in tch: rdn over 3f out: styd on same pce fnl f* **11/1**
4331 **7** *1 1/2* **Aperitif**[22] 4679 3-9-0 77 ........................ SWKelly 11 76
(WJHaggas) *hld up: n.m.r and hmpd 6f out: rdn 2f out: kpt on fnl f: nvr trbld ldrs* **9/1**[3]
3244 **8** *hd* **Lauro**[77] 3039 4-9-2 74 ........................ RWinston 10 72
(MissJACamacho) *midfield: hdwy over 4f out: rdn 3f out: no ex ins fnl f* **10/1**
1253 **9** *3/4* **Doctorate**[8] 5055 3-9-6 83 ........................ PHanagan 8 80
(EALDunlop) *midfield: hdwy over 3f out: rdn over 2f out: wknd fnl f* **14/1**
4014 **10** *3/4* **Brief Goodbye**[53] 3797 4-9-9 81 ........................ MFenton 12 76
(JohnBerry) *trckd ldrs: rdn over 2f out: wknd fnl f* **40/1**
-001 **11** *hd* **Zweibrucken (IRE)**[22] 4684 3-9-7 84 ........................ DHolland 3 78
(SKirk) *racd keenly: midfield: rdn over 3f out: wknd over 2f out* **14/1**
2301 **12** *3 1/2* **Little Bob**[30] 4444 3-8-12 75 ........................ PRobinson 7 61
(JDBethell) *s.i.s: a bhd* **16/1**
1506 **13** *2* **Baffle**[29] 4490 3-8-10 73 ........................ KDarley 9 55
(JLDunlop) *w ldr: led 1/2-way: rdn and hdd over 1f out: sn wknd* **22/1**
643 **14** *1 3/4* **Miss Monica (IRE)**[66] 3392 3-8-6 69 ........................ WRyan 14 47
(HRACecil) *hld up: rdn over 3f out: nvr on terms* **11/1**
0600 **15** *1 1/4* **Morse (IRE)**[15] 4874 3-9-8 85 ........................ DSweeney 1 60
(JAOsborne) *trckd ldrs: rdn over 3f out: wknd over 2f out* **33/1**

1m 41.5s (-4.05) **Going Correction** -0.25s/f (Firm)
**WFA** 3 from 4yo+ 5lb **15** Ran SP% **115.9**
Speed ratings: **110,108,107,106,105 105,104,103,103,102 102,98,96,94,93**CSF £21.50 CT £205.35 TOTE £5.00: £2.10, £2.50, £4.60; EX 24.70 Trifecta £173.90 Pool: £2,082.57 - 8.50 winning units..
**Owner** Peter J Davies **Bred** Michael Ng **Trained** Longton, Lancs
■ Stewards Enquiry : J P Murtagh one-day ban: used whip with excessive force (Sep 14)

**FOCUS**
A decent time for what was a competitive heat won nicely by favourite Goodbye Mr Bond. Hold-up horses dominated.

**NOTEBOOK**
**Goodbye Mr Bond** has not run a bad race all season on turf and has gone up a total of 19lb since his winning spree started back in June. In rear early, he came through with a strong run to take it up and won going away. This represented a career best effort and although set to face another rise, the style in which he won this suggests he has not done winning yet.
**African Sahara(USA)** is another who has been running consistently well of late. This was a good effort under top-weight but he has nothing on the Handicapper.
**Mr Jack Daniells(IRE)** ran a bold race from the front and was able to leave a disappointing run at Newbury behind. He is still on a fair enough mark and it would come as no surprise to see him win again.
**Stoic Leader(IRE)** has gone up 14lb since winning back in May and has not been able to defy his higher mark of late. This was another solid effort but he does not appeal as a winner waiting to happen.
**Play Master(IRE)** bounced back from a shocking effort at Ascot in July and appreciated the short break.
**Hills Of Gold** had his chance and struggled off a 4lb higher mark than when going close latest.
**Little Bob** *Official explanation: jockey reported gelding was slow away*

## 5266 RECTANGLE GROUP H'CAP 1m 3f 200y
**4:40** (4:41) (D2) (0-85,80) 3-Y-O+ **£6,996** (£2,152; £1,076; £538) **Stalls** High

Form RPR
3111 **1** **Sendintank**[4] 5190 4-8-11 68 6ex ........................ KDarley 5 84+
(SCWilliams) *hld up: rdn and hdwy over 2f out: led over 1f out: hung lft ins fnl f: sn clr* **4/5**[1]
1050 **2** *2 1/2* **Reservoir (IRE)**[15] 4888 3-8-11 77 ........................ ACulhane 6 85
(WJHaggas) *trckd ldrs: rdn and ev ch fr 3f out: nt qckn fnl f* **10/1**
2520 **3** *1 1/2* **Genghis (IRE)**[17] 4831 5-9-6 80 ........................ LFletcher(3) 7 86
(HMorrison) *racd keenly: trckd ldrs: rdn whn chalng 2f out: one pce fnl f* **5/1**[2]
2030 **4** *hd* **Allied Victory (USA)**[5] 5144 4-9-1 72 ........................ (t) DAllan 1 77
(EJAlston) *led: rdn over 2f out: hdd over 1f out: no ex ins fnl f* **25/1**

2443 **5** *hd* **Chanteloup**[29] [4492] 3-9-0 **80** ........ JPMurtagh 4 85
(JRFanshawe) *hld up: rdn and outpcd over 2f out: swtchd rt over 1f out: kpt on fnl f: nvr able to chal* **7/1**[3]

-200 **6** *3* **Golano**[13] [4950] 4-9-8 **79** ........ DHolland 3 79
(PRWebber) *prom: rdn 4f out: wknd over 2f out* **14/1**

10-6 **7** *6* **Theatre Time (USA)**[26] [4571] 4-9-6 **77** ........ PRobinson 2 68
(IanWilliams) *s.s: a bhd* **28/1**

3150 **8** *22* **Karamea (SWI)**[14] [4915] 3-8-11 **77** ........ SWKelly 8 32
(JLDunlop) *hld up: pushed along 3f out: eased whn wl btn over 1f out* **25/1**

2m 32.08s (-3.08) **Going Correction** -0.25s/f (Firm)
**WFA** 3 from 4yo+ 9lb **8** Ran SP% **111.6**
Speed ratings: **100,98,97,97,97 95,91,76**CSF £9.08 CT £24.86 TOTE £1.70: £1.10, £2.10, £1.60; EX 9.50.
**Owner** Steve Jones And Phil McGovern **Bred** K G Powter **Trained** Newmarket, Suffolk

**FOCUS**
Another good opportunity for the highly progressive Sendintank. The time was modest for the grade, however, and the form behind him is not sure to work out.

**NOTEBOOK**
**Sendintank** was able to race from the same mark as when scoring earlier in the week. Despite finding the trip a bit on the sharp side, he won comfortably, recording his fourth win in 11 days and his eighth of the campaign. He remains highly progressive.
**Reservoir(IRE)** ran well but had no chance with the well-treated winner and second was probably the best he could hope for.
**Genghis(IRE)** bettered his recent effort at York with a keeping-on third but was never going to win. He is pretty exposed and his lack of pace will always leave him vulnerable.
**Allied Victory(USA)** ran his race from the front but had no more to offer when challenged.
**Theatre Time(USA)** *Official explanation: jockey said gelding hung left in straight*
**Karamea(SWI)** *Official explanation: jockey said filly lost her action*

## 5267 THREE SISTERS H'CAP (FOR GENTLEMAN AMATEUR RIDERS) 1m 2f 120y
**5:10** (5:11) (E3) (0-70,70) 3-Y-0+ **£3,463** (£1,065; £532; £266) **Stalls** High

Form RPR

2024 **1** **Milk And Sultana**[14] [4911] 4-10-11 **56** oh4 ........ MrEDehdashti(3) 1 61
(GAHam) *hld up: hdwy over 3f out: sn chsd ldr: led over 1f out: styd on* **7/2**[2]

0054 **2** *2 ½* **Iberus (GER)**[63] [3470] 6-11-10 **69** ........ MrRStephens(3) 7 70
(SGollings) *hld up: hdwy over 3f out: chsd ldr over 1f out: edgd lft ins fnl f: styd on* **5/2**[1]

0020 **3** *4* **Jidiya (IRE)**[12] [4971] 5-11-7 **70** ........ MrTFWoodside(7) 8 64
(SGollings) *hld up: hdwy over 3f out: rdn over 2f out: hung lft over 1f out: one pce* **13/2**

/060 **4** *nk* **King Halling**[42] [4080] 5-10-11 **56** oh1 ........ (b1) MrLNewnes(3) 4 49
(RFord) *led: rdn and hdd over 1f out: sn btn* **8/1**

1-06 **5** *7* **Boing Boing (IRE)**[47] [3682] 4-10-7 **56** oh4 ........ MrASwinswood(7) 3 38
(MissSJWilton) *s.s: hld up in rr: hdwy over 3f out: wknd over 2f out* **7/1**

0300 **6** *¾* **Smart Boy Prince (IRE)**[4] [5197] 3-10-1 **58** ........ MrRCMorris(7) 5 38
(MJAttwater) *chsd ldrs tl rdn and wknd over 1f out* **20/1**

-600 **7** *6* **Chapter House (USA)**[13] [4698] 5-11-9 **65** ........ MrTGreenall 6 35
(MWEasterby) *a bhd* **6/1**[3]

0000 **8** *26* **Luxor**[18] [4808] 7-11-0 **56** oh11 ........ MrSWalker 2 —
(MrsGSRees) *chsd ldr tl over 3f out: sn wknd* **12/1**

2m 17.49s (-0.24) **Going Correction** -0.25s/f (Firm)
**WFA** 3 from 4yo+ 8lb **8** Ran SP% **114.5**
Speed ratings: **90,88,85,85,79 79,75,56**CSF £12.72 CT £52.95 TOTE £3.40: £1.10, £1.60, £2.50; EX 6.90 Place 6 £3.12, Place 5 £2.34.
**Owner** D M Drury **Bred** D Malcolm Drury **Trained** Rooks Bridge, Somerset

**FOCUS**
They went a decent clip that suited the winner, who was dropping in trip. The form looks weak, however.

**NOTEBOOK**
**Milk And Sultana**, dropping in distance, was done no harm at all by the good gallop set and came through strongly in the final furlong to win going away. This was not a strong race however and she will need to improve to follow up.
**Iberus(GER)** was well served by this trip and kept plugging on without proving a match for the winner.
**Jidiya(IRE)** shaped a little better but still needs to find some improvement from somewhere before he is winning.
**King Halling** did a bit too much too soon in the first-time blinkers and will settle better in them second time round.
T/Jkpt: £7,100 to a £1 stake. Pool: £10,000. 1.00 winning tickets. T/Plt: £3.80 to a £1 stake. Pool: £49,954.75. 9,563.35 winning tickets. T/Qpdt: £2.30 to a £1 stake. Pool: £2,583.50. 823.30 winning tickets. DO

# 4844 KEMPTON (R-H)
### Friday, September 3
**OFFICIAL GOING: Good (good to firm in places)**

## 5268 RUKBA SENATE CONSULTING EBF MAIDEN STKS (DIV I) 1m (J)
**1:35** (1:40) (D3) 2-Y-0 **£5,161** (£1,588; £794; £397) **Stalls** High

Form RPR

432 **1** **Kharish (IRE)**[22] [4689] 2-9-0 **83** ........ EAhern 3 86
(JNoseda) *swtg: prom: trckd ldr 1/2-way: chal 2f out: rdn and narrow ld 1f out: asserted nr fin* **9/4**[1]

3 **2** *¾* **Foxhaven**[22] [4681] 2-9-0 ........ MartinDwyer 1 84
(PRChamings) *led: rdn and hrd pressed 2f out: hdd narrowly 1f out: kpt on wl tl no ex nr fin* **9/1**

3 **3** *½* **Ameeq (USA)**[20] [4743] 2-9-0 ........ RHills 9 83
(MPTregoning) *lw: trckd ldr to 1/2-way: shkn up and unable qck 2f out: styd on wl again ins fnl f* **11/4**[2]

**4** *2* **Luis Melendez (USA)** 2-9-0 ........ RLMoore 7 79+
(PFICole) *w'like: scope: bit bkwd: str: chsd ldrs: shkn up and rn green 2f out: kpt on same pce fr over 1f out* **25/1**

4 **5** *1 ¾* **Bertrose**[20] [4747] 2-9-0 ........ SSanders 12 75
(JLDunlop) *lw: reluctant to enter stalls: t.k.h: hld up bhd ldrs: outpcd 2f out: kpt on ins fnl f* **9/1**

**6** *2 ½* **Esquire** 2-9-0 ........ LDettori 13 69+
(SaeedBinSuroor) *leggy: scope: tall: rangy: prom: cl up over 1f out: rdn and edgd lft: wknd* **6/1**[3]

4 **7** *2* **My Portfolio (IRE)**[14] [4913] 2-9-0 ........ SDrowne 6 64
(RCharlton) *lw: racd midfield: pushed along and nt on terms w ldrs fnl 3f* **16/1**

0 **8** *1* **Our Kes (IRE)**[91] [2655] 2-8-9 ........ DaneO'Neill 14 57
(PHowling) *s.i.s: t.k.h: hld up in rr: lost tch w ldrs fr 1/2-way* **100/1**

**9** *3 ½* **Indian Pipe Dream (IRE)** 2-9-0 ........ JFortune 10 54
(JHMGosden) *w'like: bit bkwd: hld up: a wl in rr: no ch fr over 2f out* **25/1**

30 **10** *nk* **Uncle Bulgaria (IRE)**[12] [4967] 2-9-0 ........ MHills 5 53
(GCBravery) *a towards rr: no ch fr over 2f out* **50/1**

00 **11** *5* **Picot De Say**[18] [4797] 2-8-11 ........ JFMcDonald(3) 2 42
(JohnBerry) *a wl in rr: wknd 2f out* **50/1**

0 **12** *¾* **Night Guest (IRE)**[14] [4922] 2-9-0 ........ RHughes 8 40
(RHannon) *lw: racd midfield: pushed along and lost tch w ldrs 3f out: sn wknd* **33/1**

**13** *14* **Ampelio (IRE)** 2-9-0 ........ KFallon 11 8
(SirMichaelStoute) *w'like: scope: bit bkwd: towards rr: wknd 3f out: eased: t.o* **8/1**

1m 41.21s (1.59) **Going Correction** -0.025s/f (Good) 2y crse rec **13** Ran SP% **124.3**
Speed ratings: **91,90,89,87,86 83,81,80,77,76 71,70,56**CSF £23.45 TOTE £4.00: £1.10, £3.10, £1.20; EX 29.70.
**Owner** Mrs Susan Roy **Bred** Irish National Stud **Trained** Newmarket, Suffolk

**FOCUS**
A fair maiden, but very few got into it and the front three were up with the pace throughout. The pace was modest and the winning time was moderate for the class, 0.82 seconds slower than the second division.

**NOTEBOOK**
**Kharish(IRE)** maintained his sequence of improving his finishing position by one with each start, but had to fight very hard to get the better of the dogged runner-up. Nurseries may be his best option now, whilst his style of racing suggests he will get further.
**Foxhaven ◆**, up a furlong from his debut, did very well to get across and bag the rail in front from his outside draw but set only a modest pace. Showing plenty of courage when the challengers arrived, he was only just touched off in the end and it should not be long before he gets off the mark.
**Ameeq(USA)**, should have appreciated this extra furlong, but the modest pace did him few favours as he was staying on again after getting outpaced. A proper gallop or a longer trip is what he needs.
**Luis Melendez(USA)**, out of a winning half-sister to French 1,000 Guineas winner Rose Gypsy, looked to need the experience and showed a rather exaggerated action, but he also showed plenty of promise for the future.
**Bertrose** was another not at all suited by the way the race was run and he was never closer than at the finish. He will show what he is made of when faced with a proper test of stamina.
**Esquire**, out of a champion juvenile filly in Argentina, had every chance but did not get home. He got tired and was eased, so is entitled to improve, but he does not look one of the stable's stars.

## 5269 RUKBA SENATE CONSULTING EBF MAIDEN STKS (DIV II) 1m (J)
**2:10** (2:12) (D3) 2-Y-0 **£5,161** (£1,588; £794; £397) **Stalls** High

Form RPR

5 **1** **Humourous (IRE)**[26] [4567] 2-9-0 ........ (t) LDettori 1 86
(SaeedBinSuroor) *lw: mde virtually all: rdn and hrd pressed fnl f: hld on wl* **5/2**[1]

**2** *shd* **Forward Move (IRE)** 2-9-0 ........ RHughes 9 86
(RHannon) *lengthy: t.k.h: trckd ldrs: shkn up to chse wnr over 1f out: upsides nr fin: jst hld* **20/1**

0 **3** *1 ¾* **Front Stage (IRE)**[20] [4743] 2-9-0 ........ KFallon 8 82
(SirMichaelStoute) *lw: trckd ldrs: rdn to chse wnr over 2f out to over 1f out: one pce fnl f* **9/1**

**4** *4* **Night Hour (IRE)** 2-9-0 ........ MartinDwyer 6 73+
(MPTregoning) *w'like: lw: settled towards rr: outpcd 1/2-way: nudged along 2f out: r.o fnl f: bttr for experience* **6/1**[2]

0 **5** *¾* **Art Elegant**[35] [4290] 2-9-0 ........ MHills 14 71
(BWHills) *hld up bhd ldng gp: prog on inner over 2f out: chsd ldng trio jst over 1f out: fdd* **14/1**

40 **6** *4* **Off Colour**[44] [4030] 2-9-0 ........ SSanders 5 62
(MrsAJPerrett) *dwlt: racd wd: sn chsd ldrs: rdn 2f out: wknd over 1f out* **6/1**[2]

655 **7** *1 ¼* **Silverleaf**[14] [4922] 2-8-11 ........ SHitchcott(3) 7 59
(MRChannon) *chsd wnr to over 2f out: wknd rapidly over 1f out* **10/1**

06 **8** *1* **Penalty Kick (IRE)**[14] [4922] 2-9-0 ........ (b1) NCallan 10 56
(NACallaghan) *lw: plld hrd: prom: lost pl 3f out: wknd 2f out* **10/1**

0 **9** *6* **Byron Bay**[20] [4739] 2-8-11 ........ JFMcDonald(3) 2 43
(JJBridger) *chsd ldrs: lost pl and rdn 3f out: sn struggling* **100/1**

0 **10** *6* **Loitokitok**[27] [4544] 2-9-0 ........ DaneO'Neill 3 29
(PDCundell) *dwlt: a in rr: wl bhd fnl 3f* **100/1**

6 **11** *¾* **Figaro's Quest (IRE)**[22] [4689] 2-9-0 ........ RLMoore 4 27
(PFICole) *pushed along in rr after 2f: wl bhd fnl 3f* **8/1**[3]

**12** *hd* **Silver Song** 2-9-0 ........ SDrowne 12 27
(JLDunlop) *w'like: bit bkwd: dwlt: a in rr: wl bhd fnl 3f* **20/1**

0 **13** *nk* **Eastwell Magic**[44] [4022] 2-8-9 ........ JBramhill 13 21
(JGGiven) *a wl in rr: wl bhd fnl 3f* **66/1**

**14** *8* **Brego (IRE)** 2-9-0 ........ JFortune 11 8
(JHMGosden) *str: bkwd: green to post: racd midfield early: wknd 1/2-way: t.o* **25/1**

1m 40.39s (0.77) **Going Correction** -0.025s/f (Good) 2y crse rec **14** Ran SP% **119.9**
Speed ratings: **95,94,93,89,88 84,83,82,76,70 69,69,68,60**CSF £62.81 TOTE £2.80: £1.30, £5.30, £3.20; EX 26.90.
**Owner** Godolphin **Bred** Gainsborough Stud Management Ltd **Trained** Newmarket, Suffolk

**FOCUS**
Like the first division, only an ordinary pace and it was crucial to be up with the pace. The winning time was 0.82 seconds faster than the first division, though still only ordinary for the grade. The form has provisionally been rated marginally higher.

**NOTEBOOK**
**Humourous(IRE)** appreciated the extra furlong, but the real key to this victory was being able to get across from the outside box in front and then being gifted a soft lead. As a result, he was able to keep something in reserve for the latter stages, but it was a close run thing and he would be hard pressed to confirm the form with the placed horses if they were to meet again.
**Forward Move(IRE) ◆**, a half-brother to Kindness and Turnstile out of a winner on Fibresand, showed plenty of promise on this debut and looked as though he had timed his challenge perfectly, but he could not quite get past the winner. It has to be said that his rider was not particularly busy in the last ten yards and whether that made the difference between victory and defeat or not, it did not make for great viewing. He should find compensation before long.
**Front Stage(IRE)** improved a good deal from his debut and had every chance down the home straight, but he could not quite get on terms with the front pair. A stronger pace or a longer trip would probably help him.
**Night Hour(IRE) ◆**, a half-brother to Unafraid, was the eye-catcher of the contest, making good late progress in a race dominated by those than raced close to the pace. His next outing is awaited with great interest.
**Art Elegant** performed a bit better than on his debut, but did not seem to get home even in a moderately run contest like this.
**Off Colour** does not seem to be progressing, but he did see plenty of daylight and may do better in nurseries.
**Penalty Kick(IRE)**, blinkered first time, paid the price for taking too strong a hold early in a moderately run race.

## 5270 RUKBA CANTOR SPORT EBF MAIDEN FILLIES' STKS (DIV I) 6f

2:40 (2:43) (D3) 2-Y-O £5,239 (£1,612; £806; £403) Stalls Low

| Form | | | | | RPR |
|---|---|---|---|---|---|
| 2 | 1 | | **Halle Bop**[21] 4714 2-8-11 ........ LDettori 4 | 86 |
| | | | (SaeedBinSuroor) *racd against nr side rail: mde all: gng easily 2f out: shkn up fnl f: in command after* **6/4**[1] | |
| | 2 | 1 1/4 | **Holly Springs** 2-8-11 ........ JFortune 7 | 82 |
| | | | (JHMGosden) *w'like: lengthy: trckd wnr for 2f: styd cl up: shkn up to go 2nd again jst over 1f out: styd on: a readily hld* **33/1** | |
| 0 | 3 | 3/4 | **Desert Imp**[21] 4714 2-8-11 ........ MHills 10 | 80 |
| | | | (BWHills) *racd midfield: prog over 2f out: shkn up to chse ldng pair ins fnl f: kpt on wl* **6/1**[3] | |
| | 4 | 2 | **Biriyani (IRE)** 2-8-11 ........ EAhern 6 | 74 |
| | | | (PWHarris) *w'like: trckd ldrs: pushed along and unable qck 2f out: styd on same pce fnl f* **20/1** | |
| 4 | 5 | 1 3/4 | **Neverletme Go (IRE)**[35] 4298 2-8-11 ........ SDrowne 12 | 69 |
| | | | (GWragg) *prom: chsd wnr after 2f to jst over 1f out: wknd* **5/2**[2] | |
| | 6 | 1 1/2 | **Verbier (USA)** 2-8-11 ........ NCallan 9 | 64 |
| | | | (NACallaghan) *unf: lengthy: dwlt: racd midfield: pushed along 1/2-way: one pce and no ch w ldrs* **33/1** | |
| 54 | 7 | nk | **Ellens Princess (IRE)**[21] 4705 2-8-11 ........ RLMoore 11 | 63 |
| | | | (RHannon) *trckd ldrs: rdn and effrt on outer over 2f out: wknd over 1f out* **14/1** | |
| | 8 | hd | **Diamond Katie (IRE)** 2-8-11 ........ RHughes 15 | 63 |
| | | | (RGuest) *w'like: racd on wd outside in midfield: nudged along and no prog fnl 2f* **50/1** | |
| 0 | 9 | 3/4 | **Ruby Murray**[25] 4611 2-8-11 ........ KMcEvoy 3 | 61 |
| | | | (BJMeehan) *lw: towards rr: pushed along and no prog over 2f out* **50/1** | |
| 40 | 10 | 2 1/2 | **Veritable**[32] 4399 2-8-11 ........ ADaly 1 | 53 |
| | | | (SKirk) *s.s: hld up in rr: taken to outer by 1/2-way: nudged along and no prog* **50/1** | |
| 44 | 11 | 3/4 | **Tashyra (IRE)**[22] 4670 2-8-11 ........ DaneO'Neill 13 | 51 |
| | | | (AMBalding) *pressed ldrs tl wknd 2f out* **33/1** | |
| 0 | 12 | 1 | **Lady Pilot**[43] 4060 2-8-11 ........ SSanders 14 | 48 |
| | | | (CEBrittain) *lw: racd on outer: prom tl wknd wl over 1f out* **8/1** | |
| 50 | 13 | 5 | **Blazing View (USA)**[32] 4399 2-8-11 ........ KFallon 2 | 33 |
| | | | (EALDunlop) *a in rr: detached in last pair fr 1/2-way* **25/1** | |
| 00 | 14 | 1 1/2 | **Night Club Queen (IRE)**[21] 4712 2-8-11 ........ RHills 5 | 28 |
| | | | (JWHills) *dwlt: towards rr: rdn and no rspnse over 2f out* **66/1** | |
| | 15 | 4 | **Danaatt (USA)** 2-8-11 ........ MartinDwyer 8 | 16 |
| | | | (MPTregoning) *leggy: bit bkwd: a in rr: last and struggling bdly 1/2-way* **33/1** | |

1m 11.76s (-1.31) **Going Correction** -0.275s/f (Firm) **15** Ran SP% **128.4**
Speed ratings: **97,95,94,91,89 87,86,86,85,82 81,80,73,71,66**CSF £72.10 TOTE £2.30: £1.10, £8.90, £2.50; EX 63.30.
**Owner** Godolphin **Bred** Normandie Stud Ltd **Trained** Newmarket, Suffolk

**FOCUS**
The stalls were against the stands' rail and the whole field stayed on that side. The time was fair for the type of race, 0.13 seconds faster than the second division, and there were some notable performances quite apart from the winner, who can rate higher than this.

**NOTEBOOK**
**Halle Bop** had the form to win this and used her experience to the full, bagging the nearside rail and finding plenty to hold off her pursuers. She should get further and there may be better to come.
**Holly Springs ◆**, a 120,000gns yearling out of a dual winner over the minimum trip, showed plenty of promise on this debut and was coming home in good style. She should not be hard to place, but as there is plenty of speed in her pedigree she may not get much further than this.
**Desert Imp**, an expensive failure on her debut, again started a little tardily but did not lose that much ground. She was staying on nicely towards the end and should win her maiden.
**Biriyani(IRE) ◆**, a 180,000euros half-sister to Mister Monet and Tarascon, was never far away against the stands' rail and made a very promising debut. It will be a big surprise if she does not make her mark with this experience under her belt.
**Neverletme Go(IRE)**, as on her debut, failed to justify her place in the market after holding every chance. She might do better back at five furlongs and is obviously well regarded.
**Verbier(USA)**, a half-sister to Sanbonah out of the useful Oh Nellie, was far from disgraced and should find an opportunity.
**Ellens Princess(IRE)** again showed some signs of ability and it will be interesting to see what nursery mark she gets.
**Diamond Katie(IRE) ◆**, a half-sister to Beryl, raced wide of the field. She travelled very well and was by no means knocked about in the closing stages. She is bred to appreciate further and is very much one to keep an eye on.
**Veritable** was drawn next to the rail, but she hung to her right after exiting the stalls and found herself at the back of the field. She was not unduly knocked about during the race and was subsequently found to be lame in her left fore. *Official explanation: jockey said, regarding the running and riding, his orders were to drop in and switch off filly as she had run too free last time, adding that filly had bolted to post and hung right-handed in the closing stages; trainer confirmed orders and said filly had been unsuited by making the running last time out; vet said filly finished lame on her left fore*
**Lady Pilot** probably saw too much daylight from her wide draw.

## 5271 RUKBA CANTOR SPORT EBF MAIDEN FILLIES' STKS (DIV II) 6f

3:15 (3:17) (D3) 2-Y-O £5,239 (£1,612; £806; £403) Stalls Low

| Form | | | | | RPR |
|---|---|---|---|---|---|
| 0 | 1 | | **Penkenna Princess (IRE)**[20] 4739 2-8-11 ........ SSanders 3 | 83 |
| | | | (RMBeckett) *racd against nr side rail: pressed ldr: rdn to ld narrowly over 1f out: styd on u.p* **16/1** | |
| 2 | 2 | 1/2 | **Code Orange**[83] 2876 2-8-11 ........ JFortune 10 | 82 |
| | | | (JHMGosden) *lw: mde most: rdn and hdd narrowly over 1f out: pressed wnr fnl f: a hld* **4/6**[1] | |
| | 3 | 3/4 | **Sheboygan (IRE)** 2-8-11 ........ JBramhill 4 | 79+ |
| | | | (JGGiven) *w'like: leggy: in tch: chsd ldng pair over 2f out: drvn and styd on fnl f: nvr quite able to chal* **25/1** | |
| 4 | 4 | 2 1/2 | **Ten-Cents**[6] 5131 2-8-11 ........ IMongan 1 | 72 |
| | | | (CACyzer) *settled in rr: prog over 2f out: rdn and styd on fnl f: nrst fin* **33/1** | |
| 55 | 5 | 5 | **Xeeran**[81] 2940 2-8-11 ........ NCallan 2 | 57 |
| | | | (MAJarvis) *stmbld s: chsd ldrs: rdn 1/2-way: wknd over 1f out* **10/1**[3] | |
| | 6 | 1/2 | **Loyal Love (USA)** 2-8-11 ........ LDettori 8 | 55 |
| | | | (SaeedBinSuroor) *lengthy: bit bkwd: trckd ldrs: shkn up 2f out: btn over 1f out: fdd* **4/1**[2] | |
| 00 | 7 | hd | **Follow My Lead**[73] 3176 2-8-11 ........ MHills 11 | 55 |
| | | | (BWHills) *wl in rr: struggling and bhd 1/2-way: kpt on fr over 1f out* **33/1** | |
| | 8 | nk | **Cup Of Love (USA)** 2-8-11 ........ MartinDwyer 6 | 54 |
| | | | (RGuest) *w'like: leggy: in tch: pushed along 2f out: wknd over 1f out* **50/1** | |
| 0 | 9 | 1/2 | **Bailey Gate**[21] 4714 2-8-11 ........ RHughes 12 | 52 |
| | | | (RHannon) *racd on outer: in tch: wknd wl over 1f out: eased* **10/1**[3] | |
| | 10 | 3/4 | **Daisys Girl** 2-8-11 ........ RHills 14 | 50 |
| | | | (BHanbury) *unf: bit bkwd: racd on outer: wl in tch tl wknd wl over 1f out* **25/1** | |
| 000 | 11 | 1 | **Never Away**[20] 4753 2-8-11 ........ EAhern 5 | 47 |
| | | | (NACallaghan) *racd in rr: struggling fr 1/2-way* **50/1** | |
| | 12 | 5 | **Music Teacher** 2-8-11 ........ SDrowne 13 | 32 |
| | | | (HMorrison) *w'like: bit bkwd: prom tl wknd rapidly 2f out* **14/1** | |
| | 13 | 13 | **Aleyah** 2-8-11 ........ RLMoore 9 | — |
| | | | (CFWall) *str: bkwd: s.s: a bhd: t.o 1/2-way* **50/1** | |

1m 11.89s (-1.18) **Going Correction** -0.275s/f (Firm) **13** Ran SP% **130.2**
Speed ratings: **96,95,94,91,84 83,83,83,82,81 80,73,56**CSF £28.41 TOTE £28.60: £7.10, £1.02, £9.00; EX 61.60.
**Owner** Mrs H M Chamberlain **Bred** Mill House Stud **Trained** Lambourn, Berks

**FOCUS**
As in the first division, the whole field stayed on the stands' side and the draw played its part, with low numbers favoured. The winning time was 0.13 seconds slower than the first division, but it was still respectable for the grade and the form looks fair.

**NOTEBOOK**
**Penkenna Princess(IRE)** had shown distinct signs of promise on her debut and confirmed it, despite being allowed to go off at a big price. Bagging the stands' rail from her low draw, she raced nip and tuck with the favourite the whole way and just managed to prevail after a prolonged battle. There is a mixture of speed and stamina in her pedigree and she should continue to progress.
**Code Orange** did not appear to do much wrong under a positive ride, despite being a beaten odds-on favourite. As things turned out, she may not have been helped by the draw, but equally she may simply have run into one that was too good for her on the day. She will probably benefit from an extra furlong.
**Sheboygan(IRE) ◆**, a 34,000gns yearling out of a winner over seven furlongs, ran a debut full of promise and finished right on the heels of the front pair. Normal improvement should soon see her off the mark.
**Ten-Cents** ran with credit from her rails draw, pulling well clear of the rest of the field, and would probably benefit from a bit further.
**Xeeran**, returning from a three-month break, has spoiled her chances by pulling hard in the past, but the extra furlong looked to be a bigger problem for her this time.
**Loyal Love(USA)**, a half-sister to a winner in the US out of the French 1,000 Guineas winner Always Loyal, offered only limited promise on this debut, but her next outing should tell us more.
**Bailey Gate** *Official explanation: jockey said filly suffered interference in running*

## 5272 RUKBA PAFS EBF FILLIES' CONDITIONS STKS 7f (J)

3:45 (3:45) (C2) 2-Y-O £7,308 (£2,772; £1,386; £630) Stalls High

| Form | | | | | RPR |
|---|---|---|---|---|---|
| 1 | 1 | | **Joint Aspiration**[22] 4682 2-8-5 ........ SHitchcott(3) 2 | 89 |
| | | | (MRChannon) *lw: trckd ldrs: rdn over 2f out: effrt to ld jst over 1f out: r.o wl* **3/1**[2] | |
| | 2 | 1 1/2 | **Tahrir (IRE)** 2-8-8 ........ RHills 7 | 85 |
| | | | (BWHills) *unf: dwlt: sn trckd ldrs: eased out 2f out: chal and upsides jst over 1f out: shkn up and nt pce of wnr* **20/1** | |
| 2 | 3 | 1 1/2 | **Titian Time (USA)**[20] 4747 2-8-8 ........ JFortune 5 | 81 |
| | | | (JHMGosden) *lw: pressed ldr: shkn up to ld 2f out: hdd jst over 1f out: outpcd* **11/8**[1] | |
| | 4 | 3 1/2 | **Light Of Dubai (USA)** 2-8-8 ........ LDettori 3 | 81+ |
| | | | (SaeedBinSuroor) *w'like: str: led to 2f out: wknd and eased fnl f* **7/2**[3] | |
| 6 | 5 | shd | **Marchetta**[21] 4706 2-8-8 ........ RLMoore 6 | 72 |
| | | | (PWHarris) *in tch in rr: outpcd wl over 1f out: n.d after* **33/1** | |
| | 6 | 3/4 | **Insinuation (IRE)** 2-8-8 ........ KFallon 4 | 70 |
| | | | (SirMichaelStoute) *w'like: scope: bit bkwd: dwlt: racd last: pushed along and effrt to chse ldrs 2f out: sn outpcd* **15/2** | |
| | 7 | 10 | **Grand Girl** 2-8-8 ........ ADaly 1 | 44 |
| | | | (BWDuke) *leggy: tall: s.i.s: in tch to 1/2-way: wl bhd fnl 2f* **100/1** | |

1m 26.92s (-0.35) **Going Correction** -0.025s/f (Good) **7** Ran SP% **109.8**
Speed ratings: **101,99,97,93,93 92,81**CSF £49.01 TOTE £3.50: £2.00, £4.90; EX 63.20.
**Owner** Ridgeway Downs Racing **Bred** Messinger Stud Ltd **Trained** West Ilsley, Berks

**FOCUS**
A decent winning time for the type of race and the form should work out.

**NOTEBOOK**
**Joint Aspiration** managed to maintain her unbeaten record, though that seemed unlikely when she came off the bridle before many of those around her. However, the further they went the better she was going and she was well on top at the line. The step up in trip for either the Fillies' Mile or Prix Marcel Boussac will not be a problem, but her form so far is nowhere near that level.
**Tahrir(IRE) ◆**, a 350,000gns sister to Green Channel and half-sister to Mister Sacha, moved up to hold every chance approaching the last furlong but found the more-experienced winner too strong. This was a promising debut and it should not take her long to go one better.
**Titian Time(USA)** appeared to get the run of the race, but did not find very much in front after getting the better of the long-time leader and was made to look one-paced by the front pair in the closing stages. She is worth another chance.
**Light Of Dubai(USA)**, a $1,600,000 yearling out of a high-class performer in the US, was allowed to dictate the pace, but folded rather tamely once challenged and was eased. She shaped as if she needed this and is probably capable of better.
**Marchetta**, taking on much better company this time, was not disgraced.
**Insinuation(IRE)**, a 260,000gns yearling related to several useful performers in the US on the dam's side, look badly in need of the experience and is surely capable of much better. *Official explanation: jockey said filly was slow away*

## 5273 RUKBA UBS LAING AND CRUICKSHANK H'CAP 1m 4f

4:20 (4:20) (D2) (0-85,85) 3-Y-O+ £10,249 (£3,887; £1,943; £883) Stalls High

| Form | | | | | RPR |
|---|---|---|---|---|---|
| -106 | 1 | | **Ocean Avenue (IRE)**[30] 4441 5-9-6 **82** ........ LDettori 7 | 91 |
| | | | (CAHorgan) *mde all: drew clr over 2f out: rdn over 1f out: unchal* **4/1**[2] | |
| 2314 | 2 | 2 | **Blaze Of Colour**[31] 4416 3-8-6 **77** ........ (v) KFallon 1 | 83 |
| | | | (SirMichaelStoute) *hld up in rr: prog over 4f out: drvn to chse wnr wl over 1f out: no imp* **7/2**[1] | |
| 6020 | 3 | 1 | **Dovedon Hero**[27] 4550 4-8-9 **71** oh1 ........ (b) MHills 5 | 75 |
| | | | (PJMcbride) *hld up in rr: rdn over 2f out: hanging and reluctant prog over 1f out: kpt on to take 3rd nr fin* **8/1** | |
| 0131 | 4 | nk | **Mr Tambourine Man (IRE)**[40] 4177 3-8-13 **84** ........ JFortune 6 | 88 |
| | | | (PFICole) *hld up in rr: rdn and prog over 2f out: one pce fnl f* **8/1** | |
| 6-32 | 5 | 3/4 | **Albavilla**[26] 4572 4-8-13 **75** ........ IMongan 10 | 78 |
| | | | (PWHarris) *chsd wnr for 3f: styd prom: disp 2nd again 2f out: fdd fnl f* **10/1** | |
| 21- | 6 | 4 | **Regal Setting (IRE)**[349] 5087 3-8-6 **77** ........ SSanders 2 | 73 |
| | | | (SirMarkPrescott) *settled in rr: reminder 7f out: hrd rdn and no prog 3f out* **6/1** | |
| 2055 | 7 | 1 3/4 | **Trueno (IRE)**[20] 4754 5-9-6 **82** ........ SDrowne 4 | 75 |
| | | | (LMCumani) *prom: chsd wnr over 6f out to wl over 1f out: wknd* **12/1** | |
| 1163 | 8 | hd | **Desert Island Disc**[4] 5182 7-8-10 **75** ........ JFMcDonald(3) 8 | 68 |
| | | | (JJBridger) *in tch: rdn and wknd wl over 2f out* **11/2**[3] | |

2030 **9** *17* **Leighton (IRE)**[4] 5203 4-8-12 **74**.......................................... LisaJones 3 40
(RMStronge) *t.k.h: chsd wnr after 3f to over 6f out: wknd over 3f out : t.o*
**25/1**

2m 31.67s (-3.33) **Going Correction** -0.075s/f (Good)
**WFA** 3 from 4yo+ 9lb **9** Ran SP% **114.7**
Speed ratings: **108,106,106,105,105 102,101,101,90**CSF £18.29 CT £105.64 TOTE £5.20: £2.10, £1.80, £2.60; EX 19.50.
**Owner** Mrs Wendy Gillings **Bred** Steve Starkey **Trained** Ogbourne Maisey, Wilts

**FOCUS**
A fair handicap run at a solid pace, but not many got into it.

**NOTEBOOK**
**Ocean Avenue(IRE)**, back over probably his best trip, set the pace as usual and was not hard pressed to do so. That enabled him to kick off the final bend and his rivals were never able to make up the leeway. He loves it here, especially when he can get a soft lead, and this was a decent effort off a 6lb higher mark than he has ever won off before.
**Blaze Of Colour** ran with credit off a 7lb higher mark than for her only win, but she was never going to get to the winner.
**Dovedon Hero**, who is not proving easy to win with, stayed on from the rear and probably finds a sharp 12 furlongs like this an insufficient test of stamina for him now.
**Mr Tambourine Man(IRE)**, trying this trip for the first time, threatened to get into it after turning for home but was making little impression in the closing stages and did not convince that he stayed.
**Albavilla** appeared to hold every chance and there seemed to be no excuses. She remains a maiden.
**Regal Setting(IRE)**, racing on turf for the first time and stepping up half a mile in trip, never got into the race. He was making his reappearance following a year off, but that is not normally a problem with representatives from the yard.

## 5274 RUKBA MORGAN STANLEY H'CAP — 2m
**4:50** (4:51) (E3) (0-70,72) 3-Y-O+ **£3,507** (£1,079; £539; £269) **Stalls** High

Form RPR
4032 **1** **Typhoon Tilly**[7] 5073 7-9-9 **68**.......................................... SDrowne 11 78
(CREgerton) *hld up in midfield: stdy prog over 2f out: chsd ldr over 1f out : rdn to ld jst ins fnl f: r.o wl* **6/1**[2]

2121 **2** *1 3/4* **Belle Rouge**[7] 5073 6-9-13 **72** 6ex.......................................... LDettori 8 80
(CAHorgan) *prom: effrt to ld wl over 1f out: hdd and one pce jst ins fnl f* **5/1**[1]

2411 **3** *hd* **Crocolat**[11] 4998 3-8-1 **62** 6ex.......................................... NMackay(3) 3 70
(MrsStefLiddiard) *settled wl in rr: effrt on outer over 2f out: r.o strly fnl f: too much to do* **6/1**[2]

3133 **4** *1* **Treason Trial**[9] 5037 3-7-13 **57**.......................................... LisaJones 1 64
(MrsStefLiddiard) *t.k.h: hld up in midfield: prog over 2f out: rdn and nt qckn over 1f out: one pce after* **25/1**

-062 **5** *1/2* **Majestic Vision**[31] 4424 3-8-9 **67**.......................................... RLMoore 13 73
(PWHarris) *trckd ldr: rdn over 2f out: fdd over 1f out* **14/1**

5033 **6** *3/4* **Macaroni Gold (IRE)**[111] 2126 4-8-13 **58**.......................................... SSanders 17 63
(WJarvis) *racd towards rr: rdn and effrt over 2f out: kpt on fr over 1f out: nvr rchd ldrs* **16/1**

2026 **7** *1* **Riyadh**[10] 5027 6-9-9 **68**.......................................... RFfrench 4 72
(MJohnston) *trckd ldrs: rdn and effrt over 2f out: nt qckn over 1f out: one pce after* **11/1**

0420 **8** *shd* **San Hernando**[23] 4647 4-9-9 **68**.......................................... DaneO'Neill 15 72
(DRCElsworth) *settled wl in rr: n.m.r on inner 3f out: nt clr run 2f out: eased out and r.o fnl f: no ch* **7/1**[3]

0535 **9** *4* **Beechy Bank (IRE)**[42] 4075 6-9-4 **63**.......................................... NPollard 14 62
(MrsMaryHambro) *led: rdn over 2f out: hdd wl over 1f out: wknd* **20/1**

0530 **10** *1/2* **Dance Light (IRE)**[37] 4226 5-8-13 **58**.......................................... EAhern 16 57
(TTClement) *b: trckd ldrs: rdn over 2f out: wknd over 1f out* **25/1**

4001 **11** *1* **Papeete (GER)**[10] 5019 3-7-11 **58** 6ex.......................................... JFMcDonald(3) 18 55
(MissBSanders) *settled bhd ldrs on inner: shkn up over 2f out: trapped on rail and hmpd over 1f out: no ch after* **16/1**

3065 **12** *1 3/4* **Red Scorpion (USA)**[27] 4550 5-9-4 **63**.......................................... KFallon 10 58
(WMBrisbourne) *racd wd: hld up in rr: rdn over 2f out: no prog* **8/1**

4660 **13** *2 1/2* **Moon Emperor**[51] 3851 7-9-11 **70**.......................................... KMcEvoy 5 62
(JRJenkins) *hld up in last pair: rdn 3f out: no prog* **20/1**

3554 **14** *1 1/2* **Rome (IRE)**[44] 4033 5-9-5 **64**.......................................... RHughes 9 54
(GPEnright) *sn lost pl and in rr: rdn and one pce 3f out: wknd over 1f out* **33/1**

0032 **15** *nk* **Simonovski (USA)**[42] 4082 3-8-2 **63** ow3.......................................... RMiles(3) 2 53
(SCBurrough) *t.k.h: wnt prom 10f out: wknd over 2f out* **33/1**

6100 **16** *10* **The Varlet**[7] 5073 4-9-10 **69**..........................................(t) MartinDwyer 6 47
(BICase) *reluctant to s: a last: wknd over 2f out* **66/1**

3m 29.41s (-0.95) **Going Correction** -0.075s/f (Good)
**WFA** 3 from 4yo+ 13lb **16** Ran SP% **120.2**
Speed ratings: **99,98,98,97,97 96,96,96,94,94 93,92,91,90,90 85**CSF £32.16 CT £192.21 TOTE £6.40: £2.00, £1.70, £2.20, £4.70; EX 24.50.
**Owner** Mrs Evelyn Hankinson **Bred** Blackdown Stud **Trained** Chaddleworth, Berks

**FOCUS**
A competitive staying handicap, but an ordinary pace and a modest winning time for the class.

**NOTEBOOK**
**Typhoon Tilly** was brought with a perfectly timed run to score and reverse recent Bath form with Belle Rouge. The faster ground was at least as important to him as the 6lb pull.
**Belle Rouge**, carrying a 6lb penalty for her Bath victory, looked likely to score when hitting the front over a furlong from home but could not withstand her old rival's finishing burst. This was a fine effort considering she is better with cut.
**Crocolat ◆**, racing over half a mile further than she has ever attempted before and bidding for a hat-trick after two recent victories on Fibresand, got going far too late but was finishing to some purpose under her 6lb penalty. Despite an imminent hike in the handicap, she is still relatively unexposed and can win over this sort of trip when things go her way.
**Treason Trial**, another taking a major step up in trip, had every chance and did not appear to fail through lack of stamina.
**Majestic Vision**, a maiden having only his sixth outing, did not run badly under a positive ride.
**Macaroni Gold(IRE)** made steady late progress without offering a threat and is probably being geared up for another winter campaign on the sand.
**Papeete(GER)**, one of several stepping up in trip and carrying a 6lb penalty, did not get much of a run down the home straight and would have finished quite a bit closer. *Official explanation: jockey said filly failed to get a run in the straight*
**Red Scorpion(USA)** *Official explanation: jockey said gelding was moving poorly throughout*

## 5275 RUKBA MOBILITY BUREAU APPRENTICE H'CAP — 1m (J)
**5:25** (5:29) (D2) (0-85,85) 3-Y-O+ **£7,091** (£2,182; £1,091; £545) **Stalls** High

Form RPR
1203 **1** **Arkholme**[11] 5004 3-8-8 **80**..........................................(b) MSavage(3) 15 88
(PWinkworth) *settled midfield: plld out and prog 2f out: rdn to ld last 100yds: styd on* **12/1**

0032 **2** *1* **Border Music**[20] 4738 3-8-2 **78**.......................................... TBlock(7) 5 84+
(AMBalding) *trckd ldrs: led gng easily over 2f out: rdn fnl f: hdd last 100yds* **9/2**[2]

3132 **3** *1/2* **Desert Cristal (IRE)**[10] 5024 3-8-9 **78**.......................................... DCorby 13 83
(JRBoyle) *trckd ldrs: hrd rdn and edgd lft 2f out: styd on to press ldng pair ins fnl f: hld nr fin* **10/1**[3]

0-01 **4** *1* **Pagan Prince**[6] 5135 7-9-0 **78** 6ex.......................................... LisaJones 6 81+
(JARToller) *dwlt: hld up wl in rr: brought to wd outside in st: rdn and styd on fnl 2f: no ch* **7/2**[1]

3-60 **5** *1 1/2* **Honorine (IRE)**[37] 4230 4-9-0 **78**.......................................... ABeech 9 77
(JWPayne) *dwlt: hld up wl in rr: rdn 3f out: kpt on fr over 2f out: nvr rchd ldrs* **20/1**

0106 **6** *1 1/2* **Invader**[30] 4462 8-8-8 **72**..........................................(bt) NMackay 4 68
(CEBrittain) *hld up in rr: effrt over 2f out: sme prog to chse ldrs 1f out: fdd ins fnl f* **25/1**

0030 **7** *1 3/4* **Kindlelight Debut**[27] 4551 4-8-5 **74**.......................................... MHoward(5) 3 66
(DKIvory) *hld up in rr: effrt and rdn over 2f out: one pce and n.d* **25/1**

3160 **8** *1* **Boundless Prospect (USA)**[20] 4742 5-8-8 **77**.......................................... DerekNolan(5) 1 66
(JWHills) *dwlt: hld up in rr: rdn and no prog over 2f out* **25/1**

-000 **9** *1 1/2* **Border Edge**[11] 5004 6-9-7 **85**..........................................(v) JFMcDonald 11 71
(JJBridger) *rrd and s.v.s: racd in last tl kpt on fr over 1f out: no ch* **50/1**

0064 **10** *3/4* **Iskander**[29] 4490 3-7-13 **73**..........................................(b) AMullen(5) 8 57
(KARyan) *prom: led over 2f out: hung lft and sn hdd & wknd* **7/2**[1]

5013 **11** *hd* **Moscow Times**[30] 4438 3-7-12 **72**.......................................... NataliaGemelova(5) 14 56
(DRCElsworth) *dwlt: hld up in rr: prog on inner over 2f out: wknd over 1f out* **10/1**[3]

2065 **12** *3* **Blue Patrick**[16] 4846 4-8-8 **72**.......................................... SHitchcott 7 49
(JMPEustace) *sweating profusely: led at fast pce to over 2f out: wknd* **10/1**[3]

0000 **13** *hd* **Barrantes**[19] 4772 7-8-7 **74**.......................................... NChalmers(3) 2 50
(MissSheenaWest) *pressed ldrs tl wknd over 2f out* **50/1**

1500 **14** *2* **Camberwell**[23] 4646 3-9-0 **83**.......................................... RMiles 12 55
(TGMills) *cl up tl wknd wl over 2f out* **25/1**

1m 38.82s (-0.80) **Going Correction** -0.025s/f (Good)
**WFA** 3 from 4yo+ 5lb **14** Ran SP% **121.7**
Speed ratings: **103,102,101,100,99 97,95,94,93,92 92,89,89,87**CSF £60.94 CT £592.98 TOTE £16.60: £4.10, £2.00, £4.00; EX 79.20 Place 6 £32.75, Place 5 £22.66 .
**Owner** I Russell **Bred** G And Mrs Middlebrook **Trained** Chiddingfold, Surrey

**FOCUS**
A very decent early pace in this apprentice handicap, but most of those that helped force it eventually finished up out the back and the form might not be all it seems.

**NOTEBOOK**
**Arkholme** was in no mood to get involved in the early battle for the lead and that proved to be a wise move. He was brought with his effort at just the right time and looks more effective when ridden this way.
**Border Music**, settled just off the pace, was travelling really well turning in, but may have found himself in front sooner than he wanted as the pace-setters folded. He did little wrong in the run to the line, but winner had the impetus where it mattered.
**Desert Cristal(IRE)** was always in the first half dozen and never stopped trying. She is very consistent and should be able to pick up a similar event.
**Pagan Prince**, carrying a 6lb penalty for his Windsor victory, was settled off the pace before being brought with his effort down the centre of the track, but he could never quite get to the leaders. He remains on a fair mark and a longer straight or stiffer finish seems to suit him better.
**Honorine(IRE)**, who is dropping to a more reasonable mark, never threatened the principals but still arguably ran her best race of the year so far.
**Iskander** was never far away and had every chance soon after turning in, but he started to hang under pressure and quickly dropped out. This was disappointing, but he may have done too much too soon and might be better off being held up these days.
**Blue Patrick** paid for going off too quickly.
T/Plt: £24.60 to a £1 stake. Pool: £39,435.30. 1,168.95 winning tickets. T/Qpdt: £10.40 to a £1 stake. Pool: £2,098.40. 148.40 winning tickets. JN

5276 - 5279a (Foreign Racing) - See Raceform Interactive

# 5254 BADEN-BADEN (L-H)
### Friday, September 3

**OFFICIAL GOING: Good**

## 5280a MAURICE LACROIX-TROPHY (GROUP 2) — 6f
**3:25** (3:28) 2-Y-O **£37,324** (£14,085; £7,746; £3,521)

RPR
**1** **Daring Love (GER)**[33] 2-8-9 .......................................... ABoschert 8 101
(UOstmann, Germany) *hld up, disp 3rd towards outside str, rdn 1 1/2f out, fin wl fr 1f out to ld cl home, driven out* 1

**2** *nk* **Beirut (GER)** 2-8-7 .......................................... AStarke 1 98
(PSchiergen, Germany) *trckd ldrs, pushed along to hld pl appr str, drvn & hdwy 1 1/2f out to ld over 1f out, ran on til hdd cl home* 3

**3** *3/4* **Tournedos (IRE)**[12] 4981 2-9-2 .......................................... TEDurcan 5 105
(MRChannon) *prominent, disputing 3rd straight, every chance approaching final furlong, kept on* 2

**4** *1 1/4* **Free Dreams (GER)**[33] 2-8-7 .......................................... J-PCarvalho 7 92
(MarioHofer, Germany) *tracked leaders, 5th straight, effort 1 1/2f out, stayed on at one pace to take 4th close home*

**5** *hd* **Rue D'Alsace**[63] 2-8-7 .......................................... FSanchez 4 92
(FReuterskiold, Sweden) *cl up on ins, pushed along to ld str, hdd over 1f out, kpt on under pressure til no ex cl home*

**6** *9* **Spiriton (GER)** 2-8-11 .......................................... AHelfenbein 2 69
(KWoodburn) *towards rear, pushed along and last straight, never a factor*

**7** *2 1/2* **Thai Dancer (IRE)**[96] 2-8-11 .......................................... WMongil 3 61
(WHefter, Germany) *towards rear, pushed along before half-way, 7th straight, never dangerous*

**8** *14* **Von Dutch (IRE)** 2-8-11 .......................................... ASuborics 6 19
(VChaloupka, Czech Republic) *led and set strong pace to straight, eased when beaten, virtually pulled up inside final furlong*

1m 11.16s **8** Ran SP% **132.2**
Speed ratings: .
**Owner** Gestut Auenquelle **Bred** Gestut Auenquelle **Trained** Germany

**NOTEBOOK**
**Daring Love(GER)** justified favourtism in good style. She will not run again this season and be aimed at next season's Henkel-Rennen (German 1,000 Guineas)
**Beirut(GER)** ran a fair race but was outpointed by the winners's finishing burst close home.
**Tournedos(IRE)** burdened by a penalty, he ran a fair race being up there all the way. The extra weight told in the final furlong though when the front two went on.

# 4966 FOLKESTONE (R-H)

Saturday, September 4

**OFFICIAL GOING: Good to firm (firm in places)**

The first 'matinee' meeting to be held since 2002.

## 5281 BARRETTS OF ASHFORD MAIDEN AUCTION STKS 6f

11:30 (11:31) (H5) 2-Y-O £1,372 (£392; £196) Stalls Low

Form RPR

4 **1** **Bahia Breeze**[17] 4844 2-8-7 CCatlin 5 86+
(RGuest) *mde virtually all: drew rt away fr over 2f out: unchal* **15/8**[1]

5320 **2** *7* **Avertigo**[15] 4914 2-8-9 74 RMiles(3) 4 70
(WRMuir) *mosrlt chsd wnr: easily outpcd over 2f out: jst hld on for 2nd* **12/1**

62 **3** *nk* **Tanning**[20] 4770 2-8-5 TPQueally 12 62
(HMorrison) *s.s: rcvrd into midfield 1/2-way: styd on fr over 1f out : nrst fin* **9/2**[3]

**4** *2 1/2* **Pink Bay** 2-8-4 LPKeniry(3) 3 57
(WSKittow) *racd midfield: outpcd 1/2-way: kpt on fr over 1f out* **100/1**

55 **5** *3* **Task's Muppet (IRE)**[23] 4670 2-8-4 JFMcDonald(3) 11 48
(JAOsborne) *prom: rdn and outpcd over 2f out: no ch after* **50/1**

0422 **6** *1* **Persian Carpet**[30] 4487 2-8-5 70 IMongan 1 43
(IAWood) *racd on outer: chsd ldrs: rdn 1/2-way: struggling and no ch 2f out* **3/1**[2]

0020 **7** *nk* **Yeldham Lady**[11] 5022 2-8-6 50 AMcCarthy 13 43
(JPearce) *dwlt: wl off the pce in rr: kpt on over 1f out: n.d* **25/1**

**8** *1/2* **Lord Of Adventure (IRE)** 2-8-12 PDoe 6 48
(JamiePoulton) *dwlt: a in rr* **33/1**

000 **9** *1/2* **Before The Dawn**[14] 4936 2-8-1 FPFerris(3) 14 38
(AGNewcombe) *chsd ldrs: outpcd over 2f out: wkng whn bmpd over 1f out* **25/1**

50 **10** *1* **Sunny Times (IRE)**[39] 4212 2-8-3 HayleyTurner(3) 10 37
(JWPayne) *a wl in rr* **25/1**

3464 **11** *2* **Turtle Magic (IRE)**[7] 5132 2-8-5 51 (v[1]) ADaly 2 30
(WGMTurner) *chsd ldrs: rdn 1/2-way: wkng whn hung rt over 1f out* **66/1**

0 **12** *1 1/4* **Amigra (IRE)**[14] 4936 2-8-4 DKinsella 9 25
(MissJacquelineSDoyle) *a bhd* **100/1**

600 **13** *nk* **Liameliss**[40] 4198 2-8-0 ow2 NChalmers(5) 8 25
(MAAllen) *a bhd* **100/1**

0020 **14** *17* **Comintrue (IRE)**[45] 4017 2-8-7 56 SCarson 15 —
(EJO'Neill) *t.k.h: prom 2f: sn wknd: t.o* **50/1**

1m 12.16s (-1.44) **Going Correction** -0.125s/f (Firm) **14 Ran SP% 108.5**

Speed ratings: **104,94,94,90,86 85,85,84,83,82 79,78,77,55**CSF £18.58 TOTE £2.90: £1.30, £2.90, £2.20; EX 20.70.

**Owner** F Nowell **Bred** P And Mrs Venner **Trained** Newmarket, Suffolk

**FOCUS**

Bahia Breeze destroyed the opposition in what was an ordinary affair, coming right away and recording an outstanding time for the grade of race.

**NOTEBOOK**

**Bahia Breeze**, a promising fourth in a much better race on her debut, led throughout and had it in the bag after two thirds of the race. She came right away once asked to go clear, but beating a 74-rated horse in such a fashion will do her future prospects no good at all.

**Avertigo** showed his Salisbury running to be all wrong in second but was well held by the easy winner. He is worth trying back in handicaps.

**Tanning** lost her chance of getting second with a sloppy start and was closing with every stride at the finish. Now qualified for nurseries, she should have little trouble winning in that sphere.

**Pink Bay** would no doubt have delighted connections with this debut effort as her odds suggested not much was expected of her. If building on this she can probably sneak a weak race.

**Task's Muppet(IRE)** in not much but can now run in nurseries and may be capable of a bit better in that sphere.

**Persian Carpet** was the disappointment of the race as her form entitled her to finish a clear second. However, you can always forgive a horse one bad run and she is up to winning a nursery.
*Official explanation: jockey said filly had run flat*

## 5282 LANCASTER BANDED STKS 6f

11:55 (11:59) (H5) 3-Y-O+ £1,540 (£440; £220) Stalls Low

Form RPR

4031 **1** **Yorkies Boy**[1] 5261 9-9-2 46 (p) MSavage(5) 7 61
(NEBerry) *stmbld s: hld up in midfield: stdy prog 2f out: drvn and r.o to ld nr fin* **11/2**[2]

2635 **2** *1/2* **Elsinora**[10] 5035 3-8-9 45 (b) LFletcher(3) 15 53
(HMorrison) *trckd ldrs: rdn to chal 1f out: upsides whn hung lft ins fnl f: nt run on* **14/1**

0041 **3** *nk* **Molotov**[11] 5016 4-8-12 50 NataliaGemelova(7) 14 57
(IWMcinnes) *w ldr: led after 2f: hrd pressed fnl f: hdd nr fin* **5/1**[1]

0065 **4** *1 1/2* **Poppyline**[19] 4801 4-8-13 47 (b) JFMcDonald(3) 10 49
(WRMuir) *s.s: wl in rr: prog fr 2f out: styd on fnl f : nrst fin* **16/1**

0003 **5** *1 1/4* **Mayzin (IRE)**[15] 4923 4-9-2 47 TPQueally 16 45
(RMFlower) *led for 2f: w ldr to over 1f out: wknd fnl f* **6/1**[3]

0016 **6** *1* **Little Flute**[82] 2932 3-8-13 46 PDoe 11 41
(TKeddy) *chsd ldrs: rdn over 2f out: fdd over 1f out* **20/1**

0000 **7** *2 1/2* **Moscow Mary**[32] 4414 3-8-9 45 FPFerris(3) 12 33
(AGNewcombe) *wl in rr: rdn and kpt on fnl 2f: n.d* **33/1**

0036 **8** *2 1/2* **Dexileos (IRE)**[19] 4811 5-9-0 45 (t) CCatlin 3 25
(ADWPinder) *wl in rr: outpcd and n.d fnl 2f* **25/1**

0220 **9** *3 1/2* **Cargo**[19] 4802 5-8-13 47 (tp) RMiles(3) 2 17
(BAPearce) *racd on outer: chsd ldrs: wknd 2f out* **9/1**

0026 **10** *nk* **Lake Verdi (IRE)**[22] 4727 5-9-1 46 (t) IMongan 4 15
(MissGayKelleway) *s.i.s: a wl in rr* **11/2**[2]

5250 **11** *nk* **Superchief**[120] 1935 9-9-0 45 (t) SCarson 13 13
(MissBSanders) *hld up midfield: struggling on inner 1/2-way: sn btn* **14/1**

533 **12** *1/2* **La Calera (GER)**[10] 5036 3-9-0 47 (b) OUrbina 8 14
(GCHChung) *chsd ldrs: u.p 1/2-way: wknd over 2f out* **10/1**

4500 **13** *1 3/4* **Lily Of The Guild (IRE)**[43] 4083 5-9-2 50 LPKeniry(3) 1 11
(WSKittow) *a wl in rr* **12/1**

0050 **14** *3/4* **Tamarella (IRE)**[32] 4415 4-9-1 46 AMcCarthy 9 5
(GGMargarson) *prom tl wknd rapidly wl over 1f out* **25/1**

-540 **15** *2* **Otylia**[12] 5000 4-9-3 48 MHenry 6 —
(RMHCowell) *racd midfield: wknd over 2f out* **33/1**

6040 **16** *3/4* **Pink Supreme**[13] 4968 3-8-12 48 DNolan(3) 5 —
(IAWood) *chsd ldrs: u.p and struggling 1/2-way: sn wknd* **25/1**

1m 13.37s (-0.23) **Going Correction** -0.125s/f (Firm)

**WFA** 3 from 4yo+ 2lb **16 Ran SP% 129.9**

Speed ratings: **96,95,94,92,91 89,86,83,78,78 77,77,74,73,71 70**CSF £78.27 TOTE £6.40: £2.70, £4.80, £2.60; EX 63.30.

**Owner** Paul & Ann de Weck **Bred** J And Mrs M Beddis **Trained** Earlswood, Monmouths

**FOCUS**

Average form for the grade, but two wins in as many days for Yorkies Boy, who is rated slightly better than for his win the previous day.

**NOTEBOOK**

**Yorkies Boy**, who scored his first success for over three years the previous day, is evidently in top form as he proved good enough to score here despite having stumbled coming out of the gate. He still had a bit to do at one stage, but picked up strongly in the closing stages and ended up winning going away. In this sort of form, a hat-trick cannot be discounted.

**Elsinora** has been running over farther and did not seem inconvenienced by the drop in trip. She looked a likely winner until hanging and throwing it away, and does not look one to rely on.

**Molotov** is putting a run of decent efforts together and will be winning again before long if remaining in good form.

**Poppyline** remains a maiden after 28 starts and was doing her best work late on.

**Mayzin(IRE)** had run well in a better race last time and it was a little disappointing he could not hold out in front for longer.

**Cargo** *Official explanation: jockey said gelding had blown up*

**Lake Verdi(IRE)** *Official explanation: jockey said gelding did not handle the track*

## 5283 HURRICANE APPRENTICE BANDED STKS 7f (S)

12:25 (12:26) (H5) 3-Y-O+ £1,319 (£377; £188) Stalls Low

Form RPR

4000 **1** **Savernake Brave (IRE)**[16] 4881 3-8-12 40 DCorby 1 54
(MrsHSweeting) *racd nr side w runner-up: pair clr over 2f out: drvn to assert ins fnl f* **22/1**

0003 **2** *3/4* **Crimson Star (IRE)**[13] 4968 3-8-12 40 LFletcher 2 52
(CTinkler) *racd nr side w wnr: pair clr over 2f out: one pce u.p fnl f* **12/1**

-300 **3** *5* **Nassau Street**[23] 4669 4-8-9 40 AHindley(7) 6 38
(DJSFfrenchDavis) *racd far side: last of gp: pushed along 4f out: prog against rail 2f out: kpt on to snatch 3rd last stride: no ch w ldng pa* **33/1**

0400 **4** *hd* **Coppington Flyer (IRE)**[53] 3828 4-9-2 40 (t) RMiles 14 38
(BWDuke) *disp ld far side: nt on terms fr over 2f out: one pce u.p* **8/1**

3300 **5** *hd* **Stagecoach Ruby**[30] 4469 3-8-5 40 JemmaMarshall(7) 13 37
(GLMoore) *disp ld far side: nt on terms w nr side pair over 2f out: one pce u.p* **18/1**

0050 **6** *nk* **Silistra**[19] 4802 5-8-11 40 (p) NataliaGemelova(5) 15 37
(MrsLCJewell) *trckd far side ldrs: drvn and one pce over 1f out* **16/1**

6004 **7** *3/4* **Zinging**[10] 5039 5-9-2 40 HayleyTurner 9 35
(JJBridger) *hld up in midfield far side: effrt and n.m.r over 2f out: kpt on same pce* **7/1**

6542 **8** *3/4* **Mr Uppity**[47] 3991 5-8-11 40 (e) MHalford(5) 10 33
(JulianPoulton) *chse far side ldrs: one pce u.p fnl 2f* **4/1**[1]

0415 **9** *nk* **Brandywine Bay (IRE)**[22] 4708 4-8-9 40 (p) TBlock(7) 7 32
(APJones) *hld up in rr far side: nt clr run and swtchd lft over 2f out: kpt on: no ch* **11/2**[2]

0605 **10** *3* **Balmacara**[44] 4066 5-9-2 40 ABeech 4 24
(MissKBBoutflower) *hld up in rr far side: no prog 2f out* **16/1**

1522 **11** *hd* **Tiny Tim (IRE)**[108] 2229 6-8-9 40 RJKilloran(7) 16 23
(AMBalding) *trckd far side ldrs: wknd over 1f out* **13/2**[3]

0-00 **12** *1 3/4* **Vertedanz (IRE)**[19] 4818 4-8-13 40 NChalmers(3) 11 18
(MissIECraig) *racd far side: a towards rr: no prog 2f out* **50/1**

2400 **13** *1/2* **Badou**[84] 2885 4-9-2 40 (v) JFMcDonald 5 17
(LMontagueHall) *racd on outer of far side: chsd ldrs tl wknd over 2f out* **8/1**

0500 **14** *hd* **Komena**[22] 4708 6-9-2 40 TPQueally 8 16
(JWPayne) *hld up in rr far side: effrt whn bmpd over 2f out: wknd* **14/1**

-050 **15** *2 1/2* **Rue De Paris**[15] 4926 4-8-11 40 (p) DeanWilliams(5) 12 10
(JohnAHarris) *prom far side tl wknd rapidly over 2f out* **16/1**

1m 28.15s (0.35) **Going Correction** -0.125s/f (Firm)

**WFA** 3 from 4yo+ 4lb **15 Ran SP% 130.0**

Speed ratings: **93,92,86,86,85 85,84,83,83,80 79,77,77,77,74**CSF £280.52 TOTE £35.10: £9.00, £6.50, £10.80; EX 476.10.

**Owner** P Sweeting **Bred** Denis Hackett **Trained** Marlborough, Wilts

**FOCUS**

The front two decided to race on the usually unfavoured stands' rail over this trip but it paid dividends as they finished well clear. The form as a result should be treated with caution as those far side were clearly at a disadvantage.

**NOTEBOOK**

**Savernake Brave(IRE)** went against the grain along with the runner-up and chose to race on the usually unfavoured stands' side. He looked to be a bit behind the main group on the far side at one stage, but in the final quarter mile it became evident they were on top and came right away in the final furlong. He was well suited by the trip but it is hard to gauge just what he achieved due to the track bias.

**Crimson Star(IRE)** raced along with the winner on the stands' side and, although unable to get past Savernake Brave, pulled clear of the remainder. Again though it is hard to tell what she actually achieved.

**Nassau Street** did best of those far side, coming through late to 'win' that race, but found himself behind with the stands'-side duo. This was a fair effort and he can count himself a little unlucky.

**Coppington Flyer(IRE)** was always up with the pace and ran well, just getting caught for third.

**Stagecoach Ruby** kept battling away under pressure and ran her best race for a while.

**Zinging** was a little unlucky not to get closer but would not have troubled the principals.

**Mr Uppity** had the beating of the winner on Brighton form, but the extra furlong, and a slightly below-par effort racing on the wrong side, enabled the form to be reversed.

**Brandywine Bay(IRE)** never got into it and was always in rear.

## 5284 CARL SCARROTT 40TH BIRTHDAY TRI-BANDED STKS 1m 1f 149y

12:50 (12:51) (H5) 3-Y-O £1,508 (£431; £215) Stalls Low

Form RPR

6200 **1** **Cunning Pursuit**[36] 4302 3-8-11 45 TPQueally 10 49
(MLWBell) *settled midfield: prog on inner over 2f out: led over 1f out: drvn out* **11/4**[1]

0452 **2** *1 1/4* **Lenwade**[19] 4798 3-8-1 35 AMcCarthy 4 37
(GGMargarson) *racd towards rr: drvn 3f out: prog over 1f out: chsd wnr ins fnl f: no imp nr fin* **5/1**[3]

0-00 **3** *3 1/2* **Skelthwaite**[12] 5001 3-8-1 35 JMcAuley 7 30
(MissDAMchale) *chsd ldr for 2f and again 5f out to wl over 1f out: one pce* **100/1**

6000 **4** *1 1/2* **Princess Bankes**[71] 3261 3-8-11 45 IMongan 14 37
(MissGayKelleway) *prom: rdn 3f out: one pce and btn over 1f out* **20/1**

0636 **5** 1/2 **Anisette**$^{8}$ [5080] 3-8-6 40 ........ ADaly 13 31
(JulianPoulton) *t.k.h: hld up in midfield: rdn 3f out: no prog tl kpt on ins fnl f* **10/1**

6501 **6** 1/2 **Fiddles Music**$^{10}$ [5036] 3-8-11 46 ........ CCatlin 9 35
(MissSheenaWest) *led: 3l clr over 3f out: hdd & wknd over 1f out* **4/1**$^{2}$

0302 **7** *nk* **Tshukudu**$^{11}$ [5018] 3-7-12 35 ........ JFMcDonald(3) 5 25
(MBlanshard) *racd midfield: rdn 3f out: wd bnd over 2f out: btn after: kpt on ins fnl f* **6/1**

0006 **8** 2 **Chiqitita (IRE)**$^{27}$ [4568] 3-8-4 45 ........ DerekNolan(7) 8 31
(MissMERowland) *sweating: dwlt: racd in rr: effrt on inner over 2f out: no imp over 1f out: fdd* **25/1**

0065 **9** 1 1/2 **Jaolins**$^{43}$ [4093] 3-8-6 40 ........ DKinsella 6 23
(PGMurphy) *s.s: hld up in last pair: effrt over 2f out: wknd over 1f out* **12/1**

6000 **10** 5 **Brother Cadfael**$^{30}$ [4497] 3-7-12 35 ........ (t) HayleyTurner(3) 3 9
(JohnAHarris) *racd midfield: rdn and effrt 3f out: wd bnd over 2f out: wknd* **25/1**

005 **11** 2 1/2 **Anna Gayle**$^{20}$ [4775] 3-8-11 45 ........ SCarson 11 14
(MrsAJPerrett) *prom tl wknd over 2f out* **12/1**

0000 **12** *nk* **Rumour Mill (IRE)**$^{8}$ [5080] 3-8-3 40 ........ FPFerris(3) 1 8
(NEBerry) *led to 3f out: hld up in last pair: chse ldr after 2f to 5f out: wknd over 2f out* **33/1**

0250 **13** 4 **Bretton**$^{14}$ [4940] 3-8-3 40 ........ (p) BReilly(3) 12 1
(BAPearce) *n.m.r after 1f and dropped to last pair: struggling 4f out: c v wd bnd over 2f out* **10/1**

2m 3.05s (-2.11) **Going Correction** -0.225s/f (Firm) **13** Ran SP% **127.6**
Speed ratings: **99,98,95,94,93 93,92,91,90,86 84,83,80**CSF £16.59 TOTE £3.50: £1.30, £2.00, £12.10; EX 22.00.
**Owner** Mrs Maureen Buckley **Bred** Mrs C S Knowles **Trained** Newmarket, Suffolk

**FOCUS**
Poor stuff as one would expect for the grade, the winner apart.

**NOTEBOOK**
**Cunning Pursuit** comes from a stable whose horses are in cracking form at present and, although only a moderate performer himself, proved good enough to defy favouritism. It was a weak race but he proved well suited by the drop in trip - he has been running over 1m6f and two miles - and he can land a handicap.
**Lenwade** did a lot of running to reach a challenging position and had nothing left when she needed to go again. This was not a bad effort, but she remains winless after 15 attempts.
**Skelthwaite** ran by far and away his best-ever race despite being beaten almost five lengths. Whether he can build on this is open to debate, and it will be a bad race he wins.
**Princess Bankes** was up there throughout and had her chance. This is her grade.
**Anisette** ran better back in this sort of grade.

## 5285 HAMBRIDGE RUBY BANDED STKS — 1m 1f 149y

1:20 (1:20) (H5) 4-Y-O+ — £1,711 (£489; £244) Stalls Low

Form — RPR

3300 **1** **Shamwari Fire (IRE)**$^{26}$ [4605] 4-8-13 47 ........ JFMcDonald(3) 13 52
(IWMcinnes) *settled midfield: clsd 2f out: nt clr run and swtchd lft over 1f out: drvn to ld nr fin* **14/1**

5000 **2** 1/2 **Midnight Mambo (USA)**$^{5}$ [5175] 4-8-7 40 ........ RMills(7) 9 49
(RGuest) *dwlt: sn in midfield: prog over 2f out: led over 1f out: shuffled along fnl f: hdd nr fin* **66/1**

4503 **3** 1/2 **My Maite (IRE)**$^{29}$ [4519] 5-9-1 46 ........ (tp) NDay 14 49
(RIngram) *hld up in rr: clsd 2f out: threaded through 1f out: styd on wl: nrst fin* **5/1**$^{2}$

00-1 **4** 3/4 **Royal Indulgence**$^{28}$ [4537] 4-8-12 48 ........ MSavage(5) 1 50
(WMBrisbourne) *s.s: hld up in rr: stdy prog over 2f out: effrt to press ldrs 1f out: fnd nil* **3/1**$^{1}$

-000 **5** 3 1/2 **Havantadoubt (IRE)**$^{58}$ [3670] 4-9-5 50 ........ (t) GBaker 5 45
(MRBosley) *settled in last pair and wl off the pce: rdn over 2f out: kpt on fnl f: no ch* **33/1**

2330 **6** *shd* **Miss Glory Be**$^{12}$ [5002] 6-8-11 45 ........ (p) DCorby(3) 15 40
(EROertel) *pressed ldng pair: cl up whn nt clr run on inner 2f out: fdd fnl f* **17/2**

3400 **7** 1 1/4 **Due To Me**$^{15}$ [4912] 4-9-0 45 ........ (p) IMongan 12 37
(GLMoore) *racd midfield: rdn 4f out: effrt u.p and cl up over 1f out: wknd* **12/1**

1020 **8** 3/4 **Gran Clicquot**$^{31}$ [4438] 9-8-10 48 ........ DerekNolan(7) 2 39
(GPEnright) *trckd ldrs: effrt on outer over 2f out: fdd jst over 1f out* **14/1**

2634 **9** 3/4 **Private Seal**$^{11}$ [5021] 9-9-0 45 ........ (t) ADaly 7 35
(JulianPoulton) *sn in last and wl off the pce: kpt on fnl 2f: no ch* **20/1**

0050 **10** *nk* **Margery Daw (IRE)**$^{11}$ [5021] 4-8-11 45 ........ FPFerris(3) 8 34
(PSMcentee) *pressed ldr: rdn and ev ch 2f out: wknd over 1f out* **50/1**

0400 **11** 3/4 **Ballare (IRE)**$^{43}$ [4083] 5-9-0 45 ........ (p) DKinsella 3 33
(BobJones) *racd midfield: effrt 3f out: no prog over 1f out* **20/1**

0040 **12** 1/2 **Lady Liesel**$^{128}$ [1723] 4-8-11 45 ........ HayleyTurner(3) 4 32
(JJBridger) *t.k.h: hld up in rr: c wd bnd over 2f out: no prog* **50/1**

0100 **13** 3/4 **Piquet**$^{26}$ [4604] 6-9-0 45 ........ TPQueally 6 30
(JJBridger) *prom: cl bhd ldrs whn nt clr run wl over 1f out: sn wknd* **33/1**

2020 **14** *hd* **Kindness**$^{20}$ [4771] 4-9-5 50 ........ CCatlin 10 35
(ADWPinder) *led: hanging lft fr over 3f out: hdd & wknd over 1f out* **8/1**$^{3}$

4006 **15** 1/2 **Expected Bonus (USA)**$^{19}$ [4818] 5-9-0 45 ........ RHavlin 11 29
(SCWilliams) *racd midfield: rdn and lost pl over 3f out: sn no ch* **3/1**$^{1}$

2m 2.80s (-2.36) **Going Correction** -0.225s/f (Firm) **15** Ran SP% **130.2**
Speed ratings: **100,99,99,98,95 95,94,94,93,93 92,92,91,91,91**CSF £768.22 TOTE £20.80: £6.10, £12.90, £2.10; EX 1386.60.
**Owner** Ivy House Racing **Bred** Mrs P M Kalman **Trained** Catwick, E Yorks

**FOCUS**
Average banded form, and the winner did not need to be at his best to score.

**NOTEBOOK**
**Shamwari Fire(IRE)** has been running in slightly better races and the drop back into this grade did the trick. Once returning to handicaps he will continue to struggle before no doubt returning to this grade and winning again.
**Midnight Mambo(USA)** ran well at huge odds and very nearly caused a shock. She did not find much under pressure - her jockey seemingly reluctant to get stuck into her - and she is evidently not the most 'gutsy' around.
**My Maite(IRE)** ran a similar race to last time, staying on when the race was all over. He is nearing a return to the winner's enclosure.
**Royal Indulgence**, off the mark at the 18th attempt last month, travelled nicely enough but found nothing once asked for maximum effort. He is evidently not one to place much trust in.
**Havantadoubt(IRE)** was given quite a bit to do and could not make the ground up in time.
**Miss Glory Be** had run her race when weakening out of it in the final furlong.

## 5286 SPITFIRE BANDED STKS — 1m 4f

1:45 (1:47) (H5) 3-Y-O+ — £1,718 (£491; £245) Stalls Low

Form — RPR

-005 **1** **Lysander's Quest (IRE)**$^{3}$ [5217] 6-9-7 40 ........ NDay 3 51
(RIngram) *chsd ldr after 3f: rdn over 2f out: nt qckn u.p over 1f out: forced ahd last strides* **14/1**

0420 **2** *hd* **Tintawn Gold (IRE)**$^{30}$ [4485] 4-9-9 47 ........ (p) CCatlin 16 53
(SWoodman) *hld up midfield: smooth prog over 2f out: led jst over 1f out: fnd nil in front and hdd last strides* **8/1**

0000 **3** 1/2 **Open Book**$^{92}$ [2645] 3-8-13 49 ........ LFletcher(3) 12 54
(HMorrison) *t.k.h: hld up in midfield: prog 3f out: rdn to chal 1f out: nt qckn* **33/1**

0223 **4** 1/2 **Tata Naka**$^{11}$ [5019] 4-9-4 45 ........ HayleyTurner(3) 1 49
(MrsCADunnett) *hld up in last: prog over 2f out: styd on fr over 1f out: nt rch ldrs* **6/1**$^{3}$

1300 **5** 1/2 **Cantrip**$^{26}$ [4603] 4-9-11 49 ........ SCarson 9 52
(MissBSanders) *led after 2f: rdn and hdd jst over 1f out: one pce* **8/1**

3000 **6** *nk* **Coolfore Jade (IRE)**$^{11}$ [5021] 4-9-2 40 ........ MSavage(5) 17 48
(NEBerry) *t.k.h: hld up midfield: nt clr run on inner 3f out: plld out and kpt on fnl f* **20/1**

3334 **7** 1 1/4 **Vandenberghe**$^{3}$ [5221] 5-9-2 47 ........ RKeogh(7) 14 48
(JAOsborne) *hld up in last pair: stl wl in rr and wd bnd over 2f out: styd on fr over 1f out: hopeless task* **11/4**$^{1}$

4330 **8** 1 **Absinther**$^{11}$ [5021] 7-9-11 49 ........ GBaker 4 48
(MRBosley) *s.s: hld up wl in rr: effrt on outer over 2f out: no imp on ldrs* **3/1**$^{2}$

0000 **9** 2 1/2 **Macchiato**$^{16}$ [4883] 3-8-9 40 ........ (b) JFMcDonald(3) 5 40
(RFJohnsonHoughton) *wl in rr: rdn 3f out: struggling and btn 2f out* **20/1**

2300 **10** 1 **Giko**$^{23}$ [4686] 10-9-4 35 ........ RMiles(3) 10 39
(JaneSouthcombe) *racd midfield: prog to chse ldrs 4f out: wknd over 1f out* **25/1**

0/00 **11** *shd* **Repent At Leisure**$^{6}$ [5159] 4-9-10 48 ........ RHavlin 11 41
(JulianPoulton) *prom: chsd ldng pair 5f out: drvn over 3f out: wknd over 1f out* **66/1**

4060 **12** 1 3/4 **Hilarious (IRE)**$^{10}$ [5039] 4-9-7 40 ........ (b) ADaly 15 36
(DrJRJNaylor) *t.k.h: led for 2f: styd prom tl wknd wl over 1f out* **33/1**

0000 **13** 4 **Mad Maurice**$^{30}$ [4499] 3-8-12 45 ........ (b$^{1}$) TPQueally 7 29
(BJCurley) *t.k.h: hld up wl in rr: hrd rdn and no prog over 2f out* **10/1**

0000 **14** *hd* **Purr**$^{6}$ [5153] 3-9-2 49 ........ JMcAuley 6 33
(TTClement) *racd towards rr: shkn up and no prog over 2f out: wknd* **50/1**

-260 **15** 5 **Retail Therapy (IRE)**$^{5}$ [1463] 4-9-7 45 ........ (b$^{1}$) MHenry 13 21
(MABuckley) *prom tl wknd u.p wl over 2f out* **33/1**

2m 40.04s (-0.36) **Going Correction** -0.225s/f (Firm)
**WFA** 3 from 4yo+ 9lb **15** Ran SP% **129.6**
Speed ratings: **92,91,91,91,90 90,89,89,87,86 86,85,82,82,79**CSF £119.55 TOTE £18.60: £4.80, £4.30, £8.00; EX 154.30 Place 6 £5,855.98, Place 5 £3,832.88.
**Owner** Mrs E N Nield **Bred** J M Ryan **Trained** Epsom, Surrey

**FOCUS**
Neither Lysander's Quest or Tintawn Gold wanted to win so it was down to the two jockeys. The time was modest, even for a race like this, and the winner ran to the standard of his effort the previous week.

**NOTEBOOK**
**Lysander's Quest(IRE)** was winning for the first time at the 29th attempt and it took every ounce of his jockey's strength to get him there. Not the most reliable of characters, it will be most surprising if he follows up.
**Tintawn Gold(IRE)** did not really want to win and decided she had done more than enough once getting to the lead. She is one you can afford to miss if she ever wins.
**Open Book** is probably the one to take from the race, as this represented an improvement on recent form and she is only lightly raced.
**Tata Naka** was going on at the end and could probably do with a stiffer test.
**Cantrip** went at it from the front but could not cling on despite trying. *Official explanation: jockey said filly had hung left*
**Coolfore Jade(IRE)** is an out-and-out galloper who does nothing quickly. Being held up in her run obviously would have done her no good and she could not quicken. She needs everything to go her way.
**Vandenberghe** was not given the greatest of rides and was running on without cause in the straight as he had too much ground to make up.
T/Plt: £14,893.60 to a £1 stake. Pool: £20,402.20. 0.90 winning tickets. T/Qpdt: Not won. JN

# 5262 HAYDOCK (L-H)

Saturday, September 4

**OFFICIAL GOING: Good**
Times indicate that the going was riding faster than the official version.
Wind: almost nil Weather: warm & sunny

## 5287 STANLEYBET BE FRIENDLY H'CAP — 5f

1:35 (1:39) (C1) (0-100,95) 3-Y-O+ — £21,376 (£8,108; £4,054; £1,842) Stalls Low

Form — RPR

3036 **1** **Forever Phoenix**$^{7}$ [5105] 4-9-2 92 ........ AQuinn(5) 16 106
(RMHCowell) *hld up: hdwy 1/2-way: led 1f out: r.o* **7/1**$^{2}$

0232 **2** 1 1/4 **Devise (IRE)**$^{8}$ [5071] 5-9-1 86 ........ DHolland 13 95
(MSSaunders) *chsd ldrs: led 1/2-way: rdn and hdd 1f out: nt qckn ins fnl f* **7/2**$^{1}$

6510 **3** 1/2 **Ptarmigan Ridge**$^{28}$ [4538] 8-9-1 86 ........ MFenton 12 93
(MissLAPerratt) *midfield: rdn and hdwy 2f out: r.o and edgd lft ins fnl f* **16/1**

3000 **4** 1/2 **Bond Boy**$^{8}$ [5075] 7-9-1 86 ........ FLynch 6 91
(BSmart) *bhd: rdn whn swtchd rt and hdwy over 1f out: r.o ins fnl f: nrst fin* **20/1**

2004 **5** 1/2 **Bo McGinty (IRE)**$^{33}$ [4394] 3-8-12 84 ........ PHanagan 14 88
(RAFahey) *in tch: rdn 2f out: kpt on ins fnl f: nt pce to chal* **10/1**

0400 **6** *hd* **Funfair Wane**$^{35}$ [4324] 5-9-5 90 ........ ANicholls 1 93
(DNicholls) *chsd ldrs: rdn 1/2-way: kpt on same pce fnl f* **25/1**

0000 **7** 3/4 **Whitbarrow (IRE)**$^{5}$ [5181] 5-9-7 92 ........ (b) JFEgan 11 92
(JMBradley) *prom: rdn and ev ch wl over 1f out: wknd ins fnl f* **16/1**

0600 **8** 1 1/2 **Absent Friends**$^{7}$ [5105] 7-9-1 86 ........ JEdmunds 8 81
(JBalding) *chsd ldrs tl rdn and wknd over 1f out* **16/1**

0460 **9** 1 1/4 **Maktavish**$^{9}$ [5062] 5-8-10 81 oh2 ........ (p) RWinston 4 71
(ISemple) *led: hdd 1/2-way: rdn and stl ev ch wl over 1f out: wknd fnl f* **12/1**

0600 **10** *nk* **Trinculo (IRE)**$^{6}$ [5157] 7-8-7 81 oh1 ........ (p) J-PGuillambert(3) 10 70
(NPLittmoden) *prom tl lost pl 1/2-way: n.d after* **33/1**

0301 **11** 1 1/2 **River Falcon**$^{29}$ [4510] 4-9-5 90 ........ TEDurcan 3 74
(JSGoldie) *racd on far side: midfield: rdn and outpcd 1/2-way* **9/1**$^{3}$

000U **12** *nk* **Peruvian Chief (IRE)**$^{35}$ [4324] 7-9-10 95 ........ (v) KDarley 9 78
(NPLittmoden) *s.i.s: sn pushed along towards rr: nvr on terms* **33/1**

4500 **13** *nk* **Blackheath (IRE)**$^{28}$ [4538] 8-9-2 87 ........ AlexGreaves 2 69
(DNicholls) *racd on far side: midfield: rdn and outpcd 1/2-way* **16/1**

0000 **14** 1 1/4 **Johnston's Diamond (IRE)**$^{18}$ [4837] 6-8-13 84 ........ (b$^{1}$) WSupple 7 61
(EJAlston) *hld up: rdn 1/2-way: nvr on terms* **20/1**

4034 **15** *2* **Whistler**[28] 4538 7-9-5 **90**........................(p) MHills 15 60
(JMBradley) *s.i.s: a bhd* **7/1**[2]

3033 **16** *hd* **Prince Of Blues (IRE)**[14] 4935 6-8-10 **81** oh25..............(b) SRighton 5 50
(MMullineaux) *hld up: rdn 2f out: nvr on terms* **100/1**

59.50 secs (-2.57) **Going Correction** -0.225s/f (Firm)
**WFA** 3 from 4yo+ 1lb **16** Ran SP% **117.8**
Speed ratings: **111,109,108,107,106 106,105,102,100,100 97,97,96,94,91 91**CSF £27.71 CT £308.99 TOTE £7.50: £2.10, £1.60, £3.80, £5.10; EX 24.20.
**Owner** J M Greetham **Bred** J M Greetham **Trained** Six Mile Bottom, Cambs

**FOCUS**
A decent sprint handicap with many contenders not in the best of form. Nevertheless, the form appears solid enough for the grade. The winning jockey was landing his biggest success on his first ride at the track.

**NOTEBOOK**
**Forever Phoenix** came through to lead a furlong from home to land her fifth win of the year in tidy fashion. She has been racing in better company and this effort displayed her wellbeing ahead of the Portland at Doncaster. Connections reported the filly will stay in training for one more year.
**Devise(IRE)** maintained his consistency with this effort, but he may continue to rise in the weights without winning.
**Ptarmigan Ridge**, making his third appearance in this race, put in one of his better efforts on a surface which was possibly on the fast side for him.
**Bond Boy** found this on the sharp side with the prevailing ground conditions, but on a positive note finished well to record one of his better performances considering he lost a shoe. This run offered a spot of encouragement for the autumn campaign, particularly on an easier surface. *Official explanation: jockey said gelding hung right handed and lost an off fore shoe*
**Bo McGinty(IRE)** shaped adequately towards the finish, looking as though a return to six would be beneficial. *Official explanation: jockey said gelding hung left handed from 3f out*
**Funfair Wane** was always up with the pace and this inconsistent individual ran one of his better races off his tumbling mark.
**Maktavish** *Official explanation: jockey said gelding hung right handed throughout*
**Whistler** *Official explanation: jockey said gelding slipped leaving stalls and hung right handed*

## 5288 STANLEYBET.COM OLD BOROUGH CUP STKS (HERITAGE H'CAP) 1m 6f
**2:05** (2:06) (B1) (0-105,105) 3-Y-0+ **£52,000** (£16,000; £8,000; £4,000) **Stalls** Low

Form RPR

0304 **1** **Defining**[17] 4858 5-9-3 **98**........................ JPMurtagh 1 111+
(JRFanshawe) *midfeld: hdwy 4f out: led over 1f out: sn hung lft: r.o: eased cl home* **11/1**

3512 **2** *¾* **Sergeant Cecil**[39] 4218 5-8-12 **93**........................ SDrowne 7 102
(BRMillman) *hld up: hdwy 3f out: rdn over 2f out: chsd wnr 1f out: styd on* **10/1**[3]

1111 **3** *hd* **Sendintank**[1] 5266 4-8-1 **82** 5ex........................ MartinDwyer 12 91+
(SCWilliams) *hld up: nt clr run and lost pl over 3f out: hdwy whn swtchd lft over 1f out: fin wl* **7/1**[2]

1314 **4** *shd* **Lochbuie (IRE)**[16] 4888 3-8-5 **97**........................ JFEgan 3 106
(GWragg) *in tch: rdn 4f out: hdwy over 2f out: styd on ins fnl f* **11/2**[1]

1054 **5** *½* **Millville**[18] 4831 4-8-4 **85**........................ PRobinson 11 93+
(MAJarvis) *hld up: hdwy over 1f out: r.o ins fnl f* **7/1**[2]

3520 **6** *1* **Crow Wood**[17] 4858 5-9-0 **95**........................ KMcEvoy 6 101
(JGGiven) *in tch: n.m.r and lost pl over 3f out: rallied over 1f out: styd on* **33/1**

1606 **7** *nk* **Ski Jump (USA)**[18] 4831 4-8-0 **81**........................(v) PHanagan 9 87
(RAFahey) *midfield: hdwy over 3f out: rdn over 2f out: one pce ins fnl f* **25/1**

0011 **8** *¾* **High Action (USA)**[34] 4361 4-8-9 **90**........................(t) JPSpencer 15 95
(IanWilliams) *in tch: led over 2f out: rdn and hdd over 1f out: no ex ins fnl f* **12/1**

-064 **9** *2* **Lodger (FR)**[35] 4345 4-8-8 **89**........................ RHughes 16 91
(JNoseda) *hld up: rdn over 3f out: hdwy over 2f out: swtchd lft over 1f out: no ex ins fnl f* **16/1**

-212 **10** *nk* **Loves Travelling (IRE)**[57] 3716 4-8-9 **90**........................ DHolland 4 92+
(LMCumani) *hld up: hdwy whn hmpd over 1f out: no imp fnl f* **11/2**[1]

4110 **11** *nk* **Trance (IRE)**[20] 4777 4-8-1 **87**........................ PMakin(5) 10 88
(TDBarron) *hld up: rdn over 4f out: hdwy over 3f out: one pce fnl f* **100/1**

0331 **12** *3* **Sahem (IRE)**[12] 4990 7-8-3 **84**........................ WSupple 20 81
(CJTeague) *racd keenly: prom: rdn 3f out: ev ch 2f out: wknd over 1f out* **66/1**

42-4 **13** *shd* **It's The Limit (USA)**[42] 4123 5-8-11 **92**........................ MJKinane 19 89
(MrsAJPerrett) *rrd s: a bhd* **12/1**

1061 **14** *2* **Dr Sharp (IRE)**[14] 4934 4-8-1 **82**........................ JQuinn 8 76
(TPTate) *s.i.s: midfield: hdwy over 4f out: sn rdn: wknd over 1f out* **25/1**

1060 **15** *½* **Jorobaden (FR)**[70] 3310 4-8-6 **87**........................ RMullen 2 81
(CFWall) *midfield: rdn over 3f out: wknd over 1f out: sn eased* **66/1**

5000 **16** *nk* **Trust Rule**[17] 4858 4-8-9 **90**........................ MHills 18 83
(BWHills) *towars rr: effrt over 2f out: no imp* **25/1**

006 **17** *1* **Almah (SAF)**[28] 4529 6-8-6 **86** ow1........................ RWinston 14 79
(MissVenetiaWilliams) *s.i.s: sn chsd ldrs: rdn and wknd 3f out* **66/1**

1205 **18** *½* **Bendarshaan**[22] 4715 4-8-8 **89**........................ RFfrench 17 80
(MJohnston) *in tch: rdn and wknd over 3f out* **66/1**

-004 **19** *1 ¼* **Albanov (IRE)**[14] 4932 4-8-13 **94**........................ KDarley 5 83
(MJohnston) *racd keenly: prom: rdn over 3f out: ev ch over 2f out: hmpd whn wkng over 1f out* **33/1**

2/0- **20** *2 ½* **Pushkin (IRE)**[232] 6-9-10 **105**........................ SChin 13 91
(MJohnston) *led: rdn 4f out: hdd over 2f out: wknd over 1f out* **100/1**

3m 0.43s (-5.72) **Going Correction** -0.275s/f (Firm)
**WFA** 3 from 4yo+ 11lb **20** Ran SP% **119.8**
Speed ratings: **105,104,104,104,104 103,103,102,101,101 101,99,99,98,98 98,97,97,96,95**CSF £103.06 CT £834.87 TOTE £18.10: £3.90, £2.70, £2.60, £2.10; EX 120.40 Trifecta £670.40 Part won. Pool: £944.32. 0.10 winning tickets..
**Owner** Mrs V Shelton **Bred** Mrs A J Brudenell **Trained** Newmarket, Suffolk
■ With this winner trainer James Fanshawe passed the £1 million prizemoney mark in a season for the first time in his career.
■ Stewards Enquiry : R Hughes one-day ban: careless riding (Sep 15)

**FOCUS**
A strong handicap involving some progressive types and run at a sound pace. The form is solid, being rated through the runner-up.

**NOTEBOOK**
**Defining** led over a furlong from home having travelled well throughout, to win a shade comfortably off a career-high mark. This was his first success over the trip, and with regards to the future the options are varied as the five-year-old holds an entry in the Melbourne Cup but it would be no surprise to see him over timber as he has already schooled. According to his trainer, who has a fine record over the years with the few jumpers he has sent out, he enjoys his jumping.
**Sergeant Cecil** is a much-improved performer and, with the ground drying out to his liking, ran another big race.
**Sendintank** was 14lb higher than when winning well the previous day yet looked a shade unfortunate not to land his fifth race on the bounce, having been denied a run and shuffled back in the field early in the straight before weaving through to finish well. He is a credit to connections and on this evidence he can continue to defy the Handicapper.
**Lochbuie(IRE)** appreciated the return to a sounder surface compared with that which he last encountered, and this progressive type stayed on in good style.
**Millville**, a lightly-raced four-year-old, ran on towards the end, highlighting the fact that there are races in him on turf before a possible return to the All-Weather, the sphere in which he has gained all his wins.
**Crow Wood**, fairly well exposed, was not beaten far so it would be folly to suggest he did not stay.
**Ski Jump(USA)** stayed adequately on his first mission over the trip.
**High Action(USA)** found this race a shade hot compared with his most recent assignments.
**Loves Travelling(IRE)** was hampered when trying to make a run approaching the final furlong, so never really got into the fight. This was his first time over the trip and is worth another chance.
**It's The Limit(USA)** *Official explanation: jockey said gelding reared at start*

## 5289 STANLEYBET SPRINT CUP (GROUP 1) 6f
**2:35** (2:39) (A1) 3-Y-0+ **£130,500** (£49,500; £24,750; £11,250) **Stalls** Low

Form RPR

0-11 **1** **Tante Rose (IRE)**[57] 3715 4-8-11 **111**........................ RHughes 14 121
(RCharlton) *midfield: rdn and hdwy over 1f out: r.o strly ins fnl f to ld post* **10/1**

0251 **2** *shd* **Somnus**[27] 4595 4-9-0 **118**........................ MJKinane 5 124
(TDEasterby) *a.p: rdn to ld over 1f out: hdd post* **7/1**[3]

1-30 **3** *¾* **Patavellian (IRE)**[58] 3674 6-9-0 **114**........................(b) SDrowne 4 121
(RCharlton) *dwlt: trckd ldrs: rdn over 1f out: ev ch ins fnl f: nt qckn cl home* **14/1**

5-10 **4** *1 ½* **Royal Millennium (IRE)**[27] 4595 6-9-0 **111**........................ TEDurcan 8 118+
(MRChannon) *bhd: hdwy whn nt clr run and swtchd lft over 1f out: r.o ins fnl f* **50/1**

1060 **5** *hd* **Monsieur Bond (IRE)**[27] 4595 4-9-0 **115**........................(b[1]) FLynch 19 116
(BSmart) *a.p: rdn 2f out: ev ch over 1f out: nt qckn ins fnl f* **33/1**

0513 **6** *1* **One Cool Cat (USA)**[16] 4886 3-8-12........................ JPSpencer 7 113
(APO'Brien, Ire) *midfield: rdn and hdwy over 1f out: nt pce to chal* **6/4**[1]

5315 **7** *½* **Orientor**[16] 4886 6-9-0 **115**........................ WSupple 16 112
(JSGoldie) *midfield: rdn and hdwy over 1f out: styd on one pce ins fnl f* **25/1**

4652 **8** *hd* **Welsh Emperor (IRE)**[16] 4889 5-9-0 **107**........................(b) RWinston 17 111
(TPTate) *led: rdn and hdd over 1f out: wknd ins fnl f* **66/1**

2024 **9** *½* **Ashdown Express (IRE)**[27] 4595 5-9-0 **117**........................ RMullen 13 110
(CFWall) *bhd: pushed along 1/2-way: hdwy over 1f out: edgd lft ent fnl f: styd on: nt rch ldrs* **16/1**

10-1 **10** *hd* **Ratio**[35] 4357 6-9-0........................(t) PRobinson 1 109
(JEHammond, France) *hld up: rdn and hdwy over 1f out: nt pce to chal* **18/1**

6016 **11** *¾* **Airwave**[16] 4886 4-8-11 **110**........................ KDarley 12 104
(HCandy) *trckd ldrs: rdn over 1f out: wknd ins fnl f* **16/1**

0161 **12** *nk* **Bahamian Pirate (USA)**[16] 4886 9-9-0 **110**........................ DHolland 9 106
(DNicholls) *bhd: nt clr run over 1f out: sn rdn: styd on: nvr trbld ldrs* **40/1**

2661 **13** *1* **Mac Love**[35] 4317 3-8-12 **104**........................ JFEgan 6 103
(JAkehurst) *trckd ldrs tl rdn and wknd 2f out* **100/1**

0324 **14** *nk* **Lochridge**[20] 4779 5-8-11 **101**........................ MartinDwyer 3 99
(AMBalding) *prom: rdn 2f out: sn wknd* **100/1**

5104 **15** *hd* **Tychy**[5] 5181 5-8-11 **98**........................ PHanagan 10 99
(SCWilliams) *prom: rdn 2f out: wknd over 1f out* **200/1**

4000 **16** *nk* **Capricho (IRE)**[16] 4889 7-9-0 **100**........................ JQuinn 2 101
(JAkehurst) *midfield: pushed along 1/2-way: wknd over 1f out* **150/1**

1310 **17** *¾* **Frizzante**[27] 4595 5-8-11 **115**........................ JPMurtagh 18 95
(JRFanshawe) *hld up: pushed along 2f out: nvr on terms* **13/2**[2]

-332 **18** *nk* **Cartography (IRE)**[49] 3940 3-8-12 **106**........................(t) KMcEvoy 11 97
(SaeedBinSuroor) *trckd ldrs tl rdn and wknd over 2f out* **50/1**

3015 **19** *1* **The Trader (IRE)**[27] 4595 6-9-0 **114**........................(b) DSweeney 15 94
(MBlanshard) *s.i.s: a bhd* **20/1**

1m 11.58s (-3.31) **Going Correction** -0.225s/f (Firm)
**WFA** 3 from 4yo+ 2lb **19** Ran SP% **121.2**
Speed ratings: **113,112,111,109,109 108,107,107,106,106 105,105,103,103,103 102,101,101,99**CSF £71.81 TOTE £10.40: £2.60, £3.00, £5.30; EX 80.50 Trifecta £612.10 Pool: £3793.52. 4.40 winning tickets.
**Owner** B E Nielsen **Bred** Addison Racing Ltd Inc **Trained** Beckhampton, Wilts

**FOCUS**
By no means an outstanding renewal of one of the most important six-furlong sprints in the calendar, but a record field, which confirms just how open the sprinting division is at present. One Cool Cat was backed virtually to the exclusion of all the other runners, and his presence in the field certainly added to the attendance. The winning time was unspectacular for a Group One.

**NOTEBOOK**
**Tante Rose(IRE)** did not immediately find her stride when asked to quicken but, once she did, flew home and got up in the shadow of the post. Physically she has done well from three to four and, given the way she knuckled down to her task, quickening up in the process, she has further improvement in her. She has already proven she stays seven furlongs, and it will be very interesting to see if she goes for the Prix de la Foret over that distance.
**Somnus** kept finding more for pressure and was unlucky to be collared right on the line. He deserves a lot of credit and proved he does not need a soft surface. The Prix de la Foret could be on the agenda, and it's worth remembering that on the only occasion he has been tried at the trip he had yet to recover his form.
**Patavellian(IRE)** ◆, bandaged in front and reportedly lame only a fortnight previously, was also given every chance and returned a very good effort. This should set him up perfectly for Longchamp, where he will bid for a repeat win in the Prix de l'Abbaye.
**Royal Millennium(IRE)** ◆ made good ground from the rear and, after meeting some trouble in running, was never nearer than at the finish. He may go for the Prix de la Foret.
**Monsieur Bond(IRE)** ran a fine race in first-time blinkers, racing up the stands'-side rail. He already has a place at stud next year but in the meantime is another who is likely to take his chance in the Prix de la Foret, where softer ground would be an obvious plus.
**One Cool Cat(USA)** looked magnificent in the paddock but had sweated up quite badly by the time it came to race. Held up, he was asked for a big effort two furlongs out and the response was not immediate, although he did stay on inside the final furlong after receiving a bump from Lochridge. Overall he looked short of the necessary toe for this grade.
**Orientor** was another to stay on late without looking likely to trouble the leaders.
**Welsh Emperor(IRE)** deserves a great deal of credit in running the race of his life, suggesting a another black-type affair is within his compass.
**Ashdown Express(IRE)** never got competitive and ought to have finished closer.
**Ratio** failed to land a blow.
**Airwave** found little when asked for her effort.
**Bahamian Pirate(USA)** did not get involved, but he experienced trouble in running and this effort can be forgotten.
**Frizzante** was disappointing, but her jockey reported that she had hung left throughout the race. *Official explanation: jockey said mare hung left handed throughout*

**Cartography(IRE)** failed to handle the conditions. *Official explanation: jockey said gelding lost its action 3f out*
**The Trader(IRE)** finished last but was struck into during the race. *Official explanation: trainer said gelding was struck into*

## 5290 STANLEYBET MOBILE EBF MAIDEN STKS — 6f
**3:05** (3:08) (D2) 2-Y-O — **£5,720** (£1,760; £880; £440) **Stalls** Low

| Form | | | | RPR |
|---|---|---|---|---|
| | **1** | | **Zohar (USA)** 2-9-0 ... MJKinane 12 (BJMeehan) *bhd: rdn and hdwy over 2f out: drvn to ld 1f out: r.o strly ins fnl f* **14/1** | 82+ |
| 2 | **2** | *1 1/4* | **Munaddam (USA)**[30] [4494] 2-9-0 ... WSupple 9 (SaeedBinSuroor) *s.i.s: bhd: rdn over 2f out: gd hdwy fnl f: kpt on wl cl home but nt rch wnr* **4/1**[2] | 78 |
| 0 | **3** | *3/4* | **Aviation**[17] [4844] 2-9-0 ... RHughes 6 (RHannon) *bhd: rdn over 2f out: styd on fnl f: fin wl* **50/1** | 76 |
| | **4** | *nk* | **Museeb (USA)** 2-9-0 ... JPMurtagh 11 (JLDunlop) *s.i.s: bhd: rdn 2f out: gd hdwy over 1f out: r.o wl fnl f: nt rch ldrs* **9/2**[3] | 75+ |
| 2 | **5** | *1/2* | **One Great Idea (IRE)**[29] [4507] 2-9-0 ... PHanagan 13 (TDBarron) *chsd ldrs: rdn 2f out: hung lft and wknd ins fnl f* **7/1** | 73 |
| | **6** | *nk* | **Grosvenor Square (IRE)** 2-9-0 ... KMcEvoy 8 (SaeedBinSuroor) *bhd: sn pushed along: hdwy ins fnl 2f: kpt on fnl f: nt rch ldrs* **7/2**[1] | 72 |
| 23 | **7** | *1 1/4* | **Sacranun**[49] [3925] 2-9-0 ... DHolland 3 (LMCumani) *chsd ldrs: rdn 2f out: wknd ins fnl f* **6/1** | 69 |
| 05 | **8** | *shd* | **Sydneyroughdiamond**[15] [4900] 2-9-0 ... RMullen 1 (MMullineaux) *pressed ldr tl led ins fnl 2f: hdd 1f out: sn wknd* **200/1** | 68? |
| 0 | **9** | *2 1/2* | **Shankly Bond (IRE)**[8] [5095] 2-9-0 ... FLynch 4 (BSmart) *sn pushed along in rr: sme hdwy fr over 1f out: nt a danger* **33/1** | 61 |
| 0 | **10** | *6* | **Owed**[18] [4824] 2-9-0 ... (t) TEDurcan 5 (MrsGSRees) *outpcd most of way* **200/1** | 43 |
| 520 | **11** | *nk* | **Touch Of Silk (IRE)**[78] [3031] 2-8-9 73 ... MHills 2 (BWHills) *chsd ldrs over 4f* **7/1** | 37 |
| | **12** | *3* | **Distinctive Mind** 2-9-0 ... MFenton 10 (TDEasterby) *sn led: hdd ins fnl 2f: sn wknd* **66/1** | 33 |
| | **13** | *5* | **De Bullions** 2-9-0 ... MartinDwyer 7 (AMBalding) *a outpcd* **66/1** | 18 |
| 0 | **14** | *25* | **Cool Sands (IRE)**[7] [5128] 2-9-0 ... RWinston 14 (DShaw) *s.i.s: sn rcvrd: wknd qckly 1/2-way* **200/1** | — |

1m 14.6s (-0.29) **Going Correction** -0.225s/f (Firm) — **14** Ran SP% **115.7**
Speed ratings: **92,90,89,88,88 87,86,86,82,74 74,70,63,30**CSF £66.52 TOTE £23.70: £4.90, £2.40, £9.10; EX 110.90.
**Owner** E H Jones (paints) Ltd **Bred** Gracefield Equine Et Al **Trained** Upper Lambourn, Berks

**FOCUS**
There were some decent-looking two-year-olds in this race although the bare form rates as little better than average and the time was modest. That said, a number of the runners have the scope for a good deal of improvement and the form may prove reliable.

**NOTEBOOK**
**Zohar(USA)**, a Middle Park entry, readily picked up the leaders when asked to although his head carriage was a little high, probably through greenness. To be fair, he did little wrong, despite edging left when hitting the front.
**Munaddam(USA)** travelled well for much of the race, but did not find as much when asked for a bigger effort as might have been expected. He also drifted left in the final furlong.
**Aviation** ◆ had to be given a reminder fairly early on to keep his mind on the job in hand. However, once the penny dropped, he stayed on under hands-and-heels and was never nearer than at the finish. A strong colt, he looks well up to winning a similar race.
**Museeb(USA)** ◆ did plenty of shouting in the paddock and was also green during the race. He too took a while to realise what he was here for but, when he did, ran on. He should improve for this and stay further, but given his round action he might not be so effective on quick going.
**One Great Idea(IRE)**, runner-up in similar company on his debut a month ago, seemed to have every chance but hung under pressure.
**Grosvenor Square(IRE)**, a quick-actioned colt, took a while to warm to his task, but he was another to keep on for a never-nearer finish and should improve. He will prove best on a sound surface over further.
**Sacranun** looked a little one-paced in the final two furlongs, although his jockey had trouble keeping him straight. *Official explanation: jockey said colt hung right handed throughout*
**Cool Sands(IRE)** appeared to hang to his left from halfway.

## 5291 STANLEYBET ROBERT SANGSTER SUPERIOR MILE (LISTED RACE) — 1m 30y
**3:40** (3:42) (A1) 3-Y-O+ — **£23,200** (£8,800; £4,400; £2,000) **Stalls** Low

| Form | | | | RPR |
|---|---|---|---|---|
| 21-0 | **1** | | **With Reason (USA)**[112] [2109] 6-9-2 115 ... (t) KMcEvoy 5 (SaeedBinSuroor) *mde all: rdn over 1f out: kpt on wl* **11/2**[3] | 111 |
| 35- | **2** | *1* | **Troubadour (IRE)**[45] [4038] 3-8-11 ... JPSpencer 9 (APO'Brien, Ire) *in tch: hdwy to chse wnr over 2f out: rdn over 1f out: nt qckn ins fnl f* **2/1**[1] | 109 |
| 2461 | **3** | *1 1/4* | **Audience**[16] [4887] 4-9-2 98 ... (p) JQuinn 1 (JAkehurst) *racd keenly: in tch: rdn and hdwy over 2f out: styd on same pce fnl f* **14/1** | 106 |
| 0300 | **4** | *5* | **Excelsius (IRE)**[16] [4887] 4-9-2 96 ... (b[1]) KDarley 7 (JLDunlop) *plld hrd: hld up: rdn and outpcd over 2f out: no imp on ldrs* **66/1** | 95 |
| 1215 | **5** | *1* | **Shot To Fame (USA)**[23] [4685] 5-9-7 111 ... JPMurtagh 2 (PWHarris) *trckd ldr to 5f out: rdn over 2f out: wknd over 1f out* **4/1**[2] | 97 |
| 0213 | **6** | *1 1/4* | **St Petersburg**[16] [4887] 4-9-2 101 ... DHolland 8 (MHTompkins) *trckd ldrs: chsd wnr 5f out tl over 2f out: wknd over 1f out* **9/1** | 89 |
| -110 | **7** | *6* | **Putra Pekan**[83] [2923] 6-9-5 110 ... (b) PRobinson 4 (MAJarvis) *plld hrd: hld up: rn wd and hdwy over 4f out: wknd over 2f out* **11/2**[3] | 79 |
| 2330 | **8** | *3 1/2* | **Millennium Force**[21] [4745] 6-9-2 106 ... TEDurcan 6 (MRChannon) *hld up: effrt over 2f out: no imp* **16/1** | 67 |

1m 41.8s (-3.75) **Going Correction** -0.275s/f (Firm)
**WFA** 3 from 4yo+ 5lb — **8** Ran SP% **108.1**
Speed ratings: **107,106,104,99,98 97,91,88**CSF £15.03 TOTE £5.70: £2.20, £1.20, £2.80; EX 13.70.
**Owner** Godolphin **Bred** Gainsborough Farm Inc **Trained** Newmarket, Suffolk
■ Stewards Enquiry : J P Spencer caution: used whip with whip arm above shoulder height

**FOCUS**
The first three home came clear of the others in the final two furlongs, with the winner probably not having to be at his best to win. The time was ordinary for a Listed event and neither the first two needed to run to thier best.

**NOTEBOOK**
**With Reason(USA)** made all for a fairly comfortable win. He gradually increased the pace in the straight to record a confidence-boosting win. He should give a good account of himself next time.
**Troubadour(IRE)** took the eye in the paddock, but betrayed his inexperience by hanging in behind the winner when asked for his effort.
**Audience** put in a solid effort in third place, keeping on despite being held by the first two home.
**Excelsius(IRE)** raced too keenly in first-time blinkers.
**Shot To Fame(USA)** was revved-up in the preliminaries and folded in the final quarter-mile. All of his winning form has come at seven furlongs, and has yet to conclusively prove that he is effective at this longer trip.
**Putra Pekan** raced very keenly in the early stages, but then seemed happier when his rider let him stride out on his own up the centre of the track in the straight. However, it was a short-lived period of joy. *Official explanation: jockey said horse hung right handed in home straight*

## 5292 STANLEYBET 0808 100 1221 NURSERY — 1m 30y
**4:15** (4:18) (B1) 2-Y-O — **£15,474** (£5,869; £2,934; £1,334) **Stalls** Low

| Form | | | | RPR |
|---|---|---|---|---|
| 0613 | **1** | | **Spaced (IRE)**[16] [4890] 2-9-2 **81** ... RHughes 6 (RHannon) *trckd ldrs: rdn over 2f out: led over 1f out: all out* **20/1** | 85 |
| 31 | **2** | *shd* | **Hallhoo (IRE)**[21] [4747] 2-9-2 **81** ... TEDurcan 1 (MRChannon) *in tch: hdwy whn nt clr run 2f out: sn rdn: r.o ins fnl f* **7/2**[2] | 85+ |
| 0033 | **3** | *3/4* | **Wise Dennis**[9] [5052] 2-9-0 **79** ... KMcEvoy 4 (APJarvis) *racd keenly: midfield: rdn over 2f out: r.o ins fnl f: nrst fin* **11/1** | 81 |
| 21 | **4** | *1 1/2* | **Looks Could Kill (USA)**[24] [4633] 2-9-7 **86** ... JPMurtagh 2 (GAButler) *hld up: nt clr run 2f out: hdwy over 1f out: hung lft ins fnl f: styd on wl cl home* **5/2**[1] | 85+ |
| 6541 | **5** | *hd* | **Im Spartacus**[14] [4953] 2-8-10 **75** ... MFenton 9 (IAWood) *coltish to post: a.p: rdn over 3f out: hung lft over 1f out: nt qckn ins fnl f* **16/1** | 73 |
| 133 | **6** | *2 1/2* | **Simply St Lucia**[8] [5082] 2-8-10 **75** ... RWinston 11 (JRWeymes) *led: rdn 2f out: hdd over 1f out: no ex ins fnl f* **100/1** | 68 |
| 565 | **7** | *3/4* | **Traianos (USA)**[36] [4292] 2-8-9 **79** ... NDeSouza(5) 10 (PFICole) *racd keenly: trckd ldrs: rdn over 2f out: wknd over 1f out* **33/1** | 70 |
| 3250 | **8** | *shd* | **Adoration**[58] [3677] 2-8-13 **78** ... RFfrench 5 (MJohnston) *hld up: pushed along over 3f out: styd on fnl f: nt rch ldrs* **25/1** | 69 |
| 4411 | **9** | *2 1/2* | **Night Of Joy (IRE)**[5] [5188] 2-9-8 **87** 6ex ... PRobinson 3 (MAJarvis) *racd keenly: in tch: rdn over 1f out: sn btn* **7/2**[2] | 80+ |
| 455 | **10** | *3/4* | **Turks Wood (IRE)**[24] [4649] 2-8-10 **75** ... DHolland 8 (MHTompkins) *midfield: rdn over 3f out: wknd over 1f out* **33/1** | 59 |
| 01 | **11** | *1/2* | **Ceiriog Valley**[14] [4930] 2-9-6 **85** ... MHills 7 (BWHills) *pushed along over 3f out: a bhd* **7/1**[3] | 68 |

1m 43.74s (-1.81) **Going Correction** -0.275s/f (Firm) — **11** Ran SP% **115.2**
Speed ratings: **98,97,97,95,95 92,92,92,89,88 88**CSF £84.17 CT £843.27 TOTE £21.60: £4.00, £1.70, £2.60; EX 126.60.
**Owner** de La Warr Racing **Bred** Tally-Ho Stud **Trained** East Everleigh, Wilts

**FOCUS**
Some interesting types in a decent nursery event. The form is strong and the race should produce its share of future winners.

**NOTEBOOK**
**Spaced(IRE)** ran on well for pressure once he got the gap he needed along the far rail. He should continue to run well.
**Hallhoo(IRE)** ◆ was denied a run two furlongs from home, but was possibly a little unlucky and should continue to improve.
**Wise Dennis** took a little while to get himself organised in the straight but, once it all came together, he ran on well. He certainly has ability. *Official explanation: jockey said gelding was too keen early*
**Looks Could Kill(USA)** is an attractive colt who is still learning his trade. Short of room two furlongs out, he then stayed on when switched to the far rail.
**Im Spartacus** played up when out on the track and was unruly at the start. That said he put in a solid effort.
**Simply St Lucia** may be of interest over a slightly shorter trip.
**Traianos(USA)** produced another example on the day of a horse hanging under pressure.
**Adoration** made late gains and are also capable of better again.
**Night Of Joy(IRE)** appeared to lose her action when coming under pressure. *Official explanation: jockey said the race came too soon*
**Ceiriog Valley** looked all at sea in the final two furlongs.

## 5293 STANLEY CASINOS H'CAP — 1m 2f 120y
**4:45** (4:50) (E3) (0-70,70) 3-Y-O — **£5,543** (£1,705; £852; £426) **Stalls** High

| Form | | | | RPR |
|---|---|---|---|---|
| 0501 | **1** | | **Stephano**[2] [5245] 3-8-13 **62** 3ex ... MHills 10 (BWHills) *midfield: rdn and hdwy 3f out: led over 1f out: edgd lft ins fnl f: r.o* **2/1**[1] | 79+ |
| 0223 | **2** | *3* | **Captain Marryat**[68] [3386] 3-8-10 **59** ... WSupple 4 (PWHarris) *a.p: rdn and ev ch over 1f out: nt qckn ins fnl f* **6/1**[3] | 68 |
| 0046 | **3** | *1 1/2* | **Mr Midasman (IRE)**[16] [4882] 3-8-7 **56** oh1 ... JQuinn 2 (RHollinshead) *hld up: hdwy over 3f out: rdn over 2f out: kpt on ins fnl f* **25/1** | 62 |
| 0502 | **4** | *3/4* | **Patrixtoo (FR)**[24] [4655] 3-8-11 **60** ... PRobinson 7 (MHTompkins) *led: rdn and hdd over 1f out: kpt on same pce* **10/1** | 65 |
| 0020 | **5** | *1 1/2* | **American Duke (USA)**[27] [4582] 3-9-3 **66** ... KMcEvoy 13 (BJMeehan) *in tch: rdn over 3f out: kpt on same pce fnl f* **20/1** | 69 |
| 0042 | **6** | *3/4* | **Turtle Patriarch (IRE)**[13] [4971] 3-8-11 **60** ... SDrowne 1 (MrsAJPerrett) *in tch: rdn and hdwy over 2f out: one pce ins fnl f: eased whn hld towards fin* **10/1** | 61 |
| 4520 | **7** | *2 1/2* | **Santa Caterina (IRE)**[30] [4493] 3-9-7 **70** ... KDarley 12 (JLDunlop) *racd keenly: prom: rdn and ev ch over 2f out: wknd over 1f out* **25/1** | 67 |
| 400 | **8** | *1* | **Estepona**[102] [2392] 3-9-2 **65** ... RWinston 9 (MissJACamacho) *midfield: rdn over 2f out: nvr able to chal* **33/1** | 60 |
| 0500 | **9** | *shd* | **Impulsive Bid (IRE)**[31] [4451] 3-8-7 **56** ... PHanagan 11 (JeddO'Keeffe) *midfield: rdn over 3f out: nvr trbld ldrs* **66/1** | 51 |
| 053 | **10** | *1* | **Classic Lease**[23] [4679] 3-8-12 **61** ... FLynch 8 (RHollinshead) *bhd: effrt over 3f out: no imp on ldrs* **40/1** | 55 |
| 662 | **11** | *1 3/4* | **Miss Inkha**[10] [5038] 3-8-12 **61** ... MartinDwyer 14 (RGuest) *in tch: rdn over 3f out: wknd over 2f out* **40/1** | 52 |
| 1060 | **12** | *1 3/4* | **Zaffeu**[25] [4618] 3-9-3 **66** ... (b[1]) TEDurcan 5 (NPLittmoden) *s.i.s: in rr: rdn over 2f out: nvr on terms* **50/1** | 54 |
| 1000 | **13** | *2* | **Miss Eloise**[24] [4628] 3-8-9 **58** ... MFenton 17 (TDEasterby) *stmbld s: a bhd* **50/1** | 42 |
| 001 | **14** | *6* | **Hilltop Rhapsody**[61] [3592] 3-9-6 **69** ... JPMurtagh 15 (DJDaly) *trckd ldrs: rdn over 2f out: sn wknd* **12/1** | 43 |
| 0352 | **15** | *7* | **Keeper's Lodge (IRE)**[6] [5145] 3-9-7 **70** ... DHolland 16 (BAMcmahon) *a bhd* **5/1**[2] | 32 |
| 3440 | **16** | *16* | **Supamach (IRE)**[43] [4092] 3-9-2 **65** ... JFEgan 6 (PFICole) *trckd ldrs: pushed along over 4f out: wknd over 3f out* **33/1** | — |

3300 **17** *13* **Turner**[2] 5245 3-9-7 **70**............(v[1]) RHughes 3 —
(WMBrisbourne) *s.i.s: midfield: wknd qckly 4f out: eased over 2f out* **33/1**

2m 13.54s (-4.19) **Going Correction** -0.275s/f (Firm) **17** Ran SP% **121.7**
Speed ratings: **104,101,100,100,99 98,96,96,95,95 93,92,91,86,81 70,60**CSF £11.23 CT £241.18 TOTE £2.80: £1.30, £2.00, £6.20, £2.30; EX 20.60 Place 6 £303.98, Place 5 £139.34.
**Owner** Guy Reed **Bred** G Reed **Trained** Lambourn, Berks

**FOCUS**
A modest handicap and not all that competitive, but a fair pace and sound enough form for the grade.

**NOTEBOOK**
**Stephano** confirmed he is on the upgrade by comfortably landing the finale. Based on this effort he should stay further, and provided that the Handicapper does not overreact, could go well again off his revised mark.
**Captain Marryat** appeared not to see out this extended trip.
**Mr Midasman(IRE)** had to be switched to deliver his run and was never nearer than at the finish. He appeared to put in an improved effort over the longer trip.
**Zaffeu**was a lot further behind the winner today than he had been at Redcar and, even allowing for his slow start, never looked likely to get involved.
**Miss Eloise** was sweating in the paddock and got worked up in the stalls.
**Keeper's Lodge(IRE)** seemed ill-at-ease on the going in the final three furlongs and the race may have come to soon after her Beverley effort. *Official explanation: jockey said filly was never travelling and lost her action in the home straight*
**Turner** *Official explanation: jockey said gelding moved badly*
T/Plt: £409.90 to a £1 stake. Pool: £84,863.20. 151.10 winning tickets. T/Qpdt: £80.80 to a £1 stake. Pool: £3,190.90. 29.20 winning tickets. DO

## 5268 KEMPTON (R-H)
### Saturday, September 4

**OFFICIAL GOING: Good to firm (good in places)**
Wind: nil Weather: sunny, very warm

### 5294 PENTAX "PERFECT IMAGE" H'CAP — 1m (J)
2:10 (2:11) (C1) (0-100,95) 3-Y-O — £12,145 (£4,606; £2,303; £1,047) Stalls High

| Form | | | | RPR |
|---|---|---|---|---|
| 0605 | **1** | | **Mystical Girl (USA)**[11] 5025 3-9-3 **91** ... KFallon 5 (MJohnston) *lw: mde all: rdn clr fnl f* **5/2**[1] | 101 |
| 1115 | **2** | *2* | **Diamond Lodge**[31] 4442 3-9-4 **92** ... EAhern 6 (JNoseda) *in tch: chsd wnr over 2f out: hrd rdn over 1f out: no imp* **7/2**[2] | 97 |
| 321- | **3** | *nk* | **Pedrillo**[338] 5325 3-8-13 **87** ... SSanders 4 (SirMarkPrescott) *s.s: hld up in rr: rdn and hdwy 2f out: kpt on fnl f* **9/2**[3] | 92+ |
| 1000 | **4** | *nk* | **State Dilemma (IRE)**[16] 4887 3-9-3 **91** ... RHills 10 (BWHills) *lw: towards rr: pushed along after 3f: hdwy on ins 3f out: styd on same pce fnl f* **20/1** | 95 |
| 0224 | **5** | *½* | **Jazz Scene (IRE)**[49] 3959 3-9-4 **95** ... SHitchcott(3) 7 (MRChannon) *lw: dwlt: towards rr: rdn and outpcd 1/2-way: styd on appr fnl f* **8/1** | 98 |
| -004 | **6** | *½* | **Sgt Pepper (IRE)**[56] 3751 3-9-4 **92** ... RLMoore 9 (RHannon) *mid-div: wd and outpcd st: rallied over 1f out: styd on same pce* **25/1** | 94 |
| 5204 | **7** | *1 ¾* | **Tranquil Sky**[57] 3689 3-8-6 **83** ... LPKeniry(3) 1 (NACallaghan) *chsd ldrs: hrd rdn 2f out: wknd over 1f out* **14/1** | 81 |
| 0625 | **8** | *2* | **Flip Flop And Fly (IRE)**[24] 4646 3-8-11 **85** ... JFortune 2 (SKirk) *hld up in rr: hung bdly lft to stands' rail in st: n.d* **9/1** | 78 |
| 0034 | **9** | *1 ¼* | **Surf The Net**[19] 4812 3-8-11 **85** ... (p) DaneO'Neill 8 (RHannon) *prom 5f* **33/1** | 75 |
| 5360 | **10** | *6* | **Qasirah (IRE)**[58] 3671 3-9-6 **94** ... (b) LDettori 3 (MAJarvis) *lw: jnd wnr after 2f: rdn and fnd nil over 2f out: qckly lost pl* **10/1** | 70 |

1m 37.64s (-1.98) **Going Correction** -0.20s/f (Firm) **10** Ran SP% **117.4**
Speed ratings: **101,99,98,98,97 97,95,93,92,86**CSF £10.87 CT £37.18 TOTE £3.50: £1.80, £1.80, £1.80; EX 14.80.
**Owner** T T Bloodstocks **Bred** Simon Tindall **Trained** Middleham Moor, N Yorks
■ Stewards Enquiry : E Ahern one-day ban: used whip in the incorrect place (Sep 15)

**FOCUS**
A decent handicap contested by some smart three-year-old handicappers, though the winning time was modest. The winner is ideally suited by events like this, in which she can control things from the front, and the third has a bright future.

**NOTEBOOK**
**Mystical Girl(USA)** had plenty in her favour, ridden from the front in the right company and over her optimum trip, and she was readily holding the opposition in the last 200 yards.
**Diamond Lodge** has had a fine season and again ran well, though a 5lb rise in the weights counted against her in the end.
**Pedrillo** ◆ looked on a stiffish mark for his first run of the season, but it was reasonable to expect significant improvement. Weak in the market and slowly away, he was going on at the finish and did his Cambridgeshire prospects no harm at all.
**State Dilemma(IRE)** has only won at seven furlongs but he stays this trip alright, if a little too slowly on this occasion.
**Jazz Scene(IRE)** has won only once, over six furlongs, but this run suggests he should stay a bit beyond a mile on fast ground.
**Sgt Pepper(IRE)** gets this trip well but he has not done anything special this season and on this occasion he lacked the pace to stay competitive turning for home, though being forced wide did not help.
**Flip Flop And Fly(IRE)** ruined his chance by hanging badly in the straight. There was no benefit in coming wide on this fast ground. *Official explanation: jockey said gelding hung left in straight*

### 5295 PENTAX SIRENIA STKS (GROUP 3) — 6f
2:40 (2:42) (A1) 2-Y-O — £23,200 (£8,800; £4,400; £2,000) Stalls Low

| Form | | | | RPR |
|---|---|---|---|---|
| 211 | **1** | | **Satchem (IRE)**[58] 3677 2-8-11 95 ... KFallon 5 (CEBrittain) *lw: hdwy 2f out: led over 1f out: hrd rdn: r.o* **3/1**[2] | 110 |
| 1220 | **2** | *1 ½* | **Council Member (USA)**[17] 4857 2-8-11 100 ... LDettori 1 (SaeedBinSuroor) *lw: mde most tl over 1f out: kpt on same pce* **15/8**[1] | 106 |
| 143 | **3** | *1 ½* | **Visionist (IRE)**[14] 4958 2-8-11 ... JFortune 2 (JAOsborne) *lw: in tch: effrt 2f out: kpt on fnl f* **7/1** | 101 |
| 4321 | **4** | *nk* | **Tremar**[9] 5054 2-8-11 90 ... GCarter 4 (TGMills) *w ldrs: hrd rdn over 1f out: no ex* **20/1** | 100 |
| 415 | **5** | *shd* | **Galeota (IRE)**[17] 4857 2-8-11 100 ... (p) RLMoore 7 (RHannon) *w ldrs: edgd rt and hrd rdn 2f out: no ex over 1f out* **5/1**[3] | 100 |
| 163 | **6** | *nk* | **Stagbury Hill (USA)**[16] 4872 2-8-11 100 ... RHills 3 (JWHills) *dwlt: pushed along in rr: styd on fnl f* **20/1** | 99 |
| 41 | **7** | *2* | **Sudden Dismissal (IRE)**[14] 4936 2-8-11 87 ... SSanders 8 (GAButler) *stdd s: hrd rdn over 2f out: a in rr* **12/1** | 93 |
| 1343 | **8** | *1 ¾* | **Safari Sunset (IRE)**[39] 4217 2-8-11 99 ... PDoe 6 (PWinkworth) *w ldrs 4f* **16/1** | 88 |

1m 10.87s (-2.20) **Going Correction** -0.225s/f (Firm) **8** Ran SP% **112.0**
Speed ratings: **105,103,101,100,100 100,97,95**CSF £8.63 TOTE £3.90: £1.20, £1.10, £1.50; EX 6.90 Trifecta £63.90 Pool £486.70 - 5.40 winning units..
**Owner** Sheikh Hamdan Bin Mohammed Al Maktoum **Bred** K Molloy **Trained** Newmarket, Suffolk

**FOCUS**
An improving winner and a proven runner-up give this the look of a solid Group 3, though the proximity of some others raises something of a question mark. The winning time was as you would expect for a race like this.

**NOTEBOOK**
**Satchem(IRE)** is on an upward curve and coped well with the step up in class, making a winning debut for new connections. Effective at both six and seven furlongs, he has a number of options and looks capable of winning again in Pattern company
**Council Member(USA)** left a dismal soft-ground run at York well behind and was beaten by a progressive sort. He is capable of winning a Group 3.
**Visionist(IRE)** was beaten by two decent sorts. The Mill Reef Stakes, in which he is likely to have more use made of him, is reportedly his immediate target, but a return to seven furlongs should suit him in due course.
**Tremar** did well in this better company, only losing a winning chance entering the final furlong. His handicap mark may be done no favours by this run, but he deserves to win a decent race.
**Galeota(IRE)**, wearing cheekpieces for the first time, drifted off a straight line as the race began in earnest. This ground may have been a bit lively for him.
**Stagbury Hill(USA)** found the trip too sharp, particularly on the fast ground. He needs seven furlongs at least.

### 5296 PENTAX UK SEPTEMBER STKS (GROUP 3) — 1m 4f
3:15 (3:15) (A1) 3-Y-O+ — £31,000 (£11,000; £5,500; £2,500) Stalls High

| Form | | | | RPR |
|---|---|---|---|---|
| 10-3 | **1** | | **Mamool (IRE)**[21] 4766 5-9-3 118 ... (t) LDettori 5 (SaeedBinSuroor) *lw: trckd ldr: led jst over 2f out: rdn out* **3/1**[3] | 119 |
| -211 | **2** | *½* | **Alkaased (USA)**[36] 4285 4-9-3 113 ... JFortune 1 (LMCumani) *lw: hld up: swtchd wd and effrt ent st: drvn to press wnr 1f out: kpt on* **6/4**[1] | 118 |
| 1010 | **3** | *1 ¼* | **Bandari (IRE)**[42] 4121 5-9-8 119 ... RHills 4 (MJohnston) *swtg: led tl jst over 2f out: nt qckn ins fnl f* **15/8**[2] | 121 |
| -030 | **4** | *4* | **Jagger**[17] 4858 4-9-3 101 ... EAhern 2 (GAButler) *hld up: effrt and forced wd ent st: btn over 2f out* **11/1** | 110 |

2m 31.13s (-3.87) **Going Correction** -0.075s/f (Good) **4** Ran SP% **108.1**
Speed ratings: **109,108,107,105**CSF £7.87 TOTE £2.90; EX 6.10.
**Owner** Godolphin **Bred** Sheikh Mohammed Bin Rashid Al Maktoum **Trained** Newmarket, Suffolk

**FOCUS**
A small field but a well-contested Group 3. The winning time was ordinary for the class, but the race only really developed off the turn.

**NOTEBOOK**
**Mamool(IRE)**, unpenalised for last year's Group 1 wins and so well-in at the weights, was safely on top in the last 50 yards, though he had to battle to see off his two closest pursuers. He acts on fast ground but gives the impression he would be happier with a bit more cut than this.
**Alkaased(USA)** was mixing it with two genuine Group level performers and emerged with plenty of credit, improving yet again. A Pattern race triumph should come his way.
**Bandari(IRE)**, minus the earplugs he has worn lately, ran a game race from the front, though finally giving way in the last 100 yds. He is a tough sort and takes his racing well, so a sixth Group level success is entirely possible.
**Jagger** had a tough task in this company and being forced wide on the turn was the beginning of the end. However, he was not beaten far and success in a weaker Group Three cannot be ruled out.

### 5297 PENTAX "DIGITAL CAMERA" H'CAP — 1m 2f (J)
3:50 (3:53) (D2) (0-85,84) 3-Y-O+ — £10,235 (£3,882; £1,941; £882) Stalls High

| Form | | | | RPR |
|---|---|---|---|---|
| 0340 | **1** | | **Tidal**[34] 4367 5-9-6 **83** ... LDettori 1 (AWCarroll) *prom: led 3f out: hld on wl fnl f* **14/1** | 93 |
| 0201 | **2** | *nk* | **Top Spec (IRE)**[15] 4921 3-8-6 **76** ... RLMoore 2 (RHannon) *lw: in rr: gd hdwy over 1f out: clsd on wnr ins fnl f: r.o* **20/1** | 85 |
| 6232 | **3** | *1 ¼* | **Arry Dash**[6] 5153 4-8-7 **73** ... SHitchcott(3) 9 (MRChannon) *lw: dwelt: towards rr: hdwy to chse ldrs over 1f out: styd on same pce* **8/1**[2] | 80 |
| 4354 | **4** | *½* | **Street Life (IRE)**[58] 3678 6-8-9 **72** ... GCarter 14 (WJMusson) *dwelt, bhd: nt clr run over 2f out: gd late hdwy* **10/1** | 78+ |
| 432 | **5** | *½* | **Ouninpohja (IRE)**[50] 3896 3-8-3 **73** ow1 ... DeanMcKeown 8 (GASwinbank) *lw: towards rr: effrt whn hmpd over 2f out: swtchd to far rail and hdwy wl over 1f out: one pce fnl f* **7/2**[1] | 78+ |
| 1-00 | **6** | *nk* | **Pagan Sky (IRE)**[96] 2527 5-9-7 **84** ... TPQueally 15 (JARToller) *in tch: drvn to chse wnr 2f out: no ex fnl f* **20/1** | 88 |
| 3032 | **7** | *½* | **Piri Piri (IRE)**[28] 4556 4-8-7 **70** oh1 ... CCatlin 11 (PJMcbride) *dwlt: bhd: rdn and styd on fnl 2f: nvr nrr* **25/1** | 73 |
| 0006 | **8** | *1 ½* | **Liquid Form (IRE)**[29] 4520 4-8-12 **75** ... AMcCarthy 4 (BHanbury) *b: dwelt, towards rr: rdn and hdwy wl over 1f out: no further prog fnl f* **33/1** | 75 |
| 2212 | **9** | *shd* | **Fortune's Princess**[38] 4240 3-8-7 **77** ... KFallon 17 (MJWallace) *in tch: drifted v wd st: hrd rdn 2f out: one pce* **9/1**[3] | 77 |
| 0135 | **10** | *¾* | **Fuel Cell (IRE)**[9] 5057 3-8-0 **70** ... (b) RSmith 12 (RHannon) *lw: prom tl wknd over 1f out* **25/1** | 69 |
| 2315 | **11** | *½* | **Vamp**[43] 4079 3-8-7 **77** ... SSanders 10 (RMBeckett) *mid-div: nt clr run on rail over 2f out: n.d* **25/1** | 75+ |
| 3403 | **12** | *1 ½* | **Voice Mail**[20] 4772 5-8-11 **77** ... LPKeniry(3) 6 (AMBalding) *nvr trbld ldrs* **25/1** | 72 |
| 6410 | **13** | *shd* | **Penzance**[57] 3692 3-8-10 **80** ... OUrbina 20 (JRFanshawe) *lw: chsd ldrs: nt clr run over 2f out: sn btn* **12/1** | 75+ |
| 1105 | **14** | *1* | **Sangiovese**[20] 4772 5-8-10 **76** ... LFletcher(3) 18 (HMorrison) *chsd ldrs: drvn along 3f out: sn btn* **8/1**[2] | 69 |
| 5354 | **15** | *shd* | **Leoballero**[12] 5004 4-9-2 **79** ... (t) EAhern 16 (DJDaly) *chsd ldrs tl wknd wl over 1f out* **12/1** | 72 |
| 0540 | **16** | *5* | **Best Be Going (IRE)**[18] 4831 4-8-12 **75** ... DaneO'Neill 7 (PWHarris) *in tch: rdn to chse ldrs 3f out: wknd 2f out* **12/1** | 58 |
| 32-0 | **17** | *8* | **Lasanga**[12] 5004 5-9-0 **77** ... PDoe 13 (LadyHerries) *led 3f: pressed ldr tl 3f out: sn wknd* **66/1** | 45 |
| 21-0 | **18** | *nk* | **Electrique (IRE)**[23] 4691 4-8-12 **75** ... IMongan 19 (JAOsborne) *lw: prom: led after 3f tl 3f out: sn wknd* **33/1** | 42 |
| 1302 | **19** | *dist* | **Sunisa (IRE)**[73] 3206 3-8-12 **82** ... RHills 3 (BWHills) *in tch and wd: wknd 4f out: sn bhd and vitually p.u: lame* **33/1** | — |

2m 3.29s (-2.85) **Going Correction** -0.20s/f (Firm)
**WFA** 3 from 4yo+ 7lb **19** Ran SP% **128.5**
Speed ratings: **103,102,101,101,100 100,100,99,99,98 98,96,96,95,95 91,85,85,—**CSF £275.88 CT £2417.50 TOTE £23.10: £4.90, £5.10, £2.40, £2.90; EX 280.40 Trifecta £636.00 Part won. Pool £896.98 - 0.20 winning units..
**Owner** Mrs B Quinn **Bred** Wyck Hall Stud Ltd **Trained** Wixford, Warwicks

**FOCUS**
A competitive handicap and solid form. The strong pace resulted in a number of horses arriving late from behind, which makes the winner's performance all the more meritorious. The favourite was unlucky in running and should find a similar race.

**NOTEBOOK**
**Tidal** put up a good weight-carrying performance and must be still improving. She was the only placed horse to come from those who had raced close to the strong pace.
**Top Spec(IRE)**, winner of a claimer last time, nearly repeated the feat back in handicap company, but the post came just too soon.
**Arry Dash** is reasonably handicapped at present, but this ground would have been plenty fast enough for him.
**Street Life(IRE)** was unlucky to hit trouble in running just at the point when the hold-up horses were beginning their moves. He has been running consistently well and is capable of winning this autumn.
**Ouninpohja(IRE)** was well backed for his handicap debut but had a bad run through when starting his effort from behind and, though getting amongst the chasing group on the run to the final furlong, his reserves had been used up. He can win a similar race.
**Pagan Sky(IRE)** ran well after a three-month absence and looks to have been nicely set up for a repeat of the autumn campaign that yielded two victories last year.
**Piri Piri(IRE)** was the slowest out of the stalls but came home well to keep up the good form that she has been showing this season. She has only one win to her name but a second cannot be ruled out.
**Liquid Form(IRE)** has not been at his best this season but there were signs of a revival here.
**Fortune's Princess** nearly came to the stands' rail in the straight, which was of no benefit, so this run should be ignored.
**Sunisa(IRE)** *Official explanation: after race vet found horse to be lame*

## 5298 PENTAX "LIGHT & IMAGE" CONDITIONS STKS (C&G) 7f (J)
**4:25** (4:29) (C2) 2-Y-O **£7,290** (£2,765; £1,382; £628) **Stalls** High

Form RPR
4 **1** **Storm Silk (CAN)**[21] 4739 2-8-10 .......... LDettori 4 97+
(SaeedBinSuroor) *lw: h.d.w: mde all: qcknd 2f out: smoothly drew clr: impressive* **2/1**[1]
**2** *3 ½* **Peruvian Prince (USA)** 2-8-10 .......... EAhern 6 85
(JARToller) *cmpt: b.bkwd: w wnr: outpcd and easily hld fr 2f out* **12/1**
**3** *3* **Rain Stops Play (IRE)** 2-8-10 .......... SHitchcott 8 77
(MRChannon) *leggy: unf: trckd ldrs: rdn over 2f out: one pce* **20/1**
**4** *nk* **Kerashan (IRE)** 2-8-10 .......... KFallon 5 77+
(SirMichaelStoute) *lengthy: bkwd: pressed ldrs 3f: pushed along and lost pl over 2f out: swtchd rt wl over 1f out: styd on same pce* **6/1**[2]
30 **5** *1* **Gitche Manito (IRE)**[8] 5087 2-8-10 .......... JDSmith 1 74
(AKing) *prom tl rdn and btn over 2f out* **33/1**
**6** *1 ¼* **Molem** 2-8-10 .......... RHills 3 71
(SirMichaelStoute) *cmpt: b.bkwd: hld up towards rr: rn green and rdn over 2f out: nvr nr to chal* **12/1**
**7** *2* **Pillars Of Wisdom** 2-8-10 .......... JFortune 9 66
(JLDunlop) *rangy: scope: b.bkwd: dwlt: hld up towards rr: effrt and briefly n.m.r over 2f out: no hdwy* **8/1**[3]
**8** *9* **Party Boss** 2-8-10 .......... SSanders 2 43
(CEBrittain) *wl grwn: bkwd: dwlt: outpcd in rr thrght* **25/1**

1m 26.7s (-0.57) **Going Correction** -0.20s/f (Firm) 2y crse rec **8** Ran SP% **85.7**
Speed ratings: **95,91,87,87,86 84,82,72**CSF £13.23 TOTE £1.90: £1.10, £1.90, £4.20; EX 15.00.
**Owner** Godolphin **Bred** J Everatt And Janeane Everatt **Trained** Newmarket, Suffolk

**FOCUS**
Difficult form to rate with confidence. Storm Silk was favoured by dictating the pace, while some of his rivals needed the experience, but he was impressive and looks well capable of holding his own in better company..

**NOTEBOOK**
**Storm Silk(CAN)** ◆ looked much improved from his debut, both physically and in the race. A step up in class looks inevitable, and the stylish way in which he dispatched the opposition makes him one to keep an eye on wherever he goes.
**Peruvian Prince(USA)**, a Dewhurst entry, had no chance with the impressive winner but was comfortably second-best. He should have no problem winning his maiden before going on to better things.
**Rain Stops Play(IRE)**, a 111,000euro son of Desert Prince, travelled well before being found wanting when the winner went up through the gears. Nonetheless, a satisfactory debut.
**Kerashan(IRE)**, a son of Sinndar and out of a mile winner in Ireland, shaped well without having a hard time. Improvement is likely from this May foal.
**Gitche Manito(IRE)** looks a likely sort for nurseries, having run with credit in two of his three qualifying races.
**Molem**, a Green Desert colt, needed the experience. He never looked like becoming competitive but should learn from this.
**Pillars Of Wisdom**, entered for the Royal Lodge, needs a bit more time and was not knocked about after being short of room as the race began to develop. He would not have been in the first four but should come on for the outing.

## 5299 PENTAX "PERFECT" H'CAP 6f
**4:55** (4:57) (D2) (0-85,85) 3-Y-O+ **£7,111** (£2,188; £1,094; £547) **Stalls** Low

Form RPR
-050 **1** **Thurlestone Rock**[82] 2948 4-8-11 **75** .......... CCatlin 2 84
(BJMeehan) *w ldrs stands' side: drvn to ld wl ins fnl f* **25/1**
3000 **2** *nk* **Najeebon (FR)**[7] 5124 5-8-9 **76** .......... SHitchcott(3) 3 84+
(MRChannon) *lw: outpcd and bhd stands' side: gd hdwy fnl 2f: clsng fast at fin* **8/1**[3]
30-0 **3** *hd* **Aversham**[154] 4-9-7 **85** .......... JFortune 7 93+
(RCharlton) *lw: outpcd and bhd stands' side: gd late hdwy* **20/1**
0056 **4** *¾* **Little Edward**[17] 4847 6-9-1 **82** .......... LPKeniry(3) 1 87
(BGPowell) *mid-div stands' side: hdwy to press ldrs 2f out: one pce ins fnl f* **16/1**
0631 **5** *hd* **Nivernais**[12] 5008 5-8-11 **75** .......... DaneO'Neill 12 80
(HCandy) *chsd ldrs stands' side: rdn to chal over 1f out: one pce ins fnl f* **10/1**
0610 **6** *shd* **Mr Malarkey (IRE)**[17] 4847 4-9-1 **82** .......... (b) HayleyTurner(3) 11 86
(MrsCADunnett) *racd stands' side: mde most: hrd rdn over 1f out: hdd and no ex ins fnl f* **20/1**
0100 **7** *½* **Mine Behind**[26] 4614 4-9-4 **82** .......... LDettori 17 85+
(JRBest) *lw: chsd far side ldrs: led gp over 1f out: kpt on: jst hld by stands' side* **8/1**[3]
0255 **8** *1* **Golden Dixie (USA)**[18] 4837 5-9-3 **81** .......... KFallon 5 81
(AMBalding) *chsd ldrs stands' side: no ex fnl f* **8/1**[3]
0100 **9** *½* **Wyatt Earp (IRE)**[7] 5124 3-8-9 **75** .......... EAhern 4 73
(JARToller) *lw: in tch and sn rdn along stands' side: no imp fnl 2f* **16/1**
0040 **10** *1* **Danehill Stroller (IRE)**[34] 4366 4-9-4 **82** .......... (p) SSanders 20 77+
(RMBeckett) *mid-div far side: rdn over 2f out: kpt on fnl f: no ch w stands' side* **6/1**[1]
3230 **11** *nk* **Armagnac**[21] 4742 6-9-2 **80** .......... GCarter 18 74+
(MABuckley) *bhd far side: r.o fnl f: nvr nrr* **7/1**[2]
0630 **12** *nk* **Hard To Catch (IRE)**[9] 5055 6-8-8 **77** .......... (b) MSavage(5) 6 71
(DKIvory) *b: towards rr stands' side: hdwy to chse ldrs 2f out: no ex fnl f: eased fnl 50 yds* **20/1**
1143 **13** *hd* **Savile's Delight (IRE)**[8] 5077 5-8-10 **77** .......... DNolan(3) 14 70+
(RBrotherton) *lw: prom far side: hrd rdn and edgd lft over 1f out: no ex* **12/1**
0050 **14** *½* **Treasure House (IRE)**[108] 2224 3-9-5 **85** .......... GBaker 19 76+
(JJay) *outpcd in rr far side: nvr able to chal* **33/1**
3030 **15** *1* **Miss George**[9] 5055 6-8-8 **79** .......... MHoward(7) 16 67+
(DKIvory) *b: outpcd far side: n.d* **14/1**
6010 **16** *nk* **Semenovskii**[18] 4837 4-8-9 **73** .......... (v) RLMoore 15 61+
(PWD'Arcy) *led far side gp tl wknd over 1f out* **16/1**
0004 **17** *½* **Willhewiz**[8] 5071 4-8-9 **76** .......... JFMcDonald(3) 10 62
(RMStronge) *prom stands' side 4f* **20/1**
2044 **18** *1 ¾* **Celtic Thunder**[27] 4576 3-9-3 **83** .......... RHills 13 64
(TJEtherington) *mid-div stands' side: outpcd fnl 2f* **25/1**
2010 **19** *8* **Midnight Ballard (USA)**[51] 3884 3-8-13 **79** .......... (b[1]) SCarson 9 36
(RFJohnsonHoughton) *w ldrs stands' side 3f* **33/1**

1m 11.01s (-2.06) **Going Correction** -0.225s/f (Firm)
**WFA** 3 from 4yo+ 2lb **19** Ran SP% **133.8**
Speed ratings: **104,103,103,102,102 101,101,99,99,97 97,97,96,96,94 94,93,91,80**CSF £209.15 CT £4127.67 TOTE £38.40: £5.70, £2.70, £9.90, £3.80; EX 156.80.
**Owner** N Attenborough & Mrs L Mann **Bred** B Mills **Trained** Upper Lambourn, Berks

**FOCUS**
An ordinary but competitive sprint, in which the field split, with 12 of the 19 staying stands' side. The first home in the far-side group, Mine Behind, was only seventh but beaten less than two lengths. The second and third look to be running back into form.

**NOTEBOOK**
**Thurlestone Rock**, on a winning mark and over an ideal course and distance, had plenty going for him. Freshened up by a break, he showed speed throughout, though the post came just in time.
**Najeebon(FR)** often takes a while to get going, and on this occasion another few strides would probably have seen him in front. He is handicapped to win if he can conjure up a similar performance.
**Aversham**, now with Roger Charlton after a spell in Dubai, flew home from the back along with the runner-up. Though winless since his juvenile days, he retains enough ability to be dangerous in similar events, or over another furlong.
**Little Edward** is capable of winning off his current mark and he did not fail by far here. This trip suits him well nowadays.
**Nivernais** had been raised five pounds for his win twelve days earlier and that may have been crucial in a tight finish.
**Mr Malarkey(IRE)**, five pounds above his highest winning mark, showed a lot of speed from the outset and went down narrowly in a blanket finish.
**Mine Behind**, first home on the far side, was unlucky to go down so narrowly yet finish no better than seventh. A good effort.
**Armagnac** again got going too late but he was finishing well on the unfavoured far side.

## 5300 PENTAX "OPTICAL EXCELLENCE" H'CAP 1m 6f 92y
**5:25** (5:27) (D2) (0-85,85) 3-Y-O **£6,860** (£2,111; £1,055; £527) **Stalls** High

Form RPR
3101 **1** **Leg Spinner (IRE)**[27] 4572 3-9-4 **79** .......... LDettori 6 86
(MRChannon) *lw: trckd ldr: slt ld fnl 2f: rdn out* **13/2**
2-21 **2** *hd* **Red Damson (IRE)**[14] 4939 3-9-10 **85** .......... SSanders 7 92
(SirMarkPrescott) *led tl 2f out: w wnr after: kpt on gamely* **8/1**
2213 **3** *2* **Velvet Waters**[15] 4915 3-8-10 **71** oh1 .......... SCarson 3 75
(RFJohnsonHoughton) *chsd ldrs: rdn 3f out: styd on same pce* **12/1**
1026 **4** *1 ¼* **Considine (USA)**[23] 4692 3-8-11 **72** .......... JFortune 13 74
(JMPEustace) *lw: chsd ldrs: rdn 3f out: one pce* **12/1**
4133 **5** *1* **Donastrela (IRE)**[25] 4618 3-8-5 **71** oh6 .......... (v) NChalmers(5) 2 72
(AMBalding) *b.hind: in tch: effrt 3f out: styd on same pce* **33/1**
320 **6** *shd* **Turnstile**[15] 4915 3-9-0 **75** .......... RLMoore 5 76
(RHannon) *mid-div: lost pl and dropped to rr over 5f out: rdn and styd on wl fnl 3f* **20/1**
0251 **7** *1 ¾* **Topkat (IRE)**[15] 4915 3-9-2 **77** .......... DaneO'Neill 8 75
(DRCElsworth) *lw: towards rr: hdwy 4f out: rdn and btn over 2f out* **5/1**[2]
6315 **8** *1 ½* **Silver Sash (GER)**[16] 4884 3-9-5 **80** .......... KFallon 4 76
(MLWBell) *swtg: b: hld up and bhd: hdwy and prom on outside 1/2-way: rdn and btn over 2f out* **6/1**[3]
433 **9** *hd* **Garnett (IRE)**[29] 4513 3-9-0 **75** .......... JDSmith 1 71
(AKing) *in rr: pushed along 6f out: wd and rdn st: nvr rchd ldrs* **33/1**
0046 **10** *½* **Man At Arms (IRE)**[37] 4274 3-8-12 **76** .......... SHitchcott(3) 10 71
(RHannon) *towards rr: hrd rdn over 2f out: nvr trbld ldrs* **20/1**
1522 **11** *hd* **Masked (IRE)**[31] 4441 3-9-4 **79** .......... EAhern 11 74
(JWHills) *lw: in tch tl wknd over 2f out* **3/1**[1]
5020 **12** *2 ½* **Sound Of Fleet (USA)**[16] 4888 3-9-9 **84** .......... TPQueally 9 75
(PFICole) *lw: towards rr: rdn over 3f out: sn bhd* **12/1**
0204 **13** *11* **Keep On Movin' (IRE)**[24] 4642 3-8-10 **71** .......... GCarter 12 47
(TGMills) *chsd ldrs tl wknd over 3f out* **25/1**

3m 7.09s (-3.57) **Going Correction** -0.075s/f (Good) **13** Ran SP% **122.7**
Speed ratings: **107,106,105,105,104 104,103,102,102,102 102,100,94**CSF £55.03 CT £619.00 TOTE £6.00: £2.90, £2.80, £3.50; EX 52.50 Place 6 £208.47, Place 5 £162.24.
**Owner** P D Savill **Bred** Steven Nolan **Trained** West Ilsley, Berks

**FOCUS**
A staying race of reasonable quality, though dominated by the first two home. The moderate pace only quickened half a mile from home and favoured those who had been racing handy.

**NOTEBOOK**
**Leg Spinner(IRE)** got the trip well and proved a game winner in a protracted duel with the runner-up.
**Red Damson(IRE)** gave the winner a good race in what turned into a two-horse race. He should continue to acquit himself well in similar events.
**Velvet Waters** got the trip, without ever finding the pace to trouble the first two.
**Considine(USA)** was five pounds above his highest winning mark, and that is more or less how he ran.
**Donastrela(IRE)** was six pounds out of the handicap, though admittedly ridden by an able five-pound claimer to compensate for that. Nonetheless, she might have gone close off her true mark.
**Turnstile** is worth another try at this sort of trip, for he was done by the quickening pace nearing the end of the back straight rather than lack of stamina.
**Masked(IRE)** had good claims but failed to run his race. *Official explanation: trainer had no explanation for poor form shown*
**Keep On Movin'(IRE)** *Official explanation: jockey said filly was unsuited by track and ground*
T/Plt: £133.70 to a £1 stake. Pool: £72,290.40. 394.60 winning tickets. T/Qpdt: £104.70 to a £1 stake. Pool: £2,561.60. 18.10 winning tickets. LM



The Form Book, Raceform Ltd, Compton, RG20 6NL

## $^{5095}$THIRSK (L-H)

Saturday, September 4

**OFFICIAL GOING: Firm (good to firm in places)**

The riders reported the ground was just on the quick side of good and nowhere near as firm as the official version.

Wind: Almost nil. Weather: Fine and sunny.

### 5301 RICHMOND CASTLE MAIDEN AUCTION STKS (DIV I) 7f
1:50 (1:51) (E3) 2-Y-O £3,503 (£1,078; £539; £269) Stalls Low

| Form | | | | | RPR |
|---|---|---|---|---|---|
| 52 | 1 | | **Chantaco (USA)**$^{31}$ [4432] 2-8-11 (AMBalding) *led: qcknd over 3f out: r.o wl: readily* 2/1$^{2}$ | WRyan 3 | 74+ |
| 5 | 2 | 2½ | **Bold Counsel (IRE)**$^{31}$ [4432] 2-8-7 (BJMeehan) *sn trcking wnr: effrt over 3f out: kpt on wl: no imp* 9/1 | FNorton 2 | 64 |
| 00 | 3 | 2½ | **Blushing Russian (IRE)**$^{19}$ [4804] 2-8-7 (PCHaslam) *hld up in rr: hdwy over 2f out: styd on fnl f* 12/1 | GFaulkner 5 | 58 |
| | 4 | 1½ | **Abstract Folly (IRE)** 2-8-7 (JDBethell) *lenghy: unf: bhd: hdwy over 1f out: styd on ins last* 25/1 | ACulhane 8 | 54 |
| 5 | 5 | nk | **Cayenne (GER)**$^{22}$ [4704] 2-8-6 (DMSimcock) *t.k.h in rr: swtchd outside over 2f out: hrd rdn: nvr rchd ldrs* 20/1 | DAllan 7 | 52 |
| 06 | 6 | 2½ | **Kashtanka (IRE)**$^{8}$ [5098] 2-8-7 (JJQuinn) *chsd ldrs: wknd over 1f out* 40/1 | JFanning 9 | 47 |
| 6 | 7 | ¾ | **Secret Cavern (USA)**$^{30}$ [4488] 2-8-11 (JAOsborne) *trckd ldrs: effrt over 2f out: wknd over 1f out* 7/4$^{1}$ | SWKelly 10 | 49 |
| 06 | 8 | 3½ | **Andy Mal**$^{8}$ [5095] 2-8-2 ow3 (RAFahey) *s.i.s: a in rr* 20/1 | THamilton$^{(3)}$ 4 | 34 |
| 5 | 9 | 1¼ | **Mr Marucci (USA)**$^{8}$ [5098] 2-8-8 (BEllison) *t.k.h: trckd ldrs: lost pl over 1f out* 6/1$^{3}$ | TEaves$^{(3)}$ 6 | 37 |
| | 10 | 2 | **Linzis Lad** 2-8-7 (KARyan) *tall: unf: s.i.s: sn chsng ldrs: lost pl 2f out* 28/1 | NCallan 1 | 28 |
| 00 | 11 | ¾ | **Lady Suesanne (IRE)**$^{80}$ [2985] 2-8-2 (CADwyer) *sn pushed along towards rr: bmpd over 2f out: nvr on terms* 100/1 | DaleGibson 11 | 21 |

1m 26.31s (-0.79) **Going Correction** -0.125s/f (Firm) **11 Ran SP% 121.9**

Speed ratings: **99,96,93,91,91 88,87,83,82,79 78**CSF £19.19 TOTE £3.10: £1.40, £2.00, £4.30; EX 14.30.

**Owner** The Pink Hat Racing Partnership **Bred** London Thoroughbred Services **Trained** Kingsclere, Hants

**FOCUS**

An ordinary maiden and reliable form although the well-backed winner was given his own way in front.

**NOTEBOOK**

**Chantaco(USA)**, who looked very fit indeed, set sail for home coming off the home turn and never looked in any danger. This sets him up nicely for a nursery campaign.

**Bold Counsel(IRE)**, three lengths behind the winner at Brighton, was meeting him on 3lb better terms but, even with that first outing under his belt, he was not good enough to close the gap.

**Blushing Russian(IRE)**, a moderate mover, stayed on from way off the pace and will be suited by a mile in nursery company.

**Abstract Folly(IRE)**, an April foal, was clueless but showed ability, staying on in good style late on.

**Cayenne(GER)**, who continually swished her tail in the paddock, behaved herself in the stalls this time but would not settle and then had to pull wide to find racing room.

**Kashtanka(IRE)**, having his third outing, did not improve on earlier efforts but this at least opens up the nursery route.

**Secret Cavern(USA)**, who became very warm beforehand, found nothing and this was a big disappointment after his sound initial effort.

**Mr Marucci(USA)** would not settle at all and dropped away in disappointing fashion.

### 5302 EUROPEAN BREEDERS FUND MAIDEN STKS 1m
2:25 (2:27) (D2) 2-Y-O £5,707 (£1,756; £878; £439) Stalls Low

| Form | | | | | RPR |
|---|---|---|---|---|---|
| 2 | 1 | | **Sunday Symphony**$^{22}$ [4728] 2-9-0 (SaeedBinSuroor) *trckd ldrs: effrt and hung rt over 2f out: led over 1f out: drew clr* 6/4$^{1}$ | JCarroll 9 | 88+ |
| 55 | 2 | 5 | **Mobarhen (USA)**$^{15}$ [4913] 2-8-11 (SirMichaelStoute) *led tl over 1f out: kpt on: no ch w wnr* 7/1 | NMackay$^{(3)}$ 10 | 77 |
| 660 | 3 | 1¼ | **Chinese Puzzle**$^{27}$ [4567] 2-9-0 (HRACecil) *mid-div: effrt 3f out: styd on fnl f* 10/1 | (t) WRyan 8 | 74 |
| 0 | 4 | 1 | **King Zafeen (IRE)**$^{29}$ [4523] 2-9-0 (MRChannon) *dwlt: bhd: hdwy on outer 3f out: styd on appr fnl f* 25/1 | (t) ACulhane 2 | 72+ |
| 062 | 5 | ¾ | **Nasseem Dubai (USA)**$^{8}$ [5095] 2-9-0 80 (MrsADuffield) *w ldr: ev ch tl wknd over 1f out* 5/1$^{3}$ | GGibbons 13 | 70 |
| 0 | 6 | 2 | **Truckle**$^{113}$ [2087] 2-9-0 (MJohnston) *chsd ldrs: drvn along over 3f out: lost pl over 1f out* 16/1 | JFanning 11 | 66 |
| 63 | 7 | 1½ | **Kingsholm**$^{23}$ [4689] 2-9-0 (AMBalding) *chsd ldrs: hung lft 2f out: sn wknd* 4/1$^{2}$ | NCallan 14 | 62 |
| 0 | 8 | ¾ | **Bronze Dancer (IRE)**$^{9}$ [5059] 2-9-0 (GASwinbank) *chsd ldrs: rdn and outpcd over 2f out: fdd* 100/1 | SWKelly 3 | 61 |
| | 9 | 6 | **Bodden Bay** 2-9-0 (CADwyer) *cmpt: s.i.s: nvr on terms* 100/1 | FNorton 7 | 48 |
| 00 | 10 | 1¼ | **Wiltshire (IRE)**$^{9}$ [5059] 2-8-7 (MRChannon) *s.i.s: a in rr* 100/1 | TO'Brien$^{(7)}$ 5 | 45 |
| | 11 | ¾ | **Be Bop** 2-9-0 (NTinkler) *cmpt: bit bkwd: s.i.s: a bhd* 40/1 | KimTinkler 6 | 43 |
| 00 | 12 | 1 | **Lightening Fire (IRE)**$^{37}$ [4277] 2-9-0 (TJEtherington) *rr-div: bhd fnl 3f* 100/1 | DAllan 12 | 41 |
| 43 | 13 | 3½ | **Jackadandy (USA)**$^{24}$ [4633] 2-8-11 (JHowardJohnson) *nvr on terms* 25/1 | PMulrennan$^{(3)}$ 4 | 33 |
| 4 | 14 | dist | **Rockpiler**$^{33}$ [4392] 2-8-11 (JHowardJohnson) *chsd ldrs: lost pl over 4f out: sn bhd: virtually p.u: t.o* 50/1 | TEaves$^{(3)}$ 1 | — |

1m 37.97s (-1.73) **Going Correction** -0.125s/f (Firm) 2y crse rec **14 Ran SP% 120.2**

Speed ratings: **103,98,96,95,95 93,91,90,84,83 82,81,78,—**CSF £12.06 TOTE £2.20: £1.40, £2.90, £2.90; EX 12.40.

**Owner** Godolphin **Bred** Darley **Trained** Newmarket, Suffolk

■ John Carroll's winner ended a losing run stretching back over three months and 115 mounts.

**FOCUS**

This looks reliable maiden form with the placed horses close to their pre-race best. A most decisive winner who lowered the two-year-old track record for a mile.

**NOTEBOOK**

**Sunday Symphony**, a half-brother to the Triumph Hurdle winner Made In Japan, is a big sort who stands over plenty of ground. He took a while to warm to his task and showed a tendency to hang, but in the end he came right away.

**Mobarhen(USA)**, given his own way in front, in the end proved no match.

**Chinese Puzzle** showed a fluent action going to post and stayed on in willing fashion, thoroughly appreciating the step up to a mile.

**King Zafeen(IRE)**, who showed quite a pronounced knee action, was fitted with a tongue strap this time. He ran a lot better than on his debut a month earlier and will improve again.

**Nasseem Dubai(USA)**, still carrying condition, hunted up the leader in a race run in course record time. He cried enough before stamina became an issue.

**Truckle**, whose sole previous outing was in May, has size and scope but may need more time yet.

**Kingsholm**, worst drawn, hung left under pressure and soon beat a retreat.

**Be Bop** *Official explanation: jockey said gelding hung right*

### 5303 TOTESPORT HAMBLETON CUP (H'CAP) 1m 4f
3:00 (3:00) (D2) (0-85,85) 3-Y-O+ £7,073 (£2,176; £1,088; £544) Stalls Low

| Form | | | | | RPR |
|---|---|---|---|---|---|
| 4415 | 1 | | **Night Sight (USA)**$^{3}$ [5229] 7-8-2 69 (MrsSLamyman) *hdwy to trck ldrs after 3f: led 1f out: hld on nr fin* 16/1 | RThomas$^{(5)}$ 16 | 76 |
| 436U | 2 | hd | **Sporting Gesture**$^{18}$ [4831] 7-8-10 75 (MWEasterby) *chsd ldrs: outpcd over 3f out: hdwy over 1f out: styd on wl towards fin* 10/1 | PMulrennan$^{(3)}$ 4 | 82 |
| 3541 | 3 | ¾ | **Smart John**$^{5}$ [5203] 4-8-5 72 3ex (WMBrisbourne) *in tch: swtchd outside over 2f out: styd on wl fnl f* 7/1$^{3}$ | BSwarbrick$^{(5)}$ 12 | 78 |
| 2104 | 4 | nk | **Party Ploy**$^{6}$ [5158] 6-8-5 70 (KRBurke) *chsd ldrs: led over 1f out: sn hdd and nt qckn* 12/1 | LEnstone$^{(3)}$ 8 | 75 |
| 2000 | 5 | nk | **Northside Lodge (IRE)**$^{32}$ [4416] 6-8-8 70 (PWHarris) *chsd ldrs: effrt over 2f out: kpt on fnl f* 12/1 | SWKelly 11 | 75 |
| 1220 | 6 | ¾ | **Prenup (IRE)**$^{24}$ [4642] 3-8-2 76 (LMCumani) *led: qcknd over 4f out: hdd over 1f out: kpt on same pce* 6/1$^{2}$ | NMackay$^{(3)}$ 5 | 80 |
| 0000 | 7 | nk | **Financial Future**$^{34}$ [4363] 4-8-8 70 (MJohnston) *chsd ldrs: rdn over 3f out: kpt on same pce* 16/1 | (b$^{1}$) JFanning 2 | 73 |
| 60 | 8 | ¾ | **Stallone**$^{42}$ [4155] 7-8-5 70 (NWilson) *dwlt: bhd: hdwy 3f out: kpt on: nt rch ldrs* 12/1 | THamilton$^{(3)}$ 1 | 72 |
| 4326 | 9 | nk | **Mexican Pete**$^{27}$ [4572] 4-9-3 79 (PWHiatt) *rr-div: swtchd outside over 1f out: r.o: nt rch ldrs* 25/1 | DAllan 14 | 80 |
| 10-1 | 10 | 1 | **Perelandra (USA)**$^{9}$ [5056] 4-8-6 75 (MJWallace) *bhd: effrt on ins over 2f out: kpt on: nvr nr ldrs* 16/1 | AMullen$^{(7)}$ 10 | 75 |
| 2401 | 11 | 1 | **Rutters Rebel (IRE)**$^{28}$ [4536] 3-8-1 72 (GASwinbank) *hld up in mid-field: effrt over 2f out: nvr nr to chal* 16/1 | FNorton 13 | 70 |
| 5600 | 12 | nk | **Cripsey Brook**$^{7}$ [5122] 6-9-6 82 (DonEnricoIncisa) *sn bhd and pushed along: nvr a factor* 16/1 | KimTinkler 6 | 80 |
| 3400 | 13 | shd | **Crathorne (IRE)**$^{18}$ [4831] 4-8-13 75 (JDBethell) *hld up towards rr: effrt over 2f out: nvr on terms* 11/1 | (p) ACulhane 3 | 73 |
| 4-26 | 14 | 1¾ | **Petrula**$^{111}$ [2142] 5-9-5 81 (KARyan) *in tch: drvn along over 3f out: sn btn* 25/1 | NCallan 9 | 76 |
| -211 | 15 | 5 | **Asaleeb**$^{24}$ [4642] 3-9-0 85 (EFVaughan) *chsd ldrs: lost pl over 1f out* 11/2$^{1}$ | WRyan 17 | 72 |
| 1153 | 16 | 4 | **Heneseys Leg**$^{21}$ [4760] 4-9-1 77 (JohnBerry) *a towards rr* 33/1 | LisaJones 7 | 57 |
| 0-0R | P | | **Conquering Love (IRE)**$^{41}$ [4176] 6-9-4 83 (CGrant) *rel to r: sn bhd and reminders: plld himself up bnd after 2f* 100/1 | TEaves$^{(3)}$ 15 | — |

2m 33.61s (-1.59) **Going Correction** -0.125s/f (Firm)

**WFA** 3 from 4yo+ 9lb **17 Ran SP% 123.7**

Speed ratings: **100,99,99,99,98 98,98,97,97,96 96,96,95,94,91 88,—**CSF £164.18 CT £1244.90 TOTE £21.90: £4.90, £2.40, £2.10, £3.60; EX 318.10 Trifecta £528.00 Part won. Pool of £743.70 - 0.10 winning units..

**Owner** David Fravigar-Alan Mann **Bred** Costello, Davis, Dolan And Ryan **Trained** Louth, Lincs

■ Richard Thomas's 50th career win, reducing his claim to 3lb.

**FOCUS**

In effect with Conquering Love virtually taking no part it was a 0-82 handicap and nothing came from off the pace. The winning time was modest for the class, but the form appears reliable on paper, with the first seven all running close to their mark.

**NOTEBOOK**

**Night Sight(USA)**, happier on this slightly quicker ground, took what looked a decisive advantage but in the end the post came only just in time.

**Sporting Gesture** as usual hit a flat spot, this time on the turn in. He stayed on to some effect late on and in the end was just denied.

**Smart John**, under a 3lb penalty, made his way to the outside and was closing the first two down at the line. He is a credit to his trainer.

**Party Ploy** put two below-par efforts behind him, keeping tabs on the leader and only just missing out in the end.

**Northside Lodge(IRE)**, out of sorts last time, looked back to his very best after a four-week break and his good effort confirmed his wellbeing. All his wins have been over ten furlongs, but here this trip seemed to be in his favour.

**Prenup(IRE)** settled much better in front. Stepping up the gallop starting the final turn, she kept on in willing fashion when collared.

**Financial Future**, who has slipped to a lenient mark, looked light and warm beforehand in first-time blinkers. He moved moderately to post and, though in the end this was a much better effort, lacked any sparkle.

**Stallone**, absent for six weeks, showed he is in good heart.

**Asaleeb**, 5lb higher, had to race wide to the first bend from her high draw. She kept tabs on the leader but dropped right out in most disappointing fashion.

**Conquering Love(IRE)** wanted no part of it for the second time running and a repetition will lead to a ban.

### 5304 B.D.O. STOY HAYWARD FILLIES' STKS (H'CAP) 1m
3:30 (3:31) (D2) (0-85,80) 3-Y-O+ £6,936 (£2,134; £1,067; £533) Stalls Low

| Form | | | | | RPR |
|---|---|---|---|---|---|
| 340P | 1 | | **Poppys Footprint (IRE)**$^{64}$ [3478] 3-9-5 75 (KARyan) *dwlt: hdwy on ins and nt clr run over 2f out: led over 1f out: edgd rt: hld on wl* 20/1 | NCallan 3 | 83 |
| 0650 | 2 | 1 | **Flashing Blade**$^{20}$ [4779] 4-8-13 64 (BAMcmahon) *trckd ldrs: edgd rt 2f out: nt qckn ins last* 16/1 | (t) GGibbons 2 | 70 |
| 6331 | 3 | 1¼ | **Millagros (IRE)**$^{15}$ [4903] 4-9-6 74 (ISemple) *hld up: hdwy over 2f out: styd on same pce fnl f* 8/1 | (p) TEaves$^{(3)}$ 8 | 77 |
| 2511 | 4 | ½ | **Sharp Needle**$^{27}$ [4574] 3-9-3 73 (JNoseda) *s.i.s: hdwy over 3f out: kpt on same pce fnl f* 7/2$^{2}$ | SWKelly 1 | 75+ |
| -111 | 5 | 2 | **Perle D'Or (IRE)**$^{35}$ [4318] 3-9-10 80 (WJHaggas) *chsd ldrs: drvn along over 4f out: one pce fnl 2f* 2/1$^{1}$ | ACulhane 6 | 77 |
| 6121 | 6 | hd | **Miss Madame (IRE)**$^{24}$ [4652] 3-8-10 69 (RGuest) *led after 1f: hdd over 1f out: fdd fnl f* 5/1 | NMackay$^{(3)}$ 4 | 66 |
| -510 | 7 | 1¼ | **Sharp Secret (IRE)**$^{60}$ [3609] 6-8-6 57 (JARToller) *chsd ldrs: lost pl over 4f out: swtchd outside 2f out: hung lft: nvr a threat* 12/1 | LisaJones 5 | 51 |

2011 **8** *2* **Munaawashat (IRE)**[7] [5136] 3-9-10 **80**.................... JFanning 7 69
(KRBurke) *led 1f: chsd ldr: led over 2f out tl over 1f out: wknd* **9/2**[3]

1m 38.14s (-1.56) **Going Correction** -0.125s/f (Firm)
**WFA** 3 from 4yo+ 5lb **8** Ran SP% **119.9**
Speed ratings: **102,101,99,99,97 97,95,93**CSF £300.59 CT £2789.27 TOTE £22.80: £3.30, £2.70, £2.20; EX 232.50.
**Owner** Kimian Barfly **Bred** Richard Whelan **Trained** Hambleton, N Yorks

**FOCUS**
A fair fillies' handicap run at a very strong pace early pace, although the overall time was unexceptional. The form appears ordinary for the grade.

**NOTEBOOK**
**Poppys Footprint(IRE)**, who injured herself in the stalls when last seen in action ten weeks ago, was loaded last and still had the hood on when the traps opened. She stuck to the inner and came from last to first, and if anything seemed suited by the mile.
**Flashing Blade**, back in the right grade, returned to form and made the winner pull out all the stops.
**Millagros(IRE)**, with the cheekpieces fitted again, gave a good account of herself but she looked rated to the hilt.
**Sharp Needle**, 5lb higher than when she won in handicap company two outings ago, was simply not good enough.
**Perle D'Or(IRE)**, 6lb higher, was making hard work of it some way from home and did not look at her very best.
**Miss Madame(IRE)**, keen to lead, did not handle the turn too well and, after setting a strong pace, did not last home.
**Sharp Secret(IRE)** never seemed to be galloping on an even keel and looked a tricky ride.
**Munaawashat(IRE)**, 7lb higher, was taken on for the lead and in a strongly-run race the two pacesetters finished in the last three.

## 5305 TASKMASTER (S) STKS 1m

4:05 (4:05) (F4) 3-Y-0+ £3,059 (£874; £437) **Stalls** Low

Form RPR

0206 **1** **Rymer's Rascal**[26] [4605] 12-9-0 48.................... DAllan 13 55
(EJAlston) *hld up towards rr: hdwy over 2f out: styd on to ld nr fin* **8/1**

1260 **2** *½* **Splodger Mac (IRE)**[7] [5127] 5-8-13 53.................... AReilly(7) 3 60
(NBycroft) *led: qcknd over 3f out: hdd nr fin* **3/1**[1]

4000 **3** *nk* **Efimac**[24] [4624] 4-8-9 40.................... FNorton 14 48
(NBycroft) *bhd: hdwy on ins 3f out: styd on wl ins last* **28/1**

4246 **4** *1* **Dancing Tilly**[214] [663] 6-8-6 40....................(p) THamilton(3) 2 46
(RAFahey) *in tch: sn drvn along: hdwy and n.m.r 1f out: hrd rdn and styd on* **8/1**

0006 **5** *3* **The Gambler**[8] [5081] 4-8-7 45....................(p) DFentiman(7) 12 44
(PaulJohnson) *s.i.s: hdwy on outside over 3f out: hung lft: kpt on: nvr rchd ldrs* **16/1**

0506 **6** *hd* **Abuelos**[12] [4985] 5-9-0 40.................... TWilliams 1 44
(DWThompson) *chsd ldrs: wknd fnl f* **100/1**

0450 **7** *nk* **Transcendantale (FR)**[14] [4486] 6-8-4 40.................... RThomas(5) 10 38
(MrsSLamyman) *s.i.s: hdwy 3f out: nvr nr ldrs* **9/1**

0000 **8** *shd* **Hoh's Back**[8] [5085] 5-9-0 49....................(p) LisaJones 6 43
(PaulJohnson) *hdwy on ins to chse ldrs over 4f out: fdd appr fnl f* **9/2**[2]

0050 **9** *nk* **Canlis**[2] [5238] 5-8-11 45....................(p) LEnstone(3) 15 42
(DWThompson) *mid-div: drvn along over 4f out: sme hdwy over 2f out: nvr on terms* **20/1**

0000 **10** *1 ¾* **Wild Tide**[18] [4825] 5-8-4 30.................... PPMathers(5) 9 33
(DWThompson) *mid-div: swtchd outside over 1f out: nvr on terms* **100/1**

0050 **11** *½* **Night Wolf (IRE)**[16] [4877] 4-9-0 52.................... ACulhane 4 37
(MRChannon) *hld up: hdwy over 3f out: rdn and btn over 2f out* **15/2**[3]

0500 **12** *6* **Zamyatina (IRE)**[35] [4350] 5-8-2 40.................... RKennemore(7) 8 18
(PLClinton) *chsd ldrs: hrd rdn 2f out: sn wknd* **25/1**

0460 **13** *1 ½* **Espada (IRE)**[31] [4438] 8-9-6 50....................(b) SWKelly 11 25
(JAOsborne) *chsd ldrs: lost pl over 2f out* **9/1**

0500 **14** *14* **Blue Nun**[6] [5141] 3-8-4 40....................(p) JFanning 7 —
(MrsADuffield) *chsd ldrs: lost pl 3f out: sn bhd* **50/1**

0-00 **15** *dist* **Natmsky (IRE)**[52] [3835] 5-8-11 30.................... PMulrennan(3) 5 —
(GAHarker) *chsd ldrs: drvn along over 4f out: lost pl over 2f out: sn eased and bhd: virtually p.u: t.o* **100/1**

1m 38.88s (-0.82) **Going Correction** -0.125s/f (Firm)
**WFA** 3 from 4yo+ 5lb **15** Ran SP% **120.0**
Speed ratings: **99,98,98,97,94 94,93,93,93,91 91,85,83,69,**—CSF £30.34 TOTE £6.40: £2.50, £2.00, £7.90; EX 29.80.There was no bid for the winner.
**Owner** Brian Chambers **Bred** Mrs Sara Logue And David Lewis **Trained** Longton, Lancs

**FOCUS**
A rock-bottom seller and the best horse on the day had to settle for the runner-up spot, and the form is unlikely to work out.

**NOTEBOOK**
**Rymer's Rascal**, suited by the strong pace, came home as straight as a die to put his head in front almost on the line and record his 11th career success on his 122nd outing.
**Splodger Mac(IRE)**, down in class, took what looked a decisive lead but his young rider's finishing effort lacked co-ordination and they were picked off almost on the line. This was an opportunity lost.
**Efimac**, who is only small, is hard to predict but she seemed to run out of her skin and in the end was just denied.
**Dancing Tilly**, placed three times from 25 previous starts, was having her first outing since February and was fitted with first-time cheekpieces. She made very hard work of it but this will set her up for a return to banded racing.
**The Gambler**, whose sole win was over six furlongs, has yet to prove his stamina and his attitude did not impress.
**Abuelos**, who has not won for over two years, started on terms this time but seven looks more his trip.
**Hoh's Back**, dropped in class, continues to under perform and he is now on a lengthy losing sequence.

## 5306 RJF HOMES MAIDEN STKS 6f

4:35 (4:35) (D3) 3-Y-0+ £4,114 (£1,266; £633; £316) **Stalls** High

Form RPR

0-04 **1** **Jilly Why (IRE)**[7] [5126] 3-8-7 57.................... ANicholls 6 68
(MsDeborahJEvans) *led: qcknd over 3f out: styd on wl appr fnl f* **8/1**

2020 **2** *3 ½* **Harrison's Flyer (IRE)**[36] [4309] 3-8-9 67.................... THamilton(3) 4 63
(RAFahey) *w wnr: hrd rdn and hung lft over 1f out: no imp* **6/1**[3]

0000 **3** *3 ½* **Yorke's Folly (USA)**[33] [4391] 3-8-7 45....................(v[1]) LisaJones 9 47
(CWFairhurst) *chsd ldrs: outpcd over 3f out: kpt on fnl 2f* **50/1**

5032 **4** *1* **Zwadi (IRE)**[15] [4916] 3-8-7 72.................... DSweeney 2 44
(HCandy) *w ldrs: rdn over 2f out: wknd over 1f out* **11/10**[1]

0202 **5** *1* **Roan Raider (USA)**[51] [3864] 4-8-7 57....................(v) KGhunowa(7) 5 46
(MJPolglase) *chsd ldrs: outpcd over 3f out: edgd lft and n.d after* **14/1**

30 **6** *5* **Ariesanne (IRE)**[7] [5104] 3-8-0.................... NLawes(7) 8 26
(RAFahey) *outpcd over 3f out: sme hdwy 2f out: edgd lft and fdd fnl f* **20/1**

2-63 **7** *14* **Thomas Lawrence (USA)**[17] [4845] 3-8-12 80....................(b[1]) JFanning 1 —
(PFICole) *wl outpcd and lost pl over 3f out: hung lft and nt run on: bhd fnl 2f* **10/3**[2]

0- **8** *11* **Chantilly Sunset (IRE)**[425] [3051] 3-8-7.................... JBramhill 10 —
(JBalding) *rrd s: outpcd and bhd over 3f out: sn lost tch* **66/1**

**9** *dist* **Dejeeje (IRE)** 3-8-12.................... ACulhane 7 —
(DWChapman) *s.s: sn wl bhd: t.o* **20/1**

1m 11.46s (-1.04) **Going Correction** -0.125s/f (Firm)
**WFA** 3 from 4yo 2lb **9** Ran SP% **115.7**
Speed ratings: **101,96,91,90,89 82,63,49,**—CSF £52.61 TOTE £11.90: £2.50, £1.80, £5.90; EX 55.40.
**Owner** Paul Green (Oaklea) **Bred** K And Mrs Cullen **Trained** Lydiate, Merseyside
■ A first training success for Deborah Evans.
■ Stewards Enquiry : K Ghunowa caution: careless riding

**FOCUS**
A low-grade sprint maiden and the form is not strong.

**NOTEBOOK**
**Jilly Why(IRE)** sat in front. She quickened the pace just before halfway and in the end ran out a ready winner.
**Harrison's Flyer(IRE)**, back after a five-week break, ran better than here last time but still does not look 100% straightforward.
**Yorke's Folly(USA)**, unplaced in six previous starts, is rated just 45.
**Zwadi(IRE)** had a stone in hand of the winner on official ratings but it did not work out like that at all.
**Roan Raider(USA)**, a maiden after 32 previous starts, never kept straight at any stage and his young rider must learn to keep both hands on the steering wheel.
**Thomas Lawrence(USA)**, in first-time blinkers, never went a yard at any stage and looked most reluctant. He has been a bitter disappointment after showing a fair level of form in three starts at two.
**Dejeeje(IRE)** *Official explanation: jockey said colt had a breathing problem*

## 5307 RICHMOND CASTLE MAIDEN AUCTION STKS (DIV II) 7f

5:05 (5:05) (E3) 2-Y-0 £3,493 (£1,075; £537; £268) **Stalls** Low

Form RPR

55 **1** **Easy Mover (IRE)**[19] [4797] 2-8-3.................... NMackay(3) 9 74
(RGuest) *mid-div: effrt on outer over 3f out: styd on wl appr fnl f: led nr fin* **5/1**

6226 **2** *½* **Malinsa Blue (IRE)**[14] [4958] 2-8-6 77.................... FNorton 2 73
(JAGlover) *trckd ldrs: led over 1f out: hdd and no ex nr fin* **11/4**[2]

**3** *hd* **Vancouver Gold (IRE)** 2-8-2.................... DaleGibson 3 69
(KRBurke) *lengthy: unf: dwlt: hld up: hdwy over 2f out: swtchd rt over 1f out: styd on ins last: no ex nr fin* **25/1**

00 **4** *1 ½* **Plenty Cried Wolf**[31] [4446] 2-8-4.................... THamilton(3) 10 70
(RAFahey) *w ldrs: led 2f out: sn hdd: one pce* **33/1**

00 **5** *½* **Egyptian Lady**[2] [5233] 2-7-9.................... DFentiman(7) 1 64
(RPElliott) *hld up: hdwy over 2f out: hung lft and kpt on fnl f* **33/1**

032 **6** *6* **Robinzal**[8] [5098] 2-8-11 75.................... DAllan 5 58
(TDEasterby) *led tl 2f out: wknd over 1f out* **9/2**[3]

2230 **7** *1 ¼* **Mceldowney**[28] [4527] 2-8-11 82....................(b[1]) JFanning 6 54
(MJohnston) *chsd ldrs: sn drvn along: hung lft and lost pl over 1f out: eased ins last* **9/4**[1]

**8** *½* **Sadie's Star (IRE)** 2-8-2.................... PFessey 4 44
(MDods) *leggy: unf: trckd ldrs: effrt 3f out: lost pl over 1f out* **14/1**

066 **9** *hd* **Hidden Jewel**[68] [3377] 2-8-7 48.................... GGibbons 8 49
(BAMcmahon) *sn outpcd and bhd* **25/1**

**10** *3* **Miss Bear (IRE)** 2-8-6.................... DMcGaffin 11 40
(BSmart) *lengthy: angular: swvd rt s: a bhd* **14/1**

0 **11** *2 ½* **Street Dancer (IRE)**[21] [4761] 2-8-11.................... NCallan 7 39
(JJQuinn) *mid-div: bhd and drvn along 3f out* **50/1**

1m 26.61s (-0.49) **Going Correction** -0.125s/f (Firm) **11** Ran SP% **121.2**
Speed ratings: **97,96,96,94,93 87,85,85,84,81 78**CSF £18.80 TOTE £6.30: £2.00, £1.50, £6.80; EX 21.30 Place 6 £1,102.79, Place 5 £495.02.
**Owner** Wendals Herbs Ltd **Bred** John Egan **Trained** Newmarket, Suffolk
■ Stewards Enquiry : T Hamilton two-day ban: careless riding (Sep 15-16)

**FOCUS**
A messy race and almost certainly much the weaker division. The form is difficult to evaluate with two of the first three in the betting being well beaten

**NOTEBOOK**
**Easy Mover(IRE)** is well named. Pulled wide to make her effort, she knuckled down willingly to lead almost on the line. With the runner up rated a provisional 77 she cannot expect a lenient nursery mark.
**Malinsa Blue(IRE)**, a scratchy mover, looked nailed on when hitting the front but her trainer cannot buy a winner at present.
**Vancouver Gold(IRE)**, an April foal, is a narrow type. After a tardy start and having to be switched, she finished with quite a flourish. The experience will not be lost on her, but it was quite a tough introduction.
**Plenty Cried Wolf**, who showed little on her two previous starts, seemed to appreciate the much better ground and the step up in trip.
**Egyptian Lady**, well beaten on her two previous starts, seemed to appreciate going left-handed and this was a big improvement.
**Robinzal** made this a good test but in the end he did not see it out and by a good way too.
**Mceldowney**, in first-time blinkers, was on edge and unhappy with himself beforehand. Tightened up leaving the back straight, he would not keep in a straight line under pressure and the response was limited to say the very least. He seems to be going the wrong way.

T/Plt: £4,693.50 to a £1 stake. Pool: £36,969.40. 5.75 winning tickets. T/Qpdt: £588.10 to a £1 stake. Pool: £2,424.00. 3.05 winning tickets. WG

5308 - 5311a (Foreign Racing) - See Raceform Interactive

# 5276 DOWN ROYAL (R-H)

Saturday, September 4

**OFFICIAL GOING: Flat course - firm; hurdle course - good to firm (firm in places)**

## 5312a HER MAJESTY'S PLATE 1m 4f 195y

5:40 (5:41) 3-Y-0+ £7,299 (£1,700; £750; £433)

RPR

**1** **Coat Of Honour (USA)**[28] [4540] 4-9-9.................... DPMcDonogh 3 103
(SirMarkPrescott) *settled 3rd: tk clsr order 4f out: rdn to ld over 2f out: sn strly pressed: styd on wl to draw clr ins fnl f* **4/5**[1]

**2** *4* **Lord Admiral (USA)**[20] [4784] 3-9-5 100.................... FMBerry 6 103
(CharlesO'Brien, Ire) *hld up in rr: smooth hdwy 2 1/2f out: cl 2nd and ev ch 1 1/2f out: no ex ins fnl f* **6/4**[2]

**3** *9* **Seeking Bellissimo (IRE)**[394] [3946] 4-10-0 89....................(b) PJSmullen 5 89
(DKWeld, Ire) *mod 2nd: pushed along and tk clsr order over 4f out: led 2 1/2f out: sn hdd and no ex* **5/1**[3]



The Form Book, Raceform Ltd, Compton, RG20 6NL

4 13 **Shamsada (IRE)**$^{310}$ [5840] 4-9-1 65 CatherineGannon$^{(3)}$ 1 59
(RHMacnabb, Ire) *led: clr early: rdn and strly pressed over 4f out: hdd & wknd 2 1/2f out* 40/1

2m 45.2s
**WFA** 3 from 4yo+ 10lb 4 Ran SP% 114.7
Speed ratings: CSF £2.52.
**Owner** E B Rimmer-Osborne House **Bred** Makio Shimoyashiki **Trained** Newmarket, Suffolk

**NOTEBOOK**
**Coat Of Honour(USA)** faced a fairly straightforward task and accomplished it without much fuss. He stays the mile and a half all right.
**Lord Admiral(USA)** had plenty to do against the winner on these terms, but was still very much in contention with two furlongs to race before being readily outpaced inside the last.
II

## CRAON (R-H)
### Saturday, September 4

**OFFICIAL GOING: Good to soft**

### 5313a DARLEY CRITERIUM DE L'OUEST (LISTED) 1m 55y
2:20 (2:23) 2-Y-O £15,845 (£6,338; £4,754; £3,169)

RPR

1 **Hypnotic**$^{9}$ [5051] 2-9-2 J-BEyquem 10 98
(SirMarkPrescott) *in tch towards outside, pushed along & hdwy 2 1/2f out, rdn & 3rd str, ran on to ld 1f out, kpt on wl to line, drvn out* 1

2 1 1/2 **Riverbride (USA)**$^{55}$ [3790] 2-8-13 SPasquier 12 94
(NClement, France)

3 nk **Louvain (IRE)**$^{50}$ 2-8-13 TJarnet 8 93
(RGibson, France)

4 2 **Best Horse (FR)** 2-9-2 C-PLemaire 6 92
(H-APantall, France)

5 6 **Enticer (FR)**$^{27}$ [4597] 2-9-2 PSogorb 5 79
(DGuillemin, France)

6 1 **Seulement (USA)**$^{14}$ [4963] 2-9-2 OPeslier 7 76
(CLaffon-Parias, France)

7 1 **Ascot Dream (IRE)**$^{14}$ [4964] 2-8-13 (b) YBarberot 9 71
(SWattel, France)

8 nk **Glazed Frost (FR)**$^{14}$ [4963] 2-8-13 TThulliez 11 71
(PBary, France)

9 1 1/2 **Antioche (FR)**$^{40}$ 2-9-2 (b) SMaillot 3 70
(CLaffon-Parias, France)

10 5 **Slamy (USA)** 2-8-13 IMendizabal 4 56
(J-CRouget, France)

11 12 **American Touch (FR)**$^{25}$ 2-8-13 DBoeuf 2 30
(GDoleuze, France)

1m 36.5s 11 Ran SP% 12.5
Speed ratings: .
**Owner** Cheveley Park Stud **Bred** Cheveley Park Stud Ltd **Trained** Newmarket, Suffolk

**NOTEBOOK**
**Hypnotic**, making his turf debut having previously been successful twice from four starts on the Polytrack at Lingfield, made the trip to the French Provinces well worthwhile. Eyquem is now three from four for Prescott.

## 5223 YORK (L-H)
### Sunday, September 5

**OFFICIAL GOING: Good to firm (firm in places)**
The ground was described by the riders as 'firm but no jar but showing signs of wear and tear after the Ebor meeting and racing just four days earlier'.
Wind: Almost nil. Weather: Fine, sunny and very warm.

### 5314 SARAH COGGLES NURSERY 6f 217y
2:05 (2:08) (D3) (0-85,79) 2-Y-O £5,869 (£1,806; £903; £451) Stalls Low

Form RPR

434 1 **Diamonds And Dust**$^{14}$ [4967] 2-9-5 77 PRobinson 17 82
(MHTompkins) *chsd ldrs on outer: led over 2f out: r.o wl* 7/1$^{3}$

0656 2 1 1/2 **Algorithm**$^{3}$ [5240] 2-8-0 58 RFfrench 16 59
(TDEasterby) *chsd ldrs on outside: styd on fnl 2f: tk 2nd nr fin* 16/1

340 3 nk **Game Lad**$^{9}$ [5096] 2-9-1 73 DAllan 3 76+
(TDEasterby) *dwlt: hdwy and nt clr run over 2f out: checked 1f out: styd on wl ins last* 6/1$^{2}$

044 4 shd **Aire De Mougins (IRE)**$^{63}$ [3560] 2-9-3 75 GFaulkner 11 75
(PCHaslam) *w ldrs: edgd lft and nt qckn fnl f* 12/1

1360 5 nk **Society Music (IRE)**$^{8}$ [5119] 2-9-2 74 SWKelly 4 73
(MDods) *w ldrs: edgd rt 1f out: kpt on same pce* 12/1

2510 6 3 **Ballycroy Girl (IRE)**$^{44}$ [4089] 2-9-0 72 EAhern 1 64
(ABailey) *in rr: hdwy over 3f out: sn chsng ldrs: fdd appr fnl f* 14/1

1024 7 1/2 **Monsieur Mirasol**$^{7}$ [5143] 2-9-7 79 NCallan 5 69
(KARyan) *chsd ldrs: wknd over 1f out* 10/1

452 8 nk **Enforcer**$^{15}$ [4936] 2-9-6 78 SDrowne 6 68
(WRMuir) *sn bhd and pushed along: styd on appr fnl f* 5/1$^{1}$

4500 9 1 1/4 **Tiviski (IRE)**$^{15}$ [4958] 2-9-1 73 MFenton 2 60
(EJAlston) *mid-div: effrt over 2f out: nvr nr ldrs* 33/1

0021 10 1/2 **Apetite**$^{6}$ [5192] 2-8-6 64 5ex JQuinn 12 64+
(NBycroft) *hmpd s: sn detached in last: styd on fnl 2f: nt rch ldrs* 14/1

400 11 1 1/4 **Darko Karim**$^{41}$ [4193] 2-9-6 78 (v$^{1}$) TPQueally 13 60
(DRLoder) *hmpd s: in rr whn hrd rdn and hung lft over 1f out: nvr on terms* 14/1

4331 12 3/4 **Roko**$^{13}$ [4997] 2-8-1 59 (v$^{1}$) PHanagan 14 39
(DShaw) *swvd lft s: chsd ldrs: lost pl over 1f out* 20/1

300 13 1 1/4 **General Max (IRE)**$^{22}$ [4761] 2-8-6 64 RWinston 7 41
(ACrook) *a in rr* 33/1

2500 14 2 1/2 **Selkirk Storm (IRE)**$^{19}$ [4836] 2-9-2 77 PMulrennan$^{(3)}$ 9 48
(MWEasterby) *hdwy to ld over 5f out: hdd over 2f out: sn lost pl* 33/1

1050 15 2 **Maureen's Lough (IRE)**$^{3}$ [5234] 2-7-9 56 oh3 NMackay$^{(3)}$ 10 21
(JHetherton) *led over 1f: chsd ldrs: lost pl over 1f out* 50/1

3010 16 1 1/4 **Dartanian**$^{16}$ [4909] 2-7-13 60 FPFerris$^{(3)}$ 8 22
(PDEvans) *chsd ldrs: lost pl 2f out* 20/1

4400 17 dist **English Fellow**$^{31}$ [4487] 2-8-12 70 GGibbons 15 —
(BAMcmahon) *in rr: lost pl over 3f out: sn virtually p.u: t.o* 33/1

1m 24.65s (1.34) **Going Correction** +0.075s/f (Good) 17 Ran SP% 117.1
Speed ratings: **95,93,92,92,92 89,88,88,86,86 84,83,82,79,77 75,—**CSF £99.16 CT £736.15 TOTE £5.90: £1.30, £4.40, £1.60, £4.10; EX 148.40.
**Owner** Mrs S Ashby **Bred** Whitsbury Manor Stud **Trained** Newmarket, Suffolk

**FOCUS**
The top-weight has a provisional rating of just 79 and the draw was of no importance - the first two had the widest draws.

**NOTEBOOK**
**Diamonds And Dust**, seemingly worst drawn, had plenty of use made of him. Racing with real enthusiasm, he ran out a decisive winner and is progressing nicely.
**Algorithm**, drawn one from the outside, again ran well sticking on in solid fashion. Her action suggests less firm ground will be in her favour.
**Game Lad ◆**, keen to post, missed a beat at the start then encountered traffic problems. He would have given the winner more to do with better luck, and deserves to find a similar event.
**Aire De Mougins(IRE)**, absent for two months, was taken to post quietly. He was in the thick of things throughout and kept on in willing fashion.
**Society Music(IRE)** looked in tip-top trim but did not impress at all going to post. She gave a good account of herself but looks rated to the very limit.
**Ballycroy Girl(IRE)** moved poorly to post and, though her win was on fast ground, the surface here looked a lot firmer than she cares for.
**Enforcer**, warm beforehand, struggled badly on this very quick ground but to his credit kept going all the way to the line. *Official explanation: jockey said colt was unsuited by ground*
**Apetite**, knocked over at the start, stayed on in good style to finish in mid-division.
**English Fellow** *Official explanation: jockey said colt lost its action*

### 5315 DRS FOR SONY "PREMIER" CLAIMING STKS 1m 208y
2:35 (2:36) (D3) 3-Y-O+ £6,370 (£1,960; £980; £490) Stalls Low

Form RPR

2030 1 **Calcutta**$^{29}$ [4528] 8-9-5 95 MHills 10 92
(BWHills) *hld up in tch: hdwy over 2f out: led appr fnl f: r.o wl* 11/4$^{2}$

1300 2 1 1/2 **True Night**$^{15}$ [4931] 7-8-9 83 EAhern 8 79
(DNicholls) *led: hrd pressed fr over 2f out: rdn and hdd appr fnl f: no ex* 5/1$^{3}$

1150 3 1 1/4 **Harry Potter (GER)**$^{13}$ [5004] 5-8-12 79 (v) DSweeney 4 79
(KRBurke) *trckd ldrs: effrt whn nt clr run over 1f out: styd on fnl f* 12/1

0530 4 3/4 **Cherished Number**$^{13}$ [4988] 5-8-9 70 (p) RWinston 13 75
(ISemple) *dwlt: hld up in rr: hdwy over 2f out: chsd ldrs and rdn appr fnl f: no imp ins last* 10/1

0106 5 1 1/2 **Scotty's Future (IRE)**$^{13}$ [5006] 6-8-12 72 TPQueally 6 75
(DNicholls) *trckd ldrs: keen early: drvn along and sltly outpcd 2f out: styng on whn short of room jst ins fnl f* 22/1

4314 6 nk **On Every Street**$^{29}$ [4533] 3-8-13 77 (b$^{1}$) RFfrench 2 81
(RBastiman) *cl up: chal over 2f out: ev ch tl wknd appr fnl f* 50/1

1005 7 2 1/2 **Ionian Spring (IRE)**$^{18}$ [4856] 9-9-2 91 PRobinson 12 73
(CGCox) *dwlt: hld up in rr: hdwy over 2f out: rdn over 1f out: sn btn* 9/4$^{1}$

0-30 8 6 **Dark Charm (FR)**$^{17}$ [4887] 5-9-10 90 PHanagan 11 69
(RAFahey) *hld up towards rr: pushed along 3f out: sn wknd* 7/1

1m 51.6s (1.64) **Going Correction** +0.15s/f (Good)
**WFA** 3 from 4yo+ 6lb 8 Ran SP% 109.7
Speed ratings: **98,96,95,94,93 93,91,85**CSF £15.45 TOTE £3.10: £1.50, £2.00, £2.10; EX 18.00.True Night was subject to a friendly claim.
**Owner** The Hon Mrs J M Corbett & C Wright **Bred** Campbell Stud **Trained** Lambourn, Berks

**FOCUS**
The early gallop was very modest and it developed into a three-furlong sprint. As a result the winning time was moderate for the class.

**NOTEBOOK**
**Calcutta**, best in on official figures, did not have his stamina truly tested and he recorded his 12th career win.
**True Night**, suited by the ground, was given a soft lead but in the end the winner simply proved too good. This did not conclusively prove his stamina.
**Harry Potter(GER)** had a bit to find and this bold effort will certainly not see his rating reduced - the opposite could well be the outcome.
**Cherished Number**, an in-and-out performer, had plenty to find and did well trying to come from off the pace in a falsely-run race.
**Scotty's Future(IRE)** had plenty to find and his most fertile field these days is in sellers on the All-Weather.
**On Every Street**, having his second outing for his new yard, wore blinkers this time and did as well as could be expected, as he had over a stone to find with the first two on official ratings.
**Ionian Spring(IRE)**, as usual taken very early to post, could have done with a much stronger pace but even so this was still a disappointing effort. *Official explanation: jockey said gelding unsuited by ground*

### 5316 SMITH BROTHERS H'CAP 6f 217y
3:10 (3:10) (E3) (0-70,70) 3-Y-O+ £6,197 (£1,907; £953; £476) Stalls Low

Form RPR

1164 1 **Hazewind**$^{8}$ [5120] 3-8-6 65 (vt) FPFerris$^{(3)}$ 18 76
(PDEvans) *chsd ldrs on outer: styd on to ld ins last* 10/1

0424 2 1 **Roman Maze**$^{12}$ [5020] 4-8-9 61 SWKelly 5 69
(WMBrisbourne) *trckd ldrs: nt clr run over 1f out: nt qckn ins last* 10/1

4015 3 shd **Locombe Hill (IRE)**$^{8}$ [5108] 8-8-5 64 DTudhope$^{(7)}$ 7 72
(NWilson) *t.k.h: w ldrs: led over 2f out: hdd and no ex ins last* 20/1

0606 4 1 3/4 **Kareeb (FR)**$^{18}$ [4846] 7-9-3 69 GCarter 9 72
(WJMusson) *in tch: effrt over 2f out: nt qckn fnl f* 6/1$^{2}$

0050 5 1/2 **No Grouse**$^{28}$ [4577] 4-8-12 64 (p) PHanagan 14 66
(RAFahey) *mid-div: hrd rdn over 2f out: kpt on wl fnl f* 16/1

1302 6 nk **Downland (IRE)**$^{16}$ [4928] 8-9-0 66 KimTinkler 12 67
(NTinkler) *chsd ldrs: kpt on same pce fnl f* 25/1

6000 7 1 1/4 **Banjo Bay (IRE)**$^{12}$ [5016] 6-8-13 65 AlexGreaves 4 62
(DNicholls) *chsd ldrs: kpt on one pce fnl f* 20/1

3506 8 1/2 **Sessay**$^{6}$ [5193] 3-8-12 68 ANicholls 16 64
(DNicholls) *trckd ldrs: led over 3f out tl over 2f out: one pce* 28/1

0531 9 3 1/2 **Oh Golly Gosh**$^{13}$ [5001] 3-8-10 66 (v) TEDurcan 11 53
(NPLittmoden) *s.i.s: bhd and drvn along: sme hdwy over 2f out: nvr on terms* 28/1

1051 10 3/4 **Yorkshire Blue**$^{28}$ [4577] 5-8-6 61 NMackay$^{(3)}$ 1 46
(JSGoldie) *bhd: hdwy on ins 3f out: wknd fnl f* 7/2$^{1}$

0202 11 1/2 **Bollin Edward**$^{8}$ [5126] 5-8-12 64 (v) DAllan 15 47
(TDEasterby) *sn bhd and drvn along: nvr on terms* 9/1

0-50 12 3/4 **New Wish (IRE)**$^{15}$ [4577] 4-8-9 61 TLucas 17 42
(MWEasterby) *dwlt: a towards rr* 16/1

0406 13 2 **Phluke**$^{39}$ [4242] 3-8-12 68 SCarson 10 44
(RFJohnsonHoughton) *chsd ldrs: lost pl over 2f out* 33/1

5352 14 3/4 **Bob's Buzz**$^{29}$ [4549] 4-9-2 68 RMullen 3 42
(SCWilliams) *t.k.h in rr: sme hdwy 3f out: nvr on terms* 15/2$^{3}$

-000 15 1 1/4 **Perfect Love**$^{3}$ [5244] 4-9-4 70 EAhern 13 40
(EJAlston) *led tl over 3f out: lost pl 2f out* 50/1

-004 16 3/4 **Zap Attack**$^{28}$ [4574] 4-8-5 62 MLawson$^{(5)}$ 19 30
(JParkes) *mid-div: rdn 3f out: sn lost pl* 33/1

0020 **17** ¾ **Desert Leader (IRE)**[56] [3780] 3-8-11 **67**.............................. GGibbons 8 33
(BAMcmahon) *s.i.s: sn drvn along and chsng ldrs: lost pl over 1f out* **16/1**

1m 22.94s (-0.37) **Going Correction** +0.075s/f (Good)
**WFA** 3 from 4yo+ 4lb **17** Ran SP% **122.2**
Speed ratings: **105,103,103,101,101 100,99,98,94,93 93,92,90,89,87 87,86**CSF £94.55 CT £2042.46 TOTE £15.00: £3.70, £3.70, £3.50, £2.30; EX 153.30.
**Owner** Waterline Racing Club **Bred** Gainsborough Stud Management Ltd **Trained** Pandy, Gwent

**FOCUS**
The draw again was of no consequence but it was very hard to make ground from off the pace.

**NOTEBOOK**
**Hazewind**, drawn very wide, stuck on in admirable fashion to show ahead inside the last and defy his highest-ever mark. He is a tough type, a credit to his trainer.
**Roman Maze** travelled strongly and looked unlucky not to give the winner a bit more to do, but the fact remains he boasts just one career success and that was on the All-Weather.
**Locombe Hill(IRE)** did surprisingly well considering he was very keen to get on with it. The change of stables seems to have revitalised him.
**Kareeb(FR)**, who is slipping to a lenient mark, lay a lot handier than usual but he was never doing anything like enough to take a serious hand.
**No Grouse**, who has slipped in the weights, decided to stay on when it was all over and may be worth a try over a mile.
**Downland(IRE)** is in good form of late but best on the All-Weather, he may not want the ground quite as quick as this on turf.
**Yorkshire Blue**, 4lb higher, did not look at his very best in the paddock and did not run up to scratch on ground probably firmer than he truly likes. *Official explanation: trainer said gelding was unsuited by ground*
**Bollin Edward** *Official explanation: jockey said gelding stumbled at start*
**Desert Leader(IRE)** *Official explanation: jockey said colt was slow away*

## 5317 MONKS CROSS SHOPPING PARK H'CAP 7f 205y
3:45 (3:45) (E3) (0-70,70) 3-Y-0+ **£6,828** (£2,101; £1,050; £525) **Stalls** Low

Form RPR
0020 **1** **Mount Hillaby (IRE)**[9] [5085] 4-8-6 **60**.......................... PMulrennan(3) 6 71
(MWEasterby) *trckd ldrs: led over 1f out: styd on wl u.p* **9/1**[2]
3225 **2** 1 **Tedsdale Mac**[7] [5144] 5-8-8 **59**...................................... FNorton 15 68
(NBycroft) *dwlt: bhd: gd hdwy over 2f out: rdn over 1f out: styd on wl u.p to go 2nd wl ins last: nt trble wnr* **8/1**[1]
5200 **3** ½ **Nemo Fugat (IRE)**[12] [5020] 5-8-9 **60**..............................(v) ANicholls 16 68
(DNicholls) *prom: rdn over 2f out: ch ins fnl f: no ex* **25/1**
5203 **4** ½ **Sarraaf (IRE)**[10] [5061] 8-8-13 **64**.......................................... TEDurcan 10 71
(JSGoldie) *in tch: effrt 3f out: no hdwy tl styd on wl ins fnl f* **20/1**
2000 **5** ¾ **Queen Charlotte (IRE)**[79] [3049] 5-8-13 **64**........................... JFanning 7 69
(MrsKWalton) *w ldr: led 1/2-way: rdn and hdd over 1f out: kpt on same pce* **12/1**
0330 **6** 1 **Regent's Secret (USA)**[19] [4826] 4-8-5 **59**........................ NMackay(3) 1 62
(JSGoldie) *towards rr: hdwy whn nt clr run wl over 1f out: styd on wl fnl f: nrst fin* **12/1**
5000 **7** ½ **Heversham (IRE)**[4] [5223] 3-8-11 **67**....................................... MTebbutt 4 69
(JHetherton) *midfield: rdn 3f out: chsng ldrs and keeping on u.p whn nt clr run jst ins fnl f: nvr able to chal* **33/1**
1120 **8** ½ **Santiburi Lad (IRE)**[40] [4213] 7-9-0 **68**.......................... THamilton(3) 12 68
(NWilson) *slt ld to 1/2-way: remained cl up and sn drvn along: ev ch 2f out: fdd fr over 1f out* **16/1**
1132 **9** *hd* **Bailieborough (IRE)**[10] [5061] 5-9-3 **68**........................(v) AlexGreaves 11 68
(DNicholls) *midfield: pushed along whn nt clr run over 2f out: n.d* **14/1**
0405 **10** 1 **Adobe**[20] [4802] 9-8-9 **65** ow1........................................... MSavage(5) 5 63
(WMBrisbourne) *midfield: rdn 3f out: no hdwy* **8/1**[1]
6/00 **11** ½ **Garden Society (IRE)**[37] [4293] 7-9-1 **66**.............................. GCarter 18 62
(WAO'Gorman) *dwlt: bhd: styd on u.p appr fnl f: n.d* **33/1**
4143 **12** 2 **Oscar Pepper (USA)**[28] [4574] 7-9-2 **67**...............................(v) RWinston 13 59
(TDBarron) *sn towards rr and pushed along: n.d* **9/1**[2]
3654 **13** 1¾ **Tagula Blue (IRE)**[9] [5085] 4-9-2 **67**..............................(t) DeanMcKeown 8 55
(JAGlover) *s.i.s: sn midfield: rdn over 2f out: sn btn* **12/1**
0106 **14** 1 **Dara Mac**[8] [5127] 5-8-3 **61**........................................ SuzanneFrance(7) 20 47
(NBycroft) *dwlt: bhd: kpt on fnl 2f: n.d* **40/1**
4313 **15** 1¼ **Didnt Tell My Wife**[16] [4912] 5-9-2 **67**.................................. RMullen 17 50
(CFWall) *sn pushed along: nvr bttr than mid-div* **10/1**[3]
0606 **16** ¾ **Gala Sunday (USA)**[28] [4574] 4-9-0 **65**.............................. DaleGibson 2 46
(MWEasterby) *nvr bttr than mid-div* **20/1**
3500 **17** 3 **Skibereen (IRE)**[18] [4852] 4-9-0 **65**......................................... RFfrench 19 39
(IWMcinnes) *chsd ldrs tl wknd 3f out* **50/1**
1443 **18** 2 **Fen Gypsy**[6] [5176] 6-9-2 **70**................................................. FPFerris(3) 14 39
(PDEvans) *midfield: rdn over 2f out: no hdwy: eased ent fnl f* **10/1**[3]
6163 **19** 6 **Flash Ram**[10] [5063] 3-8-8 **64**...................................................... DAllan 9 20
(TDEasterby) *chsd ldrs: rdn 3f out: no imp and sn eased* **14/1**

1m 36.28s (-1.46) **Going Correction** +0.15s/f (Good)
**WFA** 3 from 4yo+ 5lb **19** Ran SP% **126.3**
Speed ratings: **113,112,111,111,110 109,108,108,108,107 106,104,102,101,100 99,96,94,88**CSF £74.11 CT £1819.69 TOTE £11.70: £3.00, £3.00, £6.80, £3.80; EX 137.20.
**Owner** The Woodford Group Limited **Bred** Lodge Park Stud **Trained** Sheriff Hutton, N Yorks
■ Stewards Enquiry : P Mulrennan three-day ban: used whip with excessive frequency and without giving filly time to respond (Sep 16-18)

**FOCUS**
A modest handicap and only Tedsdale Mac managed to make serious ground from off the pace. However, the winning time was very smart for a race of its type.

**NOTEBOOK**
**Mount Hillaby(IRE)**, suited by the drop back in trip and totally different ground, scored in decisive fashion but she had to be hard ridden to stay in charge.
**Tedsdale Mac**, who has not won for over two years, was taking a big drop in distance. The only one to make serious ground from off the pace, he deserves to end his losing run.
**Nemo Fugat(IRE)**, who has not tasted success for over two years, is hard to predict but ran one of his occasional good races on ground that suits.
**Sarraaf(IRE)**, suited by the strong pace, has a much better record in claimers than in handicaps.
**Queen Charlotte(IRE)**, who took this a year ago on her seasonal bow from just a 1lb lower mark, was having her first outing for over 11 weeks and she has run well when fresh in the past.
**Regent's Secret(USA)** was out of luck yet again but the fact remains he is still a maiden now after 27 attempts.
**Heversham(IRE)**, whose one success was on the All-Weather, was having his second outing here in five days and was a shade unfortunate not to finish a fraction closer.
**Adobe**, who has not won for over a year, moved badly to post and never fired.
**Fen Gypsy** *Official explanation: jockey said saddle slipped*
**Flash Ram** *Official explanation: reported by vet to be lame after race*

## 5318 LAYERTHORPE VOLKSWAGEN BEETLE H'CAP 1m 5f 197y
4:20 (4:21) (D2) (0-85,85) 3-Y-0+ **£13,183** (£5,000; £2,500; £1,136) **Stalls** Low

Form RPR
1-00 **1** **Barman (USA)**[21] [4772] 5-9-4 **80**.....................................(t) JFanning 14 89
(PFICole) *trckd ldrs: styd on to ld 1f out: r.o* **25/1**
140 **2** 1¾ **Valance (IRE)**[39] [4226] 4-9-3 **79**........................................ SDrowne 10 86
(CREgerton) *chsd ldng pair: led 2f out tl 1f out: nt qckn* **7/1**[3]
0033 **3** 1½ **Skye's Folly (USA)**[28] [4578] 4-8-10 **72**.............................(b) MFenton 3 76
(JGGiven) *hdwy on ins over 3f out: kpt on same pce fnl 2f* **14/1**
0562 **4** *shd* **Maxilla (IRE)**[31] [4486] 4-8-9 **74**.......................................... NMackay(3) 7 78
(LMCumani) *hdwy after 2f: effrt over 3f out: sn chsng ldrs: one pce fnl 2f* **6/1**[2]
0226 **5** 1½ **Tilla**[9] [5093] 4-8-9 **71** oh2..................................................... JQuinn 2 73
(HMorrison) *dwlt: hld up: hdwy over 3f out: kpt on: nvr rchd ldrs* **10/1**
0265 **6** ½ **Weet For Me**[30] [4512] 8-8-10 **72**......................................... NCallan 6 74
(RHollinshead) *led tl over 8f out: led over 3f out tl 2f out: one pce* **33/1**
-040 **7** *nk* **Fourth Dimension (IRE)**[40] [4218] 5-9-5 **81**.......................... ANicholls 8 82
(DNicholls) *bhd: hdwy on wd outside over 3f out: kpt on: nvr rchd ldrs* **10/1**
6221 **8** 2½ **Jeepstar**[21] [4777] 4-9-1 **77**................................................... GGibbons 15 75
(TDEasterby) *trckd ldr: led over 8f out tl over 3f out: lost pl over 1f out* **6/1**[2]
0161 **9** 3 **Best Port (IRE)**[36] [4352] 8-8-4 **71** oh7.............................. MLawson(5) 17 64
(JParkes) *hld up: hdwy u.p over 3f out: wknd appr fnl f* **14/1**
3141 **10** 8 **Sualda (IRE)**[19] [4831] 5-9-2 **78**.......................................... PHanagan 4 60
(RAFahey) *t.k.h in mid-field: effrt over 4f out: nvr rchd ldrs: lost pl and eased over 1f out* **3/1**[1]
2211 **11** 2½ **Magic Combination (IRE)**[30] [4512] 11-9-6 **85**........... PMulrennan(3) 13 64
(LLungo) *hld up and bhd: pushed along 4f out: no rspnse: eased over 1f out* **9/1**
-140 **12** 13 **Latalomne (USA)**[21] [4772] 10-8-11 **76**.............................. THamilton(3) 1 36
(NWilson) *hld up: hdwy 6f out: lost pl over 3f out: sn bhd: eased* **25/1**

2m 56.11s (-0.29) **Going Correction** +0.15s/f (Good)
**WFA** 3 from 4yo+ 11lb **12** Ran SP% **118.2**
Speed ratings: **106,105,104,104,103 102,102,101,99,95 93,86**CSF £187.86 CT £2569.32 TOTE £24.60: £5.50, £3.10, £3.20; EX 207.00 Trifecta £5842.90 Pool: £8,229.50. 1.00 winning ticket.
**Owner** Sir George Meyrick **Bred** Allez France Stables **Trained** Whatcombe, Oxon

**FOCUS**
Just a steady gallop until turning in, but they came home well strung out.

**NOTEBOOK**
**Barman(USA)**, whose two victories last year were in claimers, travelled strongly and took this with the minimum of fuss, if anything suited by this trip.
**Valance(IRE)**, 4lb higher than when winning at Newmarket in July, was very keen to post. After taking charge, in the end he was very much second best. This trip is his bare minimum.
**Skye's Folly(USA)** gave a good account of himself but stamina looks his real strength and he is better suited by two miles plus.
**Maxilla(IRE)**, 5lb higher, did not improve for the step up in trip.
**Tilla**, 5lb higher than when narrowly denied at Salisbury two outings ago, may not want the ground quite as quick as this.
**Weet For Me**, from a stable that has been under something of a cloud, has not won for over three years and, after helping cut out the running, he kept on surprisngly well.
**Fourth Dimension(IRE)**, having just his fourth start this time, showed he is not that far off his game and his new trainer is still finding his way with him.
**Jeepstar**, 3lb higher, did not enjoy an uncontested lead this time and in the end this extended trip looked beyond him at this stage of his development.
**Sualda(IRE)**, 4lb higher, was running off a career-high mark. He never settled and, never a threat, his stamina seemed to give out in the end.
**Magic Combination(IRE)**, 6lb higher, never looked to be enjoying himself on this lightning-fast ground and in the end he completed in his own time. *Official explanation: jockey said gelding was unsuited by ground*
**Latalomne(USA)** *Official explanation: trainer said gelding finished distressed*

## 5319 ONE CALL INSURANCE MAIDEN AUCTION STKS 6f
4:50 (4:52) (E2) 2-Y-O **£10,205** (£3,140; £1,570; £785) **Stalls** Centre

Form RPR
5022 **1** **Ridder**[16] [4914] 2-8-13 81........................................................ EAhern 12 85
(DJCoakley) *midfield: effrt 2f out: hdwy appr fnl f: r.o wl u.p fnl f: led post* **5/2**[1]
**2** *shd* **Sam's Secret** 2-8-5 ........................................................ FNorton 14 77+
(JAGlover) *leggy: scope: midfield: keen early: gd hdwy over 1f out: r.o wl u.p to ld wl ins fnl f: hdd post* **20/1**
6 **3** ½ **John Robie (USA)**[43] [4124] 2-8-13 ........................................ SWKelly 5 83
(GAButler) *cl up: led over 1f out: hdd wl ins fnl f: no ex* **11/2**[3]
0 **4** 1¾ **Ingleton**[20] [4804] 2-8-10 ........................................................ GGibbons 11 75
(BAMcmahon) *prom: drvn along 2f out: edgd lft u.p appr fnl f: kpt on* **20/1**
**5** *hd* **Oceancookie (IRE)** 2-8-2 ........................................................ RMullen 6 66
(AMBalding) *rangy: unf: scope: dwlt: towards rr early: hdwy into midfield 1/2-way: rdn 2f out: kpt on wl fnl f: nvr able to chal* **33/1**
4 **6** 1¼ **Boo**[22] [4761] 2-8-13 ........................................................ JFanning 3 74
(KRBurke) *prom: ev ch over 1f out: no ex fnl f* **10/1**
**7** *hd* **Cosmic Destiny (IRE)** 2-8-5 ................................................ SDrowne 9 65
(EFVaughan) *unf: led tl hdd over 1f out: wknd fnl f* **4/1**[2]
**8** ½ **Rapid River** 2-8-2 ........................................................ RFfrench 10 61
(MrsLStubbs) *leggy: trckd ldrs: rdn 2f out: kpt on same pce* **50/1**
**9** ½ **Haenertsburg (IRE)** 2-8-2 ................................................ JBramhill 17 59
(ABerry) *rangy: scope: towards rr: hdwy into midfield 1/2-way: kpt on fnl 2f: n.d* **33/1**
5 **10** 4 **Burnley Al (IRE)**[18] [4861] 2-8-7 ........................................ PHanagan 19 52
(RAFahey) *towards rr most of way* **6/1**
**11** *nk* **Navigation (IRE)** 2-8-7 ........................................................ TEDurcan 8 51
(TJEtherington) *lengthy: unf: s.i.s: towards rr most of way* **50/1**
4 **12** ½ **Bowled Out (GER)**[9] [5089] 2-8-2 ................................................ JQuinn 7 45
(PJMcbride) *in tch tl wknd 2f out* **14/1**
**13** *nk* **Guadaloup** 2-8-5 ........................................................ KDarley 16 47
(MBrittain) *leggy: slowly away: bhd most of way* **33/1**
**14** ¾ **Birthday Star (IRE)** 2-8-10 ................................................ LisaJones 18 49
(WJMusson) *leggy: s.i.s: towards rr most of way* **66/1**
**15** *shd* **Ginger Cookie** 2-8-2 ........................................................ DAllan 15 41
(BSmart) *rangy: unf: chsd ldrs tl wknd 2f out* **33/1**
3 **16** 2½ **Bold Haze**[22] [4761] 2-8-10 ................................................ PRobinson 2 42
(MissSEHall) *midfield: rdn over 2f out: sn btn* **16/1**
00 **17** 1½ **Season Ticket (GER)**[15] [4936] 2-7-13 ........................... NMackay(3) 13 29
(WJHaggas) *chsd ldrs to 1/2-way: sn drvn along and wknd* **50/1**
**18** 3 **Woodford Wonder (IRE)** 2-8-3 ow4........................... PMulrennan(3) 1 24
(MWEasterby) *lengthy: unf: sn wl bhd* **66/1**
0 **19** 5 **Time To Succeed**[7] [5142] 2-8-10 ................................................ GParkin 4 13
(JSWainwright) *sn wl bhd* **100/1**

0 **20** *8* **Sergeant Small (IRE)**[15] 4936 2-8-10 .................................. GCarter 20 —
(JohnBerry) *sn towards rr: wknd over 2f out* **100/1**

1m 11.2s (-1.37) **Going Correction** -0.35s/f (Firm) **20** Ran SP% **132.0**
Speed ratings: **95,94,94,91,91 89,89,89,88,83 82,81,81,80,80 77,75,71,64,53**CSF £62.24 TOTE £4.10: £2.00, £6.50, £3.00; EX 99.70.
**Owner** Chris Van Hoorn **Bred** Fittocks Stud **Trained** West Ilsley, Berks

**FOCUS**
Just an ordinary maiden auction race with the first nine stacked up at the line.

**NOTEBOOK**
**Ridder**, easily the most experienced in the field, looked to be hanging fire on this firm ground but in the end he put his head in front right on the line. Rated 81, he is a sound guide to the overall value of the form.
**Sam's Secret** ◆, an April foal, is on the leg at present. A bit fizzy early on, she quickened up in good style to show ahead, but her trainer is right out of luck at present and she was nailed on the line. She richly deserves to go one better.
**John Robie(USA)** travelled strongly on just his second start and was only found lacking in the closing stages. He can surely find a race.
**Ingleton** seemed to improve on his debut effort, well suited by the step up to six.
**Oceancookie(IRE)**, a February foal, is a big type with plenty of scope. After a sluggish start she kept on in most encouraging fashion, but she is unlikely to reach her best until next year.
**Boo** again showed ability racing on totally different ground to that he had encountered on his debut.
**Cosmic Destiny(IRE)**, an April foal, is a slip of a thing. Well supported, she was always doing too much in front and in the end did not get home. A drop back to five will not be a problem, and she had clearly been showing plenty of ability ahead of this debut.
**Rapid River**, a March foal, is a decent type and she made a highly satisfactory bow.
**Haenertsburg(IRE)**, an April foal, stands over plenty of ground and showed ability, staying on steadily from the rear.
**Burnley Al(IRE)**, as on his debut here in a much better race two weeks ago, was never racing on an even keel.
**Bowled Out(GER)** *Official explanation: jockey said gelding unsuited by ground*
**Sergeant Small(IRE)** *Official explanation: trainer said gelding had been unable to act on the loose ground*

## 5320 EVENING PRESS COMPACT APPRENTICE H'CAP — 1m 2f 88y
**5:20** (5:21) (E3) (0-70,68) 3-Y-0+ — **£4,871** (£1,499; £749; £374) **Stalls** Low

Form — RPR
5044 **1** **Jake Black (IRE)**[8] 5129 4-8-8 **58**.................................... DTudhope(3) 11 — 68
(JJQuinn) *trckd ldrs: led over 2f out: r.o wl: eased towards fin* **8/1**[3]
22-0 **2** *2* **Colway Ritz**[7] 5144 10-8-11 **61**...................................... RoryMoore(3) 12 — 67
(WStorey) *s.i.s: bhd tl hdwy on wd outside over 2f out: styd on to take 2nd ins last: no ch w wnr* **10/1**
0063 **3** *1* **Mobane Flyer**[9] 5085 4-8-13 **60**............................................ PMakin 14 — 64
(RAFahey) *hld up in rr: hdwy over 4f out: styd on same pce appr fnl f* **10/3**[1]
520 **4** *2 ½* **Eton (GER)**[13] 5006 8-9-0 **68**.............................................. PJBenson(7) 9 — 68
(DNicholls) *lft in ld after 1f: hdd over 2f out: one pce* **8/1**[3]
1004 **5** *1 ¼* **Gold Guest**[22] 4736 5-8-12 **62**........................................ SJDonohoe(3) 16 — 59
(PDEvans) *bhd: hdwy on outside over 2f out: styd on fnl f* **7/1**[2]
-310 **6** *½* **Westcourt Dream**[73] 3250 4-8-4 **54** oh2......................... PPMathers(3) 1 — 50
(MWEasterby) *t.k.h: trckd ldrs: effrt over 3f out: kpt on one pce* **7/1**[2]
0004 **7** *1* **Iftikhar (USA)**[29] 4556 5-8-7 **54** oh2.............................. BSwarbrick 4 — 48
(WMBrisbourne) *s.i.s: sn chsng ldrs: fdd over 1f out* **8/1**[3]
6050 **8** *1* **Beneking**[8] 5110 4-8-4 **54** oh3......................... StephanieHollinshead(3) 13 — 46
(RHollinshead) *hld up in mid-field: hrd rdn and edgd rt over 2f out: nvr rchd ldrs* **33/1**
2500 **9** *2 ½* **Champain Sands (IRE)**[50] 3952 5-8-7 **54** oh1.................... RThomas 8 — 42
(WMBrisbourne) *in tch: effrt over 3f out: sn outpcd* **14/1**
6000 **10** *½* **Imperial Royale (IRE)**[23] 4698 3-7-9 **54**.......................(p) MHalford(5) 15 — 41
(PLClinton) *chsd ldrs: wknd over 1f out* **50/1**
0002 **11** *7* **Littlestar (FR)**[63] 3556 3-7-11 **54**.................................. DFentiman(3) 17 — 27
(ADickman) *sn bhd and drvn along: nvr a factor* **16/1**
0600 **12** *1* **Wuxi Venture**[15] 4213 9-9-1 **62**............................................. MSavage 18 — 34
(RAFahey) *a in rr* **20/1**
0006 **13** *1* **Narciso (GER)**[3] 5243 4-8-2 **54** oh5............................. DeanWilliams(5) 7 — 24
(MWEasterby) *chsd ldrs: edgd lft and wknd over 2f out* **33/1**
00-6 **14** *dist* **Quintoto**[10] 5061 4-9-1 **65**........................................ NataliaGemelova(3) 3 — —
(RAFahey) *led: swvd bdly rt: hdd and racd v wd after 1f: rn wd bnd over 4f out: sn bhd and virtually p.u: t.o* **20/1**

2m 10.48s (1.04) **Going Correction** +0.15s/f (Good)
**WFA** 3 from 4yo+ 7lb — **14** Ran SP% **120.4**
Speed ratings: **101,99,98,96,95 95,94,93,91,91 85,84,84,—**CSF £80.19 CT £323.68 TOTE £8.30: £2.80, £4.30, £1.80; EX 160.10 Place 6 £656.21, Place 5 £255.63.
**Owner** G A Lucas **Bred** Yeomanstown Stud **Trained** Settrington, N Yorks

**FOCUS**
A 0-68 apprentice handicap run at just a steady pace after the early leader almost ran off the track at the end of the first furlong.

**NOTEBOOK**
**Jake Black(IRE)** travelled strongly and had this in the bag the minute he struck the front. He will no doubt turn out soon without a penalty, and will be worthy of plenty of respect.
**Colway Ritz**, now a veteran, has not tasted success for over two years but here, on just his second outing this time, he showed that the spirit is still strong.
**Mobane Flyer**, stepping up in trip, was racing on totally different ground and he had a high draw to overcome. There may be even better to come especially on less firm ground.
**Eton(GER)**, an ideal mount for an inexperienced rider, was left with his own way in front but in the end was not up to defying top weight. Claimers seem a better option for him now.
**Gold Guest** is slipping back to a winning mark and his last two wins were on the All-Weather.
**Westcourt Dream**, who took a similar event from an 8lb lower market at Beverley in June, was very keen on his return after a ten-week break.
**Narciso(GER)** *Official explanation: jockey said gelding hung left*
**Quintoto** *Official explanation: jockey said gelding hung right in early stages*
T/Jkpt: Not won. T/Plt: £1,341.90 to a £1 stake. Pool: £84,840.02. 46.15 winning tickets. T/Qpdt: £284.30 to a £1 stake. Pool: £8,685.00. 22.60 winning tickets. WG

5321 - (Foreign Racing) - See Raceform Interactive

# 4955 CURRAGH (R-H)
Sunday, September 5

**OFFICIAL GOING: Good to firm**

## 5322a GO AND GO ROUND TOWER STKS (GROUP 3) — 6f
**2:45** (2:45) 2-Y-0 — **£36,676** (£10,760; £5,126; £1,746)

RPR
**1** **Cherokee (USA)** 2-8-11 ................................................... JPSpencer 11 — 102
(APO'Brien, Ire) *hld up towards rr: swed rt and hdwy 1 1/2f out: 2nd 1f out: r.o wl to ld on line* **5/2**[2]
**2** *shd* **Lock And Key (IRE)**[43] 4158 2-8-11 ....................... CatherineGannon 8 — 102
(EdwardLynam, Ire) *trckd ldrs: swtchd to outer 1 1/2f out: qcknd into ld over 1f out: kpt on wl: hdd on line* **10/1**
**3** *1 ½* **Indesatchel (IRE)**[15] 4958 2-9-0 ...................................... MJKinane 4 — 100
(DavidWachman, Ire) *hld up in tch on stand's rail: nt clr run fr 2f out: 4th 1f out: r.o wl* **2/1**[1]
**4** *2 ½* **Monashee Star (IRE)**[36] 4353 2-9-0 ..................................... FMBerry 3 — 93
(THogan, Ire) *led: rdn and strly pressed over 2f out: hdd over 1f out: sn no ex* **14/1**
**5** *1* **Mount Eliza (IRE)**[14] 4973 2-8-11 ................................. DPMcDonogh 6 — 87
(CharlesO'Brien, Ire) *cl up in 3rd: rdn and one pce fr 2f out* **14/1**
**6** *hd* **L'Altro Mondo (IRE)**[70] 3352 2-9-0 ...................................... TPO'Shea 5 — 89
(MHalford, Ire) *chsd ldrs in 6th: rdn and one pce fr 2f out* **8/1**[3]
**7** *nk* **Desert Tigress (USA)**[28] 4592 2-8-11 .........................(t) CO'Donoghue 2 — 85
(APO'Brien, Ire) *hld up in rr: kpt on one pce fr 2f out* **12/1**
**8** *nk* **Virginia Waters (USA)** 2-8-11 ........................................ JAHeffernan 1 — 84
(APO'Brien, Ire) *cl up on stand's rail: 2nd and chal 2f out: wknd fr 1 1/2f out* **14/1**
**9** *1 ½* **Hemaris (IRE)**[14] 4973 2-8-11 .............................................. PJSmullen 7 — 80
(MHalford, Ire) *trckd ldrs on outer: 4th 1/2-way: wknd fr 2f out* **12/1**
**10** *1 ½* **Missturner (IRE)**[21] 4783 2-8-11 ................................. NGMcCullagh 9 — 75
(MartinBrowne, Ire) *nvr a factor* **25/1**
**11** *4 ½* **Jenkins Lane (IRE)**[102] 2413 2-9-0 ................................. PShanahan 10 — 65
(CCollins, Ire) *chsd ldrs on outer: wknd fr 2f out* **8/1**[3]

1m 12.1s **Going Correction** -0.25s/f (Firm) — **11** Ran SP% **132.4**
Speed ratings: **107,106,104,101,100 99,99,99,97,95 89**CSF £32.66 TOTE £4.50: £1.80, £1.80, £1.10; DF 32.20.
**Owner** Mrs John Magnier **Bred** Strategy Bloodstock **Trained** Ballydoyle, Co Tipperary

**NOTEBOOK**
**Cherokee(USA)** put up a smart performance for a newcomer although this was not a proper Group Three. She quickened nicely when switched out and nodded it on the line. The Cheveley Park would sound a bit ambitious.
**Lock And Key(IRE)** was successful in a nursery here off 79, but has improved. She looked to have stolen this when quickening a furlong out, but was thwarted on the line.
**Indesatchel(IRE)** ran a bit below par and encountered trouble in running two furlongs out. He could not quicken a second time, but the fast ground might have been against him.
**Monashee Star(IRE)**, second off 83 in Galway nursery, ran a bit above that here.
**Mount Eliza(IRE)** should get through a maiden on this showing.
**L'Altro Mondo(IRE)** has placed efforts in better company than this.

## 5325a MOYGLARE STUD STKS (GROUP 1) (FILLIES) — 7f
**4:20** (4:20) 2-Y-0 — **£118,732** (£40,563; £19,436; £6,760)

RPR
**1** **Chelsea Rose (IRE)**[28] 4592 2-8-11 ................................. PShanahan 4 — 106
(CCollins, Ire) *trckd ldrs on outer: impr to ld 2 1/2f out: strly pressed 1f out: kpt on wl u.p* **9/1**
**2** *¾* **Pictavia (IRE)**[90] 2745 2-8-11 ................................................ KJManning 7 — 104
(JSBolger, Ire) *in tch to 3f out: 6th rdn and outpcd 2f out: r.o wl ins fnl f* **8/1**
**3** *¾* **Saoire**[21] 4783 2-8-11 ........................................................... PJSmullen 9 — 102
(MsFMCrowley, Ire) *hld up towards rr: rdn 2f out: r.o strly ins fnl f* **6/1**[3]
**4** *hd* **Umniya (IRE)**[7] 5149 2-8-11 .............................................(b[1]) ACulhane 3 — 102?
(MRChannon) *hld up: rdn 2f out: r.o wl ins fnl f* **14/1**
**5** *shd* **Belle Artiste (IRE)**[17] 4895 2-8-11 ............................(b[1]) JAHeffernan 8 — 102
(JosephCrowley, Ire) *trckd ldrs: 4th and hdwy over 2f out: 2nd and chal 1f out: wknd cl home* **33/1**
**6** *¾* **Slip Dance (IRE)**[29] 4552 2-8-11 ............................................ JFEgan 1 — 100
(EamonTyrrell, Ire) *hld up: 7th and prog over 2f out: 4th over 1f out: sn no ex* **16/1**
**7** *shd* **Silk And Scarlet**[28] 4592 2-8-11 ....................................... JPSpencer 12 — 99
(APO'Brien, Ire) *hld up towards rr: effrt on outer under 2f out: no imp: kpt on same pce* **11/8**[1]
**8** *2* **Sanserif (IRE)**[15] 4955 2-8-11 ............................................. TPO'Shea 10 — 94
(MHalford, Ire) *chsd ldrs to over 2f out: sn no ex* **20/1**
**9** *hd* **Borthwick Girl (IRE)**[45] 4060 2-8-11 ...................................... JFortune 6 — 94
(BJMeehan) *prom: 2nd and chal 3f out: wknd fr 2f out* **16/1**
**10** *shd* **Right Key (IRE)**[28] 4592 2-8-11 ................................... DPMcDonogh 5 — 94
(KevinPrendergast, Ire) *prom: cl 3rd 2 1/2f out: no ex fr 1 1/2f out* **25/1**
**11** *nk* **Jewel In The Sand (IRE)**[61] 3599 2-8-11 ............................ MJKinane 2 — 93
(RHannon) *hld up: rdn and no imp fr 2f out* **5/2**[2]
**12** *7* **Drama (IRE)**[13] 5009 2-8-11 ............................................... PCosgrave 11 — 75
(APO'Brien, Ire) *led: hdd & wknd 2 1/2f out: eased over 1f out* **33/1**

1m 24.2s **Going Correction** -0.35s/f (Firm) — **12** Ran SP% **139.0**
Speed ratings: **107,106,105,105,104 104,103,101,101,101 101,93**CSF £89.66 TOTE £15.00: £3.40, £1.90, £1.80; DF 167.60.
**Owner** Mrs A J Donnelly **Bred** Airlie Stud **Trained** The Curragh, Co Kildare
■ Stewards Enquiry : P Shanahan caution: used whip with excessive frequency

**NOTEBOOK**
**Chelsea Rose(IRE)** had beaten the favourite in a maiden at Leopardstown, but showed improvement here on her Debuntante Stakes third to Scarlet And Silk. In front from two and a half furlongs out, she kept finding plenty and will stay further.
**Pictavia(IRE)** looked well outpaced and was struggling two furlongs down, but she stayed on strongly inside the last and could have a good autumn with the Prix Marcel Boussac mentioned.
**Saoire** was supplemented for this and certainly did not disgrace herself. She would have appreciated a bit of ease and will stay further.
**Umniya(IRE)**'s published rating of 89 is a yardstick of sorts. She ran on well without ever looking a possibility.
**Belle Artiste(IRE)** was too close for this to be rated a genuine Group One contest.
**Slip Dance(IRE)** is another whose previous form is not top class.
**Silk And Scarlet** was held up as usual, but failed totally to make any impression from the two-furlong marker.
**Jewel In The Sand(IRE)**was done with fully two furlongs out. Her jockey reported that she was never travelling. *Official explanation: jockey said filly never travelled and hung left throughout*

## 5327a NOLAN & BROPHY AUCTIONEERS FLYING FIVE (GROUP 3) — 5f
**5:25** (5:29) 3-Y-0+ — **£34,330** (£10,035; £4,753; £1,584)

RPR
**1** **Ringmoor Down**[38] 4269 5-9-1 ............................................ MJKinane 7 — 111
(DWPArbuthnot) *hld up in 7th: hdwy 1 1/2f out: 2nd and chal under 1f out: led cl home: all out* **5/2**[2]
**2** *hd* **Benbaun (IRE)**[56] 3816 3-9-0 ..............................................(b) DCorby 8 — 111
(MJWallace) *3rd early: rdn to dispute ld over 2f out: def advantage 1 1/2f out: strly pressed fnl f: hdd cl home* **11/2**[3]

3 *nk* **Osterhase (IRE)**[28] [4590] 5-9-1 118....................(b) FMBerry 5 109
(JEMulhern, Ire) *led: rdn and jnd over 2f out: hdd 1 1/2f out: rallied ins fnl f* **13/8**[1]

4 *shd* **Glocca Morra (IRE)**[15] [4956] 6-9-1 99.................... KJManning 1 109
(WTFarrell, Ire) *chsd ldrs: 4th 1/2-way: 6th 1f out: kpt on wl cl home* **14/1**

5 *shd* **Ulfah (USA)**[15] [4956] 3-8-11 104.................... DPMcDonogh 6 106
(KevinPrendergast, Ire) *chsd ldrs in 6th: rdn 2f out: styd on wl u.p fnl f* **7/1**

6 *shd* **Grand Reward (USA)**[15] [4956] 3-9-0 106....................(t) JPSpencer 2 108
(APO'Brien, Ire) *hld up in rr: last 1 1/2f out: r.o wl fnl f: checked nr fin* **7/1**

7 *2* **Anna Frid (GER)**[43] [4159] 4-8-12 92.................... PJSmullen 4 97
(DKWeld, Ire) *chsd ldrs in 4th: no ex fr over 1f out* **16/1**

8 *1/2* **Moon Unit (IRE)**[28] [4590] 3-8-11 101.................... DMGrant 3 95
(HRogers, Ire) *2nd to 1/2-way: 3rd 2f out: no ex fr over 1f out* **16/1**

58.60 secs **Going Correction** -0.25s/f (Firm)
**WFA** 3 from 4yo+ 1lb **8** Ran SP% **125.5**
Speed ratings: **113,112,112,112,111 111,108,107**CSF £18.83 TOTE £3.90: £1.40, £2.00, £1.60; DF 20.30.
**Owner** Prof C D Green **Bred** Pigeon House Stud **Trained** Upper Lambourn, Berks
■ Stewards Enquiry : D Corby caution: used whip with excessve frequency

**NOTEBOOK**
**Ringmoor Down**, held up and travelling well, got into it over a furlong out and challenged gamely to get in front close home. The Prix de l'Abbaye is the target.
**Benbaun(IRE)** disputed it with two furlongs to race and had his head in front inside the last until run out of it close home. Corby was given a severe caution by the Stewards for his use of the whip.
**Osterhase(IRE)** led as usual, but never really dominated and although sustaining his effort all the way to the line the sparkle seemed to be missing.
**Glocca Morra(IRE)** ran well for a handicapper.
**Ulfah(USA)** kept on without quickening. She needs the extra furlong.
**Grand Reward(USA)** was keeping on quite well inside the last when encountering traffic problems.

5326 - 5328a (Foreign Racing) - See Raceform Interactive

## [5280]BADEN-BADEN (L-H)
### Sunday, September 5

**OFFICIAL GOING: Soft**

### 5329a GROSSER VOLKSWAGEN PREIS VON BADEN (GROUP 1) 1m 4f
**3:40** (3:46) 3-Y-O+ **£352,113** (£98,592; £52,817; £21,127)

RPR

1 **Warrsan (IRE)**[43] [4121] 6-9-6 .................... KMcEvoy 5 124
(CEBrittain) *midfield, gd hdwy on outside 4f out, 4th str, rdn wl over 1f out, drvn to ld jst ins fnl f, hung lft last 100 yards, ran on* **7/1**[3]

2 *nk* **Egerton (GER)**[35] [4385] 3-8-9 .................... AHelfenbein 4 121?
(PRau, Germany) *midfield, 5th straight, headway well over 1f out, driven to take 2nd 100 yards out, ran on* **40/1**

3 *3/4* **Shirocco (GER)**[63] [3565] 3-8-9 .................... ASuborics 9 120
(ASchutz, Germany) *midfield, hdwy 3f out, 3rd str, led over 1f out to just inside final f, wkng when crossed by winner close home* **5/1**[2]

4 *2* **Simonas (IRE)**[21] [4794] 5-9-6 .................... ABoschert 3 119
(AWohler, Germany) *dwelt, last til headway 3f out, brought wide and 10th straight, stayed on final 2f, nearest at finish* **20/1**

5 *2* **Gamut (IRE)**[43] [4121] 5-9-6 .................... KFallon 8 116
(SirMichaelStoute) *trckd ldr after 2f, led briefly appr str, 2nd straight, hard ridden and every chance over 1f out, one pace* **5/1**[2]

6 *hd* **Malinas (GER)**[21] [4794] 3-8-9 .................... AStarke 11 114
(PSchiergen, Germany) *held up, 9th straight, some progress final 1 1/2f, never nearer* **14/1**

7 *2* **Mubtaker (USA)**[22] [4746] 7-9-6 .................... RHills 6 113
(MPTregoning) *pulled his way to the lead after 1f, headed briefly on final turn, led straight to over 1f out, soon weakened* **1/1**[1]

8 *1 3/4* **Mohandas (FR)**[53] [3863] 3-8-9 .................... J-PCarvalho 2 108
(WHefter, Germany) *prominent, 6th straight, one pace from well over 1f out* **40/1**

9 *nk* **Omikron (IRE)**[21] [4794] 3-8-9 .................... MartinDwyer 7 108
(MarioHofer, Germany) *midfield, 7th straight, one pace final 2f* **22/1**

10 *8* **Well Made (GER)**[21] [4794] 7-9-6 .................... ADeVries 10 98
(HBlume, Germany) *last most of way* **33/1**

11 *2* **Dano-Mast**[35] [4380] 8-9-6 .................... FSanchez 1 95
(FPoulsen, France) *led 1f out, close up til 3f out, 8th and beaten straight* **25/1**

2m 32.79s
**WFA** 3 from 5yo+ 9lb **11** Ran SP% **123.3**
Speed ratings: .
**Owner** Saeed Manana **Bred** Saeed Manana **Trained** Newmarket, Suffolk

**NOTEBOOK**
**Warrsan(IRE)** was held up before making rapid headway around the outside on the home turn and, after taking it up soon after the furlong marker, stayed on well to the line. He did edge left and hamper the third in the last few strides, but the positions were already decided by then. At his best on fast ground, he will probably now head for the Arc, with the Japan Cup and Hong Kong International Vase possible later targets.
**Egerton(GER)** ran an amazing race for a maiden, albeit one with some classy early season form, and for a moment inside the final furlong it looked like his turn of foot might see him break his duck in Germany's biggest race.
**Shirocco(GER)** would prefer softer ground and was only 80 per cent fit according to his jockey so would be no forlorn hope in the Arc if it came up soft.
**Simonas(IRE)** plugged on steadily from a moderate position entering the short home straight and now heads Down Under for the Melbourne Cup.
**Gamut(IRE)** had finished four lengths in front of Warrsan in the King George but had no apparent excuses here having been in 'Position A' two furlongs out.
**Mubtaker(USA)** ran the first poor race of his life. Having pulled his way into the lead early on, he settled well enough but simply failed to quicken when let down at the top of the straight. Making his own running may not have been ideal, but this was still too bad to be true.

## [2668]CAPANNELLE (R-H)
### Sunday, September 5

**OFFICIAL GOING: Good**

### 5330a PREMIO REPUBBLICHE MARINARE TATTERSALLS (LISTED) (FILLIES) 7f 110y
**3:05** (3:15) 2-Y-O **£24,648** (£10,845; £5,915; £2,958)

RPR

1 **Kykuit (IRE)**[57] 2-8-9 .................... MPasquale 8 96
(LBrogi, Italy)

2 *2* **Varenka (IRE)**[25] [4625] 2-8-9 .................... SSanders 3 91
(SirMarkPrescott) *set gd pce, edged lft over 2f out, narrowly hdd under 2f out, led again briefly appr fnl f, sn hdd and one pace*

3 *3* **Vegas Queen (IRE)** 2-8-9 .................... ACorniani 5 84
(SSantella, Italy)

4 *nk* **Lasika**[93] [2668] 2-8-12 .................... MDemuro 7 86
(BGrizzetti, Italy)

5 *5* **Katie Can Dance (USA)**[57] 2-8-9 .................... LManiezzi 2 71
(RMenichetti, Italy)

6 *10* **Wild Daughter** 2-8-9 .................... GTemperini 1 48
(RBrogi, Italy)

7 *5* **Indian Hope (IRE)** 2-8-9 .................... GCossu 4 36
(LCamici, Italy)

8 *14* **Lady Fabiola (USA)** 2-8-9 .................... PBorrelli 6 —
(ATortorella, Italy)

1m 33.9s **8** Ran
Speed ratings: .
**Owner** Allevamento La Nuova Sbarra **Bred** Allevamento La Nuova Sbarra **Trained** Italy

**NOTEBOOK**
**Varenka(IRE)** tried to make all but, having determinedly turned back the challenge of Vegas Queen, had to give best to the winner in the final furlong. The fast ground was not ideal.

5331 - (Foreign Racing) - See Raceform Interactive

## [3358]LONGCHAMP (R-H)
### Sunday, September 5

**OFFICIAL GOING: Good to soft**

### 5332a NETJETS PRIX DU MOULIN DE LONGCHAMP (GROUP 1) (C&F) 1m
**2:50** (2:51) 3-Y-O+ **£120,718** (£48,296; £24,147; £12,063)

RPR

1 **Grey Lilas (IRE)**[12] [5032] 3-8-8 .................... ELegrix 7 118
(AFabre, France) *tracked leader, led entering straight (2 1/2f out), ridden out, ran on well* **10/1**

2 *1* **Diamond Green (FR)**[56] [3791] 3-8-12 .................... TGillet 11 120
(AFabre, France) *hld up, 9th str, gd hdwy appr fnl f to disp 2nd 100yds out, kpt on same pace to just hold 2nd* **10/1**

3 *nse* **Antonius Pius (USA)**[39] [4228] 3-8-12 .................... JPMurtagh 2 120
(APO'Brien, Ire) *held up in midfield, 6th straight, disputed 2nd inside final f, ran on* **12/1**

4 *nk* **Denebola (USA)**[35] [4383] 3-8-8 .................... C-PLemaire 9 115
(PBary, France) *always close up, 4th straight, went 2nd 1 1/2f out, still disputing 2nd til no extra close home* **22/1**

5 *3/4* **Whipper (USA)**[21] [4795] 3-8-12 .................... CSoumillon 5 118
(RobertCollet, France) *held up, last straight, headway on outside over 1f out, never nearer* **3/1**[1]

6 *snk* **Paolini (GER)**[112] [2156] 7-9-2 .................... EPedroza 1 116
(AWohler, Germany) *hld up towards rr, moving up on ins whn squeezed onto rails at halfway, 10th str, hdwy fr over 1f out, fin wl* **33/1**

7 *nk* **Lucky Story (USA)**[24] [4685] 3-8-12 .................... DHolland 10 117
(MJohnston) *led to straight (2 1/2f out), 4th & weakening 1 1/2f out, kept on final f* **7/2**[2]

8 *nse* **Le Vie Dei Colori**[39] [4228] 4-9-2 .................... LDettori 3 116
(LMCumani) *disputing 3rd & pulling early, 5th straight, ran on one pace final f* **11/2**

9 *1/2* **Martillo (GER)**[56] [3792] 4-9-2 .................... WMongil 8 115
(RSuerland, Germany) *8th straight, headway 2f out, disputed 2nd 1f out, one pace* **20/1**

10 *1 1/2* **American Post**[92] [2680] 3-8-12 .................... RHughes 4 113
(MmeCHead-Maarek, France) *s.i.s, sn cl up, 3rd str, disp 2nd 1 1/2f out, wkng when n.m.r just ins fnl f, not recover* **9/2**[3]

11 **Actrice (IRE)**[81] [2967] 4-8-13 .................... OPeslier 6 109
(ELellouche, France) *held up, 7th straight, hard ridden & weakened over 1f out* **25/1**

1m 37.5s **Going Correction** -0.175s/f (Firm)
**WFA** 3 from 4yo+ 5lb **11** Ran SP% **122.6**
Speed ratings: **113,112,111,111,110 110,110,110,109,108 108.**
**Owner** Gestut Ammerland **Bred** Azienda Agricola Il Tiglio Di Amelia Prevedello **Trained** France
■ A 1-2 for Andre Fabre. The winner was a supplementary entry three days before the race.

**NOTEBOOK**
**Grey Lilas(IRE)**, who looked exceptionally well in the paddock, was smartly out of the stalls she was soon well placed behind the leader. Quickening impressively early in the straight, she built up a lead of several lengths and victory never looked in doubt from the furlong marker. She is an improving filly and now heads for the Prix de l'Opera and may well end up in the Breeders' Cup Filly and Mare Turf.
**Diamond Green(FR)**, considering his wide outside draw, ran a fine race. He was among the backmarkers on entering the straight and then came with a progressive run up the centre of the track before battling on gamely to hold second place. He holds many top engagements including the Queen Elizabeth II Stakes at Ascot.
**Antonius Pius(USA)** behaved well on this occasion. He raced in mid-division before the straight, but did not have a clear run when wanting to make a forward move. In the clear one and a half furlongs out, he finished well and only failed by a fraction to take second place.
**Denebola(USA)** was always well up there galloping alongside the winner for much of the race. She could not quicken when it mattered, but still stuck to her guns throughout the final stages and her next race will be either the Prix de la Foret or something in the States.
**Lucky Story(USA)**, smartly out of the gates, was soon taken across to the rail to make the running. He did not go that quickly and was outpaced in the straight before staying on up the far rail. Connections are now likely to run him over a longer distance or with a pacemaker.

**Le Vie Dei Colori** ran far too free early on and then failed to quicken in the straight. His jockey felt strongly that a lack of early pace led to him running to below expectations and this effort is best forgotten

## 5333a PRIX DU PETIT COUVERT (GROUP 3) 5f (S)

4:10 (4:09) 3-Y-0+ £25,704 (£10,282; £7,711; £5,141)

| | | | | RPR |
|---|---|---|---|---|
| 1 | | **Pivotal Point**[36] 4324 4-8-12 (PJMakin) *always close up on rails, led well over 1f out, driven out* | LDettori 3 2 | 117 |
| 2 | 1 | **The Tatling (IRE)**[17] 4886 7-9-4 (JMBradley) *always in touch, headway to go 2nd 1f out, ran on but never able to challenge* | RLMoore 6 1 | 119 |
| 3 | 2 | **Chineur (FR)**[76] 3162 3-8-11 (MDelzangles, France) *in rear early, ran on from over 1f out to take 3rd well inside final f* | ELegrix 5 | 106 |
| 4 | snk | **Miss Emma (IRE)**[36] 4357 4-8-9 (JEHammond, France) *led over 3f out to well over 1f out, no extra final f* | TGillet 4 | 103 |
| 5 | ¾ | **Dobby Road (FR)**[36] 4357 5-8-12 (MlleVDissaux, France) *outpaced early, some progress final 1 1/2f, nearest at finish* | FSpanu 2 | 103 |
| 6 | snk | **Sister Moonshine (FR)**[36] 4357 3-8-8 (RPritchard-Gordon, France) *prominent til weakening approaching final f* | (b) CSoumillon 7 | 99 |
| 7 | snk | **Payphone**[41] 3-8-8 (PBary, France) *led 1 1/2f, still 4th 1f out, one pace, eased when beaten* | TThulliez 9 3 | 99 |
| 8 | 2 ½ | **Villadolide (FR)**[36] 4357 3-8-8 (MmeCHead-Maarek, France) *always outpaced* | C-PLemaire 1 | 90 |
| 9 | 2 | **Ela Merici (FR)**[48] 4-8-9 (MmeCBarande-Barbe, France) *dwelt, always behind* | (b) OPeslier 8 | 83 |

56.50 secs **Going Correction** -0.175s/f (Firm)
**WFA** 3 from 4yo+ 1lb **9** Ran SP% **121.3**
Speed ratings: **114,112,109,108,107 107,107,103,100.**
**Owner** R A Bernard **Bred** T R Lock **Trained** Ogbourne Maisey, Wilts

### NOTEBOOK

**Pivotal Point**, well away on the rails, settled behind the leader in the early part of the race. He took control one and a half furlongs out and stayed on well at the finish to win with something in hand. A much-improved individual, he will be allowed to take his chance in the Prix de l'Abbaye de Longchamp.
**The Tatling(IRE)** was settled behind the leading group and started to challenge for the lead one and a half furlongs out, but never looked like catching the winner. This was a decent effort as he was conceding 6lb to Pivotal Point and no doubt will also be back for the Prix de l'Abbaye in which he was third last year.
**Chineur(FR)** was waited with and came with a run up the centre of the track. He quickened really well late on to take third place in the dying stages and deserves a Group success.
**Miss Emma(IRE)**, quickly into stride, led until one and a half furlongs out but had nothing more to offer from that point.

# 5068 BATH (L-H)

## Monday, September 6

**OFFICIAL GOING: Firm**

## 5334 MITIE ENGINEERING MAIDEN AUCTION FILLIES' STKS 5f 11y

2:10 (2:18) (E4) 2-Y-O £3,108 (£888; £444) Stalls Low

| Form | | | | | RPR |
|---|---|---|---|---|---|
| 6535 | 1 | | **Arabian Dancer**[18] 4866 2-8-2 82 (MRChannon) *hld up in tch: swtchd lft and hdwy over 1f out: qcknd to ld last half f: r.o wl* | CCatlin 5 7/2[1] | 76 |
| 24 | 2 | 1 ½ | **Farthing (IRE)**[26] 4643 2-8-5 (GCBravery) *chsd ldrs: drvn to ld over 1f out: hdd and outpcd ins last* | SWhitworth 11 9/1 | 74 |
| 00 | 3 | ½ | **Doitforreel (IRE)**[21] 4804 2-8-2 (IAWood) *chsd ldrs: rdn over 2f out: pushed lft appr fnl f: kpt on one pce* | FNorton 8 12/1 | 69 |
| 2304 | 4 | ½ | **I'm Aimee**[7] 5174 2-7-13 76 (PDEvans) *sn led: rdn over 2f out: hdd over 1f out: wknd ins last* | FPFerris(3) 6 5/1[2] | 68 |
| 2 | 5 | ¾ | **Born For Dancing (IRE)**[84] 2940 2-8-8 (BWHills) *bhd: rdn 3f out: styd on u.p fr over 1f out: nt trble ldrs* | (b[1]) WSupple 2 7/1 | 71 |
| 6203 | 6 | hd | **Saucepot**[22] 4770 2-7-13 63 (MDIUsher) *pressed ldrs: ev ch 2f out: wknd fnl f* | HayleyTurner(3) 10 25/1 | 64 |
| 0 | 7 | ½ | **Little Warning**[22] 4770 2-7-13 (RMBeckett) *chsd ldrs: rdn 1/2-way: wknd ins fnl 2f* | NMackay(3) 3 10/1 | 62 |
| 04 | 8 | ¾ | **Bob's Flyer**[6] 5209 2-8-5 (JGGiven) *bhd: plld to outside and sme hdwy fr 2f out: nvr gng pce of ldrs* | TEDurcan 9 33/1 | 63 |
| 3242 | 9 | nk | **Agent Kensington**[27] 4621 2-8-2 69 (RHannon) *sn chsng ldrs: rdn 3f out: wknd ins fnl 2f* | RLMoore 1 7/2[1] | 59 |
| 02 | 10 | 1 | **Starduster**[21] 4804 2-8-2 (BRMillman) *s.i.s: a bhd* | SRighton 4 6/1[3] | 55 |
| 000 | 11 | 9 | **Eden Star (IRE)**[11] 5053 2-8-2 (DKIvory) *s.i.s: a bhd* | MartinDwyer 7 100/1 | 24 |

61.57 secs (-0.93) **Going Correction** -0.25s/f (Firm) **11** Ran SP% **122.5**
Speed ratings: **97,94,93,93,91 91,90,89,89,87 73**CSF £37.58 TOTE £4.90: £1.90, £4.20, £7.00; EX 47.20.
**Owner** Jaber Abdullah **Bred** The National Stud **Trained** West Ilsley, Berks

### FOCUS

Quite a competitive sprint maiden and probably not bad form by Bath standards - the time was fair for a race of its type and the form appears fairly solid.

### NOTEBOOK

**Arabian Dancer** returned to form and confirmed the ability she showed earlier in the season in races like the Albany Stakes and the Cherry Hinton. She had been tried at up to a mile two starts previously, but waiting tactics over the minimum trip clearly suited much better and she picked up well when switched out to get a run. She should be competitive in nurseries, but also holds a couple of entries in sales races at Newbury and Newmarket, and is the type to go well in those.
**Farthing(IRE)**, a Cheveley Park entry, was a big drifter on the exchanges in the morning, but attracted support on course. She raced quite keenly but kept on to the line and was simply beaten by a better horse. An ordinary race should come her way.
**Doitforreel(IRE)** was able to confirm the promise she showed when unlucky in running at Nottingham on her previous start and, progressing, she should make her mark in similar company this season.
**I'm Aimee** showed plenty of pace but again found a few too good for her and, still a maiden after 14 starts, she appeals as one to keep opposing.
**Born For Dancing(IRE)** had not been seen since making a promising debut in a Warwick maiden 84 days previously and was fitted with blinkers for this return. She ran respectably, but never really looked like winning.
**Saucepot** did not look to have any excuses and, rated 19lb lower than today's winner, she may do better back in nurseries.
**Little Warning**, quite well backed, showed improve form but was still well held by the principals.
**Agent Kensington** was disappointing and is exposed.
**Starduster** had today's third behind her when second at Nottingham on her previous start, but she was below form and may not have appreciated the fast ground.

## 5335 BETFRED.COM IN-RUNNING NURSERY 1m 5y

2:40 (2:50) (D2) (0-85,77) 2-Y-O £6,019 (£1,852; £926; £463) Stalls Low

| Form | | | | | RPR |
|---|---|---|---|---|---|
| 0500 | 1 | | **Clinet (IRE)**[11] 5052 2-8-7 63 (PMPhelan) *s.i.s: bhd: rdn over 4f out: gd hdwy 3f out: led jst ins fnl 2f: styd on wl* | JFEgan 3 20/1 | 66 |
| 006 | 2 | 1 ½ | **Swell Lad**[23] 4747 2-8-9 70 (PFICole) *led after 1f: rdn 3f out: edgd rt 2f out: sn hdd: styd on same pce u.p fr over 1f out* | (b[1]) NDeSouza(5) 11 12/1 | 70 |
| 220 | 3 | ¾ | **Chapter (IRE)**[25] 4689 2-9-7 77 (RHannon) *broke wl: dropped to mid-div: rdn over 4f out: styd on u.p to chse ldrs over 2f out: styd on same pce fr over 1f out* | RLMoore 1 10/3[1] | 75 |
| 2256 | 4 | shd | **Flying Pass**[17] 4914 2-9-2 72 (DJSFfrenchDavis) *bhd: rdn and hdwy over 3f out: kpt on u.p fr over 1f out but nt pce of ldrs* | SWhitworth 7 14/1 | 70 |
| 452 | 5 | 1 ¼ | **Bongoali**[10] 5083 2-8-11 67 (MRChannon) *s.i.s: bhd: rdn over 3f out: hdwy over 2f out: kpt on same pce fnl f* | CCatlin 4 7/1[3] | 62 |
| 0443 | 6 | 1 ¾ | **Zolash (IRE)**[11] 5059 2-8-6 62 (JSMoore) *chsd ldrs after 2f: rdn 3f out: one pce whn hmpd 2f out* | MartinDwyer 6 10/1 | 53 |
| 0010 | 7 | 3 ½ | **Don't Tell Trigger (IRE)**[16] 4958 2-8-6 69 (JSMoore) *chsd ldrs: rdn over 3f out: wknd fr 2f out* | DerekNolan(7) 12 8/1 | 52 |
| 0513 | 8 | 4 | **Lady Chef**[37] 4326 2-9-6 76 (BRMillman) *led 1f: styd chsng ldrs: rdn 3f out: wknd ins fnl 2f* | TEDurcan 2 4/1[2] | 51 |
| 0600 | 9 | 2 | **Spinning Coin**[9] 5114 2-8-8 67 (JGPortman) *wl bhd tl styd on fr over 3f out: n.d* | NMackay(3) 9 8/1 | 37 |
| 0300 | 10 | 4 | **Dreemon**[11] 5052 2-9-0 70 (BRMillman) *chsd ldrs: rdn over 3f out: wknd over 2f out* | FNorton 8 14/1 | 31 |
| 4000 | 11 | 1 ½ | **Make It Happen Now**[17] 4924 2-7-12 54 oh9 (SCBurrough) *t.k.h: chsd ldrs: wknd fr 3f out* | SRighton 5 66/1 | 12 |
| 060 | 12 | 4 | **Sirce (IRE)**[57] 3770 2-7-9 54 oh9 (DJCoakley) *sn bhd* | FPFerris(3) 10 66/1 | 3 |

1m 40.74s (-0.26) **Going Correction** -0.10s/f (Good) **12** Ran SP% **115.7**
Speed ratings: **97,95,94,94,93 91,88,84,82,78 76,72**CSF £234.03 CT £1017.52 TOTE £27.30: £13.30, £10.10, £2.20; EX 596.70 Trifecta £513.00 Part won. Pool: £722.56. 0.10 winning tickets..
**Owner** Wood Hall Stud Limited **Bred** Mrs J Costelloe **Trained** Shenley, Herts

### FOCUS

With the top weight rated 8lb below the ceiling for this race, the form looks ordinary but fairly solid, with the early pace strong.

### NOTEBOOK

**Clinet(IRE)** had shown ability on some of her previous seven starts, but had not been running consistently and did not look to be progressing. However, the fast pace suited ideally and, having looked to be struggling at halfway, she picked up well when pulled widest of all in the straight and was always doing enough in front. She should not go up too much for this and can continue to go well in similar events, but is one to oppose when stepped up in class.
**Swell Lad** had failed to beat a rival on his first two starts, but showed more on his previous outing and confirmed that on his nursery debut in first-time blinkers. Having set a decent pace, he looked likely to drop away when passed by the eventual winner but, to his credit, he kept on right the way to the line.
**Chapter(IRE)**, making his nursery debut, appreciated the return to decent ground and ran well, keeping on from well off the pace.
**Flying Pass**, with the visor left off on this step up to a mile, would have finished a little closer had he not been slightly hampered about two out. He has had a few chances, but is up to winning in similar company.
**Bongoali** was faced with very different conditions to those he encountered when runner-up in a heavy-ground claimer on his previous start, but ran respectably.
**Lady Chef** promised to be suited this step up in trip, but was not at her best.
**Dreemon** *Official explanation: jockey said gelding hung left*
**Sirce(IRE)** *Official explanation: trainer said filly was found to be in season*

## 5336 BETFRED "THE BONUS KING" (S) H'CAP 1m 5y

3:10 (3:19) (G4) (0-55,53) 3-4-Y-O £2,623 (£749; £374) Stalls Low

| Form | | | | | RPR |
|---|---|---|---|---|---|
| 4020 | 1 | | **Naughty Girl (IRE)**[22] 4771 4-9-0 46 (PDEvans) *chsd ldrs: wnt 2nd 2f out: led over 1f out: sn edgd lft u.p: hld on all out* | (vt) FPFerris(3) 10 5/1[3] | 54 |
| 5055 | 2 | shd | **Esperance (IRE)**[16] 4940 4-9-2 45 (JAkehurst) *s.i.s: bhd: rdn 3f out: gd hdwy over 2f out: str run to chse wnr ins last: fin wl: jst failed* | RLMoore 2 4/1[1] | 53 |
| 4003 | 3 | 1 | **Confuzed**[12] 5035 4-9-2 45 (DFlood) *t.k.h: chsd ldrs: rdn 2f out: styng on whn hmpd 1f out: kpt on again nr fin* | (e) JFEgan 5 9/1 | 51 |
| 4064 | 4 | 1 ½ | **Young Love**[12] 5035 3-8-11 45 (MissECLavelle) *mid-div: rdn 3f out: hdwy to chse ldrs 2f out: styd on one pce u.p fnl f* | RHavlin 11 11/1 | 47 |
| -000 | 5 | 1 ¼ | **Saintly Place**[18] 4868 3-8-13 50 (MRChannon) *chsd ldr: led over 2f out: sn rdn: hdd over 1f out: wknd ins last* | SHitchcott(3) 9 33/1 | 49 |
| 600 | 6 | ¾ | **Dry Wit (IRE)**[26] 4641 3-9-2 53 (RMBeckett) *bhd: rdn 3f out: styd on fnl 2f but nvr gng pce to rch ldrs* | NMackay(3) 13 16/1 | 51 |
| 1056 | 7 | hd | **City General (IRE)**[10] 5072 3-8-9 50 (JSMoore) *chsd ldrs: rdn 3f out: wknd over 1f out* | (p) LauraReynolds(7) 14 12/1 | 47 |
| 0003 | 8 | 7 | **Pererin**[32] 4497 3-8-9 46 (IAWood) *in tch: effrt and rdn 3f out: wknd qckly 2f out* | (b) HayleyTurner(3) 4 12/1 | 27 |
| 032 | 9 | 2 | **Magico**[47] 4018 3-9-2 50 (ABHaynes) *t.k.h: plld to outside and rdn 3f out: nvr a danger and sn wknd* | (b) MartinDwyer 7 11/1 | 26 |
| 4010 | 10 | 1 | **Chubbes**[13] 5021 3-9-3 51 (BJLlewellyn) *rdn 4f out: a bhd* | (b) SWhitworth 8 7/1 | 25 |
| 405 | 11 | ½ | **Ivy Moon**[32] 4477 4-8-13 45 (BJLlewellyn) *in tch 5f* | DCorby(3) 1 20/1 | 18 |
| 0000 | 12 | 7 | **Rumour Mill (IRE)**[2] 5284 3-8-6 40 (NEBerry) *led tl hdd & wknd qckly over 2f out* | (b) CCatlin 6 66/1 | — |
| 00-0 | 13 | 3 ½ | **Katz Pyjamas (IRE)**[18] 4868 3-8-11 45 (GFHCharles-Jones) *a in rr* | JoannaBadger 3 100/1 | — |

6006 **R** **Chandelier**[7] [5176] 4-9-6 **49** ..... TEDurcan 12 —
(MSSaunders) *ref to r* **9/2**[2]

1m 40.26s (-0.74) **Going Correction** -0.10s/f (Good)
**WFA** 3 from 4yo 5lb **14** Ran SP% **125.5**
Speed ratings: **99,98,97,96,95 94,94,87,85,84 83,76,73,**—CSF £25.82 CT £188.08 TOTE £6.90: £2.20, £3.30, £2.80; EX 23.50.There was no bid for the winner. Esperance was subject to a friendly claim.
**Owner** Mrs S J Lawrence **Bred** John Perotta **Trained** Pandy, Gwent
■ Stewards Enquiry : F P Ferris one-day ban: careless riding (Sep 17)

**FOCUS**
A very ordinary seller, weakened with one of the better-fancied runners, Chandelier, refusing to race.

**NOTEBOOK**
**Naughty Girl(IRE)** beat just two home after starting very slowly in a modest course and distance handicap on her previous start but, dropped in grade and away much better this time, she returned to form. However, not that consistent, she appeals as one to take on next time.
**Esperance(IRE)** not for the first time lost several lengths at the start, but he recovered well enough and only just failed to get up. He is still a maiden after 20 starts and is not the most reliable, but clearly has the ability to win a similar race.
**Confuzed**, racing beyond seven furlongs for the first time, did not get the clearest of runs but had his chance inside the final furlong and proved he got the trip.
**Young Love**, fourth in a heavy-ground seven-furlong seller at Brighton on his previous start, ran well enough stepped up in trip on ground probably a little faster than ideal.
**Saintly Place**, well held in three runs in better company over six furlongs this year, ran respectably dropped in grade and stepped up in trip, but may prove best over seven furlongs.
**Chubbes** looked to have conditions to suit, but was not at his best.
**Ivy Moon** *Official explanation: jockey said filly moved badly in race*

## 5337 BETFRED.COM NOW ONLINE H'CAP — 5f 161y
**3:40** (3:49) (E3) (0-70,69) 3-Y-0+ **£6,107** (£1,879; £939; £469) **Stalls** Low

Form — RPR

4104 **1** **Woodbury**[23] [4740] 5-8-10 **58** ..... GBaker 1 67
(MrsHSweeting) *chsd ldrs: rdn to ld 1f out: hld on wl cl home* **10/1**

6312 **2** *hd* **Jagged (IRE)**[14] [5000] 4-8-10 **58** ..... (v) TEDurcan 17 66
(JRJenkins) *pressed ldrs on outside: str challeng fr 2f out: kpt on wl fnl f but nt pce of wnr nr fin* **13/2**[1]

-600 **3** *hd* **Innstyle**[5] [5219] 3-8-7 **60** ..... SHitchcott(3) 2 67
(JLSpearing) *sn chsng ldrs: n.m.r ins fnl 2f: rdn and styd on wl fnl f f: gng on cl home* **20/1**

1005 **4** *1 1/2* **Willheconquertoo**[21] [4811] 4-9-7 **69** ..... (t) JFEgan 6 71
(AndrewReid) *sn led: rdn over 2f out: hdd 1f out: wknd nr fin* **11/1**

1006 **5** *1* **Stagnite**[4] [5253] 4-8-7 **58** ..... (p) DCorby(3) 12 57
(MrsHSweeting) *pressed ldrs: rdn over 2f out: outpcd ins fnl f* **10/1**

5400 **6** *nk* **Pulse**[4] [5253] 6-8-9 **57** ..... (p) PFitzsimons 19 55
(JMBradley) *racd on outside prom: rdn over 2f out: kpt on fnl f but nt pce of ldrs* **9/1**[3]

2400 **7** *nk* **Astrac (IRE)**[37] [4336] 13-8-7 **55** oh7 ..... JoannaBadger 10 52
(MrsALMKing) *bhd: swtchd rt to outside and hdwy over 1f out: r.o ins last but nt trble ldrs* **16/1**

0050 **8** *3/4* **Coranglais**[22] [4774] 4-8-11 **59** ..... (b) RLMoore 8 54
(JMBradley) *bhd: rdn and hdwy 2f out: kpt on fnl f but nt rch ldrs* **16/1**

0000 **9** *1/2* **Indian Bazaar (IRE)**[22] [4774] 8-8-4 **55** oh10 ..... LPKeniry(3) 7 48
(NEBerry) *pressed ldrs: rdn 2f out: wknd fnl f* **33/1**

0010 **10** *1/2* **Dellagio (IRE)**[21] [4817] 3-8-6 **56** ..... CCatlin 9 47
(CADwyer) *rdn 1/2-way: a mid-div* **14/1**

1-00 **11** *shd* **St Austell**[10] [5094] 4-9-3 **65** ..... SWhitworth 3 56
(JARToller) *s.i.s: bhd: hdwy on rails over 2f out: rdn to chse ldrs over 1f out: wknd ins last* **20/1**

0245 **12** *3/4* **Ardkeel Lass (IRE)**[12] [5040] 3-8-7 **57** ..... RHavlin 4 46
(DHaydnJones) *bhd: kpt on fr over 1f out: nt a danger* **25/1**

0010 **13** *nk* **Miss Judgement (IRE)**[5] [5219] 3-9-0 **64** ..... FNorton 15 52
(WRMuir) *bhd: kpt on fr over 1f out: nt rch ldrs* **9/1**[3]

0100 **14** *shd* **Izmail (IRE)**[16] [4935] 5-9-0 **69** ..... SJDonohoe(7) 18 56
(PDEvans) *bhd: som hdwy 2f out: nvr gng pce to rch ldrs* **20/1**

2030 **15** *1* **Compton Banker (IRE)**[28] [4614] 7-8-12 **63** ..... (b) FPFerris(3) 11 47
(PDEvans) *chsd ldrs over 3f* **8/1**[2]

30 **16** *1/2* **Musical Top (USA)**[12] [5039] 4-8-9 **57** ..... MartinDwyer 14 39
(HMorrison) *chsd ldrs over 3f* **14/1**

-000 **17** *3/4* **Ninah**[77] [3142] 3-8-5 **58** ..... HayleyTurner(3) 5 38
(JMBradley) *spd to 1/2-way* **66/1**

0056 **18** *3/4* **Florian**[12] [5035] 6-8-4 **55** ..... RMiles(3) 13 32
(TGMills) *racd on outside: a outpcd* **11/1**

69.60 secs (-1.54) **Going Correction** -0.25s/f (Firm)
**WFA** 3 from 4yo+ 2lb **18** Ran SP% **127.0**
Speed ratings: **100,99,99,97,96 95,95,94,93,93 92,91,91,91,90 89,88,87**CSF £68.81 CT £1350.66 TOTE £11.70: £3.10, £2.30, £3.90, £2.70; EX 82.60.
**Owner** P Sweeting **Bred** D R Tucker **Trained** Marlborough, Wilts

**FOCUS**
A really competitive sprint handicap, but the pace was not that strong and it proved hard to come from too far off the pace.

**NOTEBOOK**
**Woodbury** had not won on turf since August 2002 but was able to race off a mark 15lb lower than when gaining that success. Kept to the far rail throughout, she got an incredibly clear passage considering the amount of runners and was good enough to take advantage. However, she has never followed up.
**Jagged(IRE)**, in good form on Fibresand recently, continued that returned to turf, posting a good effort despite racing wide for much of the way from stall 17 - the winner and third were drawn one and two respectively. Although he was keeping on well enough at the finish, there is a strong suspicion that a bare five furlongs suits best.
**Innstyle** ran her best race of the season so far and may well have won with a clear run. She is still a maiden, but clearly has a similar race in her.
**Willheconquertoo** would have appreciated the return to proper fast ground and can have no excuses, having made much of the running.
**Stagnite**, stablemate of the Woodbury, does not win very often and again found a few too good.
**Pulse** looked to have conditions to suit, but he was not at his best and would have preferred a decent pace.
**Astrac(IRE)**, 7lb out of the handicap, did not run badly considering a stronger pace would have suited.
**Miss Judgement(IRE)** would have benefited from a better gallop.
**Compton Banker(IRE)** was one of many that would have preferred a stronger pace.

## 5338 BETFRED "WE PAY DOUBLE RESULT" MAIDEN STKS — 5f 161y
**4:10** (4:16) (D3) 3-Y-O **£3,594** (£1,106; £553; £276) **Stalls** Low

Form — RPR

200 **1** **Comeraincomeshine (IRE)**[45] [4085] 3-8-9 **62** ..... GCarter 13 61
(TGMills) *racd wd: bhd: gd hdwy over 2f out: led 1f out: drvn out* **9/1**

335 **2** *3/4* **Deuxieme (IRE)**[24] [4718] 3-8-9 72 ..... DSweeney 6 58+
(RCharlton) *s.i.s: bhd: hdwy and hung lft fr over 2f out:nt clr run: over 1f out: carried hd high and r.o ins last: fin wl* **5/2**[2]

3534 **3** *nk* **Indiana Blues**[7] [5201] 3-8-9 65 ..... MartinDwyer 4 57
(AMBalding) *w ld tl slt advantage over 3f out: rdn 2f out: hdd 1f out: nt qckn ins last* **9/4**[1]

0 **4** *1 3/4* **Superfling**[25] [4683] 3-9-0 ..... RLMoore 10 56
(RHannon) *racd on outside: bhd: rdn 3f out: r.o fr over 1f out: kpt on ins last: nt pce to rch ldrs* **20/1**

5050 **5** *nk* **Dane Rhapsody (IRE)**[25] [4674] 3-8-6 45 ..... SHitchcott(3) 2 50
(BPalling) *chsd ldrs: rdn over 2f out: n.m.r over 1f out: kpt on same pce* **20/1**

2 **6** *1 3/4* **Knead The Dough**[196] [856] 3-9-0 ..... JFEgan 1 49
(DECantillon) *slt ld tl hdd over 3f out: styd pressing ldr to 2f out: fdd fnl f* **8/1**[3]

0404 **7** *hd* **Scarlett Breeze**[15] [4968] 3-8-9 45 ..... MTebbutt 12 43
(JWHills) *in tch: kpt on fr over 1f out but nvr gng pce to rch ldrs* **20/1**

230 **8** *3/4* **Sokoke**[8] [5147] 3-8-11 ..... NMackay(3) 8 46
(RMBeckett) *chsd ldrs: rdn over 2f out: wknd qckly fnl f* **9/1**

000 **9** *1 3/4* **Imperial Wizard**[19] [4845] 3-9-0 ..... SChin 9 39
(MDIUsher) *racd wd: chsd ldrs tl wknd over 1f out* **100/1**

-400 **10** *4* **Bold Trump**[25] [4674] 3-9-0 52 ..... (v[1]) RMullen 7 25
(Jean-ReneAuvray) *early spd: rdn 1/2-way: sn bhd* **66/1**

06 **11** *1/2* **Dine 'N' Dash**[8] [5147] 3-8-11 ..... LPKeniry(3) 11 24
(AGNewcombe) *s.i.s: a outpcd* **66/1**

003 **12** *2* **Miss Monza**[17] [4916] 3-8-9 68 ..... TEDurcan 3 12
(BRMillman) *early spd* **14/1**

06- **P** **Beresford Boy**[293] [6018] 3-9-0 ..... CCatlin 5 —
(DKIvory) *s.i.s: sn lost tch: p.u ins fnl 2f* **50/1**

1m 10.23s (-0.91) **Going Correction** -0.25s/f (Firm) **13** Ran SP% **117.3**
Speed ratings: **96,95,94,92,91 89,89,88,85,80 79,77,**—CSF £29.26 TOTE £11.00: £4.90, £1.20, £1.10; EX 55.00.
**Owner** John Humphreys (turf Accountants) Ltd **Bred** Mrs Ann Egan **Trained** Headley, Surrey

**FOCUS**
Just a modest sprint maiden and the winning time was moderate for the grade. The form is held down by the proximity of the fifth and seventh.

**NOTEBOOK**
**Comeraincomeshine(IRE)**, who lost her action when well beaten at Chepstow on her previous start, returned to form with a fortunate success, making the most of the eventual runner-up's luckless run. A half-sister to the top-class miler Where Or When, this will have boosted her paddock value, but she could struggle back in handicap company if persevered with on the track.
**Deuxieme(IRE)** had shown ability on three runs over seven furlongs and had shaped as though this sort of trip would suit. However, not for the first time she was slowly away and, although recovering to get back in touch, she got stuck in behind horses and did not get in the clear until it was too late. She flew towards the finish, but did carry her head slightly awkwardly on ground that may have been a little faster than ideal and, although there is a similar race in her, she may not be one to take too short a price about.
**Indiana Blues** again found a couple too good and is not living up to expectations. She started the season rated 93 and went into this maiden rated just 65.
**Superfling**, dropped back from seven furlongs, stepped up on his debut running and appears to be progressing.
**Dane Rhapsody(IRE)** ran well but, rated just 45, she puts the form into perspective.
**Knead The Dough**, off the track since finishing second in a very ordinary Polytrack maiden 196 days previously, was well held and may do better when handicapped.
**Sokoke** showed ability on his first two starts, but was below that form for the second race in succession.
**Beresford Boy** *Official explanation: jockey said gelding lost its action*

## 5339 BETFRED IN SHOPS, ON PHONE AND ON-LINE MAIDEN FILLIES' STKS — 1m 3f 144y
**4:40** (4:42) (D3) 3-Y-O+ **£3,662** (£1,127; £563; £281) **Stalls** Low

Form — RPR

2 **1** **Simonda**[21] [4813] 3-8-10 ..... RLMoore 11 79
(MrsAJPerrett) *hld up in rr: hdwy on outside over 3f out: sn chsng ldr and edgd lft: led 2f out: clr over 1f out: pushed out* **5/4**[1]

34 **2** *8* **Tashreefat (IRE)**[54] [3843] 3-8-10 ..... WSupple 9 66
(EFVaughan) *chsd ldr tl led over 3f out: rdn and hdd 2f out: sn no ch w wnr but hld on for 2nd* **3/1**[2]

0 **3** *1/2* **Ruggtah**[109] [2243] 3-8-10 ..... TEDurcan 10 65
(MRChannon) *chsd ldrs: hmpd and lost position bnd over 3f out: sn rdn: styd on fnl f to press for 2nd cl home: no ch w wnr* **33/1**

**4** *shd* **Let's Pretend** 3-8-10 ..... RMullen 2 65
(BWHills) *slowly away: sn rcvrd and in tch: chsd ldr and rdn 3f out: styd on one pce fnl 2f* **8/1**

**5** *3 1/2* **Eurobound (USA)**[66] [3501] 3-8-10 74 ..... CCatlin 8 60
(DJDaly) *prom early: stdd rr: rdn 3f out: nvr gng pce to ldrs* **7/1**[3]

60- **6** *2* **Stormy Day**[407] [3622] 4-9-5 ..... JCrowley 1 56
(MrsAJPerrett) *t.k.h: in tch: rdn 3f out: sn wknd* **50/1**

**7** *6* **Mrs Philip**[27] 5-9-5 ..... VSlattery 7 47
(PJHobbs) *a in rr* **33/1**

2400 **8** *1 1/2* **Powerful Parrish (USA)**[36] [4368] 3-8-10 72 ..... SChin 3 44
(PFICole) *sn chsng ldrs: wknd 3f out* **14/1**

43 **9** *shd* **Sovietta (IRE)**[22] [4775] 3-8-10 ..... MartinDwyer 4 44
(RMBeckett) *chsd ldrs tl edgd rt bnd over 3f out: sn wknd* **9/1**

**10** *7* **Moon Spinner**[7] 7-9-5 ..... JFEgan 6 33
(AndrewReid) *led tl hdd over 3f out: sn wknd* **40/1**

2m 29.07s (-1.23) **Going Correction** -0.10s/f (Good)
**WFA** 3 from 4yo+ 9lb **10** Ran SP% **120.0**
Speed ratings: **100,94,94,94,91 90,86,85,85,80**CSF £4.98 TOTE £2.30: £1.10, £1.70, £5.10; EX 8.80.
**Owner** S P Tindall **Bred** Simon Tindall **Trained** Pulborough, W Sussex
■ Ryan Moore's 100th winner of the season, his maiden century.

**FOCUS**
A weak maiden and a modest time for the grade, but a decent performance from Simonda.

**NOTEBOOK**
**Simonda**, runner-up in a fair Windsor maiden on her debut, confirmed that promise to get off the mark with an emphatic success. It is hard to know quite what to make of the form, and her future looks to lie in the hands of the Handicapper, but she is at least progressing.
**Tashreefat(IRE)** was left behind by the winner in the closing stages, but is now qualified for handicaps and may do better that sphere.
**Ruggtah** would probably have been second but for being hampered about three out. This was an improvement on her debut running and she appears to be going the right way.
**Let's Pretend** recovered well from a slow start to hold a chance, but she lacked the pace to pose a threat and, a full-sister to the high-class stayer Rainbow High, she should do better over further when handicapped.


The Form Book, Raceform Ltd, Compton, RG20 6NL

**Eurobound(USA)** showed ability in three runs when trained in Ireland, including in blinkers when last seen 66 days ago. However, making her British debut, she did nothing to justify her rating of 74.
**Stormy Day** ◆ hinted at ability on this first run in 407 days and may be capable of better over further now she is qualified for a handicap mark.
**Sovietta(IRE)** *Official explanation: jockey said filly unsuited by firm ground*

## 5340 BETFRED.COM EARLY PRICES FROM 9 A.M. MAIDEN H'CAP 1m 5f 22y
**5:10** (5:10) (E3) (0-70,69) 3-Y-O+ **£3,672** (£1,130; £565; £282) **Stalls** Low

| Form | | | | RPR |
|---|---|---|---|---|
| 022- | **1** | | **Polar Tryst**[444] 2525 5-8-13 **62** ........ NMackay(3) 1<br>(LadyHerries) *stmbld stalls: sn led: rdn clr fr 2f out: drvn out fnl f* **10/3**[1] | 75 |
| 3355 | **2** | *6* | **Sunday City (JPN)**[21] 4820 3-8-13 **69** ........ RLMoore 12<br>(DRLoder) *chsd ldrs: rdn over 3f out: chsd wnr over 2f out: sn no ch but kpt on to hold 2nd* **9/2**[2] | 74 |
| 0640 | **3** | *1/2* | **Olympias (IRE)**[18] 4870 3-7-9 **54** oh2 ........ (b[1]) FPFerris(3) 11<br>(HMorrison) *bhd: hdwy and wd bnd over 3f out: rdn and hung lft 2f out: styd on fnl f to cl on 2nd but no ch w wnr* **25/1** | 58 |
| 0050 | **4** | *2 1/2* | **Lord Lahar**[7] 5175 5-8-8 **54** oh9 ........ TEDurcan 9<br>(MRChannon) *bhd: rdn 3f out: styd on fnl 2f but nvr a danger* **25/1** | 55 |
| 0002 | **5** | *1* | **Rawalpindi**[17] 4927 3-8-0 **56** ........ FNorton 4<br>(JARToller) *hld up in rr: pushed along 3f out: mod prog fnl 2f* **9/2**[2] | 55 |
| -230 | **6** | *nk* | **Seeking A Way (USA)**[25] 4692 3-8-12 **68** ........ WSupple 5<br>(JHMGosden) *chsd wnr 10f out tl over 2f out: sn wknd* **7/1**[3] | 67 |
| 4004 | **7** | *1/2* | **Spring Adieu**[13] 5019 3-8-4 **60** ........ (b[1]) MartinDwyer 2<br>(MrsAJPerrett) *chsd wnr to 10f out: rdn over 3f out: sn wknd* **14/1** | 58 |
| 4005 | **8** | *1* | **Lord Nellsson**[18] 4870 8-8-9 **58** ........ HayleyTurner(3) 3<br>(JSKing) *chsd ldrs: sn pushed along: wknd 3f out* **16/1** | 55 |
| 6U54 | **9** | *13* | **Kilindini**[25] 4693 3-8-12 **68** ........ RHavlin 10<br>(MissECLavelle) *rdn over 3f out: a in rr* **14/1** | 46 |
| 3000 | **10** | *17* | **Once (FR)**[23] 4736 4-9-8 **68** ........ (b) JFEgan 8<br>(JAOsborne) *in tch: chsd ldrs over 5f out: sn rdn: wknd qckly 4f out* **14/1** | 23 |
| 00-4 | **11** | *12* | **Embassy Sweets (USA)**[138] 1541 3-7-10 **57** ........ NDeSouza(5) 7<br>(PFICole) *sn bhd* **11/1** | — |

2m 48.37s (-2.93) **Going Correction** -0.10s/f (Good)
**WFA** 3 from 4yo+ 10lb **11** Ran SP% **113.9**
Speed ratings: **105,101,101,99,98 98,98,97,89,79 71**CSF £17.06 CT £310.43 TOTE £4.90: £1.80, £2.10, £6.80; EX 22.30 Place 6 £43.81, Place 5 £14.99 .
**Owner** Lady Herries and Friends **Bred** Angmering Park Stud **Trained** Angmering, W Sussex

**FOCUS**
A pretty moderate contest and very few got into it despite the pace appearing good, but the form should prove reliable.

**NOTEBOOK**
**Polar Tryst** had been exposed as just a modest handicapper when last seen but, returning from a 444-day break, she was better than ever. Things did not look good when she stumbled and nearly parted company with Mackay as the stalls opened, but the pair regained their composure and she ran out a most decisive winner, quickening well from the front. She looks worth having on your side, providing she goes the right way from this and is not too harshly treated by the Handicapper.
**Sunday City(JPN)** was in the right company given the level of form he had been showing in recent starts, but was once again found wanting for a turn of foot and could prove hard to win with while he is off a mark in the high 60s. That is unless he improves for racing on easier ground - he has only ever raced on ground with 'firm' in the description.
**Olympias(IRE)**, tailed off in a similar race on easy ground over two miles two on her previous start, ran better fitted with blinkers and switched to a faster surface, but did not help her chance by hanging and may be worth another try over further.
**Lord Lahar** ran respectably from 9lb out of the handicap and may do even better off his correct mark in banded company.
**Rawalpindi** ran well to be second in a moderate event on Fibresand on his previous start, but was unable to confirm that returned to turf off a 4lb higher mark. *Official explanation: trainer said gelding did not act on the firm ground*
**Seeking A Way(USA)** did not find as much as had looked likely and failed to prove her stamina.
**Kilindini** *Official explanation: jockey said gelding unsuited by the ground*
T/Jkpt: Not won. T/Plt: £61.90 to a £1 stake. Pool: £40,187.70. 473.75 winning tickets. T/Qpdt: £6.80 to a £1 stake. Pool: £2,987.30. 321.10 winning tickets. ST

# 5186 NEWCASTLE (L-H)
### Monday, September 6

**OFFICIAL GOING: Good**
Wind: lt, hlf across Weather: overcast

## 5341 EUROPEAN BREEDERS FUND MAIDEN STKS 6f
**2:30** (2:30) (D3) 2-Y-O **£4,813** (£1,481; £740; £370) **Stalls** Centre

| Form | | | | RPR |
|---|---|---|---|---|
| | **1** | | **Potent Heir (USA)** 2-9-0 ........ KMcEvoy 1<br>(SaeedBinSuroor) *trckd ldrs: shkn up over 1f out: led ins fnl f: pushed out* **2/1**[1] | 86+ |
| | **2** | *1* | **Crosspeace (IRE)** 2-9-0 ........ RFfrench 3<br>(MJohnston) *mde most to ins fnl f: kpt on same pce* **12/1** | 83 |
| 0 | **3** | *2 1/2* | **Musahim (USA)**[9] 5118 2-9-0 ........ RHills 4<br>(BWHills) *sn disputing ld: shkn up over 1f out: r.o same pce fnl f* **11/4**[3] | 75 |
| 03 | **4** | *2 1/2* | **Come On Jonny (IRE)**[10] 5096 2-9-0 ........ SSanders 10<br>(RMBeckett) *cl up tl rdn and wknd over 1f out* **5/2**[2] | 68 |
| 00 | **5** | *1 1/4* | **Antonio Stradivari (IRE)**[11] 5051 2-9-0 ........ (v[1]) NCallan 8<br>(AMBalding) *dwlt: keen and sn prom: rdn over 2f out: btn over 1f out* **12/1** | 64 |
| 00 | **6** | *nk* | **White Star Magic**[10] 5083 2-9-0 ........ PHanagan 9<br>(JRWeymes) *hld up: outpcd fr over 2f out* **66/1** | 63 |
| 60 | **7** | *4* | **Pee Jay's Dream**[74] 3248 2-9-0 ........ DaleGibson 2<br>(MWEasterby) *sn outpcd: no ch fr 1/2-way* **50/1** | 51 |
| 00 | **8** | *1* | **Falcon Goer (USA)**[10] 5096 2-8-9 ........ KimTinkler 11<br>(NTinkler) *in tch to 1/2-way: sn rdn and btn* **100/1** | 43 |
| 00 | **9** | *dist* | **Cool Cristal**[3] 5262 2-8-6 ........ PMulrennan(3) 5<br>(MWEasterby) *wnt bdly lft s: t.o thrght* **100/1** | — |
| | **10** | *7* | **Ross Is Boss** 2-8-11 ........ TEaves(3) 6<br>(CJTeague) *s.v.s: t.o thrght* **100/1** | — |

1m 13.56s (-1.48) **Going Correction** -0.325s/f (Firm) **10** Ran SP% **110.4**
Speed ratings: **96,94,91,88,86 85,80,79,—,—**CSF £25.09 TOTE £2.70: £1.20, £5.90, £1.20; EX 14.20.
**Owner** Godolphin **Bred** New Farm **Trained** Newmarket, Suffolk
■ Stewards Enquiry : K McEvoy caution: careless riding

**FOCUS**
A fair maiden that was run at a reasonable gallop and the form of the principals looks sound.

**NOTEBOOK**
**Potent Heir(USA)** , who cost $475,000 and is a brother to the high-class US juvenile Forest Heiress, made a very pleasing winning debut under a fine ride. He has no fancy entries, but there was a fair bit to like about the manner in which he quickened up late on despite running green, and it will be interesting to see where this sharp individual is entered next by his powerful connections.
**Crosspeace(IRE)** ◆, related to several middle-distance winners, turned in a sound debut display and was clear in second. The type who will need further in time, he deserves the plaudits for going close over this trip and should have no trouble winning races in the future.
**Musahim(USA)**, who showed ability on his debut at Newmarket nine days previously, was better away this time and had his chance before again running green under pressure. He appreciated this better ground and is suited by this trip at present, but does not look anything special on this evidence.
**Come On Jonny(IRE)** , popular in the ring to improve on his two previous efforts, failed to really come on for this step up in trip. He still acquitted himself with credit however, and now qualifies for nurseries where he should fare a deal better.
**Antonio Stradivari(IRE)** raced keenly in the first-time visor, but still showed his best form to date. He is now eligible for nurseries, but is an edgy character and has now been slow to break on all of his three outings.
**White Star Magic**, dropping back from a mile, turned in his most worthwhile effort to date and was keeping on in the straight under a sympathetic ride. He can be expected to improve now he qualifies for nurseries and will appreciate another furlong.

## 5342 KPMG MAIDEN STKS 5f
**3:00** (3:01) (D3) 3-Y-O+ **£3,454** (£1,063; £531; £265) **Stalls** Centre

| Form | | | | RPR |
|---|---|---|---|---|
| 6060 | **1** | | **Mutayam**[39] 4279 4-8-9 45 ........ (t) PPMathers(5) 2<br>(DANolan) *prom far side: effrt over 1f out: led wl ins fnl f: r.o* **66/1** | 52 |
| 44-0 | **2** | *1* | **Song Koi**[159] 1200 3-8-8 60 ........ MFenton 8<br>(JGGiven) *led to wl ins fnl f: kpt on towards fin* **12/1** | 43 |
| 0400 | **3** | *nk* | **Fox Covert (IRE)**[7] 5193 3-8-10 55 ........ (v) LEnstone(3) 1<br>(DWBarker) *cl up far side: effrt over 1f out: one pce ins fnl f* **5/1**[3] | 47 |
| 0503 | **4** | *nk* | **Marysienka**[21] 4810 3-8-8 68 ........ JEdmunds 11<br>(JBalding) *keen: prom far side: effrt over 1f out: one pce ins last* **7/2**[2] | 41 |
| -505 | **5** | *2* | **Aboustar**[160] 1191 4-8-9 35 ........ MLawson(5) 10<br>(MBrittain) *chsd far side ldrs: effrt over 2f out: one pce over 1f out* **50/1** | 39 |
| 420- | **6** | *1* | **Juniper Banks**[354] 5011 3-8-13 67 ........ ACulhane 5<br>(MissAStokell) *bhd far side tl hdwy over 1f out: nvr rchd ldrs* **12/1** | 35 |
| 2006 | **7** | *nk* | **Westborough (IRE)**[9] 5104 3-8-13 52 ........ (v[1]) KimTinkler 9<br>(NTinkler) *towards rr far side: rdn 1/2-way: no imp over 1f out* **12/1** | 34 |
| 4000 | **8** | *1 1/4* | **Aguilera**[24] 4701 3-8-8 30 ........ VHalliday 12<br>(MDods) *sn rdn in rr far side: sme late hdwy: nvr on terms* **100/1** | 25 |
| -000 | **9** | *1/2* | **Warren Place**[9] 5104 4-9-0 35 ........ SSanders 15<br>(JHetherton) *chsd stands side ldr: rdn to ld that gp 1f out: no ch w far side* **20/1** | 28 |
| 04 | **10** | *1 1/2* | **Raetihi**[23] 4758 3-8-8 ........ DeanMcKeown 14<br>(ASenior) *led stands side trio to 1f out: no ex* **33/1** | 18 |
| 0-00 | **11** | *1 1/2* | **Louis Prima**[35] 4391 3-8-13 35 ........ RFfrench 6<br>(MissLAPerratt) *in tch far side to over 2f out: sn btn* **50/1** | 17 |
| 40-0 | **12** | *1 3/4* | **Self Belief**[114] 2131 3-8-8 67 ........ NCallan 3<br>(MCChapman) *prom far side tl wknd fr over 2f out* **8/1** | — |
| | **13** | *13* | **Secret Of Secrets** 3-8-13 ........ JMcAuley 13<br>(LRJames) *sn outpcd stands side: nvr on terms* **33/1** | — |
| 0202 | **U** | | **Harrison's Flyer (IRE)**[2] 5306 3-8-13 67 ........ (v[1]) PHanagan 4<br>(RAFahey) *uns rdr s* **11/4**[1] | — |

60.67 secs (-0.86) **Going Correction** -0.325s/f (Firm)
**WFA** 3 from 4yo 1lb **14** Ran SP% **116.8**
Speed ratings: **93,91,90,90,87 85,85,83,82,79 77,74,53,—**CSF £692.73 TOTE £63.90: £15.40, £3.30, £1.90; EX 1371.30.
**Owner** Miss M McFadyen-Murray **Bred** Whitsbury Manor Stud **Trained** Newmains, N Lanarks

**FOCUS**
A dire contest, which saw those drawn low at an advantage, and it produced a very moderate winning time for the class of contest.

**NOTEBOOK**
**Mutayam**, who had shown little in 16 previous outings, finally put his best foot forward and lost his maiden tag. He has had problems finishing his races in the past, but this time managed to sustain his gallop to the line and did the job nicely in the end. He would be no certainty to reproduce this next time, but his confidence will be high and he is on a lowly handicap mark at present. *Official explanation: trainer said, regarding the improved form shown, gelding was better suited by being held up today*
**Song Koi** showed good early speed and only tired out of it late in the day on this return from a 159-day absence. She will improve physically for the run, but it remains to be seen whether she has trained on this year.
**Fox Covert(IRE)** again had his chance, but once more found just the same pace late on and has now gone without a win in 22 career starts.
**Marysienka** did best of those drawn high and was not beaten that far, but again ran freely and should have done better at these weights. She looks to be well worthy of a try in some form of headgear.
**Self Belief** dropped out tamely on this return from a 114-day absence.
**Harrison's Flyer(IRE)**, in the first-time visor, lost all chance at the start when rearing at the gates and getting rid of Hanagan.

## 5343 STEPHEN EASTEN H'CAP 2m 19y
**3:30** (3:30) (E3) (0-70,67) 3-Y-O+ **£3,742** (£1,151; £575; £287) **Stalls** Centre

| Form | | | | RPR |
|---|---|---|---|---|
| 0061 | **1** | | **Trilemma**[6] 5214 3-9-0 **67** 6ex ........ SSanders 6<br>(SirMarkPrescott) *hld up in tch: smooth hdwy to ld over 1f out: pushed out* **4/7**[1] | 76+ |
| 00P5 | **2** | *1 3/4* | **Madiba**[13] 5027 5-9-0 **54** ........ MFenton 2<br>(PHowling) *hld up in tch: effrt whn n.m.r over 2f out: sn outpcd: r.o fnl f: no ch w wnr* **25/1** | 61 |
| -601 | **3** | *3/4* | **Little Tobias (IRE)**[39] 4261 5-8-10 **55** ........ RThomas(5) 1<br>(AndrewTurnell) *cl up: led over 2f to over 1f out: one pce fnl f* **5/1**[2] | 61 |
| 0560 | **4** | *1/2* | **Greenwich Meantime**[10] 5100 4-9-6 **60** ........ LGoncalves 7<br>(MrsJRRamsden) *hld up ins: hdwy whn no room fr 2f to 1f out: kpt on ins last* **9/1**[3] | 66+ |
| -300 | **5** | *1/2* | **Celtic Blaze (IRE)**[6] 5214 5-9-0 **54** ........ (tp) ACulhane 3<br>(BSRothwell) *prom tl rdn and nt qckn over 1f out* **25/1** | 59 |
| 4030 | **6** | *2* | **Fantastico (IRE)**[22] 4778 4-9-1 **58** ........ (p) PMulrennan(3) 5<br>(MrsKWalton) *led to over 2f out: kpt on same pce* **14/1** | 61 |
| | **7** | *2 1/2* | **Archias (GER)**[86] 5-9-11 **65** ........ RWinston 4<br>(JJQuinn) *chsd ldrs tl wknd over 2f out* **14/1** | 65 |

3m 38.19s (3.16) **Going Correction** +0.075s/f (Good)
**WFA** 3 from 4yo+ 13lb **7** Ran SP% **111.3**
Speed ratings: **95,94,93,93,93 92,91**CSF £17.44 TOTE £1.60: £1.10, £7.60; EX 30.60.
**Owner** Mrs Sonia Rogers **Bred** Hesmonds Stud Ltd **Trained** Newmarket, Suffolk

**FOCUS**
A modest handicap that produced an ordinary time for the grade, but the winner looks better than the bare form.
**NOTEBOOK**
**Trilemma** followed-up her recent Ripon win in good style under a 6lb penalty. She has readily improved since being upped to two miles, and should be hard to beat if turning out under a penalty once more, now she has hit form and seemingly found her niche.
**Madiba** improved on his most recent efforts and can be rated slightly better than the bare form. He is capable on his day, but always seems to find a few too good.
**Little Tobias(IRE)** had very much the run of the race, but found less than looked likely at one stage and could only plug on at the same pace when it mattered. He may just find this distance beyond him and looks worth another chance when dropping slightly in trip.
**Greenwich Meantime** found himself with nowhere to go on the rail two out, and is better than he showed on this occasion. He could be close to capitalising on his declining mark, and is one to note when the market speaks in his favour.

## 5344 BET365 CALL 08000 322 365 H'CAP — 1m 2f 32y
**4:00** (4:00) (E3) (0-70,70) 3-Y-O+ — **£3,836** (£1,180; £590; £295) **Stalls** Low

Form — RPR
0505 **1** **Market Avenue**[30] 4537 5-8-9 **58** .......... RWinston 5 — 69
(RAFahey) *keen: hld up: hdwy to chse wnr 2f out: rdn and hung lft: styd on to ld towards fin* **9/2**[1]
006- **2** *1/2* **Incroyable**[330] 5499 3-8-3 **59** .......... JMackay 1 — 69+
(SirMarkPrescott) *trckd ldrs: led gng wl over 2f out: sn rdn: kpt on wl fnl f: hdd towards fin* **16/1**
4660 **3** *1 3/4* **Derwent (USA)**[21] 4808 5-8-13 **62** .......... (v[1]) SSanders 9 — 69
(JDBethell) *hld up: hdwy outside 2f out: kpt on fnl f: no imp* **12/1**
/031 **4** *hd* **Zandeed (IRE)**[9] 5127 6-8-7 **59** .......... TEaves(3) 13 — 66
(MissLAPerratt) *hld up: outpcd 1/2-way: hdwy and edgd lft over 1f out: r.o fnl f* **6/1**[2]
0010 **5** *shd* **Maritime Blues**[9] 5129 4-9-0 **63** .......... ACulhane 7 — 69
(JGGiven) *in tch: outpcd over 2f out: rallied fnl f: kpt on* **12/1**
0061 **6** *1 1/2* **Jordans Spark**[14] 4985 3-8-1 **57** .......... (p) PFessey 4 — 61
(ISemple) *keen: prom: effrt over 2f out: sn one pce* **16/1**
55-5 **7** *4* **Flight Commander (IRE)**[14] 4987 4-9-3 **66** .......... DAllan 2 — 62
(ISemple) *midfield: effrt over 2f out: sn one pce* **33/1**
1342 **8** *3 1/2* **Futoo (IRE)**[7] 5197 3-8-10 **66** .......... NPollard 12 — 55
(GMMoore) *mde most to over 2f out: wknd over 1f out* **9/2**[1]
3644 **9** *1 3/4* **Megan's Magic**[8] 5145 4-9-5 **68** .......... (be[1]) JBramhill 8 — 54
(WStorey) *missed break: effrt and hdwy over 1f out: no imp* **8/1**[3]
2160 **10** *1 1/4* **Melodian**[8] 5144 9-8-11 **65** .......... (b) MLawson(5) 6 — 49
(MBrittain) *disp ld to over 3f out: wknd over 2f out* **9/1**
55-0 **11** *1 1/4* **Bond Millennium**[216] 667 6-8-10 **59** .......... FLynch 3 — 40
(BSmart) *hld up: hdwy whn nt clr run fr over 2f out: nt rcvr* **12/1**
0004 **12** *1 3/4* **Sandy Bay (IRE)**[26] 4631 5-8-3 **57** oh26 ow1 .......... PMakin(5) 11 — 35
(ARDicken) *prom tl wknd over 2f out* **100/1**
0000 **13** *1 1/2* **Gran Dana (IRE)**[75] 3199 4-9-7 **70** .......... RFfrench 10 — 45
(MJohnston) *midfield on outside: rdn and struggling fr 4f out* **12/1**
2m 11.36s (-0.24) **Going Correction** +0.075s/f (Good)
**WFA** 3 from 4yo+ 7lb — **13** Ran SP% **118.2**
Speed ratings: **103,102,101,101,100 99,96,93,92,91 90,88,87**CSF £78.79 CT £816.32 TOTE £4.80: £2.10, £2.50, £4.50; EX 82.40.
**Owner** Market Avenue Racing Club Ltd **Bred** Mrs Nicholas Horn **Trained** Musley Bank, N Yorks
**FOCUS**
A modest handicap run at a solid pace and the form looks sound for the class.
**NOTEBOOK**
**Market Avenue** stayed on well for pressure from two out and, despite hanging, was always going to get on top of the eventual runner-up close home. She has fallen in the weights this year and this was by far her best effort of the current campaign, so she could well strike again, as she won off an 11lb higher mark last year.
**Incroyable ◆**, a big drifter in the betting for this three-year-old debut, travelled sweetly until finding her lack of a recent run against her, and could not go with the winner inside the final furlong. This was a promising reappearance, she clearly relished this longer trip and will no doubt be placed to advantage off this lowly mark by her canny trainer.
**Derwent(USA)** has lost the plot this season, but has slipped to a decent mark as a result, and this display in the first-time visor did enough to suggest he could take advantage at this level before long.
**Zandeed(IRE)**, raised 2lb for his success at Redcar nine days previously, ran as though he may be worth a try over farther.
**Futoo(IRE)** had his chance and ultimately proved disappointing. *Official explanation: jockey said gelding ran flat*
**Bond Millennium** *Official explanation: jockey said gelding was continually denied a run*

## 5345 SALTWELL SIGNS MAIDEN STKS — 1m (R)
**4:30** (4:33) (D3) 3-Y-O+ — **£3,523** (£1,084; £542; £271) **Stalls** Low

Form — RPR
23 **1** **Backgammon**[115] 2077 3-8-12 .......... SSanders 5 — 78
(DRLoder) *prom: effrt over 2f out: sn rdn: led ins fnl f: styd on wl* **5/4**[1]
02 **2** *3/4* **Thistle**[9] 5123 3-8-12 .......... KMcEvoy 7 — 76
(JHMGosden) *led: shkn up 2f out: hdd ins fnl f: kpt on* **4/1**[2]
00- **3** *7* **Lake Diva**[307] 5913 3-8-7 .......... MFenton 11 — 55
(JGGiven) *bhd: rdn 3f out: kpt on fnl f: no ch w first two* **40/1**
2522 **4** *1 1/2* **River Nurey (IRE)**[25] 4679 3-8-12 68 .......... RHills 2 — 56
(BWHills) *in tch: effrt over 2f out: no imp over 1f out* **11/2**[3]
5-2 **5** *1 1/4* **Queen's Echo**[10] 5086 3-8-6 ow2 .......... LEnstone(3) 8 — 51
(MDods) *in tch tl outpcd fr 2f out* **12/1**
3-0 **6** *1 1/4* **Nadir**[9] 5123 3-8-12 .......... RWinston 12 — 51
(PHowling) *hld up: effrt and hung lft over 2f out: sn outpcd* **7/1**
35 **7** *shd* **Medalla (FR)**[8] 5146 4-8-12 .......... MLawson(5) 1 — 50
(MBrittain) *towards rr: rdn 3f out: n.d* **14/1**
0 **8** *10* **Swinton**[10] 5086 3-8-12 .......... TWilliams 6 — 27
(MBrittain) *towards rr: rdn 4f out: nvr on terms* **40/1**
0000 **9** *1/2* **Svenson**[16] 4102 3-8-12 30 .......... PMQuinn 10 — 26
(JSWainwright) *chsd ldrs tl rdn and wknd over 2f out* **150/1**
00- **10** *9* **Forrest Gump**[336] 5420 4-9-0 .......... (b) TEaves(3) 4 — 6
(CJTeague) *chsd ldrs tl wknd fr 3f out* **150/1**
-300 **11** *dist* **Shardda**[10] 5085 4-8-9 60 .......... (t) PMulrennan(3) 9 — —
(FWatson) *mifield: rdn 4f out: wknd and eased 2f out* **33/1**
**12** *2 1/2* **Silloth Spirit** 4-9-3 .......... NPollard 3 — —
(MrsAMNaughton) *missed break: nvr on terms* **66/1**
1m 42.8s (-0.68) **Going Correction** +0.075s/f (Good)
**WFA** 3 from 4yo 5lb — **12** Ran SP% **117.3**
Speed ratings: **106,105,98,96,95 94,94,84,83,74 —,—**CSF £5.86 TOTE £2.00: £1.10, £1.50, £9.10; EX 8.50.
**Owner** Jumeirah Racing **Bred** Darley **Trained** Newmarket, Suffolk
**FOCUS**
No strength in depth to this moderate maiden. The first two came clear.
**NOTEBOOK**
**Backgammon**, who had hit the frame in his previous two outings, stayed on strongly in the final furlong to reel in the long-time leader and win a touch cosily. His immediate future lies in handicaps, but he is unexposed and could take higher order over further before the season is out.
**Thistle**, who showed improvement on his latest start at Newmarket, again turned in an improved effort and was only run out of it close home. He should have little trouble in landing a maiden, but now qualifies for handicaps and should get ten furlongs.
**Lake Diva** stayed on well, having got behind early on, and should come on a fair deal for this first run in 307 days. She now goes handicapping.
**River Nurey(IRE)**, who has had plenty of chances this season in maidens, ran a flat race and can be considered a little disappointing. This frustrating character is surely worth switching to handicaps now.
**Shardda** *Official explanation: jockey said the saddle slipped*

## 5346 ST JAMES SECURITY H'CAP — 6f
**5:00** (5:03) (F4) (0-55,55) 3-Y-O+ — **£3,005** (£858; £429) **Stalls** Centre

Form — RPR
3540 **1** **Roman Empire**[20] 4827 4-8-10 **49** .......... NCallan 12 — 60
(KARyan) *swtchd to far side after 1f: cl up: led 2f out: kpt on wl: all out* **9/1**
5103 **2** *shd* **Ballybunion (IRE)**[22] 4774 5-9-1 **54** .......... ANicholls 2 — 65
(DNicholls) *in tch far side: nt clr run over 2f to over 1f out: kpt on wl fnl f: jst failed* **13/2**[1]
5063 **3** *nk* **William's Well**[9] 5126 10-8-13 **55** .......... (b) PMulrennan(3) 5 — 65
(MWEasterby) *hld up far side: hdwy over 1f out: r.o wl fnl f: jst hld* **7/1**[2]
2404 **4** *1/2* **Lord Baskerville**[8] 5141 3-8-7 **53** .......... MLawson(5) 4 — 62
(WStorey) *prom far side: effrt over 2f out: kpt on same pce ins fnl f* **20/1**
3114 **5** *1 1/2* **On The Trail**[9] 5107 7-9-1 **54** .......... ACulhane 3 — 58
(DWChapman) *prom far side: effrt over 2f out: one pce ins fnl f* **9/1**
1003 **6** *1 1/2* **Mickledor (FR)**[10] 5081 4-8-7 **53** .......... (p) DTudhope(7) 13 — 53
(MDods) *in tch far side: rdn over 2f out: kpt on fnl f: no imp* **16/1**
065 **7** *1 3/4* **Xanadu**[30] 4557 8-8-11 **50** .......... (p) RFfrench 14 — 44
(MissLAPerratt) *cl up far side tl rdn and no ex over 1f out* **25/1**
3166 **8** *shd* **Frimley's Matterry**[9] 5126 4-8-11 **53** .......... TEaves(3) 19 — 47
(REBarr) *prom stands side: effrt over 2f out: led that gp ins fnl f: no ch w far side* **25/1**
0001 **9** *1/2* **Jedeydd**[31] 4509 7-9-2 **55** .......... (bt) RWinston 1 — 48
(MDods) *bhd far side: hdwy over 1f out: nvr rchd ldrs* **12/1**
5040 **10** *hd* **Megabond**[38] 4309 3-8-13 **54** .......... FLynch 11 — 46
(BSmart) *bhd far side tl sme late hdwy: n.d* **20/1**
1000 **11** *hd* **Flying Tackle**[43] 4181 6-8-8 **50** .......... (p) LEnstone(3) 8 — 41
(MDods) *in tch far side: rdn 2f out: sn one pce* **33/1**
-002 **12** *shd* **The Old Soldier**[77] 3148 6-8-9 **51** .......... ABeech(3) 7 — 42
(ADickman) *in tch far side tl outpcd fr 2f out* **10/1**
4004 **13** *1* **Redoubtable (USA)**[10] 5081 13-8-6 **50** .......... PMakin(5) 15 — 38
(DWChapman) *cl up stands side: led that gp over 1f out tl ins last: no ex* **33/1**
0000 **14** *1/2* **The Wizard Mul**[4] 5235 4-9-1 **54** .......... (b[1]) JBramhill 16 — 41
(WStorey) *led stands side to over 1f out: sn btn* **50/1**
0600 **15** *1/2* **Silver Seeker (USA)**[20] 4827 4-8-9 **48** .......... PFessey 9 — 33
(ARDicken) *sn bhd and rdn far side: nvr on terms* **33/1**
0000 **16** *1/2* **Quantica (IRE)**[72] 3298 5-9-2 **55** .......... KimTinkler 20 — 39
(NTinkler) *swtchd to far side over 4f out: nvr on terms* **14/1**
0400 **17** *3/4* **Turf Princess**[10] 5081 3-8-2 **50** .......... DFentiman(7) 6 — 31
(IanEmmerson) *chsd far side ldrs to 2f out: sn btn* **50/1**
0560 **18** *3* **A Teen**[3] 5261 6-8-11 **50** .......... SSanders 18 — 22
(PHowling) *in tch far side: effrt and ev ch that gp over 1f out: hung lft and sn wknd* **8/1**[3]
4000 **19** *3 1/2* **Drury Lane (IRE)**[30] 4542 4-8-10 **49** .......... (b) NPollard 10 — 11
(DWChapman) *led far side to 2f out: sn wknd* **25/1**
6500 **20** *7* **Gaiety Girl (USA)**[39] 4260 3-8-12 **53** .......... DAllan 17 — —
(TDEasterby) *in tch stands side tl wknd over 2f out* **100/1**
1m 13.02s (-2.02) **Going Correction** -0.325s/f (Firm)
**WFA** 3 from 4yo+ 2lb — **20** Ran SP% **121.1**
Speed ratings: **100,99,99,98,96 94,92,92,91,91 91,91,89,89,88 87,86,82,78,68**CSF £55.35 CT £451.90 TOTE £11.80: £2.60, £2.90, £3.00, £4.70; EX 130.00 Place 6 £61.80, Place 5 £40.78.
**Owner** Yorkshire Racing Syndicates **Bred** Mervyn Ayers And Richard Brunger **Trained** Hambleton, N Yorks
**FOCUS**
A moderate sprint which was run at a solid pace and again saw those drawn low at a distinct advantage. Nevertheless, the form appears reliable.
**NOTEBOOK**
**Roman Empire**, with his usual blinkers left off for this, showed a great attitiude to hold off his rivals close home and win his first race on turf. He deserves extra credit, as he was unfavourably drawn, but this does look about as good as he is and he may be one to take on next time.
**Ballybunion(IRE)** would probably have won but for meeting trouble two out, and can be considered unlucky. He remains in good form.
**William's Well** was finishing best of all, but again got going all too late. He has slipped to a decent mark of late and should find a race at this level. However, his style of running means he will always need luck in his races.
**Lord Baskerville**, yet to score in 19 attempts, ran his usual sound race but seems better over another furlong nowadays.
**On The Trail** could not quicken when having his chance late on and now looks firmly in the grip of the Handicapper.
**Frimley's Matterry**
T/Plt: £243.20 to a £1 stake. Pool: £33,557.00. 100.70 winning tickets. T/Qpdt: £15.20 to a £1 stake. Pool: £3,002.80. 145.90 winning tickets. RY

# 5198 WARWICK (L-H)
Monday, September 6

**OFFICIAL GOING: Good to firm**
Wind: mod against Weather: cloudy

## 5347 EUROPEAN BREEDERS FUND MAIDEN STKS (C&G) — 7f 26y
**2:20** (2:22) (D2) 2-Y-O — **£6,396** (£1,968; £984; £492) **Stalls** Low

Form — RPR
54 **1** **Walkonthewildside**[29] 4567 2-8-11 .......... (v[1]) TPQueally 1 — 78+
(DRLoder) *mde all: rdn clr over 1f out: r.o wl* **3/1**[2]
**2** *2* **Notnowcato** 2-8-11 .......... KDarley 6 — 73+
(SirMichaelStoute) *chsd wnr: rdn over 2f out: r.o one pce* **28/1**
**3** *hd* **Croix Rouge (USA)** 2-8-11 .......... RHughes 2 — 73+
(MrsAJPerrett) *a.p: rdn over 2f out: kpt on same pce* **16/1**



The Form Book, Raceform Ltd, Compton, RG20 6NL

4 **4** *1* **King's Kama**[26] 4649 2-8-11 .................... KFallon 5 77+
(SirMichaelStoute) *hld up: hdwy on ins over 3f out: rdn 2f out: nt clr run 1f out: swtchd rt ins fnl f: nt qckn* **7/4**[1]

**5** *¾* **River Alhaarth (IRE)** 2-8-11 .................... JFortune 9 68
(PWChapple-Hyam) *a.p: one pce fnl 2f* **28/1**

**6** *shd* **Compton Quay** 2-8-11 .................... JDSmith 4 68
(AKing) *dwlt: hdwy on ins over 1f out: nt rch ldrs* **50/1**

00 **7** *1* **Wujood**[29] 4567 2-8-11 .................... IMongan 11 65
(JLDunlop) *hld up: rdn over 3f out: hung lft 2f out: hdwy over 1f out: one pce fnl f* **40/1**

5 **8** *hd* **Taj India (USA)**[44] 4117 2-8-11 .................... JFanning 8 65
(MJohnston) *hld up in tch: rdn over 2f out: edgd lft 1f out: wknd ins fnl f* **17/2**[3]

00 **9** *3* **My Rascal (IRE)**[28] 4606 2-8-11 .................... AMcCarthy 13 57
(MJWallace) *a bhd* **66/1**

00 **10** *½* **Little Indy**[43] 4169 2-8-9 ow1 .................... DNolan(3) 12 57
(RBrotherton) *hld up in mid-div: rdn 3f out: wknd fnl f* **150/1**

00 **11** *1* **Wembury Point (IRE)**[23] 4747 2-8-11 .................... DaneO'Neill 14 54
(BGPowell) *s.i.s: a bhd* **125/1**

0 **12** *shd* **Savoy Chapel**[11] 5054 2-8-11 .................... DHolland 7 53
(JAOsborne) *dwlt: a bhd* **25/1**

40 **13** *½* **Tombola (FR)**[38] 4292 2-8-11 .................... SDrowne 10 52
(JLDunlop) *a bhd* **16/1**

1m 23.84s (-1.06) **Going Correction** -0.225s/f (Firm) **13** Ran SP% **101.7**
Speed ratings: **97,94,94,93,92 92,91,91,87,87 85,85,85**CSF £67.34 TOTE £3.80: £1.10, £9.00, £3.80; EX 66.20.
**Owner** M Tabor **Bred** Chippenham Lodge Stud Ltd **Trained** Newmarket, Suffolk
■ Expeditious (11/2) withdrawn (ref to ent stalls). R4 applies, deduct 15p in the £.

**FOCUS**
Probably a decent maiden with the well-backed favourite only managing fourth and several debutants shaping with immense promise. The race could be rated higher.

**NOTEBOOK**
**Walkonthewildside**, who had not quite come up to scratch in either of his first two starts, was ideally drawn for one who wanted to make the running and the first-time visor seemed to enable him to concentrate better. Always travelling well, he cleared away halfway up the straight and won cosily. He holds an entry in the Middle Park and connections clearly believe him to be smart, but he will need to improve greatly if he is to make his mark at that sort of level.
**Notnowcato**, the lesser fancied of the Stoute duo according to the betting, held a good position throughout and turned in with every chance. The lack of previous experience told in the closing stages however and he was outpaced by the winner. Bred to stay middle-distances, he looks ready for a mile and can win his maiden.
**Croix Rouge(USA)** ◆ is another who will not be seen at his best until covering a greater distance of ground - his dam won up to 12 furlongs - so he would no doubt have pleased connections with this prominent showing. He is another for whom winning a maiden should be straightforward.
**King's Kama** stepped up on the form of his debut but, as the betting suggested, was clearly expected to do better. In fairness though he was the only one of the front five to have come from behind and did not get the best of runs, so deserves another chance and will be suited by a mile.
**River Alhaarth(IRE)**, whose stable have had a cracking season with their juveniles, is bred to want a mile plus and shaped promisingly on this racecourse debut. The experience will do him good and there are races to be won with him.
**Compton Quay** ◆ was surprisingly making his debut over this trip. He is bred to be speedy, but shaped as though he was in need of every yard of it - staying on steadily under considerate riding in the closing stages. Sure to improve considerably for the outing, he can win over this trip before going on to better things.
**Wujood** needs one more outing before he can take his place in handicaps and is very much a middle-distance prospect for next term.
**Taj India(USA)**, who shaped with promise on his debut in what was an average maiden for the course at Ascot, was fully expected to show significant improvement with the run under his belt and the extra furlong. However, having sat in midfield for most of the way, he found very little for pressure and faded. Surely capable of better, he is worth another chance and may be more of a handicap type for next season.

## 5348 EUROPEAN BREEDERS FUND MAIDEN FILLIES' STKS (DIV I) 7f 26y
**2:50** (2:53) (D2) 2-Y-O **£5,954** (£1,832; £916; £458) **Stalls** Low

Form RPR

**1** **Literature (USA)** 2-8-11 .................... LDettori 8 75
(SaeedBinSuroor) *a.p: rdn over 1f out: edgd lft and led ins fnl f: r.o wl* **7/2**[2]

**2** *1¾* **Lysandra (IRE)** 2-8-11 .................... KFallon 12 71+
(SirMichaelStoute) *s.i.s: sn prom: rdn over 2f out: edgd lft over 1f out: plld out ins fnl f: r.o to take 2nd post* **5/2**[1]

0 **3** *hd* **Foxy Gwynne**[11] 5053 2-8-11 .................... DaneO'Neill 4 70
(AMBalding) *a.p: rdn 2f out: ev ch 1f out: nt qckn* **50/1**

0 **4** *nk* **Romanova (IRE)**[24] 4712 2-8-11 .................... TPQueally 1 69
(DRLoder) *led: rdn 2f out: hdd ins fnl f: nt qckn* **11/2**

04 **5** *1* **Grandma's Girl**[32] 4468 2-8-11 .................... KDarley 11 67+
(RGuest) *a.p: hung lft fr over 1f out: one pce* **13/2**

0 **6** *3½* **Slip Catch (IRE)**[16] 4936 2-8-11 .................... LisaJones 9 58
(WJarvis) *s.i.s: styd on fnl f: n.d* **50/1**

**7** *1¾* **Overjoy Way** 2-8-11 .................... JQuinn 6 54
(PRChamings) *hld up in mid-div: no hdwy fnl 3f* **66/1**

**8** *½* **Tarabut** 2-8-11 .................... JFortune 7 53
(EALDunlop) *s.s: styd on fnl f: n.d* **20/1**

6 **9** *¾* **Ponente**[24] 4712 2-8-11 .................... MHills 3 51
(BWHills) *hld up in tch: wknd over 2f out* **9/2**[3]

**10** *1½* **Piroetta** 2-8-11 .................... SDrowne 5 47
(JAOsborne) *s.i.s: a bhd* **16/1**

0 **11** *3* **Silver Dreamer (IRE)**[7] 5172 2-8-11 .................... AMcCarthy 10 39
(HSHowe) *a bhd* **100/1**

**12** *22* **Tiegs (IRE)** 2-8-8 .................... JFMcDonald(3) 2 —
(MrsALMKing) *s.s: a bhd: t.o* **100/1**

1m 23.43s (-1.47) **Going Correction** -0.225s/f (Firm) **12** Ran SP% **115.7**
Speed ratings: **99,97,96,96,95 91,89,88,87,86 82,57**CSF £11.90 TOTE £4.10: £1.10, £2.80, £12.80; EX 7.80.
**Owner** Godolphin **Bred** Ocala Stud Farm **Trained** Newmarket, Suffolk

**FOCUS**
A fair time for the grade that compares favourably with the two other juvenile maidens run over the same trip, despite this however it was not the best of the three races and does not appeal as an event that will work out all that well.

**NOTEBOOK**
**Literature(USA)** comes from a stable whose two-year-olds have been firing all season - this was their 37th juvenile winner of the year - and, having raced prominently throughout, she picked up strongly in the final furlong and came away to win in good style. Not one of the stable stars, she holds no big race entries and is likely to try and find a conditions event or small Listed race somewhere, but will need to improve if she is to follow up.
**Lysandra(IRE)** lacks any big race entries but is probably the one to take from the race for next time, as she was being scrubbed along for most of the way before finishing to good effect. She is nothing special but is in the right hands to win races.
**Foxy Gwynne** stepped up massively on her debut at Lingfield - having reportedly not faced the kickback - and was still in with a chance of winning until the final 150 yards. If building on this she should win her maiden.
**Romanova(IRE)** stepped up on her Newbury effort with a solid fourth and needs one more run to qualify for a handicap mark; she should do much better in that sphere.
**Grandma's Girl** did herself no favours by hanging under pressure, but is now able to run in nurseries. *Official explanation: jockey said filly had trouble running in home straight*
**Slip Catch(IRE)** stepped up on her debut run with keeping on sixth and is another sure to do better once handicapped.
**Ponente**, who finished ahead of Romanova at Newbury, was reported to have disliked the ground and deserves a chance to show this running to be all wrong. *Official explanation: jockey said filly was unsuited by ground and tired in latter stages*
**Piroetta** *Official explanation: jockey said filly became unbalanced in home straight*

## 5349 EUROPEAN BREEDERS FUND MAIDEN FILLIES' STKS (DIV II) 7f 26y
**3:20** (3:23) (D2) 2-Y-O **£5,954** (£1,832; £916; £458) **Stalls** Low

Form RPR

0 **1** **Sadie Thompson (IRE)**[52] 3905 2-8-11 .................... JFanning 8 77
(MRChannon) *chsd ldr: rdn to ld jst over 1f out: stmbld jst ins fnl f: r.o* **8/1**

40 **2** *hd* **Heat Of The Night**[40] 4234 2-8-11 .................... LDettori 4 76
(JLDunlop) *s.i.s: hld up: rdn and hdwy over 1f out: ev ch ins fnl f: r.o* **4/1**[2]

060 **3** *2½* **Midcap (IRE)**[24] 4706 2-8-11 73 .................... MHills 3 70
(BWHills) *hld up: hdwy on ins over 1f out: swtchd rt ins fnl f: kpt on* **14/1**

00 **4** *nk* **Ushindi (IRE)**[19] 4851 2-8-11 .................... JFortune 2 69
(MLWBell) *led: rdn and hdd jst over 1f out: no ex ins fnl f* **33/1**

**5** *nk* **Orlar (IRE)** 2-8-11 .................... SWKelly 1 69
(JAOsborne) *a.p: rdn and one pce fnl 2f* **33/1**

**6** *2* **Daliya (IRE)** 2-8-11 .................... (b[1]) KFallon 9 64
(SirMichaelStoute) *s.i.s: sn prom: rdn and hung lft over 1f out: wknd ins fnl f* **9/2**[3]

52 **7** *¾* **Lottie Dundass**[60] 3664 2-8-11 .................... DHolland 5 69+
(PWHarris) *a.p: rdn whn hmpd wl over 1f out: n.d after* **9/2**[3]

3 **8** *1¼* **Rashida**[30] 4541 2-8-11 .................... EAhern 7 59
(JNoseda) *slowly into stride: hld up in mid-div: rdn 3f out: wknd over 1f out* **5/2**[1]

0 **9** *5* **Gypsy Royal (IRE)**[63] 3588 2-8-11 .................... NDay 12 46
(RIngram) *prom: rdn 3f out: wknd wl over 1f out* **33/1**

50 **10** *1* **Polesworth**[17] 4907 2-8-4 .................... MHalford(7) 10 44
(CNKellett) *s.i.s: a bhd* **150/1**

00 **11** *19* **Winter Mist**[28] 4599 2-8-8 .................... J-PGuillambert(3) 11 —
(NPLittmoden) *a bhd: t.o* **100/1**

**12** *1* **Ciendra Girl (IRE)** 2-8-9 ow1 .................... DNolan(3) 6 —
(RBrotherton) *s.s: a bhd: t.o* **100/1**

1m 24.03s (-0.87) **Going Correction** -0.225s/f (Firm) **12** Ran SP% **114.2**
Speed ratings: **95,94,91,91,91 88,88,86,80,79 58,56**CSF £37.48 TOTE £10.70: £2.90, £2.80, £7.50; EX 44.40.
**Owner** Sheikh Mohammed **Bred** J Hanly, A Stroud And T Stewart **Trained** West Ilsley, Berks

**FOCUS**
A winning time 0.6 seconds slower than the first division, but still acceptable for the grade and in terms of form, looks the better of the two divisions.

**NOTEBOOK**
**Sadie Thompson(IRE)**, eighth on her debut at Newbury in a race that is working out extremely well - having now produced five individual winners (one at Group Three level) - was to the fore throughout under Fanning and went on willingly just over a furlong out before digging deep under pressure to hold the challenge of the second. Evidently going the right way, she will stay a mile but has plenty of speed and will be an interesting contender if taking her place in the Watership Down Stud sales race at Newbury on the 18th.
**Heat Of The Night**, hailing from a stable that has begun to emerge from a bad spell, showed her last running to be all wrong in second and was able to build on the promise of her debut. She is going the right way and looks a likely nursery type.
**Midcap(IRE)** saw her race out better than she did at Folkestone most recently and is another now eligible for nurseries. Her stable is back in form and she can pick up a small race.
**Ushindi(IRE)** ◆, another to have come from the Newbury maiden the winner ran in, showed up well for a long way and will be in her element back over a mile in nurseries.
**Orlar(IRE)** ◆, a 100,000gns purchase, hugged the rail throughout and made a very pleasing debut, staying on again having been outpaced. Her dam was related to high-class middle-distance performer Air Marshall and she looks certain to improve for a mile. There are races to be won with her.
**Daliya(IRE)**, a half-sister to Daliapour and the talented but quirky Dalampour, was making her racecourse debut in blinkers and ran around and hung under pressure. Unfortunately for connections she looks to inherited some of Dalampour's ways and as a result warrants treating with caution.
**Lottie Dundass** lost all chance after being hampered but is at least now qualified for nurseries. *Official explanation: jockey said filly suffered interference in running*
**Rashida** was disappointing even allowing for the fact she was slowly away. She is better than this and probably deserves another chance. *Official explanation: jockey said filly ran very green*

## 5350 COLOMBE CLAIMING H'CAP 1m 2f 188y
**3:50** (3:51) (F4) (0-55,53) 3-Y-O+ **£2,590** (£740; £370) **Stalls** Low

Form RPR

1045 **1** **Heathyards Pride**[57] 3774 4-8-12 **49** .................... KFallon 6 59
(RHollinshead) *hld up in tch: hdwy 4f out: rdn to ld 1f out: edgd lft ins fnl f: r.o* **5/1**[3]

0304 **2** *¾* **Icannshift (IRE)**[7] 4262 4-9-2 **53** .................... DHolland 4 62
(SDow) *led: rdn 2f out: hdd 1f out: nt qckn* **9/2**[2]

3036 **3** *3½* **Molly's Secret**[13] 5021 6-8-10 **47** .................... (b) PRobinson 9 50
(CGCox) *s.i.s: hld up and bhd: hdwy 3f out: rdn over 1f out: one pce* **9/2**[2]

2060 **4** *shd* **Enna (POL)**[12] 5035 5-8-8 **45** .................... SDrowne 11 48
(MrsStefLiddiard) *hld up: rdn and hdwy over 1f out: styd on ins fnl f* **16/1**

0506 **5** *¾* **Compton Aviator**[46] 4070 8-8-12 **49** .................... (t) LDettori 12 51
(AWCarroll) *hld up and bhd: hdwy on outside 3f out: rdn and one pce fnl 2f* **7/2**[1]

0143 **6** *½* **Ambersong**[11] 5056 6-9-0 **51** .................... JFortune 5 52
(AWCarroll) *hld up: hdwy 2f out: no imp fnl f* **5/1**[3]

20-0 **7** *1½* **Golden Fields (IRE)**[11] 4609 4-8-8 **45** .................... (b) IMongan 8 43
(MrsJCandlish) *chsd ldr tl rdn 2f out: wknd fnl f* **40/1**

0-04 **8** *6* **Mandinka**[9] 5110 4-8-0 **44** oh9 .................... SYourston(7) 1 32
(JFCoupland) *s.s: bhd: c wd st: short-lived effrt 2f out* **40/1**

3003 **9** *2* **Tancred Imp**[7] 5197 3-7-13 **44** oh4 .................... LisaJones 3 29
(DWBarker) *hld up: rdn over 3f out: bhd fnl 2f* **14/1**

0-00 **10** *2½* **Mark Your Way**[7] 5175 4-9-1 **52** .................... JQuinn 2 32
(PRChamings) *prom: rdn over 2f out: sn wknd* **50/1**

-060 **11** *3½* **Eurolink Zante (IRE)**[196] 855 8-8-13 **50** .................... EAhern 7 24
(AJChamberlain) *hld up: hdwy over 3f out: wknd 2f out* **33/1**

/00- **12** *4* **Mulsanne**[13] 2972 6-8-7 **44** oh14 .................... AMcCarthy 13 12
(PAPritchard) *prom: rdn over 3f out: sn wknd* **100/1**

0-00 **13** 1 ½ **Legion Of Honour (IRE)**[42] 4189 5-8-5 **45**................ JFMcDonald(3) 10 10
(MissSJWilton) *hld up: rdn over 2f out: sn bhd* **66/1**

2m 16.91s (-2.49) **Going Correction** -0.225s/f (Firm)
**WFA** 3 from 4yo+ 8lb **13** Ran SP% **116.7**
Speed ratings: **100,99,96,96,96 95,94,90,89,87 84,81,80**CSF £26.14 CT £109.10 TOTE £6.30: £2.20, £1.90, £1.60; EX 36.70.
**Owner** L A Morgan **Bred** L A Morgan **Trained** Upper Longdon, Staffs

**FOCUS**
Not much of a race but the winner seemed to get on better with the Fallon that he had done with amateurs recently.

**NOTEBOOK**
**Heathyards Pride** had been given a break since disappointing in a better race at Bath in July and, with the champion jockey on board, having been amateur ridden the last twice, was able to return to winning ways. He saw the trip out well enough but a mile two is likely to prove his optimum trip.
**Icannshift(IRE)**, another dropping in grade, ran well without proving quite good enough.
**Molly's Secret** always faced an uphill task once slowly away and was never getting to the front two in time.
**Enna(POL)**, who has been running over shorter, was keeping on towards the end of the race and may benefit from more positive tactics.
**Compton Aviator** was never able to get into it. *Official explanation: jockey said gelding had breathing problems*

## 5351 PREVENTION & DETECTION (HOLDINGS) / SITE SENTRY NURSERY STKS (H'CAP) 6f 21y

**4:20** (4:23) (D2) (0-85,80) 2-Y-O **£6,162** (£1,896; £948; £474) **Stalls** Low

Form RPR

022 **1** **Viking Spirit**[18] 4866 2-9-0 **73**.................... DHolland 3 87+
(PWHarris) *led over 1f: w ldr: led again over 2f out: rdn over 1f out: edgd rt ent fnl f: r.o wl* **9/2**[2]

534 **2** 3 **Cummiskey (IRE)**[42] 4191 2-9-4 **77**.................... SDrowne 12 82
(JAOsborne) *a.p: rdn over 1f out: wnt 2nd and edgd lft ins fnl f: no ch w wnr* **2/1**[1]

212 **3** 1 ¾ **Godsend**[32] 4475 2-9-4 **77**.................... DaneO'Neill 6 77
(RHannon) *bhd: rdn over 2f out: hdwy over 1f out: r.o ins fnl f* **8/1**

2564 **4** nk **Alexander Capetown (IRE)**[9] 5119 2-8-11 **70**.................... MHills 9 69
(BWHills) *hld up: swtchd rt and hdwy wl over 1f out: sn rdn: r.o one pce fnl f* **6/1**[3]

051 **5** 1 ½ **Top Form (IRE)**[45] 4099 2-9-7 **80**.................... LDettori 8 75
(EALDunlop) *led over 4f out tl over 2f out: rdn over 1f out: wknd ins fnl f* **13/2**

300 **6** ½ **Mr Kalandi (IRE)**[31] 4523 2-8-4 **63**.................... AMcCarthy 7 56
(PWD'Arcy) *s.i.s: hdwy over 4f out: rdn over 2f out: wknd jst over 1f out* **33/1**

520 **7** ¾ **Averting**[23] 4739 2-8-6 **65**.................... SCarson 2 56
(RFJohnsonHoughton) *hld up in mid-div: rdn over 2f out: no hdwy* **50/1**

5420 **8** 1 **Miss Cotswold Lady**[63] 3583 2-9-0 **73**.................... KFallon 13 61
(APJarvis) *hld up in tch: rdn wkn sltly hmpd wl over 1f out: no imp* **25/1**

033 **9** nk **Peters Delite**[10] 5084 2-8-7 **69**.................... THamilton(3) 4 56
(RAFahey) *bhd: rdn 2f out: n.d* **14/1**

6406 **10** hd **Epitomise**[33] 4439 2-8-6 **65**....................(t) JQuinn 10 51
(RMBeckett) *a in rr* **100/1**

005 **11** ¾ **Mister Aziz (IRE)**[46] 4058 2-8-6 **65**.................... JTate 5 49
(JMPEustace) *hld up: hdwy on ins over 3f out: rdn and wknd over 1f out* **50/1**

3204 **12** ½ **Piddies Pride (IRE)**[20] 4836 2-9-0 **73**.................... TPQueally 11 56
(PSMcentee) *a bhd* **16/1**

0335 **13** ¾ **Agilete**[56] 3805 2-9-2 **75**.................... ADaly 1 55
(LGCottrell) *prom tl rdn and wknd over 1f out* **20/1**

201 **14** 24 **Lucky Emerald (IRE)**[32] 4474 2-8-13 **72**.................... KDarley 14 —
(BPalling) *hld up: hung rt and lost pl bnd over 3f out: eased whn no ch over 1f out* **25/1**

1m 10.65s (-1.65) **Going Correction** -0.225s/f (Firm) 2y crse rec **14** Ran SP% **123.1**
Speed ratings: **102,98,95,95,93 92,91,90,89,89 88,87,86,54**CSF £13.26 CT £75.53 TOTE £5.00: £1.50, £1.20, £2.60; EX 17.90.
**Owner** The Masterminds **Bred** Bearstone Stud **Trained** Ringshall, Bucks

**FOCUS**
A decent time for the type of contest, 0.47 seconds faster than the two-year-old maiden over the same trip, and strong nursery form.

**NOTEBOOK**
**Viking Spirit** has been progressing with racing, and the move into nurseries enabled him to get off the mark at the fourth attempt. He was always up with the pace from his low draw and came right away late on to win cosily. There is more to come and seven furlongs is within his stamina range.
**Cummiskey(IRE)** did not have the best of draws but was strongly supported in the market nonetheless and looked a big danger early in the straight. However the winner went again and he had no response.
**Godsend** has shaped as though a seventh furlong will help the last twice now and will improve for it.
**Alexander Capetown(IRE)** has run well in similar races the last twice now and looks ready for a greater test of stamina.
**Top Form(IRE)** was given a positive ride and ran well for a long way.
**Miss Cotswold Lady** was not disgraced from her draw and was done no favours by being hampered. She has a small race in her. *Official explanation: jockey said filly unsuited by ground*
**Peters Delite** *Official explanation: jockey said colt did not handle the bend*
**Lucky Emerald(IRE)** *Official explanation: trainer's representative said filly swallowed her tongue*

## 5352 IAN WILLIAMS RACING MEDIAN AUCTION MAIDEN STKS 1m 22y

**4:50** (4:54) (F4) 3-Y-O **£3,276** (£936; £468) **Stalls** Low

Form RPR

2252 **1** **Rangoon (USA)**[23] 4741 3-9-0 77.................... RHughes 4 74
(MrsAJPerrett) *w ldr: rdn and edgd lft over 1f out: led ent fnl f: r.o* **15/8**[1]

23 **2** ¾ **Fascination Street (IRE)**[21] 4801 3-8-9 65.................... PRobinson 3 67
(MAJarvis) *led: rdn and hdd ent fnl f: nt qckn cl home* **5/2**[2]

4325 **3** 1 ¾ **Rubaiyat (IRE)**[16] 4941 3-9-0 53.................... SDrowne 5 68
(GWragg) *hld up in tch: rdn whn n.m.r and swtchd rt jst over 1f out: hung lft ins fnl f: one pce* **10/3**[3]

0045 **4** 2 **My Michelle**[19] 4850 3-8-9 62.................... KDarley 2 58
(BPalling) *hld up: rdn and hdwy over 1f out: kpt on ins fnl f* **15/2**

4000 **5** 1 ¾ **Velocitas**[93] 2688 3-9-0 54.................... DHolland 12 59
(HJCollingridge) *hld up: rdn over 3f out: wknd over 1f out* **20/1**

0005 **6** 4 **Tartiruga (IRE)**[25] 4674 3-9-0 45.................... ADaly 1 50
(LGCottrell) *hld up in tch: rdn over 2f out: sn wknd* **40/1**

000 **7** 3 ½ **Count Boris**[14] 5007 3-9-0.................... SCarson 7 42
(GBBalding) *s.i.s: sn wl bhd* **18/1**

0000 **8** 9 **Lookouthereicome**[29] 4583 3-8-9 45.................... JQuinn 9 16
(TTClement) *s.i.s: a bhd* **100/1**

05 **9** ¾ **Start Of Authority**[25] 4679 3-9-0.................... IMongan 10 20
(JGallagher) *plld hrd early: prom: rdn over 2f out: wknd over 1f out* **33/1**

-000 **10** shd **Almanac (IRE)**[18] 4880 3-9-0 49.................... TWoodley 8 19
(BPJBaugh) *a bhd* **100/1**

1m 38.44s (-0.86) **Going Correction** -0.225s/f (Firm) **10** Ran SP% **115.6**
Speed ratings: **95,94,92,90,88 84,81,72,71,71**CSF £6.36 TOTE £2.30: £1.10, £1.10, £2.00; EX 4.30.
**Owner** K Abdulla **Bred** Juddmonte Farms Inc **Trained** Pulborough, W Sussex
■ Stewards Enquiry : R Hughes caution: careless riding

**FOCUS**
A very bad maiden won by a very badly handicapped horse in a moderate time.

**NOTEBOOK**
**Rangoon(USA)** was getting off the mark at the sixth attempt and seemed well served by the mile. He is not up to his rating of 77 and needs help from the Handicapper, otherwise he is going to struggle.
**Fascination Street(IRE)** has not set the world alight since coming over from France and it will be a bad race she wins.
**Rubaiyat(IRE)** has not been getting home over farther and ran better for this drop in trip. He was hanging under pressure and is not an easy ride, but should win a race eventually off his lowly mark.
**My Michelle** ran better on this drop back in trip but has had more than enough chances.

## 5353 BOTT FOUNDERS MAIDEN AUCTION STKS 6f 21y

**5:20** (5:32) (F4) 2-Y-O **£3,598** (£1,028; £514) **Stalls** Low

Form RPR

3 **1** **The Pheasant Flyer**[13] 5015 2-8-8.................... JFMcDonald(3) 4 85
(BJMeehan) *mde all: rdn over 2f out: edgd rt ins fnl f: r.o* **7/4**[1]

6 **2** shd **King Marju (IRE)**[38] 4290 2-9-0.................... JFortune 7 88
(PWChapple-Hyam) *chsd wnr: rdn wl over 1f out: ev ch ins fnl f: r.o* **3/1**[2]

6 **3** 1 ¾ **Miss Trial**[19] 4844 2-8-6.................... PRobinson 10 74
(MAJarvis) *a.p: rdn over 1f out: one pce* **3/1**[2]

000 **4** 7 **The Keep**[7] 5200 2-8-4.................... RSmith 6 51
(RHannon) *hld up in tch: rdn over 2f out: wknd wl over 1f out* **18/1**

46 **5** ½ **Tartan Special**[19] 4861 2-8-11.................... DarrenWilliams 11 57
(KRBurke) *dwlt: t.k.h: sn mid-div: hdwy whn swtchd lft 2f out: sn rdn and wknd* **18/1**

0 **6** nk **Red Marteeney**[21] 4809 2-8-11.................... DaneO'Neill 13 56
(DRCElsworth) *hld up in tch: rdn 2f out: wknd over 1f out* **50/1**

**7** shd **Italian Touch (IRE)** 2-8-9.................... IMongan 9 54
(JAGlover) *hld up: pushed along 3f out: rdn and sme hdwy over 1f out: n.d* **66/1**

5 **8** hd **Muddy (IRE)**[8] 5154 2-8-9.................... JQuinn 3 53
(GAHuffer) *hld up in mid-div: sme hdwy over 1f out: no imp fnl f* **20/1**

**9** shd **Monica's Revenge (IRE)** 2-8-4.................... TPQueally 2 48
(RMBeckett) *s.s: nvr nrr* **66/1**

**10** nk **Blade Of Gold (IRE)** 2-8-5.................... SWKelly 1 48
(JAOsborne) *s.s: hdwy over 1f out: no imp fnl f* **22/1**

00 **11** 2 ½ **Summer Charm**[7] 5200 2-8-3.................... LisaJones 14 38
(WJarvis) *a bhd:* **66/1**

**12** 3 ½ **Nodina** 2-8-13.................... EAhern 12 38
(SCWilliams) *dwlt: a bhd* **12/1**[3]

**13** 1 **Vague Star (ITY)** 2-8-13.................... NDay 8 35
(RIngram) *bhd most of way* **40/1**

**14** 1 ¼ **Rooks Bridge (IRE)** 2-8-8.................... ADaly 5 26
(GAHam) *s.s: sn wl bhd* **100/1**

1m 11.12s (-1.18) **Going Correction** -0.225s/f (Firm) **14** Ran SP% **123.6**
Speed ratings: **98,97,95,86,85 85,85,84,84,84 80,76,74,73**CSF £6.65 TOTE £3.00: £1.10, £2.10, £2.00; EX 9.90.
**Owner** The Second Pheasant Inn Partnership **Bred** Mrs O M Weston **Trained** Upper Lambourn, Berks

**FOCUS**
A time 0.47 seconds slower than the nursery, but still a fair one for the grade of contest and probably solid form.

**NOTEBOOK**
**The Pheasant Flyer** bounced out in front and responded well to pressure to edge out King Marju in a tight finish. This represented an improvement on his debut third at Brighton and he can probably win a nursery.
**King Marju(IRE)** was dropping back from seven furlongs and ran a good race in defeat. He will stay seven and should win his maiden.
**Miss Trial**, well beaten on her debut at Kempton on soft ground, fared much better under faster conditions and could do with an extra furlong.
**The Keep** was well adrift in fourth but is now qualified for nurseries and can do better in that sphere.
**Tartan Special** is another now eligible for nurseries.
**Red Marteeney** is discreetly going the right way and should improve again next time.
**Italian Touch(IRE)** is bred to appreciate seven or maybe a mile and was keeping on steadily towards the end of the race.
**Muddy(IRE)** probably failed to show much improvement on his initial effort.
**Monica's Revenge(IRE)** was never in the the hunt after a sluggish start but can be guaranteed to improve with the run under his belt.

## 5354 CROWN FARM APPRENTICE H'CAP 2m 39y

**5:50** (5:59) (F4) (0-55,59) 3-Y-O+ **£3,169** (£905; £452) **Stalls** Low

Form RPR

2655 **1** **Lazzaz**[13] 5021 6-8-9 **46** oh1.................... PGallagher(3) 2 55
(PWHiatt) *mde all: rdn over 2f out: hld on wl cl home* **14/1**

-200 **2** ½ **Academy (IRE)**[37] 4352 9-9-7 **55**.................... NChalmers 12 63
(AndrewTurnell) *hld up: hdwy over 2f out: rdn and edgd lft over 1f out: ev ch ins fnl f: nt qckn cl home* **20/1**

3222 **3** ½ **Banningham Blaze**[3] 5257 4-8-9 **48**.................... MHalford(5) 4 56
(AWCarroll) *hld up and bhd: hdwy 2f out: styd on wl towards fin* **10/1**

6232 **4** 2 **Oops (IRE)**[6] 5214 5-8-7 **46** oh1.................... DeanWilliams(5) 11 51
(JFCoupland) *hld up: hdwy over 6f out: rdn over 4f out: nt clr run on ins jst over 1f out: swtchd rt ins fnl f: styd on* **7/2**[2]

3412 **5** nk **Bojangles (IRE)**[7] 5175 5-9-5 **53**.................... MSavage 3 58
(RBrotherton) *hld up in tch: rdn over 3f out: styd on same pce fnl 2f* **10/1**

0000 **6** ½ **Vanbrugh (FR)**[8] 5159 4-8-7 **46** oh11....................(vt) WHogg(5) 13 50
(MissDAMchale) *chsd wnr: rdn over 2f out: edgd lft over 1f out: wknd ins fnl f* **66/1**

0330 **7** ½ **Galandora**[42] 4202 4-8-11 **50**.................... TBlock(5) 6 54
(DrJRJNaylor) *hld up and bhd: hdwy 2f out: rdn over 1f out: one pce fnl f* **16/1**

3141 **8** ¾ **Salut Saint Cloud**[7] 5178 3-8-12 **59** 6ex....................(p) AQuinn 8 62
(GLMoore) *hld up: hdwy on ins over 6f out: rdn over 2f out: one pce* **13/8**[1]

643 **9** 4 **Prairie Law (GER)**[24] 4713 4-8-9 **46** oh1.................... AMullen(3) 9 44
(IanWilliams) *bhd fnl 4f* **8/1**[3]

504 **10** nk **My True Love (IRE)**[31] 4513 5-9-2 **55**.................... CJDavies(5) 7 53
(RJBaker) *bhd fnl 4f* **50/1**

1000 **11** *hd* **Court One**[7] 5205 6-8-12 **46** BSwarbrick 10 44
(RJPrice) *hld up: stdy hdwy over 6f out: wknd 4f out* **14/1**

0-60 **12** *hd* **Dingley Lass**[10] 5073 4-8-9 **46** oh1 DerekNolan(3) 5 43
(HMorrison) *prom: rdn over 4f out: wknd over 2f out* **50/1**

-050 **13** *6* **Black Swan (IRE)**[18] 4870 4-8-7 **46** oh11 StevenHarrison(5) 1 36
(GAHam) *prom tl rdn and wknd over 2f out* **100/1**

0452 **14** *1* **Heart Springs**[18] 4870 4-8-9 **46** oh1 CHaddon(3) 15 35
(DrJRJNaylor) *sltly prematurely burst through stalls and s.s: hld up: hdwy 6f out: rdn 4f out: sn wknd* **50/1**

3m 34.9s (3.09) **Going Correction** -0.225s/f (Firm)
**WFA** 3 from 4yo+ 13lb **14** Ran SP% **122.0**
Speed ratings: **83,82,82,81,81 81,80,80,78,78 78,78,75,74**CSF £275.19 CT £2924.59 TOTE £17.40: £3.30, £5.80, £2.60; EX 221.50 Place 6 £44.43, Place 5 £15.10.
**Owner** Phil Kelly **Bred** Khalid Khalifa Al Nabooda **Trained** Hook Norton, Oxon

**FOCUS**
A poor handicap and a pedestrian winning time, even for a race like this.

**NOTEBOOK**
**Lazzaz** made every yard of the running to record his first-ever turf success at the 35th attempt. He should still be on a winning mark once reassessed.
**Academy(IRE)** came from a fair way back to challenge the winner but was always being held. It is almost two years since he last won.
**Banningham Blaze** continued her fine recent run of efforts with a keeping-on third and still shows no signs of the run coming to an end.
**Oops(IRE)** is not the quickest individual around, and as a result being blocked in his run would have done him no favours. He is at his best when there is some cut in the ground.
**Bojangles(IRE)** has been running well over a mile two and coped well with this sharp rise in trip, plugging on at the one pace under pressure.
**Vanbrugh(FR)** ran better than his odds entitled him to and showed more encouraging signs for the future.
**Salut Saint Cloud** proved a very disappointing favourite, being unable to pick up once asked on this faster surface.
**Prairie Law(GER)** *Official explanation: trainer said gelding had been unsuited by being fitted with a cross noseband*
T/Plt: £55.90 to a £1 stake. Pool: £34,684.85. 452.75 winning tickets. T/Qpdt: £9.40 to a £1 stake. Pool: £2,624.60. 206.50 winning tickets. KH

## 4370 GALWAY (R-H)
### Monday, September 6

**OFFICIAL GOING: Good**

## 5357a ARDILAUN HOUSE HOTEL OYSTER STKS (LISTED RACE) 1m 4f
**4:45** (4:46) 3-Y-O+ **£27,507** (£8,070; £3,845; £1,309)

RPR

**1** **Royal Devotion (IRE)**[15] 4977 4-9-4 92 (p) TPO'Shea 5 98
(MHalford, Ire) *chsd ldrs: impr u.p to ld 3f out: sn hdd: chal ins fnl f: led 100yds out: kpt on wl* **25/1**

**2** *1/2* **Orpington**[26] 4662 3-8-12 94 PJSmullen 7 100
(DKWeld, Ire) *towards rr: rdn and prog into 6th ent st: styd on strly fnl f: wnt 2nd cl home: nt rch wnr* **9/1**

**3** *3/4* **Arch Rebel (USA)**[16] 4960 3-8-12 98 FMBerry 4 99
(NoelMeade, Ire) *chsd ldrs: prog to ld bef st: strly pressed ins fnl f: hdd 100yds out: no ex u.p and dropped to 3rd cl home* **8/1**[3]

**4** *1* **Faasel (IRE)**[12] 5050 3-8-12 97 (b) DPMcDonogh 3 97
(KevinPrendergast, Ire) *towards rr: stdy hdwy into 3rd 3f out: 4th into st: sn no ex: kpt on same pce* **10/1**

**5** *2* **Blue Corrig (IRE)**[15] 4977 4-9-7 99 (b) PCosgrave 2 94
(JosephCrowley, Ire) *rr: rdn and impr into 3rd early st: no imp and kpt on same pce fr over 1f out* **33/1**

**6** *2* **Excalibur (IRE)**[60] 3686 4-9-7 JPSpencer 9 91
(APO'Brien, Ire) *sn led: strly pressed and hdd 3f out: 5th and no ex u.p fr early st* **4/9**[1]

**7** *11* **High Priestess (IRE)**[12] 5050 5-9-4 99 JAHeffernan 1 70
(MJPO'Brien, Ire) *trckd ldrs in 3rd: rdn and no ex fr 3f out* **11/2**[2]

**8** *dist* **Silver Silence (JPN)**[60] 3686 3-8-12 90 KJManning 8 —
(JSBolger, Ire) *trckd ldrs: mainly 4th: rdn and no ex fr 3f out: bhd and eased fnl f* **25/1**

**9** *5* **Mount Grace (IRE)**[8] 5162 3-8-9 91 (b) CO'Donoghue 6 —
(JosephCrowley, Ire) *trckd ldr in 2nd: rdn fr under 4f out: sn no ex: bhd and eased fnl f* **33/1**

2m 39.2s
**WFA** 3 from 4yo+ 9lb **9** Ran SP% **128.4**
Speed ratings: CSF £244.03 TOTE £78.30: £37.10, £3.90, £3.70; DF 327.00.
**Owner** Gigginstown House Stud **Bred** Orpendale & Barronstown Stud **Trained** the Curragh, Co Kildare

**FOCUS**
A weak Listed contest with a disappointing favourite.

**NOTEBOOK**
**Royal Devotion(IRE)** appreciated this ground and came a second time to lead just under a half furlong out. She held on gamely for a surprise win and goes up 6 lb to 98. *Official explanation: trainer said, regarding the improved form shown, filly was unsuited by good to firm ground at Naas two starts ago, and was left in the stalls and slowly away last time, adding that today the filly seemed to benefit from a change of tactics, good ground and the use of cheekpieces for the first time*
**Orpington**, winner of an amateur race at the Festival meeting, stayed on well but could'nt peg back the winner.
**Arch Rebel(USA)** looked all over a winner from the turn-in but found little under pressure when headed well inside the last.
**Faasel(IRE)** stayed on up the outside but the ground had gone against him.
**Excalibur(IRE)**, with a 109 rating, looked head and shoulders above these but he was struggling with over two furlongs to race.
**High Priestess(IRE)** has had a busy time of it and was finding nothing from well before the straight.

5358 - 5361a (Foreign Racing) - See Raceform Interactive

## 4698 CATTERICK (L-H)
### Tuesday, September 7

**OFFICIAL GOING: Good to firm (firm in places)**

## 5362 BECKSIDE MAIDEN AUCTION STKS 5f 212y
**2:30** (2:30) (E4) 2-Y-O **£2,947** (£842; £421) **Stalls** Low

Form RPR

0002 **1** **Corniche Dancer**[12] 5053 2-8-8 75 ACulhane 2 68+
(MRChannon) *hld up in tch: hdwy on ins whn nt clr run briefly 2f out: r.o u.p to ld ins fnl f: all out* **5/1**[2]

504 **2** *shd* **Ringarooma**[16] 4966 2-8-4 69 KDarley 3 64+
(MHTompkins) *trckd ldrs: nt clr run briefly over 2f out: r.o u.p to chal wl ins fnl f: jst hld* **6/4**[1]

40 **3** *2* **Street Ballad (IRE)**[10] 5109 2-8-5 ABeech(3) 6 62
(MrsJRRamsden) *rr of main gp: effrt over 2f out: rdn over 1f out: r.o wl ins fnl f: nrst fin* **6/1**[3]

554 **4** *hd* **Beverley Beau**[99] 2523 2-8-0 60 KristinStubbs(7) 1 60
(MrsLStubbs) *cl up: led over 2f out tl rdn and hdd ins fnl f: no ex* **25/1**

0 **5** *1* **Lady Vee (IRE)**[21] 4824 2-8-2 DMernagh 7 52
(PDNiven) *in tch: drvn along and hdwy over 2f out: ev ch and rdn over 1f out: no ex fnl f* **12/1**

**6** *3/4* **Hannah's Dream (IRE)** 2-8-6 RFfrench 4 54
(MJohnston) *sn bhd and drvn along: kpt on u.p fnl 2f: nvr able to chal* **7/1**

0 **7** *shd* **Turn On The Style**[33] 4488 2-8-7 SChin 8 55
(RPElliott) *led tl hdd over 2f out: rdn over 1f out: fdd* **12/1**

0 **8** *10* **Flaxby**[75] 3233 2-8-9 RMullen 10 26
(JDBethell) *s.i.s: sn prom on outer: drvn along 1/2-way: sn wknd: t.o* **33/1**

0 **9** *3* **Blades Boy**[10] 5125 2-8-7 NCallan 9 15
(KARyan) *s.i.s: sn prom: sn wkng whn hmpd wl over 1f out: t.o* **14/1**

**10** *1 1/4* **Knot In Wood (IRE)** 2-8-9 GParkin 5 13
(RAFahey) *slowly away: sn t.o* **33/1**

1m 14.15s (0.15) **Going Correction** -0.075s/f (Good) **10** Ran SP% **115.2**
Speed ratings: **96,95,93,92,91 90,90,77,73,71**CSF £12.44 TOTE £4.50: £2.50, £1.10, £3.00; EX 10.00.
**Owner** Mrs A M Jones **Bred** Roseland Thoroughbreds Ltd **Trained** West Ilsley, Berks

**FOCUS**
An ordinary maiden run at a fair gallop. The first two came clear, but the form overall is modest.

**NOTEBOOK**
**Corniche Dancer**, who hails from a yard whose juveniles have struck a rich vein of form recently, stuck to her task well in the closing stages and broke her duck at the fifth time of asking. She is improving, and is better than this bare form, but she will have to progress again to be competitive off this sort of mark in nurseries.
**Ringarooma**, getting 4lb from the winner, did not get the best of runs two out, but still held every chance in the closing stages. She handled the ground and should be capable of finding a small race back over seven furlongs before the year is out.
**Street Ballad(IRE)**, dropping from seven furlongs, stayed on nicely late on without being given that hard a time. This was her best effort to date, she looks well suited by this ground and is one to keep an eye on when reverting to further, now she qualifies for nurseries.
**Beverley Beau** settled better over this extra furlong and was not disgraced in defeat, but looked very one paced when push came to shove. He is only moderate, but may improve a touch for the switch to nurseries.
**Hannah's Dream(IRE)**, bred to better over farther in the future, was slowly getting the hang of things, but looks only modest on this evidence.

## 5363 "SPONSOR A RACE AT CATTERICK" NURSERY 5f
**3:00** (3:02) (E3) (0-75,73) 2-Y-O **£3,532** (£1,087; £543; £271) **Stalls** Low

Form RPR

6045 **1** **Melandre**[88] 2860 2-8-12 **64** TWilliams 7 69
(MBrittain) *prom: led 2f out: r.o u.p* **12/1**

0040 **2** *1/2* **Lord John**[5] 5234 2-8-1 **53** (b[1]) DaleGibson 1 56
(MWEasterby) *in tch: drvn along 2f out: r.o u.p to go 2nd ins fnl f: clsng on wnr fin* **10/1**

0021 **3** *1 1/4* **Oceanico Dot Com (IRE)**[7] 5209 2-9-7 **73** 6ex FNorton 2 72
(ABerry) *chsd ldrs: drvn along 1/2-way: kpt on u.p fnl f* **3/1**[1]

0513 **4** *1/2* **Rosiella**[11] 5068 2-9-7 **73** NCallan 10 70
(MBlanshard) *towards rr: hdwy 1/2-way: kpt on u.p fnl 2f: nvr able to chal* **7/1**[3]

1005 **5** *1/2* **Rancho Cucamonga (IRE)**[22] 4803 2-9-2 **68** KDarley 8 63
(TDBarron) *midfield: drvn along 1/2-way: kpt on u.p fnl 2f* **6/1**[2]

0603 **6** *1/2* **Apologies**[9] 5143 2-9-5 **71** (b) GGibbons 9 65
(BAMcmahon) *dwlt: rr div and sn drvn along: sme hdwy u.p whn nt clr run briefly over 1f out: n.d* **7/1**[3]

5000 **7** *1 1/2* **Our Louis**[9] 5143 2-8-2 **54** RFfrench 3 42
(JSWainwright) *led tl hdd 2f out: sn btn* **25/1**

0004 **8** *2 1/2* **Cadogen Square**[31] 4559 2-7-12 **50** oh1 PMQuinn 4 30
(DWChapman) *cl up tl wknd 2f out* **16/1**

003 **9** *2 1/2* **Starlight River (IRE)**[26] 4670 2-8-12 **64** SChin 6 35
(WRMuir) *prom: nt clr run briefly wl over 2f out: sn wknd* **16/1**

060 **10** *shd* **Kerny (IRE)**[22] 4804 2-7-13 **51** PFessey 11 22
(JJQuinn) *nvr bttr than mid-div* **16/1**

0440 **11** *1 1/4* **Next Time (IRE)**[19] 4875 2-8-3 **55** RMullen 5 21
(MJPolglase) *nvr bttr than mid-div* **20/1**

0040 **12** *1 1/4* **Evanesce**[29] 4612 2-9-5 **71** ACulhane 13 33
(MRChannon) *a rr* **12/1**

050 **13** *nk* **Carmania (IRE)**[26] 4675 2-8-1 **53** DMernagh 14 14
(RPElliott) *nvr bttr than mid-div* **33/1**

0456 **14** *hd* **Ochil Hills Dancer (IRE)**[12] 5060 2-8-2 **61** (t) DFentiman(7) 12 21
(ACrook) *a rr* **20/1**

60.24 secs (-0.36) **Going Correction** -0.175s/f (Firm) **14** Ran SP% **122.7**
Speed ratings: **95,94,92,91,90 89,87,83,79,79 77,75,74,74**CSF £122.97 CT £474.06 TOTE £11.50: £3.50, £4.50, £1.10; EX 171.10.
**Owner** Mel Brittain **Bred** Barton Stud Partnership **Trained** Warthill, N Yorks

**FOCUS**
A modest nursery run at a sound gallop and the form appears fairly solid.

**NOTEBOOK**
**Melandre**, who showed ability in some fair maidens previously, scored on this handicap debut with a tenacious display. She showed no signs of the temperament that was evident at York the last twice, and is entitled to improve a little again, as this was her first run for 88 days.
**Lord John** improved for the application of blinkers and was staying on well at the death, suggesting a stiffer test will be very much in his favour next time.
**Oceanico Dot Com(IRE)**, off the mark from a decent draw at Ripon on easy ground last time, ran a sound race under her penalty on this handicap bow. However, although this track was plenty sharp enough for her, she does look fairly exposed now.

**Rosiella** did well to get involved from her wide draw but, as expected, was not suited by this drop back to the minimum trip on a sharp track. This looks to be her preferred ground.
**Rancho Cucamonga(IRE)** again left the impression she is slightly too high in the weights, and found things happening too fast for her this time.
**Apologies** proved disappointing, but is worthy of another chance back on easy ground.

## 5364 CATTERICKBRIDGE.CO.UK H'CAP — 7f
3:30 (3:30) (E3) (0-70,67) 3-Y-0+ £5,510 (£1,695; £847; £423) Stalls Low

Form — RPR
0612 **1** **Jubilee Street (IRE)**[10] 5108 5-8-13 **58** ........ ABeech(3) 14 68
(MrsADuffield) *midfield: hdwy over 1f out: styd on wl u.p fnl f: led cl home* **11/2**[1]
4500 **2** ½ **Legal Set (IRE)**[5] 5242 8-8-13 **58** ........ (t) LFletcher(3) 9 67
(MissAStokell) *prom: styd on u.p to ld ins fnl f: hdd cl home* **16/1**
4052 **3** ½ **Mission Affirmed (USA)**[19] 4882 3-9-0 **60** ........ RWinston 11 67
(TPTate) *midfield: hdwy u.p to chse ldrs appr fnl f: styd on ins last* **9/1**[3]
0142 **4** ¾ **Northern Games**[8] 5201 5-9-3 **59** ........ (b) GParkin 6 64+
(KARyan) *slowly away: bhd: hdwy over 2f out: nt clr run briefly ent fnl f: styd on wl: nvr able to chal* **11/2**[1]
0550 **5** nk **Mandarin Spirit (IRE)**[10] 5124 4-9-8 **64** ........ (b) RMullen 1 68
(GCHChung) *prom: rdn to ld over 1f out: hdd ins fnl f: no ex* **10/1**
0206 **6** nk **Cottingham (IRE)**[5] 5245 3-9-0 **60** ........ SChin 2 64
(MCChapman) *chsd ldrs: rdn over 2f out: kpt on same pce* **16/1**
1040 **7** 2½ **Aragon's Boy**[34] 4435 4-9-11 **67** ........ DAllan 8 64
(TDEasterby) *midfield: sn pushed along: rdn over 2f out: no hdwy* **11/1**
003 **8** ¾ **Washbrook**[91] 2756 3-8-12 **58** ........ ANicholls 10 53
(AndrewTurnell) *in tch: rdn 3f out: no hdwy* **18/1**
0301 **9** ½ **Saros (IRE)**[12] 5063 3-9-4 **64** ........ FLynch 17 58
(BSmart) *s.i.s: towards rr: hdwy on outer 2f out: no further prog whn bmpd appr fnl f* **9/1**[3]
6550 **10** ¾ **Dark Day Blues (IRE)**[12] 5063 3-9-2 **62** ........ DarrenWilliams 16 54
(MDHammond) *sn towards rr: n.d* **25/1**
1551 **11** 1¼ **Headland (USA)**[15] 5000 6-9-2 **58** ........ (be) ACulhane 7 46
(DWChapman) *s.i.s: towards rr most of way: n.d* **7/1**[2]
1560 **12** ½ **Rene Barbier (IRE)**[64] 3585 3-9-2 **62** ........ FNorton 4 49
(JAGlover) *midfield: rdn over 2f out: no hdwy* **16/1**
051P **13** nk **Weet Watchers**[77] 3167 4-9-6 **62** ........ NCallan 3 48
(PABlockley) *cl up: led over 4f out: rdn and hdd over 1f out: sn btn* **16/1**
-000 **14** ¾ **Orpenberry (IRE)**[34] 4451 3-8-11 **57** ........ PMQuinn 18 41
(EJAlston) *bhd most of way* **66/1**
0000 **15** nk **Named At Dinner**[6] 5223 3-9-2 **62** ........ JCarroll 12 45
(MrsADuffield) *a bhd* **100/1**
4-60 **16** 3 **Kiss The Rain**[71] 3381 4-9-1 **57** ........ GGibbons 5 32
(PABlockley) *led tl hdd over 4f out: wknd 2f out* **66/1**
-000 **17** 2½ **Cross Ash (IRE)**[46] 4093 4-9-4 **60** ........ KDarley 15 28
(RHollinshead) *nvr bttr than mid-div* **28/1**
4510 **18** 2½ **Majhool**[40] 4265 5-9-1 **57** ........ RFfrench 13 19
(IWMcinnes) *chsd ldrs tl wknd over 2f out* **20/1**

1m 26.63s (-0.87) **Going Correction** -0.075s/f (Good)
**WFA** 3 from 4yo+ 4lb — 18 Ran SP% **125.5**
Speed ratings: **101,100,99,99,98 98,95,94,94,93 91,91,90,89,89 86,83,80**CSF £91.03 CT £802.24 TOTE £8.60: £1.90, £5.30, £3.50, £1.10; EX 116.10.
**Owner** D W Holdsworth & J A McMahon **Bred** My Firebird Syndicate **Trained** Constable Burton, N Yorks

**FOCUS**
A moderate affair that was run at a reasonable pace and the form looks reasonably sound. Those drawn low were at an advantage, but the first and third were drawn high.

**NOTEBOOK**
**Jubilee Street(IRE)** bounced back to form by scoring under a fine ride from Beech. He deserves extra credit as he was drawn wide, and this was his third win over course and distance, on ground he relishes.
**Legal Set(IRE)** looked booked for success when hitting the front late on but, try as he might, could not hold off the winner winner close home. He may be able to find a race off this sort of mark and would ideally appreciate a stiff six furlongs.
**Mission Affirmed(USA)** was doing all of his best work late in the day. He looks fairly treated at present and this display suggests he could strike when upped to a mile again.
**Northern Games** lost his chance with a sluggish start and then found trouble when attempting to get involved inside the last furlong. He is worth another chance off this mark. *Official explanation: jockey said gelding missed the break*
**Mandarin Spirit(IRE)** ran his best race for some time, but had the plum draw this time and is very hard to win with.
**Headland(USA)**

## 5365 GORACING.CO.UK H'CAP — 1m 5f 175y
4:00 (4:00) (E3) (0-70,67) 3-Y-0 £5,265 (£1,620; £810; £405) Stalls Low

Form — RPR
4121 **1** **Inchpast**[27] 4630 3-9-10 **67** ........ (b) NCallan 1 77
(MHTompkins) *trckd ldrs: drvn along to ld 2f out: styd on wl* **3/1**[2]
6-12 **2** 2 **Can Can Flyer (IRE)**[9] 5144 3-9-6 **63** ........ RFfrench 6 70
(MJohnston) *cl up: led wl over 2f out: rdn: edgd rt and hdd 2f out: styd on* **10/11**[1]
0606 **3** 1¼ **Prairie Sun (GER)**[10] 4424 3-8-7 **53** oh5 ........ ABeech(3) 5 58
(MrsADuffield) *prom: ev ch and rdn over 2f out: kpt on same pce* **16/1**
4220 **4** 1½ **Munaawesh (USA)**[5] 5245 3-8-13 **56** ........ (b) ACulhane 4 59
(DWChapman) *in tch: effrt over 2f out: rdn over 1f out: no imp on ldrs* **7/1**[3]
3002 **5** 6 **Siegfrieds Night (IRE)**[10] 4457 3-9-8 **65** ........ LVickers 7 60
(MCChapman) *towards rr: drvn along and outpcd 4f out: n.d* **9/1**
0-00 **6** 1½ **Iron Temptress (IRE)**[19] 4882 3-8-13 **56** ........ DAllan 8 48
(GMMoore) *rr: drvn along and outpcd 4f out: n.d* **50/1**
2400 **7** ½ **Bold Blade**[8] 5205 3-9-0 **60** ........ LFletcher(3) 3 52
(MJPolglase) *led tl rdn and hdd wl over 2f out: wknd 2f out* **28/1**
0530 **8** 6 **Jalousie Dream**[55] 3837 3-8-10 **53** oh8 ........ PMQuinn 2 36
(GMMoore) *towards rr: drvn along and outpcd 4f out* **100/1**

3m 2.35s (-2.15) **Going Correction** -0.075s/f (Good) — 8 Ran SP% **112.2**
Speed ratings: **103,101,101,100,96 96,95,92**CSF £5.79 CT £31.28 TOTE £4.80: £1.50, £1.02, £4.00; EX 6.30.
**Owner** Marcoe Racing Welwyn **Bred** Stanley Estate And Stud Co **Trained** Newmarket, Suffolk

**FOCUS**
A modest staying handicap, but the pace was sound and the winner looks progressive.

**NOTEBOOK**
**Inchpast** followed-up on his recent success in a classified event at Beverley in the style of a progressive horse. He had no problems in reverting to this faster ground, and the extra trip was much in his favour, so he could well strike again, despite another inevitable rise in the weights for this.
**Can Can Flyer(IRE)** had the run of the race and turned in another sound effort, but could not go with the winner late on. He remains lightly-raced and may have more to offer back on an easier surface.
**Prairie Sun(GER)** produced her best effort for some time from 5lb out of the handicap. This trip just seems to stretch her and a drop back to 12 furlongs will be of benefit in the future.
**Munaawesh(USA)** shaped like a non-stayer over this trip, but was clear of the rest in fourth and could find easier opportunites to break his duck.

## 5366 'ENTERTAIN IN STYLE AT CATTERICK' MEDIAN AUCTION MAIDEN STKS — 7f
4:30 (4:30) (F4) 3-4-Y-0 £2,919 (£834; £417) Stalls Low

Form — RPR
265 **1** **River Of Babylon**[10] 5123 3-8-9 64 ........ RMullen 7 69+
(MLWBell) *hld up: in tch: hdwy to ld over 1f out: styd on strly to go clr ins fnl f* **9/4**[2]
022 **2** 4 **Revenir (IRE)**[55] 3846 3-9-0 74 ........ NCallan 1 63+
(EFVaughan) *prom: led over 1f out: sn hdd: styd on: no ch w wnr ins fnl f* **4/7**[1]
4-00 **3** 3½ **New York (IRE)**[105] 2377 3-8-9 65 ........ (t) ACulhane 3 49+
(WJHaggas) *hld up: effrt over 2f out: styd on to go 3rd ins fnl f: no imp on first 2* **11/1**[3]
0450 **4** 1¼ **Royal Awakening (IRE)**[30] 4576 3-8-9 49 ........ MLawson(5) 4 50
(REBarr) *hld up in tch: effrt over 2f out: sn rdn: styd on fnl f: n.d* **33/1**
04 **5** 3 **Government (IRE)**[82] 3015 3-8-11 ........ ABeech(3) 8 42
(MCChapman) *cl up: led after 2f tl rdn and hdd over 1f out: sn btn* **33/1**
0300 **6** 1 **Acca Larentia (IRE)**[34] 4451 3-8-9 47 ........ VHalliday 5 34
(RMWhitaker) *hld up in tch: effrt over 2f out: sn rdn: no hdwy* **66/1**
000 **7** 3 **Plattocrat**[18] 4926 4-9-4 30 ........ SChin 2 31
(RPElliott) *cl up to 1/2-way: sn wknd* **150/1**
0-00 **8** 9 **Distinctlythebest**[30] 4573 4-9-4 ........ RWinston 6 7
(FWatson) *slt ld tl hdd after 2f: sn lost pl and pushed along: rallied and ev ch over 2f out: sn rdn: wknd qckly* **200/1**

1m 26.97s (-0.53) **Going Correction** -0.075s/f (Good)
**WFA** 3 from 4yo 4lb — 8 Ran SP% **111.3**
Speed ratings: **100,95,91,90,86 85,82,71**CSF £3.64 TOTE £2.90: £1.10, £1.02, £2.70; EX 5.50.
**Owner** C Wright & The Hon Mrs J M Corbett **Bred** Floors Farming And Christopher J Heath **Trained** Newmarket, Suffolk

**FOCUS**
A poor maiden, full of disappointing types, and the field came home strung out.

**NOTEBOOK**
**River Of Babylon** proved game in fighting off the runner-up entering the final furlong before readily drawing clear. This was her first success in six attempts, she handled the ground well and could be competitive off her current mark in a handicap, but this form probably amounts to little.
**Revenir(IRE)** had his chance, but found little when push came to shove and ultimately proved disappointing. The drop in trip was against him, and he did race freely, but he looks one to have reservations about.
**New York(IRE)** ran on late, but did not really achieve much on this return from a 105-day layoff. She has now disappointed in three outings since resuming this year and looks one to avoid.
**Royal Awakening(IRE)** ran his race and needs to drop into selling class.

## 5367 'SPECIAL PACKAGE DEAL' MAIDEN STKS — 1m 3f 214y
5:00 (5:01) (D3) 3-Y-0 £3,454 (£1,063; £531; £265) Stalls Low

Form — RPR
3-5 **1** **Exclusive Danielle**[136] 1619 3-8-9 ........ ACulhane 6 73
(BWHills) *mde all: jnd 2f out: styd on wl u.p* **8/1**[3]
-230 **2** ½ **Magnetic Pole**[52] 3953 3-9-0 83 ........ RWinston 3 78
(SirMichaelStoute) *trckd wnr: disp ld 2f out: sn drvn along: no ex u.p fnl f* **4/9**[1]
2204 **3** 1 **Ganymede**[31] 4554 3-9-0 75 ........ RMullen 1 76
(MLWBell) *trckd ldrs: effrt 3f out: sn drvn along: styd on: no imp on first 2* **3/1**[2]
4 **4** 16 **Chestall**[82] 3013 3-8-7 ........ RKennemore(7) 4 50
(RHollinshead) *in tch: hung rt bnd after 4f: wknd 3f out: t.o* **50/1**
00 **5** 12 **Sweet At Heart (IRE)**[8] 5196 3-8-9 ........ NCallan 5 26
(PABlockley) *rr of main gp but in tch: drvn along over 4f out: wkng whn hmpd 3f out: t.o* **80/1**
00-0 **6** dist **Taili**[101] 2487 3-8-9 30 ........ JMcAuley 2 —
(DANolan) *slowly away: rr: drvn along after 4f: sn lost tch: wl t.o* **150/1**

2m 38.5s (-0.50) **Going Correction** -0.075s/f (Good) — 6 Ran SP% **109.2**
Speed ratings: **98,97,86,78** —CSF £11.70 TOTE £5.60: £5.40, £1.02; EX 12.60 Place 6 £5.29, Place 5 £4.32.
**Owner** John C Grant **Bred** Sir Eric Parker **Trained** Lambourn, Berks
■ Stewards Enquiry : R Kennemore one-day ban: careless riding (Sep 18)

**FOCUS**
Little strength in depth and the form looks just modest and not that sound.

**NOTEBOOK**
**Exclusive Danielle** relished this faster ground and proved game in holding off the runner-up late on to score. Although she had very much the run of the race this time, her future lies in handicaps and she has the scope to progress.
**Magnetic Pole** failed to improve as expected for this better ground and disappointed. Connections will be hoping that dropping in trip will bring about some improvement, but he was very one-paced this time and looks lazy, so headgear is an option.
**Ganymede** was never a danger to the first two and again looked a tricky ride. He remains winless after ten outings.
T/Plt: £5.70 to a £1 stake. Pool: £32,840.75. 4,199.80 winning tickets. T/Qpdt: £2.90 to a £1 stake. Pool: £2,178.70. 546.50 winning tickets. JF

# [4567] LEICESTER (R-H)
Tuesday, September 7

**OFFICIAL GOING: Good to firm (good in places)**
Wind: breezy, hlf against Weather: sunny

## 5368 EUROPEAN BREEDERS FUND FILBERT MAIDEN FILLIES' STKS — 1m 9y
2:10 (2:11) (D2) 2-Y-0 £5,681 (£1,748; £874; £437) Stalls High

Form — RPR
2 **1** **Dash To The Top**[20] 4851 2-8-11 ........ DHolland 2 79+
(LMCumani) *a in tch: tk clsr order 1/2-way: rdn over 2f out: led over 1f out: r.o wl* **15/8**[2]
04 **2** ½ **Bazelle**[61] 3664 2-8-11 ........ JFEgan 13 78
(PWD'Arcy) *a.p: rdn to press wnr fnl f: hld nr fin* **33/1**
2 **3** 3 **Celtique**[11] 5088 2-8-11 ........ KFallon 7 71
(SirMichaelStoute) *led: edgd lft and hdd over 1f out: wknd ins fnl f* **5/4**[1]
6 **4** shd **Zayn Zen**[11] 5088 2-8-11 ........ MHills 1 71
(MAJarvis) *trckd ldrs: rdn over 2f out: one pce after* **8/1**[3]
**5** nk **Interim Payment (USA)** 2-8-11 ........ RHughes 5 70
(RCharlton) *broke wl: sn hdd: chsd ldrs tl short of room over 1f out: one pce after* **20/1**



The Form Book, Raceform Ltd, Compton, RG20 6NL

6 3 1/2 **Higher Love (IRE)** 2-8-11 ........ MartinDwyer 12 63
(MLWBell) *in tch tl rdn and wknd over 1f out* 20/1

00 7 1 **Kristalchen**[20] 4851 2-8-11 ........ JFanning 3 60
(JGGiven) *bhd: nvr on terms* 66/1

00 8 1/2 **Hallowed Dream (IRE)**[11] 5088 2-8-11 ........ WSupple 9 59
(CEBrittain) *plld hrd: prom tl wknd over 1f out* 100/1

0 9 2 1/2 **Alula**[25] 4712 2-8-11 ........ PDobbs 4 54
(RHannon) *a bhd* 50/1

000 10 3/4 **Ifit (IRE)**[8] 5179 2-8-11 ........ TEDurcan 6 52
(MRChannon) *a bhd* 66/1

11 1/2 **Released (USA)** 2-8-11 ........ LDettori 11 51
(JHMGosden) *slowly away: a bhd* 16/1

05 12 nk **Kolyma (IRE)**[25] 4706 2-8-11 ........ IMongan 8 50
(JLDunlop) *a bhd* 66/1

0 13 shd **Legend Of Dance**[25] 4705 2-8-8 ........ JFMcDonald(3) 10 50
(BJMeehan) *wnt rt s: sn bhd* 66/1

1m 41.9s (-0.70) **Going Correction** -0.35s/f (Firm) **13** Ran SP% **117.6**
Speed ratings: **89,88,85,85,85 81,80,80,77,76 76,76,75**CSF £71.68 TOTE £3.50: £1.10, £8.40, £1.20; EX 49.30.
**Owner** Helena Springfield Ltd **Bred** Meon Valley Stud **Trained** Newmarket, Suffolk

**FOCUS**
A decent maiden that is certain to produce winners, although the time was only modest.

**NOTEBOOK**
**Dash To The Top**, a real eyecatcher on her debut when coming from a mile back to claim second, confirmed the promise of that effort with a hard-fought success. Entered in the Fillies' Mile, she will need to improve to play any part in that race, but is bred to appreciate a little cut in the ground and will relish the stiff finish at the Berkshire venue, so there may be worse outsiders if turning up.
**Bazelle** has run in some decent maidens and is going the right way, this being her best effort to date. Now qualified for nurseries, she should have little trouble winning in the near future.
**Celtique** was well supported in the ring and evidently expected to go one place better than when second on her debut. She led for most of the way but found disappointingly little and folded in the final furlong. She now has something to prove.
**Zayn Zen**, not knocked about when shaping with promise on her debut at Newmarket, was keeping on well again at the line having got outpaced when it mattered and should improve again for the experience. She will be winning before long.
**Interim Payment(USA)** kept on under tender handling and will improve considerably for the outing. Her stable do well with their juveniles and she is one to watch out for on soft ground.
**Higher Love(IRE)**, a 300,000 gns purchase, is held in high regard and shaped as though very much in need of softer ground and a stiffer test. She will come on for the run and is another worth looking out for toward the backend.

## 5369 GGBET.COM BETTING EXCHANGE (S) NURSERY 7f 9y
2:40 (2:41) (G4) (0-65,63) 2-Y-0 £3,038 (£868; £434) Stalls Low

Form RPR

0330 1 **Amphitheatre (IRE)**[19] 4878 2-9-6 62 ........ LDettori 8 65
(RFJohnsonHoughton) *in tch: rdn over 2f out: hdwy over 1f out: led ins fnl f: r.o* 9/2[1]

0004 2 1 **Herencia (IRE)**[11] 5097 2-8-10 52 ........ (p) IMongan 15 52
(PABlockley) *bhd: rdn 1/2-way: hdwy over 2f out: r.o u.p ins fnl f: nt rch wnr* 12/1

6060 3 shd **Lorna Dune**[19] 4878 2-9-4 60 ........ KFallon 13 60
(MrsJRRamsden) *in tch: rdn and nt qckn 1/2-way: hdwy over 1f out: r.o and hmpd cl home: fin 4th: promoted to 3rd* 9/2[1]

0020 4 nk **Debs Broughton**[29] 4612 2-9-0 56 ........ RHughes 10 55
(WJMusson) *prom: rdn to ld 2f out: hdd ins fnl f: no ex and edgd rt cl home: fin 3rd: disqualified and plcd 4th* 11/1[3]

025 5 1/2 **Slite**[10] 5132 2-8-12 54 ........ MartinDwyer 1 52
(RJHodges) *dwlt: bhd: rdn 1/2-way: hdwy whn nt clr run over 1f out: r.o ins fnl f: nrst fin* 20/1

5654 6 hd **Artadi**[6] 5218 2-8-8 50 ........ (b) CCatlin 19 47
(PMPhelan) *a.p: rdn over 2f out: styd on same pce fnl f* 14/1

2020 7 shd **Dan's Heir**[19] 4878 2-9-2 58 ........ (p) GFaulkner 16 55
(PCHaslam) *in tch: rdn over 2f out: kpt on same pce fnl f* 16/1

3604 8 hd **Orpen Annie (IRE)**[32] 4521 2-9-0 59 ........ BReilly(3) 2 56
(MissJFeilden) *in tch: hdwy 1/2-way: rdn and ev ch over 2f out: no ex ins fnl f* 14/1

2010 9 1 1/4 **Jay (IRE)**[5] 5240 2-9-4 60 ........ DHolland 7 53
(NACallaghan) *s.s: bhd: rdn over 4f out: hdwy over 2f out: one pce fnl f* 14/1

4360 10 3/4 **Tonight (IRE)**[11] 5083 2-8-10 57 ........ (b[1]) BSwarbrick(5) 4 49
(WMBrisbourne) *stmbld s: towards rr: rdn 1/2-way: kpt on fnl f: nvr nrr* 40/1

3052 11 2 1/2 **Procrastinate (IRE)**[50] 3980 2-8-12 54 ........ JFEgan 17 39
(RFFisher) *prom: rdn and ev ch over 2f out: wknd 1f out* 14/1

1040 12 3/4 **Mytton's Dream**[34] 4445 2-8-9 58 ........ AMullen(7) 14 41
(ABailey) *midfield: rdn over 2f out: nvr on terms w ldrs* 8/1[2]

0326 13 3/4 **His Majesty**[14] 5022 2-8-11 60 ........ StevenHarrison(7) 3 42
(NPLittmoden) *cl up: rdn 1/2-way: sn wknd* 25/1

0052 14 shd **Chicago Nights (IRE)**[14] 5022 2-8-5 52 ........ (p) RoryMoore(5) 5 33
(PCHaslam) *led: rdn and hdd 2f out: wknd over 1f out* 12/1

0600 15 nk **Sherbourne**[11] 5088 2-8-5 47 ........ PaulEddery 6 28
(MGQuinlan) *hld up: swtchd rt and effrt 1/2-way: eased whn no imp fnl f* 33/1

0040 16 1/2 **Lord Normacote**[11] 5090 2-9-7 63 ........ RHavlin 9 42
(CADwyer) *midfield: rdn 1/2-way: sn bhd* 20/1

0000 17 2 1/2 **Belton**[11] 5083 2-8-13 55 ........ SRighton 18 28
(RonaldThompson) *s.s: bhd: hdwy 1/2-way: rdn over 2f out: wknd over 1f out* 40/1

3500 18 4 **Be Bop Aloha**[30] 4584 2-8-12 57 ........ LEnstone(3) 11 20
(IAWood) *midfield: rdn 1/2-way: nt clr run over 2f out: sn wknd* 25/1

6150 19 1 3/4 **Sapphire Princess**[22] 4816 2-8-5 47 ........ PDoe 12 6
(IAWood) *in tch: rdn 3f out: sn n.m.r and lost pl: bhd after* 33/1

006 20 14 **Ugly Sister (USA)**[13] 5034 2-8-10 52 ........ TEDurcan 20 —
(GCBravery) *a bhd* 33/1

1m 27.89s (1.79) **Going Correction** 0.0s/f (Good) **20** Ran SP% **134.7**
Speed ratings: **89,87,87,87,86 86,86,86,84,83 81,80,79,79,78 78,75,70,68,52**CSF £278.17 CT £8.00 TOTE £1.70: £4.70, £1.80, £2.80, £; EX106.20 1.The winner was sold for 7,000gns to Claus Bjorling. Lorna Dune was claimed for £6,000 by J G M O'Shea. Slite was claim
**Owner** R F Johnson Houghton **Bred** B Ryan **Trained** Blewbury, Oxon

**FOCUS**
A weak nursery and they were well bunched up at the line. The third and fourth had their placings reversed.

**NOTEBOOK**
**Amphitheatre(IRE)** was getting off the mark at the eighth attempt. Beaten in similar company two runs back, he was racing here off a 4lb lower mark and proved good enough in what was a moderate affair.
**Herencia(IRE)** is going the right way and is up to winning off a mark in the mid-fifties.
**Lorna Dune**, dropping into this company for the first time, ran a fair race - being rewarded rewarded third having been interfered with - and should be up to winning a similar heat.
**Debs Broughton** seems at home in this grade and will win one if holding her form. She was demoted a place having hampered the chance of Lorna Dune.
**Slite** looked a real danger at one point but did not pick up as expected having been a little short of room. Although she was going on at the end, there was not much left in the tank and a return to six furlongs will be in her favour.
**Jay(IRE)** did her chances no good with a slow start and was always struggling to catch up.

## 5370 TERRY O'FARRELL MEMORIAL H'CAP 7f 9y
3:10 (3:14) (E3) (0-70,69) 3-Y-0+ £3,842 (£1,182; £591; £295) Stalls Low

Form RPR

0300 1 **Torquemada (IRE)**[26] 4687 3-8-4 55 ........ PDoe 15 71
(WJarvis) *mid-div: hdwy 2f out: led ent fnl f: r.o wl* 33/1

5503 2 1/2 **Welcome Signal**[14] 5020 4-9-2 63 ........ (p) LDettori 11 78
(JRFanshawe) *slowly away: hld up in rr: hdwy over 1f out to chse wnr fnl f: fin wl* 4/1[1]

0066 3 2 **Mount Vettore**[31] 4558 3-9-2 67 ........ KFallon 14 76
(MrsJRRamsden) *s.i.s: rdn and hdwy over 2f out: kpt on fnl f* 4/1[1]

0000 4 3 **Ticero**[55] 3849 3-9-0 65 ........ (b) TEDurcan 6 66
(CEBrittain) *in rr: hdwy whn short of room over 2f out: styd on fnl f* 50/1

3520 5 3/4 **Bob's Buzz**[2] 5316 4-9-7 68 ........ DHolland 10 67
(SCWilliams) *mde most tl hdd 3f out: rdn and wknd fnl f* 6/1[2]

0006 6 1 1/4 **Blythe Spirit**[40] 4280 5-9-0 64 ........ (p) THamilton(3) 8 60
(RAFahey) *a.p: led 3f out: hdd ent fnl f: wknd* 8/1[3]

6620 7 nk **Morag**[14] 5020 3-8-6 60 ........ LEnstone(3) 16 55
(IAWood) *chsd ldrs tl wknd appr fnl f* 25/1

-600 8 1/2 **Raheed (IRE)**[105] 2390 3-8-8 62 ........ HayleyTurner(3) 12 56
(MrsCADunnett) *chsd ldrs tl wknd wl over 1f out* 100/1

4150 9 1 **Showtime Annie**[12] 5063 3-8-10 61 ........ JFanning 19 52
(ABailey) *towards rr: sme late hdwy: nvr on terms* 33/1

1512 10 shd **Blaeberry**[30] 4574 3-9-0 65 ........ (b) JFEgan 7 56
(PLGilligan) *mid-div: short of room over 2f out: n.d after* 12/1

5100 11 1 1/4 **Carte Noire**[64] 3589 3-8-3 57 ........ JFMcDonald(3) 20 44
(JGPortman) *in tch: rdn 1/2-way: wknd over 2f out* 100/1

0345 12 hd **Fools Entire**[9] 5156 3-8-4 58 ........ (e) BReilly(3) 17 45
(JAGilbert) *prom on outside tl wknd over 1f out* 33/1

1423 13 shd **Joshua's Gold (IRE)**[5] 5235 3-8-7 58 ........ (v) WSupple 13 44
(DCarroll) *prom tl edgd lft over 2f out: sn wknd* 12/1

2405 14 hd **Elliot's Choice (IRE)**[8] 5193 3-7-12 56 ........ (b) AMullen(7) 5 42
(DCarroll) *a towards rr* 20/1

0330 15 1/2 **Scarlett Rose**[9] 5148 3-8-13 64 ........ IMongan 1 49
(DrJDScargill) *prom: rdn 1/2-way: sn bhd* 14/1

6113 16 nk **Danifah (IRE)**[6] 5219 3-8-8 62 ........ FPFerris(3) 4 46
(PDEvans) *w ldr for 3f: rdn and sn wknd* 10/1

0-00 16 dht **Five Gold (IRE)**[87] 2880 3-8-11 62 ........ MartinDwyer 2 46
(BRMillman) *in tch tl wknd over 2f out* 50/1

0121 18 3/4 **Kings Rock**[9] 5141 3-8-10 61 6ex ........ (b) RHughes 9 43
(MrsLucindaFeatherstone) *a bhd* 14/1

0000 19 25 **Senior Minister**[4] 5259 6-8-10 60 ........ RMiles(3) 18 —
(PWHiatt) *slowly away: racd alone far side in tch for over 4f: sn wknd and eased* 50/1

1m 26.07s (-0.03) **Going Correction** 0.0s/f (Good)
**WFA** 3 from 4yo+ 4lb **19** Ran SP% **128.5**
Speed ratings: **100,99,97,93,92 91,91,90,89,89 87,87,87,87,86 86,86,85,56**CSF £158.81 CT £679.04 TOTE £59.00: £9.60, £1.40, £1.90, £16.70; EX 204.80.
**Owner** Canisbay Bloodstock **Bred** Oak Lodge Stud/hamford Stud/lileagh Fox **Trained** Newmarket, Suffolk

**FOCUS**
Not the strongest of handicaps and ordinary form, but it should still produce winner at a similar level.

**NOTEBOOK**
**Torquemada(IRE)**, 13lb lower than when he started out his handicap career back in April, was finally getting off the mark causing an upset in the process. His sole start over seven furlongs prior to today had been one of his better efforts and he was well suited by reverting to it. Now he has found his best trip, he should go on from this.
**Welcome Signal** has been tried at up to a mile two, but this seems to be more his trip and he may be even better suited by the return to a mile.
**Mount Vettore** has not gone on from his early-season efforts, but things have looked better the last twice and he looks ready for the return to a mile.
**Ticero** , beaten a total of over 114 lengths in his four starts as a three-year-old prior to today, found the blinkers working much better second time round and gave by far and away his best effort to date. If going on from this he can win a low-grade affair.
**Bob's Buzz** has been in and out this season and this was definitely an out day. He failed to respond once asked to go again and is one to leave alone for the moment until showing more.
**Blythe Spirit** has been, as of yet, unable to add his name to the long list of winners the stable have sent out in recent months, but he is on his lowest-ever mark and is sure to be found a winning opportunity in the coming weeks.
**Blaeberry** *Official explanation: jockey said filly suffered interference*
**Kings Rock** *Official explanation: trainer said gelding was unsuited by the good to firm ground*

## 5371 ZURICH RISK SERVICES MAIDEN STKS 1m 1f 218y
3:40 (3:41) (D3) 3-Y-0+ £4,358 (£1,341; £670; £335) Stalls High

Form RPR

00 1 **One So Marvellous**[20] 4850 3-8-9 ........ DHolland 3 84
(LMCumani) *in tch: rdn and hdwy over 2f out: wnt 2nd over 1f out: r.o to ld cl home* 6/1

-333 2 nk **Flamboyant Lad**[20] 4850 3-9-0 79 ........ MHills 11 88
(BWHills) *trckd ldr: led over 2f out: rdn over 1f out: hdd and no ex cl home* 6/4[1]

24- 3 12 **Kabis Booie (IRE)**[316] 5798 3-9-0 ........ PaulEddery 9 66
(HRACecil) *in tch: trckd ldrs over 5f out: rdn over 2f out: wknd over 1f out* 10/1

0040 4 1/2 **Flame Queen**[9] 5156 3-8-6 64 ........ HayleyTurner(3) 10 61
(MrsCADunnett) *led: rdn and hdd over 2f out: sn btn* 18/1

3-05 5 5 **Timber Ice (USA)**[22] 4819 4-9-2 65 ........ WRyan 2 52
(HRACecil) *prom: rdn over 2f out: wknd over 1f out* 5/1[2]

4 6 hd **Bijou Dan**[53] 3899 3-8-11 ........ TEaves(3) 7 56
(ISemple) *midfield: n.m.r and lost pl over 6f out: no imp after* 16/1

000 7 3 **Surface To Air**[50] 3994 3-9-0 ........ RHavlin 8 51
(MrsPNDutfield) *towards rr: midfield over 5f out: rdn and wknd over 3f out* 50/1

8 2 1/2 **Wyvern (GER)** 3-9-0 ........ RHughes 5 46
(WJHaggas) *trckd ldrs: rdn 3f out: wknd over 2f out* 11/2[3]

00 9 16 **Cugina Nicola**[33] 4492 3-8-4 ........ RThomas(5) 13 12
(GBBalding) *a bhd* 50/1

0 **10** *7* **Abigail Adams**[17] 4954 3-8-9 .......... MartinDwyer 4 —
(PWHarris) *midfield tl wknd over 4f out* **20/1**
**11** *13* **Up The Aisle** 7-9-4 .......... LEnstone(3) 1 —
(MMullineaux) *s.i.s: a bhd* **100/1**
0-0 **12** *4* **Lady Lucinda**[9] 5146 3-8-9 .......... IMongan 12 —
(JohnAHarris) *a bhd* **100/1**
00 **13** *23* **Gentle Warning**[9] 5146 4-9-2 ..........(b[1]) SRighton 6 —
(MAppleby) *s.i.s: racd keenly: rdn over 4f out: a bhd* **150/1**

2m 5.08s (-3.32) **Going Correction** -0.35s/f (Firm)
**WFA** 3 from 4yo+ 7lb **13** Ran SP% **117.9**
Speed ratings: **99,98,89,88,84 84,82,80,67,61 51,48,29**CSF £14.75 TOTE £5.90: £2.00, £1.02, £3.40; EX 20.20.
**Owner** Helena Springfield Ltd **Bred** Meon Valley Stud **Trained** Newmarket, Suffolk

**FOCUS**
A poor maiden and the front two pulled clear of the third. The time was modest.

**NOTEBOOK**
**One So Marvellous**, virtually pulled up when losing her action most recently, got off the mark in what was a weak maiden at the third attempt under an all-out ride from Holland. She looked set to have to settle for second deep in the final furlong, but really picked up late on and got there in time. A beautifully bred filly - full-sister to the high-class performer One So Wondeful - the win is all connections were after and this would have enhanced her value as a broodmare. If racing again she is likely to struggle in handicaps.
**Flamboyant Lad** can count himself an unfortunate second as he looked to have done enough and was nabbed in the dying strides. To make things worse he pulled 12 lengths clear of the third, but his stable is back in good form and he will no doubt find a race somewhere.
**Kabis Booie(IRE)** is a very modest performer and his best hope is a switch to handicaps.
**Flame Queen** did not appear to get the trip and is another for whom a return to handicaps will help.
**Timber Ice(USA)**, the second Cecil runner, showed little and will struggle to win a race.
**Wyvern(GER)** is evidently a horse of modest ability but he should be given a chance to improve on this debut.
**Abigail Adams** again showed little and needs to improve if she is going to be winning races.

## 5372 MANMATTERS.CO.UK CONDITIONS STKS — 5f 2y
**4:10** (4:11) (C2) 3-Y-0+ **£6,165** (£2,338; £1,169; £531) **Stalls** Low

Form RPR
4304 **1** **Dragon Flyer (IRE)**[22] 4805 5-8-3 93 ow1 .......... JFEgan 6 103
(MQuinn) *a.p: strly rdn to nose ahd wl ins fnl f: all out* **10/1**
2020 **2** *nk* **Talbot Avenue**[19] 4886 6-8-7 99 .......... KFallon 4 106
(MMullineaux) *a.p: led 1/2-way: hrd rdn and hdd wl ins fnl f: kpt on* **11/4**[1]
1300 **3** *3 1/2* **Magic Glade**[88] 2859 5-8-7 86 ow3 .......... DNolan(3) 8 95
(RBrotherton) *a in front rnk: rdn and outpcd by first 2 appr fnl f* **66/1**
2006 **4** *nk* **Hidden Dragon (USA)**[24] 4759 5-8-4 94 .......... HayleyTurner(3) 12 91
(PABlockley) *in tch: edgd lft 2f out: r.o fnl f* **12/1**
3010 **5** *nk* **Continent**[10] 5105 7-9-4 107 .......... DHolland 2 101
(DNicholls) *s.i.s: in rr tl rdn and hdwy 2f out: r.o fnl f: nvr nrr* **3/1**[2]
4006 **6** *2 1/2* **Fromsong (IRE)**[59] 3723 6-8-7 95 .......... IMongan 10 80
(BRMillman) *prom rdn and wknd over 1f out* **16/1**
1-06 **7** *3/4* **Russian Valour (IRE)**[132] 1706 3-8-12 108 ..........(b[1]) JFanning 11 83
(MJohnston) *slowly away: a struggling in rr* **14/1**
0460 **8** *2* **Speed Cop**[8] 5181 4-8-2 94 ..........(v) MartinDwyer 3 64
(AMBalding) *prom tl rdn and wknd wl over 1f out* **4/1**[3]
6000 **9** *1 3/4* **Absent Friends**[3] 5287 7-8-7 86 .......... JEdmunds 1 62
(JBalding) *led to half way: wknd over 1f out* **20/1**
0040 **10** *1* **Boleyn Castle (USA)**[29] 4614 7-8-4 86 .......... FPFerris(3) 5 58
(PSMcentee) *a towards rr and nvr on terms* **40/1**
21- **11** *3 1/2* **Efistorm**[121] 3-9-3 88 .......... LDettori 9 55
(MGQuinlan) *in tch to 1/2-way: sn bhd* **20/1**
/64- **12** *2* **Forest Rail (IRE)**[565] 581 4-7-13 .......... JFMcDonald(3) 7 31
(JohnAHarris) *a bhd and nvr gng pce* **200/1**

59.58 secs (-1.35) **Going Correction** 0.0s/f (Good)
**WFA** 3 from 4yo+ 1lb **12** Ran SP% **115.0**
Speed ratings: **110,109,103,103,102 98,97,94,91,90 84,81**CSF £34.95 TOTE £12.60: £2.50, £1.60, £18.80; EX 35.10.
**Owner** Marchwood Aggregates **Bred** Miss Dara Ni Choileain **Trained** Sparsholt, Oxon

**FOCUS**
A fair event that saw the tough Dragon Flyer score a well-deserved success and the form appears surprisingly solid for a race of its type.

**NOTEBOOK**
**Dragon Flyer(IRE)** was scoring a well-deserved success having run so many good races in the past two seasons without winning. To the fore throughout, she drew alongside Talbot Avenue before sticking her head out and holding on well. This type of race will always provide her with her best chance of success as she always just falls short at Listed and Group level.
**Talbot Avenue** is a similar story to the winner in that he has run many good races in defeat in the past season or so and he was again touched off. His turn will come again one day.
**Magic Glade** was only rated 7lb inferior to the winner and was sent off at over-priced odds of 66/1. Always on the pace, he could not go with the front pair in the final furlong but held on for third. This was his first run for connections and first outing since June -he had broken blood-vessels - and although he may bounce next time - a common thing with sprinters - there is a decent race in him with something like the Ayr Gold Cup appealing as a possible target.
**Hidden Dragon(USA)** is being aimed at the Ayr Gold Cup and shaped well enough considering the distance.
**Continent** needs soft ground to be at his best and could not confirm Nottingham form with the winner.
**Russian Valour(IRE)**, an excellent sprinting juvenile, has not come back to the form of last year since being injured and had been given a break since his last dismal outing in the hope he would return in a different frame of mind. The blinkers were applied to try to spike some life back into him but, having been slow to break, he showed none of his old dash and could only keep on at the one pace, being well held. He may be worth one last chance.
**Speed Cop** is going the wrong way and again ran awfully.
**Efistorm** *Official explanation: trainer said colt was unsuited by the good to firm ground*

## 5373 EBF RACECOURSE VIDEO SERVICES MAIDEN STKS — 7f 9y
**4:40** (4:41) (D2) 2-Y-0 **£5,811** (£1,788; £894; £447) **Stalls** Low

Form RPR
5 **1** **Santa Fe (IRE)**[33] 4494 2-9-0 .......... KFallon 3 90+
(SirMichaelStoute) *in tch: rdn and hdwy over 1f out: led ins fnl f: r.o: in command towards fin* **7/1**[3]
3 **2** *hd* **Silent Jo (JPN)**[39] 4290 2-9-0 .......... LDettori 4 87
(SaeedBinSuroor) *cl up: rdn to ld 1f out: sn hdd: hld towards fin* **4/5**[1]
244 **3** *1 1/4* **Arbella**[31] 4552 2-8-9 98 .......... DHolland 17 79
(PWHarris) *in tch: hdwy over 2f out: sn rdn: ev ch ins fnl f: nt qckn towards fin* **85/40**[2]
35 **4** *2* **L'Escapade (IRE)**[19] 4872 2-9-0 .......... MartinDwyer 7 79
(AMBalding) *led: hdd 3f out: n.m.r 1f out: styd on same pce ins fnl f* **16/1**
**5** *1* **Art Royal (USA)** 2-9-0 .......... JFanning 6 77
(MrsAJPerrett) *prom: led over 2f out: rdn and hdd 1f out: no ex ins fnl f* **40/1**
00 **6** *1 1/4* **Perez (IRE)**[10] 5118 2-9-0 .......... PDobbs 13 73
(RHannon) *cl up: led 3f out: rdn and hdd over 2f out: stl ev ch over 1f out: wknd wl ins fnl f* **100/1**
40 **7** *1/2* **Heartsonfire (IRE)**[22] 4804 2-8-9 .......... PaulEddery 8 67
(PWD'Arcy) *racd keenly: hld up: hdwy over 1f out: nvr trbld ldrs* **150/1**
0 **8** *1/2* **Secret Affair**[12] 5054 2-9-0 .......... JDSmith 11 71
(AKing) *midfield: rdn over 1f out: nvr trbld ldrs* **100/1**
**9** *1/2* **Wester Lodge (IRE)** 2-9-0 .......... JTate 1 70
(JMPEustace) *bhd: pushed along over 2f out: kpt on fnl f: nvr able to chal* **100/1**
**10** *6* **Gingiefly** 2-9-0 .......... IMongan 9 55
(JLDunlop) *s.s: midfield: rdn 2f out: wknd over 1f out* **100/1**
30 **11** *2 1/2* **Road To Heaven (USA)**[48] 4030 2-9-0 .......... WRyan 5 48
(EALDunlop) *dwlt: bhd: effrt over 2f out: no imp: wknd fnl f* **33/1**
000 **12** *nk* **Liquid Lover (IRE)**[52] 3931 2-9-0 .......... RSmith 15 48
(RHannon) *in tch: rdn 3f out: sn wknd* **100/1**
**13** *1 1/4* **Red Apache (IRE)** 2-9-0 .......... JFEgan 14 45
(HJCollingridge) *bmpd s: hld up: pushed along over 2f out: wl btn over 1f out* **100/1**
**14** *shd* **Optimum (IRE)** 2-9-0 .......... RHughes 12 44
(DRLoder) *prom tl rdn and wknd 2f out* **25/1**
**15** *6* **City Trader** 2-9-0 .......... TEDurcan 10 29
(CEBrittain) *dwlt: a bhd* **100/1**

1m 26.37s (0.27) **Going Correction** 0.0s/f (Good) **15** Ran SP% **122.8**
Speed ratings: **98,97,96,94,92 91,90,90,89,82 80,79,78,78,71**CSF £12.96 TOTE £7.90: £2.10, £1.10, £1.40; EX 20.90.
**Owner** The Celle Syndicate Incorporated **Bred** Darley **Trained** Newmarket, Suffolk

**FOCUS**
A race that is hard to evaluate, although probably not much strength in depth for this maiden, only three of the 15 runners started less than 16/1 and they filled the first three paces. The time was only fair for the grade, but there were still one or two eye-catching performances.

**NOTEBOOK**
**Santa Fe(IRE)** ◆ confirmed the promise of his Yarmouth debut and appreciated the extra furlong. Despite having the stands' rail to help him, he still ran a little green yet managed to win with a bit in hand, as he only needed to be nudged out under hands-and-heels riding towards the end. There is almost certainly a lot more to come from him.
**Silent Jo(JPN)** was well supported to confirm the promise of his Goodwood debut, but found one too good and there seemed to be no excuses, though his pedigree does suggest he will do better over further in time.
**Arbella**, stepping down from Group company, had every chance but could not match the front pair in the closing stages. This was still a fair effort against the colts and she should be able to find a race back against her own sex before long.
**L'Escapade(IRE)** was given a positive ride and the way he stayed on again after getting outpaced suggests he need further than this. He could be an interesting sort for a mile nursery. *Official explanation: jockey said colt hung left in the closing stages*
**Art Royal(USA)** ◆, a 64,000euros colt out of a dual winner in the US, shaped with promise under a positive ride and did best of the newcomers. He can be expected to improve.
**Perez(IRE)** ran a bit better than in his two previous starts over this extra furlong on a sounder surface.

## 5374 FREE BETS @ GG.COM APPRENTICE H'CAP — 1m 1f 218y
**5:10** (5:11) (E3) (0-70,70) 3-Y-0+ **£4,256** (£1,309; £654; £327) **Stalls** High

Form RPR
-060 **1** **Smoothie (IRE)**[16] 4971 6-8-9 58 ..........(p) LEnstone 16 66
(IanWilliams) *hld up in rr: hdwy over 2f out: rdn to ld post* **22/1**
5440 **2** *shd* **Rani Two**[8] 5183 5-9-5 68 .......... NChalmers 1 76
(WRMuir) *hld up: hdwy over 3f out: rdn to ld wl ins fnl f: hdd post* **20/1**
5511 **3** *1/2* **Bramantino (IRE)**[6] 5229 4-8-9 58 6ex ..........(b) THamilton 8 65
(RAFahey) *hld up: hdwy over 3f out: led over 1f out: hdd wl ins fnl f: one pce* **11/4**[1]
422 **4** *nk* **Carrowdore (IRE)**[32] 4518 4-9-4 70 ..........(p) DTudhope(3) 5 76+
(GAHuffer) *a.p: short of room and swtchd lft over 1f out: again short of room ins fnl f: r.o wl cl home* **7/1**[2]
1004 **5** *1 1/2* **Kernel Dowery (IRE)**[13] 5038 4-8-8 62 ..........(e) MCoumbe(5) 6 66
(PWHarris) *trckd ldr: rdn and ev ch 2f out: edgd lft appr fnl f: wknd ins* **20/1**
5001 **6** *3* **Snowed Under**[10] 5110 3-8-0 61 ow3 .......... JCavanagh(5) 7 59
(JDBethell) *trckd ldrs: rdn and wknd appr fnl f* **25/1**
0031 **7** *nk* **Bluegrass Boy**[27] 4641 4-9-0 63 .......... RThomas 10 60
(GBBalding) *slowly away: hld up: rdn and hdwy 3f out: one pce ins fnl 2f* **12/1**
4064 **8** *nk* **Basinet**[10] 4871 6-8-7 56 oh3 .......... PMulrennan 3 53
(JJQuinn) *slowly away: hld up: hdwy over 6f out: rdn over 2f out: wknd over 1f out* **12/1**
0-60 **9** *nk* **Quintoto**[2] 5320 4-9-2 65 .......... DNolan 14 61
(RAFahey) *led: rdn over 3f out: hdd over 1f out: sn wknd* **40/1**
0304 **10** *1* **Jackie Kiely**[8] 5185 3-8-9 65 ..........(t) FPFerris 17 59
(PSMcentee) *bhd tl hdwy over 1f out: nvr on terms* **15/2**[3]
0100 **11** *1 1/4* **Ellovamul**[14] 5019 4-8-7 56 oh5 .......... PMakin 11 48
(WMBrisbourne) *mid-div: rdn over 3f out: no hdwy after* **66/1**
2413 **12** *hd* **Sienna Sunset (IRE)**[9] 5145 5-8-9 58 .......... BSwarbrick 12 50
(WMBrisbourne) *hld up: nt clr run over 2f out: no imp after* **12/1**
-405 **13** *nk* **Bluetoria**[5] 5245 3-8-12 68 .......... JFMcDonald 15 59
(JAGlover) *t.k.h: mid-div whn hmpd and lost pl 1/2-way: n.d after* **10/1**
6300 **14** *nk* **Active Account (USA)**[41] 4240 7-8-7 59 .......... AMullen(3) 9 49
(MrsHDalton) *in tch: rdn over 4f out: sn bhd* **25/1**
204 **15** *2 1/2* **Eton (GER)**[2] 5320 8-8-12 68 .......... PJBenson(7) 2 54
(DNicholls) *prom: rdn whn short of room 3f out: sn wknd* **16/1**
0635 **16** *5* **Infidelity (IRE)**[68] 3443 3-7-8 57 .......... NatalieHassall(7) 13 33
(ABailey) *a bhd* **50/1**
0016 **17** *6* **Arms Acrossthesea**[27] 4655 5-8-11 60 .......... TEaves 4 25
(JBalding) *in tch tl rdn and wknd over 3f out* **25/1**
0001 **18** *7* **Swift Alchemist**[10] 5129 4-8-7 56 ..........(p) DCorby 18 7
(MrsHSweeting) *hld up: a in rr* **12/1**
6000 **19** *12* **Brooklands Lodge (USA)**[32] 4518 3-8-1 62 ow6. StevenHarrison(5) 19 —
(MJAttwater) *s.i.s: sddle slipped 1/2-way: sn lost tch* **100/1**

2m 5.56s (-2.84) **Going Correction** -0.35s/f (Firm)
**WFA** 3 from 4yo+ 7lb **19** Ran SP% **129.0**
Speed ratings: **97,96,96,96,95 92,92,92,91,91 90,90,89,89,87 83,78,73,63**CSF £394.04 CT £1614.33 TOTE £20.00: £4.40, £5.60, £1.40, £1.50; EX 519.20 Place 6 £13.43, Place 5 £10.86.
**Owner** Miss S Howell **Bred** Miss Mary Duckett **Trained** Portway, Warwicks

**FOCUS**
A competitive if low-grade handicap and solid form, but a modest winning time for the grade.

**NOTEBOOK**

**Smoothie(IRE)**, dropping in trip, only had a couple behind him turning in and was a long way off the pace, but he weaved his way through the pack and came with a strong run to get up on the line. He has been given a chance by the Handicapper and he will not incur a penalty for this, so could be interesting if turning out again quickly.
**Rani Two**, another to have dropped to an attractive mark, seemed to have timed her effort just right and was unfortunate to have the race snatched from her. These are her ideal conditions.
**Bramantino(IRE)**, who despite his penalty was off the same mark as when winning an amateur riders' contest at York the previous week, came to win his race a furlong from home but was just worn down. He remains in good form, but faces a further 7lb hike in the handicap from the weekend.
**Carrowdore(IRE)**, never far away, did not have much room in the latter stages and had to be switched in order to get a run. The way he was finishing suggests he would have gone very close with a clear passage, but a glance at his overall record suggests he is the last horse to lump on to gain compensation.
**Kernel Dowery(IRE)** ran with credit on ground that suited, but still looks held off this mark.
**Snowed Under**, raised 6lb for winning a bad race at Beverley, had every chance but found this tougher and the faster ground may not have suited either.
**Basinet** never managed to get competitive and seems to reserve his best for hurdles these days.
**Bluetoria**, out of the first three in four previous starts, nonetheless attracted market support. She got into a bit of trouble midway through the contest and failed to make any impression when switched wide in order to get a run. As suggested by her previous start, this fast ground was probably not ideal and she is worth noting when she can get her toe in. *Official explanation: jockey said he was hampered on the bend*
**Eton(GER)** could not dominate this field and was already dropping away when hampered.
**Brooklands Lodge(USA)** *Official explanation: jockey said saddle slipped*
T/Jkpt: Not won. T/Plt: £9.60 to a £1 stake. Pool: £43,382.35. 3,269.35 winning tickets. T/Qpdt: £5.00 to a £1 stake. Pool: £2,323.60. 339.10 winning tickets. JS

## 5216 LINGFIELD (L-H)

### Tuesday, September 7

**OFFICIAL GOING: Turf course - good to firm; all-weather - standard**

Wind: lt against Weather: sunny; warm

## 5375 EBF SIS SPORTS DATA MAIDEN FILLIES' STKS (DIV I) 7f (P)

**1:50** (1:52) (D3) 2-Y-O **£5,200** (£1,600; £800; £400) **Stalls** Low

Form / RPR

1 **Promoted Deputy (USA)** 2-8-11 ........ KMcEvoy 6 76+
(SaeedBinSuroor) *neat: dwlt: sn in midfield: effrt 2f out: rdn to ld last 100yds: styd on wl* **8/15**[1]

6 2 1 **Improvise**[94] 2690 2-8-11 ........ RHills 10 70+
(CEBrittain) *trckd ldrs: effrt 2f out: rdn to ld ent fnl f: hdd and one pce last 100yds* **10/3**[2]

60 3 2 ½ **All A Dream**[18] 4924 2-8-11 ........ EAhern 4 62
(RGuest) *trckd ldrs: effrt 2f out: rdn and swtchd rt ent fnl f: kpt on one pce* **22/1**

0 4 1 **French School**[47] 4053 2-8-11 ........ SSanders 8 59
(DRLoder) *led: rdn 2f out: hdd & wknd ent fnl f* **16/1**

0 5 2 **Swift Dame (IRE)**[5] 5248 2-8-11 ........ RLMoore 9 54
(RHannon) *chsd ldr after 2f: rdn to chal 2f out: hanging bdly lft over 1f out: wkng whn carried rt ins fnl f* **14/1**[3]

0 6 ¾ **Kindlelight Dream (IRE)**[153] 1299 2-8-11 ........ DaneO'Neill 7 52
(DKIvory) *v reluctant to post: s.s: rchd midfield after 3f: outpcd over 2f out: shuffled along and one pce after* **33/1**

0 7 2 ½ **Rockys Girl**[55] 3840 2-8-11 ........ MHenry 2 46
(MJRyan) *sn pushed along in rr: effrt 3f out: sn outpcd and n.d* **50/1**

8 shd **Joyeaux** 2-8-11 ........ JFortune 5 46
(SLKeightley) *neat: chsd ldr for 2f: outpcd and btn over 2f out* **25/1**

000 9 1 **Coombe Centenary**[16] 4967 2-8-11 ........ JQuinn 1 43
(SDow) *hanging thrght: a in rr: outpcd over 2f out* **66/1**

00 10 15 **Tinker's First**[6] 5218 2-8-4 ........(p) CHaddon(7) 3 6
(WGMTurner) *a in rr: wknd 3f out: t.o* **100/1**

1m 27.14s (1.20) **Going Correction** +0.10s/f (Slow) **10** Ran SP% **116.4**
Speed ratings: **97,95,93,91,89 88,85,85,84,67**CSF £2.20 TOTE £1.40: £1.02, £1.30, £4.90; EX 2.90.
**Owner** Godolphin **Bred** Gaillardia Llc **Trained** Newmarket, Suffolk

**FOCUS**
The winning time was 0.67 seconds faster than the second division, fair enough for the grade, and the winner is likely to prove better than this.

**NOTEBOOK**
**Promoted Deputy(USA)** has an American pedigree, and won this well after missing the break slightly. It is debatable what she beat on the day, but she could not have done it any better.
**Improvise** travelled really well during the race, and made her run at the same time as winner. She was comfortably beaten by the winner, but drew nicely clear of the third and should find a maiden within her reach.
**All A Dream**, having her third outing, ran a most eye-catching race. She was raised in trip by two furlongs, and stayed on nicely behind the first two. The step up in trip seemed to bring about a much improved performance, and she is now qualified for nurseries.
**French School** broke quickly and travelled well in front, only surrendering the lead approaching the last furlong. She did a similar thing on her debut, so a drop in trip looks likely to be needed for her to be competitive at this stage.
**Swift Dame(IRE)** travelled well during the race, but ruined any chance she had by hanging in the last four furlongs. *Official explanation: jockey said filly hung left in the final 4f*
**Joyeaux**, a close coupled filly, travelled well in the race until the pace increased.

## 5376 SIS/AT THE RACES INTERNATIONAL SERVICE EBF MEDIAN AUCTION MAIDEN STKS 6f

**2:20** (2:22) (F4) 2-Y-O **£3,213** (£918; £459) **Stalls** High

Form / RPR

040 1 **Missed A Beat**[48] 4016 2-8-9 62 ........ DSweeney 9 71
(MBlanshard) *racd midfield: prog over 2f out: led jst over 1f out: rdn out* **16/1**

320 2 1 ¼ **Kanad**[86] 2904 2-9-0 77 ........(t) RHills 8 72
(BHanbury) *racd midfield: prog over 2f out: swtchd lft wl over 1f out: ev ch sn after: one pce fnl f* **15/2**[3]

3 shd **Glad Big (GER)** 2-9-0 ........ MFenton 16 72
(JAOsborne) *unf: dwlt: wl in rr: swtchd lft and prog 2f out: styd on fnl f: nvr able to chal* **33/1**

4 2 ½ **Daldini** 2-9-0 ........ SWKelly 3 64
(JAOsborne) *unf: dwlt: wl in rr: swtchd lft and prog 2f out: drvn and kpt on same pce fnl f* **16/1**

5 5 1 ¼ **Beauchamp Turbo**[12] 5053 2-9-0 ........ JPMurtagh 15 60
(GAButler) *lw: led to wl over 2f out: outpcd and btn over 1f out* **7/2**[1]

60 6 nk **Purple Door**[12] 5059 2-8-9 ........ JMackay 13 55
(RMBeckett) *dwlt: wl in rr: shuffled along and styd on steadily fnl 2f: nvr nr ldrs* **33/1**

4 7 1 ¼ **Right To Roam (IRE)**[89] 2817 2-9-0 ........(b[1]) EAhern 14 56
(JARToller) *t.k.h: w ldr: led wl over 2f out to jst over 1f out: wknd* **10/1**

5 8 1 ½ **Wotchalike (IRE)**[32] 4523 2-9-0 ........ NPollard 4 51
(DRCElsworth) *lw: pushed along and wl in rr: plugged on fnl 2f: no ch* **5/1**[2]

9 1 **Pickapeppa** 2-8-9 ........ SCarson 2 43
(RFJohnsonHoughton) *leggy: unf: mounted on crse and taken down early: pressed ldrs tl wknd over 1f out* **33/1**

0 10 ¾ **Over Tipsy**[19] 4866 2-9-0 ........ RLMoore 6 46
(RHannon) *pushed along and wl in rr: n.d* **14/1**

0 11 hd **Attishoe**[15] 5003 2-8-9 ........ SDrowne 12 40
(MissBSanders) *chsd ldrs for 4f: wknd* **12/1**

12 shd **Best Game** 2-9-0 ........ JoannaBadger 7 45
(GAButler) *w'like: b.hind: dwlt: wl in rr: rdn and struggling over 2f out* **50/1**

13 ¾ **Storyville** 2-9-0 ........ SSanders 11 43
(DRLoder) *leggy: w ldng pair to 2f out: sn wknd* **5/1**[2]

030 14 1 **San Deng**[19] 4866 2-9-0 63 ........ KMcEvoy 17 40
(WRMuir) *nvr beyond midfield: wknd 2f out* **25/1**

60 15 1 **Penang Sapphire**[19] 4866 2-9-0 ........ JFortune 10 37
(GAButler) *pressed ldrs to over 2f out: wknd* **33/1**

16 8 **April Shannon** 2-8-2 ........ NataliaGemelova(7) 5 8
(JELong) *unf: a struggling and wl in rr* **100/1**

000 17 7 **Aleshanee**[17] 4936 2-8-9 ........ JQuinn 1 —
(JRBest) *racd wd: nt on terms in midfield: wknd over 2f out: t.o* **50/1**

1m 11.76s (0.11) **Going Correction** -0.15s/f (Firm) **17** Ran SP% **123.1**
Speed ratings: **93,91,91,87,86 85,84,82,80,79 79,79,78,77,75 65,55**CSF £124.06 TOTE £15.40: £4.30, £2.00, £14.70; EX 250.40.
**Owner** The First Timers **Bred** Whitsbury Manor Stud **Trained** Upper Lambourn, Berks

**FOCUS**
A weak looking maiden won by a horse that had already raced three times, so the form is probably modest.

**NOTEBOOK**
**Missed A Beat** did not go unbacked and won quite decisively in the end. She was always niggled in midfield but, when she picked up just over a furlong out, she ran away from her rivals on a strip of ground that produced the first four home.
**Kanad**, returning from a three-month break, raced in a similar position to the winner but did not have her finishing pace. He may be best aimed at a nursery now.
**Glad Big(GER)** was held up in rear until making a mid-race move that took him closer to the centre of the track and cost him valuable ground. This was an encouraging debut and he can progress from it.
**Daldini** missed the break and was switched to the stands side. From there, he ran a similar race to his stablemate, who finished third, and looks a decent type.
**Beauchamp Turbo** broke smartly and grabbed what was thought to be the favoured stands-side rail. He showed up well until the last furlong, where he weakened disappointingly. He should be capable of better than this, as he was well backed.
**Purple Door**, who was beaten in a seller last time, ran on well approaching the last furlong. She will be interesting off a low mark in a nursery.
**Wotchalike(IRE)** was never travelling well here, and made modest late progress.
**Storyville** raced up with pace, but weakened badly approaching the last furlong.
**San Deng** *Official explanation: jockey said colt boiled over before the race and was very keen to post*
**Aleshanee** *Official explanation: jockey said filly ran too free*

## 5377 SIS PRODUCERS OF AT THE RACES NURSERY 7f

**2:50** (2:52) (£3) (0-75,75) 2-Y-O **£3,757** (£1,156; £578; £289) **Stalls** High

Form / RPR

654 1 **Mitraillette (USA)**[25] 4706 2-9-2 73 ........ NMackay(3) 17 79
(SirMichaelStoute) *lw: trckd ldrs: rdn to ld over 1f out: drvn out* **7/1**[1]

644 2 ½ **Watchmyeyes (IRE)**[19] 4866 2-9-2 73 ........ J-PGuillambert(3) 11 78
(NPLittmoden) *cl up: rdn to chal and ev ch 1f out: kpt on but a jst hld* **12/1**

404 3 2 **Seasons Estates**[26] 4682 2-8-8 62 ........ SDrowne 8 62
(BRMillman) *racd midfield: stdy prog 3f out: rdn to chse ldng pair 1f out: sn no imp* **25/1**

005 4 ½ **Rebel Rebel (IRE)**[25] 4728 2-9-0 68 ........ OUrbina 7 74+
(NACallaghan) *s.s: hld up in rr: prog over 2f out: nt clr run over 1f out and again ins fnl f: styd on* **10/1**[3]

0030 5 ½ **Gryskirk**[19] 4878 2-8-10 64 ........ JQuinn 15 62+
(PWD'Arcy) *dwlt: hld up wl in rr: swtchd rt over 1f out: rdn and r.o wl fnl f: nvr nrr* **16/1**

620 6 nk **Shaheer (IRE)**[96] 2609 2-9-5 73 ........ JFortune 18 70
(BJMeehan) *lw: trckd ldrs: rdn and outpcd over 2f out: kpt on again fnl f* **10/1**[3]

4033 7 nk **Ivana Illyich (IRE)**[17] 4953 2-9-5 73 ........ DaneO'Neill 14 69+
(SKirk) *racd midfield: pushed along over 2f out: swtchd lft over 1f out: kpt on: nvr nrr* **14/1**

010 8 hd **Hidden Chance**[11] 5090 2-9-2 70 ........ RLMoore 16 69+
(RHannon) *lw: racd on outer: in tch: effrt 2f out: no imp ldrs 1f out: eased nr fin* **8/1**[2]

1510 9 ¾ **Good Wee Girl (IRE)**[11] 5090 2-9-3 71 ........ JPMurtagh 6 67+
(PSMcentee) *trckd ldrs: pushed along over 2f out: no prog whn hmpd jst over 1f out: eased* **14/1**

636 10 shd **Fasylitator (IRE)**[14] 5015 2-9-4 72 ........ SWKelly 2 65
(JAOsborne) *lw: led and crossed fr outside draw: hdd & wknd over 1f out* **11/1**

2525 11 ¾ **Chutney Mary (IRE)**[18] 4914 2-9-2 70 ........ EAhern 5 62
(JGPortman) *lw: pressed ldr to wl over 1f out: wknd* **25/1**

6450 12 1 **Mulberry Wine**[18] 4914 2-9-4 72 ........ DSweeney 9 61
(MBlanshard) *prom tl wknd 2f out* **50/1**

2506 13 hd **Arthur Wardle (USA)**[41] 4235 2-9-2 70 ........(v[1]) JMackay 19 59
(MLWBell) *settled wl in rr: shuffled along and no real prog fr over 2f out* **16/1**

0306 14 ½ **High Chart**[29] 4612 2-9-5 73 ........ AMcCarthy 12 60
(GGMargarson) *chsd ldrs: rdn over 2f out: fdd wl over 1f out* **33/1**

005 15 hd **Danger Zone**[26] 4681 2-9-2 70 ........ SSanders 3 57
(MrsAJPerrett) *lw: pressed ldrs tl wknd over 1f out* **14/1**

5130 16 1 **He's A Diamond**[37] 4365 2-9-7 75 ........ GCarter 20 59
(TGMills) *dwlt: hld up wl in rr: no prog whn sltly hmpd over 1f out* **12/1**

6060 17 2 ½ **Imperial Miss (IRE)**[41] 4234 2-8-12 66 ........ ADaly 10 44
(BWDuke) *nvr beyond midfield: u.p and wknd 2f out* **100/1**

040 18 1 ¾ **Makepeace (IRE)**[17] 4930 2-8-9 66 ........ SHitchcott(3) 4 40
(MRChannon) *dwlt: wl in rr: struggling whn swtchd lft 2f out: wknd* **33/1**

056 19 5 **Three Aces (IRE)**[50] 3986 2-8-11 65 ........(b[1]) KMcEvoy 1 26
(RMBeckett) *taken down early: s.s: a bhd* **50/1**

224 **20** 2 ½ **Extra Mark**[96] [2627] 2-9-7 **75** NPollard 13 30
(JRBest) *sn struggling: a bhd* **10/1**[3]

1m 23.65s (-0.56) **Going Correction** -0.15s/f (Firm) **20** Ran SP% **124.9**
Speed ratings: **97,96,94,93,93 92,92,92,91,91 90,89,88,88,88 86,84,82,76,73**CSF £83.06 CT £2056.01 TOTE £10.10: £2.90, £4.30, £8.10, £5.70; EX 144.40.
**Owner** Miss K Rausing **Bred** K Rausing **Trained** Newmarket, Suffolk
■ Stewards Enquiry : J Quinn caution: careless riding

**FOCUS**
A maximum field of unexposed two-year-olds, won in decent style by Mitraillette, and the form looks strong for the type of race.

**NOTEBOOK**
**Mitraillette(USA)** is a small filly and probably won this with a little more in hand than the offical winning distance. Always up in the front rank, she eased out approaching the last furlong and won nicely. She comes from a family that stays well, and is probably a bit better than just a nursery winner.
**Watchmyeyes(IRE)**, stepped back up in trip from his last run, came to win his race but may just have bumped into a potentially decent filly. He is a nice, big type, and may improve into a decent three-year-old. However, he may find things tough off his mark, but has plenty of ability.
**Seasons Estates**, making her nursery debut, was off the bit for the most part of the race, until staying on in the closing stages.
**Rebel Rebel(IRE)** seemed to find every bit of trouble going during the race. He looks a big two-year-old and finished this race well, and is worth bearing in mind for another nursery
**Gryskirk** definitely took the eye in the race. He was faced with a wall of horses with a furlong to go, but found a route to the stands'-side rail and fairly flew home. He has had plenty of chances already, but on this evidence can register a win shortly.
**Ivana Illyich(IRE)** found her way blocked a couple of times entering that last furlong and stayed on strongly. She has plenty of ability of this evidence.
**Chutney Mary(IRE)** *Official explanation: jockey said filly was hanging*
**Three Aces(IRE)** *Official explanation: jockey said filly was reluctant to race*

## 5378 ISIS DISPLAY SYSTEM MAIDEN STKS 7f
**3:20** (3:23) (D3) 3-Y-0+ **£4,033** (£1,241; £620; £310) **Stalls** High

Form RPR
3- **1** **Kodiac**[416] [3411] 3-9-0 SSanders 5 79+
(JLDunlop) *hld up in midfield: prog over 2f out: led over 1f out: rn green but stgd on wl* **5/2**[1]
-003 **2** 1 ¾ **Great Exhibition (USA)**[100] [2505] 3-9-0 80 (t) KMcEvoy 12 74
(SaeedBinSuroor) *lw: w ldrs: rdn and ev ch over 1f out: one pce ins fnl f* **3/1**[2]
**3** *shd* **Subtle Breeze (USA)** 3-8-9 JFortune 14 69+
(JHMGosden) *lengthy: scope: b.bkwd: w ldr: led over 2f out to over 1f out: one pce fnl f* **4/1**[3]
6-3 **4** 2 **Mrs Shilling**[26] [4683] 3-8-9 OUrbina 1 63
(JRFanshawe) *racd on outer: w ldrs: ev ch wl over 1f out: fdd ins fnl f* **9/1**
2355 **5** *nk* **All Quiet**[18] [4916] 3-8-9 70 RLMoore 4 63
(RHannon) *trckd ldrs: prog to chal 2f out: hrd rdn over 1f out: fdd fnl f* **12/1**
0235 **6** 1 ½ **Text**[9] [5147] 3-9-0 65 SDrowne 8 63
(MrsStefLiddiard) *racd midfield: swtchd to outer and drvn over 2f out: no imp over 1f out* **14/1**
0000 **7** ½ **Estrella Levante**[17] [4940] 4-9-4 45 (b) EAhern 16 62?
(RMFlower) *b.hind: racd midfield: rdn and one pce fnl 2f* **100/1**
**8** *hd* **Polish Rose** 3-8-9 RHills 13 57
(EFVaughan) *w'like: bit bkwd: b.hind: trckd ldrs: shkn up and cl up 2f out: fdd over 1f out* **12/1**
000 **9** 3 ½ **Appolonious**[22] [4811] 3-9-0 DaneO'Neill 11 52
(DRCElsworth) *in tch in midfield: wknd over 1f out* **66/1**
63 **10** 2 ½ **Encora Bay**[8] [5204] 3-8-9 JQuinn 17 40
(PRChamings) *mde most to over 2f out: wknd* **16/1**
0333 **11** 1 ½ **Bahama Reef (IRE)**[31] [4546] 3-8-11 55 LPKeniry(3) 9 41
(BGubby) *w ldrs but sn pushed along: lost pl 1/2-way: sn struggling* **20/1**
- **12** 1 **Golden Bankes (IRE)** 3-8-9 DSweeney 6 34
(WGMTurner) *leggy: bit bkwd: w ldrs to over 2f out: wknd* **33/1**
**13** 2 ½ **Charlie Masters** 3-9-0 SWKelly 3 32
(PHowling) *w'like: neat: bit bkwd: dwlt: sn detached in last trio: a bhd* **66/1**
**14** 4 **Dark Parade (ARG)** 3-8-7 JJones(7) 7 21
(GLMoore) *w'like: bit bkwd: dwlt: a detached in last trio* **33/1**
**15** 4 **Nelson's Luck** 3-9-0 SCarson 2 10
(EAWheeler) *w'like: bit bkwd: dwlt: a detached in last trio* **100/1**

1m 23.33s (-0.88) **Going Correction** -0.15s/f (Firm)
**WFA** 3 from 4yo 4lb **15** Ran SP% **127.1**
Speed ratings: **99,97,96,94,94 92,91,91,87,84 83,82,79,74,70**CSF £9.95 TOTE £3.10: £1.70, £1.10, £3.30; EX 10.40.
**Owner** Prince A A Faisal **Bred** Nawara Stud Co Ltd **Trained** Arundel, W Sussex

**FOCUS**
An ordinary maiden run in a modest time and the form is possibly suspect.

**NOTEBOOK**
**Kodiac**, who looked pretty straight, was returning from a break of well over a year and won this maiden in good style. He travelled well in behind the leaders and was produced approaching the final furlong to take the lead. When hitting the front he still showed signs of greenness, so should improve on this effort. He is from a decent family who all improved with age.
**Great Exhibition(USA)** was returning from a break of 100 days, and ran a fair race. He travelled well up with the leaders, but came under pressure about two furlongs out when the pace increased. To his credit he stayed on well all the way to the line and can pick up a race of this nature, even though he has had plenty of chances.
**Subtle Breeze(USA)** showed no signs of inexperience, breaking well from the stalls and leading the field for a long way. She should have absolutely no trouble picking up that all-important win for breeding purposes, she is closely related to Balanchine, before going on to better things.
**Mrs Shilling** ran well from a wide draw, showing early pace until really flattening out in the last couple of furlongs. She may need a step up in trip on this evidence.
**All Quiet** has been running consistently well, albeit a bit disappointingly, and ran another decent race without ever looking likely to trouble the leaders. He may not be entirely straightforward either.
**Text** *Official explanation: jockey said gelding lost a front shoe*
**Estrella Levante** *Official explanation: jockey said gelding hung left*

## 5379 LADBROKES.COM H'CAP 7f (P)
**3:50** (3:51) (D2) (0-85,85) 3-Y-0+ **£6,828** (£2,101; £1,050; £525) **Stalls** Low

Form RPR
3002 **1** **Idle Power (IRE)**[11] [5077] 6-8-13 75 (p) EAhern 10 89+
(JRBoyle) *b.hind: trckd ldrs: prog over 2f out: led over 1f out: sn rdn clr: comf* **8/1**
1105 **2** 2 ½ **Warden Complex**[48] [4031] 3-9-5 85 JPMurtagh 9 93
(JRFanshawe) *racd midfield: rdn and struggling over 2f out: hanging lft over 1f out : swtchd rt and r.o wl to take 2nd last 75yds* **5/1**[1]
0300 **3** ½ **Miss George**[3] [5299] 6-9-7 83 DaneO'Neill 6 89
(DKIvory) *s.i.s: hld up in last trio: prog wl over 2f out: rdn and styd on same pce over 1f out* **14/1**
6000 **4** ½ **Mallard (IRE)**[12] [5055] 6-9-0 76 MFenton 3 81
(JGGiven) *chsd ldrs: rdn over 2f out: styd on same pce fnl f* **16/1**
0036 **5** 1 ¾ **Taranaki**[10] [5112] 6-8-10 75 LPKeniry(3) 4 75
(PDCundell) *led for 1f: styd prom: swtchd rt and rdn ent fnl f: nt qckn* **5/1**[1]
2000 **6** *shd* **Big Bradford**[10] [5120] 3-9-2 82 (b) DKinsella 5 82
(PGMurphy) *t.k.h: chsd ldr after 2f: rdn to chal 2f out: chsd wnr ent fnl f: sn wknd* **33/1**
4630 **7** *shd* **Alchemist Master**[8] [5194] 5-9-1 77 (p) DeanMcKeown 14 77
(RMWhitaker) *racd wd: hld up in midfield: outpcd over 2f out: kpt on same pce after* **12/1**
2320 **8** ¾ **Another Glimpse**[73] [3326] 6-9-2 78 (t) SSanders 7 76
(MissBSanders) *hld up in last trio: nt clr run over 2f out: kpt on fr over 1f out: no ch* **12/1**
5204 **9** *shd* **Point Of Dispute**[12] [5055] 9-9-2 78 (v) DSweeney 2 76
(PJMakin) *dwlt: t.k.h: hld up in last trio: effrt on inner 2f out: nt qckn over 1f out* **11/1**
0102 **10** *nk* **Obrigado (USA)**[12] [5055] 4-9-6 82 SWKelly 11 79
(WJHaggas) *pushed up to ld after 1f: hdd & wknd over 1f out* **7/1**[2]
1240 **11** 1 **Instant Recall (IRE)**[25] [4717] 3-9-4 84 (b) JFortune 8 78
(BJMeehan) *racd midfield: rdn and outpcd over 2f out: no prog after* **15/2**[3]
3060 **12** 5 **Freak Occurence (IRE)**[10] [5135] 3-9-0 80 (v) SDrowne 12 61
(MissECLavelle) *racd on outer in midfield: outpcd over 2f out: wknd over 1f out* **14/1**
000- **13** 3 ½ **Blackmail (USA)**[361] [4872] 6-9-2 78 (b) SCarson 13 50
(MissBSanders) *b: chsd ldrs: losing pl whn n.m.r over 2f out: wknd* **50/1**
6300 **14** 5 **Hard To Catch (IRE)**[3] [5299] 6-8-10 77 ow2 (b) MSavage(5) 1 36
(DKIvory) *b: s.s: nvr gng wl: a towards rr: wknd over 2f out* **25/1**

1m 25.5s (-0.44) **Going Correction** +0.10s/f (Slow)
**WFA** 3 from 4yo+ 4lb **14** Ran SP% **120.4**
Speed ratings: **106,103,102,102,100 99,99,98,98,98 97,91,87,81**CSF £46.94 CT £564.23 TOTE £9.40: £2.90, £2.80, £5.50; EX 66.10 Trifecta £1187.80 Part won. Pool £1,673.00. 0.60 winning units..
**Owner** The Idle B's **Bred** Mountarmstrong Stud **Trained** Epsom, Surrey

**FOCUS**
A competitive Polytrack handicap run at a decent pace and the form appears solid and reliable.

**NOTEBOOK**
**Idle Power(IRE)**, who had shown ability in two starts on this surface last year, is marginally better handicapped on sand at the moment. Always in the ideal position to strike, once he swept past the leader turning for home the race was over. He remains relatively unexposed on Polytrack and could do very well if kept on the go through the winter.
**Warden Complex** did rather give himself a lot to do one way or another and, by the time he had plotted a path through, the winner was already in the showers. He has the ability to win on this surface when things go his way.
**Miss George** stayed on well to the line and certainly ran a good deal better than on her last visit here. Her record at this track means she should be respected whenever she returns.
**Mallard(IRE)** ran his best race for a little while, but does not look that well handicapped at present.
**Taranaki** is rated 10lb lower on sand than on turf, but that is because his form on this surface does not measure up and he had every chance on this occasion, but was just not good enough. He seems to run more modest races than good ones these days.
**Big Bradford**, never far away, had every chance before being swamped inside the last furlong, but this was still not a bad effort. He has run well here before and may not be a completely lost cause, but may need to drop a bit more in the handicap.
**Alchemist Master**, racing on sand for the first time in 19 months, is much higher in the handicap now and probably found this an insufficient test of stamina.
**Another Glimpse**, held up well off the pace, never got into the race and his best efforts have come over six furlongs.
**Obrigado(USA)**, looked more relaxed than usual, was given a positive ride once again, but did not get home and the bias towards front runners was not as pronounced as at the last meeting when he finished second.
**Freak Occurence(IRE)** *Official explanation: jockey said gelding did not face the kick-back*

## 5380 EBF SIS SPORTS DATA MAIDEN FILLIES' STKS (DIV II) 7f (P)
**4:20** (4:20) (D2) 2-Y-O **£5,200** (£1,600; £800; £400) **Stalls** Low

Form RPR
64 **1** **Icing**[29] [4598] 2-8-11 SWKelly 5 77
(WJHaggas) *prom: chsd ldr 1/2-way: rdn to ld jst over 1f out: kpt on wl* **10/1**
**2** ½ **One To Win (IRE)** 2-8-11 EAhern 2 75
(JNoseda) *tall: rangy: scope: in tch: effrt over 2f out: drvn and styd on to chse wnr ins fnl f: a jst hld* **15/2**[3]
023 **3** 1 ½ **Gone Fishing (IRE)**[27] [4625] 2-8-11 80 PRobinson 9 72
(MAJarvis) *lw: lt-f: led: shkn up and hdd jst over 1f out: fnd nil* **10/11**[1]
**4** ¾ **Jalissa** 2-8-11 SDrowne 3 70
(RCharlton) *w'like: lw: rn green and in snatches: in tch 1/2-way: outpcd over 2f out: kpt on fnl f* **14/1**
6 **5** 1 ½ **Missie Baileys**[25] [4714] 2-8-8 LPKeniry(3) 6 66
(DRCElsworth) *chsd ldrs: rdn 3f out: sn outpcd: one pce after* **8/1**
**6** 1 ½ **Sand Iron (IRE)** 2-8-11 JFortune 4 62
(SLKeightley) *w'like: bit bkwd: rn green and sn detached in last pair: sme prog 3f out: outpcd over 2f out: n.d after* **66/1**
0 **7** *nk* **Zonic**[36] [4399] 2-8-8 NMackay(3) 1 62
(SirMichaelStoute) *chsd ldr to 1/2-way: rdn and wknd 2f out* **9/2**[2]
00 **8** 9 **Balletomaine (IRE)**[27] [4625] 2-8-4 KMay(7) 7 39
(BWHills) *sn detached in last pair: no prog* **20/1**

1m 27.81s (1.87) **Going Correction** +0.10s/f (Slow) **8** Ran SP% **115.5**
Speed ratings: **93,92,90,89,88 86,86,75**CSF £82.40 TOTE £16.20: £3.20, £2.00, £1.10; EX 48.60.
**Owner** Cheveley Park Stud **Bred** T J Cooper **Trained** Newmarket, Suffolk

**FOCUS**
A maiden lacking strength in depth although the third and fifth suggest the form is fair, but the winning time was 0.67 seconds slower than the first division, which is ordinary for the grade.

**NOTEBOOK**
**Icing** had at least shown some ability on this surface and the extra furlong suited her well. The form is nothing special and she is likely to find life tough outside this company, but she has now won a race and that is probably the most important thing.
**One To Win(IRE)**, a 45,000gns yearling out of a winner in France, made a promising debut to split two much more experienced fillies. The form is nothing special, but she is entitled to improve.
**Gone Fishing(IRE)**, making her sand debut after three outings on turf, had the run of the race out in front but yet again did not appear to see out this trip.
**Jalissa**, an attractive half-sister to Vintage Premium and Domirati, looked badly in need of the experience but the way she came home suggests she is not completely without ability.
**Missie Baileys** did not improve for the switch to sand.


The Form Book, Raceform Ltd, Compton, RG20 6NL

**Sand Iron(IRE)**, a plain looking half-sister to four winners out of a three-time winner in France, needed the run and may be capable of better.
**Zonic**, following her promising debut at Windsor, ran a stinker and is surely better than this.
**Balletomaine(IRE)** *Official explanation: jockey said filly did not face the kick-back*

## 5381 SISLINK UPOD "PREMIER" CLAIMING STKS 1m 2f (P)
**4:50** (4:52) (D3) 3-4-Y-0 **£5,720** (£1,760; £880; £440) **Stalls** Low

Form RPR
6540 **1** **Platinum Pirate**[17] 4940 3-8-5 61 .......................... (v) JQuinn 14 67
(KRBurke) *hld up in last pair: rapid prog on wd outside over 2f out: led 1f out: sn clr: rdn out* **14/1**
2500 **2** 1 ½ **Sewmore Character**[10] 5108 4-9-5 66 .......................... DSweeney 7 71+
(MBlanshard) *settled in rr: prog 3f out: nt clr run over 2f out to over 1f out: r.o wl to take 2nd last 100yds: nt rch wnr* **20/1**
0000 **3** 1 ½ **Red Skelton (IRE)**[47] 4065 3-8-0 75 .......................... NMackay(3) 8 59
(WJHaggas) *racd wd: hld up: prog fr 7f out: chsd ldrs 2f out: nt qckn 1f out: styd on* **16/1**
0626 **4** ½ **Sea Of Gold**[50] 3993 3-8-7 70 .......................... KMcEvoy 5 62
(HJCyzer) *settled towards rr: sme prog fr 3f out: plld out and shkn up jst over 1f out: kpt on same pce* **8/1**[3]
5056 **5** hd **Rebate**[24] 4736 4-9-0 65 .......................... (t) RLMoore 3 62
(RHannon) *lw: led: drvn and jnd 2f out: hdd & wknd 1f out* **11/4**[1]
0 **6** 1 ¾ **Bonus Points (IRE)**[19] 4880 3-8-4 .......................... LPKeniry(3) 6 59
(BJMeehan) *s.i.s: hld up wl in rr: effrt on inner 2f out: kpt on same pce* **20/1**
6123 **7** ¾ **One Upmanship**[9] 5151 3-8-10 65 .......................... EAhern 9 60
(JGPortman) *lw: cl up: rdn to chse ldng pair over 2f out: hanging and nt qckn over 1f out: wknd fnl f* **5/1**[2]
0610 **8** nk **Belisco (USA)**[5] 5245 3-9-3 69 .......................... (bt) JPMurtagh 10 67
(CADwyer) *lw: trckd ldr: chal 2f out: upsides over 1f out: fnd nil and sn wknd* **8/1**[3]
0100 **9** 2 ½ **El Chaparral (IRE)**[10] 5135 4-9-5 72 .......................... DaneO'Neill 1 57
(DKIvory) *b: settled in rr: drvn 5f out: effrt u.p over 2f out: wknd ins fnl f* **8/1**[3]
6025 **10** 4 **Kingston Town (USA)**[8] 5187 4-8-9 62 .......................... (p) J-PGuillambert(3) 4 54+
(NPLittmoden) *prom: sn pushed along: u.str.p 4f out: wkng whn hmpd jst ins fnl f* **12/1**
1550 **11** 6 **Western Roots**[45] 4142 3-8-9 72 .......................... SDrowne 11 35
(KAMorgan) *chsd ldrs: rdn and lost pl over 2f out: wknd* **12/1**
4006 **12** ½ **Devious Ayers (IRE)**[15] 4989 3-8-7 62 .......................... SSanders 13 32
(GAButler) *prom: rdn and wknd over 2f out* **16/1**
6-00 **13** 8 **Lawaaheb (IRE)**[75] 3231 3-8-12 67 .......................... NPollard 12 22
(BRJohnson) *a in rr: last and hrd rdn 5f out: t.o* **20/1**
**14** ¾ **Golden Queen** 3-8-7 .......................... ADaly 2 15
(MDIUsher) *w'like: bit bkwd: reluctant to enter stalls: in tch: rdn and wknd 4f out: t.o* **66/1**

2m 7.85s **Going Correction** +0.10s/f (Slow)
**WFA** 3 from 4yo 7lb **14 Ran SP% 126.3**
Speed ratings: **104,102,101,101,101 99,99,98,96,93 88,88,82,81**CSF £280.60 TOTE £18.30: £3.70, £7.70, £7.00; EX 843.70.Red Skelton was claimed by Debbie Evans for £6,000
**Owner** Spigot Lodge Partnership **Bred** Llety Stud **Trained** Middleham Moor, N Yorks

**FOCUS**
A fair claimer but the despite the fair pace that it suited those that were held up, the form is not that strong.

**NOTEBOOK**
**Platinum Pirate** had it to do from his outside draw, but he appreciated being held up and the leaders coming back to him in the latter stages. This was a good effort as he had a bit to find with a few at the weights, but whether he can show the same sort of form back in regular handicap company is open to question.
**Sewmore Character**, like the winner, came from well off the pace but the winner had already gone beyond recall. He is not easy to win with, but is now 6lb below his last winning mark so he could find an opportunity back in handicap company.
**Red Skelton(IRE)**, best in by 9lb on adjusted official ratings, is obviously more suited to sand than turf and ran better with the all the weight equipment left off, but is going to continue to be difficult to place.
**Sea Of Gold** stayed on in her own time towards the end and looks worth a try over further.
**Rebate** had the run of the race out in front, but folded rather tamely once challenged. As his record shows, he is very difficult to win with.
**Bonus Points(IRE)**, backed at long odds, did not perform too badly as he was at a major disadvantage with his rivals experience-wise.
**One Upmanship** had every chance but, in commom with all the others that raced up with the pace, he did not get home.
**Belisco(USA)** *Official explanation: jockey said colt was hanging left*

## 5382 SIS VITAL LINK MEDIAN AUCTION MAIDEN STKS 1m 4f (P)
**5:20** (5:24) (F4) 3-4-Y-0 **£2,891** (£826; £413) **Stalls** Low

Form RPR
3322 **1** **Dundry**[11] 5079 3-8-13 79 .......................... (p) RLMoore 8 82+
(GLMoore) *b: trckd ldr 7f out: pushed into ld wl over 2f out: drew clr fnl 2f* **13/8**[1]
0 **2** 11 **Alexei**[153] 1304 3-8-13 .......................... DaneO'Neill 2 65
(JRFanshawe) *reluctant to enter stalls: in tch: rdn and effrt 3f out: kpt on to take modest 2nd ins fnl f* **33/1**
4330 **3** 1 **Garnett (IRE)**[3] 5300 3-8-13 75 .......................... EAhern 3 63
(AKing) *led for 2f: styd prom: rdn over 3f out: chsd wnr over 2f out to ins fnl f: one pce* **3/1**[2]
**4** nk **Moaning Myrtle** 3-8-8 .......................... OUrbina 7 58
(JRFanshawe) *leggy:trckd ldrs: gng wl 3f out: shkn up and outpcd over 2f out: hanging and rn green after* **20/1**
6343 **5** 5 **Scarrabus (IRE)**[6] 5217 3-8-13 66 .......................... TQuinn 6 55
(BGPowell) *led after 2f to wl over 2f out: wknd* **9/1**
0066 **6** 1 **Sonderborg**[17] 4941 3-8-8 49 .......................... (be) LisaJones 4 48
(MissAMNewton-Smith) *cl up: rdn and lost tch 4f out* **20/1**
042 **7** 29 **Disparity (USA)**[31] 4545 3-8-9 65 ow1 .......................... JPMurtagh 1 3
(JRFanshawe) *in tch: rdn and wknd 5f out: t.o* **13/2**
**8** dist **Czech Summer (IRE)** 3-8-13 .......................... DSweeney 11 —
(RMFlower) *leggy: s.s: a bhd: wl t.o fnl 4f* **66/1**
3003 **P** **Stocking Island**[18] 4910 3-8-8 70 .......................... SSanders 5 —
(BHanbury) *p.u and dismntd after 2f* **5/1**[3]

2m 34.6s (0.36) **Going Correction** +0.10s/f (Slow)
**WFA** 3 from 4yo 9lb **9 Ran SP% 117.1**
Speed ratings: **102,94,94,93,90 89,70,—,—**CSF £70.66 TOTE £2.80: £1.02, £12.30, £1.70; EX 75.40 Place 6 £92.67, Place 5 £82.66.
**Owner** D J Deer **Bred** R J And Mrs Deer **Trained** Woodingdean, E Sussex

**FOCUS**
A weak contest, made weaker by one horse refusing to enter the stalls and the third and fourth favourites running no sort of a race. As a result this took little winning and the future does not look rosey for these apart from the winner.

**NOTEBOOK**
**Dundry** was entitled to win this on official ratings and had little difficulty forging away from this poor field from the home bend. The form is nothing special, but he obviously took to the surface well and looks as though he would get a bit further.
**Alexei**, off since his debut in April and stepping up half a mile in trip, won the separate race for second but looks slow and will not be easy to place.
**Garnett(IRE)**, given a positive ride, was made to look woefully one paced over the last half-mile. He has already been well beaten off his current handicap mark, so a hurdling campaign surely now beckons.
**Moaning Myrtle**, a very fit looking half-sister to a couple of winners, travelled well for a long way but found nothing off the bridle. She looked to need the experience and is entitled to improve, though is obviously nothing special.
**Scarrabus(IRE)** was given a positive ride, but did not get home and is beginning to look exposed.
**Sonderborg** made it 22 races without a win.
**Disparity(USA)**, who ran into a decent sort here last time, ran a shocker and this was too bad to be true.
**Stocking Island** *Official explanation: jockey said filly was lame*
T/Plt: £103.20 to a £1 stake. Pool: £28,707.45. 202.95 winning tickets. T/Qpdt: £13.40 to a £1 stake. Pool: £2,837.70. 155.65 winning tickets. JN

5383 - 5387a (Foreign Racing) - See Raceform Interactive

# [3568]SAN SIRO (R-H)
Tuesday, September 7

**OFFICIAL GOING: Good to firm**

## 5388a PREMIO ALBAIRATE 7f 110y
**1:50** (1:50) 2-Y-0 **£7,042** (£3,099; £1,690; £845)

RPR
**1** **Mac Leader (IRE)** 2-8-8 .......................... APolli 4 —
(MGQuinlan) *raced in 3rd, switched to rails 3f out, led over 2f out, hung left inside final f, ridden out (11/20F)* 1
**2** ¾ **Ritter (ITY)** 2-9-2 .......................... FJovine 3 —
(AnnalisaBorroni, Italy)
**3** 1 ½ **Della Roggia (ITY)** 2-8-5 .......................... MDemuro 2 —
(BGrizzetti, Italy)
**4** 1 ¾ **Paradise Time (USA)**[59] 2-8-5 .......................... LManiezzi 5 —
(RMenichetti, Italy)
**5** ½ **King Of Central (IRE)** 2-8-9 .......................... MTellini 1 —
(PPaciello, Italy)

1m 34.2s **5 Ran SP% 64.5**
Speed ratings: .
**Owner** Scuderia Azzurra **Bred** Pat Beirne **Trained** Newmarket, Suffolk

**NOTEBOOK**
**Mac Leader(IRE)** was found a modest race for his debut. Hitting the front over two furlongs, he showed his inexperience by hanging left but was always doing enough. Quite what he achieved is open to debate.

## 5389a PREMIO PONTENURE (UNRACED COLTS & GELDINGS) 1m
**3:55** (4:15) 2-Y-0 **£7,042** (£3,099; £1,690; £845)

RPR
**1** **Ajvazovsky (IRE)** 2-9-0 .......................... APolli 9 —
(MGQuinlan) *pressed leader til joining him 2f out, led well inside final f, ran on strongly (291/100)* 1
**2** ¾ **Ussaro (IRE)** 2-9-0 .......................... MDemuro 7 —
(BGrizzetti, Italy)
**3** 4 **Bollucoiton Bay (IRE)** 2-9-0 .......................... DVargiu 1 —
(LD'Auria, Italy)
**4** 7 **Exor (ITY)** 2-9-0 .......................... WGambarota 10 —
(LLedda, Italy)
**5** shd **Farabutt (IRE)** 2-9-0 .......................... EBotti 5 —
(ABotti, Italy)
**6** 2 ½ **Frantoio (ITY)** 2-9-0 .......................... LPanici 8 —
(MCiciarelli, Italy)
**7** 3 **Avas (GER)** 2-9-0 .......................... DPorcu 6 —
(MGuarnieri, Italy)
**8** 5 **Kirking (FR)** 2-9-0 .......................... PConvertino 2 —
(JHeloury, Italy)
**9** 1 ½ **William Conqueror (ITY)** 2-9-0 .......................... IRossi 3 —
(FContu, Italy)

1m 40.2s **9 Ran SP% 25.6**
Speed ratings: .
**Owner** A Pettinari **Bred** A Pettinari **Trained** Newmarket, Suffolk

**NOTEBOOK**
**Ajvazovsky(IRE)** was up on the pace throughout and responded well to pressure to get on top in the final 150 yards. He still has some growing to do and is likely to have a maximum of one more run this term.

## 5390a PREMIO TENUTA LA BERGAMINA (UNRACED FILLIES) 1m
**4:25** (4:50) 2-Y-0 **£7,042** (£3,099; £1,690; £845)

RPR
**1** **Roca Azul (IRE)** 2-9-0 .......................... MDemuro 10 —
(BGrizzetti, Italy)
**2** ¾ **Manhattan (ITY)** 2-9-0 .......................... IRossi 3 —
(ABotti, Italy)
**3** 3 **Epoca (IRE)** 2-9-0 .......................... APolli 1 —
(MGQuinlan) *always in touch, 6th straight, not much room on rails over 2f out, stayed on final f, nearest at finish (259/100F)* 1
**4** snk **Valkiria (IRE)** 2-9-0 .......................... DVargiu 8 —
(LD'Auria, Italy)
**5** 1 **Anna Umbra** 2-9-0 .......................... LProietti 11 —
(JHeloury, Italy)
**6** 1 ¼ **Deploia** 2-9-0 .......................... DDettori 4 —
(VFicara, Italy)
**7** ¾ **Carrara (ITY)** 2-9-0 .......................... WGambarota 12 —
(LLedda, Italy)
**8** 2 ½ **Starry Wings (IRE)** 2-9-0 .......................... PConvertino 2 —
(JHeloury, Italy)
**9** 4 **Sweet Celtic** 2-9-0 .......................... LManiezzi 5 —
(AAiello, Italy)
**10** 3 **Miss Lalla'S (IRE)** 2-9-0 .......................... AArbau 7 —
(LCamici, Italy)
**11** 8 **Lady Hernanda** 2-9-0 .......................... APitzalis 6 —
(MCiciarelli, Italy)

12 2½ **Matrice (ITY)** 2-9-0 MTellini 14 —
(PPaciello, Italy)
13 *nk* **Matimoviestar (ITY)** 2-9-0 DViola 9 —
(LauraGrizzetti, Italy)

1m 42.5s 13 Ran SP% 27.8
Speed ratings: .
**Owner** Mack Ferrer **Bred** M Parola **Trained** Italy

**NOTEBOOK**
**Epoca(IRE)** could not complete a treble for the yard but ran with promise nevertheless, as she had trouble switching off the fence when the race began in earnest and did well to snatch third close home. This was a promising initial effort.

## 4315 DONCASTER (L-H)
### Wednesday, September 8

**OFFICIAL GOING: Good (good to firm in places on straight course)**
The ground was described at the start of the day as 'just on the fast side of good' but it continued to dry out and there was a brisk tail wind in the straight.
Wind: Fresh 1/2 behind. Weather: Fine, sunny and breeze.

### 5391 EUROPEAN BREEDERS FUND CARRIE RED FILLIES' NURSERY STKS (H'CAP) 6f 110y
1:15 (1:25) (B1) 2-Y-O £26,000 (£8,000; £4,000; £2,000) Stalls High

Form RPR
351 1 **Swan Nebula (USA)**[38] 4364 2-8-13 **82** (t) LDettori 22 89
(SaeedBinSuroor) *dwlt: racd stands' side: sn prom: rdn to ld ins fnl f: r.o* **5/1**[2]
4524 2 1¾ **Indiena**[20] 4876 2-8-5 **74** CCatlin 15 76
(BJMeehan) *mde most stands' side tl hdd and unable qck ins fnl f* **16/1**
0033 3 *hd* **Bibury Flyer**[9] 5174 2-8-13 **82** TEDurcan 21 84
(MRChannon) *racd stands' side: hld up: hdwy over 1f out: r.o* **20/1**
235 4 1 **Dance Flower (IRE)**[38] 4364 2-8-8 **77** ACulhane 13 77
(MRChannon) *racd stands' side: mid-div: rdn 1/2-way: hdwy over 1f out: r.o* **12/1**
513 5 *nk* **Aberdovey**[63] 3634 2-8-8 **77** RMullen 17 76
(MLWBell) *racd stands' side: sn pushed along in rr: hdwy fnl f: nt trble ldrs* **12/1**
1065 6 *nk* **Miss Meggy**[10] 5143 2-9-7 **90** MJKinane 12 88
(TDEasterby) *racd stands' side: prom: rdn over 1f out: kpt on* **14/1**
2532 7 ¾ **Consider This**[30] 4612 2-8-13 **82** KDarley 14 78
(WMBrisbourne) *racd stands' side: chsd ldrs: rdn over 1f out: styd on same pce* **25/1**
132 8 *hd* **Highland Cascade**[73] 3343 2-8-9 **78** JTate 18 74
(JMPEustace) *racd stands' side: chsd ldrs: rdn and hung lft over 1f out: no ex* **14/1**
110 9 1¼ **Strawberry Dale (IRE)**[32] 4552 2-9-7 **90** TQuinn 4 90+
(JDBethell) *racd far side: chsd ldr tl led that gp over 4f out: rdn over 2f out: no ch w stands' side* **10/1**[3]
4620 10 1 **Molly Marie (IRE)**[20] 4890 2-8-8 **77** PRobinson 1 75+
(TDEasterby) *racd far side: chsd ldrs: rdn over 2f out: kpt on* **22/1**
45 11 ½ **African Breeze**[39] 4348 2-8-11 **80** DeanMcKeown 19 70
(RMWhitaker) *racd stands' side: dwlt: hld up: styd on ins fnl f: nvr nrr* **25/1**
3415 12 *nk* **Easy Feeling (IRE)**[18] 4958 2-9-2 **85** RHughes 3 81+
(RHannon) *led far side 2f: remained handy: styd on same pce appr fnl f* **20/1**
113 13 ½ **Lamh Eile (IRE)**[32] 4527 2-9-2 **88** NMackay(3) 16 76
(TDBarron) *racd stands' side: chsd ldrs: rdn over 2f out: wknd over 1f out* **9/2**[1]
0240 14 1½ **Miss Malone (IRE)**[39] 4326 2-8-6 **75** DaneO'Neill 5 66+
(RHannon) *racd far side: prom: chsd ldr over 2f out: wknd fnl f* **50/1**
620 15 ½ **Ghasiba (IRE)**[20] 4885 2-8-13 **82** JMackay 11 65
(CEBrittain) *racd stands' side: dwlt: outpcd* **20/1**
4320 16 1¼ **Gennie Bond**[39] 4342 2-8-10 **79** RLMoore 20 59
(RHannon) *racd stands' side: s.i.s: sn outpcd* **20/1**
0315 17 *hd* **Keep Bacckinhit (IRE)**[18] 4953 2-8-11 **80** JFortune 6 67+
(GLMoore) *racd far side: hld up: hdwy over 2f out: wknd over 1f out* **33/1**
0410 18 2½ **Apple Of My Eye**[19] 4914 2-8-6 **75** WRyan 8 56+
(JRJenkins) *racd far side: s.i.s: hld up: effrt over 2f out: nvr trbld ldrs* **40/1**
5440 19 2½ **Alvarinho Lady**[9] 5202 2-8-5 **74** PaulEddery 2 49+
(DHaydnJones) *racd far side: chsd ldrs 5f* **66/1**
0420 20 4 **On The Waterline (IRE)**[11] 5119 2-8-4 **76** FPFerris(3) 9 41+
(PDEvans) *racd far side: hld up: n.d* **40/1**
0150 21 1¾ **Dorn Dancer (IRE)**[60] 3753 2-8-12 **81** DHolland 7 42+
(DWBarker) *racd far side: chsd ldrs over 4f* **50/1**

1m 17.95s (-2.53) **Going Correction** -0.60s/f (Hard) 2y crse rec 21 Ran SP% 122.9
Speed ratings: **101,99,98,97,97 96,96,95,94,93 92,92,91,90,89 88,87,85,82,77 75**CSF £65.50 CT £1525.86 TOTE £4.50: £1.70, £4.80, £2.80, £2.70; EX 87.70 Trifecta £499.80 Part won. Pool £703.98. 0.10 winning units..
**Owner** Godolphin **Bred** Darley **Trained** Newmarket, Suffolk

**FOCUS**
A competitive nursery, as you would expect, and it was the stands' side who dominated, with the first eight home all coming from a double figure stall. The winner did it comfortably and looks well worth her place in Listed company, with further improvement anticipated.

**NOTEBOOK**
**Swan Nebula(USA)**, who had the best of the draw in 22, continued the excellent record of Godolphin juveniles this season, staying on strongly in the final furlong to score readily. Her only previous try over seven furlongs resulted in disappointment, but she is well worth trying over it again and could easily complete the hat-trick as she is improving fast.
**Indiena** got across from her draw to lead for most of the way before being passed by the winner in the final half furlong. She has plenty of pace and five furlongs or an easy six will suit ideally.
**Bibury Flyer**, having her 15th outing of the season, shows no signs of losing her form and again ran well in defeat. She was going on at the end and may well be worth trying over a seventh furlong.
**Dance Flower(IRE)** ◆, who still holds an entry in the Fillies' Mile, was probably entitled to get a little closer to Swan Nebula on Newbury form but the winner has progressed again where she has not. She is well worth trying over seven furlongs and is likely to improve for it.
**Aberdovey** ◆ was outpaced throughout and got going only in the final couple of furlongs. She was finishing strongly and an extra half a furlong should see her back winning for her in-form stable.
**Miss Meggy** proved suited by the return to this sort of trip and was going on at the end. She is on a stiff mark and is likely to continue to struggle in nurseries despite being set to drop 2lb in future.
**Consider This** looks in need of farther and was doing her best work at the death.
**Highland Cascade** was hanging under pressure and did not make things easy for her pilot.
**Strawberry Dale(IRE)** did the best of the group who stuck to the far side and deserves a little credit. She remains progressive but will not find life easy off her current mark.
**Molly Marie(IRE)** chased home Strawberry Dale on the far side and ran better than her finishing position suggests.
**Lamh Eile(IRE)** set a fair standard on the the form of her Shergar Cup Juvenile third - the form of which has worked out well - but having been up there early, gave up the ghost rather easily. This was disappointing and she now has something to prove off her mark of 88. *Official explanation: jockey said filly hung right-handed*
**Gennie Bond** was a bit disappointing given her good draw and was always labouring in rear.
**Dorn Dancer(IRE)** *Official explanation: jockey said filly was unsuited by the good, good to firm in places ground*

### 5392 £200000 ST LEGER YEARLING STKS 6f
1:50 (1:56) (B1) 2-Y-O £173,400 (£69,360; £34,680; £17,340) Stalls High

Form RPR
11 1 **Caesar Beware (IRE)**[31] 4581 2-8-11 DaneO'Neill 12 112+
(HCandy) *mid-field: hdwy u.p 2f out: sn chsng ldrs: styd on wl to ld last 100 yds: r.o strly* **13/8**[1]
2142 2 2 **Distinctly Game**[22] 4836 2-8-11 81 NCallan 17 103
(KARyan) *trckd ldrs: led over 2f out tl ins last: nt qckn* **25/1**
1262 3 1½ **Moscow Music**[21] 4860 2-8-11 100 RHughes 19 99
(MGQuinlan) *hld up: hdwy over 2f out: styd on wl fnl f* **33/1**
4 1 **Omasheriff (IRE)**[38] 2-9-2 (b) THellier 10 101
(BruceHellier, Germany) *cmpt: trckd ldrs: ev ch over 1f out: fdd last 150 yds* **33/1**
5511 5 *shd* **Claret And Amber**[19] 4909 2-8-11 THamilton 20 95
(RAFahey) *lw: sn outpcd: hdwy over 1f out: styd on wl ins last* **22/1**
312 6 *nk* **Cammies Future**[18] 4962 2-8-11 MJKinane 21 94
(PWChapple-Hyam) *led stands' side gp tl over 2f out: kpt on same pce* **16/1**[3]
13 7 *nk* **Josh**[31] 4581 2-8-11 PRobinson 18 93
(MAJarvis) *chsd ldrs: outpcd over 2f out: n.m.r over 1f out: styd on wl ins last* **16/1**[3]
2116 8 2½ **Transaction (IRE)**[22] 4836 2-8-11 TEDurcan 13 86
(JMPEustace) *chsd ldrs: kpt on same pce fnl 2f* **66/1**
42 9 ½ **Rainbow Rising (IRE)**[25] 4757 2-8-11 RWinston 4 91+
(JHowardJohnson) *racd far side: chsd ldrs: styd on to ld that gp nr fin* **66/1**
2 10 *nk* **Oligarch (IRE)**[15] 5015 2-8-11 LDettori 9 84
(NACallaghan) *swtchd rt s: chsd ldrs: outpcd over 2f out: edgd rt: nt clr run over 1f out: styd on towards fin* **22/1**
6061 11 *nk* **Dance Night (IRE)**[21] 4860 2-9-2 92 TQuinn 3 95+
(BAMcmahon) *chsd ldrs far side: nt qckn fnl 2f* **33/1**
211 12 *shd* **Persian Rock (IRE)**[27] 4671 2-8-11 DHolland 14 82
(JAOsborne) *swvd rt s: bhd tl kpt on fnl 2f* **50/1**
5333 13 *shd* **Canton (IRE)**[11] 5131 2-8-11 87 RLMoore 11 82
(RHannon) *sn in rr: kpt on fnl 2f: nvr on terms* **50/1**
4311 14 *shd* **Mimi Mouse**[46] 4150 2-8-6 79 KDarley 2 84+
(TDEasterby) *racd far side: chsd ldrs: outpcd fnl 2f* **25/1**
0433 15 *shd* **Bigalos Bandit**[8] 5213 2-8-11 91 JPMurtagh 6 88+
(JJQuinn) *mde most far side tl hdd that side towards fin* **66/1**
2214 16 *nk* **Captain Hurricane**[17] 4981 2-9-4 JFortune 15 93+
(PWChapple-Hyam) *bumped s: hld up: nvr a factor* **4/1**[2]
1201 17 *hd* **Imperial Sound**[37] 4392 2-8-11 EAhern 16 80
(TDBarron) *mid-div: effrt over 2f out: nvr a factor* **20/1**
3 18 *shd* **For Life (IRE)**[60] 3760 2-8-11 MHills 5 87+
(APJarvis) *dwlt: racd far side: n.m.r over 2f out: nvr rchd ldrs* **33/1**
0215 19 1½ **Dario Gee Gee (IRE)**[9] 5195 2-9-0 95 JCarroll 22 78
(KARyan) *sn outpcd and pushed along* **33/1**
2253 20 *nk* **Right Answer**[25] 4744 2-8-6 95 KMcEvoy 8 69
(APJarvis) *swtchd rt after 1f to r stands' side: chsd ldrs: wknd pver 1f out* **20/1**
3140 21 7 **Forzeen**[39] 4348 2-8-11 74 CCatlin 7 60+
(JAOsborne) *racd far side: in tch: lost pl over 2f out* **100/1**
0211 22 5 **Don Pele (IRE)**[54] 3907 2-9-2 84 JFEgan 1 50+
(SKirk) *racd far side: chsd ldr: wknd over 2f out* **20/1**

69.64 secs (-4.64) **Going Correction** -0.60s/f (Hard) 2y crse rec 22 Ran SP% 124.6
Speed ratings: **105,102,100,99,98 98,98,94,94,93 93,93,93,92,92 92,92,91,89,89 80,73**CSF £50.54 TOTE £2.70: £1.60, £7.70, £7.90; EX 57.80 TRIFECTA Not won..
**Owner** Mill House Partnership **Bred** Glending Bloodstock **Trained** Wantage, Oxon
■ Europe's richest 2-year-old race.

**FOCUS**
The stands' side held the call with Rainbow Rising, ninth overall, first home on the far side. Caesar Beware lowered the all-age course record set in 1995, but when set against the other races run on the straight track on the day, his time was no more than decent for the grade.

**NOTEBOOK**
**Caesar Beware(IRE)** ◆, who came here on the back of an interrupted preparation, looked to have a fair bit to do at one stage but really knuckled down and in the end won going right away. Unbeaten in three now, he deserves to take his chance at the top level though his immediate target is the Redcar Two-Year-Old Trophy, another rich prize.
**Distinctly Game**, highly progressive, went on and stuck on strongly to finish clear second-best, justifying his trainer's faith in him and enjoying a big pay day.
**Moscow Music**, stepping up in trip, stayed on really well and clearly relished the sixth furlong.
**Omasheriff(IRE)**, a winner twice, including in Listed company, in three starts in his native Germany, is not that big and continually swished his tail in the paddock. He looked a real danger when upsides coming to the final furlong, but did not really see out the trip.
**Claret And Amber**, whose Redcar nursery win has worked out well, did not impress going to post. After struggling to go the pace, he stayed on really well and will appreciate a seventh furlong and slightly slower ground.
**Cammies Future**, a moderate walker, had the stands' side rail to help him but he may not appreciate fast ground.
**Josh**, put in his place by the winner at Windsor, was tapped for toe then met traffic problems. He is the type to do better at three.
**Rainbow Rising(IRE)** was first home on the far side but only ninth overall.
**Persian Rock(IRE)** *Official explanation: jockey said colt jumped awkwardly out of the stalls*
**Captain Hurricane**, free to post, collected a bump at the start and was never a factor. He looked a bit stale and this may have been one outing too many this time. *Official explanation: jockey said colt was possibly over the top*
**Don Pele(IRE)** *Official explanation: jockey said colt hung left-handed throughout*

### 5393 TOTESPORT PORTLAND (HERITAGE H'CAP) 5f 140y
2:25 (2:32) (B1) (0-110,99) 3-Y-O+ £32,500 (£10,000; £5,000; £2,500) Stalls High

Form RPR
5060 1 **Halmahera (IRE)**[25] 4759 9-9-10 **98** NCallan 13 107
(KARyan) *racd stands' side: hld up: swtchd rt and hdwy wl over 1f out: r.o to ld nr fin* **11/1**[3]
6602 2 *hd* **Texas Gold**[9] 5181 6-8-13 **87** MartinDwyer 1 95
(WRMuir) *racd far side: chsd ldrs: led that gp over 1f out: hdd nr fin* **16/1**

5103 **3** *nk* **Ptarmigan Ridge**[4] [5287] 8-8-9 **86** NMackay(3) 8 93
(MissLAPerratt) *racd stands' side: chsd ldrs: rdn over 1f out: r.o* **33/1**

0340 **4** *nk* **Whistler**[4] [5287] 7-9-2 **90** (p) RHills 12 96
(JMBradley) *racd stands' side: hld up: hdwy and hung lft over 1f out: r.o* **40/1**

0000 **5** *½* **Whitbarrow (IRE)**[4] [5287] 5-9-4 **92** (b) JFEgan 3 97
(JMBradley) *led far side 4f: styd on* **40/1**

0361 **6** *shd* **Forever Phoenix**[4] [5287] 4-9-6 **99** 7ex AQuinn(5) 17 103+
(RMHCowell) *racd stands' side: hld up: nt clr run over 1f out: r.o ins fnl f: nvr able to chal* **8/1**[2]

6035 **7** *hd* **Corridor Creeper (FR)**[9] [5181] 7-9-7 **95** (p) RLMoore 19 99
(JMBradley) *disp ld stands' side tl led that gp over 1f out: styd on same pce ins fnl f* **14/1**

4110 **8** *nk* **Jonny Ebeneezer**[25] [4759] 5-9-2 **90** (b) LDettori 2 93
(DFlood) *racd stands' side: hld up: r.o ins fnl f: nt trble ldrs* **12/1**

0102 **9** *nk* **Mutawaqed (IRE)**[18] [4951] 6-9-2 **90** (t) EAhern 22 92+
(MAMagnusson) *lw: racd stands' side: hld up: hmpd wl over 1f out: r.o ins fnl f: nt rch ldrs* **7/1**[1]

00U0 **10** *¾* **Peruvian Chief (IRE)**[4] [5287] 7-9-7 **95** RMullen 10 94
(NPLittmoden) *racd stands' side: hld up: r.o ins fnl f: nvr nrr* **66/1**

1200 **11** *nk* **Fun To Ride**[64] [3598] 3-9-2 **92** MHills 5 90
(BWHills) *racd stands' side: chsd ldrs: rdn over 1f out: no ex* **28/1**

4006 **12** *nk* **Funfair Wane**[4] [5287] 5-9-2 **90** DHolland 4 87
(DNicholls) *racd far side: chsd ldrs: rdn over 1f out: no ex ins fnl f* **20/1**

0041 **13** *nk* **Merlin's Dancer**[40] [4291] 4-8-13 **87** ANicholls 21 83
(DNicholls) *disp ld stands' side over 4f: no ex* **7/1**[1]

-000 **14** *shd* **Pomfret Lad**[118] [2065] 6-9-8 **96** AlexGreaves 20 92
(DNicholls) *racd stands' side: mid-div: rdn over 2f out: no imp* **66/1**

1400 **15** *½* **Connect**[32] [4538] 7-9-5 **93** (b) PRobinson 15 87
(MHTompkins) *racd stands' side: hld up: n.d* **25/1**

3600 **16** *1* **Pic Up Sticks**[39] [4324] 5-9-7 **95** TEDurcan 16 86
(MRChannon) *racd stands' side: s.i.s: hld up: effrt over 1f out: no ex ins fnl f* **7/1**[1]

0141 **17** *nk* **Atlantic Viking (IRE)**[9] [5181] 9-9-10 **98** 10ex RWinston 14 88
(DNicholls) *racd stands' side: dwlt: n.d* **40/1**

5041 **18** *½* **Spanish Ace**[12] [5071] 3-8-13 **89** (b) JPMurtagh 11 77
(AMBalding) *racd stands' side: hld up: a in rr* **25/1**

1000 **19** *nk* **Raccoon (IRE)**[32] [4538] 4-9-1 **89** (v) KDarley 6 76
(TDBarron) *racd stands' side: chsd ldrs over 4f* **14/1**

0120 **20** *1¼* **Fantasy Believer**[22] [4837] 6-9-3 **94** THamilton(3) 9 77
(JJQuinn) *racd stands' side: hld up: n.d* **18/1**

0001 **21** *5* **High Voltage**[20] [4874] 3-9-6 **96** (t) DarrenWilliams 7 63
(KRBurke) *racd stands' side: chsd ldrs over 4f* **40/1**

5311 **22** *2½* **Lake Garda**[116] [2115] 3-9-3 **93** TQuinn 18 52
(BAMcmahon) *racd stands' side: chsd ldrs over 3f* **20/1**

65.64 secs (-2.45) **Going Correction** -0.60s/f (Hard) course record
**WFA** 3 from 4yo+ 2lb **22** Ran SP% **125.5**
Speed ratings: **109,108,108,107,107 107,106,106,106,105 104,104,103,103,103 101,101,100,100,98 91,88**CSF £150.91 CT £5631.52 TOTE £14.20: £3.10, £3.60, £7.50, £9.60; EX 233.30 TRIFECTA Not won..
**Owner** J Duddy And Mrs G Quinn **Bred** Mrs John McEnery **Trained** Hambleton, N Yorks
■ Stewards Enquiry : N Callan one-day ban: used whip out of stride pattern (Sep 19)

**FOCUS**
An historic third consecutive win in this prestigious handicap for Halmahera, who at the age on nine seems as good as ever. There were several hard luck stories in behind and the field finished in a heap, with the small group who raced on the far side seemingly not at too much of a disadvantage.

**NOTEBOOK**
**Halmahera(IRE)**, winner of this race for the past two seasons, made it an historic third victory off a 5lb higher mark than last year. He had not been in the best of form coming into the race, but this specialist trip brings out the best in him and Callan timed it to perfection, getting up in the closing stages to edge out the gallant Texas Gold. He will find it tough going once again now, but is as good as ever at the age of nine and may come back and make it four.
**Texas Gold** ran a blinder from stall one as, although the draw is not as important over this trip, he raced in a small group throughout the race and is the type who is much better in amongst horses. He is evidently in cracking form and deserves to win a big one.
**Ptarmigan Ridge** seems to bringing a little consistency to his game these days - running well for the second time in four days - and will be of interest if getting in the Ayr Gold Cup, especially if the going eases.
**Whistler** gets on particularly well with the Hills brothers and would have gone very close to winning had he not hung left. He ended up nearer the far side in doing so and, although 6lb higher than when last scoring, is clearly up to winning off it.
**Whitbarrow(IRE)** took the far side group along at a decent gallop and kept grinding away once passed. This was his best effort for a while and whilst it is tempting to say he can win in the near future, he is not the most consistent.
**Forever Phoenix** was unlucky not to get at least fifth, being denied a clear run when looking to make ground - and she was finishing best of all at the line. She had finished ahead of the third, fourth and fifth at Haydock on Saturday and can be counted unfortunate.
**Corridor Creeper(FR)** was doing some good late work but remains 10lb higher than when last successful.
**Jonny Ebeneezer** never got involved and the race was all over by the time he started to get going. He remains a likely sort for the Ayr Gold Cup.
**Mutawaqed(IRE)** lost all chance when hampered and was never never going to get there in time. He had been reported in excellent shape by his trainer beforehand and is sure to play a major part in races like the Ayr Gold Cup.
**Peruvian Chief(IRE)** ran better than he has of late but is not getting any younger.
**Fun To Ride** comes from an in-form stable and can be found easier opportunities that this to add to her maiden win from earlier in the season.
**Funfair Wane** failed to confirm the promise of his run at Haydock but is sure to bounce back for the Ayr Gold Cup.
**Merlin's Dancer** was well supported in the ring but ran below expectations and may have needed this first outing since July.
**Pomfret Lad** can be expected to improve for this first run since May.
**Pic Up Sticks** ran below par and was never travelling with any real zest. He is better than this but does find it hard to win.
**Lake Garda** *Official explanation: jockey said colt was squeezed for room and had no more to give*

## 5394 NATIONAL STUD NEVER SAY DIE CLUB PARK HILL STKS (GROUP 2) (F&M) 1m 6f 132y
**3:00** (3:00) (A1) 3-Y-0+ **£60,000** (£23,000; £11,500; £5,500) **Stalls** Low

Form RPR

-445 **1** **Echoes In Eternity (IRE)**[39] [4323] 4-9-3 106 (t) LDettori 3 104
(SaeedBinSuroor) *trckd ldrs: wnt 2nd 3f out: led over 1f out: r.o wl* **5/1**[3]

1232 **2** *1* **Mazuna (IRE)**[25] [4749] 3-8-5 69 RLMoore 6 103
(CEBrittain) *t.k.h in mid-field: effrt 3f out: styd on to take 2nd nr line* **100/1**

1223 **3** *½* **Bowstring (IRE)**[15] [5025] 3-8-6 97 ow1 JFortune 5 103
(JHMGosden) *trckd ldr: led over 4f out: hrd rdn: hung lft and hdd over 1f out: nt qckn* **10/1**

2321 **4** *½* **Tarakala (IRE)**[20] [4884] 3-8-5 (b) MJKinane 2 101
(JohnMOxx, Ire) *trckd ldrs: effrt over 3f out: styd on same pce fnl f* **5/2**[1]

1206 **5** *nk* **Modesta (IRE)**[20] [4888] 3-8-5 88 WRyan 4 101
(HRACecil) *hld up in rr: hdwy over 3f out: styd on same pce fnl f* **18/1**

2314 **6** *1¾* **Light Of Morn**[38] [4367] 3-8-5 92 KDarley 1 98
(RGuest) *s.s: bhd: hdwy on outside 3f out: edgd lft and kpt on fnl f* **14/1**

1211 **7** *hd* **Astrocharm (IRE)**[39] [4321] 5-9-3 103 PRobinson 7 98
(MHTompkins) *mid-field: effrt 3f out: kpt on: nvr rchd ldrs* **7/2**[2]

3-6 **8** *8* **Opera Comique (FR)**[129] [1793] 3-8-5 (t) KMcEvoy 9 87
(SaeedBinSuroor) *led: qcknd 5f out: sn hdd: weakaned over 1f out: eased* **18/1**

4003 **9** *hd* **Desert Royalty (IRE)**[20] [4884] 4-9-3 92 JPMurtagh 8 87
(EALDunlop) *hld up in rr: effrt on outer 3f out: wknd over 2f out: eased fnl f* **25/1**

2232 **10** *7* **Selebela**[20] [4884] 3-8-5 95 TEDurcan 10 77
(LMCumani) *t.k.h: trckd ldrs: drvn along over 3f out: lost pl over 2f out: eased over 1f out* **11/2**

3m 5.82s (-3.92) **Going Correction** -0.25s/f (Firm)
**WFA** 3 from 4yo+ 12lb **10** Ran SP% **114.0**
Speed ratings: **100,99,99,98,98 97,97,93,93,89**CSF £340.27 TOTE £4.20: £1.90, £8.60, £2.70; EX 253.30 Trifecta £674.80 Part won. Pool £950.48 - 0.60 winning units..
**Owner** Godolphin **Bred** Swettenham Stud **Trained** Newmarket, Suffolk

**FOCUS**
They raced into a brisk headwind for the first six furlongs. It was not a vintage renewal and time was very slow for a Group Two when set against other races on the day. The result has been taken at face value, although the proximity of 69-rated Mazuna is obviously a worry.

**NOTEBOOK**
**Echoes In Eternity(IRE)**, running beyond a mile and a quarter for the first time, travelled strongly from just off the pace. She always looked like doing more than enough, bouncing off the fast ground. This was her fourth career win and could well be her swansong.
**Mazuna(IRE)**, runner-up in a Newbury handicap from a mark of just 68, ran out of her skin, staying on willingly to snatch second spot near the line. Her trainer loves tilting at windmills, and it occasionally pays big dividends.
**Bowstring(IRE)**, stepping up in trip, went for home but she hung under pressure, possibly feeling the ground.
**Tarakala(IRE)**, on totally different ground, could only stay on in her own time, if anything appreciating the step up in trip.
**Modesta(IRE)**, unsuited by the give at York, ran much better and just missed out on some valuable black type.
**Light Of Morn** fell out of the stalls and stayed on when it was all over despite failing to keep a straight line. Two miles will suit her even better.
**Astrocharm(IRE)**, who won a handicap in May from a mark of just 73, has made remarkable progress since but this looked a bridge too far - no doubt foreseen by her owner!
**Opera Comique(FR)** was given a copybook pacemaking ride, going just quick enough to ensure those in pursuit kept a keen eye on her.
**Selebela** would not settle and was always showing a tendency to hang right. In the end her rider simply gave up. *Official explanation: jockey said filly hung right-handed throughout*

## 5395 MCKEEVER ST. LAWRENCE CONDITIONS STKS 7f
**3:35** (3:35) (C2) 2-Y-0 **£6,431** (£2,378; £1,189; £540) **Stalls** High

Form RPR

1 **1** **Librettist (USA)**[54] [3913] 2-9-1 LDettori 5 106+
(SaeedBinSuroor) *mde virtually all: qcknd over 1f out: r.o wl* **1/1**[1]

6162 **2** *1½* **Embossed (IRE)**[18] [4949] 2-9-1 100 RLMoore 1 100
(RHannon) *a.p: chsd wnr over 2f out: rdn over 1f out: sn outpcd* **10/3**[2]

1 **3** *3½* **Camacho**[53] [3946] 2-9-1 RHughes 4 91
(HRACecil) *trckd ldrs: shkn up over 1f out: hung lft and sn outpcd* **5/1**[3]

13 **4** *2* **Le Corvee (IRE)**[23] [4807] 2-9-1 JDSmith 3 86
(AKing) *hld up: rdn over 2f out: wknd over 1f out* **18/1**

31 **5** *12* **Motarassed**[46] [4143] 2-9-1 88 RHills 2 56
(JLDunlop) *s.i.s: sn chsng wnr: rdn over 2f out: sn wknd* **13/2**

1m 22.61s (-5.20) **Going Correction** -0.60s/f (Hard) 2y crse rec **5** Ran SP% **108.3**
Speed ratings: **104,102,98,96,82**CSF £4.38 TOTE £1.90: £1.40, £1.60; EX 3.40.
**Owner** Godolphin **Bred** Calumet Farm **Trained** Newmarket, Suffolk

**FOCUS**
The winner always looked in command and looks a smart prospect. The winning time was decent for the grade and a juvenile course record.

**NOTEBOOK**
**Librettist(USA)** ◆, much more settled beforehand, was still a bit keen but he always looked in charge and will have one more run this time, in the Somerville Tattersall Stakes at Newmarket, before being prepared for the 2000 Guineas.
**Embossed(IRE)**, the biggest in the field, does not do anything in a hurry but deserves credit for the way he stuck to his task. A mile will be no problem.
**Camacho**, who is not that big, lacks scope and did not impress at all going to post.
**Le Corvee(IRE)**, who had a fair bit to find, had two handlers in the paddock and showed a moderate action going to post.
**Motarassed**, a tall type, is an easy mover but he was in trouble after jumping the shadow of the airship at halfway. *Official explanation: jockey said colt jumped the shadow of the C4 air ship 3 1/2f out and was never travelling thereafter*

## 5396 THWAITES SMOOTH BEER EBF MAIDEN STKS 1m (S)
**4:10** (4:11) (D2) 2-Y-0 **£7,065** (£2,174; £1,087; £543) **Stalls** High

Form RPR

2 **1** **Monsoon Rain (USA)**[33] [4523] 2-9-0 LDettori 3 84+
(SaeedBinSuroor) *led tl over 2f out: styd on wl to ld ins last: r.o wl* **6/4**[2]

23 **2** *¾* **Shannon Springs (IRE)**[22] [4835] 2-9-0 MHills 8 82+
(BWHills) *w wnr: led and qcknd over 2f out: hdd ins last: nt qckn* **5/4**[1]

**3** *2* **Sanchi (IRE)** 2-9-0 KDarley 4 84+
(JHMGosden) *rangy: scope: hld up in rr: hdwy 2f out: styd on wl ins last* **25/1**

**4** *nk* **Spear Thistle** 2-9-0 JFortune 11 77+
(JHMGosden) *tall: unf: scope: swrved lft s: hdwy 3f out: kpt on wl fnl f* **20/1**

6 **5** *1¾* **North Shore (IRE)**[69] [3451] 2-9-0 RLMoore 2 73
(RHannon) *in tch: hdwy 3f out: outpcd appr fnl f* **14/1**

06 **6** *shd* **Asharon**[15] [5023] 2-9-0 EAhern 9 73
(CEBrittain) *chsd ldrs: drvn along over 3f out: wknd fnl f* **100/1**

**7** *5* **Subtle Affair (IRE)** 2-8-9 JPMurtagh 7 57
(MGQuinlan) *lengthy: unf: t.k.h: trckd ldrs: wknd over 1f out* **22/1**

0 **8** *½* **High Treason (USA)**[74] [3319] 2-9-0 DeanMcKeown 1 61
(JGGiven) *hld up: hdwy over 3f out: fdd fnl 2f* **66/1**

**9** *11* **Whoopsie** 2-8-9 RWinston 5 31
(JAGlover) *lengthy: unf: s.i.s: a towards rr: bhd fnl 2f* **66/1**

**10** *2 ½* **Performing Art** 2-9-0 ........ RHughes 10 31
(PWChapple-Hyam) *big: rangy: s.s: hrd rdn and hung bdly lft over 3f out: lost pl over 2f out: sn bhd* **12/1**[3]

0 **11** *3 ½* **Love From Russia**[12] 5096 2-9-0 ........ NCallan 6 23
(ABerry) *chsd ldrs: outpcd over 3f out: sn lost pl and bhd* **200/1**

1m 37.32s (-4.28) **Going Correction** -0.60s/f (Hard) 2y crse rec **11** Ran SP% **116.2**
Speed ratings: **96,95,93,92,91 91,86,85,74,72 68**CSF £3.38 TOTE £2.70: £1.10, £1.10, £4.70; EX 3.90.
**Owner** Godolphin **Bred** Ten Broeck Farm Inc **Trained** Newmarket, Suffolk
■ Stewards Enquiry : M Hills one-day ban: failed to keep straight from stalls (Sep 19)
N Callan one-day ban: failed to keep straight from stalls (Sep 20)

**FOCUS**
A decent maiden, but just a steady gallop to past halfway and backward-looking newcomers third and fourth. Another juvenile course record, and a fifth course record in all, on a day when there was a brisk tail wind on a perfectly prepared surface. However, the time was only ordinary for the grade when set against the other race times on the straight course.

**NOTEBOOK**
**Monsoon Rain(USA)** ◆, quite a tall individual, is an easy mover. He sat wide and really buckled down and was right on top at the finish. He looks a very useful prospect.
**Shannon Springs(IRE)** did not look anywhere near as well as he had done at York. Soon racing hard against the stands' side rail, he went half a length up and quickened the pace but in the end simply met one too good. He was almost certainly not at his best on the day.
**Sanchi(IRE)** ◆, bred to make a middle-distance three-year-old, stands over any amount of ground and looks far from the finished article. Given a quiet ride on this his debut, he stayed on in most encouraging fashion to take third spot near the line.
**Spear Thistle** ◆, bred for stamina on his dam's side, is up in the air and unfurnished at present. Noisy in the paddock, he showed a round action, but after going sideways at the start, he picked up nicely late on. He looks sure to win races at three.
**North Shore(IRE)**, who made a satisfactory debut at Newbury, has been absent for ten weeks since. He again showed ability and there may be even better to come in time.
**Asharon**, a moderate mover, showed more than on his first two start but became very leg-weary late on.
**Subtle Affair(IRE)**, an April foal, looks very weak at present but she showed ability, travelling strongly until tiring badly.

## 5397 THOROUGHBRED BREEDERS' ASSOCIATION CLASSIFIED STKS 1m 2f 60y
**4:45** (4:46) (C2) 3-Y-O+ **£14,053** (£4,324; £2,162; £1,081) **Stalls** Low

Form RPR

11 **1** **Tartouche**[61] 3694 3-8-12 89 ........ RLMoore 11 96+
(LadyHerries) *mid-div: pushed along 5f out: styd on wl fnl 2f: led last 50 yds* **4/1**[1]

4516 **2** *½* **Mocca (IRE)**[38] 4367 3-8-10 87 ........ JFortune 3 93
(DJCoakley) *chsd ldrs: led over 1f out: hdd and no ex towards fin* **20/1**

2200 **3** *1 ¼* **James Caird (IRE)**[32] 4540 4-9-4 84 ........ PRobinson 4 92
(MHTompkins) *hld up: hdwy 4f out: nt qckn ins last* **12/1**

1 **4** *1 ½* **Look Again**[21] 4850 3-8-11 85 ........ JPMurtagh 9 91+
(MrsAJPerrett) *trckd ldrs: ld over 3f out tl over 1f out: kpt on same pce* **11/1**

0320 **5** *¾* **Fort**[42] 4229 3-9-0 88 ........ JFanning 8 91
(MJohnston) *chsd ldr: led 4f out: sn hdd: kpt on fnl f* **14/1**

2151 **6** *1 ¼* **Posteritas (USA)**[15] 5025 3-8-11 88 ........ RHughes 5 86+
(HRACecil) *hld up towards rr: sltly hmpd 6f out: styd on fnl 2f: nt rch ldrs* **9/2**[2]

6103 **7** *nk* **Galvanise (USA)**[8] 5211 3-8-11 85 ........(t) MHills 6 85
(BWHills) *hld up and bhd: sme hdwy and nt clr run over 2f out: kpt on: nvr trbld ldrs* **10/1**

412 **8** *nk* **Literatim**[19] 4920 4-9-5 86 ........ DHolland 7 86
(LMCumani) *t.k.h in rr: rdn and hung lft over 2f out: kpt on: nvr nr ldrs* **7/1**[3]

6006 **9** *¾* **Swagger Stick (USA)**[19] 4906 3-9-0 88 ........ KDarley 12 86
(JLDunlop) *chsd ldrs: pushed along 5f out: outpcd fnl 3f* **14/1**

5300 **10** *1* **Oddsmaker (IRE)**[41] 4271 3-9-0 88 ........ DeanMcKeown 1 84
(PDEvans) *t.k.h in mid-field: kpt on fnl 2f: nvr trbld ldrs* **50/1**

1040 **11** *3* **Silent Hawk (IRE)**[18] 4950 3-8-13 87 ........(t) KMcEvoy 10 78
(SaeedBinSuroor) *trckd ldrs: rdn over 3f out: sn btn* **33/1**

1224 **12** *5* **Inchloss (IRE)**[11] 5106 3-8-11 84 ........ TQuinn 13 67
(BAMcmahon) *chsd ldrs: lost pl over 2f out* **25/1**

1300 **13** *12* **Destination Dubai (USA)**[61] 3716 3-9-2 90 ........(t) LDettori 2 50
(SaeedBinSuroor) *led: hung rt thrght: hdd 4f out: sn lost pl: eased over 1f out* **4/1**[1]

2m 7.49s (-4.27) **Going Correction** -0.25s/f (Firm)
**WFA** 3 from 4yo 7lb **13** Ran SP% **122.6**
Speed ratings: **107,106,105,104,103 102,102,102,101,100 98,94,84**CSF £91.41 TOTE £5.00: £1.90, £6.50, £4.00; EX 108.20 Place 6 £170.67, Place 5 £52.46.
**Owner** Lady Herries **Bred** Angmering Park Stud **Trained** Angmering, W Sussex

**FOCUS**
A tightly-knit classified stakes, with just 4lb seperating the whole field on official figures, but a progressive and unbeaten winner.

**NOTEBOOK**
**Tartouche** still looked short of experience but, very willing, was firmly in command at the line. She now heads for a valuable fillies' handicap at Haydock.
**Mocca(IRE)**, back in her right grade, worked hard to get her head in front but in the end had to settle for second spot.
**James Caird(IRE)**, who came good at this time of the year 12 months ago, had the ground to suit and was back on song.
**Look Again**, quite a big sort, ran really well, showing ahead early in the straight and being by no means knocked about when it was clear on the day he was not up to the task. He will make an even better four-year-old.
**Fort**, who wore a sweat sheet in the paddock on a very warm day, was in the thick of the action throughout but in the end gave the impression this trip is short of his best.
**Posteritas(USA)**, who looked very fit indeed, was left short of room just before halfway. She made ground on the outer late on but was never going to be seriously involved.
**Galvanise(USA)**, who looked most unhappy with the first-time tongue strap in the paddock, met traffic problems trying to come from the rear and was never in the argument. It transpired that he had lost a shoe. *Official explanation: jockey said colt had lost a shoe*
**Literatim**, stepping up in trip, would not settle and then hung as if feeling the quick ground.
**Oddsmaker(IRE)**, back after a six week break, was very keen and his rider did a good job of looking after him.
**Destination Dubai(USA)**, who looked ready to take on the world in the paddock, went down very keenly. In front he wanted to do nothing but hang right-handed, and he seemed to throw in the towel too easily. *Official explanation: jockey said colt hung right-handed throughout*
T/Jkpt: £2,989.60 to a £1 stake. Pool: £29,475.49. 7.00 winning tickets. T/Plt: £135.90 to a £1 stake. Pool: £95,038.40. 510.45 winning tickets. T/Qpdt: £39.10 to a £1 stake. Pool: £4,858.30. 91.75 winning tickets. CR

# 5179 EPSOM (L-H)
### Wednesday, September 8
**OFFICIAL GOING: Good (good to firm in places)**
Wind: fresh bhd Weather: sunny; warm

## 5398 PKF EBF MAIDEN STKS 1m 114y
**2:15** (2:16) (D3) 2-Y-O **£5,434** (£1,672; £836; £418) **Stalls** Low

Form RPR

3 **1** **Intrigued**[11] 5109 2-8-9 ........ SSanders 3 91+
(SirMarkPrescott) *lw: w'like: scope: lengthy: gd sort: dwlt: hld up: cl 4th st: led 2f out: hanging lft but pushed clr fr over 1f out* **4/11**[1]

2 **2** *5* **Inca Wood (UAE)**[15] 5023 2-8-9 ........ RFfrench 2 75
(MJohnston) *led for 2f: led ent st: rdn and hdd 2f out: no ch w wnr fnl f* **5/1**[2]

5 **3** *6* **Red Riot (USA)**[28] 4625 2-9-0 ........ TPQueally 4 67
(DRLoder) *trckd ldng pair: hrd rdn wl over 2f out: sn btn* **7/1**[3]

00 **4** *18* **Archie Wright**[9] 5198 2-9-0 ........ PDobbs 1 29
(RHannon) *led after 2f: hdd ent st: sn wknd and wl bhd* **33/1**

0 **5** *dist* **Yankey**[11] 5114 2-9-0 ........ KFallon 5 —
(CEBrittain) *rdn and lost tch after 2f: t.o st* **33/1**

1m 45.66s (-0.08) **Going Correction** 0.0s/f (Good) **5** Ran SP% **108.4**
Speed ratings: **100,95,90,74,**—CSF £2.46 TOTE £1.30: £1.10, £2.00; EX 2.60.
**Owner** Faisal Salman **Bred** Belgrave Bloodstock Ltd **Trained** Newmarket, Suffolk

**FOCUS**
Not a terribly competitive maiden and not the most solid form, but a pleasing performance from the winner, who is the type to do better again.

**NOTEBOOK**
**Intrigued** had run with plenty of promise on her debut at Beverley when well supported and, although not entirely at home on this track, she appreciated the step up in trip and drew clear inside the final furlong for an easy success. This well-bred filly looks capable of handling a step up in grade, and the C L Weld Stakes, which her dam won, looks an ideal target, although the Fillies' Mile over a furlong farther could also come into calculations.
**Inca Wood(UAE)** appreciated the better ground, but she could not cope with the promising winner. She finished clear of the rest, though, and looks likely to be going the handicapping route after one more run.
**Red Riot(USA)** seemed to know his job better this time, but he too looks more of a nursery type.

## 5399 MITIE GENERATION H'CAP 7f
**2:50** (2:50) (D2) (0-85,78) 3-Y-O **£9,686** (£2,980; £1,490; £745) **Stalls** Low

Form RPR

6520 **1** **Peruvian Style (IRE)**[31] 4585 3-8-13 70 ........ TPQueally 2 79
(NPLittmoden) *pressed ldr: rdn to chal 2f out: led and hanging lft 1f out: drvn out: hld on* **12/1**

3054 **2** *½* **Ask The Clerk (IRE)**[7] 5219 3-8-8 70 ........ RoryMoore(5) 6 78
(VSmith) *lw: s.s: racd in rr: 12th st: prog on outer over 2f out : r.o to press wnr wl ins fnl f: jst hld* **13/2**[2]

2061 **3** *1 ¼* **Landucci**[15] 5020 3-8-8 65 ........(t) SDrowne 12 69
(JWHills) *dwlt: racd midfield: 9th st: prog 2f out: hanging lft fr over 1f out: unable qck fnl f* **7/1**[3]

0000 **4** *hd* **Lord Links (IRE)**[25] 4738 3-9-7 78 ........ PDobbs 10 82
(RHannon) *lw: dwlt: wl in rr: 13th st: no prog tl swtchd wd 2f out: r.o wl fnl f: nrst fin* **16/1**

1243 **5** *shd* **Little Jimbob**[46] 4140 3-9-4 75 ........ RFfrench 1 79
(RAFahey) *led: hrd rdn and hdd 1f out: fdd* **11/2**[1]

3126 **6** *1 ¼* **Iphigenia (IRE)**[17] 4969 3-9-1 72 ........ LisaJones 7 72
(PWHiatt) *racd midfield: 7th st: prog and cl up 2f out: one pce whn n.m.r briefly 1f out* **16/1**

0-21 **7** *shd* **Patterdale**[23] 4801 3-9-5 76 ........ SWKelly 4 76
(WJHaggas) *chsd ldrs: 6th st: rdn and unable qck 2f out: one pce after* **17/2**

3040 **8** *½* **Hilites (IRE)**[26] 4717 3-9-3 74 ........(p) SWhitworth 8 73
(JSMoore) *settled midfield: 8th st: shuffled along and one pce fnl 2f: nvr nr ldrs* **25/1**

-221 **9** *¾* **Saviours Spirit**[200] 840 3-9-3 74 ........ KFallon 5 71
(TGMills) *chsd ldng pair: t.k.h downhill: rdn over 2f out: wknd fnl f* **8/1**

0012 **10** *2 ½* **Glebe Garden**[10] 5155 3-9-3 74 ........ SSanders 14 64
(MLWBell) *b.hind: racd wd: chsd ldrs: 5th st: rdn and wknd 2f out* **7/1**[3]

3100 **11** *½* **St Savarin (FR)**[7] 5220 3-9-5 76 ........ NPollard 11 65
(JRBest) *chsd ldrs: 4th st: rdn and wknd 2f out* **25/1**

0150 **12** *shd* **Malibu (IRE)**[27] 4691 3-9-7 78 ........(v[1]) JQuinn 9 67
(SDow) *wnt rt s: racd in last: nt gng wl ent st: no ch after: kpt on fnl f* **40/1**

1005 **13** *¾* **Sweet Reply**[18] 4938 3-9-0 71 ........ FNorton 13 58
(IAWood) *racd towards rr: 11th st: sn rdn and struggling* **25/1**

0000 **14** *hd* **Seneschal**[11] 5120 3-8-10 70 ........ SHitchcott(3) 3 56
(MRChannon) *racd towards rr: 10th st: rdn and no prog wl over 2f out: sn wknd* **10/1**

1m 23.24s (-0.71) **Going Correction** 0.0s/f (Good) **14** Ran SP% **117.9**
Speed ratings: **104,103,102,101,101 100,100,99,98,95 95,95,94,94**CSF £82.64 CT £611.87 TOTE £11.30: £3.70, £2.80, £3.90; EX 100.30.
**Owner** M C S D Racing Ltd **Bred** Forenaghts Stud **Trained** Newmarket, Suffolk
■ Stewards Enquiry : Rory Moore one-day ban: used whip with excessive frequency (Sep 19)

**FOCUS**
A competitive handicap run at a solid pace and the form looks sound.

**NOTEBOOK**
**Peruvian Style(IRE)** had his stamina to prove over this longer trip as he had done all his previous running over sprint trips, and all his winning over five furlongs. Prominent throughout, he saw it out well in the end, and connections now have more options.
**Ask The Clerk(IRE)** is as consistent as they come and once again ran well in defeat. Indeed, had he got away on terms he may well have won.
**Landucci** had shown himself able to handle a downhill track when successful at Brighton last time, but the ground was not as soft on this occasion, and he was not well drawn either, which resulted in him racing wide.
**Lord Links(IRE)**, who has dropped to a fair mark, was another who was not well drawn but he finished better than anything, passing a number of rivals inside the final furlong.
**Little Jimbob** made the most of his inside draw and set out to make every yard. He was overhauled inside the last, though, and looks high enough in the weights at the moment.
**Iphigenia(IRE)** is another who looks high enough in the handicap.
**Patterdale**, dropped 10lb since winning his maiden last time out, looks like he is going to need even more kindness.
**Saviours Spirit** is entitled to come on for this first run since February. *Official explanation: jockey said gelding was unsuited by the track*
**Glebe Garden**, who likes to lead, had no chance from her draw.

## 5400 STERLING CONSTRUCTION COMPOSITES COMPANIES EBF MEDIAN AUCTION MAIDEN STKS 6f

**3:25** (3:25) (E3) 2-Y-O **£5,486** (£1,688; £844; £422) **Stalls** High

Form RPR

22 **1** **Amica**[27] 4670 2-8-9 ................ IMongan 5 78
(GLMoore) *lw: prom: trckd ldr st: gng easily over 2f out: led wl over 1f out: 2l clr fnl f: drvn out* **5/2**[2]

**2** *1 ½* **Market Trend** 2-8-9 ................ RFfrench 8 74
(MJohnston) *w'like: scope: tall: racd wd: in tch: 5th st: shkn up and effrt 2f out: chsd wnr ins fnl f: kpt on* **6/1**

0 **3** *hd* **Regal Dream (IRE)**[44] 4191 2-9-0 ................ SDrowne 7 78
(JWHills) *hld up: 6th st: shkn up and prog 2f out: styd on fnl f* **16/1**

54 **4** *2* **Cordage (IRE)**[15] 5015 2-9-0 ................ SSanders 2 72
(GAButler) *led: rdn and hdd wl over 1f out: wknd fnl f* **15/8**[1]

630 **5** *2 ½* **Edge Of Blue**[16] 5003 2-9-0 68 ................ KFallon 4 64
(RHannon) *hanging rt: chsd ldr tl st: rdn over 2f out: wknd over 1f out* **9/2**[3]

**6** *nk* **Briannie (IRE)** 2-8-9 ................ TPQueally 6 59
(JRBoyle) *s.i.s: in tch: 4th st: rdn over 2f out: wknd over 1f out* **25/1**

0 **7** *1* **Nan Jan**[74] 3296 2-8-9 ................ NDay 3 56
(RIngram) *s.i.s: a last: rdn over 2f out: no prog* **25/1**

1m 10.84s (0.21) **Going Correction** 0.0s/f (Good) **7 Ran SP% 109.4**
Speed ratings: **98,96,95,93,89 89,88**CSF £16.14 TOTE £2.70: £1.70, £3.00; EX 7.50.
**Owner** D J Deer **Bred** D J And Mrs Deer **Trained** Woodingdean, E Sussex

**FOCUS**
Not a strong maiden, but won in decent style by Amica and the form appears reliable.

**NOTEBOOK**
**Amica** handled this step back up in trip really well. She is not very big and travelled well just off the pace, and once sent to the front never looked like being pegged back. Nurseries now beckon for her.
**Market Trend** was friendless in the market but ran a decent first race. She is a nice big type and seemed to handle the track really well, staying on in a pleasing manner to suggest she is capable of winning her maiden.
**Regal Dream(IRE)**, stepping up a furlong from his debut, showed a lot more this time. He was another to handle this difficult course well and stayed on right to the line. A normal maiden looks within his scope.
**Cordage(IRE)** was a well-backed favourite but proved disappointing. A bit keen to post, he jumped out well and set the pace to the two-furlong mark, from where he dropped away tamely. His previous maiden form was not bad and, given a step up in trip he could be interesting in a nursery.
**Edge Of Blue** hung for most of the race and looked ill at ease on the course.

## 5401 WITHERSNET CLASSIFIED STKS 1m 2f 18y

**4:00** (4:04) (C1) 3-Y-O+ **£15,367** (£5,828; £2,914; £1,324) **Stalls** Low

Form RPR

0522 **1** **Impeller (IRE)**[40] 4287 5-9-4 90 ................ SDrowne 5 99
(WRMuir) *lw: wl in tch: prog and 4th st: led over 2f out: drvn and hld on wl fnl f* **11/2**[1]

-124 **2** *nk* **Mango Mischief (IRE)**[28] 4640 3-8-10 92 ................ SSanders 8 97
(JLDunlop) *hld up: 9th st: prog and barging match w rival fr over 2f out: chsd wnr 1f out: clsd nr fin: jst hld* **7/1**[3]

-063 **3** *½* **Zonergem**[84] 2969 6-9-6 92 ................ (p) TPQueally 7 100
(LadyHerries) *midfield: lost pl and 10th st: prog and barging match w rival over 2f out: nt qckn over 1f out: r.o last 100yds* **7/1**[3]

4201 **4** *1* **Boule D'Or (IRE)**[25] 4754 3-8-11 89 ................ NDay 10 96
(RIngram) *lw: hld up towards rr: 8th st: prog to chse wnr 2f out: hld 1f out: one pce after* **8/1**

1030 **5** *5* **Wing Commander**[21] 4856 5-9-8 94 ................ RFfrench 3 91
(RAFahey) *trckd ldrs: 5th st: cl up 2f out: wknd over 1f out* **6/1**[2]

6000 **6** *3 ½* **Jazz Messenger (FR)**[20] 4887 4-9-7 93 ................ SWKelly 4 83
(GAButler) *lw: dismntd on way to post: racd midfield: 6th st: effrt over 2f out: wknd over 1f out* **7/1**[3]

2-15 **7** *1 ½* **Nuzooa (USA)**[53] 3944 3-8-10 92 ................ (b[1]) WSupple 6 77
(MPTregoning) *led: increased pce 1/2-way: hdd over 2f out: sn wknd* **8/1**

6606 **8** *5* **Foodbroker Founder**[11] 5133 4-9-6 92 ................ NPollard 12 71
(DRCElsworth) *chsd ldr: rdn 1/2-way: wknd over 2f out* **33/1**

310 **9** *9* **Nunki (USA)**[88] 2896 3-8-11 87 ................ JQuinn 1 53
(HRACecil) *lw: trckd ldrs: 3rd st: wknd rapidly over 2f out* **25/1**

4124 **10** *1 ¾* **Cold Turkey**[111] 2240 4-9-4 90 ................ SWhitworth 9 49
(GLMoore) *lw: hld up in last: shkn up and no prog over 2f out: sn bhd* **7/1**[3]

4-50 **11** *15* **Muhareb (USA)**[32] 4530 5-9-3 92 ................ J-PGuillambert[(3)] 11 24
(CEBrittain) *chsd ldrs: 7th and losing pl: st: wknd: t.o* **20/1**

2m 7.67s (-1.03) **Going Correction** 0.0s/f (Good) **11 Ran SP% 113.4**
**WFA** 3 from 4yo+ 7lb
Speed ratings: **104,103,103,102,98 95,94,90,83,81 69**CSF £40.73 TOTE £6.40: £2.50, £1.80, £2.60; EX 39.00.
**Owner** D G Clarke & C L A Edginton **Bred** P E Banahan **Trained** Lambourn, Berks

**FOCUS**
A competitive classified event and the form looks useful. The first four all ran very close to their marks, so no reason it should not work out.

**NOTEBOOK**
**Impeller(IRE)** saves his best for the downhill tracks of Goodwood, Brighton and Epsom, where his record now reads 225176221. This was the highest mark he has ever won off, and he is likely to struggle back on a more galloping track - he is entered in the Cambridgeshire at Newmarket and John Smith's Handicap at Newbury.
**Mango Mischief(IRE)**, dropping down in grade having run respectably in Listed company last time, ran another good race, but things are not going to get any easier off a mark in the mid 90s, and connections may well opt to try again to nick a bit of black type.
**Zonergem**, held up for a late run as usual, got involved in some bumping and barging with the eventual runner-up in the straight. He was making up ground on the winner at the finish and remains capable of winning off this sort of mark, but he is very much the sort who needs everything to drop just right.
**Boule D'Or(IRE)** needs a penalty to have a realistic chance of getting into the Cambridgeshire. Drawn out wide, he was travelling as well as anything early in the straight, but could not quite pick up as had looked likely. The course did not appear to suit him ideally, and he will be seen to better effect back on a more galloping track.
**Wing Commander** looks happier over a mile.
**Jazz Messenger(FR)**, a winner over the course and distance last summer, has struggled to run to his best this term.
**Nuzooa(USA)**, blinkered for the first time, looks too highly rated on what she has achieved. She had the run of the race here but was still found wanting.
**Cold Turkey**, having his first run since May, looked to be carrying a little condition and needs further.

## 5402 GROUP TWO ROBOWATCH H'CAP 1m 4f 10y

**4:35** (4:38) (D2) (0-85,83) 3-Y-O **£9,632** (£2,963; £1,481; £740) **Stalls** Centre

Form RPR

4112 **1** **Nordwind (IRE)**[28] 4648 3-9-3 79 ................ IMongan 4 87+
(PWHarris) *mde all: hrd pressed fnl 2f: urged along and hld on ins fnl f* **4/1**[2]

2103 **2** *¾* **Horner (USA)**[45] 4176 3-9-5 81 ................ JQuinn 11 88
(PFICole) *hld up in last pair: 10th st: prog on outer fr 3f out: chsd wnr ins fnl f: kpt on: a hld* **33/1**

2120 **3** *¾* **Sand And Stars (IRE)**[20] 4888 3-9-5 81 ................ MHenry 5 87
(MHTompkins) *trckd ldrs: 5th st: prog to chse wnr over 2f out: rdn and nt qckn over 1f out: one pce after* **8/1**

0105 **4** *½* **Pagan Magic (USA)**[19] 4915 3-8-13 75 ................ LisaJones 7 80
(JARToller) *settled in rr: 9th st: prog over 2f out: chsd ldng trio over 1f out: nt qckn after: kpt on* **11/1**

0-16 **5** *6* **Payola (USA)**[20] 4884 3-8-10 72 ................ SSanders 10 68
(CEBrittain) *settled in rr: 8th st: effrt over 2f out: sn outpcd by ldrs* **14/1**

1260 **6** *3* **Bienvenue**[29] 4618 3-8-11 73 ................ ADaly 3 64
(MPTregoning) *racd midfield: 6th st: sn lost pl and floundering: n.d fnl 2f* **20/1**

0005 **7** *1* **The Violin Player (USA)**[33] 4518 3-8-4 69 oh1 ........ J-PGuillambert[(3)] 1 58
(HJCollingridge) *s.i.s: sn prom: 3rd st: wknd over 2f out* **50/1**

141 **8** *6* **Hasaiyda (IRE)**[28] 4648 3-9-4 80 ................ KFallon 6 60+
(SirMichaelStoute) *racd midfield: pushed along 5f out: 7th st: rdn whn nowhere to go over 2f out: no ch after* **6/4**[1]

0460 **9** *7* **Man At Arms (IRE)**[4] 5300 3-9-0 76 ................ (p) FNorton 2 44
(RHannon) *s.s and reminders: nvr gng wl: last st: sn btn* **16/1**

5512 **10** *¾* **Cherubim (JPN)**[53] 3933 3-8-13 75 ................ TPQueally 9 42
(DRLoder) *lw: prom: 4th st: wknd wl over 2f out* **20/1**

3216 **11** *1 ¾* **Night Spot**[12] 5074 3-9-7 83 ................ SDrowne 8 47
(RCharlton) *chsd wnr to over 2f out: wknd rapidly and eased* **13/2**[3]

2m 39.8s (1.08) **Going Correction** 0.0s/f (Good) **11 Ran SP% 119.8**
Speed ratings: **96,95,95,94,90 88,88,84,79,78 77**CSF £138.16 CT £1025.79 TOTE £5.60: £1.60, £8.90, £2.50; EX 124.40.
**Owner** Mrs P W Harris **Bred** Christoph Berglar **Trained** Ringshall, Bucks

**FOCUS**
A modest winning time for the grade and the form is just fair.

**NOTEBOOK**
**Nordwind(IRE)** won under a fine tactical ride by his jockey. He was pushed along early to gain the lead and settled in front at a fairly sedate pace. Once Mongan injected the pace in the home straight the rest were always playing catch-up and could never get to him. He does have a quirky head carriage, but whether this form is reliable, given he had the run of the race, is more debatable than his attitude.
**Horner(USA)** was given a very different ride that almost paid off. He was drawn very wide, but with a few others in the race liking to make the pace he was settled right at the back of the field. He came with a strong-looking run down the straight that and never quite got there. It will be interesting to see if those tactics are adopted next time.
**Sand And Stars(IRE)** has generally made the running recently, but was another to adopt slightly different tactics. She sat just off the pace, travelling well but a bit wide at Tattenham Corner, and came with a run entering the straight but could never get to the winner. She is quite a bit higher in the Handicap than when successful in July, but continues to run well.
**Pagan Magic(USA)** was settled in midfield and had his chance down the straight, but he never looked likely to win. A drop in grade might see him go close.
**Payola(USA)**, running here after showing nothing in the Galtres Stakes, was held up in midfield and never looked like being involved at the business end of the race.
**Bienvenue** met a little bit of trouble in running, but was never close enough to be called unlucky.
**Hasaiyda(IRE)** did not seem at ease on this track and also found some minimal trouble in running. It was reported after the race that she had been struck into. *Official explanation: trainer's representative said filly had been struck into*
**Night Spot** had a poor draw for a front runner, but managed to cut out some of the early pace with the winner. He dropped away badly towards the end of the race and the jockey reported that he tired badly from half a mile out. *Official explanation: jockey said gelding tired badly 4f from home; trainer said gelding was found to have mucus in its lungs on returning home*

## 5403 CHANTON GROUP H'CAP 1m 114y

**5:10** (5:13) (D2) (0-85,84) 3-Y-O+ **£9,791** (£3,012; £1,506; £753) **Stalls** Low

Form RPR

1063 **1** **Mr Velocity (IRE)**[9] 5185 4-9-0 71 ................ KFallon 12 80+
(EFVaughan) *racd midfield: 7th st: prog over 2f out: rdn to ld 1f out: drvn out* **2/1**[1]

0015 **2** *½* **Juste Pour L'Amour**[15] 5017 4-8-12 72 ................ RMiles[(3)] 9 80+
(PLGilligan) *settled towards rr: 9th st: stdy prog 2f out: plld out and fin wl fnl f: nt rch wnr* **16/1**

5415 **3** *¾* **Franksalot (IRE)**[9] 5185 4-8-13 70 ................ SSanders 10 76
(MissBSanders) *trckd ldrs: 6th st: smooth prog to ld over 2f out: sn rdn: hdd and nt qckn 1f out* **10/1**

0010 **4** *½* **King Of Diamonds**[11] 5120 3-9-0 77 ................ WSupple 4 82
(JRBest) *dwlt: hld up wl in rr: last st: hanging lft but prog fr over 2f out: ch 1f out: nt qckn* **14/1**

0022 **5** *1* **Flint River**[15] 5017 6-9-0 74 ................ LFletcher[(3)] 1 77+
(HMorrison) *bdly hmpd after 1f and lost pl: 8th st: rdn and effrt over 2f out: one pce fr over 1f out* **7/1**[3]

14 **6** *1 ½* **Hermitage Court (USA)**[25] 4749 3-9-7 84 ................ SWKelly 7 84
(BJMeehan) *lw: t.k.h: prom: 3rd st: rdn to chal over 2f out: fdd over 1f out* **6/1**[2]

0035 **7** *2 ½* **Takes Tutu (USA)**[13] 5061 5-9-5 76 ................ (v) IMongan 3 70
(KRBurke) *hld up in rr: 11th st: rdn over 2f out: nvr rchd ldrs* **12/1**

1066 **8** *¾* **Invader**[5] 5275 8-8-12 72 ................ (bt) J-PGuillambert[(3)] 2 65
(CEBrittain) *hld up wl in rr: 12th st: shuffled along and one pce fnl 3f* **20/1**

316 **9** *2 ½* **Habanero**[25] 4756 3-9-2 79 ................ FNorton 6 67
(RHannon) *led for 1f: pressed ldr: led 3f out to over 2f out: sn wknd* **14/1**

6460 **10** *7* **Madamoiselle Jones**[11] 5135 4-8-9 66 ................ DKinsella 13 39
(HSHowe) *led after 1f and set gd pce: hdd 3f out: sn wknd* **40/1**

1531 **11** *2 ½* **Carry On Doc**[9] 5185 3-9-3 80 6ex ................ SWhitworth 8 48
(JWHills) *keen to post: racd wd: hld up towards rr: 10th st: sn no prog and btn* **8/1**

3200 **12** *1 ¼* **Whitgift Rock**[7] 5220 3-8-10 73 ................ JQuinn 11 38
(SDow) *prom: 5th st: hung rt and wknd 3f out* **33/1**

2030 **13** *6* **Mbosi (USA)**[11] 5135 3-9-1 78 ................ (b) RFfrench 5 30
(MJohnston) *plld hrd: prom: 4th st: sn wknd* **33/1**

1m 45.13s (-0.61) **Going Correction** 0.0s/f (Good) **13 Ran SP% 120.3**
**WFA** 3 from 4yo+ 6lb
Speed ratings: **102,101,100,100,99 98,96,95,93,86 84,83,78**CSF £37.03 CT £242.45 TOTE £2.80: £1.80, £5.90, £2.60; EX 46.50 Place 6 £86.15, Place 5 £80.37.
**Owner** A M Pickering **Bred** Mrs V Dubois **Trained** Newmarket, Suffolk
■ Stewards Enquiry : J Quinn four-day ban: careless riding (Sep 19-22)

**FOCUS**
A fair handicap run at a decent pace and the form is sound.
**NOTEBOOK**
**Mr Velocity(IRE)**, unlucky in running over course and distance last time, made amends off the same mark from a worse draw. He is pretty consistent overall.
**Juste Pour L'Amour** finished with a flourish but the winner had gone beyond recall. He clearly remains on a mark which his trainer can exploit.
**Franksalot(IRE)**, who is kept almost exclusively to this type of track, ran another solid race. He has never won over farther than seven furlongs.
**King Of Diamonds** made up good ground from the rear, but he did not look entirely happy on the track as he hung left throughout the final quarter mile.
**Flint River** did not run at all badly given what happened to him in the early stages.
**Hermitage Court(USA)** probably took too much out of himself by racing keenly.
**Madamoiselle Jones** *Official explanation: jockey said filly had hung right*
**Carry On Doc** may well have lost his race before the start, and he is entitled to be given the chance to prove this run all wrong. *Official explanation: jockey said colt had bolted to the start*
T/Plt: £291.30 to a £1 stake. Pool: £38,115.75. 95.50 winning tickets. T/Qpdt: £45.90 to a £1 stake. Pool: £3,049.40. 49.10 winning tickets. JN

## 5361 CHANTILLY (R-H)
### Wednesday, September 8

**OFFICIAL GOING: Good**

### 5404a PRIX D'ARENBERG (GROUP 3) — 5f 110y
2:05 (2:06) 2-Y-O — **£25,704** (£10,282; £7,711; £5,141)

RPR
1 — **Toupie**[18] [4962] 2-8-8 .......... J-BEyquem 6 — 101
(FRohaut, France) *trckd ldrs, disp 6th halfway, hdwy 2f out, rdn & pressing ldr over 1f out, ran on to ld jst ins fnl f, hld on wl*
2 snk **Crossover**[20] 2-8-8 .......... TJarnet 8 — 100
(H-APantall, France) *trckd ldrs, disp 6th halfway, hdwy on outside from 2f out, fin wl fr over 1f out, nrst at fin*
3 hd **Salut Thomas (FR)**[17] [4981] 2-8-11 ..........(b) CSoumillon 2 — 103
(RobertCollet, France) *held up, 8th on stands side half-way, effort and ran on from over 1 1/2f out, nearest at finish*
4 1½ **Great Blood (FR)**[45] [4184] 2-8-8 .......... OPeslier 4 — 95
(XThomas-Demeaulte, France) *prom and led halfway, pushed along and qcknd 2f out, rdn over 1f out, hdd jst ins fnl f, kpt on at one pace* 2
5 nk **Speciale (USA)**[38] [4381] 2-8-8 .......... C-PLemaire 1 — 94
(MmeCHead-Maarek, France) *last and outpaced to half-way, headway over 2f out to 1f out, no extra closing stages* 1
6 2 **Key Secret**[16] [5005] 2-8-8 .......... HayleyTurner 3 — 87
(MLWBell) *close up on stands rail, 3rd half-way, pushed along over 1 1/2f out, ridden and no extra from 1f out*
7 2 **Siena Gold**[18] [4962] 2-8-8 .......... JFMcDonald 9 — 80
(BJMeehan) *led 1f, disputing 4th half-way on outside, driven over 1f out, one pace*
8 snk **Countdown**[16] [5005] 2-8-11 ..........(b) TThulliez 5 — 83
(SirMarkPrescott) *disputed lead after 1f to half-way, pushed along over 1 1/2f out, outpaced* 3
9 1½ **Shifting Place**[17] [4981] 2-8-11 .......... DVargiu 7 — 78
(RMenichetti, Italy) *disputed lead after 1f to half-way, ridden and weakened from 1 1/2f out*

62.90 secs **Going Correction** -0.40s/f (Firm) — **9** Ran SP% **121.4**
Speed ratings: **106,105,105,103,103 100,97,97,95.**
**Owner** J Gispert **Bred** Haras D'Etreham And Vision Bloodstock **Trained** France

**NOTEBOOK**
**Toupie**, a brave little filly who was held up in the early part of the race, took the advantage well inside the final furlong. She fended off all challengers in good style, goes well on good or faster ground and may now be aimed at the Criterium de Maisons-Laffitte.
**Crossover** is still green but has plenty of talent. Settled behind the leading group, she ran on really well to pinch second place close home, and could now go for the Prix Eclipse.
**Salut Thomas(FR)**, an experienced two-year-old, ran another good race. Not desperately lucky inside the final furlong, his connections objected to the winner but the placings were not altered.
**Great Blood(FR)** was fast away and was one of the leaders early on, but she began to shorten her stride at the furlong marker. She still fought well to the line, though.
**Key Secret** was quickly out of the stalls and settled in second place behind the leader. She could not quicken at the furlong marker, though, and gradually dropped back.
**Siena Gold** was also well away on the outside and up with the leaders on passing the stands. She was then unable to change gear a furlong and a half out and gradually dropped away.
**Countdown**, blinkered for the first time, was also smartly out of the stalls up the centre of the track, but he was under pressure from a furlong and a half out, and his jockey felt that the colt was unbalanced throughout the race and might not have been suited by the headgear.

5405 - (Foreign Racing) - See Raceform Interactive

## 5256 CHEPSTOW (L-H)
### Thursday, September 9

**OFFICIAL GOING: Good to firm**
Runners elected to race down the centre of the track in the majority. The ground on both rails was considered "rough".
Wind: slt across becoming nil Weather: sunny and warm

### 5406 "GRAVELLS RENAULT" E B F MAIDEN STKS — 7f 16y
2:00 (2:02) (D3) 2-Y-O — **£3,620** (£1,114; £557; £278) Stalls High

Form — RPR
06 1 — **Press Express (IRE)**[13] [5091] 2-9-0 .......... CCatlin 6 — 75
(MRChannon) *w ldrs: hrd rdn fnl f: led nr fin* **4/1**[2]
6 2 nk **Fine Lady**[10] [5172] 2-8-9 .......... DHolland 3 — 69
(MJohnston) *w ldr: led 4f out: rdn over 1f out: hdd nr fin* **6/1**[3]
0 3 shd **Strike Gold**[20] [4922] 2-9-0 .......... WSupple 1 — 74
(SKirk) *hld up in tch: rdn over 1f out: ev ch wl ins fnl f: r.o* **25/1**
56 4 shd **Knightsbridge Hill (IRE)**[20] [4913] 2-9-0 .......... JDSmith 12 — 74
(AKing) *hld up in tch: rdn over 1f out: r.o ins fnl f* **8/1**
0 5 5 **Brandexe (IRE)**[7] [5248] 2-8-2 .......... KMay[(7)] 4 — 56
(BWHills) *hld up in mid-div: lost pl over 4f out: hdwy 2f out: sn no imp* **20/1**
4 6 ¾ **World Report (USA)**[22] [4861] 2-9-0 .......... PDobbs 13 — 59
(RHannon) *wnt lft s: hld up towards rr: rdn 3f out: hdwy 2f out: no further prog fnl f* **7/4**[1]
0 7 3 **Sovereign Spirit (IRE)**[20] [4922] 2-9-0 .......... IMongan 14 — 52
(PWHarris) *chsd ldrs: rdn over 3f out: no hdwy fnl 2f* **20/1**
8 nk **Piran (IRE)** 2-8-11 .......... JFMcDonald[(3)] 2 — 51
(BJMeehan) *s.s: nvr nrr* **16/1**
40 9 shd **Creative Character (USA)**[28] [4689] 2-9-0 .......... RMullen 7 — 51
(PFICole) *s.i.s: rdn and hung lft fr over 2f out: hdwy over 1f out: n.d* **12/1**
050 10 1½ **Asteem**[21] [4866] 2-9-0 55 .......... SCarson 9 — 47
(RFJohnsonHoughton) *prom tl rdn and wknd over 2f out* **33/1**
11 1¼ **Crystal Mystic (IRE)** 2-8-11 ..........(b[1]) RMiles[(3)] 11 — 44
(BPalling) *s.v.s: hdwy over 4f out: rdn over 2f out: wknd wl over 1f out* **50/1**
00 12 nk **Montjeu Baby (IRE)**[7] [5247] 2-8-9 .......... FNorton 15 — 38
(RHannon) *a bhd* **33/1**
13 2 **Back To Reality** 2-9-0 .......... DSweeney 5 — 38
(BPalling) *sn wl bhd* **33/1**
6 14 7 **Desert Moonbeam (IRE)**[29] [4637] 2-8-9 .......... RHavlin 10 — 16
(RJHodges) *prom 2f* **33/1**
6536 15 5 **Robmantra**[17] [5005] 2-9-0 70 ..........(p) SWhitworth 8 — 8
(BJLlewellyn) *led 3f: wknd over 2f out* **50/1**

1m 23.85s (0.65) **Going Correction** -0.075s/f (Good) — **15** Ran SP% **124.4**
Speed ratings: **93,92,92,92,86 85,82,82,81,80 78,78,76,68,62**CSF £25.57 TOTE £3.30: £1.50, £2.50, £12.50; EX 36.00.
**Owner** Tareq Al-Mazeedi & Adnan Bahbahani **Bred** Tareq Al Mazeedi **Trained** West Ilsley, Berks

**FOCUS**
An average maiden with little strength in depth and the early pace was only modest, but the first four finished clear.
**NOTEBOOK**
**Press Express(IRE)**, who had shown fair form in two previous outings on an easy surface, really knuckled down well to get on top close home and lose his maiden tag. He has improved with every run, had no trouble with this faster surface and a mile will hold no barriers next year, but his future lies in handicaps.
**Fine Lady**, sixth on her debut over a mile at this track ten days previously on soft ground, held every chance but just failed. This drop back in trip proved ideal and, although she is not one of her stable's leading lights, she should win her maiden at least.
**Strike Gold**, who ran distinctly green on his recent Sandown debut, turned in a much-improved effort and was only run out of it in the dying strides. This experience will do him the world of good, he already looks in need of a mile and has a future.
**Knightsbridge Hill(IRE)** was being ridden from halfway, but responded well to his rider's urgings and finished nicely on the stands'-side rail. He will do better next year, but should not be too harshly treated now he qualifies for nurseries and could be placed to advantage.
**World Report(USA)** was backed to improve on his debut effort, but was never a serious factor and looked to be feeling this quicker ground. *Official explanation: jockey said colt was never travelling*
**Creative Character(USA)** got wound up in the preliminaries and was sluggish from the gates, but was staying on under a sympathetic ride and now qualifies for nurseries.

### 5407 RENAULT KANGOO VAN MEDIAN AUCTION MAIDEN STKS — 1m 14y
2:35 (2:39) (E3) 2-Y-O — **£3,669** (£1,129; £564; £282) Stalls High

Form — RPR
03 1 — **She's My Outsider**[43] [4234] 2-8-9 .......... FNorton 14 — 77+
(IAWood) *plld hrd: a.p: led on bit over 2f out: pushed along over 1f out: readily* **9/4**[2]
44 2 1¼ **Mokaraba**[22] [4851] 2-8-9 .......... WSupple 3 — 71
(JLDunlop) *hld up in tch: rdn and ev ch over 2f out: r.o one pce* **7/4**[1]
3 nk **Solarias Quest** 2-9-0 .......... JDSmith 7 — 75
(AKing) *wnt lft s: hld up in rr: hdwy on outside over 2f out: pushed along over 1f out: styd on ins fnl f: bttr for r* **14/1**
4 ½ **Cloonavery (IRE)** 2-9-0 .......... VSlattery 11 — 74
(JAOsborne) *dwlt: hld up: hdwy over 2f out: rdn over 1f out: nt qckn ins fnl f* **20/1**
5 5 1¾ **Oasis Way (GR)**[18] [4966] 2-8-9 .......... DSweeney 13 — 65
(PRChamings) *s.i.s: sn prom: ev ch over 2f out: rdn over 1f out: one pce fnl f* **13/2**[3]
0 6 4 **Yardstick**[56] [3870] 2-9-0 .......... CCatlin 12 — 60
(SKirk) *hld up: sn mid-div: no hdwy fnl 2f* **40/1**
7 nk **Nobbler** 2-9-0 .......... SWhitworth 8 — 59
(JWHills) *s.i.s: bhd: rdn over 2f out: nvr nrr* **25/1**
0 8 ¾ **Brego (IRE)**[6] [5269] 2-9-0 .......... RHavlin 9 — 57
(JHMGosden) *led 3f: rdn over 2f out: wknd over 1f out* **40/1**
0 9 1¼ **Manorshield Minx**[39] [4364] 2-8-9 .......... IMongan 2 — 49
(SKirk) *hld up in tch: rdn over 2f out: wknd wl over 1f out* **16/1**
000 10 nk **Welsh Galaxy (IRE)**[8] [5227] 2-8-9 .......... RPrice 5 — 48
(PLGilligan) *hld up in mid-div: rdn over 2f out: wknd over 1f out* **100/1**
00 11 ½ **Volitio**[18] [4967] 2-9-0 .......... PDobbs 10 — 52
(SKirk) *w ldr: led 5f out: rdn and hdd over 2f out: wknd wl over 1f out* **66/1**
0 12 shd **Stolen**[10] [5198] 2-9-0 .......... RMullen 4 — 52
(WRMuir) *hld up in tch: rdn 3f out: wkng whn n.m.r over 1f out* **40/1**
000 13 14 **Scale The Heights (IRE)**[10] [5173] 2-9-0 .......... DHolland 1 — 17
(BWHills) *rdn over 5f out: a bhd: t.o* **12/1**
14 16 **Chestminster Girl** 2-8-9 .......... GHannon 6 — —
(APJones) *sn pushed along in rr: t.o fnl 4f* **100/1**

1m 35.8s (-0.10) **Going Correction** -0.075s/f (Good) — **14** Ran SP% **120.1**
Speed ratings: **97,95,95,94,93 89,88,88,86,86 86,86,72,56**CSF £6.05 TOTE £3.60: £1.80, £1.10, £4.70; EX 6.80.
**Owner** Lewis Caterers **Bred** R W K Lewis **Trained** Upper Lambourn, Berks

**FOCUS**
Another maiden to lack any real strength in depth and it was run at just a reasonable gallop. The first five were clear at the finish.
**NOTEBOOK**
**She's My Outsider**, who showed significant improvement on her second outing at Kempton in July, ran out a ready winner despite running keenly through the early stages. This step up in trip proved ideal and providing she learns to settle better, she could make into a fairly useful performer next year.
**Mokaraba** held every chance and has to go down as a little disappointing, as she was very one paced in the closing stages. She is the type to fare better over farther as a three-year-old, but is clearly only modest.
**Solarias Quest** fared best of the newcomers and shaped with definite promise, keeping on under tender ride close home. Handy throughout, he looked well suited by the trip and this backward gelding should find a similar event in which to get off the mark. *Official explanation: jockey said gelding was unsuited by the good to firm ground*
**Cloonavery(IRE)** posted a pleasing debut and was doing all of his best work at the finish, not given that hard a time. Like many of his yard's juveniles, he should improve a fair bit for the experience.
**Oasis Way(GR)**, who shaped encouragingly on her debut at Folkestone recently, turned in another fair effort and will no doubt fare better when handicapped.
**Scale The Heights(IRE)** *Official explanation: jockey said gelding was reluctant to race*

## 5408 RENAULT TRAFIC VAN (S) STKS 1m 14y
3:10 (3:12) (G4) 3-Y-0+ £2,765 (£790; £395) Stalls High

Form RPR

0440 **1** **Alafzar (IRE)**[16] 5017 6-9-1 55 (vt) SJDonohoe(7) 2 64
(PDEvans) *hld up: smooth hdwy over 3f out: led 2f out: edgd rt ins fnl f: pushed out* **8/1**

0000 **2** *1* **Fizzy Lady**[6] 5260 3-8-12 52 (t) RMullen 6 57
(NEBerry) *bhd: rdn and hdwy over 2f out: chsd wnr fnl f: kpt on* **33/1**

0604 **3** *2* **Mobo-Baco**[6] 5260 7-9-5 52 JFMcDonald(3) 17 57
(RJHodges) *hld up: hdwy 5f out: rdn and ev ch over 2f out: one pce fnl f* **3/1**[1]

5660 **4** *3* **Our Destiny**[6] 5258 6-9-8 56 DHolland 8 50
(AWCarroll) *hld up: rdn and hdwy over 2f out: wknd ins fnl f* **9/2**[2]

2555 **5** *1 1/4* **Dancing King (IRE)**[10] 5199 8-9-1 48 PGallagher(7) 18 47
(PWHiatt) *led: rdn and hdd 2f out: sn wknd* **6/1**[3]

1040 **6** *nk* **Over To You Bert**[27] 4713 5-9-3 45 MSavage(5) 3 47
(RJHodges) *chsd ldrs: rdn over 2f out: wknd over 1f out* **12/1**

0000 **7** *1* **Wodhill Be**[24] 4818 4-8-12 40 MTebbutt 9 34
(DMorris) *dwlt: rdn and hdwy over 1f out: one pce fnl f* **20/1**

0060 **8** *1* **Millfields Dreams**[6] 5261 5-9-8 55 IMongan 5 42
(RBrotherton) *prom: rdn over 2f out: wknd 1f out* **10/1**

4105 **9** *3* **Cayman Breeze**[30] 4617 4-9-1 57 CJDavies(7) 19 35
(JMBradley) *trckd ldr: rdn over 2f out: wknd wl over 1f out* **10/1**

-000 **10** *2* **Lyrical Lady**[90] 2836 3-8-4 45 (p) RThomas(3) 13 20
(MrsAJBowlby) *prom: rdn 3f out: sn wknd* **33/1**

0055 **11** *1* **Tamarina (IRE)**[16] 5018 3-8-7 35 (b) FNorton 10 18
(NEBerry) *prom 3f* **50/1**

-660 **12** *4* **Frixos (IRE)**[25] 4473 4-9-3 47 (b) VSlattery 12 14
(MScudamore) *prom tl rdn and wknd over 3f out* **50/1**

0000 **13** *shd* **Diaphanous**[21] 4881 6-8-5 35 LiamJones(7) 15 9
(EAWheeler) *rrd s: plld hrd: sn mid-div: hdwy 5f out: rdn and wknd over 2f out* **100/1**

**14** *2* **Lyns Resolution**[18] 4-9-3 RPrice 16 9
(DBurchell) *s.i.s: sn t.o: sme late prog: a bhd* **66/1**

0000 **15** *1/2* **Rumour Mill (IRE)**[3] 5336 3-8-9 40 RMiles(3) 1 8
(NEBerry) *racd alone towards far side: prom: rdn 3f out: wknd wl over 1f out* **50/1**

**16** *1 1/2* **Pico Alto** 3-8-7 DSweeney 7 —
(BPalling) *dwlt: a bhd* **18/1**

00 **17** *1/2* **Miss De Bois**[17] 5006 7-8-7 BSwarbrick(5) 4 —
(WMBrisbourne) *dwlt: a bhd* **66/1**

46R0 **L** **Princess Ismene**[11] 5145 3-8-12 45 SRighton 14 —
(MAppleby) *ref to r: tk no part* **66/1**

1m 34.78s (-1.12) **Going Correction** -0.075s/f (Good)
**WFA** 3 from 4yo+ 5lb **18** Ran SP% **121.7**
Speed ratings: **102,101,99,96,94 94,93,92,89,87 86,82,82,80,79 78,77,—**CSF £258.75 TOTE £7.00: £2.70, £10.30, £1.70; EX 504.70.There was no bid for the winner.
**Owner** Waterline Racing Club **Bred** His Highness The Aga Khan's Studs S C **Trained** Pandy, Gwent

**FOCUS**
Despite the size of the field this was a typically uncompetitive seller and the field were spread across the track from an early stage.

**NOTEBOOK**
**Alafzar(IRE)** , who looked all at sea on soft ground at Brighton last time, relished this faster surface and posted an authoritative display to win his first race on turf since 2002. This marked drop in class helped him stay this mile and he should continue to pay his way at this level, granted the ground is riding quick.
**Fizzy Lady** was staying on to good effect, but never looked like pegging back the winner. This is certainly her level and she was clear in second, so could find a similarly weak heat.
**Mobo-Baco** was well backed on this return to his favoured trip back in selling company, but had no obvious excuses and was well held.
**Our Destiny** shaped better on this drop in class, but was unable to quicken when it mattered over this shorter trip. If kept to this grade, he could go close when reverting to ten furlongs.
**Dancing King(IRE)** set a fair pace for a long way, but found little when push came to shove and would prefer a sharper test at this distance.

## 5409 RENAULT MASTER VAN MAIDEN STKS 1m 4f 23y
3:45 (3:45) (D3) 3-Y-0 £3,532 (£1,087; £543; £271) Stalls Low

Form RPR

00 **1** **Dune Raider (USA)**[75] 3297 3-9-0 FNorton 4 76
(KARyan) *hld up: hdwy 4f out: rdn over 2f out: r.o to ld cl home* **13/2**[3]

24 **2** *hd* **Newnham (IRE)**[17] 5007 3-8-11 NMackay(3) 5 76
(LMCumani) *led early: chsd ldr: led over 1f out: hrd rdn and hdd cl home* **6/5**[1]

2-33 **3** *7* **Market Leader**[11] 5152 3-8-9 71 (b[1]) WSupple 3 60
(MrsAJPerrett) *sn led: clr over 5f out: hdd over 1f out: wknd fnl f* **15/8**[2]

-403 **4** *9* **Dancing Bear**[112] 2250 3-9-0 60 IMongan 2 50
(JulianPoulton) *hld up: hdwy over 5f out: sn rdn: wknd 3f out* **14/1**

0-66 **5** *1 1/2* **Dream Valley (IRE)**[8] 5217 3-8-9 60 [1] DHolland 1 43
(BWHills) *a bhd* **12/1**

00 **6** *30* **Patterson (IRE)**[19] 4939 3-8-9 SWhitworth 6 —
(MMadgwick) *hld up: pushed along over 5f out: sn struggling: t.o fnl 4f* **100/1**

2m 36.64s (-1.86) **Going Correction** -0.075s/f (Good) **6** Ran SP% **108.9**
Speed ratings: **103,102,98,92,91 71**CSF £13.96 TOTE £9.70: £4.70, £1.10; EX 20.80.
**Owner** Tariq Al Nisf **Bred** F J F M Llc **Trained** Hambleton, N Yorks

**FOCUS**
This maiden was full of late-maturing three-year-olds and it was run at a fair clip in the circumstances. The first two came well clear and the form looks ordinary.

**NOTEBOOK**
**Dune Raider(USA)** , who showed very little in two outings for Sir Michael Stoute previously, won a touch cosily on this debut for new connections. He was under pressure when attempting to challenge two out, but responded strongly for his rider and always looked like getting on top. He has clearly come right of late and relished this extra distance.
**Newnham(IRE)** looked all over the winner when easing to the lead, but quickly came under pressure when the winner challenged and could not find the necessary change of gear. He is in danger of becoming a frustrating individual, but could be worth another chance back over ten furlongs and is now eligible for handicaps.
**Market Leader** , in the first-time blinkers, was soon towing the field along at a fairly brisk pace and had the run of the race, but dropped out quickly when headed two out and ultimately proved disappointing.

## 5410 TOTESPORT H'CAP 1m 2f 36y
4:20 (4:20) (E3) (0-70,70) 3-Y-0 £3,935 (£1,211; £605; £302) Stalls Low

Form RPR

002- **1** **Nuts For You (IRE)**[276] 6145 3-8-12 61 DSweeney 2 73
(RCharlton) *prom: wnt 2nd after 2f: led 2f out: r.o wl* **16/1**

5011 **2** *3/4* **Stephano**[5] 5293 3-9-2 65 6ex DHolland 10 75
(BWHills) *hld up in mid-div: hdwy 4f out: swtchd rt 2f out: chsd wnr fnl f: kpt on nr fin* **5/6**[1]

2232 **3** *2 1/2* **Captain Marryat**[5] 5293 3-8-10 59 WSupple 13 65
(PWHarris) *hld up in mid-div: lost plcd 6f out: hdwy and nt clr run over 2f out: swtchd rt over 1f out: r.o ins fnl f* **5/1**[2]

1454 **4** *nk* **Quickstyx**[10] 5197 3-9-5 68 CCatlin 4 73
(MRChannon) *t.k.h in mid-div: hdwy 4f out: rdn 3f out: one pce fnl f* **8/1**[3]

0660 **5** *hd* **Saida Lenasera (FR)**[29] 4628 3-8-11 63 NMackay(3) 1 68
(MrsPSly) *chsd ldr 2f: prom: ev ch 2f out: rdn over 1f out: wknd ins fnl f* **33/1**

5356 **6** *1 1/2* **Mustang Ali (IRE)**[34] 4518 3-9-2 65 FNorton 8 67
(SKirk) *hld up and bhd: rdn and hdwy on ins whn swtchd rt 2f out: no ex ins fnl f* **20/1**

5562 **7** *2* **Rabitatit (IRE)**[20] 4921 3-8-8 62 BSwarbrick(5) 9 60
(JGMO'Shea) *led: rdn and hdd 2f out: wknd jst over 1f out* **14/1**

0000 **8** *1* **Off Beat (USA)**[7] 5252 3-9-2 65 SCarson 11 61
(RFJohnsonHoughton) *hld up: rdn and short-lived effrt 2f out* **33/1**

4240 **9** *nk* **Uncle John**[14] 5057 3-8-9 58 VSlattery 15 54
(SKirk) *hld up in mid-div: rdn over 2f out: sn wknd* **33/1**

005 **10** *nk* **Twelve Bar Blues**[109] 2323 3-9-4 67 RHavlin 3 62
(JHMGosden) *prom: rdn over 3f out: wknd wl over 1f out* **28/1**

0000 **11** *2 1/2* **Medica Boba**[31] 4615 3-8-10 59 PDobbs 7 49
(HMorrison) *a bhd* **50/1**

5665 **12** *4* **Sierra**[8] 5223 3-8-10 62 J-PGuillambert(3) 6 45
(CEBrittain) *prom tl wknd over 2f out* **25/1**

4326 **13** *1 3/4* **Go Green**[10] 5175 3-8-7 56 oh1 (t) RMullen 14 35
(PDEvans) *s.i.s: hld up: hdwy 6f out: lost pl 5f out: n.d after* **16/1**

1040 **14** *14* **Premier Dream (USA)**[28] 4672 3-9-6 69 SWhitworth 5 22
(JGMO'Shea) *s.i.s: a bhd: t.o* **66/1**

2m 9.58s (-0.02) **Going Correction** -0.075s/f (Good) **14** Ran SP% **125.1**
Speed ratings: **97,96,94,94,94 92,91,90,90,89 87,84,83,72**CSF £28.81 CT £92.10 TOTE £20.20: £3.70, £1.10, £2.50; EX 47.90.
**Owner** Mountgrange Stud **Bred** Epona Bloodstock Ltd **Trained** Beckhampton, Wilts

**FOCUS**
A modest handicap that was run at an average gallop, but the form looks sound for the grade.

**NOTEBOOK**
**Nuts For You(IRE)** , making her handicap and three-year-old debut after a 276-day absence from the track, was not fully extended to hold off the runner-up and duly won in good style. This longer trip was very much up her street and it would be a surprise if she were not placed to strike again, but connections will be hoping to get her out quickly under a penalty, as she will no doubt go up a fair bit in the weights for this success.
**Stephano**, looking for the quickfire hat-trick, does not do anything quickly and found the winner gone beyond recall when hitting full stride. He has improved since being upped in trip, and still looks to be maturing, so it would be no surprise were he to be turned out again quickly, as he is due to take a hefty rise in the weights in the near future.
**Captain Marryat** ran up to his recent form with the second, despite not getting the best of runs, on these better terms. He continues to look in need of respite from the Handicapper, but is a decent yardstick for the grade and deserves to find a race.
**Quickstyx** stayed on under pressure, but was never a serious threat. She is reliable, but has struggled in handicaps since winning on her debut in January and probably needs to drop in the ratings.
**Saida Lenasera(FR)** tried to force the pace and registered her best effort of the current campaign.
**Premier Dream(USA)** *Official explanation: jockey said colt had a breathing problem*

## 5411 RENAULT VANS H'CAP 7f 16y
4:55 (4:56) (F4) (0-55,55) 3-Y-0+ £3,126 (£893; £446) Stalls High

Form RPR

1036 **1** **My Girl Pearl (IRE)**[6] 5261 4-8-3 47 NMackay(3) 19 55
(MSSaunders) *w ldr: led over 2f out: r.o wl* **20/1**

0122 **2** *3/4* **Pepper Road**[38] 4386 5-8-12 53 DHolland 11 59+
(RBastiman) *hld up in mid-div: nt clr run and swtchd lft over 2f out: rdn and hdwy wl over 1f out: r.o ins fnl f* **9/2**[1]

5010 **3** *nk* **Accendere**[64] 3636 3-8-10 55 RMullen 15 60
(RMBeckett) *hld up towards rr: rdn 2f out: hdwy over 1f out: r.o ins fnl f* **20/1**

0623 **4** *nk* **Armentieres**[6] 5260 3-8-4 52 (b) JFMcDonald(3) 18 56
(JLSpearing) *a.p: rdn over 2f out: r.o same pce fnl f* **10/1**

0546 **5** *1/2* **Temper Tantrum**[15] 5039 6-8-9 55 (p) MSavage(5) 17 58
(JRBest) *hld up: rdn and hdwy over 2f out: nt qckn ins fnl f* **6/1**[2]

4402 **6** *3/4* **Iced Diamond (IRE)**[7] 5235 5-8-9 50 (t) CCatlin 2 51
(WMBrisbourne) *hld up and bhd: hdwy over 1f out: rdn and qckn ins fnl f* **7/1**[3]

0304 **7** *3/4* **Captain Cloudy**[6] 5261 4-8-12 53 SWhitworth 16 52
(MMadgwick) *s.i.s: hld up and bhd: rdn and hdwy over 2f out: one pce fnl f* **20/1**

0000 **8** *1/2* **Mister Regent**[14] 5063 3-8-10 55 (b) FNorton 14 53
(KARyan) *prom: rdn over 2f out: wknd ins fnl f* **33/1**

-000 **9** *3/4* **Caerphilly Gal**[75] 3321 4-8-6 50 DCorby(3) 9 46
(PLGilligan) *prom: rdn over 1f out: wknd ins fnl f* **20/1**

4600 **10** *3/4* **Espada (IRE)**[5] 5305 8-8-9 50 (b) VSlattery 13 44
(JAOsborne) *hld up: rdn and hdd over 2f out: wknd over 1f out* **28/1**

0300 **11** *nk* **Pagan Storm (USA)**[24] 4818 4-8-6 54 KristinStubbs(7) 12 47
(MrsLStubbs) *s.i.s: hrd rdn 3f out: hdwy over 1f out: edgd lft and wknd ins fnl f* **20/1**

0311 **12** *1* **Yorkies Boy**[5] 5282 9-8-8 52 6ex (p) RThomas(3) 20 42
(NEBerry) *prom tl rdn and wknd over 2f out* **7/1**[3]

0021 **13** *hd* **Bint Royal (IRE)**[42] 4260 6-8-11 55 J-PGuillambert(3) 10 45
(MissVHaigh) *chsd ldrs: lost pl and hrd rdn 3f out: sn struggling* **12/1**

5000 **14** *1 1/2* **Logistical**[6] 5260 4-8-11 52 DSweeney 6 37
(ADWPinder) *hld up in mid-div: pushed along over 3f out: n.d after* **25/1**

5116 **15** *nk* **Extemporise (IRE)**[90] 2854 4-8-4 52 KJackson(7) 8 37
(TTClement) *bhd fnl 2f* **50/1**

0500 **16** *nk* **Parker**[37] 4425 7-8-7 51 (t) RMiles(3) 7 35
(BPalling) *chsd ldrs tl rdn and wknd wl over 1f out* **20/1**

1210 **17** *2* **Didoe**[16] 5017 5-8-10 51 JoannaBadger 4 29
(PWHiatt) *s.i.s: a bhd* **20/1**

5244 **18** *hd* **Filliemou (IRE)**[32] 4580 3-8-9 54 WSupple 5 32
(AWCarroll) *chsd ldrs: rdn 3f out: wknd 2f out* **20/1**

0060 **19** *5* **Super Song**[43] 4232 4-8-10 51 (t) IMongan 3 15
(PDEvans) *hld up: rdn and short-lived effrt on far side over 2f out* **14/1**

0000 **20** *6* **Arabian Knight (IRE)**[115] 2166 4-8-10 51 RHavlin 1 —
(RJHodges) *a bhd* **100/1**

1m 22.56s (-0.64) **Going Correction** -0.075s/f (Good)
**WFA** 3 from 4yo+ 4lb **20** Ran SP% **132.2**
Speed ratings: **100,99,98,98,97 97,96,95,94,93 93,92,92,90,90 89,87,87,81,74**CSF £96.48 CT £1947.86 TOTE £26.20: £3.90, £2.40, £4.30, £2.70; EX 203.10.

**Owner** T A Godbert **Bred** Loan And Development Corporation **Trained** Haydon, Somerset

■ Stewards Enquiry : J-P Guillambert one-day ban: used whip with excessive force (Sep 20)

**FOCUS**

The pace was only modest until halfway in this low-grade handicap. The field came down the centre of the track and a high draw proved a distinct advantage.

**NOTEBOOK**

**My Girl Pearl(IRE)**, stepping up in trip, boosted her modest strike rate with only her second win from 32 career runs. A filly who sweats up before her races, she was in front soon enough and there to be shot at, but stayed on well to hold off all challengers. She was only 2lb higher than when gaining her previous win and is unlikely to go up too much for this.

**Pepper Road** was arguably a little unlucky, as he was briefly short of room approaching the two pole. He ran on strongly inside the final furlong and a return to a mile can see him back in the winner's enclosure.

**Accendere** ran a solid race on his first try against his elders. He is worth another chance at a mile, having failed to handle soft ground on his one try at that trip.

**Armentieres**, off the same mark as when third over course and distance last week, ran well again but seems to find the seven furlongs a little too sharp.

**Temper Tantrum** ran respectably, albeit from a favourable draw, and appeared to have no excuses.

**Iced Diamond(IRE)** was still at the back of the field with a quarter of a mile to run, but he finished strongly. This was a commendable effort from a poor draw, but he is due to race off a 3lb higher mark in future handicaps.

**Captain Cloudy** looked a danger as he attempted to challenge towards the stands' side, but not for the first time he flattered to deceive.

**Mister Regent** has been given a chance by the Handicapper and showed signs of a return to form.

**Yorkies Boy**, bidding for a quickfire hat-trick under a penalty, had perhaps the best draw of all but failed to pick up. He was beaten too far out for this longer trip to be blamed.

**Extemporise(IRE)** *Official explanation: trainer said colt bled from the nose*

**Arabian Knight(IRE)** *Official explanation: jockey said gelding lost its action on two occasions*

## 5412 RENAULT CLIO VAN H'CAP — 5f 16y

**5:25** (5:28) (E3) (0-70,69) 3-Y-0+ — **£3,822** (£1,176; £588; £294) **Stalls** High

| Form | | | | | RPR |
|---|---|---|---|---|---|
| -040 | **1** | | **Inch By Inch**[43] [4232] 5-8-7 **55** oh2 (PJMakin) *a.p: rdn to ld jst over 1f out: drvn out* **40/1** | (b) CCatlin 10 | 65 |
| 0423 | **2** | ¾ | **Redwood Star**[16] [5016] 4-8-7 **55** oh1 (PLGilligan) *hmpd s: hld up and bhd: hdwy over 1f out: r.o wl ins fnl f: edgd rt nr fin: nt rch wnr* **10/1** | (e) DSweeney 5 | 62 |
| 2005 | **3** | ¾ | **College Queen**[7] [5242] 6-8-13 **61** (SGollings) *hld up in tch: nt clr run 2f out: rdn and edgd lft 1f out: r.o ins fnl f* **14/1** | WSupple 12 | 65 |
| 0301 | **4** | ½ | **Maromito (IRE)**[7] [5253] 7-8-7 **55** (RBastiman) *w ldr: led on bit over 2f out tl jst over 1f out: no ex towards fin* **2/1**[1] | DHolland 6 | 57 |
| 0500 | **5** | 1 ½ | **Coranglais**[3] [5337] 4-8-11 **59** (JMBradley) *hld up and bhd: rdn over 2f out: gd late hdwy: nrst fin* **25/1** | (b) FNorton 15 | 55 |
| 2450 | **6** | ½ | **Ardkeel Lass (IRE)**[3] [5337] 3-8-8 **57** (DHaydnJones) *bmpd s: hld up in tch: rdn over 1f out: one pce fnl f* **33/1** | RHavlin 4 | 51 |
| 6330 | **7** | nk | **Stokesies Wish**[16] [5020] 4-8-9 **60** (JLSpearing) *led: rdn and hdd over 2f out: wknd ins fnl f* **12/1** | JFMcDonald[(3)] 8 | 53 |
| 0000 | **8** | ½ | **Indian Bazaar (IRE)**[3] [5337] 8-8-4 **55** oh10 (NEBerry) *hld up in tch: lost pl over 2f out: rallied ins fnl f: n.d* **33/1** | RThomas[(3)] 1 | 46 |
| 4006 | **9** | ½ | **Pulse**[3] [5337] 6-8-9 **57** (JMBradley) *stmbld s: hdwy 1f out: one pce ins fnl f* **10/1** | (p) PFitzsimons 7 | 46 |
| 4412 | **10** | 1 | **Davids Mark**[25] [4782] 4-8-8 **56** (JRJenkins) *hld up: hdwy over 2f out: rdn and edgd lft over 1f out: wknd ins fnl f* **7/2**[2] | IMongan 16 | 41 |
| 0405 | **11** | shd | **Tomthevic**[7] [5253] 6-8-2 **55** oh9 (JMBradley) *hld up in mid-div: rdn over 1f out: no rspnse* **20/1** | BSwarbrick[(5)] 13 | 39 |
| 1000 | **12** | nk | **Izmail (IRE)**[3] [5337] 5-9-0 **69** (PDEvans) *w ldrs: rdn 2f out: wknd 1f out* **14/1** | SJDonohoe[(7)] 9 | 52 |
| 0006 | **13** | 1 | **Tappit (IRE)**[28] [4687] 5-8-4 **55** oh10 (NEBerry) *wnt rt s: prom: rdn and wknd over 1f out* **50/1** | (b) RMiles[(3)] 2 | 34 |
| 3563 | **14** | ½ | **Moritat (IRE)**[6] [5261] 4-8-7 **55** oh4 (PDEvans) *bhd: rdn over 1f out: styng on whn nt clr run ins fnl f* **8/1**[3] | (t) RMullen 14 | 32 |
| 0600 | **15** | 2 ½ | **Zambezi River**[21] [4869] 5-8-7 **55** oh15 (JMBradley) *s.i.s: a bhd* **66/1** | JoannaBadger 11 | 22 |

58.72 secs (-0.78) **Going Correction** -0.075s/f (Good)

**WFA** 3 from 4yo+ 1lb — **15** Ran SP% **126.3**

Speed ratings: **103,101,100,99,97 96,96,95,94,92 92,92,90,89,85**CSF £400.18 CT £5940.97 TOTE £33.70: £7.20, £3.80, £2.90; EX 345.30 Place 6 £30.58, Place 5 £8.99.

**Owner** Mrs Anna L Sanders **Bred** Mrs Anna L Sanders **Trained** Ogbourne Maisey, Wilts

**FOCUS**

A modest sprint which saw the bottom six runners compete from out of the handicap.

**NOTEBOOK**

**Inch By Inch**, racing from 2lb out of the handicap proper, showed a neat turn of foot when hitting the front and stuck to her task well in the closing stages to score. She has shown little since winning last July and looked firmly in the Handicapper's grip prior to this, so it goes down as a much-improved effort and she would be of interest if turned out under a penalty.

**Redwood Star**, another to race from out of the handicap, again ran her race and is in good form at present. She deserves to find another race, but has a habit of finding a few too good.

**College Queen** ran her best race for some time. She is not easy to win with, but has dropped to a realistic mark of late.

**Maromito(IRE)**, who was unpenalised for his Salisbury win a week previously, pinged out and had his chance, but could not sustain his gallop. He looks best over an extra furlong these days and should not be written off just yet.

**Coranglais**

**Davids Mark** came there to have a chance on the near side, but could only keep on at the same pace late on and was well held. This was disappointing. *Official explanation: jockey said gelding was unsuited by the good to firm ground*

T/Plt: £24.90 to a £1 stake. Pool: £30,991.15. 907.80 winning tickets. T/Qpdt: £8.50 to a £1 stake. Pool: £2,817.35. 243.30 winning tickets. KH

# 5391 DONCASTER (L-H)

### Thursday, September 9

**OFFICIAL GOING: Straight course - good to firm; round course - good (good to firm in places)**

Despite the fast times the jockeys were adamant that the ground 'was no quicker than good to firm with a brisk wind behind'.

Wind: Fresh 1/2 behind. Weather: Fine, sunny and very warm.

## 5413 BETFAIR.COM MAY HILL STKS (GROUP 2) (FILLIES) — 1m (R)

**1:15** (1:17) (A1) 2-Y-O — **£42,000** (£16,100; £8,050; £3,850) **Stalls** High

| Form | | | | | RPR |
|---|---|---|---|---|---|
| 21 | **1** | | **Playful Act (IRE)**[13] [5089] 2-8-10 90 (JHMGosden) *trckd 1st 2: qcknd to ld over 1f out: hld on wl* **8/1** | JFortune 7 | 110 |
| 11 | **2** | ¾ | **Queen Of Poland**[49] [4060] 2-8-10 (DRLoder) *lw: chsd ldrs: hdwy over 3f out: nt qckn ins last* **11/4**[1] | TPQueally 8 | 108 |
| 2121 | **3** | shd | **Maids Causeway (IRE)**[33] [4552] 2-8-13 100 (BWHills) *hdwy 3f out: sn chsng ldrs: nt qckn ins last* **9/2**[3] | MHills 5 | 111 |
| 61 | **4** | 5 | **Cassydora**[26] [4753] 2-8-10 (JLDunlop) *led after 1f: hdd over 1f out: wknd jst ins last* **15/2** | TQuinn 2 | 97 |
| 14 | **5** | hd | **Favourita**[11] [5149] 2-8-10 (CEBrittain) *reluctant to go to s: hld up in rr: drvn along over 3f out: kpt on: nvr a factor* **16/1** | JPMurtagh 4 | 96 |
| 13 | **6** | 2 | **Red Peony**[11] [5149] 2-8-10 (SirMarkPrescott) *lw: led 1f: w ldr: rdn and hung lft over 2f out: sn wknd* **7/2**[2] | SSanders 3 | 92 |
| 16 | **7** | 5 | **Windscreamer**[33] [4552] 2-8-10 (JWHills) *s.i.s: sn chsng ldrs: lost pl over 2f out* **12/1** | EAhern 1 | 81 |
| 31 | **8** | 25 | **Road Rage (IRE)**[40] [4344] 2-8-10 (EALDunlop) *unruly s: sn in rr: rdn over 3f out: sn btn: eased* **16/1** | LDettori 6 | 26 |

1m 35.4s (-5.15) **Going Correction** -0.45s/f (Firm) 2y crse rec — **8** Ran SP% **109.4**

Speed ratings: **107,106,106,101,100 98,93,68**CSF £27.68 TOTE £10.60: £3.20, £1.60, £1.90; EX 38.00 Trifecta £124.40 Pool of £648.66 - 3.70 winning tickets.

**Owner** Sangster Family **Bred** Swettenham Stud **Trained** Manton, Wilts

**FOCUS**

Not a vintage renewal, but another fast time and the form should stand up..

**NOTEBOOK**

**Playful Act(IRE)**, whose dam has already produced Echoes In Eternity and Percussionist, showed a battling spirit and may now take her chance in the Fillies' Mile at Ascot. She looks essentially a stayer and will be trained with an Oaks in view next year.

**Queen Of Poland**, who narrowly accounted for Maids Causeway at Sandown, went down fighting.

**Maids Causeway(IRE)**, meeting Queen Of Poland on 3lb worse terms, emerges the best filly in the race and showed she is progressing nicely.

**Cassydora**, who accounted for Playful Act when taking her maiden at Newmarket, could not confirm the form and seemed to have no excuse unless the much quicker ground counted against her.

**Favourita**, a handful leaving the paddock, turned round Goodwood placings with Red Peony but she looks to have a mind of her own.

**Red Peony**, a positive on the betting front. looked to have the leader covered but, when asked a serious question, she looked uncomfortable and dropped away in disappointing fashion.

**Road Rage(IRE)** proved a madam behind the stalls, rearing over backwards. She was never moving well and in the end Dettori simply allowed her to complete in her own time. *Official explanation: jockey said filly was not moving well*

## 5414 GNER PARK STKS (GROUP 2) — 7f

**1:50** (1:50) (A1) 3-Y-O+ — **£60,000** (£23,000; £11,500; £5,500) **Stalls** High

| Form | | | | | RPR |
|---|---|---|---|---|---|
| 1-21 | **1** | | **Pastoral Pursuits**[54] [3940] 3-8-10 110 (HMorrison) *dwlt: sn pushed along: hdwy over 2f out: styd on to ld jst ins last: r.o* **5/1** | SDrowne 7 | 118 |
| 5-14 | **2** | 1 ¼ | **Firebreak**[117] [2109] 5-9-4 115 (SaeedBinSuroor) *lw: racd wd trckd ldr centre: edgd rt and ev ch over 2f out: nt qckn ins last* **5/2**[1] | (t) LDettori 1 | 119 |
| 4214 | **3** | 1 ½ | **Court Masterpiece**[12] [5113] 4-9-0 110 (EALDunlop) *tracd ldrs: effrt over 2f out: nt qckn fnl f* **13/2** | KFallon 3 | 111 |
| 0505 | **4** | 1 ½ | **Golden Nun**[8] [5255] 4-8-11 104 (TDEasterby) *trckd ldrs: effrt over 2f out: kpt on to take 4th nr line* **33/1** | (b) RWinston 4 | 104 |
| 11 | **5** | ½ | **Fong's Thong (USA)**[40] [4322] 3-8-10 108 (BJMeehan) *led on stands' side: led overall over 2f out: hdd jst ins last: 4th and wkng whn eased nr fin* **9/2**[3] | JFortune 8 | 110+ |
| 4022 | **6** | nk | **Suggestive**[26] [4745] 6-9-0 111 (WJHaggas) *trckd ldrs: effrt over 2f out: carried hd high: no imp* **9/1** | (b) MHills 5 | 105 |
| 4460 | **7** | 2 ½ | **Naahy**[12] [5113] 4-9-0 107 (MRChannon) *led overall in centre tl over 2f out: wknd fnl f* **50/1** | SHitchcott 2 | 98 |
| 0-56 | **8** | 4 | **Tillerman**[43] [4228] 8-9-0 115 (MrsAJPerrett) *hld up: effrt over 2f out: nvr threatened: wknd and eased over 1f out* **7/2**[2] | RHughes 6 | 87 |

1m 21.66s (-6.15) **Going Correction** -0.525s/f (Hard) course record

**WFA** 3 from 4yo+ 4lb — **8** Ran SP% **113.9**

Speed ratings: **114,112,110,109,108 108,105,100**CSF £17.77 TOTE £6.50: £1.90, £1.30, £2.70; EX 22.90 Trifecta £121.80 Pool of £1,043.24 - 6.08 winning tickets.

**Owner** The Pursuits Partnership **Bred** Red House Stud **Trained** East Ilsley, Berks

**FOCUS**

A decent renewal run in the sort of time you would expect for a Group Two and won well by Pastoral Pursuits, who has been assessed through Firebreak and Golden Nun and could rate higher still.

**NOTEBOOK**

**Pastoral Pursuits ◆**, who as usual did his own thing in the paddock, takes time to warm to his task but in the end he was right on top, earning the plaudit of 'the best horse I have ridden' from his jockey. He was certainly not stopping at the finish and a mile will not be a problem.

**Firebreak** looked at his very best on his first outing since May. He followed Naahy wide but then tacked over to join the action on the stands' side. After being upsides he was definitely second best at the line.

**Court Masterpiece**, happy to be back on fast ground, possibly ran his best race ever. His trainer is eyeing a winter campaign with him in Dubai.

**Golden Nun** is as tough as old boots and the return to seven furlongs was not a problem, as she grabbed some valuable black-type near the line.

**Fong's Thong(USA)**, a big negative on the betting front, set a strong pace down the stands' side rail but he seemed to lose his action altogether in the closing stages, forfeiting fourth place near the line. *Official explanation: jockey said colt lost its action in the final furlong*

**Suggestive**, who prefers a lot more cover than he was able to get here, carried his head high and looked uncomfortable on the quick ground.

**Naahy** led Firebreak away from the stands'-side rail, but he was going nowhere two furlongs out and his natural front-running style is much better suited to a turning track.



The Form Book, Raceform Ltd, Compton, RG20 6NL

**Tillerman**, who had the best chance on official figures, had the ground to suit but he did not look at his very best beforehand and ran a rare tame race. *Official explanation: jockey said horse was never travelling*

## 5415 GNER DONCASTER CUP (GROUP 2) 2m 2f
**2:25** (2:25) (A1) 3-Y-0+ **£41,500** (£41,500; £11,500; £5,500) **Stalls** Low

Form RPR
303- **1** *dht* **Kasthari (IRE)**$^{137}$ [5637] 5-9-1 112........................ JPMurtagh 8 117
(JHowardJohnson) *lw: trckd ldr: chal 4f out: led over 2f out tl ins last: rallied to join ldr on line* **14/1**
-313 **1** **Millenary**$^{23}$ [4832] 7-9-4 117........................(b) TQuinn 4 120
(JLDunlop) *hld up: smooth hdwy 4f out: styd on to take narrow ld ins last: jnd post* **7/1**$^{3}$
/122 **3** *3 1/2* **Dancing Bay**$^{23}$ [4832] 7-9-1 116........................ KFallon 6 113
(NJHenderson) *trckd ldrs: smooth hdwy over 3f out: rdn and one pce fnl 2f* **5/1**$^{2}$
2302 **4** *2* **High Accolade**$^{25}$ [4794] 4-9-1 115........................(vt) MartinDwyer 2 111
(MPTregoning) *hld up: hdwy 5f out: rdn and hung lft over 3f out: one pce fnl 2f* **5/1**$^{2}$
6131 **5** *3* **Darasim (IRE)**$^{42}$ [4270] 6-9-4 115........................(v) JFanning 7 111
(MJohnston) *led: qcknd 4f out: hdd over 2f out: fdd appr fnl f* **6/4**$^{1}$
166 **6** *3/4* **Corrib Eclipse**$^{23}$ [4832] 5-9-1 106........................ JFEgan 5 107
(JamiePoulton) *hld up and bhd: effrt over 4f out: kpt on: nvr nr ldrs* **18/1**
3155 **7** *1 1/4* **Romany Prince**$^{23}$ [4832] 5-9-1 108........................ RHughes 1 105
(DRCElsworth) *hld up in rr: hdwy 9f out: sn chsng ldrs: lost pl over 2f out* **16/1**
3260 **8** *12* **Silver Gilt**$^{23}$ [4832] 4-9-1 108........................ LDettori 3 92
(JHMGosden) *trckd ldrs: effrt over 3f out: lost pl over 2f out: eased whn bhd ins last* **16/1**

3m 51.86s (-6.07) **Going Correction** -0.45s/f (Firm) **8** Ran SP% **109.5**
Speed ratings: **95,95,93,92,91 90,90,85** TRIFECTA W: M 3.8, K 8.6; Pl: M 2.7, K 4.3, 1.3; Ex: M/K 57.6, K/M 60.5; CSF: M/K 44.27, K/M 49.16; Tri: M/K/D.B 211.50, K/M/D.B 327.6.
**Owner** ElliottBros/L Neil Jones **Bred** AgaKhan/AbergwaunFm **Trained** Crook/Arundel
■ The fourth dead-heat in the Doncaster Cup, first run in 1801.

**FOCUS**
A distinctly average renewal, and a very pedestrian time for a Group Two.

**NOTEBOOK**
**Millenary**, the 2000 St Leger winner, was sharper this time. He moved up on the bridle to go a neck up but the needle was on empty near the line and in the end it was a case of two Doncaster Cup winners.
**Kasthari(IRE)**, a striking grey, really took the eye in the paddock. He had the leader covered and hit back in ultra-game fashion to share the spoils on the line. The plan is for this winner of two hurdle races to try his hand over fences this winter though that plan may now be put on the back burner.
**Dancing Bay** is in the form of his life but this ground is as quick as he wants.
**High Accolade**, runner-up in last year's St Leger, again had the visor on and this time a tongue strap was fitted. As usual he looked a tricky customer, refusing to go forward in a straight line,. However, it would be a tough call to say that he did not truly stay the extended trip.
**Darasim(IRE)** took them along but it was only once in line for home that he really stepped up the pace. He was readily brushed aside and faded noticeably late on. This was not his real form and no doubt he will bounce back.
**Corrib Eclipse**, who just stays, sat off the pace and was never going to take a hand.
**Romany Prince**, who sole career win was in a maiden race, made smooth headway at the halfway mark but in the end was the first beaten.
**Silver Gilt**does not look up to this sort of task and his action suggests he will be happier in a lesser grade with give underfoot. *Official explanation: jockey said gelding lost its action*

## 5416 JRA GOLDEN JUBILEE SCEPTRE STKS (LISTED RACE) (F&M) 7f
**3:00** (3:00) (A1) 3-Y-0+ **£19,500** (£6,000; £3,000; £1,500) **Stalls** High

Form RPR
011 **1** **Attune**$^{7}$ [5249] 3-8-6 82........................ KDarley 7 105
(BJMeehan) *chsd ldrs: drvn along 3f out: styd on to ld last 50yds* **12/1**
1104 **2** *1* **Gonfilia (GER)**$^{41}$ [4286] 4-9-1 102........................(t) LDettori 2 107+
(SaeedBinSuroor) *led far side: edgd rt and led overall over 1f out: hdd towards fin* **5/1**$^{3}$
6534 **3** *1/2* **Ithaca (USA)**$^{25}$ [4773] 3-8-7 100 ow1........................ RHughes 13 102
(HRACecil) *w ldr: led over 2f out tl over 1f out: kpt on wl ins last* **12/1**
000 **4** *3/4* **Enchanted**$^{12}$ [5121] 5-8-10 92........................ JPMurtagh 8 99
(NACallaghan) *trckd ldrs: effrt 2f out: styd on ins last* **33/1**
5525 **5** *hd* **Nyramba**$^{25}$ [4779] 3-8-7 107 ow1........................ JFortune 5 99
(JHMGosden) *chsd ldrs: kpt on wl appr fnl f* **7/2**$^{1}$
1030 **6** *1/2* **Caveral**$^{7}$ [5249] 3-8-6 95........................ EAhern 3 97
(RHannon) *dwlt: swtchd rt after s to r stands' side: hdwy over 2f out: kpt on same pce fnl f* **66/1**
1052 **7** *1/2* **Look Here's Carol (IRE)**$^{7}$ [5249] 4-8-10 91........................ KFallon 10 96
(BAMcmahon) *hld up towards rr: hdwy over 2f out: kpt on: nt rch ldrs* **10/1**
0000 **8** *1/2* **Tahirah**$^{25}$ [4773] 4-8-10 83........................ SDrowne 11 94?
(RGuest) *in rr: hdwy over 2f out: nvr nr ldrs* **50/1**
**9** *3* **The Cat's Whiskers (NZ)**$^{124}$ 4-8-10........................ PRobinson 4 86
(PWChapple-Hyam) *racd far side: chsd ldr: wknd over 1f out* **28/1**
-066 **10** *nk* **Why Dubai (USA)**$^{25}$ [4773] 3-8-6 89........................ MartinDwyer 9 86
(RHannon) *dwlt: a in rr* **66/1**
5-34 **11** *shd* **Zosima (USA)**$^{40}$ [4323] 3-8-6 107........................(t) TEDurcan 1 85
(SaeedBinSuroor) *racd far side: chsd ldr tl wknd over 1f out* **9/2**$^{2}$
**12** *shd* **Poetical (IRE)**$^{19}$ [4961] 3-8-6........................ NGMcCullagh 15 85
(MJGrassick, Ire) *a towards rr* **12/1**
4004 **13** *3* **Starbeck (IRE)**$^{27}$ [4731] 6-8-10 79........................ NCallan 6 77
(PHowling) *swtchd rt after s to r stands' side: a in rr* **100/1**
5210 **14** *dist* **Lucky Pipit**$^{41}$ [4286] 3-8-6 100........................ MHills 14 —
(BWHills) *bolted 3f gng to s: led tl over 2f out: wkng whn hmpd over 1f out: eased heavily: t.o* **11/1**
0040 **P** **Nataliya**$^{25}$ [4779] 3-8-6 102........................(v$^{1}$) SSanders 12 —
(JLDunlop) *chsd ldrs: p.u appr fnl f* **12/1**

1m 22.26s (-5.55) **Going Correction** -0.525s/f (Hard)
**WFA** 3 from 4yo+ 4lb **15** Ran SP% **117.6**
Speed ratings: **110,108,108,107,107 106,106,105,102,101 101,101,98,—,—**CSF £66.75 TOTE £15.50: £4.30, £2.50, £3.90; EX 74.90 Trifecta £787.70 Part won. Pool of £1,109.48 - 0.40 winning tickets..
**Owner** Wyck Hall Stud **Bred** Wyck Hall Stud Ltd **Trained** Upper Lambourn, Berks

**NOTEBOOK**
**Attune** is very much on the up and relishing the fast ground stayed on on willing fashion to show ahead near the line. She will stay in training next year.
**Gonfilia(GER)**, drawn one from the outside, led two others down the centre. Under her 5lb penalty, in the end she just missed out and deserves bags of credit for this.
**Ithaca(USA)**, dropping back to seven, bounced off the ground and was only found lacking in the final dash to the line.
**Enchanted** had a bit to find and ran right up to her very best on ground that is ideal for her.
**Nyramba**, with two handlers and edgy in the paddock, put a poor run last time behind her with the distance and ground conditions she prefers.
**Caveral**, who had something to find, is hard to predict but she ran out of her skin.
**Look Here's Carol(IRE)** *Official explanation: jockey said filly was unsuited by the good to firm ground*
**Tahirah** had an impossible task and seemed to run out of her skin but wether it flattered her only time will tell.
**Zosima(USA)**, a big negative on the exchanges, was taking a big drop in trip and, one of three to race wide, dropped right away.
**Starbeck(IRE)** *Official explanation: jockey said mare was unsuited by the good to firm ground*
**Lucky Pipit** attempted to bolt going to post and after making the running was hampered twice as she dropped back, and in the end was virtually pulled up. *Official explanation: jockey said filly ran too free to post*

## 5417 RALPH RAPER MEMORIAL PRINCE OF WALES CUP (NURSERY) 1m (S)
**3:35** (3:36) (B1) 2-Y-0 **£18,200** (£5,600; £2,800; £1,400) **Stalls** High

Form RPR
433 **1** **Singhalese**$^{13}$ [5088] 2-8-6 **80** ow1........................ SDrowne 9 88
(JAOsborne) *in rr: swtchd lft 2f out: styd on wl to ld last 150yds* **20/1**
0041 **2** *2* **Mighty Empire (IRE)**$^{34}$ [4524] 2-8-2 **76**........................ PRobinson 1 79
(MHTompkins) *swtchd to r stands' side after 1f: trckd ldrs: t.k.h: lf out: sn hdd and no ex* **8/1**$^{3}$
3262 **3** *1* **Sir Anthony (IRE)**$^{12}$ [5128] 2-8-13 **87**........................ FLynch 12 88+
(BSmart) *bhd: swtchd lft over 2f out: styd on wl fnl f* **33/1**
4321 **4** *1* **Kharish (IRE)**$^{6}$ [5268] 2-9-0 **88** 5ex........................ EAhern 3 87
(JNoseda) *swtchd rt after 1f to r stands' side: in rr tl styd on fnl 2f: nt rch ldrs* **6/1**$^{1}$
3105 **5** *hd* **My Princess (IRE)**$^{13}$ [5090] 2-8-1 **75**........................ MHenry 11 73
(NACallaghan) *w ldrs: led over 3f out tl 1f out: kpt on same pce* **33/1**
001 **6** *nk* **The Coires (IRE)**$^{13}$ [5091] 2-8-13 **87**........................ RHughes 5 85
(RHannon) *swtchd rt after 1f to r stands' side: w ldrs: nt qckn fnl f* **16/1**
4524 **7** *3/4* **Alright My Son (IRE)**$^{13}$ [5090] 2-8-3 **77**........................ JFEgan 10 79+
(RHannon) *trckd ldrs: nt clr run over 1f out: nt rcvr* **20/1**
354 **8** *hd* **Bunny Rabbit (USA)**$^{14}$ [5051] 2-8-13 **87**........................ LDettori 14 91+
(BJMeehan) *trckd ldrs: nt clr run fr over 2f out tl over 1f out: nt rcvr* **6/1**$^{1}$
3162 **9** *1 1/2* **Raza Cab (IRE)**$^{14}$ [5051] 2-9-7 **95**........................ KFallon 2 87
(GAHuffer) *swtchd rt after 1f to r stands' side: chsd ldrs: weakaned and eased ins last* **15/2**$^{2}$
4235 **10** *3/4* **Sea Hunter**$^{21}$ [4890] 2-8-10 **87**........................ SHitchcott$^{(3)}$ 15 78
(MRChannon) *chsd ldrs: outpcd over 2f out: kpt on fnl f* **14/1**
0023 **11** *3/4* **Tcherina (IRE)**$^{11}$ [5142] 2-7-13 **73**........................ ANicholls 7 62
(TDEasterby) *rr-div: drvn along over 3f out: nvr a factor* **25/1**
300 **12** *1* **Celestial Arc (USA)**$^{47}$ [4143] 2-7-9 **72**........................ FPFerris$^{(3)}$ 4 59
(PFICole) *swtchd rt to r stands' side after 1f: mid-div: effrt 3f out: no imp* **50/1**
441 **13** *6* **Banknote**$^{44}$ [4208] 2-8-5 **79**........................ MartinDwyer 6 53
(AMBalding) *restless in stalls: mid-div: lost pl over 3f out: sn bhd* **17/2**
3213 **14** *5* **Coleorton Dane**$^{9}$ [5212] 2-8-4 **78**........................ JFanning 13 41
(KARyan) *w ldrs: lost pl 2f out* **20/1**
0312 **15** *14* **Following Flow (USA)**$^{20}$ [4909] 2-8-9 **83**........................ KDarley 8 15+
(WJarvis) *bhd: hmpd over 2f out: nvr on terms* **14/1**
020 **16** *3 1/2* **Shrine Mountain (USA)**$^{23}$ [4835] 2-9-2 **90**........................ SSanders 16 14
(CEBrittain) *led tl over 3f out: sn hmpd: lost pl and eased over 1f out* **33/1**
12 **17** *4* **Buddy Brown**$^{29}$ [4632] 2-9-1 **89**........................ RWinston 17 4+
(JHowardJohnson) *bhd: hmpd and swtchd lft over 2f out: hung lft and eased* **9/1**

1m 36.55s (-5.05) **Going Correction** -0.525s/f (Hard) 2y crse rec **17** Ran SP% **120.1**
Speed ratings: **104,102,101,100,99 99,98,98,97,96 95,94,88,83,69 66,62**CSF £155.43 CT £5370.73 TOTE £23.80: £4.40, £2.40, £4.90, £2.30; EX 267.70.
**Owner** Paul J Dixon **Bred** G And Mrs Middlebrook **Trained** Upper Lambourn, Berks

**FOCUS**
Quite a competitive nursery run at a strong pace. A decent time and the form looks quite reliable, although there were a couple of hard-luck stories.

**NOTEBOOK**
**Singhalese** showed promise in three runs in reasonable maidens and was able to confirm that on this nursery debut, benefiting from the strong pace and getting a clearer run than some of these. A rise in the weights will make things tougher, but her trainer thinks she will be even better next year.
**Mighty Empire(IRE)**, off the mark on his nursery debut at Newmarket, ran very well from a 10lb higher mark and would have been even closer had he been better drawn in a higher stall and not raced so keenly in the early stages. There should yet be more to come.
**Sir Anthony(IRE)**, stepped up in trip, appreciated the good pace and finished well from off the pace. However, he is high enough in the weights.
**Kharish(IRE)**, racing under a 5lb penalty for his Kempton maiden success, took a little while to pick up and simply got going too late. More positive tactics may suit, and he may stay a little further - a race like the Zetland Stakes over ten furlongs could suit.
**My Princess(IRE)** fared best of those to race on the speed and emerges with credit.
**The Coires(IRE)**, off the mark over seven furlongs on soft ground at Newmarket on his previous start, looked on a stiff-enough mark for his nursery debut, but ran well on ground maybe a little faster than he would have liked.
**Alright My Son(IRE)**, supported at big odds, would have been closer with a clearer run and is better than he showed. *Official explanation: jockey said colt was denied a run*
**Bunny Rabbit(USA)** had quite a stiff mark to contend with on his nursery debut, but he would have been much closer with better luck. *Official explanation: jockey said colt was denied a clear run*
**Raza Cab(IRE)**, stepped up from seven furlongs, had no easy task under his big weight and was well held.
**Tcherina(IRE)** was 3lb lower than in future, but could not take advantage.
**Banknote** was below the form he showed to get off the mark at Beverley on his previous start.
**Following Flow(USA)** did not get a clear run and this effort is best forgotten. *Official explanation: jockey said colt was unsuited by the good to firm ground*
**Shrine Mountain(USA)** *Official explanation: jockey said colt was never travelling*
**Buddy Brown**, a Racing Post Trophy entry, should have appreciated this step up from six furlongs, but he met with some trouble and was below form. *Official explanation: jockey said colt was unsuited by the good to firm ground*

## 5418 EARTH MORTGAGES SCARBROUGH STKS (LISTED RACE) 5f
**4:10** (4:12) (A1) 2-Y-0+ **£16,250** (£5,000; £2,500; £1,250) **Stalls** High

Form RPR
1006 **1** **Celtic Mill**$^{12}$ [5121] 6-9-12 104........................(p) LDettori 6 113
(DWBarker) *mde all: hld on wl* **15/2**
0202 **2** *1/2* **Talbot Avenue**$^{2}$ [5372] 6-9-9 99........................ KFallon 7 108
(MMullineaux) *trckd ldrs: squeezed through to chal 1f out: nt qckn towards fin* **13/2**$^{3}$
1100 **3** *1 1/4* **Caribbean Coral**$^{12}$ [5105] 5-9-9 101........................ RWinston 8 103
(JJQuinn) *sn outpcd: hdwy over 2f out: swtchd lft ins last: no ex* **13/2**$^{3}$
2414 **4** *2 1/2* **Enchantment**$^{12}$ [5105] 3-9-3 101........................ JPMurtagh 2 88
(JMBradley) *w wnr: edgd lft and wknd jst ins last* **9/2**$^{2}$

0256 **5** *nk* **Bishops Court**[10] 5181 10-9-9 102........................................ SSanders 4 92
(MrsJRRamsden) *hld up: hdwy and nt clr run2f out: nvr rchd ldrs* **15/2**

6013 **6** *3/4* **Baltic King**[12] 5105 4-9-9 106..............................................(t) JFortune 3 89
(HMorrison) *sn outpcd in rr: sme hdwy 2f out: nvr nr ldrs* **6/4**[1]

2461 **7** *5* **Komac**[20] 4924 2-8-3 72.............................................................. JFEgan 1 71
(BAMcmahon) *swvd lft s: chsd ldrs: wknd over 1f out* **100/1**

0100 **8** *1 1/4* **Night Prospector**[21] 4886 4-10-2 102.............................(b[1]) PRobinson 9 71
(JWPayne) *chsd ldrs: wknd and eased over 1f out* **33/1**

0600 **9** *hd* **If Paradise**[42] 4269 3-9-11 100................................................ RHughes 5 66
(RHannon) *sn outpcd towards rr: hung lft and eased over 1f out* **40/1**

57.28 secs (-4.14) **Going Correction** -0.525s/f (Hard) course record **9** Ran SP% **114.7**
Speed ratings: **112,111,109,105,104 103,95,93,93**CSF £54.28 TOTE £5.00: £1.50, £1.90, £2.20; EX 40.30.
**Owner** P Asquith **Bred** P Asquith **Trained** Scorton, N Yorks

**FOCUS**
On paper this looked very competitive, but very few got into it, with Frankie Dettori on Celtic Mill judging the fractions perfectly from the front to smash the track record.

**NOTEBOOK**
**Celtic Mill** is a real speedster but was amazingly running over the minimum trip for just the second time in his career. Fitted with declared cheekpieces for the first time, he pinged the gates and showed enough pace to head off Enchantment. Although by no means slowing the pace significantly, Dettori did look to get a slight breather in at halfway, and the pair always had just enough left to hold off the fast-finishing runner-up - you will not see a better bit of front-running over this sort of trip. With the sprint division wide open, he has got to be worth another try in Group company.
**Talbot Avenue** had a good position in behind the eventual winner and got the spilt when he needed it, but he was not quite good enough.
**Caribbean Coral**, below form in similar company at Beverley on his previous start, would have appreciated the strong pace but he was simply unable to get to the front two.
**Enchantment**, a good fourth in this grade at Beverley on her previous start, would have appreciated this switch to a flatter track but, with eventual winner Celtic Mill keen to lead, she was ever so slightly restrained. When the pace increased, she was unable to quicken and she looks a better filly when allowed to burn her rivals off from the front. She can yet make her mark in Pattern Company.
**Bishops Court** loves a strong pace, but Dettori on the winner judged the fractions perfectly and he was unable to get competitive from off the speed.
**Baltic King**, third in similar company at Beverley on his previous start, was taken off his feet and ran below form.
**Komac** *Official explanation: jockey said colt lost its action in the final furlong*

## 5419 QUEEN'S OWN YORKSHIRE DRAGOONS LADIES DAY STKS (H'CAP) 7f
4:45 (4:45) (D2) (0-85,85) 3-Y-O+ **£7,560** (£2,326; £1,163; £581) **Stalls** High

Form RPR

6004 **1** **Borrego (IRE)**[7] 5244 4-8-6 72........................................(b) SHitchcott(3) 10 81
(CEBrittain) *swtg: w ldrs: led over 1f out: hld on towards fin* **25/1**

0616 **2** *3/4* **Arctic Desert**[12] 5135 4-9-0 77.............................................. KFallon 16 84+
(AMBalding) *chsd ldrs: nt clr run over 1f out: styd on wl ins last: nt quite rch wnr* **9/2**[1]

6025 **3** *shd* **Granston (IRE)**[12] 5120 3-8-7 74.............................................. TQuinn 14 81
(JDBethell) *chsd ldrs: hmpd over 1f out: hrd rdn and styd on fnl f* **12/1**

0210 **4** *hd* **Sawwaah (IRE)**[19] 4931 7-9-7 84.......................................... ANicholls 19 90
(DNicholls) *bhd: swtchd outside 2f out: styd on wl: nt qckn ins last* **20/1**

3504 **5** *1 1/4* **Cloud Dancer**[23] 4837 5-8-12 75.............................................. NCallan 22 78+
(KARyan) *lw: rr-div: hdwy and nt clr run over 1f out: styd on wl ins last* **6/1**[2]

2203 **6** *hd* **Bi Polar**[22] 4846 4-8-10 73.................................................... RHughes 11 75
(DRCElsworth) *mid-div: hdwy and swtchd outside over 1f out: styd on same pce* **33/1**

0400 **7** *nk* **Queens Rhapsody**[125] 1927 4-9-5 82.................................... JFanning 17 83+
(ABailey) *mid-divsion: hdwy over 2f out: nt clr run over 1f out: styd on ins last* **50/1**

503 **8** *3/4* **Distant Country (USA)**[32] 4577 5-8-9 72........................(p) SSanders 12 71+
(MrsJRRamsden) *hld up towards rr: hdwy and nt clr run over 1f out: styd on ins last* **10/1**[3]

0000 **9** *1/2* **Serieux**[17] 5004 5-9-3 80.................................................(p) JPMurtagh 15 78+
(MrsAJPerrett) *lw: hld up towards rr: hdwy and nt clr run over 1f out: kpt on wl ins last* **14/1**

4120 **10** *nk* **Concer Eto**[21] 4877 5-8-10 73..................................................(p) LDettori 8 70+
(SCWilliams) *mid-div: effrt and n.m.r 2f out: nvr rchd ldrs* **12/1**

564 **11** *shd* **Stoic Leader (IRE)**[6] 5265 4-9-3 80.......................................... JFEgan 3 77
(RFFisher) *dwlt: swtchd rt after 100yds to r stands' side: hdwy over 3f out: ev ch over 1f out: kpt on same pce* **33/1**

0600 **12** *1/2* **Desert Dreamer (IRE)**[42] 4268 3-9-4 85.................................. MHills 6 80
(BWHills) *in tch on outer: hdwy and ev ch over 1f out: no ex* **16/1**

2201 **13** *1* **Harrison Point (USA)**[33] 4549 4-9-7 84................................... JFortune 18 77+
(PWChapple-Hyam) *in tch on inner: bdly hmpd over 2f out and over 1f out: nt rcvr* **6/1**[2]

1331 **14** *1/2* **Threezedzz**[10] 5177 6-9-4 84 6ex.......................................(t) FPFerris(3) 2 75
(PDEvans) *swtchd rt after 100yds to r stands' side: w ldrs: fdd over 1f out* **14/1**

0050 **15** *shd* **Tough Love**[19] 4931 5-9-1 78............................................... TEDurcan 9 69
(TDEasterby) *in tch: effrt over 2f out: no imp* **14/1**

0300 **16** *shd* **Kindlelight Debut**[6] 5275 4-8-11 74...................................... PRobinson 7 65+
(DKIvory) *chsd ldrs: bdly hmpd and lost pl 2f out* **66/1**

0000 **17** *1/2* **Overdrawn (IRE)**[88] 2907 3-9-3 84............................................. EAhern 5 74
(JAOsborne) *s.i.s: sn bhd* **33/1**

6100 **18** *hd* **Hey Presto**[22] 4846 4-8-9 72.................................................... KDarley 21 61
(CGCox) *sn bhd* **20/1**

5643 **19** *1/2* **Sea Storm (IRE)**[19] 4931 6-9-1 78........................................(p) TPQueally 1 66
(DRMacleod) *swtchd rt after s to r stands' side: chsd ldrs: wknd over 1f out* **33/1**

2100 **20** *3 1/2* **Lord Of The East**[41] 4291 5-8-12 78.................................... TEaves(3) 13 56
(DNicholls) *led tl 2f out: hung lft and sn lost pl: eased* **50/1**

4120 **21** *8* **Efidium**[7] 5244 6-8-11 74........................................................ RWinston 4 31
(NBycroft) *a towards rr* **40/1**

1m 23.21s (-4.60) **Going Correction** -0.525s/f (Hard)
**WFA** 3 from 4yo+ 4lb **21** Ran SP% **130.1**
Speed ratings: **105,104,104,103,102 102,101,100,100,100 99,99,98,97,97 97,96,96,96,92 82**CSF £127.24 CT £1487.40 TOTE £44.80: £6.80, £1.80, £3.80, £6.30; EX 341.30 Place 6 £274.33, Place 5 £162.95.
**Owner** Monarch Thoroughbreds Racing **Bred** Sheikh Marwan Al Maktoum **Trained** Newmarket, Suffolk

■ Sam Hitchcott's 95th career win, meaning the 23-year-old has ridden out his claim.
■ Stewards Enquiry : J F Egan three-day ban: careless riding (Sep 20-22)

**FOCUS**
A really competitive handicap, but the bare form must be treated with caution as there was no end of trouble in behind. The first nine home were drawn in double figure stalls.

**NOTEBOOK**
**Borrego(IRE)** had gained both his previous wins over a mile, but showed himself effective over this trip when a promising fourth in first-time blinkers at Redcar on his previous start. One of just a handful to gain a trouble-free run, he made the most of it to gain his first win of the campaign. Although he has clearly hit form, he could be one to take on next time.
**Arctic Desert** did not convince over a mile at Windsor on his previous start but, dropped back in trip, this was much better and he may well have won with a clearer run, although he is not the only one.
**Granston(IRE)**, a little unlucky at Newmarket on his previous start, got bumped about a bit around a furlong out, but still got a clearer run than some of these.
**Sawwaah(IRE)**, tailed off at Chester on his previous start, returned to form with a good effort. He was pulled wide of all the trouble in order to get a clear run and it very nearly paid off.
**Cloud Dancer** ◆, back up in trip and returned to her favoured fast ground, was as unlucky as anything and deserves to be rated much better than the bare form.
**Bi Polar** had conditions to suit and ran respectably, especially considering he had to be switched.
**Queens Rhapsody** has never won on turf but would have been closer on this first run on fast ground with better splits.
**Distant Country(USA)** ◆, unlucky at Redcar on his previous start, again did not get a clear run. He is in good form and is worth keeping in mind.
**Serieux** has not always been at his best this year, but it was no fault of his own he could not figure this time. He is chucked in if he ever recovers the will to win.
**Concer Eto** is yet another that can be rated better than the bare form.
**Stoic Leader(IRE)** was 2lb higher than in future handicaps.
**Harrison Point(USA)**, just 1lb higher than when successful on the Polytrack on his previous start, got absolutely no run.
**Kindlelight Debut** got knocked about all over the place and it has to be hoped this does not leave a mental scar. *Official explanation: jockey said filly was denied a run*
T/Jkpt: Not won. T/Plt: £275.40 to a £1 stake. Pool: £88,410.90. 234.30 winning tickets. T/Qpdt: £65.40 to a £1 stake. Pool: £5,275.50. 59.65 winning tickets. WG

# 5398 EPSOM (L-H)
Thursday, September 9

**OFFICIAL GOING: Good to firm (good in places)**

## 5420 H & V NEWS GENERAL EBF MEDIAN AUCTION MAIDEN STKS 7f
2:15 (2:16) (E3) 2-Y-O **£5,564** (£1,712; £856; £428) **Stalls** Low

Form RPR

223 **1** **Goodwood Spirit**[26] 4739 2-9-0 79........................................ RLMoore 1 77
(JLDunlop) *lw: b. off hind: trckd ldr: chal over 4f out: slt ld 3f out: rdn 2f out: styd on wl fnl f: jst hld on* **8/11**[1]

5 **2** *shd* **Wingspeed (IRE)**[26] 4743 2-9-0 ........................................... PHanagan 3 77
(MrsAJPerrett) *lw: trckd ldrs: wnt 2nd 2f out: rdn: green and styd on fnl f: str chal cl home: nt quite get up* **5/2**[2]

**3** *5* **Chasm** 2-9-0 .................................................................................... SChin 6 65
(MJohnston) *unf: scope: bit bkwd: lengthy: prom tl rdn and outpcd 3f out: edgd lft over 2f out: styd on again fnl f but nt rch ldrs* **10/1**[3]

00 **4** *shd* **Beauchamp Trump**[10] 5179 2-9-0 ......................................... SWKelly 2 64
(GAButler) *chsd ldrs: rdn and effrt 2f out: sn outpcd* **33/1**

306 **5** *nk* **Transgress (IRE)**[26] 4739 2-9-0 69...................................... DaneO'Neill 4 64
(RHannon) *led: kpt slt ld tl hdd 3f out: outpcd 2f out* **10/1**[3]

0 **6** *6* **Bold Diktator**[26] 4743 2-9-0 ................................................. JQuinn 5 49
(WRMuir) *a bhd* **66/1**

1m 24.42s (0.47) **Going Correction** -0.05s/f (Good) **6** Ran SP% **109.1**
Speed ratings: **95,94,89,89,88 81**CSF £2.51 TOTE £1.70: £1.10, £1.70; EX 2.50.
**Owner** Goodwood Racehorse Owners Group (Ten) **Bred** P D Player **Trained** Arundel, W Sussex

**FOCUS**
An ordinary maiden in which the two market leaders had it between them from a fair way out. Goodwood Spirit was just below form in success, but the runner-up has improved a little.

**NOTEBOOK**
**Goodwood Spirit** finally got off the mark at the fourth attempt, having been a beaten favourite on his last two starts. He appreciated the extra furlong but was all out to hold on at the finish, and he will have to improve to pay his way in nursery company.
**Wingspeed(IRE)** had shaped with some promise on his debut and his trainer's horses usually come on a good deal for their first run. He kept on in game fashion to push the winner all the way, and on this evidence should be able to win a minor maiden.
**Chasm** was weak in the market for his debut but was staying on at the finish, giving hope that there is better to come.
**Beauchamp Trump** is a half-brother to Beauchamp Ribbon, a three-time winner between nine and 11 furlongs. He is now eligible for a mark, and is likely to appreciate farther in handicap company.
**Transgress(IRE)** does not appear to be progressing.

## 5421 VOKERA NURSERY 6f
2:50 (2:50) (D2) (0-85,83) 2-Y-O **£8,346** (£2,568; £1,284; £642) **Stalls** High

Form RPR

3221 **1** **Yajbill (IRE)**[16] 5015 2-9-7 83..................................................(v) JQuinn 2 99
(MRChannon) *lw: sn led: rdn 2f out: drvn clr fnl f: styd on wl* **3/1**[1]

1066 **2** *5* **Elisha (IRE)**[40] 4326 2-8-5 67.............................................. MFenton 11 68
(DMSimcock) *lw: prom: chsd wnr appr fnl 2f: outpcd fnl f but hld on wl for 2nd* **20/1**

2025 **3** *nk* **Kwame**[12] 5119 2-9-2 78..............................................................(v[1]) SWKelly 5 78
(MissECLavelle) *hung rt bnd over 4f out: chsd ldrs: rdn and kpt on fnl 2f: clsd on 2nd last half f but no ch w wnr* **10/1**

314 **4** *2 1/2* **Cusoon**[13] 5068 2-9-2 83............................................................ AQuinn(5) 14 76
(GLMoore) *lw: bhd: rdn 3f out: styd on fr over but nvr gng pace to rch ldrs* **12/1**

1242 **5** *nk* **Bold Minstrel (IRE)**[13] 5068 2-9-7 83................................... PHanagan 4 75
(MQuinn) *w wnr 1f: styd in 2nd tl rdn over 2f out: wknd ins fnl f* **10/1**

010 **6** *1/2* **Toby's Dream (IRE)**[23] 4836 2-9-6 82....................................... SChin 7 72
(MJohnston) *lw: pushed wd bnd over 4f out: rdn: hdwy and edgd lft 2f out: kpt on ins last but nt trble ldrs* **16/1**

3410 **7** *3/4* **Louphole**[24] 4803 2-9-6 82....................................................... RSmith 10 70
(PJMakin) *chsng ldrs whn pushed wd bnd over 4f out: rdn and hdwy 3f out: no imp on ldrs: wknd fnl f* **25/1**

2501 **8** *nk* **Simplify**[10] 5202 2-9-3 79 6ex.............................................(b) RLMoore 8 66
(DRLoder) *bhd: hung lft fr 3f out: styng on whn nt clr run over 1f out and ins last: eased whn no ch* **6/1**[3]

4045 **9** *hd* **Talcen Gwyn (IRE)**[13] 5078 2-9-2 78........................................ ADaly 12 64
(MFHarris) *bhd: rdn 3f out: kpt on fnl 2f: nt pce to rch ldrs* **33/1**

0300 **10** *1/2* **Storm Fury (USA)**[10] 5202 2-8-6 68..................................(b[1]) AMcCarthy 3 53
(PWChapple-Hyam) *in tch: rdn over 2f out: no imp: wknd fnl f* **25/1**

0004 **11** *shd* **Norcroft**[19] 4953 2-8-13 75.................................................(b) OUrbina 13 60
(NACallaghan) *bhd: pushed along 3f out: styd on fr over 1f out: nvr gng pce to rch ldrs* **16/1**



The Form Book, Raceform Ltd, Compton, RG20 6NL

6550 **12** *nk* **King After**[12] 5119 2-8-9 **71** NPollard 9 55
(JRBest) *hmpd after 1f: mid-div: rdn 3f out: nvr gng pce to rch ldrs: no chnace whn nt clr run 1f out and eased* **20/1**

1433 **13** *14* **Tesary**[10] 5202 2-8-13 **75** DaneO'Neill 6 17
(EALDunlop) *sddle slipped: wl bhd fnl 3f* **11/2**[2]

200 **14** *3 1/2* **Bogaz (IRE)**[31] 4598 2-8-2 **64** (v[1]) JMackay 1 —
(RMBeckett) *sn wl bhd* **12/1**

68.89 secs (-1.74) **Going Correction** -0.05s/f (Good) **14** Ran SP% **120.2**
Speed ratings: **109,102,101,98,98 97,96,96,95,95 95,94,76,71**CSF £72.81 CT £563.98 TOTE £3.20: £1.80, £5.40, £2.60; EX 108.30.
**Owner** Sheikh Ahmed Al Maktoum **Bred** N Poole And A Franklin **Trained** West Ilsley, Berks

**FOCUS**
Yajbill set a good pace from the off here and won impressively. The form behind him looks solid.

**NOTEBOOK**
**Yajbill(IRE)** ◆ put up an impressive display as he appeared to go plenty quick enough in the early stages and yet was able to draw even further clear when stepping up another gear in the straight. The visor appears to have worked wonders and Listed races could be in the agenda before long.
**Elisha(IRE)** did not get home over seven last time and found the drop back to six furlongs far more to her liking. She showed good pace to chase the leader and lost nothing in being unable to match that progressive rival's quickening effort in the final quarter mile.
**Kwame**, visored for the first time, did not handle the track but still stayed on well for third. She will be happier back on a more conventional course.
**Cusoon** was poorly drawn and looks to be crying out for seven furlongs.
**Bold Minstrel(IRE)** once again gave the impression that his best trip is five furlongs.
**Toby's Dream(IRE)** was not done any favours on the bend, but his last two starts also suggest he is plenty high enough in the handicap.
**Simplify** had a lot to do coming into the straight and was hampered in his attempt to make up ground by his tendency to hang left. *Official explanation: trainer's representative said colt had been unsuited by the good to firm ground*
**Tesary** *Official explanation: jockey said saddle slipped*

## 5422 VAILLANT FORTUNE STKS (LISTED RACE) 7f
**3:25** (3:25) (A1) 3-Y-0+ **£20,300** (£7,700; £3,850; £1,750) **Stalls** Low

Form RPR

6610 **1** **Mac Love**[5] 5289 3-8-12 **104** GCarter 5 114
(JAkehurst) *hld up in rr: gd hdwy on outside fr 2f out: rdn and str run fnl f to ld cl home* **20/1**

5111 **2** *nk* **Peter Paul Rubens (USA)**[21] 4873 3-8-12 **105** RLMoore 6 113
(PFICole) *b. off fore: lw: led after 1f: 3l clr 3f out: rdn over 2f out: kpt on but ct cl home* **13/8**[1]

3103 **3** *1 1/2* **Vanderlin**[21] 4889 5-9-2 **107** LPKeniry 8 109
(AMBalding) *trckd ldrs: hdwy on outside over 2f out: sn edgd lft: kpt on fnl f but nt rch ldrs* **4/1**[2]

0252 **4** *1/2* **Desert Destiny**[10] 5199 4-9-2 **110** (t) KMcEvoy 2 108
(SaeedBinSuroor) *lw: in tch: hdwy 2f out: n.m.r over 1f out and swtchd rt: kpt on ins last: nt pce to rch ldrs* **11/2**[3]

-160 **5** *nk* **Iqte Saab (USA)**[54] 3940 3-8-12 **102** RHills 4 107
(JLDunlop) *hld up in rr: hdwy on outside and rdn 2f out: styd on fnl f: nt rch ldrs* **10/1**

2041 **6** *shd* **Material Witness (IRE)**[12] 5112 7-9-2 **105** JQuinn 1 107
(WRMuir) *led 1f: styd chsng ldr: rdn over 2f out: wknd ins fnl f* **8/1**

0403 **7** *1 1/4* **Kings Point (IRE)**[40] 4322 3-8-12 **103** DaneO'Neill 3 106+
(RHannon) *chsd ldrs: rdn over 2f out: wknd fnl f* **20/1**

6002 **8** *5* **Royal Storm (IRE)**[33] 4553 5-9-2 **99** PHanagan 7 90
(MrsAJPerrett) *chsd ldrs: rdn over 2f out: sn outpcd: wknd over 1f out* **9/1**

1m 21.34s (-2.61) **Going Correction** -0.05s/f (Good)
**WFA** 3 from 4yo+ 4lb **8** Ran SP% **113.2**
Speed ratings: **112,111,109,109,109 108,107,101**CSF £52.09 TOTE £28.60: £4.50, £1.20, £1.70; EX 68.60.
**Owner** Vimal Khosla **Bred** Kingwood Bloodstock **Trained** Epsom, Surrey

**FOCUS**
Not a strong Listed race on paper, but fair form nevertheless.

**NOTEBOOK**
**Mac Love**, outclassed in the Haydock Sprint Cup, was stepping up to seven furlongs for the first time. He certainly saw the trip out well, coming with a late challenge to win a shade cleverly. This win should open up a few more options for connections.
**Peter Paul Rubens(USA)** soon got to the lead and injected some pace into the race. Kicked clear early in the straight, he looked to have stolen a decisive advantage, only to falter close home. He handled the track well and had no excuse on this first venture into Pattern company.
**Vanderlin** ran his usual honest race but a real end-to-end gallop would have suited him better.
**Desert Destiny** once again disappointed his supporters, although he may well have finished third with a clear run. His rider blamed the ground, but that excuse does not really wash. *Official explanation: jockey said gelding had been unsutied by the good to firm ground*
**Iqte Saab(USA)**, having his first run since July, got going far too late in the day. This track did not look suitable.
**Material Witness(IRE)** has had a good season this year but he had more to do in this grade, and his cause was probably not helped by letting the favourite take the lead from him.
**Royal Storm(IRE)** *Official explanation: jockey said horse lost its action and had become unbalanced*

## 5423 FUJITSU H'CAP 1m 2f 18y
**4:00** (4:01) (D2) (0-85,85) 3-Y-0+ **£9,400** (£3,565; £1,782; £810) **Stalls** Low

Form RPR

6-40 **1** **Resonate (IRE)**[64] 3631 6-8-8 **72** DaneO'Neill 11 86
(AGNewcombe) *hld up in tch: hdwy on outside 3f out: led over 1f out: clr ins last: readily* **9/1**

2323 **2** *2 1/2* **Arry Dash**[5] 5297 4-8-9 **73** JQuinn 4 82
(MRChannon) *lw: chsd ldrs: wnt 2nd and rdn 2f out: chal wl over 1f out: sn no ch w wnr but hld on wl for 2nd* **11/2**[2]

0300 **3** *nk* **Maystock**[119] 2062 4-8-8 **72** SWKelly 6 80+
(GAButler) *lw: bhd: hdwy on outside over 2f out: r.o wl fnl f to cl on 2nd but nvr nr wnr* **25/1**

0520 **4** *2* **Ryan's Future (IRE)**[19] 4950 4-8-11 **75** GCarter 2 80+
(JAkehurst) *s.i.s: plld hrd in rr: hdwy fr 2f out:r.o ins fnl f kpt on cl home* **10/1**

1200 **5** *nk* **Woody Valentine (USA)**[33] 4558 3-8-10 **81** SChin 3 85
(MJohnston) *chsd ldrs: rdn over 2f out: wknd ins fnl f* **13/2**[3]

1015 **6** *2 1/2* **Realism (FR)**[36] 4450 4-9-5 **83** DarrenWilliams 10 82
(PWHiatt) *chsd ldrs: led ins fnl 3f: hdd over 1f out: wknd fnl f* **16/1**

3450 **7** *hd* **Katiypour (IRE)**[10] 5183 7-8-11 **75** LisaJones 5 74
(MissBSanders) *lw: chsd ldrs: n.m.r and lost position 3f out: styd on again fr over 1f out* **11/1**

0105 **8** *1* **Danelor (IRE)**[12] 5122 6-9-7 **85** PHanagan 9 82
(RAFahey) *led 7f out: hdd rdn and hdd ins fnl 3f: wknd over 1f out* **4/1**[1]

0000 **9** *nk* **Gallery God (FR)**[13] 5074 8-8-9 **80** LSmith[(7)] 12 76
(SDow) *bhd: shkn up and kpt on fr over 1f out: gng on cl home but nt a danger* **33/1**

2404 **10** *1/2* **Scottish River (USA)**[10] 5182 5-9-0 **81** HayleyTurner[(3)] 13 76
(MDIUsher) *swtg: slowly away: bhd: sme hdwy on rails over 2f out: nvr gng pce to rch ldrs: wkng whn hit rails 1f out* **12/1**

2651 **11** *1 1/2* **Kirkham Abbey**[36] 4436 4-8-7 **71** oh2 RLMoore 8 64
(MAJarvis) *mid-div: rdn and effrt over 2f out: wknd over 1f out* **11/2**[2]

-200 **12** *1/2* **Silver City**[26] 4737 4-9-1 **79** KMcEvoy 1 71
(MrsAJPerrett) *led after 1f: hdd 7f out: wknd 3f out and n.m.r 3f out* **20/1**

5100 **13** *5* **Prairie Wolf**[26] 4737 8-8-11 **75** MFenton 7 57
(MLWBell) *swtg: sn led: hdd after 1f: styd pressing ldrs tl wknd 3f out* **16/1**

2m 9.92s (1.22) **Going Correction** -0.05s/f (Good)
**WFA** 3 from 4yo+ 7lb **13** Ran SP% **122.5**
Speed ratings: **93,91,90,89,88 86,86,85,85,85 84,83,79**CSF £58.07 CT £1223.52 TOTE £12.40: £3.00, £2.40, £8.80; EX 56.00.
**Owner** S Langridge **Bred** D H W Dobson **Trained** Yarnscombe, Devon

**FOCUS**
A decent pace to a fair handicap. Resonate was back to his best over this longer trip, and there were quite encouraging efforts from Maystock and Ryan's Future.

**NOTEBOOK**
**Resonate(IRE)**, unlucky in running last time, had never previously run over this long a trip before, but he proved well suited by it, drawing clear in the closing stages for an easy win. He is lightly raced this term and unexposed over this sort of trip.
**Arry Dash**, who is due to go up 2lb in the handicap already, does his handicap mark little good with his consistency. He also gives the impression that he is happier to follow one or two home.
**Maystock** ran a decent race over a trip short of her best. She does not appear that well handicapped on the balance of her turf form.
**Ryan's Future(IRE)** pulled hard despite the decent gallop, and although he stayed on well inside the final quarter mile, the principals had gone beyond recall.
**Woody Valentine(USA)** ran a fair race for one who looks high enough in the weights and hails from a stable not quite firing at present.
**Realism(FR)** was racing off a mark 23lb higher than when he began winning this summer, and it now looks as though the Handicapper has his measure.
**Danelor(IRE)**, who would have preferred easier ground, probably went too quick for his own good.
**Gallery God(FR)**, who needs farther, has tumbled down the weights and showed a glimmer of hope.
**Kirkham Abbey** *Official explanation: jockey said gelding became unbalanced in the final furlong*

## 5424 DENCO MAIDEN STKS 1m 114y
**4:35** (4:36) (D3) 3-Y-0 **£5,330** (£1,640; £820; £410) **Stalls** Low

Form RPR

0 **1** **Tadawul (USA)**[55] 3916 3-8-9 RHills 3 70+
(EFVaughan) *lw: mde virtually all: rdn and green whn chal fr over 2f out: edgd rt 1f out: sn rcvrd but stl green: r.o wl cl hme* **4/5**[1]

63 **2** *1 1/2* **Paintbox**[31] 4615 3-8-9 RLMoore 1 67
(MrsAJPerrett) *in tch: pushed along and hdwy fr 3f out: str chal fr over 2f out: styd pressing wnr tl outpcd ins fnl f* **9/4**[2]

**3** *3* **Sian Thomas** 3-8-9 ADaly 2 61+
(MPTregoning) *w'like: lengthy: hld up in rr: rdn over 2f out: styd on fr over 1f out to take 3rd ins last: nt trble ldrs* **20/1**

-060 **4** *1 1/2* **Sachin**[47] 4126 3-9-0 **62** DaneO'Neill 6 63
(JRBoyle) *b. hind: chsd ldr unil ins fnl 3f: outpcd fr 2f out: wknd fnl f* **20/1**

-002 **5** *2 1/2* **Native Turk (USA)**[21] 4880 3-9-0 **69** KMcEvoy 4 57
(JARToller) *chsd ldrs: rdn over 3f out: wknd over 2f out* **6/1**[3]

-560 **6** *4* **Fabuloso**[22] 4848 3-8-9 **45** JQuinn 7 44
(VSmith) *a in rr* **33/1**

0-00 **7** *nk* **Seven Shirt**[10] 5176 3-9-0 **60** PDoe 5 48
(EGBevan) *a bhd: rdn: hd high and nt run on fr over 2f out* **50/1**

1m 45.71s (-0.03) **Going Correction** -0.05s/f (Good) **7** Ran SP% **115.0**
Speed ratings: **98,96,94,92,90 86,86**CSF £2.69 TOTE £1.80: £1.10, £1.80; EX 3.80.
**Owner** Hamdan Al Maktoum **Bred** Shadwell Farm Llc **Trained** Newmarket, Suffolk

**FOCUS**
A modest maiden, run at a steady early pace, but the winner looks a bit better than the bare form suggests and the third shaped well.

**NOTEBOOK**
**Tadawul(USA)**, who had made her debut in a race which has worked out well, got off the mark despite showing distinct signs of greenness. She won with quite a bit more up her sleeve than the winning margin suggests and should be open to a fair amount of improvement. The Handicapper is unlikely to be too harsh.
**Paintbox** is bred to want middle distances and will be interesting in handicaps now that she is eligible for a mark.
**Sian Thomas**, whose breeding is a mixture of speed and stamina, made a pleasing debut, staying on without getting in a blow at the leaders. She should be suited by a more strongly-run race.
**Sachin** is exposed as a modest performer.
**Native Turk(USA)** found himself in a stronger race than the one he contested on the Southwell Fibresand last month.
**Seven Shirt** *Official explanation: jockey said gelding hung badly left*

## 5425 H & V 05 EXHIBITION H'CAP 7f
**5:10** (5:13) (E3) (0-70,70) 3-Y-0+ **£5,683** (£1,748; £874; £437) **Stalls** Low

Form RPR

5505 **1** **Mandarin Spirit (IRE)**[2] 5364 4-9-1 **64** (b) OUrbina 1 71
(GCHChung) *swtg: trckd ldr: led 4f out: rdn over 1f out: kpt on ins last: jst hld on* **5/1**[2]

0412 **2** *shd* **Jazzy Millennium**[15] 5039 7-8-9 **58** (b) GBaker 15 65
(BRMillman) *lw: led 3f: styd chsng wnr: rdn over 2f out: kpt on strly u.p fnl f: jst failed* **8/1**

3150 **3** *1* **Scarrottoo**[24] 4818 6-8-7 **56** oh1 RLMoore 9 60+
(SCWilliams) *bhd: racd wd in st fr 3f out and plenty to do: rdn and hdwy fr 2f out: str run ins last:fin wl:nt rch ldrs* **9/2**[1]

5220 **4** *hd* **Cold Climate**[27] 4727 9-8-8 **57** JMackay 14 61
(BobJones) *s.i.s: bhd: rdn 3f out: gd hdwy over 1f out:styd on wl fnl f: gng on cl home* **16/1**

2235 **5** *hd* **Lady Mo**[11] 5155 3-8-13 **66** AMcCarthy 7 69
(GGMargarson) *in tch: rdn and lost position over 3f out: kpt on fr over 1f out: r.o wl cl home* **12/1**

250 **6** *2 1/2* **Balerno**[22] 4846 5-8-12 **61** NDay 16 57
(RIngram) *in tch: rdn fr 3f out: styd on fnl 2f: no imp on ldrs ins last* **12/1**

0100 **7** *2* **Icecap**[6] 5260 4-8-7 **56** oh3 ADaly 12 47
(WGMTurner) *b: b.hind: chsd ldrs: rdn 3f out: wknd fr 2f out* **66/1**

2016 **8** *hd* **Mister Clinton (IRE)**[16] 5020 7-8-13 **62** DaneO'Neill 11 53
(DKIvory) *b: chsd ldrs: rdn over 3f out: wknd 2f out* **12/1**

005 **9** *1/2* **Lady Taverner**[46] 4168 3-8-4 **57** PHanagan 10 46
(HJCyzer) *s.i.s: bhd: rdn 3f out: styd on fr over 1f out: nvr gng pce to rch ldrs* **50/1**

2020 **10** *1/2* **Minimum Bid**[8] 5219 3-8-4 **57** JQuinn 3 45
(MissBSanders) *bhd: rdn and styd on fnl 2f: nt rch ldrs* **14/1**

0600 **11** *hd* **Hail The Chief**[10] 5185 7-9-7 **70** ........ PDoe 6 57
(JAkehurst) *sn chsng ldrs: wknd over 2f out* **12/1**
0060 **12** *2* **Danish Monarch**[8] 5219 3-8-0 **58** ow1 ........ NChalmers(5) 8 40
(ADWPinder) *mid-div: rdn 3f out: n.d* **40/1**
0004 **13** *½* **Whippasnapper**[21] 4877 4-9-2 **65** ........ NPollard 17 46
(JRBest) *chsd ldrs tl wknd fr 3f out* **14/1**
6000 **14** *¾* **Silver Chime**[7] 5242 4-9-2 **65** ........ MFenton 5 44
(DMSimcock) *a in rr* **25/1**
4001 **15** *3* **Magic Amour**[10] 5201 6-8-10 **59** 6ex ........ (v) KMcEvoy 4 29
(IanWilliams) *lw: chsd ldrs early: wknd 3f out* **13/2**[3]

1m 22.46s (-1.49) **Going Correction** -0.05s/f (Good) **15** Ran SP% **119.0**
**WFA** 3 from 4yo+ 4lb
Speed ratings: **106,105,104,104,104 101,99,98,98,97 97,95,94,93,90**CSF £42.83 CT £199.71 TOTE £6.60: £2.70, £2.70, £2.20; EX 61.70 Place 6 £20.33, Place 5 £18.41.
**Owner** Peter Tsim **Bred** W Haggas And W Jarvis **Trained** Newmarket, Suffolk

**FOCUS**
A modest handicap in which the first two home dominated throughout.

**NOTEBOOK**
**Mandarin Spirit(IRE)**, who won over the course and distance a year ago almost to the day, sweated up beforehand. It did not seem to do him any harm, though, as he took a prominent position from his good draw from the off, and held on bravely when the eventual runner-up challenged him strongly inside the last. This looks his best trip, at least on turf.
**Jazzy Millennium** did well to overcome his high draw and race with the winner at the head of affairs. He only went down narrowly and is in fine form at the moment. Ratings wise, he has not been this good since his three-year-old days.
**Scarrottoo**, winner of a claimer over the course and distance in July, gave the first two a good head start and finished fast to grab third. His style of running requires an end-to-end gallop, and he is a bit better than this bare form.
**Cold Climate**, who proved troublesome before the start, appreciated the return to a quick surface having run poorly last time out on softish ground.
**Lady Mo** was significantly worse off at the weights with Scarrottoo compared with when they last met in a claimer here in July, so in the circumstances this was not a bad effort.
**Balerno**, who was not well drawn, looks high enough in the weights at present.
**Mister Clinton(IRE)** *Official explanation: jockey said gelding had hung right*
**Silver Chime** *Official explanation: jockey said filly had been unsuited by the track*
**Magic Amour** *Official explanation: vet said gelding finished lame behind*
T/Plt: £13.50 to a £1 stake. Pool: £42,037.45. 2,272.40 winning tickets. T/Qpdt: £6.30 to a £1 stake. Pool: £2,843.40. 329.80 winning tickets. ST

## 5331 LONGCHAMP (R-H)
### Thursday, September 9

**OFFICIAL GOING: Good**

## 5432a PRIX LA ROCHETTE (GROUP 3) 7f
1:50 (1:57) 2-Y-O £25,704 (£10,282; £7,711; £5,141)

RPR
**1** **Early March**[14] 2-8-11 ........ OPeslier 4 105
(MmeCHead-Maarek, France) *made most, pushed out, ran on well* 2
**2** *1 ½* **Stop Making Sense**[13] 5102 2-8-11 ........ CSoumillon 6 101
(AFabre, France) *dwlt, sn rcng in 5th, 5th str, hdwy wl over 1f out, disp 2nd ins fnl f, stayed on without threatening wnr* 1
**3** *hd* **Osidy (USA)**[39] 4382 2-8-11 ........ GBenoist 7 101
(XNakkachdji, France) *hld up in rr, still last wl over 1f out, hdwy on outside to disp 2nd ins fnl f, kpt on same pace*
**4** *1 ½* **Corsario (FR)**[32] 4597 2-8-11 ........ MBlancpain 5 97
(CLaffon-Parias, France) *raced in 3rd to straight, went 2nd well over 1f out, 1l behind winner at distance, weakened last 100y* 3
**5** *2* **Haute Ransom (USA)**[33] 2-8-11 ........ TJarnet 1 92
(RGibson, France) *raced in 4th to straight, weakened over 1f out*
**6** *1 ½* **Catstone (FR)**[26] 2-8-11 ........ IMendizabal 2 88
(J-CRouget, France) *first to show, tracked winner to straight, weakened well over 1f out*

1m 22.2s **Going Correction** -0.05s/f (Good) **6** Ran SP% **111.5**
Speed ratings: **102,100,100,98,96 94.**
**Owner** K Abdulla **Bred** Juddmonte Farms **Trained** France

**NOTEBOOK**
**Early March**, a most attractive colt who looks likely to make his mark at the highest level, was smartly away and led throughout. Pace was added from a furlong and a half out and from that moment he never looked liked tasting defeat. He still has plenty to learn and further improvement is guaranteed, and he now goes for the Prix Jean-Luc Lagardere over the course and distance on Arc day.
**Stop Making Sense**, not too quickly into his stride, was towards the tail of the field early on. He had nowhere to go halfway up the straight and then ran on well in the final stages to take second place close home. Probably better than the bare form, it would be no surprise to see him line up for the Jean-Luc Lagardere.
**Osidy(USA)**, held up early on, quickened rapidly from halfway up the straight and looked sure to take second place until collared close home.
**Corsario(FR)**, a nice strong sort, looked very dangerous a furlong and a half out but was then one-paced as the race came to a close.

## 5433a PRIX DE LUTECE (GROUP 3) 1m 7f
2:50 (2:57) 3-Y-O £25,704 (£10,282; £7,711; £5,141)

RPR
**1** **Etendard Indien (FR)**[25] 4796 3-8-9 ........ CSoumillon 2 109
(AFabre, France) *led after 1 1/2f, set slow pace, began to quicken 5f out, ridden out, ran on well*
**2** *2* **Reefscape**[95] 2722 3-8-9 ........ TGillet 1 107
(AFabre, France) *reluctant ldr for 1 1/2f, trckd wnr to 3f out, 4th str, regained 2nd appr fnl f, nvr rchd wnr* 1
**3** *1 ½* **Double Green (IRE)**[25] 4796 3-8-6 ........ OPeslier 3 102
(FHead, France) *raced in 4th, went 3rd 4f out, 2nd 3f out to approaching final f, one pace* 2
**4** *½* **Prairie Flower (IRE)**[25] 4796 3-8-6 ........ SPasquier 4 101
(ELellouche, France) *raced in 3rd to 4f out, 5th straight, switched outside well over 1f out, kept on one pace* 3
**5** *2* **Kensington (GER)**[42] 4284 3-8-9 ........ (b) DBonilla 5 102
(AJunk, France) *held up in 5th, went 3rd on outside approaching straight, weakened well over 1f out*
**6** *6* **Jan Africa (FR)**[4] 3-8-9 ........ FSpanu 6 94
(LCharbonnier, France) *reared up start, last throughout*

3m 29.0s **Going Correction** -0.05s/f (Good) **6** Ran SP% **123.2**
Speed ratings: **62,60,60,59,58 55.**
**Owner** Baron E De Rothschild **Bred** S C Ecurie De Meautry **Trained** France

**NOTEBOOK**
**Etendard Indien(FR)**, who led from pillar to post, set a moderate pace early on and accelerated suddenly soon after entering the straight. The race was his some way out and he seemed to revel on the fastish ground. The plan is now to run him in the Prix Hubert de Chaudenay.
**Reefscape** followed the winner for nearly all the race. Caught for speed early in the straight, he then ran on again inside the final furlong. He is another who is likely to be aimed at the Hubert de Chaudenay.
**Double Green(IRE)** settled in fourth place in a slowly-run race. She moved up a gear in the straight to tackle the winner but was then unable to hold second place inside the final furlong.
**Prairie Flower(IRE)** was not very lucky at the bottom of the descent. She saw daylight two out and quickened, but was robbed of third place inside the final furlong.

## 5413 DONCASTER (L-H)
### Friday, September 10

**OFFICIAL GOING: Good to firm (firm in places)**
The ground was again on the fast side but had eased slightly and the wind had dropped. The riders reported it was standing up well to a busy three days.
Wind: Slight 1/2 against. Weather: Overcast, slight rain 1st 2 races then warm and humid.

## 5434 DBS ST LEGER YEARLING STKS 6f
1:15 (1:16) (B1) 2-Y-O £27,000 (£10,800; £5,400; £2,700) Stalls High

Form RPR
2032 **1** **Tagula Sunrise (IRE)**[8] 5241 2-8-6 81 ........ PHanagan 8 76
(RAFahey) *chsd ldrs: hrd rdn over 2f out: burst through ins last to ld nr fin* **8/1**[3]
4530 **2** *nk* **Royal Orissa**[44] 4235 2-8-11 78 ........ (t) LDettori 17 80
(DHaydnJones) *trckd ldrs: ev ch ins last: no ex nr fin* **14/1**
03 **3** *shd* **My Gacho (IRE)**[11] 5200 2-8-11 ........ RHavlin 18 80
(MrsPNDutfield) *chsd ldrs: narrow ld 100yds out: hdd nr fin* **33/1**
4010 **4** *shd* **Grand Place**[13] 5119 2-8-11 71 ........ RLMoore 3 79
(RHannon) *towards rr: hdwy over 1f out: fin strly* **33/1**
231 **5** *¾* **Dancing Rose (IRE)**[14] 5070 2-8-6 77 ........ RSmith 20 72
(CGCox) *chsd ldrs: hmpd over 1f out: kpt on wl* **8/1**[3]
3255 **6** *nk* **Rusky Dusky (USA)**[21] 4918 2-8-11 75 ........ (v[1]) DaneO'Neill 15 76
(RHannon) *w ldrs: wnt lft and rt and led over 1f out: hdd 100yds out: no ex* **33/1**
631 **7** *2* **Toffee Vodka (IRE)**[15] 5053 2-8-6 77 ........ RHills 6 65
(JWHills) *bhd: hdwy over 2f out: swtchd outside over 1f out: styd on* **14/1**
20 **8** *1* **Love Affair (IRE)**[14] 5089 2-8-6 ........ MHills 14 62
(RHannon) *rr-div: swtchd outside over 1f out: kpt on: nvr rchd ldrs* **25/1**
6200 **9** *hd* **Molly Marie (IRE)**[2] 5391 2-8-6 77 ........ TEDurcan 22 77+
(TDEasterby) *trckd ldrs on ins: posied to chal whn bdly hmpd over 1f out: nt rcvr* **7/1**[1]
2331 **10** *nk* **Breaking Shadow (IRE)**[10] 5212 2-8-11 72 ........ KDarley 7 66
(RAFahey) *chsd ldrs: wknd jst ins fnl f* **9/1**
6044 **11** *nk* **Sapphire Dream**[22] 4875 2-8-6 80 ........ RWinston 16 60
(ABailey) *led: hdd and hmpd over 1f out: nt rcvr* **9/1**
3134 **12** *1* **Missperon (IRE)**[40] 4358 2-8-6 76 ........ NCallan 2 57
(KARyan) *w ldrs: wknd 1f out* **20/1**
05 **13** *nk* **Lord Of Dreams (IRE)**[13] 5114 2-8-11 ........ KMcEvoy 11 61
(DWPArbuthnot) *in tch: effrt over 2f out: no imp* **100/1**
452 **14** *½* **Rainbow Iris**[14] 5096 2-8-6 70 ........ CCatlin 9 54
(BSmart) *bhd: sme hdwy 2f out: nvr a factor* **40/1**
0240 **15** *½* **Scrooby Baby**[15] 5052 2-8-6 72 ........ EAhern 10 53
(JAOsborne) *in tch: effrt over 2f out: nvr a threat* **66/1**
6423 **16** *1 ½* **Musico (IRE)**[29] 4671 2-8-11 74 ........ SDrowne 13 53
(BRMillman) *mid-div: effrt over 2f out: nvr on terms* **15/2**[2]
34 **17** *½* **Flying Dancer**[15] 5053 2-8-6 ........ JDSmith 4 47
(AKing) *mid-div: effrt over 2f out: nvr a factor* **50/1**
0340 **18** *1 ¾* **Melvino**[10] 5212 2-8-11 76 ........ DMernagh 1 47
(TDBarron) *in tch: effrt over 2f out: sn btn* **100/1**
452 **19** *3* **Wigwam Willie (IRE)**[13] 5125 2-8-11 75 ........ KFallon 5 38
(MJWallace) *a towards rr* **11/1**
16 **20** *6* **Striking Endeavour**[100] 2592 2-8-11 81 ........ TQuinn 12 20
(NPLittmoden) *a in rr* **20/1**
006 **21** *15* **Superstitious (IRE)**[27] 4743 2-8-11 70 ........ WRyan 21 —
(BAMcmahon) *s.i.s: sn detached in rr* **50/1**

1m 11.91s (-2.37) **Going Correction** -0.375s/f (Firm) **21** Ran SP% **120.2**
Speed ratings: **100,99,99,99,98 97,95,93,93,93 92,91,91,90,89 87,87,84,80,72 52**CSF £96.37 TOTE £10.10: £3.30, £5.10, £13.10; EX 119.00 TRIFECTA Not won..
**Owner** David M Knaggs & Mel Roberts **Bred** Thomas Doherty **Trained** Musley Bank, N Yorks
■ Stewards Enquiry : Dane O'Neill two-day ban: careless riding (Sep 21,22)

**FOCUS**
A competitive sales consolation race resulting in a blanket finish, but a rough contest in the closing stages and several hard-luck stories. The first three home were maidens going into this, so the form is no more than fair.

**NOTEBOOK**
**Tagula Sunrise(IRE)**, who had been consistent but frustrating, having been placed in five of her six previous races but beaten twice at odds-on, showed a commendable attitude to come through under a strong ride and gain her first win. She was slightly fortunate in that she switched just in time to avoid the trouble on the stands' rail, but still had work to do from that point and responded really well. A similar event at Redcar is now on the agenda.
**Royal Orissa**, whose best previous effort had been with cut in the ground, had to switch wide to deliver his challenge and did nothing wrong in defeat, having the prize snatched from him near the line. He should have no difficulty gaining consolation on this evidence.
**My Gacho(IRE)**, one of the least experienced in the field, was dropping in trip and encountering fast ground for the first time. He got an opening as Rusky Dusky drifted but, despite getting to the front, could not hold on to his advantage. He is another that should find a race before long.
**Grand Place** ◆ did well to get so close from his low draw. Settled in rear in the early stages, he picked up well from over a furlong out and was cutting down the principals' advantage with every stride late on. A winner over five furlongs, on this evidence seven should be within his compass and he can win a nursery off his current mark.
**Dancing Rose(IRE)**, racing over six for the first time, was always close to the pace but was squeezed up by Rusky Dusky on more than one occasion and showed a commendable attitude to battle past that rival. She was not beaten far and should have been closer.
**Rusky Dusky(USA)** rediscovered his early-season form in the first-time visor. Always in the front rank, he wandered about when hitting the front and caused a fair amount of havoc on his inside below the distance which cost his rider a two-day ban.
**Toffee Vodka(IRE)** never got into contention from her low draw, but was doing her best work in the closing stages and has more races in her.
**Love Affair(IRE)** was another who was keeping on without ever getting into contention.

**Molly Marie(IRE)** ◆ was the unlucky horse of the race. Travelling well on the heels of the leaders, a gap opened briefly on the rail over a furlong out, but as she went to take it the door was slammed in her face and she was lucky to stay on her feet. Having run well from a poor draw two days previously she deserves a change of luck.
**Breaking Shadow(IRE)** showed up for a long way from his low draw before fading.
**Sapphire Dream**set the pace but was just beginning to weaken when suffering at the hands of Rusky Dusky.
**Musico(IRE)** was always struggling to go the pace. *Official explanation: jockey said colt hung right handed*
**Striking Endeavour** *Official explanation: jockey said colt bled from nose*
**Superstitious(IRE)** *Official explanation: jockey said colt was unsuited by the good, good/firm in places ground*

## 5435 TOTEPOOL MALLARD STKS (H'CAP) 1m 6f 132y
**1:50** (1:51) (B1) (0-110,105) 3-Y-O+ **£23,200** (£8,800; £4,400; £2,000) **Stalls** Low

Form RPR
5421 **1** **Lost Soldier Three (IRE)**[22] 4888 3-8-1 **97** NMackay[(3)] 2 107+
(LMCumani) *trckd ldrs: hung lft and nt clr run over 3f out: styd on to ld 1f out: kpt on wl* **5/2**[1]
5122 **2** *1 1/4* **Sergeant Cecil**[6] 5288 5-8-12 **93** JFortune 5 101+
(BRMillman) *hld up and bhd: hdwy on ins and nt clr run 2f out: swtchd rt over 1f out: styd on wl: nt rch wnr* **5/1**[3]
1-00 **3** *hd* **Fantastic Love (USA)**[23] 4858 4-9-6 **101** (t) LDettori 3 109
(SaeedBinSuroor) *trckd ldrs: qcknd to ld over 2f out: hdd 1f out: no ex* **9/1**
0000 **4** *2 1/2* **Trust Rule**[6] 5288 4-8-10 **91** oh1 (tp) MHills 13 96
(BWHills) *hld up: hdwy 3f out: styd on same pce appr fnl f* **33/1**
0110 **5** *2 1/2* **High Action (USA)**[6] 5288 4-8-10 **91** oh1 (t) KDarley 10 93+
(IanWilliams) *hld up towards rr: hdwy and nt clr run over 2f out: styd on appr fnl f* **20/1**
4126 **6** *1 1/2* **Star Member (IRE)**[23] 4858 5-9-2 **97** KMcEvoy 15 97
(APJarvis) *hld up towards rr: effrt over 3f out: kpt on fnl 2f: nvr nr ldrs* **12/1**
20-2 **7** *1 1/2* **Midas Way**[20] 4932 4-9-0 **95** EAhern 12 93
(PRChamings) *chsd ldr: drvn along over 3f out: lost pl over 1f out* **20/1**
-500 **8** *1 1/2* **Heisse**[142] 1539 4-8-12 **93** RLMoore 1 89
(DRLoder) *chsd ldrs: n.m.r over 2f out: one pce* **50/1**
0404 **9** *1* **Supremacy**[13] 5111 5-9-10 **105** KFallon 4 99
(SirMichaelStoute) *led tl over 2f out: lost pl over 1f out* **20/1**
0400 **10** *1* **Santando**[23] 4858 4-8-10 **91** oh1 (v) RHills 9 84
(CEBrittain) *mid-div: effrt over 4f out: one pce fnl 3f* **25/1**
3112 **11** *shd* **Yoshka**[43] 4274 3-7-13 **92** RFfrench 14 85
(MJohnston) *chsd ldrs: drvn along over 4f out: hung lft and lost pl over 1f out: fin lame* **4/1**[2]
1000 **12** *3/4* **Bourgeois**[23] 4856 7-9-1 **96** RWinston 7 88
(TDEasterby) *mid div: gd hdwy on outside 3f out: lost pl over 1f out* **50/1**
4533 **13** *4* **Highland Games (IRE)**[34] 4529 4-8-10 **91** oh1 TQuinn 8 78
(JGGiven) *mid-div: effrt over 3f out: no imp* **20/1**
0-30 **14** *3/4* **Zibeline (IRE)**[76] 3310 7-8-10 **91** oh3 (b) DaneO'Neill 6 77
(BEllison) *s.i.s: sme hdwy over 2f out: sn lost pl* **20/1**
6000 **15** *nk* **Salsalino**[23] 4858 4-9-5 **100** JDSmith 11 85
(AKing) *chsd ldrs: lost pl over 3f out* **50/1**

3m 3.90s (-5.84) **Going Correction** -0.325s/f (Firm)
**WFA** 3 from 4yo+ 12lb **15** Ran SP% **119.4**
Speed ratings: **102,101,101,99,98 97,96,96,95,95 95,94,92,92,91**CSF £11.82 CT £96.11 TOTE £3.70: £1.90, £2.20, £2.40; EX 14.10 Trifecta £166.80 Pool: £3,032.05. 12.90 winning units..
**Owner** Sheikh Mohammed Obaid Al Maktoum **Bred** Darley **Trained** Newmarket, Suffolk

**FOCUS**
A decent handicap run at just a fair pace ina modest time, but a good winner and the first three were clear.

**NOTEBOOK**
**Lost Soldier Three(IRE)** ◆, as expected, followed up his York win in emphatic style. Despite taking a keen grip early on, he found plenty when asked to go in pursuit of the third halfway up the striaght, and was always doing enough to hold off the late surge of the runner-up. He looks likely to get further, and should make a Cup horse next season, but would be interesting if taking his chance in the Jockey Club Cup next month.
**Sergeant Cecil** ◆ has now been runner-up in three valuable 14 furlong handicaps in a row since winning at Ascot. He is obviously in peak form, and looks worth another try at two miles, with the Gordon Carter Handicap at Ascot at the end of the month a possible. The Betfred Handicap over this trip at Haydock on the same day is an alternative.
**Fantastic Love(USA)**, trying his longest trip to date, made an early strike for home and stole a couple of lengths. However, the winner always had him in his sights and he had no response when that rival challenged. It may be worth employing similar tactics back over a mile and a half.
**Trust Rule**, fitted with cheekpieces and a tongue tie, ran his best race for a while and may be capable of returning to winning form in a slightly lower grade.
**High Action(USA)** finished a little further behind the runner-up than he had at Haydock, and gives the impression that this trip is his minimum. He seems to be holding his form and looks an interesting contender for the Cesarewitch.
**Star Member(IRE)** was entitled to finish closer on his running with Fantastic Love at York, but it may be that he goes particularly well on that track and is one to bear in mind if he returns there before the end of the season.
**Supremacy**, who stays further, set an even gallop but soon capitulated once headed.
**Yoshka** should have been suited by the trip and ground, but was being niggled at on the long home turn and dropped away under pressure in the straight before being taken off the track in the horse ambulance. His previous form through Lochbuie entitled him to be in the shake-up, and one hopes the damage was not too serious. *Official explanation: jockey said colt finished lame*

## 5436 GILBEY BROTHERS SILVER MICROPHONE CONDITIONS STKS 1m 2f 60y
**2:25** (2:25) (B1) 3-5-Y-O **£11,600** (£4,400; £2,200; £1,000) **Stalls** Low

Form RPR
-345 **1** **Big Bad Bob (IRE)**[48] 4160 4-9-2 110 LDettori 3 116
(JLDunlop) *led: qcknd clr over 8f out: hrd rdn appr fnl f: hld on* **7/2**[2]
1314 **2** *3/4* **Red Fort (IRE)**[62] 3756 4-9-2 113 PRobinson 4 115
(MAJarvis) *hld up in rr: effrt 4f out: styd on to take 2nd last 100yds: nt rch wnr* **5/6**[1]
52 **3** *nk* **Bayberry (UAE)**[20] 4948 4-8-11 93 WRyan 2 109
(HRACecil) *chsd wnr: regained 2nd over 2f out: styd on* **16/1**
605 **4** *6* **Kaieteur (USA)**[55] 3936 5-9-8 111 JFortune 6 109
(BJMeehan) *chsd ldrs: wnt 2nd over 3f out: wknd over 1f out* **8/1**
1/0- **5** *9* **Artistic Lad**[434] 2964 4-9-2 KFallon 5 86
(SirMichaelStoute) *trckd ldrs: effrt over 4f out: rdn 3f out: sn btn* **7/1**[3]
13/0 **6** *1/2* **Love You Always (USA)**[157] 1286 4-9-2 92 BReilly 1 85
(MissJFeilden) *hld up: a last: bhd fnl 3f* **100/1**

2m 6.89s (-4.87) **Going Correction** -0.325s/f (Firm) **6** Ran SP% **107.3**
Speed ratings: **106,105,105,100,93 92**CSF £6.17 TOTE £3.50: £2.00, £1.10; EX 5.80.
**Owner** Windflower Overseas Holdings Inc **Bred** Windflower Overseas Holdings Inc **Trained** Arundel, W Sussex

**FOCUS**
A masterful ride from the front by Dettori on Big Bad Bob and serious reservations about how the form will work out..

**NOTEBOOK**
**Big Bad Bob(IRE)** moved fluently to post. He dropped the bit and settled in front before quickening the gallop and seizing a lead of half a dozen lengths. He was coming to the end of his tether in the closing stages but was never in any danger of being caught. Dettori at his tactical best.
**Red Fort(IRE)**, whose best form has been on the firm, moved to post as if his shoes were a couple of sizes too small. Settled out the back, he stayed on to take second inside the last but was never going to reach the enterprisingly ridden winner.
**Bayberry(UAE)**, who had a fair bit to find, was the only one to try and keep tabs on the winner and is probably flattered by this.
**Kaieteur(USA)**, who would have eaten these at his best, has been out of sorts this year and here had the blinkers left off. He went in pursuit of the winner but never seemed to be putting his heart into it. He is one to have severe reservations about now.
**Artistic Lad**, who won his sole backend outing at two, had just one run last year. He returned looking very fit but in truth showed very little. The mere fact that he is being perservered with suggests he has been showing a fair bit at home.
**Love You Always(USA)**, who changed hands at Newmarket Sales for just 10,000gns, was out of his depth but was rewarded for just turning up.

## 5437 SGB CHAMPAGNE STKS (GROUP 2) (C&G) 7f
**3:00** (3:00) (A1) 2-Y-O **£60,000** (£23,000; £11,500; £5,500) **Stalls** High

Form RPR
1 **1** **Etlaala**[27] 4743 2-8-10 RHills 3 117+
(BWHills) *dwlt: hld up in rr: nt clr run over 2f out and over 1f out: swtchd outside: r.o strly to ld last 75yds* **6/1**[3]
211 **2** *1/2* **Iceman**[87] 2954 2-9-1 100 KFallon 2 117
(JHMGosden) *swvd rt s: sn pushed along: hdwy over 3f out: styd on to ld jst ins last: hdd and no ex wl ins last* **5/2**[1]
12 **3** *2 1/2* **Oude (USA)**[24] 4835 2-8-10 LDettori 9 106
(SaeedBinSuroor) *trckd ldrs: t.k.h: led over 2f out tl jst ins last: sn outpcd* **5/2**[1]
3212 **4** *1 1/4* **Wilko (USA)**[28] 4716 2-8-10 100 EAhern 5 103
(JNoseda) *chsd ldrs: drvn along and sltly outpcd over 2f out: swtchd rt appr fnl f: styd on* **16/1**
5112 **5** *nk* **Grand Marque (IRE)**[30] 4639 2-8-10 96 RLMoore 7 102
(RHannon) *chsd ldrs: outpcd and lost pl over 3f out: styd on appr fnl f* **50/1**
11 **6** *1 1/2* **Elliots World (IRE)**[24] 4835 2-8-10 JFanning 1 98
(MJohnston) *swtg: trckd ldrs: chal 2f out: sn fdd* **11/2**[2]
5223 **7** *nk* **Mister Genepi**[11] 5179 2-8-10 86 SDrowne 10 97
(WRMuir) *hld up towards rr: kpt on fnl 2f: nvr nr ldrs* **100/1**
41 **8** *2* **Jonquil (IRE)**[42] 4290 2-8-10 JFortune 12 92
(JHMGosden) *chsd ldrs: rdn over 2f out: sn wl outpcd* **11/1**
32 **9** *5* **Surwaki (USA)**[21] 4922 2-8-10 PRobinson 11 80
(CGCox) *led: hung rt and hdd over 3f out: lost pl over 2f out* **100/1**
110 **10** *1 1/2* **Leo's Lucky Star (USA)**[20] 4949 2-8-10 KDarley 6 76
(MJohnston) *w ldr: led over 3f out tl over 2f out: sn lost pl* **16/1**

1m 23.33s (-4.48) **Going Correction** -0.375s/f (Firm) **10** Ran SP% **110.9**
Speed ratings: **110,109,106,105,104 103,102,100,94,93**CSF £20.05 TOTE £7.40: £2.30, £1.30, £1.40; EX 26.50 Trifecta £71.30 Pool: £1,837.88. 18.30 winning units..
**Owner** Hamdan Al Maktoum **Bred** Matthews Breeding And Racing Ltd **Trained** Lambourn, Berks
■ Barry Hills' fifth Champagne Stakes success.

**FOCUS**
A decent renewal and a creditable winning time for the grade. Although the proximity of Grande Marque and Mister Genepi undermines the form to a degree, the first two look smart, especially the impressive winner, who had to quicken twice to get out of jail.

**NOTEBOOK**
**Etlaala** ◆, a real athlete, made an awkward exit from the stalls. A shade free in the rear, he met serious traffic problems twice before quickening down the outside to take the prize near the line. Although in receipt of 5lb, he still looked the best horse on the day and he sets the standard for next year's 2,000 Guineas.
**Iceman** ◆, absent since the Coventry, is a very laid back individual and was soon being pushed along after coming out of the stalls sideways. Knuckling down in willing fashion, he showed ahead just inside the last and went down fighting, pulling clear of the rest in the process. The way he runs a mile will suit him ideally and, as he was giving the winner 5lb, he remains a top prospect.
**Oude(USA)**, quite a tall, leggy type, is a much better mover than his sire. He wouldn't drop his bit and in the end the first two were simply too good for him at this stage of his development. He will do better in time, providing he learns to settle.
**Wilko(USA)** lacks size and scope but is very tough and is one of the keys to the overall value of the form.
**Grand Marque(IRE)**, who ran over a mile last time, was tapped for toe at halfway. He appears to have shown improved form and deserves credit for the way he stuck to his task, but he is now exposed as left wanting at this level.
**Elliots World(IRE)**, an edgy type, became very warm beforehand. Drawn one, he had no rail to help him this time and still very much up in the air, he will make a better three-year-old.
**Mister Genepi**, already beaten in nursery company, was out of his depth but far from disgraced. Indeed this quite attractive individual appeared to show much improved form.
**Jonquil(IRE)**, a May foal, stands over a fair amount of ground and is the type to give a better account of himself at this level at three.
**Surwaki(USA)** *Official explanation: jockey said colt hung right from one and a half furlongs out*
**Leo's Lucky Star(USA)**, a big sort, has a round action. The family tend not to progress after a bright start.

## 5438 ORDERIT-ONLINE.COM TROY STKS (LISTED RACE) 1m 4f
**3:35** (3:35) (A1) 3-Y-O+ **£19,500** (£6,000; £3,000; £1,500) **Stalls** Low

Form RPR
-051 **1** **Distinction (IRE)**[62] 3757 5-9-6 111 KFallon 2 117+
(SirMichaelStoute) *lw: trckd ldrs: effrt over 3f out: edgd lft and led over 1f out: styd on wl* **5/2**[1]
6533 **2** *3/4* **Compton Bolter (IRE)**[13] 5133 7-9-1 109 EAhern 6 111
(GAButler) *led: qcknd over 3f out: hdd over 1f out: kpt on wl* **11/2**
4312 **3** *1 1/2* **Swift Tango (IRE)**[13] 5111 4-9-6 102 PHanagan 3 114?
(EALDunlop) *hld up in rr: effrt and nt clr run over 2f out: styd on to take 3rd nr line* **10/1**
0256 **4** *nk* **Delsarte (USA)**[20] 4932 4-9-1 106 (vt[1]) LDettori 1 108
(SaeedBinSuroor) *hld up: hdwy over 3f out: styd on same pce fnl 2f* **5/1**[3]
-135 **5** *3* **Starry Lodge (IRE)**[34] 4530 4-9-1 96 JFortune 7 103+
(LMCumani) *chsd ldr: rdn over 2f out: styng on same pce whn checked appr fnl f* **9/2**[2]
-440 **6** *1/2* **Franklins Gardens**[12] 5170 4-9-1 108 PRobinson 5 103
(MHTompkins) *chsd ldrs: one pce fnl 2f* **9/2**[2]

0206 **7** *5* **Private Charter**$^{110}$ [2329] 4-9-1 105 MHills 4 95
(BWHills) *hld up in tch: outpcd over 3f out: wknd over 1f out: eased ins last* **20/1**

2m 29.62s (-6.08) **Going Correction** -0.325s/f (Firm) **7** Ran SP% **110.8**
Speed ratings: **107,106,105,105,103 102,99**CSF £15.45 TOTE £3.70: £2.10, £3.10; EX 18.60.
**Owner** Highclere Thoroughbred Racing Ltd **Bred** Orpendale And Minch Bloodstock **Trained** Newmarket, Suffolk

**FOCUS**
Very good form for a Listed race, up to Group Three standard at least.

**NOTEBOOK**
**Distinction(IRE)**, who looked at his very best, was running over a shorter trip than ideal and made hard work of it, but was firmly in command at the line and booked his ticket to Australia for the Caulfield and Melbourne Cups.
**Compton Bolter(IRE)** took them along and went for home early in the straight. He never flinched but in the end was definitely second best.
**Swift Tango(IRE)** ◆ had something to find under his penalty and ran out of room at a crucial stage but snatched third place on the line and is clearly in very good heart. This represents improved form and he will be well treated in the totesport Ascot Final Fling Handicap.
**Delsarte(USA)**, tried in a visor, ran a lot better but his effort lacked anything in the way of sparkle.
**Starry Lodge(IRE)**, who likes to go left-handed, was closely matched with Swift Tango on Epsom running but his chance had slipped when the winner left him short of room. His trainer has an eye on an American campaign with him this backend.
**Franklins Gardens** appreciated the much better ground and ran his best race so far this year on his fourth start.
**Private Charter** has now run well below his best on three successive starts and presumably has a problem.

## 5439 CENTEX FAIRCLOUGH HOMES TROPHY (CONDITIONS STKS) 1m (R)

**4:10** (4:10) (C2) 3-Y-O **£8,700** (£3,300; £1,650; £750) **Stalls** High

Form RPR

-550 **1** **Secret Charm (IRE)**$^{84}$ [3033] 3-8-6 110 MHills 9 108
(BWHills) *w ldr: led 5f out: qcknd over 2f out: hld on gamely* **11/2**$^{3}$

5033 **2** *½* **Milk It Mick**$^{22}$ [4873] 3-8-11 107 KFallon 2 112
(JAOsborne) *t.k.h: hdwy 4f out: chal over 1f out: edgd rt and no ex wl ins last* **9/2**$^{2}$

21- **3** *1* **Mansfield Park**$^{398}$ [3994] 3-8-6 100 KMcEvoy 3 105
(SaeedBinSuroor) *s.i.s: drvn along over 3f out: swtchd outside over 1f out: styd on ins last* **11/2**$^{3}$

12-5 **4** *hd* **Fantastic View (USA)**$^{148}$ [1410] 3-8-11 113 RLMoore 1 109
(RHannon) *trckd ldrs: edgd rt and lft and kpt on same pce fnl f* **6/1**

11- **5** *1 ¾* **Oriental Warrior**$^{335}$ [5483] 3-8-11 RHills 4 105
(MPTregoning) *trckd ldrs: kpt on same pce fnl 2f* **8/1**

0242 **6** *2* **Moonlight Man**$^{33}$ [4570] 3-8-11 100 DaneO'Neill 6 101
(RHannon) *led tl 5f out: one pce fnl 3f* **14/1**

3000 **7** *8* **Miss Childrey (IRE)**$^{12}$ [5162] 3-8-6 (t) DMGrant 7 77
(FrancisEnnis, Ire) *hld up towards rr: effrt 3f out: sn outpcd: wknd over 1f out* **66/1**

1-1 **8** *4* **Thajja (IRE)**$^{140}$ [1587] 3-9-2 98 LDettori 8 78
(JLDunlop) *t.k.h on outer: stdd and dropped bk over 4f out: rdn over 2f out: sn lost pl* **11/4**$^{1}$

150- **9** *1 ¼* **Tarot Card**$^{328}$ [5642] 3-8-6 104 PHanagan 5 65
(BWHills) *hld up towards rr: effrt over 3f out: sn btn* **33/1**

1m 36.07s (-4.48) **Going Correction** -0.325s/f (Firm) course record **9** Ran SP% **112.1**
Speed ratings: **109,108,107,107,105 103,95,91,90**CSF £29.25 TOTE £6.80: £2.00, £1.40, £2.00; EX 31.60.
**Owner** Maktoum Al Maktoum **Bred** Gainsborough Stud Management Ltd **Trained** Lambourn, Berks

**FOCUS**
A good conditions event, up to Listed grade, run in a reasonable time. A game effort by Secret Charm and a sound performance from Milk It Mick, although he is not quite as good as he was. The next three all ran well too after their breaks.

**NOTEBOOK**
**Secret Charm(IRE)**, who had taken on the mighty Attraction in all three previous outings this season, appreciated the drop in grade and, again ridden positively, stuck to her task bravely to hold off the runner-up. She will no doubt return to Pattern company after this, and the Joel Stakes is a possibility, although connections may be tempted by the Sun Chariot Stakes if the big guns go elsewhere.
**Milk It Mick** has not really gone on from his surprise Dewhurst victory but really came to himself in the autumn at two and could well do so again. Although he did not see out the finish quite as well as the winner, he was up against a useful rival and did little wrong.
**Mansfield Park** ◆ is the one to take out of the race. Having her first start since strolling home in a Redcar maiden in 2003, this beautifully-bred sister to Cape Cross showed signs of inexperience before keeping on steadily in the closing stages. She should have no trouble winning races, and connections will no doubt be looking for a Pattern race for her.
**Fantastic View(USA)**, best in on official ratings, seemed to get a good lead from the winner and his stable companion, but did not find as much as looked likely. However, this was his first outing since the Craven Stakes, and he can be expected to improve a little for the outing.
**Oriental Warrior**, yet another returning from a long absence, was on the heels of the leaders from the start but, after looking beaten, ran on again as if getting a second wind. He is another who should benefit from the run.
**Moonlight Man**trying this trip for the first time, had a difficult task on official ratings and got in a duel for the lead with the winner. Not surprisingly he paid the penalty, but he is a consistent sort and deserves to pick up another race, although he falls in the twilight zone between handicaps and conditions events.
**Thajja(IRE)**, another returning from a break, was made favourite despite stepping up in class on the fastest ground he has yet encountered. He was very keen early and then totally lost his place on the home turn, from which point he had no chance of getting back into the argument. A return to easy ground may be in his favour, but he will need to be more amenable if he is to progress.
*Official explanation: jockey said colt ran too free*
**Tarot Card** *Official explanation: jockey said filly hung right handed throughout*

## 5440 WILFREDA BEEHIVE H'CAP 5f

**4:45** (4:47) (D2) (0-85,85) 3-Y-O+ **£6,500** (£2,000; £1,000; £500) **Stalls** High

Form RPR

4066 **1** **Malapropism**$^{14}$ [5071] 4-8-12 78 SHitchcott$^{(3)}$ 17 88
(MRChannon) *trckd ldrs: n.m.r over 1f out: led 1f out: edgd lft: jst hld on* **13/2**$^{2}$

3006 **2** *shd* **Beyond The Clouds (IRE)**$^{13}$ [5107] 8-8-10 73 (p) RWinston 10 83
(JSWainwright) *trckd ldrs: chal 1f out: carried lft ins last: jst denied* **12/1**

3100 **3** *¾* **Midnight Parkes**$^{8}$ [5242] 5-8-7 70 MHenry 3 77+
(EJAlston) *led on far side: kpt on wl fnl f* **33/1**

0521 **4** *hd* **Currency**$^{26}$ [4774] 7-9-0 77 RLMoore 19 83
(JMBradley) *sn bhd and drvn along: hdwy over 1f out: styd on strly ins last* **6/1**$^{1}$

6500 **5** *hd* **Zarzu**$^{23}$ [4847] 5-8-11 77 RThomas$^{(3)}$ 21 82
(CRDore) *bhd: hdwy whn nt clr run over 1f out: styd on ins last* **16/1**

5101 **6** *shd* **Marshallspark (IRE)**$^{34}$ [4534] 5-8-8 71 PHanagan 15 76
(RAFahey) *in rr: hdwy over 1f out: kpt on wl ins last* **10/1**

0420 **7** *¾* **Inter Vision (USA)**$^{33}$ [4577] 4-9-2 82 ABeech$^{(3)}$ 7 84
(ADickman) *swtchd rt and r stands' side: chsd ldrs: nt qckn fnl f* **16/1**

3633 **8** *½* **Paddywack (IRE)**$^{23}$ [4855] 7-8-9 72 (b) JFanning 1 72
(DWChapman) *s.i.s: racd far side: hdwy 2f out: styd on fnl f* **16/1**

3502 **9** *nk* **Dispol Katie**$^{23}$ [4862] 3-9-3 81 NCallan 6 80+
(TDBarron) *w ldr far side: nt qckn fnl f* **11/1**

0050 **10** *nk* **Matty Tun**$^{34}$ [4538] 5-9-6 83 JBramhill 22 81
(JBalding) *in rr: n.m.r over 1f out: styd on ins last* **8/1**$^{3}$

3050 **11** *nk* **Wanchai Lad**$^{76}$ [3293] 3-9-7 85 ANicholls 2 81+
(DNicholls) *racd far side: trckd ldrs: nt qckn appr fnl f* **33/1**

003 **12** *hd* **Musical Fair**$^{15}$ [5062] 4-8-12 75 FNorton 13 71
(JAGlover) *trckd ldrs: nt clr run over 1f out: kpt on* **10/1**

2110 **13** *hd* **True Magic**$^{15}$ [5062] 3-8-10 74 KMcEvoy 18 69
(JDBethell) *w ldrs: one pce fnl 2f* **14/1**

0020 **14** *hd* **Dancing Mystery**$^{14}$ [5071] 10-9-1 78 (b) GBaker 4 72+
(EAWheeler) *racd far side: trckd ldrs: effrt 2f out: one pce* **16/1**

2135 **15** *nk* **Trick Cyclist**$^{20}$ [4952] 3-8-8 72 SDrowne 5 65+
(AMBalding) *s.s: racd far side: nvr trbld ldrs* **25/1**

050L **16** *1 ¼* **Piccled**$^{34}$ [4538] 6-9-6 83 TEDurcan 16 71
(EJAlston) *s.s: hdwy over 2f out: nvr a factor* **25/1**

1000 **17** *shd* **Silver Prelude**$^{25}$ [4810] 3-9-4 82 PRobinson 11 69
(DKIvory) *w ldrs: wknd over 1f out* **33/1**

0000 **18** *shd* **Palawan**$^{14}$ [5071] 8-8-7 70 CCatlin 14 57
(AMBalding) *led stands' side tl hdd & wknd 1f out* **50/1**

**19** *1 ¼* **Calypso Dancer (FR)**$^{22}$ 4-8-9 72 KDarley 20 54
(TDBarron) *s.i.s: a in rr* **25/1**

-060 **20** *2 ½* **Fyodor (IRE)**$^{90}$ [2877] 3-9-1 79 EAhern 12 51
(WJHaggas) *w ldrs: wkng whn hmpd and eased 150yds out* **33/1**

58.74 secs (-2.68) **Going Correction** -0.375s/f (Firm)
**WFA** 3 from 4yo+ 1lb **20** Ran SP% **128.4**
Speed ratings: **106,105,104,104,104 103,102,101,101,100 100,100,99,99,98 96,96,96,94,90**CSF £76.97 CT £2496.76 TOTE £8.30: £1.90, £3.80, £9.00, £2.30; EX 108.00 Place 6 £51.86, Place 5 £6.57.
**Owner** Michael A Foy **Bred** Michael A Foy **Trained** West Ilsley, Berks

**FOCUS**
A competitive sprint handicap in which the runners split into two groups, with a marginal advantage enjoyed by those drawn high. Solid form, but not outstanding.

**NOTEBOOK**
**Malapropism** has been generally consistent, despite not winning since last November, yet had dropped a total of 10lb since the start of the season. Appreciating the flat track and fast ground, he put up a game effort to resist the persistent challenge of the runner-up. He should not go up much for this and can win again if the rain stays away.
**Beyond The Clouds(IRE)** has not scored since winning this event two years ago. However, he delivered a determined challenge, despite the winner leaning on him in the closing stages, and only just lost out. He is currently on his lowest mark for a long while and, with the cheekpieces seemingly helping to bring about some improvement, he can end that long losing run before long.
**Midnight Parkes** ◆ deserves plenty of credit for his effort, as he did best of those racing on the far side of the track and was not beaten far in any case. He is only 3lb above the mark he won off at Pontefract in July, and could well gain compensation if better drawn next time.
**Currency** has been running well over longer trips of late and possibly found five furlongs on this track and fast ground on the short side. He remains in good heart and is one to keep on the right side in the short term.
**Zarzu** did not get the best of passages and did well to get so close. He is slipping back to a winning mark.
**Marshallspark(IRE)** stepping back up in grade and off a 6lb higher mark than when winning last time, ran with plenty of credit over a trip that is on the short side for him.
**Inter Vision(USA)**, switched from his low draw to race nearside, was close to the pace throughout and ran a fine race. A return to his favourite track, Ripon, may well see him back to winning ways.
**Paddywack(IRE)**, second home on the far side, is in decent form at present and will appreciate a little more cut in the ground.
**Dancing Mystery**, who has run some of his best races in the autumn, raced with enthusiasm, and the Handicapper seems to have given him a chance.
**Piccled** seems to have developed a habit of missing the break, and that makes winning these sort of races very difficult.
T/Jkpt: Not won. T/Plt: £57.30 to a £1 stake. Pool: £94,420.25. 1,201.45 winning tickets. T/Qpdt: £6.60 to a £1 stake. Pool: £6,697.10. 744.25 winning tickets. WG

# 4948 SANDOWN (R-H)

Friday, September 10

**OFFICIAL GOING: Good (good to firm in places on round course)**
Wind: almost nil Weather: dull

## 5441 MARSHALL ARTS EBF MAIDEN STKS 5f 6y

**2:00** (2:01) (D2) 2-Y-O **£5,538** (£1,704; £852; £426) **Stalls** High

Form RPR

6262 **1** **Unreal**$^{11}$ [5202] 2-8-9 80 RHughes 6 76+
(BWHills) *trckd ldrs: plld out over 1f out: chal and edgd rt ins fnl f: pushed into ld last 75yds* **3/1**$^{1}$

43 **2** *½* **Park Approach (IRE)**$^{18}$ [5003] 2-8-9 SWKelly 3 75+
(JNoseda) *t.k.h: led over 3f out: rdn fnl f: hdd and one pce last 75yds* **4/1**$^{3}$

604 **3** *¾* **Alexia Rose (IRE)**$^{26}$ [4776] 2-8-9 61 WSupple 4 72
(ABerry) *lw: dwlt: plld hrd early: hld up in last pair: rdn and prog over 1f out: styd on wl fnl f* **33/1**

030 **4** *½* **Encouragement**$^{14}$ [5070] 2-8-9 75 JPMurtagh 5 70+
(RHannon) *led to over 3f out: styd cl up: effrt over 1f out: n.m.r ins fnl f: one pce* **11/1**

0 **5** *hd* **Cesar Manrique (IRE)**$^{18}$ [5003] 2-9-0 ACulhane 8 75+
(BWHills) *t.k.h: hld up in last pair: effrt on inner 2f out: nt clr run after: kpt on* **40/1**

2 **6** *1 ½* **Rubies**$^{14}$ [5070] 2-8-9 SCarson 7 64+
(RFJohnsonHoughton) *lw: s.i.s: t.k.h and jnd ldr over 3f out: losing pl whn hmpd ins fnl f* **10/3**$^{2}$

**7** *2* **Small Stakes (IRE)** 2-9-0 SSanders 9 62
(PJMakin) *str: bit bkwd: settled in midfield: pushed along over 2f out: rn green and no prog* **3/1**$^{1}$

**8** *5* **Windwood (IRE)** 2-9-0 DHolland 2 45
(JWHills) *w'like: s.i.s: a in rr: rdn and rn green 1/2-way: wknd* **20/1**

**9** *1* **Elms Schoolboy** 2-9-0 JTate 1 41
(JMPEustace) *unf: s.i.s: t.k.h and sn cl up: wknd 2f out* **33/1**

64.36 secs (2.17) **Going Correction** +0.25s/f (Good) **9** Ran SP% **114.5**
Speed ratings: **92,91,90,89,88 86,83,75,73**CSF £14.53 TOTE £3.70: £1.70, £1.80, £5.40; EX 18.70.
**Owner** K Abdulla **Bred** Juddmonte Farms **Trained** Lambourn, Berks
■ Stewards Enquiry : R Hughes caution: careless riding

**FOCUS**
A messy race in which there was no great gallop on early. Suspect form, with Alexia Rose uncomfortably close.

**NOTEBOOK**
**Unreal** is a half-sister to Illustrator and Trace Clip, who both failed to live up to their early potential. She won this modest event well enough, but was the most experienced runner in the field, and it remains to be seen whether she will follow in the family tradition, or go on from this.
**Park Approach(IRE)**, beaten by the draw on her last start, did not settle off the steady gallop but was only overhauled well inside the last. She is now eligible for a mark and will be suited by a stronger pace in handicap company.
**Alexia Rose(IRE)**, who showed her true form last time, was another who struggled with the steady early pace. Ridden differently this time, she would also have preferred a stronger gallop, and she too looks likely to be more effective in handicap company.
**Encouragement** enjoyed the run of the race in a contest not run at a break-neck gallop.
**Cesar Manrique(IRE)** finished a long way behind Park Approach on his debut at Windsor, but he got a lot closer to the filly on this occasion, and would have finished even nearer had he enjoyed a clear run inside the final two furlongs.
**Rubies** was done no favours by the winner as she crossed in front of her, but she was beating a retreat at the time.
**Small Stakes(IRE)**, whose dam was a high-class two-year-old and won the Flying Childers Stakes, has Group race entries and was supported in the market for this debut. He ran green on the outside - not the place to be - but it was still disappointing that he was unable to land a blow in this fairly modest contest. He is surely better than this. *Official explanation: trainer said colt had mucus in his lungs*
**Windwood(IRE)** *Official explanation: jockey said colt hung left*

## 5442 CLEAR CHANNEL CLASSIFIED STKS 5f 6y
**2:35** (2:38) (D2) 3-Y-O+ **£6,776** (£2,085; £1,042; £521) **Stalls** High

Form RPR
5300 **1** **Dame De Noche**$^{15}$ [5062] 4-9-3 85 ACulhane 4 93
(JGGiven) *lw: chsd ldng pair: rdn 2f out: squeezed through to ld jst over 1f out: sn clr* **5/1**
1163 **2** 1 1/2 **Royal Challenge**$^{14}$ [5071] 3-9-0 79 SSanders 5 86
(GAButler) *lw: trckd ldr: rdn 2f out: fnd little and btn ins fnl f: jst hld on for 2nd* **5/2**$^{1}$
0001 **3** *hd* **Fiddle Me Blue**$^{31}$ [4622] 3-8-11 77 JPMurtagh 2 82
(HMorrison) *hld up in 4th: rdn 2f out: hanging and no prog tl styd on ins fnl f* **13/2**
2020 **4** *hd* **Domirati**$^{40}$ [4366] 4-9-3 82 DHolland 3 86+
(RCharlton) *lw: hld up in 5th: effrt on inner 2f out: nt clr run over 1f out and again ins fnl f: styd on* **4/1**$^{3}$
4520 **5** 1 1/2 **Bohola Flyer (IRE)**$^{46}$ [4194] 3-8-11 78 RHughes 1 76
(RHannon) *hld up in last: shkn up over 1f out: kpt on: nvr on terms w ldrs* **20/1**
0564 **6** 1 1/4 **Little Edward**$^{6}$ [5299] 6-9-0 82 LPKeniry$^{(3)}$ 6 76
(BGPowell) *led to jst over 1f out: wknd* **3/1**$^{2}$

62.30 secs (0.11) **Going Correction** +0.25s/f (Good) **6** Ran **SP% 108.3**
**WFA** 3 from 4yo+ 1lb
Speed ratings: **109,106,106,105,103 101**CSF £16.59 TOTE £6.80: £3.00, £1.70; EX 17.50.
**Owner** The G-Guck Group **Bred** Woodditton Stud Ltd **Trained** Willoughton, Lincs

**FOCUS**
A pretty tight affair on the ratings. Dame de Noche was well treated on some form and did not need to be at her best to win.

**NOTEBOOK**
**Dame De Noche** ran well in the Stewards' Sprint Handicap but had been largely disappointing otherwise this term. She was best in at the weights in this contest, though, and her stamina over longer trips saw her draw clear inside the last. Hopefully this will have done her confidence some good, and she could well be set for a trip to Ayr for the Silver Cup now.
**Royal Challenge** has not really progressed as expected since winning a tactical affair here in July. This was still a fair effort, though, on ground which was easier than he would have liked. This was still a fair effort, though, on ground which was easier than he would have liked.
**Fiddle Me Blue**, another who would not have appreciated the morning rain, got closer to Royal Challenge than she had at Goodwood on identical terms.
**Domirati**, although still without a win on turf, is a consistent type and would have finished closer had he enjoyed a clear run next to the far-side rail.
**Bohola Flyer(IRE)** found everything happening a bit too quickly over the minimum trip and will appreciate a return to six.
**Little Edward** has dropped 15lb in the handicap this turf season and continues below his best.

## 5443 WHATSONWEMBLEY.COM H'CAP 1m 14y
**3:10** (3:11) (C1) (0-100,98) 3-Y-O **£12,151** (£4,609; £2,304; £1,047) **Stalls** High

Form RPR
5552 **1** **Free Trip**$^{30}$ [4646] 3-8-12 89 RHughes 2 101
(JHMGosden) *lw: trckd ldr: gng easily 2f out: led over 1f out: sn clr: rdn out* **5/1**$^{3}$
1412 **2** 1 1/2 **Take A Bow**$^{22}$ [4887] 3-9-7 98 JQuinn 4 107
(PRChamings) *lw: trckd ldrs: rdn 2f out: styd on to chse wnr jst ins fnl f: nvr able to chal* **9/4**$^{1}$
4113 **3** *hd* **Royal Prince**$^{33}$ [4570] 3-8-12 89 JPMurtagh 1 98
(JRFanshawe) *hld up in last: effrt over 2f out: rdn and r.o fr over 1f out: no ch to chal* **5/1**$^{3}$
51 **4** 2 **Stream Of Gold (IRE)**$^{26}$ [4781] 3-8-12 89 SSanders 5 93
(SirMichaelStoute) *hld up in last pair: prog over 2f out: clsd on ldrs over 1f out: wknd ins fnl f* **11/2**
1300 **5** 3 1/2 **Barathea Dreams (IRE)**$^{71}$ [3452] 3-8-7 84 oh1 JFEgan 3 80
(JSMoore) *led and set str pce: clr 1/2-way: hdd & wknd over 1f out* **20/1**
1100 **6** 1 1/2 **Master Marvel (IRE)**$^{85}$ [3001] 3-8-12 89 DHolland 7 81
(MJohnston) *lw: chsd ldng pair: rdn 1/2-way: lost pl and struggling over 2f out* **9/2**$^{2}$
4046 **7** 1/2 **Sew'N'So Character (IRE)**$^{13}$ [5106] 3-8-11 88 DSweeney 6 79
(MBlanshard) *s.i.s: in tch: rdn 3f out: wknd 2f out* **10/1**

1m 41.71s (-2.21) **Going Correction** -0.10s/f (Good) **7** Ran **SP% 111.5**
Speed ratings: **107,105,105,103,99 98,97**CSF £15.83 TOTE £6.80: £2.50, £1.60; EX 16.70.
**Owner** K Abdulla **Bred** Juddmonte Farms **Trained** Manton, Wilts

**FOCUS**
A decent handicap run at a good pace. The principals are all progressive and the form looks strong.

**NOTEBOOK**
**Free Trip** reversed recent course form with Take A Bow over this longer trip and on these better terms. He travelled particularly well throughout and quickened up in style. This was a good performance off a career-high mark.
**Take A Bow**, 7lb worse off with Free Trip compared with when he beat that rival by three lengths over seven furlongs here last month, was unable to confirm his superiority under these different conditions. The Handicapper may just have his measure now.
**Royal Prince** also looks to have plenty to do off his current mark, but got the longer trip well. Perhaps this performance will open up some new options for connections.
**Stream Of Gold(IRE)** came with a promising challenge but then dropped out inside the last like a non-stayer. His maiden win was over this trip, though, and perhaps it is simply a case of the Handicapper having overreacted to that success.
**Barathea Dreams(IRE)** made it a true test at the trip, setting a strong pace from the off. Considering this was his first run for ten weeks, it was not a bad effort.
**Master Marvel(IRE)** is becoming disappointing.

## 5444 3A H'CAP 7f 16y
**3:45** (3:45) (D2) (0-85,83) 3-Y-O+ **£8,724** (£2,684; £1,342; £671) **Stalls** High

Form RPR
2300 **1** **Armagnac**$^{6}$ [5299] 6-9-5 80 ACulhane 6 89
(MABuckley) *racd towards rr: rdn wl over 2f out: prog u.p over 1f out: led last 75yds: hld on gamely* **8/1**$^{3}$
210- **2** *nk* **Sattam**$^{329}$ [5616] 5-9-2 77 (v) RHughes 10 86+
(MPTregoning) *hld up wl in rr: effrt and hmpd 2f out: prog but hanging over 1f out: squeezed through to chal nr fin: jst hld* **12/1**
0055 **3** *nk* **Binanti**$^{15}$ [5055] 4-9-5 80 JQuinn 8 87
(PRChamings) *lw: racd midfield: stdy prog to ld over 1f out: drvn fnl f: edgd lft and hdd last 75yds* **11/2**$^{1}$
116 **4** 1 1/4 **Pintle**$^{45}$ [4220] 4-8-13 74 JPMurtagh 5 78
(JLSpearing) *trckd ldr: led 2f out: rdn and hdd over 1f out: one pce fnl f* **7/1**$^{2}$
0-00 **5** 3/4 **Gems Bond**$^{29}$ [4672] 4-8-7 75 DerekNolan$^{(7)}$ 13 77
(JSMoore) *sn midfield: rdn over 2f out: effrt over 1f out: kpt on same pce* **50/1**
-600 **6** *shd* **Anuvasteel**$^{114}$ [2224] 3-8-9 74 JFEgan 2 76+
(NACallaghan) *hld up in last pair: hmpd 2f out: nt clr run over 1f out: styd on ins fnl f: no ch to rcvr* **12/1**
31- **7** *nk* **Maren (USA)**$^{368}$ [4776] 3-9-4 83 (t) WSupple 4 86+
(EFVaughan) *racd midfield: shkn up over 2f out: sme prog over 1f out: nt rch ldrs: eased last 100yds* **11/1**
21 **8** 3/4 **Serre Chevalier (IRE)**$^{50}$ [4063] 3-9-0 79 DHolland 3 78
(PWHarris) *trckd ldng gp: prog and 2f out: nt clr run briefly over 1f out: one pce fnl f* **8/1**$^{3}$
0100 **9** 1 1/4 **Lockstock (IRE)**$^{91}$ [2834] 6-8-7 71 RMiles$^{(3)}$ 1 67
(MSSaunders) *racd wd: towards rr: rdn over 2f out: plugged on one pce: n.d* **33/1**
1000 **10** *hd* **Omaha City (IRE)**$^{42}$ [4287] 10-8-7 71 LPKeniry$^{(3)}$ 15 66+
(BGubby) *hld up towards rr: sme prog on inner 2f out: styng on whn hmpd jst ins fnl f: no ch after* **20/1**
1000 **11** *shd* **Music Maid (IRE)**$^{8}$ [5249] 6-8-7 68 oh4 DKinsella 9 63
(HSHowe) *hld up in last pair: rdn and effrt on outer over 2f out: no imp on ldrs: kpt on* **20/1**
6031 **12** 2 **Waterside (IRE)**$^{14}$ [5077] 5-9-7 82 IMongan 7 72
(GLMoore) *lw: prom: rdn over 2f out: wknd over 1f out* **7/1**$^{2}$
5340 **13** 5 **Great Scott**$^{21}$ [4906] 3-9-1 80 (b$^{1}$) SChin 12 57
(MJohnston) *prom tl wknd 2f out* **14/1**
6540 **14** *nk* **Lifted Way**$^{21}$ [4920] 5-9-1 76 SSanders 11 52
(PRChamings) *led to 2f out: wknd* **9/1**
1520 **15** 1 3/4 **Goodenough Mover**$^{21}$ [4917] 8-9-4 82 HayleyTurner$^{(3)}$ 14 53
(JSKing) *prom: wknd rapidly jst over 1f out* **14/1**

1m 29.34s (-1.75) **Going Correction** -0.10s/f (Good) **15** Ran **SP% 124.1**
**WFA** 3 from 4yo+ 4lb
Speed ratings: **106,105,105,103,103 102,102,101,100,100 99,97,91,91,89**CSF £98.65 CT £585.93 TOTE £10.60: £3.20, £5.30, £2.30; EX 176.30.
**Owner** C C Buckley **Bred** M F Kentish **Trained** Castle Bytham, Lincs
■ Stewards Enquiry : J Quinn one-day ban: careless riding (Sep 21)

**FOCUS**
A competitive handicap, run at a fast pace, which suited those who were held up. One or two hard-luck stories, but the form looks solid enough.

**NOTEBOOK**
**Armagnac** ran two good races over this trip last month and appreciated the return to seven furlongs. The fast pace played into his hands and it would be foolish to believe that he could reproduce this form unless guaranteed similar conditions. He may run at Newbury on Saturday under a penalty.
**Sattam**, making a belated seasonal reappearance, is a difficult ride as he appears to be at his best when weaving between horses. His challenge was inevitably delayed on this occasion by a failure to get a clear run, but he stayed on well for second. This was a promising comeback but he still does not look one to take a short price about.
**Binanti**, 5lb lower than for his last turf run and 9lb lower than for his last win, was another suited by the way the race was run. He had the lead a furlong out, but was denied by the late challenge of the first two.
**Pintle** can take plenty of credit for doing best of those who raced up with the strong pace. This is her trip, and it was not in her favour that the course had a little rain in the morning. The Handicapper may not have her measure yet.
**Gems Bond** is looking better handicapped nowadays, and he will probably be happier back over a mile.
**Anuvasteel** ◆, returning from a four-month break, enjoyed little luck in running and would surely have contested the places with a clear run. He is well handicapped at present and should be kept in mind for a similar contest.
**Maren(USA)** may have finished fifth had his rider not let her more or less coast home inside the last.
**Omaha City(IRE)** had the race run to suit but did not enjoy the best luck in running. Short of room next to the far rail, he would have finished a bit closer with a clear passage.

## 5445 MEAN FIDDLER MAIDEN STKS 1m 2f 7y
**4:20** (4:25) (D3) 3-Y-O **£5,564** (£1,712; £856; £428) **Stalls** High

Form RPR
3-6 **1** **Maraakeb (FR)**$^{76}$ [3297] 3-9-0 WSupple 7 91+
(JHMGosden) *lw: mde all: clr and gng wl 2f out: shkn up and 6l clr ins fnl f: unchal* **3/1**$^{3}$
5 **2** 3 **Barathea Blue**$^{56}$ [3922] 3-9-0 SCarson 4 78
(PWHarris) *chsd ldrs: outpcd 3f out: styd on to dispute 2nd pl fr over 1f out: no ch w wnr* **25/1**
5 **3** *shd* **Neath**$^{18}$ [5007] 3-8-9 SSanders 1 73
(MrsAJPerrett) *settled wl in rr: outpcd over 4f out: prog fr 3f out: disp 2nd pl over 1f out: kpt on* **12/1**
0 **4** 7 **Kipsigis (IRE)**$^{23}$ [4850] 3-9-0 JQuinn 2 65
(LadyHerries) *towards rr: outpcd 4f out: plugged on fnl 2f: n.d* **66/1**
3 **5** 2 1/2 **Parliament Square (IRE)**$^{150}$ [1382] 3-9-0 TPQueally 8 60
(DRLoder) *lw: mostly chsd wnr: hrd rdn and no imp over 2f out: wknd over 1f out* **2/1**$^{1}$
U0- **6** 2 1/2 **Tizi Ouzou (IRE)**$^{322}$ [5722] 3-8-9 IMongan 5 50
(JLDunlop) *rn green in last: rdn and wl bhd 4f out: no ch after* **100/1**
**7** 6 **Ardere (USA)** 3-8-9 RHughes 3 39
(HRACecil) *leggy: prom: disp 2nd pl 7f out to over 3f out: wknd and eased* **12/1**

8 *13* **Katayeb (IRE)** 3-8-9 ........................................ DHolland 9 14
(MPTregoning) *w'like: leggy: s.s: a in rr: no ch fnl 3f* **10/1**

33 **9** *8* **Red Sail**[40] 4369 3-8-9 ........................................ JPMurtagh 6 —
(JRFanshawe) *b.hind: lw: chsd ldrs: rdn over 3f out: wknd rapidly over 2f out* **11/4[2]**

2m 8.60s (-1.58) **Going Correction** -0.10s/f (Good) **9** Ran SP% **115.8**
Speed ratings: **102,99,99,93,91 89,85,74,68**CSF £72.00 TOTE £3.90: £1.50, £3.50, £2.60; EX 69.90.

**Owner** Hamdan Al Maktoum **Bred** Shadwell Estate Company Limited **Trained** Manton, Wilts

**FOCUS**
Not a great maiden, weakened by the failure of the first two in the betting to run their races.

**NOTEBOOK**
**Maraakeb(FR)**, a beaten favourite on his last two starts, was returning from almost 11 weeks off. He dominated from the start , though, and ran out a clear winner, being value for more than the winning margin, and although this race probably did not take much winning, he could be interesting in handicap company this autumn on softer ground.

**Barathea Blue**, whose full-brother Barathea Blazer stays two miles, gives the impression that this is a minimum trip for him.

**Neath** was not knocked about in pursuit of the winner and once again gave the impression that there is better to come from her, probably in handicap company.

**Kipsigis(IRE)** showed little on his debut and merely kept on from the rear to pick up a cheap fourth place on this occasion.

**Parliament Square(IRE)** had been on the missing list since April, and the fact that he was pretty weak in the market suggested great things were not expected of him. He found little once the tap was turned.

**Ardere(USA)** *Official explanation: jockey said filly's saddle slipped*

**Katayeb(IRE)** cost 560,000gns and is a half-sister to five winners, notably top-class middle-distance performer White Muzzle, Elfaslah, the dam of Dubai World Cup winner Almutawakel, and German Group Two winner Fair Question. With that sort of breeding connections will be very keen to get a win into her, but she showed little on this debut.

**Red Sail** got upset beforehand and ran way below her best. *Official explanation: jockey said filly was upset in Stalls*

## 5446 DC ENTERTAINMENT H'CAP — 1m 2f 7y
**4:55** (4:57) (D2) (0-85,81) 3-Y-O — **£8,619** (£2,652; £1,326; £663) **Stalls** High

Form RPR

2012 **1** **Top Spec (IRE)**[6] 5297 3-9-2 **76** ........................................ RHughes 8 83
(RHannon) *s.s: t.k.h: hld up in rr: prog to ld over 1f out: sn jnd: rdn to assert last 150yds* **7/2[1]**

4124 **2** *¾* **Spring Jim**[42] 4300 3-9-5 **79** ........................................ JPMurtagh 7 84
(JRFanshawe) *dwlt: racd in rr: rdn over 2f out: hanging and nt qckn: r.o fnl f to take 2nd last stride* **4/1[2]**

0322 **3** *shd* **Border Music**[7] 5275 3-8-11 **78** ........................................ TBlock(7) 3 83
(AMBalding) *lw: hld up in last pair: smooth prog 2f out: jnd wnr jst over 1f out: shkn up and one pce ins fnl f* **7/1**

21-3 **4** *nk* **Star Of Light**[56] 3910 3-9-0 **77** ........................................ JFMcDonald(3) 5 81
(BJMeehan) *t.k.h: hld up in midfield: rdn and nt qckn 2f out: styd on ins fnl f: nrst fin* **11/2[3]**

2104 **5** *4* **Rondelet (IRE)**[11] 5183 3-9-7 **81** ........................................ SSanders 2 78
(RMBeckett) *lw: settled midfield: gng wl enough over 2f out: rdn and nt qckn wl over 1f out: one pce after* **11/2[3]**

3310 **6** *1* **Secret Flame**[51] 4032 3-9-2 **76** ........................................ ACulhane 4 71
(WJHaggas) *t.k.h: hld up midfield: rdn and outpcd 2f out: one pce after* **8/1**

2110 **7** *1 ¼* **Jakarmi**[62] 3746 3-8-13 **76** ........................................ RMiles(3) 10 69
(BPalling) *prom: jnd ldr 2f out: wknd fnl f* **25/1**

2015 **8** *nk* **Wychbury (USA)**[41] 4338 3-8-13 **73** ........................................ TPQueally 9 65
(MJWallace) *t.k.h: hld up bhd ldrs: effrt to chal over 1f out: sn wknd* **25/1**

01 **9** *6* **Boot 'n Toot**[33] 4583 3-9-2 **76** ........................................ JFEgan 6 57
(CACyzer) *a towards rr: rdn and struggling 3f out* **25/1**

4220 **10** *3* **Antigiotto (IRE)**[38] 4416 3-9-4 **78** ........................................ (b[1]) DHolland 1 53
(LMCumani) *sn trckd ldr: led 3f out to over 1f out: wkng rapidly whn hmpd ins fnl f* **20/1**

2336 **11** *4* **Tree Tops**[40] 4368 3-8-12 **72** ........................................ WSupple 11 39
(JHMGosden) *prom: cl up over 2f out: sn wknd rapidly* **16/1**

0000 **12** *nk* **Live Wire Lucy (USA)**[25] 4806 3-8-13 **73** ........................................ SWKelly 12 40
(CTinkler) *led to 3f out: wknd rapidly* **100/1**

2m 10.72s (0.54) **Going Correction** -0.10s/f (Good) **12** Ran SP% **119.8**
Speed ratings: **93,92,92,92,88 88,87,86,82,79 76,76**CSF £16.36 CT £94.90 TOTE £4.10: £1.60, £2.80, £2.00; EX 17.30 Place 6 £85.38, Place 5 £40.50.

**Owner** The Hill Top Partnership **Bred** Mrs Jacqueline Donnelly **Trained** East Everleigh, Wilts

■ Stewards Enquiry : R Hughes one-day ban: used whip above shoulder height (Sep 21)

**FOCUS**
A steady early gallop and a sprint for home resutling in a moderate time, but the first three all came from the back of the field.

**NOTEBOOK**
**Top Spec(IRE)**, successful in a claimer over this course and distance last month, fell out of the stalls, raced keenly and proved difficult to steer rounding the bend at the end of the back straight. Despite all this, he picked up well from the rear when the sprint for home began and battled on well to outpoint the eventual runner-up inside the final furlong. There could be more to come from him.

**Spring Jim** let the winner get first run and took a while to hit top gear. He stayed on well but it was all too late.

**Border Music** did not appear to get home over this longer trip, although this is also the third time in a row he has only made the frame having looked a possible winner at one stage. He may be one to have reservations about.

**Star Of Light** did not show the same acceleration as the first two but stayed on well to finish on their heels. He got the longer trip well.

**Rondelet(IRE)** is better suited by a race run at a strong all-round gallop.

**Secret Flame** raced keenly off the steady early pace and could not match the acceleration of the principals in the straight.

**Boot 'n Toot** was not persevered with after an ambitious run up the inner was blocked.

T/Plt: £376.20 to a £1 stake. Pool: £43,602.35. 84.60 winning tickets. T/Qpdt: £63.10 to a £1 stake. Pool: £3,014.60. 35.35 winning tickets. JN

# 5233 CARLISLE (R-H)
### Saturday, September 11

**OFFICIAL GOING: Back straight - good to firm; remainder - firm (good to firm in places)**
Wind: fairly strong, hlf against Weather: cloudy but bright

## 5447 CANTOR FITZGERALD MEMORIAL MEDIAN AUCTION MAIDEN STKS — 6f 192y
**11:10** (11:13) (H5) 2-Y-O — **£1,554** (£444; £222) **Stalls** High

Form RPR

4230 **1** **Secret Pact (IRE)**[29] 4700 2-9-0 75 ........................................ RFrench 3 69+
(MJohnston) *chsd ldrs: carried wd bnd over 4f out: sn pushed along: rallied to ld over 1f out: pushed clr* **3/1[1]**

250 **2** *3* **Kumala Ocean (IRE)**[20] 4966 2-8-9 62 ........................................ GParkin 15 53
(PABlockley) *midfield: effrt and prom whn hmpd wl over 1f out: kpt on fnl f: no ch w wnr* **12/1**

404 **3** *hd* **Harrys House**[12] 5186 2-8-11 68 ........................................ PMulrennan(3) 1 57
(JJQuinn) *keen: prom: effrt whn blkd wl over 1f out: sn one pce* **9/2[3]**

543 **4** *½* **Ignition**[12] 5198 2-8-4 67 ........................................ BSwarbrick(5) 8 51
(WMBrisbourne) *keen: led over 4f out: wandered and hdd over 1f out: nt qckn* **7/2[2]**

5300 **5** *1* **Singhalongtasveer**[15] 5097 2-9-0 49 ........................................ JBramhill 14 54
(WStorey) *cl up: ev ch and edgd lft wl over 1f out: sn one pce* **33/1**

000 **6** *1 ½* **Wembury Point (IRE)**[5] 5347 2-8-11 ........................................ TEaves(3) 2 50
(BGPowell) *in tch: effrt over 2f out: outpcd fnl f* **11/1**

004 **7** *¾* **Plenty Cried Wolf**[7] 5307 2-8-11 71 ........................................ THamilton(3) 7 48
(RAFahey) *chsd ldrs: rdn whn blkd wl over 1f out: sn no ex* **6/1**

0 **8** *1 ½* **Bodden Bay**[7] 5302 2-9-0 ........................................ DaleGibson 6 44
(CADwyer) *midfield: rdn 1/2-way: no imp fr 2f out* **33/1**

**9** *½* **Calfraz** 2-9-0 ........................................ GFaulkner 11 43
(MDHammond) *sn outpcd: sme hdwy over 1f out: nvr on terms* **33/1**

0P **10** *4* **Specialise**[43] 4304 2-8-9 ........................................ TWilliams 10 28
(DWBarker) *missed break: nvr on terms* **80/1**

**11** *shd* **Demolition Frank** 2-9-0 ........................................ PMQuinn 4 32
(MDHammond) *s.i.s: n.d* **33/1**

0 **12** *12* **Brave Tara (IRE)**[15] 5095 2-8-9 ........................................ ANicholls 12 —
(TDEasterby) *keen: led tl rn wd bnd over 4f out: sn rdn and lost pl* **50/1**

**13** *¾* **Casalese** 2-9-0 ........................................ MTebbutt 5 —
(MDHammond) *sn outpcd: nvr on terms* **33/1**

0000 **14** *2 ½* **Itsa Monkey (IRE)**[13] 5142 2-8-11 49 ........................................ (b) DNolan(3) 9 —
(MJPolglase) *a bhd* **50/1**

1m 29.38s (2.28) **Going Correction** -0.05s/f (Good) **14** Ran SP% **115.6**
Speed ratings: **84,80,80,79,78 76,76,74,73,69 69,55,54,51**CSF £35.64 TOTE £3.60: £1.10, £6.30, £2.20; EX 50.00.

**Owner** Jumeirah Racing **Bred** Mrs Vanessa Hutch **Trained** Middleham Moor, N Yorks

**FOCUS**
A very modest race comprising mainly exposed sorts but a decisive success by Secret Pact, who should prove equally effective over a mile, but the proximity of the fifth holds down the form.

**NOTEBOOK**
**Secret Pact(IRE)**, who looked in good shape, put a poor effort behind him and showed that stamina was his strong suit with a decisive success. He may be a bit better than the bare form, should prove equally effective over a mile and he may well be capable of further improvement.

**Kumala Ocean(IRE)** looks a bit better than the bare form as he ran out of room at a crucial stage and, although it is doubtful he would have beaten the winner, will be of interest in modest handicap company around this trip.

**Harrys House** looks a fairly reliable yardstick who again gave his running. However, he is an edgy sort who again failed to settle and he is likely to continue to look vulnerable in this grade or in handicaps from his current mark.

**Ignition**, on his toes in the paddock, did too much too soon in the race and, although he is in capable hands, he may be suited by easier ground and will have to settle better if he is to progress.

**Singhalongtasveer** had the run of the race and performed creditably in the face of a stiff task. However, his proximity does hold this form down and it remains to be seen whether this will be reproduced next time.

**Wembury Point(IRE)** was not disgraced in the face of a stiffish task, but is another that is likely to continue to look vulnerable in this grade.

**Brave Tara(IRE)** *Official explanation: jockey said filly did not handle bend*

## 5448 CANTOR SPORT MAIDEN CLAIMING STKS — 6f 192y
**11:40** (11:45) (H5) 3-Y-O+ — **£1,543** (£441; £220) **Stalls** High

Form RPR

0400 **1** **Megabond**[5] 5346 3-8-12 54 ........................................ (p) DMcGaffin 6 63+
(BSmart) *mde all: drvn clr fr 2f out: eased towards fin* **5/1[2]**

4344 **2** *4* **Nicholas Nickelby**[14] 5104 4-8-13 53 ........................................ (p) LFletcher(5) 5 53
(MJPolglase) *chsd ldrs: rdn 3f out: kpt on fnl f: no ch w wnr* **4/1[1]**

0400 **3** *1* **Firebird Rising (USA)**[13] 5141 3-8-2 50 ........................................ PMakin(5) 14 45
(TDBarron) *chsd wnr: rdn over 2f out: sn one pce* **8/1**

0330 **4** *2 ½* **Sophrano (IRE)**[12] 5177 4-9-0 55 ........................................ PBradley 1 42
(PABlockley) *in tch: rdn over 3f out: one pce fr 2f out* **10/1**

-400 **5** *nk* **Magari**[19] 5002 3-8-7 53 ........................................ JBramhill 3 38
(JGGiven) *midfield: drvn over 3f out: no imp fr 2f out* **25/1**

0300 **6** *1 ¾* **Festive Chimes (IRE)**[23] 4868 3-8-4 52 ........................................ PMulrennan(3) 7 34
(JJQuinn) *hld up: drvn over 3f out: nvr rchd ldrs* **12/1**

0000 **7** *1 ¼* **Named At Dinner**[4] 5364 3-8-12 55 ........................................ MTebbutt 9 35
(MrsADuffield) *in tch: rdn over 2f out: sn no imp* **11/1**

0-0 **8** *3* **Mazram**[31] 4624 5-8-4 ........................................ (b[1]) THamilton(3) 12 19
(IWMcinnes) *dwlt and early reminders: sme late hdwy: nvr on terms* **66/1**

0430 **9** *4* **Memory Man**[45] 4236 3-8-12 65 ........................................ DKinsella 13 17
(WRMuir) *plld hrd: cl up tl wknd over 2f out* **11/2[3]**

0504 **10** *nk* **From The North (IRE)**[40] 4391 3-8-7 50 ow3 ........................................ (v) ABeech(3) 10 14
(ADickman) *prom to 3f out: sn rdn and btn* **8/1**

0035 **11** *11* **Ragazzi (IRE)**[23] 4880 3-8-10 60 ........................................ DMernagh 8 —
(TDBarron) *towards rr: drvn 1/2-way: sn btn* **20/1**

P **12** *dist* **Deangate (IRE)**[83] 3121 3-8-12 ........................................ (t) RFitzpatrick 2 —
(PTMidgley) *bhd and outpcd: struggling fr 1/2-way* **100/1**

-440 **P** **Micklegate**[60] 3817 3-8-2 58 ........................................ BSwarbrick(5) 4 —
(JDBethell) *bhd: rdn and no ch whn broke down bdly and p.u over 2f out* **7/1**

1m 27.88s (0.78) **Going Correction** -0.05s/f (Good)
**WFA** 3 from 4yo+ 4lb **13** Ran SP% **123.0**
Speed ratings: **93,88,87,84,84 82,80,77,72,72 59,—,—**CSF £25.37 TOTE £8.00: £2.60, £1.30, £3.60; EX 38.40.The winner was claimed by C. Dwyer for £6,000.

**Owner** The Bond Girls Partnership **Bred** S And Mrs Hartwell **Trained** Hambleton, N Yorks



The Form Book, Raceform Ltd, Compton, RG20 6NL

**FOCUS**
A poor and uncompetitive event in which the early gallop was on the decent side but this race is unlikely to be throwing up too many future winners.
**NOTEBOOK**
**Megabond**, returned to seven furlongs and tried in cheekpieces, showed the right attitude and improved form to go clear in the straight. He was claimed by Chris Dwyer and, given this style of racing, will be interesting returned to sand this winter.
**Nicholas Nickelby** has yet to win but looks a fairly reliable yardstick and seemed to run his race with the cheekpieces back on. On this evidence the return to a mile should be in his favour.
**Firebird Rising(USA)** bettered her two most recent efforts back on a sound surface and was not disgraced in terms of form, but did leave the impression that she may have been saving something for herself on this very quick ground.
**Sophrano(IRE)**, who had a fair chance at the weights, was not totally disgraced, but the fact that he has yet to win and his inconsistency means he would not be one to place too much faith in.
**Magari**, well beaten on her All-Weather debut last time, fared better but, although worth a try over further, she is not going to be the easiest to place successfully.
**Festive Chimes(IRE)**, back up in trip and back on a sound surface, left the impression that a stiffer test of stamina would have been in her favour.
**Ragazzi(IRE)** *Official explanation: jockey said gelding tried to pull up*
**Micklegate** *Official explanation: jockey said filly lost her action behind and pulled up*

## 5449 CANTOR INDEX BANDED STKS — 1m 1f 61y
**12:10** (12:14) (H5) 3-Y-0+ — **£1,536** (£439; £219) **Stalls** High

Form — RPR
2464 **1** **Dancing Tilly**[7] 5305 6-9-1 40 ....(p) THamilton(3) 12 — 48
(RAFahey) *hld up: rdn 4f out: hdwy 2f out: edgd rt and led ins fnl f: r.o* **7/2**[1]
0530 **2** 3 **Campbells Lad**[14] 5110 3-8-7 40 .... PPMathers(5) 11 — 42
(ABerry) *prom: led 2f out: hdd and wandered ins fnl f: no ex* **12/1**
20U4 **3** 1 ¾ **Merlins Profit**[19] 4985 4-9-4 40 .... LEnstone 16 — 39+
(MDods) *chsd ldrs: rdn whn nt clr run over 2f and over 1f out: one pce fnl f* **6/1**[2]
4506 **4** 1 **Eddies Jewel**[14] 5110 4-9-4 40 .... GParkin 5 — 37
(JSWainwright) *keen: cl up: ev ch over 2f out: no ex over 1f out* **17/2**
5066 **5** hd **Abuelos**[7] 5305 5-9-4 40 .... TWilliams 8 — 36
(DWThompson) *prom: rdn over 2f out: one pce over 1f out* **20/1**
/60- **6** 1 ½ **Never Promise (FR)**[12] 5237 6-8-13 40 ....(v) AMedeiros(5) 9 — 33
(CRoberts) *hld up: effrt u.p over 2f out: no imp over 1f out* **11/1**
5000 **7** nk **Stepastray**[14] 5129 7-8-11 40 ....(v) DTudhope(7) 7 — 33
(REBarr) *midfield on outside: effrt over 2f out: edgd rt and sn no imp* **12/1**
U0-6 **8** 5 **Night Mail**[249] 456 4-9-4 40 .... TLucas 2 — 23
(MWEasterby) *racd wd in rr: outpcd 4f out: n.d after* **22/1**
0043 **9** 1 ½ **Erupt**[12] 5187 11-8-13 45 .... MLawson(5) 6 — 20
(REBarr) *bhd: rdn and effrt centre 2f out: nvr rchd ldrs* **7/1**[3]
-000 **10** 5 **Hormuz (IRE)**[12] 8-9-4 40 .... ANicholls 15 — 10
(PaulJohnson) *led to 2f out: sn btn* **10/1**
0050 **11** 2 ½ **Lark In The Park (IRE)**[27] 4771 4-8-13 40 ....(t) BSwarbrick(5) 4 — 5
(WMBrisbourne) *hld up: outpcd over 4f out: n.d after* **11/1**
0600 **12** ½ **Daimajin (IRE)**[26] 4818 5-9-1 40 .... ABeech(3) 1 — 4
(MrsLucindaFeatherstone) *prom to 3f out: sn rdn and btn* **16/1**
0300 **13** 3 **Lady Stratagem**[9] 5238 5-9-4 40 .... GFaulkner 3 — —
(EWTuer) *chsd ldrs to 2f out: sn rdn and btn* **20/1**
0000 **14** 4 **Coco Point Breeze**[20] 4972 3-8-9 40 ....(b[1]) PMulrennan(3) 10 — —
(JGGiven) *keen: trckd ldrs tl wknd 2f out* **50/1**
0400 **15** 3 **Bevier**[12] 5175 10-9-1 40 .... LFletcher(3) 13 — —
(TWall) *midfield: hmpd and lost pl after 2f: struggling fr 1/2-way* **8/1**

1m 57.97s (-0.06) **Going Correction** -0.05s/f (Good) — **15** Ran SP% **127.6**
**WFA** 3 from 4yo+ 6lb
Speed ratings: **98,95,93,92,92 91,91,86,85,80 78,78,75,72,69**CSF £46.56 TOTE £4.30: £1.60, £2.70, £2.70; EX 34.90.
**Owner** The 'We Believe In Miracles' Partnership **Bred** G And Mrs Whittaker **Trained** Musley Bank, N Yorks

**FOCUS**
A poor race in which the pace was sound, but one in which the winner was getting off the mark at the 27th attempt. This race, rated through the runner-up, is unlikely to be throwing up many winners.
**NOTEBOOK**
**Dancing Tilly**, back to a more suitable trip, put her best foot forward to win at the 27th attempt. She may be a bit better than the bare form as she was one of the few to make ground from off the pace at this meeting. She should continue to give a good account at up to middle distances.
**Campbells Lad**, back on a sound surface, ran right up to his best, despite looking a less than easy ride on this firm ground. His record suggests he is not certain to reproduce this next time, though.
**Merlins Profit**, back on a sound surface, did not get the run of the race and looks better than the bare form. However, a record of no wins from 16 starts shows he is not one to be placing maximum faith in.
**Eddies Jewel** ran creditably given he did not really settle in the early stages, but he is another whose record suggests he is not one to be placing any great level of faith in.
**Abuelos**, an inconsistent sort who has not won for over two years, was not disgraced in a weak event but did not really appeal as a winner waiting to happen.
**Never Promise(FR)** was not totally disgraced on this first Flat run of the year with the visor back on, but is likely to continue to look vulnerable in anything but the worst events.
**Coco Point Breeze** *Official explanation: jockey said filly hung left and had breathing problem on pulling up*
**Bevier** *Official explanation: jockey said gelding suffered interference on first bend*

## 5450 CANTORINDEX.CO.UK BANDED STKS — 7f 200y
**12:40** (12:44) (H5) 4-Y-0+ — **£1,554** (£444; £222) **Stalls** High

Form — RPR
6003 **1** **Penwell Hill (USA)**[45] 4246 5-8-12 50 .... PMakin(5) 9 — 58
(TDBarron) *mde all: rdn and hld on wl fnl f* **13/2**[3]
3020 **2** ½ **Baby Barry**[29] 4702 7-8-11 47 .... ABeech(3) 13 — 54
(MrsGSRees) *trckd ldrs: rdn over 2f out: kpt on fnl f* **6/1**[2]
3001 **3** ¾ **Shamwari Fire (IRE)**[7] 5285 4-8-13 49 .... LFletcher(3) 15 — 54
(IWMcinnes) *in tch: rdn over 2f out: hung lft over 1f out: r.o ins last* **9/2**[1]
3045 **4** ½ **Tokewanna**[27] 4771 4-8-11 49 ....(t) PPMathers(5) 12 — 53
(WMBrisbourne) *hld up: effrt outside over 2f out: one pce ins fnl f* **9/1**
0000 **5** 1 ¾ **Hoh's Back**[7] 5305 5-8-12 45 ....(p) ANicholls 11 — 45
(PaulJohnson) *towards rr: hdwy 2f out: kpt on fnl f: no imp* **12/1**
1000 **6** 3 **Night Market**[18] 5021 6-8-12 50 .... MLawson(5) 14 — 43
(NWilson) *hld up: effrt and hung rt 2f out: no imp fnl f* **12/1**
6110 **7** hd **Sennen Cove**[26] 4818 5-8-12 45 ....(t) GFaulkner 8 — 38
(RBastiman) *midfield: stdy hdwy 3f out: rdn and nt qckn fr 2f out* **8/1**
0000 **8** 3 ½ **Lucky Largo (IRE)**[22] 4901 4-8-12 48 ....(b) J-PGuillambert(3) 2 — 33
(MissLAPerratt) *prom to 2f out: sn rdn and btn* **33/1**
0200 **9** 1 **Gemini Lady**[70] 3520 4-8-12 45 .... MTebbutt 17 — 27
(MrsGSRees) *stdd s: rdn over 2f out: nt pce to chal* **33/1**
000- **10** 3 ½ **Master Nimbus**[408] 3733 4-8-13 49 .... PMulrennan(3) 1 — 23
(JJQuinn) *bhd: rdn 1/2-way: n.d* **66/1**
30-0 **11** ½ **Well Connected (IRE)**[9] 5237 4-8-12 45 .... LEnstone 3 — 18
(BSmart) *in tch tl wknd fr 2f out* **20/1**
0543 **12** hd **Jessie**[68] 3586 5-8-12 45 ....(v) KimTinkler 16 — 18
(DonEnricoIncisa) *s.i.s: struggling 1/2-way: sme hdwy over 1f out: nvr on terms* **12/1**
4000 **13** 1 ½ **Good Time Bobby**[27] 4782 7-8-6 45 ow1 .... JDO'Reilly(7) 6 — 15
(JO'Reilly) *cl up to 2f out: sn rdn and btn* **20/1**
0626 **14** ¾ **Skiddaw Jones**[22] 4901 4-9-0 47 .... DMernagh 5 — 14
(MissLAPerratt) *in tch to over 2f out: wknd* **12/1**
000- **15** ¾ **Touch Of Ebony (IRE)**[304] 3735 5-8-10 48 .... AMedeiros(5) 7 — 14
(CRoberts) *towards rr: rdn 3f out: sn btn* **12/1**
0000 **16** 2 **Ash Laddie (IRE)**[21] 3804 4-8-12 45 ....(b[1]) GParkin 4 — 6
(JSWainwright) *a bhd* **100/1**
0005 **17** 22 **Trusted Instinct (IRE)**[18] 5026 4-9-3 50 ....(p) DaleGibson 10 — —
(CADwyer) *chsd ldrs tl wknd over 2f out* **66/1**

1m 40.38s (0.38) **Going Correction** -0.05s/f (Good) — **17** Ran SP% **124.8**
Speed ratings: **96,95,94,94,92 89,89,85,84,81 80,80,79,78,77 75,53**CSF £43.27 TOTE £8.60: £3.60, £2.10, £1.70; EX 67.90.
**Owner** Mrs Liz Jones **Bred** Costello, O'Rourke & Simon **Trained** Maunby, N Yorks

**FOCUS**
Another low-grade event in which once again those racing up with the pace held the edge over those ridden with more restraint.
**NOTEBOOK**
**Penwell Hill(USA)** is not as good on turf as on sand, but ran right up to his best after enjoying the run of the race against the inside rail. He seems best when able to dominate and should continue to go well at a modest level.
**Baby Barry** had the run of the race and performed creditably, but his losing run and his inconsistency means he would not be one to be lumping on at shortish odds next time.
**Shamwari Fire(IRE)** had conditions and the draw in his favour and ran creditably. He is not the most reliable but is capable of winning again in this company.
**Tokewanna**, down in grade, looks a bit better than the bare form as she made her ground away from the inside rail, but her record suggests she is one to tread carefully with.
**Hoh's Back**, dropped in grade, was not disgraced in a race that suited those racing prominently. However, he is not the most consistent and will remain one to tread carefully with.
**Night Market** is best around this trip on a sound surface but, while not disgraced, again looked a less than easy ride and his inconsistency means he is not the best betting proposition around.
**Trusted Instinct(IRE)** *Official explanation: jockey said colt lost his action two and a half furlongs out*

## 5451 CANTORSPORT.CO.UK TRI-BANDED STKS — 7f 200y
**1:10** (1:12) (H5) 3-Y-0 — **£1,505** (£430; £215) **Stalls** High

Form — RPR
6450 **1** **Calculaite**[19] 5000 3-9-2 45 .... ABeech(3) 17 — 67+
(MrsGSRees) *w ldr: led over 4f out: drew clr fr 2f out: eased ins fnl f* **6/1**
1343 **2** 10 **Roman The Park (IRE)**[44] 4259 3-9-5 45 .... PMQuinn 5 — 44
(TDEasterby) *in tch: hung lft and chsd wnr 2f out: no imp* **7/2**[1]
6004 **3** ½ **Bargain Hunt (IRE)**[50] 4102 3-9-5 45 .... JBramhill 9 — 43
(WStorey) *in tch: effrt over 2f out: one pce* **9/1**
0 **4** 1 **Primatech (IRE)**[30] 4674 3-9-5 45 ....(p) PFitzsimons 3 — 41
(KAMorgan) *hld up: rdn over 2f out: sn no imp* **33/1**
0060 **5** ½ **Chiqitita (IRE)**[7] 5284 3-8-12 40 ow1 .... LFletcher(3) 13 — 35
(MissMERowland) *hld up midfield: effrt over 2f out: one pce* **20/1**
0-00 **6** 1 **Ballin Rouge**[68] 3582 3-8-6 35 ....(t) PMulrennan(3) 15 — 27
(TJFitzgerald) *hld up: drvn over 3f out: no imp fr 2f out* **50/1**
3651 **7** hd **Courant D'Air (IRE)**[14] 1594 3-8-9 40 .... RoryMoore(5) 12 — 32
(PCHaslam) *midfield: rdn 3f out: nvr able to chal* **5/1**[2]
-500 **8** ¾ **Aggi Mac**[22] 4925 3-8-7 40 .... SuzanneFrance(7) 11 — 30
(AndrewTurnell) *bhd: hdwy wd over 2f out: sn no imp* **20/1**
5000 **9** ½ **Delta Lady**[12] 5187 3-8-11 40 .... J-PGuillambert(3) 2 — 29
(RBastiman) *hld up: hdwy and hung rt 2f out: sn no ex* **33/1**
4000 **10** 3 ½ **Cellino**[23] 4868 3-9-0 40 .... ANicholls 4 — 21
(AndrewTurnell) *midfield: rdn over 3f out: btn 2f out* **12/1**
0564 **11** 8 **Grele (USA)**[9] 5237 3-9-5 45 .... LEnstone 6 — 7
(RHollinshead) *chsd ldrs to 2f out: sn btn* **11/2**[3]
-050 **12** 1 **Noble Desert (FR)**[19] 5000 3-9-2 45 .... BReilly(3) 10 — 5
(RGuest) *prom tl wknd over 2f out* **16/1**
0000 **13** 1 **Svenson**[5] 5345 3-8-9 30 .... PBradley 14 — —
(JSWainwright) *keen: led to over 4f out: wknd fr 2f out* **66/1**
0460 **14** 5 **Lord Wishingwell (IRE)**[20] 4968 3-8-9 35 ....(v) GParkin 1 — —
(JSWainwright) *sn struggling* **12/1**
3340 **15** 10 **Monkey Or Me (IRE)**[14] 5110 3-8-9 35 .... RFitzpatrick 7 — —
(PTMidgley) *s.i.s: nvr on terms* **14/1**

1m 40.09s (0.09) **Going Correction** -0.05s/f (Good) — **15** Ran SP% **125.4**
Speed ratings: **97,87,86,85,85 84,83,83,82,79 71,70,69,64,54**CSF £26.23 TOTE £8.30: £3.00, £1.80, £2.90; EX 42.60.
**Owner** Maggie and Eric Hemming **Bred** Capt J H Wilson **Trained** Sollom, Lancs

**FOCUS**
A fairly open race on paper but a much-improved effort, and above average for the grade, from Calculaite, who may be able to hold his own in slightly stronger company.
**NOTEBOOK**
**Calculaite**, back on turf and returned to this trip, turned in a much-improved effort to beat a fairly reliable yardstick with even more in hand than the winning margin suggests. He may be able to hold his own in slightly stronger company and will be interesting if turned out on the All-Weather later in the year.
**Roman The Park(IRE)** did not look entirely happy under these conditions but she is a fairly reliable yardstick who looks the best guide to the worth of this form. She knows how to win and should continue to give a good account.
**Bargain Hunt(IRE)**, an unreliable and fully-exposed maiden, again had his limitations exposed and this inconsistent maiden remains one to place minimal faith in.
**Primatech(IRE)**'s form to date is modest at best but, while again well beaten tried in the cheekpieces for the first time, left the impression that a stiffer test of stamina would suit.
**Chiqitita(IRE)**, a poor and inconsistent maiden, did not leave the impression that that elusive first win was imminent.
**Ballin Rouge** may prove suited by a stiffer test of stamina in due course but again achieved little.

## 5452 CANTORSPORT.CO.UK BANDED STKS — 5f
**1:40** (1:43) (H5) 3-Y-0+ — **£1,512** (£432; £216) **Stalls** High

Form — RPR
3340 **1** **Loughlorien (IRE)**[35] 4557 5-8-11 49 .... DTudhope(7) 8 — 57
(REBarr) *in tch: effrt over 2f out: led wl ins fnl f: r.o* **5/1**[2]
0000 **2** nk **Flying Tackle**[5] 5346 6-9-5 50 ....(p) LEnstone 10 — 57
(MDods) *hld up midfield: effrt over 1f out: disp ld wl ins fnl f: jst hld* **10/1**
0413 **3** 1 **Molotov**[7] 5282 4-9-2 50 .... LFletcher(3) 14 — 53
(IWMcinnes) *cl up: led over 2f out to wl ins fnl f: no ex* **5/2**[1]

4000 **4** 1/2 **Astrac (IRE)**[5] 5337 13-9-3 48 ........ PMQuinn 4 49
(MrsALMKing) *hld up midfield: effrt over 1f out: kpt on fin* **10/1**

1550 **5** *nk* **Robwillcall**[27] 4782 4-8-11 47 ........ (p) PPMathers(5) 17 47
(ABerry) *led to over 2f out: one pce fnl f* **8/1**[3]

04-0 **6** 3 **Suitcase Murphy (IRE)**[236] 561 3-8-10 45 ........ ABeech(3) 11 33
(MsDeborahJEvans) *in tch tl rdn and one pce fr over 1f out* **33/1**

0000 **7** 3/4 **Massey**[22] 4905 8-9-2 47 ........ (v) DMernagh 5 32
(TDBarron) *in tch: drvn after 2f: sn one pce* **12/1**

-000 **8** *hd* **Hi Darl**[30] 4674 3-8-8 45 ........ RoryMoore(5) 13 29
(WMBrisbourne) *sn bhd: hdwy fnl f: n.d* **40/1**

6500 **9** 3/4 **Pirlie Hill**[25] 4827 4-9-2 47 ........ GParkin 12 28
(MissLAPerratt) *chsd ldrs tl rdn and outpcd appr fnl f* **12/1**

0100 **10** *nk* **Petana**[39] 4422 4-9-4 49 ........ (p) JoannaBadger 16 29
(MDods) *bhd: hdwy appr fnl f: n.d* **20/1**

0060 **11** *shd* **Rosie's Result**[15] 5081 4-8-10 48 ........ JemmaMarshall(7) 7 27
(MTodhunter) *bhd: rdn over 2f out: sn no imp* **16/1**

0000 **12** *nk* **John O'Groats (IRE)**[23] 4881 6-9-2 47 ........ ANicholls 15 25
(DWChapman) *prom tl rdn and wknd over 1f out* **12/1**

640- **13** 1 3/4 **Las Ramblas (IRE)**[348] 5272 7-9-3 48 ........ (tp) PBradley 3 19
(DANolan) *bhd: hung rt and struggling fr 1/2-way* **50/1**

0663 **14** 1/2 **Royal Windmill (IRE)**[35] 4557 5-8-13 47 ........ PMulrennan(3) 2 16
(MDHammond) *racd wd: rdn and struggling fr 1/2-way* **10/1**

0-00 **15** 3 **O'l Lucy Broon**[37] 4489 3-9-3 49 ........ (v1) RFitzpatrick 1 6
(JSGoldie) *racd wd in rr: rdn and wknd fr 1/2-way* **40/1**

61.32 secs (-0.18) **Going Correction** -0.05s/f (Good)
**WFA** 3 from 4yo+ 1lb **15** Ran SP% **127.1**
Speed ratings: **99,98,96,96,95 90,89,89,88,87 87,87,84,83,78**CSF £54.71 TOTE £6.70: £2.60, £3.30, £1.60; EX 87.20 Place 6 £27.48, Place 5 £16.10..
**Owner** P Cartmell **Bred** John Yarr **Trained** Seamer, N Yorks

**FOCUS**
The first three came into this race with solid recent handicap form, so the race should prove sound, and once again those that raced up with the pace seemed to be at an advantage.

**NOTEBOOK**
**Loughlorien(IRE)**, back in trip, ran right up to his best on this first start for his new stable, and this fairly consistent sort should continue to give a good account at a modest level.
**Flying Tackle** has never been the most reliable but had the race run to suit and performed right up to his recent best under ideal conditions. He would not be one to take a short price about next time given his record, though.
**Molotov**, who had the run of the race, looks a good guide to the level of this form and, given the way he travelled for much of the way, appeals as the type to win more races in low-grade company.
**Astrac(IRE)** has not won for nearly a year but again ran creditably from his low draw. He is the type that needs things to fall just right but is capable of winning a race in this grade.
**Robwillcall** is not the most reliable but ran creditably under suitable conditions from his favourable draw. It remains to be seen whether this will be reproduced next time, though.
**Suitcase Murphy(IRE)**, a poor maiden, did not really leave the impression that a first win was imminent.
**Massey** shaped as though a stiffer test of stamina would have suited.
**Hi Darl** *Official explanation: trainer's representative said filly was in season*
T/Plt: £15.80 to a £1 stake. Pool: £20,426.75. 941.25 winning tickets. T/Qpdt: £5.50 to a £1 stake. Pool: £1,877.10. 248.30 winning tickets. RY

# 4930 CHESTER (L-H)

## Saturday, September 11

**OFFICIAL GOING: Good**
The ground was near perfect after 7mm of rain overnight.
Wind: slt across Weather: occasional showers

## 5453 HALLOWS ASSOCIATES NURSERY — 7f 2y
**1:55** (1:55) (C2) (0-95,92) 2-Y-0 **£8,141** (£2,505; £1,252; £626) **Stalls** Low

Form — RPR

14 **1** **Comic Strip**[54] 3983 2-9-3 **88** ........ MHills 7 97+
(SirMarkPrescott) *hld up: hdwy over 3f out: rdn over 1f out: led ins fnl f: r.o wl* **11/4**[2]

1210 **2** 1 1/2 **Rowan Lodge (IRE)**[14] 5119 2-8-9 **80** ow1 ........ NCallan 1 83
(MHTompkins) *led over 1f: w ldr: led over 3f out: rdn over 1f out: hdd ins fnl f: nt qckn* **6/1**

1602 **3** 5 **Dahteer (IRE)**[21] 4933 2-9-7 **92** ........ CCatlin 2 83
(MRChannon) *w ldr: led over 5f out tl over 3f out: rdn wl over 1f out: wknd fnl f* **9/4**[1]

2302 **4** *hd* **Langston Boy**[16] 5052 2-8-2 **73** ........ RMullen 3 63
(MLWBell) *a.p: rdn and n.m.r on ins over 1f out: wknd fnl f* **7/1**

1656 **5** 1 1/4 **Bolton Hall (IRE)**[14] 5119 2-8-12 **83** ........ RWinston 5 70
(RAFahey) *prom: outpcd wl over 2f out: styd on ins fnl f* **9/2**[3]

543 **6** 5 **Transvestite (IRE)**[70] 3531 2-8-4 **75** ........ WRyan 6 50
(JWHills) *a bhd* **9/1**

1300 **7** 8 **Gortumblo**[42] 4325 2-8-12 **86** ........ DCorby(3) 4 41
(DJSFfrenchDavis) *hld up: rdn over 3f out: sn struggling* **20/1**

1m 27.11s (-1.18) **Going Correction** -0.175s/f (Firm) **7** Ran SP% **117.2**
Speed ratings: **99,97,91,91,89 84,75**CSF £20.35 TOTE £3.90: £2.30, £3.10; EX 30.60.
**Owner** Neil Greig - Osborne House **Bred** Floors Farming And Side Hill Stud **Trained** Newmarket, Suffolk

**FOCUS**
A nursery run at a decent gallop.

**NOTEBOOK**
**Comic Strip** had disappointed on slightly softer ground when not appearing to handle the bend at Beverley. He fully justified the decision to come to this tight track on his debut in a handicap.
**Rowan Lodge(IRE)**, carrying a pound overweight, came clear of the others and was certainly not inconvenienced by the return to seven.
**Dahteer(IRE)**, out of his depth when previously tried at this trip, is probably more effective over six at the moment.
**Langston Boy** failed to deliver when the gap came and is another who may be better back at six.
**Bolton Hall(IRE)** ◆, quite highly tried since his debut win, shaped as though he is worth a try at a mile.

## 5454 TOTESPORT HENRY GEE FILLIES' STKS (LISTED RACE) (F&M) — 6f 18y
**2:25** (2:26) (A1) 3-Y-0+ **£20,300** (£7,700; £3,850; £1,750) **Stalls** Low

Form — RPR

5032 **1** **Simianna**[14] 5105 5-8-13 97 ........ (p) RWinston 1 101
(ABerry) *a.p: nt clr run over 1f out: squeezed through to ld wl ins fnl f: r.o* **9/2**[2]

0-44 **2** 1/2 **Blue Dream (IRE)**[23] 4893 4-8-13 ........ (p) MHills 4 100
(THogan, Ire) *chsd ldr: rdn over 1f out: ev ch ins fnl f: r.o* **14/1**

112- **3** *shd* **Pearl Grey**[431] 3074 3-8-11 108 ........ (t) JCarroll 2 99
(SaeedBinSuroor) *hld up in mid-div: hdwy and swtchd rt over 1f out: sn rdn: kpt on ins fnl f* **4/1**[1]

4225 **4** 1 1/4 **Fruit Of Glory**[21] 4951 5-8-13 95 ........ WRyan 3 95
(JRJenkins) *led: rdn jst over 1f out: hdd and no ex wl ins fnl f* **7/1**

0541 **5** 1 1/4 **Goldeva**[27] 4779 5-9-2 105 ........ DSweeney 5 95
(RHollinshead) *hld up and bhd: hdwy whn nt clr run and swtchd lft over 1f out: r.o* **11/2**[3]

2140 **6** 3 **And Toto Too**[27] 4773 4-8-13 75 ........ (b) DNolan 7 83?
(PDEvans) *s.i.s: bhd: rdn over 2f out: hdwy on ins jst over 1f out: n.d* **33/1**

0421 **7** 1 **Paradise Isle**[35] 4531 3-8-11 100 ........ RMullen 12 80
(CFWall) *hld up and bhd: stdy hdwy on outside over 3f out: rdn over 1f out: wknd ins fnl f* **6/1**

2012 **8** 1 3/4 **Rise**[10] 5219 3-8-11 70 ........ (b) DKinsella 11 74
(AndrewReid) *hld up in mid-div: rdn over 2f out: lost pl and nt clr run over 1f out: btn whn sltly hmpd ins fnl f* **66/1**

1040 **9** *shd* **Tychy**[7] 5289 5-8-13 97 ........ NCallan 8 74
(SCWilliams) *chsd ldrs: rdn over 2f out: wknd over 1f out* **11/2**[3]

3000 **10** 1 1/2 **Dowager**[14] 5121 3-8-11 96 ........ (b1) CCatlin 6 70
(RHannon) *a bhd* **16/1**

0410 **11** 6 **Grey Pearl**[43] 4286 5-8-13 86 ........ DarrenWilliams 10 52
(MissGayKelleway) *prom: rdn over 2f out: wknd over 1f out* **25/1**

1m 13.33s (-2.55) **Going Correction** -0.175s/f (Firm)
**WFA** 3 from 4yo+ 2lb **11** Ran SP% **116.6**
Speed ratings: **110,109,109,107,105 101,100,98,98,96 88**CSF £63.91 TOTE £4.90: £1.80, £2.70, £2.00; EX 83.40 Trifecta £205.50 Pool: £781.70. 2.70 winning tickets.
**Owner** T G & Mrs M E Holdcroft **Bred** Cobhall Court Stud **Trained** Cockerham, Lancs

**FOCUS**
A fast time for this quite competitive listed event with a low draw proving vital.

**NOTEBOOK**
**Simianna**, who only cost 1,000 gns as a yearling, took her career earnings to over £120,000. Making the most of the inside draw, she wriggled through when the gap eventually came.
**Blue Dream(IRE)**, tried in cheekpieces, ran a fine race over what appears to be her optimum distance.
**Pearl Grey** ◆ had not been seen since finishing lame when second to Attraction in last year's Cherry Hinton. Forced to come down the outside in the straight, she showed her wellbeing and is obviously on the way back.
**Fruit Of Glory** does not mind forcing the pace and only gave best in the closing stages.
**Goldeva**, not inconvenienced by the overnight rain, got going too late after not getting the best of passages.
**Tychy** *Official explanation: jockey said mare hung left; trainer's representative said mare was unsuited by good ground*

## 5455 LEGAT OWEN EBF MAIDEN STKS — 7f 2y
**3:00** (3:01) (D3) 2-Y-0 **£5,085** (£1,564; £782; £391) **Stalls** Low

Form — RPR

2 **1** **Dhaular Dhar (IRE)**[15] 5091 2-9-0 ........ MHills 1 88+
(BWHills) *mde all: qckd clr and rdn over 1f out: easily* **2/5**[1]

60 **2** 11 **Layed Back Rocky**[21] 4930 2-9-0 ........ CCatlin 6 52
(MMullineaux) *chsd wnr: rdn over 2f out: sn btn* **33/1**

04 **3** 2 1/2 **Lake Wakatipu**[25] 4824 2-8-9 ........ RMullen 2 40
(MMullineaux) *hld up: rdn over 2f out: sme hdwy ins fnl f* **14/1**

0000 **4** 1 **The Terminator (IRE)**[11] 5209 2-9-0 35 ........ NCallan 3 42
(ABerry) *prom: rdn 3f out: wknd over 1f out* **40/1**

**5** *nk* **Polar Passion** 2-8-9 ........ DSweeney 5 36
(RHollinshead) *fly-jmpd s: a bhd* **25/1**

**6** *shd* **Tavalu (USA)** 2-9-0 ........ JCarroll 4 40
(SaeedBinSuroor) *hld up: hdwy 4f out: rdn over 2f out: wknd over 1f out* **4/1**[2]

30 **7** 5 **Oxford Street Pete (IRE)**[21] 4930 2-9-0 ........ ADaly 7 25
(ABailey) *stdd s: sn swtchd to ins rail: sme hdwy over 4f out: rdn over 3f out: wknd wl over 1f out* **10/1**[3]

1m 27.64s (-0.65) **Going Correction** -0.175s/f (Firm) **7** Ran SP% **116.4**
Speed ratings: **96,83,80,79,79 78,73**CSF £23.82 TOTE £1.40: £1.10, £7.70; EX 25.80.
**Owner** Maktoum Al Maktoum **Bred** Gainsborough Stud Management Ltd **Trained** Lambourn, Berks

**FOCUS**
A modest and uncompetitive maiden, weakened by the performance of the second favourite and the proximity of the fourth. The time was half a second slower than the opening nursery.

**NOTEBOOK**
**Dhaular Dhar(IRE)** built on the promise of his debut and could hardly have been more impressive. However, he had nothing to beat with the Godolphin newcomer proving a flop.
**Layed Back Rocky** improved on his two previous starts but that is not saying a lot.
**Lake Wakatipu** stayed on for third over this longer trip but the winner had long gone.
**The Terminator(IRE)** had cut no ice in his previous outings.
**Tavalu(USA)**, a well-bred colt who will eventually need a mile and a half, proved a disappointment on his debut.

## 5456 UNIVERSITY OF LIVERPOOL H'CAP — 1m 7f 195y
**3:35** (3:36) (E3) (0-70,70) 3-Y-0+ **£5,236** (£1,611; £805; £402) **Stalls** Low

Form — RPR

232/ **1** **Rooftop Protest (IRE)**[27] 4792 7-9-4 **63** ........ (t) MHills 5 77+
(THogan, Ire) *mde all: qcknd over 4f out: rdn clr over 2f: styd on wl* **4/1**[1]

0003 **2** 8 **Irish Blade (IRE)**[14] 5116 3-8-10 **68** ........ DSweeney 8 72
(HCandy) *a.p: rdn 4f out: wnt 2nd ins fnl f: no ch w wnr* **13/2**[3]

2606 **3** 1 1/4 **Red Sun**[30] 4686 7-8-11 **56** ........ (t) DaleGibson 9 59
(JMackie) *t.k.h: a.p: wnt 2nd over 5f out: rdn over 4f out: no imp fnl 2f* **6/1**[2]

1600 **4** 1/2 **Isa'Af (IRE)**[12] 5203 5-9-7 **66** ........ DarrenWilliams 15 68
(PWHiatt) *hld up in tch: rdn and one pce fnl 2f* **25/1**

2340 **5** 1 **Northern Nymph**[62] 3782 5-9-1 **65** ........ StephanieHollinshead(5) 1 66
(RHollinshead) *hld up in tch: rdn and one pce fnl 2f* **16/1**

2530 **6** 1 **Ellway Heights**[24] 4849 7-8-11 **56** oh5 ........ RMullen 2 56
(WMBrisbourne) *hld up: stdy hdwy on ins over 4f out: n.m.r on ins over 1f out: no further prog* **14/1**

0-10 **7** *shd* **Arabian Moon (IRE)**[15] 5074 8-9-8 **70** ........ DNolan(3) 16 69
(RBrotherton) *bhd tl styd on fr jst over 1f out: nvr nrr* **25/1**

0003 **8** *hd* **Redspin (IRE)**[16] 5058 4-8-8 **60** ........ DerekNolan(7) 4 59
(JSMoore) *hld up in tch: outpcd over 4f out: no real prog fnl 2f* **10/1**

6100 **9** 1 3/4 **Teorban (POL)**[12] 5205 5-8-11 **56** oh1 ........ WRyan 6 53
(DJSFfrenchDavis) *chsd wnr tl over 5f out: wknd wl over 1f out: eased whn btn fnl f* **16/1**

4002 **10** *nk* **Henry Island (IRE)**[12] 5205 11-8-13 **58** ........ DKinsella 11 55
(MrsAJBowlby) *hld up: dropped rr 4f out: n.d after* **15/2**

00/4 **11** 3/4 **Regency Red (IRE)**[9] 5243 6-8-6 **56** oh10 ........ BSwarbrick(5) 7 52
(WMBrisbourne) *hld up: rdn over 3f out: no rspnse* **25/1**

5102 **12** *hd* **Diamond Orchid (IRE)**[23] 4603 4-8-12 **57** ........ (v) LisaJones 3 53
(PDEvans) *s.i.s: a bhd* **8/1**

4444 **13** *2* **Gallant Boy (IRE)**[20] 4971 5-9-5 **64**....................(vt) NCallan 14 57
(PDEvans) *s.i.s: a bhd* **9/1**
2066 **14** *1 3/4* **Darn Good**[12] 5205 3-8-9 **67**....................(b) JCarroll 10 58
(RHannon) *bhd: rdn over 7f out: short-lived effrt over 4f out* **16/1**
00-0 **15** *dist* **Subadar Major**[11] 5214 7-8-8 **56** oh26.................... HayleyTurner(3) 12 —
(MrsGSRees) *prom tl rdn and wknd qckly over 5f out: t.o* **100/1**

3m 32.1s (-1.68) **Going Correction** +0.025s/f (Good)
**WFA** 3 from 4yo+ 13lb **15** Ran SP% **126.4**
Speed ratings: **105,101,100,100,99 99,99,98,98,97 97,97,96,95,**—CSF £29.02 CT £162.61 TOTE £3.10: £1.70, £2.70, £2.80; EX 49.90.
**Owner** M G Byrne **Bred** J Costelloe **Trained** Nenagh, Co. Tipperary

**FOCUS**
An ordinary handicap with the winner waiting in front, and nothing was able to come from off the pace. the proximity of several racing from out of the handicap suggests the form is not that sound.

**NOTEBOOK**
**Rooftop Protest(IRE)**, 25lb higher than the first of his three wins in Ireland this summer, had it sewn up turning for home under a canny ride from the front.
**Irish Blade(IRE)** is shaping like an out and out stayer and would have preferred a more truly run race.
**Red Sun**, dropped 4lb after a couple of disappointing efforts with give in the ground, has won in the soft over hurdles.
**Isa'Af(IRE)** was back to a mark only a couple of pounds higher than when he won at Nottingham in July.
**Northern Nymph** could not get past the placed horses let alone bother the winner.
**Ellway Heights**, trying a longer trip, should by no means be considered unlucky.
**Teorban(POL)** *Official explanation: jockey said gelding tired in latter stages and was unsuited by the good ground*

## 5457 EUROPEAN BREEDERS FUND CONDITIONS STKS 7f 122y
**4:05** (4:05) (C2) 2-Y-O **£7,734** (£2,744; £1,372; £623) **Stalls** Low

Form RPR
110 **1** **Johnny Jumpup (IRE)**[21] 4949 2-9-0 93.................... NCallan 3 96
(RMBeckett) *hld up in tch: rdn over 2f out: led 1f out: r.o wl* **5/2**[2]
13 **2** *2 1/2* **Hachita (USA)**[31] 4645 2-8-9 83.................... WRyan 1 85
(HRACecil) *led: hdd jst over 3f out: rdn 2f out: kpt on to retake 2nd towards fin* **11/2**
010 **3** *1 1/4* **Country Rambler (USA)**[65] 3672 2-9-0 98.................... MHills 2 87
(BWHills) *chsd ldr: led jst over 3f out: rdn 2f out: hdd 1f out: wknd ins fnl f* **11/8**[1]
1 **4** *3 1/2* **Personify**[73] 3424 2-9-0 .................... JCarroll 4 79
(SaeedBinSuroor) *s.i.s and wnt rt: hld up: rdn over 2f out: sn struggling* **7/2**[3]

1m 35.62s (0.87) **Going Correction** +0.025s/f (Good) **4** Ran SP% **108.3**
Speed ratings: **96,93,92,88**CSF £14.28 TOTE £3.80; EX 18.40.
**Owner** Mr & Mrs A Briars **Bred** Mill House Stud **Trained** Lambourn, Berks

**FOCUS**
A strong juvenile conditions race, but only a modest pace for this interesting event, which raises doubts.

**NOTEBOOK**
**Johnny Jumpup(IRE)**, a useful sort, does like to get his toe in and only ran because the ground eased overnight. His trainer subsequently explained that it was even too soft for him in the Solario Stakes at Sandown last time.
**Hachita(USA)**, caught a shade flat-footed entering the home straight, seems ready to tackle a mile.
**Country Rambler(USA)** won on fast ground at Warwick and perhaps the slight ease in the going was against her.
**Personify** is bred to be suited by this longer trip but proved a disappointment.

## 5458 RECTANGLE GROUP H'CAP 5f 16y
**4:40** (4:41) (D2) (0-85,80) 3-Y-O+ **£6,770** (£2,083; £1,041; £520) **Stalls** Low

Form RPR
-041 **1** **Jilly Why (IRE)**[7] 5306 3-8-5 **67**.................... BSwarbrick(5) 6 80
(MsDeborahJEvans) *a.p: rdn to ld jst over 1f out: drvn out* **10/1**
3010 **2** *1 1/4* **Kings College Boy**[14] 5107 4-8-12 **68**....................(b) DaleGibson 4 76
(RAFahey) *chsd ldrs: rdn whn n.m.r on ins 2f out: r.o ins fnl f: nt trble wnr* **5/1**[2]
2311 **3** *3 1/2* **Beauvrai**[12] 5184 4-9-7 **77**....................(b) OUrbina 8 72
(GCHChung) *chsd ldrs: rdn wl over 1f out: one pce* **9/2**[1]
1200 **4** *3/4* **Frascati**[21] 4935 4-9-1 **76**.................... PPMathers(5) 9 69
(ABerry) *hld up in tch: lost pl after 1f: plld out over 1f out: hdwy fnl f: r.o* **9/1**
0000 **5** *3/4* **Izmail (IRE)**[2] 5412 5-8-13 **69**.................... NCallan 1 59
(PDEvans) *led: rdn and hdd jst over 1f out: wknd ins fnl f* **11/2**[3]
2000 **6** *nk* **Sir Ernest (IRE)**[12] 5181 3-8-7 **71**.................... DTudhope(7) 5 60
(MJPolglase) *hld up: rdn and hdwy over 1f out: no ex ins fnl f* **16/1**
0004 **7** *shd* **Hello Roberto**[22] 4929 3-8-7 **71**.................... KGhunowa(7) 12 60
(MJPolglase) *s.i.s: hdwy on ins over 2f out: one pce fnl f* **20/1**
0552 **8** *1* **Strensall**[16] 5062 7-9-7 **77**.................... CCatlin 13 62
(REBarr) *hld up: sn bhd: stdy hdwy fnl f: nvr nr to chal* **20/1**
0000 **9** *3/4* **Sir Don (IRE)**[18] 5020 5-8-10 **66** oh5....................(v) JBramhill 7 48
(DNicholls) *s.v.s: hdwy on ins jst over 1f out: n.d* **25/1**
0330 **10** *hd* **Prince Of Blues (IRE)**[7] 5287 6-8-10 **66** oh10....................(b) LEnstone 2 48
(MMullineaux) *prom: rdn 3f out: wknd jst over 1f out* **14/1**
0200 **11** *2 1/2* **Rectangle (IRE)**[44] 4279 4-8-10 **66**.................... ANicholls 10 39
(DNicholls) *prom: lost pl after 1f: c wd st: sn bhd* **12/1**
0000 **12** *nk* **Johnston's Diamond (IRE)**[7] 5287 6-9-10 **80**.................... MHills 16 51
(EJAlston) *sn bhd* **11/1**
0000 **13** *2 1/2* **Chico Guapo (IRE)**[16] 5062 4-8-11 **67**....................(b) WRyan 3 29
(JAGlover) *prom 3f* **6/1**

62.39 secs (0.41) **Going Correction** +0.225s/f (Good)
**WFA** 3 from 4yo+ 1lb **13** Ran SP% **125.6**
Speed ratings: **105,103,97,96,95 94,94,92,91,91 87,86,82**CSF £60.82 CT £267.35 TOTE £14.40: £3.70, £2.30, £2.10; EX 77.70.
**Owner** Paul Green (Oaklea) **Bred** K And Mrs Cullen **Trained** Lydiate, Merseyside
■ Stewards Enquiry : K Ghunowa caution: careless riding

**FOCUS**
A modest sprint handicap in which the first two appeared to have stiff tasks, and therefore the race has been rated conservatively.

**NOTEBOOK**
**Jilly Why(IRE)** showed her all-the-way win in a fast-ground Thirsk maiden to be no fluke. A filly in form, she is on the upgrade.
**Kings College Boy**, 7lb higher than when successful over course and distance in soft ground last month, had to check briefly at the quarter-mile marker. He would probably not have beaten the winner in any case.
**Beauvrai** had been raised 5lb for his back-to-back wins in six furlong claimers.
**Frascati**, disappointing on soft ground here last time, could never recover after losing a good early position.
**Izmail(IRE)**, making a quick reappearance, likes the top of the ground and would not have been helped by the overnight rain.
**Sir Ernest(IRE)** always goes well here but was unable to sustain his effort.
**Sir Don(IRE)** *Official explanation: jockey said gelding froze in the stalls and missed break*
**Prince Of Blues(IRE)** *Official explanation: jockey said gelding lost his action*
**Chico Guapo(IRE)** *Official explanation: jockey said gelding hung to right*

## 5459 ASTBURY WREN INSURANCE BROKERS H'CAP 1m 2f 75y
**5:10** (5:11) (E3) (0-70,70) 3-Y-O+ **£5,688** (£1,750; £875; £437) **Stalls** High

Form RPR
0241 **1** **Milk And Sultana**[8] 5267 4-8-10 **59**.................... ADaly 7 67
(GAHam) *hld up: stdy hdwy over 4f out: rdn to ld last strides* **14/1**
4032 **2** *nk* **Young Rooney**[9] 5237 4-9-5 **68**....................(p) LEnstone 15 75
(MMullineaux) *led: rdn 3f out: hdd last strides* **20/1**
0463 **3** *1* **Mr Midasman (IRE)**[7] 5293 3-8-0 **56** oh1.................... DaleGibson 1 61
(RHollinshead) *hld up in tch: wnt 2nd over 3f out: rdn over 2f out: nt qckn ins fnl f* **8/1**
6350 **4** *1/2* **Infidelity (IRE)**[4] 5374 3-7-12 **57**....................(p) HayleyTurner(3) 2 61+
(ABailey) *s.i.s: stdy hdwy on ins over 4f out: nt clr run 2f out: sn swtchd rt: rdn and edgd lft ins fnl f: kpt* **25/1**
5001 **5** *1 1/4* **Secluded**[17] 5038 4-9-5 **68**....................(b) RMullen 4 70
(EFVaughan) *s.i.s: hld up: stdy hdwy over 4f out: rdn over 2f out: one pce ins fnl f* **7/1**[3]
6041 **6** *7* **Giunchiglio**[22] 4911 5-9-2 **70**.................... BSwarbrick(5) 6 58
(WMBrisbourne) *hld up: rdn and hdwy on outside over 1f out: n.d* **20/1**
2400 **7** *1 3/4* **Desert Image (IRE)**[32] 4618 3-8-9 **68**.................... DCorby(3) 5 53
(CTinkler) *hld up and bhd: rdn over 2f out: rdn and hdwy on ins wl over 1f out: n.d* **33/1**
0211 **8** *1 1/2* **Mcqueen (IRE)**[12] 5175 4-9-3 **66**.................... DSweeney 11 48
(MrsHDalton) *wnt prom after 2f: rdn over 4f out: wknd 3f out* **9/2**[2]
2454 **9** *3/4* **Head To Kerry (IRE)**[13] 5153 4-8-7 **56** oh1....................(p) WRyan 9 37
(DJSFfrenchDavis) *bhd: rdn and sme hdwy on ins over 1f out: nvr nr ldrs* **7/1**[3]
000- **10** *3* **Investment Affair (IRE)**[368] 4790 4-8-11 **60**.................... JCarroll 10 35
(DMccain) *a bhd* **50/1**
5051 **11** *2* **Market Avenue**[5] 5344 5-9-1 **64** 6ex.................... DarrenWilliams 17 35
(RAFahey) *s.i.s: sn in tch and sddle slipped: lost pl 3f out: eased over 1f out* **8/1**
0441 **12** *7* **Jake Black (IRE)**[6] 5320 4-8-2 **58**.................... DTudhope(7) 14 16
(JJQuinn) *prom tl rdn and wknd over 2f out* **3/1**[1]
0 **13** *3 1/2* **Armatore (USA)**[52] 4028 4-9-5 **68**.................... ANicholls 3 19
(EROertel) *chsd ldr tl rdn over 3f out: wknd over 2f out* **100/1**
0412 **14** *8* **Havetoavit (USA)**[9] 5245 3-8-9 **65**.................... CCatlin 16 —
(JDBethell) *prom 5f* **10/1**
0000 **15** *1/2* **Luxor**[8] 5267 7-8-7 **56** oh11.................... LisaJones 13 —
(MrsGSRees) *bhd fnl 4f* **66/1**
5224 **16** *7* **Killala (IRE)**[34] 4568 4-8-8 **57** oh1 ow1.................... NCallan 12 —
(RNBevis) *s.i.s: a in rr* **33/1**

2m 13.83s (1.28) **Going Correction** +0.225s/f (Good)
**WFA** 3 from 4yo+ 7lb **16** Ran SP% **129.9**
Speed ratings: **103,102,101,101,100 94,93,92,91,89 87,82,79,72,72 66**CSF £281.13 CT £2420.90 TOTE £19.30: £3.50, £3.40, £2.20, £4.60; EX 213.20 Place 6 £76.41, Place 5 £22.71..
**Owner** D M Drury **Bred** D Malcolm Drury **Trained** Rooks Bridge, Somerset

**FOCUS**
A competitive handicap run in a heavy shower. The form is modest.

**NOTEBOOK**
**Milk And Sultana**, raised 3lb, proved the old adage that it pays to follow a filly in form.
**Young Rooney** again adopted front-running tactics and quickly crossed over from his high draw. Still a maiden, he hardly deserved to get picked off at the death.
**Mr Midasman(IRE)** turned in another solid performance over what now appears to be his best trip.
**Infidelity(IRE)** performed a lot better with the cheekpieces back on.
**Secluded** was eventually anchored by the 4lb rise in the weights for his victory in first-time blinkers in the heavy at Brighton.
**Market Avenue** *Official explanation: jockey said saddle slipped*
**Armatore(USA)** *Official explanation: jockey said gelding was unsuited by good ground*
**Killala(IRE)** *Official explanation: trainer said gelding spread a plate during the race and was found to be lame*
T/Plt: £143.90 to a £1 stake. Pool: £46,993.05. 238.35 winning tickets. T/Qpdt: £20.80 to a £1 stake. Pool: £2,319.00. 82.30 winning tickets. KH

# 5434 DONCASTER (L-H)
Saturday, September 11

**OFFICIAL GOING: Straight course - firm (good to firm in places); round course - good to firm**
The going had dried out overnight and it was described by the riders as 'very fast, almost firm'. The wind had swung round into a headwind in the straight.
Wind: Fresh 1/2 against. Weather: Fine and sunny.

## 5460 GNER CONDITIONS STKS 6f
**1:35** (1:36) (C2) 2-Y-O **£6,609** (£2,345; £1,172; £533) **Stalls** High

Form RPR
4155 **1** **Galeota (IRE)**[7] 5295 2-9-1 100.................... RLMoore 1 104
(RHannon) *led: qcknd over 3f out: rdn over 1f out: styd on wl* **4/1**[3]
22 **2** *2* **Rajwa (USA)**[24] 4861 2-8-11 ....................(t) KMcEvoy 4 94
(SaeedBinSuroor) *trckd wnr: chal over 1f out: sn rdn and hung rt: wknd ins last* **6/4**[1]
14U3 **3** *2 1/2* **Obe Gold**[31] 4632 2-9-1 89.................... KFallon 5 90
(MRChannon) *chsd ldrs: outpcd 1/2-way: swtchd outside over 1f out: kpt on same pce: nvr able chal* **8/1**
614 **4** *13* **Reqqa**[12] 5195 2-9-1 .................... RHills 2 51
(MJohnston) *trckd ldrs: drvn along over 3f out: lost pl over 1f out: sn bhd* **7/4**[2]

1m 12.52s (-1.76) **Going Correction** -0.20s/f (Firm) **4** Ran SP% **107.5**
Speed ratings: **103,100,97,79**CSF £10.29 TOTE £5.80; EX 11.70.
**Owner** J A Lazzari **Bred** W Maxwell Ervine **Trained** East Everleigh, Wilts

**FOCUS**
This turned out to be a disappointing event. The winner was given his own way and showed a much better attitude than the runner-up.

**NOTEBOOK**
**Galeota(IRE)**, down in grade, had his own way in front and showed a willing attitude. He should continue to give a good account of himself.
**Rajwa(USA)** looked to have the winner covered but, after moving upsides, his response was very limited to say the least.
**Obe Gold** had a fair bit to find and was always making very hard work of it.

**Reqqa**, very much up in the air, was the first under pressure and he dropped right out in most disappointing fashion. This was simply too bad to be true. *Official explanation: trainer's representative was unable to offer any explanation for poor form shown*

## 5461 LADBROKES.COM STKS (H'CAP) 1m 2f 60y

**2:05** (2:06) (B1) (0-110,105) 3-Y-O+ **£17,400** (£6,600; £3,300; £1,500) **Stalls** Low

Form RPR

364 **1** **Colisay**$^{35}$ [4528] 5-9-1 **99** ... KFallon 4 108
(EFVaughan) *trckd ldrs: styd on wl to ld 1f out: hld on wl* **4/1$^{2}$**

023 **2** *nk* **Courageous Duke (USA)**$^{36}$ [4520] 5-8-9 **93** ... SSanders 2 101
(JNoseda) *trckd ldrs: effrt over 2f out: styd on wl appr fnl f: no ex ins last* **9/2$^{3}$**

1-65 **3** *1¼* **Roehampton**$^{128}$ [1901] 3-8-6 **97** ...(v$^{1}$) MartinDwyer 1 103
(SirMichaelStoute) *trckd ldr: t.k.h: led over 2f out: hdd 1f out: styd on same pce* **16/1**

5536 **4** *¾* **Bonecrusher**$^{35}$ [4540] 5-9-7 **105** ...(v) RLMoore 7 110
(DRLoder) *s.s: hdwy over 4f out: kpt on same pce appr fnl f* **4/1$^{2}$**

4-00 **5** *¾* **Weecandoo (IRE)**$^{49}$ [4118] 6-8-7 **91** oh7 ... GCarter 6 95
(CNAllen) *chsd ldrs: outpcd and drvn along over 4f out: kpt on one pce fnl 2f* **33/1**

0-04 **6** *1¼* **Famous Grouse**$^{12}$ [5180] 4-9-0 **98** ... DHolland 5 99
(RCharlton) *led: hdd over 2f out: wknd fnl f* **12/1**

3462 **7** *2½* **Blue Sky Thinking (IRE)**$^{15}$ [5099] 5-8-8 **92** ... SWKelly 8 89
(KRBurke) *trckd ldrs: effrt over 2f out: hung lft and lost pl over 1f out* **7/1**

6051 **8** *1* **Polygonal (FR)**$^{36}$ [4520] 4-8-10 **94** ... JFortune 3 89
(MrsJRRamsden) *hld up: hdwy on ins 3f out: rdn and wknd 2f out* **3/1$^{1}$**

2m 9.33s (-2.43) **Going Correction** -0.15s/f (Firm)
**WFA** 3 from 4yo+ 7lb **8** Ran SP% **112.2**
Speed ratings: **103,102,101,101,100 99,97,96**CSF £21.44 CT £253.21 TOTE £4.70: £1.60, £2.10, £3.60; EX 25.00 Trifecta £282.00 Pool: £913.80. 2.30 winning tickets..
**Owner** M Hawkes **Bred** Patrick Eddery Ltd **Trained** Newmarket, Suffolk

**FOCUS**

In effect just a 0-105 handicap and the winning time was modest for the grade. The form looks a bit messy but has been rated around the first two.

**NOTEBOOK**

**Colisay**, with the visor left off, had the ground to suit and if anything appreciated the step up in trip. However, a 7lb penalty will make it tough for him in the Cambridgeshire.

**Courageous Duke(USA)**, meeting Polygonal on much better terms, stuck to his guns and in the end was just held at bay. He too looks Cambridgeshire bound.

**Roehampton**, absent since the Chester Vase, took a keen grip on the heels of the leader in a first-time visor. He went on and stuck to his task when headed.

**Bonecrusher** ambled out of the stalls and, though not beaten that far in the end, in truth he never looked a real threat.

**Weecandoo(IRE)**, last on both her previous starts this time, did well considering she was running from 7lb out of the handicap.

**Famous Grouse**, who has a round action, made the running but he has yet to make his mark in handicap company and in the end, on this fast ground, was found sadly lacking. *Official explanation: jockey said gelding was unsuited by the good to firm ground*

**Blue Sky Thinking(IRE)** is better on Polytrack and, with grass under his feet, he seems to struggle to see out this trip.

**Polygonal(FR)**, heavily opposed on the track, was 9lb higher and stopped in two strides. He was found to be lame afterwards. *Official explanation: vet said gelding was lame*

## 5462 PORCELANOSA STKS (H'CAP) 1m (S)

**2:40** (2:40) (B1) (0-110,108) 3-Y-O+ **£17,400** (£6,600; £3,300; £1,500) **Stalls** High

Form RPR

0301 **1** **Calcutta**$^{6}$ [5315] 8-8-11 **98** 3ex ... RHills 12 107
(BWHills) *hld up: hdwy over 1f out: styd on wl to ld towards fin* **8/1**

020- **2** *nk* **Funfair**$^{413}$ [3589] 5-9-2 **103** ... RLMoore 8 111
(MrsAJPerrett) *trckd ldrs: led over 1f out: hdd towards fin* **14/1**

310/ **3** *shd* **Desert Star**$^{693}$ [5370] 4-8-11 **98** ... KFallon 5 106
(SirMichaelStoute) *trckd ldrs: n.m.r over 2f out: ev ch ins last: no ex nr line* **8/1**

6240 **4** *shd* **Flighty Fellow (IRE)**$^{35}$ [4540] 4-8-7 **94** oh2 ...(b) GCarter 14 102
(TDEasterby) *in rr: hdwy 2f out: ev ch wl ins last: no ex* **20/1**

1520 **5** *nk* **Mine (IRE)**$^{23}$ [4889] 6-9-7 **108** ...(v) TQuinn 2 115
(JDBethell) *hld up: hdwy on far side to chal over 1f out: nt qckn wl ins last* **13/2$^{2}$**

4104 **6** *1* **Blue Spinnaker (IRE)**$^{24}$ [4856] 5-9-1 **102** ... SWKelly 15 107
(MWEasterby) *lw: bhd: hdwy over 1f out: styd on ins last* **6/1$^{1}$**

4000 **7** *nk* **Lundy's Lane (IRE)**$^{63}$ [3756] 4-8-7 **94** ... SSanders 7 98
(CEBrittain) *s.i.s: styd on fnl 2f: one pce ins last* **25/1**

1212 **8** *¾* **Welcome Stranger**$^{38}$ [4442] 4-8-7 **94** oh2 ... DHolland 3 96
(JMPEustace) *in tch: hdwy to chal 1f out: kpt on same pce* **15/2$^{3}$**

4010 **9** *nk* **Pentecost**$^{30}$ [4685] 5-9-2 **106** ... LPKeniry$^{(3)}$ 6 107
(AMBalding) *lw: hld up in rr: effrt 2f out: kpt on: nvr rchd ldrs* **8/1**

-530 **10** *shd* **Bayeux (USA)**$^{98}$ [2672] 3-8-8 **100** ...(t) KMcEvoy 9 101
(SaeedBinSuroor) *w ldrs: led 2f out: sn hdd and fdd* **8/1**

1362 **11** *4* **Will He Wish**$^{12}$ [5194] 8-8-4 **94** oh5 ...(b) RThomas$^{(3)}$ 13 86
(SGollings) *w ldrs: led over 3f out tl 2f out: wknd fnl f* **14/1**

4444 **12** *½* **Isidore Bonheur (IRE)**$^{66}$ [3639] 3-8-6 **98** ... DaneO'Neill 11 89
(BWHills) *chsd ldrs: outpcd fnl 2f* **50/1**

4140 **13** *2½* **Always Esteemed (IRE)**$^{23}$ [4887] 4-8-11 **98** ... MartinDwyer 4 83
(GWragg) *chsd ldrs: lost pl over 1f out* **16/1**

02-0 **14** *3* **Roskilde (IRE)**$^{48}$ [4178] 4-8-11 **98** ... JFortune 1 76
(MRChannon) *racd wd: w ldrs: lost pl over 1f out* **33/1**

-010 **15** *6* **Aqualung**$^{91}$ [2896] 3-8-2 **94** oh2 ... FNorton 10 58
(BWHills) *led tl over 3f out: sn lost pl and bhd* **33/1**

1m 37.74s (-3.86) **Going Correction** -0.20s/f (Firm)
**WFA** 3 from 4yo+ 5lb **15** Ran SP% **119.5**
Speed ratings: **111,110,110,110,110 109,108,108,107,107 103,103,100,97,91**CSF £106.58 CT £952.98 TOTE £8.70: £2.30, £4.10, £3.00; EX 145.40 Trifecta £1017.10 Part won. Pool £1,432.62 - 0.10 winning tickets..
**Owner** The Hon Mrs J M Corbett & C Wright **Bred** Campbell Stud **Trained** Lambourn, Berks

**FOCUS**

A blanket finish, but a good quality field and the form should prove reliable.

**NOTEBOOK**

**Calcutta**, who won this in 1999 and 2001, was turning out for the fifth successive year. His confidence boosted by his recent victory in a valuable claimer at York, he showed a nice turn of foot to put his head in front where it matters. He is a great credit to his trainer.

**Funfair**, absent for over a year, was having his first outing for his new stable. As usual loaded with a blanket, he was just edged out after showing ahead. This will put him spot on for the Cambridgeshire.

**Desert Star**, absent since contesting the Dewhurst at two, looked fighting fit and in the end was only just found wanting. He showed he retains his ability and has lost time to make up for.

**Flighty Fellow(IRE)**, third last year, had run over a mile and a quarter on his previous starts.This trip looks his bare minimum now.

**Mine(IRE)**, winner of both his previous outings here, had the strong pace he needs but, drawn one from the outside, he tended to hang right and did not give his rider full co-operation. He would have been better coming between horses. *Official explanation: jockey said horse hung right handed*

**Blue Spinnaker(IRE)** looked at his very best but found this trip just too sharp.

**Lundy's Lane(IRE)**, now a gelding, has slipped to a lenient mark but is on a long losing run.

**Always Esteemed(IRE)** *Official explanation: jockey said gelding was unsuited by firm, good to firm places ground*

**Aqualung** *Official explanation: jockey said colt had a breathing problem*

## 5463 BETFAIR.COM ST LEGER STKS (GROUP 1) (ENTIRE COLTS & FILLIES) 1m 6f 132y

**3:15** (3:17) (A1) 3-Y-O **£240,000** (£92,000; £46,000; £22,000) **Stalls** Low

Form RPR

2241 **1** **Rule Of Law (USA)**$^{25}$ [4833] 3-9-0 120 ...(t) KMcEvoy 9 122
(SaeedBinSuroor) *lw: set mod pce: shkn up and led over 2f out: fnd ex ins last: gamely* **3/1$^{1}$**

-131 **2** *hd* **Quiff**$^{24}$ [4859] 3-8-11 119 ... KFallon 4 119
(SirMichaelStoute) *lw: trckd ldrs: nt clr run on ins and swtchd outside over 2f out: styd on to chal last 100yds: no ex nr line* **3/1$^{1}$**

-360 **3** *1½* **Tycoon**$^{25}$ [4834] 3-9-0 ...(t) DHolland 6 120
(APO'Brien, Ire) *dwlt: hld up in last pl: stdy hdwy over 2f out: styd on ins last* **6/1$^{3}$**

-221 **4** *1* **Maraahel (IRE)**$^{46}$ [4215] 3-9-0 112 ... RHills 5 119
(SirMichaelStoute) *trckd ldrs: effrt 3f out: styd on same pce appr fnl f* **8/1**

-443 **5** *hd* **Mikado**$^{24}$ [4858] 3-9-0 ... JFortune 7 118
(APO'Brien, Ire) *trckdwnr: drvn along 3f out: styd on same pce* **25/1**

00- **6** *1½* **Darsalam (IRE)**$^{13}$ 3-9-0 ... SChin 10 116
(AShavuyev, Czech Republic) *chsd ldrs: rdn and sltly outpcd over 3f out: kpt on wl fnl 2f* **33/1**

-323 **7** *3* **Go For Gold (IRE)**$^{25}$ [4833] 3-9-0 ... SSanders 1 113
(APO'Brien, Ire) *chsd ldrs: rdn over 3f out: sn outpcd* **12/1**

3352 **8** *6* **Let The Lion Roar**$^{25}$ [4833] 3-9-0 118 ...(v) TQuinn 2 105
(JLDunlop) *t.k.h in rr: hdwy over 3f out: rdn and lost pl over 2f out* **9/2$^{2}$**

1311 **9** *nk* **Frank Sonata**$^{56}$ [3927] 3-9-0 105 ... RLMoore 8 104
(MGQuinlan) *towards rr: pushed along 6f out: nvr a factor* **16/1**

3m 6.29s (-3.45) **Going Correction** -0.15s/f (Firm) **9** Ran SP% **113.9**
Speed ratings: **103,102,102,101,101 100,99,95,95**CSF £11.48 TOTE £4.30: £1.80, £2.00, £2.20; EX 18.60 Trifecta £86.10 Pool: £4,897.83. 40.38 winning tickets..
**Owner** Godolphin **Bred** R E Sangster And Ben Sangster **Trained** Newmarket, Suffolk
■ Godolphin's fourth win in the St Leger. Kerrin McEvoy was the first Australian to win the race since Ron Hutchinson in 1969.

**FOCUS**

The field looked up to scratch, but the other riders played into McEvoy's hands by allowing Rule Of Law to dictate a modest pace. The time was very moderate indeed for a Classic, given the conditions, and with the form horses first and second he did not need to improve to win.

**NOTEBOOK**

**Rule Of Law(USA)** looked in tip-top trim and floated to post on this fast ground. Dropping anchor in front, he wound up the gallop for a second time with over two furlongs left to run and in the end simply would not be denied. Very tough, he may now go for the Arc, but will return next year when he will be campaigned over a mile and a half. His rider deserves full marks.

**Quiff**, whose participation was in doubt until late on after the rain missed the Town Moor, found herself trapped on the rail halfway up the straight. Pulled four horses wide, she was almost upsides inside the last but just missed out. She is a big filly who has yet to fill to her frame and hopefully will be kept in training at four. Her trainer must wonder what he has to do to win the St Leger, the only domestic classic which has escaped his grasp, for Quiff was his fifth runner-up.

**Tycoon**, a lot cooler and more settled than at York, was ridden with the patience of Job. His rider only really asked him for his effort coming to the final furlong. Unbalanced for a couple of strides, he stayed on inside the last despite a hint of hanging left. To suggest that he did not stay is nonsense. Indeed he would have been suited by a stronger pace and stiffer test.

**Maraahel(IRE)** again accounted for Go For Gold but this trip looked to stretch him to the very limit at this stage of his development. Quite a big sort, he should make an even better four-year-old.

**Mikado**, ridden a lot closer to the pace, had finished behind Maraahel and Go For Gold at Goodwood and this is as good as he is.

**Darsalam(IRE)**, a half-brother to the 1994 winner Moonax, was sold cheaply out of Mark Johnston's stable after finishing tailed off in two outings at two. A winner five times in Eastern Europe, including the Czech Derby and St Leger, he fully justified his place in the line-up and excelled himself. He looks essentially a stayer.

**Go For Gold(IRE)**, a half-brother to the 2001 winner Milan, had finished runner-up behind Maraahel at Goodwood and third behind the winner at York. This may be as good as he is.

**Let The Lion Roar**, half-brother to the 2000 winner Millenary, was on edge and stirred up beforehand. He pulled like a train and, when asked to improve, he wanted to do nothing but hang right. He has the ability but his attitude lets him down. *Official explanation: jockey said colt ran too free due to the slow early pace and hung right handed in home straight*

**Frank Sonata**, much improved at three, prefers much easier ground but this looked basically a bridge too far. *Official explanation: jockey said colt was unsuited by good to firm ground firm places in straight*

## 5464 POLYPIPE FLYING CHILDERS STKS (GROUP 2) 5f

**3:45** (3:50) (A1) 2-Y-O **£42,000** (£16,100; £8,050; £3,850) **Stalls** High

Form RPR

6110 **1** **Chateau Istana**$^{66}$ [3640] 2-8-12 98 ...(t) SSanders 7 109
(NPLittmoden) *chsd ldrs: styd on to ld appr fnl f: r.o wl* **11/1**

0103 **2** *2* **Tournedos (IRE)**$^{8}$ [5280] 2-9-1 100 ... TQuinn 3 105
(MRChannon) *trckd ldrs: styd on appr fnl f: no imp* **11/2$^{2}$**

1630 **3** *¾* **Kissing Lights (IRE)**$^{23}$ [4885] 2-8-9 100 ... DHolland 12 97
(MLWBell) *sn outpcd: hdwy over 1f out: styd on ins last* **20/1**

2125 **4** *1* **Amazin**$^{43}$ [4288] 2-8-12 97 ... RLMoore 4 96
(RHannon) *s.s: bhd: hdwy 2f out: kpt on fnl f* **16/1**

3352 **5** *1¾* **Bond City (IRE)**$^{11}$ [5213] 2-8-12 95 ... DMcGaffin 10 90
(BSmart) *trckd ldrs: effrt 2f out: styd on same pce* **33/1**

11 **6** *hd* **Sumora (IRE)**$^{28}$ [4744] 2-8-9 ... JFortune 9 86
(GAButler) *led tl 2f out: wknd appr fnl f* **11/8$^{1}$**

6115 **7** *½* **Pitch Up (IRE)**$^{28}$ [4752] 2-8-12 87 ...(b$^{1}$) GCarter 11 88
(TGMills) *chsd ldrs: kpt on same pce appr fnl f* **33/1**

1344 **8** *shd* **Bunditten (IRE)**$^{71}$ [3481] 2-8-9 96 ... FNorton 5 84
(AndrewReid) *sn chsng ldrs: fdd over 1f out* **25/1**

3430 **9** *nk* **Safari Sunset (IRE)**$^{7}$ [5295] 2-8-12 99 ... RSmith 6 86
(PWinkworth) *chsd ldrs: lost pl over 1f out* **33/1**

5130 **10** *nk* **Skywards**$^{46}$ [4217] 2-8-12 100 ...(t) KMcEvoy 2 85
(SaeedBinSuroor) *w ldrs: led 2f out: hung lft: hdd over 1f out: sn btn* **7/1$^{3}$**

1104 **11** *hd* **Beckermet (IRE)**$^{24}$ [4860] 2-8-12 100 ... KFallon 8 84
(RFFisher) *w ldrs: edgd lft 2f out: lost pl over 1f out* **11/2$^{2}$**

60.36 secs (-1.06) **Going Correction** -0.20s/f (Firm) **11** Ran SP% **117.0**
Speed ratings: **100,96,95,94,91 90,90,89,89,88 88**CSF £65.55 TOTE £13.00: £2.90, £2.30, £3.60; EX 60.00 Trifecta £737.20 Part won. Pool: £1,038.32. 0.50 winning tickets..
**Owner** Ivan Allan **Bred** High Bramley Grange Stud Ltd **Trained** Newmarket, Suffolk

**FOCUS**
An up-to-scratch renewal, and the form looks solid, though the time was modest for a juvenile Group Two. The first four home were all stepping back from six furlongs.

**NOTEBOOK**
**Chateau Istana** returned to form after a disappointing run at Newmarket, which was attributed to an infection. Tongue-tied for the first time, he was a decisive winner, showing much improved form. Fast ground seems a must, and there is no reason why he should not get the sixth furlong.
**Tournedos(IRE)**, back in trip, made his move at the same time as the winner but could not match that rival in the final furlong. Conceding 3lb, this was a decent effort.
**Kissing Lights(IRE)**, another who has been running over six furlongs, had to wait for a run otherwise she might well have finished second. A stiffer test over five furlongs or return to six would be of benefit. *Official explanation: jockey said filly was denied a clear run*
**Amazin** missed the break and did well to finish as close as he did. A return to six furlongs will suit him.
**Bond City(IRE)** ran a fair race but is exposed now. He has not run over six furlongs since his debut but could be worth another try at that trip.
**Sumora(IRE)**, tackling colts for the first time, travelled well in a narrow lead but did not find much when tackled. A return to waiting tactics may suit her better. *Official explanation: jockey said filly ran too free in early stages*
**Pitch Up(IRE)**, blinkered for the first time, ran creditably on ground which would have been faster than ideal. *Official explanation: jockey said colt was unsuited by the firm, good to firm places ground*
**Skywards**, racing on the outside, took a slight lead with two to run but was not helping his rider and was quickly on the retreat. *Official explanation: jockey said colt hung left in final two furlongs*
**Beckermet(IRE)** *Official explanation: jockey said gelding was never travelling*

## 5465 TORNE VALLEY FARM & COUNTRY STORE H'CAP — 1m 4f

**4:20** (4:22) (B1) (0-110,104) 3-Y-O+ **£13,795** (£4,244; £2,122; £1,061) **Stalls** Low

Form — RPR

1120 **1** **Mutasallil (USA)**[35] 4540 4-9-3 **100**........(t) RHills 9 — 110+
(SaeedBinSuroor) *led: qcknd over 4f out: narrowly hdd 1f out: kpt on wl to ld nr fin* **9/2**[2]

2600 **2** *shd* **Pagan Dance (IRE)**[24] 4858 5-8-9 **92**........(p) RLMoore 8 — 102
(MrsAJPerrett) *hld up in tch: effrt 2f out: narrow ld 1f out: hung lft: hdd nr fin* **9/2**[2]

0111 **3** *5* **Wunderwood (USA)**[48] 4163 5-9-7 **104**........ SSanders 6 — 106
(LadyHerries) *trckd ldrs: chal over 2f out: fdd over 1f out* **7/4**[1]

4440 **4** *2 1/2* **Bagan (FR)**[25] 4831 5-8-7 **90** oh3........ KMcEvoy 1 — 88
(HRACecil) *hld up in tch: rdn over 2f out: kpt on: nvr rchd ldrs* **10/1**

2543 **5** *2* **Hello It's Me**[14] 5106 3-7-10 **91** oh3 ow1........ RThomas(3) 5 — 86
(HJCollingridge) *chsd ldrs: effrt over 3f out: wknd 2f out* **7/1**[3]

011/ **6** *2 1/2* **Total Turtle (IRE)**[729] 4584 5-9-6 **103**........ JFortune 3 — 94
(PFICole) *dwlt: hld up in rr: nvr on terms* **12/1**

0400 **7** *3* **Turbo (IRE)**[25] 4831 5-8-8 **91**........(p) SCarson 4 — 77
(GBBalding) *hld up in rr: sme hdwy on wd outside over 2f out: nvr on terms* **12/1**

0040 **8** *1 3/4* **Albanov (IRE)**[7] 5288 4-8-10 **93**........ KFallon 2 — 76
(MJohnston) *trckd ldrs: effrt over 3f out: lost pl over 2f out* **14/1**

2m 29.15s (-6.55) **Going Correction** -0.15s/f (Firm)
**WFA** 3 from 4yo+ 9lb — **8** Ran SP% **116.4**
Speed ratings: **115,114,111,109,108 106,104,103**CSF £25.53 CT £48.25 TOTE £5.40: £2.00, £2.00, £1.40; EX 30.90.
**Owner** Godolphin **Bred** Shadwell Farm Llc **Trained** Newmarket, Suffolk

**FOCUS**
A decent handicap and a very smart time indeed for the grade. The first two finished clear and the race could be rated a few pounds higher, although it is hard to see why Pagan Dance would have improved.

**NOTEBOOK**
**Mutasallil(USA)** reverted to front-running tactics on this step up in trip. Winding up the pace turning into the home straight, he gamely held off a half-hearted challenge from the runner-up. He is capable of a further improvement.
**Pagan Dance(IRE)**, tackling this trip for the first time since finishing second to Wunderwood in the Duke Of Edinburgh at Royal Ascot, was 12lb better off with that rival here. He had every chance, but put his head in the air and was denied by a tougher opponent. He has yet to win a handicap although has plenty of decent form in that sphere.
**Wunderwood(USA)**, another 5lb higher on this return to a mile and a half, had his chance but was left behind quite easily by the first two in the final furlong.
**Bagan(FR)**, who was 3lb out of the handicap, ran a better race on this faster ground but could never get in a blow.
**Hello It's Me**, 3lb out of the handicap for this step up in grade, was found wanting over this longer trip.
**Total Turtle(IRE)** had not run since beating Doncaster Cup dead-heater Kasthari in the Mallard Handicap at this meeting two years ago. Resuming from a 12lb higher mark, he could never get into the hunt over an inadequate trip but this was a satisfactory return to action.
**Turbo(IRE)** *Official explanation: jockey said gelding was unsuited by good to firm ground*
**Albanov(IRE)** *Official explanation: jockey said gelding would not let itself down on the ground*

## 5466 TRILOGY NIGHTCLUB DONCASTER NURSERY — 7f

**4:55** (4:57) (D2) (0-85,84) 2-Y-O **£7,280** (£2,240; £1,120; £560) **Stalls** High

Form — RPR

2262 **1** **Malinsa Blue (IRE)**[7] 5307 2-8-12 **75**........ FNorton 11 — 83
(JAGlover) *mid-div: hdwy over 1f out: r.o wl to ld last 100yds: hld on wl* **20/1**

3210 **2** *3/4* **Turnaround (GER)**[25] 4836 2-9-1 **78**........ JFortune 4 — 84+
(MrsJRRamsden) *hld up in rr: stdy hdwy on stands' side 2f out: r.o wl: no ex wl ins last* **8/1**

6423 **3** *3/4* **Cerebus**[9] 5240 2-8-10 **73**........ KFallon 10 — 77
(NPLittmoden) *chsd ldrs: no ex ins last* **4/1**[1]

312 **4** *1 1/2* **Zomerlust**[11] 5212 2-9-3 **80**........ RWinston 6 — 80
(JJQuinn) *hld up: effrt over 2f out: styd on fnl f* **5/1**[2]

5312 **5** *3/4* **Dove Cottage (IRE)**[23] 4890 2-8-2 **68**........ RThomas(3) 14 — 66
(WSKittow) *lw: w ldrs: led over 3f out tl over 1f out: kpt on same pce* **7/1**[3]

515 **6** *hd* **Dry Ice (IRE)**[54] 3983 2-9-7 **84**........ DaneO'Neill 2 — 82
(HCandy) *lw: trckd ldrs: led over 1f out: hdd ins last: wknd* **8/1**

2351 **7** *5* **Secret History (USA)**[15] 5098 2-8-12 **75**........ RHills 15 — 60
(MJohnston) *chsd ldrs: drvn along over 2f out: lost pl over 1f out* **10/1**

031 **8** *1 1/2* **Cape Quest**[31] 4637 2-9-6 **83**........ RLMoore 9 — 65
(RHannon) *w ldrs: wknd over 1f out* **7/1**[3]

6514 **9** *2 1/2* **Treat Me Wild (IRE)**[22] 4914 2-8-10 **73**........ RSmith 12 — 48
(RHannon) *mid-div: drvn along over 3f out: no imp* **25/1**

0360 **10** *nk* **Along The Nile**[11] 5212 2-8-7 **70**........ MartinDwyer 1 — 45
(MrsJRRamsden) *reluctant to r and t.o: hdwy fnl 2f: nvr nrr* **20/1**

400 **11** *1/2* **Vision Victory (GER)**[95] 2758 2-7-7 **61** oh1........ DFox(5) 8 — 34
(TPTate) *stmbld and lost pl after 1f: sn bhd* **66/1**

0130 **12** *shd* **Three Pennies**[41] 4365 2-8-9 **72**........ SWKelly 5 — 45
(MDods) *t.k.h: led over 3f: sn wknd* **50/1**

500 **13** *5* **Tiffin Deano (IRE)**[71] 3476 2-7-6 **62**........ DFentiman(7) 7 — 23
(PCHaslam) *chsd ldrs: lost pl over 2f out: sn bhd* **66/1**

61 **14** *2 1/2* **Love And Laughter (IRE)**[41] 4359 2-8-12 **75**........ SSanders 13 — 29
(TDEasterby) *chsd ldrs: lost pl over 2f out: sn bhd* **7/1**[3]

1m 27.43s (-0.38) **Going Correction** -0.20s/f (Firm) — **14** Ran SP% **123.8**
Speed ratings: **94,93,92,90,89 89,83,82,79,78 78,78,72,69**CSF £168.40 CT £807.24 TOTE £23.40: £4.60, £3.70, £1.90; EX 317.70 Place 6 £440.02, Place 5 £82.63..
**Owner** Mrs Andrea M Mallinson **Bred** Martin Donovan **Trained** Carburton, Notts

**FOCUS**
A decent nursery and the form looks very solid. The first six finished clear.

**NOTEBOOK**
**Malinsa Blue(IRE)** quickened up well from just off the pace to take command and was always going to hold the runner-up. Probably on the upgrade, she has an action that suggests this sort of ground is ideal.
**Turnaround(GER)** was gradually switched over to the stands' side from his low draw. He was briefly short of room and was left with plenty to do, but came home in good style. While he is not straightforward, he looks capable of making amends over this trip.
**Cerebus**, a pound higher, ran a solid race but could not produce a change of gear in the final furlong. This looks her trip.
**Zomerlust**, who stayed on quite nicely, can be ridden more positively now he has proved his stamina at this trip and is probably capable of a bit better.
**Dove Cottage(IRE)**, just a pound higher than when runner-up at the Ebor meeting, ran up to form on this different ground.
**Dry Ice(IRE)**, under topweight, travelled well before striking the front but was worn down inside the last.
**Three Pennies** *Official explanation: jockey said filly was too keen in early stages*
**Love And Laughter(IRE)** *Official explanation: jockey said filly was unsuited by the firm, good to firm places ground*
T/Plt: £680.20 to a £1 stake. Pool: £97,984.75. 105.15 winning tickets. T/Qpdt: £35.50 to a £1 stake. Pool: £7,116.60. 148.15 winning tickets. WG

# 5147 GOODWOOD (R-H)

Saturday, September 11

**OFFICIAL GOING: Good to firm**

## 5467 EUROPEAN BREEDERS FUND GG RACING CLUB MAIDEN STKS — 1m

**2:00** (2:02) (D2) 2-Y-O **£5,629** (£1,732; £866; £433) **Stalls** High

Form — RPR

**1** **Emile Zola** 2-8-9........ NDeSouza(5) 12 — 76
(MPTregoning) *leggy: trckd ldrs: clsd 2f out: eased out jst over 1f out: nudged along and styd on to ld last stride* **12/1**

05 **2** *shd* **Eva Soneva So Fast (IRE)**[15] 5091 2-9-0........ JQuinn 14 — 76
(JLDunlop) *dwlt: sn rcvrd and prom: trckd ldr 3f out: drvn to ld narrowly last 100yds: hdd fnl stride* **7/2**[2]

**3** *nk* **Royal Jet** 2-9-0........ ACulhane 7 — 79+
(MRChannon) *lengthy: unf: lw: dwlt: wl in rr and rn green: rdn and prog 3f out: swtchd to inner and r.o fnl f: gaining fast at fin* **7/1**[3]

6 **4** *hd* **Tamatave (IRE)**[29] 4728 2-9-0........(t) WSupple 9 — 75
(SaeedBinSuroor) *lw: t.k.h: trckd ldr: led 3f out: hrd pressed fnl 2f: hdd and one pce last 100yds* **5/2**[1]

**5** *3/4* **Loch Quest (IRE)** 2-9-0........ JFanning 4 — 73
(MrsAJPerrett) *w'like: trckd ldrs: effrt and cl up 2f out: one pce and hld fnl f* **16/1**

0 **6** *3* **Tiamo**[29] 4730 2-8-11........ FPFerris(3) 2 — 67
(MHTompkins) *prom: cl up 2f out: wknd fnl f* **20/1**

**7** *6* **Honour High** 2-9-0........ IMongan 5 — 53
(LadyHerries) *w'like: str: lost pl over 5f out: rdn and struggling over 3f out: no ch after* **12/1**

00 **8** *1* **In Dream'S (IRE)**[68] 3588 2-9-0........ EAhern 1 — 51
(BGubby) *led to 3f out: wknd over 2f out* **33/1**

**9** *nk* **Raise A Tune (IRE)** 2-9-0........ VSlattery 10 — 51
(JAOsborne) *str: settled in rr: drvn and struggling over 3f out* **25/1**

**10** *shd* **Groundcover** 2-9-0........ SDrowne 6 — 50+
(MrsAJPerrett) *w'like: scope: lengthy: bit bkwd: outpcd in last after 2f: wl bhd 3f out: nvr a factor* **8/1**

**11** *2 1/2* **Sole Agent (IRE)** 2-9-0........ RBrisland 3 — 45
(GLMoore) *w'like: dwlt: a in last pair: bhd fnl 3f* **20/1**

04 **12** *4* **Pralin Star (IRE)**[17] 5034 2-9-0........ GBaker 13 — 36
(MrsHSweeting) *hld up towards rr: gng wl 3f out: sn rdn and wknd rapidly* **50/1**

1m 42.69s (2.42) **Going Correction** +0.15s/f (Good) — **12** Ran SP% **113.9**
Speed ratings: **93,92,92,92,91 88,82,81,81,81 78,74**CSF £48.21 TOTE £12.30: £3.20, £1.90, £2.20; EX 54.60.
**Owner** Sheikh Mohammed **Bred** Snailwell Stud Co Ltd **Trained** Lambourn, Berks

**FOCUS**
A modest maiden with only about a length covering the first five home. The race is rated through the runner-up, suggesting the form is not exceptional.

**NOTEBOOK**
**Emile Zola**, a half-brother to useful miler Pole Star, was well drawn for this debut but is bred to do much better over farther as a three-year-old, so it was surprising that he had the speed to win here. His rider had to wait to switch him approaching the final furlong, but he responded well and stayed on to win with more in hand than the margin suggests. He has a future.
**Eva Soneva So Fast(IRE)**, who is improving with every run, had not run on ground as quick as this before but was well drawn. He had just taken the eventual fourth's measure when the winner came with his well-timed run, and now looks nursery bound.
**Royal Jet**, a half-brother to several middle-distance winners, notably smart older filly Red Carnation, Red Fort, and November Handicap winner Red Wine, is clearly bred to do much better over farther next year. He shaped with plenty of promise, finishing well having run green.
**Tamatave(IRE)** ran a solid race in what was admittedly a modest event, leading from early in the straight until losing three places inside the final half furlong.
**Loch Quest(IRE)**, who cost $150,000, is a half-brother to a multiple sprint winner in the USA. His stable's juveniles usually come on quite a bit for their first run.
**Tiamo** ran much better than he did on his debut on this quicker ground.

## 5468 CHICHESTER OBSERVER H'CAP — 7f

**2:35** (2:37) (C1) (0-100,99) 3-Y-O+ **£12,553** (£4,761; £2,380; £1,082) **Stalls** High

Form — RPR

5110 **1** **Ettrick Water**[49] 4120 5-8-13 **94**........(v) NMackay(3) 12 — 109
(LMCumani) *trckd clr ldrs: prog 2f out: rdn to ld jst over 1f out: sn in command* **9/1**

0003 **2** *1 3/4* **Boston Lodge**[44] 4273 4-9-4 **96**........(v) EAhern 8 — 106
(GABulter) *racd midfield: rdn over 2f out: prog wl over 1f out: chsd wnr ins fnl f: no imp* **12/1**

-031 **3** *nk* **Golden Sahara (IRE)**[44] [4273] 3-9-2 **98**..............................(t) WSupple 11 107
(SaeedBinSuroor) *lw: trckd clr ldrs: clsd gng wl 2f out: effrt over 1f out: r.o but nt pce of wnr* **8/1[3]**

1112 **4** *1 ¼* **Pango**[21] [4931] 5-8-8 **86**.......................................... SDrowne 3 92
(HMorrison) *racd midfield: rdn and effrt 2f out: styd on fr over 1f out: nvr able to chal* **8/1[3]**

3202 **5** *1* **Jedburgh**[23] [4873] 3-9-3 **99**.......................................... IMongan 13 102
(JLDunlop) *lw: trckd ldng pair: led over 2f out: hdd jst over 1f out: wknd ins fnl f* **5/1[1]**

4023 **6** *hd* **Kool (IRE)**[14] [5112] 5-8-6 **89**.......................................... NDeSouza(5) 7 92+
(PFICole) *horse stl wearing hood as stalls opened: towards rr: effrt over 2f out : shuffled along and kpt on fnl f* **12/1**

315 **7** *½* **Nashaab (USA)**[22] [4908] 7-8-9 **90**.......................................... FPFerris(3) 5 92+
(PDEvans) *racd towards rr: rdn and struggling 3f out: r.o ins fnl f: no ch* **33/1**

0000 **8** *hd* **Master Robbie**[28] [4742] 5-8-1 **86**.......................................... TO'Brien(7) 9 87
(MRChannon) *racd on outer in midfield: effrt over 2f out: one pce and no imp on ldrs* **20/1**

0020 **9** *shd* **Royal Storm (IRE)**[2] [5422] 5-9-7 **99**.......................................... JCrowley 10 100
(MrsAJPerrett) *lw: chsd ldr to 3f out: sn chsd new ldr: upsides over 1f out: wknd fnl f* **10/1**

0660 **10** *½* **Vindication**[76] [3337] 4-8-7 **88**..............................(t) RMiles(3) 2 87
(JRFanshawe) *hld up in last trio: gng easily over 2f out: nudged along and hanging rt fnl 2f: nvr nr ldrs* **25/1**

0000 **11** *shd* **Sir George Turner**[35] [4530] 5-9-0 **92**.......................................... JFanning 15 91+
(MJohnston) *chsd clr ldrs: clsd 2f out: nt clr run twice over 1f out: wknd ins fnl f* **33/1**

0022 **12** *nk* **Digital**[14] [5112] 7-8-12 **90**.......................................... ACulhane 14 88
(MRChannon) *dwlt: t.k.h and hld up in midfield: rdn 3f out: no prog* **7/1[2]**

0000 **13** *1* **Barbajuan (IRE)**[56] [3943] 3-8-10 **92**..............................(b) SWhitworth 1 88
(NACallaghan) *racd in last pair: rdn 3f out: no real prog* **50/1**

0030 **14** *2 ½* **Uhoomagoo**[43] [4287] 6-8-9 **94**..............................(b) AMullen(7) 4 83
(KARyan) *nvr gng wl in last pair: hrd rdn 3f out: no ch after* **11/1**

-500 **15** *2 ½* **Grizedale (IRE)**[14] [5112] 5-8-12 **90**..............................(t) JQuinn 6 73
(JAkehurst) *hld up wl in rr: rdn 3f out: wknd 2f out* **20/1**

2031 **16** *2 ½* **Pizazz**[45] [4236] 3-8-7 **92**..............................(b) JFMcDonald(3) 16 68
(BJMeehan) *led at breaknk pce to over 2f out: wknd rapidly over 1f out* **7/1[2]**

1m 26.25s (-1.78) **Going Correction** +0.15s/f (Good)
**WFA** 3 from 4yo+ 4lb **16** Ran SP% **127.9**
Speed ratings: **116,114,113,112,111 110,110,110,109,109 109,108,107,104,102 99**CSF £108.64 CT £925.09 TOTE £11.20: £3.60, £3.70, £2.00, £2.20; EX 149.50.
**Owner** Mrs E H Vestey **Bred** Wickfield Farm Partnership **Trained** Newmarket, Suffolk

**FOCUS**
A competitive handicap run at a strong pace in a cracking time. There was little trouble in running and the form looks solid.

**NOTEBOOK**
**Ettrick Water** likes to lead but Pizazz went off so fast that he could never entertain the hope of making the running. It did not seem to bother him, though, as he picked up well inside the final quarter mile to go on and win well, showing significantly improved form. He had not been hit too hard by the Handicapper for his last win and raced off just a 2lb higher mark.
**Boston Lodge** ran his usual sort of race to finish in the places again.
**Golden Sahara(IRE)**, 5lb worse off with Boston Lodge compared with their last meeting here when he had that rival behind him, looked to be travelling well entering the final furlong but the winner found a change of pace which he could not match.
**Pango** ran a respectable race but the Handicapper may just have his measure for the time being.
**Jedburgh** was well drawn and ran a solid race given that he chased the strong pace. He does himself few favours, handicap-mark wise, with his consistency, though.
**Kool(IRE)** ran well given what happened at the start, but he is another whose consistency means that he is done few favours by the Handicapper.
**Royal Storm(IRE)**, making a quick reappearance, did not help himself by chasing such a strong pace.
**Vindication**, off the track for almost 11 weeks due to a minor injury, was poorly drawn and never got into the race. His rider was easy on him and there should be better to come with this run under his belt.
**Uhoomagoo** *Official explanation: jockey said gelding was never travelling*
**Pizazz** set a ridiculously fast pace which gave him no chance of getting home.

## 5469 STARDOM STKS (LISTED RACE) 1m
3:05 (3:08) (A1) 2-Y-O **£14,500** (£5,500; £2,750; £1,250) **Stalls** High

Form RPR

146 **1** **Hearthstead Wings**[65] [3672] 2-8-11 99.......................................... JFanning 4 98
(MJohnston) *swtg: mde virtually all: rdn 2f out: def advantage 1f out: styd on wl* **10/3[2]**

0442 **2** *1 ¼* **Destinate (IRE)**[22] [4919] 2-8-11 100.......................................... EAhern 3 96
(RHannon) *lw: trckd ldng pair: rdn 3f out: nt qckn: styd on ins fnl f: tk 2nd last stride* **9/2[3]**

3214 **3** *shd* **Capable Guest (IRE)**[25] [4835] 2-8-11 100.............................. ACulhane 1 95
(MRChannon) *w wnr: rdn wl over 2f out: hld fnl f: lost 2nd last stride* **2/1[1]**

3 **4** *nk* **Nice Tune**[9] [5247] 2-8-6.......................................... JQuinn 2 90
(CEBrittain) *hld up in last pair: pushed along and no prog 2f out: rdn and styd on fnl f: nvr nrr* **10/1**

1004 **5** *1 ¼* **Alta Petens**[41] [4365] 2-8-6 77.......................................... SDrowne 6 87
(MLWBell) *trckd ldng pair: rdn over 2f out: cl up over 1f out: fdd fnl f* **20/1**

215 **6** *3 ½* **Park Law (IRE)**[51] [4060] 2-8-6 89.......................................... RHavlin 5 79
(JHMGosden) *b. hind: hld up in last pair: rdn wl over 2f out: no prog and btn wl over 1f out* **10/3[2]**

1m 41.26s (0.99) **Going Correction** +0.15s/f (Good) **6** Ran SP% **111.5**
Speed ratings: **101,99,99,99,98 94**CSF £18.14 TOTE £4.80: £2.50, £2.50; EX 20.90.
**Owner** Hearthstead Homes Ltd **Bred** M P B Bloodstock Ltd **Trained** Middleham Moor, N Yorks

**FOCUS**
Not a strong Listed race and the pace was only modest, suggesting the form is ordinary for the grade. Reservations about how it will work out.

**NOTEBOOK**
**Hearthstead Wings** is bred to stay well on his sire's side, and the step up to a mile brought about the improvement required. Given his own way in front, he did not go a mad gallop, and kept on resolutely to see the trip out well.
**Destinate(IRE)** finished behind the winner in the Superlative Stakes and once again had to follow him home. He ran a solid race but will have to find improvement from somewhere to win at this level.
**Capable Guest(IRE)**, fourth in the Acomb Stakes last time out, a race whose form has taken one or two knocks of late, had his chance but was outstayed.
**Nice Tune**, pitched in at the deep end on only her second start having finished third in a Salisbury maiden nine days earlier, was staying on well at the finish to be closest at the line. She could surely win a maiden on this form, but her trainer does not always take the easy route, and black type may be the aim.
**Alta Petens** was beaten in a nursery last time and her performance does not do a lot for the value of the form.
**Park Law(IRE)** ran poorly again and has questions to answer now.

## 5470 MIRROR IMAGE STKS (H'CAP) 1m 1f
3:40 (3:41) (C1) (0-100,97) 3-Y-O+ **£13,877** (£4,270; £2,135; £1,067) **Stalls** High

Form RPR

0065 **1** **Gold History (USA)**[14] [5106] 3-8-10 **92**.......................................... JFanning 9 102
(MJohnston) *trckd ldng pair: led over 1f out and kicked on: drvn fnl f: hld on* **10/1**

0300 **2** *hd* **King's County (IRE)**[56] [3937] 6-9-0 **93**.......................................... NMackay(3) 2 103
(LMCumani) *hld up midfield: prog 2f out: chsd wnr over 1f out: kpt on ins fnl f: jst hld* **10/1**

0040 **3** *nk* **Chinkara**[46] [4214] 4-8-10 **89**.......................................... JFMcDonald(3) 7 98+
(BJMeehan) *t.k.h: hld up midfield: nt clr run over 2f out to over 1f out: plld out and hanging rt: r.o fnl f: gaining fin* **7/1[2]**

3-11 **4** *1* **Exterior (USA)**[15] [5076] 3-8-9 **91**.......................................... SDrowne 10 98
(MrsAJPerrett) *lw: trckd ldrs: rdn over 2f out: nt pce to chal over 1f out: styd on ins fnl f* **9/4[1]**

6051 **5** *1* **Krugerrand (USA)**[19] [5004] 5-8-13 **89**.......................................... EAhern 5 94
(WJMusson) *trckd ldrs: effrt over 2f out: disp 2nd pl over 1f out to ins fnl f: no ex* **8/1[3]**

6200 **6** *hd* **Alrafid (IRE)**[46] [4214] 5-8-9 **85**.......................................... IMongan 6 90
(GLMoore) *hld up towards rr: rdn over 2f out: no prog tl styd on u.p fnl f* **12/1**

2300 **7** *½* **Consonant (IRE)**[23] [4887] 7-8-13 **89**.......................................... SRighton 1 93
(DGBridgwater) *hld up in last: sme prog 3f out: sn rdn: styd on ins fnl f: n.d* **25/1**

01- **8** *8* **Vaughan**[310] [5932] 3-8-10 **92**.......................................... ACulhane 11 80
(MrsAJPerrett) *s.i.s: hld up in last trio: rdn 3f out: sn struggling* **14/1**

0300 **9** *1 ½* **Tuning Fork**[14] [5134] 4-8-12 **88**.......................................... JQuinn 4 73
(JAkehurst) *led: rdn and hdd over 1f out: wknd and heavily eased fnl f* **14/1**

3200 **10** *nk* **Maghanim**[44] [4273] 4-9-7 **97**.......................................... WSupple 8 81
(JLDunlop) *lw: hld up in last trio: shkn up over 2f out: sn wknd* **8/1[3]**

0014 **11** *1 ½* **Langford**[35] [4543] 4-8-7 **86**.......................................... FPFerris(3) 3 67
(MHTompkins) *lw: plld hrd: trckd ldr to 2f out: wknd rapidly* **8/1[3]**

1m 56.35s (-0.51) **Going Correction** +0.15s/f (Good)
**WFA** 3 from 4yo+ 6lb **11** Ran SP% **119.7**
Speed ratings: **108,107,107,106,105 105,105,98,96,96 95**CSF £107.81 CT £768.55 TOTE £14.70: £4.40, £4.20, £2.60; EX 141.90.
**Owner** Abdulla Buhaleeba **Bred** W S Farish And E J Hudson Jr Irrevocable Trust **Trained** Middleham Moor, N Yorks

**FOCUS**
A decent handicap, although recent winning form was thin on the ground. The form looks sound.

**NOTEBOOK**
**Gold History(USA)** did not get to the front but his rider appeared happy enough to track the leader. 2lb lower than at Beverley, he is suited by fast ground, and the drop back from ten furlongs was in his favour, but he had little in hand at the finish.
**King's County(IRE)** put a couple of poor performances during the summer behind him on this return from an eight-week break, and could be one to look out for this autumn as he goes well with cut in the ground.
**Chinkara**, back over the intermediate trip he has won over twice before, travelled well but the gap just did not come for him early enough. He finished well enough, but all too late, and he remains 5lb higher than for his last win.
**Exterior(USA)** was a clear-cut winner over the course and distance on soft ground last time, but the Handicapper's reaction was to put him up 8lb. Conditions were very different this time.
**Krugerrand(USA)** did not look to have been overpunished by the Handicapper for his Windsor success, but he is the type who has to be delivered late and needs everything to fall just right.
**Alrafid(IRE)** looks held off his current mark.
**Tuning Fork** *Official explanation: jockey said colt hung right*

## 5471 STARLIT STKS (LISTED RACE) 6f
4:15 (4:15) (A1) 3-Y-O+ **£17,400** (£6,600; £3,300; £1,500) **Stalls** Low

Form RPR

**1** **Var (USA)**[253] 5-9-0..............................(b) JQuinn 2 112
(CEBrittain) *w'like: lengthy: wnt rt s: mde all: rdn over 1f out: styd on wl fnl f* **16/1**

2323 **2** *1 ½* **Ruby Rocket (IRE)**[49] [4159] 3-8-7 105.......................................... SDrowne 7 102
(HMorrison) *in tch: chsd wnr over 2f out: drvn over 1f out: kpt on but no imp fnl f* **11/8[1]**

0405 **3** *½* **So Will I**[28] [4745] 3-9-2 106.......................................... WSupple 1 110
(MPTregoning) *in tch: rdn 2f out: sn chsd ldng pair: styd on same pce* **7/2[2]**

0 **4** *1 ½* **Lydgate (USA)**[88] [2955] 4-9-7 106..............................(t) EAhern 6 108
(SaeedBinSuroor) *b: lw: racd on outer: hld up: shkn up 2f out: one pce and no imp* **4/1[3]**

0306 **5** *1 ½* **Colonel Cotton (IRE)**[50] [4091] 5-9-0 98.......................................... ACulhane 3 97
(NACallaghan) *squeezed out s: racd last: rdn over 2f out: no hdwy* **14/1**

5002 **6** *3* **Atavus**[14] [5121] 7-9-0 92.......................................... AMcCarthy 5 88
(GGMargarson) *chsd wnr to over 2f out: sn lost pl u.p* **9/1**

2005 **P** **Coconut Penang (IRE)**[14] [5121] 4-9-0 93.......................................... SWhitworth 4 —
(PWChapple-Hyam) *in tch: hrd rdn 2f out: stmbld and broke down 1f out: p.u ins fnl f: dead* **12/1**

1m 12.2s (-0.64) **Going Correction** +0.15s/f (Good)
**WFA** 3 from 4yo+ 2lb **7** Ran SP% **114.6**
Speed ratings: **110,108,107,105,103 99,**—CSF £38.88 TOTE £11.80: £2.40, £1.70; EX 31.90.
**Owner** Mohammed Rashid **Bred** Dr John Eaton **Trained** Newmarket, Suffolk

**FOCUS**
Var got the run of the race but should not be considered a lucky winner. The form has provisionally been taken at face value, but there is a doubt about how solid it will prove.

**NOTEBOOK**
**Var(USA)**, making his debut in this country, was having his first run since January. He did get the run of the race, but he was a clear winner and, given the weakness of the sprinting division, it should not come as a total surprise that a multiple winner from the USA is capable of ruffling a few feathers in Pattern grade over here. He may run in the Dubai Duty Free Cup at Newbury.
**Ruby Rocket(IRE)**appeared to have plenty in hand of her rivals on official ratings, and in fairness she did beat all her rivals with form in this country, but she found the ex-American winner too strong. Her trainer subsequently reported that she had done little work since coming back from Ireland seven weeks earlier, so she should come on for this run.
**So Will I** has not really progressed since his win in this grade at Newbury in the spring.
**Lydgate(USA)**, another ex-American performer, had been off the track since Royal Ascot. He had a bit on his plate under his penalty and made heavy weather of it on the outside of the pack. His rider suggested that the pace had not been strong enough for him.
**Colonel Cotton(IRE)** is a difficult horse to win with at the best of times and had plenty to do in this company.

**Coconut Penang(IRE)** was in the process of running a decent race when breaking down badly. Sadly, he had to be destroyed.

## 5472 RACING UK LIVE ON 432 STKS (H'CAP) 2m
**4:50** (4:50) (D2) (0-85,85) 3-Y-O+ **£6,938** (£2,135; £1,067; £533) **Stalls** High

Form RPR

0154 **1** **Land 'n Stars**[66] 3644 4-9-2 **79** ................ RMiles[(3)] 3 89
(JamiePoulton) *cl up: effrt to ld 2f out: drvn fnl f: hld on* **15/2**

0200 **2** *hd* **Escayola (IRE)**[63] 3725 4-9-11 **85** ................(v) WSupple 12 95
(WJHaggas) *t.k.h: hld up: prog 3f out: drvn 2f out: styd on to press wnr wl ins fnl f: jst hld* **7/1**[3]

250- **3** *1 ¼* **Corton (IRE)**[393] 4143 5-9-6 **80** ................ EAhern 6 88
(PFICole) *wl in tch: trckd ldrs gng easily over 3f out: led briefly over 2f out: sn rdn to chse wnr: no ex ins fnl f* **33/1**

0260 **4** *5* **Riyadh**[8] 5274 6-8-11 **71** oh5................ JFanning 11 73
(MJohnston) *dwlt: hld up last of main gp: prog and cruising 3f out: sn fnd nil and lost pl: one pce over 1f out* **11/1**

003 **5** *1* **Enhancer**[26] 4819 6-8-10 **73**................ JFMcDonald[(3)] 14 74
(MrsLCJewell) *lw: hld up in tch: prog to chse ldrs over 4f out: rdn and btn 2f out* **33/1**

6344 **6** *nk* **Pope's Hill (IRE)**[15] 5100 3-7-9 **71**................(b[1]) NMackay[(3)] 5 71
(LMCumani) *settled towards rr: effrt on outer 4f out: rdn and no hdwy over 2f out* **9/1**

2300 **7** *½* **Theatre (USA)**[15] 5093 5-9-3 **77**................ AMcCarthy 1 77
(JamiePoulton) *chsd ldrs: rdn over 5f out: sn lost pl: wl bhd 3f out: kpt on again fnl f* **16/1**

14-3 **8** *1* **Aurelia**[40] 4389 3-8-4 **77**................ JQuinn 13 76
(SirMarkPrescott) *dwlt: hld up in rr: prog to trck ldrs 3f out: sn rdn: wknd 2f out* **6/1**[2]

0141 **9** *3 ½* **Stoop To Conquer**[13] 5152 4-9-3 **77**................ IMongan 7 71
(JLDunlop) *lw: t.k.h: led after 6f to 6f out: rdn over 3f out: steadily wknd* **7/1**[3]

4043 **10** *3* **Almizan (IRE)**[21] 4934 4-9-8 **82**................(v) ACulhane 9 73
(MRChannon) *in tch: rdn 5f out: struggling and btn over 3f out* **9/2**[1]

01 **11** *1* **Magical Quest**[36] 4513 4-9-11 **85**................ SDrowne 8 75
(MrsAJPerrett) *led at stdy pce for 6f: styd prom: wknd fr over 2f out* **8/1**

0004 **12** *2* **Establishment**[13] 5152 7-8-11 **71** oh8................ SWhitworth 4 58
(CACyzer) *hld up: slipped bdly and nrly uns rdr bnd 12f out: nt rcvr* **33/1**

0311 **13** *2* **Moonshine Beach**[12] 5205 6-8-6 **71**................ AQuinn[(5)] 10 56
(PWHiatt) *prom: led 6f out to over 2f out: wknd rapidly* **8/1**

3m 31.59s (0.93) **Going Correction** +0.15s/f (Good) **13** Ran SP% **124.5**
**WFA** 3 from 4yo+ 13lb
Speed ratings: **103,102,102,99,99 99,98,98,96,95 94,93,92**CSF £60.97 CT £1644.17 TOTE £9.30: £2.90, £3.00, £10.20; EX 127.60.
**Owner** Kenneth Wilkinson **Bred** C A Cyzer **Trained** Telscombe, E Sussex

**FOCUS**
A fair handicap, but they went very steadily in the early stages and it turned into something of a sprint. As a result the form has not been rated as highly as it might have been.

**NOTEBOOK**
**Land 'n Stars** was successful in a tactical affair at Ascot earlier in the season and once again showed that he is very effective when the early pace is not strong. He is an intended runner in the Cesarewitch, but the pace is likely to be much quicker at Newmarket.
**Escayola(IRE)**, returning from a mid-season break, ran on well for second and would probably have preferred a stronger pace. He is at his best when the ground is like this.
**Corton(IRE)** was making a belated seasonal reappearance and shaped with plenty of promise. He saw this longer trip out well off this steady gallop and, although his ability to see it out in a more strongly-run affair remains in question, this was a promising return to action.
**Riyadh** was travelling well with two furlongs to run, but he found nothing under pressure and is one to be wary of these days.
**Enhancer**, stepping up in trip on his handicap debut, could only find the one pace in the closing stages and would probably have preferred a stronger all-round pace.
**Pope's Hill(IRE)** did not improve for the first-time blinkers.
**Stoop To Conquer** raced too keenly off the slow early pace.
**Almizan(IRE)** was surprisingly made favourite on ground he has never shown a liking for. His record on good to firm now reads 44054980.
**Establishment** *Official explanation: jockey said gelding slipped on first right hand bend*

## 5473 PLANTATION STKS (H'CAP) 5f
**5:25** (5:26) (E3) (0-70,70) 3-Y-O **£3,495** (£1,075; £537; £268) **Stalls** Low

Form RPR

0212 **1** **Who's Winning (IRE)**[9] 5253 3-9-6 **69**................ JFanning 1 80
(BGPowell) *racd nr side: mde all: gng easily 2f out: rdn and kpt on fnl f* **4/1**[1]

2602 **2** *1* **Sir Loin**[14] 5104 3-8-11 **60**................(v[1]) ACulhane 16 67
(NTinkler) *racd on wd outside: in tch: drvn to go 2nd over 1f out: styd on ins fnl f: a hld* **9/1**

0-40 **3** *hd* **King Egbert (FR)**[26] 4810 3-8-7 **56**................ WSupple 3 62
(AWCarroll) *lw: outpcd and pushed along in rr over 3f out: prog u.p over 1f out: styd on: nrst fin* **25/1**

3040 **4** *¾* **Urban Rose**[28] 4740 3-8-11 **60**................(tp) MHenry 13 63
(RMHCowell) *racd in rr: sme prog 2f out: styd on fnl f: nrst fin* **25/1**

0015 **5** *¾* **Tizzy's Law**[14] 5117 3-9-2 **65**................ JQuinn 7 65
(MABuckley) *wnt rt s and bmpd: chsd ldrs: rdn 2f out: one pce fr over 1f out* **11/1**

0000 **6** *¾* **Dolce Piccata**[30] 4688 3-9-4 **70**................(b) JFMcDonald[(3)] 6 67
(BJMeehan) *mostly chsd wnr: drvn 2f out: fdd jst over 1f out* **14/1**

1420 **7** *½* **Maluti**[26] 4800 3-8-4 **56** oh1................ NMackay[(3)] 8 51
(RGuest) *hmpd s: last and detached fr rest: sme prog 1/2-way: nt clr run over 1f out: kpt on fnl f* **11/1**

0061 **8** *½* **La Vie Est Belle**[14] 5117 3-9-1 **64**................ GBaker 10 57
(BRMillman) *lw: prom: rdn 1/2-way: fdd over 1f out* **13/2**[3]

5U06 **9** *nk* **Melody King**[23] 4874 3-8-9 **61**................(v) FPFerris[(3)] 15 53
(PDEvans) *s.i.s: racd in centre: chsd ldrs to 1/2-way: sn struggling* **14/1**

4500 **10** *nk* **Cut And Dried**[35] 4547 3-9-0 **63**................ SWhitworth 9 54
(DMSimcock) *bmpd s: a towards rr: no prog over 1f out* **25/1**

0060 **11** *2 ½* **Baylaw Star**[12] 5193 3-8-8 **64**................(b[1]) AMullen[(7)] 2 45
(KARyan) *lw: racd nr side: chsd ldrs 2f: struggling fr 1/2-way* **14/1**

4005 **12** *nk* **Must Be So**[37] 4469 3-8-0 **56** oh26................(t) CHaddon[(7)] 11 36
(JJBridger) *sn rdn: struggling in rr fr 1/2-way* **50/1**

424 **13** *nk* **Short Chorus**[30] 4688 3-8-9 **58**................(p) IMongan 4 36
(JBalding) *racd midfield: rdn and lost pl over 2f out: no ch after* **10/1**

0203 **14** *½* **Imperium**[14] 5117 3-9-4 **67**................ SDrowne 12 43
(MrsStefLiddiard) *racd towards centre: chsd ldrs 3f: wknd* **14/1**

100 **15** *hd* **Dave (IRE)**[18] 5020 3-8-8 **62**................ NDeSouza[(5)] 5 38
(JRBest) *prom to 1/2-way: wknd u.str.p* **6/1**[2]

5015 **16** *1 ¼* **Simpsons Mount (IRE)**[91] 2889 3-9-3 **66**................ EAhern 14 37
(RMFlower) *mounted on crse: s.i.s: racd centre: chsd ldrs to 1/2-way: wknd* **14/1**

59.64 secs (0.59) **Going Correction** +0.15s/f (Good) **16** Ran SP% **130.2**
Speed ratings: **101,99,99,97,96 95,94,93,93,92 88,88,87,87,86 84**CSF £40.61 CT £875.05 TOTE £5.10: £1.90, £2.10, £6.70, £6.30; EX 50.60 Place 6 £466.38, Place 222.02..
**Owner** Tony Head and Caroline Andrus **Bred** Colin Kennedy **Trained** Morestead, Hants

**FOCUS**
A modest handicap and ordinary form, although it looks sound enough for the level.

**NOTEBOOK**
**Who's Winning(IRE)**, a well-backed favourite, has been in good form of late and made the most of his favourable stands'-side draw to make every yard. He is equally effective over six furlongs.
**Sir Loin** ran well from his wide draw, showing good speed througout. The first-time visor appeared to have a positive effect, and while in this form he should soon break his duck.
**King Egbert(FR)** stayed on late in the day to run his best race to date. On this evidence he could be worth another try over six furlongs.
**Urban Rose**, wearing cheekpieces for the first time, kept on well from her wide draw to post a creditable effort.
**Tizzy's Law** ran a fair race on ground plenty quick enough.
**Dolce Piccata** has dropped 22lb in the handicap this term and looks to need even more mercy.
**Maluti**, squeezed out at the start, made good progress to reach a challenging position but was then denied a clear run. He would have finished closer given more luck.
**Simpsons Mount(IRE)** *Official explanation: jockey said gelding hung left*
T/Plt: £1,922.50 to a £1 stake. Pool: £50,301.90. 19.10 winning tickets. T/Qpdt: £125.60 to a £1 stake. Pool: £2,733.60. 16.10 winning tickets. JN

# 5058 MUSSELBURGH (R-H)
Saturday, September 11
**OFFICIAL GOING: Good (good to firm in places)**

## 5474 TOTESPORT.COM H'CAP 1m
**1:50** (1:50) (C1) (0-100,94) 3-Y-O **£15,103** (£5,728; £2,864; £1,302) **Stalls** Low

Form RPR

2153 **1** **Flipando (IRE)**[14] 5120 3-8-13 **86**................ MFenton 6 94
(TDBarron) *trckd ldrs: hdwy to ld over 2f out: sn rdn: drvn ins last and kpt on gamely* **7/2**[2]

5131 **2** *½* **Mrs Moh (IRE)**[37] 4490 3-8-11 **84**................ JMackay 5 91
(TDEasterby) *chsd ldrs: hdwy 3f out: chal wl over 1f out and sn rdn ev ch tl drvn and wandered ins last: no ex nr fin* **9/2**[3]

3502 **3** *1 ¼* **Penrith (FR)**[19] 4988 3-8-13 **86**................ RFfrench 8 90
(MJohnston) *chsd ldr: effrt over 2f out and sn rdn: ev ch tl drvn and one pce wl ins last* **10/3**[1]

13 **4** *2* **United Nations**[141] 1587 3-9-7 **94**................(v[1]) TPQueally 3 94
(DRLoder) *in tch: hdwy 3f out: sn rdn and kpt on same pce appr last* **7/1**

0004 **5** *¾* **Parkview Love (USA)**[28] 4737 3-8-8 **88**................ WHogg[(7)] 2 86
(MJohnston) *bhd: hdwy over 2f out: sn rdn and kpt on u.p fnl f: nrst fin* **11/1**

-010 **6** *½* **Redwood Rocks (IRE)**[123] 2019 3-8-9 **82**................ FLynch 1 79
(BSmart) *led: rdn along 3f out: sn hdd and grad wknd* **16/1**

6666 **7** *8* **Kelucia (IRE)**[42] 4322 3-9-6 **93**................ PaulEddery 7 71
(JSGoldie) *s.i.s: a rr* **12/1**

435 **8** *16* **Mister Marmaduke**[16] 5062 3-8-4 **80** oh1................ TEaves[(3)] 4 21
(ISemple) *chsd ldrs on inner: rdn along 3f out: sn wknd and eased fnl f* **8/1**

1m 41.21s (-1.49) **Going Correction** -0.025s/f (Good) **8** Ran SP% **109.0**
Speed ratings: **106,105,104,102,101 101,93,77**CSF £17.69 CT £49.53 TOTE £4.80: £1.40, £1.60, £1.50; EX 19.50.
**Owner** Mrs J Hazell **Bred** Denis McDonnell **Trained** Maunby, N Yorks

**FOCUS**
A decent handicap but the top weight was rated 6lb below the ceiling for this race and the form looks ordinary for the grade.

**NOTEBOOK**
**Flipando(IRE)** had never raced beyond seven furlongs and had gained both his previous wins over six furlongs, but he stayed this trip well and ran out a determined winner. He has more options open to him now he has proved his stamina and is progressing.
**Mrs Moh(IRE)** only just failed to defy a 4lb rise in the weights for her recent Haydock success. She is also progressing and remains one to keep on the right side of.
**Penrith(FR)** simply appeared to lack the pace of the front two in the closing stages and looks well worth another try over further.
**United Nations**, not seen since disappointing at Sandown 141 days previously, was fitted with a visor for his return but again failed to build on his Wood Ditton success. He may be best watched for the time being.
**Parkview Love(USA)** was a Listed winner at two and started this season rated 104, but he is not progressing and was again well held. However, he was staying on in the closing stages and may be worth a try over ten furlongs.
**Mister Marmaduke** *Official explanation: jockey said gelding moved badly throughout*

## 5475 JOHN SMITH'S EXTRA SMOOTH MEDIAN AUCTION MAIDEN STKS 5f
**2:20** (2:21) (E3) 2-Y-O **£4,095** (£1,260; £630; £315) **Stalls** Low

Form RPR

30 **1** **Folga**[33] 4607 2-8-9 ................ JMackay 6 68
(JGGiven) *keen: trckd ldrs: hdwy and pushed along 1/2-way: rdn to ld 1f out: styd on* **20/1**

040 **2** *1* **Bob's Flyer**[5] 5334 2-8-9 ................ RFfrench 1 64
(JGGiven) *chsd ldrs: pushed along and hdwy over 1f out: swtchd rt and rdn ins last: kpt on* **12/1**

00 **3** *1* **Percheron (IRE)**[15] 5098 2-9-0 ................ GGibbons 8 66
(PABlockley) *cl up: effrt 2f out and ev ch tl rdn and one pce ins last* **100/1**

522 **4** *¾* **Howards Princess**[19] 4986 2-8-9 73................ TPQueally 2 58
(JSGoldie) *chsd ldrs tl outpcd 1/2-way: swtchd rt: rdn and hdwy over 1f out: sn drvn and one pce fnl f* **5/2**[2]

3 **5** *1* **Pedlar Of Dreams (IRE)**[56] 3950 2-8-9 ................ MFenton 3 54
(TDBarron) *chsd ldrs: rdn along 1/2-way: drvn and no imp appr last* **15/8**[1]

4036 **6** *1 ¼* **Llamadas**[9] 5233 2-8-11 67................(b) TEaves[(3)] 4 55
(MDods) *s.i.s: a rr* **13/2**

02 **7** *shd* **Bond Puccini**[11] 5209 2-9-0 ................ FLynch 7 55
(BSmart) *qckly away and sn led: swtchd lft to stands rail after 1f: rdn along 2f out: drvn and hdd 1f out: sn wknd* **9/2**[3]

04 **8** *1 ¼* **Thornber Court (IRE)**[12] 5192 2-8-9 ................ PaulEddery 5 45
(ABerry) *s.i.s: a rr* **33/1**

61.84 secs (1.44) **Going Correction** +0.175s/f (Good) **8** Ran SP% **111.3**
Speed ratings: **95,93,91,90,89 87,86,84**CSF £219.85 TOTE £26.70: £4.80, £2.40, £13.30; EX 180.10.

**Owner** Peter Onslow **Bred** P Onslow **Trained** Willoughton, Lincs

**FOCUS**

A weak maiden and the from does not appear worth a great deal and should not be taken at face value, with the first three in the betting appearing to run below form.

**NOTEBOOK**

**Folga** offered some promise on her debut when with a different trainer, but failed to build on that next time. Having her first start for James Given, she posted a career-best effort to get off the mark in decisive fashion. She should not be too harshly treated for this success and can get competitive in ordinary nurseries.

**Bob's Flyer** found this easier than the Bath maiden she contested on her previous start and found only her stablemate too good. A similarly minor race may come her way.

**Percheron(IRE)** travelled quite well, but he found little under pressure and carried his head high. This did, however, represent improved form.

**Howards Princess** had appeared to be going the right way but this was disappointing. A step up in trip should suit, but she does not look worthy of her rating of 73.

**Pedlar Of Dreams(IRE)** failed to build on the promise she showed on her debut at Ripon.

**Bond Puccini** had today's runner-up behind when second at Ripon on his previous start, so this has to be considered disappointing. However, he is now qualified for a handicap mark and may do better in that sphere.

## 5476 BLISS MAIDEN AUCTION STKS — 7f 30y

**2:50** (2:51) (E3) 2-Y-O — **£4,075** (£1,254; £627; £313) **Stalls** Low

| Form | | | | RPR |
|---|---|---|---|---|
| 5543 | **1** | | **Profit's Reality (IRE)**[25] 4824 2-8-11 77 ... GGibbons 4<br>(PABlockley) *trckd ldng pair: hdwy over 2f out: rdn to ld over 1f out: clr ins last* **7/2**[2] | 80 |
| 2300 | **2** | *2 ½* | **Mceldowney**[7] 5307 2-8-10 77 ... RFfrench 7<br>(MJohnston) *led: rdn along 2f out: drvn and hdd over 1f out: kpt on same pce ins last* **11/2**[3] | 73 |
| 063 | **3** | *4* | **Fadael (IRE)**[34] 4579 2-8-5 72 ... MFenton 2<br>(PWD'Arcy) *trckd ldng pair: effrt on outer over 2f out: sn rdn and kpt on same pce* **11/2**[3] | 58 |
| 0 | **4** | *½* | **Mangrove Cay (IRE)**[20] 4966 2-8-10 ... TPQueally 5<br>(DRLoder) *cl up: effrt and evc hance over 2f out: sn rdn and btn wl over 1f out* **6/5**[1] | 62 |
| 0565 | **5** | *4* | **Scorpio Sally (IRE)**[14] 5109 2-8-3 63 ... JMackay 6<br>(MDHammond) *sn rdn along and a outpcd in rr* **16/1** | 45 |
| 00 | **6** | *½* | **Ansells Legacy (IRE)**[21] 4930 2-8-10 ... FLynch 1<br>(ABerry) *s.i.s: a rr* **25/1** | 51 |
| 00 | **7** | *12* | **Smiling Starduster (IRE)**[19] 4997 2-8-5 ow1 ... TEaves(3) 3<br>(DCarroll) *sn rdn along and a rr* **66/1** | 20 |

1m 29.94s (0.41) **Going Correction** -0.025s/f (Good) **7** Ran SP% **109.7**

Speed ratings: **96,93,88,88,83 82,69**CSF £20.88 TOTE £4.70: £2.00, £2.70; EX 17.40.

**Owner** Phones Direct Partnership **Bred** Michael Munnelly **Trained** Southwell, Notts

**FOCUS**

This looked a fair event on paper, but only the winner ran to his rating. The placed horses failed to justify their marks, and the proximity of the last two tempers confidence, suggesting most of these will probably be maidens for a little while yet.

**NOTEBOOK**

**Profit's Reality(IRE)** had been shaping as tough in need of this trip and, finally given a chance over it, he ran out a comfortable winner. He looks high enough in the handicap and could yet go up for this success, but appeals as the type to do well in nurseries.

**Mceldowney**, with the blinkers left off this time, ran well enough from the front but was simply no match for the winner. A minor race should come his way.

**Fadael(IRE)**, dropped back from a mile, was well held and did not show enough to justify her rating of 72.

**Mangrove Cay(IRE)**, who won his race on the wrong side on his debut at Folkestone, did not build on that effort and may do better when handicapped.

**Scorpio Sally(IRE)** may find things easier in nurseries, although her rating of 63 looks high enough.

## 5477 KRONENBOURG NURSERY — 1m

**3:25** (3:28) (E3) (0-75,73) 2-Y-O — **£6,942** (£2,136; £1,068; £534) **Stalls** Low

| Form | | | | RPR |
|---|---|---|---|---|
| 0006 | **1** | | **Succession**[13] 5142 2-8-11 **63** ... JMackay 8<br>(SirMarkPrescott) *trckd ldng pair: hdwy to ld over 2f out: rdn clr appr last: styd on* **7/1**[3] | 75+ |
| 056 | **2** | *2* | **Kerry's Blade (IRE)**[25] 4824 2-8-11 **63** ... GFaulkner 9<br>(PCHaslam) *towards rr: gd hdwy on outer over 2f out: rdn and styd on wl fnl f* **16/1** | 71 |
| 633 | **3** | *3 ½* | **Dancing Shirl**[15] 5083 2-7-13 **58** ... LeanneKershaw(7) 6<br>(CWFairhurst) *bhd: swtchd outside and hdwy 2f out: sn rdn and kpt on fnl f: nrst fin* **33/1** | 58 |
| 430 | **4** | *1 ½* | **Lodgician (IRE)**[46] 4208 2-9-1 **70** ... THamilton(3) 13<br>(JJQuinn) *dwlt: hdwy and in tch 1/2-way: effrt over 2f out: sn rdn and kpt on same pce appr last* **12/1** | 67 |
| 6406 | **5** | *2* | **Royal Flynn**[16] 5059 2-8-10 **65** ... TEaves(3) 4<br>(MDods) *bhd tl styd on fnl 2f: nrst fin* **33/1** | 57 |
| 0410 | **6** | *3* | **Lisa Mona Lisa (IRE)**[22] 4909 2-9-2 **73** ... MLawson(5) 7<br>(VSmith) *chsd ldrs: rdn along 3f out: drvn 2f out and sn one pce* **10/1** | 59 |
| 0002 | **7** | *nk* | **Diatonic**[78] 3278 2-8-10 **62** ... MFenton 3<br>(DCarroll) *behind tl styd on fnl 2f* **33/1** | 47 |
| 4646 | **8** | *1 ¾* | **Zantero**[9] 5234 2-8-10 **62** ... GGibbons 14<br>(RPElliott) *chsd ldng pair: hdwy over 2f out: sn rdn: drvn and hung rt ent last: sn wknd* **6/1**[2] | 43+ |
| 500 | **9** | *¾* | **Dover Street**[51] 4048 2-8-10 **62** ... PaulEddery 11<br>(PWD'Arcy) *bhd tl sme late hdwy* **7/1**[3] | 41 |
| 3323 | **10** | *shd* | **Brace Of Doves**[38] 4445 2-9-0 **71** ... PMakin(5) 1<br>(TDBarron) *cl up: effrt over 2f out and ev ch tl rdn and wandered wl over 1f out: sn wknd* **4/1**[1] | 50 |
| 0056 | **11** | *2* | **Davy Crockett**[44] 4256 2-9-3 **69** ... FLynch 5<br>(BSmart) *led: rdn along 3f out: drvn and hdd over 2f out: wknd over 1f out* **11/1** | 44 |
| 056 | **12** | *1 ½* | **Speagle (IRE)**[58] 3870 2-8-11 **63** ... TPQueally 10<br>(EJO'Neill) *in tch on inner: rdn along 3f out: sn wknd* **20/1** | 35 |
| 2305 | **13** | *½* | **Exit Smiling**[42] 4326 2-9-6 **72** ... RFfrench 2<br>(MJohnston) *chsd ldrs: rdn along 3f out: sn wknd* **9/1** | 42 |
| 6510 | **14** | *3* | **Uredale (IRE)**[38] 4445 2-9-0 **66** ... MTebbutt 12<br>(MrsADuffield) *a rr* **25/1** | 30 |

1m 42.6s (-0.10) **Going Correction** -0.025s/f (Good) **14** Ran SP% **117.7**

Speed ratings: **99,97,93,92,90 87,86,84,84,84 82,80,80,77**CSF £103.30 CT £3381.07 TOTE £9.00: £3.30, £7.70, £5.60; EX 210.60.

**Owner** Dr Catherine Wills **Bred** St Clare Hall Stud **Trained** Newmarket, Suffolk

■ Stewards Enquiry : G Gibbons caution: careless riding

**FOCUS**

Succession showed herself ahead of the Handicapper on this nursery debut and should progress, but the form is pretty modest in behind, with the possible exception of Zantero, and this is not a race to get carried away with.

**NOTEBOOK**

**Succession ◆**, well held in for runs in maidens, showed significant improvement on her nursery debut to get off the mark in good style. She wandered around under pressure and her rider had to be quite hard on her, suggesting she was not doing that much in front. Well handicapped and open to further improvement, she should follow up under a penalty and will probably rack up a sequence. *Official explanation: trainer's representative said, regarding the improved form shown, filly benefited from the good ground*

**Kerry's Blade(IRE)**, making her nursery debut, like the winner showed improved form and looks up to winning a similar event. However, he is flattered to get so close to Succession and it is probably worth remembering he was beaten in a maiden claimer two starts previously.

**Dancing Shirl**, beaten in claiming company on her two previous starts, ran respectably on her nursery debut, but was never really a threat and may be best watched until she steps up to ten furlongs.

**Lodgician(IRE)**, well held in three runs in maidens, did not run a bad race on his nursery debut but does look on a high enough mark.

**Royal Flynn**, beaten in a seven-furlong seller on his previous start, gives a good guide to the strength of the form.

**Lisa Mona Lisa(IRE)** was a long way below form on this first run over a mile.

**Zantero**, racing over a mile for the first time, may have done a little bit too much to take up a prominent position and could be worth another chance.

**Brace Of Doves** had been running consistently and promised to be suited by this step up to a mile, but he was most disappointing.

**Uredale(IRE)** *Official explanation: jockey said colt was never travelling*

## 5478 STEPHEN HAY ASSOCIATES MAIDEN STKS — 1m

**3:55** (3:55) (D3) 3-Y-O — **£4,065** (£1,251; £625; £312) **Stalls** Low

| Form | | | | RPR |
|---|---|---|---|---|
| 3052 | **1** | | **Just A Fluke (IRE)**[19] 4987 3-9-0 72 ... RFfrench 5<br>(MJohnston) *hld up in tch: pushed along 3f out: sn rdn and hdwy over 1f out: drvn to ld ins last: kpt on* **5/4**[1] | 71 |
| 335 | **2** | *nk* | **The Number**[16] 5063 3-8-11 64 ... TEaves(3) 2<br>(ISemple) *held up in tch: hdwy 3f out: led over 1f out: sn rdn and hung lft and rt: hdd ins last: drvn and styd on towards fin* **9/1** | 70 |
| 4500 | **3** | *3* | **Graceful Air (IRE)**[9] 5236 3-8-6 52 ... THamilton(3) 4<br>(JRWeymes) *chsd ldin g pair: hdwy 3f out: rdn and ev ch 2f out tl drvn and one pce ent last* **25/1** | 58 |
| 024- | **4** | *shd* | **Five Years On (IRE)**[267] 6212 3-9-0 73 ... MFenton 6<br>(WJHaggas) *led 2f: cl up tl led again over 3f out: rdn 2f out: sn drvn and hdd over 1f out: wknd* **15/8**[2] | 63 |
| 0 | **5** | *2* | **Harrycat (IRE)**[14] 5123 3-9-0 ... JMackay 1<br>(VSmith) *trckd ldrs: hdwy on outer 3f out and ev ch tl rdn: wandered and wknd over 1f out* **11/2**[3] | 58 |
| 4000 | **6** | *10* | **Colloseum**[35] 4537 3-8-7 52 ... KristinStubbs(7) 3<br>(TJEtherington) *dwlt: rapid hdwy to ld after 2f: hdd over 3f out and sn wknd* **100/1** | 35 |

1m 42.59s (-0.11) **Going Correction** -0.025s/f (Good) **6** Ran SP% **109.4**

Speed ratings: **99,98,95,95,93 83**CSF £12.63 TOTE £2.00: £1.60, £2.50; EX 7.00.

**Owner** Maktoum Al Maktoum **Bred** Gainsborough Stud Management Ltd **Trained** Middleham Moor, N Yorks

**FOCUS**

Yet another weak maiden that is rated through the runner-up, and not a race to dwell on.

**NOTEBOOK**

**Just A Fluke(IRE)** was well regarded to at two, but he has never really delivered on the racecourse and, although finally winning, he only scraped home and remains no more than a fair performer.

**The Number** ran very well considering he would have been 8lb better off with the winner in a handicap and clearly has a minor race in him, although this will not have done his rating any good.

**Graceful Air(IRE)**, a long-standing maiden rated just 52, ran creditably but gives a good guide to the strength of the form.

**Five Years On(IRE)**, last of four when a beaten favourite on his final start at two 267 days previously, was again below his best on this step up from five furlongs and he has it to prove now.

**Harrycat(IRE)** was again well held and should find things easier when he is handicapped.

## 5479 WATCH LIVE ON RACING UK H'CAP — 1m 6f

**4:30** (4:30) (E3) (0-70,66) 3-Y-O+ — **£6,812** (£2,096; £1,048; £524) **Stalls** High

| Form | | | | RPR |
|---|---|---|---|---|
| -054 | **1** | | **Minivet**[19] 4990 9-8-8 **51** ... PMulrennan(3) 3<br>(RAllan) *trckd ldrs: hdwy 5f out: chal over 2f out: sn rdn and led over 1f out: drvn out* **11/1** | 63 |
| 0022 | **2** | *3* | **Sharadi (IRE)**[14] 5116 3-9-1 **66** ... JoannaBadger 7<br>(VSmith) *led: rdn along 3f out: hdd wl over 1f out and n.m.r: kpt on u.p fnl f* **9/2**[2] | 74 |
| 2062 | **3** | *3* | **Most Definitely (IRE)**[42] 4352 4-9-8 **62** ... MFenton 8<br>(TDEasterby) *midfield: smooth hdwy 5f out: chal on bit 2f out: shkn up to ld briefly over 1f out: sn rdn and one pce* **5/1**[3] | 67 |
| 0021 | **4** | *1 ¼* | **Turn Of Phrase (IRE)**[9] 5238 5-9-3 **60** ... (v) THamilton(3) 4<br>(RAFahey) *hld up: hdwy over 4f out: effrt to chse ldrs over 2f out: sn rdn and no imp* **2/1**[1] | 63 |
| 0505 | **5** | *5* | **The Ring (IRE)**[48] 4174 4-9-8 **65** ... (v[1]) TEaves(3) 5<br>(KGReveley) *keen: trckd ldrs: pushed along over 6f out: rdn over 4f out and btn 3f out* **7/1** | 62 |
| 0-50 | **6** | *6* | **Rhetorical**[16] 5057 3-8-4 **55** ... JMackay 1<br>(SirMarkPrescott) *chsd ldr: rdn along 1/2-way: drvn and wknd over 4f out* **7/1** | 45 |
| 560- | **7** | *3* | **Culcabock (IRE)**[136] 5534 4-8-11 **51** oh1 ... GFaulkner 2<br>(PMonteith) *a rr* **40/1** | 38 |
| 3125 | **8** | *9* | **Cosmic Case**[16] 5058 9-8-11 **51** oh3 ... TPQueally 9<br>(JSGoldie) *chsd ldrs: rdn along on inner 6f out: sn wknd* **10/1** | 27 |
| 00-6 | **9** | *11* | **Bridge Pal**[42] 4328 4-8-12 **52** ... RFfrench 6<br>(PMonteith) *chsd ldrs 5f: sn lost pl and bhd* **66/1** | 15 |

3m 4.83s (-0.77) **Going Correction** -0.025s/f (Good)

**WFA** 3 from 4yo+ 11lb **9** Ran SP% **114.5**

Speed ratings: **101,99,97,96,94 90,88,83,77**CSF £59.42 CT £281.90 TOTE £20.00: £2.60, £1.60, £1.70; EX 71.80 Place 6 £1,248.53, Place 5 £935.12..

**Owner** R Allan **Bred** Sir Thomas Pilkington **Trained** Cornhill-on-Tweed, Northumberland

**FOCUS**

A moderate staying handicap and ordinary form, but at least the pace was good which gives the race a solid appearance.

**NOTEBOOK**

**Minivet** had not won on the Flat since September 1999, but he offered promise returned to the level at Hamilton on his previous start and was able to confirm that, with the strong pace playing into his hands.

**Sharadi(IRE)**, still a maiden, ran respectably on ground slightly faster than ideal but just keeps finding one too good.

**Most Definitely(IRE)** did not find quite as much as had looked likely under pressure and remains a maiden after 18 starts.
**Turn Of Phrase(IRE)**, 6lb higher than when successful at Carlisle on his previous start, should have been suited by this step back up in trip but turned in a disappointing effort.
**The Ring(IRE)** failed to return to form in a first-time visor.
T/Plt: £2,417.70 to a £1 stake. Pool: £33,451.40. 10.10 winning tickets. T/Qpdt: £66.00 to a £1 stake. Pool: £2,330.20. 26.10 winning tickets. JR

5480 - (Foreign Racing) - See Raceform Interactive

# 4783 LEOPARDSTOWN (L-H)

## Saturday, September 11

**OFFICIAL GOING: Good to firm**

## 5481a 02 KILTERNAN STKS (LISTED RACE) 1m 2f
**2:20** (2:20) 3-Y-0+ **£27,507** (£8,070; £3,845; £1,309)

RPR
1 **Acropolis (IRE)**[315] 5883 3-8-12 100 ....(t) JPSpencer 4 107+
(APO'Brien, Ire) *hld up in rr: 5th appr st: hdwy into 3rd 1f out: edgd lft cl home: led nr fin* **2/1**[1]
2 ½ **Lord Admiral (USA)**[7] 5312 3-8-12 100 .... JPMurtagh 5 103
(CharlesO'Brien, Ire) *attempted to make all: qcknd ent st: strly pressed ins fnl f: hdd nr fin* **10/1**
3 ½ **Trefflich (GER)**[18] 5029 3-8-12 107 .... MJKinane 6 102
(JohnMOxx, Ire) *settled 3rd: 4th after 1/2-way: rdn st: 2nd and swtchd rt 1f out: 3rd whn bmpd cl home: kpt on* **7/2**[3]
4 1½ **Misty Heights**[13] 5162 3-8-13 103 .... PShanahan 1 100
(DKWeld, Ire) *hld up: last and pushed along 3f out: kpt on st* **10/1**
5 ¾ **Napper Tandy (IRE)**[76] 3355 4-9-5 106 ....(b) KJManning 3 98
(JSBolger, Ire) *trckd ldrs in 4th: impr into 3rd after 1/2-way: chal appr st: no ex fr 2f out* **9/2**
6 1 **Medicinal (IRE)**[34] 4587 3-9-2 107 ....(b) PJSmullen 2 100
(DKWeld, Ire) *trckd ldrs in 2nd: rdn ent st: 4th and no ex whn checked 1f out: eased* **3/1**[2]

2m 4.40s **Going Correction** -0.425s/f (Firm)
**WFA** 3 from 4yo 7lb 6 Ran SP% **116.9**
Speed ratings: **107,106,106,105,104 103**CSF £23.55 TOTE £3.60: £2.00, £4.60; DF 63.20.
**Owner** Michael Tabor **Bred** Quay Bloodstock & Samac Ltd **Trained** Ballydoyle, Co Tipperary

**NOTEBOOK**
**Acropolis(IRE)**, making a belated reapperance, was well supported and showed an effective turn of foot. Inclined to hang in left when challenging to lead close home, he predictably survived the Stewards' inquiry. He does not look an entirely straightforward ride, but should be capable of stepping up on this.
**Lord Admiral(USA)**paid his Down Royal conqueror Coat Of Honour a substantial tribute.
**Trefflich(GER)** left his disappointing run in bad ground at Tralee well behind him. He made contact with the winner close home but could hardly be considered unlucky.
**Misty Heights** had plenty to do turning for home, she took a few smacks and ran on to some extent but was never able to challenge the colts.
**Napper Tandy(IRE)** had his chance turning in but this remains a bogey track for him.
**Medicinal(IRE)** was beaten when finding trouble just over a furlong down and was eased.

## 5483a BAILEYS IRISH CHAMPION STKS (GROUP 1) 1m 2f
**3:30** (3:30) 3-Y-0+ **£407,746** (£133,098; £62,676; £20,422)

RPR
1 **Azamour (IRE)**[88] 2956 3-8-11 118 .... MJKinane 8 126
(JohnMOxx, Ire) *hld up in rr: 7th and rdn ent st: 4th 1f out: r.o strly to ld nr fin* **8/1**
2 ½ **Norse Dancer (IRE)**[25] 4834 4-9-4 .... JFEgan 1 125
(DRCElsworth) *trckd ldrs in 4th: impr into 2nd 1 1/2f out: led under 1f out: kpt on wl: hdd nr fin* **20/1**
3 nk **Powerscourt**[28] 4768 4-9-4 117 ....(b[1]) JPSpencer 2 124
(APO'Brien, Ire) *cl up in 2nd: led ent st: sn qcknd clr: strly pressed over 1f out: hdd under 1f out: kpt on* **11/1**
4 ¾ **Grey Swallow (IRE)**[76] 3353 3-8-11 124 .... PJSmullen 6 123
(DKWeld, Ire) *settled 5th: prog early st: 3rd 1 1/2f out: no imp ins fnl f: kpt on* **9/2**[2]
5 ½ **Rakti**[70] 3540 5-9-4 .... PRobinson 4 122
(MAJarvis) *s.i.s: hld up in 6th: kpt on u.p st* **5/1**[3]
6 2 **Imperial Dancer**[10] 5225 6-9-4 .... SHitchcott 7 118
(MRChannon) *towards rr: last into st: rdn and no imp* **66/1**
7 ¾ **Doyen (IRE)**[49] 4121 4-9-4 .... LDettori 3 —
(SaeedBinSuroor) *settled 3rd: 2nd and effrt ent st: no imp fr 2f out: wknd and eased ins fnl f* **4/5**[1]
8 15 **Millstreet**[25] 4834 5-9-4 ....(t) TEDurcan 5 —
(SaeedBinSuroor) *led: hdd ent st: wknd qckly: eased fnl f* **100/1**

2m 1.90s **Going Correction** -0.425s/f (Firm)
**WFA** 3 from 4yo+ 7lb 8 Ran SP% **117.1**
Speed ratings: **117,116,116,115,115 113,113,101**CSF £133.67 TOTE £10.90: £1.80, £2.90, £1.50; DF 152.90.
**Owner** H H Aga Khan **Bred** H H Aga Khan **Trained** Currabeg, Co Kildare

**NOTEBOOK**
**Azamour(IRE)** looked in tremendous shape physically on his first appearance since Royal Ascot. Held up, he came from off the pace on the outside, delivering a sustained challenge to get on top close home as jockeyship played a major role. He got this longer trip well and Newmarket's Dubai Champion Stakes appears the next likely option.
**Norse Dancer(IRE)** ran fourth on the inside of the favourite, holding his position throughout. Closing early in the straight, he led just inside the last and looked like springing a major shock. He pulled out plenty but appeared to prick his ears and idle briefly and was picked off in the last few strides.
**Powerscourt** ran second and stole a couple of lengths early in the straight as the Godolphin pacemaker weakened. Headed inside the last furlong, he could not quicken a second time but ran on gamely enough.
**Grey Swallow(IRE)** gave the impression beforehand that however he fared in the race there would be a bit more to come and he performed like that. He made smooth enough progress early in the straight and was third with over a furlong and a half to race. He kept on without being abused, on ground that might have been a bit fast for him, and has to be the prime contender from his age group in the Arc.
**Rakti** missed the kick, apparently banging his head when leaving the stalls. He had two behind him for most of the race and just kept on at the one pace under pressure over the last furlong and a half. He certainly was not disgraced but this was not one of his going days.
**Imperial Dancer** ran on well from behind without ever promising to get on terms.
**Doyen(IRE)**, although able to hold third place during the race, was never really travelling and was on offer from three furlongs out. Second briefly as they turned for home, he dropped away from the two-furlong marker. There was no apparent physical reason for this disappointment, and it was too bad for it simply to have been the trip. Connections were mystified, but their immediate inclination was to abandon thoughts of running him in the Arc and sign him off for the season. *Official explanation: jockey said colt failed to quicken when asked and felt flat from thereon*

## 5484a COOLMORE FUSAICHI PEGASUS MATRON STKS (GROUP 1) (F&M) 1m
**4:10** (4:10) 3-Y-0+ **£119,014** (£34,788; £16,478; £5,492)

RPR
1 **Soviet Song (IRE)**[45] 4228 4-9-2 .... JPMurtagh 7 124
(JRFanshawe) *hld up in 5th: hdwy appr st: 2nd 1 1/2f out: rdn to chal ins fnl f: led 100 yds out: comf* **8/13**[1]
2 ½ **Attraction**[27] 4795 3-8-11 .... KDarley 5 123
(MJohnston) *attempted to make all: clr ent st: strly pressed fnl f: hdd 100 yds out: no ex* **7/2**[2]
3 5 **Phantom Wind (USA)**[43] 4286 3-8-11 .... RHughes 3 111
(JHMGosden) *trckd ldrs in 3rd: 2nd early st: mod 3rd and no ex fnl f* **9/1**
4 4½ **Red Feather (IRE)**[56] 3959 3-8-11 106 ....(t) NGMcCullagh 1 101
(EdwardLynam, Ire) *chsd ldrs in 2nd: 3rd and rdn early st: 4th and no ex fr over 1f out* **20/1**
5 3½ **Yesterday (IRE)**[322] 5771 4-9-2 114 .... JPSpencer 8 93+
(APO'Brien, Ire) *chsd ldrs in 4th: 5th into st: sn no ex* **7/1**[3]
6 9 **Livadiya (IRE)**[13] 5162 8-9-2 103 .... KJManning 4 —
(HRogers, Ire) *a bhd: no imp st* **50/1**

1m 36.8s **Going Correction** -0.425s/f (Firm)
**WFA** 3 from 4yo+ 5lb 6 Ran SP% **113.4**
Speed ratings: **121,120,115,111,107 98**CSF £3.15 TOTE £1.70: £1.30, £2.10; DF 2.90.
**Owner** Elite Racing Club **Bred** Elite Racing Club **Trained** Newmarket, Suffolk

**NOTEBOOK**
**Soviet Song(IRE)** looked to have an enormous task turning for home, but she went a four-length second with just over a furlong and a half to race and got up inside the last 50yds to confirm her superiority over Attraction a shade snugly. Following this third successive Group One win in little more than two months connections will now choose between the Queen Elizabeth II Stakes or the Sun Chariot.
**Attraction** looked on good terms with herself beforehand and bounced out in front. She maintained her clear lead to the straight and the winner was her only challenger from under two furlongs out. She swished her tail under pressure inside the last but kept on bravely until finding no more once headed.
**Phantom Wind(USA)** was toiling throughout the last furlong and a half but was beaten by two outstanding fillies.
**Red Feather(IRE)** ran second but was done with early in the straight.
**Yesterday(IRE)** struggled over an inadequate trip on this her first race since a life-threatening attack of colic during the winter, but was not disgraced in the circumstances.
**Livadiya(IRE)** was totally outclassed.

5485 - 5487a (Foreign Racing) - See Raceform Interactive

# VELIEFENDI

## Saturday, September 11

**OFFICIAL GOING: Firm**

## 5488a TOPKAPI TROPHY (GROUP 2) (C&F) 1m
**2:30** (2:39) 3-Y-0+ **£83,799** (£33,520; £16,760; £8,380)

RPR
1 **Luxor (TUR)** 4-9-6 .... EYavuz 16 108
(ACoskan, Turkey) 1
2 nse **Sabirli (TUR)** 3-8-12 .... HKaratas 7 105
(CKurt, Turkey) 2
3 ½ **Ribella (IRE)** 5-9-3 .... YAkagac 9 104
(UKarakoca, Turkey)
4 nk **Lindholm (GER)**[101] 2608 5-9-6 .... THellier 14 106
(WernerGlanz, Germany) 3
5 1 **Iania (IRE)**[27] 4-9-3 .... EPedroza 8 101
(RRohne, Germany)
7 ½ **Rockets 'n Rollers (IRE)**[23] 4889 4-9-6 .... PDobbs 5 103
(RHannon) *led to 2f out, kept on one pace*
8 ½ **Corriolanus (GER)**[20] 4984 4-9-6 .... OPeslier 1 102
(PMitchell) *4th early, hampered on rail and lost place half-way, 12th straight, stayed on steadily final 2f*
9 2 **Arlecchina (GER)**[20] 4984 4-9-3 .... TJarnet 2 95
(UStoltefuss, Germany)
10 hd **Flier's Fantasy (TUR)** 5-9-6 .... NSen 3 98
(ACoflkan, Turkey) 1
11 ½ **Mary Ellen (IRE)**[364] 6-9-3 .... EValcin 11 94
(LBerkol, Turkey)
12 ½ **Dexterity (USA)**[34] 4595 6-9-6 .... C-PLemaire 6 96
(H-APantall, France)
13 nse **Bebek Cafe (TUR)** 4-9-3 .... SBoyraz 12 92
(ROzyigit, Turkey)
14 1 **Hasilat** 4-9-6 .... OSezik 4 93
(EPaparan, Turkey)
15 ¾ **Abdulbey (IRE)** 4-9-6 .... NKonu 15 92
(UAysel, Turkey)

1m 35.2s
**WFA** 3 from 4yo+ 5lb 15 Ran SP% **239.4**
Speed ratings: .
**Owner** L Kitapci **Bred** M Kitapci **Trained** Turkey

**NOTEBOOK**
**Rockets 'n Rollers(IRE)** ran an honest race, making the running, but could not match the pace of the leaders in the last quarter mile.
**Corriolanus(GER)** lost a prominent pitch before halfway before making up ground again in the closing stages. He needs further.

## 5489a BOSPHORUS CUP (GROUP 2) (C&F) 1m 4f
**3:30** (3:37) 3-Y-0+ **£83,799** (£33,520; £16,760; £8,380)

RPR
1 **Senex (GER)**[48] 4183 4-9-6 .... WMongil 6 119
(HBlume, Germany)
2 ½ **Maktub (ITY)**[41] 4380 5-9-6 .... TJarnet 1 118
(MAJarvis) *tracked leader, led 1 1/2f out, headed 100y out, ran on*
3 1 **Touch Of Land (FR)**[69] 3567 4-9-6 .... C-PLemaire 10 116
(H-APantall, France)

4 1 1/2 **Dayano (GER)**[48] 4183 3-8-10 EPedroza 9 2 113
(AWohler, Germany)
5 nse **Ultramar (TUR)** 5-9-6 HKaratas 4 114
(VBoztas, Turkey)
6 3 **Kaneko (TUR)** 3-8-10 YAkagac 8 108
(TAlkan, Turkey)
7 8 **Mity Dancer (GER)**[20] 4980 4-9-3 THellier 11 94
(DKRichardson, Germany)
8 nse **Grand Ekinoks (TUR)**[168] 1144 6-9-6 (b) SAkdi 2 1 97
(BTaskan, Turkey)
9 2 1/2 **Scream To Scream (IRE)** 4-9-6 SBoyraz 3 3 94
(TAvci, Turkey)
10 nk **Sweet Mistress (IRE)** 4-9-3 (b) SKaya 7 90
(TKose, Turkey)
11 1 **Altinordu (TUR)** 3-8-10 FCakar 5 91
(ADutal, Turkey)

2m 26.47s
**WFA** 3 from 4yo+ 9lb **11** Ran SP% **209.2**
Speed ratings: .
**Owner** Stall Meerbusch **Bred** H Greis **Trained** Germany

**NOTEBOOK**
**Senex(GER)** needs firm ground. Moving up from fourth place to challenge a furlong and a half out, he always looked to be going just better than Maktub, but could not be called the definite leader until 100 yards from home. The Hong Kong Vase is now on his agenda.
**Maktub(ITY)** chased the leader until going on three furlongs out. He did not go down without a fight when Senex drew alongside but, just as in the Gran Premio di Milano, eventually had to settle for second. A third meeting with the winner in the Hong Kong Vase is a possibility.

# 5467 GOODWOOD (R-H)

Sunday, September 12

**OFFICIAL GOING: Good to firm**

## 5490 CELER ET AUDAX NURSERY STKS (H'CAP) 6f

**2:00** (2:02) (D2) (0-85,85) 2-Y-O **£5,655** (£1,740; £870; £435) **Stalls** Low

Form RPR
1 **1** **Cyclical**[20] 4986 2-9-7 **85** LDettori 4 95
(GAButler) *str: lw: settled in last pair: prog on outer 2f out: rdn over 1f out: led ent fnl f: sn in command* **3/1**[2]
5342 **2** 1 1/2 **Cummiskey (IRE)**[6] 5351 2-8-13 **77** SDrowne 7 82
(JAOsborne) *lw: trckd ldrs: led wl over 1f out: flashed tail whn rdn: hdd ent fnl f: nt qckn* **7/4**[1]
5252 **3** 1 1/2 **Cree**[16] 5078 2-7-12 **62** oh3 LisaJones 9 63
(WRMuir) *pressed ldr: led wl over 2f out to wl over 1f out: one pce u.p* **10/1**
325 **4** 1 1/4 **Peeptoe (IRE)**[19] 5015 2-8-11 **75** TQuinn 6 72
(JLDunlop) *settled in rr: prog on outer over 2f out: drvn over 1f out: fdd ins fnl f* **11/2**[3]
2040 **5** 2 1/2 **Piddies Pride (IRE)**[6] 5351 2-8-6 **73** FPFerris(3) 3 62
(PSMcentee) *swtg: chsd ldrs: hrd rdn over 2f out: struggling and btn wl over 1f out* **14/1**
6444 **6** 7 **Kempsey**[16] 5078 2-7-12 **65** (p) JFMcDonald(3) 8 33
(JJBridger) *prom: lost pl and rdn over 2f out: hanging and wknd over 1f out: eased* **16/1**
3456 **7** 10 **Elsie Wagg (USA)**[42] 4358 2-8-7 **71** ow1 KFallon 1 9
(MJWallace) *cl up for 2f: sn outpcd and drvn: wl btn over 2f out* **10/1**
1550 **8** 5 **Trempjane**[43] 4326 2-9-2 **80** RHughes 5 3
(RHannon) *led to wl over 2f out: wknd rapidly* **33/1**

1m 14.3s (1.46) **Going Correction** +0.25s/f (Good) **8** Ran SP% **110.4**
Speed ratings: **100,98,96,94,91 81,68,61**CSF £7.99 CT £40.09 TOTE £3.30: £1.40, £1.10, £2.60; EX 7.60 Trifecta £34.20 Pool of £705.50 - 14.60 winning units..
**Owner** Cheveley Park Stud **Bred** Cheveley Park Stud Ltd **Trained** Blewbury, Oxon

**FOCUS**
A strong nursery with the first two both well treated. Cyclical could be hard for the handicapper to pin down.

**NOTEBOOK**
**Cyclical**, who confirmed market support when winning in a small field on his debut, faced no easy task on this nursery bow off a mark of 85 so did well for one so inexperienced to come through and win going away. He will need to continue improving to follow up but as he is lightly raced this is a distinct possibility.
**Cummiskey(IRE)** had every chance in second and was probably a little unlucky to come up against the winner. He will find easier races.
**Cree** ran well on this first try at six furlongs and will be home back on a softer surface.
**Peeptoe(IRE)** has failed to show any improvement the last twice and is beginning to look exposed.
**Piddies Pride(IRE)**, in great form earlier in the season, seems to have lost her form and may need a break.
**Elsie Wagg(USA)** *Official explanation: vet said filly had a higher heart rate than normal*
**Trempjane** *Official explanation: jockey said filly stopped very quickly in final furlong*

## 5491 TOTEPOOL STKS (H'CAP) 6f

**2:35** (2:35) (C1) (0-100,98) 3-Y-O+ **£15,300** (£5,803; £2,901; £1,319) **Stalls** Low

Form RPR
6022 **1** **Texas Gold**[4] 5393 6-9-0 **89** SDrowne 8 101+
(WRMuir) *trckd ldng trio: smooth prog 2f out: led jst over 1f out: sn rdn clr* **7/2**[2]
0600 **2** 1 3/4 **Cd Europe (IRE)**[29] 4759 6-8-10 **85** (p) RWinston 7 90+
(JJQuinn) *hld up in last pair: pushed along 2f out: nt clr run over 1f out: r.o to take 2nd last stride* **17/2**
0U00 **3** shd **Peruvian Chief (IRE)**[4] 5393 7-9-3 **92** KFallon 13 97
(NPLittmoden) *lw: chsd ldrs: rdn 2f out: styd on ins fnl f: no ch w wnr* **10/1**
1344 **4** hd **Two Step Kid (USA)**[43] 4324 3-9-7 **98** EAhern 1 102+
(JNoseda) *lw: sn trckd ldng pair: nt clr run over 1f out to ins fnl f: styd on nr fin* **5/2**[1]
0000 **5** shd **Spliff**[29] 4750 3-8-12 **89** DaneO'Neill 11 93
(HCandy) *pressed ldr: rdn to ld 2f out: hdd jst over 1f out: no ch w wnr: lost 3 pls nr fin* **20/1**
-000 **6** 1/2 **Impressive Flight (IRE)**[17] 5062 5-8-8 **83** RLMoore 4 86
(TDBarron) *towards rr: pushed along 1/2-way: struggling 2f out: kpt on ins fnl f* **9/1**
3043 **7** 1/2 **Mystic Man (FR)**[11] 5224 6-8-13 **88** NCallan 6 89+
(KARyan) *b: towards rr: rdn 2f out: nt clr run over 1f out to ins fnl f: kpt on* **5/1**[3]
2322 **8** 2 **Devise (IRE)**[8] 5287 5-8-10 **88** RMiles(3) 12 83
(MSSaunders) *hld up in last: prog on outer 3f out: hrd rdn and wknd 1f out* **9/1**
0100 **9** hd **Corps De Ballet (IRE)**[44] 4294 3-8-10 **87** TQuinn 9 81
(JLDunlop) *led to 2f out: cl up jst over 1f out: sn wknd* **33/1**

1m 12.62s (-0.22) **Going Correction** +0.25s/f (Good)
**WFA** 3 from 4yo+ 2lb **9** Ran SP% **114.8**
Speed ratings: **111,108,108,108,108 107,106,104,103**CSF £33.06 CT £272.25 TOTE £3.70: £1.30, £2.70, £2.30; EX 29.90 Trifecta £371.90 Pool of £4,295.40 - 8.20 winning units..
**Owner** C L A Edginton **Bred** Coln Valley Stud **Trained** Lambourn, Berks

**FOCUS**
A deserved win for Texas Gold who showed no ill-effects from his gallant second earlier in the week. Solid form, with the fifth and sixth setting the standard.

**NOTEBOOK**
**Texas Gold**, tough and consistent, came into this on the back of a brave effort in the Portland Handicap at Doncaster earlier in the week. Always going strongly, he came right away once asked to go and now looks set to run a big race in the Ayr Gold Cup if the going rides fast.
**Cd Europe(IRE)** bounced back to some kind of form with a staying-on second and is seemingly back to something like his best. He goes on soft ground and can win a race at the backend.
**Peruvian Chief(IRE)** ran one of his better races and is on a winning mark.
**Two Step Kid(USA)** was probably unlucky not to get second as he had no room when he wanted it and finished well once getting going. He does everything in his races to suggest he requires seven furlongs and looks well worth trying over it.
**Spliff** ran better and will find easier opportunities.
**Impressive Flight(IRE)** is gradually coming back into form and is one to watch out for later in the season.
**Devise(IRE)** *Official explanation: jockey said gelding ran too free early on*

## 5492 SELECT RACING UK ON SKY 432 STKS (GROUP 3) 1m 1f 192y

**3:05** (3:11) (A1) 3-Y-O+ **£29,000** (£11,000; £5,500; £2,500) **Stalls** High

Form RPR
1043 **1** **Alkaadhem**[44] 4285 4-9-0 107 (b[1]) WSupple 8 114
(MPTregoning) *trckd ldrs: gng easily 3f out: effrt to ld over 1f out: edgd lft but sn clr* **11/2**[3]
-302 **2** 2 1/2 **Battle Chant (USA)**[13] 5180 4-9-0 102 RLMoore 6 109
(MrsAJPerrett) *uns rdr and bolted bef s: hld up: prog 3f out: n.m.r over 1f out: plld out and kpt on to take 2nd on line* **16/1**
3052 **3** shd **Salselon**[11] 5225 5-9-0 118 (b) KFallon 4 109
(LMCumani) *hld up in tch: pushed along and no rspnse 3f out: effrt to chse wnr 1f out: fnd little and no imp* **7/2**[2]
0112 **4** 5 **Muqbil (USA)**[36] 4539 4-9-0 114 RHills 7 99
(JLDunlop) *lw: sn trckd ldr: chal and upsides 3f out: edgd rt over 1f out : sn wknd* **11/8**[1]
2020 **5** 1 1/4 **Vespone (IRE)**[29] 4768 4-9-0 112 (t) LDettori 3 97
(SaeedBinSuroor) *lw: led: jnd 3f out: bmpd over 1f out: sn hdd & wknd* **7/2**[2]
-014 **6** 3/4 **Pawn Broker**[15] 5134 7-9-0 109 DaneO'Neill 1 96
(DRCElsworth) *hld up in last pair: pushed along 3f out: no rspnse and btn 2f out* **16/1**
5300 **7** 12 **Sir Haydn**[22] 4950 4-9-0 62 EAhern 2 73?
(JRJenkins) *prom over 6f: wknd* **100/1**

2m 6.54s (-1.14) **Going Correction** +0.25s/f (Good) **7** Ran SP% **114.7**
Speed ratings: **114,112,111,107,106 106,96**CSF £82.38 TOTE £6.70: £2.80, £6.10; EX 77.00 Trifecta £362.20 Pool of £918.28 - 1.80 winning units..
**Owner** Hamdan Al Maktoum **Bred** Meon Valley Stud **Trained** Lambourn, Berks

**FOCUS**
Only fair Group 3 form with Muqbil running below par and neither of the other two highest-rated horses, Salselon and Vespone, showing any desire for the game and running below capabilities. The seventh was not beaten far considering he was outclassed and limits the form to some extent.

**NOTEBOOK**
**Alkaadhem**, sporting the first-time blinkers, comes from a stable who had their first winner for a while the previous day and showed further signs of them coming back to form with a smooth success. Always travelling well, he brushed aside Muqbil before going away in the final furlong. Whether the headgear will have the same effect next time is open to debate.
**Battle Chant(USA)** was unlucky not to get closer to the winner as he was short of room when he wanted to go and momentarily lost his footing just over a furlong out. He ran on well to just snatch second once getting into the clear and is going the right way.
**Salselon** has plenty of ability but not much will to go with it and was just done for second. He will struggle to win in the near future.
**Muqbil(USA)** was very disappointing, running a long way below form and folding tamely. This was an out-of-character effort and he deserves a chance to show this running to be all wrong.
**Vespone(IRE)** has no desire to win these days and willingly gave up the chase once coming under pressure and getting a bump.

## 5493 FEGENTRI WORLD CUP OF NATIONS STKS (H'CAP) (AMATEUR RIDERS) (FOR THE RICHMOND BRISSAC TROPHY) 1m 1f

**3:40** (3:44) (E3) (0-70,69) 3-Y-O+ **£6,789** (£2,089; £1,044; £522) **Stalls** High

Form RPR
0313 **1** **Fantasy Crusader**[27] 4818 5-10-7 **55** oh3 (p) MrCFais 2 65
(JAGilbert) *prom: led 2f out: rdn over 1f out: jst hld on* **5/1**[1]
0643 **2** nk **Cormorant Wharf (IRE)**[38] 4479 4-11-3 **65** MrCVonBallmoos 8 74
(TEPowell) *lw: chsd ldrs: clsd fr 2f out: chsd wnr ins fnl f: gaining at fin* **10/1**
3040 **3** 1 3/4 **Jackie Kiely**[5] 5374 3-10-11 **65** MissJPatterson 11 71
(PSMcentee) *settled in rr: last over 3f out: styd on steadily after: tk 3rd nr fin* **10/1**
-112 **4** 1 1/4 **Barton Sands (IRE)**[17] 5056 7-11-7 **69** (t) MrFOllivaud 4 72
(AndrewReid) *b: b.hind: towards rr: prog on outer 3f out: chsd wnr over 1f out: bmpd along and hld ent fnl f: wknd* **8/1**
1402 **5** nk **Lord Chamberlain**[9] 5260 11-10-7 **55** (b) MrSWalker 5 57
(JMBradley) *s.i.s: wl in rr: sme prog on inner over 2f out: hrd rdn and one pce over 1f out* **7/1**
3042 **6** 2 **Icannshift (IRE)**[6] 5350 4-10-7 **55** oh2 MsAmyHerbert 12 53
(SDow) *led: drew clr 4f out: hdd 2f out: wknd fnl f* **6/1**[2]
0130 **7** 3 1/2 **Wind Chime (IRE)**[43] 4327 7-11-4 **66** MlleCGatta 9 57
(AGNewcombe) *nvr beyond midfield: outpcd and btn 2f out* **13/2**[3]
3105 **8** 3/4 **Billy Bathwick (IRE)**[9] 5258 7-10-11 **59** MissNVolz 1 49
(JMBradley) *prom: grad wknd over 2f out* **12/1**
0050 **9** 2 **Phred**[9] 5259 4-10-7 **55** (t) MsCWilliams 7 41
(RFJohnsonHoughton) *chsd ldrs: rdn and wknd 3f out* **8/1**
0500 **10** 3 **Regulated (IRE)**[16] 5069 3-10-3 **57** MissMelanieSauer 6 37
(DBFeek) *a wl in rr* **50/1**
6200 **11** 1 **Morag**[5] 5370 3-10-6 **60** MrCDeSmet 3 38
(IAWood) *sn prom: ev ch 2f out: wknd rapidly* **12/1**


The Form Book, Raceform Ltd, Compton, RG20 6NL

0403 **12** *1* **Canni Thinkaar (IRE)**[22] 4940 3-10-5 **59**..........(p) MissCelineMonfort 10 35
(PButler) *racd midfield: bmpd along 1/2-way: sn struggling* **25/1**

1m 59.9s (3.04) **Going Correction** +0.25s/f (Good)
**WFA** 3 from 4yo+ 6lb **12** Ran SP% **118.4**
Speed ratings: **96,95,94,93,92 91,87,87,85,82 81,81**CSF £54.94 CT £493.31 TOTE £6.90: £2.30, £3.10, £3.10; EX 78.20.
**Owner** The Fantasy Fellowship **Bred** J R C And Mrs Wren **Trained** Hargrave, Suffolk
■ This event was won by Italy's Cristiano Fais for the third consecutive year.

**FOCUS**
A novelty race with a variable standard of jockeyship. They went a good gallop, but this is ordinary form.

**NOTEBOOK**
**Fantasy Crusader** was to the fore of the main bunch throughout and went on at the two pole before galloping on strongly to hold the challenge of the fast-finishing second. He should continue to run well.
**Cormorant Wharf(IRE)** finished strongly and would have got there in a few more strides. He has dropped over a stone in the ratings this season and should be winning soon if building on this.
**Jackie Kiely** came from a long way back to claim third and may have been flattered as he ran on through tiring rivals.
**Barton Sands(IRE)** had been beaten in a seller most recently and faced a stiff task. He momentarily looked a threat but folded late on.
**Lord Chamberlain** ran well enough but has had his win for the turf season.
**Icannshift(IRE)** probably did a bit too much too soon in going off in front at a decent gallop.

## 5494 LESLEY DOLPHIN EUROPEAN BREEDERS FUND MAIDEN STKS 6f
**4:15** (4:17) (D2) 2-Y-O **£5,538** (£1,704; £852; £426) **Stalls** Low

Form RPR

2 **1** **Wazir (USA)**[60] 3847 2-9-0 .............................. LDettori 5 81
(JHMGosden) *lw: mde most to 2f out: rdn and looked in trble over 1f out: rallied to ld nr fin* **4/11**[1]

6 **2** *½* **Aberdeen (IRE)**[17] 5051 2-9-0 .............................. RLMoore 3 79
(PMitchell) *lw: racd in rr: prog over 2f out: pressed ldr over 1f out: fnd little and hld tl kpt on nr fin* **12/1**[3]

**3** *shd* **Dr Zalo** 2-9-0 .............................. DSweeney 6 79+
(PJMakin) *w'like: trckd ldrs: prog to ld 2f out: looked wnr 1f out: tired and hdd nr fin* **14/1**

00 **4** *½* **Archie Glenn**[97] 2736 2-9-0 .............................. PMcCabe 7 77
(MSSaunders) *racd in rr: rdn 1/2-way: prog 2f out: wandered fnl 2f: kpt on but nvr able to chal* **25/1**

03 **5** *3 ½* **Aviation**[8] 5290 2-9-0 .............................. RHughes 8 67
(RHannon) *trckd ldrs: pushed along 1/2-way: rdn and no imp over 1f out : fdd and eased* **5/1**[2]

000 **6** *4* **Chek Oi**[60] 3847 2-9-0 .............................. SDrowne 2 55
(WRMuir) *trckd ldrs: cl up 2f out: sn wknd: eased fnl f* **50/1**

00 **7** *8* **Kirkhammerton (IRE)**[19] 5015 2-9-0 .............................. VSlattery 4 31
(JAOsborne) *outpcd in last: a bhd* **25/1**

666 **8** *nk* **Dominer (IRE)**[69] 3570 2-9-0 40..............................(p) CCatlin 1 30
(JMBradley) *w ldr over 2f out: sn wknd* **66/1**

1m 14.5s (1.66) **Going Correction** +0.25s/f (Good) **8** Ran SP% **115.5**
Speed ratings: **98,97,97,96,91 86,75,75**CSF £5.89 TOTE £1.40: £1.02, £2.70, £3.00; EX 5.60.
**Owner** H R H Princess Haya Of Jordan **Bred** Newgate Stud Farm **Trained** Manton, Wilts

**FOCUS**
A fair maiden that was won by hot favourite Wazir, albeit not in the manner expected. The first four were clear and the form looks solid enough despite the muddling finish.

**NOTEBOOK**
**Wazir(USA)**, runner-up on his debut in what is turning out to be a very decent polytrack maiden at Lingfield - third, fourth and fifth all won next time - appeared to face a simple task in trying to add himself to the list of winners. However he found himself outpaced and unable to go with Dr Zalo from around two furlongs out and looked beaten as he dropped back, only for Dettori to get him together and come with a strong late run to end up winning with a little in hand. Evidently in need of seven furlongs plus, he should not be too harshly treated by the handicapper and can pick up a nursery.
**Aberdeen(IRE)** ran on well to snatch second on the line and left his debut running behind. He is up to winning a maiden but in the long run will make up into a better handicapper.
**Dr Zalo ◆** comes from a stable more than capable of producing a juvenile to score first time up and he looked for all the world as though he was going to make a successful introduction when going on. He appeared to blow up though in the closing stages and was eventually nabbed. A winner waiting to happen, he travelled extremely well here for a debutant and will be effective over the minimum trip.
**Archie Glenn** put up an improved effort and is now eligible for nurseries.
**Aviation** failed to build on his decent Haydock effort but should not be harshly treated for handicaps.

## 5495 ADENSTAR MAIDEN STKS 1m 1f 192y
**4:50** (4:52) (D2) 3-Y-O **£6,955** (£2,140; £1,070; £535) **Stalls** High

Form RPR

3- **1** **Corsican Native (USA)**[319] 5825 3-9-0 .............................. RHughes 5 91+
(MrsAJPerrett) *str: scope: lw: mde all: set stdy pce: rdn 2f out: rn green but drew rt away fr over 1f out* **15/8**[1]

030 **2** *9* **Royal Lustre**[20] 5007 3-9-0 67.............................. LDettori 6 68
(JHMGosden) *lw: chsd wnr: rdn and easily outpcd fnl 2f* **5/2**[2]

0300 **3** *1 ¾* **Polar Dancer**[30] 4710 3-8-9 53.............................. SDrowne 2 60
(MrsAJPerrett) *wl in tch: cl up and rdn over 2f out: sn outpcd and btn* **13/2**

3- **4** *7* **Tyup Pompey (IRE)**[361] 4989 3-8-11 .............................. LPKeniry(3) 8 51
(DRCElsworth) *lw: trckd ldng pair: cl up 2f out: wknd rapidly* **8/1**

66 **5** *10* **Montgomery**[14] 5151 3-9-0 .............................. SWhitworth 9 32
(AGNewcombe) *s.s: nvr gng wl in rr: wl bhd fnl 3f* **14/1**

**6** *1 ¼* **Mariday** 3-9-0 .............................. PaulEddery 1 30
(LadyHerries) *w'like: dwlt: sn in tch: pushed along and wknd over 4f out* **5/1**[3]

000- **7** *12* **Kwai Baby (USA)**[449] 2566 3-8-6 .............................. JFMcDonald(3) 4 2
(JJBridger) *bit bkwd: in tch over 6f: sn wknd* **50/1**

2m 11.36s (3.68) **Going Correction** +0.25s/f (Good) **7** Ran SP% **113.1**
Speed ratings: **95,87,86,80,72 71,62**CSF £6.58 TOTE £2.70: £1.80, £1.90; EX 6.90.
**Owner** K Abdulla **Bred** Juddmonte Farms Inc **Trained** Pulborough, W Sussex

**FOCUS**
The winner was impressive, but this was a modest maiden lacking strength in depth, and the field came home at long intervals.

**NOTEBOOK**
**Corsican Native(USA)**, who has been given time grow into his big frame, was allowed to take them along at his own pace and really powered away once asked to, coasting home by nine lengths. He did not beat much and it will be interesting to see how he does from a likely mark in the mid-80s.
**Royal Lustre** is not up to much but can be placed to advantage in low-grade handicaps if connections opt to persevere.
**Polar Dancer**, a stablemate of the winner, often shapes over this trip as if farther is required, but does not appear to stay it when tried. She has ability and will find a race off her lowly mark.
**Tyup Pompey(IRE)** stopped sharply in the final furlong or so and has something to prove after this.
**Mariday**, gambled from 16/1 into 5/1, showed absolutely nothing and the money was clearly misguided. He will need to show more than this if he is to be winning at even the lowest level.

## 5496 SEABEACH APPRENTICE STKS (H'CAP) 1m
**5:25** (5:25) (E3) (0-70,69) 3-Y-O+ **£3,530** (£1,086; £543; £271) **Stalls** High

Form RPR

4632 **1** **Johannian**[13] 5176 6-9-7 **69**.............................. LFletcher 4 78
(JMBradley) *settled in last pair: gd prog on wd outside wl over 1f out: rdn to ld last 75yds* **12/1**

5002 **2** *¾* **Mythical Charm**[16] 5080 5-8-7 **55** oh7..............................(t) JFMcDonald 13 62
(JJBridger) *dwlt: sn rcvrd and midfield: prog to ld over 2f out: hrd rdn over 1f out: hdd last 75yds* **20/1**

4225 **3** *½* **Kelseas Kolby (IRE)**[11] 5222 4-8-9 **57**.............................. DNolan 11 63
(PButler) *racd towards rr: prog 2f out: rdn to chse ldr briefly ins fnl f: kpt on same pce* **20/1**

2125 **4** *¾* **Burgundy**[13] 5183 7-9-2 **64**..............................(b) TPQueally 17 68
(PMitchell) *dwlt: racd last pair: rdn 1/2-way: prog on inner u.p over 2f out: styd on fnl f: nrst fin* **11/2**[2]

0042 **5** *1* **Oh So Rosie (IRE)**[23] 4912 4-8-5 **58**..............................(p) DerekNolan(5) 6 60
(JSMoore) *settled rr: prog 3f out: chsd ldr 2f out to ins fnl f : fdd* **14/1**

2001 **6** *½* **Londoner (USA)**[11] 5222 6-8-12 **60**.............................. LisaJones 16 61
(SDow) *led after 2f to over 2f out: sn outpcd: one pce after* **6/1**[3]

4040 **7** *½* **Alchera**[15] 5135 3-8-2 **60**.............................. CHaddon(5) 7 60
(RFJohnsonHoughton) *hld up in rr: nt clr run over 2f out tl swtchd lft ins fnl f: kpt on: no ch* **16/1**

1665 **8** *1* **Trevian**[192] 959 3-9-0 **67**.............................. BReilly 3 65
(SCWilliams) *chsd ldrs: rdn 2f out: fdd fr over 1f out* **20/1**

2426 **9** *1* **Spirit's Awakening**[23] 4920 5-8-12 **60**.............................. SHitchcott 14 55
(JAkehurst) *trckd ldrs: cl up and rdn 2f out: fdd over 1f out* **7/2**[1]

0510 **10** *4* **Little Englander**[46] 4238 4-8-7 **58**.............................. NChalmers(3) 5 44
(HCandy) *dwlt: a towards rr: rdn and struggling over 2f out* **16/1**

0353 **11** *2 ½* **Knickyknackienoo**[11] 5222 3-8-6 **59**.............................. LPKeniry 15 39
(AGNewcombe) *prom tl wknd over 2f out* **8/1**

0406 **12** *nk* **Lord Of The Sea (IRE)**[14] 5150 3-8-6 **59**.............................. RMiles 10 39
(JamiePoulton) *a in rr: rdn on outer 3f out: no prog* **20/1**

0421 **13** *1 ¾* **Otago (IRE)**[10] 5236 3-8-5 **58**.............................. FPFerris 1 34
(JRBest) *led for 2f: wknd 3f out* **8/1**

0023 **14** *2 ½* **Jarvo**[16] 5092 3-8-9 **62**.............................. J-PGuillambert 12 32
(NPLittmoden) *prom tl wknd u.p 3f out* **12/1**

1m 41.43s (1.16) **Going Correction** +0.25s/f (Good)
**WFA** 3 from 4yo+ 5lb **14** Ran SP% **127.0**
Speed ratings: **104,103,102,102,101 100,100,99,98,94 91,91,89,86**CSF £243.97 CT £4777.31 TOTE £14.30: £4.30, £7.00, £6.80; EX 264.20 Place 6 £163.65, Place 5 £119.78.
**Owner** Ms A M Williams **Bred** J R And Mrs P Good **Trained** Sedbury, Gloucs

**FOCUS**
Solid form for the grade and a welcome return to winning ways for Johannian.

**NOTEBOOK**
**Johannian**, racing off a 29lb lower mark than when last successful well over two years ago, had everything go his way and made some neat headway around runners to take it up and win going away deep inside the final furlong. If holding this level of form he can win again off a higher mark.
**Mythical Charm** is without a win in roughly a year now but has run well the last twice, finishing second on both occasions, and her level of consistency should see her rewarded before long.
**Kelseas Kolby(IRE)** continues to run consistently without winning.
**Burgundy** was doing his best work at the finish and continues to run well.
**Oh So Rosie(IRE)** ran well but was gunned down by a couple of late finishers.
**Alchera** was a little unlucky not to get closer, being denied a run and getting into the clear all too late.
**Trevian** *Official explanation: vet said gelding was struck into behind*
**Spirit's Awakening** was a bit disappointing and remains without a win in almost two years.
T/Jkpt: £4,639.40 to a £1 stake. Pool: £32,672.50. 5.00 winning tickets. T/Plt: £270.90 to a £1 stake. Pool: £67,879.85. 182.85 winning tickets. T/Qpdt: £74.70 to a £1 stake. Pool: £3,243.30. 32.10 winning tickets. JN

5497 - 5499a (Foreign Racing) - See Raceform Interactive

# 5432 LONGCHAMP (R-H)
Sunday, September 12

**OFFICIAL GOING: Soft**

## 5500a PRIX NIEL CASINO BARRIERE D'ENGHIEN (GROUP 2) (C&F) 1m 4f
**2:15** (2:17) 3-Y-O **£44,155** (£17,042; £8,134; £5,423)

RPR

**1** **Valixir (IRE)**[60] 3863 3-9-2 .............................. ELegrix 6 118
(AFabre, France) *racd in 4th, 2nd and pushed along 2f out, rdn to chal appr fnl f, ran on to ld cl home, driven out*

**2** *nse* **Prospect Park**[77] 3359 3-9-2 .............................. OPeslier 2 118
(CLaffon-Parias, France) *racd in 3rd, led ent str, pushed along 2f out, joined appr fnl f, ran on & led again inside final f, hdd cl home* 2

**3** *1* **Bago (FR)**[26] 4834 3-9-2 .............................. TGillet 3 117
(JEPease, France) *hld up in 5th, pushed along 2f out and hdwy to chase ldrs, kept on fnl f but not reach leading pair* 1

**4** *nk* **Lord Du Sud (FR)**[98] 2722 3-9-2 .............................. IMendizabal 4 116
(J-CRouget, France) *raced in 6th, pushed along and ran on steadily from 1 1/2f out to go 3rd, stayed on to line*

**5** *6* **Blue Canari (FR)**[98] 2722 3-9-2 .............................. TThulliez 8 108
(PBary, France) *held up, 7th straight, some late headway but never a threat* 3

**6** *10* **Mister Farmer (FR)**[40] 4431 3-9-2 .............................. CSoumillon 7 94
(NBranchu, France) *held up in last, effort 2f out, never a threat*

**7** *6* **Primaxis (IRE)**[40] 3-9-2 .............................. MBlancpain 1 85
(CLaffon-Parias, France) *led, joined 7f out, headed entering straight, one pace*

**8** *5* **Alnitak (USA)**[77] 3360 3-9-2 ..............................(b) C-PLemaire 5 78
(JEPease, France) *raced in 2nd, joined leader 7f out, driven approaching straight, soon weakened*

2m 29.4s **Going Correction** -0.025s/f (Good) **8** Ran SP% **118.6**
Speed ratings: **115,114,114,114,110 103,99,96**.
**Owner** Lagardere Family **Bred** S N C Lagardere Elevage **Trained** France

NOTEBOOK

**Valixir(IRE)** looked exceptionally well in the paddock and won this Arc trial in good style, value for more than the winning margin as he did nothing once hitting the front. Fourth early on travelling strongly, he made a forward move from one and a half out and took the lead well inside the final furlong before battling on bravely to keep his advantage. A colt who has improved during the year, he now goes for the Arc de Triomphe and looks the best of the French challenge with further improvement to come.

**Prospect Park**, dropped in behind his pacemaker, he went for the line early in the straight. He stayed at the head of affairs until inside the final furlong and then battled on gamely before finally being beaten on the nod. It was a good trial and he lost nothing in defeat. He is another that will go for the Arc.

**Bago(FR)** was being niggled at for some time during the 12 furlongs and looked outpaced when things quickened up at the two-furlong marker. Then he found another gear and was closing on the winner and runner-up throughout the final furlong. Connections were a little confused by his run and there are no plans for him at the moment. Faster ground may be the key.

**Lord Du Sud(FR)**, held up in sixth position for much of the early part of the race, he began to make progress from two out and came with his run on the far rail. He was rather short of room as the race came to an end and the outing will have done him a lot of good. He will taske on the principals again in the Arc.

## 5501a PRIX VERMEILLE FOUQUET'S BARRIERE (GROUP 1) (FILLIES) 1m 4f
**2:50** (2:52) 3-4-Y-O **£100,599** (£40,246; £20,123; £10,053)

RPR

1 **Sweet Stream (ITY)**[36] [4566] 4-9-2 .......... TGillet 6 112
(JEHammond, France) *mid-div, pushed along 4f out, tk clsr order on rail ent str, effort and ran on to chal over 1f out, ridden out* **16/1**

2 ½ **Royal Fantasy (GER)**[36] [4566] 4-9-2 .......... EBotti 2 111
(HSteinmetz, Germany) *mid-div, pushed along and 5th str, rdn and ran on to challenge over 1f out, every chance inside final f, ran on* **16/1**

3 ½ **Pride (FR)**[21] [4982] 4-9-2 .......... DBonilla 13 110
(ADeRoyer-Dupre, France) *held up in last, pushed along over 1 1/2f out, driven and finished well final furlong to go 3rd close home* **14/1**

4 snk **Vallera (GER)**[21] [4980] 3-8-7 .......... ABoschert 11 110
(UOstmann, Germany) *mid-div, effort on outside over 2f out, ran on under pressure fr over 1f out and went 3rd briefly, stayed on* **16/1**

5 hd **Diamond Tango (FR)**[19] [5033] 3-8-7 .......... OPeslier 7 109
(AFabre, France) *held up, some late headway but never dangerous* **16/1**

6 snk **Silverskaya (USA)**[19] [5033] 3-8-7 .......... IMendizabal 3 109
(J-CRouget, France) *mid-division, stayed on closing stages, nearest at finish* **9/1**[3]

7 hd **Visorama (IRE)**[36] [4566] 4-9-2 .......... ELegrix 12 109
(AFabre, France) *held up, never a threat* **12/1**

8 shd **Latice (IRE)**[91] [2925] 3-8-7 .......... CSoumillon 4 109
(J-MBeguigne, France) *trckd ldrs in 4th on rail, led ent straight, ridden and ran on 1 1/2f out til headed 100yds out, no extra* **11/10**[1]

9 2½ **Whortleberry (FR)**[21] [4982] 4-9-2 ..........(b) C-PLemaire 5 105
(FRohaut, France) *mid-division, effort over 2f out, ran on til outpaced from over 1f out* **12/1**

10 6 **Lune D'Or (FR)**[36] [4566] 3-8-7 .......... TJarnet 10 96
(RGibson, France) *in touch, 6th straight, soon pushed along, one pace* **7/2**[2]

11 **Anabaa Republic (FR)**[19] [5033] 3-8-7 .......... TThulliez 1 —
(FDoumen, France) *always towards rear* **50/1**

12 **Gloirez (FR)**[64] 3-8-7 .......... SPasquier 8 —
(PDemercastel, France) *held up in last, pushed along straight, never dangerous* **66/1**

13 **Pilgrim Of Grace (FR)**[22] 3-8-7 .......... SMaillot 9 —
(RGibson, France) *led to straight, weakened once headed* **150/1**

2m 29.5s **Going Correction** -0.025s/f (Good)
**WFA** 3 from 4yo 9lb **13** Ran SP% **129.5**
Speed ratings: **115,114,114,114,114 114,113,113,112,108 108,108,108.**
**Owner** Team Valor **Bred** Paolo Torrente **Trained** France

NOTEBOOK

**Sweet Stream(ITY)** needed riding virtually throughout this race. She was always one of the last and still had plenty to do on the rail entering the straight, but under strong persuasion she gradually cut the others down and the gap opened up beautifully for her at exactly the right moment. She hit the front half a furlong out and stayed on well. She is not in the Arc and will now probably be campaigned in the States.

**Royal Fantasy(GER)**, in mid-division for the early part of the race, she made a forward move at the furlong and a half marker and stayed on but could not quicken with the winner. She is now likely to go for the Prix de Royallieu in October.

**Pride(FR)** can be considered unlucky. At the tail of the field early on, she had to be checked 300 yards out and was again short of room a little later. She finished best of all and was in front 20 yards after the post. Highly rated by her trainer, she could be allowed to take her chance in the Arc de Triomphe.

**Vallera(GER)**, eighth when the field settled down after the start, she was asked for an effort halfway up the straight. She stayed on to the line but could not quicken as well as the three in front of her. She is another possible for the Royallieu.

**Latice(IRE)**, the unbeaten winner of the Prix de Diane, was making her first appearance since. She looked sure to win when going on early in the straight, but she was swallowed up in the final furlong and gave the impression she did not quite stay.

## 5502a PRIX FOY GRAY D'ALBION BARRIERE (GROUP 2) (C&F) 1m 4f
**3:20** (3:26) 4-Y-O+ **£44,155** (£17,042; £8,134; £5,423)

RPR

1 **Policy Maker (IRE)**[70] [3567] 4-9-2 .......... OPeslier 4 119
(ELellouche, France) *made all, pushed along 2f out, ran on well final furlong, readily* 1

2 2 **Short Pause**[70] [3567] 5-9-2 .......... TGillet 3 116
(AFabre, France) *disputed 2nd, 2nd and pushed along straight, ridden over 1f out, stayed on but not pace of winner* 3

3 1½ **Nysaean (IRE)**[15] [5134] 5-9-2 .......... JFortune 1 114
(RHannon) *disputed 2nd, 3rd straight, pushed along over 2f out, ran on steadily to line*

4 ¾ **Polish Summer**[70] [3567] 7-9-2 .......... CSoumillon 2 113
(AFabre, France) *raced in last, pushed along 2f out, no impression* 2

2m 38.7s **Going Correction** -0.025s/f (Good) **4** Ran SP% **108.8**
Speed ratings: **84,82,81,81.**
**Owner** Ecurie Wildenstein **Bred** Dayton Investments Ltd **Trained** France

NOTEBOOK

**Policy Maker(IRE)** was given a beautiful waiting-in-front ride. After setting a sound pace in the early stages, he quickened very rapidly from two out and stayed on to win with something in hand. He is a solid individual who should give a good account of himself in the Arc.

**Short Pause** galloped behind the winner throughout. Caught for pace when things quickened up in the straight, he stayed on at one paced through the final furlong. He is a very consistent and genuine individual.

**Nysaean(IRE)** was third throughout. Slightly short of room on the descent before the straight, he was another caught for speed before staying on at the same pace. He never threatened the winner and runner-up.

**Polish Summer** has never won at Longchamp and he never really looked happy on this occasion. He was last throughout, outpaced in the straight, and not given a hard time when the writing was on the wall. He is probably best on a left-handed track.

## 5503a PRIX GLADIATEUR ROYAL THALASSO BARRIERE (GROUP 3) 1m 7f 110y
**4:35** (4:35) 4-Y-O+ **£25,704** (£10,282; £7,711; £5,141)

RPR

1 **Westerner**[70] [3567] 5-9-6 .......... OPeslier 6 120
(ELellouche, France) *hld up, disp 5th str, hdwy over 2f out, chal 1 1/2f out rdn to ld 1f out, ran on wl to hold chal of 2nd cl home* 1

2 snk **Cut Quartz (FR)**[21] [4983] 7-8-13 .......... TJarnet 2 113
(RGibson, France) *in tch, 4th on ins str, pushed along and hdwy 1 1/2f out, fin strongly and ev ch fnl f, ran on*

3 2½ **Clear Thinking**[21] [4983] 4-8-13 .......... CSoumillon 8 111
(AFabre, France) *prominent, 2nd half-way, pushed along to lead 2f out to 1f out, kept on* 3

4 2 **Le Carre (USA)**[112] [2337] 6-8-11 .......... IMendizabal 1 107
(ADeRoyer-Dupre, France) *raced in last, ridden straight, stayed on closing stages to take 4th*

5 snk **Gold Medallist**[21] [4983] 4-9-4 .......... JFortune 3 113
(DRCElsworth) *led to 2f out, ridden and rallied when headed til no extra from 1f out* 2

6 1 **Clety (FR)**[21] [4983] 8-8-11 ..........(b) TThulliez 7 105
(FDoumen, France) *in touch, 3rd and pushed along straight, under pressure 1 1/2f out, stayed on at one pace to line*

7 ¾ **Epopee (IRE)**[125] 4-8-8 .......... J-BEyquem 4 102
(FRohaut, France) *held up, never dangerous*

8 1½ **Affirmative Action (IRE)**[40] [4431] 4-8-11 .......... TGillet 5 103
(JEPease, France) *held up, disputing 5th straight, pushed along 2f out, unable to quicken*

3m 26.6s **Going Correction** +0.275s/f (Good) **8** Ran SP% **121.7**
Speed ratings: **108,107,106,105,105 105,104,103.**
**Owner** Ecurie Wildenstein **Bred** Dayton Investments Ltd **Trained** France

NOTEBOOK

**Westerner** had a perfect comeback race. Free early on, he then settled in sixth place and was going easily when the field entered the straight. Brought up the centre of the track, he hit the front from one and a half out and then stayed on to win with a little in hand, despite his jockey dropping his whip. He now goes on to the Prix du Cadran.

**Cut Quartz(FR)** a very genuine performer who rarely runs a bad race. Third for sometime he slipped through on the far rail running into the final furlong and a half and challenged the winner throughout the final stages. Connections are not sure whether he will take his chance in the Cadran.

**Clear Thinking** followed the long-time leader before taking control of the race 300 yards from the finish. Immediately joined by the winner, he was unable to quicken inside the final furlong.

**Le Carre(USA)** put in his best work at the finish. At the tail of the field early on he didn't fire until entering the straight. He still had plenty to do at the furlong marker and put in a fantastic burst of acceleration as the race came to an end.

**Gold Medallist** this was a slightly disappointing run by the Kergorlay winner. Taken into the lead from the start he set a true pace but he was under pressure early in the straight. For the last two furlongs he just kept going at the same speed on the rail. No plans for him at the moment.

# TABY (R-H)
Sunday, September 12

**OFFICIAL GOING: Dirt course - fast; turf course - good to firm**

## 5504a NICKES MINNESLOPNING (LISTED) (DIRT) 1m (D)
**2:15** (2:24) 3-Y-O+ **£11,646** (£5,823; £2,795; £1,863)

RPR

1 **Vortex**[36] [4528] 5-9-4 .......... NCordrey 4 —
(MissGayKelleway) *tracked leader, led 2f out, one length clear 1f out, all out, just held on (67/100F)* 1

2 hd **Hovman (DEN)**[21] [4984] 5-9-4 .......... MLarsen 7 —
(MsCErichsen, Norway) 2

3 2 **Hanzano (IRE)**[10] 6-9-4 .......... KAndersen 10 —
(AreHyldmo, Norway)

4 1½ **Nicki Hill (NOR)**[10] 8-9-4 .......... MSantos 2 —
(ALund, Norway)

5 1½ **Oregon**[346] 5-9-4 .......... FJohansson 3 —
(WidoNeuroth, Norway)

6 6 **Magic Fact**[364] [4927] 7-9-4 .......... P-AGraberg 6 —
(BHallencreutz, Sweden)

7 2½ **Jubilation**[129] [1954] 5-9-4 .......... FSanchez 1 —
(FReuterskiold, Sweden)

8 3 **Rotulo (ARG)**[129] [1954] 6-9-4 .......... FDiaz 9 —
(DiegoLowther, Sweden)

9 1 **Golden Gift**[364] [4927] 6-9-4 ..........(b) ANicholls 8 —
(FReuterskiold, Sweden)

10 dist **Sufian**[809] 5-9-4 .......... YvonneDurant 5 —
(BNeuman, Sweden)

1m 39.9s **10** Ran SP% **87.8**
Speed ratings: .
**Owner** Coriolis Partnership **Bred** Juddmonte Farms **Trained** Newmarket, Suffolk

NOTEBOOK

**Vortex** tracked the pace-setting Golden Gift, but when that one dropped away he was left in front two furlongs out and had to be hard driven throughout the closing stages to hold Hovman's late thrust. Better when held up until the last minute, he is now set to make an ambitious Japanese raid on the Grade 3 Mushashino Stakes over a mile at Tokyo on October 30 then the Japan Cup Dirt at the same course four weeks later.

## 5505a TABY OPEN SPRINT CHAMPIONSHIP (GROUP 3) 5f 165y
**3:15** (3:20) 3-Y-O+ **£31,056** (£15,528; £7,453; £4,970)

RPR

1 **Steve's Champ (CHI)**[21] 4-9-4 ..........(b) FDiaz 7 110
(RuneHaugen, Norway) *made all, driven out* 3

2 1 **Waquaas**[35] 8-9-4 .......... KAndersen 2 107
(RoyArneKvisla, Sweden) *last to half-way, progress 3f out, finished well*

3 hd **Musadif (USA)**[45] 6-9-4 ........ FJohansson 11 106
(RoyArneKvisla, Sweden) *mid-division, headway to chase winner 1f out, lost 2nd last strides* 2

4 1 **Shawdon**[45] 9-9-4 ........ FSanchez 8 103
(FReuterskiold, Sweden) *mid-division, some progress from over 1f out, never nearer*

5 hd **Proud Boast**[36] 4526 6-9-0 ........ SSanders 9 98
(DNicholls) *behind until 2f out, stayed on well*

6 1 **Pipoldchap (CHI)**[35] 4-9-4 ........(b) MSantos 5 99
(FCastro, Sweden) *started well, tracked winner to half-way, gradually faded* 1

7 1 **Fire Up The Band**[24] 4886 5-9-4 ........ ANicholls 1 96
(DNicholls) *close up to 2f out, one pace*

8 1 ½ **Lores Joy (ARG)**[71] 3552 5-9-4 ........ MLarsen 6 91
(DiegoLowther, Sweden) *third to half-way, gradually weakened*

9 1 ½ **Rex (IRE)**[129] 1953 7-9-4 ........(b) MMartinez 3 86
(FCastro, Sweden) *never nearer than mid-division* 2

10 hd **King Quantas (IRE)**[364] 4928 6-9-4 ........ NCordrey 4 85
(OStenstrom, Sweden) *close up to half-way*

11 2 ½ **Damachida (IRE)**[129] 1953 5-9-4 ........ RSkrzydlo 10 77
(EvaSundbye, Sweden) *always behind*

66.20 secs 11 Ran SP% **147.5**
Speed ratings: .
**Owner** Lagulise Racing **Bred** Haras Matancilla **Trained** Norway

**NOTEBOOK**
**Proud Boast** was always trailing and had too much ground to make up. She kept on well enough but was always being held.
**Fire Up The Band** was a bit disappointing as he failed to put up much of a fight once asked for his effort.

## 5506a STOCKHOLM CUP INTERNATIONAL (GROUP 3) 1m 4f
3:45 (3:47) 3-Y-O+ **£31,056** (£15,528; £7,453; £4,970)

RPR

1 **Collier Hill**[25] 4858 6-9-4 ........ DeanMcKeown 3 110
(GASwinbank) *in rear to 4f out, good progress to challenge final f, led last stride* 3

2 shd **Foreign Affairs**[28] 4784 6-9-4 ........ SSanders 2 110
(SirMarkPrescott) *tried to make all, set good pace, caught last stride* 2

3 2 **Mandrake El Mago (CHI)**[21] 4984 5-9-4 ........ MSantos 7 107
(FCastro, Sweden) *held up in mid-division, challenged from 2f out, every chance 1f out, unable to quicken* 1

4 1 **Alpino Chileno (ARG)**[21] 4984 5-9-4 ........(b) FDiaz 6 105
(RuneHaugen, Norway) *raced in mid-division, stayed on final 2f but never able to challenge*

5 ½ **Santiago Matias (CHI)**[42] 4380 5-9-4 ........(b) MMartinez 1 104
(FCastro, Sweden) *towards rear til making some late headway*

6 2 **Royal Experiment (USA)**[21] 4984 5-9-4 ........ FJohansson 9 101
(WidoNeuroth, Norway) *tracked leader to 2f out, soon weakened*

7 ½ **Honeysuckle Player (SWE)**[21] 4984 6-9-4 ........ YvonneDurant 5 100
(FReuterskiold, Sweden) *mid-division to half-way*

8 1 ½ **Year Two Thousand**[21] 4984 6-9-4 ........ JJohansen 4 98
(ALund, Norway) *raced in 3rd to 2f out, weakened quickly*

9 4 **Cayman Venture (IRE)**[748] 4182 4-9-4 ........ KAndersen 10 91
(MKahn, Sweden) *mid-division to half-way*

2m 27.8s 9 Ran SP% **128.2**
Speed ratings: .
**Owner** R H Hall & Ashley Young **Bred** George Strawbridge **Trained** Melsonby, N Yorks

**NOTEBOOK**
**Collier Hill** defied fears about the fast ground. In the rear for the first mile, he challenged Foreign Affairs a furlong out and got his nose in front in the shadow of the post to give Alan Swinbank his first Pattern success. He has various options, including the Canadian International, but will definitely not be returning to hurdling.
**Foreign Affairs** cut out the running and, battling on gamely when pressed by Collier Hill throughout the final furlong, only gave best in the last couple of strides.
**Mandrake El Mago(CHI)** is the highest-rated horse in Scandinavia but does not really stay a mile and a half.

# 5334 BATH (L-H)
## Monday, September 13

**OFFICIAL GOING: Good**
The ground had eased after 10mm of rain overnight.
Wind: fresh against Weather: heavy downpours after races 3 and 5.

## 5507 SHARP MINDS BETFAIR MEDIAN AUCTION MAIDEN STKS 5f 161y
2:30 (2:31) (E3) 2-Y-O **£3,614** (£1,112; £556; £278) **Stalls** Low

Form RPR

43 1 **Bahamian Magic**[44] 4334 2-9-0 ........ TPQueally 8 78
(DRLoder) *t.k.h: a.p: rdn over 2f out: r.o to ld cl home* **7/2**[2]

066 2 ½ **Lighted Way**[17] 5070 2-8-6 64 ........ LPKeniry(3) 4 71
(AMBalding) *t.k.h: w ldr: rdn to ld 2f out: hdd cl home* **20/1**

3 ½ **Inka Dancer (IRE)** 2-8-6 ........ FPFerris(3) 11 69
(BPalling) *s.s: wl bhd whn rdn over 3f out: gd hdwy over 1f out: fin wl* **66/1**

52 4 1 **Disguise**[50] 4172 2-9-0 ........ MHills 3 71
(BWHills) *led: hdd and rdn 2f out: nt qckn ins fnl f* **11/8**[1]

5 ½ **Chinalea (IRE)** 2-9-0 ........ RSmith 9 69
(CGCox) *s.i.s: sn chsng ldrs: rdn and kpt on same pce fnl 2f* **5/1**[3]

0 6 1 ¼ **Edge Of Italy**[18] 5054 2-8-9 ........ SWhitworth 6 60
(KBell) *hld up and bhd: hdwy jst over 1f out: r.o* **100/1**

0635 7 1 **Il Pranzo**[39] 4474 2-9-0 71 ........ JFEgan 2 62
(SKirk) *wnt lft s: chsd ldrs: rdn and no hdwy fnl 2f* **14/1**

006 8 shd **Perez (IRE)**[6] 5373 2-9-0 ........ PDobbs 10 62
(RHannon) *mid-div: rdn over 2f out: no imp* **14/1**

9 9 **Latin Express (IRE)** 2-9-0 ........ MartinDwyer 5 32
(WRMuir) *prom: rdn over 2f out: wknd wl over 1f out* **9/1**

10 5 **Rosie Muir** 2-8-9 ........ DSweeney 7 —
(MrsALMKing) *s.s: rdn 3f out: a bhd* **100/1**

11 18 **Saturday's Child (FR)** 2-8-6 ........ RMiles(3) 1 —
(MSSaunders) *s.s: sn t.o* **100/1**

1m 12.87s (1.73) **Going Correction** +0.175s/f (Good) 11 Ran SP% **113.6**
Speed ratings: **95,94,93,92,91 90,88,88,76,69 45**CSF £72.42 TOTE £3.80: £1.70, £7.00, £24.50; EX 90.10.
**Owner** Lucayan Stud **Bred** M C Collins **Trained** Newmarket, Suffolk

**FOCUS**
This is just fairly useful form, although the race could possibly be rated a few pounds higher.
**NOTEBOOK**
**Bahamian Magic** needed every yard of this extended five furlongs and confirmed he really wants a shade further.
**Lighted Way**, in contrast to the winner, will probably be suited by a return to the bare minimum distance. This was a much improved run but her handicap mark will suffer as a result.
**Inka Dancer(IRE)** ◆ lost far more ground at the start than the distance she was beaten by and also lost her off-fore shoe. She looks a ready-made future winner in this sort of company. *Official explanation: jockey said filly lost an off fore shoe*
**Disguise** may have found the drop back to a slightly shorter trip against him.
**Chinalea(IRE)** ◆, a half-brother to a couple of winners abroad, was not unduly knocked about on his debut. Improvement can be expected when he tackles further.
**Edge Of Italy**, virtually unrideable on her debut, showed signs of ability over an inadequate trip.

## 5508 SHARP MINDS WINNERS WELCOME MAIDEN STKS 1m 5y
3:00 (3:01) (D3) 2-Y-O **£3,662** (£1,127; £563; £281) **Stalls** Low

Form RPR

02 1 **Rumbalara**[14] 5179 2-8-9 ........ JFortune 7 74
(JHMGosden) *mde virtually all: rdn 2f out: flashed tail ins fnl f: all out* **15/8**[2]

02 2 nk **Silver Highlight (CAN)**[39] 4498 2-8-9 ........ MartinDwyer 4 74
(AMBalding) *a.p: rdn 2f out: r.o ins fnl f* **1/1**[1]

0 3 ¾ **Battledress (IRE)**[17] 5091 2-8-9 ........ NDeSouza(5) 2 77
(MPTregoning) *hld up in mid-div: rdn over 3f out: outpcd 2f out: styd on wl towards fin* **7/1**[3]

4 hd **Rightful Ruler** 2-9-0 ........ MHills 3 77
(BWHills) *hld up and bhd: rdn over 2f out: hdwy over 1f out: styd on wl towards fin* **14/1**

6 5 hd **Spill A Little**[73] 3483 2-9-0 ........ SHitchcott 8 76
(MRChannon) *plld hrd: sn w wnr: ev ch 2f out: no ex towards fin* **20/1**

00 6 6 **Moshkil (IRE)**[24] 4913 2-9-0 ........ SDrowne 6 63
(MPTregoning) *prom: pushed along over 4f out: rdn 3f out: wknd over 1f out* **25/1**

000 7 19 **Fire At Will**[16] 5132 2-9-0 ........ RLMoore 9 21
(AWCarroll) *sn bhd* **100/1**

0 8 2 **Mount Arafat**[14] 5173 2-9-0 ........ ADaly 11 17
(MSalaman) *dwlt: wl bhd fnl 4f* **100/1**

9 shd **Lambriggan Lad** 2-9-0 ........ PDobbs 10 17
(MissVictoriaRoberts) *hld up in mid-div: rdn over 3f out: sn struggling* **100/1**

10 2 ½ **Edith Bankes** 2-8-2 ........ CHaddon(7) 1 —
(WGMTurner) *s.s: a wl bhd* **100/1**

0 11 24 **Ciendra Girl (IRE)**[7] 5349 2-8-9 ow3 ........ DNolan(3) 5 —
(RBrotherton) *hld up: rdn over 4f out: sn bhd: t.o* **100/1**

1m 43.3s (2.30) **Going Correction** +0.175s/f (Good) 11 Ran SP% **117.5**
Speed ratings: **95,94,93,93,93 87,68,66,66,63 39**CSF £3.92 TOTE £3.20: £1.20, £1.10, £2.00; EX 5.30.
**Owner** Peter Maher **Bred** Sir Eric Parker **Trained** Manton, Wilts

**FOCUS**
With the first five finishing in a heap, only time will tell the value of this form. The third to seventh horses inclusive all showed significant improvement.
**NOTEBOOK**
**Rumbalara**, stepping up from seven, again flashed her tail in the closing stages but her attitude could not be faulted.
**Silver Highlight(CAN)** stuck to her task and confirmed the opinion that she is going to need middle distances next year.
**Battledress(IRE)** improved significantly on his debut and is another who will come into his own when tackling longer distances at a three-year-old.
**Rightful Ruler** is a half-brother to mile and a half winner Haile Selassie. Making a satisfactory debut, he shaped like one who is eventually going to require that sort of trip.
**Spill A Little** ran too freely and this was a good effort in the circumstances.

## 5509 SHARP MINDS BETFAIR: BEST ODDS NURSERY 5f 161y
3:30 (3:30) (E4) (0-75,75) 2-Y-O **£3,108** (£888; £444) **Stalls** Low

Form RPR

1 1 **Arbors Little Girl**[34] 4620 2-8-4 58 ........ ADaly 9 66
(BRMillman) *hld up and bhd: swtchd rt and hdwy 2f out: hung lft 1f out: hung lft and led ins fnl f: r.o wl* **9/2**[1]

011 2 1 ¾ **Monashee Rose (IRE)**[18] 5060 2-9-4 75 ........ NMackay(3) 10 77
(JSMoore) *hld up in tch: led jst over 2f out: sn rdn: hdd and no ex ins fnl f* **9/2**[1]

4000 3 1 ¼ **Perianth (IRE)**[35] 4601 2-8-7 61 ........ KFallon 11 61+
(BJMeehan) *a.p: rdn over 2f out: bmpd and n.m.r 1f out: ev ch whn hmpd ins fnl f: nt rcvr* **9/1**

0042 4 1 **Majestical (IRE)**[34] 4620 2-8-6 60 ........ SDrowne 4 55
(WRMuir) *led: hdd jst over 2f out: sn rdn: one pce fnl f* **8/1**[3]

3044 5 ¾ **I'm Aimee**[7] 5334 2-8-12 73 ........ SJDonohoe(7) 6 65
(PDEvans) *hld up in mid-div: rdn over 2f out: hdwy over 1f out: nt rch ldrs* **6/1**[2]

6605 6 ½ **Atsos (IRE)**[29] 4770 2-9-0 68 ........ RLMoore 12 59
(RHannon) *dwlt: bhd tl hdwy jst over 1f out: r.o* **9/1**

050 7 shd **Cross My Shadow (IRE)**[14] 5198 2-8-9 63 ........(t) SHitchcott 3 53
(MFHarris) *prom tl rdn and wknd over 1f out* **25/1**

360 8 3 **Mister Bell**[52] 4081 2-8-6 60 ........ DSweeney 8 41
(JGMO'Shea) *s.s: nvr nrr* **50/1**

2036 9 1 ¾ **Saucepot**[7] 5334 2-8-9 63 ........ TQuinn 2 38
(MDIUsher) *plld hrd: prom tl wknd wl over 1f out* **11/1**

555 10 2 **Task's Muppet (IRE)**[9] 5281 2-8-4 61 ........ JFMcDonald(3) 5 30
(JAOsborne) *chsd ldrs: rdn over 2f out: wknd wl over 1f out* **12/1**

440 11 ½ **Tashyra (IRE)**[10] 5270 2-8-10 64 ........ MartinDwyer 1 31
(AMBalding) *s.i.s: rdn over 2f out: sn struggling* **10/1**

2060 12 nk **Dreamer's Lass**[20] 5015 2-7-13 56 ........ FPFerris(3) 7 22
(JMBradley) *prom: rdn over 2f out: wknd wl over 1f out* **25/1**

1m 12.53s (1.39) **Going Correction** +0.175s/f (Good) 12 Ran SP% **116.5**
Speed ratings: **97,94,93,91,90 90,89,85,83,80 80,79**CSF £22.64 CT £153.03 TOTE £5.50: £2.50, £2.30, £3.20; EX 14.10.
**Owner** Dr Ian R Shenkin **Bred** Mrs M Shenkin **Trained** Kentisbeare, Devon
■ Stewards Enquiry : A Daly one-day ban: careless riding (Sep 24)

**FOCUS**
A modest nursery with the first two the only previous winners in the field.
**NOTEBOOK**
**Arbors Little Girl**, who landed a seller over the bare five here on her debut, showed why she was a springer in the market that day. She interfered twice with the third and her rider was given a one-day ban.
**Monashee Rose(IRE)** may not have been helped by the overnight rain in her bid to complete a hat-trick off a 3lb higher mark.

**Perianth(IRE)** may well have been third best on merit despite the fact he was twice done no favours by the winner. He seemed to appreciate this return to a shorter distance.
**Majestical(IRE)**, 3lb better off than when pipped on the post by Arbors Little Girl here last time, may not have found the extended trip in his favour. *Official explanation: jockey said gelding hung right*
**I'm Aimee**, dropped 3lb, is fully exposed and is always going to be vulnerable to the improvers.
**Atsos(IRE)** was not helped by missing the break but needs at least a full six furlongs by the look of it.
**Cross My Shadow(IRE)** *Official explanation: jockey said colt hung right*

## 5510 SHARP MINDS BETFAIR: BACK AND LAY H'CAP — 1m 5y
**4:00** (4:01) (E3) (0-70,70) 3-Y-O — **£3,701** (£1,139; £569; £284) **Stalls** Low

| Form | | | | RPR |
|---|---|---|---|---|
| 6030 | **1** | | **Master Mahogany**[10] 5259 3-8-13 **59** ... SDrowne 9 **11/1**<br>(RJHodges) *a.p: led wl over 2f out: sn rdn: drvn out* | 66 |
| 4006 | **2** | ½ | **Desert Hawk**[15] 5153 3-9-6 **66** ... RLMoore 7 **16/1**<br>(RHannon) *hld up in mid-div: rdn 4f out: hdwy on outside over 2f out: r.o ins fnl f* | 72 |
| 0025 | **3** | *shd* | **Fleet Anchor**[25] 4868 3-8-10 **56** oh4 ... JFEgan 14 **10/1**<br>(JMBradley) *stdd s: sn wl bhd: rdn over 3f out: hdwy over 2f out: r.o ins fnl f* | 62 |
| 045 | **4** | *nk* | **Capitole (IRE)**[29] 4781 3-9-1 **61** ... (v¹) PMcCabe 8 **17/2**<br>(EFVaughan) *hld up and bhd: hdwy 2f out: sn rdn: kpt on ins fnl f* | 66 |
| 0-65 | **5** | 1 | **Kinbrace**[70] 3589 3-8-13 **59** ... MartinDwyer 12 **11/2**[2]<br>(MPTregoning) *hld up and bhd: gd hdwy over 3f out: ev ch over 2f out: sn rdn: no ex ins fnl f* | 62 |
| 0553 | **6** | 2½ | **Trois Etoiles (IRE)**[39] 4477 3-8-10 **56** oh1 ... KFallon 1 **3/1**[1]<br>(JWHills) *hld up in mid-div: hdwy over 2f out: swtchd lft 1f out: wknd ins fnl f* | 53 |
| 3060 | **7** | 1¾ | **Ali Deo**[28] 4817 3-9-10 **70** ... (p) TPQueally 10 **14/1**<br>(WJHaggas) *prom: rdn over 2f out: wknd wl over 1f out* | 63 |
| 5306 | **8** | 4 | **Beauty Of Dreams**[15] 5141 3-8-11 **57** ... SHitchcott 4 **8/1**[3]<br>(MRChannon) *hld up in tch: rdn and btn whn hmpd on ins over 2f out* | 41 |
| 4000 | **9** | 1¼ | **Zuri (IRE)**[33] 4641 3-8-13 **62** ... NMackay(3) 5 **12/1**<br>(LMCumani) *prom: rdn 3f out: wknd wl over 1f out: eased fnl f* | 43 |
| 360- | **10** | *nk* | **Royal Zephyr (USA)**[345] 5369 3-9-4 **64** ... JMackay 3 **14/1**<br>(SirMarkPrescott) *hld up in mid-div: rdn 3f out: sn bhd* | 44 |
| 0000 | **11** | 3 | **My Sunshine (IRE)**[12] 5222 3-8-10 **56** oh2 ... MHills 2 **33/1**<br>(BWHills) *a bhd* | 29 |
| 3500 | **12** | 12 | **Charlie Tango (IRE)**[12] 5223 3-9-4 **64** ... (b¹) TQuinn 13 **8/1**[3]<br>(NTinkler) *plld hrd: led over 6f out tl wl over 2f out: wknd qckly* | 10 |
| 60-0 | **13** | *dist* | **Romantic Drama (IRE)**[14] 5201 3-8-10 **56** oh1 ... DSweeney 6 **66/1**<br>(MrsALMKing) *led over 1f: wknd qckly 3f out: eased fnl 2f* | — |

1m 43.18s (2.18) **Going Correction** +0.175s/f (Good) **13** Ran SP% **121.9**
Speed ratings: **96,95,95,95,94 91,89,85,84,84 81,69,—**CSF £178.81 CT £1881.76 TOTE £13.30: £4.30, £6.80, £2.90; EX 251.80.
**Owner** Villagers Five **Bred** C J Hill **Trained** Charlton Adam, Somerset

**FOCUS**
A modest winning time for the grade and ordinary form, with five of the runners out of the handicap proper.

**NOTEBOOK**
**Master Mahogany** had run well when third over course and distance last month and held on to score with little to spare.
**Desert Hawk** will appreciate a return to further with these more patient tactics adopted.
**Fleet Anchor**, 4lb 'wrong', was dropped out at the start on this first attempt at a mile. Now he has proved he stays the trip, he can be ridden a bit closer to the pace in future and further improvement can be expected.
**Capitole(IRE)**, switched off in the first-time visor, settled well and can be ridden more aggressively in the headgear from now on.
**Kinbrace** was reported to have hung left by her rider and may not have been putting it all in. *Official explanation: jockey said filly hung left*
**Trois Etoiles(IRE)** again faded in the closing stages and could be worth a try back at seven.
**Charlie Tango(IRE)** *Official explanation: jockey said gelding run too free early on*

## 5511 SHARP MINDS BETFAIR MAIDEN FILLIES' STKS — 1m 2f 46y
**4:30** (4:31) (D3) 3-Y-O — **£3,536** (£1,088; £544; £272) **Stalls** Low

| Form | | | | RPR |
|---|---|---|---|---|
| 3 | **1** | | **Batik (IRE)**[33] 4644 3-8-8 ... NMackay(3) 9 **2/1**[2]<br>(LMCumani) *hld up: rdn over 4f out: swtchd rt and hdwy wl over 1f out: styd on to ld cl home* | 76+ |
| 3204 | **2** | 1 | **Uig**[16] 5136 3-8-11 74 ... JFortune 1 **13/2**[3]<br>(HSHowe) *led: rdn 2f out: edgd rt ins fnl f: hdd cl home* | 75 |
| 2024 | **3** | *nk* | **Principessa**[24] 4910 3-8-11 70 ... TQuinn 4 **11/1**<br>(BPalling) *chsd ldr: rdn over 1f out: ev ch fnl f: nt qckn* | 74 |
| 4 | **4** | 7 | **Go Supersonic**[23] 4954 3-8-11 ... KFallon 6 **7/4**[1]<br>(SirMichaelStoute) *prom: rdn over 3f out: wknd 1f out* | 61+ |
| 2-43 | **5** | 5 | **Tenny's Gold (IRE)**[94] 2842 3-8-11 70 ... MHills 2 **7/1**<br>(BWHills) *hld up: hdwy over 6f out: rdn over 3f out: wknd over 2f out* | 51 |
| 0 | **6** | 6 | **Key In**[152] 1395 3-8-11 ... SDrowne 5 **40/1**<br>(BWHills) *a bhd* | 40 |
| 0000 | **7** | 1 | **Zarneeta**[10] 5257 3-8-11 40 ... RSmith 8 **200/1**<br>(WDeBest-Turner) *a bhd* | 38 |
| 4000 | **8** | ½ | **Mystic Moon**[19] 5036 3-8-11 40 ... RLMoore 3 **100/1**<br>(JRJenkins) *a in rr* | 37 |
| 0 | **9** | 2½ | **Gold Relic (USA)**[70] 3592 3-8-11 ... MartinDwyer 7 **33/1**<br>(AMBalding) *a in rr* | 32 |

2m 10.7s (-0.30) **Going Correction** +0.175s/f (Good) **9** Ran SP% **110.7**
Speed ratings: **108,107,106,101,97 92,91,91,89**CSF £14.20 TOTE £2.50: £1.10, £2.20, £3.80; EX 12.90.
**Owner** Aston House Stud **Bred** Aston House Stud **Trained** Newmarket, Suffolk

**FOCUS**
Modest form, but a strong gallop led to a smart winning time for the type of race.

**NOTEBOOK**
**Batik(IRE)** really appreciated the extra quarter-mile and eventually found her stamina enabling her to pull it out of the fire. She could be interesting in handicaps given that the assessor cannot be too harsh on her for this.
**Uig** ensured there would be no hanging about. She did not help her cause by drifting into the centre of the course which is a cardinal sin here. *Official explanation: jockey said filly hung right*
**Principessa** may have been intimidated a little when the runner-up started to drift right, but lack of a turn of foot was the real problem.
**Go Supersonic**, trying a longer trip, never appeared to be going particularly well in this strongly-run race.

## 5512 SHARP MINDS PHONE 0870 90 80 121 H'CAP — 5f 161y
**5:00** (5:00) (E3) (0-70,69) 3-Y-O+ — **£5,883** (£1,810; £905; £452) **Stalls** Low

| Form | | | | RPR |
|---|---|---|---|---|
| 6150 | **1** | | **Oeuf A La Neige**[31] 4707 4-9-2 **64** ... OUrbina 3 **25/1**<br>(GCHChung) *hld up and bhd: rdn and hdwy over 1f out: r.o to ld nr fin* | 73 |
| 0003 | **2** | *nk* | **Roman Quintet (IRE)**[30] 4748 4-8-12 **60** ... TQuinn 5 **7/1**[3]<br>(DWPArbuthnot) *a.p: led ins fnl f: hdd nr fin* | 68 |
| 2000 | **3** | ½ | **Double M**[11] 5253 7-9-3 **65** ... (v) ADaly 4 **14/1**<br>(MrsLRichards) *rdr slow to remove blindfold and s.s: bhd tl rdn and hdwy over 1f out: r.o ins fnl f* | 71 |
| 3122 | **4** | *nk* | **Jagged (IRE)**[7] 5337 4-8-10 **58** ... (v) KFallon 6 **2/1**[1]<br>(JRJenkins) *led: edgd rt towards stands' side fr jst over 2f out: hdd ins fnl f: nt qckn* | 63 |
| 0060 | **5** | *nk* | **Pulse**[4] 5412 6-8-8 **56** ... (p) PFitzsimons 13 **16/1**<br>(JMBradley) *a.p: ev ch whn carried rt towards stands' side fr wl over 1f out: nt qckn ins fnl f* | 60 |
| 2010 | **6** | ½ | **Sewmuch Character**[21] 5008 5-9-7 **69** ... DSweeney 8 **33/1**<br>(MBlanshard) *hld up in tch: rdn over 1f out: one pce fnl f* | 71 |
| 1041 | **7** | 1 | **Woodbury**[7] 5337 5-9-2 **64** 6ex ... GBaker 12 **10/1**<br>(MrsHSweeting) *hld up: hdwy over 2f out: sn rdn: hmpd on stands' rail ins fnl f: nt rcvr* | 63+ |
| 6003 | **8** | ½ | **Innstyle**[7] 5337 3-8-7 **57** ... SHitchcott 2 **6/1**[2]<br>(JLSpearing) *hld up and bhd: hdwy whn nt clr run over 2f out: rdn over 1f out: one pce* | 54+ |
| 0102 | **9** | 2 | **Taboor (IRE)**[17] 5094 6-8-11 **59** ... (bt) MartinDwyer 1 **8/1**<br>(JWPayne) *bhd: rdn 3f out: n.d* | 49 |
| 1050 | **10** | *nk* | **Cayman Breeze**[4] 5408 4-8-9 **57** ... JFEgan 7 **33/1**<br>(JMBradley) *hld up in tch: rdn and wknd wl over 1f out* | 46 |
| 0065 | **11** | 2½ | **Stagnite**[7] 5337 4-8-4 **57** ... (p) NChalmers(5) 11 **14/1**<br>(MrsHSweeting) *prom tl rdn and wknd 2f out* | 37 |
| 5004 | **12** | 1¼ | **Formalise**[11] 5253 4-8-4 **55** oh1 ... (p) RThomas(3) 9 **8/1**<br>(GBBalding) *prom tl wknd 2f out* | 31 |
| 6040 | **13** | 3 | **Pure Imagination (IRE)**[12] 5219 3-8-8 **58** ... RLMoore 10 **25/1**<br>(JMBradley) *dwlt: hdwy over 3f out: rdn over 2f out: wknd over 1f out* | 23 |

1m 12.15s (1.01) **Going Correction** +0.175s/f (Good)
**WFA** 3 from 4yo+ 2lb **13** Ran SP% **124.2**
Speed ratings: **100,99,98,98,98 97,96,95,92,92 89,87,83**CSF £193.00 CT £1664.38 TOTE £38.40: £9.00, £2.50, £3.50; EX 415.30 Place 6 £530.62, Place 5 £140.79.
**Owner** G C H Chung **Bred** Gainsborough Stud Management Ltd **Trained** Newmarket, Suffolk

**FOCUS**
An unsatisfactory affair with the runners fanning out after the pacemaker came across the course more by accident than design. The form is ordinary.

**NOTEBOOK**
**Oeuf A La Neige** came through to snatch it late in the day over a trip on the short side for him.
**Roman Quintet(IRE)** does seem to be knocking on the door at the moment.
**Double M**, whose rider had difficulty removing the hood as the stalls opened, lost far more ground than the margin of his defeat. He has to be considered unlucky.
**Jagged(IRE)** did not help his cause by gradually drifting right across the track.
**Pulse** had little option but to come across the course with the winner, and it is hard to say whether he was unlucky.
**Sewmuch Character** was again running off a mark 7lb higher than when landing a classified event at Folkestone a month ago.
**Woodbury**, was the main sufferer in a messy race. Although she may not have won, she would have finished closer with a trouble-free run.
**Cayman Breeze** *Official explanation: jockey said gelding had its head up and was never travelling*
T/Plt: £789.10 to a £1 stake. Pool: £40,756.50. 37.70 winning tickets. T/Qpdt: £327.70 to a £1 stake. Pool: £2,878.70. 6.50 winning tickets. KH

# 5474 MUSSELBURGH (R-H)
Monday, September 13

**OFFICIAL GOING: Good to firm (good in places)**

## 5513 SHARP MINDS BETFAIR MAIDEN AUCTION STKS — 5f
**2:20** (2:20) (E3) 2-Y-O — **£3,386** (£1,042; £521; £260) **Stalls** Low

| Form | | | | RPR |
|---|---|---|---|---|
| 00 | **1** | | **Blades Boy**[6] 5362 2-8-8 ow1 ... NCallan 1 **16/1**<br>(KARyan) *mde all: rdn over 1f out: hung rt ins last: drvn and jst hld on* | 61 |
| 0526 | **2** | *nk* | **Hymn Of Victory (IRE)**[69] 3605 2-8-7 72 ... JFanning 5 **7/2**[2]<br>(TJEtherington) *outpcd and bhd after 1f: hdwy 2f out: swtchd lft and rdn over 1f out: styd on strly ins last: jst failed* | 59 |
| 0520 | **3** | *shd* | **Procrastinate (IRE)**[6] 5369 2-8-10 54 ... RWinston 4 **10/1**<br>(RFFisher) *chsd ldrs: rdn along 2f out: hdwy over 1f out: swtchd rt ins last and styd on wl u.p* | 62 |
| 0402 | **4** | 3½ | **Bob's Flyer**[2] 5475 2-8-8 ... MFenton 7 **6/4**[1]<br>(JGGiven) *chsd ldrs on outer: effrt 2f out:snrdn and one pce appr last* | 47 |
| | **5** | 1 | **Our Little Secret (IRE)** 2-8-2 ... FNorton 2 **8/1**<br>(ABerry) *cl up: effrt 2f out and ev ch tl rdn and wknd 1f out* | 38 |
| 0 | **6** | 3½ | **Compton Classic**[55] 4003 2-8-10 ... TEaves(3) 6 **50/1**<br>(JSGoldie) *sn outpcd and bhd* | 37 |
| 0 | **7** | 4 | **Miss Jellybean (IRE)**[108] 2458 2-8-4 ow2 ... PMulrennan(3) 3 **5/1**[3]<br>(NTinkler) *cl up: ev ch 2f out: sn rdn and wknd appr last* | 17 |

61.37 secs (0.97) **Going Correction** -0.05s/f (Good) **7** Ran SP% **106.9**
Speed ratings: **90,89,89,83,82 76,70**CSF £62.11 TOTE £27.20: £10.40, £1.80; EX 268.90.
**Owner** Crown Select **Bred** Crown Select **Trained** Hambleton, N Yorks

**FOCUS**
A messy race and modest form, with the winner only improving a stone to score. A modest winning time for the grade, 1.71 seconds slower than the nursery.

**NOTEBOOK**
**Blades Boy**, who had missed the break on both his previous outings, pinged out to make all and lose his maiden tag at the third attempt. This certainly looks to be his trip, and although this was a weak heat, he is learning all the time. *Official explanation: trainer's representative said, regarding the improved form shown, gelding appreciated the drop back to 5f*
**Hymn Of Victory(IRE)** picked up strongly under pressure when switched late on and would have won with a little further. This drop back a furlong was not in his favour and he could find a similarly weak event when reverting to six furlongs.
**Procrastinate(IRE)** stayed on strongly for pressure and was not beaten at all far. This was a much-improved effort and he was clear of the rest, but he has been inconsistent to date and would not be certain to reproduce this form.
**Bob's Flyer**, runner-up over course and distance two days previously, failed to reproduce that form and probably found this coming too soon.



The Form Book, Raceform Ltd, Compton, RG20 6NL

**Miss Jellybean(IRE)** dropped out tamely having held a chance two out, and failed to build on her York debut in May. *Official explanation: jockey said filly hung right handed in final two furlongs*

## 5514 SHARP MINDS: BEST ODDS "PREMIER" CLAIMING STKS 1m 1f
**2:50** (2:50) (D2) 3-Y-0+ **£6,916** (£2,128; £1,064; £532) **Stalls** Low

Form RPR

1121 **1** **The Prince**[15] 5151 10-8-13 79 ..... CCatlin 7 75
(IanWilliams) *hld up in rr: hdwy 4f out: rdn to ld over 1f out: styd on strly* **4/1**[1]

6261 **2** *3* **Barking Mad (USA)**[21] 5006 6-9-9 85 ..... MFenton 3 79
(MLWBell) *led: rdn along over 2f out: drvn and hdd over 1f out: kpt on same pce* **4/1**[1]

3103 **3** *½* **Todlea (IRE)**[13] 5210 4-9-7 76 ..... SWKelly 11 76
(JAOsborne) *dwlt: sn prom: effrt to chal over 2f out: sn rdn and ev ch tl drvn and one pce ov er 1f out* **8/1**

1065 **4** *¾* **Scotty's Future (IRE)**[8] 5315 6-9-10 72 ..... JFanning 8 78
(DNicholls) *hld up and bhd: hdwy 3f out: rdn along wl over 1f out: kpt on ins last* **25/1**

-300 **5** *1* **Dark Charm (FR)**[8] 5315 5-9-5 90 ..... THamilton(3) 10 74
(RAFahey) *trckd ldrs: pushed along over 3f out: rdn over 2f out: drvn and one pce appr last* **9/1**

2034 **6** *shd* **Sarraaf (IRE)**[8] 5317 8-8-11 64 ..... RWinston 1 62
(JSGoldie) *hld up towards rr: hdwy over 2f out: swtchd lft and rdn over 1f out: sn one pce* **14/1**

2421 **7** *3½* **Yenaled**[18] 5061 7-8-9 72 ..... DonnaCaldwell(7) 5 60
(KARyan) *s.i.s and bhd: hdwy on outer 3f out: sn rdn and no imp* **9/2**[2]

5304 **8** *½* **Tedstale (USA)**[13] 5211 6-9-5 77 ..... (b) WSupple 4 62
(TDEasterby) *in tch: effrt over 2f out: sn rdn along and no hdwy* **11/2**[3]

6446 **9** *3½* **Phoenix Nights (IRE)**[17] 5099 4-8-7 52 ..... PPMathers(5) 9 48
(ABerry) *in tch: hdwy on inner 3f out: rdn over 2f out and sn btn* **150/1**

-640 **10** *¾* **Ambushed (IRE)**[19] 3796 8-8-6 50 ..... PMulrennan(3) 6 44
(PMonteith) *chsd ldrs: rdn along 3f out: sn wknd* **150/1**

0 **11** *dist* **Lange Bleu (FR)**[134] 1786 5-8-9 ..... ANicholls 2 —
(MrsSCBradburne) *prom to 1/2-way: sn lost pl and bhd fnl 3f* **200/1**

1m 52.26s (-0.94) **Going Correction** -0.15s/f (Firm) **11** Ran SP% **107.0**
Speed ratings: **98,95,94,94,93 93,90,89,86,85** —CSF £17.16 TOTE £4.40: £1.90, £1.50, £2.70; EX 10.70.
**Owner** Patrick Kelly **Bred** Bottisham Heath Stud **Trained** Portway, Warwicks

**FOCUS**
Strong form for the grade and the pace was fair. The Prince did not need to be at his best to score and is hard to assess accurately at the moment.

**NOTEBOOK**
**The Prince**, winner of this event in 2003, could have been called the winner some way out and duly scored in fine style. He has now won his last six outings at this level in Britain, so is clearly in excellent heart and should continue to be hard to beat.
**Barking Mad(USA)** got the run of the race in front, but had no answer to the winner when challenged entering the final furlong. He ran up to his recent sound form in this grade and should be placed to find a similar race once again.
**Todlea(IRE)** turned in another sound effort, but lacked a change of gear when it mattered. He can strike in this grade, but needs all to fall right and has trouble finishing his races.
**Scotty's Future(IRE)** looked laboured for most of the way, but was doing all of his best work late on and was not disgraced at the weights. He can be found easier opportunities at this level, but is not easy to predict.
**Dark Charm(FR)**, best in at the weights, was woefully one-paced in the straight and has gone badly the wrong way since his excellent third in the Lincoln in March.
**Yenaled**, successful in this grade over course and distance for this rider last time, was never a factor after missing the break and has to be considered disappointing.
**Tedstale(USA)** failed to improve for this drop in grade and ran a flat race. He again suggested he may be worth a try over further.

## 5515 SHARP MINDS BETFAIR BET IN RUNNING NURSERY 5f
**3:20** (3:25) (C1) (0-95,93) 2-Y-0 **£13,728** (£4,224; £2,112; £1,056) **Stalls** Low

Form RPR

0213 **1** **Oceanico Dot Com (IRE)**[6] 5363 2-7-13 **71** oh3 ow1 ..... FNorton 12 74
(ABerry) *a.p: effrt 2f out: rdn over 1f out: styd on to ld wl ins last* **12/1**

4510 **2** *nk* **Smiddy Hill**[18] 5060 2-8-3 **82** ..... AMullen(7) 8 84
(RBastiman) *cl up: led after 1 1/2f: rdn over 1f out: hdd and nt qckn wl ins last* **16/1**

2310 **3** *shd* **Moth Ball**[14] 5202 2-8-11 **83** ..... SWKelly 3 85
(JAOsborne) *hmpd s: a chsng ldrs: rdn wl over 1f out: styd on u.p ins last* **5/1**[1]

0450 **4** *1¼* **Talcen Gwyn (IRE)**[4] 5421 2-8-6 **78** ..... ANicholls 5 75
(MFHarris) *hmpd s and sn wl bhd: hdwy wl over 1f out: styd on strly ins last: nrst fin* **50/1**

212 **5** *shd* **Graze On**[15] 5143 2-8-12 **84** ..... RWinston 10 81
(JJQuinn) *towards rr: hdwy 2f out: sn rdn and swtchd rt over 1f out: kpt on fnl f* **10/1**

2010 **6** *nk* **Imperial Sound**[5] 5392 2-9-7 **93** ..... PFessey 4 89
(TDBarron) *hmpd s: sn chsng ldrs: rdn 2f out: drvn and hung lft over 1f out: one pce* **7/1**[3]

3122 **7** *nk* **Wise Wager (IRE)**[25] 4875 2-8-2 **77** ..... THamilton(3) 7 72
(RAFahey) *led 1 1/2f: cl up tl rdn along 2f out and grad wknd* **6/1**[2]

4610 **8** *1½* **Annatalia**[58] 3938 2-8-9 **81** ..... CCatlin 2 71+
(BJMeehan) *hmpd s and towards rr: hdwy 2f out: effrt and clsng whn hmpd over 1f out: nt rcvr* **15/2**

2215 **9** *shd* **Gifted Gamble**[44] 4325 2-8-8 **80** ..... NCallan 13 69
(KARyan) *in tch on outer: rdn along 2f out: wknd over 1f out* **25/1**

10 **10** *nk* **Gloved Hand**[89] 2970 2-9-3 **89** ..... MFenton 9 77
(JGGiven) *midfield: rdn along 2f out: no hdwy* **10/1**

4013 **11** *1* **Nova Tor (IRE)**[24] 4918 2-9-1 **87** ..... IMongan 1 72+
(NPLittmoden) *wnt rt s: prom tl rdn along 2f out and sn wknd* **5/1**[1]

331 **12** *5* **Trim Image**[32] 4670 2-7-11 **74** ..... BSwarbrick(5) 11 41
(HAlexander) *racd wd: bhd fr 1/2-way* **50/1**

5632 **13** *¾* **Wonderful Mind**[18] 5060 2-8-2 **74** ..... (b) WSupple 6 39
(TDEasterby) *chsd ldrs: rdn along 2f out: wknd over 1f out* **10/1**

59.66 secs (-0.74) **Going Correction** -0.05s/f (Good) **13** Ran SP% **120.5**
Speed ratings: **103,102,102,100,100 99,99,96,96,96 94,86,85** CSF £189.20 CT £1127.58 TOTE £21.40: £4.50, £5.10, £2.40; EX 385.80 Trifecta £416.20 Pool £703.50, 1.20 w/u.
**Owner** The Red And The Green **Bred** Mrs C Hartery **Trained** Cockerham, Lancs
■ Stewards Enquiry : P Fessey one-day ban: careless riding (Sep 25)

**FOCUS**
A competitive nursery which was run at a solid gallop and the form looks sound, although several were hampered at the start.

**NOTEBOOK**
**Oceanico Dot Com(IRE)**, not disgraced on her nursery debut under a penalty six days previously, was handy throughout and produced a tenacious display to score. She is progressing well and is clearly a brave filly, so could be placed to win more races at this level.
**Smiddy Hill** got to the lead this time and ran much better as a result. She lacked a change of gear late on, but went down fighting and this is her true form.
**Moth Ball** probably lost it at the start, as he was flying late on and was not beaten at all far. This drop back a furlong was not ideal, but he relished this faster ground and can make amends when facing a stiffer test.
**Talcen Gwyn(IRE)** was another to lose momentum at the start and lost ground, but he really picked up for his rider at halfway and was finishing best of all. He can be rated better than the bare form and it goes down as a much-improved effort.
**Graze On** was not able to go with the early pace, but stuck to his task well from halfway and ran another solid race. He looks worthy of a try at an extra furlong.
**Imperial Sound** was not disgraced under topweight, having met trouble at the start.
**Wise Wager(IRE)** had her chance, but found just the same pace when asked to win his race. She looks weighted to the hilt at present, but should find easier opportunities. *Official explanation: jockey said filly finished lame*
**Nova Tor(IRE)** caused the mayhem at the start and then proved disappointing through the race. This quick ground may have accounted for her poor effort. *Official explanation: jockey said filly hung right handed throughout*

## 5516 SHARP MINDS BETFAIR BACK AND LAY MAIDEN AUCTION STKS 1m
**3:50** (3:50) (E3) 2-Y-0 **£3,413** (£1,050; £525; £262) **Stalls** Low

Form RPR

265 **1** **Lithos**[10] 5264 2-8-13 77 ..... SWKelly 1 80
(JAOsborne) *hld up: tk clsr order 1/2-way: swtchd ins and effrt 2f out: rdn to ld appr last and kpt on* **10/3**[2]

42 **2** *2* **Maneki Neko (IRE)**[28] 4797 2-8-10 ..... NCallan 6 73
(MHTompkins) *trckd ldrs: hdwy over 3f out: led over 2f out and sn rdn: drvn and hdd appr last: one pce* **10/11**[1]

3440 **3** *3* **Blackcomb Mountain (USA)**[25] 4890 2-8-2 68 ..... ANicholls 2 58
(MFHarris) *cl up tl carried bdly wd bnd after 3f and bhd: hdwy to chse ldng pair over 2f out: sn rdn and kpt on same pce apprlast* **8/1**

0326 **4** *3* **Eskdale (IRE)**[14] 5186 2-8-7 67 ..... PMulrennan(3) 4 60
(RFFisher) *chsd ldrs: rdn along 3f out: sn drvn and one pce* **13/2**[3]

0 **5** *3½* **Geordie Dancer (IRE)**[11] 5233 2-8-8 ..... PPMathers(5) 7 55
(ABerry) *dwlt: sn cl up: lft in ld bnd after 3f: rdn along and hdd over 2f out: sn wknd* **33/1**

000 **6** *9* **Bella Plunkett (IRE)**[14] 5200 2-7-11 ..... BSwarbrick(5) 5 24
(WMBrisbourne) *disp ld tl led and rn v wd bnd after 3f: sn bhd* **20/1**

1m 41.84s (-0.86) **Going Correction** -0.15s/f (Firm) **6** Ran SP% **107.6**
Speed ratings: **98,96,93,90,86 77** CSF £6.16 TOTE £3.90: £1.50, £1.40; EX 7.10.
**Owner** J McGarry **Bred** Ecurie Haras De Beauvoir **Trained** Upper Lambourn, Berks
■ Stewards Enquiry : S W Kelly caution: careless riding

**FOCUS**
A modest affair and field came home well strung out. The form ought to stand up, however.

**NOTEBOOK**
**Lithos**, who looked useful on his debut in August, but had subsequently disappointed the last twice, showed his true colours and won readily. This faster ground was right up his street and he could progress in nurseries over this trip.
**Maneki Neko(IRE)** held every chance if good enough over this longer distance, but could only muster the same pace when it mattered. He is learning all the time and seemed to get this trip, so should not be written off and is now eligible for nurseries.
**Blackcomb Mountain(USA)**, stepping up in trip, again looked far from straightforward, but deserves credit for getting so close having been badly interefered with on the turn out of the back straight.
**Eskdale(IRE)** was found wanting over this longer trip and back on fast ground. He looks in need of another drop into plating company.
**Bella Plunkett(IRE)** *Official explanation: jockey said filly hung badly left handed on bend leaving back straight*

## 5517 SHARP MINDS BETFAIR MUSSELBURGH GOLD CUP (A H'CAP) 1m 4f
**4:20** (4:20) (D2) (0-85,84) 3-Y-0+ **£10,108** (£3,110; £1,555; £777) **Stalls** High

Form RPR

2210 **1** **Jeepstar**[8] 5318 4-9-3 **77** ..... MFenton 8 85
(TDEasterby) *mde all: rdn along over 2f out: drvn and edgd lft and rt ent last: r.o gamely* **4/1**[2]

1314 **2** *¾* **Mr Tambourine Man (IRE)**[10] 5273 3-9-1 **84** ..... CCatlin 10 91
(PFICole) *hld up in tch: hdwy on inner over 2f out: rdn over 1f out: drvn ins last and kpt on wl* **11/2**[3]

3310 **3** *½* **Sahem (IRE)**[9] 5288 7-9-9 **83** ..... WSupple 5 89
(CJTeague) *trckd ldrs: hdwy on outer to chal 2f out and ev ch tl drvn and nt qckn wl ins last* **20/1**

5313 **4** *hd* **Easibet Dot Net**[27] 4830 4-8-9 **69** oh3 ..... (p) RWinston 2 75?
(ISemple) *hld up in tch: hdwy 2f out: effrt and shkn up ent last: kpt on towards fin* **20/1**

1003 **5** *hd* **Merrymaker**[15] 5144 4-8-5 **70** ..... PPMathers(5) 1 75
(WMBrisbourne) *dwlt: hld up and bhd: hdwy on outer over 2f out: rdn over 1f out kpt on same pce ins last* **12/1**

4010 **6** *½* **Rutters Rebel (IRE)**[9] 5303 3-8-2 **71** ..... PFessey 4 76
(GASwinbank) *trckd ldrs on inner: effrt over 2f out: sn rdn and n.m.r whn swtchd lft ins last: kpt on same pce* **16/1**

6060 **7** *¾* **Ski Jump (USA)**[9] 5288 4-9-4 **81** ..... (v) THamilton(3) 3 84
(RAFahey) *hld up in tch: hdwy over 2f out: rdn wl over 1f out: wknd ent last* **6/1**

2010 **8** *3* **Baileys Dancer**[31] 4729 3-8-12 **81** ..... JFanning 6 80
(MJohnston) *chsd wnr: rdn along 3f out: drvn and wknd 2f out* **12/1**

4111 **9** *2* **Jack Of Trumps (IRE)**[17] 5074 4-9-4 **78** ..... FNorton 7 73
(GWragg) *hld up in touc h: hdwy 4f out: effrt to chal over 2f out and ev ch tl rdn and wknd wl over 1f out* **5/2**[1]

2m 35.21s (-2.81) **Going Correction** -0.15s/f (Firm)
**WFA** 3 from 4yo+ 9lb **9** Ran SP% **109.0**
Speed ratings: **103,102,102,102,101 101,101,99,97** CSF £23.75 CT £346.88 TOTE £6.20: £1.30, £2.00, £3.50; EX 29.80.
**Owner** Miss E Jeeps And Partners **Bred** P D And Mrs Player **Trained** Great Habton, N Yorks
■ Stewards Enquiry : P P Mathers four-day ban: used whip with excessive frequency (Sep 24-27)

**FOCUS**
A tight handicap run at just an ordinary pace, that produced a bunch finish.

**NOTEBOOK**
**Jeepstar**, winner of this event last year off a 6lb lower mark, really dug deep late on to repel his challengers having looked like folding two out and scored under a well-judged ride from Fenton. This was a very brave performance and he should continue to pay his way, but could be vulnerable off a higher mark in the future.
**Mr Tambourine Man(IRE)**, again held up to get this trip, ran another solid race off this career-high mark. He should find easier opportunites and is worth perservering with over the trip, but may just remain vulnerable to an improver off his current rating.
**Sahem(IRE)** turned in a decent effort under topweight and firmly put behind him a disappointing effort at Haydock last time. This trip is on the short side, so he could well defy this mark when reverting to further.

**Easibet Dot Net** was held up this time and it seemed to work, as he turned in another sound effort. He deserves extra credit, as he was 4lb out of the weights, and he is clearly in good form at present.
**Merrymaker** ran his race, but now looks firmly within the Handicapper's grasp.
**Ski Jump(USA)** shaped like a non-stayer over this trip. He is well treated at present, but is in need of a shorter trip.
**Jack Of Trumps(IRE)** looked to be holding every chance over two out, but quickly fell in a hole and ran well below his best. He has it all to prove now.

## 5518 SHARP MINDS BETFAIR PHONE 0870 90 80 121 CLASSIFIED STKS 1m

4:50 (4:50) (F3) 3-Y-0+ £3,523 (£1,084; £542; £271) Stalls Low

Form RPR

0633 **1** **Mobane Flyer**[8] 5320 4-9-0 60 THamilton(3) 3 71
(RAFahey) *trckd ldrs: hdwy 3f out: rdn to ld over 1f out: drvn ins last and jst hld on* **5/1**[2]

5-00 **2** *shd* **Bond Millennium**[7] 5344 6-9-3 59 FNorton 1 71
(BSmart) *hld up towards rr: gd hdwy on outer over 2f out: rdn to chal over 1f out: sn drvn and kpt on: jst hld* **17/2**

4240 **3** *1 1/2* **Newcorp Lad**[11] 5236 4-9-3 59 JFanning 6 67
(MrsGSRees) *trckd ldng pair: smooth hdwy to ld over 2f out: rdn and edgd rt wl over 1f out: sn hdd and kpt on same pce ent last* **7/1**[3]

5002 **4** *hd* **Legal Set (IRE)**[6] 5364 8-9-0 57 (t) LFletcher(3) 10 67
(MissAStokell) *chsd ldrs: hdwy 2f out: sn rdn and kpt on same pce appr last* **14/1**

4230 **5** *2* **Joshua's Gold (IRE)**[6] 5370 3-8-5 57 DTudhope(7) 5 62
(DCarroll) *bhd: gd hdwy on outer over 2f out: sn rdn and kpt on fnl f: nrst fin* **20/1**

-514 **6** *nk* **Commitment Lecture**[132] 1875 4-9-0 57 (t) SWKelly 7 59
(MDods) *midfield: hdwy 3f out: rdn along 2f out: sn one pce* **12/1**

33-0 **7** *1 1/4* **Beamish Prince**[40] 4449 5-9-3 57 MFenton 9 59
(GMMoore) *bhd tl styd on fnl 2f: nvr a factor* **33/1**

2003 **8** *shd* **Nemo Fugat (IRE)**[8] 5317 5-9-3 60 (v) ANicholls 12 58
(DNicholls) *led: rdn along 3f out: hdd over 2f out and grad wknd* **9/2**[1]

1320 **9** *shd* **Anthemion (IRE)**[27] 4826 7-9-3 60 DMcGaffin 2 58
(MrsJCMcgregor) *midfield: effrt on outer 3f out: sn rdn along and no imp* **16/1**

0330 **10** *1 1/4* **Louisiade (IRE)**[35] 4610 3-8-12 60 WSupple 4 55
(TDEasterby) *chsd ldr: rdn along 3f out: wknd fnl 2f* **10/1**

3306 **11** *shd* **Regent's Secret (USA)**[8] 5317 4-9-0 59 PMulrennan(3) 13 55
(JSGoldie) *midfield: hdwy 3f out: rdn and edgd rt 2f out: sn wknd* **10/1**

0314 **12** *nk* **Zandeed (IRE)**[7] 5344 6-9-3 59 PFessey 11 54
(MissLAPerratt) *a rr* **12/1**

6606 **13** *14* **Wood Dalling (USA)**[11] 5235 6-9-3 54 RWinston 14 22
(ISemple) *chsd ldrs: rdn along over 3f out: wkng whn n.m.r 2f out: sn bhd and eased* **16/1**

1m 40.0s (-2.70) **Going Correction** -0.15s/f (Firm)
**WFA** 3 from 4yo+ 5lb **13** Ran SP% **117.6**
Speed ratings: **107,106,105,105,103 102,101,101,101,100 100,99,85**CSF £46.45 TOTE £5.90: £2.70, £1.80, £3.70; EX 43.60.
**Owner** P N Devlin **Bred** Cheveley Park Stud Ltd **Trained** Musley Bank, N Yorks

**FOCUS**
A moderate handicap, but it produced a smart time for the class. The form looks very solid for the grade.

**NOTEBOOK**
**Mobane Flyer** proved game late on to hold off the runner-up and gained a deserved success. He enjoyed racing handy over this shorter trip and he could follow up on this, as he was rated 20lb higher as a three-year-old, when trained by Dermot Weld in Ireland.
**Bond Millennium** showed the benefit of his recent comeback from a seven-month lay-off and only lost out by a whisker. This was his best effort for a long time and a reproduction of this would see him hard to beat next time.
**Newcorp Lad**, who disappointed in the first-time visor latest, had every chance, but did not see his race out that well. This was much more like his true form and he can find a samll race off this mark.
**Legal Set(IRE)** posted a creditable effot over a trip that stretches him. He could be about to strike when dropped back in trip.
**Nemo Fugat(IRE)** paid for setting too strong a gallop and is capable of better than this when reverting to more patient tactics and a sharper test.
**Zandeed(IRE)** *Official explanation: jockey said gelding was never travelling*

## 5519 SHARP MINDS BETFAIR H'CAP 2m

5:20 (5:20) (E3) (0-70,66) 3-Y-0+ £3,359 (£1,033; £516; £258) Stalls Low

Form RPR

0222 **1** **Sharadi (IRE)**[2] 5479 3-9-3 66 NCallan 4 82
(VSmith) *trckd ldr: hdwy to ld wl over 2f out: sn rdn clr* **2/1**[1]

2325 **2** *6* **Spring Breeze**[16] 5130 3-8-3 52 (v[1]) PFessey 5 61
(MDods) *led: rdn along 4f out: hdd wl over 2f out: sn drvn and kpt on same pce* **11/2**

1444 **3** *10* **Sonoma (IRE)**[20] 5027 4-9-11 61 MFenton 2 58
(MLWBell) *in tch: rdn along over 5f out: drvn over 3f out: sn no imp* **7/2**[2]

1060 **4** *hd* **Gargoyle Girl**[20] 3236 7-9-8 58 WSupple 1 55
(JSGoldie) *hld up and bhd: hdwy over 3f out: sn rdn along and nvr nr ldrs* **9/2**[3]

5300 **5** *12* **Dance Light (IRE)**[10] 5274 5-9-6 56 JFanning 6 38
(TTClement) *chsd first two: rdn along 5f out: drvn and wknd 3f out* **8/1**

6060 **6** *19* **Millennium Hall**[18] 5058 5-9-9 59 RWinston 3 18
(PMonteith) *a rr* **8/1**

3m 30.28s (-3.42) **Going Correction** -0.15s/f (Firm)
**WFA** 3 from 4yo+ 13lb **6** Ran SP% **111.3**
Speed ratings: **102,99,94,93,87 78**CSF £13.10 TOTE £3.20: £1.70, £2.60; EX 14.20 Place 6 £108.83, Place 5 £33.62.
**Owner** R J Baines **Bred** His Highness The Aga Khan's Studs S C **Trained** Exning, Suffolk

**FOCUS**
A weak staying handicap which was run at a fair pace. The two three-year-olds had it to themselves.

**NOTEBOOK**
**Sharadi(IRE)**, runner-up over 14 furlongs at this track just two days previously, gained a deserved success and won in style over this longer trip. Granted this was a very moderate affair, but he is clearly in good form and should continue to give a good account of himself, even though he will go up in the ratings for this.
**Spring Breeze**, racing in a visor for the first time, ran very much up to form, back over this longer trip. He is proving a hard horse to win with and is still a maiden after 12 outings, but he was well clear in second.
**Sonoma(IRE)** has to go down as disappointing, as she had plenty in her favour, and was beaten with no obvious excuses.
**Gargoyle Girl**, a comfortable winner over hurdles last time, never posed a serious threat from off the pace and is probably best kept over hurdles now.
**Millennium Hall** *Official explanation: jockey said gelding ran flat*
T/Jkpt: Not won. T/Plt: £128.70 to a £1 stake. Pool: £41,190.55. 233.55 winning tickets. T/Qpdt: £28.60 to a £1 stake. Pool: £3,080.50. 79.50 winning tickets. JR

# 5239 REDCAR (L-H)

## Monday, September 13

**OFFICIAL GOING: Firm (good to firm in places)**

## 5520 SHARP MINDS WINNERS WELCOME NURSERY 5f

2:10 (2:12) (E3) (0-75,75) 2-Y-0 £4,225 (£1,300; £650; £325) Stalls Centre

Form RPR

2230 **1** **Connotation**[18] 5052 2-8-12 66 (v[1]) LDettori 11 73
(PWD'Arcy) *dwlt: rr: hdwy over 1f out: r.o wl u.p to ld clsng stages* **8/1**

41 **2** *1/2* **Clove (USA)**[49] 4191 2-9-7 75 RHughes 15 80
(BWHills) *dwlt: led after 1f: rdn over 1f out: hdd clsng stages: no ex* **2/1**[1]

0402 **3** *1/2* **Lord John**[6] 5363 2-7-13 53 (b) DaleGibson 3 56
(MWEasterby) *wnt lft s: sn cl up: rdn over 1f out: disp ld ins last: no ex clsng stages* **13/2**[3]

6105 **4** *2* **Hopelessly Devoted**[11] 5234 2-7-11 56 RoryMoore(5) 7 51
(PCHaslam) *cl up: ev ch and rdn appr fnl f: fdd ins last* **14/1**

4233 **5** *1 1/4* **Bond Babe**[13] 5209 2-9-0 68 SSanders 8 58
(BSmart) *led 1f: remained cl up tl rdn and wknd appr fnl f* **9/2**[2]

2450 **6** *3/4* **Hillside Heather (IRE)**[15] 5143 2-8-10 64 (p) DeanMcKeown 12 51
(ABerry) *midfield: kpt on u.p fnl f* **7/1**

0000 **7** *nk* **Our Louis**[6] 5363 2-8-0 54 RFfrench 13 40
(JSWainwright) *prom: rdn 2f out: sn btn* **25/1**

5004 **8** *1* **Paris Bell**[32] 4676 2-8-10 64 KDarley 1 46
(TDEasterby) *dwlt and hmpd s: midfield: drvn along 1/2-way: no hdwy* **12/1**

0460 **9** *hd* **Gogetter Girl**[18] 5054 2-8-12 66 (p) TEDurcan 5 47
(JGallagher) *midfield: fdrvn along 1/2-way: no hdwy* **25/1**

0040 **10** *1/2* **Cadogen Square**[6] 5363 2-7-12 52 oh3 PMQuinn 9 31
(DWChapman) *s.i.s: sn midfield: drvn along 1/2-way: no hdwy* **50/1**

0550 **11** *3/4* **Kilmovee**[11] 5234 2-8-13 67 EAhern 10 43
(NTinkler) *midfield: drvn along 1/2-way: sn btn* **25/1**

0500 **12** *3* **Carmania (IRE)**[6] 5363 2-7-6 53 DFentiman(7) 6 17
(RPElliott) *sn bhd* **40/1**

6000 **13** *2 1/2* **Paula Jo**[29] 4776 2-7-12 52 oh7 (p) DMernagh 14 6
(JSWainwright) *midfield to 1/2-way: sn bhd* **50/1**

056 **14** *3 1/2* **Isitloveyourafter (IRE)**[46] 4277 2-7-12 52 oh2 JQuinn 2 —
(RPElliott) *dwlt and hmpd s: sn wl bhd* **50/1**

57.78 secs (-0.92) **Going Correction** -0.475s/f (Firm) **14** Ran SP% **122.7**
Speed ratings: **88,87,86,83,81 80,79,77,77,76 75,70,66,61**CSF £23.35 CT £117.58 TOTE £7.60: £2.80, £1.10, £2.40; EX 23.90.
**Owner** Hyperion Bloodstock **Bred** Millsec Limited **Trained** Newmarket, Suffolk

**FOCUS**
Solid nursery form, and a modest winning time given the conditions.

**NOTEBOOK**
**Connotation** did not get home over seven furlongs last time and appreciated the drop back to the minimum trip. Visored for the first time, she came from the back to lead close home in a race run into a headwind.
**Clove(USA)** did not look to have been set too stiff a task by the Handicapper based on her Windsor maiden success but, having made most of the running, was headed close home. This was the quickest ground she has encountered to date.
**Lord John** ran well again in the blinkers and clearly the headgear is having the desired effect.
**Hopelessly Devoted** won her claimer in heavy ground and she seemed to handle these very different conditions well in the circumstances.
**Bond Babe** would have preferred an uncontested lead but was forced to surrender that role to the favourite.
**Hillside Heather(IRE)** is struggling off her current mark.

## 5521 SHARP MINDS BETFAIR/EUROPEAN BREEDERS FUND MAIDEN FILLIES' STKS 6f

2:40 (2:42) (D3) 2-Y-0 £3,926 (£1,208; £604; £302) Stalls Centre

Form RPR

0 **1** **Amalie (IRE)**[11] 5248 2-8-11 SSanders 5 88+
(CEBrittain) *s.i.s: hdwy and cl up 1/2-way: drvn to ld over 1f out: sn clr: eased cl home* **7/2**[3]

4 **2** *3* **May Morning (IRE)**[17] 5070 2-8-11 RHughes 12 76
(BWHills) *cl up: rdn 2f out: kpt on fnl f: no ch w wnr* **5/2**[1]

20 **3** *1/2* **Rasseem (IRE)**[17] 5070 2-8-11 LDettori 4 75
(SaeedBinSuroor) *led tl hdd over 1f out: sn btn* **11/4**[2]

3 **4** *6* **Branston Lily**[37] 4532 2-8-11 DeanMcKeown 10 55
(GASwinbank) *chsd ldrs: rdn 2f out: sn outpcd by ldng trio* **8/1**

**5** *1 1/4* **Kindling** 2-8-11 RFfrench 3 51
(MJohnston) *sn bhd: drvn along 1/2-way: hdwy over 1f out: styd on fnl f: n.d* **12/1**

**6** *nk* **Nepal (IRE)** 2-8-11 DMernagh 1 50
(TDBarron) *midfield: drvn along 1/2-way: no hdwy* **16/1**

**7** *1/2* **Musardiere** 2-8-11 LGoncalves 7 48
(MrsJRRamsden) *sn bhd: rn green: kpt on fnl f: n.d* **28/1**

00 **8** *1/2* **Mercari**[65] 3741 2-8-11 NPollard 11 47
(GMMoore) *chsd ldrs: drvn along 1/2-way: sn wknd* **66/1**

**9** *6* **Sorceress** 2-8-11 TEDurcan 6 27
(JGallagher) *midfield: drvn along 1/2-way: no hdwy: wknd over 1f out* **50/1**

0 **10** *13* **Graceful Flight**[17] 5096 2-8-11 RFitzpatrick 8 —
(PTMidgley) *midfield to 1/2-way: sn bhd: t.o* **100/1**

**11** *4* **Factual Lady** 2-8-11 KDarley 13 —
(TDEasterby) *slowly away: a wl bhd: t.o* **16/1**

**12** *25* **Sterling Supporter** 2-8-11 LEnstone 9 —
(DWThompson) *prom early: sn towards rr: faltered over 3f out: sn eased: t.o* **50/1**

69.39 secs (-2.31) **Going Correction** -0.475s/f (Firm) 2y crse rec **12** Ran SP% **117.9**
Speed ratings: **96,92,91,83,81 81,80,79,71,54 49,15**CSF £12.29 TOTE £3.10: £1.30, £1.40, £1.20; EX 12.70.
**Owner** Saeed Manana **Bred** John T L Jones, W McMinn And Live Foal Inc **Trained** Newmarket, Suffolk

**FOCUS**
A juvenile course record time and the form picks came clear, suggesting the form is sound.

**NOTEBOOK**
**Amalie(IRE)** had shaped with promise on her debut and came clear to win this fair maiden in good style. She looks capable of handling a step up in grade, although her trainer is prone to pitching his charges in at the deep end once they show some ability.

**May Morning(IRE)** appreciated the step up in trip and confirmed her debut form with Rasseem, although nowhere near as convincingly, but the winner had too many guns for her on this occasion. Her stable is back in form now, and she should find her maiden on this evidence.
**Rasseem(IRE)** got bogged down in softish ground at Bath last time and preferred this quicker surface. She got much closer to May Morning than at Bath, finishing clear of the rest, and nurseries are now an option for connections.
**Branston Lily** could not live with the first three but ran another encouraging race, suggesting she will pay her way once handicapped.
**Kindling**, a half-sister to four winners, was starting over a short-enough trip given her breeding and can be expected to improve with time.
**Musardiere**, a half-sister to smart middle-distance performer Montalban, was too green to do herself justice on her debut, and in any case is bred to need much farther.
**Sterling Supporter** *Official explanation: vet said filly was sore behind*

## 5522 SHARP MINDS BETFAIR : BEST ODDS/EUROPEAN BREEDERS FUND MAIDEN STKS (FOR THE DOUBLE TRIGGER TROPHY) 1m 1f

**3:10** (3:11) (D3) 2-Y-O **£3,926** (£1,208; £604; £302) **Stalls** Low

| Form | Pos | Dist | Horse | Jockey | RPR |
|---|---|---|---|---|---|
| 23 | 1 | | **Spear (IRE)**[24] 4900 2-9-0 (DRLoder) *mde all: rdn over 2f out: hrd pressed fnl f: hld on wl* **7/2**[2] | SSanders 4 | 80 |
| 34 | 2 | *shd* | **Haatmey**[24] 4900 2-9-0 (MRChannon) *trckd ldrs: rdn 3f out: disp ld ins fnl f: jst hld* **6/1** | TEDurcan 6 | 80 |
| 6603 | 3 | 2 ½ | **Chinese Puzzle**[9] 5302 2-9-0 71 (HRACecil) *hld up: hdwy u.p 3f out: chsd first 2 fr over 1f out: no imp ins last* **11/4**[1] | (t) RHughes 11 | 74 |
| 06 | 4 | *nk* | **Lunar Sky (USA)**[30] 4753 2-8-9 (CEBrittain) *hld up: hdwy u.p 3f out: chsd ldrs over 1f out: kpt on same pce ins last* **5/1**[3] | JQuinn 9 | 68 |
| | 5 | 3 | **Timber Scorpion (UAE)** 2-9-0 (MJohnston) *cl up: rdn over 3f out: fdd fnl 2f* **9/1** | RFfrench 5 | 66 |
| 00 | 6 | 2 ½ | **Trigony (IRE)**[17] 5095 2-9-0 (TDEasterby) *trckd ldrs tl outpcd 4f out: n.d after* **100/1** | KDarley 3 | 60 |
| 20 | 7 | *nk* | **Double Kudos (FR)**[22] 4966 2-9-0 (JGGiven) *trckd ldrs: rdn 3f out: sn btn* **11/2** | LDettori 8 | 59 |
| 0 | 8 | 3 | **Indonesia**[15] 5142 2-9-0 (MJohnston) *sn towards rr: drvn along 4f out: no hdwy* **33/1** | DeanMcKeown 10 | 52 |
| 0 | 9 | 1 ¼ | **Be Bop**[9] 5302 2-9-0 (NTinkler) *dwlt: midfield whn short of room 1/2-way: in rr and drvn along 4f out: no hdwy* **80/1** | KimTinkler 7 | 49 |
| | 10 | 3 | **Cabopino Lad (USA)** 2-9-0 (MrsLStubbs) *s.i.s: rr: drvn along 4f out: no hdwy* **66/1** | JoannaBadger 1 | 42 |

1m 52.44s (-0.96) **Going Correction** -0.15s/f (Firm) 2y crse rec **10 Ran SP% 111.9**
Speed ratings: **98,97,95,95,92 90,90,87,86,83**CSF £23.37 TOTE £2.80: £1.50, £1.60, £1.30; EX 19.30.
**Owner** Highclere Thoroughbred Racing XXIV **Bred** Sir Evelyn De Rothschild **Trained** Newmarket, Suffolk

**FOCUS**
This was a real stamina test for these two-year-olds, and given the proximity of the 71-rated Chinese Puzzle in third, not overly strong form.

**NOTEBOOK**
**Spear(IRE)** did not handle the soft ground at Ayr last time but found these quick conditions far more suitable. He had threatened to be suited by the step up in trip and on this evidence he could develop into a Zetland Stakes contender, although he will have to improve again to take a hand at Newmarket.
**Haatmey**, one place behind the winner at Ayr last time, had to accept being beaten by that rival again. He only lost out narrowly, though, and is clearly not short on stamina. He is eligible to run in handicap company now.
**Chinese Puzzle**, only rated 71, looked sure to be suited by the step up in trip, but it was surprising to see him supported into favouritism. His performance does not do a lot for the value of the form.
**Lunar Sky(USA)** ran in a decent Newmarket maiden last time and looked to hold a solid chance on that effort. This was the first time she had taken on the colts, but she was still a bit disappointing. She got the longer trip well enough, though.
**Timber Scorpion(UAE)**, whose dam is a three-parts sister to high-class sprinter Millstream, is not necessarily bred to stay well, but this was not a bad debut and he will certainly come on for the experience.
**Trigony(IRE)** ran a better race on this step up in trip, and can now be given a mark.

## 5523 SHARP MINDS BETFAIR : BACK & LAY H'CAP 1m 6f 19y

**3:40** (3:40) (E3) (0-70,73) 3-Y-O+ **£7,553** (£2,324; £1,162; £581) **Stalls** Low

| Form | Pos | Dist | Horse | Jockey | RPR |
|---|---|---|---|---|---|
| 1211 | 1 | | **Inchpast**[6] 5365 3-9-1 73 6ex (MHTompkins) *trckd ldrs: hdwy to ld 3f out: styd on wl u.p* **7/4**[1] | (b) LDettori 8 | 83+ |
| 0623 | 2 | ½ | **Most Definitely (IRE)**[2] 5479 4-9-1 62 (TDEasterby) *hld up in rr: hdwy 2f out: styd on u.p to go 2nd ins fnl f: nt rch wnr* **6/1**[3] | TEDurcan 5 | 68 |
| 3004 | 3 | 1 ½ | **Distant Cousin**[45] 4297 7-8-9 56 (MABuckley) *cl up: upsides gng wl over 2f out: rdn over 1f out: no ex fnl f* **20/1** | (v) ACulhane 2 | 60 |
| 1610 | 4 | ¾ | **Best Port (IRE)**[8] 5318 8-8-12 64 (JParkes) *in tch: drvn to take clsr order 3f out: ev ch and rdn over 1f out: kpt on same pce* **7/1** | MLawson(5) 1 | 67 |
| -100 | 5 | 1 | **Etching (USA)**[103] 2590 4-8-13 60 (JRFanshawe) *hld up: drvn along and hdwy over 2f out: chsng ldrs and rdn whn hung rt ent fnl: no ex* **12/1** | RHughes 6 | 61 |
| 6013 | 6 | *nk* | **Masterman Ready**[15] 5159 3-8-8 66 (PWHarris) *prom: short of room briefly over 3f out: sn chsng ldrs and drvn along: no hdwy* **5/1**[2] | EAhern 4 | 67 |
| 3524 | 7 | 3 | **East Cape**[15] 5144 7-8-9 56 oh11 (DonEnricoIncisa) *hld up: drvn along 3f out: no hdwy* **25/1** | KimTinkler 10 | 53? |
| 0660 | 8 | *nk* | **Lawrence Of Arabia (IRE)**[20] 5027 4-8-11 58 (SirMarkPrescott) *led: rdn 4f out: hdd 3f out: sn wknd* **5/1**[2] | SSanders 7 | 54 |
| /000 | 9 | *dist* | **Dr Cool**[15] 5152 7-8-9 56 oh1 (JAkehurst) *hld up in rr: rdn over 4f out: lost tch 3f out: t.o* **50/1** | JQuinn 9 | — |

3m 4.52s (-0.48) **Going Correction** -0.15s/f (Firm)
**WFA** 3 from 4yo+ 11lb **9 Ran SP% 114.7**
Speed ratings: **95,94,93,93,92 92,90,90,—**CSF £12.15 CT £154.18 TOTE £2.60: £1.40, £1.30, £3.60; EX 12.70.
**Owner** Marcoe Racing Welwyn **Bred** Stanley Estate And Stud Co **Trained** Newmarket, Suffolk

**FOCUS**
Not a strong handicap and a moderate time for the grade.

**NOTEBOOK**
**Inchpast** is improving all the time and notched up the hat-trick in determined style. He was racing off a mark 18lb higher than for the first of his four wins this season, and looks likely to stay two miles.
**Most Definitely(IRE)**, who is still a maiden, was finishing runner-up for the eighth time in 19 starts. He needs to be brought with as late a challenge as possible and looks one for win-only punters to avoid.
**Distant Cousin** has only one win on turf to his name, and that was over two years ago. He had less to do in this grade and ran accordingly, but remains difficult to win with.
**Best Port(IRE)** has enjoyed a successful season, winning half of his starts, but the Handicapper may just have his measure now.
**Etching(USA)** was returning from a 103-day layoff and the betting suggested no great things were expected of her, despite having gone well fresh in the past.
**Masterman Ready** may have been flattered by his win in a modest affair run at a steady pace last month.
**Dr Cool** *Official explanation: jockey said gelding lost its action*

## 5524 SHARP MINDS BETFAIR (S) H'CAP 1m 2f

**4:10** (4:10) (G4) (0-55,50) 3-5-Y-O **£3,515** (£1,081; £540; £270) **Stalls** Low

| Form | Pos | Dist | Horse | Jockey | RPR |
|---|---|---|---|---|---|
| 3306 | 1 | | **Defana**[16] 5130 3-8-9 48 (MDods) *nvr far away: effrt 3f out: rdn over 1f out: styd on u.p to ld wl ins fnl f* **12/1** | LEnstone 12 | 54 |
| 2003 | 2 | ¾ | **Plausabelle**[16] 5110 3-8-9 48 (TDEasterby) *cl up: led 3f out: styd on u.p: hdd wl ins fnl f: no ex* **7/1**[3] | (b) EAhern 6 | 53 |
| 5400 | 3 | 2 ½ | **Athollbrose (USA)**[62] 3822 3-8-10 49 (TDEasterby) *prom: ev ch and rdn 2f out: no ex* **7/1**[3] | (b) KDarley 13 | 49 |
| 0552 | 4 | ¾ | **Esperance (IRE)**[7] 5336 4-8-13 45 (JAkehurst) *midfield: hdwy u.p to chse ldrs over 2f out: kpt on same pce* **2/1**[1] | SSanders 10 | 43 |
| 3006 | 5 | 2 ½ | **Acca Larentia (IRE)**[6] 5366 3-8-5 47 (RMWhitaker) *midfield: hdwy 3f out: in tch and rdn 2f out: no further prog* **16/1** | HayleyTurner(3) 16 | 41 |
| 5002 | 6 | *shd* | **Antony Ebeneezer**[43] 4189 5-8-8 40 (CRDore) *hld up: hdwy over 3f out: in tch and rdn 2f out: no further prog* **5/1**[2] | JBramhill 4 | 33 |
| 0000 | 7 | 2 | **Myannabanana (IRE)**[14] 5197 3-8-6 45 (JRWeymes) *chsd ldrs: drvn along and outpcd over 3f out: n.d after* **12/1** | (v) JQuinn 5 | 35 |
| 0500 | 8 | 1 | **Canlis**[9] 5305 5-8-8 40 (DWThompson) *led tl rdn and hdd 3f out: sn btn* **8/1** | RFfrench 3 | 28 |
| 0605 | 9 | 3 | **Mr Moon**[16] 5110 3-8-0 39 oh9 (JParkes) *s.i.s: rr div most of way: n.d* **20/1** | LisaJones 14 | 21 |
| 6060 | 10 | 5 | **Russalka**[26] 4853 3-8-11 50 (JulianPoulton) *sn bhd* **12/1** | (v) ACulhane 8 | 23 |
| -000 | 11 | 2 ½ | **Great Blasket (IRE)**[17] 5072 3-8-6 48 (EJO'Neill) *prom tl wknd 4f out* **16/1** | J-PGuillambert(3) 2 | 16 |
| 0600 | 12 | 4 | **Dame Nova (IRE)**[48] 4207 3-7-10 40 (PCHaslam) *midfield: outpcd and rdn 4f out: sn bhd* **20/1** | RoryMoore(5) 1 | — |
| 0000 | 13 | 11 | **Alpha Zeta**[46] 4259 3-8-1 40 (CWThornton) *bhd most of way* **50/1** | DaleGibson 15 | — |
| 000- | 14 | 21 | **Amaretto Express (IRE)**[156] 4731 5-8-8 40 (REBarr) *sn bhd: t.o* **50/1** | GParkin 7 | — |

2m 5.43s (-1.37) **Going Correction** -0.15s/f (Firm)
**WFA** 3 from 4yo+ 7lb **14 Ran SP% 134.4**
Speed ratings: **99,98,96,95,93 93,92,91,88,84 82,79,70,54**CSF £101.37 CT £662.00 TOTE £16.50: £4.70, £2.40, £2.80; EX 102.40.There was no bid for the winner. Plausabelle was claimed by Michael Kelly for £6,000
**Owner** Denton Hall Racing Ltd **Bred** Mrs E McKee **Trained** Piercebridge, Co Durham

**FOCUS**
Only three previous winners in what was a poor race, which has been rated negatively.

**NOTEBOOK**
**Defana**, who has been tried at a variety of trips this season, had shown enough to suggest that a moderate race of this nature was within his ability, and he stayed on best of all to score at the tenth attempt.
**Plausabelle** had never previously run as well as this on fast ground, but she seemed to handle the conditions well enough on this occasion.
**Athollbrose(USA)** put up a better performance on his first start in selling company, and may have found his grade.
**Esperance(IRE)** did not blow it at the start this time but was never able to pick up the leaders. He has now been beaten on each of his three starts in selling grade, and on each occasion he started at 4-1 or shorter.
**Acca Larentia(IRE)** did not perform too badly given the huge stamina worries over this longer trip.
**Antony Ebeneezer** has yet to win a race on turf in 22 starts.

## 5525 SHARP MINDS PHONE 0870 90 80 121 MAIDEN STKS 7f

**4:40** (4:40) (D3) 3-Y-O+ **£3,497** (£1,076; £538; £269) **Stalls** Centre

| Form | Pos | Dist | Horse | Jockey | RPR |
|---|---|---|---|---|---|
| 3656 | 1 | | **Moors Myth**[28] 4813 3-9-0 73 (BWHills) *mde all: rdn clr over 1f out: unchal* **7/2**[2] | RHughes 1 | 67 |
| 0240 | 2 | 7 | **Borodinsky**[17] 5086 3-8-9 47 (REBarr) *cl up: rdn 3f out: outpcd by wnr over 1f out* **25/1** | MLawson(5) 5 | 48 |
| 5036 | 3 | 3 ½ | **Speed Racer**[17] 5086 3-8-9 49 (DonEnricoIncisa) *prom early: drvn along and outpcd 1/2-way: kpt on u.p fnl f* **33/1** | KimTinkler 3 | 34 |
| 5-52 | 4 | *shd* | **M For Magic**[17] 5081 5-8-11 45 (CWFairhurst) *rr of main gp: kpt on u.p fr over 1f out: n.d* **12/1**[3] | KPierrepont(7) 8 | 38 |
| | 5 | *hd* | **Eshaadeh (USA)** 3-8-9 (SaeedBinSuroor) *trckd ldrs: rdn 3f out: flashed tail and sn btn* **1/3**[1] | (t) LDettori 4 | 33 |
| -660 | 6 | 4 | **Comic Tales**[32] 4674 3-9-0 45 (MMullineaux) *slowly away: wl bhd most of way* **100/1** | (b) SRighton 9 | 27 |
| 0 | 7 | 28 | **Dejeeje (IRE)**[9] 5306 3-9-0 (DWChapman) *sn wl bhd: lost tch fr 1/2-way: t.o and eased fnl f* **100/1** | ACulhane 6 | — |

1m 21.9s (-3.00) **Going Correction** -0.475s/f (Firm)
**WFA** 3 from 4yo+ 4lb **7 Ran SP% 113.7**
Speed ratings: **98,90,86,85,85 81,49**CSF £61.97 TOTE £4.10: £1.10, £6.30; EX 104.80.
**Owner** K Abdulla **Bred** Juddmonte Farms **Trained** Lambourn, Berks

**FOCUS**
An uncompetitive maiden run in a modest time for the grade. The winner had nothing to beat with the odds-on favourite running badly.

**NOTEBOOK**
**Moors Myth** was perhaps helped by the drop back in trip, but his stable is back in form now and, as it turned out, this race took little winning, with the odds-on favourite failing to deliver and his three nearest pursuers all rated plating class.
**Borodinsky** is pretty exposed as a moderate maiden but collected over £1,000 for finishing runner-up ahead of equally poor performers.
**Speed Racer**, who began the year rated 62, has looked regressive this term, and this performance did nothing to alter that view.
**M For Magic** has been running well this summer in very moderate company and would be better employed back in low-grade handicaps.
**Eshaadeh(USA)**, whose dam was a smart juvenile and is a half-sister to top-class middle-distance horses Unfuwain, Nashwan and Nayef, was all the rage on her belated debut, but she completely failed to impress, being under pressure a long way out, flashing her tail and trailing home well beaten.

**5526** **SHARP MINDS BETFAIR APPRENTICE H'CAP** **6f**
**5:10** (5:10) (E3) (0-70,73) 3-Y-O+ **£3,749** (£1,153; £576; £288) **Stalls** Centre

Form RPR
3200 **1** **Bowling Along**[18] 5063 3-7-10 **57**........................ TDean(7) 2 66
(MESowersby) *in tch: hdwy over 1f out: r.o wl u.p to ld ins fnl f* **33/1**
1145 **2** 3/4 **On The Trail**[7] 5346 7-7-12 **54**........................ LiamJones(4) 1 61
(DWChapman) *chsd ldrs: chal appr fnl f: no ex u.p ins last* **9/1**
0544 **3** hd **Winthorpe (IRE)**[48] 4211 4-8-12 **68**........................ KGhunowa(4) 16 74
(JJQuinn) *midfield: rdn over 1f out: r.o wl u.p ins fnl f: nrst fin* **9/1**
0240 **4** 3/4 **Flying Bantam (IRE)**[14] 5193 3-8-8 **69**........................ NLawes(7) 14 73
(RAFahey) *cl up: led 1/2-way: bmpd ent fnl f: sn hdd: no ex* **14/1**
0000 **5** nk **Banjo Bay (IRE)**[8] 5316 6-8-6 **65**........................ PJBenson(7) 5 68
(DNicholls) *midfield: effrt whn nt clr run over 1f out: kpt on fnl f: nvr able to chal* **8/1**
3340 **6** 1 1/2 **Snow Bunting**[11] 5242 6-8-5 **61**........................ TBlock(4) 9 60
(JeddO'Keeffe) *towards rr: kpt on u.p fr over 1f out: n.d* **9/2**[2]
0411 **7** 1/2 **Jilly Why (IRE)**[2] 5458 3-9-1 **73** 6ex........................ RJKilloran(4) 13 70
(MsDeborahJEvans) *midfield: rdn 2f out: no real hdwy* **5/1**[3]
020 **8** nk **Haulage Man**[37] 4542 6-8-6 **58**........................(p) WHogg 10 54
(DEddy) *missed break: rr div: kpt on u.p fr over 1f out: n.d* **4/1**[1]
0000 **9** 5 **Global Achiever**[108] 2455 3-8-6 **60**........................ DeanWilliams 3 41
(GCHChung) *cl up: rdn 2f out: sn btn* **33/1**
3036 **10** 1 **Finger Of Fate**[28] 4800 4-7-9 **54** oh9........................(b) MNem(7) 8 32
(MJPolglase) *mde most tl hdd 1/2-way: wknd over 1f out* **33/1**
0015 **11** 1 1/4 **Mimic**[26] 4854 4-8-12 **68**........................ RMills(4) 15 43
(RGuest) *towards rr most of way* **12/1**
3200 **12** 3/4 **Park Ave Princess (IRE)**[12] 5223 3-8-4 **58**........................ JDO'Reilly 11 30
(MJPolglase) *s.i.s: sn rdn in rr: n.d* **20/1**
1140 **13** 3/4 **Simply The Guest (IRE)**[151] 1427 5-8-0 **59**........................(t) JaniceWebster(7) 4 29
(DonEnricoIncisa) *sn rr div* **66/1**
000- **14** nk **Whittle Warrior**[353] 5194 4-8-9 **65**........................ KPierrepont(4) 6 34
(CWFairhurst) *cl up tl wknd 2f out* **66/1**
0326 **15** 1 **Pride Of Kinloch**[37] 4557 4-8-1 **57**........................ AReilly(4) 7 23
(JHetherton) *missed break: a rr div* **16/1**

69.25 secs (-2.45) **Going Correction** -0.475s/f (Firm)
**WFA** 3 from 4yo+ 2lb **15 Ran SP% 122.8**
Speed ratings: **97,96,95,94,94 92,91,91,84,83 81,80,79,79,77**CSF £299.83 CT £2984.85 TOTE £52.70: £10.40, £3.40, £3.40; EX 431.90 Place 6 £65.71, Place 5 £46.91.
**Owner** Keith Brown Properties (hull) Ltd **Bred** T E Pocock **Trained** Goodmanham, E Yorks
■ The first winner for Tolly Dean.

**FOCUS**
A very ordinary handicap run in a modest time for the class. The form looks sound for the grade.

**NOTEBOOK**
**Bowling Along** has only run on ground officially described as firm three times since her debut, and her record on such a surface now reads 121. Clearly she revels on a fast surface.
**On The Trail** ran a solid race, getting this easy six furlongs well. Unfortunately, his handicap mark will not be done any good by this effort.
**Winthorpe(IRE)** has been running creditably this summer without getting his head in front, and once again ran a sound race off what has to be regarded as a fair mark.
**Flying Bantam(IRE)**, a consistent animal, has finished runner-up six times in 14 starts. He had his chance again but lost the lead inside the last.
**Banjo Bay(IRE)** ran a more promising race. Things did not fall right on this occasion but he shaped with promise, and he is certianly well handicapped.
**Snow Bunting** is usually running on all too late at the end of a race, and it was no different on this occasion.
**Jilly Why(IRE)**, having her third run in the space of ten days and second within the last two days, may have been feeling the effects of her recent efforts.
**Haulage Man**, for whom there was money in the ring, has been backed on more than one occasion this season and once again let his supporters down.
T/Plt: £67.50 to a £1 stake. Pool: £36,383.90. 393.10 winning tickets. T/Qpdt: £38.00 to a £1 stake. Pool: £1,955.40. 38.00 winning tickets. JF

5527 - 5529a (Foreign Racing) - See Raceform Interactive

## 2701 BELMONT PARK (L-H)
Sunday, September 12

**OFFICIAL GOING: Good**

**5530a** **GARDEN CITY BREEDERS' CUP H'CAP (GRADE 1) (FILLIES)** **1m 1f**
**10:12** (10:14) 3-Y-O **£100,559** (£22,346; £11,173; £5,587)

RPR
**1** **Lucifer's Stone (USA)**[91] 3-8-6........................(b) JSantos 2 115
(LindaRice, U.S.A) **92/10**
**2** 1 1/4 **Barancella (FR)**[19] 5033 3-8-4........................ JChavez 3 110
(FHead, France) **25/1**
**3** 3/4 **Noahs Ark (IRE)**[28] 4787 3-8-4........................ JCastellano 6 109
(DKWeld, Ire) *raced in 2nd til led narrowly 3f out til inside final f, one pace* **69/10**
**4** nk **Necklace**[29] 4767 3-8-10........................ JPSpencer 1 114
(APO'Brien, Ire) *started slowly, in touch in last, effort and taken to outside 2f out, ran on but no impression on leaders* **18/10**[2]
**5** 3/4 **Mambo Slew (USA)**[20] 3-8-6........................ EPrado 5 109
(PLBiancone, U.S.A) **43/10**[3]
**6** 9 **Torrestrella (IRE)**[91] 2925 3-8-10........................ CNakatani 4 96
(ChristopheClement, U.S.A) **7/4**[1]
**7** 5 **Saratoga Sugar (USA)** 3-8-4........................ TFarina 7 80
(PLBiancone, U.S.A) **43/10**[3]

1m 48.88s **7 Ran SP% 136.1**
Speed ratings: .
**Owner** Solaris Stable **Bred** Mega Stable **Trained** North America

## 5404 CHANTILLY (R-H)
Monday, September 13

**OFFICIAL GOING: Good**

**5532a** **PRIX D'AUMALE (GROUP 3) (FILLIES)** **1m**
**1:20** (1:20) 2-Y-O **£25,704** (£10,282; £7,711; £5,141)

RPR
**1** **Birthstone**[17] 2-8-9........................ C-PLemaire 3 104+
(H-APantall, France) *close up, 3rd straight, led 1 1/2f out, pushed out, easily* 1
**2** 1 1/2 **Portrayal (USA)**[23] 4964 2-8-9........................ CSoumillon 2 101
(AFabre, France) *raced in 4th, pushed along and slightly outpaced over 2f out, headway 1 1/2f out, went 2nd 100 yards out, kept on* 1
**3** 2 **Faint Heart (IRE)**[21] 5009 2-8-9........................ TJarnet 1 96
(DavidWachman, Ire) *held up in 5th, switched to outside and headway 1 1/2f out, went 2nd inside final furlong, lost 2nd and one pace final 100y*
**4** 3 **Lonesome Me (FR)**[36] 2-8-9........................ TThulliez 4 90
(PBary, France) *reluctant leader for 1 1/2f, raced in 2nd, led again entering straight, headed 1 1/2f out, weakened inside final furlong* 2
**5** shd **Victoria Page (FR)**[24] 2-8-9........................ OPeslier 6 89
(J-MBeguigne, France) *missed break, led after 1 1/2f, set slow pace, headed entering straight, disputed lead again 2f out to 1 1/2f out, weakened* 3
**6** 1 1/2 **Pretty Soon (FR)** 2-8-9........................ IMendizabal 5 86
(J-CRouget, France) *held up in last, headway on inside to chase leaders over 1 1/2f out, not much room to inside final furlong, not recover*

1m 38.9s **Going Correction** -0.15s/f (Firm) **6 Ran SP% 171.5**
Speed ratings: **103,101,99,96,96 94.**
**Owner** Sheikh Mohammed **Bred** Darley **Trained** France

**NOTEBOOK**
**Birthstone** showed an impressive turn of foot to take this Group Three in comfortable fashion. She could well be top-class and may now be aimed at the Marcel Boussac.
**Portrayal(USA)** got slightly outpaced early in the straight before running on again near the finish, and she was never really a threat to the winner.
**Faint Heart(IRE)** looked to have every chance but just lacked a change of pace.
**Lonesome Me(FR)** did not help her chance by racing ran freely and gradually dropped out of contention.

5533 - (Foreign Racing) - See Raceform Interactive

## 5246 SALISBURY (R-H)
Tuesday, September 14

**OFFICIAL GOING: Soft (heavy in places)**
The stands' rail between the six and seven furlong marker was dolled off due to being virtually waterlogged. Runners raced down the centre throughout the day.

**5534** **RACING UK ON CHANNEL 432 MEDIAN AUCTION MAIDEN STKS (DIV I)** **6f 212y**
**1:40** (1:41) (E3) 2-Y-O **£3,666** (£1,128; £564; £282) **Stalls** Centre

Form RPR
**1** **Brecon** 2-8-9........................ TQuinn 8 72
(DRCElsworth) *bhd: rdn: green and hdwy fr 3f out: str run fr over 1f out: sn edgd rt but kpt on wl to ld last strides* **12/1**
6 **2** nk **Hawridge Star (IRE)**[82] 3240 2-9-0........................ WSupple 5 76
(WSKittow) *bhd: rdn and hdwy over 2f out: styd on wl to ld ins fnl f: ct last strides* **9/1**
**3** 1/2 **Astronomical (IRE)** 2-9-0........................ MHills 2 75
(BWHills) *bhd: stdy hdwy over 3f out to ld ins fnl 2f: sn pushed along: hdd ins fnl f: kpt on same pce* **15/2**
**4** 1/2 **Villarrica (USA)** 2-8-9........................ KFallon 4 69+
(SirMichaelStoute) *s.i.s: sn rcvrd and in tch: rdn and kpt on fr over 1f out: styd on ins last: kpt on cl home* **7/2**[1]
60 **5** 1 1/4 **Tohama**[17] 5109 2-8-9........................ RLMoore 10 66
(JLDunlop) *chsd ldrs: rdn 3f out: swtchd lft 1f out but nt clr run: kpt same pce ins last* **5/1**[2]
40 **6** 1/2 **Tiggers Touch**[12] 5248 2-8-9........................ DaneO'Neill 1 64
(BRMillman) *led 2f: styd w ldr tl led again 3f out: hdd ins fnl 2f: kpt on same pce ins last* **7/1**
0 **7** 5 **Best Game**[7] 5376 2-9-0........................ JFortune 6 57
(GABulter) *pressed ldrs 3f: styd prom: rdn over 3f out: wknd wl over 1f out* **50/1**
0 **8** 1 **Whitland**[33] 4681 2-9-0........................(t) RHavlin 9 55
(MrsPNDutfield) *s.i.s: bhd: rdn over 3f out: kpt on fr over 1f out but nvr gng pce to rch ldrs* **100/1**
5 **9** 1 3/4 **Samson Quest**[55] 4023 2-9-0........................ MartinDwyer 7 51
(AMBalding) *chsd ldrs: led 5f out: hdd 3f out: wknd qckly fr 2f out* **6/1**[3]
**10** 2 1/2 **Final Promise** 2-9-0........................ SCarson 15 45
(GBBalding) *bhd: nvr gng pce to rch ldrs* **50/1**
00 **11** 1 3/4 **Rum Creek**[50] 4193 2-9-0........................ PDobbs 3 41
(SKirk) *chsd ldrs over 4f* **33/1**
0 **12** 10 **Patronofconfucius (IRE)**[66] 3726 2-9-0........................ DSweeney 13 17
(JRBoyle) *chsd ldrs tl wknd qckly 2f out* **66/1**
000 **13** 1 1/4 **Gold Majesty**[54] 4040 2-8-9........................ SHitchcott 12 9
(MRChannon) *chsd ldrs to 1/2-way* **50/1**
**14** 6 **Mel's Moment (USA)** 2-9-0........................ SDrowne 11 —
(MrsAJPerrett) *s.i.s: sn in tch: wknd 1/2-way* **10/1**

1m 33.78s (4.78) **Going Correction** +0.725s/f (Yiel) **14 Ran SP% 115.5**
Speed ratings: **101,100,100,99,98 97,91,90,88,85 83,72,70,64**CSF £107.95 TOTE £15.00: £3.20, £2.80, £2.70; EX 216.70.
**Owner** K J Mercer & Mrs S Mercer **Bred** Usk Valley Stud **Trained** Whitsbury, Hants

**FOCUS**
A decent time for the grade, 1.38 seconds faster than the second division - mainly down the the fact they went no gallop in the latter - and definitely the better of the two. The form as it stands is only fair.

**NOTEBOOK**
**Brecon**, whose trainer tends to introduces some of his nicer horses at this course - Island Sands, Norse Dancer and Gold Medallist to name but a few - made a highly encouraging debut, getting up close home to win a shade cosily having run green. She picked up strongly once switched towards the stands' side to come with her winning run and although she has no major targets for the remainder of the campaign, can be expected to improve from two to three and will get further.
**Hawridge Star(IRE)** confirmed the promise of his debut run here with a keeping-on second. He clearly benefited from the break between runs and with further improvement to come should be able to win this year.
**Astronomical(IRE)** ◆, whose stable have come back to form in recent weeks, is bred to stay middle distances so he deserves credit for being beaten under a length over this trip on his racecourse debut. Sure to improve for the outing, he can pick up a maiden.
**Villarrica(USA)** ◆, whose dam is related to the likes of Galileo, Urban Ocean and Black Sam Bellamy, shaped as though very much in need of the experience and can be expected to improve massively on this next time. A mile will suit this daughter of Selkirk and it will be surprising if she does not win her maiden.
**Tohama**, unlucky in running at Beverley last time, was there if good enough today but lacked the pace. She is more of a handicap type.
**Tiggers Touch** is now qualified for nurseries and should do better in that sphere.

## 5535 RACING UK ON CHANNEL 432 MEDIAN AUCTION MAIDEN STKS (DIV II) 6f 212y

**2:10** (2:13) (E3) 2-Y-O £3,666 (£1,128; £564; £282) **Stalls** Centre

| Form | | | | | RPR |
|---|---|---|---|---|---|
| 43 | 1 | | **Palatinate (FR)**$^{18}$ [5087] 2-9-0 .......... DaneO'Neill 4 | | 78+ |
| | | | (HCandy) *t.k.h: hld up rr: stdy hdwy over 2f out: chsd ldr 1f out: hrd drvn and styd on to ld cl home* | **9/4**$^{1}$ | |
| 50 | 2 | *nk* | **Wotchalike (IRE)**$^{7}$ [5376] 2-9-0 .......... JFortune 12 | | 77+ |
| | | | (DRCElsworth) *led until: hdd over 3f out: led again 2f out: kpt on u.p tl hdd and nt qckn cl home* | **11/2**$^{3}$ | |
| 3 | 3 | *1 ½* | **Salinja (USA)**$^{51}$ [4172] 2-9-0 .......... SDrowne 5 | | 73+ |
| | | | (MrsAJPerrett) *chsd ldrs: rdn to chal 2f out: kpt on same pce fr over 1f out* | **5/2**$^{2}$ | |
| 5 | 4 | *3 ½* | **Zeena**$^{17}$ [5115] 2-8-9 .......... MartinDwyer 10 | | 60 |
| | | | (MPTregoning) *bhd: pushed along and styd on fr over 2f out: kpt on fnl f but nt pce of ldrs* | **7/1** | |
| 00 | 5 | *½* | **Byron Bay**$^{11}$ [5269] 2-8-11 .......... JFMcDonald$^{(3)}$ 1 | | 64 |
| | | | (JJBridger) *pressed ldrs tl led over 3f out: hdd 2f out: wknd fnl f* | **100/1** | |
| 5660 | 6 | *¾* | **Merrymadcap (IRE)**$^{15}$ [5173] 2-9-0 63.......... TQuinn 6 | | 62 |
| | | | (MBlanshard) *bhd: rdn over 3f out: kpt on fr over 1f out and styd on cl home: nt a danger* | **33/1** | |
| 000 | 7 | *hd* | **Election Seeker (IRE)**$^{17}$ [5114] 2-9-0 .......... RLMoore 11 | | 62 |
| | | | (GLMoore) *chsd ldrs: rdn and one pce 3f out: kpt on again u.p fnl f but nvr a danger* | **20/1** | |
| 00 | 8 | *1 ¼* | **Monad (IRE)**$^{15}$ [5198] 2-8-9 .......... RHavlin 13 | | 54 |
| | | | (MrsPNDutfield) *chsd ldrs: rdn over 2f out: sn outpcd* | **100/1** | |
| 0 | 9 | *¾* | **Backstreet Lad**$^{33}$ [4681] 2-9-0 .......... GBaker 3 | | 57 |
| | | | (BRMillman) *s.i.s: bhd: pushed along 3f out: styd on fr over 1f out and kpt on ins last but nvr a danger* | **50/1** | |
| 00 | 10 | *1* | **Manorshield Minx**$^{5}$ [5407] 2-8-9 .......... PDobbs 8 | | 49 |
| | | | (SKirk) *chsd ldrs tl wknd 2f out* | **20/1** | |
| 0 | 11 | *hd* | **Grand Girl**$^{11}$ [5272] 2-8-9 .......... ADaly 14 | | 49 |
| | | | (BWDuke) *s.i.s: outpcd most of way* | **100/1** | |
| 0 | 12 | *2* | **Thorny Mandate**$^{33}$ [4682] 2-9-0 .......... SCarson 9 | | 49 |
| | | | (RFJohnsonHoughton) *in tch: rdn to chse ldrs over 2f out: wknd wl over 1f out* | **50/1** | |
| | 13 | *2* | **Mister Troubridge** 2-8-11 .......... RThomas$^{(3)}$ 2 | | 44 |
| | | | (GBBalding) *chsd ldrs early: bhd fr 1/2-way* | **16/1** | |

1m 35.16s (6.16) **Going Correction** +0.725s/f (Yiel) **13** Ran SP% **112.5**

Speed ratings: **93,92,90,86,86 85,85,83,83,81 81,79,77**CSF £12.84 TOTE £2.90: £1.20, £2.20, £1.20; EX 14.90.

**Owner** Crichel Racing **Bred** Crichel Estates Ltd And Crichel Farms Ltd **Trained** Wantage, Oxon

**FOCUS**

This was the weaker division, although not much should be read into the time difference as they went a modest gallop in this heat. The first three dominated and finished clear, and time may tell that they are more superior to the remainder than they are able to have been rated. The bare form is only fairly good.

**NOTEBOOK**

**Palatinate(FR)** clearly acts on this ground but connections expect him to be much better on a faster surface so he can be rated a deal better than the bare form. It took him some time to get going but he picked up strongly in the final furlong and ended up winning with a little in hand. Still quite weak, better can be expected at three on fast ground in handicaps.

**Wotchalike(IRE)** fared better back up in trip and was only caught in the closing stages. Now qualified for nurseries, he will stay a mile and should be placed to good advantage in that sphere.

**Salinja(USA)**, whose debut run came in an ordinary maiden Newmarket for the track, ran well without setting the world alight and will do better once handicapped.

**Zeena** was suited to this extra furlong and improved on her initial effort. Her stable are sneaking the odd winner in again now but she will not be winning until eligible for handicaps. *Official explanation: jockey said filly hung left handed*

**Byron Bay** is another who will find life easier in handicaps.

**Backstreet Lad** was noted making good late headway having fluffed the start and could win if making the transition to nurseries in the coming weeks after one more run. His stable's juveniles are in particularly good order at present. *Official explanation: jockey said colt missed break*

## 5536 SYDENHAMS MAIDEN STKS 6f

**2:40** (2:41) (D2) 2-Y-O £5,843 (£1,798; £899; £449) **Stalls** Centre

| Form | | | | | RPR |
|---|---|---|---|---|---|
| 42 | 1 | | **Loaderfun (IRE)**$^{64}$ [3808] 2-9-0 .......... DaneO'Neill 2 | | 90+ |
| | | | (HCandy) *mde all: qcknd clr over 1f out: easily* | **2/1**$^{1}$ | |
| | 2 | *5* | **Anchor Date** 2-9-0 .......... RHughes 4 | | 75+ |
| | | | (BWHills) *s.i.s: hld up in rr: hdwy: nt clr run and swtchd rt over 1f out: chsd wnr ins last but no ch* | **5/1** | |
| 5 | 3 | *3 ½* | **Desert Demon (IRE)**$^{59}$ [3946] 2-9-0 .......... MHills 1 | | 64+ |
| | | | (BWHills) *plld hrd: chsd ldrs: rdn 2f out: disp 2nd over 1f out but no ch w wnr: wknd ins last* | **11/4**$^{2}$ | |
| 22 | 4 | *1* | **Drum Dance (IRE)**$^{95}$ [2846] 2-9-0 .......... SCarson 5 | | 61 |
| | | | (RFJohnsonHoughton) *chsd ldrs: disp 2nd fr over 2f out: nvr gng pce of wnr: wknd fnl f* | **4/1**$^{3}$ | |
| 55 | 5 | *hd* | **Auwitesweetheart**$^{18}$ [5070] 2-8-9 .......... SDrowne 9 | | 56 |
| | | | (BRMillman) *chsd wnr: rdn and no imp 2f out: no ch fr over 1f out and wknd ins last* | **12/1** | |
| 6 | 6 | *½* | **Wood Spirit (IRE)**$^{124}$ [2057] 2-8-9 .......... RHavlin 7 | | 54 |
| | | | (MrsPNDutfield) *s.i.s: bhd: sn pushed along: rdn over 3f out: styd on ins last but nvr a danger* | **16/1** | |
| | 7 | *¾* | **Belle Chanson** 2-8-9 .......... DSweeney 3 | | 52 |
| | | | (JRBoyle) *rr but in tch: swtchd rt and sme hdwy over 1f out:nvr gng pce to rch ldrs and sn wknd* | **33/1** | |
| 0000 | 8 | *3* | **Play Up Pompey**$^{17}$ [5114] 2-8-11 58.......... JFMcDonald$^{(3)}$ 8 | | 48 |
| | | | (JJBridger) *in tch: rdn and effrt over 2f out: wkng whn hmpd over 1f out* | **100/1** | |

1m 19.54s (4.60) **Going Correction** +0.725s/f (Yiel) **8** Ran SP% **114.2**

Speed ratings: **98,91,86,85,85 84,83,79**CSF £12.51 TOTE £2.50: £1.10, £1.60, £1.50; EX 12.50.

**Owner** Paul & Linda Dixon **Bred** Mrs L A Sadler **Trained** Wantage, Oxon

**FOCUS**

They went a crawl early and Loaderfun was given an easy time before quickening up best on ground he liked. As a result the form is worth treating with caution, although the winner could be significantly underrated on the bare form.

**NOTEBOOK**

**Loaderfun(IRE)** was allowed to take them along at a steady gallop, causing his two main rivals Desert Demon and Drum Dance to run very freely, and quickened up by far the best when the race began to hot up. He reversed Leicester form with Drum Dance by some way and the form does want treating with caution, but nonetheless this progressive colt clearly has bundles of speed and connections are keen to find a novice event to follow up in.

**Anchor Date ◆**, the lesser fancied of the Hills pair according to the betting, was not given the most tactically astute ride and by the time he came with his run the winner had flown. He pulled a healthy way ahead of the third though and was the clear second best. He is a maiden winner waiting to happen. *Official explanation: jockey said he was unable to get a run approaching final furlong*

**Desert Demon(IRE)** took a fair old tug in the early stages and ruined his chance. Back in a truly-run race he will show this running to be all wrong.

**Drum Dance(IRE)**, who did not quite live up to expectations in the early part of the season - twice finishing second - should have relished the combination of six furlongs and soft ground, but he too took a strong hold and found little for pressure. He is now eligible for nurseries and should be seen to better effect in that sphere.

**Wood Spirit(IRE)** *Official explanation: trainer said filly was unsuited by ground, soft, heavy in places*

## 5537 HERBERT H HARRISON 90TH BIRTHDAY MAIDEN FILLIES' STKS 1m

**3:10** (3:13) (D3) 3-Y-O £5,726 (£1,762; £881; £440) **Stalls** High

| Form | | | | | RPR |
|---|---|---|---|---|---|
| 022 | 1 | | **Zameyla (IRE)**$^{96}$ [2818] 3-8-11 74.......... PRobinson 4 | | 86 |
| | | | (MAJarvis) *trckd ldrs: swtchd far side to ld ins fnl 3f: drvn clr fr over 1f out* | **10/3**$^{2}$ | |
| 2 | 2 | *5* | **Woodland Glade**$^{32}$ [4718] 3-8-11 .......... JFortune 11 | | 76 |
| | | | (RHannon) *chsd ldrs: styd centre crse and rdn to chse wnr over wl over 2f out: sn no imp: kpt on for clr 2nd* | **11/4**$^{1}$ | |
| 6323 | 3 | *4* | **Ela Paparouna**$^{38}$ [4551] 3-8-11 72.......... DaneO'Neill 7 | | 68 |
| | | | (HCandy) *w ldr: led over 4f out: hdd and styd centre crse ins fnl 3f: sn outpcd but hld on for clr 3rd* | **10/3**$^{2}$ | |
| -04 | 4 | *4* | **Dandygrey Russett (IRE)**$^{134}$ [1827] 3-8-11 .......... RLMoore 1 | | 60 |
| | | | (GLMoore) *s.i.s: bhd: rdn and sme hdwy over 3f out: n.d and sn one pce* | **10/1** | |
| 6L33 | 5 | *nk* | **Elusive Kitty (USA)**$^{22}$ [4987] 3-8-11 68.......... KFallon 6 | | 59 |
| | | | (GAButler) *s.i.s: sn in tch: rdn to chse ldrs over 3f out: sn no btn: no ch fnl 2f* | **13/2**$^{3}$ | |
| 50 | 6 | *7* | **Cemgraft**$^{38}$ [4554] 3-8-11 .......... SDrowne 5 | | 45 |
| | | | (MissECLavelle) *bhd: mod hdwy fnl 2f* | **33/1** | |
| 0- | 7 | *¾* | **She's A Fox**$^{323}$ [5785] 3-8-11 .......... PDobbs 3 | | 44 |
| | | | (AWCarroll) *broke wl: sn bhd* | **100/1** | |
| 0 | 8 | *5* | **Sabander Bay (USA)**$^{25}$ [4916] 3-8-11 .......... RHavlin 9 | | 34 |
| | | | (JHMGosden) *s.i.s: sn chsng ldrs: wknd 3f out* | **20/1** | |
| 4400 | 9 | *24* | **Supamach (IRE)**$^{10}$ [5293] 3-8-11 63.......... TQuinn 12 | | — |
| | | | (PFICole) *pressed ldrs 4f: wknd over 3f out* | **25/1** | |
| 0 | 10 | *1 ¼* | **Mad**$^{13}$ [5217] 3-8-11 .......... SCarson 10 | | — |
| | | | (AndrewReid) *sn drvn to ld: hdd over 4f out: sn wknd* | **66/1** | |

1m 48.63s (5.66) **Going Correction** +0.725s/f (Yiel) **10** Ran SP% **109.3**

Speed ratings: **100,95,91,87,86 79,78,73,49,48**CSF £11.32 TOTE £4.10: £1.60, £1.10, £1.50; EX 9.40.

**Owner** Sheikh Ahmed Al Maktoum **Bred** Gerard Callanan **Trained** Newmarket, Suffolk

**FOCUS**

An average maiden but the winner is capable of leaving this form behind.

**NOTEBOOK**

**Zameyla(IRE)**, turned over at odds of 2/5 on firm ground on her most recent outing back in June, has not been easy to train but this contrasting surface suited her ideally. Robinson took her across to the far rail around three furlongs out - unraced on since the last meeting here early in the month - and it evidently worked as she ran out an authoritative winner. This well-bred filly has got the all-important win under her belt now and she can probably add to it if the ground remains in her favour.

**Woodland Glade** has run well on both occasions now - twice finishing second - and can be expected to improve for a faster surface.

**Ela Paparouna**, a half-sister to the stable's high-class sprinter Kyllachy, has nowhere near as much speed and continues to frustrate.

**Dandygrey Russett(IRE)** is very much a handicap type and should get a reasonable mark.

**Elusive Kitty(USA)** is one to continue to leave alone until showing more.

**Cemgraft** *Official explanation: jockey said, regarding the running and riding, orders were to drop in and get the filly to settle as she had ran too free last time out, adding that she was outpaced after 2f and stayed on past beaten horses; trainer added filly was dropping in trip today and would probably go up in trip in the future*

**Supamach(IRE)** *Official explanation: jockey said filly lost her action*

## 5538 MILFORD HALL HOTEL CLAIMING STKS 1m 4f

**3:40** (3:40) (E3) 3-Y-O £3,497 (£1,076; £538; £269) **Stalls** High

| Form | | | | | RPR |
|---|---|---|---|---|---|
| 3420 | 1 | | **Fort Churchill (IRE)**$^{15}$ [5203] 3-9-5 71.......... (b) PRobinson 9 | | 82+ |
| | | | (MHTompkins) *mde all: c clr fr 3f out: drvn fnl f: unchal* | **3/1**$^{2}$ | |
| 0000 | 2 | *13* | **Persian Genie (IRE)**$^{27}$ [4849] 3-8-6 60.......... RHavlin 2 | | 51 |
| | | | (GBBalding) *chsd ldrs: styd on to take 2nd ins fnl 2f but nvr in contention w wnr* | **12/1** | |
| 3260 | 3 | *3* | **Go Green**$^{5}$ [5410] 3-8-1 55.......... (t) FPFerris$^{(3)}$ 6 | | 45 |
| | | | (PDEvans) *bhd: hdwy 6f out: rdn 3f out: styd on fnl 2f but nvr nr ldrs* | **7/1** | |
| 2005 | 4 | *1 ¾* | **Varuni (IRE)**$^{68}$ [3669] 3-8-7 57.......... TQuinn 5 | | 45 |
| | | | (JGPortman) *prom: chsd wnr 3f out but no ch:wknd and lost 2nd ins fnl 2f* | **9/1** | |
| 0 | 5 | *1 ¾* | **Silken John (IRE)**$^{120}$ [2168] 3-9-0 .......... GBaker 1 | | 50 |
| | | | (JGPortman) *bhd: rdn over 3f out: mod hdwy fnl 2f* | **50/1** | |
| 5045 | 6 | *nk* | **Pangloss (IRE)**$^{17}$ [5116] 3-9-2 62.......... (b) RLMoore 3 | | 51 |
| | | | (GLMoore) *bhd: rdn and mod prog 3f out: nvr nr ldrs: wknd and hung rt ins fnl 2f* | **11/4**$^{1}$ | |
| 0600 | 7 | *1 ¼* | **Signora Panettiera (FR)**$^{71}$ [3572] 3-8-4 40.......... SHitchcott 4 | | 38 |
| | | | (MRChannon) *in tch: rdn 4f out: sn btn* | **25/1** | |
| 2104 | 8 | *nk* | **Hoh Bleu Dee**$^{18}$ [5092] 3-8-10 73.......... JFortune 7 | | 43 |
| | | | (SKirk) *rr but in tch: sme hdwy 4f out: wknd fr 3f out* | **4/1**$^{3}$ | |
| 00 | 9 | *3* | **Charing Cross (IRE)**$^{13}$ [5217] 3-8-9 .......... RBrisland 8 | | 38 |
| | | | (GLMoore) *bhd: no ch whn hmpd and stmbld ins fnl 2f* | **25/1** | |
| 0-0 | 10 | *3* | **Pagan Ceremony (USA)**$^{15}$ [5196] 3-8-11 .......... SDrowne 10 | | 36 |
| | | | (MrsAJPerrett) *chsd wnr to 3f out: sn wknd* | **25/1** | |

2m 43.86s (7.51) **Going Correction** +0.725s/f (Yiel) **10** Ran SP% **115.4**

Speed ratings: **103,94,92,91,90 89,88,88,86,84**CSF £35.99 TOTE £4.20: £1.50, £4.00, £2.20; EX 39.40.The winner was claimed by Henry Rix for £31,000

**Owner** P H Betts **Bred** P H Betts **Trained** Newmarket, Suffolk

**FOCUS**

A modest claimer overall but the winner demolished them and was in a league of his own.

**NOTEBOOK**

**Fort Churchill(IRE)** was given a fine ride by Robinson who took them along throughout, and the partnership powered away down the straight. He was the proven best horse in the race at this sort of trip and should be capable of winning again back in handicap company.

**Persian Genie(IRE)** does everything to suggest she needs farther and has a low-grade handicap in her.

**Go Green** ran as well as could have been expected.

**Pangloss(IRE)** did not look the keenest under pressure - hanging to his right - and is never one to take a short price about.
**Hoh Bleu Dee** was never going to get this distance and folded in the straight as expected.
**Charing Cross(IRE)** *Official explanation: jockey said he clipped heels with horse in front*

## 5539 AXMINSTER CARPETS NURSERY — 1m
**4:10** (4:12) (D3) (0-85,80) 2-Y-O — **£5,076** (£1,562; £781; £390) **Stalls** High

Form — RPR

400 **1** **Something Exciting**[12] [5247] 2-8-12 **71** ... JFortune 7 — 78
(DRCElsworth) *bhd: swtchd lft to outside and rapid hdwy over 1f out: str run fnl f to ld cl home: sn clr: readily* **12/1**

645 **2** 1 3/4 **William Tell (IRE)**[11] [5256] 2-8-10 **76** ... TDean(7) 5 — 79
(MRChannon) *bhd: hdwy 3f out: slt ld 2f out: hung lft over 1f out: sn hdd: kpt on to chal wl ins last:nt pce of wnr cl home* **25/1**

3665 **3** nk **Guinea A Minute (IRE)**[26] [4878] 2-7-13 **61** ... HayleyTurner(3) 4 — 63
(MLWBell) *chsd ldrs: chal over 2f out: stl upsides whn hung lft over 1f out: rallied to chal ins last: one pce cl home* **11/1**

01 **4** nk **Bathwick Finesse (IRE)**[11] [5256] 2-9-6 **79** ... GBaker 8 — 80
(BRMillman) *in tch: hdwy over 2f out: rdr dropped whip ins fnl 2f: slt ld over 1f out:kpt narrow advantage tl hdd and one pce cl home* **12/1**

3565 **5** 2 1/2 **Hawridge King**[19] [5052] 2-8-9 **68** ... WSupple 11 — 64
(WSKittow) *chsd ldrs: rdn over 2f out: kpt on same pce ins fnl f* **20/1**

402 **6** 8 **Scarlet Invader (IRE)**[33] [4682] 2-9-7 **80** ... TQuinn 6 — 58
(JLDunlop) *bhd: rdn over 2f out: nvr gng pce to rch ldrs* **7/1**[3]

41 **7** hd **Torrens (IRE)**[15] [5173] 2-9-6 **79** ... KFallon 10 — 57
(MJohnston) *in tch: sn pushed along: chsd ldrs u.p 3f out: wknd qckly fr 2f out* **13/8**[1]

560 **8** 1 3/4 **Bespoke**[41] [4454] 2-8-3 **62** ... JMackay 2 — 36
(SirMarkPrescott) *s.i.s: sn drvn and chsd ldrs: wknd qckly 2f out* **10/1**

564 **9** 3/4 **Sir Monty (USA)**[17] [5114] 2-9-0 **73** ... SDrowne 1 — 45
(MrsAJPerrett) *trckd ldrs: pushed along 3f out: sn wknd* **13/2**[2]

6521 **10** 1 1/4 **Briannsta (IRE)**[15] [5198] 2-9-7 **80** ... SHitchcott 12 — 50
(MRChannon) *led after 1f: hdd 2f out: sn wknd* **9/1**

055 **11** 8 **Worth A Grand (IRE)**[42] [4413] 2-8-4 **66** ... RThomas(3) 3 — 18
(JWMullins) *led 1f: styd pressing ldrs tl wknd 3f out* **20/1**

600 **12** 3 **Benedict Bay**[51] [4166] 2-8-11 **70** ... SCarson 13 — 15
(GBBalding) *rdn over 3f out: a in rr* **40/1**

1m 50.07s (7.10) **Going Correction** +0.725s/f (Yiel) — **12 Ran SP% 122.5**
Speed ratings: **93,91,90,90,88 80,79,78,77,76 68,65**CSF £289.99 CT £3383.66 TOTE £13.30: £3.10, £5.80, £3.90; EX 169.10.
**Owner** Setsquare Recruitment **Bred** R E Crutchley **Trained** Whitsbury, Hants

**FOCUS**
A useful nursery where the front five pulled eight lengths clear of the remainder. The form looks fairly strong.

**NOTEBOOK**
**Something Exciting**, making her nursery debut, returned to something like the form that saw her finish fourth on her debut in a good maiden at Newbury - race that produced seven individual winners - and clearly found the ground of no inconvenience. She came with a strong late challenge to get on top in the final 100 yards and win going away. David Elsworth likes her and expects further improvement next season granted a stiffer test of stamina.
**William Tell(IRE)** left his previous form behind with a gallant second, just being done for speed by the winner in the final half-furlong. His trainer's juveniles are in tip-top form at the moment and he looks up to contributing towards the hot-streak back on a faster surface.
**Guinea A Minute(IRE)** improved on previous efforts in third and rewarded each-way supporters.
**Bathwick Finesse(IRE)** may well have been placed had her rider not lost his whip just inside the two pole, and consolidated her Chepstow maiden win.
**Hawridge King** should probably have been a little closer as he was short of room when the pace quickened and could not get going in time. He will stay farther and can win once venturing into handicaps. He pulled right away from the sixth-placed horse.
**Scarlet Invader(IRE)**, although bred to go on the ground, ran arguably his worst race to date on it and deserves another chance back on better ground.
**Torrens(IRE)** was reported to have never been travelling and will be much better suited by a sound surface. His trainer's horses are a bit in and out and he deserves another chance. *Official explanation: trainer said colt was never travelling*
**Bespoke** was a little disappoitning but is surely capable of better.
**Sir Monty(USA)** deserves another chance back on better ground.
**Briannsta(IRE)** *Official explanation: jockey said colt was unsuited by the soft, heavy in places ground*

## 5540 WADWORTH 6X CLASSIFIED STKS — 1m
**4:40** (4:42) (E3) 3-Y-0+ — **£5,570** (£1,714; £857; £428) **Stalls** High

Form — RPR

35-3 **1** **High Reserve**[17] [5123] 3-8-10 70 ... OUrbina 8 — 47+
(JRFanshawe) *stmbld stalls: sn rcvrd and trckd ldrs: hemmed in fr 2f out tl swtchd lft over 1f out:qcknd to ld nr fin: readily* **11/4**[2]

3000 **2** 1 **Giko**[10] [5286] 10-9-1 35 ... HayleyTurner(3) 2 — 48
(JaneSouthcombe) *led: rdn over 2f out: kpt on wl: hdd and nt pce of wnr nr fin* **100/1**

5430 **3** 1 3/4 **Parnassian**[15] [5185] 4-9-1 70 ... RThomas(3) 1 — 45
(GBBalding) *in tch: hdwy to chse ldrs over 2f out: hung rt and wnt 2nd ins last: styd on same pce* **7/4**[1]

0006 **4** 3/4 **Lakota Brave**[185] [1011] 10-9-4 70 ... SDrowne 4 — 43
(MrsStefLiddiard) *chsd ldrs: wnt 2nd over 3f out: sn rdn: outpcd ins fnl f* **16/1**

0650 **5** 2 **Blue Patrick**[11] [5275] 4-9-1 70 ... LFletcher(3) 3 — 39
(JMPEustace) *s.i.s: bhd: rdn over 3f out: kpt on ins fnl f but nvr gng pce to rch ldrs* **8/1**

1641 **6** shd **Hazewind**[9] [5316] 3-9-2 65 ... (vt) FPFerris(3) 5 — 49+
(PDEvans) *chsd ldr tl over 3f out: styd prom and sn rdn:wknd fnl f* **7/2**[3]

0000 **7** 5 **Oh Boy (IRE)**[12] [5252] 4-9-4 67 ... DaneO'Neill 6 — 29
(RHannon) *bhd: rdn over 3f out: sme hdwy over 2f out: sn wknd* **12/1**

1m 48.78s (5.81) **Going Correction** +0.725s/f (Yiel)
**WFA** 3 from 4yo+ 5lb — **7 Ran SP% 110.9**
Speed ratings: **99,98,96,95,93 93,88**CSF £140.54 TOTE £3.20: £1.90, £6.50; EX 101.10.
**Owner** Helena Springfield Ltd **Bred** Meon Valley Stud **Trained** Newmarket, Suffolk
■ Stewards Enquiry : S Drowne caution: careless riding
F P Ferris caution: allowed gelding to coast home with no assistance

**FOCUS**
A race to treat with real caution as the 35-rated Giko was beaten just a length in second.

**NOTEBOOK**
**High Reserve** had shown plenty of ability in three runs in maiden company and was the best off at the weights by some way on her first run outside of that grade but, despite doing enough to get off the mark, she did not run to her rating of 70. She is by no means a world-beater and is no sure thing to follow up, but is clearly better than the bare form would suggest as a stronger pace would have suited and she had to be switched wide for a run.
**Giko** was allowed his own way out in front and, with stamina for much further, saw this testing mile out better than most. Rated just 35, he holds the form down.
**Parnassian** kept the eventual winner blocked in for much of the closing stages, but simply had no answer when that one was finally in the clear. He was unable to quicken in the conditions off the modest gallop.
**Lakota Brave** amazingly at the age of ten had never previously run on ground softer than good. He did not appear to mind conditions too much, but was another who simply found it hard to quicken and should be sharper for this first run in 185 days. He ought to be spot on for the forthcoming All-Weather season.
**Blue Patrick**, well backed, looked to be going nicely in last place for much of the way but found nothing when switched round the entire field for his run and did not appear to handle the ground at all. Both his previous wins came on a decent surface.
**Hazewind** was kept tight against the far rail by Lakota Brave in the closing stages and was squeezed up late on, but he was by no means unlucky and was simply unable to produce his best in the conditions.
**Oh Boy(IRE)** was another who only had winning form on fast ground and was never really going under these very different conditions.

## 5541 SALISBURYRACECOURSE.CO.UK H'CAP — 6f 212y
**5:10** (5:13) (E3) (0-70,70) 3-Y-0+ — **£3,842** (£1,182; £591; £295) **Stalls** Centre

Form — RPR

0546 **1** **Fearby Cross (IRE)**[17] [5124] 8-8-9 **61** ... (b) KFallon 7 — 71
(WJMusson) *stdd s: bhd: gd hdwy on outside over 2f out: hrd drvn to ld last half f: edgd lft: r.o strly* **7/2**[1]

43-5 **2** 1 **Young Alex (IRE)**[12] [5252] 6-8-8 **65** ... (v[1]) PMakin(5) 4 — 72
(MCPipe) *hld up in rr: stdy hdwy over 2f out: styd on to ld jst ins fnl f: hdd: edgd lft and one pce last half f* **8/1**[3]

5020 **3** 1 3/4 **Dr Synn**[24] [4938] 3-8-10 **66** ... SHitchcott 3 — 69
(JAkehurst) *trckd ldrs: led appr fnl 2f: rdn over 1f out: hdd ins last: kpt on same pce* **11/1**

4040 **4** 2 1/2 **Majik**[141] [1665] 5-8-0 **59** ... LiamJones(7) 2 — 55
(DJSFfrenchDavis) *chsd ldrs: chal over 2f out tl over 1f out: wknd ins last* **14/1**

6000 **5** 2 **Emerald Fire**[22] [5008] 5-8-5 **60** ... LPKeniry(3) 9 — 51
(AMBalding) *in tch: rdn over 2f out: kpt on fnl f but nvr gng pce of ldrs* **12/1**

05-0 **6** 1 1/4 **Russian Symphony (USA)**[160] [1295] 3-8-13 **69** ... (b[1]) SDrowne 10 — 57
(CREgerton) *bhd: pushed along 3f out: styd on wl fnl f but nvr gng pce to rch ldrs* **40/1**

5500 **7** nk **Blue Daze**[27] [4848] 3-8-3 **59** ... RLMoore 15 — 47
(RHannon) *bhd: rdn and hdwy opn outside over 2f out: nvr gng pce to rch ldrs* **16/1**

6060 **8** 3/4 **Sundried Tomato**[159] [1313] 5-9-1 **70** ... LFletcher(3) 5 — 56
(PWHiatt) *led tl rdn and hdd appr fnl 2f: wknd over 1f out* **14/1**

1000 **9** shd **Gallery Breeze**[21] [5017] 5-9-1 **67** ... (p) VSlattery 11 — 52
(JLSpearing) *mid-div: rdn and styd on same pce fr over 2f out* **40/1**

0300 **10** hd **Ben Lomand**[15] [5201] 4-8-8 **60** ... ADaly 8 — 45
(BWDuke) *chsd ldrs: rdn 3f out: styd on same pce fnl 2f* **25/1**

0540 **11** 3/4 **Cheese 'n Biscuits**[19] [5055] 4-8-13 **65** ... (p) JFortune 16 — 48
(GLMoore) *bhd: sme hdwy on rails over 2f out: nvr rchd ldrs* **11/1**

1210 **12** 1 1/4 **Kings Rock**[7] [5370] 3-8-1 **60** ... (b) HayleyTurner(3) 1 — 40
(MrsLucindaFeatherstone) *slowly into strude: sn chsng ldrs: wknd fr 2f out* **16/1**

04-1 **13** 1 3/4 **Poule De Luxe (IRE)**[155] [1352] 3-8-13 **69** ... TQuinn 13 — 45
(JLDunlop) *chsd ldrs tl wknd 2f out* **4/1**[2]

0036 **14** 1 **Terraquin (IRE)**[12] [5252] 4-8-6 **61** ... (v[1]) JFMcDonald(3) 12 — 34
(JJBridger) *chsd ldrs: n.m.r over 2f out: sn lost pl and bhd* **9/1**

0055 **15** 3 **Tipsy Lady**[24] [4954] 3-8-6 **62** ... DaneO'Neill 6 — 28
(DRCElsworth) *nvr bttr than mid-div* **12/1**

/3-0 **16** 5 **Corbel (USA)**[17] [5123] 4-8-10 **65** ... J-PGuillambert(3) 14 — 18
(MissGayKelleway) *a in rr* **40/1**

1m 33.15s (4.15) **Going Correction** +0.725s/f (Yiel)
**WFA** 3 from 4yo+ 4lb — **16 Ran SP% 131.6**
Speed ratings: **105,103,101,99,96 95,94,94,93,93 92,91,89,88,84 79**CSF £33.28 CT £295.04 TOTE £5.40: £1.60, £2.30, £3.10, £4.20; EX 41.30 Place 6 £211.55, Place 5 £45.28.
**Owner** Mrs Rita Brown **Bred** William Webb **Trained** Newmarket, Suffolk

**FOCUS**
An ordinary handicap. Fearby Cross was on a winning mark and cashed in with the blinkers back on.

**NOTEBOOK**
**Fearby Cross(IRE)**, having the blinkers on for the first time since October 1999 when his one run in them had no real effect, seemed to take more notice of them now he is an eight-year-old and he came with a powerful late run to win going away. Hardly consistent, he is not one to rely on to repeat the effort.
**Young Alex(IRE)** is best on a faster surface and ran well considering. The first-time visor did not have much effect but he is sure to be placed to score again by Pipe.
**Dr Synn** is on a winnable mark and will be winning sooner rather than later.
**Majik** was not good enough on the day.
**Emerald Fire** was doing her best work at the finish and saw out the trip well.
**Russian Symphony(USA)** ran his best race to date and, being only a three-year-old, can be expected to do better still.
**Ben Lomand** *Official explanation: jockey said gelding hung right*
**Poule De Luxe(IRE)** ran below form and deserves another chance back on a better surface.
T/Plt: £224.60 to a £1 stake. Pool: £36,443.80. 118.40 winning tickets. T/Qpdt: £52.90 to a £1 stake. Pool: £2,811.60. 39.30 winning tickets. ST

# 5301 THIRSK (L-H)
Tuesday, September 14

**OFFICIAL GOING: Good (good to firm in places)**

## 5542 PENYGHENT MEDIAN AUCTION MAIDEN STKS — 6f
**2:30** (2:34) (E4) 2-Y-O — **£3,272** (£935; £467) **Stalls** High

Form — RPR

6435 **1** **Taras Treasure (IRE)**[37] [4575] 2-8-9 71 ... RWinston 6 — 71
(JJQuinn) *trckd ldrs: effrt whn nt clr run 2f out: r.o u.p to ld fnl 100yds* **5/2**[1]

**2** 1 **Monkey Madge** 2-8-9 ... FLynch 8 — 68
(BSmart) *cl up: led over 2f out: rdn and hdd fnl 100yds: no ex* **7/1**[2]

0 **3** 1 1/4 **Orpen Wide (IRE)**[54] [4048] 2-8-9 ... DFox(5) 2 — 69
(MCChapman) *cl up: ev ch and rdn ent fnl f: no ex ins last* **100/1**

00 **4** 3 **Owed**[10] [5290] 2-9-0 ... DaleGibson 13 — 60
(MrsGSRees) *dwlt: towards rr: hdwy and hung lft 2f out: kpt on fnl f: nvr able to chal* **33/1**

5656 **5** 1 1/2 **Sound And Vision (IRE)**[82] [3233] 2-9-0 66 ... (b[1]) SWKelly 5 — 56
(MDods) *slt ld tl hdd over 2f out: kpt on same pce* **7/1**[2]

0 **6** 1 1/4 **Mossmann Gorge**[113] 2352 2-9-0 .............................. DeanMcKeown 4 52
(GASwinbank) *s.i.s: sn midfield: rdn 2f out: no hdwy whn hmpd appr fnl f* **20/1**

26 **7** 2 **Able Charlie (GER)**[36] 4606 2-9-0 .............................. ACulhane 12 46+
(MrsJRRamsden) *rrd s and v.s.a: wl bhd tl styd on appr fnl f: n.d* **5/2**[1]

00 **8** shd **Street Dancer (IRE)**[10] 5307 2-9-0 .............................. MFenton 7 46
(JJQuinn) *cl up: short of room over 3f out: chsd ldrs after: fdd fnl 2f* **100/1**

**9** nk **Komreyev Star** 2-9-0 .............................. PHanagan 11 45
(RAFahey) *sn towards rr* **8/1**[3]

0 **10** 3 **Independent Spirit**[73] 3531 2-8-11 .............................. THamilton(3) 1 36
(RPElliott) *sn towards rr* **66/1**

000 **11** 2 **Mark Your Card**[13] 5227 2-8-9 .............................. KDarley 10 25
(TDEasterby) *s.i.s: sn midfield: rdn over 2f out: wknd over 1f out* **22/1**

**12** 11 **Avizandum (IRE)** 2-9-0 .............................. JFanning 9 —
(TJEtherington) *sn bhd: t.o* **50/1**

00 **13** dist **Kimberley Hall**[14] 5209 2-8-9 .............................. GGibbons 3 —
(JAGlover) *bolted loose bef s: slowly away and hung lft: sn t.o* **40/1**

1m 12.84s (0.34) **Going Correction** -0.075s/f (Good) **13** Ran SP% **113.2**
Speed ratings: **94,92,91,87,85 83,80,80,80,76 73,58,**—CSF £18.41 TOTE £3.60: £1.20, £1.80, £21.30; EX 18.90.
**Owner** Tara Leisure **Bred** Yeomanstown Stud **Trained** Settrington, N Yorks

**FOCUS**
This was not the strongest of maidens, weakened by joint-favourite Able Charlie missing the break, but was won in good style by Taras Treasure. The handicapper looks to have her covered, however.

**NOTEBOOK**
**Taras Treasure(IRE)** was entitled to be involved in the finish given her previous form, and duly won this comfortably. Always travelling fairly well in mid-pack, she picked up when a gap came in the last furlong between the two leaders and won going away. This may not have been the strongest of events so the merit of the form is not easy to assess, but it looks like a step back up in trip maybe worth another try.
**Monkey Madge** probably came out of the race with as much credit as the winner. Making her debut, she showed plenty of pace and travelled well in the lead until giving best close home. Given normal progression, she should find a maiden on this evidence.
**Orpen Wide(IRE)** improved markedly from his debut, where he missed the break. He was well away, from a moderate draw, and showed fair pace until a furlong and a half out where he showed a bit of greenness. A small maiden over the minimum trip should be within his capabilities.
**Owed** was held up in midfield early on, but then hung for most of the race out to the left, eventually finishing up in the middle of the track. He is now qualified for nurseries and his future probably lies there. *Official explanation: jockey said colt hung left from half way*
**Sound And Vision(IRE)**, fitted with first-time blinkers, showed a lot of early pace until headed and stayed on well enough to the line. He could be difficult place, but a drop to five furlongs may help if the blinkers were to work a second time.
**Mossmann Gorge** ran a little green, and got hampered by another runner, but stayed on well enough to the line. He is well related to some decent sprinters and can progress.
**Able Charlie(GER)** completely missed the break, and this run can be ignored.
**Komreyev Star** showed a modicum of ability.
**Independent Spirit** *Official explanation: jockey said gelding hung throughout the race*

## 5543 BROUGH CASTLE MAIDEN STKS — 7f
**3:00** (3:05) (D3) 2-Y-O — **£4,342** (£1,336; £668; £334) **Stalls** Low

Form — RPR

62 **1** **Hadrian (IRE)**[47] 4263 2-9-0 .............................. JFanning 3 83
(MJohnston) *mde all: rdn 2f out: drvn and kpt on wl fnl f* **9/4**[1]

4320 **2** nk **Mozafin**[15] 5186 2-9-0 79 .............................. (v[1]) ACulhane 10 82
(MRChannon) *a.p: chsd wnr fr 1/2-way: rdn over 2f out: drvn and styd on ins last* **7/1**

**3** 1 1/4 **David Junior (USA)** 2-9-0 .............................. RHills 5 79
(BJMeehan) *in tch: rdn along 1/2-way: hdwy 3f out and sn rdn: kpt on same pce u.p fnl 2f* **5/2**[2]

005 **4** 7 **Halla San**[18] 5096 2-9-0 .............................. LGoncalves 7 62
(MrsJRRamsden) *stdd s and bhd: hdwy 3f out: swtchd outside and styd on wl fnl f* **25/1**

2 **5** shd **Lord Mayfair (USA)**[28] 4824 2-9-0 .............................. RWinston 12 61
(TDBarron) *chsd ldrs: rdn over 2f out: sn drvn and wknd wl over 1f out* **4/1**[3]

00 **6** hd **Shankly Bond (IRE)**[10] 5290 2-9-0 .............................. FLynch 13 61
(BSmart) *midfield: hdwy to chse ldrs 3f out: sn rdn and wknd wl over 1f out* **50/1**

00 **7** 3/4 **Bronze Dancer (IRE)**[10] 5302 2-9-0 .............................. DeanMcKeown 6 59
(GASwinbank) *keen: towards rr: hdwy 3f out: sn no imp* **100/1**

00 **8** 1 1/2 **Royal Wedding**[27] 4861 2-9-0 .............................. KDarley 1 55
(DRLoder) *chsd ldrs: rdn along 3f ut: drvn 2f out and sn wknd* **9/1**

00 **9** 9 **Keyalzao (IRE)**[38] 4559 2-8-9 .............................. LEnstone 8 28
(ACrook) *a rr* **150/1**

**10** 1 1/2 **Sooyou Sir (IRE)** 2-9-0 .............................. GGibbons 2 29
(MrsADuffield) *midfield: rdn along 1/2-way: sn wknd* **80/1**

**11** 3 1/2 **Lillas Forest** 2-9-0 .............................. GFaulkner 11 20
(PCHaslam) *s.i.s: a rr* **100/1**

06 **12** 5 **Dancing Deano (IRE)**[17] 5125 2-9-0 .............................. PHanagan 4 8
(RMWhitaker) *a rr* **33/1**

1m 25.88s (-1.22) **Going Correction** -0.075s/f (Good) **12** Ran SP% **114.5**
Speed ratings: **103,102,101,93,93 92,92,90,80,78 74,68**CSF £17.46 TOTE £3.40: £1.30, £2.00, £1.70; EX 17.40.
**Owner** Highclere Thoroughbred Racing XXIII **Bred** Lady Halifax **Trained** Middleham Moor, N Yorks

**FOCUS**
A useful winning time for the grade.

**NOTEBOOK**
**Hadrian(IRE)** had the best form coming into this race and, given a positive ride from a good draw, won this is good style. Rushed up to lead early, he was always holding the rest of the field up the home straight. Connections believe he is maturing all the time, and it remains to be seen what the Handicapper does with him to influence where me may go next.
**Mozafin**, who was visored for the first time, was beaten at odds-on last time and looked one to have reservations about prior to this. He was niggled along from some way out but, to his credit, almost pulled the winner back in towards the line. Whether he repeats this form is open to question given his previous profile and he could be difficult to place.
**David Junior(USA)**, making his debut, did not appear to handle the turn particularly well but ran on well down the home straight. He has a very decent American turf pedigree, and should be capable of building on this decent first effort.
**Halla San**, stepping up in trip again, was held up at the rear until making headway around the turn. He stayed on nicely from an unpromising position, and appeals as a likely type for a nursery at a stiffer course and another step up in trip.
**Lord Mayfair(USA)** did not have the best of draws but did manage to get to the front rank. After getting outpaced early in the straight, he stayed on fairly well to finish in a bunch behind the clear leaders. His debut run has worked out very well, and he is worth another chance to confirm that promise. *Official explanation: jockey said gelding hung left in straight*
**Shankly Bond(IRE)** ran a fair race, albeit never looking likely to be involved, and is now qualified for nurseries.
**Royal Wedding** was travelling well into the straight but found nothing from there on in. He appears to be regressing. *Official explanation: jockey said colt hung left*

## 5544 RACING UK ON CHANNEL 432 H'CAP — 1m
**3:30** (3:34) (E3) (0-70,70) 3-Y-O+ — **£4,555** (£1,401; £700; £350) **Stalls** Low

Form — RPR

0040 **1** **Huxley (IRE)**[52] 4142 5-9-5 70 .............................. (t) GFaulkner 1 81+
(MGQuinlan) *dwlt: sn midfield: hdwy on bit to join ldrs 2f out: led over 1f out: shkn up jst ins fnl f: styd on wl: comf* **12/1**

0000 **2** 2 **Heversham (IRE)**[9] 5317 3-8-9 65 .............................. DeanMcKeown 7 71
(JHetherton) *in tch: hdwy 3f out: jnd ldrs 2f out: ev ch appr fnl f: outpcd by wnr ins last* **16/1**

1552 **3** 1/2 **Hula Ballew**[12] 5236 4-8-11 62 .............................. (p) SWKelly 6 67
(MDods) *in tch: hdwy to chse ldrs 2f out: sn rdn: styd on fnl f* **7/1**[3]

1060 **4** 3/4 **Dara Mac**[9] 5317 5-8-5 61 ow2 .............................. SuzanneFrance(7) 2 66
(NBycroft) *midfield: hdwy 3f out: ch and rdn over 1f out: no ex ins fnl f* **16/1**

6440 **5** 3/4 **Megan's Magic**[8] 5344 4-9-2 67 .............................. (be) JBramhill 8 69+
(WStorey) *slowly away: bhd: hdwy u.p 2f out: swtchd rt jst ins fnl f: styd on wl: nvr able to chal* **14/1**

0005 **6** shd **Queen Charlotte (IRE)**[9] 5317 5-8-13 64 .............................. JFanning 5 65
(MrsKWalton) *cl up: led 1/2-way: rdn and hdd over 1f out: no ex* **6/1**[1]

4050 **7** hd **Adobe**[9] 5317 9-8-13 64 .............................. ACulhane 10 65
(WMBrisbourne) *midfield: effrt over 2f out: styd on fnl f: n.d* **11/1**

1436 **8** 1 1/2 **Gifted Flame**[12] 5236 5-9-2 67 .............................. RWinston 9 64
(TDBarron) *s.i.s: hld up towards rr: hdwy into midfield 3f out: effrt 2f out: sn rdn: no further prog fnl f* **13/2**[2]

06 **9** 3/4 **Inchdura**[41] 4447 6-9-1 66 .............................. KimTinkler 16 62
(NTinkler) *dwlt: sn midfield: drvn along over 3f out: no hdwy* **14/1**

0200 **10** 1 1/4 **Time To Remember (IRE)**[42] 4425 6-8-6 57 .............................. PHanagan 11 50
(RAFahey) *hld up towards rr: keen early: kpt on fnl 2f: n.d* **7/1**[3]

0050 **11** 1/2 **Wessex (USA)**[47] 4258 4-9-0 68 .............................. TEaves(3) 4 60
(JamesMoffatt) *prom: rdn 2f out: sn wknd* **33/1**

6000 **12** 1 3/4 **Atlantic Ace**[49] 4220 7-8-12 63 .............................. FLynch 12 51
(BSmart) *hld up: sme hdwy 3f out: no further prog* **8/1**

0063 **13** 1/2 **Movie King (IRE)**[41] 4450 5-8-9 60 .............................. DaleGibson 14 46
(SGollings) *led tl hdd 1/2-way: wknd 2f out* **16/1**

0003 **14** 11 **Grandma Lily (IRE)**[137] 1750 6-8-3 61 .............................. DTudhope(7) 18 22
(MCChapman) *towards rr most of way: t.o* **33/1**

4505 **15** nk **Magical Mimi**[45] 4318 3-8-8 64 .............................. DarrenWilliams 13 24
(JeddO'Keeffe) *chsd ldrs: rdn over 3f out: wknd over 2f out: t.o* **33/1**

5200 **16** 6 **Sharaab (USA)**[41] 4443 3-8-12 68 .............................. (t) RHills 17 15
(BHanbury) *sn bhd: t.o* **16/1**

1m 38.16s (-1.54) **Going Correction** -0.075s/f (Good)
**WFA** 3 from 4yo+ 5lb **16** Ran SP% **125.4**
Speed ratings: **104,102,101,100,100 99,99,98,97,96 95,93,93,82,82 76**CSF £193.71 CT £952.46 TOTE £14.50: £3.10, £3.40, £1.80, £4.30; EX 310.90.
**Owner** Liam Mulryan **Bred** Leonard H Macmahon **Trained** Newmarket, Suffolk

**FOCUS**
An open handicap won easily by Huxley, who was value for more than the winning margin. The general form is sound but unexceptional.

**NOTEBOOK**
**Huxley(IRE)** won this with plenty in hand. After travelling smoothly throughout the race, and pushed clear a furlong out, he ran right away from the rest of the field. He is well handicapped on his Irish form, and it would be no surprise to see him turned out quickly in an attempt to make use of his mark before getting pushed up the handicap again.
**Heversham(IRE)** has been dropping down the weights and ran another sound race. He was never going to trouble the winner but, after travelling well for a long way, stayed on respectably to the line and clearly is in good heart.
**Hula Ballew**, 3lb higher than her last run and 11lb above her last winning mark, does not look the easiest of rides but you can not knock her consistency this season.
**Dara Mac** often runs well at this course, only two wins have come at Thirsk, travelled well through the race. He was pulled wide to challenge and stayed on to the line after coming under pressure. He looks to be a touch high in the Handicap at the moment.
**Megan's Magic** missed the break, as is normal with her, and made some fair headway up the home straight. She still remains 7lb higher than her last win, and will be continually hampered by missing the break She would be of interest if tried at a stiffer course, on this evidence.
**Queen Charlotte(IRE)** made most of the running, from a decent draw, but had nothing left at the business end of the race. *Official explanation: jockey said mare hung right in the final two furlongs*
**Adobe** ran his usual race, and his handicapped to win soon if the ground stays fast.
**Gifted Flame** travelled well, held up off the pace, and came with a chance up the inside rail a just over a furlong out. He was never quite getting there, and was not overly persevered with when he clearly was not going to be involved. His winning form has been at a track with an uphill finish, and would be interesting if returned to one of those courses next time given he is close to a winning mark.
**Time To Remember(IRE)** is extremely well-handicapped at the moment and ran an eye-catching race. Given that he has shown his best form at sprinting distances, this trip was always likely to test him. He was held up at the back and made late headway, when given his head, and would be of interest if dropped back in trip. Given his overall profile he is not one to trust, but there is little doubt he is well handicapped.

## 5545 ROGAN'S SEAT MAIDEN STKS — 1m
**4:00** (4:01) (D3) 3-Y-O — **£4,186** (£1,288; £644; £322) **Stalls** Low

Form — RPR

**1** **Iktibas** 3-9-0 .............................. (t) RHills 5 89+
(SaeedBinSuroor) *sn led: pushed clr 3f out: unchal* **8/15**[1]

4060 **2** 9 **True (IRE)**[17] 5108 3-8-9 58 .............................. RWinston 4 60
(MrsSLamyman) *hld up: hdwy 1/2-way: rdn 2f out: kpt on u.p: no ch w wnr* **4/1**[2]

04-0 **3** 4 **The Rip**[92] 2934 3-9-0 70 .............................. KDarley 2 56
(TDEasterby) *prom: chsd wnr 1/2-way:sn rdn along and one pce* **18/1**

0 **4** 3/4 **Jonnyem**[12] 5237 3-9-0 .............................. DeanMcKeown 1 54
(GASwinbank) *hld up: hdwy 3f out: sn rdn and plodded on same pce fnl 2f* **40/1**

-000 **5** 1 1/2 **Fifth Column (USA)**[46] 4303 3-9-0 60 .............................. LEnstone 7 51
(DWThompson) *chsd ldrs: rdn along over 3f out: sn wknd* **66/1**

460 **6** 9 **The Nibbler**[38] 4545 3-9-0 52 .............................. MHenry 6 30
(GCHChung) *a rr* **20/1**

0040 **7** 6 **Unprecedented (IRE)**[112] 2392 3-9-0 50 .............................. (v) JFanning 9 16
(TTClement) *chsd wnr: rdn along 1/2-way: sn wknd* **33/1**

0- **8** 1/2 **Attack Minded**[432] 3121 3-9-0 .............................. TWilliams 3 15
(LRJames) *s.i.s and a b ehind* **200/1**

-400 **9** *5* **Top Line Dancer (IRE)**[98] 2756 3-9-0 65..........................(t) ACulhane 8 3
(MDHammond) *a rr* **11/1**[3]

1m 38.64s (-1.06) **Going Correction** -0.075s/f (Good) **9** Ran SP% **111.0**
Speed ratings: **102,93,89,88,86 77,71,71,66**CSF £2.41 TOTE £1.40: £1.50, £1.10, £1.80; EX 3.30.
**Owner** Godolphin **Bred** Shadwell Estate Company Limited **Trained** Newmarket, Suffolk

**FOCUS**
As uncompetitive a maiden as you can get and the favourite had this won a long way out. The time was fair enough considering he could have won by further had he wanted.

**NOTEBOOK**
**Iktibas**, a half-brother to ten-furlong winner Khams-Alhawas out of the high-class Bint Shadayid, appeared to face a straightforward task on this debut and completed it with ease, making all the running and pulling right away from a modest field. He obviously has some talent, but his true ability remains untested and the fact that he has not appeared before now suggests things have not been straightforward with him.
**True(IRE)** has plenty of experience and it was that as much as anything that enabled her to run on into a remote second. She appeared to run above herself on official ratings, but that means little in a one-sided contest like this and she remains a maiden after 12 attempts.
**The Rip**, lightly raced this term, was close enough turning for home but did not look that enthusiastic about trying to bridge the gap to the winner. Even a filly who has looked reluctant in the past was able to get past him into second and he looks one to treat with caution.
**Jonnyem**, who only made his racecourse debut 12 days earlier, did not achieve a great deal in finishing a well-beaten fourth but may improve a bit for further.
**Top Line Dancer(IRE)** again ran poorly and, despite the application of a tongue tie, was reported to have a breathing problem. *Official explanation: jockey said colt had breathing problem*

## 5546 BUCKDEN PIKE H'CAP 1m 4f
**4:30** (4:33) (F4) (0-55,55) 3-Y-0+ **£3,209** (£917; £458) **Stalls** Low

Form RPR
1304 **1** **Ego Trip**[43] 4389 3-8-9 **52**..........................(b[1]) DaleGibson 11 64
(MWEasterby) *chsd ldrs: drvn along over 4f out: led over 2f out: styd on wl u.p* **12/1**
4 **2** *1* **Wild Power (GER)**[11] 5258 6-9-2 **55**.......................... BSwarbrick(5) 5 65
(JGMO'Shea) *midfield: smooth hdwy over 2f out: rdn over 1f out: styd on to go 2nd ins fnl f: no imp on wnr* **11/1**
5204 **3** *1 ¾* **Theatre Tinka (IRE)**[42] 4424 5-9-7 **55**..........................(p) FLynch 9 62+
(RHollinshead) *hld up in rr: hdwy 3f out: midfield whn nt clr run 2f out: styd on wl u.p fr over 1f out: nrst fin* **7/1**[3]
1246 **4** *nk* **Broughton Knows**[141] 1668 7-9-4 **52**..........................(b) KDarley 10 59
(MissGayKelleway) *hld up: hdwy 5f out: chal over 2f out: ev ch and rdn over 1f out: no ex fnl f* **14/1**
2204 **5** *1* **Munaawesh (USA)**[7] 5365 3-8-11 **54**..........................(b) ACulhane 14 59
(DWChapman) *slowly away: hmpd after 2f: hld up: hmpd over 3f out: gd hdwy over 2f out: ev ch and rdn over 1f out: no ex* **11/1**
0025 **6** *hd* **Muslin**[12] 5243 3-8-11 **54**.......................... SWKelly 17 59
(JRFanshawe) *midfield: hdwy over 3f out: ev ch and rdn over 1f out: kpt on same pce* **15/2**
0/66 **7** *1 ½* **All Bleevable**[43] 4397 7-8-12 **46** oh6.......................... JBramhill 13 48
(MrsSLamyman) *midfield: sme hdwy and in tch over 2f out: sn rdn: no further prog* **50/1**
5202 **8** *½* **Sovereign State (IRE)**[12] 5243 7-9-2 **50**..........................(p) LEnstone 16 52
(DWThompson) *midfield: hdwy 3f out: in tch 2f out: no further prog* **14/1**
5010 **9** *2* **Chevin**[12] 5243 5-8-12 **46**.......................... PHanagan 8 44
(RAFahey) *hld up: pushed along whn hmpd over 3f out: n.d* **13/2**[2]
1152 **10** *1 ¼* **Let It Be**[17] 5130 3-8-1 **51**.......................... NeilBrown(7) 12 47
(KGReveley) *chsd ldrs: pushed along 4f out: fdd fnl 3f* **5/1**[1]
0U-0 **11** *¾* **Amalfi Coast**[17] 5110 5-9-0 **48**.......................... GFaulkner 4 43
(WSCunningham) *cl up: led over 3f out tl hdd over 2f out: fdd* **100/1**
P000 **12** *½* **Grande Terre (IRE)**[27] 4848 3-8-12 **55**.......................... MFenton 2 49
(JGGiven) *midfield tl wknd over 2f out* **66/1**
6430 **13** *4* **Prairie Law (GER)**[8] 5354 4-8-12 **46** oh1.......................... ANicholls 7 34
(IanWilliams) *sn bhd: n.d* **14/1**
3106 **14** *½* **Westcourt Dream**[9] 5320 4-9-1 **52**.......................... PMulrennan(3) 6 39
(MWEasterby) *prom tl rdn and wknd 3f out* **16/1**
-202 **15** *3 ½* **Fairy Monarch (IRE)**[76] 3411 5-9-1 **49**..........................(p) RFitzpatrick 18 31
(PTMidgley) *midfield: drvn along and no hdwy whn stmbld over 3f out* **25/1**
0300 **16** *shd* **Awwal Marra (USA)**[17] 5110 4-8-12 **46** oh1.......................... DeanMcKeown 3 27
(EWTuer) *prom tl wknd over 3f out* **50/1**
1100 **17** *6* **Dial Square**[29] 4818 3-8-9 **52**.......................... JFanning 15 24
(PHowling) *bhd most of way* **40/1**
0/10 **18** *5* **Woodwind Down**[56] 4007 7-9-0 **48**.......................... RWinston 1 12
(MTodhunter) *led: pushed along 5f out: hdd over 3f out: wknd qckly: sn bhd and eased* **25/1**
350- **19** *2 ½* **Mister Merlin (IRE)**[471] 2020 3-8-2 **52** oh1 ow6.......... DTudhope(7) 19 12
(DCarroll) *a bhd* **100/1**

2m 34.95s (-0.25) **Going Correction** -0.075s/f (Good)
**WFA** 3 from 4yo+ 9lb **19** Ran SP% **122.0**
Speed ratings: **97,96,95,94,94 94,93,91,91,90 90,87,87,84,84 80,77,75,75**CSF £129.14 CT £1009.22 TOTE £16.00: £4.80, £5.00, £2.30, £2.30; EX 269.50.
**Owner** K Hodgson & Mrs J Hodgson **Bred** K And Mrs Hodgson **Trained** Sheriff Hutton, N Yorks

**FOCUS**
A low-grade handicap and the pace was modest, but a very competitive contest nonetheless.

**NOTEBOOK**
**Ego Trip**, blinkered for the first time, came with his effort soon after turning for home. With a couple of his nearest dangers hanging their chances away and another finding little off the bridle, racing against the inside rail was probably a big help to him and he saw the trip out much better than he had in his previous start.
**Wild Power(GER)**, not for the first time, travelled well before not finding as much as had looked likely. This trip may have stretched him a bit, but he does not look one to lump on to go one better over any distance.
**Theatre Tinka(IRE)** made up a great deal of ground in the latter stages and could be worth keeping in mind for a similar contest on softer ground before going back on to sand during the winter.
**Broughton Knows**, reappearing after a five-month break, came to win his race halfway up the home straight but no sooner had he got there than he started to hang about and chucked it away. He is yet to win on turf and looks much happier on sand.
**Munaawesh(USA)** did not enjoy the smoothest of passages, but still came with his effort on the wide outside at just the right time. However, he tended to hang over to the nearside under pressure and had nothing more to offer. He is yet to win after 20 attempts.
**Muslin** had every chance, but looked short of pace in the closing stages and may not have been suited by the drop back in trip.
**Let It Be** was close enough turning in, but dropped out rather tamely over the last couple of furlongs and there seemed no obvious excuse.
**Woodwind Down** *Official explanation: jockey said mare hung left in straight*

## 5547 SCARBOROUGH CASTLE H'CAP 6f
**5:00** (5:07) (F4) (0-55,55) 3-Y-O **£3,085** (£881; £440) **Stalls** High

Form RPR
4003 **1** **Fox Covert (IRE)**[8] 5342 3-9-0 **53**..........................(v) LEnstone 1 60
(DWBarker) *mde all far side: rdn wl over 1f out: styd on* **7/1**[2]
0060 **2** *1 ½* **Westborough (IRE)**[8] 5342 3-8-13 **52**..........................(t) KimTinkler 2 55
(NTinkler) *trckd ldrs far side: hdwy to chse wnr 2f out: sn rdn and kpt on* **20/1**
4-06 **3** *½* **Suitcase Murphy (IRE)**[3] 5452 3-8-2 **46** oh1.............. BSwarbrick(5) 19 47
(MsDeborahJEvans) *trckd ldrs stands side: hdwy 2f out: rdn and styd on wl fnl f* **12/1**
2530 **4** *¾* **Yamato Pink**[11] 5261 3-8-12 **51**.......................... SWKelly 17 50
(MrsHSweeting) *cl up stands side: led that gp 2f out: sn rdn and evc hance tl nt qckn ins last* **6/1**[1]
0003 **5** *nk* **Yorke's Folly (USA)**[10] 5306 3-8-7 **46** oh1..........................(v) RWinston 5 44
(CWFairhurst) *chsd ldrs far side: rdn 2f out: kpt on same pce appr last* **20/1**
5000 **6** *hd* **Sea Fern**[47] 4279 3-8-7 **46** oh1.......................... PFessey 12 43
(DEddy) *in tch stands side: hdwy 2f out: rdn and n.m.r over 1f out: kpt on same pce* **16/1**
5040 **7** *1* **From The North (IRE)**[3] 5448 3-8-8 **50**..........................(p) ABeech(3) 7 44
(ADickman) *in tch far side: rdn along 2f out: kpt on same pce* **33/1**
3206 **8** *shd* **Uhuru Peak**[36] 4610 3-8-11 **53**..........................(b[1]) PMulrennan(3) 18 47
(MWEasterby) *reminders s and sn prom stands side: led that gp 1/2-way: rdn: wandered and hdd 2f out: sn drvn and wknd 1f out* **6/1**[1]
2330 **9** *¾* **Tsarbuck**[23] 4968 3-8-8 **47**.......................... GFaulkner 14 39
(RMHCowell) *chsd ldrs stands side: rdn 2f out: drvn and one pce appr last* **10/1**
2005 **10** *nk* **Vittorioso (IRE)**[40] 4484 3-8-7 **46** oh1.......................... DarrenWilliams 11 37
(MissGayKelleway) *towards rr stand side: swtchd rt to stands rail 1/2-way: styd on appr last: nrst fin* **20/1**
033 **11** *¾* **Red Hot Ruby**[66] 3739 3-8-7 **46**.......................... PHanagan 3 35
(RAFahey) *chsd ldrs far side: rdn along over 2f out: sn btn* **15/2**[3]
0605 **12** *hd* **Schinken Otto (IRE)**[12] 5237 3-8-4 **46** oh1.......................... TEaves(3) 10 34
(JMJefferson) *towards rr stands side: hdwy over 2f out: sn rdn and no imp* **33/1**
3000 **13** *2 ½* **Turkish Delight**[13] 5219 3-9-2 **55**.......................... ACulhane 13 35
(JBalding) *cl up stands side: rdn along 2f out and sn wknd* **12/1**
4400 **14** *3 ½* **Appetina**[16] 5156 3-9-2 **55**..........................(b[1]) KDarley 6 25
(JGGiven) *hmpd s and a rr stands side* **12/1**
30-0 **15** *1* **Faites Vos Jeux**[16] 5141 3-8-7 **46** oh1.......................... DaleGibson 8 13
(CNKellett) *chsd wnr far side: rdn along 1/2-way and sn wknd* **33/1**
3060 **16** *½* **Open Mind**[15] 5193 3-8-9 **48**.......................... DeanMcKeown 15 13
(EJAlston) *dwlt: sn led stands side gp: rdn along and hdd 1/2-way: sn wknd* **20/1**
054 **17** *5* **Lottie**[45] 4316 3-8-7 **46** oh1.......................... JFanning 16 —
(MissVHaigh) *a rr stands side* **40/1**
0 **18** *5* **Hallahoise Hydro (IRE)**[15] 5193 3-9-0 **53**.......................... MFenton 20 —
(BSRothwell) *s.i.s and a rr stands side* **18/1**
-000 **19** *7* **Big Tom (IRE)**[17] 5104 3-8-3 **49**.......................... DTudhope(7) 4 —
(DCarroll) *chsd ldrs far side to 1/2-way: sn lost pl and bhd* **33/1**

1m 11.95s (-0.55) **Going Correction** -0.075s/f (Good) **19** Ran SP% **129.4**
Speed ratings: **100,98,97,96,95 95,94,94,93,92 91,91,88,83,82 81,74,68,58**CSF £149.67 CT £1729.68 TOTE £8.40: £2.30, £5.40, £3.40, £1.50; EX 107.20 Place 6 £82.12, Place 5 £42.55.
**Owner** D W Barker **Bred** John O Browne **Trained** Scorton, N Yorks

**FOCUS**
A competitive if modest sprint handicap. The field split into two with the slightly larger group racing stands' side, but despite the first two home coming from the two lowest stalls there was not a great deal in it.

**NOTEBOOK**
**Fox Covert(IRE)**, a long-standing maiden, led the far-side group the whole way from his rails draw and stayed on well to finally get off the mark at the 23rd attempt. He has made the frame off much higher marks than this in the past so could strike again now that he knows how to win, especially if allowed an uncontested lead.
**Westborough(IRE)**, another long-standing maiden, came through to chase the winner home on the far side but could never get on terms. This was a fair effort, but we have been here before with him and he has not managed to capitalise on it.
**Suitcase Murphy(IRE)** finished strongly to win the separate race on the stands' side. This was by some way his best effort yet and he looks capable of winning a similar contest off this sort of mark.
**Yamato Pink**, who had to be walked all the way to the start, made good use of her high draw and soon bagged the stands' rail in front. However, she tended to hang away from the rail as she came under pressure and had nothing more to offer inside the last furlong.
**Yorke's Folly(USA)**, never far away over on the far side, seems to have improved a little for the fitting of a visor and has now run two creditable races in succession.
**Sea Fern** has now finished out of the frame in all eight of his starts, but was staying on quite well here and was not completely disgraced.
**Uhuru Peak**, dropping back from a mile, was given a positive ride in the stands'-side group but looked a horrible ride, hanging all over the track in the second half of the contest. He may prefer easier ground, but after this effort he cannot be supported with any confidence whatsoever.
**Tsarbuck** showed up for a while, but does look a much better horse on Fibresand.
**Red Hot Ruby** *Official explanation: jockey said filly hung left throughout*
**Hallahoise Hydro(IRE)** *Official explanation: jockey said gelding lost his action*
T/Plt: £90.30 to a £1 stake. Pool £36,411.00, 294.20 winning tickets T/Qpdt: £22.60 to a £1 stake. Pool £2,648.00, 86.65 winning tickets JF

# 5154 YARMOUTH (L-H)
Tuesday, September 14

**OFFICIAL GOING: Good to firm changing to good after race 1 (2.20)**
Wind: Fresh across Weather: Cloudy with rain after the first race until just before the third, giving way to sunny spells.

## 5548 JACK LEADER CHALLENGE TROPHY FILLIES' NURSERY 7f 3y
**2:20** (2:23) (D2) (0-85,81) 2-Y-O **£5,772** (£1,776; £888; £444) **Stalls** High

Form RPR
0061 **1** **Succession**[3] 5477 2-8-9 **69** 6ex.......................... SSanders 7 76
(SirMarkPrescott) *mde all: rdn and edgd lft over 1f out: jst hld on* **9/4**[1]
0333 **2** *½* **Bibury Flyer**[6] 5391 2-9-7 **81**.......................... TEDurcan 6 87
(MRChannon) *hld up: hdwy over 2f out: shkn up ins fnl f: r.o* **11/2**[3]
004 **3** *1 ½* **Miss Patricia**[32] 4714 2-9-0 **74**.......................... NCallan 14 76
(JGPortman) *hld up: hdwy to chse wnr over 2f out: rdn and ev ch over 1f out: unable qck ins fnl f* **20/1**
0120 **4** *1 ½* **Whatatodo**[17] 5119 2-8-12 **72**.......................... JQuinn 1 70
(MLWBell) *chsd ldrs: rdn over 1f out: styd on same pce ins fnl f* **20/1**

0430 **5** *1* **Azuree (IRE)**[31] 4752 2-8-7 **67**........(b) JFEgan 5 62
(RHannon) *trckd ldrs: rdn over 1f out: styd on same pce* **50/1**

504 **6** *7* **Flaunting It (IRE)**[17] 5115 2-8-3 **63**........ CCatlin 16 39
(JAOsborne) *prom: rdn over 2f out: wknd over 1f out* **33/1**

032 **7** *hd* **Velveteen Rabbit**[32] 4706 2-9-0 **74**........ LDettori 12 49
(SaeedBinSuroor) *hld up: rdn over 2f out: sn wknd* **9/2**[2]

0526 **8** *½* **Lateral Thinker (IRE)**[19] 5052 2-8-10 **70**........ KMcEvoy 3 44
(JAOsborne) *chsd wnr over 4f: wknd over 1f out* **16/1**

503 **9** *nk* **Theas Dance**[17] 5115 2-8-5 **65**........ TPQueally 4 38
(DRLoder) *s.s: hdwy over 2f out: wknd wl over 1f out* **10/1**

2361 **10** *1* **Lakesdale (IRE)**[13] 5218 2-7-12 **58**........ AMcCarthy 8 29
(MissDMountain) *chsd ldrs 5f* **20/1**

0000 **11** *¾* **Never Away**[11] 5271 2-7-13 **59**........ DKinsella 10 28
(NACallaghan) *dwlt: hld up: wknd over 2f out* **66/1**

443 **12** *10* **Grezie**[143] 1607 2-8-0 **60**........ RFfrench 15 —
(JRBest) *sn pushed along in rr: wknd 3f out* **28/1**

4050 **13** *3½* **Tantien**[12] 5240 2-8-0 **60**........ LisaJones 11 —
(JohnAHarris) *chsd ldrs over 4f* **66/1**

14 **14** *7* **Krynica (USA)**[61] 3865 2-9-7 **81**........ EAhern 13 —
(SirMichaelStoute) *hld up in tch: wkng whn n.m.r wl over 1f out* **10/1**

1m 28.35s (1.85) **Going Correction** +0.20s/f (Good) **14** Ran SP% **114.0**
Speed ratings: **97,96,94,93,91 83,83,83,82,81 80,69,65,57**CSF £11.43 CT £195.28 TOTE £3.40: £1.30, £2.00, £5.40; EX 16.60.
**Owner** Dr Catherine Wills **Bred** St Clare Hall Stud **Trained** Newmarket, Suffolk

**FOCUS**
This looks strong, reliable nursery form, with the first five well clear.

**NOTEBOOK**
**Succession**, off the mark in clear-cut fashion over a mile on her handicap debut at Musselburgh, was 4lb well-in under her 6lb penalty and followed up over this shorter trip. She had to work quite hard, but remains one to have on your side as she could well be turned out to run off the same mark again.
**Bibury Flyer** has been running well all season, including when third in a very competitive six-furlong Doncaster nursery on her previous start. Stepped up to seven furlongs for the first time, she ran yet another fine race and proved her stamina in the process. She always seems to find one or two too good for her, but she has more options open to her now she gets seven furlongs.
**Miss Patricia** showed ability in three runs in maidens and confirmed that promise switched to a handicap. There could be a similar race in her, or maybe a minor event back in maiden company.
**Whatatodo**, dropped in class, ran well from a 10lb higher mark than when winning on her handicap debut.
**Azuree(IRE)**, 4lb lower than when running last over five furlongs on her nursery debut on her previous start, ran better over these extra two furlongs but did not quite do enough to suggest she is about to strike.
**Velveteen Rabbit** had shown fair form in maiden company, but this was disappointing and represented a step back.
**Never Away** ◆ beat just six home in four runs in maiden company, but caught the eye on this nursery debut. Towards the rear, she was beginning to make ground when the pace was quickening but got stopped in her run and could not recover thereafter. She is at the right end of the handicap and could be better than she has shown.
**Krynica(USA)** *Official explanation: jockey said filly's saddle slipped*

## 5549 TRETT CONSULTING CLAIMING STKS 1m 3f 101y
**2:50** (2:52) (F4) 3-Y-O **£3,024** (£864; £432) **Stalls** Low

Form RPR

2456 **1** **Our Emmy Lou**[22] 4998 3-8-5 60 ow1........ SSanders 1 66
(SirMarkPrescott) *hld up: hdwy over 4f out: led over 1f out: sn clr* **7/2**[2]

4300 **2** *7* **Fu Fighter**[17] 5116 3-8-11 68........ LDettori 7 61
(JAOsborne) *swtchd to r alone and wd after 1f: led 8f out: rdn and hdd over 2f out: styd on same pce* **11/4**[1]

0404 **3** *2* **Maria Bonita (IRE)**[24] 4940 3-8-2 63........(b) JQuinn 4 49
(RMBeckett) *hld up in tch: led over 2f out: rdn and hdd over 1f out: edgd lft and wknd fnl f* **4/1**[3]

0035 **4** *hd* **Hinode (IRE)**[20] 5037 3-8-13 60........ TPQueally 6 59
(JARToller) *hld up: rdn over 4f out: styd on appr fnl f: nvr trbld ldrs* **16/1**

062P **5** *½* **Auroville**[24] 4940 3-8-11 57........ RMullen 10 56
(MLWBell) *led over 3f: remained handy tl rdn and wknd over 1f out* **14/1**

5060 **6** *8* **Duke's View (IRE)**[21] 5021 3-8-13 53........ EAhern 2 46
(MrsAJPerrett) *chsd ldrs: lost pl over 4f out: hdwy 3f out: hung lft and wknd 2f out* **14/1**

0300 **7** *3* **Lillianna (IRE)**[15] 5197 3-8-6 60........ WRyan 5 34
(HRACecil) *chsd ldrs: rdn over 3f out: wknd wl over 1f out* **11/2**

4500 **8** *1¼* **Royal Starlet**[17] 5116 3-8-8 45........ IMongan 8 34
(MrsAJPerrett) *hld up in tch: rdn over 4f out: wknd 2f out* **33/1**

0600 **9** *2½* **Zaffeu**[10] 5293 3-9-9 65........(b) TEDurcan 9 45
(NPLittmoden) *s.s: bhd: effrt over 3f out: sn wknd* **16/1**

0000 **10** *22* **Brooklands Lodge (USA)**[7] 5374 3-8-4 56........(p) PDoe 3 —
(MJAttwater) *chsd ldrs 8f* **33/1**

-003 **11** *1½* **Skelthwaite**[10] 5284 3-9-2 35........ WHogg(7) 11 7
(MissDAMchale) *chsd ldrs 8f* **100/1**

2m 31.6s (4.20) **Going Correction** +0.35s/f (Good) **11** Ran SP% **116.2**
Speed ratings: **98,92,91,91,90 85,82,82,80,64 63** CT £4.40 TOTE £1.90: £1.50, £1.70, £; EX17.40 1.Fu Fighter was claimed by Mr C. L. Popham for £9000. Maria Bonita (IRE) was claimed by Mr A. Grinter for £7000. Our Emmy Lou was the subject of a
**Owner** Lady Roborough **Bred** Blackdown Stud **Trained** Newmarket, Suffolk

**FOCUS**
A pretty moderate claimer and the winner is the only one worth taking from the race on this evidence.

**NOTEBOOK**
**Our Emmy Lou** ◆ had not really been progressing in more competitive events recently, including in blinkers on Fibresand on his previous start, but this drop in grade proved the answer and she got off the mark in emphatic fashion. Retained by her current connections, she can win a handicap on this evidence.
**Fu Fighter**, dropped in grade and trip, was taken wide soon after the start and had a clear lead when rejoining the main field, but it made little difference - he was simply beaten by a better horse. All he did was stay and a return to further may suit.
**Maria Bonita(IRE)**, racing over her furthest trip to date, was the best off at the weights but she found very little under pressure and was disappointing.
**Hinode(IRE)** ran his best race to date over a mile on Fibresand and these conditions did not bring out the best in him.
**Auroville** had a bit to find with some of these at the weights and well beaten.
**Lillianna(IRE)**, dropped in grade and stepped up in trip, found nothing under pressure.
**Brooklands Lodge(USA)** *Official explanation: jockey said filly was coughing post race*

## 5550 TOTEPLACEPOT SPRINT H'CAP 5f 43y
**3:20** (3:27) (D2) (0-85,83) 3-Y-O+ **£9,331** (£3,539; £1,769; £804) **Stalls** High

Form RPR

1000 **1** **Mine Behind**[10] 5299 4-8-13 **82**........ LDettori 1 94+
(JRBest) *sn pushed along in rr: hdwy 1/2-way: rdn to ld ins fnl f: r.o wl* **4/1**[1]

1005 **2** *1½* **Tony The Tap**[17] 5124 3-8-12 **82**........ TPQueally 4 89
(NACallaghan) *mid-div: outpcd 1/2-way: r.o ins fnl f: no ch w wnr* **9/1**

0030 **3** *½* **Musical Fair**[4] 5440 4-8-6 **75**........ FNorton 8 80
(JAGlover) *hld up: hdwy 1/2-way: rdn over 1f out: styd on* **12/1**

0000 **4** *nk* **Absent Friends**[7] 5372 7-9-0 **83**........ KMcEvoy 9 87
(JBalding) *w ldr: rdn and ev ch over 1f out: styd on same pce ins fnl f* **16/1**

1420 **5** *¾* **Foley Millennium (IRE)**[18] 5094 6-8-5 **74**........ NPollard 11 75
(MQuinn) *led: hung lft and hdd ins fnl f: wknd nr fin* **20/1**

0013 **6** *¾* **Fiddle Me Blue**[4] 5442 3-8-7 **77**........(v[1]) JQuinn 5 76
(HMorrison) *dwlt: stmbld sn after s: bhd: r.o ins fnl f: nvr nrr* **8/1**

0661 **7** *½* **Malapropism**[4] 5440 4-8-5 **81** 3ex........ BO'Neill(7) 15 78
(MRChannon) *hld up in tch: rdn over 1f out: hung lft and nt run on* **11/2**[2]

4001 **8** *1½* **Prime Recreation**[16] 5157 7-8-2 **71**........ LisaJones 10 63
(PSFelgate) *chsd ldrs to 1/2-way* **20/1**

1000 **9** *5* **Salviati (USA)**[18] 5071 7-8-11 **80**........ PFitzsimons 6 54
(JMBradley) *s.s: n.d* **20/1**

0006 **10** *½* **Polish Emperor (USA)**[18] 5094 4-8-6 **75** ow1........(e) NCallan 2 47
(PWHarris) *chsd ldrs over 3f* **6/1**[3]

0502 **11** *nk* **Gone'N'Dunnett (IRE)**[21] 5016 5-8-0 **69** oh9........(v) AMcCarthy 3 40
(MrsCADunnett) *chsd ldrs: rdn 1/2-way: wknd wl over 1f out* **40/1**

6106 **12** *½* **Mr Malarkey (IRE)**[10] 5299 4-8-13 **82**........(b) CCatlin 7 51
(MrsCADunnett) *chsd ldrs 3f* **14/1**

64.06 secs (1.36) **Going Correction** +0.35s/f (Good)
**WFA** 3 from 4yo+ 1lb **12** Ran SP% **107.7**
Speed ratings: **103,100,99,99,98 96,96,93,85,84 84,83**CSF £30.48 CT £294.78 TOTE £4.90: £2.60, £2.90, £3.30; EX 35.20 Trifecta £346.30 Pool £, w/u.
**Owner** M Folan R Lees R Crampton **Bred** Hesmonds Stud Ltd **Trained** Hucking, Kent

**FOCUS**
A competitive sprint handicap run at a good pace, and the first three home came from off the pace. This is fair form.

**NOTEBOOK**
**Mine Behind**, who won the race on his side yet was only seventh at Kempton on his previous start, gained compensation with a most decisive success. He would have to be of interest next time off the back of this performance, but has never followed up and was below form for his next two starts when he last won.
**Tony The Tap** continued his good recent run of form with a fine effort, but he picked up a little too late and may be slightly better over six furlongs.
**Musical Fair**, just 2lb higher than when last successful, has gained all of her previous wins with firm in the ground description, so this was a decent effort. *Official explanation: jockey said filly hung left*
**Absent Friends** has not won for over a year and has dropped 15lb in the weights since the start of the season, but this was a promising run and he could well be ready to exploit his current mark - he was last successful in a handicap off a 1lb higher mark.
**Foley Millennium(IRE)** ran an honest race and was not beaten that far, but the handicapper may just have got to grips with him now. However, he is rated just 45 on the All-Weather and must be followed should he bid to exploit that mark.
**Fiddle Me Blue** missed the kick in the first-time visor and then stumbled, and this was a very good effort considering. *Official explanation: jockey said filly was never travelling*
**Malapropism** did not run to the form he showed to win at Doncaster on his previous start and probably would have preferred faster ground.
**Polish Emperor(USA)**, again well backed, could not dominate and was not at his best.

## 5551 THOMAS PRIOR MAIDEN STKS 6f 3y
**3:50** (3:54) (D3) 3-Y-O+ **£4,095** (£1,260; £630; £315) **Stalls** High

Form RPR

0332 **1** **Instinct**[26] 4868 3-8-12 58........ LDettori 1 65
(RHannon) *hld up in tch: chsd ldr over 1f out: sn rdn: styd on to ld post* **2/1**[1]

2202 **2** *shd* **Stargem**[16] 5147 3-8-7 64........ JQuinn 2 60
(JPearce) *led: racd keenly: rdn and hdd post* **5/2**[3]

0026 **3** *2½* **Antigua Bay (IRE)**[22] 5001 3-8-7 70........ LisaJones 7 52
(JARToller) *chsd ldr over 4f out to over 1f out: styd on same pce* **9/4**[2]

6000 **4** *6* **Raheed (IRE)**[7] 5370 3-8-12 62........(v[1]) AMcCarthy 6 39
(MrsCADunnett) *chsd ldrs over 4f* **14/1**

**5** *21* **Nopleazinu** 4-8-9........ JoannaBadger 5 —
(MrsNMacauley) *s.s: hung lft and wknd 1/2-way* **40/1**

**6** *8* **Terenure Girl** 3-8-7........ NCallan 4 —
(PSFelgate) *s.s: sme hdwy over 3f out: sn wknd* **16/1**

1m 15.68s (2.08) **Going Correction** +0.35s/f (Good)
**WFA** 3 from 4yo 2lb **6** Ran SP% **107.7**
Speed ratings: **100,99,96,88,60 49**CSF £6.66 TOTE £2.20: £1.50, £1.40; EX 5.90.
**Owner** Jim Horgan **Bred** The Queen **Trained** East Everleigh, Wilts

**FOCUS**
A very weak maiden with the whole field disappointing to an extent.

**NOTEBOOK**
**Instinct**, who won the race on the wrong side when runner-up at Chepstow on his previous start, was able to gain compensation, despite having 11lb to find at the weights with the eventual runner-up. He was a touch keen early on, but had enough left in the closing stages and just got up under a determined Dettori drive. With the Handicapper likely to have his way, he would have to be of interest under a penalty.
**Stargem** had 11lb in hand of the eventual winner at the weights but, despite appearing to have every possible chance, that one was just too strong. He may not be quite as good as his mark of 64 would suggest.
**Antigua Bay(IRE)**, a beaten favourite on Fibresand on her previous start, was again disappointing, lacking a change of pace when it was most needed.
**Raheed(IRE)** did not run to his rating of 62 in a first-time visor.
**Nopleazinu** showed nothing.
**Terenure Girl** also showed nothing.

## 5552 RACING WELFARE (S) STKS 7f 3y
**4:20** (4:25) (G4) 3-Y-O **£2,723** (£778; £389) **Stalls** High

Form RPR

00 **1** **Zalebe**[15] 5204 3-8-7........ JQuinn 1 53
(JPearce) *hld up: hdwy and hung lft over 2f out: rdn to ld ins fnl f: r.o* **20/1**

0005 **2** *nk* **Saintly Place**[8] 5336 3-8-12 50........ TEDurcan 7 57
(MRChannon) *chsd ldrs: led over 2f out: sn rdn: hdd ins fnl f: r.o* **10/1**

2040 **3** *3* **Yashin (IRE)**[18] 5092 3-8-12 57........ LDettori 8 49
(MHTompkins) *led: hdd over 5f out: remined handy tl outpcd over 2f out: styd on fnl f* **7/2**[1]

6352 **4** *nk* **Elsinora**[10] 5282 3-8-7 45 (b) DKinsella 18 44
(HMorrison) *a.p: rdn over 2f out: styd on same pce fnl f* **8/1**
05 **5** *2* **Bulberry Hill**[184] 1022 3-8-12 TPQueally 12 43
(MGQuinlan) *hld up in tch: rdn over 2f out: styd on same pce appr fnl f* **12/1**
5006 **6** *1 ¼* **David's Girl**[18] 5092 3-8-4 40 BReilly(3) 2 35
(DMorris) *chsd ldrs: rdn 1/2-way: wknd fnl f* **40/1**
0-0 **7** *1 ¼* **Mannyman (IRE)**[15] 5204 3-8-7 GCarter 13 32
(WJarvis) *trckd ldrs: racd keenly: rdn and wknd fnl f* **25/1**
0013 **8** *hd* **Shinko Femme (IRE)**[16] 5141 3-8-12 51 WRyan 6 36
(NTinkler) *hld up: sme hdwy over 1f out: nvr trbld ldrs* **9/2**[3]
0340 **9** *5* **Killoch Place (IRE)**[63] 3822 3-8-12 40 (v) FNorton 5 23
(JAGlover) *dwlt: hld up: n.d* **20/1**
0006 **10** *2* **Tardis**[40] 4497 3-8-7 45 RMullen 10 13
(MLWBell) *prom over 5f* **20/1**
0034 **11** *5* **Wings Of Morning (IRE)**[26] 4879 3-9-0 63 DNolan(3) 17 10
(DCarroll) *sn outpcd* **12/1**
1000 **12** *nk* **Mitzi Caspar**[22] 5002 3-8-12 45 (b[1]) JFEgan 11 4
(PLGilligan) *hld up: rdn over 2f out: sn wknd* **40/1**
0002 **13** *1* **Indrani**[21] 5026 3-8-0 40 NataliaGemelova(7) 16 —
(JohnAHarris) *led over 5f out: hdd over 2f out: wknd over 1f out* **25/1**
0403 **14** *2 ½* **Molinia**[29] 4817 3-8-7 51 (t) SSanders 14 —
(RMBeckett) *s.s: a bhd* **4/1**[2]
0-0 **15** *dist* **Chantilly Sunset (IRE)**[10] 5306 3-8-7 JEdmunds 3 —
(JBalding) *chsd ldrs: rdn 1/2-way: sn wknd* **66/1**

1m 29.0s (2.50) **Going Correction** +0.35s/f (Good) **15 Ran SP% 124.3**
Speed ratings: **99,98,95,94,92 91,89,89,83,81 75,75,74,71,**—CSF £196.62 TOTE £18.00: £3.50, £3.80, £2.90; EX 416.60.There was no bid for the winner. Saintly Place was claimed by Trevor Sleath for £6000

**Owner** T H Rossiter **Bred** T H Rossiter **Trained** Newmarket, Suffolk

**FOCUS**
Just ordinary form for this seller, but it should work out at a similar level.

**NOTEBOOK**
**Zalebe** had been well held in two starts in maiden company, but did show improvement on her previous start when not beaten that far. Dropped significantly in grade, she was supported at big odds and justified the interest with a narrow win. She should not be too harshly treated for this given the runner-up is rated just 50 and could well continue her progression in low-grade handicaps, possibly over a mile.
**Saintly Place** appreciated this drop back from a mile and, now his optimum conditions have been established, he could well find a similar event.
**Yashin(IRE)** was favoured by the weights on this drop into selling company, but he seemed to hit a flat spot and could not pose a threat to the front two.
**Elsinora**, runner-up in banded company over six furlongs on her previous start, did not look straightforward in the early stages but seemed to run her race and can have no real excuses.
**Bulberry Hill**, supported on this drop in grade, offered some promise and may find a very minor race if he continues to go the right way.
**Shinko Femme(IRE)** never landed a blow and was below form for the second race in succession.
**Mitzi Caspar** *Official explanation: jockey said filly had breathing problem*
**Molinia** had run well in a handicap over course and distance on her previous start so this was disappointing. *Official explanation: jockey said filly did not handle eased ground*

## 5553 ELM CONTRACTS CONDITIONS STKS 6f 3y
4:50 (4:51) (C2) 3-Y-0+ **£9,048** (£3,432; £1,716; £780) **Stalls** High

Form RPR
0000 **1** **Dowager**[3] 5454 3-8-1 96 FNorton 4 103
(RHannon) *racd centre: a.p: led over 1f out: rdn out* **12/1**
4400 **2** *¾* **Country Reel (USA)**[31] 4745 4-8-8 110 (vt) LDettori 5 106
(SaeedBinSuroor) *racd centre: hld up: hdwy over 2f out: rdn to chse wnr over 1f out: styd on* **1/1**[1]
3065 **3** *1 ¼* **Colonel Cotton (IRE)**[3] 5471 5-8-8 98 (v) WRyan 8 102
(NACallaghan) *racd centre: hld up: hdwy over 2f out: styd on same pce fnl f* **6/1**[3]
0005 **4** *2* **Whitbarrow (IRE)**[6] 5393 5-8-8 90 (b) JFEgan 2 96
(JMBradley) *racd centre: led: hung lft thrght: rdn and hdd over 1f out: wknd ins fnl f* **7/2**[2]
5- **5** *3 ½* **Flushing Meadows (USA)**[366] 4930 3-8-6 (t) KMcEvoy 7 86
(SaeedBinSuroor) *racd centre: hld up: effrt over 2f out: wknd over 1f out* **7/1**
0400 **6** *2* **Boleyn Castle (USA)**[7] 5372 7-8-8 86 (b[1]) TPQueally 9 80
(PSMcentee) *racd alone stands' side: w ldr 4f: sn wknd* **33/1**
-060 **7** *3 ½* **Russian Valour (IRE)**[7] 5372 3-8-13 108 (b) SSanders 6 76
(MJohnston) *racd centre: dwlt: sn prom: wknd over 2f out* **20/1**
64-0 **8** *17* **Forest Rail (IRE)**[7] 5372 4-8-3 LisaJones 3 13
(JohnAHarris) *racd centre: chsd ldr tl wknd 1/2-way* **200/1**

1m 14.47s (0.87) **Going Correction** +0.35s/f (Good)
**WFA** 3 from 4yo+ 2lb **8 Ran SP% 114.9**
Speed ratings: **108,107,105,102,98 95,90,68**CSF £24.58 TOTE £16.60: £2.50, £1.20, £1.90; EX 34.70.

**Owner** Plantation Stud **Bred** Plantation Stud **Trained** East Everleigh, Wilts

**FOCUS**
A good conditions race and the form looks reliable, even though Country Reel failed to run to his Group-race form.

**NOTEBOOK**
**Dowager**, mainly well below form this season, including in blinkers on her previous start, bounced right back with the headgear left off this time. This is likely to have boosted her confidence and she looks worthy of another chance in Listed company.
**Country Reel(USA)** should have won this judged on his fourth in the Golden Jubilee, but he has been below form in recent contests and the drop in grade failed to do the trick.
**Colonel Cotton(IRE)** ◆ ran well considering these small fields do not always play to his strengths and he could be one to keep in mind for something like the Rous Stakes at Newmarket, a Listed race he won last year.
**Whitbarrow(IRE)**, a good fifth in the Portland on his previous start, had quite a bit to find at the weights and proved unable to quicken.
**Flushing Meadows(USA)** ◆, making his debut for Saeed Bin Suroor having been switched from Godolphin's American operation, shaped with more promise than his finishing position might suggest. He simply lacked the pace of some of these and should improve for a step back up in trip and better ground. *Official explanation: jockey said colt was not suited by good ground*
**Boleyn Castle(USA)**, who raced alone against the stands'-side rail, was well beaten but did have it to do at the weight anyway.
**Russian Valour(IRE)** had every chance but dropped right out of contention and is one to avoid now.

## 5554 BENNETTS ELECTRICAL TOSHIBA H'CAP 1m 3f 101y
5:20 (5:21) (E3) (0-70,70) 3-Y-0+ **£6,037** (£1,857; £928; £464) **Stalls** Low

Form RPR
0-02 **1** **Circassian (IRE)**[25] 4915 3-8-10 67 SSanders 5 89+
(SirMarkPrescott) *a.p: chsd ldr over 3f out: rdn to ld over 1f out: styd on wl* **2/1**[1]
-040 **2** *4* **Kind Emperor**[16] 5158 7-8-13 62 AMackay 11 70
(PLGilligan) *led: clr 4f out: rdn and hdd over 1f out: no ex* **33/1**
224 **3** *1 ¼* **Carrowdore (IRE)**[7] 5374 4-9-7 70 (p) IMongan 7 76
(GAHuffer) *hld up: hdwy over 2f out: nt trble ldrs* **6/1**[3]
2302 **4** *2 ½* **Great View (IRE)**[15] 5203 5-9-4 67 (v) LDettori 2 69
(MrsALMKing) *hld up: hdwy over 3f out: rdn over 1f out: no ex fnl f* **13/2**
1013 **5** *1 ¼* **Wellington Hall (GER)**[15] 5203 6-9-4 67 AMcCarthy 15 67
(PWChapple-Hyam) *hld up in tch: rdn over 2f out: styd on same pce* **9/2**[2]
2306 **6** *2 ½* **Blazing The Trail (IRE)**[81] 3274 4-9-1 64 EAhern 3 60
(JWHills) *hld up: hdwy over 3f out: wknd fnl f* **25/1**
-200 **7** *hd* **Perfect Punch**[82] 3232 5-9-3 66 RMullen 10 62
(CFWall) *chsd ldrs 9f* **33/1**
3020 **8** *1 ¾* **Field Spark**[16] 5144 4-8-9 58 (p) FNorton 12 51
(JAGlover) *hld up: sme hdwy over 1f out: n.d* **20/1**
0320 **9** *hd* **Piri Piri (IRE)**[10] 5297 4-9-6 69 SWhitworth 1 62
(PJMcbride) *s.i.s: hld up: sme hdwy over 1f out: n.d* **8/1**
0110 **10** *shd* **Zeis (IRE)**[48] 4240 4-9-4 67 (t) JFEgan 9 59
(AndrewReid) *s.i.s: hld up: sme hdwy over 1f out: n.d* **40/1**
0000 **11** *12* **Mi Odds**[65] 3781 8-8-13 62 JoannaBadger 8 35
(MrsNMacauley) *chsd ldrs over 8f* **66/1**
1050 **12** *nk* **Billy Bathwick (IRE)**[2] 5493 7-8-10 59 CCatlin 6 32
(JMBradley) *chsd ldrs 9f* **33/1**
4010 **13** *1 ¼* **Ellina**[45] 4346 3-8-8 65 JQuinn 13 36
(JPearce) *hld up: n.d* **25/1**
034 **14** *2* **Dream Alive**[16] 5146 3-8-13 70 (t) NCallan 14 38
(MBlanshard) *prom: rdn over 3f out: wknd 2f out* **33/1**
0603 **15** *1* **Pending (IRE)**[20] 5038 3-8-12 69 (p) KMcEvoy 4 35
(JRFanshawe) *hld up: a in rr* **20/1**
0520 **16** *8* **Zawrak (IRE)**[45] 4333 5-8-12 61 RFfrench 16 14
(IWMcinnes) *mid-div: wknd 4f out* **40/1**

2m 29.69s (2.29) **Going Correction** +0.35s/f (Good)
**WFA** 3 from 4yo+ 8lb **16 Ran SP% 125.6**
Speed ratings: **105,102,101,99,98 96,96,95,95,95 86,86,85,83,82 77**CSF £91.13 CT £372.50 TOTE £3.00: £1.20, £10.80, £1.80, £1.60; EX 133.70 Place 6 £16.20, Place 5 £9.55.

**Owner** Lady Katharine Watts **Bred** Barouche Stud Ireland Ltd **Trained** Newmarket, Suffolk

**FOCUS**
A modest handicap run at a decent gallop with Great View trying to steal it from the front. Fair form for the grade.

**NOTEBOOK**
**Circassian(IRE)**, a promising second at Salisbury on his previous start, was able to confirm that to get off the mark with a wide-margin success. He should follow up under a penalty and promises to improve again for staying trips.
**Kind Emperor** nearly stole it under positive ride but was no match for the well-handicapped winner.
**Carrowdore(IRE)** again ran respectably, but has now finished in the first four in his last eight starts without winning.
**Great View(IRE)** did not run a bad race but was not suited by the way the race was run.
**Wellington Hall(GER)** appeared to have conditions to suit, but was not at his best.
**Zeis(IRE)** *Official explanation: jockey said gelding had a breathing problem*
**Billy Bathwick(IRE)** *Official explanation: jockey said gelding got very tired*
**Dream Alive** *Official explanation: jockey said colt got very tired*
T/Jkpt: Not won. T/Plt: £16.10 to a £1 stake. Pool: £50,787.15. 2,299.75 winning tickets. T/Qpdt: £7.00 to a £1 stake. Pool: £2,336.70. 246.10 winning tickets. CR

# 5141 BEVERLEY (R-H)
## Wednesday, September 15

**OFFICIAL GOING: Good to firm (firm in places)**
The jockeys reckoned the ground was 'only just on the fast side of good'..
Wind: Moderate 1/2 against. Weather: Fine and sunny.

## 5555 BRECKS SAAB MAIDEN STKS (DIV I) 5f
1:50 (1:50) (D3) 2-Y-0 **£4,208** (£1,295; £647; £323) **Stalls** High

Form RPR
40 **1** **Space Maker**[90] 3003 2-9-0 RMullen 11 85
(MLWBell) *lw: mde all: rdn clr wl over 1f out: kpt on* **10/3**[2]
5000 **2** *6* **Waggledance (IRE)**[13] 5233 2-8-11 56 (p) TEaves(3) 3 64
(JSWainwright) *prom: rdn along to chse wnr over 1f out: sn drvn and no imp* **20/1**
063 **3** *nk* **Ben Casey**[13] 5241 2-9-0 66 FLynch 1 63
(BSmart) *chsd ldrs: rdn along 2f out: sn drvn and kpt on same pce* **5/1**[3]
6 **4** *6* **Danethorpe Lady (IRE)**[15] 5209 2-8-9 DarrenWilliams 2 37
(DShaw) *swtchd rt s: midfield and rdn along 1/2-way: styd on u.p appr last* **50/1**
05 **5** *nk* **Russian Rio (IRE)**[13] 5233 2-9-0 GFaulkner 10 41
(PCHaslam) *cl up: rdn along 1/2-way: sn wknd* **3/1**[1]
**6** *2 ½* **Boppys Dream** 2-8-9 PHanagan 4 27
(RAFahey) *w'like: bit bkwd: bhd tl sme late hdwy* **7/1**
**7** *shd* **Lugana Point** 2-9-0 FNorton 8 32
(JBalding) *w'like: scope: bit bkwd: bhd tl sme late hdwy* **33/1**
05 **8** *1* **Hamburg Springer (IRE)**[79] 3370 2-9-1 ow4 LFletcher(3) 9 32
(MJPolglase) *dwlt: towards rr: hdwy 1/2-way: sn rdn and wknd* **100/1**
**9** *1 ¾* **Holiday Cocktail** 2-9-0 PMQuinn 5 22
(SCWilliams) *rangy: bit bkwd: v s.i.s: a rr* **20/1**
040 **10** *shd* **Lucy Parkes**[31] 4776 2-8-9 51 MHenry 6 17
(EJAlston) *chsd ldrs on outer: bdly hmpd 1/2-way: bhd after* **10/1**
**11** *1 ½* **Primarily** 2-9-0 RWinston 7 17
(ABerry) *lengthy: unf: dwlt: a rr* **12/1**
**12** *6* **Amazing Grace Mary** 2-8-9 JBramhill 12 —
(SRBowring) *cmpt: chsd ldrs: rdn and hung bdly lft 1/2-way: sn bhd* **16/1**

63.30 secs (-0.70) **Going Correction** -0.175s/f (Firm) **12 Ran SP% 115.3**
Speed ratings: **98,88,87,78,77 73,73,72,69,69 66,57**CSF £73.85 TOTE £3.30: £1.40, £4.80, £2.70; EX 81.70.

**Owner** H E Sheikh Rashid Bin Mohammed **Bred** Fourways Bloodstock **Trained** Newmarket, Suffolk

**FOCUS**
A modest maiden in which very few got involved. A slightly faster time than the second division and the form looks solid enough.


The Form Book, Raceform Ltd, Compton, RG20 6NL

**NOTEBOOK**
**Space Maker** had disappointed last time but had an excuse as he was found to be lame afterwards. A change of tactics from a good draw saw him in a better light, and he made every yard. Although this race did not take a lot of winning, he looks to be going the right way.
**Waggledance(IRE)** seemed to improve for the fitting of cheekpieces, but his performance only underlines the modest overall level of this form.
**Ben Casey** did not fare too badly from the worst draw, but he would be better employed in nursery company.
**Danethorpe Lady(IRE)** probably did not improve on her debut performance.
**Russian Rio(IRE)** had run with promise last time but, although well drawn and backed into favouritism, did not get to the front and was beaten with a fair way to run. On the plus side he is now eligible for a mark.
**Amazing Grace Mary** *Official explanation: jockey said filly hung left throughout*

## 5556 RACING UK ON CHANNEL 432 (S) NURSERY — 7f 100y

**2:20** (2:21) (F4) (0-65,58) 2-Y-O — **£3,146** (£899; £449) **Stalls** High

Form — RPR

0000 **1** **Belton**[8] 5369 2-9-4 **55** ... KMcEvoy 15 — 56
(RonaldThompson) *mid-div: hdwy on outside over 2f out: r.o to ld last 75yds* **20/1**

0500 **2** *nk* **Maureen's Lough (IRE)**[10] 5314 2-8-13 **50** ... RWinston 7 — 50
(JHetherton) *chsd ldrs: led over 1f out: hdd and no ex wl ins last* **7/1**[2]

0003 **3** *hd* **Outrageous Flirt (IRE)**[16] 5192 2-8-8 **45** ... PHanagan 11 — 45
(ADickman) *trckd ldrs: swtchd rt to chal jst ins last: no ex nr fin* **9/1**

0500 **4** *1 ½* **Mr Maxim**[20] 5059 2-9-6 **57** ... DeanMcKeown 10 — 53
(RMWhitaker) *sn chsng ldrs: effrt over 2f out: styd on ins last* **12/1**

0060 **5** *1 ½* **Fransiscan**[19] 5083 2-8-8 **45** ... (p) GFaulkner 5 — 37
(PCHaslam) *mid-div: styd on appr fnl f: nt rch ldrs* **33/1**

0665 **6** *½* **Miss Good Time**[39] 4559 2-8-8 **45** ... (b) JBramhill 16 — 36
(JGGiven) *mid-div: hdwy over 2f out: styd on same pce: nvr rchd ldrs* **8/1**[3]

0400 **7** *½* **Cadogen Square**[2] 5520 2-8-12 **49** ... JFanning 12 — 39
(DWChapman) *led tl over 4f out: edgd lft and kpt on same pce fnl 2f* **12/1**

5000 **8** *¾* **Desert Buzz (IRE)**[19] 5097 2-9-5 **56** ... (p) MTebbutt 4 — 44
(JHetherton) *trckd ldr: led over 4f out tl over 1f out: wknd ins last* **14/1**

0046 **9** *1 ½* **Lanas Turn**[19] 5097 2-9-1 **52** ... (b) GGibbons 14 — 37
(TDEasterby) *unruly s: mid-div: kpt on fnl 2f: nvr nr ldrs* **10/1**

0000 **10** *3 ½* **Admittance (USA)**[19] 5095 2-9-7 **58** ... ACulhane 13 — 35
(MrsJRRamsden) *mid-div: effrt over 2f out: nvr nr ldrs* **9/2**[1]

0000 **11** *5* **Itsa Monkey (IRE)**[4] 5447 2-8-12 **49** ... (b) RMullen 8 — 14
(MJPolglase) *s.i.s: a in rr* **20/1**

6425 **12** *2* **Riverweld**[74] 3506 2-9-6 **57** ... NPollard 3 — 17
(GMMoore) *sltly hmpd s: sn chsng ldrs: wknd over 2f out* **12/1**

0530 **13** *2 ½* **Fold Walk**[19] 5097 2-8-9 **46** ... DaleGibson 6 — —
(MWEasterby) *s.i.s: a bhd* **25/1**

5000 **14** *1 ¾* **Be Bop Aloha**[8] 5369 2-9-6 **57** ... NCallan 2 — 7
(IAWood) *sn chsng ldrs: lost pl over 2f out* **28/1**

6403 **15** *1 ¼* **Justenjoy Yourself**[22] 5022 2-8-9 **46** ... FNorton 1 — —
(CADwyer) *a bhd* **12/1**

406 **16** *28* **Zanderido**[56] 4009 2-8-10 **50** ... PMulrennan(3) 9 — —
(BSRothwell) *bhd: eased fnl f: t.o* **16/1**

1m 34.61s (0.31) **Going Correction** -0.175s/f (Firm) — **16** Ran SP% **124.0**
Speed ratings: **91,90,90,88,87 86,85,85,83,79 73,71,68,66,65 33**CSF £148.06 CT £1434.28 TOTE £26.20: £4.30, £1.50, £2.00, £4.20; EX 261.10.The winner was bought in for 4,000gns. Be Bop Aloha was claimed by John Berry for £6,000.
**Owner** J M Phillips **Bred** R G Percival **Trained** Stainforth, S Yorks

**FOCUS**
A poor-quality, if competitive contest. The form looks reliable enough. Comparing the winning time with the slowly-run fillies' maiden over the same trip is misleading, but a comparison with the later maiden auction event puts this contest more into perspective.

**NOTEBOOK**
**Belton**, well beaten in all five of his previous starts including at this level, had to improve a good deal in order to win even a poor contest like this. Brought with a sustained late challenge down the outside, there seemed no fluke about it and he must have just been slow to come to hand. *Official explanation: trainer said, regarding the improved form shown, colt was entitled to win this modest contest*
**Maureen's Lough(IRE)**, a fair sort at this level, has gone well here in the past and ran another game race having been close to the pace from the off. She seems to stand her racing well and could be the type to do well at a modest level on sand through the winter.
**Outrageous Flirt(IRE)**, stepping up in trip, came through with her effort on the inside of the front pair inside the last furlong, but could not quite go through with it. Stamina was not a problem, but she may appreciate easier ground.
**Mr Maxim** had every chance, but even this stiff track could not offset his lack of pace. He looks a real stayer and needs further.
**Fransiscan**, with cheekpieces replacing a visor, looks another woefully lacking pace, but may be worth keeping in mind for a modest middle-distance handicap on Fibresand during the winter.
**Miss Good Time** did not make any great improvement for the step up in trip.
**Desert Buzz(IRE)** did not get home after being given a positive ride and is still to make the frame after eight attempts.
**Admittance(USA)** was well backed to make the most of the drop in grade, but never got into the race at all.
**Zanderido** *Official explanation: jockey said gelding was never travelling*

## 5557 MAC AND LENI MEMORIAL H'CAP — 1m 100y

**2:50** (2:50) (F4) (0-55,55) 3-Y-O+ — **£3,684** (£1,133; £566; £283) **Stalls** High

Form — RPR

6-03 **1** **Emperor's Well**[22] 5021 5-9-2 **55** ... (b) TLucas 5 — 69
(MWEasterby) *mde all: rdn clr wl over 1f out: styd on* **20/1**

1000 **2** *2* **Time To Regret**[13] 5236 4-8-8 **50** ... TEaves(3) 17 — 60
(JSWainwright) *trckd ldrs on inner: hdwy 2f out: sn rdn: styd on ent last* **22/1**

3000 **3** *nk* **Golden Spectrum (IRE)**[13] 5235 5-8-5 **51** ... PJBenson(7) 15 — 60
(DNicholls) *trckd ldrs: hdwy 3f out: rdn wl over 1f out: kpt on ins last* **20/1**

2602 **4** *¾* **Splodger Mac (IRE)**[11] 5305 5-9-0 **53** ... FNorton 16 — 61
(NBycroft) *chsd wnr: rdn along 2f out: drvn over 1f out: wknd ins last* **9/2**[2]

1211 **5** *1* **Boppys Princess**[26] 4902 3-8-11 **55** ... PHanagan 12 — 60+
(RAFahey) *towards rr: hdwy 3f out: chsd ldrs whn rdn and edgd rt over 1f out: kpt on ins last* **3/1**[1]

5000 **6** *nk* **Champain Sands (IRE)**[10] 5320 5-8-9 **53** ... BSwarbrick(5) 13 — 58
(WMBrisbourne) *trckd ldrs on inner: effrt and nt clr run over 1f out: kpt on* **25/1**

1000 **7** *¾* **Sedge (USA)**[50] 4209 4-9-1 **54** ... RFitzpatrick 9 — 57
(PTMidgley) *hld up towards rr: hdwy 3f out: rdn: edgd rt and n.m.r wl over 1f out: kpt on same pce u.p appr last* **50/1**

0640 **8** *nk* **Basinet**[8] 5374 6-9-0 **53** ... (p) RWinston 3 — 56+
(JJQuinn) *s.i.s and bhd: swtchd rt and hdwy whn nt clr run wl over 1f out: kpt on fnl f* **14/1**

5555 **9** *3* **Apache Point (IRE)**[13] 5235 7-9-0 **53** ... KimTinkler 10 — 49
(NTinkler) *trckd ldrs on outer: pushed along 3f out: sn rdn and wknd 2f out* **8/1**

2100 **10** *1 ½* **Didoe**[6] 5411 5-8-12 **51** ... JoannaBadger 14 — 44
(PWHiatt) *keen: chsd ldng pair: rdn along 3f out: sn wknd* **16/1**

6061 **11** *½* **Mon Secret (IRE)**[13] 5235 6-9-2 **55** ... FLynch 8 — 47
(BSmart) *a rr* **14/1**

5400 **12** *1* **Pas De Surprise**[41] 4479 6-8-11 **50** ... ACulhane 7 — 40
(PDEvans) *midfield: effrt on outer 3f out: sn rdn and wknd* **6/1**[3]

000- **13** *1* **Aqribaa (IRE)**[305] 5135 6-8-10 **52** ... PMulrennan(3) 11 — 40
(AJLockwood) *s.i.s: a rr* **33/1**

3300 **14** *nk* **Weakest Link**[41] 4489 3-8-11 **55** ... NCallan 4 — 42
(EJAlston) *in tch: rdn along over 3f out: sn wknd* **25/1**

1623 **15** *¾* **Senor Eduardo**[14] 5229 7-9-1 **54** ... KMcEvoy 2 — 40
(SGollings) *a rr* **16/1**

1m 45.36s (-1.94) **Going Correction** -0.175s/f (Firm)
**WFA** 3 from 4yo+ 5lb — **15** Ran SP% **120.1**
Speed ratings: **102,100,99,98,97 97,96,96,93,92 91,90,89,89,88**CSF £375.21 CT £8781.97 TOTE £20.90: £5.10, £7.40, £9.00; EX 477.10.
**Owner** M W Easterby **Bred** M W Easterby And K Hodgson **Trained** Sheriff Hutton, N Yorks

**FOCUS**
A big field for this modest handicap, but a fine tactical ride on the winner meant that not many got into it. That said, the form looks sound enough.

**NOTEBOOK**
**Emperor's Well** has improved with each start since returning from his break and won this in good style under a well-judged front-running ride. This was a good effort from his low draw and there are fewer better tactical riders than his veteran jockey.
**Time To Regret**, back on a winning mark, was never far away, but the winner's injection of pace approaching the last furlong left him with ground to make up and there was little he could do about it.
**Golden Spectrum(IRE)**, with the visor left off, ran as though he would have preferred a greater test, but a losing run stretching back well over two years despite a tumbling handicap mark tempers enthusiasm.
**Splodger Mac(IRE)** looks a better horse when able to dominate, but the winner soon put paid to that.
**Boppys Princess**, in such good form of late, could never land a serious blow and the way the race was run was probably as big a handicap to her as the faster ground and 4lb higher mark.
**Champain Sands(IRE)** was not totally disgraced considering he is better over further, but remains a maiden after 20 attempts.
**Basinet** would have found this an insufficient test of stamina given the way the race was run.

## 5558 BRECKS SAAB MAIDEN STKS (DIV II) — 5f

**3:25** (3:26) (F4) 2-Y-O — **£4,208** (£1,295; £647; £323) **Stalls** High

Form — RPR

4342 **1** **Juantorena**[12] 5262 2-9-0 **83** ... RMullen 6 — 75
(MLWBell) *lw: chsd ldr: hung rt over 1f out: chal jst ins last: led post* **10/11**[1]

25 **2** *shd* **One Great Idea (IRE)**[11] 5290 2-9-0 ... PHanagan 7 — 75
(TDBarron) *swtg: led: wnt rt after 100 yds: kpt on wl fnl f: jst ct* **7/2**[2]

**3** *1 ¼* **Golden Asha** 2-8-9 ... FNorton 1 — 65+
(NACallaghan) *rangy: unf: s.s: rn green and bhd: hdwy over 2f out: styd on wl ins last: fin strly* **25/1**

5544 **4** *1 ¼* **Beverley Beau**[8] 5362 2-8-7 **60** ... KristinStubbs(7) 5 — 66
(MrsLStubbs) *swtg: chsd ldrs: kpt on same pce appr fnl f* **22/1**

06 **5** *7* **Ms Three**[23] 4999 2-8-9 ... JoannaBadger 8 — 36
(RFord) *sltly hmpd after 100yds: chsd ldrs: wknd over 1f out* **100/1**

0035 **6** *2* **Molly Dancer**[16] 5174 2-8-9 **67** ... CCatlin 9 — 29
(MRChannon) *chsd ldrs: lost pl over 1f out* **10/1**

0 **7** *shd* **Storm Chase (USA)**[20] 5053 2-9-0 ... KMcEvoy 10 — 34
(APJarvis) *hmpd after 100yds: in tch: effrt over 2f out: sn btn* **11/2**[3]

0 **8** *nk* **Distinctive Mind**[11] 5290 2-9-0 ... GGibbons 11 — 33
(TDEasterby) *hmpd after 100yds: sn chsng ldrs: lost pl 2f out* **22/1**

**9** *1 ½* **Grandma Ryta** 2-8-9 ... TLucas 4 — 23
(JohnBerry) *cmpt: s.i.s: sn chsng ldrs: wknd over 2f out* **50/1**

**10** *nk* **Spring Time Girl** 2-8-6 ... TEaves(3) 12 — 22
(BEllison) *cmpt: s.i.s: sn wl bhd* **33/1**

**11** *3 ½* **Pretty Woman (IRE)** 2-8-9 ... NPollard 2 — 9
(SCWilliams) *bkwd: s.s: sn wl bhd* **33/1**

63.46 secs (-0.54) **Going Correction** -0.175s/f (Firm) — **11** Ran SP% **120.5**
Speed ratings: **97,96,94,92,81 78,78,77,75,74 69**CSF £3.85 TOTE £1.90: £1.10, £1.60, £8.50; EX 5.20.
**Owner** H E Sheikh Rashid Bin Mohammed **Bred** C J Mills **Trained** Newmarket, Suffolk

**FOCUS**
A slightly slower time than the first division, but still par for the class. The race has been rated through the fourth.

**NOTEBOOK**
**Juantorena** broke his duck at the seventh attempt but he never looked that happy and in the end it was a very close-run thing.
**One Great Idea(IRE)**, who sweated up badly at the start, made a bee-line for the far rail causing plenty of havoc in his wake. He stuck on really well and was in the end only just denied.
**Golden Asha ◆**, a backward-looking February foal, is a half-sister to Enchanted. Worst drawn and slowly away, she was clueless when first asked a question but the penny dropped and she put in some sterling late work. She should improve a good deal and looks a much better mid-term prospect than the two ahead of her at the line.
**Beverley Beau**, who is not very big, was on his toes in the paddock and became very warm. He seemed to appreciate the drop back to five but this may be as good as he is and his proximity puts a question mark over the overall value of the form.
**Ms Three** had been well beaten in a seller on the All-Weather on her previous start.
**Storm Chase(USA)**, still carrying plenty of condition, was knocked right back early on and was never travelling thereafter. *Official explanation: jockey said colt was slow away and ran green in early stages*

## 5559 EUROPEAN BREEDERS FUND MAIDEN FILLIES' STKS — 7f 100y

**3:55** (3:55) (D3) 2-Y-O — **£5,804** (£1,786; £893; £446) **Stalls** High

Form — RPR

6 **1** **Verbier (USA)**[12] 5270 2-8-11 ... FNorton 7 — 68
(NACallaghan) *trckd ldr: hdwy to chal 2f out: sn led: rdn over 1f out and styd on wl* **9/2**[3]

6 **2** *1* **Hannah's Dream (IRE)**[8] 5362 2-8-11 ... JFanning 8 — 66
(MJohnston) *led: rdn along over 2f out: hdd wl over 1f out: kpt on u.p ins last* **9/1**

**3** *¾* **Sharaiji Blossom (USA)** 2-8-11 ... KMcEvoy 12 — 64+
(SaeedBinSuroor) *rangy: lengthy: hld up: hdwy 3f out: pushed along and edgd rt 2f out: styd on ins last: nrst fin* **10/3**[2]

0 **4** *nk* **Shamrock Bay**[53] 4137 2-8-11 ... JBramhill 4 — 63
(JGGiven) *chsd ldrs: rdn along wl over 1f out: drvn and one pce ins last* **25/1**

05 **5** ½ **Pearl's A Singer (IRE)**[28] 4851 2-8-11 .................................. RMullen 3 62
(MLWBell) *chsd ldrs on outer: effrt 2f out: sn rdn and kpt on same pce* **9/1**

0 **6** *nk* **Ecologically Right**[19] 5096 2-8-11 ...................................... ACulhane 10 61
(MrsJRRamsden) *trckd ldrs on inner: hdwy over 2f out: shkn up and edgd rt over 1f out: 3rd whn eased ins last* **10/1**

2 **7** *1* **Naivety**[19] 5089 2-8-8 ................................................... J-PGuillambert(3) 2 58
(CEBrittain) *hld up in rr: effrt and hdwy over 2f out: sn rdn and no imp* **15/8**[1]

60 **8** *hd* **Tamora**[45] 4364 2-8-11 ................................................ NCallan 9 58
(APJarvis) *chsd ldng pair: rdn along over 2f out: sn wknd* **16/1**

0 **9** *nk* **Tetra Sing (IRE)**[16] 5186 2-8-11 ....................................... GFaulkner 1 57
(PCHaslam) *a rr* **50/1**

1m 36.19s (1.89) **Going Correction** -0.175s/f (Firm) **9** Ran SP% **116.8**
Speed ratings: **82,80,80,79,79 78,77,77,77**CSF £44.98 TOTE £5.40: £1.60, £2.20, £1.70; EX 59.50.
**Owner** Mrs Doreen Tabor **Bred** Chelston Ireland, Ltd **Trained** Newmarket, Suffolk

**FOCUS**
No gallop until once in line for home resulting in a very slow time indeed for the grade, 3.82 seconds slower than the later maiden auction event, and consequently modest form.

**NOTEBOOK**
**Verbier(USA)** improved for the experience and the step up in trip and at the line was right on top. She should improve again.
**Hannah's Dream(IRE)** had clearly learnt plenty first time. Given her own way in front, she deserves credit for the way she fought back and should improve again.
**Sharaiji Blossom(USA)**, a May foal, is long in the back and stands over plenty of ground. Unusually for one from this stable she did not look in peak condition and was very inexperienced. Putting in her best work at the finish, there should be a fair bit better to come especially next year.
**Shamrock Bay**, a half-sister by Celtic Swing to Dancing Bay, showed a lot more than on her debut and will improve again.
**Pearl's A Singer(IRE)**, drawn on the outer, again showed ability and she is now qualified for nurseries.
**Ecologically Right** tended to hang and didn't look to be really striding out. She was clinging on to third spot when eased in the final stages. She will show her true worth in handicap company at three. *Official explanation: jockey said filly was continually denied a clear run*
**Naivety**, soon in a bad position, looked all at sea on the home turn and this track seemed all against her. This is best forgotten. *Official explanation: jockey said filly was unsuited by track*

## 5560 KATIE AND PAUL WEDDING CELEBRATION H'CAP 1m 4f 16y
**4:30** (4:30) (E3) (0-70,70) 3-Y-O **£5,635** (£1,734; £867; £433) **Stalls** High

Form RPR

2043 **1** **Wing Collar**[13] 5245 3-9-2 **65** .............................................. GGibbons 1 74
(TDEasterby) *chsd ldrs: led over 1f out: kpt on wl* **7/1**

-051 **2** 1¾ **Argentum**[28] 4853 3-8-7 **56** ................................................ ACulhane 5 62
(LadyHerries) *mid-div: drvn along over 4f out: styd on to go 2nd 1f out: no imp* **9/4**[1]

0250 **3** *2* **Golden Drift**[13] 5245 3-8-10 **59** .......................................... RFrench 3 62
(GWragg) *chsd ldrs: drvn along over 4f out: kpt on one pce fnl 2f* **16/1**

2133 **4** ½ **Hearthstead Dream**[15] 5214 3-9-7 **70** ................................. KMcEvoy 12 72
(JDBethell) *hld up towards rr: hdwy on outer over 2f out: kpt on wl: nt rch ldrs* **6/1**[3]

6661 **5** *hd* **Prelude**[16] 5197 3-8-7 **61** ................................................ BSwarbrick(5) 7 63
(WMBrisbourne) *hld up in tch: effrt over 2f out: hung rt over 1f out: one pce* **12/1**

4544 **6** 1¾ **Quickstyx**[6] 5410 3-9-5 **68** ................................................ CCatlin 10 67
(MRChannon) *rr-div: hdwy 3f out: kpt on: nt rch ldrs* **9/1**

0200 **7** *1* **Royal Distant (USA)**[14] 5223 3-9-2 **65** ................................. DaleGibson 6 62
(MWEasterby) *racd in last pl: hdwy on ins over 2f out: nvr nr ldrs* **16/1**

5024 **8** 2½ **Patrixtoo (FR)**[11] 5293 3-8-11 **60** ......................................... NCallan 11 53
(MHTompkins) *t.k.h in front: led tl over 1f out: sn wknd* **11/2**[2]

3206 **9** *7* **Kythia (IRE)**[16] 5203 3-9-7 **70** ............................................. JFanning 4 52
(HMorrison) *chsd ldrs: lost pl over 1f out: eased ins last* **12/1**

-006 **10** *9* **Iron Temptress (IRE)**[8] 5365 3-8-7 **56** ............................(b[1]) NPollard 14 24
(GMMoore) *t.k.h in rr: nvr on terms* **50/1**

0-06 **11** 1¾ **Sweep The Board (IRE)**[37] 4615 3-8-13 **62** ........................ RWinston 9 27
(APJarvis) *chsd ldrs: lost pl over 2f out* **40/1**

5550 **12** *1* **Chara**[34] 4692 3-8-13 **62** .................................................... RMullen 8 25
(JRJenkins) *hld up towards rr: effrt 3f out: sn lost pl* **16/1**

2m 37.97s (-1.33) **Going Correction** -0.175s/f (Firm) **12** Ran SP% **120.4**
Speed ratings: **97,95,94,94,94 92,92,90,85,79 78,78**CSF £23.34 CT £253.49 TOTE £8.20: £2.00, £1.50, £6.20; EX 21.50.
**Owner** Mr and Mrs J D Cotton **Bred** B Freiha **Trained** Great Habton, N Yorks

**FOCUS**
A routine handicap run at a modest pace which did not help a few. The fifth home sets the standard.

**NOTEBOOK**
**Wing Collar**, back over probably his best trip, has run well in all four of his starts on this track in the past and stayed on very well towards the line to record his first victory at the 12th attempt. He has already been schooled over hurdles.
**Argentum**, on faster ground and racing over his longest trip to date, was well backed to follow up his Nottingham victory off a 4lb higher mark, but he came off the bridle a long way out and probably did well to get as close as he did. The modest pace would not have suited him at all and he is worth another chance in a truly-run race.
**Golden Drift**, still a maiden, had every chance but was held towards the end and it will be a moderate race she wins.
**Hearthstead Dream**, stepping back from two miles, stayed on from well off the pace but was never getting there quickly enough. A stronger pace would have suited him, but alternatively he may be worth a try over a trip of around 14 furlongs.
**Prelude**, raised 5lb for her Ripon win, would not have been inconvenienced by this longer trip but may prefer softer ground.
**Quickstyx**, trying her longest trip to date, could never land a blow and may be worth another chance in a more strongly-run race over this trip.
**Patrixtoo(FR)** probably did too much too soon which compromised his chances of seeing out this longer trip on such a stiff track.

## 5561 THANK YOU TO THE STALLS HANDLERS MAIDEN AUCTION STKS 7f 100y
**5:00** (5:02) (E3) 2-Y-O **£3,620** (£1,114; £557; £278) **Stalls** High

Form RPR

222 **1** **King's Account (USA)**[12] 5256 2-8-9 82 .................................. JFanning 10 82+
(MJohnston) *mde all: rdn clr 2f out: styd on wl* **1/1**[1]

00 **2** 2½ **Stancomb Wills (IRE)**[19] 5087 2-8-9 ....................................... NCallan 11 74
(MHTompkins) *chsd wnr fr 1/2-way: rdn and edgd lft wl over 1f ou: sn no imp* **10/1**

**3** 3½ **Zagreus (GER)** 2-8-10 ........................................................ PMulrennan(3) 8 70
(MWEasterby) *rangy: unf: chsd ldrs: hdwy on inner 3f out: rdn 2f out and kpt on same pce* **50/1**

00 **4** *1* **Killena Boy (IRE)**[30] 4809 2-8-9 .......................................... MTebbutt 7 64
(WJarvis) *chsd ldrs: rdn along over 3f out: sn one pce* **33/1**

**5** 1¾ **Paparaazi (IRE)** 2-8-7 ........................................................ PHanagan 9 57
(RAFahey) *rangy: scope: swvd bdly lft s and bhd: hdwy on inner 3f out: rdn and no imp fnl 2f* **16/1**

560 **6** ½ **Satin Rose**[19] 5098 2-8-4 54 ................................................ GGibbons 4 53
(TDEasterby) *a rr* **33/1**

63 **7** *shd* **Red Rudy**[19] 5095 2-8-9 ..................................................... KMcEvoy 3 58
(RMBeckett) *towards rr: effrt over 3f out: sn rdn and no hdwy* **3/1**[2]

53 **8** *6* **Askwith (IRE)**[19] 5098 2-8-9 .............................................. CCatlin 6 44
(JDBethell) *chsd wnr to 1/2-way: sn rdn along and lost pl: bhd fnl 2f* **7/1**[3]

600 **9** *11* **Golden Squaw**[19] 5098 2-8-2 47 .........................................(b[1]) PMQuinn 5 11
(TDEasterby) *a bhd* **66/1**

05 **10** *10* **Yankey**[7] 5398 2-8-4 ......................................................... J-PGuillambert(3) 2 —
(CEBrittain) *midfield: rdn along 1/2-way: sn lost pl and bhd* **66/1**

1m 32.37s (-1.93) **Going Correction** -0.175s/f (Firm) **10** Ran SP% **113.3**
Speed ratings: **104,101,97,96,94 93,93,86,73,62**CSF £11.66 TOTE £1.70: £1.02, £2.10, £30.60; EX 7.90.
**Owner** Brian Yeardley Continental Ltd **Bred** Barnett Enterprises **Trained** Middleham Moor, N Yorks

**FOCUS**
Very few got involved in this and the winner posted a very smart time indeed for the grade, 3.82 seconds than the earlier fillies' maiden. The form is fairly good and the winner can rate higher.

**NOTEBOOK**
**King's Account(USA)** jumped out well from his good draw and never saw another rival. He deserved to get his head in front after a number of good efforts in defeat and hopefully he can now build on this.
**Stancomb Wills(IRE)**, well drawn, appreciated this quicker ground and ran his best race to date. He is now eligible for a mark and should have better opportunites in handicap company.
**Zagreus(GER)**, whose dam is a half-sister to Mutamam, is from a stable whose juveniles usually come on for their first run. He shaped with promise and looks the type who will do better next year when he has strengthened up.
**Killena Boy(IRE)** was stepping up in trip from six furlongs and appeared to get the trip alright, without ever threatening the principals.
**Paparaazi(IRE)**, from a stable in form, lost ground at the start and in the circumstances did not shape too badly in staying on for fifth.
**Red Rudy** was not well drawn but this was still a very disappointing effort. On the plus side, he is now eligible for handicaps.
**Askwith(IRE)** was well positioned for a good final placing but for some reason dropped out very tamely from three furlongs out.

## 5562 SUBSCRIBE TO RACING UK ON 08700 860432 H'CAP 5f
**5:35** (5:35) (E3) (0-70,69) 3-Y-O+ **£4,092** (£1,259; £629; £314) **Stalls** High

Form RPR

1000 **1** **Compton Plume**[18] 5107 4-9-0 **62** ........................................ DaleGibson 3 71
(WHTinning) *mid-divsion: hdwy on outer 2f out: styd on wl to laed last 50yds* **33/1**

2000 **2** ¾ **Torrent**[43] 4422 9-8-7 **55** oh2 ...............................................(b) JFanning 13 61
(DWChapman) *chsd ldrs: nt qckn wl ins last* **25/1**

4100 **3** *nk* **Malahide Express (IRE)**[74] 3524 4-8-9 **57** ............................ NCallan 16 62
(EJAlston) *led tl hdd and no ex wl ins last* **9/1**[3]

0024 **4** ½ **Online Investor**[22] 5016 5-9-0 **62** ....................................... AlexGreaves 17 65
(DNicholls) *dwlt: hdwy over 2f out: edgd rt over 1f out: no ex ins last* **13/2**[2]

4044 **5** ½ **Obe One**[13] 5242 4-9-5 **67** .................................................. FLynch 2 68+
(ABerry) *sn bhd: hdwy on outer over 1f out: styd on wl towards fin* **14/1**

6010 **6** *hd* **Bettys Pride**[46] 4331 5-8-4 **55** oh3 ...................................... PMulrennan(3) 15 55
(MDods) *rrd s: bhd tl hdwy 2f out: styd on strly ins last* **14/1**

4006 **7** *nk* **Twice Upon A Time**[20] 5062 5-8-13 **61** ................................. FNorton 12 60
(BSmart) *chsd ldrs: keeping on same pce whn n.m.r ins last* **12/1**

4006 **8** *nk* **Tally (IRE)**[26] 4926 4-9-3 **65** ............................................. GGibbons 7 63
(MJPolglase) *bhd: hdwy on outer over 1f out: kpt on wl: nt rch ldrs* **25/1**

3030 **9** ½ **Soaked**[18] 5107 11-8-11 **59** ..................................................(b) ACulhane 18 55
(DWChapman) *mid-div: kpt on fnl 2f: nt rch ldrs* **13/2**[2]

5503 **10** ½ **Brigadier Monty (IRE)**[18] 5107 6-8-7 **55** oh2 ........................ CCatlin 20 49
(MrsSLamyman) *in tch: n.m.r on inner over 1f out: kpt on: nvr rchd ldrs* **4/1**[1]

0400 **11** *1* **Tuscan Flyer**[17] 5157 6-8-10 **58** ..........................................(b) RFrench 9 48
(RBastiman) *mid-div: kpt on appr fnl f: nvr nr ldrs* **20/1**

202U **12** *nk* **Harrison's Flyer (IRE)**[9] 5342 3-9-0 **66** ................................ TEaves(3) 10 54
(RAFahey) *swvd lft s: bhd: sme hdwy on wd outside 2f out: nvr a factor* **20/1**

1003 **13** *shd* **Midnight Parkes**[5] 5440 5-9-7 **69** ....................................... MHenry 8 57+
(EJAlston) *stembled s: bhd: nt clr run over 1f out: nvr on terms* **11/1**

000 **14** 3½ **Tommy Smith**[18] 5107 6-9-6 **68** ...........................................(b) RWinston 14 42+
(JSWainwright) *chsd ldrs: hung both ways: n.m.r and wknd 1f out* **9/1**[3]

6505 **15** *hd* **Abelard (IRE)**[38] 4576 3-8-11 **60** ........................................ PHanagan 4 33
(RAFahey) *a in rr* **25/1**

6020 **16** ½ **He's A Rocket (IRE)**[29] 4828 3-8-6 **55** .............................(b) DarrenWilliams 19 26
(KRBurke) *chsd ldrs: lost pl over 1f out* **9/1**[3]

0060 **17** *1* **Count Cougar (USA)**[43] 4422 4-8-7 **55** oh2 ........................... JMcAuley 11 22
(SPGriffiths) *chsd ldrs: lost pl 2f out: eased* **100/1**

63.06 secs (-0.94) **Going Correction** -0.175s/f (Firm)
**WFA** 3 from 4yo+ 1lb **17** Ran SP% **131.0**
Speed ratings: **100,98,98,97,96 96,95,95,94,93 92,91,91,86,85 84,83**CSF £706.24 CT £8051.67 TOTE £53.20: £8.90, £6.40, £2.50, £2.40; EX 1605.70 Place 6 £586.95, Place 5 £287.30 .
**Owner** W H Tinning **Bred** Mrs D A La Trobe **Trained** Thornton-le-Clay, N Yorks

**FOCUS**
A modest sprint handicap and very ordinary form, but a good performance by the winner to overcome his poor draw - only two of the previous 23 races of 16 runners or more over this trip had been won by a horse drawn in single figures.

**NOTEBOOK**
**Compton Plume** was not as well drawn as he was here last time, but the ground was more in his favour on this occasion. Nevertheless, this was still a cracking effort from stall three, and he came from off the pace to lead close home.
**Torrent** is a difficult horse to predict but this proved to be one of his going days and he ran right up to his recent best.
**Malahide Express(IRE)**, returning from a mid-season break and well drawn, raced keenly in front in the early stages but he held onto his lead well until collared late on. He is a very consistent performer.
**Online Investor**, well drawn, is running well now that he has dropped to a fair mark, but he remains difficult to win with.
**Obe One** does not have a good strike-rate but he is largely consistent. He was staying on really well at the finish and this was a top effort from his coffin-box draw.
**Bettys Pride** lost her race at the start and in the circumstances did not fare too badly.
**Brigadier Monty(IRE)** is a difficult horse to win with and, although in theory he was well drawn, his style of running requires plenty of luck in running, and he did not get it.

**Tommy Smith** *Official explanation: jockey said gelding hung both ways*
T/Plt: £1,020.10 to a £1 stake. Pool: £31,164.90. 22.30 winning tickets. T/Qpdt: £134.20 to a £1 stake. Pool: £2,277.50. 12.55 winning tickets. JR

## 5441 SANDOWN (R-H)
### Wednesday, September 15

**OFFICIAL GOING: Good**
Wind: nil Weather: fine and sunny

### 5563 QUEEN ELIZABETH'S FOUNDATION CHARITY DAY H'CAP — 5f 6y
**2:30** (2:31) (D2) (0-85,83) 3-Y-O — **£8,303** (£2,554; £1,277; £638) **Stalls** High

Form — RPR
0045 **1** **Bo McGinty (IRE)**[11] 5287 3-9-7 **83** .......... GParkin 11 — 90
(RAFahey) *lw: chsd ldng pair: rdn 2f out: styd on u.p to ld last 75yds* **6/1**[2]
113 **2** *shd* **Out After Dark**[12] 5263 3-9-5 **81** .......... RSmith 3 — 88
(CGCox) *racd midfield: rdn 2f out: styd on wl fnl f: nt quite rch wnr* **5/1**[1]
4010 **3** *nk* **Mirasol Princess**[18] 5117 3-8-11 **73** .......... DaneO'Neill 12 — 79
(DKIvory) *hld up wl in rr: taken to outer 3f out: prog over 1f out: styd on wl fnl f: jst unable to chal* **16/1**
0523 **4** *½* **Skyharbor**[25] 4952 3-9-0 **76** .......... (v[1]) MartinDwyer 6 — 80
(AMBalding) *disp ld: rdn 2f out: def advantage ins fnl f: hdd last 75yds* **10/1**[3]
0440 **5** *nk* **Celtic Thunder**[11] 5299 3-9-6 **82** .......... RHavlin 13 — 85
(TJEtherington) *lw: chsd ldng pair: rdn 2f out: styd on fnl f: nvr able to chal* **16/1**
1000 **6** *nk* **Beejay**[33] 4717 3-8-6 **73** .......... NDeSouza(5) 9 — 75
(PFICole) *chsd ldrs: rdn 2f out: prog jst over 1f out: kpt on but nvr rchd ldrs* **25/1**
-001 **7** *hd* **Red Sovereign**[70] 3628 3-8-13 **75** .......... SSanders 4 — 76
(IAWood) *b.hind: racd on outer in midfield: effrt over 1f out: kpt on same pce* **14/1**
5603 **8** *hd* **Handsome Cross (IRE)**[47] 4289 3-9-4 **80** .......... JFortune 15 — 80
(HMorrison) *lw: disp ld tl fnl f: fdd nr fin* **5/1**[1]
0004 **9** *hd* **Four Amigos (USA)**[18] 5117 3-9-0 **76** .......... TQuinn 1 — 76+
(JGGiven) *hld up wl in rr fr outside draw: effrt whn hmpd jst over 1f out: styd on ins fnl f: nrst fin* **14/1**
0000 **10** *½* **Silver Prelude**[5] 5440 3-9-6 **82** .......... SDrowne 10 — 80
(DKIvory) *racd on inner in midfield: lost pl and rdn 2f out: kpt on again last 100yds* **20/1**
5034 **11** *nk* **Marysienka**[9] 5342 3-8-7 **69** oh1 .......... (p) JEdmunds 5 — 66
(JBalding) *b: racd midfield: effrt 2f out: chsng ldrs 1f out: no ex* **33/1**
21 **12** *½* **Kool Acclaim**[35] 4653 3-9-0 **76** .......... OUrbina 7 — 71
(SCWilliams) *dwlt: sn in tch towards rr: rdn 2f out: no imp on ldrs* **10/1**[3]
1415 **13** *hd* **Ivory Lace**[34] 4688 3-9-1 **77** .......... DSweeney 8 — 71
(SWoodman) *hld up wl in rr: prog on inner over 1f out: styng on whn nt clr run ins fnl f: lost several pls nr fin* **25/1**
2004 **14** *2 ½* **Snow Wolf**[30] 4810 3-9-3 **79** .......... MFenton 2 — 64
(JMBradley) *racd on outer: chsd ldrs: lost pl and hanging rt over 1f out: no ch after* **25/1**
4203 **15** *5* **Tregarron**[16] 5193 3-8-11 **73** .......... RLMoore 14 — 40
(RHannon) *moved scratchily to post: nvr gng wl: last and bhd fr 1/2-way* **6/1**[2]

61.75 secs (-0.44) **Going Correction** +0.025s/f (Good) — **15** Ran **SP% 124.4**
Speed ratings: **104,103,103,102,102 101,101,100,100,99 99,98,98,94,86**CSF £34.35 CT £482.57 TOTE £7.40: £2.50, £2.40, £7.80; EX 29.90.
**Owner** Paddy McGinty & Bo Turnbull **Bred** Stephen Breen **Trained** Musley Bank, N Yorks

**FOCUS**
A competitive three-year-old handicap, with an exciting finish. The field were well bunched at the line, however, and the form cannot rate that highly. The time was almost the same as that for the subsequent claimer.

**NOTEBOOK**
**Bo McGinty(IRE)** was settled just off the front pace before asserting in the last furlong. He had just enough left in the tank to hold off a lot of late challenges, however the jockey reported he was idling in front. He does act really well at these stiff courses and should be capable of progressing a bit more.
**Out After Dark**, who did not have the best of draws, sat in midfield until picking up well in the last furlong. He appears to like a stiff course, given limited evidence, and can progress again.
**Mirasol Princess** was unable to utilise her favourable draw as she missed the break, which has now happened in her last three races. The jockey quickly switched to the middle of the track, for a clear run, and she flew home. She is fairly handicapped at the moment, but will always find it hard to win if she continues to miss the break.
**Skyharbor**, in a first-time visor, raced off to share the clear lead until fading inside the final furlong. He has been in consistent form since his move from Dandy Nicholls, but as a result is steadily climbing the handicap again.
**Celtic Thunder**, dropping back in trip, was being niggled slightly from two furlongs out but stayed on respectably up the hill. He still has the slight look of being a bit high in the handicap at the moment, even though he has run some decent races from around this mark.
**Beejay** ran a fair race, finishing on the heels of the leaders. She was under pressure a little way out, and was switched a few times, but stayed on nicely to finish close up. She looks to be returning to some kind of form after a few disappointments this season.
**Red Sovereign**, returning from a ten-week break, ran a sound race. She travelled nicely in midfield until the distance, where she was not overly persevered with up the hill. If she progresses after her break, she should be capable of regaining the winning thread soon.
**Handsome Cross(IRE)**, who was well backed from a good draw, helped to cut out a decent early pace and did not quite get home.
**Four Amigos(USA)** was settled in midfield, and was slightly hampered when making his challenge about two furlongs out. He finished really well and looks in good heart.
**Kool Acclaim**, having only her third run, ran with some credit. She never looked likely to get involved in the finish but was not knocked about when her chance was gone. She could be worth another chance.
**Ivory Lace** came with a sweeping run up the rail only to find all kinds of trouble. She looked particularly unlucky on the day. *Official explanation: jockey said filly was unlucky in running*
**Tregarron** was detached pretty early in the race, and was never a factor.

### 5564 QUEEN ELIZABETH'S FOUNDATION "PREMIER" CLAIMING STKS — 5f 6y
**3:05** (3:05) (D3) 3-Y-0+ — **£5,590** (£1,720; £860; £430) **Stalls** High

Form — RPR
606 **1** **Ok Pal**[28] 4855 4-9-7 72 .......... JFortune 11 — 87
(TGMills) *lw: mde virtually all: rdn and styd on wl fnl f* **13/2**[3]
-206 **2** *1 ¾* **First Order**[30] 4805 3-9-6 100 .......... SSanders 5 — 81
(SirMarkPrescott) *sn trckd ldrs: effrt to chse wnr over 1f out: rdn and no imp fnl f* **11/8**[1]
5150 **3** *¾* **Further Outlook (USA)**[16] 5181 10-9-2 87 .......... DaneO'Neill 1 — 73
(DKIvory) *b: b.hind: dwlt: hld up in rr: prog 2f out: hanging rt but styd on fnl f* **5/1**[2]
0400 **4** *½* **Man Crazy (IRE)**[36] 4617 3-8-0 50 .......... (b) JMackay 12 — 56
(RMBeckett) *chsd ldrs: rdn 2f out: kpt on same pce* **25/1**
5060 **5** *1 ½* **Borzoi Maestro**[16] 5184 3-8-5 69 .......... (p) RMiles(3) 2 — 59
(JLSpearing) *t.k.h: sn trckd ldrs: rdn over 1f out: nt qckn* **25/1**
0036 **6** *½* **Tender (IRE)**[24] 4970 4-8-6 48 .......... (p) SDrowne 7 — 54
(MrsStefLiddiard) *nvr beyond midfield: no prog over 1f out: one pce* **20/1**
0040 **7** *½* **Hello Roberto**[4] 5458 3-8-7 71 .......... MartinDwyer 9 — 54
(MJPolglase) *dwlt: towards rr: rdn over 2f out: no imp on ldrs after* **10/1**
0005 **8** *hd* **Our Gamble (IRE)**[42] 4437 3-8-3 65 ow1 .......... RLMoore 10 — 49
(RHannon) *lw: nvr beyond midfield: rdn and no prog 2f out* **16/1**
5000 **9** *1 ½* **Black Oval**[39] 4548 3-8-3 45 ow2 .......... PDoe 4 — 44
(SDow) *lw: wl in rr: effrt on outer 1/2-way: sn no prog* **100/1**
0040 **10** *½* **Willhewiz**[11] 5299 4-9-4 73 .......... (v) LPKeniry(3) 8 — 59
(RMStronge) *w wnr to 2f out: wknd* **13/2**[3]
0000 **11** *2 ½* **Alizar (IRE)**[14] 5219 3-8-0 53 .......... RSmith 3 — 30
(SDow) *b.hind: a in rr: rdn and struggling 1/2-way* **66/1**
0 **12** *8* **Master Rat**[16] 5204 3-9-1 .......... RHavlin 6 — 16
(RJHodges) *chsd ldrs to halfway: wknd rapidly* **100/1**

61.77 secs (-0.42) **Going Correction** +0.025s/f (Good)
**WFA** 3 from 4yo+ 1lb — **12** Ran **SP% 116.3**
Speed ratings: **104,101,100,99,96 96,95,94,92,91 87,74** CT £7.00 TOTE £1.90: £1.30, £1.60, £; EX17.10 1.The winner was subject to a friendly claim. Alizar was claimed by R. Guest for £5,000. First Order was claimed by A. Re
**Owner** Sherwoods Transport Ltd **Bred** Sherwoods Transport Ltd **Trained** Headley, Surrey

**FOCUS**
A decent enough claimer on paper, won by a once well-regarded sprinter, but the principals were below their best and the form is clearly held down by the fourth and sixth.

**NOTEBOOK**
**Ok Pal**, who was rated 28lb behind the favourite, pinged out from his decent draw and made all up the rail. He has had his problems since his promising juvenile days, but he is fairly treated now if the Handicapper does not over-react to this.
**First Order** has to be considered disappointing given his rating. He has not been running to his best recently, and is not one to trust implicitly after this result. Andrew Reid claimed him from the race, and it will be interesting to see what plans he has for this once decent animal.
**Further Outlook(USA)** did not have a great draw, and missed the break. He travelled well up the middle of the course until coming under pressure over a furlong out, and then started to hang to the right. Ideally he likes more cut in the ground.
**Man Crazy(IRE)** was never travelling that enthusiastically but stayed on well up the hill. Her proximity to the favourite casts doubts on the form.
**Borzoi Maestro** pulled hard up the centre of the track, and had little left at the business end of the race.
**Willhewiz** helped cut out a decent pace from a good draw, but weakened badly in the last two furlongs.
**Master Rat** *Official explanation: jockey said gelding hung both ways*

### 5565 HALEWOOD INTERNATIONAL FUTURES NOVICE STKS — 7f 16y
**3:35** (3:37) (D2) 2-Y-O — **£10,192** (£3,136; £1,568; £784) **Stalls** High

Form — RPR
31 **1** **Linngari (IRE)**[20] 5051 2-9-4 93 .......... RLMoore 2 — 92+
(SirMichaelStoute) *lw: trckd ldr: led over 2f out: pushed clr over 1f out: easily* **8/15**[1]
551 **2** *3 ½* **Easy Mover (IRE)**[11] 5307 2-8-11 76 .......... SSanders 3 — 76
(RGuest) *trckd ldng pair: rdn to chse wnr over 1f out: no imp* **6/1**[3]
213 **3** *2 ½* **Minnesota (USA)**[35] 4639 2-9-4 85 .......... DaneO'Neill 5 — 77
(HCandy) *lw: led to over 2f out: grad wknd* **4/1**[2]
0215 **4** *hd* **Kalmini (USA)**[16] 5188 2-8-13 76 .......... SHitchcott 4 — 72
(MRChannon) *lw: chsd ldng pair: rdn wl over 2f out: sn struggling* **12/1**

1m 31.64s (0.55) **Going Correction** -0.10s/f (Good) — **4** Ran **SP% 107.2**
Speed ratings: **92,88,85,84**CSF £4.06 TOTE £1.50; EX 3.20.
**Owner** H H Aga Khan **Bred** His Highness The Aga Khan's Studs S C **Trained** Newmarket, Suffolk

**FOCUS**
A decent novice event and a decisive winner, but a modest winning time for the class.

**NOTEBOOK**
**Linngari(IRE)** ran out an extremely impressive winner, from three previous winners. The form of his Lingfield victory had already been franked and he looks to be going the right way. Connections are sure to place him to good advantage and he should stay middle distances as a three-year-old.
**Easy Mover(IRE)** won a maiden last time from a subsequent decent nursery winner, but was no match for the favourite. She did finish nicely clear of the other two runners and is entitled to improve again.
**Minnesota(USA)** helped to make the running, but had nothing to offer when the first two swept past. He could be difficult to place now, after running with credit in two decent novice events, but has the look of making a decent staying three-year-old given his pedigree.
**Kalmini(USA)** missed the break badly after her jockey was still removing her hood as the stalls opened. From there on in she was always fighting a losing battle and ran as well as could have been reasonably expected.

### 5566 MAN GROUP FILLIES' H'CAP — 1m 14y
**4:10** (4:13) (D2) (0-85,83) 3-Y-O — **£8,334** (£2,564; £1,282; £641) **Stalls** High

Form — RPR
0-1 **1** **Porthcawl**[25] 4954 3-9-2 **75** .......... SSanders 3 — 84
(MrsAJPerrett) *trckd ldrs: effrt 2f out: rdn to ld over 1f out: styd on wl* **8/1**
0004 **2** *1 ¼* **Zerlina (USA)**[14] 5220 3-9-2 **75** .......... PDoe 7 — 81
(WJMusson) *n.m.r s: hld up last: rapid prog on outer over 2f out: chal and upsides jst over 1f out: one pce fnl f* **16/1**
2312 **3** *shd* **Nouveau Riche (IRE)**[34] 4684 3-9-4 **77** .......... SDrowne 1 — 83
(HMorrison) *prom: led 2f out to over 1f out: kpt on same pce* **12/1**
0340 **4** *¾* **Enford Princess**[13] 5249 3-9-9 **82** .......... RLMoore 4 — 86
(RHannon) *lw: hld up in rr: nt clr run 2f out and swtchd to outer: styd on fnl f: nt rch ldrs* **10/1**
3011 **5** *hd* **Flying Adored**[17] 5150 3-9-7 **80** .......... TQuinn 5 — 84
(JLDunlop) *hld up in rr: prog on outer over 2f out: cl up 1f out: one pce after* **6/1**[2]
1-00 **6** *1 ¼* **Taminoula (IRE)**[17] 5150 3-9-4 **77** .......... DaneO'Neill 6 — 78+
(MrsAJPerrett) *lw: hld up in rr: effrt on inner and nt clr run 2f out: swtchd lft and styd on fnl f* **20/1**
1125 **7** *nk* **Our Jaffa (IRE)**[14] 5220 3-9-10 **83** .......... MFenton 14 — 83
(DJDaly) *b.hind: sn chsd ldrs: rdn on inner whn n.m.r over 1f out: no ch after* **11/1**
5056 **8** *nk* **Mrs Pankhurst**[81] 3320 3-8-12 **71** .......... RHills 12 — 70+
(BWHills) *t.k.h: hld up midfield: rdn whn bdly hmpd and nrly fell over 1f out: nt rcvr* **33/1**
1323 **9** *1 ¼* **Desert Cristal (IRE)**[12] 5275 3-9-5 **78** .......... Wenkaya 10 — 75+
(JRBoyle) *lw: t.k.h: trckd ldrs: rdn whn hmpd and nrly uns rdr over 1f out: unbalanced and wknd fnl f* **12/1**
6130 **10** *2* **Citrine Spirit (IRE)**[105] 2587 3-9-1 **74** .......... JFortune 9 — 66
(JHMGosden) *t.k.h: sn hld up in rr: shkn up and no prog 2f out* **11/1**

3131 **11** *3½* **Kryssa**[38] 4580 3-9-2 **75** ........ IMongan 11 59+
(GLMoore) *hld up midfield: rdn and effrt whn hmpd over 1f out: nt rcvr* **7/1**

1112 **12** *¾* **Pickle**[48] 4266 3-9-7 **80** ........ MartinDwyer 13 62+
(SCWilliams) *led after 2f to 2f out: wkng whn hmpd over 1f out* **11/2**[1]

5212 **13** *13* **Sea Nymph (IRE)**[18] 5136 3-9-5 **78** ........ JMackay 2 30
(SirMichaelStoute) *led for 2f: styd prom: wknd 2f out: lost action over 1f out: t.o* **13/2**[3]

1m 42.04s (-1.88) **Going Correction** -0.10s/f (Good) **13** Ran SP% **121.3**
Speed ratings: **105,103,103,102,102 101,101,100,99,97 94,93,80**CSF £131.50 CT £1586.50 TOTE £8.50: £2.60, £5.30, £3.40; EX 201.30.
**Owner** Usk Valley Stud **Bred** K J Mercer **Trained** Pulborough, W Sussex
■ Stewards Enquiry : P Doe two-day ban: careless riding (Sep 26,27)

**FOCUS**
An ordinary fillies' handicap, but one that featured several improving types. Several runners lost their chance in the scrimmaging approaching the furlong marker, which gives the form a messy appearance.

**NOTEBOOK**
**Porthcawl**, off the mark on her seasonal debut in a modest course maiden, is clearly a progressive filly and was able to defy her mark of 75. Undoubtedly helped by some trouble in behind, she stuck her neck out when pressed and was always holding the second. She seems effective on most ground types and with further improvement anticipated could score again.
**Zerlina(USA)** ran much her best race of the season over seven furlongs back on the polytrack earlier in the month and was able to build on that back on the turf. Having been a long way behind turning in, she made relentless headway around the outer of the field to throw down a challenge to Porthcawl but her effort in reaching a challenging position told in the final half furlong. She saw the trip out better than she had done earlier in the season and looks an obvious future winner.
**Nouveau Riche(IRE)** continues to go the right way and has yet to run a bad race in five attempts. She shapes as though a slightly stiffer test would help.
**Enford Princess** has been struggling in handicaps but would have been closer here with an uninterrupted run.
**Flying Adored**, on a hat-trick following two cosy wins, was 6lb higher than when winning her most recent race and that seemed to anchor her in this more competitive race.
**Taminoula(IRE)** ◆, 9lb better off with Flying Adored on their Goodwood running, was much better suited by this sounder surface and may have reversed the form with a clear run. She is on a winning mark and is one to look out for in the coming weeks.
**Our Jaffa(IRE)** was done no favours by the bumping that went on but would not have been winning anyhow.
**Mrs Pankhurst** ◆, whose stable have come back to form in recents weeks, travelled well before hitting a flat spot, but was running on nicely when badly squeezed for room and having to be snatched up. She seems on a reasonable mark and is another worth watching out for.
**Desert Cristal(IRE)** had just come under pressure when badly hampered and losing all chance. This run should be ignored.
**Citrine Spirit(IRE)** looked as though she would improve on this effort after her break.
**Kryssa** lost her chance when hampered. *Official explanation: jockey said filly lost her momentum, having suffered interference*
**Pickle** had run her race when getting hampered.
**Sea Nymph(IRE)** lost her action and deserves another chance. *Official explanation: jockey said filly lost her action*

## 5567 QUEEN ELIZABETH'S FOUNDATION E B F MAIDEN STKS 1m 14y
**4:40** (4:45) (D2) 2-Y-O **£6,873** (£2,115; £1,057; £528) **Stalls** High

Form RPR

4 **1** **Mutajammel (FR)**[19] 5091 2-9-0 ........ RHills 4 86
(SirMichaelStoute) *lw: trckd ldng trio: effrt on outer over 2f out: rdn to ld over 1f out: edgd lft but styd on gamely* **13/8**[1]

434 **2** *¾* **Golden Fury**[13] 5246 2-9-0 87 ........ SSanders 1 84
(JLDunlop) *hld up in 5th pl: prog on outer to chal over 1f out: carried lft ins fnl f: a jst hld* **11/4**[3]

4 **3** *2* **Luis Melendez (USA)**[12] 5268 2-9-0 ........ RLMoore 7 80
(PFICole) *lw: trckd ldng pair: shkn up over 2f out: rn green after: kpt on same pce* **2/1**[2]

0 **4** *1¼* **Fantorini (USA)**[46] 4315 2-9-0 ........ JFortune 6 77
(JHMGosden) *led: rdn over 2f out: hdd over 1f out: fdd ins fnl f* **20/1**

**5** *1¾* **Cave Of The Giant (IRE)** 2-9-0 ........ TQuinn 8 73
(TDMccarthy) *leggy: s.s: last tl sme prog 2f out: no imp on ldrs tl r.o strly last 100yds: bttr for experience* **33/1**

000 **6** *5* **Snow Tempest (USA)**[60] 3931 2-8-11 ........ RMiles(3) 3 62
(TGMills) *a in last trio: rdn and struggling over 2f out* **50/1**

0 **7** *nk* **Ustad (IRE)**[19] 5087 2-9-0 ........ PDoe 2 61
(JLDunlop) *scope: settled in last trio: shkn up and btn over 2f out* **16/1**

000 **8** *6* **Wiltshire (IRE)**[11] 5302 2-8-7 ........ LHarman(7) 5 48
(MRChannon) *pressed ldr: rdn and stl upsides jst over 2f out: wknd rapidly* **100/1**

1m 43.14s (-0.78) **Going Correction** -0.10s/f (Good) **8** Ran SP% **114.6**
Speed ratings: **99,98,96,95,93 88,87,81**CSF £6.30 TOTE £2.50: £1.10, £1.40, £1.10; EX 5.30.
**Owner** Hamdan Al Maktoum **Bred** 6 C Stallions Limited **Trained** Newmarket, Suffolk

**FOCUS**
Not the greatest maiden the course has ever hosted, but the form looks fairly sound.

**NOTEBOOK**
**Mutajammel(FR)**, a promising fourth on his debut in a race that is working out well, was never far off the pace and although it took him plenty of time to get on top, he showed a good attitude and ultimately won with a little in hand. The runner-up's rating of 87 flatters him so it would be unwise to get carried away but he is a nice colt who will stay further and very much looks the type to improve again. Something like the Zetland Stakes at Newmarket later in the season may prove the ideal target.
**Golden Fury** is a bit exposed now after four starts and while he is up to winning a maiden, his mark of 87 will not make life easy for him in handicaps as he has not really done enough to earn it.
**Luis Melendez(USA)** shaped with promise on his debut at Kempton and still showed signs of inexperience. He is going the right way but strikes as the type to find one too good again next time.
**Fantorini(USA)** left a dismal display on his debut behind in fourth. He did not go down without a fight, but once headed appeared to get a little tired and can be expected to improve again next time.
**Cave Of The Giant(IRE)**, whose stable are hardly renowned for their juveniles, fluffed the start and showed signs of inexperience until the penny dropped late on and he finished the race well. Sure to come on for the experience, he may be able to sneak an ordinary maiden somewhere.
**Ustad(IRE)** is likely to do better in handicaps next season.
**Wiltshire(IRE)** had run well to a point and clearly has ability, but it was a little worrying how sharply he stopped. Having said that though, his dam was more of a sprinter and a drop back in trip may be required.

## 5568 QUEEN ELIZABETH'S FOUNDATION H'CAP 1m 2f 7y
**5:15** (5:16) (D2) (0-85,83) 3-Y-0+ **£8,533** (£2,625; £1,312; £656) **Stalls** High

Form RPR

**1** **Diego Cao (IRE)**[109] 3-8-9 **78** ........ RLMoore 8 87
(GLMoore) *b.hind: trckd ldrs: rdn to cl 2f out: drvn ahd last 100yds: styd on wl* **50/1**

4604 **2** *½* **Go Tech**[46] 4319 4-8-12 **74** ........ TQuinn 9 82
(TDEasterby) *hld up in rr: prog on outer 2f out: rdn to chal ent fnl f: styd on but a hld* **12/1**

3233 **3** *¾* **Dream Magic**[16] 5183 6-9-1 **77** ........ MartinDwyer 4 84
(MJRyan) *mde most: kpt on wl whn hrd pressed 2f out: hdd and one pce last 100yds* **7/1**[3]

0145 **4** *1¾* **Freeloader (IRE)**[18] 5135 4-9-2 **78** ........ RHills 11 82
(JWHills) *hld up wl in rr: prog on outer 2f out: rdn jst over 1f out: kpt on same pce ins fnl f* **7/1**[3]

3232 **5** *nk* **Arry Dash**[6] 5423 4-8-13 **75** ........ SHitchcott 12 78
(MRChannon) *settled midfield: rdn over 2f out: prog over 1f out: kpt on: nvr able to chal* **11/2**[2]

0041 **6** *1¼* **Another Choice (IRE)**[17] 5158 3-8-9 **78** ........ (t) DaneO'Neill 3 79
(NPLittmoden) *settled towards rr: prog 2f out: one pce fnl f* **16/1**

0433 **7** *nk* **Impersonator**[18] 5135 4-9-0 **76** ........ PDoe 10 76
(JLDunlop) *sn trckd ldng pair: chal over 2f out: upsides tl wknd jst over 1f out* **10/1**

1113 **8** *½* **Unsuited**[61] 3909 5-8-0 **69** oh1 ........ NataliaGemelova(7) 5 68
(JELong) *settled in rr: rdn and no prog over 2f out: styd on fnl f: nrst fin* **14/1**

2343 **9** *¾* **Recount (FR)**[17] 5158 4-8-13 **75** ........ IMongan 13 73
(JRBest) *chsd clr ldrs: rdn over 2f out: in tch but btn whn hmpd over 1f out: fdd* **25/1**

4136 **10** *¾* **Jacaranda (IRE)**[31] 4772 4-8-9 **71** ........ SDrowne 1 67
(MrsALMKing) *lw: settled wl in rr: rdn over 2f out: one pce and no prog* **20/1**

2240 **11** *1* **Hatch A Plan (IRE)**[26] 4915 3-8-3 **72** ........ JMackay 15 66
(RMBeckett) *racd midfield: effrt on inner over 2f out: sn no prog and btn* **25/1**

1410 **12** *nk* **Hasaiyda (IRE)**[7] 5402 3-8-11 **80** ........ JFortune 14 74
(SirMichaelStoute) *dwlt: hld up towards rr: rdn and effrt wl over 2f out: no prog wl over 1f out* **3/1**[1]

2005 **13** *¾* **Competitor**[17] 5153 3-8-0 **69** oh4 ........ DKinsella 7 61
(JAkehurst) *chsd ldrs: rdn over 4f out: wknd over 2f out* **33/1**

1004 **14** *1½* **War Owl (USA)**[35] 4634 7-8-11 **73** ........ SSanders 16 63
(IanWilliams) *dwlt: a wl in rr: rdn and struggling over 2f out* **12/1**

4104 **15** *9* **Supreme Salutation**[18] 5135 8-9-0 **83** ........ MHoward(7) 6 56
(DKIvory) *pressed ldr: sddle slipped after 2f: lost pl qckly fr 3f out* **14/1**

321- **16** *1½* **Lord Eurolink (IRE)**[363] 5012 10-8-7 **72** ........ FPFerris(3) 2 42
(MHTompkins) *a in last trio: hrd rdn and btn 3f out* **25/1**

2m 8.67s (-1.51) **Going Correction** -0.10s/f (Good)
**WFA** 3 from 4yo+ 7lb **16** Ran SP% **130.3**
Speed ratings: **102,101,101,99,99 98,98,97,97,96 95,95,94,93,86 85**CSF £573.26 CT £4713.81 TOTE £71.00: £8.80, £2.30, £2.00, £2.40; EX 653.10 Place 6 £100.22, Place 5 £42.93.

**Owner** Vetlab Supplies Ltd **Bred** Kildaragh Stud **Trained** Woodingdean, E Sussex
■ Stewards Enquiry : P Doe caution: careless riding

**FOCUS**
A shock winner in Ex-French Diego Cao. The form is sound enough, but not strong for the track.

**NOTEBOOK**
**Diego Cao(IRE)**, whose three runs prior to this had come in France, looked to be starting out life in this country on a stiff enough mark of 78, but he proved many people wrong and caused an upset in fending off Go Tech close home to grab the spoils. He is reportedly a lazy worker who had shown little at home, but assuming this is no flash in the pan connections have a decent handicapper on their hands. Bought with a view to going jumping, he may make up into a fair hurdler.
**Go Tech** has not won for around two years now and always seems to lack that winning kick in a finish.
**Dream Magic** remains in good form and his turn will come if he can maintain this level of form.
**Freeloader(IRE)** made some good late headway but he could not go again once getting within striking distance.
**Arry Dash** has proved a bit disappointing this season as he looked the sort to do well, and he is another who finds it hard to win.
**Unsuited**, returning from a break, ran well enough to suggest she can get competitive off this mark when back on her favoured soft ground.
**Hasaiyda(IRE)** has disappointed the last twice now and is best left alone until showing more.
**War Owl(USA)** *Official explanation: jockey said gelding pulled up sore*
**Supreme Salutation** *Official explanation: jockey said gelding's saddle slipped*
T/Plt: £82.10 to a £1 stake. Pool: £49,524.65. 440.25 winning tickets. T/Qpdt: £20.70 to a £1 stake. Pool: £2,705.10. 96.35 winning tickets. JN

# 5548 YARMOUTH (L-H)
### Wednesday, September 15

**OFFICIAL GOING: Good (good to soft in places in straight)**
After 2mm of rain overnight the ground eased, but there didn't appear to be much bias in the draw.
Wind: Slight half behind Weather: Fine

## 5569 EUROPEAN BREEDERS FUND MAIDEN FILLIES' STKS 6f 3y
**2:10** (2:13) (D3) 2-Y-O **£5,216** (£1,605; £802; £401) **Stalls** High

Form RPR

**1** **Divinely Decadent (IRE)** 2-8-11 ........ KFallon 1 86+
(PWChapple-Hyam) *dwlt: hld up: hdwy over 2f out: led ins fnl f: r.o* **7/1**[3]

00 **2** *2* **Peppermint Tea (IRE)**[75] 3476 2-8-11 ........ PRobinson 14 80
(MLWBell) *mde most over 4f: styd on same pce* **40/1**

03 **3** *shd* **Desert Imp**[12] 5270 2-8-11 ........ MHills 12 80
(BWHills) *chsd ldrs: led over 1f out: hdd and no ex ins fnl f* **13/8**[1]

44 **4** *2½* **Ten-Cents**[12] 5271 2-8-11 ........ DHolland 3 72
(CACyzer) *chsd ldrs: rdn over 1f out: styd on same pce* **8/1**

**5** *¾* **Fashion House (USA)** 2-8-11 ........ LDettori 5 70
(SaeedBinSuroor) *swvd rt s: chsd ldrs: styd on same pce appr fnl f* **5/1**[2]

00 **6** *1¾* **Lady Pilot**[12] 5270 2-8-11 ........ JPMurtagh 4 65
(CEBrittain) *w ldr: rdn and hung lft over 1f out: wknd ins fnl f* **11/1**

0 **7** *½* **Depressed**[20] 5053 2-8-11 ........ JFEgan 11 63
(AndrewReid) *chsd ldrs: rdn and hung lft over 1f out: sn wknd* **50/1**

5 **8** *nk* **Qawaafil (USA)**[85] 2876 2-8-11 ........ WSupple 10 62
(EALDunlop) *hld up: sme hdwy over 1f out: nvr trbld ldrs* **25/1**

**9** *1¼* **Magic Flo** 2-8-11 ........ SWhitworth 2 58
(GCBravery) *mid-div: pushed along 1/2-way: n.d* **66/1**

**10** *1* **Pesquera** 2-8-11 ........ KDarley 6 55
(JNoseda) *hmpd s: hdwy over 2f out: wknd over 1f out* **20/1**

**11** *3* **Neferura** 2-8-11 ........ SWKelly 16 46
(WJHaggas) *sn outpcd* **40/1**

000 **12** *¾* **Lady Suesanne (IRE)**[11] 5301 2-8-11 ........ WRyan 17 44
(CADwyer) *bhd fr 1/2-way* **150/1**

13 4 **Frambroise** 2-8-11 ............ (v[1]) TPQueally 8 32
(DRLoder) *hmpd s: sn prom: rdn and wknd over 1f out* **16/1**
14 ½ **Lady Lakota** (IRE) 2-8-8 ............ JFMcDonald(3) 7 31
(APJarvis) *hmpd s: bhd fr 1/2-way* **50/1**
15 1¼ **Lasting Image** 2-8-11 ............ AMcCarthy 9 27
(SCWilliams) *s.s and swvd lft s: a bhd* **50/1**
16 shd **Four Pleasure** 2-8-11 ............ TEDurcan 13 27
(CADwyer) *s.i.s: a in rr* **50/1**
0 17 2 **Assured (IRE)**[47] 4292 2-8-11 ............ JQuinn 15 21
(PWD'Arcy) *s.i.s: sn pushed along: bhd fr 1/2-way* **66/1**

1m 13.6s **Going Correction** -0.075s/f (Good) **17** Ran SP% **117.6**
Speed ratings: **97,94,94,90,89 87,86,86,84,83 79,78,73,72,70 70,68**CSF £266.29 TOTE £8.90: £2.50, £10.50, £1.10; EX 544.60.
**Owner** Mrs Sue Catt **Bred** Albert Sherwood **Trained** Newmarket, Suffolk

**FOCUS**
Fairly strong form and it should prove reliable. The winner could make her mark at Listed level or higher.

**NOTEBOOK**
**Divinely Decadent(IRE)**, who is from the same family as the high-class Vinnie Roe, took a while to grasp what was required, but was well on top in the end. She will stay further than this and is sure to have learnt plenty from the experience.
**Peppermint Tea(IRE)**, a half-sister to a 10-furlong winner, is going the right way, and left the impression a step up in trip will bring about further improvement.
**Desert Imp** again flattered briefly and is clearly nothing special.
**Ten-Cents** should do better when stepping up in trip in nursery company.
**Fashion House(USA)** free to post, was very green as the stalls opened and dived away to her right, hampering several of her rivals. Not knocked about when her race had gone, she should be capable of better. *Official explanation: jockey said filly ran too freely to post*

## 5570 EUROPEAN BREEDERS FUND/NORTON PESKETT LEGAL SERVICES MAIDEN STKS 7f 3y
**2:40** (2:46) (D3) 2-Y-O **£5,255** (£1,617; £808; £404) **Stalls** High

Form RPR
5 1 **Home Affairs**[61] 3913 2-9-0 ............ KFallon 4 83+
(SirMichaelStoute) *s.i.s: racd towards far side: hld up: hdwy 1/2-way: led over 2f out: r.o wl* **8/13**[1]
0 2 3 **Notability (IRE)**[33] 4728 2-9-0 ............ PRobinson 7 76
(MAJarvis) *racd stands' side: led that gp: rdn over 1f out: styd on same pce* **25/1**
3 nk **Alqaahir (USA)** 2-9-0 ............ LDettori 9 75
(SaeedBinSuroor) *s.i.s: racd towards far side: hld up: hdwy over 2f out: rdn to chse wnr over 1f out: no imp* **9/2**[2]
4 ¾ **Burgundian (USA)** 2-9-0 ............ TEDurcan 8 73
(JNoseda) *racd stands' side: chsd ldrs: rdn and ev ch over 1f out: styd on same pce* **25/1**
0 5 2 **Allied Cause**[32] 4753 2-8-6 ............ NMackay(3) 6 63
(LMCumani) *racd towards far side: chsd ldrs: rdn over 1f out: wknd ins fnl f* **10/1**[3]
6 1¾ **Treble Seven (USA)** 2-8-9 ............ MHills 12 59
(CEBrittain) *racd stands' side: chsd ldrs: ev ch 2f out: wknd fnl f* **20/1**
7 ¾ **Phi (USA)** 2-9-0 ............ KDarley 5 62
(SirMichaelStoute) *mde most towards far side over 4f: wknd fnl f* **33/1**
8 shd **Eskimo's Nest** 2-8-9 ............ SWKelly 11 57
(WJHaggas) *dwlt: swtchd to r towards far side: sn prom: wknd over 1f out* **100/1**
0 9 ¾ **Selika (IRE)**[18] 5118 2-9-0 ............ WRyan 14 60
(MHTompkins) *racd stands' side: hld up in tch: wknd over 1f out* **150/1**
6 10 hd **Boxhall (IRE)**[19] 5087 2-9-0 ............ JPMurtagh 1 59
(PWHarris) *racd towards far side: hld up: wknd wl over 1f out* **12/1**
50 11 shd **Muddy (IRE)**[9] 5353 2-9-0 ............ WSupple 13 59
(GAHuffer) *racd stands' side: chsd ldrs: rdn over 2f out: wknd over 1f out* **66/1**
00 12 9 **Mambazo**[27] 4866 2-9-0 ............ JFEgan 2 36
(SCWilliams) *racd towards far side: chsd ldr over 4f: wknd wl over 1f out* **100/1**
13 1¾ **Missy Cinofaz** 2-8-9 ............ TPQueally 10 27
(IAWood) *racd stands' side: bhd fnl 3f* **100/1**
14 shd **Mont Saint Michel (IRE)** 2-9-0 ............ DHolland 3 32
(GWragg) *racd towards far side: lost action and and wl bhd over 5f out* **25/1**

1m 26.26s (-0.24) **Going Correction** -0.075s/f (Good) **14** Ran SP% **121.3**
Speed ratings: **98,94,94,93,91 89,88,88,87,87 86,76,74,74**CSF £27.47 TOTE £1.60: £1.10, £3.60, £1.70; EX 18.40.
**Owner** K Abdulla **Bred** Juddmonte Farms **Trained** Newmarket, Suffolk

**FOCUS**
The field split into two, but there did not appear to be any great advantage to either side. A mixed bag of talent on show and those at the back help govern the level of the form, but all in all probably a fair maiden.

**NOTEBOOK**
**Home Affairs** had clearly learnt from his debut and was well on top in the end. There is almost certainly plenty more to come from him.
**Notability(IRE)**, who was colty in the paddock, won the race on his side, and provided he can keep his mind on the job should have no trouble winning his maiden.
**Alqaahir(USA)**, a half-brother to Queen Anne Stakes winner Intikhab, showed enough to suggest he can pay his way in due course. *Official explanation: jockey said colt was slowly away*
**Burgundian(USA)**, a $350,000 half-brother to a winner in the USA, didn't shape at all badly and he is sure to be all the wiser next time.
**Allied Cause** still looks to be learning and should do better when stepping up in trip.
**Treble Seven(USA)**, a half-sister to Group 2 winner Double Knot, is out of a mare that won over ten furlongs as a three-year-old. Having had every chance she just got tired in the ground, and is sure to come on for the experience.
**Mont Saint Michel(IRE)** *Official explanation: jockey said horse lost its action*

## 5571 DANNY WRIGHT (S) STKS 1m 2f 21y
**3:15** (3:15) (G4) 3-4-Y-0 **£2,632** (£752; £376) **Stalls** Low

Form RPR
4522 1 **Lenwade**[11] 5284 3-8-5 40 ............ AMcCarthy 5 45
(GGMargarson) *chsd ldrs: led over 1f out: rdn out* **11/1**
5000 2 nk **Skibereen (IRE)**[10] 5317 4-9-3 65 ............ DHolland 4 49
(IWMcinnes) *a.p: rdn over 2f out: r.o* **5/1**[2]
0 3 3 **Golden Queen**[8] 5381 3-7-12 ............ AshleighHorton(7) 3 39
(MDIUsher) *a.p: chsd ldr over 4f out: led over 2f out: rdn and hdd over 1f out: no ex wl ins fnl f* **100/1**
0005 4 nk **Romeo's Day**[19] 5069 3-8-10 40 ............ (v) TEDurcan 2 44
(MRChannon) *led: clr 4f out: hdd over 2f out: no ex ins fnl f* **16/1**
664 5 1¼ **Port Sodrick**[39] 4545 3-8-7 62 ............ HayleyTurner(3) 1 41
(MDIUsher) *chsd ldr over 5f: n.m.r over 1f out: no ex ins fnl f* **7/1**[3]
0013 6 nk **Shamwari Fire (IRE)**[4] 5450 4-9-5 49 ............ JFMcDonald(3) 8 46
(IWMcinnes) *hld up: hdwy over 3f out: styd on same pce appr fnl f* **7/1**[3]
5040 7 1¾ **Soviet Spirit**[21] 5036 3-8-0 51 ............ DFox(5) 6 33
(CADwyer) *hld up in tch: rdn over 2f out: styd on same pce appr fnl f* **16/1**
0401 8 nk **Oktis Morilious (IRE)**[19] 5069 3-9-1 55 ............ LDettori 9 42
(AWCarroll) *dwlt: hld up: effrt over 2f out: n.d* **9/4**[1]
0460 9 9 **Soviet Sceptre (IRE)**[19] 5092 3-8-10 62 ............ KFallon 10 21
(MissDMountain) *hld up: plld hrd: hung rt and wknd 2f out* **5/1**[2]
3000 10 3 **Fox Hollow (IRE)**[53] 4128 3-8-10 35 ............ JQuinn 7 15
(MJHaynes) *hld up: a in rr* **66/1**

2m 11.91s (3.94) **Going Correction** +0.075s/f (Good)
**WFA** 3 from 4yo 7lb **10** Ran SP% **111.7**
Speed ratings: **87,86,84,84,83 82,81,81,74,71** CT £8.20 TOTE £2.10: £2.00, £39.60, £; EX76.10 1.The winner was bought in for 10,400gns. Golden Queen was subject to a friendly claim. Oktis Morilious was claimed by Mr C. Dore for
**Owner** The Lenwade Partnership **Bred** Stetchworth Park Stud Ltd **Trained** Newmarket, Suffolk

**FOCUS**
A poor contest and a moderate winning time, even for a seller.

**NOTEBOOK**
**Lenwade** finally got off the mark at the 16th attempt, which speaks volumes for her rivals.
**Skibereen(IRE)**, like the winner, is exposed as moderate, but he did at least try to make a fight of it.
**Golden Queen** is at least open to improvement, but she will need to improve if she is to get off the mark.
**Romeo's Day** had plenty of use made of him, but failed to get home.
**Port Sodrick**, taking a drop in class, didn't have much room on the inside, but that can hardly be used as an excuse.
**Oktis Morilious(IRE)** never looked likely at any stage to follow up his Bath win.

## 5572 TOTEJACKPOT STKS (H'CAP) (FOR THE GOLDEN JUBILEE TROPHY) 1m 2f 21y
**3:45** (3:49) (D2) (0-85,84) 3-Y-O+ **£10,561** (£3,249; £1,624; £812) **Stalls** Low

Form RPR
2234 1 **Tata Naka**[11] 5286 4-8-4 **66** oh21 ............ HayleyTurner(3) 7 73
(MrsCADunnett) *hld up in tch: led 2f out: drvn out* **100/1**
6504 2 1 **River Treat (FR)**[49] 4236 3-8-12 **78** ............ JFEgan 2 83
(GWragg) *hld up: hdwy over 2f out: r.o* **16/1**
5300 3 nk **Winners Delight**[32] 4749 3-8-13 **79** ............ KDarley 13 84
(APJarvis) *hld up in tch: plld hrd: rdn over 1f out: r.o* **6/1**[2]
3150 4 1½ **Vamp**[11] 5297 3-8-9 **75** ............ JQuinn 5 77+
(RMBeckett) *hld up: nt clr run over 2f out: r.o ins fnl f: nt rch ldrs* **20/1**
0060 5 hd **Liquid Form (IRE)**[11] 5297 4-9-0 **73** ............ KFallon 3 75+
(BHanbury) *hld up: nt clr run over 2f out: r.o fnl f: nvr trbld ldrs* **9/2**[1]
4504 6 1½ **Vantage (IRE)**[19] 5076 3-8-11 **77** ............ (b) TEDurcan 1 76
(NPLittmoden) *hld up: rdn over 2f out: styd on: nt pce to chal* **20/1**
4401 7 ½ **Stretton (IRE)**[15] 5211 6-9-7 **80** ............ LDettori 12 78
(JDBethell) *chsd ldrs: n.m.r and lost pl wl over 1f out: nt rcvr* **9/2**[1]
0113 8 hd **Trew Class**[55] 4049 3-8-11 **77** ............ PRobinson 4 75
(MHTompkins) *chsd ldrs: rdn over 2f out: wknd ins fnl f* **8/1**
21-5 9 hd **Baltic Blazer (IRE)**[104] 2624 4-9-2 **75** ............ DHolland 14 72
(PWHarris) *chsd ldr: rdn over 3f out: wknd ins fnl f* **9/1**
3225 10 5 **Grey Clouds**[35] 4634 4-9-6 **79** ............ WSupple 8 67
(TDEasterby) *hld up: rdn over 3f out: wkng whn hmpd over 2f out* **13/2**[3]
11 nk **Lady's View (USA)**[31] 4785 3-9-4 **84** ............ JPMurtagh 15 72
(DJDaly) *s.i.s: sn chsng ldrs: wknd over 1f out* **20/1**
0404 12 2½ **Flame Queen**[8] 5371 3-8-0 **66** oh4 ............ LisaJones 9 49
(MrsCADunnett) *plld hrd and sn led: hdd 2f out: wknd fnl f* **66/1**
-400 13 14 **Donna Vita**[32] 4749 3-9-3 **83** ............ TPQueally 11 41
(PWChapple-Hyam) *hld up: rdn 1/2-way: wknd over 3f out* **20/1**

2m 8.92s (0.95) **Going Correction** +0.075s/f (Good)
**WFA** 3 from 4yo+ 7lb **13** Ran SP% **112.5**
Speed ratings: **99,98,97,96,96 95,95,94,94,90 90,88,77**CSF £1139.20 CT £10641.83 TOTE £66.40: £9.80, £5.40, £2.80; EX 639.10 TRIFECTA Not won..
**Owner** Andy Middleton **Bred** Ivyclose Ltd **Trained** Hingham, Norfolk

**FOCUS**
A moderate winning time for the grade, and a difficult race to rate with the winner much improved.

**NOTEBOOK**
**Tata Naka**, who was 21lb out of the handicap, had a trouble-free run, unlike quite a few of her rivals.
**River Treat(FR)** stayed this longer trip well enough, and although not an easy ride should be capable of scoring again.
**Winners Delight** did himself no favours by racing too keenly early on.
**Vamp** got going far too late having had no daylight, and must surely have gone close with a clear run.
**Liquid Form(IRE)**, 6lb lower than his last winning mark, looks to be coming back to form.
**Stretton(IRE)** was going as well as anything before being shuffled back through the pack by the struggling Trew Class.
**Grey Clouds** turned in a rare poor performance and clearly had an off day.

## 5573 JOHN MUSKER FILLIES' STKS (LISTED RACE) 1m 2f 21y
**4:20** (4:21) (A1) 3-Y-O+ **£17,400** (£6,600; £3,300; £1,500) **Stalls** Low

Form RPR
1632 1 **Polar Jem**[45] 4367 4-8-13 98 ............ AMcCarthy 5 98
(GGMargarson) *mde virtually all: rdn over 1f out: r.o gamely* **5/2**[2]
2240 2 ½ **Shamara (IRE)**[68] 3699 4-8-13 90 ............ JPMurtagh 4 97
(CFWall) *hld up in tch: rdn to chse wnr over 1f out: r.o* **18/1**
1112 3 2 **La Persiana**[22] 5025 3-8-6 100 ............ KDarley 11 94
(WJarvis) *trckd ldrs: racd keenly: rdn over 1f out: styd on same pce ins fnl f* **15/8**[1]
1644 4 1¼ **Silk Fan (IRE)**[13] 5249 3-8-6 95 ............ DHolland 9 91
(PWHarris) *s.i.s: hld up: hdwy over 2f out: no imp fnl f* **11/2**[3]
2115 5 4 **Dami (USA)**[30] 4806 3-8-6 77 ............ (p) TPQueally 3 84
(CEBrittain) *prom: rdn over 3f out: outpcd fnl 2f* **40/1**
010 6 nk **Boot 'n Toot**[5] 5446 3-8-6 76 ............ JFEgan 6 84?
(CACyzer) *hld up: rdn over 3f out: nvr trbld ldrs* **100/1**
-005 7 nk **Weecandoo (IRE)**[4] 5461 6-8-13 84 ............ GCarter 12 83
(CNAllen) *hld up: n.d* **33/1**
2150 8 1 **Crystal (IRE)**[22] 5025 3-8-6 93 ............ MHills 7 81
(BJMeehan) *chsd wnr 8f: sn wknd* **8/1**
4130 9 2½ **Olivia Rose (IRE)**[46] 4343 5-8-13 83 ............ JQuinn 8 77
(JPearce) *hld up: rdn over 3f out: n.d* **33/1**
3401 10 2 **Tidal**[11] 5297 5-8-13 88 ............ LDettori 10 73
(AWCarroll) *prom over 7f* **10/1**

0/30 **11** *20* **Rainbow Queen**[28] [4856] 4-8-13 **88** ........ KFallon 1 37
(SirMichaelStoute) *trckd ldrs: rdn over 3f out: wknd 2f out* **20/1**

2m 7.26s (-0.71) **Going Correction** +0.075s/f (Good)
**WFA** 3 from 4yo+ 7lb **11** Ran SP% **118.3**
Speed ratings: **105,104,103,102,98 98,98,97,95,93 77**CSF £43.43 TOTE £3.70: £1.50, £5.20, £1.20; EX 43.20.
**Owner** Norcroft Park Stud **Bred** Norcroft Park Stud **Trained** Newmarket, Suffolk

**FOCUS**
Not a strong Listed contest with little strength in depth. The winner did not have to run up to her best to score and the fifth and sixth hold the form down.

**NOTEBOOK**
**Polar Jem** is a tough filly who was allowed a soft lead, and she never looked likely to be reeled in despite the persistent challenge from the runner-up.
**Shamara(IRE)**, who hit form this time last year, turned in a solid effort on these terms.
**La Persiana** was plenty keen enough early on and may have done better had there been more of a gallop.
**Silk Fan(IRE)**, although not beaten far, left the impression that this trip was just beyond her.
*Official explanation: jockey said filly was slowly away*
**Dami(USA)** had plenty to find at this level, but was far from disgraced.
**Boot 'n Toot** didn't have the best of runs, but despite that still looked to leave her maiden form well behind here.
**Tidal** *Official explanation: jockey said filly was not suited by the good, good to soft ground*
**Rainbow Queen** *Official explanation: jockey said filly stumbled twice about two furlongs out*

## 5574 SEA-DEER LEVY BOARD H'CAP — 1m 3y
4:50 (4:50) (D2) (0-85,85) 3-Y-O+ **£7,685** (£2,915; £1,457; £662) **Stalls** High

Form RPR
1000 **1** **Little Venice (IRE)**[23] [5004] 4-9-7 **82** ........ KDarley 2 91
(CFWall) *w ldr: rdn to ld 1f out: r.o* **20/1**
6321 **2** *¾* **Johannian**[3] [5496] 6-8-5 **69** ........ NMackay(3) 9 76
(JMBradley) *hld up: hdwy over 1f out: r.o: too much too do* **3/1**[1]
0220 **3** *shd* **Brazilian Terrace**[18] [5136] 4-8-11 **75** ........ HayleyTurner(3) 13 82
(MLWBell) *chsd ldrs: rdn over 2f out: r.o* **16/1**
1200 **4** *shd* **Concer Eto**[6] [5419] 5-8-12 **73** ........ (p) LDettori 5 80
(SCWilliams) *trckd ldrs: rdn over 1f out: r.o* **5/1**[3]
5006 **5** *¾* **H Harrison (IRE)**[20] [5055] 4-9-4 **79** ........ LVickers 8 84
(IWMcinnes) *led: hung lft and hdd 1f out: no ex* **25/1**
-110 **6** *shd* **Salinor**[84] [3198] 4-9-5 **80** ........ KFallon 12 85
(EFVaughan) *hld up: pushed along 1/2-way: nt clr run ins fnl f: r.o* **7/2**[2]
0534 **7** *¾* **Rafferty (IRE)**[37] [4613] 5-9-6 **81** ........ (b) DHolland 4 84
(CEBrittain) *trckd ldrs: rdn over 1f out: no ex ins fnl f* **8/1**
6240 **8** *nk* **Red Sahara (IRE)**[18] [5136] 3-8-11 **77** ........ SWKelly 6 79
(WJHaggas) *chsd ldrs: rdn over 2f out: one pce fnl f* **25/1**
6004 **9** *1 ¼* **Star Sensation (IRE)**[22] [5017] 4-8-9 **77** ........ MCoumbe(7) 10 76
(PWHarris) *s.s: rdn over 2f out: n.d* **20/1**
5560 **10** *hd* **Tiber Tiger (IRE)**[16] [5185] 4-8-11 **72** ........ (b) TEDurcan 11 71
(NPLittmoden) *s.i.s: hld up: rdn 1/2-way: n.d* **16/1**
0104 **11** *3 ½* **King Of Diamonds**[7] [5403] 3-8-11 **77** ........ WSupple 14 68
(JRBest) *hld up: rdn over 1f out: sn wknd* **8/1**

1m 39.25s (-0.45) **Going Correction** -0.075s/f (Good)
**WFA** 3 from 4yo+ 5lb **11** Ran SP% **115.1**
Speed ratings: **99,98,98,98,97 97,96,96,94,94 91**CSF £74.50 CT £1018.33 TOTE £23.20: £5.00, £1.50, £3.40; EX 77.10.
**Owner** Hintlesham SPD Partners **Bred** Limestone Stud **Trained** Newmarket, Suffolk

**FOCUS**
Quite a competitive handicap, but the pace was only steady which resuted in a modest winning time for the class. The bunch finish suggests that the form is nothing special.

**NOTEBOOK**
**Little Venice(IRE)** had pretty much the run of the race up front and may be flattered by this effort.
**Johannian**, ridden with plenty of confidence, never looked likely to peg back the winner, who got first run. There will be other days for him.
**Brazilian Terrace** left behind her a poor effort last time, but the Handicapper knows how good she is.
**Concer Eto**, unbeaten in his two previous starts here, wasn't really suited to the steady pace.
**H Harrison(IRE)** had something of a soft time of things up front, but he didn't look that keen when push came to shove.
**Salinor**, who was returning after a break, was doing his best work late on.

## 5575 TELETEXT "HANDS AND HEELS" APPRENTICE H'CAP — 7f 3y
5:25 (5:25) (F4) (0-55,55) 3-Y-O+ **£3,036** (£867; £433) **Stalls** High

Form RPR
2060 **1** **Halcyon Magic**[61] [3911] 6-8-4 **46** ........ (b) LauraPike(5) 6 57
(MWigham) *chsd ldrs: led ins fnl f: edgd lft: r.o* **14/1**
0640 **2** *¾* **Feast Of Romance**[71] [3615] 7-8-4 **46** oh1 ........ (b) TBlock(5) 7 55
(GAHuffer) *led tl hdd ins fnl f: r.o* **40/1**
5054 **3** *1 ¾* **Linden's Lady**[13] [5235] 4-8-6 **50** ........ TDean(7) 1 54
(JRWeymes) *chsd ldrs: edgd rt over 1f out: styd on same pce* **12/1**
0361 **4** *½* **My Girl Pearl (IRE)**[6] [5411] 4-9-1 **52** 6ex ........ WHogg 5 55
(MSSaunders) *chsd ldrs: ev ch over 1f out: no ex* **13/2**[3]
0310 **5** *1* **Lucefer (IRE)**[16] [5176] 6-8-10 **52** ........ JemmaMarshall(5) 4 52
(GCHChung) *hld up: swtchd lft and hdwy over 2f out: styd on same pce fnl f* **8/1**
P015 **6** *shd* **Taiyo**[30] [4818] 4-8-4 **46** ........ RJKilloran(5) 9 46
(JWPayne) *chsd ldrs: shkn up over 1f out: no ex* **12/1**
2230 **7** *¾* **Blakeseven**[185] [1020] 4-8-6 **48** ........ ARutter(5) 13 46
(WJMusson) *chsd ldrs: styd on same pce appr fnl f* **20/1**
5465 **8** *nk* **Temper Tantrum**[6] [5411] 6-9-4 **55** ........ (p) HPoulton 11 52
(JRBest) *s.i.s: hld up: styd on ins fnl f: nvr nrr* **9/2**[2]
4025 **9** *shd* **Lord Chamberlain**[3] [5493] 11-9-1 **55** ........ (b) CJDavies(3) 16 52
(JMBradley) *s.i.s: bhd: r.o ins fnl f: nvr nrr* **10/1**
6000 **10** *2 ½* **Indian Lily**[33] [4708] 3-8-3 **49** ow2 ........ SO'Hara(5) 15 40
(CFWall) *n.d* **50/1**
0/33 **11** *½* **Hammer Of The Gods (IRE)**[22] [5026] 4-8-4 **46** oh1 ..... (t) AHindley(5) 10 35
(JulianPoulton) *chsd ldrs: edgd lft over 2f out: wknd over 1f out* **25/1**
1206 **12** *¾* **Zonnebeke**[21] [5036] 3-8-0 **46** ........ BO'Neill(5) 3 33
(MrsCADunnett) *s.i.s: hdwy 1/2-way: wknd over 1f out* **25/1**
0610 **13** *1* **Wood Fern (UAE)**[12] [5260] 4-8-5 **49** ........ TO'Brien(7) 8 34
(MRChannon) *mid-div: wknd over 1f out* **33/1**
-000 **14** *½* **Maureen Ann**[40] [4511] 4-8-6 **48** ........ KPierrepont(5) 14 32
(TJFitzgerald) *n.d* **20/1**
4003 **15** *½* **Charlottebutterfly**[23] [5008] 4-8-11 **53** ........ KJackson(5) 2 35
(TTClement) *chsd ldrs over 4f* **12/1**
1503 **16** *17* **Scarrottoo**[6] [5425] 6-9-4 **55** ........ DeanWilliams 12 —
(SCWilliams) *prom 5f: eased fnl f: sddle slipped* **7/2**[1]

1m 25.75s (-0.75) **Going Correction** -0.075s/f (Good)
**WFA** 3 from 4yo+ 4lb **16** Ran SP% **128.2**
Speed ratings: **101,100,98,97,96 96,95,95,95,92 91,90,89,89,88 69**CSF £509.20 CT £6775.37 TOTE £16.10: £3.00, £7.30, £2.80, £2.10; EX 644.00 Place 6 £128.29, Place 5 £79.09.
**Owner** The Magic Partnership **Bred** Lawrence Shepherd **Trained** Newmarket, Suffolk

**FOCUS**
An ordinary contest which suited those that raced close to the pace. The form looks solid for the grade.

**NOTEBOOK**
**Halcyon Magic**, the winner of this two years ago, had little difficulty repeating the trick off a 10lb lower mark.
**Feast Of Romance** showed plenty of pace on this return to action, and although he has yet to strike on turf, is more than capable.
**Linden's Lady**, who has been in fair form of late, continues to slide down the weights.
**My Girl Pearl(IRE)** ran well enough under her penalty, on ground which could well have been slower than ideal.
**Lucefer(IRE)** came out best of those to come from off the pace.
**Scarrottoo** *Official explanation: jockey said gelding's saddle slipped*
T/Jkpt: Not won. T/Plt: £149.80 to a £1 stake. Pool: £50,687.00. 246.85 winning tickets. T/Qpdt: £70.90 to a £1 stake. Pool: £2,788.50. 29.10 winning tickets. CR

# 5388 SAN SIRO (R-H)
Wednesday, September 15

**OFFICIAL GOING: Soft**

## 5576a PREMIO MOTTALCIATA (F&M) — 1m 2f
2:50 (3:00) 3-Y-O+ **£12,324** (£5,423; £2,958; £1,479)

RPR
**1** **Windy Britain**[22] [5025] 5-9-2 ........ CColombi 5 98
(LMCumani) *2nd early on inside, 5th straight, ridden to lead 100y out, ran on well*
**2** *1* **Holy Moon (IRE)**[87] [3137] 4-9-2 ........ EBotti 8 96
(ABotti, Italy)
**3** *¾* **Noble Stella (GER)**[325] [5780] 3-8-9 ........ MDemuro 9 95
(BGrizzetti, Italy)
**4** *7* **Barmad Di San Jore (ITY)**[311] [5965] 3-8-9 ........ MMonteriso 6 83
(JHeloury, Italy)
**5** *7* **Musical Score**[87] [3137] 5-9-2 ........ DVargiu 3 70
(MGonnelli, Italy)
**6** *2 ½* **Brain Storm (IRE)**[451] [2621] 4-9-2 ........ PAgus 7 66
(GRomano, Italy)
**7** *2 ½* **Supereva (IRE)**[87] [3137] 4-9-2 ........ SMulas 1 62
(BGrizzetti, Italy)

2m 6.90s
**WFA** 3 from 4yo+ 7lb **7** Ran
Speed ratings: .
**Owner** Scuderia Giocri **Bred** Scuderia Giocri **Trained** Newmarket, Suffolk

**NOTEBOOK**
**Windy Britain** has been struggling of late back in Britain and appreciated this less demanding test to score readily. This would have done her confidence good and it would come as no surprise to see her repeat the trick back home.

## 5577a PREMIO PIZZORLA (MAIDEN) (FILLIES) — 7f
4:20 (4:43) 2-Y-O **£7,042** (£3,099; £1,690; £845)

RPR
**1** **Miss Hanks (IRE)** 2-8-11 ........ DVargiu 8 —
(LMCumani) *raced in 5th, challenged 1f out, led 150 yards out, ridden out*
**2** *1* **Natikhab**[77] [3436] 2-9-0 ........ DPorcu 11 —
(MGuarnieri, Italy)
**3** *1 ¼* **Manhattan (ITY)**[8] [5390] 2-9-0 ........ EBotti 1 —
(ABotti, Italy)
**4** *3* **Sphynx (GER)** 2-8-11 ........ MTellini 5 —
(RRohne, Germany)
**5** *nse* **Risata** 2-9-0 ........ AArbau 13 —
(LLedda, Italy)
**6** *1 ¼* **East Of Shannon (IRE)** 2-8-10 ........ JDHillis 9 —
(WernerGlanz, Germany)
**7** *1 ¾* **Dragozza (ITY)** 2-9-0 ........ MLatorre 7 —
(AMorazzoni, Italy)
**8** *4* **Nord's Cadeaux (IRE)** 2-9-0 ........ MDemuro 4 —
(BGrizzetti, Italy)
**9** *1 ¾* **Royal Claudette (ITY)** 2-9-0 ........ SUrru 12 —
(RMenichetti, Italy)
**10** *hd* **Zachela (IRE)** 2-9-0 ........ FJovine 10 —
(AnnalisaBorroni, Italy)
**11** *8* **Valhalling** 2-9-0 ........ LManiezzi 6 —
(MCiciarelli, Italy)
**12** *1 ¼* **Bandiera (GER)** 2-8-11 ........ MPregel 2 —
(WFigge, Germany)
**13** *1 ½* **Matrice (ITY)**[8] [5390] 2-9-0 ........ AParravani 3 —
(PPaciello, Italy)

1m 28.8s **13** Ran
Speed ratings: .
**Owner** Allevamento La Nuova Sbarra **Bred** Castello Di Razza Ascagnano S A S **Trained** Newmarket, Suffolk

**NOTEBOOK**
**Miss Hanks(IRE)** made a pleasing start to her career with a cosy win but probably failed to achieve much. She will finds things tougher once upped in grade.

# $^{4900}$AYR (L-H)

Thursday, September 16

**OFFICIAL GOING: Good to soft changing to soft after race 4 (3.40)**

Wind: str across Weather: raining throughout

## 5578 AUDI A4 MAIDEN AUCTION STKS 6f

**2:10** (2:12) (E3) 2-Y-O **£3,458** (£1,064; £532; £266) **Stalls** High

| Form | | | Horse | Jockey | RPR |
|---|---|---|---|---|---|
| 04 | 1 | | **Ingleton**$^{11}$ 5319 2-8-7 | GGibbons 18 | 81 |
| | | | (BAMcmahon) *mde virtually all: pushed along 2f out: hld on wl* | **5/1**$^{2}$ | |
| | 2 | hd | **Real Quality (USA)** 2-8-11 | DeanMcKeown 3 | 84 |
| | | | (ISemple) *dwlt: bhd: swtchd and hdwy ins over 1f out: ev ch wl ins fnl f: jst hld: improve* | **66/1** | |
| 0 | 3 | 2 ½ | **Captain Johnno (IRE)**$^{35}$ 4682 2-8-9 (b$^{1}$) | KDarley 13 | 75 |
| | | | (DRLoder) *w ldrs tl rdn and nt qckn fnl f* | **16/1** | |
| 2 | 4 | 2 | **Moon Forest (IRE)**$^{17}$ 5198 2-8-7 | ACulhane 6 | 67 |
| | | | (PWChapple-Hyam) *midfield on outside: effrt over 2f out: edgd rt and one pce over 1f out* | **1/1**$^{1}$ | |
| 60 | 5 | 2 ½ | **Hits Only Cash**$^{41}$ 4507 2-8-9 | NCallan 16 | 61 |
| | | | (PABlockley) *prom tl rdn and nt qckn fr 2f out* | **33/1** | |
| 06 | 6 | 2 | **Compton Classic**$^{3}$ 5513 2-8-6 | NMackay$^{(3)}$ 14 | 55 |
| | | | (JSGoldie) *keen: hld up: shkn up and hdwy fr 2f out: nvr nrr* | **100/1** | |
| 0 | 7 | 5 | **Haenertsburg (IRE)**$^{11}$ 5319 2-7-13 ow2 | PPMathers$^{(5)}$ 11 | 35 |
| | | | (ABerry) *prom tl outpcd fr 2f out* | **50/1** | |
| 4460 | 8 | ¾ | **Sweet Marguerite**$^{14}$ 5240 2-8-2 60 | CCatlin 17 | 31 |
| | | | (TDEasterby) *w ldrs tl wknd over 1f out* | **33/1** | |
| | 9 | 1 ¾ | **Blacknyello Bonnet (USA)** 2-8-4 | JFanning 15 | 28 |
| | | | (MJohnston) *dwlt: sn prom: rdn and wknd fr 2f out* | **20/1** | |
| 54 | 10 | ¾ | **High Petergate (IRE)**$^{14}$ 5241 2-8-6 | TLucas 10 | 28 |
| | | | (MWEasterby) *prom: outpcd 1/2-way: n.d after* | **33/1** | |
| | 11 | ¾ | **Orpendonna (IRE)** 2-8-4 | PFessey 1 | 23 |
| | | | (KARyan) *bhd on outside: hdwy 2f out: sn no imp* | **14/1** | |
| 0000 | 12 | 2 ½ | **Slate Grey**$^{41}$ 4507 2-8-7 57 (v$^{1}$) | DarrenWilliams 7 | 19 |
| | | | (KRBurke) *hld up: outpcd over 3f out: n.d after* | **100/1** | |
| | 13 | 3 ½ | **Stanley Arthur** 2-8-9 | ANicholls 2 | 10 |
| | | | (DNicholls) *bhd and sn outpcd: sme hdwy over 1f out: n.d* | **66/1** | |
| 0 | 14 | ½ | **Enborne Again (IRE)**$^{19}$ 5125 2-8-7 | PHanagan 9 | 7 |
| | | | (RAFahey) *bhd on ins: no ch fr 1/2-way* | **25/1** | |
| 0305 | 15 | 3 | **Mytton's Bell (IRE)**$^{21}$ 5059 2-7-13 65 | HayleyTurner$^{(3)}$ 12 | — |
| | | | (ABailey) *w ldrs: sddle slipped sn after s: wknd fr 1/2-way* | **10/1**$^{3}$ | |
| | 16 | 3 ½ | **Mount Kellet (IRE)** 2-8-9 | DHolland 4 | — |
| | | | (JGGiven) *s.i.s: a bhd* | **25/1** | |
| | 17 | 2 ½ | **Sonic Anthem (USA)** 2-9-0 | AlexGreaves 5 | — |
| | | | (DNicholls) *towards rr: outpcd fr 1/2-way* | **50/1** | |
| 6340 | 18 | nk | **Shatin Leader**$^{21}$ 5060 2-8-2 59 | DaleGibson 8 | — |
| | | | (MissLAPerratt) *racd on outside: prom to 1/2-way: sn btn* | **50/1** | |

1m 14.41s (0.69) **Going Correction** +0.05s/f (Good) **18** Ran SP% **120.4**

Speed ratings: **97,96,93,90,87 84,78,77,74,73 72,69,64,64,60 55,52,51**CSF £311.79 TOTE £5.50: £1.60, £15.30, £3.40; EX 447.10.

**Owner** J C Fretwell **Bred** Thomas Trafford **Trained** Hopwas, Staffs

**FOCUS**

Only ordinary maiden form with little strength in depth, but there were a couple of nice performances with regards to the future.

**NOTEBOOK**

**Ingleton**, who improved from his first to second run, stepped up again with the rail to race against and just found enough to hold off the challenge of Real Quality. He seemingly likes to race from the front and, with his effectiveness on this sort of ground proven, can pick up a nursery in the coming weeks.

**Real Quality(USA)** is related to winners, but his stable's juveniles are usually unsighted on their debuts, so the fact that he ran such a big race suggests he is a fair performer in the making. He looked sure to get past the winner in the final furlong, but lack of previous experience told and he was just denied. Sure to improve for the outing, he can win an ordinary maiden.

**Captain Johnno(IRE)**, sporting the first-time blinkers having disappointed on his debut, ran a much better race and will appreciate the return to seven furlongs.

**Moon Forest(IRE)** was a little disappointing and found this drop back in trip against him. He is more of a handicap type for next season.

**Hits Only Cash** is now qualified for nurseries and should do better in that sphere.

**Compton Classic** is another now eligible for nurseries and he can probably sneak a small one.

**Blacknyello Bonnet(USA)** looked too green and inexperienced to do himself justice and will make a better three-year-old.

**Mytton's Bell(IRE)** *Official explanation: jockey said saddle slipped*

## 5579 ALL NEW AUDI A6 H'CAP 5f

**2:40** (2:43) (E3) (0-70,68) 3-Y-0+ **£7,202** (£2,216; £1,108; £554) **Stalls** High

| Form | | | Horse | Jockey | RPR |
|---|---|---|---|---|---|
| 5000 | 1 | | **Blueberry Rhyme**$^{40}$ 4542 5-8-7 54 oh2 (v) | NCallan 27 | 64 |
| | | | (PABlockley) *cl up stands side: led that gp wl over 1f out: hld on wl* | **50/1** | |
| 106 | 2 | ½ | **Strawberry Patch (IRE)**$^{14}$ 5242 5-8-10 57 (p) | PFessey 26 | 65 |
| | | | (MissLAPerratt) *chsd stands side ldrs: effrt 2f out: kpt on fnl f* | **20/1** | |
| 2411 | 3 | 1 ¼ | **Hout Bay**$^{19}$ 5107 7-9-6 67 | PHanagan 22 | 71 |
| | | | (RAFahey) *midfield stands side: rdn 1/2-way: effrt over 1f out: kpt on: nrst fin* | **13/2**$^{2}$ | |
| 0102 | 4 | hd | **Kings College Boy**$^{5}$ 5458 4-9-7 68 (b) | DaleGibson 1 | 71 |
| | | | (RAFahey) *cl up far side: rdn to ld that gp ins fnl f: kpt on: hld by stands side* | **14/1** | |
| 3024 | 5 | shd | **Sharp Hat**$^{30}$ 4828 10-9-2 63 | ACulhane 5 | 66 |
| | | | (DWChapman) *led far side to ins fnl f: kpt on same pce* | **25/1** | |
| 5060 | 6 | hd | **Sessay**$^{11}$ 5316 3-9-3 65 | PMQuinn 16 | 67 |
| | | | (DNicholls) *towards rr stands side: hdwy 2f out: r.o fnl f* | **33/1** | |
| 0312 | 7 | nk | **Mister Mal (IRE)**$^{19}$ 5107 8-8-11 58 | JFanning 3 | 59 |
| | | | (BEllison) *dwlt: sn in tch far side: ev ch that gp over 1f out: nt qckn* | **10/1** | |
| 0605 | 8 | 1 ¼ | **Brantwood (IRE)**$^{19}$ 5107 4-8-8 55 (t) | GGibbons 12 | 51 |
| | | | (BAMcmahon) *midfield stands side: rdn 1/2-way: r.o fnl f: no imp* | **16/1** | |
| 2121 | 9 | 1 | **Trojan Flight**$^{14}$ 5242 3-9-5 67 | RWinston 19 | 60 |
| | | | (MrsJRRamsden) *hld up stands side: rdn and effrt 2f out: nt pce to chal* | **3/1**$^{1}$ | |
| 5003 | 10 | ½ | **Sweet Cando (IRE)**$^{20}$ 5094 3-8-11 59 (p) | DHolland 20 | 50 |
| | | | (MissLAPerratt) *hld up stands side: rdn 1/2-way: no imp* | **50/1** | |
| 5052 | 11 | hd | **Aahgowangowan (IRE)**$^{20}$ 5101 5-9-2 63 (t) | SWKelly 23 | 53 |
| | | | (MDods) *led stands side to wl over 1f out: nt qckn* | **16/1** | |
| 0202 | 12 | hd | **Blue Power (IRE)**$^{27}$ 4929 3-8-12 60 | DarrenWilliams 2 | 49 |
| | | | (KRBurke) *chsd far side ldrs tl rdn and no ex over 1f out* | **50/1** | |
| 1032 | 13 | hd | **Ballybunion (IRE)**$^{10}$ 5346 5-8-7 54 | ANicholls 24 | 43 |
| | | | (DNicholls) *bhd stands side tl hdwy over 1f out: n.d* | **9/1**$^{3}$ | |
| 0043 | 14 | nk | **Mystery Pips**$^{44}$ 4422 4-8-7 54 oh9 (v) | KimTinkler 21 | 42 |
| | | | (NTinkler) *chsd stands side ldrs tl outpcd wl over 1f out* | **100/1** | |
| 5505 | 15 | ½ | **Robwillcall**$^{5}$ 5452 4-8-7 54 oh7 | PBradley 6 | 40 |
| | | | (ABerry) *chsd far side ldrs tl outpcd wl over 1f out* | **100/1** | |
| 0633 | 16 | shd | **William's Well**$^{10}$ 5346 10-8-8 55 (b) | KDarley 14 | 41 |
| | | | (MWEasterby) *midfield stands side: outpcd 1/2-way: n.d after* | **20/1** | |
| 6530 | 17 | hd | **College Maid (IRE)**$^{14}$ 5242 7-8-7 57 (v) | NMackay$^{(3)}$ 7 | 42 |
| | | | (JSGoldie) *bhd far side: rdn 1/2-way: n.d* | **33/1** | |
| 2000 | 18 | ¾ | **Rectangle (IRE)**$^{5}$ 5458 4-9-5 66 | AlexGreaves 15 | 48 |
| | | | (DNicholls) *prom stands side tl hung lft and outpcd fr 2f out* | **50/1** | |
| 40-0 | 19 | ¾ | **Las Ramblas (IRE)**$^{5}$ 5452 7-8-8 54 oh6 ow4 (tp) | DNolan$^{(3)}$ 25 | 37 |
| | | | (DANolan) *bhd stands side: nvr on terms* | **100/1** | |
| 0000 | 20 | 1 | **Regal Song (IRE)**$^{19}$ 5107 8-8-13 60 (b) | DMcGaffin 4 | 36 |
| | | | (TJEtherington) *bhd far side: effrt u.p over 2f out: sn no imp* | **100/1** | |
| 0601 | 21 | shd | **Mutayam**$^{10}$ 5342 4-8-2 54 3ex oh3 (t) | PPMathers$^{(5)}$ 10 | 29 |
| | | | (DANolan) *in tch far side tl wknd fr 2f out* | **66/1** | |
| 0410 | 22 | 1 | **Roman Mistress (IRE)**$^{19}$ 5107 4-9-5 66 (b) | TLucas 17 | 38 |
| | | | (TDEasterby) *dwlt: a bhd stand side* | **33/1** | |
| 5000 | 23 | 2 ½ | **Spy Master**$^{52}$ 4185 6-8-4 54 oh19 (tp) | HayleyTurner$^{(3)}$ 18 | 17 |
| | | | (JParkes) *a bhd stands side* | **100/1** | |
| 0000 | 24 | hd | **Viewforth**$^{19}$ 5126 6-8-12 59 (b) | CCatlin 9 | 21 |
| | | | (JSGoldie) *hld up far side: rdn and wknd fr 1/2-way* | **14/1** | |
| 5006 | 25 | 2 ½ | **Champagne Cracker**$^{27}$ 4904 3-9-0 62 | JCarroll 8 | 15 |
| | | | (MissLAPerratt) *hld up far side: rdn 1/2-way: sn btn* | **100/1** | |
| 2000 | 26 | dist | **Silver Mascot**$^{33}$ 4751 5-8-7 57 | TEaves$^{(3)}$ 11 | — |
| | | | (ISemple) *bolted bef s: racd stands side: lost tch fr 1/2-way* | **66/1** | |

60.19 secs (-0.24) **Going Correction** +0.05s/f (Good)

**WFA** 3 from 4yo+ 1lb **26** Ran SP% **126.2**

Speed ratings: **103,102,100,99,99 98,98,96,95,94 94,93,93,93,92 92,91,90,89,87 87,86,82,81,77** —CSF £870.61 CT £4147.30 TOTE £96.60: £15.80, £5.40, £2.30, £3.90; EX 604.10 TRIFECTA Not won..

**Owner** Nigel Shields **Bred** Red House Stud **Trained** Southwell, Notts

**FOCUS**

Solid handicap form, but a shock winner in Blueberry Rhyme, who led them home on what appeared to be the slightly favoured stands' side.

**NOTEBOOK**

**Blueberry Rhyme** has been well held in recent starts, but bounced back to form with a bang from his good draw, causing a huge upset in the process. This was his first-ever success in handicap company and, if he is able to build on it, may be able to win again for current connections. *Official explanation: trainer said, regarding the improved form shown, gelding appreciated today's softer going*

**Strawberry Patch(IRE)** has been in good form of late and ran another fine race. Despite being 4lb higher than when winning at Newbury, he should continue to run well.

**Hout Bay** is another in-form sprinter and he was gaining with every stride at the line. He was running from out of the handicap and has not finished winning yet.

**Kings College Boy**, a stablemate of the third, 'won' the race far side and deserves some credit. He should continue to run well.

**Sharp Hat** took them along on the far side and stuck to the task well.

**Sessay** was finishing to good effect and, despite still being a maiden, will get his head in front eventually.

**Silver Mascot** *Official explanation: jockey said gelding ran flat after bolting to the start*

## 5580 AUDI TT CHASE EUROPEAN BREEDERS FUND NOVICE STKS 1m

**3:10** (3:11) (D2) 2-Y-O **£5,408** (£1,664; £832; £416) **Stalls** Low

| Form | | | Horse | Jockey | RPR |
|---|---|---|---|---|---|
| 311 | 1 | | **Thunderwing (IRE)**$^{20}$ 5082 2-9-4 91 | DarrenWilliams 5 | 93+ |
| | | | (KRBurke) *trckd ldng pair: hdwy to ld wl over 2f out: drvn clr fnl f* | **7/4**$^{1}$ | |
| 51 | 2 | 2 ½ | **Rocamadour**$^{18}$ 5142 2-9-2 88 | ACulhane 3 | 86 |
| | | | (MRChannon) *trckd ldr: hdwy and ev ch over 2f out: one pce fnl f* | **9/4**$^{2}$ | |
| 015 | 3 | 1 ½ | **Fenrir**$^{19}$ 5128 2-9-2 83 | RWinston 4 | 83 |
| | | | (JRWeymes) *hld up in tch: hdwy and ch 2f out: outpcd fnl f* | **25/1**$^{3}$ | |
| 515 | 4 | ½ | **Melrose Avenue (USA)**$^{26}$ 4959 2-9-5 | JFanning 1 | 85 |
| | | | (MJohnston) *wnt rt s and hung rt thrght: led to wl over 2f out: sn outpcd: n.d after* | **7/4**$^{1}$ | |

1m 44.63s (1.51) **Going Correction** +0.05s/f (Good) **4** Ran SP% **107.3**

Speed ratings: **94,91,90,89**CSF £5.90 TOTE £3.00; EX 6.00.

**Owner** Market Avenue Racing Club Ltd **Bred** Agricola Del Parco **Trained** Middleham Moor, N Yorks

**FOCUS**

With Melrose Avenue disappointing again, Thunderwing might not have achieved as much as first impressions suggest. Nevertheless, he remains a progressive colt who could win at a higher level given these conditions.

**NOTEBOOK**

**Thunderwing(IRE)**, a promising third on his debut before winning the next twice, acts well with cut in the ground and was able to make it three in a row. He ultimately did not beat much, as Melrose Avenue ran below par, but is going the right way and deserves a crack at a better race.

**Rocamadour** improved on maiden form and stuck to his task well in second. He is on a stiff mark for what he has actually achieved.

**Fenrir** ran better than his odds suggested he would and was still there with every chance two out. He is quietly progressive but will not find life easy in nurseries.

**Melrose Avenue(USA)**, regarded earlier in the season as one of his powerful stable's better juveniles, has run shockingly the last twice now, and the fact he has hung on both occasions suggests he may have a problem of some sort. *Official explanation: jockey said colt hung right handed throughout*

## 5581 NEW AYR AUDI "PREMIER" CLAIMING STKS 1m 1f 20y

**3:40** (3:43) (D2) 3-Y-0+ **£7,033** (£2,164; £1,082; £541) **Stalls** Low

| Form | | | Horse | Jockey | RPR |
|---|---|---|---|---|---|
| 1211 | 1 | | **The Prince**$^{3}$ 5514 10-9-2 79 | CCatlin 7 | 70+ |
| | | | (IanWilliams) *bhd: hdwy centre over 2f out: led ins fnl f: r.o wl* | **7/4**$^{1}$ | |
| 4346 | 2 | 1 ¼ | **Donna's Double**$^{17}$ 5187 9-8-10 49 (p) | KDarley 17 | 61 |
| | | | (DEddy) *prom: effrt over 2f out: chal over 1f out to ins fnl f: kpt on* | **25/1** | |
| 5304 | 3 | 1 | **Cherished Number**$^{11}$ 5315 5-9-10 70 (p) | RWinston 2 | 73 |
| | | | (ISemple) *in tch: effrt over 2f out: r.o fnl f* | **10/1** | |
| 4210 | 4 | hd | **Yenaled**$^{3}$ 5514 7-9-5 72 | NCallan 8 | 68 |
| | | | (KARyan) *hld up: hdwy 2f out: rdn and r.o fnl f* | **10/1** | |
| 4020 | 5 | ½ | **Cat's Whiskers**$^{16}$ 5211 5-9-10 79 | DaleGibson 10 | 72 |
| | | | (MWEasterby) *cl up: led over 2f out to ins fnl f: no ex* | **7/1**$^{3}$ | |
| 2245 | 6 | 2 | **Spree Vision**$^{23}$ 4830 8-8-10 47 (v) | PHanagan 3 | 54 |
| | | | (PMonteith) *midfield: effrt and cl up over 2f out: one pce fnl f* | **66/1** | |
| 0545 | 7 | ½ | **York Cliff**$^{208}$ 844 6-8-11 76 | PPMathers$^{(5)}$ 14 | 59 |
| | | | (WMBrisbourne) *bhd tl hdwy over 1f out: n.d* | **14/1** | |
| 0654 | 8 | hd | **Scotty's Future (IRE)**$^{3}$ 5514 6-9-10 72 | JFanning 9 | 66 |
| | | | (DNicholls) *hld up: hdwy 2f out: no imp fnl f* | **12/1** | |
| 0346 | 9 | 4 | **Sarraaf (IRE)**$^{3}$ 5514 8-9-2 64 | ACulhane 12 | 50 |
| | | | (JSGoldie) *hld up midfield: effrt over 2f out: sn outpcd* | **20/1** | |
| 4000 | 10 | ½ | **Pas De Surprise**$^{1}$ 5557 6-8-8 50 ow1 | DNolan$^{(3)}$ 5 | 44 |
| | | | (PDEvans) *cl up tl wknd over 2f out* | **50/1** | |

0040 **11** *2* **Soller Bay**[19] [5127] 7-9-5 69 .......... DarrenWilliams 4 48
(KRBurke) *led to over 2f out: sn rdn and btn* **25/1**

0602 **12** *1 1/2* **Travelling Band (IRE)**[18] [5151] 6-9-8 72 .......... (v) DHolland 11 48
(AMBalding) *hld up: rdn over 2f out: sn btn* **6/1[2]**

4000 **13** *shd* **Crathorne (IRE)**[12] [5303] 4-9-7 71 .......... (p) NMackay(3) 15 50
(JDBethell) *hld up: rdn over 3f out: sn btn* **16/1**

5630 **14** *6* **Ben Hur**[18] [5151] 5-9-2 72 .......... SWKelly 13 30
(WMBrisbourne) *cl up tl wknd over 2f out* **20/1**

0005 **15** *8* **Business Matters (IRE)**[14] [5239] 4-9-2 .......... HayleyTurner(3) 6 17
(MsRebeccaBowden, Ire) *towards rr: rdn 4f out: sn btn* **100/1**

/600 **16** *dist* **Axford Lord**[27] [4905] 4-8-9 45 .......... (v) TEaves(3) 1 —
(ACWhillans) *keen: prom to 4f out: sn btn* **100/1**

**17** *dist* **Lexicon** 4-9-5 .......... JCarroll 16 —
(MissLucindaVRussell) *s.v.s: t.o thrght* **150/1**

2m 0.63s (4.09) **Going Correction** +0.325s/f (Good) **17** Ran SP% **124.9**
Speed ratings: **94,92,92,91,91 89,89,88,85,84 83,81,81,76,69** —,—CSF £61.30 TOTE £2.60: £1.50, £4.40, £3.40; EX 59.50.
**Owner** Patrick Kelly **Bred** Bottisham Heath Stud **Trained** Portway, Warwicks

**FOCUS**
A decent claimer, but a modest time for the grade and the sixth anchors the form.

**NOTEBOOK**
**The Prince** has had a fruitful season in this company and was recording his fourth win of the season. Although he has a reputation of being a bit soft, he seems in great spirits and could easily win again.
**Donna's Double** ran a good race and was only claimed in the final furlong. The winner had a ton in hand on him at the weights so this has to go down as an excellent effort.
**Cherished Number** has been a bit disappointing this season, not being able to get his head in front, and he still seems to find it hard enough going in this company. He should win one eventually however.
**Yenaled** was doing his best work at the finish.
**Cat's Whiskers** was a little disappointing and remains without a win in over two years.
**York Cliff** was unlucky not to get closer as he had nowhere to go when trying to come with a run. If going the right way from this seasonal debut, he should have little trouble winning in this grade.
**Travelling Band(IRE)** continues to frustrate and failed to run to form with The Prince.
**Lexicon** *Official explanation: jockey said filly hung right throughout*

## 5582 AUDI A8 CLASSIC H'CAP 1m

**4:10** (4:11) (D2) (0-85,80) 3-Y-O **£6,851** (£2,108; £1,054; £527) **Stalls** Low

Form RPR

0411 **1** **Eboracum (IRE)**[15] [5223] 3-9-2 **75** .......... (b) KDarley 10 82
(TDEasterby) *cl up: led over 2f out: styd on gamely* **7/1[3]**

1500 **2** *1* **Showtime Annie**[9] [5370] 3-8-7 **66** oh5 .......... RWinston 4 71
(ABailey) *trckd ldrs: effrt over 2f out: r.o fnl f* **25/1**

4114 **3** *1 1/2* **Silverhay**[32] [4780] 3-8-13 **72** .......... JFanning 5 74
(TDBarron) *led to over 2f out: kpt on same pce fnl f* **11/2[2]**

1002 **4** *3/4* **Alfonso**[19] [5120] 3-9-4 **77** .......... DHolland 8 78
(BWHills) *hld up: hdwy centre over 1f out: nvr able to chal* **6/4[1]**

6431 **5** *3/4* **Tytheknot**[17] [5189] 3-9-1 **74** .......... (p) PHanagan 7 73
(JeddO'Keeffe) *hld up: hdwy 3f out: rdn and one pce fr 2f out* **25/1**

3410 **6** *1 1/4* **Bright Sun (IRE)**[19] [5120] 3-9-0 **73** .......... KimTinkler 6 70
(NTinkler) *plld hrd: in tch: rdn 2f out: sn one pce* **10/1**

1112 **7** *3* **She's Our Lass (IRE)**[27] [4902] 3-9-0 **80** .......... DTudhope(7) 11 71
(DCarroll) *hld up: hdwy outside over 2f out: btn over 1f out* **9/1**

3160 **8** *6* **Neon Blue**[14] [5244] 3-8-10 **72** .......... HayleyTurner(3) 2 51
(RMWhitaker) *trckd ldrs tl wknd fr 2f out* **25/1**

2-15 **9** *1 3/4* **West Highland Way (IRE)**[91] [3017] 3-9-2 **78** .......... TEaves(3) 3 53
(ISemple) *keen: hld up in tch: rdn 3f out: sn btn* **25/1**

40P1 **10** *2* **Poppys Footprint (IRE)**[12] [5304] 3-9-6 **79** .......... NCallan 1 50
(KARyan) *hld up: rdn 3f out: sn btn* **12/1**

05-0 **11** *dist* **Glencairn Star**[171] [1174] 3-8-4 **66** oh2 .......... NMackay(3) 9 —
(JSGoldie) *bhd: lost tch fr 1/2-way* **33/1**

1m 45.36s (2.24) **Going Correction** +0.325s/f (Good) **11** Ran SP% **113.0**
Speed ratings: **101,100,98,97,97 95,92,86,85,83** —CSF £169.41 CT £1042.30 TOTE £5.10: £1.90, £5.10, £2.20; EX 170.50.
**Owner** Mrs K Arton **Bred** Tullamaine Castle Stud **Trained** Great Habton, N Yorks

**FOCUS**
A tight handicap that was run at a reasonable pace and the form looks sound for the grade, although the presence of the runner-up raises doubts.

**NOTEBOOK**
**Eboracum(IRE)** was handy throughout and stuck to her task gamely from over a furlong out to run out a ready winner over trip that very much suits. This was her third straight success, so she is clearly progressing fast and could have more to offer still while in this current mood.
**Showtime Annie**, whose form had tailed off since scoring over course and distance in May, emerged as a real threat when pressing the winner late on, but she could not sustain her gallop to the line. This was a much-improved effort, considering she was 5lb out of the weights, and she looks to be hitting top form again.
**Silverhay** was soon taking taking them along at a reasonable gallop and deserves credit for keeping to his task once headed. He can find another race off this sort of mark, but looks vulnerable to an improver.
**Alfonso** got going all too late over this extra furlong and ultimately proved disappointing. A drop back to seven would very much suit and he is worthy of another chance when ridden more prominently.
**Tytheknot**, in the cheekpices for the first time, was travelling nicely three out, but could not quicken with the principals over this shorter trip. He should get closer when reverting to ten furlongs and is one to keep an eye on.
**Poppys Footprint(IRE)** *Official explanation: jockey said filly was unsuited by soft ground*

## 5583 ALLROAD CHALLENGE H'CAP 7f 50y

**4:40** (4:41) (E3) (0-70,70) 3-Y-O+ **£7,055** (£2,171; £1,085; £542) **Stalls** Low

Form RPR

0153 **1** **Locombe Hill (IRE)**[11] [5316] 8-8-8 **64** .......... DTudhope(7) 2 75
(NWilson) *keen: mde all: rdn and hld on wl fnl f* **7/1[2]**

1424 **2** *shd* **Northern Games**[9] [5364] 5-8-12 **61** .......... (b) NCallan 9 72
(KARyan) *plld hrd in midfield: smooth hdwy over 2f out: effrt and ev ch ins fnl f: jst hld* **14/1**

2400 **3** *2 1/2* **Sharoura**[14] [5242] 8-8-12 **64** .......... TEaves(3) 11 69
(RAFahey) *trckd ldrs: rdn over 2f out: one pce over 1f out* **25/1**

2020 **4** *5* **Bollin Edward**[11] [5316] 5-9-1 **64** .......... (v) ACulhane 6 56
(TDEasterby) *trckd ldrs: rdn over 2f out: one pce over 1f out* **16/1**

3026 **5** *1/2* **Downland (IRE)**[11] [5316] 8-9-3 **66** .......... KimTinkler 7 57
(NTinkler) *midfield: effrt over 2f out: kpt on fnl f: no imp* **12/1**

3163 **6** *2* **Pertemps Magus**[18] [5155] 4-9-0 **63** .......... (p) PHanagan 4 49
(RAFahey) *hld up midfield: rdn over 3f out: no imp fr 2f out* **7/1[2]**

3200 **7** *2* **Anthemion (IRE)**[3] [5518] 7-8-11 **60** .......... DMcGaffin 1 41
(MrsJCMcgregor) *prom tl outpcd fr 2f out* **50/1**

0143 **8** *3/4* **Branston Tiger**[17] [5201] 5-9-1 **64** .......... (v) DHolland 17 43
(PDEvans) *towards rr: rdn over 3f out: n.d* **10/1[3]**

4142 **9** *1/2* **Scotland The Brave**[27] [4903] 4-9-7 **70** .......... CCatlin 16 48
(JDBethell) *in tch tl wknd over 2f out* **14/1**

0034 **10** *1/2* **Rare Coincidence**[21] [5063] 3-8-8 **63** .......... (t) DNolan(3) 13 39
(RFFisher) *bhd: effrt over 2f out: n.d* **33/1**

2044 **11** *3* **Bundy**[62] [3923] 8-9-0 **63** .......... RWinston 8 32
(MDods) *hld up: effrt over 2f out: nvr able to chal* **25/1**

4242 **12** *6* **Roman Maze**[11] [5316] 4-8-12 **61** .......... SWKelly 3 15
(WMBrisbourne) *towards rr: rdn 1/2-way: sn btn* **10/1[3]**

0510 **13** *3 1/2* **Yorkshire Blue**[11] [5316] 5-8-9 **61** .......... NMackay(3) 14 6
(JSGoldie) *hld up: rdn 1/2-way: sn btn* **14/1**

0262 **14** *3 1/2* **Fair Shake (IRE)**[14] [5242] 4-9-6 **69** .......... (v) KDarley 5 5
(DEddy) *bhd: rdn 1/2-way: nvr on terms* **13/2[1]**

2042 **15** *10* **Merdiff**[28] [4877] 5-8-7 **61** .......... PPMathers(5) 10 —
(WMBrisbourne) *cl up tl wknd over 2f out* **14/1**

0000 **16** *2 1/2* **Sir Don (IRE)**[5] [5458] 5-8-12 **61** .......... ANicholls 18 —
(DNicholls) *dwlt: sn prom: rdn and wknd over 2f out* **33/1**

0200 **17** *14* **Desert Leader (IRE)**[11] [5316] 3-9-1 **67** .......... GGibbons 15 —
(BAMcmahon) *sn bhd: nvr on terms* **50/1**

0-01 **18** *3* **Constable Burton**[154] [1425] 3-8-13 **65** .......... JFanning 12 —
(MrsADuffield) *midfield: rdn over 3f out: sn btn* **33/1**

1m 33.76s (1.29) **Going Correction** +0.325s/f (Good)
**WFA** 3 from 4yo+ 3lb **18** Ran SP% **117.2**
Speed ratings: **105,104,102,96,95 93,91,90,89,89 85,78,74,70,59 56,40,37**CSF £89.08 CT £2355.35 TOTE £8.80: £2.10, £3.00, £7.10, £3.60; EX 238.70.
**Owner** Ian W Glenton **Bred** Rathbarry Stud **Trained** Malton, N Yorks

**FOCUS**
A modest handicap that saw the field well strung out at the finish. The form is ordinary but the first three came clear.

**NOTEBOOK**
**Locombe Hill(IRE)**, despite taking a pull early on, bravely made all to score a narrow success. He found plenty for pressure when pressed inside the final furlong, clearly relished the underfoot conditions and has done well since joining his current stable, but may be one to take on off a higher mark next time.
**Northern Games** came there with every chance travelling strongly two out, but try as he might could not get on top of the winner inside the closing stages. He remains in good form and a reproduction of this run should he him strike again at this level before too long.
**Sharoura** turned in an improved effort and was clear of the rest, but again shaped as though this trip is slightly beyond her.
**Bollin Edward** found little when asked for an effort and only kept on at the same pace. He is a very frustrating performer.
**Roman Maze** *Official explanation: jockey said gelding was unsuited by soft ground*
**Fair Shake(IRE)**, whose latest effort gave him an obvious chance in this, was never really going on this softer ground and ran well below par. *Official explanation: jockey said gelding was unsuited by soft ground*
**Merdiff** *Official explanation: jockey said gelding was unsuited by the soft ground*
**Sir Don(IRE)** *Official explanation: jockey said gelding was unsuited by soft ground*
**Constable Burton** *Official explanation: jockey said gelding had no more to give*

## 5584 AUDI A3 STKS (H'CAP) (FOR THE KILKERRAN CUP) 1m 2f 192y

**5:10** (5:13) (E3) (0-70,70) 3-Y-O+ **£3,250** (£1,000; £500; £250) **Stalls** Low

Form RPR

1311 **1** **Artistic Style**[20] [5085] 4-9-2 **68** .......... TEaves(3) 11 84+
(BEllison) *hld up midfield: hdwy to ld over 1f out: pushed out: comf* **10/3[1]**

4124 **2** *2 1/2* **Dance To My Tune**[14] [5245] 3-8-9 **65** .......... DaleGibson 16 74
(MWEasterby) *midfield: smooth hdwy 3f out: effrt and chsd wnr over 1f out: edgd rt ins fnl f: no ch w wnr* **14/1**

5063 **3** *2* **Champion Lion (IRE)**[124] [2120] 5-9-4 **67** .......... CCatlin 3 73
(MRChannon) *hld up: smooth hdwy 3f out: effrt over 1f out: r.o same pce fnl f* **11/1**

5501 **4** *6* **Lucayan Dancer**[23] [5021] 4-8-8 **57** .......... JFanning 12 52
(DNicholls) *in tch: smooth hdwy to dispute ld wl over 1f out: sn rdn and no ex* **8/1[3]**

3140 **5** *1/2* **Zandeed (IRE)**[3] [5518] 6-8-10 **59** .......... PFessey 8 54
(MissLAPerratt) *bhd: rdn over 3f out: hdwy over 1f out: sn no imp* **20/1**

345 **6** *1/2* **Kid'Z'Play (IRE)**[24] [4990] 8-8-13 **65** .......... (p) NMackay(3) 6 59
(JSGoldie) *sn led and mde most to over 2f out: sn outpcd* **12/1**

-024 **7** *2* **Loaded Gun**[15] [5229] 4-8-2 **56** oh2 .......... PPMathers(5) 2 46
(WMBrisbourne) *prom: effrt over 2f out: sn rdn and no ex* **20/1**

0105 **8** *5* **Maritime Blues**[10] [5344] 4-9-0 **63** .......... DeanMcKeown 14 45
(JGGiven) *hld up: rdn 3f out: nvr able to chal* **16/1**

0325 **9** *nk* **Jolizero**[18] [5159] 3-8-6 **62** .......... ACulhane 9 43
(PWChapple-Hyam) *chsd ldrs tl wknd over 2f out* **8/1[3]**

4103 **10** *hd* **Mount Benger**[19] [5129] 4-8-13 **62** .......... (p) RWinston 7 43
(RMBeckett) *hld up: rdn over 3f out: sn n.d* **14/1**

0000 **11** *3* **Lucky Largo (IRE)**[5] [5450] 4-8-0 **56** oh8 .......... (b) LeanneKershaw(7) 4 32
(MissLAPerratt) *keen: in tch tl rdn and wknd over 2f out* **100/1**

6-40 **12** *3* **The Fairy Flag (IRE)**[124] [2121] 6-8-5 **57** .......... (p) HayleyTurner(3) 18 28
(ABailey) *trckd ldrs: led over 2f out to over 1f out: sn btn* **25/1**

0416 **13** *5* **Giunchiglio**[5] [5459] 5-9-7 **70** .......... SWKelly 17 32
(WMBrisbourne) *bhd: rdn 4f out: sn btn* **33/1**

360- **14** *12* **Tarawan**[396] [4204] 8-9-7 **70** .......... (v) DHolland 10 12
(AMBalding) *bhd: rdn on outside 4f out: nvr on terms* **33/1**

3500 **15** *9* **King's Envoy (USA)**[20] [5085] 5-8-10 **59** .......... DMcGaffin 13 —
(MrsJCMcgregor) *hld up: rdn over 3f out: sn btn* **100/1**

2600 **16** *3* **Nakwa (IRE)**[62] [3902] 6-9-2 **65** .......... NCallan 15 —
(EJAlston) *disp ld to over 2f out: sn wknd* **20/1**

0000 **17** *13* **Repulse Bay (IRE)**[21] [5058] 6-8-7 **56** oh11 .......... KDarley 5 —
(JSGoldie) *sn lost tch: t.o* **33/1**

1552 **18** *4* **Calatagan (IRE)**[15] [5229] 5-9-6 **69** .......... PHanagan 1 —
(JMJefferson) *plld hrd: cl up tl wknd fr 3f out: eased whn no ch* **7/1[2]**

2m 29.46s (6.14) **Going Correction** +0.65s/f (Yiel)
**WFA** 3 from 4yo+ 7lb **18** Ran SP% **122.0**
Speed ratings: **103,101,99,95,95 94,93,89,89,89 87,84,81,72,65 63,54,51**CSF £44.51 CT £475.10 TOTE £4.00: £1.50, £2.60, £2.80, £2.70; EX 52.90 Place 6 £1,075.52, Place 5 £247.46.
**Owner** Mr & Mrs D A Gamble **Bred** Juddmonte Farms **Trained** Norton, N Yorks

**FOCUS**
A modest handicap, but the pace was sound and the form looks reliable for the class. Good efforts from the first three, who pulled well clear of the rest.

**NOTEBOOK**
**Artistic Style** ◆ readily quickened clear when asked to win his race approaching the final furlong and was not fully extended to score. He does love this soft ground and should improve again when upped to 12 furlongs. This was his fourth success in his last five outings and he is clearly progressing fast, so could well have a decent prize in him before the year is out.
**Dance To My Tune** travelled as well as the winner for most of the way, but could not match his turn of foot when asked up with him late on. This was a solid effort and reproduction of this form would be good enough to see her strike again, as long as there is cut in the ground.

**Champion Lion(IRE)** turned in a sound effort on this return from his 124-day absence. He is clearly on a fair mark at present and is entitled to improve for this outing, but has only scored once in 19 starts, and is generally one to take on.
**Lucayan Dancer** was still going well a the top of the straight, but lacked a change of gear when it mattered and was well held. He remains well treated on his best form and can be found easier opportunities at this level.
**Zandeed(IRE)** never looked a serious threat on this quick reappearance and may have found the ground against him.
**Maritime Blues** *Official explanation: jockey said gelding had no more to give*
**Jolizero** *Official explanation: jockey said gelding had no more to give*
**Repulse Bay(IRE)** *Official explanation: jockey said gelding had a breathing problem*
**Calatagan(IRE)** *Official explanation: jockey said gelding was unsuited by soft ground*
T/Jkpt: Not won. T/Plt: £1,478.30 to a £1 stake. Pool: £56,195.75. 27.75 winning tickets. T/Qpdt: £79.70 to a £1 stake. Pool: £3,700.30. 34.35 winning tickets. RY

## 4776 PONTEFRACT (L-H)

### Thursday, September 16

**OFFICIAL GOING: Firm**
The going was described as 'like the M62, no give at all'.
Wind: Slight 1/2 behind. Weather: Fine and sunny.

### 5585 BETFAIR.COM APPRENTICE SERIES (ROUND 4) H'CAP 1m 2f 6y
2:20 (2:20) (F4) (0-55,55) 3-Y-0+ £3,604 (£1,109; £554; £277) Stalls Low

Form RPR
0-40 **1** **Time Marches On**[199] 943 6-8-2 **40**............(t) NeilBrown(5) 14 48
(KGReveley) *stdd s: racd in last pl: hdwy on wd outside over 3f out: styd on to ld 1f out: drew clr* **20/1**
2503 **2** *5* **Islands Farewell**[20] 5080 4-8-9 **49**............ PJBenson(7) 3 48
(DNicholls) *in tch: kpt on appr fnl f: tk 2nd nr line* **8/1**
32-0 **3** *nk* **First Eagle**[258] 406 5-8-0 **40**............(v) HFellows(7) 6 38
(ALForbes) *mid-div: hdwy to go 2nd over 1f out: sn hdd: no ex* **22/1**
0-14 **4** *3/4* **Royal Indulgence**[12] 5285 4-9-1 **48**............ DFentiman 13 45
(WMBrisbourne) *s.s: hdwy on outer over 2f out: hung lft and one pce appr fnl f* **9/2**[2]
4500 **5** *3 1/2* **Turftanzer (GER)**[17] 5187 5-8-0 **40** oh10............(t) JaniceWebster(7) 4 30
(DonEnricoIncisa) *chsd ldrs: one pce fnl 2f* **50/1**
0000 **6** *nk* **Lucky Archer**[56] 4042 11-8-12 **45**............ CHaddon 12 34
(IanWilliams) *hld up in rr: hdwy 4f out: chsng ldrs on inner whn hmpd over 1f out: nt rcvr* **20/1**
0006 **7** *2 1/2* **Dubai Dreams**[24] 5002 4-8-7 **45**............(t) RJKilloran(5) 7 30
(SRBowring) *chsd ldrs: wnt 2nd over 3f out: wknd over 1f out* **9/1**
5000 **8** *3 1/2* **Tyzack (IRE)**[31] 4817 3-8-11 **55**............ KPierrepont(5) 9 33
(JBalding) *t.k.h: led after 1f: hdd over 1f out: sn wknd* **16/1**
2604 **9** *1/2* **Late Arrival**[34] 4698 7-8-7 **40**............ AMullen 1 17
(MDHammond) *bhd: pushed along 4f out: nvr on terms* **4/1**[1]
4000 **10** *21* **Banners Flying (IRE)**[14] 5243 4-8-9 **45**............ KGhunowa(3) 2 —
(DWChapman) *a in rea: lost tch over 2f out* **33/1**
-003 **11** *4* **Sixtilsix (IRE)**[26] 4941 3-8-6 **45**............ DeanWilliams 5 —
(HAlexander) *led 1f: chsd ldrs: lost pl 3f out: wl bhd fnl f* **16/1**
-000 **12** *16* **Reign Of Fire (IRE)**[15] 5222 3-8-11 **53**............ KMay(3) 8 —
(JWHills) *sn bhd and pushed along: lost tch over 2f out* **18/1**
-034 **13** *1 3/4* **Wake Up Henry**[98] 2802 3-8-9 **55**............(v[1]) RKingscote(7) 10 —
(RCharlton) *t.k.h: trckd ldrs: lost pl over 2f out: sn bhd* **6/1**[3]
0400 **U** **Dispol Evita**[36] 4642 5-8-12 **45**............ HPoulton 11 —
(JamiePoulton) *hld up towards rr: rn wd bnd: slipped and uns rdr 6f out* **9/1**

2m 12.5s (-1.41) **Going Correction** -0.10s/f (Good)
**WFA** 3 from 4yo+ 6lb **14** Ran SP% **119.4**
Speed ratings: **101,97,96,96,93 93,91,88,87,71 67,55,53,**—CSF £162.25 CT £3554.89 TOTE £25.60: £7.60, £2.50, £7.40; EX 219.50.
**Owner** Mrs M B Thwaites **Bred** Mrs M B Thwaites **Trained** Lingdale, N Yorks
■ A first winner for Keith Reveley who has taken the licence over from mother Mary.
■ Stewards Enquiry : K Pierrepont caution: careless riding

**FOCUS**
A 0-55 apprentice handicap, a seller in all but name, and they seemed to go off very fast and the first four home came from off the pace.

**NOTEBOOK**
**Time Marches On**, last seen in action in March when he was reported to have a breathing problem, was dropped in at the start and made his effort on the wide outside. The leaders had gone off very fast and in the end he swept clear.
**Islands Farewell**, a maiden after nine previous starts, stuck on to take second near the line and if anything appreciated the step up in trip.
**First Eagle**, absent since January, was having his first outing on turf since 2002. A maiden now after 27 starts, he usually plies his trade on the All-Weather, but both Southwell and Wolverhampton are out of action at present.
**Royal Indulgence**, 5lb higher than Ayr, is a habitual slow starter.
**Turftanzer(GER)**, whose sole win was over two years ago, was far from disgraced from 10lb out of the handicap.
**Lucky Archer**, a pensioner who has not won for over three years, was poking his head up the inner when chopped off. He might well have finished runner-up.
**Late Arrival**, whose two wins were over seven furlongs, never went a yard.

### 5586 REG VARDY ROTHERHAM RENAULT MEDIAN AUCTION MAIDEN STKS 5f
2:50 (2:52) (E3) 2-Y-0 £4,124 (£1,269; £634; £317) Stalls Low

Form RPR
**1** **Seamus Shindig** 2-9-0............ DaneO'Neill 5 87+
(HCandy) *str: cmpt: led early: w ldr: led 1f out: kpt on wl* **3/1**[2]
6043 **2** *3/4* **Alexia Rose (IRE)**[6] 5441 2-8-9 63............ WSupple 1 79
(ABerry) *swtg: hld up: effrt over 2f out: chal 1f out: no ex ins last* **12/1**
2 **3** *1 3/4* **Sam's Secret**[11] 5319 2-8-9............ FNorton 2 73
(JAGlover) *sn led: qcknd over 2f out: hdd 1f out: fdd ins last* **4/5**[1]
05 **4** *3/4* **Cesar Manrique (IRE)**[6] 5441 2-9-0............ MHills 4 75
(BWHills) *t.k.h: trckd ldrs: effrt 2f out: sn outpcd: styd on fnl f* **6/1**[3]
4 **5** *8* **Aynsley**[13] 5262 2-8-9............ MHenry 6 42
(MAJarvis) *w ldrs: drvn along over 2f out: lost pl over 1f out: eased and bhd* **12/1**

63.68 secs (-0.12) **Going Correction** -0.10s/f (Good) **5** Ran SP% **110.2**
Speed ratings: **96,94,92,90,78**CSF £32.08 TOTE £4.90: £1.40, £3.40; EX 70.40.
**Owner** Henry Candy **Bred** R S A Urquhart **Trained** Wantage, Oxon

**FOCUS**
A steady pace to past halfway but a first-time-out winner of some potential.

**NOTEBOOK**
**Seamus Shindig**, an April foal, is not very big but he is well put together. Despite looking to be feeling the very firm ground, in the end he did more than enough. His target is the sales race at Doncaster next month.
**Alexia Rose(IRE)**, having her second outing within a week, looked very light and was sweating. She went down fighting and must be as hard as nails. Now rated 73, she is the key to the value of the form.
**Sam's Secret** did not look as well as she had done at York and, after setting sail for home, she was leg weary near the line.
**Cesar Manrique(IRE)**, out of luck when behind Alexia Rose at Sandown, took a keen hold as a result of the lack of pace. Staying on when it was all over, he either needs a sixth furlong or an end-to-end gallop. He can now ply his trade in nursery company.
**Aynsley** did not improve at all on her initial outing and dropped right away in most disappointing fashion.

### 5587 JOHN AND DIANE'S 50TH BIRTHDAY BASH (S) H'CAP 1m 4y
3:20 (3:20) (F4) (0-55,52) 3-Y-0+ £3,604 (£1,109; £554; £277) Stalls Low

Form RPR
2060 **1** **Vermilion Creek**[41] 4511 5-8-13 **49**............(p) KFallon 15 58
(RHollinshead) *hld up and bhd: hdwa on outer over 2f out: styd on to ld last 50yds* **6/1**[1]
2061 **2** *nk* **Rymer's Rascal**[12] 5305 12-8-12 **48**............ WSupple 8 56
(EJAlston) *hld up in mid-div: hdwy over 2f out: led 1f out: hdd and no ex towards fin* **8/1**[3]
5005 **3** *1 1/2* **Encounter**[19] 5129 8-8-2 **45**............ DFentiman(7) 3 50+
(JHetherton) *hld up in mid-div: hdwy and nt clr run over 1f out: styd on ins last* **7/1**[2]
0005 **4** *hd* **Super Dominion**[27] 4925 7-8-11 **47**............(p) DaneO'Neill 4 51
(RHollinshead) *hld up and bhd: hdwy on outer over 2f out: edgd lft over 1f out: kpt on same pce ins last* **20/1**
5555 **5** *2 1/2* **Dancing King (IRE)**[7] 5408 8-8-7 **48**............ PMakin(5) 1 46
(PWHiatt) *led tl 1f out: fdd* **9/1**
0000 **6** *2* **Delta Lady**[5] 5451 3-8-0 **40**............ MHenry 7 34
(RBastiman) *bhd: gd hdwy and hung lft over 1f out: nvr rchd ldrs* **50/1**
0601 **7** *1 1/4* **Alpine Hideaway (IRE)**[26] 4624 11-8-13 **49**............(p) GParkin 19 40
(JSWainwright) *chsd ldrs: drvn along over 2f out: wknd appr fnl f* **16/1**
4004 **8** *3/4* **Tancred Arms**[43] 4447 8-7-11 **40**............(v) DonnaCaldwell(7) 11 29
(DWBarker) *s.s: hdwy on wd outside 2f out: nvr nr ldrs* **25/1**
0-05 **9** *1 1/4* **Wonder Wolf**[39] 4573 3-8-8 **48**............ RFfrench 18 34
(RAFahey) *chsd ldrs: wknd over 1f out* **12/1**
0201 **10** *shd* **Naughty Girl (IRE)**[10] 5336 4-8-13 **52** 6ex............(vt) FPFerris(3) 5 38
(PDEvans) *chsd ldrs: wknd over 1f out* **9/1**
1-03 **11** *3/4* **Millkom Elegance**[17] 4605 5-8-2 **45**............(b) AMullen(7) 12 29
(KARyan) *mid-div: hdwy over 2f out: wknd over 1f out* **7/1**[2]
0000 **12** *3* **Dispol Verity**[61] 3954 4-8-5 **41** ow1............ SHitchcott 2 18
(WMBrisbourne) *in tch: effrt over 2f out: lost pl over 1f out* **33/1**
0004 **13** *3/4* **Summer Special**[17] 5187 4-8-9 **45**............ LEnstone 17 21
(DWBarker) *chsd ldrs: sn rdn along: lost pl over 1f out* **20/1**
3505 **14** *nk* **Ace-Ma-Vahra**[24] 5000 6-8-4 **40**............ JBramhill 10 15
(SRBowring) *mid-div: drvn along over 4f out: nvr a factor* **16/1**
4500 **15** *6* **Transcendantale (FR)**[12] 5305 6-8-1 **40**............ RThomas(3) 14 1
(MrsSLamyman) *a in rr* **16/1**
6000 **16** *3* **Peartree House (IRE)**[31] 4818 10-8-4 **40**............ NPollard 13 —
(DWChapman) *chsd ldrs: lost pl 2f out* **20/1**
-600 **17** *2 1/2* **Delightful Gift**[76] 3471 4-8-9 **45**............ TWilliams 16 —
(MBrittain) *chsd ldrs: wkng whn heavily eased appr fnl f* **50/1**

1m 45.55s (-0.05) **Going Correction** -0.10s/f (Good)
**WFA** 3 from 4yo+ 4lb **17** Ran SP% **120.7**
Speed ratings: **96,95,94,94,91 89,88,87,86,86 85,82,81,81,75 72,69**CSF £46.37 CT £359.59 TOTE £4.50: £1.90, £2.10, £1.70, £6.80; EX 34.80.There was no bid for the winner.
**Owner** M Johnson **Bred** R Hollinshead And M Johnson **Trained** Upper Longdon, Staffs

**FOCUS**
An ordinary seller run at a strong early gallop and the first four home came from off the pace. The second provides the key to the form, which looks reasonable.

**NOTEBOOK**
**Vermilion Creek**, with the cheekpieces back on, wanted no part of the fast and furious pace. Picking up ground on the outside, she put her head in front where it really matters. No one rides this track better than the champion.
**Rymer's Rascal**, a sprightly veteran, possibly hit the front sooner than expected and was edged out near the line.
**Encounter**, who needs everything to fall just right, met traffic problems and in the end did well to finish on the heels of the first two.
**Super Dominion**, stablemate of the winner, gave a good account of himself but, while Southwell and Wolverhampton are out of action, banded racing looks his best shot.
**Dancing King(IRE)** went off like Paula Radcliffe and it was just a question of time before he was reeled in. At least he completed the course!
**Delta Lady**, a handful going to the start, looks a real madam but this was her best effort for some time.
**Alpine Hideaway(IRE)** was last seen in action finishing second in a selling hurdle at Market Rasen.

### 5588 DIXON RENAULT FILLIES' STKS (H'CAP) 6f
3:50 (3:50) (D2) (0-85,83) 3-Y-0+ £6,795 (£2,091; £1,045; £522) Stalls Low

Form RPR
1005 **1** **Saristar**[18] 5148 3-9-4 **82**............ KFallon 2 97+
(PFICole) *led 1f: led over 2f out: clr 1f out: r.o wl* **5/1**[3]
4216 **2** *2 1/2* **Maddie's A Jem**[18] 5157 4-8-13 **75**............ WRyan 1 82
(JRJenkins) *hld up in rr: hdwy on ins over 1f out: styd on to take 2nd ins last: no ch w wnr* **8/1**
0600 **3** *1/2* **Favour**[54] 4134 4-8-7 **69** oh2............ JFEgan 3 75+
(MrsJRRamsden) *hld up: hdwy and nt clr run over 1f out: styd on ins last* **7/1**
0100 **4** *1 1/4* **Obe Bold (IRE)**[17] 5193 3-8-5 **69** oh2............ FNorton 6 71
(ABerry) *chsd ldrs: drvn along over 2f out: one pce* **25/1**
0006 **5** *3/4* **Impressive Flight (IRE)**[4] 5491 5-9-7 **83**............ WSupple 8 83
(TDBarron) *dwlt: hdwy and nt clr run over 1f out: kpt on ins last: nvr nr ldrs* **7/2**[1]
3231 **6** *2* **Lake Charlotte (USA)**[19] 5104 3-8-6 **70**............(t) NPollard 7 64
(DRLoder) *t.k.h: hdwy over 2f out: wknd fnl f* **13/2**
2421 **7** *1/2* **Complication**[72] 3606 4-8-8 **70**............(b) LisaJones 9 62
(JARToller) *lost pl after 2f: n.d after* **4/1**[2]
0460 **8** *8* **Consensus (IRE)**[19] 5107 5-8-9 **71**............ TWilliams 5 39
(MBrittain) *t.k.h: led after 1f: hdd over 2f out: hung lft and lost pl over 1f out: eased* **8/1**

40-0 **9** *1* **Scarlet Empress**[34] 4717 3-8-7 71 ...................................... DaneO'Neill 4 36
(RHannon) *chsd ldrs: rdn over 2f out: lost pl over 1f out* **33/1**

1m 16.41s (-0.89) **Going Correction** -0.10s/f (Good)
**WFA** 3 from 4yo+ 2lb **9** Ran SP% **113.7**
Speed ratings: **101,97,97,95,94 91,91,80,79**CSF £43.74 CT £230.05 TOTE £4.50: £1.80, £2.70, £2.60; EX 53.90.
**Owner** R A Instone **Bred** R A Instone **Trained** Whatcombe, Oxon

**FOCUS**
They went no great pace and the winner rather stole the race at the head of the straight. The impression is that the form is not that strong.

**NOTEBOOK**
**Saristar**, who had failed to stay seven furlongs on her two most recent runs, kicked on entering the straight and soon had her race won. She seems pretty versatile when it comes to ground conditions.
**Maddie's A Jem**, returning to this trip, made good progress along the inside rail once in line for home but the winner had already flown.
**Favour**, back down to this trip, was a couple of pounds out of the handicap. A keen filly, and no easy ride, she was going on at the finish after having to wait for a clear run, but the winner was beyond recall.
**Obe Bold(IRE)** gained her Redcar win last month off 7lb lower, including the 2lb she was out of the handicap here, and this was a respectable effort.
**Impressive Flight(IRE)** was slowly away, as is often the case, and needed to be switched right to get a run in the short home straight. She is well handicapped now, having begun the season 11lb higher, and there will be other days for her.
**Lake Charlotte(USA)**, who had her tongue tied down, won only a poor maiden at Beverley and was found wanting on this handicap bow. An easy six furlongs could be her optimum trip.
**Complication** had been absent since landing a better race than this over course and distance in July from a 5lb lower mark.

## 5589 PHIL BULL TROPHY CONDITIONS STKS — 2m 1f 216y
4:20 (4:20) (C2) 3-Y-0+ **£9,210** (£3,405; £1,702; £774) **Stalls** Low

Form RPR
1666 **1** **Corrib Eclipse**[7] 5415 5-9-10 106 ...................................... JFEgan 4 102+
(JamiePoulton) *trckd ldr: led 5f out: rdn over 2f out: styd on wl fnl f* **6/4**[1]
/0-0 **2** *1 3/4* **Pushkin (IRE)**[12] 5288 6-9-2 100 ...................................... KFallon 2 93+
(MJohnston) *hld up: effrt over 3f out: wnt 2nd over 2f out: 1 l down 1f out: no real imp* **3/1**[3]
4332 **3** *15* **Vicars Destiny**[20] 5100 6-8-11 64 ...................................... DaneO'Neill 5 71
(MrsSLamyman) *hld up in last pl: hdwy to chse ldrs 5f out: wl outpcd fnl 3f* **16/1**
12-0 **4** *10* **One Off**[25] 4977 4-9-2 90 ...................................... JMackay 6 65
(SirMarkPrescott) *trckd ldrs: chal 5f out: wknd over 2f out: sn bhd* **2/1**[2]
4445 **5** *21* **Jamaican Flight (USA)**[124] 2126 11-8-13 45 .................. RThomas(3) 1 42
(MrsSLamyman) *led tl 5f out: sn lost pl: t.o 2f out* **25/1**

3m 57.07s (-5.93) **Going Correction** -0.10s/f (Good)
**WFA** 3 from 4yo+ 13lb **5** Ran SP% **108.1**
Speed ratings: **109,108,101,97,87**CSF £6.08 TOTE £2.10: £1.20, £1.90; EX 6.90.
**Owner** M Ioannou **Bred** J Godfrey **Trained** Telscombe, E Sussex

**FOCUS**
An uncompetitive conditions race, but the pace was sound and this was a good test of stamina.

**NOTEBOOK**
**Corrib Eclipse**, his stamina assured, was wound up passing the three-furlong pole and stayed on that bit stronger than the runner-up. He is not easy to place on the Flat, being a few pounds below Pattern level, but is an interesting novice hurdle prospect for the new season.
**Pushkin(IRE)**, beaten a head by Give Notice in the Group One Prix du Cadran at Longchamp two years ago when trained by Elie Lellouche, has had a spell in the Middle East since. Having his second run for Johnston, he delivered his challenge in the straight but found the favourite too tough a nut to crack.
**Vicars Destiny**, who had a great deal on at the weights, plugged on to finish a well-beaten third without ever threatening to take a hand.
**One Off** had 8lb to find with the winner on official figures. He challenged with five to run as the pacesetter dropped away, but was unable to get to the front and faded on the approach to the straight as his stamina gave out.
**Jamaican Flight(USA)**, having his first run for four months, had an impossible task at the weights, but did a good job of pacemaking before dropping away.

## 5590 HARRATTS RENAULT CLASSIFIED STKS — 1m 4y
4:50 (4:50) (D2) 3-Y-0+ **£6,938** (£2,135; £1,067; £533) **Stalls** Low

Form RPR
4046 **1** **Jay Gee's Choice**[17] 5177 4-9-2 82 ...................................... SHitchcott 8 90
(MRChannon) *led: qcknd over 3f out: hdd over 2f out: regained ld 1f out: hld on towards fin* **11/2**[3]
14 **2** *1/2* **Namroc (IRE)**[68] 3750 3-9-1 85 ...................................... KFallon 3 92+
(EFVaughan) *trckd ldrs: drvn along and outpcd over 2f out: styd on wl ins last: nt quite rch wnr* **11/8**[1]
3120 **3** *1/2* **Anna Pallida**[27] 4906 3-8-9 82 ...................................... DaneO'Neill 7 85
(PWHarris) *trckd ldr: chal over 3f out: led over 2f out: wandered and hdd 1f out: no ex ins last* **7/2**[2]
640 **4** *3 1/2* **Stoic Leader (IRE)**[7] 5419 4-9-0 78 ...................................... JFEgan 2 78
(RFFisher) *hld up: styd on fnl 2f: nvr on terms* **7/1**
1000 **5** *3 1/2* **Intricate Web (IRE)**[40] 4540 8-9-0 80 ...................................... WSupple 4 70
(EJAlston) *trckd ldrs: outpcd over 2f out: n.d after* **9/1**
1360 **6** *10* **Les Arcs (USA)**[17] 4831 4-9-0 76 ...................................... FNorton 6 47
(RCGuest) *t.k.h: trckd ldrs: lost pl over 2f out: wknd over 1f out* **12/1**
30-0 **7** *12* **Humid Climate**[27] 4908 4-9-0 78 ...................................... GParkin 1 19
(RAFahey) *v rel to r: a detached in last* **50/1**

1m 43.62s (-1.98) **Going Correction** -0.10s/f (Good)
**WFA** 3 from 4yo+ 4lb **7** Ran SP% **111.9**
Speed ratings: **105,104,104,100,97 87,75**CSF £12.92 TOTE £7.30: £2.80, £1.40; EX 17.60.
**Owner** John Guest **Bred** The Lavington Stud **Trained** West Ilsley, Berks

**FOCUS**
A decent classified stakes and fair form. The winner set a moderate pace until quickening things up with over three to run.

**NOTEBOOK**
**Jay Gee's Choice**, under a good ride from Hitchcott, who recently rode out his claim, rallied bravely after being headed to notch his first win for nearly two years. He appreciated the firm ground and had no problem with the mile.
**Namroc(IRE)** was a little outpaced by the leaders as the pace lifted but was keeping on strongly inside the last. One to keep on the right side, he will be suited by a stronger pace over this trip and promises to stay a bit farther.
**Anna Pallida** went on before the turn but was headed at the furlong pole. Battling on, but coming quite close to the winner and rolling about under pressure, she had no more to give in the last 50 yards and was caught for second too.
**Stoic Leader(IRE)** is holding his form well after a busy season but is not easy to place from his current mark.
**Intricate Web(IRE)**, who is more effective over ten furlongs, has gone off the boil in recent runs.
**Les Arcs(USA)** had run poorly over hurdles on his most recent appearance.

## 5591 LADY BALK MAIDEN STKS — 1m 2f 6y
5:20 (5:20) (D3) 3-Y-0+ **£5,629** (£1,732; £866; £433) **Stalls** Low

Form RPR
3332 **1** **Flamboyant Lad**[9] 5371 3-9-0 79 ...................................... MHills 2 89+
(BWHills) *trckd ldr: led over 2f out: clr 1f out: eased nr fin* **8/11**[1]
2302 **2** *10* **Magnetic Pole**[9] 5367 3-9-0 83 ...................................... (b[1]) KFallon 4 67+
(SirMichaelStoute) *led: shkn up over 2f out: fnd nthing and sn hdd* **6/4**[2]
0203 **3** *6* **Jidiya (IRE)**[13] 5267 5-9-6 68 ...................................... JFEgan 5 56
(SGollings) *trckd ldng pair: pushed along over 5f out: sn outpcd and nvr a threat* **14/1**[3]
0 **4** *dist* **Silloth Spirit**[10] 5345 4-9-6 ...................................... NPollard 1 —
(MrsAMNaughton) *s.i.s: pushed along after 3f: t.o 3f out* **125/1**
0 **5** *10* **Up The Aisle**[9] 5371 7-9-6 ...................................... LEnstone 3 —
(MMullineaux) *chsd ldrs: pushed along after 3f: sn lost tch: t.o 3f out* **100/1**

2m 10.55s (-3.36) **Going Correction** -0.10s/f (Good)
**WFA** 3 from 4yo+ 6lb **5** Ran SP% **106.4**
Speed ratings: **109,101,96,—,—**CSF £1.85 TOTE £1.70: £1.10, £1.10; EX 1.90 Place 6 £414.75, Place 5 £49.41.
**Owner** Maktoum Al Maktoum **Bred** Gainsborough Stud Management Ltd **Trained** Lambourn, Berks

**FOCUS**
An uncompetitive maiden and a match on paper, but run at a decent pace. Easy enough for the favourite, with his market rival putting up little resistance when headed.

**NOTEBOOK**
**Flamboyant Lad** deserved his win after a string of placed efforts and had no problem with the trip, but did not have to be at his best to score in this weakly-contested event.
**Magnetic Pole** raced rather freely in the first-time headgear and was quickly beaten once headed. He had a pound in hand of the favourite on official adjusted ratings, but is not going the right way and does not look one to rely on.
**Jidiya(IRE)** had plenty to find with the two three-year-olds on these terms and ran as well as could be expected, plugging on over a trip short of his best.
**Silloth Spirit** struggled past his fellow no-hoper on the home turn to pick up £433.
T/Plt: £699.30 to a £1 stake. Pool: £35,304.95. 36.85 winning tickets. T/Qpdt: £15.40 to a £1 stake. Pool: £3,544.00. 169.70 winning tickets. WG

# 5569 YARMOUTH (L-H)
Thursday, September 16

**OFFICIAL GOING: Good (good to soft in places)**
Wind: Fresh across Weather: Fine and sunny

## 5592 EUROPEAN BREEDERS FUND MAIDEN STKS — 1m 3y
2:30 (2:31) (D3) 2-Y-O **£5,099** (£1,569; £784; £392) **Stalls** High

Form RPR
0 **1** **Red Admiral (USA)**[27] 4922 2-9-0 ...................................... LDettori 10 89+
(SaeedBinSuroor) *trckd ldr tl led over 3f out: styd on wl* **6/1**[2]
0 **2** *2* **Clasp**[68] 3726 2-9-0 ...................................... RMullen 4 83
(MLWBell) *hld up: hdwy over 3f out: rdn over 2f out: styd on same pce fnl f* **13/2**[3]
20 **3** *nk* **Oligarch (IRE)**[8] 5392 2-9-0 ...................................... JPMurtagh 8 82
(NACallaghan) *a.p: chsd wnr 3f out: sn rdn: no ex ins fnl f* **5/6**[1]
**4** *nk* **Clueless** 2-9-0 ...................................... TPQueally 1 81+
(WJHaggas) *hld up: hdwy and hung rt over 1f out: r.o* **25/1**
**5** *6* **Force Nine (USA)** 2-9-0 ...................................... EAhern 6 68
(JNoseda) *dwlt: hld up: hdwy 1/2-way: wknd over 1f out* **16/1**
6 **6** *2* **Gidam Gidam (IRE)**[15] 5228 2-9-0 ...................................... RLMoore 9 64
(CEBrittain) *prom: rdn 1/2-way: wknd 2f out* **25/1**
**7** *1/2* **River Card** 2-8-9 ...................................... PRobinson 3 58
(MHTompkins) *hld up: nvr trbld ldrs* **33/1**
**8** *1* **Kahira (IRE)** 2-8-9 ...................................... SSanders 7 55
(MLWBell) *hld up: n.d* **20/1**
04 **9** *nk* **King Zafeen (IRE)**[12] 5302 2-9-0 ...................................... (t) TEDurcan 2 60
(MRChannon) *s.i.s: hld up: hdwy over 3f out: wknd over 1f out* **9/1**
0 **10** *7* **Prophet's Calling (IRE)**[52] 4198 2-9-0 ...................................... JMcAuley 11 44
(MissDAMchale) *led over 4f: wknd 2f out* **150/1**

1m 40.36s (0.66) **Going Correction** +0.10s/f (Good) **10** Ran SP% **114.1**
Speed ratings: **100,98,97,97,91 89,88,87,87,80**CSF £40.49 TOTE £5.40: £1.80, £2.10, £1.10; EX 58.10.
**Owner** Godolphin **Bred** Newgate Stud Farm **Trained** Newmarket, Suffolk

**FOCUS**
A decent pace for this maiden and the time was fair for the grade, mking the form look strong and reliable. The whole field raced down the stands' side of the track and the front four finished a long way clear of the rest.

**NOTEBOOK**
**Red Admiral(USA)**, a half-brother to six winners including Yorkshire, looked a different horse to the one who flopped so badly at Sandown on his debut. Content to get a lead until well past halfway, he then saw his race out much better than his nearest rivals and should go on from here.
**Clasp** improved a good deal on his Ascot debut, but although staying on was never going to get to the winner. He should be able to win an ordinary maiden.
**Oligarch(IRE)**, stepping up two furlongs in trip, not for the first time was well backed to get off the mark but was always being held by the winner despite holding every chance. He is not as good as some people obviously think he is.
**Clueless ◆**, a 26,000gns yearling out a full-sister to User Friendly, looked to need the experience and was off the bridle a long way out, but he was doing some sterling work over the last couple of furlongs and would have been second with a little further to go. He should be a different proposition next time.
**Force Nine(USA)**, who fetched 80,000gns as a two-year-old, ran a fair race until getting tired late on and ought to improve.
**River Card**, a half-sister to dual juvenile winner Light Fingered out of Light Hand, who won ten times including one over hurdles, was ultimately well beaten but also hinted at ability and can be expected to do better in time.

## 5593 RACING WELFARE (S) NURSERY — 1m 3y
3:00 (3:04) (G4) (0-65,64) 2-Y-O **£2,618** (£748; £374) **Stalls** High

Form RPR
0604 **1** **Lorna Dune**[9] 5369 2-9-3 60 ...................................... DSweeney 14 62
(JGMO'Shea) *racd stands' side: a.p: led over 1f out: rdn out* **10/1**[3]
6040 **2** *1 1/2* **Orpen Annie (IRE)**[9] 5369 2-8-13 59 ...................................... BReilly(3) 16 58
(MissJFeilden) *racd stands' side: hld up: hdwy over 2f out: sn rdn: hung lft and ev ch over 1f out: styd on same pce ins fnl f* **16/1**
0200 **3** *1/2* **Yeldham Lady**[12] 5281 2-8-7 50 ...................................... (p) JQuinn 15 48
(JPearce) *racd stands' side: hld up: hdwy over 2f out: rdn over 1f out: one pce ins fnl f* **12/1**

4506 **4** *3* **Tip Toes (IRE)**[34] 4699 2-7-9 **45** .......... TDean[(7)] 10 36
(MRChannon) *racd stands' side: chsd ldrs: led that gp over 5f out: rdn and hdd over 1f out: no ex* **40/1**

0203 **5** *2* **Debs Broughton**[9] 5369 2-8-13 **56** .......... RMullen 4 51+
(WJMusson) *racd far side: hld up: hdwy over 2f out: led that gp ins fnl f: no ch w stands' side* **8/1**[2]

6546 **6** *1 1/4* **Artadi**[9] 5369 2-8-7 **50** .......... (b) TPQueally 7 42+
(PMPhelan) *racd far side: chsd ldrs: led that gp 2f out: hdd and no ex ins fnl f* **12/1**

0400 **7** *3* **Lord Normacote**[9] 5369 2-9-3 **63** .......... (b[1]) J-PGuillambert[(3)] 13 40
(CADwyer) *racd stands' side: chsd ldrs: hung lft and wknd wl over 1f out* **33/1**

3600 **8** *3* **Tonight (IRE)**[9] 5369 2-8-9 **57** .......... BSwarbrick[(5)] 11 28
(WMBrisbourne) *led stands' side: hdd over 5f out: wknd over 2f out* **25/1**

4436 **9** *1 1/4* **Zolash (IRE)**[10] 5335 2-8-12 **62** .......... DerekNolan[(7)] 9 38+
(JSMoore) *racd far side: prom over 6f* **8/1**[2]

0506 **10** *1 1/4* **Dramatic Review (IRE)**[20] 5083 2-9-7 **64** .......... (p) GFaulkner 8 37+
(PCHaslam) *racd far side: chsd ldrs: led that gp 3f out to 2f out: sn wknd* **20/1**

0033 **11** *1 1/4* **Lara's Girl**[20] 5097 2-8-8 **51** .......... PDoe 12 13
(IAWood) *racd stands's ide: prom over 5f* **16/1**

056 **12** *1 1/4* **Champagne Rossini (IRE)**[24] 4997 2-9-3 **60** .......... RLMoore 2 28+
(MCChapman) *led far side 5f: wknd wl over 1f out* **20/1**

3610 **13** *1 1/2* **Lakesdale (IRE)**[2] 5548 2-9-1 **58** .......... OUrbina 5 22+
(MissDMountain) *racd far side: chsd ldrs over 5f* **8/1**[2]

6000 **14** *shd* **Sherbourne**[9] 5369 2-8-4 **47** .......... PaulEddery 3 11+
(MGQuinlan) *racd far side: bhd fnl 3f* **33/1**

01 **15** *1* **Beaumont Girl (IRE)**[20] 5097 2-8-12 **55** .......... LDettori 6 17+
(GASwinbank) *racd far side: hld up: hdwy over 3f out: wknd wl over 1f out* **15/8**[1]

0000 **16** *24* **Lord Chalfont (IRE)**[18] 5142 2-7-5 **41** oh11 .......... (b) MNem[(7)] 1 —
(MJPolglase) *racd far side: swvd lft s: sn prom: wknd 3f out* **150/1**

1m 42.8s (3.10) **Going Correction** +0.10s/f (Good) **16** Ran SP% **126.7**
Speed ratings: **88,86,86,83,81 79,76,73,72,71 70,68,67,67,66 42**CSF £154.79 CT £1219.52 TOTE £9.50: £2.20, £4.40, £2.10, £4.00; EX 162.50.The winner was bought in for 6,800gns.
**Owner** Gary Roberts **Bred** Mrs D O Joly **Trained** Elton, Gloucs

**FOCUS**
A poor two-year-old seller run in a time 2.44 seconds slower than the opening maiden, but still competitive thanks to the number of runners. The field split into two with a distinct advantage held by those on the stands' side.

**NOTEBOOK**
**Lorna Dune** had suggested in her most recent start, when she had several of these rivals behind her, that she would appreciate this longer trip and duly did so for her new connections. This was a poor race though, influenced by a significant track bias, and she will surely struggle outside this grade.
**Orpen Annie(IRE)**, who had finished just over a length behind Lorna Dune in her most recent start, was no better off at the weights and ran almost exactly to form with that rival. She seemed to stay the extra furlong well enough, but was another drawn on the right side as things turned out.
**Yeldham Lady** has been racing over six furlongs of late and, although she seemed to run well enough to make the frame over this trip, she may be a bit flattered given the way the race was run.
**Tip Toes(IRE)**, yet to make the first three in seven previous starts including several at this level, made much of the running against the stands' rail but was completely exposed for speed in the latter stages. With the advantage held by those who raced stands' side, her final placing flatters her somewhat.
**Debs Broughton**, who actually finished in front of Lorna Dune at Leicester before being demoted for interference, had no chance over on the far side of the track as things turned out, but deserves credit for leading that group home and looks well capable of winning a similar event.
**Artadi**, another in this field to have run in the Leicester selling nursery won by Amphitheatre, ran to an almost identical level of form using Debs Broughton as a guide, but like that rival was compromised by the track bias and should be rated a bit better than her finishing position.
**Zolash(IRE)** was third home over on the far side so deserves to be rated a little better than his finishing position, but he may be better suited by seven.
**Beaumont Girl(IRE)** *Official explanation: jockey said filly had a breathing problem*

## 5594 JOHN SLAPP BOOKMAKERS NORWICH NOVICE STKS 6f 3y
**3:30** (3:31) (D2) 2-Y-O **£6,747** (£2,076; £1,038; £519) **Stalls** High

Form RPR

130 **1** **Josh**[8] 5392 2-9-5 .......... PRobinson 4 91
(MAJarvis) *s.i.s: sn chsng ldrs: swtchd lft over 2f out: led over 1f out: sn edgd rt: rdn out* **10/3**[3]

21 **2** *nk* **Army Of Angels (IRE)**[50] 4239 2-9-5 .......... (t) LDettori 1 91
(SaeedBinSuroor) *trckd ldr: chal over 2f out: rdn whn hmpd 1f out: r.o* **10/11**[1]

1400 **3** *1 1/2* **Island Swing (IRE)**[17] 5202 2-8-13 78 .......... SDrowne 3 80
(JLSpearing) *hld up in tch: effrt over 1f out: styd on* **50/1**

1563 **4** *shd* **Roodeye**[14] 5250 2-8-11 96 .......... JPMurtagh 2 84+
(RFJohnsonHoughton) *led over 4f: hmpd 1f out: nt rcvr* **9/4**[2]

1m 14.8s (1.20) **Going Correction** +0.10s/f (Good) **4** Ran SP% **108.2**
Speed ratings: **96,95,93,93**CSF £6.88 TOTE £3.60; EX 6.60.
**Owner** T G & Mrs M E Holdcroft **Bred** Bearstone Stud **Trained** Newmarket, Suffolk
■ Stewards Enquiry : P Robinson three-day ban: careless riding (Sep 27-29)

**FOCUS**
A decent little event run at a sound pace, although the proximity of the 78-rated Island Swing casts doubt on the overall level of the form.

**NOTEBOOK**
**Josh**, who ran a decent race at Doncaster last time, is at his best with some cut in the ground. He edged right in the closing stages, causing Roodeye to be squeezed on the rail, but he won on merit and survived a Stewards' enquiry. He is likely to be stepped up in grade now, but his trainer reiterated that the colt needs soft ground to be seen at his best.
**Army Of Angels(IRE)**, who came here rather than contest a Listed race at Ayr the following day, travelled well and had his chance, but the winner had his measure when he edged right in front of him and, although he rallied, he never looked like making up the ground. Perhaps a faster surface would have suited him better.
**Island Swing(IRE)**, well held in nurseries of late, ran a good race at the weights, and her performance casts some doubt on the quality of the form.
**Roodeye**, placed in Listed company last time, showed plenty of speed next to the rail, but she had been passed when hampered a furlong out. She rallied again close home but the race was already effectively over.

## 5595 R M LEVITT "ANOTHER YEAR IN PRACTICE" H'CAP 2m
**4:00** (4:02) (D2) (0-85,85) 3-Y-O+ **£9,225** (£3,499; £1,749; £795) **Stalls** High

Form RPR

3605 **1** **High Point (IRE)**[20] 5093 6-9-0 **75** .......... JPMurtagh 7 83
(GPEnright) *a.p: rdn over 2f out: styd on to ld towards fin* **13/2**[3]

5010 **2** *1/2* **Astyanax (IRE)**[26] 4934 4-9-1 **76** .......... SSanders 12 83
(SirMarkPrescott) *chsd ldrs: led over 3f out: hrd rdn fnl f: hdd towards fin* **9/1**

1541 **3** *1* **Land 'n Stars**[5] 5472 4-9-10 **85** 6ex .......... PDoe 3 91
(JamiePoulton) *chsd ldrs: lost pl over 4f out: nt clr run 3f out: hdwy u.p over 1f out: styd on* **7/1**

1663 **4** *1* **Marine City (JPN)**[17] 5191 3-7-8 **72** .......... (p) DFox[(5)] 10 77
(MAJarvis) *mid-div: rn in snatches: dropped rr 6f out: swtchd rt over 1f out: r.o: nt trble ldrs* **10/1**

2000 **5** *1 1/2* **King Flyer (IRE)**[53] 4174 8-8-11 **75** .......... BReilly[(3)] 8 78
(MissJFeilden) *hld up: hdwy over 2f out: one pce fnl f* **14/1**

0321 **6** *shd* **Typhoon Tilly**[13] 5274 7-8-12 **73** .......... SDrowne 11 76
(CREgerton) *hld up: hdwy 1/2-way: rdn to chse ldr over 2f out: no ex fnl f* **4/1**[1]

6156 **7** *1 1/2* **Hathlen (IRE)**[20] 5100 3-8-2 **75** .......... JQuinn 6 76
(MRChannon) *hld up: hdwy 1/2-way: lost pl over 5f out: hdwy u.p over 1f out: nt trble ldrs* **20/1**

-551 **8** *1/2* **Patrixprial**[18] 5159 3-8-5 **78** .......... PRobinson 5 79
(MHTompkins) *mid-div: rdn over 3f out: styd on same pce fnl 2f* **6/1**[2]

1326 **9** *2* **Thewhirlingdervish (IRE)**[40] 4550 6-9-7 **82** .......... TEDurcan 4 80
(TDEasterby) *chsd ldrs: rdn over 3f out: wknd wl over 1f out* **8/1**

00-0 **10** *3/4* **Halland**[47] 4345 6-9-4 **82** .......... J-PGuillambert[(3)] 2 79
(NPLittmoden) *hld up: hdwy over 3f out: wknd 2f out* **50/1**

6213 **11** *12* **Tudor Bell (IRE)**[71] 3621 3-8-10 **83** .......... DSweeney 1 66
(JGMO'Shea) *led 2f: remained handy tl wknd over 2f out* **16/1**

5120 **12** *1 3/4* **Cherubim (JPN)**[8] 5402 3-8-2 **75** .......... TPQueally 13 56
(DRLoder) *led after 2f: hdd over 3f out: wknd wl over 1f out* **33/1**

603- **13** *6* **King Eider**[147] 5730 5-9-10 **85** .......... RLMoore 9 59
(BEllison) *hld up: hdwy over 3f out: sn wknd* **14/1**

3m 31.41s (1.41) **Going Correction** +0.225s/f (Good)
**WFA** 3 from 4yo+ 12lb **13** Ran SP% **119.2**
Speed ratings: **105,104,104,103,103 102,102,101,100,100 94,93,90**CSF £62.59 CT £427.81 TOTE £7.80: £2.70, £3.10, £3.00; EX 96.10.
**Owner** The Aedean Partnership **Bred** Ballymacoll Stud Farm Ltd **Trained** Lewes, E Sussex
■ Stewards Enquiry : T P Queally caution: allowed filly to coast home with no assistance from saddle

**FOCUS**
A competitive staying handicap, and the first three are all in the Cesarewitch.

**NOTEBOOK**
**High Point(IRE)**, another 2lb lower, likes a bit of cut in the ground and stayed on well to lead close home. He may struggle again when reassessed, though, as he has always seemed to struggle off marks in the high 70s.
**Astyanax(IRE)** took over the running with three furlongs to go and appeared to have stolen a decisive advantage but, despite Sanders throwing everything at the horse, he was just outpointed close home. He may need a break after this big effort.
**Land 'n Stars**, carrying a 6lb penalty, ran well in defeat as he did not enjoy the best of runs. He had to wait for the gaps to appear but, once in the clear, stayed on well. He is holding his form well.
**Marine City(JPN)**, fitted with cheekpieces for the first time and stepping up from a mile and a half, had plenty to do with a quarter mile to run, but came home well. She ran in snatches for much of the race and is clearly not straightforward, but the ability is there.
**King Flyer(IRE)** ran a more promising race than of late and is currently back on his last winning mark.
**Typhoon Tilly** has never won off a mark higher than 70 in 17 starts. *Official explanation: jockey said that gelding lost its action*
**Patrixprial** was disappointing on his first start over two miles as the trip should have suited.

## 5596 LOTTIE AND ALBERT BOTTON MEMORIAL NURSERY 1m 3y
**4:30** (4:33) (E3) (0-75,75) 2-Y-O **£4,043** (£1,244; £622; £311) **Stalls** High

Form RPR

0054 **1** **Rebel Rebel (IRE)**[9] 5377 2-9-0 **68** .......... LDettori 8 80
(NACallaghan) *racd centre: hld up: hdwy over 2f out: led over 1f out: r.o wl* **2/1**[1]

005 **2** *3 1/2* **Tomobel**[17] 5198 2-8-6 **60** .......... PRobinson 7 64
(MHTompkins) *racd centre: sn chsng ldr: rdn over 2f out: styd on same pce fnl f* **20/1**

552 **3** *nk* **Mobarhen (USA)**[12] 5302 2-9-5 **73** .......... RHills 1 77+
(SirMichaelStoute) *racd far side: hld up: hdwy over 3f out: led that gp over 2f out: sn rdn clr: no ch w centre gp* **9/2**[2]

4006 **4** *3* **Union Jack Jackson (IRE)**[28] 4878 2-8-11 **65** .......... MFenton 9 62
(JGGiven) *led centre over 6f: no ex* **50/1**

300 **5** *1 1/2* **Uncle Bulgaria (IRE)**[13] 5268 2-8-11 **65** .......... SWhitworth 11 59
(GCBravery) *racd stands' side: chsd ldrs: rdn over 2f out: no imp* **33/1**

0562 **6** *6* **Kerry's Blade (IRE)**[5] 5477 2-8-9 **63** .......... GFaulkner 20 44
(PCHaslam) *racd stands' side: chsd ldrs: led that gp and hung lft over 2f out: sn hdd & wknd* **7/1**[3]

064 **7** *1/2* **Big Hoo Hah**[17] 5172 2-8-13 **67** .......... KMcEvoy 6 46
(CACyzer) *racd centre: bhd: styd on fnl f: nvr nrr* **40/1**

16 **8** *1 1/2* **Pon My Soul (IRE)**[41] 4521 2-8-11 **65** .......... TPQueally 13 41
(MGQuinlan) *racd stands' side: hld up: n.d* **33/1**

044U **9** *3* **Sharp N Frosty**[17] 5188 2-8-4 **63** .......... BSwarbrick[(5)] 16 33
(WMBrisbourne) *racd stands' side: nvr nrr* **66/1**

0305 **10** *2* **Gryskirk**[9] 5377 2-8-10 **64** .......... JQuinn 14 29
(PWD'Arcy) *racd stands' side: mid-div: hdwy 3f out: wknd 2f out* **16/1**

5100 **11** *4* **Good Wee Girl (IRE)**[9] 5377 2-9-3 **71** .......... JPMurtagh 19 27
(PSMcentee) *led stands' side over 5f: sn wknd* **20/1**

050 **12** *1 3/4* **Captain Margaret**[17] 5200 2-9-0 **68** .......... (p) RLMoore 18 20
(JPearce) *racd stands' side: a in rr* **33/1**

034 **13** *1* **Young Mick**[18] 5142 2-9-5 **73** .......... AMcCarthy 4 23
(GGMargarson) *racd far side: chsd ldr tl led wl over 2f out: sn hdd & wknd* **33/1**

005 **14** *2 1/2* **Terminate (GER)**[23] 5023 2-8-13 **67** .......... SSanders 12 12
(SirMarkPrescott) *racd stands' side: mid-div: hdwy over 3f out: wknd 2f out* **9/2**[2]

1300 **15** *1* **He's A Diamond**[9] 5377 2-9-7 **75** .......... GCarter 5 18
(TGMills) *swtchd to r centre over 6f out: prom over 5f* **50/1**

555 **16** *3/4* **Silver Visage (IRE)**[89] 3083 2-8-6 **63** .......... (b[1]) BReilly[(3)] 17 4
(MissJFeilden) *racd stands' side: a in rr* **50/1**

4525 **17** *3* **Bongoali**[10] 5335 2-8-6 **67** .......... TDean[(7)] 3 —
(MRChannon) *racd far side: chsd ldrs over 4f* **33/1**

0024 **18** *hd* **Countrywide Sun**[28] 4878 2-8-4 **61** .......... (p) J-PGuillambert[(3)] 2 —
(NPLittmoden) *led far side over 5f: sn wknd* **40/1**

054 **19** *8* **Tit For Tat**[20] 5095 2-8-7 **61** .......... SDrowne 10 —
(JGGiven) *s.i.s: racd centre: sn prom: hung lft and wknd 3f out* **50/1**

6550 **20** *2* **Silverleaf**[13] 5269 2-9-4 **72** .......... TEDurcan 15 —
(MRChannon) *racd stands' side: a in rr* **40/1**

1m 40.75s (1.05) **Going Correction** +0.10s/f (Good) **20** Ran SP% **129.0**
Speed ratings: **98,94,94,91,89 83,83,81,78,76 72,70,69,67,66 65,62,62,54,52**CSF £50.48 CT £184.78 TOTE £3.70: £1.30, £3.90, £1.80, £10.40; EX 89.40.
**Owner** Six Star Racing **Bred** William P Fogarty **Trained** Newmarket, Suffolk

**FOCUS**
Probably a fair nursery. They were well strung out at the finish and those that raced towards the centre of the track had the edge.
**NOTEBOOK**
**Rebel Rebel(IRE)**, unlucky in running on his handicap debut, was sent off a short price to make amends. He ran out an authoritative winner and connections may well turn him out under a penalty at Lingfield next week, as he is likely to go up a fair amount for this easy win.
**Tomobel**, making her handicap debut, appreciated the step up to a mile and, although no match for the easy winner, came clear of the rest of her group. She looks perfectly capable of winning a nursery on this evidence.
**Mobarhen(USA)** was unfortunate to be badly drawn as it turned out and, although he finished well clear of his group on the far side, the centre group had the edge. He is another who looks capable of defying this sort of mark in handicap company.
**Union Jack Jackson(IRE)** left his average performance on the Fibresand behind with a sound effort from the front and, although his pedigree is geared more towards sprinting, he saw the trip out quite well.
**Uncle Bulgaria(IRE)**, another making his handicap debut, did best of the stands'-side group to win that race. He finished well clear of the rest and should be found easier opportunities than this.
**Kerry's Blade(IRE)** ran well last time but, despite showing good pace, was well held at the finish in this stronger race.
**Silver Visage(IRE)** *Official explanation: jockey said saddle slipped*
**Countrywide Sun** *Official explanation: jockey said gelding hung right*

## 5597 BBC LOOK EAST H'CAP — 6f 3y
**5:00** (5:02) (F4) (0-55,55) 3-Y-0+ — **£3,369** (£962; £481) **Stalls** High

Form — RPR
0400 **1** — **Kew The Music**[13] 5261 4-8-8 **49** (v) TEDurcan 9 — 61
(MRChannon) *dwlt: outpcd: hdwy to ld 1f out: rdn out* **20/1**
0000 **2** *nk* **Mutassem (FR)**[15] 5219 3-8-9 **52** PDoe 14 — 63
(TKeddy) *hld up: hdwy over 1f out: rdn and ev ch ins fnl f: r.o* **50/1**
0000 **3** *3 ½* **Laurel Dawn**[19] 5107 6-8-7 **55** WHogg(7) 6 — 56
(IWMcInnes) *chsd ldrs: rdn over 1f out: styd on same pce* **14/1**
4133 **4** *3* **Molotov**[5] 5452 4-8-2 **50** NataliaGemelova(7) 18 — 42
(IWMcInnes) *led 5f: wknd ins fnl f* **15/2**[3]
4024 **5** *½* **Kennington**[18] 5157 4-8-9 **50** JoannaBadger 16 — 40
(MrsCADunnett) *chsd ldrs: rdn over 2f out: wknd fnl f* **12/1**
0000 **6** *shd* **Quantica (IRE)**[10] 5346 5-9-0 **55** MFenton 7 — 45
(NTinkler) *mid-div: rdn over 2f out: hung lft and wknd over 1f out* **8/1**
1452 **7** *1 ¼* **On The Trail**[3] 5526 7-8-13 **54** SSanders 2 — 40
(DWChapman) *chsd ldrs: rdn over 2f out: hung rt and wknd over 1f out* **6/1**[2]
0560 **8** *shd* **Florian**[10] 5337 6-9-0 **55** GCarter 10 — 41
(TGMills) *chsd ldrs: rdn over 2f out: wknd over 1f out* **28/1**
3255 **9** *shd* **Enjoy The Buzz**[13] 5261 5-8-10 **51** RLMoore 4 — 36
(JMBradley) *hld up: hdwy over 2f out: wknd over 1f out* **10/1**
3110 **10** *1 ¾* **Yorkies Boy**[7] 5411 9-8-9 **53** (p) RMiles(3) 5 — 33
(NEBerry) *mid-div: rdn over 2f out: sn wknd* **12/1**
0262 **11** *1 ¾* **Salon Prive**[13] 5261 4-9-0 **55** LDettori 15 — 30
(CACyzer) *w ldr over 3f: wknd over 1f out* **7/2**[1]
5000 **12** *½* **Star Fern**[114] 2377 3-8-9 **52** EAhern 8 — 25
(RMHCowell) *dwlt hld up: rdn 1/2-way: n.d* **50/1**
5310 **13** *shd* **Pretty Kool**[13] 5260 4-8-11 **52** KMcEvoy 11 — 25
(SCWilliams) *chsd ldrs 4f* **9/1**
0106 **14** *1 ½* **Doctor Dennis (IRE)**[65] 3828 7-8-10 **51** (v) AMcCarthy 12 — 20
(JPearce) *prom 4f* **25/1**
1120 **15** *nk* **Baytown Flyer**[124] 2123 4-8-10 **51** TPQueally 1 — 19
(PSMcentee) *sn bhd* **33/1**
4050 **16** *½* **Tomthevic**[7] 5412 6-8-10 **51** PFitzsimons 20 — 17
(JMBradley) *chsd ldrs over 4f* **25/1**
5000 **17** *2 ½* **Warlingham (IRE)**[45] 4403 6-8-13 **54** RMullen 17 — 13
(PHowling) *chsd ldrs over 3f* **20/1**
0-04 **18** *5* **Montana**[31] 4801 4-9-0 **55** SDrowne 19 — —
(JLSpearing) *prom 4f* **22/1**
0000 **19** *2* **Forzenuff**[71] 3636 3-8-8 **51** DSweeney 3 — —
(JRBoyle) *mid-div: rdn over 2f out: sn wknd* **50/1**

1m 14.3s (0.70) **Going Correction** +0.10s/f (Good) **19** Ran SP% **134.4**
**WFA** 3 from 4yo+ 2lb
Speed ratings: **99,98,93,89,89 89,87,87,87,84 82,81,81,79,79 78,75,68,66**CSF £791.10 CT £13790.48 TOTE £21.60: £4.30, £20.20, £4.10, £3.20; EX 1520.70 Place 6 £543.82, Place 5 £143.94.
**Owner** Miss Bridget Coyle **Bred** Miss B Coyle **Trained** West Ilsley, Berks

**FOCUS**
A competitive if modest handicap but the form looks reasonable for the grade. The field were spread across the track, but occupied the middle to stands' side and gave the far rail a wide berth. Considering the size of the field, there was a healthy margin between the second and the fourth horses.
**NOTEBOOK**
**Kew The Music**, badly out of form this year, has tumbled down the handicap and returned to form with a bang. He came from almost last down the centre of the track and pulled right away with the runner-up as the early leaders fell in a heap. The form is modest, but he could follow up if this signals a general return to form, as a penalty will still leave him well below the mark off which he started the season.
**Mutassem(FR)**, never better than sixth in seven previous outings, has been in freefall down the handicap though he had no chance from his draw at Lingfield last time. Berthed much better on this occasion, he looked like scoring when swooping through against the stands' rail a furlong out, but the winner down the centre of the track just saw his race out the better. This looks to be his best trip.
**Laurel Dawn**, never far away, ran with credit and although well held by the front pair, still finished clear of the others. He has never won beyond five furlongs, though this was one of his best-ever efforts over this trip.
**Molotov** set a decent gallop and still had a decent advantage over a furlong from home, but then ran out of gas. He does look better over five or an easy six.
**Kennington**, with the headgear left off, raced prominently for a long way but was easily shaken off in the latter stages. This was his 16th outing of the season and he may need a rest.
**Quantica(IRE)** has been mostly out of form over the last couple of seasons, though to be fair he has rarely had his favoured soft ground. This was a bit better and he is becoming reasonably handicapped.
**On The Trail**, who is not being allowed to let the grass grow under his feet, showed his usual good early pace but faced a stiff task from his low draw and had nothing more to offer over the last furlong and a half.
**Salon Prive** was well backed to get off the mark at the tenth attempt, but folded rather tamely in the second half of the contest. *Official explanation: jockey said gelding lost a front shoe*
**Forzenuff** *Official explanation: jockey said colt lost its action*
T/Plt: £1,021.00 to a £1 stake. Pool: £41,961.15. 30.00 winning tickets. T/Qpdt: £164.20 to a £1 stake. Pool: £2,907.50. 13.10 winning tickets. CR

# 5578 AYR (L-H)
Friday, September 17

**OFFICIAL GOING: Soft**

## 5602 AON CONSULTING HARRY ROSEBERY STKS (LISTED RACE) — 5f
**2:05** (2:07) (A1) 2-Y-O — **£17,400** (£6,600; £3,300; £1,500) **Stalls** High

Form — RPR
1106 **1** — **Prince Charming**[27] 4962 2-8-11 98 JFanning 12 — 105
(JHMGosden) *trckd ldrs gng wl: led over 1f out: shkn up and hld on wl* **6/1**[2]
3120 **2** *1* **Mary Read**[34] 4744 2-8-9 100 FLynch 3 — 100
(BSmart) *slt ld to over 1f out: r.o fnl f: hld towards fin* **10/1**[3]
0610 **3** *2* **Dance Night (IRE)**[9] 5392 2-9-2 100 GGibbons 4 — 100
(BAMcmahon) *w ldrs: rdn 2f out: one pce fnl f* **6/1**[2]
350 **4** *¾* **Next Time Around (IRE)**[94] 2959 2-8-11 97 RWinston 10 — 92
(MrsLStubbs) *prom: rdn over 2f out: kpt on fnl f* **20/1**
1040 **5** *1 ½* **Beckermet (IRE)**[6] 5464 2-9-0 100 JFEgan 11 — 90
(RFFisher) *w ldrs tl rdn and no ex over 1f out* **20/1**
121 **6** *½* **Sundance (IRE)**[17] 5213 2-8-11 98 JQuinn 1 — 85
(HJCollingridge) *in tch on outside: effrt 2f out: sn one pce* **5/1**[1]
4416 **7** *1 ¼* **Key Secret**[9] 5404 2-8-6 93 HayleyTurner 9 — 76
(MLWBell) *sn rdn in midfield: no imp fr 2f out* **10/1**[3]
3110 **8** *2* **Mimi Mouse**[9] 5392 2-8-6 88 KDarley 8 — 69
(TDEasterby) *hmpd sn after s: nvr rchd ldrs* **25/1**
4213 **9** *2* **Sentiero Rosso (USA)**[18] 5195 2-8-11 96 TEaves 7 — 67
(BEllison) *sn pushed along in rr: n.d* **6/1**[2]
144 **10** *2* **Notjustaprettyface (USA)**[29] 4885 2-8-6 100 SDrowne 2 — 55
(HMorrison) *racd wd in rr: struggling fr 1/2-way* **5/1**[1]
0564 **11** *nk* **Handsome Lady**[22] 5060 2-8-6 75 PHanagan 5 — 54
(ISemple) *towards rr: rdn 1/2-way: sn btn* **50/1**
4106 **12** *6* **Theatre Of Dreams**[17] 5213 2-8-11 86 ANicholls 6 — 38
(DNicholls) *plld hrd and sn prom: rdn and wknd fr 2f out* **66/1**

60.85 secs (0.42) **Going Correction** +0.225s/f (Good) **12** Ran SP% **111.2**
Speed ratings: **105,103,100,99,96 95,93,90,87,84 83,74**CSF £55.82 TOTE £7.40: £2.40, £3.90, £2.60; EX 81.70 Trifecta £391.70 Part won. Pool: £551.00. 0.50 winning units..
**Owner** Sheikh Mohammed **Bred** Mrs R D Peacock **Trained** Manton, Wilts
■ Stewards Enquiry : G Gibbons one-day ban: careless riding (Sep 28)

**FOCUS**
A useful field and a taking performance from Prince Charming, who was value for more than the winning margin. Sound efforts too from the placed horses.
**NOTEBOOK**
**Prince Charming** had the run of the race next to the favoured stands rail but did the job in very smooth fashion and won with more in hand than the official margin suggested. He goes particularly well on easy ground and looks worth a try in stronger company, granted suitable conditions.
**Mary Read**, back on easy ground, confirmed herself a useful performer and ran right up to her best. She is a consistent sort who should continue to give a good account when the emphasis is on speed.
**Dance Night(IRE)**, conceding weight all round, had conditions to suit and showed that his last run from an unfavourable draw had not done him any justice. He is a fair performer with cut in the ground but does look vulnerable to progressive sorts, so may not be the easiest to place successfully.
**Next Time Around(IRE)**, absent since June, ran right up to his best back on easy ground and left the impression that the step up to six furlongs would be in his favour. He looks capable of winning a similar event granted a stiffer test.
**Beckermet(IRE)** ran creditably back on an easy surface but was again held by Dance Night. Although a sounder surface may have helped, he may not be the easiest to place successfully from now on.
**Sundance(IRE)** is a good sort on looks and came into the race with a progressive profile but was a shade disappointing in this stronger grade, even allowing for the fact that his wide draw was no help. The step up to six furlongs will suit and he is not one to write off yet.
**Key Secret** again left the impression that she is worth a try over six furlongs.
**Mimi Mouse**, well beaten from an unfavourable draw at Doncaster, shaped as though a bit better than the bare result and is well worth another chance.
**Notjustaprettyface(USA)** *Official explanation: trainer's representative had no explanation for the poor form shown*

## 5603 TOTESPORT AYR SILVER CUP (H'CAP) — 6f
**2:35** (2:41) (B1) 3-Y-O+ — **£18,049** (£6,846; £3,423; £1,556) **Stalls** High

Form — RPR
3311 **1** — **Eisteddfod**[28] 4917 3-9-3 **87** NDeSouza(5) 22 — 98+
(PFICole) *midfield stands side: effrt and drvn over 2f out: rallied to ld ins fnl f: styd on* **8/1**[2]
6002 **2** *¾* **Cd Europe (IRE)**[5] 5491 6-9-8 **85** (p) RWinston 14 — 94
(JJQuinn) *bhd stands side: hdwy 2f out: kpt on wl fnl f: a hld* **14/1**
0000 **3** *hd* **Johnston's Diamond (IRE)**[6] 5458 6-9-7 **84** JQuinn 28 — 93
(EJAlston) *cl up stands side: led that gp 2f out: hdd ins fnl f: r.o* **33/1**
0513 **4** *hd* **Balakiref**[20] 5124 5-8-10 **73** SDrowne 26 — 81+
(MDods) *prom stands side: nt clr run over 2f out: rdn and r.o fnl f* **9/1**[3]
4000 **5** *2* **Queens Rhapsody**[8] 5419 4-9-5 **82** JFanning 24 — 84
(ABailey) *prom stands side: rdn over 2f out: kpt on same pce fnl f* **20/1**
2211 **6** *1* **Fonthill Road (IRE)**[20] 5124 4-9-4 **81** 3ex PHanagan 6 — 80+
(RAFahey) *hld up in tch far side: smooth hdwy 2f out: led that gp ins fnl f: kpt on wl: no ch w stands side* **10/1**
1245 **7** *1 ½* **Machinist (IRE)**[21] 5075 4-9-5 **82** AlexGreaves 11 — 77+
(DNicholls) *led far side tl hdd and no ex ins fnl f* **16/1**
6005 **8** *¾* **Sierra Vista**[14] 5263 4-9-2 **79** LEnstone 13 — 71
(DWBarker) *chsd stands side ldrs: rdn over 2f out: one pce over 1f out* **50/1**
2266 **9** *2* **Million Percent**[68] 3778 5-9-0 **77** DarrenWilliams 25 — 63
(KRBurke) *chsd stands side ldrs tl rdn and nt qckn fr 2f out* **18/1**
0030 **10** *hd* **Native Title**[48] 4324 6-9-9 **86** ANicholls 3 — 72+
(DNicholls) *in tch far side: effrt 2f out: no imp fnl f* **22/1**
0445 **11** *nk* **Obe One**[2] 5562 4-7-12 **66** PPMathers(5) 9 — 51+
(ABerry) *hld up far side: rdn over 2f out: no imp fnl f* **33/1**
0430 **12** *hd* **Mystic Man (FR)**[5] 5491 6-9-10 **87** NCallan 27 — 71
(KARyan) *prom stands rail: nt clr run over 2f out: sn rdn and no imp* **7/1**[1]
105 **13** *½* **Zoom Zoom**[106] 2628 4-8-9 **75** J-PGuillambert(3) 16 — 58
(MrsLStubbs) *bhd stands side: drvn 1/2-way: sme late hdwy: nvr on terms* **25/1**
0400 **14** *½* **Hilites (IRE)**[9] 5399 3-8-2 **74** (p) DerekNolan(7) 17 — 55
(JSMoore) *bhd stands side tl sme late hdwy: nvr on terms* **100/1**
2460 **15** *½* **Rising Shadow (IRE)**[29] 4874 3-9-3 **82** KDarley 12 — 62+
(RAFahey) *prom far side tl rdn and outpcd fr 2f out* **66/1**

1332 **16** ½ **Pieter Brueghel (USA)**[34] [4759] 5-9-9 **86**.................... PDoe 20 64
(DNicholls) *led stands side to 2f out: sn rdn and btn* **12/1**

0226 **17** *nk* **Kirkby's Treasure**[27] [4931] 6-8-12 **75**.................... FLynch 4 52+
(ABerry) *bhd far side: rdn 1/2-way: nvr rchd ldrs* **40/1**

4356 **18** *1* **Cd Flyer (IRE)**[21] [5075] 7-9-6 **86**.................... TEaves(3) 1 60+
(BEllison) *trckd far side ldrs tl outpcd fr 2f out* **25/1**

0311 **19** *shd* **Bond Playboy**[20] [5126] 4-8-3 **66**.................... GGibbons 19 40
(BSmart) *bhd and sn rdn stands side: nvr on terms* **16/1**

3564 **20** 3½ **Sir Desmond**[21] [5075] 6-9-0 **77**....................(p) JMackay 5 40+
(RGuest) *sn rdn along towards rr far side: n.d* **33/1**

2356 **21** 1½ **Ellens Academy (IRE)**[16] [5224] 9-9-9 **86**.................... FNorton 2 45+
(EJAlston) *trckd far side ldrs to 2f out: sn rdn and btn* **33/1**

2065 **22** ½ **Skip Of Colour**[83] [3293] 4-8-8 **71**.................... DeanMcKeown 21 28
(PABlockley) *dwlt: effrt u.p 1/2-way stands side: sn btn* **33/1**

0060 **23** *1* **Indian Spark**[31] [4837] 10-8-12 **75**.................... JFEgan 23 29
(JSGoldie) *in tch stands side tl wknd over 2f out* **20/1**

2550 **24** *hd* **Golden Dixie (USA)**[13] [5299] 5-9-4 **81**.................... ACulhane 8 35+
(AMBalding) *cl up far side to 2f out: sn btn* **25/1**

5400 **25** *hd* **Cheese 'n Biscuits**[3] [5541] 4-8-2 **68**....................(p) HayleyTurner(3) 18 21
(GLMoore) *a bhd stands side* **50/1**

5000 **26** *10* **Blackheath (IRE)**[13] [5287] 8-9-3 **87**.................... PJBenson(7) 10 10+
(DNicholls) *prom far side to 1/2-way: sn lost tch* **66/1**

1m 13.9s (0.18) **Going Correction** +0.225s/f (Good)
**WFA** 3 from 4yo+ 2lb **26** Ran SP% **124.5**
Speed ratings: **107,106,105,105,102 101,99,98,95,95 95,94,94,93,92 92,91,90,90,85 83,83,81,81,81 67**CSF £88.43 CT £3546.78 TOTE £6.00: £1.80, £3.80, £8.20, £2.50; EX 125.80 Trifecta £4139.70 Part won. Pool: £5,830.61. 0.10 winning units..
**Owner** Elite Racing Club **Bred** Elite Racing Club **Trained** Whatcombe, Oxon

**FOCUS**
A competitive event run at a decent pace and one in which the stands' side group held the clear edge over the 11 that raced on the far side. The winner is a progressive sort who looks capable of holding his own in better company.

**NOTEBOOK**
**Eisteddfod** ◆, a most progressive sort, had conditions to suit and turned in his best effort yet returned to sprinting. He should prove equally effective back over seven furlongs and appeals strongly as the type to win more races.
**Cd Europe(IRE)** is not the most consistent but ran right up to his recent best in the favoured stands' side group from his moderate draw. His style of racing means he needs things to fall right but he is capable of winning again from his current mark.
**Johnston's Diamond(IRE)**, much better drawn than at Chester last time, had slipped in the weights, had the run of the race and ran right up to his best. He was 7lb badly in here in this early-closing race, but may not have the opportunity to race off the lower mark before the Handicapper addresses the situation.
**Balakiref** has shown improved form since being dropped to sprinting and ran as well as he has ever done. He did not get the best of runs at a crucial stage, so may be better than the bare result, and he can win again when things fall right.
**Queens Rhapsody** has not won since February last year but ran creditably from his favourable draw. However he left the impression that the return to seven furlongs would be in his favour.
**Fonthill Road(IRE)** ◆, a progressive performer, travelled strongly for a long way and fared the best of those to race on the far side. He has a good strike rate and appeals as the type to win more races.
**Machinist(IRE)** has improved since being dropped to sprint distances for his current stable and is another that looks a bit better than the bare form, as he finished second best of those that raced on the far side. He looks the type to win more races.
**Blackheath(IRE)** *Official explanation: trainer said gelding lost its action*

## 5604 JAMES BARR EUROPEAN BREEDERS FUND MAIDEN STKS 7f 50y
**3:05** (3:12) (D2) 2-Y-O £**5,512** (£1,696; £848; £424) **Stalls** Low

Form RPR

2 **1** **Market Trend**[9] [5400] 2-8-9 .................... JFanning 13 81
(MJohnston) *w ldr: rdn to ld wl over 1f out: kpt on wl u.p fnl f* **15/8**[1]

5320 **2** 1¼ **Consider This**[9] [5391] 2-8-9 82.................... KDarley 3 78
(WMBrisbourne) *mde most tl hdd over 2f out: rallied u.p to chse wnr fnl f: kpt on: no imp* **10/3**[2]

0625 **3** *3* **Nasseem Dubai (USA)**[13] [5302] 2-9-0 76.................... JQuinn 9 76
(MrsADuffield) *keen: trckd ldrs: led over 2f out: rdn and hdd wl over 1f out: no ex* **13/2**[3]

05 **4** *2* **Brandexe (IRE)**[8] [5406] 2-8-9 .................... ACulhane 11 66
(BWHills) *s.i.s: towards rr: drvn along 1/2-way: kpt on u.p fnl f: nvr able to chal* **11/1**

0 **5** *hd* **Thorntoun Piccolo**[28] [4900] 2-8-9 .................... PHanagan 6 66
(JSGoldie) *towards rr: hdwy into midfield over 2f out: kpt on u.p fnl f: n.d* **33/1**

0 **6** 3½ **Rainbow Treasure (IRE)**[16] [5228] 2-8-6 .................... TEaves(3) 1 57
(JSGoldie) *in tch: hdwy to chse ldrs 3f out: rdn 2f out: sn btn* **33/1**

**7** 2½ **Bestbyfar (IRE)** 2-9-0 .................... NCallan 2 56
(JGGiven) *in tch: rdn 3f out: sn btn* **16/1**

**8** *11* **Mays Dream** 2-8-9 .................... ANicholls 10 25
(DNicholls) *s.i.s: sn wl bhd: t.o* **25/1**

**9** *4* **Plungington Tavern (IRE)** 2-9-0 .................... DeanMcKeown 5 20
(PABlockley) *slowly away: a bhd: lost tch over 2f out: t.o* **66/1**

**10** *9* **Degree Of Honor (FR)** 2-8-9 .................... RWinston 12 —
(JGGiven) *trckd ldrs: effrt over 3f out: no imp: lost pl and eased over 2f out: t.o* **25/1**

**11** ½ **Victor Buckwell** 2-9-0 .................... JFEgan 7 —
(BEllison) *slowly away: bhd: lost tch over 2f out: t.o* **8/1**

1m 36.73s (4.26) **Going Correction** +0.55s/f (Yiel) **11** Ran SP% **111.6**
Speed ratings: **97,95,92,89,89 85,82,70,65,55 54**CSF £6.77 TOTE £2.30: £1.50, £1.50, £2.20; EX 5.60.
**Owner** Maktoum Al Maktoum **Bred** Gainsborough Stud Management Ltd **Trained** Middleham Moor, N Yorks

**FOCUS**
Just an ordinary maiden, and the pace was only fair. However, Market Trend is heading in the right direction and may be capable of better in handicaps.

**NOTEBOOK**
**Market Trend** fully confirmed debut promise on this first run on soft and over a trip that had looked likely to suit. She is likely to stay a mile and may well be capable of further improvement when sent into handicaps.
**Consider This** looks a fairly reliable yardstick who ran right up to her best on this first run over seven, back in this less competitive race. She is starting to look exposed but is certainly capable of picking up a small race away from progressive sorts.
**Nasseem Dubai(USA)**, back in trip and back on easier ground, ran creditably but is starting to look exposed and may not be the easiest to place in this grade, or indeed in handicap company from his current mark.
**Brandexe(IRE)** ◆ was anything but disgraced and left the impression that she would be capable of better granted a stiffer test of stamina. She is one to keep an eye on now she is qualified for a handicap mark.
**Thorntoun Piccolo** bettered her debut effort and appeals as the type that may be capable of better in ordinary handicap company granted a stiffer test of stamina in due course.
**Rainbow Treasure(IRE)** improved on her first run and looks the type to do better in ordinary company when qualifield for handicaps.
**Bestbyfar(IRE)** is related to winners and, although well beaten on this racecourse debut, is entitled to improve for the experience.
**Degree Of Honor(FR)** *Official explanation: jockey said filly lost her action turning into the straight*
**Victor Buckwell** *Official explanation: jockey said colt felt weak and finished tired*

## 5605 HBG PROPERTIES H'CAP 5f
**3:40** (3:41) (D2) (0-85,85) 3-Y-O+ £**6,975** (£2,146; £1,073; £536) **Stalls** High

Form RPR

4113 **1** **Hout Bay**[1] [5579] 7-8-7 **70** oh3.................... PHanagan 5 82
(RAFahey) *hld up: hdwy 2f out: led ins fnl f: r.o wl* **8/1**

0005 **2** 1¼ **Mr Wolf**[21] [5094] 3-8-9 **73**.................... LEnstone 6 81
(DWBarker) *w ldr: led briefly ins fnl f: kpt on* **20/1**

50L0 **3** *hd* **Piccled**[7] [5440] 6-9-6 **83**.................... SDrowne 15 90
(EJAlston) *dwlt: hld up: hdwy 2f out: ev ch ins fnl f: no ex towards fin* **28/1**

6330 **4** *shd* **Paddywack (IRE)**[7] [5440] 7-8-9 **72**....................(b) ACulhane 1 79
(DWChapman) *hld up: hdwy over 1f out: swtchd and kpt on fnl f* **16/1**

6000 **5** 1½ **Trinculo (IRE)**[13] [5287] 7-8-9 **75**....................(be) J-PGuillambert(3) 4 76
(NPLittmoden) *racd alone towards far side: rdn and one pce fr over 1f out* **33/1**

6302 **6** *nk* **Highland Warrior**[28] [4904] 5-8-8 **71**.................... JFEgan 2 71
(JSGoldie) *s.i.s: hdwy whn nt clr run wl over 1f out: kpt on fnl f: nrst fin* **14/1**

0000 **7** ½ **Artie**[31] [4837] 5-9-7 **84**.................... RWinston 10 83
(TDEasterby) *chsd ldrs tl rdn and nt qckn over 1f out* **7/1**[3]

0000 **8** ½ **Pax**[14] [5263] 7-9-2 **79**.................... ANicholls 9 76
(DNicholls) *hld up: effrt on outside 2f out: sn no imp* **33/1**

2003 **9** *hd* **Plateau**[18] [5181] 5-9-6 **83**.................... AlexGreaves 16 79
(DNicholls) *prom: rdn and hung lft 2f out: sn outpcd* **6/1**[1]

2000 **10** ½ **Brave Burt (IRE)**[18] [5181] 7-9-3 **80**.................... JFanning 14 74
(DNicholls) *led stands rail to ins fnl f: sn btn* **10/1**

5020 **11** ½ **Dispol Katie**[7] [5440] 3-9-3 **81**.................... NCallan 12 74
(TDBarron) *in tch: lost pl 1/2-way: n.d after* **11/1**

1024 **12** *nk* **Kings College Boy**[1] [5579] 4-8-7 **70** oh2....................(b) DaleGibson 3 62
(RAFahey) *hld up: rdn 1/2-way: nvr rchd ldrs* **14/1**

5624 **13** 2½ **Misaro (GER)**[18] [5193] 3-8-9 **73**.................... DeanMcKeown 8 56
(PABlockley) *in tch on outside: rdn and hung lft 1/2-way: sn outpcd* **14/1**

4600 **14** ¾ **Maktavish**[13] [5287] 5-8-12 **78**....................(p) TEaves(3) 11 58
(ISemple) *cl up to 2f out: sn btn* **13/2**[2]

0500 **15** *8* **Wanchai Lad**[7] [5440] 3-9-7 **85**.................... KDarley 13 37
(DNicholls) *midfield: rdn 1/2-way: btn over 1f out* **11/1**

60.70 secs (0.27) **Going Correction** +0.225s/f (Good)
**WFA** 3 from 4yo+ 1lb **15** Ran SP% **117.0**
Speed ratings: **106,104,103,103,101 100,99,99,98,97 97,96,92,91,78**CSF £161.88 CT £4263.53 TOTE £10.80: £3.20, £6.70, £5.60; EX 426.90.
**Owner** Northumbria Leisure Ltd **Bred** Mrs Mary Taylor **Trained** Musley Bank, N Yorks
■ Stewards Enquiry : J-P GuillambertE one-day ban: failed to keep straight from stalls (Sep 28)

**FOCUS**
They all raced centre to stands' side here, with one exception. This is solid handicap form, and Hout Bay put up another improved performance.

**NOTEBOOK**
**Hout Bay**, turned out quickly after a creditable run at this course the previous day, showed the right attitude to win his fourth race from only nine starts for his current stable, showing significantly improved form in the process. He rarely wins by very far and may be able to keep a step ahead of the handicapper in the near future.
**Mr Wolf** is a speedy sort who got a bit closer to the winner than he had done at Newmarket on his previous start. He seems particularly effective on easy ground and looks capable of winning again away from progressive sorts.
**Piccled** has become a most unreliable betting proposition in recent times but again showed that he retains enough ability to win more races. Whether this will be reproduced next time remains to be seen, though.
**Paddywack(IRE)** extended his run of creditable efforts and looked unlucky not to have finished a bit closer, as he had to switch to get a run in the closing stages. He should continue to give a good account.
**Trinculo(IRE)** ran well considering he was taken on his own towards the far side. However, he is inconsistent and has a modest strike rate, so is by no means sure to reproduce this next time.
**Highland Warrior** ran a typical race in that he lost ground at the start and met trouble in running. He is capable of winning from his current mark but remains one to tread carefully with.

## 5606 KNIGHT FRANK NURSERY 6f
**4:15** (4:16) (D2) (0-85,85) 2-Y-O £**7,046** (£2,168; £1,084; £542) **Stalls** High

Form RPR

032 **1** **Je Suis Belle**[20] [5115] 2-8-5 **69**.................... ACulhane 6 72
(BWHills) *trckd ldrs: effrt 2f out: styd on to ld last stride* **7/2**[2]

1340 **2** *shd* **Missperon (IRE)**[7] [5434] 2-8-12 **76**....................(p) NCallan 8 79
(KARyan) *cl up: led ins fnl f: kpt on: hdd last stride* **10/1**

4444 **3** *nk* **Dispol Isle (IRE)**[15] [5233] 2-8-1 **65**.................... PFessey 5 67
(TDBarron) *prom: effrt and ev ch ins fnl f: kpt on: hld cl home* **8/1**[3]

5134 **4** ¾ **Generous Option**[17] [5212] 2-9-6 **84**.................... JFanning 10 84
(MJohnston) *mde most to ins fnl f: kpt on same pce* **10/3**[1]

1150 **5** *hd* **Word Perfect**[17] [5212] 2-9-7 **85**.................... DaleGibson 7 88+
(MWEasterby) *hld up: nt clr run over 2f out: edgd lft over 1f out: r.o fnl f* **20/1**

1500 **6** *nk* **Dorn Dancer (IRE)**[9] [5391] 2-9-3 **81**.................... LEnstone 9 79
(DWBarker) *prom: effrt over 2f out: one pce over 1f out* **33/1**

0024 **7** *4* **Favouring (IRE)**[28] [4918] 2-8-0 **64**.................... PHanagan 2 50
(RAFahey) *hld up: effrt over 2f out: wknd appr fnl f* **7/2**[2]

450 **8** *4* **African Breeze**[9] [5391] 2-8-13 **80**.................... HayleyTurner(3) 1 54
(RMWhitaker) *dwlt: effrt on outside 1/2-way: wknd over 1f out* **12/1**

540 **9** *4* **Middle Eastern**[15] [5233] 2-8-4 **68**.................... DeanMcKeown 11 30
(PABlockley) *w ldrs tl wknd over 1f out* **20/1**

5035 **10** *6* **Unlimited**[18] [5202] 2-8-5 **69**.................... JQuinn 4 13
(MrsADuffield) *hung lft thrght: prom to 1/2-way: sn lost pl* **16/1**

1m 15.79s (2.07) **Going Correction** +0.225s/f (Good) **10** Ran SP% **113.8**
Speed ratings: **95,94,94,93,93 92,87,82,76,68**CSF £36.04 CT £259.57 TOTE £2.90: £1.40, £3.40, £2.50; EX 58.40.
**Owner** Guy Reed **Bred** G Reed **Trained** Lambourn, Berks
■ Stewards Enquiry : P Fessey two-day ban: used whip with excessive frequency (Sep 28-29)

**FOCUS**
Not a strongly run race and less than two lengths covered the first six home. However, the principals were all close to form.

**NOTEBOOK**

**Je Suis Belle**, who goes well on easy ground, has improved with every outing and turned in her best effort yet on this nursery debut. She shapes as though the step up to seven furlongs would suit and she is likely to win more races.

**Missperon(IRE)**, back in nursery company, ran right up to her best with the cheekpieces on for the first time. This easier ground seemed to suit and she looks capable of winning a similar event.

**Dispol Isle(IRE)**, upped in trip for this nursery debut, ran creditably on her first run on soft ground. She is consistent and should continue to give a good account.

**Generous Option** ran creditably on this nursery debut but left the impression that the step up to seven furlongs would be in her favour. She looks capable of winning again, granted a stiffer test.

**Word Perfect**is better than the bare form as she would have been suited by a stronger pace and was continually denied room in the last half of the race. She may well have been unlucky and is capable of winning again. *Official explanation: jockey said filly was continually denied a run*

**Dorn Dancer(IRE)** was not disgraced but her form has a patchy look to it and she is likely to continue to look vulnerable in this type of event from her current mark.

## 5607 WESTSOUND H'CAP — 1m 2f

**4:50** (4:50) (D2) (0-85,85) 3-Y-0+ — **£7,056** (£2,171; £1,085; £542) **Stalls** Low

Form — RPR

-235 **1** **Straw Bear (USA)**$^{25}$ [4988] 3-8-9 **77** ... JMackay 4 — 90+
(SirMarkPrescott) *in tch: pushed along whn nt clr run and lost pl over 3f out: gd hdwy 2f out: styd on wl u.p to ld clsng stages* **13/2**$^{1}$

0214 **2** ½ **Trouble Mountain (USA)**$^{18}$ [5194] 7-8-9 **71** ... JFEgan 11 — 83
(MWEasterby) *hld up: gd hdwy over 2f out: led over 1f out: styd on wl u.p: hdd clsng stages: no ex* **7/1**$^{2}$

3310 **3** 5 **Aperitif**$^{14}$ [5265] 3-8-9 **77** ... JQuinn 19 — 81
(WJHaggas) *trckd ldrs: led over 2f out: hdd over 1f out: sn rdn and btn* **12/1**

5152 **4** 1¾ **Opening Ceremony (USA)**$^{19}$ [5158] 5-8-13 **75** ... PHanagan 5 — 76
(RAFahey) *hld up midfield: hdwy over 2f out: chsd ldrs over 1f out: no further prog* **9/1**$^{3}$

2330 **5** 1 **Lennel**$^{18}$ [5182] 6-8-6 **71** ... (b) HayleyTurner$^{(3)}$ 13 — 70
(ABailey) *hld up towards rr: hdwy 3f out: styd on u.p fnl 2f: nvr able to chal* **16/1**

3000 **6** ¾ **Strong Hand**$^{18}$ [5194] 4-8-10 **72** ... DaleGibson 9 — 70
(MWEasterby) *hld up: gd hdwy over 2f out: in tch over 1f out: no further prog* **16/1**

3010 **7** 2 **Little Bob**$^{14}$ [5265] 3-8-5 **73** ... JFanning 16 — 67
(JDBethell) *hld up: hdwy u.p 2f out: kpt on fnl f: n.d* **40/1**

2063 **8** 1 **Qualitair Wings**$^{20}$ [5127] 5-8-10 **72** ... DMcGaffin 1 — 64
(JHetherton) *hld up: gd hdwy 3f out: ev ch and rdn 2f out: sn btn* **20/1**

2510 **9** 3½ **Rotuma (IRE)**$^{17}$ [5211] 5-8-13 **75** ... (b) LEnstone 7 — 62
(MDods) *in tch: pushed along 4f out: no hdwy* **16/1**

5100 **10** 2½ **Burning Moon**$^{20}$ [5106] 3-9-3 **85** ... (v$^{1}$) KDarley 20 — 67
(JNoseda) *in tch: drvn along over 3f out: no hdwy* **20/1**

-000 **11** hd **Urowells (IRE)**$^{33}$ [4777] 4-9-7 **83** ... (v$^{1}$) SDrowne 6 — 65
(EALDunlop) *led 2f: remained prom: ev ch and rdn 2f out: sn btn* **20/1**

530- **12** 6 **Neckar Valley (IRE)**$^{347}$ [5423] 5-9-1 **77** ... GParkin 12 — 49
(RAFahey) *rr div: sme late hdwy: n.d* **50/1**

1136 **13** 1 **Jimmy Byrne (IRE)**$^{17}$ [5211] 4-8-13 **78** ... TEaves$^{(3)}$ 3 — 48
(BEllison) *midfield: drvn along over 3f out: no hdwy* **12/1**

630/ **14** ¾ **Lewis Island (IRE)**$^{148}$ [5234] 5-9-4 **80** ... JCarroll 2 — 49
(BEllison) *rr div most of way: n.d* **33/1**

3530 **15** 6 **Go Solo**$^{18}$ [5185] 3-8-7 **75** ... ACulhane 8 — 34
(BWHills) *chsd ldrs: rdn 3f out: sn wknd* **25/1**

-260 **16** 2 **Petrula**$^{13}$ [5303] 5-9-4 **80** ... (b) NCallan 10 — 35
(KARyan) *cl up: disp ld over 4f out tl wknd over 2f out* **16/1**

5400 **17** 5 **Low Cloud**$^{25}$ [4988] 4-8-11 **73** ... FNorton 15 — 20
(JJQuinn) *s.i.s: a rr div* **66/1**

2010 **18** hd **Nevada Desert (IRE)**$^{18}$ [5194] 4-8-11 **73** ... (p) DeanMcKeown 18 — 19
(RMWhitaker) *cl up: led over 4f out tl hdd over 2f out: wknd qckly* **16/1**

3614 **19** dist **Bessemer (JPN)**$^{28}$ [4906] 3-9-2 **84** ... RWinston 17 — —
(ISemple) *midfield tl wknd qckly 3f out: virtually p.u: t.o* **7/1**$^{2}$

1050 **20** 25 **Hiawatha (IRE)**$^{37}$ [4634] 5-8-10 **72** ... GGibbons 14 — —
(PABlockley) *led after 2f tl hdd over 4f out: wknd qckly over 3f out: virtually p.u: t.o* **50/1**

2m 14.12s (1.93) **Going Correction** +0.55s/f (Yiel)
**WFA** 3 from 4yo+ 6lb — **20** Ran SP% **122.1**
Speed ratings: **105,104,100,99,98 97,96,95,92,90 90,85,84,84,79 77,73,73,—,—**CSF £42.57 CT £546.41 TOTE £7.50: £1.60, £2.20, £3.30, £3.30; EX 43.50.
**Owner** Chris Jenkins **Bred** Cyril Humphris **Trained** Newmarket, Suffolk
■ Stewards Enquiry : J F Egan one-day ban: careless riding (Sep 28)

**FOCUS**

This looked a fair handicap and the form is solid. Straw Bear improved several pounds and can rate higher still.

**NOTEBOOK**

**Straw Bear(USA)** ◆ turned in an improved effort on this first run over this trip and looks a bit better than the bare form, as he was shuffled down the field turning for home. He shapes as though he will stay a mile and a half and is the type to win more races.

**Trouble Mountain(USA)**, returned to this more suitable trip, had the race run to suit and ran his best race all year, finishing clear of the remainder. He goes on any ground and is mainly a consistent sort so should continue to give a good account.

**Aperitif**, upped to this trip for the first time, did not really get home and left the impression that the drop back to a mile would be in his favour.

**Opening Ceremony(USA)**, a proven performer on soft ground, had the race run to suit but was again a bit below her best returned to handicap company.

**Lennel**, returned to the scene of his win in July, was not disgraced in a race that was run to suit, but this showed that he does need things to fall just right.

**Strong Hand**, who had conditions to suit, has slipped to a fair mark and ran well for a long way. She is one to keep an eye on around this trip with cut in the ground.

**Bessemer(JPN)** *Official explanation: trainer's representative said gelding had a breathing problem*

**Hiawatha(IRE)** *Official explanation: jockey had no explanation for the poor performance*

## 5608 STRACHANS MOTOR GROUP H'CAP (FOR THE EGLINTON & WINTON CHALLENGE CUP) — 2m 1f 105y

**5:20** (5:20) (D2) (0-85,80) 3-Y-0+ — **£6,830** (£2,101; £1,050; £525) **Stalls** Low

Form — RPR

211 **1** **Strangely Brown (IRE)**$^{37}$ [4647] 3-8-5 **71** ... PHanagan 8 — 79+
(SCWilliams) *keen early: hld up: hdwy outside over 2f out: led ins fnl f: styd on wl* **13/8**$^{1}$

0312 **2** 1¼ **Late Opposition**$^{18}$ [5190] 3-8-4 **70** ... (v) FNorton 3 — 77
(EALDunlop) *trckd ldr: led over 2f out: hdd ins fnl f: flashed tail and hld whn edgd lft cl home* **6/1**

240 **3** 1 **Historic Place (USA)**$^{63}$ [3912] 4-9-12 **80** ... SDrowne 2 — 86
(GBBalding) *prom: effrt over 2f out: one pce fnl f* **9/1**

0021 **4** shd **Master Wells (IRE)**$^{21}$ [5100] 3-8-13 **79** ... ACulhane 6 — 85
(JDBethell) *hld up in tch: effrt whn n.m.r over 2f and ins fnl f: keeping on whn no room cl home* **7/2**$^{2}$

/005 **5** 2½ **Ebinzayd (IRE)**$^{18}$ [5190] 8-9-3 **71** ... JFanning 5 — 74
(LLungo) *led to over 2f out: one pce fnl f* **25/1**

6/0- **6** 6 **Alam (USA)**$^{207}$ [5274] 5-9-6 **74** ... LEnstone 1 — 71
(PMonteith) *prom to over 2f out: sn btn* **66/1**

1556 **7** 1¾ **Toni Alcala**$^{18}$ [5190] 5-9-1 **72** ... DNolan$^{(3)}$ 4 — 67
(RFFisher) *hld up in tch: rdn 3f out: sn btn* **25/1**

5003 **8** shd **Kristensen**$^{31}$ [4831] 5-9-9 **77** ... (p) KDarley 7 — 72
(DEddy) *hld up: rdn wl over 2f out: sn btn* **11/2**$^{3}$

4m 5.91s (11.14) **Going Correction** +0.55s/f (Yiel)
**WFA** 3 from 4yo+ 12lb — **8** Ran SP% **109.2**
Speed ratings: **95,94,93,93,92 89,89,89**CSF £10.54 CT £57.63 TOTE £2.30: £1.20, £2.10, £2.00; EX 8.40 Place 6 £369.90, Place 5 £153.27.
**Owner** J T and K Worsley **Bred** Barry Noonan **Trained** Newmarket, Suffolk

**FOCUS**

Only a steady pace in the conditions and a modest time, but another improved effort from Strangely Brown, who remains one to keep on the right side.

**NOTEBOOK**

**Strangely Brown(IRE)** ◆, up 6lb, had a trouble-free passage on the outside and turned in an improved effort to confirm his effectiveness on soft ground. A more strongly run race would suit and he still looks progressive.

**Late Opposition** may not be entirely straightforward but once again did little wrong against a progressive rival. He should continue to give a good account around this trip.

**Historic Place(USA)**, upped in trip, ran creditably in a race that did not really place maximum emphasis on stamina. However, he is going to have to improve to beat progressive rivals from his current mark.

**Master Wells(IRE)** had conditions to suit and could have been expected to improve for the step up in trip but he did not get chance to show what he was capable of in this messy race and he is well worth another chance.

**Ebinzayd(IRE)** had the run of the race but was beaten on merit and is likely to continue to look vulnerable in handicaps from his current mark.

**Alam(USA)**, unproven over this trip on the Flat, was soundly beaten on this first start since February.

T/Jkpt: £28,472.00 to a £1 stake. Pool: £40,101.50. 1.00 winning ticket. T/Plt: £256.30 to a £1 stake. Pool: £76,637.10. 218.20 winning tickets. T/Qpdt: £22.00 to a £1 stake. Pool: £4,535.10. 152.40 winning tickets. RY

# 4742 NEWBURY (L-H)

Friday, September 17

**OFFICIAL GOING: Good (good to firm in places)**

## 5609 EBF DUBAI TENNIS CHAMPIONSHIPS MAIDEN STKS — 6f 8y

**1:20** (1:22) (D2) 2-Y-0 — **£6,646** (£2,045; £1,022; £511) **Stalls** Centre

Form — RPR

2 **1** **Newsround**$^{20}$ [5118] 2-9-0 ... PRobinson 9 — 92+
(MAJarvis) *lw: mde all: shkn up over 1f out: sn clr: easily* **2/5**$^{1}$

**2** 2½ **Oranmore Castle (IRE)** 2-9-0 ... MHills 5 — 85+
(BWHills) *w'like: scope: lengthy: gd sort: t.k.h: hld up in rr: stdy hdwy over 2f out to chse wnr over 1f out: no imp but kpt on enco* **10/1**$^{3}$

0 **3** 5 **Ask For Rain**$^{15}$ [5247] 2-8-9 ... DHolland 11 — 65
(BWHills) *bhd: hdwy fr 3f out: rdn and edgd lft 2f out: kpt on same pce fnl f* **33/1**

**4** ¾ **Awaaser (USA)** 2-8-9 ... RHills 8 — 62
(MPTregoning) *w'like: prom: chsd wnr over 2f out tl over 1f out but nvr a danger: wknd fnl f* **6/1**$^{2}$

40 **5** ½ **Methodical**$^{27}$ [4936] 2-8-9 ... RMullen 2 — 61
(IAWood) *lw: bhd: pushed along and hdwy over 2f out: kpt on fnl f but nvr a danger* **50/1**

00 **6** 1¾ **Sir Bluebird (IRE)**$^{20}$ [5118] 2-9-0 ... RHughes 10 — 61
(RHannon) *chsd ldr to 3f out: sn rdn: wknd ins fnl 2f* **66/1**

**7** ½ **Pagan Quest** 2-9-0 ... LisaJones 4 — 59
(JARToller) *s.i.s: rdn and sme hdwy fr 3f out: nvr nr ldrs and wknd ins fnl 2f* **16/1**

000 **8** 1½ **Worth Abbey**$^{32}$ [4809] 2-9-0 ... DaneO'Neill 6 — 55
(RHannon) *prom: chsd wnr 3f out tl over 2f out: sn rdn and wknd* **66/1**

**9** 5 **Speedy Spirit** 2-8-9 ... SWhitworth 7 — 35
(MSalaman) *w'like: bkwd: s.i.s: a bhd* **100/1**

**10** 4 **Jubilee Coin** 2-8-6 ... RThomas$^{(3)}$ 1 — 23
(GBBalding) *bkwd: in tch: rdn 1/2-way: sn wknd* **66/1**

1m 13.42s (-0.95) **Going Correction** -0.10s/f (Good) — **10** Ran SP% **111.1**
Speed ratings: **102,98,92,91,90 88,87,85,78,73**CSF £4.47 TOTE £1.40: £1.10, £2.50, £3.20; EX 4.70.
**Owner** Sheikh Mohammed **Bred** Meon Valley Stud **Trained** Newmarket, Suffolk

**FOCUS**

Strong maiden form. The race was run at a sound gallop in a decent time, and the field came home well strung out.

**NOTEBOOK**

**Newsround** confirmed the promise of his recent Newmarket debut by making all for a bloodless success. He has plenty of early pace, should get seven furlongs this year and looks potentially smart, so deserves a crack at Pattern company now.

**Oranmore Castle(IRE)**, a 150,000 euros gns purchase, took a strong hold on this debut and ran green as grass early on, but gradually got the hang of things and shaped encouragingly in the closing stages. He was unlucky to run into such a promising winner and was clear in second, so will have little trouble winning his maiden assuming he learns to settle.

**Ask For Rain** was again none too smartly away, but improved on her recent Salisbury debut over this slightly shorter trip. She will not be seen at her best until next year, but her future looks to lie in handicaps.

**Awaaser(USA)**, whose dam is half-sister to Musidora winner Marillette and classy British and American performer Storm Trooper, was smartly away and shaped with promise, but paid for trying to go with the winner from halfway. She will come on for this outing and should go closer next time, but is unlikely to fulfill her potential until racing over farther in due course.

**Methodical**, who had shown fair form in two previous outings over the trip, was hard ridden from an early stage, but was keeping on nicely in the final stages. She will do better over another furlong and now qualifies for handicaps.

**Sir Bluebird(IRE)** showed early pace, but could not sustain his gallop and was running on empty in the latter stages. He should fare better in nurseries.

## 5610 DUBAI DUTY FREE CUP (LISTED RACE) 7f (S)
1:50 (1:51) (A1) 3-Y-0+ £17,400 (£6,600; £3,300; £1,500) Stalls Centre

Form RPR
0200 **1** **Royal Storm (IRE)**[6] 5468 5-9-0 99 ........ DHolland 12 108
(MrsAJPerrett) *lw: racd stands side and led that gp after 2f: rdn: edgd lft and tk overall ld appr fnl f: kpt on wl u.p* **16/1**
41-0 **2** *½* **Meshaheer (USA)**[139] 1758 5-9-0 105 ........ (t) RHills 4 107
(SaeedBinSuroor) *racd far side: hld up:nt clr run 2f out:swtchd lft and hdwy over 1f out: str run to chse wnr ins last: no imp nr fin* **12/1**
1110 **3** *½* **Lucky Spin**[49] 4286 3-8-6 102 ........ RLMoore 6 101
(RHannon) *racd far side: chsd ldrs: led that gp over 2f out: hdd overall appr fnl f: styd on same pce* **10/1**
4-54 **4** *½* **Azarole (IRE)**[111] 2476 3-8-11 106 ........ JPMurtagh 3 104
(JRFanshawe) *racd far side and chsd ldrs: rdn over 2f out: kpt on same pce ins fnl f* **12/1**
5120 **5** *½* **Oasis Star (IRE)**[55] 4140 3-8-6 89 ........ TQuinn 11 98
(PWHarris) *lw: racd stands side and sn chsng ldrs: rdn over 2f out: kpt on same pce fnl f* **33/1**
0226 **6** *1* **Suggestive**[8] 5414 6-9-0 111 ........ (b) MHills 8 101
(WJHaggas) *racd far side: hld up in rr: rdn over 2f out: styd on u.p fnl f but nt trble ldrs* **9/2**[1]
0416 **7** *1 ½* **Material Witness (IRE)**[8] 5422 7-9-0 105 ........ MartinDwyer 5 97
(WRMuir) *racd far side and led that gp tl over 2f out: styd chsng ldrs tl wknd ins fnl f* **16/1**
4030 **8** *1 ½* **Kings Point (IRE)**[8] 5422 3-8-11 103 ........ RHughes 14 93
(RHannon) *racd stands side: in tch: rdn over 2f out: wknd fnl f* **33/1**
016- **9** *½* **Sabbeeh (USA)**[329] 5731 3-8-11 110 ........ (t) LDettori 13 91
(SaeedBinSuroor) *lw: racd stands side and led that gp 2f: styd prom tl wknd over 1f out* **5/1**[2]
0301 **10** *½* **Zonus**[27] 4931 3-8-11 100 ........ (b) KFallon 1 90
(BWHills) *racd far side: bhd: rdn and hdwy to chse ldrs over 2f out: wknd appr fnl f* **6/1**[3]
0660 **11** *nk* **Lago D'Orta (IRE)**[36] 4685 4-9-0 99 ........ PRobinson 9 89
(CGCox) *s.i.s: racd stands side: sn in tch: rdn over 2f out: sn wknd* **16/1**
0400 **12** *2* **Bahiano (IRE)**[48] 4322 3-8-11 104 ........ TEDurcan 7 84
(CEBrittain) *racd far side: chsd ldrs until rdn and wknd over 2f out* **33/1**
0310 **13** *shd* **Pizazz**[6] 5468 3-8-11 92 ........ (b) JFortune 10 84
(BJMeehan) *racd stands side: chsd ldrs: rdn 3f out: wknd 2f out* **50/1**
0136 **14** *2 ½* **Rum Shot**[19] 5171 3-8-11 108 ........ DaneO'Neill 2 77
(HCandy) *s.i.s: racd far side: hdwy over 2f out: sn rdn and wknd* **15/2**

1m 24.64s (-2.58) **Going Correction** -0.10s/f (Good)
**WFA** 3 from 4yo+ 3lb **14** Ran SP% **113.8**
Speed ratings: **110,109,108,108,107 106,104,103,102,102 101,99,99,96**CSF £180.21 TOTE £19.50: £7.60, £5.10, £2.50; EX 370.30 Trifecta £526.70 Part won. Pool: £741.86. 0.10 winning units..
**Owner** The Cloran Family **Bred** E Campion **Trained** Pulborough, W Sussex

**FOCUS**
This Listed race was run at a decent gallop, but it was a bit messy as they raced in two groups until merging in the closing stages. The solid handicap form of Royal Storm and Oasis Star sets the standard.

**NOTEBOOK**
**Royal Storm(IRE)** soon adopted his usual position at the head of affairs and responded gamely to pressure when challenged late on to score a deserved success. He is very tough and this was a career-best effort, but he is going to be increasingly hard to place now.
**Meshaheer(USA)**, off since disappointing at Haydock in May, turned in a much-improved effort, but could not get to the winner inside the final furlong, try as he might. He is a headstrong character, but retains his ability and could be placed to win a similar event before the season is out.
**Lucky Spin** proved her Goodwood running to be all wrong and showed her true colours on this more conventional track. She can find another race at this level now her confidence has been boosted.
**Azarole(IRE)**, who has had a soft palate operation since disappointing at Kempton in May, posted a solid effort on this comeback and will improve plenty for the outing. He is one to keep an eye on.
**Oasis Star(IRE)** was not at all disgraced on this first try at Pattern level and confirmed her latest running to be all wrong. She will take a rise in the ratings for this, however.
**Suggestive**, best in on BHB figures, failed to run up to that mark and was a little disappointing. He is smart on his day, but needs things to fall right and is generally one to take on.
**Sabbeeh(USA)** was handy for a long way on this belated seasonal reappearance, but dropped out when asked for maximum effort. He will need to improve plenty for this outing if he is to figure at this level again.
**Zonus** never looked like following-up on his Chester success in this much better race. He could struggle off his new mark when reverting to handicaps.
**Rum Shot** flattered briefly two out, but was soon treading water and dropped out tamely. This was way below the form of his third in the Hungerford on his penultimate outing and he may be better back at six furlongs, although he has plenty to prove now. *Official explanation: trainer said colt lost its action*

## 5611 DUBAI DUTY FREE ARC TRIAL (GROUP 3) 1m 3f 5y
2:20 (2:20) (A1) 3-Y-0+ £29,000 (£11,000; £5,500; £2,500) Stalls High

Form RPR
12-1 **1** **Sights On Gold (IRE)**[18] 5180 5-9-2 114 ........ (t) LDettori 3 118+
(SaeedBinSuroor) *hld up in rr: swtchd rt and hdwy ins fnl 3f: lft in ld and rdn ins fnl 2f: kpt on wl fnl f* **3/1**[1]
3036 **2** *1* **Imperial Dancer**[5] 5483 6-9-2 110 ........ TEDurcan 7 116
(MRChannon) *hld up in rr: hdwy to chse ldrs 3f out: hung rt and chsd wnr ins fnl 2f: edgd lft ins last: kpt on cl home* **7/2**[2]
5332 **3** *1* **Compton Bolter (IRE)**[7] 5438 7-9-2 109 ........ DHolland 4 114
(GAButler) *chsd ldrs: rdn over 3f out: kpt on same pce fnl 2f* **11/1**
114 **4** *½* **Day Flight**[103] 2722 3-8-9 114 ........ RHughes 8 113
(JHMGosden) *lw: hld up in rr: hdwy and n.m.r ins fnl 3f: chsd ldrs 2f out: kpt on same pce fnl f* **7/2**[2]
2113 **5** *1 ½* **Albinus**[62] 3927 3-8-9 104 ........ (b) MartinDwyer 1 111
(AMBalding) *sn chsng ldr: led ins fnl 3f: rdn: hung bdly rt and hdd ins fnl 2f: nt rcvr* **14/1**
453 **6** *6* **Nysaean (IRE)**[5] 5502 5-9-5 112 ........ RLMoore 5 104
(RHannon) *hld up rr: rdn and hdwy 3f out: wknd qckly fr 2f out: dismntd* **20/1**
-224 **7** *8* **Westmoreland Road (USA)**[15] 5251 4-9-2 106 ........ JPMurtagh 2 88
(MrsAJPerrett) *lw: s.i.s: sn drvn to ld: hdd ins fnl 3f: sn btn* **12/1**
0234 **8** *30* **Always First**[31] 4833 3-8-9 110 ........ KFallon 6 40
(SirMichaelStoute) *in tch: rdn and wkng whn hmpd ins fnl 3f: eased* **5/1**[3]

2m 18.07s (-4.74) **Going Correction** -0.10s/f (Good)
**WFA** 3 from 4yo+ 7lb **8** Ran SP% **113.6**
Speed ratings: **113,112,111,111,110 105,99,78**CSF £13.44 TOTE £4.30: £1.80, £1.40, £2.30; EX 16.40 Trifecta £46.90 Pool: £568.90. 8.60 winning units..
**Owner** Godolphin **Bred** Moyglare Stud Farm Ltd **Trained** Newmarket, Suffolk

**FOCUS**
A decent enough field for the first running of this former Listed race under Group Three status, and a winning time in keeping with its new level. The form has been rated through Compton Bolter.

**NOTEBOOK**
**Sights On Gold(IRE)** followed-up his comeback success at Epsom 18 days previously in good style on this step back up to Group level, looking value for more than the bare margin. He coped with the extra distance and could have been called the winner some way out, after the leader hung badly right. He is open to further improvement, and while he may not be one of his stable's leading lights, he may be able to find a Group Two over this sort of trip.
**Imperial Dancer**, who escaped a penalty for his Group One success in Italy in 2003, turned in another solid effort and is a reliable yardstick at this level. However, he is not the easiest to win with, and may have found this coming too soon after the Irish Champion Stakes only six days previously.
**Compton Bolter(IRE)**, who took this in 2003 when it was still under Listed status, ran another soid race in defeat. He deserves to find a similar event, but will probably need to drop back to Listed level in order to do so.
**Day Flight**, last seen when fourth in the French Derby in June, has to go down as slightly disappointing. He was travelling as well as any two out, but failed to find much off the bridle on this ground, which may not have been as soft as he prefers. He will come on for this and remains lightly raced, but has a bit to prove now nevertheless.
**Albinus** looked booked for a place at least, until he again showed his quirks and hung violently to his right, losing all chance in the process. He is very talented, but not one to place any real faith in at present, although he may do better at four if staying in training. *Official explanation: jockey said colt hung right*
**Nysaean(IRE)** ran below his best on ground quicker than ideal.
**Westmoreland Road(USA)** was rushed up to lead after a sluggish start and raced freely at the head of affairs, before fading tamely when challenged as the race got serious. This was another disappointing display and he is in danger of becoming regressive. *Official explanation: trainer had no explanation for the poor form shown*
**Always First** ran below his Great Volitgeur form and continues to frustrate.

## 5612 HAYNES, HANSON AND CLARK CONDITIONS STKS (C&G) 1m (S)
2:55 (2:55) (B1) 2-Y-0 £10,873 (£4,020; £2,010; £913) Stalls Centre

Form RPR
2111 **1** **Merchant (IRE)**[21] 5090 2-8-10 99 ........ RMullen 4 92+
(MLWBell) *lw: trckd ldrs: drvn to ld ins fnl 2f: sn hung lft: hung rt ins last and wnt lft cl home: readily* **4/5**[1]
**2** *2 ½* **Noble Duty (USA)** 2-8-10 ........ LDettori 5 87
(SaeedBinSuroor) *w'like: gd sort: hld up rr but in tch: stdy hdwy to chse wnr over 1f out: kpt on wl but no imp ins last* **5/2**[2]
2541 **3** *¾* **Mastman (IRE)**[29] 4872 2-9-1 85 ........ (t) JFortune 3 90
(BJMeehan) *trckd ldr: rdn to chal ins fnl 3f: kpt on same pce fnl f* **14/1**
**4** *¾* **Pittsburgh** 2-8-10 ........ KFallon 1 83
(AMBalding) *str: gd sort: chsd ldrs:rdn 3f out: swtchd rt over 1f out and kpt on again u.p ins last* **11/1**
5 **5** *3* **Takhleed (USA)**[22] 5051 2-8-10 ........ RHills 2 77
(MPTregoning) *lw: led tl hdd ins fnl 2f: wknd fnl f* **8/1**[3]

1m 40.25s (-0.58) **Going Correction** -0.10s/f (Good) **5** Ran SP% **110.2**
Speed ratings: **98,95,94,94,91**CSF £3.01 TOTE £1.70: £1.10, £1.70; EX 2.90.
**Owner** H E Sheikh Rashid Bin Mohammed **Bred** John Foley **Trained** Newmarket, Suffolk

**FOCUS**
Just a fair renewal of an event that boasts a righ heritage. The form might not be that solid, but they came home well strung out and it has provisionally been assessed positively.

**NOTEBOOK**
**Merchant(IRE)** continued his rise up the ranks and won with authority, despite hanging badly both ways after hitting the front. He has improved out of all recognition since the ground eased and this was his fourth straight success. This earned him a crack at Group level, with his trainer sighting as a likely target the Group One Gran Criterium in Italy, where he should get his favoured conditions.
**Noble Duty(USA)**, a son of the great Dubai Millenium out of a mare who was a dual Listed winner in the US, made a very pleasing debut. He looked a real threat to the winner when produced from off the pace, but tired late on and was not given too hard a time. He has a future and could make up into a decent performer next year over further. In the meantime a maiden is there for the taking.
**Mastman(IRE)** was prominent throughout and held every chance if good enough, but the penalty for winning a novice event last time was always going to make it tough. This was no disgrace, but he will not be the easiest horse to place now.
**Pittsburgh** turned in a promising debut display and ran on again late in the day after showing a bit of inexperience. He should improve a great deal for the outing and ought to have no trouble winning a maiden, although he will not be seen at his best until next year.
**Takhleed(USA)**, slowly away on his Lingfield debut in August, pinged out this time to lead, but found only the one pace under pressure and was well beaten in the end. He may be capable of better in time, but in the short term might benefit from a shorter trip.

## 5613 DUBAI DUTY FREE FULL OF SURPRISES EBF FILLIES' CONDITIONS STKS 7f (S)
3:30 (3:30) (B1) 2-Y-0 £11,386 (£4,040; £2,020; £918) Stalls Centre

Form RPR
1 **1** **Shanghai Lily (IRE)**[35] 4712 2-8-13 ........ KFallon 5 100+
(SirMichaelStoute) *lw: hld up in 4th but wl in tch: hdwy to ld ins fnl 2f: pushed clr fnl f: comf* **4/7**[1]
0210 **2** *2 ½* **Sharp As A Tack (IRE)**[19] 5149 2-8-8 83 ........ (b[1]) JFortune 2 89
(BJMeehan) *led: pushed along 3f out: hdd ins fnl 2f: flashed tail u.p ins last: no ch w wnr but kpt on to hold 2nd* **14/1**
2 **3** *¾* **Tahrir (IRE)**[14] 5272 2-8-8 ........ RHills 3 87
(BWHills) *trckd ldr: rdn to chal over 2f out: outpcd fr over 1f out* **11/4**[2]
1 **4** *6* **Annals**[20] 5115 2-8-13 ........ DaneO'Neill 6 77
(HCandy) *racd in cl 3rd tl disp 2nd 1/2-way: sn rdn: wknd ins fnl 2f* **15/2**[3]

1m 26.09s (-1.13) **Going Correction** -0.10s/f (Good) **4** Ran SP% **108.8**
Speed ratings: **102,99,98,91**CSF £8.82 TOTE £1.40; EX 8.10.
**Owner** Cheveley Park Stud **Bred** Mrs Monica Hackett **Trained** Newmarket, Suffolk

**FOCUS**
A useful time for the type of race. The winner looks sure to make her mark in Pattern company, but the form behind her perhaps wants treating with a degree of caution.

**NOTEBOOK**
**Shanghai Lily(IRE)**, who looked potentially smart when landing her maiden at this track on her debut in August, followed up in fine style, showing a decent turn of foot. She again ran green and will improve plenty as a result of this outing, so fully deserves a crack at Pattern company now. She should have no trouble in getting a mile next year, but in the meantime has the Rockfel as her likely target.
**Sharp As A Tack(IRE)**, last of 12 when tried in Group company last time, showed her true colours back at this more realistic level and time may tell she lost very little in defeat, although she was getting 5lb from the winner. The blinkers had the desired effect and she should be placed to score again.
**Tahrir(IRE)**, a promising second on her debut at Kempton a fortnight previously, got outpaced when the race got serious but again showed a fair amount of ability. She should have no trouble winning her maiden at least.
**Annals** dropped out quickly when put under pressure and was a little disappointing. She may be best forgiven this run and could leave it behind when faced with a stiffer test.

## 5614 DUBAI DUTY FREE FOUNDATION H'CAP 7f (S)

4:05 (4:06) (D2) (0-85,85) 3-Y-O+ £7,914 (£2,435; £1,217; £608) Stalls Centre

| Form | | | | RPR |
|---|---|---|---|---|
| 5660 | **1** | | **Chateau Nicol**[55] 4122 5-9-3 **81** ... TQuinn 18<br>(BGPowell) *mid div: gd hdwy fr 2f out: str run fnl f: led last stride* **20/1** | 90 |
| 2000 | **2** | *shd* | **Blue Trojan (IRE)**[25] 5004 4-8-12 **83** ... JDaly(7) 4<br>(SKirk) *led: hung lft to r along far rail over 2f out: sn pushed along and 3l clr: shkn up ins last: eased and ct last stride* **16/1** | 92+ |
| 26-1 | **3** | *shd* | **Mutamared (USA)**[116] 2367 4-9-4 **82** ... RHills 21<br>(MPTregoning) *lw: hld up mid div: gd hdwy fr 2f out: chsd wnr ins last: fin strly: jst failed* **5/1**[2] | 90+ |
| 0000 | **4** | *½* | **Serieux**[8] 5419 5-9-2 **80** ...(p) JPMurtagh 23<br>(MrsAJPerrett) *bhd: hdwy fr 2f out: styd on u.p fnl f: gng on cl home* **7/1**[3] | 87 |
| 0204 | **5** | *nk* | **In The Pink (IRE)**[19] 5155 4-8-7 **71** oh1 ... SHitchcott 17<br>(MRChannon) *lw: slowly ins stride: bhd: stl plenty to do 2f out: rapid hdwy over 1f out: fin wl* **25/1** | 77 |
| 0152 | **6** | *¾* | **Juste Pour L'Amour**[9] 5403 4-8-3 **72** ... DFox(5) 14<br>(PLGilligan) *chsd ldrs: wnt 2nd and rdn 2f out: no imp on ldr but kpt on ins fnl f* **12/1** | 76 |
| 3001 | **7** | *shd* | **Armagnac**[7] 5444 6-9-7 **85** 6ex ... DaneO'Neill 20<br>(MABuckley) *bhd: hdwy over 1f out: kpt on fnl f: nt pce of ldrs* **16/1** | 89 |
| 2002 | **8** | *1 ¾* | **Winning Venture**[18] 5177 7-9-3 **81** ...(p) DHolland 6<br>(AWCarroll) *chsd ldrs: rdn over 2f out: styd on same pce fnl f* **16/1** | 81 |
| 6162 | **9** | *nk* | **Arctic Desert**[8] 5419 4-8-13 **77** ... KFallon 13<br>(AMBalding) *b.: in tch: hdwy 3f out: drvn to chse ldrs 2f out: sn one pce: wknd ins fnl f* **10/3**[1] | 76 |
| 0000 | **10** | *hd* | **Omaha City (IRE)**[7] 5444 10-8-4 **71** oh1 ... LPKeniry(3) 8<br>(BGubby) *swtg: chsd ldrs: rdn over 2f out: wknd ins fnl f* **40/1** | 69 |
| 6064 | **11** | *nk* | **Kareeb (FR)**[12] 5316 7-8-7 **71** oh2 ... RMullen 24<br>(WJMusson) *bhd: hdwy over 1f out: kpt on but nt trble ldrs* **12/1** | 69 |
| 0004 | **12** | *½* | **Craiova (IRE)**[34] 4742 5-8-9 **80** ... KMay(7) 19<br>(BWHills) *sn in tch: rdn to chse ldrs 3f out: wknd ins fnl f* **12/1** | 76 |
| 0000 | **13** | *nk* | **Just Fly**[30] 4846 4-8-8 **72** ... SWhitworth 5<br>(SKirk) *bhd: sme hdwy 2f out: nvr gng pce to trble ldrs* **40/1** | 67 |
| 3103 | **14** | *2* | **Corky (IRE)**[27] 4938 3-8-10 **77** ... RLMoore 26<br>(RHannon) *bhd: rdn over 3f out: kpt on fr over 1f out but n.d* **16/1** | 67 |
| 3536 | **15** | *1 ½* | **Ammenayr (IRE)**[28] 4917 4-8-11 **75** ... GCarter 2<br>(TGMills) *chsd ldrs tl wknd 2f out* **50/1** | 61 |
| 0000 | **16** | *¾* | **Border Edge**[14] 5275 6-9-1 **82** ...(v) ABeech(3) 3<br>(JJBridger) *chsd ldrs: rdn over 3f out: wknd over 1f out* **66/1** | 66 |
| -640 | **17** | *hd* | **Go Bananas**[16] 5220 3-9-1 **82** ... JFortune 25<br>(BJMeehan) *bhd tl sme hdwy fnl 2f* **33/1** | 66 |
| 0400 | **18** | *nk* | **Danehill Stroller (IRE)**[13] 5299 4-9-2 **80** ...(p) MartinDwyer 12<br>(RMBeckett) *t.k.h: chsd ldrs 5f* **33/1** | 63 |
| 5646 | **19** | *½* | **Little Edward**[7] 5442 6-9-4 **82** ... RHughes 9<br>(BGPowell) *s.i.s: t.k.h: a bhd* **50/1** | 64 |
| 4240 | **20** | *1 ¼* | **Quantum Leap**[55] 4122 7-8-8 **72** ...(v) LisaJones 16<br>(SDow) *chsd ldr tl 2f out: sn wknd* **50/1** | 51 |
| 3000 | **21** | *nk* | **Kindlelight Debut**[8] 5419 4-8-8 **72** ... PRobinson 15<br>(DKIvory) *chsd ldrs over 4f* **33/1** | 50 |
| 010- | **22** | *nk* | **Caledonian (IRE)**[272] 6222 3-9-1 **82** ... NPollard 22<br>(DRCElsworth) *a in rr* **66/1** | 59 |
| 0300 | **23** | *½* | **Flying Express**[22] 5055 4-9-4 **82** ... MHills 1<br>(BWHills) *chsd ldrs over 4f* **33/1** | 58 |
| 0555 | **24** | *7* | **Tribute (IRE)**[29] 4874 3-8-6 **73** ... TEDurcan 10<br>(KARyan) *chsd ldrs 4f* **33/1** | 31 |

1m 25.23s (-1.99) **Going Correction** -0.10s/f (Good)

**WFA** 3 from 4yo+ 3lb **24** Ran SP% **135.9**

Speed ratings: **107,106,106,106,105 105,104,102,102,102 101,101,101,98,97 96,95,95,95,93 93,92,92,84**CSF £303.53 CT £1903.14 TOTE £29.30: £6.70, £5.50, £2.30, £2.30; EX 822.40.

**Owner** Basingstoke Commercials **Bred** Aston House Stud **Trained** Morestead, Hants

■ Stewards Enquiry : J Daly 28-day ban: failed to ride out for first place (Sep 28-30, Oct 1-2,4-27)

**FOCUS**

A strong handicap run at a solid pace. The form looks sound, even though the winner must be considered a shade lucky.

**NOTEBOOK**

**Chateau Nicol** really picked up for pressure two out and stayed on strongly to collar the leader close home. He was aided by the runner-up being eased a shade late on, but this was a solid effort, especially as he was without his usual visor and was returning from a 55-day break. This was the highest mark he has won off and he is a very useful performer when things go his way.

**Blue Trojan(IRE)** looked booked for success when going clear, after hanging to the far side rail two out, but his rider eased slightly close home and he was caught on the line. He would have won with stronger handling and he might be the type to run well at fair odds in the Cambridgeshire if making the cut.

**Mutamared(USA)** ◆, a headstrong character when trained by Godolphin and making his handicap bow, clearly goes well fresh and showed a strong turn of foot approaching the final furlong, only just missing out on the line. He settled better this time, and it will be surprising if he fails to make amends in a similar race before the end of the season.

**Serieux**, who has dropped 13lb since resuming this season, turned in his best effort for sometime and has clearly found his mark. The cheekpieces have helped recently and he is capable of winning a similar event, but he is not the easiest horse to predict.

**In The Pink(IRE)** once again dented her cause with a sluggish start, but was really motoring close home and produced another sound effort. She can be found easier opportunites off this sort of mark, but always needs things to fall right.

**Juste Pour L'Amour** can have no excuses, but confirmed his recent well-being with a solid display and was not beaten far. Suspicion remains that he is best at a mile now, however.

**Armagnac** turned in a very respectable effort under his penalty and was clear of the rest. He may struggle to score off this mark, but should continue to pay his way in handicaps.

**Arctic Desert**, who looked most unlucky at Doncaster last time, ran below his best and was disappointing. He does look tricky, but remains well treated on his best form.

## 5615 DUBAI GRAND PRIX H'CAP 1m 3f 5y

4:40 (4:42) (D2) (0-85,85) 3-Y-O+ £7,220 (£2,221; £1,110; £555) Stalls High

| Form | | | | RPR |
|---|---|---|---|---|
| 6020 | **1** | | **Solo Flight**[20] 5122 7-9-7 **85** ... RLMoore 6<br>(HMorrison) *s.i.s: hld up in rr: stdy hdwy over 2f out: drvn and str run fnl f to ld last strides* **25/1** | 93 |
| 131- | **2** | *nk* | **Tip The Dip (USA)**[359] 5152 4-9-6 **84** ... JFortune 11<br>(JHMGosden) *h.d.w: sn trcking ldr: rdn over 3f out: led ins fnl 2f: kpt on wl u.p: ct last strides* **10/1** | 92 |
| -314 | **3** | *½* | **Cellarmaster (IRE)**[34] 4754 3-8-8 **79** ... KFallon 7<br>(EFVaughan) *in tch: rdn and hdwy over 2f out: chsd ldr ins fnl f: kpt on but nt qckn cl home* **7/1**[3] | 86 |
| 0212 | **4** | *hd* | **Compton Drake**[18] 5185 5-8-8 **72** ... LDettori 5<br>(GAButler) *lw: t.k.h: chsd ldrs: rdn over 2f out: styd on fnl f but nt qckn cl home* **4/1**[2] | 79 |
| 3016 | **5** | *½* | **Flotta**[18] 5182 5-9-4 **82** ... SHitchcott 12<br>(MRChannon) *hld up in rr: hdwy on rails fr 3f out: rdn and styd on to chse ldrs over 1f out: one pce last half f* **20/1** | 88 |
| 14 | **6** | *2* | **Deep Purple**[27] 4950 3-9-0 **85** ... MartinDwyer 3<br>(MPTregoning) *lw: s.i.s: sn mid-div: rdn: edgd lft and one pce over 2f out: styd on again fnl f but nt trble ldrs* **3/1**[1] | 88 |
| 31 | **7** | *1* | **Daze**[28] 4910 3-8-5 **76** ow1 ... RHills 15<br>(SirMichaelStoute) *chsd ldrs: rdn over 2f out: wknd ins fnl f* **10/1** | 77 |
| 3-45 | **8** | *½* | **Petrosa (IRE)**[37] 4641 4-8-7 **71** oh1 ... TQuinn 13<br>(DRCElsworth) *s.i.s: plld hrd in rr: pushed along and hdwy fr 2f out: kpt on ins last but nt trble ldrs* **16/1** | 71 |
| 00-5 | **9** | *nk* | **Seeyaaj**[12] 4572 4-9-1 **79** ... WRyan 14<br>(JonjoO'Neill) *s.i.s: bhd: pushed along and styd on wl fnl 2f: nt rch ldrs* **40/1** | 79 |
| 0356 | **10** | *nk* | **Nawow**[128] 2047 4-8-10 **74** ... DHolland 9<br>(PDCundell) *hld up in rr: hdwy to chse ldrs over 2f out: wknd over 1f out* **10/1** | 74 |
| 5310 | **11** | *hd* | **Rasid (USA)**[17] 5211 6-9-0 **78** ... DaneO'Neill 2<br>(CADwyer) *b.near fore: s.i.s: sn in tch: rdn 3f out: sn outpcd: kpt on again ins last* **25/1** | 77 |
| 2000 | **12** | *½* | **Anticipating**[18] 5182 4-9-3 **81** ... RMullen 16<br>(AMBalding) *slowly away: plld hrd: bhd most of way* **25/1** | 79 |
| 1016 | **13** | *shd* | **Cause Celebre (IRE)**[63] 3908 3-8-7 **78** ... MHills 4<br>(BWHills) *led tl hdd ins fnl 2f: wknd over 1f out* **25/1** | 76 |
| 4100 | **14** | *1 ¼* | **Penzance**[13] 5297 3-8-10 **81** ow1 ... JPMurtagh 1<br>(JRFanshawe) *chsd ldrs: rdn 3f out: wknd over 2f out* **10/1** | 77 |
| 3232 | **15** | *½* | **Sir Laughalot**[102] 1624 4-8-7 **71** oh1 ... TEDurcan 8<br>(MissECLavelle) *chsd ldrs tl wknd over 2f out* **33/1** | 66 |

2m 22.27s (-0.54) **Going Correction** -0.10s/f (Good)

**WFA** 3 from 4yo+ 7lb **15** Ran SP% **125.3**

Speed ratings: **97,96,96,96,95 94,93,93,93,92 92,92,92,91,91**CSF £248.86 CT £1969.17 TOTE £33.40: £5.80, £3.80, £3.30; EX 193.70 Place 6 £55.39, Place 5 £45.16.

**Owner** Lady Hardy **Bred** S Wingfield Digby **Trained** East Ilsley, Berks

**FOCUS**

A decent handicap and the first five were clear at the finish. However, there was no real early pace and it produced a modest time for the grade.

**NOTEBOOK**

**Solo Flight** turned in a much-improved display to score his first success for two years under a fine ride from Moore. He deserves extra credit for carrying top-weight and despite not getting his favoured fast gallop this time. However, it is hard to predict what he will do next time as he has never managed to win back-to-back races in the past.

**Tip The Dip(USA)** ◆, not seen since winning off a 4lb lower mark a year previously, made a very promising reappearance and went down fighting. This effort leaves his shrewd yard with plenty of options, and he could win a decent handicap this year.

**Cellarmaster(IRE)** posted another solid effort and enjoyed the underfoot condtions. He is still open to further progression this season and would not mind easier ground.

**Compton Drake** did well to finish so close after running too keenly early on. This trip looks to be his optimum and he can be placed to advantage off this mark.

**Flotta** ran feeely through the early stages and would have been better suited by a stronger early gallop. He did well in the circumtances and was clear of the rest.

**Deep Purple** was not disgraced on this, his third outing, and he still looked green this time. He can do better with further experience and is far from one to write off.

**Daze** was put in her place on this handicap debut, but remains lightly-raced and should be found easier opportunities.

T/Plt: £64.70 to a £1 stake. Pool: £50,409.35. 568.20 winning tickets. T/Qpdt: £8.30 to a £1 stake. Pool: £3,815.60. 336.40 winning tickets. ST

# [4850] NOTTINGHAM (L-H)

## Friday, September 17

**OFFICIAL GOING: Good to soft**

The going was described as 'good to soft' on the straight course and 'definitely soft' on the round course with the home turn rail put back 12 yards.

Wind: Almost nil. Weather: Overcast, light rain 1st 3 races.

## 5616 SARREGO MEMORIAL EBF MAIDEN STKS 6f 15y

2:10 (2:11) (D2) 2-Y-O £6,337 (£1,950; £975; £487) Stalls Low

| Form | | | | RPR |
|---|---|---|---|---|
| | **1** | | **The Abbess** 2-8-9 ... DSweeney 7<br>(HCandy) *leggy: unf: scope: hld up in tch: shkn up over 2f out: led wl ins fnl f: r.o* **10/1** | 80+ |
| 3 | **2** | *1 ½* | **Sound The Drum (USA)**[37] 4637 2-9-0 ... KMcEvoy 14<br>(JHMGosden) *chsd ldr tl led over 3f out: hdd and unable qckn wl ins fnl f* **7/4**[1] | 80 |
| | **3** | *1 ½* | **Three Degrees (IRE)** 2-8-4 ... NChalmers(5) 5<br>(RMBeckett) *lengthy: unf: s.s: outpcd: hdwy and hung lft over 1f out: r.o: nt rch ldrs* **50/1** | 71+ |
| 44 | **4** | *3* | **Etaar**[37] 4625 2-9-0 ... WSupple 11<br>(EALDunlop) *s.i.s: hld up: hdwy over 2f out: styd on same pce fnl f* **4/1**[3] | 67 |
| 0 | **5** | *2 ½* | **Cavalarra**[14] 5262 2-9-0 ... EAhern 10<br>(BWHills) *chsd ldrs: rdn over 1f out: wknd ins fnl f* **20/1** | 59 |
| 3 | **6** | *1 ¼* | **Beaune**[14] 5262 2-9-0 ... SWKelly 3<br>(WJHaggas) *chsd ldrs: rdn over 1f out: wknd ins fnl f* **9/4**[2] | 55 |
| | **7** | *nk* | **Leighton Buzzard** 2-9-0 ... RHavlin 1<br>(PWChapple-Hyam) *rangy: unf: s.s: outpcd: styd on ins fnl f: nvr nrr* **20/1** | 54 |
| | **8** | *2* | **Eforetta (GER)** 2-8-9 ... MTebbutt 6<br>(DJWintle) *s.i.s: hld up: n.d* **66/1** | 43 |
| 0 | **9** | *½* | **Italian Touch (IRE)**[11] 5353 2-9-0 ... IMongan 16<br>(JAGlover) *s.s: n.d* **40/1** | 47 |
| 000 | **10** | *¾* | **Sonntag Blue (IRE)**[39] 4598 2-9-0 ... TPQueally 4<br>(JAOsborne) *hld up: n.d* **66/1** | 45 |
| 30 | **11** | *1 ¼* | **Queue Up**[44] 4454 2-9-0 ... MFenton 8<br>(JGGiven) *led: hdd over 3f out: wknd over 1f out* **25/1** | 41 |
| | **12** | *½* | **Temple Belle Xpres** 2-8-9 ... JBramhill 12<br>(SRBowring) *neat: unf: prom over 3f* **66/1** | 34 |
| 00 | **13** | *5* | **Preskani**[28] 4924 2-9-0 ... RFitzpatrick 2<br>(MrsNMacauley) *prom: lost pl over 4f out: wknd 1/2-way* **100/1** | 24 |
| 000 | **14** | *2* | **Kirkhammerton (IRE)**[5] 5494 2-9-0 ... VSlattery 15<br>(JAOsborne) *s.s: outpcd* **100/1** | 18 |

600 **15** 2½ **Just Bonnie**[32] 4809 2-9-0 35 PFitzsimons 13 11
(JMBradley) *s.s: hdwy over 4f out: wknd 1/2-way* **100/1**

1m 15.91s (1.11) **Going Correction** +0.125s/f (Good) **15** Ran SP% **121.4**
Speed ratings: **97,95,93,89,85 84,83,80,80,79 77,76,70,67,64**CSF £26.17 TOTE £11.80: £3.00, £1.60, £16.50; EX 24.10.
**Owner** Girsonfield Ltd **Bred** Girsonfield Ltd **Trained** Wantage, Oxon

**FOCUS**
An ordinary maiden in which they all raced towards the far side. Not a race to get carried away about, although the winner, from a stable with a strong hand on the juvenile front, is a filly of potential.

**NOTEBOOK**
**The Abbess**, an April foal, is very much on the leg and still far from the finished article. She came from off the pace to win going away and should build on this first-time success.
**Sound The Drum(USA)**, third in a Salisbury maiden that has yet to throw up a winner or even another placed horse, was the paddock pick but after showing ahead at halfway he had no answer when the filly swept by on his outside near the line.
**Three Degrees(IRE)**, a February foal, is bred for stamina not speed. She looked very immature beforehand but finished in good style after a sluggish start. This will have taught her plenty but she will not be at her best until next year.
**Etaar**, absent for five weeks, ran much better and at least he is now qualified for a nursery mark.
**Cavalarra** showed a fair bit more than on his debut two weeks earlier.
**Beaune**, who looked very fit, had finished five places ahead of Cavalarra at Haydock.
**Leighton Buzzard**, a March foal, showed ability on his debut and can do better in time.

## 5617 ZIMINSKI GOLDEN WEDDING CELEBRATION NURSERY 6f 15y
**2:45** (2:48) (E3) (0-75,79) 2-Y-O **£4,403** (£1,355; £677; £338) **Stalls** Low

Form RPR
0221 **1** **Viking Spirit**[11] 5351 2-9-11 **79** 6ex IMongan 11 94+
(PWHarris) *racd stands' side: chsd ldrs: led that gp and overall ldr wl over 1f out: r.o wl: eased nr fin* **2/1**[1]
4330 **2** 2½ **Tesary**[8] 5421 2-9-7 **75** EAhern 4 76
(EALDunlop) *racd far side: trckd ldrs: led that gp over 2f out: r.o* **11/1**
6036 **3** 1¼ **Apologies**[10] 5363 2-8-13 **72** (b) NChalmers(5) 10 69
(BAMcmahon) *racd far side: chsd ldrs: rdn over 1f out: styd on same pce ins fnl f* **16/1**
0104 **4** 1½ **Grand Place**[7] 5434 2-9-3 **71** PDobbs 1 64
(RHannon) *hld up: hdwy 2f out: no imp fnl f* **5/1**[2]
11 **5** ½ **Arbors Little Girl**[4] 5509 2-8-10 **64** 6ex ADaly 14 62+
(BRMillman) *racd stands' side: hld up in tch: rdn over 1f out: outpcd over 1f out* **13/2**[3]
5134 **6** 1 **Rosiella**[10] 5363 2-9-5 **73** DSweeney 5 61
(MBlanshard) *racd far side: s.i.s: sn prom: rdn over 2f out: no ex fnl f* **16/1**
4040 **7** nk **Gaudalpin (IRE)**[64] 3886 2-8-11 **65** AMcCarthy 8 52
(MJAttwater) *racd far side: chsd ldrs over 4f* **66/1**
6500 **8** 1¼ **Twice Nightly**[22] 5059 2-8-9 **63** KMcEvoy 3 46
(JDBethell) *racd far side: prom over 4f* **25/1**
6443 **9** shd **Pennestamp (IRE)**[25] 5005 2-8-11 **65** RHavlin 6 48
(MrsPNDutfield) *led far side over 3f: wknd over 1f out* **25/1**
0101 **10** shd **Marcela Zabala**[24] 5022 2-8-1 **58** NMackay(3) 2 41
(JGGiven) *racd far side: hld up: styd on ins fnl f: nvr nrr* **25/1**
4600 **11** nk **Gogetter Girl**[4] 5520 2-8-12 **66** (p) MFenton 12 55+
(JGallagher) *racd stands' side: s.i.s: hld up: rdn over 2f out: n.d* **80/1**
4034 **12** 3 **Indibraun (IRE)**[22] 5059 2-8-13 **72** (p) RoryMoore(5) 9 45
(PCHaslam) *racd far side: chsd ldrs over 4f* **25/1**
432 **13** hd **Sister Gee (IRE)**[53] 4187 2-8-7 **61** WSupple 16 40+
(RHollinshead) *racd stands' side: w ldrs tl led 1/2-way: hdd 2f out: wknd over 1f out* **50/1**
2051 **14** 1½ **Megell (IRE)**[32] 4816 2-8-11 **65** TPQueally 17 40+
(MGQuinlan) *mde most stands' side to 1/2-way: edgd rt over 2f out: wknd over 1f out* **33/1**
560 **15** shd **Peopleton Brook**[62] 3938 2-8-13 **67** SWKelly 15 41+
(DWPArbuthnot) *racd stands' side: hld up in tch: plld hrd: rdn and wknd 2f out* **50/1**
660 **16** nk **Joe Jo Star**[15] 5233 2-8-3 **57** PBradley 20 31+
(PABlockley) *racd stands' side: s.i.s: nt clr run over 2f out: a in rr* **33/1**
2620 **17** 1¼ **Haroldini (IRE)**[42] 4521 2-8-11 **65** JEdmunds 7 28
(JBalding) *racd far side: chsd ldrs: rdn 1/2-way: wknd wl over 1f out* **28/1**
0055 **18** 5 **Rancho Cucamonga (IRE)**[10] 5363 2-9-0 **68** SSanders 13 23+
(TDBarron) *racd stands' side: chsd ldrs over 4f* **12/1**
5200 **19** 1½ **Averting**[11] 5351 2-8-11 **65** (b[1]) SCarson 19 15+
(RFJohnsonHoughton) *racd stands' side: w ldrs to 1/2-way: n.m.r and wknd over 2f out* **40/1**

1m 15.83s (1.03) **Going Correction** +0.125s/f (Good) **19** Ran SP% **124.9**
Speed ratings: **98,94,93,91,90 89,88,86,86,86 86,82,82,80,79 79,77,71,69**CSF £21.24 CT £305.93 TOTE £2.30: £1.20, £3.90, £3.70, £1.80; EX 41.50.
**Owner** The Masterminds **Bred** Bearstone Stud **Trained** Ringshall, Bucks

**FOCUS**
They split into two almost equal groups with stalls one to 10 towards the far side. The form has been assessed as if two separate races, with the stands' side, from which the winner emerged, given 7lb.

**NOTEBOOK**
**Viking Spirit**, a grand type, had been hoisted 11lb after Warwick. He made light of a 6lb penalty here, winning by almost six lengths on the stands' side, and will still be of real interest when reassessed.
**Tesary**, whose saddle slipped last time, led them home on the far side but was no match for the fast improving winner on the other wing. She looks rated to the hilt.
**Apologies**, improved since being fitted with blinkers, has shown he can handle easy ground and he seemed to appreciate the step up to six.
**Grand Place** ran a creditable race, but his 9lb rise after Doncaster looks harsh to say the very least.
**Arbors Little Girl**, a lightly-made filly, was making a quick return and finished second best on the stands' side.
**Pennestamp(IRE)** *Official explanation: jockey said colt hung right-handed*

## 5618 IBETX.COM SPORTS BETTING EXCHANGE FILLIES' H'CAP 6f 15y
**3:15** (3:17) (E3) (0-70,70) 3-Y-0+ **£4,150** (£1,277; £638; £319) **Stalls** Low

Form RPR
3300 **1** **Stokesies Wish**[8] 5412 4-8-8 **60** BSwarbrick(5) 17 70
(JLSpearing) *towards rr stands side: hdwy 1/2-way: rdn over 1f out: styd on to ld ins last* **16/1**
6256 **2** ¾ **Yomalo (IRE)**[44] 4459 4-9-3 **64** CCatlin 19 72
(RGuest) *bhd stand side: swtchd lft and hdwy 2f out: sn rdn: kpt on wl fnl f* **14/1**
10-4 **3** ½ **Riquewihr**[27] 4937 4-8-13 **60** TPQueally 9 66
(DRLoder) *racd far side: in tch: hdwy 2f out: rdn and ev ch ins last: kpt on* **8/1**[2]
0610 **4** 1 **La Vie Est Belle**[6] 5473 3-9-1 **64** AMcCarthy 5 67
(BRMillman) *led far side gp: rdn along and ev ch over 1f out: sn drvn and hdd: no ex towards fin* **20/1**
543 **5** hd **Asbo**[19] 5147 4-8-8 **58** DCorby(3) 20 61
(DrJDScargill) *hld up stands side: hdwy 2f out: sn rdn and kpt on ins last: nrst fin* **16/1**
0410 **6** 1 **Woodbury**[4] 5512 5-9-3 **64** 6ex GBaker 15 64
(MrsHSweeting) *in tch stands side: effrt 2f out: sn rdn and kpt on ins last* **14/1**
-301 **7** nk **Cefira (USA)**[118] 2290 3-9-4 **67** MHenry 8 66
(MHTompkins) *towards rr far side: hdwy wl over 1f out: sn rdn and kpt on ins last* **14/1**
4132 **8** ¾ **Tancred Times**[25] 5008 9-9-3 **64** SSanders 13 61
(CFWall) *sn led stand side: rdn along and hdd over 2f out: led again over 1f out: drvn: hdd & wknd ins last* **13/2**[1]
6560 **9** shd **Generous Gesture (IRE)**[26] 4969 3-9-3 **66** WSupple 14 62
(MLWBell) *chsd ldrs stand side: rdn along over 2f out: grad wknd* **33/1**
0000 **10** hd **Silver Chime**[8] 5425 4-9-2 **63** (b[1]) MFenton 10 59
(DMSimcock) *chsd ldrs far side: rdn wl over 2f out and grad wknd* **66/1**
3000 **11** nk **Stormy Nature (IRE)**[20] 5124 3-9-7 **70** PDobbs 7 65
(PWHarris) *cl up far side: rdn along over 2f out: wknd over 1f out* **16/1**
4200 **12** 1½ **Gojo (IRE)**[102] 2741 3-9-5 **68** DSweeney 4 58
(BPalling) *chsd ldrs far side: rdn along over 2f out: sn wknd* **33/1**
0200 **13** 1¼ **Ballinger Express**[38] 4622 4-8-10 **62** (b) NChalmers(5) 16 48
(AMBalding) *in tch stands side: effrt over 2f out: sn rdn along and no imp* **33/1**
1145 **14** ½ **United Spirit (IRE)**[16] 5219 3-9-1 **64** (b) EAhern 3 49
(MAMagnusson) *racd far side: nvr a factor* **13/2**[1]
0053 **15** ½ **College Queen**[8] 5412 6-9-0 **61** SCarson 6 44
(SGollings) *chsd ldrs far side: rdn over 2f out and sn wknd* **10/1**[3]
0526 **16** 1 **Darla (IRE)**[16] 5219 3-9-6 **69** KMcEvoy 11 49
(JWPayne) *prom stands side: hdwy to ld over 2f out: sn rdn: hdd & wknd over 1f out* **8/1**[2]
0000 **17** shd **Party Princess (IRE)**[18] 5193 3-8-9 **58** IMongan 1 38
(JAGlover) *chsd ldrs far side: rdn along over 2f out and sn wknd* **16/1**
0100 **18** nk **Miss Judgement (IRE)**[11] 5337 3-8-12 **64** RMiles(3) 18 43
(WRMuir) *chsd ldrs stands side: rdn over 2f out: sn wknd* **14/1**
5120 **19** 1¼ **Diamond Shannon (IRE)**[73] 3615 3-8-9 **58** JoannaBadger 2 34
(DCarroll) *s.i.s: a bhd far side* **33/1**
605- **20** 5 **Wall Street Runner**[450] 2680 3-8-6 **62** NataliaGemelova(7) 12 23
(CADwyer) *a rr: eased fnl fnl* **50/1**

1m 15.21s (0.41) **Going Correction** +0.125s/f (Good) **20** Ran SP% **128.2**
**WFA** 3 from 4yo+ 2lb
Speed ratings: **102,101,100,99,98 97,97,96,95,95 95,93,91,90,90 88,88,88,86,80**CSF £217.26 CT £1992.95 TOTE £16.30: £3.50, £3.30, £2.50, £7.20; EX 333.90.
**Owner** Byron J Stokes **Bred** B J Stokes **Trained** Kinnersley, Worcs
■ Stewards Enquiry : A McCarthy caution: careless riding

**FOCUS**
A modest 0-70 fillies' handicap, but solid enough form. They split into two even groups but at the finish they covered the whole width of the track.

**NOTEBOOK**
**Stokesies Wish**, winner of just one of her previous 30 starts, appreciated getting her toe in and stayed on in dour style from off the pace.
**Yomalo(IRE)** came good at the backend last year, winning twice, and is now just 2lb higher than for her last success.
**Riquewihr**, having just her fourth career start and only her second for her present trainer, did best of those that raced exclusively towards the far side.
**La Vie Est Belle**, 4lb higher than when making all at Goodwood on her penultimate start, showed bags of toe to take them along on the far side. A drop back to five will be no problem.
**Asbo**, a maiden after seven previous starts, stayed on hard up against the stands' side rail and will be suited by a step up to seven.
**Tancred Times**, raised 3lb, took them along on the stands' side but after regaining the lead, she tired markedly near the line. She has won at up to seven furlongs and has shown form on easy ground but she is all speed and conditions turned against her here.
**United Spirit(IRE)** was never a factor and her rider blamed the ease in the ground. *Official explanation: jockey said filly was unsuited by today's good to soft ground*
**College Queen** *Official explanation: jockey said mare was unsuited by today's good to soft ground*
**Darla(IRE)** *Official explanation: jockey said filly ran freely in the early stages*
**Party Princess(IRE)** *Official explanation: jockey said filly suffered interference in running*
**Miss Judgement(IRE)** *Official explanation: jockey said filly was unsuited by today's good to soft ground*
**Wall Street Runner** *Official explanation: jockey said saddle slipped*

## 5619 STORA ENSO/REEL PAPER COMPANY H'CAP 1m 6f 15y
**3:50** (3:51) (D2) (0-85,86) 3-Y-0+ **£12,034** (£3,702; £1,851; £925) **Stalls** Low

Form RPR
21-6 **1** **Regal Setting (IRE)**[14] 5273 3-8-6 **77** SSanders 3 93+
(SirMarkPrescott) *trckd ldrs on inner: hdwy 4f out: chsd ldr 3f out and sn rdn along: drvn over 1f out: styd on to ld ins last: kpt on* **7/1**[3]
-221 **2** 1¼ **Mr Ed (IRE)**[26] 4441 6-9-5 **80** (p) KMcEvoy 6 89
(PBowen) *hld up and wl bhd: hdwy on outer 3f out: str run over 1f out: rdn and ev ch ins last: no ex towards fin* **7/2**[1]
5203 **3** 1¼ **Genghis (IRE)**[14] 5266 5-9-2 **80** LFletcher(3) 13 87
(HMorrison) *led: rdn clr over 4f out: drvn over 1f out: hdd & wknd ins last* **14/1**
0333 **4** 1½ **Skye's Folly (USA)**[12] 5318 4-8-11 **72** (b) MFenton 4 77
(JGGiven) *hld up towards rr: hdwy 3f out: rdn over 2f out: styd on appr last* **11/1**
36U2 **5** 2½ **Sporting Gesture**[13] 5303 7-9-1 **76** TPQueally 5 78
(MWEasterby) *in tch: pushed along and outpcd over 5f out: hdwy on inner 3f out: sn rdn and kpt on same pce appr last* **14/1**
0225 **6** 1½ **Bucks**[28] 4911 7-8-11 **79** MHoward(7) 15 79
(DKIvory) *midfield: hdwy 1/2-way: rdn along to chse ldrs 3f out: drvn wl over 1f out and sn one pce* **14/1**
1100 **7** 3½ **Trance (IRE)**[13] 5288 4-9-6 **86** PMakin(5) 10 81
(TDBarron) *hld up and bhd: hdwy on outer over 3f out: rdn along 2f out and sn n o imp* **20/1**
6533 **8** ¾ **Serramanna**[18] 5196 3-8-1 **72** PaulEddery 9 66
(HRACecil) *a midfield: rdn along over 4f out and no hdwy* **16/1**
4631 **9** nk **Redi (ITY)**[36] 4673 3-7-11 **71** NMackay(3) 1 65
(LMCumani) *chsd ldng pair: hdwy 3f out: rdn 2f out and grad wknd* **5/1**[2]
4000 **10** 4 **Mamcazma**[21] 5093 6-9-10 **85** MTebbutt 11 74
(DMorris) *midfield: hdwy and in tch 1/2-way: rdn along over 3f out and wknd fnl 2f* **25/1**
51/0 **11** 1¼ **Fait Le Jojo (FR)**[44] 4441 7-9-10 **85** EAhern 16 72
(PJHobbs) *chsd ldng pair: rdn along 3f out: grad wknd fnl 2f* **40/1**

0600 **12** *shd* **Ski Jump (USA)**[4] [5517] 4-9-3 **81**................................(v) THamilton(3) 12 68
(RAFahey) *trckd ldrs: rdn along 4f out: drvn and btn over 2f out* **12/1**
4232 **13** *27* **Obay**[37] [4636] 3-9-0 **85**................................ WSupple 2 37
(EALDunlop) *a towards rr* **14/1**
2656 **14** *1 1/2* **Weet For Me**[12] [5318] 8-8-11 **72**................................ DSweeney 18 22
(RHollinshead) *chsd ldr: rdn along 4f out: sn wknd* **33/1**
0200 **15** *3/4* **Sound Of Fleet (USA)**[13] [5300] 3-8-11 **82**................................ PDobbs 7 31
(PFICole) *a bhd* **28/1**
4050 **16** *23* **Qudrah (IRE)**[24] [5025] 4-9-3 **78**................................ RFfrench 17 —
(EJO'Neill) *s.i.s: a rr* **100/1**
6000 **17** *dist* **Teresa**[27] [4934] 4-8-10 **71**................................ IMongan 8 —
(JLDunlop) *midfield: pushed along 1/2-way: sn lost pl and behind when virtually p.u 3f out* **16/1**

3m 4.37s (-2.83) **Going Correction** 0.0s/f (Good)
**WFA** 3 from 4yo+ 10lb **17** Ran SP% **124.3**
Speed ratings: **108,107,106,105,104 103,101,101,100,98 97,97,82,81,81 67,—**CSF £29.67 CT £349.48 TOTE £11.10: £3.30, £1.40, £4.50, £3.10; EX 41.00.
**Owner** W E Sturt - Osborne House **Bred** R G Patton **Trained** Newmarket, Suffolk

**FOCUS**
A fair handicap run at a sound pace on ground now described as 'definitely soft'. Third-placed Genghis set a decent standard, and Mr Ed improved again on his Kempton form. The unexposed Regal Setting looked value for extra and is one to keep on the right side of.

**NOTEBOOK**
**Regal Setting(IRE)**, having just his fourth career start and only his second this year, improved for the step up in trip and showed a willing attitude. Two miles will suit him even better and he remains completely unexposed as a stayer.
**Mr Ed(IRE)**, fresh from his triumph in a valuable handicap hurdle at Newton Abbot, was racing from a mark 6lb higher than Kempton. Last of all on the home turn, he stayed on in willing fashion down the wide outside. The trip was on the sharp side for him and connections are expecting a big run from him in the Cesarewitch.
**Genghis(IRE)**, a maiden after eight previous starts, was given an enterprising ride and picked up the gallop turning in. This was his sixth placed effort and he deserves to break his duck.
**Skye's Folly(USA)**, who finds this trip his bare minimum, again gave a good account of himself but he receives no mercy.
**Sporting Gesture** as usual hit a flat spot on the home turn. He stuck on in his own time and lack of stamina was not a factor.
**Bucks** ran as well as could be expected considering the rain had turned the ground against him.
**Trance(IRE)** did not impress at all with his action going to post.
**Teresa** *Official explanation: jockey said filly hung right-handed throughout*

## 5620 EUROPEAN BREEDERS FUND TRENT MAIDEN STKS 1m 54y
4:25 (4:26) (D2) 2-Y-O **£6,314** (£1,943; £971; £485) **Stalls** Centre

Form RPR
3503 **1** **Catch A Star**[71] [3675] 2-8-6 80................................ NMackay(3) 7 73
(NACallaghan) *dwlt: hld up: hdwy over 2f out: swtchd rt over 1f out: r.o to ld post* **9/1**
33 **2** *nk* **Banchieri**[16] [5228] 2-9-0................................ KMcEvoy 6 77
(SaeedBinSuroor) *sn pushed along in rr: hdwy over 3f out: rdn and ev ch ins fnl f: r.o* **85/40**[2]
0 **3** *hd* **Speightstown**[28] [4922] 2-9-0................................ SSanders 3 77
(PFICole) *led after 1f: rdn over 1f out: hdd post* **8/1**[3]
50 **4** *shd* **Mutamaasek (USA)**[35] [4728] 2-9-0................................ WSupple 9 77
(JLDunlop) *trckd ldrs: rdn over 1f out: ev ch ins fnl f: r.o* **20/1**
05 **5** *3/4* **Moonmaiden**[18] [5172] 2-8-9................................ CCatlin 4 70
(MRChannon) *a.p: chsd ldr over 2f out: rdn and ev ch over 1f out: unable qckn towards fin* **33/1**
**6** *2* **Fen Game (IRE)** 2-9-0................................ RHavlin 10 71
(JHMGosden) *rangy: unf: chsd ldrs: rdn and nt clr run wl over 1f out: styd on same pce fnl f* **40/1**
4 **7** *3/4* **Given A Choice (IRE)**[42] [4523] 2-9-0................................ IMongan 1 69
(JGGiven) *hld up in tch: plld hrd: rdn over 3f out: styd on same pce fnl f* **5/4**[1]
50 **8** *1 1/2* **Silsong (USA)**[18] [5198] 2-8-9................................ RSmith 2 61
(BRMillman) *led 1f: rdn over 2f out: styd on same pce* **150/1**
3 **9** *2* **Red River Rock (IRE)**[26] [4967] 2-9-0................................ EAhern 8 61
(CTinkler) *broke wl: lost pl over 6f out: bhd whn rn wd over 4f out* **14/1**
0 **10** *8* **Irish Ballad**[24] [5023] 2-9-0................................ MFenton 11 44
(PWHarris) *sn bhd* **50/1**
**11** *dist* **Miss Defying** 2-8-6................................ RMiles(3) 5 —
(RCurtis) *rangy: bkwd: s.s: outpcd* **125/1**

1m 48.58s (2.18) **Going Correction** +0.175s/f (Good) **11** Ran SP% **117.8**
Speed ratings: **96,95,95,95,94 92,91,90,88,80** —CSF £27.73 TOTE £11.20: £2.20, £1.10, £2.90; EX 37.20.
**Owner** M Tabor **Bred** Haras Du Gazon **Trained** Newmarket, Suffolk

**FOCUS**
A modest gallop early on, contributing to a slow time and a bunch finish. It was nevertheless still quite a test of stamina in the soft ground.

**NOTEBOOK**
**Catch A Star**, easily the most experienced in the field, recovered from a sluggish start and was persuaded to put her head in front right on the line. Fully exposed, she has a BHB rating of 80.
**Banchieri**, third at Leicester and York on his two previous start, did nothing at all wrong and just missed out.
**Speightstown**, a big, rangy type, went on and quickened the gallop and in the end just missed out. He looks essentially a stayer.
**Mutamaasek(USA)**, who looked very fit indeed, put a below par effort last time behind him and is now qualified for nurseries.
**Moonmaiden**, who looked on the light side, ran her best race so far on her third start, but her proximity to the winner will rule out a lenient nursery mark.
**Fen Game(IRE)**, a February foal, stands over plenty of ground. Fitted with a cross noseband, he seemed to have problems making the turn then was going nowhere when left short of racing room. He will make a better three-year-old.
**Given A Choice(IRE)**, a big, well-made sort, took a keen grip then seemed to wander and run green. A stronger pace and less soft ground would have suited him better but basically he is a three-year-old in the making. *Official explanation: jockey said colt was unsuited by the ground and slow early pace*
**Silsong(USA)** seemed to run a lot better than on her first two starts but the lack of pace early on may have flattered her.

## 5621 HBLB CITY LIFE MAGAZINE MAIDEN STKS 1m 54y
5:00 (5:01) (D3) 3-Y-O **£4,966** (£1,528; £764; £382) **Stalls** Centre

Form RPR
-235 **1** **Cantarna (IRE)**[73] [3607] 3-8-9 73................................ RFfrench 12 75
(JMackie) *cl up: led over 3f out: rdn wl over 1f out: drvn ins last and kpt on* **9/2**[3]
4-3 **2** *1/2* **Meneef (USA)**[57] [4069] 3-9-0................................ WSupple 5 79
(MPTregoning) *led: hdd over 3f out: rdn and n.m.r ent last: kpt on wl towards fin* **7/2**[2]
645 **3** *1* **Coppice (IRE)**[26] [4972] 3-8-11 74................................ NMackay(3) 4 77
(LMCumani) *a.p: effrt over 2f out: rdn and edgd lft over 1f out: sn drvn and no ex towards fin* **11/2**
**4** *1 1/4* **All Blue (IRE)** 3-9-0................................(t) KMcEvoy 6 74
(SaeedBinSuroor) *tall: lt-f: in tch: hdwy 3f out: rdn to chse ldrs 2f out: kpt on same pce ent last* **8/1**
5555 **5** *1 1/4* **Beautiful Noise**[37] [4650] 3-8-9 49................................(b) MTebbutt 16 67?
(DMorris) *midfield: hdwy 3f out: rdn along 2f out: kpt on u.p fnl f* **33/1**
**6** *3/4* **Miss Polaris** 3-8-9................................ MFenton 13 65
(PWHarris) *rangy: unf: bhd tl hdwy on outer 2f out: styd on wl fnl f: nrst fin* **25/1**
3 **7** *1 3/4* **Subtle Breeze (USA)**[10] [5378] 3-8-9................................ RHavlin 2 61
(JHMGosden) *chsd ldrs: rdn along 3f out: drvn wl over 1f out and grad wknd* **11/4**[1]
**8** *1/2* **Cirrious** 3-8-9................................ DSweeney 11 60
(BPalling) *lengthy: unf: towards rr: hdwy 3f out: rdn and hung lft 2f out: sn no imp* **100/1**
**9** *3/4* **Bobby Charles** 3-9-0................................ TPQueally 10 64
(DrJDScargill) *s.i.s: bhd tl sme late hdwy* **80/1**
**10** *1* **Portmeirion** 3-8-9................................ SSanders 3 57
(EFVaughan) *in tch: rdn along 3f out: drvn 2f out and sn wknd* **12/1**
004 **11** *1* **Eijaaz (IRE)**[75] [3554] 3-9-0 67................................ PDobbs 7 60
(GCBravery) *a rr* **66/1**
3 **12** *3/4* **Sian Thomas**[8] [5424] 3-8-9................................ ADaly 8 53
(MPTregoning) *midfield: rdn along 3f out: sn outpcd* **20/1**
**13** *2 1/2* **Desiree (IRE)** 3-8-2................................ FrancesPickard(7) 9 48
(JohnBerry) *s.i.s: a rr* **150/1**
5-0 **14** *nk* **Royal Flight**[158] [1352] 3-9-0................................ EAhern 1 52
(PWHarris) *chsd ldrs: rdn along 3f out: sn wknd* **28/1**
0 **15** *24* **Kikis Girls (IRE)**[55] [4141] 3-8-2................................ JBrennan(7) 14 —
(MWigham) *s.i.s: a bhd* **150/1**

1m 47.13s (0.73) **Going Correction** +0.175s/f (Good) **15** Ran SP% **121.3**
Speed ratings: **103,102,101,100,99 98,96,96,95,94 93,92,90,89,65**CSF £19.35 TOTE £6.20: £1.90, £1.40, £1.90; EX 18.40.
**Owner** Gwen K Dot.com **Bred** Newberry Stud Farm Ltd **Trained** Church Broughton, Derbys

**FOCUS**
A very modest maiden with the 73-rated winner appreciating the soft ground and the second and third getting in each others' way. The proximity of the 49-rated fifth offers further grounds for caution.

**NOTEBOOK**
**Cantarna(IRE)**, absent for 10 weeks after a below-par effort over further on firm ground at Pontefract, showed battling qualities and in the end did just enough. She seemed to really appreciate getting her toe in.
**Meneef(USA)**, disappointing on his return, was crowded by the third and was almost certainly unlucky not to break his duck on his third career start.
**Coppice(IRE)**, only fifth when odds-on at Folkestone, ran better dropped back in trip but persisted in edging left under pressure, getting in the way of the runner-up.
**All Blue(IRE)**, whose dam won the Sun Chariot Stakes, is a tall, lightly-made gelding. He showed only limited ability on his belated debut but at least the experience will have taught him something.
**Beautiful Noise**, having her 11th career start, would have met the winner on 24lb better terms in a handicap and her proximity anchors the overall value of the form.
**Miss Polaris**, a backward-looking newcomer, took a while to get the hang of things but she did stay on in good style very late in the day. The experience will have done her a power of good and she can improve, especially over further.
**Subtle Breeze(USA)**, who continually swished her tail in the paddock, did not improve on her reappearance effort just 10 days earlier. The step up to a mile and soft ground were clearly not to her liking.

## 5622 IBETX.COM - THE PUNTER'S CHOICE MADAME JONES CLASSIFIED STKS 1m 1f 213y
5:30 (5:30) (E3) 3-Y-O+ **£4,111** (£1,265; £632; £316) **Stalls** Low

Form RPR
06-2 **1** **Incroyable**[11] [5344] 3-8-9 59................................ SSanders 4 72+
(SirMarkPrescott) *trckd ldrs: hdwy to chse ldr over 2f out: rdn wl over 1f out: drvn ins last: styd on to ld nr line* **4/5**[1]
0223 **2** *nk* **Mambina (USA)**[14] [5258] 3-8-9 59................................ CCatlin 6 71
(MRChannon) *led: rdn along over 2f out: drvn over 1f out: headed and no ex nr line* **8/1**[3]
5040 **3** *5* **Wrenlane**[16] [5223] 3-8-9 60................................ THamilton(3) 15 65
(RAFahey) *dwlt and swtchd lft s: sn in tch: hdwy to chse ldrs over 2f out: sn rdn and kpt on same pce* **16/1**
2411 **4** *1/2* **Milk And Sultana**[6] [5459] 4-9-7 59................................ ADaly 12 67
(GAHam) *towards rr: hdwy 3f out: rdn 2f out: kpt on appr last* **15/2**[2]
0403 **5** *5* **Jomus**[14] [5259] 3-8-9 58................................ RMiles(3) 5 55
(LMontagueHall) *s.i.s and bhd: hdwy on outer 3f out: rdn and kpt on fnl 2f: nrst fin* **28/1**
2066 **6** *1/2* **Cottingham (IRE)**[10] [5364] 3-8-9 59................................ BReilly(3) 11 54
(MCChapman) *hld up in rr: hdwy 3f out: rdn along 2f out: kpt on fnl f: nrst fin* **28/1**
4130 **7** *2* **Sienna Sunset (IRE)**[10] [5374] 5-8-10 58................................ BSwarbrick(5) 13 48
(WMBrisbourne) *a towards rr* **14/1**
4410 **8** *1/2* **Jake Black (IRE)**[6] [5459] 4-8-11 58................................ DTudhope(7) 8 50
(JJQuinn) *prom: rdn along 3f out: drvn 2f out and sn wknd* **9/1**
0-50 **9** *1 1/2* **Royal Approach**[81] [3379] 3-8-9 60................................ DSweeney 9 44
(MBlanshard) *a rr* **80/1**
-000 **10** *1/2* **Airgusta (IRE)**[130] [1998] 3-8-12 59................................ SCarson 2 46
(CPMorlock) *prom: rdn along over 3f out and sn wknd* **80/1**
4340 **11** *1/2* **Cryfield**[15] [5236] 7-9-4 59................................ KimTinkler 10 45
(NTinkler) *a rr* **25/1**
-000 **12** *23* **Saharan Song (IRE)**[88] [3156] 3-8-9 59................................ EAhern 3 —
(BWHills) *chsd ldrs: rdn along 4f out: sn wknd* **25/1**
0160 **13** *3* **Arms Acrossthesea**[10] [5374] 5-9-4 60................................ JEdmunds 7 —
(JBalding) *in tch: rdn along 1/2-way: sn wknd and bhd fnl 3f* **50/1**

2m 12.34s (-8.50) **Going Correction** +0.375s/f (Good)
**WFA** 3 from 4yo+ 6lb **13** Ran SP% **120.0**
Speed ratings: **103,102,98,98,94 93,92,91,90,90 89,71,69**CSF £6.91 TOTE £1.50: £1.10, £1.30, £4.10; EX 10.90 Place 6 £78.93, Place 5 £38.81 .
**Owner** Lady O'Reilly **Bred** Biddestone Stud And Partner **Trained** Newmarket, Suffolk

**FOCUS**
A modest classified stakes, but a sound pace considering the soft ground and solid form. The first two finished clear of two horses that had been in fair form, and Incroyable can build on this.

**NOTEBOOK**
**Incroyable**, raised to an official mark of 63 after her reappearance second at Newcastle, made very hard work of mastering a 59-rated maiden. She is game but will need to improve again to add to this success in handicap company.

**Mambina(USA)**, seeking her first success on her 13th start, took them along at a sound pace and in the end was only just worn down. She deserves a first success but even in such modest company, it is proving elusive.
**Wrenlane**, suited by the give, was stepping up in trip but was still not good enough.
**Milk And Sultana**, seeking a hat-trick, was racing on a totally different surface. Attempting to make ground from the rear down the outside, she was never going to land a blow.
**Jomus** again hinted at a return to form despite his rider reporting that he disliked the soft ground. *Official explanation: trainer said gelding had been unsuited by the good to soft ground*
**Cottingham(IRE)** ran well and the extended trip did not seem to be a problem.
T/Plt: £103.40 to a £1 stake. Pool: £33,052.95. 233.35 winning tickets. T/Qpdt: £35.30 to a £1 stake. Pool: £2,376.70. 49.80 winning tickets. JR

5623 - 5625a (Foreign Racing) - See Raceform Interactive

## 5602 AYR (L-H)

### Saturday, September 18

**OFFICIAL GOING: Soft (heavy in places on bottom bend)**

## 5626 TSG FIRTH OF CLYDE STKS (GROUP 3) 6f

**2:00** (2:00) (A1) 2-Y-O **£23,200** (£8,800; £4,400; £2,000) **Stalls** High

Form RPR
0113 **1** **Golden Legacy (IRE)**[30] 4876 2-8-8 96 PHanagan 1 103
(RAFahey) *hld up: hdwy whn n.m.r over 1f out: styd on to ld wl ins fnl f* **7/1**
1001 **2** *nk* **Nufoos**[20] 5143 2-8-8 94 WSupple 10 102
(MJohnston) *trckd ldrs: rdn over 2f out: ev ch ins fnl f: one pce whn blkd cl home: fin 3rd: plcd 2nd* **15/8**[1]
1252 **3** *3/4* **Castelletto**[16] 5250 2-8-8 98 GGibbons 11 102
(BAMcmahon) *led after 2f: hdd wl ins fnl f: edgd lft: kpt on: fin 2nd: demoted to 3rd* **13/2**[3]
0656 **4** *2 1/2* **Miss Meggy**[10] 5391 2-8-11 88 (v[1]) KDarley 5 95
(TDEasterby) *w ldrs tl rdn and nt qckn fr over 1f out* **16/1**
210 **5** *1 1/4* **Dance Away**[35] 4744 2-8-8 97 DHolland 2 89
(MLWBell) *hld up: effrt and swtchd over 1f out: no imp fnl f* **8/1**
1036 **6** *1/2* **Golden Anthem (USA)**[58] 4060 2-8-8 90 JQuinn 9 87
(JPearce) *in tch: effrt over 2f out: nt qckn over 1f out* **16/1**
3511 **7** *8* **Swan Nebula (USA)**[10] 5391 2-8-8 82 (t) KMcEvoy 8 63
(SaeedBinSuroor) *prom: effrt over 2f out: wknd over 1f out* **5/1**[2]
2152 **8** *14* **Madame Topflight**[28] 4962 2-8-8 93 ACulhane 6 21
(MrsGSRees) *in tch tl rdn and wknd over 2f out* **14/1**
1304 **9** *3* **World At My Feet**[18] 5213 2-8-8 87 FNorton 7 12
(NBycroft) *led 2f: prom tl wknd over 2f out* **33/1**

1m 17.36s (3.64) **Going Correction** +0.70s/f (Yiel) 9 Ran SP% **109.8**
Speed ratings: **103,101,102,98,96 95,85,66,62**CSF £18.85 TOTE £9.40: £2.80, £1.50, £2.10; EX 25.90 Trifecta £64.30 Pool £299.30 - 3.30 winning units..
**Owner** P N Devlin **Bred** E Tynan **Trained** Musley Bank, N Yorks
■ Stewards Enquiry : G Gibbons three-day ban: careless riding (Sep 29-30, Oct 1)

**FOCUS**
Just an ordinary renewal, and the form looks only Listed level. Although the time was acceptable for a juvenile Group Three, the pace in the early stages was steady and only a length covered the first three home.

**NOTEBOOK**
**Golden Legacy(IRE)** ◆ has done nothing but improve and she turned in her best effort on this first attempt on testing ground. However, she will have to improve again to play a part in the Cheveley Park, which is reportedly her next intended target. Her style of racing suggests she should stay seven furlongs and she may well be capable of better.
**Nufoos**, back up in trip and on the softest ground she has encountered to date, ran creditably upped in grade and was promoted a place after suffering inteference in the closing stages. This represented her best effort to date and she should continue to run well kept away from the better juveniles.
**Castelletto** got stirred up in the preliminaries but had the run of the race against the stands'-side rail and proved she is at least as good on soft as on a sound surface. She was demoted for causing inteference late on and is likely to remain vulnerable to progressive sorts in this type of event.
**Miss Meggy** looked to have a tough task back in Group company but ran creditably in the first-time visor. However, she may not be the easiest to place successfully in either Pattern company or from her current mark in nurseries.
**Dance Away** showed her latest Newbury running to be all wrong on this first start on testing ground and on her first run over this trip. She may be better than the bare form given the way this race unfolded, but she is another that is not going to be easy to place.
**Golden Anthem(USA)** was not disgraced back on testing ground but, while she has had her limitations exposed in Listed and Group company, she did shape as though the return to seven furlongs would be in her favour.
**Swan Nebula(USA)**, a progressive sort on a sound surface, looked to have a bit to find in this stronger grade but dropped out tamely on this first run on a testing surface. She is worth another chance back on more suitable ground when returned to nursery company. *Official explanation: trainer said filly was unsuited by the soft ground*
**Madame Topflight** *Official explanation: jockey said filly boiled over at the start*

## 5627 TOTEPOOL AYRSHIRE H'CAP 1m

**2:35** (2:35) (C1) (0-100,93) 3-Y-O+ **£12,267** (£4,653; £2,326; £1,057) **Stalls** Low

Form RPR
2130 **1** **Young Mr Grace (IRE)**[19] 5194 4-8-8 80 DAllan 11 91
(TDEasterby) *w ldr: led over 3f out: pushed out* **8/1**
2245 **2** *1 1/4* **Jazz Scene (IRE)**[14] 5294 3-9-3 93 ACulhane 1 101
(MRChannon) *cl up: rdn over 2f out: kpt on fnl f: no ch w wnr* **4/1**[2]
0000 **3** *1 1/2* **Sir George Turner**[7] 5468 5-9-3 89 JFanning 2 94
(MJohnston) *prom: rdn 3f out: kpt on fnl f* **9/1**
0110 **4** *1/2* **Everest (IRE)**[55] 4178 7-8-10 85 TEaves(3) 3 89
(BEllison) *hld up: rdn 3f out: kpt on fnl f: no imp* **7/2**[1]
1060 **5** *1 1/2* **Tony Tie**[26] 4988 8-8-10 82 DHolland 8 83
(JSGoldie) *in tch: effrt over 2f out: no imp fnl f* **14/1**
3000 **6** *shd* **Oddsmaker (IRE)**[10] 5397 3-8-10 86 DeanMcKeown 10 87
(PDEvans) *keen: chsd ldrs: effrt over 2f out: wknd ins fnl f* **9/1**
0305 **7** *1* **Wing Commander**[10] 5401 5-9-7 93 PHanagan 7 92
(RAFahey) *hld up: effrt outside over 2f out: nvr able to chal* **6/1**[3]
1503 **8** *3* **Harry Potter (GER)**[13] 5315 5-8-7 79 (v) DarrenWilliams 9 72
(KRBurke) *hld up in tch: effrt over 2f out: wknd over 1f out* **10/1**
400- **9** *5* **Duke Of Modena**[322] 5873 7-8-11 86 RThomas(3) 4 69
(GBBalding) *hld up in tch: rdn over 2f out: n.d* **12/1**
1500 **10** *3 1/2* **Chappel Cresent (IRE)**[32] 4837 4-9-7 93 ANicholls 5 69
(DNicholls) *led to over 3f out: wknd over 2f out* **50/1**

1m 48.63s (5.51) **Going Correction** +0.725s/f (Yiel)
**WFA** 3 from 4yo+ 4lb 10 Ran SP% **113.0**
Speed ratings: **101,99,98,97,96 96,95,92,87,83**CSF £38.74 CT £300.04 TOTE £10.50: £3.20, £1.70, £3.10; EX 44.90 Trifecta £409.50 Part won. Pool £576.80 - 0.90 winning units..
**Owner** Norman Jackson **Bred** Michael Greany **Trained** Great Habton, N Yorks

**FOCUS**
A steady early pace not surprisingly resulted in modest time for a race of its type, even allowing for the conditions. It played to the strengths of those racing up with the pace, and the bare form does not look reliable.

**NOTEBOOK**
**Young Mr Grace(IRE)**, was proven in the conditions and turned in his best effort yet after very much enjoying the run of the race. Although he may be a shade flattered given the way the race unfolded, he is a reliable sort who should continue to give a good account when allowed to dominate.
**Jazz Scene(IRE)** is a consistent sort who ran well after enjoying the run of the race. However, she is likely to continue to look vulnerable to progressive or well-handicapped sorts in this type of event.
**Sir George Turner** has been essentially disappointing but had the run of the race and performed creditably. He shaped as though a stiffer test of stamina over this trip would have suited, but the fact that he has not won for nearly three years is a concern.
**Everest(IRE)** ◆ disappointed at Pontefract last time but shaped as though in better form than this bare result would imply after his short break. He goes on most ground and is worth keeping an eye on in similar company when a better gallop looks likely.
**Tony Tie**, a dual course and distance winner this year, seems to have gone off the boil at present and, although not disgraced having been well placed in a steadily-run race, is likely to remain vulnerable from his current mark in this type of event.
**Oddsmaker(IRE)**, back to a more suitable trip and on ground he likes, again took a good hold but, although enjoying the run of the race, continues below his best.
**Wing Commander** shaped as though in better form than this result gives him credit for, as he was dropped out in a steadily-run race and attempted to make his ground on the wide outside. He has not been the most consistent but is not one to write off yet.
**Chappel Cresent(IRE)** *Official explanation: jockey said gelding finished tired*

## 5628 TOTESPORT AYR GOLD CUP (HERITAGE H'CAP) 6f

**3:10** (3:11) (B1) 3-Y-O+ **£70,000** (£26,551; £13,275; £6,034) **Stalls** High

Form RPR
0060 **1** **Funfair Wane**[10] 5393 5-8-6 90 PDoe 8 106
(DNicholls) *mde all centre: sn clr: rdn and flashed tail ins fnl f: hld on wl* **33/1**
1200 **2** *2* **Fantasy Believer**[10] 5393 6-8-8 95 THamilton(3) 16 105
(JJQuinn) *in tch stands side: hdwy to chse wnr over 1f out: edgd lft: no ex wl ins fnl f* **14/1**
0105 **3** *2 1/2* **Continent**[11] 5372 7-9-10 108 DHolland 18 111+
(DNicholls) *hld up stands side: n.m.r over 2f out: hdwy and swtchd over 1f out: r.o fnl f* **18/1**
1020 **4** *nk* **Mutawaqed (IRE)**[10] 5393 6-8-6 90 (t) KMcEvoy 20 92
(MAMagnusson) *bhd stands side tl hdwy over 1f out: kpt on fnl f: no imp* **8/1**[1]
516 **5** *1/2* **Quito (IRE)**[35] 4745 7-9-8 106 (b) ACulhane 23 106+
(DWChapman) *dwlt: hld up stands side: repeatedly denied room fr 1/2-way tl ins fnl f: r.o strly: no ch w ldrs* **11/1**[2]
2014 **6** *1 1/2* **Onlytime Will Tell**[17] 5224 6-8-7 91 JFanning 10 87
(DNicholls) *cl up stands side: effrt over 2f out: one pce over 1f out* **33/1**
0064 **7** *1/2* **Hidden Dragon (USA)**[11] 5372 5-8-10 94 GFaulkner 6 88
(PABlockley) *prom centre: effrt 2f out: sn one pce* **33/1**
0100 **8** *3/4* **Zilch**[40] 4614 6-8-13 97 SSanders 24 89
(MLWBell) *midfield stands side: effrt u.p over 2f out: no imp over 1f out* **8/1**[1]
0000 **9** *1* **Capricho (IRE)**[14] 5289 7-9-1 99 JQuinn 4 88
(JAkehurst) *hld up far side: hdwy over 2f out: no ex over 1f out* **33/1**
2035 **10** *2* **Tom Tun**[17] 5224 9-9-1 99 (b) TLucas 27 82
(JBalding) *chsd stands side ldrs: effrt over 2f out: btn appr fnl f* **14/1**
0000 **11** *2* **Raccoon (IRE)**[10] 5393 4-8-5 89 (t) KDarley 28 66
(TDBarron) *w stands side ldrs tl outpcd fr 2f out* **20/1**
5001 **12** *1/2* **Chookie Heiton (IRE)**[21] 5105 6-9-4 105 7ex TEaves(3) 25 80
(ISemple) *midfield stands side: rdn over 2f out: n.d* **16/1**
5040 **13** *1/2* **Circuit Dancer (IRE)**[17] 5224 4-8-9 93 FLynch 26 67
(ABerry) *in tch tl outpcd over 2f out* **33/1**
0004 **14** *hd* **Bond Boy**[14] 5287 7-8-4 88 GGibbons 17 61
(BSmart) *bhd stands side: hdwy over 2f out: sn rdn and no ex* **16/1**
0100 **15** *1/2* **Cardinal Venture (IRE)**[72] 3673 6-8-9 93 NCallan 22 65
(KARyan) *w stands side ldrs to 2f out: sn btn* **11/1**[2]
4415 **16** *1 1/2* **King's Caprice**[21] 5112 3-8-0 89 RThomas(3) 7 56
(GBBalding) *hld up in tch centre: effrt over 2f out: sn btn* **33/1**
4440 **17** *shd* **Glaramara**[28] 4931 3-8-6 95 HayleyTurner(3) 11 62
(ABailey) *in tch on outside of stands side gp: rdn and edgd lft over 2f out: sn outpcd* **50/1**
3010 **18** *1* **River Falcon**[14] 5287 4-8-6 90 WSupple 9 54
(JSGoldie) *chsd wnr in centre to over 1f out: sn btn* **50/1**
4000 **19** *1 1/4* **Connect**[10] 5393 7-8-6 93 (b) FPFerris(3) 5 53
(MHTompkins) *hld up centre: rdn over 2f out: sn btn* **100/1**
4-40 **20** *3* **Philharmonic**[74] 3598 3-9-0 100 PHanagan 15 51
(RAFahey) *hld up in tch on outside of stands side: hdwy over 2f out: hung lft and sn btn* **14/1**
1000 **21** *1 3/4* **Fire Up The Band**[6] 5505 5-9-1 99 (v) ANicholls 13 45
(DNicholls) *prom stands side: rdn and hung lft over 2f out: wknd* **20/1**
0000 **22** *1/2* **Pomfret Lad**[10] 5393 6-8-12 96 AlexGreaves 21 40
(DNicholls) *towards rr stands side: rdn 1/2-way: sn btn* **66/1**
1100 **23** *1 3/4* **Jonny Ebeneezer**[10] 5393 5-8-6 90 (b) FNorton 1 29
(DFlood) *hld up: rdn over 2f out: sn btn* **33/1**
1511 **24** *14* **Prince Aaron (IRE)**[21] 5121 4-8-12 96 7ex GCarter 3 —
(CNAllen) *hld up centre: rdn and wknd fr over 2f out* **12/1**[3]

1m 16.15s (2.43) **Going Correction** +0.70s/f (Yiel)
**WFA** 3 from 4yo+ 2lb 24 Ran SP% **120.1**
Speed ratings: **111,108,105,104,103 101,101,100,98,96 93,92,92,92,91 89,89,87,86,82 79,79,76,58**CSF £380.85 CT £8407.52 TOTE £53.70: £11.70, £4.40, £4.50, £2.10; EX 865.40 TRIFECTA Not won..
**Owner** Mrs Jean Keegan & D Nicholls **Bred** J K Keegan **Trained** Sessay, N Yorks
■ A tremendous training performance from David Nicholls, who was winning the race for the fourth time in the last five years.

**FOCUS**
The whole field raced centre to stands' side and very few got involved. The time was fair for a race like this and the form is solid, as one would expect, with the runner-up providing the key.

**NOTEBOOK**
**Funfair Wane**, the winner of this race in 2002, has not been the most predictable since but had been shaping as though retaining plenty of ability and turned in a tremendous display of front-running. He remains a very useful sprinter on his day but, given his record since his previous win, is not one to bank on next time.

**Fantasy Believer** had not been at his best on fast ground (effective on a sound surface) on his last couple of starts, but ran right up to his best from his middle draw back on this testing surface. He also filled the same placing in the Stewards Cup at Goodwood and should continue to go well in the better handicaps over this trip.
**Continent**, a dual Group One winner and having his first run in handicap company for well over two years, was briefly short of room when about to make an effort but ran at least as well as he has done all year. He is still a smart performer with cut in the ground, but his style of racing means he needs things to fall just right.
**Mutawaqed(IRE)** is a very capable handicapper on his day and he ran right up to his recent best in a race where the leaders did not come back to the field. He goes on most ground and is capable of winning a decent handicap when things go his way.
**Quito(IRE)** ◆, the winner of this race from a 14lb lower mark in 2003, had reportedly suffered an interrupted preparation and was the main eyecatcher. He would almost certainly have given the winner something to think about with a clear run and, although effective over seven, a strongly-run race over six furlongs with cut in the ground are his requirements. His style of racing means he needs things to drop right, but he looks capable of winning another decent handicap.
**Onlytime Will Tell**, who broke a lengthy losing run last month, goes well with cut in the ground and ran right up to that recent best. He stays seven furlongs and should continue to give a good account.
**Hidden Dragon(USA)** has slipped in the weights and confirmed he retains plenty of ability with his best effort of the year. He travelled strongly for much of the way and, although vulnerable to progressive or well-handicapped sorts from this mark, is one to keep an eye on back on a sound surface.
**Zilch** was not surprisingly well supported given the testing conditions were very much in his favour, but he never looked like adding to his three successes this term. He has come a long way this year but does look a shade high in the weights at present.
**Prince Aaron(IRE)** *Official explanation: jockey said gelding was unsuited by the soft ground*

## 5629 WEATHERBYS BANK STKS (REGISTERED AS THE DOONSIDE CUP) (LISTED RACE) 1m 2f 192y

**3:45** (3:45) (A1) 3-Y-O+ **£17,400** (£6,600; £3,300; £1,500) **Stalls** Low

| Form | | | | RPR |
|---|---|---|---|---|
| 111 | **1** | | **Into The Dark**[17] 5226 3-8-4 **114** (vt) KMcEvoy 6<br>(SaeedBinSuroor) *trckd ldr: led over 4f out: clr fnl f: styd on* **5/4**[2] | 117 |
| 1140 | **2** | *5* | **Percussionist (IRE)**[83] 3353 3-8-11 **118** KDarley 1<br>(JHMGosden) *in tch: drvn along over 4f out: disp 2nd over 3f out: outpcd over 2f out: styd on u.p to regain 2nd ins fnl f* **1/1**[1] | 119+ |
| 5364 | **3** | *½* | **Bonecrusher**[7] 5461 5-8-11 **105** (v) SSanders 3<br>(DRLoder) *s.i.s: hld up: hdwy to chse wnr over 3f out: ch 2f out: flashed tail u.p and no ex appr last* **9/1**[3] | 108 |
| 0005 | **4** | *28* | **Howards Dream (IRE)**[49] 4328 6-8-11 **30** (t) DAllan 5<br>(DANolan) *bhd: lost tch over 3f out: t.o* **500/1** | 60? |
| 0000 | **5** | *14* | **Society Times (USA)**[23] 5061 11-8-11 **30** (t) PPMathers 4<br>(DANolan) *led tl hdd over 4f out: wknd qckly 3f out: t.o* **500/1** | 36? |
| 3202 | **6** | *dist* | **Court Of Appeal**[32] 4831 7-8-11 **90** (t) TEaves 2<br>(BEllison) *in tch tl wknd qckly over 4f out: sn t.o* **25/1** | — |

2m 27.85s (4.53) **Going Correction** +0.725s/f (Yiel)
**WFA** 3 from 5yo+ 7lb **6 Ran SP% 108.7**
Speed ratings: **112,108,108,87,77** —CSF £2.59 TOTE £2.20: £1.40, £1.20; EX 3.10.
**Owner** Godolphin **Bred** Gainsborough Stud Management Ltd **Trained** Newmarket, Suffolk

**FOCUS**
A race that did not take as much winning as seemed likely, with Percussionist turning in a laboured performance, but another step in the right direction for Into the Dark. The pace was only fair and threw up the sort of time you would expect for the grade given the conditions.

**NOTEBOOK**
**Into The Dark** ◆ has come a very long way in a short time and, although his main rivals failed to deliver for one reason or another, impressed once again with the way he went through the race. He remains a very useful prospect and is well worth a further step up in grade.
**Percussionist(IRE)**, tailed off in the Irish Derby when last seen in June, looked to have conditions to suit but turned in a laboured display and, although he will be suited by the return to further, looks one to have reservations about.
**Bonecrusher**, up in trip and on testing ground, had a bit to find at the weights but once again did not convince with his effort off the bridle. He may be suited by more cover in a more strongly-run race but remains one to tread carefully with.
**Howards Dream(IRE)**, who faced an impossible task at the weights, is flattered by his proximity to the first three.
**Society Times(USA)** faced an impossible task on these terms.
**Court Of Appeal** faced a stiff task at the weights but ran no sort of race even so. He will be much happier back on less testing ground. *Official explanation: jockey said gelding finished distressed*

## 5630 TOTESPORT.COM NURSERY 1m

**4:15** (4:15) (C1) (0-95,96) 2-Y-O **£12,319** (£4,672; £2,336; £1,062) **Stalls** Low

| Form | | | | RPR |
|---|---|---|---|---|
| 141 | **1** | | **Comic Strip**[7] 5453 2-9-8 **96** SSanders 10<br>(SirMarkPrescott) *hld up in midfield: smooth hdwy to ld over 2f out: drvn out* **10/3**[2] | 103+ |
| 312 | **2** | *1* | **Hallhoo (IRE)**[14] 5292 2-8-11 **85** ACulhane 1<br>(MRChannon) *trckd ldrs: ch 3f out: sn rdn and outpcd: styd on wl u.p to go 2nd ins fnl f: clsng on wnr fin* **3/1**[1] | 90 |
| 214 | **3** | *3½* | **Looks Could Kill (USA)**[14] 5292 2-8-12 **86** PHanagan 6<br>(GAButler) *hld up: gd hdwy to join ldrs 3f out: ev ch and rdn over 1f out: no ex* **10/3**[2] | 84 |
| 1204 | **4** | *2* | **Catwalk Cleric (IRE)**[19] 5202 2-8-12 **86** KDarley 8<br>(MJWallace) *chsd ldrs: rdn over 2f out: kpt on same pce* **20/1** | 80 |
| 4433 | **5** | *1¼* | **Young Thomas (IRE)**[19] 5188 2-7-12 **72** oh2 JQuinn 3<br>(MLWBell) *prom: ev ch 3f out: sn rdn: kpt on same pce* **20/1** | 64 |
| 023 | **6** | *1¼* | **Takhmin (IRE)**[57] 4078 2-8-10 **84** WSupple 2<br>(MJohnston) *led 2f: remained cl up: led again 3f out: sn hdd: outpcd whn hmpd 2f out: n.d after* **12/1** | 73 |
| 5106 | **7** | *8* | **Ballycroy Girl (IRE)**[13] 5314 2-7-9 **72** oh1 HayleyTurner(3) 7<br>(ABailey) *midfield: effrt and sme hdwy 3f out: rdn and swtchd lft over 2f out: sn btn* **25/1** | 45 |
| 4550 | **8** | *2* | **Turks Wood (IRE)**[14] 5292 2-7-9 **72** (b[1]) FPFerris(3) 11<br>(MHTompkins) *dwlt: towards rr: effrt and sme hdwy over 3f out: sn rdn and btn* **50/1** | 41 |
| 0100 | **9** | *4* | **John Forbes**[55] 4166 2-8-10 **87** TEaves(3) 5<br>(BEllison) *hld up: effrt over 3f out: sn btn* **25/1** | 48 |
| 0210 | **10** | *1¼* | **Apetite**[13] 5314 2-8-0 **74** oh12 ow2 FNorton 4<br>(NBycroft) *slowly away: a bhd* **66/1** | 33 |
| 1 | **11** | *5* | **Gypsy Johnny**[77] 3505 2-8-11 **85** (v[1]) DHolland 9<br>(MLWBell) *dwlt: towards rr: gd hdwy to ld after 2f: hdd 3f out: wknd qckly* **8/1**[3] | 34 |

1m 50.02s (6.90) **Going Correction** +0.925s/f (Soft) **11 Ran SP% 110.6**
Speed ratings: **102,101,97,95,94 93,85,83,79,77 72**CSF £11.47 CT £32.99 TOTE £4.50: £2.20, £1.80, £1.60; EX 16.70 Trifecta £47.00 Pool £496.60 - 7.50 winning units..
**Owner** Neil Greig - Osborne House **Bred** Floors Farming And Side Hill Stud **Trained** Newmarket, Suffolk

■ Stewards Enquiry : J Quinn caution: careless riding
D Holland one-day ban: used whip when colt was showing no response and was out of contention (Sep 29)

**FOCUS**
A decent nursery, run at a fair pace in the conditions, and very strong form. The winner is one to keep on the right side and is good enough to win at Listed level.

**NOTEBOOK**
**Comic Strip** ◆ is a progressive sort who turned in his best effort yet upped to this trip and on the softest ground he has encountered. He won with a bit in hand and, given his connections and the manner of this win, appeals as the type to hold his own in stronger company.
**Hallhoo(IRE)** has progressed with every outing and turned in his best effort on this first start away from a sound surface. He should stay further and there is no reason why he should not continue to go well.
**Looks Could Kill(USA)** finished further behind Halhoo than at Haydock, even on these better terms but, given that he travelled strongly for much of the way, may prove better suited by less testing ground. He is well worth another chance.
**Catwalk Cleric(IRE)**, who has winning form on soft ground, ran creditably on this first try above sprint distances but he will have to improve to win in similar company from his current mark.
**Young Thomas(IRE)** was again not disgraced but again had his limitations exposed in this type of event and, on this evidence, will be well suited by a drop in grade.
**Takhmin(IRE)**'s latest form worked out well but, although not knocked about on this nursery debut and first run over this trip, did not really shape as though he would be winning from this sort of mark in similar company in the near future.
**Gypsy Johnny**, who created a favourable impression on his debut was surprisingly tried in a visor for this handicap debut but dropped out tamely in the testing conditions. He is not one to write off just yet.

## 5631 KEYLINE BUILDERS MERCHANTS H'CAP (FOR THE WEIR MEMORIAL TROPHY) 7f 50y

**4:50** (4:51) (D2) (0-85,85) 3-Y-O+ **£12,616** (£4,785; £2,392; £1,087) **Stalls** Low

| Form | | | | RPR |
|---|---|---|---|---|
| 3020 | **1** | | **Azreme**[27] 4969 4-8-8 **72** ACulhane 14<br>(DKIvory) *hld up: hdwy to ld ins fnl f: hld on wl* **14/1** | 83 |
| 6430 | **2** | *nk* | **Sea Storm (IRE)**[9] 5419 6-8-12 **76** GCarter 7<br>(DRMacleod) *bhd: hdwy 2f out: r.o fnl f* **25/1** | 87 |
| 0023 | **3** | *1* | **Watching**[22] 5075 7-9-4 **82** PHanagan 4<br>(RAFahey) *hld up: hdwy over 2f out: r.o fnl f* **9/2**[2] | 90 |
| -300 | **4** | *1¼* | **Bandos**[86] 3235 4-8-10 **74** (t) DAllan 1<br>(ISemple) *keen: led: styd alone far rail but overall ldr ent st: hdd and no ex ins fnl f* **66/1** | 79 |
| 0033 | **5** | *nk* | **Marshman (IRE)**[19] 5177 5-8-13 **80** FPFerris(3) 6<br>(MHTompkins) *hld up: hdwy u.p 2f out: r.o ins last* **10/1** | 84 |
| 2146 | **6** | *1* | **Hills Of Gold**[15] 5265 5-8-13 **77** DHolland 11<br>(MWEasterby) *prom: effrt over 2f out: r.o same pce fnl f* **15/2** | 79 |
| 5004 | **7** | *7* | **Ulysees (IRE)**[29] 4904 5-8-7 **71** WSupple 5<br>(ISemple) *keen in tch: effrt over 2f out: hung lft and outpcd over 1f out* **20/1** | 55 |
| 4012 | **8** | *¾* | **Khanjar (USA)**[18] 5210 4-9-0 **78** DarrenWilliams 9<br>(KRBurke) *dwlt: hld up: effrt outside over 2f out: nvr rchd ldrs* **20/1** | 60 |
| 0004 | **9** | *¾* | **Namroud (USA)**[28] 4931 5-8-8 **75** THamilton(3) 2<br>(RAFahey) *chsd ldrs tl outpcd fr 2f out* **7/1**[3] | 55 |
| 5002 | **10** | *1* | **Smirfys Systems**[50] 4308 5-8-9 **73** NCallan 10<br>(WMBrisbourne) *hld up: hdwy and ev ch over 2f out: wknd over 1f out* **66/1** | 51 |
| 5000 | **11** | *3½* | **Wanchai Lad**[1] 5605 3-9-1 **82** PDoe 8<br>(DNicholls) *w ldr tl wknd fr 2f out* **66/1** | 51 |
| 3002 | **12** | *hd* | **True Night**[13] 5315 7-9-5 **83** AlexGreaves 3<br>(DNicholls) *chsd ldrs tl wknd over 2f out* **20/1** | 52 |
| 1034 | **13** | *8* | **Flur Na H Alba**[15] 5263 5-9-0 **81** (p) TEaves(3) 16<br>(ISemple) *in tch: effrt over 2f out: sn rdn and btn* **33/1** | 30 |
| 0042 | **14** | *14* | **Hurricane Floyd (IRE)**[19] 5184 6-8-10 **74** (b[1]) SSanders 15<br>(DFlood) *midfield on outside: rdn over 2f out: sn btn* **14/1** | — |
| 3432 | **15** | *14* | **Albashoosh**[36] 4727 6-8-7 **71** ANicholls 17<br>(DNicholls) *cl up tl wknd over 2f out* **10/1** | — |
| /4-5 | **16** | *1¾* | **Lady Mytton**[154] 1469 4-9-6 **84** JFanning 12<br>(ABailey) *hld up: lost tch fr 3f out* **100/1** | — |
| 5301 | **17** | *16* | **Presumptive (IRE)**[37] 4690 4-9-4 **82** (b[1]) KDarley 13<br>(RCharlton) *bhd: lost tch fr 1/2-way* **4/1**[1] | — |
| 6015 | **18** | *dist* | **King Harson**[22] 5077 5-9-7 **85** (v) KMcEvoy 18<br>(JDBethell) *midfield: rdn over 3f out: sn lost pl* **25/1** | — |

1m 38.04s (5.57) **Going Correction** +0.925s/f (Soft)
**WFA** 3 from 4yo+ 3lb **18 Ran SP% 124.3**
Speed ratings: **105,104,103,102,101 100,92,91,90,89 85,85,76,60,44 42,24,**—CSF £332.57 CT £1886.38 TOTE £18.40: £3.30, £5.10, £1.90, £18.30; EX 391.50.
**Owner** Halcyon Partnership **Bred** Miss Helen Mary Ann Omersa **Trained** Radlett, Herts

**FOCUS**
A strong pace in the conditions meant this race favoured those coming from off the pace. Despite that the form looks sound.

**NOTEBOOK**
**Azreme** goes particularly well on testing ground and, with the race run to suit, ran right up to his best under a well-judged ride. It remains to be seen whether things will pan out as well back on a sounder surface next time.
**Sea Storm(IRE)** looked a bit better than the bare form of his latest run at Doncaster when poorly drawn and returned to something like his best in a race that was run to suit. He has been largely consistent and should continue to give a good account.
**Watching**, who handles soft ground, ran creditably for his in-form stable back over this longer trip. He has been in decent heart of late but his losing run, that stretches back to July 2000, has to be a concern.
**Bandos** ◆, a dual course and distance winner on fast ground last year, shaped as though a fair bit better than the bare result as he fared the best of those that raced up with the strong pace and raced on his own on the far rail in the straight. He is not the most straightforward but looks capable of winning again from this mark back on fast ground.
**Marshman(IRE)** extended his run of creditable efforts in a race that was run to suit. He is effective on Polytrack and should continue to give a good account, but his win record means he is not one to be going in head down for.
**Hills Of Gold** shaped as though a bit better than the bare result as he raced up with the strong pace throughout over a trip that is a bare minimum. He seems a reliable sort who should continue to give a good account.
**Ulysees(IRE)** did not improve for the return to this longer trip in a race that placed the emphasis on stamina but, although the drop back to six will suit, does not look the most straightforward of characters.
**Hurricane Floyd(IRE)** *Official explanation: jockey said saddle slipped*
**Albashoosh** *Official explanation: jockey said gelding ran too free in the early stages*
**Lady Mytton** *Official explanation: trainer said filly was in season*
**Presumptive(IRE)** *Official explanation: jockey said colt lost its action after 2f*
**King Harson** *Official explanation: trainer's representative had no explanation for the poor run*

**5632** **GLASGOW AUDI - THE WORLD'S LARGEST AUDI CENTRE H'CAP** **1m 5f 13y**
**5:20** (5:20) (D2) (0-85,83) 3-Y-O+ **£8,284** (£2,549; £1,274; £637) **Stalls** Low

Form RPR
1113 **1** **Elusive Dream**[30] 4888 3-9-1 **81** SSanders 6 102+
(SirMarkPrescott) *hld up in tch: hdwy to ld over 2f out: edgd rt: styd on strly* **1/2**[1]
3115 **2** *5* **Lets Roll**[30] 4888 3-9-3 **83** DeanMcKeown 9 91
(CWThornton) *hld up: hdwy over 2f out: edgd lft over 1f out: kpt on: nt rch wnr* **11/2**[2]
-145 **3** *2* **Faayej (IRE)**[28] 4950 4-9-12 **83** (p) WSupple 3 88
(SirMichaelStoute) *trckd ldrs: effrt over 2f out: outpcd over 1f out* **7/1**[3]
0-10 **4** *nk* **Perelandra (USA)**[14] 5303 4-9-1 **72** NCallan 4 77
(MJWallace) *hld up in tch: smooth hdwy to dispute ld over 2f out: sn rdn: no ex over 1f out* **66/1**
0035 **5** *7* **Merrymaker**[5] 5517 4-8-8 **70** PPMathers(5) 1 65
(WMBrisbourne) *prom: rdn over 2f out: sn outpcd: n.d after* **25/1**
3305 **6** *nk* **Lennel**[1] 5607 6-8-9 **69** (b) HayleyTurner(3) 7 63
(ABailey) *hld up: outpcd 4f out: n.d after* **16/1**
3300 **7** *1 1/2* **Nessen Dorma (IRE)**[67] 3821 3-9-3 **83** DHolland 8 75
(JGGiven) *led to over 2f out: sn btn* **33/1**
103 **8** *dist* **Tomasino**[22] 5100 6-8-13 **70** (t) KDarley 5 —
(KGReveley) *trckd ldrs: rdn over 3f out: sn struggling* **16/1**

3m 6.94s (11.09) **Going Correction** +0.925s/f (Soft) **8** Ran SP% **114.6**
**WFA** 3 from 4yo+ 9lb
Speed ratings: **102,98,97,97,93 93,92,**—CSF £3.58 CT £9.26 TOTE £1.60: £1.10, £1.80, £2.30; EX 4.00 Place 6 £57.80, Place 5 £37.97..
**Owner** Cheveley Park Stud **Bred** Cheveley Park Stud Ltd **Trained** Newmarket, Suffolk

**FOCUS**
A decent handicap and one in which the progressive three-year-olds dominated. The pace was not a strong one, but the winner looks capable of going in again and the form behind looks sound.

**NOTEBOOK**
**Elusive Dream** has improved with every outing and confirmed recent superiority over Lets Roll. He will be going up in the weights again, but is a good sort on looks and may well be capable of better. He remains one to keep on the right side.
**Lets Roll**, who got closer to the winner than at York, ran creditably without ever threatening to make a challenge. A stronger gallop over this trip would have suited him and he should continue to give a good account.
**Faayej(IRE)**, tried in cheekpieces on this first run over this longer trip, had the run of the race and was not disgraced but looks vulnerable to progressive sorts from his current mark.
**Perelandra(USA)** travelled strongly for a long way but found little off the bridle in these testing conditions. He will be more of interest back on a sound surface but he may not be the most straightforward.
**Merrymaker**, a bit better than the bare form at Musselburgh last week, was a long way below that level back on very testing ground. He looks vulnerable in this grade from his current mark.
**Lennel**, turned out for the second successive day, was well below his best in a race that was not really run to suit over a trip further than ideal.
**Tomasino** *Official explanation: jockey said gelding was unsuited by the soft ground*
T/Plt: £135.40 to a £1 stake. Pool: £92,851.90. 500.30 winning tickets. T/Qpdt: £25.80 to a £1 stake. Pool: £4,936.90. 141.40 winning tickets. RY

## 5362 CATTERICK (L-H)
Saturday, September 18

**OFFICIAL GOING: Firm (good to firm in places)**
The ground was described by the riders as 'firm but with no jar' after four days without any significant rain.
Wind: Fresh 1/2 against. Weather: Fine and sunnyy.

**5633** **EUROPEAN BREEDERS FUND MAIDEN STKS** **5f 212y**
**1:55** (1:56) (D3) 2-Y-O **£4,212** (£1,296; £648; £324) **Stalls** Low

Form RPR
53 **1** **Leslingtaylor (IRE)**[21] 5125 2-9-0 GParkin 10 70+
(JJQuinn) *hld up on outer: bit slipped 1/2-way: hdwy 2f out: rdn to ld 1f out: sn clr* **7/2**[2]
200 **2** *3* **Mas O Menos (IRE)**[79] 3444 2-8-9 NChalmers(5) 4 54
(MsDeborahJEvans) *cl up: led 1/2-way: rdn along 2f out: hdd 1f out: sn one pce* **50/1**
**3** *3/4* **On Action (USA)** 2-8-11 ABeech(3) 9 52
(MrsADuffield) *cmpt: chsd ldrs: effrt and pushed along whn n.m.r 2f out: swtchd lft and rdn over 1f out: styd on ins last* **20/1**
**4** *hd* **Balkan Leader (USA)** 2-9-0 JCarroll 3 51
(SaeedBinSuroor) *w'like: leggy: dwlt: sn chsng ldrs on inner: hdwy over 2f out: sn rdn and kpt on same pce appr last* **4/7**[1]
**5** *3 1/2* **Missin Margot** 2-8-4 BSwarbrick(5) 1 35
(MsDeborahJEvans) *cmpt: bit bkwd: dwlt: hdwy to chse ldrs 1/2-way: sn rdn along and wknd 2f out* **25/1**
**6** *2* **Katie's Biscuit** 2-8-9 NPollard 8 29
(IanEmmerson) *cmpt: bkwd: s.i.s: a rr* **40/1**
00 **7** *1/2* **Love From Russia**[10] 5396 2-9-0 DaleGibson 7 32
(ABerry) *sn led: hdd 1/2-way: sn rdn along and wknd* **66/1**
5 **8** *3/4* **Dispol Charm (IRE)**[18] 5209 2-8-9 PFessey 6 25
(TDBarron) *chsd ldrs to 1/2-way: sn lost pl and bhd* **12/1**[3]
**9** *8* **Ekaterina** 2-8-9 JBramhill 2 —
(WStorey) *leggy: unf: s.i.s: a bhd* **40/1**

1m 14.02s (0.02) **Going Correction** -0.20s/f (Firm) **9** Ran SP% **110.5**
Speed ratings: **91,87,86,85,81 78,77,76,66**CSF £147.84 TOTE £7.50: £1.10, £10.50, £4.10; EX 213.10.
**Owner** Derrick Bloy **Bred** Mrs Peggy Kelly **Trained** Settrington, N Yorks

**FOCUS**
A modest maiden and a moderate time for the grade and, with the Godolphin favourite flopping, it almost certainly took little winning.

**NOTEBOOK**
**Leslingtaylor(IRE)**, very much up in the air, did really well after his bit pulled right through his mouth at the halfway mark. It probably took little winning and his future depends on getting a realistic nursery mark.
**Mas O Menos(IRE)** was found to have a sore throat when finishing last in a claimer at Haydock 11 weeks earlier.
**On Action(USA)**, a February foal, is a close-coupled individual. He knew his job and was probably second best on merit.
**Balkan Leader(USA)**, a May foal, is rather on the leg but he looked different class in the paddock and showed a good action going to post. After missing a beat at the start he made very hard work of it and in the end looked to have no excuse. Surely he is capable of better than he showed here.
**Missin Margot**, a February foal, is bred exclusively for speed but she looked short of peak condition on her debut.
**Katie's Biscuit**, a backward newcomer, was a handful to load.
**Dispol Charm(IRE)** *Official explanation: jockey said filly did not handle the track*

**5634** **SCORTON (S) STKS** **1m 5f 175y**
**2:25** (2:25) (G4) 3-Y-O **£2,993** (£855; £427) **Stalls** Low

Form RPR
1400 **1** **Pepe (IRE)**[29] 4927 3-8-11 **54** (p) RFrench 9 57
(RHollinshead) *trckd ldrs: hdwy 5f out: ev ch 2f out: sn rdn: drvn and styd on wl fnl f to ld nr fin* **9/1**
0622 **2** *hd* **Zuleta**[22] 5069 3-8-0 **45** BSwarbrick(5) 7 51
(JGMO'Shea) *hld up in tch: hdwy 1/2-way: led over 2f out: rdn over 1f out: drvn ins last: hdd and no ex nr fin* **7/2**[1]
0300 **3** *6* **Calomeria**[30] 4870 3-8-0 **54** (b) NChalmers(5) 11 42
(RMBeckett) *led: rdn along over 3f out: hdd over 2f out and sn one pce* **7/2**[1]
6000 **4** *7* **Signora Panettiera (FR)**[4] 5538 3-8-5 **40** JCarroll 3 33
(MRChannon) *hld up towards rr: hdwy 5f out: rdn along 3f out: nvr nr ldrs* **8/1**[3]
3050 **5** *6* **Bonjour Bond (IRE)**[32] 4825 3-8-10 **45** (p) DMcGaffin 8 29
(BSmart) *chsd ldrs: rdn along over 5f out: drvn and wknd over 3f out* **12/1**
4000 **6** *1/2* **Bold Blade**[11] 5365 3-8-9 **55** DTudhope(7) 4 34
(MJPolglase) *a rr* **4/1**[2]
0 **7** *1* **Parisi Princess**[20] 5146 3-8-5 JEdmunds 1 22
(GPKelly) *a rr: bhd fnl 4f* **100/1**
0060 **8** *11* **Iron Temptress (IRE)**[3] 5560 3-8-5 **53** NPollard 6 7
(GMMoore) *chsd ldrs: rdn along 5f out: sn wknd* **12/1**
0000 **9** *5* **Myannabanana (IRE)**[5] 5524 3-8-7 **45** (v) ABeech(3) 2 5
(JRWeymes) *cl up: rdn along over 4f out and sn wknd* **16/1**
5640 **10** *20* **Weaver Spell**[62] 3371 3-8-3 **35** (v[1]) AMullen(7) 5 —
(JRNorton) *midfield: rdn along 1/2-way: sn wknd and bhd fnl 4f* **100/1**
0-00 **11** *30* **Amar (CZE)**[219] 746 3-8-10 **35** GParkin 12 —
(PABlockley) *a bhd: t.o fnl 4f* **33/1**

3m 2.96s (-1.54) **Going Correction** -0.20s/f (Firm) **11** Ran SP% **111.7**
Speed ratings: **96,95,92,88,85 84,84,77,75,63 46**CSF £38.30 TOTE £8.70: £2.70, £1.10, £2.00; EX 44.40.There was no bid for the winner.
**Owner** J D Graham **Bred** Paul Starr **Trained** Upper Longdon, Staffs

**FOCUS**
A rock-bottom seller, with the winner showing his first form on turf. A race unlikely to provide many pointers to future events.

**NOTEBOOK**
**Pepe(IRE)**, who took a handicap at Southwell in April from a mark of just 49, did not go without market support and did just enough to take a poor race even by selling race standards.
**Zuleta**, who has changed stables, seemed to be worried out of it by the winner.
**Calomeria**, who looked reluctant on the way to post, took them along at a sound pace but dropped away tamely and is one to have severe reservations about.
**Signora Panettiera(FR)**, who seems to be going the wrong way, has now finished unplaced in ten starts and she did not prove her stamina here.
**Bonjour Bond(IRE)**, who ran over a mile last time, had the cheekpieces on but he was on the retreat turning in.
**Bold Blade** seems better on the All-Weather, his two career wins have been on the artificial surfaces.
**Weaver Spell** *Official explanation: trainer said gelding was unsuited by the firm, good to firm in places ground*

**5635** **WEATHERBYS BANK SEPTEMBER STKS (H'CAP)** **1m 3f 214y**
**3:00** (3:02) (E3) (0-70,73) 3-Y-O+ **£7,190** (£2,212; £1,106; £553) **Stalls** Low

Form RPR
-021 **1** **Circassian (IRE)**[4] 5554 3-9-7 **73** 6ex JCarroll 13 81+
(SirMarkPrescott) *trckd ldrs: hdwy 1/2-way: led over 2f out and sn rdn: drvn over 1f out:hld on wl* **5/6**[1]
2-02 **2** *hd* **Colway Ritz**[13] 5320 10-9-3 **61** JBramhill 5 69
(WStorey) *hld up: stdy hdwy over 4f out: effrt on outer 2f out: sn rdn and ev ch ins last: drvn and nt qckn towards fin* **14/1**
5604 **3** *1* **Greenwich Meantime**[12] 5343 4-9-2 **60** LGoncalves 4 66
(MrsJRRamsden) *hld up in midfield: hdwy on inner over 2f out: rdn to chal and ev ch ent last tl drvn and no ex towards fin* **8/1**[3]
1335 **4** *nk* **Donastrela (IRE)**[14] 5300 3-8-9 **66** (v) NChalmers(5) 9 72
(AMBalding) *trckd ldrs: pushed along and sltly outpcd 3f out: sn rdn and styd on wl fnl f: nrst fin* **11/1**
4000 **5** *5* **Sadler's Pride (IRE)**[17] 5229 4-9-2 **60** DMernagh 10 58
(AndrewTurnell) *prom: rdn along 3f out: drvn and wknd over 1f out* **50/1**
00 **6** *hd* **Stallone**[14] 5303 7-9-5 **70** DTudhope(7) 11 68
(NWilson) *hld up in midfld:hdwy n outer over 3f out: rdn along 2f out: sn drvn and no imp over 1f out* **16/1**
2100 **7** *2* **Trusted Mole (IRE)**[47] 4397 6-8-7 **56** oh1 BSwarbrick(5) 14 50
(WMBrisbourne) *midfield: hdwy to chse ldrs 5f out: rdn along over 2f out: drvn and wknd wl over 1f out* **40/1**
0003 **8** *3* **Red Skelton (IRE)**[11] 5381 3-8-3 **60** PMakin(5) 3 50
(MsDeborahJEvans) *s.i.s and bhd tl styd on fnl 2f: nvr a factor* **28/1**
06-4 **9** *nk* **Smirfys Dance Hall (IRE)**[50] 4306 4-8-13 **57** NPollard 8 46
(WMBrisbourne) *hld up in midfield: hdwy over 4f out: rdn along and hung lft wl over 1f out: sn wknd* **50/1**
2252 **10** *1/2* **Tedsdale Mac**[13] 5317 5-9-2 **60** RFfrench 1 48
(NBycroft) *trckd ldrs on inner: rdn along 3f out: drvn 2f out and sn wknd* **7/1**[2]
6000 **11** *2* **Sovereign Dreamer (USA)**[43] 4518 4-9-12 **70** (t) DaleGibson 7 55
(PFICole) *cl up: led after 5f: rdn along over 3f out: hdd over 2f out and sn wknd* **25/1**
00-0 **12** *2* **Spitfire Bob (USA)**[239] 590 5-8-10 **61** AMullen(7) 12 43
(MESowersby) *a rr* **66/1**
0440 **13** *12* **Bond May Day**[58] 4045 4-9-4 **62** DMcGaffin 6 25
(BSmart) *s.i.s: a rr* **40/1**
0000 **14** *15* **Financial Future**[14] 5303 4-9-4 **69** (b) WHogg(7) 2 8
(MJohnston) *led 5f: prominen tl rdn along 1/2-way and sn wknd: bhd fnl 3f* **20/1**

2m 36.14s (-2.86) **Going Correction** -0.20s/f (Firm)
**WFA** 3 from 4yo+ 8lb **14** Ran SP% **121.4**
Speed ratings: **101,100,100,100,96 96,95,93,93,92 91,90,82,72**CSF £12.89 CT £67.55 TOTE £1.60: £1.10, £3.30, £3.00; EX 13.70.
**Owner** Lady Katharine Watts **Bred** Barouche Stud Ireland Ltd **Trained** Newmarket, Suffolk

**FOCUS**
An ordinary handicap and modest form behind the winner, who is better than the bare form suggests.

**NOTEBOOK**
**Circassian(IRE)**, with a 6lb penalty for his four lengths Yarmouth success just four days earlier, made very hard work of it but this tight track and quick ground were not in his favour. In the end he had to dig deep.

**Colway Ritz** confirmed he was back to form at York last time and here, on his 98th start, he almost upset the hot-pot.
**Greenwich Meantime**, dropped in trip, made his effort on the inner and was only found wanting inside the last. He does not look entirely straightforward however, and he has now won just one of his 16 career starts.
**Donastrela(IRE)**, 9lb higher than her last success, is in good form at present and on this showing is well worth a try over further.
**Sadler's Pride(IRE)** has slipped 12lb since his handicap bow but is still struggling to make much impact.
**Sovereign Dreamer(USA)** *Official explanation: jockey said colt had a breathing problem*

## 5636 CONSTANT SECURITY NURSERY 7f
3:35 (3:37) (E3) (0-75,75) 2-Y-0 **£7,572** (£2,330; £1,165; £582) **Stalls** Low

Form RPR
2301 **1** **Secret Pact (IRE)**[7] 5447 2-9-7 **75** RFfrench 3 79
(MJohnston) *cl up: led halfway: rdn clr wl over 1f out: kpt on* **9/2**[1]
4131 **2** ¾ **Caitlin (IRE)**[16] 5240 2-9-5 **73** DMcGaffin 5 75
(BSmart) *chsd ldrs: hdwy 2f out: rdn to chse wnr and hung lft ins last: kpt on* **5/1**[2]
6562 **3** ¾ **Algorithm**[13] 5314 2-8-5 **59** JBramhill 1 59
(TDEasterby) *chsd ldrs on inner: hdwy 2f out: sn rdn and kpt on fnl f* **7/1**[3]
3600 **4** *shd* **Along The Nile**[7] 5466 2-9-2 **70** LGoncalves 8 70
(MrsJRRamsden) *hld up in tch: hdwy over 2f out: rdn over 1f out: styd on wl fnl f* **14/1**
500 **5** ½ **Wayward Shot (IRE)**[34] 4776 2-8-4 **58** DaleGibson 17 57+
(MWEasterby) *midfield: hdwy 2f out: sn rdn and styng on whn hmpd ins last: nrst fin* **50/1**
6460 **6** 1¼ **Zantero**[7] 5477 2-7-12 **59** DFentiman[(7)] 18 55
(RPElliott) *midfield: hdwy on outer 2f out: sn rdn and kpt on fnl f: nrst fin* **16/1**
3230 **7** 1 **Brace Of Doves**[7] 5477 2-8-11 **70** PMakin[(5)] 11 63+
(TDBarron) *midfield: hdwy over 2f out: rdn and styng on whn hmpd ins last: nt rcvr* **14/1**
2502 **8** ½ **Kumala Ocean (IRE)**[7] 5447 2-8-10 **64** PBradley 10 56
(PABlockley) *cl up: rdn and ch 2f out: sn drvn and grad wknd* **12/1**
1663 **9** 3 **Pro Tempore**[16] 5234 2-8-7 **64** ABeech[(3)] 15 48
(MrsJRRamsden) *keen: racd wd: hdwy over 2f out: sn rdn and no imp* **7/1**[3]
5434 **10** ½ **Ignition**[7] 5447 2-8-6 **65** BSwarbrick[(5)] 4 48
(WMBrisbourne) *dwlt: sn in tch: rdn along over 2f out and sn wknd* **16/1**
4304 **11** *nk* **Lodgician (IRE)**[7] 5477 2-9-0 **68** GParkin 9 50
(JJQuinn) *s.i.s: hdwy 2f out: sn rdn and nt rch ldrs* **14/1**
0300 **12** ½ **Dishdasha (IRE)**[41] 4567 2-8-3 **57** ow3 JEdmunds 16 38
(CRDore) *chsd ldrs: rdn over 2f out: sn wknd* **80/1**
0560 **13** 2½ **Strathtay**[23] 5059 2-8-1 **60** NChalmers[(5)] 6 35
(PCHaslam) *s.i.s: a rr* **40/1**
625 **14** *nk* **Just Do It (UAE)**[19] 5173 2-9-7 **75** JCarroll 12 49
(MRChannon) *s.i.s: a rr* **16/1**
0366 **15** ¾ **Llamadas**[7] 5475 2-8-13 **67** (b) PFessey 13 39
(MDods) *a rr* **25/1**
010 **16** *nk* **Beaumont Girl (IRE)**[2] 5593 2-8-1 **55** MHenry 7 26
(GASwinbank) *midfield whn n.m.r on inner after 2f: sn lost pl and bhd* **14/1**
064 **17** 1¼ **Paris Heights**[21] 5128 2-9-0 **68** DMernagh 2 36
(RMWhitaker) *led to 1/2-way: sn wknd* **33/1**
460 **18** 5 **King Henrik (USA)**[61] 3974 2-8-7 **61** NPollard 14 17
(ACrook) *a rr* **66/1**

1m 26.34s (-1.16) **Going Correction** -0.20s/f (Firm) **18** Ran SP% **125.8**
Speed ratings: **98,97,96,96,95 94,93,92,89,88 88,87,84,84,83 83,81,76**CSF £25.23 CT £141.28 TOTE £5.80: £3.30, £1.70, £2.40, £5.90; EX 16.00.
**Owner** Jumeirah Racing **Bred** Mrs Vanessa Hutch **Trained** Middleham Moor, N Yorks

**FOCUS**
A tight-knit nursery with the first four all drawn in single figures. The form looks solid, although not much to get excited about with regard to the future.

**NOTEBOOK**
**Secret Pact(IRE)** is at last starting to fulfill the promise he showed early. He had it in the bag before the final furlong but in the end had to be kept right up to his work. Progressing nicely, he is well worth a try in a slightly higher grade.
**Caitlin(IRE)**, 3lb higher, again looked a tricky ride but she kept finding something and in the end made the winner work hard.
**Algorithm** is in good form and again gave the impression that she may be better suited by a mile.
**Along The Nile**, who forfeited many lengths at the start at Doncaster, started on terms this time and stuck on in good style late on. A slightly stiffer test will be in his favour.
**Wayward Shot(IRE)**, who had a poor draw, was making no real impression when left short of racing room inside the last when the runner-up tightened up those on her inside.
**Zantero** deserves credit as he had the worst stall of all.
**Brace Of Doves** was sticking on in his own time when tightened up inside the last. A stiffer track might suit him better.
**Paris Heights** *Official explanation: jockey said gelding became unbalanced in the home straight*

## 5637 JOHN GILL LIMITED CHRYSLER JEEP MAIDEN STKS 7f
4:05 (4:06) (D3) 3-Y-0 **£3,406** (£1,048; £524; £262) **Stalls** Low

Form RPR
232 **1** **Fascination Street (IRE)**[12] 5352 3-8-9 65 MHenry 10 55
(MAJarvis) *chsd ldrs: rdn along 2f out: styd on ent last to ld last 100 yds* **7/2**[2]
5343 **2** 1 **Indiana Blues**[12] 5338 3-8-4 63 NChalmers[(5)] 4 53
(AMBalding) *led: rdn clr wl over 1f out: drvn ins last: hdd and no ex last 100 yds* **7/2**[2]
0324 **3** 1½ **Zwadi (IRE)**[14] 5306 3-8-9 72 DaleGibson 1 49
(HCandy) *cl up: rdn wl over 1f out: drvn and wknd ent last* **3/1**[1]
0545 **4** *nk* **Danettie**[29] 4910 3-8-4 62 BSwarbrick[(5)] 6 48
(WMBrisbourne) *chsd ldrs: rdn along over 2f out: kpt on u.p fnl f* **25/1**
6440 **5** 1¾ **Beamsley Beacon**[20] 5141 3-9-0 45 NPollard 9 48
(IanEmmerson) *prom: rdn along wl over 2f out: sn drvn and one pce* **100/1**
-400 **6** *hd* **Strawberry Fair**[59] 4032 3-8-9 70 (t) JCarroll 3 42
(SaeedBinSuroor) *sn outpcd and bhd: rdn along 1/2-way: sme late hdwy* **5/1**
-220 **7** 4 **Rosacara**[65] 3875 3-8-9 68 (t) RFfrench 2 32
(DJDaly) *chsd ldrs to 1/2-way: sn rdn along and wknd* **9/2**[3]
5000 **8** 4 **Aggi Mac**[7] 5451 3-8-2 35 (e) SuzanneFrance[(7)] 5 21
(AndrewTurnell) *s.i.s: a bhd* **66/1**
04 **9** *hd* **Jonnyem**[4] 5545 3-9-0 PFessey 8 25
(GASwinbank) *bhd fr 1/2-way* **33/1**

1m 26.26s (-1.24) **Going Correction** -0.20s/f (Firm) **9** Ran SP% **113.6**
Speed ratings: **99,97,96,95,93 93,89,84,84**CSF £15.52 TOTE £4.40: £1.90, £1.50, £1.10; EX 18.80.
**Owner** N R A Springer **Bred** James Egan and David Hanley **Trained** Newmarket, Suffolk

**FOCUS**
A very modest maiden fillies' race with the fifth rated just 45 and a slow time anchoring the form.

**NOTEBOOK**
**Fascination Street(IRE)**, over a trip that is her bare minimum, showed a good attitude and broke her duck at the eighth attempt.
**Indiana Blues**, highly tried at two, came wide once in line for home and in the end had to settle for a place, her fourth on her 12th attempt.
**Zwadi(IRE)**, well below her best at Thirsk, ran better but her handicap mark of 72 flatters her.
**Danettie**, who ran over a mile and a half on her previous start, seemed to find this trip on the sharp side.
**Beamsley Beacon**, placed just once in 13 previous starts, has an official rating of just 45 and puts a cloud over the overall value of the race.
**Strawberry Fair**, favourite on her first three starts, had finished last of ten at Sandown and she must be a bitter disappointment.
**Rosacara**, tailed off when favourite in a handicap at Epsom on her previous start ten weeks earlier, again ran poorly. *Official explanation: jockey said filly hung right in the last 3f*

## 5638 RICHMOND H'CAP 1m 7f 177y
4:40 (4:40) (F4) (0-55,58) 3-Y-0+ **£3,091** (£883; £441) **Stalls** Low

Form RPR
3252 **1** **Spring Breeze**[5] 5519 3-8-3 **52** (v) DTudhope[(7)] 11 62+
(MDods) *mde all: pushed clr 4f out: easily* **11/2**[2]
60 **2** 5 **Bushido (IRE)**[25] 4698 5-9-4 **53** MLawson[(5)] 2 57
(MrsSJSmith) *midfield: hdwy 5f out: rdn to chse ldr fnl 2f: kpt on* **18/1**
6013 **3** 4 **Little Tobias (IRE)**[12] 5343 5-9-10 **54** DMernagh 18 53
(AndrewTurnell) *trckd ldrs: hdwy 5f out: rdn along over 3f out: drvn and one fnl 2* **11/1**
2324 **4** 6 **Oops (IRE)**[12] 5354 5-9-1 **48** ABeech[(3)] 1 40
(JFCoupland) *trckd ldrs: hdwy 1/2-way: rdn along to chse wnr over 3f out: drvn and wknd 2f out* **5/1**[1]
311 **5** 5 **Super Fellow (IRE)**[34] 4778 10-9-2 **46** oh1 JBramhill 10 32
(CNKellett) *s.i.s and bhd: rdn along 1/2-way: styd on fnl 3f: nvr a factor* **10/1**
0060 **6** *hd* **Narciso (GER)**[13] 5320 4-9-5 **49** DaleGibson 13 35
(MWEasterby) *towards rr: hdwy and rdn along over 4f out: styd on u.p fnl 2f: nvr a factor* **10/1**
0650 **7** 3 **Theatre Belle**[16] 5243 3-8-5 **47** GParkin 4 29
(TDEasterby) *prom: rdn along over 3f out: grad wknd fnl 3f* **66/1**
1534 **8** ¾ **Peter's Imp (IRE)**[19] 4578 9-9-2 **46** oh1 PBradley 20 27
(ABerry) *a towards rr* **16/1**
0043 **9** ½ **Rouge Et Noir**[16] 5243 6-9-0 **51** (t) NeilBrown[(7)] 15 32
(KGReveley) *s.i.s and bhd tl sme late hdwy* **10/1**
-506 **10** 4 **Rhetorical**[7] 5479 3-8-8 **50** PFessey 17 26
(SirMarkPrescott) *chsd wnr: rdn along 1/2-way: wknd over 4f out* **9/1**
1421 **11** 3½ **Shotley Dancer**[20] 5145 5-9-5 **49** DMcGaffin 16 21
(NBycroft) *in tch: rdn along 1/2-way: drvn over 3f out and sn outpcd* **16/1**
2024 **12** 1¾ **Doctor John**[40] 4609 7-9-2 **46** oh1 MHenry 6 16
(AndrewTurnell) *a rr* **33/1**
0040 **13** *shd* **Paint The Lily (IRE)**[64] 3919 3-8-12 **54** RFfrench 14 23
(FWatson) *bhd fr 1/2-way* **100/1**
-000 **14** ¾ **Caper**[16] 5238 4-9-2 **46** oh6 JEdmunds 7 15
(RHollinshead) *midfield: rdn along and bhd fr 1/2-way* **100/1**
0041 **15** 1¼ **Zan Lo (IRE)**[16] 5243 4-9-3 **50** PAspell[(3)] 5 17
(BSRothwell) *a rr* **16/1**
04-0 **16** 13 **Needwood Spirit**[16] 5238 9-9-2 **46** oh11 NPollard 12 —
(MrsAMNaughton) *a bhd* **100/1**
0504 **17** 21 **Lord Lahar**[12] 5340 5-9-3 **47** JCarroll 19 —
(MRChannon) *chsd ldrs: rdn along 1/2-way: sn lost pl and bhd whn eased fnl 2f* **25/1**
0-00 **18** *dist* **Subadar Major**[7] 5456 7-8-11 **46** oh16 PMakin[(5)] 9 —
(MrsGSRees) *in tch: rdn along 1/2-way: sn lost pl and bhd whn eased fnl 2f* **100/1**
2002 **P** **Academy (IRE)**[12] 5354 9-9-9 **58** NChalmers[(5)] 3 —
(AndrewTurnell) *in rr whn p.u lame after 6f* **8/1**[3]

3m 26.25s (-5.15) **Going Correction** -0.20s/f (Firm)
**WFA** 3 from 4yo+ 12lb **19** Ran SP% **123.9**
Speed ratings: **104,101,99,96,94 93,92,92,91,89 88,87,87,86,86 79,69,—,—**CSF £98.26 CT £1067.41 TOTE £8.20: £2.40, £5.90, £4.10, £2.10; EX 211.80.
**Owner** Sheridan Fabrications Ltd **Bred** W P Churchward, D J Bloodstock And C Hue-Will **Trained** Piercebridge, Co Durham
■ Danny Tudhope, 18, was aboard his 20th winner reducing his claim to 5lb.

**FOCUS**
A 0-58 handicap run at a strong early pace, but the winner got the run of the race.

**NOTEBOOK**
**Spring Breeze**, making a quick return, made every yard and stepped it up from the front on the final turn and was soon in no danger. He just stays and stays and has already been schooled over hurdles.
**Bushido(IRE)**, better known as a hurdler, has slipped to a lenient mark and finished clear second best. Five times a winner over timber, an even stiffer test will be in his favour.
**Little Tobias(IRE)**, who took this a year ago from a 7lb lower mark, kept tabs on the winner but was left behind once in line for home.
**Oops(IRE)**, 6lb higher than his last success, does not do a lot under pressure.
**Super Fellow(IRE)**, who made a tardy start, was never in the contest and the ground was plenty quick enough for him. *Official explanation: jockey said gelding was unsuited by the firm, good to firm in places ground*
**Narciso(GER)**, a springer in the market, stayed on when it was all over but was never a factor.
**Caper** *Official explanation: trainer's rerpesentative said gelding returned injured*
**Subadar Major** *Official explanation: jockey said gelding lost its action*

## 5639 CATTERICKBRIDGE.CO.UK FILLIES' H'CAP 7f
5:10 (5:16) (F4) (0-55,55) 3-Y-0+ **£3,043** (£869; £434) **Stalls** Low

Form RPR
0210 **1** **Bint Royal (IRE)**[9] 5411 6-9-6 **55** MHenry 5 63
(MissVHaigh) *mde virtually all: rdn clr wl over 1f out: drvn ins last: jst hld on* **8/1**[3]
5-05 **2** *hd* **Dubaian Mist**[116] 2380 3-8-9 **52** NChalmers[(5)] 1 59
(AMBalding) *chsd ldrs on inner: hdwy 2f out: sn rdn: styd on strly ins last* **10/1**
0454 **3** *nk* **Tokewanna**[7] 5450 4-8-7 **47** (t) BSwarbrick[(5)] 10 54
(WMBrisbourne) *s.i.s and bhd: wd st and gd hdwy 2f out: rdn and hung lft ins last: styd on wl* **7/1**[2]

2000 **4** *hd* **Gemini Lady**[7] 5450 4-8-11 **46** oh1 ....................(b[1]) JCarroll 2 52
(MrsGSRees) *in tch: hdwy 2f out: sn rdn: styd on wl fnl f: nrst fin* **25/1**

0036 **5** *1* **Mickledor (FR)**[12] 5346 4-8-10 **52** ....................(p) DTudhope(7) 9 55
(MDods) *midfield: hdwy 2f out: sn rdn and styd on fnl f: nrst fin* **7/1**[2]

5360 **6** *nk* **Spring Dancer**[40] 4605 3-8-2 **47** ....................(t) AMullen(7) 8 50
(TJFitzgerald) *s.i.s and bhd: hdwy on outer 2f out: styng on whn n.m.r ins last: nrst fin* **10/1**

0000 **7** *1 1/4* **Maureen Ann**[3] 5575 4-8-13 **48** .................... DMcGaffin 7 47
(TJFitzgerald) *towards rr: hdwy and swtchd rt wl over 1f out: sn rdn and one pce ins last* **14/1**

0543 **8** *shd* **Linden's Lady**[3] 5575 4-8-12 **50** .................... ABeech(3) 11 49
(JRWeymes) *dwlt and topwards rr: gd hdwy on outer 2f out: rdn and ch ent last: sn drvn and wknd* **5/1**[1]

3006 **9** *1 1/2* **Festive Chimes (IRE)**[7] 5448 3-8-12 **50** ....................(p) PFessey 15 45
(JJQuinn) *cl up: rdn over 2f out: drvn and wkng whn n.m.r over 1f out* **28/1**

-026 **10** *1 1/2* **Katy O'Hara**[194] 990 5-8-11 **46** oh1 .................... NPollard 3 37
(MissSEHall) *s.i.s and bhd tl styd on appr last* **20/1**

1000 **11** *1/2* **Miss Wizz**[26] 5000 4-8-6 **46** oh1 ....................(p) MLawson(5) 16 36
(WStorey) *chsd ldrs: rdn 2f out: sn wknd* **25/1**

30-0 **12** *1 1/4* **Passion Fruit**[17] 5223 3-9-3 **55** .................... RFfrench 17 41
(CWFairhurst) *in tch: hdwy to chse ldrs over 2f out: sn rdn and wknd wl over 1f out* **50/1**

1250 **13** *1/2* **Cut Ridge (IRE)**[16] 5235 5-9-5 **54** .................... GParkin 13 39
(JSWainwright) *cl up: rdn over 2f out and sn wknd* **10/1**

4003 **14** *3 1/2* **Firebird Rising (USA)**[7] 5448 3-8-4 **47** .................... PMakin(5) 14 22
(TDBarron) *a rr* **10/1**

0660 **15** *1 3/4* **Susiedil (IRE)**[67] 3828 3-8-11 **49** .................... DaleGibson 12 20
(PWHarris) *a rr* **16/1**

003 **16** *19* **Through The Slips (USA)**[26] 5001 3-8-13 **51** .................... JBramhill 6 —
(JGGiven) *chsd ldrs: rdn along and lost pl 1/2-way: sn bhd and eased* **20/1**

1m 25.94s (-1.56) **Going Correction** -0.20s/f (Firm)
**WFA** 3 from 4yo+ 3lb **16** Ran SP% **124.3**
Speed ratings: **100,99,99,99,98 97,96,96,94,92 92,90,90,86,84 62**CSF £79.22 CT £628.57 TOTE £6.80: £2.20, £2.40, £2.60, £3.10; EX 41.60 Place 6 £31.74, Place 5 £6.13..
**Owner** Miss V Haigh **Bred** Gainsborough Stud Management Ltd **Trained** Bawtry, S Yorks

**FOCUS**
A moderate fillies' handicap run at a flat-out early gallop, but only average form for the grade.

**NOTEBOOK**
**Bint Royal(IRE)** capitalised on a favourable draw but after holding a decisive advantage in the end the post came only just in time.
**Dubaian Mist**, having her first outing since May and just her fifth start in all, in the end was just denied and there is surely a race to be won with her at the bottom level.
**Tokewanna**, well supported, made her effort on the wide outside but she edged left inside the last, causing traffic problems on her inside.
**Gemini Lady**, in first-time blinkers, ran a lot better than of late but she has yet to hit the target now in 18 starts.
**Mickledor(FR)**, whose two wins were over six furlongs, if anything seemed to appreciate the extra yardage here.
**Spring Dancer**, better suited by the shorter trip and much faster ground, ran a lot better and was a shade unfortunate not to finish closer.
**Linden's Lady**, who has not tasted success for over two years, was on the retreat when slightly tightened up inside the last.
T/Plt: £27.20 to a £1 stake. Pool: £26,288.60. 703.60 winning tickets. T/Qpdt: £6.50 to a £1 stake. Pool: £2,178.10. 245.45 winning tickets. JR

## 5375 LINGFIELD (L-H)
### Saturday, September 18

**OFFICIAL GOING: Standard**
Wind: almost nil Weather: fine

### 5640 WELNEY MAIDEN AUCTION STKS 7f (P)
**11:30** (11:30) (H5) 2-Y-O £1,491 (£426; £213) **Stalls** Low

Form RPR

30 **1** **Elrafa Mujahid**[31] 4851 2-8-4 .................... LisaJones 8 65
(JulianPoulton) *trckd ldrs: pushed along 1/2-way: effrt over 1f out: coaxed along and kpt on to ld nr fin* **4/1**[1]

3 **2** *nk* **Pinafore**[28] 4936 2-8-3 .................... TPQueally 10 63
(HMorrison) *mde most: hrd rdn over 1f out: hdd nr fin* **4/1**[1]

0050 **3** *1 3/4* **Danger Zone**[11] 5377 2-8-12 66 .................... PDobbs 4 68
(MrsAJPerrett) *trckd ldrs gng easily: effrt over 1f out: drvn and one pce fnl f* **12/1**[3]

**4** *hd* **Bird Over** 2-8-3 .................... JMackay 3 58
(RMBeckett) *rr of main gp: prog over 2f out: shkn up and styd on fnl f: nrst fin* **40/1**

5 **5** *1* **Oceancookie (IRE)**[13] 5319 2-8-6 .................... RMullen 6 59
(AMBalding) *pushed along in rr over 4f out: prog over 2f out: clsd on ldrs 1f out: one pce fnl f* **4/1**[1]

52 **6** *1 1/2* **Bold Counsel (IRE)**[14] 5301 2-8-12 ....................(b[1]) JFortune 13 61
(BJMeehan) *prom: chsd ldr wl over 2f out to 1f out: wknd* **4/1**[1]

0 **7** *5* **Bonnabee (IRE)**[27] 4966 2-8-5 .................... DKinsella 9 42
(CFWall) *racd wd: hld up in rr: nt clr run over 2f out: shuffled along and kpt on fnl f: do bttr* **25/1**

4033 **8** *4* **Phlaunt**[24] 5034 2-8-3 68 .................... SCarson 5 30
(RFJohnsonHoughton) *rdn in rr over 4f out: struggling over 2f out* **9/1**[2]

0 **9** *4* **Touch Of Spice**[33] 4809 2-8-9 .................... RHavlin 12 26
(JRJenkins) *racd midfield: rdn 3f out: sn btn* **66/1**

000 **10** *3* **Silver Creek**[19] 5200 2-8-4 .................... DFox(5) 11 18
(IAWood) *chsd ldr to wl over 2f out: wknd* **33/1**

000 **11** *3 1/2* **Summer Charm**[12] 5353 2-8-9 ow2 .................... MTebbutt 7 9
(WJarvis) *settled in last and sn detached fr main gp: nvr nr ldrs* **40/1**

**12** *2 1/2* **Sperrin Valley (IRE)** 2-8-2 .................... RMiles(3) 1 —
(JSMoore) *detached in last pair after 2f: rdn and no prog* **66/1**

0 **13** *2* **Rooks Bridge (IRE)**[12] 5353 2-8-8 .................... ADaly 2 —
(GAHam) *chsd ldrs tl wknd rapidly over 2f out* **66/1**

06 **L** **Kindlelight Dream (IRE)**[11] 5375 2-8-8 ow8 .................... MHoward(7) 14 —
(DKIvory) *ref to r: tk no part* **33/1**

1m 26.04s (0.10) **Going Correction** -0.05s/f (Stan) **14** Ran SP% **116.8**
Speed ratings: **97,96,94,94,93 91,85,81,76,73 69,66,64,—**CSF £16.97 TOTE £5.50: £1.80, £1.70, £4.50; EX 23.10.
**Owner** Giovanni Favarulo & Manan Khawaja **Bred** R S A Urquhart **Trained** Kentford, Suffolk

**FOCUS**
Modest form, but a decent winning time for the type of contest and solid enough for the grade.

**NOTEBOOK**
**Elrafa Mujahid**, who had shown promise over a mile at this track on her debut, enjoyed the decent gallop over this shorter trip and proved game in getting up near the line. She will be suited by the return to further in due course and could do better next year.
**Pinafore** stepped up on her debut effort over this longer trip and was only just denied. This was a decent effort and she did very well to sustain her gallop, having set the brisk pace for most of the way. A similar event is hers for the taking.
**Danger Zone** turned is his best effort to date. Travelling best of all turning for home, he found less than expected under pressure and could only find the one pace when it mattered. He could be worth another try in a nursery off this mark and he enjoyed this surface.
**Bird Over**, a late foal and a cheap purchase, made a pleasing debut. She ran green early on, but looked better the further she went and was staying on nicely towards the end.
**Oceancookie(IRE)** ran below the form of her York debut over this extra furlong. She had trouble going the early pace and has a bit to prove now.
**Bold Counsel(IRE)** failed to build on his recent Thirsk outing in the first-time blinkers. However, he was not helped by his wide draw and now qualifies for nurseries.
**Bonnabee(IRE)** again showed signs of ability, despite nothing going her way this time, and can be rated better than the bare form.

### 5641 TITCHWELL BANDED STKS 1m (P)
**11:55** (11:56) (H5) 3-Y-O+ £1,491 (£426; £213) **Stalls** High

Form RPR

-356 **1** **Levantine (IRE)**[179] 1090 7-8-7 40 .................... KirstyMilczarek(7) 3 54+
(MissJFeilden) *trckd ldrs gng easily: no room on inner over 2f out and trapped on rails over 1f out: fnlly got through and r.o to ld last* **12/1**

0032 **2** *1/2* **Crimson Star (IRE)**[14] 5283 3-8-10 40 .................... DKinsella 4 47
(CTinkler) *trckd ldrs: rdn to ld 2f out: clr ins fnl f: hdd and outpcd last 50yds* **5/1**[3]

0604 **3** *2 1/2* **Enna (POL)**[12] 5350 5-9-0 40 .................... RHavlin 2 41
(MrsStefLiddiard) *racd midfield: rdn 3f out: prog and swtchd rt over 1f out: styd on to take 3rd ins fnl f* **9/2**[2]

/0-0 **4** *2 1/2* **Ragasah**[63] 3934 6-9-0 40 .................... LisaJones 5 36
(EROertel) *led to over 3f out: rdn and outpcd over 2f out: n.d after* **33/1**

1-05 **5** *nk* **Denise Best (IRE)**[19] 5175 6-8-11 40 ....................(p) DNolan(3) 12 35
(MissKMGeorge) *s.i.s: rdn thrght: last pair tl kpt on fr over 1f out: nrst fin* **5/1**[3]

0650 **6** *1 1/4* **Desert Fury**[22] 5081 7-9-0 40 .................... TPQueally 11 32
(RBastiman) *s.i.s: sn pushed along in rr: drvn and struggling over 3f out: kpt on one pce u.p* **11/4**[1]

0004 **7** *1/2* **Catch The Fox**[22] 5080 4-9-0 40 .................... ADaly 8 31
(JJBridger) *racd in last pair: nvr a factor* **11/1**

0000 **8** *hd* **Estrella Levante**[11] 5378 4-9-0 40 ....................(b) SCarson 6 30
(RMFlower) *pressed ldr: led over 3f out and kicked on: hdd & wknd 2f out* **16/1**

060/ **9** *3/4* **Tap Dancer (IRE)**[770] 3024 6-8-7 40 .................... AHindley(7) 10 29
(BGPowell) *t.k.h: trckd ldrs tl rdn and wknd wl over 2f out* **33/1**

0004 **10** *2 1/2* **Rathmullan**[44] 4469 5-8-7 40 ....................(b) LiamJones(7) 7 23
(EAWheeler) *chsd ldrs: rdn and btn over 2f out: hanging and reluctant over 1f out* **16/1**

0000 **11** *1/2* **Explicit (IRE)**[26] 5001 3-8-10 40 .................... JMackay 1 22
(GCBravery) *rdn in midfield whn hmpd on inner 5f out: struggling after* **33/1**

-000 **L** **Singularity**[19] 3932 4-8-11 40 ....................(b) BReilly(3) 9 —
(KFClutterbuck) *ref to r: tk no part* **66/1**

1m 40.82s (1.27) **Going Correction** -0.05s/f (Stan)
**WFA** 3 from 4yo+ 4lb **12** Ran SP% **116.3**
Speed ratings: **91,90,88,85,85 83,83,83,82,80 79,—**CSF £68.00 TOTE £11.90: £3.00, £1.90, £2.00; EX 62.70.
**Owner** City Racing Club **Bred** Gainsborough Stud Management Ltd **Trained** Exning, Suffolk
■ The first winner for apprentice Kirsty Milczarek.

**FOCUS**
Only average form for the grade, but a slow time, even for a banded contest.

**NOTEBOOK**
**Levantine(IRE)** proved he goes best fresh, and did very well to overcome trouble on the rail in the straight to score. He is better then the bare form and clearly in good heart, but is inconsistent and may be one to take on next time.
**Crimson Star(IRE)** ◆ had every chance, but could not match the winner's turn of foot when pressed late on. She has been slowly going the right way, is still lightly-raced and should soon go one better in this grade.
**Enna(POL)** ran another sound race and looked suited to this surface, but may need to revert to further in order to score.
**Ragasah** set the ordinary pace, until lacking the necessary change of gear and she finished well held.
**Denise Best(IRE)** gave herself a very stiff task with a sluggish start from her wide berth. She is capable of better.
**Desert Fury** was another who faced a stiff task when blowing the start from his wide draw. He is a frustrating performer.
**Catch The Fox** *Official explanation: jockey said gelding hung both ways*

### 5642 AMY & JESSICA RIX BANDED STKS 7f (P)
**12:20** (12:20) (H5) 3-Y-O+ £1,701 (£486; £243) **Stalls** Low

Form RPR

4460 **1** **Sylva Royal (IRE)**[26] 5000 3-8-12 49 .................... J-PGuillambert(3) 4 59
(CEBrittain) *racd midfield: pushed along and prog fr 3f out: rdn to ld last 150yds: styd on wl* **12/1**

4000 **2** *1 1/2* **Ballare (IRE)**[14] 5285 5-9-5 50 ....................(v) TWilliams 5 56
(BobJones) *prom: rdn to ld 2f out: hdd and one pce last 150yds* **5/1**[2]

4501 **3** *1 3/4* **Calculaite**[7] 5451 3-9-2 55 .................... RoryMoore(5) 14 56
(MrsGSRees) *prom: rdn to chal 2f out: nt qckn and btn fnl f* **3/1**[1]

0000 **4** *2* **Pirouettes (IRE)**[40] 4604 4-9-0 45 .................... LisaJones 3 41
(EROertel) *dwlt: racd in rr: sme prog on inner 3f out: kpt on fr over 1f out: n.d* **25/1**

2560 **5** *3* **Labelled With Love**[66] 3848 4-9-3 48 ....................(t) VVenkaya 2 36
(JRBoyle) *dwlt: plld hrd and sn chsd ldrs: urged along and unbalanced over 1f out: wknd* **28/1**

0600 **6** *nk* **Averami**[36] 4708 3-8-9 50 ....................(b[1]) RJKilloran(7) 13 38
(AMBalding) *settled wl in rr: pushed along 3f out: kpt on fnl f: no ch* **28/1**

5430 **7** *1/2* **Loch Laird**[15] 5260 9-8-11 49 .................... CHaddon(7) 10 35
(MMadgwick) *settled in rr: rdn and struggling 3f out: no ch after: plugged on* **8/1**

0156 **8** *nk* **Taiyo**[3] 5575 4-9-4 49 .................... RHavlin 1 35
(JWPayne) *chsd ldrs: rdn 3f out: grad wknd u.p* **10/1**

0000 **9** *1/2* **Logistical**[9] 5411 4-8-10 47 ow1 .................... CCavanagh(7) 7 32
(ADWPinder) *s.s: a wl in rr and struggling* **16/1**

0004 **10** *1/2* **Bold Wolf**[26] 5000 3-8-11 48 .................... DCorby(3) 11 31
(JLSpearing) *chsd ldrs: hrd rdn 3f out: sn wknd* **7/1**[3]

000- **11** ¾ **Spinetail Rufous (IRE)**[598] 410 6-9-3 48........................(bt) SCarson 8 29
(DFlood) *led: gng easily 3f out: hdd 2f out: folded tamely* **7/1**[3]
5000 **12** 5 **Soul Provider (IRE)**[22] 5092 3-8-6 45........................(p) RMiles(3) 12 13
(MJAttwater) *nvr beyond midfield: u.p and wl in rr 3f out* **25/1**
00-0 **13** 9 **Spring Whisper (IRE)**[252] 490 3-8-10 49........................(b[1]) DFox(5) 9 —
(CADwyer) *a towards rr: bhd and struggling 1/2-way* **28/1**
0005 **14** 9 **Hagley Park**[39] 4622 5-8-13 47........................ DNolan(3) 6 —
(MissKMGeorge) *prom: hrd rdn over 3f out: sn wknd: eased fnl f* **25/1**

1m 25.87s (-0.07) **Going Correction** -0.05s/f (Stan)
**WFA** 3 from 4yo+ 3lb **14 Ran SP% 122.3**
Speed ratings: **98,96,94,92,88 88,87,87,86,86 85,79,69,59**CSF £66.14 TOTE £11.20: £3.10, £3.10, £1.80; EX 82.40.
**Owner** Eddy Grimstead Ltd **Bred** Kildaragh Stud **Trained** Newmarket, Suffolk

**FOCUS**
A typical contest for the grade that saw the field come home well strung out. The form is fair for the level and the runner-up sets the standard.

**NOTEBOOK**
**Sylva Royal(IRE)**, dropping in class, responded gamely for pressure three out and stayed on nicely to collar her rivals late on and win this going away. She is clearly only moderate, but remains lightly-raced and has the scope to progress back up in a higher grade.
**Ballare(IRE)**, with the visor replacing the cheekpieces this time, could offer no more when headed by the winner in the final furlong, but was nicely clear in second and could go one better at this level when upped to a mile.
**Calculaite**, a facile winner at this level at Carlisle last time, could not find a change of pace when it mattered and was well held this time. He had the worst of the draw however, and still turned in a sound effort, so is not one to discard just yet.
**Pirouettes(IRE)**, with the tongue tie left off, would have been closer with a better start and turned in an improved effort over this shorter trip.

## 5643 FILEY MAIDEN CLAIMING STKS 1m 2f (P)
**12:50** (12:51) (H5) 3-Y-0+ **£1,487** (£425; £212) **Stalls** Low

Form RPR
0056 **1** **Ryan's Bliss (IRE)**[27] 4972 4-8-12 45........................ RMiles(3) 9 56
(TDMccarthy) *prom: trckd ldr 6f out: led over 3f out and sn clr: hrd rdn over 1f out: kpt on* **4/1**[2]
0400 **2** 3 **Zalkani (IRE)**[19] 5175 4-8-13 57........................ AHindley(7) 8 56
(BGPowell) *hld up in rr: outpcd over 4f out: prog over 3f out: chsd clr wnr over 2f out: hrd rdn and kpt on: nvr able to chal* **7/2**[1]
0-32 **3** 8 **Lady Lakshmi**[142] 1728 4-8-8 40........................(t) CHaddon(7) 7 36
(MMadgwick) *dwlt: settled in rr: outpcd over 4f out: rdn over 3f out: kpt on to take 3rd nr fin* **8/1**
0644 **4** ½ **Young Love**[12] 5336 3-8-9 45........................ RHavlin 6 35
(MissECLavelle) *racd midfield: outpcd over 4f out: effrt to chse clr ldng pair over 1f out: no imp: lost 3rd nr fin* **13/2**[3]
0 **5** 2 **Dark Parade (ARG)**[11] 5378 3-8-7........................ JJones(7) 14 37
(GLMoore) *last and detached early: reminder 1/2-way: prog whn hmpd on inner over 2f out: swtchd wd and styd on fnl f* **33/1**
0060 **6** 1¼ **Ricky Martan**[51] 4259 3-8-9 45 ow2........................ DNolan(3) 4 32
(GCBravery) *chsd ldrs: outpcd over 4f out: rdn and one pce fnl 3f* **20/1**
000- **7** shd **Damask Dancer (IRE)**[364] 5089 5-9-4 45........................(p) PMcCabe 12 32
(JASupple) *trckd ldrs: outpcd over 4f out: effrt 3f out: no prog fnl 2f* **33/1**
0500 **8** 1¼ **Margery Daw (IRE)**[14] 5285 4-8-8 45........................ JBrennan(7) 3 27
(PSMcentee) *taken down early: reluctant and rdn early: chsd ldrs: no ch whn hmpd on inner 2f out* **10/1**
0050 **9** nk **Anna Gayle**[14] 5284 3-8-7 40........................ SCarson 13 24
(MrsAJPerrett) *a towards rr: rdn and struggling over 4f out* **20/1**
06 **10** 9 **Bonus Points (IRE)**[11] 5381 3-8-11........................(b[1]) DCorby(3) 1 15
(BJMeehan) *led and sn clr: wknd and hdd over 3f out* **4/1**[2]
430- **11** 5 **Trigger Mead**[392] 4365 4-8-11 50........................ DKinsella 11 —
(MrsStefLiddiard) *dwlt: a in rr: lost tch over 4f out: t.o* **16/1**
0 **12** 3½ **Jimmy Hay**[78] 3487 3-8-1........................ VictoriaHill(7) 5 —
(JCFox) *a bhd: last and tailing off over 4f out* **66/1**
6000 **13** 2½ **Akiramenai (USA)**[36] 4708 4-8-8 45........................ KristinStubbs(7) 2 —
(MrsLStubbs) *chsd ldr to 6f out: wknd rapidly 3f out: t.o* **25/1**
-000 **14** 5 **Seagold**[10] 2882 3-8-5 45........................(b) TWilliams 10 —
(AEJones) *chsd ldrs to 1/2-way: wknd rapidly: t.o* **66/1**

2m 7.02s (-0.83) **Going Correction** -0.05s/f (Stan)
**WFA** 3 from 4yo+ 6lb **14 Ran SP% 123.9**
Speed ratings: **101,98,92,91,90 89,89,88,87,80 76,73,71,67**CSF £17.55 TOTE £6.30: £2.00, £1.30, £2.60; EX 31.40.
**Owner** James Ryan **Bred** A F O'Callaghan **Trained** Godstone, Surrey

**FOCUS**
A modest claimer but a reasonable time for the grade, 2.75 seconds faster than the following banded contest.

**NOTEBOOK**
**Ryan's Bliss(IRE)**, who came into this still looking for her first success after 20 outings, relished this drop in class and won nicely. This was decent effort at the weights, she can score again at this level and acts well on this surface.
**Zalkani(IRE)**, the subject of serious support on this drop in class, was a clear second best, but never looked serious threat to the winner. He has the ability to score at this level, but is a tricky ride and not one to trust.
**Lady Lakshmi** got badly outpaced over this shorter trip and was staying on all too late. She can find a race at this level, but it will be over further.
**Young Love** shaped like a non-stayer over this extra distance.
**Dark Parade(ARG)** blew his chance at the start, but looked better the further he went and could have been placed, buit for meeting trouble two out. He is much better than this and is one to keep an eye on.
**Bonus Points(IRE)** went off at a suicidal pace in the first-time blinkers and had nothing left when challenged turning for home.

## 5644 SLIMBRIDGE BANDED STKS 1m 2f (P)
**1:15** (1:17) (H5) 3-Y-0+ **£1,281** (£366; £183) **Stalls** Low

Form RPR
3005 **1** **Stagecoach Ruby**[14] 5283 3-8-10 35........................ RBrisland 12 41
(GLMoore) *plld hrd: trckd ldrs: eased to outer over 1f out: shkn up to ld last 100yds: comf* **12/1**
6- **2** 1½ **Sammagefromtenesse (IRE)**[65] 3890 7-9-2 35........................(p) TWilliams 5 38
(AEJones) *trckd ldrs: prog to ld wl over 2f out: drvn over 1f out: hdd and one pce last 100yds* **10/1**
4564 **3** 1¾ **Smarter Charter**[52] 4250 11-8-9 35........................ KristinStubbs(7) 9 35+
(MrsLStubbs) *settled in rr: nudged along and r.o fr over 1f out: nrst fin* **6/1**[2]
**4** 1¾ **Maeveen (IRE)**[105] 2695 4-8-11 35........................(e[1]) RoryMoore(5) 8 32
(VSmith) *trckd ldrs: prog to chse ldr over 2f out to ins fnl f: fdd* **12/1**
0603 **5** ¾ **Kalanisha (IRE)**[71] 3712 4-8-13 35........................(b) DCorby(3) 11 30
(JohnBerry) *dwlt: sn chsd ldrs: rdn wl over 2f out: lost pl wl over 1f out: no ch after* **3/1**[1]
00-5 **6** shd **Street Games**[37] 4669 5-9-2 35........................ SRighton 6 30
(DGBridgwater) *t.k.h: hld up towards rr: hmpd on inner 5f out: prog to chsd ldrs over 1f out: wknd ins fnl f* **7/1**[3]
0-05 **7** ¾ **Mac's Elan**[30] 4869 4-8-13 35........................ LFletcher(3) 10 28
(ABCoogan) *racd midfield: effrt and cl up 2f out: fnd nil and btn over 1f out* **16/1**
0-00 **8** nk **Prince Ivor**[13] 1231 4-8-13 35........................(vt) BReilly(3) 13 28
(MJGingell) *trckd ldrs: cl up 2f out: wknd u.p fnl f* **66/1**
0400 **9** 2 **Lady Liesel**[14] 5285 4-8-13 35........................ J-PGuillambert(3) 4 24
(JJBridger) *a towards rr: rdn and no prog over 2f out* **16/1**
4-63 **10** 8 **Tomsk (IRE)**[37] 4669 4-8-13 35........................ DNolan(3) 1 9
(MissKMGeorge) *s.s: t.k.h: in tch in rr: u.p and btn over 2f out: wknd* **6/1**[2]
3020 **11** 7 **Tshukudu**[14] 5284 3-8-10 35........................ SCarson 14 —
(MBlanshard) *led to over 7f out: wknd over 3f out* **16/1**
6000 **12** ½ **Daimajin (IRE)**[7] 5449 5-8-9 35........................(v[1]) DerekNolan(7) 3 —
(MrsLucindaFeatherstone) *dwlt: racd freely and led over 7f out: sn clr: hdd & wknd rapidly over 2f out* **10/1**
0600 **13** 5 **Costa Del Sol (IRE)**[27] 4968 3-8-7 35........................(p) RMiles(3) 2 —
(JJBridger) *t.k.h: hld up in rr: n.m.r on inner over 5f out: wknd over 3f out* **25/1**
0030 **U** **Skelthwaite**[4] 5549 3-8-10 35........................ JMcAuley 7 —
(MissDAMchale) *trckd ldrs: disputing 5th pl whn stmbld and uns rdr 5f out* **28/1**

2m 9.77s (1.92) **Going Correction** -0.05s/f (Stan)
**WFA** 3 from 4yo+ 6lb **14 Ran SP% 126.1**
Speed ratings: **90,88,87,86,85 85,84,84,82,76 70,70,66,—**CSF £131.08 TOTE £7.30: £2.90, £3.60, £3.20; EX 77.20.
**Owner** Richard Dean **Bred** Mrs Jacqueline Conroy **Trained** Woodingdean, E Sussex

**FOCUS**
A rock-bottom event and a moderate time, even for a race like this, being 2.75 seconds slower than the preceding claimer. The form can be ignored away from similar events.

**NOTEBOOK**
**Stagecoach Ruby**, who hinted at a return to form in this grade last time, won cosily and proved she gets this trip. She can strike again now she has more options over this distance, although she beat very little.
**Sammagefromtenesse(IRE)** ran up to his recent level of form, but held no chance with the winner. This will sharpen him up for a forthcoming hurdling campaign.
**Smarter Charter** only got into his full stride when the race was beyond him and continues to frustrate, but retains his ability despite his veteran status.
**Maeveen(IRE)** stepped up on his recent efforts on this debut for new connections in the eyeshield.
**Kalanisha(IRE)**, dropping back in trip and well-backed in the betting ring, never looked like landing the gamble on this first run for new connections.

## 5645 MINSMERE BANDED STKS 2m (P)
**1:45** (1:46) (H5) 3-Y-0+ **£1,494** (£427; £213) **Stalls** Low

Form RPR
0045 **1** **Habitual (IRE)**[44] 4499 3-8-10 49........................ J-PGuillambert(3) 7 56+
(SirMarkPrescott) *wl plcd: trckd ldng pair over 4f out: shkn up to ld over 1f out: sn clr* **9/4**[1]
0401 **2** 3½ **Indian Chase**[30] 4870 7-9-7 45........................ LVickers 8 48
(DrJRJNaylor) *racd midfield: prog to chse ldrs over 3f out: rdn over 2f out: styd on to take 2nd ins fnl f* **7/1**[3]
040- **3** 2 **Cody**[6] 5500 5-9-7 45........................(t) TWilliams 4 46
(GAHam) *prom: jnd ldr over 5f out: drvn 3f out: stl upsides over 1f out: one pce* **25/1**
3646 **4** shd **Vanilla Moon**[44] 4499 4-9-7 45........................(v) PMcCabe 2 45
(JRJenkins) *led for 3f: led again 6f out: sn jnd: hdd and outpcd over 1f out* **14/1**
3300 **5** 1 **Galandora**[12] 5354 4-9-5 50........................ NataliaGemelova(7) 6 49
(DrJRJNaylor) *dwlt: hld up in rr: prog into midfield over 3f out: drvn and one pce after* **7/1**[3]
00-0 **6** 2 **Icey Run**[43] 4513 4-9-7 45........................ SRighton 11 42
(DGBridgwater) *racd towards rr: sme prog on inner over 2f out: n.d fr over 1f out* **33/1**
0003 **7** nk **Open Book**[14] 5286 3-8-13 49 ow3........................ LFletcher(3) 1 49
(HMorrison) *trckd ldrs: lost pl over 5f out: prog again over 4f out: rdn and no imp over 2f out* **11/2**[2]
4060 **8** 2½ **Maximinus**[54] 4196 4-9-5 50........................ RLucey-Butler(7) 10 44
(MMadgwick) *racd in rr: outpcd over 4f out: no imp on ldrs after* **12/1**
2500 **9** 3 **Bretton**[14] 5284 3-8-4 45........................ RoryMoore(5) 5 35
(BAPearce) *hld up in last: prog on outer to chse ldrs over 3f out: wknd over 2f out* **25/1**
0004 **10** 3½ **Joely Green**[44] 4467 7-9-0 45........................(p) StevenHarrison(7) 3 31
(NPLittmoden) *a in rr: rdn and struggling over 4f out* **7/1**[3]
3005 **11** 13 **Cantrip**[14] 5286 4-9-11 49........................ SCarson 14 19
(MissBSanders) *prom tl wknd 4f out: t.o* **12/1**
0-00 **12** nk **Curragh Gold (IRE)**[33] 4808 4-9-2 47........................ AmyBaker(7) 13 17
(MrsPNDutfield) *chsd ldrs: pushed along 5f out: sn wknd: t.o* **50/1**
00/ **13** 6 **Cold Encounter (IRE)**[40] 4306 9-9-9 50........................ DCorby(3) 9 13
(RMStronge) *hld up in rr: prog into midfield 5f out: sn wknd: t.o* **50/1**
0/00 **14** dist **Ash Hab (USA)**[17] 5221 6-9-0 45........................(b) DerekNolan(7) 12 —
(ABHaynes) *led after 3f: sn clr: wknd and hdd 6f out: sn wl t.o* **50/1**

3m 29.0s (0.42) **Going Correction** -0.05s/f (Stan)
**WFA** 3 from 4yo+ 12lb **14 Ran SP% 122.2**
Speed ratings: **96,94,93,93,92 91,91,90,88,87 80,80,77,—**CSF £16.93 TOTE £3.50: £1.60, £2.10, £7.30; EX 26.90 Place 6 £95.46, Place 5 £46.24..
**Owner** P J McSwiney - Osborne House **Bred** Rathasker Stud **Trained** Newmarket, Suffolk

**FOCUS**
A poor staying contest that saw the field finish strung out behind the facile winner, who is capable of better.

**NOTEBOOK**
**Habitual(IRE)** was always travelling like the winner and only had to be pushed out to score a most comfortable first success. He enjoyed this return to two miles and he can be rated value for more than the official winning margin, so should be placed to advantage once more by his in-form yard.
**Indian Chase**, who improved to win at Chepstow last time, ran another sound race and lost little in defeat this time. He is in good form and should go close if returning in this grade next time.
**Cody** made a respectable return to the Flat, but did not really see out this trip too well.
**Vanilla Moon** again looked very one-paced when push came to shove and is seriously struggling to find her optimum trip. She remains winless after 22 outings.
**Open Book** failed to build on her latest effort in this grade and disappointed. However, she may be worth chancing again at this level when racing again over slightly shorter.
T/Plt: £44.00 to a £1 stake. Pool: £21,528.65. 356.95 winning tickets. T/Qpdt: £9.00 to a £1 stake. Pool: £1,424.60. 116.20 winning tickets. JN

5609 **NEWBURY** (L-H)

Saturday, September 18

**OFFICIAL GOING: Good changing to good to soft after race 3 (2.50)**

## 5646 DUBAI DUTY FREE GOLF WORLD CUP MAIDEN STKS 7f (S)

1:50 (1:51) (D2) 2-Y-O £6,240 (£1,920; £960; £480) Stalls Centre

Form RPR

6 **1** **Esquire**[15] 5268 2-9-0 .......... LDettori 3 91+
(SaeedBinSuroor) *h.d.w: mde all: pushed along and qcknd clr appr fnl f: readily* **5/1**

4 **2** *1 3/4* **Museeb (USA)**[14] 5290 2-9-0 .......... RHills 15 87
(JLDunlop) *prom: chsd wnr over 2f out: kpt on wl but no imp fnl f* **3/1**[1]

**3** *1 1/2* **Alfie Noakes** 2-9-0 .......... PRobinson 2 83
(MrsAJPerrett) *scope: bkwd: s.i.s: bhd: hdwy fr 3f out: styd on wl fr over 1f out to take 3rd cl home but nvr gng pce of ldrs* **25/1**

4 **4** *shd* **Top The Charts**[22] 5087 2-9-0 .......... RLMoore 8 83
(RHannon) *chsd wnr 3f: rdn over 2f out: kpt on fnl f but nvr gng pce of ldrs* **9/2**[3]

**5** *1 1/4* **Sparkwell** 2-9-0 .......... RHughes 1 80
(BWHills) *lw: str: bkwd: s.i.s: sn rcvrd: hdwy 4f out: drvn to go 3rd over 1f out but nt pce to rch ldrs: wknd qckly fnl 100yds* **8/1**

**6** *5* **Barbary Coast (FR)** 2-9-0 .......... MartinDwyer 13 67
(WRMuir) *w'like: s.i.s: bhd: pushed along 1/2-way: styd on fnl 2f but n.d* **80/1**

**7** *1 1/4* **In The Lead (USA)** 2-8-9 .......... TQuinn 10 59
(JLDunlop) *w'like: in tch tl pushed along and outpcd over 3f out: styd on again fr over 1f out* **50/1**

3 **8** *1 1/2* **Rain Stops Play (IRE)**[14] 5298 2-9-0 .......... CCatlin 7 60
(MRChannon) *prom: chsd wnr 4f out tl over 2f out: sn wknd* **16/1**

0 **9** *3* **Piran (IRE)**[9] 5406 2-9-0 .......... JFortune 12 53
(BJMeehan) *chsd ldrs tl wknd over 2f out* **66/1**

**10** *1/2* **Bulwark (IRE)** 2-9-0 .......... EAhern 4 51
(MrsAJPerrett) *neat: nvr bttr than mid-div* **25/1**

**11** *3/4* **King Gabriel (IRE)** 2-9-0 .......... RSmith 11 50
(DJSFfrenchDavis) *w'like: nvr bttr than mid-div* **100/1**

2 **12** *3/4* **Count Kristo**[35] 4743 2-9-0 .......... DaneO'Neill 9 48
(CGCox) *chsd ldrs: rdn and btn 3f out* **4/1**[2]

00 **13** *2 1/2* **Over Tipsy**[11] 5376 2-9-0 .......... PDobbs 16 41
(RHannon) *in tch 4f* **100/1**

**14** *1 3/4* **Planet (IRE)** 2-8-11 .......... NMackay(3) 6 37
(SirMichaelStoute) *w'like: scope: bit bkwd: s.i.s: sme hdwy into mid-div 4f out: n.d and sn bhd* **22/1**

**15** *3 1/2* **Atacama Star** 2-8-11 .......... LPKeniry(3) 14 28
(BGPowell) *lengthy: bkwd: b.off hind: slowly away: rdn and sme hdwy into mid-div 1/2-way: sn wknd* **50/1**

**16** *10* **Chiracahua (IRE)** 2-9-0 .......... RWinston 5 —
(BJMeehan) *str: bkwd: chsd ldrs tl wknd fr 3f out* **66/1**

1m 26.52s (-0.70) **Going Correction** -0.125s/f (Firm) **16** Ran SP% **119.0**

Speed ratings: **99,97,95,95,93 88,86,84,81,80 80,79,76,74,70 58**CSF £18.46 TOTE £5.10: £1.90, £2.30, £6.20; EX 25.00.

**Owner** Godolphin **Bred** Darley **Trained** Newmarket, Suffolk

**FOCUS**

An impressive winner, but only a few notable performances further down the field. They raced centre to far side and those that were more towards the far rail appeared to have an advantage.

**NOTEBOOK**

**Esquire**, all the better for his Kempton debut, made every yard over this shorter trip and was not hard pressed to put daylight between himself and his rivals. He does not look top class, but still has improvement in him and may be up to winning in lesser Pattern company next season.

**Museeb(USA)** improved from his debut over this extra furlong and deserves credit for doing best of those drawn high. He did tend to hang a bit late on, suggesting easier ground would suit, and should not be hard to place.

**Alfie Noakes ◆**, a 36,000gns full brother to Crimson Dancer, was drawn on the right side as things turned out but still deserves plenty of credit for finishing where he did considering he missed the break. He looks sure to improve.

**Top The Charts** did not appear to improve much from his debut and had his chance, but should be able to find an ordinary maiden.

**Sparkwell**, a half-brother to Salcombe, ran a creditable debut until appearing to blow up inside the last furlong. He should come on for this.

**Barbary Coast(FR)**, a 105,000euros yearling from the same family as Verveine, Vallee Enchantee and Vespone, ended up well beaten by the front quintet, but showed enough to suggest he will probably do better in the longer term.

**Count Kristo** ran to nothing like the form of his debut over course and distance and is much better than this. *Official explanation: trainer said colt was weak*

## 5647 DUBAI INTERNATIONAL AIRPORT WORLD TROPHY (GROUP 3) 5f 34y

2:20 (2:21) (A1) 3-Y-O+ £29,000 (£11,000; £5,500; £2,500) Stalls Centre

Form RPR

0322 **1** **The Tatling (IRE)**[13] 5333 7-9-4 116.......... RLMoore 6 119
(JMBradley) *lw: in tch: rdn and hdwy to chse ldr 1f out: styd on strly u.p to ld last strides* **5/1**[2]

1 **2** *hd* **Var (USA)**[7] 5471 5-8-13 ..........(b) RHills 1 113
(CEBrittain) *lw: racd wd tl jnd ldrs 3f out: led over 1f out: styd on wl u.p fnl f: ct last strides* **10/1**

0160 **3** *1 1/4* **Airwave**[14] 5289 4-8-10 108.......... TQuinn 7 106
(HCandy) *bhd: n.m.r and swtchd lft to outside 2f out: styd on wl u.p ins last but nt pce of ldrs* **5/1**[2]

0221 **4** *nk* **Texas Gold**[6] 5491 6-8-13 89.......... MartinDwyer 10 108
(WRMuir) *bhd: rdn 2f out: hdwy over 1f out: r.o ins last and fin wl but nt pce to rch ldrs* **16/1**

1211 **5** *1 1/4* **Pivotal Point**[13] 5333 4-9-2 113.......... LDettori 5 106
(PJMakin) *lw: chsd ldrs: rdn 1/2-way: outpcd ins fnl f* **5/2**[1]

1-50 **6** *1/2* **Majestic Missile (IRE)**[51] 4269 3-8-12 112.......... JFortune 4 101
(WJHaggas) *bhd: n.m.r and swtchd lft over 1f out: kpt on ins fnl f but nvr gng pce to rch ldrs* **10/1**

2022 **7** *3/4* **Talbot Avenue**[9] 5418 6-8-13 101.......... PDobbs 3 99
(MMullineaux) *b. in tch: rdn 1/2-way: wknd fnl f* **33/1**

0061 **8** *shd* **Celtic Mill**[9] 5418 6-8-13 107..........(p) LEnstone 8 98
(DWBarker) *sn led: hdd over 1f out: wknd ins last* **16/1**

6303 **9** *1/2* **High Reach**[49] 4324 4-8-13 94.......... RMullen 11 97
(TGMills) *chsd ldrs: rdn and one pce whn nt clr run and snatched up last half f* **20/1**

1642 **10** *shd* **Boogie Street**[51] 4269 3-8-12 110..........(t) RHughes 9 96
(RHannon) *sn pressing ldr: stl upsides appr fnl f: wknd ins last* **8/1**[3]

1003 **11** *nk* **Caribbean Coral**[9] 5418 5-8-13 100.......... RWinston 2 95
(JJQuinn) *a outpcd* **14/1**

60.68 secs (-1.97) **Going Correction** -0.125s/f (Firm)

**WFA** 3 from 4yo+ 1lb **11** Ran SP% **117.3**

Speed ratings: **110,109,107,107,105 104,103,103,102,102 101**CSF £54.20 TOTE £5.80: £2.00, £3.40, £1.90; EX 87.40 Trifecta £948.40 Part won. Pool £1,335.90 - 0.90 winning units..

**Owner** Dab Hand Racing **Bred** Patrick J Power **Trained** Sedbury, Gloucs

**FOCUS**

Apart from the runner-up, the field came straight over to the stands' rail from the stalls. The winning time was ordinary for a Group Three, suggesting the leaders may have gone off too quick.

**NOTEBOOK**

**The Tatling(IRE)** got the strong early pace he needs and was brought with a sustained effort to get up right on the line. His chance looks as good as any should he line up for the Abbaye.

**Var(USA)**, down a furlong from Goodwood and up in class, was kept wide of his field from his low draw during the early stages and was one of three forcing the early pace. He eventually managed to get the lead on his own, but that gave the winner something to aim at and he was nailed almost on the line. This was a fine effort and there should be more to come from him, especially when he is able to dominate.

**Airwave**, switched off out the back, had to be manoeuvred towards the outside in order to get a run and although she was gradually reeling the front pair in, she never looked like getting there. She still continues to fall just short at this level these days.

**Texas Gold** is in good form at present and ran a blinder considering he was around 20lb badly in with the best of these on adjusted official ratings. This effort will not have helped his handicap mark, but a repeat could see him pick up a Listed contest.

**Pivotal Point** was 4lb worse in with The Tatling after beating him in France, but even allowing for that his effort lacked sparkle.

**Majestic Missile(IRE)** did not have the clearest of runs, but even so this effort backs up the theory that he may not have trained on.

**Celtic Mill** was given no peace out in front and that eventually told.

**Boogie Street** helped force the early pace before fading. He looks a better horse on faster ground and when getting the lead on his own.

## 5648 WATERSHIP DOWN STUD SALES (FILLIES) 6f 110y

2:50 (2:53) (B1) 2-Y-O £146,150 (£58,460; £29,230; £14,615) Stalls Centre

Form RPR

1 **1** **Salamanca**[36] 4714 2-8-9 .......... LDettori 18 92
(SKirk) *lw: racd stands side: rdn and hdwy over 1f out: styd on wl u.p to ld last stride* **5/1**[1]

5351 **2** *shd* **Arabian Dancer**[12] 5334 2-7-12 .......... CCatlin 21 81
(MRChannon) *racd stands side: in tch: rdn to ld 1f out: styd on wl u.p: ct last stride* **13/2**[2]

5664 **3** *shd* **Umniya (IRE)**[13] 5325 2-8-8 ..........(v) TQuinn 16 90+
(MRChannon) *racd stands side: bhd: hdwy over 1f out: swtchd lft ins last and r.o strly to chal last strides: jst failed* **8/1**[3]

3332 **4** *1 1/4* **Bibury Flyer**[4] 5548 2-8-8 .......... RHavlin 19 87
(MRChannon) *racd stands side: bhd: hdwy over 1f out: r.o ins last: nt rch ldrs* **14/1**

62 **5** *1/2* **Love Thirty**[20] 5154 2-9-0 .......... RHills 24 92?
(MRChannon) *racd stands side: chsd ldrs: str chal fr ins fnl 2f: outpcd ins last* **33/1**

0045 **6** *3/4* **Alta Petens**[7] 5469 2-7-12 .......... JMackay 8 74
(MLWBell) *racd far side: chsd ldrs: led that gp 1f out but nvr gng pce of stands side* **12/1**

0 **7** *1 1/4* **Diamond Katie (IRE)**[15] 5270 2-8-4 .......... EAhern 22 76
(RGuest) *racd stands side: s.i.s: bhd: hdwy over 1f out: r.o wl fnl f: nt rch ldrs* **33/1**

14 **8** *shd* **Baltic Dip (IRE)**[84] 3316 2-8-11 .......... RHughes 4 83
(RHannon) *lw: racd far side: slowly away and lost 6l: gd hdwy fr 2f out: kpt on fnl f but nt pce to rch ldrs* **8/1**[3]

3215 **9** *shd* **Justaquestion**[20] 5149 2-8-5 .......... LEnstone 7 77
(IAWood) *lw: racd far side: bhd: hdwy fr 2f out: kpt on fnl f but nt pce to rch ldrs* **13/2**[2]

0223 **10** *nk* **Shosolosa (IRE)**[39] 4621 2-8-2 .......... DKinsella 26 73
(BJMeehan) *racd stands side: pressed ldrs and chal fr 2f out tl 1f out: wknd ins last* **66/1**

2 **11** *shd* **Holly Springs**[15] 5270 2-9-0 .......... JFortune 2 84
(JHMGosden) *lw: racd far side and led that gp tl hdd 1f out: wknd ins last* **12/1**

0002 **12** *nk* **Musical Day**[21] 5109 2-8-6 .......... RWinston 11 76
(BJMeehan) *racd far side: pressed ldrs tl wknd fnl f* **40/1**

6211 **13** *nk* **Lady Le Quesne (IRE)**[58] 4041 2-8-7 .......... MartinDwyer 27 76
(AMBalding) *led stands side tl hdd over 1f out: sn wknd* **16/1**

22 **14** *1/2* **Honey Ryder**[33] 4815 2-8-8 .......... TPQueally 25 75
(DRLoder) *racd stands side: bhd: rdn and effrt 2f out: nvr gng pce to rch ldrs* **20/1**

023 **15** *hd* **County Clare**[35] 4753 2-8-8 .......... RMullen 14 75
(AMBalding) *racd stands side: sn pressing ldr: wknd fnl f* **25/1**

55 **16** *1* **Oasis Way (GR)**[9] 5407 2-8-2 .......... LisaJones 20 66
(PRChamings) *racd stands side: bhd: sme hdwy fr over 1f out: nt rch ldrs* **100/1**

2S31 **17** *hd* **Miss Cassia**[22] 5078 2-8-8 .......... PDobbs 13 72
(RHannon) *racd far side: bhd: styd on fr over 1f out: nt a danger* **66/1**

460 **18** *hd* **Authenticate**[16] 5247 2-8-6 .......... ADaly 5 69
(BAMcmahon) *racd far side: in tch over 4f* **100/1**

46 **19** *2 1/2* **Casterossa**[19] 5202 2-8-10 .......... WRyan 6 66
(DHaydnJones) *racd far side: sn outpcd* **100/1**

0350 **20** *1 1/2* **Madhavi**[40] 4612 2-8-6 ..........(b[1]) DaneO'Neill 9 58
(RHannon) *racd far side: pressed ldrs to 2f out: wknd fnl f* **40/1**

0515 **21** *3/4* **Top Form (IRE)**[12] 5351 2-8-11 .......... PRobinson 12 61
(EALDunlop) *racd far side: chsd ldrs 4f* **50/1**

3200 **22** *1 1/2* **Gennie Bond**[10] 5391 2-8-8 .......... RLMoore 23 54
(RHannon) *racd stands side: outpcd most of way* **40/1**

4226 **23** *3/4* **Persian Carpet**[14] 5281 2-7-12 .......... NMackay 15 42
(IAWood) *racd far side: sn outpcd* **100/1**

2420 **24** *nk* **Agent Kensington**[12] 5334 2-7-13 ow1.......... RSmith 1 42
(RHannon) *racd far side: spd over 4f* **66/1**

3060 **25** *shd* **High Chart**[11] 5377 2-8-2 .......... DFox 17 45
(GGMargarson) *racd stands side: sn bhd* **100/1**

0021 **26** *21* **Corniche Dancer**[11] 5362 2-8-6 .......... LPKeniry 10 —
(MRChannon) *racd stands side: slowly away: a bhd* **100/1**

1m 20.09s **26** Ran SP% **127.7**

Speed ratings: CSF £31.16 TOTE £5.60: £2.40, £3.20, £2.60; EX 40.90 Trifecta £182.00 Pool £1,000.20 - 3.90 winning units..

**Owner** Wood Street Syndicate **Bred** D P Martin **Trained** Upper Lambourn, Berks

■ Stewards Enquiry : C Catlin two-day ban: used whip without giving filly time to respond and with excessive force (Sep 29, Oct 4)

T Quinn caution: used whip without giving filly time to respond

**FOCUS**
Difficult form to assess with confidence, as is often the case in these valuable sales races, especially with the field splitting into two and the stands' side group appearing to hold an advantage. This must have been as close to a triple dead-heat as you can possibly get. With this being the first ever race over this trip on the track, no speed figures can be calculated.

**NOTEBOOK**
**Salamanca**, winner of her only previous start and with Dettori a late replacement, was brought with her effort on the stands' side over a furlong from home and battled on really well. It took the judge a very long time to announce her as the winner, which shows that she had nothing in hand, but her preparation had been interrupted by an infected joint. She was also the most lightly raced in the field so is entitled to still have some improvement in her.
**Arabian Dancer** would probably have preferred faster ground, but still put up a fine effort and it was only by the skin of her teeth that she was denied. With her trainer having saddled the third, fourth and fifth also, he probably did not know whether to laugh or cry.
**Umniya(IRE)**, fourth in the Group One Moyglare Stud Stakes last time, was just about last and under the cosh two furlongs from home, but then suddenly kicked into gear and finished to such purpose between the front pair after having to be switched that she would have won in another half-stride. Considering her ability, it is surprising she has only won once from 11 starts.
**Bibury Flyer** stayed on to finish a highly creditable fourth and earn some decent prize money for connections. She is very consistent, but finds winning difficult, having scored only once yet finished in the first three on 11 other occasions in 17 starts.
**Love Thirty** ◆ had every chance and ran a cracker considering this was by some margin the toughest opposition she had faced and she was conceding weight to the majority of the field. She should not take long in winning.
**Alta Petens** ◆, stepping back from a mile, was always close up over on the far side and ended up the clear winner of that group. A repeat of this should see her winning again.
**Diamond Katie(IRE)** ◆, as on her debut, very much caught the eye with the way she was staying on. When she is stepped up to seven furlongs or more she should start to show her true ability.
**Baltic Dip(IRE)** ◆, off since June, effectively lost her chance at the start and was soon a long way behind. She did well to finish where she did and must have gone close with a level break. *Official explanation: jockey said filly reared in the stalls as the gates opened*
**Justaquestion** ran with credit and was third home over on the far side, although only ninth overall.
**Gennie Bond** *Official explanation: trainer's representative said filly had been struck into*

## 5649 DUBAI DUTY FREE MILL REEF STKS (GROUP 2) 6f 8y
3:25 (3:26) (A1) 2-Y-0 £40,600 (£15,400; £7,700; £3,500) Stalls Centre

Form RPR
1551 **1** **Galeota (IRE)**[7] [5460] 2-8-12 100 ... RLMoore 6 110
(RHannon) *lw: mde all: rdn and qcknd fr 2f out: kpt on wl fnl f* **7/1**
2325 **2** *1* **Mystical Land (IRE)**[27] [4981] 2-8-12 100 ... (v[1]) LDettori 5 107
(JHMGosden) *in tch: rdn and hdwy 2f out: chsd wnr over 1f out: kpt on ins last but no imp nr fin* **10/3**[2]
21 **3** *shd* **Rebuttal (USA)**[31] [4844] 2-8-12 ... JFortune 3 107
(BJMeehan) *lw: hld up in rr: nt clr run and swtchd lft fr over 1f out: styd on strly u.p ins last to press for 2nd: nt rch wnr* **8/1**
1322 **4** *2 ½* **Salsa Brava (IRE)**[30] [4885] 2-8-9 100 ... TPQueally 1 96
(NPLittmoden) *lw: bhd: rdn and hdwy over 2f out: chsd ldrs 1f out: outpcd ins last* **3/1**[1]
1200 **5** *1 ¾* **Royal Alchemist**[20] [5149] 2-8-9 94 ... ADaly 7 91
(MDIUsher) *chsd ldrs: rdn ins fnl 3f: outpcd fr over 1f out* **50/1**
513 **6** *¾* **One Putra (IRE)**[28] [4933] 2-8-12 91 ... PRobinson 9 92
(MAJarvis) *trckd ldr to 2f out: sn rdn: wknd fnl f* **6/1**
12 **7** *¾* **Andronikos**[31] [4857] 2-8-12 ... TQuinn 2 89
(PFICole) *lw: in tch: drvn to chse wnr 2f out tl over 1f out: wknd qckly ins last* **4/1**[3]
64 **8** *1 ¼* **Ocean Gift**[35] [4743] 2-8-12 ... MartinDwyer 4 86
(DRCElsworth) *sn outpcd in rr* **50/1**
0010 **9** *1* **Doctor's Cave**[27] [4981] 2-8-12 89 ... RHills 8 83
(CEBrittain) *disp 2nd 4f: wknd qckly over 1f out* **66/1**

1m 13.84s (-0.53) **Going Correction** +0.10s/f (Good) **9** Ran SP% **111.4**
Speed ratings: **107,105,105,102,99 98,97,96,94**CSF £28.96 TOTE £8.00: £2.20, £1.50, £2.80; EX 38.20 Trifecta £226.10 Pool £764.38 - 2.40 winning units..
**Owner** J A Lazzari **Bred** W Maxwell Ervine **Trained** East Everleigh, Wilts

**FOCUS**
Not a strong renewal of this race, but the winning time was as you would expect for a race of its type in the deteriorating conditions. The whole field raced stands' side.

**NOTEBOOK**
**Galeota(IRE)** seems to be improving and utilised the same tactics that had proved successful at Doncaster the previous week, despite the different ground and rise in class. He may not be an easy horse to place next season with his Group Two penalty and may be forced to take on the best, but at least this victory makes him a valuable asset.
**Mystical Land(IRE)**, visored for the first time, came through to hold very chance a furlong out but could not get to the winner and only just held on to second. This was his fourth placing in Group company and this looks as good as he is.
**Rebuttal(USA)**, proven in soft ground, was held up off the pace but had to be switched to the outside in order to get a run. Once in the clear he finished to some purpose and only just failed to snatch second. He will be very interesting when stepped up a furlong.
**Salsa Brava(IRE)** had every chance against the boys, but was firmly put in her place by the front three in the last furlong. She had run well in soft ground at York, but may prove better on a faster surface over an extra furlong.
**Royal Alchemist** ran with some credit over this shorter trip, but again looked short of Group class.
**One Putra(IRE)**, proven on the ground, found this step up in class too much.
**Andronikos**, who had the winner behind him when runner-up in similar ground in the Gimcrack, was well below that from here. *Official explanation: trainer had no explanation for the poor form shown*

## 5650 JOHN SMITH'S STKS (HERITAGE H'CAP) 1m 2f 6y
4:00 (4:00) (B1) (0-105,107) 3-Y-0+ £58,000 (£22,000; £11,000; £5,000) Stalls High

Form RPR
-036 **1** **Spuradich (IRE)**[56] [4118] 4-8-9 90 ... NMackay[(3)] 7 102+
(LMCumani) *lw: trckd ldrs: led over 1f out: hung lft u.p ins last: drvn out* **14/1**
2500 **2** *¾* **Jabaar (USA)**[18] [5211] 6-8-5 83 ... TPQueally 12 94
(MWEasterby) *chsd ldrs: n.m.r and swtchd rt over 1f out: chsd wnr ins last but no imp nr fin* **18/1**
1046 **3** *¾* **Blue Spinnaker (IRE)**[7] [5462] 5-9-10 102 ... RWinston 14 114+
(MWEasterby) *mid-div: hdwy fr 4f out: styng on to chse ldrs whn hmpd and swtchd rt ins last: kpt on but nt rcvr* **14/1**
-006 **4** *1* **Pagan Sky (IRE)**[14] [5297] 5-8-6 84 ... LisaJones 1 92
(JARToller) *s.i.s: bhd: hdwy over 3f out: sn rdn: styd on fr over 1f out but nt rch ldrs* **20/1**
6051 **5** *hd* **Gatwick (IRE)**[21] [5106] 3-9-9 107 5ex ... TQuinn 3 114+
(MRChannon) *lw: mid-div: n.m.r 2f out and again over 1f out: swtchd rt and styd on strly: fin wl but nt rch ldrs* **10/3**[1]
2350 **6** *nk* **Dumaran (IRE)**[30] [4887] 6-8-12 90 ... CCatlin 11 97
(WJMusson) *chsd ldrs: rdn over 2f out: styd on same pce fnl f* **14/1**
0060 **7** *1 ½* **Swagger Stick (USA)**[10] [5397] 3-8-4 88 ... (b[1]) DKinsella 20 92
(JLDunlop) *chsd ldrs: rdn and one pce whn bmpd over 1f out: wknd ins last* **25/1**
0015 **8** *½* **Telemachus**[18] [5211] 4-8-7 85 ... (b) JMackay 8 88
(JGGiven) *led 1f: styd chsng ldr tl led again wl over 3f out: hdd over 1f out: wknd ins last* **20/1**
5115 **9** *¾* **Spanish Don**[53] [4214] 6-9-0 95 ... LPKeniry[(3)] 15 97
(DRCElsworth) *bhd: hdwy over 2f out: kpt on fnl f but nvr gng pce to rch ldrs* **12/1**
4015 **10** *hd* **Desert Quest (IRE)**[28] [4932] 4-9-2 94 ... (b) MartinDwyer 13 96
(AMBalding) *s.i.s: bhd: pushed along over 3f out: kpt on fnl 2f but n.d* **25/1**
0140 **11** *shd* **Langford**[7] [5470] 4-8-8 86 ... RHills 5 87
(MHTompkins) *bhd: hdwy 3f out: chsng ldrs and one pce whn pushed rt over 1f out: sn wknd* **66/1**
1-11 **12** *1 ½* **Sky Quest (IRE)**[35] [4737] 6-8-13 91 ... (tp) RLMoore 9 90
(PWHarris) *bhd: rdn and sme hdwy 3f out: nvr gng pce to rch ldrs and wknd fr 2f out* **11/1**[3]
4000 **13** *1 ¼* **Turbo (IRE)**[7] [5465] 5-8-13 91 ... (p) SCarson 2 88
(GBBalding) *bhd tl mod prog fnl 2f* **20/1**
3200 **14** *nk* **Keelung (USA)**[17] [5226] 3-8-4 88 ... PRobinson 6 84
(MAJarvis) *lw: led after 1f tl hdd wl over 3f out: wknd ins fnl 2f* **14/1**
0300 **15** *1 ¾* **Thyolo (IRE)**[49] [4322] 3-8-13 97 ... RSmith 19 90
(CGCox) *nvr bttr than mid-div* **25/1**
1242 **16** *3* **Hawridge Prince**[21] [5133] 4-9-3 95 ... LDettori 17 82
(LGCottrell) *lw: chsd ldrs tl rdn and wknd qckly 2f out: eased whn btn fnl f* **7/2**[2]
0042 **17** *11* **Counsel's Opinion (IRE)**[42] [4530] 7-9-8 100 ... RMullen 16 68
(CFWall) *s.i.s: bhd most of way* **14/1**
0000 **18** *dist* **Camp Commander (IRE)**[21] [5112] 5-9-0 92 ... (t) RHughes 18 —
(CEBrittain) *in tch 6f: sn wknd: t.o* **33/1**

2m 8.16s (-0.55) **Going Correction** +0.275s/f (Good)
**WFA** 3 from 4yo+ 6lb **18** Ran SP% **130.2**
Speed ratings: **113,112,111,111,110 110,109,109,108,108 108,106,105,105,104 101,93,**—CSF £230.54 CT £3610.16 TOTE £23.50: £5.60, £6.10, £3.80, £3.40; EX 613.90 Trifecta £894.20 Part won. Pool £1,259.52 - 0.20 winning units..
**Owner** Scuderia Rencati Srl **Bred** Azienda Agricola Francesca **Trained** Newmarket, Suffolk
■ Stewards Enquiry : T P Queally three-day ban: careless riding (Sep 29,30, Oct 1)
N Mackay two-day ban: careless riding (Sep 29, Oct 4)

**FOCUS**
A very competitive handicap run at a decent pace, and a useful time for the grade given the conditions. There were traffic problems for a few, but the form is solid and should work out.

**NOTEBOOK**
**Spuradich(IRE)**, a major gamble in this race last year when returning lame, was off a 3lb lower mark this time and made no mistake despite being a market drifter on this occasion. He did hang to his left after hitting the front over a furlong out, hampering the third, but how much it affected the result is debatable.
**Jabaar(USA)** ◆, with the headgear left off this time, was never far away. He had to switch the avoid the weakening Telemachus inside the last furlong and may have gone very close otherwise, but is certainly capable of winning a decent race off this mark.
**Blue Spinnaker(IRE)**, ran a fine race off a stiff mark, especially as he would have preferred the rain to have stayed away. Off the bridle some way out, he never stopped responding and was still staying on when the winner crossed in front of him inside the last furlong. He would not have won without the interference, but would probably have beaten his stable companion.
**Pagan Sky(IRE)** stayed on well in the closing stages and posted a good effort on ground that was probably easier than ideal.
**Gatwick(IRE)** ◆ faced a stiff task against his elders off this mark, but finished in such good style that he must have gone very close but for running into all sorts of trouble in the last couple of furlongs. He remains in good heart and should be on anyone's Cambridgeshire shortlist.
**Dumaran(IRE)** found the ground had come right for him and ran a decent race as a result. Despite a losing run stretching back nearly two years, the Handicapper has been very slow to drop him.
**Telemachus** was given a positive ride under conditions that suit, but was never able to quite dominate on his own and was a spent force inside the last furlong.
**Sky Quest(IRE)** would not have been helped by the softening ground.
**Keelung(USA)** was unable to dominate in a race of this quality.
**Hawridge Prince** was 15lb higher than for his last win yet still theoretically 10lb well in following his second in a Windsor Listed race. While he was probably flattered there, he had shown good handicap form off marks in the 90s and this was clearly too bad to be true. *Official explanation: trainer said gelding was never travelling and hung right*
**Counsel's Opinion(IRE)** *Official explanation: jockey said gelding did not feel right*
**Camp Commander(IRE)** *Official explanation: jockey said horse was hanging right*

## 5651 SCOTTISH COURAGE BERKSHIRE BREWERY SILVER JUBILEE CONDITIONS STKS 1m 1f
4:35 (4:35) (B2) 3-Y-0+ £8,948 (£3,308; £1,654; £752) Stalls High

Form RPR
0100 **1** **Pentecost**[7] [5462] 5-8-11 106 ... MartinDwyer 3 114
(AMBalding) *lw: racd in 3rd: smooth hdwy to led 2f out: pushed out ins last* **4/1**[3]
0362 **2** *¾* **Checkit (IRE)**[18] [5215] 4-8-11 110 ... JFortune 4 113
(MRChannon) *hld up in 4th: hdwy over 2f out: sn chsng wnr: kpt on u.p but no imp cl home* **7/4**[1]
6-63 **3** *6* **Island Sound**[19] [5180] 7-8-11 99 ... TQuinn 1 101
(DRCElsworth) *led: sn clr: rdn 3f out: hdd 2f out: sn btn* **5/1**
-200 **4** *5* **Parasol (IRE)**[105] [2678] 5-8-11 111 ... (v) LDettori 2 91
(DRLoder) *lw: b.hind: trckd ldr: chal 3f out: rdn: hung lft and nt run on 2f out* **5/2**[2]
0046 **5** *nk* **Sgt Pepper (IRE)**[14] [5294] 3-8-6 89 ... RLMoore 5 90
(RHannon) *rdn 3f out: a bhd* **16/1**

1m 55.71s (1.36) **Going Correction** +0.275s/f (Good)
**WFA** 3 from 4yo+ 5lb **5** Ran SP% **107.5**
Speed ratings: **104,103,98,93,93**CSF £10.89 TOTE £5.30: £2.40, £1.50; EX 14.20.
**Owner** J C, J R And S R Hitchins **Bred** Miss S N Ralphs **Trained** Kingsclere, Hants

**FOCUS**
A strong pace, but a messy contest and Pentecost may have won by default.

**NOTEBOOK**
**Pentecost** may have found the ground softer and the trip further than ideal, but he did get the decent pace he needs and picked up well when asked. The key to this victory though, may have been that he was up against one rival who rarely wins, one who went off too quick in the conditions, another one who looked reluctant, and one who had little chance on official ratings. All in all the form looks very suspect.
**Checkit(IRE)**, held up early, looked as though he might prove a problem to the winner approaching the last furlong, but could never quite get there. He is kept very busy and keeps on collecting prize money, but finds winning hard these days.
**Island Sound** usually makes the running and likes this ground, but the way he capitulated halfway up the home straight suggests he may have done too much too soon in the conditions.



The Form Book, Raceform Ltd, Compton, RG20 6NL

**Parasol(IRE)**, off since June, had every chance but when put under pressure he carried his head awkwardly and looked very reluctant. He looks to have fallen out of love with the game and perhaps he would be better off racing on sand in Dubai or on dirt Stateside.
**Sgt Pepper(IRE)** faced a stiff task at the weights and ran accordingly.

## 5652 JOHN SMITH'S WOOLSTON TRADES AND LABOUR CLUB H'CAP 7f (S)
**5:05** (5:13) (D2) (0-85,84) 3-Y-O **£7,586** (£2,334; £1,167; £583) **Stalls** Centre

Form RPR
2530 **1** **Doctorate**[15] 5265 3-9-4 **81** ... EAhern 2 91
(EALDunlop) *racd far side: chsd ldrs tl tk overall ld over 1f out: drvn out ins last* **22/1**
152 **2** 1 ½ **Night Air (IRE)**[16] 5244 3-8-13 **76** ... TPQueally 16 82
(DRLoder) *racd centre: in tch: hdwy to chse ldrs 2f out: chsd wnr and hung lft u.p ins last: swtchd rt: nt rcvr* **10/1**
3630 **3** *hd* **Primo Way**[79] 3455 3-9-5 **82** ... LDettori 15 88+
(BWHills) *lw: racd centre: bhd: hdwy over 2f out: styd on to chse ldrs ins last: kpt on cl home* **6/1**[1]
0555 **4** ½ **Star Pupil**[19] 5177 3-8-10 **73** ... (v) MartinDwyer 1 77
(AMBalding) *lw: racd far side: chsd ldrs: led overall 2f out: hdd over 1f out: one pce ins last* **33/1**
0000 **5** 1 ¾ **Seneschal**[10] 5399 3-8-0 **70** oh3 ... TO'Brien[(7)] 17 70
(MRChannon) *racd centre and bhd: hdwy fr 2f out: styd on wl fnl f but nvr gng pce to rch ldrs* **40/1**
3321 **6** *nk* **Kali**[91] 3106 3-8-13 **76** ... DaneO'Neill 22 75+
(RCharlton) *racd stands side: in tch: rdn and kpt on fnl 2f: nt go pce of far side* **12/1**
3331 **7** ¾ **Farewell Gift**[31] 4845 3-9-3 **80** ... (v) RHughes 21 77+
(RHannon) *racd stands side: chsd ldrs: rdn over 2f out: one pce ins last* **25/1**
0004 **8** *shd* **Lord Links (IRE)**[10] 5399 3-9-1 **78** ... PDobbs 27 75+
(RHannon) *racd stands side: chsd ldrs: rdn over 2f out: styd on same pce ins last* **33/1**
1144 **9** 1 **Keyaki (IRE)**[25] 5024 3-9-2 **79** ... RMullen 24 73+
(CFWall) *racd stands side: s.i.s: bhd: hdwy fr 2f out: kpt on wl fnl f but nt rch ldrs* **25/1**
2210 **10** 1 **Saviours Spirit**[10] 5399 3-8-6 **72** ... RMiles[(3)] 13 64
(TGMills) *racd centre crse and led that gp 5f: stl ev ch whn hung rt over 1f out: wknd ins last* **33/1**
-035 **11** ½ **Truman**[85] 3261 3-8-7 **70** ... LisaJones 23 60+
(JARToller) *racd stands side: bhd: rdn 1/2-way: kpt on fnl f but n.d* **50/1**
2311 **12** *nk* **Violet Park**[36] 4731 3-8-12 **75** ... JFortune 3 64
(BJMeehan) *racd far side: chsd ldrs: rdn over 2f out: wknd ins fnl f* **15/2**[3]
1515 **13** *nk* **Stevedore (IRE)**[20] 5150 3-8-10 **73** ... RWinston 8 62
(BRMillman) *racd far side and led that gp tl hdd 2f out: wknd fnl f* **20/1**
4114 **14** ¾ **General Feeling (IRE)**[20] 5150 3-8-6 **76** ... JDWalsh[(7)] 14 63
(SKirk) *racd centre crse: in tch: styd on one pce fnl 2f* **40/1**
4-1 **15** ½ **Ashwaaq (USA)**[156] 1419 3-9-1 **78** ... RHills 18 63+
(JLDunlop) *racd stands side: s.i.s: bhd: kpt on fnl 2f but n.d* **12/1**
0600 **16** 1 **Freak Occurence (IRE)**[11] 5379 3-9-0 **77** ... (v) RHavlin 26 60
(MissECLavelle) *racd far side: chsd ldrs 5f* **25/1**
1-66 **17** 1 ½ **Chanterelle (IRE)**[36] 4731 3-9-7 **84** ... PRobinson 19 63
(JLDunlop) *racd centre: chsng ldrs whn hmpd and wknd over 1f out* **33/1**
5-13 **18** 1 ¾ **Enrapture (USA)**[20] 5148 3-9-2 **79** ... RLMoore 10 53
(MrsAJPerrett) *lw: racd centre: chsd ldrs 5f* **7/1**[2]
0340 **19** ½ **Surf The Net**[14] 5294 3-9-5 **82** ... (v[1]) RSmith 7 55
(RHannon) *racd far side: n.d* **66/1**
0542 **20** ½ **Ask The Clerk (IRE)**[10] 5399 3-8-4 **72** ... RoryMoore[(5)] 20 44+
(VSmith) *racd stands side: in tch over 4f* **12/1**
44-1 **21** 1 ¼ **Vonadaisy**[19] 5204 3-8-7 **70** ... TQuinn 4 39
(WJHaggas) *racd far side: s.i.s: sn in tch: rdn: hung lft and wknd 2f out* **14/1**
1200 **22** 1 ¼ **Pick Of The Crop**[159] 1357 3-8-9 **72** ... WRyan 6 37
(JRJenkins) *racd far side: s.i.s: a in rr* **50/1**
600 **23** 2 ½ **Pine Bay**[84] 3304 3-8-5 **71** oh6 ow1 ... LPKeniry[(3)] 11 30
(BGubby) *racd centre: bhd fr 1/2-way* **100/1**
1-00 **24** 3 **Soliniki**[58] 4051 3-8-13 **76** ... SCarson 25 27+
(JAOsborne) *racd stands side and led that gp 5f: sn wknd* **66/1**
1403 **25** *nk* **Mr Jack Daniells (IRE)**[15] 5265 3-8-9 **75** ... (b[1]) NMackay[(3)] 9 25
(WRMuir) *racd far side: chsd ldrs over 4f* **10/1**

1m 27.72s (0.50) **Going Correction** +0.15s/f (Good) **25** Ran **SP% 131.7**
Speed ratings: **103,101,101,100,98 98,97,97,96,94 94,93,93,92,92 91,89,87,86,86 84,83,80,77,76**CSF £207.03 CT £1540.86 TOTE £39.80: £7.30, £3.30, £2.50, £7.00; EX 495.30 Place 6 £154.24, Place 5 £67.25..
**Owner** P G Goulandris **Bred** Chippenham Lodge Stud Ltd **Trained** Newmarket, Suffolk

**FOCUS**
By this stage the ground had become quite testing. They split into three groups early on, though the centre and far side groups merged towards the end and it was they that held the advantage.

**NOTEBOOK**
**Doctorate**, who had gained his only previous victory on soft ground, found conditions had come just right. Racing towards the far side, he eventually won with a bit in hand and would obviously not mind if it stayed wet during the autumn. He did show some promise on his Polytrack debut and there are some tasty handicaps at around this trip on that surface during the winter.
**Night Air(IRE)** ◆, making his handicap debut and on soft ground for the first time, came with a steady late run down the centre, but was making little impression on the winner when appearing to take a bad step about 20 yards from the line. He still has some scope and can win a similar contest off this mark.
**Primo Way** is not the easiest to predict, but he has form on the ground and has gone well fresh in the past so the break of around 11 weeks was not a negative. Held up at the back of the centre group, he ran on steadily over the last couple of furlongs but the winner had already gone beyond recall.
**Star Pupil** made his effort over on the far side along with the winner, but did not see his race out as well as that rival and is still looking for his first win.
**Seneschal**, 3lb out of the handicap, has been badly out of form this year after showing promise at two. Staying on well down the centre of the track towards the end, this was by far his best effort of the campaign so far having dropped 24lb since the start of the season.
**Kali** ◆, off since winning a Warwick maiden in June, had not been raised in the weights for that and deserves credit for emerging best of those to race stands' side. There should be a similar contest in her.
**Farewell Gift** did not find the visor working a second time, but to be fair he was at a disadvantage racing on the stands' side in this contest, so may be worth another chance.
**Lord Links(IRE)** ran another fair race from a disadvantageous draw and looks to be returning to form.
**Saviours Spirit** *Official explanation: trainer said gelding was unsuited by the good to soft ground*
**General Feeling(IRE)** *Official explanation: trainer said gelding had a breathing problem*
T/Plt: £289.50 to a £1 stake. Pool: £79,259.30. 199.85 winning tickets. T/Qpdt: £50.20 to a £1 stake. Pool: £4,062.50. 59.80 winning tickets. ST

# 5347 WARWICK (L-H)
## Saturday, September 18

**OFFICIAL GOING: Good to soft**
The ground was much softer than expected after 10mm of rain overnight.
Wind: slt across Weather: an odd light shower

## 5653 GALLIONS MAIDEN STKS 7f 26y
**2:10** (2:11) (D3) 2-Y-O **£4,494** (£1,383; £691; £345) **Stalls** Low

Form RPR
32 **1** **Red Affleck (USA)**[22] 5087 2-9-0 ... AMcCarthy 1 83
(PWChapple-Hyam) *mde all: rdn 2f out: drvn out* **4/6**[1]
64 **2** 1 ¼ **Belly Dancer (IRE)**[93] 3021 2-8-4 ... NDeSouza[(5)] 8 74
(PFICole) *sn chsng ldrs: swtchd rt 2f out: wnt 2nd jst over 1f out: r.o one pce* **13/2**[2]
65 **3** 1 ¾ **Marchetta**[15] 5272 2-8-9 ... SWKelly 9 70
(PWHarris) *w wnr: rdn over 2f out: lost 2nd jst over 1f out: one pce* **15/2**[3]
2550 **4** *nk* **Dante's Diamond (IRE)**[19] 5202 2-9-0 75 ... GBaker 5 74
(FJordan) *hld up in tch: rdn 3f out: kpt on towards fin* **16/1**
0 **5** 3 **Royal Mougins**[63] 3946 2-9-0 ... SWhitworth 7 67
(GWragg) *bhd: rdn and hdwy on outside over 1f out: nvr trbld ldrs* **66/1**
6 **6** 2 **Briannie (IRE)**[10] 5400 2-8-9 ... DSweeney 13 57
(JRBoyle) *chsd ldrs tl wknd over 1f out* **33/1**
**7** 1 ½ **Mr Mayfair (IRE)** 2-9-0 ... PFitzsimons 2 58
(JAOsborne) *s.i.s: rdn and sme hdwy on ins over 1f out: n.d* **50/1**
**8** 1 ½ **Blue Torpedo (USA)** 2-9-0 ... JCrowley 12 54
(MrsAJPerrett) *s.i.s: in rr: rdn 3f out: styd on fnl f: nvr nrr* **33/1**
**9** 1 ¼ **Esrar (IRE)** 2-9-0 ... OUrbina 6 51
(MPTregoning) *s.i.s: sn mid-div: lost pl 3f out: n.d after* **10/1**
0 **10** *nk* **Great General (IRE)**[20] 5154 2-9-0 ... RFitzpatrick 10 50
(SLKeightley) *prom: rdn over 2f out: wknd over 1f out* **150/1**
**11** 1 **Empangeni** 2-9-0 ... IMongan 4 48
(JLDunlop) *sn outpcd* **40/1**
60 **12** *nk* **Zoripp (IRE)**[49] 4315 2-9-0 ... SChin 11 47
(JGGiven) *hld up in mid-div: lost pl 3f out: sn rdn and btn* **50/1**
00 **13** 5 **Savoy Chapel**[12] 5347 2-9-0 ... VSlattery 3 35
(JAOsborne) *s.i.s: a bhd* **100/1**

1m 26.75s (1.85) **Going Correction** +0.20s/f (Good) **13** Ran **SP% 115.4**
Speed ratings: **97,95,93,93,89 87,85,84,82,82 81,80,75**CSF £4.55 TOTE £1.30: £1.10, £2.20, £2.10; EX 7.00.
**Owner** Dr J Wilson,Tom McNaughton,John Porter **Bred** Calumet Farm **Trained** Newmarket, Suffolk

**FOCUS**
A fairly strong maiden for the track and a race that can be expected to produce a few winners.

**NOTEBOOK**
**Red Affleck(USA)** had shown he could handle the soft at Newmarket last time and probably had less to do. His trainer thinks he will be suited by further.
**Belly Dancer(IRE)** was suited by the step up from the minimum trip on this first outing for three months. She stuck to her task and is capable of going one better in similar company.
**Marchetta** was back in the right sort of grade but lacked the acceleration to keep tabs on the winner.
**Dante's Diamond(IRE)** was tackling this trip for the first time and gave the impression he will appreciate a mile.
**Royal Mougins** improved significantly on his debut and seems to be going the right way. A longer trip will help.

## 5654 BEECHY BANK CLASSIFIED STKS 1m 4f 134y
**2:40** (2:40) (G4) 3-Y-O+ **£3,101** (£886; £443) **Stalls** Low

Form RPR
6551 **1** **Lazzaz**[12] 5354 6-8-13 50 ... PGallagher[(7)] 6 59
(PWHiatt) *chsd ldr: rdn over 3f out: led over 2f out: drvn out* **9/2**[2]
2223 **2** ½ **Banningham Blaze**[12] 5354 4-8-10 50 ... MHalford[(7)] 2 55
(AWCarroll) *hld up and bhd: hdwy over 4f out: rdn over 2f out: styd on fnl f: no ex towards fin* **4/1**[1]
532- **3** 1 ¼ **Croix De Guerre (IRE)**[13] 5328 4-9-6 50 ... (b) VSlattery 7 56+
(PJHobbs) *hld up: rdn over 5f out: hdwy over 1f out: styd on wl ins fnl f* **4/1**[1]
0660 **4** 3 **Tasneef (USA)**[54] 4196 5-9-6 50 ... (b) SWhitworth 1 52
(TDMccarthy) *led: rdn and hdd over 2f out: wknd ins fnl f* **13/2**[3]
6150 **5** 2 **Top Trees**[22] 5073 6-9-6 50 ... IMongan 13 49
(WSKittow) *s.s: hld up and bhd: hdwy over 6f out: rdn over 3f out: wknd fnl f* **13/2**[3]
4220 **6** 3 **Lunar Lord**[44] 4473 8-9-1 49 ... NDeSouza[(5)] 11 44
(DBurchell) *hld up and bhd: hdwy on ins 4f out: rdn over 2f out: wknd over 1f out* **8/1**
0600 **7** 5 **Lahob**[33] 4820 4-9-6 50 ... SWKelly 3 37
(PHowling) *prom: rdn over 6f out: wknd 3f out* **40/1**
0030 **8** 3 ½ **Caliban (IRE)**[19] 5205 6-9-6 46 ... RFitzpatrick 4 31
(IanWilliams) *hld up towards rr: rdn over 6f out: sn struggling* **14/1**
0605 **9** 3 ½ **Fight The Feeling**[84] 3300 6-9-6 45 ... (v) OUrbina 12 26
(JWUnett) *hld up in tch: rdn over 3f out: wknd over 2f out* **14/1**
4300 **10** 3 ½ **Wodhill Hope**[33] 4820 4-9-3 45 ... AMcCarthy 9 18
(DMorris) *mid-div: rdn over 4f out: sn bhd* **100/1**
0000 **11** 4 **Ocean Rock**[58] 4055 3-8-11 50 ... PaulEddery 5 15
(CAHorgan) *a bhd* **25/1**
-000 **12** 22 **Lord Greystoke (IRE)**[15] 5259 3-8-11 48 ... DSweeney 8 —
(CPMorlock) *hld up and bhd: rdn 6f out: no rspnse: t.o* **80/1**
0000 **13** 15 **High View (USA)**[22] 5080 3-8-11 49 ... GBaker 10 —
(FJordan) *prom: rdn over 5f out: wknd over 4f out: t.o* **100/1**

2m 49.62s (6.32) **Going Correction** +0.475s/f (Yiel)
**WFA** 3 from 4yo+ 9lb **13** Ran **SP% 118.8**
Speed ratings: **99,98,97,96,94 93,89,87,85,83 81,67,58**CSF £22.24 TOTE £6.50: £2.40, £1.50, £1.90; EX 12.60.
**Owner** Phil Kelly **Bred** Khalid Khalifa Al Nabooda **Trained** Hook Norton, Oxon

**FOCUS**
A tight classified event on paper, but only a few were able to get competitive in the yielding ground.

**NOTEBOOK**
**Lazzaz** made it back-to-back wins at Warwick over this shorter trip, with the rain-softened ground putting the emphasis on stamina.
**Banningham Blaze** was 5lb better off than when a length and a half behind the winner over two miles here last time. Her rider got into a bit of a tangle with his reins on the home turn, and the ground that would have been plenty soft enough for her.
**Croix De Guerre(IRE)**, the winner of a couple of weak novice hurdles in the summer, found his stamina really coming into play in the closing stages. He is another who in theory would not have been helped by the overnight rain.

**Tasneef(USA)** eventually paid the penalty for getting this field well strung out on the softest ground he has ever encountered.
**Top Trees** would have preferred the top of the ground.
**Lunar Lord** would not have been beaten for stamina over this trip.

## 5655 ELECTROLUX NURSERY — 7f 26y
**3:15** (3:16) (D3) (0-85,81) 2-Y-O — **£4,621** (£1,422; £711; £355) **Stalls** Low

| Form | | | | | | RPR |
|---|---|---|---|---|---|---|
| 200 | **1** | | **Danehill Willy (IRE)**[22] 5091 2-8-6 **71** (NACallaghan) *in tch: hrd rdn and hdwy on ins over 1f out: r.o to ld wl ins fnl f* | NDeSouza(5) 1 | **4/1**[1] | 77 |
| 4105 | **2** | 3/4 | **Brooklime (IRE)**[18] 5212 2-9-2 **76** (JAOsborne) *led: rdn over 2f out: hdd and no ex wl ins fnl f* | SWKelly 3 | **9/2**[2] | 80 |
| 656 | **3** | 3 1/2 | **Eltizaam (USA)**[19] 5179 2-9-2 **76** (EALDunlop) *hld up in tch: rdn over 2f out: kpt on same pce fnl f* | OUrbina 4 | **13/2**[3] | 71 |
| 401 | **4** | 3/4 | **Fong Shui**[27] 4967 2-9-7 **81** (PJMakin) *hld up: rdn over 2f out: swtchd rt and hdwy over 1f out: one pce ins fnl f* | DSweeney 5 | **4/1**[1] | 75 |
| 5004 | **5** | nk | **Aberdeen Park**[87] 3192 2-8-8 **68** (MrsHSweeting) *prom: rdn over 2f out: wknd ins fnl f* | JoannaBadger 9 | **28/1** | 61 |
| 5004 | **6** | 1 | **Grand Option**[19] 5198 2-8-9 **69** (BWDuke) *hld up in rr: rdn and c wd st: nvr trbld ldrs* | (b) GBaker 10 | **16/1** | 59 |
| 0565 | **7** | 1 | **High Dyke**[19] 5200 2-8-12 **72** (DHaydnJones) *prom: rdn over 2f out: wknd fnl f* | SWhitworth 2 | **10/1** | 60 |
| 3006 | **8** | 3/4 | **Mr Kalandi (IRE)**[12] 5351 2-7-13 **59** (PWD'Arcy) *hld up in mid-div: rdn over 2f out: sn bhd* | AMcCarthy 8 | **8/1** | 45 |
| 004 | **9** | 7 | **Asaateel (IRE)**[19] 5173 2-8-13 **73** (JLDunlop) *w ldr: rdn over 2f out: wknd over 1f out* | IMongan 7 | **8/1** | 41 |

1m 26.37s (1.47) **Going Correction** +0.20s/f (Good) **9** Ran SP% **112.2**
Speed ratings: **99,98,94,93,92 91,90,89,81**CSF £21.08 CT £111.74 TOTE £4.60: £1.20, £2.00, £2.20; EX 30.00.
**Owner** T Mohan **Bred** Patrick J Farrington **Trained** Newmarket, Suffolk

**FOCUS**
A run-of-the-mill nursery, but reliable form that should throw up its share of winners.

**NOTEBOOK**
**Danehill Willy(IRE)** responded well to his rider's urgings in the short home straight. He is crying out for a mile, and a more galloping course will probably suit him better.
**Brooklime(IRE)** was not inconvenienced by the extra furlong and the front-running tactics very nearly paid off.
**Eltizaam(USA)** may now be ready for another crack at a mile.
**Fong Shui** could have found the rain-softened ground against him.
**Aberdeen Park**, another who seems best on a sounder surface, was having her first outing for nearly three months.

## 5656 ZACHARY WHITE CLAIMING STKS — 7f 26y
**3:50** (3:50) (E3) 3-Y-O — **£3,753** (£1,155; £577; £288) **Stalls** Low

| Form | | | | | | RPR |
|---|---|---|---|---|---|---|
| 6000 | **1** | | **Morse (IRE)**[15] 5265 3-9-7 83 (JAOsborne) *led 1f: led over 4f out: rdn 2f out: drvn out* | SWKelly 6 | **9/2**[2] | 73 |
| 0-60 | **2** | 1 | **Penel (IRE)**[171] 1214 3-8-8 58 (BRMillman) *a.p: rdn wl over 1f out: kpt on ins fnl f* | PFitzsimons 1 | **28/1** | 57 |
| 534 | **3** | shd | **Tetcott (IRE)**[29] 4916 3-7-10 72 (MPTregoning) *hld up in tch: rdn 2f out: kpt on ins fnl f* | NDeSouza(5) 2 | **2/1**[1] | 50 |
| 3500 | **4** | hd | **Queenstown (IRE)**[33] 4817 3-8-4 60 (BJMeehan) *w ldrs: rdn and ev ch 2f out: nt qckn ins fnl f* | (b) RFitzpatrick 10 | **14/1** | 52 |
| 4203 | **5** | 1 3/4 | **Reidies Choice**[16] 5244 3-9-7 73 (JGGiven) *hld up: rdn and hdwy on outside over 1f out: one pce fnl f* | IMongan 4 | **6/1**[3] | 65 |
| 2000 | **6** | 3/4 | **Head Boy**[15] 5259 3-8-6 55 (SDow) *bhd: rn wd ent st: hdwy over 1f out: nt rch ldrs* | SWhitworth 9 | **12/1** | 48 |
| 26 | **7** | 1 3/4 | **Knead The Dough**[12] 5338 3-8-6 (DECantillon) *prom: rdn 2f out: wknd over 1f out* | AMcCarthy 13 | **16/1** | 43 |
| 2460 | **8** | nk | **Sweet Pickle**[17] 5219 3-8-11 63 (DJCoakley) *hld up: hdwy on ins 2f out: sn rdn: no imp fnl f* | OUrbina 14 | **20/1** | 47 |
| 1000 | **9** | 9 | **Baker Of Oz**[36] 4726 3-8-10 72 (RHannon) *a bhd* | PaulEddery 5 | **7/1** | 23 |
| -000 | **10** | hd | **Five Gold (IRE)**[11] 5370 3-8-11 55 (BRMillman) *s.s: hung rt thrght: a bhd* | GBaker 7 | **16/1** | 23 |
| 0005 | **11** | 5 | **Commander Bond**[18] 5210 3-8-6 60 (BSmart) *led after 1f tl over 4f out: rdn over 2f out: sn wknd* | DSweeney 8 | **20/1** | 5 |
| 0 | **12** | nk | **Pico Alto**[9] 5408 3-7-13 (BPalling) *a bhd* | JoannaBadger 3 | **100/1** | — |
| 0- | **13** | 1/2 | **Pearl Island (USA)**[390] 4453 3-8-7 (DJWintle) *s.i.s: a bhd* | FrancesPickard(7) 11 | **50/1** | 11 |

1m 26.8s (1.90) **Going Correction** +0.20s/f (Good) **13** Ran SP% **120.3**
Speed ratings: **97,95,95,95,93 92,90,90,80,79 74,73,73**CSF £135.09 TOTE £5.50: £2.10, £11.50, £1.30; EX 179.50.
**Owner** Turf 2000 Limited **Bred** Auriga Partnership **Trained** Upper Lambourn, Berks

**FOCUS**
A fair event for the grade, but nothing came from off the pace and the form looks messy and unreliable.

**NOTEBOOK**
**Morse(IRE)** found the combination of a drop in grade on softer ground enabling him to bounce back to form. *Official explanation: trainer said, regarding the improved form shown, colt had benefited from today's drop in class*
**Penel(IRE)**, tried in blinkers when last seen at the end of March, seems worth another try at a mile now.
**Tetcott(IRE)**, dropped in class, may require further on a course as easy as this.
**Queenstown(IRE)**, fitted with a hood in addition to the regular blinkers, had no excuses.
**Reidies Choice** would have preferred faster ground on this descent into a claimer.
**Head Boy** could never land a blow after taking the scenic route off the home turn.
**Five Gold(IRE)** *Official explanation: jockey said gelding had hung right-handed throughout*

## 5657 CERS H'CAP — 1m 22y
**4:25** (4:26) (D3) (0-70,70) 3-Y-O+ — **£3,887** (£1,196; £598; £299) **Stalls** Low

| Form | | | | | | RPR |
|---|---|---|---|---|---|---|
| 6540 | **1** | | **Tagula Blue (IRE)**[13] 5317 4-9-1 **64** (JAGlover) *s.s: hld up and bhd: hdwy 3f out: swtchd rt 2f out: rdn and hung lft over 1f out: led ins fnl f: r.o wl* | (t) JCrowley 4 | **12/1** | 76 |
| 1356 | **2** | 3 | **Here To Me**[20] 5148 3-8-10 **70** (RHannon) *led early: prom: rdn to ld over 1f out: hdd ins fnl f: one pce* | PGallagher(7) 5 | **10/1** | 76 |
| 0000 | **3** | 1 3/4 | **Motu (IRE)**[21] 5108 3-8-11 **64** (JLDunlop) *hld up: rdn and hdwy over 2f out: edgd lft 1f out: one pce* | (b[1]) SWKelly 17 | **20/1** | 66 |
| 5213 | **4** | 1/2 | **Ali Bruce**[40] 4602 4-8-10 **64** (GLMoore) *sn led: rdn and hdd over 1f out: wknd ins fnl f* | AQuinn(5) 3 | **5/1**[2] | 65 |
| 5024 | **5** | shd | **Elidore**[19] 5176 4-9-2 **68** (BPalling) *t.k.h: sn w ldr: rdn 3f out: wknd wl over 1f out* | J-PGuillambert(3) 6 | **10/1** | 69 |
| 3130 | **6** | 2 1/2 | **Didnt Tell My Wife**[13] 5317 5-9-4 **67** (CFWall) *hld up and bhd: hdwy on ins 3f out: rdn whn hmpd over 1f out: no further prog* | SWhitworth 1 | **13/2**[3] | 68+ |
| 04-0 | **7** | nk | **Bathwick Bruce (IRE)**[19] 5176 6-9-0 **63** (BRMillman) *prom: rdn over 2f out: wknd fnl f* | GBaker 9 | **14/1** | 58 |
| 0-53 | **8** | 2 1/2 | **Zonic Boom (FR)**[145] 1675 4-8-13 **62** (JRFanshawe) *hld up: rdn 2f out: sme hdwy over 1f out: nvr trbld ldrs* | OUrbina 16 | **4/1**[1] | 52+ |
| 0341 | **9** | nk | **Liberty Royal**[16] 5252 5-9-2 **65** (PJMakin) *dwlt: hdwy over 3f out: rdn and wkng whn n.m.r wl over 1f out* | (p) DSweeney 13 | **8/1** | 54 |
| 0060 | **10** | 1 3/4 | **Bold Phoenix (IRE)**[40] 4610 3-8-11 **69** (EFVaughan) *hld up in mid-div: hdwy on ins over 3f out: rdn 2f out: sn wknd* | NDeSouza(5) 8 | **50/1** | 55 |
| 0500 | **11** | hd | **Adobe**[4] 5544 9-8-9 **63** ow1 (WMBrisbourne) *hld up: lost pl over 3f out: rdn over 2f out: nvr nr ldrs* | MSavage(5) 15 | **20/1** | 48 |
| 0025 | **12** | 7 | **Anna Walhaan (IRE)**[35] 2878 5-9-0 **70** (IanWilliams) *hld up and bhd: hdwy on outside whn forced wd bnd over 3f out: n.d after* | DeanWilliams(7) 7 | **20/1** | 41 |
| 0050 | **13** | 3/4 | **Mountcharge (IRE)**[33] 4806 3-9-3 **70** (GAHuffer) *hld up: rdn and short-lived effrt on outside bnd over 3f out* | IMongan 11 | **22/1** | 39 |
| -000 | **14** | 3/4 | **Bonsai (IRE)**[48] 4369 3-8-12 **65** (RTPhillips) *a bhd* | (t) AMcCarthy 10 | **40/1** | 32 |
| -600 | **15** | 6 | **Quintoto**[11] 5374 4-8-11 **63** (RAFahey) *chsd ldrs: rdn over 3f out: sn wknd* | DNolan(3) 12 | **20/1** | 18 |
| 144- | **16** | 1 1/2 | **Scalloway (IRE)**[100] 3425 4-9-5 **68** (DJWintle) *a in rr* | VSlattery 2 | **33/1** | 20 |
| 0360 | **17** | 5 | **Sister Sophia (USA)**[20] 5155 4-8-10 **59** (WJMusson) *s.i.s: sn rcvrd: prom tl wknd 3f out* | PaulEddery 14 | **25/1** | — |

1m 42.53s (3.23) **Going Correction** +0.475s/f (Yiel)
**WFA** 3 from 4yo+ 4lb **17** Ran SP% **128.2**
Speed ratings: **102,99,97,96,96 94,93,91,91,89 89,82,81,80,74 73,68**CSF £114.54 CT £2488.85 TOTE £17.60: £3.50, £3.40, £8.00, £1.50; EX 172.30.
**Owner** Boston R S Ian Bennett **Bred** Michael Conlon **Trained** Carburton, Notts

**FOCUS**
A modest, open-looking handicap, in which the winner returned to form helped by a big drop in the weights. The form is ordinary for the grade.

**NOTEBOOK**
**Tagula Blue(IRE)**, who is far from straightforward, overcame his habitual slow start to give his rider his first winner on the Flat since he was an apprentice.
**Here To Me**, back up to a mile, does not seem to know how to run a bad race.
**Motu(IRE)** ran well from his wide draw in the first-time blinkers.
**Ali Bruce** likes to force the pace but is better suited to seven furlongs.
**Elidore** paid the penalty for running too freely.
**Didnt Tell My Wife** would have finished a bit closer had he not become the meat in the sandwich.

## 5658 EDWARD JOSEPH H'CAP — 1m 2f 188y
**4:55** (4:55) (F4) (0-55,58) 3-Y-O+ — **£3,606** (£1,030; £515) **Stalls** Low

| Form | | | | | | RPR |
|---|---|---|---|---|---|---|
| 4125 | **1** | | **Bojangles (IRE)**[12] 5354 5-8-11 **53** (RBrotherton) *a.p: led over 3f out: clr over 2f out: rdn wl over 1f out: drvn out* | DNolan(3) 10 | **4/1**[1] | 63 |
| 0002 | **2** | 1 | **Gustavo**[26] 5002 3-8-8 **54** (BWHills) *a.p: chsd wnr jst over 1f out: sn rdn: hung lft ins fnl f: nt qckn* | (b) OUrbina 5 | **13/2**[3] | 62 |
| 050 | **3** | 2 | **Duc's Dream**[54] 4196 6-8-12 **51** (DMorris) *a.p: rdn over 3f out: one pce fnl 2f* | PaulEddery 11 | **16/1** | 56 |
| 1-20 | **4** | 1/2 | **Killing Me Softly**[62] 804 3-8-5 **51** (JGallagher) *a.p: rdn over 3f out: one pce fnl 2f* | RFitzpatrick 16 | **33/1** | 55 |
| 4004 | **5** | 1 | **Ribbons And Bows (IRE)**[19] 5175 4-8-12 **51** (CACyzer) *hld up: hdwy over 4f out: lost pl 3f out: sn rdn: styd on fnl f* | DSweeney 7 | **14/1** | 53 |
| 436- | **6** | 4 | **My Last Bean (IRE)**[169] 5920 7-8-13 **55** (BSmart) *prom: rdn over 2f out: wknd over 1f out* | LFletcher(3) 13 | **16/1** | 51 |
| 3030 | **7** | 1/2 | **Kalou (GER)**[19] 4616 6-8-8 **47** (BJCurley) *hld up and bhd: rdn and sme hdwy 3f out: no real prog fnl 2f* | SWKelly 17 | **9/2**[2] | 42 |
| 6604 | **8** | 2 | **Our Destiny**[9] 5408 6-8-7 **53** (AWCarroll) *hld up in mid-div: hdwy over 3f out: rdn 2f out: sn wknd* | MHalford(7) 8 | **12/1** | 44 |
| 0005 | **9** | 2 1/2 | **Havantadoubt (IRE)**[14] 5285 4-8-9 **48** (MRBosley) *hld up towards rr: rdn 3f out: swtchd rt wl over 1f out: nvr nr ldrs* | (t) GBaker 14 | **25/1** | 35 |
| 0140 | **10** | 2 | **Got To Be Cash**[22] 5085 5-8-10 **54** (WMBrisbourne) *hld up: hdwy on ins whn nt clr run over 3f out: rdn over 2f out: sn wknd* | MSavage(5) 9 | **14/1** | 38 |
| 0006 | **11** | 1 | **Cuddles (FR)**[15] 5258 5-9-1 **54** (KOCunningham-Brown) *s.v.s: hld up: hdwy 4f out: rdn over 2f out: wknd wl over 1f out* | (b[1]) SWhitworth 19 | **16/1** | 36 |
| 200- | **12** | 4 | **Mighty Pip (IRE)**[353] 5308 8-8-10 **49** (MRBosley) *hld up and bhd: rdn 3f out: no rspnse* | JoannaBadger 18 | **33/1** | 24 |
| 4050 | **13** | 2 | **Violet Avenue**[20] 5156 3-8-7 **53** (JGGiven) *hld up in mid-div: rdn 3f out: wknd 2f out* | (b[1]) SChin 15 | **28/1** | 25 |
| 3-31 | **14** | 6 | **Be Wise Girl**[154] 1465 3-8-9 **55** (JGGiven) *racd wd early: led: hdd over 3f out: sn rdn: wknd qckly 2f out* | IMongan 20 | **17/2** | 17 |
| -000 | **15** | 1/2 | **Whispering Valley**[27] 4972 4-8-13 **52** ow2 (MrsAJPerrett) *hld up and bhd: hdwy on ins 4f out: rdn 3f out: wknd 2f out* | JCrowley 4 | **80/1** | 13 |
| 0000 | **16** | 29 | **Must Be Magic**[31] 4849 7-8-11 **53** (HJCollingridge) *hld up: stdy hdwy over 5f out: wknd over 4f out: t.o* | (v) J-PGuillambert(3) 12 | **25/1** | — |
| 2000 | **17** | 6 | **Forge Lane (IRE)**[28] 4941 3-8-5 **56** ow3 (GLMoore) *hld up in tch: rdn and wknd over 4f out: t.o* | (p) AQuinn(5) 1 | **25/1** | — |
| 3406 | **18** | 7 | **Fairland (IRE)**[91] 3088 5-8-8 **47** (SDow) *dwlt: a bhd: t.o* | PFitzsimons 3 | **16/1** | — |

2m 23.91s (4.51) **Going Correction** +0.475s/f (Yiel)
**WFA** 3 from 4yo+ 7lb **18** Ran SP% **128.7**
Speed ratings: **102,101,99,99,98 95,95,94,92,90 90,87,85,81,80 59,55,50**CSF £28.29 CT £398.27 TOTE £5.10: £1.60, £3.10, £5.00, £9.40; EX 25.50 Place 6 £25.65, Place 5 £23.16..
**Owner** Alan Solomon **Bred** C H Wacker Iii **Trained** Elmley Castle, Worcs

**FOCUS**
Another wide-open modest handicap. The form makes sense although the winner got the run of the race.

**NOTEBOOK**
**Bojangles(IRE)**, who seems versatile with regard to distance, was not inconvenienced by the overnight rain. Slipping his field off the home turn, he stole enough of an advantage to hold on.
**Gustavo**, trying a longer trip, looked set to pick up the winner until hanging left in the closing stages.
**Duc's Dream** was certainly not disgraced on ground softer than he prefers.
**Killing Me Softly**, who failed to take to hurdling, was having his first run on turf on the Flat and is unexposed.
**Ribbons And Bows(IRE)** ◆ likes this sort of ground but really wants further. She has dropped to a useful mark.
**Kalou(GER)**, returning to the Flat after a couple of runs over hurdles, never got into the race. He is capable of better.
**Be Wise Girl** *Official explanation: jockey said filly blew up*
**Fairland(IRE)** *Official explanation: jockey said gelding had a breathing problem*
T/Plt: £85.90 to a £1 stake. Pool: £30,856.20. 262.05 winning tickets. T/Qpdt: £26.00 to a £1 stake. Pool: £1,358.60. 38.60 winning tickets. KH

5659 - (Foreign Racing) - See Raceform Interactive

## 5321 CURRAGH (R-H)

Saturday, September 18

**OFFICIAL GOING: Straight course - yielding; round course - good (good to firm in places)**

### 5660a LAND ROVER H'CAP (PREMIER HANDICAP) 5f
2:35 (2:36) 3-Y-0+ **£25,214** (£7,397; £3,524; £1,200)

RPR
1 **Jacks Estate (IRE)**[7] 5482 9-8-11 94........................ CPGeoghegan(7) 16 103
(AdrianMcguinness, Ire) *trckd ldrs on outer: 4th and chal over 1f out: 2nd ins fnl f: led 100yds out* **12/1**
2 3/4 **Moon Unit (IRE)**[13] 5327 3-9-10 101........................(p) JPMurtagh 2 107
(HRogers, Ire) *cl up in 2nd: led 2f out: strly pressed fnl f: hdd 100yds out: kpt on* **14/1**
3 1/2 **Tigim (IRE)**[44] 4506 5-8-12 91........................ MCHussey(3) 10 96
(PeterHenley, Ire) *s.i.s and towards rr: 10th over 1f out: r.o wl* **8/1**[2]
4 shd **Belleinga (IRE)**[30] 4896 3-7-9 77........................ PBBeggy(5) 1 81
(TFLacy, Ire) *sn trckd ldrs in 4th: 5th 1 1/2f out: kpt on ins fnl f* **7/1**[1]
5 hd **Rydal (USA)**[28] 4952 3-8-10 87........................(b) DPMcDonogh 6 90
(GAButler) *trckd ldrs: 6th 2f out: 5th and kpt on ins fnl f* **7/1**[1]
6 3/4 **Budelli (IRE)**[13] 5324 7-8-1 82........................(b) RPCleary(5) 7 83
(MHalford, Ire) *led: hdd 2f out: 3rd 1f out: sn no ex* **7/1**[1]
7 3/4 **Tiger Royal (IRE)**[83] 3350 8-9-8 98........................(b) PJSmullen 11 96
(DKWeld, Ire) *towards rr: kpt on fr over 1f out* **10/1**
8 nk **Symboli West (USA)**[94] 2995 4-8-12 88........................ MJKinane 5 85
(JohnMOxx, Ire) *mid-div: 8th after 1/2-way: kpt on one pced fr 2f out* **9/1**[3]
9 nk **Step Back (IRE)**[14] 5309 11-8-8 84........................ FMBerry 12 80
(GerardKeane, Ire) *cl up in 3rd: rdn 1 1/2f out: wknd fnl f* **14/1**
10 hd **Fairy Pass (IRE)**[13] 5324 3-7-7 77........................ CDHayes(7) 8 72
(GMLyons, Ire) *nvr a factor: kpt on ins fnl f* **16/1**
11 hd **Lupine (IRE)**[13] 5324 5-8-9 85........................ KJManning 14 79
(GWRobinson, Ire) *towards rr: sme prog whn checked over 1f out: no ex* **14/1**
12 nk **Amiata**[85] 3285 4-8-4 80........................ WMLordan 13 73
(DeclanGillespie, Ire) *chsd ldrs on outer: 8th 2f out: sn no ex* **14/1**
13 shd **Mrs St George (IRE)**[42] 4526 3-8-8 85........................ KFallon 4 78
(JGBurns, Ire) *chsd ldrs to 2f out: sn no ex* **11/1**
14 nk **Assigh Lady (IRE)**[13] 5324 6-8-1 80........................ CatherineGannon(3) 9 72
(DesmondMcdonogh, Ire) *nvr a factor* **12/1**
15 1 **Libras Child (IRE)**[13] 5324 5-8-6 82........................ NGMcCullagh 3 70
(PDelaney, Ire) *chsd ldrs on stand's side: no ex fr 2f out* **8/1**[2]
16 1 1/2 **Lone Plainsman**[27] 4975 3-7-11 79........................ DJMoran(5) 15 62
(PFO'Donnell, Ire) *chsd ldrs on outer: wknd fr over 2f out* **14/1**

60.50 secs **Going Correction** +0.025s/f (Good)
**WFA** 3 from 4yo+ 1lb **16 Ran SP% 141.7**
Speed ratings: **109,107,107,106,106 105,104,103,103,102 102,102,101,101,99 97**CSF £196.98 CT £1531.18 TOTE £17.30: £3.10, £3.10, £2.10, £2.10; DF 379.90.
**Owner** Pinheads Pizza Syndicate **Bred** Robert J Cotter **Trained** Lusk, Co Dublin

**NOTEBOOK**
**Jacks Estate(IRE)** appreciated the drop back in trip and defied a high draw for his first success of the year. *Official explanation: trainer said, regarding the improved form shown, gelding is a Curragh specialist and the left-handed track and firm ground did not suit last time out at Leopardstown, a course he has rarely performed well on*
**Moon Unit(IRE)** has been acquitting herself reasonably in Group Three company and went close in this drop back in class. She liked the give in the ground and there should be an opportunity soon.
**Tigim(IRE)** was 8lb higher for his Tipperary success last month and, after a sluggish start, ran on strongly inside the last once he got an opening.
**Belleinga(IRE)** was a wide-margin winner of a Tipperary sprint maiden last time. She had to sit and suffer on the inner until a gap appeared for her inside the last.
**Rydal(USA)** went with the pace but was struggling a furlong and a half down and, although keeping on, could not raise a final effort.

### 5661a BALLYGALLON STUD RENAISSANCE STKS (GROUP 3) 6f
3:05 (3:06) 3-Y-0+ **£34,330** (£10,035; £4,753; £1,584)

RPR
1 **Royal Millennium (IRE)**[14] 5289 6-9-5........................ TEDurcan 6 115
(MRChannon) *hld up in tch: hdwy 2f out: 3rd over 1f out: led ins fnl f: kpt on wl* **7/2**[1]
2 1/2 **Moss Vale (IRE)**[30] 4886 3-9-0........................ MHills 8 111
(BWHills) *prom: 3rd on stand's rail 1/2-way: swtchd over 1f out: kpt on wl ins fnl f* **6/1**[3]
3 nk **Grand Reward (USA)**[13] 5327 3-9-0 106........................(bt[1]) JPSpencer 9 110
(APO'Brien, Ire) *hld up: hdwy on outer 1 1/2f out: kpt on wl ins fnl f* **7/1**
4 shd **Glocca Morra (IRE)**[13] 5327 6-9-2 102........................ KJManning 5 109
(WTFarrell, Ire) *trckd ldrs: 5th 1/2-way: 2nd 2f out: led over 1f out: hdd ins fnl f: no ex cl home* **8/1**
5 3/4 **Dangle (IRE)**[11] 5386 3-8-11 98........................ FMBerry 10 104
(EdwardLynam, Ire) *trckd ldrs: 4th 1/2-way: kpt on same pce fr 1 1/2f out* **12/1**
6 hd **Ulfah (USA)**[13] 5327 3-8-11 104........................ DPMcDonogh 11 103
(KevinPrendergast, Ire) *led: rdn and hdd over 1f out: sn no ex* **7/1**
7 4 **Ruby Rocket (IRE)**[7] 5471 3-8-11........................ KFallon 2 91
(HMorrison) *chsd ldrs early: no imp fr 1 1/2f out: kpt on same pce* **9/2**[2]
8 3 **Millybaa (USA)**[21] 5121 4-8-13........................ JPMurtagh 4 82
(RGuest) *chsd ldrs: no imp fr 2 1/2f out* **16/1**
9 2 **Hanabad (IRE)**[7] 5482 4-9-2 104........................(b) MJKinane 1 79
(JohnMOxx, Ire) *hld up: rdn and no imp fr over 2f out* **8/1**
10 3 **Newton (IRE)**[95] 2956 3-9-0 106........................ PCosgrave 3 70
(APO'Brien, Ire) *a bhd* **16/1**
11 1 1/2 **Anna Frid (GER)**[13] 5327 4-8-13 93........................(b[1]) PShanahan 7 63
(DKWeld, Ire) *chsd ldrs on outer: no ex fr 2f out: eased fnl f* **16/1**
12 nk **Wathab (IRE)**[25] 5029 3-9-0 104........................(bt[1]) PJSmullen 12 65
(DKWeld, Ire) *prom: 2nd 1/2-way: wknd qckly fr 2f out* **14/1**

1m 13.1s **Going Correction** +0.025s/f (Good)
**WFA** 3 from 4yo+ 2lb **12 Ran SP% 133.9**
Speed ratings: **111,110,109,109,108 108,103,99,96,92 90,90**CSF £28.01 TOTE £4.00: £1.70, £2.50, £3.00; DF 23.90.
**Owner** Jackie & George Smith **Bred** Mrs G Smith **Trained** West Ilsley, Berks

**FOCUS**
A fair Group Three, with the winner suited by the drop in grade.

**NOTEBOOK**
**Royal Millennium(IRE)** found this company much more congenial than the Group One class he has been competing in. He quickened inside the last to effectively seal it in a matter of strides.
**Moss Vale(IRE)** was close up throughout although having to switch from the inner over a furlong out. He ran on well towards the end.
**Grand Reward(USA)** ran on well in the closing stages to be nearest at the finish. First-time blinkers did not exactly revitalise him, but he did not shirk.
**Glocca Morra(IRE)** remains difficult to place in that limbo land between handicaps and Group company.
**Dangle(IRE)** liked the ground but could never get in blow from over a furlong out despite keeping on.
**Ulfah(USA)** worked her way over to the stands' side in trying to make all, but found little when headed over a furlong out.
**Ruby Rocket(IRE)** showed plenty of pace but had run out of fuel with less than two furlongs to race.
**Millybaa(USA)** ran prominently to halfway before fading.
**Wathab(IRE)** continues to disappoint despite the application of first-time blinkers.

### 5662a IRISH FIELD ST. LEGER (GROUP 1) 1m 6f
3:40 (3:45) 3-Y-0+ **£118,732** (£40,563; £19,436; £6,760)

RPR
1 **Vinnie Roe (IRE)**[34] 4784 6-9-8 117........................(b) PJSmullen 5 124+
(DKWeld, Ire) *settled 4th: 3rd fr over 5f out: impr to chal travelling easily ent st: led over 2f out: clr over 1f out: easily* **7/2**[1]
2 2 1/2 **Brian Boru**[27] 4983 4-9-8 115........................(t) JPSpencer 14 119
(APO'Brien, Ire) *mid-div: 7th 5f out: impr into mod 4th over 2f out: 2nd and kpt on wl fr over 1f out* **7/2**[1]
3 1/2 **First Charter**[32] 4832 5-9-8........................ KFallon 13 118
(SirMichaelStoute) *a.p: 2nd fr 6f out: rdn to ld ent st: hdd over 2f out: sn outpcd: kpt on u.p fnl f* **5/1**[3]
4 3/4 **Dubai Success**[35] 4746 4-9-8........................ MHills 10 117
(BWHills) *trckd ldrs in 5th: 4th 5f out: 3rd over 2f out: kpt on same pce* **10/1**
5 hd **Alcazar (IRE)**[93] 2998 9-9-8........................ MFenton 9 117
(HMorrison) *trckd ldrs: 5th after 1/2-way: outpcd ent st: kpt on wl fnl f* **14/1**
6 2 **Two Miles West (IRE)**[34] 4784 3-8-12 104........................(t) JAHeffernan 7 114
(APO'Brien, Ire) *rr of mid-div: 8th 1/2-way: 7th appr st: kpt on same pce* **10/1**
7 3 1/2 **Media Puzzle (USA)**[41] 4587 7-9-8 106........................(b) PShanahan 11 109
(DKWeld, Ire) *hld up in rr: styd on fr over 3f out* **20/1**
8 3 **Orange Touch (GER)**[21] 5111 4-9-8........................ JPMurtagh 4 105
(MrsAJPerrett) *led: rdn and hdd ent st: wknd fr 2f out* **9/2**[2]
9 3/4 **Cruzspiel**[66] 3862 4-9-8 108........................(b) MJKinane 2 104
(JohnMOxx, Ire) *hld up: prog into 6th 5f out: no ex bef st* **33/1**
10 2 1/2 **Blue Corrig (IRE)**[12] 5357 4-9-8 97........................(b) PCosgrave 12 101
(JosephCrowley, Ire) *a bhd* **100/1**
11 10 **Jagger**[14] 5296 4-9-8........................ DPMcDonogh 3 87
(GAButler) *a bhd* **33/1**
12 25 **Chimes At Midnight (USA)**[54] 4204 7-9-8 70......(b) CatherineGannon 1 52
(LukeComer, Ire) *6th early: wknd qckly 1/2-way: t.o* **100/1**
13 1 **Napoleon (IRE)**[20] 5166 3-8-12 83........................(bt) CO'Donoghue 6 50
(APO'Brien, Ire) *sn 2nd: 3rd 1/2-way: wknd qckly fr 6f out: t.o* **100/1**

3m 3.90s **Going Correction** +0.025s/f (Good)
**WFA** 3 from 4yo+ 10lb **13 Ran SP% 117.8**
Speed ratings: **102,100,100,99,99 98,96,94,94,93 87,73,72**CSF £14.40 TOTE £3.90: £1.50, £1.40, £2.30; DF 13.20.
**Owner** Seamus Sheridan **Bred** Mrs Virginia Moeran **Trained** The Curragh, Co Kildare
■ Vinnie Roe is the first horse since the European Pattern was instituted in 1971 to win the same Group One race four times.

**FOCUS**
A well-contested renewal of this all-aged Classic, but Vinnie Roe scored easily in a race he has made his own.

**NOTEBOOK**
**Vinnie Roe(IRE)** looked lean and hard for this incredible fourth successive victory in the race. Cruising coming down the hill, he led just over two furlongs out and had soon pulled away. The rain came at the right time, but at this time of year this is his course and he has made the race his own. He was greyhound thin for this, only his third appearance of the season. The Arc and Melbourne remain in abeyance.
**Brian Boru** made eyecatching headway from over two furlongs down. He went second a furlong out and kept on strongly without ever looking likely to trouble the winner. He is likely to go to Melbourne to fly the Ballydoyle flag for the first time in the Cup. He is a kilo below Vinnie Roe in the Flemington weights.
**First Charter** took over early in the straight but was readily outpaced when headed by the winner. He kept on under pressure but was not happy in the ground.
**Dubai Success** put in a short-lived effort before the two-furlong marker which petered away quickly.
**Alcazar(IRE)** is feeling his years and could only stay on at the one pace, but he could still be a Prix Royal-Oak possibility.
**Two Miles West(IRE)** engendered market support but made little impression after turning for home.
**Media Puzzle(USA)** had an easy time of it, staying on in his own time over the last quarter mile without being bustled unduly.
**Orange Touch(GER)** rather surprisingly adopted front running tactics. Headed turning for home, he was soon struggling.
**Jagger** never promised at any stage and trailed in.

## 5500 LONGCHAMP (R-H)

Saturday, September 18

**OFFICIAL GOING: Good to soft**

### 5666a PRIX DES CHENES (GROUP 3) (C&G) 1m

1:15 (1:16) 2-Y-0 **£25,704** (£10,282; £7,711; £5,141)

RPR

1 **Helios Quercus (FR)**[39] 2-9-2 ........ ARoussel 1 107
(CDiard, France) *in touch disputing 4th straight, pushed along & headway to challenge 1 1/2f out, led just inside final f, ran on gamely*

2 *snk* **Musketier (GER)**[25] 2-9-2 ........ TThulliez 3 107
(PBary, France) *held up, disputing 6th straight, ran on from over 1f out, went 2nd close home, nearest at finish* 1

3 *nk* **Vatori (FR)**[49] 2-9-2 ........ SPasquier 7 106
(PDemercastel, France) *in touch, disputing 6th straight, effort & ran on from 1 1/2f out, stayed on*

4 *snk* **Capable Guest (IRE)**[7] 5469 2-9-2 ........ SHitchcott 6 106
(MRChannon) *pushed along before halfway, headway approaching straight, 3rd straight, driven to lead over 1f out to just ins fnl f, stay*

5 *3* **King Kasyapa (IRE)**[46] 2-9-2 ........ CSoumillon 5 99
(AFabre, France) *raced in last, disputing 4th straight, never a threat* 2

6 *3* **Le Reveur**[18] 2-9-2 ........ OPeslier 2 92
(MmeCHead-Maarek, France) *led after 1f to over 1f out, weakened* 3

7 *6* **Hypnotic**[14] 5313 2-9-2 ........ J-BEyquem 4 79
(SirMarkPrescott) *led 1f, 2nd til under pressure & slightly hampered entering straight, soon weakened*

1m 40.6s **Going Correction** +0.125s/f (Good) **7 Ran SP% 131.5**
Speed ratings: **109,108,108,108,105 102,96.**
**Owner** T Maudet **Bred** D Chassagneux **Trained** France

**NOTEBOOK**
**Helios Quercus(FR)**, an experienced and consistent provincial colt, deserved this Group success and he is certainly a force to be reckoned with over this distance. Having been settled in third place early on, he went to the head of affairs one furlong out and then stayed on bravely to hold the favourite. He will now be upped again in class and go for the Criterium International at Saint-Cloud.
**Musketier(GER)** still lacks experience and was not completely at ease at the bottom of the descent, where he still had plenty to do. He made a lot of progress in the final furlong and a half to finish best of all. A Group race should come his way before the end of the season.
**Vatori(FR)** was outpaced early in the straight and then came to join the leaders at the furlong marker. He then fought on gamely to the line.
**Capable Guest(IRE)** came with a promising run on the outside to take the lead early in the straight. He then crossed to the far rail and stuck to his guns throughout the closing stages.
**Hypnotic** in second position for much of this race, struggled once things warmed up in the straight. The jockey felt he did not settle and had a breathing problem on this occasion, and he certainly ran well below his best form.

### 5667a PRIX DU PRINCE D'ORANGE (GROUP 3) 1m 2f

2:20 (2:19) 3-Y-0 **£25,704** (£10,282; £7,711; £5,141)

RPR

1 **Delfos (IRE)**[28] 4965 3-9-0 ........ MBlancpain 4 113
(CLaffon-Parias, France) *raced in 2nd, challenged over 1f out, joined leader approaching final f, led just inside final f, ran on well* 2

2 *1 1/2* **Apsis**[340] 5569 3-8-12 ........ CSoumillon 2 108
(AFabre, France) *prominent, 4th on rail straight, effort in centre over 1f out, finished well final f, nearest at finish* 1

3 *1 1/2* **Lyonels Glory**[20] 5168 3-9-0 ........ C-PLemaire 9 108
(USuter, Germany) *led to just inside final furlong, kept on*

4 *1/2* **Dalicia (GER)**[78] 3504 3-8-9 ........ ABoschert 1 102
(PRau, Germany) *mid-division, disputing 5th straight, ridden & ran on from 1 1/2f out to go 4th inside final f*

5 *1 1/2* **Green Noon (FR)**[25] 5032 3-8-9 ........ SDrowne 7 99
(CLerner, France) *prominent, 3rd straight, pushed along 1 1/2f out, no extra inside final f*

6 *2 1/2* **Artiste Royal (IRE)**[28] 4965 3-8-12 ........(b) OPeslier 5 98
(ELellouche, France) *held up, 7th straight, never dangerous*

7 *3* **Ershaad (USA)**[20] 5169 3-8-12 ........ TGillet 8 92
(JEHammond, France) *held up in rear, disputing last & pushed along straight, no impression* 3

8 *nk* **Trinity Joy**[25] 5032 3-8-9 ........(b) TJarnet 3 89
(RGibson, France) *mid-division, disputing 5th straight, effort 1 1/2f out, soon one pace*

9 *8* **Islero Noir (FR)**[28] 4965 3-8-12 ........ SPasquier 6 77
(YDeNicolay, France) *mid-division, lost place & disputing last straight, never able to challenge*

2m 9.40s **Going Correction** +0.45s/f (Yiel) **9 Ran SP% 122.5**
Speed ratings: **113,111,110,110,109 107,104,104,97.**
**Owner** L Marinopoulos **Bred** Stilvi Compania Financiera S A **Trained** France

**NOTEBOOK**
**Delfos(IRE)** had a perfect run. Second early on, he took control just before the furlong marker and was not extended to win his second Group race of the season. Ten furlongs seems to be his ideal distance, and if he runs again this season it will be in the Hollywood Derby. The colt will stay in training as a four-year-old.
**Apsis**, considering he has been off the track for 11 months, put up a good show. He was not given a hard time and raced in fourth place before making his effort halfway up the straight. He hung a little left in the latter stages but never threatened the winner. This outing will have done the power of good and he has been entered in both the Arc and Champion Stakes.
**Lyonels Glory** tried to make all the running and kept up the good work until the furlong marker. He then stayed on one paced in the closing stages.
**Dalicia(GER)** was putting in her best work at the finish. She had been towards the tail of the field early on but, could not quite get to third place.

### 5668a PRIX DU PIN (GROUP 3) 7f

3:00 (3:02) 3-Y-0+ **£25,704** (£10,282; £7,711; £5,141)

RPR

1 **Comete (FR)**[100] 5-8-12 ........ DBonilla 1 108
(MCesandri, France) *in touch, disputing 5th on inside straight, headway to chase leader 2f out, ridden to lead 1 1/2f out, ridden out*

2 *2* **Puppeteer**[20] 5171 4-9-5 ........ CSoumillon 11 110
(ADeRoyer-Dupre, France) *held up, disputing last straight, headway on outside from over 1 1/2f out, went 2nd inside final f, ran on* 3

3 *hd* **Keltos (FR)**[20] 5169 6-9-1 ........ MBlancpain 4 105
(CLaffon-Parias, France) *held up, good headway from 2f out, disputed 2nd fnl f, no extra when slightly short of room close home, fin 4th, hd, placed* 1

4 *hd* **Millennium Force**[14] 5291 6-9-1 ........ SHitchcott 8 105
(MRChannon) *in touch, 4th straight, led 2 1/2f out, headed 1 1/2f out, kept on under pressure, went right close home, fin 3rd, 2l & hd,*

5 *1* **Autumn Glory (IRE)**[20] 5169 4-9-5 ........ SDrowne 6 106
(GWragg) *prominent, disputing 5th straight, pushed along 2f out, ran on steadily but never challenged leaders*

6 *nk* **Ashkawar (IRE)**[100] 5-9-1 ........ DBoeuf 10 101
(ELibaud, France) *prominent, disputing 2nd straight, pressed leader 2 1/2f out, ridden & no extra from 1 1/2f out*

7 *1/2* **Night Chapter**[20] 5171 3-8-12 ........ C-PLemaire 2 100
(MmeCHead-Maarek, France) *mid-division, 8th straight, kept on one pace without threatening*

8 *1 1/2* **Almond Mousse (FR)**[20] 5169 5-8-12 ........ SMaillot 3 93
(RobertCollet, France) *prominent, disputing 2nd straight, pushed along over 2f out & lost place, one pace*

9 *2 1/2* **Ventalle (SPA)**[100] 4-9-1 ........ MBorregoGarcia-Penuelas 7 89
(ASanchez, Spain) *held up, never a factor*

10 *1* **Dobby Road (FR)**[13] 5333 5-9-1 ........ FSpanu 5 87
(MlleVDissaux, France) *mid-division, 7th straight, one pace from 2f out*

11 **Sunday Doubt (USA)**[83] 3361 3-8-12 ........ OPeslier 9 87
(MmeCHead-Maarek, France) *held up, 10th on outside straight, effort over 2f out, no impression* 2

12 **She Breeze**[140] 1776 4-8-12 ........ TThulliez 12 84
(VCaruso, Italy) *led to 2 1/2f out*

1m 20.1s **Going Correction** -0.075s/f (Good)
**WFA** 3 from 4yo+ 3lb **12 Ran SP% 122.1**
Speed ratings: **113,110,110,110,109 108,108,106,103,102 102,102.**
**Owner** Mme J-C Bouret **Bred** Jean-Claude Bouret **Trained** Italy

**NOTEBOOK**
**Comete(FR)** this Lyon-trained mare was running in a Group race for the first time and she had previously lifted a handicap. Given a fine ride, she was second until making a forward move running into the final furlong. Once in control she went on to win with plenty in hand. She could be supplemented into the Prix de la Foret and if not will be retired to stud.
**Puppeteer** held up early on came with a strong late run from one and a half out and pinched second place close home. It was a decent effort considering the weights. The colt has been sold and will now continue his career in the United States.
**Keltos(FR)** had an awful lot to do at the entrance to the straight. He made his run up the far rail and was slightly hampered when making his challenge, so was promoted into third position. This ex-stallion is still showing good form on the racecourse.
**Millennium Force**, tucked in behind the leader, he went to the head of affairs two out but could do nothing when the winner made her challenge. He lost second place close home and was then demoted for interfering with Keltos. Connections felt he might have hit the front a little too soon.
**Autumn Glory(IRE)**, never far from the leaders, was one paced for the last furlong and a half. Compared with Deauville, the ground was not in his favour on this occasion, and he now goes for the Premio Vittorio di Capua in Milan next month.

## 4985 HAMILTON (R-H)

Sunday, September 19

**OFFICIAL GOING: Soft (good to soft in places)**

### 5669 BELLWAY HOMES MAIDEN STKS 1m 65y

2:25 (2:26) (D2) 2-Y-0 **£5,863** (£1,804; £902; £451) **Stalls** High

Form RPR

224 1 **Love Palace (IRE)**[18] 5228 2-9-0 85 ........ JFanning 5 95
(MJohnston) *mde all: drew clr fr 1/2-way: pushed out* **8/13**[1]

4 2 *9* **Kames Park (IRE)**[16] 5264 2-9-0 ........ RWinston 4 77
(ISemple) *hld up: hdwy to chse wnr over 2f out: kpt on: no imp* **13/2**[3]

42 3 *3 1/2* **Haiban**[29] 4930 2-9-0 ........ PHanagan 2 70
(GAButler) *keen early: prom tl outpcd fr over 2f out* **11/2**[2]

46 4 *4* **Boo**[14] 5319 2-9-0 ........ DarrenWilliams 1 62
(KRBurke) *prom: chsd wnr over 3f to over 2f out: sn btn* **12/1**

2 5 *5* **Alani (IRE)**[20] 5186 2-8-9 ........ MFenton 3 47
(JeddO'Keeffe) *chsd wnr to over 3f out: edgd rt and sn btn* **14/1**

0 6 *8* **Imperioli**[42] 4567 2-9-0 ........ GGibbons 6 36
(PABlockley) *in tch: outpcd 1/2-way: sn btn* **66/1**

7 *3/4* **Peter Roughley (IRE)** 2-9-0 ........ PBradley 7 35
(ABerry) *unruly bef s: bhd: struggling fr 1/2-way* **100/1**

1m 51.47s (2.17) **Going Correction** +0.20s/f (Good) **7 Ran SP% 107.5**
Speed ratings: **97,88,84,80,75 67,66**CSF £4.33 TOTE £1.50: £1.10, £2.50; EX 5.00.
**Owner** M Doyle **Bred** Horse Breeding Company **Trained** Middleham Moor, N Yorks

**FOCUS**
A very weak maiden with little strength in depth behind the winner who could be rated higher.

**NOTEBOOK**
**Love Palace(IRE)**, back up in trip, was faced with by far his easiest task to date and did the job nicely. His current rating of 85 should not change too much, if at all, and he should not be opposed lightly if going down the nursery route.
**Kames Park(IRE)** did not improve at all on his debut running and still looked badly in need of the experience. He did not have the pace to ever pose a threat to the eventual winner, and carried his head high under pressure in the closing stages. All he did was stay and is probably best watched until he goes handicapping over further
**Haiban** eight lengths behind Love Palace on his debut over this course and distance, was very one paced and beaten even further this time. He should find things easier now he is qualified for a mark.
**Boo** had shown ability in two runs over six furlongs, but was below form over this testing mile. It is hard to know quite why he was stepped up significantly in trip, but this run does qualify him for a handicap mark.
**Alani(IRE)**, runner-up in an ordinary and unreliable maiden at Newcastle on his debut, ran nowhere near that form and looks best watched for the time being.

### 5670 GALA CASINOS MERCHANT CITY 2-Y-O FINAL (NURSERY) (FOR THE LORD HAMILTON OF DALZELL TROPHY) 6f 5y

2:55 (2:58) (B1) 2-Y-0 **£12,087** (£4,584; £2,292; £1,042) **Stalls** High

Form RPR

3221 1 **Windy Prospect**[31] 4878 2-9-6 89 ........ MFenton 15 99
(PABlockley) *mde virtully all: edgd lft wl ins fnl f: hld on wl* **9/2**[1]

2150 2 *shd* **Gifted Gamble**[6] 5515 2-8-11 80 ........ RWinston 5 90
(KARyan) *midfield: hdwy on outside 2f out: r.o wl fnl f: jst hld* **16/1**

5431 **3** 1 **Profit's Reality (IRE)**[8] [5476] 2-8-12 **81**.............................. GGibbons 11 88
(PABlockley) *in tch: rdn 1/2-way: rallied over 1f out: keeping on one pce whn n.m.r wl ins fnl f* **5/1**[2]

412 **4** 2½ **Hansomelle (IRE)**[17] [5234] 2-8-6 **75**.............................. DaleGibson 6 74
(BMactaggart) *midfield: effrt over 2f out: edgd rt over 1f out: no imp ins fnl f* **9/1**

3002 **5** 5 **Mceldowney**[8] [5476] 2-8-7 **76**.............................. JFanning 9 60
(MJohnston) *prom: rdn 1/2-way: outpcd fr 2f out* **7/1**[3]

4520 **6** ½ **Rainbow Iris**[9] [5434] 2-7-12 **70**.............................. FPFerris(3) 3 53
(BSmart) *prom: rdn 1/2-way: no imp whn hmpd over 1f out: sn btn* **16/1**

1616 **7** ½ **Tequila Sheila (IRE)**[31] [4876] 2-9-1 **84**.............................. DarrenWilliams 2 65
(KRBurke) *hld up: rdn and edgd rt over 2f out: n.d* **20/1**

0500 **8** 1¾ **Kristikhab (IRE)**[17] [5234] 2-7-13 **68** oh14 ow1.............................. PFessey 13 44
(ABerry) *disp ld to 2f out: sn rdn and btn* **66/1**

3400 **9** 1¼ **Monashee Prince (IRE)**[22] [5119] 2-8-9 **78**.............................. SSanders 7 50
(JRBest) *towards rr: drvn over 3f out: nt pce to chal* **20/1**

420 **10** 9 **Invertiel (USA)**[30] [4900] 2-8-11 **80**.............................. PHanagan 14 25
(ISemple) *dwlt: sn midfield: rdn and wknd fr over 2f out* **16/1**

4560 **11** shd **Ochil Hills Dancer (IRE)**[12] [5363] 2-7-5 **67** oh8..........(t) DFentiman(7) 4 12
(ACrook) *sn bhd: nvr on terms* **66/1**

0210 **12** 1 **Make Us Flush**[19] [5212] 2-8-5 **74**.............................. FNorton 12 16
(ABerry) *blkd s: sn outpcd: no ch fr 1/2-way* **12/1**

1050 **13** ¾ **No Commission (IRE)**[17] [5234] 2-8-2 **71**.............................. RFfrench 10 11
(RFFisher) *sn bhd: struggling after 2f* **25/1**

2240 **14** 5 **Extra Mark**[12] [5377] 2-8-3 **72**.............................. ANicholls 8 —
(JRBest) *hung rt thrght: sn wl bhd* **16/1**

1m 13.91s (0.81) **Going Correction** +0.20s/f (Good) **14** Ran SP% **104.9**
Speed ratings: **102,101,100,97,90 89,89,86,85,73 73,71,70,64**CSF £55.26 CT £278.03 TOTE £4.90: £1.70, £6.30, £3.00; EX 73.80 Trifecta £732.40 Pool of £50,237.95 - 48.70 winning units..

**Owner** bellhouseracing.com **Bred** T J Cooper **Trained** Southwell, Notts
■ Stewards Enquiry : F P Ferris one-day ban: failed to keep straight stalls (Oct 4)
Darren Williams one-day ban: failed to keep straight stalls (Oct 4)

**FOCUS**
A competitive race with good prizemoney, a reasonable contest and reliable enough given they went a strong pace and the first three pulled clear.

**NOTEBOOK**
**Windy Prospect**, 5lb higher than when winning an ordinary nursery over seven furlongs on Fibresand on previous start, made this a real test returned to turf and dropped in trip, and just lasted home. He is getting better and could well defy another rise in the weights.
**Gifted Gamble** had not progressed since winning his maiden, but returned to his best with a fine effort. He would have won in another stride and, a tough sort, he should continue to go well in similar company for the remainder of the season.
**Profit's Reality(IRE)**, a stablemate of the winner, would have appreciated the strong pace given that he was dropping back from seven furlongs, but he could just never quite get there. A step back up in trip should suit.
**Hansomelle(IRE)** had never previously raced on ground softer than good, and posted no more than a creditable performance.
**Mceldowney**, racing on soft ground for the first time, did not appear suited by this drop back in trip.
**Invertiel(USA)** *Official explanation: jockey said colt hung left throughout*
**Extra Mark** *Official explanation: jockey said gelding hung right-handed throughout*

## 5671 BETFAIR.COM FLOWER OF SCOTLAND STKS (LISTED RACE) (F&M) 5f 4y
3:30 (3:30) (A1) 3-Y-0+ **£20,300** (£7,700; £3,850; £1,750) **Stalls** High

Form RPR

1111 **1** **Kind (IRE)**[65] [3914] 3-8-11 89.............................. RHughes 5 91+
(RCharlton) *trckd ldrs gng wl: shkn up and squeezed through to ld wl ins fnl f: comf* **8/1**

2360 **2** ½ **Autumn Pearl**[52] [4269] 3-8-11 97.............................. SSanders 10 89
(MAJarvis) *mde most to wl ins fnl f: kpt on* **5/1**[2]

2004 **3** ¾ **Frascati**[8] [5458] 4-8-12 76.............................. FLynch 2 87
(ABerry) *prom: effrt and edgd rt over 1f out: ev ch ins last: flashed tail and hld towards fin* **100/1**

4144 **4** 1¼ **Enchantment**[10] [5418] 3-8-11 100.............................. RLMoore 11 83
(JMBradley) *w ldr tl rdn and nt qckn ins fnl f* **7/2**[1]

0321 **5** 1½ **Simianna**[8] [5454] 5-9-2 97..............................(p) RWinston 7 82
(ABerry) *bhd: rdn 1/2-way: hdwy over 1f out: nrst fin* **6/1**[3]

3616 **6** 1 **Forever Phoenix**[11] [5393] 4-8-12 98.............................. EAhern 1 75
(RMHCowell) *hld up: effrt 2f out: no imp fnl f* **5/1**[2]

1300 **7** ¾ **Baron Rhodes**[22] [5105] 3-8-11 80.............................. TEaves 8 72
(JSWainwright) *cl up tl rdn and wknd 1f out* **100/1**

004 **8** 3 **Enchanted**[10] [5416] 5-8-12 92.............................. ACulhane 4 62
(NACallaghan) *bhd and sn rdn along: nvr rchd ldrs* **20/1**

1-00 **9** ½ **Smart Hostess**[18] [5224] 5-8-12 91.............................. PHanagan 3 61
(JJQuinn) *midfield: rdn over 2f out: wknd over 1f out* **20/1**

-506 **10** nk **Sister Moonshine (FR)**[14] [5333] 3-8-11 ..............................(b) JFanning 6 60
(RPritchard-Gordon, France) *prom tl rdn and wknd over 1f out: stmbld and fell after fin* **14/1**

3041 **11** 2 **Dragon Flyer (IRE)**[12] [5372] 5-8-12 98.............................. FNorton 9 53
(MQuinn) *towards rr: effrt u.p over 2f out: btn over 1f out* **15/2**

60.80 secs (-0.46) **Going Correction** +0.20s/f (Good)
**WFA** 3 from 4yo+ 1lb **11** Ran SP% **110.9**
Speed ratings: **111,110,109,107,104 103,101,97,96,95 92**CSF £43.38 TOTE £8.10: £2.00, £1.90, £5.80; EX 58.60.
**Owner** K Abdulla **Bred** Juddmonte Farms **Trained** Beckhampton, Wilts

**FOCUS**
A Listed race to treat with caution as, despite the fact the principals appeared to pretty much run their races, the third horse is rated just 76. At least the time was fair for the type of race.

**NOTEBOOK**
**Kind(IRE)**, highly progressive in lesser events earlier in the year, was coming back from a 65-day break. She had never previously run over the minimum trip but the good pace helped her settle and, showing plenty of willingness to take a tight gap when making her move, she picked up nicely. This was a significant boost to her paddock value, but she is improving all the time and there will be plenty more opportunities for her on the track.
**Autumn Pearl**, racing for the first time in 52 days, loved the testing ground and can have no excuses.
**Frascati**, rated just 76 and having her 40th start, really does hold the form down. Given that she is sure to take a significant rise in the weights for this, she would have to be of interest in a handicap before she is reassessed, but may be best watched to see if she can repeat this.
**Enchantment** is at her best when able to dominate, but again she was ever so slightly restrained.
**Simianna**, successful in this grade over six furlongs at Chester on her previous start, was not ideally suited by this drop in trip, but the ground suited and she ran respectably.
**Forever Phoenix**, unlucky in the Portland Handicap on her previous start, was unable to repeat that returned to Listed company.

## 5672 SUPER SUNDAY "PREMIER" CLAIMING STKS 1m 1f 36y
4:05 (4:07) (D2) 3-4-Y-0 **£8,248** (£2,538; £1,269; £634) **Stalls** High

Form RPR

2440 **1** **Lauro**[16] [5265] 4-8-6 72.............................. RWinston 2 81
(MissJACamacho) *in tch: effrt over 2f out: led over 1f out: pushed clr* **2/1**[1]

3321 **2** 5 **Magic Sting**[16] [5258] 3-8-10 75.............................. JMackay 5 80
(MLWBell) *keen: prom: effrt over 2f out: kpt on fnl f: no ch w wnr* **2/1**[1]

-001 **3** ¾ **Familiar Affair**[19] [5210] 3-8-11 78.............................. RLMoore 8 79
(TDBarron) *keen: cl up: led over 2f to over 1f out: outpcd ins fnl f* **3/1**[2]

5620 **4** 3½ **Rabitatit (IRE)**[10] [5410] 3-7-6 60..............................(p) NataliaGemelova(7) 4 60
(JGMO'Shea) *led to over 2f out: wknd over 1f out* **12/1**

0640 **5** 9 **Iskander**[16] [5275] 3-8-8 72..............................(b) JCarroll 1 51
(KARyan) *hld up: rdn 3f out: nvr able to chal* **11/1**[3]

P140 **6** 22 **Banana Grove (IRE)**[19] [5210] 3-8-8 68.............................. FLynch 3 7
(ABerry) *hld up in tch: rdn over 3f out: sn btn* **33/1**

3146 **7** 1½ **On Every Street**[14] [5315] 3-9-4 77..............................(b) RFfrench 7 14
(RBastiman) *keen: cl up tl wknd fr 3f out* **33/1**

0060 **8** hd **Devine Light (IRE)**[52] [4260] 4-8-4 50..............................(p) PHanagan 9 —
(BMactaggart) *hld up in tch: rdn 4f out: sn btn* **66/1**

2m 3.95s (4.35) **Going Correction** +0.50s/f (Yiel)
**WFA** 3 from 4yo 5lb **8** Ran SP% **115.1**
Speed ratings: **100,95,94,91,83 64,62,62**CSF £6.09 TOTE £2.70: £1.10, £1.20, £1.60; EX 6.60.
**Owner** Shangri-La Racing Club **Bred** Mrs S Camacho **Trained** Norton, N Yorks

**FOCUS**
A reasonable claimer run at no more than an ordinary pace, but sound form on paper.

**NOTEBOOK**
**Lauro** had never previously won beyond a mile or raced on ground this soft, but she was best off at the weights and took advantage in good style, coping well with the conditions.
**Magic Sting**, 6lb wrong at the weights with the eventual winner, should not have been inconvenienced by the conditions and can have no real excuse.
**Familiar Affair**, claimed out of Bryan Smart's yard for £20,000 after winning a claimer on his previous start, did not find as much as had looked likely and was not at his best. This ground may have been too soft for him.
**Rabitatit(IRE)** gained both her previous wins on fast ground and did not run to form under these very different conditions in first-time cheekpieces.
**Iskander** was beaten a long way and looked to hate the ground.
**Banana Grove(IRE)** *Official explanation: jockey said gelding had no more to give*
**On Every Street** *Official explanation: jockey said gelding had no more to give*
**Devine Light(IRE)** *Official explanation: jockey said filly had no more to give*

## 5673 HAMILTON PARK CLASSIFIED STKS 1m 65y
4:40 (4:45) (C2) 3-Y-0+ **£10,166** (£3,128; £1,564; £782) **Stalls** High

Form RPR

21-3 **1** **Pedrillo**[15] [5294] 3-8-12 87.............................. SSanders 7 108+
(SirMarkPrescott) *trckd ldrs: shuffled bk 3f out: smooth hdwy over 2f out: led ins fnl f: pushed out: readily* **8/11**[1]

1312 **2** 5 **Mrs Moh (IRE)**[8] [5474] 3-8-8 86.............................. DAllan 2 91
(TDEasterby) *cl up: led over 2f out to ins last: no ch w wnr* **3/1**[2]

6140 **3** 3 **Bessemer (JPN)**[2] [5607] 3-8-10 84.............................. RWinston 4 87
(ISemple) *keen: sn cl up: led over 3f to over 2f out: wknd over 1f out* **7/1**[3]

6404 **4** 6 **Stoic Leader (IRE)**[3] [5590] 4-9-0 78.............................. PHanagan 1 75
(RFFisher) *hld up in tch: rdn 3f out: edgd rt and outpcd fr 2f out* **10/1**

**5** 9 **King Summerland**[95] 7-9-0 50.............................. RFfrench 3 57?
(BMactaggart) *set stdy pce to over 3f out: sn btn* **150/1**

4460 **6** 3½ **Phoenix Nights (IRE)**[6] [5514] 4-8-9 52.............................. PPMathers(5) 6 50
(ABerry) *hld up in tch: rdn 3f out: sn btn* **150/1**

1m 51.77s (2.47) **Going Correction** +0.50s/f (Yiel)
**WFA** 3 from 4yo+ 4lb **6** Ran SP% **105.8**
Speed ratings: **107,102,99,93,84 80**CSF £2.65 TOTE £1.50: £1.10, £1.90; EX 2.30.
**Owner** Hesmonds Stud **Bred** Hesmonds Stud Ltd **Trained** Newmarket, Suffolk

**FOCUS**
Not a very competitive classified event, but a taking effort from Pedrillo and the runner-up provides a line to the form.

**NOTEBOOK**
**Pedrillo** ◆ did not have things go his way and dropped towards the rear of the small field three out, but he was good enough to overcome the minor trouble and eventually won nicely, with his rider always oozing confidence. This was a good effort and he is the one to beat if he gets in the Cambridgeshire, for which he has picked up a 5lb penalty.
**Mrs Moh(IRE)** has been progressing well in recent runs, winning two of her last four starts. Encountering her softest ground to date, she did little wrong but was no match for the evidently well-handicapped winner.
**Bessemer(JPN)**, dropped back from ten furlongs, did not run badly but has yet to really prove his effectiveness on this sort of ground.
**Stoic Leader(IRE)** has had a busy season and was not at his best.
**King Summerland** was out of his depth.
**Phoenix Nights(IRE)** was also out of his depth.

## 5674 SCOTTISH RACING H'CAP 6f 5y
5:10 (5:15) (E3) (0-70,70) 3-Y-0 **£5,135** (£1,580; £790; £395) **Stalls** High

Form RPR

0400 **1** **Pure Imagination (IRE)**[6] [5512] 3-8-9 **58**.............................. RLMoore 8 71+
(JMBradley) *bhd and sn rdn along: hdwy to ld appr fnl f: edgd rt: hld on wl* **20/1**

0540 **2** 2½ **Thornaby Green**[24] [5063] 3-8-8 **62**.............................. PMakin(5) 11 67
(TDBarron) *cl up: rdn 1/2-way: rallied ins fnl f: nt rch wnr* **11/2**[3]

5651 **3** 1 **Mecca's Mate**[23] [5101] 3-8-8 **57**.............................. LEnstone 16 59
(DWBarker) *keen: trckd ldrs: led 2f out: hdd appr fnl f: no ex ins last* **5/1**[2]

1210 **4** 1½ **Trojan Flight**[3] [5579] 3-9-4 **67**.............................. RWinston 9 65+
(MrsJRRamsden) *midfield: effrt over 2f out: ch over 1f out: outpcd ins fnl f* **15/8**[1]

0050 **5** 1½ **Piccolo Prince**[20] [5193] 3-9-3 **66**.............................. EAhern 5 59
(EJAlston) *bhd tl styd on fr over 1f out: nrst fin* **14/1**

0600 **6** 1 **Baylaw Star**[8] [5473] 3-8-12 **61**.............................. DMernagh 2 51
(KARyan) *racd stands side: prom: hung to centre and ch 2f out: outpcd over 1f out* **25/1**

5150 **7** 5 **Best Desert (IRE)**[21] [5156] 3-9-1 **64**.............................. GGibbons 6 39
(JRBest) *dwlt: bhd tl styd on fnl f: nrst fin* **14/1**

0030 **8** hd **Sweet Cando (IRE)**[3] [5579] 3-8-10 **59**..............................(p) SSanders 12 33
(MissLAPerratt) *towards rr: rdn 1/2-way: n.d* **10/1**

0200 **9** 1¼ **Mind Alert**[50] [4340] 3-9-1 **64**..............................(b[1]) DAllan 14 35
(TDEasterby) *mde most to 2f out: sn btn* **20/1**

6000 **10** 6 **Vademecum**[17] [5244] 3-9-7 **70**.............................. FLynch 15 23
(BSmart) *w ldrs to over 1f out: sn btn* **16/1**

4440 **11** ¾ **Kamenka**[20] [5193] 3-9-4 **67**.............................. PHanagan 3 17
(RAFahey) *swtchd to far side sn after s: midfield: hung rt 1/2-way: sn btn* **16/1**

1004 **12** *1 1/2* **Obe Bold (IRE)**[3] 5588 3-9-4 **67**....(t) FNorton 13 13
(ABerry) *dwlt: a bhd* **20/1**

4410 **13** *2* **Troodos Jet**[22] 5126 3-8-10 **64**.... PPMathers(5) 1 4
(ABerry) *chsd stands side ldr: outpcd fr 1/2-way* **50/1**

00-0 **14** *10* **Solar Prince (IRE)**[25] 5048 3-8-4 **56** oh8.... FPFerris(3) 10 —
(HAlexander) *in tch to over 2f out: sn rdn and btn* **100/1**

-000 **15** *3* **Louis Prima**[13] 5342 3-8-7 **56** oh26.... RFfrench 4 —
(MissLAPerratt) *a bhd* **100/1**

1m 15.53s (2.43) **Going Correction** +0.50s/f (Yiel) **15** Ran SP% **123.1**
Speed ratings: **103,99,98,96,94 93,86,86,84,76 75,73,70,57,53**CSF £122.16 CT £671.26 TOTE £24.60: £5.50, £1.90, £2.10; EX 218.20 Place 6 £27.91, Place 5 £21.81.
**Owner** Dab Hand Racing **Bred** Azienda Agricola Valle Falcone Srl **Trained** Sedbury, Gloucs

**FOCUS**
Just a moderate sprint handicap in which the runner-up sets the standard and the winner appears progressive.

**NOTEBOOK**
**Pure Imagination(IRE)**, 6lb lower than when first running in a handicap, got off the mark at the ninth attempt under conditions that clearly suit well. Now he has got his head in front, he is just the type to go in again. *Official explanation: trainer said, regarding the improved form shown, gelding appreciated the softer ground*
**Thornaby Green** gained both his previous wins on fast ground, but this surface did not appear to inconvenience him too much and he ran well off a mark just 1lb higher than when last successful.
**Mecca's Mate**, 2lb higher than getting off the mark over five furlongs at Thirsk, ran respectably but may not have been entirely suited by this step up in trip.
**Trojan Flight** just lacked the pace to pose a serious threat and this ground could have been soft enough.
**Piccolo Prince** came from an unpromising position to take fifth and ran creditably in the circumstances.
**Vademecum** *Official explanation: jockey said gelding was unsuited by the ground*
T/Jkpt: Not won. T/Plt: £23.80 to a £1 stake. Pool: £54,715.75. 1,671.80 winning tickets. T/Qpdt: £8.80 to a £1 stake. Pool: £2,461.60. 205.30 winning tickets. RY

5675 - 5677a (Foreign Racing) - See Raceform Interactive

# 5659 CURRAGH (R-H)

Sunday, September 19

**OFFICIAL GOING: Good (yielding in straight)**

## 5678a DUNNES STORES NATIONAL STKS (GROUP 1) (ENTIRE COLTS & FILLIES) 7f

3:45 (3:45) 2-Y-O **£124,929** (£40,422; £19,295; £6,619)

RPR

**1** **Dubawi (IRE)**[73] 3672 2-9-0 .... LDettori 2 122+
(SaeedBinSuroor) *settled 2nd: led travelling best under 2f out: rdn and qcknd clr fr over 1f out: impressive* **8/13[1]**

**2** *3* **Berenson (IRE)**[29] 4955 2-9-0 .... WMLordan 1 114
(TStack, Ire) *settled 5th: 4th 1/2-way: 3rd and rdn over 2f out: kpt on u.p to mod 2nd ins fnl f* **12/1**

**3** *1 1/2* **Russian Blue (IRE)**[28] 4981 2-9-0 113.... JPSpencer 3 111
(APO'Brien, Ire) *led: hdd under 2f out: sn rdn and one pce: no ex ins fnl f* **5/1[3]**

**4** *3* **Democratic Deficit (IRE)**[29] 4959 2-9-0 111.... KJManning 6 103
(JSBolger, Ire) *chsd ldrs: 3rd 1/2-way: 4th 2f out: one pce* **9/2[2]**

**5** *2 1/2* **In Excelsis (USA)**[92] 3071 2-9-0 .... JPMurtagh 5 97
(APO'Brien, Ire) *s.i.s and hld up in rr: prog into mod 5th 1 1/2f out: sn no ex* **16/1**

**6** *nk* **Elusive Double (IRE)**[29] 4959 2-9-0 105.... PJSmullen 4 96
(DKWeld, Ire) *3rd early: lost pl after 1/2-way: no imp fr over 2f out* **12/1**

**7** *shd* **Rowan Tree**[53] 4227 2-9-0 100.... (b[1]) JAHeffernan 7 96
(APO'Brien, Ire) *hld up in 6th: rdn and no imp fr over 2f out* **16/1**

1m 24.8s **Going Correction** -0.025s/f (Good) **7** Ran SP% **123.9**
Speed ratings: **116,112,110,107,104 104,104**CSF £11.73 TOTE £1.80: £1.10, £2.90; DF 17.70.
**Owner** Godolphin **Bred** Darley **Trained** Newmarket, Suffolk

**FOCUS**
A highly-impressive display from Dubawi who, at this stage, is rated the best juvenile around.

**NOTEBOOK**
**Dubawi(IRE)**, a supplementay entry, retained his unbeaten record with a very classy performance, and though he edged left and then right once he got in front there was no intractability, just greenness. He achieved the highest juvenile RPR of the season so far and looks an outstanding prospect for next year, when he will make just as much appeal for the 2000 Guineas as the Derby.
**Berenson(IRE)** came through to take second without ever getting on terms with the winner. This was a fine effort from a colt having just his second race, and he looks a good prospect in his own right.
**Russian Blue(IRE)** was precocious earlier in the season but his front-running tactics were a bit of a surprise. Once headed by the winner he was quickly done. This might have been too far at this stage.
**Democratic Deficit(IRE)** proved totally incapable of confirming previous form with Russian Blue.
**In Excelsis(USA)** was struggling from halfway.
**Elusive Double(IRE)** was already struggling at halfway.
**Rowan Tree** played little part.

## 5679a IRISH NATIONAL STUD BLANDFORD STKS (GROUP 2) (F&M) 1m 2f

4:15 (4:17) 3-Y-O+ **£59,507** (£17,394; £8,239; £2,746)

RPR

**1** **Monturani (IRE)**[28] 4982 5-9-3 .... TEDurcan 13 111
(GWragg) *trckd ldrs: 4th 1/2-way: 2nd and chal ent st: led over 2f out: strly pressed fnl f: kpt on wl u.p* **12/1**

**2** *1/2* **Kinnaird (IRE)**[47] 4430 3-8-11 .... (t) KDarley 9 110
(PCHaslam) *prom: 3rd 1/2-way: 2nd and rdn 2f out: chal fnl f: kpt on wl* **10/1**

**3** *shd* **All Too Beautiful (IRE)**[63] 3968 3-8-11 109.... JPSpencer 2 110+
(APO'Brien, Ire) *towards rr: 10th appr st: hdwy 2f out: 4th 1 1/2f out: styd on wl ins fnl f* **11/2[3]**

**4** *2* **Red Bloom**[18] 5225 3-8-11 .... KFallon 3 106+
(SirMichaelStoute) *mid-div: 7th 1/2-way: rdn and outpcd ent st: 8th 1 1/2f out: 6th 1f out: styd on* **13/8[1]**

**5** *1 1/2* **Tropical Lady (IRE)**[35] 4786 4-9-3 110.... KJManning 12 103
(JSBolger, Ire) *hld up: 9th 1/2-way: hdwy into 4th early st: 3rd 1 1/2f out: no ex fnl f* **10/1**

**6** *3 1/2* **New Morning (IRE)**[39] 4640 3-8-11 .... PRobinson 10 97
(MAJarvis) *led: jnd 1/2-way: regained ld appr st: hdd over 2f out: sn no ex* **12/1**

**7** *2* **Livadiya (IRE)**[8] 5484 8-9-3 102.... JPMurtagh 4 93
(HRogers, Ire) *towards rr: prog on outer ent st: 6th 2f out: no ex fr over 1f out* **16/1**

**8** *2 1/2* **Leonor Fini (IRE)**[21] 5162 3-8-11 97.... DPMcDonogh 1 88
(KevinPrendergast, Ire) *s.i.s and bhd: rdn and one pce fr 4f out* **25/1**

**9** *nk* **Baraka (IRE)**[134] 1963 3-8-11 110.... JAHeffernan 8 87
(APO'Brien, Ire) *nvr a factor: one pce st* **8/1**

**10** *1 1/2* **Hazarista (IRE)**[32] 4859 3-8-11 112.... MJKinane 11 96+
(JohnMOxx, Ire) *chsd ldrs in 5th: wknd early st* **9/2[2]**

**11** *3 1/2* **Blue Reema (IRE)**[21] 5162 4-9-3 96.... (tp) TPO'Shea 6 78
(MHalford, Ire) *chsd ldrs in 6th: rdn over 4f out: sn wknd* **25/1**

**12** *6* **Cache Creek (IRE)**[21] 5162 6-9-3 107.... FMBerry 5 67
(PHughes, Ire) *a bhd* **12/1**

**13** *25* **Lucky (IRE)**[119] 2330 3-8-11 103.... PCosgrave 7 19
(APO'Brien, Ire) *cl up: disp ld 1/2-way: hdd & wknd appr st: eased fr 2f out* **20/1**

2m 5.40s **Going Correction** -0.025s/f (Good)
**WFA** 3 from 4yo+ 6lb **13** Ran SP% **142.4**
Speed ratings: **115,114,114,112,111 108,107,105,105,103 101,96,76**CSF £147.43 TOTE £41.60: £7.60, £3.80, £2.00; DF 328.00.
**Owner** Mrs R Philipps **Bred** Mrs Rebecca Philipps **Trained** Newmarket, Suffolk

**FOCUS**
A well-contested Group Two event that saw a welcome win for the genuine Monturani.

**NOTEBOOK**
**Monturani(IRE)**, who has been performing well in similar company all season, was very brave in front over the last two furlongs and deserved this first win for well over two years.
**Kinnaird(IRE)** had every chance over the last quarter mile but was continually denied by the winner.
**All Too Beautiful(IRE)** was given plenty to do for a filly with no stamina doubts. She stayed on strongly inside the last and different tactics might just have seen a different result.
**Red Bloom** was all at sea early in the straight and had no chance in the last furlong and a half. She stayed on again but too late.
**Tropical Lady(IRE)** looked very leg weary inside the last.
**New Morning(IRE)** cried enough when headed two furlongs down.
**Livadiya(IRE)** kept on late without ever getting on terms.
**Baraka(IRE)** was never in a position to threaten.
**Hazarista(IRE)** dropped out very tamely in the straight. *Official explanation: vet said filly was struck into from behind*

## 5680a ST. BERNARD BLENHEIM STKS (LISTED RACE) 6f

4:45 (4:45) 2-Y-O **£25,214** (£7,397; £3,524; £1,200)

RPR

**1** **Ad Valorem (USA)**[14] 5328 2-9-0 .... JPSpencer 5 108+
(APO'Brien, Ire) *settled 3rd: cl 2nd and chal under 2f out: led over 1f out: r.o wl* **9/4[1]**

**2** *1* **Indesatchel (IRE)**[14] 5322 2-9-0 109.... MJKinane 1 105
(DavidWachman, Ire) *trckd ldrs in 4th: swtchd rt 1 1/2f out: 3rd 1f out: kpt on* **9/4[1]**

**3** *1/2* **Cupid's Glory**[24] 5052 2-9-0 .... DPMcDonogh 4 104
(SirMarkPrescott) *cl up in 2nd: led under 2f out: sn strly pressed: hdd over 1f out: no ex ins fnl f* **5/2[2]**

**4** *4 1/2* **Belle Artiste (IRE)**[14] 5325 2-8-11 104.... (b) JAHeffernan 6 87
(JosephCrowley, Ire) *trckd ldrs in 5th: 4th and no imp fr 1 1/2f out: one pce* **8/1[3]**

**5** *3* **Man O World (IRE)**[84] 3352 2-9-4 99.... PJSmullen 3 85
(DKWeld, Ire) *hld up in rr: effrt and no imp fr 2f out* **12/1**

**6** *3 1/2* **L'Altro Mondo (IRE)**[14] 5322 2-9-0 102.... TPO'Shea 2 71
(MHalford, Ire) *led: rdn and hdd under 2f out: sn wknd* **12/1**

1m 13.9s **Going Correction** -0.025s/f (Good) **6** Ran SP% **116.6**
Speed ratings: **104,102,102,96,92 87**CSF £8.08 TOTE £2.50: £1.60, £2.00; DF 5.50.
**Owner** Mrs John Magnier **Bred** Calumet Farm **Trained** Ballydoyle, Co Tipperary

**FOCUS**
A decent display from the promising Ad Valorem and strong form for the grade.

**NOTEBOOK**
**Ad Valorem(USA)** travelled well throughout but took a while to get on top before quickening up nicely. The Middle Park is on the agenda, but he would prefer better ground than this.
**Indesatchel(IRE)** was not too keen on the softened ground but ran well in the circumstances and might better this effort.
**Cupid's Glory** was surprisingly well supported and flattered when leading under two furlongs down. He could not match the winner's pace when headed.
**Belle Artiste(IRE)** was comfortably held from a furlong and a half out.
**Man O World(IRE)** found this company too warm.
**L'Altro Mondo(IRE)** made the running but with no benefit to himself.

## 5681a IRISH BREEDERS FOAL LEVY STKS 6f 63y

5:15 (5:16) 2-Y-O **£75,246** (£29,394; £18,107; £10,582)

RPR

**1** **Slip Dance (IRE)**[14] 5325 2-8-10 103.... JFEgan 1 97+
(EamonTyrrell, Ire) *trckd ldrs: 5th 1/2-way: 3rd and hdwy 2f out: 2nd over 1f out: led ins fnl f: drew clr* **11/4[2]**

**2** *2* **All Night Dancer (IRE)**[39] 4657 2-8-4 81.... WMLordan 7 83
(DavidWachman, Ire) *a.p: led over 2f out: hdd ins fnl f: kpt on* **14/1**

**3** *3/4* **Makuti (IRE)**[15] 5311 2-8-4 .... NGMcCullagh 4 81
(MJGrassick, Ire) *2nd early: 3rd 1/2-way: 4th and outpcd over 1f out: kpt on u.p* **14/1**

**4** *1* **Miss Sally (IRE)**[22] 5137 2-8-1 .... TPO'Shea 10 75
(MHalford, Ire) *chsd ldrs in 7th: 5th and rdn over 1f out: kpt on* **14/1**

**5** *hd* **Tournedos (IRE)**[8] 5464 2-9-1 .... TEDurcan 8 89
(MRChannon) *trckd ldrs: impr into 2nd 2f out: 3rd u.p over 1f out: sn no ex* **11/8[1]**

**6** *shd* **Nova Tor (IRE)**[6] 5515 2-8-7 .... (p) PJSmullen 2 82+
(NPLittmoden) *chsd ldrs: 6th 1/2-way: swtchd rt 1f out: kpt on same pce* **14/1**

**7** *2* **Monashee Star (IRE)**[14] 5322 2-8-9 94.... FMBerry 6 76
(THogan, Ire) *led: rdn and hdd over 2f out: sn no ex* **6/1[3]**

**8** *1* **Imperial Brief (IRE)**[28] 4973 2-8-9 .... DPMcDonogh 3 74
(KevinPrendergast, Ire) *towards rr: rdn and no imp fr 2f out* **20/1**

**9** *1/2* **Sanfrancullinan (IRE)**[24] 5065 2-8-10 66.... MJKinane 5 73
(MHalford, Ire) *a towards rr* **20/1**

**10** *13* **Wavertree Warrior (IRE)**[39] 4649 2-8-12 .... J-PGuillambert 9 37
(NPLittmoden) *chsd ldrs to 1/2-way: sn rdn and wknd: eased fnl f* **10/1**

1m 18.4s **Going Correction** -0.025s/f (Good) **10** Ran SP% **128.3**
Speed ratings: **93,90,89,88,87 87,84,83,82,65**CSF £46.22 TOTE £4.60: £1.60, £5.60, £7.90; DF 132.80.
**Owner** M McLoughlin **Bred** Mary Rose Hayes **Trained** Ireland

**NOTEBOOK**
**Slip Dance(IRE)** was quite impressive and there was only one winner from a furlong out, dismissing fears regarding the ground. She is better than the face value of this result.
**All Night Dancer(IRE)** has not been raised from her mark of 81 but this was a career-best effort.

**Makuti(IRE)** improved on her Down Royal maiden win.
**Tournedos(IRE)** did not run to anything near his best and the ground, rather than the quick reappearance after Doncaster, might have been to blame.
**Nova Tor(IRE)** found this stretching her a bit too far but she was not disgraced.
**Wavertree Warrior(IRE)** was outclassed.

5682 - (Foreign Racing) - See Raceform Interactive

## 3972 FRANKFURT (L-H)

Sunday, September 19

**OFFICIAL GOING: Good**

### 5683a MERRILL LYNCH EURO-CUP (GROUP 2) 1m 2f
4:00 (4:20) 3-Y-O+ **£26,761** (£10,563; £5,282; £3,169)

RPR

1 **Soldier Hollow**[23] 4-8-13 ........ WMongil 4 113
(PSchiergen, Germany) *always prominent, 2nd straight, led 1 1/2f out, ran on well* 1

2 1 1/4 **Fight Club (GER)**[77] 3565 3-8-6 ........ AStarke 5 110
(ASchutz, Germany) *mid-division, disputing 3rd straight, ridden to chase winner 1 1/2f out, kept on but no impression* 2

3 2 **Morbidezza (GER)**[23] 4-8-9 ........ LHammer-Hansen 2 103
(MTrinker, Germany) *held up, 6th straight, stayed on under pressure final 1 1/2f to take 3rd closing stages* 3

4 nk **Near Honor (GER)**[63] 3972 6-8-13 ........ THellier 1 107
(TimGibson, Germany) *led to 1 1/2f out, one pace*

5 1 **Anolitas (GER)**[23] 4-8-13 ........(b) NRichter 3 105
(UOstmann, Germany) *raced in 5th, one pace final 2f*

6 1/2 **Lysuna (GER)**[23] 4-8-9 ........ RonanThomas 6 100
(ATrybuhl, Germany) *always in rear, beaten 2f out*

7 4 **Apeiron (GER)**[29] 4965 3-8-6 ........ J-PCarvalho 7 96
(MarioHofer, Germany) *close up on outside, disputing 3rd straight, one pace final 1 1/2f*

2m 13.91s
**WFA** 3 from 4yo+ 6lb 7 Ran SP% **113.0**
Speed ratings: .
**Owner** Gestut Park Wiedingen **Bred** Car Colston Hall Stud **Trained** Germany

**NOTEBOOK**
**Soldier Hollow** completed a Group race hat-trick with a convincing victory. He will dip his toes in Group 1 water in the Premio Roma in Italy in November and stay in training as a five-year-old.

## 5406 CHEPSTOW (L-H)

Monday, September 20

**OFFICIAL GOING: Heavy**

1.5mil of rain overnight and another 3mil during the morning made conditions very testing.
Wind: fresh across Weather: fine

### 5687 ALLPRINT MEDIAN AUCTION MAIDEN STKS (DIV I) 7f 16y
2:20 (2:21) (F4) 2-Y-0 **£3,066** (£876; £438) **Stalls High**

Form RPR

1 **Songerie** 2-8-9 ........ SSanders 1 84+
(SirMarkPrescott) *hld up: hdwy over 2f out: led wl over 1f out: sn edgd rt: pushed clr* **7/4**[1]

62 2 5 **Mystery Lot (IRE)**[39] 4681 2-8-9 ........ JDSmith 2 73
(AKing) *hld up in tch: ev ch wl over 1f out: sn carried rt: one pce* **5/2**[2]

50 3 5 **Scent**[18] 5248 2-8-9 ........ IMongan 8 62
(JLDunlop) *hld up: swtchd lft and hdwy 2f out: wknd over 1f out* **11/1**

0 4 4 **Crystal Mystic (IRE)**[11] 5406 2-8-11 ........(b) FPFerris(3) 3 58
(BPalling) *led: rdn and hdd wl over 1f out: sn wknd* **40/1**

5 1 3/4 **Turnover** 2-8-6 ........ DCorby(3) 5 49
(MJWallace) *s.i.s: bhd: rdn over 3f out: sme late hdwy* **25/1**

000 6 3 **Little Indy**[14] 5347 2-8-11 ........ DNolan(3) 12 48
(RBrotherton) *prom: rdn 3f out: wknd over 1f out* **100/1**

03 7 1/2 **Strike Gold**[11] 5406 2-9-0 ........ TPQueally 6 47
(SKirk) *chsd ldr tl rdn over 2f out: sn wknd* **7/2**[3]

0 8 3/4 **Monica's Revenge (IRE)**[14] 5353 2-8-4 ........ NChalmers(5) 4 40
(RMBeckett) *prom 5f* **20/1**

9 5 **Patrician Dealer** 2-9-0 ........ VSlattery 7 34
(MSSaunders) *s.s: rdn over 5f out: a bhd* **33/1**

00 10 6 **Young Boldric**[35] 4809 2-8-11 ........ LPKeniry(3) 10 21
(KBell) *bhd fnl 4f* **66/1**

11 5 **Oakley Absolute** 2-9-0 ........ DaneO'Neill 9 10
(RHannon) *s.s: rdn over 3f out: a bhd* **14/1**

1m 30.05s (6.85) **Going Correction** +0.875s/f (Soft) 11 Ran SP% **118.6**
Speed ratings: **95,89,83,79,77 73,73,72,66,59 53**CSF £5.84 TOTE £2.50: £1.20, £1.10, £2.60; EX 9.80.
**Owner** Miss K Rausing **Bred** Miss K Rausing **Trained** Newmarket, Suffolk

**FOCUS**
Little strength in depth to this maiden, but a highly promising winner and the time was 0.27 seconds faster than the second division and fair for the grade in the conditions.

**NOTEBOOK**
**Songerie** made a very promising winning debut and clearly relished the underfoot conditions. She was not fully extended to score, should improve a deal for the outing and could make up into a fairly smart performer next year over middle-distances.
**Mystery Lot(IRE)** was again unlucky to bump into an above-average rival, but still acquitted himself with credit and was well clear of the rest. A switch to nurseries should bring success.
**Scent** appreciated this return to soft ground, but was firmly put in her place by the front pair. This looks about as far as she wants to go for now and she could possibly do better in nurseries.
**Crystal Mystic(IRE)** showed the benefit of her recent debut over course and distance and broke much better this time. She is going the right way and shaped as though a drop in trip would be very much in her favour.
**Turnover** showed some ability on this debut and should know more next time.
**Strike Gold** failed by some way to build on his recent improved effort over course and distance and has to go down as disappointing. However, he now qualifies for a nursery mark and could do better back on a sound surface.

### 5688 ALLPRINT MEDIAN AUCTION MAIDEN STKS (DIV II) 7f 16y
2:55 (2:55) (F4) 2-Y-0 **£3,059** (£874; £437) **Stalls High**

Form RPR

0 1 **Karlu (GER)**[65] 3931 2-9-0 ........ IMongan 7 73
(JLDunlop) *s.s: sn rcvrd: hld up: rdn and hdwy over 2f out: swtchd rt over 1f out: led ins fnl f: r.o* **2/1**[2]

2 1/2 **Spectait** 2-9-0 ........ SSanders 2 72
(SirMarkPrescott) *dwlt: hld up and bhd: hdwy 3f out: sn rn green and hung lft: styd on wl ins fnl f: bttr for r* **8/1**[3]

03 3 shd **Duroob**[32] 4866 2-9-0 ........ WSupple 11 72
(EALDunlop) *hld up in mid-div: hdwy over 3f out: led 1f out: rdn and hdd ins fnl f: r.o* **7/4**[1]

0 4 2 1/2 **Miss Sudbrook (IRE)**[41] 4621 2-8-9 ........ MFenton 10 61
(DHaydnJones) *hld up in tch: led wl over 2f out: rdn and edgd lft jst over 1f out: sn hdd: one pce* **100/1**

5 1/2 **Maxamillion (IRE)** 2-9-0 ........ TPQueally 8 65
(SKirk) *s.s: bhd: rdn over 3f out: hdwy over 2f out: ev ch 1f out: sn edgd lft: no ex* **8/1**[3]

6 3 **Valiant Act (IRE)** 2-8-9 ........ CCatlin 6 53
(DMSimcock) *prom: rdn over 2f out: wknd ins fnl f* **20/1**

0 7 1/2 **Dewin Coch**[21] 5198 2-8-9 ........ BSwarbrick(5) 5 57
(WMBrisbourne) *led over 1f: w ldr: rdn and ev ch over 1f out: carried lft jst ins fnl f: wknd* **25/1**

00 8 3 1/2 **Grand Girl**[6] 5535 2-8-9 ........ ADaly 12 45
(BWDuke) *nvr trbld ldrs* **40/1**

0 9 11 **Flower Seeker**[21] 5198 2-8-9 ........ SWhitworth 9 20
(CTinkler) *s.s: a bhd* **66/1**

00 10 7 **Southern Tide (USA)**[42] 4611 2-8-11 ........ NMackay(3) 3 10
(JJSheehan) *w ldr: led over 5f out tl wl over 2f out: sn wknd* **25/1**

00 11 21 **Brego (IRE)**[11] 5407 2-9-0 ........(b[1]) RHavlin 1 —
(JHMGosden) *hld up in tch: rdn and wknd 3f out: t.o* **16/1**

1m 30.32s (7.12) **Going Correction** +0.875s/f (Soft) 11 Ran SP% **115.2**
Speed ratings: **94,93,93,90,89 86,85,81,69,61 37**CSF £16.38 TOTE £2.60: £1.30, £2.80, £1.10; EX 13.50.
**Owner** Pat Eddery Racing (Rainbow Quest) **Bred** Gestut Hof Iserneichen **Trained** Arundel, W Sussex

**FOCUS**
A modest maiden and the time was 0.27 seconds slower than the first division, but it was still adequate in the conditions. The form is difficult to assess at this stage.

**NOTEBOOK**
**Karlu(GER)** took time to hit his full stride, but picked up strongly when switched to challenge and was comfortably on top close home. This was a fair effort on only his second start, he handled the going well and, as he comes from the same family as dual Classic herione Kazzia, should do better over further next year.
**Spectait**, a gelding whose dam won over sprint trips as a juvenile, made a very pleasing debut and was really motoring close home. He was not at all given a hard time and should learn plenty from this, so would have serious prospects of reversing this form in the future.
**Duroob**, who showed significant improvement from his debut last time, had his chance, but failed to see his race out as well as the front pair. He will get this trip better on a less-testing surface and, while he failed to improve this time, he should do now he qualifies for nurseries.
**Miss Sudbrook(IRE)** turned in a much-improved effort on this second start and only tired out of contention late in the day. This soft ground helped and she is the type to keep progressing with more racing.
**Maxamillion(IRE)** was fairly well-backed for this debut, but gave himself a stiff task with a slow start and running green through the early stages. He still showed ability from halfway and should know more next time.
**Brego(IRE)** *Official explanation: jockey said gelding was unsuited by heavy ground*

### 5689 EUROPEAN BREEDERS FUND MAIDEN STKS 6f 16y
3:30 (3:31) (D3) 2-Y-0 **£3,571** (£1,099; £549; £274) **Stalls High**

Form RPR

4 1 **Daldini**[13] 5376 2-9-0 ........ TPQueally 5 78
(JAOsborne) *hld up in tch: hdwy over 2f out: rdn to ld over 1f out: drvn out* **3/1**[2]

004 2 1/2 **Archie Glenn**[8] 5494 2-9-0 ........ PMcCabe 2 77
(MSSaunders) *t.k.h: led 3f: w ldrs: rdn and ev ch fnl f: r.o* **4/1**[3]

6 3 3 1/2 **Inagh**[98] 2940 2-8-6 ........ DCorby(3) 8 62
(MJWallace) *prom: led 3f out: rdn and hdd over 1f out: one pce* **33/1**

56 4 nk **Rapid Romance (USA)**[58] 4137 2-8-9 ........ WSupple 6 61
(EALDunlop) *hld up: sn in tch: hdwy over 2f out: kpt on same pce fnl f* **11/1**

5 6 **Devil's Island** 2-9-0 ........ SSanders 7 50
(SirMarkPrescott) *hld up: pushed along over 1f out: no rspnse* **4/1**[3]

06 6 9 **Mytori**[35] 4807 2-8-9 ........ SWhitworth 1 20
(DShaw) *wnt lft s: sn prom: wknd over 2f out* **100/1**

7 1 **Flying Highest** 2-8-9 ........ DaneO'Neill 4 17
(HCandy) *in tch: rdn over 2f out: sn wknd* **15/8**[1]

1m 18.21s (6.01) **Going Correction** +0.875s/f (Soft) 7 Ran SP% **112.0**
Speed ratings: **94,93,88,88,80 68,66**CSF £14.74 TOTE £3.90: £1.30, £2.10; EX 20.50.
**Owner** Paul J Dixon **Bred** Mrs J A Gawthorpe **Trained** Upper Lambourn, Berks

**FOCUS**
The first two came clear in what was probably just a modest maiden, but the form appears reliable.

**NOTEBOOK**
**Daldini**, who showed definite promise when staying on late on his recent debut, confirmed that effort was no fluke and won well on this much softer ground. He was well-backed for this and has clearly improved, so could be the type to acquit himself well at a higher level.
**Archie Glenn** ran keen early on, but stuck to his task from halfway and made the winner pull out all the stops in the closing stages. He proved he goes on soft ground and now looks well worth a switch to nurseries.
**Inagh**, absent since getting outpaced over five furlongs on her debut in June, put up an improved display and looked suited by this trip. It is unlikely that we will see the best of her until she is eligible for nurseries.
**Rapid Romance(USA)** could not find a change of gear on this much slower ground and pretty much ran up to the form of her previous outings. She will fare better now she qualifies for nurseries.
**Devil's Island**, half-brother to high-class miler Gateman and the 2001 Hunt Cup winner Suprise Encounter, was easy to back for this debut and ran a tame race. However, his sire mainly has fast ground performers and this colt is almost certainly capable of better.
**Flying Highest**, half-sister to several sprint winners, looked all at sea on this ground and proved disappointing. She could leave the form behind when racing on a sound surface, but she has a lot to prove now nonetheless. *Official explanation: trainer said filly was unsuited by heavy ground*

## 5690 ALLPRINT NURSERY 5f 16y
**4:00** (4:01) (E3) (0-75,72) 2-Y-O **£4,134** (£1,272; £636; £318) **Stalls** High

Form RPR
2523 **1** **Cree**[8] [5490] 2-8-8 **59** SSanders 6 66
(WRMuir) *trckd ldrs: swtchd rt wl over 1f out: led ent fnl f: rdn and veered rt ins fnl: r.o wl* **2/1**[1]
0662 **2** *2* **Lighted Way**[7] [5507] 2-8-9 **63** LPKeniry(3) 11 63
(AMBalding) *a.p: led over 2f out: rdn and hdd ent fnl f: nt qckn* **5/2**[2]
420 **3** *shd* **Knock Bridge (IRE)**[98] [2947] 2-9-0 **65** JoannaBadger 10 65
(PDEvans) *s.s: hdwy jst over 1f out: r.o wl towards fin* **16/1**
5360 **4** *1 3/4* **Robmantra**[11] [5406] 2-8-12 **63** (p) SWhitworth 2 57
(BJLlewellyn) *hld up: sn bhd: hdwy jst over 1f out: rdn and r.o ins fnl f* **33/1**
2400 **5** *1 1/4* **Miss Malone (IRE)**[12] [5391] 2-9-6 **71** DaneO'Neill 7 60
(RHannon) *led over 2f: sn rdn: wknd ins fnl f* **4/1**[3]
0550 **6** *1/2* **Worth A Grand (IRE)**[6] [5539] 2-8-12 **66** JFMcDonald(3) 5 53
(JWMullins) *broke wl: rdn and lost pl over 3f out: styng on whn nt clr run ins fnl f* **16/1**
5606 **7** *hd* **Limonia (GER)**[28] [5003] 2-9-0 **65** CCatlin 1 52
(DKIvory) *wnt lft s: sn prom: rdn 2f out: wknd ins fnl f* **11/1**
3310 **8** *3/4* **Roko**[15] [5314] 2-8-8 **59** (v) WSupple 8 43
(DShaw) *hld up in mid-div: rdn over 2f out: btn whn edgd lft 1f out* **12/1**
2543 **9** *2* **Lady Erica**[117] [2405] 2-8-8 **59** LEnstone 9 36
(KRBurke) *w ldrs tl wknd over 1f out* **20/1**

64.31 secs (4.81) **Going Correction** +0.875s/f (Soft) **9** Ran SP% **117.4**
Speed ratings: **96,92,92,89,87 87,86,85,82**CSF £7.23 CT £60.93 TOTE £3.10: £1.20, £1.20, £7.30; EX 5.60.
**Owner** Inflite Partners **Bred** Miss G Abbey **Trained** Lambourn, Berks

**FOCUS**
A modest nursery run at a fair clip in the conditions, but the form is worth treating with a degree of caution.

**NOTEBOOK**
**Cree** dug deep when asked to win his race over one out and stayed on nicely in the condtions to post a much-deserved success. He is a versatile sort who should be capable of further success this season as he is at the right end of the handicap to progress.
**Lighted Way** held every chance on this nursery debut, but failed to quicken on this drop back in trip and was well held in the end. She has the ability to find a race off this mark, but needs to step up another furlong in order to do so.
**Knock Bridge(IRE)**, runner-up in a seller on her penultimate outing, stayed on best of all in the closing stages and turned in an improved effort on this handicap bow. This drop back to five furlongs was probably against her and she could get closer when reverting to six.
**Robmantra** could not quicken on this ground, but still managed to improve on his recent efforts on this drop back in trip. He clearly likes this track.
**Miss Malone(IRE)** failed to find a change of gear on this testing ground when it mattered. She has lost her form somewhat of late, but is capable of better and may drop again in the weights as a result of this.

## 5691 ARTHUR LLEWELLYN JENKINS CLASSIFIED STKS 7f 16y
**4:30** (4:31) (G4) 3-Y-0+ **£3,087** (£882; £441) **Stalls** High

Form RPR
3000 **1** **Semper Paratus (USA)**[17] [5261] 5-9-3 47 (b) MTebbutt 17 57
(VSmith) *hld up: hdwy over 2f out: sn rdn: carried rt fnl f: led cl home* **4/1**[1]
1640 **2** *nk* **Zhitomir**[18] [5235] 6-9-3 48 LEnstone 15 56
(MDods) *hld up: rdn 3f out: hdwy wl over 1f out: carried rt ins fnl f* **5/1**[3]
5650 **3** *nk* **Amber Fox (IRE)**[41] [4619] 3-8-11 45 RHavlin 5 52
(PDEvans) *hld up: hdwy over 3f out: led over 2f out: rdn over 1f out: edgd rt fnl f: hdd cl home* **50/1**
6100 **4** *2* **Wood Fern (UAE)**[5] [5575] 4-9-3 49 CCatlin 13 50
(MRChannon) *a.p: ev ch over 2f out: rdn over 1f out: one pce* **12/1**
0601 **5** *shd* **Halcyon Magic**[5] [5575] 6-8-10 46 (b) LauraPike(7) 19 50
(MWigham) *racd stands' side: hld up and bhd: hdwy over 2f out: r.o ins fnl f* **7/1**
-000 **6** *1/2* **Seven Shirt**[11] [5424] 3-8-11 50 RMiles(3) 10 49
(EGBevan) *w ldrs: led and edgd to far rail over 3f out: hdd over 2f out: sn rdn: one pce* **50/1**
5000 **7** *nk* **Night Worker**[24] [5072] 3-9-0 45 DaneO'Neill 18 48
(RHannon) *hld up: rdn and hdwy over 2f out: wknd wl ins fnl f* **25/1**
3614 **8** *1 1/4* **My Girl Pearl (IRE)**[5] [5575] 4-8-11 50 NMackay(3) 16 42+
(MSSaunders) *prom: lost pl over 3f out: kpt on fnl f* **9/2**[2]
0360 **9** *hd* **Dexileos (IRE)**[16] [5282] 5-8-12 45 (t) NChalmers(5) 20 44
(ADWPinder) *s.s: racd stands' side: hdwy over 2f out: wknd over 1f out* **33/1**
0000 **10** *1* **Pharoah's Gold (IRE)**[18] [5236] 6-9-3 48 (p) SWhitworth 4 42
(DShaw) *bhd: rdn over 2f out: hdwy jst over 1f out: n.d* **14/1**
4500 **11** *6* **Barabella (IRE)**[17] [5261] 3-8-11 47 VSlattery 2 24
(RJHodges) *hld up and bhd: short-lived effrt over 2f out* **25/1**
0500 **12** *2 1/2* **Chatshow (USA)**[44] [4548] 3-9-0 50 IMongan 12 21
(AWCarroll) *prom tl wknd over 1f out* **10/1**
0600 **13** *nk* **Super Song**[11] [5411] 4-9-0 48 (vt[1]) FPFerris(3) 14 20
(PDEvans) *t.k.h: led over 5f out tl over 3f out: rdn over 2f out: sn wknd* **16/1**
0024 **14** *10* **Back In Spirit**[32] [4881] 4-9-3 40 (t) GGibbons 11 —
(BAMcmahon) *led over 1f: prom: rdn over 2f out: wknd wl over 1f out* **33/1**
0000 **15** *16* **Dream Of Dubai (IRE)**[30] [4941] 3-8-8 48 (b[1]) HayleyTurner(3) 7 —
(PMitchell) *s.i.s: a bhd: t.o* **40/1**
0066 **16** *7* **Emperor Cat (IRE)**[29] [4968] 3-9-0 45 PBradley 6 —
(PABlockley) *chsd ldrs tl wknd over 2f out: t.o* **40/1**

1m 31.13s (7.93) **Going Correction** +0.875s/f (Soft)
**WFA** 3 from 4yo+ 3lb **16** Ran SP% **119.1**
Speed ratings: **89,88,88,86,85 85,85,83,83,82 75,72,72,60,42 34**CSF £20.81 TOTE £6.00: £1.80, £3.40, £7.80; EX 20.90.
**Owner** Exeter Stables Partnership **Bred** Lantern Hill Farm Llc **Trained** Exning, Suffolk

**FOCUS**
A very moderate time for the class, but basically a seller and slower than both divisions of the two-year-old maiden, as the first three came clear. Again a high draw proved an advantage.

**NOTEBOOK**
**Semper Paratus(USA)**, who had dropped in the ratings of late, showed a fair turn of foot on this testing ground and proved game in holding off the runner-up close home en-route to success. This return to seven furlongs worked the oracle and he could win again of this sort of mark if encountering this surface once again.
**Zhitomir** advertised his liking for cut in the ground and went down fighting. This was an improved effort and he is clearly in good form, but is not certain to reproduce this form next time.
**Amber Fox(IRE)** improved on all known form and was not beaten at all far. She did by far the best of those drawn low and clearly enjoyed the underfoot conditions, so looks well worth another try at this trip in order to break her duck.
**Wood Fern(UAE)** had his chance, but could not quicken with the principals when it mattered. He is best on this ground, but very hard to win with.
**Halcyon Magic** would have fared better with a more positive ride and can be rated better then the bare form.
**Seven Shirt** *Official explanation: jockey said gelding was unsuited by the heavy ground*
**My Girl Pearl(IRE)** looked to find this ground too testing and could not pick up when well placed to strike before halfway. She remains in fair form and would prefer a return to a sound surface.
**Dexileos(IRE)** *Official explanation: jockey said gelding missed break*
**Chatshow(USA)** *Official explanation: jockey said gelding was unsuited by heavy ground*
**Back In Spirit** *Official explanation: jockey said gelding had a breathing problem*
**Dream Of Dubai(IRE)** *Official explanation: jockey said filly was hit on head in stalls*

## 5692 COUNTRY LAND & BUSINESS ASSOCIATION RACEDAY 2ND OCTOBER H'CAP 1m 2f 36y
**5:00** (5:04) (F4) (0-55,55) 3-Y-O **£3,348** (£956; £478) **Stalls** Low

Form RPR
0003 **1** **Cotton Easter**[21] [5175] 3-8-7 **49** RThomas(3) 8 56
(MrsAJBowlby) *hld up: hdwy over 3f out: sn rdn: led over 1f out: r.o wl* **3/1**[1]
0056 **2** *1 1/2* **Tartiruga (IRE)**[14] [5352] 3-8-7 **46** oh1 ADaly 5 50
(LGCottrell) *uns rdr and bolted bef s: t.k.h: led after 1f tl over 6f out: led 3f out: sn rdn: hdd over 1f out: nt qckn* **8/1**
0 **3** *5* **Charlottine (IRE)**[54] [4251] 3-9-1 **54** (p) SSanders 1 50
(MPSunderland, Ire) *hld up in tch: hdwy 4f out: rdn 2f out: wknd over 1f out* **7/1**[3]
0002 **4** *3* **Fizzy Lady**[11] [5408] 3-8-11 **50** (t) CCatlin 7 41
(NEBerry) *hld up in rr: hdwy 3f out: swtchd rt over 1f out: no further prog* **9/1**
0004 **5** *1 1/2* **Farnborough (USA)**[24] [5072] 3-8-6 **48** RMiles(3) 12 36
(RJPrice) *stdd s: hld up in rr: hdwy on outside over 3f out: rdn over 1f out: wknd fnl f* **7/1**[3]
0000 **6** *1 1/4* **Pleasure Seeker**[24] [5092] 3-8-13 **52** IMongan 4 38
(MDIUsher) *hld up: rdn and hdwy on ins over 4f out: wknd over 1f out* **33/1**
0006 **7** *8* **Amwell Brave**[25] [5057] 3-9-2 **55** TPQueally 3 28
(JRJenkins) *hld up: hdwy over 5f out: rdn over 3f out: wknd over 2f out* **7/1**[3]
4005 **8** *7* **Acuzio**[39] [4680] 3-8-11 **55** BSwarbrick(5) 2 16
(WMBrisbourne) *prom tl rdn and wknd over 3f out* **12/1**
5060 **9** *1 3/4* **Stylish Dancer**[30] [4939] 3-8-7 **46** oh1 RHavlin 10 4
(MBlanshard) *hld up in mid-div: rdn over 3f out: bhd fnl 2f* **25/1**
060P **10** *3/4* **Unintentional**[39] [4673] 3-8-10 **52** DNolan(3) 6 8
(RBrotherton) *prom: led over 6f out tl to 3f out: wknd wl over 1f out* **33/1**
-630 **11** *nk* **Mr Strowger**[24] [5072] 3-8-7 **46** oh1 WSupple 13 2
(ACharlton) *led 1f: prom tl wknd over 3f out* **25/1**
2400 **12** *18* **Uncle John**[11] [5410] 3-9-2 **55** DaneO'Neill 9 —
(SKirk) *prom tl wknd over 3f out: t.o* **5/1**[2]

2m 20.64s (11.04) **Going Correction** +1.10s/f (Soft) **12** Ran SP% **121.5**
Speed ratings: **99,97,93,91,90 89,82,77,75,75 74,60**CSF £27.05 CT £158.00 TOTE £4.80: £1.60, £3.40, £1.60; EX 50.10.
**Owner** The Reg Partnership **Bred** S R Hope And D Erwin **Trained** Kingston Lisle, Oxon

**FOCUS**
A very weak handicap with no strength in depth that saw the first two come clear, but cannot be rated highly.

**NOTEBOOK**
**Cotton Easter**, who showed her first worthwhile form over course and distance last time, again improved on this testing ground and ran out a ready winner. She is clearly improving and the manner in which she won this suggests she has more to offer, so she should be able to find plenty of opportunities on this sort of ground.
**Tartiruga(IRE)**, bred to relish this ground, did well considering he bolted to the start and ran way too keen early on. He is tricky, but has an engine and could break his duck at this level when putting it all together.
**Charlottine(IRE)**, making her British debut, turned in a respectable effort and enjoyed this ground. She got the trip well enough.
**Fizzy Lady**, who stayed on over a mile at this track last time when second in a seller, failed to really improve on this step up in trip. She is best at a mile and could be given another chance back in plating compnay.
**Farnborough(USA)** failed to pick up on this ground and is capable of better back on a sound surface. *Official explanation: jockey said gelding was unsuited by heavy ground*
**Uncle John** dropped out most alarmingly when holding a chance three out. Something may well have been amiss.

## 5693 JUMP SEASON BEGINS HERE SATURDAY 2ND OCTOBER H'CAP 1m 14y
**5:30** (5:32) (E3) (0-70,70) 3-Y-O **£3,986** (£1,226; £613; £306) **Stalls** High

Form RPR
1130 **1** **Danifah (IRE)**[13] [5370] 3-8-11 **63** DNolan(3) 8 73
(PDEvans) *mde all: rdn over 1f out: drvn out* **12/1**
0401 **2** *1 1/4* **Smoothly Does It**[21] [5176] 3-9-0 **66** RThomas(3) 13 73
(MrsAJBowlby) *hld up and bhd: hdwy over 3f out: rdn 2f out: r.o one pce fnl f* **2/1**[1]
432 **3** *3* **Premier Rouge**[22] [5156] 3-9-4 **67** SSanders 3 68
(EFVaughan) *hld up: hdwy 4f out: rdn 3f out: chsd wnr 2f out tl no ex ins fnl f* **7/2**[2]
0660 **4** *3/4* **Night Frolic**[22] [5156] 3-8-10 **59** TPQueally 1 59
(JWHills) *hld up in tch: chsd wnr 3f out tl rdn 2f out: wknd ins fnl f* **12/1**
0253 **5** *8* **Fleet Anchor**[7] [5510] 3-8-7 **56** oh4 CCatlin 14 40
(JMBradley) *t.k.h: prom: rdn 3f out: wknd wl over 1f out* **8/1**[3]
3660 **6** *1* **Ligne D'Eau**[32] [4868] 3-8-4 **56** oh3 FPFerris(3) 9 38
(PDEvans) *hld up in mid-div: hdwy 3f out: sn rdn: wknd wl over 1f out* **25/1**
0030 **7** *2* **Waziri (IRE)**[25] [5057] 3-9-4 **70** LFletcher(3) 6 48
(HMorrison) *prom tl rdn and wknd over 2f out* **12/1**
003 **8** *4* **Primeshade Promise**[46] [4478] 3-8-8 **57** RPrice 12 27
(DBurchell) *hld up and bhd: hdwy 3f out: sn rdn: wknd 2f out* **33/1**
-062 **9** *10* **Suchwot (IRE)**[139] [1874] 3-8-9 **58** RHavlin 11 8
(FJordan) *s.i.s: rdn over 3f out: a bhd* **16/1**
0062 **10** *nk* **Desert Hawk**[7] [5510] 3-9-3 **66** DaneO'Neill 7 15
(RHannon) *rdn 3f out: a bhd* **10/1**
050 **11** *shd* **Ink In Gold (IRE)**[21] [5196] 3-8-7 **56** oh1 PBradley 2 5
(PABlockley) *hld up in mid-div: bhd fnl 3f* **40/1**
2400 **12** *8* **Green Ridge**[79] [3524] 3-8-8 **60** HayleyTurner(3) 10 —
(MissAMNewton-Smith) *hld up in tch: rdn 3f out: sn wknd* **28/1**

1100 **13** *6* **Athboy**[82] 3419 3-9-2 **68**......(v) DCorby[(3)] 4 —
(MJWallace) *hld up in rr: rdn over 3f out: lost tch 2f out* **20/1**

1m 42.52s (6.62) **Going Correction** +0.875s/f (Soft) **13** Ran SP% **122.2**
Speed ratings: **101,99,96,96,88 87,85,81,71,70 70,62,56**CSF £34.95 CT £112.34 TOTE £13.20: £3.80, £1.40, £1.10; EX 63.00 Place 6 £14.20, Place 5 £10.30.
**Owner** E A R Morgans **Bred** Rocklow Stud **Trained** Pandy, Gwent

**FOCUS**
A modest handicap featuring largely out-of-form types. However the pace was solid and the form appears sound for the grade.

**NOTEBOOK**
**Danifah(IRE)**, one of few to come into this in good form, again advertised her liking for this track and readily made all over this longer trip. This was a much-improved effort, but when she is able to dominate a field she is a much better performer. *Official explanation: trainer said, regarding the improved form shown, filly was unable to dominate on her previous run*
**Smoothly Does It**, winner over course and distance last time, gave her all in trying to follow-up off this 4lb higher mark. He could not quicken in this sticky ground, but remains in good heart and may not be weighted out of scoring again just yet.
**Premier Rouge**, making his handicap debut, turned in another fair effort and again suggested he will be seen in a a better light when racing over ten furlongs.
**Night Frolic** managed to improve on recent efforts, and had no trouble on the ground, but looked very one-paced late on. She is a tricky sort.
**Fleet Anchor** paid late on for pulling too hard throught the early stages and never looked like getting home on this ground.
**Athboy** *Official explanation: jockey said the gelding hung left*
T/Plt: £40.40 to a £1 stake. Pool: £33,370.00. 602.35 winning tickets. T/Qpdt: £20.80 to a £1 stake. Pool: £2,367.90. 84.00 winning tickets. KH

## 5294 KEMPTON (R-H)
### Monday, September 20
**OFFICIAL GOING: Good to firm (last race abandoned due to unsafe ground)**

## 5694 NORMAN HILL MEMORIAL EBF MAIDEN FILLIES' STKS (DIV I) 7f (J)
2:10 (2:10) (D3) 2-Y-0 **£5,265** (£1,620; £810; £405) **Stalls** High

Form RPR

**1** **Fen Shui (UAE)** 2-8-11 ...... LDettori 7 86+
(SaeedBinSuroor) *lengthy: scope: lw: cl up: led 2f out: sn clr: easily* **3/1**[1]

6 **2** *6* **Abide (FR)**[18] 5247 2-8-11 ...... RHughes 8 73+
(RHannon) *lw: disp ld to 2f out: clr of rest but no ch w wnr after: eased nr fin* **11/2**[3]

**3** *1 1/4* **Phoebe Woodstock (IRE)** 2-8-11 ...... EAhern 4 68+
(PWHarris) *unf: lw: racd midfield: pushed along 1/2-way: swtchd lft over 1f out: styd on wl fnl f* **20/1**

**4** *1 1/2* **Witwatersrand (IRE)** 2-8-11 ...... MHills 10 69+
(BWHills) *tall: str: bit bkwd: dwlt and wnt rt s: hld up wl in rr: nt clr run over 2f out and over 1f out: styd on wl fnl f: bttr for* **16/1**

**5** *1/2* **Shiny Thing (USA)** 2-8-11 ...... DKinsella 6 60
(AKing) *tall: str: bit bkwd: racd midfield: pushed along and prog on outer over 2f out: one pce over 1f out* **33/1**

505 **6** *3/4* **Rosapenna (IRE)**[42] 4598 2-8-11 64...... DHolland 9 58
(CFWall) *stmbld bdly s: wl in rr: nt clr run over 2f out: styd on fnl f: nrst fin: uns rdr after fin* **33/1**

**7** *nk* **Best About** 2-8-11 ......(t) RLMoore 12 57
(DRLoder) *leggy: dwlt: trckd ldrs: shkn up 2f out: chsd clr ldng pair over 1f out: wknd fnl f* **11/1**

5 **8** *1* **Papality**[74] 3675 2-8-11 ...... TQuinn 1 55
(WJarvis) *disp ld to over 2f out: wknd over 1f out* **4/1**[2]

**9** *1* **Ti Adora (IRE)** 2-8-11 ...... AMcCarthy 11 52
(PWChapple-Hyam) *leggy: lw: cl up: shkn up over 2f out: wknd over 1f out* **12/1**

**10** *1/2* **Zaville** 2-8-11 ...... MHenry 13 51
(MAJarvis) *lengthy: scope: bit bkwd: disp ld to 3f out: hanging and wknd wl over 1f out* **25/1**

**11** *nk* **Royal Jelly** 2-8-11 ...... JFortune 2 50
(JHMGosden) *lengthy: lw: dwlt: wl in rr: hanging bdly and reminder 2f out: no prog* **12/1**

**12** *nk* **Miss Tolerance (USA)** 2-8-11 ...... KFallon 14 50
(SirMichaelStoute) *leggy: dwlt: sn disp ld to over 2f out: wknd over 1f out* **11/1**

0 **13** *3/4* **Smart Dawn**[121] 2300 2-8-11 ...... SHitchcott 15 48
(CTinkler) *trckd ldrs tl wknd 2f out* **66/1**

**14** *24* **Pavilion** 2-8-11 ...... FNorton 3 —
(BJMeehan) *lt-f: dwlt: a wl in rr: t.o* **33/1**

00 **15** *3 1/2* **Rockys Girl**[13] 5375 2-8-11 ...... KDarley 5 —
(MJRyan) *a wl in rr: t.o* **50/1**

1m 27.44s (0.17) **Going Correction** +0.125s/f (Good) **15** Ran SP% **119.2**
Speed ratings: **104,97,95,94,93 92,92,91,89,89 89,88,87,60,56**CSF £17.12 TOTE £3.50: £1.50, £2.50, £8.10; EX 23.60.
**Owner** Godolphin **Bred** Darley **Trained** Newmarket, Suffolk

**FOCUS**
A very smart winning time indeed for the type of race being 1.74 seconds faster than the second division and an impressive winner in Fen Shui. A race sure to produce winners.

**NOTEBOOK**
**Fen Shui(UAE)**, whose stable's juveniles continue to thrive, recorded an impressive debut performance - going right away in the final furlong. Dettori always had her up on the pace and, although this was probably not a great maiden, she will stay a mile and should hold her own at a higher level.
**Abide(FR)**, a fairly promising sixth in only an ordinary maiden on her debut, proved no match for the winner but held the remainder comfortably and should win an average maiden. In the long run she should pay her way in handicaps.
**Phoebe Woodstock(IRE)** ◆ comes from a successful family that includes Leporello, and she would have given connections plenty of hope for the future with a staying on third. She was being encouraged for most of the way and it was not until late she got going. A mile will suit in time and she looks a ready-made maiden scorer.
**Witwatersrand(IRE)** ◆, who looked very much in need of the experience both physically and mentally, was another who was doing her best work at the death and she would have been closer had she had a clear passage through. She is another winner waiting to happen.
**Shiny Thing(USA)** comes from a predominently jumping stable that does very well with the juveniles they have, and this one can be expected to improve for the run. If going the right way she has a maiden in her.
**Rosapenna(IRE)** ◆ has been given a very fair mark of 64, but was having one more run in maiden company before taking up nursery engagements. She practically lost the race at the start when going down on her nose and was short of room when trying to come with a run. She looks a certain nursery winner of this sort of mark. *Official explanation: vet said filly lost an off hind shoe; jockey said filly stumbled leaving stalls*
**Best About** did not shape without promise and can be expected to improve.
**Papality** was disappointing and looks more of a nursery type.
**Ti Adora(IRE)** looked in need of the outing and is in the right hands to win races.
**Zaville** is bred to do better with time and distance and is very much a three-year-old staying handicapper in the making.
**Royal Jelly** did not look straightforward but deserves another chance to show what she can do.
**Miss Tolerance(USA)** comes from a top stable and many of her owner's runners tend to improve with time.

## 5695 NORMAN HILL MEMORIAL EBF MAIDEN FILLIES' STKS (DIV II) 7f (J)
2:45 (2:47) (D3) 2-Y-0 **£5,265** (£1,620; £810; £405) **Stalls** High

Form RPR

2 **1** **Quickfire**[66] 3904 2-8-11 ...... KFallon 2 79
(SirMichaelStoute) *hdw: lw: dwlt: t.k.h and rn green: cl up: led over 2f out: hung bdly lft fnl f and ended on nr side rail: pushed out* **8/13**[1]

4 **2** *1 3/4* **Love Always**[18] 5247 2-8-11 ...... LDettori 3 75
(MrsAJPerrett) *lw: dwlt: sn cl up: effrt to chse wnr over 1f out: styd on but no real imp* **4/1**[2]

**3** *1* **Aunt Julia** 2-8-11 ...... RHughes 8 72
(RHannon) *str: lw: racd midfield: prog 2f out: disp 2nd pl over 1f out: nudged along and styd on* **50/1**

**4** *3/4* **Seven Magicians (USA)** 2-8-11 ...... KDarley 10 70
(SirMichaelStoute) *w'like: hld up rr: n.m.r on inner 1/2-way: shuffled along 2f out: styd on steadily fnl f: bttr for experience* **25/1**

0 **5** *1/2* **Pickapeppa**[13] 5376 2-8-11 ...... SCarson 4 69
(RFJohnsonHoughton) *trckd ldr: led 1/2-way: shkn up and hdd over 2f out: fdd fnl f* **66/1**

**6** *3/4* **Clara Bow (IRE)** 2-8-11 ...... MHills 5 67
(BWHills) *rangy: lw: racd green on outer: trckd ldrs: pushed along and kpt on one pce fnl 2f* **10/1**[3]

**7** *3 1/2* **Danzare** 2-8-11 ...... RHills 11 58
(MPTregoning) *w'like: s.s: wl in rr: sme prog into midfield over 2f out: one pce after* **16/1**

65 **8** *hd* **Missie Baileys**[13] 5380 2-8-11 ...... JFortune 1 58
(DRCElsworth) *rn green in rr: kpt on fr over 1f out: n.d* **33/1**

**9** *hd* **Sign Of Luck (IRE)** 2-8-11 ...... DHolland 14 57
(CEBrittain) *unf: prom tl wknd 2f out* **20/1**

**10** *2* **Franela** 2-8-11 ...... RLMoore 6 52
(DRLoder) *cmpt: dwlt: t.k.h in rr: sme prog 2f out: wknd fnl f* **33/1**

**11** *3* **Ballet Ballon (USA)** 2-8-11 ...... MHenry 13 45
(MAJarvis) *str: bit bkwd: rn v green in last w plenty of tail swishing: nvr a factor* **25/1**

0 **12** *3 1/2* **In The Shadows**[24] 5068 2-8-11 ...... TEDurcan 7 36
(WSKittow) *dwlt: t.k.h in midfield: wknd over 2f out* **100/1**

**13** *3 1/2* **Roma Valley (FR)** 2-8-11 ...... EAhern 9 27
(RGuest) *neat: bit bkwd: racd midfield: lost pl and rdn 1/2-way: in rr after* **66/1**

0600 **14** *4* **Mystery Maid (IRE)**[68] 3840 2-8-11 45...... AMcCarthy 12 —
(HSHowe) *racd v freely: led to 1/2-way: wknd rapidly over 2f out* **100/1**

1m 29.18s (1.91) **Going Correction** +0.125s/f (Good) **14** Ran SP% **122.2**
Speed ratings: **94,92,90,90,89 88,84,84,84,81 78,74,70,65**CSF £2.72 TOTE £1.60: £1.02, £1.50, £9.80; EX 4.30.
**Owner** K Abdulla **Bred** Juddmonte Farms Ltd **Trained** Newmarket, Suffolk

**FOCUS**
This was probably the lesser of the two divisions - the time being 1.74 seconds slower confirming this - but it looks sound enough on paper and should still produce winners nonetheless.

**NOTEBOOK**
**Quickfire**, second on her debut at Newbury in a race that is not working out all that well, just about did enough to hold on having hung sharply left in the final furlong, ending up on the stands' rail. This was not a strong race and she will need to up her game significantly to win in a higher grade.
**Love Always** showed an improvement in form on her debut run and will stay a mile. There is a maiden in her.
**Aunt Julia** made a pleasing start to her career - staying on takingly under tender handling to get third. Had she been given a harder time of things she could have been much closer and, although going off here at odds of 50/1, is clearly capable of winning races. *Official explanation: jockey said filly hung left*
**Seven Magicians(USA)** ◆, the Stoute second string, was lacking in experience and did not get much luck in running before finishing strongly to threaten for a place. Bound to improve with the run under her belt, a mile will suit and she too can win her maiden.
**Pickapeppa** ran well for a long way and is a likely type for handicaps next season.
**Clara Bow(IRE)** looked badly in need of the experience and, on a softer surface towards the backend, can win a maiden.
**Danzare**, whose stable remain someway below their best form at the minute, shaped well enough and will be seen to better effect at three.
**Missie Baileys** is now qualified for nurseries and will do better in that sphere.
**Sign Of Luck(IRE)**, a Cheveley Park entrant, dropped away disappointingly and is surely capable of better.
**Ballet Ballon(USA)** was rightly not given a hard time on this debut as she looked badly in need of the outing. She will know more next time but may be more of a three-year-old.
**Roma Valley(FR)**, one of her Arc winning sire Sagamix's first runners in this country, did not know enough at this stage of her career to get competitive and middle-distance handicaps at three beckon.

## 5696 DENNIS HUTCHINGS EBF MAIDEN STKS 1m (J)
3:20 (3:23) (D3) 2-Y-0 **£5,304** (£1,632; £816; £408) **Stalls** High

Form RPR

**1** **Australian** 2-9-0 ...... JFortune 11 80+
(JHMGosden) *lengthy: lw: green to post: trckd ldrs: led over 2f out: drvn out fnl f* **8/1**

4 **2** *nk* **Kerashan (IRE)**[16] 5298 2-9-0 ...... KFallon 6 80
(SirMichaelStoute) *lw: trckd ldrs: rdn 2f out: no real imp tl picked up last 100yds: clsng at fin* **2/1**[2]

354 **3** *nk* **L'Escapade (IRE)**[13] 5373 2-9-0 85...... DHolland 2 79
(AMBalding) *trckd ldrs: effrt 2f out: rdn to dispute 2nd pl 1f out: kpt on* **7/1**[3]

**4** *nk* **The Composer** 2-9-0 ...... FNorton 10 78
(MBlanshard) *gd sort: rangy: str: bit bkwd: detached in last: rdn over 2f out: gd prog fnl f: fin best of all* **66/1**

**5** *shd* **Ashkal Way (IRE)** 2-9-0 ...... EAhern 12 78
(EALDunlop) *w'like: bit bkwd: reminders sn after s: cl up: rdn to dispute 2nd pl over 1f out: one pce u.p* **25/1**

**6** *2* **Unfurled (IRE)** 2-9-0 ...... TQuinn 7 74
(JLDunlop) *leggy: unf: dwlt: racd in rr: prog on inner over 2f out: chsd ldrs 1f out: fdd ins fnl f* **14/1**

006 **7** *1 1/2* **Golden Dynasty**[21] 5173 2-9-0 ...... RHughes 1 70
(RHannon) *racd wd 1st 3f: prom: pushed along and cl up 2f out: fdd fnl f* **50/1**

00 **8** *4* **Loitokitok**$^{17}$ 5269 2-9-0 ........ SCarson 4 62
(PDCundell) *dwlt: t.k.h: in tch tl wknd 2f out* **66/1**

33 **9** *1* **Ameeq (USA)**$^{17}$ 5268 2-9-0 ........ RHills 9 59
(MPTregoning) *lw: led: hung lft and hdd over 2f out: sn wknd* **1/1**$^{1}$

0 **10** *10* **Mothecombe Dream (IRE)**$^{43}$ 4567 2-9-0 ........ KDarley 8 37
(BJMeehan) *t.k.h: trckd ldr to 3f out: wknd rapidly* **66/1**

1m 41.73s (2.11) **Going Correction** +0.125s/f (Good) 2y crse rec **10** Ran SP% **123.9**
Speed ratings: **94,93,93,93,93 91,89,85,84,74**CSF £25.74 TOTE £9.50: £2.60, £1.20, £2.10; EX 34.10.

**Owner** Sheikh Mohammed **Bred** Cheveley Park Stud Ltd **Trained** Manton, Wilts

**FOCUS**

Nothing more than a fair maiden, but appears sound enough rated through the third.

**NOTEBOOK**

**Australian**, a 125,000gns yearling, is bred to want all of this trip and, having had an ideal sit just off the leaders, took it up over two furlongs out and dug deep under strong pressure to hold the challengers and make a successful debut. Entered in the Racing Post Trophy, he is open to improvement - ran green on way to post and in race itself - and is probably worth his place in the line-up at Doncaster. However, he did have a hard enough introduction and it remains to be seen if he goes the right way from it.

**Kerashan(IRE)** improved on his course debut form and was gaining on the winner with every stride at the finish. He is capable of winning his maiden but in the long run looks more of a handicap type for next season.

**L'Escapade(IRE)** has shown a decent level of form on all starts and will find life easier in nurseries.

**The Composer** was a real eyecatcher, coming from a mile back to finish best of all and just be denied a place. This was a pleasing debut and, although not necessarily bred to stay this sort of trip, looks a likely future winner. The negative though is that he is certain to be underpriced next time and he would be one to take on if too short in the betting.

**Ashkal Way(IRE)** was given early reminders to wake him up and take a prominent position, and he kept grinding away down the straight to not be beaten far at all. There should be more to come from him.

**Unfurled(IRE)** is likely to make up into a middle-distance handicapper next season and is unlikely to do much as a juvenile.

**Golden Dynasty** ran well for a long way and can now compete nurseries.

**Ameeq(USA)**, whose stable remain out of form, was well supported but hung under pressure and dropped out tamely suggesting all may not have been well. *Official explanation: jockey said colt hung left*

## 5697 RENAULT MASTER VAN STKS (H'CAP) 6f

**3:50** (3:55) (D2) (0-85,85) 3-Y-O **£8,420** (£2,590; £1,295; £647) **Stalls** Centre

Form RPR

2121 **1** **Who's Winning (IRE)**$^{9}$ 5473 3-8-10 **74** ........ TQuinn 4 88
(BGPowell) *lw: racd nr side: mde virtually all: rdn and styd on wl fnl f* **9/1**

1000 **2** *1 ¼* **Wyatt Earp (IRE)**$^{16}$ 5299 3-8-10 **74** ........ KDarley 1 84
(JARToller) *lw: hld up rr of nr side gp: rdn and prog 2f out: chsd wnr ent fnl f: no imp nr fin* **12/1**

1431 **3** *3 ½* **Chimali (IRE)**$^{19}$ 5219 3-8-9 **73** ........(v) EAhern 9 73
(JNoseda) *pressed wnr nr side: rdn and hld over 1f out: lost 2nd and fdd fnl f* **13/2**$^{2}$

410 **4** *½* **Kostar**$^{38}$ 4717 3-8-12 **76** ........ RSmith 2 74
(CGCox) *racd nr side: in tch: effrt and cl up 2f out: fdd fnl f* **25/1**

6220 **5** *1* **The Jobber (IRE)**$^{32}$ 4874 3-9-0 **78** ........ FNorton 12 73+
(MBlanshard) *lw: racd far side: trckd ldr: led gp 2f out: in command fnl f but no ch w nr side* **16/1**

5205 **6** *¾* **Bohola Flyer (IRE)**$^{10}$ 5442 3-9-0 **78** ........ RHughes 3 71
(RHannon) *trckd nr side ldrs: drvn and lost pl 2f out: n.d after* **12/1**

1660 **7** *nk* **Extra Cover (IRE)**$^{19}$ 5220 3-8-2 **71** oh2........(b) NDeSouza$^{(5)}$ 7 63
(NACallaghan) *s.s: rr of nr side gp: rdn 1/2-way: one pce after* **33/1**

1632 **8** *hd* **Royal Challenge**$^{10}$ 5442 3-9-1 **79** ........ LDettori 11 70+
(GAButler) *restless stalls: rrd s: hld up rr of far side gp: progess over 1f out: chsd ldr nr fin: no ch* **3/1**$^{1}$

0500 **9** *nk* **Totally Yours (IRE)**$^{17}$ 5263 3-9-4 **82** ........ PaulEddery 8 72
(WRMuir) *trckd nr side ldrs to 2f out: wknd over 1f out* **33/1**

2030 **10** *½* **Tregarron**$^{5}$ 5563 3-8-9 **73** ........ RLMoore 6 62
(RHannon) *lw: racd nr side in rr: rdn over 2f out: no prog* **20/1**

6230 **11** *hd* **Bathwick Bill (USA)**$^{68}$ 3845 3-9-3 **81** ........ JFortune 14 69+
(BRMillman) *t.k.h: hld up far side: rdn 2f out: styd on ins fnl f: no ch* **20/1**

6000 **12** *hd* **Desert Dreamer (IRE)**$^{11}$ 5419 3-9-4 **82** ........ MHills 10 70+
(BWHills) *racd far side: in tch: chsd ldr over 1f out tl wknd wl ins fnl f* **7/1**$^{3}$

5234 **13** *½* **Skyharbor**$^{5}$ 5563 3-8-12 **76** ........(v) DHolland 5 62
(AMBalding) *racd on outer of nr side gp: chsd ldrs for 4f* **8/1**

0006 **14** *2* **Big Bradford**$^{13}$ 5379 3-9-7 **85** ........(b) DKinsella 16 65+
(PGMurphy) *led far side gp to 2f out: wknd* **20/1**

0350 **15** *2 ½* **Cherokee Nation**$^{31}$ 4926 3-8-7 **71** oh1........ KFallon 13 44+
(PWD'Arcy) *dwlt: hld up far side: rdn and no prog 2f out: eased ins fnl f* **12/1**

1m 12.15s (-0.92) **Going Correction** -0.075s/f (Good) **15** Ran SP% **124.9**
Speed ratings: **103,101,96,96,94 93,93,93,92,91 91,91,90,88,84**CSF £104.36 CT £777.38 TOTE £10.10: £2.80, £4.80, £2.80; EX 144.60.

**Owner** Tony Head and Caroline Andrus **Bred** Colin Kennedy **Trained** Morestead, Hants

■ Stewards Enquiry : D Kinsella one-day ban: failed to keep straight from stalls (Oct 4)

**FOCUS**

A fair, competitive handicap where the stands' side had a clear advantage and Who's Winning ran out an easy winner, but the form looks decent for the grade despite the field splitting.

**NOTEBOOK**

**Who's Winning(IRE)** practically made all on the stands' side and came away in the final half furlong to win nicely. He is an in-form sprinter who still has more to offer and could easily complete the hat-trick.

**Wyatt Earp(IRE)** came from the back of the stands' group to throw down a brief challenge to the winner but he was soon brushed aside. This was a decent effort.

**Chimali(IRE)** ran well for a long way but was left behind in the final half furlong. A return to the minimum may help.

**Kostar** made no show on his handicap debut, but this was a much better effort and he can win again if building on this.

**The Jobber(IRE)** can feel hard done-by as he won the race far side with a bit in hand but was well behind the stands' bunch. He has been a bit in-and-out but is useful on his day.

**Bohola Flyer(IRE)** kept on without threatening.

**Royal Challenge** fared second best of the far-side group and deserves a little credit.

**Desert Dreamer(IRE)** was disappointing and this drop back in trip did not seem the answer.

## 5698 RENAULT TRAFIC VAN H'CAP 1m (J)

**4:20** (4:26) (D2) (0-85,84) 3-Y-O+ **£10,278** (£3,162; £1,581; £790) **Stalls** High

Form RPR

0002 **1** **Blue Trojan (IRE)**$^{3}$ 5614 4-9-7 **83** ........ DHolland 9 98
(SKirk) *lw: chsd ldrs: rdn to ld wl over 1f out: hung lft 1f out: styd on wl* **6/1**$^{1}$

0000 **2** *1 ¼* **Just Fly**$^{3}$ 5614 4-8-10 **72** ........ RLMoore 7 84
(SKirk) *lw: hld up midfield: prog on outer over 2f out: pressed wnr and carried lft 1f out: no imp ins fnl f* **33/1**

10-2 **3** *4* **Sattam**$^{10}$ 5444 5-9-3 **79** ........(v) RHills 1 82+
(MPTregoning) *lw: dwlt: hld up wl in rr and swtchd to inner: prog 2f out: nt look keen but styd on to take 3rd ins fnl f* **8/1**$^{3}$

2031 **4** *hd* **Arkholme**$^{17}$ 5275 3-8-12 **83** ........(b) MSavage$^{(5)}$ 16 85
(PWinkworth) *hld up midfield: prog 2f out: styd on same pce fnl f* **14/1**

2030 **5** *shd* **Lorien Hill (IRE)**$^{30}$ 4938 3-8-7 **73** ........ MHills 6 75
(BWHills) *settled wl in rr: rdn over 2f out: prog on outer over 1f out: styd on: nrst fin* **25/1**

-014 **6** *shd* **Pagan Prince**$^{17}$ 5275 7-9-2 **78** ........ LisaJones 8 80
(JARToller) *racd on outer in midfield: prog 2f out: styd on same pce fnl f* **8/1**$^{3}$

1042 **7** *¾* **Dr Thong**$^{22}$ 5150 3-8-12 **83** ........ NDeSouza$^{(5)}$ 15 83
(PFICole) *lw: plld hrd: trckd ldr: led 3f out to wl over 1f out: wknd ins fnl f* **9/1**

0041 **8** *nk* **Borrego (IRE)**$^{11}$ 5419 4-8-13 **75** ........(b) SHitchcott 10 74
(CEBrittain) *swtg: hld up midfield: effrt 2f out: one pce fnl f* **16/1**

1454 **9** *1* **Giocoso (USA)**$^{21}$ 5177 4-9-4 **80** ........ KDarley 4 77
(BPalling) *w ldrs: rdn to chal 2f out: wknd ins fnl f* **16/1**

500 **10** *nk* **Dance On The Top**$^{21}$ 5185 6-8-13 **75** ........(t) JFortune 11 71
(JRBoyle) *hld up towards rr: rdn and sme prog on inner over 1f out: no imp fnl f* **16/1**

0000 **11** *1 ¾* **Music Maid (IRE)**$^{10}$ 5444 6-8-7 **69** oh5........ AMcCarthy 14 61
(HSHowe) *dwlt: wl in rr: kpt on one pce fnl 2f: nvr rchd ldrs* **33/1**

4153 **12** *hd* **Franksalot (IRE)**$^{12}$ 5403 4-8-8 **70** ........ TQuinn 3 62
(MissBSanders) *racd wd in midfield: effrt over 2f out: fnd nil and btn over 1f out* **16/1**

1033 **13** *3* **Todlea (IRE)**$^{7}$ 5514 4-9-0 **76** ........ LDettori 20 74+
(JAOsborne) *prom: rdn to chal 2f out: hld whn lost action and heavily eased ins fnl f* **6/1**$^{1}$

1040 **14** *shd* **Supreme Salutation**$^{5}$ 5568 8-9-0 **83** ........ MHoward$^{(7)}$ 2 68
(DKIvory) *trckd ldrs: shkn up over 2f out: wknd wl over 1f out* **33/1**

0430 **15** *1 ¼* **Ile Michel**$^{91}$ 3159 7-9-0 **76** ........ DKinsella 18 58
(JGMO'Shea) *racd towards rr: no prog on inner over 2f out: wknd over 1f out* **33/1**

1216 **16** *14* **Miss Madame (IRE)**$^{16}$ 5304 3-8-3 **69** ........ MHenry 19 19
(RGuest) *led to 3f out: wknd rapidly over 2f out: t.o* **25/1**

0100 **17** *17* **Molcon (IRE)**$^{33}$ 4846 3-9-4 **84** ........ WRyan 17 —
(NACallaghan) *dwlt: a bhd: t.o* **20/1**

31-0 **18** *1 ¾* **Maren (USA)**$^{10}$ 5444 3-9-2 **82** ........(t) KFallon 12 —
(EFVaughan) *dwlt: a in rr: rdn and no prog over 2f out: virtually p.u fnl f* **13/2**$^{2}$

1m 39.25s (-0.37) **Going Correction** +0.125s/f (Good)
**WFA** 3 from 4yo+ 4lb **18** Ran SP% **128.5**
Speed ratings: **106,104,100,100,100 100,99,99,98,98 96,96,93,92,91 77,60,58**CSF £214.51 CT £1648.62 TOTE £7.00: £2.00, £7.10, £2.00, £3.00; EX 168.20 TRIFECTA Not won..

**Owner** The Ex Katy Boys **Bred** Patrick Cassidy **Trained** Upper Lambourn, Berks

**FOCUS**

A fair, competitive handicap and a one-two for trainer Sylvester Kirk. The form looks solid enough and the time was reasonable.

**NOTEBOOK**

**Blue Trojan(IRE)**, who should have won at Newbury at the weekend - his inexperienced rider eased down towards the finish and he got caught - made no mistake in his bid for compensation and ran out a good winner from his stable companion. Going the right way, he has a decent race in him.

**Just Fly**, a stablemate of the winner, pulled clear of the third and can probably count himself a little hard done by. This represented a return to form and he has a similar race in him.

**Sattam** stayed on well to take third but not for the first time looked far from straightforward and is not one to make a habit of backing.

**Arkholme** was doing his best work towards the finish and probably stepped up on his course win last time.

**Lorien Hill(IRE)** ran a slightly improved race and shaped well on this step back up in trip, if anything running as though a stiffer test would suit.

**Pagan Prince** was keeping on steadily at the line but may be finding his current mark a little high.

**Todlea(IRE)** was already beginning to look in trouble when losing his action but can probably be given another chance.

**Maren(USA)** ran very disappointingly and stopped as though something was amiss.

## 5699 RENAULT KANGOO VAN EBF CLASSIFIED STKS 1m 4f

**4:50** (4:59) (C1) 3-Y-O+ **£12,267** (£4,653; £2,326; £1,057) **Stalls** High

Form RPR

3252 **1** **Camrose**$^{21}$ 5183 3-8-9 89 ........ JFortune 1 98
(JLDunlop) *lw: trckd ldrs: effrt to chal wl over 1f out: hrd rdn to ld on line* **14/1**

212 **2** *shd* **Elmustanser**$^{45}$ 4520 3-9-0 95 ........(t) LDettori 13 103
(SaeedBinSuroor) *lw: prom: effrt to ld 2f out: hrd pressed over 1f out: hdd on line* **4/1**$^{1}$

4133 **3** *2* **Credit (IRE)**$^{19}$ 5226 3-8-9 90 ........ KFallon 10 95
(RHannon) *lw: hld up bhd ldrs: hrd rdn and nt qckn 2f out: kpt on fnl f* **5/1**$^{2}$

01-0 **4** *hd* **Vaughan**$^{9}$ 5470 3-8-9 90 ........ KDarley 6 94
(MrsAJPerrett) *trckd ldrs: rdn over 3f out: unable qck over 2f out: styd on fnl f* **16/1**

-101 **5** *nk* **Vinando**$^{57}$ 4167 3-8-13 94 ........(t) MHills 4 98
(CREgerton) *trckd ldr to over 2f out: one pce u.p* **10/1**

5-60 **6** *4* **Lunar Exit (IRE)**$^{75}$ 3641 3-8-11 92 ........ EAhern 5 90
(LadyHerries) *hld up midfield: rdn over 2f out: no prog* **25/1**

1061 **7** *hd* **Ocean Avenue (IRE)**$^{17}$ 5273 5-9-3 88 ........ DHolland 12 87
(CAHorgan) *lw: led to 2f out: wknd over 1f out* **17/2**$^{3}$

0122 **8** *2* **Secretary General (IRE)**$^{19}$ 5226 3-8-13 94 ........ TQuinn 11 88+
(PFICole) *lw: settled in rr: rdn over 2f out: hanging and no prog* **5/1**$^{2}$

0055 **9** *nk* **Tizzy May (FR)**$^{23}$ 5133 4-9-8 95 ........ TEDurcan 3 89+
(RHannon) *hld up in rr: rdn and no prog over 2f out* **25/1**

125 **10** *2* **Wait For The Will (USA)**$^{23}$ 5111 8-9-3 90 ........(b) RLMoore 9 80+
(GLMoore) *hld up wl in rr: shkn up and no prog over 2f out* **12/1**

1516 **11** *8* **Posteritas (USA)**$^{12}$ 5397 3-8-6 88 ........ RHughes 8 65
(HRACecil) *settled in last trio: sltly hmpd 4f out: wknd 2f out* **10/1**

3125 **S** **Larkwing (IRE)**$^{19}$ 5226 3-8-9 88 ........ FNorton 2 —
(GWragg) *settled in rr: 10th and in tch whn slipped up 4f out* **9/1**

0/0- **S** **Hasty Prince**$^{143}$ 4881 6-9-3 88 ........ JMackay 14 —
(JonjoO'Neill) *dwlt: settled in last: in tch whn slipped up 4f out* **20/1**

2m 33.83s (-1.17) **Going Correction** +0.125s/f (Good)
**WFA** 3 from 4yo+ 8lb **13** Ran SP% **124.7**
Speed ratings: **108,107,106,106,106 103,103,102,101,100 95,—,—**CSF £70.62 TOTE £17.60: £4.80, £2.20, £2.50; EX 124.80 Place 6 £92.90, Place 5 £46.68.



The Form Book, Raceform Ltd, Compton, RG20 6NL

**Owner** Nicholas Cooper **Bred** Normandie Stud Ltd **Trained** Arundel, W Sussex

**FOCUS**

A decent and typically tight classified event run at a sound pace, and a great finish between the front two in a race that is likely to work out well.

**NOTEBOOK**

**Camrose** has yet to run a bad race this season and seemed well-suited by the return to this stiffer test, just nosing it on the line having looked held. He evidently has a will to win and further improvement cannot be ruled out given an additional couple of furlongs.

**Elmustanser** has yet to finish out of the two in four career starts, and looked as though he had done enough on first impression as they crossed the line, but lost out on the bob. His rating does not make things easy for him but he is steadily progressing.

**Credit(IRE)** has filled this position the last three times now and, while he is building a consistent profile, does not look a winner waiting to happen and will probably continue to find at least one too good.

**Vaughan ◆**, who looked promising when winning his maiden at two, had no been seen for quite a while until reappearing at Goodwood earlier in the month, and was expected to be well served by the extra three furlongs. Close to the leaders throughout, he simply had no change of pace when things stared to heat up and dropped back before plugging on again to just miss out on a place. His trainer does well with this type of horse and he can be expected to improve again from three to four, with something the the 2005 Ebor looking a speculative long-term target.

**Vinando**, an easy winner when last seen at Ascot in July, is entitled to improve for this and will be suited by a stiffer test.

**Lunar Exit(IRE)** has struggled off this mark to date and needs to drop a few more pounds in the weights before he gets competitive.

**Ocean Avenue(IRE)** was unable to carry out his front-running tactics to quite the same effect as last time.

**Posteritas(USA)** *Official explanation: jockey said filly was never travelling*

**Hasty Prince** slipped up on the bend partly as a result of trying to avoid the other faller.

**Larkwing(IRE)** fell independently on the same bend as Hasty Prince. This caused the last race to be abandoned.

## 5700 DALKIA ETS&LANDSECURITIES TRILLIUM MAIDEN STKS — 1m 4f

() (D3) 3-Y-O £

T/Jkpt: Not won. T/Plt: £62.00 to a £1 stake. Pool: £46,141.45. 543.20 winning tickets. T/Qpdt: £35.80 to a £1 stake. Pool: £3,048.40. 62.90 winning tickets. JN

# 5368 LEICESTER (R-H)

## Monday, September 20

**OFFICIAL GOING: Good to soft**

Race times suggested the ground on the straight course was Good with the round course a little easier.

Wind: Fresh behind Weather: Fine

## 5701 IBETX.COM - THE PUNTER'S CHOICE FILLIES' NURSERY — 5f 218y

**2:00** (2:00) (D2) (0-85,84) 2-Y-O **£5,759** (£1,772; £886; £443) **Stalls** Low

| Form | | | | | RPR |
|---|---|---|---|---|---|
| 416 | 1 | | **Magical Romance (IRE)**[58] 4119 2-9-6 **83** (BJMeehan) *mde all: rdn clr over 1f out: eased nr fin* | RWinston 8 **13/2**[3] | 94+ |
| 0045 | 2 | 3 | **Aberdeen Park**[2] 5655 2-8-5 **68** (MrsHSweeting) *dwlt: hld up: hdwy 1/2-way: rdn over 1f out: edgd lft ins fnl f: styd on same pce* | PDoe 10 **25/1** | 70 |
| 1320 | 3 | ½ | **Highland Cascade**[12] 5391 2-8-12 **75** (JMPEustace) *chsd ldrs: rdn over 2f out: no ex fnl f* | JTate 4 **12/1** | 75 |
| 555 | 4 | ¾ | **Xeeran**[17] 5271 2-7-8 **62** (MAJarvis) *hld up: hdwy over 1f out: nt rch ldrs* | DFox(5) 12 **9/1** | 60 |
| 0000 | 5 | nk | **Aspen Ridge (IRE)**[32] 4866 2-7-12 **61** oh4 (CTinkler) *chsd ldrs: rdn over 2f out: styd on same pce appr fnl f* | PHanagan 7 **40/1** | 58 |
| 4233 | 6 | nk | **Cerebus**[9] 5466 2-8-11 **74** (NPLittmoden) *hld up: hdwy over 2f out: hrd rdn over 1f out: no imp* | RMullen 1 **5/1**[2] | 70 |
| 21 | 7 | 2 | **Epiphany**[44] 4532 2-9-7 **84** (EALDunlop) *hld up: pushed along over 3f out: hdwy over 2f out: no ex fnl f* | KMcEvoy 5 **7/1** | 74 |
| 5644 | 8 | hd | **Alexander Capetown (IRE)**[14] 5351 2-8-6 **69** (BWHills) *plld hrd and prom: rdn over 2f out: wknd fnl f* | ACulhane 11 **9/2**[1] | 58 |
| 0253 | 9 | ¾ | **Kwame**[11] 5421 2-9-1 **78** (MissECLavelle) *chsd ldrs: rdn over 2f out: wknd fnl f* | (v) SDrowne 6 **9/1** | 65 |
| 1300 | 10 | 4 | **Three Pennies**[9] 5466 2-8-5 **68** ow1 (MDods) *prom over 3f* | SWKelly 9 **40/1** | 43 |
| 0004 | 11 | 5 | **The Keep**[14] 5353 2-7-12 **64** oh3 ow3 (RHannon) *prom: rdn 1/2-way: sn wknd* | RThomas(3) 13 **33/1** | 24 |
| 540 | 12 | 2½ | **Ellens Princess (IRE)**[17] 5270 2-8-9 **72** (RHannon) *chsd ldrs over 3f* | PDobbs 2 **14/1** | 24 |
| 5042 | 13 | 2 | **Ringarooma**[13] 5362 2-8-6 **69** (MHTompkins) *prom over 3f* | PRobinson 3 **7/1** | 15 |

1m 12.06s (-1.34) **Going Correction** -0.025s/f (Good) **13** Ran **SP% 119.2**

Speed ratings: **107,103,102,101,100 100,97,97,96,91 84,81,78**CSF £165.38 CT £1957.91 TOTE £10.50: £3.10, £16.60, £4.50; EX 500.80.

**Owner** F C T Wilson **Bred** Quay Bloodstock And Samac Ltd **Trained** Upper Lambourn, Berks

**FOCUS**

The stalls were against the stands' rail and the whole field raced that side. A decent pace and cracking winning time for the type of contest, so the form appears strong and should work out.

**NOTEBOOK**

**Magical Romance(IRE)**, racing for the first time since her modest effort in the Princess Margaret, was quickly away and made every yard to win with plenty in hand. She looks well worth stepping back up again in grade.

**Aberdeen Park** certainly improved a good deal on her previous form and deserves extra credit as she was rather stuck out in the centre of the track. On this showing she will have little difficulty winning a nursery.

**Highland Cascade** was never far away and ran her race, but may prefer faster ground.

**Xeeran**, making her nursery debut and yet to make the frame, saw the trip out much better this time and looks capable of winning off this mark.

**Aspen Ridge(IRE)**, another yet to make the frame and making her nursery debut, was not totally disgraced but she is not seeing her races out at present.

**Cerebus** was not done any favours by the drop back to six and ran accordingly.

**Epiphany**, having only her third start, had her limitations exposed on this nursery debut, but she may prefer faster ground and should not be written off just yet.

**Alexander Capetown(IRE)** dropped away rather tamely after holding a good early position and is starting to look exposed.

## 5702 GOLDEN HAND (S) STKS — 7f 9y

**2:30** (2:33) (G4) 3-Y-O **£3,073** (£878; £439) **Stalls** Low

| Form | | | | | RPR |
|---|---|---|---|---|---|
| 0040 | 1 | | **Inescapable (USA)**[17] 5260 3-8-11 49 (WRMuir) *chsd ldr: rdn over 2f out: styd on u.p to ld wl ins fnl f* | SDrowne 7 **33/1** | 57 |
| 6000 | 2 | 1 | **Absolutely Soaked (IRE)**[40] 4655 3-8-6 54 (DrJDScargill) *led: rdn over 1f out: hdd wl ins fnl f* | (b[1]) KMcEvoy 10 **7/1**[3] | 49 |
| 2035 | 3 | ½ | **Red Rocky**[54] 4241 3-8-6 45 (RHollinshead) *chsd ldrs: rdn over 2f out: styd on* | (p) RFfrench 13 **8/1** | 48 |
| U060 | 4 | shd | **Melody King**[9] 5473 3-9-2 58 (PDEvans) *prom: rdn over 2f out: styd on* | (b) RWinston 18 **5/1**[1] | 58 |
| 0600 | 5 | hd | **Russalka**[7] 5524 3-7-13 50 (JulianPoulton) *outpcd: hdwy over 1f out: r.o* | MHalford(7) 5 **20/1** | 47 |
| 5000 | 6 | ½ | **Blue Daze**[6] 5541 3-8-11 59 (RHannon) *chsd ldrs: rdn over 2f out: styd on* | PDobbs 1 **7/1**[3] | 51 |
| 0050 | 7 | ½ | **Vittorioso (IRE)**[6] 5547 3-8-8 45 (MissGayKelleway) *prom: rdn over 2f out: styd on same pce ins fnl f* | BReilly(3) 6 **20/1** | 50 |
| 055 | 8 | 3½ | **Bulberry Hill**[6] 5552 3-8-11 (MGQuinlan) *mid-div: rdn over 2f out: nvr trbld ldrs* | DRMcCabe 16 **16/1** | 41 |
| 5330 | 9 | 1 | **La Calera (GER)**[16] 5282 3-8-11 45 (GCHChung) *prom: rdn over 2f out: wknd fnl f* | OUrbina 20 **10/1** | 41+ |
| 0000 | 10 | hd | **Named At Dinner**[9] 5448 3-8-11 50 (MrsADuffield) *s.s: hdwy over 4f out: rdn over 2f out: wknd over 1f out* | (b[1]) RMullen 17 **40/1** | 38 |
| 0000 | 11 | ¾ | **Capetown Girl**[31] 4905 3-8-11 52 (KRBurke) *s.i.s: sn prom: rdn and wknd over 1f out* | DarrenWilliams 19 **9/1** | 36 |
| 0000 | 12 | 4 | **Orpenberry (IRE)**[13] 5364 3-8-11 50 (EJAlston) *mid-div: rdn 1/2-way: wknd over 2f out* | DAllan 3 **20/1** | 25 |
| 0000 | 13 | 7 | **Mac The Knife (IRE)**[83] 3391 3-9-2 50 (AWCarroll) *bhd: hdwy over 2f out: wknd over 1f out* | ACulhane 15 **20/1** | 12 |
| 0540 | 14 | 5 | **Lottie**[6] 5547 3-8-6 45 (MissVHaigh) *sn outpcd* | PDoe 12 **50/1** | — |
| 05- | 15 | ¾ | **Munaahej (IRE)**[380] 4715 3-8-11 (KAMorgan) *chsd ldrs over 4f* | PHanagan 11 **11/2**[2] | — |
| 6000 | 16 | 4 | **Power Nap**[44] 4562 3-8-6 40 (NTinkler) *dwlt and swvd lft s: outpcd* | (b[1]) GCarter 9 **66/1** | — |
| 060 | 17 | 10 | **Scooby Dooby Do**[21] 5193 3-8-6 49 (RMWhitaker) *sn outpcd* | (p) SWKelly 4 **33/1** | — |
| | 18 | dist | **Nippy Nipper** 3-8-6 (MQuinn) *dwlt and hmpd s: outpcd* | NPollard 8 **33/1** | — |

1m 27.32s (1.22) **Going Correction** -0.025s/f (Good) **18** Ran **SP% 126.9**

Speed ratings: **92,90,90,90,89 89,88,84,83,83 82,78,70,64,63 58,47,**—CSF £235.41 TOTE £48.30: £17.90, £2.30, £3.00; EX 600.70.The winner was bought in for 4,500 gns.

**Owner** M J Caddy **Bred** J R Perrotta **Trained** Lambourn, Berks

**FOCUS**

A poor contest and a modest winning time, even for a race like this, 0.3 seconds slower than the following two-year-old novice event, and the form is unlikely to prove reliable.

**NOTEBOOK**

**Inescapable(USA)**, who had no chance from his draw at Chepstow last time as things turned out, appreciated being dropped into a seller for the first time and ground out a victory after looking held for much of the way. This was a bad race though and he will be fortunate to find another one like it.

**Absolutely Soaked(IRE)**, another dropped into a seller and blinkered for the first time, was also dropping back from middle distances and her jockey rightly tried to make full use of her stamina. She looked like succeeding for a long time too, but just found the winner too strong inside the last half-furlong. Even this trip looked right on the limit.

**Red Rocky**, already placed a couple of times in this grade, was given a positive ride as usual. Although not able to lead on her own, she ran her race and is a guide to the level of the form.

**Melody King**, racing over this trip for only the second time on his 21st start, was taking a substantial drop in grade and that as much as anything probably helped him get as close as he did. In stronger company he would remain a doubtful stayer.

**Russalka** found this trip too short and did not get going until it was too late. She is exposed as moderate, but does have some form on Fibresand and may be worth a try at this level on that surface over a bit further during the winter.

**Blue Daze** would probably have preferred faster ground, but nonetheless has become very disappointing and even this drop in class did not bring about any great improvement.

**Vittorioso(IRE)** *Official explanation: jockey said gelding hung left*

**Munaahej(IRE)**, racing for the first time in a year after having shown ability in two starts for Barry Hills as a juvenile, was well backed on this considerable drop in grade but showed little. It is too early to write him off completely for a similar event, especially on easier ground, though he obviously has questions to answer. *Official explanation: jockey said gelding hung left*

**Power Nap** *Official explanation: jockey said filly pulled up lame*

**Scooby Dooby Do** *Official explanation: jockey said filly hung left*

**Nippy Nipper** *Official explanation: jockey said filly felt wrong during the race*

## 5703 EBF KEGWORTH NOVICE STKS — 7f 9y

**3:05** (3:05) (D2) 2-Y-O **£5,408** (£1,664; £832; £416) **Stalls** Low

| Form | | | | | RPR |
|---|---|---|---|---|---|
| 154 | 1 | | **Pivotal Flame**[30] 4949 2-9-5 100 (BAMcmahon) *hld up in tch: chsd ldr 1/2-way: rdn to ld over 1f out: hung lft ins fnl f: styd on* | GCarter 6 **7/4**[2] | 91 |
| 41 | 2 | 1 | **Haunting Memories (IRE)**[33] 4861 2-9-5 (MAJarvis) *sn led: hung rt thrght: rdn and hdd over 1f out: hmpd ins fnl f: unable qck* | PRobinson 1 **8/13**[1] | 89 |
| 03 | 3 | 5 | **Orpen Wide (IRE)**[6] 5542 2-8-12 (MCChapman) *chsd ldr to 1/2-way: outpcd fnl 2f* | KMcEvoy 3 **50/1** | 69 |
| 1001 | 4 | 5 | **Happy Event**[24] 5068 2-9-4 86 (BRMillman) *chsd ldrs over 4f* | GBaker 5 **16/1**[3] | 63 |
| | 5 | dist | **Court Ruler** 2-8-8 (RJPrice) *s.i.s: outpcd* | OUrbina 4 **150/1** | — |
| | 6 | 1¾ | **Silver Court** 2-8-8 (RJPrice) *swvd rt s: sn outpcd* | PHanagan 7 **100/1** | — |

1m 27.02s (0.92) **Going Correction** -0.025s/f (Good) **6** Ran **SP% 107.8**

Speed ratings: **93,91,86,80,**— —CSF £2.85 TOTE £2.70: £1.10, £1.10; EX 3.80.

**Owner** R L Bedding **Bred** Cheveley Park Stud Ltd **Trained** Hopwas, Staffs

■ Stewards Enquiry : G Carter caution: careless riding

**FOCUS**

Six runners, but a match according to the market and so it proved. A steady early pace resulted in a very modest winning time for the grade, despite being 0.3 seconds faster than the three-year-old seller, and therefore slightly messy.

**NOTEBOOK**

**Pivotal Flame**, dropping back from Group company, always had his market rival in his sights and the pair battled it out over the last couple of furlongs. They got very close in the closing stages, but he proved the stronger in the run to the line and was the winner on merit.

**Haunting Memories(IRE)** was given a positive ride over this longer trip, but hung away from the stands' rail as the race unfolded. He got very close to the eventual winner, with the result that his rider had problems trying to use his whip, and was eventually worried out of it. A combination of a gusty wind and drying ground may have counted against him, and he should be given another chance when conditions are more suitable. *Official explanation: jockey said colt hung right*

**Orpen Wide(IRE)** finished a clear third best, but the way the race was run did not mean he conclusively proved he stayed this longer trip and a literal interpretation of this effort might adversely affect his provisional nursery mark.

**Happy Event** did not see out this longer trip.

## 5704 BETTING WITH IBETX.COM H'CAP 5f 2y

3:40 (3:41) (D2) (0-85,88) 3-Y-O+ £7,264 (£2,235; £1,117; £558) Stalls Low

Form RPR

4602 1 **Endless Summer**[30] 4935 7-8-12 **76** .......... PDoe 12 92+
(AWCarroll) *racd stands' side: chsd ldrs: led over 1f out: r.o* **4/1**[1]

061 2 1 **Ok Pal**[5] 5564 4-9-0 **78** 6ex .......... GCarter 8 90
(TGMills) *racd stands' side: led over 3f: styd on* **8/1**[3]

0200 3 nk **Dancing Mystery**[10] 5440 10-8-13 **77** .......... (b) PRobinson 7 88
(EAWheeler) *racd stands' side: chsd ldrs: swtchd rt over 1f out: styd on* **14/1**

0001 4 1 **Mine Behind**[6] 5550 4-9-10 **88** 6ex .......... KMcEvoy 3 96+
(JRBest) *racd stands' side: hld up: hdwy over 1f out: r.o* **4/1**[1]

3304 5 shd **Paddywack (IRE)**[3] 5605 7-8-8 **72** .......... (b) ACulhane 4 79
(DWChapman) *racd stands' side: s.i.s: hdwy over 1f out: r.o* **5/1**[2]

2422 6 ¾ **Never Without Me**[22] 5157 4-8-2 **71** oh6 .......... PMakin(5) 2 76
(JFCoupland) *racd stands' side: chsd ldrs: rdn over 1f out: styd on same pce* **8/1**[3]

0062 7 nk **Beyond The Clouds (IRE)**[10] 5440 8-8-12 **76** .......... (p) RWinston 1 80
(JSWainwright) *racd stands' side: rdn over 1f out: styd on same pce* **12/1**

2000 8 ½ **Law Breaker (IRE)**[19] 5224 6-9-4 **85** .......... BReilly(3) 15 87
(JAGilbert) *racd centre: chsd ldrs: rdn over 1f out: styd on same pce* **20/1**

0020 9 nk **Devon Flame**[24] 5075 5-8-13 **77** .......... SDrowne 5 78
(RJHodges) *racd stands' side: chsd ldrs: rdn over 1f out: no ex* **16/1**

0000 10 4 **Turibius**[52] 4291 5-8-9 **73** .......... (v) SWKelly 10 59
(TEPowell) *racd stands' side: hld up: rdn over 1f out: n.d* **20/1**

3100 11 nk **Parkside Pursuit**[52] 4291 6-8-9 **73** .......... PFitzsimons 16 58
(JMBradley) *racd centre: chsd ldrs over 3f* **25/1**

3300 12 ½ **Prince Of Blues (IRE)**[9] 5458 6-8-0 **71** oh15 .......... (p) LiamJones(7) 14 54
(MMullineaux) *racd centre: w ldrs over 3f: wknd fnl f* **66/1**

3520 13 ¾ **Prince Cyrano**[24] 5094 5-8-8 **72** .......... RMullen 11 53+
(WJMusson) *rrd s: racd stands' side: outpcd* **14/1**

0500 14 hd **Treasure House (IRE)**[16] 5299 3-9-1 **80** .......... GBaker 17 60
(JJay) *racd alone far side: w ldrs over 3f* **40/1**

0053 15 nk **Lets Get It On (IRE)**[72] 3737 3-8-9 **74** .......... DarrenWilliams 6 53
(JJQuinn) *racd stands' side: outpcd* **28/1**

2000 16 3½ **The Fisio**[30] 4935 4-8-5 **72** .......... (v) TEaves(3) 13 38
(SGollings) *unruly stalls: racd stands' side: mid-div: rdn 1/2-way: sn wknd* **33/1**

59.60 secs (-1.33) **Going Correction** -0.025s/f (Good)
**WFA** 3 from 4yo+ 1lb **16** Ran SP% **129.5**
Speed ratings: **109,107,106,105,105 103,103,102,102,95 95,94,93,93,92 86**CSF £35.37 CT £432.75 TOTE £5.60: £1.10, £2.70, £3.60, £1.70; EX 57.40.
**Owner** Seasons Holidays **Bred** Juddmonte Farms **Trained** Wixford, Warwicks

**FOCUS**
A competitive sprint run at a decent pace and a fair winning time for the grade so the form looks solid. The vast majority of the field raced towards the stands' side, though one raced alone on the far side.

**NOTEBOOK**
**Endless Summer**, recently disqualified from his 2000 Richmond Stakes victory after revelations over his actual age, scored his first victory since and was well backed to do so. The way he travelled, plus his trainer's record at reviving horses like him, suggests he will not take so long before winning again this time.
**Ok Pal**, carrying a 6lb penalty for his victory in a Sandown claimer five days earlier, ran a fine race under a positive ride and only the winner proved too strong. This was his best effort away from the Esher track, but things will not get any easier as he is sue to go up another 3lb at the weekend.
**Dancing Mystery** came home strongly and this was certainly one of his better recent performances. He has become well handicapped on his best form and could well nick another race like this before too long.
**Mine Behind**, bidding to follow up his Yarmouth victory under a 6lb penalty, did not get going until it was too late. Despite his Yarmouth victory over an extended five, he is probably better over six.
**Paddywack(IRE)** continues to run with great credit despite being kept very busy. He is still 4lb above his last winning mark, but it would still be no surprise to see him hit the bullseye before too long.
**Never Without Me** did about as well as could be expected from 6lb out of the handicap. He has been in fine form on Fibresand this year so he is likely to be kept going beyond the end of the turf season.
**Turibius** *Official explanation: jockey said gelding was unsuited by ground*
**Prince Cyrano** lost all chance at the start. *Official explanation: jockey said gelding reared at start and missed break*
**Treasure House(IRE)** raced on his own over on the far side from his high draw and ended up well beaten, but was a 40/1 shot in any case so it proved little.

## 5705 HENRY ALKEN CLAIMING STKS 1m 1f 218y

4:10 (4:10) (E3) 3-4-Y-O £4,251 (£1,308; £654; £327) Stalls High

Form RPR

5401 1 **Platinum Pirate**[13] 5381 3-8-2 65 .......... (v) RoryMoore(5) 7 69
(KRBurke) *hld up: hdwy to ld over 2f out: rdn over 1f out: r.o* **5/1**[2]

2603 2 ½ **Go Green**[6] 5538 3-7-5 54 .......... (t) NataliaGemelova(7) 6 59
(PDEvans) *s.i.s: sn chsng ldrs: rdn over 1f out: r.o* **8/1**

0036 3 2½ **Ephesus**[20] 5210 4-9-3 76 .......... (v) ACulhane 10 68
(MissGayKelleway) *a.p: rdn over 1f out: edgd rt: no ex ins fnl f* **7/2**[1]

52-2 4 ½ **Tricky Venture**[22] 5146 4-8-8 73 .......... PMakin(5) 12 63
(PWHiatt) *chsd ldrs: rdn whn nt clr run 1f out: styd on same pce* **5/1**[2]

3/ 5 ½ **Selkirk Grace**[703] 5341 4-9-7 .......... PHanagan 1 70
(KAMorgan) *s.s: hld up: hdwy over 1f out: styd on* **7/1**

4000 6 nk **Grand Wizard**[31] 4911 4-8-9 60 .......... RMullen 8 57
(WJarvis) *hld up: outpcd 4f out: styd on ins fnl f: nt trble ldrs* **33/1**

0565 7 nk **Rebate**[13] 5381 4-8-9 58 .......... (t) PDobbs 5 57
(RHannon) *plld hrd and prom: rdn over 2f out: no ex fnl f* **6/1**[3]

3/06 8 5 **Love You Always (USA)**[10] 5436 4-9-4 92 .......... BReilly(3) 3 69+
(MissJFeilden) *chsd ldrs: rdn and hung rt fr over 3f out: wknd over 1f out* **12/1**

0501 9 6 **Ivory Coast (IRE)**[27] 5018 3-8-2 57 .......... (b) PDoe 11 36
(WRMuir) *mde most over 7f: wknd over 1f out* **14/1**

10 25 **Indian's Landing (IRE)**[105] 2743 3-9-1 .......... RWinston 4 4
(MichaelCunningham, Ire) *hld up: wknd over 4f out* **40/1**

340- P **Rustic Charm (IRE)**[106] 5935 4-8-12 67 .......... ANicholls 9 —
(MissKMarks) *hld up: rdn over 4f out: sn wknd: t.o whn p.u ins fnl f* **25/1**

2m 10.18s (1.78) **Going Correction** +0.20s/f (Good)
**WFA** 3 from 4yo 6lb **11** Ran SP% **117.0**
Speed ratings: **100,99,97,97,96 96,96,92,87,67** —CSF £43.68 TOTE £5.60: £2.10, £3.10, £1.20; EX 28.50.
**Owner** Spigot Lodge Partnership **Bred** Llety Stud **Trained** Middleham Moor, N Yorks

**FOCUS**
A moderate claimer run at an ordinary pace and the form amounts to little.

**NOTEBOOK**
**Platinum Pirate** had a bit to find at the weights with a few of these, but at least came into this in form. Kept wide of his field down the home straight, he proved too good despite holding his head up and dossing in front, but is not the type to lump on to complete the hat-trick.
**Go Green**, who was not that well in at the weights, goes well in these types of races and performed well again, but was still unable to take advantage of the winner's antics in the closing stages.
**Ephesus**, one of those more favourably treated at the weights, had every chance but his effort flattened out in the last furlong and he would probably have preferred faster ground.
**Tricky Venture**, second-best in at the weights, would probably have finished third had he not run out of room against the inside rail passing the furlong pole and looks capable of winning a similar contest.
**Selkirk Grace** ◆, not seen since making a promising debut for Ed Dunlop almost two years ago, stayed on from well off the pace and can still be placed to advantage.
**Grand Wizard** probably found this trip too short, but has been very disappointing since returning to turf this year.
**Rebate** probably did too much early and continues to disappoint.
**Love You Always(USA)** was by some way best in at the weights based on his juvenile form for Mark Johnston, but judged on this season's efforts is nothing like the same horse now. *Official explanation: jockey said gelding hung right*
**Ivory Coast(IRE)** *Official explanation: jockey said filly ran too keen early on*
**Rustic Charm(IRE)** *Official explanation: jockey said filly pulled up lame*

## 5706 HIGHFIELDS CLASSIFIED STKS 1m 9y

4:40 (4:40) (D2) 3-Y-O+ £7,260 (£2,234; £1,117; £558) Stalls High

Form RPR

0221 1 **Zameyla (IRE)**[6] 5537 3-8-13 74 .......... PRobinson 10 84+
(MAJarvis) *chsd ldrs: led 2f out: edgd lft ins fnl f: rdn out: eased nr fin* **11/4**[1]

5452 2 1 **Honest Injun**[24] 5092 3-8-10 72 .......... SWKelly 9 79
(JGMO'Shea) *hld up: hdwy over 3f out: rdn over 1f out: styd on* **9/1**

3330 3 ½ **Master Theo (USA)**[18] 5244 3-8-10 73 .......... RWinston 6 78
(HJCollingridge) *a.p: rdn and ev ch 2f out: styd on same pce ins fnl f* **25/1**

3615 4 ½ **Riska King**[18] 5236 4-9-0 72 .......... PHanagan 7 77
(RAFahey) *hld up: hdwy over 3f out: rdn over 1f out: styd on same pce ins fnl f* **7/1**

1000 5 1 **St Savarin (FR)**[12] 5399 3-8-10 74 .......... RFfrench 5 75
(JRBest) *hld up: hdwy over 2f out: rdn and hung rt ins fnl f: styd on same pce* **33/1**

01 6 1¾ **Tadawul (USA)**[11] 5424 3-8-7 75 .......... KMcEvoy 1 68
(EFVaughan) *hld up: hdwy 3f out: lost pl and hmpd wl over 1f out: styd on ins fnl f* **4/1**[3]

4005 7 nk **The Bonus King**[31] 4928 4-9-0 75 .......... GBaker 8 70
(JJay) *led 6f: wknd ins fnl f* **40/1**

3460 8 ½ **Weet A Head (IRE)**[46] 4490 3-8-10 75 .......... ACulhane 4 69
(RHollinshead) *chsd ldrs: rdn and ev ch 2f out: wknd ins fnl f* **12/1**

5200 9 ¾ **Fiveoclock Express (IRE)**[37] 4751 4-8-11 71 .......... (p) TEaves(3) 2 68
(MissGayKelleway) *hld up: hdwy over 5f out: hung lft and wknd over 1f out* **16/1**

3041 10 2 **Crail**[31] 4912 4-9-0 75 .......... SDrowne 3 64
(CFWall) *chsd ldrs: rdn over 3f out: wknd 2f out* **7/2**[2]

1m 42.54s (-0.06) **Going Correction** +0.20s/f (Good)
**WFA** 3 from 4yo 4lb **10** Ran SP% **114.2**
Speed ratings: **108,107,106,106,105 103,102,102,101,99**CSF £27.22 TOTE £3.80: £1.10, £3.40, £11.40; EX 36.80 Place 6 £174.80, Place 5 £26.21.
**Owner** Sheikh Ahmed Al Maktoum **Bred** Gerard Callanan **Trained** Newmarket, Suffolk

**FOCUS**
Probably not a bad little classified event and the time was quite reasonable for the grade, confirming the solid appearance of the form on paper.

**NOTEBOOK**
**Zameyla(IRE)** still appears to be improving and was very game after hitting the front two furlongs from home. The ground had obviously not dried to too much for her and there may be a bit more to come when conditions allow.
**Honest Injun**, who is yet to win on turf, would probably have preferred softer ground but performed with credit and this effort again suggested he is worth another try over a bit further.
**Master Theo(USA)** ran a very creditable race, but usually finds a couple to beat him and did so again. He is becoming frustrating, but there is probably a small race in him, possibly back on sand.
**Riska King** had every chance, but is yet to win over this trip and lacked pace where it matters.
**St Savarin(FR)** put in a better performance after three modest efforts, but all four of his wins have been over seven furlongs and he could never quite land a blow.
**Tadawul(USA)**, having only her third start, was inclined to run in snatches and is almost certainly better than this.
**Crail** should have had no problem with these conditions and this was too bad to be true.
T/Plt: £254.10 to a £1 stake. Pool: £34,792.15. 99.95 winning tickets. T/Qpdt: £6.70 to a £1 stake. Pool: £2,790.70. 306.50 winning tickets. CR

5707 - 5709a (Foreign Racing) - See Raceform Interactive

# 5555 BEVERLEY (R-H)

### Tuesday, September 21

**OFFICIAL GOING: Good to firm (firm in places)**
Wind: Fresh 1/2 against. Weather: Fine and sunny but very wind.

## 5710 RACING UK ON CHANNEL 432 (S) STKS 1m 4f 16y

2:10 (2:10) (G4) 3-Y-O+ £3,503 (£1,078; £539; £269) Stalls High

Form RPR

0/40 1 **Regency Red (IRE)**[10] 5456 6-9-0 46 .......... BSwarbrick(5) 6 56
(WMBrisbourne) *hld up in midfield: hdwy 5f out: led 2f out and sn rdn clr: kpt on* **9/1**

0533 2 7 **Staff Nurse (IRE)**[29] 4998 4-9-0 35 .......... KimTinkler 11 40
(DonEnricoIncisa) *wl bhd 1/2-way: hdwy 3f out: rdn and styd on fnl 2f: nrst fin* **10/1**

0610 3 1 **Righty Ho**[19] 5243 10-9-3 48 .......... KristinStubbs(7) 7 48
(WHTinning) *hld up in midfield: hdwyover 4f out: effrt to chse wnr over 1f out sn one pce* **8/1**[3]

0006 4 1½ **Coolfore Jade (IRE)**[17] 5286 4-9-0 40 .......... MSavage(5) 8 41
(NEBerry) *trckd ldrs: hdwy 4f out: effrt and ev ch over 2f out: sn rdn: edgd rt and btn* **10/1**

6300 5 hd **Our Imperial Bay (USA)**[18] 5257 5-9-10 40 .......... (p) ADaly 2 46
(MrsJCandlish) *rdn along and wl bhd 1/2-way: hdwy u.p 3f out: drvn and styd on fnl 2f: nrst fin* **16/1**

0-32 6 1¾ **Forbearing (IRE)**[61] 4042 7-9-5 62 .......... DSweeney 10 38
(JGMO'Shea) *in tch: rdn along over 3f out: drvn and no imp 2f out* **7/2**[2]

5306 7 6 **Ellway Heights**[10] 5456 7-9-5 51 .......... SWKelly 3 28
(WMBrisbourne) *led 1f: cl up tl led 3f out: sn rdn: hdd 2f out and sn wknd* **13/8**[1]

0-00 **8** *6* **Golden Fields (IRE)**$^{15}$ 5350 4-9-0 45................................(b) MFenton 5 14
(MrsJCandlish) *cl up: led after 1f: rdn along 4f out: hdd 3f out and sn wknd* **25/1**

00 **9** *13* **Shameless**$^{23}$ 5146 7-8-12 ..................................................(t) RKeogh(7) 1 —
(HAlexander) *chsd ldrs: rdn along 4f out: sn wknd* **80/1**

**10** *hd* **Modulor (FR)**$^{31}$ 12-9-5 ...................................................... TWilliams 12 —
(LRJames) *a rr: t.o fr 1/2-way* **40/1**

/00- **11** *3/4* **Benvolio**$^{9}$ 4161 7-8-12 ............................................ NataliaGemelova(7) 4 —
(IWMcinnes) *chsd ldrs: rdn along over 4f out: sn wknd* **66/1**

2m 41.02s (1.72) **Going Correction** -0.05s/f (Good) **11** Ran SP% **114.5**
Speed ratings: **92,87,86,85,85 84,80,76,67,67 67**CSF £90.42 TOTE £13.60: £3.60, £1.90, £2.40; EX 130.90.Forbearing was claimed by F.Jordan for £6,000.
**Owner** Mrs J M Russell **Bred** Patrick J Burke **Trained** Great Ness, Shropshire

**FOCUS**
A poor seller featuring some very disappointing types and a slow time after a steady gallop over the opening mile. However, the winner came clear and the placed horses were close to form, suggesting the form is fairly sound for the grade.

**NOTEBOOK**
**Regency Red(IRE)**, who on official figures had plenty to find, was well backed at long odds. Rated just 46, he had this won in a matter of strides ending his trainer's recent drought.
**Staff Nurse(IRE)** was out of contention until picking up in the final quarter mile and she snatched second place near the line.
**Righty Ho**, who had plenty to find, likes it around here and kept on up the wide outside only losing out on second spot in the closing stages.
**Coolfore Jade(IRE)**, well backed despite facing a very stiff task, was bang in contention once in line for home but he came off a straight line under pressure and did not pull out much.
**Our Imperial Bay(USA)** struggled badly to keep up and was soon flat out. He stayed on up the hill but was never going to seriously enter the argument.
**Forbearing(IRE)**, having his first outing for his new trainer, was weak in the market. He made ground on the wide outside but was going up and down in the same place in the final two furlongs. His best days look history now but he was claimed yet again.
**Ellway Heights**, dropped in grade, went on and stepped up the gallop but once collared he fell away like the leaves in the strong wind and reportedly bled. *Official explanation: jockey said gelding bled from nose*

## 5711 CHILDREN IN NEED PANTOMIME HORSE RACE NOVICE STKS 5f
**2:40** (2:40) (D3) 2-Y-O **£5,512** (£1,696; £848; £424) **Stalls** High

Form RPR
13 **1** **Sharplaw Star**$^{97}$ 2970 2-9-0 ...................................................... MHills 5 91+
(WJHaggas) *hld up in tch: smooth hdwy 2f out: sheken up to ld ins last: pushed clr* **8/13**$^{1}$

40 **2** *2* **Cutlass Gaudy**$^{48}$ 4454 2-8-12 ............................................ DSweeney 6 82
(RHollinshead) *dwlt and bhd: swtchd lft and hdwy over 1f out: styd on wl towards fin* **100/1**

201 **3** *nk* **Safsoof (USA)**$^{57}$ 4187 2-9-5 93.......................................... KMcEvoy 1 88
(SaeedBinSuroor) *chsd ldr: rdn: edgd rt and sltly outpcd 2f out: kpt on u.p fnl f* **11/4**$^{2}$

2106 **4** *nk* **Bold Marc (IRE)**$^{64}$ 3975 2-9-4 88................................ DarrenWilliams 4 86
(KRBurke) *chsd ldrs: rdn along 2f out: drvn and one pce appr last* **16/1**

2425 **5** *nk* **Bold Minstrel (IRE)**$^{12}$ 5421 2-9-2 83.................................... RWinston 2 83
(MQuinn) *led: rdn along 2f out: drvn and hdd ins last: sn wknd* **20/1**

100 **6** *6* **Gloved Hand**$^{8}$ 5515 2-9-0 89............................................... ACulhane 7 60+
(JGGiven) *chsd ldrs: rdn along and wkng whn n.m.r wl over 1f out: eased* **9/1**$^{3}$

64.91 secs (0.91) **Going Correction** +0.10s/f (Good) **6** Ran SP% **110.2**
Speed ratings: **96,92,92,91,91 81**CSF £54.13 TOTE £1.50: £1.10, £16.70; EX 55.00.
**Owner** Miss Tina Miller **Bred** Angmering Park Stud **Trained** Newmarket, Suffolk

**FOCUS**
Just a steady gallop but in the end the winner was most convincing, as she was entitled to be. The surprise runner-up raises doubts, but the fourth and fifth provide the best guide to the value of the form.

**NOTEBOOK**
**Sharplaw Star**, considered not at her best when third in the Queen Mary, had to be shaken up to make sure but was firmly in command at the line. She may now bid for the Cornwallis Stakes at Salisbury.
**Cutlass Gaudy**, the rank outsider of the field, stuck on well to snatch second spot near the line. This was have blown his potential lenient nursery mark out of the water.
**Safsoof(USA)**, drawn one, was on his toes beforehand on his first outing for two months. After looking uncomfortable and being tapped for toe, he stayed on again in the closing stages. The All-Weather surfaces possibly put less strain on him.
**Bold Marc(IRE)**, excitable in the blustery conditions beforehand, was having his first outing for nine weeks.
**Bold Minstrel(IRE)** had something to find and after setting up the race for the winner he tired inside the last.
**Gloved Hand**, who could not be given away in the market, has gone downhill since her first time out win.

## 5712 VIOLET AND EDDIE SMITH MEMORIAL CONDITIONS STKS 5f
**3:15** (3:17) (C2) 3-Y-O+ **£8,746** (£3,317; £1,658; £754) **Stalls** High

Form RPR
0136 **1** **Baltic King**$^{12}$ 5418 4-8-9 104...............................................(t) SDrowne 5 116+
(HMorrison) *hld up: hdwy and nt clr run 2f out: swtchd lft over 1f out and qckd wl to ld ins last: sn clr* **7/4**$^{1}$

6000 **2** *3 1/2* **If Paradise**$^{12}$ 5418 3-8-5 98............................................... RThomas(3) 6 102
(RHannon) *prom: hdwy on inner over 1f out: rdn to ld briefly ent last: sn hdd and drvn: nt match pce of wnr* **14/1**

5200 **3** *hd* **Dazzling Bay**$^{38}$ 4759 4-8-9 99..................................................(b) DAllan 9 101
(TDEasterby) *hld up in rr: swtchd outside and gd hdwy wl over 1f out: rdn and styd on wl fnl f* **7/2**$^{2}$

0653 **4** *nk* **Colonel Cotton (IRE)**$^{7}$ 5553 5-8-9 97...............................(v) SWKelly 12 100+
(NACallaghan) *towards rr: hdwy and trcking ldrs whn hmpd over 1f out: sn rdn and styd on ins last* **7/2**$^{2}$

6000 **5** *3 1/2* **Bonus (IRE)**$^{87}$ 3324 4-8-9 98................................................. MHills 1 86
(WJHaggas) *in tch on outer: effrt 2f out: rdn and edgd rt over 1f out: sn one pce* **14/1**

0000 **6** *1 1/4* **Blue Crush (IRE)**$^{26}$ 5062 3-8-3 85....................................... PHanagan 2 76
(KRBurke) *chsd ldrs: rdn along 2f out: wknd over 1f out* **66/1**

0004 **7** *nk* **Absent Friends**$^{7}$ 5550 7-8-9 83........................................... KMcEvoy 10 80
(JBalding) *led and sn clr: rdn over 1f out: hdd ent fnl f and sn wknd* **6/1**$^{3}$

4100 **8** *1 1/2* **Grey Pearl**$^{10}$ 5454 5-9-0 86...............................................(tp) MFenton 11 79
(MissGayKelleway) *chsd ldrs: rdn along and outpcd fr 1/2-way* **25/1**

5520 **9** *1* **Strensall**$^{10}$ 5458 7-8-7 76 ow1............................................ TEaves(3) 8 77+
(REBarr) *chsd ldrs: rdn along halwfay: wknd wl over 1f out* **40/1**

0620 **10** *5* **Beyond The Clouds (IRE)**$^{1}$ 5704 8-8-9 76......................(p) RWinston 3 50+
(JSWainwright) *dwlt: sn prom: chsd ldr 1/2-way: sn rdn and wkng whn heavily eased over 1f out* **20/1**

63.49 secs (-0.51) **Going Correction** +0.10s/f (Good)
**WFA** 3 from 4yo+ 1lb **10** Ran SP% **121.0**
Speed ratings: **108,102,102,101,96 94,93,91,89,81**CSF £29.96 TOTE £2.90: £1.30, £2.50, £2.40; EX 42.80.
**Owner** Thurloe Thoroughbreds Viii **Bred** R F And Mrs Knipe **Trained** East Ilsley, Berks

**FOCUS**
A good conditions event and decent, sound form for the grade.

**NOTEBOOK**
**Baltic King**, not at his best at Doncaster, had to switch to find room but in the end came right away. He is clearly right at the top of his game now and deserves a crack at something better.
**If Paradise**, who has been struggling to make much impact, ran a lot better but he may continue to prove hard to place.
**Dazzling Bay**, last at halfway, stayed on when switched wide. This marked a return to form but he has his quirks nowadays.
**Colonel Cotton(IRE)**, whose one success last year was in October, stayed on after having his path blocked by the winner over a furlong out.
**Bonus(IRE)**, absent since June, has changed stables in the interim.
**Blue Crush(IRE)** has been bang out of form but this was slightly more encouraging.
**Absent Friends**, who took this in 2002, was runner-up last year but he is not in the same sort of form this time.
**Beyond The Clouds(IRE)** *Official explanation: jockey said gelding lost his action*

## 5713 PAUL AND LUCY WOOLFITT HAPPY ANNIVERSARY H'CAP 7f 100y
**3:45** (3:46) (E3) (0-70,70) 3-Y-O+ **£5,086** (£1,565; £782; £391) **Stalls** High

Form RPR
4360 **1** **Gifted Flame**$^{7}$ 5544 5-8-13 **67**............................................. PMakin(5) 16 76
(TDBarron) *in tch: hdwy to trckd ldrs 1/2-way: squeezed through to ld 11/2f out: sn rdn and styd on* **5/1**$^{1}$

6-34 **2** *1* **Mrs Shilling**$^{14}$ 5378 3-8-13 **65**............................................ RWinston 15 72+
(JRFanshawe) *trckd ldrs: hdwy 2f out: rdn and n.m.r over 1f out: kpt on u.p ins last* **8/1**$^{3}$

6300 **3** *1* **Alchemist Master**$^{14}$ 5379 5-9-7 **70**...................................(p) KMcEvoy 4 74+
(RMWhitaker) *hld up towards rr: stdy hdwy over 2f out: effrt whn hmpd and swtchd lft over 1f out: fin strly* **11/1**

0505 **4** *shd* **No Grouse**$^{16}$ 5316 4-9-0 **63**............................................(p) PHanagan 2 67
(RAFahey) *towards rr: hdwy on outer 2f out: rdn over 1f out: kpt on wl fnl f* **11/1**

0000 **5** *hd* **Prince Of Gold**$^{24}$ 5108 4-8-13 **62**.......................................(p) DSweeney 6 65+
(RHollinshead) *trckd ldrs: hdwy on inner whn nt clr run and swtchd lft over 1f out: sn rdn and kpt on* **25/1**

3400 **6** *1 1/4* **Cryfield**$^{4}$ 5622 7-8-10 **59**.................................................(v) KimTinkler 10 59
(NTinkler) *in tch: hdwy whn hmpd over 1f out: sn rdn and kpt on ins last* **20/1**

0604 **7** *1/2* **Dara Mac**$^{7}$ 5544 5-8-3 **59**........................................... SuzanneFrance(7) 14 58
(NBycroft) *midfield: effrt 2f out: sn rdn and n.m.r over 1f out: swtchd ins and styng on whn hit in face w whip: one pce after* **14/1**

6121 **8** *nk* **Jubilee Street (IRE)**$^{14}$ 5364 5-8-10 **62**................................. ABeech(3) 9 60
(MrsADuffield) *hed up: hdwy on outer 2f out: rdn and hung rt over 1f out: sn wknd* **13/2**$^{2}$

0024 **9** *5* **Legal Set (IRE)**$^{8}$ 5518 8-8-4 **60**...........................................(t) DTudhope(7) 8 46+
(MissAStokell) *chsd ldrs: rdn along 2f out: drvn whn hmpd and wknd over 1f out* **16/1**

0201 **10** *1 1/2* **Mount Hillaby (IRE)**$^{16}$ 5317 4-9-0 **63**....................................... TLucas 7 45+
(MWEasterby) *led: edgd rt bnd after 2f: sn rn wd and hdd: rdn along and ch wl over 1f out: sn edgd rt and wknd* **13/2**$^{2}$

3405 **11** *3* **Nearly A Fool**$^{30}$ 4969 6-9-6 **69**...........................................(v) NPollard 13 43
(GGMargarson) *cl up: led after 2f: rdn along 2f out: sn hdd and grad wknd* **20/1**

6060 **12** *3/4* **Gala Sunday (USA)**$^{16}$ 5317 4-8-11 **60**.............................. DaleGibson 3 33
(MWEasterby) *a rr* **28/1**

5200 **13** *2* **Zawrak (IRE)**$^{7}$ 5554 5-8-5 **61**.............................(v) NataliaGemelova(7) 12 29
(IWMcinnes) *slowly away and a rr* **14/1**

0043 **14** *1* **Captain Saif**$^{68}$ 3871 4-9-4 **70**............................................ THamilton(3) 5 35
(NWilson) *dwlt: a bhd* **16/1**

0000 **15** *17* **Atlantic Ace**$^{7}$ 5544 7-9-0 **63**.............................................(p) DMcGaffin 11 —+
(BSmart) *cl up whn hmpd after 2f: remained prom and ch whn rdn along and hmpd over 1f out: nt rcvr* **12/1**

1m 32.98s (-1.32) **Going Correction** -0.05s/f (Good)
**WFA** 3 from 4yo+ 3lb **15** Ran SP% **120.7**
Speed ratings: **105,103,102,102,102 100,100,100,94,92 89,88,86,84,65**CSF £40.72 CT £438.51 TOTE £5.60: £2.30, £2.10, £3.80; EX 47.20.
**Owner** Raymond Miquel **Bred** Taker Bloodstock **Trained** Maunby, N Yorks

**FOCUS**
A 0-70 handicap run at a sound pace, but plenty encountering traffic problems and the form appears slightly messy and is rated accordingly.

**NOTEBOOK**
**Gifted Flame**, drawn hard against the running rail, raced a lot more prominently than usual and as a result avoided the traffic problems encountered by those trying to come from off the pace. He rather idled in front and scored with a something in hand.
**Mrs Shilling**, on her handicap debut, was quite keen early on. Tightened up at a crucial stage, she stuck on to claim second spot but in truth was never making any real impression on the winner.
**Alchemist Master**, 7lb higher than his last win, came in for market support. Off the pace and hard at work at halfway, he was forced to pull wide before finishing best of all. *Official explanation: jockey said gelding was denied clear run until final furlong*
**No Grouse** is finding his feet in his new stable and stayed on from off the pace down the wide outside.
**Prince Of Gold**, off the boil, is slipping to a good mark and here he had no luck in running at all.
**Cryfield** usually runs well here but he met traffic problems when trying to improve and he is proving very hard to win with.
**Dara Mac**, who prefers more give underfoot, had a luckless run.

## 5714 BRIAN MERRINGTON MEMORIAL STKS (H'CAP) 1m 1f 207y
**4:20** (4:21) (F4) (0-55,61) 3-Y-O+ **£3,680** (£1,132; £566; £283) **Stalls** High

Form RPR
-031 **1** **Emperor's Well**$^{6}$ 5557 5-9-7 **61** 6ex.......................................(b) TLucas 5 72
(MWEasterby) *set stdy pce: qckd over 2f out: rdn clr over 1f out: kpt on* **15/2**

1624 **2** *1/2* **Life Is Beautiful (IRE)**$^{19}$ 5238 5-8-8 **48**.............................. RWinston 15 58+
(WHTinning) *midfield: hdwy on inner 2f out: nt clr run and swtchd lft over 1f out: sn rdn and styd on wl fnl f* **7/1**$^{3}$

6230 **3** *nk* **Senor Eduardo**$^{6}$ 5557 7-9-0 **54**.......................................... ANicholls 14 63
(SGollings) *chsd ldrs: rdn 2f out: drvn and kpt on appr last* **25/1**

42 **4** *1 1/4* **Wild Power (GER)**$^{7}$ 5546 6-9-1 **55**...................................... DSweeney 13 62
(JGMO'Shea) *in tch: hdwy 2f out: rdn over 1f out: kpt on u.p ins last* **5/1**$^{1}$

0002 **5** *1* **Time To Regret**6 5557 4-8-7 **50** .......... TEaves(3) 19 55+
(JSWainwright) *towards rr: hdwy 2f out: nt clr run and swtchd rt over 1f out: sn rdn and kpt on wl towards fin* **10/1**

6001 **6** *½* **Royal Racer (FR)**47 4485 6-8-12 **52** .......... (b) NPollard 2 56
(JRBest) *chsd ldrs: rdn along 2f out: drvn and one pce appr last* **16/1**

6010 **7** *shd* **Alpine Hideaway (IRE)**5 5587 11-8-9 **49** .......... (p) DAllan 9 53
(JSWainwright) *midfield: hdwy 2f out: sn rdn along and kpt on same pce* **33/1**

2020 **8** *1* **Fairy Monarch (IRE)**7 5546 5-8-9 **49** .......... (p) RFitzpatrick 16 51
(PTMidgley) *bhd: hdwy 2f out: sn rdn alonga nd kpt on fnl f: nrst fin* **20/1**

0136 **9** *½* **Shamwari Fire (IRE)**6 5571 4-8-9 **49** .......... RFfrench 18 50
(IWMcinnes) *midfield: hdwy 2f out: sn rdn and n.m.r over 1f out: one pce* **12/1**

1000 **10** *nk* **Ellovamul**14 5374 4-8-6 **51** .......... PMakin(5) 12 51
(WMBrisbourne) *midield: effrt 2f out: sn rdn alonga nd no imp* **20/1**

0440 **11** *nk* **Hirayna**28 5021 5-8-8 **48** .......... SWKelly 10 48
(WMBrisbourne) *midfield: hdwy over 2f out: sn rdn along and nvr a factor* **14/1**

4000 **12** *1½* **Dance Party (IRE)**86 3348 4-9-1 **55** .......... DaleGibson 4 52
(MWEasterby) *a rr* **22/1**

0041 **13** *½* **Grand Rapide**25 5072 3-8-8 **54** .......... SDrowne 3 50
(JLSpearing) *chsd ldrs: rdn along 2f out: grad wknd over 1f out* **14/1**

0500 **14** *¾* **Beneking**16 5320 4-8-9 **49** .......... ACulhane 17 43
(RHollinshead) *towards rr: hdwy over 2f out: n.m.r wl over 1f out: nt rcvr* **14/1**

00-0 **15** *1¾* **Aqribaa (IRE)**6 5557 6-8-9 **52** .......... PMulrennan(3) 11 43
(AJLockwood) *s.i.s: a rr* **40/1**

3462 **16** *½* **Donna's Double**5 5581 9-8-9 **49** .......... (p) KDarley 6 39
(DEddy) *in tch on outer: hdwy over 2f out: sn rdn and wknd wl over 1f out* **6/1**2

U-00 **17** *3* **Amalfi Coast**7 5546 5-8-3 **50** ow2 .......... DTudhope(7) 7 34
(WSCunningham) *a rr* **100/1**

303- **18** *8* **Sheer Focus (IRE)**325 5881 6-8-1 **48** .......... (p) NataliaGemelova(7) 1 17
(IWMcinnes) *cl up: rdn along 3f out: sn wknd* **40/1**

0000 **19** *nk* **Uno Mente**34 4852 5-8-8 **48** .......... (v) KimTinkler 8 17
(DonEnricoIncisa) *a bhd* **40/1**

2m 4.62s (-2.58) **Going Correction** -0.05s/f (Good)
**WFA** 3 from 4yo+ 6lb **19** Ran SP% **126.8**
Speed ratings: **108,107,107,106,105 105,105,104,103,103 103,102,101,101,99 99,97,90,90**CSF £53.61 CT £1288.94 TOTE £7.60: £2.80, £2.00, £3.70, £1.90; EX 40.50.
**Owner** M W Easterby **Bred** M W Easterby And K Hodgson **Trained** Sheriff Hutton, N Yorks

**FOCUS**
In effect a 0-61 handicap with the winner again given a masterful ride from the front. Those close up appeared to run to expectations making the form looks sound.

**NOTEBOOK**
**Emperor's Well**, drawn just four from the outside, was bounced out of the stalls and was soon able to drop anchor in front. Quickening up the pace coming off the home turn, he never looked in danger though in the end there was precious little left in the locker.
**Life Is Beautiful(IRE)**, who has won five of her 11 previous starts here, met traffic problems. She stayed on in willing fashion to snatch second spot near the line and will no doubt be back here next year to add to her record.
**Senor Eduardo**, back up to a more suitable trip, would have appreciated better ground but he deserves credit for the way he stuck to his task.
**Wild Power(GER)**, very warm beforehand on a day when the strong wind kept the temperature down, is in poor form for his new yard.
**Time To Regret**, ridden to stay the trip, met traffic problems and did well to finish so close. He needs a much more positive ride.
**Royal Racer(FR)**, drawn wide, kept tabs on the winner and had no excuse.
**Grand Rapide** *Official explanation: jockey said filly was unsuited by ground*
**Beneking** *Official explanation: jockey said gelding was denied a clear run*

## 5715 SUBSCRIBE TO RACING UK ON 08700 860432 H'CAP 1m 100y
4:50 (4:50) (E3) (0-70,68) 3-Y-O £4,355 (£1,340; £670; £335) **Stalls High**

Form RPR

3010 **1** **Pella**19 5252 3-9-2 **63** .......... DSweeney 12 71
(MBlanshard) *midfield: hdwy 3f out: swtchd rt and rdn over 1f out: styd on to ld last 100 yds* **9/1**

0002 **2** *nk* **Heversham (IRE)**7 5544 3-9-4 **65** .......... DaleGibson 17 72
(JHetherton) *trckd ldrs: hdwy over 2f out: rdn to ld over 1f out: drvn ins last: hdd last 100 yds: kpt on* **5/1**1

6361 **3** *nk* **Princess Galadriel**23 5155 3-9-0 **61** .......... KDarley 16 67
(JRBest) *dwlt and bhd: pushed along 1/2-way: hdwy and swtchd ins 2f out: swtchd lft over 1f out and styd on strly fnl f* **6/1**2

5000 **4** *¾* **Charlie Tango (IRE)**8 5510 3-9-3 **64** .......... RWinston 6 70+
(NTinkler) *bhd: hdwy on inner 2f out: nt clr run and swtchd lft over 1f out: sn rdn and kpt on* **14/1**

5130 **5** *1¼* **Kingsmaite**19 5242 3-9-6 **67** .......... (b) JBramhill 14 69
(SRBowring) *led: rdn along over 2f out: drvn and hdd over 1f out: grad wknd* **12/1**

5450 **6** *¾* **Charmatic (IRE)**23 5145 3-9-4 **65** .......... SDrowne 5 66
(JAGlover) *towards rr: hdwy on outer 2f out: sn rdn and kpt on fnl f: nrst fin* **7/1**3

2305 **7** *nk* **Joshua's Gold (IRE)**8 5518 3-8-3 **57** .......... (v) DTudhope(7) 10 57
(DCarroll) *t.k.h: chsd ldrs: hdwy 2f out: rdn and hung rt over 1f out: sn drvn and wknd* **9/1**

6500 **8** *1¼* **Kalishka (IRE)**59 4138 3-8-11 **58** .......... (b1) ANicholls 9 55
(AndrewTurnell) *towards rr: pushed along and hdwy 3f out: sn rdn: kpt on fnl f* **33/1**

5500 **9** *nk* **Dark Day Blues (IRE)**14 5364 3-8-12 **59** .......... DarrenWilliams 11 56
(MDHammond) *chsd ldrs: rdn over 2f out: sn wknd* **33/1**

-000 **10** *¾* **Sion Hill (IRE)**19 5244 3-9-0 **68** .......... JDO'Reilly(7) 3 63
(JO'Reilly) *keen: chsd ldrs on outer: rdn along 2f out: sn wknd* **66/1**

0454 **11** *¾* **Capitole (IRE)**8 5510 3-9-0 **61** .......... (v) KMcEvoy 7 55
(EFVaughan) *bhd: rdn along over 2f out: nvr a factor* **7/1**3

6220 **12** *1¾* **Cayman Calypso (IRE)**22 5197 3-9-3 **64** .......... PHanagan 15 54
(JMJefferson) *midfield: hdwy on inner 2f out: rdn and wknd over 1f out* **16/1**

10-6 **13** *shd* **Freddie Freccles**258 466 3-9-4 **65** .......... MFenton 13 55
(JGGiven) *chsd ldrs on inner: rdn along over 2f out: wknd wl over 1f out* **33/1**

0602 **14** *1½* **True (IRE)**7 5545 3-8-8 **58** .......... RThomas(3) 2 45
(MrsSLamyman) *a towards rr* **14/1**

040 **15** *1¼* **Spes Bona (USA)**43 4615 3-8-12 **59** .......... ACulhane 4 43
(WJHaggas) *a rr* **14/1**

-525 **16** *8* **It Must Be Speech**172 1235 3-8-13 **60** .......... RFitzpatrick 1 27
(SLKeightley) *bhd fr 1/2-way* **40/1**

6020 **17** *5* **Always Flying (USA)**70 3817 3-8-11 **61** .......... PMulrennan(3) 8 18
(NWilson) *in tch on outer: rdn along and wd st: sn bhd* **20/1**

1m 46.95s (-0.35) **Going Correction** -0.05s/f (Good) **17** Ran SP% **127.0**
Speed ratings: **99,98,98,97,96 95,95,94,93,93 92,90,90,88,87 79,74**CSF £52.05 CT £244.84 TOTE £10.30: £2.30, £1.60, £1.70, £4.10; EX 55.60 Place 6 £78.90, Place 5 £16.32.
**Owner** The Pella Partnership **Bred** Whitsbury Manor Stud **Trained** Upper Lambourn, Berks

**FOCUS**
In effect a 0-68 handicap run at just a steady pace. The form is sound for the grade but unexceptional.

**NOTEBOOK**
**Pella** stuck on in game fashion after having to change course to show ahead near the line.
**Heversham(IRE)**, in good form for his new yard, worked hard to get his head in front but he had no answer to the winner's sustained late burst.
**Princess Galadriel**, who made a tardy start, met traffic problems trying to improve from the rear before finishing best of all. If anything this extended distance was in her favour.
**Charlie Tango(IRE)**, with the headgear dispensed with, settled a lot better and did well to finish as close as he did after meeting trouble in running. *Official explanation: jockey said gelding hung right handed in straight*
**Kingsmaite**, keen in front, took them along but was never going to see it out, especially on this stiff, uphill finish with a strong wind blowing in his face.
**Charmatic(IRE)**, whose yard is finding form, stayed on in her own time and will be hoping for some easy ground this backend.
T/Plt: £172.30 to a £1 stake. Pool: £42,349.50. 179.40 winning tickets. T/Qpdt: £14.90 to a £1 stake. Pool: £4,362.90. 216.10 winning tickets. JR

# 2689 NEWMARKET (R-H)
Tuesday, September 21

**OFFICIAL GOING: Good to firm**
Wind: Strong behind Weather: Overcast

## 5716 ROBINSONS MERCEDES-BENZ MEDIAN AUCTION MAIDEN STKS 1m
2:20 (2:23) (E3) 2-Y-O £4,358 (£1,341; £670; £335) **Stalls Centre**

Form RPR

2 **1** **Forward Move (IRE)**18 5269 2-9-0 .......... RLMoore 7 93+
(RHannon) *chsd ldr tl led 1/2-way: rdn clr over 1f out* **2/1**1

3 **2** *5* **My Putra (USA)**34 4861 2-9-0 .......... TQuinn 4 81
(PFICole) *a.p: chsd wnr over 2f out: outpcd over 1f out* **5/1**2

55 **3** *shd* **Patronage**22 5179 2-9-0 .......... KFallon 9 80
(MLWBell) *s.i.s: sn prom: rdn over 2f out: styd on same pce appr fnl f* **11/2**3

**4** *1½* **Maidanni (USA)** 2-9-0 .......... LDettori 11 77
(SaeedBinSuroor) *chsd ldrs: rdn over 2f out: no ex appr fnl f* **5/1**2

0 **5** *1¾* **Robeson**94 3093 2-8-11 .......... LPKeniry(3) 15 72
(DMSimcock) *trckd ldrs: styd on same pce fnl 2f* **100/1**

3 **6** *nk* **Royal Jet**10 5467 2-9-0 .......... DHolland 18 71
(MRChannon) *hld up: rdn 1/2-way: hdwy over 2f out: edgd rt and no imp appr fnl f* **7/1**

00 **7** *3* **Scarp (USA)**25 5091 2-9-0 .......... EAhern 8 64
(JNoseda) *chsd ldrs tl wknd over 1f out* **50/1**

**8** *1¼* **Eloquent Knight (USA)** 2-9-0 .......... SSanders 1 61
(WRMuir) *s.i.s: nvr nrr* **33/1**

**9** *1¼* **Penny Wedding (IRE)** 2-8-9 .......... WRyan 10 53+
(JRFanshawe) *s.i.s: sn outpcd: nvr nrr* **33/1**

0 **10** *2½* **Three Boars**41 4649 2-9-0 .......... JFortune 2 51
(WJarvis) *nvr trbld ldrs* **66/1**

**11** *nk* **Royal Sailor (IRE)** 2-9-0 .......... JTate 5 51
(JMPEustace) *mid-div: wknd over 2f out* **50/1**

000 **12** *1¾* **Speedie Rossini (IRE)**30 4967 2-9-0 .......... (b1) AMcCarthy 6 46
(SCWilliams) *led to 1/2-way: wknd over 2f out* **66/1**

**13** *nk* **Swords** 2-9-0 .......... CCatlin 13 46
(DJDaly) *s.s: outpcd* **66/1**

**14** *4* **Ross Moor** 2-9-0 .......... PRobinson 14 36
(MrsAJPerrett) *dwlt: hdwy 1/2-way: wknd over 2f out* **9/1**

**15** *2* **Chief Dipper** 2-9-0 .......... TPQueally 17 31
(PJMcbride) *chsd ldrs over 5f* **66/1**

**16** *6* **Fantastic Luck (IRE)** 2-9-0 .......... GCarter 16 16+
(JLDunlop) *dwlt: outpcd* **40/1**

**17** *6* **Polish Index** 2-9-0 .......... TEDurcan 12 1
(JRJenkins) *dwlt: outpcd* **100/1**

**18** *3* **La Musique** 2-9-0 .......... JMackay 3 —
(PJMcbride) *s.s: outpcd* **66/1**

1m 35.7s (-3.70) **Going Correction** -0.45s/f (Firm) 2y crse rec **18** Ran SP% **126.2**
Speed ratings: **100,95,94,93,91 91,88,87,85,83 83,81,81,77,75 69,63,60**CSF £11.29 TOTE £3.50: £1.20, £1.60, £2.50; EX 16.70.
**Owner** The Queen **Bred** The Queen **Trained** East Everleigh, Wilts

**FOCUS**
A reasonable maiden, run in marginally the fastest time of the three races over a mile, and a really impressive performance fror Forward Move who looks potentially Group class.

**NOTEBOOK**
**Forward Move(IRE)** ◆, only just denied on his debut under a considerate ride over this trip at Kempton, showed significant improvement on that form to get off the mark in impressive fashion, quickening up smartly. He does not have any fancy entries at this stage, but looks Group class and could be worth keeping in mind for something like the Autumn Stakes, a race his stable won last year with Fantastic View. However, connections are leaning towards either the Zetland Stakes or Horris Hill.
**My Putra(USA)**, a fair third on his debut over six furlongs at York, would have appreciated this step up to a mile but just lacked the change of pace shown by the winner. He is still learning and there should be more to come.
**Patronage** was again slowly away but recovered well enough, the winner simply had too much speed in the closing stages. A promising sort, he is now qualified for a handicap mark and promises to improve for a little further.
**Maidanni(USA)**, a $425,000 first known foal out of a triple winner in the USA, looked to have every chance. He showed plenty of ability and is up to winning a minor maiden on this evidence, but he will need to improve to win at a top track.
**Robeson** showed nothing on his only previous start in June so this represents significant improvement. Handled by a good first-season trainer, he is clearly progressing and is one to have on your side.
**Royal Jet**, not beaten far when third on his debut over this trip at Goodwood, did not step up on that effort but still offered promise. He was never a threat to the winner, but was keeping on well at the finish and is the type to improve with time and distance.
**Ross Moor**, a half-brother to the very useful five-furlong juvenile Spliff out of a smart sprinting two-year-old, it was a surprise to see him make his debut over a mile and he was well held. However, his purchase price nearly doubled this year to 60,000gns and, sent off at single-figure odds in what was a decent maiden, he can be given another chance.

## 5717 ROBINSONS MERCEDES-BENZ EBF MAIDEN FILLIES' STKS 1m

2:50 (2:54) (D2) 2-Y-O £5,538 (£1,704; £852; £426) Stalls Centre

Form RPR

23 1 **Titian Time (USA)**[18] 5272 2-8-11 .......... JFortune 11 84
(JHMGosden) *mde all: rdn out* **11/4**[1]

000 2 1 1/4 **Hallowed Dream (IRE)**[14] 5368 2-8-11 .......... TPQueally 8 81
(CEBrittain) *a.p: plld hrd: rdn over 1f out: chsd wnr fnl f: styd on* **66/1**

3 1 1/4 **Russian Revolution** 2-8-11 ..........(t) LDettori 12 78
(SaeedBinSuroor) *chsd wnr: rdn over 2f out: styd on same pce fnl f* **11/4**[1]

5 4 1/2 **Tamalain (USA)**[19] 5248 2-8-11 .......... RLMoore 4 77
(MrsAJPerrett) *chsd ldrs: rdn over 2f out: styd on same pce fnl f* **7/1**[2]

5 3/4 **Ayam Zaman (IRE)** 2-8-11 .......... PRobinson 6 75+
(MAJarvis) *hld up: plld hrd: outpcd over 2f out: r.o ins fnl f: nt rch ldrs* **33/1**

042 6 nk **Bazelle**[14] 5368 2-8-11 83 .......... SSanders 9 74
(PWD'Arcy) *chsd ldrs: rdn over 2f out: no ex fnl f* **15/2**[3]

7 nk **Basserah (IRE)** 2-8-11 .......... RHills 10 73
(BWHills) *s.s: sn chsng ldrs: rdn over 2f out: no ex fnl f* **25/1**

8 6 **Dancinginthedouds (IRE)** 2-8-11 .......... TQuinn 5 58+
(JLDunlop) *s.s: bhd: sme hdwy over 1f out: nvr trbld ldrs* **10/1**

0 9 5 **Red Duchess**[19] 5247 2-8-11 .......... KFallon 7 46
(SirMichaelStoute) *hld up: rdn 1/2-way: wknd over 2f out* **8/1**

10 1/2 **Shades Of Green** 2-8-11 .......... DHolland 14 44
(NACallaghan) *prom: lost pl 6f out: hdwy 1/2-way: wknd over 2f out* **33/1**

00 11 1/2 **Our Kes (IRE)**[18] 5268 2-8-11 .......... JMackay 13 43
(PHowling) *hld up: bhd fnl 3f* **100/1**

0 12 1 **Cup Of Love (USA)**[18] 5271 2-8-11 .......... EAhern 1 41
(RGuest) *hld up: hdwy over 5f out: wknd over 2f out* **66/1**

13 1 **Queen Tomyra (IRE)** 2-8-8 .......... NMackay(3) 3 38
(LMCumani) *s.s: hld up: sme hdwy over 3f out: wknd over 2f out* **16/1**

14 3 **Tale Of Dubai (USA)** 2-8-11 .......... CCatlin 15 31
(SaeedBinSuroor) *chsd ldrs over 5f* **33/1**

15 8 **Queen's Dancer** 2-8-11 .......... TEDurcan 2 11
(MRChannon) *s.i.s: outpcd* **50/1**

1m 36.22s (-3.18) **Going Correction** -0.45s/f (Firm) 2y crse rec **15 Ran SP% 122.3**
Speed ratings: **97,95,94,94,93 92,92,86,81,81 80,79,78,75,67** CSF £267.48 TOTE £3.70: £1.30, £34.70, £1.80; EX 245.90.
**Owner** Lady Bamford & The Sangster Family **Bred** Swettenham Stud **Trained** Manton, Wilts

**FOCUS**
Probably quite a good maiden with plenty of strength in depth - there were plenty of promising types in behind that look capable of improving past the principals. Hallowed Dream benefited from racing up with the steady pace as the first four home were all close to the pace.

**NOTEBOOK**
**Titian Time(USA)**, who had shown promise on two runs over seven furlongs, benefited from this step up to a mile and did what was required to get off the mark. Some of those in behind her may well progress past her in time, but she is improving herself and could be hard to beat if turned out in a nursery, although the temptation must now be to aim for some black type.
**Hallowed Dream(IRE)** had run to an RPR of just 60 on her three previous runs, so her proximity is a slight worry. However, she just looks like a typical Clive Brittain improver and clearly benefited from racing up with the modest gallop.
**Russian Revolution**, a half-sister to a useful ten-furlong three-year-old winner, out of a smart middle-distance performer, is entered in the Derby. This was a respectable debut and, with improvement, she should soon be winning.
**Tamalain(USA)**, who offered promise despite running green on her debut over seven furlongs at Salisbury, did not improve greatly and looked to find this tougher.
**Ayam Zaman(IRE)** ◆, a 95,000gns half-sister to three-year-old middle-distance winners, never threatened the principals but was noted keeping on well close home and should be capable of significant improvement in time.
**Bazelle** failed to justify her rating of 83 and that does look very harsh. A minor maiden is within her grasp, but she could struggle in handicaps off a mark in the 80s.
**Basserah(IRE)** ◆, a 45,000gns foal, half-sister to a juvenile winner over a mile, made an eye-catching debut without being given a hard time. She should progress and looks worth following.
**Dancinginthedouds(IRE)** ◆, a full-sister to St Leger winner Millenary, and half-sister to the 2004 Derby third Let The Lion Roar, would not have appreciated the modest gallop and looks capable of much better than she showed. She is one to keep an eye on.
**Red Duchess**, well held on her debut at Salisbury, again failed to get competitive.
**Shades Of Green** ◆, a half-sister to several winners in France, showed more ability than her finishing position would suggest.
**Cup Of Love(USA)** ◆ was not given a hard time once her chance had gone and should be capable of better, probably when she is handicapped.

## 5718 SCOTTISH EQUITABLE EBF MAIDEN STKS (C&G) 7f

3:25 (3:28) (D2) 2-Y-O £5,681 (£1,748; £874; £437) Stalls Centre

Form RPR

6 1 **Grosvenor Square (IRE)**[17] 5290 2-8-11 .......... LDettori 8 90+
(SaeedBinSuroor) *mde all: shkn up over 1f out: r.o wl* **2/1**[1]

344 2 4 **Councellor (FR)**[56] 4219 2-8-11 81 .......... RLMoore 5 79
(RHannon) *chsd wnr: rdn over 2f out: outpcd over 1f out* **5/1**[2]

0 3 2 1/2 **Pillars Of Wisdom**[17] 5298 2-8-11 .......... JFortune 1 72
(JLDunlop) *chsd ldrs: rdn over 2f out: styd on same pce appr fnl f* **14/1**

5 4 1 1/4 **Spanish Ridge (IRE)**[38] 4747 2-8-11 .......... TQuinn 13 69
(JLDunlop) *chsd ldrs: rdn over 2f out: styd on same pce appr fnl f* **13/2**

5 3 **Registrar** 2-8-11 .......... SSanders 12 60+
(MrsAJPerrett) *s.s: hdwy 5f out: wknd over 1f out* **14/1**

0 6 3/4 **Cost Analysis (IRE)**[25] 5091 2-8-11 .......... PRobinson 2 58
(MAJarvis) *chsd ldrs: rdn over 2f out: wknd over 1f out* **9/1**

7 5 **King's Majesty (IRE)** 2-8-11 .......... KFallon 9 52+
(SirMichaelStoute) *prom 5f* **6/1**[3]

8 1/2 **Trafalgar Square** 2-8-11 .......... EAhern 4 43
(RGuest) *hld up: wknd over 2f out: hung rt over 1f out* **25/1**

9 1 3/4 **Mineral Star (IRE)** 2-8-11 .......... NCallan 11 38
(MHTompkins) *dwlt: hld up: wknd over 2f out* **33/1**

10 3/4 **Jostle** 2-8-11 ..........(t) TPQueally 10 36
(DRLoder) *s.s: a bhd* **25/1**

11 5 **Green Pirate** 2-8-11 .......... DRMcCabe 6 23
(DRLoder) *plld hrd and prom: wknd over 2f out* **50/1**

12 3/4 **Linda's Colin (IRE)** 2-8-11 .......... DHolland 3 21
(PWD'Arcy) *s.s: hld up: wknd over 2f out* **16/1**

13 shd **Shatin Star** 2-8-11 .......... OUrbina 7 20
(GCHChung) *s.s: outpcd* **50/1**

1m 22.95s (-3.52) **Going Correction** -0.45s/f (Firm) 2y crse rec **13 Ran SP% 121.4**
Speed ratings: **102,97,94,93,89 88,83,82,80,79 74,73,73** CSF £10.87 TOTE £2.80: £1.50, £1.80, £4.10; EX 16.00.
**Owner** Godolphin **Bred** Darley **Trained** Newmarket, Suffolk

**FOCUS**
Probably not a great maiden, but the time was decent for the class and the race should produce winners. Again it proved hard to come from off the pace.

**NOTEBOOK**
**Grosvenor Square(IRE)** confirmed the promise he showed on his debut over six furlongs at Haydock, with this step up in trip suiting well. This Derby entry very much got the run of the race and the runner-up is beginning to look exposed, but he is a nice prospect nonetheless.
**Councellor(FR)**, back up in trip, did not look to do that much wrong, the winner is just a better horse.
**Pillars Of Wisdom**, who offered promise on his debut in a Kempton conditions event, again showed ability and is going the right way.
**Spanish Ridge(IRE)** failed to improve on his debut running, but did not exactly run badly.
**Registrar**, a half-brother to a seven-furlong three-year-old winner, out of a winner over the same trip, made a respectable debut and should improve.
**Cost Analysis(IRE)** looked to step up on his debut effort and is going the right way.
**King's Majesty(IRE)** ◆, a 240,000euros half-brother to 2000 Guineas winner Island Sands, looked in need of the experience and should be capable of much better in future. He is the one to take from the race.
**Linda's Colin(IRE)** *Official explanation: jockey said colt hung left throughout*

## 5719 UAE EQUESTRIAN AND RACING FEDERATION NURSERY 1m

4:30 (4:30) (C1) (0-95,94) 2-Y-O £13,884 (£4,272; £2,136; £1,068) Stalls Centre

Form RPR

3540 1 **Bunny Rabbit (USA)**[12] 5417 2-9-0 87 .......... LDettori 2 94
(BJMeehan) *a.p: rdn to ld over 1f out: hdd ins fnl f: rallied to ld nr fin* **2/1**[1]

5240 2 hd **Alright My Son (IRE)**[12] 5417 2-8-3 76 .......... RLMoore 8 83
(RHannon) *w ldr tl led 3f out: rdn and hdd over 1f out: rallied to ld ins fnl f: hdd nr fin* **5/1**[2]

0410 3 2 **King Of Blues (IRE)**[31] 4953 2-8-3 76 ow1 ..........(t) EAhern 9 78
(MAMagnusson) *chsd ldrs: rdn over 2f out: styd on same pce fnl f* **25/1**

51 4 hd **Donyana**[19] 5247 2-8-13 86 .......... PRobinson 13 87
(MAJarvis) *racd alone: w ldrs: rdn over 2f out: styd on same pce ins fnl f* **5/1**[2]

063 5 2 **Penny Island (IRE)**[24] 5114 2-8-1 74 .......... DKinsella 7 70
(AKing) *chsd ldrs: rdn over 2f out: styd on same pce appr fnl f* **20/1**

2125 6 shd **Spirit Of France (IRE)**[45] 4527 2-9-7 94 .......... DHolland 5 90
(MJohnston) *led 5f: rdn over 1f out: no ex* **10/1**

0412 7 1 1/4 **Mighty Empire (IRE)**[12] 5417 2-8-7 80 .......... NCallan 10 73
(MHTompkins) *hld up: hdwy over 3f out: sn rdn: no ex appr fnl f* **6/1**[3]

045 8 nk **Grandma's Girl**[15] 5348 2-7-9 71 oh1 .......... NMackay(3) 12 63
(RGuest) *prom: lost pl over 6f out: n.d after* **20/1**

0062 9 1 1/2 **Swell Lad**[15] 5335 2-7-10 72 .......... JFMcDonald(3) 1 60
(PFICole) *chsd ldrs: rdn over 2f out: wknd over 1f out* **25/1**

1403 10 hd **Shivaree**[38] 4757 2-9-0 87 .......... TEDurcan 4 75
(MRChannon) *prom over 6f* **25/1**

0010 11 5 **Velvet Heights (IRE)**[22] 5188 2-8-12 85 .......... GCarter 3 60
(JLDunlop) *s.i.s: hld up: a in rr* **25/1**

0040 12 12 **Norcroft**[12] 5421 2-7-11 73 ..........(b) FPFerris(3) 6 18
(NACallaghan) *prom over 5f* **40/1**

066 13 6 **Asharon**[13] 5396 2-8-7 80 .......... SSanders 11 10
(CEBrittain) *dwlt: hdwy over 5f out: wknd over 2f out* **33/1**

1m 35.98s (-3.42) **Going Correction** -0.45s/f (Firm) 2y crse rec **13 Ran SP% 120.3**
Speed ratings: **99,98,96,96,94 94,93,92,91,91 86,74,68** CSF £9.93 CT £203.65 TOTE £3.10: £1.60, £2.00, £4.80; EX 16.10 Trifecta £323.40 Pool of £3,097.65 - 6.80 winning units.
**Owner** Gold Group International Ltd **Bred** Gainesway Thoroughbreds Ltd **Trained** Upper Lambourn, Berks

**FOCUS**
A fair nursery that ended up producing a really tight finish and the form looks reliable for the grade.

**NOTEBOOK**
**Bunny Rabbit(USA)**, who was well-backed after an unlucky run last time, finished behind two of this field in his last race, but overturned that form with a clearer run. Travelling well just in behind the lead, he made his move a furlong and a half out and looked to be going clear until the second battled back bravely. He appears to be progressing, but how far he can go now is down to the Hhandicapper.
**Alright My Son(IRE)** was 3lb worse off with the winner, given their troubled run last time out, but emerges from the race with as much credit as that colt. He helped cut out a decent pace and stayed on resolutely up the hill, only giving best in the last half furlong. He is still a maiden, but on this evidence should not stay that way for much longer given similar conditions.
**King Of Blues(IRE)**, disappointing on a soft surface last time, bounced back to his best form on this much quicker surface. He travelled kindly in midfield and stayed on nicely up the middle of the course without ever looking likely to pick up the first two. This looks to be his ideal conditions at this time.
**Donyana** was ridden away from the main body of the field, in an attempt to find better ground, and ran a decent race there on her own. Her maiden form has been enhanced and looks fairly good, so she should be capable of improving off this effort.
**Penny Island(IRE)** has some fairly solid juvenile form and ran with credit in what may have been a decent nursery. He looks to stay well on this evidence and is capable of picking up a mile nursery somewhere.
**Spirit Of France(IRE)** helped to cut out the early pace, and stayed involved until being outpaced about one and a half furlongs out. He looked likely to drop away tamely until hitting the rising ground and running on well again. On this evidence he needs some help from the Handicapper before winning again.
**Mighty Empire(IRE)** finished in front of the principals last time out, but was never going to trouble those two today. He travelled well in midfield before staying on at one pace up the hill. On this evidence he is weighted up to his best form.
**Grandma's Girl** was never competitive at any stage, but made a little late progress when the race was over as a contest. A weak nursery could see her go close at this distance.
**Velvet Heights(IRE)** *Official explanation: jockey said colt was unsuited by the good to firm ground*
**Asharon** *Official explanation: jockey said colt was unsuited by the good to firm ground*

## 5720 LOUISE STEEL MEDIAN AUCTION MAIDEN STKS 6f

5:00 (5:02) (E3) 2-Y-O £4,212 (£1,296; £648; £324) Stalls Centre

Form RPR

62 1 **King Marju (IRE)**[15] 5353 2-9-0 .......... JFortune 1 87
(PWChapple-Hyam) *chsd ldr: rdn to ld over 1f out: r.o wl* **10/11**[1]

62 2 1 1/4 **Improvise**[14] 5375 2-8-9 .......... SSanders 7 78
(CEBrittain) *chsd ldrs: rdn over 1f out: r.o* **8/1**[2]

0304 3 hd **Encouragement**[11] 5441 2-8-9 75 .......... RLMoore 13 77
(RHannon) *led over 4f: no ex nr fin* **8/1**[2]

4 3 1/2 **Kenmore** 2-9-0 .......... KFallon 2 71+
(BWHills) *s.i.s: hld up: hung rt 2f out: hdwy over 1f out: r.o* **8/1**[2]

3202 5 3/4 **Kanad**[14] 5376 2-9-0 77 ..........(t) RHills 6 68
(BHanbury) *chsd ldrs: rdn over 2f out: styd on same pce appr fnl f* **12/1**[3]

0 6 1 **Pacific Pirate (IRE)**[24] 5118 2-9-0 .......... TPQueally 11 65
(MGQuinlan) *chsd ldrs over 4f* **25/1**

7 3/4 **Born For Diamonds (IRE)** 2-8-9 .......... EAhern 5 58+
(BWHills) *hld up: r.o ins fnl f: nvr trbld ldrs* **33/1**

8 ½ **Silver Bark** 2-8-9 ........ LDettori 3 56
(EALDunlop) *trckd ldrs tl wknd over 1f out* **12/1**³

9 1¼ **Pamir (IRE)** 2-8-11 ........ NMackay⁽³⁾ 8 57
(LMCumani) *s.i.s: sn pushed along in rr: hdwy over 2f out: hung rt and wknd over 1f out* **25/1**

10 ½ **Hawkes Bay** 2-9-0 ........ PRobinson 4 55
(MHTompkins) *s.i.s: outpcd: styd on ins fnl f: nvr nrr* **33/1**

11 ½ **Perfect Solution (IRE)** 2-8-9 ........ LisaJones 12 49
(JARToller) *prom to 1/2-way* **33/1**

460 12 2½ **Classic Guest**[19] [5247] 2-8-9 60 ........ TEDurcan 10 41
(MRChannon) *chsd ldrs over 4f* **50/1**

13 9 **Branston Penny** 2-8-9 ........ DHolland 9 11
(JGGiven) *sn outpcd* **50/1**

1m 10.49s (-2.60) **Going Correction** -0.45s/f (Firm) **13** Ran SP% **121.5**
Speed ratings: **99,97,97,92,91 90,89,88,86,86 85,82,70**CSF £7.93 TOTE £1.90: £1.10, £2.50, £2.60; EX 10.70.

**Owner** Bryan Fry **Bred** T Stewart **Trained** Newmarket, Suffolk

**FOCUS**
A fair median auction stakes for the course with the third providing the level of the form.

**NOTEBOOK**
**King Marju(IRE)** had been running well in maiden company and made no mistake. Always up with the pace, he forged clear just over a furlong out and was always holding the third in the final furlong. He remains progressive and should be able to be competitive in a nursery.

**Improvise** ran well on the All Weather last time, and translated that improvement to the turf. She came under pressure early in the race and looked to be going nowhere until really picking up when hitting the rising ground. She is now handicapped and could be a nursery type, possibly over a furlong longer.

**Encouragement** broke well and was leading for most of the race. Along with the winner, she came clear until weakening slightly up the hill. This was a solid effort again and should be capable of winning sooner rather than later on this evidence.

**Kenmore** missed the break and ran green throughout the race. When Fallon got him straightened out he finished nicely up the hill, and comes out of the race as an eyecatcher.

**Kanad** has been running respectably this season without looking a star. He again travelled well in the race until the pressure was applied, where he stayed on at the one pace. He looks to be a nursery type.

**Pacific Pirate(IRE)** was always up with the pace, but could only finish at one paced from the dip.

**Born For Diamonds(IRE)** travelled well in the race until becoming a bit unbalanced at the dip. From there he stayed on strongly up the hill and the race will have brought him on.

**Silver Bark** shaped as though she has ability. She travelled really well through the race, getting close to the lead at one point, but found very little when push came to shove. If that can be put down to inexperience this was a promising effort, and she can win her maiden in due course.

## 5721 ROBINSONS MERCEDES-BENZ NURSERY 6f
**5:30** (5:31) (D2) (0-85,84) 2-Y-O **£5,577** (£1,716; £858; £429) **Stalls** Centre

Form RPR

31 1 **The Pheasant Flyer**[15] [5353] 2-9-4 **81** ........ JFortune 5 92
(BJMeehan) *mde virtually all: drvn out* **3/1**¹

160 2 1¼ **Elgin Marbles**[43] [4601] 2-9-3 **80** ........ RLMoore 6 87
(RHannon) *chsd wnr: rdn and ev ch over 1f out: unable qck nr fin* **16/1**

01 3 *shd* **Penkenna Princess (IRE)**[18] [5271] 2-9-7 **84** ........ SSanders 1 91
(RMBeckett) *chsd ldrs: rdn over 1f out: r.o* **5/1**

3150 4 1 **Keep Baccknihit (IRE)**[13] [5391] 2-8-10 **78** ........ AQuinn⁽⁵⁾ 3 81
(GLMoore) *chsd ldrs: rdn over 2f out: styd on* **12/1**

0240 5 1¾ **Monsieur Mirasol**[16] [5314] 2-8-12 **75** ........ NCallan 8 73
(KARyan) *chsd ldrs: rdn over 2f out: no ex fnl f* **7/1**

2301 6 2½ **Connotation**[8] [5520] 2-8-9 **72** 6ex ........ (v) LDettori 2 62
(PWD'Arcy) *hld up: hdwy over 2f out: wknd over 1f out* **4/1**³

0100 7 *shd* **Prospect Court**[24] [5119] 2-9-2 **79** ........ TQuinn 9 68
(JDBethell) *prom over 4f* **16/1**

0440 8 *nk* **First Rule**[66] [3930] 2-8-9 **72** ........ EAhern 10 60
(CFWall) *chsd ldrs over 4f* **20/1**

2102 9 2½ **Rowan Lodge (IRE)**[10] [5453] 2-9-7 **84** ........ PRobinson 4 64
(MHTompkins) *prom over 3f* **7/2**²

000 10 4 **Welsh Galaxy (IRE)**[12] [5407] 2-7-7 **61** oh8 ........ DFox⁽⁵⁾ 7 28
(PLGilligan) *sn outpcd* **50/1**

1m 10.52s (-2.57) **Going Correction** -0.45s/f (Firm) **10** Ran SP% **122.6**
Speed ratings: **99,97,97,95,93 90,90,89,86,81**CSF £56.28 CT £248.32 TOTE £3.40: £1.60, £3.60, £1.90; EX 58.70 Place 6 £8.04, Place 5 £5.70.

**Owner** The Second Pheasant Inn Partnership **Bred** Mrs O M Weston **Trained** Upper Lambourn, Berks

**FOCUS**
A strong-looking nursery and the form looks reliable for the grade.

**NOTEBOOK**
**The Pheasant Flyer** was always up with the pace and won going away. His form looks rock solid, having beaten a winner earlier in the card and finishing third behind a subsequent nursery winner on his debut, and as long as the Handicapper does not hit him hard for this win he can score again. He remains progressive.

**Elgin Marbles** came back to form after a break of over a month and a return to a quicker turf surface. He appeared to get in front in the last furlong, but could not fend off the winner's final burst. This looks to be his favoured trip and going on the evidence so far.

**Penkenna Princess(IRE)** ran a fine race given that due to her draw she raced away from the front two, and more-or-less on her own. She looks to be progressing nicely and is still open to plenty of improvement. A step up in grade, on this evidence, would not be out of the question.

**Keep Bacckinhit(IRE)**, drawn badly last time and did not act on the soft the time before, was always in the leading pack until getting outpaced around two furlongs out. She finished well up the hill and could probably do with a return to seven furlongs. She is one to keep an eye on if he returning to that the trip on a quick surface before the end of the season.

**Monsieur Mirasol** was pushed along early and stayed on up the hill without ever threatening. Her better form is with much more cut, so she has excuses given the ground.

**Connotation** raced up the unfavoured stands side and looked a little bit quirky during the race before dropping away.

**Rowan Lodge(IRE)** *Official explanation: jockey said colt was unsuited by the good to firm ground*

T/Jkpt: £201.20 to a £1 stake. Pool: £20,411.50. 72.00 winning tickets. T/Plt: £12.90 to a £1 stake. Pool: £50,697.85. 2,861.90 winning tickets. T/Qpdt: £5.30 to a £1 stake. Pool: £2,651.30. 366.40 winning tickets. CR

5722 - 5726a (Foreign Racing) - See Raceform Interactive

# 4184 MAISONS-LAFFITTE (R-H)
Tuesday, September 21

**OFFICIAL GOING: Good**

## 5727a LA COUPE DE MAISONS-LAFFITTE (GROUP 3) (STRAIGHT COURSE) 1m 2f (S)
**2:50** (2:47) 3-Y-O+ **£25,704** (£10,282; £7,711; £5,141)

RPR

1 **Fair Mix (IRE)**[23] [5170] 6-9-1 ........ SPasquier 10 119+
(MRolland, France) *always in touch on outside, driven to lead 1 1/2f out, ridden out, ran on well*

2 *snk* **Marshall (FR)**[62] [4039] 4-8-12 ........ MBlancpain 8 115
(CLaffon-Parias, France) *held up in rear, headway on outside well over 1f out, hard ridden and every chance 100y out, unable to quicken close home*

3 2½ **Special Kaldoun (IRE)**[38] [4766] 5-9-1 ........ DBoeuf 3 114
(DSmaga, France) *midfield, stayed on at one pace under pressure final f* ³

4 2 **Bailador (IRE)**[23] [5170] 4-9-1 ........ CSoumillon 5 110
(AFabre, France) *held up in rear, headway tracking 2nd from well over 1f out, one pace final f* ²

5 2 **Binary File (USA)**[30] [4984] 6-8-12 ........ IMendizabal 7 103
(SJensen, Denmark) *disputed 2nd on outside, led 2f out to 1 1/2f out, soon weakened*

6 1½ **Vassilievsky (IRE)**[125] [2233] 3-8-6 ........ OPeslier 11 101
(ELellouche, France) *held up in rear, stayed on from over 1f out, never near to challenge*

7 4 **Martaline**[23] [5170] 5-8-12 ........ TGillet 9 93
(AFabre, France) *disputed 2nd til weakened over 1f out* ¹

8 2 **Denominado (ARG)**[128] [2163] 5-8-12 ........ J-LMartinez 4 90
(GBindella, Spain) *led to 2f out, soon weakened*

9 3 **Look Honey (IRE)**[38] [4766] 4-8-12 ........ (b) TThulliez 1 84
(CLerner, France) *midfield, brief effort 2f out, soon weakened*

10 *snk* **Ecole D'Art (USA)**[85] [3389] 3-8-6 ........ MSautjeau 2 84
(AFabre, France) *disputed 2nd on rails til weakened 2f out*

1m 59.4s **Going Correction** -0.80s/f (Hard)
**WFA** 3 from 4yo+ 6lb **10** Ran SP% **119.4**
Speed ratings: **113,112,110,109,107 106,103,101,99,99**.
**Owner** Mme J Shalam **Bred** Snc Lagardere Elevage **Trained** France

**NOTEBOOK**
**Fair Mix(IRE)** had his ground on this occasion and made full use of it to repeat his victory of two years ago. Sixth early on, he made a forward move two out to take the advantage a furlong later and ran on under strong pressure to hold the runner-up, but always appeared to have something in hand. He will now go to Italy for the Jockey Club Gold Cup in Milan on October 17 and then the Premio Roma the following month. He will then go off to the Far East for a second tilt at the Hong Kong Vase.
**Marshall(FR)** came out of the pack one and a half furlongs out to put in a determined challenge, but could never quite peg back the winner and was being held as the race came to an end.
**Special Kaldoun(IRE)**, who is not at his best on this slightly faster ground, did not appear on the scene until the latter stages. He did make up some late ground but never threatened the winner and runner-up. He now goes for the Prix Dollar or a second attempt to win the Prix Daniel Wildenstein.
**Bailador(IRE)** was held up early on then outpaced when things warmed up, but ran on again during the final furlong. He may well be better suited by a longer trip.

# 5490 GOODWOOD (R-H)
Wednesday, September 22

**OFFICIAL GOING: Good**

## 5728 MACPHIE FOODSERVICE CLASSIFIED STKS 1m 4f
**2:20** (2:21) (D2) 3-Y-O+ **£6,873** (£2,115; £1,057; £528) **Stalls** Low

Form RPR

1212 1 **Belle Rouge**[19] [5274] 6-9-0 74 ........ LDettori 13 80+
(CAHorgan) *trckd ldrs: led appr fnl 2f: sn pushed along: hld on wl fnl f* **3/1**¹

3560 2 ½ **Nawow**[5] [5615] 4-9-3 74 ........ DHolland 11 82
(PDCundell) *bhd: hdwy fr 3f out: hrd drvn and kpt on fr over 1f out: fin wl to take 2nd last strides: nt rch wnr* **16/1**

0244 3 *shd* **Dr Cerullo**[23] [5203] 3-8-9 73 ........ SSanders 4 82
(CTinkler) *hld up in rr: plenty to do 3f out: hdwy on outside over 2f out: str run u.p fnl f:nt rch wnr and lost 2nd last strides* **14/1**

1200 4 1¼ **Wasted Talent (IRE)**[23] [5182] 4-9-0 75 ........ (v) PHanagan 15 77
(JGPortman) *t.k.h: in tch: hdwy to ld 7f out: rdn 3f out: hdd appr fnl 2f: styd chasing ldrs tl outpcd ins last* **14/1**

5540 5 2 **Mad Carew (USA)**[53] [4327] 5-9-3 73 ........ (b) RLMoore 14 77
(GLMoore) *bhd: hdwy 3f out: n.m.r on ins and swtchd lft ins fnl 2f: kpt on ins last but nvr gng pce to rch ldrs* **14/1**

2043 6 ½ **Ganymede**[15] [5367] 3-8-9 75 ........ KFallon 16 76
(MLWBell) *sn led: hdd 7f out: styd chsng ldr: drvn to chal appr fnl 2f: wknd fnl f* **12/1**

1054 7 1¼ **Pagan Magic (USA)**[14] [5402] 3-8-9 75 ........ PRobinson 9 74
(JARToller) *chsd ldrs: rdn and hung rt 2f out: wknd fnl f* **7/1**²

-325 8 1½ **Albavilla**[19] [5273] 4-9-0 74 ........ TQuinn 3 68
(PWHarris) *t.k.h: in tch: outpcd 4f out: rdn and kpt on fnl 2f but nvr gng pce to trble ldrs* **8/1**³

2133 9 *shd* **Velvet Waters**[18] [5300] 3-8-6 71 ........ SCarson 5 68
(RFJohnsonHoughton) *chsd ldrs: rdn over 2f out: wknd over 1f out* **10/1**

2000 10 *hd* **Silver City**[13] [5423] 4-9-3 73 ........ PDobbs 2 71
(MrsAJPerrett) *s.i.s: hld up in rr: rdn and styd on fr over 2f out: n.d* **25/1**

3003 11 1 **Maystock**[13] [5423] 4-9-0 73 ........ JFortune 6 66
(GAButler) *slowly away: bhd: rdn and modest hdwy fnl 2f* **9/1**

0050 12 4 **Bukit Fraser (IRE)**[26] [5093] 3-8-9 75 ........ MHills 1 63
(PFICole) *a in rr* **14/1**

1250 13 3½ **Miss Pebbles (IRE)**[32] [4950] 4-9-0 73 ........ MartinDwyer 12 54
(SCWilliams) *in tch: rdn over 3f out: wknd qckly 2f out* **16/1**

0001 14 5 **Abington Angel**[21] [5217] 3-8-6 75 ........ (b) RWinston 7 46
(BJMeehan) *lw: rel to r and rdn sn after s: a bhd* **16/1**

330- 15 5 **Mumbling (IRE)**[291] [6130] 6-8-10 69 ........ AHindley⁽⁷⁾ 10 41
(BGPowell) *sn bhd* **50/1**

1200 **16** *7* **Linens Flame**[111] 2631 5-9-3 73 ........................................ DSweeney 8 30
(BGPowell) *lw: chsd ldrs: wknd 4f out* **50/1**

2m 39.43s (0.50) **Going Correction** +0.15s/f (Good)
**WFA** 3 from 4yo+ 8lb **16** Ran SP% **127.5**
Speed ratings: **104,103,103,102,101 101,100,99,99,99 98,95,93,90,86 82**CSF £57.11 TOTE £3.50: £1.70, £5.70, £6.80; EX 128.50.
**Owner** Mrs B Woodford **Bred** Whitsbury Manor Stud **Trained** Ogbourne Maisey, Wilts

**FOCUS**
A competitive event that was run at a solid gallop. The form looks sound for the class.

**NOTEBOOK**
**Belle Rouge** used her proven stamina to great effect from her useful draw and ran out a ready winner. She has been really progressive at this trip and beyond this season, is yet to run a bad race and was winning this off a 20lb higher mark than when successful in April. Value for more than the bare margin, she has not stopped winning yet and connections will have one eye on her very appealing All-Weather rating.
**Nawow** ◆ was staying on with real effect late in the day, but never really looked like getting there. This showed the benefit of his recent comeback from a break at Newbury last time, and he could be placed to strike off this mark, especially if facing a stiffer test.
**Dr Cerullo** did not help himself by rearing on leaving the stalls and still had it all to do on the turn for home, but really picked up under pressure and finished well. He looks well worth a try over further now and is on a fair mark.
**Wasted Talent(IRE)** was given a good ride from the front and only faded out of it late on. She looks weighted to her best, but looks worth a shot over further and could do better over hurdles this winter.
**Mad Carew(USA)** was short of room when full of running two out, but had his chance if good enough and may have found this trip stretching him. This was still not a bad effort and he can be found better opportunities over slightly shorter. *Official explanation: jockey said gelding hung both ways*
**Ganymede** had every chance if good enough, but again looked tricky under pressure and failed to see this trip out all that well. He is seriously frustrating horse and may need to be gelded in order to progress.
**Pagan Magic(USA)** failed to find the necessary change of gear when asked to pick up in the straight and was a little disappointing.
**Maystock** lost her chance at the start and is capable of a lot better. *Official explanation: jockey said filly reared on leaving the stalls and was slowly away*

## 5729 RICH'S PRODUCTS CORPORATION EBF MAIDEN STKS 1m

**2:55** (2:56) (D2) 2-Y-O **£5,551** (£1,708; £854; £427) **Stalls** High

Form RPR

05 **1** **Wingman (IRE)**[21] 5228 2-9-0 ........................................ KFallon 2 90
(JWHills) *lw: hld up in rr: stdy hdwy fr 3f out: trckd ldr appr fnl f: qcknd to ld last strides: readily* **16/1**

32 **2** *nk* **Foxhaven**[19] 5268 2-9-0 ........................................ MartinDwyer 5 89
(PRChamings) *led: hdd over 5f out:styd w ldr tl led again over 3f out: shkn up and 3l clr over 1f out: kpt on wl tl ct cl home* **7/2[2]**

45 **3** *7* **Bertrose**[19] 5268 2-9-0 ........................................ SSanders 10 74
(JLDunlop) *bhd: hdwy over 2f out: kpt on fr over 1f out to take 3rd wl ins last but no ch w ldrs* **12/1**

4 **4** *3/4* **Spear Thistle**[14] 5396 2-9-0 ........................................ JFortune 9 72
(JHMGosden) *chsd ldrs: rdn over 2f out: no imp and sn outpcd* **2/1[1]**

2203 **5** *shd* **Chapter (IRE)**[16] 5335 2-9-0 77 ........................................ RLMoore 4 72
(RHannon) *chsd ldrs: wnt 2nd over 2f out but nvr gng pce to chal: lost 2nd over 1f out and sn outpcd* **16/1**

00 **6** *1 1/4* **Water Pistol**[19] 5256 2-9-0 ........................................ PRobinson 6 69
(MrsAJPerrett) *bhd: pushed along on ins and kpt on fnl 2f: nvr gng pce to rch ldrs* **66/1**

05 **7** *shd* **Art Elegant**[19] 5269 2-9-0 ........................................ MHills 11 71+
(BWHills) *hld up in rr: hdwy on outside fr 3f out: trckd ldrs 2f out: shkn up and sn outpcd* **20/1**

5 **8** *6* **Loch Quest (IRE)**[11] 5467 2-9-0 ........................................ LDettori 7 56
(MrsAJPerrett) *chsd ldrs: rdn 3f out: wknd 2f out* **6/1[3]**

65 **9** *nk* **Spill A Little**[9] 5508 2-9-0 ........................................ SHitchcott 8 55
(MRChannon) *lw: trckd ldr tl led over 5f out: hdd over 3f out: wknd qckly ins fnl 2f* **16/1**

22 **10** *3* **Inca Wood (UAE)**[14] 5398 2-8-9 ........................................ DHolland 1 43
(MJohnston) *chsd ldrs: rdn over 2f out: sn wknd* **7/1**

**11** *1 3/4* **Huboob (FR)** 2-9-0 ........................................ RHills 3 44
(MPTregoning) *w'like: scope: bit bkwd: s.i.s: sn rdn: green and a bhd* **16/1**

1m 42.01s (1.74) **Going Correction** +0.15s/f (Good) **11** Ran SP% **119.8**
Speed ratings: **97,96,89,88,88 87,87,81,81,78 76**CSF £72.79 TOTE £20.20: £5.90, £1.90, £4.20; EX 202.10.
**Owner** D M Kerr **Bred** Newtown Stud And T J Pabst **Trained** Upper Lambourn, Berks

**FOCUS**
A decent maiden that was run at a fair pace and the first two came well clear of the rest and the form looks strong.

**NOTEBOOK**
**Wingman(IRE)** relished this extra furlong and quickened up nicely late on to collar the long-time leader and win with a bit up his sleeve. This was his best effort to date, but he had previously shown ability in two outings and looks capable of doing better still next year over further.
**Foxhaven** ◆ made another bold bid from the front, but could not quicken again when the winner came at him close home. This was another solid effort and he now qualifies for a nursery mark, but certainly has the ability to win a maiden at any rate. It is interesting that his yard saddled their stable star Take A Bow to finish second in this last season, and this colt may prove as good or better next year over further.
**Bertrose** ran slightly below the form of his latest effort behind Foxhaven, but still turned in a sound effort and now qualifies for an all-important nursery mark. Better things can be expected of this colt as a three-year-old and he will have no problem in staying further.
**Spear Thistle**, who showed temperament on his recent Doncaster debut as well as definite ability, proved more straightforward this time, but was well held by the principals. He did however, shape as though he will do much better when faced with a stiffer test.
**Chapter(IRE)** is in danger of becoming a disappointing sort, but he really does look in need of further on this evidence. He is reliable enough and gives the form a solid look.
**Water Pistol** is bred to be much more effective at longer distances and now qualifies for handicaps, so could prove a deal better when things are in his favour.
**Art Elegant** was given far from a hard time in the straight and is one to keep a close eye on now he is eligible for nurseries.
**Loch Quest(IRE)** probably ran up to form of his recent debut over course and diatance, but may do better when dropped back a furlong and is not one to write off.

## 5730 SHARP COMMERCIAL MICROWAVE OVEN STKS H'CAP 6f

**3:30** (3:31) (D2) (0-85,82) 3-Y-0+ **£7,072** (£2,176; £1,088; £544) **Stalls** Low

Form RPR

6021 **1** **Endless Summer**[2] 5704 7-9-9 **82** 6ex ........................................ PDoe 8 93
(AWCarroll) *hld up in rr: hdwy and n.m.r over 1f out: qcknd to ld ins last: comf* **11/2[2]**

1016 **2** *1* **Marshallspark (IRE)**[12] 5440 5-8-12 **71** ........................................ PHanagan 12 79
(RAFahey) *lw: chsd ldrs: led 1f out: sn rdn and hdd: styd on same pce* **12/1**

0002 **3** *1 1/4* **Najeebon (FR)**[18] 5299 5-9-5 **78** ........................................ SHitchcott 20 82
(MRChannon) *lw: in tch: hdwy to chse ldrs 2f out: rdn to chal 1f out: kpt on same pce ins last* **11/2[2]**

0000 **4** *1* **Turibius**[2] 5704 5-8-9 **73** ........................................ (v) AQuinn(5) 16 74
(TEPowell) *sn chsng ldrs: rdn and effrt 2f out: styd on same pce ins last* **33/1**

5214 **5** *1/2* **Currency**[12] 5440 7-9-4 **77** ........................................ RLMoore 6 77
(JMBradley) *b: bhd: sn pushed along: hdwy over 1f out: fin wl but nt rch ldrs* **8/1[3]**

022 **6** *hd* **Kingscross**[19] 5263 6-9-7 **80** ........................................ DSweeney 5 79
(MBlanshard) *hld up in rr: hdwy 2f out: nt clr run over 1f out: kpt on wl fnl f but nvr gng pce of ldrs* **14/1**

0600 **7** *1/2* **Fyodor (IRE)**[12] 5440 3-8-13 **74** ........................................ RHills 10 72
(WJHaggas) *hld up in rr: hdwy over 1f out: kpt on ins last but nvr gng pce to rch ldrs* **50/1**

0010 **8** *1 1/2* **Canterloupe (IRE)**[26] 5075 6-9-3 **76** ........................................ SSanders 18 69
(PJMakin) *chsd ldrs tl led 2f out: hdd 1f out: sn wknd* **12/1**

2340 **9** *hd* **Skyharbor**[2] 5697 3-9-1 **76** ........................................ (v) MartinDwyer 9 69
(AMBalding) *chsd ldrs: outpcd 1/2-way: kpt on again fnl f* **33/1**

1224 **10** *1/2* **High Ridge**[51] 4403 5-8-12 **71** ........................................ (p) LDettori 11 62
(JMBradley) *s.i.s: bhd: rdn 1/2-way: kpt on fnl f but n.d* **5/1[1]**

0501 **11** *3/4* **Thurlestone Rock**[18] 5299 4-9-5 **78** ........................................ JFortune 14 67
(BJMeehan) *chsd ldrs: rdn over 2f out: wknd fnl f* **14/1**

4150 **12** *1/2* **Ivory Lace**[7] 5563 3-9-2 **77** ........................................ KFallon 13 64
(SWoodman) *bhd: rdn over 2f out: hung lft fr over 1f out and nvr gng pce to rch ldrs* **20/1**

4410 **13** *1 1/2* **Undeterred**[54] 4291 8-9-2 **75** ........................................ DMernagh 4 58
(TDBarron) *lw: racd stands side: led that gp ins last but no ch w main gp fr 1/2-way* **20/1**

0021 **14** *3/4* **Swinbrook (USA)**[89] 3262 3-9-5 **80** ........................................ LisaJones 1 61
(JARToller) *racd stands side: led that gp 2f out but no ch w main gp fr 1/2-way* **25/1**

0100 **15** *nk* **Semenovskii**[18] 5299 4-8-13 **72** ........................................ DHolland 3 52
(PWD'Arcy) *pressed ldrs tl wknd over 1f out* **12/1**

0100 **16** *2* **Michelle Ma Belle (IRE)**[26] 5075 4-9-1 **74** ........................................ (b) MHills 7 48
(SKirk) *racd stands side: outpcd* **25/1**

4000 **17** *nk* **Danehill Stroller (IRE)**[5] 5614 4-9-2 **80** ........................................ (p) NDeSouza(5) 2 53
(RMBeckett) *lw: led stands side 4f: no ch w maiden gp fr 1/2-way* **25/1**

5201 **18** *4* **Peruvian Style (IRE)**[14] 5399 3-8-13 **74** ........................................ RWinston 17 35
(NPLittmoden) *led 1f: styd w ldr tl over 2f out* **16/1**

5005 **19** *2 1/2* **Zarzu**[12] 5440 5-9-1 **77** ........................................ RThomas(3) 19 30
(CRDore) *b: b.hind: led after 1f: hdd 2f out: sn wknd* **20/1**

1m 12.86s (0.02) **Going Correction** +0.15s/f (Good)
**WFA** 3 from 4yo+ 2lb **19** Ran SP% **134.5**
Speed ratings: **105,103,102,100,100 99,99,97,96,96 95,94,92,91,91 88,88,82,79**CSF £66.10 CT £411.17 TOTE £7.10: £2.30, £3.70, £1.70, £8.70; EX 99.80 Trifecta £705.50 w/u.
**Owner** Seasons Holidays **Bred** Juddmonte Farms **Trained** Wixford, Warwicks

**FOCUS**
A competitive sprint handicap that saw those drawn high at a distinct advantage. The form is solid for the grade.

**NOTEBOOK**
**Endless Summer**, back to winning ways at Leicester two days previously, readily followed-up under his 6lb penalty. His current connections look to have found the key to him, and he should take plenty of beating if they can find him another race under a penalty before the Handicapper can have his say.
**Marshallspark(IRE)** relished this return to six furlongs and turned in another solid effort in defeat. He is clearly in great form and is not weighted out of winning again just yet.
**Najeebon(FR)**, who had shown improvement last time at Kempton, ran right up to form and should find a similar race before the season is out.
**Turibius** improved greatly for this extra furlong and more positive tactics. He could be about to hit top form and is on a fair mark.
**Currency** struggled to go the early pace, but again finished with gusto and is a solid yardstick in this grade.
**Kingscross** soon tracked across to the far side and was in the process of mounting a challenge when finding trouble entering the last furlong. He would not have won, but is slightly better than the bare form, and continues in good heart.
**High Ridge** blew his chance at the start and was never really going this time. He remains at the right end of the handicap, but has a bit to prove now. *Official explanation: jockey said gelding was never travelling*

## 5731 MERBURY CATERING CONSULTANTS FOUNDATION STKS (LISTED RACE) 1m 1f 192y

**4:05** (4:05) (A1) 3-Y-0+ **£17,400** (£6,600; £3,300; £1,500) **Stalls** High

Form RPR

0431 **1** **Alkaadhem**[10] 5492 4-9-3 107 ........................................ (b) RHills 6 118
(MPTregoning) *lw: hld up in tch: hdwy to trck ldr 2f out: pushed along and qcknd to ld 1f out: c clr ins last: readily* **6/4[1]**

2304 **2** *3 1/2* **Privy Seal (IRE)**[87] 3360 3-8-8 107 ........................................ JFortune 1 108
(JHMGosden) *lw: chsd ldrs: wnt 2nd over 5f out: led over 2f out: rdn and hdd 1f out: kpt on but no ch w wnr ins last* **12/1**

3022 **3** *nk* **Battle Chant (USA)**[10] 5492 4-9-0 102 ........................................ RLMoore 4 108
(MrsAJPerrett) *hld up in tch: rdn 3f out: styd on to chse ldrs fr 2f out: nvr gng pce to chal and one pce fnl f* **11/2[3]**

641 **4** *1 1/4* **Colisay**[11] 5461 5-9-0 102 ........................................ KFallon 3 105
(EFVaughan) *lw: chsd ldr tl over 5f out: rdn over 3f out: styd on same pce fnl 2f* **15/2**

3501 **5** *3/4* **Naheef (IRE)**[25] 5133 5-9-0 109 ........................................ (vt) LDettori 8 104
(SaeedBinSuroor) *lw: led: rdn and hdd over 2f out: styd in tch tl wknd ins last* **2/1[2]**

1340 **6** *3/4* **Skidmark**[133] 2043 3-8-8 97 ........................................ SSanders 2 103
(DRCElsworth) *t.k.h in rr: kpt on fnl 2f but n.d* **33/1**

6100 **7** *nk* **Corriolanus (GER)**[11] 5488 4-9-0 103 ........................................ DHolland 7 102
(PMitchell) *bhd: styd on fnl 2f: nvr a danger* **33/1**

30- **8** *27* **Bayadere (GER)**[371] 5000 4-8-9 ........................................ MHenry 5 46
(VSmith) *in tch tl wknd qckly fr 4f out* **100/1**

2m 11.62s (3.94) **Going Correction** +0.15s/f (Good)
**WFA** 3 from 4yo+ 6lb **8** Ran SP% **115.0**
Speed ratings: **90,87,86,85,85 84,84,62**CSF £20.87 TOTE £2.60: £1.30, £2.10, £1.70; EX 25.60.
**Owner** Hamdan Al Maktoum **Bred** Meon Valley Stud **Trained** Lambourn, Berks

**FOCUS**
A reasonable enough Listed contest, but Naheef was allowed to set a very steady pace and the race did not really get under way until the final half mile. That would explain why the time was remarkably slow for a race of this class.

**NOTEBOOK**

**Alkaadhem**, who beat the third horse in a Group Three over course and distance ten days previously, readily quickened clear when asked to win his race and did not have to be at his best to register a fourth course success. The application of blinkers the last twice has clearly been the making of him and, although he clearly loves this track, connections have yet to get to the bottom of him. He could make a much better four-year-old and is due to campaign in Dubai next spring.
**Privy Seal(IRE)** turned in a pleasing effort on this return from an 87-day break, and this effort leaves connections with plenty of further options this coming autumn. He should improve for easier ground and would make a nice four-year-old if staying in training.
**Battle Chant(USA)** was again doing all of his best work late in the day and would have been suited by a stronger early pace. He ran below the form of his recent Group effort with the winner, despite these better terms, but he still has to convince he truly sees out this trip and may do better over slightly shorter.
**Colisay** ran too freely through the early stages on this first try in Listed company and was not disgraced in the circumstances. He will do better with a stronger gallop and could find a race at this level over the trip.
**Naheef(IRE)**, successful in Listed company over an extended mile three at Windsor on his previous start, was allowed to do his own thing out in front. However, he could offer little when the pace began to increase and has to be considered disappointing.
**Skidmark** ◆ progressed into a smart performer on Polytrack earlier in the year, but has yet to confirm that on turf. However, this was his first run in 133 days and he had little chance given how the race was run. He can yet make his mark on turf.
**Corriolanus(GER)** was given a ridiculous ride, held up and virtually detached off what was a very slow early pace. This was a good effort in the circumstances. *Official explanation: jockey said colt had hung right*

## 5732 CROSSE & BLACKWELL STKS (H'CAP) 1m 3f
**4:40** (4:40) (D2) (0-85,85) 3-Y-O **£7,065** (£2,174; £1,087; £543) **Stalls** Low

Form RPR

1121 **1** **Nordwind (IRE)**[14] 5402 3-9-5 **83**........................ LDettori 1 94+
(PWHarris) *w ldr 2f: styd in 2nd tl led over 3f out: pushed clr 2f out: kpt on strly fnl f* **2/1**[1]

501 **2** *1 ½* **Qudraat (IRE)**[23] 5196 3-9-2 **80**........................ RHills 7 93+
(EFVaughan) *lw: hld up rr: nt clr run 3f out: swtchd lft to outside over 2f out: str run to chse wnr ins last:edgd rt: kpt on: no imp* **7/1**[3]

-156 **3** *5* **Goodwood Finesse (IRE)**[24] 5152 3-8-10 **74**........................ SSanders 5 75
(JLDunlop) *in tch: rdn and hdwy over 2f out: outpcd fnl f but hld on for 3rd* **20/1**

5020 **4** *hd* **Prime Powered (IRE)**[23] 5183 3-9-7 **85**........................(p) RLMoore 9 86
(GLMoore) *s.i.s: bhd: hdwy over 2f out: styd on u.p fnl f but nvr nr ldrs* **15/2**

1100 **5** *6* **Jakarmi**[12] 5446 3-8-9 **73**........................ PHanagan 2 64
(BPalling) *bhd: rdn 3f out: kpt on fnl 2f but nvr in contention* **20/1**

4330 **6** *4* **Gjovic**[93] 3160 3-8-8 **72**........................ RWinston 4 57
(BJMeehan) *chsd ldrs: rdn over 3f out: wknd ins fnl 2f* **20/1**

3142 **7** *hd* **Mr Tambourine Man (IRE)**[9] 5517 3-9-1 **84**........................ NDeSouza(5) 10 68
(PFICole) *bhd: hdwy 3f out: chsd ldrs 3f out: wknd 2f out* **5/1**[2]

1-00 **8** *3* **Quartino**[33] 4915 3-9-5 **83**........................(b[1]) JFortune 11 63
(JHMGosden) *bhd: hdwy on ins to ld 6f out: hdd over 3f out: wknd over 2f out* **33/1**

6450 **9** *½* **Absolutelythebest (IRE)**[41] 4692 3-9-2 **80**........................ DHolland 3 59
(EALDunlop) *bhd most of way* **25/1**

0341 **10** *½* **Wedding Cake (IRE)**[21] 5216 3-8-9 **73**........................ KFallon 12 51
(SirMichaelStoute) *lw: chsd ldrs: ridden 4f out: n.m.r and wknd 3f out* **7/1**[3]

6213 **11** *2 ½* **Michabo (IRE)**[26] 5074 3-9-2 **80**........................ TQuinn 8 54
(DRCElsworth) *lw: plld hrd: mde most tl hdd 6f out: wknd qckly 3f out* **9/1**

30-3 **12** *¾* **Lomapamar**[26] 5079 3-9-0 **78**........................ PRobinson 6 51
(MrsAJPerrett) *chsd ldrs over 7f* **20/1**

2m 27.15s (1.04) **Going Correction** +0.15s/f (Good) **12** Ran SP% **122.6**
Speed ratings: **102,100,97,97,92 89,89,87,87,86 84,84**CSF £14.65 CT £229.59 TOTE £3.40: £1.40, £3.00, £4.50; EX 28.30.
**Owner** Mrs P W Harris **Bred** Christoph Berglar **Trained** Ringshall, Bucks

**FOCUS**
A decent-enough handicap for the grade, and really good efforts from the front two, and the form of the principals should work out.

**NOTEBOOK**
**Nordwind(IRE)**, 4lb higher than when winning at Epsom on his previous start, made it four wins from his last five starts in decisive fashion. His attitude has looked questionable in the past, but he was willing enough and, always well placed by Dettori, he got a decisive first run on the eventual runner-up and made the most of it. Things could have been closer, but he was still well clear of the remainder and, with this representing a career-best effort, he is clearly still improving. Connections think he could make up into a Cup horse one day, but something like the November Handicap is probably a realistic target in the meantime.
**Qudraat(IRE)**, off the mark in a Ripon maiden on his previous start, was not given a very good ride and probably should have finished much closer. He had to be switched wide round the entire field while the eventual winner was making his move, and then proceeded to run green under pressure, hanging right under a left-hand drive. This will have taught him plenty and there should be improvement to come.
**Goodwood Finesse(IRE)**, dropped three furlongs in trip, ran her best race since winning her maiden but the principals were far too good.
**Prime Powered(IRE)** simply plugged on without looking like a particularly enthusiastic character.
**Jakarmi**, having his second race back after a beak, did not run badly but has a little way to go to return to winning form.
**Mr Tambourine Man(IRE)** was not at his best and is a better horse on really fast ground.
**Absolutelythebest(IRE)** *Official explanation: jockey said colt did not get a clear run*
**Wedding Cake(IRE)**, off the mark in decent enough fashion in just an ordinary Polytrack maiden on her previous start, looked on a reasonable enough mark for her handicap debut but ran a very lacklustre race.
**Michabo(IRE)** was unable to build on the promise of his recent course effort after racing keenly.

## 5733 PREMIER FOODS CLAIMING STKS (H'CAP) 1m
**5:15** (5:18) (F4) (0-55,55) 3-Y-O+ **£3,542** (£1,090; £545; £272) **Stalls** High

Form RPR

0202 **1** **Baby Barry**[11] 5450 7-8-8 **47**........................ SSanders 8 56
(MrsGSRees) *hld up mid-div: hdwy over 2f out: rdn to ld ins last: hld on wl* **8/1**

6043 **2** *nk* **Mobo-Baco**[13] 5408 7-8-13 **52**........................ KFallon 14 60
(RJHodges) *mid-div: hdwy 2f out: nt clr run and swtchd rt appr fnl f: str run on rail ins last but nt rch wnr* **13/2**[1]

0000 **3** *¾* **Colemanstown**[25] 5108 4-9-0 **53**........................ PHanagan 17 60
(BEllison) *chsd ldrs: rdn to ld 1f out: sn hdd: kpt on same pce* **15/2**[3]

3040 **4** *1* **Captain Cloudy**[13] 5411 4-8-12 **51**........................ GBaker 16 55
(MMadgwick) *chsd ldrs: rdn to chal wl over 1f out: styd on same pce ins last* **33/1**

0426 **5** *nk* **Icannshift (IRE)**[10] 5493 4-9-2 **55**........................ DHolland 18 59
(SDow) *led: rdn over 2f out: hdd 1f out: outpcd ins last* **7/1**[2]

2240 **6** *shd* **Midshipman**[23] 5175 6-9-0 **53**........................(vt) RLMoore 15 56
(AWCarroll) *hld up in rr: hdwy on ins over 2f out: styng on whn hmpd over 1f out: sn one pce* **9/1**

6234 **7** *nk* **Armentieres**[13] 5411 3-8-4 **52**........................(b) BSwarbrick(5) 2 55
(JLSpearing) *bhd: rdn and hdwy over 2f out: styd on u.p ins last but nt rch ldrs* **16/1**

5065 **8** *nk* **Compton Aviator**[16] 5350 8-8-10 **49**........................(tp) PDobbs 13 51
(AWCarroll) *chsd ldrs: rdn over 2f out: wknd fnl f* **33/1**

3105 **9** *¾* **Lucefer (IRE)**[7] 5575 6-8-6 **52**........................ DeanWilliams(7) 10 52
(GCHChung) *swtg: mid-div: hdwy fr 2f out: nt rch ldrs* **11/1**

600 **10** *5* **Bertocelli**[20] 5245 3-8-12 **55**........................ AMcCarthy 12 44
(GGMargarson) *lw: mid-div: rdn over 2f out: nvr gng pce to trble ldrs* **12/1**

6200 **11** *shd* **Blue Quiver (IRE)**[23] 5175 4-9-0 **53**........................ LDettori 3 42
(CAHorgan) *bhd: sme hdwy whn nt clr run 2f out: n.d* **14/1**

0220 **12** *nk* **Cafe Americano**[24] 5147 4-8-9 **48**........................(e) DSweeney 6 36
(DWPArbuthnot) *t.k.h: hld up in rr: sme hdwy on outside 3f out: n.d and sn wknd* **40/1**

3006 **13** *11* **Smart Boy Prince (IRE)**[19] 5267 3-8-5 **53**........................ PMakin(5) 20 16
(MJAttwater) *chsd ldrs over 5f* **33/1**

0000 **14** *4* **Learned Lad (FR)**[57] 4220 6-8-9 **48**........................ PDoe 4 1
(JamiePoulton) *chsd ldrs over 5f* **33/1**

0000 **15** *4* **Meelup (IRE)**[19] 5260 4-8-12 **51**........................(p) VSlattery 7 —
(JaneSouthcombe) *lw: bhd most of way* **40/1**

056 **16** *10* **Land Of Nod (IRE)**[19] 5259 3-8-10 **53**........................(v) JFortune 11 —
(GAButler) *bhd: brief effrt on ins fr 3f out: n.m.r and sn wknd* **14/1**

0040 **17** *5* **Private Jessica**[30] 5002 3-8-7 **50**........................ RWinston 5 —
(JRFanshawe) *chsd ldrs 5f* **33/1**

1m 41.13s (0.86) **Going Correction** +0.15s/f (Good)
**WFA** 3 from 4yo+ 4lb **17** Ran SP% **113.5**
Speed ratings: **101,100,99,98,98 98,98,97,97,92 92,91,80,76,72 62,57**CSF £41.90 CT £232.79 TOTE £6.40: £1.90, £1.10, £2.40, £5.70; EX 23.20.
**Owner** S B Partnership **Bred** Capt J H Wilson **Trained** Sollom, Lancs
■ Mac's Talisman (4/1F) withdrawn at start on vet's advice. R4 applies, deduct 20p in the £.
■ Stewards Enquiry : K Fallon one-day ban: used whip in the forehand position down the shoulder and without allowing sufficient time for response (Oct 4); caution: careless riding

**FOCUS**
A competitive claimer run at a good pace, but moderate form as the previous effort of the winner testifies.

**NOTEBOOK**
**Baby Barry**, runner-up in a banded race at Carlisle on his previous start, stepped up on that effort to run out a narrow winner. He is clearly in good form, but his recent winning record does not inspire much confidence of a follow up.
**Mobo-Baco**, a beaten favourite when third in a Chepstow seller on his previous start, improved on that effort under a determined ride, but the winner got first run.
**Colemanstown** got a good run up the far rail and posted one of his best efforts of the season.
**Captain Cloudy**, racing over a mile for just the third time, did not find as much as had looked likely and may do better ridden with restraint over this trip.
**Icannshift(IRE)** does most of racing over ten furlongs these days, but showed plenty of pace on this drop in trip to make good use of his draw near the rail; he was simply unable to sustain the good gallop he set.
**Midshipman**, dropped in grade and trip, was a shade unlucky as Moore went for an ambitious run up the rail and did have to stop riding, but he would not have won.
**Blue Quiver(IRE)** *Official explanation: jockey said gelding had a breathing problem and lost its action*
**Land Of Nod(IRE)** *Official explanation: jockey said filly was unsuited by the good ground*
**Private Jessica** *Official explanation: jockey said filly was unsuited by the good going*

## 5734 WESTLER FOODS APPRENTICE STKS (H'CAP) 5f
**5:45** (5:48) (E3) (0-70,69) 3-Y-O+ **£3,462** (£1,065; £532; £266) **Stalls** Low

Form RPR

0401 **1** **Inch By Inch**[13] 5412 5-8-10 **60**........................(b) AQuinn(3) 7 71
(PJMakin) *hld up rr: hdwy and nt clr run 1f out: swtchd rt and rapid hdwy ins last: qcknd to ld nr fin* **9/1**

4150 **2** *¾* **One Way Ticket**[20] 5253 4-9-7 **68**........................(p) LFletcher 8 76
(JMBradley) *led: rdn 2f out: ct cl home* **14/1**

-050 **3** *shd* **Flaran**[30] 5008 4-8-7 **57**........................ NDeSouza(3) 11 65
(EFVaughan) *chsd ldrs: rdn over 2f out: styd on wl and str chal ins fnl f: no ex cl home* **12/1**

1340 **4** *nk* **Byo (IRE)**[20] 5253 6-9-2 **68**........................ DeanWilliams(5) 13 75
(MQuinn) *pressed ldr: rdn to chal fr 1f out: nt qckn cl home* **14/1**

0605 **5** *1* **Borzoi Maestro**[7] 5564 3-9-7 **69**........................(p) ABeech 3 72
(JLSpearing) *in tch: hdwy 2f out: styd on ins fnl f but nt pce to rch ldrs* **16/1**

0060 **6** *½* **Madrasee**[26] 5075 6-9-1 **62**........................ DNolan 2 63
(LMontagueHall) *bhd: styd on fr over 1f out: kpt on ins last but nt rch ldrs* **7/1**[3]

0003 **7** *nk* **Double M**[9] 5512 7-9-1 **65**........................(v) RThomas(3) 16 65
(MrsLRichards) *lw: mid-div: hdwy over 1f out: styng on whn hmpd wl ins last: nt rcvr* **9/4**[1]

-403 **8** *hd* **King Egbert (FR)**[11] 5473 3-8-1 **56**........................ TDean(7) 9 55
(AWCarroll) *bhd: hdwy and swtchd rt 1f out: one pce ins last* **10/1**

3014 **9** *2* **Maromito (IRE)**[13] 5412 7-8-11 **63**........................ AMullen(5) 15 55
(RBastiman) *s.i.s: bhd: hdwy 3f out: pressed ldrs over 1f out: wknd ins last* **5/1**[2]

0600 **10** *shd* **Golden Bounty**[41] 4687 5-8-9 **61**........................ PGallagher(5) 5 53
(RHannon) *s.i.s: bhd: hdwy over 1f out out: styd on ins last but n.d* **25/1**

6000 **11** *½* **Margalita (IRE)**[63] 4034 4-8-13 **60**........................(bt) LisaJones 14 50
(PMitchell) *chsd ldrs tl wknd over 1f out* **33/1**

0000 **12** *1 ¼* **Palawan**[12] 5440 8-8-9 **63**........................(p) RJKilloran(7) 10 49
(AMBalding) *b: chsd ldrs tl wknd ins fnl 2f* **16/1**

0404 **13** *½* **Urban Rose**[11] 5473 3-8-7 **58**........................(tp) PMakin(3) 6 42
(RMHCowell) *racd stands side: a outpcd* **16/1**

0000 **14** *5* **Indian Bazaar (IRE)**[13] 5412 8-8-2 **54** oh6........................ MHalford(5) 1 20
(NEBerry) *lw: racd stands side: a outpcd* **25/1**

4502 **15** *3 ½* **Avit (IRE)**[43] 4622 4-8-0 **54** oh14........................ KirstyMilczarek(7) 4 7
(PLGilligan) *bmpd s: racd stands side and a outpcd* **28/1**

59.26 secs (0.21) **Going Correction** +0.15s/f (Good)
**WFA** 3 from 4yo+ 1lb **15** Ran SP% **131.8**
Speed ratings: **104,102,102,102,100 99,99,98,95,95 94,92,92,84,78**CSF £135.12 CT £1560.92 TOTE £8.70: £2.70, £6.00, £3.90; EX 206.10 Place 6 £199.32, Place 5 £61.97.
**Owner** Mrs Anna L Sanders **Bred** Mrs Anna L Sanders **Trained** Ogbourne Maisey, Wilts
■ Stewards Enquiry : A Quinn one-day ban: careless riding (Oct 4)

**FOCUS**
A modest sprint handicap but the form, although ordinary, looks reliable. The majority of runners raced middle to far side, but there was no draw bias.



The Form Book, Raceform Ltd, Compton, RG20 6NL

**NOTEBOOK**
**Inch By Inch ◆**, 5lb higher than when winning at Chepstow on her previous start, followed up in good style, picking up smartly when a gap finally appeared. In the form of her life, she would avoid a penalty if turned out before she is reassessed and should complete the hat-trick.
**One Way Ticket** returned to form with a solid effort, but the winner was just too strong in the closing stages.
**Flaran** ran respectably and can win a similar race whilst in this sort of form, although he does look better suited to six furlongs.
**Byo(IRE)** was not quite at his best and may have preferred a faster surface.
**Borzoi Maestro** ran well off a rating 4lb higher than in future and could do even better if turned out off his new mark of 65.
**Madrasee** is much better when racing on the pace, so this was a good effort in the circumstances.
**Double M**, apparently unlucky at Bath on his previous start, was unable to confirm that despite appearing to have conditions to suit. He was slightly hampered, but would not have been much closer.
**King Egbert(FR)** was not quite at his best, but still did enough to suggest he has the ability to win a similar event.
**Maromito(IRE)** was 8lb higher than when winning at Salisbury two starts previously, and when a beaten favourite at Chepstow last time. He did not help his chances with a slow start and was not at his best.
T/Jkpt: Not won. T/Plt: £109.20 to a £1 stake. Pool: £66,364.00. 443.25 winning tickets. T/Qpdt: £14.70 to a £1 stake. Pool: £4,336.70. 217.20 winning tickets. ST

## 5640 LINGFIELD (L-H)
### Wednesday, September 22

**OFFICIAL GOING: Turf course - good to firm; all-weather - standard**

## 5735 ROSE MAIDEN AUCTION STKS (DIV I) 1m (P)
2:10 (2:11) (E3) 2-Y-O £3,454 (£1,063; £531; £265) Stalls High

Form RPR
0 **1** **Raise A Tune (IRE)**[11] 5467 2-8-10 SWKelly 6 74
(JAOsborne) *sn led and set stdy pce: rdn 2f out: kpt on wl fnl f* **33/1**
6442 **2** *nk* **Watchmyeyes (IRE)**[15] 5377 2-8-7 77 J-PGuillambert(3) 8 73+
(NPLittmoden) *t.k.h: hld up bhd ldrs: c wd bnd 2f out: effrt over 1f out: r.o to press wnr last 100yds: too much to do* **11/10[1]**
050 **3** *1 1/2* **Lord Of Dreams (IRE)**[12] 5434 2-8-11 68 KMcEvoy 7 71
(DWPArbuthnot) *trckd wnr: rdn 2f out: hld 1f out: one pce and lost 2nd last 100yds* **4/1[2]**
02 **4** *1/2* **Krasivi's Boy (USA)**[25] 5114 2-8-8 IMongan 11 67
(GLMoore) *trckd ldng pair: effrt 2f out: rdn and one pce fr over 1f out* **4/1[2]**
00 **5** *1 1/4* **Katana**[25] 5114 2-8-2 FNorton 5 58
(IAWood) *cl up: rdn over 2f out: one pce u.p fr over 1f out* **25/1**
**6** *6* **Indian Dove (IRE)** 2-8-5 EAhern 2 48
(GAButler) *racd in rr: pushed along 1/2-way: outpcd 3f out: no ch after* **11/1[3]**
**7** *1 1/4* **Moonstruck** 2-8-9 JTate 9 49
(JMPEustace) *racd in rr: pushed along 1/2-way: outpcd 3f out: no ch after* **20/1**
00 **8** *1 1/4* **Legend Of Dance**[15] 5368 2-8-0 JFMcDonald(3) 3 40
(BJMeehan) *a wl in rr: rdn and struggling over 3f out* **33/1**
6 **9** *3/4* **African Emperor (FR)**[84] 3424 2-8-8 NCallan 4 44
(WJarvis) *chsd ldrs: rdn 3f out: wknd over 2f out* **33/1**
06 **10** *shd* **Fly Me To Dunoon (IRE)**[24] 5154 2-8-3 (v) RMullen 1 39
(KRBurke) *racd midfield: rdn and outpcd 3f out: sn wknd* **50/1**
0000 **11** *9* **Secret Diva (IRE)**[21] 5218 2-8-1 40 DKinsella 10 17
(MrsPNDutfield) *racd wd: lost pl after 2f: detached in last over 3f out: t.o* **66/1**

1m 40.77s (1.22) **Going Correction** -0.05s/f (Stan) 11 Ran SP% **116.8**
Speed ratings: **91,90,89,88,87 81,80,78,78,78 69**CSF £67.22 TOTE £54.70: £11.50, £1.02, £2.30; EX 90.80.
**Owner** H Rosenblatt and D Margolis **Bred** Denis Bergin **Trained** Upper Lambourn, Berks

**FOCUS**
A race run at a crawl early resulting in a modest time for the grade, 1.19 seconds slower than the second division. Just fair form and, because of the way the race was run, the form is somewhat dubious.

**NOTEBOOK**
**Raise A Tune(IRE)**, beaten a long way on his debut at Goodwood earlier this month, was sent into the lead after a furlong or so and, once there, set only a moderate pace. Gradually winding things up rounding the home bend, he established an advantage that his nearest pursuers were just unable to bridge. This was an unsatisfactory contest and he will be fortunate to find his future rivals always so accommodating.
**Watchmyeyes(IRE)**, trying a mile for the first time, became slightly outpaced when the winner quickened things up from the home bend and, though he tried his best, just had too much leeway to make up. A stronger pace would have suited him.
**Lord Of Dreams(IRE)** was always close to the pace, but was another who would almost certainly have preferred a stronger gallop as he lacked toe where it mattered. This was still a fair effort using the official rating of the runner-up as a guide, and he could be interesting in a mile nursery off this mark.
**Krasivi's Boy(USA)** was not suited by the modest pace, but still looks as though he is a bit better on turf and may be worth noting for a nursery on that surface with cut in the ground.
**Katana**, never far away, was caught short of pace when the tempo quickened, which was not surprising for a filly with a middle-distance pedigree. She still finished clear of the others and is not without hope.
**Secret Diva(IRE)** *Official explanation: jockey said filly was hanging right throughout*

## 5736 AIR HARRODS H'CAP 5f
2:45 (2:45) (F4) (0-55,56) 3-Y-0+ £3,000 (£857; £428) Stalls High

Form RPR
0106 **1** **Bettys Pride**[7] 5562 5-8-11 52 SWKelly 19 62
(MDods) *dwlt: sn prom nr side: rdn to ld ins fnl f: edgd lft: kpt on* **13/2[2]**
0605 **2** *1* **Pulse**[9] 5512 6-9-0 55 (p) PFitzsimons 20 61
(JMBradley) *racd against nr side rail: hld up bhd ldrs: shkn up and nt qckn over 1f out: styd on to take 2nd nr fin* **7/1[3]**
5203 **3** *hd* **Valiant Romeo**[24] 5157 4-8-13 54 (p) RFfrench 18 59
(RBastiman) *taken down early: mde most nr side to ins fnl f: one pce* **5/1[1]**
0500 **4** *shd* **Certa Cito**[81] 3524 4-8-12 53 (b[1]) FNorton 14 58
(DFlood) *racd midfield: prog 1/2-way: rdn to chal over 1f out: upsides ins fnl f: one pce after* **12/1**
1100 **5** *1/2* **Yorkies Boy**[6] 5597 9-8-10 56 ow3 (p) MSavage(5) 8 59+
(NEBerry) *racd midfield and towards centre: nt clr run 2f out and swtchd rt: styd on fnl f: nvr able to chal* **25/1**
2550 **6** *nk* **Enjoy The Buzz**[6] 5597 5-8-10 51 CCatlin 15 53
(JMBradley) *racd nr side: sn wl bhd: rdn and styd on fnl 2f: nrst fin* **9/1**
0600 **7** *1* **Millfields Dreams**[13] 5408 5-8-9 53 ow1 DNolan(3) 9 51
(RBrotherton) *pressed ldrs: rdn 2f out: fdd ins fnl f* **33/1**
4050 **8** *hd* **Elliot's Choice (IRE)**[15] 5370 3-8-8 53 LPKeniry(3) 11 50
(RMStronge) *chsd ldrs: rdn 2f out: no imp fr over 1f out* **33/1**
0200 **9** *3/4* **He's A Rocket (IRE)**[7] 5562 3-8-10 55 (b) HayleyTurner(3) 12 49
(KRBurke) *racd midfield: rdn over 2f out: no prog over 1f out* **20/1**
5005 **10** *nk* **Coranglais**[13] 5412 4-8-11 55 (b) RMiles(3) 4 48
(JMBradley) *racd centre: sn wl bhd: styd on u.p fnl f: nrst fin* **14/1**
0002 **11** *nk* **Flying Tackle**[11] 5452 6-8-8 54 ow1 (p) DTudhope(5) 6 45+
(MDods) *s.s: hld up wl in rr: nt clr run 2f out: styng on whn squeezed out jst ins fnl f: nt rcvr* **12/1**
0 **12** *3/4* **Chantelle (IRE)**[20] 5253 4-8-12 53 (b) TPQueally 16 41
(SKirk) *dwlt: sn rdn to stay in tch: no real prog fnl 2f* **8/1**
0031 **13** *3/4* **Fox Covert (IRE)**[8] 5547 3-8-13 55 6ex (v) LEnstone 5 40
(DWBarker) *racd centre: w ldrs over 3f: wknd* **10/1**
0040 **14** *nk* **Formalise**[9] 5512 4-8-13 54 (p) SDrowne 7 38
(GBBalding) *reluctant to go to post: racd centre: w ldrs over 3f: wknd* **20/1**
0000 **15** *hd* **Turkish Delight**[8] 5547 3-8-13 55 ACulhane 13 38
(JBalding) *nvr beyond midfield: rdn and struggling 2f out* **25/1**
0000 **16** *hd* **Smokin Joe**[21] 5219 3-8-11 53 (b[1]) GBaker 2 36
(JRBest) *dwlt: racd centre: sn wl bhd: no prog* **25/1**
5031 **17** *1* **Rehia**[51] 4393 3-8-4 53 DerekNolan(7) 17 32
(JWHills) *pressed ldrs to 1/2-way: sn wknd u.p* **20/1**
4-02 **18** *nk* **Song Koi**[16] 5342 3-8-13 55 MFenton 10 32
(JGGiven) *racd centre: w ldrs 3f: wknd* **20/1**
5-00 **19** *3 1/2* **The Baroness (IRE)**[34] 4881 4-8-7 51 DCorby(3) 3 14
(EROertel) *racd centre: nvr on terms: wl bhd over 1f out* **33/1**

58.12 secs (-0.75) **Going Correction** -0.075s/f (Good)
**WFA** 3 from 4yo+ 1lb 19 Ran SP% **134.2**
Speed ratings: **103,101,101,100,100 99,98,97,96,96 95,94,93,92,92 92,90,89,84**CSF £47.87 CT £209.60 TOTE £11.80: £2.10, £1.90, £2.40, £4.30; EX 46.00.
**Owner** Betty's Brigade **Bred** Raffin Stud And Raimon Bloodstock **Trained** Piercebridge, Co Durham

**FOCUS**
Low-grade stuff where the draw appeared to play its part in the result, despite which the form appears solid for the level.

**NOTEBOOK**
**Bettys Pride**, enjoying a slight drop in grade, regained the winning thread with the aid of what seemed a distinct draw advantage. Settled just behind the pace, she made her move a furlong out and had enough to repel all raiders. She remains well handicapped on her old form.
**Pulse** enjoyed a good passage on the favoured side of the draw, and had every chance. He is more than capable of winning off this mark, but finds it difficult to get his head in front.
**Valiant Romeo** shows a lot of pace, and made the most of his favoured draw. He was another in the race who appreciated a slight drop in grade and should have no problem winning a sprint somewhere under similar conditions. He still remains a maiden however, but the application of cheekpieces seems to have improved him.
**Certa Cito**, on her first run for the stable, was settled in midfield and came under pressure about a furlong out. She has form at six furlongs and stayed on well to suggest a return to that trip will see her competitive next time.
**Yorkies Boy**, carrying 3lb overweight, had not shown much in two recent runs since his winning spell but ran better this time. This trip is short of his recent best, so a return to six furlongs may see him a bit more competitive next time, although he is still higher in the handicap than for those two recent wins.
**Enjoy The Buzz** got behind early but finished well to suggest a step back up to six furlongs will see him go close. He is still slightly high in the weights, however.
**Coranglais** was well behind from a poor draw at halfway, but finished fairly well through beaten horses in the last furlong. From this evidence he could do with a stiffer course at this distance, even given his moderate draw.
**Flying Tackle** was held up towards the rear, and got squeezed out a couple of times when making a challenge. It is difficult to know how unlucky he was, but he probably would not have troubled the winner even with a clear run. That said, he is still in good heart judging on this effort.
**Chantelle(IRE)** was well backed before the race, but showed very little during it. This was only her second run in England since moving from Ireland, and she is close to her only winning mark.
**Fox Covert(IRE)** showed good early pace, but on the day had no chance from the draw.
**Formalise** had a few ideas of his own going to post, but showed decent pace through the early stages from a disadvantageous draw only to fade away like most who were drawn that side.

## 5737 DAHLIA H'CAP 6f
3:20 (3:25) (E3) (0-70,70) 3-Y-0 £3,675 (£1,130; £565; £282) Stalls High

Form RPR
5041 **1** **Glencalvie (IRE)**[37] 4817 3-9-5 68 (v) EAhern 5 75+
(JNoseda) *hld up in rr and racd on outer: pushed along 1/2-way: prog u.p over 1f out: styd on to ld nr fin* **5/1[1]**
6310 **2** *hd* **Fission**[202] 965 3-9-7 70 FNorton 13 76
(MrsStefLiddiard) *taken down early: reluctant to enter stalls: prom gng easily: led 2f out: hdd jst over 1f out: kpt on again nr fin* **33/1**
0360 **3** *hd* **Piccleyes**[37] 4811 3-8-11 60 (b) RHughes 3 65
(RHannon) *settled midfield: prog fr 2f out: drvn to ld jst over 1f out: hdd nr fin* **20/1**
0613 **4** *shd* **Landucci**[14] 5399 3-9-2 65 (t) SDrowne 6 70
(JWHills) *hld up rr: rdn and prog 2f out: styd on ins fnl f: jst hld* **13/2[3]**
3001 **5** *hd* **Torquemada (IRE)**[15] 5370 3-8-11 60 KMcEvoy 8 65+
(WJarvis) *hld up in last pair: effrt but nt clr run thrght fnl 2f: r.o wl nr fin: unlucky* **9/1**
2260 **6** *shd* **Cyfrwys (IRE)**[40] 4717 3-8-11 60 (t) DKinsella 17 64+
(BPalling) *t.k.h: trckd ldrs: nt clr run wl over 1f out and swtchd lft: rdn to chal fnl f: no ex nr fin* **16/1**
5-06 **7** *1* **Russian Symphony (USA)**[8] 5541 3-9-6 69 (b) TEDurcan 14 70
(CREgerton) *racd towards rr: lost pl and in last trio over 2f out: swtchd lft and effrt over 1f out: kpt on: nvr able to chal* **20/1**
3504 **8** *1* **Whistful (IRE)**[40] 4707 3-9-2 65 RMullen 10 63
(CFWall) *dwlt: sn in midfield: rdn 2f out: one pce and no imp* **10/1**
0301 **9** *nk* **Moon Legend (USA)**[53] 4351 3-9-0 66 HayleyTurner(3) 4 63
(WJarvis) *dwlt: racd in last pair and nt gng wl: swtchd to outer and effrt 2f out: kpt on: n.d* **25/1**
0150 **10** *shd* **Simpsons Mount (IRE)**[11] 5473 3-9-3 66 SWKelly 12 63
(RMFlower) *mounted on crse: s.i.s: racd midfield: rdn 2f out: one pce after* **20/1**
5260 **11** *1/2* **Darla (IRE)**[5] 5618 3-9-6 69 TPQueally 9 65
(JWPayne) *pressed ldrs: rdn over 1f out: wknd fnl f* **14/1**
0420 **12** *hd* **Ace Club**[21] 5219 3-9-1 64 ACulhane 20 59+
(WJHaggas) *hld up bhd ldrs: lost pl over 2f out: nt clr run after and no prog* **8/1**
1301 **13** *3/4* **Danifah (IRE)**[2] 5693 3-9-3 69 6ex FPFerris(3) 19 62
(PDEvans) *mde most to 2f out: wknd fnl f* **6/1[2]**
0050 **14** *nk* **Iltravitore (IRE)**[20] 5253 3-8-8 60 LPKeniry(3) 18 52+
(DRCElsworth) *dwlt: hld up wl in rr: nt clr run 2f out: no ch after* **33/1**

0030 **15** *shd* **Innstyle**[9] 5512 3-9-1 **64** ADaly 2 55
(JLSpearing) *hld up towards rr gng easily: rdn and fnd nil over 1f out: wknd* **20/1**
3021 **16** *½* **Growler**[24] 5147 3-9-7 **70** (v) IMongan 15 60+
(JLDunlop) *hld up towards rr: nt clr run fr 2f out: no ch* **7/1**
0300 **17** *5* **Bella Tutrice (IRE)**[39] 4740 3-9-4 **67** NCallan 16 42
(IAWood) *pressed ldr to 2f out: wknd rapidly* **33/1**

1m 12.06s (0.41) **Going Correction** -0.075s/f (Good) **17** Ran SP% **131.3**
Speed ratings: **94,93,93,93,93 92,91,90,89,89 89,88,87,87,87 86,79**CSF £188.89 CT £3173.51 TOTE £3.90: £2.50, £8.80, £5.40, £2.30; EX 250.10.
**Owner** Mrs Susan Roy **Bred** Top Of The Form Syndicate **Trained** Newmarket, Suffolk

**FOCUS**
A moderate sprint with a blanket finish but the form, rated through the placed horses, appears sound.

**NOTEBOOK**
**Glencalvie(IRE)**, 9lb higher than his last win and dropping back a furlong, would have been huge odds to take this race early on. He was held up in rear and looked to be struggling until finding his feet at halfway and finishing really well. Whilst this was not the greatest event, he is still open to improvement and should not be hit hard again by the Handicapper given the margin and manner of victory.
**Fission**, having her first run for Stef Liddiard, was really reluctant to enter the stalls but fairly flew out of them when they opened. She travelled best of all to two furlongs out, where she was headed, but picked up again inside the final furlong. This was her first run for 202 days and she is entitled to come on from it. Given that she stays seven furlongs well, she will be interesting next time as long as she does not 'bounce'.
**Piccleyes** raced in the pack and came to have every chance in the final furlong. He could not quite sustain his run to the line, weakening close home, and this represents a far better effort than he has been producing recently.
**Landucci** settled in midfield and came with his run a furlong out. He held every chance and looks to still be in good heart, and a step back up in trip could help him off his current mark.
**Torquemada(IRE)** was one of a few unlucky horses in the race, but at least he got a run. Held up at the back of the field, he met all kinds of trouble as horses started to make challenges, and had to switch a number of times. Given a clearer run he would probably have won, and can be counted an unlucky loser. He stays seven furlongs well so the drop back in trip probably made things difficult for him, and a return to seven or a stiff six looks the next port of call. *Official explanation: jockey said colt was denied a clear run in closing stages*
**Cyfrwys(IRE)** travelled well in the pack and came to have every chance inside the last furlong. She has been hinting at ability and should not be far off breaking her maiden tag on this effort. *Official explanation: trainer said filly was struck into behind*
**Russian Symphony(USA)** finished fairly well up the centre of the track having had a decent draw. He has shown ability at seven furlongs so this drop in trip probably did not help.
**Simpsons Mount(IRE)** *Official explanation: jockey said gelding was denied a clear run*
**Ace Club** was another not to have the best of runs. Having grabbed the favoured rails side, he travelled well in just behind the pace. When the race began in earnest he could never find a way through and was not given a hard time when his chance was gone.
**Danifah(IRE)** showed a lot of early pace, from a good draw, but faded badly two furlongs out.
**Growler** was well drawn and held up behind a wall of horses. As the complexion of the race changed he had absolutely nowhere to go, and this run can safely be forgotten. Until his chance went, he looked to travelling kindly and remains in good heart. *Official explanation: jockey said gelding hung right throughout*

## 5738 POLYANTHUS NURSERY 7f
**3:55** (4:01) (E4) (0-75,75) 2-Y-O **£3,367** (£962; £481) **Stalls** High

Form RPR
0541 **1** **Rebel Rebel (IRE)**[6] 5596 2-9-6 **74** 6ex OUrbina 7 83+
(NACallaghan) *prom gng easily: led 2f out: shkn up and clr 1f out: comf* **4/5**[1]
3336 **2** *2* **Tumbleweed Galore (IRE)**[26] 5090 2-9-2 **73** JFMcDonald(3) 1 74
(BJMeehan) *pushed along in rr early: prog on outer fr 1/2-way: drvn to chse wnr 1f out: kpt on* **16/1**
2500 **3** *1* **Tybalt**[20] 5240 2-8-8 **62** (v[1]) IMongan 4 60
(PWHarris) *bmpd s: racd midfield: rdn and effrt over 2f out: styd on fr over 1f out: nvr able to chal* **40/1**
0030 **4** *¾* **Resistance Heroine**[23] 5172 2-9-5 **73** SDrowne 17 71+
(EALDunlop) *hld up midfield gng wl: shkn up wl over 1f out: styd on same pce fnl f* **16/1**
0044 **5** *shd* **Royal Pardon**[20] 5234 2-8-3 **57** JMackay 20 53
(MLWBell) *racd against nr side rail: chsd ldrs: rdn over 2f out: kpt on one pce* **10/1**[3]
0406 **6** *shd* **He's A Star**[52] 4365 2-8-7 **61** RSmith 3 57
(RHannon) *bmpd s: wl in rr: rdn and prog on outer fr over 2f out: nrst fin* **33/1**
0560 **7** *1* **Three Aces (IRE)**[15] 5377 2-8-0 **59** ow1 (b) NChalmers(5) 12 52
(RMBeckett) *dwlt: hld up in last trio: shkn up over 2f out: r.o against nr side rail fnl f: nvr nrr* **66/1**
3605 **8** *¾* **Society Music (IRE)**[17] 5314 2-9-6 **74** (b[1]) SWKelly 5 65
(MDods) *bmpd s: sn led: mde most to 2f out: wknd fnl f* **16/1**
360 **9** *nk* **Coconut Squeak**[26] 5098 2-8-9 **63** MFenton 18 54
(JGGiven) *w ldr to 2f out: wknd fnl f* **25/1**
0330 **10** *nk* **Ivana Illyich (IRE)**[15] 5377 2-9-4 **72** CCatlin 16 69+
(SKirk) *racd midfield: rdn 3f out: nt clr run 2f out: one pce and n.d after* **7/1**[2]
5436 **11** *½* **Transvestite (IRE)**[11] 5453 2-9-4 **72** (v[1]) EAhern 6 66+
(JWHills) *chsd ldrs: drvn 3f out: stl cl up over 1f out: wknd fnl f* **20/1**
5040 **12** *shd* **Mabella (IRE)**[23] 5202 2-8-9 **63** TPQueally 10 54+
(BRMillman) *hld up midfield: reminders over 2f out: no prog tl eased to outer and styd on ins fnl f* **40/1**
0006 **13** *nk* **Wembury Point (IRE)**[11] 5447 2-8-8 **62** SWhitworth 19 50
(BGPowell) *w ldrs over 4f: wknd* **40/1**
0500 **14** *2½* **Lady Luisa (IRE)**[19] 5256 2-8-6 **60** RMullen 14 41
(JSMoore) *a wl in rr: rdn and no prog over 2f out* **50/1**
6606 **15** *hd* **Merrymadcap (IRE)**[8] 5535 2-8-9 **63** FNorton 15 44
(MBlanshard) *nvr beyond midfield: rdn and struggling wl over 2f out* **16/1**
0046 **16** *nk* **Grand Option**[4] 5655 2-9-1 **69** (b) ADaly 2 49
(BWDuke) *racd alone in centre: on terms w ldrs over 4f: wknd* **33/1**
6056 **17** *nk* **Atsos (IRE)**[9] 5509 2-9-0 **68** RHughes 13 47
(RHannon) *hld up midfield: lost pl then hmpd over 2f out: no ch after* **20/1**
6300 **18** *¾* **Shujune Al Hawaa (IRE)**[33] 4907 2-8-10 **64** TEDurcan 9 41
(MRChannon) *settled in rr: rdn 3f out: no prog* **50/1**
630 **19** *9* **Chicken Soup**[23] 5179 2-9-7 **75** KMcEvoy 8 30
(JAOsborne) *chsd ldrs for 5f: wknd and heavily eased over 1f out* **10/1**[3]
4200 **20** *¾* **Miss Cotswold Lady**[16] 5351 2-9-2 **70** NCallan 11 23
(APJarvis) *reluctant to go to post: prom to 1/2-way: sn lost pl and bhd* **25/1**

1m 24.5s (0.29) **Going Correction** -0.075s/f (Good) **20** Ran SP% **145.6**
Speed ratings: **95,92,91,90,90 90,89,88,88,87 87,87,86,83,83 83,83,82,71,71**CSF £17.43 CT £447.66 TOTE £2.00: £1.10, £4.10, £8.40, £6.10; EX 28.80.
**Owner** Six Star Racing **Bred** William P Fogarty **Trained** Newmarket, Suffolk

**FOCUS**
A fair handicap but a race full of trouble, apart from another impressive performance by the winner, who is well treated at present.

**NOTEBOOK**
**Rebel Rebel(IRE)** is improving at a rate of knots, and won this as he liked. Connections are now toying with the idea of running him again on Sunday in a decent nursery at Ascot where, as long as the ground does not get too firm, he is likely to hold a strong chance. He gets seven furlongs well and should stay a mile.
**Tumbleweed Galore(IRE)** was outpaced early on but really found his stride in the closing stages. He has some fairly useful maiden and nursery form to his name, and will be unlucky to keep bumping into such decent two-year-olds. He deserves to pick up a race over seven or even a mile, given the way he finished here.
**Tybalt** was always being niggled in midfield, but stayed on well to the line. He did hang slightly right again in the final furlong but would not have finished any closer with a straight run.
**Resistance Heroine** was slightly unlucky. She travelled well up the rail only to find nowhere to go at the crucial stage of the race. Once she extricated herself she stayed on well to the line, suggesting she is capable of winning off her current mark. *Official explanation: jockey said filly was denied a clear run*
**Royal Pardon** had the perfect pitch up against the rail. Even with her feather weight she was being pushed along from at least three furlongs out, and looks to need atleast seven furlongs if not a mile already in a slightly lower grade.
**He's A Star** got bumped leaving the stalls and seemed to lose interest as he needed plenty of stoking. He gradually made his way back through the field, where he met trouble in running a couple of times, and finished well. Unfortunately he always seems to miss the break and get detached, so a stiffer course is more likely to suit rather than a step up in trip.
**Three Aces(IRE)** missed the break and struggled early. She was another to finish well up the rail. *Official explanation: jockey said filly missed the break*
**Society Music(IRE)**, in first-time blinkers, was at the head of the field until fading inside the last furlong. He is probably a bit high in the handicap at the moment.
**Ivana Illyich(IRE)**, for the second race running, found all sorts of trouble in the last furlong. She is probably more than capable of winning off this mark but needs to find a clear passage to make use of it.
**Transvestite(IRE)** *Official explanation: jockey said colt was denied a clear run*
**Mabella(IRE)** already looks as though she wants at least a mile if not further. She is not devoid of ability, but looks like another step up in trip is needed.
**Atsos(IRE)** was reported as hanging left for all of the race by his jockey. *Official explanation: jockey said gelding hung left throughout*
**Chicken Soup** reportedly stumbled and lost his action when fading badly from halfway. *Official explanation: jockey said colt stumbled and lost action*

## 5739 PANSY CLASSIFIED STKS 1m 2f (P)
**4:30** (4:31) (D2) 3-Y-O+ **£6,987** (£2,150; £1,075; £537) **Stalls** Low

Form RPR
2124 **1** **Compton Drake**[5] 5615 5-9-4 **72** EAhern 13 87
(GAButler) *hld up last: sme prog 3f out: gd hdwy 2f out: led ins fnl f: sn in command* **3/1**[1]
3044 **2** *1¼* **Ma Yahab**[20] 5239 3-8-9 **72** NMackay(3) 4 85
(LMCumani) *hld up midfield: prog gng wl 3f out: rdn to ld briefly ent fnl f: sn outpcd by wnr* **8/1**
4500 **3** *3* **Katiypour (IRE)**[13] 5423 7-9-4 **75** SCarson 5 79
(MissBSanders) *trckd ldrs gng wl: prog to ld over 2f out: hrd rdn and hdd ent fnl f: one pce* **11/1**
3060 **4** *1¾* **Doctored**[37] 4806 3-8-9 **75** (b) FPFerris(3) 9 76
(PDEvans) *settled wl in rr: rdn and outpcd over 3f out: effrt and kpt on fr over 1f out: n.d* **33/1**
3106 **5** *1* **Secret Flame**[12] 5446 3-8-9 **74** ACulhane 10 71
(WJHaggas) *settled towards rr: prog 3f out: hrd rdn and hanging lft over 1f out: fdd ins fnl f* **7/1**[3]
1310 **6** *hd* **Kryssa**[7] 5566 3-8-9 **75** IMongan 2 71
(GLMoore) *settled in rr: n.m.r on inner over 2f out: drvn and hanging lft over 1f out: one pce* **8/1**
0045 **7** *2½* **Love Triangle (IRE)**[42] 4648 3-8-12 **74** RHughes 8 69
(DRCElsworth) *trckd ldr to 6f out: styd prom: wknd and eased over 1f out* **20/1**
1524 **8** *shd* **Opening Ceremony (USA)**[5] 5607 5-8-12 **75** THamilton(3) 6 66
(RAFahey) *settled in rr: rdn 3f out: sn outpcd: n.d after* **7/1**[3]
1-00 **9** *3½* **Electrique (IRE)**[18] 5297 4-9-4 **72** SWKelly 7 62
(JAOsborne) *cl up: prog to ld 6f out: hdd over 2f out: wknd over 1f out* **33/1**
3026 **10** *nk* **Silvaline**[25] 5122 5-8-13 **72** DTudhope(5) 14 62
(TKeddy) *racd midfield: pushed along over 4f out: lost pl and struggling 3f out* **11/2**[2]
5650 **11** *5* **Convince (USA)**[39] 4749 3-8-12 **74** SDrowne 11 52
(MABuckley) *settled rr: rdn and struggling 3f out: wknd* **50/1**
2000 **12** *2½* **Whitgift Rock**[14] 5403 3-8-12 **73** TPQueally 3 47
(SDow) *led to 6f out: wknd wl over 2f out* **20/1**
5500 **13** *¾* **Internationalguest (IRE)**[24] 5158 5-9-4 **75** (b) NPollard 1 46
(GGMargarson) *prom: pushed along 1/2-way: sn lost pl: no ch over 2f out* **12/1**
3626 **14** *5* **Magic Amigo**[24] 5158 3-8-12 **74** TEDurcan 12 36
(JRJenkins) *trckd ldrs tl wknd wl over 2f out* **33/1**

2m 5.40s (-2.45) **Going Correction** -0.05s/f (Stan)
**WFA** 3 from 4yo+ 6lb **14** Ran SP% **123.9**
Speed ratings: **107,106,103,102,101 101,99,99,96,96 92,90,89,85**CSF £25.64 TOTE £3.50: £1.20, £3.20, £3.50; EX 36.10.
**Owner** Erik Penser **Bred** Meon Valley Stud **Trained** Blewbury, Oxon

**FOCUS**
A decent contest of its type and the pace was sound. The form is fair and solid for the grade.

**NOTEBOOK**
**Compton Drake** ◆ had a very wide draw to overcome, but he is an effective performer from off the pace so that did not matter so much. Last at halfway, he was fortunate that the gaps appeared when he wanted them, but he took full advantage and came with a sustained run down the outside to score. He has now won twice and finished second once from just three starts here and probably has not finished yet.
**Ma Yahab**, a frustrating performer making his debut on the surface, travelled noticeably well and had every chance, but the winner had the impetus down the middle of the track and wore him down. He looks well worth another try on Polytrack.
**Katiypour(IRE)** travelled well before being rushed up to hit the front approaching the final bend and tried to kick away from his rivals, but he did not do a great deal in front and was soon swamped by the front pair. He has the ability to win again on this surface if held onto a little longer.
**Doctored**, who looks to be on a stiff mark and is yet to win on Polytrack, kept staying on and may need further on this surface.
**Secret Flame** looked like getting involved coming to the home bend, but did not find much after turning in and did not improve for the switch to sand.
**Kryssa**, trying this trip for the first time, did not really prove one way or the another that she stayed.
**Electrique(IRE)** *Official explanation: jockey said gelding lost its action*


The Form Book, Raceform Ltd, Compton, RG20 6NL

**Silvaline**, a winner over course and distance in his last outing on sand, never managed to get into the race from his outside draw.

## 5740 MARIGOLD FILLIES' H'CAP 1m (P)
**5:05** (5:07) (E3) (0-70,70) 3-Y-O+ **£3,519** (£1,082; £541; £270) **Stalls** High

Form RPR

2651 **1** **River Of Babylon**[15] 5366 3-9-3 **70** RMullen 7 77
(MLWBell) *t.k.h: hld up midfield: prog to chse ldr wl over 2f out : drvn to ld 1f out: styd on* **6/1**[3]

3260 **2** *1* **Island Rapture**[23] 5185 4-9-6 **69** EAhern 8 74
(JARToller) *s.i.s: hld up rr: nt clr run over 2f out: hrd rdn and prog over 1f out: r.o to take 2nd last strides* **13/2**

0000 **3** *hd* **Kindlelight Debut**[5] 5614 4-9-5 **68** NCallan 11 73
(DKIvory) *hld up rr and racd on outer: rdn and prog to chse ldng pair 2f out: kpt on u.p fnl f* **16/1**

-066 **4** *½* **Morning After**[62] 4067 4-9-5 **68** RHughes 5 71
(JRFanshawe) *prom: led over 3f out: rdn and hdd 1f out: lost 2 pls nr fin* **5/1**[2]

4-10 **5** *nk* **Vonadaisy**[4] 5652 3-9-3 **70** (b[1]) ACulhane 6 73
(WJHaggas) *trckd ldrs: rdn whn n.m.r over 2f out: styd on u.p fnl f: nrst fin* **14/1**

6-25 **6** *shd* **Grand Apollo**[101] 2911 3-9-3 **70** KMcEvoy 9 72
(JHMGosden) *led to over 3f out: outpcd over 2f out: rdn over 1f out: kpt on again fnl f* **7/1**

0060 **7** *½* **Cuddles (FR)**[4] 5658 5-9-5 **68** (v) TPQueally 10 69
(KOCunningham-Brown) *settled in rr: rdn on outer over 2f out: prog u.p over 1f out: nrst fin* **25/1**

0040 **8** *shd* **Starbeck (IRE)**[13] 5416 6-9-3 **66** PMcCabe 2 67
(PHowling) *s.s: in rr: rdn 3f out: styd on u.p fr over 1f out: nrst fin* **9/1**

1406 **9** *3 ½* **And Toto Too**[11] 5454 4-9-4 **70** (b) FPFerris(3) 12 63
(PDEvans) *chsd ldrs: rdn 3f out: struggling and btn 2f out* **7/2**[1]

3020 **10** *5* **Efrhina (IRE)**[24] 5153 4-9-5 **68** (p) SDrowne 1 50
(MrsStefLiddiard) *led to over 3f out: wknd over 2f out* **14/1**

1005 **11** *2* **Lilli Marlane**[47] 4520 4-9-6 **69** WRyan 3 46
(NACallaghan) *mostly last: stl last but looked gng wl enough over 1f out: eased ins fnl f: do bttr* **14/1**

0560 **12** *½* **Blonde En Blonde (IRE)**[46] 4549 4-9-4 **67** (b) IMongan 4 43
(NPLittmoden) *racd midfield: rdn over 3f out: wknd wl over 1f out* **16/1**

1m 39.1s (-0.45) **Going Correction** -0.05s/f (Stan)
**WFA** 3 from 4yo+ 4lb **12** Ran SP% **124.6**
Speed ratings: **100,99,98,98,98 97,97,97,93,88 86,86**CSF £47.32 CT £613.34 TOTE £7.60: £3.00, £2.70, £6.10; EX 89.50.
**Owner** C Wright & The Hon Mrs J M Corbett **Bred** Floors Farming And Christopher J Heath **Trained** Newmarket, Suffolk

**FOCUS**
A modest fillies' handicap run at a steady early pace which only picked up after halfway, giving the form a slightly suspect feel.

**NOTEBOOK**
**River Of Babylon**, raised 6lb for her Catterick maiden victory and making her sand debut, was keen enough early but was always in the ideal place to strike and saw her race out well. Her confidence is high at present.
**Island Rapture** finds this trip inadequate on this surface and the modest early pace was no help either, but to her credit she did her level best to get to the winner and just ran out of ground. She is a winner over ten furlongs here and a return to that trip should see her scoring again.
**Kindlelight Debut ◆**, who showed ability on this surface as a juvenile, has only run once here in the meantime but has now slipped to a decent mark and this effort suggests there is a race to be won with her on Polytrack.
**Morning After** ran her race under a positive ride, but could not contain the winner and was run out of the places in the dying strides. She is still to fully convince over this trip.
**Vonadaisy**, blinkered for the first time, ran into a bit of traffic on the home bend before staying on in the home straight. She may be able to find a modest event on this surface.
**Grand Apollo** set a modest gallop until past halfway and as things turned out she may have been better setting a stronger pace. She is less exposed than her rivals and is worth another chance.
**Cuddles(FR)** appeared to finish in eye-catching style down the outside, but her overall record suggests caution.
**And Toto Too** had every chance and there seemed no obvious excuse. *Official explanation: vet said filly was coughing post-race*
**Lilli Marlane ◆**, making her sand debut, was given a very negative ride and was never put under any real pressure at any stage. Her rider gave up plenty soon enough and, whilst she is not very consistent, she is certainly a lot better than this. *Official explanation: jockey said filly was denied a clear run at any stage*

## 5741 ROSE MAIDEN AUCTION STKS (DIV II) 1m (P)
**5:35** (5:36) (E3) 2-Y-O **£3,454** (£1,063; £531; £265) **Stalls** High

Form RPR

04 **1** **Raffish**[23] 5200 2-8-7 JTate 4 71
(JMPEustace) *mostly chsd clr ldr: rdn 3f out: clsd to ld wl over 1f out: hrd pressed fnl f: jst hld on* **9/2**[3]

4620 **2** *shd* **Ragged Glory (IRE)**[33] 4913 2-8-10 76 (v[1]) RHughes 10 74
(RHannon) *racd midfield: rdn to chse clr ldng trio over 2f out: styd on over 1f out: hung lft but clsd nr fin: jst failed* **6/1**

564 **3** *½* **Pollito (IRE)**[23] 5179 2-8-7 77 JFMcDonald(3) 7 73
(BJMeehan) *trckd ldrs: effrt over 2f out: hung lft u.p over 1f out: kpt on nr fin* **7/4**[1]

00 **4** *½* **Amigra (IRE)**[18] 5281 2-7-8 (b[1]) JDoyle(7) 8 63
(MissJacquelineSDoyle) *racd freely: led and sn clr: hdd wl over 1f out: battled on wl and w wnr fnl f: no ex nr fin* **50/1**

**5** *2* **Kangrina** 2-8-5 JMackay 5 62+
(SirMarkPrescott) *in tch: pushed along 4f out: outpcd over 3f out: styd on fr over 1f out: nrst fin* **7/2**[2]

00 **6** *2* **Prince Vettori**[19] 5256 2-8-9 EAhern 1 62
(DJCoakley) *settled in rr: outpcd 3f out: no ch after: modest late prog* **33/1**

**7** *¾* **Soft Focus (IRE)** 2-8-2 CCatlin 11 53
(JAOsborne) *racd midfield: rdn and effrt 3f out: no prog and btn 2f out* **14/1**

000 **8** *¾* **Monad (IRE)**[8] 5535 2-7-9 AmyBaker(7) 3 52
(MrsPNDutfield) *prom tl wknd over 2f out* **33/1**

06 **9** *½* **Yardstick**[13] 5407 2-8-8 SWhitworth 9 57
(SKirk) *racd midfield: rdn over 4f out: one pce over 2f out: wknd fnl f* **14/1**

**10** *7* **Royal Game** 2-8-9 TPQueally 6 42
(DRLoder) *dwlt: a in rr: bhd fnl 3f* **6/1**

0 **11** *dist* **Autumn Daze**[44] 4599 2-7-12 FPFerris(3) 2 —
(MJRyan) *dwlt: plld hrd and chsd ldrs to 1/2-way: sn wknd: t.o* **50/1**

1m 39.58s (0.03) **Going Correction** -0.05s/f (Stan) **11** Ran SP% **123.3**
Speed ratings: **97,96,96,95,93 91,91,90,89,82** —CSF £32.66 TOTE £5.60: £2.70, £2.90, £1.10; EX 36.10 Place 6 £84.88, Place 5 £60.03.
**Owner** Blue Peter Racing 5 **Bred** P And Mrs Venner **Trained** Newmarket, Suffolk

**FOCUS**
A decent pace thanks to Amigra and a fair time for the grade, 1.19 seconds faster than the first division.

**NOTEBOOK**
**Raffish** appreciated the step up to a mile in a strongly run race, but was off the bridle some way out and had to work very hard to get on top of the clear leader. He managed to do so well inside the last furlong, but then only managed to hang on by the skin of his teeth. He may be capable of a bit more improvement.
**Ragged Glory(IRE)**, visored for the first time on this switch to sand, appreciated the return to a faster surface. Making ground steadily from the home bend, he put in a determined finish but it was half a stride too late. He might be interesting in a nursery over this trip on a sound surface.
**Pollito(IRE)** had every chance on this switch to sand, but was inclined to hang in behind the eventual winner and could not quite land a telling blow. He is another who may be suited by a switch to nursery company.
**Amigra(IRE)**, well beaten in two previous outings on turf, ran a phenomenal race on this step up in trip. Setting off at a rate of knots and quickly establishing a clear lead, she looked sure to finished out with the washing when the pack caught up with her starting the home turn, but she then found more and was not shaken off until well inside the last furlong. She obviously possesses ability and it will be interesting to see what nursery mark she gets.
**Kangrina ◆**, first foal of a dual-winner in Germany, is bred to get further and the way she stayed on offered plenty of promise for the future.
T/Plt: £36.80 to a £1 stake. Pool: £32,467.55. 642.35 winning tickets. T/Qpdt: £15.90 to a £1 stake. Pool: £2,046.10. 94.80 winning tickets. JN

5742 - 5744a (Foreign Racing) - See Raceform Interactive

# 5034 BRIGHTON (L-H)
### Thursday, September 23

**OFFICIAL GOING: Firm (good to firm in places)**
Race times suggested that the ground was not as fast as the official description and they appeared to be kicking the top off.
Wind: Fresh across Weather: Cloudy becoming sunny

## 5745 DJMT MAGNOTHERAPY HORSE RUG NURSERY 5f 213y
**2:10** (2:10) (D3) (0-85,84) 2-Y-O **£4,173** (£1,284; £642; £321) **Stalls** Low

Form RPR

3103 **1** **Moth Ball**[10] 5515 2-9-7 **84** DHolland 6 91
(JAOsborne) *trckd ldr: led jst over 1f out: hrd rdn: r.o* **4/5**[1]

0662 **2** *1 ½* **Elisha (IRE)**[14] 5421 2-8-5 **68** CCatlin 2 70
(DMSimcock) *led: hrd rdn and hdd jst over 1f out: kpt on same pce ins fnl f* **4/1**[2]

4200 **3** *1* **Safendonseabiscuit**[24] 5202 2-8-7 **70** JFEgan 1 69
(SKirk) *chsd ldng pair: hrd rdn and hld whn hung lft fnl 2f: styd on nr fin* **16/1**

1220 **4** *6* **Ronnies Lad**[66] 3987 2-8-0 **63** FNorton 7 43
(AndrewReid) *bhd and rdn along: styd on fnl 2f: nt trble ldrs* **33/1**

0210 **5** *¾* **Corniche Dancer**[5] 5648 2-8-10 **73** TEDurcan 8 50
(MRChannon) *in tch: hrd rdn and outpcd 2f out: btn whn hung lft over 1f out* **12/1**[3]

0000 **6** *1* **Gurrun**[32] 4966 2-8-4 **67** RLMoore 3 41
(NACallaghan) *bhd and rdn along: mod hdwy over 1f out: nvr nr to chal* **20/1**

5242 **7** *1 ½* **Mulberry Lad (IRE)**[51] 4413 2-8-5 **68** (bt) MartinDwyer 9 37
(WRMuir) *hdwy and prom after 1f: hrd rdn over 2f out: sn wknd* **12/1**[3]

0500 **8** *1* **Asteem**[14] 5406 2-7-6 **62** oh6 ow1 CHaddon(7) 5 28
(RFJohnsonHoughton) *outpcd: a wl bhd* **40/1**

3000 **9** *3* **Gortumblo**[12] 5453 2-9-3 **80** (b[1]) TQuinn 4 37
(DJSFfrenchDavis) *in tch to 1/2-way* **12/1**[3]

1m 10.3s (0.20) **Going Correction** +0.175s/f (Good) **9** Ran SP% **114.7**
Speed ratings: **105,103,101,93,92 91,89,88,84**CSF £3.85 CT £27.15 TOTE £1.70: £1.10, £2.10, £2.20; EX 6.10.
**Owner** Mountgrange Stud **Bred** Stratford Place Stud **Trained** Upper Lambourn, Berks

**FOCUS**
A decent all-round pace resulting in a very smart winning time for the class. The principals were at the forefront throughout and very few got into the race. The front three finished a long way clear of the others, making this strong form for the track and the grade and therefore the form looks solid.

**NOTEBOOK**
**Moth Ball** appreciated the return to six and, even though he had to fight hard to get the better of the runner-up, the winning time and the margin between the front three and the others suggests he ran right up to form.
**Elisha(IRE)** pinged the gates and made sure the favourite had to dig deep in order to get the better of her. A return to five could see her winning again.
**Safendonseabiscuit** had excuses for modest efforts in his last two starts and returned to something like his previous form, but not for the first time was inclined to hang under pressure. The ability is there, but he does not look straightforward.
**Ronnies Lad**, runner-up in a couple of claimers here, is finding nursery company much more taxing.
**Corniche Dancer** seems to have gone badly the wrong way since her Catterick victory.

## 5746 BOC SUREFLOW (S) STKS 5f 59y
**2:40** (2:40) (G4) 2-Y-O **£2,583** (£738; £369) **Stalls** Low

Form RPR

0000 **1** **Wiltshire (IRE)**[8] 5567 2-8-4 LHarman(7) 1 54
(MRChannon) *disp 2nd pl: drvn along 1/2-way: slt ld over 1f out: hld on wl* **16/1**

1466 **2** *hd* **Von Wessex**[26] 5132 2-8-11 58 (p) AQuinn(5) 2 58
(WGMTurner) *led: hung rt 2f out: narrowly hdd over 1f out: str chal fnl f: jst hld* **12/1**

0066 **3** *2* **Queen's Glory (IRE)**[42] 4671 2-8-6 57 MartinDwyer 6 41
(WRMuir) *s.s: bhd tl hdwy 2f out: chal over 1f out: one pce ins fnl f* **7/2**[3]

006 **4** *2 ½* **Baileys Applause**[40] 4752 2-8-6 63 (b) FNorton 5 33
(CADwyer) *disp 2nd pl: sltly hmpd and swtchd lft 2f out: hung lft and chal over 1f out: no ex* **7/4**[1]

**5** *1 ¾* **Eidsfoss (IRE)** 2-8-11 DHolland 4 31
(NACallaghan) *s.i.s: rn green towards rr: effrt and sltly hmpd wl over 1f out: nvr nr to chal* **2/1**[2]

06 **6** *2* **Imperatrice**[22] 5218 2-8-6 CCatlin 3 19
(RMHCowell) *s.i.s: mid-div: rdn and no hdwy fnl 2f* **20/1**

00 **7** *2* **Sartaena (IRE)**[42] 4670 2-8-3 (b[1]) FPFerris(3) 9 12
(RMBeckett) *wnt lft s: hdwy to dispute 2nd pl after 1f: sltly hmpd and wknd 2f out* **33/1**

6060 **8** *11* **Jonny Fox'S (IRE)**[31] 5003 2-8-11 48................................(b) TEDurcan 8 —
(JGallagher) *rrd s and missed break: a wl bhd* **40/1**

63.46 secs (1.19) **Going Correction** +0.175s/f (Good) **8** Ran SP% **115.6**
Speed ratings: **97,96,93,89,86 83,80,62**CSF £180.44 TOTE £16.60: £4.60, £3.00, £1.50; EX 112.60.There was no bid for the winner. Eidsfoss was claimed by R. J. Francis for £5,600.
**Owner** M Channon **Bred** John Perotta **Trained** West Ilsley, Berks
■ Leon Harman's first career winner.

**FOCUS**
Another race where not that many got into it. A few of the runners took several positions during the contest, switching out to the centre of the track and then switching back inside, though the winner raced close to the inside rail throughout. The winning time was decent for a two-year-old seller, but the form is rated no more than average for the grade.

**NOTEBOOK**
**Wiltshire(IRE)**, beaten at least 17 lengths in four previous outings, was taking a big drop in both class and trip. He was off the bridle much earlier than most but, sticking to the inside rail, his stamina came into play and he responded well to pressure to narrowly prevail. Six furlongs may turn out to be his best trip and this is his grade.
**Von Wessex** was always up there, but whether by accident or design found himself racing out in the centre of the track. Despite that, he kept on trying right to the line and was only just held off. The return to a faster surface was a help after three defeats on soft ground, but race times suggest it was not as fast as officially described. *Official explanation: jockey said gelding was hanging right*
**Queen's Glory(IRE)**, the subject of significant market support, was the only one to get into the race from off the pace but had nothing more to offer inside the last furlong. She has proved very disappointing after showing early promise.
**Baileys Applause**, taking a big drop in class, was always up with the pace but, after switching positions a couple of times which may not have always been deliberate, she was a spent force passing the furlong pole.
**Eidsfoss(IRE)**, a 34,000euros foal out of a half-sister to a Listed winner in France, was fancied according to the market but he was slow to leave the stalls and could never get into the race. He may not be very good, but he should have learned something from this.
**Jonny Fox'S(IRE)** *Official explanation: jockey said gelding was hanging left*

## 5747 EUROPEAN BREEDERS FUND MAIDEN STKS 6f 209y
**3:10** (3:10) (D3) 2-Y-O **£4,871** (£1,499; £749; £374) **Stalls** Low

Form RPR
000 **1** **Lola Sapola (IRE)**[27] 5089 2-8-9 ................................ RLMoore 1 71
(NACallaghan) *outpcd and bhd: stdy hdwy 2f out: styd on wl to ld nr fin* **25/1**
305 **2** *1* **Gitche Manito (IRE)**[19] 5298 2-9-0 76................................ JDSmith 4 73
(AKing) *w ldrs: led over 5f out and set str pce: hrd rdn 2f out: tired ins fnl f: ct nr fin* **14/1**
63 **3** *2* **Miss Trial**[17] 5353 2-8-9 ................................ PRobinson 7 63
(MAJarvis) *led over 1f: chsd ldng pair: drvn to chal over 1f out: no ex fnl 100 yds* **11/8**[2]
52 **4** *7* **Wingspeed (IRE)**[14] 5420 2-9-0 ................................ DHolland 5 50
(MrsAJPerrett) *pressed ldr: hrd rdn over 2f out: hung bdly lft and wknd wl over 1f out* **1/1**[1]
060 **5** *9* **Pussy Cat**[21] 5248 2-8-9 50................................ CCatlin 3 22
(KOCunningham-Brown) *outpcd: a bhd* **66/1**
**6** *2* **Sergeant Lewis** 2-9-0 ................................ SWKelly 6 21
(JAOsborne) *dwlt: rn green: fair 4th tl wknd over 2f out* **12/1**[3]

1m 24.21s (1.61) **Going Correction** +0.175s/f (Good) **6** Ran SP% **111.8**
Speed ratings: **97,95,93,85,75 73**CSF £285.08 TOTE £18.50: £5.10, £5.60; EX 141.10.
**Owner** Jeremy Gompertz **Bred** Jeremy Gompertz **Trained** Newmarket, Suffolk

**FOCUS**
A strange contest, run at a decent pace and the winner came from last, which suggests the early leaders had gone off too quick; that said , the race looks reasonable on paper.

**NOTEBOOK**
**Lola Sapola(IRE)** had finished well beaten in her three starts to date, though the form of her last two outings has worked out very well. Her chances of winning this looked slim at halfway, but she got stronger as the race progressed whilst the front runners faded and, brought out to the centre of the track, got up well inside the last furlong. The way the race was run does raise questions over the true value of the form, but she is obviously going the right way.
**Gitche Manito(IRE)** did best of those that forced the pace, but had no answer to the winner's finishing thrust. He would probably be better off in nurseries though, as he will always be vulnerable to an improver in races like this.
**Miss Trial** should have appreciated the extra furlong, but was probably done no favours by getting caught up in the early battle for the lead and had little left at the business end.
**Wingspeed(IRE)**, one of three helping force the pace from the start, looked very awkward on the track in the latter part of the contest which was surprising considering he had run so well at Epsom last time. *Official explanation: jockey said colt was hanging left*

## 5748 BETDAQ.COM GLOBAL BETTING EXCHANGE CLASSIFIED STKS 7f 214y
**3:40** (3:40) (F3) 3-Y-O **£3,476** (£1,069; £534; £267) **Stalls** Low

Form RPR
4210 **1** **Otago (IRE)**[11] 5496 3-9-0 58................................ TQuinn 1 71
(JRBest) *sn stdd bk into midfield: rdn and hdwy 2f out: drvn to ld ins fnl f* **4/1**[2]
5555 **2** *nk* **Beautiful Noise**[6] 5621 3-8-11 49................................(b) MTebbutt 4 67
(DMorris) *hld up in tch: drvn to chal over 1f out: kpt on* **10/1**
1000 **3** *2 ½* **Mister Trickster (IRE)**[35] 4871 3-9-0 60................................ LisaJones 8 65
(RDickin) *dwelt: soon chasing ldrs: drvn to ld over 1f out: hdd ins fnl f: no ex* **16/1**
3060 **4** *nk* **Beauty Of Dreams**[10] 5510 3-8-11 57................................ CCatlin 7 61
(MRChannon) *towards rr: styd on u.p fnl 2f: nrst fin* **7/1**[3]
-003 **5** *1* **New York (IRE)**[16] 5366 3-8-11 60................................(t) DHolland 6 59
(WJHaggas) *mde most tl hrd rdn and hdd over 1f out: no ex* **7/1**[3]
0000 **6** *½* **Off Beat (USA)**[14] 5410 3-9-0 60................................ SCarson 10 61
(RFJohnsonHoughton) *dwlt: towards rr: hrd rdn 3f out: nvr rchd ldrs* **16/1**
1000 **7** *1 ½* **Carte Noire**[16] 5370 3-8-8 54................................(p) FPFerris(3) 12 54
(JGPortman) *prom 3f: lost pl and hrd rdn 3f out: kpt on again nr fin* **25/1**
0050 **8** *nk* **Lady Taverner**[14] 5425 3-8-11 54................................ SWhitworth 5 53
(HJCyzer) *dwelt: towards rr: rdn and sme hdwy over 2f out: no further prog* **20/1**
3344 **9** *nk* **Archerfield (IRE)**[20] 5259 3-8-11 58................................(t) RLMoore 9 53
(JWHills) *bhd: swtchd lft and drvn into midfield 2f out: edgd lft: no further prog* **7/2**[1]
5500 **10** *6* **Fisby**[21] 5252 3-9-0 60................................ JFEgan 2 42
(SKirk) *jnd ldrs after 2f: wknd over 1f out: eased whn btn* **12/1**
4001 **11** *nk* **Megabond**[12] 5448 3-8-9 60................................(p) DFox(5) 3 41
(CADwyer) *prom over 5f* **10/1**
0420 **12** *1 ½* **Trifti**[40] 4738 3-9-0 56................................ NCallan 11 38
(CACyzer) *sn chsng ldrs: wknd over 2f out: btn whn hung lft over 1f out* **20/1**

1m 36.07s (1.07) **Going Correction** +0.175s/f (Good) **12** Ran SP% **118.2**
Speed ratings: **101,100,98,97,96 96,94,94,94,88 88,86**CSF £42.33 TOTE £5.20: £1.70, £3.20, £6.00; EX 42.30.
**Owner** Mrs L M Askew **Bred** W J Hamilton **Trained** Hucking, Kent

**FOCUS**
A moderate classified event run at an ordinary pace and again the runners raced middle to far side.

**NOTEBOOK**
**Otago(IRE)** was switched off this time and the tactics proved spot on as he came through under strong pressure to score. His victory backs up the opinion that the ground was not as fast as officially described. *Official explanation: trainer said, regarding the improved form shown, gelding was drawn one of 14 last time and jockey made too much use of his mount*
**Beautiful Noise**, who had finished unplaced in all 11 of her previous outings, for the second race in a row ran much better than her official rating entitled her to. Even with a record like hers she would be interesting in a handicap off her current mark.
**Mister Trickster(IRE)**, who has done nothing since his Chepstow win, ran better this time and looked the likely winner coming to the last furlong, but he then hung left over to the inside rail and had nothing more to offer. He looks better suited by seven.
**Beauty Of Dreams** made up a lot of late ground, but was never going to get there and is probably better suited by a stiffer mile.
**New York(IRE)** made the running and was kept out in the centre of the track, but was beaten passing the furlong pole. She looks very moderate and does not appear to see out this trip.
**Archerfield(IRE)** has been running with credit on undulating tracks, including here, in recent months and this represented a step backwards. *Official explanation: jockey said filly did not act on the firm, good to firm in places ground*
**Fisby** *Official explanation: jockey said gelding moved badly throughout*
**Trifti** *Official explanation: jockey said gelding hung left throughout*

## 5749 BETDAQ.CO.UK MAIDEN STKS 7f 214y
**4:10** (4:11) (D3) 3-Y-O+ **£3,513** (£1,081; £540; £270) **Stalls** Low

Form RPR
5-2 **1** **Southern Bazaar (USA)**[109] 2706 3-8-13 ................................(t) RHughes 6 73+
(BWHills) *prom: led 3f out: shkn up 2f out: pushed out* **5/4**[1]
030 **2** *1* **Olivander**[103] 2887 3-8-13 74................................(bt) NCallan 7 71
(RMBeckett) *plld hrd: w ldrs: led over 4f out tl 3f out: kpt on: a hld* **4/1**[2]
L335 **3** *¾* **Elusive Kitty (USA)**[9] 5537 3-8-9 68 ow1................................(t) DHolland 9 65
(GAButler) *led over 3f: styd on same pce fnl 2f* **9/2**[3]
3600 **4** *1 ¼* **Ground Patrol**[99] 2988 3-8-13 62................................(t) RLMoore 5 66
(GLMoore) *in tch: effrt over 2f out: hrd rdn over 1f out: one pce* **12/1**
0 **5** *6* **Polish Rose**[16] 5378 3-8-8 ................................ MartinDwyer 1 48
(EFVaughan) *in tch: rdn 3f out: btn 2f out* **5/1**
00 **6** *10* **Royal Logic**[97] 3044 3-8-8 ................................ TEDurcan 8 25
(MRChannon) *in tch 5f* **33/1**
05 **7** *13* **Dark Parade (ARG)**[5] 5643 3-8-6 ................................ JJones(7) 3 —
(GLMoore) *wnt lft s: t.k.h early: lost tch 1/2-way* **66/1**
**8** *14* **Little Miss Lili** 3-8-8 ................................ AMcCarthy 2 —
(GGMargarson) *s.s: rdn in rr after 3f: wl bhd fnl 3f* **25/1**

1m 36.79s (1.79) **Going Correction** +0.175s/f (Good) **8** Ran SP% **115.3**
Speed ratings: **98,97,96,95,89 79,66,52**CSF £6.43 TOTE £2.00: £1.40, £1.10, £1.70; EX 9.00.
**Owner** K Abdulla **Bred** Juddmonte Farms Inc **Trained** Lambourn, Berks

**FOCUS**
A weak maiden overall and a moderate early pace resulted in a modest winning time for the grade. The principals were at the front from the start and very few got into it.

**NOTEBOOK**
**Southern Bazaar(USA)**, whose three outings to date have been well spaced out, was always up with the pace and, despite tending to hang away from the inside rail, saw his race out perfectly well. He does not look anything special, but the track was probably not ideal and he should find his niche in handicaps.
**Olivander**, making his debut for the yard and racing for the first time since June, was plenty keen enough early thanks to the moderate pace but kept battling away against a much more progressive rival. He is not straightforward, but has now run well in both of his starts here.
**Elusive Kitty(USA)** was always up there, but lacked a change of gear where it mattered and is now totally exposed.
**Ground Patrol**, another to have changed yards since his last outing in June, tried to get into the race over the last couple of furlongs, but lacked the pace to do so over a trip that looks short of his best. He has already shown ability on Polytrack and looks a likely type for modest ten-furlong handicaps on that surface throughout the winter.
**Polish Rose** did not improve for the extra furlong.

## 5750 BETDAQ.COM H'CAP 1m 1f 209y
**4:40** (4:42) (F4) (0-55,51) 3-Y-O **£2,643** (£755; £377) **Stalls** High

Form RPR
0301 **1** **Daydream Dancer**[38] 4798 3-9-2 **49**................................(b) RSmith 5 57
(CGCox) *in tch: effrt and briefly nt clr run 2f out: r.o to ld ins fnl f: won gng away* **7/2**[2]
5030 **2** *2 ½* **Cobalt Blue (IRE)**[27] 5072 3-9-4 **51**................................(p) JFEgan 8 54
(WJHaggas) *w ldr: led 5f out and drvn 3 l ahd: hdd and no ex ins fnl f* **5/1**[3]
5221 **3** *1 ¼* **Lenwade**[8] 5571 3-8-13 **46** 6ex................................ AMcCarthy 7 47
(GGMargarson) *dwlt: towards rr: rdn 5f out: hdwy over 2f out: drvn to chse ldrs over 1f out: one pce* **15/2**
300 **4** *5* **Hana Dee**[27] 5072 3-9-2 **49**................................ TEDurcan 4 40
(MRChannon) *hld up towards rr: rdn over 3f out: styd on fnl 2f* **14/1**
0606 **5** *2* **Larad (IRE)**[41] 4713 3-8-6 **46**................................(b) LauraReynolds(7) 2 33
(JSMoore) *s.i.s: bhd: stdy hdwy over 1f out: nt rch ldrs* **14/1**
50-0 **6** *6* **Melinda's Girl**[143] 1844 3-9-2 **49**................................ NCallan 1 25
(APJarvis) *t.k.h: led 5f: sn rdn: hung lft and wknd over 1f out* **16/1**
5016 **7** *1 ¼* **Fiddles Music**[19] 5284 3-8-13 **46**................................ CCatlin 10 20
(MissSheenaWest) *t.k.h: prom tl hrd rdn and wknd wl over 1f out* **11/1**
3204 **8** *9* **Mr Belvedere**[33] 4941 3-9-4 **51**................................ JMackay 3 7
(AJLidderdale) *chsd ldrs to 1/2-way* **7/1**
5640 **9** *15* **African Star**[25] 5153 3-9-3 **50**................................(p) RLMoore 6 —
(MrsAJPerrett) *nvr moving fluently: sn chsng ldrs: lost action 3f out: eased* **3/1**[1]
0650 **10** *1 ¼* **Breaking The Rule (IRE)**[36] 4853 3-9-0 **47**................................ DaneO'Neill 9 —
(PRWebber) *n.d: no ch fnl 2f* **40/1**

2m 4.97s (2.43) **Going Correction** +0.175s/f (Good) **10** Ran SP% **118.1**
Speed ratings: **97,95,94,90,88 83,82,75,63,62**CSF £21.80 CT £124.94 TOTE £3.30: £1.60, £2.60, £2.10; EX 25.00.
**Owner** The Grey Lady Partnership **Bred** Haras Du Gazon **Trained** Lambourn, Berks

**FOCUS**
A sound pace, but a moderate contest and they finished well strung out. The first three had finished one-two-three in an identical contest here last month and the only difference this time was that the positions of the second and third were reversed.

**NOTEBOOK**
**Daydream Dancer** confirmed the form with both the second and third off a 2lb higher mark compared with their meeting here last month. That seemed unlikely at one stage though, as she was one of the first off the bridle, but she got stronger as the race progressed and was well on top at the line.

**Cobalt Blue(IRE)** was given a good, if ultimately unsuccessful ride, as he tried to nick the race from the front with a sudden injection of pace half a mile out and had most of his rivals in trouble. The winner gradually wore him down, but nonetheless full marks to his rider for at least attempting a bit of enterprise.
**Lenwade**, whose recent selling victory meant she was meeting Daydream Dancer on 9lb worse terms for a head defeat here last month, was off the bridle some way out but stayed on to finish a respectable third.
**Hana Dee**, trying this trip for the first time, was ridden to get it but never looked like getting to the leaders.
**Larad(IRE)**, who is effective under these conditions, never looked like taking a hand but still gives the impression he is capable of better on his day.
**African Star** seemed to go wrong passing the three-furlong pole and was found to be lame. *Official explanation: vet said colt finished lame*

## 5751 ALEXANDER CATERING AMATEUR RIDERS' MAIDEN H'CAP 1m 3f 196y
**5:10** (5:11) (F4) (0-55,55) 3-Y-0+ **£2,587** (£739; £369) **Stalls** High

Form RPR
4240 **1** **Tom Bell (IRE)**[49] 4473 4-10-8 **49**.................. MrEDehdashti 10 59+
(JGMO'Shea) *a gng wl: trckd ldrs: wnt 2nd 5f out: led 3f out: sn clr: easily* **11/2**[3]
5032 **2** *4* **Islands Farewell**[7] 5585 4-10-5 **49**.................. MissKellyHarrison(3) 8 51
(DNicholls) *hld up in midfield: effrt over 2f out: wnt 2nd over 1f out: no ch w wnr* **3/1**[1]
0004 **3** *6* **Princess Bankes**[19] 5284 3-9-4 **46** oh1.................. MissEJTuck(7) 11 38
(MissGayKelleway) *rrd s: hdwy 1/2-way: chsd wnr over 2f out tl over 1f out: no ex* **25/1**
0000 **4** *5* **Madame Marie (IRE)**[22] 5221 4-10-2 **48**.................. MrDHutchison(5) 3 32
(SDow) *s.s: bhd: sme hdwy 4f out: no imp* **12/1**
536- **5** *4* **Eachy Peachy (IRE)**[399] 4319 5-10-0 **46** oh11.......... MissKManser(5) 7 24
(JRBest) *travelled wl in midfield: effrt and hrd rdn over 2f out: fnd little* **12/1**
-400 **6** *7* **Greek Star**[54] 4346 3-9-4 **46** oh1.................. MissSHarler(7) 6 13
(KAMorgan) *chsd ldrs 8f* **20/1**
2030 **7** *7* **Colonnade**[150] 1668 5-10-2 **46**.................. MrsNWilson(3) 9 2
(NWilson) *bhd most of way: passed btn horses* **16/1**
2366 **8** *shd* **Waltzing Beau**[22] 5221 3-9-11 **46** oh1.................. MrSWalker 5 1
(BGPowell) *chsd ldrs to 1/2-way* **10/3**[2]
0-40 **9** *3/4* **Karakum**[56] 3774 5-9-12 **46** oh6.................. MrGTumelty(7) 12 —
(AJChamberlain) *s.s: sn in midfield: rdn 5f out: n.d fnl 4f* **33/1**
0005 **10** *3/4* **Autumn Flyer (IRE)**[44] 4618 3-10-0 **54**.................. MissNadineForde(5) 1 7
(CGCox) *prom 9f* **15/2**
-005 **11** *4* **Lasser Light (IRE)**[27] 5079 4-11-0 **55**.................. MissEJJones 4 2
(DGBridgwater) *prom to 1/2-way: bhd fnl 4f* **20/1**
0606 **12** *4* **Duke's View (IRE)**[9] 5549 3-10-1 **53**..................(b) MissLJHarwood(3) 2 —
(MrsAJPerrett) *sn rdn up to ld: pushed along 5f out: hdd 3f out: wknd qckly* **14/1**

2m 35.74s (3.64) **Going Correction** +0.175s/f (Good)
**WFA** 3 from 4yo+ 8lb **12** Ran SP% **119.5**
Speed ratings: **94,91,87,84,81 76,72,71,71,70 68,65**CSF £21.29 CT £389.30 TOTE £9.10: £2.10, £1.60, £9.90; EX 30.60 Place 6 £792.41, Place 5 £605.91.
**Owner** K W Bell **Bred** John O'Connor **Trained** Elton, Gloucs

**FOCUS**
A terrible contest run at an even pace and margins that would have been more appropriate for a jumps contest. This is likely to have minimal bearing on future events.

**NOTEBOOK**
**Tom Bell(IRE)** could be called the winner a long way out, and once he cruised to the front the race was over. This trip and good ground look his ideal conditions, but this was such a bad contest that the form probably means little.
**Islands Farewell**, trying this trip for the first time, was ridden to get it and was produced at the right time had he been good enough, but the fact was that the winner was different gear. This effort did not really confirm his stamina.
**Princess Bankes**, another trying this trip for the first time, was close enough to the eventual winner two furlongs from home but did not appear to stay.
**Madame Marie(IRE)** stayed on without ever offering a threat and is beginning to look tripless as well as one-paced.
**Waltzing Beau** had the form to do better than this and was disappointing. *Official explanation: trainer said gelding ran flat*
T/Plt: £741.00 to a £1 stake. Pool: £35,481.35. 34.95 winning tickets. T/Qpdt: £112.10 to a £1 stake. Pool: £2,667.40. 17.60 winning tickets. LM

# 5585 PONTEFRACT (L-H)
## Thursday, September 23

**OFFICIAL GOING: Firm**
The ground was described as 'very firm' despite 1/2" water being put down the previous day. It was showing signs of wear and tear after a busy year.
Wind: Fresh 1/2 behind. Weather: Fine and dry but windy.

## 5752 EUROPEAN BREEDERS FUND POPPIN LANE MAIDEN STKS 6f
**2:30** (2:42) (D2) 2-Y-0 **£5,733** (£1,764; £882; £441) **Stalls** Low

Form RPR
24 **1** **Wise Owl**[26] 5118 2-9-0.................. KDarley 10 82+
(MJohnston) *cl up: led over 2f out: sn pushed clr: easily* **8/15**[1]
**2** *4* **Circumspect (IRE)** 2-9-0.................. GFaulkner 4 70
(PCHaslam) *dwlt: in tch whn j. faller over 3f out: hdwy to chse wnr over 1f out: sn rdn and kpt on: no ch w wnr* **66/1**
00 **3** *3 1/2* **Zonic**[16] 5380 2-8-9.................. KFallon 5 55+
(SirMichaelStoute) *chsd ldrs: rdn along and edgd lft 2f out: styd on ins last* **4/1**[2]
**4** *1 1/4* **Grand Show** 2-9-0.................. IMongan 8 56
(PWHarris) *dwlt: sn trcking ldrs: hdwy over 2f out: sn rdn and wknd over 1f out* **12/1**[3]
3 **5** *3/4* **On Action (USA)**[5] 5633 2-8-11.................. ABeech(3) 2 54
(MrsADuffield) *led: rdn along and hdd over 2f out: sn drvn and wknd wl over 1f out* **20/1**
0 **6** *10* **Knot In Wood (IRE)**[16] 5362 2-9-0.................. PHanagan 6 24
(RAFahey) *trckd ldrs: effrt over 2f out: sn rdn and outpcd* **40/1**
0 **7** *6* **Isle Dream**[21] 5241 2-8-2.................. KPierrepont(7) 7 —
(JBalding) *cl up: rdn along 1/2-way: wknd 2f out* **100/1**
**8** *1 3/4* **Cliffie (IRE)** 2-9-0.................. SRighton 3 —
(JHetherton) *sn outpaced and bhd fr 1/2-way* **66/1**
**B** **Baileys Honour** 2-8-9.................. RFfrench 9 —
(MJohnston) *rdn along in rr whn b.d over 3f out* **22/1**
**F** **Matsunosuke** 2-9-0.................. DeanMcKeown 1 —
(ABCoogan) *dwlt: sn trcking ldrs tl stmbld and fell over 3f out* **66/1**

1m 15.27s (-2.03) **Going Correction** -0.40s/f (Firm) **10** Ran SP% **109.9**
Speed ratings: **97,91,87,85,84 71,63,60,—,—**CSF £64.43 TOTE £1.50: £1.02, £10.40, £1.20; EX 39.30.
**Owner** Sheikh Mohammed **Bred** Darley **Trained** Middleham Moor, N Yorks

**FOCUS**
By no means a great maiden, but there were a few who offered promise behind the fairly decent Wise Owl and this race should produce winners.

**NOTEBOOK**
**Wise Owl** failed to build on an encouraging debut run when only fourth on easy ground at Newmarket on his previous start, but this was much better. He was admittedly faced with his easiest task to date, but he won in good style and, on the upgrade, he is one to have on your side.
**Circumspect(IRE)** ◆, an 11,000gns half-brother to a seven-furlong two-year-old winner, made a very promising debut. One of the last to leave the stalls, he was forced to jump over the fallen horse at halfway and had just one behind when the eventual winner was getting into a challenging position, but he kept on for pressure and was ultimately clear in second. A promising sort, he will have learnt plenty from this and he should soon be winning.
**Zonic**, very disappointing when upped to seven furlongs and switched to Polytrack on her previous start, ran a little better but was simply not good enough to go with the front two, and may do better now she is qualified for a handicap mark.
**Grand Show** ◆ is a half-brother to a dual five-furlong two-year-old winner who later proved useful over a mile, a smart sprinter and a winning miler. He looked likely to pose a threat when making headway inside the final three furlongs, but was simply unable to sustain his effort and probably just needed this. There should be better to come.
**On Action(USA)** failed to build on the promise of his debut effort and may do better when handicapped.

## 5753 RACING UK ON CHANNEL 432 FILLIES' NURSERY 1m 4y
**3:00** (3:31) (D2) (0-85,85) 2-Y-0 **£5,603** (£1,724; £862; £431) **Stalls** Low

Form RPR
310 **1** **Glorious Step (USA)**[33] 4964 2-9-7 **85**.................. JFortune 8 87+
(JHMGosden) *s.i.s and bhd: hdwy wl over 1f out: swtchd rt and rdn ent last: edgd lft and styd on wl to ld last 75 yds* **7/2**[2]
2354 **2** *nk* **Dance Flower (IRE)**[15] 5391 2-8-13 **77**.................. ACulhane 3 78
(MRChannon) *trckd ldrs: hdwy over 2f out: rdn to ld over 1f out: drvn ins last: hdd and no ex last 75 yds* **7/2**[2]
0546 **3** *2* **Patxaran (IRE)**[24] 5188 2-7-11 **66**.................. RoryMoore(5) 10 63
(PCHaslam) *trckd ldrs: hdwy over 2f out: rdn and edgd lft over 1f out and ins last: kpt on* **25/1**
520 **4** *1/2* **Lottie Dundass**[17] 5349 2-8-9 **73**.................. EAhern 13 69
(PWHarris) *in tch: hdwy over 2f out: sn rdn and jockey lost whip over 1f out kpt on ins last* **12/1**[3]
1 **5** *shd* **Ratukidul (FR)**[41] 4705 2-9-2 **80**.................. KFallon 5 80+
(SirMichaelStoute) *in tch: shuffled bk bnd after 2f: pushed along in rr whn nt clr run over 2f out: hdwy over 1f out: hld whn n.m.r ins last* **6/4**[1]
4403 **6** *1* **Blackcomb Mountain (USA)**[10] 5516 2-8-4 **68**.................. ANicholls 2 61
(MFHarris) *led 3f: cl up tl led again 2f out: sn rdn and hdd over 1f out: grad wknd* **28/1**
403 **7** *1 1/4* **Street Ballad (IRE)**[16] 5362 2-8-3 **67**.................. TPQueally 9 58
(MrsJRRamsden) *in tch: rdn along 2f out: sn drvn and one pce* **16/1**
0633 **8** *2* **Fadael (IRE)**[12] 5476 2-8-1 **65**.................. PHanagan 6 51
(PWD'Arcy) *in tch on inner: hdwy to chse ldrs 3f out: rdn over 1f out: hld whn n.m.r and eased ins last* **22/1**
4340 **9** *2 1/2* **Burton Ash**[21] 5240 2-8-8 **72**.................. MFenton 1 53
(JGGiven) *dwlt: sn cl up on inner: led after 3f tl rdn and hdd 2f out: sn wknd* **25/1**
0650 **10** *3/4* **Sahara Mist (IRE)**[38] 4804 2-7-9 **62** oh17.................. HayleyTurner(3) 4 41
(DShaw) *chsd ldrs: rdn along over 2f out: sn wknd* **150/1**
0065 **11** *3* **Kashmar Flight**[85] 3406 2-7-12 **62** oh3.................. DaleGibson 7 35
(TDEasterby) *a rr* **25/1**

1m 43.46s (-11.00) **Going Correction** -0.40s/f (Firm) **11** Ran SP% **118.0**
Speed ratings: **94,93,91,91,91 90,88,86,84,83 80**CSF £14.84 CT £271.74 TOTE £4.60: £2.00, £1.90, £6.90; EX 20.00.
**Owner** Saif Ali **Bred** Classic Lines Partnership **Trained** Manton, Wilts

**FOCUS**
Quite a competitive nursery and the form looks decent for the grade and sound.

**NOTEBOOK**
**Glorious Step(USA)** had been progressing nicely until flopping in a heavy-ground French Group Three on her latest outing. Dropped in grade and faced with very different conditions, she returned to form to gain her second win from just four starts. Time could show that she was particularly well-in off a mark of 85.
**Dance Flower(IRE)**, stepped up in trip from six and a half furlongs, was only just pegged back and ran a very brave race in defeat. A tough sort, she is clearly quite versatile and has more than enough ability to win a race, but it is just worth remembering she has been a beaten favourite twice already.
**Patxaran(IRE)** failed to get home over this trip on soft ground on her previous start but, returned to a faster surface, she ran much better and has a little race in her off her current mark in the 60s.
**Lottie Dundass**, who found only subsequent Richmond Stakes winner Montgomery's Arch too good on her second start, made a respectable handicap debut but did not show any improvement.
**Ratukidul(FR)**, off the mark in just an ordinary seven-furlong Folkestone maiden on her debut, was entitled to have finished closer as she found herself in a very unpromising position when the pace quickened and met some trouble in running. *Official explanation: jockey said filly lost her action in the closing stages*
**Sahara Mist(IRE)** *Official explanation: jockey said filly hung left throughout*

## 5754 S B HONDA H'CAP 5f
**3:30** (4:01) (E3) (0-70,70) 3-Y-0+ **£4,243** (£1,305; £652; £326) **Stalls** Low

Form RPR
1500 **1** **Blue Maeve**[21] 5242 4-8-9 **58**.................. SRighton 4 73
(JHetherton) *sn led: rdn clr wl over 1f out: drvn ins last: jst hld on* **16/1**
2104 **2** *1/2* **Trojan Flight**[4] 5674 3-9-3 **67**.................. KFallon 2 80
(MrsJRRamsden) *bhd and sn pushed along: hdwy 2f out: swtchd rt and rdn over 1f out: styd on strly fnl f: jst failed* **5/2**[1]
4000 **3** *hd* **Tuscan Flyer**[8] 5562 6-8-9 **58**..................(b) DarrenWilliams 3 70
(RBastiman) *chaased wnr: rdn wl over 1f out: kpt on u.p fnl f* **14/1**
0320 **4** *3/4* **Ballybunion (IRE)**[7] 5579 5-8-7 **56** oh1.................. ANicholls 6 65
(DNicholls) *midfield: hdwy 2f out: sn rdn and kpt on fnl f: nrst fin* **15/2**
4450 **5** *1 1/4* **Obe One**[6] 5603 4-9-4 **67**.................. FLynch 5 71
(ABerry) *bhd: hdwy 2f out: sn rdn and kpt on fnl f: nrst fin* **7/1**[3]
0360 **6** *1* **Fitzwarren**[21] 5242 3-8-9 **59**.................. EAhern 8 59
(NBycroft) *chsd ldrs: rdn and outpcd 2f out: kpt on ins last* **66/1**
0030 **7** *nk* **Midnight Parkes**[8] 5562 5-9-7 **70**.................. MHenry 9 69
(EJAlston) *towards rr: rdn along and hdwy 1/2-way: kpt on ins last: nvr a factor* **10/1**
0244 **8** *1* **Online Investor**[8] 5562 5-8-13 **62**.................. SSanders 14 57
(DNicholls) *dwlt and towards rr tl sme late hdwy* **10/1**

2025 **9** ¾ **Roan Raider (USA)**[19] 5306 4-8-8 **57**................................(v) MFenton 1 49
(MissVHaigh) *chsd ldrs on inner: rdn along over 2f out and sn one pce* **40/1**

4001 **10** ¾ **Kew The Music**[7] 5597 4-8-7 **55** 6ex oh1........................(v) SHitchcott 17 45
(MRChannon) *s.i.s and bhd tl sme late hdwy* **16/1**

0650 **11** *1* **Stagnite**[10] 5512 4-8-3 **57**..............................................(p) NChalmers(5) 10 42
(MrsHSweeting) *chsd ldrs: rdn along 2f out: sn wknd* **40/1**

0000 **12** ½ **Chico Guapo (IRE)**[12] 5458 4-9-1 **64**................................ RWinston 13 47
(JAGlover) *cl up: rdn along 2f out: grad wknd* **25/1**

062 **13** 2½ **Strawberry Patch (IRE)**[7] 5579 5-8-5 **57**....................(p) NMackay(3) 11 30
(MissLAPerratt) *dwlt: a rr* **11/2**[2]

0 **14** 2½ **Calypso Dancer (FR)**[13] 5440 4-9-4 **67**................................ KDarley 12 30
(TDBarron) *in tch on outer: rdn along over 2f out: sn wknd* **33/1**

5020 **15** 3½ **Gone'N'Dunnett (IRE)**[9] 5550 5-8-8 **60**.................(p) HayleyTurner(3) 16 9
(MrsCADunnett) *a rr* **33/1**

0500 **16** 2½ **Erracht**[38] 4800 6-8-11 **60**......................................................... GBaker 15 —
(MrsHSweeting) *a rr* **50/1**

60.84 secs (-2.96) **Going Correction** -0.40s/f (Firm) course record
**WFA** 3 from 4yo+ 1lb **16** Ran SP% **122.9**
Speed ratings: **107,106,105,104,102 101,100,99,97,96 95,94,90,86,80 76**CSF £53.63 CT £492.54 TOTE £20.40: £3.00, £1.30, £2.70, £2.20; EX 79.80 Trifecta £812.00 Part won. Pool of £1,143.73 - 0.40 winning tickets..
**Owner** R G Fell **Bred** P J And Mrs Nolan **Trained** Malton, N Yorks

**FOCUS**
A competitive sprint handicap, but not that many got into it and the form is just moderate although solid enough for the level.

**NOTEBOOK**
**Blue Maeve**, 7lb higher than when gaining his only previous win, showed good pace from his low draw and, given an easy enough time up front, he was able to sustain his challenge to the line. He had little in hand, but will always be worthy of respect over five furlongs on ground with firm in the description - his form figures given those conditions read 84211.
**Trojan Flight** simply lacked the early pace of the winner and, although finishing with his usual flourish, it was not quite enough. He is the type to keep improving and can win more races, but he is never a very good price (he has been sent off favourite on his last seven starts) and it is probably best to look elsewhere.
**Tuscan Flyer** has not been running very consistently this season, but this was one of his better efforts off a mark 3lb higher than in future.
**Ballybunion(IRE)**, disappointing on easy ground at Ayr on his previous start, appreciated the return to a faster surface and ran respectably.
**Obe One**, 2lb higher than in future, can have no real excuse as he was near the eventual runner-up in the early stages.
**Strawberry Patch(IRE)** was 3lb well-in but did not pick up at all and maybe this ground was fast enough for him.

## 5755 DALBY SCREW-DRIVER H'CAP 1m 2f 6y
**4:00** (4:30) (C1) (0-100,92) 3-Y-O+ **£12,006** (£4,554; £2,277; £1,035) **Stalls** Low

Form RPR

6042 **1** **Go Tech**[8] 5568 4-8-7 **75** oh1................................................ GGibbons 3 84
(TDEasterby) *hld up: stdy hdwy 1/2-way: rdn over 1f out: styd on wl to ld ins last: edgd rt and drvn out* **7/1**

2003 **2** 1¼ **James Caird (IRE)**[15] 5397 4-9-5 **87**...................................... JFortune 5 94
(MHTompkins) *hld up: hdwy 3f out: rdn 2f out: styd on wl fnl f* **3/1**[3]

0045 **3** *hd* **Parkview Love (USA)**[12] 5474 3-8-12 **86**............................. KDarley 2 92
(MJohnston) *led: rdn along over 2f out: hdd jst over 1f out: drvn and rallied ins last: styng on towards fin* **18/1**

2120 **4** *hd* **Adaikali (IRE)**[54] 4343 3-8-13 **87**............................................ KFallon 8 93
(SirMichaelStoute) *trckd ldrs: hdwy 3f out: rdn to ld briefly 1f out: sn drvn and hdd: wknd last 100 yds* **85/40**[1]

030/ **5** *2* **Torcello (IRE)**[696] 5493 6-9-7 **89**............................................ MFenton 4 91
(GWragg) *trckd ldr: hdwy to chal over 2f out: rdn to ld briefly over 1f out: sn hdd and drvn: wknd ins last* **50/1**

0404 **6** *hd* **Selective**[26] 5112 5-9-6 **88**...................................................... EAhern 7 90
(EFVaughan) *hld up in rr: hdwy on inner whn hmpd over 2f out and nt rcvr* **20/1**

1115 **7** 1½ **Masafi (IRE)**[50] 4435 3-9-4 **92**.............................................. SSanders 1 91
(SirMarkPrescott) *trckd ldrs: pushed along and edgd lft 2f out: sn rdn and wknd* **11/4**[2]

2250 **8** *14* **Grey Clouds**[8] 5572 4-8-11 **79**................................................. DAllan 6 51
(TDEasterby) *a rr* **18/1**

2m 10.3s (-3.61) **Going Correction** -0.40s/f (Firm)
**WFA** 3 from 4yo+ 6lb **8** Ran SP% **113.4**
Speed ratings: **98,97,96,96,95 94,93,82**CSF £27.84 CT £361.65 TOTE £8.60: £1.70, £1.60, £3.10; EX 25.20.
**Owner** Ryedale Partners No 4 **Bred** A G Nicholson **Trained** Great Habton, N Yorks

**FOCUS**
Just the eight runners, but a decent enough race and the form looks good but not outstanding. However, the early pace was pretty modest and, as a result, the winning time was slow for the grade - 0.72 seconds slower than the 0-60 classified stakes over the same trip.

**NOTEBOOK**
**Go Tech** had not won for two years and was simply not doing enough to win a race but, 2lb lower than in future, this was more like it. He was a little keen in the early stages under a patient ride, but found plenty when asked and proved brave to come between horses with his effort in the straight. He is in good order, but his win-to-runs record does not inspire confidence of a follow up.
**James Caird(IRE)** has run some big races this season but remains without win since scoring in the apprentice race on this card the previous year. Racing off a career-high mark, he ran his race and found only the back-to-form winner too good. He deserves to win, but is creeping up the weights without doing so.
**Parkview Love(USA)** ◆, without a win since scoring in a six-furlong Listed event last year, appreciated this step up to ten furlongs and ran one of his best races of the year on ground possibly a little faster than ideal, sticking on right the way to the line. This was a good effort and he could well be ready to strike.
**Adaikali(IRE)** was not quite at his best despite appearing to have conditions to suit and had every chance in the race itself. It was disappointing that he was unable to sustain his effort, and it may well be that he needs producing very late.
**Torcello(IRE)**, racing for the first time in 696 days, made a very pleasing return to action and clearly retains plenty of ability. If he goes the right way from this, he has races in him.
**Selective** would have been closer had he not been slightly hampered by the eventual winner on the final bend, but he was not that unlucky.
**Masafi(IRE)** appeared found out by a combination of a hectic campaign and a mark 17lb higher than when last winning a handicap. He may now be put away until next season and should benefit from a lengthy break, but he will need to improve to get competitive off a mark in the 90s when we next see him.
**Grey Clouds** *Official explanation: jockey said filly was never travelling*

## 5756 EUROPEAN BREEDERS FUND FRIER WOOD MAIDEN STKS 1m 4y
**4:30** (5:01) (D2) 2-Y-O **£5,577** (£1,716; £858; £429) **Stalls** Low

Form RPR

3324 **1** **Little Miss Gracie**[33] 4963 2-8-9 85............................................ KFallon 1 87+
(ABHaynes) *cl up: led after 11/2f: qcknd clr 2f out: v easily* **11/8**[1]

**2** *5* **Amazing Valour (IRE)** 2-9-0 .................................................. KDarley 9 75
(MJohnston) *chsd ldrs: rdn along 3f out: drvn and kpt on fnl f: no ch w wnr* **14/1**

**3** *nk* **Mujazaf** 2-9-0 ................................................................ ACulhane 2 74
(MRChannon) *in tch: hdwy to chse wnr wl over 1f out: sn drvn and btn* **11/4**[2]

**4** 3½ **Travel Tip (USA)** 2-9-0 ..................................................... JFortune 8 69+
(JHMGosden) *s.i.s and bhd tl modest late hdwy* **7/1**

0 **5** *1* **Optimum (IRE)**[16] 5373 2-9-0 ............................................. TPQueally 5 64
(DRLoder) *in tch: drvn along 3f out: sn btn* **25/1**

00 **6** 2½ **Sovereign Spirit (IRE)**[14] 5406 2-9-0 ...................................... IMongan 4 59
(PWHarris) *bhd fr 1/2-way* **25/1**

**7** 2½ **Red Opera** 2-9-0 ............................................................ SSanders 3 53
(SirMarkPrescott) *dwlt: hld up: a bhd* **9/2**[3]

0 **8** 2½ **Caribbean Dancer (USA)**[26] 5109 2-8-9 ................................ RWinston 7 43
(MJohnston) *led 11/2f: cl up tl rdn along 3f out and sn wknd* **25/1**

1m 44.09s (-1.51) **Going Correction** -0.40s/f (Firm) **8** Ran SP% **117.7**
Speed ratings: **91,86,85,82,81 78,76,73**CSF £23.19 TOTE £2.10: £1.10, £3.90, £1.60; EX 16.20.
**Owner** AbacusAliciaHardenAndrewHaynesRacing Ltd **Bred** Keith Wills **Trained** Collingbourne Ducis, Wilts
■ A first training success for Andrew Haynes, who took over the licence from Paul Burgoyne.

**FOCUS**
This looked a reasonable maiden on paper, but it was effectively a one-horse race with newcomers in second, third and fourth all running too green to challenge the emphatic winner. However, the placed horses may be able to find the improvement they need to win maidens.

**NOTEBOOK**
**Little Miss Gracie**, fourth to Berkhamsted in French Listed race on her debut for her current trainer having shown promise in reasonable maidens, put her experience to good use and the result never looked in doubt. With the second, third and fourth all running green on what was their racecourse debuts, the manner of success does flatter her a little, but she is clearly going the right way and should have a leading chance in a Group Three at Deauville, her next intended target.
**Amazing Valour(IRE)**, a 40,000gns half-brother to three winners, out of a ten-furlong winner in France, was very easy to back and was too inexperienced to ever pose a threat to the winner. He should be capable of significant improvement.
**Mujazaf**, a 150,000gns first foal out of a seven-furlong two-year-old winner, has been given a Derby entry and was quite well supported. He was never quite going the pace of the eventual winner but shaped as though the experience would bring him on.
**Travel Tip(USA)**, a half-brother to a multiple winner in the USA, out of a Stakes winner from the same country, was never really competitive after starting slowly and is another who should improve significantly for the experience.
**Optimum(IRE)** stepped up on his debut running, but did not achieve a great deal and may do better when handicapped.
**Sovereign Spirit(IRE)** travelled quite well but found nothing. He is, however, now qualified for a handicap mark.
**Red Opera**, a half-brother to the top-class two-year-old/miler Grand Lodge, is entered in the Derby. Easy enough to back on course but still short enough to suggest he is expected to make the grade as a two-year-old, he showed nothing. However, he is surely capable of better and do not rule out significant improvement.
**Caribbean Dancer(USA)**, $55,000 yearling, half-sister to several winners in the US, including two useful turf winners, dropped right out after trying to mix it with the eventual winner.

## 5757 BETFAIR.COM APPRENTICE SERIES CLASSIFIED STKS (FINAL ROUND) 1m 2f 6y
**5:00** (5:31) (F3) 3-Y-O+ **£4,202** (£1,293; £646; £323) **Stalls** Low

Form RPR

5014 **1** **Lucayan Dancer**[7] 5584 4-8-7 57.................................... PJBenson(7) 16 68
(DNicholls) *hld up and bhd: hdwy over 2f out: rdn to chse ldr ent last: hung lft and styd on to ld last 100 yds* **5/1**[3]

0666 **2** ¾ **Cottingham (IRE)**[6] 5622 3-8-8 59............................................ WHogg 2 67
(MCChapman) *trckd ldng pair: hdwy 4f out: led 3f out and rdn clr wl over 1f out: drvn and wknd ins last: hdd and no ex last 100 yds* **20/1**

0016 **3** 2½ **Snowed Under**[16] 5374 3-8-3 58.................................... JCavanagh(5) 3 62
(JDBethell) *in tch: hdwy to chse ldr 2f out: sn rdn and kpt on same pce appr last* **10/1**

2232 **4** ¾ **Mambina (USA)**[6] 5622 3-7-12 59........................................ TO'Brien(7) 9 58
(MRChannon) *hld up: hdwy over 4f out: chsd ldrs 2f out: sn rdn and one pce* **4/1**[2]

4561 **5** *3* **Our Emmy Lou**[9] 5549 3-8-4 60........................................ SArcher(7) 13 58
(SirMarkPrescott) *in tch: rdn along 3f out: sn outpcd* **11/4**[1]

3000 **6** *11* **Active Account (USA)**[16] 5374 7-9-0 57...........................(b[1]) AMullen 1 34
(MrsHDalton) *chsd ldrs: rdn along 1/2-way: sn outpcd* **33/1**

2341 **7** 3½ **Tata Naka**[8] 5572 4-8-12 45............................................ LauraPike(5) 12 31
(MrsCADunnett) *hld up and bhd: sme hdwy 3f out: sn rdn and nvr a factor* **8/1**

-401 **8** 1½ **Time Marches On**[7] 5585 6-9-1 40................................(t) NeilBrown(5) 7 31
(KGReveley) *hld up and bhd: effrt on outer and sme hdwy 2f out: nvr a factor* **12/1**

5005 **9** 3½ **Turftanzer (GER)**[7] 5585 5-8-7 30........................(t) JaniceWebster(7) 14 18
(DonEnricoIncisa) *in tch on outer: rdn along over 4f out and sn btn* **100/1**

-040 **10** *hd* **Mandinka**[17] 5350 4-8-7 35................................................ JBrennan(7) 6 18
(JFCoupland) *rdr lost iron s: a rr* **100/1**

0240 **11** 1¼ **Legal Set (IRE)**[2] 5713 8-9-0 60................................(t) SuzanneFrance 8 15
(MissAStokell) *led: rdn along over 3f out: sn hdd & wknd* **25/1**

6204 **12** *6* **Rabitatit (IRE)**[4] 5672 3-8-5 60............................................ DFentiman 10 —
(JGMO'Shea) *prom: rdn along 1/2-way: sn wknd* **12/1**

2m 9.58s (-4.33) **Going Correction** -0.40s/f (Firm)
**WFA** 3 from 4yo+ 6lb **12** Ran SP% **112.4**
Speed ratings: **101,100,98,97,95 86,83,82,79,79 78,73**CSF £89.61 TOTE £6.30: £2.10, £4.00, £3.50; EX 208.00 Place 6 £59.76, Place 5 £45.91.
**Owner** Lucayan Stud **Bred** The National Stud Owner Breeders Club Ltd **Trained** Sessay, N Yorks
■ Irish-based apprentice Paul Benson's first winner. Sterling Guarantee (9/1) w/d, ref to ent stalls, R4 deduct 10p in the £.

**FOCUS**
A very moderate classified event and it is hard to see anything progressing like last year's winner, James Caird.

**NOTEBOOK**
**Lucayan Dancer**, successful on soft ground at Brighton just two starts previously, handled this much faster surface well and gained his third career win under a well-judged ride.
**Cottingham(IRE)**, whose only previous win came over a mile on Fibresand in a banded maiden, nearly stole this under a positive ride from Hogg.

**Snowed Under** seems to go well for Cavanagh and ran another good race. He gained his only previous win on easy ground, but a fast surface would not appear to bother him.
**Mambina(USA)** did not run badly, but she has yet to prove herself fully effective on fast ground and is quite simply just a hard horse to win with.
**Our Emmy Lou**, due to be raised to a mark of 68 following her runaway win in a Yarmouth claimer on her previous start, was left behind when the pace increased and was disappointing. She shapes as though a return to further and easier ground will suit.
**Mandinka** *Official explanation: jockey said he lost his irons in the early stages*
T/Jkpt: £9,577.50 to a £1 stake. Pool: £13,489.50. 0.50 winning units. £6,744.75 carried over to Ascot 24/09 (3.05). T/Plt: £68.80 to a £1 stake. Pool: £51,998.10. 551.10 winning units. T/Qpdt: £22.00 to a £1 stake. Pool: £2,709.40. 90.80 winning units. JR

5758 - 5760a (Foreign Racing) - See Raceform Interactive

# 4526 ASCOT (R-H)

Friday, September 24

**OFFICIAL GOING: Good to firm (good in places)**

## 5761 SODEXHO EUROPEAN BREEDERS FUND CLASSIFIED STKS 1m 2f
**2:00** (2:02) (C1) 3-Y-O+ **£15,167** (£5,753; £2,876; £1,307) **Stalls High**

Form RPR
3000 **1** **Destination Dubai (USA)**[16] 5397 3-8-10 90 (vt) LDettori 2 96
(SaeedBinSuroor) *lw: taken down early: sn trckd ldr: rdn to ld 1f out: hld on wl* **9/1**
232 **2** ½ **Courageous Duke (USA)**[13] 5461 5-9-6 94 EAhern 7 99
(JNoseda) *trckd ldng pair: effrt to chal and upsides over 1f out: pressed wnr fnl f: a hld* **8/1[3]**
5221 **3** ¾ **Impeller (IRE)**[16] 5401 5-9-4 92 SDrowne 8 96
(WRMuir) *lw:t.k.h early in midfield: effrt 2f out: styd on fr over 1f out : jst unable to chal* **9/1**
2014 **4** nk **Boule D'Or (IRE)**[16] 5401 3-8-10 89 NDay 11 93+
(RIngram) *t.k.h early: hld up towards rr: effrt 2f out: rdn and r.o fnl f: too much to do* **25/1**
-500 **5** hd **Muhareb (USA)**[16] 5401 5-9-2 90 TPQueally 3 93
(CEBrittain) *swtg: led to 1f out: one pce fnl f* **40/1**
5162 **6** ¾ **Mocca (IRE)**[16] 5397 3-8-7 88 MartinDwyer 6 88
(DJCoakley) *t.k.h early: racd midfield: rdn over 3f out: no prog tl styd on fnl f: nvr able to chal* **16/1**
41-1 **7** ½ **Border Castle**[27] 5122 3-8-10 89 KFallon 1 90
(SirMichaelStoute) *lw: sn chsd ldrs: rdn over 2f out: one pce and no imp* **7/4[1]**
0651 **8** nk **Gold History (USA)**[13] 5470 3-9-0 94 DHolland 12 94
(MJohnston) *settled towards rr: rdn over 2f out: kpt on fr over 1f out: n.d* **11/1**
0121 **9** ¾ **Top Spec (IRE)**[14] 5446 3-8-10 80 RLMoore 13 88
(RHannon) *dwlt: hld up in last: rdn over 2f out: kpt on same pce: n.d* **25/1**
1242 **10** 1 **Mango Mischief (IRE)**[16] 5401 3-8-7 90 RHughes 4 83
(JLDunlop) *lw: t.k.h early: racd wd towards rr: one pce and no imp on ldrs fnl 2f* **9/2[2]**
100- **11** nk **Sharmy (IRE)**[89] 725 8-9-6 94 TEDurcan 9 90
(IanWilliams) *t.k.h early: hld up in rr: last and rdn over 2f out: one pce after* **66/1**
6060 **12** 3 **Foodbroker Founder**[16] 5401 4-9-2 90 JFortune 10 80
(DRCElsworth) *t.k.h early: prom: rdn 2f out: wknd over 1f out* **66/1**
140- **13** ¾ **Sailing Through**[91] 5484 4-9-1 92 RMiles(3) 5 81
(RDickin) *t.k.h early: hld up midfield: wknd 2f out* **66/1**

2m 7.70s (-1.03) **Going Correction** +0.05s/f (Good)
**WFA** 3 from 4yo+ 6lb **13 Ran SP% 114.5**
Speed ratings: **106,105,105,104,104 104,103,103,102,101 101,99,98**CSF £71.72 TOTE £7.50: £2.20, £2.80, £2.90; EX 96.20.
**Owner** Godolphin **Bred** Calumet Farm **Trained** Newmarket, Suffolk

**FOCUS**
The pace was not strong, putting several key horses at a disadvantage, so the form overall is a bit muddling. While Destination Dubai ran to form, the placed horses were all a few pounds off their best.

**NOTEBOOK**
**Destination Dubai(USA)** has a tendency to hang under pressure and has not always looked the most genuine, but there was nothing wrong with his attitude here and he was able to provide connections with yet another winner at the course. This represented arguably his best effort to date and, as a three-year-old, he is open to further improvement.
**Courageous Duke(USA)** sat just off the leaders and came through with his challenge but was always just being held off by the winner. He was 7lb higher than when last successful and currently looks held by the handicapper, a situation that is unlikely to improve anytime soon.
**Impeller(IRE)** got his head in front for the first time in roughly a year at Epsom and came into this with confidence on a high. He would ideally have prefered a faster gallop and was never quite getting there in time, but it was still another decent run.
**Boule D'Or(IRE)** ◆, a progressive three-year-old with a turn of foot on his day, was another who would have prefered them to go a bit quicker up front and he too was doing all his best work too late in the day. He goes on most ground and may be an interesting contender for the Cambridgeshire off a low-weight.
**Muhareb(USA)** ◆ ran without doubt his best race of the season, off a 2lb lower mark than when last successful. Once returning to a mile four, he can get back to winning ways.
**Mocca(IRE)** was unable to get going in time and might appreciate being ridden more aggressively in future, as she does stay this trip well.
**Border Castle**, off an 8lb higher mark than when winning on his seasonal return, ran below par and seemed to find the rise too much, although his wide draw and the 'bounce' factor may also have played their parts. He is surely a little bit better than this.
**Gold History(USA)** is at his best when able to dominate and did not seem to appreciate being ridden from behind.
**Top Spec(IRE)** had a stiff task at the weights and did well to finish so close.
**Mango Mischief(IRE)** raced towards the outside from her low draw and never got competitive. This was not her form.

## 5762 PRICEWATERHOUSECOOPERS STKS (H'CAP) 6f 110y(R)
**2:30** (2:36) (C1) (0-100,100) 3-Y-O **£15,787** (£5,988; £2,994; £1,361) **Stalls High**

Form RPR
1360 **1** **Khabfair**[23] 5224 3-9-2 95 JPMurtagh 10 105
(MrsAJPerrett) *lw: trckd ldng pair: rdn over 1f out: hanging lft fnl f but drvn ahd last strides* **9/2[1]**
1222 **2** hd **Compton's Eleven**[36] 4874 3-9-0 93 SHitchcott 8 102
(MRChannon) *led to over 4f out: led again over 1f out: wandered u.p: hdd last strides* **6/1[2]**
3131 **3** 1 ¼ **Majors Cast (IRE)**[23] 5220 3-8-12 91 EAhern 6 97+
(JNoseda) *lw: racd wd towards rr: plenty to do and rdn 2f out: styd on wl fr over 1f out: nrst fin* **15/2**
0034 **4** ½ **Bentley's Ball (USA)**[41] 4750 3-8-9 88 RLMoore 13 93
(RHannon) *led over 4f out to over 1f out: one pce fnl f* **8/1**
1205 **5** nk **Oasis Star (IRE)**[7] 5610 3-8-10 89 DHolland 11 93
(PWHarris) *sn chsd ldrs: rdn over 2f out: kpt on u.p: nvr able to chal* **13/2[3]**
1132 **6** hd **Out After Dark**[9] 5563 3-8-7 86 oh5 RSmith 3 90
(CGCox) *racd midfield: rdn and effrt over 1f out: sme prog ent fnl f: one pce last 100yds* **14/1**
3-12 **7** hd **Mr Lambros**[223] 770 3-8-7 86 oh1 MartinDwyer 14 90+
(AMBalding) *s.s: racd in last trio: effrt 2f out: styng on but no ch whn nt clr run nr fin* **16/1**
0145 **8** 1 **Rydal (USA)**[6] 5660 3-8-8 87 (b) JFortune 9 88
(GAButler) *b.hind: racd midfield: rdn and effrt over 1f out: nt qckn ent fnl f: fdd nr fin* **25/1**
-605 **9** ½ **Bravo Maestro (USA)**[128] 2224 3-9-0 93 TQuinn 12 93
(DWPArbuthnot) *b: racd towards rr: rdn over 2f out: nvr on terms w ldrs* **14/1**
3210 **10** nk **Apex**[23] 5224 3-8-9 88 KFallon 2 87
(EALDunlop) *rrd s and slowly away: racd last trio: sme prog whn nt clr run 1f out: no ch after* **12/1**
2266 **11** 1 **Doitnow (IRE)**[27] 5120 3-8-6 88 THamilton(3) 7 84
(RAFahey) *racd midfield: rdn over 2f out: wknd over 1f out* **16/1**
0052 **12** 1 ¼ **Tony The Tap**[10] 5550 3-8-4 86 oh4 FPFerris(3) 4 79
(NACallaghan) *b.hind: s.s: a last trio: n.m.r on inner 3f out: no prog* **14/1**
0051 **13** nk **Saristar**[8] 5588 3-8-4 88 6ex NDeSouza(5) 5 80
(PFICole) *plld hrd: trckd ldng pair tl wknd 2f out* **14/1**

1m 20.21s **13 Ran SP% 118.6**
Speed ratings: CSF £29.73 CT £201.12 TOTE £5.10: £2.00, £2.30, £3.10; EX 26.10 Trifecta £163.20 Pool of £1,558.78 - 6.78 winning units.
**Owner** Star Pointe Ltd & Arlington Bloodstock **Bred** Peter Hodgson **Trained** Pulborough, W Sussex

**FOCUS**
The draw played its part here, not surprisingly as they were racing around a bend, but this was a decent sprint handicap and the form looks solid enough.

**NOTEBOOK**
**Khabfair** has held his form well this season and despite hanging a little when maximum pressure was apllied, just did enough to nose out Compton's Eleven. He continues to go the right way and may make Listed grade next season.
**Compton's Eleven**, who has been in cracking form of late, suffered another heartbreakingly narrow defeat. In his last three runs he has been beaten a head on two occasions and a short head on the other. He deserves a change of luck.
**Majors Cast(IRE)** came from a long way back to snatch third and may have got there in another half furlong. This was his first try at the trip and while effective at it, returning to seven will suit.
**Bentley's Ball(USA)** has looked in the grip of the handicapper for most of the season, but he seems to be finding his feet now and has run solid races on his last three appearances. He will be suited by a return to seven furlongs.
**Oasis Star(IRE)** is a tough, genuine mare who has yet to run a bad race all season. This was her eighth run of the term and she could not get going in time, so will prove suited by the return to seven furlongs.
**Out After Dark** is creeping up the handicap but continues ot run well and was only beaten around two lengths. He should continue to pay his way.
**Mr Lambros** ◆, having his first start since February and first on the turf, was the real eyecatcher of the race, as having raced freely in the early stages, he found himself tight for room when trying to come with a run and had to settle for seventh - going past the line with a bit still left in the tank. Provided he avoids the 'bounce' factor, he has the look of an obvious future winner.
**Rydal(USA)** travelled nicely but did not find as much as had once looked likely.
**Bravo Maestro(USA)** ◆ had not been seen since May and made a pleasing reappearance, without setting the world alight. He is fully entitled to leave this form behind though and may have a decent backend handicap in him.

## 5763 PRINCESS ROYAL JOHN DOYLE STKS (GROUP 3) (F&M) 1m 4f
**3:05** (3:05) (A1) 3-Y-O+ **£29,000** (£11,000; £5,500; £2,500) **Stalls High**

Form RPR
2322 **1** **Mazuna (IRE)**[16] 5394 3-8-6 97 RLMoore 3 107
(CEBrittain) *hld up in last pair: gd prog over 2f out: drvn to ld last 100yds: jst hld on* **14/1**
1-31 **2** shd **My Renee (USA)**[53] 4406 4-9-0 NGMcCullagh 6 107
(MJGrassick, Ire) *lw: trckd ldrs: rdn and prog to ld over 1f out: hdd last 100yds: rallied wl: jst pipped* **5/2[1]**
1542 **3** 1 ½ **Hidden Hope**[48] 4566 3-8-6 109 TEDurcan 4 104+
(GWragg) *t.k.h: trckd ldr 4f: cl up and rdn whn n.m.r over 1f out: kpt on same pce* **9/2[3]**
2636 **4** 1 ½ **Summitville**[33] 4980 4-9-0 102 DHolland 2 102
(JGGiven) *lw: t.k.h: trckd ldr after 4f: led wl over 2f out: hrd rdn and hdd over 1f out: one pce* **10/1**
2110 **5** 6 **Astrocharm (IRE)**[16] 5394 5-9-3 103 LDettori 8 95
(MHTompkins) *settled towards rr: rdn and no rspnse over 2f out: no ch after* **7/1**
6321 **6** 1 ½ **Polar Jem**[9] 5573 4-9-0 98 AMcCarthy 7 90
(GGMargarson) *led to wl over 2f out: wknd* **8/1**
2010 **7** 2 ½ **Beneventa**[48] 4566 4-9-3 110 RHughes 10 92+
(JLDunlop) *t.k.h: prom tl wknd 2f out* **7/2[2]**
-410 **8** 2 **Castagna (USA)**[36] 4884 3-8-6 85 WRyan 9 86+
(HRACecil) *t.k.h early: lost pl after 4f: last and struggling fr 1/2-way* **50/1**

2m 30.24s (-3.32) **Going Correction** +0.05s/f (Good)
**WFA** 3 from 4yo+ 8lb **8 Ran SP% 110.3**
Speed ratings: **113,112,111,110,106 105,104,102**CSF £45.78 TOTE £15.90: £3.00, £1.40, £1.80; EX 41.20 Trifecta £224.90 Pool of £3,739.22 - 11.80 winning units.
**Owner** Saeed Manana **Bred** B Freiha **Trained** Newmarket, Suffolk

**FOCUS**
Only an ordinary Group 3, but the time was fair and it was fought out by two progressive fillies with only a short head separating them at the line. Mazuna clearly was not flattered by her 100-1 second in the Park Hill.

**NOTEBOOK**
**Mazuna(IRE)** has improved out of all recognition the last twice - going from being beaten in a handicap off a mark of 69, to placing and now winning in Group company. Quite where the improvement has come from is a mystery but she is clearly here to stay at this level and having come with a strong challenge, did just enough to hold the favourite.
**My Renee(USA)**, a progressive Irish-trained filly who has a course and distance win to her name, was rightly made favourite in what was an ordinary Group 3 and only just got nailed on the line. She had reportedly missed work the previous week with a stone bruise, and that may have been crucial. She may race in the States in order to take advantage of the fast ground she prefers.
**Hidden Hope** is a fair performer at this level but lacked the pace of the front two on the run to the line. She is ideally suited by a softer surface.
**Summitville** is without a win since her two-year-old days and continues to find at least a couple too good at this level.
**Astrocharm(IRE)** seems to have stopped improving now, but she has had a long season.
**Polar Jem** ran a rare disappointing race but this trip does stretch her.

**Beneventa** seems to have lost her for for the time being. *Official explanation: jockey said filly ran flat*
**Castagna(USA)** was running out of her grade.

## 5764 BOLLINGER CHAMPAGNE CHALLENGE SERIES FINAL H'CAP (GENTLEMAN AMATEUR RIDERS) 1m 4f

**3:40** (3:40) (D2) (0-85,84) 3-Y-0+ **£7,033** (£2,164; £1,082; £541) **Stalls** High

Form RPR

4155 **1** **Skylarker (USA)**[25] 5182 6-11-2 **74**.......... MrLJefford 4 86
(WSKittow) *lw: prom: chsd ldr 3f out: shkn up to ld over 1f out: styd on wl* **20/1**

2033 **2** *3* **Genghis (IRE)**[7] 5619 5-11-5 **80**.......... MrJJBest(3) 10 87
(HMorrison) *trckd ldr: led 1/2-way: rdn and hdd over 1f out: one pce* **5/1**[3]

0211 **3** *1 3/4* **Tender Falcon**[25] 5182 4-11-7 **82**.......... MrJamesWhite(3) 8 86+
(RJHodges) *lw: hld up midfield: effrt and nt clr run over 2f out: hld in by rival 2f out to over 1f out: styd on fnl f: nrst fin* **9/2**[2]

4151 **4** *1 3/4* **Night Sight (USA)**[20] 5303 7-10-10 **71**.......... MrJJMorgan(3) 7 73
(MrsSLamyman) *racd midfield: rdn and effrt over 2f out: kpt on one pce* **11/1**

1360 **5** *3/4* **Jacaranda (IRE)**[9] 5568 4-10-13 **71**.......... MrSWalker 5 71
(MrsALMKing) *hld up in rr: prog 3f out: bored into rival fr 2f out to over 1f out: one pce* **33/1**

4040 **6** *3/4* **Scottish River (USA)**[15] 5423 5-11-5 **80**.......... MrLNewnes(3) 9 79
(MDIUsher) *s.i.s: sn midfield: chsd ldrs 3f out: pushed along and no rspnse 2f out* **20/1**

0542 **7** *1/2* **Iberus (GER)**[21] 5267 6-10-3 **68**.......... MrTFWoodside(7) 13 66
(SGollings) *prom: chsd ldng pair 2f out: wknd jst over 1f out* **20/1**

2256 **8** *nk* **Bucks**[7] 5619 7-11-7 **84** ow5.......... MrMichaelMurphy(5) 2 82
(DKIvory) *racd wd thrght: towards rr: no ch 2f out: kpt on fnl f* **14/1**

5413 **9** *1* **Smart John**[20] 5303 4-10-9 **72**.......... MrCDavies(5) 14 68
(WMBrisbourne) *lw: hld up wl in rr: effrt over 2f out: one pce and nvr rchd ldrs* **13/2**

4440 **10** *1 1/4* **Kylkenny**[23] 5229 9-10-12 **70**.......... (t) MrJRees 1 64
(HMorrison) *stdd s: hld up in last: hmpd 4f out: plugged on fnl 2f: hopeless task* **25/1**

5540 **11** *4* **Rome (IRE)**[21] 5274 5-10-5 **68** oh6.......... MrJPemberton(5) 3 56
(GPEnright) *a wl in rr: bmpd along furiously and no prog 3f out* **40/1**

22-1 **12** *8* **Polar Tryst**[18] 5340 5-11-0 **72**.......... MrTGreenall 16 47
(LadyHerries) *led to 1/2-way: wknd rapidly over 2f out* **4/1**[1]

2460 **13** *1* **Danakil**[25] 5182 9-10-11 **74**.......... MrDHutchison(5) 15 48
(SDow) *prom tl wknd 4f out* **14/1**

100- **14** *5* **Constantine**[144] 5287 4-11-4 **76**.......... MrEDehdashti 12 42
(GLMoore) *a in rr: rdn and wknd 4f out* **25/1**

2m 34.54s (0.98) **Going Correction** +0.05s/f (Good)
**WFA** 3 from 4yo+ 8lb **14** Ran SP% **117.2**
Speed ratings: **98,96,94,93,93 92,92,92,91,90 87,82,81,78**CSF £106.25 CT £542.15 TOTE £27.30: £5.70, £2.10, £2.20; EX 132.30.
**Owner** Midd Shire Racing **Bred** P Pritchard **Trained** Blackborough, Devon
■ Stewards Enquiry : Mr James White seven-day ban: improper riding (Nov 12,16,22,29,30, Dec 27, Jan 7)

**FOCUS**
A weak race for the course, but sound enough form of its type. The first two enjoyed the run of the race.

**NOTEBOOK**
**Skylarker(USA)** ran out an easy winner of what was a weak race for the course. Always up on the pace, he came right away.
**Genghis(IRE)** has run many good races in defeat this season but remains winless. His turn will come eventually and he may be the type to make a better hurdler.
**Tender Falcon** would have appreciated a stronger pace but was unlucky not to get closer, as he finished strongly, having been short of room and unable to get a run. He remains in good form but will need to continue to progress to defy his rising mark.
**Night Sight(USA)** is another in-form character and he may have benefited from a more positive ride.
**Jacaranda(IRE)** returned to a bit of form but did himself no favours by lugging into Tender Falcon for about a furlong.
**Polar Tryst**, up 10lb for winning a weak maiden handicap at Bath on her return from more than a year off, failed to run her race and may have 'bounced'. *Official explanation: trainer was unable to offer any explanation for poor form shown*

## 5765 ALLIED IRISH BANK (GB) MAIDEN STKS 7f (R)

**4:15** (4:17) (D2) 2-Y-0 **£7,475** (£2,300; £1,150; £575) **Stalls** High

Form RPR

3 **1** **David Junior (USA)**[10] 5543 2-9-0.......... RHills 2 83+
(BJMeehan) *lw: mde virtually all: rdn wl over 1f out: rn green and edgd lft but styd on wl* **1/1**[1]

**2** *3/4* **Macabre** 2-9-0.......... LDettori 1 81
(SaeedBinSuroor) *lt-f: pressed wnr after 1f: persistent chal fr over 1f out: styd on but a jst hld* **9/4**[2]

**3** *6* **Giant's Rock (IRE)** 2-9-0.......... JFortune 3 66
(GAButler) *w'like: uns rdr bef gng into stalls: rn green: cl up tl outpcd wl over 1f out* **12/1**

**4** *nk* **Bonfire** 2-9-0.......... DHolland 4 65
(MJohnston) *b.bkwd: rangy: rn green and in snatches: chsd ldrs tl outpcd 2f out* **10/1**

**5** *1 1/4* **Dart Along (USA)** 2-9-0.......... RHughes 5 62
(RHannon) *b.bkwd: strong: scope: plld hrd and snatched up after 1f: rdn in last over 2f out: no prog* **7/1**[3]

1m 29.69s **5** Ran SP% **110.1**
Speed ratings: CSF £3.45 TOTE £2.00: £1.20, £1.60; EX 3.90.
**Owner** Roldvale Limited **Bred** A I Appleton **Trained** Upper Lambourn, Berks

**FOCUS**
Four of the five runners were newcomers, and the pace was only steady, so a hard race to assess with confidence. David Junior was the only member of the field with previous experience, yet he still looked very green.

**NOTEBOOK**
**David Junior(USA)**, very highly regarded by connections, did not have the know-how to win on his debut, but this time he was soon sent into the lead by Richard Hills. Although only looking workmanlike in winning, was still green and gave the impression he was only just doing enough. There should be more to come from him and a mile will suit, so he looks worthy of a step up in class.
**Macabre**, a Derby entrant, made the favourite work hard for his win and would no doubt have pleased connections with his effort. He pulled six lengths clear of the third and should have little bother picking up an ordinary maiden.
**Giant's Rock(IRE)** ◆, who unseated his rider before entering the stalls, looked badly in need of the experience and lacked the pace of the front pair. Sure to benefit greatly for the run, he too can win his maiden, possibly over a mile.
**Bonfire** ◆ was typical of one of his stable's juvenile debutants - running green and simply lacking the know-how to get competitive at the business end. Mark Johnston tends to introduce some of his better juveniles here, and he can be expected to leave this form behind in time.
**Dart Along(USA)** pulled too hard to do himself justice and will hopefully settle better next time.

## 5766 WEST END & METROPOLITAN LTD H'CAP 1m (R)

**4:50** (4:51) (D2) (0-85,85) 3-Y-0 **£7,181** (£2,209; £1,104; £552) **Stalls** High

Form RPR

0253 **1** **Granston (IRE)**[15] 5419 3-8-11 **75**.......... TQuinn 15 84
(JDBethell) *lw: t.k.h: hld up midfield: plld out and prog over 1f out: edgd rt and jnd ldr ins fnl f: led nr fin* **10/1**

2202 **2** *nk* **Evaluator (IRE)**[32] 5004 3-9-7 **85**.......... KFallon 4 93
(TGMills) *trckd ldrs: effrt to ld over 1f out: edgd rt and jnd ins fnl f: hdd nr fin* **6/1**

0042 **3** *1 1/2* **Cello**[28] 5076 3-9-0 **78**.......... (t) PDobbs 16 83
(RHannon) *t.k.h: hld up towards rr: prog wl over 1f out: carried hd high and edgd lft but styd on to take 3rd on line* **25/1**

3223 **4** *shd* **Border Music**[14] 5446 3-9-2 **80**.......... DHolland 11 84+
(AMBalding) *lw: settled wl in rr: nt clr run 2f out and over 1f out: prog fnl f: styd on wl nr fin* **11/2**[3]

0060 **5** *shd* **Alekhine (IRE)**[55] 4319 3-9-4 **82**.......... (e) EAhern 12 86
(PWHarris) *hld up wl in rr: stl in last trio 2f out: gd prog fr over 1f out: got clr run through fnl f: nrst fin* **14/1**

311 **6** *1/2* **New Order**[26] 5148 3-9-0 **78**.......... RHughes 13 83+
(BWHills) *lw: led for 1f: cl up after: rdn to chal and upsides over 1f out: hld whn nt clr run ins fnl f* **5/1**[2]

3-1 **7** *3/4* **Kodiac**[17] 5378 3-9-4 **82**.......... LDettori 2 83
(JLDunlop) *lw: trckd ldrs: bmpd over 2f out: hanging rt but prog to press ldrs 1f out: fnd nil after* **11/4**[1]

6061 **8** *nk* **Jath**[31] 5024 3-9-2 **80**.......... LisaJones 6 81
(JulianPoulton) *dwlt and squeezed out s: wl in rr: rdn over 2f out: prog on outer fnl f: nt rch ldrs* **20/1**

0006 **9** *hd* **Forthright**[23] 5220 3-9-5 **83**.......... (b[1]) RHills 17 83
(CEBrittain) *dwlt: t.k.h: hld up wl in rr: swtchd to outer over 2f out: kpt on: no ch* **20/1**

-040 **10** *1 3/4* **Gravardlax**[132] 2107 3-9-4 **82**.......... JFortune 9 78
(BJMeehan) *wl in rr: rdn over 2f out: one pce and nvr rchd ldrs* **33/1**

0010 **11** *nk* **Zweibrucken (IRE)**[21] 5265 3-9-5 **83**.......... JFEgan 8 86+
(SKirk) *trckd ldrs: effrt and cl up gng wl whn nt clr run over 1f out: btn whn hmpd ent fnl f* **66/1**

146 **12** *1* **Hermitage Court (USA)**[16] 5403 3-9-6 **84**.......... SWKelly 18 77
(BJMeehan) *wl in rr: n.m.r on inner over 3f out: rdn and no real prog over 2f out* **25/1**

-006 **13** *2 1/2* **Taminoula (IRE)**[9] 5566 3-8-13 **77**.......... JPMurtagh 5 64
(MrsAJPerrett) *lw: n.m.r s: towards rr: prog on outer and bmpd over 2f out: chsd ldrs over 1f out: sn wknd* **14/1**

3005 **14** *nk* **Barathea Dreams (IRE)**[14] 5443 3-9-3 **81**.......... MartinDwyer 7 68+
(JSMoore) *lw: racd freely: led after 1f to over 1f out: wkng whn hmpd ent fnl f* **20/1**

1500 **15** *1 1/4* **Malibu (IRE)**[16] 5399 3-8-12 **76**.......... PDoe 1 60+
(SDow) *lw: chsd ldr to 2f out: wkng whn hmpd ent fnl f* **66/1**

0000 **16** *1 1/4* **Overdrawn (IRE)**[15] 5419 3-9-2 **80**.......... TPQueally 3 61
(JAOsborne) *hld up wl in rr: rdn and no prog over 2f out* **50/1**

3160 **17** *8* **Habanero**[16] 5403 3-9-0 **78**.......... RLMoore 14 40
(RHannon) *chsd ldrs: rdn 3f out: wknd 2f out* **33/1**

1m 41.28s (-1.76) **Going Correction** +0.05s/f (Good) **17** Ran SP% **128.2**
Speed ratings: **110,109,108,108,108 107,106,106,106,104 104,103,100,100,99 97,89**CSF £64.32 CT £1549.49 TOTE £14.80: £2.90, £1.90, £4.60, £1.90; EX 101.40 Place 6 £68.99, Place 5 £20.89.
**Owner** The Four Players Partnership **Bred** Yeomanstown Stud **Trained** Middleham Moor, N Yorks

**FOCUS**
A decent handicap run in a good time and a cracking finish, but messy, with several hard-luck stories. The first two both improved a little, and several of those further back can be rated better than the bare form

**NOTEBOOK**
**Granston(IRE)** has been doing all his racing over seven furlongs of late and was well suited by this return to a mile. He was winning here off a 2lb higher mark than when last successful and this is his best trip.
**Evaluator(IRE)** has finished second in four of his last five starts and deserves a change of luck. He might benefit from a return to seven furlongs. *Official explanation: jockey said colt was hanging left throughout*
**Cello** has run many of his best races on softer ground and this fast surface did not suit so he deserves extra credit for finishing where he did.
**Border Music** was unlucky not to finish closer and still ran well considering this ground would have been too fast for him. He is quietly progressive and can win when returning to a slower surface.
**Alekhine(IRE)** was doing his best work at the death and a return to a mile two should see him return to winning ways.
**New Order** would not have won but may have been fourth had she got a clear run. She had been progressive prior to this and, although 7lb higher than when winning at Goodwood, can win again.
**Kodiac** was disappointing and failed to improve for this move into handicap company. He was hanging under pressure and may have had something amiss, so is possibly worth another chance. *Official explanation: jockey said colt lost his action*
**Jath** will be much more at home back on softer going and ran very well considering. She is lightly-raced and has more to offer.
**Zweibrucken(IRE)** did not enjoy much luck in running and is better than this.
T/Jkpt: Not won. T/Plt: £101.70 to a £1 stake. Pool: £87,005.10. 624.50 winning tickets. T/Qpdt: £15.30 to a £1 stake. Pool: £5,022.80. 241.80 winning tickets. JN

# 5287 HAYDOCK (L-H)

Friday, September 24

**OFFICIAL GOING: Heavy (soft in places)**
Wind: nil Weather: sunny

## 5767 BARRY CASE NORTH WEST LTD NURSERY 6f

**1:50** (1:52) (C1) 2-Y-0 **£10,868** (£3,344; £1,672; £836) **Stalls** Centre

Form RPR

0321 **1** **Tagula Sunrise (IRE)**[14] 5434 2-8-3 **77**.......... PHanagan 4 83
(RAFahey) *in tch: effrt and n.m.r wl over 1f out: sn rdn and styd on strly ins last to ld last 100 yds* **9/2**[1]

2215 **2** *1 3/4* **Harvest Warrior**[71] 3865 2-9-7 **95**.......... DAllan 15 96
(TDEasterby) *in tch: gd hdwy to ld 2f out: rdn over 1f out: drvn ins last: hdd and no ex last 100 yds* **16/1**

6023 **3** ¾ **Dahteer (IRE)**[13] [5453] 2-9-4 **92** ACulhane 3 91
(MRChannon) *chsd ldrs: effrt 2f out: sn rdn and kpt on same pce fnl f* **10/1**

21 **4** ½ **Throw The Dice**[50] [4487] 2-8-13 **87** NCallan 14 84
(KARyan) *hld up in tch: gd hdwy over 2f out: chal over 1f out and ev ch tl rdn and one pce fnl f* **11/2**[2]

0401 **5** *hd* **Missed A Beat**[17] [5376] 2-8-2 **76** WSupple 2 72
(MBlanshard) *chsd ldrs: rdn along 2f out: drvn and one pce fnl f* **33/1**

2100 **6** 1 ¼ **Make Us Flush**[5] [5670] 2-8-0 **74** FNorton 9 67
(ABerry) *hld up and bhd: hdwy 2f out: rdn over 1f out: styd on ins last: nrst fin* **12/1**

5304 **7** ½ **Celtic Spa (IRE)**[34] [4958] 2-8-9 **83** KDarley 6 74
(MrsPNDutfield) *in tch: rdn along over 2f out: kpt on same pce appr last* **8/1**

050 **8** 5 **Sydneyroughdiamond**[20] [5290] 2-8-1 **75** SRighton 8 51
(MMullineaux) *led: rdn along and hdd 2f out: sn wknd* **50/1**

340 **9** *nk* **Flying Dancer**[14] [5434] 2-7-12 **72** oh2 DKinsella 7 47
(AKing) *hld up in tch: effrt over 2f out: sn rdn and no imp* **50/1**

5000 **10** *nk* **Selkirk Storm (IRE)**[19] [5314] 2-7-12 **72** DaleGibson 12 46
(MWEasterby) *midfield: rdn along over 2f out: n.d* **12/1**

2315 **11** ½ **Dancing Rose (IRE)**[14] [5434] 2-8-2 **76** PRobinson 1 49
(CGCox) *chsd ldrs: rdn along over 2f out: sn wknd* **6/1**[3]

0500 **12** ½ **Cross My Shadow (IRE)**[11] [5509] 2-7-11 **74** oh9 ow2...(t) RThomas(3) 5 45
(MFHarris) *cl up: rdn along over 2f out: sn wknd* **100/1**

3555 **13** ½ **Mitchelland**[42] [4700] 2-7-12 **72** oh5...(v) DMernagh 10 42
(JamesMoffatt) *cl up: rdn along 1/2-way: wknd over 2f out* **50/1**

5000 **14** 1 ¼ **Tiviski (IRE)**[19] [5314] 2-7-13 **73** oh2 ow1 JQuinn 11 39
(EJAlston) *chsd ldrs: rdn along 1/2-way: sn wknd* **33/1**

1160 **15** 7 **Transaction (IRE)**[16] [5392] 2-9-1 **89** JTate 13 34
(JMPEustace) *racd wd: chsd ldrs: rdn along over 2f out and sn wknd* **10/1**

1m 17.89s (3.00) **Going Correction** +0.45s/f (Yiel) **15** Ran SP% **111.2**
Speed ratings: **98,95,94,94,93 92,91,84,84,83 83,82,81,80,70**CSF £67.80 CT £670.40 TOTE £6.20: £2.50, £4.20, £3.20; EX 72.10.
**Owner** David M Knaggs & Mel Roberts **Bred** Thomas Doherty **Trained** Musley Bank, N Yorks

**FOCUS**
A competitive nursery run at a decent enough pace, and the form looks strong. A race that should work out well.

**NOTEBOOK**
**Tagula Sunrise(IRE)**, off the mark in DBS St Leger Yearling Stakes at Doncaster on her previous start, followed up on her nursery debut in decisive fashion, handling the ground particularly well. She has really got the hang of things now and could win again in this grade, although connections may be temped to go for the Redcar Two-Year-Old Trophy.
**Harvest Warrior**, racing for the first time in 71 days, relished the ground and ran a cracking race under a positive ride, only giving way late on to the fast-finishing winner. Entitled to come on for the run, he could be worth keeping on your side for the remainder of the season under similar conditions, although he will not exactly be easy to place off a mark in the high 90s.
**Dahteer(IRE)** gained both his previous wins on ground with firm in the description, but he appeared to handle the testing conditions and ran well.
**Throw The Dice**, off the mark in a course and distance maiden that has not worked out very well, ran respectably in this much better contest, but did not find as much as had looked likely and may have got bogged down a little in this very testing ground. He is held in quite high regard and can be given another chance on less extreme going.
**Missed A Beat** had only ever raced on good to firm ground, but she did not appear to mind these very different conditions too much and acquitted herself creditably. She is going the right way and should continue to run well in nurseries.
**Make Us Flush** would have appreciated this ground but just got going a little too late. Not a bad effort in one the best races she has contested to date.
**Celtic Spa(IRE)** appeared to have conditions to suit but, although not running badly, she was not quite at her best.
**Dancing Rose(IRE)**, an unlucky fifth behind today's winner in a Sales race on her previous start, ran a long below that form and this ground must have been too soft for her, although she did win her maiden on an easy surface.
**Mitchelland** *Official explanation: jockey said filly ran too freely early on*

## 5768 VALE UK H'CAP — 1m 2f 120y
**2:20** (2:20) (D2) (0-85,85) 3-Y-O+ **£11,003** (£3,385; £1,692; £846) **Stalls** High

Form RPR

2351 **1** **Straw Bear (USA)**[7] [5607] 3-8-12 **83** 6ex SSanders 11 106+
(SirMarkPrescott) *trckd ldng pair: smooth hdwy to ld 3f out: pushed clr wl over 1f out: easily* **15/8**[1]

0460 **2** 5 **Sew'N'So Character (IRE)**[14] [5443] 3-9-0 **85** NCallan 9 94
(MBlanshard) *in tch: hdwy to trck ldrs over 4f out: rdn to chse wnr 2f out: sn drvn and no imp* **20/1**

2142 **3** 1 ¼ **Trouble Mountain (USA)**[7] [5607] 7-8-4 **71** PMulrennan(3) 16 78
(MWEasterby) *hld up and bhd: hdwy on outer over 3f out: rdn and hung lft wl over 1f out: sn drvn and kpt on same pce* **11/2**[2]

1002 **4** 2 ½ **Cruise Director**[136] [2022] 4-9-7 **85** RMullen 4 89+
(WJMusson) *hld up and bhd: hdwy 3f out: rdn along and styng on whn n.m.r ent last: nrst fin* **14/1**

2110 **5** 2 ½ **Mcqueen (IRE)**[13] [5459] 4-8-0 **71** oh5 AMullen(7) 3 70
(MrsHDalton) *dwlt: sn midfield on inner: hdwy 3f out: swtchd outside 2f out and sn rdn: drvn and kpt on same pce appr last* **20/1**

0005 **6** 1 **Intricate Web (IRE)**[8] [5590] 8-9-2 **80** DAllan 5 77
(EJAlston) *hld up towards rr: hdwy over 3f out: sn rdn along: kpt on fnl 2f: nvr nr ldrs* **25/1**

1200 **7** 1 ½ **Santiburi Lad (IRE)**[19] [5317] 7-8-2 **71** oh4 DTudhope(5) 1 65
(NWilson) *led 4f: prom tl rdn along 3f out: grad wknd* **33/1**

40-6 **8** 1 ¼ **Brooklyn's Gold (USA)**[193] [768] 9-9-0 **78** LEnstone 19 70
(IanWilliams) *bhd tl styd on fnl 3f* **50/1**

4201 **9** *shd* **Fort Churchill (IRE)**[10] [5538] 3-8-6 **77** 6ex...(b) PHanagan 7 69
(BEllison) *prom: led after 4f: rdn along and hdd 3f out: sn wknd* **6/1**[3]

355 **10** 1 ¼ **Safirah**[47] [4583] 3-8-2 **73** ow1 PRobinson 2 63
(MAJarvis) *in tch: rdn along 3f out: sn no imp* **20/1**

0214 **11** *hd* **Templet (USA)**[22] [5236] 4-8-5 **72**...(b) TEaves(3) 10 61
(ISemple) *chsd ldrs: rdn along over 3f out: grad wknd fnl 2f* **33/1**

4050 **12** 2 ½ **Dower House**[160] [1460] 9-8-12 **76** DMernagh 15 61
(AndrewTurnell) *a towards rr* **66/1**

2006 **13** 1 **Golano**[21] [5266] 4-8-12 **76**...(v[1]) DaneO'Neill 6 60
(PRWebber) *dwlt: sn chsng ldrs: rdn along over 4f out and sn wknd* **33/1**

2333 **14** 1 **Dream Magic**[9] [5568] 6-8-13 **77** MHenry 18 59
(MJRyan) *bhd fr 1/2-way* **14/1**

-213 **15** 12 **Triple Jump**[35] [4906] 3-8-4 **75** WSupple 17 36
(TDEasterby) *in tch: effrt over 4f out: sn rdn along and wknd over 2f out* **12/1**

-060 **16** *hd* **Sunny Glenn**[90] [3315] 6-9-2 **80** PMcCabe 8 41
(SimonEarle) *s.i.s: a rr* **66/1**

2000 **17** 13 **Akash (IRE)**[24] [5211] 4-9-7 **85** KDarley 14 24
(MJohnston) *chsd ldrs: rdn along 1/2-way: wknd 4f out* **40/1**

10-0 **18** 14 **Adjawar (IRE)**[41] [4754] 6-9-2 **80** RWinston 12 —
(JJQuinn) *a rr* **100/1**

1-44 **19** ½ **Kings Empire**[77] [3706] 3-8-11 **82**...(t) KMcEvoy 13 —
(DCarroll) *in tch whn hmpd and lost pl after 1 1/2f: bhd after* **66/1**

2m 17.25s (-0.48) **Going Correction** +0.15s/f (Good)
**WFA** 3 from 4yo+ 7lb **19** Ran SP% **122.3**
Speed ratings: **107,103,102,100,98 98,97,96,96,95 94,93,92,91,82 82,73,63,62**CSF £46.14 CT £189.90 TOTE £2.80: £1.30, £4.20, £1.70, £3.60; EX 38.90 Trifecta £217.60 Pool of £551.88 - 1.8 winning tickets.
**Owner** Chris Jenkins **Bred** Cyril Humphris **Trained** Newmarket, Suffolk

**FOCUS**
Just a fair handicap, but much improved form from Straw Bear, who is progressing into a very useful performer.

**NOTEBOOK**
**Straw Bear(USA)** ◆, who showed improved form when winning a similar event on soft ground over ten furlongs at Ayr on his previous start, progressed again under his 6lb penalty to follow up very easily. Making up into a very useful performer, he should complete the hat-trick.
**Sew'N'So Character(IRE)**, with just a six-furlong maiden win to his name well over a year previously, seemed to handle conditions well and ran a big race - he was just unfortunate to bump into such a well-handicapped rival.
**Trouble Mountain(USA)**, beaten just half a length by today's winner at Ayr on his previous start, was weighted to reverse that placing, racing off a mark 4lb lower than in future. He was put firmly in his place, which confirms just how fast Straw Bear is progressing.
**Cruise Director** ◆ ran a very encouraging first race in 136 days over a trip just short of his best and could be in for a good autumn.
**Mcqueen(IRE)** returned to reasonable form with a respectable effort from 5lb out of the handicap.
**Intricate Web(IRE)** did not run badly and is due to be dropped 2lb.
**Fort Churchill(IRE)**, claimed out of Mark Tompkins' yard after winning a Salisbury claimer by 13 lengths on his previous start, was 3lb well-in under his 6lb penalty for that success. Despite appearing to have conditions to suit, he ran a most disappointing race and has something to prove now.
**Dower House** *Official explanation: jockey said gelding was unsuited by heavy (soft in places) ground*

## 5769 BETFRED IN-RUNNING ON SPORTS H'CAP — 1m 30y
**2:50** (2:50) (C1) (0-100,97) 3-Y-O+ **£18,739** (£7,108; £3,554; £1,615) **Stalls** Low

Form RPR

6250 **1** **St Andrews (IRE)**[48] [4528] 4-9-5 **94** PRobinson 6 111+
(MAJarvis) *trckd ldrs gng wl: smooth hdwy to ld 2f out: rdn clr appr last: styd on strly* **9/4**[1]

3004 **2** 7 **Excelsius (IRE)**[20] [5291] 4-9-7 **96**...(b) KDarley 1 98
(JLDunlop) *s.i.s: plld hrd and sn in tch: pushed along and hdwy whn edgd lft 3f out: drvn and styd on fnl f* **11/1**

1055 **3** 1 ¼ **Imperialistic (IRE)**[25] [5194] 3-9-0 **93**...(p) SSanders 8 93
(KRBurke) *hld up: hdwy on outer 3f out: rdn wl over 2f out: sn drvn: edgd lft and one pce over 1f out* **3/1**[2]

0230 **4** 1 **Gift Horse**[80] [3597] 4-8-11 **86** RWinston 5 84
(JRFanshawe) *hld up towards rr: swtchd outside and hdwy over 2f out: rdn over 1f out and sn one pce* **6/1**

1301 **5** 3 ½ **Young Mr Grace (IRE)**[6] [5627] 4-8-11 **86** 6ex DAllan 10 77
(TDEasterby) *chsd clr ldr: effrt and ev ch 3f out: sn rdn and wknd fnl 2f* **5/1**[3]

0322 **6** 1 ¾ **Young Rooney**[13] [5459] 4-8-7 **82** oh12...(b[1]) LEnstone 2 69
(MMullineaux) *led and sn clr: rdn along 3f out: hdd 2f out and sn wknd* **25/1**

3620 **7** 1 ½ **Will He Wish**[13] [5462] 8-8-11 **89**...(b) TEaves(3) 9 73
(SGollings) *chsd ldrs: rdn along 3f out: wknd 2f out* **20/1**

6044 **8** 3 ½ **Resplendent One (IRE)**[55] [4322] 3-9-4 **97** KMcEvoy 3 74
(TGMills) *chsd ldrs on inner: rdn along and wkng whn hmpd 3f out: sn bhd* **16/1**

053- **9** 6 **Camille Pissarro (USA)**[332] [5814] 4-9-0 **89** DaneO'Neill 4 54
(DJWintle) *a rr* **40/1**

4/0- **10** 9 **Northern Desert (IRE)**[493] [1742] 5-9-7 **96** DarrenWilliams 7 43
(PWHiatt) *chsd ldrs over 3f out and sn wknd* **100/1**

1m 44.37s (-1.18) **Going Correction** +0.15s/f (Good)
**WFA** 3 from 4yo+ 4lb **10** Ran SP% **113.0**
Speed ratings: **111,104,102,101,98 96,95,91,85,76**CSF £26.18 CT £76.52 TOTE £3.40: £1.20, £3.00, £1.60; EX 37.50 Trifecta £102.10 Pool of £733.72 - 5.10 winning tickets.
**Owner** Team Havana **Bred** P D Savill **Trained** Newmarket, Suffolk

**FOCUS**
This looked competitive enough on paper, but St Andrews relished the ground and destroyed them in a respectable time. The runner-up has been rated up to this year's best, but the form further behind is not that solid.

**NOTEBOOK**
**St Andrews(IRE)** has been promising to produce a performance like this and, with the testing ground clearly in his favour, he delivered in some style. This form is Listed class, and he would have a big chance in the Cambridgeshire under a 5lb penalty if there is some cut in the ground.
**Excelsius(IRE)** was again inclined to race keenly in the blinkers, and he was no match whatsoever for the emphatic winner. A slightly disappointing effort considering conditions appeared ideal and he may need to come down in the weights a little more.
**Imperialistic(IRE)**, a little unlucky when not beaten far in a competitive handicap at Ripon on her previous start, had the cheekpieces back on but did not really build on that effort.
**Gift Horse** had never previously raced on ground easier than good and could only find the one pace under pressure.
**Young Mr Grace(IRE)** did not run to the form he showed to win when getting the run of the race at Ripon on his previous start, even allowing for his penalty.
**Resplendent One(IRE)** *Official explanation: jockey said he suffered interference in running*

## 5770 SUBSCRIBE TO RACING UK ON 08700 860432 MAIDEN STKS — 1m 30y
**3:25** (3:26) (D3) 3-Y-O+ **£3,679** (£1,132; £566; £283) **Stalls** Low

Form RPR

2 **1** **Musicanna**[111] [2693] 3-8-9...(t) RWinston 17 59+
(JRFanshawe) *towards rr: edgd lft and hdwy over 3f out: swtchd rt over 1f out: r.o to ld wl ins fnl f* **5/2**[1]

6350 **2** 1 ¾ **Foolish Groom**[54] [4360] 3-9-0 66 WSupple 10 60
(RHollinshead) *in tch: rdn and edgd lft over 2f out: styd on to ld briefly ins fnl f: hld towards fin* **11/2**

5200 **3** 3 **Santa Caterina (IRE)**[20] [5293] 3-8-9 69 SSanders 13 49+
(JLDunlop) *hld up: hdwy over 3f out: rdn over 2f out: one pce fr over 1f out* **11/4**[2]

-435 **4** *shd* **Tenny's Gold (IRE)**[11] [5511] 3-8-9 70 ACulhane 2 49
(BWHills) *trckd ldrs: wnt 2nd over 3f out: rdn over 2f out: ev ch ins fnl f: no ex towards fin* **9/2**[3]

0005 **5** 2 **The Loose Screw (IRE)**[51] 4444 6-9-4 35............................(p) KDarley 4 53?
(GMMoore) *led after 2f: rdn over 3f out: hdd ins fnl f: sn hmpd whn btn* **100/1**

00P0 **6** 2 ½ **Dances With Angels (IRE)**[73] 3827 4-8-13 35.................. PMQuinn 16 40
(JWUnett) *midfield: rdn and edgd lft over 3f out: kpt on one pce fnl 2f* **66/1**

**7** 1 **Dovedale**[87] 4-8-13 ................................................ VSlattery 9 38
(MrsMaryHambro) *s.i.s: hld up: rdn over 3f out: kpt on fnl f: nvr able to chal* **100/1**

00 **8** 1 ½ **Warbreck**[85] 3448 3-9-0 .................................................(b[1]) PHanagan 15 40
(CREgerton) *s.i.s: bhd: kpt on fnl f: nvr on terms* **33/1**

0000 **9** 2 **Aggi Mac**[6] 5637 3-8-2 35........................................(e) SuzanneFrance(7) 6 31
(AndrewTurnell) *s.i.s: sn in tch: rdn and wknd over 2f out* **100/1**

**10** ¾ **Alghaazy (IRE)** 3-8-11 .......................................... NMackay(3) 14 35
(LMCumani) *hld up: pushed along 3f out: nvr nr to chal* **10/1**

**11** 3 ½ **Bodfari Dream** 3-8-9 ............................................... LEnstone 18 23
(MMullineaux) *s.s: a bhd* **100/1**

**12** 1 **Delta Star** 4-8-13 ..................................................... NCallan 8 21
(KARyan) *in tch: rdn over 3f out: wknd 2f out* **25/1**

P00- **13** ¾ **Carnt Spell**[332] 5822 3-9-0 ........................................ ANicholls 7 24
(MsDeborahJEvans) *led 2f: remained prom: rdn over 3f out: wknd 2f out* **100/1**

**14** 1 ½ **Jack's Check** 3-9-0 ................................................ RMullen 12 21
(NTinkler) *s.s: a bhd* **100/1**

600 **15** 2 **Classic Expression**[36] 4880 3-8-9 45.......................... GGibbons 1 12
(BAMcmahon) *in tch: rdn and wknd over 4f out* **33/1**

0-0 **16** 5 **Pearl Island (USA)**[6] 5656 3-9-0 .............................. MTebbutt 3 7
(DJWintle) *s.s: a towards rr* **100/1**

**17** 19 **Marburyanna** 4-8-13 .............................................. SRighton 5 —
(MMullineaux) *in tch: lost pl after 3f: n.d after* **100/1**

1m 47.43s (1.88) **Going Correction** +0.15s/f (Good)
**WFA** 3 from 4yo+ 4lb **17 Ran SP% 117.0**
Speed ratings: **96,94,91,91,89 86,85,84,82,81 77,76,76,74,72 67,48**CSF £15.01 TOTE £3.30: £1.90, £2.00, £1.80; EX 23.60.
**Owner** Abdulla Buhaleeba **Bred** P D And Mrs Player **Trained** Newmarket, Suffolk

**FOCUS**
They went a good pace, but this is a weak maiden and the form is held down by the poor horses in fifth and sixth. It looks unlikely to produce many winners outside the lower grades, but the winner is better than the bare form.

**NOTEBOOK**
**Musicanna**, a five-length second to subsequent St James' Palace Stakes sixth Castleton in June on her only previous start, was fitted with a tongue tie for her return. Drawn very wide, she had to be dropped in and soon had plenty to do, but she found enough under pressure and eventually won going away. She did not need to reproduce her debut form to beat a gelding rated just 66, but things did not go her way and she is better than the bare form.
**Foolish Groom**, with both the tongue tie and cheekpieces left off, ran well but always looked like being reeled in by the winner when that one hit top stride.
**Santa Caterina(IRE)**, having her first run on ground easier than good and dropped two and a half furlongs in trip, just plugged on at the one pace. She appeared to handle the ground well enough, but should be suited by a return to further.
**Tenny's Gold(IRE)** can have no real excuses and did little to justify her rating of 70.
**The Loose Screw(IRE)**, rated 35, helps put the form into perspective.
**Alghaazy(IRE)**, a 65,000euro, half-brother to a useful miler, could never pose a threat. This would have been quite a test for a newcomer and he can be given another chance.
**Bodfari Dream** *Official explanation: jockey said he was hit in the face by filly as gates opened*

## 5771 VISITSTHELENS.COM MAIDEN FILLIES' STKS 6f

**4:00** (4:00) (D3) 2-Y-O £3,679 (£1,132; £566; £283) **Stalls** Centre

Form RPR

0432 **1** **Alexia Rose (IRE)**[8] 5586 2-8-11 73........................................ FLynch 13 82
(ABerry) *cl up: led 1/2-way: rdn: flashed tail and wandered ins last: styd on* **4/1**[3]

2000 **2** 2 ½ **Molly Marie (IRE)**[14] 5434 2-8-11 77.................................. DAllan 10 75
(TDEasterby) *in tch: effrt and hdwy 2f out: rdn to chse wnr over 1f out: kpt on* **6/4**[1]

6 **3** 1 **Squaw Dance**[39] 4809 2-8-11 ............................................ PHanagan 5 72
(WJHaggas) *towards rr: hdwy over 2f out: rdn over 1f out: kpt on same pce fnl f* **15/8**[2]

6 **4** 1 ½ **Sand Iron (IRE)**[17] 5380 2-8-11 ....................................... RFitzpatrick 3 67
(SLKeightley) *chsd ldrs: rdn along over 2f out: kpt on same pce approaching last* **25/1**

0 **5** shd **Danzatrice**[21] 5262 2-8-8 .................................................. TEaves(3) 7 67
(CWThornton) *hld up towards rr: hdwy over 2f out: kpt on wl fnl f: nrst fin* **50/1**

0 **6** shd **Joyeaux**[17] 5375 2-8-11 ............................................... RHavlin 2 66
(SLKeightley) *led to 1/2-way: sn rdn along and grad wknd fnl 2f* **50/1**

**7** 6 **Taragan** 2-8-7 ............................................................... RWinston 4 44
(JJQuinn) *s.i.s and bhd tl sme late hdwy* **50/1**

5500 **8** hd **Kilmovee**[11] 5520 2-8-11 67.................................................. ACulhane 8 48
(NTinkler) *cl up: rdn along 1/2-way: wknd fnl 2f* **33/1**

**9** ½ **Stevmarie Star** 2-8-7 ................................................... FNorton 9 42
(JAGlover) *s.i.s: a towards rr* **33/1**

05 **10** 1 **Swallow Falls (IRE)**[54] 4359 2-8-11 ................................. LEnstone 1 43
(DMccain) *chsd ldrs: rdn along 1/2-way: sn wknd* **33/1**

5 **11** 5 **Polar Passion**[13] 5455 2-8-11 ......................................... WSupple 14 28
(RHollinshead) *in tch on outer to 1/2-way: sn outpcd and bhd fnl 2f* **50/1**

**12** 2 **Lirage** 2-8-7 ........................................................... SRighton 12 18
(MMullineaux) *a rr* **100/1**

**13** 1 ½ **Just Elizabeth** 2-8-5 ow1........................................... PMulrennan(3) 6 15
(MESowersby) *wnt lft s: rdn along in midfield 1/2-way: sn wknd* **40/1**

**14** 12 **Witchy Vibes** 2-8-7 ................................................ GGibbons 11 —
(MAppleby) *outpcd and bhd fr 1/2-way* **100/1**

1m 17.92s (3.03) **Going Correction** +0.45s/f (Yiel) **14 Ran SP% 119.7**
Speed ratings: **97,93,92,90,90 90,82,81,81,79 73,70,68,52**CSF £9.57 TOTE £5.10: £1.80, £1.30, £1.10; EX 10.50.
**Owner** Pisani Plc **Bred** Sonarc Bloodstock **Trained** Cockerham, Lancs

**FOCUS**
No strength in depth, and just three horses were sent off at single-figure odds. A deserved first success for Alexia Rose, but a suspicion that runner-up Molly Marie would prefer faster ground.

**NOTEBOOK**
**Alexia Rose(IRE)**, runner-up on firm ground in a Pontefract maiden on her previous start, relished these drastically different conditions and got off the mark in most decisive fashion, despite flashing her tail and hanging when in the clear. Given that the runner-up is rated 77, she is likely to take a sharp rise in the weights and would therefore be of interest if turned out in a nursery under a penalty.
**Molly Marie(IRE)**, very unlucky when a beaten favourite in the DBS St Leger Yearling Stakes on her previous start, was unable to confirm that and simply lacked the change of pace shown by the winner in these testing conditions.
**Squaw Dance**, a promising enough sixth of 17 in an ordinary Windsor maiden on her debut 39 days previously, was clearly expected to improve on that and did so. She lacked the pace of the front two and should appreciate a step up to seven furlongs.
**Sand Iron(IRE)**, dropped a furlong in trip and switched from Polytrack to turf, ran respectably and showed enough ability to suggest there is a small race in her, although it may well come when she is handicapped.
**Danzatrice** stepped up on her debut running and is going the right way.
**Joyeaux** did not quite last home, but still offered promise. She will probably do better when handicapped and is one to keep in mind if she drops to the minimum trip.

## 5772 TELINDUS MAIDEN STKS (C&G) 6f

**4:35** (4:38) (D3) 2-Y-O £3,523 (£1,084; £542; £271) **Stalls** Centre

Form RPR

3 **1** **Dramaticus**[143] 1871 2-8-11 ............................................ SSanders 7 89+
(DRLoder) *hld up: hdwy over 2f out: led over 1f out: r.o* **7/2**[1]

**2** 1 ¾ **Rio Riva** 2-8-11 .......................................................... RWinston 6 84+
(MissJACamacho) *s.s: towards rr: hdwy 2f out: wnt 2nd ins fnl f: styd on: nt rch wnr* **14/1**

5 **3** 2 ½ **Breathing Fire**[27] 5118 2-8-11 ...................................... RMullen 5 76
(WJMusson) *s.i.s: trckd ldrs: rdn over 1f out: styd on same pce* **9/2**[2]

230 **4** 2 **Sacranun**[20] 5290 2-8-8 .............................................. NMackay(3) 11 70
(LMCumani) *midfield: rdn over 1f out: kpt on: nt pce to chal* **9/2**[2]

0 **5** 3 **Primarily**[9] 5555 2-8-11 ............................................... FLynch 10 61
(ABerry) *dwlt: bhd: sn pushed along: effrt over 1f out: nvr able to chal* **100/1**

25 **6** nk **Lord Mayfair (USA)**[10] 5543 2-8-11 ................................ PHanagan 3 60
(TDBarron) *led: rdn and hdd over 2f out: wknd 1f out* **7/2**[1]

605 **7** ½ **Hits Only Cash**[8] 5578 2-8-11 ....................................... PBradley 8 59
(PABlockley) *hld up: pushed along over 2f out: nvr on terms* **100/1**

3 **8** ¾ **Glad Big (GER)**[17] 5376 2-8-11 ..................................... MFenton 1 57
(JAOsborne) *restless in stalls: prom: led over 2f out: hdd over 1f out: sn wknd* **13/2**[3]

**9** 3 ½ **Golden Square** 2-8-11 ................................................ WSupple 2 46
(BJMeehan) *s.s: rn green: a bhd* **20/1**

0 **10** 5 **Diamond Heritage**[73] 3818 2-8-11 ................................. FNorton 4 31
(JAGlover) *trckd ldrs: rdn over 2f out: wknd over 1f out* **100/1**

**11** nk **Ruman (IRE)** 2-8-11 ................................................... NCallan 12 30
(MJAttwater) *wnt rt s: in tch: rdn and wknd over 1f out* **100/1**

0 **12** 13 **El Potro**[24] 5209 2-8-11 ............................................... GGibbons 9 —
(BAMcmahon) *trckd ldrs: rdn over 2f out: wknd over 1f out* **25/1**

1m 17.41s (2.52) **Going Correction** +0.45s/f (Yiel) **12 Ran SP% 113.4**
Speed ratings: **101,98,95,92,88 88,87,86,81,75 74,57**CSF £49.85 TOTE £3.90: £1.90, £2.60, £2.00; EX 45.80.
**Owner** Derek And Jean Clee **Bred** D D And Mrs Jean P Clee **Trained** Newmarket, Suffolk

**FOCUS**
The pace was good, resutling in a creditable time, and they finished well strung out. This has provisionally been rated strong maiden form from the principals.

**NOTEBOOK**
**Dramaticus**, beaten at odds on in similar conditions at Warwick on his only previous outing 143 days previously, gained compensation with a straightforward success, travelling well and finding plenty on ground he bred to relish. He is still in the Middle Park, but in the meantime connections must be tempted by his entry in the Redcar Two-Year-Old Trophy, especially if the mud is flying.
**Rio Riva** ♦, a half-brother to high-class six-furlong juvenile River Belle, was supported at big odds beforehand. He recovered well from a slow start and showed good tactical speed to get into a challenging position as the pace quickened, but he simply met one too good on the day. A very promising debut from a colt who looks well up to winning a similar event.
**Breathing Fire**, who made a promising debut in a decent Newmarket maiden, again ran creditably and looks to be going the right way.
**Sacranun** again failed to produce a turn of foot and may be worth trying over seven furlongs.
**Primarily** showed improved form for the step up in trip and switch to easier ground and is getting the hang of things. He should progress again could be an interesting type for back-end nurseries.
**Lord Mayfair(USA)** showed up well early on, but was unable to sustain his effort and was disappointing, even allowing for having gone off quite fast. *Official explanation: jockey said gelding became upset in stalls*
**Hits Only Cash** should find things easier in nurseries, possibly over a little further.
**Glad Big(GER)** did not improve on his promising debut and this ground may have been against him.
**El Potro** *Official explanation: jockey said colt was tired in drying ground*

## 5773 RACING UK ON CHANNEL 432 H'CAP 1m 3f 200y

**5:10** (5:10) (E3) (0-70,74) 3-Y-O+ £3,885 (£1,195; £597; £298) **Stalls** High

Form RPR

6-50 **1** **Ivy League Star (IRE)**[112] 2665 3-8-7 62.............................. ACulhane 7 78+
(BWHills) *midfield: hdwy whn nt clr run over 2f out: swtchd rt over 1f out: r.o to ld cl home* **50/1**

3111 **2** nk **Artistic Style**[8] 5584 4-9-10 74 6ex.................................. TEaves(3) 14 84+
(BEllison) *midfield: hdwy over 2f out: led over f out: hdd cl home* **11/4**[2]

620 **3** 3 ½ **Miss Inkha**[20] 5293 3-8-6 61........................................... JQuinn 10 66
(RGuest) *prom: lost pl over 5f out: rallied over 3f out: led briefly over 1f out: no ex ins fnl f* **66/1**

0211 **4** ½ **Circassian (IRE)**[6] 5635 3-9-4 73 6ex............................... SSanders 13 77+
(SirMarkPrescott) *midfield: rdn on wd outside and hung lft over 3f out: hdwy over 2f out: kpt on fnl f* **7/4**[1]

5113 **5** ½ **Bramantino (IRE)**[17] 5374 4-9-4 65.................................(b) PHanagan 6 69
(RAFahey) *in tch: hdwy 3f out: rdn over 2f out: one pce fnl f* **11/1**

004 **6** ¾ **Onward To Glory (USA)**[39] 4819 4-9-4 65........................ KMcEvoy 3 68
(JLDunlop) *hld up: hdwy over 3f out: rdn over 2f out: no ex ins fnl f* **66/1**

-122 **7** hd **Can Can Flyer (IRE)**[17] 5365 3-8-13 68.............................. KDarley 16 70
(MJohnston) *chsd ldrs: rdn 4f out: wknd 1f out* **7/1**[3]

0000 **8** 1 ¾ **Karathaena (IRE)**[143] 1857 4-8-5 55................................ PMulrennan(3) 4 55
(MESowersby) *midfield: rdn and hdwy over 2f out: wknd fnl f* **100/1**

6503 **9** nk **Sudden Flight (IRE)**[37] 4849 7-9-6 67................................ RHavlin 19 67
(PDEvans) *hld up: rdn over 3f out: hdwy over 2f out: one pce fnl f* **11/1**

0532 **10** ½ **General**[28] 5085 7-9-2 66................................................ RThomas(3) 1 65
(CRDore) *sn led: hdd over 5f out: rdn to regain ld over 2f out: hdd over 1f out: sn wknd* **14/1**

000 **11** 5 **Estepona**[20] 5293 3-8-8 63............................................. GParkin 5 55
(MissJACamacho) *bhd: rdn over 3f out: sme late hdwy: nvr trbld ldrs* **66/1**

0030 **12** 1 **Red Skelton (IRE)**[6] 5635 3-8-5 60..................................... ANicholls 12 50+
(MsDeborahJEvans) *in rr: rdn and nt clr run over 2f out: sn swtchd rt: sme late hdwy: nvr trbld ldrs* **50/1**

5123 **13** 3 **Danebank (IRE)**[28] 5073 4-8-7 54....................................(p) DaleGibson 8 40
(JMackie) *in tch: rdn and wknd over 2f out* **22/1**

0050 **14** *8* **Sun Hill**[132] 2116 4-9-6 **67** DSweeney 18 42
(MBlanshard) *a bhd* **50/1**
1500 **15** *2½* **Archie Babe (IRE)**[23] 5229 8-9-5 **66** RWinston 2 38
(JJQuinn) *cl up: rdn 4f out: sn wknd* **16/1**
5-50 **16** *9* **Flight Commander (IRE)**[18] 5344 4-9-3 **64** DAllan 17 23
(ISemple) *in tch: rdn over 3f out: sn wknd* **66/1**
0040 **17** *2½* **Anduril**[29] 5057 3-8-5 **60** (b[1]) JTate 9 15
(JMPEustace) *racd keenly: midfield: hdwy to ld over 5f out: rdn and hdd over 2f out: sn wknd* **100/1**
050 **18** *10* **Celebre Citation (IRE)**[27] 5123 3-8-5 **60** (t) RMullen 15 1
(JRFanshawe) *a bhd* **50/1**
0523 **19** *9* **Super King**[25] 5189 3-8-11 **66** FNorton 20 —
(NBycroft) *midfield: bmpd 6f out: bhd after* **50/1**
656/ **20** *6* **Desert City**[533] 5297 5-9-4 **65** DaneO'Neill 11 —
(PRWebber) *in tch: rdn and wknd 4f out* **100/1**

2m 36.84s (1.68) **Going Correction** +0.15s/f (Good)
**WFA** 3 from 4yo+ 8lb **20** Ran SP% **127.8**
Speed ratings: **100,99,97,97,96 96,96,95,94,94 91,90,88,83,81 75,73,67,61,57**CSF £185.94 CT £9310.61 TOTE £48.70: £6.60, £1.40, £10.00, £1.20; EX 417.90 Place 6 £7.53, Place 5 £2.79.
**Owner** D M James **Bred** Orpendale **Trained** Lambourn, Berks

**FOCUS**
They went a decent pace and the form looks very reliable for the grade. The finish was dominated by two well-treated horses.

**NOTEBOOK**
**Ivy League Star(IRE)**, well beaten on her handicap debut on Fibresand when last seen 112 days previously, left that form behind to get off the mark, despite still looking in need of the experience. There should be plenty more to come and it will be disappointing if she does not add to this.
**Artistic Style**, 2lb well-in under his 6lb penalty, was racing over his furthest trip and ran a game race in defeat under his big weight - he did not fail through lack of stamina. Still progressing, he should be competitive off higher marks.
**Miss Inkha**, runner-up on heavy ground at Brighton two starts back, again showed her liking for a slog and ran well.
**Circassian(IRE)**, chasing the hat-trick off a 4lb lower than in future, was forced to come widest of all with his effort and could only muster the one pace.
**Bramantino(IRE)** ran respectably off a mark 7lb higher than when last successful.
**General** *Official explanation: jockey said gelding hung right-handed*
T/Plt: £8.10 to a £1 stake. Pool: £49,593.95. 4,422.85 winning tickets. T/Qpdt: £3.00 to a £1 stake. Pool: £2,543.70. 607.70 winning tickets. JR

5774 - 5777a (Foreign Racing) - See Raceform Interactive

## 5761 ASCOT (R-H)

Saturday, September 25

**OFFICIAL GOING: Good to firm (firm in places)**
Wind: nil Weather: steady rain first four races

### 5778 HACKNEY EMPIRE ROYAL LODGE STKS (GROUP 2) (C&G) 1m (R)
1:55 (1:56) (A1) 2-Y-O **£58,000** (£22,000; £11,000; £5,000) **Stalls** High

Form RPR
121 **1** **Perfectperformance (USA)**[45] 4639 2-8-11 100 LDettori 1 112+
(SaeedBinSuroor) *lw: trckd ldrs: effrt to ld wl over 1f out: edgd rt and hrd pressed ent fnl f: rdn and in command last 100yds* **4/6**[1]
**2** *1½* **Scandinavia (USA)**[56] 4355 2-8-11 JPSpencer 6 109
(APO'Brien, Ire) *w'like: scope: hld up in rr: prog over 1f out: edgd rt and chsd wnr jst over 1f out: str chal sn after: hld last 100yds* **8/1**[3]
2124 **3** *1¼* **Wilko (USA)**[15] 5437 2-8-11 100 EAhern 8 112+
(JNoseda) *trckd ldrs: effrt to chal 2f out: unable qck and hld whn n.m.r twice over 1f out: styd on ins fnl f* **7/1**[2]
116 **4** *½* **Elliots World (IRE)**[15] 5437 2-8-11 KDarley 7 105
(MJohnston) *sweating: led: rdn and hdd wl over 1f out: fdd ins fnl f* **9/1**
23 **5** *1¾* **Frith (IRE)**[57] 4292 2-8-11 MHills 5 101
(BWHills) *settled in last: rdn over 2f out: kpt on fnl f: n.d* **25/1**
030 **6** *¾* **Kandidate**[49] 4527 2-8-11 90 SSanders 3 99
(CEBrittain) *lw: hld up in last trio: effrt on outer over 2f out: one pce and no imp* **80/1**
1125 **7** *1¾* **Grand Marque (IRE)**[15] 5437 2-8-11 96 KFallon 4 96
(RHannon) *chsd ldrs: rdn 3f out: lost pl and btn 2f out* **14/1**
6251 **8** *nk* **Berkhamsted (IRE)**[35] 4963 2-8-11 100 DHolland 2 95
(JAOsborne) *pressed ldr: chal 2f out: losing pl and btn whn bdly hmpd over 1f out* **20/1**

1m 41.89s (-1.15) **Going Correction** +0.10s/f (Good) **8** Ran SP% **110.1**
Speed ratings: **109,107,106,105,104 103,101,101**CSF £5.81 TOTE £1.60: £1.10, £1.40, £1.90; EX 5.40 Trifecta £19.80 Pool: £1,140.74. 40.78 winning units..
**Owner** Godolphin **Bred** Brushwood Stable **Trained** Newmarket, Suffolk

**FOCUS**
Just an average renewal of this Group Two, but run a third of a second faster than the following fillies' contest. Perfectperformance built on his solid conditions race form, and Wilko and Elliots World give the race a solid look.

**NOTEBOOK**
**Perfectperformance(USA)** ◆ is progressing well and took the step up from Listed to Group company in his stride. Always in a good position, he went on early in the straight and resisted the challenge of the runner-up to score going away. He is likely to take his chance in the Racing Post Trophy next, and while a strict interpretation of this form through the third and fourth puts him a few pounds behind the likes of Etlaala and Iceman, he is going the right way. His style of racing suggests he will stay middle distances next season.
**Scandinavia(USA)** was taking a big step up in class but made the transition with little difficulty and ran his best race yet. He followed the winner through and looked as if he might prevail at the furlong pole, but had nothing in reserve in the closing stages. He should continue to progress and it would be no surprise with his pedigree if he was aimed at the Kentucky Derby next season.
**Wilko(USA)**is a most consistent performer and a good yardstick. He again ran his race but was squeezed up when trying to deliver a challenge halfway up the straight, but for which he would have finished closer. He has been in the frame in all six Pattern events he has contested, and deserves to win one. Races such as the Horris Hill and Somerville Tattersall Stakes will possibly provide his best chance.
**Elliots World(IRE)** was again warm beforehand, but ran better than he had at Doncaster and seemed suited by the switch to forcing tactics. In the end he was well held, but he may be better as a three-year-old, when hopefully he will be more relaxed.
**Frith(IRE)** was stepping up from maiden company and ran on in the straight without ever looking likely to land a blow. His pedigree suggests he will be a better horse next year over middle distances, and he should have no difficulty winning races.
**Kandidate** had a fair amount to find on the evidence of his previous form, but at least reversed Newbury placings with Grand Marque. He should be capable of winning a maiden on what he has shown so far.
**Grand Marque(IRE)** finished much further behind the winner than he had at Salisbury, and looks out of his depth at this level. He is in danger of becoming a 'twilight' horse.
**Berkhamsted(IRE)**, a Listed winner in France last time, raced prominently but was just beginning to lose his pitch when becoming the worst sufferer in some buffeting halfway up the straight. If none the worse he can return to winning ways, given a slight drop in class and some cut in the ground.

### 5779 MEON VALLEY STUD FILLIES' MILE (GROUP 1) 1m (R)
2:30 (2:31) (A1) 2-Y-O **£116,000** (£44,000; £22,000; £10,000) **Stalls** High

Form RPR
211 **1** **Playful Act (IRE)**[16] 5413 2-8-10 90 JFortune 2 113
(JHMGosden) *lw: mde all: drvn 2l clr wl over 1f out: styd on u.p* **11/4**[2]
1213 **2** *1* **Maids Causeway (IRE)**[16] 5413 2-8-10 100 MHills 8 111
(BWHills) *prom: rdn to chse wnr over 2f out: kpt on fnl f but a hld* **7/1**[3]
21 **3** *¾* **Dash To The Top**[18] 5368 2-8-10 DHolland 6 110+
(LMCumani) *lw: wl in tch: effrt whn hmpd jst over 2f out: styd on again fnl f* **16/1**
**4** *shd* **Mona Lisa**[41] 4783 2-8-10 JPSpencer 4 112+
(APO'Brien, Ire) *w'like: trckd ldrs: effrt whn bdly hmpd jst over 2f out: rallied over 1f out: styd on ins fnl f* **14/1**
1 **5** *2* **Shohrah (IRE)**[64] 4074 2-8-10 RHills 1 105
(MPTregoning) *dwlt: settled in rr: effrt on outer over 2f out: sn rdn and no imp on ldrs* **10/1**
11 **6** *shd* **Joint Aspiration**[22] 5272 2-8-10 TEDurcan 7 104
(MRChannon) *dwlt: settled towards rr: rdn over 2f out: one pce and no prog over 1f out* **20/1**
1 **7** *1¾* **Echelon**[28] 5118 2-8-10 KFallon 5 104+
(SirMichaelStoute) *lw: dwlt: rn in snatches in rr: effrt on outer whn nt clr run 2f out: one pce and no ch whn nt clr run ent fnl f* **15/8**[1]
311 **8** *3* **Dubai Surprise (IRE)**[27] 5149 2-8-10 100 LDettori 3 94
(DRLoder) *chsd wnr to over 2f out: wkng whn sltly hmpd sn after* **7/1**[3]
6200 **9** *7* **Ghasiba (IRE)**[17] 5391 2-8-10 82 SSanders 9 78+
(CEBrittain) *last whn n.m.r and snatched up after 2f: lost tch w rest over 3f out* **100/1**

1m 42.22s (-0.82) **Going Correction** +0.10s/f (Good) **9** Ran SP% **113.8**
Speed ratings: **108,107,106,106,104 104,102,99,92**CSF £22.09 TOTE £4.00: £1.60, £2.30, £3.40; EX 21.40 Trifecta £253.10 Pool: £2,210.92. 6.20 winning units..
**Owner** Sangster Family **Bred** Swettenham Stud **Trained** Manton, Wilts

**FOCUS**
A decent renewal of this important juvenile fillies' contest, but a roughish race behind the all-the-way winner. With the first two running close to their May Hill form and the time only a third of a second slower than the preceding colts' event the form looks solid.

**NOTEBOOK**
**Playful Act(IRE)** ◆ is progressing well with racing and confirmed Doncaster placings with the runner-up, who was 3lb better off. She is a game sort and, as a full-sister to Percussionist, is likely to go into the winter as favourite for the Oaks. Connections report she will go directly for the 1000 Guineas before Epsom, but it would not be the biggest surprise if Godolphin stepped in to buy her, as they did with her half-sister Echoes In Eternity.
**Maids Causeway(IRE)** is proving a most consistent performer, having won twice and never out of the first three in her four other races. The Rockfel is a possibility and, if her new owner resisits the temptation to ship her home to the States, she has Classic potential.
**Dash To The Top** ◆, representing the sponsors, was taking a big step up in class and showed distinct signs of inexperience by running around in the straight, doing a couple of her rivals no favours in the process. She has plenty of stamina influences in her pedigree, although her dam only stayed ten furlongs, and could well develop into an Oaks contender.
**Mona Lisa** ◆, cost 1.25m guineas but had been beaten at odds on on both her previous outings, ran a fine race considering she was knocked right back early in the straight. She showed plenty of tenacity to get back into the frame and should have no difficulty winning decent races. She is likely to be one of her yard's principal Oaks contenders.
**Shohrah(IRE)**, a rangy sort, had the outside draw and was forced to race wide. She kept on without ever looking likley to reach the principals, and at this stage appeals as the type to be suited by the York and Doncaster in the second half of next season rather than Epsom.
**Joint Aspiration**, a dual winner but stepping up in grade, had her limitations exposed at this level. She may appreciate a softer surface.
**Echelon**, favourite on the strength of her debut success from a subsequent winner and the fact that connections have several other high class juvenile fillies, seemed to find this step up too much for her at this stage. She was not helped by being hampered twice in the straight, and deserves another chance, possibly at a slightly lower level.
**Dubai Surprise(IRE)** was somewhat disappointing after her Goodwood Group Three win, but the much quicker ground may have been the reason.

### 5780 GNER DIADEM STKS (GROUP 2) 6f (R)
3:00 (3:03) (A1) 3-Y-O+ **£58,000** (£22,000; £11,000; £5,000) **Stalls** High

Form RPR
2115 **1** **Pivotal Point**[7] 5647 4-9-0 100 SSanders 6 119
(PJMakin) *lw: t.k.h: trckd ldr: led over 1f out: sn rdn clr* **11/2**[2]
1603 **2** *3* **Airwave**[7] 5647 4-8-11 108 JPSpencer 4 107+
(HCandy) *lw: hld up rr: smooth prog 2f out: effrt jst over 1f out: chsd wnr ins fnl f: one pce* **4/1**[1]
3221 **3** *1¼* **The Tatling (IRE)**[7] 5647 7-9-4 116 RLMoore 12 110
(JMBradley) *trckd ldrs: gng wl 2f out: rdn and one pce over 1f out* **6/1**[3]
0610 **4** *hd* **Celtic Mill**[7] 5647 6-9-0 104 (p) DHolland 2 106
(DWBarker) *led: rdn and hdd over 1f out: one pce fnl f* **12/1**
4002 **5** *1¾* **Country Reel (USA)**[11] 5553 4-9-0 110 (t) LDettori 10 100
(SaeedBinSuroor) *prom: rdn 2f out: outpcd and btn over 1f out* **7/1**
0000 **6** *1* **Capricho (IRE)**[7] 5628 7-9-0 99 RHughes 7 97
(JAkehurst) *stdd s: hld up in last pair: stdy prog on inner 2f out: shkn up over 1f out: nt pce to rch ldrs* **40/1**
2411 **7** *¾* **Ringmoor Down**[20] 5327 5-8-11 108 TQuinn 1 92
(DWPArbuthnot) *lw: racd in last pair: rdn 3f out: no prog tl kpt on fnl f* **9/1**
3215 **8** *½* **Simianna**[6] 5671 5-8-11 97 (p) TEDurcan 3 91
(ABerry) *t.k.h early: racd wd: chsd ldrs: lost pl and rdn over 2f out: n.d after* **50/1**
6101 **9** *nk* **Mac Love**[16] 5422 3-8-12 103 GCarter 11 93
(JAkehurst) *chsd ldrs: pushed along and outpcd whn nt clr run briefly over 1f out: no ch after* **12/1**
5054 **10** *1¾* **Golden Nun**[16] 5414 4-8-11 104 (b) RWinston 9 85
(TDEasterby) *chsd ldrs: rdn over 2f out: wknd over 1f out: eased fnl f* **25/1**
0-10 **11** *nk* **Ratio**[21] 5289 6-9-0 (t) PRobinson 8 87
(JEHammond, France) *lw: midfield whn no room and snatched up after 1f: toiling in rr after* **11/2**[2]
1200 **12** *3½* **Steenberg (IRE)**[79] 3674 5-9-0 111 NCallan 5 76
(MHTompkins) *racd midfield: rdn 1/2-way: hanging and wknd 2f out* **12/1**

1m 13.55s **Going Correction** 0.0s/f (Good)
**WFA** 3 from 4yo+ 2lb **12** Ran SP% **118.9**
Speed ratings: CSF £27.43 TOTE £6.00: £2.30, £1.90, £2.30; EX 28.00 Trifecta £82.40 Pool: £2,079.36. 17.90 winning units..
**Owner** R A Bernard **Bred** T R Lock **Trained** Ogbourne Maisey, Wilts

**FOCUS**

Traditionally a competitive sprint, but run on the round track due to the redevelopment of the course, so a new experience for many. Pivotal Point was a clear-cut winner and continues on the upgrade.

**NOTEBOOK**

**Pivotal Point** ◆, who has really progressed this summer, turned this competitive contest on paper into something of a procession. Connections blamed his defeat the previous week on the loose ground at Newbury (it had evidently been nearer good to firm than the official good to soft when he won at Longchamp) and he reversed placings with old rival The Tatling in no uncertain manner. The Prix de l'Abbaye will only tempt if the rain stays away, and Hong Kong at the end of the year is a more appealing option if he is invited. Whatever his fate this season, he will be a major contender for sprint honours in 2005.

**Airwave**, who finished ahead of the winner at Newbury the previous week, brought down the curtain on her career with another fine effort, despite apparently not handling the bend into the straight. Winner of the Cheveley Park at two, the Temple Stakes at three, and a Listed event this season, she will attract huge interest at the December sales.

**The Tatling(IRE)** ◆, who beat the first two at Newbury the previous week, ran another decent race but looks much more effective over five. He will now go to the Prix de l'Abbaye, in which he finished third last year, and is likely to have the race run to suit.

**Celtic Mill**, as usual set off in front, and when headed stuck to his task quite well. He is in the form of his life at present, and it would be no surprise if he won again before the season is out, especially on a flat track. *Official explanation: jockey said gelding slipped coming out of stalls and hung right in home straight*

**Country Reel(USA)**, who has not quite proved himself up to this level, ran well enough under a positive ride but will need to drop back in grade if he is to score again in the near future.

**Capricho(IRE)** ◆, better known as a handicapper although he has a German Group Three to his name, ran a decent race on this occasion and looks as if he is returning to form. He is one to bear in mind for a lesser contest in the coming weeks.

**Ringmoor Down**, dropped out as usual, was too far back turning in and merely ran on past beaten rivals. It will be no surprise to see her turn out for the Abbaye next weekend, when she can be expected to fare better than she did here if the ground is not too soft. *Official explanation: jockey said mare slipped coming out of stalls*

**Ratio**, who has been somewhat inconsistent of late, was squeezed out early in the race which ended his chance. This run can be ignored, and he would be much more interesting if turning up at Longchamp next weekend with the headgear re-applied.

## 5781 TOTEJACKPOT ON SATURDAY STKS (HERITAGE H'CAP) 7f (R)

**3:35** (3:37) (B1) 3-Y-O+ **£40,600** (£15,400; £7,700; £3,500) **Stalls** High

Form RPR

110 **1** **Kehaar**[58] 4273 3-8-6 **93** .......... EAhern 12 107+
(MAMagnusson) *lw: trckd ldng gp: effrt on inner over 1f out: swept into ld last 150yds: sn clr: impressive* **13/2**[3]

0236 **2** *1 3/4* **Kool (IRE)**[14] 5468 5-8-5 **89** .......... RLMoore 6 98
(PFICole) *lw: hld up towards rr: prog on outer over 2f out: hrd rdn to chal 1f out: outpcd by wnr* **12/1**

5205 **3** *1* **Mine (IRE)**[14] 5462 6-9-10 **108** ..........(v) TQuinn 5 114
(JDBethell) *hld up wl in rr: effrt on outer 2f out: styd on wl fr over 1f out: nrst fin* **9/1**

1300 **4** *shd* **Traytonic**[42] 4750 3-9-0 **101** .......... JPMurtagh 7 107
(JRFanshawe) *racd midfield: rdn and effrt 2f out: styd on fnl f: unable to chal* **12/1**

4600 **5** *1/2* **Naahy**[16] 5414 4-9-9 **107** .......... SHitchcott 15 112
(MRChannon) *led: drvn 2f out: kpt on wl tl hdd & wknd last 150yds* **25/1**

1101 **6** *1/2* **Ettrick Water**[14] 5468 5-8-12 **99** 5ex ..........(v) NMackay(3) 9 102
(LMCumani) *lw: settled towards rr: rdn over 2f out: kpt on same pce fr over 1f out: n.d* **4/1**[1]

5521 **7** *nk* **Free Trip**[15] 5443 3-8-7 **94** 5ex .......... RHughes 8 97
(JHMGosden) *racd wd: prom: effrt on outer to chal over 1f out: upsides ent fnl f: wknd* **6/1**[2]

4000 **8** *nk* **Bahiano (IRE)**[8] 5610 3-9-3 **104** .......... DHolland 3 106
(CEBrittain) *hld up in last: rdn wl over 2f out: prog on outer fnl f: nrst fin* **50/1**

3003 **9** *nk* **Millennium Force**[7] 5668 6-9-8 **106** .......... TEDurcan 14 107+
(MRChannon) *lw: dwlt: wl in rr: effrt on inner whn nt clr run over 1f out: kpt on fnl f: no ch* **16/1**

3066 **10** *1/2* **Greenslades**[42] 4742 5-8-9 **93** .......... SSanders 10 93+
(PJMakin) *trckd ldrs: nt clr run 2f out to jst over 1f out: no ch to rcvr* **12/1**

0032 **11** *1 3/4* **Boston Lodge**[14] 5468 4-8-12 **96** ..........(v) JFortune 2 91+
(GAButler) *dwlt: hld up in last pair: effrt whn nt clr run on inner over 1f out: no ch after* **12/1**

0300 **12** *1 1/2* **Uhoomagoo**[14] 5468 6-8-10 **94** ..........(b) NCallan 4 85
(KARyan) *sn drvn in last trio: styng on whn nt clr run then hmpd over 1f out: no ch* **16/1**

5000 **13** *2* **Grizedale (IRE)**[14] 5468 5-8-6 **90** ..........(t) JFEgan 16 75
(JAkehurst) *t.k.h: trckd ldr: nt clr run briefly over 2f out: sn chalng: wknd over 1f out* **25/1**

2001 **14** *1 1/2* **Royal Storm (IRE)**[8] 5610 5-9-6 **104** 5ex .......... MJKinane 13 85
(MrsAJPerrett) *lw: prom: rdn to chal 2f out: wknd rapidly fnl f* **10/1**

4160 **15** *3 1/2* **Material Witness (IRE)**[8] 5610 7-9-7 **105** .......... MartinDwyer 11 77
(WRMuir) *prom tl wknd rapidly wl over 1f out* **25/1**

1m 27.15s

**WFA** 3 from 4yo+ 3lb **15** Ran SP% **122.7**

Speed ratings: CSF £80.10 CT £734.17 TOTE £8.40: £2.70, £4.70, £2.40; EX 161.20 Trifecta £1955.50 Part won. Pool: £2,754.60. 0.40 winning units..

**Owner** East Wind Racing Ltd **Bred** Watership Down Stud **Trained** Upper Lambourn, Berks

**FOCUS**

A typically competitive handicap, run on the round course, although the draw did not appear to have significant effect. Kehaar looks potentially Pattern class, but while the form overall should prove reliable, few behind him have the profile of imminent winners.

**NOTEBOOK**

**Kehaar** ◆ had a temperature only days after his sole defeat at Goodwood, so was not necessarily beaten by the track and draw there. He bounced back after a break to take this competitive handicap in great style and is potentially in the same sort of class as Mister Monet, who he had previously beaten at Newmarket. Connections will be looking forward to 2005. *Official explanation: trainer said, regarding the improved form shown, colt was running a temperature subsequent to its run last time which may have explained the poor form shown*

**Kool(IRE)** had been beaten by several of these in recent races, despite some creditable efforts. He ran a fine race but came up against something special this time. A turning seven seems to suit him.

**Mine(IRE)** ran his usual genuine race, but looks in the Handicapper's grip off his current mark. However, a return to a straight track will be more in his favour.

**Traytonic**, who has raced mostly over six furlongs in the last year, ran well enough on this step back up in distance without ever landing a blow. If he holds his form, the Wentworth Stakes at Doncaster on the last day of the season looks right up his street.

**Naahy**, as usual set the pace, but was treading water when collared by the winner entering the last furlong. He is probably better off in small-field Group Threes or Listed races off his current mark.

**Ettrick Water**, who came into this in good form, has now been beaten on all three starts at this track, during which time he has won three of his four other races. This was a fair effort, but he just seems less suited by this course than others and it would be no surprise to see him bounce back next time.

**Free Trip**, up in class, dropped in trip and carrying a penalty for his recent win, nevertheless ran a decent race until fading late on. He has held his form well this season and may do even better in 2005.

**Bahiano(IRE)** never reached a challenging position, but is due to race off a 4lb lower mark in future. He will be interesting if returned to Polytrack, as his All-Weather rating is just 92, and he has already won on that surface. *Official explanation: jockey said colt was struck into*

**Greenslades** saw no daylight at all until too late, and this can be ignored.

**Boston Lodge** *Official explanation: jockey said gelding reared up in stalls*

**Uhoomagoo** did not get much of a run and this effort can be ignored.

**Grizedale(IRE)** *Official explanation: jockey said gelding lost its action*

**Royal Storm(IRE)** was one of several to be prominent early that finished up out the back. *Official explanation: jockey said horse was struck into*

**Material Witness(IRE)**was another who dropped right out after helping force the pace. *Official explanation: trainer said gelding ran flat as colt had a lot of racing recently*

## 5782 QUEEN ELIZABETH II STKS (SPONSORED BY NETJETS) (GROUP 1) 1m (R)

**4:10** (4:15) (A1) 3-Y-O+ **£145,000** (£55,000; £27,500; £12,500) **Stalls** High

Form RPR

-105 **1** **Rakti**[14] 5483 5-9-1 122 .......... PRobinson 13 128+
(MAJarvis) *lw: sn trckd ldr: led over 2f out: drew 3l clr wl over 1f out: drvn and hld on fnl f* **9/2**[3]

1-20 **2** *1/2* **Lucky Story (USA)**[20] 5332 3-8-11 118 .......... DHolland 6 127
(MJohnston) *prom: rdn wl over 2f out: chsd wnr wl over 1f out: grad clsd fnl f: a hld* **16/1**

0110 **3** *2 1/2* **Refuse To Bend (IRE)**[59] 4228 4-9-1 121 ..........(t) LDettori 3 121+
(SaeedBinSuroor) *lw: settled towards rr: prog over 2f out: chsd ldng pair over 1f out: kpt on same pce fnl f* **4/1**[2]

3022 **4** *1 1/4* **Nayyir**[28] 5113 6-9-1 120 .......... JFortune 5 118+
(GAButler) *dwlt: hld up in last: prog on outer 2f out: styd on fnl f: nrst fin* **11/1**

1 **5** *4* **Ace (IRE)**[41] 4786 3-8-11 .......... JPSpencer 1 109
(APO'Brien, Ire) *lw: tall: scope: racd wd in midfield: rdn and hanging rt 2f out: sn btn* **12/1**

2111 **6** *1 1/4* **Soviet Song (IRE)**[14] 5484 4-8-12 120 .......... JPMurtagh 8 103
(JRFanshawe) *racd midfield: eased out and rdn 2f out: no rspnse and btn after* **5/2**[1]

115 **7** *1 1/4* **Fong's Thong (USA)**[16] 5414 3-8-11 108 ..........(t) PJSmullen 4 103
(BJMeehan) *lost pl after 3f: n.m.r and dropped to last 1/2-way: effrt and nt clr run over 2f out: sme prog over 1f out: nvr a factor* **50/1**

2222 **8** *4* **Diamond Green (FR)**[20] 5332 3-8-11 .......... CSoumillon 11 94
(AFabre, France) *settled in rr: gng wl enough over 2f out: rdn wl over 1f out: wknd* **8/1**

3053 **9** *2 1/2* **Antonius Pius (USA)**[20] 5332 3-8-11 ..........(t) KFallon 12 88
(APO'Brien, Ire) *t.k.h: wl plcd: rdn 2f out: fnd nil and sn wknd* **14/1**

4122 **10** *4* **Norse Dancer (IRE)**[14] 5483 4-9-1 121 .......... JFEgan 14 79
(DRCElsworth) *nvr gng wl and pushed along in rr after 2f: no ch* **11/1**

2-05 **11** *3* **Blatant**[198] 5-9-1 112 ..........(vt) KMcEvoy 7 72
(SaeedBinSuroor) *led to over 2f out: wknd* **100/1**

1m 39.82s (-3.22) **Going Correction** +0.10s/f (Good)

**WFA** 3 from 4yo+ 4lb **11** Ran SP% **117.7**

Speed ratings: **120,119,117,115,111 110,109,105,102,98 95**CSF £74.30 TOTE £5.90: £2.50, £3.40, £1.90; EX 83.80 Trifecta £562.20 Pool: £5,780.64. 7.30 winning units..

**Owner** Gary A Tanaka **Bred** Azienda Agricola Rosati Colarieti **Trained** Newmarket, Suffolk

**FOCUS**

A well up-to-standard renewal of this Group One, run in a decent time. Rakti had everything fall right and won well from a revitalised Lucky Story, whose close second rates the best three-year-old form of the season. However, there were some notable absentees and Soviet Song, Diamond Green and Norse Dancer all failed to run their races.

**NOTEBOOK**

**Rakti**, whose refusal to settle in recent races over ten furlongs had cost him, got a good lead from the Godolphin pacemaker and the faster pace helped him. Having got first run on his rivals, he had enough stamina to last home and equal the feat of former compatriot Falbrav in this race last year. The Breeders' Cup Mile is being suggested for him next, but his tendency to miss the break will not make things easy for him in the USA, and he also has the option of the Emirates Airline Champion Stakes or a race in Kyoto, Japan, before the Hong Kong Cup.

**Lucky Story(USA)** ◆, on the fastest ground he has faced this season, bounced back to form with a tremendous effort. He was always close to the pace, as he likes to be, and he was the only one able to go in pursuit of the winner in the last furlong. He was gaining all the way to the line, and in finishing clear of the rest he recorded the best 3-y-o RPR of the season so far. It will not be long before he is back in the winner's enclosure, and he shapes as if the extra distance of the Champion Stakes will suit him well.

**Refuse To Bend(IRE)** was held up and had to make his run on the wide outside, and made little impression on the winner from halfway up the straight. He is likely to represent connections in the Emirates Airline Champion Stakes, where he may meet at least one of those in front of him.

**Nayyir** ◆ has been performing well this season without winning. Previously thought of as a seven-furlong specialist, he has not run over that trip this season, but may get the chance in the Challenge Stakes at Newmarket, a race in which he has been first and second in the last two seasons.

**Ace(IRE)**, who took the Group Three Desmond Stakes last time, was unbeaten coming into this but was taking on the best at the trip. However, he performed with credit and could well be a force at this level next season.

**Soviet Song(IRE)**, who was going for a Group One four-timer, put up a lacklustre effort and may well have had enough for the season. That said, she owes nobody anything and she will be a very valuable broodmare prospect when she eventually goes to stud.

**Fong's Thong(USA)**'s previous form in this country suggested that this task would be beyond him. That proved correct but he was not disgraced, especially as he appeared to have been squeezed out and was hampered in his run. He should be capable of winning another Pattern race given a sound surface. *Official explanation: jockey said colt lost its action*

**Diamond Green(FR)**, who has been running consistently at the highest level all season, was another to run flat. Perhaps he can bounce back on an easier surface.

**Antonius Pius(USA)**, broke well and was quite free in the early stages despite the good pace. However, he paid the penalty and dropped away quickly in the straight.

**Norse Dancer(IRE)**, who had narrowly beaten Lucky Story at Salisbury and finished ahead of Rakti at Leopardstown, ran a rare poor race. His last three efforts on this track have been disappointing, but he may well have gone over the top.

## 5783 KLEENEX ROSEMARY STKS (H'CAP) (LISTED RACE) (F&M) 1m (R)

**4:45** (4:50) (A1) (0-110,104) 3-Y-O+ **£17,400** (£6,600; £3,300; £1,500) **Stalls** High

Form RPR

112 **1** **Tarfah (USA)**[36] 4906 3-8-6 **90** .......... SSanders 9 98+
(GAButler) *lw: t.k.h: trckd ldr after 3f: led over 2f out and kicked on: edgd lft ins fnl f: hld on* **4/1**[2]

5103 **2** *hd* **Golden Island (IRE)**[23] 5249 3-8-3 **87** oh2 RLMoore 1 94
(JWHills) *lw: dwlt: hld up: in last pair 3f out: prog and threaded through fnl 2f: clsd on wnr nr fin: jst hld* **25/1**

21-3 **3** *1* **Mansfield Park**[15] 5439 3-9-2 **100** LDettori 10 105
(SaeedBinSuroor) *lw: sn trckd ldrs: chsd wnr 2f out: hld ins fnl f: lost 2nd nr fin* **13/8**[1]

-340 **4** *hd* **Soldera (USA)**[34] 4982 4-9-7 **101** JPMurtagh 4 106
(JRFanshawe) *hld up wl in rr: prog on inner 2f out: cl up ins fnl f: hld whn nt clr run nr fin* **14/1**

1050 **5** *3* **Flowerdrum (USA)**[32] 5025 4-8-8 **88** KDarley 11 86
(WJHaggas) *racd midfield: lost pl and in last pair over 2f out: styd on fr over 1f out: no imp ldrs* **12/1**

4552 **6** *3 ½* **Moon Dazzle (USA)**[41] 4773 3-9-6 **104** DHolland 13 94
(WJHaggas) *cl up: n.m.r after 3f: wknd wl over 1f out* **8/1**[3]

4461 **7** *1* **Brindisi**[41] 4773 3-9-2 **100** MHills 7 87
(BWHills) *swtg: hld up: effrt on wd outside over 2f out: no imp ldrs over 1f out* **16/1**

0006 **8** *2 ½* **Convent Girl (IRE)**[23] 5249 4-8-7 **87** oh2 RHavlin 5 69
(MrsPNDutfield) *dwlt: racd midfield: rdn over 2f out: wknd wl over 1f out* **20/1**

454 **9** *½* **Treasure The Lady (IRE)**[27] 5162 3-8-12 **96** (t) MJKinane 3 76
(JohnMOxx, Ire) *hld up towards rr: rdn over 2f out: no prog: wknd over 1f out* **14/1**

0-11 **10** *1 ¼* **Porthcawl**[10] 5566 3-8-3 **87** oh8 PRobinson 6 65+
(MrsAJPerrett) *snatched up after 1f and dropped to rr: effrt 3f out: wknd 2f out: no ch whn nt clr run sn after* **11/1**

0123 **11** *shd* **Three Secrets (IRE)**[35] 4948 3-8-8 **92** AMcCarthy 12 69
(PWChapple-Hyam) *chsd ldr: snatched up after 3f: wknd 2f out* **33/1**

4360 **12** *5* **Cote Quest (USA)**[41] 4773 4-8-10 **90** KFallon 8 56
(SCWilliams) *lw: trckd ldrs tl wknd 2f out* **50/1**

3055 **13** *7* **Crystal Curling (IRE)**[26] 5180 3-8-13 **97** (t) MartinDwyer 2 47
(BWHills) *racd freely: led to over 2f out: wknd rapidly* **50/1**

1m 42.12s (-0.92) **Going Correction** +0.10s/f (Good)
**WFA** 3 from 4yo 4lb **13 Ran SP% 119.9**
Speed ratings: **108,107,106,106,103 100,99,96,96,94 94,89,82** CSF £109.69 CT £232.53 TOTE £4.90: £1.80, £6.00, £1.60; EX 173.60 Trifecta £248.80 Pool: £2,348.68. 6.70 winning units..
**Owner** Abdulla Al Khalifa **Bred** Sheik A Bin I Alkahlifa **Trained** Blewbury, Oxon
■ Stewards Enquiry : Martin Dwyer three-day ban: careless riding (Oct 6-8)

**FOCUS**
A decent Listed fillies' handicap, but run only fractionally faster than the juvenile fillies earlier and slower than the juvenile colts. Nevertheless the first four were clear and the form appears reasonable for the grade.

**NOTEBOOK**
**Tarfah(USA)**, a course and distance winner on her belated debut, had found the soft ground and longer trip too much last time. Back at a mile and on fast going, she was given a positive ride and looks progressive. She can rate better than this and should have further success in Pattern company next season.
**Golden Island(IRE)**, who ran well behind subsequent Listed winner Attune at Salisbury, was back up in trip and earned some valuable black type to go with her decent pedigree.
**Mansfield Park**, a well-backed favourite, chased the winner early in the straight but seemed to wander and failed to pick up. She is still inexperienced and this was a step up in grade, but she has earned some black type now and can be found a confidence-booster in a lower-grade event.
**Soldera(USA)**, dropped in class, having contested Group One and Two races since last summer, got a good run up the rail but should have finished closer, as she was crossed by the drifting winner in the closing stages. She did best of the older fillies and is capable of winning a Group Three.
**Flowerdrum(USA)** had a difficult task against these fillies and stayed on from the rear, by which time the first four were clear.
**Moon Dazzle(USA)** finshed ahead of Golden Island and Flowerdrum at Bath and could have been expected to run better than this, even though she suffered some interference.
**Porthcawl** did not get the best of runs after being squeezed out early on, and can be forgiven this.
**Three Secrets(IRE)** was another to suffer in the early scrimmaging.
**Crystal Curling(IRE)**, caused some early interference, which resulted in an enforced holiday for her rider.

## 5784 CAPLAN GORDON CARTER STKS (H'CAP) 2m 45y
**5:20** (5:23) (C1) (0-100,93) 3-Y-0+ **£13,650** (£4,200; £2,100; £1,050) **Stalls** High

Form RPR

2002 **1** **Escayola (IRE)**[14] 5472 4-9-7 **88** (v) JFEgan 14 99
(WJHaggas) *lw: racd midfield: prog to trck ldrs 2f out: plld out over 1f out: drvn to ld last 100yds: readily* **7/1**[3]

0000 **2** *½* **Mamcazma**[8] 5619 6-8-13 **80** TEDurcan 8 91
(DMorris) *prom: drvn to ld over 1f out: hdd last 100yds: kpt on wl* **33/1**

0-20 **3** *3* **Midas Way**[15] 5435 4-9-12 **93** LDettori 2 100
(PRChamings) *trckd ldr after 4f to 9f out: styd prom: rdn and unable qck over 2f out: styd on again fnl f* **16/1**

2-40 **4** *hd* **It's The Limit (USA)**[21] 5288 5-9-10 **91** MJKinane 5 98
(MrsAJPerrett) *settled wl in rr: plenty to do whn rdn 2f out: styd on wl fnl f: nrst fin* **16/1**

1-50 **5** *¾* **Tempsford (USA)**[136] 2047 4-9-5 **86** SSanders 13 92
(SirMarkPrescott) *lw: t.k.h: trckd ldr for 4f: styd prom: rdn to ld 2f out: hdd over 1f out: one pce* **15/2**

50-3 **6** *nk* **Corton (IRE)**[14] 5472 5-9-1 **82** JFortune 12 88
(PFICole) *sn settled in midfield: effrt and sme prog over 3f out: one pce fnl 2f* **16/1**

0015 **7** *1 ¼* **Mana D'Argent (IRE)**[59] 4226 7-9-7 **88** DHolland 3 92
(MJohnston) *settled in last trio: drvn and effrt on outer over 2f out: plugged on but no ch* **4/1**[2]

1112 **8** *1 ¼* **Peak Of Perfection (IRE)**[37] 4888 3-8-11 **90** PRobinson 10 93
(MAJarvis) *led: rdn and hdd 2f out: wknd fnl f* **7/2**[1]

0060 **9** *nk* **Almah (SAF)**[21] 5288 6-9-4 **85** (b) MartinDwyer 4 87
(MissVenetiaWilliams) *dwlt: pushed along in rr early: plld way to press ldr 9f out to 2f out: wknd* **100/1**

0640 **10** *1 ½* **Lodger (FR)**[21] 5288 4-9-7 **88** EAhern 1 89
(JNoseda) *lw: racd towards rr: rdn and short-lived effrt on inner 2f out: sn no prog* **20/1**

3260 **11** *¾* **Thewhirlingdervish (IRE)**[9] 5595 6-8-13 **80** TQuinn 16 80
(TDEasterby) *prom: lost pl 4f out: struggling fnl 2f* **14/1**

3000 **12** *2 ½* **Theatre (USA)**[14] 5472 5-8-12 **79** oh4 AMcCarthy 9 76
(JamiePoulton) *settled in rr: rdn 7f out: no prog on outer over 2f out* **33/1**

1402 **13** *5* **Valance (IRE)**[20] 5318 4-9-0 **81** JPMurtagh 7 78+
(CREgerton) *racd midfield: rdn over 3f out: wknd over 1f out: eased* **16/1**

0-02 **14** *5* **Stance**[59] 4226 5-8-12 **79** (p) RLMoore 15 64
(GLMoore) *a towards rr: rdn 5f out: wl btn over 2f out* **10/1**

150- **15** *2 ½* **Mac**[385] 4713 4-9-9 **90** (b[1]) KMcEvoy 11 72
(MPTregoning) *dwlt: a last: rdn 1/2-way: wl bhd fnl 3f* **33/1**

5330 **P** **Highland Games (IRE)**[15] 5435 4-9-8 **89** KDarley 6 —
(JGGiven) *p.u after 5f* **25/1**

3m 34.03s (-0.81) **Going Correction** +0.10s/f (Good)
**WFA** 3 from 4yo+ 12lb **16 Ran SP% 124.2**
Speed ratings: **106,105,104,104,103 103,103,102,102,101 101,99,97,94,93** —CSF £238.20 CT £3574.61 TOTE £9.30: £2.40, £6.10, £2.90, £4.60; EX 232.80 Trifecta £1382.40 Part won. Pool: £1,947.12. 0.50 winning units. Place 6 £54.24, Place 5 £47.61.
**Owner** Mrs M Findlay **Bred** Rozelle Bloodstock **Trained** Newmarket, Suffolk

**FOCUS**
A sound enough pace in this established Cesarewitch trial, and the first two came clear. The winner looks the sort who will be suited by the Newmarket test.

**NOTEBOOK**
**Escayola(IRE)**, narrowly beaten at Goodwood last time, won this in the manner of a thorough stayer. He has picked up a 5lb penalty for the Cesarewitch, but looks to have been trained with that race in mind and connections will be praying for a dry spell as he needs the ground fast.
**Mamcazma** has dropped 15lb in the handicap after some disappointing efforts this season. He came to win his race but has never scored over this far and was just outstayed. He is likely to go back up a few pounds after this, but connections may be able to find an opportunity for him at around 14 furlongs before the season is out.
**Midas Way**, another whose best form is at shorter, appeared to 'bounce' last time but ran a creditable race this time, despite being left behind by the principals. It will be no surprise to see him re-oppose on better terms with the winner at Newmarket, although he has stamina to prove.
**It's The Limit(USA)** ◆, a lightly-raced individual, was having only his third outing of the season and trying his longest trip to date. Held up at the back, he came with a strong late run and appeals as the sort that will appreciate the longer trip at Newmarket.
**Tempsford(USA)**, returning from four and a half months off, ran too free up with the pace and paid the penalty in the closing stages. He should be more settled next time and, on a fair mark, could be of interest if re-opposing at Newmarket.
**Corton(IRE)**, who returned from over a year's absence last time, did not run a bad race but appears better suited by shorter trips or a sharper track. *Official explanation: jockey said gelding slipped on bend*
**Mana D'Argent(IRE)** loves this track, but got behind and never looked like reducing the deficit.
**Peak Of Perfection(IRE)**, 8lb higher than for his last win, set the pace but capitulated rather tamely early in the straight, as if the trip is beyond him at this stage of his career. *Official explanation: jockey said gelding hung left in home straight*
**Thewhirlingdervish(IRE)** *Official explanation: jockey said gelding was unsuited by the uneven pace*
**Valance(IRE)** *Official explanation: jockey said gelding ran too free*
**Highland Games(IRE)** *Official explanation: jockey said gelding was lame*
T/Jkpt: £9,804.80 to a £1 stake. Pool: £27,619.25. 2.00 winning tickets. T/Plt: £84.80 to a £1 stake. Pool: £126,878.30. 1,091.25 winning tickets. T/Qpdt: £36.40 to a £1 stake. Pool: £5,357.15. 108.90 winning tickets. JN

# 5767 HAYDOCK (L-H)
## Saturday, September 25

**OFFICIAL GOING: Soft (heavy in places)**
Most of the action tended to unfold up the centre of the track.
Wind: Slight against Weather: Rain giving way to sunny spells

## 5785 BETFRED THE BONUS KING H'CAP 1m 6f
**2:15** (2:15) (C1) (0-100,95) 3-Y-0+ **£15,097** (£5,726; £2,863; £1,301) **Stalls** Low

Form RPR

1-61 **1** **Regal Setting (IRE)**[8] 5619 3-8-1 **82** JMackay 6 92+
(SirMarkPrescott) *chsd ldrs: pushed along over 5f out: led over 2f out: edgd lft fnl f: drvn out* **6/5**[1]

-356 **2** *¾* **Big Moment**[60] 4218 6-9-10 **95** SWKelly 3 104
(MrsAJPerrett) *s.i.s: hld up: hdwy over 3f out: chsd wnr over 1f out : hung lft and nt qckn ins fnl f* **15/2**[3]

1000 **3** *2* **Trance (IRE)**[8] 5619 4-8-8 **84** PMakin[(5)] 1 90
(TDBarron) *chsd ldrs: rdn over 2f out: styd on same pce appr fnl f* **20/1**

0112 **4** *13* **Hezaam (USA)**[29] 5074 3-8-3 **84** WSupple 7 74
(JLDunlop) *sn led: rdn and hdd over 2f out: sn wknd* **11/4**[2]

2050 **5** *nk* **Bendarshaan**[21] 5288 4-9-1 **86** SChin 4 75
(MJohnston) *chsd ldrs: rdn over 3f out: wknd over 1f out* **20/1**

5206 **6** *3* **Crow Wood**[21] 5288 5-9-10 **95** IMongan 5 80
(JGGiven) *trckd ldr: racd keenly: rdn and ev ch over 2f out: wknd over 1f out* **9/1**

103- **7** *dist* **Bollin Thomas**[434] 3408 6-8-10 **81** oh1 GGibbons 2 —
(TDEasterby) *hld up: rdn 6f out: wknd over 4f out* **14/1**

3m 8.26s (2.11) **Going Correction** +0.45s/f (Yiel)
**WFA** 3 from 4yo+ 10lb **7 Ran SP% 110.1**
Speed ratings: **111,110,109,102,101 100,**—CSF £10.11 TOTE £2.10: £1.70, £3.30; EX 9.90.
**Owner** W E Sturt - Osborne House **Bred** R G Patton **Trained** Newmarket, Suffolk

**FOCUS**
A steady early pace which only picked up once in line for home, but the form looks fairly sound.

**NOTEBOOK**
**Regal Setting(IRE)** tended to run his race his snatches, but there is no doubt he does have plenty of ability and is one to keep on the right side of.
**Big Moment** turned in a solid effort under his big weight, considering he did not get the strong pace he needs at this trip and, on ground which could well have been soft enough for him. Although down the field in two previous efforts in the Cesarewitch, he will go into this year's race fresher than most and is certainly worthy of consideration where the likely strong pace will play to his strengths.
**Trance(IRE)** stuck to his task well enough on ground softer than ideal.
**Hezaam(USA)** was a major disappointment, dropping out tamely having set no more than an ordinary gallop, and is surely better than he showed here. *Official explanation: vet said colt was wrong behind*
**Bendarshaan** found conditions too testing for him.
**Crow Wood** was always doing a little too much to last home in the ground.

## 5786 AKZO NOBEL H'CAP 6f
**2:45** (2:46) (C1) (0-100,96) 3-Y-O **£20,553** (£6,324; £3,162; £1,581) **Stalls** Centre

Form RPR

3111 **1** **Eisteddfod**[8] 5603 3-9-2 **93** NDeSouza[(5)] 8 112+
(PFICole) *a.p: rdn to ld over 1f out: edgd lft ins fnl f: r.o* **7/4**[1]

4431 **2** *½* **Solar Power (IRE)**[22] 5263 3-8-12 **84** JDSmith 3 101+
(JRFanshawe) *hld up: swtchd rt and hdwy over 1f out: rdn and ev ch ins fnl f: r.o* **9/2**[2]

0341 **3** *6* **Imperial Echo (USA)**[26] 5193 3-8-12 **84** PFessey 7 83
(TDBarron) *s.i.s: hdwy 4f out: led over 1f out: sn hdd: wknd ins fnl f* **20/1**

0051 **4** *1 ¾* **Partners In Jazz (USA)**[24] 5224 3-8-12 **89** PMakin[(5)] 10 82
(TDBarron) *w ldrs: led over 2f out: rdn and hdd over 1f out: sn wknd* **8/1**[3]

0451 **5** *½* **Bo McGinty (IRE)**[10] 5563 3-9-0 **86** GParkin 11 78
(RAFahey) *chsd ldrs: rdn whn hmpd over 1f out: n.d after* **14/1**

0004 **6** *1 ¼* **Danzig River (IRE)**[37] 4874 3-9-3 **89**........ RMullen 5 77
(BWHills) *hld up: rdn over 1f out: nvr trbld ldrs* **14/1**

1150 **7** *½* **Commando Scott (IRE)**[37] 4874 3-9-5 **91**........ FLynch 6 78
(ABerry) *led 1f: remained handy tl wknd over 1f out* **10/1**

0001 **8** *shd* **Morse (IRE)**[7] 5656 3-8-11 **83**........ SWKelly 12 69
(JAOsborne) *w ldrs: led over 3f out to over 2f out: wknd over 1f out* **16/1**

4110 **9** *8* **Jilly Why (IRE)**[12] 5526 3-8-3 **82** oh10........ CHaddon(7) 9 44
(MsDeborahJEvans) *led 5f out: hdd over 3f out: wknd over 1f out* **50/1**

21-0 **10** *3 ½* **Efistorm**[18] 5372 3-9-2 **88**........ WSupple 1 40
(MGQuinlan) *hld up: hdwy over 2f out: wknd over 1f out* **50/1**

0005 **11** *2 ½* **Spliff**[13] 5491 3-9-3 **89**........ DSweeney 2 33
(HCandy) *hld up: hdwy over 2f out: wknd over 1f out* **10/1**

0010 **12** *¾* **High Voltage**[17] 5393 3-9-10 **96**........(t) IMongan 4 38
(KRBurke) *prom: rdn 1/2-way: wkng whn n.m.r wl over 1f out* **16/1**

1m 17.64s (2.75) **Going Correction** +0.45s/f (Yiel) **12** Ran SP% **117.6**
Speed ratings: **99,98,90,88,87 85,85,84,74,69 66,65**CSF £8.53 CT £116.94 TOTE £2.40: £1.40, £1.80, £6.50; EX 12.40.
**Owner** Elite Racing Club **Bred** Elite Racing Club **Trained** Whatcombe, Oxon
■ Stewards Enquiry : J D Smith two-day ban: careless riding (Oct 6-7)

**FOCUS**
A decent contest in which the front pair came nicely clear, both continuing to look progressive. However, a surprisingly modest time.

**NOTEBOOK**
**Eisteddfod** continues on an upward curve and, while his days in handicaps will be limited now, he looks sure to hold his own at Listed level.
**Solar Power(IRE)** has really come into her own since dropped to sprinting, and was probably unlucky to come up against a fast-improving sort. There will certainly be other days for her.
**Imperial Echo(USA)** did himself no favours by missing the break and, although well beaten in the end, probably was not disgraced.
**Partners In Jazz(USA)** came out best of those to race up with the pace. *Official explanation: jockey said colt hung left-handed in closing stages*
**Bo McGinty(IRE)** may well have finished third had he not been squeezed out as the runner-up made progress.
**Danzig River(IRE)** still looks to need some help from the Handicapper.

## 5787 BETFRED.COM H'CAP — 5f
**3:15** (3:16) (C1) (0-100,100) 4-Y-0+ **£20,176** (£6,208; £3,104; £1,552) **Stalls** Centre

Form RPR

1000 **1** **Jonny Ebeneezer**[7] 5628 5-8-7 **89**........(be) HayleyTurner(3) 8 101
(DFlood) *hld up: swtchd lft and hdwy over 1f out: led ins fnl f: r.o wl* **14/1**

3404 **2** *2* **Whistler**[17] 5393 7-8-11 **90**........(p) PFitzsimons 9 96
(JMBradley) *hld up: hdwy and hung lft fnl f: nt run on towards fin* **8/1**

0350 **3** *1* **Corridor Creeper (FR)**[17] 5393 7-8-10 **94**........(p) PMakin(5) 4 97
(JMBradley) *trckd ldrs tl led 1/2-way: rdn and hdd ins fnl f: unable qck* **11/2**[2]

0100 **4** *1* **River Falcon**[7] 5628 4-8-9 **88**........ WSupple 1 88
(JSGoldie) *hld up in tch: rdn over 1f out: styd on same pce* **9/1**

1503 **5** *1* **Further Outlook (USA)**[10] 5564 10-8-7 **86** oh4........ DSweeney 6 83
(DKIvory) *mde most to 1/2-way: no ex fnl f* **12/1**

0003 **6** *hd* **Johnston's Diamond (IRE)**[8] 5603 6-8-7 **86** oh1........ JQuinn 11 82
(EJAlston) *chsd ldrs: rdn 1/2-way: styd on same pce appr fnl f* **6/1**[3]

033 **7** *5* **Ptarmigan Ridge**[17] 5393 8-8-8 **87**........ MFenton 10 68
(MissLAPerratt) *trckd ldrs: rdn over 1f out: sn wknd* **7/2**[1]

2565 **8** *1 ¾* **Bishops Court**[16] 5418 10-9-7 **100**........ IMongan 3 76
(MrsJRRamsden) *chsd ldrs over 3f: b.b.v.* **13/2**

0054 **9** *hd* **Whitbarrow (IRE)**[11] 5553 5-8-11 **90**........(b) SWKelly 7 66
(JMBradley) *chsd ldrs over 3f* **14/1**

0000 **10** *1 ¾* **Henry Hall (IRE)**[26] 5181 8-8-10 **89**........ KimTinkler 5 59
(NTinkler) *mid-div: sn pushed along: wknd wl over 1f out* **25/1**

0040 **11** *22* **Absent Friends**[4] 5712 7-8-7 **86** oh3........ RMullen 2 —
(JBalding) *w ldrs tl lost pl over 3f out: sn bhd* **25/1**

62.75 secs (0.68) **Going Correction** +0.45s/f (Yiel) **11** Ran SP% **115.1**
Speed ratings: **112,108,107,105,104 103,95,92,92,89 54**CSF £118.92 CT £702.52 TOTE £13.50: £3.20, £2.60, £2.30; EX 126.60.
**Owner** Mrs Ruth M Serrell **Bred** John Purcell **Trained** Upper Lambourn, Berks

**FOCUS**
A decent handicap and there was plenty of pace on, but the race was full of exposed types. The runner-up is the guide to the level of the form.

**NOTEBOOK**
**Jonny Ebeneezer** is a quirky customer who takes a bit of knowing, but Turner sat quiet on him and produced him at the right time to win off his highest mark. He may not have stopped winning just yet. *Official explanation: trainer said, regarding the improved form shown, gelding is an inconsistent sort*
**Whistler**, just as he had at Doncaster, hung most of the way across the course, and while he clearly has plenty of ability, he is not without his quirks.
**Corridor Creeper(FR)** did best of those to race up with the pace, but he will have done himself no favours with the Handicapper.
**River Falcon** ran his race, but the Handicapper knows just how good he is.
**Further Outlook(USA)** had his ideal conditions but, 4lb out of the weights, at this level that was always going to be too much for him to overcome.
**Johnston's Diamond(IRE)** has found life difficult this term and, although there were better signs at Ayr last time, he was unable to build on that.
**Ptarmigan Ridge**, 9lb higher than when landing this last year, had his ideal conditions and no excuses.
**Bishops Court** was reported to have bled from the nose. *Official explanation: trainer's representative said gelding bled from nose*

## 5788 EUROPEAN BREEDERS FUND "REPROCOLOR" FILLIES' H'CAP — 1m 2f 120y
**3:50** (3:50) (C1) (0-100,91) 3-Y-0+ **£19,827** (£6,100; £3,050; £1,525) **Stalls** Low

Form RPR

5602 **1** **La Sylphide**[25] 5211 7-9-10 **82**........ SWKelly 7 91
(GMMoore) *mde all: rdn over 1f out: styd on gamely* **9/2**[3]

111 **2** *¾* **Tartouche**[17] 5397 3-9-12 **91**........ JQuinn 1 99+
(LadyHerries) *hld up in tch: chsd wnr over 2f out: sn rdn: styd on* **10/3**[2]

1222 **3** *¾* **Charnock Bates One (IRE)**[42] 4760 3-8-7 **72**........ GGibbons 3 79
(TDEasterby) *s.i.s: hld up: hdwy over 3f out: rdn and hung lft fr over 1f out: styd on* **13/2**

1522 **4** *1 ¼* **Fling**[43] 4729 3-9-4 **83**........ RMullen 2 88
(JRFanshawe) *s.s: hld up: outpcd over 3f out: styd on u.p fnl f: nvr able to chal* **11/4**[1]

3123 **5** *nk* **Nouveau Riche (IRE)**[10] 5566 3-8-12 **77**........ IMongan 5 81
(HMorrison) *chsd ldrs: rdn over 2f out: styd on u.p* **15/2**

5115 **6** *shd* **Light Wind**[55] 4367 3-9-7 **86**........ WSupple 4 90
(MrsAJPerrett) *prom: chsd wnr 8f out: rdn over 2f out: styd on same pce appr fnl f* **8/1**

2042 **7** *5* **Uig**[12] 5511 3-8-9 **74**........ MFenton 6 69
(HSHowe) *prom: racd keenly: lost pl 6f out: rdn and wknd over 1f out* **20/1**

2m 21.39s (3.66) **Going Correction** +0.45s/f (Yiel)
**WFA** 3 from 7yo 7lb **7** Ran SP% **108.9**
Speed ratings: **104,103,102,102,101 101,98**CSF £17.88 TOTE £5.80: £2.30, £2.40; EX 13.40.
**Owner** Geoff & Sandra Turnbull **Bred** H Young **Trained** Middleham Moor, N Yorks

**FOCUS**
Quite a competitive contest despite the small field, but it was run at only a steady pace and three lengths covered six of the seven runners.

**NOTEBOOK**
**La Sylphide**, 9lb higher than when making all in this contest last year, followed up in similar fashion. Allowed a soft time of things up front, she gradually wound things up turning for home and showed plenty of resolution to hold off the persistent runner-up.
**Tartouche** turned in a solid effort under her big weight, especially as the lack of a decent pace would hardly have played to her strengths.
**Charnock Bates One(IRE)** was again found out by a lack of a change of gear, and may have done better with a stronger pace.
**Fling**, who fell out of the stalls, got caught flat-footed when the pace picked up and only consented to stay on when the race was all but over. She will be better suited by a return to 12 furlongs.
**Nouveau Riche(IRE)** appeared to stay this longer trip well enough, although better ground may have helped her even more.
**Light Wind**, who stays further than this, was not suited by the steady pace.

## 5789 EUROPEAN BREEDERS FUND SODEXHO MAIDEN FILLIES' STKS — 1m 30y
**4:20** (4:23) (D2) 2-Y-0 **£5,573** (£1,715; £857; £428) **Stalls** Low

Form RPR

0230 **1** **Tcherina (IRE)**[16] 5417 2-8-11 73........ GGibbons 8 76
(TDEasterby) *hld up in tch: led 3f out: hdd over 2f out: rallied to ld over 1f out: rdn out* **11/2**[3]

6 **2** *1 ¾* **Higher Love (IRE)**[18] 5368 2-8-11........ RMullen 2 73
(MLWBell) *dwlt: hld up: hdwy over 3f out: led over 2f out: hdd over 1f out: unable qck ins fnl f* **5/2**[1]

**3** *3* **Limit (IRE)** 2-8-11........ JQuinn 6 67
(MRChannon) *s.s: hld up: hdwy over 3f out: rdn and ev ch over 2f out: styd on same pce appr fnl f* **7/2**[2]

0 **4** *6* **Sideshow**[38] 4851 2-8-11........(v[1]) DRMcCabe 4 55
(DRLoder) *disp ld to 1/2-way: hung lft wl over 2f out: wknd over 1f out* **12/1**

64 **5** *¾* **Hill Fairy**[40] 4807 2-8-11........ JMackay 5 53
(TPTate) *disp ld tl led 1/2-way: hdd 3f out: wknd wl over 1f out* **9/1**

043 **6** *10* **Lake Wakatipu**[14] 5455 2-8-11 57........ LEnstone 1 33
(MMullineaux) *chsd ldrs: bmpd wl over 2f out: sn wknd* **25/1**

5 **7** *2 ½* **Napapijri (FR)**[29] 5089 2-8-11........ WSupple 7 28
(DPKeane) *s.i.s: hld up: wknd 3f out* **8/1**

5 **8** *6* **Orlar (IRE)**[19] 5349 2-8-11........ SWKelly 3 16
(JAOsborne) *plld hrd and prom: hmpd wl over 2f out: sn eased* **6/1**

1m 49.83s (4.28) **Going Correction** +0.45s/f (Yiel) **8** Ran SP% **113.1**
Speed ratings: **96,94,91,85,84 74,72,66**CSF £19.22 TOTE £6.10: £1.70, £1.70, £1.60; EX 21.10.
**Owner** Mr & Mrs W J Williams **Bred** Ken Carroll **Trained** Great Habton, N Yorks

**FOCUS**
This did not look a strong contest and the field finished well strung out in the conditions, despite the pace only being a moderate one.

**NOTEBOOK**
**Tcherina(IRE)** had the edge in experience over her rivals and that counted for plenty on this surface.
**Higher Love(IRE)** looked all over the winner when going on, but for one reason or another did not find as much as she looked like doing.
**Limit(IRE)**, whose dam was a juvenile winner in France, showed promise for the future.
**Sideshow** looked a real madam in the first-time visor.
**Hill Fairy** will have more options open to her now in nurseries.
**Orlar(IRE)** *Official explanation: jockey said filly ran too freely early on, suffered interference and subsequently felt wrong*

## 5790 EBF BETFRED IN-SHOP ON-PHONE ON-LINE MAIDEN STKS (C&G) — 1m 30y
**4:55** (4:56) (D2) 2-Y-0 **£5,720** (£1,760; £880; £440) **Stalls** Low

Form RPR

3202 **1** **Mozafin**[11] 5543 2-8-11 82........(v) JQuinn 2 80
(MRChannon) *mde virtually all: clr 1/2-way: rdn over 1f out: edgd rt ins fnl f: wnt lft nr fin: all out* **11/10**[1]

40 **2** *1 ¼* **Love Beauty (USA)**[81] 3601 2-8-11........ SChin 6 78
(MJohnston) *chsd wnr: rdn and hung lft over 3f out: styd on u.p* **8/1**

3 **3** *shd* **Solarias Quest**[16] 5407 2-8-11........ JDSmith 5 77
(AKing) *hld up in tch: rdn over 2f out: styd on* **3/1**[2]

**4** *4* **Kong (IRE)** 2-8-11........ IMongan 3 69
(JLDunlop) *s.s: hld up: rdn and rn green 1/2-way: nvr trbld ldrs* **4/1**[3]

**5** *9* **Emerald Destiny (IRE)** 2-8-11........ WSupple 4 51
(DCarroll) *plld hrd and prom: wknd over 3f out* **22/1**

602 **6** *¾* **Layed Back Rocky**[14] 5455 2-8-11 62........ LEnstone 1 50
(MMullineaux) *chsd ldrs over 5f* **25/1**

1m 49.61s (4.06) **Going Correction** +0.45s/f (Yiel) **6** Ran SP% **111.9**
Speed ratings: **97,95,95,91,82 81**CSF £10.87 TOTE £2.10: £1.40, £3.30; EX 11.90 Place 6 £32.63, Place 5 £19.98.
**Owner** Jaber Abdullah **Bred** Floors Farming And Beckhampton Stables Ltd **Trained** West Ilsley, Berks

**FOCUS**
The winner set a fair standard and had the run of the race. The form looks reasonable, although the winner did not need to be at his best to score.

**NOTEBOOK**
**Mozafin** made the most of his experience and looked to have things well under control from some way out, although he had little in reserve at the line. Fully exposed, he looks sure to find life difficult in the future, and will certainly need placing with care.
**Love Beauty(USA)** given a break since disappointing at Headquarters back in July, stuck to his task well enough having looked in trouble some way out. There is still time for him to make his mark this term.
**Solarias Quest** looked as though an even stiffer test would suit.
**Kong(IRE)**, a half-brother to the high-class juvenile Preseli, as well as the 1000 Guineas runner-up Snowfire, was too green to do himself justice. There should be plenty of improvement to come.
T/Plt: £43.40 to a £1 stake. Pool: £53,471.10. 889.20 winning tickets. T/Qpdt: £19.00 to a £1 stake. Pool: £1,815.60. 70.50 winning tickets. CR

## [5694]KEMPTON (R-H)

Saturday, September 25

**OFFICIAL GOING: Good to firm (good in places) changing to good (good to firm in places) after 1.25 (race 5)**

Wind: lt across Weather: lt rain last 3 races

### 5791 BOOK NOW FOR THE CHRISTMAS FESTIVAL BANDED STKS 1m 2f (J)

11:25 (11:30) (H5) 3-Y-0+ £1,564 (£447; £223) Stalls High

Form RPR

6043 **1** **Enna (POL)**[7] 5641 5-9-4 45 TQuinn 1 52
(MrsStefLiddiard) *lw: t.k.h: making hdwy whn swtchd lft over 2f out: str run on outside to ld over 1f out: readily* **12/1**

4641 **2** 2 **Dancing Tilly**[14] 5449 6-9-2 46 (p) THamilton(3) 15 49
(RAFahey) *mid-div: hdwy 3f out: styd on to go 2nd fnl 50yds* **11/2**[3]

5033 **3** ½ **My Maite (IRE)**[21] 5285 5-9-5 46 (vt) NDay 17 48
(RIngram) *lw: t.k.h: in tch: rdn over 2f out: chsd wnr 1f out tl fnl 50yds* **9/2**[2]

2001 **4** 3½ **Cunning Pursuit**[21] 5284 3-9-3 50 KFallon 13 46
(MLWBell) *lw: in tch: rdn over 3f out: one pce after* **2/1**[1]

6010 **5** shd **Mister Completely (IRE)**[32] 5021 3-9-0 47 MartinDwyer 2 42
(JRBest) *racd wd: in tch: rdn 3f out: nt qckn fnl 2f* **12/1**

4005 **6** ½ **Maid The Cut**[29] 5072 3-8-12 45 ADaly 4 39
(ADSmith) *towards rr: rdn and hdwy over 2f out: wknd over 1f out* **20/1**

-000 **7** ½ **Artzola (IRE)**[50] 4517 4-9-8 49 DHolland 14 43
(CAHorgan) *b.hind: mid-div: rdn over 2f out: wknd over 1f out* **25/1**

1000 **8** nk **Piquet**[21] 5285 6-9-4 45 GBaker 10 38
(JJBridger) *in tch: rdn over 3f out: no hdwy after* **33/1**

0300 **9** nk **Nuzzle**[65] 4045 4-9-4 45 SHitchcott 8 37
(MQuinn) *trckd ldr tl rdn over 3f out: wknd 2f out* **20/1**

0024 **10** nk **Fizzy Lady**[5] 5692 3-8-12 50 (t) MSavage(5) 19 42
(NEBerry) *v.s.a: nvr on terms* **16/1**

6555 **11** ½ **Rojabaa**[58] 4042 5-9-0 48 SHaddon(7) 16 39+
(WGMTurner) *b: stdd s: a in rr* **20/1**

0050 **12** ½ **Glendale**[83] 3556 3-8-10 50 MHoward(7) 6 40
(DKIvory) *chsd ldrs: ridde 3f out: wknd over 1f out* **33/1**

6000 **13** ½ **Sunset Dreamer (USA)**[119] 2484 3-9-2 49 RLMoore 5 38
(PMitchell) *a.p: led over 2f out: hdd & wknd qckly over 1f out* **33/1**

4060 **14** hd **Fairland (IRE)**[7] 5658 5-8-12 46 LSmith(7) 9 35
(SDow) *wnt lft s: bdly hmpd and rdr lost iron after 3f: nvr a factor after* **20/1**

0000 **15** ¾ **Indian Lily**[10] 5575 3-8-12 45 CCatlin 11 32
(CFWall) *prom: rdn over 3f out: wknd 2f out* **33/1**

1640 **16** 8 **Piste Bleu (FR)**[58] 3774 4-9-7 48 JoannaBadger 7 20
(RFord) *hld up: a in rr* **20/1**

4030 **17** 7 **Jade Star (USA)**[61] 4190 4-9-1 49 (p) DerekNolan(7) 3 8
(ABHaynes) *sn led: hdd over 2f out: wknd qckly* **25/1**

450 **18** 12 **Tregenna**[28] 5123 3-9-0 47 MHenry 12 —
(RMHCowell) *hld up in rr: hung lft ande eased ins fnl 2f* **33/1**

2m 8.03s (1.89) **Going Correction** +0.05s/f (Good)
**WFA** 3 from 4yo+ 6lb **18** Ran SP% **134.4**
Speed ratings: **94,92,92,89,89 88,88,88,87,87 87,86,86,86,85 79,73,64**CSF £69.13 TOTE £14.20: £5.50, £1.90, £1.90; EX 55.40.
**Owner** Valley Fencing **Bred** Sk Jaroszowka **Trained** Great Shefford, Berks

**FOCUS**
A very moderate race but a good performance from Enna, who came with a powerful late challenge to claim her first win in this country. The form is ordinary for the grade.

**NOTEBOOK**
**Enna(POL)** looked at home in this grade last time and the step back up to a more suitable trip did the trick. She came with a strong, well-timed run and ended up winning easily. She is capable of winning outside of this grade and looks to be finding her feet at last.
**Dancing Tilly**, easy winner of a slightly lesser race at Carlisle earlier in the month, ran creditably for her bang in-form stable but was never getting to the winner.
**My Maite(IRE)** lost second in the closing stages and was filling this position for the third consecutive outing.
**Cunning Pursuit**, a winner in this grade at Folkestone earlier in the month, failed to run to form and may have found the extra 5lb a bit too much.
**Mister Completely(IRE)** is an in-and-out performer but this was one of his better efforts.
**Fizzy Lady** *Official explanation: jockey said filly resented tongue strap and was slowly away*

### 5792 JUMP RACING HERE 23RD OCTOBER MAIDEN AUCTION STKS 1m (J)

11:55 (12:01) (H5) 2-Y-0 £1,522 (£435; £217) Stalls High

Form RPR

526 **1** **Bold Counsel (IRE)**[7] 5640 2-8-12 65 CCatlin 11 66
(BJMeehan) *trckd ldr: led over 3f out: narrowly hdd over 1f out: rallied u.p to ld again cl home* **8/1**[3]

**2** nk **Ghaill Force** 2-8-12 NCallan 2 65
(JGPortman) *w'like: strong: s.i.s: hld up: hdwy over 3f out: rdn to ld over 1f out: hdd cl home* **66/1**

0500 **3** hd **Cabin Fever**[24] 5218 2-8-1 55 DFox(5) 7 59
(JCFox) *mid-div: hdwy 3f out: hung rt but ev ch ent fnl f: nt go by* **50/1**

53 **4** 1½ **Maktu**[26] 5173 2-8-11 KFallon 8 61
(PFICole) *a.p: ev ch 2f out: one pce after* **10/11**[1]

500 **5** nk **Sunny Times (IRE)**[21] 5281 2-8-6 51 JFEgan 16 55
(JWPayne) *in rr tl styd on fnl 2f: nvr nrr* **16/1**

00 **6** 1 **Bonnabee (IRE)**[7] 5640 2-8-5 LisaJones 9 52
(CFWall) *slowly away in rr tl hdwy 3f out: styd on ins fnl 2f: nvr nrr* **20/1**

6U **7** hd **Tranquilizer**[28] 5114 2-8-6 (t) EAhern 12 52
(DJCoakley) *chsd ldrs: rdn over 2f out: one pce after* **12/1**

053 **8** 1¼ **Kapaje**[34] 4966 2-8-5 70 JoannaBadger 4 49
(PDEvans) *hld up: hdwy to chse ldrs over 3f out: wknd over 1f out* **6/1**[2]

00 **9** 1¼ **Whitland**[11] 5534 2-8-12 (t) RHavlin 20 53
(MrsPNDutfield) *plld hrd: prom: one pce fnl 2f* **50/1**

05 **10** 1 **Lady Vee (IRE)**[18] 5362 2-8-2 THamilton(3) 10 44
(PDNiven) *chsd ldrs: rdn over 2f out: sn wknd* **20/1**

5002 **11** 1½ **Beau Marche**[24] 5218 2-8-11 61 (p) MartinDwyer 3 46
(IAWood) *hld up in rr: rdn over 3f out: nvr on terms* **16/1**

000 **12** 3 **Manorshield Minx**[11] 5535 2-8-6 DHolland 13 35
(SKirk) *in tch tl wknd 2f out* **14/1**

303 **13** 2½ **Cois Na Tine Eile**[84] 3506 2-8-1 51 ow2 NChalmers(5) 14 27
(MsDeborahJEvans) *a bhd* **33/1**

000 **14** 4 **Blue Spectrum (IRE)**[50] 4521 2-8-5 DerekNolan(7) 5 26
(JSMoore) *mid-div: bhd fnl 3f* **66/1**

00 **15** 3½ **Tiger Hunter**[24] 5218 2-8-2 KristinStubbs(7) 18 16
(PHowling) *mid-div: wknd over 2f out* **100/1**

00 **16** 7 **Touch Of Spice**[7] 5640 2-8-9 WRyan 6 —
(JRJenkins) *led tl hdd over 3f out: sn wknd* **100/1**

**17** 12 **Millquista D'Or** 2-8-3 RThomas(3) 19 —
(GAHam) *w'like: leggy: slowly away: a bhd* **50/1**

**18** 2½ **Miss Dinamite** 2-8-3 AMcCarthy 17 —
(MJAttwater) *w'like: wnt rt s: a bhd* **66/1**

**19** 4 **Charlieslastchance** 2-8-3 ADaly 1 —
(JJBridger) *w'like: leggy: a bhd* **66/1**

1m 41.69s (2.07) **Going Correction** +0.05s/f (Good) 2y crse rec **19** Ran SP% **130.2**
Speed ratings: **91,90,90,89,88 87,87,86,85,84 82,79,77,73,69 62,50,48,44**CSF £490.79 TOTE £11.20: £2.60, £26.30, £13.40; EX 757.80.
**Owner** Racegoers Club Owners Group **Bred** Liam Reidy **Trained** Upper Lambourn, Berks

**FOCUS**
A cracking finish to what was a weak maiden, and the winner did not need to improve to score a narrow victory.

**NOTEBOOK**
**Bold Counsel(IRE)** had near enough the best turf form on offer and was only made as big as 8/1 as a result of a slightly disappointing effort most recently on the Polytrack. He was fortunate enough to be found a weak maiden and, having been prominent throughout, battled back gamely once headed to get up in the dying strides. Off a mark in the mid-to-high 60s, he should be competitive in nurseries.
**Ghaill Force** has more of a sprinting pedigree, but saw the mile out well enough on this racecourse debut, just not as strongly as the winner. At 66/1 this was clearly not expected, and it remains to be seen if he can prove this was no fluke.
**Cabin Fever** could be said to have thrown the race away, as she had every chance until hanging under pressure, and seeming to want to do anything but go by the line in front. This step up in trip suited, but she is evidently not one to trust.
**Maktu**, along with the winner, had the best form on offer and was understandably made a short-priced favourite. Having looked to have every chance, he was simply outpaced and clearly wants an even stiffer test, even at this early stage of his career.
**Sunny Times(IRE)** ran a better race and it will be disappointing if she can not get competitive in nurseries off a mark in the low 50s.
**Bonnabee(IRE)** is now qualified for a mark and will be much more at home in handicaps.
**Kapaje** was disappointing and appeared not to stay. She is going to struggle off what looks a very harsh mark of 70 for what she has actually achieved.

### 5793 RACING UK ON CHANNEL 432 BANDED STKS 6f

12:25 (12:29) (H5) 3-Y-0+ £1,491 (£426; £213) Stalls Centre

Form RPR

00-0 **1** **Spinetail Rufous (IRE)**[7] 5642 6-9-0 40 (b) JFEgan 2 53
(DFlood) *wnt lft s: hdwy stands' side 1/2-way: led overall over 1f out: r.o wl* **12/1**

0322 **2** 1 **Crimson Star (IRE)**[7] 5641 3-8-12 40 CCatlin 4 50+
(CTinkler) *lw: a.p stands' side: r.o to go 2nd ins fnl f* **11/2**[2]

0003 **3** 3½ **Angel Isa (IRE)**[58] 4257 4-8-11 40 (v[1]) THamilton(3) 5 40
(RAFahey) *sn led stands' gp to over 3f out: kpt on one pce fnl f* **9/1**

4200 **4** 1¼ **Danakim**[49] 4534 7-9-0 40 DHolland 17 36+
(JRWeymes) *lw: trckd overall ldr far side tl led that gp over 1f out: kpt on* **7/1**[3]

5420 **5** 1 **Mr Uppity**[21] 5283 5-9-0 40 (e) TQuinn 3 33
(JulianPoulton) *b.hind: in tch stands' side: swtchd rt over 2f out: wknd fnl f* **9/2**[1]

0040 **6** 2½ **Zinging**[21] 5283 5-9-0 40 (v) ADaly 6 25
(JJBridger) *prom stands' side: one pce fnl 2f* **20/1**

5020 **7** shd **Avit (IRE)**[3] 5734 4-9-0 40 RPrice 12 25+
(PLGilligan) *a mid-div on far side* **14/1**

-000 **8** nk **Old Harry**[49] 4548 4-9-0 40 MartinDwyer 20 24+
(PCRitchens) *overall ldr on far side: tl hdd & wknd over 1f out* **20/1**

5660 **9** ½ **Jasmine Pearl (IRE)**[34] 4968 3-8-12 40 SWhitworth 8 23
(TMJones) *racd stands' side and led that gp over 3f out tl hdd by wnr over 1f out* **33/1**

-063 **10** ½ **Suitcase Murphy (IRE)**[11] 5547 3-8-12 45 NCallan 18 21+
(MsDeborahJEvans) *chsd ldrs far side: rdn 2f out: wknd 1f out* **7/1**[3]

6000 **11** shd **Zambezi River**[16] 5412 5-9-0 40 RLMoore 19 21+
(JMBradley) *chsd ldrs far side: rdn 2f out: sn btn* **16/1**

4000 **12** 1 **Badou**[21] 5283 4-9-0 40 PDobbs 13 18+
(LMontagueHall) *towrds rr far side: rdn 2f out: nvr on terms* **25/1**

0050 **13** 2½ **Bahamian Belle**[68] 3991 4-8-7 40 JBrennan(7) 14 10+
(PSMcentee) *mid-div on far side: wknd over 1f out* **33/1**

0600 **14** 5 **Pardon Moi**[34] 4968 3-8-12 40 AMcCarthy 16 —+
(MrsCADunnett) *mid-div on far side: rdn 2f out: eased whn btn* **16/1**

0000 **15** 1 **Daimajin (IRE)**[7] 5644 5-8-11 40 (v) DNolan(3) 1 —
(MrsLucindaFeatherstone) *racd stands' side: bhd fnl 2f* **33/1**

0500 **16** 1½ **Lady Predominant**[29] 5072 3-8-9 40 BReilly(3) 9 —
(GFBridgwater) *t.k.h on stands' side: bhd fr 1/2-way* **66/1**

2200 **17** nk **Beaver Diva**[54] 4387 3-8-7 40 BSwarbrick(5) 11 —+
(WMBrisbourne) *hld up in rr far side: a bhd* **25/1**

4510 **18** 1 **Sotonian (HOL)**[81] 3616 11-9-0 40 LisaJones 7 —
(PSFelgate) *racd centre of crse: bhd fr 1/2-way* **20/1**

/0-0 **19** shd **Society Pet**[36] 4916 5-8-7 40 DerekNolan(7) 10 —
(DGBridgwater) *racd centre of crse: bhd fr 1/2-way* **66/1**

1m 12.25s (-0.82) **Going Correction** -0.20s/f (Firm)
**WFA** 3 from 4yo+ 2lb **19** Ran SP% **128.5**
Speed ratings: **97,95,91,89,88 84,84,84,83,82 82,81,78,71,70 68,67,66,66**CSF £70.24 TOTE £17.40: £4.20, £2.40, £4.10; EX 60.80.
**Owner** Miss J Wickens **Bred** Michael Coogan **Trained** Upper Lambourn, Berks

**FOCUS**
An average event for the grade, but Spinetail Rufous proved well suited by this drop in trip and can win again if able to hold this level of form. The group racing on the far side looked at a disadvantage.

**NOTEBOOK**
**Spinetail Rufous(IRE)** ran out of stamina very quickly when trying to make all over seven furlongs at Lingfield last week, and the drop back to six proved ideal. He was forced to sit in early, but made good headway to lead just over a furlong out and record his first win since February 2001. If he can hold this level of form he can probably win again.
**Crimson Star(IRE)** is fully effective from six furlongs to a mile, but was found wanting for speed when the race really got going and shapes as though seven may be her ideal trip.
**Angel Isa(IRE)** has run much better the last twice and can pick up a small race for her in-form stable if continuing to run to this level.
**Danakim** was done no favours by the draw and did best of those racing on the far side.
**Mr Uppity** remains a maiden after 26 starts and is not one to make a habit of backing.
**Suitcase Murphy(IRE)** ran a long way below the form that saw him finish third at Thirsk last time.

## 5794 KEMPTON FOR CHRISTMAS PARTIES TRI-BANDED STKS 7f (J)
12:55 (1:00) (H5) 3-Y-O £1,505 (£430; £215) Stalls High

Form RPR

0400 **1** **Dante's Devine (IRE)**[51] 4489 3-9-5 45 VSlattery 15 52
(ABailey) *b: trckd ldrs: led 1f out: rdn out* **20/1**

3524 **2** *nk* **Elsinora**[11] 5552 3-9-2 45 (b) LFletcher(3) 17 51
(HMorrison) *chsd ldrs: ev ch 1f out: no imp after* **11/2**[2]

0066 **3** *1 3/4* **David's Girl**[11] 5552 3-8-11 40 BReilly(3) 8 41
(DMorris) *towards rr: hdwy wl over 1f out: fin strly: nvr nrr* **20/1**

6030 **4** *3/4* **Emaradia**[32] 5016 3-9-2 45 DNolan(3) 13 44
(AWCarroll) *led tl 4f out: led again over 2f out: rdn and hdd 1f out: one pce after* **12/1**

5606 **5** *3/4* **Fabuloso**[16] 5424 3-9-5 45 NCallan 1 42
(VSmith) *a in tch: nt qckn ins fnl 2f* **10/1**

-000 **6** *1/2* **Silver Island**[44] 4669 3-9-5 45 MHenry 16 41
(RMHCowell) *towards rr tl styd on ins fnl 2f* **33/1**

6503 **7** *hd* **Amber Fox (IRE)**[5] 5691 3-9-2 45 FPFerris(3) 10 41
(PDEvans) *in tch: rdn over 2f out: no hdwy after* **7/1**

0051 **8** *nk* **Stagecoach Ruby**[7] 5644 3-9-5 45 RBrisland 5 40
(GLMoore) *in tch: rdn over 2f out: one pce after* **12/1**

0060 **9** *nk* **Whiplash (IRE)**[29] 5072 3-9-5 45 (b) CCatlin 14 39
(KOCunningham-Brown) *hmpd leaving stalls: in rr tl sme prog fnl 2f: n.d* **20/1**

4000 **10** *1* **Royaltea**[23] 5237 3-9-0 45 NChalmers(5) 12 36
(MsDeborahJEvans) *chsd ldrs: rdn over 2f out: wknd over 1f out* **25/1**

4030 **11** *nk* **Pappy (IRE)**[22] 5261 3-9-5 45 PDobbs 11 35
(AWCarroll) *bhd and nvr on terms* **6/1**[3]

0001 **12** *1 1/4* **Savernake Brave (IRE)**[21] 5283 3-9-5 45 GBaker 3 32
(MrsHSweeting) *s.i.s: racd wd and sn in tch: led 4f out tl hdd over 2f out: rdn and sn wknd* **11/4**[1]

6000 **13** *hd* **Joans Jewel**[34] 4968 3-9-5 45 (p) AMcCarthy 6 31
(GGMargarson) *b.hind: mid-div: hung lft 2f out: sn btn* **33/1**

0000 **14** *1/2* **Imperial Wizard**[19] 5338 3-9-5 45 ADaly 7 30
(MDIUsher) *b: a in rr* **50/1**

3000 **15** *nk* **Welsh Empress**[22] 5260 3-9-5 45 RPrice 9 29
(PLGilligan) *played up in stalls and v.s.a: a struggling in rr* **20/1**

0000 **16** *nk* **Hi Darl**[14] 5452 3-9-0 45 BSwarbrick(5) 2 29
(WMBrisbourne) *a bhd* **25/1**

-000 **17** *4* **Court Chancellor**[56] 4337 3-9-5 45 (b) JFEgan 4 18
(PMitchell) *a bhd and hung rt thrght: eased appr fnl f* **33/1**

1m 28.37s (1.10) **Going Correction** +0.05s/f (Good) **17** Ran SP% **130.8**
Speed ratings: **95,94,92,91,90 90,90,89,89,88 87,86,86,85,85 85,80**CSF £121.82 TOTE £24.00: £7.90, £2.40, £7.20; EX 83.90.
**Owner** Raymond Gomersall **Bred** Kilfrush Stud Ltd **Trained** Little Budworth, Cheshire

**FOCUS**
A race contested mainly by frustrating characters, and the form does not look that solid, even for this grade.

**NOTEBOOK**
**Dante's Devine(IRE)**, off since finishing in mid-division in a decent sprint handicap at Haydock in early August, had the step up in trip/drop in grade in his favour and held a perfect position throughout. He had to dig deep to land the spoils, but is open to further improvement.
**Elsinora** remains a maiden after 14 starts, but does not want for lack of trying and deserves to get her head in front.
**David's Girl** is another who struggles to win and she was doing her best work when the race was all over.
**Emaradia** had her chance.
**Fabuloso** could do with stepping back up in trip.
**Silver Island** ran by far and away his best race to date but has yet to establish a suitable trip.
**Savernake Brave(IRE)** spent most of the race out wide and clearly did himself no favours as he ran a shocker.
**Imperial Wizard** *Official explanation: jockey said gelding suffered slight interference just after start*
**Court Chancellor** *Official explanation: jockey said gelding hung left throughout*

## 5795 SUBSCRIBE TO RACING UK ON 08700 860432 BANDED STKS 1m (J)
1:25 (1:31) (H5) 3-Y-O+ £1,589 (£454; £227) Stalls High

Form RPR

0000 **1** **Caerphilly Gal**[16] 5411 4-9-1 47 DFox(5) 7 55
(PLGilligan) *a in tch: hdwy 3f out: led over 1f out: r.o wl* **16/1**

3561 **2** *1 1/2* **Levantine (IRE)**[7] 5641 7-9-0 48 KirstyMilczarek(7) 12 53+
(MissJFeilden) *a.p: swtchd lft 2f out: edgd lft but chsd wnr fnl f* **10/1**

0666 **3** *1/2* **Sonderborg**[18] 5382 3-9-4 49 (b) LisaJones 3 52
(MissAMNewton-Smith) *slowly away: hld up in rr: hdwy over 1f out: r.o wl fnl f: nvr nrr* **33/1**

**4** *nk* **Idle Journey (IRE)**[32] 5030 3-9-3 48 VSlattery 6 51
(MScudamore) *slowly away: t.k.h in mid-div: rdn over 3f out: styd on fnl 2f* **14/1**

4543 **5** *nk* **Tokewanna**[7] 5639 4-9-2 48 (t) BSwarbrick(5) 2 50
(WMBrisbourne) *racd wd in mid-div: styd on fnl 2f* **12/1**

5550 **6** *2 1/2* **Marnie**[41] 4771 7-9-6 47 SHitchcott 19 43
(JAkehurst) *hld up: rdn 1/2-way: styd on one pace fnl 2f* **12/1**

0560 **7** *shd* **City General (IRE)**[19] 5336 3-8-11 49 (p) DerekNolan(7) 4 45
(JSMoore) *lw: chsd ldr: led 3f out: hdd appr fnl f: wknd qckly ins* **25/1**

1004 **8** *shd* **Wood Fern (UAE)**[5] 5691 4-9-6 47 CCatlin 20 43
(MRChannon) *a towards rr: nvr on terms* **8/1**[2]

0022 **9** *2* **Mythical Charm**[13] 5496 5-10-0 55 (t) ADaly 14 46
(JJBridger) *v.s.a: in rr: brief effrt 3f out: nvr on terms* **3/1**[1]

4600 **10** *nk* **Magic Warrior**[51] 4479 4-9-9 50 PMcCabe 9 41
(JCFox) *a in rr* **33/1**

6005 **11** *2* **Russalka**[5] 5702 3-8-9 47 MHalford(7) 8 33
(JulianPoulton) *in rr: sme hdwy over 2f out: edgd rt and wknd fnl f* **20/1**

0200 **12** *1/2* **Gran Clicquot**[21] 5285 9-9-6 47 SWhitworth 18 32
(GPEnright) *a in rr* **16/1**

0004 **13** *2 1/2* **Gemini Lady**[7] 5639 4-9-6 47 (b) AMcCarthy 17 26
(MrsGSRees) *lw: mid-div: rdn over 2f out: sn wknd* **16/1**

0400 **14** *2* **Prince Valentine**[32] 5021 3-9-4 49 (b) MartinDwyer 15 23
(DBFeek) *mid-div: rdn 1/2-way: swtchd rt over 2f out: no hdwy after* **33/1**

6060 **15** *5* **Indian Blaze**[47] 4604 10-9-8 49 JFEgan 13 12
(AndrewReid) *lw: b.hind: in tch: rdn 3f out: wknd 2f out* **10/1**

4400 **16** *5* **Hirayna**[4] 5714 5-9-7 48 GBaker 5 —
(WMBrisbourne) *prom tl rdn and wknd over 2f out* **9/1**[3]

6106 **17** *3* **Faith Healer (IRE)**[51] 4470 3-9-5 50 (b) NCallan 11 —
(VSmith) *led tl hdd 3f out: sn wknd* **12/1**

-000 **18** *4* **St Tropez (IRE)**[17] 3368 3-9-0 48 (b) LPKeniry(3) 16 —
(MrsAJHamilton-Fairley) *a bhd* **50/1**

0100 **19** *6* **Albadi**[61] 4199 3-9-2 50 (b) J-PGuillambert(3) 1 —
(CEBrittain) *trckd ldrs on wd outside: rdn over 3f out: sn wknd* **20/1**

1m 40.86s (1.24) **Going Correction** +0.05s/f (Good)
**WFA** 3 from 4yo+ 4lb **19** Ran SP% **135.8**
Speed ratings: **95,93,93,92,92 89,89,89,87,87 85,84,82,80,75 70,67,63,57**CSF £170.48 TOTE £15.80: £5.00, £4.50, £5.40; EX 657.20.
**Owner** T Williams **Bred** D J And Mrs Deer **Trained** Newmarket, Suffolk

**FOCUS**
A tight-looking contest, but the placed horses ran to recent form and the form appears sound.

**NOTEBOOK**
**Caerphilly Gal**, taking a drop in grade, had conditions to suit and was favoured by the extra furlong. She stayed on strongly to win going away and there may well be more to come from her at the distance.
**Levantine(IRE)**, a winner on the Polytrack the previous week, was done for speed by the winner and could only keep on at the one pace.
**Sonderborg** fluffed her lines coming out of the stalls and as a result she could never get into a good position and had to come from a fair way back. She remains a winless after 23 attempts.
**Idle Journey(IRE)**, making his British debut, was doing his best work towards the finish and should show the benefit of this run. He can pay his way.
**Tokewanna** is another who is still a maiden and she has had plenty of chances.
**Marnie** ◆ is back on a winning mark and may be one to watch out for in the coming weeks.
**Mythical Charm**, who got a little warm beforehand, totally blew it at the start and was never going to get involved. *Official explanation: jockey said mare was slowly away*
**Indian Blaze** *Official explanation: jockey said gelding lost his action*
**Hirayna** *Official explanation: jockey said mare did not act on the Good (Good to Firm in places) ground*
**Faith Healer(IRE)** *Official explanation: jockey said filly was never travelling*

## 5796 BUY YOUR JUMP MEMBERSHIP NOW BANDED STKS 1m 4f
2:00 (2:02) (H5) 3-Y-O+ £1,571 (£449; £224) Stalls High

Form RPR

5106 **1** **Theatre Lady (IRE)**[52] 4457 6-9-5 47 FPFerris(3) 3 57
(PDEvans) *mid-div: hdwy over 2f out: led over 1f out: sn clr: comf* **20/1**

5556 **2** *1 3/4* **Make My Hay**[34] 4971 5-9-6 45 MartinDwyer 9 52
(JGallagher) *mid-div: hdwy over 2f out: wnt 2nd wl ins fnl f: nvr nrr* **6/1**[2]

0030 **3** *1/2* **Open Book**[7] 5645 3-8-12 48 LFletcher(3) 15 54
(HMorrison) *a in tch: chsd ldrs over 2f out: wnt 2nd 1f out tl wl ins fnl f* **20/1**

6604 **4** *3/4* **Tasneef (USA)**[7] 5654 5-9-10 49 SWhitworth 7 54
(TDMccarthy) *trckd ldrs: wnt 2nd 1/2-way: led 4f out: hdd approachiung fnl f: one pce after* **8/1**[3]

2232 **5** *1* **Banningham Blaze**[7] 5654 4-9-8 50 DNolan(3) 14 53
(AWCarroll) *hld up: hdwy over 2f out: styd on: nvr nr to chal* **9/2**[1]

0200 **6** *nk* **Fairy Monarch (IRE)**[4] 5714 5-9-8 47 (p) RFitzpatrick 12 50
(PTMidgley) *hld up in rr: rdn and hdwy 3f out: styd on one pce* **25/1**

3340 **7** *3* **Vandenberghe**[21] 5286 5-9-0 46 RKeogh(7) 5 44
(JAOsborne) *hld up in rr: hdwy over 2f out: one pce after* **12/1**

0100 **8** *3/4* **Chevin**[11] 5546 5-9-3 45 THamilton(3) 13 42
(RAFahey) *prom tl outpcd over 3f out: nvr a factor after* **10/1**

0051 **9** *3/4* **Lysander's Quest (IRE)**[21] 5286 6-9-7 46 NDay 8 42
(RIngram) *in rr tl mde sme late hdwy* **20/1**

1203 **10** *1/2* **Montosari**[24] 5221 5-9-7 46 JFEgan 1 41+
(PMitchell) *mid-div: no hdwy fnl 2f* **12/1**

5060 **11** *nk* **Rhetorical**[7] 5638 3-8-13 49 J-PGuillambert(3) 10 43
(SirMarkPrescott) *led after 1f: hdd 4f out: wknd wl over 1f out* **10/1**

2206 **12** *shd* **Lunar Lord**[7] 5654 8-9-7 46 RPrice 20 40
(DBurchell) *in tch: rdn and outpcd over 3f out: nvr on terms after* **25/1**

0606 **13** *hd* **Ricky Martan**[7] 5643 3-8-9 45 LPKeniry(3) 2 39
(GCBravery) *prom tl rdn and wknd over 1f out* **66/1**

1436 **14** *3/4* **Ambersong**[19] 5350 6-9-10 49 PDobbs 16 42
(AWCarroll) *slowly away: a in rr* **14/1**

/401 **15** *nk* **Regency Red (IRE)**[4] 5710 6-9-8 46 BSwarbrick(5) 6 44
(WMBrisbourne) *mid-div: rdn over 3f out: sn bhd* **8/1**[3]

0002 **16** *6* **Giko**[11] 5540 10-9-8 47 LisaJones 18 29
(JaneSouthcombe) *a in rr* **20/1**

0-00 **17** *12* **Spring Whisper (IRE)**[7] 5642 3-8-7 45 DFox(5) 4 8
(CADwyer) *mid-div: rdn 2f out: wknd* **50/1**

0050 **18** *hd* **Havantadoubt (IRE)**[7] 5658 4-9-6 45 (t) GBaker 19 8
(MRBosley) *a bhd* **50/1**

4202 **19** *12* **Tintawn Gold (IRE)**[21] 5286 4-9-8 47 (p) CCatlin 11 —
(SWoodman) *a in rr* **20/1**

50-0 **20** *dist* **Mister Merlin (IRE)**[11] 5546 3-8-12 45 NPollard 17 —
(DCarroll) *t.k.h: led for 1f: trckd ldr to 1/2-way: sn hrd rdn and wknd qckly: t.o* **66/1**

2m 35.43s (0.43) **Going Correction** +0.05s/f (Good)
**WFA** 3 from 4yo+ 8lb **20** Ran SP% **133.3**
Speed ratings: **100,98,98,98,97 97,95,94,94,93 93,93,93,92,92 88,80,80,72,—**CSF £129.76 TOTE £14.60: £4.70, £2.70, £7.50; EX 96.30 Place 6 £10,927.54, Place 5 £3,990.27.
**Owner** Waterline Racing Club **Bred** Terry Keaney **Trained** Pandy, Gwent

**FOCUS**
This looked solid form for the level and the drop in grade did the trick for Theatre Lady, who ran out a cosy winner.

**NOTEBOOK**
**Theatre Lady(IRE)** has been running in vastly better races than this and the drop in grade/return to a mile four proved just the job. She ran out a cosy winner in the end and should continue to pay her way.
**Make My Hay**, who looked a bit unlucky when coming from a mile back at Folkestone latest, was again doing his best work at the line and the logical step is a rise in distance.
**Open Book** has shown improved form either side of a poor run on the Fibresand and she is evidently better on turf.
**Tasneef(USA)** has been going the wrong way for a while now and does not see out his races that well.
**Banningham Blaze** was finishing out of the first three for the first time since July, but still ran creditably and may simply have been given a bit much to do.
**Chevin** *Official explanation: jockey said mare hung left*
**Montosari** *Official explanation: jockey said gelding was unsuited by the Good (Good to Firm in places) ground*
**Regency Red(IRE)** *Official explanation: jockey said gelding did not act on the Good (Good to Firm in places) ground*
**Giko** *Official explanation: jockey said gelding lost his action on the Good (Good to Firm in places) ground; trainer said gelding slipped during race, lost its action and was never travelling*
**Tintawn Gold(IRE)** *Official explanation: jockey said filly lost her action on the Good (Good to Firm in places) ground*
T/Plt: £4,980.90 to a £1 stake. Pool: £22,516.45. 3.30 winning tickets. T/Qpdt: £878.70 to a £1 stake. Pool: £1,781.20. 1.50 winning tickets. JS

# [5209]RIPON (R-H)

## Saturday, September 25

**OFFICIAL GOING: Good to firm**

After morning rain on watered ground the going was described by the jockeys as 'just on the easy side of good', certainly softer than the official version.

Wind: Moderate 1/2 behind. Weather: Fine.

## 5797 WEATHERBYS BANK NURSERY 5f

1:50 (1:52) (D2) (0-85,80) 2-Y-O £10,335 (£3,180; £1,590; £795) Stalls High

Form RPR

4504 1 **Talcen Gwyn (IRE)**[12] 5515 2-9-3 **76**.......................... ANicholls 14 79
(MFHarris) *dwlt: sn in tch: swtchd lft and hdwy 2f out: rdn to chal ent last: styd on to ld last 75 yds* **11/1**

0451 2 *nk* **Melandre**[18] 5363 2-8-10 **69**.......................... TWilliams 10 71
(MBrittain) *a.p: rdn to ld over 1f out: drvn ins last: hdd and no ex last 75 yds* **10/1**

6100 3 *1 3/4* **Chilly Cracker**[50] 4508 2-8-6 **65**.......................... DaleGibson 11 61
(RHollinshead) *led: rdn along over 2f out: hdd over 1f out: kpt on same pce u.p ins last* **33/1**

0365 4 *nk* **Skiddaw Wolf**[65] 4046 2-8-4 **63**.......................... TPQueally 2 58
(BSmart) *s.i.s and towards rr: pushed along and hdwy 1/2-way: rdn wl over 1f out: styd on strly ins last: nrst fin* **22/1**

6320 5 *nk* **Wonderful Mind**[12] 5515 2-9-0 **73**..........................(b) DAllan 12 67
(TDEasterby) *cl up: rdn and ev ch over 1f out: sn drvn and wknd ins last* **12/1**

2131 6 *1 1/4* **Oceanico Dot Com (IRE)**[12] 5515 2-9-1 **74**.......................... FNorton 15 64
(ABerry) *chsd ldrs: rdn along wl over 1f out: sn one pce* **7/2**[1]

1416 7 *1/2* **Baymist**[27] 5143 2-8-8 **67**.......................... TLucas 13 55
(MWEasterby) *chsd ldrs: rdn and hung lft 2f out: sn wknd* **20/1**

6100 8 *1/2* **Annatalia**[12] 5515 2-9-2 **78**.......................... JFMcDonald(3) 8 64
(BJMeehan) *dwlt and towards rr: hdwy over 2f out: rdn and kpt on ins last nvr afactor* **4/1**[2]

5224 9 *nk* **Howards Princess**[14] 5475 2-8-7 **69**.......................... TEaves(3) 1 54
(JSGoldie) *wnt lft s and bhd: hdwy 2f out: sn rdn and kpt on ins last: nvr a factor* **16/1**

0112 10 *nk* **Monashee Rose (IRE)**[12] 5509 2-9-4 **77**.......................... DaneO'Neill 5 61
(JSMoore) *a towards rr* **15/2**

6565 11 *2* **Bolton Hall (IRE)**[14] 5453 2-9-7 **80**.......................... PHanagan 6 57
(RAFahey) *hld up: a rr* **13/2**[3]

5262 12 *1 1/4* **Hymn Of Victory (IRE)**[12] 5513 2-8-7 **66**.......................... SDrowne 3 39
(TJEtherington) *a towards rr* **20/1**

2002 13 *1 3/4* **Mas O Menos (IRE)**[7] 5633 2-8-4 **66** ow1.......................... PMulrennan(3) 4 32
(MsDeborahJEvans) *chsd ldrs: rdn along 1/2-way: sn wknd* **33/1**

0400 14 *1/2* **Lucy Parkes**[10] 5555 2-7-12 **57** oh6.......................... DMernagh 9 22
(EJAlston) *bhd fr 1/2-way* **50/1**

050 15 *1 1/2* **Hamburg Springer (IRE)**[10] 5555 2-7-13 **58** oh12 ow1..... SRighton 16 17
(MJPolglase) *sn outpcd and bhd* **66/1**

60.95 secs (0.75) **Going Correction** +0.10s/f (Good) **15** Ran SP% **121.5**

Speed ratings: **98,97,94,94,93 91,90,90,89,89 86,84,81,80,78**CSF £107.93 CT £3517.19 TOTE £10.80: £2.90, £3.60, £8.10; EX 138.90.

**Owner** D K Watkins **Bred** Paul Smyth **Trained** Paxford, Gloucs

**FOCUS**

A fair nursery in which they raced in one group down the far side. The form looks solid enough with the placed horses setting the standard.

**NOTEBOOK**

**Talcen Gwyn(IRE)**, out of luck at Musselburgh, buckled down in willing fashion to show ahead near the line and end his rider's drought. A May foal, he should make a useful three-year-old.

**Melandre**, taken to post early, is settling down well. She worked hard to get her head in front but was edged out near the line.

**Chilly Cracker**, from a stable in top form, ran right up to her best but she looks rated to the limit now.

**Skiddaw Wolf** almost bolted to the post. Dropped in at the start, after taking a while to pick up she was putting in all her best work at the finish.

**Wonderful Mind**, with the blinkers on again, was again found lacking in the closing stages.

**Oceanico Dot Com(IRE)**, 3lb higher, was unable to confirm Musselburgh placings with the winner, who was out of luck there.

**Baymist** *Official explanation: jockey said filly was unsuited by the good to firm ground and hung left-handed throughout*

**Annatalia**, out of luck at Musselburgh, is only small and after a tardy start was never a factor.

**Mas O Menos(IRE)** *Official explanation: jockey said gelding hung right-handed throughout*

## 5798 HOMESALE NETWORK H'CAP 6f

2:20 (2:20) (E3) (0-70,70) 3-Y-0+ £5,096 (£1,568; £784; £392) Stalls Low

Form RPR

0066 1 **Blythe Spirit**[18] 5370 5-8-8 **62**..........................(p) PHanagan 7 78+
(RAFahey) *hld up stands side: gd hdwy 2f out: rdn to ld ins last: kpt on wl* **7/1**[2]

5006 2 *2 1/2* **Vigorous (IRE)**[52] 4452 4-8-2 **63**.......................... AMullen(7) 3 72
(MTodhunter) *trckd ldrs stands side: hdwy and overall ldr 11/2h out: sn rdn: hdd ins last: kpt on* **33/1**

0005 3 *shd* **Prince Of Gold**[8] 5713 4-8-8 **62**..........................(p) SDrowne 11 71
(RHollinshead) *towards rr far side: hdwy wl over 1f out: sn rdn and styd on wl fnl f: nrst fin* **25/1**

0203 4 *1/2* **Dr Synn**[11] 5541 3-8-10 **66**.......................... PDoe 6 73
(JAkehurst) *hld up stands side: swtchd lft and hdwy wl over 1f out: sn rdn and kpt on ins last: nrst fin* **25/1**

2101 5 *1* **Bint Royal (IRE)**[7] 5639 6-8-4 **58**.......................... FNorton 17 62
(MissVHaigh) *trckd ldrs far side: hdwy 2f out: rdn over 1f out: kpt on ins last* **11/1**

2001 6 *nk* **Bowling Along**[12] 5526 3-7-11 **60**.......................... TDean(7) 13 63
(MESowersby) *in tch far side: swtchd lft and hdwy centre wl over 1f out: sn rdn and kpt on fnl f* **18/1**

0010 7 *1* **Magic Amour**[16] 5425 6-8-3 **57**..........................(b[1]) SRighton 4 57
(IanWilliams) *chsd ldrs stands side: rdn 2f out: drvn and one pce ent last* **22/1**

0500 8 *1/2* **Wessex (USA)**[11] 5544 4-8-11 **65**..........................(v[1]) DMernagh 18 64
(JamesMoffatt) *hld up far side: swtchd lft and hdwy 2f out: sn rdn and kpt on fnl f* **50/1**

0001 9 *1/2* **Compton Plume**[10] 5562 4-8-13 **67**.......................... DaleGibson 9 64
(WHTinning) *towards rr far side: rdn along 1/2-way: kpt on u.p appr last* **20/1**

1600 10 *nk* **Desert Arc (IRE)**[77] 3747 6-8-10 **64**.......................... DAllan 5 60
(WMBrisbourne) *prom stands side: rdn along 2f out: grad wknd* **50/1**

4046 11 *hd* **Val De Maal (IRE)**[26] 5201 4-8-10 **67**.......................... TEaves(3) 20 63
(GCHChung) *led far side gp: pushed along and hdd over 2f out: grad wknd appr last* **12/1**

4226 12 *nk* **Never Without Me**[5] 5704 4-8-8 **65**.......................... PMulrennan(3) 14 60
(JFCoupland) *trckd ldrs far side: hdwy to ld that gp over 2f out: sn rdn: hdd and grad wknd* **13/2**[1]

0060 13 *1* **Tally (IRE)**[10] 5562 4-8-9 **63**.......................... DaneO'Neill 10 55
(MJPolglase) *chsd ldrs far side: rdn along over 2f out: grad wknd* **28/1**

0005 14 *1/2* **Banjo Bay (IRE)**[12] 5526 6-8-9 **63**.......................... ANicholls 16 53
(DNicholls) *hld up far side: nvr a factor* **13/2**[1]

5443 15 *1* **Winthorpe (IRE)**[12] 5526 4-9-0 **68**.......................... DarrenWilliams 15 55
(JJQuinn) *in tch far side: rdn along 2f out: sn wknd* **15/2**[3]

0245 16 *nk* **Sharp Hat**[9] 5579 10-8-9 **63**.......................... ACulhane 1 49
(DWChapman) *led stands side gp: overall ldr 1/2-way: rdn along and hdd 11/2 f out: sn wknd* **12/1**

4050 17 *nk* **Mynd**[28] 5107 4-8-7 **61** ow2..........................(p) VHalliday 2 46
(RMWhitaker) *cl up stands side: rdn along 2f over 2f out: sn wknd* **25/1**

0000 18 *3/4* **Attacca**[26] 5193 3-7-11 **60**..........................(b) DFentiman(7) 12 43
(JRWeymes) *prom far side: rdn along over 2f out: sn wknd* **100/1**

5006 19 *3/4* **Mister Sweets**[36] 4928 5-8-11 **70**.......................... DTudhope(5) 8 51
(DCarroll) *a rr stands side* **33/1**

0002 20 *nk* **Torrent**[10] 5562 9-7-12 **57**..........................(b) RoryMoore(5) 19 37
(DWChapman) *cl up far side: led that gp over 2f out: sn rdn: hdd & wknd* **14/1**

1m 12.87s (-0.03) **Going Correction** +0.10s/f (Good)

**WFA** 3 from 4yo+ 2lb **20** Ran SP% **121.5**

Speed ratings: **104,100,100,99,98 98,96,96,95,95 94,94,93,92,91 90,90,89,88,87**CSF £226.56 CT £5489.29 TOTE £10.70: £2.70, £9.90, £4.80, £3.30; EX 456.60.

**Owner** The Matthewman Partnership **Bred** W Haggas And W Jarvis **Trained** Musley Bank, N Yorks

**FOCUS**

A fair handicap in which they split into two groups with the first two home on the stands' side. The winner could be well treated, even after re-assessment.

**NOTEBOOK**

**Blythe Spirit**, who has won at up to a mile, is not easy to predict but he was in the right frame of mind and took this in most decisive fashion. He has won from a stone higher mark in the past and will still be worthy of close interest when he is re-assesed.

**Vigorous(IRE)** has come down 10lb in the ratings and was having his first outing for her new trainer.

**Prince Of Gold**, making a quick reappearance, has a high cruising speed and came out best of the far side group on this drop in trip.

**Dr Synn**, a maiden after ten previous starts, appreciated the give underfoot. Despite flashing his tail he was putting in all his best work at the finish.

**Bint Royal(IRE)**, unable to dominate this time, came out second best on the far side.

**Bowling Along**, 3lb higher, seemed to find herself rather marooned up the centre.

**Wessex(USA)** *Official explanation: jockey gelding was unsuited by the good to firm ground*

**Never Without Me**, having his second outing in five weeks, found this a bridge too far.

**Banjo Bay(IRE)**, meeting Bowling Along on better terms compared with Redcar, never figured.

## 5799 SPORTINGOPTIONS.CO.UK COMMISSION CUTTERS H'CAP 6f

2:55 (2:55) (C1) (0-100,99) 3-Y-0+ £12,255 (£4,648; £2,324; £1,056) Stalls Low

Form RPR

6000 1 **Pic Up Sticks**[17] 5393 5-9-1 **93**.......................... ACulhane 2 106
(MRChannon) *racd stands' side: hld up: hdwy over 2f out: led 1f out: r.o wl* **6/1**[2]

3560 2 *1* **Ellens Academy (IRE)**[8] 5603 9-8-7 **85** oh1.......................... FNorton 3 95
(EJAlston) *racd stands' side: hld up in rr: hdwy 2f out: styd on wl to take 2nd nr line* **20/1**

-000 3 *nk* **Smart Hostess**[6] 5671 5-8-10 **91**.......................... TEaves(3) 8 100
(JJQuinn) *chsd ldrs: kpt on wl fnl f* **25/1**

0000 4 *1/2* **Artie**[8] 5605 5-8-7 **85** oh2.......................... DaneO'Neill 13 93
(TDEasterby) *led on far side: kpt on wl fnl f* **20/1**

0-03 5 *nk* **Aversham**[21] 5299 4-8-9 **87**.......................... SDrowne 6 94
(RCharlton) *racd stands' side: trckd ldrs: led over 1f out: sn hdd and no ex* **11/2**[1]

2002 6 *1* **Fantasy Believer**[7] 5628 6-9-6 **98**.......................... PHanagan 7 102
(JJQuinn) *racd stands' side: trckd ldrs: styd on same pce appr fnl f* **11/2**[1]

0065 7 *hd* **Impressive Flight (IRE)**[9] 5588 5-8-7 **85** oh3.......................... DMernagh 11 88
(TDBarron) *dwlt: racd far side: hld up: hdwy to join ldr that side over 1f out: kpt on same pce* **20/1**

0002 8 *shd* **Marsad (IRE)**[24] 5224 10-8-9 **87**.......................... PDoe 4 90
(JAkehurst) *racd stands' side: trckd ldrs: effrt 2f out: kpt on same pce* **12/1**

0640 9 *1 1/2* **Hidden Dragon (USA)**[7] 5628 5-8-12 **90**..........................(p) GFaulkner 10 88
(PABlockley) *swtchd lft after s and racd stands' side: w ldrs: one pce appr fnl f* **8/1**

4200 10 *shd* **Inter Vision (USA)**[15] 5440 4-8-4 **85** oh4..........................(p) PMulrennan(3) 9 83
(ADickman) *racd stands' side: led that side tl over 2f out: weakaned appr fnl f* **20/1**

3320 11 *1/2* **Pieter Brueghel (USA)**[8] 5603 5-8-8 **86**.......................... ANicholls 1 83+
(DNicholls) *hung rt thrght: racd stands' side: w ldr: led that gp over 2f out tl over 1f out: sn btn* **8/1**

U003 12 *2* **Peruvian Chief (IRE)**[13] 5491 7-9-0 **92**..........................(b) TPQueally 12 83
(NPLittmoden) *racd far side: chsd ldr tl lost pl over 1f out: eased ins last* **16/1**

1145 13 *3* **Raymond's Pride**[140] 1956 4-8-0 **85** oh3..........................(b) AMullen(7) 5 67
(KARyan) *racd stands' side: in rr: hrd drvn over 3f out: sn bhd* **50/1**

2003 14 *5* **Dazzling Bay**[4] 5712 4-9-7 **99**..........................(b) DAllan 14 66
(TDEasterby) *reluctant to go to s: racd far side: chsd ldrs: lost pl 2f out: eased* **15/2**[3]

1m 12.4s (-0.50) **Going Correction** +0.10s/f (Good) **14** Ran SP% **117.5**

Speed ratings: **107,105,105,104,104 102,102,102,100,100 99,97,93,86**CSF £126.19 CT £2851.29 TOTE £7.20: £2.60, £4.80, £7.00; EX 103.80.

**Owner** A Ball & W Harrison-Allan **Bred** J P Coggan **Trained** West Ilsley, Berks

**FOCUS**

In effect a 0-99 handicap and they split into two groups with the first three home racing on the stands' side. The form looks solid, being rated through the runner-up and fourth.

**NOTEBOOK**

**Pic Up Sticks**, who needed the outing at Doncaster after missing some work, was in peak form and recorded his fourth career win in convincing fashion. Getting his head in front again will have done him a power of good.

**Ellens Academy(IRE)**, who has not tasted success for almost a year, keeps running well in this grade but as a result receives precious little relief.

**Smart Hostess ◆**, unsuited by the soft at Hamilton, showed a welcome return to form and last year she clocked up three wins in October.

**Artie** dominated the smaller group on the far side. Despite a tendency to hang left, he kept on all the way to the line despite lacking company in the closing stages. *Official explanation: jockey said gelding hung left-handed in the final 2f*

**Aversham**, having his second outing for his new trainer in three weeks after seven months on the sidelines, was a bit keen to post. After taking charge on the stands' side, he did not last home.
**Fantasy Believer**, 3lb higher, ran a bit flat after his fine effort at Ayr just seven days earlier. An admirable type, he will bounce back.
**Pieter Brueghel(USA)** wanted to do nothing but hang right throughout. *Official explanation: jockey said gelding hung right-handed throughout*
**Dazzling Bay** was most reluctant to go the start and once there was reluctant to go behind the stalls. His temperament seems to be getting the better of him.

## 5800 ARK DE TRIUMPH FILLIES' MAIDEN AUCTION STKS 5f
3:25 (3:25) (E3) 2-Y-O **£4,102** (£1,262; £631; £315) **Stalls** High

Form RPR
3330 **1** **Angelofthenorth**[37] 4875 2-8-4 63 .................. TPQueally 12 65
(JDBethell) *sn overall ldr stands side: rdn clr wl over 1f out: drvn ins last: jst hld on* **8/1**[3]
040 **2** *nk* **Thornber Court (IRE)**[14] 5475 2-8-4 56 .................. FNorton 10 64
(ABerry) *s.i.s: sn in tch stands side: hdwy wl over 1f out: rdn and styd on wl fnl f* **100/1**
3 **3** *shd* **Pivotal's Princess (IRE)**[72] 3868 2-8-6 .................. DaneO'Neill 4 70+
(BAMcmahon) *lw: hld up stands side: nt clr run and swtchd lft 2f out: gd hdwy swtchd rt 1f out: str run ins last: edgd rt nr fin* **3/1**[1]
4024 **4** *1 3/4* **Bob's Flyer**[12] 5513 2-8-8 67 .................. PHanagan 11 61
(JGGiven) *towards rr: hdwy 2f out: rdn over 1f out: kpt on fnl f* **8/1**[3]
2205 **5** *1 3/4* **Lady Hopeful (IRE)**[71] 3898 2-8-6 62 ow5 .................. TEaves(3) 1 56
(RPElliott) *chsd wnr stands side: rdn along 2f out: sn wknd* **20/1**
0 **6** *2 1/2* **Daisys Girl**[22] 5271 2-8-6 .................. SDrowne 9 45
(BHanbury) *towards rr stands side: rdn along 1/2-way: kpt on appr last: nvr nr ldrs* **6/1**[2]
4600 **7** *1/2* **Sweet Marguerite**[9] 5578 2-8-6 55 .................. DAllan 16 43+
(TDEasterby) *led far side gp: rdn along over 2f out: no ch w stands side* **20/1**
00 **8** *3/4* **Bahamian Bay**[63] 4149 2-8-2 .................. TWilliams 8 36
(MBrittain) *chsd ldrs stands side: rdn along 2f out: sn wknd* **80/1**
**9** *5* **Time For Mee** 2-7-13 .................. JFMcDonald(3) 2 19
(RAFahey) *neat: unf: a rr stands side* **33/1**
054 **10** *1* **Ashes (IRE)**[123] 2388 2-8-7 64 ow3 ..................(b[1]) DarrenWilliams 7 20
(KRBurke) *chsd ldrs stands side: rdn along 1/2-way: sn wknd* **10/1**
6 **11** *1/2* **Boppys Dream**[10] 5555 2-8-2 .................. DMernagh 5 13
(RAFahey) *a rr stands side* **28/1**
00 **12** *1 1/4* **Brave Tara (IRE)**[14] 5447 2-8-4 .................. PMQuinn 13 11
(TDEasterby) *chsd ldr far side: rdn along 1/2-way: sn outpcd* **100/1**
0 **13** *1 1/2* **Courtintime**[127] 2268 2-8-4 .................. ANicholls 3 6
(TDEasterby) *in tch stands side: rdn along and wkng whn hmpd 2f out: sn bhd* **50/1**
0 **14** *hd* **Woodford Wonder (IRE)**[20] 5319 2-8-4 ow5 .......... PMulrennan(3) 14 8
(MWEasterby) *racd far side: bhd fr 1/2-way* **100/1**
00 **15** *15* **Agreat Dayoutwithu**[25] 5209 2-8-2 .................. JMcAuley 15 —
(PTMidgley) *racd far side: bhd fr 1/2-way* **100/1**
0603 **P** **Lady Dan (IRE)**[23] 5233 2-8-4 65 .................. DaleGibson 6 —
(MWEasterby) *chsd ldrs stands side: rdn along 1/2-way: wkng whn lost action and p.u lame wl over 1f out* **3/1**[1]

60.91 secs (0.71) **Going Correction** +0.10s/f (Good) **16** Ran SP% **118.7**
Speed ratings: **98,97,97,94,91 87,86,85,77,76 75,73,70,70,46** —CSF £655.33 TOTE £11.00: £2.20, £10.30, £2.10; EX 446.50.
**Owner** J Hamilton **Bred** Jephanil **Trained** Middleham Moor, N Yorks

**FOCUS**
A modest maiden won by a filly with a provisional rating of just 63. The standard is moderate and most of these will be plying their trade in ordinary handicaps.
**NOTEBOOK**
**Angelofthenorth**, who lost her action on her previous start, has plenty of speed and in the end did just enough to get off the mark at the seventh attempt.
**Thornber Court(IRE)**, already beaten in claimers and sellers, would have met the winner on much better terms in a nursery and in the end just missed out.
**Pivotal's Princess(IRE)**, absent for ten weeks, looked in tip-top condition and was unlucky not to land the spoils. She deserves to find a similar race but this was basically a fine opportunity lost.
**Bob's Flyer**, an exciteable type, had two handlers in the paddock. She only got going late on but may not be straightforward.
**Lady Hopeful(IRE)**, absent for two months, had the visor left off.
**Daisys Girl**, from a stable struggling for winners, stayed on late despite a marked tendency to hang right. *Official explanation: jockey said filly hung right throughout*
**Courtintime** *Official explanation: jockey said filly became unbalanced on the undulations*
**Agreat Dayoutwithu** *Official explanation: jockey said filly bled from the nose*
**Lady Dan(IRE)** did not impress at all going to post and seemed to suffer a severe knee injury. *Official explanation: vet said filly pulled up lame*

## 5801 A RHODES HAULAGE MAIDEN STKS (DIV I) 6f
4:00 (4:00) (D3) 3-Y-O+ **£4,071** (£1,252; £626; £313) **Stalls** Low

Form RPR
6326 **1** **Kensington (IRE)**[106] 2836 3-9-0 64 .................. SDrowne 10 63
(RGuest) *wnt rt s: sn trcking ldrs: hdwy to ld 1f out: rdn clr ins last* **2/1**[1]
00-0 **2** *4* **Forrest Gump**[19] 5345 4-8-13 .................. TEaves(3) 2 51
(CJTeague) *towards rr: hdwy over 2f out: sn rdn: styd on u.p ins last: no ch w wnr* **80/1**
4253 **3** *3/4* **Brain Washed**[28] 5104 3-8-9 67 .................. DAllan 1 44
(TDEasterby) *cl up: rdn 2f out: drvn ent last and kpt on same pce* **3/1**[3]
050- **4** *1/2* **Aegean Mist**[439] 3269 4-8-11 40 .................. SRighton 9 42
(MMullineaux) *led: rdn along 2f out: drvn and hdd 1f out: sn wknd* **50/1**
-524 **5** *3/4* **M For Magic**[12] 5525 5-8-9 45 .................. KPierrepont(7) 3 45
(CWFairhurst) *chsd ldrs: rdn along 2f out: sn drvn and one pce appr last* **9/1**
6005 **6** *nk* **Pay Time**[56] 4351 5-8-8 35 .................. PMulrennan(3) 12 39
(REBarr) *dwlt: sn in tch: effrt and rdn along 2f out: sn no imp* **33/1**
5000 **7** *1* **Caribbean Blue**[57] 4309 3-8-6 40 ..................(v[1]) JFMcDonald(3) 8 36
(RMWhitaker) *chsd ldrs: swtchd lft and rdn along over 2f out: sn drvn and btn* **14/1**
-060 **8** *shd* **Russian Symphony (USA)**[3] 5737 3-9-0 65 ..................(b) ACulhane 13 41
(CREgerton) *chsd ldrs: rdn along over 2f out: sn wknd* **9/4**[2]
0040 **9** *6* **Designer City (IRE)**[28] 5104 3-8-9 35 .................. FNorton 11 18
(ABerry) *sn rdn along in rr: outpcd and bhd fr 1/2-way* **33/1**
0 **10** *dist* **Secret Of Secrets**[19] 5342 3-9-0 .................. JMcAuley 5 —
(LRJames) *swtg: sn rdn along in rr: outpcd and bhd fr 1/2-way* **22/1**

1m 14.28s (1.38) **Going Correction** +0.10s/f (Good)
**WFA** 3 from 4yo+ 2lb **10** Ran SP% **119.2**
Speed ratings: **94,88,87,87,86 85,84,84,76,**—CSF £191.03 TOTE £3.30: £1.30, £7.20, £1.60; EX 281.00.
**Owner** M Sakal **Bred** Mountarmstrong Stud **Trained** Newmarket, Suffolk

**FOCUS**
A poor maiden and the slowest of five races run over the trip, but a most decisive winner and they all raced down the stands' side.
**NOTEBOOK**
**Kensington(IRE)** ◆, absent since flopping when favourite in a handicap at Chepstow in June, is a big colt and stood out like a beacon in the fog in the paddock. He travelled supremely well and had only to be sent about his job to forge clear inside the last.
**Forrest Gump**, unplaced in three previous starts, had the headgear left off and this marked a big step up.
**Brain Washed**, who had the best of the draw, hung right throughout and does not look straightfoward. She looks harshly treated with an official rating of 67. *Official explanation: jockey said filly hung right-handed throughout*
**Aegean Mist**, placed once in 15 previous starts and often beaten in selling company, was having her first outing for 14 months and her first for her new stable. Her official rating of just 40 will shoot up after this.
**M For Magic**, who has run at up to a mile three in the past, was having his 22nd outing and this is surely too sharp for him.
**Pay Time**, a maiden after 15 previous starts, is rated just 35.
**Russian Symphony(USA)**, a close-up seventh at Lingfield just three days earlier, scratched his way to post and was one of the first beaten.

## 5802 NIDDERDALE NOVICE STKS 6f
4:35 (4:35) (D2) 2-Y-O **£10,022** (£2,505) **Stalls** Low

Form RPR
0103 **1** **Country Rambler (USA)**[14] 5457 2-8-12 94 .................. KMay(7) 1 93+
(BWHills) *mde all: rdn along over 2f out: sn clr* **9/4**[2]
421 **2** *16* **Loaderfun (IRE)**[11] 5536 2-9-5 100 .................. DaneO'Neill 2 45+
(HCandy) *trckd wnr: pushed along over 2f out: sn rdn and btn whn eased over 1f out* **2/5**[1]

1m 12.94s (0.04) **Going Correction** +0.10s/f (Good) **2** Ran SP% **102.2**
Speed ratings: **103,81** TOTE £2.50.
**Owner** Ahmed Buhaleeba **Bred** M & B Delfiner Et Al **Trained** Lambourn, Berks

**FOCUS**
What turned out to be a one-horse race was run in a surprisingly good time under the circumstances.
**NOTEBOOK**
**Country Rambler(USA)**, a most likeable individual, jumped off and set a strong pace and was about five lengths up when the rider of the below-par runner-up accepted the inevitable. Six furlongs suits him well and he should continue to give a good account of himself at this level.
**Loaderfun(IRE)**, edgy at the start, ran no race at all and in the end was allowed to complete in his own time. This was simply too bad to be true. *Official explanation: trainer's representative had no explanation for the poor form shown*

## 5803 A RHODES HAULAGE MAIDEN STKS (DIV II) 6f
5:05 (5:05) (D2) 3-Y-O+ **£4,063** (£1,250; £625; £312) **Stalls** Low

Form RPR
2404 **1** **Flying Bantam (IRE)**[12] 5526 3-9-0 68 .................. PHanagan 3 76
(RAFahey) *t.k.h: mde all: kpt on wl fnl f* **9/4**[2]
3352 **2** *1 3/4* **Deuxieme (IRE)**[19] 5338 3-8-9 72 .................. SDrowne 2 66
(RCharlton) *hld up: hdwy over 2f out: edgd rt appr fnl f: no real imp* **7/4**[1]
5-2 **3** *4* **Bluebok**[26] 5204 3-9-0 .................. TPQueally 9 59
(DRLoder) *trckd ldrs: effrt 2f out: wl outpcd fnl f* **7/2**[3]
00- **4** *1/2* **Rose Of York (IRE)**[213] 2303 4-8-8 .................. TEaves(3) 5 52
(TDWalford) *sn outpcd and bhd: hdwy 2f out: styd on ins last* **66/1**
3442 **5** *2 1/2* **Nicholas Nickelby**[14] 5448 4-9-2 52 ..................(p) DaneO'Neill 12 56+
(MJPolglase) *swvd rt s: chsd ldrs: wkng whn n.m.r appr fnl f* **10/1**
20-6 **6** *1/2* **Juniper Banks**[19] 5342 3-9-0 62 .................. ACulhane 10 48
(MissAStokell) *chsd ldrs: wknd fnl f* **25/1**
04 **7** *5* **Grey Fortune**[29] 5086 5-8-11 .................. TWilliams 1 28
(MBrittain) *w ldrs: wknd over 1f out* **50/1**
0- **8** *2* **Dorisima (FR)**[372] 5029 3-8-6 ..................(e[1]) PMulrennan(3) 6 22
(MWEasterby) *sn outpcd and bhd* **50/1**
**9** *1 1/2* **Kussharro**[107] 3-9-0 .................. DMernagh 8 23
(BruceHellier, Germany) *w ldrs: drvn along 3f out: lost pl over 1f out* **16/1**
0006 **10** *8* **Sea Fern**[11] 5547 3-9-0 45 .................. ANicholls 7 —
(DEddy) *outpcd and drvn along 3f out: lost pl 2f out: sn bhd and eased* **66/1**

1m 13.75s (0.85) **Going Correction** +0.10s/f (Good)
**WFA** 3 from 4yo+ 2lb **10** Ran SP% **115.1**
Speed ratings: **98,95,90,89,86 85,79,76,74,63** CSF £6.28 TOTE £4.60: £1.30, £1.20, £2.00; EX 8.20 Place 6 £3,172.61, Place 5 £390.85.
**Owner** The Matthewman Partnership **Bred** Robinski Bloodstock Limited **Trained** Musley Bank, N Yorks
■ Stewards Enquiry : S Drowne caution: careless riding

**FOCUS**
A modest maiden but the better of the two divisions and the faster too, though still relatively weak and lacking any strength in depth.
**NOTEBOOK**
**Flying Bantam(IRE)**, runner-up six times in 14 previous starts, was certainly not winning out of turn and he made the most of a good opportunity.
**Deuxieme(IRE)** had 9lb in hand of the winner on official figures but it did not work out that way. Very keen to post, she came off a straight line under pressure and at the finish was very much second best.
**Bluebok**, having just his third-ever start and dropped back in trip, was hopelessly outpaced by the first two in the closing stages.
**Rose Of York(IRE)**, pulled up in a selling hurdle and well beaten in two starts on the Flat last year, has changed stables and ran as if she will need at least a mile in handicap company.
**Nicholas Nickelby**, on his 14th start, had finished well beaten in a claimer last time.
**Juniper Banks**, a keen type, did not improve for the step up to six.
T/Plt: £3,248.90 to a £1 stake. Pool: £38,943.35. 8.75 winning tickets. T/Qpdt: £59.90 to a £1 stake. Pool: £2,362.60. 29.15 winning tickets. JR

5804 - 5807a (Foreign Racing) - See Raceform Interactive

# [4794] COLOGNE (R-H)
Saturday, September 25

**OFFICIAL GOING: Soft**

## 5808a EUROPA STEHER-PREIS (LISTED) 1m 7f
3:35 (3:41) 3-Y-O+ **£9,155** (£2,817; £1,408; £704)

RPR
**1** **No Refuge (IRE)**[24] 5254 4-9-2 ..................(b[1]) THellier 6 109
(SirMarkPrescott) *raced in 4th, switched to challenge 2 1/2f out, led over 1 1/2f out, ran on well. (28/10)* 1
**2** *2* **Le Royal (GER)** 4-9-2 .................. OPeslier 5 107
(HJGroschel, Germany)

3 2 **Liquido (GER)**[24] 5254 5-9-4 ........ ADeVries 1 107
(HSteinmetz, Germany)
4 hd **Kasus (GER)**[24] 5254 6-9-2 ........ AStarke 7 105
(PVovcenko, Germany)
5 3/4 **Bailamos (GER)**[39] 4832 4-9-6 ........ WMongil 2 108
(PSchiergen, Germany)
6 2 **Altamirano (GER)** 5-9-2 ........ IFerguson 3 102
(WBaltromei, Germany)
7 21 **Lisibila (GER)**[452] 2882 6-8-12 ........ J-PCarvalho 4 77
(FrauJMayer, Germany)

3m 22.83s 7 Ran SP% **26.3**
Speed ratings: .
**Owner** W E Sturt - Osborne House III **Bred** Cathal M Ryan **Trained** Newmarket, Suffolk

**NOTEBOOK**
**No Refuge(IRE)** reacted well to the application of blinkers to score with a degree of comfort. Stamina is his strong suit and the Cesarewitch looks tailor-made for him.

## 5809a GROSSE EUROPA-MEILE (GROUP 2) 1m
4:05 (4:13) 3-Y-0+ **£28,169** (£10,563; £4,225; £2,817)

RPR
1 **Eagle Rise (IRE)**[29] 4-9-1 ........ THellier 4 113
(ASchutz, Germany) *raced in 4th, switched to outside over 2f out, led narrowly over 1f out, held on well* 2
2 nk **Putra Pekan**[21] 5291 6-9-1 ........(b) OPeslier 5 113
(MAJarvis) *led til headed over 1f out, dropped back to 3rd, rallied gamely under strong driving to regain 2nd 100yds out, ran on* 3
3 1 **Assiun (GER)**[25] 5215 3-8-9 ........ FilipMinarik 1 109
(PSchiergen, Germany) *held up on inside, 6th straight, headway on inside when not much room approaching final f, stayed on to take 3rd close home* 1
4 nk **Peppercorn (GER)**[35] 7-9-1 ........ AStarke 3 110
(UOstmann, Germany) *raced in 3rd, disputed lead briefly over 1f out, edged right and headed, one pace closing stages*
5 3 1/2 **Ryono (USA)**[27] 5169 5-9-1 ........ TCastanheira 2 103
(PLautner, Germany) *held up in last, headway to go 5th straight, one pace final 2f*
6 nk **Lazio (GER)**[55] 4378 3-8-9 ........ ADeVries 6 100
(ATrybuhl, Germany) *raced in 2nd, weakened 2f out*
7 3 **Moon Over Miami (GER)**[97] 3134 3-8-9 ........ JBojko 7 94
(FrauEMader, Germany) *always in rear*

1m 41.06s
**WFA** 3 from 4yo+ 4lb 7 Ran SP% **131.9**
Speed ratings: .
**Owner** Baron G Von Ullmann **Bred** Baron G Von Ullmann **Trained** Germany

**NOTEBOOK**
**Eagle Rise(IRE)** was switched to the centre of the track in the last two furlongs, and may have found the best ground, so that move was instrumental in providing Hellier with the 1,000th success of his riding career. The Premio Ribot in Rome on November 7 could be his next outing.
**Putra Pekan** made the running and looked set to be swamped when challenged on both sides at the distance. However, responding to fierce pressure that earned Peslier a fine for excessive use of the whip, he battled on gamely and was only narrowly denied.

# 5778 ASCOT (R-H)
## Sunday, September 26

**OFFICIAL GOING: Good to firm**
Wind: lt against Weather: mostly fine

## 5810 RIGGS BANK NURSERY 7f (R)
2:00 (2:02) (B1) 2-Y-0 **£12,644** (£4,796; £2,398; £1,090) **Stalls** High

Form RPR
0333 1 **Wise Dennis**[22] 5292 2-8-6 **80** ........ KMcEvoy 3 92
(APJarvis) *lw: racd wd: dwlt: hld up in rr: prog on outer over 2f out: led over 1f out: hanging lft but sn clr: pushed out* **10/1**[3]
5411 2 1 3/4 **Rebel Rebel (IRE)**[4] 5738 2-8-3 **84** 5ex ........ AMullen(7) 9 94+
(NACallaghan) *swtg: dwlt: wl in rr and nt gng wl: effrt and swtchd lft over 1f out: r.o to take 2nd ins fnl f: no ch wnr* **15/8**[1]
165 3 3 **Sky Crusader**[48] 4601 2-8-9 **83** ........ SDrowne 12 83
(RIngram) *swtg: prom: effrt 2f out: upsides over 1f out: one pce fnl f* **40/1**
5415 4 1/2 **Im Spartacus**[22] 5292 2-8-1 **75** ........(p) MartinDwyer 8 74
(IAWood) *lw: chsd ldng pair to over 2f out: rdn and nt qckn: styd on again ins fnl f* **33/1**
2231 5 hd **Goodwood Spirit**[17] 5420 2-8-7 **81** ........ TQuinn 4 80
(JLDunlop) *stmbld bdly s: in tch in rr: rdn and struggling over 2f out: styd on fnl f* **12/1**
1052 6 3/4 **Brooklime (IRE)**[8] 5655 2-8-6 **80** ........ SWKelly 10 77
(JAOsborne) *pressed ldr: upsides over 1f out: fdd ins fnl f* **16/1**
4341 7 shd **Diamonds And Dust**[21] 5314 2-8-8 **82** ........ PRobinson 2 78
(MHTompkins) *mde most to over 1f out: wknd fnl f* **10/1**[3]
2110 8 3/4 **Persian Rock (IRE)**[18] 5392 2-9-0 **88** ........ LDettori 11 83
(JAOsborne) *s.i.s: sn midfield: hrd rdn 2f out: chsd ldrs over 1f out: wknd ins fnl f* **9/2**[2]
5512 9 3/4 **Easy Mover (IRE)**[11] 5565 2-8-0 **77** ........ NMackay(3) 5 70
(RGuest) *settled midfield: effrt on inner 2f out: chsd ldrs over 1f out: wknd fnl f* **16/1**
1052 10 2 1/2 **Al Qudra (IRE)**[49] 4581 2-9-7 **95** ........ JFortune 7 81
(BJMeehan) *racd midfield: u.p and losing pl 2f out* **20/1**
0016 11 1 1/2 **The Coires (IRE)**[17] 5417 2-8-12 **86** ........ RHughes 13 69
(RHannon) *dwlt: a in rr: struggling fr 1/2-way* **12/1**
3144 12 1/2 **Cusoon**[17] 5421 2-8-6 **80** ........ RLMoore 1 61
(GLMoore) *b.hind: racd on outer: a towards rr: struggling in last pair 3f out* **14/1**

1m 28.95s 12 Ran SP% **115.1**
Speed ratings: CSF £27.51 CT £748.69 TOTE £13.00: £3.30, £1.30, £14.50; EX 40.30.
**Owner** Quadrillian Partnership **Bred** J And Mrs Bowtell **Trained** Twyford, Bucks

**FOCUS**
A competitive nursery run at a decent pace and the front two came from right out the back of the field. The form looks strong for the grade.

**NOTEBOOK**
**Wise Dennis** has been threatening to win a race in recent starts, but has usually left his effort too late. However, on this occasion he was well suited by the strong pace and stiff track and, with an uninterrupted run down the outside, hit the front in plenty of time before scoring with some comfort. He stays further and should find other opportunities.
**Rebel Rebel(IRE)**, bidding for a quick hat-trick, started short enough considering he was apprentice-ridden for the first time and racing off a 10lb higher mark. Things did not look good for him from an early stage, as he got very warm and was not travelling well once under way, but he gathered himself together and ran on to finish a clear second best. He did have to switch in order to get a racing, but it would be pushing things to day it cost him the race.
**Sky Crusader** did best of those who raced prominently and did not fail through lack of stamina this time.
**Im Spartacus**, wearing cheekpieces for the first time, put up a fair effort off his new inflated mark, but does not have the same amount of scope as those that finished ahead of him.
**Goodwood Spirit** almost sent his rider over his head leaving the stalls, so he did well to finish as close as he did. *Official explanation: jockey said colt slipped on leaving the stalls*
**Brooklime(IRE)** emerged with credit as he was involved in a speed duel from the start and his best previous form has been on easier ground.
**Persian Rock(IRE)** was trying this trip for the first time and did not appear to stay.

## 5811 MILES AND MORRISON OCTOBER STKS (LISTED RACE) (F&M) 7f (R)
2:35 (2:36) (A1) 3-Y-0+ **£17,400** (£6,600; £3,300; £1,500) **Stalls** High

Form RPR
123- 1 **Badminton**[360] 5332 3-8-8 107 ........(t) LDettori 6 104+
(SaeedBinSuroor) *lw: wl plcd: prog over 2f out: rdn to ld over 1f out: clr fnl f* **11/4**[1]
12-3 2 3 **Pearl Grey**[15] 5454 3-8-8 104 ........(t) KMcEvoy 2 96
(SaeedBinSuroor) *hld up midfield: effrt on outer over 2f out: r.o to chse wnr ins fnl f: no imp* **7/1**
0000 3 3/4 **Tahirah**[17] 5416 4-8-11 85 ........ SDrowne 1 94
(RGuest) *sn last: rdn and prog on outer 2f out: styd on wl fnl f: nrst fin* **50/1**
2100 4 3/4 **Lucky Pipit**[17] 5416 3-8-8 100 ........ MHills 5 92
(BWHills) *led to over 1f out: fdd ins fnl f* **20/1**
01- 5 1 1/4 **Thaminah (USA)**[323] 5948 3-8-8 87 ........ RHills 4 89
(MPTregoning) *bit bkwd: prom: chsd ldr 3f out to wl over 1f out: fdd fnl f* **9/2**[3]
3121 6 1/2 **Delphie Queen (IRE)**[78] 3751 3-8-8 102 ........ JFEgan 11 87
(SKirk) *lw: t.k.h: hld up last trio: hung lft and c wd into st: prog 2f out: carried hd high and no imp over 1f out* **7/2**[2]
345- 7 1/2 **Voile (IRE)**[360] 5332 3-8-8 105 ........ DaneO'Neill 9 86
(RHannon) *swtg: racd midfield: rdn 3f out: sn outpcd: kpt on same pce* **25/1**
-442 8 7 **Blue Dream (IRE)**[15] 5454 4-8-11 ........(p) JPMurtagh 3 67
(THogan, Ire) *prom: chsd ldr 4f out to 3f out: wknd over 2f out* **12/1**
0400 9 shd **Starbeck (IRE)**[4] 5740 6-8-11 79 ........ SWKelly 7 67
(PHowling) *b: b.hind: s.s: sn midfield: rdn 3f out: wknd over 2f out* **100/1**
0520 10 6 **Look Here's Carol (IRE)**[17] 5416 4-8-11 92 ........ KFallon 12 51
(BAMcmahon) *s.i.s: a towards rr and nt gng wl: wknd 2f out : eased fnl f* **12/1**
0306 11 3/4 **Caveral**[17] 5416 3-8-8 94 ........ RLMoore 10 49
(RHannon) *racd midfield: lost pl and struggling over 3f out: sn no ch: eased fnl f* **25/1**
0000 12 6 **Miss Childrey (IRE)**[16] 5439 3-8-8 ........ TQuinn 8 32
(DJSFfrenchDavis) *chsd ldr for 3f: wknd 3f out: eased over 1f out* **66/1**

1m 27.96s
**WFA** 3 from 4yo+ 3lb 12 Ran SP% **111.9**
Speed ratings: CSF £19.30 TOTE £3.60: £1.60, £2.00, £10.80; EX 15.70.
**Owner** Godolphin **Bred** Darley **Trained** Newmarket, Suffolk

**FOCUS**
An interesting Listed contest, run at a decent pace in a time almost exactly a second quicker than the opening nursery. The form is limited by the proximity of the third and is ordinary for the grade.

**NOTEBOOK**
**Badminton ◆**, not seen since finishing third in the Cheveley Park a year ago, was making her debut for Godolphin and was travelling like a winner from a long way out. She impressed with the way she put daylight between herself and her rivals and can now go on and make up for lost time.
**Pearl Grey**, trying this trip for the first time, stepped up from her reappearance and came through to finish a clear second best, but was completely outclassed by her stablemate.
**Tahirah**, unplaced in six previous starts this season, ran very well to finish amongst a group of much higher-rated three-year-olds and would be interesting if her sights were lowered a little, but form shown in these types of races can be very misleading.
**Lucky Pipit** established her usual position out front, but could not withstand this quality of opposition.
**Thaminah(USA)**, not seen since winning a Doncaster maiden ten months ago, ran well until lack of a recent race took its toll. This was only the third race of her career, so she is entitled to come on for it.
**Delphie Queen(IRE)**, returning from a short break, came very wide indeed entering the home straight, but you cannot afford to do that here and it was no surprise to her effort flattened out.

## 5812 BARNARDO'S CUMBERLAND LODGE STKS (GROUP 3) 1m 4f
3:10 (3:10) (A1) 3-Y-0+ **£29,000** (£11,000; £5,500; £2,500) **Stalls** High

Form RPR
3024 1 **High Accolade**[17] 5415 4-9-0 114 ........(vt) MartinDwyer 8 114
(MPTregoning) *lw: pushed up to chse ldr after 1f: led 4f out: drvn and hdd 2f out: hmpd on inner 1f out: rallied to ld last 75yds: hld on* **3/1**[2]
0655 2 nk **Self Defense**[39] 4858 7-9-0 102 ........ KFallon 9 114
(PRChamings) *trckd ldng pair: effrt to ld 2f out: hanging rt and idled in front: hdd last 75yds* **9/1**
0103 3 3/4 **Bandari (IRE)**[22] 5296 5-9-5 119 ........ RHills 5 117
(MJohnston) *swtg: racd in 5th: shkn up 3f out: prog to chse ldng pair over 1f out: hanging rt fnl f: clsng nr fin* **7/4**[1]
3323 4 4 **Compton Bolter (IRE)**[9] 5611 7-9-0 106 ........ JFortune 6 106
(GABUtler) *led to 4f out: stl upsides 2f out: outpcd over 1f out* **11/1**
1124 5 1 1/4 **Muqbil (USA)**[14] 5492 4-9-0 114 ........ WSupple 3 104
(JLDunlop) *hld up in 8th: effrt 3f out: no imp on ldrs fr 2f out* **9/1**
4406 6 nk **Franklins Gardens**[16] 5438 4-9-0 105 ........ PRobinson 2 103
(MHTompkins) *b: racd in 7th: shkn up and outpcd over 2f out: no ch after: keeping on nr fin* **33/1**
5 7 1 1/2 **The Khamsin (DEN)**[15] 5-9-0 ........ EAhern 7 101
(MsCErichsen, Norway) *lengthy: str: lw: chsd ldng trio to 3f out: wkng whn n.m.r 2f out* **100/1**
-644 8 shd **Alpino Chileno (ARG)**[14] 5506 5-9-0 ........(b) FDiaz 4 101
(RuneHaugen, Norway) *str: racd in 6th: lost pl 5f out: struggling fnl 4f* **66/1**
3354 9 1 1/2 **Persian Majesty (IRE)**[58] 4285 4-9-0 113 ........(b1) JPMurtagh 1 98
(PWHarris) *bolted to post: s.v.s: t.k.h and hld up in last: effrt 3f out: wknd wl over 1f out* **6/1**[3]

2m 33.21s (-0.35) **Going Correction** +0.225s/f (Good) 9 Ran SP% **109.4**
Speed ratings: **110,109,109,106,105 105,104,104,103**CSF £27.05 TOTE £3.60: £1.50, £2.00, £1.40; EX 33.60 Trifecta £51.40 Pool: £1,905.78. 26.28 winning tickets.
**Owner** Lady Tennant **Bred** Deerfield Farm **Trained** Lambourn, Berks
■ High Accolade was winning this race for the second year in succession.

**FOCUS**
Areasonable renewal but an ordinary pace and an unspectacular time for a Group Three, 0.83 seconds slower than the later handicap. The form is very mixed with the runner-up performing above himself.

**NOTEBOOK**
**High Accolade**, who took this event last year, was winning his first race since. He had to be brave too, as he looked held by the runner-up and was also quite seriously hampered by that rival passing the furlong pole, but battled back gamely to regain the advantage. With his favoured fast ground less and less likely to prevail from now on, that is probably him finished for the season.
**Self Defense**, racing over the shortest trip he has attempted since arriving from France, looked all over the winner when taking it up inside the last two furlongs, but he hung to his right, hampering the eventual winner, and was never quite getting there.
**Bandari(IRE)** was ridden more patiently this time, but he took a long time to hit top gear when asked and was never quite going to get there.
**Compton Bolter(IRE)**, runner-up to High Accolade in this last year, set the pace and did his best to hang on but found the front trio too strong. He continues to fall short at this level.
**Muqbil(USA)**, trying this trip for the first time, never offered a threat.
**Franklins Gardens** is still some way short of the form he was showing early last year.
**Persian Majesty(IRE)** was full of himself beforehand and then walked out of the stalls, so it was no surprise to see him fail to run his race.

## 5813 NICK CHEYNE FAREWELL STKS (H'CAP) 1m (R)
3:45 (3:48) (C1) (0-100,98) 3-Y-O+ £12,791 (£4,852; £2,426; £1,102) Stalls High

Form RPR

2120 **1** **Welcome Stranger**[15] [5462] 4-9-2 **92**........ LFletcher(3) 3 103
(JMPEustace) *racd far side to 1/2-way in 6th of gp: effrt on outer over 2f out: drvn and r.o to ld over 1f out: in command fnl f* **16/1**

1-10 **2** *2* **Thaija (IRE)**[16] [5439] 3-9-7 **98**........ RHills 6 105
(JLDunlop) *racd far side to 1/2-way in 7th of gp: effrt on outer over 2f out: prog to chal over 1f out: nt pce of wnr fnl f* **16/1**

2404 **3** *1 1/4* **Flighty Fellow (IRE)**[15] [5462] 4-9-7 **94**........(b) GCarter 1 98
(TDEasterby) *racd far side to 1/2-way and last of gp: stl in last trio and rdn over 2f out: r.o over 1f out: nrst fin* **14/1**

1133 **4** *1 1/4* **Royal Prince**[16] [5443] 3-8-12 **89**........(t) JPMurtagh 10 90
(JRFanshawe) *swtg: racd far side to 1/2-way in 5th of gp: hrd rdn 3f out: kpt on and cl up 2f out: no ex after* **9/2**[2]

1400 **5** *1* **Langford**[8] [5650] 4-8-13 **86**........ PRobinson 4 85
(MHTompkins) *t.k.h: racd far side to 1/2-way and trckd ldr: rdn to ld 2f out: edgd lft and hdd over 1f out: fdd* **40/1**

2231 **6** *nk* **Grand But One (IRE)**[83] [3587] 3-8-10 **87**........ MHills 14 85
(BWHills) *lw: racd nr side: trckd ldr: led gp and in 3rd whn gps merged over 3f out: drvn and cl up over 1f out: fdd fnl f* **12/1**

2006 **7** *1 1/2* **Alrafid (IRE)**[15] [5470] 5-8-11 **84**........ IMongan 12 79
(GLMoore) *lw: racd nr side: hld up in 4th of gp: hmpd whn gps merged over 3f out: sn rdn: one pce after* **25/1**

150 **8** *1/2* **Nashaab (USA)**[15] [5468] 7-9-0 **90**........ FPFerris(3) 7 84
(PDEvans) *racd nr side: hld up in 5th of gp: drvn in last trio over 2f out: styd on fr over 1f out: n.d* **20/1**

5340 **9** *1/2* **Rafferty (IRE)**[11] [5574] 5-8-7 **80** oh1........(b) EAhern 8 72
(CEBrittain) *racd far side to 1/2-way: t.k.h: trckd ldng pair: in 4th whn gps merged over 2f out: losing pl whn n.m.r 2f out* **25/1**

1124 **10** *3* **Pango**[15] [5468] 5-8-13 **86**........ SDrowne 11 71
(HMorrison) *racd nr side: chsd ldng pair: sltly hmpd whn gps merged over 3f out: btn 2f out: eased ins fnl f* **6/1**[3]

3000 **11** *8* **Tuning Fork**[15] [5470] 4-8-13 **86**........(p) LDettori 5 53
(JAkehurst) *racd far side to 1/2-way: overall ldr: hdd 2f out: wknd and eased fnl f* **12/1**

0004 **12** *5* **Serieux**[9] [5614] 5-8-7 **80**........(p) RLMoore 9 36
(MrsAJPerrett) *lw: racd nr side: hld up last of gp: last trio and rdn 3f out: sn btn: eased over 1f out* **4/1**[1]

2406 **13** *7* **Psychiatrist**[72] [3906] 3-9-7 **98**........ RHughes 13 37
(RHannon) *lw: led nr side gp over 4f: hmpd whn gps merged over 3f out and lost pl: eased fnl 2f* **14/1**

0031 **14** *7* **Norton (IRE)**[37] [4920] 7-9-7 **94**........ JFortune 2 17
(TGMills) *racd far side to 1/2-way: chsd ldng trio: cl enough 3f out: sn wknd: virtually p.u ins fnl f* **7/1**

1m 41.85s (-1.19) **Going Correction** +0.225s/f (Good)
**WFA** 3 from 4yo+ 4lb **14** Ran SP% **120.3**
Speed ratings: **114,112,110,109,108 108,106,106,105,102 94,89,82,75**CSF £239.12 CT £3650.83 TOTE £21.00: £5.70, £4.40, £3.50; EX 411.70 Trifecta £1139.60 Part won. Pool: £1,605.20. 0.10 winning tickets..
**Owner** H R Moszkowicz **Bred** Henry And Mrs Rosemary Moszkowicz **Trained** Newmarket, Suffolk

**FOCUS**
A competitive handicap and a smart winning time for the grade, suggesting the form is decent. The field split into two racing down the side of the track, with the larger group of eight racing towards the outside and taking the 'Willie Carson' route under the trees. They appeared to hold the advantage too, with the first five home coming from that side.

**NOTEBOOK**
**Welcome Stranger ◆**, with trip and ground in his favour, raced under the trees early and was brought with his effort down the wide outside, showing a sharp turn of foot to score. This was a fine effort to win off a 16lb higher mark than for his last win in a handicap and he still looks to be improving.
**Thajja(IRE) ◆**, making his handicap debut, probably found the ground just about acceptable despite the official description and ran much better than at Doncaster. He still has plenty of scope and can return to winning ways on an easy surface.
**Flighty Fellow(IRE)** was finishing in good style, but too late. Even this stiff mile looks an insufficient test of stamina, but he is still in the Cambridgeshire where the trip would be perfect.
**Royal Prince** is running well despite being 10lb higher than for his last win and ran another solid race in the first-time tongue tie.
**Langford** did not help his chances by pulling hard early and, although he just about forced his head in front soon after turning for home, he then had nothing more to offer.
**Grand But One(IRE)**, making his handicap debut, did best of those who stuck to the inside in the early stages. Unraced at two, he still has a little scope and can do better.
**Serieux** seems not to run two races alike these days and this was a modest effort.
**Norton(IRE)** *Official explanation: jockey said gelding had hung badly*

## 5814 TOTESPORT ASCOT FINAL FLING STKS (HERITAGE H'CAP) 1m 4f
4:20 (4:21) (B1) 3-Y-O+ £34,800 (£13,200; £6,600; £3,000) Stalls High

Form RPR

3205 **1** **Fort**[18] [5397] 3-7-13 **88**........ NMackay(3) 9 106
(MJohnston) *t.k.h: cl up: prog to ld over 3f out: rdn and styd on strly fnl 2f: comf* **16/1**

1131 **2** *2 1/2* **Elusive Dream**[8] [5632] 3-7-13 **85** 4ex........ JMackay 7 99
(SirMarkPrescott) *lw: dwlt: sn prom: trckd ldr after 5f to 4f out: rdn over 3f out: chsd wnr wl over 1f out: no imp* **9/4**[1]

1222 **3** *3* **Sergeant Cecil**[16] [5435] 5-9-1 **93**........ JFortune 12 102
(BRMillman) *lw: dwlt: hld up in last trio: rdn and prog 3f out: styd on fnl 2f: chsd ldng pair 1f out: no imp* **11/2**[2]

6002 **4** *1 3/4* **Pagan Dance (IRE)**[15] [5465] 5-9-0 **92**........(p) RLMoore 14 98
(MrsAJPerrett) *lw: dwlt: racd midfield: rdn and effrt 3f out: hanging rt fr 2f out: chsd ldng pair over 1f out: fnd nil* **15/2**

2302 **5** *1 1/4* **Grampian**[24] [5251] 5-9-10 **102**........ TQuinn 2 106
(JGGiven) *hld up rr: effrt on outer 2f out: styd on: nrst fin* **25/1**

43/4 **6** *shd* **Ovambo (IRE)**[29] [5133] 6-9-8 **100**........ DSweeney 5 104
(PJMakin) *dwlt: hld up towards rr: rdn and effrt on outer over 2f out: no prog over 1f out* **33/1**

0004 **7** *1 1/2* **Trust Rule**[16] [5435] 4-8-12 **90**........(tp) MHills 4 92
(BWHills) *racd wd in midfield: rdn 3f out: no real prog* **14/1**

0320 **8** *3/4* **Top Seed (IRE)**[39] [4858] 3-9-2 **102**........ TEDurcan 10 102
(MRChannon) *chsd ldrs: rdn 3f out: wknd over 1f out* **50/1**

0050 **9** *1 1/4* **Weecandoo (IRE)**[11] [5573] 6-8-6 **84**........ GCarter 3 82
(CNAllen) *swtg: hld up in last pair: drvn and struggling 3f out* **50/1**

0165 **10** *hd* **Flotta**[9] [5615] 5-8-5 **83**........ SHitchcott 13 81
(MRChannon) *swtg: dwlt: hld up in rr: effrt but little ch whn hmpd on inner 2f out: no ch after* **25/1**

6011 **11** *4* **Tawny Way**[44] [4729] 4-8-13 **91**........ SDrowne 6 83
(WJarvis) *led to over 3f out: wknd 2f out* **8/1**

4220 **12** *1 1/4* **Nawamees (IRE)**[61] [4218] 6-8-10 **88**........(p) RHughes 11 78
(GLMoore) *trckd ldrs: 4th and wl in tch 3f out: nudged along and losing pl whn squeezed out 2f out: eased* **25/1**

-653 **13** *7* **Roehampton**[15] [5461] 3-8-11 **97**........(v) KFallon 8 76
(SirMichaelStoute) *t.k.h: trckd ldr for 5f: snatched up 5f out: wknd over 2f out* **12/1**

2120 **14** *12* **Loves Travelling (IRE)**[22] [5288] 4-8-12 **90**........ LDettori 15 49
(LMCumani) *racd midfield: drvn and wknd 3f out* **6/1**[3]

2m 32.38s (-1.18) **Going Correction** +0.225s/f (Good)
**WFA** 3 from 4yo+ 8lb **14** Ran SP% **122.0**
Speed ratings: **112,110,108,107,106 106,105,104,103,103 101,100,95,87**CSF £49.59 CT £237.02 TOTE £20.20: £6.00, £1.60, £2.30; EX 95.80 Trifecta £594.00 Pool: £6,860.76. 8.20 winning tickets.
**Owner** Highclere Thoroughbred Racing IX **Bred** Floors Farming **Trained** Middleham Moor, N Yorks

**FOCUS**
A decent pace for this competitive and valuable handicap and the time was fair for the grade, 0.83 seconds faster than the Cumberland Lodge. As a result the form looks reasonably solid.

**NOTEBOOK**
**Fort ◆** has been missing out this season, but back over his best trip he won this in great style to record his first victory since his racecourse debut. Bearing in mind his trainer's skill with older handicappers, it would be no surprise to see him do even better next term.
**Elusive Dream**, carrying a 4lb penalty for his Ayr victory, did not help his chances at all by starting slowly and then taking a fierce hold when moving up to hold a prominent position. The fact that he still managed to finish clear second best shows how talented he is, and there are plenty more races to be won with him.
**Sergeant Cecil**, 7lb higher than for his last win, was doing all his best work late and looks better over further these days.
**Pagan Dance(IRE)** had every chance, but inside the last couple of furlongs he again looked as though he was not willing to exert himself too much.
**Grampian** ran another decent race and stayed on to finish a respectable fifth, but is getting no help from the Handicapper as a result, still being 8lb higher than for his last win two and a half years ago.
**Ovambo(IRE)** ran with credit, but despite gradually dropping down the weights is still 10lb higher than for his last win.
**Tawny Way**, bidding for a hat-trick and whose price halved due to significant market support, was able to enjoy an uncontested lead but was still not good enough.
**Roehampton** was right on the heels of the leaders when running into trouble approaching the home bend and there was no way back.
**Loves Travelling(IRE)**, off a 10lb higher mark than for his last win, was popular in the market but ran no sort of race. *Official explanation: jockey said gelding lost its action*

## 5815 TOM MCGEE FENWOLF STKS (LISTED RACE) 2m 45y
4:55 (4:55) (A1) 3-Y-O+ £17,850 (£6,600; £3,300; £1,500) Stalls High

Form RPR

3041 **1** **Defining**[22] [5288] 5-9-3 105........ JPMurtagh 4 111
(JRFanshawe) *lw: trckd ldng pair: wnt 2nd over 4f out: rdn to ld over 1f out: styd on wl* **2/1**[1]

3123 **2** *2 1/2* **Swift Tango (IRE)**[16] [5438] 4-9-6 106........ LDettori 5 111
(EALDunlop) *lw: s.s: hld up in 4th: clsd over 3f out: rdn to chse wnr jst over 1f out: fnd nil and a hld* **5/2**[2]

4040 **3** *2 1/2* **Supremacy**[16] [5435] 5-9-3 103........ KFallon 6 105
(SirMichaelStoute) *led: kicked on 1/2-way: hrd rdn and hdd over 1f out: one pce* **4/1**[3]

6661 **4** *2 1/2* **Corrib Eclipse**[10] [5589] 5-9-3 106........ JFEgan 2 102
(JamiePoulton) *trckd ldr: rdn 6f out: lost 2nd over 4f out: one pce u.p* **9/2**

11/6 **5** *dist* **Total Turtle (IRE)**[15] [5465] 5-9-3 100........ JFortune 1 —
(PFICole) *s.s: hld up in last: rdn 4f out: sn btn: virtually p.u fnl f* **12/1**

3m 35.71s (0.87) **Going Correction** +0.225s/f (Good) **5** Ran SP% **107.8**
Speed ratings: **106,104,103,102,—**CSF £6.92 TOTE £3.30: £1.70, £1.70; EX 6.00 Place 6 £85.04, Place 5 £47.09.
**Owner** Mrs V Shelton **Bred** Mrs A J Brudenell **Trained** Newmarket, Suffolk
■ The last race run at the old Ascot. The course will undergo a major refit before reopening, hopefully in summer 2006.

**FOCUS**
With just the five runners, the pace was moderate and the winning time was therefore modest for a Listed contest. The first two were helped to get home by the slow pace, and as a result the form is not convincing.

**NOTEBOOK**
**Defining** had not really proved one way or the other that he stays this trip when seventh in the Northumberland Plate, but that became academic when the pace proved to be modest. Always travelling well, he seized the initiative soon after turning for home and the move proved decisive. Despite this victory, the jury is still out over his stamina.
**Swift Tango(IRE)**, trying this trip for the first time, travelled really well but, when asked for maximum effort, did not find anything like as much off the bridle as had looked likely. Despite the modest pace, he may not have stayed.
**Supremacy**, winner of this race last year, set a modest pace before quickening things up at halfway and looked to have established a decisive advantage racing up from Swinley Bottom, but he could never shake his rivals off completely and was swamped for toe once into the home straight.
**Corrib Eclipse** stays all day, so the modest gallop was no help to him at all and it was no surprise to see him struggling to keep up when the tempo increased. It was only his bottomless stamina that enabled him to finish as close as he did.
**Total Turtle(IRE)**, having his second run back after a two-year layoff, ran as though his problems have returned. *Official explanation: jockey said gelding was never travelling*

T/Jkpt: Not won. T/Plt: £90.30 to a £1 stake. Pool: £102,422.10. 827.65 winning tickets. T/Qpdt: £25.50 to a £1 stake. Pool: £5,872.30. 170.40 winning tickets. JN

# 5513 MUSSELBURGH (R-H)

Sunday, September 26

**OFFICIAL GOING: Good to firm (good in places)**

## 5816 CRITERION PUB CHALLENGE MAIDEN AUCTION STKS — 5f

2:25 (2:25) (E3) 2-Y-O — £4,095 (£1,260; £630; £315) Stalls Low

Form — RPR

4506 **1** **Hillside Heather (IRE)**[13] 5520 2-8-3 61........................(p) PHanagan 10 — 69
(ABerry) *hld up towards rr: hdwy 1/2-way: rdn over 1f out: led ins last: styd on wl* **9/2**[2]

00 **2** 1 ½ **Turn On The Style**[19] 5362 2-8-8 ........................ SChin 8 — 69
(RPElliott) *trckd lesders: hdwy 1/2-way: rdn to ld over 1f out: drvn and hdd ins last: nt qckn* **33/1**

242 **3** 1 **Farthing (IRE)**[20] 5334 2-8-8 74........................ DHolland 2 — 65
(GCBravery) *cl up: rdn and ev ch 2f out: drvn and one pce ent last* **5/4**[1]

05 **4** ½ **Orphan (IRE)**[71] 3925 2-8-7 ........................ DarrenWilliams 1 — 63
(KRBurke) *sn led: rdn along 2f out: drvn and hdd over 1f: wknd ins last* **9/2**[2]

5444 **5** nk **Beverley Beau**[11] 5558 2-8-0 68........................ KristinStubbs(7) 9 — 61
(MrsLStubbs) *in tch on outer: effrt 2f out: sn rdn and one pce* **11/1**[3]

065 **6** ½ **Ms Three**[11] 5558 2-8-3 ........................ JoannaBadger 4 — 56
(RFord) *dwlt and sn pushed along: hdwy 2f out: styd on u.p fnl f: nrst fin* **100/1**

0260 **7** 4 **Ducal Diva**[24] 5241 2-7-9 60........................ DFentiman(7) 6 — 41
(JRWeymes) *prom: ev ch 2f out: sn rdn and wknd* **20/1**

6 **8** ½ **In Rhubarb**[66] 4064 2-8-1 ........................ NataliaGemelova(7) 7 — 45
(IWMcinnes) *s.i.s and outpcd in rr tl sme late hdwy* **50/1**

0002 **9** 3 ½ **Waggledance (IRE)**[11] 5555 2-8-7 66........................(p) TEaves(3) 5 — 35
(JSWainwright) *cl up: rdn along over 2f out: sn drvn and wknd* **14/1**

5203 **10** 1 ½ **Procrastinate (IRE)**[13] 5513 2-8-10 68........................ RWinston 3 — 29
(RFFisher) *cl up: rdn along 1/2-way: sn wknd* **16/1**

61.15 secs (0.75) **Going Correction** +0.025s/f (Good) — **10** Ran SP% **112.3**
Speed ratings: **95,92,91,90,89 88,82,81,76,73**CSF £141.67 TOTE £7.10: £1.90, £3.90, £1.10; EX 165.00.
**Owner** Hillside Racing **Bred** Miss Annette McMahon **Trained** Cockerham, Lancs

**FOCUS**
A pretty modest maiden, with Farthing failing to run near her rating of 74, and the form is messy and unsatisfactory.

**NOTEBOOK**
**Hillside Heather(IRE)** went into this with quite a regressive profile, having dropped 8lb in the handicap since she was allotted a mark. However, returned to maiden company, she was able to confirm the promise of her earlier starts. She will probably move back up in the weights for this, and would therefore command respect of turned out in a nursery under a penalty.
**Turn On The Style**, dropped a furlong in trip, stepped up on his first two efforts and would appear to be progressing. He is now qualified for a handicap mark.
**Farthing(IRE)**, runner-up to the subsequent Watership Down second Arabian Dancer at Bath on her previous start, did not run to that form and was disappointing.
**Orphan(IRE)** showed improved form over six furlongs on soft ground on his previous start, but did not really go on from that under these very different conditions.
**Beverley Beau** did not run to his rating of 68 despite appearing to have every chance.

## 5817 ROYAL SCOTS "PREMIER" CLAIMING STKS — 1m 4f

3:00 (3:00) (D3) 3-Y-0+ — £5,395 (£1,660; £830; £415) Stalls High

Form — RPR

2104 **1** **Yenaled**[10] 5581 7-9-5 72........................ NCallan 6 — 62
(KARyan) *hld up in tch: hdwy on inner 3f out: led 2f out: rdn and styd on wl fnl f* **7/2**[2]

4620 **2** 1 ¾ **Donna's Double**[5] 5714 9-9-1 52........................(p) KDarley 2 — 55
(DEddy) *hld up in tch: hdwy on bit 3f out: ev ch 2f out: sn rdn and kpt on same pce* **11/1**

0040 **3** 7 **Sandy Bay (IRE)**[20] 5344 5-9-0 30........................ PFessey 1 — 43?
(ARDicken) *trckd ldrs: hdwy 3 out: sn rdn: drvn and outpcd wl over 1f out* **100/1**

-104 **4** ¾ **Perelandra (USA)**[8] 5632 4-9-2 71........................ DHolland 4 — 44
(MJWallace) *set stdy pce: qcknd over 3f out: sn rdn and edgd lft: drvn and hdd 2f out: sn hung bdly lft and btn* **4/5**[1]

0431 **5** nk **On Cloud Nine**[23] 5257 3-8-0 62........................ BSwarbrick(5) 3 — 40
(JGMO'Shea) *keen: trckdldr: hdwy to chal 3f out: sn rdn and ev ch tl drvn and wknd wl over 1f out* **9/2**[3]

2636 **6** 1 ¼ **Winslow Boy (USA)**[28] 5159 3-8-13 59........................ LEnstone 5 — 46
(PMonteith) *trckd ldng pair: effrt 3f out: sn rdn and wknd 2f out* **16/1**

2m 43.7s (5.68) **Going Correction** -0.15s/f (Firm)
**WFA** 3 from 4yo+ 8lb — **6** Ran SP% **111.2**
Speed ratings: **75,73,69,68,68 67**CSF £37.31 TOTE £4.60: £2.10, £3.30; EX 16.70.
**Owner** The Fishermen **Bred** R S A Urquhart **Trained** Hambleton, N Yorks

**FOCUS**
With Perelandra not at her best, this claimer did not take a lot of winning. They went no gallop early and the winning time was very slow for the grade, suggesting the form may be worth ignoring.

**NOTEBOOK**
**Yenaled** had never previously won beyond ten furlongs, but he got the trip well off the steady pace and did not run have to run to his mark to win. He remains one to have on your side at this level.
**Donna's Double**, without a win since June 2002, had 16lb to find with the eventual winner at the weights, but acquitted himself very creditably. He has never won over a trip this far, but the steady early pace ensured stamina was not a premium and he finished well. A good effort.
**Sandy Bay(IRE)** had several mountains to climb on the figures, but he ran above himself to finish a creditable third. However, this run flatters him.
**Perelandra(USA)** was 2lb ahead of the winner on the adjusted official figures but ran a very disappointing race. She found nothing when challenged and did not help her rider by hanging quite badly to her left. She looks best watched for the time being. *Official explanation: jockey said filly was unsuited by the fast ground and also hung left-handed from 3f out*
**On Cloud Nine**, claimed out of Michael Bell's yard after winning a similar race at Chepstow on her previous start, was below form on her debut for new connections. This ground may have been fast enough, but she has it to prove now.

## 5818 MUSSELBURGH NEWS H'CAP — 7f 30y

3:35 (3:36) (D2) (0-85,81) 3-Y-0+ — £6,780 (£2,086; £1,043; £521) Stalls Low

Form — RPR

4302 **1** **Sea Storm (IRE)**[8] 5631 6-9-7 79........................ RWinston 8 — 87
(DRMacleod) *trckd ldrs: hdwy over 2f out: rdn over 1f out: str run to ld last 100 yds* **7/1**[3]

1411 **2** ½ **Hartshead**[24] 5244 5-9-3 78........................ PMulrennan(3) 12 — 85
(GASwinbank) *trckd ldrs on inner: hdwy over 2f out: n.m.r and swtchd lft over 1f out: sn rdn and kpt on fnl f* **5/1**[2]

2260 **3** hd **Kirkby's Treasure**[9] 5603 6-9-3 75........................ KDarley 1 — 81
(ABerry) *stdd s and bhd: hdwy on outer over 2f out: rdn and ev ch whn hung bdly lft ins last: styd on* **8/1**

6460 **4** ½ **Ballyhurry (USA)**[69] 3977 7-8-6 67........................ TEaves(3) 6 — 72
(JSGoldie) *towards rr: hdwy over 2f out: rdn over 1f out: styd on ins last: nrst fin* **14/1**

2040 **5** ½ **Tranquil Sky**[22] 5294 3-9-5 80........................ DHolland 10 — 83+
(NACallaghan) *hld up: hdwy 2f out: swtchd ins and rdn over 1f out: swtchd lft and n.m.r ins last: kpt on* **8/1**

5045 **6** nk **Cloud Dancer**[17] 5419 5-9-3 75........................ NCallan 9 — 78
(KARyan) *hld up: hdwy over 2f out: rdn and ch over 1f out: sn drvn and no ex ins last* **4/1**[1]

4044 **7** shd **Stoic Leader (IRE)**[7] 5673 4-9-5 77........................ PHanagan 3 — 79
(RFFisher) *trckd ldrs: effrt 2f out: sn rdn to chse ldr ent last: sn drvn and evey ch tl wknd towards fin* **16/1**

0065 **8** nk **H Harrison (IRE)**[7] 5574 4-9-3 78........................ THamilton(3) 4 — 80
(IWMcinnes) *midfield: hdwy on outer over 2f out: rdn wl over 1f out: kpt on same pce ins last* **16/1**

4350 **9** nk **Mister Marmaduke**[15] 5474 3-9-3 78........................ DAllan 13 — 79
(ISemple) *prom: hdwy to ld 2f out: sn rdn: drvn ent last: hdd & wknd last 100 yds* **33/1**

2016 **10** 9 **Samuel Charles**[24] 5244 6-8-12 75........................ BSwarbrick(5) 7 — 51
(WMBrisbourne) *cl up: rdn wl over 2f out: drvn and wknd over 1f out* **25/1**

0106 **11** 8 **Redwood Rocks (IRE)**[15] 5474 3-9-6 81........................ FLynch 11 — 36
(BSmart) *led: rdn along 3f out: hdd 2f out: drvna nd wkng whn hmpd over 1f out* **16/1**

0360 **12** 12 **Finger Of Fate**[13] 5526 4-8-4 65 oh20........................(b) JFMcDonald(3) 14 — —
(MJPolglase) *s.i.s: a bhd* **100/1**

3003 **P** **Alchemist Master**[5] 5713 5-8-12 70........................(p) ACulhane 5 — —
(RMWhitaker) *hld up towards rr: effrt and sme hdwy 3f out: sn rdn and wkng whn p.u lame and dismntd over 1f out* **7/1**[3]

1m 29.11s (-0.42) **Going Correction** -0.15s/f (Firm)
**WFA** 3 from 4yo+ 3lb — **13** Ran SP% **116.0**
Speed ratings: **96,95,95,94,94 93,93,93,92,82 73,59,—**CSF £40.02 CT £298.39 TOTE £10.40: £3.50, £2.60, £1.80; EX 47.70.
**Owner** Maurice W Chapman **Bred** Dan Daly **Trained** Lauder, Borders
■ Stewards Enquiry : N Callan caution: careless riding

**FOCUS**
A really competitive handicap for the grade but, although the pace was good, they finished well bunched and the time was modest for the class, suggesting the form is ordinary.

**NOTEBOOK**
**Sea Storm(IRE)**, runner-up in a competitive 18-runner handicap at Ayr on his previous start, continues in good heart and was able to go one place better. He is one to have on your side whilst in this sort of form.
**Hartshead**, successful on four of his last five starts, showed a tremendous attitude to take some tight gaps, but simply had no an answer to the winner's late burst. He must be kept on the right side of until showing signs of losing his form.
**Kirkby's Treasure** had plenty to do when hanging over to the near-side rail, but seemed to appreciate having something to run against and flew home. *Official explanation: jockey said gelding hung left-handed in the home straight*
**Ballyhurry(USA)** ran an encouraging race off a mark 3lb lower than when last successful, and is one to keep in mind for similar events.
**Tranquil Sky** may have finished closer with better luck, but he has quite simply had a disappointing season. *Official explanation: jockey said filly was denied a clear run*
**Cloud Dancer** proved unable to gain compensation for a very unlucky run at Doncaster on her previous start.
**Mister Marmaduke** ◆ has shaped as though ready to win a couple of times this year, and this was another very encouraging run. He found himself in front soon enough and, despite still being clear well inside the final furlong, he was swamped. He is one to keep an eye on.
**Redwood Rocks(IRE)** *Official explanation: jockey said gelding suffered interference*
**Finger Of Fate** *Official explanation: jockey said gelding lost its action*
**Alchemist Master** *Official explanation: trainer's representative said gelding finished distressed*

## 5819 ROYAL SCOTS CLUB CUP NURSERY — 1m

4:10 (4:13) (D2) (0-85,85) 2-Y-O — £5,501 (£1,692; £846; £423) Stalls Low

Form — RPR

0611 **1** **Succession**[12] 5548 2-8-12 76........................ DHolland 5 — 86
(SirMarkPrescott) *mde all: rdn along 2f out: styd on wl* **4/5**[1]

01 **2** 1 ¾ **I'm So Lucky**[80] 3679 2-9-7 85........................ KDarley 4 — 91
(MJohnston) *in tch: hdwy 1/2-way: rdn to chse wnr appr last: sn drvn and kpt on* **7/2**[2]

1312 **3** 1 **Caitlin (IRE)**[8] 5636 2-8-11 75........................ FLynch 3 — 79
(BSmart) *trckd wnr: effrt to chal over 2f out: sn rdn: drvn and one pce ent last* **7/1**[3]

5623 **4** 6 **Algorithm**[8] 5636 2-7-12 62 oh3........................ DMernagh 7 — 53
(TDEasterby) *hld up in tch: pushed along over 3f out: rdn 2f out and sn no imp* **14/1**

01 **5** 4 **Just Waz (USA)**[27] 5186 2-8-6 70........................ ACulhane 6 — 52
(RMWhitaker) *hld up: effrt over 3f out: sn rdn along and no hdwy* **16/1**

5002 **6** 7 **Maureen's Lough (IRE)**[11] 5556 2-7-12 62 oh9........................ SRighton 1 — 29
(JHetherton) *chsd ldng pair: rdn along over 2f out: sn wknd* **50/1**

4142 **7** 2 ½ **Mount Ephram (IRE)**[67] 4010 2-8-8 72........................ PHanagan 8 — 33
(RFFisher) *s.i.s and b ehind: hdwy 3f out: sn rdn and wknd 2f out* **50/1**

0153 **8** 11 **Fenrir**[10] 5580 2-9-5 83........................ RWinston 2 — 20
(JRWeymes) *in tch: hdwy 3f out: sn rdn and wknd wl over 1f out: bhd whn eased fnl f* **20/1**

1m 40.34s (-2.36) **Going Correction** -0.15s/f (Firm) 2y crse rec — **8** Ran SP% **111.5**
Speed ratings: **105,103,102,96,92 85,82,71**CSF £3.41 CT £9.71 TOTE £1.80: £1.10, £1.20, £1.70; EX 3.90.
**Owner** Dr Catherine Wills **Bred** St Clare Hall Stud **Trained** Newmarket, Suffolk

**FOCUS**
This only really concerned three horses and the front two are particularly nice types. The time was very smart time for the class, 0.44 seconds faster than the 0-75 classified stakes for older horses over the same trip, suggesting the form is strong for the grade.

**NOTEBOOK**
**Succession**, 7lb higher than when winning at Yarmouth on her previous start, completed the hat-trick returned to the course and distance she started her winning run over. Although she had to be pushed right out, this was her most straightforward win to date.
**I'm So Lucky**, not seen since getting off the mark at Warwick in a race that has worked out quite well 80 days previously, ran a creditable race but was always just be held by the winner. Lightly raced, he should develop into a pretty useful performer.
**Caitlin(IRE)**, 5lb higher than when winning at Redcar two starts previously, ran a very creditable race in finishing third to a couple of nice, progressive types and the step up to a mile clearly suited well.

**Algorithm**, stepped up a furlong in trip, did not run to the form she showed when beaten just three quarters of a length by Caitlin on her previous start. *Official explanation: jockey said filly was unsuited by the good to firm ground*
**Just Waz(USA)**, off the mark in a muddling soft-ground maiden at Newcastle on his previous start, found this a much tougher test stepped up a furlong in trip.
**Mount Ephram(IRE)** *Official explanation: jockey said gelding missed the break*
**Fenrir** *Official explanation: jockey said colt was unsuited by the good to firm ground*

## 5820 SUNDAY MAIL JOE PUNTER H'CAP 2m
**4:45** (4:45) (D2) (0-85,77) 3-Y-0+ **£6,886** (£2,119; £1,059; £529) **Stalls** Low

Form RPR
0102 1 **Astyanax (IRE)**[10] 5595 4-9-12 **77** ..... DHolland 6 87
(SirMarkPrescott) *mde all: rdn along over 2f out: styd on strly* **3/1**[2]
0030 2 *7* **Kristensen**[9] 5608 5-9-7 **75** ..... (p) JFMcDonald(3) 1 77
(DEddy) *hld up: hdwy 1/2-way: effrt on outer 3f out: sn rdn and kpt on same pce fnl 2f* **7/1**[3]
11 3 *1 3/4* **Strangely Brown (IRE)**[9] 5608 3-8-13 **76** ..... PHanagan 3 76
(SCWilliams) *trckd ldrs: hdwy on inner over 3f out: chsd wnr over 2f out: sn rdn and btn* **1/1**[1]
5560 4 *nk* **Toni Alcala**[9] 5608 5-9-0 **68** ..... PMulrennan(3) 5 68
(RFFisher) *hld up: hdwy over 3f out: rdn along over 2f out and sn one pce* **10/1**
40 5 *7* **Pilgrims Progress (IRE)**[34] 4990 4-9-7 **72** ..... RWinston 4 63
(DWThompson) *a rr* **33/1**
1560 6 *2* **Hathlen (IRE)**[10] 5595 3-8-10 **73** ..... ACulhane 2 62
(MRChannon) *chsd wnr: rdn along over 3f out: drvn and wknd over 2f out* **14/1**

3m 32.5s (-1.20) **Going Correction** -0.15s/f (Firm)
**WFA** 3 from 4yo+ 12lb **6** Ran SP% **106.2**
Speed ratings: **97,93,92,92,88 87**CSF £20.70 TOTE £4.10: £2.00, £2.30; EX 22.60.
**Owner** Lady Katharine Watts **Bred** P D Player **Trained** Newmarket, Suffolk

**FOCUS**
With Strangely Brown not quite at his best, this did not take a lot of winning, but still a decent performance from Astyanax. The early pace was steady and the time was modest for the grade, suggesting the overall form is not that strong.

**NOTEBOOK**
**Astyanax(IRE)**, only just denied over this trip at Yarmouth on his previous start, made no mistake under a good front-running ride from Holland. The Handicapper may hit him hard for this, so he would have to be of interest if turned out under a penalty. He is the type to relish the stamina test of the Cesarewitch.
**Kristensen** ran respectably, he was simply no match for the winner and does not win very often.
**Strangely Brown(IRE)**, chasing the four-timer off a 5lb higher mark, did not help his chance by racing keenly and found little off the bridle. He had quite a hard race last time and that may just have left its mark.
**Toni Alcala** has had a good year - winning four times - but recent efforts suggest he is not at his best at present.
**Pilgrims Progress(IRE)** may not have appreciated ground this fast.

## 5821 RSP CONSULTING CLASSIFIED STKS 1m
**5:15** (5:15) (D2) 3-Y-0+ **£6,864** (£2,112; £1,056; £528) **Stalls** Low

Form RPR
0631 1 **Mr Velocity (IRE)**[18] 5403 4-9-2 75 ..... DHolland 11 78
(EFVaughan) *in tch on inner: swtchd lft and hdwy over 2f out: rdn wl over 1f out: chsd ldr ins last: drvn and styd on to ld nr line* **7/4**[1]
6125 2 *nk* **Summer Shades**[41] 4812 6-8-8 71 ..... BSwarbrick(5) 4 74
(WMBrisbourne) *chsd ldrs: gd hdwy 3f out: led 2f out: rdn over 1f out: drvn and edgd rt wl ins last: hdd nr fin* **20/1**
3313 3 *1/2* **Millagros (IRE)**[22] 5304 4-8-13 74 ..... (p) PHanagan 3 73
(ISemple) *hld up: hdwy on outer over 2f out: sn rdn: drvn ent last and styd on wl towards fin* **8/1**
1526 4 *hd* **Juste Pour L'Amour**[9] 5614 4-8-13 74 ..... HayleyTurner(3) 6 75
(PLGilligan) *hld up in rr: hdwy on wd outside over 2f out: rdn wl over 1f out: styd on ins last: nrst fin* **6/1**[3]
4522 5 *3/4* **Honest Injun**[6] 5706 3-8-12 72 ..... RWinston 8 74
(JGMO'Shea) *cl up: led over 4f out: rdn over 2f out: sn hdd: ev ch ent last: drvn: hld and n.m.r whn eased last 50 yds* **14/1**
0016 6 *shd* **Top Dirham**[64] 4134 6-9-2 72 ..... DaleGibson 1 73
(MWEasterby) *bhd: hdwy 3f out: rdn over 2f out: styd on appr last: nrst fin* **6/1**[3]
2325 7 *hd* **Arry Dash**[11] 5568 4-9-2 75 ..... (v[1]) ACulhane 10 73
(MRChannon) *prom: rdn along 3f out: drvn 2f out: one pce appr last* **9/2**[2]
2000 8 *3/4* **Anthemion (IRE)**[10] 5583 7-9-2 58 ..... DMcGaffin 5 71?
(MrsJCMcgregor) *chsd ldrs: rdn along over 2f out: grad wknd fr over 1f out* **100/1**
0000 9 *3* **Rarefied (IRE)**[29] 5127 3-8-12 74 ..... DAllan 9 64
(TDEasterby) *towards rr: hdwy on inner over 3f out: rdn to chse ldrs over 2f out: sn wknd* **33/1**
6405 10 *1* **Iskander**[7] 5672 3-8-12 72 ..... (b) NCallan 7 62
(KARyan) *m idfield: rdn along 3f out: sn no imp* **16/1**
6000 11 *11* **Silver Seeker (USA)**[20] 5346 4-9-2 45 ..... PFessey 2 37
(ARDicken) *a rr* **150/1**
0600 12 *dist* **Devine Light (IRE)**[7] 5672 4-8-10 50 ..... PMulrennan(3) 12 —
(BMactaggart) *led 3f: rdn along over 3f out: sn wknd: bhd and eased over 1f out* **100/1**

1m 40.78s (-1.92) **Going Correction** -0.15s/f (Firm)
**WFA** 3 from 4yo+ 4lb **12** Ran SP% **117.1**
Speed ratings: **103,102,102,102,101 101,100,100,97,96 85,—**CSF £44.87 TOTE £2.80: £1.30, £3.50, £2.30; EX 83.10 Place 6 £65.97, Place 5 £44.71.
**Owner** A M Pickering **Bred** Mrs V Dubois **Trained** Newmarket, Suffolk

**FOCUS**
Quite a tight classified event; the pace was just ordinary and they finished well bunched, with the eighth anchoring the form.

**NOTEBOOK**
**Mr Velocity(IRE)** had a good chance at the weights and was able to follow up his recent Epsom success, although he took an age to get there. He should not go up too much for this and, clearly improving, the hat-trick cannot be ruled out.
**Summer Shades** had her ideal conditions and was just denied. In this form, she is up to winning in similar company.
**Millagros(IRE)**, the best off at the weights, appeared to run her race and did not seem to have any excuses.
**Juste Pour L'Amour**, back up in trip from seven furlongs, ran a respectable race and continues in good form.
**Honest Injun**, with just a Fibresand maiden win to his name, would have been closer had he not been short of room in the last furlong. *Official explanation: jockey said colt was denied a clear run approaching the line*
**Top Dirham** had conditions to suit on his return from a 64-day break and ran creditably.
**Arry Dash**, dropped in trip and fitted with a visor for the first time, was well held.
**Anthemion(IRE)** *Official explanation: jockey said gelding was denied a clear run approaching the line*
**Devine Light(IRE)** *Official explanation: jockey said filly hung left-handed throughout*
T/Plt: £49.30 to a £1 stake. Pool: £40,733.60. 602.55 winning tickets. T/Qpdt: £12.20 to a £1 stake. Pool: £2,769.20. 167.35 winning tickets. JR

# 5808 COLOGNE (R-H)
Sunday, September 26

**OFFICIAL GOING: Soft**

## 5822a IVG-EUROSELECT-PREIS - STUTENRENNEN (LISTED) (F&M) 1m 4f
**1:30** (1:31) 3-Y-0+ **£9,155** (£2,817; £1,408; £704)

RPR
1 **Aviane (GER)** 3-8-9 ..... ABoschert 1 80
(WHickst, Germany)
2 *1/2* **Gemini Diamond (IRE)**[20] 5356 4-9-5 ..... (b) NGMcCullagh 8 82
(MJGrassick, Ire) *soon led, headed after 2f, raced in 2nd til led again 2f out, narrow lead til headed and outpaced 100 yards out SP 74-10*
3 *1* **Trullitti (IRE)**[30] 5079 3-8-9 ..... SSanders 6 78
(JLDunlop) *held up, 9th straight, stayed on from 1 1/2f out to take 3rd on line SP 128-10*
4 *hd* **Top Call (GER)**[70] 3973 3-8-9 ..... AStarke 5 78
(ASchutz, Germany)
5 *2* **Sinaada (GER)** 3-8-9 ..... AngelaKull-Hohn 2 75
(WHefter, Germany)
6 *3/4* **Just Before (GER)** 3-8-9 ..... WMongil 7 74
(HBlume, Germany)
7 *1 1/4* **Morettina (GER)**[56] 4-9-5 ..... KKerekes 11 74
(WernerGlanz, Germany)
8 *4* **Loachapoka (GER)** 3-8-9 ..... ASchikora 3 66
(PSchiergen, Germany)
9 *9* **Antique Rose (GER)**[35] 4980 4-9-5 ..... ADeVries 4 54
(HSteinmetz, Germany)
10 *shd* **Danse D'Ecole (USA)** 3-8-9 ..... C-PLemaire 9 52
(H-APantall, France)
11 *3 1/2* **Silver Sash (GER)**[22] 5300 3-8-9 ..... RMullen 12 47
(MLWBell) *mid-division, 8th and weakening straight SP 138-10*

2m 35.21s
**WFA** 3 from 4yo 8lb **11** Ran
Speed ratings: .
**Owner** Stall Blanchelande **Bred** Benedikt Fassbinder **Trained** Germany

**NOTEBOOK**
**Trullitti(IRE)** making the step up to Listed company after breaking her maiden last time, she was rewarded with valuable black type. However, do not expect her to repeat the trick back in Britain.
**Silver Sash(GER)** was unfancied and ran accordingly.

## 5823a OPPENHEIM-STUTEN-MEILE (GROUP 3) (F&M) 1m
**3:05** (3:05) 3-Y-0+ **£22,535** (£7,042; £3,521; £2,113)

RPR
1 **Secret Melody (FR)**[38] 4899 3-8-12 ..... C-PLemaire 2 102
(H-APantall, France) *tracked leader, 2nd straight, strong challenge from distance to lead last stride*
2 *shd* **Snow Goose**[46] 4640 3-8-12 ..... SSanders 1 102
(JLDunlop) *tried to make all, caught last stride* **3**
3 *2 1/2* **Kitcat (GER)** 3-8-12 ..... ASchikora 4 97
(PSchiergen, Germany) *held up on inside, 8th straight, good run on inside to go 3rd distance, never troubled first two* **1**
4 *1 3/4* **Chrisiida (GER)**[140] 1983 3-8-12 ..... NRichter 3 94
(ASchutz, Germany) *always prominent, 3rd straight, kept on one pace from approaching final furlong*
5 *3/4* **New Princess (GER)**[98] 3134 5-9-3 ..... WMongil 7 93
(HHorwart, Germany) *mid-division, 6th straight, kept on*
6 *3* **Avenir Rubra (GER)**[88] 3434 4-9-3 ..... JBojko 10 87
(FrauEMader, Germany) *held up towards rear, 9th straight, some headway from 2f out*
7 *1/2* **Nicolaia (GER)**[88] 3434 4-9-3 ..... ADeVries 12 86
(HSteinmetz, Germany) *held up, 10th straight, never dangerous*
8 *2 1/2* **Ripley (GER)**[88] 3434 4-9-3 ..... J-PCarvalho 11 81
(MarioHofer, Germany) *last to straight and always behind*
9 *2* **Nostrana (GER)**[322] 5963 5-9-3 ..... AHelfenbein 6 77
(PRau, Germany) *prominent, 5th straight, soon beaten*
10 *hd* **Freedom (GER)**[112] 2723 3-8-12 ..... AStarke 8 76
(ASchutz, Germany) *raced in 7th to straight, beaten 2f out* **2**
11 *1/2* **Fair Dream (GER)** 3-8-12 ..... ABoschert 5 75
(MarioHofer, Germany) *prominent, 4th straight, soon beaten*

1m 40.07s
**WFA** 3 from 4yo+ 4lb **11** Ran SP% **131.6**
Speed ratings: .
**Owner** Lady O'Reilly **Bred** Petra Bloodstock Agency **Trained** France

**NOTEBOOK**
**Secret Melody(FR)** timed her challenge to perfection and showed a good attitude in just nosing out Snow Goose.
**Snow Goose** made a brave attempt to make all, and lost little in defeat. She is certainly capable of winning a stakes race.

## 5824a IVG - PREIS VON EUROPA (GROUP 1) 1m 4f
**4:20** (4:24) 3-Y-0+ **£66,901** (£24,648; £11,972; £5,634)

RPR
1 **Albanova**[42] 4794 5-9-2 ..... SSanders 1 111
(SirMarkPrescott) *broke well & settled in touch, headway well over 2f out, driven & challenged over 1f out, led close home, driven out* **14/10**[1]
2 *1/2* **Saldentigerin (GER)**[28] 5168 3-8-6 ..... AStarke 8 108
(PSchiergen, Germany) *led after 1f and soon 3 lengths clear setting good pace, joined over 1f out, ran on til headed close home* **29/10**[2]
3 *3/4* **Darsalam (IRE)**[15] 5463 3-8-10 ..... ABoschert 3 111
(AShavuyev, Czech Republic) *led 1f, raced in 2nd, pushed along approaching straight, driven 3f out to chase leader, ran on steadily to line, nearest at* **87/10**
4 *1/2* **Egerton (GER)**[21] 5329 3-8-10 ..... AHelfenbein 2 110
(PRau, Germany) *held up, stayed on in centre from over 2f out, nearest at finish* **37/10**



The Form Book, Raceform Ltd, Compton, RG20 6NL

5 *7* **Deva (GER)**[35] 4980 5-9-2 .................................................... KKerekes 6 98
(DRonge, Germany) *mid-ivision, never a danger* **29/1**
6 *3* **Well Made (GER)**[21] 5329 7-9-6 .................................................... WMongil 7 97
(HBlume, Germany) *in touch, pushed along 2 1/2f out, no impression* **79/10**[3]
7 *1 3/4* **Longridge (GER)**[30] 6-9-6 .................................................... J-PCarvalho 4 95
(MarioHofer, Germany) *mid-division, pushed along straight, no imprssion* **24/1**
8 *6* **Soterio (GER)**[25] 5254 4-9-6 .................................................... IFerguson 5 86
(WBaltromei, Germany) *held up, never a threat* **106/10**
9 *3* **Dano-Mast**[21] 5329 8-9-6 .................................................... THellier 9 81
(FPoulsen, France) *always in rear* **193/10**

2m 36.12s
**WFA** 3 from 4yo+ 8lb 9 Ran SP% **112.4**
Speed ratings: .
**Owner** Miss K Rausing **Bred** Miss K Rausing **Trained** Newmarket, Suffolk
■ Stewards Enquiry : S Sanders two-day ban: excessive use of the whip

**FOCUS**
A third successive Group One win for Albanova.

**NOTEBOOK**
**Albanova** had to work hard in the final stages but ultimately gained another deserved Group One victory, though her jockey did receive a two-day ban for excessive use of the whip. A credit to connections, she may run in the Premio Roma in November, and will be retired at the end of the season.
**Saldentigerin(GER)** had the favourite stretched after setting a testing pace, and battled well in the final stages before finally finding the British raider too good.
**Darsalam(IRE)** has carried all before him in Central Europe this season, and ran an excellent race. Impressing with his attitude in the closing stages, he could take a decent late-season prize on the continent on this showing.

# 5507 BATH (L-H)
## Monday, September 27

**OFFICIAL GOING: Good (good to firm in places)**
Wind: fresh against Weather: overcast

## 5825 UNIVERSITY AND LITERARY CLUB/EUROPEAN BREEDERS FUND MAIDEN STKS 5f 161y
**2:10** (2:11) (D3) 2-Y-O **£4,433** (£1,364; £682; £341) **Stalls Low**

Form RPR
22 **1** **Munaddam (USA)**[23] 5290 2-9-0 .................................................... LDettori 8 94+
(SaeedBinSuroor) *chsd ldr: led wl over 1f out: drew clr fnl f: comf* **4/9**[1]
26 **2** *5* **Rubies**[17] 5441 2-8-9 .................................................... JFortune 15 73
(RFJohnsonHoughton) *chsd ldrs: rdn 2f out: wnt 2nd ins fnl f: no ch w wnr* **12/1**
03 **3** *1 3/4* **Regal Dream (IRE)**[19] 5400 2-9-0 .................................................... RHills 12 72
(JWHills) *hld up: hdwy 2f out: sn rdn: one pce fnl f* **14/1**
3 **4** *3/4* **Inka Dancer (IRE)**[14] 5507 2-8-6 .................................................... FPFerris(3) 1 65
(BPalling) *a.p: rdn 3f out: swtchd rt jst over 1f out: one pce* **12/1**
5 **5** *1/2* **Chinalea (IRE)**[14] 5507 2-9-0 .................................................... RSmith 9 68
(CGCox) *a.p: rdn wl over 1f out: one pce* **9/1**[2]
2556 **6** *2 1/2* **Rusky Dusky (USA)**[17] 5434 2-9-0 77 ....................................(v) RLMoore 11 60
(RHannon) *led: rdn and hdd wl over 1f out: wkng whn n.m.r on ins ins fnl f* **10/1**[3]
0 **7** *1/2* **Windwood (IRE)**[17] 5441 2-9-0 .................................................... SDrowne 10 58
(JWHills) *mid-div: rdn over 2f out: no hdwy* **100/1**
0000 **8** *1 3/4* **Gold Majesty**[13] 5534 2-8-9 45 .................................................... CCatlin 16 48
(MRChannon) *hld up: rdn over 2f out: no imp* **100/1**
0 **9** *shd* **Will The Till**[53] 4474 2-8-11 .................................................... DCorby(3) 3 52
(JMBradley) *bhd: rdn over 3f out: no ch whn edgd rt over 1f out* **100/1**
0050 **10** *3/4* **Amalgam (IRE)**[66] 4095 2-8-4 40 .................................................... BSwarbrick(5) 14 45
(MrsPNDutfield) *rdn over 2f out: a bhd* **100/1**
00 **11** *2 1/2* **Gypsy Royal (IRE)**[21] 5349 2-8-9 .................................................... NDay 6 37
(RIngram) *bhd: rdn and short-lived effrt 2f out* **125/1**
**12** *1 1/2* **Moonside** 2-8-6 .................................................... RThomas(3) 13 32
(GBBalding) *a bhd* **100/1**
00 **13** *4* **Blade Runner (IRE)**[39] 4866 2-8-9 .................................................... MFenton 4 19
(DHaydnJones) *in tch: sltly hmpd on ins over 3f out: sn bhd* **66/1**
04 **14** *3/4* **Open Verdict (IRE)**[79] 3729 2-9-0 ....................................(t) DarrenWilliams 7 21
(APJarvis) *bmpd s: plld hrd: sn chsng ldrs: rdn and wknd 2f out* **33/1**
000 **15** *3 1/2* **Our Nigel (IRE)**[30] 5132 2-9-0 .................................................... TEDurcan 5 10
(MrsPNDutfield) *towards rr whn stmbld after 1f: rdn over 2f out: no rspnse* **100/1**
000 **16** *dist* **Rum Creek**[13] 5534 2-9-0 .................................................... JFEgan 2 —
(SKirk) *s.i.s: outpcd: t.o* **66/1**

1m 12.74s (1.60) **Going Correction** +0.275s/f (Good) **16 Ran SP% 123.1**
Speed ratings: **100,93,91,90,89 86,85,83,82,81 78,76,71,70,65** —CSF £7.23 TOTE £1.50: £1.02, £2.30, £3.50; EX 9.60.
**Owner** Godolphin **Bred** Shadwell Farm Llc **Trained** Newmarket, Suffolk

**FOCUS**
An ordinary maiden, but easy winner Munaddam should leave the form behind and could be Pattern class. The form behind looks reasonably sound.

**NOTEBOOK**
**Munaddam(USA)** set a good standard on the form of his two previous runs and looked to have been found a relatively simple task to lose his maiden status. Never far off the lead, he swept clear in the final furlong and was always in total control. He looks worthy of a step up in grade and, although he will stay seven furlongs, looks quite comfy at this trip for the time being.
**Rubies** showed her latest effort to be all wrong with a keeping on second. She was no match for the winner, but has a similar race in her.
**Regal Dream(IRE)** has now shown a fair level of ability on all three starts and may find further improvement for a soft surface. He is an obvious future winner and is now qualified for nurseries.
**Inka Dancer(IRE)**, a shock 66/1 third here on her debut when she lost a shoe, confirmed that run to be no fluke in fourth and will find easier opportunities.
**Chinalea(IRE)** ran pretty much to form with Inka Dancer and he too will find easier winning opportunities.
**Rusky Dusky(USA)** did not run to his mark of 77 and looks regressive.
**Windwood(IRE)** was noted making a little late headway and one more run will see him qualified for a mark.
**Gold Majesty** ◆ wants farther and will find life easier in nurseries off her very competitive mark of 45.
**Amalgam(IRE)** *Official explanation: jockey said filly was hanging right*
**Rum Creek** *Official explanation: vet said colt was lame*

## 5826 LETHEBY & CHRISTOPHER H'CAP 2m 1f 34y
**2:40** (2:42) (E3) (0-70,70) 3-Y-0+ **£3,577** (£1,100; £550; £275) **Stalls Low**

Form RPR
0660 **1** **Darn Good**[16] 5456 3-8-7 **65** ....................................(b) RLMoore 8 76
(RHannon) *hld up: hdwy over 8f out: rdn to ld 2f out: drvn out* **16/1**
1000 **2** *2* **Teorban (POL)**[16] 5456 5-8-10 **56** oh1 .................................................... ADaly 14 65
(DJSFfrenchDavis) *hld up and bhd: hdwy over 8f out: styd on to take 2nd ins fnl f: nt rch wnr* **50/1**
3110 **3** *5* **Moonshine Beach**[16] 5472 6-9-10 **70** .................................................... DarrenWilliams 13 73
(PWHiatt) *a.p: led over 8f out: rdn over 3f out: hdd 2f out: wknd ins fnl f* **8/1**[3]
0020 **4** *2 1/2* **Henry Island (IRE)**[16] 5456 11-8-11 **57** .................................................... SDrowne 16 57
(MrsAJBowlby) *hld up in tch: hdwy over 6f out: rdn 3f out: wknd ins fnl f* **14/1**
3405 **5** *1/2* **Northern Nymph**[16] 5456 5-9-4 **64** .................................................... JFortune 18 63
(RHollinshead) *hld up in tch: hdwy 8f out: ev ch 3f out: sn rdn: wknd over 1f out* **14/1**
2604 **6** *5* **Riyadh**[16] 5472 6-9-6 **66** .................................................... RFfrench 17 59
(MJohnston) *hld up and bhd: hdwy 7f out: rdn over 4f out: no real prog fnl 2f* **8/1**[3]
0050 **7** *1/2* **Lord Nellsson**[6] 5340 8-8-10 **56** .................................................... VSlattery 19 48
(JSKing) *hld up: hdwy over 9f out: rdn over 4f out: wknd over 2f out* **33/1**
1055 **8** *3* **Anyhow (IRE)**[47] 4642 7-9-0 **63** .................................................... DNolan(3) 9 52
(MissKMGeorge) *hld up and bhd: hdwy on outside over 3f out: sn rdn: wknd over 1f out* **22/1**
3301 **9** *14* **Most-Saucy**[26] 5221 8-8-5 **56** .................................................... BSwarbrick(5) 11 28
(IAWood) *bhd: rdn over 4f out: nvr nr ldrs: eased whn no ch fnl f* **12/1**
320 **10** *10* **Claradotnet**[32] 5058 4-9-2 **62** .................................................... TEDurcan 7 22
(MRChannon) *hld up towards rr: hdwy over 6f out: rdn over 4f out: wknd 3f out* **12/1**
0230 **11** *3/4* **Circus Maximus (USA)**[26] 5221 7-8-10 **56** oh3 ....................(p) CCatlin 2 15
(IanWilliams) *a bhd* **16/1**
6063 **12** *13* **Red Sun**[16] 5456 7-8-10 **56** ....................................(t) TPQueally 3 —
(JMackie) *led 5f: led over 9f out tl over 8f out: rdn and wknd 6f out* **9/2**[2]
410- **13** *3* **Kaluana Court**[415] 3986 8-9-5 **68** .................................................... RThomas(3) 12 8
(RJPrice) *hld up: hdwy over 8f out: wknd over 3f out* **16/1**
40-3 **14** *2 1/2* **Cody**[9] 5645 5-8-10 **56** oh11 .................................................... SRighton 15 —
(GAHam) *prom tl wknd 4f out* **50/1**
500- **15** *20* **Blau Grau (GER)**[291] 1463 7-8-3 **56** oh16 .................................................... MHalford(7) 6 —
(NEBerry) *a bhd* **100/1**
6403 **16** *1 1/2* **Olympias (IRE)**[21] 5340 3-7-9 **56** oh3 ....................................(b) FPFerris(3) 5 —
(HMorrison) *a bhd* **20/1**
1004 **17** *12* **Komoto**[33] 5037 3-8-2 **60** ....................................(b[1]) MartinDwyer 20 —
(GAButler) *prom tl rdn and wknd over 5f out* **50/1**
1005 **18** *13* **Etching (USA)**[14] 5523 4-9-0 **60** .................................................... LDettori 1 —
(JRFanshawe) *hld up towards rr: rdn over 4f out: sn struggling* **7/2**[1]
-042 **19** *10* **Royal Prodigy (USA)**[176] 759 5-8-13 **59** .................................................... MFenton 10 —
(RJHodges) *bhd fnl 8f* **25/1**
1043 **20** *dist* **Rolex Free (ARG)**[24] 5257 6-8-10 **56** oh5 ....................................(v) JFEgan 4 —
(DFlood) *chsd ldr: led after 5f tl rdn and hdd over 9f out: wknd qckly over 6f out: t.o* **22/1**

3m 52.91s (3.31) **Going Correction** +0.275s/f (Good)
**WFA** 3 from 4yo+ 12lb **20 Ran SP% 136.1**
Speed ratings: **103,102,99,98,98 95,95,94,87,83 82,76,75,73,64 63,58,52,47,**—CSF £706.39 CT £6757.09 TOTE £22.80: £5.80, £10.00, £2.80, £5.60; EX 2727.30.
**Owner** J E Garrett **Bred** Mrs Patricia Conway **Trained** East Everleigh, Wilts

**FOCUS**
This looked a competitive race beforehand but they came home at lengthy intervals having gone a fair gallop and the form should prove reliable.

**NOTEBOOK**
**Darn Good**, back down to a winning mark after a couple of lacklustre efforts, made good headway from the rear of the field before coming through to take it up just over quarter of a mile out and powering away to win comfortably. Likely to go back up for this, he will need to find further improvement to follow up.
**Teorban(POL)** defied odds of 50/1 by running a huge race in second. He was finishing well having been held up and, if able to build on this, is on a good mark, so may be one to keep an eye on.
**Moonshine Beach**, who has had a fruitful time of it this season, in contrast to the front two was up with the pace all the way and did not have enough left to go again when challenged. He is still on a reasonable mark and one could not rule out him winning again. *Official explanation: jockey said gelding hung right*
**Henry Island(IRE)**, 7lb lower than when last successful over a year ago, is not getting any better at the age of 11, and he ran well enough without suggesting he is about to strike.
**Northern Nymph** has yet to win in 22 starts on turf and does not look like putting an end to that anytime soon.
**Riyadh**, although still capable of paying his way, has no desire for the game and is a shadow of what he used to be capable of.
**Most-Saucy**, who seems more at home over this sort of trip these days, won a weaker race at Lingfield last time and found this tougher heat beyond her. Back in a lesser race, she can add to her admirable record.
**Red Sun** ran no sort of race and is better than this.
**Komoto** *Official explanation: jockey said gelding hung right*
**Etching(USA)**, slightly unlucky when fifth on his most recent outing, was never going at any stage and looks best left alone until showing more. *Official explanation: jockey said filly had breathing problems*

## 5827 WORKPLACE SOLUTIONS/EUROPEAN BREEDERS FUND MAIDEN STKS 1m 2f 46y
**3:10** (3:13) (D3) 2-Y-O **£4,537** (£1,396; £698; £349) **Stalls Low**

Form RPR
342 **1** **Haatmey**[14] 5522 2-9-0 76 .................................................... TEDurcan 2 87
(MRChannon) *hld up: hdwy over 3f out: sn swtchd rt: rdn to ld jst over 2f out: r.o wl* **5/1**
42 **2** *3 1/2* **Master Cobbler (IRE)**[69] 4003 2-9-0 .................................................... JFortune 6 81
(GAButler) *s.s: hld up: hdwy over 2f out: rdn and chsd wnr wl over 1f out: no imp* **4/1**[3]
66 **3** *8* **Gidam Gidam (IRE)**[11] 5592 2-9-0 .................................................... RHills 1 66
(CEBrittain) *s.i.s: bhd: rdn over 2f out: hdwy over 1f out: styd on fnl f: n.d* **40/1**
03 **4** *shd* **Battledress (IRE)**[14] 5508 2-9-0 .................................................... MartinDwyer 4 66
(MPTregoning) *s.i.s: sn in tch: hdwy over 1f out: ev ch over 2f out: sn rdn: wknd over 1f out* **7/2**[2]
00 **5** *nk* **Northanger Abbey (IRE)**[68] 4030 2-9-0 .................................................... RLMoore 3 66
(JHMGosden) *hld up: hdwy over 5f out: rdn 3f out: wknd wl over 1f out* **25/1**
33 **6** *9* **The Duke Of Dixie (USA)**[31] 5091 2-9-0 .................................................... LDettori 10 49
(PFICole) *hld up: hdwy 6f out: rdn and wknd 4f out* **9/4**[1]

5 **7** 1 1/4 **Timber Scorpion (UAE)**14 [5522] 2-9-0 ............ RFfrench 11 47
(MJohnston) *led: rdn and hdd jst over 2f out: sn wknd* **14/1**

0 **8** hd **Back To Reality**18 [5406] 2-8-11 ............ FPFerris(3) 7 47
(BPalling) *a bhd: no ch fnl 4f* **100/1**

53 **9** nk **Red Riot (USA)**19 [5398] 2-9-0 ............ TPQueally 8 46
(DRLoder) *prom: rdn over 4f out: wknd jst over 2f out* **16/1**

0002 **10** 5 **Inchcape Rock**28 [5173] 2-9-0 78 ............ IMongan 5 37
(LGCottrell) *prom: jnd ldr 5f out: rdn over 2f out: sn wknd* **20/1**

00 **11** dist **Mount Arafat**14 [5508] 2-9-0 ............(t) ADaly 9 —
(MSalaman) *prom: lost pl 5f out: sn bhd: t.o* **150/1**

2m 12.12s (1.12) **Going Correction** +0.275s/f (Good) **11** Ran SP% **114.9**
Speed ratings: **106,103,96,96,96 89,88,88,87,83** —CSF £23.70 TOTE £6.40: £1.70, £2.00, £8.70; EX 22.30.
**Owner** Sheikh Ahmed Al Maktoum **Bred** Darley **Trained** West Ilsley, Berks

**FOCUS**
A very smart time indeed for the grade of contest, 0.25 seconds faster than the following maiden for older fillies and solid form for the grade. The winner did it very well indeed and looks a likely sort for the Zetland Stakes at Newmarket.

**NOTEBOOK**
**Haatmey ◆**, who had shown fair form in three previous starts, was able to supplement his name to the ever-growing list of recent Mick Channon-trained juvenile winners, and he did it in the shape of a real stayer. Although he will need to improve, the Zetland Stakes at Newmarket is never the strongest of events and, with his stable having won the race last term, that would look an obvious target and he will go there with a solid each-way chance.
**Master Cobbler(IRE)**, who was taking a huge step up in trip having previously competed over five and six furlongs, saw it out well enough and pulled eight lengths clear of the third. He has an ordinary maiden at his mercy.
**Gidam Gidam(IRE) ◆** gave an improved effort with a staying on third and can win his maiden over this trip. He will make up into a decent staying handicapper next term.
**Battledress(IRE)** comes from a stable that is just beginning to show signs of something like a revival in form, and she was not disgraced in fourth. She is another middle-distance handicapper in the making.
**Northanger Abbey(IRE)** showed his first worthwhile piece of form and, as his dam won at up to 2m2f, great improvement can be expected from two to three and when stepping up in distance.
**The Duke Of Dixie(USA)** was bitterly disappointing and although beaten too early for the run to be blamed on the distance, it was probably too stiff a test at this stage of his career and he deserves another chance. *Official explanation: jockey said colt was never travelling*
**Timber Scorpion(UAE)** is not bred to stay and simply looks slow.

## 5828 LETHEBY & CHRISTOPHER MAIDEN FILLIES' STKS — 1m 2f 46y
3:40 (3:42) (D3) 3-Y-O+ £3,552 (£1,093; £546; £273) Stalls Low

Form RPR

2 **1** **Namat (IRE)**25 [5239] 3-8-10 ............ RHills 2 74
(MPTregoning) *hld up in tch: hdwy over 3f out: rdn over 2f out: styd on to ld last strides* **5/2**1

0243 **2** hd **Principessa**14 [5511] 3-8-7 70 ............ FPFerris(3) 11 74
(BPalling) *led: rdn jst over 2f out: hdd last strides* **6/1**

0200 **3** 5 **Efrhina (IRE)**5 [5740] 4-9-2 68 ............ SDrowne 3 65
(MrsStefLiddiard) *hld up: sn bhd: hdwy over 2f out: styd on fnl f: nvr trbld ldrs* **9/1**

**4** 1 1/4 **Angry Bark (USA)**99 3-8-10 ............ RSmith 7 62
(HSHowe) *a.p: wnt 2nd 7f out: rdn over 2f out: wknd fnl f* **40/1**

30 **5** hd **Sian Thomas**10 [5621] 3-8-10 ............ MartinDwyer 13 62+
(MPTregoning) *hld up and bhd: rdn over 2f out: hdwy over 1f out: n.d* **33/1**

632 **6** nk **Paintbox**18 [5424] 3-8-10 69 ............ RLMoore 14 61
(MrsAJPerrett) *hld up and bhd: c wd ent st: rdn and hdwy over 2f out: nvr able to chal* **5/1**3

34 **7** 3 1/2 **Play Bouzouki**30 [5123] 3-8-10 ............ LDettori 15 55
(LMCumani) *hld up: hdwy 3f out: rdn over 1f out: wknd fnl f* **4/1**2

0 **8** 6 **Mrs Philip**21 [5339] 5-9-2 ............ VSlattery 1 43
(PJHobbs) *s.i.s: hdwy on ins 7f out: rdn over 4f out: sn wknd* **66/1**

520 **9** 1 1/2 **Wait For Spring (USA)**30 [5123] 3-8-10 69 ............ JFortune 10 40
(JHMGosden) *hld up: hdwy 5f out: rdn over 3f out: wknd 2f out* **12/1**

2040 **10** 3 **Al Shuua**32 [5057] 3-8-10 70 ............ TEDurcan 12 35
(CEBrittain) *prom: rdn over 3f out: wknd over 2f out* **25/1**

0 **11** 8 **Favourable**133 [2182] 3-8-10 ............ TPQueally 5 19
(AWCarroll) *prom tl rdn and wknd 3f out* **50/1**

42 **12** shd **Pleasant**35 [5007] 3-8-10 ............ IMongan 4 19
(LGCottrell) *s.i.s: a bhd* **9/1**

06 **13** 5 **Pins 'n Needles (IRE)**121 [2486] 3-8-10 ............ JFEgan 8 10
(CACyzer) *a bhd* **66/1**

03 **14** 6 **Golden Queen**12 [5571] 3-8-3 ............ AshleighHorton(7) 9 —
(MDIUsher) *hld up: lost pl 7f out: bhd fnl 5f* **100/1**

00 **15** 15 **Observation**161 [1507] 3-8-10 ............ ADaly 6 —
(MrsJCandlish) *hld up in tch: n.m.r and lost pl 5f out: bhd fnl 3f* **66/1**

2m 12.37s (1.37) **Going Correction** +0.275s/f (Good)
**WFA** 3 from 4yo+ 6lb **15** Ran SP% **123.9**
Speed ratings: **105,104,100,99,99 99,96,91,90,88 81,81,77,72,60** CSF £17.29 TOTE £3.40: £1.60, £2.20, £2.80; EX 32.70.
**Owner** Hamdan Al Maktoum **Bred** Shadwell Estate Company Limited **Trained** Lambourn, Berks

**FOCUS**
A pretty poor maiden, with many of the principals having an off day and the race is rated through the runner-up.

**NOTEBOOK**
**Namat(IRE)** confirmed the promise of her debut second at Redcar with a game win - getting up in the shadows of the post to claim the long-time leader Principessa. She is likely to get a mark in the mid-70's but connections will probably favour a crack at Listed company. Either way she will need to improve to win again and strikes as the type to struggle.
**Principessa** remains a maiden after 12 starts, but one could not help but feel sorry for her as she had led for most of the way and looked to have done enough until wilting near the line. Her day will come but she is not one to follow.
**Efrhina(IRE)** was backed in the ring as though a decent run was expected and she plugged on to reward each-way punters.
**Angry Bark(USA)** was making her British debut having had two spins in France and she ran well enough to suggest she can win at a low level.
**Sian Thomas** is now qualified for handicaps and can do better in that sphere.
**Paintbox** was given a lot to do by her rider and never got into contention. She is better than this.
**Play Bouzouki** was another not given the best tactical ride and she was always trailing. This was her third run in a maiden and better can be expected of her now she is eligible for handicaps. *Official explanation: jockey said filly failed to handle bend*
**Pleasant**, like Play Bouzouki, was having her third run in a maiden and ran below par. She should do better in handicaps. *Official explanation: jockey said filly hung left*

## 5829 BET365 CALL 08000 322 365 H'CAP — 1m 5y
4:10 (4:10) (E3) (0-70,69) 3-Y-O £3,521 (£1,083; £541; £270) Stalls Low

Form RPR

0604 **1** **Sachin**18 [5424] 3-9-0 62 ............ MartinDwyer 14 70
(JRBoyle) *hld up: rdn and hdwy over 2f out: led over 1f out: all out* **33/1**

0620 **2** 1/2 **Desert Hawk**7 [5693] 3-9-4 66 ............ RLMoore 11 73
(RHannon) *hld up and bhd: hdwy on outside 3f out: rdn and ev ch over 1f out: r.o* **11/1**

-420 **3** 1/2 **Barons Spy (IRE)**88 [3452] 3-9-3 65 ............ RHills 16 71
(AWCarroll) *hld up in rr: hdwy on outside over 2f out: ev ch over 1f out: rdn and nt qckn ins fnl f* **20/1**

24-4 **4** shd **Five Years On (IRE)**16 [5478] 3-9-2 64 ............ MFenton 6 70
(WJHaggas) *hld up and bhd: smooth hdwy over 2f out: ev ch over 1f out: sn rdn: nt qckn ins fnl f* **7/1**3

1120 **5** 2 1/2 **The Fun Merchant**61 [4242] 3-9-6 68 ............ LDettori 15 68
(JPearce) *hld up and bhd: stdy hdwy on ins whn n.m.r 2f out: rdn over 1f out: kpt on same pce fnl f* **9/2**1

0301 **6** 1/2 **Master Mahogany**14 [5510] 3-8-13 61 ............ SDrowne 4 60
(RJHodges) *a.p: led 2f out: rdn and hdd over 1f out: wknd fnl f* **11/2**2

0500 **7** 3/4 **Fit To Fly (IRE)**39 [4882] 3-9-3 65 ............ IMongan 13 62
(MrsJCandlish) *hld up in tch: rdn 4f out: ev ch 2f out: wknd jst over 1f out* **16/1**

0550 **8** 1 1/2 **Dan Di Canio (IRE)**25 [5245] 3-8-10 61 ............(t) DCorby(3) 12 55
(PWHarris) *hld up in mid-div: hdwy over 3f out: rdn over 2f out: wknd over 1f out* **33/1**

2356 **9** 1 3/4 **Text**20 [5378] 3-9-3 65 ............(v1) JFEgan 1 55
(MrsStefLiddiard) *prom tl rdn and wknd 2f out* **16/1**

2420 **10** 1 3/4 **Scriptorium**47 [4655] 3-9-0 62 ............ TPQueally 9 47
(LMCumani) *w ldr: led over 4f out: rdn and hdd 2f out: wknd over 1f out* **7/1**3

-630 **11** 3/4 **Zazous**53 [4478] 3-9-1 63 ............ JDSmith 8 47
(AKing) *bhd fnl 5f* **40/1**

0004 **12** nk **Ticero**20 [5370] 3-9-1 63 ............(b) TEDurcan 3 46
(CEBrittain) *a bhd* **12/1**

6502 **13** 11 **The Way We Were**65 [4147] 3-9-7 69 ............ JFortune 10 27
(TGMills) *led over 3f: rdn and wknd over 2f out* **9/2**1

0000 **14** 3 **Live Wire Lucy (USA)**17 [5446] 3-9-3 65 ............ CCatlin 2 16
(CTinkler) *a in rr* **66/1**

6264 **15** 2 **Sea Of Gold**20 [5381] 3-9-3 68 ............ FPFerris(3) 5 14
(HJCyzer) *chsd ldrs: rdn over 3f out: sn wknd* **20/1**

1m 43.67s (2.67) **Going Correction** +0.275s/f (Good) **15** Ran SP% **123.9**
Speed ratings: **97,96,96,95,93 92,92,90,88,87 86,86,75,72,70** CSF £351.29 CT £7303.84 TOTE £54.40: £11.00, £3.00, £6.40; EX 472.20.
**Owner** Epsom Sorts **Bred** Jephanil **Trained** Epsom, Surrey

**FOCUS**
Only a modest handicap, the form looks fairly sound at a limited level and should produce the odd winner.

**NOTEBOOK**
**Sachin** improved on some pretty modest form to take this modest handicap. He showed a good attitude in winning and gave everything, so that counts in his favour and he could possibly improve again now he has got his head in front.
**Desert Hawk** has not really gone on as expected but did at least leave behind a poor run at Chepstow.
**Barons Spy(IRE)** is of more interest than either of the front two with regards to the future, as he is unexposed and this represented an improved effort on what was his first outing since July.
**Five Years On(IRE)** travelled well and looked a live threat at one stage, but his progress through the field levelled out and he could only plug on. He evidently has a small race in him.
**The Fun Merchant** was doing his best work at the death and was unlucky not to get closer. He looks capable of winning off this mark.
**Master Mahogany** did not quite see his race out and may have done a little too much in the early stages of the race.
**Scriptorium** had his chance and continues to disappoint.
**The Way We Were** is down to a winning mark but he ran as though something was amiss. *Official explanation: jockey said colt ran flat*

## 5830 LETHEBY & CHRISTOPHER APPRENTICE MAIDEN H'CAP — 1m 5y
4:40 (4:41) (F4) (0-55,55) 3-Y-O+ £2,679 (£765; £382) Stalls Low

Form RPR

005 **1** **Blake Hall Lad (IRE)**31 [5092] 3-8-9 55 ............ DeanWilliams(3) 12 61
(MissJFeilden) *hld up: hdwy over 3f out: sn rdn: led and edgd lft ins fnl f: r.o* **16/1**

5003 **2** 1/2 **Graceful Air (IRE)**16 [5478] 3-8-9 52 ............(p) DFentiman 5 57
(JRWeymes) *chsd ldrs: rdn 2f out: r.o ins fnl f* **6/1**2

4005 **3** nk **Magari**16 [5448] 3-8-0 50 ............ RKingscote(7) 2 54
(JGGiven) *s.i.s: sn chsng ldrs: rdn 3f out: r.o ins fnl f* **25/1**

300 **4** hd **Musical Top (USA)**21 [5337] 4-8-11 55 ............ TBlock(5) 9 59
(HMorrison) *hld up: rdn 2f out: hdwy jst over 1f out: kpt on wl towards fin* **12/1**

3300 **5** nk **Ask The Driver**65 [4128] 3-8-8 51 ............(b1) DerekNolan 16 54
(DJSFfrenchDavis) *hld up and bhd: rdn 3f out: hdwy 2f out: kpt on ins fnl f* **9/1**

000/ **6** 1/2 **Dark Society**592 [857] 6-8-8 52 ............ TDean(5) 3 54
(AWCarroll) *s.i.s: bhd: rdn over 2f out: hdwy 1f out: nt rch ldrs* **25/1**

0200 **7** shd **Kindness**23 [5285] 4-8-11 50 ............ PGallagher 1 52
(ADWPinder) *led early: chsd ldr: led 4f out: rdn over 1f out: hdd ins fnl f: no ex cl home* **7/1**3

-000 **8** 1 **Doringo**105 [2950] 3-8-4 52 ............ RJKilloran(5) 13 52
(JLSpearing) *chsd ldrs: rdn and ev ch over 1f out: swtchd rt ins fnl f: one pce* **25/1**

0000 **9** 2 1/2 **Hold Up**53 [4496] 3-8-5 53 ............ KirstyMilczarek(5) 7 47
(MissJFeilden) *s.i.s: hdwy on outside over 3f out: sn rdn: wknd over 1f out* **12/1**

0000 **10** 3/4 **Ninah**21 [5337] 3-8-5 53 ............ JemmaMarshall(5) 15 45
(JMBradley) *hld up and bhd: hdwy on outside over 3f out: rdn wl over 1f out: wknd fnl f* **25/1**

4425 **11** 1 1/2 **Nicholas Nickelby**2 [5803] 4-8-13 52 ............(p) KristinStubbs 4 41
(MJPolglase) *prom: rn wd bnd over 4f out: rdn 2f out: sn wknd* **5/1**1

0000 **12** hd **Imperial Royale (IRE)**22 [5320] 3-8-5 51 ............(p) MHalford(3) 10 39
(PLClinton) *bhd: rdn and short-lived effrt 3f out* **14/1**

5-00 **13** 12 **Royal Flight**10 [5621] 3-8-2 50 ............ MCoumbe(5) 6 11
(PWHarris) *hld up in mid-div: rdn over 3f out: sn struggling* **10/1**

0000 **14** nk **My Sunshine (IRE)**14 [5510] 3-8-2 50 ............(b1) KMay(5) 14 10
(BWHills) *sn led: hdd 4f out: rdn 3f out: wknd 2f out* **11/1**

0000 **15** 2 **Whispering Valley**9 [5658] 4-8-8 47 ............ ThomasYeung 8 2
(MrsAJPerrett) *bhd fnl 4f* **20/1**



The Form Book, Raceform Ltd, Compton, RG20 6NL

4-66 **16** 1 ½ **Maid For Life (IRE)**[29] 5145 4-9-1 **54**................................ MLawson 11 6
(MJWallace) *s.i.s: rdn 4f out: a in rr* **12/1**
1m 44.65s (3.65) **Going Correction** +0.275s/f (Good)
**WFA** 3 from 4yo+ 4lb **16** Ran SP% **126.6**
Speed ratings: **92,91,91,91,90 90,90,89,86,85 84,84,72,71,69 68**CSF £105.43 CT £2482.89 TOTE £29.20: £5.40, £1.10, £5.30, £3.50; EX 58.60 Place 6 £1,705.60, Place 5 £1,294.66.
**Owner** Blake Hall Lad Partnership **Bred** Mark Clarke **Trained** Exning, Suffolk

**FOCUS**
A weak affair run in a very slow time and the form is more or less plating class.

**NOTEBOOK**
**Blake Hall Lad(IRE)** took what was a weak affair on this handicap debut and seemed to improve for the step up in trip. Whether he can build on this is questionable but, if he can, can probably supplement this. *Official explanation: trainer said, regarding the improved form shown, gelding may have benefited from the step up in trip*
**Graceful Air(IRE)** was always being held by the winner and remains winless after 23 starts. She had cheekpieces on here but they made no real difference.
**Magari** was gaining at the line, but she is a filly of limited ability who will struggle to get her head in front.
**Musical Top(USA)** falls into the same category as the third and has yet to find a suitable trip.
**Ask The Driver** has not gone on this season but this run in the first-time blinkers did seem to offer some encouragement for the future.
**Dark Society**, having his first start for well over two years, ran well and was closing at the line, but the odds of him 'bouncing' next time look very high. As a result he may be one to watch out for the time after.
**Nicholas Nickelby** failed to confirm Carlisle form with third-placed Magari and evidently had an off day.
T/Plt: £1,795.10 to a £1 stake. Pool: £38,608.25. 15.70 winning tickets. T/Qpdt: £297.30 to a £1 stake. Pool: £3,335.30. 8.30 winning tickets. KH

# [5669]HAMILTON (R-H)
## Monday, September 27
**OFFICIAL GOING: Soft (good to soft in places)**

## 5831 FAMOUS GROUSE EBF MEDIAN AUCTION MAIDEN STKS 1m 65y
**2:20** (2:21) (E3) 2-Y-O **£4,273** (£1,315; £657; £328) **Stalls** High

Form RPR
2 **1** **Kiswahili**[74] 3870 2-8-9 .......................................... SSanders 5 86+
(SirMarkPrescott) *trckd ldrs: hdwy 1/2-way: led 21/2f out: sn clr: easily* **2/5**[1]
0444 **2** 9 **Aire De Mougins (IRE)**[22] 5314 2-9-0 75................... GFaulkner 3 71
(PCHaslam) *trckd ldrs: hdwy 1/2-way: rdn to chse wnr over 1f out: sn drvn and no imp* **8/1**[3]
62 **3** 3 ½ **Fine Lady**[18] 5406 2-8-9 .......................................... DHolland 8 59
(MJohnston) *led: rdn along and hdd 21/2f out: sn drvn and wknd wl over 1f out* **4/1**[2]
00 **4** 1 ¼ **Last Pioneer (IRE)**[31] 5095 2-9-0 ............................ PHanagan 2 64+
(TPTate) *bhd: hdwy on inner over 3f out: rdn over 2f out and kpt on same pce* **66/1**
5 **5** 5 **Eastern Mandarin**[31] 5083 2-8-11 ........................ PMulrennan[(3)] 4 52
(DEddy) *in tch: pushed along 3f out: rdn over 2f out and sn btn* **50/1**
0 **6** 7 **Jeffslottery**[31] 5098 2-9-0 ........................................ RWinston 1 38
(JRWeymes) *stdd s: a rr* **100/1**
0 **7** ¾ **Casalese**[16] 5447 2-9-0 .............................................. FLynch 7 36
(MDHammond) *a rr* **100/1**
6606 **8** 2 ½ **Forpetesake**[30] 5128 2-9-0 58.................................... ANicholls 6 31
(MsDeborahJEvans) *prom: rdn along 1/2-way: sn wknd* **100/1**
1m 51.25s (1.95) **Going Correction** +0.20s/f (Good) **8** Ran SP% **109.0**
Speed ratings: **98,89,85,84,79 72,71,69**CSF £3.76 TOTE £1.40: £1.02, £1.30, £1.20; EX 3.90.
**Owner** Miss K Rausing **Bred** Miss K Rausing **Trained** Newmarket, Suffolk
■ Seb Sanders bags his 150th winner of the season.

**FOCUS**
No strength in depth to this maiden and the field finished well strung out behind the facile winner.

**NOTEBOOK**
**Kiswahili** confirmed the promise of her debut at Epsom in July and ran out an easy winner on this much softer ground. The step up to a mile was to her advantage and she can be rated value for much more than the official winning margin, so looks the type to progress to a high level over middle-distances as a three-year-old.
**Aire De Mougins(IRE)** stuck to his task well when under pressure and finished a clear second. This extra furlong suited and he is one to look out for when switching to nurseries.
**Fine Lady** had her chance and probably ran up to the form of her previous outing at Chepstow. She has not really progressed in three outings, but could be the type to improve for a switch to nurseries and looked to find this ground plenty soft enough.
**Last Pioneer(IRE)** was again none too smartly away, but kept on well enough in the latter stages over this extra furlong. He will no doubt fare better next term in handicaps.

## 5832 SAM COLLINGWOOD-CAMERON CONDITIONS STKS 6f 5y
**2:50** (2:51) (B1) 3-Y-O+ **£12,174** (£4,617; £2,308; £1,049) **Stalls** Centre

Form RPR
6520 **1** **Welsh Emperor (IRE)**[23] 5289 5-9-5 107........................(b) DHolland 6 109
(TPTate) *mde virtually all: rdn along wl over 1f out: styd on strly u.p ins last* **2/1**[2]
3320 **2** 1 ¾ **Cartography (IRE)**[23] 5289 3-8-7 106...............................(t) KMcEvoy 8 94
(SaeedBinSuroor) *trckd ldrs: hdwy over 2f out: rdn over 1f out: drvn and kpt on same pce ins last* **15/8**[1]
0036 **3** nk **Johnston's Diamond (IRE)**[2] 5787 6-8-9 85.................. DAllan 1 93
(EJAlston) *a rpominent: effrt and ev ch 2f out: sn rdn and kpt on same pce ent last* **20/1**
0400 **4** ¾ **Circuit Dancer (IRE)**[9] 5628 4-8-9 89.............................. FLynch 4 91
(ABerry) *dwlt and bhd: hdwy 1/2-way: rdn wl over 1f out: drvn and no imp fnl f* **33/1**
-400 **5** 1 ½ **Philharmonic**[9] 5628 3-8-7 98.................................... PHanagan 7 86
(RAFahey) *in tch: rdn along 1/2-way: kpt on u.p fnl f: nrst fin* **8/1**
0601 **6** 5 **Funfair Wane**[9] 5628 5-8-9 98.................................... ANicholls 2 71
(DNicholls) *cl up: rdn along 1/2-way: sn wknd* **4/1**[3]
6010 **7** 11 **Mutayam**[11] 5579 4-8-12 50...............................................(t) JMcAuley 3 41
(DANolan) *a rr* **200/1**
0-00 **8** 12 **Las Ramblas (IRE)**[11] 5579 7-8-9 45...............................(bt) PMakin 9 2
(DANolan) *a rr* **500/1**
000- **9** 5 **Second Wind**[373] 5058 9-8-9 40.........................................(tp) CHaddon 5 —
(DANolan) *in tch: rdn along and outpcd 1/2-way: sn bhd* **500/1**
1m 12.62s (-0.48) **Going Correction** +0.20s/f (Good)
**WFA** 3 from 4yo+ 2lb **9** Ran SP% **107.8**
Speed ratings: **111,108,108,107,105 98,83,67,61**CSF £5.29 TOTE £3.00: £1.10, £1.20, £2.60; EX 7.30.
**Owner** Mrs Sylvia Clegg **Bred** Times Of Wigan Ltd **Trained** Tadcaster, N Yorks
■ Stewards Enquiry : J McAuley caution: used whip while out of contention

**FOCUS**
A decent conditions event that was run at a stop-start pace. The form behind the front pair looks worth treating with a degree of caution.

**NOTEBOOK**
**Welsh Emperor(IRE)** relished this return to a testing surface and duly took advantage in grand style, making nearly all of the running to score. This was a decent performance in giving weight away to some very useful rivals, and he was aided by a canny ride from Holland. When he gets his conditions he is a very tough horse to pass, and he will now most likely head to France for a Group Three next.
**Cartography(IRE)**, weighted to reverse his recent Haydock form with the winner, ran a solid race on ground that was clearly against him. He is a tough sort but tends to find one too good, and he really does deserve to score this year, but needs faster ground in order to do so.
**Johnston's Diamond(IRE)** ran a blinder at the weights and will look very well treated on this form when reverting to handicaps off this sort of mark. However, he is not the easiest to win with and may be slightly flattered.
**Circuit Dancer(IRE)** recovered well from a sluggish start and turned in a very respectable display at the weights. A return to faster ground could see him strike again in handicaps off this mark.
**Philharmonic** took time to find his full stride and was never a serious factor. He has not really progressed, but may do better next year and is not one to write off just yet.
**Funfair Wane**, back to his best when taking the Ayr Gold Cup for the second time when making all latest, was unable to dominate this time and ran below par. This was disappointing, even allowing for the fact he has never strung together back-to-back victories, and he has a lot to prove now. That said, he owes connections nothing.

## 5833 HAMILTON PARK APPRENTICE SERIES FINAL H'CAP 6f 5y
**3:20** (3:21) (E3) (0-70,70) 4-Y-0+ **£4,270** (£1,314; £657; £328) **Stalls** Centre

Form RPR
0360 **1** **Yorker (USA)**[30] 5108 6-8-8 57...............................(b[1]) NataliaGemelova 7 67
(MsDeborahJEvans) *mde all: rdn clr and hung bdly rt 2f out: styd on* **33/1**
1531 **2** 1 ¾ **Locombe Hill (IRE)**[11] 5583 8-9-6 69.............................. DTudhope 12 74
(NWilson) *promient: rdn along over 2f out: drvn and edgd lft ins last: kpt on* **11/4**[1]
0000 **3** ½ **Viewforth**[11] 5579 6-7-13 56 oh4.....................................(b) JCurrie[(8)] 5 60
(JSGoldie) *dwlt: sn trcking ldrs: effrt 2f out: sn rdn and kpt on fnl f* **15/2**
0004 **4** ½ **Flying Edge (IRE)**[51] 4542 4-8-7 56 oh4.................................. JDO'Reilly 4 58
(EJAlston) *racd wd: a.p: rdn along over 2f out: one pce fnl f* **12/1**
0600 **5** ¾ **Sundried Tomato**[13] 5541 5-9-5 68................................... PMakin 6 68
(PWHiatt) *cl up: rdn along 1/2-way: drvn and one pce fnl 2f* **9/2**[2]
0365 **6** ½ **Mickledor (FR)**[9] 5639 4-8-7 56 oh4.................................(p) CHaddon 1 54
(MDods) *towards rr: hdwy over 2f out: kpt on ins last: nrst fin* **20/1**
0440 **7** ½ **Bundy**[11] 5583 8-8-12 61........................................... RoryMoore 9 58
(MDods) *midfield: rdn along over 2f out: kpt on u.p fnl f* **7/1**
2620 **8** hd **Fair Shake (IRE)**[11] 5583 4-9-6 69.......................................(p) AMullen 2 65
(DEddy) *s.i.s: a rr* **5/1**[3]
0200 **9** 1 ¾ **Pays D'Amour (IRE)**[38] 4904 7-8-7 56 oh4................ LeanneKershaw 8 47
(MissLAPerratt) *chsd ldrs: rdn along 1/2-way: sn wknd* **50/1**
0065 **10** 1 ¾ **Indian Music**[31] 5081 7-8-0 59 oh11 ow3................................. CEly[(10)] 10 45
(ABerry) *in tch: rdn along 1/2-way: sn wknd* **33/1**
0040 **11** 6 **Ulysees (IRE)**[9] 5631 5-9-7 70...............................................(v[1]) WHogg 3 38
(ISemple) *chsd ldrs: rdn alon g over 2f out and sn wknd* **12/1**
1m 14.42s (1.32) **Going Correction** +0.20s/f (Good) **11** Ran SP% **113.8**
Speed ratings: **99,96,96,95,94 93,93,92,90,88 80**CSF £115.94 CT £793.07 TOTE £42.60: £13.00, £1.60, £2.00; EX 563.50.
**Owner** Men Behaving Badly **Bred** Dinwiddie Farm **Trained** Lydiate, Merseyside

**FOCUS**
A modest handicap run at a solid pace and ordinary form, with the runner up setting the standard.

**NOTEBOOK**
**Yorker(USA)** pinged out of the gates and, despite hanging over to the rail under pressure two out, made all in good style. The blinkers clearly had the desired effect and he could look well-treated on his best form, should the headgear have the same effect in the future.
**Locombe Hill(IRE)** was not able to dominate as her prefers and that ultimately cost him back-to-back successes. He remains in good form and is not one to write off.
**Viewforth** stayed on well after a sluggish start, but never looked a serious threat. However, this was a good effort from 4lb out of the weights.
**Flying Edge(IRE)** was not disgraced in defeat from his low draw considering he was 4lb out of the handicap. He could be about to hit top form and is better on faster ground.
**Sundried Tomato** had his chance and has to go down as slightly disappointing. He is undoubtedly well-handicapped on his best form, but has a bit to prove now.
**Fair Shake(IRE)** lost his chance at the start and is capable of better.

## 5834 TOTESPORT BUTTONHOOK H'CAP 1m 5f 9y
**3:50** (3:50) (C1) (0-100,97) 3-Y-0+ **£12,011** (£4,556; £2,278; £1,035) **Stalls** High

Form RPR
1250 **1** **Zeitgeist (IRE)**[61] 4229 3-7-13 87.................................... NMackay[(3)] 2 94
(LMCumani) *hld up: hdwy to trck ldrs 1/2-way: effrt over 1f out: rdn ins last: styd on to ld post* **2/1**[2]
0400 **2** shd **Albanov (IRE)**[16] 5465 4-9-2 92.......................................... DHolland 5 99
(MJohnston) *cl up: rdn along over 3f out: drvn over 1f out: styd on gamely to ld nr fin: hdd post* **7/1**[3]
1400 **3** nk **Protective**[26] 5226 3-8-0 85................................................ PHanagan 7 92
(JGGiven) *hld up: gd hdwy 3f out: rdn to ld over 1f out: drvn: hdd and no ex nr fi nish* **20/1**
3162 **4** 4 **Gold Ring**[40] 4858 4-9-7 97................................................ SCarson 3 98
(GBBalding) *led: pushed along 3f out: rdn 2f out: hdd over 1f out and sn wknd* **15/8**[1]
0-02 **5** ½ **Pushkin (IRE)**[11] 5589 6-9-6 96.......................................... SChin 1 96
(MJohnston) *trckd ldrs: effrt 4f out: rdn along and ch over 2f out: sn drvn and wknd wl over 1f out* **7/1**[3]
3103 **6** 5 **Sahem (IRE)**[14] 5517 7-8-4 83........................................ TEaves[(3)] 6 76
(CJTeague) *a rr* **9/1**
/0-6 **7** 6 **Alam (USA)**[10] 5608 5-8-7 83 oh13.................................... KDarley 4 68
(PMonteith) *prom: pushed along whn n.m.r on inner and lost pl 1/2-way: bhd after* **66/1**
2m 55.55s (2.15) **Going Correction** +0.20s/f (Good)
**WFA** 3 from 4yo+ 9lb **7** Ran SP% **109.4**
Speed ratings: **101,100,100,98,97 94,91**CSF £14.80 TOTE £3.50: £2.10, £3.00; EX 18.50.
**Owner** L Marinopoulos **Bred** Sir Eric Parker **Trained** Newmarket, Suffolk

**FOCUS**
A decent handicap on paper, but the pace was modest and it produced an ordinary winning time for the grade. The first three came clear and the runner-up is the guide to the form.

**NOTEBOOK**
**Zeitgeist(IRE)** really knuckled down inside the final furlong and stuck his head out to lead on the line. This was more like the form that saw him develop into a progressive horse in the summer, and he got the trip well in the conditions, so could improve further for another step up in trip on better ground.

**Albanov(IRE)** improved greatly on his most recent efforts and was only just denied success. He has looked high in the weights since joining his current connections, but may be about to strike top form and should be well suited by a return to further.
**Protective** turned in a greatly-improved effort and was not beaten at all far. He did not see out this longer trip too well, but clearly relished the ground and will be well suited by reverting to slightly shorter. However, he is certain to rise in the weights for this.
**Gold Ring** had his chance from the front, but got outpaced when the race became serious and would have been better served by setting a stronger gallop. He is better than this, but has a bit to prove now.
**Pushkin(IRE)** failed to run up to his best on this softer ground and over this much shorter trip. He can improve with a much stiffer test and is not one to write off just yet.

## 5835 FAMOUS GROUSE H'CAP — 1m 65y
**4:20** (4:22) (D2) (0-85,89) 3-Y-O+ — **£7,055** (£2,170; £1,085; £542) **Stalls** High

Form — RPR

3103 **1** **Aperitif**[10] 5607 3-8-13 **77** ... PHanagan 7 — 96+
(WJHaggas) *dwlt and towards rr: gd hdwy 1/2-way: effrt to join ldrs over 2f out: rdn to ld ent last and sn clr: rdn out* **7/2**[1]

0006 **2** *5* **Strong Hand**[10] 5607 4-8-9 **72** ... PMulrennan(3) 8 — 81
(MWEasterby) *trckd ldrs gng wl: smooth hdwy 3f out: led over 2f out: rdn and jnd over 1f out: hdd ent last: kpt on same pce* **7/1**[3]

3043 **3** *4* **Cherished Number**[11] 5581 5-8-10 **70** ... (b[1]) RWinston 2 — 71
(ISemple) *dwlt and towards rr: hdwy over 3f out: rdn 2f out: styd on appr last* **12/1**

0521 **4** *1 3/4* **Just A Fluke (IRE)**[16] 5478 3-8-7 **71** ... KDarley 11 — 69
(MJohnston) *hld up towards rr: hdxway 3f out: rdn and kpt on fnl 2f: nvr nr ldrs* **11/1**

0630 **5** *3/4* **Qualitair Wings**[10] 5607 5-8-12 **72** ... DMcGaffin 10 — 68
(JHetherton) *s.i.s: sn in tch: rdn along to chse ldrs over 3f out: drvn 2f out and sn wknd* **14/1**

4401 **6** *hd* **Blonde Streak (USA)**[80] 3714 4-8-13 **78** ... PMakin(5) 9 — 74
(TDBarron) *cl up: rdn along over 3f out: drvn over 2f out and grad wknd* **6/1**[2]

0605 **7** *3 1/2* **Tony Tie**[9] 5627 8-9-3 **80** ... NMackay(3) 1 — 69
(JSGoldie) *hld up and bhd tl sme late hdwy* **25/1**

0100 **8** *1 1/4* **Nevada Desert (IRE)**[10] 5607 4-8-9 **72** ... (p) HayleyTurner(3) 5 — 58
(RMWhitaker) *chsd ldrs: rdn along over 3f out: sn wknd* **14/1**

0000 **9** *6* **Urowells (IRE)**[10] 5607 4-9-4 **78** ... (v) SSanders 12 — 52
(EALDunlop) *cl up: rdn along 4f out: wknd 3f out* **20/1**

3606 **10** *1/2* **Les Arcs (USA)**[11] 5590 4-9-0 **74** ... DHolland 13 — 47
(RCGuest) *led: rdn along and hdd 2f out: sn drvn and wknd 2f out* **33/1**

2211 **11** *2* **Zameyla (IRE)**[7] 5706 3-9-11 **89** 6ex ... NCallan 6 — 58
(MAJarvis) *chsd ldrs: hdwy over 4f out: led 3f out: sn rdn: hdd over 2f out and sn wknd* **7/1**[3]

3400 **12** *2 1/2* **Great Scott**[17] 5444 3-8-13 **77** ... SChin 4 — 41
(MJohnston) *midfield: rdn along over 4f out: sn wknd* **33/1**

00-0 **13** *nk* **Duke Of Modena**[9] 5627 7-9-10 **84** ... SCarson 14 — 48
(GBBalding) *hld up: a bhd* **16/1**

0014 **14** *dist* **Creskeld (IRE)**[30] 5127 5-8-10 **70** oh2 ... FLynch 3 — —
(BSmart) *chsd ldrs on outer: pushed along after 2f: rdn and lost pl qckly over 4f out: sn bhd and virtually p.u fnl 2f* **20/1**

1m 49.4s (0.10) **Going Correction** +0.20s/f (Good)
**WFA** 3 from 4yo+ 4lb — **14** Ran SP% **116.0**
Speed ratings: **107,102,98,96,95 95,91,90,84,84 82,79,79,—**CSF £23.39 CT £268.73 TOTE £3.90: £1.50, £3.60, £2.30; EX 47.20.
**Owner** Stretton Manor Stud **Bred** A B Barraclough **Trained** Newmarket, Suffolk

**FOCUS**
A fairly competitive handicap run at a sound pace. The form is worth treating with a degree of caution, but the winner looks capable of better still.

**NOTEBOOK**
**Aperitif ◆**, despite getting outpaced as the tempo increased before two out, ran out a most ready winner on this drop back to a mile. He had conditions in his favour this time, but looks to have struck form with a vengeance and could be one to follow while at this end of the handicap.
**Strong Hand**, beaten behind the winner last time on the same terms, could not go with Aperitif when challenged late on, but turned in another improved effort nonetheless and was well clear in second. She can be placed to advantage off this mark.
**Cherished Number** kept on in the straight and would have got closer but for a sluggish start. He has dropped 11lb since resuming this season and has proved disappointing on occasions, but could be placed to strike off this mark and has found some consistency of late.
**Just A Fluke(IRE)** again looked none too willing when push came to shove around two out, but stayed on under maximum pressure to the line. He is a fiendishly difficult ride.
**Qualitair Wings** lost her chance of following up last year's success in this event at the start.
**Blonde Streak(USA)** had his chance on this return from an 80-day break, but ran as though this would bring him on plenty.
**Zameyla(IRE)** paid late on for chasing the pace and faded out of it under her big weight. She could do better, but it looks like the Handicapper may just have caught up with her now.
**Creskeld(IRE)** *Official explanation: jockey said gelding felt wrong behind*

## 5836 SCOTTISH RACING MAIDEN STKS — 1m 1f 36y
**4:50** (4:51) (D3) 3-Y-O — **£5,609** (£1,726; £863; £431) **Stalls** High

Form — RPR

**1** **Reem One (IRE)** 3-8-9 ... NCallan 7 — 75
(MAJarvis) *trckd ldrs: smooth hdwy 1/2-way: chal over 2f out and sn rdn: drvn and styd on to ld ins last* **10/3**[1]

3326 **2** *1 1/2* **Bubbling Fun**[51] 4562 3-8-9 66 ... SSanders 4 — 72
(EALDunlop) *led: jnd and rdn along 3f out: drvn and 11/2 l up whn wandered: put hd in air and hdd ins last: one pce* **7/2**[2]

2200 **3** *3 1/2* **Antigiotto (IRE)**[17] 5446 3-8-11 76 ... (v[1]) NMackay(3) 3 — 70
(LMCumani) *trckd ldrs: effrt over 3f out: rdn over 2f out and sn one pce* **7/2**[2]

00-3 **4** *7* **Lake Diva**[21] 5345 3-8-9 61 ... DHolland 8 — 51
(JGGiven) *chsd ldr: rdn along over 3f out: sn drvn and wknd over 2f out* **12/1**

6250 **5** *1 1/2* **Aston Lad**[30] 5130 3-8-11 50 ... PMulrennan(3) 5 — 53
(MDHammond) *bhd tl sme late hdwy* **25/1**

-336 **6** *5* **Par Indiana (IRE)**[110] 2783 3-8-9 57 ... PHanagan 9 — 38
(ISemple) *a rr* **14/1**

46 **7** *3 1/2* **Bijou Dan**[20] 5371 3-9-0 ... RWinston 2 — 36
(ISemple) *a rr* **33/1**

**8** *2* **Trebello** 3-9-0 ... KDarley 6 — 32
(MJohnston) *a rr* **9/2**[3]

2m 2.86s (3.26) **Going Correction** +0.20s/f (Good) — **8** Ran SP% **106.9**
Speed ratings: **93,91,88,82,81 76,73,71**CSF £13.13 TOTE £4.30: £1.60, £1.50, £1.40; EX 12.30.
**Owner** Sheikh Ahmed Al Maktoum **Bred** Darley **Trained** Newmarket, Suffolk

**FOCUS**
A modest maiden that saw the field well strung out at the finish. It was a very moderate time for the class of contest and the form appears ordinary.

**NOTEBOOK**
**Reem One(IRE)**, whose dam is half-sister to the smart, but enigmatic Aramram, made a belated winning debut, knuckling down really well close home and having no problems with this ground. She should improve for this and will not be too harshly treated in handicaps.
**Bubbling Fun** looked the most likely winner two out, but again found less than expected when push came to shove and got worried out of it by the winner late on. She is reliable enough, but remains very hard to win with, despite the fact she may need it faster underfoot.
**Antigiotto(IRE)** failed to improve for the application of the visor and looked very one paced close home. She has had plenty of chances.
**Lake Diva** tired late on over this slightly longer trip on the ground and is capable of better. She could be interesting off her current mark in handicaps, when encountering quicker ground.
**Trebello**, half-brother to the high-class US mile winner Katdogawn, showed very little on this belated debut and needs more experience before realising his potential.

## 5837 RACING UK ON CHANNEL 432 CLASSIFIED STKS — 5f 4y
**5:20** (5:22) (D3) 3-Y-O — **£4,143** (£1,275; £637; £318) **Stalls** Centre

Form — RPR

1500 **1** **Jadan (IRE)**[39] 4874 3-9-2 74 ... DAllan 3 — 82
(EJAlston) *trckd ldrs gng wl: effrt to chal ent last: rdn and qcknd to ld nr fin* **16/1**

1100 **2** *nk* **Jilly Why (IRE)**[2] 5786 3-8-11 72 ... NCallan 1 — 75
(MsDeborahJEvans) *cl up: led 2f out: rdn o ver 1f out: drvn: hdd and nt qckn nr fin* **20/1**

0132 **3** *1* **Morgan Lewis (IRE)**[37] 4952 3-8-12 69 ... DHolland 7 — 73
(GBBalding) *in tch: rdn along 1/2-way: hdwy over 1f out: drvn and hung right ins last: kpt on* **9/4**[1]

040 **4** *1 3/4* **Icenaslice (IRE)**[40] 4862 3-8-4 70 ... DTudhope(5) 4 — 63
(JJQuinn) *in tch: rdn along over 2f out: drvn and kpt on appr last* **14/1**

1112 **5** *1* **Wunderbra (IRE)**[30] 5117 3-8-10 74 ... (t) HayleyTurner(3) 2 — 64
(MLWBell) *keen: trckd ldrs: effrt and ev ch 2f out: sn rdn and wknd appr last* **3/1**[2]

0052 **6** *hd* **Mr Wolf**[10] 5605 3-8-12 73 ... TEaves(3) 5 — 65
(DWBarker) *led: rdn along and hdd 2f out: drvn over 1f out and grad wknd* **9/2**[3]

0040 **7** *7* **Four Amigos (USA)**[12] 5563 3-9-3 75 ... SSanders 8 — 43
(JGGiven) *hld up: effrt 2f out: sn rdn and wknd* **5/1**

0010 **8** *6* **Finders Keepers**[26] 5220 3-9-0 72 ... KDarley 6 — 19
(EALDunlop) *dwlt: a rr* **20/1**

61.33 secs (0.07) **Going Correction** +0.20s/f (Good) — **8** Ran SP% **112.7**
Speed ratings: **107,106,104,102,100 100,89,79**CSF £270.96 TOTE £13.70: £3.40, £5.60, £1.40; EX 153.30 Place 6 £11.38, Place 5 £11.37.
**Owner** Derrick Mossop **Bred** Michael Rourke **Trained** Longton, Lancs

**FOCUS**
A tight classified sprint that produced a decent time for the grade of contest. However, the form looks ordinary.

**NOTEBOOK**
**Jadan(IRE)** improved on recent efforts and showed a neat turn of foot in the conditions to get on top near the line. If he can maintain this mood, he would be very hard to beat under a penalty and looks best at this trip.
**Jilly Why(IRE)** , well beaten from out of the handicap at Haydock two days previously, ran very much up to her best and was clear of the rest. She could go in again of this sort of mark, back on better ground.
**Morgan Lewis(IRE)** lost his chance by again hanging to his right under pressure late on and ran below par. He can be given another chance back over another furlong, and remains on a handy-looking mark, but is starting to show signs of temperament.
**Icenaslice(IRE)** turned in a respectable effort and is capable of scoring off this sort of mark, but shaped as though she would appreciate a stiffer test.
**Wunderbra(IRE)** paid late on for pulling too hard through the early stages and ran below her best. She has been in fantastic form of late, but the Handicapper looks to be catching up with her.
**Mr Wolf** had his chance, in his ideal condtions, but faded tamely under pressure form two out and was disappointing.
**Four Amigos(USA)** found very little when push came to shove from off the pace and continues to frustrate.
T/Plt: £30.80 to a £1 stake. Pool: £41,754.55. 988.80 winning tickets. T/Qpdt: £20.70 to a £1 stake. Pool: £2,481.70. 88.60 winning tickets. JR

# 5131 WINDSOR (R-H)
### Monday, September 27

**OFFICIAL GOING: Good to firm**
The stands' rail was moved out by six yards over the last six furlongs and it appeared to eradicate the usual bias towards high number draws.
Wind: light behind Weather: overcast

## 5838 EUROPEAN BREEDERS FUND MAIDEN STKS (DIV I) — 1m 67y
**2:00** (2:00) (D3) 2-Y-O — **£5,239** (£1,612; £806; £403) **Stalls** High

Form — RPR

03 **1** **Speightstown**[10] 5620 2-9-0 ... TQuinn 6 — 69
(PFICole) *lw: prom: rn wd bnd over 4f out and lost pl: effrt to press ldr 2f out: drvn to ld 1f out: all out* **5/4**[1]

**2** *nk* **Mr Aitch (IRE)** 2-9-0 ... DaneO'Neill 9 — 69
(JAOsborne) *gd sort: tall: str: bit bkwd: hld up: lft prom bnd over 4f out: sn led: shkn up and hanging lft 2f out: hdd 1f out: kpt on* **16/1**

0 **3** *2* **Gingiefly**[20] 5373 2-9-0 ... SWKelly 8 — 64
(JLDunlop) *in tch: lft in ld over 4f out: sn hdd: styd cl up: one pce over 1f out* **33/1**

000 **4** *1/2* **Our Kes (IRE)**[6] 5717 2-8-9 ... KFallon 1 — 58
(PHowling) *t.k.h: sn prom: rn wd bnd over 4f out: effrt to chal over 2f out: one pce sn after* **33/1**

00 **5** *shd* **Piran (IRE)**[9] 5646 2-8-11 ... JFMcDonald(3) 12 — 63
(BJMeehan) *t.k.h: trckd ldrs: rdn over 3f out: kpt on u.p fr over 1f out* **16/1**

**6** *2* **Gabanna (USA)** 2-9-0 ... EAhern 4 — 58
(SaeedBinSuroor) *w'like: in tch: pushed along and outpcd 3f out: one pce and n.d after* **9/2**[3]

**7** *2* **Dizzy Future** 2-9-0 ... WRyan 10 — 54
(WJarvis) *str: lw: s.i.s: hld up in rr: styng on steadily whn nt clr run over 1f out: nvr nrr: bttr for experience* **20/1**

0 **8** *1/2* **Overjoy Way**[21] 5348 2-8-9 ... JQuinn 11 — 58+
(PRChamings) *trckd ldr: virtually carried off the crse bnd over 4f out: rdn to rcvr over 2f out: fdd over 1f out* **25/1**

000 **9** *nk* **Mambazo**[12] 5570 2-9-0 ... WSupple 7 — 52
(SCWilliams) *s.i.s: hld up in rr: shuffled along 2f out: nvr on terms* **66/1**

10 11 **Solar Falcon** 2-8-9 ........ SWhitworth 5 23
(AGNewcombe) *lengthy: unf: s.v.s: a wl in rr: jst in tch 3f out: wknd* **33/1**

0 11 dist **Takemetoyourheart**[32] 5054 2-8-9 ........ FNorton 2 —
(IAWood) *prom: rn wd bnd over 4f out: sn wknd: t.o* **66/1**

3 12 25 **Croix Rouge (USA)**[21] 5347 2-9-0 ........ RHughes 3 —
(MrsAJPerrett) *led: virtually rn off the crse bnd over 4f out: nt rcvr: t.o* **3/1**[2]

1m 46.01s (0.41) **Going Correction** -0.075s/f (Good) **12** Ran SP% **119.8**
Speed ratings: **94,93,91,91,91 89,87,86,86,75** —,—CSF £23.93 TOTE £2.30: £1.10, £4.30, £6.90; EX 32.30.
**Owner** Sir Martyn Arbib **Bred** Martyn Arbib **Trained** Whatcombe, Oxon

**FOCUS**
A marginally slower time than the second division and ordinary for the grade, but the mayhem on the home bend would have affected the time and possibly the result, giving it a messy look, so the principals should not be judged too harshly.

**NOTEBOOK**
**Speightstown** was probably not suited by these sharp bends, and the fact he ran very wide turning for home may not have been totally caused by the antics of the leaders. Despite that, he knuckled down once on to the straighter parts of the course and battled on well to score. He can be considered a bit better than the official margin in view of how much ground he lost turning in, and will be suited by a return to a more galloping track.
**Mr Aitch(IRE)** is a 77,000gns half-brother to three winners including Soyuz, and out of a Listed winner. He suddenly went from racing in the pack to disputing the lead following the melee turning for home, but stayed on really well from that point, despite showing signs of greenness, and was just outbattled. He showed more than enough ability to suggest he will be winning races, though his pedigree suggests this will be as far as he wants.
**Gingiefly**, up a furlong from his debut, found himself in front when the leaders ran off the track turning for home, but stayed on well to make the frame and should eventually make his mark when stepped up to middle-distances.
**Our Kes(IRE)** had finished unplaced in her three previous outings, for which she started 100/1 every time. However, the booking of the champion jockey suggested she was capable of better and this was certainly an improved effort, especially as she was one of those caught up in the problems on the home bend.
**Piran(IRE)** was tracking the leaders when he had a real problem taking the sharp home bend, running wide and causing problems for a couple on his outside. He managed to stay in contention though and kept on at one pace to the line. This was an improved effort and he may have a small contest in him.
**Gabanna(USA)**, a $1,200,000 half-brother to Roosevelt and Five Dynasties, showed a little ability but will have to improve a good deal once faced with a longer trip in order to justify his price tag.
**Overjoy Way** ◆ was tracking the leader when all but carried out by him on the home bend, losing a good six lengths. She did very well to get herself back into contention before not surprisingly running out of gas, and can be considered a lot better than her final placing.
**Croix Rouge(USA)** took the field along until cocking his jaw and virtually running off the course turning for home. He obviously has his quirks, but a more galloping track should see him in a better light.

## 5839 DINE IN THE CASTLE RESTAURANT TODAY NURSERY 5f 10y
**2:30** (2:34) (D2) (0-85,84) 2-Y-O **£5,768** (£1,775; £887; £443) **Stalls** High

Form RPR

1400 1 **Forzeen**[19] 5392 2-9-3 **80** ........ EAhern 5 87
(JAOsborne) *lw: trckd ldrs: rdn and prog to ld 1f out: styd on wl* **14/1**

020 2 ¾ **Starduster**[21] 5334 2-8-2 **65** ........ RMullen 6 69
(BRMillman) *v s.i.s: gd spd on wd outside to rcvr by 1/2-way: hanging lft but chal 1f out: kpt on fnl f: jst hld* **25/1**

4100 3 nk **Louphole**[18] 5421 2-9-1 **78** ........ DSweeney 2 81
(PJMakin) *lw: w ldrs: led wl over 1f out to 1f out: one pce fnl f* **25/1**

0105 4 ½ **Withering Lady (IRE)**[31] 5068 2-8-12 **75** ........ RHavlin 8 76
(MrsPNDutfield) *settled midfield: eased towards outer and prog over 1f out: styd on same pce* **25/1**

301 5 hd **Folga**[16] 5475 2-8-7 **70** ........ JMackay 7 71
(JGGiven) *led: hanging thrght: hdd wl over 1f out: one pce after* **33/1**

S310 6 hd **Miss Cassia**[9] 5648 2-8-10 **73** ........ PDobbs 13 74+
(RHannon) *pushed along on inner in midfield: u.p 2f out: styng on but no ch whn rn out of room nr fin* **16/1**

0424 7 ½ **Majestical (IRE)**[14] 5509 2-7-12 **61** oh1 ........ LisaJones 11 59
(WRMuir) *lw: pressed ldrs: rdn over 2f out: nt clr run briefly jst over 1f out : one pce after* **20/1**

3460 8 ½ **Empire's Ghodha**[44] 4752 2-9-4 **84** ........ (b) JFMcDonald(3) 18 81+
(BJMeehan) *n.m.r on inner over 3f out and dropped to rr: effrt whn nt clr run over 1f out: styd on ins fnl f* **14/1**

412 9 ½ **Clove (USA)**[14] 5520 2-9-1 **78** ........ RHughes 19 80+
(BWHills) *s.i.s: t.k.h: wl in rr: taken towards outer and prog 2f out: nt rch ldrs fnl f* **7/2**[1]

1120 10 ¾ **Monashee Rose (IRE)**[2] 5797 2-8-7 **77** ........ DerekNolan(7) 17 72+
(JSMoore) *t.k.h: hld up towards rr: shkn up 2f out: styd on ins fnl f: n.d* **12/1**

441 11 1 ¼ **Danzili Bay**[25] 5241 2-8-12 **80** ........ NChalmers(5) 14 68
(RMBeckett) *towards rr: rdn 2f out: one pce and no imp on ldrs* **5/1**[3]

3540 12 ½ **Ruby's Dream**[61] 4243 2-8-6 **69** ........ SWKelly 4 55
(JMBradley) *pressed ldrs to 2f out: wknd* **50/1**

4446 13 1 ¾ **Kempsey**[15] 5490 2-8-0 **63** ........ (p) SWhitworth 10 43
(JJBridger) *racd midfield: hmpd 1/2-way: struggling fnl 2f* **50/1**

5500 14 2 ½ **King After**[18] 5421 2-8-4 **67** ........ WSupple 9 38
(JRBest) *plld hrd early: hld up in rr: rdn and struggling 1/2-way* **20/1**

0600 15 hd **High Chart**[9] 5648 2-8-4 **67** ........ (t) AMcCarthy 12 37
(GGMargarson) *b.hind: nvr on terms w ldrs: u.p 2f out: wknd fnl f* **20/1**

1346 16 2 **Rosiella**[10] 5617 2-8-9 **72** ........ FNorton 20 35
(MBlanshard) *a towards rr: n.m.r wl over 1f out: no ch after* **8/1**

2000 17 1 **Averting**[10] 5617 2-7-13 **62** oh5 ow1 ........ (b) JQuinn 15 22
(RFJohnsonHoughton) *a wl in rr* **40/1**

2304 18 2 **Beautiful Mover (USA)**[32] 5054 2-8-10 **73** ........ KFallon 16 61+
(JWHills) *lost pl on inner after 1f: hmpd 1/2-way: sn no ch* **4/1**[2]

59.63 secs (-1.57) **Going Correction** -0.20s/f (Firm) **18** Ran SP% **132.0**
Speed ratings: **104,102,102,101,101 100,100,99,98,97 95,94,91,87,87 84,82,79**CSF £339.32 CT £4342.51 TOTE £22.90: £4.20, £9.70, £5.70, £7.30; EX 2597.20.
**Owner** Cavendish Racing **Bred** James Clark **Trained** Upper Lambourn, Berks

**FOCUS**
A very competitive nursery and unusually those drawn low held the advantage. The winning time was decent for a race of its type and the form looks solid.

**NOTEBOOK**
**Forzeen**, totally outclassed in the St Leger Yearling Sales race at Doncaster last time, was back in a more realistic grade and was always in a good position to strike. He saw his race out well, and the minimum trip and a sound surface appear to bring out the best in him.
**Starduster** ◆, a maiden making her nursery debut, was forced to make her effort wide of the field. Under normal circumstances that would have been a negative, but low-number stalls had the call in this contest and that helped her get as close as she did. The ground must have been less quick than at Bath and, given similar conditions, she should be able to find a similar contest.
**Louphole** ◆ is not short of early pace and showed that from the gates, though he was not able to dominate on his own, so did very well to hang in there to the bitter end. He should find other opportunities, especially when able to establish an uncontested lead.
**Withering Lady(IRE)** was another to run a fine race down the centre of the track and is retaining her form well.
**Folga**, making her nursery debut, showed blinding early pace but, despite starting from a single-figure draw, continually edged to her right and ended up on the nearside rail. Under the circumstances this was a pleasing effort.
**Miss Cassia** ◆ did best of those drawn high and may have finished fourth had she not run out of room in the last few strides. Her only win came on soft ground, so she may well find a similar contest before the season is out.
**Clove(USA)** was drawn very high, but missed the break and had to manoeuvre out wide in order to see daylight. She had to do a lot of running to get there and was therefore never able to offer a threat. *Official explanation: jockey said filly missed break*
**Averting** *Official explanation: jockey said colt missed break*
**Beautiful Mover(USA)**, well backed, broke well enough but was already losing places when getting bumped about at halfway. She has not built on her promising debut. *Official explanation: jockey said filly lost her action in the final furlong*

## 5840 EUROPEAN BREEDERS FUND MAIDEN STKS (DIV II) 1m 67y
**3:00** (3:01) (D2) 2-Y-O **£5,226** (£1,608; £804; £402) **Stalls** High

Form RPR

052 1 **Eva Soneva So Fast (IRE)**[16] 5467 2-9-0 80 ........ JQuinn 6 78
(JLDunlop) *lw: trckd ldr: chal and upsides fr 4f out: narrow ld u.p over 1f out: styd on wl* **5/4**[1]

0 2 ½ **Phi (USA)**[12] 5570 2-9-0 ........ KFallon 1 77
(SirMichaelStoute) *led: rdn over 2f out: narrowly hdd over 1f out: kpt on wl but hld ins fnl f* **13/8**[2]

3 5 **Kinrande (IRE)** 2-9-0 ........ DSweeney 11 68+
(PJMakin) *lw: hld up in rr: pushed along over 2f out: r.o fnl f to take 3rd nr fin* **25/1**

0 4 nk **Hoh My Darling**[31] 5088 2-8-9 ........ RMullen 7 60
(MLWBell) *in tch: outpcd and pushed along over 3f out: effrt to dispute 3rd pl 2f out: kpt on* **12/1**

54 5 ¾ **Zeena**[13] 5535 2-8-4 ........ NDeSouza(5) 8 59
(MPTregoning) *t.k.h: trckd ldng pair: outpcd over 3f out: one pce fnl 2f* **10/1**[3]

6 7 **War Pennant** 2-9-0 ........ SHitchcott 2 48
(MRChannon) *rangy: bit bkwd: chsd ldrs: outpcd over 3f out: wknd 2f out* **25/1**

7 2 **Hawridge Sensation** 2-9-0 ........ WSupple 10 44
(LGCottrell) *str: bkwd: t.k.h: trckd ldng pair: outpcd over 3f out: wknd over 2f out* **33/1**

000 8 2 ½ **Savoy Chapel**[9] 5653 2-9-0 ........ SWKelly 9 38
(JAOsborne) *in tch: outpcd over 3f out: sn btn* **100/1**

9 7 **Stunning Spark** 2-8-6 ........ RMiles(3) 4 18
(TDMccarthy) *w'like: bkwd: dwlt: detached in last: outpcd 1/2-way: bhd after* **100/1**

10 4 **Dunlows Minstrel** 2-9-0 ........ OUrbina 3 14
(MissDMountain) *w'like: bkwd: dwlt: a in rr: wknd 3f out* **33/1**

1m 45.87s (0.27) **Going Correction** -0.075s/f (Good) **10** Ran SP% **114.9**
Speed ratings: **95,94,89,89,88 81,79,76,69,65**CSF £3.13 TOTE £2.10: £1.10, £1.40, £4.30; EX 4.60.
**Owner** Eurostrait Ltd **Bred** John O'Connor **Trained** Arundel, W Sussex

**FOCUS**
A two-horse race according to the market, the pair having the race to themselves from a long way out and nothing else got into it, making the form appear sound enough. A marginally faster time than the first division, but still only ordinary for the grade.

**NOTEBOOK**
**Eva Soneva So Fast(IRE)** maintained his progressive profile and showed admirable courage at the end of the protracted battle with the runner-up. He should develop into a nice middle-distance handicapper next year.
**Phi(USA)** was able to set his own pace but, although he kept trying in the protracted battle with the favourite up the home straight, he had to admit defeat in the last half-furlong. He should be able to find a similar maiden, but does not look amongst the best juveniles from the yard.
**Kinrande(IRE)** ◆, a half-brother to three winners including a Listed winner in France, stayed on under a hands-and-heels ride to snatch third at a respectable distance. He did not have a hard race and should repay the kindness in time.
**Hoh My Darling** appeared to find even this trip inadequate and is likely to improve over further once handicapped.
**Zeena**, stepping up in trip again, looks a stayer and now qualifies for a handicap mark.
**Hawridge Sensation** *Official explanation: jockey said gelding hung right and was very green*

## 5841 NATIONAL HUNT RACING RETURNS TO WINDSOR H'CAP 1m 67y
**3:30** (3:30) (E3) (0-70,70) 3-Y-O+ **£3,636** (£1,118; £559; £279) **Stalls** High

Form RPR

0000 1 **Omaha City (IRE)**[10] 5614 10-9-3 **69** ........ FNorton 12 77
(BGubby) *swtg: trckd ldrs: effrt over 1f out: r.o to ld wl ins fnl f* **11/1**

0002 2 nk **Just Fly**[7] 5698 4-9-4 **70** ........ KFallon 13 78
(SKirk) *settled wl in rr: stdy prog fr over 2f out: threaded way through to ld ins fnl f: sn hdd and nt qckn* **5/4**[1]

-450 3 ¾ **Petrosa (IRE)**[10] 5615 4-9-3 **69** ........ TQuinn 10 75
(DRCElsworth) *lw: hld up last pair: rdn and prog on outer over 2f out: styd on wl fnl f: unable to chal* **8/1**[2]

0010 4 ¾ **Hilltop Rhapsody**[23] 5293 3-8-13 **69** ........ NPollard 14 73
(DJDaly) *prom: rdn to chal 2f out: upsides ent fnl f: one pce* **14/1**

1000 5 hd **Lockstock (IRE)**[17] 5444 6-9-4 **70** ........ (p) DaneO'Neill 1 74
(MSSaunders) *pushed up to chse ldr: rdn to chal 2f out: upsides ent fnl f: one pce* **16/1**

3005 6 ½ **Kabeer**[49] 4602 6-8-11 **63** ........ DRMcCabe 8 66
(PSMcentee) *led: rdn over 2f out: hdd and fdd jst ins fnl f* **33/1**

0400 7 ½ **Duelling Banjos**[97] 3177 5-8-11 **63** ........ SHitchcott 6 65
(JAkehurst) *bit bkwd: settled in rr: rdn 3f out: effrt on wd outside 2f out: no imp ldrs fnl f* **16/1**

0-02 8 hd **Charlie Bear**[130] 2251 3-8-12 **68** ........ EAhern 7 69
(EALDunlop) *t.k.h: trckd ldrs: rdn over 2f out: cl up jst over 1f out: fdd fnl f* **10/1**[3]

0160 9 ½ **Mister Clinton (IRE)**[18] 5425 7-8-9 **61** ........ DSweeney 4 61
(DKIvory) *b: racd midfield: rdn and effrt over 2f out: no imp ldrs over 1f out* **20/1**

6000 10 nk **Hail The Chief**[18] 5425 7-9-1 **67** ........ SWhitworth 3 66
(JAkehurst) *racd midfield: rdn over 2f out: nt qckn and no imp after* **25/1**

5055 11 ½ **Mamore Gap (IRE)**[28] 5176 6-8-12 **64** ........ RHughes 5 62
(RHannon) *hld up last pair: sme prog over 2f out: no hdwy over 1f out* **16/1**

2000 12 1 ½ **Zariano**[25] 5252 4-8-10 **65** ........ LPKeniry(3) 9 60
(RMStronge) *racd midfield: rdn 3f out: lost pl and btn wl over 1f out* **33/1**

5600 **13** 2½ **Tiber Tiger (IRE)**[12] 5574 4-9-1 **70**........................(p) J-PGuillambert(3) 11 59
(NPLittmoden) *hld up midfield: lost pl and rdn wl over 2f out: n.d after* **10/1**[3]

0660 **14** *nk* **Invader**[19] 5403 8-9-3 **69**........................(bt) JQuinn 2 57
(CEBrittain) *a in rr: rdn and no prog 3f out* **16/1**

1m 43.51s (-2.09) **Going Correction** -0.075s/f (Good)
**WFA** 3 from 4yo+ 4lb **14** Ran SP% **126.8**
Speed ratings: **107,106,105,105,105 104,104,103,103,103 102,101,98,98**CSF £25.26 CT £129.98 TOTE £17.10: £4.30, £1.30, £2.00; EX 34.90.
**Owner** Brian Gubby Ltd **Bred** Brownstown Stud Farm **Trained** Bagshot, Surrey

**FOCUS**
An ordinary handicap and a one-horse market, despite looking competitive on paper, with the betting showing 8/1 bar one. A decent pace and a fair winning time for the grade and the form looks sound.

**NOTEBOOK**
**Omaha City(IRE)** is a law unto himself and more than twice the age of the other placed horses, whilst five of his seven previous wins have come at Goodwood. However, he is capable of decent form on his day and was brought with a well-timed run to spoil the party for favourite backers.
**Just Fly** started an amazingly short price for a race like this, especially as he was on a losing run of 15. Given plenty to do before gradually weaving his way through the field, to be fair his run was delivered at just the right time and he was just unlucky that he met Omaha City on a going day. He is undoubtedly well handicapped at present, but is proving expensive to follow.
**Petrosa(IRE)** finished in good style down the centre of the track and put up a good performance over a trip probably short of her best, but she does not look straightforward and is still a maiden after ten attempts.
**Hilltop Rhapsody** looked happier back at a mile and ran well under a positive ride. She did not run at two and remains comparatively lightly raced, so may still be capable of some improvement over this trip.
**Lockstock(IRE)** was always up with the pace and was not beaten far, but still looks a bit too high in the handicap.
**Kabeer** set a decent pace, but did not quite get home. Despite having been placed in a bumper, he may be better over a furlong shorter.

## 5842 TANGERINE H'CAP — 1m 3f 135y
**4:00** (4:02) (D2) (0-85,85) 3-Y-O **£7,100** (£2,184; £1,092; £546) **Stalls** Low

Form RPR

0210 **1** **Ringsider (IRE)**[30] 5106 3-9-5 **83**........................ RHughes 9 93+
(GAButler) *s.i.s: hld up midfield: prog 2f out: plld out over 1f out: hrd rdn to ld ins fnl f: r.o wl* **11/2**[3]

1212 **2** ¾ **Quarrymount**[28] 5191 3-8-7 **71** oh1........................ JMackay 10 79
(SirMarkPrescott) *lw: led: rdn over 2f out: hdd and outpcd ins fnl f* **10/3**[1]

1504 **3** 1¾ **Vamp**[12] 5572 3-8-11 **75**........................ RMullen 11 80
(RMBeckett) *hld up midfield: rdn and effrt over 2f out: styd on fr over 1f out : nvr able to chal* **6/1**

2214 **4** 1 **Sunny Lady (FR)**[85] 3557 3-8-13 **77**........................ EAhern 1 81
(EALDunlop) *hld up midfield: effrt over 2f out: chsd ldrs over 1f out: one pce after* **14/1**

1660 **5** *hd* **Graham Island**[100] 3078 3-9-5 **83**........................ FNorton 6 86
(GWragg) *hld up last pair: sme prog over 2f out: swtchd rt ent fnl f: kpt on: nvr rchd ldrs* **20/1**

1130 **6** *shd* **Trew Class**[12] 5572 3-8-13 **77**........................ TQuinn 4 80
(MHTompkins) *mostly chsd ldr to jst over 1f out: fdd fnl f* **16/1**

5046 **7** 5 **Vantage (IRE)**[12] 5572 3-8-8 **75**........................(b) J-PGuillambert(3) 12 70
(NPLittmoden) *t.k.h: hld up midfield: rdn 3f out: looked reluctant and btn 2f out* **20/1**

-515 **8** ¾ **Daring Aim**[58] 4321 3-9-7 **85**........................ KFallon 5 79
(SirMichaelStoute) *swtg: reluctant to enter stalls: rel to r and set off last: prog and prom after 4f: rdn and fnd nil 3f out: btn after* **4/1**[2]

0106 **9** ¾ **Rutters Rebel (IRE)**[14] 5517 3-8-7 **71**........................ KimTinkler 7 64
(NTinkler) *settled rr: rdn over 3f out: no prog* **16/1**

1420 **10** ½ **Mr Tambourine Man (IRE)**[5] 5732 3-9-2 **85**........................ NDeSouza(5) 3 77
(PFICole) *lw: restless stalls: plld hrd in midfield: prog to press ldrs 2f out: wknd rapidly over 1f out* **7/1**

1005 **11** 3 **Jakarmi**[5] 5732 3-8-6 **73**........................ RMiles(3) 8 60
(BPalling) *hld up in detached last: reminder over 1f out: a bhd* **33/1**

3221 **12** 10 **Dundry**[20] 5382 3-9-7 **85**........................(p) DaneO'Neill 2 56
(GLMoore) *prom: lost pl on outer and rdn 3f out: wknd rapidly 2f out* **16/1**

2m 28.36s (-1.74) **Going Correction** -0.075s/f (Good) **12** Ran SP% **122.0**
Speed ratings: **102,101,100,99,99 99,96,95,95,94 92,86**CSF £24.23 CT £117.95 TOTE £7.90: £3.30, £1.40, £1.90; EX 46.60 Trifecta £461.20 Pool of £5,586.57 - 8.60 winning units.
**Owner** S A O'Donoghue & M V Deegan **Bred** Airlie Stud **Trained** Blewbury, Oxon

**FOCUS**
A fair handicap run at an even pace and the form appears sound for the grade.

**NOTEBOOK**
**Ringsider(IRE)**, trying his longest trip to date and back on his favoured surface, was ridden to get it and produced a decent turn of foot to nail the favourite. He still appears to be improving.
**Quarrymount** was able to get his own way out in front and managed to keep most of his rivals at bay, but the progressive winner proved too strong. He is steadily climbing the handicap, but his prospects of winning again depend on whether he can dominate his rivals at least as much as whether conditions are suitable.
**Vamp**, trying this trip for the first time, was pulled wide for her effort and stayed on without being able to land a blow. She did not appear to fail through lack of stamina, but one thing she must have is fast ground.
**Sunny Lady(FR)** had every chance, but had nothing more to offer inside the last furlong. She is consistent and a good guide to the value of the form.
**Graham Island ◆**, off since June, stayed on in the latter stages without having a hard race. He has faced some stiff tasks this season and became disappointing, but if he can build on this he may be able to add to his solitary maiden victory.
**Trew Class** was given a positive ride, but did not appear to see out this longer trip. *Official explanation: jockey said filly did not stay*
**Daring Aim**, dropping down from Pattern company, looks a horrible ride. Less than keen to enter the stalls, she was also reluctant to leave them and showed her displeasure by swishing her tail early. She did manage to get into a prominent position, but found little when put under pressure and is definitely one to avoid at all costs.
**Jakarmi** *Official explanation: jockey said gelding hung right throughout*

## 5843 WINDSOR-RACECOURSE.CO.UK (S) STKS — 1m 2f 7y
**4:30** (4:33) (E3) 3-Y-O **£3,532** (£1,087; £543; £271) **Stalls** Low

Form RPR

4600 **1** **Soviet Sceptre (IRE)**[12] 5571 3-8-11 **60**........................ RMiles(3) 13 62
(MissDMountain) *hld up off the pce: prog 4f out: led 2f out: clr over 1f out: pushed out* **12/1**

U0-6 **2** 3 **Tizi Ouzou (IRE)**[17] 5445 3-8-9........................ TQuinn 1 52
(JLDunlop) *lw: hld up wl off the pce: prog on outer 3f out: chsd wnr over 1f out: no imp* **8/1**

060 **3** *nk* **Bonus Points (IRE)**[9] 5643 3-8-11 **57**........................ JFMcDonald(3) 5 56
(BJMeehan) *trckd ldrs: rdn and outpcd 3f out: prog again 2f out: styd on same pce* **14/1**

000 **4** 7 **Bertocelli**[5] 5733 3-9-0 **55**........................ JMackay 3 43
(GGMargarson) *lw: mde most and set str pce: rn wd bnd 5f out and jnd: hdd & wknd 2f out* **9/2**[1]

3300 **5** 1 **La Calera (GER)**[7] 5702 3-9-1 **45**........................(p) OUrbina 11 42
(GCHChung) *prom: rdn 3f out: wknd over 1f out* **14/1**

0500 **6** *nk* **Vittorioso (IRE)**[7] 5702 3-8-11 **40**........................ BReilly(3) 7 40
(MissGayKelleway) *b: b.hind: trckd ldrs: stdy prog gng wl 4f out: wknd 2f out* **20/1**

3061 **7** *nk* **Defana**[14] 5524 3-9-6 **53**........................(p) SWKelly 2 46
(MDods) *prom: prog to join ldr over 4f out: disp after tl wknd 2f out* **9/2**[1]

665 **8** ¾ **Montgomery**[15] 5495 3-9-0 **48**........................ SWhitworth 10 38
(AGNewcombe) *dwlt: wl bhd: shkn up 4f out: no prog tl r.o fr over 1f out* **25/1**

6645 **9** *hd* **Port Sodrick**[12] 5571 3-9-0 **60**........................ KFallon 15 38
(MDIUsher) *s.i.s: wl in rr and nt gng wl: drvn 4f out: sme prog 3f out: no imp 2f out: wknd* **5/1**[2]

0054 **10** 2 **Romeo's Day**[12] 5571 3-9-0 **40**........................(v) SHitchcott 4 34
(MRChannon) *prom: rdn over 4f out: wknd u.p over 2f out* **13/2**[3]

5000 **11** *nk* **Regulated (IRE)**[15] 5493 3-9-6 **54**........................ MTebbutt 12 39
(DBFeek) *dwlt: wl in rr: sme prog on outer over 2f out: no imp on ldrs* **33/1**

2050 **12** ¾ **Another Con (IRE)**[37] 4940 3-9-1 **48**........................(v[1]) EAhern 8 33
(PHowling) *chsd ldr to over 5f out: wknd over 3f out* **10/1**

0000 **13** 5 **Harry Came Home**[24] 5259 3-8-11 **30**........................(b) LPKeniry(3) 9 23
(JCFox) *a wl in rr: drvn and struggling 4f out* **66/1**

0 **14** 9 **Charlie Masters**[20] 5378 3-9-0........................ AMcCarthy 6 5
(PHowling) *off the pce in midfield: rn wd bnd 5f out: sn wknd* **66/1**

00 **15** *dist* **Jimmy Hay**[9] 5643 3-8-9........................ DFox(5) 14 —
(JCFox) *b.hind: dwlt: a bhd: rn wd bnd 5f out: sn wl t.o* **66/1**

2m 6.96s (-1.34) **Going Correction** -0.075s/f (Good) **15** Ran SP% **123.6**
Speed ratings: **102,99,99,93,92 92,92,91,91,90 89,89,85,78,—**CSF £101.54 TOTE £16.20: £5.70, £3.20, £4.10; EX 242.00.The winner was bought in for 6,400gns. Tizi Ouzou (IRE) was bought by Martin Pipe for £6,000.
**Owner** David Fremel **Bred** Barnane Stud **Trained** Newmarket, Suffolk

**FOCUS**
A fair contest for a seller and a solid pace, but a huge margin after the third horse suggests there is little optimism for the majority of the field.

**NOTEBOOK**
**Soviet Sceptre(IRE)**, well beaten in a similar contest last time on his first try at the trip, settled better this time and was brought through to hit the front passing the quarter-mile pole. Despite starting his effort on the outside, he hung right over to the stands' rail, but was always clear and scored with authority. A strong pace looks the key to him. *Official explanation: trainer said, regarding the improved form shown, colt had run on from the front today and had appreciated the strong gallop*
**Tizi Ouzou(IRE)**, taking a big drop in class, showed her first sign of ability on her fourth outing, though she could never get to the winner. She now joins Martin Pipe and will presumably be seen over hurdles next.
**Bonus Points(IRE)**, dropped in grade and having his first run on turf, settled better with the blinkers left off and plugged on to finish third. He pulled right away from the rest and this effort suggests he has the ability to win a similar event, but he did show a high head carriage which sounds a note of caution.
**Bertocelli**, dropped in grade, set the pace but is still to prove he stays this trip and did not get home.
**La Calera(GER)**, trying this trip for the first time, did not see it out.
**Defana**, under similar conditions to his Redcar victory, had every chance but dropped away disappointingly over the last couple of furlongs.
**Jimmy Hay** *Official explanation: jockey said gelding hung very badly throughout*

## 5844 WINDSOR FIREWORKS EXTRAVAGANZA SAT 6TH NOVEMBER MAIDEN STKS (DIV I) — 6f
**5:00** (5:00) (D3) 3-Y-O+ **£4,160** (£1,280; £640; £320) **Stalls** High

Form RPR

6000 **1** **Pine Bay**[9] 5652 3-8-7 **63**........................ FNorton 1 64
(BGubby) *lw: trckd ldrs: effrt 2f out: rdn to ld jst ins fnl f: hld on* **9/1**

**2** ½ **Soul Dance** 3-8-7........................(t) DSweeney 7 63
(PJMakin) *leggy: unf: settled in rr: stdy prog 2f out: rdn to chal ins fnl f and hanging lft: hld nr fin* **15/2**

2000 **3** 1¾ **Ballinger Express**[10] 5618 4-8-9 **57**........................(b) WRyan 6 57+
(AMBalding) *stl wearing hood whn stalls opened and lost 8l: rcvrd and in tch 1/2-way: effrt on outer 2f out: shkn up and nt qckn over 1* **11/4**[1]

0050 **4** *nk* **Called Up**[68] 4024 3-8-12 **68**........................ DaneO'Neill 2 61
(HCandy) *w ldr: led 2f out to jst ins fnl f: one pce* **5/1**[3]

-602 **5** 2 **Penel (IRE)**[9] 5656 3-8-12 **62**........................ PFitzsimons 5 55
(BRMillman) *lw: mde most to 2f out: fdd u.p* **10/3**[2]

00- **6** *hd* **Clearing Sky (IRE)**[310] 6045 3-8-7........................ EAhern 11 50
(JRBoyle) *bkwd: chsd ldrs: rdn over 2f out: no imp over 1f out* **25/1**

0000 **7** 1 **Diaphanous**[18] 5408 6-8-2 **30**........................ LiamJones(7) 8 47?
(EAWheeler) *plld hrd: hld up bhd ldrs: wknd jst over 1f out* **66/1**

**8** 1½ **Duxford** 3-8-12........................ JQuinn 10 47
(DKIvory) *str: bkwd: dwlt: rn green in last pair: nvr a factor* **16/1**

04 **9** 1 **Superfling**[21] 5338 3-8-12........................ PDobbs 3 44
(RHannon) *w ldr to 2f out: hrd rdn and wknd* **6/1**

6 **10** 6 **Terenure Girl**[13] 5551 3-8-7........................ LisaJones 9 21
(PSFelgate) *t.k.h: hld up: wknd over 2f out* **33/1**

1m 12.68s (-1.19) **Going Correction** -0.20s/f (Firm)
**WFA** 3 from 4yo+ 2lb **10** Ran SP% **116.6**
Speed ratings: **99,98,96,95,92 92,91,89,88,80**CSF £73.48 TOTE £14.70: £3.80, £2.50, £1.60; EX 164.70.
**Owner** Brian Gubby Ltd **Bred** J W Ford **Trained** Bagshot, Surrey
■ A first-ever double for trainer Brian Gubby after a career of nearly 30 years.

**FOCUS**
A poor race in the main, especially with the favourite losing it at the start, though the front two may be capable of more. The winning time was also moderate for the class, 0.52 seconds slower than the second division and the form is very limited.

**NOTEBOOK**
**Pine Bay**, unplaced in her four previous starts, has not enjoyed the best of health and has been tried over as far as ten furlongs. This shorter trip seemed to suit her much better and she held on well, but even though this was a poor contest she has the advantage of being comparatively unexposed.
**Soul Dance**, making a belated debut, had little to recommend her on pedigree but obviously has some ability and ran on well despite showing signs of greenness inside the last furlong. Her trainer is notoriously patient with his horses and should find an opportunity for her.

**Ballinger Express** started favourite despite being out of form in recent outings, but that all became academic at the start as she still had the blindfold on when the gates opened and lost a huge amount of ground. She did manage to get into the race down the outside in the middle of the contest, but had nothing more to offer after that. This incident means that she and her half-brother Ballinger Ridge have both been embroiled in controversy this year. *Official explanation: jockey said filly's blindfold became stuck as gates opened was slowly away*
**Called Up** raced up with the pace for much of the way, but was well held in the closing stages and does not seem to be progressing.
**Penel(IRE)**, dropping back to six, was given a positive ride but did not get home. He has been tried over as far as a mile and looks tripless.

## 5845 WINDSOR FIREWORKS EXTRAVAGANZA SAT 6TH NOVEMBER MAIDEN STKS (DIV II) 6f
**5:30** (5:30) (D3) 3-Y-0+ **£4,160** (£1,280; £640; £320) **Stalls** High

Form RPR
3432 **1** **Indiana Blues**[9] 5637 3-8-2 63 NChalmers(5) 6 68
(AMBalding) *lw: cl up: rdn to ld over 1f out: kpt on fnl f* **4/1**[2]
23 **2** 3/4 **Millinsky (USA)**[25] 5253 3-8-7 56 KFallon 4 66
(RGuest) *trckd ldrs: prog to chal 2f out: pressed wnr fnl f : nt qckn* **11/8**[1]
4 **3** 3/4 **Future Deal**[45] 4718 3-8-7 TQuinn 10 64
(CAHorgan) *lw: hld up in tch: prog 2f out: hanging lft fr over 1f out: kpt on but nvr able to chal* **4/1**[2]
0030 **4** 2 1/2 **Charlottebutterfly**[12] 5575 4-8-6 52 JFMcDonald(3) 11 56
(TTClement) *chsd ldrs: bmpd 2f out: rdn and one pce after* **16/1**
5020 **5** 1 3/4 **Imtalkinggibberish**[40] 4845 3-8-12 79 WRyan 1 56
(JRJenkins) *lw: prom: led over 3f out to over 1f out: wknd* **7/1**[3]
0000 **6** nk **Appolonious**[20] 5378 3-8-12 55 (t) NPollard 9 55
(DRCElsworth) *outpcd and bhd: nt gng wl 1/2-way: styd on fr over 1f out: nvr nrr* **66/1**
555 **7** 1 1/4 **All Quiet**[20] 5378 3-8-7 67 RHughes 5 46
(RHannon) *chsd ldrs tl wknd rapidly over 1f out* **8/1**
0030 **8** 3/4 **Miss Monza**[21] 5338 3-8-7 62 WSupple 7 44
(BRMillman) *a towards rr: outpcd and struggling over 2f out* **50/1**
0602 **9** nk **Westborough (IRE)**[13] 5547 3-8-12 52 (t) KimTinkler 8 48
(NTinkler) *nvr on terms: struggling fr 1/2-way* **33/1**
06-P **10** 11 **Beresford Boy**[21] 5338 3-8-12 DaneO'Neill 2 15
(DKIvory) *dwlt: outpcd and a wl bhd* **66/1**
00 **11** 1 3/4 **Tanne Blixen**[28] 5204 3-8-5 ow1 LPKeniry(3) 3 6
(PSFelgate) *led to over 3f out: swtchd lft 2f out: wknd rapidly* **66/1**

1m 12.16s (-1.71) **Going Correction** -0.20s/f (Firm)
**WFA** 3 from 4yo 2lb **11** Ran SP% **121.0**
Speed ratings: **103,102,101,97,95 94,93,92,91,77 74**CSF £10.05 TOTE £5.50: £1.40, £1.30, £2.60; EX 18.60.
**Owner** J C Smith **Bred** Littleton Stud **Trained** Kingsclere, Hants

**FOCUS**
A modest contest lacking strength in depth and an ordinary time for the class, despite being 0.52 seconds faster than the first division and looking more solid that that contest.

**NOTEBOOK**
**Indiana Blues** has been knocking on the door for some time now, and seemed better suited by this trip than the seven she ran over at Catterick last time. She was always holding the favourite in the closing stages, and connections will be very relieved to have got a win out of her.
**Millinsky(USA)** started favourite despite being badly in with a few on official ratings, including the winner. Trying this trip for the first time, she battled on well enough but the winner saw her race out that much better. Given the winning margin, it would be hard to say the extra furlong was the reason for her defeat.
**Future Deal**, stepping back a furlong from her belated debut, made her effort down the outside and stayed on well, but the drop in trip did not seem to do her any favours.
**Charlottebutterfly** took a hefty bump just after halfway that knocked her sideways, but she is already exposed as a modest maiden so it would be unwise to make too many excuses for her.
**Imtalkinggibberish**, officially the highest rated of these by some margin, ran fast until entering the last furlong and was already beaten when slightly running out of room. Connections must be ruing running him at Royal Ascot, as it completely ruined his handicap mark.
**All Quiet** *Official explanation: jockey said filly got struck into*
**Beresford Boy** *Official explanation: jockey said trainer lost his action*
T/Jkpt: Not won. T/Plt: £2,080.90 to a £1 stake. Pool: £38,483.20. 13.50 winning tickets. T/Qpdt: £18.80 to a £1 stake. Pool: £3,346.00. 131.10 winning tickets. JN

# 5616 NOTTINGHAM (L-H)
## Tuesday, September 28

**OFFICIAL GOING: Good to firm (good in places)**
Although the stalls were on the far side in the straight, the races tended to unfold more towards the centre, or even the stands' side.
Wind: Slight against Weather: Overcast

## 5846 EUROPEAN BREEDERS FUND MAIDEN FILLIES' STKS 1m 54y
**2:10** (2:12) (D2) 2-Y-0 **£6,370** (£1,960; £980; £490) **Stalls** Centre

Form RPR
3 **1** **Sharaiji Blossom (USA)**[13] 5559 2-8-11 LDettori 12 78
(SaeedBinSuroor) *mde all: rdn wl over 1f out: styd on ins last* **11/8**[1]
64 **2** 1 1/2 **Zayn Zen**[21] 5368 2-8-11 MHills 17 75
(MAJarvis) *trckd ldrs: hdwy 3f out: rdn wl over 1f out: kpt on same pce fnl f* **4/1**[2]
0 **3** 1/2 **Orpendonna (IRE)**[12] 5578 2-8-11 NCallan 2 74
(KARyan) *trckd ldrs: hdwy on inner to chal over 3f out: rdn 2f out and ev ch tl drvn and one pce ins last* **22/1**
**4** 1 3/4 **Rill** 2-8-11 RHughes 13 70
(JHMGosden) *trckd ldrs: hdwy 3f out: rdn wl over 1f out: kpt on same pce ent last* **33/1**
**5** 3 **Fearless Spirit (USA)** 2-8-11 JFortune 4 67+
(JHMGosden) *s.i.s and bhd: hdwy on outer 3f out: rdn and edgd lft wl over 1f out: kpt on: nrst fin* **15/2**
2 **6** nk **Mansiya**[54] 4480 2-8-11 SSanders 5 63
(CEBrittain) *chsd wnr: hung rt bnd after 3f: rdn along 3f out: wknd wl over 1f out* **13/2**[3]
**7** 3/4 **Natalie Jane (IRE)** 2-8-11 PHanagan 16 61+
(GAButler) *s.i.s and b ehind: hdwy wl over 2f out: kpt on appr last: nrst fin* **40/1**
**8** 1 1/4 **Kiama** 2-8-11 KFallon 9 58+
(HMorrison) *trckd ldrs: n.m.r and sltly hmpd bnd after 3f: sn pushed along and wknd wl over 2f out* **20/1**
**9** nk **Lujain Rose** 2-8-11 SDrowne 7 58+
(HMorrison) *in tch: pushed along over 3f out: rdn over 2f out and sn no hdwy* **50/1**
00 **10** 1 3/4 **Jenna Stannis**[26] 5247 2-8-6 NChalmers(5) 6 54
(RMBeckett) *in tch: rdn along over 3f out: grad wknd* **40/1**
**11** 1 **Gambling Spirit** 2-8-11 DaneO'Neill 3 52
(HCandy) *towards rr: hdwy 3f out: sn pushed along and no imp fnl 2f* **16/1**
**12** 2 1/2 **Danita Dancer (IRE)** 2-8-11 DHolland 10 46
(BPalling) *towards rr: pushed along 1/2-way: no hdwy* **40/1**
00 **13** 1 **Alula**[21] 5368 2-8-11 RLMoore 8 44
(RHannon) *midfield on inner: rdn along over 3f out: sn wknd* **33/1**
00 **14** 1 **Assured (IRE)**[13] 5569 2-8-11 (p) TQuinn 18 42
(PWD'Arcy) *in tch: rdn along over 3f out: wknd 2f out* **100/1**
04 **15** 2 **Calamari (IRE)**[31] 5109 2-8-11 JQuinn 11 37
(MrsADuffield) *a towards rr* **40/1**
0 **16** shd **Whoopsie**[20] 5396 2-8-11 FNorton 14 37
(JAGlover) *chsd ldrs: rdn along over 3f out: sn wknd* **100/1**
**17** 1 **Treasury (IRE)** 2-8-11 TPQueally 15 35
(CEBrittain) *s.i.s: a rr* **66/1**
**18** 1 3/4 **Glads Image** 2-8-11 CCatlin 1 31
(DJDaly) *sn outpaced and a rr* **100/1**

1m 45.84s (-0.56) **Going Correction** 0.0s/f (Good) **18** Ran SP% **124.3**
Speed ratings: **102,100,100,98,95 94,94,92,92,90 89,87,86,85,83 83,82,80**CSF £5.55 TOTE £2.50: £1.70, £1.30, £7.80; EX 10.70.
**Owner** Godolphin **Bred** Gaines-Gentry Thoroughbreds **Trained** Newmarket, Suffolk

**FOCUS**
Not a strong contest and they did not appear to go that quick, yet the winning time was very good for a race of its type.

**NOTEBOOK**
**Sharaiji Blossom(USA)** had clearly learnt from her debut and had plenty of use made of her. While this may not have taken a deal of winning, she is at least open to improvement.
**Zayn Zen** did not appear to want to let herself down on the fast ground.
**Orpendonna(IRE)**, a half-sister to stayer Alberich, proved well suited by this step up in trip and, while she may not be good enough to win her maiden, she should have no trouble making her mark in handicaps.
**Rill**, a half-sister to Araglin, a winner under both codes, as well as juvenile winner Ciel, did not shape at all badly and looks sure to benefit from the experience.
**Fearless Spirit(USA)**, a half-sister to the high-class Rodrigo De Triano, was very green on this racecourse debut. A lengthy filly, she should come on no end from this.
**Mansiya** looked to find this trip beyond her.
**Calamari(IRE)** *Official explanation: jockey said filly ran too freely in the early stages*

## 5847 MIDLANDS RACING - 9 GREAT VENUES MAIDEN FILLIES' STKS (DIV I) 6f 15y
**2:40** (2:41) (D3) 2-Y-0 **£4,751** (£1,462; £731; £365) **Stalls** Low

Form RPR
06 **1** **Ecologically Right**[13] 5559 2-8-11 TQuinn 6 77
(MrsJRRamsden) *chsd ldrs: rdn to ld ins fnl f: r.o* **6/1**[3]
65 **2** 1 1/2 **Entertaining**[46] 4705 2-8-11 DaneO'Neill 13 72
(HCandy) *led: rdn over 1f out: hung lft and hdd ins fnl f* **11/4**[1]
00 **3** 2 1/2 **Midnight Lace**[80] 3741 2-8-11 RLMoore 8 65
(RHannon) *chsd ldr: rdn over 2f out: no ex fnl f* **16/1**
5 **4** 2 1/2 **E Bride (USA)**[100] 3116 2-8-11 MFenton 4 57
(JGGiven) *s.i.s: hdwy 1/2-way: no ex fnl f* **14/1**
0 **5** 1 1/2 **Born For Diamonds (IRE)**[7] 5720 2-8-11 MHills 11 53
(BWHills) *s.i.s: pushed along 1/2-way: styng on whn hung lft ins fnl f: nvr trbld ldrs* **11/2**[2]
**6** nk **Turkana Girl** 2-8-11 SDrowne 1 52
(GWragg) *sn outpcd: hdwy over 2f out: wknd ins fnl f* **18/1**
50 **7** 1 **Qawaafil (USA)**[13] 5569 2-8-11 RHills 7 49
(EALDunlop) *chsd ldrs: rdn 1/2-way: wknd over 1f out* **15/2**
06 **8** 2 1/2 **Lady Hen**[62] 4243 2-8-11 EAhern 9 41
(MJWallace) *hld up: effrt over 2f out: wknd over 1f out* **14/1**
35 **9** 3 **Pedlar Of Dreams (IRE)**[17] 5475 2-8-11 PHanagan 10 32+
(TDBarron) *prom: lost pl over 4f out: n.d after* **9/1**
0 **10** 2 **Temple Belle Xpres**[11] 5616 2-8-11 SWKelly 3 26
(SRBowring) *chsd ldrs 4f* **100/1**
**11** 1/2 **La Cygne Blanche (IRE)** 2-8-11 JoannaBadger 5 25
(MrsNMacauley) *s.s: hung lft over 1f out: a bhd* **100/1**
00 **12** 1 **Mochaccino (IRE)**[28] 5209 2-8-8 HayleyTurner(3) 12 22
(DShaw) *sn outpcd* **50/1**
**13** 9 **Snowdrift** 2-8-11 KFallon 2 —
(DJDaly) *dwlt: sn prom: wknd over 2f out* **11/1**

1m 15.6s (0.80) **Going Correction** 0.0s/f (Good) **13** Ran SP% **114.9**
Speed ratings: **94,92,88,85,83 82,81,78,74,71 70,69,57**CSF £21.73 TOTE £6.50: £2.20, £1.10, £9.20; EX 22.90.
**Owner** W J Gredley **Bred** Middle Park Stud Ltd **Trained** Sandhutton, N Yorks

**FOCUS**
An ordinary contest and just fair form in which most of these will have to go the handicap route if they are to get off the mark. The winning time was slightly faster than the second division, but still only average for the grade.

**NOTEBOOK**
**Ecologically Right**, a poor mover in her slower paces showed the right attitude to get her head in front. Her future clearly lies in the hands of the Handicapper.
**Entertaining** had no excuses, but will have more options open to her now in handicap company.
**Midnight Lace**, a half-sister to the useful pair Tadeo and Attache, looks to be going the right way and will certainly have more openings to her now in handicaps.
**E Bride(USA)** looks the sort to do better with another year on her back.
**Born For Diamonds(IRE)** looked to find things happening too quickly for him and looks in need of a stiffer test.
**Turkana Girl**, a half-sister to a juvenile winner in Italy, showed promise despite looking in need of both the outing and experience.
**Qawaafil(USA)** will have more options open to her now in handicaps.

## 5848 MIDLANDS RACING - 9 GREAT VENUES MAIDEN FILLIES' STKS (DIV II) 6f 15y
**3:10** (3:17) (D3) 2-Y-0 **£4,751** (£1,462; £731; £365) **Stalls** Low

Form RPR
**1** **Bon Nuit (IRE)** 2-8-11 SDrowne 9 81
(GWragg) *s.i.s and behiund: hdwy over 2f out: styd on to ld ins last: r.o* **25/1**
00 **2** 1 3/4 **Nan Jan**[20] 5400 2-8-11 (t) NCallan 5 76
(RIngram) *prom: hdwy over 2f out: led 11/2f out: sn rdn: hdd and nt qckn ins last* **50/1**
5242 **3** 1/2 **Indiena**[20] 5391 2-8-11 77 JFortune 12 74
(BJMeehan) *trckd ldrs: hdwy 1/2-way: chal 2f out and ev ch tl rdn and one pce ent last* **1/1**[1]

4 2½ **Gimasha** 2-8-11 ........ TEDurcan 2 67
(MRChannon) *cl up: led over 3f out: rdn along and hdd 11/2f out: sn wknd* **5/1**[3]

0 **5** 3½ **Musardiere**[15] [5521] 2-8-11 ........ LGoncalves 8 56
(MrsJRRamsden) *bhd: hdwy 2f out: swtchd rt over 1f out: styd on ins last: nrst fin* **66/1**

203 **6** *shd* **Rasseem (IRE)**[15] [5521] 2-8-11 76 ........ LDettori 11 56
(SaeedBinSuroor) *chsd ldrs: rdn along wl over 2f out: sn edgd lft and btn* **7/2**[2]

**7** ¾ **Arous (FR)** 2-8-11 ........ SSanders 1 59+
(JLDunlop) *in tch: pushed along over 2f out: no hdwy* **12/1**

0 **8** 9 **Amazing Grace Mary**[13] [5555] 2-8-11 ........(b[1]) SWKelly 7 26
(SRBowring) *led: rdn along and hdd over 3f out: sn wknd* **100/1**

**9** 1¼ **Jolie (IRE)** 2-8-11 ........ LisaJones 10 23
(RDickin) *s.i.s and bhd: hdwy 1/2-way: in tch 2f out: sn riden and wknd* **80/1**

**10** 1¾ **Petite Girl** 2-8-11 ........ CCatlin 3 17
(JLSpearing) *squeezed out s: a bhd* **50/1**

000 **11** *nk* **Kimberley Hall**[14] [5542] 2-8-11 ........ MHenry 13 17
(JAGlover) *sn outpcd and bhd fr 1/2-way* **100/1**

05 **12** *dist* **Swift Dame (IRE)**[21] [5375] 2-8-11 ........ RHughes 4 —
(RHannon) *prom centre: hung bdly lft after 2f and sn bhd* **33/1**

1m 15.76s (0.96) **Going Correction** 0.0s/f (Good) **12** Ran SP% **112.0**
Speed ratings: **93,90,90,86,82 81,80,68,67,64 64,**—CSF £762.23 TOTE £30.40: £5.80, £10.70, £1.10; EX 459.20.
**Owner** Howard Spooner **Bred** Michael Dargan **Trained** Newmarket, Suffolk

**FOCUS**
With the market leaders below their best this probably didn't take as much winning as it should have, although the form looks fairly solid on paper. A slightly slower time than the first division and only average for the grade.

**NOTEBOOK**
**Bon Nuit(IRE)**, a half-sister to several winners, did this well without having to do too much. She is open to plenty of improvement.
**Nan Jan** found improvement for the first-time tongue tie and, if building on this, should find a little race.
**Indiena** could not take advantage of what looked a soft opening and looks to have something to prove now.
**Gimasha** taken down steadily to post, showed plenty of pace on the way back, and should benefit from the experience.
**Musardiere** is never going to be effective over sprint trips, but is one to keep an eye on when tackling handicappers over further.
**Rasseem(IRE)**, off the bridle some way out was already beaten when short of room around the two-furlong marker. She looks to have something to prove now.
**Arous(FR)**, a half-sister to the high-class Dandoun, is only small and will do well to find a race of any description.
**Swift Dame(IRE)** *Official explanation: jockey said filly hung violently left making her unrideable*

## 5849 RACING UK ON CHANNEL 432 CLASSIFIED STKS 6f 15y
**3:40** (3:46) (F3) 3-Y-O+ **£3,874** (£1,192; £596; £298) **Stalls** Low

Form RPR

4011 **1** **Inch By Inch**[6] [5734] 5-8-6 60 ........(b) AQuinn(5) 8 73+
(PJMakin) *wnt rt s: sn swtchd to r stands' side: chsd ldrs: led over 1f out: sn clr: eased towards fin* **3/1**[1]

3603 **2** 1¾ **Piccleyes**[6] [5737] 3-8-12 60 ........(b) RLMoore 18 65
(RHannon) *racd stands' side: hld up: hdwy over 1f out: r.o* **10/1**

0030 **3** 1½ **Grandma Lily (IRE)**[14] [5544] 6-8-6 60 ........ DTudhope(5) 20 58
(MCChapman) *racd stands' side: hld up: hdwy over 1f out: edgd lft ins fnl f: r.o* **33/1**

1004 **4** *nk* **Firework**[29] [5184] 6-9-0 57 ........(p) TQuinn 13 60
(JAkehurst) *racd stands' side: w ldrs: rdn and ev ch over 1f out: styd on same pce* **33/1**

5510 **5** 1¼ **Headland (USA)**[21] [5364] 6-9-0 58 ........(be) ACulhane 12 56
(DWChapman) *racd stands' side: hld up: styd on ins fnl f: nvr trbld ldrs* **40/1**

4600 **6** *hd* **Sweet Pickle**[10] [5656] 3-8-9 58 ........ TPQueally 11 52
(DJCoakley) *racd stands' side: chsd ldrs: rdn over 2f out: styd on same pce appr fnl f* **33/1**

046 **7** *nk* **Ziet D'Alsace (FR)**[55] [4437] 4-8-11 59 ........ LDettori 15 51
(AWCarroll) *dwlt: racd stands' side: hld up: swtchd lft and hdwy over 2f out: styd on same pce fnl f* **14/1**

1334 **8** 1¼ **Tuscarora (IRE)**[26] [5252] 5-8-11 60 ........ JFortune 4 48
(AWCarroll) *unruly stalls: swtchd to racd stands' side: hld up: hdwy 2f out: styd on same pce appr fnl f* **5/1**[2]

5600 **9** ¾ **Rene Barbier (IRE)**[21] [5364] 3-8-12 59 ........ FNorton 19 48
(JAGlover) *racd stands' side: chsd ldrs: rdn whn nt clr and lost pl over 2f out: n.d after* **50/1**

0016 **10** ¾ **Bowling Along**[3] [5798] 3-8-6 60 ........ TEaves(3) 9 43
(MESowersby) *s.i.s: racd stands' side: hld up: effrt 1/2-way: nvr trbld ldrs* **22/1**

0200 **11** 1¼ **Gone'N'Dunnett (IRE)**[5] [5754] 5-9-0 60 ........(p) DaneO'Neill 14 42
(MrsCADunnett) *racd stands' side: w ldrs: rdn and ev ch over 1f out: sn wknd* **33/1**

4122 **12** ½ **Jazzy Millennium**[19] [5425] 7-9-0 59 ........(b) DHolland 7 41
(BRMillman) *racd stands' side: hld up: hdwy over 2f out: wknd fnl f* **7/1**[3]

6050 **13** 1¼ **Kallista's Pride**[26] [5253] 4-8-11 58 ........(v) KFallon 17 34
(JRBest) *swvd lft s: racd stands' side: sn led: edgd lft and hdd over 1f out: sn wknd* **16/1**

5140 **14** 2 **Shamrock Tea**[54] [4489] 3-8-12 59 ........ PHanagan 16 31
(RAFahey) *s.s: racd stands' side: hld up: hdwy 1/2-way: wknd 2f out* **16/1**

645 **15** 1¾ **Victoriana**[31] [5104] 3-8-9 57 ........ JQuinn 3 54+
(HJCollingridge) *racd far side: chsd ldrs: rdn over 1f out: led that gp wl ins fnl f: no ch w stands' side* **40/1**

-000 **16** ¾ **St Austell**[22] [5337] 4-9-0 58 ........ SSanders 5 64+
(JARToller) *racd far side: chsd ldrs: led that gp over 1f out: no ch w stands' side* **16/1**

0040 **17** ½ **Zap Attack**[23] [5316] 4-8-9 58 ........ MLawson(5) 6 53+
(JParkes) *racd far side: chsd ldrs over 4f* **50/1**

3606 **18** *nk* **Fitzwarren**[5] [5754] 3-8-12 59 ........(v) EAhern 2 52+
(NBycroft) *racd far side: chsd ldrs over 4f* **40/1**

-060 **19** 1¼ **Mrs Spence**[141] [1992] 3-8-9 58 ........ TLucas 1 45+
(MWEasterby) *led far side over 4f: sn wknd* **14/1**

1m 14.19s (-0.61) **Going Correction** 0.0s/f (Good) **19** Ran SP% **121.6**
**WFA** 3 from 4yo+ 2lb
Speed ratings: **104,101,99,99,97 97,96,95,94,93 91,90,89,86,84 83,82,82,80**CSF £28.48 TOTE £4.00: £1.80, £2.80, £7.50; EX 27.60.
**Owner** Mrs Anna L Sanders **Bred** Mrs Anna L Sanders **Trained** Ogbourne Maisey, Wilts

**FOCUS**
An ordinary event and the stands' side had much the best of this with the five to race on the far side filling the last five places. This wasn't as competitive as the numbers suggested, although it appeared to be run at a fair clip and the runner-up sets the standard.

**NOTEBOOK**
**Inch By Inch** is a mare in flying form at present and won with far more in hand than the verdict suggested.
**Piccleyes** turned in a sound enough effort and, while he may not be the easiest of rides, he is more than capable.
**Grandma Lily(IRE)** showed a bit more sparkle than of late and is one to keep an eye on when the All-Weather season gets going.
**Firework** turned in a sound enough effort at the weights.
**Rene Barbier(IRE)** *Official explanation: jockey said gelding was denied a clear run*

## 5850 ROSELAND GROUP AUTUMN H'CAP 2m 9y
**4:10** (4:10) (D2) (0-85,83) 3-Y-O **£10,514** (£3,235; £1,617; £808) **Stalls** Low

Form RPR

0611 **1** **Trilemma**[22] [5343] 3-8-10 72 ........ SSanders 1 91+
(SirMarkPrescott) *hld up in tch: hdwy on bit over 3f out: shkn up to ld over 1f out: rdn and edgd lft ent last: drvn out* **1/1**[1]

2331 **2** 2½ **Race The Ace**[31] [5116] 3-9-1 77 ........ LDettori 6 87+
(JLDunlop) *trckd ldrs: hdwy to ld over 3f out: rdn over 2f out: sn drvn and hdd over 1f out: kpt on same pce* **15/8**[2]

6634 **3** 3 **Marine City (JPN)**[12] [5595] 3-8-5 72 ........(p) DFox(5) 5 77
(MAJarvis) *hld up: hdwy on outer over 3f out: rdn and hung lft 2f out: sn drvn and one pce* **7/1**[3]

2130 **4** 16 **Tudor Bell (IRE)**[12] [5595] 3-9-5 81 ........ DSweeney 3 67
(JGMO'Shea) *chsd clr ldr: pushed along over 5f out: rdn 4f out and sn wknd* **33/1**

3303 **5** 2 **Garnett (IRE)**[21] [5382] 3-8-8 70 ........ DHolland 7 53
(AKing) *in tch: hdwy 6f out: led briefly 4f out: sn rdn and hdd: drvn and wknd 3f out* **33/1**

1314 **6** 4 **Richtee (IRE)**[29] [5191] 3-8-10 72 ........ PHanagan 2 51
(RAFahey) *hld up in rr: hdwy 5f out: rdn over 3f out and sn btn* **14/1**

-000 **7** *dist* **Quartino**[6] [5732] 3-9-7 83 ........(b) JFortune 4 —
(JHMGosden) *led and sn clr: rdn along over 6f out: drvn and hdd 4f out: wknd rapidly and sn bhd* **50/1**

3m 30.04s (-3.46) **Going Correction** 0.0s/f (Good) **7** Ran SP% **111.8**
Speed ratings: **108,106,105,97,96 94,**—CSF £2.86 TOTE £1.80: £1.10, £2.00; EX 3.00.
**Owner** Mrs Sonia Rogers **Bred** Hesmonds Stud Ltd **Trained** Newmarket, Suffolk

**FOCUS**
A fair handicap and not that much strength in depth, but there was plenty of pace on and the front three finished nicely clear and looks generally progressive.

**NOTEBOOK**
**Trilemma** continues to progress and the manner of her victory suggested there should be plenty more to come.
**Race The Ace**, like the winner is a progressive type. He seems to handle most types of ground and although beaten here, should not find it too difficult to get back to winning ways.
**Marine City(JPN)**, just as she did at Yarmouth, looks a difficult ride.
**Tudor Bell(IRE)** was beaten too far out for stamina to have been an issue and looks some way below his best at present.
**Garnett(IRE)**
**Richtee(IRE)** *Official explanation: jockey said filly choked on pulling up*

## 5851 LETHEBY & CHRISTOPHER MAIDEN STKS 1m 54y
**4:40** (4:45) (D3) 3-Y-O+ **£4,985** (£1,534; £767; £383) **Stalls** Centre

Form RPR

2-2 **1** **Baboosh (IRE)**[44] [4781] 3-8-9 ........ LDettori 4 74
(JRFanshawe) *a.p: chsd ldr over 1f out: rdn to ld wl ins fnl f* **11/4**[2]

022 **2** 1½ **Thistle**[22] [5345] 3-9-0 76 ........ JFortune 1 76
(JHMGosden) *s.i.s: sn led: rdn over 1f out: hdd wl ins fnl f* **11/4**[2]

0-22 **3** 2 **Admiral Compton**[88] [3487] 3-9-0 77 ........ KFallon 10 71
(EFVaughan) *hld up: hdwy over 3f out: rdn whn hmpd 2f out: no imp fnl f* **11/8**[1]

0 **4** 5 **Lyns Resolution**[19] [5408] 4-9-4 ........ RPrice 8 60
(DBurchell) *prom: rdn over 2f out: wknd over 1f out* **200/1**

0-0 **5** 1¼ **Eva Jean**[134] [2182] 3-8-9 ........ RLMoore 7 52
(HMorrison) *mid-div: rdn 1/2-way: nvr trbld ldrs* **20/1**[3]

0 **6** *nk* **Cirrious**[11] [5621] 3-8-9 ........ SWKelly 5 51
(BPalling) *s.i.s: sn prom: rdn over 3f out: wknd over 1f out* **40/1**

0363 **7** ¾ **Speed Racer**[15] [5525] 3-8-9 45 ........ KimTinkler 2 50
(DonEnricoIncisa) *chsd ldrs: rdn 1/2-way: wknd 2f out* **66/1**

0 **8** 2½ **Moon Spinner**[22] [5339] 7-8-13 ........ SDrowne 11 44
(AndrewReid) *s.i.s: outpcd* **66/1**

0 **9** *nk* **Rabbit**[50] [4615] 3-8-9 ........ SRighton 3 43
(MrsALMKing) *chsd ldr over 6f out: rdn and hung lft 2f out: sn wknd* **100/1**

5 **10** ½ **Nopleazinu**[14] [5551] 4-8-13 ........ JoannaBadger 9 42
(MrsNMacauley) *s.s: outpcd* **200/1**

0-0 **11** 1¾ **She's A Fox**[14] [5537] 3-8-9 ........ ACulhane 12 38
(AWCarroll) *unruly at post: dwlt: sn outpcd* **150/1**

000 **12** 6 **Constructor**[27] [5217] 3-9-0 ........ DSweeney 13 29
(CACyzer) *unruly stalls: hld up: bhd fr 1/2-way* **66/1**

04 **13** 8 **Silloth Spirit**[12] [5591] 4-9-4 ........ NPollard 6 11
(MrsAMNaughton) *dwlt: outpcd* **250/1**

1m 44.58s (-1.82) **Going Correction** 0.0s/f (Good)
**WFA** 3 from 4yo+ 4lb **13** Ran SP% **110.2**
Speed ratings: **109,107,105,100,99 98,98,95,95,94 93,87,79**CSF £9.48 TOTE £2.90: £1.10, £1.10, £1.10; EX 8.10.
**Owner** Lord Halifax **Bred** Lord Halifax **Trained** Newmarket, Suffolk

**FOCUS**
An ordinary contest lacking strength in depth, but it appeared to be soundly run and those favoured in the betting had the race to themselves.

**NOTEBOOK**
**Baboosh(IRE)** confirmed the promise shown in previous runs and was well on top in the end. However, with the runner-up and third rated in the high 70s she cannot expect any favours from the Handicapper.
**Thistle** was again found out by the lack of a change of pace. A step up in trip may offset that.
**Admiral Compton** is becoming a frustrating animal, and was already making hard work of things when hampered at around the two-furlong marker.

## 5852 BETTING WITH IBETX.COM NURSERY 1m 1f 213y
**5:10** (5:11) (E3) (0-75,72) 2-Y-O **£3,948** (£1,215; £607; £303) **Stalls** Low

Form RPR

060 **1** **Penalty Kick (IRE)**[25] [5269] 2-9-3 68 ........ KFallon 12 75+
(NACallaghan) *sn trcking ldrs: hdwy on inner over 2f out: rdn to ld over 1f out: sn clr: eased nr fin* **9/2**[1]

2564 **2** 1 1/2 **Flying Pass**22 5335 2-9-7 **72** ........ TQuinn 4 71
(DJSFfrenchDavis) *hld up towards rr: hdwy 3f out: rdn 2f out: styd on strly ins last* **11/1**

5001 **3** *shd* **Clinet (IRE)**22 5335 2-9-4 **69** ........ CCatlin 14 68
(PMPhelan) *held up and bhd: hdwy wl over 2f out: swtchd rt and rdn over 1f out: styd on wl fnl f* **10/1**

0100 **4** 1/2 **Hidden Chance**21 5377 2-9-2 **67** ........ RHughes 7 65
(RHannon) *cl up: led 3f out: rdn 2f out: drvn and hdd over 1f out: grad wknd* **11/1**

0330 **5** *shd* **Cava Bien**27 5227 2-9-5 **70** ........ MFenton 8 68
(JGGiven) *in tch: pushed along and lost pl over 4f out: swtchd wd and rdn 2f out: styd on wl fnl f: nrst fin* **33/1**

5463 **6** 1 1/2 **Patxaran (IRE)**5 5753 2-8-10 **66** ........ RoryMoore(5) 6 61
(PCHaslam) *in tch: hdwy to chse ldrs over 3f out: rdn and hung lft 2f out: sn drvn and sn one pce* **9/1**

3000 **7** 1 1/4 **Celestial Arc (USA)**19 5417 2-9-3 **68** ........ RLMoore 16 61+
(PFICole) *hld up and bhd: hdwy wl over 2f out: styd on appr last: nrst fin* **8/1**

5250 **8** 1 1/4 **Bongoali**12 5596 2-8-12 **63** ........ SHitchcott 1 54
(MRChannon) *in tch: effrt and rdn along 3f out: drvn and one pce fnl 2f* **14/1**

063 **9** 3/4 **You Found Me**29 5172 2-9-2 **67** ........ EAhern 2 56
(CTinkler) *in tch: effrt and hdwy over 3f out: sn rdn and wkng whn n.m.r 2f out* **15/2**3

350 **10** 1 **Dancer's Serenade (IRE)**66 4131 2-9-5 **70** ........ PHanagan 9 58
(TPTate) *hld up and bhd: styd on fnl 2f: nvr a factor* **66/1**

500 **11** *hd* **Silsong (USA)**11 5620 2-9-0 **65** ........ RSmith 5 52
(BRMillman) *chsd ldrs on inner: rdn along over 2f out: sn drvn and wknd wl over 1f out* **33/1**

6041 **12** 1 **Lorna Dune**12 5593 2-9-1 **66** ........(v1) DSweeney 11 51
(JGMO'Shea) *chsd ldrs: hdwy 3f out: rdn over 2f out: ev ch tl drvn and wknd wl over 1f out* **20/1**

6206 **13** 1 3/4 **Shaheer (IRE)**21 5377 2-9-6 **71** ........ JFortune 15 53
(BJMeehan) *chsd ldrs: rdn along over 3f out: snd riven and wknd 2f out* **5/1**2

064 **14** *nk* **Lunar Sky (USA)**15 5522 2-9-7 **72** ........ SSanders 10 54
(CEBrittain) *in tch: hdwy on outer to chse ldrs 3f out: rdn and hung lft 2f out: sn wknd* **12/1**

045 **15** 1/2 **Comical Errors (USA)**32 5095 2-9-5 **70** ........ GFaulkner 3 51
(PCHaslam) *s.i.s a bhd: hdwy 3f out: sn rdn and wknd* **28/1**

655 **16** 8 **Scorpio Sally (IRE)**17 5476 2-8-12 **63** ........ ACulhane 13 29
(MDHammond) *led: rdn along and hdd 3f out: sn wknd* **66/1**

2m 12.71s (3.21) **Going Correction** 0.0s/f (Good) **16** Ran SP% **124.9**
Speed ratings: **87,85,85,85,85 84,83,82,81,80 80,79,78,78,77 71**CSF £51.96 CT £485.03 TOTE £5.60: £2.10, £2.50, £2.60, £5.10; EX 90.70.
**Owner** John Livock Bloodstock Limited **Bred** Bernard Cooke **Trained** Newmarket, Suffolk
■ Stewards Enquiry : Rory Moore one-day ban: careless riding (Oct 9)

**FOCUS**
Not a great race, and the pace was only steady which resulted in a moderate winning time, although the winner can rate a little higher.

**NOTEBOOK**
**Penalty Kick(IRE)** without the blinkers this time, left his previous form behind on this first venture into handicap company. He won with something in hand and it will be a surprise if he cannot build on this.
**Flying Pass** stayed this trip well enough and looked to run somewhere near his best.
**Clinet(IRE)**, closely matched with the runner-up on Bath running, was set a fair bit to do and did well to finish as close as she did.
**Hidden Chance** does not look to be progressing with racing.
**Cava Bien** has ability but, he looked a difficult ride and may not be one to rely on.

## 5853 BACK OR LAY WITH IBETX.COM H'CAP 1m 1f 213y
5:40 (5:40) (E3) (0-70,70) 3-Y-0+ **£4,195** (£1,291; £645; £322) **Stalls** Low

Form RPR

6510 **1** **Kirkham Abbey**19 5423 4-9-6 **69** ........ KDarley 8 76
(MAJarvis) *hld up: hdwy over 3f out: hung lft over 1f out: rdn to ld ins fnl f: r.o* **10/1**

0003 **2** 3/4 **Planters Punch (IRE)**33 5057 3-8-13 **68** ........ KFallon 3 74
(RHannon) *a.p: chsd ldr 1/2-way: rdn to ld 2f out: hdd and unable qck ins fnl f* **11/2**3

1000 **3** 3/4 **Factual Lad**29 5183 6-9-7 **70** ........ GBaker 6 75
(BRMillman) *a.p: rdn over 2f out: styd on* **28/1**

1124 **4** *hd* **Barton Sands (IRE)**16 5493 7-9-6 **69** ........(t) SDrowne 2 73
(AndrewReid) *hld up: hdwy over 2f out: styd on* **16/1**

0633 **5** *hd* **Champion Lion (IRE)**12 5584 5-9-4 **67** ........ SHitchcott 4 75+
(MRChannon) *hld up: hdwy over 2f out: nt clr run over 1f out: r.o ins fnl f: nt trble ldrs* **7/2**1

0402 **6** 1 **Kind Emperor**14 5554 7-9-1 **64** ........ AMackay 9 66
(PLGilligan) *led 8f: no ex ins fnl f* **12/1**

5046 **7** 1/2 **Sahaat**25 5257 6-8-13 **65** ........ RThomas(3) 16 66
(CRDore) *plld hrd and prom: rdn over 1f out: styd on same pce* **40/1**

3000 **8** 1 **Sir Haydn**16 5492 4-8-13 **62** ........(v) RLMoore 10 61
(JRJenkins) *hld up: hdwy over 2f out: nt rch ldrs* **12/1**

0510 **9** 1 1/2 **Market Avenue**17 5459 5-9-0 **63** ........ PHanagan 7 59+
(RAFahey) *hld up in tch whn hmpd over 1f out: wknd ins fnl f* **9/2**2

3200 **10** 3 **Piri Piri (IRE)**14 5554 4-9-4 **67** ........ SWhitworth 12 58
(PJMcbride) *dwlt: hld up: nvr nrr* **10/1**

0 **11** 3/4 **Darab (POL)**52 4556 4-9-0 **63** ........(p) EAhern 1 52
(RMHCowell) *chsd ldrs over 8f* **100/1**

0000 **12** 1 **Once (FR)**22 5340 4-9-2 **65** ........(b) SWKelly 14 52
(JAOsborne) *sn pushed along in rr: n.d* **66/1**

6603 **13** *shd* **Derwent (USA)**22 5344 5-8-13 **62** ........(v) SSanders 15 49
(JDBethell) *hld up: rdn and hung lft over 2f out: a in rr* **9/1**

0060 **14** *nk* **Caroubier (IRE)**29 5203 4-9-3 **66** ........ TEDurcan 11 52
(JGallagher) *sn pushed along: a in rr* **40/1**

-420 **15** 1 **Big Bertha**244 618 6-9-4 **67** ........ MFenton 5 52
(JohnBerry) *chsd ldrs 8f* **33/1**

2m 9.78s (0.28) **Going Correction** 0.0s/f (Good) **15** Ran SP% **119.0**
**WFA** 3 from 4yo+ 6lb
Speed ratings: **98,97,96,96,96 95,95,94,93,90 90,89,89,89,88**CSF £60.44 CT £1510.69 TOTE £15.00: £2.80, £3.70, £8.30; EX 67.10 Trifecta £488.20 Pool £1,031.50, 1.50 w/u. Place 6 £7.01, Place 5 £5.08.
**Owner** P D Savill **Bred** Highclere Stud Ltd **Trained** Newmarket, Suffolk

**FOCUS**
Another ordinary contest run at a steady pace, which resulted in a modest winning time for the class. However, the placed horses give the form a solid look.

**NOTEBOOK**
**Kirkham Abbey** has done his fair share of winning, for one of his ability. However, he again gave signs that he is far from a straightforward ride.
**Planters Punch(IRE)** looked as though he had matters under control when going on, only to be worn down in the latter stages. This looks as good as he is.
**Factual Lad** turned in a solid-enough effort and is not far off his last winning mark.
**Barton Sands(IRE)**, who has yet to win in handicap company, did not have the strong pace he needs.
**Champion Lion(IRE)** is one to keep in mind for a similar contest, for he had no luck in running.
*Official explanation: jockey said gelding was denied a clear run in the final furlong*
**Once(FR)** *Official explanation: jockey said gelding lost its action*
T/Jkpt: Not won. T/Plt: £11.10 to a £1 stake. Pool: £47,863.50. 3,140.90 winning tickets. T/Qpdt: £2.90 to a £1 stake. Pool: £2,537.60. 641.80 winning tickets. CR

5854 - (Foreign Racing) - See Raceform Interactive

# 5341 NEWCASTLE (L-H)
Wednesday, September 29

**OFFICIAL GOING: Good to firm**

## 5855 BENFIELD MOTORS RENAULT MAIDEN AUCTION STKS (DIV I) 7f
2:10 (2:11) (F4) 2-Y-0 **£2,961** (£846; £423) **Stalls** Centre

Form RPR

0560 **1** **Davy Crockett**18 5477 2-8-8 67 ow1 ........ DMcGaffin 4 69
(BSmart) *cl up far side: rdn to ld 1f out: hld on wl* **8/1**3

0002 **2** *hd* **Grand Welcome (IRE)**35 5034 2-8-7 71 ........(b) SWKelly 7 67
(CTinkler) *led far side: hdd 1f out: rallied and edgd rt ins last: jst hld* **14/1**

0040 **3** *shd* **Plenty Cried Wolf**18 5447 2-8-7 68 ........ THamilton(3) 10 70
(RAFahey) *led stands side trio: rdn over 2f out: drifted lft and styd on wl fnl f: jst hld* **12/1**

4 **4** 2 **Abstract Folly (IRE)**25 5301 2-8-10 ........ KMcEvoy 6 65
(JDBethell) *prom: rdn over 2f out: one pce over 1f out* **7/2**2

3 **5** 3/4 **Vancouver Gold (IRE)**25 5307 2-8-5 ........ DaleGibson 5 58
(KRBurke) *trckd far side ldrs: rdn over 2f out: one pce over 1f out* **1/1**1

06 **6** 8 **Liability (IRE)**28 5227 2-8-2 ........ KimTinkler 2 43+
(NTinkler) *chsd far side ldrs to 2f out: sn wknd* **20/1**

**7** 4 **Maynooth Prince (IRE)** 2-8-13 ........ JCarroll 8 36
(HAlexander) *hld up far side: outpcd after 2f: n.d after* **40/1**

R **8** 1 **Continental Flyer (IRE)**51 4606 2-8-8 ........(b1) VHalliday 1 29
(MDods) *prom far side tl wknd over 2f out* **66/1**

**9** 3 **Showtime Faye** 2-8-3 ow1 ........ RMullen 11 16
(ABailey) *cl up stands side tl rdn and outpcd over 2f out* **20/1**

0 **10** 1 1/2 **Fraambuoyant (IRE)**105 2985 2-8-2 ........ RFfrench 9 11
(CWFairhurst) *cl up stands side tl wknd fr over 2f out* **100/1**

**11** 17 **Sergeant Shinko (IRE)** 2-8-7 ........ LEnstone 3 —
(MDods) *s.i.s: sn wl bhd far side* **33/1**

1m 26.7s (-1.32) **Going Correction** -0.40s/f (Firm) **11** Ran SP% **115.1**
Speed ratings: **91,90,90,88,87 78,73,72,69,67 48**CSF £98.03 TOTE £8.80: £2.30, £2.70, £3.60; EX 57.50.
**Owner** J M & Mrs E E Ranson **Bred** Longdon Stud Ltd **Trained** Hambleton, N Yorks

**FOCUS**
A modest maiden in which the majority of runners raced far side and the placed horses provide the level of the form. Of the three who stayed stands' side, Plenty Cried Wolf fared best in third. The time was ordinary for the class despite being 0.7 seconds faster than the second division.

**NOTEBOOK**
**Davy Crockett**, well beaten on his debut for Bryan Smart in a Musselburgh nursery, left that form behind to get off the mark. A rise in the weights for this success is very possible and he has to be taken on back in handicap company.
**Grand Welcome(IRE)**, runner-up in an ordinary heavy-ground Brighton maiden on his previous outing, coped well with these faster conditions and was just denied. There is a minor race in him, but he looks high enough in the handicap off a mark of 71.
**Plenty Cried Wolf** was one of just three horses to race stands' side and ran a fine race in the circumstances, pulling a mile clear on his side and only being beaten narrowly by the far side, despite hanging across the track in the closing stages.
**Abstract Folly(IRE)**, who ran green when fourth on his debut, again showed inexperience and is probably best watched until he is handicapped.
**Vancouver Gold(IRE)** had a hard enough race when third on her debut and this represented a step back. *Official explanation: jockey said filly hung left handed from half way*

## 5856 BENFIELD MOTORS RENAULT MAIDEN AUCTION STKS (DIV II) 7f
2:40 (2:41) (F4) 2-Y-0 **£2,954** (£844; £422) **Stalls** Centre

Form RPR

000 **1** **Bronze Dancer (IRE)**15 5543 2-8-7 ........ RWinston 5 68+
(GASwinbank) *hld up: hdwy 1/2-way. effrt: n.m.ra nd swtchd lft 2f out: rdn to chse ldr over 1f out: styd on to ld nr fin* **5/1**3

6 **2** *hd* **Nepal (IRE)**16 5521 2-8-5 ........ DMernagh 8 63
(TDBarron) *trckd ldrs: hdwy to ld wl over 1f out: sn rdn: drvn ins last: hdd and no ex nr fin* **10/1**

04 **3** 3 **Rudaki**31 5154 2-8-10 ........ MTebbutt 3 60
(MGQuinlan) *hld up and bhd: hdwy over 2f out: styd on appr last* **7/2**2

500 **4** 2 1/2 **Tahlal (IRE)**30 5200 2-8-10 63 ........ ACulhane 10 54
(MrsADuffield) *led after 1f: rdn along over 2f out: hdd wl over 1f out and grad wknd* **9/1**

0 **5** 1 1/4 **Sadie's Star (IRE)**25 5307 2-8-6 ow1 ........ SWKelly 2 47
(MDods) *towards rr: hdwy over 2f out: kpt on appr last* **33/1**

0500 **6** 1 **Aza Wish (IRE)**120 2550 2-8-2 60 ........ SRighton 9 40
(MsDeborahJEvans) *chsd ldrs on outer: rdn along over 2f out: sn one pce* **14/1**

05 **7** 3/4 **Geordie Dancer (IRE)**16 5516 2-8-13 ........ FLynch 7 49
(ABerry) *sn cl up: rdn along over 2f out: sn edgd rt and wknd* **12/1**

0 **8** 1/2 **Blacknyello Bonnet (USA)**13 5578 2-8-8 ........ KDarley 1 43
(MJohnston) *led 1f: prom tl rdn along a nd wknd wl over 1f out* **15/2**

5 **9** 2 1/2 **Paparaazi (IRE)**14 5561 2-8-4 ........ THamilton(3) 6 36
(RAFahey) *s.i.s and swvd violently righht s: a bhd* **10/3**1

000 **10** 5 **Season Ticket (GER)**24 5319 2-8-2 ........ JMackay 4 18
(WJHaggas) *chsd ldrs: rdn along after 3f: sn wknd* **10/1**

1m 27.4s (-0.62) **Going Correction** -0.40s/f (Firm) **10** Ran SP% **119.2**
Speed ratings: **87,86,83,80,79 77,77,76,73,67**CSF £55.45 TOTE £5.40: £1.60, £4.00, £2.00; EX 74.30.
**Owner** J Yates **Bred** Lisieux Stud **Trained** Melsonby, N Yorks

**FOCUS**
The form looks modest and the time was just that for the grade - 0.7 seconds slower than the first division.

**NOTEBOOK**

**Bronze Dancer(IRE)** had not shown much on his three previous starts, including in a seller on his debut, but this was his easiest task since that first run and he gained a narrow success. He had to wait for a gap, but was always going well and found enough when in the clear. His immediate future lies in the hands of the Handicapper.

**Nepal(IRE)**, well beaten in a six-furlong Redcar maiden on her debut, stepped up on that effort. She got first run on the eventual winner and her proximity does flatter her a little, but she is progressing.

**Rudaki**, up a furlong in trip, was settled well off the pace and simply took too long to get going.

**Tahlal(IRE)** did not look to have any real excuses and may do better in handicaps.

**Sadie's Star(IRE)** looked to improve on her debut running but may best best watched until she is qualified for a handicap mark.

**Blacknyello Bonnet(USA)** offered little, but do not rule out improvement when she is handicapped.

**Paparaazi(IRE)** swerved badly to her right after coming out of the stalls and, after re-joining the main field, was far too keen.

**Season Ticket(GER)** showed nothing, but is now qualified for a handicap mark.

## 5857 REG VARDY STONEYGATE RENAULT EBF MAIDEN STKS 6f

**3:10** (3:11) (D3) 2-Y-O **£4,556** (£1,402; £701; £350) **Stalls** Centre

Form RPR

2 **1** **Crosspeace (IRE)**[23] 5341 2-9-0 ........ RFrench 13 87+
(MJohnston) *trckd ldrs: hdwy 2f out: rdn to ld ins last: styd on wl* **4/5**[1]

**2** *1 3/4* **Desert Chief** 2-9-0 ........ RHills 12 79+
(SaeedBinSuroor) *trckd ldrs: hdwy 2f out: rdn to ld over 1f out: hdd and nt qckn ins last* **5/2**[2]

03 **3** *2 1/2* **Kool Ovation**[54] 4507 2-9-0 ........ DAllan 8 71
(ADickman) *cl up: led 1/2-way: rdn and hdd over 1f out: kpt on same pce* **25/1**

00 **4** *3* **Flaxby**[22] 5362 2-9-0 ........ JCarroll 5 62
(JDBethell) *in tch: hdwy over 2f out: sn rdn and one pce fr wl over 1f out* **100/1**

06 **5** *nk* **Mossmann Gorge**[15] 5542 2-9-0 ........ RWinston 3 61
(GASwinbank) *towards rr: hdwy over 2f out: kpt on ins last: nrst fin* **40/1**

0 **6** *3/4* **Navigation (IRE)**[24] 5319 2-9-0 ........ KMcEvoy 6 59
(TJEtherington) *led to 1/2-way: rdn along over 2f out: grad wknd* **25/1**

5400 **7** *1 1/2* **Kaggamagic**[27] 5234 2-9-0 65 ........ SWKelly 9 55
(JRNorton) *in tch: effrt over 2f out: sn rdn and no imp* **33/1**

5 **8** *1 3/4* **Devil's Island**[9] 5689 2-9-0 ........ JMackay 10 61+
(SirMarkPrescott) *s.i.s and bhd tl styd on fnl 2f* **14/1**

34 **9** *shd* **Branston Lily**[16] 5521 2-8-9 ........ ACulhane 11 44
(MrsJRRamsden) *midfield: rdn along over 2f out: no hdwy* **10/1**[3]

**10** *1 3/4* **Pebble Mill (IRE)** 2-9-0 ........ KDarley 14 44
(MJohnston) *dwlt: a rr* **12/1**

00 **11** *nk* **Enborne Again (IRE)**[13] 5578 2-9-0 ........ GParkin 7 43
(RAFahey) *in tch tl rdn along and wknd 1/2-way* **66/1**

**12** *1* **Champagne Lujain** 2-9-0 ........ TLucas 4 40
(MWEasterby) *s.i.s: a bhd* **100/1**

0 **13** *1 1/4* **Komreyev Star**[15] 5542 2-8-11 ........ THamilton(3) 2 36
(RAFahey) *midfield: rdn along 1/2-way: wknd over 2f out* **33/1**

**14** *dist* **Cayman King** 2-9-0 ........ DMernagh 1 —
(RCraggs) *sn outpcd and wl b ehind fr 1/2-way* **100/1**

1m 12.35s (-2.69) **Going Correction** -0.40s/f (Firm) 2y crse rec **14 Ran SP% 128.1**
Speed ratings: **101,98,95,91,90 89,87,85,85,83 82,81,79,**—CSF £2.77 TOTE £1.70: £1.10, £1.60, £3.50; EX 4.30.
**Owner** Favourites Racing **Bred** Patrick Jones **Trained** Middleham Moor, N Yorks

**FOCUS**

The front two are nice sorts, but this was a weak maiden overall which does not make it easy to rate. The winning time was fair for the grade.

**NOTEBOOK**

**Crosspeace(IRE)**, runner-up over course and distance on his debut, confirmed that promise and got off the mark with a straightforward success. He is bred to appreciate much further and is a nice prospect.

**Desert Chief**, a half-brother the useful six to seven-furlong juvenile Oriental Warrior, out of a mile Group winner in Italy, made a pleasing debut, but the winner was just too good. There is a similar race in him.

**Kool Ovation** again showed plenty of pace and also the ability to win a race. This trip seemed fine, the front two were simply too strong.

**Flaxby**, tailed off over this trip at Catterick on his previous start, showed that running to be wrong with a much-improved performance. He is bred to be suited by this sort of trip, but seems very one paced.

**Mossmann Gorge** again showed promise without posing a threat to the principals. Now qualified for a handicap mark, he could improve.

## 5858 RENAULT TRAFIC EBF MAIDEN STKS 1m (R)

**3:40** (3:43) (D3) 2-Y-O **£4,615** (£1,420; £710; £355) **Stalls** Low

Form RPR

32 **1** **Glen Ida**[26] 5264 2-9-0 ........ RMullen 11 90+
(MLWBell) *prom: rdn to ld over 1f out: kpt on wl* **3/1**[2]

64 **2** *3/4* **Tamatave (IRE)**[18] 5467 2-9-0 ........(t) KMcEvoy 3 88+
(SaeedBinSuroor) *led: pushed along over 2f out: hdd over 1f out: rallied: hld towards fin* **5/1**[3]

4342 **3** *5* **Golden Fury**[14] 5567 2-9-0 85 ........ KDarley 2 76
(JLDunlop) *trckd ldrs: rdn 2f out: kpt on same pce* **6/4**[1]

04 **4** *1* **Globe Trekker (USA)**[28] 5227 2-8-9 ........ RFrench 8 68
(JamesMoffatt) *cl up tl rdn and one pce fr 2f out* **12/1**

3 **5** *nk* **Chasm**[20] 5420 2-9-0 ........ RHills 5 72
(MJohnston) *in tch: effrt over 2f out: outpcd over 1f out* **9/1**

**6** *2 1/2* **Blue Bajan (IRE)** 2-9-0 ........ DMernagh 7 66
(AndrewTurnell) *dwlt and checked after 1f: effrt fr rr over 2f out: no imp* **14/1**

**7** *nk* **Vocative (GER)** 2-8-4 ........ RoryMoore(5) 6 60
(PCHaslam) *towards rr: drvn 1/2-way: nvr rchd ldrs* **50/1**

5000 **8** *3* **Artic Fox**[28] 5227 2-9-0 52 ........(b[1]) RWinston 4 58
(TDEasterby) *hld up: rdn over 2f out: hung lft and btn over 1f out* **100/1**

0 **9** *8* **Red Opera**[6] 5756 2-9-0 ........ JMackay 9 38
(SirMarkPrescott) *hld up: rdn over 3f out: sn btn* **25/1**

**10** *1* **Our Wildest Dreams** 2-8-9 ........ TWilliams 12 30
(CWFairhurst) *bhd and sn pushed along: nvr on terms* **100/1**

00 **11** *2 1/2* **Tetra Sing (IRE)**[14] 5559 2-8-9 ........ GFaulkner 1 24
(PCHaslam) *prom tl rdn and wknd over 2f out* **100/1**

**12** *3 1/2* **Sake (IRE)** 2-9-0 ........(t) ACulhane 10 20
(NTinkler) *bhd: rdn over 3f out: sn btn* **100/1**

1m 41.91s (-1.57) **Going Correction** -0.275s/f (Firm) **12 Ran SP% 115.8**
Speed ratings: **96,95,90,89,88 86,86,83,75,74 71,68**CSF £17.59 TOTE £4.30: £1.30, £1.30, £1.40; EX 17.00.
**Owner** Andrew Buxton & B J Warren **Bred** Mrs C L Parker **Trained** Newmarket, Suffolk

**FOCUS**

Not a bad maiden and decent enough efforts from the front two in pulling so far clear, giving the form a sound appearance. The first five home were never far off the pace.

**NOTEBOOK**

**Glen Ida** did not show improved form from his debut when beaten into second at Haydock on his previous start, but there was nothing wrong with this effort and he did just enough to get off the mark at the third attempt. His future looks in the hands of the Handicapper.

**Tamatave(IRE)**, not beaten far into fourth in a modest maiden at Goodwood on his previous start, appeared to improve on that effort in making sure the winner had a proper race and pulling so far clear of the remainder. He should win a maiden this year, but is a nice staying prospect.

**Golden Fury** was not at his best in third and again did very little to justify his current rating.

**Globe Trekker(USA)** benefited from racing up with the pace to finish fourth, but simply lacked a change of pace. This run qualified her for a handicap mark.

**Chasm**, third on his debut in seven-furlong Epsom maiden, did not improve. He may do better when handicapped.

## 5859 RENAULT CLIO H'CAP 1m 3y(S)

**4:10** (4:16) (E3) (0-70,68) 3-Y-O+ **£3,758** (£1,156; £578; £289) **Stalls** Centre

Form RPR

2403 **1** **Newcorp Lad**[16] 5518 4-9-1 59 ........(p) ACulhane 16 76+
(MrsGSRees) *mde all stands side: overall ldr and clr 2f out: unchal* **8/1**[3]

6640 **2** *5* **Intavac Boy**[55] 4489 3-8-9 57 ........ GFaulkner 15 62
(CWThornton) *cl up stands side: rdn over 2f out: kpt on: no ch w wnr* **20/1**

6331 **3** *2 1/2* **Mobane Flyer**[16] 5518 4-9-2 63 ........ THamilton(3) 13 62
(RAFahey) *hld up in tch stands side: rdn over 2f out: kpt on fnl f: no imp* **5/1**[1]

3460 **4** *nk* **Sarraaf (IRE)**[13] 5581 8-9-5 63 ........ VHalliday 19 62
(JSGoldie) *in tch stands side: rdn over 2f out: kpt on same pce* **16/1**

5550 **5** *1 1/2* **Apache Point (IRE)**[14] 5557 7-8-7 51 ........ KimTinkler 4 46
(NTinkler) *prom far side: rdn to ld that gp ins fnl f: no ch w stands side* **20/1**

3352 **6** *hd* **The Number**[18] 5478 3-9-2 64 ........ ANicholls 3 59
(ISemple) *midfield far side: rdn over 2f out: kpt on fnl f: no imp* **16/1**

55-6 **7** *shd* **Beacon Blue (IRE)**[112] 2774 3-9-1 63 ........ KDarley 6 57
(MJohnston) *wl bhd far side tl hdwy over 1f out: nvr rchd ldrs* **20/1**

-002 **8** *1* **Bond Millennium**[16] 5518 6-9-4 62 ........ FLynch 1 54
(BSmart) *bhd far side: hdwy over 1f out: nrst fin* **6/1**[2]

5000 **9** *1/2* **Dark Day Blues (IRE)**[8] 5715 3-8-11 59 ........ MTebbutt 20 50
(MDHammond) *hld up stands side: rdn over 2f out: nt pce to chal* **50/1**

1222 **10** *1/2* **Pepper Road**[20] 5411 5-8-10 54 ........(p) RFrench 7 44
(RBastiman) *cl up far side: led that gp 2f out to ins fnl f: sn btn* **5/1**[1]

5523 **11** *2 1/2* **Hula Ballew**[15] 5544 4-9-4 62 ........(p) SWKelly 17 46
(MDods) *swtchd to far side after 1f: hld up midfield: rdn over 2f out: sn n.d* **12/1**

5002 **12** *3/4* **Showtime Annie**[13] 5582 3-9-6 68 ........ RWinston 5 50
(ABailey) *in tch far side tl outpcd fr 2f out* **12/1**

0400 **13** *2* **Aragon's Boy**[22] 5364 4-9-7 65 ........ DAllan 10 43
(TDEasterby) *cl up far side tl wknd over 1f out* **14/1**

0000 **14** *1 3/4* **Ace Coming**[43] 4826 3-9-1 63 ........(b) JMackay 11 37
(DEddy) *dwlt: bhd far side: nvr on terms* **33/1**

3050 **15** *1/2* **Joshua's Gold (IRE)**[8] 5715 3-8-4 57 ........(v) DTudhope(5) 8 30
(DCarroll) *led far side to 2f out: sn btn* **16/1**

4044 **16** *3/4* **Lord Baskerville**[23] 5346 3-7-13 52 ........ RoryMoore(5) 14 23
(WStorey) *prom stands side tl rdn and wknd over 2f out* **20/1**

030 **17** *4* **Washbrook**[22] 5364 3-8-9 57 ........ JCarroll 2 19
(AndrewTurnell) *towards rr far side: rdn over 3f out: nvr on terms* **33/1**

1m 38.96s (-2.24) **Going Correction** -0.40s/f (Firm)
**WFA** 3 from 4yo+ 4lb **17 Ran SP% 125.3**
Speed ratings: **95,90,87,87,85 85,85,84,83,83 80,80,78,76,75 75,71**CSF £165.72 CT £898.80 TOTE £10.30: £2.20, £4.70, £2.70, £3.80; EX 333.80.
**Owner** Red Rose Partnership **Bred** Mrs P P Dunn **Trained** Sollom, Lancs

**FOCUS**

An ordinary handicap and a modest winning time for the class, although the winner was returning to last year's form.

**NOTEBOOK**

**Newcorp Lad**, sporting first-time cheekpieces, absolutely ran away with this. The draw looked to play a part in his procession, however he did readily outpoint his nearside rivals very early in the contest. He has a history of not running two races alike so whether he will show this form next time is questionable. The victory did not seem totally unexpected though, as he was well backed prior to the race.

**Intavac Boy**, who was stepping up in trip by two furlongs, would have won this nicely had the winner not turned up. He is still open to improvement, as he is only three and has had only five races so far. He should pick up a maiden if not a handicap before the end of the season.

**Mobane Flyer** had beaten the winner last time out, but on these revised terms could not get within hailing distance of him. He ran his race but may be a busy September caught up with him on this occasion.

**Sarraaf(IRE)**, returning to handicaps from claimers, ran a fair race on the favoured side. He basically finds it very difficult to get his head in front despite his consistency.

**Apache Point(IRE)**, who was the first to finish on the far side, never had an earthly chance of winning the race given the draw bias on the day, but won the private battle on his flank. He is steadily dropping down the handicap and, although fairly consistent, does find it difficult to get his head in front.

**The Number** ran a fair race on the wrong side. He made late headway to finish close up to the winner on the far side and looks to be form. Given an level playing field next time, he can be competitive off this handicap mark.

**Beacon Blue(IRE)**, who was dropping down four furlongs from her last start, was well behind until making some late headway. It appears connections are still trying to find her best trip and it would not be surprising to see her next run over ten furlongs on this evidence.

**Bond Millennium** never had any chance of winning on his side, but ran his race all the same. Held up at the back on his side, he came through the field late on to finish on the heels of those horses. He appears to be in good form still.

**Pepper Road** was always up with the pace on the far side, but faded at the business end of the race.

**Hula Ballew** made the wrong decision from the stalls. He had what ended up a perfect draw only to switch to the far side and ruin any chance he had. This run can be safely forgotten for future purposes.

**Washbrook** *Official explanation: jockey said gelding had a breathing problem*

## 5860 RENAULT VANS H.B.L.B. H'CAP 2m 19y

**4:40** (4:41) (E3) (0-70,69) 3-Y-O **£3,480** (£1,070; £535; £267) **Stalls** Centre

Form RPR

5231 **1** **Princess Kiotto**[72] 3984 3-9-3 62 ........ DAllan 11 72+
(TDEasterby) *hld up midfield: hdwy to ld 2f out: drvn out* **3/1**[1]

0010 **2** *1* **Restart (IRE)**[27] 5243 3-8-13 58 ........ GFaulkner 4 67
(PCHaslam) *in tch: hdwy and ev ch over 1f out: kpt on: hld towards fin* **20/1**

2654 **3** 3½ **Vicario**[29] 5214 3-9-1 **60**........................ RMullen 12 65
(MLWBell) *chsd ldrs: effrt and ev ch 2f out: sn rdn and one pce* **10/1**
4010 **4** nk **Oktis Morilious (IRE)**[14] 5571 3-8-7 **55**........................ RThomas(3) 8 60
(CRDore) *hld up: hdwy over 2f out: kpt on fnl f: no imp* **25/1**
1520 **5** 3 **Let It Be**[15] 5546 3-8-10 **55** oh4........................ ACulhane 13 56
(KGReveley) *hld up: rdn and swtchd over 2f out: nrst fin* **12/1**
2521 **6** 2½ **Spring Breeze**[11] 5638 3-8-10 **60**........................(v) DTudhope(5) 9 58
(MDods) *cl up: led over 3f to 2f out: sn outpcd* **7/2**[2]
5446 **7** 1 **Quickstyx**[14] 5560 3-9-8 **67**........................ KMcEvoy 7 64
(MRChannon) *chsd ldrs: effrt and ch 2f out: sn rdn and outpcd* **8/1**
0451 **8** 14 **Habitual (IRE)**[11] 5645 3-9-1 **60**........................ JMackay 10 40
(SirMarkPrescott) *in tch: drvn 4f out: outpcd fr 3f out* **9/2**[3]
0025 **9** 2½ **Siegfrieds Night (IRE)**[22] 5365 3-9-2 **64**........................ J-PGuillambert(3) 1 41
(MCChapman) *hld up: rdn 4f out: btn over 2f out* **25/1**
5433 **10** 3 **Kyber**[47] 4703 3-9-0 **62**........................ DNolan(3) 5 35
(RFFisher) *hld up: rdn over 3f out: nvr on terms* **33/1**
5000 **11** 9 **Lucky Piscean**[32] 5110 3-8-10 **55** oh3........................ RFfrench 3 18
(CWFairhurst) *bhd: lost tch fr 1/2-way* **100/1**
0000 **12** 28 **Grande Terre (IRE)**[15] 5546 3-8-10 **55** oh5........................ RWinston 2 —
(JGGiven) *a bhd* **66/1**
3552 **13** 1¾ **Sunday City (JPN)**[23] 5340 3-9-10 **69**........................ KDarley 6 —
(DRLoder) *led to over 3f out: sn btn and eased* **11/1**

3m 30.01s (-5.02) **Going Correction** -0.275s/f (Firm) **13** Ran SP% **119.5**
Speed ratings: **101,100,98,98,97 95,95,88,87,85 81,67,66**CSF £71.18 CT £547.53 TOTE £4.40: £1.70, £5.90, £3.10; EX 105.90.
**Owner** Roy Matthews **Bred** R Matthews **Trained** Great Habton, N Yorks

**FOCUS**
A low-grade staying event, where the leaders appeared to set a decent early pace and the form looks sound.

**NOTEBOOK**
**Princess Kiotto** ◆ is lucky to be racing at all after suffering a near fatal injury last-time-out. She enjoyed being settled behind a good early pace and came to win her race two furlongs out. She is definitely going the right way and should progress from this.
**Restart(IRE)** ◆, having his first try at two miles, looked to appreciate this step up in trip. Always travelling powerfully in midfield, he came to win his race only to find the winner a touch too strong. Off this mark he should have little problem picking up a modest staying event somewhere soon.
**Vicario** was always close to the pace and stayed on fairly well to the line. He looks as though this is about his grade and can go close in a similar event next time.
**Oktis Morilious(IRE)** was stepping up in trip by fully four furlongs further than he had ever raced at before. He made up a lot of late headway and, if he could sit closer to the pace, a similar event event could be won with him.
**Let It Be** was well behind until making headway up the straight. This was her first attempt at two miles and from out of the handicap, and she looks the sort who could do with a stiff track whereever she races.
**Spring Breeze** probably paid the price for sitting close to a good early pace. Given he was a wide-margin winner last time, this was a slightly disappointing effort. He may want an uncontested lead to be at his most effective.
**Quickstyx** sat close to the early pace and was not overly perservered with when her chance was gone. This was her first attempt at two miles and she did not seem to stay, but she is probably high enough in the weights for what she has achieved.
**Habitual(IRE)** hacked up in banded company last time, but ran more in keeping with his previous efforts in this better grade. Perhaps a return to Lingfield's All-Weather may bring about some improvement again.
**Sunday City(JPN)** made much of the running at a decent early pace, but found nothing on entering the straight. *Official explanation: jockey said colt lost his action*

## 5861 EUROPEAN BREEDERS FUND RENAULT MASTER CLASSIFIED STKS 7f
**5:10** (5:11) (D3) 3-Y-0+ **£5,551** (£1,708; £854; £427) **Stalls** Centre

Form RPR
64 **1** **Pintle**[19] 5444 4-9-0 73........................ KMcEvoy 10 83+
(JLSpearing) *led 3f: cl up tl led again over 2f out: rdn clr wl over 1f out: kpt on* **2/1**[1]
2035 **2** 2½ **Reidies Choice**[11] 5656 3-9-0 73........................ JMackay 9 78
(JGGiven) *dwlt and bhd: gd hdwy on inner 2f out: rdn to chse wnr ent last: kpt on* **8/1**
2045 **3** 2½ **In The Pink (IRE)**[12] 5614 4-8-12 71........................ ACulhane 4 67
(MRChannon) *towards rr: hdwy over 2f out: sn rdn and kpt on same pce* **4/1**[2]
050 **4** ¾ **Zoom Zoom**[12] 5603 4-8-12 71........................ J-PGuillambert(3) 3 67
(MrsLStubbs) *prom on outer: effrt over 2f out: sn rdn and kpt on same pce* **16/1**
3004 **5** 1¾ **Bandos**[11] 5631 4-9-3 73........................(t) DAllan 8 65
(ISemple) *cl up: led after 3f: rdn along and hdd over 2f out: sn drvn and wknd* **10/1**
5130 **6** 2½ **Menai Straights**[75] 3895 3-8-10 65 ow2........................ DNolan(3) 6 57
(RFFisher) *a towards rr* **100/1**
0210 **7** 1¼ **Growler**[7] 5737 3-8-11 70........................(v) KDarley 7 52
(JLDunlop) *chsd ldrs: rdn along wl over 2f out: sn wknd* **8/1**
0410 **8** hd **Borrego (IRE)**[9] 5698 4-9-5 75........................(b) RHills 1 56
(CEBrittain) *hld up in tch: rr: effrt and pushed along wl over 2f out: nvr a factor* **13/2**[3]
1006 **9** 1½ **Acomb**[53] 4543 4-9-5 75........................ DaleGibson 5 52
(MWEasterby) *chsd ldrs: rdn along 3f out: sn wknd* **14/1**
2400 **10** 21 **Red Sahara (IRE)**[14] 5574 3-8-13 75........................(b[1]) SWKelly 2 —
(WJHaggas) *chsd ldrs: rdn along 3f out: sn wknd* **11/1**

1m 24.78s (-3.24) **Going Correction** -0.40s/f (Firm)
**WFA** 3 from 4yo 3lb **10** Ran SP% **119.9**
Speed ratings: **102,99,96,95,93 90,89,88,87,63**CSF £19.57 TOTE £3.30: £1.40, £1.90, £1.80; EX 15.80.
**Owner** Robert Heathcote **Bred** R And Mrs Heathcote **Trained** Kinnersley, Worcs
■ Stewards Enquiry : K McEvoy one-day ban: failed to keep straight from stalls (Oct 10)

**FOCUS**
This fair handicap was run in a decent time with Pintle winning with plenty in hand, but the form is ordinary for the grade.

**NOTEBOOK**
**Pintle** had this won from a long way out. Pintle and McEvoy clearly get on really well and, as long as the Handicapper does not overly punish her for this, which he may do given the ease of victory, she is capable of winning again.
**Reidies Choice** was well backed in the run up to the race and ran a strange race. He was behind for the majority of the race before scything through the field to get closest to the easy winner. He has not won since his debut, but this is probably his best run for a while and he may be best on straight courses.
**In The Pink(IRE)** was held up off the pace, as is usual for her, and came with her customary late run. She was never going to get to the winner but, ran as well as she has been doing recently. A bigger field and strong pace may suit her for the future, even though she has won in relatively small fields.
**Zoom Zoom** was always close to the pace, but did not go on from his position. He looked a bit unenthusiastic, but this may have been due to quicker ground than he likes.
**Bandos** raced close to the pace, but was readily left behind when the winner went clear. He is close to a winning mark however.
**Menai Straights** got well behind early and ran on close home.
**Growler** fell out of the stalls and was always being niggled along. This was a disappointing effort on recent form, with no real excuse apart from being a lot higher in the handicap than when winning at Goodwood. *Official explanation: jockey said gelding was unsuited by good to firm ground*
**Borrego(IRE)** ran no race at all with no explanation put forward.

## 5862 RENAULT KANGOO H'CAP 5f
**5:40** (5:40) (E3) (0-70,69) 3-Y-0+ **£4,011** (£1,234; £617; £308) **Stalls** Centre

Form RPR
5013 **1** **Playful Dane (IRE)**[27] 5242 7-9-1 **68**........................ DTudhope(5) 8 86
(WSCunningham) *cl up: led 2f out: rdn clr appr last: comf* **4/1**[1]
5050 **2** 2½ **Abelard (IRE)**[14] 5562 3-8-4 **56**........................(v[1]) THamilton(3) 14 64
(RAFahey) *dwlt and towards rr: hdwy 2f out:rdn and styd on fnl f* **14/1**
5001 **3** 1 **Blue Maeve**[6] 5754 4-9-2 **64** 6ex........................ SRighton 10 68
(JHetherton) *led: rdn along and hdd 2f out: sn drvn and kpt on same pce* **13/2**[3]
3204 **4** 2½ **Ballybunion (IRE)**[6] 5754 5-8-7 **55**........................ ANicholls 2 49
(DNicholls) *chsd ldrs: effrt 2f out: sn rdn and kpt on same pce appr last* **5/1**[2]
0062 **5** nk **Vigorous (IRE)**[4] 5798 4-8-8 **63**........................ AMullen(7) 6 56
(MTodhunter) *swtchd rt s and sn rdn along in rr: hdwy wl over 1f out: styd on ins last: nrst fin* **13/2**[3]
5300 **6** ¾ **College Maid (IRE)**[13] 5579 7-8-1 **56**........................(b) JCurrie(7) 13 46
(JSGoldie) *bhd tl styd on appr last: nrst fin* **25/1**
330 **7** hd **Lady Protector**[42] 4854 5-8-9 **57**........................ DaleGibson 12 46
(JBalding) *cl up: rdn along 2f out: drvn and wknd over 1f out* **12/1**
0250 **8** 1½ **Roan Raider (USA)**[6] 5754 4-8-9 **57**........................(v) MTebbutt 11 40
(MissVHaigh) *chsd ldrs: rdn along 2f out: grad wknd* **33/1**
2000 **9** nk **Mind Alert**[10] 5674 3-9-1 **64**........................(b) DAllan 15 46
(TDEasterby) *chsd ldrs: rdn along over 2f out: sn wknd* **33/1**
4600 **10** ½ **Consensus (IRE)**[13] 5588 5-9-7 **69**........................ TWilliams 3 49
(MBrittain) *racd alone far side: prom tl rdn 2f out and grad wknd* **14/1**
6003 **11** shd **Favour**[13] 5588 4-9-5 **67**........................ RWinston 7 46
(MrsJRRamsden) *midfield: rdn along over 2f out: sn btn and eased* **9/1**
1061 **12** 1¼ **Bettys Pride**[7] 5736 5-8-11 **59** 6ex........................ SWKelly 9 33
(MDods) *dwlt and towards rr: hdwy 1/2-way: sn rdn and wknd* **7/1**
4400 **13** 1¼ **Fayrz Please (IRE)**[187] 1111 3-8-6 **55**........................ JoannaBadger 4 24
(MCChapman) *chsd ldrs: rdn along 1/2-way: sn wknd* **100/1**
0000 **14** 4 **Perfect Love**[24] 5316 4-9-0 **62**........................ LEnstone 5 15
(EJAlston) *a rr* **100/1**
0-00 **15** 17 **Self Belief**[23] 5342 3-8-10 **62**........................ J-PGuillambert(3) 1 —
(MCChapman) *s.i.s: a rr* **100/1**

59.02 secs (-2.51) **Going Correction** -0.40s/f (Firm)
**WFA** 3 from 4yo+ 1lb **15** Ran SP% **120.7**
Speed ratings: **104,100,98,94,93 92,92,90,89,88 88,86,84,78,50**CSF £59.45 CT £371.53 TOTE £5.20: £1.70, £6.10, £2.60; EX 92.80 Place 6 £85.47, Place 5 £13.68.
**Owner** Ann And David Bell **Bred** Omicida Syndicate **Trained** Hutton Rudby, N Yorks

**FOCUS**
An ordinary handicap and a race where the true five-furlong horses seemed to hold sway. The third and fourth came into the race in good form and give a good indicator of the level.

**NOTEBOOK**
**Playful Dane(IRE)** had a an good draw for a horse that likes to race up with the pace, and made full use of it. He won this with something in hand and looks to be improving at the age of seven.
**Abelard(IRE)** returned to something like his juvenile form in the first-time visor. He can find a low-grade sprint somewhere off this mark, as long as the visor has a similar effect next time. A stiffer track may suit him better as well.
**Blue Maeve** showed some good early pace and only lost second place to close home. He looks to be in good form at this time and a return to a sharp five furlongs can see him go close again.
**Ballybunion(IRE)** did not have the best of draws so was forced to come up the centre of the track. He finished well and is probably better over another furlong.
**Vigorous(IRE)** did not get into the race until too late after being switched early. He stays further than this five and might find things easier if stepped back up to six furlongs next time.
**College Maid(IRE)** got behind early on, but finished fairly well up the favoured side. She generally needs further nowadays and finds it difficult to win.
**Consensus(IRE)** was manoeuvred to the far rail, which had been a big disadvantage all day, and never had a chance of being involved.
**Favour** did not improve from her last run, which was after a break.The drop down in trip probably did not help either as she stays six furlongs very well.
**Bettys Pride**, who was raised back up in grade after winning at Lingfield, found this task a lot tougher. She seems suited by racing at a slightly lower level.
T/Plt: £156.60 to a £1 stake. Pool: £34,851.15. 162.40 winning tickets. T/Qpdt: £6.10 to a £1 stake. Pool: £3,146.10. 380.80 winning tickets. RY

# 5846 NOTTINGHAM (L-H)
## Wednesday, September 29

**OFFICIAL GOING: Good to firm**
After a dry night the ground was altered to Good To Firm.
Wind: Almost nil Weather: Cloudy

## 5863 IBETX.COM - LIFE IS A GAMBLE APPRENTICE (S) H'CAP 1m 1f 213y
**2:20** (2:38) (G4) (0-55,53) 3-Y-0 **£2,666** (£761; £380) **Stalls** Low

Form RPR
0240 **1** **Fizzy Lady**[4] 5791 3-8-6 **50**........................ ThomasYeung(5) 13 57
(NEBerry) *hld up: hdwy and hung lft over 2f out: styd on to ld wl ins fnl f* **8/1**[3]
0060 **2** ½ **Smart Boy Prince (IRE)**[7] 5733 3-8-9 **53**........................ WHogg(5) 10 59
(MJAttwater) *led: rdn over 1f out: hdd wl ins fnl f* **25/1**
0105 **3** 1 **Mister Completely (IRE)**[4] 5791 3-8-8 **47**........................ LPKeniry 8 51
(JRBest) *chsd ldrs: rdn over 1f out: ev ch ins fnl f: no ex nr fin* **9/2**[2]
6222 **4** hd **Zuleta**[11] 5634 3-8-5 **47**........................(v[1]) BSwarbrick(3) 9 51
(JGMO'Shea) *prom: rdn 1/2-way: hung lft over 2f out: styd on nr fin* **4/1**[1]
4004 **5** 3 **Valiant Air (IRE)**[7] 3371 3-8-5 **44** oh4........................(b) PMulrennan 16 42
(JRWeymes) *hld up: styd on appr fnl f: nvr nrr* **14/1**
0065 **6** nk **Acca Larentia (IRE)**[16] 5524 3-8-6 **45**........................ LisaJones 15 42
(RMWhitaker) *hld up: hdwy and hung lft over 1f out: nvr nrr* **14/1**
0000 **7** 1 **Myannabanana (IRE)**[11] 5634 3-8-0 **44** oh4........................(v) DFentiman(5) 6 44+
(JRWeymes) *hld up: hdwy over 3f out: styng on same pce whn hmpd over 1f out* **28/1**

0000 **8** *2* **Named At Dinner**[9] 5702 3-8-11 **50**..........(v[1]) ABeech 5 42
(MrsADuffield) *chsd ldrs: rdn over 2f out: wkng whn hung lft over 1f out* **20/1**

6065 **9** *1* **Larad (IRE)**[6] 5750 3-8-0 **46**..........(b) LauraReynolds(7) 2 36
(JSMoore) *s.i.s: bhd: styd on ins fnl f: nvr nrr* **8/1**[3]

0550 **10** *nk* **Bulberry Hill**[9] 5702 3-8-6 **45**.......... DCorby 1 34
(MGQuinlan) *hld up: effrt over 2f out: n.d* **10/1**

0000 **11** *hd* **Lord Greystoke (IRE)**[11] 5654 3-8-1 **45**..........(b[1]) PPMathers(5) 11 34
(CPMorlock) *chsd ldrs: hung lft over 2f out: sn wknd* **66/1**

5640 **12** *7* **Grele (USA)**[18] 5451 3-8-1 **45**.......... StephanieHollinshead(5) 12 21
(RHollinshead) *hld up: effrt over 3f out: wknd over 2f out* **10/1**

0000 **13** *6* **Reign Of Fire (IRE)**[13] 5585 3-8-4 **48**..........(v[1]) DerekNolan(5) 14 12
(JWHills) *hld up: a in rr* **33/1**

6000 **14** *nk* **Livia (IRE)**[10] 3193 3-8-6 **45**..........(v[1]) FPFerris 7 9
(JGPortman) *chsd ldrs over 6f* **40/1**

6250 **15** *8* **Buchanan Street (IRE)**[41] 4867 3-8-6 **45**..........(bt) TEaves 4 —
(JGMO'Shea) *s.i.s: a in rr* **20/1**

0006 **16** *1* **Prince Renesis**[36] 5018 3-8-6 **48**.......... PMakin(3) 3 —
(IWMcinnes) *hld up: a in rr* **66/1**

2m 9.34s (-0.16) **Going Correction** -0.175s/f (Firm) **16** Ran SP% **117.1**
Speed ratings: **93,92,91,91,89 89,88,86,85,85 85,79,75,74,68** CSF £197.43 CT £1008.59 TOTE £9.80: £2.40, £7.50, £1.80, £1.10; EX 227.70.There was no bid for the winner.
**Owner** Leeway Group Limited **Bred** Baydon House Stud **Trained** Earlswood, Monmouths
■ The first winner in Britain for Hong Kong-born apprentice Thomas Yeung.

**FOCUS**
A poor handicap with nine of the 15 runners wearing some form of headgear, there were plenty of dodgy performers on show. Although the form looks reasonable it is very limited for the grade.

**NOTEBOOK**
**Fizzy Lady**, who resented the tongue-tie last time, was much happier without it, although she did not look the easiest of rides for an apprentice.
**Smart Boy Prince(IRE)** turned in a solid-enough effort and proved very brave, but he is much happier on the Fibresand.
**Mister Completely(IRE)** has been running well enough recently, for one of his ability, and he had his chance.
**Zuleta** looks something of a monkey, even allowing for the trip being on the sharp side for her.
**Valiant Air(IRE)**, pulled up in a couple of recent outings over timber, looked to find this trip too sharp.
**Acca Larentia(IRE)** does not do anything quickly and may be worth a try over further.
**Buchanan Street(IRE)** *Official explanation: jockey said colt spread a plate and had breathing problems*

## 5864 CITY LIFE MAGAZINE FILLIES' NOVICE AUCTION STKS 6f 15y
**2:50** (3:07) (F3) 2-Y-O **£3,718** (£1,144; £572; £286) **Stalls** High

Form RPR

2130 **1** **Rockburst**[41] 4890 2-8-10 75.......... DarrenWilliams 8 93+
(KRBurke) *chsd ldrs: led over 3f out: rdn over 1f out: r.o: eased nr fin* **10/1**

23 **2** *1 ½* **Sam's Secret**[13] 5586 2-8-6 .......... FNorton 2 85
(JAGlover) *s.i.s: hdwy over 2f out: chsd wnr and hung lft over 1f out: styd on* **9/2**[3]

145 **3** *5* **Encanto (IRE)**[51] 4612 2-8-12 82.......... JFEgan 11 76
(JSMoore) *chsd ldrs: rdn and hung lft over 2f out: styd on same pce appr fnl f* **9/2**[3]

400 **4** *2 ½* **Heartsonfire (IRE)**[22] 5373 2-8-2 67.......... JQuinn 5 58
(PWD'Arcy) *prom: chsd wnr 1/2-way tl wknd over 1f out* **20/1**

221 **5** *1 ¼* **Amica**[21] 5400 2-8-10 82.......... SSanders 7 62
(GLMoore) *chsd ldrs over 3f* **15/8**[1]

0 **6** *2 ½* **Tanzanite (IRE)**[47] 4712 2-8-4 .......... WSupple 4 49
(DWPArbuthnot) *chsd ldrs 4f* **66/1**

6100 **7** *7* **Spree (IRE)**[64] 4217 2-9-0 92.......... RHughes 9 38
(RHannon) *led: hdd over 3f out: sn rdn and wknd* **7/2**[2]

64 **8** *hd* **Danethorpe Lady (IRE)**[14] 5555 2-8-4 .......... LisaJones 10 27
(DShaw) *prom over 3f* **150/1**

6000 **9** *3* **Dancing Moonlight (IRE)**[60] 4334 2-8-1 35.......... BSwarbrick(5) 1 20
(MrsNMacauley) *sn outpcd* **250/1**

**10** *25* **Small Time Blues (IRE)** 2-8-4 .......... RFitzpatrick 6 —
(MJPolglase) *dwlt: outpcd* **100/1**

1m 13.89s (-0.91) **Going Correction** -0.175s/f (Firm) **10** Ran SP% **110.8**
Speed ratings: **99,97,90,87,85 82,72,72,68,35** CSF £50.76 TOTE £21.80: £2.80, £1.30, £1.70; EX 58.60.
**Owner** Mrs Sally L Jones **Bred** J A And Mrs Duffy **Trained** Middleham Moor, N Yorks

**FOCUS**
With the market leaders failing to perform, this may not have taken as much winning as it should have. However, the winner won with something in hand and could well be on the upgrade. The winning time was decent for a race of its type and the form appears very decent for the grade.

**NOTEBOOK**
**Rockburst**, back on her favoured fast surface having been found out by the slow ground at York, fairly sluiced up. The ground is clearly the key to her, and while conditions remain on the fast side she looks capable of adding to this.
**Sam's Secret** soon made her way across to the stands' side rail and was the only one to try and make a race of it in the final 250 yards. Although well held, there was no disgrace in this and an ordinary maiden should come her way.
**Encanto(IRE)** was much more settled at the start this time, although she looked to run a little flat in the race itself and may have had enough for the time being.
**Heartsonfire(IRE)** is struggling to find a trip that suits.
**Amica** was very disappointing having been off the bridle at halfway.
**Spree(IRE)** ran no sort of race and clearly has plenty to prove now. *Official explanation: jockey said filly had no more to give*

## 5865 EUROPEAN BREEDERS FUND MAIDEN STKS 5f 13y
**3:20** (3:32) (D2) 2-Y-O **£5,973** (£1,838; £919; £459) **Stalls** High

Form RPR

**1** **Rock Dove (IRE)** 2-8-9 .......... SSanders 9 75+
(SirMarkPrescott) *s.i.s: sn chsng ldrs: rdn over 1f out: r.o to ld post* **11/4**[1]

524 **2** *shd* **Disguise**[16] 5507 2-9-0 78..........(t) RHughes 12 77
(BWHills) *w ldrs: led and edgd lft 2f out: sn rdn: hdd post* **11/4**[1]

0 **3** *1 ½* **Vague Star (ITY)**[23] 5353 2-9-0 .......... NDay 1 72
(RIngram) *chsd ldrs: rdn and ev ch over 1f out: no ex towards fin* **66/1**

5 **4** *¾* **Malaika**[29] 5213 2-8-4 .......... StephanieHollinshead(5) 5 64
(RHollinshead) *trckd ldrs: rdn over 1f out: no ex ins fnl f* **20/1**

00 **5** *¾* **Little Warning**[23] 5334 2-8-9 .......... JQuinn 16 62
(RMBeckett) *hld up: rdn and edgd lft over 1f out: styd on ins fnl f: nrst fin* **25/1**

000 **6** *½* **Mercari**[16] 5521 2-8-6 .......... TEaves(3) 4 60
(GMMoore) *chsd ldrs: rdn over 1f out: styd on same pce* **50/1**

3254 **7** *1* **Peeptoe (IRE)**[17] 5490 2-8-9 72.......... LDettori 7 56
(JLDunlop) *chsd ldrs: rdn 1/2-way: wknd fnl f* **3/1**[2]

00 **8** *1* **Italian Touch (IRE)**[12] 5616 2-9-0 .......... FNorton 8 58
(JAGlover) *prom: lost pl over 3f out: styd on ins fnl f* **50/1**

00 **9** *shd* **Distinctive Mind**[14] 5558 2-9-0 .......... JFEgan 14 57
(TDEasterby) *s.s: hdwy over 1f out: n.d* **66/1**

0 **10** *nk* **Leighton Buzzard**[12] 5616 2-8-9 .......... ThomasYeung(5) 17 56
(PWChapple-Hyam) *outpcd: r.o ins fnl f: nvr nrr* **14/1**[3]

0 **11** *2 ½* **Elms Schoolboy**[19] 5441 2-9-0 .......... JTate 3 48
(JMPEustace) *mid-div: rdn 1/2-way: sn lost pl* **66/1**

63 **12** *½* **Anfield Dream**[89] 3491 2-9-0 .......... WRyan 15 46
(JRJenkins) *prom to 1/2-way* **14/1**[3]

00 **13** *½* **Katie Killane**[63] 4243 2-8-9 .......... VSlattery 2 39
(MWellings) *led: hung lft: hdd & wknd over 1f out* **100/1**

**14** *2* **Crux** 2-8-11 .......... PMulrennan(3) 11 37
(CWThornton) *s.s: outpcd* **25/1**

**15** *6* **Waterfront Dancer** 2-9-0 .......... WSupple 6 16
(JRBest) *s.i.s: outpcd* **20/1**

60.66 secs (-1.14) **Going Correction** -0.175s/f (Firm) **15** Ran SP% **118.3**
Speed ratings: **102,101,99,98,97 96,94,93,92,92 88,87,86,83,74** CSF £8.99 TOTE £3.90: £2.00, £1.50, £7.20; EX 18.50.
**Owner** Sir Edmund Loder **Bred** Sir E J Loder **Trained** Newmarket, Suffolk

**FOCUS**
A fair maiden and the runner-up set a fair standard, but the proximity of the third casts a doubt over the form.

**NOTEBOOK**
**Rock Dove(IRE)**, who is from the same family as champion sprinter Marwell, did what was required. She is sure to have learnt from the experience, and is almost certain to go on to better things.
**Disguise**, tackling his fastest surface to date, did nothing wrong and was only just denied. The first time tongue-tie clearly suited and, although he has been shown up in ordinary maidens, he does have a little race in him.
**Vague Star(ITY)**, a half-brother to five winners, found plenty of improvement from his debut. If this effort can be believed, he should be able to find a small race somewhere.
**Malaika** travelled really well on the heels of the leaders until getting a little unbalanced in the closing stages. From a prolific winning family, she looks sure to pay her way in time.
**Little Warning** shaped as though she would appreciate an extra furlong, although, she did not look that happy on the surface. *Official explanation: jockey said filly lost her action 1 1/2f out*
**Peeptoe(IRE)** again failed to deliver and has become disappointing.

## 5866 ERIC POTTER CLARKSON H'CAP 1m 1f 213y
**3:50** (3:56) (D2) (0-85,89) 3-Y-O+ **£12,125** (£3,730; £1,865; £932) **Stalls** Low

Form RPR

-605 **1** **Honorine (IRE)**[26] 5275 4-8-13 **75**.......... JFEgan 9 86
(JWPayne) *hld up: hdwy over 2f out: rdn and hung lft fr over 1f out: styd on u.p to ld wl ins fnl f* **33/1**

001 **2** *1* **One So Marvellous**[22] 5371 3-8-7 **75**.......... OUrbina 2 84
(LMCumani) *chsd ldrs: rdn over 2f out: led 1f out: hdd wl ins fnl f* **8/1**[2]

3511 **3** *nk* **Straw Bear (USA)**[5] 5768 3-9-7 **89** 6ex.......... SSanders 4 97
(SirMarkPrescott) *chsd ldr tl led over 2f out: rdn and hdd 1f out: styng on same pce whn n.m.r towards fin* **4/6**[1]

3100 **4** *1 ¼* **Nunki (USA)**[21] 5401 3-9-3 **85**..........(v[1]) WRyan 13 91?
(HRACecil) *led over 7f: styng on same pce whn hmpd towards fin* **33/1**

5204 **5** *1 ½* **Ryan's Future (IRE)**[20] 5423 4-8-13 **75**.......... LDettori 16 78
(JAkehurst) *hld up: hdwy 6f out: rdn over 2f out: styd on same pce appr fnl f* **8/1**[2]

301 **6** *½* **Clipperdown (IRE)**[56] 4455 3-8-6 **74**.......... NCallan 5 76
(PWHarris) *chsd ldrs: rdn over 2f out: styd on same pce appr fnl f* **16/1**

0604 **7** *shd* **Doctored**[7] 5739 3-8-4 **75**..........(b) FPFerris(3) 1 77
(PDEvans) *chsd ldrs: hrd rdn over 2f out: styd on same pce appr fnl f* **25/1**

0156 **8** *½* **Realism (FR)**[20] 5423 4-9-6 **82**.......... DarrenWilliams 11 83
(PWHiatt) *hld up in tch: plld hrd: outpcd over 2f out: styd on ins fnl f* **33/1**

2-00 **9** *½* **Star Of Normandie (USA)**[242] 649 5-9-3 **79**.......... AMcCarthy 10 79
(GGMargarson) *hld up: effrt over 2f out: nvr trbld ldrs* **100/1**

4-05 **10** *1 ¾* **Don't Sioux Me (IRE)**[80] 3590 6-9-4 **80**.......... LisaJones 7 77
(CRDore) *s.i.s: hld up: n.d* **100/1**

1300 **11** *shd* **Olivia Rose (IRE)**[14] 5573 5-9-7 **83**.......... JQuinn 3 80
(JPearce) *hld up: effrt over 2f out: sn edgd lft and wknd* **33/1**

0605 **12** *3 ½* **Liquid Form (IRE)**[14] 5572 4-8-11 **73**.......... RHughes 12 63
(BHanbury) *prom over 7f* **10/1**[3]

0-00 **13** *nk* **Humid Climate**[13] 5590 4-8-13 **78**.......... TEaves(3) 14 67
(RAFahey) *hld up: a in rr* **50/1**

-005 **14** *4* **Gems Bond**[19] 5444 4-8-4 **73**.......... DerekNolan(7) 6 55
(JSMoore) *slowly in to stride: hld up: hdwy over 3f out: wknd wl over 1f out* **33/1**

**15** *2 ½* **Zalam (IRE)**[28] 5230 4-8-12 **74**.......... PBradley 15 51
(PABlockley) *s.i.s: a bhd* **50/1**

2m 8.13s (-1.37) **Going Correction** -0.175s/f (Firm)
**WFA** 3 from 4yo+ 6lb **15** Ran SP% **121.6**
Speed ratings: **98,97,96,95,94 94,94,93,93,92 92,89,88,85,83** CSF £267.14 CT £439.17 TOTE £36.70: £6.50, £2.20, £1.10; EX 368.60.
**Owner** Mrs R A C Vigors **Bred** Mrs Rebecca Phillips **Trained** Newmarket, Suffolk

**FOCUS**
A decent handicap but a modest winning time for the grade, only just over a second quicker than the seller, suggesting the form is only ordinary for the level.

**NOTEBOOK**
**Honorine(IRE)** proved well suited by this step up in trip, and showed she still has the heart for a battle.
**One So Marvellous** took a while to get the better of Straw Bear, only to get mugged towards the finish. She can find compensation.
**Straw Bear(USA)**, due to go up 8lb shortly, was found out on this faster surface.
**Nunki(USA)**, sharpened up by the first-time visor, had no excuses and this looks as good as he is.
**Ryan's Future(IRE)**, stuck out wide from his draw, did not do too bad in the circumstances. A winner on the Polytrack, he will find other openings.
**Clipperdown(IRE)** may have been better suited by a stronger pace, and is certainly worth another try over this trip.

## 5867 RACING UK ON CHANNEL 432 MAIDEN STKS 1m 1f 213y
**4:20** (4:25) (D3) 3-Y-O+ **£5,063** (£1,558; £779; £389) **Stalls** Low

Form RPR

52 **1** **Barathea Blue**[19] 5445 3-9-0 .......... SSanders 5 73
(PWHarris) *chsd ldrs: led 3f out: rdn and hdd over 1f out: rallied to ld 1f out: styd on u.p* **7/4**[1]

0002 **2** *¾* **Skibereen (IRE)**[14] 5571 4-9-6 57.......... JFEgan 15 72?
(MrsAMThorpe) *hld up: hdwy and hung lft fr over 2f out: styd on reluctantly* **33/1**

-530 **3** *hd* **Zonic Boom (FR)**[11] 5657 4-9-6 61.......... OUrbina 4 71
(JRFanshawe) *chsd ldrs: rdn and ev ch 1f out: styd on* **11/2**[3]

4 **4** *hd* **All Blue (IRE)**[12] 5621 3-9-0 ........ (t) LDettori 12 71
(SaeedBinSuroor) *chsd ldrs: rdn to ld over 1f out: edgd lft and hdd 1f out: nt run on nr fin* **15/8**[2]

4523 **5** *2* **Mouftari (USA)**[39] 4939 3-9-0 80 ........ (b[1]) MHills 1 67
(BWHills) *sn led: hdd 3f out: sn rdn: no ex fnl f* **8/1**

0454 **6** *1 ¾* **My Michelle**[23] 5352 3-8-6 57 ........ FPFerris(3) 6 59
(BPalling) *mid-div: outpcd over 3f out: styd on ins fnl f* **33/1**

**7** *3* **Fender** 3-9-0 ........ (b[1]) RHughes 2 58
(HRACecil) *hdwy over 6f out: rdn 4f out: wknd 2f out* **16/1**

**8** *5* **Cumbrian Knight (IRE)**[152] 6-9-3 ........ TEaves(3) 11 49
(JMJefferson) *s.i.s: hld up: rdn 4f out: sn wknd* **80/1**

00 **9** *½* **Parisi Princess**[11] 5634 3-8-9 ........ JEdmunds 7 43
(GPKelly) *hld up: hdwy 4f out: sn rdn and wknd* **150/1**

0040 **10** *2* **Iftikhar (USA)**[24] 5320 5-9-6 52 ........ NCallan 13 44
(WMBrisbourne) *hld up: rdn over 4f out: n.d* **50/1**

**11** *7* **Pilca (FR)**[143] 4-9-6 ........ LVickers 9 31
(IWMcinnes) *chsd ldrs over 7f* **100/1**

**12** *9* **Rambo Blue** 4-9-6 ........ WSupple 14 14
(AWCarroll) *s.i.s: hld up: wknd over 4f out* **100/1**

0 **13** *dist* **Little Miss Lili**[6] 5749 3-8-9 ........ AMcCarthy 10 —
(GGMargarson) *dwlt: outpcd* **100/1**

2m 9.02s (-0.48) **Going Correction** -0.175s/f (Firm)
**WFA** 3 from 4yo+ 6lb **13** Ran SP% **120.9**
Speed ratings: **94,93,93,93,91 90,87,83,83,81 76,68,**—CSF £68.78 TOTE £3.10: £1.10, £5.70, £2.00; EX 62.30.
**Owner** David & Elaine Long **Bred** Mrs John Trotter **Trained** Ringshall, Bucks

**FOCUS**
This didn't look a great maiden and was steadily run, which produced a moderate winning time for the class of contest, only 0.32 seconds faster than the seller.

**NOTEBOOK**
**Barathea Blue** made really hard work of this, but this trip is obviously the bare minimum for him and he can show improvement when he faces a stiffer test.
**Skibereen(IRE)** is exposed as moderate, which speaks volumes for those who finished behind him.
**Zonic Boom(FR)** stayed this longer trip well enough, but the way it was run hardly put the emphasis on stamina.
**All Blue(IRE)** found very little off the bridle and is clearly one of the yard's lesser lights.
**Mouftari(USA)** continues to disappoint and the first-time blinkers did little for him.
**Parisi Princess** *Official explanation: trainer said filly coughed after race*

## 5868 FASTEST GROWING EXCHANGE IBETX.COM H'CAP 1m 54y
**4:50** (4:51) (E3) (0-70,69) 3-Y-O+ **£4,511** (£1,388; £694; £347) **Stalls** Centre

Form RPR

4260 **1** **Spirit's Awakening**[17] 5496 5-8-6 58 ........ FPFerris(3) 1 68
(JAkehurst) *mde all: rdn over 1f out: styd on gamely* **11/2**[2]

0213 **2** *½* **Dont Call Me Derek**[31] 5156 3-8-12 65 ........ SSanders 10 74
(SCWilliams) *hld up: rdn 1/2-way: hdwy over 1f out: edgd lft: r.o* **9/2**[1]

0065 **3** *nk* **Gay Romance**[30] 5197 3-8-9 62 ........ MHills 2 70
(BWHills) *chsd ldrs: rdn and ev ch fr over 1f out: unable qck towards fin* **18/1**

5100 **4** *3 ½* **Little Englander**[17] 5496 4-8-5 57 ........ LPKeniry(3) 6 57+
(HCandy) *hld up: nt clr run over 3f out: hdwy over 1f out: r.o* **16/1**

0401 **5** *hd* **Zafarshah (IRE)**[26] 5259 5-8-10 64 ........ BSwarbrick(5) 12 64
(PDEvans) *hld up: rdn over 3f out: r.o ins fnl f: nt rch ldrs* **22/1**

2321 **6** *shd* **Fascination Street (IRE)**[11] 5637 3-8-12 65 ........ MHenry 7 64
(MAJarvis) *chsd ldrs: rdn over 2f out: styd on same pce appr fnl f* **12/1**

/000 **7** *1 ¼* **Garden Society (IRE)**[24] 5317 7-9-0 63 ........ FNorton 14 60
(WAO'Gorman) *hld up: swtchd rt and hdwy 2f out: nt rch ldrs* **20/1**

0523 **8** *¾* **Mission Affirmed (USA)**[22] 5364 3-8-8 61 ........ JQuinn 3 56
(TPTate) *s.i.s: hld up: hdwy 4f out: rdn over 2f out: wknd over 1f out* **8/1**

1600 **9** *nk* **Mister Clinton (IRE)**[2] 5841 7-8-12 61 ........ JFEgan 8 55
(DKIvory) *chsd ldrs: rdn over 3f out: wknd over 1f out* **16/1**

4060 **10** *¾* **Phluke**[24] 5316 3-8-12 65 ........ LisaJones 16 57
(RFJohnsonHoughton) *chsd ldrs over 6f* **33/1**

3424 **11** *nk* **Dagola (IRE)**[50] 4619 3-8-13 66 ........ RSmith 9 58
(CGCox) *prom: rdn over 2f out: wkng whn n.m.r over 1f out* **10/1**

0306 **12** *½* **Scientist**[62] 4266 3-9-2 69 ........ LDettori 13 60
(JHMGosden) *hld up: hdwy over 3f out: wknd over 1f out* **7/1**[3]

5000 **13** *2 ½* **Adobe**[11] 5657 9-8-6 60 ........ PPMathers(5) 4 45
(WMBrisbourne) *hld up: hdwy 1/2-way: wknd 2f out* **16/1**

**14** *½* **Kaymich Perfecto**[109] 4-9-0 63 ........ SChin 15 47
(RMWhitaker) *hld up: a in rr* **100/1**

2200 **15** *hd* **Blue Mariner**[61] 4301 4-9-4 67 ........ NCallan 11 50
(PWHarris) *hld up: stmbld over 5f out: a in rr* **40/1**

0420 **16** *4* **Merdiff**[13] 5583 5-8-11 60 ........ RHughes 17 34
(WMBrisbourne) *prom: rdn over 3f out: edgd lft and wknd wl over 1f out* **12/1**

2200 **17** *1 ½* **Cayman Calypso (IRE)**[8] 5715 3-8-8 64 ........ TEaves(3) 5 35
(JMJefferson) *hld up: hdwy over 3f out: wknd over 2f out* **100/1**

1m 43.4s (-3.00) **Going Correction** -0.175s/f (Firm)
**WFA** 3 from 4yo+ 4lb **17** Ran SP% **121.0**
Speed ratings: **108,107,107,103,103 103,102,101,101,100 100,99,97,96,96 92,90**CSF £27.97 CT £440.39 TOTE £8.90: £1.80, £1.70, £4.80, £4.20; EX 29.60 Place 6 £28.22, Place 5 £14.43.
**Owner** Canisbay Bloodstock **Bred** Canisbay Bloodstock Ltd **Trained** Epsom, Surrey

**FOCUS**
This ordinary handicap consisted mainly of exposed sorts, but it was soundly run and produced a decent winning time for the class, giving it a sound appearance.

**NOTEBOOK**
**Spirit's Awakening** does not win that often, but you cannot fault his attitude and he should not suffer too much for this victory.
**Dont Call Me Derek** had plenty to do turning for home, but he stuck on well enough only to find the post arriving too soon. Just as effective on the Fibresand, he will find other openings.
**Gay Romance**, unlike his rivals, is still open to a little improvement, and showed enough to suggest he has a small race in him.
**Little Englander** did not have the best of runs, but he can hardly be called unlucky.
**Zafarshah(IRE)** lacks consistency, but he had a fair bit to do in the last two furlongs and deserves some credit for finishing as close as he did.
**Fascination Street(IRE)** had no excuses and this is about as good as she is.
T/Plt: £75.20 to a £1 stake. Pool: £35,264.95. 341.95 winning tickets. T/Qpdt: £10.30 to a £1 stake. Pool: £2,274.10. 162.20 winning tickets. CR

# 5534 SALISBURY (R-H)
## Wednesday, September 29

**OFFICIAL GOING: Good to soft (good in places) changing to good to soft after race 2 (3.00)**
The false running rail that was present for the last meeting was removed and those drawn on the far side looked to be holding an advantage.
Wind: almost nil Weather: lt rain

## 5869 AXMINSTER CARPETS APPRENTICE H'CAP 1m 1f 198y
**2:30** (2:30) (E3) (0-70,69) 3-Y-O+ **£3,950** (£1,215; £607; £303) **Stalls** High

Form RPR

0205 **1** **American Duke (USA)**[25] 5293 3-8-11 65 ........ DFox 11 79+
(BJMeehan) *lw: sn led: hdd over 5f out: styd pressing ldrs tl led again jst ins fnl 2f: drvn clr over 1f out: eased nr fin* **10/1**

4402 **2** *5* **Rani Two**[22] 5374 5-9-7 69 ........ NChalmers 17 72
(WRMuir) *in tch: chsd ldrs fr 4f out: chal over 2f out: kpt on but no ch w wnr fnl f* **8/1**[2]

1340 **3** *nk* **Dickie Deadeye**[28] 5229 7-8-11 69 ........ FrancesHarper(10) 10 72
(GBBalding) *lw: chsd ldrs: led over 5f out: hdd over 4f out: styd pressing ldrs: one pce fr over 1f out* **12/1**

1306 **4** *nk* **Critical Stage (IRE)**[39] 4479 5-8-8 61 ........ MHalford(5) 16 63
(JDFrost) *bhd: swtchd lft over 4f out: styd on fr over 1f out: fin wl but nt rch ldrs* **14/1**

0310 **5** *1 ¼* **Bluegrass Boy**[22] 5374 4-8-12 63 ........ PGallagher(3) 6 67+
(GBBalding) *b.font: bhd: hmpd over 4f out: styd on fnl 2f: nt rch ldrs* **14/1**

0050 **6** *½* **Competitor**[14] 5568 3-8-9 63 ........ (p) AQuinn 8 62
(JAkehurst) *chsd ldrs: rdn over 2f out: sn one pce* **25/1**

0500 **7** *¾* **Billy Bathwick (IRE)**[15] 5554 7-8-5 58 ........ LiamJones(5) 2 56
(JMBradley) *chsd ldrs: led over 4f out: hdd ins fnl 2f: wknd fnl f* **33/1**

566 **8** *1 ¼* **Rollswood (USA)**[39] 4939 4-9-0 62 ........ MSavage 7 57
(PRHedger) *b.front: in tch: rdn fr 4f out: nvr gng pce to trble ldrs* **14/1**

0601 **9** *¾* **Smoothie (IRE)**[22] 5374 6-8-9 60 ........ (p) CHaddon(3) 18 54
(IanWilliams) *s.i.s: bhd: sme hdwy on outside fnl 2f: n.d* **9/1**[3]

0015 **10** *1 ¾* **Farriers Charm**[32] 5136 3-8-12 66 ........ NDeSouza 15 57
(DJCoakley) *lw: chsd ldrs: rdn to chal over 2f out: wknd over 1f out* **10/1**

3066 **11** *¾* **Blazing The Trail (IRE)**[15] 5554 4-8-8 61 ........ KMay(5) 13 51
(JWHills) *nvr bttr than mid-div* **7/1**[1]

6050 **12** *1 ½* **Secret Jewel (FR)**[42] 4849 4-9-5 67 ........ (p) MLawson 12 54
(LadyHerries) *s.i.s: bhd: hmpd over 4f out: nvr in contention after* **50/1**

0045 **13** *1 ¼* **Kernel Dowery (IRE)**[22] 5374 4-8-6 62 ........ (e) MCoumbe(8) 14 47
(PWHarris) *lw: chsd ldrs: rdn 3f out: wknd 2f out* **14/1**

2060 **14** *2* **Kythia (IRE)**[14] 5560 3-8-8 67 ........ TBlock(5) 4 48
(HMorrison) *nvr bttr than mid-div* **20/1**

4114 **15** *5* **Milk And Sultana**[12] 5622 4-8-9 62 ........ DeanWilliams(5) 1 34
(GAHam) *bhd most of way* **10/1**

1130 **16** *8* **Unsuited**[14] 5568 5-9-3 68 ........ NataliaGemelova(3) 9 26
(JELong) *a in rr* **12/1**

60-0 **17** *dist* **Tarawan**[13] 5584 8-8-11 67 ........ (v) RJKilloran(8) 5 —
(AMBalding) *s.i.s: a in rr: t.o* **33/1**

2253 **18** *16* **Kelseas Kolby (IRE)**[17] 5496 4-8-6 57 ........ KristinStubbs(3) 3 —
(PButler) *wd bnd over 6f out: a in rr: t.o* **33/1**

2m 9.78s (1.46) **Going Correction** +0.20s/f (Good)
**WFA** 3 from 4yo+ 6lb **18** Ran SP% **122.3**
Speed ratings: **102,98,97,97,96 96,95,94,93,92 91,90,89,88,84 77,—,—**CSF £80.28 CT £989.96 TOTE £12.10: £2.40, £2.80, £3.40, £4.50; EX 94.30.
**Owner** Grays, Jaye & Connolly **Bred** A R Dragone **Trained** Upper Lambourn, Berks
■ Stewards Enquiry : M Savage four-day ban: careless riding (Oct 10-13)

**FOCUS**
A typically tight and tricky looking apprentice handicap that was run at a solid gallop, and the winner looks improved.

**NOTEBOOK**
**American Duke(USA)** was on the pace from the off on the inside rail and ran out a most decisive winner under his capable young rider. He has taken time to find his level, but looks capable of building on this first success off his mark and clearly relished the underfoot conditions.
**Rani Two** had her chance, but lacked the turn of foot to go with the winner when it mattered. This was yet another sound effort however, and she can win a similar event off this mark when reverting to faster ground. *Official explanation: trainer's representative said mare was struck into*
**Dickie Deadeye** looked to be travelling better than the winner before two out, but found less than looked likely off the bridle for his inexperienced jockey. This was a more encouraging effort however, he relished this ground, and he could go closer once again with stronger handling.
**Critical Stage(IRE)** did not get the best of runs over two out and did enough to suggest that he could find another race on the All-Weather during the winter.
**Bluegrass Boy** , winner over course and distance on his penultimate start, stayed on late in the day but was never a serious threat on this unsuitably soft ground.
**Smoothie(IRE)** was given a lot to do and got going all too late in the day. He never looked like following up his recent Leicester success and is capable of better.
**Blazing The Trail(IRE)** was well below par and never got into it from off the gallop.
**Unsuited** *Official explanation: trainer said mare had a breathing problem*
**Kelseas Kolby(IRE)** *Official explanation: trainer said gelding was lame*

## 5870 E.B.F./SUBSCRIBE TO RACING UK ON 08700 860432 MAIDEN STKS (DIV I) 1m
**3:00** (3:03) (D2) 2-Y-O **£5,804** (£1,786; £893; £446) **Stalls** High

Form RPR

4 **1** **The Composer**[9] 5696 2-9-0 ........ KFallon 13 81
(MBlanshard) *lw: a.p: chal 2f out: strly rdn to ld ins fnl f: styd on dourly* **7/4**[1]

502 **2** *½* **Wotchalike (IRE)**[15] 5535 2-9-0 79 ........ TQuinn 8 80
(DRCElsworth) *chsd ldr: led over 3f out: responded wl u.p whn chal 2f out: hdd ins fnl f: no ex nr fin* **3/1**[2]

**3** *2 ½* **Plea Bargain** 2-9-0 ........ RHavlin 15 78+
(JHMGosden) *leggy: sn pushed along: short of room and swtchd lft over 2f out: styd on ins fnl 2f: no ch w first 2* **20/1**

0 **4** *5* **Mister Elegant**[100] 3157 2-9-0 ........ SWhitworth 14 64
(JLSpearing) *mid-div: hdwy over 2f out: sn rdn: wknd ins fnl f* **50/1**

05 **5** *shd* **Royal Mougins**[11] 5653 2-9-0 ........ SDrowne 7 63
(GWragg) *slowly away: plugged on one pce fnl 2f: nvr nrr* **15/2**[3]

**6** *3 ½* **Mt Desert** 2-9-0 ........ JFortune 11 56
(JHMGosden) *lenghty: scope: slowly away: sme hdwy 2f out: nvr on terms* **10/1**

0 **7** *1* **Oakley Absolute**[9] 5687 2-9-0 ........ DaneO'Neill 2 53
(RHannon) *led to over 3f out: wknd wl over 1f out* **66/1**

| Form | Pos | Dist | Horse | Jockey | RPR |
|---|---|---|---|---|---|
| | 8 | 3 1/2 | **Marhaba Million (IRE)** 2-9-0 (MRChannon) *unf: leggy: chsd ldrs tl wknd ins fnl 2f* **20/1** | SHitchcott 3 | 46 |
| | 9 | 1/2 | **Palace Walk (FR)** 2-9-0 (AMBalding) *w'like: scope: v.s.a: nvr on terms* **20/1** | MartinDwyer 1 | 45 |
| 00 | 10 | nk | **Backstreet Lad**[15] 5535 2-9-0 (BRMillman) *lw: hld up: a towards rr* **50/1** | GBaker 10 | 44 |
| 0 | 11 | nk | **Silver Song**[26] 5269 2-9-0 (JLDunlop) *bit bkwd: in tch tl wknd 2f out* **66/1** | IMongan 9 | 43 |
| | 12 | 1 3/4 | **Barbirolli** 2-9-0 (JHMGosden) *tall: str: scope: lw: s.i.s: a bhd* **12/1** | (t) RLMoore 5 | 39 |
| | 13 | 5 | **Emerald Dancer** 2-8-9 (HMorrison) *lenghty: unf: a bhd* **25/1** | MFenton 12 | 23 |
| 00 | 14 | 7 | **Smart Dawn**[9] 5694 2-8-9 (CTinkler) *in tch: sn rdn: dropped rr 1/2-way* **100/1** | PHanagan 6 | 8 |
| 00 | 15 | 9 | **Night Guest (IRE)**[26] 5268 2-9-0 (RHannon) *a struggling in rr* **66/1** | PDobbs 4 | — |

1m 43.85s (0.88) **Going Correction** +0.05s/f (Good) **15** Ran SP% **117.4**
Speed ratings: **97,96,94,89,88 85,84,80,80,80 79,78,73,66,57**CSF £5.51 TOTE £2.70: £1.30, £1.40, £6.60; EX 7.80.
**Owner** Mrs C J Ward **Bred** D A And Mrs Hicks **Trained** Upper Lambourn, Berks

**FOCUS**
A fair maiden that produced a marginally slower time than the second division and average form for the grade.

**NOTEBOOK**
**The Composer**, an imposing colt, confirmed the promise of his recent Kempton debut and really knuckled down well under Fallon to grind down the runner-up near the line. Although speedily-bred, he clearly has stamina in abundance and can be expected to get further as a three-year-old. This softer ground was no barrier and he looks useful prospect.
**Wotchalike(IRE)**, narrowly denied over seven furlongs at this track last time, had every chance, but failed to see his race out as well as the winner. He is clearly suited by soft ground and has the ability to win a similar event, but is starting to look exposed and may need to switch to nurseries now.
**Plea Bargain** ◆, a 425,000gns purchase, stayed on promisingly under a sympathetic ride on this debut. He readily made up ground when switched for a run inside two out and was in turn well clear of the rest. He should have little difficulty in winning his maiden, could be better suited to a faster surface, and will stay middle distances next year.
**Mister Elegant** improved significantly on his debut in June over this longer trip and looks the type to fare better once handicapped.
**Royal Mougins** ran very much to the form of his recent Haydock outing over this extra furlong and now qualifies for a nursery mark.
**Mt Desert** can be expected to leave this debut form behind in due course.

## 5871 E.B.F./SUBSCRIBE TO RACING UK ON 08700 860432 MAIDEN STKS (DIV II) 1m

**3:30** (3:35) (D2) 2-Y-O **£5,785** (£1,780; £890; £445) **Stalls** High

| Form | Pos | Dist | Horse | Jockey | RPR |
|---|---|---|---|---|---|
| 4 | 1 | | **Night Hour (IRE)**[26] 5269 2-9-0 (MPTregoning) *lw: sn trcking ldr: chal over 3f out: led appr fnl 2f: drvn and hld on gamely fnl f* **3/1**[3] | MartinDwyer 3 | 87 |
| | 2 | 1 1/2 | **Top Gear** 2-9-0 (DRCElsworth) *w'like: scope: s.i.s: bhd: hdwy 3f out: out: styd on strly fnl f: tk 2nd last strides but nt rch wnr* **10/1** | TQuinn 10 | 84 |
| 44 | 3 | shd | **Top The Charts**[11] 5646 2-9-0 (RHannon) *lw: sn slt ld:hdd over 2f out:styd pressing wnr and chal ins fnl f: outpcd nr fin and lost 2nd last strides* **11/4**[2] | RLMoore 8 | 83 |
| | 4 | 3/4 | **Bureaucrat** 2-9-0 (JHMGosden) *tall: str: scope: s.i.s: bhd: hdwy 3f out: drvn and styd on fr over 1f out: kpt on ins last: nt pce to rch ldrs* **50/1** | RHavlin 5 | 82 |
| 5330 | 5 | 2 1/2 | **Subyan Dreams**[31] 5149 2-8-9 95 (PWChapple-Hyam) *lw: t.k.h: chsd ldrs: drvn to chal over 2f out: edgd rt and outpcd jst ins last: eased whn no ch nr fin* **9/4**[1] | KFallon 14 | 71 |
| 0 | 6 | 6 | **Indian Pipe Dream (IRE)**[26] 5268 2-9-0 (JHMGosden) *bhd: pushed along over 3f out: kpt on fr over 1f out but n.d* **50/1** | PDobbs 15 | 63 |
| 0 | 7 | 8 | **Honour High**[18] 5467 2-9-0 (LadyHerries) *t.k.h: stdd rr after 1f: pushed along over 4f out: n.d after* **50/1** | IMongan 9 | 46 |
| 000 | 8 | 6 | **Voir Dire**[40] 4913 2-9-0 (MrsPNDutfield) *bhd: sn pushed along: nvr nrr* **66/1** | NPollard 7 | 32 |
| 6 | 9 | 4 | **Kristinor (FR)**[61] 4292 2-9-0 (JRFanshawe) *t.k.h: chsd ldrs: rdn 3f out: sn wknd* **7/1** | MFenton 12 | 24 |
| 0 | 10 | 4 | **Oneiro Way (IRE)**[40] 4922 2-9-0 (PRChamings) *awkward stalls: chsd ldrs tl wknd over 3f out* **50/1** | EAhern 11 | 26+ |
| 6 | 11 | 1 1/2 | **Tavalu (USA)**[18] 5455 2-9-0 (SaeedBinSuroor) *s.i.s: sn rcvrd: chsd ldrs 5f out: wknd qckly 3f out* **20/1** | SDrowne 1 | 11 |
| 00 | 12 | 3 1/2 | **Flower Seeker**[9] 5688 2-8-9 (CTinkler) *early spd: bhd fr 1/2-way* **100/1** | PHanagan 2 | — |
| 000 | 13 | 2 1/2 | **South O'The Border**[40] 4922 2-9-0 (TGMills) *swtg: a in rr* **100/1** | GCarter 13 | — |
| 000 | 14 | 8 | **Garance**[30] 5172 2-8-9 (RHannon) *t.k.h: broke wl: sn bhd* **66/1** | DaneO'Neill 4 | — |

1m 43.76s (0.79) **Going Correction** +0.05s/f (Good) **14** Ran SP% **126.4**
Speed ratings: **98,96,96,95,93 87,79,73,69,65 63,60,57,49**CSF £31.55 TOTE £4.30: £1.70, £2.30, £1.60; EX 45.20.
**Owner** Greenbay Stables Ltd **Bred** C H Wacker Iii **Trained** Lambourn, Berks

**FOCUS**
This maiden looked the stronger of the two divisions and it was run in a marginally faster time than the first. The first five came clear at the finish and the third sets the standard.

**NOTEBOOK**
**Night Hour(IRE)**, who shaped with promise from off the pace on his debut, was much smarter from the gates this time and showed a good attitude when sticking to his task under maximum pressure to get on top close home. His entry in the Dewhurst Stakes looks ambitious at this stage, but he is clearly progressing nicely and could make up into a fairly decent performer over further next year.
**Top Gear** ◆, whose stable saddled the winner in divisions of this race in 1999 and 2002, made a highly-pleasing debut. He was only really asked for an effort approaching the final furlong and finished strongly, so could have troubled the winner with little further to go. He will come on for this, has scope, and looks sure to win races.
**Top The Charts** was rushed up to dispute the lead early on and only tired out of contention in the closing stages. He got this extra furlong well enough and will be one to look for when switching to nurseries, for which he is now qualified. *Official explanation: jockey said colt hung left*
**Bureaucrat** ◆, half-brother to several winners, made a very promising debut and would surely have gone closer but for fluffing the start. He should come on plenty for this and looked well suited by the trip.
**Subyan Dreams** seemed to be going as well as any two out, but found less than looked likely when asked for an effort and failed to get home in these conditions. She is in danger of going the wrong way, but should be given another chance back on a sound surface and will be suited by a drop back to seven furlongs.
**Indian Pipe Dream(IRE)** was gradually getting the hang of things in the straight and was not at all knocked about. He will be capable of much better with more experience under his belt.
**Kristinor(FR)** again left the impression that he is a headstrong character, but could do better in time. *Official explanation: trainer said colt finished distressed*

## 5872 PORTWAY EBF NOVICE STKS 6f 212y

**4:00** (4:02) (D2) 2-Y-O **£5,668** (£1,744; £872; £436) **Stalls** High

| Form | Pos | Dist | Horse | Jockey | RPR |
|---|---|---|---|---|---|
| 410 | 1 | | **Sudden Dismissal (IRE)**[25] 5295 2-9-2 95 (GAButler) *lw: a in tch: qcknd to ld appr fnl f: pushed out* **5/2**[1] | PHanagan 8 | 93 |
| 31 | 2 | 1 3/4 | **Sant Jordi**[44] 4809 2-9-2 80 (BJMeehan) *led tl hdd appr fnl f: nt pce of wnr* **5/1**[2] | JFMcDonald(3) 7 | 92 |
| 2 | 3 | 1 1/2 | **Notnowcato**[23] 5347 2-8-12 (SirMichaelStoute) *trckd ldrs: hrd rdn 2f out: kpt on one pce fnl f* **5/2**[1] | KFallon 3 | 81 |
| 431 | 4 | 1 1/2 | **Palatinate (FR)**[15] 5535 2-9-2 80 (HCandy) *s.i.s: hdwy 2f out: swtchd rt over 1f out: swtchd lft ins fnl f: kpt on* **8/1**[3] | DaneO'Neill 9 | 81 |
| 035 | 5 | 1/2 | **Aviation**[17] 5494 2-8-12 78 (RHannon) *in tch tl rdn and one pce fnl f* **14/1** | RLMoore 5 | 76 |
| 33 | 6 | 3 | **Fairmile**[47] 4730 2-8-12 (PWHarris) *t.k.h: sn in tch: swtchd lft over 1f out: wknd ins fnl f* **5/1**[2] | EAhern 2 | 73+ |
| 6 | 7 | 3 | **Compton Quay**[23] 5347 2-8-12 (AKing) *bkwd: t.k.h: in tch: rdn and lost tch over 2f out* **33/1** | JDSmith 6 | 60 |
| 0 | 8 | 1 | **Final Promise**[15] 5534 2-8-12 (GBBalding) *prom tl rdn and wknd 2f out* **100/1** | SCarson 11 | 58 |
| 0 | 9 | 5 | **Mister Troubridge**[15] 5535 2-8-12 (GBBalding) *a bhd* **66/1** | SDrowne 12 | 45 |
| 60 | 10 | nk | **Desert Moonbeam (IRE)**[20] 5406 2-8-7 (RJHodges) *a bhd* **100/1** | NPollard 10 | 39 |
| 0 | 11 | 12 | **April Shannon**[22] 5376 2-8-0 (JELong) *bkwd: trckd ldr tl wknd 1/2-way: sn bhd: eased ins fnl f* **100/1** | NataliaGemelova(7) 4 | 9 |

1m 30.3s (1.30) **Going Correction** +0.05s/f (Good) **11** Ran SP% **115.7**
Speed ratings: **94,92,90,88,88 84,81,80,74,73 60**CSF £15.06 TOTE £3.50: £1.60, £1.40, £1.90; EX 16.80.
**Owner** The Schtum Partnership **Bred** Skymarc Farm And Castlemartin Stud **Trained** Blewbury, Oxon

**FOCUS**
A reasonable race for the grade and competitive enough on paper, but the early pace was very steady and as a result few of these could quicken and land a serious blow. The form looks fairly good on paper with winner, fourth and fifth setting the standard.

**NOTEBOOK**
**Sudden Dismissal(IRE)** appreciated this drop from Group Three company and won well. He is clearly held in some regard by connections given that he has already been tried in Pattern company and, with the promise of even better to come, especially in a more strongly-run race, he is one to keep on the right side of.
**Sant Jordi** was unable to follow up his win in a competitive Windsor maiden returning from a 44-day absence, and was slightly below his best. He found himself somewhat reluctantly in front and, after racing a little keenly, was simply unable to quicken sufficiently in the sprint to the line. He can be given another chance in a more truly-run affair.
**Notnowcato** had shaped well when runner-up on his debut in a reasonable Warwick maiden, but did not have the race run to suit and was unable to build on that. He was well placed for the dash, but was quite simply outpaced by the front two and should be capable of better in a stronger-run race.
**Palatinate(FR)** simply lacked the speed to pose a threat having been held up off the modest pace. He is better than this.
**Aviation** was made to look pretty one paced on this step up from six furlongs and did little to justify his rating of 78, even allowing for the way the race was run.
**Fairmile** is better than the bare form as he was stuck out wide all the way and would definitely not have been suited by the gallop. He is now qualified for a handicap mark.
**Compton Quay** failed to improve on his promising debut, never really looking like picking up. He is capable of better and may be one to keep in mind for handicaps.

## 5873 AVERTI CONDITIONS STKS 6f

**4:30** (4:30) (C1) 2-Y-O **£9,831** (£3,729; £1,864; £847) **Stalls** High

| Form | Pos | Dist | Horse | Jockey | RPR |
|---|---|---|---|---|---|
| 2211 | 1 | | **Yajbill (IRE)**[20] 5421 2-9-1 95 (MRChannon) *s.i.s: sn rcvrd to ld after half a f: 4l clr over 3f out: drvn whn chal over 1f out: hld on readily cl home* **5/2**[2] | (v) KFallon 2 | 99 |
| 5115 | 2 | nk | **Claret And Amber**[21] 5392 2-8-12 97 (RAFahey) *lw: chsd ldrs: pushed along over 3f out: chsd wnr 2f out: rdn to chal over 1f out: no imp but rallied again cl home* **15/8**[1] | PHanagan 5 | 95 |
| 00 | 3 | 4 | **Montecito**[27] 5248 2-8-7 (RHannon) *bhd: pushed along over 2f out: styd on fr over 1f out to and tk 3rd ins last but nvr gng pce to rch ldrs* **80/1** | PDobbs 3 | 78 |
| 3611 | 4 | nk | **Angel Sprints**[32] 5131 2-8-13 90 (LGCottrell) *led half a f: styd chsng wnr to 2f out: outpcd appr fnl f* **20/1** | ADaly 1 | 83 |
| 4212 | 5 | 3 1/2 | **Marching Song**[32] 5119 2-9-1 91 (RHannon) *lw: s.i.s: bhd: swtchd lft to outside 3f out and rdn: nvr gng pce to rch ldrs* **6/1** | RLMoore 6 | 75 |
| 2 | 6 | shd | **Something (IRE)**[44] 4809 2-8-12 (TGMills) *lw: chsd ldrs: pushed along and edgd rt 2f out: no imp on ldrs whn hung rt again ins last* **11/4**[3] | GCarter 4 | 71+ |

1m 14.82s (-0.12) **Going Correction** +0.05s/f (Good) **6** Ran SP% **110.3**
Speed ratings: **102,101,96,95,91 91**CSF £7.32 TOTE £3.50: £1.70, £2.40; EX 6.40.
**Owner** Sheikh Ahmed Al Maktoum **Bred** N Poole And A Franklin **Trained** West Ilsley, Berks
■ Stewards Enquiry : G Carter four-day ban: dropped hands and lost fifth place (Oct 10-13)

**FOCUS**
An intriguing little conditions event for juveniles that had not won at Pattern level and it featured four previous winners amongst the six-strong field. The form looks strong for the grade and not far short of Listed class.

**NOTEBOOK**
**Yajbill(IRE)**, an improved performer since the application of the visor the last twice, who overcame a slow start to just about make all the running to land the hat-trick in game style. He is a tough, relentless galloper who is fast progressing and he had no problems with this much slower ground, so looks well worthy of a crack at Pattern level now in search of the four-timer.
**Claret And Amber** ◆ was rousted to go the early pace, yet kept to his task well and had his chance, but could not pass the winner try as he might. He continues to go the right way and, on this evidence, a return to seven furlongs can see him get back to winning ways.
**Montecito** turned in a much-improved effort and was staying on well late over what really does look an inadequate trip. He now qualifies for nurseries and should fare better in that sphere over further.



The Form Book, Raceform Ltd, Compton, RG20 6NL

**Angel Sprints** , who came into this looking for the hat-trick, was unable to dominate in this better race and that ultimately cost her. She can be found easier opportunities and was not at all disgraced.
**Marching Song** had his chance, but weakened dramatically in the closing stages. He was not that well in at the weights and can do better back on a sound surface in nurseries.
**Something(IRE)** faced a stiff task on this second outing and found little off the bridle when asked to improve on this testing ground. He has scope and it is unlikely that we will see the best of him until next year.

## 5874 CATISFIELD HINTON & STUD H'CAP 6f
**5:00** (5:01) (D2) (0-85,85) 3-Y-O+ **£9,516** (£3,609; £1,804; £820) **Stalls** High

Form RPR
5200 **1** **Goodenough Mover**[19] 5444 8-8-10 **80**.................... HayleyTurner(3) 10 91
(JSKing) *pressed ldr tl led over 2f out: drvn and hld on wl fnl f* **33/1**
5000 **2** *1 ¾* **Totally Yours (IRE)**[9] 5697 3-8-13 **82**.................................. EAhern 17 88
(WRMuir) *chsd ldrs: rdn over 2f out: styd on ins last and tk 2nd nr fin but no imp on wnr* **66/1**
612 **3** *hd* **Ok Pal**[9] 5704 4-9-0 **81**................................................. GCarter 4 86
(TGMills) *sn led: hdd over 2f out: styd chsng wnr: one pce ins last and lost 2nd nr fin* **25/1**
0226 **4** *hd* **Kingscross**[7] 5730 6-8-13 **80**............................................ KFallon 16 85+
(MBlanshard) *hld up in rr: hdwy on rails over 2f out: nt clr run fr wl over 1f out tl ins last: kpt on but nt rcvr* **9/1**[3]
0000 **5** *½* **Danehill Stroller (IRE)**[7] 5730 4-8-10 **77**............................ MFenton 18 80+
(RMBeckett) *hld up in rr: nt clr run and swtchd rt over 1f out: swtchd lft jst ins last and fin wl: nt rcvr* **20/1**
0046 **6** *hd* **Caustic Wit (IRE)**[26] 5263 6-9-3 **84**..............................(p) SDrowne 11 86
(MSSaunders) *chsd ldrs: rdn over 2f out: one pce ins last* **25/1**
0211 **7** *½* **Endless Summer**[7] 5730 7-9-1 **82** 6ex.................................. PDoe 20 83+
(AWCarroll) *hld up in tch: hdwy on rails 2f out: chsd ldrs over 1f out: styng on same pce whn n.m.r wl ins last* **7/2**[1]
2116 **8** *1* **Fonthill Road (IRE)**[12] 5603 4-9-1 **82**............................. PHanagan 12 80+
(RAFahey) *lw: mid-div: n.m.r 2f out: rdn and swtchd lft jst ins last: kpt on cl home* **7/2**[1]
5500 **9** *¾* **Golden Dixie (USA)**[12] 5603 5-8-11 **78**......................... MartinDwyer 15 74
(AMBalding) *chsd ldrs: rdn 3f out: outpcd fr over 1f out* **25/1**
0023 **10** *1* **Najeebon (FR)**[7] 5730 5-8-11 **78**...................................... SHitchcott 7 71+
(MRChannon) *bhd: riden and n.m.r 2f out: styd on fnl f but n.d* **11/1**
2300 **11** *2* **Bathwick Bill (USA)**[9] 5697 3-8-12 **81**.................................... GBaker 8 68
(BRMillman) *pressed ldrs: rdn 2f out: wknd fnl f* **66/1**
2134 **12** *1 ½* **Presto Shinko (IRE)**[51] 4614 3-9-0 **83**............................. RLMoore 19 65
(RHannon) *lw: in tch: ridddena dn wkng whn bmpd and veered lft ins fnl f* **7/1**[2]
2145 **13** *2 ½* **Currency**[7] 5730 7-8-10 **77**............................................ PFitzsimons 1 52
(JMBradley) *b.front: bhd: rdn over 2f out: nvr gng pce to rch ldrs* **25/1**
321- **14** *2* **Great Fox (IRE)**[337] 5818 3-8-10 **79**.......................................(t) RPrice 9 48
(PLGilligan) *chsd ldrs: rdn over 2f out: wknd and hung lft sn after* **33/1**
0210 **15** *½* **Swinbrook (USA)**[7] 5730 3-8-11 **80**................................... DaneO'Neill 3 47
(JARToller) *a outpcd* **40/1**
0000 **16** *3* **Law Breaker (IRE)**[9] 5704 6-9-1 **85**............................... BReilly(3) 14 43
(JAGilbert) *nvr bttr than mid-div* **25/1**
000- **17** *5* **Avening**[23] 4-9-0 **81**..................................................(bt) PDobbs 5 24+
(JEHammond, France) *chsd ldrs over 3f* **9/1**[3]
0060 **18** *¾* **Big Bradford**[9] 5697 3-9-2 **85**.........................................(b) DKinsella 6 26
(PGMurphy) *lw: a bhd* **66/1**
365 **19** *3* **Taranaki**[22] 5379 6-9-4 **85**.............................................. SCarson 2 17+
(PDCundell) *chsd ldrs 1/2-way: sn wknd* **18/1**

1m 14.58s (-0.36) **Going Correction** +0.05s/f (Good)
**WFA** 3 from 4yo+ 2lb **19** Ran SP% **127.3**
Speed ratings: **104,101,101,101,100 100,99,98,97,95 93,91,87,85,84 80,73,72,68**CSF £1409.08 CT £43068.12 TOTE £56.30: £6.90, £14.50, £5.20, £2.30; EX 1508.10 TRIFECTA Not won..
**Owner** D Goodenough Removals & Transport **Bred** G Foster **Trained** Broad Hinton, Wilts

**FOCUS**
A decent-enough sprint for the grade that saw the entire field go over to the far side, which resulted in a fair amount of hard-luck stories, and the form should be treated with a degree of caution.

**NOTEBOOK**
**Goodenough Mover** pinged out to bag the lead on the far rail and make most of the running to score. He is best when able to dominate and was winning this off a 13lb higher mark than when scoring on his turf reappearance in May, so deserves full credit. However, connections will be very keen to turn him out under a penalty, as he will most likely struggle off a higher mark. *Official explanation: trainer had no explanation for the improved form shown*
**Totally Yours(IRE)** turned in an improved effort and was finishing well on the rail. She had a decent draw this time, but could be about to regain her form and has clearly fallen to a fair mark.
**Ok Pal** continues in good form and did by far the best of those drawn in single figures. He saw out this extra furlong in the testing conditions, but does look best at the minimum trip and could well make amends when reverting to that distance.
**Kingscross** was tight for room on several occasions on the rail and can be considered better than the bare form. He has crept up the handicap without winning, but remains in great form and deserves to taste success once more.
**Danehill Stroller(IRE)** ◆ was unlucky. He suffered serious traffic problems throughout on the rail, but flew once in the clear and would surely have gone close with an unhindered passage. He is on a decent mark and can be placed to gain compensation over this trip.
**Caustic Wit(IRE)** had his chance and ran a sound race, but continues to look in the Handicapper's grip.
**Endless Summer** , chasing a hat-trick under his penalty, was another to suffer traffic problems and is better than his placing suggests.
**Fonthill Road(IRE)** was another who had no luck and can do better than this. *Official explanation: jockey said gelding hung right*
**Great Fox(IRE)** showed good early pace on this belated reappearance and should come on a bundle for this outing.
**Big Bradford** *Official explanation: jockey said gelding was unsuited by good to soft ground*

## 5875 SOVEREIGN WINDOWS & CONSERVATORIES H'CAP 1m 6f 15y
**5:30** (5:30) (E3) (0-70,70) 3-Y-O+ **£4,078** (£1,254; £627; £313) **Stalls** Far side

Form RPR
0032 **1** **Irish Blade (IRE)**[18] 5456 3-8-13 **69**.................................. DSweeney 6 82
(HCandy) *lw: b.hind: trckd ldrs: led over 3f out: clr over 1f out: comf* **12/1**
2000 **2** *3 ½* **Perfect Punch**[15] 5554 5-9-5 **65**....................................... SDrowne 10 73
(CFWall) *lw: a in tch: rdn to chse wnr fnl 2f* **50/1**
0625 **3** *1 ¼* **Majestic Vision**[26] 5274 3-8-11 **67**.................................. RLMoore 4 73
(PWHarris) *lw: led tl hdd over 3f out: styd on one pce* **8/1**
0426 **4** *1 ½* **Penny Stall**[45] 4778 3-8-7 **63**............................................ TQuinn 9 67
(JLDunlop) *mid-div: hdwy to chse ldrs 3f out: kpt on one pce* **11/1**
6260 **5** *1 ¼* **Aoninch**[30] 5203 4-9-1 **61**........................................... SWhitworth 20 64
(MrsPNDutfield) *hld up: hdwy over 2f out: styd on: nvr nrr* **25/1**
0015 **6** *3* **Silver Prophet (IRE)**[30] 5203 5-9-6 **66**................................ GBaker 17 65
(MRBosley) *trckd ldrs: rdn 3f out: one pce after* **33/1**
5602 **7** *2 ½* **Nawow**[7] 5728 4-9-9 **69**................................................ KFallon 3 65
(PDCundell) *hld up: riden and hdwy over 3f out: btn over 2f out* **11/4**[1]
0512 **8** *1* **Argentum**[14] 5560 3-8-3 **59**........................................... PHanagan 7 53
(LadyHerries) *lw: hld up in mid-div: lost tch 2f out* **15/2**[3]
2265 **9** *1 ½* **Tilla**[24] 5318 4-9-6 **69**............................................... LFletcher(3) 8 61
(HMorrison) *bhd and nvr on terms* **7/1**[2]
-043 **10** *shd* **Innocent Rebel (USA)**[38] 4972 3-8-12 **68**............................ EAhern 5 60
(EALDunlop) *t.k.h: in tch: sme hdwy 3f out but short of room sn after and readily btn* **25/1**
-003 **11** *hd* **Flamenco Bride**[56] 4441 4-9-10 **70**................................ DaneO'Neill 12 62
(DRCElsworth) *lw: racd mid-div: no ch fnl 2f* **14/1**
0000 **12** *3* **Western (IRE)**[42] 4849 4-9-0 **60**....................................... GCarter 16 48
(JAkehurst) *hld in rr: a bhd* **25/1**
4046 **13** *hd* **Saxe-Coburg (IRE)**[33] 5073 7-8-10 **56** oh1............................. ADaly 1 44
(GAHam) *reluctan to r: a bhd* **33/1**
0064 **14** *¾* **Snow's Ride**[30] 5205 4-9-0 **60**................................. MartinDwyer 13 47
(WRMuir) *mid-div: wknd over 2f out* **9/1**
120- **15** *2 ½* **Shush**[364] 5308 6-9-1 **61**........................................... SHitchcott 11 45
(CEBrittain) *a bhd* **50/1**
0500 **16** *½* **Blue Hills**[32] 5116 3-8-4 **63**........................................ RMiles(3) 2 46
(PWHiatt) *trckd ldrs: weakeneing whn hmpd over 2f out* **100/1**
0320 **17** *½* **Simonovski (USA)**[26] 5274 3-8-3 **59**.................................. PDoe 15 41
(SCBurrough) *plld hrd: a bhd* **66/1**
0354 **18** *1 ¼* **Hinode (IRE)**[15] 5549 3-8-4 **60**...................................... NPollard 14 41
(JARToller) *a bhd* **50/1**
4200 **19** *shd* **San Hernando**[26] 5274 4-9-8 **68**...................................... MFenton 19 49
(DRCElsworth) *hld up: racd wd: wl bhd fnl 4f* **14/1**

3m 7.60s (1.60) **Going Correction** +0.20s/f (Good)
**WFA** 3 from 4yo+ 10lb **19** Ran SP% **127.2**
Speed ratings: **103,101,100,99,98 97,95,95,94,94 93,92,92,91,90 90,89,89,88**CSF £538.66 CT £5041.65 TOTE £14.00: £3.20, £10.90, £2.50, £3.70; EX 415.20 Place 6 £133.37, Place 5 £43.57.
**Owner** Thurloe Thoroughbreds V **Bred** Maurice Burns **Trained** Wantage, Oxon
■ Stewards Enquiry : K Fallon one-day ban: careless riding (Oct 10)

**FOCUS**
A modest staying handicap that featured largely out-of-form performers and the gallop was only moderate. Despite this the form appears solid enough.

**NOTEBOOK**
**Irish Blade(IRE)** ◆ , who came into this on the back of two respectable efforts in defeat, tracked the modest pace, until readily going for home on the final bend and never looked in danger from that point. Granted he had the run of the race and was given a well-judged ride, but there was a lot to like about the way in which he won and he could go in under a penalty.
**Perfect Punch** turned in an improved effort for this step up in trip, which now gives his connections further options, but he can be hard to predict.
**Majestic Vision** did well to keep on for third, having looked like folding when challenged for the lead turning for home. He looked suited to this trip and this was his best effort to date.
**Penny Stall** kept on at the one pace in the straight and would have been better served by a stronger gallop.
**Aoninch** came from a long way back, having been set a lot to do from off the pace, and reached fourth place a furlong out before tiring.
**Nawow** failed to pick up under pressure and has to go down as disappointing. He failed to build on his decent effort at Goodwood as expected over this longer trip, and connections will be hoping a spell over hurdles brings about improvement.
**Argentum** shaped like a non-stayer on his first attempt over this longer trip. *Official explanation: jockey said gelding was unsuited by good to soft ground*
T/Jkpt: Not won. T/Plt: £63.80 to a £1 stake. Pool: £47,984.50. 548.80 winning tickets. T/Qpdt: £30.70 to a £1 stake. Pool: £2,419.90. 58.30 winning tickets. ST

# 4973 FAIRYHOUSE (R-H)
Wednesday, September 29

**OFFICIAL GOING: Good to yielding**

## 5878a EL GRAN SENOR STKS (LISTED) 7f
**3:30** (3:31) 2-Y-O **£22,922** (£6,725; £3,204; £1,091)

RPR
**1** **Gaff (USA)**[167] 2-9-0 ............................................ PJSmullen 4 96+
(DKWeld, Ire) *broke wl: settled 2nd: checked and dropped to 5th 1/2-way: 4th and swtchd early st: 2nd ins fnl f: led cl home* **6/1**
**2** *½* **Zelkova (IRE)**[23] 5358 2-9-0 96.......................................... FMBerry 1 95
(MsFMCrowley, Ire) *sn led: hdd 1/2-way: remained cl up: chal fr 2f out: ev ch ins fnl f: no ex nr fin* **4/1**[2]
**3** *shd* **Ridder**[24] 5319 2-9-0 ................................................ JAHeffernan 7 95
(DJCoakley) *hld up: 5th on outer over 1 1/2f out: 4th ins fnl f: r.o wl* **20/1**
**4** *nk* **Only Make Believe**[31] 5160 2-9-0 .................................... KJManning 3 94
(JSBolger, Ire) *3rd early: led 1/2-way: strly pressed st: kpt on u.p: hdd cl home* **9/4**[1]
**5** *1 ½* **Bibury Flyer**[11] 5648 2-8-11 ........................................... TEDurcan 5 87
(MRChannon) *hld up in rr: kpt on st wout threatening ldrs* **7/1**
**6** *1 ½* **Allexina**[13] 5598 2-8-11 ................................................ MJKinane 8 84
(JohnMOxx, Ire) *trckd ldrs: 4th into st: sn no ex* **11/2**[3]
**7** *1* **Crystal View (IRE)**[9] 5709 2-8-11 95........................... DPMcDonogh 6 81
(KevinPrendergast, Ire) *s.i.s: sn in tch: 3rd 1/2-way: rdn early st: wknd fr 2f out* **4/1**[2]

1m 30.0s **7** Ran SP% **117.7**
Speed ratings: CSF £31.36 TOTE £14.20: £4.90, £2.50; DF 93.50.
**Owner** L W Heiligbrodt **Bred** Earlie Irving Mack **Trained** The Curragh, Co Kildare

**NOTEBOOK**
**Gaff(USA)** overcame trouble in running to win on his Irish debut. He showed a nice turn of foot to challenge between horses and led close home. This was a strange sort of race but he is highly regarded by his trainer. On his only other outing he had finished seventh of ten in a four and a half furlong race at Keeneland back in April.
**Zelkova(IRE)** has run in varied company to earn his rating, but had every chance until finding the winner too strong.
**Ridder** ran on well inside the last furlong and emerged with credit, as this run looked way above his York win.
**Only Make Believe** edged ahead at halfway but looked likely to hold on inside the last, only to succumb in the closing stages.
**Bibury Flyer** was having her 18th outing of the season, with just one success to show for it. She kept on well over the last furlong and a half without ever threatening.
**Allexina** was beaten fully two furlongs out.

**Crystal View(IRE)**, a wide-margin winner of a valuable Listowel nursery in bad ground nine days previously, might just have had enough for the time being. She missed the kick and although in contention at halfway, was not a factor in the straight.

5879 - 5883a (Foreign Racing) - See Raceform Interactive

# 5728 GOODWOOD (R-H)

Thursday, September 30

**OFFICIAL GOING: Good (good to firm in places)**

Jockeys stayed far side in the first couple of races, but came up the middle in the third before deciding the far side was best in the final four races.

Wind: slt against Weather: morning rain; overcast becoming bright

## 5885 3663 NURSERY STKS (H'CAP) 1m

2:05 (2:08) (D2) (0-85,83) 2-Y-O £5,200 (£1,600; £800; £400) Stalls High

Form RPR

4001 **1** **Something Exciting**[16] 5539 2-9-5 **78** TQuinn 12 87+
(DRCElsworth) *hld up in rr: pushed along in rr over 3f out: hdwy 2f out: str run to ld ins fnl f: won gng away* **14/1**

3011 **2** 1 1/2 **Secret Pact (IRE)**[12] 5636 2-9-6 **79** RFrench 18 84
(MJohnston) *mde most tl rdn and hdd ins fnl f: nt pce of wnr* **15/2**

6111 **3** 1 **Succession**[4] 5819 2-9-10 **83** 7ex SSanders 6 86
(SirMarkPrescott) *racd on outside: trckd ldr: chal 2f out: tl no ex and one pce ins fnl f* **3/1**[1]

3125 **4** 1 1/4 **Dove Cottage (IRE)**[19] 5466 2-8-8 **67** DKinsella 4 67
(WSKittow) *a.p: rdn over 2f out: styd on fnl f* **20/1**

61 **5** hd **Verbier (USA)**[15] 5559 2-9-2 **75** FNorton 11 75
(NACallaghan) *in tch: short of room and swtchd rt over 2f out: r.o wl fnl f* **9/2**[3]

3000 **6** hd **Shujune Al Hawaa (IRE)**[8] 5738 2-8-5 **64** (v[1]) CCatlin 5 63
(MRChannon) *mid-div: effrt over 1f out: nt pce to chal* **66/1**

21 **7** nk **Innocent Splendour**[39] 4966 2-9-7 **80** LDettori 14 79
(EALDunlop) *bhd and rdn sn after 1/2-way: styd on fnl f* **4/1**[2]

061 **8** nk **Press Express (IRE)**[21] 5406 2-9-6 **79** SHitchcott 10 77
(MRChannon) *t.k.h: prom tl wknd appr fnl f* **25/1**

4066 **9** 1/2 **He's A Star**[8] 5738 2-8-2 **61** RSmith 20 58
(RHannon) *a mid-div and nvr nr to chal* **16/1**

605 **10** 1 **Tohama**[16] 5534 2-9-1 **74** JQuinn 7 72+
(JLDunlop) *hld up in rr: reminders over 2f out: mde sme late hdwy* **25/1**

300 **11** 1/2 **Flag Point (IRE)**[39] 4967 2-9-2 **75** DaneO'Neill 17 69
(JLDunlop) *a bhd* **50/1**

2154 **12** 1 1/2 **Kalmini (USA)**[15] 5565 2-9-2 **75** (v[1]) TEDurcan 13 65
(MRChannon) *mid-div: sn pushed along bhd fnl 3f* **33/1**

055 **13** 6 **Pearl's A Singer (IRE)**[15] 5559 2-8-12 **71** RMullen 2 48
(MLWBell) *a in rr* **33/1**

301 **14** 5 **Jamaaron**[33] 5114 2-9-4 **77** RHughes 9 43
(RHannon) *slowly away: bit slipped c over to stands' side 3f out: sn wl bhd* **16/1**

0000 **15** 1 **Election Seeker (IRE)**[16] 5535 2-8-7 **65** ow1 PDobbs 16 30
(GLMoore) *a bhd* **66/1**

4500 **16** 8 **Mulberry Wine**[23] 5377 2-8-7 **66** DSweeney 19 12
(MBlanshard) *mid-div: bhd fnl 3f* **33/1**

564 **17** 17 **Knightsbridge Hill (IRE)**[21] 5406 2-9-4 **77** DHolland 15 —
(AKing) *in tch: prom tl wknd 2f out: eased ins fnl f* **16/1**

1m 42.07s (1.80) **Going Correction** +0.275s/f (Good) 17 Ran SP% **125.5**
Speed ratings: **102,100,99,98,98 97,97,97,96,95 95,93,87,82,81 73,56**CSF £107.53 CT £424.48 TOTE £15.60: £2.70, £2.10, £1.80, £5.80; EX 71.70.
**Owner** Setsquare Recruitment **Bred** R E Crutchley **Trained** Whitsbury, Hants

**FOCUS**

A decent nursery run at a reasonable pace; the form looks very solid and this race should produce plenty of winners. They raced towards the far side in the straight.

**NOTEBOOK**

**Something Exciting**, off the mark on her nursery debut over this trip on soft ground at Salisbury, followed up off a 7lb higher mark. She was well on top at the finish, but took a while to get going and is type to keep improving with time and distance. Her trainer may now look for some black type for her and the Zetland Stakes looks a realistic target, especially with the extra two furlongs at Newmarket almost sure to suit.

**Secret Pact(IRE)**, chasing the hat-trick off a 4lb higher mark than when successful in a Catterick nursery on his previous start, ran a fine race in defeat, only just failing to make virtually every yard at quite a decent pace. There should yet be more to come.

**Succession**, attempting the four-timer off a mark 7lb higher than when winning in good style at Musselburgh on her previous start, soon had a good position from her low draw but did not quite go through with her effort. A recent busy spell and rise in the weights may just have caught up with her.

**Dove Cottage(IRE)** continues in good form, but may just benefit from a slight drop in class.

**Verbier(USA)**, supported and off the mark over an extended seven furlongs at Beverley on her previous start, acquitted herself with credit in this tougher heat.

**Shujune Al Hawaa(IRE)**, fitted with a visor for the first time on this step up in trip, improved on recent efforts off a mark 6lb higher than in future. Her stable have their juveniles in great form and she would have to be of interest if turned out to run off her new mark.

**Innocent Splendour**, off the mark in an ordinary Folkestone maiden on her previous start, could never land a blow stepped up to a mile. She can be given another chance.

**Tohama** ◆ was very eye-catching. She met trouble when looking to make her effort and had to be switched inside for a run, but was never going to get back on terms with the principals and was not knocked about thereafter. She has plenty of ability and is one to follow.

**Jamaaron** *Official explanation: jockey said bit slipped through colt's mouth*

**Knightsbridge Hill(IRE)** *Official explanation: jockey said colt hung left throughout*

## 5886 EUROPEAN BREEDERS FUND KENT RELIANCE BUILDING SOCIETY CLASSIFIED STKS 1m

2:35 (2:37) (C2) 3-Y-O+ £6,960 (£2,640; £1,320; £600) Stalls High

Form RPR

3230 **1** **Desert Cristal (IRE)**[15] 5566 3-8-9 78 LDettori 10 88
(JRBoyle) *trckd ldr: led 2f out: r.o wl: readily* **7/1**[3]

2005 **2** 2 **Woody Valentine (USA)**[21] 5423 3-8-12 80 SChin 3 86
(MJohnston) *in tch: hrd rdn over 1f out to go 2nd ins fnl f* **12/1**

0461 **3** 1 1/2 **Jay Gee's Choice**[14] 5590 4-9-7 85 SHitchcott 1 88
(MRChannon) *led: rdn over 3f out: hdd 2f out: no ex and lost 2nd ins fnl f* **10/1**

0314 **4** 1 **Arkholme**[10] 5698 3-9-1 83 (b) PDoe 7 84
(PWinkworth) *in rr and sn pushed long: styd on ins fnl 2f: nvr nr to chal* **12/1**

0040 **5** 1 **Serieux**[4] 5813 5-9-2 80 (p) SDrowne 6 78
(MrsAJPerrett) *t.k.h: rdn 3f out: no hdwy fnl 2f* **7/1**[3]

3404 **6** 1/2 **Enford Princess**[15] 5566 3-8-11 82 RHughes 2 76
(RHannon) *in tch: rdn 2f out: one pce after* **10/1**

0553 **7** 1 1/4 **Binanti**[20] 5444 4-9-3 81 JQuinn 12 75
(PRChamings) *hld up: hdwy over 2f out: wknd ins fnl f* **8/1**

0-23 **8** nk **Sattam**[10] 5698 5-9-2 79 (v) WSupple 9 74
(MPTregoning) *plld hrd: a bhd* **5/1**[2]

10-0 **9** 2 1/2 **Caledonian (IRE)**[13] 5614 3-8-12 79 TQuinn 4 68
(DRCElsworth) *a bhd* **50/1**

1565 **10** 1/2 **Najaaba (USA)**[146] 1931 4-8-12 82 BReilly[(3)] 5 66
(MissJFeilden) *in rr: rdn 3f out: nvr on terms* **33/1**

1300 **11** 1 1/2 **Taruskin (IRE)**[84] 3671 3-9-2 84 DHolland 11 67
(NACallaghan) *trckd ldrs tl outpcd 2f out: eased whn btn fnl f* **25/1**

1106 **12** 3 1/2 **Salinor**[15] 5574 4-9-2 79 SSanders 8 55
(EFVaughan) *bhd: effrt 2f out: sn btn* **7/2**[1]

1m 40.49s (0.22) **Going Correction** +0.275s/f (Good)
**WFA** 3 from 4yo+ 4lb 12 Ran SP% **117.3**
Speed ratings: **109,107,105,104,103 103,101,101,98,98 96,93**CSF £85.61 TOTE £6.00: £2.10, £2.90, £2.90; EX 147.60.
**Owner** John Hopkins (t/a South Hatch Racing) **Bred** Illuminatus Investments **Trained** Epsom, Surrey

**FOCUS**

A tight race on the figures with just 4lb separating the entire field on the figures, but the form looks ordinary if sound enough. They raced just off the far rail in the straight.

**NOTEBOOK**

**Desert Cristal(IRE)** gained her only previous win over seven furlongs on fast ground, but this mile on good ground proved ideal and she doubled her career tally in emphatic fashion. She might have one more run this year and, in this form, would have to be looked at closely.

**Woody Valentine(USA)** has gained his last two wins over ten furlongs, so this was a decent effort dropped back in trip and he looks to be returning to form.

**Jay Gee's Choice**, successful in a similar event at Pontefract on his previous start, had every chance of following up.

**Arkholme** continues in good heart, but he was simply unable to get on terms with the principals. Waiting tactics appear to suit and they could be worth employing over ten furlongs.

**Serieux**, a beaten favourite at Ascot on his previous start, was again below form and remains without a win since April 2003. *Official explanation: jockey said horse was unsuited by good, good to firm ground*

**Enford Princess** is proving quite frustrating.

**Binanti**, a beaten favourite at Sandown on his previous start, travelled quite well but found little under pressure.

**Sattam** can be quite tricky and was far too keen. *Official explanation: jockey said gelding ran too free*

**Salinor** failed to build on the promise he showed on his return form a break at Yarmouth on his previous start and ran too bad to be true. *Official explanation: jockey said gelding was never travelling from 4f out*

## 5887 ANGLO IRISH BANK STKS (H'CAP) 7f

3:10 (3:11) (D2) (0-85,85) 3-Y-O+ £6,500 (£2,000; £1,000; £500) Stalls High

Form RPR

0021 **1** **Idle Power (IRE)**[23] 5379 6-8-13 **77** (p) LDettori 2 89
(JRBoyle) *trckd ldrs: led wl over 1f out: pushed out fnl f* **4/1**[2]

2004 **2** nk **Concer Eto**[15] 5574 5-8-9 **73** (p) WSupple 13 84
(SCWilliams) *t.k.h: hld up in mid-div: hdwy over 2f out to press wnr ins fnl f: nt go by* **10/1**

2036 **3** 1 1/2 **Bi Polar**[21] 5419 4-8-8 **72** CCatlin 10 79+
(DRCElsworth) *hld up in rr: hdwy over 1f out: str run to go 3rd ins fnl f* **7/1**[3]

650 **4** 3/4 **Taranaki**[1] 5874 6-9-2 **85** NDeSouza[(5)] 16 90
(PDCundell) *a.p: ev ch 2f out: no ex fnl f* **8/1**

5150 **5** 1 1/4 **Stevedore (IRE)**[12] 5652 3-8-5 **72** GCarter 5 74
(BRMillman) *in tch: rdn over 2f out: one pce fnl f* **25/1**

2400 **6** hd **Quantum Leap**[13] 5614 7-8-7 **71** oh1 (v) DHolland 3 72
(SDow) *in rr: mde sme late hdwy* **33/1**

0000 **7** hd **Master Robbie**[19] 5468 5-9-6 **84** SHitchcott 9 85
(MRChannon) *bhd tl hdwy over 2f out: fdd fnl f* **10/1**

0000 **8** 1 1/4 **Border Edge**[13] 5614 6-8-13 **77** (v) GBaker 4 75
(JJBridger) *in tch: one pce ins fnl 2f* **40/1**

1000 **9** 1 3/4 **Hey Presto**[21] 5419 4-8-8 **72** ow1 DaneO'Neill 7 65
(CGCox) *bhd tl hdwy over 2f out: wknd ins fnl f* **33/1**

2100 **10** 1/2 **Instructor**[121] 2560 3-8-8 **75** RHughes 14 67
(RHannon) *led: hdd wl over 1f out: wknd* **33/1**

0040 **11** shd **Star Sensation (IRE)**[15] 5574 4-8-11 **75** SSanders 8 67
(PWHarris) *slowly away: a bhd* **14/1**

6006 **12** 1 1/2 **Anuvasteel**[20] 5444 3-8-6 **73** FNorton 11 61
(NACallaghan) *in tch: rdn over 2f out: wknd over 1f out* **7/2**[1]

0310 **13** 1 1/4 **Waterside (IRE)**[20] 5444 5-9-2 **80** EAhern 1 64
(GLMoore) *in tch on outside: rdn 3f out: wknd over 1f out* **16/1**

0612 **14** shd **Sabrina Brown**[32] 5148 3-8-6 **73** ow1 RHavlin 6 57
(GBBalding) *mid-div: rdn over 2f out: sn btn* **12/1**

2010 **15** 8 **Just A Glimmer**[135] 2206 4-9-1 **82** LPKeniry[(3)] 12 45
(LGCottrell) *trckd ldrs: rdn over 2f out: wknd qckly wl over 1f out and eased* **14/1**

-050 **16** 3/4 **Betty Stogs (IRE)**[28] 5249 3-8-10 **77** RSmith 15 38
(CGCox) *v.s.a: a bhd* **50/1**

1m 28.72s (0.69) **Going Correction** +0.275s/f (Good)
**WFA** 3 from 4yo+ 3lb 16 Ran SP% **128.0**
Speed ratings: **107,106,104,104,102 102,102,100,98,98 98,96,94,94,85 84**CSF £43.51 CT £297.24 TOTE £4.80: £1.60, £2.80, £2.60, £2.70; EX 62.70.
**Owner** The Idle B's **Bred** Mountarmstrong Stud **Trained** Epsom, Surrey

**FOCUS**

A fair handicap, but the early pace was just steady and the form is a bit messy. They were spread out all over the track in the straight, but the middle was the place to be.

**NOTEBOOK**

**Idle Power(IRE)**, successful over seven furlongs on Lingfield's Polytrack on his previous start, followed up returned to turf off just a 2lb higher mark. Given that he appeared to idle in front, he is value for a little more than the winning margin and, unlikely to go up too much for this, remains one to have on your side.

**Concer Eto** has gained all of his previous six wins with firm in the going description, but handled this ground just fine and looked the most likely winner a furlong out, the winner just found more under pressure.

**Bi Polar** ran another respectable race, especially considering a stronger end-to-end gallop would have suited, but he remains with just a maiden win to his name.

**Taranaki**, last of 19 over six furlongs at Salisbury the previous day, left that form behind with a creditable effort. His draw against the rail proved of very little advantage with the main group racing down the centre of the track, and he was simply unable to sustain his effort.

**Stevedore(IRE)** had conditions to suit and did not appear to have any excuses.

**Master Robbie** raced more towards the far side than the middle in the straight and ran creditably in the circumstances.

**Instructor** raced towards the far side in the straight and had no chance with those down the middle of the track.

**Anuvasteel** failed to build on the promise he showed off the back of a break when unlucky at Goodwood on his previous start and was disappointing.
**Sabrina Brown** *Official explanation: trainer said filly was lame behind the following morning*

## 5888 CITIGROUP CHARLTON HUNT SUPREME STKS (GROUP 3) 7f
3:40 (3:43) (A1) 3-Y-O+ **£29,000** (£11,000; £5,500; £2,500) **Stalls** High

Form RPR
1010 **1** **Mac Love**[5] 5780 3-8-9 106 GCarter 7 117
(JAkehurst) *t.k.h: hld up in rr: hdwy 2f out: rdn to ld appr fnl f: r.o wl* **14/1**
1033 **2** *2* **Vanderlin**[21] 5422 5-8-12 105 LPKeniry 9 112
(AMBalding) *hld up in tch: wnt 2nd appr fnl f: r.o but no imp* **16/1**
3201 **3** *shd* **Polar Way**[31] 5199 5-8-12 114 RHughes 2 112
(MrsAJPerrett) *hld up in rr: stdy hdwy 2f out: ev ch ent fnl f: r.o one pce* **5/1**[3]
4053 **4** *1* **So Will I**[19] 5471 3-8-9 106 (p) WSupple 11 109
(MPTregoning) *in tch: kpt on one pce fnl f* **11/1**
1036 **5** *2* **Kheleyf (USA)**[46] 4795 3-8-13 111 LDettori 4 108
(SaeedBinSuroor) *t.k.h: led briefly over 1f out: wknd ins fnl f* **2/1**[1]
2143 **6** *1* **Court Masterpiece**[21] 5414 4-8-12 110 SSanders 6 101
(EALDunlop) *hld up in rr: hdwy whn nt clr run and swtchd rt appr fnl f: no further hdwy* **3/1**[2]
0300 **7** *½* **Kings Point (IRE)**[13] 5610 3-8-9 100 (b[1]) DaneO'Neill 3 100
(RHannon) *trckd ldrs: rdn and wknd over 1f out* **50/1**
2266 **8** *hd* **Suggestive**[13] 5610 6-8-12 110 (b) DHolland 10 100
(WJHaggas) *towards rr: rdn over 3f out: btn 2f out* **7/1**
0010 **9** *shd* **Royal Storm (IRE)**[5] 5781 5-8-12 105 SDrowne 8 99
(MrsAJPerrett) *led after 1f: hdd wl over 1f out: wknd qckly* **16/1**
5400 **10** *20* **Rockets 'n Rollers (IRE)**[19] 5488 4-8-12 102 PDobbs 1 47
(RHannon) *a bhd: rdn and btn 2f out: eased ent fnl f* **50/1**
0026 **11** *5* **Atavus**[19] 5471 7-8-12 92 JMackay 5 34
(GGMargarson) *led for 1f: prom tl wknd and short of room over 1f out: eased 1f out* **50/1**

1m 28.19s (0.16) **Going Correction** +0.275s/f (Good)
**WFA** 3 from 4yo+ 3lb **11** Ran SP% **120.1**
Speed ratings: **110,107,107,106,104 103,102,102,102,79 73**CSF £219.28 TOTE £17.60: £3.30, £3.60, £1.80; EX 126.50.
**Owner** Vimal Khosla **Bred** Kingwood Bloodstock **Trained** Epsom, Surrey
■ Stewards Enquiry : D Holland one-day ban: used whip with excessive frequency (Oct 11)

**FOCUS**
An average Group Three contest run in an ordinary time, with Mac Love and Vanderlin running to a similar level of form to that they showed when first and third in an Epsom Listed race earlier in the month. The field raced towards the near-side rail in the straight.

**NOTEBOOK**
**Mac Love**, a really tough sort, he has been a little inconsistent this season but has, on the main, been progressing and gained his first Group success in good style, despite having raced very keenly. Just a small horse with 26 races under his belt going into this, he is not an obvious improver, but this was career best and he is one to keep on the right side of.
**Vanderlin** had his ideal conditions, but has never won in this grade and, despite doing his best, he was again just found out. He pretty much ran to the form he showed to be third to today's winner in an Epsom Listed race on his previous start.
**Polar Way** found this tougher than the Warwick conditions race he won on his previous outing, but still ran a solid race and would have gone much closer with better luck in running.
**So Will I**, with cheekpieces on for the first time, ran better than his finishing position suggests as he was forced to make his challenge widest of all (quite a way of the near side rail) and just lacked a decisive change of pace in the circumstances.
**Kheleyf(USA)** has not really gone on from his Jersey Stakes success and this was something of a lacklustre effort. A return to faster ground may suit. *Official explanation: jockey said colt was unsuited by good, good to firm going*
**Court Masterpiece**, third in a Group Two at Doncaster on his previous start, got stopped when looking to make his challenge and is much better than the bare form would suggest.
**Suggestive** was again below his best and is not easy to predict.
**Rockets 'n Rollers(IRE)** *Official explanation: jockey said colt was never travelling*

## 5889 LLOYDS TSB DRESS REHEARSAL STKS (H'CAP) 2m
4:15 (4:15) (E3) (0-70,71) 3-Y-O+ **£3,250** (£1,000; £500; £250) **Stalls** High

Form RPR
0136 **1** **Masterman Ready**[17] 5523 3-8-13 **66** EAhern 1 74
(PWHarris) *hld up early: hdwy to ld over 6f out: hdd over 2f out: rallied to ld again 1f out: drvn out* **7/1**[3]
6004 **2** *½* **Isa'Af (IRE)**[19] 5456 5-9-5 **65** PMakin[(5)] 5 73
(PWHiatt) *trckd ldrs: led over 2f out: hdd 1f out: hrd rdn and no imp cl home* **7/2**[2]
0000 **3** *4* **Medica Boba**[21] 5410 3-8-2 **55** JMackay 6 58
(HMorrison) *hld up: rdn 4f out: plugged on one pce to go 3rd ins fnl f* **33/1**
6601 **4** *2½* **Darn Good**[3] 5826 3-9-4 **71** 6ex (b) RHughes 8 71
(RHannon) *in rr: rdn 3f out: kpt on one pce but nvr a danger* **5/2**[1]
0050 **5** *10* **Cantrip**[12] 5645 4-8-10 **51** oh6 JQuinn 7 39
(MissBSanders) *in tch: t.k.h: rdn over 3f out: one pce after* **16/1**
0516 **6** *11* **Garston Star**[41] 4927 3-8-2 **62** DerekNolan[(7)] 9 37
(JSMoore) *sn led: hdd over 6f out: rdn over 3f out: sn btn* **12/1**
3435 **7** *12* **Scarrabus (IRE)**[23] 5382 3-8-12 **65** TQuinn 3 25
(BGPowell) *hld up in rr: nvr got into r* **11/1**
1030 **8** *1½* **Illeana (GER)**[62] 4302 3-8-0 **53** FNorton 2 12
(WRMuir) *hld up: rdn over 3f out: wl bhd fnl 3f* **16/1**
232 **9** *dist* **Champagne Shadow (IRE)**[29] 5216 3-8-12 **65** (b) LDettori 4 —
(GLMoore) *hld up in rr: lost tch: over 3f out and eased to walk over 2f out: t.o* **7/2**[2]

3m 34.56s (3.90) **Going Correction** +0.275s/f (Good)
**WFA** 3 from 4yo+ 12lb **9** Ran SP% **116.2**
Speed ratings: **101,100,98,97,92 87,81,80,—**CSF £31.96 CT £763.80 TOTE £10.80: £2.30, £2.20, £12.80; EX 40.40.
**Owner** The Mastermen **Bred** Miss G J Abbey **Trained** Ringshall, Bucks

**FOCUS**
A moderate heat, but they went a decent pace and a good effort from Masterman Ready, who was never far away and really had to battle for this. They raced near side in the straight, but the form is modest and not sure to work out.

**NOTEBOOK**
**Masterman Ready** ◆, racing over two miles for the first time, deserves plenty of credit for this given that he was always close to a decent pace and committed for home a long way out. He then had two battles, one to see off long-time leader Garston Star (who eventually dropped right out) and then one to get the better of Isa'Af in the closing stages. As a result, he is value for more than the winning margin and could follow up.
**Isa'Af(IRE)** came to win his race, he was simply outstayed by the winner. Still a good effort to finish clear of the rest, albeit a moderate bunch.
**Medica Boba**, racing beyond ten furlongs for the first time, posted her best effort to date, but will need to improve again to win a similar race.
**Darn Good** was unable to run to the form he showed to win a competitive but slightly muddling affair at Bath on his previous outing under a 6lb penalty.
**Cantrip**, twice a winner over a mile and a half, failed to prove her stamina for this trip.
**Garston Star** *Official explanation: jockey said gelding did not stay*
**Illeana(GER)** *Official explanation: trainer reported filly did not stay trip*
**Champagne Shadow(IRE)** *Official explanation: jockey said colt lost his action*

## 5890 EUROPEAN BREEDERS FUND PADDY POWER MEDIAN AUCTION MAIDEN FILLIES' STKS 6f
4:50 (4:53) (D3) 2-Y-O **£3,250** (£1,000; £500; £250) **Stalls** Low

Form RPR
625 **1** **Love Thirty**[12] 5648 2-8-11 94 TEDurcan 7 78+
(MRChannon) *trckd ldr: led 2f out: edgd rt uner press: jst hld on* **5/6**[1]
**2** *shd* **Cape Columbine** 2-8-11 TQuinn 2 78+
(DRCElsworth) *hld up: hdwy over 1f out: fin fast fnl f: jst failed* **11/2**[3]
5250 **3** *2* **Chutney Mary (IRE)**[23] 5377 2-8-11 68 EAhern 10 72
(JGPortman) *led tl hdd 2f out: r.o but nt pce of first 2* **16/1**
220 **4** *2* **Honey Ryder**[12] 5648 2-8-11 83 SSanders 11 66
(DRLoder) *trckd ldrs: rdn 2f out: wknd ins fnl f* **7/2**[2]
0 **5** *3½* **Silver Bark**[9] 5720 2-8-11 LDettori 5 56
(EALDunlop) *in tch: rdn 2f out: wknd over 1f out* **10/1**
**6** *nk* **Tapa** 2-8-8 LPKeniry[(3)] 8 55
(AMBalding) *outpcd and a towards rr* **40/1**
**7** *3½* **Flying Heart** 2-8-11 CCatlin 3 44
(MRChannon) *outpcd thrght* **25/1**
0 **8** *1* **Belle Chanson**[16] 5536 2-8-11 DSweeney 9 41
(JRBoyle) *s.i.s: sn prom on outside: wknd wl over 1f out* **40/1**
**9** *4* **Flaunt N Flirt** 2-8-11 WSupple 4 29
(MPTregoning) *slowly away and wnt rt s: rn green and a bhd* **12/1**
0 **10** *5* **Jubilee Coin**[13] 5609 2-8-11 SDrowne 1 14
(GBBalding) *t.k.h: hld up: wl bhd fnl 2f* **66/1**

1m 14.1s (1.26) **Going Correction** +0.15s/f (Good) **10** Ran SP% **125.0**
Speed ratings: **97,96,94,91,86 86,81,80,75,68**CSF £6.48 TOTE £1.90: £1.10, £1.90, £3.00; EX 6.70.
**Owner** John Livock Bloodstock Limited **Bred** Major And Mrs R B Kennard And Whitsbury Manor St **Trained** West Ilsley, Berks

**FOCUS**
Not much strength in depth with the winner scoring despite being well below his previous form, but a very promising debut from Cape Columbine. They all stayed near side.

**NOTEBOOK**
**Love Thirty**, who ran a blinder when fifth under a big weight in the Watership Down Stud Sales race on her previous outing, should have found this easier but only scraped home after idling in front. She will be seen to better effect back in a more strongly-run race when she can get a longer lead, but may not be easy to place off a mark in the 90s.
**Cape Columbine** ◆, a 33,000gns, half-sister to Group-class sprinter Cape Of Good Hope, made a very pleasing debut. She took a while to pick up, but was really motoring at the finish and only just failed to get up. She should improve considerably for the run and is likely to be winning soon.
**Chutney Mary(IRE)**, thoroughly exposed, had every chance against the near-side rail but was simply left behind by two better horses.
**Honey Ryder**, well held and behind today's winner in the Watership Down Stud Sales race, did not run to her mark of 83 dropped in grade and was very disappointing.
**Silver Bark** did not really improve on her promising debut effort and may do better when handicapped.

## 5891 SUTTON BUSINESS CENTRE MAIDEN STKS 1m 1f 192y
5:20 (5:21) (D2) 3-Y-O **£6,500** (£2,000; £1,000; £500) **Stalls** Low

Form RPR
**1** **Double Deputy (IRE)** 3-9-0 (t) LDettori 7 78+
(SaeedBinSuroor) *led for 1f: restrained bhd ldrs: led over 2f out: rdn clr appr fnl f: easily* **7/4**[2]
**2** *4* **Day Care** 3-9-0 RHughes 4 70+
(MrsAJPerrett) *s.i.s: sn trckd ldr: rdn over 2f out: kpt on but nt pce of wnr* **5/4**[1]
3003 **3** *1* **Polar Dancer**[18] 5495 3-8-9 55 SDrowne 2 63
(MrsAJPerrett) *in tch: rdn and kpt on one pce to go 3rd ins fnl f* **14/1**
005 **4** *¾* **Danze Romance**[45] 4813 3-8-9 64 TQuinn 1 62
(JLDunlop) *in rr: hdwy fr 3f out: styd on but nvr nr to chal* **16/1**
0302 **5** *1¼* **Royal Lustre**[18] 5495 3-9-0 67 RHavlin 8 65
(JHMGosden) *t.k.h: led 5f out: sn clr: rdn and hdd over 2f out: one pce after* **6/1**[3]
000 **6** *17* **Charing Cross (IRE)**[16] 5538 3-9-0 RBrisland 6 32
(GLMoore) *bhd: brief effrt over 2f out: sn wl btn* **50/1**
**7** *5* **Tank (IRE)** 3-8-9 NChalmers[(5)] 9 23
(MissSheenaWest) *a bhd* **33/1**
0 **8** *3½* **Elzees**[257] 553 3-9-0 VVenkaya 5 16
(DRCElsworth) *a bhd* **66/1**
00-0 **9** *12* **Kwai Baby (USA)**[18] 5495 3-8-9 35 ADaly 3 —
(JJBridger) *a bhd* **100/1**
00 **10** *3½* **King's Minstrel (IRE)**[131] 2311 3-9-0 PDoe 10 —
(RRowe) *slowly away: t.k.h and led after 1f: hdd 5f outrdn and wknd over 3f out* **66/1**

2m 11.45s (3.77) **Going Correction** +0.275s/f (Good) **10** Ran SP% **116.5**
Speed ratings: **95,91,91,90,89 75,71,69,59,56**CSF £4.19 TOTE £2.90: £1.50, £1.30, £2.00; EX 4.20 Place 6 £302.22, Place 5 £150.52.
**Owner** Godolphin **Bred** Gainsborough Stud Management Ltd **Trained** Newmarket, Suffolk

**FOCUS**
Just an ordinary maiden for the track, run in a modest time and not that competitive, with the third and fourth setting the standard. They all raced near side in the straight, although the winner was a little way off the rail.

**NOTEBOOK**
**Double Deputy(IRE)**, a half-brother to the top-class two-year-old, later high-class six-to-eight furlong performer Lend A Hand, out of a winner over a mile and a half, had to be stoked up to hit top gear, but powered away in the closing stages and simply outclassed these rivals. He should improve and promises to get further.
**Day Care**, a half-brother to a couple of ten-furlong winners out of a middle-distance winner in France, did not find as much as had looked off the bridle, given that Hughes looked pretty confident while the eventual winner was hard at work two out. This was still a promising-enough debut, although he will need to improve next time.
**Polar Dancer**, rated just 55, ran above her mark but still puts the form into perspective. She will be better off in handicap company, especially before she is reassessed.
**Danze Romance** never really posed a serious threat and may do better over further in handicaps.
**Royal Lustre** did not last home under a positive ride and it is hard to believe he is a half-brother to Lammtarra.
T/Plt: £354.10 to a £1 stake. Pool: £53,414.80. 110.10 winning tickets. T/Qpdt: £45.00 to a £1 stake. Pool: £3,621.50. 59.50 winning tickets. JS

# 5716 NEWMARKET (R-H)

Thursday, September 30

**OFFICIAL GOING: Good (good to firm in places) changing to good (good to soft in places) after 2.25 (race 3)**

Wind: Slight against Weather: Showers

## 5892 UNICOIN HOMES NOEL MURLESS STKS (LISTED RACE) 1m 6f

1:15 (1:16) (A1) 3-Y-O £17,400 (£6,600; £3,300; £1,500) Stalls Centre

Form RPR

1132 1 **Tungsten Strike (USA)**[54] 4550 3-8-12 86 MartinDwyer 4 110
(MrsAJPerrett) *led: hit rails after 3f: hdd over 2f out: rallied to ld 1f out: hung lft ins fnl f: styd on* **22/1**

11 2 2 **Carte Diamond (USA)**[83] 3716 3-8-12 96 KDarley 2 107
(MJohnston) *lw: chsd wnr tl led over 2f out: rdn and hdd 1f out: hung lft and no ex ins fnl f* **7/1**[3]

3144 3 3 **Lochbuie (IRE)**[26] 5288 3-8-12 98 JFEgan 5 103
(GWragg) *lw: hld up: hdwy over 5f out: rdn over 3f out: styd on same pce fnl 2f* **9/2**[2]

4211 4 nk **Lost Soldier Three (IRE)**[20] 5435 3-8-12 104 KFallon 3 103
(LMCumani) *lw: hld up: rdn over 3f out: no imp fnl 2f* **8/11**[1]

2010 5 5 **Massif Centrale**[65] 4215 3-8-12 98 RLMoore 7 96
(DRCElsworth) *chsd ldrs: rdn over 3f out: wknd over 1f out* **20/1**

0440 6 5 **Mutafanen**[33] 5106 3-8-12 103 RHills 6 89
(EALDunlop) *hld up: rdn over 3f out: wknd 2f out* **9/1**

1040 7 dist **Anousa (IRE)**[34] 5093 3-9-1 91 JPMurtagh 1 —
(PHowling) *chsd ldrs: rdn over 4f out: wknd over 3f out* **50/1**

2m 56.93s (-3.39) **Going Correction** +0.05s/f (Good) **7 Ran SP% 109.7**

Speed ratings: **111,109,108,107,105 102,—**CSF £150.10 TOTE £22.00: £5.20, £2.10; EX 107.60.

**Owner** John Connolly **Bred** Minster Stud **Trained** Pulborough, W Sussex

**FOCUS**

The form is probably not that easy to rate and possibly not the most reliable with Tungsten Strike being allowed his own way up front - it paid to be on the pace all afternoon - and although possibly flattered, is still a progressive gelding. Carte Diamond is the one to take from the race, being a lightly-raced colt open to masses of improvement. The winning time was fair for a race of its type.

**NOTEBOOK**

**Tungsten Strike(USA)**, who has been progressive at a lesser level, but is proven at two miles and Dwyer made plenty of use of his extra stamina by taking a clear early lead. Having gradually come back to the field, he was headed by Carte Diamond running into the final quarter mile, but dug deep and his superior stamina won him the day despite hanging in the final 100 yards. This win results in him getting a 7lb penalty for the Cesarewitch which should leave him on 7st 11lb, but odds of around 12/1 look a little skinny as he has an extra couple of furlongs to go and may lack the experience of some of the hardened handicappers.

**Carte Diamond(USA)** ◆, who only started out his racing career back in June, had won both his maiden and handicap, a good effort for one so inexperienced, and had been off since then. He led the main pack throughout and closed down the winner to take it up approaching the two pole. However, he was unable to stay with the winner when that rival found extra and had to settle for second. Clearly a highly-progressive colt, he will stay this trip better with another season under his belt and has the making of a Group class performer.

**Lochbuie(IRE)** continues to go the right way and is another who has realistic chances of being able to score at this level with a little further improvement.

**Lost Soldier Three(IRE)**, who has gone up a total of 17lb in his last three outings - winning competitive handicaps the last twice - ran rather flat and failed to pick up when asked to go about his work by Fallon, eventually running on all too late. He is better than this but may be feeling the effects of a long first season, and could ideally do with a break.

**Massif Centrale** has now failed to run a race in three attempts at Listed/Group level. He is in the horrible position of being too high in the weights to win a handicap and not good enough at this stage to win at this sort of level.

**Mutafanen** has taken a dip in form recently but has had a long season.

**Anousa(IRE)**, despite facing an impossible task with the 3lb penalty, should have ran better and finished tailed-off. *Official explanation: jockey said colt hung badly left-handed throughout*

## 5893 ROLLS-ROYCE MOTOR CARS LONDON ROUS STKS (LISTED RACE) 5f

1:50 (1:53) (A1) 3-Y-O+ £17,400 (£6,600; £3,300; £1,500) Stalls High

Form RPR

3300 1 **Nights Cross (IRE)**[32] 5171 3-8-11 101 (v) ACulhane 13 106
(MRChannon) *chsd ldr: rdn over 1f out: r.o to ld wl ins fnl f* **11/1**

001 2 ½ **Steve's Champ (CHI)**[18] 5505 4-9-4 (b) JPMurtagh 16 110
(RuneHaugen, Norway) *w'like: b.hind: led: rdn over 1f out: hdd wl ins fnl f* **12/1**

1361 3 1¼ **Baltic King**[9] 5712 4-8-12 104 (t) RLMoore 8 100
(HMorrison) *w.hind: hld up: hdwy and nt clr run over 1f out: r.o ins fnl f : nt rch ldrs* **5/2**[1]

2214 4 1 **Texas Gold**[12] 5647 6-8-12 106 MartinDwyer 9 96
(WRMuir) *lw: a.p: rdn and edgd rt over 1f out: styd on same pce* **11/2**[2]

0010 5 ½ **Red Sovereign**[15] 5563 3-8-6 74 MFenton 15 89?
(IAWood) *b.hind: chsd ldrs: rdn over 1f out: edgd lft and no ex ins fnl f* **100/1**

0 6 nk **The Cat's Whiskers (NZ)**[21] 5416 4-8-7 PRobinson 14 88
(PWChapple-Hyam) *swtg: hld up: hdwy and nt clr run over 1f out: r.o* **33/1**

0410 7 ½ **Dragon Flyer (IRE)**[11] 5671 5-8-7 98 JFEgan 11 86
(MQuinn) *lw: prom: rdn 1/2-way: nt clr run 2f out: styd on same pce fnl f* **25/1**

0040 8 shd **Millybaa (USA)**[12] 5661 4-8-7 93 RWinston 4 86
(RGuest) *hld up: hdwy 1/2-way: styd on same pce fnl f* **25/1**

0601 9 nk **Halmahera (IRE)**[22] 5393 9-8-12 101 NCallan 3 90
(KARyan) *b.hind: sn outpcd: r.o ins fnl f: nrst fin* **9/1**

3030 10 2 **High Reach**[12] 5647 4-8-12 94 KFallon 12 83
(TGMills) *chsd ldrs: rdn over 1f out: wknd ins fnl f* **6/1**[3]

0065 11 shd **Proud Boast**[18] 5505 6-8-7 90 KDarley 1 77
(DNicholls) *sn outpcd* **16/1**

5000 12 ¾ **Green Manalishi**[31] 5181 3-8-11 87 RHills 5 80
(DWPArbuthnot) *hld up: n.d* **25/1**

0050 13 ½ **Zarzu**[8] 5730 5-8-12 77 RThomas 10 78
(CRDore) *b: chsd ldrs over 3f* **100/1**

0000 14 nk **Silver Prelude**[15] 5563 3-8-11 80 IMongan 2 77
(DKIvory) *b: b.hind: lw: sn outpcd* **66/1**

6534 15 ½ **Colonel Cotton (IRE)**[9] 5712 5-8-12 97 (v) WRyan 7 75
(NACallaghan) *sn bhd* **11/1**

59.46 secs (-0.95) **Going Correction** +0.05s/f (Good)

**WFA** 3 from 4yo+ 1lb **15 Ran SP% 116.4**

Speed ratings: **109,108,106,104,103 103,102,102,101,98 98,97,96,96,95**CSF £123.95 TOTE £12.30: £3.20, £3.40, £1.80; EX 173.60 Trifecta £1049.80 Pool: £3,253.09. 2.20 winning units..

**Owner** Ridgeway Downs Racing **Bred** Tim Taylor **Trained** West Ilsley, Berks

**FOCUS**

A competitive Listed heat where it paid to be up on the pace, though the time was unexceptional for a Listed contest and the form is dubious, being somewhat held down by 74-rated Red Sovereign.

**NOTEBOOK**

**Nights Cross(IRE)**, who is proven over five furlongs with cut in the ground, did not get home over six most recently and this proved a much more suitable test. He was never far off the pace and he came with a strong run inside the last furlong to get up in the final 50 yards. He takes his racing extremely well and is the type to win again in a similar event this backend, but reportedly heads to the Horses-In-Training sales.

**Steve's Champ(CHI)**, a smart front-runner in his homeland, made no show when down the field at Chester earlier in the season, but this was much more his form and he went very close to landing a hat-trick. He went at it from the start and was not stopping at the line - he has won over seven and a half furlongs - but the winner just had a bit too much in the finish.

**Baltic King** is a smart performer on his day and he ran well - doing all his best work in the final furlong. His best performances have come at courses with a stiffer finish and Ascot is probably his ideal course but, unfortunately for him, there is no racing there until 2006.

**Texas Gold**, who could have done without the rain, ran another sound race and seems to have successfully made the leap from handicapper to Pattern sprinter. Better can be expected of him back on fast ground, but that is going to be hard to come by at this time of year.

**Red Sovereign** had absolutely no chance at the weights and her overall level of form fell way short of the standard required. However, having been up with the pace throughout she managed to hold her position and ran way above herself in fifth. Evidently flattered by the run, she will need to be turned out again quickly if she is to make the most of her current mark as a sharp rise looks imminent.

**The Cat's Whiskers(NZ)**, who did not see out seven furlongs on her British debut at Doncaster most recently, ran well on this drop in trip but, judging by the way she finished, six furlongs may prove to be her distance. *Official explanation: jockey said filly reared on leaving stalls and was slowly away*

**Dragon Flyer(IRE)** may have been a little unlucky not to get closer as she was denied a clear passage when she was trying to get back into it. *Official explanation: jockey said saddle slipped*

**Halmahera(IRE)** found this trip too sharp and was never getting there in time.

**High Reach** dropped out disappointingly and may have found the change in going against him. *Official explanation: jockey said gelding lost his action in final furlong*

**Colonel Cotton(IRE)** *Official explanation: jockey said gelding suffered interference in running and was denied a clear run in closing stages*

## 5894 SKY BET CHEVELEY PARK STKS (GROUP 1) (FILLIES) 6f

2:25 (2:25) (A1) 2-Y-O £110,606 (£41,954; £20,977; £9,535) Stalls High

Form RPR

4161 1 **Magical Romance (IRE)**[10] 5701 2-8-11 83 RWinston 4 107
(BJMeehan) *chsd ldr: rdn and ev ch fr over 1f out: r.o to ld nr fin* **40/1**

11 2 nk **Suez**[28] 5250 2-8-11 100 PRobinson 7 106
(MAJarvis) *led: rdn over 1f out: hdd towards fin* **4/1**[2]

111 3 nk **Damson (IRE)**[53] 4589 2-8-11 KFallon 5 106
(DavidWachman, Ire) *chsd ldrs: rdn and ev ch fr over 1f out: r.o* **10/11**[1]

1131 4 ½ **Golden Legacy (IRE)**[12] 5626 2-8-11 PHanagan 2 104
(RAFahey) *lw: hld up: hdwy over 1f out: r.o* **16/1**

6261 5 hd **Slip Dance (IRE)**[11] 5681 2-8-11 JFEgan 6 103
(EamonTyrrell, Ire) *gd sort: lw: chsd ldrs: rdn and ev ch whn n.m.r 1f out: styd on* **40/1**

1211 6 3½ **Soar**[42] 4885 2-8-11 100 JPMurtagh 3 93
(JRFanshawe) *h.d.w: unruly stalls: s.i.s: hld up: effrt over 1f out: wknd ins fnl f* **4/1**[2]

1110 7 3½ **Jewel In The Sand (IRE)**[25] 5325 2-8-11 100 RLMoore 1 82
(RHannon) *lw: hld up: rdn over 2f out: wknd over 1f out* **12/1**[3]

1m 12.61s (-0.48) **Going Correction** +0.05s/f (Good) **7 Ran SP% 110.8**

Speed ratings: **105,104,104,103,103 98,93**CSF £180.31 TOTE £27.20: £6.30, £2.50; EX 76.70.

**Owner** F C T Wilson **Bred** Quay Bloodstock And Samac Ltd **Trained** Upper Lambourn, Berks

**FOCUS**

There was a going change soon after this race and that may have contributed to the shock result. Hard to know what to make of the form of this Group One event with the 40/1 winner having been favoured by the way the race was run and the hot favourite failing to run her race in third. The winning time was just slightly slower than would be expected for a race of its type in the conditions, and the form appears below the normal standard for the race.

**NOTEBOOK**

**Magical Romance(IRE)**, who evidently ran below par when last of six behind Soar in the Princess Margaret back in July on unsuitably fast ground, had got back to winning ways on her nursery debut Leicester and again with cut in the ground, caused a huge shock in just getting the better of Suez to land this Group One contest. On the pace throughout, she dropped back to third when Damson made her move around runners, but she stuck out her neck and came back through to score. Bred to be more of a miler, she should improve from two to three and, although maybe not having the make up of a classic Guineas winner, has to merit respect for the spring showpiece.

**Suez**, two from two coming into the race - with maiden and Listed wins - bagged the far rail and stuck to her task well under pressure - not giving in to the winner. Her two wins came on a sound surface and there should be more to come from her on decent ground.

**Damson(IRE)**, the top filly this summer over this sort of distance - winner of the Queen Mary and Phoenix Stakes - has been on the go since April and, combined with the fact the ground was softer than ideal, ran a below-par race. She momentarily looked set to take it up but never quite got to the front. She is bred to get the Guineas distance, and will be suited by a return to quicker conditions, but needs to leave this form behind if she is to take the opening 2005 fillies' classic.

**Golden Legacy(IRE)** came into this as an in-form filly on the back of a Group Three win and improved again to run a big race close up in fourth. She is more of an out-and-out sprinter and will struggle in the early part of next season as a result of precious little opportunities for three-year-old sprinting fillies.

**Slip Dance(IRE)** got much closer to Damson than she had when fourth behind her in June - further emphasising the below-par running of the favourite - and continues to have a profitable season.

**Soar** ran a below-par race and that can probably be put down to her playing up before the start, then being slowly away and held up in a race where it paid to be on the pace. She is better than this and has a fair chance of making the grade as a sprinter next term. *Official explanation: jockey said filly ran flat*

**Jewel In The Sand(IRE)** has fallen short of what is required at Group One level the last twice, and dropped away on what was the softest ground she has encountered to date. *Official explanation: jockey said filly was never travelling*

## 5895 SOMERVILLE TATTERSALL STKS (GROUP 3) (C&G) 7f

3:00 (3:01) (A1) 2-Y-O £34,800 (£13,200; £6,600; £3,000) Stalls High

Form RPR

01 1 **Diktatorial**[41] 4922 2-8-9 MartinDwyer 9 104
(AMBalding) *lw: sn led: hdd over 2f out: rallied to ld ins fnl f: drvn out* **3/1**[2]

2110 2 nk **Crimson Sun (USA)**[43] 4857 2-8-9 97 RHills 1 103
(SaeedBinSuroor) *trckd ldrs: led over 2f out: rdn and hdd ins fnl f: r.o* **12/1**

2230 3 shd **Mister Genepi**[20] 5437 2-8-9 95 PHanagan 4 103
(WRMuir) *lw: hld up: hdwy over 1f out: r.o* **33/1**

51 4 ½ **Santa Fe (IRE)**[23] 5373 2-8-9 91 KFallon 6 102
(SirMichaelStoute) *lw: a.p: rdn over 1f out: nt much ins fnl f: styd on* **11/2**[3]

2623 **5** 3/4 **Moscow Music**[22] 5392 2-8-9 **100** ... RWinston 8 100
(MGQuinlan) *s.i.s: hld up: hdwy 1/2-way: rdn over 1f out: n.m.r ins fnl f: no ex towards fin* **16/1**

021 **6** 5 **Kings Quay**[48] 4716 2-8-12 **100** ... RLMoore 5 90
(RHannon) *lw: prom: rdn 1/2-way: wknd fnl f* **9/1**

1 **7** 2 **Subpoena**[29] 5228 2-8-9 ... PRobinson 2 82
(MAJarvis) *hld up: racd keenly: rdn and wknd over 1f out* **7/4**[1]

041 **8** shd **Chief Scout**[34] 5087 2-8-9 **83** ... MHills 7 82
(BJMeehan) *chsd ldr: rdn and ev ch over 2f out: wknd over 1f out* **25/1**

541 **9** 15 **Walkonthewildside**[24] 5347 2-8-9 **83** ... KDarley 3 45
(DRLoder) *hld up: racd keely: rdn and wknd over 1f out* **12/1**

1m 26.0s (-0.47) **Going Correction** +0.05s/f (Good) **9** Ran SP% **114.8**
Speed ratings: **104,103,103,102,102 96,94,94,76**CSF £38.42 TOTE £4.20: £1.40, £3.30, £9.10; EX 56.50 Trifecta £858.40 Part won. Pool: £1,209.12. 0.40 winning units..
**Owner** Tweenhills Thurloe **Bred** Mrs D O Joly **Trained** Kingsclere, Hants

**FOCUS**
It again paid to be on the pace in a race that just about lived up to Group Three standard, including time-wise, and was not as strong as many recent renewals; the fifth sets the standard.

**NOTEBOOK**
**Diktatorial**, impressive winner of a maiden that is beginning to work out at Sandown, was able to make the successful transition to Group company with a hard-fought win. Always on the pace, he looked beaten when passed approaching the two pole, but galloped on resolutely and came back through to land the spoils. Although not neccessarily bred to stay a mile, he shapes as though he should and has more to offer at a similar level.
**Crimson Sun(USA)** had shown himself to be useful in previous starts despite disappointing on very soft ground at York, and this step up to seven furlongs brought about improvement. Fast ground over seven furlongs or a mile will prove to be his ideal conditions and he looks up to this grade.
**Mister Genepi**, beaten six and a half lengths when last seen in the Champagne Stakes, again ran better than he was forecast to and had looked a likely winner at one stage. He remains a maiden but is probably Listed class.
**Santa Fe(IRE)**, narrow winner of his maiden at Leicester, had his chance and was not good enough to win on the day, but still ran creditably and better can be expected back on a faster surface.
**Moscow Music** ran another sound race but is not good enough to win at this sort of level and too high in the weights to get competitive in handicaps.
**Kings Quay** did not run his race and there is no obvious excuse as the rain he wanted arrived. Undoubtedly better than this, he has been on the go a while and may be worth putting away until next season, as his sire was a top-class three-year-old and there should be more to come from him.
**Subpoena**, impressive winner of an ordinary maiden on his debut at York, was surprisingly made a short-priced favourite and ran way below market expectations. Presumably a lot better than this, being held up in this ground would have counted against him and he should make a better three-year-old. *Official explanation: jockey said colt hung left throughout*

## 5896 NGK SPARK PLUGS NURSERY STKS (H'CAP) 6f
3:30 (3:36) (B1) (0-95,93) 2-Y-O **£13,806** (£4,248; £2,124; £1,062) **Stalls** High

Form RPR

U33 **1** **Obe Gold**[19] 5460 2-9-4 **90** ...(v) ACulhane 4 103
(MRChannon) *chsd ldrs: led over 3f out: rdn clr over 1f out: edgd lft wl ins fnl f: r.o* **20/1**

602 **2** 1 3/4 **Elgin Marbles**[9] 5721 2-8-8 **80** ... RLMoore 12 87
(RHannon) *h.d.w: a.p: chsd wnr 2f out: r.o* **10/1**

11 **3** 1 3/4 **Cyclical**[18] 5490 2-9-6 **92** ... JPMurtagh 11 94
(GAButler) *lw: s.i.s: hld up: hdwy and nt clr run over 1f out: nt rch ldrs* **9/4**[1]

3124 **4** shd **Zomerlust**[19] 5466 2-8-7 **79** ... RWinston 9 81
(JJQuinn) *chsd ldrs: rdn over 2f out: styd on same pce fnl f* **14/1**

5302 **5** nk **Royal Orissa**[20] 5434 2-8-8 **80** ...(t) MartinDwyer 1 81+
(DHaydnJones) *s.i.s: hld up: edgd lft and r.o ins fnl f: nrst fin* **12/1**

3310 **6** 3 **Breaking Shadow (IRE)**[20] 5434 2-8-6 **78** ... PHanagan 7 70
(RAFahey) *lw: hld up: rdn over 1f out: r.o ins fnl f: nt trble ldrs* **14/1**

2211 **7** 1/2 **Viking Spirit**[13] 5617 2-9-7 **93** ... IMongan 3 83+
(PWHarris) *h.d.w: prom: rdn over 1f out: sn edgd rt and wknd* **4/1**[2]

2102 **8** 1/2 **Turnaround (GER)**[19] 5466 2-8-9 **81** ... JFEgan 2 70
(MrsJRRamsden) *lw: hld up: hdwy 1/2-way: wknd over 1f out* **12/1**

1111 **9** 3/4 **Coleorton Dancer**[33] 5119 2-9-3 **89** ... NCallan 10 76
(KARyan) *lw: prom: lost pl over 4f out: rallied and hmpd wl over 1f out: wknd fnl f* **13/2**[3]

1306 **10** 1 1/2 **Nova Tor (IRE)**[11] 5681 2-9-1 **87** ...(p) PRobinson 8 69
(NPLittmoden) *led: hdd over 3f out: wknd over 1f out* **33/1**

0106 **11** 5 **Toby's Dream (IRE)**[21] 5421 2-8-7 **79** ... KDarley 6 46
(MJohnston) *prom: rdn and edgd rt over 1f out: sn wknd* **33/1**

431 **12** 17 **Bahamian Magic**[17] 5507 2-8-11 **83** ... KFallon 5 —
(DRLoder) *prom over 3f* **12/1**

1m 13.05s (-0.04) **Going Correction** +0.05s/f (Good) **12** Ran SP% **120.2**
Speed ratings: **102,99,97,97,96 92,92,91,90,88 81,59**CSF £206.77 CT £640.14 TOTE £21.10: £4.60, £2.90, £1.70; EX 141.40.
**Owner** BDR Partnership **Bred** Mrs M Mason **Trained** West Ilsley, Berks

**FOCUS**
A decent nursery won by Obe Gold, who deserved to get his head in front again after several good efforts in defeat. The race is rated through the second and fifth and should produce winners.

**NOTEBOOK**
**Obe Gold**, although exposed, was almost certain to run his race under ideal conditions and, having taken it up with three to run, stayed on strongly to win well. A tough and consistent colt, he will go up for this, but one could not rule out a successful venture into Listed company, either here or abroad, before the season is out.
**Elgin Marbles** has now run well in course and distance nurseries the last twice, and evidently has a race in him off this sort of mark.
**Cyclical**, a winner on both his starts prior to this, was doing his best work late having been held up and short of somewhere to go when trying to make ground. This was a good effort and he is clearly capable of winning again off this sort of mark.
**Zomerlust**, proven under the conditions, has twice now shaped as if in need of further and the seventh furlong can bring about improvement.
**Royal Orissa** was doing his best work late and deserves credit for his effort on ground that may not have suited.
**Breaking Shadow(IRE)** was another unable to get into it in time and was unable to reverse form with Royal Orissa.
**Viking Spirit**, up 14lb from when winning last time, found it too big an ask and found no extra under pressure.
**Coleorton Dancer**, bidding for a five-timer, was trying to get into it although looking held when hampered.
**Bahamian Magic** *Official explanation: jockey said colt felt wrong*

## 5897 JRA GOLDEN JUBILEE MAIDEN STKS (C&G) 1m
4:05 (4:14) (D2) 2-Y-O **£8,498** (£2,615; £1,307; £653) **Stalls** High

Form RPR

60 **1** **Pevensey (IRE)**[57] 4454 2-8-11 ...(b[1]) KDarley 6 89
(JHMGosden) *lw: a.p: led 2f out: sn rdn and edgd rt: styd on* **50/1**

33 **2** nk **Salinja (USA)**[16] 5535 2-8-11 ... JPMurtagh 8 89
(MrsAJPerrett) *hld up in tch: rdn over 2f out: r.o ins fnl f* **6/1**

4 **3** 1 1/4 **Clueless**[14] 5592 2-8-11 ... KFallon 12 86
(WJHaggas) *lw: unruly stalls: chsd ldrs: rdn over 1f out: styd on* **9/4**[1]

**4** 1 **Alrafidain (IRE)** 2-8-11 ... RHills 5 84+
(MJohnston) *gd sort: hld up: hdwy over 3f out: chsd wnr over 1f out: tl no ex ins fnl f* **14/1**

40 **5** 2 **Given A Choice (IRE)**[13] 5620 2-8-11 ... ACulhane 2 79
(JGGiven) *lw: trckd ldrs tl led over 2f out: sn hdd: wknd ins fnl f* **5/1**[3]

0 **6** nk **Mel's Moment (USA)**[16] 5534 2-8-11 ... IMongan 15 79
(MrsAJPerrett) *led: hdd over 6f out: remained handy: rdn and ev ch 2f out: wknd ins fnl f* **100/1**

3 **7** 3 **Astronomical (IRE)**[16] 5534 2-8-11 ... MHills 9 72
(BWHills) *lw: chsd ldrs: outpcd over 2f out: n.d after* **7/2**[2]

0 **8** 1 1/2 **Swords**[9] 5716 2-8-11 ... SWhitworth 7 69
(DJDaly) *hld up: outpcd over 3f out: n.d* **100/1**

**9** 6 **Cavan Gael (FR)** 2-8-11 ... RWinston 11 56
(PHowling) *w'like: scope: hld up: hdwy and n.m.r 1/2-way: wknd over 2f out* **50/1**

033 **10** 1 1/4 **Orpen Wide (IRE)**[10] 5703 2-8-8 ...(t) ABeech[(3)] 3 53
(MCChapman) *lw: led over 6f out: hdd over 2f out: rdn and wknd over 1f out* **100/1**

**11** 2 **Sandy's Legend (USA)** 2-8-11 ... WRyan 13 48
(JHMGosden) *leggy: w'like: sn outpcd* **25/1**

**12** nk **Sparkford (USA)** 2-8-11 ... RLMoore 10 48
(JHMGosden) *str: scope: bkwd: dwlt: outpcd* **8/1**

000 **13** 4 **Southern Tide (USA)**[10] 5688 2-8-11 ... MFenton 4 39
(JJSheehan) *s.i.s: outpcd* **100/1**

**14** hd **Gold Gun (USA)** 2-8-11 ... PRobinson 1 39
(MAJarvis) *leggy: scope: lw: dwlt: outpcd* **12/1**

**15** 3 **Dream Along** 2-8-11 ... MartinDwyer 14 54+
(MrsAJPerrett) *cmpt: bit bkwd: s.s: a wl bhd* **25/1**

1m 39.9s (0.50) **Going Correction** +0.05s/f (Good) **15** Ran SP% **125.0**
Speed ratings: **99,98,97,96,94 94,91,89,83,82 80,80,76,75,72**CSF £335.58 TOTE £67.90: £12.40, £2.50, £1.90; EX 432.50.
**Owner** Jumeirah Racing **Bred** Barronstown Stud And Orpendale **Trained** Manton, Wilts

**FOCUS**
A difficult race to rate but at present it appears ordinary maiden form, with Pevensey popping up at 50/1.

**NOTEBOOK**
**Pevensey(IRE)**, beaten a total of nearly 36 lengths in his two starts prior to this, had the blinkers on for the first time and it made a huge difference. Always to the fore, he found plenty under pressure and should pay his way in handicaps if the headgear continues to have the same effect.
**Salinja(USA)** has now shown fair place form on all three starts and has a maiden in her if being found a slightly less-competitive maiden.
**Clueless**, who was doing his best work late on his debut, played up in the stalls and again got going too late. He as an ordinary maiden in him.
**Alrafidain(IRE)** ◆, a 110,000gns purchase, made some good headway mid-race to sit handily on the outside of the field and committed over a furlong out, but no sooner had he got near the lead, than he appeared to get a little tired and ultimately faded. Not necessarily bred to appreciate a mile at this stage of his career, he showed enough speed to suggest he will be fully effective at seven furlongs and can win his maiden.
**Given A Choice(IRE)** has not gone on from his promising debut fourth in two subsequent starts and has shown a few of the habits his half-brother Bandari possesses - getting warm and being a bit edgy. Undoubtedly better than he has shown so far, there may be better to come from him at three.
**Mel's Moment(USA)** showed her debut effort to be all wrong and was up on the pace throughout. With another run under her belt she will be eligible to run in handicaps.
**Astronomical(IRE)** did not go on from his initial effort and may be more of a handicap type for next season, although it would come as no surprise to see him bounce back in a backend maiden.

## 5898 NEWMARKET RACECOURSES FILLIES' H'CAP 6f
4:40 (4:45) (C1) (0-100,100) 3-Y-O+ **£11,957** (£4,535; £2,267; £1,030) **Stalls** High

Form RPR

4210 **1** **Paradise Isle**[19] 5454 3-9-7 **100** ... KDarley 8 108
(CFWall) *w ldr tl led over 2f out: drvn out* **14/1**

4312 **2** 1/2 **Solar Power (IRE)**[5] 5786 3-8-5 **84** ... OUrbina 6 91+
(JRFanshawe) *swtg: hld up: hdwy over 1f out: r.o: nt rch wnr* **5/6**[1]

6166 **3** 1/2 **Forever Phoenix**[11] 5671 4-9-2 **98** ... AQuinn[(5)] 3 103
(RMHCowell) *lw: chsd ldrs: rdn over 1f out: r.o* **10/1**[3]

3001 **4** nk **Dame De Noche**[20] 5442 4-8-8 **85** ... KFallon 7 89
(JGGiven) *prom: pushed along 1/2-way: rdn over 1f out: r.o* **6/1**[2]

4200 **5** 1/2 **Valjarv (IRE)**[47] 4750 3-8-12 **91** ...(b) IMongan 10 94
(NPLittmoden) *lw: dwlt: outpcd: hdwy over 1f out: r.o* **20/1**

0510 **6** 1/2 **Saristar**[6] 5762 3-8-10 **89** ... ACulhane 11 90
(PFICole) *led over 3f: rdn over 1f out: no ex ins fnl f* **12/1**

2254 **7** 2 1/2 **Fruit Of Glory**[19] 5454 5-9-3 **94** ... WRyan 1 88
(JRJenkins) *chsd ldrs: rdn over 1f out: wknd ins fnl f* **12/1**

0650 **8** 2 **Impressive Flight (IRE)**[5] 5799 5-8-7 **84** oh2...(b[1]) PHanagan 2 72
(TDBarron) *swtg: hld up: hdwy over 3f out: hung rt and wknd over 1f out* **14/1**

2020 **9** 7 **Cusco (IRE)**[28] 5249 3-8-9 **88** ... RLMoore 4 55
(RHannon) *sn pushed along in rr: hdwy 4f out: wknd 2f out* **16/1**

1-50 **10** dist **Firebelly**[53] 4570 3-8-11 **90** ...(v) NCallan 9 —
(MJWallace) *lw: prom tl lost pl wl over 3f out: sn bhd* **33/1**

1m 13.1s (0.01) **Going Correction** +0.05s/f (Good)
**WFA** 3 from 4yo+ 2lb **10** Ran SP% **120.2**
Speed ratings: **101,100,99,99,98 97,94,91,82,**—CSF £26.91 CT £140.20 TOTE £16.20: £3.60, £1.20, £3.00; EX 34.50 Place 6 £1,687.63, Place 5 £130.57.
**Owner** The Equema Partnership **Bred** Jeremy Green And Sons **Trained** Newmarket, Suffolk

**FOCUS**
A decent sprint handicap won by Paradise Isle, who appreciated the return to more aggressive tactics. The time was modest though, being slower than both two-year-old contests over the same trip, suggesting the form is not that strong.

**NOTEBOOK**
**Paradise Isle**, given an excellent front-running ride when making all to win at the Shergar Cup meeting, had to be held-up from a poor draw at Chester most recently and, back under more aggressive tactics, was able to return to winning ways - holding on gamely in the closing stages. Her rating entitles her to have a crack at Listed level and, as she is effective with cut in the ground, that may not be a bad idea.

**Solar Power(IRE)**, who ran a very good race to finish second to the highly-progressive Eisteddfod at Haydock most recently, was made a very short price to gain compensation and was unfavoured by being held up. He was closing with every stride at the line, but it was all too late.
**Forever Phoenix** has had a long hard season but shows no signs of losing her form, and she too was edging ever nearer at the finish.
**Dame De Noche** seems to have been converted into a sprinter this season but, having won over five furlongs last time, found this tougher assignment a little too much.
**Valjarv(IRE)** has had a disappointing season and does not look like putting an end to that anytime soon.
**Cusco(IRE)** *Official explanation: jockey said filly tired badly on Good to Soft ground*
**Firebelly** *Official explanation: jockey said filly lost her action*
T/Jkpt: Not won. T/Plt: £731.30 to a £1 stake. Pool: £70,175.95. 70.05 winning tickets. T/Qpdt: £40.30 to a £1 stake. Pool: £5,251.00. 96.40 winning tickets. CR

5899 - 5906a (Foreign Racing) - See Raceform Interactive

## 5735 LINGFIELD (L-H)

Friday, October 1

**OFFICIAL GOING: Turf course - good to firm; all-weather - standard**
Wind: light behind Weather: overcast

### 5907 JOE HOLLYWOOD 50TH BIRTHDAY MAIDEN STKS (DIV I) 1m 5f (P)
**1:30** (1:30) (D3) 3-Y-O+ **£3,818** (£1,175; £587; £293) **Stalls** Low

Form RPR
034 **1** **Shastye (IRE)**[77] 3922 3-8-8 73 RHavlin 10 73+
(JHMGosden) *a gng wl: hld up in rr: smooth prog over 3f out: led jst over 1f out: sn wl clr* **10/1**
35 **2** *7* **Parliament Square (IRE)**[21] 5445 3-8-13 WSupple 3 68
(DRLoder) *trckd ldrs: smooth prog 3f out: led briefly over 1f out: sn outpcd by wnr* **11/2**[3]
06 **3** *shd* **Key In**[18] 5511 3-8-8 TQuinn 11 63
(BWHills) *settled rr: pushed along and prog over 3f out: styd on same pce fr over 1f out* **50/1**
04 **4** *2* **Kipsigis (IRE)**[21] 5445 3-8-13 JQuinn 2 68+
(LadyHerries) *hld up midfield: shuffled along and effrt 3f out: styng on whn nt clr run over 1f out and ins fnl f* **16/1**
02 **5** *hd* **Alexei**[24] 5382 3-8-13 OUrbina 13 65
(JRFanshawe) *racd wd in midfield: prog to press ldrs 2f out: shkn up and fdd over 1f out* **12/1**
-332 **6** *hd* **Dalisay (IRE)**[41] 4939 3-8-8 74 RWinston 4 60
(SirMichaelStoute) *led: rdn and reluctant bnd 2f out: hanging and hdd over 1f out: nt run on* **9/4**[1]
0/5- **7** *3/4* **Red Rackham (IRE)**[633] 249 4-9-7 TEDurcan 8 64
(JNicol) *prom: lost pl 7f out: detached in rr and rdn 3f out: one pce u.p after* **14/1**
6660 **8** *1/2* **Simon's Seat (USA)**[38] 5027 5-9-7 58 SWKelly 7 63
(PHowling) *s.s and reminders: wl in rr: rdn over 3f out: sn outpcd: kpt on* **33/1**
-05 **9** *nk* **Sunshine On Me**[41] 4939 3-8-8 RMullen 5 58+
(CFWall) *dwlt: hld up in rr: gng wl enough on inner and sme prog over 2f out: nt clr run and snatched up over 1f out: do bttr* **33/1**
4435 **10** *3 1/2* **Chanteloup**[28] 5266 3-8-8 80 DaneO'Neill 9 53
(JRFanshawe) *prom: chsd ldr 3f out to 2f out: wknd rapidly over 1f out* **3/1**[2]
**11** *nk* **Explosive Fox (IRE)**[61] 4373 3-8-13 67 MTebbutt 12 57
(VSmith) *hld up: a in rr: lost tch wl over 2f out* **20/1**
4 **12** *nk* **Lyes Green**[50] 4673 3-8-10 NChalmers(3) 1 57
(RMBeckett) *prom tl wknd wl over 2f out* **40/1**
0 **13** *1/2* **Irish Playwright (IRE)**[57] 4478 4-9-7 VSlattery 14 56
(DGBridgwater) *hld up in rr: rdn 4f out: struggling and detached 3f out* **66/1**
0-00 **14** *7* **Pagan Ceremony (USA)**[17] 5538 3-8-13 SDrowne 6 46
(MrsAJPerrett) *chsd ldr to 3f out: wknd rapidly* **66/1**

2m 44.84s (-3.24) **Going Correction** -0.175s/f (Stan)
**WFA** 3 from 4yo+ 8lb **14** Ran SP% **118.5**
Speed ratings: **102,97,97,96,96 96,95,95,95,93 92,92,92,88**CSF £60.00 TOTE £14.50: £3.00, £2.90, £9.00; EX 195.50.
**Owner** Skara Glen Stables **Bred** Skara Glen Stables **Trained** Manton, Wilts

**FOCUS**
A modest maiden and not particularly strong form, as the pace looked ordinary and the winning time was only 0.02 seconds slower than the second division. Only a couple, including the winner, offered any encouragement for the future.

**NOTEBOOK**
**Shastye(IRE)**, making her debut on the surface following a three-month break, seems to have matured in the meantime as she was always going well and absolutely bolted up. The longer trip suited and she has a future as a staying handicapper.
**Parliament Square(IRE)**, up three furlongs in trip and making his sand debut, had every chance when a nice big gap appeared for him against the inside rail turning for home, but the winner's turn of foot made him look very one paced. He can now be handicapped, which may be a better option for him now.
**Key In**, another sand debutante, made up quite a bit of late ground but even this trip looked inadequate. Handicaps over even further beckon.
**Kipsigis(IRE)** ◆, another making his sand debut and taking a major step up in trip, may well have finished in the places had he not run into traffic problems in the home straight. He can now be handicapped and could be very interesting in that sphere at around this trip. *Official explanation: jockey said gelding had hung right throughout*
**Alexei** had every chance, but was firmly put in his place in the straight and the race he finished runner-up in here last time is not working out.
**Dalisay(IRE)** was given a positive ride, but did not impress with her attitude from the home bend as she hung, put her head in the air, and was easily swept aside. She looks one to have severe reservations about.
**Sunshine On Me** can be counted a few lengths better than her final position, as she was staying on when running into a dead end in the home straight.
**Chanteloup** had every chance on this sand debut, but did not appear to see out this longer trip and looks exposed.

### 5908 EUROPEAN BREEDERS FUND TURF MAIDEN STKS 5f
**2:00** (2:02) (D3) 2-Y-O **£4,251** (£1,308; £654; £327) **Stalls** High

Form RPR
2233 **1** **Dane's Castle (IRE)**[46] 4803 2-8-11 75 (b) JFMcDonald(3) 10 79
(BJMeehan) *hanging lft: mde all: clr w runner-up bef 1/2-way: rdn 2f out: kpt on* **9/2**[2]
25 **2** *1 1/4* **Born For Dancing (IRE)**[25] 5334 2-8-9 DaneO'Neill 9 70
(BWHills) *hanging lft thrght: chsd wnr: clr of rest bef 1/2-way: rdn and no imp 2f out: kpt on* **8/1**
03 **3** *3/4* **Captain Johnno (IRE)**[15] 5578 2-9-0 (v[1]) WSupple 8 72
(DRLoder) *wnt lft s: hanging lft thrght: outpcd and swtchd to outer 3f out: rdn and styd on fr over 1f out: nrst fin* **11/2**[3]
5566 **4** *1 3/4* **Rusky Dusky (USA)**[4] 5825 2-9-0 77 (b[1]) PDobbs 7 66
(RHannon) *chsd ldrs: outpcd bef 1/2-way: no imp after* **11/2**[3]
0 **5** *3/4* **Nodina**[25] 5353 2-9-0 NCallan 6 63
(SCWilliams) *reluctant to enter stalls: outpcd: rdn and sme prog over 1f out: n.d* **33/1**
06 **6** *3* **Daisys Girl**[6] 5800 2-8-9 (b[1]) SDrowne 2 48
(BHanbury) *reluctant to enter stalls: dwlt: outpcd and bhd: styd on fnl f* **20/1**
3 **7** *1/2* **Golden Asha**[16] 5558 2-8-9 RMullen 1 46
(NACallaghan) *chsd ldrs: outpcd bef 1/2-way: struggling after* **9/4**[1]
0 **8** *1/2* **Forest Delight (IRE)**[39] 5003 2-8-9 CCatlin 4 44
(CTinkler) *chsd ldng pair: outpcd bef 1/2-way: wknd over 1f out* **14/1**
0 **9** *5* **Waterfront Dancer**[2] 5865 2-9-0 GBaker 3 32
(JRBest) *outpcd: a wl bhd* **66/1**
0 **10** *shd* **Pretty Woman (IRE)**[16] 5558 2-8-9 NPollard 5 26
(SCWilliams) *dwlt: outpcd: a wl bhd* **10/1**

58.96 secs (0.09) **Going Correction** 0.0s/f (Good) **10** Ran SP% **115.8**
Speed ratings: **99,97,95,93,91 87,86,85,77,77**CSF £39.20 TOTE £6.10: £1.80, £2.60, £2.80; EX 25.70.
**Owner** Ed McCormack **Bred** Tally-Ho Stud **Trained** Upper Lambourn, Berks

**FOCUS**
A fair maiden run at a decent pace in which the draw had a major effect despite the size of the field. The first five home came from stalls 10, 9, 8, 7 and 6 in that order. The form looks reasonably sound with the placed horses close to pre-race marks.

**NOTEBOOK**
**Dane's Castle(IRE)**, with the plum draw against the stands' rail, utilised his early speed and had his rivals well stretched from a long way out. He never looked in any danger of defeat and should be able to make his mark back in nursery company when allowed to dominate.
**Born For Dancing(IRE)**, with the blinkers left off this time, was always in second place but could never quite reel the winner in. She still ran a bit green and now qualifies for nurseries.
**Captain Johnno(IRE)** ◆, despite starting from stall eight, missed the break and was therefore forced to make his effort down the wide outside. He made up a lot of ground in the latter stages and emerges with plenty of credit as this shorter trip did him no favours, especially on a sharp track like this. He now qualifies for a handicap mark and is well worth noting back over further.
**Rusky Dusky(USA)** showed early speed from his high draw, but did not get home and looks exposed.
**Nodina** improved a little from his debut without looking a winner waiting to happen.
**Golden Asha** was disappointing after her promising debut, but this is a very different track to Beverley and the number one stall would not have helped. Still, she has questions to answer now.

### 5909 BOOK A BOX AT LINGFIELD NURSERY 7f
**2:35** (2:37) (E3) (0-75,75) 2-Y-O **£3,776** (£1,162; £581; £290) **Stalls** High

Form RPR
4043 **1** **Seasons Estates**[24] 5377 2-8-8 62 PDoe 9 67
(BRMillman) *trckd ldrs: led 2f out: drvn and kpt on wl fnl f* **10/1**
0452 **2** *1/2* **Aberdeen Park**[11] 5701 2-8-12 66 GBaker 14 70
(MrsHSweeting) *dwlt: hld up midfield: prog to press wnr wl over 1f out: ev ch fnl f: nt qckn nr fin* **6/1**[1]
0500 **3** *1 1/4* **Captain Margaret**[15] 5596 2-8-7 61 (t) JQuinn 15 62+
(JPearce) *wl in rr: last 3f out: u.p and stl bhd whn swtchd lft over 1f out: r.o fnl f: nrst fin* **25/1**
0030 **4** *shd* **Starlight River (IRE)**[24] 5363 2-8-8 62 DKinsella 10 63
(WRMuir) *pressed ldr: rdn over 2f out: kpt on same pce fr over 1f out* **33/1**
6563 **5** *1/2* **Eltizaam (USA)**[13] 5655 2-9-7 75 WSupple 3 74
(EALDunlop) *dwlt: racd centre: wl in tch: effrt 2f out: one pce fnl f* **7/1**[2]
0603 **6** *hd* **Midcap (IRE)**[25] 5349 2-9-2 70 DaneO'Neill 11 69
(BWHills) *dwlt: hld up wl in rr: gd prog 2f out: pressed ldrs ent fnl f: one pce after* **12/1**
006 **7** *nk* **Lady Pilot**[16] 5569 2-9-2 70 TEDurcan 13 68
(CEBrittain) *chsd ldrs: rdn and effrt over 2f out: kpt on same pce* **11/1**
066 **8** *1 1/4* **Go Mo (IRE)**[36] 5053 2-9-3 71 MFenton 6 66
(SKirk) *wl in rr: rdn 3f out: prog and barged through 1f out: keeping on but no ch whn nt clr run nr fin* **16/1**
3000 **9** *shd* **Dreemon**[25] 5335 2-8-13 67 SWKelly 17 62
(BRMillman) *pressed ldr: rdn and upsides over 2f out: wknd over 1f out* **25/1**
3053 **10** *nk* **Fortnum**[42] 4914 2-8-4 61 RThomas(3) 18 55
(RHannon) *cl up: rdn over 2f out: fdd over 1f out* **6/1**[1]
3000 **11** *1 3/4* **Storm Fury (USA)**[22] 5421 2-8-5 64 ThomasYeung(5) 20 64+
(PWChapple-Hyam) *trckd ldrs: nt clr run on inner fr 2f out and lost pl: n.d after* **16/1**
005 **12** *nk* **Byron Bay**[17] 5535 2-8-11 68 RMiles(3) 19 60+
(JJBridger) *dwlt: sn midfield: effrt on outer over 2f out: chsd ldrs over 1f out: sn wknd* **25/1**
0430 **13** *nk* **Lily Lenat**[83] 3727 2-9-4 72 (p) DSweeney 16 60
(JRBoyle) *led to 2f out: wknd* **14/1**
623 **14** *1/2* **Tanning**[27] 5281 2-8-11 65 SDrowne 5 62+
(HMorrison) *racd centre: chsd ldrs: rdn and lost pl 3f out: one pce and no ch whn bmpd 1f out* **15/2**[3]
030 **15** *nk* **Northern Secret**[35] 5095 2-9-2 70 RMullen 12 56
(AMBalding) *a in rr: rdn and struggling 1/2-way* **14/1**
003 **16** *15* **Guyana (IRE)**[53] 4599 2-9-3 71 CCatlin 1 20
(SKirk) *racd centre: chsd ldrs to 1/2-way: wknd: t.o* **20/1**
5600 **17** *1 1/2* **Peopleton Brook**[14] 5617 2-8-6 63 JFMcDonald(3) 2 8
(DWPArbuthnot) *racd alone far side: wl on terms for 5f: wknd rapidly and eased: t.o* **50/1**

1m 25.24s (1.03) **Going Correction** 0.0s/f (Good) **17** Ran SP% **124.3**
Speed ratings: **94,93,92,91,91 91,90,89,89,88 86,86,86,85,85 68,66**CSF £63.85 CT £1495.50 TOTE £14.60: £2.10, £1.90, £4.70, £11.90; EX 99.50.
**Owner** Seasons Holidays **Bred** Old Mill Stud **Trained** Kentisbeare, Devon

**FOCUS**
A competitive nursery, though the pace did not look that strong, but the form looks solid at a modest level. The majority of the field raced centre to stands' side, though one stayed far side and that finished last.

**NOTEBOOK**
**Seasons Estates**, who ran well here last time, was drawn in the centre but managed to get a good position just behind the leaders for much of the way. After taking the lead, she was able to get right over to the stands' rail and that may have proved decisive. She seems to be improving with racing.
**Aberdeen Park** ◆, whose second place behind Magical Romance at Leicester last time has since been spectacularly boosted by the winner, was possibly unlucky as she was making her effort more towards the centre of the track whilst her main rival was tight against the stands' rail in the run to the line. This faster ground was not a problem and she deserves to make amends.

**Captain Margaret** ◆, unplaced in all four of her previous starts, finished with quite a flourish and looks capable of winning a similar contest over this trip on a stiffer track or back over a mile.
**Starlight River(IRE)**, trying a longer trip, seemed to see it out well enough but would probably have preferred easier ground.
**Eltizaam(USA)** ran with credit considering she was rather marooned down the middle of the track. Her best previous run had come with cut in the ground.
**Midcap(IRE)**, making her nursery debut, came through to hold every chance at the furlong pole before flattening out.
**Fortnum** dropped away after holding a prominent position, but may prefer easier ground.
**Storm Fury(USA)** *Official explanation: jockey said gelding had been denied a clear run*
**Byron Bay** *Official explanation: jockey said colt had been unsuited by the good to firm going*

## 5910 ENTERPRISE INNS "PREMIER" CLAIMING STKS 6f
3:10 (3:12) (D2) 2-Y-O £6,061 (£1,865; £932; £466) Stalls High

Form RPR
3600 **1** **Coconut Squeak**[9] 5738 2-8-1 63 JMackay 15 65
(JGGiven) *mde virtually all: shkn up and clr over 1f out: rdn out* **14/1**
0 **2** *2* **Atacama Star**[13] 5646 2-8-12 AHindley(7) 18 77
(BGPowell) *racd midfield: prog u.p 2f out: hanging lft but styd on to chse wnr ins fnl f: nvr able to chal* **33/1**
115 **3** *¾* **Arbors Little Girl**[14] 5617 2-8-8 66 ADaly 10 64
(BRMillman) *racd midfield: rdn over 2f out: prog over 1f out: styd on wl fnl f: nrst fin* **5/2**[1]
4003 **4** *½* **Island Swing (IRE)**[15] 5594 2-9-0 81 SDrowne 1 69
(JLSpearing) *racd midfield: prog over 2f out: chsd wnr over 1f out to ins fnl f: one pce* **7/1**[2]
4430 **5** *1¾* **Pennestamp (IRE)**[14] 5617 2-8-6 65 RHavlin 3 55
(MrsPNDutfield) *racd in centre: wl on terms: shkn up and outpcd 2f out: one pce after* **20/1**
5260 **6** *½* **Lateral Thinker (IRE)**[17] 5548 2-8-9 68 SWKelly 12 57
(JAOsborne) *racd midfield: rdn wl over 2f out: one pce fnl 2f* **7/1**[2]
4005 **7** *1¾* **Miss Malone (IRE)**[11] 5690 2-8-6 71 PDobbs 2 49
(RHannon) *racd midfield: rdn wl over 2f out: one pce and no imp on ldrs* **10/1**[3]
0003 **8** *1* **Perianth (IRE)**[18] 5509 2-8-8 62 JFMcDonald(3) 9 51
(BJMeehan) *racd towards rr: outpcd over 2f out: kpt on same pce after* **10/1**[3]
3653 **9** *½* **Goldhill Prince**[46] 4816 2-8-2 63 (p) CHaddon(7) 5 47
(WGMTurner) *racd in centre: wl on terms w ldrs: wknd 2f out* **20/1**
00 **10** *2* **Bodden Bay**[20] 5447 2-8-8 ow1 NCallan 19 40
(CADwyer) *wl in rr: outpcd fr 1/2-way* **66/1**
6060 **11** *1* **Merrymadcap (IRE)**[9] 5738 2-8-13 65 (b1) DaneO'Neill 4 42
(MBlanshard) *dwlt: racd centre: midfield tl wknd 2f out* **25/1**
052 **12** *3* **Hiamovi (IRE)**[39] 4997 2-8-8 64 AQuinn(5) 16 33
(RMHCowell) *pressed wnr to over 2f out: wknd* **20/1**
06 **13** *½* **Red Marteeney**[25] 5353 2-9-5 TQuinn 8 38
(DRCElsworth) *a wl in rr* **20/1**
0001 **14** *1¼* **Wiltshire (IRE)**[8] 5746 2-8-3 60 ow1 LHarman(7) 13 25
(MRChannon) *racd midfield: bmpd along over 2f out: wkng whn nt clr run over 1f out* **20/1**
0031 **15** *1¾* **Ruby Muja**[34] 5132 2-8-4 62 MFenton 6 14
(MissECLavelle) *chsd ldrs tl wknd 2f out* **12/1**
**16** *2* **After The Snow (IRE)** 2-8-0 ow1 CCatlin 17 4
(IAWood) *dwlt: sn t.o* **33/1**
066 **17** *shd* **Imperatrice**[8] 5746 2-8-0 (p) MHenry 7 3
(RMHCowell) *dwlt: a wl in rr* **33/1**
6 **18** *2* **Sergeant Lewis**[8] 5747 2-8-9 VSlattery 20 6
(JAOsborne) *dwlt: a wl in rr* **25/1**
20 **19** *7* **Killington (IRE)**[36] 5053 2-8-11 RWinston 14 —
(GAButler) *chsd ldrs over 3f: wknd rapidly: t.o* **12/1**

1m 12.07s (0.42) **Going Correction** 0.0s/f (Good) **19** Ran SP% **135.6**
Speed ratings: **97,94,93,92,90 89,87,86,85,82 81,77,76,75,72 70,69,67,57**CSF £433.12 TOTE £15.80: £4.60, £25.00, £1.80; EX 800.80.The winner was subject to a friendly claim.
**Owner** Moneyleague Ltd **Bred** P D And Mrs Player **Trained** Willoughton, Lincs

### FOCUS
A big field, but probably not that competitive with only three of the 19 runners starting at single-figure prices. The pace was only ordinary and the draw again played its part, but the first and third give the form a reliable look.

### NOTEBOOK
**Coconut Squeak**, dropping in class and trip, was given a positive ride from her good draw and had the race won at the furlong pole. Sprinting looks to be her game and she should find other opportunities at a modest level.
**Atacama Star**, well beaten in what looked a hot Newbury maiden on his debut, found this much more his level and ran much better as a result despite still looking green. Normal improvement should see him off the mark in similar company.
**Arbors Little Girl**, who ran better than her form figure would suggest at Nottingham last time when bidding for a hat-trick, was doing all her best work late and may prefer a stiffer six now.
**Island Swing(IRE)** was favoured by the weights, but even so probably did well to finish so close from such a poor draw.
**Pennestamp(IRE)** deserves credit, as he was rather caught out in the centre of the track for much of the way and even this sharp six looked to stretch his stamina.
**Red Marteeney** *Official explanation: jockey said colt had never been travelling*
**Killington(IRE)** *Official explanation: jockey said gelding lost its action*

## 5911 EUROPEAN BREEDERS FUND AWT MAIDEN STKS 6f (P)
3:45 (3:48) (D3) 2-Y-O £4,381 (£1,348; £674; £337) Stalls Low

Form RPR
35 **1** **Emerald Lodge**[28] 5262 2-9-0 (v1) SWKelly 4 80
(JNoseda) *w ldr: led 4f out: clr wl over 1f out: drvn out* **12/1**
0 **2** *2½* **Bolodenka (IRE)**[53] 4611 2-9-0 RMullen 9 73
(WJMusson) *sn wl off the pce in midfield: prog fr 1/2-way: shkn up and r.o to take 2nd ins fnl f: no ch w wnr* **8/1**[3]
**3** *1¾* **El Rey Del Mambo (USA)** 2-9-0 SDrowne 11 67
(GAButler) *prom: chsd wnr over 2f out: no imp: lost 2nd and one pce ins fnl f* **13/8**[1]
**4** *½* **Scripted** 2-9-0 JMackay 5 66
(SirMarkPrescott) *pushed along to chse ldrs: outpcd over 2f out: one pce after* **16/1**
40 **5** *5* **Right To Roam (IRE)**[24] 5376 2-9-0 JQuinn 6 51+
(JARToller) *outpcd and wl off the pce: modest late prog* **25/1**
3 **6** *nk* **World Music (USA)**[35] 5070 2-8-9 TEDurcan 3 45
(SaeedBinSuroor) *prom: rdn over 3f out: sn struggling: wknd 2f out* **2/1**[2]
0 **7** *5* **Chiracahua (IRE)**[13] 5646 2-9-0 RWinston 2 35
(BJMeehan) *led to 4f out: chsd wnr to over 2f out: wknd* **33/1**
**8** *¾* **Wiz In** 2-9-0 MHenry 8 33
(TKeddy) *s.s: outpcd and a bhd* **33/1**
**9** *nk* **Silver Swing** 2-9-0 DaneO'Neill 7 32
(WJHaggas) *dwlt: outpcd and a wl bhd* **20/1**
**10** *4* **Girlsweekend** 2-8-9 PDoe 10 15
(MrsLJMongan) *uns rdr bef ent stalls: s.s: a wl bhd* **33/1**
**11** *1¼* **Just Cliff** 2-9-0 NCallan 1 16
(WRMuir) *chsd ldrs to 1/2-way: wknd rapidly* **66/1**
**12** *11* **Miss Hermione** 2-8-9 JMcAuley 12 —
(MrsCADunnett) *dwlt: a wl bhd: t.o* **50/1**

1m 12.24s (-0.68) **Going Correction** -0.175s/f (Stan) **12** Ran SP% **117.0**
Speed ratings: **97,93,91,90,84 83,76,75,75,70 68,53**CSF £95.45 TOTE £20.10: £3.70, £2.00, £1.20; EX 140.20.
**Owner** Hesmonds Stud **Bred** M P B Bloodstock Ltd **Trained** Newmarket, Suffolk

### FOCUS
An uncompetitive maiden on paper with 8/1 bar two, but it did not work out that way. The pace was solid and the winner looks a nice prospect, with the runner-up and fifth providing the best guide to the level of the form.

### NOTEBOOK
**Emerald Lodge**, up a furlong for this sand debut, took well to the first-time visor and bolted up when given his head. His trainer has won with some nice juveniles on this surface over the years, and this colt looks to have a future.
**Bolodenka(IRE)**, from a yard not noted for its juveniles, improved from his debut and, although never in the same parish as the winner, showed enough to suggest he can win a race on this surface. His pedigree suggests he would not get much further than this.
**El Rey Del Mambo(USA)**, who fetched 95,000gns as a two-year-old, is out of a three-time winner in the USA and was well backed to make a winning debut. He had every chance and should improve, but does not look anything special on this evidence.
**Scripted**, a half-brother to three winners including Palawan, was not disgraced but looked to need the experience and should do much better in time.
**Right To Roam(IRE)** was surprisingly taken off his feet considering his speedy pedigree.
**World Music(USA)** was very disappointing on this switch to sand and something must have been amiss. *Official explanation: jockey said filly had no more to give in the final furlong*

## 5912 H.B.L.B. LADBROKES.COM H'CAP 7f (P)
4:20 (4:20) (D2) (0-85,84) 3-Y-O £7,046 (£2,168; £1,084; £542) Stalls Low

Form RPR
12 **1** **Polar Magic**[41] 4938 3-8-10 73 DaneO'Neill 1 85+
(JRFanshawe) *s.i.s: hld up in rr: prog over 2f out: swept into ld jst over 1f out: r.o wl* **3/1**[1]
-004 **2** *2* **Outer Hebrides**[134] 2239 3-8-13 76 (t) WSupple 4 83
(DRLoder) *chsd ldrs: effrt over 2f out: rdn to ld briefly over 1f out: outpcd by wnr fnl f* **14/1**
0002 **3** *shd* **Wyatt Earp (IRE)**[11] 5697 3-8-11 74 TEDurcan 5 81
(JARToller) *hld up in rr: prog 2f out: r.o wl fnl f: no ch w wnr* **6/1**[3]
3216 **4** *1* **Kali**[13] 5652 3-8-13 76 DSweeney 3 80
(RCharlton) *hld up midfield: swtchd rt and prog over 1f out: r.o one pce fnl f* **13/2**
0130 **5** *2½* **Moscow Times**[28] 5275 3-8-6 72 LPKeniry(3) 9 70
(DRCElsworth) *settled wl in rr: effrt on outer 2f out: one pce and no ch w ldrs* **20/1**
0000 **6** *shd* **Fancy Foxtrot**[48] 4742 3-9-4 84 (p) JFMcDonald(3) 7 81
(BJMeehan) *dwlt: racd in last: prog on inner fr 1/2-way: chsng ldrs whn no room twice over 1f out: nt rcvr* **8/1**
6561 **7** *5* **Moors Myth**[18] 5525 3-8-10 73 SDrowne 6 57
(BWHills) *prom: chsd ldng pair over 2f out: wknd over 1f out* **10/1**
2150 **8** *nk* **Bridgewater Boys**[32] 5193 3-8-12 75 (b) NCallan 10 58
(KARyan) *a in rr: rdn and struggling 1/2-way* **10/1**
0100 **9** *nk* **Midnight Ballard (USA)**[27] 5299 3-8-13 76 (b) TQuinn 11 59
(RFJohnsonHoughton) *led for 2f: chsd ldr to over 1f out: wknd rapidly* **33/1**
-000 **10** *1¼* **Benny The Ball (USA)**[122] 2549 3-8-12 75 MFenton 13 54
(NPLittmoden) *dwlt: racd wd in midfield: lost pl and rdn 1/2-way: no ch after* **20/1**
0120 **11** *shd* **Glebe Garden**[23] 5399 3-9-1 78 RMullen 12 57
(MLWBell) *chsd ldrs tl wknd wl over 1f out* **25/1**
1-00 **12** *2½* **Little Ridge (IRE)**[28] 5263 3-8-11 77 LFletcher(3) 2 50
(HMorrison) *led after 2f to over 1f out: wknd rapidly* **50/1**
0411 **13** *nk* **Glencalvie (IRE)**[9] 5737 3-8-11 74 6ex (v) SWKelly 8 46
(JNoseda) *pushed along in rr 4f out: struggling and wl btn over 2f out* **5/1**[2]

1m 24.2s (-1.74) **Going Correction** -0.175s/f (Stan) **13** Ran SP% **123.5**
Speed ratings: **102,99,99,98,95 95,89,89,89,87 87,84,84**CSF £46.74 CT £215.31 TOTE £2.90: £1.80, £4.40, £3.10; EX 71.90.
**Owner** R C Thompson **Bred** Cheveley Park Stud Ltd **Trained** Newmarket, Suffolk

### FOCUS
A fair handicap run at a true gallop and the front four finished clear. Those in the frame behind the winner give the form a sound appearance.

### NOTEBOOK
**Polar Magic** ◆, making his sand debut after two starts on soft ground on turf, won this with a very impressive turn of foot. He is still very lightly raced having not made his racecourse debut until June and could go on to even better things.
**Outer Hebrides**, whose only previous win came on Fibresand as a two-year-old, was having his first start since May. Fitted with a tongue-tied rather than a visor, he was always in the right place and hit the front at the right time, but the winner's turn of foot blew him away. He should be able to find another race on sand.
**Wyatt Earp(IRE)**, trying his longest trip to date on this sand debut, certainly did not fail through lack of stamina and the way he finished suggested he would get even further.
**Kali** ◆, who has been running consistently well and has placed form on this surface, can be considered unlucky not to do even better as she was carried back on the home bend when travelling well and then had to be switched a couple of times in order to get a run. She can win on this surface.
**Moscow Times** probably needs a mile these days.
**Fancy Foxtrot** travelled well and was close enough against the inside rail turning in, but then completely ran out of room and this effort can be ignored. *Official explanation: jockey said colt had been denied a clear run*
**Midnight Ballard(USA)** *Official explanation: jockey said gelding had hung right in the home straight*
**Glencalvie(IRE)**, bidding for a hat-trick on this sand debut and raised 6lb, ran no sort of race and the different surface seems the most obvious reason.

## 5913 JOE HOLLYWOOD 50TH BIRTHDAY MAIDEN STKS (DIV II) 1m 5f (P)
4:55 (4:55) (D2) 3-Y-O+ £3,799 (£1,169; £584; £292) Stalls Low

Form RPR
0-22 **1** **Meissen**[93] 3417 3-8-8 76 TQuinn 5 75
(EFVaughan) *led after 2f to 8f out: pressed ldr after: led again over 2f out: drvn out and hld on* **11/4**[1]

2306 **2** ½ **Seeking A Way (USA)**[25] 5340 3-8-8 66 .......... RHavlin 11 74
(JHMGosden) *hld up in rr: stdy prog over 4f out: chsd ldng pair over 2f out: wnt 2nd ent fnl f: clsd nr fin: a hld* **7/1**

0424 **3** 4 **Samaria (GER)**[32] 5196 3-8-8 72 .......... (v[1]) JQuinn 4 69
(CFWall) *led for 2f: ld again 8f out: rdn and hdd over 2f out: fdd fnl f* **4/1**[2]

0 **4** 2½ **Helm (IRE)**[160] 1612 3-8-13 .......... PDoe 1 70
(RRowe) *s.i.s: towards rr: rdn 5f out: prog on outer over 4f out: chsd ldrs 2f out: one pce u.p* **40/1**

03 **5** 2½ **Ruggtah**[25] 5339 3-8-8 .......... TEDurcan 14 62
(MRChannon) *towards rr: rdn over 4f out: no imp on ldrs over 2f out: one pce* **7/1**

**6** 1 **Jonanaud**[191] 5-9-4 .......... FPFerris(3) 9 65
(HJManners) *dwlt: sn trckd ldrs: rdn over 3f out: fdd over 2f out* **16/1**

-400 **7** 6 **Verasi**[104] 3107 3-8-13 64 .......... RMullen 2 60+
(GLMoore) *chsd ldrs: rdn over 4f out: wknd over 2f out* **16/1**

0 **8** 1 **Riviera Red (IRE)**[55] 4554 4-9-7 .......... AMcCarthy 10 56
(LMontagueHall) *chsd ldrs: pushed along 8f out: styd in tch u.p tl wknd over 2f out* **33/1**

6 **9** shd **Mariday**[19] 5495 3-8-13 .......... PaulEddery 12 55
(LadyHerries) *wl in rr: rdn over 5f out: sn lost tch w ldrs* **16/1**

-0 **10** 17 **Grand Music (IRE)**[55] 4554 4-9-2 .......... (b[1]) AQuinn(5) 8 32
(JJSheehan) *dwlt: a in rr: rdn and struggling over 6f out: t.o* **66/1**

4 **11** 30 **Moaning Myrtle**[24] 5382 3-8-8 .......... DaneO'Neill 7 —
(JRFanshawe) *t.k.h: trckd ldng pair to 5f out: wknd rapidly: t.o* **11/2**[3]

0 **12** dist **Czech Summer (IRE)**[24] 5382 3-8-13 .......... (b[1]) DSweeney 6 —
(RMFlower) *dwlt: racd midfield: rdn and wknd 6f out: wl t.o* **100/1**

0-30 **13** dist **Lomapamar**[9] 5732 3-8-8 78 .......... SDrowne 13 —
(MrsAJPerrett) *racd wd in midfield: rdn and wknd 6f out: sn wl t.o: eased 3f out* **9/1**

**14** dist **Helixalot (IRE)** 3-8-10 .......... DCorby(3) 3 —
(GPEnright) *dwlt: a last pair: hrd rdn and wknd over 6f out: wl t.o* **66/1**

2m 44.82s (-3.26) **Going Correction** -0.175s/f (Stan)
**WFA** 3 from 4yo+ 8lb **14** Ran SP% **124.1**
Speed ratings: **103,102,100,98,97 96,92,92,92,81 63,—,—,—**CSF £22.69 TOTE £4.20: £1.30, £4.00, £1.80; EX 17.60.
**Owner** B H Voak **Bred** B H Voak **Trained** Newmarket, Suffolk

**FOCUS**
Another modest maiden run at an ordinary pace and the time was just 0.02 seconds faster than the first division. They finished well spread out which suggests those outside the placings are going to struggle.

**NOTEBOOK**
**Meissen**, off since June, helped share the pace for most of the way and, after getting the better of the other front-runner, stayed on dourly to repel the runner-up. The proximity of a rival rated 10lb lower than her suggests the form is not great, but she stays well and should hold her own in modest middle-distance handicaps.
**Seeking A Way(USA)** is very one-paced, but she does stay and that enabled her to get so close having been given a patient ride. She may be flattered to have split two higher-rated rivals though, and will continue to be hard to place.
**Samaria(GER)**, visored for the first time, was given a positive ride, but the winner was always hassling her and she probably did well to hang in there for as long she did. She is starting to look exposed and, vulnerable in races like this, so may be better off in handicaps.
**Helm(IRE)**, not seen since his racecourse debut for Luca Cumani in April and gelded in the meantime, was not completely disgraced and is presumably being readied for a hurdling campaign.
**Ruggtah** did not improve for the switch to sand.
**Moaning Myrtle**, who showed some promise on her debut here last month, was close enough over half a mile from home, but then quickly came off the bridle and was virtually pulled up as though something was amiss. *Official explanation: jockey said filly had run too freely and had hung left under pressure*
**Lomapamar** *Official explanation: jockey said filly finished distressed*

## 5914 LINGFIELD-RACECOURSE.CO.UK APPRENTICE CLASSIFIED STKS 1m 4f (P)
5:25 (5:25) (F3) 3-Y-0+ **£3,532** (£1,087; £543; £271) **Stalls** Low

Form RPR

2464 **1** **Broughton Knows**[17] 5546 7-8-10 54 .......... (b) AKirby(7) 12 66
(MissGayKelleway) *dwlt: t.k.h and hld up in rr: prog 3f out: plenty to do over 1f out: rdn and r.o wl to ld last 50yds* **14/1**

0004 **2** 1 **King Of Knight (IRE)**[33] 5156 3-8-10 59 .......... ABeech 8 64
(GProdromou) *hld up midfield: prog 3f out: rdn to ld over 1f out: hdd and outpcd last 50yds* **20/1**

0005 **3** 2 **King Flyer (IRE)**[15] 5595 8-9-3 60 .......... (e[1]) BReilly 15 61
(MissJFeilden) *hld up midfield: prog over 3f out: led over 2f out to over 1f out: one pce* **11/2**[2]

6031 **4** 1¼ **Scott**[42] 4927 3-8-5 60 .......... CHaddon(5) 11 59
(JJay) *racd midfield: prog on outer to press ldrs 2f out: sn outpcd: kpt on* **7/1**

0231 **5** ½ **Willhego**[36] 5057 3-8-10 60 .......... RThomas 7 58
(JRBest) *trckd ldrs: effrt over 2f out: one pce u.p over 1f out* **6/1**[3]

3250 **6** 1¼ **Jolizero**[15] 5584 3-8-5 60 .......... ThomasYeung(5) 13 56
(PWChapple-Hyam) *racd freely: led after 2f to over 2f out: wknd over 1f out* **5/1**[1]

0256 **7** 2 **Chocolate Boy (IRE)**[109] 2930 5-9-0 60 .......... AQuinn(3) 16 53
(GLMoore) *wl in rr: stl in last pair over 2f out: prog on inner over 1f out : no ch* **16/1**

0416 **8** ½ **State Of Balance**[30] 5222 6-9-0 60 .......... LPKeniry 3 49
(KBell) *dwlt: racd towards rr: rdn over 2f out: sn outpcd and btn* **14/1**

5615 **9** nk **Our Emmy Lou**[8] 5757 3-8-0 58 .......... SArcher(7) 2 49
(SirMarkPrescott) *led for 2f: cl up after: wknd rapidly over 1f out* **5/1**[1]

4034 **10** 2 **Dancing Bear**[22] 5409 3-8-7 57 .......... (b[1]) JFMcDonald(3) 6 49
(JulianPoulton) *t.k.h: hld up midfield: rdn and effrt over 2f out: nt rch ldrs: wknd over 1f out* **50/1**

0000 **11** 1½ **Raheel (IRE)**[30] 5222 4-9-0 58 .......... (t) MSavage(3) 14 46
(PMitchell) *dwlt: hld up in rr: prog 3f out: hrd rdn and wknd over 2f out* **33/1**

0426 **12** 3 **Turtle Patriarch (IRE)**[27] 5293 3-8-10 59 .......... RMiles 10 42
(MrsAJPerrett) *prom: chsd ldr 5f out: losing pl whn n.m.r over 2f out: wknd* **10/1**

0-40 **13** ½ **Embassy Sweets (USA)**[25] 5340 3-8-4 55 .......... NDeSouza(3) 4 38
(PFICole) *chsd ldrs: wknd on inner over 2f out* **33/1**

0550 **14** 8 **Chanfron**[57] 4473 3-8-7 52 .......... DFox(3) 5 28
(BRMillman) *chsd ldrs: wkng whn squeezed out over 2f out* **50/1**

10P0 **15** 7 **Our Little Rosie**[57] 4493 3-8-0 56 .......... APutland(7) 9 14
(MBlanshard) *racd wd: a in rr: lost tch 4f out: t.o* **50/1**

0460 **P** **Saxe-Coburg (IRE)**[2] 5875 7-9-3 55 .......... DNolan 1 —
(GAHam) *rel to r: t.o whn p.u after 2f* **20/1**

2m 31.99s (-2.25) **Going Correction** -0.175s/f (Stan)
**WFA** 3 from 4yo+ 7lb **16** Ran SP% **125.1**
Speed ratings: **100,99,98,97,96 96,94,94,94,92 91,89,89,84,79** —CSF £277.35 TOTE £15.70: £5.30, £8.20, £3.00; EX 455.20 Place 6 £324.65, Place 5 £58.50.
**Owner** A J Clarke **Bred** Broughton Bloodstock **Trained** Newmarket, Suffolk
■ A winner for jockey Adam Kirby on his first-ever ride.

**FOCUS**
A modest contest and only an ordinary pace. The winner is improving but there is little solid to go on and the form would not be sure to work out.

**NOTEBOOK**
**Broughton Knows**, who completed a four-timer in banded company on sand at the beginning of the year, was only having his second race for his current yard. He gradually crept closer as the race progressed, and still looked to have it to do when the runner-up went clear turning in, but his rider did not panic and the combination found a smart turn of foot to settle it. This was a cracking effort from his pilot having his first-ever ride.
**King Of Knight(IRE)**, looking for his first win on his tenth start and making his sand debut, was given a copybook ride and looked to have timed it right when sent clear starting up the home straight, but he reckoned without Broughton Knows on a going day and the combination were mugged.
**King Flyer(IRE)**, wearing an eyeshield for the first time, came to lead on the home bend, but lacked the pace to make it count and could only plug on for third. This would have been an inadequate test of stamina for him.
**Scott**, raised 10lb for his Southwell win, lacked pace where it mattered and is probably better suited by the slower Fibresand.
**Willhego** was trying this trip for the first time, but did not really prove his stamina one way or the other.
**Jolizero**, a maiden after nine attempts, was trying Polytrack for the first time but almost certainly did too much too soon.
**Our Emmy Lou** did not improve for the switch to Polytrack and does not look one of the stable's stars.
**Chanfron** *Official explanation: trainer said gelding had been struck into*
T/Plt: £368.70 to a £1 stake. Pool: £33,210.30. 65.75 winning tickets. T/Qpdt: £18.50 to a £1 stake. Pool: £3,640.60. 145.30 winning tickets. JN

# 5892 NEWMARKET (R-H)
### Friday, October 1

**OFFICIAL GOING: Good**
Although the stalls were in the centre of the course, some of the runners tended to race apart, but there appeared to be no advantage to be gained.
Wind: Slight across Weather: Cloudy

## 5915 BEECH HOUSE STUD EBF MAIDEN STKS 7f
1:15 (1:17) (D2) 2-Y-O **£8,628** (£2,655; £1,327; £663) **Stalls** Centre

Form RPR

**1** **Rob Roy (USA)** 2-9-0 .......... KFallon 8 86+
(SirMichaelStoute) *gd sort: hld up: hdwy over 2f out: led over 1f out: r.o wl* **4/1**[1]

**2** 2½ **Fortunate Isle (USA)** 2-8-9 .......... AMedeiros(5) 11 80+
(BWHills) *w'like: bit bkwd: a.p: shkn up over 1f out: styd on same pce* **66/1**

**3** ½ **Tharua (IRE)** 2-8-9 .......... EAhern 17 74+
(EALDunlop) *leggy: lt-f: hld up: hdwy over 2f out: rdn over 1f out: styd on* **66/1**

0 **4** ¾ **Sarem (USA)**[48] 4747 2-9-0 .......... RHills 7 77+
(MPTregoning) *hld up: hdwy over 1f out: r.o: nt trble ldrs* **7/1**[3]

5 **5** shd **Dart Along (USA)**[7] 5765 2-9-0 .......... RHughes 22 76
(RHannon) *led over 5f: no ex* **25/1**

**6** 1 **Bravemore (USA)** 2-9-0 .......... KDarley 21 74+
(BJMeehan) *w'like: scope: chsd ldrs: ev ch 2f out: styd on same pce approaching fnl f* **14/1**

**7** 1¾ **Mpenzi** 2-8-9 .......... SCarson 18 65+
(JLDunlop) *gd sort: uns rdr and cantered to post: dwlt: outpcd: hdwy over 1f out: r.o* **50/1**

6 **8** ½ **Barbary Coast (FR)**[13] 5646 2-9-0 .......... JFEgan 14 68
(WRMuir) *hld up: hdwy over 2f out: wknd over 1f out* **20/1**

6 **9** 1 **Fen Game (IRE)**[14] 5620 2-9-0 .......... RLMoore 6 66
(JHMGosden) *lw: hld up in tch: rdn over 2f out: edgd rt and wknd over 1f out* **15/2**

**10** shd **Goose Chase** 2-9-0 .......... DHolland 3 66+
(MLWBell) *neat: prom over 5f* **20/1**

**11** hd **Miss Particular (IRE)** 2-8-9 .......... MHills 9 60+
(BWHills) *lt-f: scope: s.i.s: hld up: styd on appr fnl f: nvr nrr* **12/1**

**12** 5 **Harlestone Linn** 2-9-0 .......... PaulEddery 1 53
(JLDunlop) *w'like: hld up: hdwy over 2f out: edgd rt and wknd over 1f out* **66/1**

**13** ¾ **Daniella** 2-8-9 .......... WRyan 20 46
(RGuest) *w'like: bkwd: mid-div: rdn over 2f out: wknd over 1f out* **66/1**

**14** shd **Bachelor Affair** 2-9-0 .......... MartinDwyer 2 50
(WJarvis) *gd sort: lw: s.s: hld up: hdwy over 2f out: sn wknd* **50/1**

**15** ½ **Crown Of Medina** 2-9-0 .......... JPMurtagh 4 49
(PWHarris) *w'like: scope: b.nr hind: sn outpcd* **25/1**

0 **16** ½ **Sugitani (USA)**[30] 5228 2-9-0 .......... (t) LDettori 15 48
(SaeedBinSuroor) *chsd ldrs over 5f* **10/1**

**17** nk **Causeway Girl (IRE)** 2-8-9 .......... SWhitworth 16 42
(DMSimcock) *leggy: unf: scope: mid-div: lost pl 1/2-way: sn bhd* **66/1**

5 **18** 1¼ **Art Royal (USA)**[24] 5373 2-9-0 .......... SSanders 10 44
(MrsAJPerrett) *prom over 4f* **9/2**[2]

**19** nk **Queen Of Iceni** 2-8-9 .......... IMongan 5 38
(JLDunlop) *w'like: scope: s.s: outpcd* **50/1**

**20** ½ **Rainbow Sky** 2-8-2 .......... KMay(7) 23 37
(BWHills) *w'like: prom over 4f* **66/1**

00 **21** ½ **High Treason (USA)**[23] 5396 2-9-0 .......... ACulhane 24 41
(JGGiven) *chsd ldrs over 5f* **50/1**

**22** shd **Expeditious (USA)** 2-9-0 .......... (t) KMcEvoy 13 41
(SaeedBinSuroor) *leggy: scope: prom over 4f* **20/1**

0 **23** hd **Four Pleasure**[16] 5569 2-8-9 .......... FNorton 12 35
(CADwyer) *lw: slowly into stride: hdwy 1/2-way: sn wknd* **100/1**

1m 26.57s (0.10) **Going Correction** 0.0s/f (Good) **23** Ran SP% **125.7**
Speed ratings: **99,96,95,94,94 93,91,90,89,89 89,83,82,82,82 81,81,79,79,78 78,78,77**CSF £288.80 TOTE £4.90: £2.30, £19.00, £28.40; EX 264.00.
**Owner** Philip Newton **Bred** Millsec, Ltd **Trained** Newmarket, Suffolk

**FOCUS**

This race has thrown up some decent performers in the past, and it looks to have produced another one in Rob Roy. The race is not easy to rate with the principals all debutants, but the form looks reasonably good for the grade.

**NOTEBOOK**

**Rob Roy(USA)** ♦, a $300,000 yearling, is related to a couple of top-class performers in France and the USA. He came with quite a reputation and did not disappoint, although he did look about a bit when going on. Plenty more will be heard of him.

**Fortunate Isle(USA)**, a late foal, is a half-brother to useful performers Island Light and L'Oiseau d' Argent. From the stable that sent out last year's winner, there was plenty to like about this debut, but he looks the sort to do better with another year on his back.

**Tharua(IRE)**, who is out of a maiden mare, came from a fair way back and gave the impression she will be suited by a stiffer test next term.

**Sarem(USA)** is still learning, but showed showed enough to suggest he can make his mark in due course.

**Dart Along(USA)** had clearly learnt from his debut, but it looks as though he will need his sights lowering if he is to get off the mark.

**Bravemore(USA)**, who is out of an unraced half-sister to several winners in the USA, did enough to suggest she can pay her way in time.

**Mpenzi**did herself no damage having got rid of her rider on the way to post. Picking up in good style when the race was all but over, she should improve no end for the experience.

**Bachelor Affair** ran much better than his final position suggested.

**Art Royal(USA)** folded tamely and was clearly not right. *Official explanation: trainer was unable to offer any explanation for poor form shown*

## 5916 FISHPOOLS FURNISHINGS GODOLPHIN STKS (LISTED RACE) 1m 4f

**1:50** (1:51) (A1) 3-Y-O+ **£17,400** (£6,600; £3,300; £1,500) **Stalls** Centre

Form RPR

2060 **1** **Private Charter**[21] 5438 4-9-0 102 (p) MHills 5 109
(BWHills) *lw: mde all: lft to r alons on far side over 5f out: all out* **16/1**

-003 **2** *hd* **Fantastic Love (USA)**[21] 5435 4-9-0 103 (t) KMcEvoy 4 109
(SaeedBinSuroor) *lw: chsd wnr: c centre over 5f out: rdn and hung lft over 1f out: hung rt ins fnl f: hung lft towards fin: r.o* **10/3**[2]

1-0P **3** *½* **Shanty Star (IRE)**[123] 2533 4-9-0 105 KDarley 1 108
(MJohnston) *lw: s.i.s: sn chsng ldrs: c centre over 5f out: rdn over 2f out: hmpd over 1f out: styd on* **20/1**

3146 **4** *2½* **Light Of Morn**[23] 5394 3-8-2 93 MartinDwyer 3 99
(RGuest) *hld up: c centre over 5f out: effrt over 1f out: no imp fnl f* **12/1**[3]

-144 **5** *¾* **Razkalla (USA)**[188] 1144 6-9-0 113 LDettori 2 103
(SaeedBinSuroor) *b: prom: c centre over 5f out: rdn over 2f out: no ex fnl f* **4/7**[1]

2m 31.51s (-1.95) **Going Correction** 0.0s/f (Good)
**WFA** 3 from 4yo+ 7lb **5** Ran SP% **105.1**
Speed ratings: **106,105,105,103,103**CSF £60.44 TOTE £10.90: £3.10, £1.60; EX 54.30.
**Owner** Sangster Family & Partners **Bred** W And R Barnett Ltd **Trained** Lambourn, Berks

**FOCUS**

A messy contest with four of the five runners electing to race down the centre for the last five furlongs. A modest time for a Listed contest and the form is below average for the grade.

**NOTEBOOK**

**Private Charter**, who had promised so much, finally delivered. The first-time cheekpieces clearly had the desired effect, although he did have something of a soft lead.

**Fantastic Love(USA)** led the other runners towards the centre and, had he consented to run in a straight line rather than ducking and diving, he may well have got up.

**Shanty Star(IRE)**, given a break and gelded since disappointing in the spring, looked a little ring-rusty and should be much sharper for the outing.

**Light Of Morn** looked to run her race, but may have done better still had there been more pace on.

**Razkalla(USA)** arrived at the start with a tongue-strap which had not been declared, and his trainer was fined £240. He should have beaten his rivals on these terms, but folded tamely and was later reported to have needed the race. *Official explanation: trainer said gelding weakened in final furlong, having not run for 188 days*

## 5917 SHADWELL STUD JOEL STKS (GROUP 3) 1m

**2:25** (2:27) (A1) 3-Y-O+ **£29,000** (£11,000; £5,500; £2,500) **Stalls** Centre

Form RPR

-220 **1** **Polar Ben**[97] 3318 5-9-0 111 JPMurtagh 2 115+
(JRFanshawe) *hld up: hdwy over 2f out: r.o to ld towards fin* **16/1**

0523 **2** *¾* **Salselon**[19] 5492 5-9-0 116 (b) LDettori 5 118+
(LMCumani) *lw: s.i.s: bhd: hdwy to ld over 1f out: nt run on and hdd towards fin* **11/2**[2]

20-2 **3** *1¼* **Funfair**[20] 5462 5-9-0 104 RLMoore 1 110
(MrsAJPerrett) *lw: hld up: hdwy over 2f out: rdn and ev ch over 1f out: styd on same pce ins fnl f* **11/1**

0060 **4** *¾* **Tout Seul (IRE)**[50] 4685 4-9-0 105 SCarson 3 109
(RFJohnsonHoughton) *hld up: hdwy over 2f out: rdn over 1f out: styd on same pce* **33/1**

5501 **5** *2* **Secret Charm (IRE)**[21] 5439 3-8-8 110 MHills 11 101
(BWHills) *chsd ldr tl led over 3f out: hdd over 1f out: wknd towards fin* **8/1**

4213 **6** *1* **Grand Passion (IRE)**[47] 4786 4-9-0 106 JFEgan 9 102
(GWragg) *mid-div: rdn 1/2-way: hdwy over 2f out: wknd ins fnl f* **16/1**

3622 **7** *hd* **Checkit (IRE)**[13] 5651 4-9-0 110 ACulhane 7 101
(MRChannon) *lw: prom: rdn to chse ldr over 2f out: wknd ins fnl f* **7/1**[3]

1001 **8** *11* **Pentecost**[13] 5651 5-9-0 110 MartinDwyer 6 76
(AMBalding) *lw: hld up: rdn over 1f out: sn wknd* **10/1**

-314 **9** *2½* **Red Feather (IRE)**[20] 5484 3-8-11 (t) NGMcCullagh 13 70
(EdwardLynam, Ire) *led over 4f: wknd over 2f out* **25/1**

0111 **10** *¾* **Attune**[22] 5416 3-8-8 99 KDarley 12 66
(BJMeehan) *chsd ldrs tl wknd wl over 1f out* **16/1**

35-2 **11** *½* **Troubadour (IRE)**[12] 5676 3-8-11 JPSpencer 10 67
(APO'Brien, Ire) *wl grwn: prom: rdn over 2f out: wknd over 1f out* **5/1**[1]

2155 **12** *nk* **Shot To Fame (USA)**[27] 5291 5-9-3 111 EAhern 4 70
(PWHarris) *prom over 5f* **16/1**

10/3 **13** *hd* **Desert Star**[20] 5462 4-9-0 99 KFallon 8 66
(SirMichaelStoute) *lw: s.i.s: sn prom: rdn over 3f out: wknd over 2f* **15/2**

1m 37.33s (-2.07) **Going Correction** 0.0s/f (Good)
**WFA** 3 from 4yo+ 3lb **13** Ran SP% **115.2**
Speed ratings: **110,109,108,107,105 104,104,93,90,89 89,89,88**CSF £98.02 TOTE £17.70: £4.10, £2.80, £3.30; EX 79.50 Trifecta £2469.90 Part won. Pool: £3,478.86. 0.90 winning units..
**Owner** Simon Gibson **Bred** Worksop Manor Stud **Trained** Newmarket, Suffolk

**FOCUS**

Unfortunately the race will go down as the one Salselon threw away, rather than Polar Ben winning. An ordinary time for a Group Three, but reasonably decent form for the grade and sound enough with the fourth setting the standard.

**NOTEBOOK**

**Polar Ben** looked destined for the runner-up spot when Salselon dug his toes in, thinking he had done enough.

**Salselon** is much better suited to a straight track, and finally looked to have got his act together when swooping to go clear inside the final furlong. However, there was one trick left up his sleeve and he put the brakes on about 50 yards from the line to turn certain victory into defeat. He is clearly a high-class animal, but which animal remains open to doubt.

**Funfair** took the step up in class in his stride, and it will be a surprise if he cannot add to his tally at this level.

**Tout Seul(IRE)**, back to the scene of his greatest moment, again left the impression this trip is just beyond him.

**Secret Charm(IRE)**, a winner at this meeting last year was not disgraced, but she looks as though she will difficult to place at this level.

**Grand Passion(IRE)** had something to find with the best of these, but ran as well as could be expected.

**Checkit(IRE)** looked to run a little flat and may not have got over his hard race at Newbury last time.

**Troubadour(IRE)** dropped away tamely with no apparent excuse. *Official explanation: jockey said colt lost his action and prefers faster ground*

## 5918 SHADWELL STUD MIDDLE PARK STKS (GROUP 1) (ENTIRE COLTS) 6f

**3:00** (3:01) (A1) 2-Y-O **£110,606** (£41,954; £20,977; £9,535) **Stalls** Centre

Form RPR

1 **1** **Ad Valorem (USA)**[12] 5680 2-8-11 JPSpencer 4 121
(APO'Brien, Ire) *gd sort: lw: trckd ldrs: led over 1f out: drvn out* **9/2**[2]

213 **2** *¾* **Rebuttal (USA)**[13] 5649 2-8-11 PJSmullen 1 119
(BJMeehan) *hld up: hdwy over 2f out: rdn and ev ch ins fnl f: r.o* **9/1**[3]

2112 **3** *2½* **Iceman**[21] 5437 2-8-11 100 KFallon 6 111
(JHMGosden) *hld up: outpcd 1/2-way: hung rt and r.o ins fnl f: nvr trbld ldrs* **9/4**[1]

2111 **4** *nk* **Satchem (IRE)**[27] 5295 2-8-11 LDettori 9 110
(CEBrittain) *lw: hld up in tch: rdn over 2f out: styd on same pce fnl f* **9/2**[2]

2333 **5** *½* **Russian Blue (IRE)**[12] 5678 2-8-11 JPMurtagh 7 109
(APO'Brien, Ire) *gd sort: leggy: trckd ldr tl led over 2f out: rdn and hdd over 1f out: styd on same pce* **9/1**[3]

1301 **6** *1* **Josh**[15] 5594 2-8-11 PRobinson 2 106
(MAJarvis) *lw: hld up: hdwy over 2f out: rdn and edgd rt over 1f out: no ex* **33/1**

31 **7** *1* **Dramaticus**[7] 5772 2-8-11 SSanders 3 103
(DRLoder) *hld up: hdwy over 2f out: n.m.r over 1f out: nvr trbld ldrs* **14/1**

1061 **8** *shd* **Prince Charming**[14] 5602 2-8-11 98 KMcEvoy 8 102
(JHMGosden) *lw: led over 3f: wknd fnl f* **14/1**

1101 **9** *hd* **Chateau Istana**[20] 5464 2-8-11 98 (t) KDarley 5 102
(NPLittmoden) *prom: n.m.r over 1f out: wknd ins fnl f* **16/1**

1m 12.19s (-0.90) **Going Correction** 0.0s/f (Good) **9** Ran SP% **109.3**
Speed ratings: **106,105,101,101,100 99,97,97,97**CSF £40.39 TOTE £5.30: £1.30, £2.90, £1.50; EX 49.90 Trifecta £407.50 Pool: £1,492.44. 2.60 winning units..
**Owner** Mrs John Magnier **Bred** Calumet Farm **Trained** Ballydoyle, Co Tipperary
■ Aidan O'Brien's first Group One winner in Britain this year.

**FOCUS**

This did not look the strongest of Group Ones and produced only an ordinary time for a race of its class. That said the form looks solid with the fourth the guide.

**NOTEBOOK**

**Ad Valorem(USA)**, impressive in both of his starts in Ireland, passed his stiffest test yet with a workmanlike display. He recieved a 14/1 quote for the Guineas after this, but he has plenty of natural speed and is not certain to stay the stiff mile.

**Rebuttal(USA)**, third in the Mill Reef Stakes on his previous outing, handled this step up in class well and was only just touched off. He looks progressive and his racing style suggests he will get further.

**Iceman** looked to be crying out for a return to seven furlongs, so the Dewhurst would appear to be the logical target.

**Satchem(IRE)**, closely matched with Iceman through Council Member, ran his race but gave the impression he will be happier by a return to an extra furlong.

**Russian Blue(IRE)** was the only runner to come into this with Group One form. While he is a consistent colt, he is just found wanting at this level.

**Josh** was not disgraced on this step up in class.

**Dramaticus** had no luck in running and is certainly worth another shot at the big boys.

## 5919 GREENE KING IPA CHAMPIONS BEER H'CAP 1m 4f

**3:35** (3:37) (C1) (0-100,100) 3-Y-O+ **£12,300** (£4,665; £2,332; £1,060) **Stalls** Centre

Form RPR

1015 **1** **Vinando**[11] 5699 3-8-8 **94** (t) LDettori 16 105
(CREgerton) *a.p: chsd ldr over 2f out: rdn to ld ins fnl f: styd on* **12/1**

5/00 **2** *nk* **Manorson (IRE)**[118] 2681 5-8-7 **86** oh1 (t) EAhern 17 96
(MAMagnusson) *b: led clr 4f out: rdn and hdd ins fnl f: styd on* **12/1**

0201 **3** *1½* **Solo Flight**[14] 5615 7-8-8 **87** RLMoore 4 95
(HMorrison) *hld up: hdwy over 3f out: rdn over 1f out: styd on same pce* **20/1**

3/46 **4** *2½* **Ovambo (IRE)**[5] 5814 6-9-7 **100** SSanders 12 104
(PJMakin) *lw: hld up: hdwy over 4f out: rdn over 2f out: styd on same pce appr fnl f* **20/1**

0064 **5** *1* **Pagan Sky (IRE)**[13] 5650 5-8-7 **86** oh3 LisaJones 14 88
(JARToller) *lw: hld up: hdwy over 3f out: styd on* **20/1**

2051 **6** *nk* **Fort**[5] 5814 3-8-4 **93** 6ex NMackay(3) 3 95
(MJohnston) *hld up in tch: rdn over 3f out: styd on same pce fnl 2f* **4/1**[1]

125S **7** *½* **Larkwing (IRE)**[11] 5699 3-8-2 **88** FNorton 11 89
(GWragg) *prom: rdn over 4f out: styd on same pce fnl 2f* **12/1**

1-04 **8** *nk* **Vaughan**[11] 5699 3-8-5 **91** ow1 KDarley 8 92
(MrsAJPerrett) *chsd ldrs: rdn over 2f out: wknd fnl f* **12/1**

03-0 **9** *¾* **King Eider**[15] 5595 5-8-7 **86** oh3 PHanagan 13 85
(BEllison) *plld hrd and prom: lost pl 3f out: styd on ins fnl f* **50/1**

31-2 **10** *1¾* **Tip The Dip (USA)**[14] 5615 4-8-7 **86** oh1 KMcEvoy 15 83
(JHMGosden) *chsd ldr over 9f: wknd over 1f out* **13/2**[3]

5000 **11** *5* **Heisse**[21] 5435 4-8-12 **91** RHughes 5 80
(DRLoder) *s.s: sn prom: rdn over 2f out: wknd over 1f out: eased ins fnl f* **66/1**

3450 **12** *1½* **Prins Willem (IRE)**[45] 4831 5-8-8 **87** (vt[1]) KFallon 1 73
(JRFanshawe) *hld up: hdwy u.p over 3f out: wknd 2f out* **12/1**

0545 **13** *4* **Millville**[27] 5288 4-8-7 **86** oh1 PRobinson 10 66
(MAJarvis) *hld up: rdn over 4f out: n.d* **9/2**[2]

-046 **14** *3½* **Famous Grouse**[20] 5461 4-9-5 **98** DHolland 6 72
(RCharlton) *hld up: rdn over 5f out: a in rr* **40/1**

4404 **15** *9* **Bagan (FR)**[20] 5465 5-8-7 **86** WRyan 9 46
(HRACecil) *hld up: hdwy over 3f out: sn wknd* **25/1**

-606 **16** *nk* **Lunar Exit (IRE)**[11] 5699 3-8-6 **92** (b[1]) JFEgan 2 51
(LadyHerries) *prom: rdn 1/2-way: wknd over 4f out* **50/1**

5005 **17** *8* **Muhareb (USA)**[7] 5761 5-8-11 **90**........ JPMurtagh 7 37
(CEBrittain) *lw: chsd ldrs over 8f* **16/1**

2m 30.5s (-2.96) **Going Correction** 0.0s/f (Good)
**WFA** 3 from 4yo+ 7lb **17** Ran SP% **121.8**
Speed ratings: **109,108,107,106,105 105,104,104,104,103 99,98,96,93,87 87,82**CSF £133.72 CT £2862.83 TOTE £11.60: £3.20, £4.50, £2.80, £4.70; EX 297.50.
**Owner** Mrs Evelyn Hankinson **Bred** Miss K Rausing **Trained** Chaddleworth, Berks

**FOCUS**
Quite a competitive handicap on paper, but very few got into it. The form looks solid enough and the winner is progressive.

**NOTEBOOK**
**Vinando** continues on the upgrade, and with better to come over a little further looks one to keep on the right side of.
**Manorson(IRE)** had a soft time of things up front and looked to have stolen this. However, although collared up the hill, he did stick on bravely and proved beyond doubt that he does stay this far. The November Handicap could be a possible target for him.
**Solo Flight** sixth in this race last year, did not really have the race run to suit, but still performed with credit.
**Ovambo(IRE)** still looks to be in the grip of the Handicapper.
**Pagan Sky(IRE)** could never get competitive, but is certainly worth another try at this trip.
**Fort** was a little disappointing under his penalty, but the way the race was run hardly suited him, and he is certainly worth another chance.
**Larkwing(IRE)**, like so many in this contest, could have done with a stronger pace.
**Tip The Dip(USA)** *Official explanation: jockey said colt hung left in latter stages*
**Lunar Exit(IRE)** *Official explanation: jockey said felt wrong*
**Muhareb(USA)** *Official explanation: jockey said gelding had a breathing problem*

## 5920 TAITTINGER CHAMPAGNE E B F CLASSIFIED STKS 1m
**4:10** (4:12) (C1) 3-Y-0+ **£11,971** (£4,540; £2,270; £1,032) **Stalls** Centre

Form RPR
1334 **1** **Royal Prince**[5] 5813 3-8-11 89........ JPMurtagh 2 103
(JRFanshawe) *racd centre: hld up: hdwy over 2f out: led that gp and edgd rt 1f out: r.o to be overall ldr nr fin* **13/2**[2]
1511 **2** *½* **Dawn Surprise (USA)**[35] 5099 3-8-11 93........(t) LDettori 10 102+
(SaeedBinSuroor) *lw: led far side duo and overall ldr: clr of that pair 3f out: rdn over 1f out: hdd nr fin* **5/4**[1]
1100 **3** *1 ¾* **Ace Of Hearts**[32] 5194 5-9-0 90........ EAhern 4 98
(CFWall) *lw: racd centre: chsd ldrs tl led that gp over 1f out: sn hdd: styd on same pce* **12/1**
2452 **4** *2* **Jazz Scene (IRE)**[13] 5627 3-9-0 93........ ACulhane 1 96
(MRChannon) *racd centre: sn pushed along in rr: outpcd over 2f out: r.o ins fnl f: nt trble ldrs* **8/1**[3]
1665 **5** *2 ½* **Appalachian Trail (IRE)**[54] 4570 3-8-11 87........ PHanagan 3 88
(ISemple) *racd centre: chsd ldrs: rdn over 1f out: wknd ins fnl f* **14/1**
1250 **6** *2 ½* **Our Jaffa (IRE)**[16] 5566 3-8-8 83........ PRobinson 8 79
(DJDaly) *b.hind: led centre over 6f: sn wknd* **33/1**
0004 **7** *nk* **State Dilemma (IRE)**[27] 5294 3-8-11 90........ MHills 5 81
(BWHills) *h.d.w: racd centre: trckd ldrs: rdn over 2f out: wknd over 1f out* **14/1**
134 **8** *9* **United Nations**[20] 5474 3-8-13 92........(v) SSanders 7 63
(DRLoder) *racd centre: chsd ldr tl wknd wl over 1f out* **11/1**
6050 **9** *20* **Bravo Maestro (USA)**[7] 5762 3-9-0 93........ KFallon 6 18
(DWPArbuthnot) *b: s.i.s: racd centre: hld up: rdn and wknd over 2f out* **12/1**
0-0 **10** *¾* **Marko Jadeo (IRE)**[22] 5428 6-9-1 91........ RHughes 11 14
(KAMorgan) *lw: chsd ldr far side tl wknd 3f out: eased* **25/1**

1m 37.59s (-1.81) **Going Correction** 0.0s/f (Good)
**WFA** 3 from 5yo+ 3lb **10** Ran SP% **112.7**
Speed ratings: **109,108,106,104,102 99,99,90,70,69**CSF £14.39 TOTE £7.20: £2.10, £1.20, £3.30; EX 18.70.
**Owner** Abdulla Buhaleeba **Bred** Snailwell Stud Co Ltd **Trained** Newmarket, Suffolk

**FOCUS**
The field split into two with just a pair of them racing next to the far rails, with no advantage to either group. The pace was decent and the form looks solid, with the third setting the standard.

**NOTEBOOK**
**Royal Prince** confirmed himself a decent performer and showed a nice turn of foot to get up in the final strides. Now he has proven he stays this far, there should be plenty of opportunities for him.
**Dawn Surprise(USA)**, taken across to the far rails, may have been a little unlucky for she had nothing to race with for much of the trip.
**Ace Of Hearts** ran a solid-enough race, but he is not going to be easy to place off his current mark.
**Jazz Scene(IRE)** did not do much to help his rider and looks one to have reservations about.
**Appalachian Trail(IRE)** without the visor this time, looks out of sorts at present.
**Bravo Maestro(USA)** *Official explanation: jockey said colt had a breathing problem*
**Marko Jadeo(IRE)** *Official explanation: jockey said gelding ran too free to post*

## 5921 REG DAY MEMORIAL H'CAP 7f
**4:45** (4:46) (C1) (0-100,100) 3-Y-0+ **£12,277** (£4,656; £2,328; £1,058) **Stalls** Centre

Form RPR
5555 **1** **Wizard Of Noz**[35] 5099 4-9-0 **93**........(b[1]) EAhern 6 106
(JNoseda) *a.p: led 1f out: rdn out* **12/1**
3540 **2** *1* **Leoballero**[27] 5297 4-8-7 **86** oh7........(t) JFEgan 2 96
(DJDaly) *lw: hld up: hung rt and hdwy over 1f out: r.o* **20/1**
0001 **3** *1* **Jonny Ebeneezer**[6] 5787 5-8-13 **95** 6ex........(be) HayleyTurner[(3)] 16 103
(DFlood) *hld up: hdwy over 1f out: r.o: hung lft nr fin* **12/1**
0000 **4** *¾* **Master Robbie**[1] 5887 5-8-7 **86** oh2........ SHitchcott 3 92
(MRChannon) *a.p: rdn over 2f out: styd on* **16/1**
0220 **5** *hd* **Digital**[20] 5468 7-8-9 **88**........ ACulhane 1 93
(MRChannon) *hld up: hdwy over 1f out: r.o* **12/1**
0660 **5** *dht* **Greenslades**[6] 5781 5-9-0 **93**........ SSanders 15 98
(PJMakin) *hld up in tch: rdn over 1f out: ev ch ins fnl f: nt clr run and no ex towards fin* **7/2**[1]
10-0 **7** *nk* **Fremen (USA)**[188] 1125 4-9-0 **93**........ KFallon 10 98+
(SirMichaelStoute) *lw: chsd ldrs: nt clr run over 1f out: rna on* **8/1**[3]
5301 **8** *1* **Doctorate**[13] 5652 3-8-5 **86**........ KDarley 14 88
(EALDunlop) *lw: chsd ldrs: rdn to ld over 1f out: rdr dropped reins and hdd 1f out: no ex ins fnl f* **11/1**
6600 **9** *1 ½* **Vindication**[20] 5468 4-8-5 **87**........(t) NMackay[(3)] 13 85
(JRFanshawe) *hld up: rdn over 1f out: styd on same pce* **10/1**
0200 **10** *hd* **Colour Wheel**[72] 4031 3-8-8 **89**........(vt[1]) RHughes 11 87
(RCharlton) *chsd ldr: rdn and ev ch whn hmpd over 1f out: wknd ins fnl f* **40/1**
-500 **11** *shd* **Asia Winds (IRE)**[29] 5249 3-8-9 **90**........ MHills 5 87
(BWHills) *lw: hld up: n.d* **33/1**
0000 **12** *½* **Pomfret Lad**[13] 5628 6-8-13 **92**........ JPMurtagh 7 88
(DNicholls) *mde most over 5f: wknd ins fnl f* **25/1**
2025 **13** *shd* **Jedburgh**[20] 5468 3-9-2 **97**........ IMongan 12 93
(JLDunlop) *chsd ldrs: rdn and ev ch whn hung lft over 1f out: sn wknd* **8/1**[3]
0313 **14** *2* **Golden Sahara (IRE)**[20] 5468 3-9-4 **99**........(t) LDettori 4 90
(SaeedBinSuroor) *lw: hld up: wknd over 1f out* **5/1**[2]
6305 **15** *1 ½* **Mazepa (IRE)**[130] 2372 4-9-0 **93**........ RLMoore 8 80
(NACallaghan) *lw: chsd ldrs: rdn over 2f out: sn wknd* **33/1**

1m 25.38s (-1.09) **Going Correction** 0.0s/f (Good)
**WFA** 3 from 4yo+ 2lb **15** Ran SP% **124.4**
Speed ratings: **106,104,103,102,102 102,102,101,99,99 99,98,98,96,94**CSF £243.58 CT £3003.38 TOTE £16.80: £4.30, £9.10, £3.80; EX 140.40 Place 6 £276.70, Place 5 £105.31.
**Owner** C Fox & J Wright **Bred** T R Lock And R Gibbons **Trained** Newmarket, Suffolk

**FOCUS**
A competitive handicap run at a sound pace making the form look solid and reliable.

**NOTEBOOK**
**Wizard Of Noz** has found life difficult since winning on his debut, but the fitting of blinkers clearly had the desired effect and, now he has got his head in front again, may be capable of following up.
**Leoballero** does not always produce, but there is no doubt he does have ability.
**Jonny Ebeneezer** is a much-improved performer, and although beaten here probably turned in his best-ever effort.
**Master Robbie**, none the worse for his run the day before, is well treated on his best form.
**Greenslades** does not win as often as he should, and again flattered only to deceive.
**Digital** has gone over a year without winning, but there were plenty of encouraging signs and there is still time for him to put matters right.
**Fremen(USA)** *Official explanation: jockey said colt hung left and did not get a clear run*
T/Jkpt: Not won. T/Plt: £558.30 to a £1 stake. Pool: £80,392.00. 105.10 winning tickets. T/Qpdt: £52.60 to a £1 stake. Pool: £6,966.90. 97.90 winning tickets. CR

# 5854 CHANTILLY (R-H)
Friday, October 1

**OFFICIAL GOING: Good**

## 5922a PRIX ECLIPSE (GROUP 3) 6f
**1:50** (1:49) 2-Y-0 **£25,704** (£10,282; £7,711; £5,141)

RPR
**1** **Tremar**[27] 5295 2-8-11........ GCarter 7 108+
(TGMills) *raced in 2nd, led half-way, pushed along and ran on over 2f out, ran on well final furlong, comfortably*
**2** *1 ½* **Crossover**[23] 5404 2-8-8........ TJarnet 6 100
(H-APantall, France) *in touch on outside, ran on to chase leader over 2f out, ridden over 1f out, stayed on but not pace of winner*
**3** *nk* **Nipping (IRE)**[10] 5726 2-8-8........ OPeslier 2 99
(RobertCollet, France) *tracked leaders, 3rd half-way, stayed on to line final stages* **2**
**4** *1 ½* **Salut Thomas (FR)**[23] 5404 2-8-11........(b) CSoumillon 3 98
(RobertCollet, France) *raced in last, ridden and stayed on final 1 1/2f out to take 4th but never dangerous* **2**
**5** *nk* **Million Wishes**[19] 2-8-8........ TGillet 1 94
(JEPease, France) *held up, pushed along over 2f out, unable to quicken* **3**
**6** *6* **Princesse Jasmine (FR)**[25] 2-8-8........ TThulliez 4 76
(YDeNicolay, France) *in touch til weakened 2f out*
**7** *1* **Speciale (USA)**[23] 5404 2-8-8........ C-PLemaire 5 73
(MmeCHead-Maarek, France) *led to half-way, weakened from over 2f out* **1**

1m 11.2s **Going Correction** -0.15s/f (Firm) **7** Ran SP% **152.9**
Speed ratings: **102,100,99,97,97 89,87.**
**Owner** T Jacobs **Bred** Mrs Mary Taylor **Trained** Headley, Surrey

**NOTEBOOK**
**Tremar**, not disgraced in Group Three company back in Britain latest, stepped up again and won this slightly weaker race with any amount in hand. He came with a strong run in the final third of the race and was not stopping at the line. Evidently a progressive sort, he takes his racing well and is worthy of a crack at something better.
**Crossover** finished to good effect but the race had already been decided. She is still a maiden and should have little trouble winning an ordinary heat.
**Nipping(IRE)**, off the mark in Listed company latest, had her chance and could have done with softer ground.

5923 - 5924a (Foreign Racing) - See Raceform Interactive

# 5745 BRIGHTON (L-H)
Saturday, October 2

**OFFICIAL GOING: Good**
Wind: str; half across Weather: overcast; shower mid-meeting

## 5925 BETFRED.COM IN-RUNNING MAIDEN AUCTION STKS 5f 213y
**11:05** (11:05) (H5) 2-Y-0 **£1,452** (£415; £207) **Stalls** Low

Form RPR
0020 **1** **Beau Marche**[7] 5792 2-8-10 61........ IMongan 3 69
(IAWood) *trckd ldr: strly rdn appr fnl f: led post* **28/1**
32 **2** *shd* **Pinafore**[14] 5640 2-8-3 ow1........ RLMoore 2 62
(HMorrison) *led: rdn appproaching fnl f: kpt on: hdd post* **1/2**[1]
0 **3** *3* **Moonfleet (IRE)**[75] 3983 2-8-4........ ANicholls 1 54
(MFHarris) *hld up in tch: sltly short of room 1/2-way: styd on one pce ins fnl 2f: nvr nrr* **50/1**
202 **4** *6* **Avertigo**[28] 5281 2-8-11 73........ TEDurcan 6 43
(WRMuir) *in tch: rdn over 2f out: wknd appr fnl f* **3/1**[2]
0 **5** *nk* **Vino Venus**[47] 4797 2-8-1 ow1........ NChalmers[(3)] 5 35
(MissSheenaWest) *s.i.s: hdwy on outside 1/2-way: sn rdn: wknd wl over 1f out* **16/1**
00 **6** *¾* **Dewin Coch**[12] 5688 2-8-7........ SWhitworth 4 36
(WMBrisbourne) *t.k.h: in rr: rdn 1/2-way: wl bhd fnl 2f* **12/1**[3]

1m 13.21s (3.11) **Going Correction** +0.35s/f (Good) **6** Ran SP% **110.7**
Speed ratings: **93,92,88,80,80 79**CSF £42.53 TOTE £8.50: £5.00, £1.10; EX 21.90.
**Owner** Christopher Shankland **Bred** Alan Spargo Ltd **Trained** Upper Lambourn, Berks
■ Stewards Enquiry : I Mongan three-day ban: used whip with excessive force (Oct 13-15)
R L Moore one-day ban: excessive use of the whip (Oct 13)

**FOCUS**
A moderate maiden and the form is just ordinary, despite an improved effort from the winner.

**NOTEBOOK**
**Beau Marche**, dropping back from a mile, produced a tenacious display to get off the mark at the sixth attempt. This was by far his best display to date, he reversed his Lingfield form with the runner-up and could have more to offer over this trip in nurseries.

**Pinafore** pinged out and only just failed to make all on this third outing. On previous form she looked to have an outstanding chance to score, but although she ran below her best, she did nothing wrong in defeat. It is possible that she could improve for a switch to nurseries now, and should not be too harshly treated.
**Moonfleet(IRE)**, off since finishing tailed off on her debut in July, did the best of those to come from off the pace, but never looked a threat. She was clear in second and, although she looks just moderate, should improve again for this outing.
**Avertigo** set the standard on form, but ran way below his current mark of 73 and has to go down as very disappointing.

## 5926 BETFRED.COM NOW ONLINE MAIDEN CLAIMING STKS 6f 209y

**11:35** (11:35) (H5) 3-Y-0+ **£1,522** (£435; £217) **Stalls** Low

| Form | | | | RPR |
|---|---|---|---|---|
| 5242 | **1** | | **Elsinora**[7] 5794 3-8-6 45 (v) RLMoore 18<br>(HMorrison) *hld up: gd hdwy 2f out: led 1f out: sn clr* **5/2**[1] | 50 |
| 0000 | **2** | *5* | **Wodhill Be**[23] 5408 4-9-2 40 PaulEddery 12<br>(DMorris) *bhd tl hdwy 2f out: r.o to chse easy wnr fnl f* **16/1** | 45 |
| 0040 | **3** | *nk* | **Catch The Fox**[14] 5641 4-9-4 35 HayleyTurner(3) 17<br>(JJBridger) *towards rr: swtchd rt after 2f: hdwy on outside 1f out: r.o strly: nvr nrr* **10/1**[3] | 49 |
| 0500 | **4** | *1 1/2* | **Bahamian Belle**[7] 5793 4-8-5 35 JBrennan(7) 9<br>(PSMcentee) *a.p: led 2f out: weakned and hdd 1f out* **25/1** | 36 |
| 3400 | **5** | *hd* | **Roving Vixen (IRE)**[59] 4460 3-8-3 40 RMiles(3) 1<br>(JLSpearing) *led tl hdd 2f out: no ex after* **14/1** | 32 |
| 003 | **6** | *1 3/4* | **Shaamit's All Over**[118] 1918 5-8-11 30 MSavage(5) 5<br>(BAPearce) *s.i.s: sn in tch: rdn 2f out: hung lft and hit rail over 1f out: no ch after* **20/1** | 35 |
| 2300 | **7** | *1 1/2* | **Blakeseven**[17] 5575 4-9-7 46 (b[1]) SWhitworth 2<br>(WJMusson) *t.k.h: prom tl wknd over 1f out* **5/2**[1] | 36 |
| 4600 | **8** | *5* | **Lord Wishingwell (IRE)**[21] 5451 3-9-5 30 PMcCabe 6<br>(JSWainwright) *prom tl rdn and wknd wl over 1f out* **16/1** | 23 |
| 000- | **9** | *nk* | **Dangerous Dave**[614] 399 5-9-5 40 PDoe 10<br>(JamiePoulton) *prom: rdn 2f out: wknd fnl f* **33/1** | 21 |
| 0000 | **10** | *1/2* | **Court Chancellor**[7] 5794 3-9-5 40 (b) IMongan 11<br>(PMitchell) *sn rdn alon: nvr bttr than mid-div* **66/1** | 21 |
| 0000 | **11** | *1 1/2* | **Military Two Step (IRE)**[120] 2660 3-9-1 50 LEnstone 7<br>(KRBurke) *prom to 1/2-way* **12/1** | 13 |
| 000 | **12** | *1* | **Till There Was You**[72] 4044 3-7-13 CHaddon(7) 15<br>(WGMTurner) *in tch on outside tl rdn and wknd 2f out* **66/1** | 2 |
| 0-00 | **13** | *1* | **Mazram**[21] 5448 5-8-12 (b) RFfrench 16<br>(IWMcinnes) *in tch tl rdn 4f out: sn bhd* **50/1** | 3 |
| 006 | **14** | *1 1/4* | **Royal Logic**[9] 5749 3-9-0 45 TEDurcan 13<br>(MRChannon) *bmpd s and a bhd* **12/1** | 4 |
| 0320 | **15** | *2* | **Magico**[26] 5336 3-8-12 48 DerekNolan(7) 4<br>(ABHaynes) *rrd up leaving stalls: a bhd* **9/1**[2] | 4 |
| | **16** | *26* | **Dunlea (IRE)**[6] 2105 8-9-0 35 (v) BReilly(3) 14<br>(MJGingell) *wnt lft s and sn wl bhd: virtually p.u 2f out: t.o* **66/1** | — |

1m 26.23s (3.63) **Going Correction** +0.35s/f (Good)
**WFA** 3 from 4yo+ 2lb **16** Ran SP% **128.0**
Speed ratings: **93,87,86,85,85 83,81,75,75,74 72,71,70,69,66 37**CSF £50.43 TOTE £4.00: £1.80, £4.80, £3.10; EX 65.80.Elsinora was claimed by A. G. Juckes for £3,000.
**Owner** John R Goddard And John Steel **Bred** J Goddard And J Steel **Trained** East Ilsley, Berks

**FOCUS**
A dire contest with the third setting the standard, but the winner did the job nicely and may be capable of better.

**NOTEBOOK**
**Elsinora** ◆, with the visor replacing the blinkers this time, produced a neat turn of foot when asked to win her race over one out and scored comfortably under a well-judged ride from Moore. She could easily build on this first success if kept to this grade, and her confidence will be high after this.
**Wodhill Be** broke much better than had been the case the last twice and turned in an improved display as a result over this more suitable trip. She is hard to predict, but on this form could find a similarly weak heat.
**Catch The Fox** was brought wide to deliver his challenge and never looked a threat at any stage. He is one to avoid, but this is clearly his level.
**Bahamian Belle** had her chance from the front, but dropped out of contention tamely when challenged late on. She has fallen in the ratings of late and a return to six furlongs could see her go close at this level.
**Roving Vixen(IRE)** *Official explanation: jockey said filly had run too freely*
**Blakeseven** paid for running way too keen in the first-time blinkers and weakened badly late in the straight. He is capable of better, but is very hard to predict.
**Dunlea(IRE)** *Official explanation: jockey said gelding ducked left leaving stalls*

## 5927 BETFRED "THE BONUS KING" BANDED STKS 7f 214y

**12:05** (12:05) (H5) 3-Y-0+ **£1,673** (£478; £239) **Stalls** Low

| Form | | | | RPR |
|---|---|---|---|---|
| 4454 | **1** | | **Magic Verse**[38] 5036 3-8-12 46 RLMoore 5<br>(RGuest) *a in tch: hdwy over 2f out: led jst ins fnl f: drvn clr* **13/2** | 62 |
| 0001 | **2** | *4* | **Caerphilly Gal**[7] 5795 4-9-0 50 DFox(5) 14<br>(PLGilligan) *a.p: led briefly over 1f out: tl jst ins fnl f: nt pce of wnr* **4/1**[1] | 57 |
| 1360 | **3** | *3/4* | **Shamwari Fire (IRE)**[11] 5714 4-9-4 49 RFfrench 6<br>(IWMcinnes) *a in tch: rdn 3f out: styd on one pce ins fnl 2f* **8/1** | 54 |
| 5612 | **4** | *2* | **Levantine (IRE)**[7] 5795 7-8-10 48 KirstyMilczarek(7) 3<br>(MissJFeilden) *rrd s but led after 1f: rdn and hdd appr fnl f: wknd ins fnl f* **11/2**[3] | 49 |
| 0053 | **5** | *3* | **Encounter**[16] 5587 8-8-11 45 RMiles(3) 1<br>(JHetherton) *racd wd and in rr: styd on u.p fnl 2f but nvr nr to chal* **9/2**[2] | 39 |
| 0030 | **6** | *1 1/2* | **Pererin**[26] 5336 3-8-11 45 LEnstone 13<br>(IAWood) *towards rr and nvr on terms* **16/1** | 35 |
| 6600 | **7** | *3/4* | **Susiedil (IRE)**[14] 5639 3-8-4 45 MCoumbe(7) 10<br>(PWHarris) *a towards rr and nvr on terms* **25/1** | 34 |
| 0401 | **8** | *1 1/2* | **Inescapable (USA)**[12] 5702 3-9-5 53 TPQueally 8<br>(WRMuir) *led for 1f: rdn over 2f out: wknd wl over 1f out* **14/1** | 38 |
| 0050 | **9** | *1 1/4* | **Beltane**[29] 5259 6-9-1 46 PDoe 12<br>(WDeBest-Turner) *alowly into stride and a bhd* **22/1** | 28 |
| 0040 | **10** | *nk* | **Wood Fern (UAE)**[7] 5795 4-8-8 46 TO'Brien(7) 9<br>(MRChannon) *a bhd* **11/1** | 28 |
| 0602 | **11** | *hd* | **Love Of Life**[61] 4387 3-9-1 49 LisaJones 15<br>(JulianPoulton) *v.s.a and a struggling in rr* **12/1** | 30 |
| 4000 | **12** | *shd* | **Lady Liesel**[14] 5644 4-8-11 45 HayleyTurner(3) 11<br>(JJBridger) *hld up in tch: rdn 1/2-way: wknd over 2f out* **40/1** | 26 |
| 03-0 | **13** | *3* | **Sheer Focus (IRE)**[11] 5714 6-8-11 47 (p) NataliaGemelova(5) 2<br>(IWMcinnes) *trckd ldrs: rdn 3f out: sn wknd* **20/1** | 21 |

1m 40.07s (5.07) **Going Correction** +0.525s/f (Yiel)
**WFA** 3 from 4yo+ 3lb **13** Ran SP% **122.0**
Speed ratings: **95,91,90,88,85 83,83,81,80,79 79,79,76**CSF £31.78 TOTE £7.00: £2.40, £2.30, £2.50; EX 45.90.
**Owner** Eugene Lismonde **Bred** Miss Nathalie Lismonde **Trained** Newmarket, Suffolk

**FOCUS**
Very few got into this poor event and the field were well strung out behind the comfortable winner at the finish. The race is rated through the third.

**NOTEBOOK**
**Magic Verse** relished this drop in grade and posted a commanding display to break her duck at the eighth time of asking. She was helped by the recent ease in the ground, was suited by this trip and would have excellent claims of following up in this grade.
**Caerphilly Gal** could not go with the winner when challenged inside the last furlong and was well held. However, she confirmed recent form with Levantine despite being on worse terms and posted another creditable effort.
**Shamwari Fire(IRE)** lacked the turn of foot over this shorter trip to get serious, but at least improved on recent outings and appreciated the drop in class. *Official explanation: jockey said gelding hung left throughout*
**Levantine(IRE)** ran very much to the form of her recent Kempton encounter with the runner-up, despite these better terms. She remains in fair form, but always seems at her best when returning from a break.
**Encounter** was not helped by having to race wide throughout and can do better, but is a very hard horse to catch right and has now gone 30 outings without winning.
**Pererin**

## 5928 BETFRED "WE PAY DOUBLE RESULT" BANDED STKS 1m 1f 209y

**12:35** (12:37) (H5) 3-Y-0+ **£1,498** (£428; £214) **Stalls** High

| Form | | | | RPR |
|---|---|---|---|---|
| 0540 | **1** | | **Romeo's Day**[5] 5843 3-8-3 40 ow1 (v) TO'Brien(7) 17<br>(MRChannon) *mid-div: hdwy 1/2-way: edgd lft and led over 2f out: hrd rdn: jst hld on* **12/1** | 48 |
| 2213 | **2** | *shd* | **Lenwade**[9] 5750 3-8-4 40 DFox(5) 1<br>(GGMargarson) *s.i.s: t.k.h: hmpd over 2f out: hrd rdn to chal strly thrght fnl f: jst failed* **7/1** | 47 |
| 6365 | **3** | *2* | **Anisette**[28] 5284 3-8-9 40 LisaJones 7<br>(JulianPoulton) *slowly away and sn pushed along: making hdwy whn short of room and swtchd rt over 2f out: styd on to go 3rd ins fnl f* **16/1** | 43+ |
| 0562 | **4** | *1/2* | **Tartiruga (IRE)**[12] 5692 3-8-9 45 SWhitworth 2<br>(LGCottrell) *plld hrd: a.p: one pce fnl 2f* **11/2**[2] | 43 |
| 00-0 | **5** | *shd* | **Mighty Pip (IRE)**[14] 5658 8-9-0 45 GBaker 9<br>(MRBosley) *bhd tl hdwy 2f out: styd on: nvr nrr* **5/1**[1] | 42 |
| 0U43 | **6** | *5* | **Merlins Profit**[21] 5449 4-9-0 40 LEnstone 13<br>(MDods) *in tch tl no hdwy fnl 2f* **10/1** | 33 |
| 5104 | **7** | *2 1/2* | **Mr Whizz**[20] 5257 7-8-7 40 (p) DerekNolan(7) 11<br>(APJones) *hld up in mid-div: effrt 2f out: eased whn btn fnl f* **6/1**[3] | 29 |
| 0000 | **8** | *7* | **Zarneeta**[19] 5511 3-8-9 40 PDoe 18<br>(WDeBest-Turner) *prom tl wknd over 2f out* **40/1** | 16 |
| 60/0 | **9** | *nk* | **Tap Dancer (IRE)**[14] 5641 6-8-7 35 AHindley(7) 20<br>(BGPowell) *prom: led 1/2-way: hdd over 2f out: wknd qckly* **33/1** | 16 |
| 00-0 | **10** | *1 3/4* | **Blau Grau (GER)**[5] 5826 7-8-10 40 ow1 MSavage(5) 10<br>(NEBerry) *sn bhd and nvr on terms after* **33/1** | 14 |
| 0404 | **11** | *3/4* | **Morning Hawk (USA)**[33] 5178 3-8-9 35 (b) DSweeney 4<br>(JSMoore) *a bhd* **25/1** | 11 |
| 0064 | **12** | *shd* | **Coolfore Jade (IRE)**[11] 5710 4-8-11 40 ABeech(3) 12<br>(NEBerry) *trckd ldr: rdn 1/2-way: sn wknd* **9/1** | 11 |
| 0600 | **13** | *1 1/2* | **Hilarious (IRE)**[28] 5286 4-8-11 40 RThomas(3) 15<br>(DrJRJNaylor) *mid-div: bhd fnl 3f* **16/1** | 8 |
| 0200 | **14** | *1 3/4* | **Tshukudu**[14] 5644 3-8-9 35 DKinsella 14<br>(MBlanshard) *sn rdn: in tch tl wknd 3f out* **33/1** | 5 |
| 5000 | **15** | *1 1/4* | **Margery Daw (IRE)**[14] 5643 4-8-7 40 (b[1]) JBrennan(7) 16<br>(PSMcentee) *mid-div: wknd 3f out* **25/1** | 3 |
| 0600 | **16** | *11* | **Geography (IRE)**[146] 1644 4-8-11 40 (p) DNolan(3) 5<br>(PButler) *a bhd* **33/1** | — |
| 0030 | **17** | *9* | **Bontadini**[102] 3173 5-9-0 40 PaulEddery 3<br>(DMorris) *mid-div: wknd 3f out* **14/1** | — |
| -000 | **18** | *10* | **Spring Whisper (IRE)**[7] 5796 3-8-6 40 (v) J-PGuillambert(3) 19<br>(CADwyer) *led to 1/2-way: wknd 4f out* **33/1** | — |
| -000 | **19** | *25* | **Prince Ivor**[13] 5644 4-8-11 35 (vt) BReilly(3) 6<br>(MJGingell) *bhd: t.o sn after 1/2-way* **50/1** | — |

2m 9.80s (7.26) **Going Correction** +0.525s/f (Yiel)
**WFA** 3 from 4yo+ 5lb **19** Ran SP% **130.8**
Speed ratings: **91,90,89,88,88 84,82,77,77,75 75,74,73,72,71 62,55,47,27**CSF £89.82 TOTE £16.70: £4.90, £2.70, £5.30; EX 359.80.
**Owner** Heart Of The South Racing **Bred** Michael Ng **Trained** West Ilsley, Berks
■ The first winner for apprentice Tom O'Brien.
■ Stewards Enquiry : T O'Brien caution: careless riding

**FOCUS**
A modest time and ordinary form, rated through the placed horses, and the field came home well and truly strung out.

**NOTEBOOK**
**Romeo's Day** proved very game in just holding off the runner-up close home to score a first success at the 16th attempt. He looked to be idling a touch after hitting the front and could have a little more to offer in this grade, but is not one to lump on for a follow-up bid.
**Lenwade** ◆ has to go down as unlucky. She again started slowly and met serious trouble two out, but flew to join the winner late on and only just failed to get her head in front. She has to be of interest next time in this grade and should make amends.
**Anisette** did her chances no good with a very sluggish start, but stayed on well enough in the straight and is worth another try over this trip.
**Tartiruga(IRE)** was aided by the recent ease in the going, but ran way too keen through the early stades and had nothing more to give when it mattered late on. He has an engine, but is too headstrong for his own good at present.
**Mighty Pip(IRE)** was well backed in the ring, but failed to improve for this drop in class and never looked like justifying favourtism. *Official explanation: jockey said gelding was never travelling on good ground (loose on top) in first half of the race*
**Mr Whizz** found very little under pressure and looks in need of a break.
**Tshukudu** *Official explanation: jockey said filly hung left throughout*

## 5929 BETFRED IN SHOPS, ON PHONE AND ONLINE BANDED STKS 7f 214y

**1:05** (1:06) (H5) 3-Y-0+ **£1,498** (£428; £214) **Stalls** Low

| Form | | | | RPR |
|---|---|---|---|---|
| 150 | **1** | | **Delcienne**[65] 4259 3-8-8 45 ABeech(3) 12<br>(GGMargarson) *mid-div: rdn and hdwy 2f out: led 1f out: drvn clr* **7/2**[2] | 53 |
| 5605 | **2** | *5* | **Labelled With Love**[14] 5642 4-9-0 45 (t) DSweeney 2<br>(JRBoyle) *prom: led 5f out: hdd 1f out: nt pce of wnr* **3/1**[1] | 42 |
| 0040 | **3** | *3/4* | **Rathmullan**[14] 5641 5-8-7 35 LiamJones(7) 10<br>(EAWheeler) *bhd: hdwy 3f out: wnt 3rd ins fnl f: nvr nr to chal* **18/1** | 40 |
| 0406 | **4** | *1* | **Zinging**[7] 5793 5-9-0 40 GBaker 4<br>(JJBridger) *mid-div: stdy hdwy 1/2-way: wknd ins fnl f* **5/1**[3] | 37 |
| 6000 | **5** | *6* | **Kumakawa**[151] 1863 6-8-7 40 MHoward(7) 6<br>(DKIvory) *mid-div: rdn over 3f out: wknd over 1f out* **12/1** | 24 |

3330 **6** *nk* **Dundonald**[136] 2228 5-9-0 35 (t) SRighton 11 23
(MAppleby) *mid-div: c stands side over 3f out: sn btn* **12/1**
0500 **7** *6* **Noble Desert (FR)**[21] 5451 3-8-4 40 RMills(7) 1 9
(RGuest) *in tch whn bdly hmpd over 4f out: rallied to regain pl: wknd wl over 1f out* **33/1**
0000 **8** *shd* **Lyrical Lady**[23] 5408 3-8-8 40 RThomas(3) 5 9
(MrsAJBowlby) *towards rr: weakeneing whn hmpd wl over 1f out: eased* **25/1**
3440 **9** *½* **Mahlstick (IRE)**[113] 2836 6-8-11 40 RMiles(3) 7 8
(DWPArbuthnot) *in tch: rdn 3f out: sn wknd* **14/1**
/000 **10** *1½* **Thwaab**[55] 4574 12-9-0 40 (v) LEnstone 9 4
(FWatson) *a bhd: c over to stands side over 3f out: nvr on terms* **20/1**
0040 **11** *4* **Vizulize**[182] 1244 5-8-11 45 DNolan(3) 3 —
(AWCarroll) *led tl hdd over 5f out: c over to stands side: wknd 2f out* **11/2**
-300 **12** *dist* **Crusty Lily**[114] 2823 8-8-9 30 AQuinn(5) 8 —
(RMHCowell) *s.i.s: sn in tch but lost pl over 3f out and dropped out qckly: t.o* **22/1**

1m 42.2s (7.20) **Going Correction** +0.525s/f (Yiel)
**WFA** 3 from 4yo+ 3lb **12** Ran SP% **122.5**
Speed ratings: **85,80,79,78,72 71,65,65,65,63 59,**—CSF £14.17 TOTE £4.30: £1.90, £1.40, £6.00; EX 13.00.
**Owner** The Del Boys **Bred** Castlemans Farms **Trained** Newmarket, Suffolk
■ Stewards Enquiry : D Sweeney five-day ban: careless riding (Oct 13-17)

**FOCUS**
A weak event run at just a modest gallop and a poor time, even for a banded contest. The winner and second may be capable of improving again, but the form is average in the main for the grade.

**NOTEBOOK**
**Delcienne** readily quickened clear when asked to win her race approaching the final furlong and scored with plenty in hand. She clearly has a liking for this track and really appreciated this drop into banded class, so could well follow-up in this grade while in this current mood.
**Labelled With Love**, well backed for this return to turf, was handy throughout and had very much the run of the race, but was found out by the winner when challenged and could not quicken. A similar effort could see him go one better in this grade, and he may stay a little further.
**Rathmullan**, held up to get the trip and without his usual blinkers, ran on without being a serious threat and improved on recent displays.
**Zinging**, with the visor removed for this, found little for pressure late on over this longer trip and weakened badly. He continues out of form.
**Mahlstick(IRE)** *Official explanation: jockey said gelding was unsuited by good ground (loose on top)*
**Thwaab** *Official explanation: jockey said gelding was unsuited by good ground (loose on top)*
**Vizulize** was not disgraced on this return from a 182-day layoff and is one to keep an eye on for a similar event, as he showed up well for a long way before tiring from two out.

## 5930 BETFRED.COM EARLY PRICES FROM 10AM BANDED STKS 5f 213y
1:40 (1:41) (H5) 3-Y-0+ £1,515 (£433; £216) Stalls Low

Form RPR
0-01 **1** **Spinetail Rufous (IRE)**[7] 5793 6-9-3 48 (b) PDoe 14 60
(DFlood) *trckd ldr: a gng wl: c over to stand side: led 1f out: r.o wl* **9/2[2]**
2200 **2** *2* **Cargo**[28] 5282 5-8-12 46 (bt) RMiles(3) 7 52
(BAPearce) *led: cmae over to stands: side: hdd 1f out: nt pce of wnr* **16/1**
5000 **3** *2½* **Chatshow (USA)**[12] 5691 3-8-10 45 DNolan(3) 13 44
(AWCarroll) *sn rdn in mid-div: hdwy over 2f out: hrd rdn and one pce fnl f* **20/1**
0600 **4** *3* **Tuscan Treaty**[78] 3911 4-8-11 45 (v) BReilly(3) 11 35
(TTClement) *slowly away: mde sme hdwy ins fnl 2f* **25/1**
0060 **5** *nk* **Tappit (IRE)**[23] 5412 5-8-7 45 MHalford(7) 12 34
(NEBerry) *prom tl one pce ins fnl 2f* **33/1**
5304 **6** *shd* **Yamato Pink**[18] 5547 3-9-4 50 GBaker 9 38
(MrsHSweeting) *hld up: effrt over 2f out: one pce after* **5/1[3]**
5400 **7** *hd* **Otylia**[28] 5282 4-8-9 45 (v[1]) AQuinn(5) 1 33
(RMHCowell) *chsd ldrs: styd far side: rdn over 2f out: wknd over 1f out* **66/1**
0304 **8** *hd* **Night Cap (IRE)**[56] 4548 5-8-11 45 J-PGuillambert(3) 5 32
(TDMccarthy) *towards rr and nvr on terms* **13/2**
0004 **9** *2* **Astrac (IRE)**[21] 5452 13-9-3 48 PaulEddery 15 29
(MrsALMKing) *hld up: nvr on terms: fin lame* **10/1**
1060 **10** *2½* **Doctor Dennis (IRE)**[16] 5597 7-9-2 50 (v) ABeech(3) 16 24
(JPearce) *hld up: nvr got into r* **4/1[1]**
0003 **11** *3* **Flapdoodle**[41] 4970 6-9-0 45 (b) LEnstone 6 10
(AWCarroll) *prom: rdn 1/2-way: sn wknd* **11/1**
1056 **12** *4* **Gentle Response**[158] 1692 4-9-0 45 (v[1]) SWhitworth 8 —
(BRJohnson) *a bhd* **20/1**
0000 **13** *4* **Queen Of Bulgaria (IRE)**[72] 4052 3-8-13 45 PMcCabe 3 —
(JPearce) *plld hrd early: sn bhd and outpcd* **33/1**
4040 **14** *½* **Scarlett Breeze**[26] 5338 3-8-6 45 DerekNolan(7) 2 —
(JWHills) *prom tl wknd wl over 1f out: eased ins fnl f* **10/1**
0055 **15** *15* **Run On**[58] 4472 6-9-0 45 (b[1]) SRighton 4 —
(DGBridgwater) *sn bhd: eased over 1f out* **25/1**

1m 13.14s (3.04) **Going Correction** +0.525s/f (Yiel)
**WFA** 3 from 4yo+ 1lb **15** Ran SP% **125.2**
Speed ratings: **100,97,94,90,89 89,89,88,86,82 78,73,68,67,47**CSF £70.22 TOTE £6.10: £2.40, £4.50, £6.10; EX 110.30 Place 6 £209.54, Place 5 £143.03.
**Owner** Miss J Wickens **Bred** Michael Coogan **Trained** Upper Lambourn, Berks

**FOCUS**
A fair event for the grade that was run at a sound pace and the form looks reasonable.

**NOTEBOOK**
**Spinetail Rufous(IRE)** followed-up his recent win in this grade at Kempton in good style. He has really found his feet for current connections since switching to the turf, and should be hard to beat when going for the hat-trick, if kept to this lowly level.
**Cargo**, with the blinkers replacing the cheekpieces this time, had the run of the race, but was a sitting duck for the winner late on. He was clear in second however, and although he finds it hard to win, certainly deserves to end his long losing run.
**Chatshow(USA)** turned in by far his best effort for some time and responded well to pressure entering the last furlong. He was in turn clear of the rest and a return to fast ground can see him improve again.
**Tuscan Treaty**, off since July, blew her chance at the start, but showed enough to suggest that she can improve for this and get closer over another furlong.
**Yamato Pink** could not quicken under pressure and ran below her best. *Official explanation: jockey said filly was unsuited by good ground*
**Otylia** *Official explanation: jockey said filly had a breathing problem*
**Astrac(IRE)** *Official explanation: jockey said gelding finished lame*
**Doctor Dennis(IRE)** was gambled into favouritsism on a track he goes well at, but failed to get competitive and has to go down as disappointing.
**Flapdoodle** *Official explanation: jockey said mare was unsuited by good ground*
T/Plt: @76.50 to a £1 stake. Pool: 18,664.10 - 177.90 winning tickets T/Qpdt: @46.70 to a £1 stake. Pool: 1,823.30 - 28.85 winning tickets JS

# 5420 EPSOM (L-H)
Saturday, October 2

**OFFICIAL GOING: Good (good to soft in places on round course, good to firm in places on sprint course)**
The course was dolled off, particularly on the inside of the track, to protect the ground for next year, and overnight rain had eased the going.
Wind: blustery, half behind Weather: mostly fine

## 5931 RHT 40TH ANNIVERSARY CONDITIONS STKS 1m 114y
2:05 (2:05) (C2) 2-Y-0 £9,117 (£3,458; £1,729; £786) Stalls Low

Form RPR
1411 **1** **Comic Strip**[14] 5630 2-8-11 100 JMackay 2 91+
(SirMarkPrescott) *s.i.s: trckd ldng pair: styd far side st: led 2f out: rdn fnl f: comf* **2/5[1]**
512 **2** *2½* **Rocamadour**[16] 5580 2-8-11 87 TEDurcan 3 86
(MRChannon) *trckd ldr: c nr side st: rdn and styd on same pce fnl 2f: no ch w wnr* **10/1[3]**
4124 **3** *1½* **Fiefdom (IRE)**[71] 4100 2-8-11 98 RFfrench 1 83
(MJohnston) *led: styd far side st: rdn and hdd 2f out: one pce* **8/1[2]**
62 **4** *nk* **Aberdeen (IRE)**[20] 5494 2-8-11 RLMoore 5 82
(PMitchell) *hld up in 4th pl: nt handle downhill 4f out: c nr side st: one pce fnl 2f* **16/1**
1 **5** *15* **Emile Zola**[21] 5467 2-8-11 HayleyTurner(3) 4 54
(MPTregoning) *dwlt: hld up last: styd far side st: lost tch over 2f out* **8/1[2]**

1m 48.17s (2.43) **Going Correction** +0.35s/f (Good) **5** Ran SP% **108.6**
Speed ratings: **103,100,99,99,85**CSF £5.01 TOTE £1.40: £1.10, £3.20; EX 4.10.
**Owner** Neil Greig - Osborne House **Bred** Floors Farming And Side Hill Stud **Trained** Newmarket, Suffolk

**FOCUS**
A decent juvenile contest run at a reasonable pace, but slightly messy form-wise with the winner not having to be at his best to score. Despite the small field, they split into two groups in the straight and there did not appear to be much between them.

**NOTEBOOK**
**Comic Strip**, who was well supported at short odds, had no worries on account of the rain-softened ground or the trip and won as his price suggested he should. He may well go abroad now, but if put away should make a very useful three-year-old.
**Rocamadour**, one of two to come stands' side in the straight, has run all his races on easy ground. He ran above his official mark and seems to be progressing with experience.
**Fiefdom(IRE)**, who had been absent since a below-par effort at Epsom in July, set the pace but was well beaten by the winner. The Handicapper is likely to drop him a few pounds after this.
**Aberdeen(IRE)**, stepping up in trip for this third outing, seemed unhappy on the track and came stands' side. He looks capable of winning races and now qualifies for a handicap mark. *Official explanation: jockey said colt hung both ways*
**Emile Zola**, whose Goodwood form received a boost earlier in the week, was relatively unfancied but was never going on this softer ground and is clearly better than this effort indicates.

## 5932 ICON DISPLAY NURSERY 5f
2:40 (2:40) (D2) (0-85,86) 2-Y-0 £10,348 (£3,184; £1,592; £796) Stalls High

Form RPR
1003 **1** **Louphole**[5] 5839 2-9-0 77 DSweeney 1 85
(PJMakin) *trckd ldrs: effrt 2f out: rdn to ld last 100yds: styd on wl* **8/1[3]**
0202 **2** *1* **Starduster**[5] 5839 2-7-11 65 DFox(5) 5 70
(BRMillman) *racd wd and sn off the pce: clsd fr 1/2-way: rdn over 1f out: styd on to take 2nd last 75yds: no imp on wnr* **7/1[2]**
5102 **3** *¾* **Smiddy Hill**[19] 5515 2-9-7 84 RFfrench 4 86
(RBastiman) *prom: led over 1f out: hdd and one pce last 100yds* **8/1[3]**
5231 **4** *shd* **Cree**[12] 5690 2-7-12 64 HayleyTurner(3) 7 66
(WRMuir) *trckd ldrs: hrd rdn over 1f out: kpt on same pce fnl f* **7/1[2]**
1044 **5** *½* **Grand Place**[15] 5617 2-8-11 74 RLMoore 9 74
(RHannon) *chsd ldrs: eased towards outer over 1f out: styd on fnl f: nvr able to chal* **4/1[1]**
4255 **6** *1½* **Bold Minstrel (IRE)**[11] 5711 2-9-6 83 IMongan 6 78
(MQuinn) *led to over 1f out: fdd u.p* **14/1**
3205 **7** *1¼* **Wonderful Mind**[7] 5797 2-8-9 72 (b) TPQueally 10 62
(TDEasterby) *w ldr to 2f out: losing pl whn n.m.r jst over 1f out* **12/1**
4001 **8** *½* **Forzeen**[5] 5839 2-9-6 86 6ex DCorby(3) 2 75
(JAOsborne) *sn outpcd and wl off the pce: no prog tl styd on fnl f* **9/1**
4512 **9** *1¼* **Melandre**[7] 5797 2-8-10 73 TWilliams 11 57
(MBrittain) *s.i.s: sn chsd ldrs: rdn and hanging over 1f out: wknd* **7/1[2]**
5041 **10** *1½* **Talcen Gwyn (IRE)**[7] 5797 2-9-5 82 ANicholls 3 61
(MFHarris) *s.s: rdn to stay in tch after 2f: struggling over 1f out* **10/1**
5150 **11** *1½* **Top Form (IRE)**[14] 5648 2-9-0 77 TEDurcan 8 51
(EALDunlop) *s.s: outpcd and a wl bhd* **20/1**

55.70 secs (0.02) **Going Correction** +0.05s/f (Good) **11** Ran SP% **117.9**
Speed ratings: **101,99,98,98,97 94,92,92,90,87 85**CSF £63.24 CT £468.52 TOTE £9.70: £2.40, £2.70, £2.70; EX 110.10.
**Owner** Ten Of Hearts **Bred** Mrs P Harford **Trained** Ogbourne Maisey, Wilts

**FOCUS**
A fair nursery run in a decent time and producing a close finish. The form looks solid for the grade and may even prove better than rated.

**NOTEBOOK**
**Louphole**, better off with both Forzeen and Starduster compared with Windsor, reversed the placings emphatically. He did well to score from the number one stall, asserting late on and, previously a winner at Brighton, seems well suited by a sharp track and the minimum trip. There could be more to come.
**Starduster** ◆, 1lb worse off with the winner for beating him half a length at Windsor, struggled to handle this sharp track and was doing her best work at the end. She looks well capable of winning a nursery back on a more conventional track.
**Smiddy Hill** is pretty consistent at this level and again ran her race. However, her best efforts have been on flat tracks with fast ground, and she may have another small contest in her if she is lucky enough to get those conditions before the end of the season.
**Cree**, up 5lb for his Chepstow win, did not perform badly in this higher grade without looking likely to score. He would have appreciated softer ground.
**Grand Place**, backed down to favourite, had beaten Cree four lengths in a maiden earlier in the season and ran close to that form without ever being able to land a blow. He may need a return to six now.
**Bold Minstrel(IRE)**, another fairly consistent performer, ran his race from the front before tiring.
**Wonderful Mind** got the stands' rail early, but on this ground could not sustain his effort.
**Forzeen**, who had beaten the first two at Windsor, could not go the early pace and did not look as well suited by this rain-softened ground.
**Talcen Gwyn(IRE)** *Official explanation: jockey said colt was unsuited by track*
**Top Form(IRE)** *Official explanation: jockey said filly was unsuited by track*

## 5933 SODEXHO PRESTIGE H'CAP 5f
**3:10** (3:11) (C1) (0-100,98) 3-Y-O+ **£17,400** (£6,600; £3,300; £1,500) **Stalls** High

Form RPR

2250 **1** **Jayanjay**[33] 5181 5-8-4 **84** oh3 RThomas(3) 11 93
(MissBSanders) *bmpd s: racd against nr side rail and hld up: nt clr run 2f out: str burst fnl f to ld last strides* **17/2**

3503 **2** *nk* **Corridor Creeper (FR)**[7] 5787 7-9-3 **94** (p) RLMoore 4 102
(JMBradley) *pressed ldrs: rdn and narrow ld jst over 1f out: hdd last strides* **11/2**[2]

4100 **3** *1 1/4* **Dragon Flyer (IRE)**[2] 5893 5-9-7 **98** IMongan 3 102
(MQuinn) *mde most to jst over 1f out: one pce fnl f* **12/1**

0030 **4** *1/2* **Caribbean Coral**[14] 5647 5-9-4 **98** THamilton(3) 5 100
(JJQuinn) *dwlt: sn chsd ldrs: rdn over 1f out: styd on same pce fnl f* **3/1**[1]

1000 **5** *1/2* **Corps De Ballet (IRE)**[20] 5491 3-8-7 **84** TPQueally 1 84
(JLDunlop) *s.i.s: sn chsd ldrs: rdn over 1f out: styd on same pce* **25/1**

6610 **6** *1* **Malapropism**[18] 5550 4-8-0 **84** oh2 TDean(7) 13 80
(MRChannon) *w ldrs to over 1f out: edgd lft and fdd fnl f* **10/1**

0006 **7** *1/2* **Blue Crush (IRE)**[11] 5712 3-8-7 **84** oh2 DSweeney 7 79
(KRBurke) *w ldrs over 3f: wknd fnl f* **25/1**

0000 **8** *shd* **Henry Hall (IRE)**[7] 5787 8-8-9 **86** KimTinkler 9 80
(NTinkler) *trckd ldrs: nt clr run 2f out to 1f out: one pce after* **7/1**[3]

0540 **9** *3/4* **Whitbarrow (IRE)**[7] 5787 5-8-12 **89** PDoe 12 80
(JMBradley) *w ldrs to over 1f out: losing pl whn n.m.r sn after* **7/1**[3]

0043 **10** *1/2* **Frascati**[13] 5671 4-8-7 **84** oh2 TEDurcan 6 74
(ABerry) *mistimed s: a in rr: rdn and struggling 2f out* **14/1**

4006 **11** *1* **Boleyn Castle (USA)**[18] 5553 7-8-0 **84** oh4 (b) JBrennan(7) 10 70
(PSMcentee) *wnt rt s: pushed along to keep in tch after 2f: wknd over 1f out* **20/1**

1000 **12** *4* **No Time (IRE)**[140] 2132 4-8-10 **90** ow3 LFletcher(3) 2 62
(MJPolglase) *racd on outer: chsd ldrs to 1/2-way: sn u.p and btn* **25/1**

55.59 secs (-0.09) **Going Correction** +0.05s/f (Good) **12** Ran SP% **115.7**
Speed ratings: **102,101,99,98,97 96,95,95,94,93 91,85**CSF £50.46 CT £566.47 TOTE £10.20: £3.20, £1.80, £5.20; EX 70.70.
**Owner** Peter Crate **Bred** P D Crate **Trained** Epsom, Surrey

**FOCUS**
A decent, competitive sprint, but run only fractionally faster than the preceding nursery. However the form is solid for the grade.

**NOTEBOOK**
**Jayanjay** loves these switchback tracks, handles cut in the ground and, after travelling well on the rail, a gap opened for him in the final furlong and he took full advantage. He has crept up the handicap and will go up again for this, but is always one to be reckoned with when he gets his favoured conditions.
**Corridor Creeper(FR)** has been running well all season without scoring, but has crept up the handicap as a result. Testimony of that is that his last win was when beating Jayanjay over course and distance in August 2003, and he was 9lb higher on this occasion. He was only just caught this time which makes it difficult for the assessor to give him any respite.
**Dragon Flyer(IRE)** is the epitome of a 'twilight' performer, being not quite good enough to win in Pattern company and too highly rated to win handicaps. The Handicapper has shown some mercy but, as at Leicester, her best opportunities lie in conditions races. *Official explanation: jockey said mare hung left throughout*
**Caribbean Coral**, who won the Vodafone Dash on his only previous visit here, was unsurprisingly made favourite. He ran well on this return to handicap company, and did not help his chance by missing a beat at the start.
**Corps De Ballet(IRE)** ◆, dropping back from six furlongs and tackling ground with some give for the first time, did not perform at all badly given that she was another to miss the break. She may find a winning opportunity before the season is out.
**Malapropism** ran his usual honest race, but would have preferred the rain to have stayed away.
**Blue Crush(IRE)** again gave the impression that she is finding her feet in this country and, already 20lb below her mark at the end of last season, will be interesting in a lower grade if dropped a few pounds more.
**Henry Hall(IRE)**, last year's winner, was 3lb lower but has not won since and did not get the run of the race this time.
**Whitbarrow(IRE)** apparently does not like being crowded and seems best with an uncontested lead; he got neither on this occasion.

## 5934 BMS GROUP H'CAP 1m 114y
**3:45** (3:46) (D2) (0-85,82) 3-Y-O **£9,433** (£3,578; £1,789; £813) **Stalls** Low

Form RPR

1032 **1** **Ridge Boy (IRE)**[30] 5252 3-8-11 **72** RLMoore 4 81
(RHannon) *mde virtually all: kicked on 3f out: drvn 3l clr over 1f out: kpt on* **4/1**[1]

-514 **2** *1 1/2* **Desert Reign**[59] 4443 3-8-10 **71** DSweeney 1 76
(APJarvis) *settled midfield: 5th st: effrt over 2f out: styd on to take 2nd nr fin: n.d to wnr* **4/1**[1]

0040 **3** *hd* **Lord Links (IRE)**[14] 5652 3-8-13 **77** RThomas(3) 9 82
(RHannon) *t.k.h: mostly chsd wnr: rdn over 2f out: one pce over 1f out: lost 2nd nr fin* **12/1**

1120 **4** *3/4* **Pickle**[17] 5566 3-9-2 **80** RMiles(3) 11 83
(SCWilliams) *hld up and racd on outer: 8th st: c to nr side: prog 2f out: chsd ldrs and hung lft fnl f: kpt on* **7/1**[2]

0403 **5** *1 3/4* **Jackie Kiely**[20] 5493 3-8-0 **68** oh3 (t) JBrennan(7) 2 68
(PSMcentee) *hld up rr: 9th st: outpcd over 2f out: styd on over 1f out: no ch* **14/1**

160 **6** *shd* **Davorin (JPN)**[31] 5220 3-9-5 **80** TPQueally 10 80
(DRLoder) *reluctant to enter stalls: dwlt: racd on outer in midfield: 6th st: drvn 3f out: one pce fnl 2f* **25/1**

5310 **7** *shd* **Carry On Doc**[24] 5403 3-9-3 **78** SWhitworth 7 77
(JWHills) *t.k.h: hld up rr: 11th st: effrt on outer over 2f out: kpt on same pce: no imp ldrs* **8/1**[3]

4106 **8** *1 3/4* **Bright Sun (IRE)**[16] 5582 3-8-11 **72** KimTinkler 5 68
(NTinkler) *plld hrd: hld up midfield: 7th st: rdn and no prog over 2f out* **12/1**

0150 **9** *1/2* **Wychbury (USA)**[22] 5446 3-8-9 **73** DCorby(3) 12 68
(MJWallace) *prom: 4th st: rdn and no imp over 2f out: fdd* **20/1**

5420 **10** *2 1/2* **Ask The Clerk (IRE)**[14] 5652 3-8-11 **72** ANicholls 8 61
(VSmith) *hld up: last st and c to nr side: no prog* **10/1**

1600 **11** *1 1/2* **Burley Flame**[35] 5120 3-9-3 **78** MFenton 3 64
(JGGiven) *t.k.h: prom: 3rd st: wknd wl over 1f out* **10/1**

1-00 **12** *1 1/4* **Maren (USA)**[12] 5698 3-9-7 **82** (t) TEDurcan 6 66
(EFVaughan) *dwlt: hld up: 10th st: sn struggling and btn* **10/1**

1m 48.68s (2.94) **Going Correction** +0.35s/f (Good) **12** Ran SP% **121.5**
Speed ratings: **100,98,98,97,96 96,96,94,94,91 90,89**CSF £18.67 CT £184.35 TOTE £4.60: £2.40, £1.70, £3.50; EX 14.70.
**Owner** Mrs Chris Harrington **Bred** Mrs Chris Harrington **Trained** East Everleigh, Wilts

**FOCUS**
A fair handicap run at a modest early pace which the winner dictated, and only two of the field came stands' side in the straight. The third gives a line to the form which does not appear that strong.

**NOTEBOOK**
**Ridge Boy(IRE)**, given a fine ride, dictated the pace and, slipping his field early in the straight, did enough to hold on. He had adopted similar tactics when scoring his previous win at Windsor, and they clearly suit.
**Desert Reign**, whose win in a course and distance maiden handicap in July has produced eight subsequent winners, was unsurprisingly backed down to joint favourite. After being held up he was doing his best work at the finish, but proved no threat to the winner.
**Lord Links(IRE)** ◆, stepping up in trip, was keen early but stuck to his guns in the straight. He has dropped in the handicap and is showing clear signs that he is on the way back.
**Pickle**, whose hat-trick in July included a win over seven furlongs here, was one of two to come stands' side early in the straight, but ended up drifting back down the hill to join the others. Although that cost her ground, she would not have won in any case and looks in the Handicapper's grip at present.
**Jackie Kiely** had been raised 3lb for his decent Goodwood effort, and never really got competitive on this occasion. It may be worth giving him a break and bringing him back on the All-Weather later in the winter.
**Davorin(JPN)** is only lightly raced but does not seem in love with the game. Despite being a brother to Diktat, it may be that the gelding operation is needed for him to apply himself.
**Carry On Doc**, a previous course and distance winner, did not settle at the steady early pace and never got into contention.

## 5935 INTERNATIONAL MORTGAGE PLANS APPRENTICE DERBY H'CAP 1m 4f 10y
**4:20** (4:22) (E3) (0-70,70) 3-Y-O+ **£6,958** (£2,141; £1,070; £535) **Stalls** Centre

Form RPR

0015 **1** **Nounou**[41] 4971 3-8-2 **63** MHalford(5) 8 75
(DJDaly) *settled midfield: 8th st: prog 3f out: rdn to ld over 1f out : styd on wl* **20/1**

3056 **2** *2* **Lennel**[14] 5632 6-9-4 **67** (b) LEnstone 9 76
(ABailey) *settled wl in rr: detached in 11th and drvn st: swtchd rt 2f out: styd on strly to take 2nd ins fnl f: nvr nrr* **14/1**

503 **3** *2 1/2* **Duc's Dream**[14] 5658 6-8-7 **56** oh5 BReilly 10 61
(DMorris) *trckd ldrs: 4th st: prog to ld over 2f out: hdd over 1f out: wknd ins fnl f* **20/1**

243 **4** *5* **Carrowdore (IRE)**[18] 5554 4-9-0 **70** (p) TBlock(7) 13 68
(GAHuffer) *trckd ldr: 6th st: in tch over 2f out: sn outpcd: wknd fnl f* **13/2**[2]

1251 **5** *2* **Bojangles (IRE)**[14] 5658 5-8-9 **58** DNolan 15 53
(RBrotherton) *led to 1/2-way: sn rdn: 3rd st: lost pl and struggling over 2f out: one pce after* **10/1**

1254 **6** *1/2* **Burgundy**[20] 5496 7-9-1 **64** (b) ABeech 1 58
(PMitchell) *hld up in rr: 10th st: prog 3f out: drvn to chse clr ldng pair over 1f out: wknd* **12/1**

3354 **7** *3/4* **Donastrela (IRE)**[14] 5635 3-8-7 **66** (v) NChalmers(3) 3 59
(AMBalding) *trckd ldrs: lost pl 1/2-way: 9th and struggling st: kpt on fnl 2f: no ch* **12/1**

0022 **8** *5* **Skibereen (IRE)**[3] 5867 4-8-8 **57** J-PGuillambert 4 42
(MrsAMThorpe) *dwlt: racd midfield: 7th st: rdn and btn wl over 2f out* **8/1**[3]

3024 **9** *1/2* **Great View (IRE)**[18] 5554 5-9-3 **66** (b) HayleyTurner 7 51
(MrsALMKing) *prom: 5th st: wknd wl over 2f out* **12/1**

00-0 **10** *3* **Touch Of Ebony (IRE)**[21] 5450 5-8-4 **56** oh11 AMedeiros(3) 6 36
(CRoberts) *prom: chsd ldr over 4f out: wknd 3f out* **50/1**

0/00 **11** *1* **Knocktopher Abbey**[34] 5151 7-8-2 **56** (b) DeanWilliams(5) 12 35
(AGNewcombe) *dwlt: a in last trio: t.o ent st: kpt on* **20/1**

6-21 **12** *5* **Incroyable**[15] 5622 3-8-10 **66** TPQueally 14 37
(SirMarkPrescott) *prom: led 1/2-way: kicked on ent st: hdd & wknd rapidly over 2f out* **6/4**[1]

001- **13** *2* **Tass Heel (IRE)**[350] 5635 5-8-2 **56** oh2 ThomasYeung(5) 5 24
(WJarvis) *a in rr: t.o in last trio ent st* **25/1**

00-0 **14** *1 1/2* **Blackmail (USA)**[25] 5379 6-8-8 **57** (b) RThomas 11 23
(MissBSanders) *a in rr: t.o in last trio ent st* **33/1**

2m 42.23s (3.51) **Going Correction** +0.35s/f (Good)
**WFA** 3 from 4yo+ 7lb **14** Ran SP% **126.3**
Speed ratings: **102,100,99,95,94 94,93,90,89,87 87,83,82,81**CSF £267.27 CT £5610.80 TOTE £39.60: £6.60, £3.80, £6.70; EX 396.10.
**Owner** Miss Anita Farrell **Bred** Downclose Stud **Trained** Newmarket, Suffolk

**FOCUS**
A modest affair but run at a fair gallop and the principals came from off the pace. The form is ordinary but appears solid enough, rated through the placed horses, while the winner is unexposed.

**NOTEBOOK**
**Nounou**, who won a similar race on easy ground at Folkestone under today's rider, was ridden more positively on his second attempt at this trip and picked up really well to win decisively. He is lightly raced and seems to be going the right way.
**Lennel**, whose form appeared to be tailing off prior to this, did not look interested early on but picked up in the stragth to hunt up the winner. He handled the rain-softened ground on this occasion, but does not want genuine soft going.
**Duc's Dream**, who has run many of his best races at Yarmouth, handled this very different course and ran with credit. He has one more chance this season back on his favourite track, as he is too highly rated for the regional meeting in a fortnight.
**Carrowdore(IRE)** ran his usual consistent race and is a decent guide to the form, but his sole victory was over two years ago.
**Bojangles(IRE)**set the early gallop and kept on in the straight, faring best of those to race up with the pace.
**Great View(IRE)** *Official explanation: jockey said gelding ran flat*
**Incroyable**, who narrowly beat the winner of the following maiden at Nottingham in her previous outing, was a well-backed favourite but, after taking the advantage at halfway, found nothing when tackled early in the straight. No doubt a reason for this disappointing performance will eventually come to light. *Official explanation: jockey said filly became unbalanced in latter stages of race*

## 5936 WOODHURST CONSTRUCTION MAIDEN STKS 1m 2f 18y
**4:55** (4:55) (D3) 3-Y-O **£5,369** (£1,652; £826; £413) **Stalls** Low

Form RPR

2324 **1** **Mambina (USA)**[9] 5757 3-8-9 63 TEDurcan 2 74
(MRChannon) *trckd ldrs: 4th st: prog to ld over 2f out: idled in front and coaxed along fr over 1f out* **4/1**[3]

0420 **2** *1 3/4* **Uig**[7] 5788 3-8-9 72 PDoe 7 71
(HSHowe) *led at gd pce: shkn up and hdd over 2f out: nt qckn and a hld after* **7/2**[2]

0223 **3** *hd* **News Sky (USA)**[61] 4396 3-9-0 79 RLMoore 3 75
(BWHills) *cl up: wnt 2nd st: rdn and fnd little over 2f out: one pce after* **5/2**[1]

0222 **4** *2 1/2* **Revenir (IRE)**[25] 5366 3-8-11 72 DCorby(3) 1 71
(EFVaughan) *hld up in last pair: 6th st: rdn and no rspnse 3f out: one pce after* **4/1**[3]

3353 **5** ½ **Elusive Kitty (USA)**[9] 5749 3-8-9 66 (t) RFfrench 4 65
(GAButler) *hld up in last: rdn bef st: sn in trble* **7/1**
4300 **6** 2 **My Pension (IRE)**[34] 5156 3-9-0 60 IMongan 5 66
(PHowling) *cl up: wnt 3rd ent st: rdn and wknd over 2f out* **20/1**
-000 **7** *dist* **Lawaaheb (IRE)**[25] 5381 3-9-0 63 (p) SWhitworth 6 —
(BRJohnson) *chsd ldr tl 5th and wkng ent st: sn t.o* **33/1**
2m 12.87s (4.17) **Going Correction** +0.35s/f (Good) 7 Ran SP% **111.0**
Speed ratings: **97,95,95,93,93 91,**—CSF £17.23 TOTE £4.50: £2.90, £2.10; EX 19.00.
**Owner** R A Scarborough **Bred** Michael Jojlity And Robert Scarborough **Trained** West Ilsley, Berks

**FOCUS**
A modest maiden with a couple of disappointing types. The form is nothing special but the winner is progressing.

**NOTEBOOK**
**Mambina(USA)**, who is best with cut in the ground, finally got the reward for some creditable efforts in the last couple of months. Despite appearing to have a difficult taks on official ratings, she was always travelling nicely, picked up when asked and had matters in control from that point. Likely to go up a fair amount for this, she may be capable of winning a small handicap if turned out under a penalty.
**Uig**, as she likes to, set the pace and stuck to her task once headed. She does not look particularly well handicapped, but there are some modest maidens at this time of year and she may be able to find one.
**News Sky(USA)** is beginning to look frustrating and found little at the business end in a race he was entitled to win comfortably on official ratings. It would be no surprise to see him fitted with headgear next time.
**Revenir(IRE)**, runner-up in his three previous races, like the favourite is developing into a frustrating sort. He appeared to get the trip but is another who may need trying in headgear, although a return to Polytrack, where he lost out to a subsequent three-time winner, may be the answer.
**Elusive Kitty(USA)**, returning to this longer trip, was held up and never got into contention.

## 5937 IBETX.COM CLASSIFIED STKS 7f
**5:30** (5:31) (D2) 3-Y-0+ **£10,452** (£3,216; £1,608; £804) **Stalls** Low

Form RPR
2600 **1** **Bettalatethannever (IRE)**[52] 4646 3-9-0 82 JMackay 9 103
(SDow) *hld up and racd wd: 6th st: smooth prog to ld over 1f out: sn wl clr* **14/1**
502B **2** 6 **Manaar (IRE)**[74] 4006 4-9-3 83 TEDurcan 8 88
(JNoseda) *racd towards rr: 8th and rdn st: styd on fr over 2f out: tk modest 2nd last strides* **10/1**
0650 **3** *nk* **H Harrison (IRE)**[6] 5818 4-9-0 78 (p) RFfrench 7 84
(IWMcinnes) *trckd ldng pair: cruised up to join ldr wl over 2f out: shkn up and fnd nil over 1f out: chsd wnr after: lost 2nd last stri* **16/1**
4613 **4** 1¾ **Jay Gee's Choice**[2] 5886 4-9-5 85 SWhitworth 3 85
(MRChannon) *led for 1f: led again over 3f out: hdd and outpcd over 1f out* **11/2**[3]
0420 **5** *hd* **Dr Thong**[12] 5698 3-9-1 83 RLMoore 6 82
(PFICole) *chsd ldrs: 5th and pushed along st: rdn and one pce over 2f out* **11/4**[1]
0140 **6** 5 **Brief Goodbye**[29] 5265 4-8-11 79 DCorby(3) 4 66
(JohnBerry) *chsd ldrs: 4th st: rdn 3f out: wknd over 2f out* **25/1**
-120 **7** 1 **Mr Lambros**[8] 5762 3-9-0 85 NChalmers(3) 10 69
(AMBalding) *t.k.h: hld up in rr: 7th st: rdn and wknd over 2f out* **4/1**[2]
0020 **8** 8 **True Night**[14] 5631 7-9-2 82 PDoe 1 45
(DNicholls) *rdn to ld after 1f: hdd & wknd over 3f out* **7/1**
1322 **9** 19 **Dumnoni**[49] 4756 3-8-9 80 IMongan 2 —
(JulianPoulton) *s.i.s: detached in last: wl bhd fnl 3f: t.o* **6/1**
2104 **10** 4 **Sawwaah (IRE)**[23] 5419 7-9-5 85 ANicholls 5 —
(DNicholls) *hld up: 9th and rdn st: sn wknd: t.o* **9/1**
1m 23.33s (-0.62) **Going Correction** +0.05s/f (Good)
**WFA** 3 from 4yo+ 2lb 10 Ran SP% **124.3**
Speed ratings: **105,98,97,95,95 89,88,79,57,53**CSF £155.17 TOTE £19.00: £3.90, £3.40, £3.10; EX 157.50 Place 6 £824.12, Place 5 £630.66.
**Owner** J R May **Bred** Mick McGinn **Trained** Epsom, Surrey

**FOCUS**
A typically tight classified event on paper, but a runaway winner in a very good time for the grade, making the form look decent for the grade.

**NOTEBOOK**
**Bettalatethannever(IRE)**, twice a winner on Polytrack earlier in the season, was returning from a short break and, on his first encounter with rain-softened ground, absolutely destroyed his rivals for pace in the closing stages. Rated 10lb higher on the All-Weather, he looks a strong candidate to follow up under a penalty, given similar conditions.
**Manaar(IRE)**, last seen when brought down at Ayr in July, kept on in the closing stages and this will have helped restore his confidence.
**H Harrison(IRE)**, who had a couple of pounds to find on official ratings, put up a creditable effort but, after taking the lead going well, was brushed aside by the winner. His best form has been on fast ground and Polytrack does not seem to suit, so he may find opportunities limited.
**Jay Gee's Choice** won the early battle for the lead with True Night, but in the end it cost him, as he had nothing in reserve to repel the challenges in the straight.
**Dr Thong**, appreciates some cut in the ground and put up a fair effort. Softer ground and a drop of a couple of pounds in the weights may work for him.
**Mr Lambros**, was very keen early and never got involved. He may well have bounced after his good return last time, and is one to keep in mind when returned to Polytrack.
**Dumnoni** *Official explanation: jockey said filly was unsuited by track and good, good to firm going*
**Sawwaah(IRE)** *Official explanation: jockey said gelding was unsuited by track*
T/Plt: £1,634.50 to a £1 stake. Pool: £32,354.30. 14.45 winning tickets. T/Qpdt: £415.10 to a £1 stake. Pool: £1,963.50. 3.50 winning tickets. JN

# 5915 NEWMARKET (R-H)
Saturday, October 2

**OFFICIAL GOING: Good (good to soft in places)**
There appeared to be little advantage in the draw.
Wind: First two races strong across, remainder strong behind. Weather: Cloudy with sunny spells.

## 5938 EUROPEAN BREEDERS FUND JERSEY LILY FILLIES' NURSERY 7f
**2:00** (2:01) (B1) 2-Y-0 **£25,268** (£7,775; £3,887; £1,943) **Stalls** Centre

Form RPR
314 **1** **Wedding Party**[37] 5052 2-9-5 79 JPMurtagh 11 86
(MrsAJPerrett) *racd centre: chsd ldrs: led over 1f out: hung lft ins fnl f: rdn out* **9/1**[3]
200 **2** 1¼ **Love Affair (IRE)**[22] 5434 2-8-11 71 KDarley 13 75
(RHannon) *racd centre: a.p: rdn over 1f out: r.o* **20/1**
5031 **3** *shd* **Catch A Star**[15] 5620 2-9-3 80 NMackay(3) 10 84
(NACallaghan) *racd centre: s.s: hld up: hdwy over 1f out: edgd lft ins fnl f: r.o* **7/1**[2]
0020 **4** *hd* **Musical Day**[14] 5648 2-9-4 78 SSanders 15 81
(BJMeehan) *lw: racd far side: chsd ldrs: rdn over 1f out: r.o* **25/1**
2230 **5** *hd* **Shosolosa (IRE)**[14] 5648 2-8-7 70 JFMcDonald(3) 8 73
(BJMeehan) *racd centre: hld up in tch: rdn and ev ch over 1f out: edgd lft ins fnl f: styd on* **14/1**
642 **6** *nk* **Belly Dancer (IRE)**[14] 5653 2-8-9 74 NDeSouza(5) 6 76
(PFICole) *racd towards stands' side: led that gp: rdn over 1f out: styd on* **16/1**
2110 **7** ¾ **Lady Le Quesne (IRE)**[14] 5648 2-9-6 80 MartinDwyer 14 80
(AMBalding) *led centre over 5f: no ex ins fnl f* **25/1**
2123 **8** 2 **Godsend**[26] 5351 2-9-2 76 RHughes 16 71
(RHannon) *lw: racd centre: chsd ldrs: rdn over 2f out: wknd ins fnl f* **12/1**
6310 **9** ½ **Toffee Vodka (IRE)**[22] 5434 2-8-13 73 RHills 9 67
(JWHills) *racd centre: hld up: hdwy and edgd rt over 1f out: nvr trbld ldrs* **12/1**
5135 **10** 1½ **Aberdovey**[24] 5391 2-9-3 77 RMullen 1 67
(MLWBell) *racd towards stands' side: hld up: hmpd over 5f out: hdwy over 2f out: no ex fnl f* **11/1**
641 **11** ½ **Icing**[25] 5380 2-9-1 75 PHanagan 7 64
(WJHaggas) *racd towards stands' side: hld up: hmpd over 5f out: n.d* **20/1**
2621 **12** ¾ **Malinsa Blue (IRE)**[21] 5466 2-9-6 80 FNorton 5 67
(JAGlover) *racd towards stadns' side: hld up: sme hdwy over 1f out: sn wknd* **16/1**
0321 **13** 2 **Je Suis Belle**[15] 5606 2-8-11 71 MHills 3 53
(BWHills) *racd towards stand's side: hld up: rdn over 2f out: wknd over 1f out* **10/1**
2336 **14** *shd* **Cerebus**[12] 5701 2-9-0 74 DHolland 4 56
(NPLittmoden) *racd towards stands' side: chsd ldr: rdn over 2f out: wknd over 1f out* **20/1**
3542 **15** *dist* **Dance Flower (IRE)**[9] 5753 2-9-7 81 KFallon 12 —
(MRChannon) *lw: racd centre: chsd ldrs: rdn over 2f out: wknd and virtually p.u over 1f out* **6/1**[1]
3123 **P** **Caitlin (IRE)**[6] 5819 2-9-1 75 DMcGaffin 2 —
(BSmart) *racd towards stands' side: w ldr tl p.u over 5f out: lame* **10/1**
1m 27.18s (0.71) **Going Correction** -0.05s/f (Good) 16 Ran SP% **119.1**
Speed ratings: **93,91,91,91 90,89,87,86,85 84,83,81,81,**— —CSF £182.53 CT £1329.89 TOTE £11.00: £2.50, £5.00, £2.10, £9.10; EX 161.90 TRIFECTA Not won..
**Owner** Cheveley Park Stud **Bred** Cheveley Park Stud Ltd **Trained** Pulborough, W Sussex
■ Stewards Enquiry : J P Murtagh three-day ban: careless riding (Oct 13-15)

**FOCUS**
A strong-looking nursery in which the field split into two, one group racing in the centre and the other on the stands' side, before the groups converged down the stands' side in the final furlong. The centre-field group came out on top.

**NOTEBOOK**
**Wedding Party** kept on strongly once striking the front despite edging left and costing Murtagh a suspension. Reverting to turf, she clearly had no problem with the easier ground or the seventh furlong.
**Love Affair(IRE)** appreciated the return to seven furlongs and was running on well at the death. She can win a similar event.
**Catch A Star** missed the break, and did very well in the circumstances to reach her final position. The return to a mile ought to suit her.
**Musical Day**, from a yard whose juveniles are in top form at present, was suited by underfoot conditions and the return to this trip and ran a solid race.
**Shosolosa(IRE)** was slightly hampered by the winner approaching the furlong pole, but for which she would have made the frame. This was a decent effort on her first try at seven furlongs.
**Belly Dancer(IRE)** ◆ , better for her recent return to action after a three-month break, ran a commendable race, as the others in the smaller stands'-side group finished well beaten.
**Lady Le Quesne(IRE)** is bred to stay this sort of trip but, after adopting her customary trail-blazing tactics, she appeared not to see it out.
**Malinsa Blue(IRE)**, 5lb higher than at Doncaster, was unsuited by this easier ground and raced up the unfavoured side too.
**Dance Flower(IRE)** seemed to lose her action and was all but pulled up. *Official explanation: jockey said filly pulled up lame*

## 5939 FINNFOREST OH SO SHARP STKS (LISTED RACE) (FILLIES) 7f
**2:35** (2:36) (A1) 2-Y-0 **£14,500** (£5,500; £2,750; £1,250) **Stalls** Centre

Form RPR
013 **1** **Penkenna Princess (IRE)**[11] 5721 2-8-9 84 PHanagan 9 103
(RMBeckett) *hld up: hdwy 3f out: led 1f out: rdn out* **25/1**
145 **2** ½ **Favourita**[23] 5413 2-8-9 99 TQuinn 1 102
(CEBrittain) *lw: trckd ldrs: n.m.r and lost pl wl over 1f out: rallied fnl f: r.o* **10/1**
140 **3** 1¾ **Borthwick Girl (IRE)**[27] 5325 2-8-9 MHills 10 97
(BJMeehan) *w ldrs tl led 2f out: rdn and hdd 1f out: styd on same pce ins fnl f* **16/1**
140 **4** ½ **Baltic Dip (IRE)**[14] 5648 2-8-9 94 RHughes 3 96
(RHannon) *led 5f: no ex fnl f* **7/1**[3]
6643 **5** *nk* **Umniya (IRE)**[14] 5648 2-8-9 100 (v) KFallon 5 95
(MRChannon) *s.i.s: sn pushed along in rr: swtchd rt and hdwy over 1f out: nt rch ldrs* **9/2**[2]
11 **6** *nk* **Salamanca**[14] 5648 2-8-9 94 JFEgan 8 95
(SKirk) *lw: chsd ldrs: rdn over 1f out: no ex fnl f* **4/1**[1]
0456 **7** 2½ **Alta Petens**[14] 5648 2-8-9 85 RMullen 12 88
(MLWBell) *hld up: hdwy over 1f out: nt trble ldrs* **50/1**
4155 **8** *nk* **All For Laura**[30] 5250 2-8-9 95 MartinDwyer 2 88
(DRLoder) *chsd ldrs: rdn over 1f out: wknd ins fnl f* **10/1**
1 **9** *hd* **Divinely Decadent (IRE)**[17] 5569 2-8-9 AMcCarthy 7 87
(PWChapple-Hyam) *hld up: rdn and nt clr run over 2f out: nvr trbld ldrs* **7/1**[3]
410 **10** 2½ **Miss L'Augeval**[34] 5149 2-8-9 77 DHolland 13 81
(GWragg) *hld up in tch: rdn over 1f out: wknd fnl f* **33/1**
1150 **11** ½ **Jane Jubilee (IRE)**[34] 5149 2-8-9 93 KDarley 4 80
(MJohnston) *w ldr: rdn over 2f out: wknd over 1f out* **25/1**
22 **12** 1¾ **Elizabethan Age (FR)**[30] 5248 2-8-9 SSanders 14 75
(DRLoder) *lw: hld up: hdwy over 1f out: wknd ins fnl f* **12/1**
2005 **13** 1¾ **Royal Alchemist**[14] 5649 2-8-9 94 ADaly 11 71
(MDIUsher) *lw: hld up: rdn 1/2-way: wknd over 1f out* **20/1**
0366 **14** ½ **Golden Anthem (USA)**[14] 5626 2-8-9 92 JQuinn 6 70
(JPearce) *hld up: rdn 1/2-way: wknd over 1f out* **50/1**
1m 26.22s (-0.25) **Going Correction** -0.05s/f (Good) 14 Ran SP% **114.3**
Speed ratings: **99,98,96,95,95 95,92,91,91,88 88,86,84,83**CSF £232.12 TOTE £30.40: £7.80, £3.50, £4.20; EX 354.00 Trifecta £770.60 Part won. Pool £1,085.40. 0.20 winning units..
**Owner** Mrs H M Chamberlain **Bred** Mill House Stud **Trained** Lambourn, Berks

**FOCUS**
This is average Listed-race form. The whole field tacked over to the stands' side, with those racing closest to the rail seemingly at an advantage.

**NOTEBOOK**
**Penkenna Princess(IRE)** had no problem with the rise in grade or the seventh furlong and, quickening up to lead after travelling nicely, she was always going to hold the runner-up. A progressive filly, she would be of interest if returning to this track for the Rockfel Stakes in a fortnight.
**Favourita** was briefly short of room below the distance and by the time she was in the clear the winner had taken first run, although she cannot be classed as unlucky. This trip looks a bare minimum for her.
**Borthwick Girl(IRE)**, returning to a more suitable level after tackling the Group One Moyglare Stud Stakes, preferred this easier ground and turned around Curragh form with Umniya. This was another solid effort this week from a Meehan two-year-old.
**Baltic Dip(IRE)** was away on terms this time and took the field along, but this was a stiff test at the trip and she did not see it out as well as some of the others.
**Umniya(IRE)** was having her 12th run of the campaign, but has just one win to show for it. Once again doing her best work late on, she was not helped by having to switch to the outer to make her effort.
**Salamanca**, who had three of these behind her when inching home at Newbury, had her chance, but did not see out the extra half-furlong. *Official explanation: jockey said filly hung right*
**Divinely Decadent(IRE)**, who was still green on this second run, was keeping on after the breaks did not really come for her.
**Elizabethan Age(FR)** improved from the rear when pulled wide but her effort petered out in disappointing fashion.
**Royal Alchemist** *Official explanation: jockey said filly lost his action*

## 5940 KINGDOM OF BAHRAIN SUN CHARIOT STKS (GROUP 1) (F&M) 1m
3:15 (3:18) (A1) 3-Y-0+ £116,000 (£44,000; £22,000; £10,000) Stalls Centre

Form RPR
1202 **1** **Attraction**[21] 5484 3-8-11 119 KDarley 3 123
(MJohnston) *mde all: rdn over 1f out: r.o gamely: edgd lft towards fin* **11/4**[3]
0311 **2** *nk* **Chic**[35] 5113 4-9-0 117 KFallon 1 122
(SirMichaelStoute) *lw: bhd: hdwy 1/2-way: rdn to chse wnr fnl f: sn ev ch: edgd lft towards fin: r.o* **9/4**[1]
-543 **3** *1 1/2* **Nebraska Tornado (USA)**[62] 4383 4-9-0 RHughes 5 119
(AFabre, France) *leggy: trckd wnr: rdn over 2f out: styd on same pce fnl f* **5/2**[2]
2224 **4** *5* **Majestic Desert**[48] 4795 3-8-11 113 DHolland 4 107
(MRChannon) *lw: chsd ldrs: rdn over 2f out: edgd rt and wknd ins fnl f* **11/2**
32 **5** *14* **Miss Mambo (USA)**[13] 5676 3-8-11 JPMurtagh 2 75
(DKWeld, Ire) *sn outpcd* **14/1**

1m 36.27s (-3.13) **Going Correction** -0.05s/f (Good)
**WFA** 3 from 4yo 3lb **5 Ran SP% 108.1**
Speed ratings: **113,112,111,106,92**CSF £8.95 TOTE £3.10: £1.90, £1.90; EX 6.70.
**Owner** Duke Of Roxburghe **Bred** Floors Farming **Trained** Middleham Moor, N Yorks
■ This event, run over ten furlongs until 1999, had Group One status for the first time and produced a memorable race.

**FOCUS**
A newly instituted Group One, and the sort of time you would expect for a race of its type, making the form look solid. The field raced up the far rail.

**NOTEBOOK**
**Attraction**, who missed the Queen Elizabeth II Stakes as the track at Ascot had been watered, only ran here after her trainer and rider had walked the course, but despite the reservations over the ground she ended a fine season with a victory. Taken over to the far rail and setting a brisk pace, she saw off the French filly before repelling the favourite in tenacious style. She will stay in training at four, when it would be no surprise to see her running over shorter trips.
**Chic** was given the go-ahead to run after a minor injury scare. Again soon off the bridle and pushed along, she came through to hold every chance but found the Guineas winner too tough a nut to crack, although she lost nothing in defeat and this run confirms her as a true Group One filly. She is set to stay in training at four, and the Lockinge Stakes, won by former stablemate Russian Rhythm this year, looks an obvious target.
**Nebraska Tornado(USA)**, who proved awkward to load into the stalls, tracked Attraction going easily, but could only keep on at the same pace when brought under pressure. She is a high-class filly at this trip but is probably best at ten furlongs.
**Majestic Desert**, a few pounds below the best of her sex, was always up against it in this company, but only conceded defeat in the final furlong.
**Miss Mambo(USA)**, previously trained in France, was having her second run for the Weld stable. Quickly outpaced, she always brought up the rear.

## 5941 TOTESPORT CAMBRIDGESHIRE (HERITAGE H'CAP) 1m 1f
3:55 (4:01) (B1) 3-Y-0+ £75,400 (£28,600; £14,300; £6,500) Stalls Centre

Form RPR
1150 **1** **Spanish Don**[14] 5650 6-8-7 95 LPKeniry(3) 3 109
(DRCElsworth) *racd stands' side: a.p: rdn over 1f out: r.o to ld nr fin* **100/1**
4122 **2** *nk* **Take A Bow**[22] 5443 3-8-9 98 JQuinn 7 111
(PRChamings) *racd stands' side: a.p: rdn to ld 1f out: hdd nr fin* **25/1**
1422 **3** *1 1/4* **Fine Silver (IRE)**[65] 4271 3-8-7 96 TQuinn 5 107
(PFICole) *racd stands' side: chsd ldr tl led that gp over 3f out: rdn and hdd 1f out: styd on same pce* **25/1**
0463 **4** *nk* **Blue Spinnaker (IRE)**[14] 5650 5-9-0 102 PMulrennan(3) 18 112
(MWEasterby) *racd centre: chsd ldrs: rdn over 2f out: hung lft and r.o ins fnl f* **16/1**
3054 **5** *3/4* **Unshakable (IRE)**[44] 4887 5-8-8 93 FNorton 29 102
(BobJones) *b.hind: lw: racd far side: plld hrd and prom: rdn over 2f out: r.o to ld that gp wl ins fnl f* **33/1**
3000 **6** *hd* **Blythe Knight (IRE)**[45] 4856 4-9-3 102 (p) RHills 26 110
(EALDunlop) *racd centre: chsd ldr: led that gp and edgd lft over 1f out: hdd wl ins fnl f* **100/1**
0515 **7** *hd* **Gatwick (IRE)**[14] 5650 3-9-4 107 SHitchcott 31 115
(MRChannon) *lw: racd far side: hld up: rdn over 2f out: hdwy over 1f out: r.o* **9/1**[2]
0021 **8** *1/2* **Blue Trojan (IRE)**[12] 5698 4-8-2 87 3ex ow1 JFEgan 34 94
(SKirk) *racd far side: led: hdd over 7f out: led that gp again over 3f out: hdd and no ex wl ins fnl f* **16/1**
4040 **9** *3/4* **El Coto**[44] 4887 4-9-1 100 (b) GGibbons 14 106
(BAMcmahon) *racd centre: hld up: hdwy over 1f out: r.o* **40/1**
0000 **10** *3/4* **Lundy's Lane (IRE)**[21] 5462 4-8-9 94 MHills 2 98
(CEBrittain) *racd stands' side: chsd ldrs: rdn over 2f out: styd on same pce fnl f* **20/1**
2213 **11** *hd* **Impeller (IRE)**[8] 5761 5-8-10 95 5ex SDrowne 27 99
(WRMuir) *racd far side: led that gp over 7f out: tl over 3f out: rdn over 1f out: styd on same pce* **33/1**
3002 **12** *1 3/4* **King's County (IRE)**[21] 5470 6-8-5 93 NMackay(3) 33 93
(LMCumani) *racd far side: hld up: hdwy over 1f out: no ex ins fnl f* **16/1**
1060 **13** *shd* **Putra Kuantan**[64] 4287 4-8-13 98 OUrbina 20 98
(MAJarvis) *led centre over 7f: edgd lft and no ex* **66/1**
500 **14** *nk* **Nashaab (USA)**[6] 5813 7-8-5 90 (v) LisaJones 17 89
(PDEvans) *racd centre: s.i.s: hld up: n.d* **100/1**
0223 **15** *hd* **Vicious Warrior**[33] 5194 5-7-10 86 BSwarbrick(5) 35 85
(RMWhitaker) *lw: racd far side: plld hrd and prom: rdn over 2f out: styd on same pce appr fnl f* **33/1**
-420 **16** *hd* **Able Baker Charlie (IRE)**[77] 3937 5-8-8 93 KFallon 28 92
(JRFanshawe) *racd far side: prom: rdn over 3f out: styd on same pce fnl 2f* **14/1**
3214 **17** *1 1/4* **Ice Palace**[39] 5025 4-8-11 96 JPMurtagh 24 92
(JRFanshawe) *racd centre: prom: rdn over 2f out: btn over 1f out* **14/1**
2501 **18** *nk* **St Andrews (IRE)**[8] 5769 4-9-0 99 5ex PRobinson 23 94
(MAJarvis) *racd centre: prom over 7f* **10/1**[3]
4005 **19** *3/4* **Langford**[6] 5813 4-7-12 86 FPFerris(3) 21 80
(MHTompkins) *racd centre: plld hrd and prom: wknd wl over 1f out* **100/1**
050- **20** *1 3/4* **Diamond Max (IRE)**[63] 6-8-0 85 JoannaBadger 10 75
(JLEyre, Spain) *led stands' side over 5f: wknd wl over 1f out* **100/1**
3050 **21** *shd* **Wing Commander**[14] 5627 5-8-9 94 (v) PHanagan 12 84
(RAFahey) *racd stands' side: chsd ldrs: rdn over 2f out: sn wknd* **80/1**
1-31 **22** *3* **Pedrillo**[13] 5673 3-8-3 92 5ex SSanders 16 76
(SirMarkPrescott) *racd centre: trckd ldrs: racd keenly: hung rt and wknd 2f out* **7/2**[1]
4613 **23** *3* **Audience**[28] 5291 4-8-13 98 (p) DHolland 6 76
(JAkehurst) *racd stands' side: hld up: effrt over 2f out: sn wknd* **25/1**
0403 **24** *1 3/4* **Chinkara**[21] 5470 4-8-1 89 JFMcDonald(3) 25 64
(BJMeehan) *racd centre: hld up: effrt over 3f out: wknd 2f out* **25/1**
0633 **25** *1* **Zonergem**[24] 5401 6-8-7 92 (p) RHughes 32 65
(LadyHerries) *racd far side: hld up: wknd over 2f out* **22/1**
0146 **26** *1/2* **Pawn Broker**[20] 5492 7-9-10 109 PFitzsimons 22 81
(DRCElsworth) *lw: racd centre: s.i.s: hld up: a in rr* **100/1**
0515 **27** *1* **Krugerrand (USA)**[21] 5470 5-8-4 89 RMullen 8 59
(WJMusson) *racd stands' side: s.i.s: hld up: rdn over 2f out: sn wknd* **66/1**
-010 **28** *shd* **Thihn (IRE)**[168] 1456 9-8-9 94 ADaly 19 64
(JLSpearing) *racd centre: hld up: plld hrd: wknd over 2f out* **50/1**
53-0 **29** *3* **Camille Pissarro (USA)**[8] 5769 4-8-4 89 DKinsella 9 53
(DJWintle) *racd stands' side: hld up: rdn over 3f out: sn wknd* **100/1**
2304 **30** *2 1/2* **Gift Horse**[8] 5769 4-8-1 86 AMcCarthy 13 45
(JRFanshawe) *lw: racd centre: prom over 6f* **50/1**
1104 **31** *3* **Everest (IRE)**[14] 5627 7-8-1 86 ow1 MartinDwyer 30 39
(BEllison) *racd centre: hld up: wknd over 2f out* **16/1**
3506 **R** **Dumaran (IRE)**[14] 5650 6-7-12 90 AMullen(7) 15 —
(WJMusson) *rrd and hit hd on stalls: concussed: tk no part* **50/1**

1m 49.8s (-2.11) **Going Correction** -0.05s/f (Good)
**WFA** 3 from 4yo+ 4lb **32 Ran SP% 131.0**
Speed ratings: **107,106,105,105,104 104,104,103,103,102 102,100,100,100,100 100,99,98,98,96 96,93,91,89,88 88**CSF £1826.03 CT £21536.87 TOTE £75.40: £14.20, £7.10, £6.40, £4.70; EX 2238.30 Trifecta £6390.60 Part won. Pool £9.000.82, 0.30 winning units..
**Owner** Richard J Cohen **Bred** Juddmonte Farms **Trained** Whitsbury, Hants
■ Spanish Don, at 100/1, was the joint longest-priced winner in the history of the race along with Pullover in 1932.

**FOCUS**
An ultra-competitive Cambridgeshire as one would expect and the field split into three groups, with the first three home all racing on the stands' side. The form is typically strong and rock-solid. There was a strong bias in favour of those that raced prominently - as there had been all week - and the winner was recording one of the biggest shocks in the history of the race.

**NOTEBOOK**
**Spanish Don**, a very useful performer on his day who possesses a change of pace, has had a good season and came into this overpriced at 100/1. Having evidently progressed from his first start since July when ninth at Newbury, he raced on the favoured stands' side and came with a strong late challenge to deny three-year-old Take A Bow. Rated 102 a couple of years ago when with Philip Mitchell, he has come right back to his best since moving to Elsworth - going up over 20lb - and, although now a six-year-old, looks capable of further improvement and is surely worth his place back in Listed company.
**Take A Bow** has had a real profitable season - winning three times to date - and he has now finished second on each of his last three outings. Never far away on the stands' side, he came through to take it up about a furlong out and looked set to score, only for Spanish Don to come through and grab him close home. This was without doubt a career highlight for this rapidly improving three-year-old, and he will not need to improve much to make his mark at Listed level.
**Fine Silver(IRE)**, another improving three-year-old, was never far away and looked a huge threat when coming through to lead, but he had no answer to the front pair's respective challenges and had to settle for third. He should continue to go the right way and has a decent handicap in him. *Official explanation: jockey said colt hung right*
**Blue Spinnaker(IRE)** did the best of those drawn down the middle and can be rated better than the bare form, as he hung badly to the stands' side and was motoring at the finish. However, he has a tendency to finish all too late over this trip, and despite his solid profile in these valuable handicaps, looks weighted to his best at present. A return to ten furlongs could bring about some improvement.
**Unshakable(IRE)** loves these big-field handicaps and, racing off a mark 5lb higher than when last successful, he ran a blinder to win the race on the far side. He is always one to have on your side in this type of race.
**Blythe Knight(IRE)**, in the cheekpieces for the first time, turned in another solid effort and improved greatly on his recent displays. This trip still looks slightly on the short side for him however, he saw daylight plenty early enough this time and remains a difficult horse to win with off his current rating.
**Gatwick(IRE)** ran a fine race in finishing second on the unfavoured far-side group. He looks well worth another try in Pattern company, and something like the Newmarket Darley Stakes, a Listed race over this course and distance later in month, could be a race to aim at.
**Blue Trojan(IRE)**, 4lb well-in under his 3lb penalty, emerges with plenty of credit. Given a positive ride on the far side of the track, he appeared to lead the entire field at one stage and was simply unable to sustain such a big effort. He is improving.
**El Coto**, with the blinkers back on, ran his usual solid race and can be considered a little unlucky as he did well to make up ground from the unfavoured middle group. He is one to keep an eye on when getting his favoured soft ground, but will need to improve in order to score off this mark. *Official explanation: jockey said colt finished lame*
**Lundy's Lane(IRE)** has dropped to a decent mark and will find easier winning opportunities than this. He ran well without ever threatening.
**Impeller(IRE)**, 3lb wrong at the weights, ran creditably to be fourth in the far side.
**King's County(IRE)**, 1lb well-in, did not run badly to finish fifth on the far side and is in good form.
**Putra Kuantan** showed up well for a long way down the centre of the track, but was struggling once the principals went for home. He will find easier races to win than this.
**Vicious Warrior** pulled too hard for his own good in the early stages, and it was too his credit that he was still grinding away at the death.
**Able Baker Charlie(IRE)**, one of the main fancies coming into the race, had his chance but would have preferred faster ground. *Official explanation: jockey said gelding was never travelling*
**Ice Palace**

**St Andrews(IRE)**, whose latest success looked to give him a good opportunity in this, was disappointing even allowing for the fact he had to race down the centre of the track. It is possible he may have finished closer on softer ground, which looks the key to him, but he will most likely struggle to win off his new mark in future handicaps.
**Langford** was always going to find this test stretching his stamina.
**Pedrillo**, subject of a big public gamble and bidding to give his yard back-to-back wins in this event, ran too keen through the early parts and never looked like landing the gamble. This was disappointing, but he is a lightly-raced horse who may be best kept to smaller fields for the short-term and he could leave this form behind in due course. *Official explanation: jockey said gelding was never travelling*
**Zonergem** *Official explanation: jockey said gelding was unsuited by Good, Good to Soft in places ground.*
**Everest(IRE)**, who has sound form in handicaps such as this, never showed from off the pace and remains weighted to the hilt. *Official explanation: jockey said gelding bled from nose*

## 5942 KENNETT H'CAP — 1m 2f
4:30 (4:37) (C1) (0-100,93) 3-Y-O — **£12,138** (£4,604; £2,302; £1,046) **Stalls** Centre

Form — RPR
3321 **1** **Flamboyant Lad**[16] 5591 3-8-8 **80** ... MHills 16 — 91
(BWHills) *racd far side: w ldr: led that gp 2f out: r.o wl* — **11/2**[1]
3-1 **2** ½ **Corsican Native (USA)**[20] 5495 3-9-4 **90** ... RHughes 17 — 100
(MrsAJPerrett) *racd far side: trckd ldrs: styd on wl fnl f: no ex towards fin* — **8/1**[3]
0144 **3** 1¾ **Boule D'Or (IRE)**[8] 5761 3-9-3 **89** ... NDay 5 — 96
(RIngram) *lw: racd stands' side: trckd ldrs: styd on to ld that gp jst ins last: hld by 1st 2 far side* — **17/2**
142 **4** nk **Namroc (IRE)**[16] 5590 3-9-1 **87** ... RMullen 14 — 93
(EFVaughan) *racd far side: chsd ldrs: outpcd over 2f out: kpt on wl fnl f* — **11/2**[1]
0000 **5** 1 **Barbajuan (IRE)**[21] 5468 3-8-12 **87** ... NMackay(3) 3 — 92
(NACallaghan) *racd stands' side: hld up: hdwy over 2f out: styd on fnl f* — **25/1**
621 **6** shd **Countrywide Luck**[30] 5237 3-9-1 **87** ... DHolland 6 — 91
(NPLittmoden) *lw: racd far side: chsd ldrs: outpcd fnl 2f* — **20/1**
1155 **7** hd **Dami (USA)**[17] 5573 3-8-8 **80** ... (p) SSanders 9 — 84
(CEBrittain) *racd stands' side: w ldrs: led that gp 3f out: edgd lft and hdd jst ins last: one pce* — **25/1**
5120 **8** nk **Motive (FR)**[87] 3641 3-9-4 **90** ... KFallon 4 — 97+
(SirMichaelStoute) *lw: racd stands' side: hld up: hdwy and n.m.r on ins over 2f out: styng on whn hmpd jst ins last: nt rcvr* — **6/1**[2]
1006 **9** ½ **Master Marvel (IRE)**[22] 5443 3-9-0 **86** ... JPMurtagh 1 — 88+
(MJohnston) *led stands' side tl 3f out: wkng whn hmpd on ins jst ins last* — **16/1**
2406 **10** 1 **Dancing Lyra**[50] 4709 3-9-2 **88** ... SDrowne 2 — 89
(JWHills) *racd stands' side: chsd ldrs: kpt on fnl f* — **25/1**
0453 **11** shd **Parkview Love (USA)**[9] 5755 3-9-0 **86** ... KDarley 12 — 86
(MJohnston) *led far side gp tl 2f out: sn wknd* — **14/1**
5435 **12** 2½ **Hello It's Me**[21] 5465 3-9-1 **87** ... JQuinn 10 — 83
(HJCollingridge) *racd far side: hld up: effrt over 2f out: sn btn* — **14/1**
0310 **13** ¾ **Iktitaf (IRE)**[133] 2281 3-8-13 **85** ... RHills 8 — 79
(JHMGosden) *racd stands' side: chsd ldrs: lost pl over 1f out* — **16/1**
4440 **14** 1 **Isidore Bonheur (IRE)**[21] 5462 3-9-7 **93** ... MartinDwyer 7 — 85
(BWHills) *racd stands' side: w ldrs: wknd over 1f out* — **50/1**
0465 **15** nk **Sgt Pepper (IRE)**[14] 5651 3-9-3 **89** ... JFEgan 11 — 81
(RHannon) *racd far side: chsd ldrs: lost pl over 1f out* — **33/1**
2240 **16** 1 **Inchloss (IRE)**[24] 5397 3-8-11 **83** ... TQuinn 13 — 73
(BAMcmahon) *racd far side: hld up: effrt over 2f out: sn wknd* — **25/1**
2000 **17** ¾ **Keelung (USA)**[14] 5650 3-9-0 **86** ... (p) PRobinson 15 — 74
(MAJarvis) *racd stands' side: chsd ldrs: edgd lft 2f out: sn lost pl* — **20/1**

2m 3.40s (-2.29) **Going Correction** -0.05s/f (Good) — **17** Ran SP% **121.6**
Speed ratings: **107,106,105,104,104 104,103,103,103,102 102,100,99,99,98 97,97**CSF £41.86 CT £379.06 TOTE £5.60: £1.60, £2.90, £2.20, £2.60; EX 33.90.
**Owner** Maktoum Al Maktoum **Bred** Gainsborough Stud Management Ltd **Trained** Lambourn, Berks

**FOCUS**
Quite a competitive contest with the field splitting into two, and no real advantage to either side. This looks solid and useful handicap form that should work out, and the principals can rate higher.

**NOTEBOOK**
**Flamboyant Lad**, having taken a while to get his head in front, seems to have got the hang of things now. He showed the right attitude and appears to be on the upgrade, and with further improvement likely over an extra furlong or two, he will have plenty of opportunities.
**Corsican Native(USA)** ran a solid race for one lacking in experience, and this good-looking individual is the sort to do better still with another year on his back.
**Boule D'Or(IRE)**, who is holding his form well, came out best of those to race on the stands' side.
**Namroc(IRE)** has a progressive profile and proved well suited by this stiffer test. He should make a decent four-year-old.
**Barbajuan(IRE)**, who has found life tough this term, was without the blinkers he has worn on his last three runs, and showed a bit more promise than of late.
**Countrywide Luck** was far from disgraced on this first venture into handicap company, and will certainly find easier openings than he faced here.
**Motive(FR)** was just beginning to get competitive when all but knocked over. There will be other days for him. *Official explanation: jockey said colt suffered interference in running*

## 5943 SUFFOLK INSULATION AND RENOVATION SERVICES EBF MAIDEN FILLIES' STKS — 6f
5:05 (5:10) (D2) 2-Y-O — **£8,206** (£2,525; £1,262; £631) **Stalls** Centre

Form — RPR
6 **1** **Loyal Love (USA)**[29] 5271 2-8-11 ... JPMurtagh 12 — 88
(SaeedBinSuroor) *mde all far side: r.o wl* — **12/1**
**2** 2½ **Discuss (USA)** 2-8-11 ... KFallon 2 — 81+
(SirMichaelStoute) *unf: scope: gd sort: s.s: racd centre: hld up: hdwy over 1f out: led that gp ins fnl f: r.o wl: no ch w far side* — **5/2**[2]
00 **3** 2 **Diamond Katie (IRE)**[11] 5648 2-8-11 ... TQuinn 9 — 75
(RGuest) *racd centre: chsd ldr tl led that gp over 1f out: hdd and unable qck ins fnl f* — **10/1**[3]
33 **4** ½ **Ahdaaf (USA)**[70] 4137 2-8-11 ... PRobinson 4 — 73
(JLDunlop) *racd centre: prom: rdn over 1f out: styd on same pce* — **14/1**
**5** ½ **Archeology (USA)** 2-8-11 ... KDarley 13 — 72
(SaeedBinSuroor) *w'like: bkwd: racd far side: chsd wnr: rdn over 1f out: sn outpcd* — **16/1**
0230 **6** 1¼ **County Clare**[14] 5648 2-8-11 86 ... MartinDwyer 6 — 68
(AMBalding) *racd centre: chsd ldrs: rdn over 1f out: no ex* — **14/1**
3043 **7** nk **Encouragement**[11] 5720 2-8-11 75 ... RHughes 8 — 67
(RHannon) *led centre over 4f: wknd ins fnl f* — **16/1**
**8** ½ **Lady Doris Watts** 2-8-11 ... SHitchcott 10 — 65
(MRChannon) *leggy: racd centre: hld up: effrt over 1f out: n.d* — **50/1**
**9** 1 **Alhaadh (USA)** 2-8-11 ... RHills 7 — 62+
(JHMGosden) *w'like: s.s: racd centre: hld up: hdwy over 1f out: wknd ins fnl f* — **7/4**[1]
0 **10** 1½ **Rock Fever (IRE)**[104] 3123 2-8-11 ... SDrowne 3 — 58
(MJWallace) *b.hind: racd centre: sn outpcd* — **80/1**
5 **11** 1½ **Lilting Prose (IRE)**[75] 3992 2-8-11 ... DHolland 5 — 53
(RHannon) *racd centre: hld up: rdn over 1f out: n.d* — **33/1**
6 **12** 5 **Treble Seven (USA)**[17] 5570 2-8-11 ... SSanders 11 — 38
(CEBrittain) *b.: racd far side: chsd ldrs 4f* — **16/1**
00 **13** 1 **Ruby Murray**[29] 5270 2-8-8 ... LPKeniry(3) 1 — 35
(BJMeehan) *racd centre: chsd ldrs: rdn over 2f out: sn wknd* — **66/1**

1m 12.6s (-0.49) **Going Correction** -0.05s/f (Good) — **13** Ran SP% **120.3**
Speed ratings: **101,97,95,94,93 92,91,90,89,87 85,78,77**CSF £41.93 TOTE £12.50: £2.70, £1.70, £2.90; EX 72.10.
**Owner** Godolphin **Bred** Gainsborough Farm Llc **Trained** Newmarket, Suffolk

**FOCUS**
The field split into two and the winner always looked to be holding the call. This looked a strong maiden that should produce its fair share of winners.

**NOTEBOOK**
**Loyal Love(USA)**, whose debut run received a boost earlier in the day when Penkenna Princess took the fillies' Listed race, had clearly come on a bundle for that experience. A late foal, she should continue to improve, will be suited by further in time and looks to have a bright future.
**Discuss(USA)**, a half-sister to Group Three winner Dance Dress as well as middle-distance winners Colophony and Conclude, was the youngest of these having not been foaled until 26th May. She shaped with plenty of promise, despite being green, and should have no trouble paying her way.
**Diamond Katie(IRE)** had shown enough in her two previous outings to suggest she could win her maiden and, although outpointed, time may tell she was taking on a couple of fair performers.
**Ahdaaf(USA)** looks as though she will benefit from a step up in trip.
**Archeology(USA)**, who is related to a couple of useful juveniles in the States, did not shape at all badly over what will eventually turn out to be an inadequate trip.
**County Clare** set a fair standard for the others in this, but proved something of a disappointment. While she is certainly up to winning her maiden, she will need her sights lowering.
**Alhaadh(USA)** appeared in need of both the outing and the experience, and should do better in time.

## 5944 NGK SPARK PLUGS H'CAP — 1m 6f
5:35 (5:45) (D2) (0-85,80) 3-Y-O — **£8,245** (£2,537; £1,268; £634) **Stalls** Centre

Form — RPR
2122 **1** **Quarrymount**[5] 5842 3-8-11 **70** ... SSanders 10 — 87+
(SirMarkPrescott) *hld up in tch: led on bit over 2f out: clr over 1f out: styd on strly* — **7/2**[1]
2010 **2** 6 **Fort Churchill (IRE)**[8] 5768 3-9-3 **76** ... (b) JPMurtagh 7 — 84
(BEllison) *sn led: rdn and hdd over 2f out: styd on same pce appr fnl f* — **11/1**
2221 **3** 2½ **Sharadi (IRE)**[19] 5519 3-8-12 **71** ... DHolland 9 — 76
(VSmith) *hld up: hdwy u.p over 3f out: styd on same pce fnl 2f* — **9/2**[3]
310 **4** nk **Daze**[15] 5615 3-9-1 **74** ... KFallon 8 — 78
(SirMichaelStoute) *trckd ldr: rdn and ev ch over 2f out: wknd fnl f* — **6/1**
13 **5** 5 **Strangely Brown (IRE)**[6] 5820 3-9-3 **76** ... MartinDwyer 1 — 73
(SCWilliams) *prom: rdn over 2f out: wknd over 1f out* — **4/1**[2]
3003 **6** 5 **Winners Delight**[17] 5572 3-9-7 **80** ... KDarley 2 — 70
(APJarvis) *hld up: hdwy over 3f out: wknd over 2f out* — **14/1**
4600 **7** 1¾ **Man At Arms (IRE)**[24] 5402 3-8-13 **72** ... (p) RHughes 11 — 60
(RHannon) *chsd ldrs: rdn over 5f out: wknd over 2f out* — **25/1**
5014 **8** hd **Bill Bennett (FR)**[95] 3396 3-9-7 **80** ... OUrbina 6 — 67
(JJay) *hld up: rdn over 3f out: wknd over 2f out* — **20/1**
5220 **9** ¾ **Masked (IRE)**[28] 5300 3-9-6 **79** ... TQuinn 12 — 65
(JWHills) *hld up: effrt over 3f: sn wknd* — **12/1**
6040 **10** 15 **Doctored**[3] 5866 3-8-13 **75** ... (b) FPFerris(3) 5 — 40
(PDEvans) *hld up: rdn over 5f out: wknd over 3f out* — **33/1**
3122 **11** 24 **Late Opposition**[15] 5608 3-8-12 **71** ... (v) SDrowne 4 — 3
(EALDunlop) *chsd ldrs tl wknd over 3f out* — **9/1**

2m 55.9s (-4.42) **Going Correction** -0.05s/f (Good) — **11** Ran SP% **118.9**
Speed ratings: **110,106,105,104,102 99,98,98,97,89 75**CSF £42.33 CT £179.35 TOTE £4.10: £2.00, £4.10, £2.20; EX 59.50 Place 6 £2,756.15, Place 5 £683.45.
**Owner** Lady Fairhaven **Bred** Lord Fairhaven **Trained** Newmarket, Suffolk

**FOCUS**
A fair handicap that looked competitive enough on paper, but it was one-way traffic in the end. The pace was solid and the time was decent for the grade, giving the form a sound look.

**NOTEBOOK**
**Quarrymount** found plenty of improvement for the step up in trip and had this in safe keeping from some way out. While he is sure to face the wrath of the Handicapper, it will be a surprise if he cannot add to this.
**Fort Churchill(IRE)** appeared to stay this longer trip well enough, which will open up other doors for him.
**Sharadi(IRE)**, tackling better company than of late, was far from disgraced off this higher mark, over a trip probably short of his best.
**Daze** looked to find this trip beyond her.
**Strangely Brown(IRE)** looked to run a little flat and, having been on the go since February, may be in need of a break.
T/Jkpt: Not won. T/Plt: £4,152.70 to a £1 stake. Pool: £112,067.15. 19.70 winning tickets. T/Qpdt: £58.60 to a £1 stake. Pool: £7,079.10. 89.30 winning tickets. CR

# 5520 REDCAR (L-H)
Saturday, October 2

**OFFICIAL GOING: Good to firm (firm in places)**
The going was described as 'loose on top but good to firm underneath' and there was a brisk wind which contributed to the fast times.
Wind: Fresh 1/2 behind. Weather: Changeable, overcast and windy.

## 5945 TETLEY'S SMOOTH H'CAP — 1m
1:45 (1:45) (E3) (0-70,72) 3-Y-O+ — **£8,382** (£2,579; £1,289; £644) **Stalls** Centre

Form — RPR
3030 **1** **Mistress Twister**[31] 5223 3-8-13 **67** ... PFessey 16 — 78
(TDBarron) *midfield: outpcd over 3f out: rallied 2f out: led wl ins fnl f: r.o* — **33/1**
0663 **2** ½ **Mount Vettore**[25] 5370 3-8-13 **67** ... DaneO'Neill 14 — 77
(MrsJRRamsden) *hld up: hdwy outside over 2f out: led appr fnl f: edgd rt ins: hdd wl ins last: r.o* — **11/2**[2]
3060 **3** 1½ **Regent's Secret (USA)**[19] 5518 4-8-5 **56** ... (p) WSupple 20 — 62
(JSGoldie) *hld up: rdn over 2f out: hdwy whn n.m.r and hung lft over 1f out: r.o fnl f* — **25/1**

4031 **4** *nk* **Newcorp Lad**[3] 5859 4-9-0 **65** 6ex.....(p) ACulhane 18 71+
(MrsGSRees) *sn pushed along midfield: hdwy and chsng ldrs whn n.m.r over 1f out: kpt on ins last* **4/1**[1]

0400 **5** *2 ½* **Alchera**[20] 5496 3-8-6 **60**.....SCarson 5 60
(RFJohnsonHoughton) *prom: rdn to ld briefly over 1f out: no ex fnl f* **25/1**

1500 **6** *½* **Best Desert (IRE)**[13] 5674 3-8-8 **62**.....DarrenWilliams 26 61
(JRBest) *dwlt: hld up: rdn and outpcd 1/2-way: rallied 2f out: kpt on: no imp fnl f* **33/1**

4040 **7** *2* **Flame Queen**[17] 5572 3-8-6 **60**.....JMcAuley 2 54
(MrsCADunnett) *led to over 1f out: sn rdn and btn* **40/1**

0000 **8** *nk* **Atlantic Ace**[11] 5713 7-8-8 **59**.....(p) FLynch 10 53
(BSmart) *hld up midfield: effrt over 2f out: no imp over 1f out* **20/1**

6040 **9** *1* **Dara Mac**[11] 5713 5-8-5 **63** ow2.....SuzanneFrance(7) 17 54
(NBycroft) *bhd tl styd on fr 2f out: n.d* **50/1**

-626 **10** *3* **Heart's Desire (IRE)**[30] 5239 3-9-0 **68**.....WRyan 9 52
(BWHills) *prom: rdn 3f out: wknd fr 2f out* **33/1**

2520 **11** *nk* **Tedsdale Mac**[14] 5635 5-8-8 **59**.....CCatlin 24 43
(NBycroft) *hld up: rdn over 3f out: kpt on over 1f out: nvr rchd ldrs* **12/1**[3]

5120 **12** *1 ½* **Blaeberry**[25] 5370 3-8-10 **64**.....(b) SWKelly 8 44
(PLGilligan) *wnt lft s: cl up: rdn and wandered 1/2-way: wknd fr 2f out* **20/1**

0440 **13** *nk* **Lord Baskerville**[3] 5859 3-8-2 **56** oh4.....JBramhill 27 35
(WStorey) *hld up: rdn over 3f out: n.d* **66/1**

0000 **14** *¾* **Anthemion (IRE)**[6] 5821 7-8-4 **58**.....TEaves(3) 15 36
(MrsJCMcgregor) *in tch: outpcd 1/2-way: n.d after* **20/1**

3601 **15** *nk* **Gifted Flame**[11] 5713 5-9-2 **72**.....PMakin(5) 6 49
(TDBarron) *bmpd s: hld up: smooth hdwy 3f out: rdn and wknd over 1f out* **14/1**

546- **16** *1* **Pearson Glen (IRE)**[327] 5971 5-8-6 **57** oh2 ow1.....RWinston 25 32
(GASwinbank) *hld up: rdn 1/2-way: n.d* **33/1**

0003 **17** *1* **Golden Spectrum (IRE)**[17] 5557 5-8-5 **56** oh5.....PMQuinn 3 28
(DNicholls) *midfield: rdn 1/2-way: sn btn* **28/1**

1542 **18** *nk* **Prime Offer**[39] 5020 8-9-0 **65**.....NCallan 21 37
(JJay) *chsd ldrs tl rdn and wknd fr over 2f out* **12/1**[3]

6024 **19** *hd* **Splodger Mac (IRE)**[17] 5557 5-7-12 **56** oh3.....AReilly(7) 23 27
(NBycroft) *bhd: rdn 1/2-way: nvr on terms* **28/1**

2150 **20** *1 ¾* **Zarin (IRE)**[30] 5236 6-8-5 **56** oh4.....NPollard 12 23
(DWChapman) *chsd ldrs to over 3f out: sn btn* **50/1**

0200 **21** *nk* **Orangino**[46] 4827 6-7-12 **56** oh11.....RKennemore(7) 11 23
(JSHaldane) *chsd ldrs tl wknd fr 3f out* **100/1**

0060 **22** *shd* **Mister Sweets**[7] 5798 5-8-12 **68**.....(t) DTudhope(5) 13 34
(DCarroll) *s.s: nvr on terms* **20/1**

0022 **23** *½* **Heversham (IRE)**[11] 5715 3-8-12 **66**.....MTebbutt 1 31
(JHetherton) *midfield: rdn over 3f out: sn btn* **14/1**

4000 **24** *1 ½* **Cashneem (IRE)**[85] 3698 6-8-11 **62**.....DAllan 4 24
(WMBrisbourne) *hld up: rdn 1/2-way: sn btn* **20/1**

0600 **25** *13* **Gala Sunday (USA)**[11] 5713 4-8-5 **56** oh1.....DaleGibson 7 —
(MWEasterby) *dwlt: effrt 1/2-way: sn rdn and btn* **50/1**

3616 **26** *12* **Rahjel Sultan**[166] 1502 6-8-8 **59**.....(t) GCarter 19 —
(BAMcmahon) *bhd: rdn 1/2-way: sn btn* **50/1**

1m 35.06s (-2.64) **Going Correction** -0.375s/f (Firm)
**WFA** 3 from 4yo+ 3lb **26 Ran SP% 127.0**
Speed ratings: **98,97,96,95,93 92,90,90,89,86 86,84,84,83,83 82,81,80,80,79 78,78,78,76,63 51**CSF £161.19 CT £4685.23 TOTE £47.00: £7.60, £2.40, £7.80, £1.50; EX 437.20.
**Owner** Dave Scott **Bred** Mrs F A Veasey **Trained** Maunby, N Yorks

**FOCUS**
A modest handicap and they raced in one group towards the centre. The winning time was modest and the form is ordinary, rated through the runner-up.

**NOTEBOOK**
**Mistress Twister**, a maiden after seven previous starts, proved suited by the trip and the ground and showed a battling attitude to claim the prize near the line.
**Mount Vettore**, very keen to post, has slipped to a handy mark but basically this was a prize simply thrown away, as he hung badly right when in front inside the last.
**Regent's Secret(USA)**, fitted with cheekpieces, was again out of luck and surely deserves to break his duck.
**Newcorp Lad**, with no rail to run against, was making very hard work of this some way from home. He would have been even more closely concerned in the finish but for running out of racing room coming to the final furlong. His trainer has another six days before his revised rating kicks in.
**Alchera**, who won from a 16lb higher mark last year, has been bang out of form this time but this was a lot more encouraging.
**Best Desert(IRE)**, slipping down the weights, had the ground in his favour and ran better than of late.
**Pearson Glen(IRE)** *Official explanation: trainer said gelding had a breathing problem*
**Splodger Mac(IRE)** *Official explanation: jockey said gelding finished lame*
**Rahjel Sultan** *Official explanation: trainer said gelding was unsuited by fast early pace*

## 5946 EUROPEAN BREEDERS FUND MAIDEN FILLIES' STKS 7f
2:20 (2:21) (D3) 2-Y-O **£4,550** (£1,400; £700; £350) **Stalls** Centre

Form RPR

3 **1** **Sheboygan (IRE)**[29] 5271 2-8-11.....JBramhill 1 81
(JGGiven) *mde all: rdn and edgd lft wl over 1f out: styd on wl fnl f* **4/1**[3]

**2** *¾* **Her Own Kind (JPN)** 2-8-11.....KMcEvoy 6 80
(SaeedBinSuroor) *dwlt and towards rr: stdy hdwy 3f out: rdn to chse wnr ent last: edgd lft and kpt on* **3/1**[1]

4 **3** *2* **Villarrica (USA)**[18] 5534 2-8-11.....RWinston 2 75
(SirMichaelStoute) *dwlt: sn prom:effrt and ev ch 2f out: sn rdn and kpt on same pce ent last* **10/3**[2]

5 **4** *½* **Kindling**[19] 5521 2-8-11.....SChin 12 73
(MJohnston) *trckd ldrs: hdwy over 2f out and sn ev ch: rdn wl over 1f out and kpt on same pce* **22/1**

402 **5** *shd* **Heat Of The Night**[26] 5349 2-8-11 75.....DaneO'Neill 4 73
(JLDunlop) *cl up: effrt to challeng over 2f out: sn rdn and ev ch tl drvn and one pce appr last* **13/2**

**6** *3 ½* **Madge** 2-8-11.....RHavlin 7 64
(JHMGosden) *sn outpcd and rdn along in rr: hdwy 2f out: kpt on appr last: nt rch ldrs* **12/1**

055 **7** *1* **Moonmaiden**[15] 5620 2-8-11 77.....ACulhane 10 62
(MRChannon) *cl up: rdn along over 2f out: grad wknd* **7/1**

5 **8** *2* **Sweet Potato (IRE)**[35] 5125 2-8-11.....PFessey 8 57
(TDBarron) *keen: hld up towards rr: effrt over 2f out and no imp* **66/1**

0 **9** *1 ¼* **Neferura**[17] 5569 2-8-11.....SWKelly 9 54
(WJHaggas) *a rr* **66/1**

6 **10** *shd* **Katie's Biscuit**[14] 5633 2-8-11.....NPollard 5 53
(IanEmmerson) *cl up: rdn along 1/2-way: sn wknd* **150/1**

05 **11** *1 ½* **Musardiere**[4] 5848 2-8-11.....LGoncalves 3 50
(MrsJRRamsden) *hld up: a rr* **28/1**

000 **12** *10* **Keyalzao (IRE)**[18] 5543 2-8-4.....DFentiman(7) 11 25
(ACrook) *dwlt: sn chsng ldrs: rdn along 1/2-way and sn wknd* **200/1**

600 **13** *dist* **Kalika (IRE)**[108] 2985 2-8-11 35.....NCallan 13 —
(MsDeborahJEvans) *racd wd: in tch to 1/2-way: sn outpcd and bhd* **150/1**

1m 23.53s (-1.37) **Going Correction** -0.375s/f (Firm) **13 Ran SP% 114.2**
Speed ratings: **92,91,88,88,88 84,83,80,79,79 77,66,**—CSF £15.14 TOTE £5.90: £2.00, £1.70, £1.60; EX 27.10.
**Owner** David Eiffe **Bred** David Eiffe **Trained** Willoughton, Lincs
■ Stewards Enquiry : J Bramhill one-day ban: failed to keep straight from stalls (Oct 13)

**FOCUS**
A decent maiden for the track run at a strong early gallop and the form should stand up.

**NOTEBOOK**
**Sheboygan(IRE)**, stepping up to seven, made every yard and should hold her own in a higher grade.
**Her Own Kind(JPN)** ◆, a tall, rangy filly, is a half-sister to the St Leger winner Mutafaweq. After missing a beat at the start, she warmed to her work and in the end made the winner dig deep. She looks a very promising type who will be suited by much further at three.
**Villarrica(USA)**, who raced on the wide outside, was hard at work at halfway and in the end was simply not good enough. She should make her mark at three especially on easier ground.
**Kindling** ran a lot better than on her debut here two weeks earlier. She still looked very inexperienced and there should be even better to come.
**Heat Of The Night**, having her fourth start, is already rated 75.
**Madge** was very green and only got going late in the day. This will have taught her plenty.
**Kalika(IRE)** *Official explanation: jockey said filly lost her action*

## 5947 BETFAIR.COM TWO-YEAR-OLD TROPHY (LISTED RACE) 6f
2:55 (2:55) (A1) 2-Y-O **£128,412** (£48,708; £24,354; £11,070) **Stalls** Centre

Form RPR

331 **1** **Obe Gold**[2] 5896 2-8-3 89.....(v) CCatlin 24 100
(MRChannon) *mde virtually all: edgd lft ins fnl f: drvn out* **15/2**[2]

111 **2** *1* **Caesar Beware (IRE)**[24] 5392 2-8-9.....DaneO'Neill 8 103
(HCandy) *a cl up: rdn and ev ch over 1f out: no ex wl ins fnl f* **4/7**[1]

2150 **3** *1 ½* **Dario Gee Gee (IRE)**[24] 5392 2-8-7 95 ow1.....NCallan 2 97
(KARyan) *cl up: rdn over 2f out: kpt on same pce ins fnl f* **33/1**

1031 **4** *½* **Moth Ball**[9] 5745 2-9-0 83.....SWKelly 25 102
(JAOsborne) *chsd ldrs: rdn over 2f out: one pce over 1f out* **33/1**

0621 **5** *½* **Beaver Patrol (IRE)**[42] 4958 2-8-9 100.....SCarson 16 96
(RFJohnsonHoughton) *prom: rdn over 2f out: kpt on same pce fr over 1f out* **11/1**[3]

1541 **6** *¾* **Pivotal Flame**[12] 5703 2-9-2 100.....GCarter 10 100
(BAMcmahon) *dwlt: hld up: hdwy 2f out: kpt on fnl f: nrst fin* **18/1**

1505 **7** *shd* **Word Perfect**[15] 5606 2-8-7 85.....DaleGibson 21 91
(MWEasterby) *in tch tl rdn and nt qckn fr 2f out* **100/1**

41 **8** *nk* **Bahia Breeze**[28] 5281 2-8-4 89.....WRyan 3 87
(RGuest) *prom tl rdn and outpcd fr 2f out* **12/1**

2130 **9** *2 ½* **Sentiero Rosso (USA)**[15] 5602 2-8-9 96.....KMcEvoy 20 85
(BEllison) *cl up tl rdn and wknd wl over 1f out* **66/1**

3525 **10** *shd* **Bond City (IRE)**[21] 5464 2-8-9 95.....FLynch 9 84
(BSmart) *midfield: effrt over 2f out: btn over 1f out* **50/1**

1502 **11** *hd* **Gifted Gamble**[13] 5670 2-8-9 80.....(p) RWinston 11 84
(KARyan) *bhd: effrt and hung lft over 2f out: nvr rchd ldrs* **66/1**

2152 **12** *hd* **Harvest Warrior**[8] 5767 2-8-9 95.....DAllan 15 83
(TDEasterby) *in tch: rdn and edgd lft 2f out: sn outpcd* **22/1**

5634 **13** *1 ½* **Roodeye**[16] 5594 2-8-7 96.....WSupple 18 77
(RFJohnsonHoughton) *prom: outpcd over 2f out: n.d after* **33/1**

3040 **14** *shd* **World At My Feet**[14] 5626 2-8-1 87.....PFessey 23 70
(NBycroft) *midfield: effrt over 2f out: btn wl over 1f out* **125/1**

2405 **15** *1 ½* **Monsieur Mirasol**[11] 5721 2-8-9 79.....(b[1]) JCarroll 14 74
(KARyan) *bhd: rdn 1/2-way: nvr rchd ldrs* **125/1**

1254 **16** *7* **Amazin**[21] 5464 2-8-12 95.....PDobbs 7 56
(RHannon) *in tch tl wknd fr over 2f out* **25/1**

2125 **17** *shd* **Russian Rocket (IRE)**[57] 4514 2-8-6 79.....JMcAuley 5 49
(MrsCADunnett) *midfield: outpcd whn hung bdly lft 2f out* **100/1**

06 **18** *¾* **Cilla's Smile**[29] 5262 2-7-12.....PMQuinn 12 39
(MABuckley) *prom tl rdn and wknd 2f out* **200/1**

3 **19** *¾* **Second Reef**[43] 4924 2-8-6.....GParkin 19 45
(RAFahey) *sn pushed along in rr: no ch fr 1/2-way* **125/1**

6000 **20** *nk* **Gogetter Girl**[15] 5617 2-8-1 66.....(p) JBramhill 4 39
(JGallagher) *a bhd* **250/1**

0650 **21** *2 ½* **Lowestoft Playboy**[70] 4124 2-9-2 67.....SChin 6 47
(MrsCADunnett) *prom to 1/2-way: sn rdn and btn* **200/1**

500 **22** *5* **Forest Viking (IRE)**[70] 4149 2-8-9 58.....DMernagh 22 25
(JSWainwright) *a bhd* **200/1**

0 **23** *dist* **Ross Is Boss**[26] 5341 2-8-4 ow1.....TEaves 17 —
(CJTeague) *s.i.s: sn t.o* **250/1**

4610 **P** **Komac**[23] 5418 2-8-12 72.....ACulhane 13 —
(BAMcmahon) *in tch 2f: sn lost pl: p.u over 2f out* **200/1**

68.84 secs (-2.86) **Going Correction** -0.375s/f (Firm) 2y crse rec **24 Ran SP% 125.8**
Speed ratings: **104,102,100,100,99 98,98,97,94,94 94,93,91,91,89 80,80,79,78,77 74,67,**—,—CSF £11.14 TOTE £8.20: £2.70, £1.10, £8.40; EX 18.60.
**Owner** BDR Partnership **Bred** Mrs M Mason **Trained** West Ilsley, Berks

**FOCUS**
A decent renewal of this valuable contest in which the layers went 22/1 bar five. They raced in one group towards the centre and the time was acceptable for the grade, giving the form a solid look.

**NOTEBOOK**
**Obe Gold**, much improved by the visor, was making a quick reappearance, having won at Newmarket two days previously, and must be as hard as nails. He simply would not be denied and in the end was a worthy winner of this rich prize.
**Caesar Beware(IRE)** carried new colours after being sold to Sheikh Rashid, Sheikh Mohammed's son. He went much more freely than at Doncaster, but on this occasion never looked like picking up to the same effect and in the end had to settle for second best. He will be better suited by seven furlongs and less firm ground, but opportunities for him at three may prove thin on the ground.
**Dario Gee Gee(IRE)**, rated 95, ran out of his skin especially considering he much prefers easier ground.
**Moth Ball**, who had plenty to find, ran out of his skin especially considering for most of the race he found himself rather marooned towards the stands' side.
**Beaver Patrol(IRE)** was far from disgraced, but the impression was that he will be happier on less quick ground than he encountered here.
**Pivotal Flame** did really well, making serious inroads in the second half of the contest after being last out of the stalls. His two best efforts have been with give in the ground so he deserves plenty of credit for this.
**Word Perfect** did well considering she had a mountain to climb on official ratings.
**Bahia Breeze** found this an aweful lot tougher but to her credit was far from disgraced. The experience will not be lost on her.
**Harvest Warrior** *Official explanation: jockey said colt hung left handed from half way*
**Russian Rocket(IRE)** *Official explanation: jockey said gelding hung left handed from half way*
**Komac** *Official explanation: jockey said colt lost his action*

## 5948 BETFAIR.COM GUISBOROUGH STKS (LISTED RACE) 7f
3:25 (3:26) (A1) 3-Y-O+ £17,400 (£6,600; £3,300; £1,500) Stalls Centre

Form RPR

1042 **1** **Gonfilia (GER)**[23] [5416] 4-9-0 102........(t) KMcEvoy 10 111
(SaeedBinSuroor) *cl up: led 3f out: rdn wl over 1f ot: styd on strly ins last* **2/1**[1]

-505 **2** 1 3/4 **Twilight Blues (IRE)**[91] [3537] 5-9-0 103........ SWKelly 3 106
(JNoseda) *hld up: hdwy 1/2-way: chsd wnr 2f out: rdn and ev ch over 1f out: drvn and one pce ins last* **11/2**[3]

1605 **3** 1 **Iqte Saab (USA)**[23] [5422] 3-8-12 100........ WSupple 2 104
(JLDunlop) *hld up: swtchd lft and hdwy over 2f out: sn rdn and kpt on fnl f* **8/1**

2421 **4** 1 3/4 **Vortex**[20] [5504] 5-9-3 105........(t) NCordrey 5 102
(MissGayKelleway) *cl up: pushed along over 2f out: rdn wl over 1f out and kpt on same pce* **7/2**[2]

5343 **5** 2 1/2 **Ithaca (USA)**[23] [5416] 3-8-7 98........ WRyan 8 87
(HRACecil) *cl up: rdn along over 2f out: sn rdn and wknd wl over 1f out* **7/1**

0-30 **6** shd **Orcadian**[78] [3906] 3-8-12 101........ JTate 9 92
(JMPEustace) *hld up in tch: hdwy over 2f out: sn rdn and no imp appr last* **25/1**

2150 **7** 1 **Simianna**[7] [5780] 5-8-12 97........(p) RWinston 4 87
(ABerry) *hld up in rr: hdwy over 2f out: sn rdn and no imp fr over 1f out* **16/1**

1004 **8** 3 1/2 **Lucky Pipit**[6] [5811] 3-8-7 98........ ACulhane 6 75
(BWHills) *led: pushed along and hdd 3f out: rdn over 2f out and sn wknd* **10/1**

2426 **9** 1/2 **Moonlight Man**[22] [5439] 3-8-12 100........ PDobbs 1 78
(RHannon) *cl up: rdn along 1/2-way and sn wknd* **20/1**

0003 **10** 8 **Kindlelight Debut**[10] [5740] 4-8-9 70........ NCallan 7 52
(DKIvory) *wnt lft s: sn prom: rdn along 1/2-way and sn wknd* **150/1**

1m 21.04s (-3.86) **Going Correction** -0.375s/f (Firm)
**WFA** 3 from 4yo+ 2lb **10** Ran SP% **118.8**
Speed ratings: **107,105,103,101,99 98,97,93,93,84**CSF £13.36 TOTE £2.60: £1.60, £2.10, £2.90; EX 23.60.
**Owner** Godolphin **Bred** Gestut Auenquelle **Trained** Newmarket, Suffolk

**FOCUS**
A tight-knit Listed event with just 5lb covering all but one runner on official ratings. The winning time was ordinary for a Listed contest but the form looks sound enough.

**NOTEBOOK**
**Gonfilia(GER)**, already the winner of three races, including a Listed race and a Group Three, this season, travelled best throughout and in the end won going away. She must be a pleasure to train.
**Twilight Blues(IRE)**, absent since July, relished this fast type of ground and was the only one to seriously bustle up the winner. He has not tasted success since his York win last year but the ground will shortly turn against him.
**Iqte Saab(USA)** put three below-par efforts behind him and he may now be more effective over a mile.
**Vortex**, giving weight away all round, has proved in the past he is effective on turf but nine of his ten career wins have been on the All-Weather.
**Ithaca(USA)**, a major negative on the exchanges, had finished just behind the winner at Doncaster last time but it was a different story here.
**Orcadian** had been absent since a below-par effort at Newbury in July. This was only his third start this time and he presumably has his problems.
**Simianna**, who had something to find, was trying seven furlongs for the first time for a year.

## 5949 SHEPHERD CONSTRUCTION CLASSIFIED STKS 5f
4:00 (4:01) (E3) 3-Y-O+ £7,228 (£2,224; £1,112; £556) Stalls Centre

Form RPR

0060 **1** **Polish Emperor (USA)**[18] [5550] 4-9-2 73........(e) NCallan 13 86
(PWHarris) *wnt rt s: w ldrs: led 1/2-way: drvn out* **8/1**[2]

0131 **2** 3/4 **Playful Dane (IRE)**[3] [5862] 7-9-0 68........ DTudhope(5) 2 86
(WSCunningham) *prom: effrt 2f out: kpt on ins fnl f* **15/8**[1]

1160 **3** 1 1/4 **Nanna (IRE)**[54] [4608] 3-8-10 68........ FLynch 1 72
(RHollinshead) *disp ld to 2f out: rdn and kpt on same pce ins fnl f* **14/1**

6000 **4** 1 **Fyodor (IRE)**[10] [5730] 3-9-0 71........ SWKelly 5 72
(WJHaggas) *midfield: rdn after 2f: kpt on u.p fnl f* **14/1**

4205 **5** 1/2 **Foley Millennium (IRE)**[18] [5550] 6-9-2 73........ RWinston 4 72
(MQuinn) *led to 1/2-way: cl up: kpt on same pce fnl f* **10/1**[3]

4300 **6** 2 **Lualua**[54] [4608] 3-8-10 72........ PMakin(5) 14 63
(TDBarron) *dwlt: bhd tl hdwy appr fnl f: nrst fin* **12/1**

0600 **7** 1 **Indian Spark**[15] [5603] 10-9-0 71........ WSupple 10 58
(JSGoldie) *sn outpcd: sme late hdwy: nvr on terms* **12/1**

0350 **8** hd **Smirfys Party**[40] [5008] 6-8-13 48........(v) PMQuinn 6 56
(DNicholls) *in tch to 2f out: sn rdn and btn* **25/1**

0103 **9** 1/2 **Mirasol Princess**[17] [5563] 3-9-0 74........ DaneO'Neill 8 55
(DKIvory) *checked s: sn outpcd: n.d* **10/1**[3]

0340 **10** 2 **Scottish Exile (IRE)**[50] [4727] 3-8-10 70........(v) DarrenWilliams 15 43
(KRBurke) *midfield: rdn 1/2-way: sn btn* **25/1**

0600 **11** 1 1/2 **Count Cougar (USA)**[17] [5562] 4-8-13 50........ DaleGibson 7 40
(SPGriffiths) *chsd ldrs to 1/2-way: sn rdn and btn* **200/1**

0054 **12** 3/4 **Smirfys Night**[48] [4782] 5-8-13 49........ JBramhill 9 37
(DNicholls) *sn outpcd: nvr on terms* **33/1**

0000 **13** 7 **Miss Ceylon**[52] [4626] 4-8-10 35........ JMcAuley 3 6
(SPGriffiths) *s.i.s: a struggling* **200/1**

1000 **14** 1/2 **Catch The Cat (IRE)**[37] [5062] 5-8-12 72........(v) TEaves(3) 16 9
(JSWainwright) *sn wl bhd: nvr on terms* **14/1**

56.82 secs (-1.88) **Going Correction** -0.375s/f (Firm) **14** Ran SP% **111.1**
Speed ratings: **100,98,96,95,94 91,89,89,88,85 82,81,70,69**CSF £19.02 TOTE £10.80: £3.10, £1.50, £1.90; EX 37.10.
**Owner** Edrich, Graves, Harris **Bred** Chevington Stud **Trained** Ringshall, Bucks

**FOCUS**
Another competitive affair and decent form for the level, which looks solid for the grade.

**NOTEBOOK**
**Polish Emperor(USA)**, who is standing up well to a busy season, raced wide, towards the stands' side. Five furlongs on fast ground is his cup of tea and he made the most of the opportunity. *Official explanation: trainer's representative said, regarding the improved form shown, gelding was better suited by the fast ground on this occasion*
**Playful Dane(IRE)**, who had to give weight away all round, was unable to dominate and went down fighting. He is clearly right at the top of his game at present.
**Nanna(IRE)**, who raced wide down the far side, returned to form after two rather disappointing efforts.
**Fyodor(IRE)**, who has struggled this year, ran better sticking on really well in the closing stages. Six may suit him better now.
**Foley Millennium(IRE)**, already a winner five times this year, is currently rated 11lb higher than for his last handicap success.
**Lualua**, who scored on his debut, has failed to hit the back of the net in ten starts since and here the visor was left off.
**Smirfys Party**, who had a mountain to climb on official ratings, seemed to run out of his skin.
**Mirasol Princess** *Official explanation: jockey said filly ran flat*

## 5950 BOOK YOUR CHRISTMAS PARTY AT REDCAR RACECOURSE H'CAP 1m 2f
4:35 (4:35) (D2) (0-85,85) 3-Y-O+ £9,516 (£2,928; £1,464; £732) Stalls Low

Form RPR

0421 **1** **Go Tech**[9] [5755] 4-9-0 78........ DAllan 6 91+
(TDEasterby) *hld up in midfield: smooth hdwy over 3f out: qcknd to ld 1f out: sn rdn clr* **7/2**[1]

0005 **2** 3 **St Savarin (FR)**[12] [5706] 3-8-4 73........ DaleGibson 9 79
(JRBest) *hld up towards rr: hdwy 4f out: swtchd lft and rdn over 2f out: styd on wl fnl f* **33/1**

3226 **3** shd **Young Rooney**[8] [5769] 4-8-7 71 oh1........ SChin 4 77
(MMullineaux) *led: rdn along 3f out: drvn and hdd 1f out: kpt on same pce* **20/1**

0000 **4** 1 1/2 **Rarefied (IRE)**[6] [5821] 3-8-5 74........ WSupple 1 77
(TDEasterby) *hld up: hdwy over 3f out: swtchd rt over 2f out: sn rdn and kpt on same pce appr last* **14/1**

1514 **5** nk **Night Sight (USA)**[8] [5764] 7-8-7 71 oh1........ RWinston 2 73
(MrsSLamyman) *trckd ldrs: effrt and hdwy 3f out: rdn 2f out and sn one pce* **7/1**

06 **6** 3 1/2 **Stallone**[14] [5635] 7-8-3 72 oh5 ow1........(t) DTudhope(5) 8 68
(NWilson) *dwlt: hld up in rr: hdwy on inner over 3f out: rdn wl over 1f out: sn no imp* **12/1**

2612 **7** 9 **Barking Mad (USA)**[19] [5514] 6-9-7 85........ ACulhane 3 64
(MLWBell) *chsd ldng pair: hdwy and cl up over 3f out: rdn wl over 2f out and sn wknd* **5/1**[3]

0160 **8** 3 1/2 **Cause Celebre (IRE)**[15] [5615] 3-8-8 77........ WRyan 7 49
(BWHills) *a rr* **14/1**

5042 **9** 1 1/4 **River Treat (FR)**[17] [5572] 3-8-11 80........ DaneO'Neill 11 50
(GWragg) *hld up: hdwy on outer to chse ldrs over 3f out: rdn along and wknd over 2f out* **11/1**

3330 **10** 1 **Dream Magic**[8] [5768] 6-9-1 79........ GCarter 5 47
(MJRyan) *chsd ldrs: rdn along 4f out: sn wknd* **15/2**

0111 **11** 6 **Double Vodka (IRE)**[48] [4780] 3-8-4 73........ DMernagh 10 29
(MrsJRRamsden) *plld hrd: racd wd: cl up tl lost pl 4f out and sn bhd* **4/1**[2]

2m 3.06s (-3.74) **Going Correction** -0.25s/f (Firm)
**WFA** 3 from 4yo+ 5lb **11** Ran SP% **120.2**
Speed ratings: **104,101,101,100,100 97,90,87,86,85 80**CSF £123.53 CT £2051.67 TOTE £4.80: £1.80, £8.30, £4.90; EX 123.30.
**Owner** Ryedale Partners No 4 **Bred** A G Nicholson **Trained** Great Habton, N Yorks

**FOCUS**
A fair handicap for the prizemoney run at a sound pace and the form should stand up.

**NOTEBOOK**
**Go Tech**, 3lb higher, was ridden with bags of confidence and, bouncing off the ground, could be named the winner the moment he moved into second place with over two furlongs left to run. He is clearly in great heart and is not the first to bounce back at four after a good season at two.
**St Savarin(FR)**, often a front-runner, was waited with over this extended trip. Making his effort down the wide outside, he stayed on to snatch second spot on the line but, like the rest, had no earthly chance with the winner.
**Young Rooney** set the pace and went for home three furlongs out. He keeps running well, but the fact remains that he has yet to hit the target in 16 attempts now.
**Rarefied(IRE)**, stepping up in trip, made a tardy start. Putting in his best work at the finish, he may be worth a try over even further but he does not look altogether straightforward.
**Night Sight(USA)** as usual travelled strongly, but he now looks in the Handicapper's grip.
**Stallone**, 5lb out of the handicap, showed he is in good heart.
**Double Vodka(IRE)**, drawn one off the outside, pulled far too hard for his own good on his first outing for seven weeks. Hopefully this will have taken the freshness away. *Official explanation: jockey said gelding ran too free*

## 5951 REDCAR RACECOURSE CONFERENCE & BANQUETING CENTRE H'CAP 1m 6f 19y
5:10 (5:10) (E3) (0-70,70) 3-Y-O+ £4,270 (£1,314; £657; £328) Stalls Low

Form RPR

3316 **1** **Red Forest (IRE)**[34] [5144] 5-9-6 67........(t) DaleGibson 8 76
(JMackie) *trckd ldrs: hdwy to ld 4f out: rdn clr 2f out: styd on wl* **11/2**

6232 **2** 2 1/2 **Most Definitely (IRE)**[19] [5523] 4-9-3 64........ DAllan 5 70
(TDEasterby) *hld up in rr: hdwy over 4f out: rdn to chse wnr 2f out: sn drvn: edgd lft and no imp ent last* **4/1**[1]

6104 **3** 2 **Best Port (IRE)**[19] [5523] 8-8-11 63........ MLawson(5) 1 66
(JParkes) *hld up in rr: hdwy on outer 3f out: rdn over 2f out: kpt on ins last: nrst fin* **5/1**[3]

0203 **4** shd **Dovedon Hero**[29] [5273] 4-9-9 70........(b) GCarter 7 73
(PJMcbride) *hld up in tch: hdwy 4f out: rdn and ev ch over 2f out: sn drvn and one pce* **11/2**

-022 **5** 6 **Colway Ritz**[14] [5635] 10-9-2 63........ JBramhill 2 57
(WStorey) *trckd ldrs: hdwy on inner 4f out: sn rdn and wknd wl over 2f out* **6/1**

2503 **6** nk **Golden Drift**[17] [5560] 3-8-3 59........ CCatlin 6 53
(GWragg) *chsd ldrs: rdn along 4f out: wknd3f out* **9/1**

2316 **7** 6 **Spitting Image (IRE)**[32] [5214] 4-9-0 61........ ACulhane 3 46
(KGReveley) *led: rdn and hdd 4 out: sn wknd* **9/2**[2]

0043 **8** 15 **Distant Cousin**[19] [5523] 7-8-9 56........(v) DaneO'Neill 4 20
(MABuckley) *chsd ldr: rdn along 4f out: sn wknd* **10/1**

3m 0.17s (-4.83) **Going Correction** -0.25s/f (Firm)
**WFA** 3 from 4yo+ 9lb **8** Ran SP% **119.0**
Speed ratings: **103,101,100,100,96 96,93,84**CSF £28.99 CT £119.25 TOTE £9.20: £2.40, £1.60, £1.70; EX 42.20 Place 6 £15.45, Place 5 £6.45.
**Owner** P Riley **Bred** Olympic B'Stock Ltd, Freynestown B'Stock And B Hi **Trained** Church Broughton, Derbys

**FOCUS**
A modest staying contest that did not take much winning, run at just a fair gallop with the winner in the end getting first bite of the cherry.

**NOTEBOOK**
**Red Forest(IRE)** travelled strongly on the ground he loves and, sent for home with over two furlongs left to run, was never in any danger. His rider deserves top marks.
**Most Definitely(IRE)** turned in another sound performance, but his record now reads no wins from 20 starts with nine silver medals.
**Best Port(IRE)** could have done with the leaders going off a shade faster. He hung left when asked to improve, but in the end stayed on and just missed out on second spot.
**Dovedon Hero**, suited by the trip and the ground, is now 7lb lower than his last win a year ago. He travelled strongly, but when asked a question wanted to do nothing but hang left.
**Colway Ritz** did not run anywhere near as well as on his last two starts.
**Golden Drift**, stepping up in trip, was one of the first to come off the bridle.

**Spitting Image(IRE)**, just 2lb higher than when winning over two miles here in August, took them along but was swallowed up once in line for home.
T/Plt: £22.10 to a £1 stake. Pool: £39,381.55. 1,300.05 winning tickets. T/Qpdt: £10.40 to a £1 stake. Pool: £2,197.50. 155.50 winning tickets. JR

## 2662 WOLVERHAMPTON (A.W) (L-H)
Saturday, October 2

**OFFICIAL GOING: Standard**
The was the first meeting at Dunstall Park on Polytrack with the circumference of the course having been increased by 41 yards.
Wind: nil Weather: clear

### 5952 PARKSTONE GROUP QUALITY ASSURED CLAIMING STKS 7f 32y(P)
7:00 (7:01) (F3) 3-Y-O+ £3,458 (£1,064; £532; £266) Stalls High

Form RPR
0160 1 **Samuel Charles**[6] 5818 6-8-11 75 BSwarbrick(5) 7 83
(WMBrisbourne) *a.p: wnt 2nd over 3f out: rdn over 2f out: led wl ins fnl f: drvn out* **6/1**[3]
0010 2 nk **Morse (IRE)**[7] 5786 3-9-8 78 SWKelly 11 90
(JAOsborne) *sn led: rdn over 2f out: hdd wl ins fnl f* **5/1**[2]
0004 3 3 1/2 **Mallard (IRE)**[25] 5379 6-9-6 75 MFenton 8 77
(JGGiven) *hld up in tch: rdn and one pce fnl 2f* **3/1**[1]
1060 4 2 1/2 **Tre Colline**[37] 5055 5-9-10 76 GBaker 10 75
(NTinkler) *hld up in rr: hdwy on outside over 2f out: sn rdn: edgd lft jst ins fnl f: no imp* **10/1**
4300 5 2 **Ile Michel**[12] 5698 7-9-6 72 DSweeney 6 65
(JGMO'Shea) *hld up: rdn and sme hdwy over 2f out: nvr nr ldrs* **20/1**
1-00 6 3 **Dvinsky (USA)**[65] 4268 3-9-8 85 PHanagan 9 62
(GAButler) *hld up and bhd: rdn over 3f out: hdwy over 2f out: wknd 1f out* **6/1**[3]
0600 7 3/4 **Cashel Mead**[141] 2091 4-9-1 75 ADaly 5 51
(JLSpearing) *led early: chsd ldr tl over 3f out: rdn and wknd 2f out* **20/1**
4555 8 1 1/2 **Linning Wine (IRE)**[11] 5151 8-9-6 94 SCarson 4 52
(BGPowell) *hld up: rdn over 3f out: bhd fnl 2f* **6/1**[3]
00 9 hd **Moon Spinner**[4] 5851 7-8-3 FNorton 2 34
(AndrewReid) *pushed along 4f out: a bhd* **33/1**
0420 10 6 **Hurricane Floyd (IRE)**[14] 5631 6-9-10 74 (b) TPQueally 1 40
(DFlood) *s.i.s: rdn 3f out: a bhd* **10/1**

1m 29.51s
**WFA** 3 from 4yo+ 2lb 10 Ran SP% **115.2**
Speed ratings: CSF £34.58 TOTE £7.40: £2.10, £1.70, £1.60; EX 31.80.
**Owner** J F Thomas **Bred** Sheikh Mohammed Obaid Al Maktoum **Trained** Great Ness, Shropshire

**FOCUS**
A fair claimer but not many got into it. With this being a new surface and new distances being used, no speed figures will be calculated until there is sufficent data available.

**NOTEBOOK**
**Samuel Charles**, already a winner on the Polytrack, does have the trait of carrying his head high but his resolution can never be faulted.
**Morse(IRE)**, back in the right sort of grade, likes to force the pace and hardly deserved to be beaten.
**Mallard(IRE)**, four times a winner here on Fibresand, has also scored once on the Polytrack. He had no excuses on this drop in class.
**Tre Colline** seems more effective at a mile these days.
**Ile Michel** found this trip on the short side.
**Dvinsky(USA)** was reported by his rider to have had a breathing problem on this drop in grade for his All-Weather debut. *Official explanation: jockey said colt had a breathing problem*
**Linning Wine(IRE)** *Official explanation: jockey said gelding lost his action*
**Hurricane Floyd(IRE)** *Official explanation: jockey said saddle slipped*

### 5953 GUINNESS MEDIAN AUCTION MAIDEN STKS 5f 216y(P)
7:30 (7:32) (F3) 2-Y-O £4,309 (£1,326; £663; £331) Stalls Low

Form RPR
0 1 **Manic**[70] 4124 2-8-9 GGibbons 3 66
(AndrewReid) *a.p: rdn and wnt 2nd over 2f out: edgd lft 1f out: r.o to ld wl ins fnl f* **33/1**
4 2 1 1/2 **Pink Bay**[28] 5281 2-8-9 FNorton 5 61
(WSKittow) *prom: lost pl over 3f out: rdn and hdwy over 2f out: swtchd rt ins fnl f: r.o* **9/1**
00 3 3/4 **Depressed**[17] 5569 2-8-9 JFEgan 4 59
(AndrewReid) *sn led: clr 2f out: rdn over 1f out: hdd and no ex wl ins fnl f* **14/1**
00 4 1 **First Rhapsody (IRE)**[117] 2730 2-8-2 KristinStubbs(7) 13 56
(TJEtherington) *hld up: sn bhd: hdwy fr jst over 1f out: nrst fin* **100/1**
04 5 hd **Mangrove Cay (IRE)**[21] 5476 2-9-0 TPQueally 9 60
(DRLoder) *a.p: hrd rdn over 2f out: one pce* **9/2**[2]
06 6 1 3/4 **Edge Of Italy**[19] 5507 2-8-9 DSweeney 10 50
(KBell) *hld up: hdwy over 3f out: rdn over 2f out: wknd fnl f* **20/1**
5 7 4 **Missin Margot**[14] 5633 2-8-9 PHanagan 12 38
(MsDeborahJEvans) *sn bhd: rdn 3f out: nvr nr ldrs* **40/1**
00 8 3/4 **Prophet's Calling (IRE)**[16] 5592 2-9-0 LisaJones 1 41
(MissDAMchale) *chsd ldrs tl wknd over 4f out* **100/1**
000 9 5 **Preskani**[15] 5616 2-8-7 (p) CHaddon(7) 11 25
(MrsNMacauley) *prom: hung rt and lost pl after 1f: wl bhd fnl 3f* **100/1**
04 10 5 **Miss Sudbrook (IRE)**[12] 5688 2-8-9 MFenton 2 5
(DHaydnJones) *led early: chsd ldr tl wknd over 2f out* **6/1**[3]
2 11 3 1/2 **Spectait**[12] 5688 2-9-0 SWKelly 7 —
(SirMarkPrescott) *s.i.s: outpcd* **8/11**[1]
0 12 9 **Randalls Touch**[29] 5262 2-8-9 BSwarbrick(5) 6 —
(BDLeavy) *prom: rdn and lost pl over 3f out: sn bhd* **100/1**

1m 17.1s 12 Ran SP% **121.1**
Speed ratings: CSF £304.00 TOTE £25.20: £4.40, £2.90, £3.10; EX 514.10.
**Owner** A S Reid **Bred** A S Reid **Trained** Mill Hill, London NW7

**FOCUS**
A poor maiden with the odds-on favourite running no race at all, and the form is just modest for the level.

**NOTEBOOK**
**Manic** appreciated the extra furlong in an event which probably did not take much winning.
**Pink Bay** is crying out for a step up to seven.
**Depressed**, a stable companion of the winner, is worth dropping back to the minimum trip if ridden like this.
**First Rhapsody(IRE)** ◆, off course for nearly four months, was given a lot to do and is worth bearing in mind over further with stronger handling.
**Mangrove Cay(IRE)** lacked the required turn of foot on this drop back from seven.
**Edge Of Italy** had shaped as though he needed at least this trip at Bath last time.
**Spectait**, who was granted permission not to come into the paddock, is obviously not straightforward. His rider reported that his mount had banged his head against the starting stalls. *Official explanation: jockey said gelding banged his head on stalls*

### 5954 DINE AT DUNSTALL PARK (S) STKS 5f 20y(P)
8:00 (8:07) (G4) 2-Y-O £2,597 (£742; £371) Stalls Low

Form RPR
0244 1 **Bob's Flyer**[7] 5800 2-8-7 65 ow1 KFallon 9 64
(JGGiven) *a.p: rdn over 1f out: edgd lft and led jst ins fnl f: r.o wl* **5/2**[1]
3660 2 3 1/2 **Llamadas**[14] 5636 2-8-11 64 (v1) JFEgan 3 56
(MDods) *hld up and bhd: swtchd rt over 2f out: gd hdwy fnl f: r.o wl* **7/1**
5 3 1 **Our Little Secret (IRE)**[19] 5513 2-8-6 FNorton 11 48
(ABerry) *sn chsng ldr: rdn 2f out: ev ch 1f out: one pce* **14/1**
2600 4 1/2 **Ducal Diva**[6] 5816 2-7-13 60 DFentiman(7) 1 46
(JRWeymes) *led: rdn wl over 1f out: hdd jst ins fnl f: no ex* **14/1**
5550 5 nk **Mitchelland**[8] 5767 2-8-11 65 PHanagan 4 50
(JamesMoffatt) *bhd: rdn and hdwy over 1f out: nt rch ldrs* **6/1**
50 6 3 **William James**[33] 5179 2-8-11 SWKelly 5 39
(MJWallace) *wnt rt s: sn hmpd: outpcd: nvr nrr* **25/1**
0 7 nk **Mount Kellet (IRE)**[16] 5578 2-8-11 MFenton 10 38
(JGGiven) *chsd ldrs: rdn over 3f out: wknd 2f out* **20/1**
45 8 1 1/2 **Aynsley**[16] 5586 2-8-7 ow1 NCallan 8 29
(MAJarvis) *hdwy over 3f out: rdn 2f out: wknd 1f out* **11/2**[3]
2000 9 1/2 **Bogaz (IRE)**[23] 5421 2-8-11 61 GGibbons 2 31
(PABlockley) *prom: rdn and lost pl over 3f out: sn bhd* **9/2**[2]
000 10 3/4 **Wilford Maverick (IRE)**[72] 4048 2-8-11 AMcCarthy 12 29
(MJAttwater) *prom: rdn over 2f out: sn wknd* **40/1**
2000 11 3 **Miss Cotswold Lady**[10] 5738 2-8-6 65 (v1) TPQueally 7 13
(APJarvis) *rdn over 3f out: sn bhd* **10/1**
00 12 1 3/4 **Independent Spirit**[18] 5542 2-8-8 PMulrennan(3) 6 12
(RPElliott) *bmpd s: outpcd* **50/1**

63.44 secs 12 Ran SP% **127.3**
Speed ratings: CSF £20.76 TOTE £3.10: £1.70, £2.50, £2.10; EX 26.20.The winner was sold for 7,000gns to J G M O'Shea. Llamadas was claimed by Mrs Stef Liddiard for £6000
**Owner** D Maloney **Bred** Helshaw Grange Stud And Graham White **Trained** Willoughton, Lincs

**FOCUS**
A run-of-the-mill seller that could be rated a little higher but with few of the field running to form a cautious approach has been taken.

**NOTEBOOK**
**Bob's Flyer** took advantage of a drop in grade and changed hands for 7,000 guineas after winning going away.
**Llamadas**, wearing a visor instead of the blinkers, was claimed for £6,000 after finishing an eye-catching second. A return to six is called for.
**Our Little Secret(IRE)** was 5lb better off than when a length behind the winner on his debut at Musselburgh last month.
**Ducal Diva**, down in class for this switch to the sand, is not short of speed but barely stays five furlongs.
**Mitchelland**, a five-furlong winner on heavy ground, requires further on a surface like this.
**William James** *Official explanation: jockey said gelding hung left throughout*

### 5955 MARTIN COLLINS ENTERPRISES H'CAP 1m 141y(P)
8:30 (8:35) (E3) (0-70,70) 3-Y-O+ £5,112 (£1,573; £786; £393) Stalls Low

Form RPR
6154 1 **Riska King**[12] 5706 4-9-3 **65** PHanagan 9 75
(RAFahey) *hld up: rdn and hdwy 3f out: hrd rdn to ld ins fnl f: r.o* **4/1**[2]
0206 2 1/2 **Almond Willow (IRE)**[31] 5223 3-9-2 **68** SWKelly 13 77
(JNoseda) *flashed tail intermittently: a.p: led 4f out: rdn 3f out: hdd and nt qckn ins fnl f* **10/1**
2602 3 3/4 **Island Rapture**[10] 5740 4-9-7 **69** JFEgan 4 76
(JARToller) *hld up and bhd: hdwy on wd outside over 2f out: hung lft fr over 1f out: r.o ins fnl f* **6/1**[3]
6416 4 nk **Hazewind**[18] 5540 3-9-1 **70** (vt) FPFerris(3) 6 76
(PDEvans) *hld up in tch: rdn 3f out: kpt on ins fnl f* **7/1**
0404 5 1 1/2 **Moonshaft (USA)**[40] 4987 3-9-1 **67** SSanders 11 70
(EALDunlop) *hld up and bhd: hdwy on outside 3f out: sn rdn: one pce fnl f* **20/1**
0050 6 1 3/4 **The Bonus King**[12] 5706 4-9-5 **67** GBaker 5 67
(JJay) *chsd ldr: rdn and lost 2nd over 2f out: wknd ins fnl f* **20/1**
0600 7 1/2 **Ali Deo**[19] 5510 3-9-1 **67** (p) TPQueally 8 65
(WJHaggas) *hld up: stdy hdwy 5f out: rdn and wnt 2nd over 2f out: wknd ins fnl f* **14/1**
0004 8 7 **Charlie Tango (IRE)**[11] 5715 3-9-0 **66** MFenton 7 50
(NTinkler) *s.i.s: rdn 3f out: a bhd* **16/1**
-105 9 1/2 **Vonadaisy**[10] 5740 3-9-2 **68** (b) ACulhane 3 51
(WJHaggas) *prom: nt clr run and lost pl over 3f out: sn rdn and bhd* **9/1**
3560 10 1 1/2 **Text**[5] 5829 3-9-2 **68** (p) FNorton 2 48
(MrsStefLiddiard) *hld up and bhd: nt clr run on ins over 3f out: no ch after* **20/1**
1252 11 2 1/2 **Summer Shades**[6] 5821 6-9-1 **63** KFallon 12 37
(WMBrisbourne) *hld up: stdy hdwy 5f out: wknd over 3f out* **11/4**[1]
5500 12 15 **Western Roots**[25] 5381 3-9-3 **69** NCallan 1 12
(KAMorgan) *led: hdd 4f out: sn hmpd on ins: rdn 3f out: sn bhd* **40/1**

1m 51.47s
**WFA** 3 from 4yo+ 4lb 12 Ran SP% **121.8**
Speed ratings: CSF £42.53 CT £247.50 TOTE £7.00: £2.50, £3.10, £1.90; EX 41.70.
**Owner** Market Avenue Racing Club Ltd **Bred** D R Tucker **Trained** Musley Bank, N Yorks
■ Stewards Enquiry : Non-Runner £450 fine: gelding doubly delcared
S W Kelly one-day ban: careless riding (Oct 13)

**FOCUS**
A ordinary but competitive handicap rated through the third and fourth, and fairly reliable for the grade.

**NOTEBOOK**
**Riska King**, 2lb lower than when winning at Beverley in August, had not previously been at his best on sand. He answered his rider's every call.
**Almond Willow(IRE)**, making her Polytrack debut, is a bit of a tail swisher but her attitude could not be faulted.
**Island Rapture** came the scenic route and then drifted towards the far rail in the home straight. The stretch nine furlongs here will suit her better.
**Hazewind** ran a sound race in trying to defy a career-high mark.
**Moonshaft(USA)** was dropping back in distance for this first try on sand.
**The Bonus King** seems more effective over seven.
**Charlie Tango(IRE)** *Official explanation: jockey said he suffered interference on last bend*
**Summer Shades** *Official explanation: trainer had no explanation for the poor form shown*

## 5956 WEATHERBYS BANK H'CAP — 1m 4f 50y(P)
9:00 (9:03) (E3) (0-70,70) 3-Y-O+ £5,204 (£1,601; £800; £400) Stalls Low

Form RPR

0355 **1** **Merrymaker**[14] 5632 4-9-9 **69**.................................... KFallon 4 83
(WMBrisbourne) *hld up: hdwy 3f out: sn rdn: led jst ins fnl f: r.o wl* **9/2**[2]

-401 **2** *5* **Resonate (IRE)**[23] 5423 6-9-4 **64**.................................... DaneO'Neill 9 71
(AGNewcombe) *t.k.h in tch: rdn to ld jst over 1f out: hdd jst ins fnl f: one pce* **4/1**[1]

1140 **3** *½* **Milk And Sultana**[3] 5869 4-9-6 **66**.................................... ADaly 1 72
(GAHam) *hld up in tch: rdn over 2f out: kpt on fnl f* **14/1**

2003 **4** *hd* **Efrhina (IRE)**[5] 5828 4-9-4 **64**.................................... FNorton 6 70
(MrsStefLiddiard) *hld up and bhd: hdwy on outside over 1f out: r.o ins fnl f* **20/1**

-501 **5** *nk* **Ivy League Star (IRE)**[8] 5773 3-9-3 **70**.................................... ACulhane 10 75
(BWHills) *hld up in tch: jinked rt and lost pl paddock exit over 7f out: hdwy over 3f out: rdn over 2f out: styd on one pce fnl f* **8/1**

4400 **6** *1* **Jadeeron**[135] 2235 5-9-4 **64**....................................(p) LisaJones 2 68
(MissDAMchale) *led 2f: prom tl wknd 3f out* **14/1**

4220 **7** *1* **Alpine Special (IRE)**[37] 5058 3-9-3 **70**.................................... GFaulkner 11 72
(PCHaslam) *hld up: sme hdwy 2f out: sn rdn: no imp* **12/1**

0000 **8** *1 ¾* **Crathorne (IRE)**[16] 5581 4-9-9 **69**....................................(p) TPQueally 3 69
(JDBethell) *a.p: led over 3f out: rdn over 2f out: hdd jst over 1f out: wknd ins fnl f* **20/1**

1100 **9** *4* **Zeis (IRE)**[18] 5554 4-9-5 **65**....................................(t) JFEgan 5 59
(AndrewReid) *rdn over 5f out: a bhd* **20/1**

2110 **10** *1 ½* **Quedex**[66] 4226 8-9-1 **64**.................................... RMiles(3) 8 55
(RJPrice) *prom tl wknd over 3f out* **5/1**[3]

02-1 **11** *5* **Nuts For You (IRE)**[23] 5410 3-9-2 **69**.................................... DSweeney 12 53
(RCharlton) *led after 2f: rdn and hdd over 2f out: wknd over 1f out* **4/1**[1]

4544 **12** *dist* **Port 'n Starboard**[36] 5079 3-9-1 **68**.................................... SSanders 7 —
(CACyzer) *hld up and bhd: hdwy on outside over 4f out: hung bdly rt bnd over 3f out: sn bhd: t.o fnl 2f* **25/1**

2m 42.12s
**WFA** 3 from 4yo+ 7lb **12** Ran SP% **125.1**
Speed ratings: CSF £22.83 CT £244.73 TOTE £6.20: £2.10, £2.20, £3.20; EX 53.50.
**Owner** The Blacktoffee Partnership **Bred** Hascombe And Valiant Studs **Trained** Great Ness, Shropshire

**FOCUS**
An ordinary handicap that looked pretty competitive beforehand but it eventually did not turn out that way. The fourth and sixth set the standard and the winner looks well suited by the surface.

**NOTEBOOK**
**Merrymaker** took to this surface like a duck to water and ran out a convincing winner. He can defy a penalty on a surface that clearly suits.
**Resonate(IRE)**, again up in distance, appeared to stay well enough especially considering he ran too freely.
**Milk And Sultana**, 7lb higher than for the second of her back-to-back wins last month, was reverting to a longer distance for this first outing on the Polytrack.
**Efrhina(IRE)**, unsuited by the soft when previously tried at this trip, does appear to need at least a mile and a half now.
**Ivy League Star(IRE)** raised 8lb for his heavy ground win a Haydock, will stay further on a surface this quick. *Official explanation: jockey said filly had steering problems*
**Jadeeron** had finished lame when last seen back in May.
**Zeis(IRE)** *Official explanation: jockey said gelding had a breathing problem*
**Quedex** *Official explanation: jockey said gelding had no more to give*
**Nuts For You(IRE)** *Official explanation: trainer said he had no explanation for poor form shown*
**Port 'n Starboard** *Official explanation: jockey said gelding hung badly left throughout and pulled himself up*

## 5957 WOOD BROTHERS H'CAP — 1m 1f 103y(P)
9:30 (9:32) (F4) (0-55,55) 3-Y-O £2,935 (£838; £419) Stalls Low

Form RPR

2115 **1** **Boppys Princess**[17] 5557 3-9-2 **55**.................................... PHanagan 5 63
(RAFahey) *hld up and bhd: rdn and hdwy over 2f out: edgd lft over 1f out: r.o u.p to ld last strides* **4/1**[2]

0005 **2** *nk* **Velocitas**[26] 5352 3-9-1 **54**.................................... JFEgan 8 61
(HJCollingridge) *hld up and bhd: hdwy on outside over 3f out: rdn wl over 1f out: r.o ins fnl f* **33/1**

3253 **3** *hd* **Rubaiyat (IRE)**[26] 5352 3-9-2 **55**.................................... FNorton 11 62
(GWragg) *hld up in tch: rdn to ld wl over 1f out: sn edgd lft: ct last strides* **7/2**[1]

5013 **4** *3 ½* **Calculaite**[14] 5642 3-9-2 **55**.................................... SSanders 4 55
(MrsGSRees) *led: rdn and hdd wl over 1f out: wknd wl ins fnl f* **13/2**

5-00 **5** *1* **Mr Lewin**[51] 4680 3-9-1 **54**.................................... DarrenWilliams 6 52
(RAFahey) *prom: rdn over 2f out: wknd fnl f* **14/1**

2210 **6** *½* **Turks And Caicos (IRE)**[79] 3881 3-9-2 **55**.................................... GFaulkner 3 52
(PCHaslam) *hld up in mid-div: hdwy on ins 2f out: one pce fnl f* **10/1**

0000 **7** *nk* **Imperial Royale (IRE)**[5] 5830 3-8-12 **51**....................................(p) GGibbons 1 47
(PLClinton) *hld up in mid-div: lost pl on ins over 3f out: swtchd rt wl over 1f out: styd on fnl f: n.d* **50/1**

-310 **8** *½* **Be Wise Girl**[14] 5658 3-9-1 **54**.................................... MFenton 10 49
(JGGiven) *plld hrd: sn chsng ldr: disp ld over 4f out tl rdn 2f out: flashed tail and wknd jst over 1f out* **14/1**

3504 **9** *10* **Infidelity (IRE)**[21] 5459 3-8-13 **52**.................................... VSlattery 12 27
(ABailey) *hld up: stdy hdwy 5f out: rdn and wknd over 2f out* **8/1**

5536 **10** *½* **Trois Etoiles (IRE)**[19] 5510 3-9-1 **54**....................................(v[1]) KFallon 7 28
(JWHills) *t.k.h in tch: n.m.r bnd 7f out: rdn over 2f out: btn whn lost action and eased over 1f out* **9/2**[3]

-050 **11** *1 ¼* **Blue Viking (IRE)**[96] 3379 3-8-5 **51**.................................... DFentiman(7) 13 23
(JRWeymes) *a bhd* **50/1**

0410 **12** *¾* **Grand Rapide**[11] 5714 3-9-1 **54**.................................... NCallan 9 24
(JLSpearing) *a bhd* **11/1**

-100 **13** *12* **Poker**[29] 5260 3-9-0 **53**.................................... ACulhane 2 —
(MrsJCandlish) *prom: rdn over 4f out: wknd over 3f out* **16/1**

2m 3.34s **13** Ran SP% **128.4**
Speed ratings: CSF £142.46 CT £525.94 TOTE £6.20: £2.60, £11.10, £1.90; EX 345.10 Place 6 £294.02, Place 5 £175.86.
**Owner** Mrs S Bond **Bred** Mrs Sylvia Bond **Trained** Musley Bank, N Yorks

**FOCUS**
A low-grade affair won by a filly in fine form. The third and fifth set the standard, which is very limited.

**NOTEBOOK**
**Boppys Princess** continues on the crest of a wave despite having gone up a total of 15lb for her three wins during the summer. She got the longer trip well on this first run on sand.
**Velocitas** ◆ had not been seen on this surface since cutting little ice on his debut nearly a year ago. This was a big improvement and he is capable of going one better in a similar event.
**Rubaiyat(IRE)**, 5lb higher than when just touched off on this surface at Lingfield in July, seemed likely to hold on until worn down near the line.
**Calculaite** may have found this trip just beyond him but was 9lb higher than when last in a handicap.
**Mr Lewin**, trying his luck on the All-Weather, gave the impression he failed to get home over this longer trip.
**Turks And Caicos(IRE)**, returning after a summer break, may find he needs further on a surface like this.
**Trois Etoiles(IRE)** *Official explanation: jockey said filly lost her action*
T/Plt: £830.90 to a £1 stake. Pool £35,968.35, 31.60 winning units T/Qpdt: £21.50 to a £1 stake. Pool £1,987.80, 68.25 winning units KH

5958 - 5960a (Foreign Racing) - See Raceform Interactive

5675

# CURRAGH (R-H)
Saturday, October 2

**OFFICIAL GOING: Yielding to soft**

## 5961a C L WELD PARK STKS (GROUP 3) (FILLIES) — 7f
4:00 (4:00) 2-Y-O £36,676 (£10,760; £5,126; £1,746)

RPR

**1** **Jazz Princess (IRE)**[26] 5358 2-8-11 94.................................... NGMcCullagh 4 109
(MrsJohnHarrington, Ire) *mde all: rdn and styd on wl fr over 2f out: clr fr over 1f out* **12/1**

**2** *3* **Saoire**[27] 5325 2-8-11 106.................................... MJKinane 3 102
(MsFMCrowley, Ire) *trckd ldrs: 5th 2f out: sn rdn: 3rd 1 1/2f out: kpt on ins fnl f wout troubling wnr* **10/3**[3]

**3** *1 ½* **Virginia Waters (USA)**[14] 5665 2-8-11 .................................... JAHeffernan 7 98
(APO'Brien, Ire) *trckd ldrs on far rail: 3rd bef 1/2-way: 2nd 3f out: rdn and no imp fr 2f out: no ex fnl f* **5/1**

**4** *2* **Adaala (USA)**[19] 5527 2-8-11 84.................................... DPMcDonogh 9 93
(KevinPrendergast, Ire) *hld up: 5th and rdn under 2f out: 4th and swtchd rt 1 1/2f out: kpt on fnl f* **10/1**

**5** *6* **Perfect Memory (IRE)**[61] 4410 2-8-11 82.................................... TPO'Shea 1 78
(JamesJKelly, Ire) *chsd ldrs: 3rd over 2f out: sn no ex* **25/1**

**6** *½* **Fuerta Ventura (IRE)**[19] 5527 2-8-11 75.................................... PShanahan 5 77
(KJCondon, Ire) *hld up towards rr: kpt on same pce fr over 2f out* **50/1**

**7** *nk* **Faint Heart (IRE)**[19] 5532 2-8-11 .................................... WMLordan 2 72
(DavidWachman, Ire) *prom: 4th and rdn 3f out: sn no ex* **10/1**

**8** *2* **Pictavia (IRE)**[27] 5325 2-8-11 107.................................... KJManning 6 57
(JSBolger, Ire) *sn prom: 2nd and rdn 1/2-way: wknd fr 3f out* **3/1**[2]

**9** *6* **Songerie**[12] 5687 2-8-11 .................................... EAhern 8 57
(SirMarkPrescott) *nvr travelling wl: drvn along early: bhd fr 2 1/2f out* **5/2**[1]

1m 26.7s **Going Correction** +0.05s/f (Good) **9** Ran SP% **125.0**
Speed ratings: **108,104,102,100,93 93,93,93,93**CSF £57.82 TOTE £12.80: £3.40, £1.40, £2.30; DF 126.50.
**Owner** T Curran **Bred** Kill Na Moragh Stud **Trained** Stud Moone, Co Kildare
■ A first Group winner on the Flat for Jessica Harrington.
■ Stewards Enquiry : E Ahern 21-day ban: improper conduct - hit out at rival jockey following weigh in (Oct 13,14,16,17,20,23-27,31, Mar 20,24,26-28, Apr 3,6,7,10,14)

**NOTEBOOK**
**Jazz Princess(IRE)** completed the hat-trick in good style on this step up in grade following wins at Sligo and Galway. Well suited by soft ground, she will not run again this year. Quoted at 33/1 for the 1000 Guineas, whether she is up to that class remains to be seen, but she is going the right way.
**Saoire**, third in the Moyglare Stud Stakes, gives a good line to the value of the form although this was her first attempt on soft ground.
**Virginia Waters(USA)** seems to be progressing and handled the step back up in class, although no match for the first two. She will appreciate further next season.
**Songerie**, winner of Chepstow maiden on heavy ground on her debut, but was never going and it is possible she bounced, or had some other sort of problem.

## 5962a STANLEYBET DIAMOND STKS (LISTED RACE) — 1m 2f
4:30 (4:31) 3-Y-O+ £25,214 (£7,397; £3,524; £1,200)

RPR

**1** **Mikado**[21] 5463 3-9-0 115.................................... CO'Donoghue 4 117
(APO'Brien, Ire) *led: strly pressed 2f out: hdd briefly under 1f out: rallied u.p to regain ld: styd on wl* **10/3**[2]

**2** *1 ½* **Ecomium (IRE)**[172] 1382 3-9-0 .................................... EAhern 7 114
(JNoseda) *trckd ldrs in 5th: smooth hdwy into 2nd ent st: chal fr 2f out: led briefly under 1f out: sn hdd and kpt on* **9/2**[3]

**3** *1 ½* **Mingun (USA)**[410] 4269 4-9-5 113.................................... JAHeffernan 15 112
(APO'Brien, Ire) *settled 2nd: 3rd and rdn to chal early st: kpt on wl wout threatening fnl f* **6/1**

**4** *4 ½* **Dashing Home (IRE)**[14] 5663 5-9-5 99.................................... PCosgrave 2 104
(NoelMeade, Ire) *hld up: styd on wl on outer fr 1 1/2f out* **16/1**

**5** *shd* **Jade Quest (IRE)**[41] 4977 4-9-9 100.................................... WJO'Connor 9 107
(CharlesO'Brien, Ire) *trckd ldrs in 6th: dropped to 10th ent st: kpt on fr 2f out* **20/1**

**6** *1* **Trefflich (GER)**[21] 5481 3-9-0 107.................................... MJKinane 13 102
(JohnMOxx, Ire) *mid-div: 9th 1/2-way: prog early st: 4th 1 1/2f out: sn no ex* **10/1**

**7** *½* **Emmas Princess (IRE)**[14] 5663 4-9-2 93.................................... NGMcCullagh 5 98
(EdwardLynam, Ire) *hld up: kpt on fr 1 1/2f out* **25/1**

**8** *1 ½* **Tipperary All Star (FR)**[13] 5676 4-9-5 106.................................... TPO'Shea 11 98
(MHalford, Ire) *trckd ldrs in 3rd: 5th and rdn early st: no ex 1 1/2f out* **16/1**

**9** *4 ½* **Cold Cold Woman**[21] 5486 3-8-11 92.................................... FMBerry 3 87
(JohnMOxx, Ire) *trckd ldrs: 7th appr 1/2-way: no imp st* **16/1**

**10** *¾* **Tropical Lady (IRE)**[13] 5679 4-9-9 110.................................... KJManning 8 92
(JSBolger, Ire) *rr of mid-div: 8th and effrt under 2f out: sn no ex* **8/1**

**11** *1 ½* **Tolpuddle (IRE)**[13] 5676 4-9-9 108.................................... WMLordan 14 90
(TStack, Ire) *trckd ldrs in 4th: rdn ent st: wknd fr 2f out* **3/1**[1]

**12** *5* **Blue Reema (IRE)**[13] 5679 4-9-2 95....................................(tp) JMO'Dwyer 1 74
(MHalford, Ire) *nvr a factor* **33/1**

**13** *13* **Blue Corrig (IRE)**[14] 5662 4-9-5 96....................................(b) MCHussey 10 53
(JosephCrowley, Ire) *s.i.s and a bhd: trailing st* **25/1**

**14** *3 ½* **Bella Estella (GER)**[167] 3-8-11 .................................... DPMcDonogh 6 44
(FFlood, Ire) *a bhd: trailing st* **50/1**

2m 11.4s **Going Correction** +0.525s/f (Yiel)
**WFA** 3 from 4yo+ 5lb **14** Ran SP% **135.8**
Speed ratings: **113,111,110,107,106 106,106,106,106,106 106,106,106,106**CSF £20.41 TOTE £6.10: £2.40, £2.40, £2.50; DF 64.60.
**Owner** Mrs John Magnier **Bred** Gerald W Leigh **Trained** Ballydoyle, Co Tipperary

**NOTEBOOK**
**Mikado**, third in the Ebor and fifth in the St Leger, appreciated the drop in class to take this. He was given a positive ride over this shorter distance and outstayed his rivals. He should do even better as a four-year-old.
**Ecomium(IRE)** had not been seen since making a winning debut at Newmarket in April despite a number of good entries. He ran with plenty of credit on this step up in grade and, like the winner, is likely to be a decent horse next season.
**Mingun(USA)**, whose winning sequence came to an end in the 2003 Juddmonte International, had not been seen since. In the circumstances ran a fair race and may yet fulfil his potential.

5963 - 5964a (Foreign Racing) - See Raceform Interactive

# 5666 LONGCHAMP (R-H)
## Saturday, October 2

**OFFICIAL GOING: Good**
The going appeared to be riding much faster than the official description.

## 5965a PRIX CHAUDENAY CASINO BARRIERE DE MENTON (GROUP 2) 1m 7f
**1:15** (1:15) 3-Y-O **£42,148** (£16,268; £7,764; £5,176)

RPR
1 **Reefscape**[23] 5433 3-9-2 TGillet 2 118
(AFabre, France) *broke well, settled 5th on inside, closed up 4f out, 3rd straight, quickened to lead 150y out, ridden out* 3
2 *2* **Lord Du Sud (FR)**[20] 5500 3-9-2 IMendizabal 3 117+
(J-CRouget, France) *held up early, went 2nd over 7f out, led 2f out to 150 yards out, one pace* 1
3 *5* **Percussionist (IRE)**[14] 5629 3-9-2 LDettori 1 110
(JHMGosden) *first to show, settled in 4th, close 5th straight on outside, stayed on at one pace final 2f* 2
4 *1* **Orpington**[26] 5357 3-9-2 PJSmullen 7 108
(DKWeld, Ire) *held up in 6th, kept on under pressure from over 1f out, never near to challenge*
5 *3* **Prairie Flower (IRE)**[23] 5433 3-8-13 OPeslier 4 102
(ELellouche, France) *led after 1f, headed 2f out, soon weakened*
6 *2 1/2* **Kensington (GER)**[23] 5433 3-9-2 (b) DBonilla 5 102
(AJunk, France) *held up in rear, last straight, never a factor*
7 *2* **Etendard Indien (FR)**[23] 5433 3-9-2 CSoumillon 6 99
(AFabre, France) *tracked leader to over 7f out, 4th straight, weakened well over 1f out* 2

3m 8.10s **Going Correction** -0.20s/f (Firm) 7 Ran SP% **120.4**
Speed ratings: **112,110,108,107,106 104,103.**
**Owner** K Abdulla **Bred** Juddmonte Farms **Trained** France

**NOTEBOOK**
**Reefscape**, given a patient ride, he ultimately won with plenty in hand. A fast ground specialist, he may now head for the Prix Royal-Oak at the end of the month.
**Lord Du Sud(FR)** moved smoothly to the head of affairs and looked the winner halfway up the straight, but he was unable to quicken like the winner and is much more effective on softer ground.
**Percussionist(IRE)** made a forward move at the bottom of the hill, but was outpaced early in the straight and could only run on at the one pace. He is another better suited by a soft surface.
**Orpington** was putting in his best work as the race came to an end. He now heads for the Tote Cesarewitch, in which he must go well off his low weight.

## 5966a PRIX DE ROYALLIEU HOTEL DU GOLF BARRIERE (GROUP 2) (F&M) 1m 4f 110y
**2:20** (2:21) 3-Y-O+ **£42,148** (£16,268; £7,764; £5,176)

RPR
1 **Samando (FR)**[19] 5533 4-9-1 SPasquier 8 111
(FDoumen, France) *held up in touch, disputing 5th straight, pushed along and headway over 2f out, led over 1 1/2f out, headed briefly inside*
2 *snk* **Russian Hill**[19] 5533 4-9-1 TGillet 5 111
(AFabre, France) *held up, disputing 8th straight, shaken up 2f out, driven to chase leaders 1 1/2f out, led briefly inside final f, ran on*
3 *1 1/2* **Behkara (IRE)**[41] 4983 4-9-1 CSoumillon 7 109
(ADeRoyer-Dupre, France) *held up, disputing 8th straight, shaken up 2f out, driven to chase leaders 1 1/2f out, ran on to take 3rd inside final f* 1
4 *3/4* **Diamond Tango (FR)**[20] 5501 3-8-7 OPeslier 9 107
(AFabre, France) *prominent, 3rd straight, pushed along 2f out, pressing leader 1 1/2f out, ridden and no extra final f* 2
5 *shd* **Reverie Solitaire (IRE)**[19] 5533 3-8-7 MBlancpain 10 107
(CLaffon-Parias, France) *held up, last straight, stayed on final stages but never dangerous*
6 *1* **Australie (IRE)**[40] 3-8-7 TJarnet 3 106
(RGibson, France) *held up, 10th straight, never a factor*
7 *1 1/2* **Royal Fantasy (GER)**[20] 5501 4-9-1 EBotti 6 104
(HSteinmetz, Germany) *prominent early, disputing 5th straight, one pace from 1 1/2f out* 3
8 *2 1/2* **Anabaa Republic (FR)**[20] 5501 3-8-7 ELegrix 1 100
(FDoumen, France) *in touch, 4th straight, pushed along 2f out, unable to quicken*
9 *nk* **Queen Astrid (IRE)**[34] 5162 4-9-1 PJSmullen 4 99
(DKWeld, Ire) *led, pushed along entering straight, headed 2f out, weakened steadily*
10 *1 1/2* **Buoyant (IRE)**[27] 5331 3-8-7 DBonilla 2 97
(FHead, France) *in touch, disputing 5th straight, weakened over 1f out*
11 **Echoes In Eternity (IRE)**[24] 5394 4-9-8 LDettori 11 104
(SaeedBinSuroor) *soon prominent, 2nd straight, ran on to lead briefly 2f out to over 1 1/2f out, soon ridden and weakened* 2

2m 39.4s
**WFA** 3 from 4yo 7lb 11 Ran SP% **125.2**
Speed ratings: .
**Owner** H Wirth **Bred** Barry Root **Trained** France

**NOTEBOOK**
**Samando(FR)** was brought with a perfectly timed late run and stayed on bravely in the dying stages. A consistent filly, she has blossomed at exactly the right time and could now go for the E P Taylor Stakes in Canada.
**Russian Hill** looked the likely winner inside the final furlong but was just run out of things in the final stages. She would have preferred a faster early pace.
**Behkara(IRE)**, who won at this meeting last year, was one paced throughout the final furlong, but this outing will put her spot on for the Royal-Oak, in which she was third in 2003.
**Diamond Tango(FR)**, heavily backed, looked dangerous one and a half out but did not go through with her effort and may not have been suited by the fastish surface.
**Echoes In Eternity(IRE)** gradually dropped out of contention to finish last. This was a disappointing effort, but it may simply have been one race too many.

## 5967a PRIX DANIEL WILDENSTEIN CASINO BARRIERE LA ROCHELLE (GROUP 2) 1m
**2:50** (2:53) 3-Y-O+ **£42,148** (£16,268; £7,764; £5,176)

RPR
1 **Cacique (IRE)**[46] 4834 3-8-12 CSoumillon 9 117
(AFabre, France) *held up, 8th straight, headway on outside 2f out, led distance, ran on well* 1
2 *1/2* **Hurricane Alan (IRE)**[35] 5113 4-9-3 LDettori 1 118
(RHannon) *held up on inside, 6th straight, headway on rails over 2f out, led 1 1/2f out to distance, kept on steadily*
3 *hd* **Mister Sacha (FR)**[34] 5169 3-8-12 IMendizabal 6 115
(J-CRouget, France) *held up, 9th straight, tracked winner from 2f out, stayed on under pressure final f, just missed 2nd* 3
4 *1 1/2* **Asti (IRE)**[24] 5405 3-8-8 OPeslier 3 108
(ELellouche, France) *always close up, 3rd straight, stayed on at same pace final 2f*
5 *hd* **Keltos (FR)**[14] 5668 6-9-1 MBlancpain 7 111+
(CLaffon-Parias, France) *held up, 7th straight, ran on final f, nearest finish*
6 *nse* **Grandes Illusions (FR)**[34] 5169 3-8-8 DBoeuf 10 107?
(DSmaga, France) *held up in rear, 10th straight, headway on outside from 2f out, nearest at finish*
7 *snk* **Polar Bear**[44] 4889 4-9-1 PJSmullen 4 111
(WJHaggas) *held up in rear, last straight, headway on inside from 2f out, kept on but never reached challenging position*
8 *1 1/2* **My Risk (FR)**[48] 4795 5-9-1 C-PLemaire 8 108
(J-MBeguigne, France) *closed up before halfway, 5th straight, every chance well over 1f out, one pace* 2
9 *1* **Baqah (IRE)**[48] 4795 3-8-10 DBonilla 11 103
(FHead, France) *rushed up to press leader after 1f, settled in 2nd, every chance 1 1/2f out, soon weakened*
10 *6* **Hovman (DEN)**[20] 5504 5-9-1 MLarsen 2 91
(MsCErichsen, Norway) *led to 1 1/2f out*
11 **Eclipse West (ARG)**[130] 5-9-3 TJarnet 5 —
(RGibson, France) *4th straight, soon weakened*

1m 37.5s **Going Correction** -0.20s/f (Firm)
**WFA** 3 from 4yo+ 3lb 11 Ran SP% **126.8**
Speed ratings: **112,111,111,109,109 109,109,107,106,100 100.**
**Owner** K Abdulla **Bred** Juddmonte Farms **Trained** France

**NOTEBOOK**
**Cacique(IRE)**, back to his best distance and on his favourite ground, was produced at exactly the right moment and won in a resolute manner. The Breeders' Cup Mile is now on the cards.
**Hurricane Alan(IRE)** put up another game display. He still had plenty to do at the bottom of the hill, but slipped through on the far rail and battled well to the line to take second.
**Mister Sacha(FR)** looked extremely dangerous when making his challenge up the centre of the track but, despite sticking to his task, he lost second place with a few yards left to run. He stays in training and will continue to be raced over this distance, or even slightly shorter.
**Asti(IRE)** did not have the best of luck at the entrance to the straight, but made up late ground.
**Keltos(FR)** ◆ got no luck in running and hardly came off the bridle as a result. He should have finished much closer.
**Polar Bear** had plenty to do at the entrance to the straight and made some late progress up the far rail. His jockey felt the firm ground was not in his favour.

## 5968a PRIX DOLLAR CASINO BARRIERE DE MONTREUX (GROUP 2) 1m 1f 165y
**3:20** (3:23) 3-Y-O+ **£42,148** (£16,268; £7,764; £5,176)

RPR
1 **Touch Of Land (FR)**[21] 5489 4-9-4 C-PLemaire 3 122
(H-APantall, France) *held up, 10th straight, progress on outside over 1 1/2f out, ridden to challenge over 1f out, led inside final f, driven ou*
2 *nk* **Gateman**[35] 5134 7-9-0 TJarnet 4 117
(MJohnston) *close up, disputing 2nd straight, ridden to lead 1 1/2f out, headed inside final f, ran on* 2
3 *1* **Special Kaldoun (IRE)**[11] 5727 5-9-0 DBoeuf 1 115
(DSmaga, France) *midfield, 6th on inside straight, headway over 2f out, driven and every chance 1f out, kept on* 2
4 *1* **Valentino (FR)**[26] 5361 5-9-0 IMendizabal 11 113
(ADeRoyer-Dupre, France) *held up in last, went 4th inside final f, nearest finish*
5 *2 1/2* **Shakis (IRE)**[15] 4-9-0 TGillet 2 108
(JEHammond, France) *held up, disputing 6th straight, driven and stayed on at same pace closing stages*
6 *2* **Simple Exchange (IRE)**[49] 4769 3-9-0 PJSmullen 5 110
(DKWeld, Ire) *always midfield, never a threat* 3
7 *1/2* **Sights On Gold (IRE)**[15] 5611 5-9-0 LDettori 7 104
(SaeedBinSuroor) *in touch, disputing 4th straight, kept on until weakened inside final f* 1
8 *3/4* **Kindjhal (FR)**[34] 5170 4-9-0 SPasquier 10 102
(ELellouche, France) *midfield, lost place entering straight, never a factor*
9 *1 1/2* **Weightless**[181] 1261 4-9-0 TThulliez 6 99
(PBary, France) *led, pressed 2f out, headed 1 1/2f out, no extra* 3
10 *3/4* **Binary File (USA)**[11] 5727 6-9-0 ELegrix 8 98
(SJensen, Denmark) *midfield, never dangerous*
11 *6* **Morning Eclipse**[26] 5361 4-9-0 OPeslier 9 87
(MmeCHead-Maarek, France) *prominent, disputing 2nd straight, shaken up 2f out, soon weakened*
12 *nk* **Maxwell (FR)**[13] 4-9-0 CSoumillon 12 86
(MmeCHead-Maarek, France) *prominent, disputing 4th straight, beaten over 1 1/2f out*

1m 58.3s **Going Correction** -0.20s/f (Firm)
**WFA** 3 from 4yo+ 5lb 12 Ran SP% **125.7**
Speed ratings: **117,116,115,115,113 111,111,110,109,108 103,103.**
**Owner** Gary A Tanaka **Bred** Unknown **Trained** France

**NOTEBOOK**
**Touch Of Land(FR)**, giving weight to the rest of the field and racing for the first time since a trip to Turkey, posted an excellent performance. He had plenty to do when entering the straight, but was brought with a perfectly timed late run. Apparently he does not travel that well but connections are now looking at the Hong Kong Cup.
**Gateman** ran yet another extremely game race. He looked the likely winner a furlong out but was caught with 50 metres left to run. He may well be allowed to take his chance in the Champion Stakes before going for a Group One in Italy.
**Special Kaldoun(IRE)** was held up for a late challenge as usual and came to attack the winner at the furlong marker, but he did not run on in his usual manner on ground faster than ideal.
**Valentino(FR)** had plenty to do entering the straight and never really threatened the first three.

**Sights On Gold(IRE)** had his chance but began to fade from a furlong and a half out. His rider reported afterwards that he choked.

## 5969a PRIX CHARLES LAFFITTE HERMITAGE BARRIERE (LISTED) (FILLIES) 1m 2f
**3:50** (3:53) 3-Y-O **£15,845** (£6,338; £4,754; £3,169)

RPR
1 **Flip Flop (FR)**[27] 5331 3-8-12 ............ C-PLemaire 11 100
(DProd'Homme, France)
2 ¾ **Miss France (FR)**[27] 5331 3-9-2 ............ SPasquier 1 102
(ELellouche, France)
3 *snk* **Bright Abundance (USA)**[44] 4899 3-8-12 ............ MBlancpain 5 98
(CLaffon-Parias, France)
4 *nk* **Cattiva Generosa**[62] 4383 3-9-2 ............ TJarnet 8 101
(RGibson, France)
5 *1* **Sandbox (IRE)**[27] 5331 3-8-12 ............ TThulliez 9 96
(PBary, France)
6 *2* **October Moon (FR)**[26] 3-8-12 ............ DBoeuf 2 92
(MlleHVanZuylen, France)
7 *nk* **Iles Marquises (IRE)**[100] 3258 3-8-12 ............ CSoumillon 4 92
(AFabre, France)
8 *½* **Mainly Monroe (IRE)** 3-9-2 ............ DBonilla 7 95
(TSatra, Czech Republic)
9 *2* **Blue Oasis (IRE)**[34] 5162 3-8-12 ............ PJSmullen 3 87
(RGuest) *held up in midfield, 7th straight, kept on at one pace*
10 *3* **Colony Band (USA)**[111] 2925 3-9-2 ............ OPeslier 10 86
(MmeCHead-Maarek, France)
P **Glen Innes (IRE)**[120] 2641 3-9-2 ............ LDettori 6 —
(DRLoder) *led after 2f, headed over 3f out, 3rd straight, soon weakened, pulled up in final f*

2m 4.50s **Going Correction** -0.20s/f (Firm) **11 Ran**
Speed ratings: **106,105,105,105,104 102,102,102,100,98** —.
**Owner** P Barbe **Bred** T Watanabe **Trained** France

**NOTEBOOK**
**Blue Oasis(IRE)** never looked dangerous.
**Glen Innes(IRE)** tried to go from pillar to post but was soon in trouble at the entrance to the straight and completely dropped out of contention.

# 5576 SAN SIRO (R-H)
Saturday, October 2
**OFFICIAL GOING: Good to firm**

## 5970a PREMIO FEDERICO TESIO (GROUP 3) 1m 3f
**3:50** (4:00) 4-Y-O+ **£38,250** (£20,272; £10,885; £5,443)

RPR
1 **Without Connexion (IRE)**[107] 3030 5-8-12 ............ DVargiu 2 113
(PBary, France) *held up in midfield, 5th straight, headway over 2f out, led 1 1/2f out, ran on well*
2 *2½* **Serenus (GER)**[36] 6-8-12 ............ MTellini 7 109
(GKussatz, Germany) *set strong pace, headed 1 1/2f out, kept on same pace*
3 *4* **One Little David (GER)** 4-8-12 ............ WMongil 3 103
(HSteinmetz, Germany) *pressed leader early, settled in 2nd, every chance 1 1/2f out, one pace*
4 *¾* **Solista**[496] 1857 4-8-12 ............ SMulas 9 101
(BGrizzetti, Italy) *held up, last straight, headway final 2f, never near to challenge*
5 *nk* **Nordhal**[685] 5740 5-8-12 ............ MDemuro 6 101
(BGrizzetti, Italy) *7th straight, one pace final 3f*
6 *1¾* **Landinium (ITY)**[104] 3137 5-8-9 ............ CColombi 1 95
(VValiani, Italy) *held up, 8th straight, always behind*
7 *9* **Fielding (IRE)**[125] 2509 4-8-12 ............ GTemperini 4 84
(RBrogi, Italy) *raced in 3rd, weakened over 2f out*
8 *1½* **Monetary (GER)**[205] 1002 4-8-8 ............ MMonteriso 5 77
(ECharpy, UAE) *6th straight, behind final 2f*
9 *1¼* **Prince Troy (GER)**[496] 1856 5-9-1 ............ IRossi 8 82
(WernerGlanz, Germany) *prominent, 4th straight, soon weakened*

2m 14.8s **9 Ran**
Speed ratings: .
**Owner** Wattlefield Hall Stud **Bred** Niarchos Family **Trained** France

**NOTEBOOK**
**Without Connexion(IRE)**, whose runs in France have mainly been with cut in the ground, had gained his only previous Pattern win on fast, and this ground seemed to suit him as he won decisively.
**Serenus(GER)**, third in this last season, went one place better. He made the running and burnt off the rest but was not able to trouble the winner in the closing stages.

# 5598 TIPPERARY
Sunday, October 3
**OFFICIAL GOING: Heavy**

## 5971a DANEHILL DANCER TIPPERARY STKS (LISTED) 5f
**2:15** (2:16) 2-Y-O **£27,507** (£8,070; £3,845; £1,309)

RPR
1 **Kay Two (IRE)**[45] 4895 2-9-0 99............ DPMcDonogh 6 99
(MsFMCrowley, Ire) *a.p: 2nd and rdn 2f out: led over 1f out: clr ins fnl f: comf* **3/1**[1]
2 *2* **Tournedos (IRE)**[14] 5681 2-9-7 ............ SHitchcott 4 99
(MRChannon) *chsd ldrs: 3rd 2f out: kpt on u.p to go 2nd wl ins fnl f* **4/1**[2]
3 *hd* **Dancing Duchess (IRE)**[17] 5600 2-8-11 81............ CO'Donoghue 5 88
(OwenWeldon, Ire) *chsd ldrs: 4th 2f out: kpt on u.p ins fnl f* **6/1**
4 *1½* **Rare Cross (IRE)**[77] 3965 2-8-11 90............ JAHeffernan 3 83
(JosephGMurphy, Ire) *led: rdn and hdd over 1f out: no ex ins fnl f* **10/1**
5 *2* **Nebraska Lady (IRE)**[36] 5137 2-8-11 ............ NGMcCullagh 2 76
(PatrickMartin, Ire) *chsd ldrs: 5th after 1/2-way: no imp fr 1 1/2f out* **11/2**
6 *2* **Monashee Rose (IRE)**[6] 5839 2-8-11 ............ EAhern 1 69
(JSMoore) *chsd ldrs: 5th appr 1/2-way: no ex fr 2f out* **14/1**
7 *1½* **Tamworth (IRE)**[14] 5675 2-9-0 ............ PShanahan 7 67
(KJCondon, Ire) *s.i.s: nvr a factor* **33/1**
8 *nk* **Fairest Cape (USA)** 2-8-11 ............(t) PCosgrave 8 62
(APO'Brien, Ire) *in tch on stands side: wknd fr 2f out* **5/1**[3]
9 *13* **Kurkova (IRE)**[15] 5659 2-8-11 ............ MCHussey 9 17
(TARegan, Ire) *s.i.s: nvr a factor* **50/1**

63.40 secs **9 Ran SP% 112.0**
Speed ratings: CSF £14.25 TOTE £3.20: £1.10, £1.70, £1.50; DF 8.70.
**Owner** Hugh B McGahon **Bred** Roger A Ryan **Trained** Curragh, Co Kildare

**NOTEBOOK**
**Kay Two(IRE)** showed he handles soft ground when a course and distance winner on his previous outing, and gained his first Pattern success in good style. He looks progressive under these conditions.
**Tournedos(IRE)** has been busy travelling since winning the Molecomb, paying his second visit to Ireland along with trips to Deauville and Baden-Baden. He is quite versatile with regard to trip and ground, and may pick up a similar contest before the season is out.
**Dancing Duchess(IRE)**, who won a course and distance nursery on soft ground off a mark of 74 on her previous outing, was 7lb higher here and although she may be improving, tends to hold the form down.

## 5972a COOLMORE HOME OF CHAMPIONS CONCORDE STKS (GROUP 3) 7f 100y
**3:15** (3:16) 3-Y-O+ **£36,619** (£10,704; £5,070; £1,690)

RPR
1 **Hamairi (IRE)**[49] 4786 3-8-12 109............ TPO'Shea 9 111
(JohnMOxx, Ire) *trckd ldrs: 3rd 1/2-way: 2nd early st: rdn to over ld 1f out: styd on wl* **7/2**[1]
2 *2½* **Fearn Royal (IRE)**[9] 5776 5-8-11 98............ CO'Donoghue 1 102
(PeterCasey, Ire) *trckd ldrs: 6th into st: 5th and rdn over 1 1/2f out: 3rd 1f out: styd on wl* **12/1**
3 *½* **Poetical (IRE)**[24] 5416 3-8-9 98............ NGMcCullagh 6 101
(MJGrassick, Ire) *attempted to make all: edgd clr early st: hdd over 1f out: sn no ex* **14/1**
4 *3* **Dangle (IRE)**[15] 5661 3-8-9 101............ EAhern 5 94
(EdwardLynam, Ire) *prom: 4th 1/2-way: rdn and one pced st* **12/1**
5 *3* **Millennium Force**[8] 5781 6-9-0 ............ SHitchcott 3 90
(MRChannon) *hld up: prog after 1/2-way: 6th 1 1/2f out: kpt on same pce* **13/2**
6 *2* **Megec Blis (IRE)**[26] 5386 3-8-9 96............ WMLordan 7 83
(DKWeld, Ire) *settled 2nd: rdn ent st: sn wknd* **12/1**
7 *11* **One More Round (USA)**[62] 4405 6-9-0 107............ PShanahan 12 60
(DKWeld, Ire) *hld up in tch: 7th 1/2-way: no imp st* **8/1**
8 *1½* **Newton (IRE)**[15] 5661 3-8-12 106............ PCosgrave 8 57
(APO'Brien, Ire) *towards rr: no imp st* **12/1**
9 *1½* **Abunawwas (IRE)**[77] 3967 4-9-0 109............ DPMcDonogh 4 54
(KevinPrendergast, Ire) *chsd ldrs: 5th 1/2-way: rdn and wknd early st* **5/1**[2]
10 *2½* **Desert Fantasy (IRE)**[43] 4956 5-9-0 108............(bt) JAHeffernan 10 48
(CRoche, Ire) *a bhd* **6/1**[3]
11 *3* **Queen Of Palms (IRE)**[14] 5676 3-8-9 102............ MCHussey 2 38
(KevinPrendergast, Ire) *s.i.s: hld up in tch: impr into 7th ent st: sn rdn and wknd* **8/1**
12 *14* **Jemmy's Brother (IRE)**[171] 1431 3-8-12 92............ CatherineGannon 11 9
(GMLyons, Ire) *nvr a factor: wknd bef st* **25/1**

1m 43.5s
**WFA** 3 from 4yo+ 2lb **12 Ran SP% 130.0**
Speed ratings: CSF £52.78 TOTE £4.00: £1.60, £4.30, £5.60; DF 43.70.
**Owner** H H Aga Khan **Bred** H H Aga Khan's Stud Sc **Trained** Currabeg, Co Kildare

**NOTEBOOK**
**Hamairi(IRE)**, runner up in similar races on fast ground on his two previous outings, has previously shown ability to handle the track and soft going and took his first Group race in good fashion. He is progressive and looks capable of making up into a classy performer if kept in training next season.
**Fearn Royal(IRE)**, a proven soft-ground performer, has now been runner-up in four of his last six races and is entitled to win one, although his consistency does not help his rating.
**Poetical(IRE)**, stepping up in grade and tackling testing ground for the first time, made a bold bid to lead throughout but ultimately was not good enough.
**Millennium Force** who is best with cut in the ground, may have found these conditions a little too testing. He is now on a losing run stretching back 18 months, although much of the ability is still there.
**Abunawwas(IRE)** *Official explanation: jockey said colt did not handle the ground*

5973 - (Foreign Racing) - See Raceform Interactive

# 3134 DORTMUND (R-H)
Sunday, October 3
**OFFICIAL GOING: Good**

## 5974a GROSSER PREIS DER DORTMUNDER STADTWERKE - DEUTSCHES ST.LEGER (GROUP 2) 1m 6f
**4:05** (4:08) 3-Y-O **£43,662** (£17,606; £8,803; £3,873)

RPR
1 **Darsalam (IRE)**[7] 5824 3-9-2 ............ FilipMinarik 6 —
(AShavuyev, Czech Republic) *chased leader to straight, led 2f out, headed inside final f, rallied to regain lead close home* 2
2 *nk* **Sword Roche (GER)**[119] 2723 3-8-12 ............ J-PCarvalho 3 —
(MarioHofer, Germany) *held up in rear, last straight, rapid headway to lead inside final furlong, headed close home*
3 *2* **Fiepes Winged (GER)** 3-9-2 ............(b) WMongil 5 —
(MarioHofer, Germany) *led til headed 2f out, kept on same pace*
4 *nse* **Quartier Latin (USA)** 3-9-2 ............ AStarke 1 —
(ASchutz, Germany) *held up, 6th straight, stayed on final 2f, just missed 3rd* 3
5 *2½* **Thanksgiving (GER)** 3-8-12 ............ AGoritz 2 —
(PRau, Germany) *raced in midfield, 4th straight, one pace final 2f*
6 *1¼* **Luttis Champ (GER)**[78] 3-9-2 ............ JBojko 7 —
(HSteinmetz, Germany) *raced in 3rd to straight, no extra from 2f out* 3
7 *19* **Absolut Power (GER)**[63] 4377 3-9-2 ............ EPedroza 4 —
(AWohler, Germany) *raced in 4th til weakening 3f out, tailed off* 1

3m 4.01s **7 Ran SP% 132.9**
Speed ratings: .
**Owner** Turan Stables **Bred** Liscannor Stud Ltd **Trained** The Czech Republic

**NOTEBOOK**
**Darsalam(IRE)**, winner of the Czech Derby and St Leger earlier in the season, has since run well in the Doncaster St Leger and the all-aged Preis Von Europa. He gained a deserved success in this Group Two, and showed courage to get back in front after looking sure to be beaten. He has a good attitude which should help him win more good races.

## [4596] HOPPEGARTEN (R-H)

Sunday, October 3

**OFFICIAL GOING: Good**

### 5975a VOLKSWAGEN-PREIS DER DEUTSCHEN EINHEIT (GROUP 3) 1m 2f

**3:40** (3:42) 3-Y-0+ **£22,535** (£6,866; £6,866; £2,465)

RPR

1 **Omikron (IRE)**[28] 5329 3-8-12 ........ MartinDwyer 2 113
(MarioHofer, Germany) *always in touch, 4th straight, quickened to lead 2f out, held on well* 1

2 ¾ **Anna Victoria (GER)**[27] 5361 4-9-0 ........ DVSmith 5 109
(GSybrecht, Germany) *held up, 6th straight, ran on strongly from 2f out to dispute 2nd approaching final f, kept on*

2 *dht* **Salonhonor (GER)**[35] 5168 3-8-12 ........ IFerguson 9 112
(AndreasLowe, Germany) *always prominent, 3rd straight, went 2nd 2f out, joined by Anna Victoria approaching final f, kept on*

4 3 ½ **Fruhlingssturm**[36] 5134 4-9-4 ........ MO'Reilly 7 107
(MAJarvis) *held up, 5th straight, one pace final 2f* 2

5 ½ **Rajpute (GER)**[37] 4-9-4 ........ LHammer-Hansen 1 106
(DrABolte, Germany) *last to straight, some late headway, nearest at finish*

6 *nk* **Sweet Wake (GER)**[35] 5168 3-8-12 ........ NRichter 4 104
(MarioHofer, Germany) *mid-division, 6th straight, one pace* 3

7 2 **Near Honor (GER)**[14] 5683 6-9-4 ........ WPanov 8 102
(PVovcenko, Germany) *chased leader to straight, weakened quickly from 2f out*

8 2 ½ **Tofastforyou** 7-9-4 ........ SaraSlot 3 97
(GSjolin, Sweden) *midfield til weakening from 3f out*

9 2 **Mariella (GER)**[42] 4980 3-8-7 ........ PRoberts 6 88
(CVonDerRecke, Germany) *set good pace, headed 2f out, weakened quickly*

2m 5.00s
**WFA** 3 from 4yo+ 5lb **9** Ran SP% **128.9**
Speed ratings: .
**Owner** Stall Jenny **Bred** Gestut Wittekindshof **Trained** Germany

**NOTEBOOK**

**Fruhlingssturm** raced in midfield and, when the first three kicked for home two furlongs out, was unable to go with them.

## [5965] LONGCHAMP (R-H)

Sunday, October 3

**OFFICIAL GOING: Good**

The going appeared to be riding much faster than the official description.

### 5976a PRIX DU CADRAN CASINO LES PRINCES BARRIERE DE CANNES (GROUP 1) 2m 4f

**1:15** (1:17) 4-Y-0+ **£80,479** (£32,197; £16,099; £8,042)

RPR

1 **Westerner**[21] 5503 5-9-2 ........ OPeslier 3 117+
(ELellouche, France) *prominent, 3rd half-way, 2nd and challenged straight, led over 2f out, pushed clear over 1 1/2f out, easily* **8/13**[1]

2 3 **Cut Quartz (FR)**[21] 5503 7-9-2 ........ TJarnet 5 114
(RGibson, France) *held up, disputing 4th straight, headway over 1 1/2f out, ridden and stayed on to take 2nd from over 1f out* **12/1**

3 1 **Le Carre (USA)**[21] 5503 6-9-2 ........ IMendizabal 7 113
(ADeRoyer-Dupre, France) *in touch, pushed along and disputing 4th on outside straight, ridden & ran on steadily to take 3rd from over 1 1/2f out* **40/1**

4 2 **Dancing Bay**[24] 5415 7-9-2 ........ KFallon 6 111
(NJHenderson) *held up, disputing 4th straight, stayed on final stages but never a threat* **7/1**[3]

5 3 **Holy Orders (IRE)**[42] 4977 7-9-2 ........(b) DJCondon 2 108
(WPMullins, Ire) *held up in last, never threatened* **25/1**

6 2 ½ **Darasim (IRE)**[24] 5415 6-9-2 ........(v) KDarley 1 106
(MJohnston) *pushed along to race in close 2nd, led over 3f out to over 2f out, no extra once headed* **7/2**[2]

7 10 **Anak Pekan**[66] 4270 4-9-2 ........ PRobinson 8 96
(MAJarvis) *led to over 3f out, 3rd and weakening straight* **20/1**

8 10 **Clear Thinking**[21] 5503 4-9-2 ........ CSoumillon 4 86
(AFabre, France) *reluctant to load, held up in touch, disputing 4th straight, effort and soon weakened from over 2f out* **25/1**

4m 19.8s **8** Ran SP% **119.2**
Speed ratings: .
**Owner** Ecurie Wildenstein **Bred** Dayton Investments Ltd **Trained** France

**FOCUS**

Not a vintage renewal of this prestigious race, but Westerner had little trouble following up last year's win despite conditions being vastly different.

**NOTEBOOK**

**Westerner**, arguably the top stayer in Europe, travelled like a dream throughout and totally outclassed the opposition. After racing behind the leading group for much of the race, he quickened like a top-class horse when asked to go on and will now try and land back-to-back victories in the Prix Royal-Oak. He will be trained for the Gold Cup at York next year and even at this early stage, is the one to beat. Significantly, his last two wins have both been gained without removing his earplugs.

**Cut Quartz(FR)** came through to launch his challenge a furlong and a half out and ran on well to take second place without ever looking likely to reach the winner. Considering he is a soft ground horse, this was a decent effort and the Royal-Oak could be in his programme.

**Le Carre(USA)** was being ridden rounding the final turn and, although staying on gamely, he could only find the one pace. He is another who prefers cut and given his odds, this was a smart effort.

**Dancing Bay** has been running well in Group Two company and ran on from two out to take fourth place late on. Another who could have done with softer ground, he will now go for the Jockey Club Cup.

**Holy Orders(IRE)**, a very inconsistent performer who is capable of top form on his day, kept on without ever getting involved and ran well.

**Darasim(IRE)** has now run below par the last twice and never looked happy - being pushed along to take a prominent early position - and did not put much of a fight up once asked for maximum effort. He might have fared better without Anak Pekan in the line-up, but he could probably do with a rest. He stays in training.

**Anak Pekan** was smartly away and soon in the lead, but his effort petered out early in the straight and he did not look happy on the firm ground. This was a big ask and he will be better off back down in grade.

### 5977a PRIX DE L'ABBAYE DE LONGCHAMP MAJESTIC BARRIERE (GROUP 1) 5f (S)

**1:55** (1:57) 2-Y-0+ **£80,479** (£32,197; £16,099; £8,042)

RPR

1 **Var (USA)**[15] 5647 5-9-11 ........(b) LDettori 13 121
(CEBrittain) *made all, ridden over 1 1/2f out, driven out* **8/1**[3]

2 ½ **The Tatling (IRE)**[8] 5780 7-9-11 ........ RLMoore 14 119
(JMBradley) *raced in 7th, headway on outside to go 2nd inside final f, ran on but not reach winner* **5/1**[2]

3 1 **Royal Millennium (IRE)**[15] 5661 6-9-11 ........ TEDurcan 4 115
(MRChannon) *towards rear early, headway on inside before halfway, switched right 1 1/2f out, ran on well final f to take 3rd last strid* **10/1**

4 *nk* **Osterhase (IRE)**[28] 5327 5-9-11 ........(b) FMBerry 8 114
(JEMulhern, Ire) *raced in 2nd on inside, joined for 2nd over 1 1/2f out, lost 2nd inside final f and 3rd last strides* **16/1**

5 1 ½ **Avonbridge**[45] 4886 4-9-11 ........(b) JFortune 9 109
(RCharlton) *always front rank, ridden to dispute 2nd over 1 1/2f out, one pace final f* **9/1**

6 *nse* **Orientor**[29] 5289 6-9-11 ........ JPMurtagh 5 109
(JSGoldie) *tracked Osterhase on inside in 4th or 5th, stayed on under pressure final 1 1/2f* **28/1**

7 ½ **Patavellian (IRE)**[29] 5289 6-9-11 ........(b) SDrowne 10 107
(RCharlton) *midfield, kept on final 2f but never near leaders* **7/2**[1]

8 *hd* **Ringmoor Down**[8] 5780 5-9-8 ........ TQuinn 6 103
(DWPArbuthnot) *towards rear early, headway when hampered before halfway, switched inside, stayed on from over 1f out* **12/1**

9 1 **Bahamian Pirate (USA)**[29] 5289 9-9-11 ........ SSanders 7 103
(DNicholls) *always midfield* **20/1**

10 *snk* **Continent**[15] 5628 7-9-11 ........ DHolland 2 102
(DNicholls) *in rear, headway when checked 1f out, r.o* **20/1**

11 2 ½ **Raffelberger (GER)**[32] 5255 3-9-11 ........ ASuborics 12 93
(MarioHofer, Germany) *speed 3f* **33/1**

12 1 ½ **Ratio**[8] 5780 6-9-11 ........(b) TGillet 11 88
(JEHammond, France) *s.i.s, always towards rear* **14/1**

13 *hd* **Lucky Strike**[32] 5255 6-9-11 ........ ADeVries 15 87
(ATrybuhl, Germany) *close up on outside early, weakened halfway* **33/1**

14 1 ½ **The Trader (IRE)**[29] 5289 6-9-11 ........(b) KFallon 1 82
(MBlanshard) *s.i.s, held up in last, always behind* **8/1**[3]

15 3 **Grand Reward (USA)**[15] 5661 3-9-11 ........(b) JPSpencer 3 71
(APO'Brien, Ire) *s.i.s, always in rear* **25/1**

55.00 secs **Going Correction** -0.40s/f (Firm) **15** Ran SP% **123.1**
Speed ratings: **117,116,114,114,111 111,110,110,108,108 104,102,101,99,94**.
**Owner** Mohammed Rashid **Bred** Dr John Eaton **Trained** Newmarket, Suffolk

**FOCUS**

A field largely made up of British runners and a race well up to its Group One status. A cracking effort from former American sprinter Var, who has created an excellent impression since joining Clive Brittain.

**NOTEBOOK**

**Var(USA)** landed an enormous gamble on the pari-mutuel, and did it in style. Quickly away from his wide draw, he made virtually every yard and when shaken up a furlong out he was always holding The Tatling. His ever popular trainer has done a fantastic job under difficult circumstances and the five-year-old is now expected to go for the Hong Kong Sprint. He faces a formidable opponent in Silent Witness, but fast ground will not be aa problem and his early pace and ability to see out his race well will stand him in good stead.

**The Tatling(IRE)**, who has proven course and distance form, started to surge from one and a half out but could not quite get to the winner. He has had a busy time recently and connections felt he would have preferred more cover, but he appreciated the firmish ground. He is an intended runner in Hong Kong again.

**Royal Millennium(IRE)** finished the race in great style, having been well in rear early, and just ran out of time. He is a versatile sort who deserves to win a decent race, probably back over a bit further.

**Osterhase(IRE)** has emerged as one of Ireland's leading sprinters this season and ran an excellent race in fourth. He broke well near the rail and showed bags of speed, then stuck to his task well without being able to hold off a couple of the finishers.

**Avonbridge**, very quickly into his stride, was up with the leaders early on but, like Osterhase, just could not fend off the late comers. This was a good effort.

**Orientor**, who would have ideally preferred some cut in the ground, got a nice tow through from Osterhase but was unable to pick up as well as he may have done had the ground been softer.

**Patavellian(IRE)** had much quicker conditions to contend with than when winning this in 2003 and failed to obtain a good early position. He simply failed to make the ground up quick enough, and this was a bit disappointing.

**Ringmoor Down** has really progressed this season and looked the type to run a big race but was badly interfered with about a furlong and a half out and had no chance to get back into the race in time. She kept on well, to her credit, and is better than the bare result.

**Bahamian Pirate(USA)**, a regular in this race, could have done with the ground being much softer and lacked the necessary pace to get competitive.

**Continent**, winner of this race back in 2002, had made a little progress by the halfway stage but was then blocked at the furlong marker before running on again. Another for whom the ground may have been too fast.

**Ratio** could have been expected to fare a little better and never made a move.

**The Trader(IRE)** has some classy form in France and was second here last year, but this time he ran a rare bad race. Slowly away, he never picked up any ground at all. This was nothing like his form.

**Grand Reward(USA)**, like The Trader, never went a yard and simply lacked the speed.

### 5978a PRIX DE L'OPERA CASINO BARRIERE D'ENGHIEN (GROUP 1) (FILLIES) 1m 2f

**2:30** (2:30) 3-Y-0+ **£100,599** (£40,246; £20,123; £10,053)

RPR

1 **Alexander Goldrun (IRE)**[99] 3331 3-8-12 ........ KJManning 3 118
(JSBolger, Ire) *held up, progress from over 2f out, pushed along to chase leaders 1 1/2f out, ran on to lead 100yds out, pushed out* **6/1**[2]

2 1 **Grey Lilas (IRE)**[28] 5332 3-8-12 ........ ELegrix 10 116
(AFabre, France) *prominent, 2nd straight, pushed along to lead 2f out, driven over 1f out, headed 100 yards out, no extra* **10/11**[1]

3 1 ½ **Walkamia (FR)**[27] 5361 4-9-2 ........ CSoumillon 7 112
(AFabre, France) *led after 1f, pushed along straight, headed 2f out, kept on* **14/1**

4 1 ½ **Yesterday (IRE)**[22] 5484 4-9-2 ........ JPSpencer 2 109
(APO'Brien, Ire) *held up in mid-division, pushed along 1 1/2f out, ridden and stayed on inside final furlong* **6/1**[2]

5 1 1/2 **Actrice (IRE)**[28] 5332 4-9-2 ........ OPeslier 4 106
(ELellouche, France) *held up, disputing 8th on outside straight, pushed along and headway over 1 1/2f out, no extra inside final furlong* **14/1**

6 hd **Whortleberry (FR)**[21] 5501 4-9-2 ........ C-PLemaire 1 106
(FRohaut, France) *led 1f, 3rd and pushed along straight, stayed on under pressure until no extra close home* **10/1**[3]

7 2 1/2 **Shapira (GER)**[147] 1983 3-8-12 ........ JPalik 5 106+
(AndreasLowe, Germany) *mid-division, 4th straight, weakened over 1f out* **20/1**

8 nk **Menhoubah (USA)**[46] 4859 3-8-12 ........ RLMoore 6 102
(CEBrittain) *mid-division, disputing 5th straight, soon pushed along, no impression* **50/1**

9 shd **Green Noon (FR)**[15] 5667 3-8-12 ........ SDrowne 8 101
(CLerner, France) *in touch, disputing 8th straight, soon ridden and outpaced* **33/1**

10 2 1/2 **Vallera (GER)**[21] 5501 3-8-12 ........ TGillet 9 97
(UOstmann, Germany) *held up, last straight, pushed along over 2f out, no impression* **12/1**

2m 2.30s **Going Correction** -0.225s/f (Firm)
**WFA** 3 from 4yo+ 5lb **10 Ran SP% 120.7**
Speed ratings: **114,113,112,110,109 109,107,107,107,105.**
**Owner** Mrs N O'Callaghan **Bred** Dermot Cantillon **Trained** Coolcullen, Co Carlow

**FOCUS**
A good renewal of this race that went the way of Irish-trained runner Alexander Goldrun, who came through to claim favourite Grey Lilas in the final half furlong.

**NOTEBOOK**
**Alexander Goldrun(IRE)** has shown herself to be a high-class filly this season, with her second to star filly Attraction in the Irish 1000 Guineas arguably being the highlight. This was a well deserved first win at this level, staying on strongly to reverse previous Chantilly form with the runner-up. She bided her time before making her challenge in the straight and ultimately ran out a very game winner. She could possibly go to Hollywood Park later in the year and probably stays in training.
**Grey Lilas(IRE)**, successful in Group One company last time when beating Diamond Green, was settled just behind the leaders and took the advantage halfway up the straight, but she was just unable to quicken like the winner. Possibly not suited by the fast ground, she may go for the Hong Kong Mile and she stays in training next year.
**Walkamia(FR)** stuck to her task to the bitter end on ground that might have been a little lively. This represented a step up on previous form.
**Yesterday(IRE)**, a high-class three-year-old, had been off with injury in the early part of the season and made her seasonal reappearance only last month. Slightly hampered turning into the straight, she ran on bravely as the race came to an end, without having the necessary pace. Despite being reported to have been training well, it is still possible she will come on again for this. Third in last seasons Breeders' Cup Filly & Mare Turf, it is not hard to see her going well again.
**Actrice(IRE)**, disappointing at the course last month behind Grey Lilas, ran a much better race this time and stepped up on previous form.
**Menhoubah(USA)** made little progress in the straight.
**Green Noon(FR)** has not gone on at all from her juvenile form and continues to run disappointingly.

## 5979a PRIX MARCEL BOUSSAC ROYAL BARRIERE DEAUVILLE (GROUP 1) (FILLIES) 1m
**3:05** (3:07) 2-Y-O **£100,599** (£40,246; £20,123; £10,053)

RPR

1 **Divine Proportions (USA)**[42] 4981 2-8-11 ........ C-PLemaire 4 114+
(PBary, France) *tracked leaders, disputing 2nd straight, pulled out and challenged approaching final f, led 1f out, ridden clear* **8/11**[1]

2 2 **Titian Time (USA)**[12] 5717 2-8-11 ........ JFortune 3 107
(JHMGosden) *led, pushed along and ran on over 2f out, ridden and stayed on gamely under pressure to line, just held 2nd* **25/1**

3 nse **Fraloga (IRE)**[25] 2-8-11 ........ CSoumillon 10 107
(AFabre, France) *prominent, disputing 2nd straight, driven over 2f out, ran on from over 1f out, just missed 2nd* **10/1**

4 1/2 **Intrigued**[25] 5398 2-8-11 ........ SSanders 7 106
(SirMarkPrescott) *towards rear, disputing 6th on inside straight, outpaced over 1 1/2f out, ridden & stayed on final f to take 4th* **9/1**[3]

5 snk **Portrayal (USA)**[20] 5532 2-8-11 ........ OPeslier 9 106
(AFabre, France) *went right leaving stalls but soon racing in touch, disputing 6th straight, ran on at one pace to line but never troubled l* **18/1**

6 nk **Queen Of Poland**[24] 5413 2-8-11 ........ LDettori 1 105
(DRLoder) *held up in touch, disputing 4th straight, ridden and under pressure 2f out, stayed on at one pace* **5/1**[2]

7 snk **Gorella (FR)**[43] 4964 2-8-11 ........ ELegrix 2 105
(JDeRoualle, France) *held up, last straight, effort over 1 1/2f out, never dangerous* **33/1**

8 1 1/2 **New Largue (USA)**[11] 2-8-11 ........ TJarnet 6 101
(RobertCollet, France) *prominent, disputing 4th straight, outpaced from 2f out* **66/1**

9 2 1/2 **Mirabilis (USA)**[24] 2-8-11 ........ RHughes 5 96
(AFabre, France) *held up, 9th straight, never a factor* **11/1**

10 3 **Cours De La Reine (IRE)**[43] 4964 2-8-11 ........ KFallon 8 89
(PWChapple-Hyam) *behind, 8th straight, never in contention* **16/1**

1m 36.7s **Going Correction** -0.225s/f (Firm) **10 Ran SP% 121.4**
Speed ratings: **115,113,112,112,112 112,111,110,107,104.**
**Owner** Niarchos Family **Bred** Flaxman Holding Ltd **Trained** France

**FOCUS**
An impressive display from new 1000 Guineas favourite Divine Proportions, who represented a trainer and an owner who have magnificent records in the race. She quickened up smartly to win well.

**NOTEBOOK**
**Divine Proportions(USA)**, successful over five to six furlongs on her four previous starts, was stepping up two furlongs and there was always going to be a nagging doubt about whether she would race too keenly in the early stages, wanting to go a bit faster. However, she was given a good ride - tucked in behind the long-time leader - and although she was hemmed in by Fraloga in the straight, she found an an impressive change of gear once extricated. Surviving a Stewards' enquiry, she remains unbeaten, even against colts, and although connections would not commit her firmly for Newmarket, she was rightly made favourite for the 1000 Guineas.
**Titian Time(USA)**, coming into this on the back of maiden win, ran a great race considering her inexperience. She tried to go from pillar to post but was simply unable to quicken when the winner came sweeping past. She stuck to her guns though and a Group race should come her way.
**Fraloga(IRE)** came into this as a promising filly, having won her previous start impressively, and she ran well. A stiffer test of stamina will suit and as she still showed signs of greeness here, better can be expected at three.
**Intrigued**, whose trainer knows the time of day when he gets a good horse, was an interesting runner and did nothing to suggest she was out of place. Perhaps not given the greatest ride, she was doing her best work at the finish and could develop into an Oaks contender next year.
**Portrayal(USA)** gives the form a solid look as she was the most experienced filly in the line-up and was staying on at the end.
**Queen Of Poland** had a bit to find with some of these and ran as well as could have been expected. She was a little one paced in the latter stages but was at least going on at the end.
**Mirabilis(USA)** was disappointing given the manner of her previous win and it is safe to assume she is better than this.
**Cours De La Reine(IRE)**, who lost her maiden tag in a Group Three at Deauville in August, made no show and finished a remote last, apparently failing to act on the track and the firm ground.

## 5980a PRIX JEAN-LUC LAGARDERE (GROUP 1) (C&F) 7f
**3:45** (3:45) 2-Y-O **£140,838** (£56,345; £28,173; £14,074)

RPR

1 **Oratorio (IRE)**[43] 4959 2-9-0 ........ JPSpencer 1 118
(APO'Brien, Ire) *prominent, 3rd straight, dropped back but then driven and ran on from 2f out, challenged strongly 1f out, led final strides* **5/2**[2]

2 snk **Early March**[24] 5432 2-9-0 ........ OPeslier 6 117
(MmeCHead-Maarek, France) *led after 1 1/2f, headed over 1 1/2f out, ridden and rallied to lead again briefly just inside final f, ran on* **11/4**[3]

3 nse **Layman (USA)**[42] 4981 2-9-0 ........ CSoumillon 4 117
(AFabre, France) *led 1 1/2f, led again over 1 1/2f out, headed just inside final furlong briefly, led again til headed final strides* **7/4**[1]

4 2 1/2 **Montgomery's Arch (USA)**[65] 4288 2-9-0 ........ JFortune 3 111
(PWChapple-Hyam) *in touch, 4th straight, ridden over 1 1/2f out, stayed on final stages but no impression on leading trio* **10/1**

5 1 **Democratic Deficit (IRE)**[14] 5678 2-9-0 ........ KJManning 5 108
(JSBolger, Ire) *5th straight, shaken up to chase leaders 2f out, ridden and pressing leaders 1 1/2f out, no extra from over 1f out* **20/1**

6 3/4 **Tony James (IRE)**[46] 4857 2-9-0 ........ SSanders 2 106
(CEBrittain) *raced in 4th, last but still well in touch straight, effort in centre over 1 1/2f out, unable to quicken* **14/1**

1m 19.3s **Going Correction** -0.225s/f (Firm) **6 Ran SP% 112.1**
Speed ratings: **111,110,110,107,106 105.**
**Owner** Mrs John Magnier & M Tabor **Bred** Barronstown Stud & Orpendale **Trained** Ballydoyle, Co Tipperary

**FOCUS**
A fantastic finish to this Group One event, with the Aidan O'Brien-trained Oratorio nipping up the inside of the two French runners to land the spoils.

**NOTEBOOK**
**Oratorio(IRE)** had already shown himself to be a solid Group Two performer and stepped up on previous efforts to take this Group One contest from a couple of very promising sorts. Having appeared to get a little outpaced halfway up the straight, he picked up well under strong pressure and got a dream run up the inside after Early March hung off the rail. A very tough sort, he was quoted at 20-1 for next year's 2000 Guineas and deserves a chance to enhance his claims for the race in the Dewhurst.
**Early March**, bidding to follow up connections' win in the race with American Post last year, went off at a decent gallop and was given a breather early in the straight, but Peslier probably allowed them to get to him too easily and he may well have won had he kicked a bit earlier. Hanging off the rail and allowing the winner up his inside added insult to injury, but he still emerges from the race with much credit. There is more to come from him and he will make a better three-year-old over a mile.
**Layman(USA)** ran a game race in defeat, but the front two were just too strong. Likely to be suited by a straight track and longer distance, odds of around 20-1for the 2000 Guineas make no appeal at all.
**Montgomery's Arch(USA)** got outpaced when things quickened up and then ran on steadily as things came to a close. This represented a step up in form and he is going the right way.
**Democratic Deficit(IRE)** was entitled to get a little closer to Oratorio on Curragh form and ran a little below par.
**Tony James(IRE)** was outpaced early on and never really landed a blow. He is not up to this grade, but does have the scope to make a better three-year-old.

## 5981a PRIX DE L'ARC DE TRIOMPHE LUCIEN BARRIERE (GROUP 1) (ENTIRE COLTS & FILLIES) 1m 4f
**4:30** (4:31) 3-Y-O+ **£643,831** (£257,577; £128,789; £64,338)

RPR

1 **Bago (FR)**[21] 5500 3-8-11 ........ TGillet 5 129
(JEPease, France) *held up, 9th straight on inside, switched left and headway over 2f out, went 2nd 1f out, led final 50yds, ran on well* **10/1**

2 1/2 **Cherry Mix (FR)**[35] 5170 3-8-11 ........ CSoumillon 1 128
(AFabre, France) *close up, 4th straight, quickened to lead just over 1 1/2f out, 2l clear appr final f, headed and no extra 50yds out* **33/1**

3 1 **Ouija Board**[77] 3968 3-8-8 ........ JPMurtagh 9 123+
(EALDunlop) *held up, 14th straight, not much room 2f out, strong run down outside from 1 1/2f out to go 3rd 100yds out, stayed on* **7/1**[3]

4 2 **Acropolis (IRE)**[22] 5481 3-8-11 ........ JPSpencer 19 123
(APO'Brien, Ire) *in rear, 15th straight, ran on towards inside under pressure from over 1 1/2f out to take 4th on line* **100/1**

5 shd **North Light (IRE)**[98] 3353 3-8-11 ........ KFallon 12 123
(SirMichaelStoute) *led, joined 6f out til led again 3f out, headed just over 1 1/2f out, lost 4th on line* **9/2**[1]

6 1/2 **Vallee Enchantee (IRE)**[71] 4121 4-9-2 ........ SPasquier 16 120+
(ELellouche, France) *held up on outside, 16th straight, stayed on down outside final 1 1/2f, nearest finish* **14/1**

7 snk **Latice (IRE)**[21] 5501 3-8-8 ........ MJKinane 13 121+
(J-MBeguigne, France) *midfield, 7th on ins straight, switched off rail 2f out, headway when n.m.r 1 1/2f out, switched left and stayed on* **28/1**

8 2 1/2 **Silverskaya (USA)**[21] 5501 3-8-8 ........ IMendizabal 6 115+
(J-CRouget, France) *held up in last, steady headway down inside final 2f, nearest finish* **66/1**

9 1/2 **Warrsan (IRE)**[28] 5329 6-9-5 ........ KMcEvoy 8 118
(CEBrittain) *held up in rear, 18th straight, stayed on steadily down outside final 1 1/2f* **9/1**

10 shd **Valixir (IRE)**[21] 5500 3-8-11 ........ ELegrix 20 117
(AFabre, France) *midfield, 12th straight, effort on outside 2f out, kept on at same pace* **9/1**

11 nk **Execute (FR)**[154] 1804 7-9-5 ........ DBoeuf 17 117
(JEHammond, France) *close up, 6th straight, tracking leader on inside over 1 1/2f out, 4th 1f out, weakened* **66/1**

12 1/2 **Blue Canari (FR)**[21] 5500 3-8-11 ........ C-PLemaire 3 118+
(PBary, France) *held up, 13th straight, stayed on at same pace final 2f* **40/1**

13 1/2 **Pride (FR)**[21] 5501 4-9-2 ........ TJarnet 10 113
(ADeRoyer-Dupre, France) *midfield, 11th straight, slightly hampered and lost place just over 2f out, stayed on final f* **33/1**

14 snk **Imperial Dancer**[16] 5611 6-9-5 ........ TEDurcan 15 115
(MRChannon) *held up in rear, 17th straight, kept on under pressure final 1 1/2f* **100/1**

15 hd **Mamool (IRE)**[29] 5296 5-9-5 ........ LDettori 14 115
(SaeedBinSuroor) *close up on outside, 5th straight, one pace final 1 1/2f* **11/1**

16 1/2 **Prospect Park**[21] 5500 3-8-11 ........ OPeslier 2 113
(CLaffon-Parias, France) *prominent, 3rd straight, went 2nd briefly 2f out, weakened* **10/1**

17 8 **Tap Dance City (USA)**[98] 7-9-5 ........ TSato 18 102
(SSasaki, Japan) *pressed leader til disputed lead 6f out, pushed along and headed 3f out, 2nd straight, soon weakened* **10/1**

18 1 1/2 **Grey Swallow (IRE)**[22] 5483 3-8-11 ........ PJSmullen 11 98
(DKWeld, Ire) *midfield on outside, 8th straight, effort and edged left just over 2f out, soon weakened* **5/1**[2]

19 10 **Policy Maker (IRE)**[21] 5502 4-9-5 ........ TThulliez 4 83
(ELellouche, France) *close up, 10th straight, weakened over 2f out* **131/10**

2m 25.0s **Going Correction** -0.225s/f (Firm)
**WFA** 3 from 4yo+ 7lb **19** Ran SP% **136.4**
Speed ratings: **122,121,121,119,119 119,119,117,117,117 116,116,116,116,116 115,110,109,102.**
**Owner** Niarchos Family **Bred** Famille Niarchos **Trained** France

**FOCUS**
A fair renewal of this historic race with the French, English and Irish Derby winners all in the line-up, as well as many of the key French trial winners. However, the race went to Bago, who returned to his brilliant best on his favoured fast ground after his bubble had appeared to burst with defeats in the Juddmonte and the Niel.

**NOTEBOOK**
**Bago(FR)**, who had not quite lived up to expectations in unsuitably soft conditions in top company the last twice, relished this faster surface and bounced right back to his best to add his name to the illustrious roll of honour for this race. In rear early, he did not get the clearest of runs at the entrance to the straight, but picked up strongly once in the clear and ran on gamely to lead well inside the final furlong, just missing out on the track record by 0.4 of a second. A sound surface is the key to this son of Nashwan, and he may go for the Breeders' Cup Classic. He is likely to stay in training next season.
**Cherry Mix(FR)** has been climbing the ranks and came into this on the back of an impressive Group Two win. Unfortunately for this fellow though, the ground went against him, so it is to his credit that he managed to run such a huge race. Never far off the lead, he quickened impressively early on in the straight and built up a lead of a couple of lengths, only to be cut down once Bago hit overdrive. There are no fixed plans for him at the moment but he will make a smashing four-year-old, with improvement still to come.
**Ouija Board** confirmed herself as the best middle-distance filly in Europe with a storming run in third. She did not have the best of luck in her run, as she was being kept in from some way out and was hampered two furlongs from home, when ready to make her final effort. There are more top races to be won with this dual Oaks winner and the Filly & Mare Turf would look an obvious target. She may stay in training as a four-year-old.
**Acropolis(IRE)**, who has nothing better than a Listed race to his name, ran way above himself in fourth and deserves masses of credit. Drawn almost worst of all and lacking the pace to get a position, he was still among the backmarkers into the straight, he passed horse after horse under strong pressure up the rail. Obviously a high-class performer in the making, assuming this was no fluke, he should improve again from three to four.
**North Light(IRE)**, winner of this year's Epsom Derby, found the ground too fast when disappointing in the Irish equivalent and again could have done with softer here. He made much of the early running, together with the Japanese runner, and stretched out soon after entering the straight, but was just one paced towards the end and had no more to offer. He is likely to stay in training at four, when the Arc will be his main target and will be unlucky if the ground is as fast as this again.
**Vallee Enchantee(IRE)** bounced right back to something like her best and was finishing to good effect.
**Latice(IRE)** was unlucky not to finish closer and showed her previous running to be all wrong back on this more suitable ground.
**Silverskaya(USA)** was another doing her best work at the death and ran better than her odds suggested she would.
**Warrsan(IRE)** lost his early pitch and was shuffled back through the pack to be nearly last. For such a strong galloper as himself, this ended any chance he had, the run should be ignored. He could now be aimed races like the Japan Cup and Hong Kong Vase.
**Valixir(IRE)**, a highly progressive colt who came into this on the back of victory in the Prix Niel, had the worst draw of all and with the fast ground going against him, stood little chance of winning. He raced keenly, to make matters worse, and would not let himself down on the ground when asked for maximum effort. The run is best ignored and he remains a high-class prospect for next season, when he is sure to feature prominently in many good races.
**Blue Canari(FR)**, winner of the French Derby, never got into it but was going on at the finish.
**Pride(FR)**, formerly trained by Gerard Butler, did not get the best of luck in running and was well held.
**Imperial Dancer** was always towards the tail of the field and did not really run on in the straight.
**Mamool(IRE)** was still well there one and a half out, but faded soon after and connections felt the ground was too lively.
**Prospect Park**, just nosed out by Valixir in the Prix Niel, held a good position throughout from his low draw but was a spent force once the dash for the line began. He is better than this and should make a good four-year-old.
**Tap Dance City(USA)** did too much too early and could not keep up the gallop, which make the efforts of North Light - who went with him - even better.
**Grey Swallow(IRE)** had an interrupted preparation and did not run his race. He had shown in the Irish Derby, and again in the shorter Irish Champion Stakes, that he is top-class three-year-old and there should be more to come from him next season.
**Policy Maker(IRE)**, easy winner of the Prix Foy - a shambles of a trial with three runners dawdling around - could not cut it in this better race but this was still too bad to be true.

## NAKAYAMA
Sunday, October 3

**OFFICIAL GOING: Heavy**

### 5982a SPRINTERS STKS (GRADE 1) 6f (T)
**7:40** (7:40) 3-Y-O+ **£507,480** (£203,075; £127,600; £72,974)

RPR

1 **Calstone Light O (JPN)**[364] 6-9-0 ........ NOnishi 5 126?
(HOneda, Japan) **15/2**

2 4 **Durandal (JPN)**[189] 5-9-0 ........ KenichiIkezoe 1 116
(MSakaguchi, Japan) **36/10**[2]

3 nk **Cape Of Good Hope**[87] 3674 6-9-0 ........ BPrebble 12 115
(DOughton, Hong Kong) **24/1**

4 1 1/4 **Win Radius (JPN)**[119] 6-9-0 ........ KatsuharuTanaka 16 112
(KazuoFujisawa, Japan) **155/10**

5 nse **Silky Lagoon (JPN)**[189] 4-8-10 ........ YShibata 15 108
(MIkegami, Japan) **52/1**

6 nse **Keeneland Swan (USA)**[189] 5-9-0 ........ HShii 14 112
(HideyukiMori, Japan) **94/10**

7 nk **She Is Tosho (JPN)**[189] 4-8-10 ........ ENakadate 13 107
(ATsurudome, Japan) **62/10**[3]

8 2 **Tamamo Hot Play (JPN)** 3-8-10 ........ RWada 8 103
(KMinai, Japan) **53/1**

9 1/2 **Sunningdale (JPN)**[189] 5-9-0 ........ YFukunaga 3 105
(TSetoguchi, Japan) **23/10**[1]

10 1/2 **Silver Zetto (IRE)** 3-8-10 ........ YYoshida 2 101
(KTadokoro, Japan) **102/1**

11 1 1/4 **Golden Cast (JPN)**[511] 4-9-0 ........ YTake 9 100
(KHashiguchi, Japan) **63/10**

12 nse **Wonder Seattle (JPN)** 5-9-0 ........ HKitamura 10 100
(SYuasa, Japan) **65/1**

13 3/4 **Ashdown Express (IRE)**[29] 5289 5-9-0 ........ HGoto 6 98
(CFWall) *mid-division, badly hampered over 1f out, not recover* **37/1**

14 1 1/4 **Namura Big Time (JPN)**[176] 3-8-10 ........ TEda 4 92
(YTamura, Japan) **38/1**

15 5 **Cafe Bostonian (USA)**[189] 5-9-0 ........ YOkabe 7 83
(YMatsuyama, Japan) **53/1**

16 3 1/2 **Fayr Jag (IRE)**[32] 5255 5-9-0 ........ NYokoyama 11 74
(TDEasterby) *mid-division til weakened well over 1f out* **41/1**

69.90 secs
**WFA** 3 from 4yo+ 1lb **16** Ran SP% **126.7**
Speed ratings: .
**Owner** S Shimizu **Bred** Oshima Bokujo **Trained** Japan

**NOTEBOOK**
**Cape Of Good Hope** would have preferred firmer ground, but proved yet again what a versatile and consistent performer he is, staying on strongly in the closing stages to almost catch the runner-up.
**Ashdown Express(IRE)**suffered traffic problems in the home straight and would have preferred faster ground.
**Fayr Jag(IRE)** raced in midfield but could not pick up on the ground.

## 5684 BELMONT PARK (L-H)
Saturday, October 2

**OFFICIAL GOING: Turf course - yielding; dirt course - fast**

### 5985a JOE HIRSCH TURF CLASSIC INVITATIONAL (GRADE 1) 1m 4f
**10:12** (10:14) 3-Y-O+ **£251,397** (£83,799; £41,899; £20,950)

RPR

1 **Kitten's Joy (USA)**[49] 4769 3-8-9 ........ JRVelazquez 5 128
(DaleRomans, U.S.A) **24/10**[2]

2 2 1/2 **Magistretti (USA)**[21] 4-9-0 ........(b) EPrado 4 122
(PLBiancone, U.S.A) **17/10**[1]

3 3/4 **Tycoon**[21] 5463 3-8-9 ........ JPSpencer 6 123
(APO'Brien, Ire) **92/10**

4 3 **Request For Parole (USA)**[21] 5-9-0 ........ CVelasquez 2 116
(SHough, U.S.A) **29/2**

5 2 1/4 **Polish Summer**[20] 5502 7-9-0 ........ GaryStevens 7 113
(AFabre, France) **84/10**

6 1 1/2 **Kicken Kris (USA)**[49] 4768 4-9-0 ........ JCastellano 1 111
(MMatz, U.S.A) **4/1**[3]

7 dist **Maktub (ITY)**[21] 5489 5-9-0 ........ JChavez 3 —
(MAJarvis) **23/1**

2m 29.97s
**WFA** 3 from 4yo+ 7lb **7** Ran SP% **117.5**
Speed ratings: .
**Owner** Kenneth L & Sarah K Ramsey **Bred** Kenneth L & Sarah K Ramsey **Trained** USA

**NOTEBOOK**
**Kitten's Joy(USA)** hit the front a furlong out and demonstrated a fine turn of foot to quicken away. America has lacked a real top notch turf performer over the past few years, but this son of El Prado, who has won eight of his nine starts on grass, looks like the real deal and will be difficult to beat in the Breeders' Cup Turf.
**Magistretti(USA)** has clearly benefitted from using medication since crossing the Atlantic. Taking up the running passing the half mile pole, he was comprehensively outpaced by the winner in the closing stages and Biancone is in no hurry to take him on again in the Breeders' Cup.
**Tycoon** raced in sixth in the early stages but moved up to third, within three lengths of the lead, two furlongs out. He kept on steadily thereafter to post a solid US debut, but would have preferred a stronger pace.
**Maktub(ITY)** set a sedate gallop, but was passed by Magistretti with half a mile to run and his fuel guage immediately registered empty. Firm ground would have been more suitable and maybe all his recent travelling had taken its toll.

## 5752 PONTEFRACT (L-H)
Monday, October 4

**OFFICIAL GOING: Good to firm**
After 9mm overnight rain on watered ground the going was described by the jockeys as 'near perfect, just kicking the top off slightly'.
Wind: Fresh 1/2 behind. Weather: Fine and sunny.

### 5988 EUROPEAN BREEDERS FUND CLAXTON BAY MAIDEN STKS 1m 2f 6y
**2:20** (2:23) (D2) 2-Y-O **£5,590** (£1,720; £860; £430) **Stalls** Low

Form RPR

5 **1** **Ayam Zaman (IRE)**[13] 5717 2-8-9 ........ PRobinson 4 85+
(MAJarvis) *trckd ldrs: qcknd to ld over 1f out: sn clr: eased nr fin* **5/4**[1]

36 **2** 2 1/2 **Royal Jet**[13] 5716 2-9-0 ........(v[1]) ACulhane 15 80
(MRChannon) *chsd ldrs: wnt 2nd over 1f out: no ch w wnr* **5/1**[2]

50 **3** 9 **Majestic Movement (USA)**[44] 4930 2-9-0 ........ RHavlin 7 64
(JHMGosden) *chsd ldrs: kpt on same pce fnl 2f* **12/1**

5000 **4** 1 1/4 **Dover Street**[23] 5477 2-9-0 59 ........ NCallan 13 62
(PWD'Arcy) *chsd ldrs on outer: one pce fnl 2f* **50/1**

504 **5** 3 1/2 **Mutamaasek (USA)**[17] 5620 2-9-0 84 ........ RHills 12 55
(JLDunlop) *chsd ldrs: led 2f out: sn hdd & wknd* **5/1**[2]

**6** 1 1/4 **Numero Due** 2-9-0 ........ PMQuinn 9 53
(GMMoore) *cmpt: unf: bhd: sme hdwy on outer over 1f out: nvr on terms* **50/1**

5004 **7** 1 3/4 **Mr Maxim**[19] 5556 2-9-0 57 ........ FLynch 5 50
(RMWhitaker) *w ldr: led 3f out tl 2f out: sn wknd* **50/1**

2 **8** shd **Amazing Valour (IRE)**[11] 5756 2-9-0 ........ KDarley 8 50
(MJohnston) *s.i.s: bhd: reminders and sme hdwy over 4f out: nvr nr ldrs* **7/1**[3]

00 **9** 3½ **Three Boars**$^{13}$ 5716 2-9-0 ........ RWinston 6 43
(WJarvis) *chsd ldrs: wknd over 2f out* **50/1**

3030 **10** 1½ **Cois Na Tine Eile**$^{9}$ 5792 2-8-9 51 ........ ANicholls 11 36
(MsDeborahJEvans) *s.i.s: nvr a factor* **100/1**

060 **11** ¾ **Yardstick**$^{12}$ 5741 2-9-0 65 ........ MHills 3 39
(SKirk) *mid-div: drvn along 4f out: nvr a factor* **33/1**

005 **12** 6 **Northanger Abbey (IRE)**$^{7}$ 5827 2-9-0 ........ JCarroll 2 29
(JHMGosden) *led tl 3f out: lost pl over 1f out: sn bhd* **20/1**

0 **13** 1¼ **Sooyou Sir (IRE)**$^{20}$ 5543 2-9-0 ........ JQuinn 14 26
(MrsADuffield) *a in rr* **100/1**

5 **14** 1¼ **Emerald Destiny (IRE)**$^{9}$ 5790 2-8-9 ........ DTudhope$^{(5)}$ 1 24
(DCarroll) *mid-div: lost pl over 3f out* **66/1**

6060 **15** 14 **Forpetesake**$^{7}$ 5831 2-8-11 58 ........ DCorby$^{(3)}$ 10 —
(MsDeborahJEvans) *a bhd* **125/1**

2m 14.18s (0.27) **Going Correction** +0.025s/f (Good) **15 Ran SP% 117.8**
Speed ratings: **99,97,89,88,86 85,83,83,80,79 78,74,73,72,60**CSF £6.60 TOTE £1.90: £1.10, £1.10, £4.40; EX 4.90.
**Owner** Saif Ali **Bred** Dr T A Ryan **Trained** Newmarket, Suffolk

**FOCUS**
A stiff test for juveniles with the first two clear and a quite impressive winner. The form is held down somewhat by the proximity of the fourth and seventh.

**NOTEBOOK**
**Ayam Zaman(IRE)** ♦, bred to make a middle-distance three-year-old, settled much better and had this won in a matter of strides, being value for double the official margin. She can go on to much better things.
**Royal Jet**, bred for stamina on his dam's side, was sharpened up by a visor and seemed to improve on his first two efforts, finishing clear second best.
**Majestic Movement(USA)** did not see out the trip anywhere near as well as the first two and does not seem to be progressing.
**Dover Street**, a keen type, is not progressing and already has a provisional rating of just 59.
**Mutamaasek(USA)** took it up turning on but his stamina soon seemed to give out completely.
**Numero Due**, a March foal and a son of Sinndar, lacks size and scope but made a satisfactory debut.
**Amazing Valour(IRE)** was never going at any stage.
**Yardstick** *Official explanation: jockey said colt hung left handed throughout*
**Northanger Abbey(IRE)** *Official explanation: jockey said colt had no more to give*

## 5989 MARAVAL NURSERY — 6f
2:50 (2:53) (E3) (0-75,73) 2-Y-O — £4,416 (£1,359; £679; £339) Stalls Low

Form — RPR

2003 **1** **Safendonseabiscuit**$^{11}$ 5745 2-9-4 70 ........ MHills 9 81
(SKirk) *sn led: rdn clr over 1f out: styd on strly* **8/1**

0550 **2** 4 **Rancho Cucamonga (IRE)**$^{17}$ 5617 2-8-12 64 ........ (v$^{1}$) KDarley 17 63
(TDBarron) *midfield: hdwy on outer over 2f out: rdn over 1f out: styd on ins last: nrst fin* **14/1**

5554 **3** shd **Xeeran**$^{14}$ 5701 2-8-9 61 ........ PRobinson 6 60
(MAJarvis) *trckd ldrs: hdwy over 2f out: rdn wl over 1f out: kpt on same pce fnl f* **11/2**$^{2}$

4305 **4** ¾ **Azuree (IRE)**$^{20}$ 5548 2-8-13 65 ........ (b) PDobbs 5 62
(RHannon) *towards rr: hdwy 1/2-way: rdn along towards inner wl over 1f out: kpt onsame pce ins last* **16/1**

2560 **5** ½ **Ming Vase**$^{35}$ 5188 2-8-3 60 ........ DTudhope$^{(5)}$ 11 55
(DCarroll) *in tch: rdn along wl over 1f out: kpt on u.p ins last* **66/1**

0240 **6** 1½ **Favouring (IRE)**$^{17}$ 5606 2-8-7 62 ........ (v$^{1}$) THamilton$^{(3)}$ 10 53
(RAFahey) *cl up: rdn along 2f out: drvn over 1f out and grad wknd* **7/1**$^{3}$

3403 **7** hd **Game Lad**$^{29}$ 5314 2-9-7 73 ........ DAllan 7 63
(TDEasterby) *towards rr: hdwy into midfield 1/2-way: sn rdn along: swtchd outside wl over 1f out: kpt on u.p: nt rch ldrs* **9/2**$^{1}$

6630 **8** ¾ **Pro Tempore**$^{16}$ 5636 2-8-12 64 ........ FNorton 3 52
(MrsJRRamsden) *hld up in tch: effrot and hdwy on inner wl over 1f out: rdn and no imp ent last* **8/1**

614 **9** ¾ **Pauline's Prince**$^{70}$ 4186 2-9-4 70 ........ NCallan 16 56
(RHollinshead) *sn prom: effrt to chse wnr over 1f out: sn rdn and wknd ins last* **25/1**

0030 **10** nk **Perianth (IRE)**$^{3}$ 5910 2-8-7 62 ........ JFMcDonald$^{(3)}$ 14 47
(BJMeehan) *midfield: hdwy 2f out: sn rdn and hld whn n.m.r over 1f out* **12/1**

2100 **11** 1¼ **Apetite**$^{16}$ 5630 2-8-8 60 ........ JQuinn 4 41
(NBycroft) *dwlt and bhd tl styd on fnl 2f: nvr a factor* **25/1**

600 **12** hd **Pee Jay's Dream**$^{28}$ 5341 2-8-7 59 ........ DaleGibson 15 39
(MWEasterby) *wnt rt s: a rr* **50/1**

3040 **13** 1 **Lodgician (IRE)**$^{16}$ 5636 2-9-0 66 ........ RWinston 8 43
(JJQuinn) *bhd fr 1/2-way* **20/1**

6565 **14** ½ **Sound And Vision (IRE)**$^{20}$ 5542 2-8-11 63 ........ (b) SWKelly 12 39
(MDods) *a rr* **25/1**

020 **15** ½ **Bond Puccini**$^{23}$ 5475 2-8-11 63 ........ FLynch 2 37
(BSmart) *prom: sn rdn along and lost pl: midfield whn jinked and hit rail: sn bhd* **16/1**

540 **16** ¾ **High Petergate (IRE)**$^{18}$ 5578 2-8-7 62 ........ PMulrennan$^{(3)}$ 13 34
(MWEasterby) *a rr* **25/1**

0640 **17** ¾ **Paris Heights**$^{16}$ 5636 2-8-11 63 ........ ACulhane 1 33
(RMWhitaker) *a rr* **50/1**

0006 **18** 24 **Mill By The Stream**$^{60}$ 4498 2-8-4 56 ........ ANicholls 18 —
(APJarvis) *chsd ldrs on outer: rdn along 1/2-way: sn wknd* **20/1**

1m 17.16s (-0.14) **Going Correction** +0.025s/f (Good) **18 Ran SP% 124.7**
Speed ratings: **101,95,95,94,93 91,91,90,89,89 87,87,85,85,84 83,82,50**CSF £102.07 CT £702.92 TOTE £9.40: £2.30, £3.30, £1.90, £4.30; EX 143.70.
**Owner** J B R Leisure Ltd **Bred** J Redmond **Trained** Upper Lambourn, Berks

**FOCUS**
A modest heat but a decent time for the class of contest and solid form for the grade.

**NOTEBOOK**
**Safendonseabiscuit**, whose Bath third has since been advertised by the winner, shot clear once in line for home to break his duck at the ninth attempt. Connections would be well advised to have him out soon under a penalty but apparently the plan is to wait for the Autumn Auction race at Newmarket.
**Rancho Cucamonga(IRE)**, drawn one off the outside, did well in a first-time visor considering she was always playing catch up. In the end she stayed on just well enough to snatch second spot.
**Xeeran**, fourth behind the subsequent Cheveley Park winner in a nursery at Leicester, again gave a good account of herself but this may be as good as she is.
**Azuree(IRE)**, 2lb lower, looked very fit indeed but did not improve for the drop back in trip.
**Ming Vase**, who ran over a mile last time, found this too sharp.
**Favouring(IRE)**, in a first-time visor, dropped away in the closing stages and his best efforts have been on much softer ground.
**Game Lad**, a big type, struggled to go the pace and did not really have the run of the race. He should come into his own next year. *Official explanation: jockey said colt hung right handed*
**Sound And Vision(IRE)** *Official explanation: jockey said gelding lost an off fore shoe*
**Bond Puccini** *Official explanation: jockey said colt suffered interference three furlongs out*
**Mill By The Stream** *Official explanation: jockey said colt had no more to give*

## 5990 TOTEPLACEPOT H'CAP — 1m 4y
3:20 (3:20) (D2) (0-85,85) 3-Y-O — £9,669 (£3,667; £1,833; £833) Stalls Low

Form — RPR

0042 **1** **Zerlina (USA)**$^{19}$ 5566 3-8-8 75 ........ JQuinn 8 87
(WJMusson) *dwlt: hld up: hdwy and swtchd outside over 1f out: r.o to ld last 100yds* **7/1**$^{3}$

2435 **2** 2 **Little Jimbob**$^{26}$ 5399 3-8-5 75 ........ THamilton$^{(3)}$ 4 82
(RAFahey) *led: qcknd over 4f out: hdd and no ex ins last* **9/2**$^{2}$

1110 **3** 1 **Double Vodka (IRE)**$^{2}$ 5950 3-8-6 73 ........ PRobinson 1 78
(MrsJRRamsden) *stdd s: hld up: hdwy 3f out: chal over 1f out: styd on same pce* **15/8**$^{1}$

231 **4** 3 **Backgammon**$^{28}$ 5345 3-8-11 78 ........ TPQueally 2 76
(DRLoder) *trckd ldrs: drvn along over 2f out: one pce appr fnl f* **9/2**$^{2}$

4200 **5** nk **Saffron Fox**$^{51}$ 4760 3-8-12 79 ........ (p) ACulhane 7 76
(JGPortman) *bhd and pushed along: styd on fnl f: nvr a threat* **16/1**

2351 **6** 7 **Cantarna (IRE)**$^{17}$ 5621 3-8-7 74 ow1 ........ NCallan 12 55
(JMackie) *w ldrs: lost pl over 1f out* **7/1**$^{3}$

4-10 **7** shd **Ashwaaq (USA)**$^{16}$ 5652 3-8-9 76 ........ RHills 11 57
(JLDunlop) *s.i.s: sn chsng ldrs: drvn along over 4f out: lost pl over 2f out* **9/1**

1m 44.92s (-0.68) **Going Correction** +0.025s/f (Good) **7 Ran SP% 112.0**
Speed ratings: **104,102,101,98,97 90,90**CSF £36.54 CT £81.59 TOTE £7.70: £4.00, £2.80; EX 29.50 Trifecta £126.00 Pool: £532.76. 3.00 winning units..
**Owner** G Howard-Spink **Bred** Bricklow Ltd **Trained** Newmarket, Suffolk

**FOCUS**
A race decimated by five non-runners but still a reasonable event. The pace was a fair one and the form appears sound.

**NOTEBOOK**
**Zerlina(USA)** has dropped to a favourable mark and showed a smart turn of foot to pick off her rivals after being given a patient ride. Now that she has found her form she could win again, though soft ground would be a problem.
**Little Jimbob** again made a bold bid to make all the running, but ran into a filly in form. He is very consistent.
**Double Vodka(IRE)**, making a quick reappearance, had every chance but lacked pace where it mattered. Perhaps this trip on fast ground was an insufficient test of stamina for him.
**Backgammon**, making his handicap debut, was in a good position to strike had he been good enough but failed to deliver. This was his first try on fast ground and perhaps he needs it softer.
**Saffron Fox** found this trip too sharp and was always struggling at the back. Only her stamina enabled her to beat two home.
**Cantarna(IRE)** was disappointing, but her best form has been on easier ground.
**Ashwaaq(USA)** ran a modest race for the second time following her five-month break, though this would have been the fastest surface she has encountered.

## 5991 TRINIDAD & TOBAGO H'CAP — 2m 1f 22y
3:50 (3:50) (E3) (0-70,70) 3-Y-O+ — £4,182 (£1,287; £643; £321) Stalls Low

Form — RPR

1103 **1** **Moonshine Beach**$^{7}$ 5826 6-9-5 70 ........ PMakin$^{(5)}$ 5 79
(PWHiatt) *trckd ldrs: hdwy to ld 3f out: rdn clr wl over 1f out: drvn ins last and hld on wl* **11/1**

4113 **2** ¾ **Crocolat**$^{31}$ 5274 3-8-9 66 ........ FNorton 8 74+
(MrsStefLiddiard) *hld up and bhd: hdwy on inner and pushed along 4f out: rdn and styng on whn n.m.r over 1f out: drvn and kpt on ins last* **5/1**$^{2}$

3323 **3** 1 **Vicars Destiny**$^{18}$ 5589 6-9-4 64 ........ RWinston 6 71
(MrsSLamyman) *hld up and bhd: stdy hdwy on inner 4f out: rdn to chse wnr over 1f out: sn drvn and kpt on ins last* **10/1**

6046 **4** 1½ **Riyadh**$^{7}$ 5826 6-9-6 66 ........ KDarley 11 71
(MJohnston) *midfield: hdwy 4f out: rdn to chse ldrs over 1f out: drvn and one pce ins last* **8/1**

3115 **5** 5 **Super Fellow (IRE)**$^{16}$ 5638 10-8-3 56 oh11 ........ MHalford$^{(7)}$ 7 56
(CNKellett) *s.i.s and bhd: gd hdwy into midfield after 6f: rdn along over 4f out: styd on fnl 2f: nvr rch ldrs* **16/1**

0104 **6** 1 **Oktis Morilious (IRE)**$^{5}$ 5860 3-7-13 56 oh1 ........ LisaJones 14 55
(CRDore) *hld up: gd hdwy to join ldrs 1/2-way: rdn along over 3f out: sn drvn and grad wknd* **20/1**

1032 **7** 3 **Crackleando**$^{50}$ 4778 3-8-2 59 ........ JBramhill 9 54
(NPLittmoden) *led: rdn along 4f out: hdd 3f out: sn drvn and wknd fnl 2f* **16/1**

602 **8** shd **Bushido (IRE)**$^{16}$ 5638 5-8-10 56 oh1 ........ LEnstone 13 51
(MrsSJSmith) *chsd ldrs: rdn along over 4f out: drvn and wknd 2f out* **15/2**$^{3}$

0025 **9** 13 **Rawalpindi**$^{28}$ 5340 3-7-13 56 oh1 ........ DaleGibson 3 37
(JARToller) *midfield: rdn along over 4f out: sn btn* **25/1**

5024 **10** 1¾ **Accepting**$^{10}$ 3363 7-8-10 56 oh3 ........ (b) NCallan 1 35
(JMackie) *in tch on inner: hdwy to chse ldrs over 4f out: rdn and btn 3f out* **14/1**

5563 **11** 5 **Muzio Scevola (IRE)**$^{98}$ 3363 3-8-5 62 ........ SHitchcott 4 36
(MRChannon) *a rr* **28/1**

0102 **12** 1¾ **Restart (IRE)**$^{5}$ 5860 3-8-1 58 ........ JQuinn 12 30
(PCHaslam) *trckd ldrs: hdwy and cl up 1/2-way: rdn along over 3f out: sn rdn and wknd* **7/2**$^{1}$

5604 **13** 17 **Toni Alcala**$^{8}$ 5820 5-9-5 68 ........ PMulrennan$^{(3)}$ 2 21
(RFFisher) *trckd ldrs on inner: pushed along and lost pl 1/2-way: sn bhd* **16/1**

0133 **14** 5 **Little Tobias (IRE)**$^{16}$ 5638 5-8-10 56 oh3 ........ DMernagh 10 3
(AndrewTurnell) *chsd ldrs: rdn along 5f out: drvn and wknd over 3f out* **25/1**

3m 50.75s (0.25) **Going Correction** +0.025s/f (Good)
**WFA** 3 from 5yo+ 11lb **14 Ran SP% 119.4**
Speed ratings: **100,99,99,98,96 95,94,94,88,87 84,84,76,73**CSF £61.43 CT £581.03 TOTE £14.10: £4.70, £2.70, £2.20; EX 78.50.
**Owner** Ken Read **Bred** Lawrence Shepherd **Trained** Hook Norton, Oxon

**FOCUS**
A modest, if fairly competitive, staying handicap and the pace was ordinary but the third sets a reliable standard.

**NOTEBOOK**
**Moonshine Beach** continues in great form and being sent a few lengths clear on the home bend proved a race-winning move. This was his fifth win since July and it may not be his last considering he is effective on most types of ground, though the Handicapper is still to have his say.
**Crocolat** may have been unlucky as, after being given a positive ride, she was stopped in her run a couple of times in the last three furlongs, yet was cutting into the winner's lead at the line and would have gone very close with a clear run. She is yet to win on turf and is on a career-high mark, but she is relatively unexposed and this effort shows that she can win off it.
**Vicars Destiny** stayed on dourly in the closing stages to make the frame without ever looking like winning, but that has been the story with her in recent months.

**Riyadh** stays all day and plugged on for fourth, but is without a win in well over two years.
**Super Fellow(IRE)** appreciates a thorough test of stamina, but needs softer ground to slow the others down and under these conditions it was a struggle to reach his final placing.
**Bushido(IRE)** was the gamble of the race, but was disappointing under conditions which should have suited.
**Restart(IRE)** ran well over two miles at Newcastle last time, but the way he dropped out after holding a prominent position suggested he did not stay this longer trip on such a stiff track.
**Little Tobias(IRE)** *Official explanation: jockey said gelding hung left from 6 furlongs out*

## 5992 BUCCOO REEF "PREMIER" CLAIMING STKS — 1m 4y
4:20 (4:20) (D3) 3-Y-0 — **£5,564** (£1,712; £856; £428) **Stalls** Low

Form — RPR

2316 **1** **Grand But One (IRE)**[8] 5813 3-9-5 87 ...... MHills 12 — 88
(BWHills) *sn trcking ldrs: styd on to ld last 100yds: drvn out* **9/2**[2]

-210 **2** *1 1/4* **Patterdale**[26] 5399 3-8-12 74 ...... KDarley 13 — 78
(WJHaggas) *rr-div: hdwy over 2f out: styd on to take 2nd nr line* **9/1**

3502 **3** *hd* **Foolish Groom**[10] 5770 3-8-4 68 ...... JQuinn 6 — 70
(RHollinshead) *dwlt: sn trcking ldrs: led 1f out: hdd and no ex ins last* **16/1**

4050 **4** *nk* **Iskander**[8] 5821 3-8-9 71 ......(b) JCarroll 15 — 74
(KARyan) *bhd: hdwy on outer over 2f out: kpt on same pce ins last* **20/1**

4000 **5** *1/2* **Great Scott**[7] 5835 3-8-4 77 ...... PRobinson 4 — 68
(MJohnston) *chsd ldrs: kpt on same pce appr fnl f* **7/1**

0060 **6** *1* **Forthright**[10] 5766 3-8-11 81 ......(b) DaleGibson 1 — 73
(CEBrittain) *sn chsng ldrs: hdwy to ld over 2f out: hdd 1f out: wknd ins last* **4/1**[1]

0-00 **7** *6* **Passion Fruit**[16] 5639 3-7-13 50 ...... LisaJones 9 — 47
(CWFairhurst) *bhd: sme hewady on outer over 2f out: nvr nr ldrs* **80/1**

5300 **8** *5* **Go Solo**[17] 5607 3-8-9 74 ...... ACulhane 16 — 49+
(BWHills) *rr-div: hdwy on outer over 2f out: wknd fnl f* **12/1**

6202 **9** *6* **Desert Hawk**[7] 5829 3-8-4 66 ...... NPollard 8 — 26
(RHannon) *in tch: effrt 3f out: wknd 2f out* **14/1**

03-4 **10** *1/2* **Romaric (USA)**[35] 5199 3-9-0 84 ......(v) JBramhill 5 — 35
(JRNorton) *s.i.s: hdwy to chse ldrs 4f out: lost pl 2f out* **33/1**

0013 **11** *1* **Familiar Affair**[15] 5672 3-8-10 78 ...... NCallan 7 — 29
(TDBarron) *led over 1f: led 5f out tl over 2f out: lost pl over 1f out* **6/1**[3]

515- **12** *3* **On The Wing**[346] 5726 3-8-9 78 ...... RWinston 10 — 21
(APJarvis) *bhd: drvn along 4f out: nvr a factor* **18/1**

0000 **13** *2* **Cheverak Forest (IRE)**[33] 5223 3-8-4 55 ...... KimTinkler 11 — 11
(DonEnricoIncisa) *a bhd* **50/1**

2100 **14** *dist* **Kings Rock**[20] 5541 3-8-4 58 ......(b) TPQueally 2 — —
(MrsLucindaFeatherstone) *w ldr: led over 6f out tl 5f out: sn hrd rdn and lost pl: t.o 2f out* **33/1**

1m 45.9s (0.30) **Going Correction** +0.025s/f (Good) — **14** Ran **SP% 114.3**
Speed ratings: **99,97,97,97,96 95,89,84,78,78 77,74,72,—**CSF £40.08 TOTE £5.60: £2.60, £2.10, £4.50; EX 44.70.
**Owner** Enton Thoroughbred Racing 2 **Bred** Musaid Abo Salim **Trained** Lambourn, Berks
■ Stewards Enquiry : N Pollard caution: careless riding

### FOCUS
A well above average claimer run at a furious early gallop, but they paid for it later on and the winning time was modest for the class. Quite a large field, but a few had no chance at the weights.

### NOTEBOOK
**Grand But One(IRE)**, who ran better at Ascot last time than it may have seemed, was only fairly well in at the weights in this, but came from off the cracking gallop to score in clear-cut fashion. The problem is that he would have been worse off with the second, third and fourth in a handicap so he may have to try and find another race like this.
**Patterdale**, who had a bit to find with several of these at the weights, saw this trip out better than might have been expected.
**Foolish Groom** is still a maiden after nine attempts, but deserves some credit for this effort considering his best previous form has come on softer ground and he was by no means best in at the weights.
**Iskander** seemed to run up to form under conditions that suit, but he has flattered to deceive in the past.
**Great Scott**, best in on adjusted official ratings, ran alright but has become very disappointing.
**Forthright** led the main bulk of the field chasing the two clear leaders, but no sooner had he forged his way to the front rounding the home turn than the cavalry arrived and he was swamped. He is becoming a very hard horse to place.
**Familiar Affair**, best when gaining an uncontested lead, had his chances scuppered by the attentions of Kings Rock.

## 5993 BLANCHISSEUSE H'CAP — 1m 4f 8y
4:50 (4:51) (F4) (0-55,55) 3-Y-0+ — **£3,640** (£1,120; £560; £280) **Stalls** Low

Form — RPR

0451 **1** **Heathyards Pride**[28] 5350 4-8-13 **52** ...... NCallan 5 — 65
(RHollinshead) *hld up: gd hdwy over 3f out: rdn to chse ldrs over 1f out: styd on wl fnl f to ld last 75yds* **12/1**

1230 **2** *1 1/2* **Danebank (IRE)**[10] 5773 4-8-13 **52** ......(p) DaleGibson 16 — 63
(JMackie) *hld up: gd hdwy on outer over 3f out: rdn to ld 2f out and sn clr: drvn ins last: hdd and no ex last 75 yds* **7/1**[2]

0030 **3** *3* **Wyoming**[37] 5116 3-8-9 **55** ...... ACulhane 18 — 61
(JARToller) *hld up: pushed along over 4f out: rdn and hdwy 2f out: sn chsng ldr: drvn and one pce ins last* **11/1**

0200 **4** *2 1/2* **Field Spark**[20] 5554 4-8-13 **55** ......(p) PMulrennan(3) 17 — 57
(JAGlover) *stdd s and bhd: gd hdwy over 3f out: rdn 2f out: kpt on appr last: nrst fin* **12/1**

033 **5** *nk* **Duc's Dream**[2] 5935 6-8-12 **51** ...... PaulEddery 11 — 53
(DMorris) *hld up in tch: pushed along 4f out: rdn wl over 2f out and kpt on same pce* **13/2**[1]

0002 **6** *5* **Persian Genie (IRE)**[20] 5538 3-8-9 **55** ...... RHavlin 2 — 49
(GBBalding) *hld up: gd hdwy on outer to chse ldrs 3f out: sn rdn and wknd fnl 2f* **20/1**

2303 **7** *3/4* **Senor Eduardo**[13] 5714 7-9-2 **55** ...... ANicholls 15 — 48
(SGollings) *in tch: hdwy 3f out: sn rdn and no imp fnl 2f* **12/1**

6202 **8** *2* **Donna's Double**[8] 5817 9-8-13 **52** ......(p) KDarley 6 — 41
(DEddy) *hld up: hdwy on outer 4f out: rdn along to chse ldrs 3f out: sn drvn and btn* **8/1**[3]

5511 **9** *5* **Lazzaz**[16] 5654 6-8-8 **54** ...... PGallagher(7) 8 — 35
(PWHiatt) *trckd ldrs: effrt over 3f out and ev ch tl rdn 2f out and sn wknd* **8/1**[3]

0000 **10** *1 3/4* **Karathaena (IRE)**[10] 5773 4-8-13 **55** ...... TEaves(3) 9 — 34
(MESowersby) *in tch: hdwy to ld over 3f out: sn rdn: hdd 2f out and sn wknd* **33/1**

0410 **11** *10* **Zan Lo (IRE)**[16] 5638 4-8-10 **49** ...... RWinston 1 — 12
(BSRothwell) *hld up: hdwy over 3f out: sn rdn along and no further prog* **33/1**

3060 **12** *1/2* **Ellway Heights**[13] 5710 7-8-12 **51** ...... FNorton 12 — 13
(WMBrisbourne) *midfield: hdwy on outer to trck ldrs 1/2-way: rdn over 3f out and sn wknd* **12/1**

0000 **13** *2* **Ellovamul**[13] 5714 4-8-6 **50** ...... PMakin(5) 3 — 9
(WMBrisbourne) *a towards rr* **25/1**

5000 **14** *hd* **Beneking**[13] 5714 4-8-5 **49** ...... StephanieHollinshead(5) 4 — 7
(RHollinshead) *midfield: gd hdwy 4f out: chsd ldrs over 2f out: sn rdn and wknd* **33/1**

200- **15** *9* **Iron Warrior (IRE)**[325] 1104 4-9-2 **55** ...... NPollard 14 — —
(GMMoore) *chsd ldng pair: rdn along over 4f out and sn wknd* **50/1**

-400 **16** *2* **Dreams Forgotten (IRE)**[31] 5259 4-8-13 **55** ...... ABeech(3) 13 — —
(GGMargarson) *prom: rdn along over 3f out: drvn over 2f out and sn wknd* **40/1**

0620 **17** *1 1/2* **Bravely Does It (USA)**[44] 4934 4-9-2 **55** ...... SWKelly 10 — —
(WMBrisbourne) *led: rdn along and hdd 4f out: sn wknd* **16/1**

36-6 **18** *7* **My Last Bean (IRE)**[16] 5658 7-9-0 **53** ...... FLynch 7 — —
(BSmart) *cl up: rdn to ld briefly 4f out: sn hdd & wknd* **10/1**

2m 38.94s (-1.11) **Going Correction** +0.025s/f (Good)
**WFA** 3 from 4yo+ 7lb — **18** Ran **SP% 124.0**
Speed ratings: **104,103,101,99,99 95,95,93,90,89 82,82,81,81,75 73,72,68**CSF £87.46 CT £975.32 TOTE £13.10: £4.30, £2.10, £3.40, £4.20; EX 123.40.
**Owner** L A Morgan **Bred** L A Morgan **Trained** Upper Longdon, Staffs
■ Stewards Enquiry : A Nicholls one-day ban: careless riding (Oct 15)

### FOCUS
A low-grade handicap, but very competitive and the pace was decent, making the form slightly above average for the level.

### NOTEBOOK
**Heathyards Pride**, raised 3lb for his Warwick victory, had no problem with the longer trip and saw his race out well. He has already won on sand so looks the ideal type for a winter campaign in middle-distance handicaps.
**Danebank(IRE)** returned to form back on a sound surface and looked like winning soon after turning for home, but the winner found a decisive turn of foot and he was already getting the worst of the argument when jumping a newspaper Dayjur-style about 20 yards from the line.
**Wyoming**, a maiden after eight attempts coming into this, had every chance but tended to lug into the inside rail in the home straight and may not want the ground as fast as this.
**Field Spark** had the whole field in front of him starting the final bend and ran on past beaten horses without ever being able to get on terms. He is dropping to a decent mark.
**Duc's Dream**, making a quick reappearance, has dropped to a mark 2lb lower than for his last win and ran a fair race. With his favoured fast ground less and less likely to prevail as the autumn progresses, his best chance of further success is likely to be at Southwell where he has won four times.
**Persian Genie(IRE)** would have preferred softer ground.

## 5994 CARONI MAIDEN STKS — 1m 4y
5:20 (5:21) (D3) 3-Y-0 — **£5,616** (£1,728; £864; £432) **Stalls** Low

Form — RPR

6 **1** **Miss Polaris**[17] 5621 3-8-9 ...... MFenton 3 — 79+
(PWHarris) *trckd ldrs: effrt on inner whn nt clr run and hmpd over 1f out: swtchd rt: styd on wl to ld nr fin* **10/1**

3230 **2** *1/2* **Pinching (IRE)**[80] 3916 3-8-9 73 ......(v) WRyan 7 — 72
(HRACecil) *w ldrs: upsides fnl f: no ex nr fin* **6/1**[3]

4-32 **3** *shd* **Meneef (USA)**[17] 5621 3-9-0 76 ...... RHills 4 — 77
(MPTregoning) *led: rdn and qcknd over 2f out: edgd lft over 1f out: hdd nr fin* **7/4**[1]

-342 **4** *nk* **Mrs Shilling**[13] 5713 3-8-9 67 ...... RWinston 11 — 71
(JRFanshawe) *trckd ldrs too t.k.h: effrt and upisdes 1f out: bmpd and wknd nr fin* **11/4**[2]

6020 **5** *5* **True (IRE)**[13] 5715 3-8-6 56 ...... TEaves(3) 9 — 60
(MrsSLamyman) *t.k.h in rr: hdwy 2f out: nvr nr ldrs* **28/1**

05 **6** *1/2* **Harrycat (IRE)**[23] 5478 3-9-0 ...... JQuinn 10 — 63
(VSmith) *mid-div: kpt on fnl f: nvr a threat* **25/1**

4464 **7** *1 3/4* **Slavonic (USA)**[122] 2648 3-9-0 73 ......(b) NCallan 12 — 59
(KARyan) *trckd ldrs: effrt over 2f out: wknd over 1f out* **7/1**

**8** *2* **Mtilly** 3-8-9 ...... KDarley 5 — 50
(MJohnston) *lengthy: unf: chsd ldrs: lost pl bnd after 2f: bhd fnl 2f* **33/1**

5552 **9** *2 1/2* **Beautiful Noise**[11] 5748 3-8-9 60 ......(b) ACulhane 6 — 44
(DMorris) *trckd ldrs: outpcd over 2f out: lost pl over 1f out* **14/1**

0 **10** *11* **Jack's Check**[10] 5770 3-8-11 ...... PMulrennan(3) 1 — 24
(NTinkler) *dwlt: hld up in rr: effrt over 3f out: wl bhd fnl 2f* **100/1**

1m 46.54s (0.94) **Going Correction** +0.025s/f (Good) — **10** Ran **SP% 116.8**
Speed ratings: **96,95,95,95,90 89,87,85,83,72**CSF £66.65 TOTE £14.60: £3.10, £1.80, £4.90; EX 68.60 Place 6 £269.29, Place 5 £191.23.
**Owner** Cool Customers **Bred** Al Dahlawi Stud Co Ltd **Trained** Ringshall, Bucks
■ The Tote place dividend of £4.90 applies to Harrycat who was originally announced as third by the Judge.
■ Stewards Enquiry : R Hills two-day ban: careless riding (Oct 15,17)

### FOCUS
A modest winning time for the grade and little to choose between the first four at the line. The next five home behind the winner were close to their best and the form is limited but sound.

### NOTEBOOK
**Miss Polaris** had clearly learnt plenty first time. Going for an audacious run up the inner once in line for home, she found the door slammed in her face and had to pull two horses wide. She came between horses to lead almost on the line and will improve again especially over further.
**Pinching(IRE)**, placed in three of her previous five starts, looked to be saving something for herself and in the end just missed out. She is proving very frustrating.
**Meneef(USA)**, allowed to set his own pace, swung wide for two or three strides coming off the home turn, tempting the rider of the winner to try his luck up his inside. He only just missed out in the end and did nothing at all wrong.
**Mrs Shilling**, a keen type, went to post early. She was one of four upsides inside the last, but had no more to give when pushed sideways by the winner near the line. Rated 67, a strong-run handicap over seven might be her best chance of breaking her duck.
**True(IRE)**, a maiden after 13 previous starts, had plenty to find on official ratings.
**Harrycat(IRE)**, having his third outing, gave every indication that he is capable of better now he is qualified to try his hand in handicap company.

T/Jkpt: Not won. T/Plt: £792.80 to a £1 stake. Pool: £44,042.30. 40.55 winning tickets. T/Qpdt: £108.00 to a £1 stake. Pool: £3,140.70. 21.50 winning tickets. JR

# [5838]WINDSOR (R-H)

Monday, October 4

**OFFICIAL GOING: Soft**

The far side of the track in the straight was by far the fastest area of the track, as those that opted to stay stands' side were well beaten.

Wind: Moderate half behind Weather: Fine

## 5995 CANONS STOKE POGES NURSERY — 1m 67y

2:30 (2:30) (E3) (0-75,75) 2-Y-O — £3,630 (£1,117; £558; £279) Stalls High

Form — RPR

034 1 **Come On Jonny (IRE)**[28] 5341 2-9-4 **72** DHolland 9 77
(RMBeckett) *lw: t.k.h: chsd ldrs: led over 3f out: drvn out* **14/1**

3510 2 ½ **Secret History (USA)**[23] 5466 2-9-3 **71** RFfrench 3 75
(MJohnston) *prom: chal fnl 3f: kpt on* **14/1**

4000 3 2½ **Darko Karim**[29] 5314 2-9-6 **74** SSanders 4 73
(DRLoder) *towards rr: hdwy 4f out: one pce fnl 2f* **40/1**

0503 4 2 **Lord Of Dreams (IRE)**[12] 5735 2-9-2 **70** RLMoore 11 64
(DWPArbuthnot) *lw: bhd: hdwy whn hmpd over 2f out: drifted lft: styd on same pce* **11/1**

0601 5 1½ **Penalty Kick (IRE)**[6] 5852 2-9-6 **74** 6ex LDettori 10 65
(NACallaghan) *prom: hrd rdn over 2f out: sn outpcd* **6/4**[1]

550 6 1¾ **Oasis Way (GR)**[16] 5648 2-9-4 **72** MartinDwyer 2 59
(PRChamings) *bhd: hdwy 3f out: no ex fnl 2f* **20/1**

5642 7 shd **Flying Pass**[6] 5852 2-9-2 **70** SWhitworth 14 57
(DJSFfrenchDavis) *bhd: hrd rdn and sme hdwy 2f out: nt pce to chal* **10/1**

0660 8 ½ **Go Mo (IRE)**[3] 5909 2-9-3 **71** JFEgan 13 57
(SKirk) *mid-div: hrd rdn over 2f out: sn btn* **9/1**[3]

6250 9 nk **Just Do It (UAE)**[16] 5636 2-8-12 **66** TEDurcan 7 51
(MRChannon) *s.s: sn in midfield: rdn and no hdwy whn hung lft fnl 2f* **25/1**

0450 10 3 **Grandma's Girl**[13] 5719 2-8-13 **67** EAhern 1 45
(RGuest) *prom over 5f* **16/1**

5130 11 1½ **Lady Chef**[28] 5335 2-9-7 **75** AMcCarthy 6 50
(BRMillman) *chsd ldrs 5f* **40/1**

4230 12 8 **Musico (IRE)**[24] 5434 2-9-5 **73** SDrowne 5 30
(BRMillman) *t.k.h in midfield: btn whn bmpd 2f out: eased whn no ch fnl f* **8/1**[2]

0620 13 5 **Swell Lad**[13] 5719 2-9-1 **69** (b) TQuinn 12 15
(PFICole) *lw: led tl over 3f out: hrd rdn and wkng whn wnt lft over 2f out: eased whn no ch fnl f* **14/1**

1m 46.96s (1.36) **Going Correction** +0.05s/f (Good) **13** Ran SP% **117.9**

Speed ratings: **95,94,92,90,88 86,86,86,85,82 81,73,68**CSF £185.65 CT £7404.83 TOTE £13.40: £3.20, £4.00, £11.40; EX 180.40.

**Owner** A E Frost **Bred** Mountarmstrong Stud **Trained** Lambourn, Berks

**FOCUS**

A fair nursery run at a reasonable pace in which they raced middle to far side in the straight; the first two home came up the middle. The form appears ordinary.

**NOTEBOOK**

**Come On Jonny(IRE)**, who showed ability in three runs in maiden company over six furlongs, improved as expected for this step up in trip and switch to nursery company. He should not go up too much for this and looks capable of winning again.

**Secret History(USA)**, who won her maiden on easy ground, appreciated these conditions on this step up to a mile and returned to form with a solid effort.

**Darko Karim** showed little on his handicap debut over seven furlongs on fast ground with a visor fitted but, with the headgear left off and faced with very different conditions, he ran his best race to date.

**Lord Of Dreams(IRE)**, who made his challenge against the far-side rail, made a respectable nursery debut and has the ability to win a similar race.

**Penalty Kick(IRE)** scored well on his nursery debut at Nottingham on his previous start, but that was over ten furlongs on decent ground and he was unable to reproduce that level under these very different conditions.

**Oasis Way(GR)** again showed ability and is not one to write off just yet. *Official explanation: jockey said filly hung right*

**Go Mo(IRE)** was well held, but he attracted support and may be capable of better. *Official explanation: jockey said colt had a breathing problem*

**Musico(IRE)** *Official explanation: jockey said colt hung right*

**Swell Lad** *Official explanation: jockey said colt lost his action*

## 5996 EUROPEAN BREEDERS FUND MAIDEN STKS (DIV I) — 6f

3:00 (3:03) (D3) 2-Y-O — £5,213 (£1,604; £802; £401) Stalls High

Form — RPR

226 1 **Hanseatic League (USA)**[50] 4776 2-9-0 **82** LDettori 4 78
(MJohnston) *mde virtually all: rdn over 1f out: hld on nr fin* **3/1**[1]

2 nk **Puya** 2-8-9 DaneO'Neill 8 72
(HCandy) *rangy: scope: bit bkwd: s.s: bhd tl hdwy 2f out: shkn up and rn green over 1f out: fin wl: bttr for experience* **7/1**

0 3 1¾ **Pesquera**[19] 5569 2-8-9 EAhern 1 67
(JNoseda) *prom: jnd wnr 2f out: one pce ins fnl f* **9/1**

0 4 2½ **Guildenstern (IRE)**[73] 4081 2-9-0 SDrowne 12 64
(HMorrison) *jnd main gp on far side after 1f: sn outpcd: styd on fnl 2f: nt rch ldrs* **6/1**[3]

000 5 1¾ **In Dream'S (IRE)**[23] 5467 2-8-11 LPKeniry(3) 3 59
(BGubby) *lw: chsd ldrs: no ex fnl 2f* **25/1**

6 nk **Babe Maccool (IRE)** 2-9-0 SSanders 11 58
(BWHills) *leggy: scope: jnd main gp on far side after 1f: chsd ldrs: no ex fnl 2f* **13/2**

66 7 1½ **Briannie (IRE)**[16] 5653 2-8-9 MartinDwyer 2 49
(JRBoyle) *mid-div: rdn and no hdwy fnl 2f* **20/1**

4460 8 1¾ **Kempsey**[7] 5839 2-9-0 **63** ADaly 9 48
(JJBridger) *sn racing alone stands' side: spd to 1/2-way: n.d fnl 2f* **25/1**

65 9 3 **North Shore (IRE)**[26] 5396 2-9-0 RLMoore 7 39
(RHannon) *swvd lft s: mid-div after 2f: wknd 2f out* **7/2**[2]

0 10 6 **Eforetta (GER)**[17] 5616 2-8-9 VSlattery 5 16
(DJWintle) *bhd fnl 2f* **50/1**

11 9 **Formidable Will (FR)** 2-9-0 RSmith 10 —
(CGCox) *str: bkwd: s.s: outpcd: sn wl bhd* **20/1**

1m 15.0s (1.13) **Going Correction** +0.10s/f (Good) **11** Ran SP% **116.5**

Speed ratings: **96,95,93,89,87 87,85,82,78,70 58**CSF £22.07 TOTE £2.70: £1.70, £2.40, £2.50; EX 35.80.

**Owner** Sheikh Mohammed **Bred** Darley **Trained** Middleham Moor, N Yorks

**FOCUS**

Just an ordinary maiden and an average time for the class, despite being more than a second slower than the second division. They raced far side in the straight and the winner ran somewhere near his debut effort.

**NOTEBOOK**

**Hanseatic League(USA)**, a beaten favourite on his last two starts, made no mistake this time on this first run beyond five furlongs. However, he does looks high enough in the weights judged on this performance and could be one to take on in a competitive nursery.

**Puya**, a half-sister to the high-class multiple sprint winner Gorse, was easy enough to back on course but made a very pleasing debut. She showed signs of inexperience, but still got to within a neck of a horse rated 82 and should soon be winning.

**Pesquera** stepped up on her debut effort and is clearly progressing.

**Guildenstern(IRE)**, well held on his debut when his saddle slipped 73 days previously, duly improved on that effort but may just be more of a handicap type.

**In Dream'S(IRE)**, hailing from an in-form stable, ran his best race to date and could be capable of even better now he is qualified for a mark.

**Babe Maccool(IRE)**, a 50,000gns half-brother to a winning three-year-old in Norway, out of a half-sister to the dam of High Chaparral, offered some promise and should improve.

**North Shore(IRE)** did not help his chance by swerving badly as the stalls opened and was well held. He is now though, qualified for a handicap mark.

## 5997 MORELLI CLASSIFIED STKS — 1m 3f 135y

3:30 (3:30) (D3) 3-Y-O+ — £4,966 (£1,528; £764; £382) Stalls Low

Form — RPR

2121 1 **Belle Rouge**[12] 5728 6-9-5 **75** LDettori 9 87
(CAHorgan) *in tch: effrt 3f out: styd on u.p to ld ins fnl f* **11/4**[2]

1221 2 2 **Quarrymount**[2] 5944 3-9-2 **70** SSanders 12 88
(SirMarkPrescott) *prom: led over 3f out tl ins fnl f: one pce* **10/11**[1]

3250 3 2 **Albavilla**[12] 5728 4-9-2 **72** RLMoore 2 78
(PWHarris) *prom: jnd ldr over 3f out: no ex fnl f* **16/1**

6020 4 5 **Nawow**[5] 5875 4-9-8 **75** DHolland 10 77
(PDCundell) *lw: in tch: effrt and hrd rdn over 2f out: no imp* **14/1**

2400 5 nk **Hatch A Plan (IRE)**[19] 5568 3-8-10 **70** (p) RMullen 3 72
(RMBeckett) *towards rr: fair 5th and styng on u.p whn hmpd on far rail over 1f out* **33/1**

-334 6 2 **Royal Bathwick (IRE)**[38] 5074 4-9-3 **73** GBaker 6 69
(BRMillman) *lw: s.i.s: in rr tl sme hdwy and hrd rdn over 2f out: nt pce to chal* **18/1**

3-00 7 1¼ **Montecristo**[103] 3199 11-8-11 **71** RMills(7) 8 68
(RGuest) *bit bkwd: sn wl bhd: styd on fnl 2f* **66/1**

3403 8 1 **Dickie Deadeye**[5] 5869 7-9-3 **69** SDrowne 7 66
(GBBalding) *prom over 8f* **12/1**[3]

4440 9 1¼ **Gallant Boy (IRE)**[23] 5456 5-9-3 **63** (vt) RHughes 5 64
(PDEvans) *b: mid-div: rdn and btn over 2f out* **25/1**

3605 10 4 **Jacaranda (IRE)**[10] 5764 4-9-3 **70** DSweeney 4 58
(MrsALMKing) *lw: chsd ldrs 8f* **20/1**

0400 11 17 **Soller Bay**[18] 5581 7-9-3 **67** JFEgan 1 34
(KRBurke) *led and set gd pce tl wknd over 3f out: eased whn no ch fnl 2f* **25/1**

2m 32.0s (1.90) **Going Correction** +0.40s/f (Good)

**WFA** 3 from 4yo+ 7lb **11** Ran SP% **121.4**

Speed ratings: **109,107,106,103,102 101,100,99,99,96 85**CSF £5.39 TOTE £3.90: £1.60, £1.10, £3.80; EX 8.10.

**Owner** Mrs B Woodford **Bred** Whitsbury Manor Stud **Trained** Ogbourne Maisey, Wilts

**FOCUS**

A reasonable classified event run at a decent pace and fought out by two horses at the top of their game and the form looks sound enough on paper. They all came far side in the straight, although some sooner than others and Quarrymount was one of those who took his time.

**NOTEBOOK**

**Belle Rouge** is being brilliantly handled, having finished in the first two on her last 12 starts and has now won five times this season, all under today's jockey. There should yet be more to come and a race at Newbury could be next on the agenda. Should she get too high in handicap on turf, she will have no bother in exploiting an All-Weather rating of just 60, unless the Handicapper amends it in the meantime, as her form figures on Polytrack read 221.

**Quarrymount**, due to be raised to a mark of 82 following six-length Newmarket success, took longer to get over the far side than the eventual winner and appeared to go for home too soon. He would therefore be one to keep in mind next time, even off his new mark.

**Albavilla** had never previously raced on ground this soft, but she handled conditions well enough and was just beaten by two better horses.

**Nawow** has just a maiden win to his name on the Flat and continues below his best.

**Hatch A Plan(IRE)**, with cheekpieces on for the first time, ran better than he has been on his last couple of outings and would have been closer had he not been hampered in the closing stages.

**Soller Bay** *Official explanation: jockey said gelding got tired and had no more to give*

## 5998 NATIONAL HUNT RACING RETURNS TO WINDSOR H'CAP — 1m 2f 7y

4:00 (4:00) (D2) (0-85,85) 3-Y-O — £7,077 (£2,177; £1,088; £544) Stalls Low

Form — RPR

-513 1 **Day To Remember**[36] 5150 3-9-4 **85** DHolland 2 95
(EFVaughan) *led after 2f: rdn clr over 2f out: jnd ins fnl f: hld on wl* **4/1**[1]

0416 2 nk **Another Choice (IRE)**[19] 5568 3-8-11 **78** (t) TEDurcan 5 87
(NPLittmoden) *prom: hrd rdn over 1f out: drew level 100 yds out: nt qckn nr fin* **9/1**

0115 3 1¼ **Flying Adored**[19] 5566 3-8-13 **80** TQuinn 8 87
(JLDunlop) *chsd ldrs: hrd rdn over 1f out: styd on fnl f* **5/1**[3]

1 4 2½ **Diego Cao (IRE)**[19] 5568 3-9-3 **84** RLMoore 12 87
(GLMoore) *lw: prom: hrd rdn over 1f out: one pce* **9/2**[2]

3212 5 2 **Magic Sting**[15] 5672 3-8-5 **75** HayleyTurner(3) 9 74
(MLWBell) *b: plld hrd in rr: hdwy on bit 4f out: rdn over 2f out: sn btn* **4/1**[1]

4012 6 1 **Smoothly Does It**[14] 5693 3-8-4 **71** oh2 JFEgan 11 69
(MrsAJBowlby) *mid-div: nt handle bnd and dropped rr 1/2-way: kpt on steadily fnl 2f: n.d* **7/1**

0006 7 1¼ **Over The Rainbow (IRE)**[35] 5183 3-8-13 **80** (p) SSanders 6 75
(BWHills) *in tch: outpcd 3f out: sn btn* **9/1**

40-0 8 15 **Buzz Buzz**[110] 2971 3-8-4 **71** oh3 JMackay 7 41
(CEBrittain) *lw: stdd in rr s: rdn and lost tch 3f out* **25/1**

323- 9 6 **English Rocket (IRE)**[331] 5950 3-8-6 **73** EAhern 1 33
(DJSFfrenchDavis) *bit bkwd: plld hrd: led 2f: prom tl wknd qckly over 2f out* **25/1**

2m 12.03s (3.73) **Going Correction** +0.40s/f (Good) **9** Ran SP% **115.0**

Speed ratings: **101,100,99,97,96 95,94,82,77**CSF £40.19 CT £180.31 TOTE £4.90: £1.60, £2.90, £2.40; EX 58.20.

**Owner** Racing For Gold **Bred** Stratford Place Stud **Trained** Newmarket, Suffolk

**FOCUS**

A fair handicap, but the pace was ordinary and the race does not appear particularly strong, although the first two are progressive. They raced far side in the straight.

**NOTEBOOK**

**Day To Remember**, slightly disappointing on his handicap debut at Goodwood on his previous start, improved for this step up from a mile and ran out a determined winner. Unlikely to go up much for this, there could be more to come.

**Another Choice(IRE)**, with conditions in his favour, came to win his race but the eventual winner found more under pressure. A decent effort off a mark 6lb higher than when last winning and he seems to be improving.

**Flying Adored**, racing beyond a mile for the first time, appeared to get the trip as, although no match for the front two, he was clear of the remainder.

**Diego Cao(IRE)**, who caused a surprise when winning on his British debut over this trip at Sandown, was not quite at that level of form off a 6lb higher mark. However, he is the type to improve with time and is one to keep on the right side of.

**Magic Sting** had conditions to suit, but he did not help his chance by racing keenly and he looks high enough in the weights.

**English Rocket(IRE)** *Official explanation: jockey said gelding was unsuited by Soft ground*

## 5999 ATTHERACES.COM MAIDEN STKS — 1m 2f 7y

4:30 (4:31) (D3) 3-Y-O+ — £4,485 (£1,380; £690; £345) Stalls Low

| Form | Pos | Btn | Horse | Jockey | RPR |
|---|---|---|---|---|---|
| 3242 | 1 | | **Mikao (IRE)**[33] [5217] 3-9-0 78 — (MHTompkins) *lw: led 2f: led over 2f out tl over 1f out: led ins fnl f: drvn out* 4/1[2] | DHolland 5 | 68 |
| 0-22 | 2 | nk | **Zakfree (IRE)**[35] [5189] 3-9-0 66 — (NPLittmoden) *in tch: effrt 3f out: slt ld over 1f out tl ins fnl f: kpt on* 14/1 | (b) TEDurcan 11 | 67 |
| 0000 | 3 | 9 | **Zarneeta**[2] [5928] 3-8-9 40 — (WDeBest-Turner) *prom: hrd rdn 2f out: sn outpcd* 100/1 | PDoe 4 | 47? |
| 5-46 | 4 | 1 1/4 | **Residential**[37] [5123] 3-9-0 64 — (MrsAJPerrett) *lw: t.k.h: chsd ldrs: pushed along 4f out: hrd rdn and btn 2f out* 8/1 | RHughes 9 | 50 |
| 4503 | 5 | 1/2 | **Petrosa (IRE)**[7] [5841] 4-9-0 69 — (DRCElsworth) *lw: hdwy and rn wd bnd at 1/2-way: rdn to chse ldrs over 2f out: one pce* 5/2[1] | TQuinn 3 | 44 |
| -050 | 6 | shd | **Mac's Elan**[16] [5644] 4-9-5 35 — (ABCoogan) *hdwy 5f out: chsd ldrs 3f out: hrd rdn and no ex fnl 2f* 25/1 | LDettori 1 | 49? |
| 0 | 7 | 5 | **River Of Diamonds**[37] [5123] 3-9-0 — (RGuest) *mid-div: lost pl 1/2-way: sme late hdwy* 16/1 | MartinDwyer 15 | 40 |
| 420 | 8 | 2 1/2 | **Pleasant**[7] [5828] 3-8-9 — (LGCottrell) *chsd ldrs over 7f* 14/1 | SDrowne 7 | 31 |
| -044 | 9 | 3/4 | **Dandygrey Russett (IRE)**[20] [5537] 3-8-9 63 — (GLMoore) *mid-div: hmpd bnd at 1/2-way and dropped to rr: styd on fnl 2f* 8/1 | RLMoore 19 | 30 |
| 3-06 | 10 | 1 1/2 | **Nadir**[28] [5345] 3-9-0 65 — (PHowling) *mid-div to rr thrght: rdn 1/2-way: n.d* 14/1 | EAhern 18 | 32 |
| 00 | 11 | 1 1/4 | **Mrs Philip**[7] [5828] 5-9-0 — (PJHobbs) *sn bhd: rdn 4f out: mod hdwy 2f out: nvr trbld ldrs* 66/1 | VSlattery 13 | 25 |
| | 12 | shd | **Pacific Run (USA)** 3-8-11 — (BJMeehan) *leggy: led after 2f tl wknd over 2f out* 20/1 | LPKeniry(3) 8 | 30 |
| 0-00 | 13 | 2 | **Diequest (USA)**[42] [5007] 3-9-0 — (JamiePoulton) *towards rr whn rn wd bnd into st: nvr a factor* 33/1 | JFEgan 2 | 26 |
| 0 | 14 | 3 | **Desiree (IRE)**[17] [5621] 3-8-2 — (JohnBerry) *bkwd: bhd most of way* 66/1 | FrancesPickard(7) 16 | 16 |
| 3360 | 15 | 3 1/2 | **Tree Tops**[24] [5446] 3-8-9 69 — (JHMGosden) *prom: hrd rdn 2f out: wknd qckly* 7/1[3] | JFortune 10 | 10 |
| 00 | 16 | 6 | **Just Dashing**[65] [4337] 5-8-12 — (JELong) *bhd fr 1/2-way* 100/1 | HPoulton(7) 14 | 5 |
| 000- | 17 | 3 | **Zorn**[558] [806] 5-9-5 35 — (PHowling) *chsd ldrs over 6f* 100/1 | RMullen 17 | — |
| | 18 | dist | **Mister Chalk** 3-8-11 — (TKeddy) *rangy: b: s.s: sn t.o* 66/1 | J-PGuillambert(7) 12 | — |

2m 11.0s (2.70) **Going Correction** +0.40s/f (Good) — 18 Ran SP% 128.2

**WFA** 3 from 4yo+ 5lb

Speed ratings: **105,104,97,96,96 96,92,90,89,88 87,87,85,83,80 75,73,—**CSF £58.32 TOTE £4.60: £1.90, £4.20, £35.40; EX 41.20.

**Owner** Ben Allen **Bred** Kildaragh Stud **Trained** Newmarket, Suffolk

**FOCUS**

A weak maiden that only concerned two horses from a long way out, but the form is anchored by the proximity of the third and sixth. They all raced far side in the straight.

**NOTEBOOK**

**Mikao(IRE)** handled the conditions better than most of these and was able to confirm the promise of his earlier efforts to get off the mark. Things will be tougher in future, but his ability to handle soft ground will be an advantage this backend.

**Zakfree(IRE)** has not always looked that straightforward, but there was nothing wrong with this effort considering he would have been 12lb better off with the eventual winner had this been a handicap.

**Zarneeta** has not progressed from her promising debut when third at 100/1 in a six-furlong fast-ground Leicester maiden, but this was encouraging and she may find her level in banded company.

**Residential** is not progressing and he failed to improve for the step up from a mile.

**Petrosa(IRE)** had never previously raced on ground softer than good and was a long way below form.

**Dandygrey Russett(IRE)** was a long way below the form she had shown on her three previous starts.

**Tree Tops** is not progressing and this was one of her worst efforts to date.

## 6000 EUROPEAN BREEDERS FUND MAIDEN STKS (DIV II) — 6f

5:00 (5:00) (D3) 2-Y-O — £5,213 (£1,604; £802; £401) Stalls High

| Form | Pos | Btn | Horse | Jockey | RPR |
|---|---|---|---|---|---|
| 4200 | 1 | | **On The Waterline (IRE)**[26] [5391] 2-8-9 72 — (PDEvans) *mde all: drvn clr over 1f out: r.o wl* 12/1 | (v[1]) SDrowne 5 | 78 |
| 6 | 2 | 3 | **Daliya (IRE)**[28] [5349] 2-8-9 — (SirMichaelStoute) *chsd ldrs: hung lft 2f out: styd on to take 2nd ins fnl f* 9/1[3] | (v[1]) DHolland 11 | 69 |
| 0 | 3 | 1 | **Pamir (IRE)**[13] [5720] 2-8-7 — (LMCumani) *a.p: one pce fnl 2f* 33/1 | AHamblett(3) 7 | 71 |
| | 4 | 2 | **Marhoon (USA)** 2-9-0 — (EFVaughan) *str: bkwd: in tch: rdn and styd on same pce fnl 2f* 50/1 | TEDurcan 1 | 65 |
| 3 | 5 | 1/2 | **Dr Zalo**[22] [5494] 2-9-0 — (PJMakin) *prom: hrd rdn over 1f out: no ex* 5/2[2] | SSanders 3 | 64 |
| | 6 | 1 1/4 | **Patternmaker (USA)** 2-9-0 — (WJarvis) *wl grwn: bit bkwd: dwlt: towards rr: rdn and hdwy over 2f out: no imp* 40/1 | TQuinn 2 | 60 |
| 2 | 7 | 2 1/2 | **Anchor Date**[20] [5536] 2-9-0 — (BWHills) *stdd s and swtchd to far rail: towards rr: rdn over 2f out: rchd ldrs* 10/11[1] | RHughes 12 | 52 |
| | 8 | 2 1/2 | **Halcyon Express (IRE)** 2-9-0 — (PFICole) *lengthy: unf: scope: bit bkwd: in tch over 3f* 16/1 | LDettori 4 | 45 |
| 000 | 9 | nk | **Laurollie**[31] [5256] 2-8-9 — (DrJRJNaylor) *a bhd* 100/1 | ADaly 6 | 39 |
| 0 | 10 | 5 | **Silver Swing**[3] [5911] 2-9-0 — (WJHaggas) *dwlt: a towards rr* 33/1 | DaneO'Neill 8 | 29 |
| 00 | 11 | 12 | **Ciendra Girl (IRE)**[21] [5508] 2-8-6 — (RBrotherton) *towards rr: drvn along 1/2-way: nvr a factor* 100/1 | HayleyTurner(3) 9 | — |
| 032 | 12 | 5 | **Stan's Girl**[141] [2140] 2-8-9 60 — (IAWood) *lw: racd alone stands' rail: bhd fnl 2f* 25/1 | PDoe 10 | — |

1m 13.96s (0.09) **Going Correction** +0.10s/f (Good) — 12 Ran SP% 120.6

Speed ratings: **103,99,97,95,94 92,89,86,85,78 62,56**CSF £111.26 TOTE £16.30: £3.40, £1.90, £6.60; EX 135.70.

**Owner** M W Lawrence **Bred** M W Lawrence **Trained** Pandy, Gwent

**FOCUS**

Just a fair maiden, but a very smart time for the grade, over a second quicker than the first division and the first two set a reasoanble standard. Only one horse stayed stands' side in the straight and was well beaten.

**NOTEBOOK**

**On The Waterline(IRE)** had been below form on her last couple of starts but, fitted with a visor for the first time, this was much better and she got off the mark in most decisive fashion. She is one to keep on the right side of if the headgear continues to have a positive effect.

**Daliya(IRE)**, with a visor replacing blinkers, did not look entirely straightforward and failed to improve on her debut running.

**Pamir(IRE)** just about improved on his debut effort and should continue to go the right way, especially when handicapped.

**Marhoon(USA)** ◆, a half-brother to a mile three-year-old winner and unbeaten UAE sprinter/miler Mannjam, looks the one to take from this modest race. He will need to improve, but seems almost sure to do so and should not be underestimated in future.

**Dr Zalo**, a very promising third of his six on his debut on fast ground at Goodwood, ran nowhere near that form faced with very different conditions. *Official explanation: jockey was unable to offer any explanation for poor form shown; trainer said gelding finished lame*

**Anchor Date**, a very promising second under similar conditions on his debut at Salisbury, was simply unable to land a blow having been dropped in and is much better than he was able to show. *Official explanation: jockey said colt colt ran free to post*

**Stan's Girl** opted to take her chance on the stands' side, but the gamble did not pay off.

## 6001 WINDSOR FIREWORKS EXTRAVAGANZA ON SAT 6TH NOVEMBER H'CAP — 6f

5:30 (5:30) (E3) (0-70,70) 3-Y-O+ — £3,647 (£1,122; £561; £280) Stalls High

| Form | Pos | Btn | Horse | Jockey | RPR |
|---|---|---|---|---|---|
| 501 | 1 | | **Oeuf A La Neige**[21] [5512] 4-9-2 **68** — (GCHChung) *hld up in midfield: hdwy 2f out: led 1f out: hld on wl* 16/1 | OUrbina 20 | 76 |
| 0032 | 2 | hd | **Roman Quintet (IRE)**[21] [5512] 4-8-10 **62** — (DWPArbuthnot) *towards rr: hdwy and nt clr run over 1f out: jnd wnr fnl 75 yds: r.o* 10/1 | TQuinn 1 | 69 |
| 1430 | 3 | 1 1/2 | **Branston Tiger**[18] [5583] 5-8-11 **63** — (PDEvans) *a.p: nt qckn fnl f* 8/1[3] | (v) TEDurcan 7 | 66 |
| 2506 | 4 | nk | **Missus Links (USA)**[103] [3211] 3-9-3 **70** — (RHannon) *lw: chsd ldrs: rdn and n.m.r over 1f out: rallied and kpt on nr fin* 33/1 | RHughes 15 | 72 |
| 3001 | 5 | hd | **Stokesies Wish**[17] [5618] 4-8-8 **65** — (JLSpearing) *chsd ldrs: drvn to ld 2f out: hdd 1f out: one pce* 16/1 | BSwarbrick(5) 3 | 66 |
| 0006 | 6 | hd | **Extremely Rare (IRE)**[44] [4952] 3-8-11 **64** — (MSSaunders) *a.p: one pce fnl f* 50/1 | EAhern 18 | 65 |
| 30-1 | 7 | 1 1/4 | **Go Go Girl**[153] [1855] 4-9-3 **69** — (LGCottrell) *hld up in rr: hdwy over 1f out: nrst fin* 16/1 | SDrowne 13 | 66 |
| 4001 | 8 | nk | **Pure Imagination (IRE)**[15] [5674] 3-8-12 **65** — (JMBradley) *towards rr: rdn and hdwy 2f out: no imp fnl f* 7/1[2] | RLMoore 4 | 61 |
| -010 | 9 | nk | **Siraj**[38] [5094] 5-8-3 **62** — (PSMcentee) *a.p: no ex fnl f* 50/1 | JBrennan(7) 12 | 57 |
| 6005 | 10 | shd | **Sundried Tomato**[7] [5833] 5-8-13 **68** — (PWHiatt) *a.p: no ex fnl f* 8/1[3] | LFletcher(3) 11 | 63 |
| 2240 | 11 | shd | **High Ridge**[12] [5730] 5-9-4 **70** — (JMBradley) *in rr: effrt and swtchd rt wl over 1f out: nt rch ldrs* 20/1 | (p) DaneO'Neill 8 | 65 |
| 1600 | 12 | 1/2 | **Full Spate**[35] [5201] 9-9-3 **69** — (JMBradley) *mid-div: effrt 2f out: no imp* 16/1 | JFEgan 14 | 62 |
| 0040 | 13 | 3/4 | **Whippasnapper**[25] [5425] 4-8-8 **63** — (JRBest) *lw: s.s amd swtchd lft: bhd: effrt and hrd rdn over 1f out: nt trble ldrs* 9/1 | LPKeniry(3) 17 | 54 |
| 3321 | 14 | nk | **Instinct**[20] [5551] 3-8-7 **60** — (RHannon) *in tch: rdn whn hmpd over 1f out: sn hld* 20/1 | RSmith 10 | 50 |
| 6020 | 15 | 2 1/2 | **After The Show**[49] [4810] 3-9-2 **69** — (JRJenkins) *lw: led tl 2f out: wknd over 1f out* 33/1 | MartinDwyer 9 | 52 |
| 4200 | 16 | 1 | **Ace Club**[12] [5737] 3-8-10 **63** — (WJHaggas) *in tch: rdn whn hmpd on rail over 1f out: n.d after* 6/1[1] | LDettori 2 | 43 |
| 3010 | 17 | 3/4 | **Cefira (USA)**[17] [5618] 3-8-12 **65** — (MHTompkins) *mid-div: outpcd fnl 2f* 20/1 | DHolland 16 | 42 |
| 2034 | 18 | hd | **Dr Synn**[9] [5798] 3-8-13 **66** — (JAkehurst) *s.s: rdn along: a in rr* 12/1 | PDoe 5 | 43 |
| 2000 | 19 | 1/2 | **Gojo (IRE)**[17] [5618] 3-8-10 **63** — (BPalling) *towards rr: effrt 2f out: sn wknd* 25/1 | SSanders 6 | 38 |
| 3024 | 20 | 9 | **Cerulean Rose**[38] [5094] 5-9-3 **69** — (AWCarroll) *racd alone stands' rail: bhd fr 1/2-way* 10/1 | JFortune 19 | 17 |

1m 13.95s (0.08) **Going Correction** +0.10s/f (Good) — 20 Ran SP% 136.3

**WFA** 3 from 4yo+ 1lb

Speed ratings: **103,102,100,100,100 99,98,97,97,97 97,96,95,95,91 90,89,89,88,76**CSF £166.56 CT £1444.17 TOTE £20.40: £4.00, £3.00, £2.50, £9.40; EX 742.00 Place 6 £1,807.56, Place 5 £140.13.

**Owner** G C H Chung **Bred** Gainsborough Stud Management Ltd **Trained** Newmarket, Suffolk

**FOCUS**

A modest but competitive sprint handicap in which one horse raced alone stands' side, but was well beaten. The form is somewhat messy and the runner-up was again somewhat unlucky.

**NOTEBOOK**

**Oeuf A La Neige** had never previously raced on ground this soft and had the highest stall of all to overcome, but was still able to follow up his recent Bath success off a 4lb higher mark and is in the form of his life.

**Roman Quintet(IRE)** continues in cracking form but again just found one too good. Clear of the rest, his luck could well change soon.

**Branston Tiger** ran a solid race, but was well held by the front two and remains without a handicap win since May 2003.

**Missus Links(USA)** had never previously raced on ground this soft, but he seemed to handle conditions and would have been even closer with better luck.

**Stokesies Wish** found this tougher than Nottingham handicap she won on her previous start, racing off a 5lb higher mark.

**Pure Imagination(IRE)** ran respectably off a 7lb higher mark than when successful at Hamilton on his previous start.

**Sundried Tomato** looked like being in the mix, but could not sustain his effort.

**Whippasnapper** should not have minded these conditions, but he was never a threat after starting slowly.
**Ace Club** can be forgiven this, as he got no run when he most needed it. *Official explanation: jockey said gelding was checked 2f out*
**Cefira(USA)** *Official explanation: jockey said filly was unsuited by the Soft ground*
**Gojo(IRE)** *Official explanation: trainer said filly finished lame*
**Cerulean Rose** tried her luck on her own stands' side, but had no chance the way things worked out.

T/Plt: £1,445.80 to a £1 stake. Pool: £42,086.85. 21.25 winning tickets. T/Qpdt: £67.00 to a £1 stake. Pool: £4,159.00. 45.90 winning tickets. LM

# 5633 CATTERICK (L-H)

## Tuesday, October 5

**OFFICIAL GOING: Good (good to firm in places)**

The going was reckoned to be good to firm at the start but after the heavy showers it became soft on the bends and cut-up aginst the inside rail.
Wind: Strong 1/2 behind. Weather: Very windy with heavy bluster showers.

## 6002 LANCASHIRE MAIDEN STKS (DIV I) — 5f

**2:10** (2:10) (D3) 2-Y-O — **£3,425** (£1,054; £527; £263) **Stalls** Low

Form — RPR

4043 **1** **Harrys House**[24] 5447 2-9-0 67 ... RWinston 6 — 77+
(JJQuinn) *chsd ldr: led over 1f out: styd on wl: eased nr fin* **9/1**[3]

0400 **2** *1 1/4* **Gaudalpin (IRE)**[18] 5617 2-8-9 61 ... AMcCarthy 8 — 62
(MJAttwater) *trckd ldrs: hung lft 1f out: kpt on: no imp* **22/1**

0402 **3** *nk* **Thornber Court (IRE)**[10] 5800 2-8-9 66 ... FNorton 11 — 61
(ABerry) *chsd ldrs: effrt over 1f out: styd on ins last* **14/1**

054 **4** *3* **Orphan (IRE)**[9] 5816 2-9-0 ... DarrenWilliams 2 — 55
(KRBurke) *led tl over 1f out: wknd ins last* **20/1**

402 **5** *3 1/2* **Cutlass Gaudy**[14] 5711 2-9-0 82 ... DSweeney 7 — 43
(RHollinshead) *mid-div: effrt over 2f out: no imp* **7/2**[2]

630 **6** *1 1/4* **Underthemistletoe (IRE)**[73] 4149 2-8-9 55 ... FLynch 10 — 33
(BSmart) *chsd ldrs: wknd over 1f out* **50/1**

4 **7** *1/2* **Cavorting**[173] 1412 2-9-0 ... SSanders 5 — 37
(DRLoder) *mid-div: effrt and hung rt over 2f out: nvr a threat: wl btn whn eased ins last* **8/11**[1]

**8** *nk* **Passionately Royal** 2-8-11 ... THamilton(3) 1 — 36
(RAFahey) *cmpt: s.i.s: bhd tl sme late hdwy* **20/1**

0 **9** *1/2* **Grandma Ryta**[20] 5558 2-8-9 ... LisaJones 3 — 29
(JohnBerry) *bhd fnl 2f* **100/1**

6640 **10** *3* **Serene Pearl (IRE)**[47] 4878 2-8-9 53 ... (t) DAllan 4 — 18
(GMMoore) *a in rr* **150/1**

**11** *5* **Lady Edge (IRE)** 2-8-6 ... PMulrennan(3) 12 — 1
(MWEasterby) *leggy: unf: s.s: a bhd and out of tch* **50/1**

60.09 secs (-0.51) **Going Correction** -0.10s/f (Good) **11** Ran SP% **116.2**
Speed ratings: **100,98,97,92,87 85,84,83,83,78 70**CSF £177.94 TOTE £8.00: £2.80, £4.00, £3.80; EX 165.30.
**Owner** N Bulmer **Bred** N Bulmer **Trained** Settrington, N Yorks

**FOCUS**
A modest maiden and, with the first two in the betting flopping, this probably took little winning with a 61-rated horse runner-up. A fair time for the grade though, 1.71 seconds faster than the second division.

**NOTEBOOK**
**Harrys House**, whose last two runs were over seven, had the leader covered and always looked in total command, value three lengths.
**Gaudalpin(IRE)**, dropping back in trip, clung on to second spot despite a tendency to hang.
**Thornber Court(IRE)** showed her much-improved Ripon effort was no fluke and a less sharp track will be in her favour.
**Orphan(IRE)**, a tall type, shows bags of toe but struggles to see it out. He will be stronger next year.
**Cutlass Gaudy**, given a provisional rating of 82 after his 100/1 second at Beverley, found this downhill track a totally different cup of tea and was never travelling. *Official explanation: jockey said colt was unsuited by undulating track*
**Underthemistletoe(IRE)**, absent since July, has not built on the promise she showed on her debut.
**Cavorting**, absent since Newmarket in April, has been gelded in the interim. Again fitted with a cross noseband, he did not impress at all to post and give his rider little help persisting in hanging right. *Official explanation: jockey said gelding was never travelling and hung right handed in closing stages*

## 6003 TOTEEXACTA FILLIES' NURSERY STKS (H'CAP) — 7f

**2:40** (2:42) (D2) (0-85,82) 2-Y-O — **£7,260** (£2,234; £1,117; £558) **Stalls** Low

Form — RPR

4124 **1** **Hansomelle (IRE)**[16] 5670 2-9-0 **75** ... DaleGibson 6 — 78
(BMactaggart) *trckd ldrs: hdwy 2f out: rdn over 1f out: styd on to ld ins last: kpt on* **10/1**

1055 **2** *nk* **My Princess (IRE)**[26] 5417 2-9-0 **75** ... KFallon 9 — 81+
(NACallaghan) *in tch: hdwy over 2f out: sn rdn: drvn and styng on whn bdly hmpd ins last: kpt on wl; fin 3rd, plcd 2nd* **4/1**[1]

004 **3** *1/2* **Ushindi (IRE)**[29] 5349 2-8-8 **69** ... JMackay 15 — 71
(MLWBell) *chsd ldrs on outer: hdwy 2f out: rdn to ld over 1f out: hung bdly lft and hdd ins last: kpt on; fin 2nd, nk: disq: plcd 3rd* **20/1**

6160 **4** *nk* **Tequila Sheila (IRE)**[16] 5670 2-9-6 **81** ... DarrenWilliams 12 — 81
(KRBurke) *hld up: hdwy over 2f out: rdn over 1f out: styd on ins last: nrst fin* **25/1**

4443 **5** *1* **Dispol Isle (IRE)**[18] 5606 2-8-4 **65** ... PFessey 3 — 63
(TDBarron) *chsd ldrs: sltly outpcd 1/2-way: rdn and kpt on fnl 2f* **11/1**

2503 **6** *nk* **Chutney Mary (IRE)**[5] 5890 2-8-7 **68** ow1 ... NCallan 2 — 65
(JGPortman) *led: rdn along over 2f out: drvn and hdd over 1f out: kpt on* **17/2**

21 **7** *1/2* **Market Trend**[18] 5604 2-9-7 **82** ... KDarley 17 — 81+
(MJohnston) *midfield: hdwy over 2f out: sn rdn and styng on whn n.m.r ins last: nrst fin* **5/1**[2]

210 **8** *1 1/4* **Epiphany**[15] 5701 2-9-7 **82** ... (t) SSanders 10 — 77+
(EALDunlop) *hld up and bhd: stdy hdwy 2f out: sn rdn and kpt on same pce ins last* **8/1**[3]

6234 **9** *3/4* **Algorithm**[9] 5819 2-7-13 **60** ow1 ... RFfrench 7 — 51
(TDEasterby) *chsd ldrs: rdn along over 2f out: drvn over 1f out and grad wknd* **10/1**

4340 **10** *1 1/2* **Ignition**[17] 5636 2-7-10 **62** ow2 ... BSwarbrick(5) 14 — 49
(WMBrisbourne) *midfield: hdwy and wd st: sn rdn and kpt on fnl 2f: nt rch ldrs* **33/1**

4030 **11** *1 3/4* **Street Ballad (IRE)**[12] 5753 2-8-3 **64** ... FNorton 13 — 46
(MrsJRRamsden) *bhd tl sme late hdwy* **20/1**

4460 **12** *7* **Missed Turn**[50] 4797 2-7-9 **59** oh12 ... FPFerris(3) 18 — 24
(JMPEustace) *a rr* **100/1**

0400 **13** *1 1/4* **Evanesce**[28] 5363 2-8-6 **67** ... SHitchcott 1 — 29
(MRChannon) *chsd ldrs: rdn over 2f out: wknd wl over 1f out* **22/1**

2055 **14** *1/2* **Lady Hopeful (IRE)**[10] 5800 2-7-7 **61** ... DFentiman(7) 4 — 22
(RPElliott) *cl up: rdn along 3f out: wknd 2f out* **33/1**

5006 **15** *9* **Dorn Dancer (IRE)**[18] 5606 2-9-4 **79** ... LEnstone 8 — 17
(DWBarker) *s.i.s: a rr* **16/1**

031 **16** *9* **Daisy Bucket**[41] 5034 2-8-9 **70** ... CCatlin 11 — —
(DMSimcock) *a rr* **16/1**

0400 **17** *7* **Summer Silks**[33] 5240 2-7-12 **59** oh2 ... LisaJones 5 — —
(RAFahey) *sn rdn along in midfield: lost pl after 2f and bhd after* **50/1**

1m 28.29s (0.79) **Going Correction** +0.175s/f (Good) **17** Ran SP% **123.1**
Speed ratings: **102,101,101,100,99 99,98,97,96,94 92,84,83,82,72 62,54**CSF £44.97 CT £842.91 TOTE £11.70: £2.30, £1.50, £4.50, £6.90; EX 72.70.
**Owner** Corsby Racing **Bred** J Beckett **Trained** Hawick, Borders
■ The placings of the second and third were reversed after accidental interference.

**FOCUS**
An average nursery in which the strong, blustery wind was a significant factor in the second past the post ducking and diving and causing mayhem behind her. However, the time was decent for the type of race and the principals ran close to previous form.

**NOTEBOOK**
**Hansomelle(IRE)**, who is progressing nicely, proved suited by the step up to seven and she was left with a clear passage on the inside whilst there was carnage in lanes two and three.
**My Princess(IRE)**, well supported, looked to be going nowhere until knocked sideways by the runner-up. That seemed to wake her up and she would have been in front with a bit further to go. A return to a mile should see her gain compensation.
**Ushindi(IRE)**, who is bred to make a middle-distance three-year-old, is on the up and, but for ducking and diving, must have opened her account on her nursery bow. She swerved badly left into the wind inside the last, leaving the way clear for the winner to gain the day.
**Tequila Sheila(IRE)** put two poor efforts behind her and on this showing a slightly stiffer test of stamina will play to her strengths.
**Dispol Isle(IRE)**, stepping up in trip, seemed to relish every yard of the extra furlong.
**Chutney Mary(IRE)**, hoisted 8lb after her improved showing at Goodwood, capitalised on her favourable draw to lead but she had no more to give when hampered in the melee caused by the runner-up inside the last.
**Market Trend**, drawn one from the outside, had work to do turning in but was staying on in resolute fashion when forced sideways inside the last. It transpired that her rider knocked a foot leaving the stalls, injuring a toe, and he had to give up his remaining brides.
**Lady Hopeful(IRE)** *Official explanation: jockey said filly lost her action*
**Dorn Dancer(IRE)** *Official explanation: jockey said filly was never travelling*
**Daisy Bucket** *Official explanation: jockey said filly lost her action*

## 6004 CUMBRIA MEDIAN AUCTION MAIDEN STKS (DIV I) — 5f 212y

**3:10** (3:11) (F4) 3-Y-O — **£1,881** (£1,881; £418) **Stalls** Low

Form — RPR

2606 **1** *dht* **Cyfrwys (IRE)**[13] 5737 3-8-6 60 ... FPFerris(3) 10 — 66
(BPalling) *w ldrs: chal over 1f out: styd on towards fin* **15/8**[2]

606 **1** **Sessay**[19] 5579 3-9-0 65 ... ANicholls 6 — 71
(DNicholls) *w ldr: led over 1f out: jnd on line* **1/1**[1]

5330 **3** *7* **Shaymee's Girl**[156] 1788 3-8-4 52 ... BSwarbrick(5) 1 — 45
(MsDeborahJEvans) *led tl over 1f out: wknd ins last* **12/1**[3]

3000 **4** *2* **Weakest Link**[20] 5557 3-9-0 51 ... DAllan 5 — 44
(EJAlston) *mid-div: kpt on fnl 2f* **14/1**

0-00 **5** *shd* **Faites Vos Jeux**[21] 5547 3-8-2 40 ... MHalford(7) 2 — 39
(CNKellett) *chsd ldrs: outpcd fnl 2f* **50/1**

0000 **6** *shd* **Svenson**[24] 5451 3-8-11 30 ... TEaves(3) 9 — 43?
(JSWainwright) *in tch: edgd lft over 1f out: nvr rchd ldrs* **100/1**

-0 **7** *2* **Golden Bankes (IRE)**[28] 5378 3-8-9 ... DSweeney 4 — 32
(WGMTurner) *bhd: sme hdwy 2f out: nvr on terms* **16/1**

00 **8** *11* **Miss Chancelot**[66] 4351 3-8-9 ... RFfrench 7 — —
(SPGriffiths) *a towards rr: bhd fnl 2f* **100/1**

4000 **9** *9* **Fayrz Please (IRE)**[6] 5862 3-9-0 55 ... SChin 8 — —
(MCChapman) *a bhd* **33/1**

-000 **10** *13* **Quintillion**[106] 3146 3-9-0 40 ... KFallon 3 — —
(TJEtherington) *s.i.s: a in last: bhd and eased fnl 2f* **40/1**

1m 14.16s (0.16) **Going Correction** +0.175s/f (Good) **10** Ran SP% **114.3**
Speed ratings: **105,105,95,93,92 92,90,75,63,46** TRIFECTA Win: Ses 1.00, Cyf 1.40; Plc: Ses 1.10, Cyf 1.80, 2.60; Ex: Ses/Cyf 1.8, Cyf/Ses 2.3; CSF: Ses/Cyf 1.39, Cyf/Ses 1.93.
**Owner** P Crane, A Barker & S Short **Bred** Miss A J Rawding And P M Crane **Trained** Sessay, N Yorks

**FOCUS**
A very moderate sprint maiden, with the first pair clear and basically to form but with the sixth rated just 30 a little close. The time was decent for the grade though, 1.16 seconds faster than the second division.

**NOTEBOOK**
**Sessay**, who would have preferred easier ground, was a neck up and seemingly in charge inside the last but at the line it was just a share of first prize.
**Cyfrwys(IRE)**, who had exactly the same chance as the favourite on official figures, found a fraction extra to share the spoils right on the line.
**Shaymee's Girl**, taken to post early, took them along but was very leg weary inside the last.
**Weakest Link**, who has run poorly on his two most recent starts after a lengthy break, shaped better and the All-Weather seems to suit him better.
**Faites Vos Jeux** has been well beaten in three starts this year.
**Svenson** is now with his third trainer and has yet to be placed in eight starts now.
**Fayrz Please(IRE)** *Official explanation: jockey said gelding lost his action after first furlong*

## 6005 SKYRAM H'CAP — 1m 7f 177y

**3:40** (3:41) (F4) (0-55,54) 3-Y-O+ — **£3,053** (£872; £436) **Stalls** Low

Form — RPR

2125 **1** **Mercurious (IRE)**[47] 4883 4-9-2 **45** ... DaleGibson 13 — 53
(JMackie) *hld up and bhd: stdy hdwy over 5f out: rdn to chse ldrs 2f out: styd on ins last to ld nr line* **12/1**

0240 **2** *hd* **Doctor John**[17] 5638 7-8-13 **45** ... DCorby(3) 9 — 53
(AndrewTurnell) *in tch: hdwy to chse ldrs after 6f: pushed along 4f out: rdn 2f out: styd on to ld wl ins last: hdd and no ex nr fin* **20/1**

42-3 **3** *1/2* **Totally Scottish**[168] 1534 8-9-2 **45** ... SSanders 17 — 52
(KGReveley) *hld up towards rr: gd hdwy on outer over 5f out: wd st and rdn to ld over 2f out: drvn 1f out: hdd wl ins last: kpt on* **8/1**[3]

2325 **4** *6* **Banningham Blaze**[10] 5796 4-9-2 **48** ... DNolan(3) 18 — 48
(AWCarroll) *hld up towards rr: stdy hdwy 5f out: rdn to chse ldrs 2f out: sn drvn and no imp appr last* **10/1**

/50- **5** *nk* **Simlet**[139] 4481 9-9-2 **45** ... GFaulkner 12 — 44
(EWTuer) *hld up in rr: hdwy over 4f out: rdn over 2f out: styd on same pce* **50/1**

0P52 **6** *4* **Madiba**[29] 5343 5-9-11 **54** ... KFallon 3 — 49
(PHowling) *midfield: smooth hdwy on inner 5f out: effrt and ev ch over 2f out: sn rdn and wknd* **13/2**[1]

0003 **7** 3½ **Nod's Star**[38] 5130 3-8-5 **45** .................... RFrench 1 35
(MissJACamacho) *trckd ldrs: gd hdwy on inner to ld over 5f out: rdn along and hdd over 2f out: grad wknd* **16/1**

500- **8** 1¾ **Lake 'O' Gold**[127] 3134 5-9-4 **47** .................... TWilliams 4 35
(DWThompson) *bhd: hdwy over 4f out: sn rdn along and kpt on fnl 2f: nvr a factor* **80/1**

3244 **9** nk **Oops (IRE)**[17] 5638 5-9-3 **46** .................... DAllan 2 34
(JFCoupland) *prom: rdn along 1/2-way: wknd over 5f out* **7/1**[2]

2045 **10** 2½ **Munaawesh (USA)**[21] 5546 3-9-0 **54** ....................(b) ACulhane 8 39
(DWChapman) *hld up towards rr: effrt and hdwy 5f out: sn rdn along and nvr a factor* **12/1**

0300 **11** 5 **Red Skelton (IRE)**[11] 5773 3-8-12 **52** .................... IMongan 14 31
(MsDeborahJEvans) *hld up in rr: hdwy on outer 1/2-way: disp ld 4f out: wd st and ev ch tl rdn and wknd 2f out* **20/1**

4010 **12** 3 **Regency Red (IRE)**[10] 5796 6-9-0 **48** .................... BSwarbrick(5) 7 23
(WMBrisbourne) *s.i.s: a rr* **16/1**

130- **13** 1 **Own Line**[428] 3837 5-8-13 **45** .................... THamilton(3) 20 19
(JHetherton) *midfield: rdn along 6f out: sn wknd* **20/1**

3005 **14** 14 **Dance Light (IRE)**[22] 5519 5-9-10 **53** ....................(v¹) EAhern 11 10
(TTClement) *in tch: rdn along 1/2-way: sn wknd* **16/1**

3103 **15** 5 **Astromancer (USA)**[36] 5205 4-9-6 **49** .................... NCallan 10 —
(MHTompkins) *in tch: rdn along after 5f: lost pl and bhd fr 1/2-way* **7/1**[2]

-000 **16** 1¼ **Amalfi Coast**[14] 5714 5-8-11 **45** .................... DTudhope(5) 6 —
(WSCunningham) *prom: rdn alon g 6f out: sn wknd* **100/1**

04-0 **17** 3 **Seattle Prince (USA)**[42] 5027 6-9-8 **51** .................... ANicholls 5 —
(SGollings) *a rr* **33/1**

4455 **18** 10 **Jamaican Flight (USA)**[19] 5589 11-9-2 **45** .................... RWinston 19 —
(MrsSLamyman) *led: rdn along 1/2-way: hdd over 5f out and sn wknd* **16/1**

/00- **19** shd **Ensemble**[444] 2265 4-9-2 **45** oh5 .................... CCatlin 15 —
(DMSimcock) *in tch: rdn along 1/2-way: sn wknd* **100/1**

0-35 **20** 27 **Bien Good**[80] 3955 3-8-5 **48** ow3 .................... TEaves(3) 16 —
(KGReveley) *bhd fr 1/2-way* **50/1**

3m 34.74s (3.34) **Going Correction** +0.175s/f (Good)
**WFA** 3 from 4yo+ 11lb **20** Ran SP% **121.8**
Speed ratings: **98,97,97,94,94 92,90,89,89,88 85,84,83,76,74 73,72,67,67,53**CSF £242.13 CT £2042.93 TOTE £16.40: £3.80, £6.20, £2.50, £1.70; EX 514.60.
**Owner** Gwen K Dot.com **Bred** Miss Jill Finegan **Trained** Church Broughton, Derbys
■ Stewards Enquiry : K Fallon caution: careless riding

**FOCUS**
The inside rail was becoming cut up and the vast majority came wide off the home turn. A modest handicap but a decent pace led to most of the principals challenging from off the pace. The form, rated through the third, is not particularly strong.

**NOTEBOOK**
**Mercurious(IRE)**, twice a winner over two miles on the Fibresand, was gaining her first victory on turf. She appreciated the good gallop and came from off the pace to secure the win inside the last.
**Doctor John**, another chasing his first win on turf, looked to have it to do off this mark but it was only close home that he gave way.
**Totally Scottish**, who is still searching for his first win on the Flat, ran another good race in defeat and is entitled to come on for this first run since April.
**Banningham Blaze** enjoyed the decent pace and stayed on well for a place again. She continues to run to a consistent level.
**Simlet** had a nice pipe-opener prior to a return to jumping.
**Madiba** has a poor strike-rate.
**Red Skelton(IRE)** *Official explanation: jockey said gelding hung right handed*
**Dance Light(IRE)** *Official explanation: jockey said mare would not face first time visor*
**Astromancer(USA)** *Official explanation: jockey said filly was never travelling*

## 6006 NOTTINGHAMSHIRE H'CAP 1m 3f 214y
**4:10** (4:13) (E3) (0-70,70) 3-Y-O **£3,628** (£1,116; £558; £279) **Stalls** Low

Form RPR

2132 **1** **Dont Call Me Derek**[6] 5868 3-9-5 **65** .................... SSanders 20 84
(SCWilliams) *hld up: hdwy 6f out: led 2f out: all out* **4/1**[1]

3041 **2** shd **Ego Trip**[21] 5546 3-8-12 **58** ....................(b) DaleGibson 12 77
(MWEasterby) *mid-div: hdwy 6f out: chal over 1f out: r.o* **10/1**

0100 **3** 9 **Ellina**[21] 5554 3-9-3 **63** .................... KFallon 10 67
(JPearce) *rr-div: hdwy 7f out: sn chsng ldrs: one pce appr fnl f* **12/1**

6662 **4** nk **Cottingham (IRE)**[12] 5757 3-8-13 **59** .................... SChin 7 63
(MCChapman) *chsd ldrs: upsides 2f out: one pce* **16/1**

6605 **5** hd **Saida Lenasera (FR)**[26] 5410 3-9-3 **63** .................... ACulhane 1 67
(MrsPSly) *chsd ldrs: outpcd 2f out: kpt on fnl f* **33/1**

4460 **6** 1¾ **Quickstyx**[6] 5860 3-9-7 **67** .................... CCatlin 6 68
(MRChannon) *mid-div: hdwy on ins over 2f out: kpt on same pce* **14/1**

1220 **7** shd **Can Can Flyer (IRE)**[11] 5773 3-9-6 **66** .................... RFfrench 5 67
(MJohnston) *led early: chsd ldrs: one pce fnl 2f* **5/1**[2]

3230 **8** ½ **Lucky Arthur (IRE)**[67] 4307 3-8-10 **56** .................... DSweeney 19 56
(JGMO'Shea) *rr-div: hdwy 6f out: one pce fnl 2f* **25/1**

1440 **9** 2½ **Music Mix (IRE)**[36] 5197 3-9-2 **62** ....................(v¹) EAhern 15 58
(EALDunlop) *trckd ldrs: led 7f out: hdd 2f out: sn btn* **22/1**

6615 **10** 1¼ **Prelude**[20] 5560 3-9-1 **61** .................... SWKelly 11 55
(WMBrisbourne) *in tch: hrd rdn 3f out: nvr a threat* **16/1**

-000 **11** 2 **Abbeygate**[45] 4939 3-8-11 **60** ....................(t) J-PGuillambert(3) 16 51
(TKeddy) *rr-div: sme hdwy 3f out: nvr on terms* **66/1**

4-03 **12** 3 **The Rip**[21] 5545 3-8-11 **57** .................... DAllan 14 43
(TDEasterby) *mid-div: rdn 6f out: nvr a threat* **33/1**

6032 **13** 6 **Go Green**[15] 5705 3-8-10 **56** oh2 ....................(t) NCallan 8 32
(PDEvans) *a bhd* **12/1**

2406 **14** 4 **Baawrah**[94] 3543 3-9-5 **65** .................... RWinston 3 35
(MTodhunter) *s.i.s: a bhd* **14/1**

5250 **15** 2 **It Must Be Speech**[14] 5715 3-8-11 **57** .................... RFitzpatrick 13 24
(SLKeightley) *bhd: sme hdwy 4f out: sn lost pl* **50/1**

2432 **16** 1¾ **Principessa**[8] 5828 3-9-7 **70** .................... FPFerris(3) 2 34
(BPalling) *reminders after s: sn led: hdd 7f out: lost pl 4f out* **8/1**[3]

0-40 **17** 8 **Crociera (IRE)**[155] 1843 3-9-3 **63** .................... PRobinson 4 14
(MHTompkins) *chsd ldrs: lost pl 5f out: sn bhd* **16/1**

040 **18** dist **Jonnyem**[17] 5637 3-8-7 **56** oh4 .................... PMulrennan(3) 9 —
(GASwinbank) *bhd: t.o 3f out: virtually p.u* **25/1**

0620 **19** 6 **Suchwot (IRE)**[15] 5693 3-8-7 **56** .................... THamilton(3) 18 —
(FJordan) *bhd and drvn along: t.o 3f out: virtually p.u* **40/1**

**F** **Cambo (FR)**[158] 3-8-10 **56** oh1 .................... JoannaBadger 17 —
(RFord) *bhd whn fell bnd 7f out* **50/1**

2m 41.57s (2.57) **Going Correction** +0.175s/f (Good) **20** Ran SP% **129.0**
Speed ratings: **98,97,91,91,91 90,90,90,88,87 86,84,80,77,76 75,69,—,—,—**CSF £40.45 CT £466.91 TOTE £5.40: £1.70, £1.90, £2.50, £4.00; EX 54.60 Trifecta £341.20 Pool of £816.98 - 1.70 winning tickets.
**Owner** The Chummy Northerners **Bred** Whitsbury Manor Stud **Trained** Newmarket, Suffolk

**FOCUS**
A modest handicap in which they all avoided the cut-up ground on the inner in the home straight. The first two were clear giving the impression they have improved.

**NOTEBOOK**
**Dont Call Me Derek** had his stamina to prove over this longer distance, but saw it out really well. He looks open to more improvement and this win opens up further opportunities.
**Ego Trip** looks to be on the upgrade and only narrowly failed to follow up his recent Thirsk victory off a 6lb higher mark. He finished well clear of the rest and, while he will go up again for this, he could soon return to the winner's enclosure.
**Ellina** returned to form back off her last winning mark.
**Cottingham(IRE)** ran well enough but did not look a proper stayer over this longer trip.
**Saida Lenasera(FR)** has still to conclusively prove that this is the trip she wants.
**Quickstyx** ran well enough back over a more suitable trip.
**Music Mix(IRE)** *Official explanation: jockey said colt was unsuited by good, good to firm in places ground*
**Go Green** *Official explanation: jockey said filly was unsuited by good, good to firm in places ground*

## 6007 DERBYSHIRE APPRENTICE H'CAP 5f 212y
**4:40** (4:43) (F4) (0-55,55) 3-Y-O+ **£2,961** (£846; £423) **Stalls** Low

Form RPR

4520 **1** **On The Trail**[19] 5597 7-8-10 **54** .................... PMakin(3) 2 63
(DWChapman) *sn led: rdn wl over 1f out: styd on strly ins last* **7/1**[3]

3401 **2** 1¾ **Loughlorien (IRE)**[24] 5452 5-8-8 **54** .................... DTudhope(5) 7 58
(REBarr) *in tch: hdwy to chse wnr wl over 1f out: sn rdn and edgd lft ins last: kpt on same pce* **8/1**

0003 **3** 1½ **Laurel Dawn**[19] 5597 6-8-8 **54** .................... NataliaGemelova(5) 13 53+
(IWMcinnes) *bhd: gd hdwy on outer 2f out: sn rdn and kpt on appr last* **8/1**

6330 **4** 1¼ **Amanda's Lad (IRE)**[63] 4422 4-8-12 **53** .................... DNolan 10 49
(MCChapman) *hld up and bhd: hdwy over 2f out: swtchd rt and rdn over 1f out: styd on ins last: nrst fin* **16/1**

6330 **5** ¾ **William's Well**[19] 5579 10-9-0 **55** ....................(b) PMulrennan 8 48
(MWEasterby) *stdd s and bhd: hdwy 2f out: sn rdn and kpt on ins last: nrst fin* **8/1**

1005 **6** 1¼ **Yorkies Boy**[13] 5736 9-8-11 **55** ....................(p) BSwarbrick(3) 6 45
(NEBerry) *hld up in rr: hdwy 2f out: sn rdn and kpt on same pce appr last* **10/1**

2500 **7** 1 **Roan Raider (USA)**[6] 5862 4-8-13 **54** ....................(v) LEnstone 5 41
(MissVHaigh) *chsd ldrs: rdn over 2f out: grad wknd* **16/1**

600 **8** ¾ **Kiss The Rain**[28] 5364 4-8-8 **54** ....................(v) MLawson(5) 14 38
(PABlockley) *bhd: hdwy and swtchd rt wl over 1f out: sn rdn and no imp ent last* **33/1**

5030 **9** 2 **Brigadier Monty (IRE)**[20] 5562 6-8-12 **53** .................... SHitchcott 12 31
(MrsSLamyman) *stdd s and bhd: sme hdwy on inner 2f out: sn rdn and nvr a factor* **9/1**

5630 **10** nk **Moritat (IRE)**[26] 5412 4-8-13 **54** .................... FPFerris 1 31
(PDEvans) *cl up: rdn wl over 2f out: sn wknd* **6/1**[2]

0000 **11** ½ **Cross Ash (IRE)**[28] 5364 4-8-5 **53** .................... RKennemore(7) 3 29
(RHollinshead) *chsd ldrs: rdn wl over 2f out and sn wknd* **40/1**

2000 **12** nk **Time To Remember (IRE)**[21] 5544 6-9-0 **55** .................... THamilton 4 30
(RAFahey) *chsd ldrs: rdn 2f out: sn wknd* **11/2**[1]

0060 **13** 2 **Highland Lass**[43] 5008 3-8-10 **55** .................... NChalmers(3) 11 24
(MrsHSweeting) *a rr* **16/1**

0000 **14** 2 **Global Achiever**[22] 5526 3-8-10 **55** ....................(t) AQuinn(3) 9 18
(GCHChung) *slwoly into stride: rapid hdwy on inner to chse ldrs after 2f: n ot much room 1/2-way: sn rdn and wknd* **16/1**

1m 14.97s (0.97) **Going Correction** +0.175s/f (Good)
**WFA** 3 from 4yo+ 1lb **14** Ran SP% **123.5**
Speed ratings: **100,97,95,94,93 91,90,89,86,85 85,84,82,79**CSF £63.80 CT £481.99 TOTE £7.80: £2.10, £2.70, £4.90; EX 42.70.
**Owner** J M Chapman **Bred** Ian Bellamy **Trained** Stillington, N Yorks

**FOCUS**
An ordinary sprint handicap with the runner-up to his recent best the guide to the level of the form.

**NOTEBOOK**
**On The Trail** bounced out well from his low draw and made almost all. He is a moderate performer but has a fair strike-rate, having now won 15 times from 79 starts, and trained by a master at keeping mature sprinters interested.
**Loughlorien(IRE)**, a winner in banded grade last time, had his chance but did not see his race out as well as the winner. He does not look that well handicapped at present, but does tend to run well at this track.
**Laurel Dawn**, who is happier over the minimum trip, was poorly drawn and could only stay on when the race was all over.
**Amanda's Lad(IRE)** was another handicapped by a wide draw.
**William's Well** could not get into contention from off the pace. He is probably better on a straight track.
**Moritat(IRE)** seems to have lost his way after a good spell in late summer.
**Time To Remember(IRE)**, made favourite on this drop back in trip, could not repeat his Glorious Goodwood effort and has not won since June 2003.

## 6008 LANCASHIRE MAIDEN STKS (DIV II) 5f
**5:10** (5:15) (F4) 2-Y-O **£3,415** (£1,051; £525; £262) **Stalls** Low

Form RPR

002 **1** **Turn On The Style**[9] 5816 2-9-0 .................... SChin 11 64
(RPElliott) *unruly s: w ldrs: led over 1f out: wandered and swvd lft jst ins last: hld on nr fin* **9/2**[3]

000 **2** nk **Benny The Bus**[49] 4824 2-9-0 .................... ACulhane 3 63
(MrsGSRees) *chsd ldrs: styd on and upsides whn bdly bmpd jst ins last: jst hld nr fin* **33/1**

**3** 2½ **Revien (IRE)** 2-9-0 .................... IMongan 9 54
(GAHuffer) *lengthy: chsd ldrs: outpcd and lost pl after 2f: hdwy over 1f out: kpt on ins last* **3/1**[2]

5000 **4** nk **Tiffin Deano (IRE)**[24] 5466 2-9-0 56 .................... GFaulkner 7 53
(PCHaslam) *outpcd and rdn over 2f out: hung lft and styd on fnl f* **16/1**

0633 **5** ½ **Ben Casey**[20] 5555 2-9-0 66 .................... FLynch 1 51
(BSmart) *led tl over 1f out: wknd ins last* **6/4**[1]

50 **6** 4 **Missin Margot**[3] 5953 2-8-4 .................... BSwarbrick(5) 8 32
(MsDeborahJEvans) *chsd ldrs: wknd over 1f out* **33/1**

60 **7** 1¾ **In Rhubarb**[9] 5816 2-8-9 .................... NataliaGemelova(5) 4 31
(IWMcinnes) *swvd rt s: outpcd over 2f out: n.d after* **50/1**

**8** shd **Ammirare** 2-8-9 .................... RWinston 10 26
(CWThornton) *leggy: unf: s.s: bhd tl sme late hdwy: nvr on terms* **11/1**

0060 **9** 3½ **Gloria Nimbus**[86] 3770 2-8-9 50 .................... SRighton 6 14
(MMullineaux) *sltly hmpd s: t.k.h: trckd ldrs: lost pl over 2f out* **80/1**

5430 **10** *3* **Lady Erica**[15] 5690 2-8-9 57........................................(v[1]) DarrenWilliams 2 3
(KRBurke) *chsd ldr: lost pl over 1f out: eased* **12/1**

61.80 secs (1.20) **Going Correction** -0.10s/f (Good) **10** Ran SP% **114.2**
Speed ratings: **86,85,81,81,80 73,71,70,65,60**CSF £140.75 TOTE £7.40: £2.30, £6.90, £1.80; EX 142.60.
**Owner** The Haydock Badgeholders **Bred** J And Mrs Bowtell **Trained** Formby, Lancs

**FOCUS**
An ordinary maiden run in a very slow time for the grade, 1.71 seconds (hand timed) slower than the first division, and the weaker of the two divisions, with the winner not having to be at his best to score.

**NOTEBOOK**
**Turn On The Style**, who looked suited by the drop back to five last time, built on that promise by going one better. He gave the eventual runner-up a hefty bump inside the last, but the incident probably made no difference to the result.
**Benny The Bus** showed a lot more than he had on his first three starts, when he failed to beat a single rival.
**Revien(IRE)**, a well-made newcomer, did not impress at all going to post. He ran green and should come on for the experience.
**Tiffin Deano(IRE)** looks likely to continue to struggle in this sort of grade and may need some more leniency from the Handicapper.
**Ben Casey** set a fair standard in what was a very ordinary maiden, but he failed to run up to his best. *Official explanation: jockey said colt hung right handed throughout*
**Lady Erica** *Official explanation: jockey said filly hung right handed*

## 6009 CUMBRIA MEDIAN AUCTION MAIDEN STKS (DIV II) 5f 212y
**5:40** (5:43) (F4) 3-Y-O **£2,917** (£833; £416) **Stalls** Low

Form RPR
6020 **1** **Westborough (IRE)**[8] 5845 3-9-0 52..............................(t) KimTinkler 7 60
(NTinkler) *chsd ldrs: rdn over 2f out: led 1f out: kpt on wl* **16/1**
260 **2** *2* **Knead The Dough**[17] 5656 3-9-0 55.............................. AMcCarthy 3 54
(DECantillon) *led: styd far side in home st: hdd 1f out: no ex* **8/1**
4400 **3** *2 ½* **Kamenka**[16] 5674 3-8-6 65.............................. THamilton(3) 8 42
(RAFahey) *chsd ldrs: one pce fnl 2f* **5/2**[2]
5040 **4** *1* **Whistful (IRE)**[13] 5737 3-8-9 63.............................. SSanders 10 39
(CFWall) *racd v wd: chsd ldrs: rdn over 2f out: one pce* **6/4**[1]
6606 **5** *1 ½* **Comic Tales**[22] 5525 3-9-0 40..............................(p) LEnstone 9 39
(MMullineaux) *dwlt: sn drvn along: outpcd and lost pl over 4f out: hrd rdn and kpt on fnl 2f* **50/1**
2533 **6** *1 ¾* **Brain Washed**[10] 5801 3-8-9 59.............................. RWinston 6 29
(TDEasterby) *outpcd and lost pl over 4f out: n.d after* **9/2**[3]
045 **7** *3* **Government (IRE)**[28] 5366 3-9-0 45.............................. SChin 1 25
(MCChapman) *chsd ldrs: outpcd and lost pl over 4f out: no ch after* **40/1**
**8** *1 ½* **Miss Prim** 3-8-9.............................. JEdmunds 4 15
(GPKelly) *s.i.s: nvr on terms: styd far side in home st* **40/1**

1m 15.32s (1.32) **Going Correction** +0.175s/f (Good) **8** Ran SP% **110.6**
Speed ratings: **98,95,92,90,88 86,82,80**CSF £124.59 TOTE £15.40: £3.10, £2.30, £1.10; EX 73.60 Place 6 £443.53, Place £67.28.
**Owner** Mr Venning, Mr Parks & Mr Raybould **Bred** Ballyhane Stud **Trained** Langton, N Yorks

**FOCUS**
Only the runner-up and the last horse home stayed on the far-side rail in the home straight. The time was acceptable for the grade, despite being 1.16 seconds slower than the first division, but the form is no better than plating class.

**NOTEBOOK**
**Westborough(IRE)**, a moderate performer having his 20th career start, finally got off the mark. He is fully exposed and found a bad race.
**Knead The Dough**, less exposed than most of the others, had his chance but probably did himself no favours by remaining on the far side.
**Kamenka** had every chance on the figures but she has been out of form of late and could not take advantage of this opportunity.
**Whistful(IRE)**, another who had a good shout at the weights, was disappointing, although she was drawn widest of all and raced on the outside.
**Comic Tales** is only plating class.
**Brain Washed**, who has dropped 13lb in the ratings since July, should have finished closer than she did.
T/Jkpt: Not won. T/Plt: £190.10 to a £1 stake. Pool: £50,549.95. 194.10 winning tickets. T/Qpdt: £8.60 to a £1 stake. Pool: £4,718.50. 401.40 winning tickets. JR

5907
# LINGFIELD (L-H)
Wednesday, October 6
**OFFICIAL GOING: Standard**

## 6010 MENZIES DISTRIBUTION EBF MAIDEN STKS (DIV I) 7f (P)
**1:50** (1:50) (D3) 2-Y-O **£4,251** (£1,308; £654; £327) **Stalls** Low

Form RPR
0 **1** **Blue Torpedo (USA)**[18] 5653 2-9-0.............................. RLMoore 1 78
(MrsAJPerrett) *trckd ldrs: effrt on inner over 1f out: rdn to ld last 100yds: styd on wl* **25/1**
5 **2** *¾* **Optimus (USA)**[41] 5054 2-9-0.............................. JFortune 11 76
(GAButler) *gd sort: dwlt: settled towards rr: plenty to do 2f out: hrd rdn and r.o strly fnl f: hopeless task* **4/1**[2]
2 **3** *1 ¼* **Mutanabi (USA)**[58] 4599 2-9-0.............................. LDettori 4 73
(SaeedBinSuroor) *lw: led: 2l clr 2f out: shkn up fnl f: hdd and jinked rt last 100yds: fnd nil* **4/7**[1]
**4** *1* **Angel Rays** 2-8-9.............................. DHolland 5 66
(GAButler) *leggy: unf: trckd ldrs: effrt over 2f out: cl up 1f out: one pce* **16/1**
**5** *1 ¼* **Postgraduate (IRE)** 2-9-0.............................. SDrowne 8 67
(HMorrison) *unf: bit bkwd: trckd ldrs: effrt to chse ldr wl over 2f out: pushed along and fdd fnl f* **33/1**
60 **6** *1 ½* **Compton Quay**[7] 5872 2-9-0.............................. RHughes 12 64
(AKing) *lw: s.s: settled in last trio: pushed along and styd on steadily fr over 1f out: do bttr* **33/1**
00 **7** *shd* **Meditation**[77] 4023 2-8-9.............................. FNorton 9 58
(IAWood) *pushed along in midfield: struggling 3f out: kpt on fr over 1f out* **33/1**
**8** *1 ¼* **High Card** 2-9-0.............................. JTate 7 60
(JMPEustace) *leggy: bkwd: s.i.s: rn green in midfield: shkn up and one pce fnl 2f* **66/1**
**9** *3 ½* **Aggravation** 2-9-0.............................. ANicholls 6 52+
(AndrewReid) *w'like: bkwd: b.hind: dwlt: t.k.h early: nvr beyond midfield: wknd over 1f out* **50/1**
06 **10** *½* **Lama Albarq (USA)**[62] 4481 2-9-0.............................. RHills 10 50
(EALDunlop) *racd midfield: losing pl whn rn v wd bnd 2f out: no ch after* **33/1**



**11** *1 ¼* **Lake Chini (IRE)** 2-9-0.............................. PRobinson 3 52+
(MAJarvis) *w'like: bit bkwd: s.s: hld up towards rr: brief effrt over 2f out: sn wknd* **12/1**[3]
00 **12** *5* **Red Opera**[7] 5858 2-9-0.............................. SSanders 14 35
(SirMarkPrescott) *gd sort: last and rdn over 4f out: bhd after* **40/1**
00 **13** *3* **In The Shadows**[16] 5695 2-8-9.............................. NCallan 13 22
(WSKittow) *a last trio: rdn over 4f out: sn bhd* **100/1**
0 **14** *11* **Aramat**[44] 5003 2-8-4.............................. NataliaGemelova(5) 2 —
(JRBoyle) *w ldr after 1f to 3f out: wknd rapidly: t.o* **100/1**

1m 24.95s (-0.99) **Going Correction** -0.125s/f (Stan) **14** Ran SP% **120.7**
Speed ratings: **100,99,97,96,95 93,93,91,87,87 85,80,76,64**CSF £118.60 TOTE £29.00: £5.80, £1.50, £1.02; EX 158.40.
**Owner** A D Spence **Bred** Star Thoroughbreds **Trained** Pulborough, W Sussex

**FOCUS**
A fair time for the grade, 0.27 seconds faster than the second division.

**NOTEBOOK**
**Blue Torpedo(USA)**, whose trainer's runners usually come on a good deal for their debuts, put up a much improved display, picking off the favourite inside the last. He may have been lucky to beat the runner-up, though.
**Optimus(USA)**, who had shown promise on his debut, was given plenty to do having been dropped out. He finished like a train on the outside and probably should have won, and looks sure to go one better before long.
**Mutanabi(USA)**, a well-backed favourite stepping up a furlong, was soon sent into the lead and attempted to make all. He looked in trouble early in the straight though, and dropped back to third inside the last. He does not look anything special on this evidence.
**Angel Rays**, a half-sister to Grade Three placed National Park and dual Listed grade winner Film Script, was conceding previous racecourse experience to the first three and in the circumstances performed with plenty of credit. Middle distances will suit her in time.
**Postgraduate(IRE)**, a half-brother to juvenile winner Bella Tutrice, shaped with some promise before weakening out of it inside the last.
**Compton Quay** has now had the required three runs for a mark and can be expected to do better once he switches to handicaps.
**Lama Albarq(USA)** *Official explanation: jockey said colt hung right*

## 6011 MENZIES DISTRIBUTION EBF MAIDEN STKS (DIV II) 7f (P)
**2:20** (2:22) (D3) 2-Y-O **£4,238** (£1,304; £652; £326) **Stalls** Low

Form RPR
23 **1** **Qadar (IRE)**[124] 2644 2-9-0..............................(t) RHills 9 75+
(MPTregoning) *lw: sn trckd ldr: shkn up to ld jst over 1f out: hanging lft but sn clr* **10/11**[1]
4 **2** *2 ½* **Balkan Leader (USA)**[18] 5633 2-9-0.............................. LDettori 10 69
(SaeedBinSuroor) *led: rdn 2f out: hdd and one pce jst over 1f out* **5/1**[3]
**3** *hd* **Desert Lightning (IRE)** 2-9-0.............................. EAhern 2 68
(JNoseda) *leggy: lengthy: unf: prom: rdn 2f out: unable qck over 1f out: kpt on* **3/1**[2]
0 **4** *4* **Missy Cinofaz**[21] 5570 2-8-9.............................. FNorton 4 53
(IAWood) *prom: rdn over 2f out: wknd fnl f* **100/1**
0 **5** *2* **Precious Sammi**[90] 3665 2-9-0.............................. NCallan 12 53
(JulianPoulton) *dwlt: sn trckd ldrs: effrt over 2f out: wknd over 1f out* **100/1**
0 **6** *nk* **Magic Flo**[21] 5569 2-8-9.............................. SWhitworth 7 48
(GCBravery) *t.k.h: trckd ldrs: wknd over 1f out* **50/1**
**7** *shd* **Daybreaking (IRE)** 2-9-0.............................. SCarson 3 52
(RFJohnsonHoughton) *w'like: bkwd: racd midfield: effrt over 2f out: wknd over 1f out* **66/1**
0 **8** *1 ¾* **Planet (IRE)**[18] 5646 2-9-0.............................. KFallon 5 48+
(SirMichaelStoute) *awkward s: racd towards rr: pushed along 1/2-way: no prog and btn over 2f out* **14/1**
**9** *nk* **Heathwood (IRE)** 2-9-0.............................. JFortune 1 47
(JHMGosden) *w'like: scope: bit bkwd: s.s: hld up wl in rr: detached fr main gp over 2f out: nudged along and kpt on steadily fr over 1f* **25/1**
05 **10** *1 ½* **Optimum (IRE)**[13] 5756 2-9-0.............................. TPQueally 6 43
(DRLoder) *settled towards rr: lost tch w main gp over 2f out* **40/1**
50 **11** *½* **Devil's Island**[7] 5857 2-9-0.............................. SSanders 8 42
(SirMarkPrescott) *dwlt: hld up wl in rr: wl off the pce over 2f out: c wd bnd sn after: no ch* **28/1**
**12** *1* **Song Sparrow** 2-8-9.............................. DHolland 14 35+
(GAButler) *neat: small: a wl in rr: struggling fr 3f out* **66/1**
**13** *hd* **Blue Hedges** 2-9-0.............................. JQuinn 11 39
(HJCollingridge) *w'like: scope: tall: s.s: hld up in last: wl bhd over 2f out: shuffled along and one pce over 1f out* **100/1**
**14** *2 ½* **Celtic Promise (IRE)** 2-8-9.............................. RLMoore 13 28
(MrsAJPerrett) *unf: sn pushed along: a struggling in rr* **25/1**

1m 25.22s (-0.72) **Going Correction** -0.125s/f (Stan) **14** Ran SP% **122.2**
Speed ratings: **99,96,95,91,89 88,88,86,86,84 83,82,82,79**CSF £5.54 TOTE £1.80: £1.10, £1.70, £1.90; EX 6.50.
**Owner** Hamdan Al Maktoum **Bred** Martin Francis **Trained** Lambourn, Berks

**FOCUS**
A creditable time for the grade, despite being 0.27 seconds slower than the first division.

**NOTEBOOK**
**Qadar(IRE)**, unlucky to run into the Derby favourite Dubawi on his last start, had been given a break since and was found an easier opportunity here. He duly got off the mark in good style and looks likely to develop into a very useful performer next year. He is reportedly unlikely to have another race this season as a fast surface suits him best.
**Balkan Leader(USA)** made his debut at Catterick, suggesting connections did not believe he was anything special. He was easily brushed aside by the winner in the straight and this performance confirmed the earlier impression.
**Desert Lightning(IRE)** cost 120,000gns as a yearling and is entered in the Dewhurst. He ran a promising race as he was conceding racecourse experience to the first two, but the Group One entry looks optimistic at this stage.
**Missy Cinofaz**, whose dam is a half-sister to high-class middle-distance filly Mezzogiorno, improved a good deal on her debut performance at Yarmouth.
**Precious Sammi** was seen off when the pace quickened entering the straight.
**Heathwood(IRE)**, a half-brother to a couple of winners in Lahooq and Wood Fern, looked in need of the experience and is likely to do better in time. *Official explanation: jockey said colt dwelt in stalls*
**Blue Hedges** *Official explanation: jockey said colt missed break*

## 6012 SUN NURSERY 6f (P)
**2:50** (2:50) (D2) (0-85,83) 2-Y-O **£5,655** (£1,740; £870; £435) **Stalls** Low

Form RPR
032 **1** **Fantaisiste**[41] 5054 2-8-13 75.............................. SSanders 2 79+
(SirMarkPrescott) *mde all: rdn and hrd pressed over 1f out: drvn out* **2/1**[1]
4310 **2** *½* **Bahamian Magic**[6] 5896 2-9-7 83.............................. LDettori 1 85
(DRLoder) *lw: cl up: chsd wnr over 2f out: drvn to chal over 1f out: kpt on but a hld* **11/4**[2]

4360 **3** ½ **Transvestite (IRE)**$^{14}$ 5738 2-8-8 **70**.....(v) EAhern 6 71
(JWHills) *chsd ldrs: rdn over 2f out: styd on wl fnl f: nrst fin* **8/1**
6360 **4** ¾ **Fasylitator (IRE)**$^{29}$ 5377 2-8-7 **69**..... SWKelly 8 67
(JAOsborne) *settled in last trio: effrt 2f out: plld out and styd on wl fnl f: nrst fin* **9/2**$^{3}$
4300 **5** *nk* **Lily Lenat**$^{5}$ 5909 2-8-10 **72**.....(p) DSweeney 5 69
(JRBoyle) *mostly chsd wnr to over 2f out: one pce u.p* **33/1**
2420 **6** *nk* **Mulberry Lad (IRE)**$^{13}$ 5745 2-8-3 **65**.....(b) DKinsella 10 64+
(WRMuir) *dwlt: sn midfield: prog on inner 2f out: chal jst over 1f out: squeezed out ins fnl f: wknd* **33/1**
6253 **7** ½ **Nasseem Dubai (USA)**$^{19}$ 5604 2-9-2 **78**..... JQuinn 11 73
(MrsADuffield) *hld up towards rr: effrt over 2f out: styng on one pce whn no room last 50yds* **12/1**
0300 **8** *4* **San Deng**$^{29}$ 5376 2-7-13 **61** ow1..... FNorton 3 44
(WRMuir) *dwlt: hld up towards rr: effrt over 2f out: fdd over 1f out: eased* **66/1**
644 **9** *5* **General Haigh**$^{46}$ 4936 2-8-10 **72**..... WSupple 7 40
(JRBest) *chsd ldrs: lost pl 1/2-way: wknd 2f out* **16/1**
006 **10** *2* **Sir Bluebird (IRE)**$^{19}$ 5609 2-8-6 **68**..... RLMoore 4 30
(RHannon) *lw: sn rdn: a bhd* **12/1**
1440 **11** *1* **Gee Bee Em**$^{70}$ 4235 2-8-10 **75**..... LPKeniry$^{(3)}$ 9 34
(GPEnright) *racd wd: prom to over 2f out: wknd rapidly* **33/1**

1m 12.1s (-0.82) **Going Correction** -0.125s/f (Stan) **11** Ran SP% **120.9**
Speed ratings: **100,99,98,97,97 96,96,90,84,81 80**CSF £7.48 CT £37.46 TOTE £3.30: £1.10, £2.10, £3.40; EX 7.30.
**Owner** Miss K Rausing **Bred** Miss K Rausing **Trained** Newmarket, Suffolk
■ Stewards Enquiry : S Sanders caution: careless riding

**FOCUS**
Not much winning form on view but the winner had run into a subsequent Group winner last time.

**NOTEBOOK**
**Fantaisiste**, runner-up to a subsequent Group Three winner last time, really needs farther than this but she still proved good enough off what looked a very reasonable mark. She should not go up too much for this win and looks likely to progress further as she steps up in trip.
**Bahamian Magic** put a below-par run at Newmarket behind him and made the winner pull out all the stops. This was a good performance under top weight and he should continue to run well. *Official explanation: jockey said colt felt wrong*
**Transvestite(IRE)**, who had started to look as though he was going backwards, ran a decent race on his first attempt on Polytrack, finishing well down the outside.
**Fasylitator(IRE)**, another finishing well towards the end of the race, appreciated the drop back to six.
**Lily Lenat** did not get home over seven last time and appeared suited by the return to sprinting.
**Mulberry Lad(IRE)** looked to have a good chance of a place entering the last, but he faded badly inside the final furlong.

## 6013 SPORT NEWSPAPERS LTD H'CAP 1m 4f (P)
**3:20** (3:20) (E3) (0-70,70) 3-Y-0+ **£3,680** (£1,132; £566; £283) **Stalls** Low

Form RPR
01 **1** **Mith Hill**$^{56}$ 4629 3-8-12 **68**..... EAhern 9 77+
(EALDunlop) *trckd ldrs: pushed along over 3f out: effrt 2f out: rdn to ld last 150yds: hld on* **10/1**
6310 **2** ½ **Redi (ITY)**$^{19}$ 5619 3-8-11 **70**..... NMackay$^{(3)}$ 7 78+
(LMCumani) *racd midfield: prog 2f out: r.o to take 2nd wl ins fnl f: nt rch wnr* **6/1**$^{2}$
005 **3** ¾ **Baranook (IRE)**$^{62}$ 4492 3-8-11 **67**..... JFortune 16 74+
(PWHarris) *led: rdn over 2f out: hdd last 150yds: kpt on* **20/1**
1342 **4** *hd* **Regal Gallery (IRE)**$^{91}$ 3638 6-9-7 **70**..... LDettori 2 76+
(CAHorgan) *settled towards rr: plenty to do 2f out: plld out over 1f out: r.o fnl f: too much to do* **2/1**$^{1}$
234- **5** *1* **Strathspey**$^{380}$ 5130 5-9-3 **69**..... LPKeniry$^{(3)}$ 12 74
(PJMcbride) *trckd ldrs: smooth prog to chal over 2f out: fdd fnl f* **50/1**
4006 **6** ½ **Jadeeron**$^{4}$ 5956 5-9-1 **64**.....(p) LisaJones 13 68
(MissDAMchale) *t.k.h: prom: chsd ldr over 3f out: chal over 1f out: wknd fnl f* **20/1**
5660 **7** *1* **Rollswood (USA)**$^{7}$ 5869 4-8-13 **62**.....(tp) SWhitworth 4 64
(PRHedger) *b: hld up in last trio: effrt over 2f out: styd on fr over 1f out: n.d* **16/1**
4400 **8** 1 ½ **Gallant Boy (IRE)**$^{2}$ 5997 5-8-7 **59**.....(vt) FPFerris$^{(3)}$ 10 59
(PDEvans) *b.: hld up in rr: rdn and effrt over 2f out: styd on fnl f: no ch* **9/1**
5002 **9** ¾ **Sewmore Character**$^{29}$ 5381 4-9-5 **68**..... DSweeney 8 67
(MBlanshard) *lw: dwlt: hld up wl in rr: kpt on fr over 1f out: no ch* **12/1**
0040 **10** ½ **Eijaaz (IRE)**$^{19}$ 5621 3-8-9 **65**..... CCatlin 15 63
(GCBravery) *mostly chsd ldr to over 3f out: fdd u.p* **50/1**
0000 **11** *hd* **Raheel (IRE)**$^{5}$ 5914 4-8-9 **58**.....(bt$^{1}$) DHolland 5 56
(PMitchell) *s.s: hld up in last: detached 5f out: stl last 2f out: nudged along and r.o fnl f: nvr nr ldrs* **20/1**
6-42 **12** 1 ½ **Precious Mystery (IRE)**$^{43}$ 5019 4-8-11 **60**..... KFallon 6 55
(AKing) *t.k.h: prom tl wknd over 2f out* **7/1**$^{3}$
2000 **13** ½ **Surdoue**$^{163}$ 1675 4-9-2 **65**..... NPollard 11 59
(PHowling) *racd wd towards rr: effrt over 2f out: wknd wl over 1f out* **40/1**
5000 **14** 2 ½ **Billy Bathwick (IRE)**$^{7}$ 5869 7-8-9 **58**..... RLMoore 1 48
(JMBradley) *racd midfield: lost pl on inner and struggling over 2f out* **20/1**
0420 **15** *5* **Disparity (USA)**$^{29}$ 5382 3-8-9 **65**.....(t) WRyan 3 47
(JRFanshawe) *hld up in rr: no prog 3f out: bhd after* **25/1**
506 **16** *nk* **Cemgraft**$^{22}$ 5537 3-8-9 **65**..... SDrowne 14 47
(MissECLavelle) *chsd ldrs: rdn over 4f out: sn struggling* **20/1**

2m 36.11s (1.87) **Going Correction** -0.125s/f (Stan) **16** Ran SP% **126.8**
**WFA** 3 from 4yo+ 7lb
Speed ratings: **88,87,87,87,86 86,85,84,83,83 83,82,82,80,77 76**CSF £62.05 CT £1211.37 TOTE £7.40: £2.80, £1.70, £2.70, £1.10; EX 75.60 Trifecta £520.00 Pool £878.96. 1.20 winning units.
**Owner** Mohammed Jaber **Bred** Floors Farming, Hmh Management Ltd And John Warren **Trained** Newmarket, Suffolk

**FOCUS**
Not much pace on in the early stages and a very slow time for the class of race.

**NOTEBOOK**
**Mith Hill** raced in touch off a steady gallop and was in the right position to pick up the leaders as they turned into the straight. The step up in trip appeared to offset the slow pace and he came home well. He should be even better suited by a strongly-run race.
**Redi(ITY)** could have done with a stronger gallop as he finished well from off the pace, but the winner had gone beyond recall.
**Baranook(IRE)**, a half-brother to top-class middle-distance performer Pentire, was making his handicap debut and stepping up in trip. He enjoyed the run of the race in a slowly-run affair and had no excuse.
**Regal Gallery(IRE)**, a well-backed favourite on her return from a three-month break, was racing off a 5lb higher mark than when beaten last time. She was given plenty to do given the way the race was run and is capable of better.
**Strathspey**, returning from a year's absence, usually runs her race but she has a poor strike-rate.
**Jadeeron** is another with a poor strike-rate.
**Rollswood(USA)**, held up towards the rear in a steadily-run event, was another unsuited by the way the race was run.
**Raheel(IRE)**, who never got involved on this occasion, could have done with a stronger pace. *Official explanation: jockey said gelding ran too free in first time blinkers*
**Precious Mystery(IRE)** *Official explanation: jockey said filly hung right in final furlong*

## 6014 DAWSON NEWS (S) STKS 1m (P)
**3:50** (3:51) (G4) 3-Y-0+ **£2,688** (£768; £384) **Stalls** High

Form RPR
3540 **1** **Analyze (FR)**$^{61}$ 3872 6-9-0 67..... RLMoore 8 68
(BGPowell) *hld up: prog to trck ldrs 2f out: wnt 2nd ins fnl f: r.o to ld nr fin* **4/1**$^{3}$
0001 **2** *nk* **Omaha City (IRE)**$^{9}$ 5841 10-9-5 69..... FNorton 9 72
(BGubby) *trckd ldrs gng easily: led over 1f out and kicked 2l clr: kpt on but hdd nr fin* **11/4**$^{1}$
006R **3** *5* **Chandelier**$^{30}$ 5336 4-9-2 50..... LPKeniry$^{(3)}$ 3 61
(MSSaunders) *s.v.s: wl in rr: prog 3f out: hanging lft over 1f out: kpt on one pce to take 3rd wl ins fnl f* **25/1**
6600 **4** 1 ¾ **Extra Cover (IRE)**$^{16}$ 5697 3-9-2 67.....(b) LDettori 6 56
(NACallaghan) *s.i.s: sn w ldr: led over 2f out: hdd over 1f out: nt run on* **13/2**
0000 **5** *1* **Gallery Breeze**$^{22}$ 5541 5-9-0 65.....(b) VSlattery 5 49
(JLSpearing) *led after 2f: mde most to over 2f out: wknd over 1f out* **14/1**
0000 **6** *6* **Its Ecco Boy**$^{72}$ 4185 6-9-5 53..... SWKelly 10 40
(PHowling) *racd in rr: outpcd 3f out: no ch after: kpt on* **40/1**
0020 **7** 3 ½ **Rockley Bay (IRE)**$^{33}$ 5261 3-8-11 57.....(t) DSweeney 2 27
(PJMakin) *chsd ldrs: outpcd fr 3f out: no ch fnl 2f* **25/1**
4401 **8** *1* **Alafzar (IRE)**$^{27}$ 5408 6-9-5 62.....(bt) KFallon 7 30
(PDEvans) *trckd ldrs: rdn 3f out: wknd 2f out: eased fnl f* **3/1**$^{2}$
5555 **9** *2* **Dancing King (IRE)**$^{20}$ 5587 8-9-0 46..... PMakin$^{(5)}$ 1 25
(PWHiatt) *led for 2f: prom tl wknd 2f out* **20/1**
0400 **10** *10* **Soviet Spirit**$^{21}$ 5571 3-8-1 48.....(b$^{1}$) DFox$^{(5)}$ 4 —
(CADwyer) *s.s: rcvrd and prom after 2f: wknd 3f out* **50/1**
00 **11** ¾ **Pico Alto**$^{18}$ 5656 3-8-3.....(t) FPFerris$^{(3)}$ 12 —
(BPalling) *a wl in rr* **100/1**
0040 **12** *3* **Ticero**$^{9}$ 5829 3-8-11 63.....(b) SSanders 11 —
(CEBrittain) *racd wd: chsd ldrs: rdn bef 1/2-way: sn wknd* **16/1**

1m 37.72s (-1.83) **Going Correction** -0.125s/f (Stan)
**WFA** 3 from 4yo+ 3lb **12** Ran SP% **115.4**
Speed ratings: **104,103,98,96,95 89,86,85,83,73 72,69**CSF £13.83 TOTE £5.80: £1.10, £1.80, £8.00; EX 18.30.There was no bid for the winner. Extra Cover was claimed by Ms D J Evans for £5,500
**Owner** The Arkle Bar Partnership **Bred** London Thoroughbred Services Ltd **Trained** Morestead, Hants

**FOCUS**
A true pace and a decent time for a seller. The field finished well strung out.

**NOTEBOOK**
**Analyze(FR)**, whose five previous victories have all come over ten furlongs, was very much suited by the strong pace and was travelling best from a long way out. It did look as though he may be stuck in a pocket starting up the home straight, but a gap appeared just in time for him to reel in the runner-up. He still has the ability to win outside of this grade.
**Omaha City(IRE)** was a little surprisingly dropped into a seller considering he showed at Windsor last week that he can still win in 0-70 company. He travelled well and made his bid at just the right time, but despite doing nothing wrong was mugged near the line. Despite his age he is still very lightly raced on this surface, and there are plenty of other races like this here in the coming months.
**Chandelier** handicapped himself with a tardy start, but did stay on past weakening rivals to grab third. He has bits of form on this surface and could find a similar contest if breaking on terms.
**Extra Cover(IRE)**, kept wide of the inside rail as his rider likes to do here, needs his effort timing to perfection and probably found himself in front much sooner than ideal.
**Gallery Breeze** was given a positive ride and ran her race, but this trip looks too far. A similar contest should be within her compass back over seven.
**Alafzar(IRE)** has a good record here, so this tame effort was disappointing. *Official explanation: jockey said gelding made a noise*
**Ticero** *Official explanation: jockey said gelding stopped quickly*

## 6015 HIGG'S INTERNATIONAL MAIDEN STKS (DIV I) 1m (P)
**4:20** (4:20) (D3) 3-Y-0+ **£3,809** (£1,172; £586; £293) **Stalls** High

Form RPR
-223 **1** **Admiral Compton**$^{8}$ 5851 3-9-0 77.....(v$^{1}$) KFallon 4 72
(EFVaughan) *lw: prom: led over 3f out: drvn wl clr fr 2f out: unchal* **1/1**$^{1}$
0 **2** *4* **Duxford**$^{9}$ 5844 3-9-0..... JQuinn 6 63
(DKIvory) *dwlt: in tch: prog to chse wnr over 2f out: no imp* **50/1**
4044 **3** *2* **Hunter's Valley**$^{35}$ 5223 3-8-9 65..... RHughes 10 53
(RHannon) *hld up rr: prog over 2f out: kpt on one pce over 1f out* **7/1**$^{3}$
5063 **4** *nk* **Song Of Vala**$^{53}$ 4756 3-9-0 74.....(t) SDrowne 8 58
(RCharlton) *lw: sn trckd ldrs: rdn to dispute 2nd pl over 2f out: one pce* **11/4**$^{2}$
000 **5** ½ **Warbreck**$^{12}$ 5770 3-9-0.....(b) RLMoore 9 56
(CREgerton) *sn drvn in last: stl wl bhd over 2f out: kpt on one pce* **33/1**
65 **6** *1* **Magic Spin**$^{37}$ 5204 4-8-12..... SCarson 7 49
(RFJohnsonHoughton) *hld up towards rr: pushed along whn nt clr run over 2f out: no imp ldrs* **25/1**
4 **7** *3* **Angry Bark (USA)**$^{9}$ 5828 3-8-9..... RSmith 5 42
(HSHowe) *trckd ldrs: wnt prom over 3f out: wknd over 2f out* **14/1**
0/ **8** 1 ½ **King At Last**$^{774}$ 4139 5-9-3..... DSweeney 12 44
(KBell) *racd on outer: in tch to 3f out* **50/1**
00 **9** 1 ¼ **Mad**$^{22}$ 5537 3-8-9..... ANicholls 1 36
(AndrewReid) *b.hind: led to over 4f out: sn lost pl and struggling* **66/1**
000- **10** *2* **Bebopskiddly**$^{391}$ 4834 3-9-0..... EAhern 11 36
(BGPowell) *dwlt: a struggling and wl in rr* **40/1**
2640 **11** *5* **Sea Of Gold**$^{9}$ 5829 3-8-9 68.....(v$^{1}$) CCatlin 3 20
(HJCyzer) *led to over 4f out: wknd rapidly* **14/1**
**12** *7* **Son And Heir (IRE)** 3-9-0..... PaulEddery 2 9
(NJHawke) *w'like: s.s: plld hrd and sn prom: wknd 1/2-way* **50/1**

1m 37.98s (-1.57) **Going Correction** -0.125s/f (Stan)
**WFA** 3 from 4yo+ 3lb **12** Ran SP% **119.1**
Speed ratings: **102,98,96,95,95 94,91,89,88,86 81,74**CSF £84.43 TOTE £1.80: £1.10, £6.70, £2.80; EX 73.10.
**Owner** Racing For Gold **Bred** Mrs N F M Sampson **Trained** Newmarket, Suffolk

**FOCUS**
Not the most competitive of maidens and an ordinary time for the class, despite being 1.5 seconds faster than the second division.

**NOTEBOOK**

**Admiral Compton** took well to the Polytrack and was booted right out straightening up for home as though Fallon really wanted it. He had the form to win this as he did, and his best option may be to come back here for a handicap now that he is proven on the surface.

**Duxford** improved a good deal from his turf debut over this extra two furlongs and finished a clear second best. His proximity might be considered as holding the form down but, using the official marks of the winner and the fourth as a guide, it might be wise to give him the benefit of the doubt, so there may be a small race in him.

**Hunter's Valley**, an exposed maiden on turf, did not improve for the switch to Polytrack and probably merely repeated her grass form. She is gradually dropping in the weights and will eventually reach a mark she can win off.

**Song Of Vala**, another making his sand debut, continues to flatter to deceive.

**Warbreck** was always struggling to go the pace, but did pick off a few stragglers in the closing stages. Considering his breeding and his 250,000gns price tag he looks very disappointing, but he does give the impression there is some ability there and a longer trip and handicap company may see him start to show it.

## 6016 W H SMITH NEWS APPRENTICE H'CAP — 6f (P)

**4:50** (4:51) (E3) (0-70,70) 3-Y-0 — **£3,482** (£1,071; £535; £267) **Stalls** Low

Form — RPR

1500 **1** — **Simpsons Mount (IRE)**14 5737 3-8-13 **65** ... DTudhope(3) 6 — 75+
(RMFlower) *hld up rr: prog 3f out: nt clr run and swtchd rt over 1f out : r.o to ld fnl 50yds* — **16/1**

2100 **2** *1* **Saviours Spirit**18 5652 3-9-4 **70** ... AMullen(3) 2 — 77
(TGMills) *lw: trckd ldrs: effrt on inner 2f out: led ins fnl f: hdd fnl 50yds* — **4/1**2

2600 **3** *1* **Darla (IRE)**14 5737 3-9-4 **67** ... NChalmers 8 — 71
(JWPayne) *trckd ldrs: prog to ld over 1f out: hdd and one pce ins fnl f* — **12/1**

1500 **4** *hd* **Ivory Lace**14 5730 3-9-0 **68** ... AKirby(5) 1 — 71
(SWoodman) *hld up in rr: gd prog over 1f out: chsd ldrs ins fnl f: one pce nr fin* — **8/1**

6104 **5** *2 ½* **La Vie Est Belle**19 5618 3-8-11 **63** ... StephanieHollinshead(3) 4 — 59
(BRMillman) *mde most to over 1f out: wknd fnl f* — **15/2**

3261 **6** *hd* **Kensington (IRE)**11 5801 3-9-1 **64** ... PMakin 3 — 59
(RGuest) *racd midfield on inner: effrt 2f out: no prog and btn over 1f out* — **7/2**1

4640 **7** *1* **Multiple Choice (IRE)**33 5261 3-8-10 **64** ...(bt) StevenHarrison(5) 9 — 56
(NPLittmoden) *chsd ldrs: wknd over 1f out* — **25/1**

0526 **8** *½* **Ever Cheerful**207 1008 3-8-10 **66** ...(p) SHaddon(7) 5 — 57
(WGMTurner) *bit bkwd: mostly chsd ldr to 2f out: bmpd along and wknd* — **20/1**

0006 **9** *1 ½* **Dolce Piccata**25 5473 3-9-5 **68** ...(b) NDeSouza 11 — 54
(BJMeehan) *racd v wd: lost pl and struggling 1/2-way* — **10/1**

3000 **10** *½* **Bella Tutrice (IRE)**14 5737 3-9-1 **64** ...(p) BSwarbrick 10 — 49
(IAWood) *lw: racd wd: in tch to over 2f out* — **25/1**

3403 **11** *1 ¾* **Dandouce**54 4707 3-9-2 **68** ... ThomasYeung(3) 7 — 48
(PWChapple-Hyam) *racd wd: chsd ldrs over 3f: wknd* — **11/2**3

0000 **F** **Gojo (IRE)**2 6001 3-8-9 **63** ...(p) RMills(5) 12 — —
(BPalling) *racd v wd: nvr on terms: wl in rr whn stmbld and fell over 1f out* — **33/1**

1m 11.69s (-1.23) **Going Correction** -0.125s/f (Stan) — **12** Ran SP% **118.5**

Speed ratings: **103,101,100,100,96 96,95,94,92,91 89,**—CSF £75.59 CT £828.35 TOTE £11.80: £3.50, £2.80, £3.50; EX 171.40.

**Owner** C Simpson,Z Mount,T J Lowe,R M Flower **Bred** Thomas Heatrick **Trained** Jevington, E Sussex

**FOCUS**

A decent pace for this apprentice handicap and a nasty incident on the home turn.

**NOTEBOOK**

**Simpsons Mount(IRE)** can be a bit of a character, but has run well here before and he did not lose as much ground at the start as he sometimes can. Given a very confident ride, he had to wait to get a clear run but, once he did, fairly flew home to snatch the race out of the fire. He has the ability, but would not be guaranteed to repeat this next time.

**Saviours Spirit** returned to form on a surface he handles well following a couple of recent sighters on turf. Although doing nothing wrong, he had the race snatched from him near the line and can win a similar contest off this sort of mark.

**Darla(IRE)**, one place behind Simpsons Mount on turf here last month, was 1lb better off but was beaten a little further on this different surface and remains a maiden after 12 attempts.

**Ivory Lace**, who has form on this surface, is rated 7lb lower on sand than on turf and ran well enough to suggest she can be placed to advantage.

**La Vie Est Belle** established her usual place at the head of affairs and tried to lead the whole way, but did not get home.

**Kensington(IRE)**, making his sand debut, started favourite on account of his Ripon victory last time, but that was a poor race and his limits were well exposed.

**Ever Cheerful**, reappearing after a seven-month break, ran as if needing it.

**Dandouce**, placed a couple of times here just under a year ago, did not run up to that form this time.

**Gojo(IRE)** took a very wide course until clipping heels and taking a nasty fall straightening up for home. *Official explanation: trainer said filly finished lame*

## 6017 HIGG'S INTERNATIONAL MAIDEN STKS (DIV II) — 1m (P)

**5:20** (5:20) (E3) 3-Y-0+ — **£3,809** (£1,172; £586; £293) **Stalls** High

Form — RPR

0243 **1** — **Noora (IRE)**46 4954 3-8-9 69 ... RHills 8 — 66
(MPTregoning) *hld up in rr: prog wl over 1f out: str run to ld last 75yds: sn clr* — **13/2**

2533 **2** *1 ¼* **Rubaiyat (IRE)**4 5957 3-9-0 55 ... SDrowne 7 — 68
(GWragg) *prom: pushed into ld over 1f out: hdd and outpcd last 75yds* — **9/1**

322 **3** *1 ¼* **Kauri Forest (USA)**67 4316 3-9-0 83 ...(t) LDettori 4 — 65
(JRFanshawe) *hld up midfield: clsd on ldrs over 1f out: shkn up and one pce fnl f* — **6/4**1

3303 **4** *¾* **Master Theo (USA)**16 5706 3-9-0 73 ... JQuinn 6 — 63
(HJCollingridge) *t.k.h: hld up in tch: clsng on ldrs whn nt clr run over 1f out: one pce fnl f* — **6/1**3

24- **5** *1 ¾* **Authority (IRE)**445 3413 4-9-3 ... SSanders 1 — 59
(LadyHerries) *dwlt: hld up in rr: prog on inner 2f out: chsd ldrs 1f out: shuffled along and lost pl: do bttr* — **14/1**

30 **6** *1* **Subtle Breeze (USA)**19 5621 3-8-9 ... JFortune 3 — 52
(JHMGosden) *led: hanging rt fr 1/2-way: hdd & wknd over 1f out* — **7/2**2

4060 **7** *nk* **Lord Of The Sea (IRE)**17 5496 3-9-0 59 ... PDoe 10 — 56
(JamiePoulton) *mostly chsd ldr to over 1f out: wknd* — **33/1**

0000 **8** *5* **Zuri (IRE)**23 5510 3-8-6 58 ... NMackay(3) 12 — 40
(LMCumani) *hld up rr: outpcd and btn over 2f out* — **40/1**

00 **9** *1 ¼* **Charlie Masters**9 5843 3-9-0 ... LisaJones 11 — 42
(PHowling) *a wl in rr: lost tch over 2f out* — **66/1**

0 **10** *4* **Kajul**55 4683 3-8-9 ... PaulEddery 5 — 28
(CAHorgan) *dwlt: t.k.h and hld up in rr: wknd 3f out* — **100/1**

40-0 **11** *30* **Kiniska**124 2647 3-8-6 60 ... FPFerris(3) 2 — —
(BPalling) *plld hrd: prom tl wknd rapidly over 3f out: virtually p.u over 1f out* — **40/1**

1m 39.48s (-0.07) **Going Correction** -0.125s/f (Stan)

**WFA** 3 from 4yo 3lb — **11** Ran SP% **116.8**

Speed ratings: **95,93,92,91,90 89,88,83,82,78 48**CSF £60.80 TOTE £7.10: £2.60, £3.20, £1.10; EX 41.60 Place 6 £3.97, Place 5 £3.51.

**Owner** Khalil Alsayegh **Bred** Shadwell Estate Company Limited **Trained** Lambourn, Berks

**FOCUS**

A modest pace and a moderate time for the grade, 1.5 seconds slower than the first division.

**NOTEBOOK**

**Noora(IRE)** found the switch to sand and being given a much more patient ride paying dividends as she found a decent turn of foot to take the spoils. This did not look a great race though, especially in view of the winning time and, as she may go up in the weights for beating some much higher rated rivals, she seems likely to struggle in handicap company.

**Rubaiyat(IRE)** appeared to run very well at the weights, but he has plenty of form on this surface and looked like scoring until having the race snatched from him. Hopefully the Handicapper will not take this effort at face value.

**Kauri Forest(USA)** had an outstanding chance on official ratings, but does not look straightforward and, after being produced with his effort, did not find that much off the bridle. He looks one to treat with caution.

**Master Theo(USA)** did not have much room to play with in the home straight, but in reality lacked the pace to get him out of it. A longer trip may be what he needs.

**Authority(IRE)** ◆, off the track for 15 months, was bang there racing down the home straight and this was a good effort after such a long layoff. He can now be handicapped.

**Subtle Breeze(USA)** was given a positive ride on this switch to sand, but looked very awkward around the bends and was swamped in the home straight. She can now be handicapped, but has questions to answer. *Official explanation: jockey said filly hung badly right*

**Kiniska** *Official explanation: jockey said filly lost her action*

T/Jkpt: Not won. T/Plt: £5.50 to a £1 stake. Pool: £45,422.80. 5,969.90 winning tickets. T/Qpdt: £5.80 to a £1 stake. Pool: £2,328.80. 295.20 winning tickets. JN

# 5952 WOLVERHAMPTON (A.W) (L-H)

Thursday, October 7

**OFFICIAL GOING: Standard**

Wind: Slight across Weather: Fine

## 6020 HOLIDAY INN GARDEN COURT MAIDEN AUCTION STKS (DIV I) 1m 141y(P)

**1:50** (1:57) (E4) 2-Y-0 — **£2,947** (£842; £421) **Stalls** Low

Form — RPR

4422 **1** — **Watchmyeyes (IRE)**15 5735 2-8-12 77 ... KFallon 7 — 80+
(NPLittmoden) *chsd ldrs: led over 2f out: rdn clr and hung rt over 1f out: all out* — **7/4**1

0 **2** *shd* **Linda's Colin (IRE)**16 5718 2-8-9 ... MFenton 4 — 77
(PWD'Arcy) *a.p: rdn and nt clr run wl over 1f out: r.o* — **50/1**

0204 **3** *½* **Musical Day**5 5938 2-8-7 78 ow1 ... DHolland 3 — 74+
(BJMeehan) *chsd ldrs: rdn over 3f out: nt clr run and outpcd over 2f out: r.o ins fnl f* — **15/8**2

5 **4** *2* **Kangrina**15 5741 2-8-7 ... SSanders 2 — 70
(SirMarkPrescott) *led: hdd over 5f out: led over 3f out: hdd over 2f out: sn edgd rt: no ex ins fnl f* — **4/1**3

50 **5** *6* **Mr Marucci (USA)**33 5301 2-8-7 ... TEaves(3) 5 — 60
(BEllison) *s.i.s: sn pushed along in rr: styd on appr fnl f: n.d* — **50/1**

**6** *2 ½* **Kergolay (IRE)** 2-8-9 ... SDrowne 13 — 54
(WRMuir) *s.i.s: n.d* — **50/1**

0 **7** *3* **Soft Focus (IRE)**15 5741 2-8-4 ... CCatlin 6 — 42
(JAOsborne) *hld up: effrt over 2f out: n.d* — **25/1**

00 **8** *3* **Monica's Revenge (IRE)**17 5687 2-8-4 ... TPQueally 11 — 36
(RMBeckett) *hld up: hdwy over 5f out: wknd over 2f out* — **66/1**

0030 **9** *1 ¼* **Dixie Queen (IRE)**36 5227 2-8-6 62 ow1 ...(b1) SWKelly 12 — 35
(MDods) *s.i.s: hmpd over 5f out: n.d* — **50/1**

0 **10** *hd* **Mountain Breeze**40 5109 2-8-3 ... LisaJones 1 — 32
(DShaw) *sn pushed along and prom: wknd over 5f out* — **100/1**

350 **11** *¾* **Good Investment**48 4900 2-8-10 69 ... GFaulkner 8 — 37
(PCHaslam) *chsd ldrs: led over 5f out: hdd over 3f out: wknd over 2f out* — **10/1**

1m 52.42s — **11** Ran SP% **114.4**

Speed ratings: CSF £98.02 TOTE £2.60: £1.10, £10.80, £1.20; EX 72.60.

**Owner** V And J Properties **Bred** Sea Syndicate **Trained** Newmarket, Suffolk

**FOCUS**

Fairly good form, of a similar standard to the other division. A good pace, and not many got into it with the front four all holding prominent positions from the off. The winning time was 0.55 seconds faster than the second division.

**NOTEBOOK**

**Watchmyeyes(IRE)**, who already has Polytrack form on the board, appreciated the stronger pace and established a decent advantage straightening up for home, only to nearly throw it away by hanging violently over to the stands' rail and just holding on by the skin of his teeth. He is value for much more than the winning margin, but is obviously not straightforward.

**Linda's Colin(IRE)** improved a good deal from his debut and finished well against the inside rail after running green on the home turn and having to switch in order to get a run. He is a little flattered by his proximity to the winner, but still showed more than enough to suggest he will soon be winning.

**Musical Day**, well supported following her improved effort in a decent Newmarket nursery five days earlier, was finishing best of all but gave the impression that even this longer trip was an insufficient test on this different surface.

**Kangrina** was given a positive ride, but was done for foot in the latter stages and did not really improve on her debut effort.

**Mr Marucci(USA)** was not totally disgraced and is likely to do better now that he can be handicapped.

**Good Investment** was racing on sand for the first time and held a prominent position early, but gradually dropped away and looks regressive.

## 6021 HOLIDAY INN GARDEN COURT MAIDEN AUCTION STKS (DIV II) 1m 141y(P)

**2:20** (2:23) (E4) 2-Y-0 — **£2,940** (£840; £420) **Stalls** Low

Form — RPR

4 **1** — **Cloonavery (IRE)**28 5407 2-8-11 ... LDettori 4 — 80
(JAOsborne) *hld up: hdwy over 3f out: led wl over 1f out: edgd rt 1f out: drvn out* — **2/1**1

05 **2** *¾* **Desperation (IRE)**38 5186 2-8-8 ... DarrenWilliams 13 — 75
(KRBurke) *chsd ldrs: rdn and ev ch over 2f out: r.o* — **10/1**

600 **3** *3 ½* **Tamora**22 5559 2-8-4 65 ... FNorton 10 — 64
(APJarvis) *chsd ldrs: led over 2f out: hdd wl over 1f out: styd on same pce fnl f* — **16/1**



The Form Book, Raceform Ltd, Compton, RG20 6NL

0 **4** ½ **Danzare**[17] 5695 2-8-0 ........ NDeSouza(5) 11 64
(MPTregoning) *mid-div: hmpd over 6f out: styd on appr fnl f: nt trble ldrs* **6/1**[3]

6330 **5** 1¾ **Fadael (IRE)**[14] 5753 2-8-6 64........ MFenton 6 61
(PWD'Arcy) *chsd ldrs: hmpd over 6f out: rdn over 3f out: hung lft over 1f out: styd on same pce* **6/1**[3]

0403 **6** 1 **Plenty Cried Wolf**[8] 5855 2-8-7 68........ THamilton(3) 1 63
(RAFahey) *led: rdn and hdd over 2f out: wknd over 1f out* **8/1**

0 **7** ½ **Overtop Way (GR)**[38] 5200 2-8-9 ........ TPQueally 5 61
(PRChamings) *s.i.s: bhd: styd on appr fnl f: nvr nrr* **66/1**

5626 **8** 1½ **Kerry's Blade (IRE)**[21] 5596 2-8-9 66........ GFaulkner 2 58+
(PCHaslam) *mid-div: rdn over 3f out: nvr trbld ldrs* **4/1**[2]

00 **9** 10 **Stolen**[28] 5407 2-8-8 ........ SDrowne 3 36+
(WRMuir) *chsd ldrs 6f* **100/1**

00 **10** ¾ **Harry's Simmie (IRE)**[63] 4487 2-8-3 ........ DaleGibson 7 29
(RHollinshead) *mid-div: dropped rr over 5f out: sn bhd* **100/1**

0 **11** *nk* **Sergeant Shinko (IRE)**[8] 5855 2-8-8 ........(b[1]) LEnstone 8 33
(MDods) *sn pushed along in rr: wknd 4f out* **100/1**

0 **12** 10 **Magdelaine**[50] 4851 2-8-6 ........ JFEgan 12 —
(PMPhelan) *hdwy over 6f out: wknd over 2f out* **80/1**

63 **13** 13 **Inagh**[17] 5689 2-8-4 ........ CCatlin 9 —
(MJWallace) *bhd fr 1/2-way* **25/1**

1m 51.87s **13** Ran SP% **117.5**
Speed ratings: CSF £23.10 TOTE £2.90: £1.40, £4.90, £6.10; EX 22.20.
**Owner** David N Reynolds and Chris Watkins **Bred** Horse Breeding Company **Trained** Upper Lambourn, Berks
■ Stewards Enquiry : F Norton one-day ban: careless riding (Oct 18)

**FOCUS**
Surprisingly good form for what looked on paper an ordinary maiden. It was run in a time 0.55 seconds slower than the first division.

**NOTEBOOK**
**Cloonavery(IRE)** came on from his debut and saw his race out well despite still showing distinct signs of greenness. He should eventually make his mark in handicap company over a bit further.
**Desperation(IRE)** showed a lot more than he did on Fibresand on his debut under a positive ride over this longer trip and kept battling right to the line. There should be a race in him on this surface and handicaps are an option for him now.
**Tamora** ran better on this switch to sand following a couple of modest efforts on turf. She could be interesting off her current mark in handicap company on this surface.
**Danzare** ran with credit, especially as she met some trouble entering the back straight. There is almost certainly better to come from her.
**Fadael(IRE)** did not perform too badly considering she got messed about at the beginning of the back straight. Her handicap mark looks more realistic now based on what she has achieved and that may be a better option than races like this.
**Plenty Cried Wolf** did not seem to see out the extra furlong.
**Kerry's Blade(IRE)** did not improve for the switch to Polytrack.
**Magdelaine** *Official explanation: jockey said filly had a breathing problem*

## 6022 COME FLOODLIT RACING THIS SATURDAY "PREMIER" CLAIMING STKS 5f 216y(P)
**2:50** (2:57) (D2) 2-Y-O **£5,616** (£1,728; £864; £432) **Stalls** Low

Form RPR

0010 **1** **Forzeen**[5] 5932 2-9-7 80........ LDettori 12 84
(JAOsborne) *chsd ldrs: led over 1f out: rdn and hdd ins fnl f: rallied to ld towards fin* **11/4**[1]

2105 **2** *hd* **Corniche Dancer**[14] 5745 2-8-6 70........ ACulhane 13 68
(MRChannon) *hld up in tch: rdn to chal over 1f out: led ins fnl f : hdd towards fin* **6/1**

0363 **3** 1½ **Apologies**[20] 5617 2-9-2 73........(b) GGibbons 7 74
(BAMcmahon) *chsd ldrs: rdn and ev ch over 1f out: styd on same pce ins fnl f* **11/2**[3]

0 **4** 5 **Chief Dipper**[16] 5716 2-8-5 ........ TPQueally 1 48
(PJMcbride) *chsd ldrs: led 4f out: rdn and hdd over 2f out: wknd over 1f out* **100/1**

00 **5** *nk* **Windwood (IRE)**[10] 5825 2-8-11 ........ SDrowne 9 53
(JWHills) *prom: rdn over 2f out: wknd over 1f out* **66/1**

0340 **6** *nk* **Indibraun (IRE)**[20] 5617 2-8-4 70........ NPollard 6 45
(PCHaslam) *led 2f: remained handy tl wknd 2f out* **12/1**

44 **7** 1 **Bond Finesse (IRE)**[152] 1960 2-8-8 ........ CCatlin 8 46
(BSmart) *s.i.s: outpcd: nvr nrr* **20/1**

60 **8** 2 **African Emperor (FR)**[15] 5735 2-8-0 ........ FPFerris(3) 10 35
(WJarvis) *chsd ldrs: rdn 1/2-way: sn wknd* **66/1**

405 **9** ½ **Piddies Pride (IRE)**[25] 5490 2-7-9 69........ HayleyTurner(3) 11 29
(PSMcentee) *dwlt: outpcd* **7/1**

36 **10** *shd* **Beaune**[20] 5616 2-9-7 ........ KFallon 2 51
(WJHaggas) *chsd ldrs: led over 2f out: rdn and hdd over 1f out: wknd and eased fnl f* **7/2**[2]

1006 **11** 5 **Make Us Flush**[13] 5767 2-8-7 72........ FNorton 4 22
(ABerry) *mid-div: sn pushed along: wknd over 2f out* **10/1**

**12** ¾ **Val D'Isere** 2-8-8 ........ JFMcDonald(3) 5 24
(BJMeehan) *s.s: outpcd* **33/1**

000 **13** *hd* **Bodden Bay**[6] 5910 2-7-12 ........ DFox(5) 3 15
(CADwyer) *sn outpcd* **100/1**

1m 15.81s **13** Ran SP% **120.5**
Speed ratings: CSF £19.06 TOTE £4.40: £2.30, £1.40, £2.60; EX 18.80.
**Owner** Cavendish Racing **Bred** James Clark **Trained** Upper Lambourn, Berks

**FOCUS**
A wide range of abilities in this claimer, but the pace was good and the front three pulled a mile clear of the others. This looks strong form.

**NOTEBOOK**
**Forzeen**, not that well in on adjusted official ratings, appreciated the return to a faster surface and responded well to pressure to get back up and win after looking likely to be swallowed up.
**Corniche Dancer**, who ran well on Polytrack on her only previous try, looked to have timed her effort just right down the wide outside but was worried out of it. This was an improvement on her last two efforts, but she does not look that consistent.
**Apologies** ran creditably on this sand debut and pulled right away from the others, but may appreciate a slower surface than this.
**Chief Dipper**, down two furlongs in trip from his debut, performed much better this time but will need to improve as much again in order to win a race.
**Windwood(IRE)** probably did not achieve much, but does at least now qualify for a handicap mark.
**Indibraun(IRE)** showed his usual early speed, but gradually faded and is yet to match his turf form on sand.
**Piddies Pride(IRE)** has been kept very busy, but did not take to the sand at the first time of asking.
**Beaune** showed up for a while, but eventually dropped away very tamely.
**Bodden Bay** *Official explanation: jockey said gelding did not handle kickback*

## 6023 WOLVERHAMPTON-RACECOURSE.CO.UK NOVICE STKS 5f 20y(P)
**3:20** (3:23) (D3) 2-Y-O **£4,212** (£1,296; £648; £324) **Stalls** Low

Form RPR

5250 **1** **Bond City (IRE)**[5] 5947 2-9-2 94........ FLynch 1 87
(BSmart) *chsd ldrs: rdn to ld wl ins fnl f: r.o* **2/1**[1]

2556 **2** ¾ **Bold Minstrel (IRE)**[5] 5932 2-9-2 83........ FNorton 11 84
(MQuinn) *a.p: chsd ldr over 2f out: rdn to ld 1f out: hdd wl ins fnl f* **10/1**

3016 **3** 3 **Connotation**[16] 5721 2-8-11 72........(b[1]) LDettori 5 69
(PWD'Arcy) *hld up in tch: rdn and edgd lft over 1f out: styd on same pce* **10/1**

003 **4** 1½ **Depressed**[5] 5953 2-8-7 ........ JFEgan 2 60
(AndrewReid) *led: rdn and hdd 1f out: sn wknd* **16/1**

1120 **5** 2½ **Countdown**[29] 5404 2-9-10 92........ SSanders 8 68
(SirMarkPrescott) *s.s: outpcd: styd on appr fnl f: nvr nrr* **11/4**[2]

00 **6** 1½ **Cool Sands (IRE)**[33] 5290 2-8-12 ........ DarrenWilliams 12 51
(DShaw) *s.s: styd on appr fnl f: nrst fin* **100/1**

4221 **7** 1¾ **Paris Tapis**[45] 4999 2-8-0 60........ JBrennan(7) 3 40
(PSMcentee) *prom to 1/2-way* **20/1**

1000 **8** *nk* **Annatalia**[12] 5797 2-9-0 76........ KFallon 7 45
(BJMeehan) *prom to 1/2-way* **10/3**[3]

5310 **9** 9 **Eternally**[77] 4046 2-8-12 57........(v[1]) RLMoore 6 12
(RMHCowell) *dwlt: outpcd* **25/1**

1000 **10** ½ **Town House**[68] 4348 2-8-7 70........ ACulhane 4 5
(BPJBaugh) *chsd ldrs to 1/2-way* **40/1**

00 **11** ½ **Waterfront Dancer**[6] 5908 2-8-12 ........ TPQueally 10 8
(JRBest) *sn outpcd* **100/1**

000 **12** 1¼ **Katie Killane**[8] 5865 2-8-7 ........(p) SCarson 9 —
(MWellings) *hld up: wknd 1/2-way* **100/1**

62.41 secs **12** Ran SP% **121.2**
Speed ratings: CSF £23.29 TOTE £3.70: £1.50, £3.60, £3.40; EX 28.20.
**Owner** R C Bond **Bred** David Ryan **Trained** Hambleton, N Yorks

**FOCUS**
A decent novice event run at a good clip and they finished well spread out.

**NOTEBOOK**
**Bond City(IRE)**, who has been taking on Pattern company in recent outings, found this level more to his liking and took to the surface well at the first time of asking. There are more races to be won with him on this surface, though there may not be that many opportunities for him.
**Bold Minstrel(IRE)** would have been 11lb better off with the winner in a handicap and found his finish too strong, but this was a decent sand debut nonetheless. He looks well worth another try here with similar tactics.
**Connotation**, wearing blinkers rather than a visor, ran as though she would prefer a slightly stiffer test, but she has been tried over as far as seven without success and does not look straightforward.
**Depressed**, who ran well at the opening meeting here, again tried to lead all the way in this better race. She was eventually collared, but this was still another fair effort against this company and her yard are sure to find an opportunity.
**Countdown**, like the winner stepping down from Pattern company, not for the first time missed the break and never managed to get seriously involved. He does not look an easy ride.
**Annatalia**, making her sand debut, broke well enough but was unable to hold her position and gradually faded.

## 6024 SPONSOR A RACE H'CAP 1m 141y(P)
**3:50** (3:51) (F4) (0-55,55) 3-Y-O+ **£3,038** (£868; £434) **Stalls** Low

Form RPR

0201 **1** **Nautical**[5] 5260 6-9-0 55........ LDettori 8 75+
(AWCarroll) *hld up: hdwy over 2f out: led over 1f out: edgd lft ins fnl f: rdn clr* **4/1**[1]

0460 **2** 3 **Ziet D'Alsace (FR)**[9] 5849 4-8-12 53........ RLMoore 9 64
(AWCarroll) *s.i.s: hld up: hdwy 2f out: rdn to chse wnr fnl f: no imp* **12/1**

4650 **3** 1¼ **Temper Tantrum**[22] 5575 6-8-13 54........(p) TPQueally 12 62
(JRBest) *hld up: hdwy over 2f out: rdn and n.m.r over 1f out: styd on same pce* **7/1**[3]

0010 **4** 3 **Dubonai (IRE)**[35] 5235 4-8-13 54........ CCatlin 6 56
(AndrewTurnell) *w ldr: led over 6f out: rdn: edgd rt and hdd over 1f out: wknd ins fnl f* **10/1**

5146 **5** 2 **Commitment Lecture**[24] 5518 4-9-0 55........(t) SWKelly 2 53
(MDods) *chsd ldrs: rdn 1/2-way: edgd lft over 2f out: wknd over 1f out* **12/1**

4150 **6** 5 **Danger Bird (IRE)**[76] 4096 4-9-0 55........ KFallon 4 42
(RHollinshead) *chsd ldrs: swtchd rt 4f out: rdn and wknd over 1f out* **8/1**

5100 **7** 6 **Sharp Secret (IRE)**[33] 5304 6-8-12 53........ LisaJones 3 28
(JARToller) *led: hdd over 6f out: wkng whn n.m.r over 2f out* **14/1**

2021 **8** 1½ **Baby Barry**[15] 5733 7-8-13 54........ SSanders 10 26
(MrsGSRees) *hld up: hdwy over 3f out: wknd over 2f out* **4/1**[1]

0500 **9** 2 **Phred**[25] 5493 4-8-13 54........(t) SCarson 1 21
(RFJohnsonHoughton) *chsd ldrs: lost pl over 6f out: sn bhd* **25/1**

3131 **10** ¾ **Fantasy Crusader**[25] 5493 5-9-0 55........(p) DaneO'Neill 11 21
(JAGilbert) *chsd ldrs: rdn over 3f out: wknd over 1f out* **11/2**[2]

0000 **11** 2 **Pharoah's Gold (IRE)**[17] 5691 6-9-0 55........(be[1]) DarrenWilliams 5 17
(DShaw) *hld up: hdwy and hmpd 4f out: rdn and wknd 3f out* **20/1**

0000 **12** 8 **Senior Minister**[30] 5370 6-8-11 55........ RMiles(3) 13 —
(PWHiatt) *chsd ldrs 6f* **66/1**

2240 **13** 9 **Killala (IRE)**[26] 5459 4-8-10 54........ LPKeniry(3) 7 —
(RNBevis) *hld up in tch: hmpd and wknd 4f out* **33/1**

1m 51.02s **13** Ran SP% **123.2**
Speed ratings: CSF £53.79 CT £337.18 TOTE £5.10: £2.20, £4.50, £2.50; EX 75.50.
**Owner** Gary J Roberts **Bred** Sheikh Mohammed Bin Rashid Al Maktoum **Trained** Wixford, Warwicks
■ A one-two for Tony Carroll.

**FOCUS**
A modest contest, but a decent pace. The winning time was faster than both divisions of the two-year-old maiden, but that is only to be expected.

**NOTEBOOK**
**Nautical**, pulled up over hurdles since his Chepstow victory, was given a patient ride but came home in great style and can win again in this mood.
**Ziet D'Alsace(FR)**, rated 6lb lower on sand than on turf, ran her best race so far on this surface under a patient ride and looks up to winning off this sort of mark.
**Temper Tantrum** has won over this trip, but does look a bit better over shorter and, having looked to be the one to beat turning for home, could do nothing about the winner's finishing burst.
**Dubonai(IRE)** did best of those that raced prominently, but just looks held off his current mark.
**Commitment Lecture** did not get home and might be happier on an easier surface on turf.
**Danger Bird(IRE)** has shown all her best sand form on Fibresand and also might have just needed this after nearly three months off. *Official explanation: jockey said filly hung both ways*
**Baby Barry** seemed to find this extended mile beyond the limits of his stamina. *Official explanation: jockey said gelding was never travelling*

## 6025 DINE AT DUNSTALL PARK H'CAP — 1m 4f 50y(P)
**4:20** (4:20) (E3) (0-70,71) 3-Y-0+ — **£3,558** (£1,094; £547; £273) **Stalls** Low

Form — RPR

1321 **1** **Dont Call Me Derek**[2] 6006 3-9-1 **71** 6ex........ RLMoore 7 — 88+
(SCWilliams) *hld up: hdwy over 3f out: led over 2f out: sn rdn clr: edgd lft over 1f out: styd on* **5/4**[1]

2034 **2** *4* **Dovedon Hero**[5] 5951 4-9-7 **70**........(b) SSanders 8 — 81+
(PJMcbride) *hld up: hdwy over 3f out: rdn to chse wnr over 1f out: styd on* **9/2**[2]

0034 **3** *6* **Efrhina (IRE)**[5] 5956 4-9-1 **64**........ FNorton 9 — 65
(MrsStefLiddiard) *hld up: hdwy over 2f out: sn rdn and outpcd* **11/1**

4160 **4** *nk* **Giunchiglio**[21] 5584 5-9-4 **67**........ KFallon 2 — 68
(WMBrisbourne) *hld up in tch: rdn over 2f out: sn outpcd* **10/1**

1044 **5** *¾* **Party Ploy**[33] 5303 6-9-6 **69**........ DarrenWilliams 6 — 68
(KRBurke) *led: rdn and hdd over 2f out: wknd over 1f out* **7/1**[3]

**6** *¾* **Sweetwater (GER)**[16] 4-9-7 **70**........ SDrowne 1 — 68
(MrsStefLiddiard) *prom: rdn over 3f out: wknd over 1f out* **33/1**

1000 **7** *1 ¾* **Zeis (IRE)**[5] 5956 4-8-13 **65**........(t) LFletcher(3) 3 — 60
(AndrewReid) *hld up: hdwy over 2f out: nvr trbld ldrs* **33/1**

1050 **8** *1 ½* **Maritime Blues**[21] 5584 4-8-12 **61**........ ACulhane 11 — 54
(JGGiven) *chsd ldrs: rdn whn hmpd over3f out: sn wknd* **14/1**

-100 **9** *hd* **Arabian Moon (IRE)**[26] 5456 8-9-3 **69**........ DNolan(3) 12 — 62
(RBrotherton) *hld up: hdwy over 4f out: rdn and wknd over 2f out* **25/1**

0000 **10** *shd* **Vin Du Pays**[9] 5205 4-9-7 **70**........ DSweeney 10 — 62
(MBlanshard) *chsd ldrs: rdn over 3f out: wknd 2f out* **33/1**

0-06 **11** *½* **Mister Arjay (USA)**[120] 2775 4-9-4 **70**........ TEaves(3) 5 — 62
(BEllison) *hld up: rdn and wknd 3f out* **40/1**

-105 **12** *6* **Modesty Blaise (SWE)**[224] 900 4-9-3 **66**........ LDettori 4 — 48
(CAHorgan) *s.i.s: hld up: a in rr* **8/1**

2m 43.04s
**WFA** 3 from 4yo+ 7lb — **12 Ran SP% 125.4**
Speed ratings: CSF £6.79 CT £48.01 TOTE £2.10: £1.30, £2.10, £1.50; EX 9.80 Trifecta £116.60 Pool: £867.70. 5.28 winning units..
**Owner** The Chummy Northerners **Bred** Whitsbury Manor Stud **Trained** Newmarket, Suffolk

**FOCUS**
Only an ordinary pace for this handicap, which was not all that competitive with front pair proving different class to the others.

**NOTEBOOK**
**Dont Call Me Derek**, turned out again quickly, has thrived since being stepped up to this trip and, making light of his 6lb penalty, absolutely bolted up. He would be a very short price if turned out again soon.
**Dovedon Hero ◆**, given a patient ride, followed the winner through but, although pulling right away from the others, could make little impression on him. This was still a fair sand debut over an inadequate trip and he should be winning races on this surface under more favourable conditions.
**Efrhina(IRE)**, who ran with credit here at the opening meeting five days earlier, had every chance, but she lacks pace where it matters and remains a maiden after 13 attempts on the Flat. She needs a stronger pace, or perhaps an even longer trip may be the answer.
**Giunchiglio** was left behind from the home bend and is another that would probably have preferred a stronger pace.
**Party Ploy** took quite a hold in front and that may have counted against him late on.

## 6026 COME RACING SATURDAY NIGHT AT DUNSTALL PARK H'CAP — 5f 216y(P)
**4:50** (4:51) (E3) (0-70,70) 3-Y-0+ — **£3,448** (£1,061; £530; £265) **Stalls** Low

Form — RPR

0661 **1** **Blythe Spirit**[12] 5798 5-9-1 **69**........(p) KFallon 12 — 79
(RAFahey) *hld up: hdwy over 2f out: rdn and edgd lft over 1f out: led ins fnl f: r.o wl: eased nr fin* **11/8**[1]

5205 **2** *1 ¼* **Bob's Buzz**[30] 5370 4-9-2 **70**........ SSanders 2 — 76+
(SCWilliams) *s.s: hdwy over 4f out: led over 1f out: hdd and unable qck ins fnl f:* **9/2**[2]

3002 **3** *1 ¼* **Silent Storm**[48] 4926 4-8-13 **67**........ FLynch 7 — 69
(HJCyzer) *w ldrs: rdn over 2f out: edgd over 1f out: styd on same pce ins fnl f* **14/1**

0054 **4** *5* **Willheconquertoo**[31] 5337 4-9-1 **69**........(t) FNorton 5 — 56
(AndrewReid) *w ldr over 4f: wknd ins fnl f* **12/1**

6055 **5** *1 ¾* **Borzoi Maestro**[15] 5734 3-8-9 **67**........(p) RMiles(3) 9 — 49
(JLSpearing) *chsd ldrs: rdn over 2f out: wknd fnl f* **14/1**

0400 **6** *¾* **Whippasnapper**[3] 6001 4-8-12 **66**........ LDettori 10 — 46
(JRBest) *s.i.s: styd on ins fnl f: nvr nrr* **8/1**

5000 **7** *3 ½* **Landing Strip (IRE)**[44] 5016 4-8-9 **66**........ FPFerris(3) 3 — 35
(JMPEustace) *led: rdn and hdd over 1f out: wknd ins fnl f* **25/1**

0000 **8** *¾* **Chairman Bobby**[35] 5242 6-8-10 **64**........ LEnstone 11 — 31
(DWBarker) *chsd ldrs over 3f* **25/1**

0460 **9** *½* **Val De Maal (IRE)**[12] 5798 4-8-11 **65**........ OUrbina 13 — 31
(GCHChung) *hld up: riddejn over 2f out: sn wknd* **12/1**

0600 **10** *hd* **Tally (IRE)**[12] 5798 4-8-10 **64**........ GGibbons 8 — 29
(MJPolglase) *prom over 3f* **14/1**

3-00 **11** *2 ½* **Phrenologist**[135] 2379 4-8-11 **65**........ SDrowne 1 — 22
(AndrewReid) *prom: rdn 1/2-way: wknd 2f out* **50/1**

5000 **12** *5* **Ronnie From Donny (IRE)**[35] 5242 4-8-12 **66**........ DaneO'Neill 4 — 8
(BEllison) *dwlt: outpcd* **6/1**[3]

1m 15.04s
**WFA** 3 from 4yo+ 1lb — **12 Ran SP% 130.7**
Speed ratings: CSF £8.15 CT £72.24 TOTE £2.70: £1.20, £1.80, £4.40; EX 10.40 Place 6 £17.87, Place 5 £13.11.
**Owner** The Matthewman Partnership **Bred** W Haggas And W Jarvis **Trained** Musley Bank, N Yorks

**FOCUS**
A fair pace for this handicap and the market got it spot-on. An ordinary handicap but the form looks solid enough.

**NOTEBOOK**
**Blythe Spirit**, raised 7lb for his Ripon victory and making his sand debut, was off the bridle some way from home, but once he was switched left he found a decent turn of foot against the inside rail and won with a bit in hand.
**Bob's Buzz**, very well backed, travelled well for much of the way and without the favourite would have been a clear winner. He obviously likes this surface, but is unlikely to be such a generous price if seen on it again.
**Silent Storm**, still a maiden, ran up to form and kept staying on, but may need an extra furlong on a fast surface like this.
**Willheconquertoo** could not get the lead on his own and his chance was probably affected as a result.
**Borzoi Maestro** is dropping down the handicap, but is not at the top of his game at present and he does look better on Fibresand.
**Whippasnapper**, weak in the market, was struggling from the start and never managed to land a serious blow. He is capable of better. *Official explanation: jockey said gelding was never travelling*

T/Jkpt: £111.10 to a £1 stake. Pool: £27,564.00. 176.00 winning tickets. T/Plt: £13.50 to a £1 stake. Pool: £47,873.65. 2,588.30 winning tickets. T/Qpdt: £7.90 to a £1 stake. Pool: £2,827.60. 261.80 winning tickets. CR

6030 - 6034a (Foreign Racing) - See Raceform Interactive

# 3566 SAINT-CLOUD (L-H)
Thursday, October 7

**OFFICIAL GOING: Good**

## 6035a PRIX THOMAS BRYON (GROUP 3) — 1m
**1:20** (1:23) 2-Y-O — **£25,704** (£10,282; £7,711; £5,141)

RPR

**1** **Vatori (FR)**[19] 5666 2-8-11........ SPasquier 3 — 106
(PDemercastel, France) *raced in 3rd, ridden to disputed lead 100y out, led post* 2

**2** *nse* **Guillaume Tell (IRE)**[16] 2-8-11........ C-PLemaire 4 — 106
(PDemercastel, France) *raced in 2nd til led approaching final f, joined 100y out, headed post*

**3** *1* **Stop Making Sense**[28] 5432 2-8-11........ CSoumillon 2 — 104
(AFabre, France) *held up in 4th, headway on inside to track leaders but not much room 2f out til switched right 100y out, ran on* 1

**4** *4* **Campo Bueno (FR)**[41] 5102 2-8-11........ MBlancpain 1 — 95
(XNakkachdji, France) *led, ridden over 1 1/2f out, headed approaching final f, weakened*

**5** *5* **Osidy (USA)**[28] 5432 2-8-11........ GBenoist 5 — 84
(XNakkachdji, France) *missed break, last throughout, effort & no response 1 1/2f out, eased inside final f* 3

1m 43.2s — **5** Ran SP% **130.7**
Speed ratings: .
**Owner** Ecurie Bader **Bred** A-J Quesny, P Joubert & L Favre **Trained** France

**NOTEBOOK**
**Vatori(FR)**, whose full-brother Hightori won this race in 1999, got up on the line to deny his stablemate. He is now likely to go for the Criterium de Saint-Cloud and will appreciate the longer trip.
**Guillaume Tell(IRE)**, given every possible chance, was second for much of the race before taking the advantage a furlong out. He ran on bravely and failed by inches to hold his stablemate.
**Stop Making Sense** has to be considered unlucky. He was hemmed in on the rail before finding space running into the final furlong. Once extracted, he ran on but the race was over by the time he engaged top gear. He definitely looks Group material.
**Campo Bueno(FR)** acted as pacemaker and did his job well until a furlong and a half out.

# 5869 SALISBURY (R-H)
Friday, October 8

**6036 Meeting Abandoned** - Waterlogged

Meeting switched from Ascot.

# 5314 YORK (L-H)
Friday, October 8

**OFFICIAL GOING: Good**

The riders reported the ground was 'on the easy side of good and a bit loose on top'.

Wind: Moderate 1/2 against. Weather: Fine but overcast at times.

## 6042 ACORN WEB OFFSET STKS (NURSERY) — 6f
**2:05** (2:07) (C2) 2-Y-O — **£9,698** (£2,984; £1,492; £746) **Stalls** Centre

Form — RPR

041 **1** **Ingleton**[22] 5578 2-8-3 **77**........ GGibbons 9 — 92+
(BAMcmahon) *lw: cl up: led 1/2-way: rdn clr over 1f out: styd on wl* **9/1**

41 **2** *3* **Daldini**[18] 5689 2-8-6 **80**........ TPQueally 10 — 86
(JAOsborne) *sn pushed along towards rr: hdwy 1/2-way: rdn along 2f out: kpt on fnl f* **11/1**

5050 **3** *1* **Word Perfect**[6] 5947 2-8-11 **85**........ DaleGibson 11 — 88
(MWEasterby) *chsd ldrs: rdn over 2f out: sn drvn and one pce appr last* **11/2**[2]

1020 **4** *1 ½* **Rowan Lodge (IRE)**[17] 5721 2-8-10 **84**........ PRobinson 14 — 83
(MHTompkins) *midfield: pushed along 2f out: sn rdn and kpt on ins last: nrst fin* **16/1**

5206 **5** *hd* **Rainbow Iris**[19] 5670 2-7-9 **72** oh6........ FPFerris(3) 8 — 70
(BSmart) *led: hdd 1/2-way and sn pushed along: rdn 2f out and grad wknd* **33/1**

1064 **6** *1 ½* **Bold Marc (IRE)**[17] 5711 2-8-12 **86**........ DarrenWilliams 4 — 79
(KRBurke) *midfield: effrt over 2f out: sn rdn and no imp* **33/1**

5650 **7** *shd* **Bolton Hall (IRE)**[13] 5797 2-8-4 **78**........ PHanagan 5 — 71
(RAFahey) *broke wl: sn hld up in rr: smooth hdwy over 2f out: kpt on: nvr nr ldrs* **12/1**

1316 **8** *1 ¼* **Oceanico Dot Com (IRE)**[13] 5797 2-8-0 **74**........ FNorton 6 — 63
(ABerry) *chsd ldrs: rdn along 2f out: sn wknd* **14/1**

0233 **9** *2 ½* **Dahteer (IRE)**[14] 5767 2-9-4 **92**........ ACulhane 13 — 74
(MRChannon) *swtg: midfield: rdn along over 2f out: no hdwy* **15/2**

2125 **10** *½* **Graze On**[25] 5515 2-8-9 **83**........ RWinston 2 — 63
(JJQuinn) *a rr* **6/1**[3]

1000 **11** *½* **John Forbes**[20] 5630 2-8-5 **82**........(b[1]) TEaves(3) 7 — 61
(BEllison) *swtg: s.i.s: a rr* **66/1**

5160 **12** *nk* **Piper Lily**[91] 3704 2-8-4 **78**........ WSupple 12 — 56
(MBlanshard) *midfield: rdn along 1/2-way: sn btn* **66/1**

1000 **13** *½* **Prospect Court**[17] 5721 2-8-2 **76**........(b[1]) CCatlin 15 — 52
(JDBethell) *chsd ldrs on outer: rdn along over 2f out: sn wknd* **33/1**

241 **14** *6* **Wise Owl**[15] 5752 2-9-0 **88**........ KDarley 3 — 46
(MJohnston) *chsd ldrs: pushed along 1/2-way: sn rdn and wknd wl over 1f out* **9/2**[1]

0520 **15** *½* **Al Qudra (IRE)**[12] 5810 2-9-7 **95**........(b[1]) JFortune 1 — 52
(BJMeehan) *prom: rdn along over 2f out: sn wknd* **20/1**

1m 13.65s (1.08) **Going Correction** +0.30s/f (Good) — **15** Ran SP% **114.8**
Speed ratings: **104,100,98,96,96 94,94,92,89,88 87,87,86,78,78**CSF £92.23 CT £594.63 TOTE £10.70: £3.60, £3.70, £2.40; EX 90.10.
**Owner** J C Fretwell **Bred** Thomas Trafford **Trained** Hopwas, Staffs

**FOCUS**
A competitive nursery run in a decent time and a clear-cut winner. The form looks sure to stand up well and the winner will be very interesting under a penalty.

**NOTEBOOK**
**Ingleton ◆**, quite a big type, looked outstandingly well. He travelled supremely well and took this with a fair bit to spare. He looks a step or two ahead of the Handicapper.
**Daldini**, having just his third start and facing a tough task, showed a very scratchy action going down. Struggling to go the pace, he was putting in all his best work in the closing stages and will be well suited by a step up to seven and the easier the ground the better for him.
**Word Perfect**, very much on her toes in the paddock, confirmed that she is in very good form.
**Rowan Lodge(IRE)**, suited by the ease in the ground, stayed on from way off the pace and did well to get so close.
**Rainbow Iris**, 6lb out of the handicap, showed plenty of toe but persisted in hanging left.
**Bolton Hall(IRE)**, who started life in nurseries from a 9lb higher mark, seemed to be ridden with another day, possibly next year, in mind.
**Dahteer(IRE)** became very warm beforehand and did not impress at all to post.
**Wise Owl**, a lazy walker, showed a fluent action going down but was soon hard at work and in the end he dropped right away. This was too bad to be true. *Official explanation: trainer was unable to offer any explanation for poor form shown*

## 6043 GARBUTT & ELLIOTT H'CAP — 1m 2f 88y
**2:40** (2:41) (C2) (0-85,84) 3-Y-O+ — **£11,047** (£3,399; £1,699; £849) **Stalls** Low

Form — RPR
4211 **1** **Go Tech**[6] 5950 4-9-7 **84** 6ex .......... DAllan 13 — 96
(TDEasterby) *hld up in mid-div: effrt over 2f out: led over 1f out: r.o wl* **4/1**[1]
000- **2** *1 ½* **Beat The Heat (IRE)**[160] 5463 6-8-7 **77** .......... LeanneKershaw(7) 12 — 86
(JeddO'Keeffe) *swtg: prom: hdwy to ld 3f out: hdd over 1f out: kpt on wl* **66/1**
4010 **3** *¾* **Stretton (IRE)**[23] 5572 6-9-3 **80** .......... PRobinson 7 — 89+
(JDBethell) *hld up towards rr: hdwy and nt clr run over 2f out: swtchd outside and hdwy over 1f out: r.o* **8/1**[3]
6000 **4** *¾* **Ski Jump (USA)**[21] 5619 4-9-2 **79** .......... (v) PHanagan 9 — 85
(RAFahey) *chsd ldrs: styd on fnl f* **10/1**
6000 **5** *½* **Cripsey Brook**[34] 5303 6-9-2 **79** .......... KimTinkler 20 — 84
(DonEnricoIncisa) *in rr: hdwy over 2f out: swtchd lft: styd on wl ins last* **20/1**
0550 **6** *shd* **Trueno (IRE)**[35] 5273 5-9-1 **81** .......... NMackay(3) 11 — 86
(LMCumani) *lw: mid-div: smooth hdwy over 2f out: shkn up over 1f out: kpt on same pce* **11/1**
2600 **7** *nk* **Petrula**[21] 5607 5-9-0 **77** .......... (b) NCallan 5 — 82
(KARyan) *prom: styd on same pce fnl 2f* **16/1**
2045 **8** *1 ¼* **Ryan's Future (IRE)**[9] 5866 4-8-12 **75** .......... GCarter 19 — 77
(JAkehurst) *s.s: bhd: hdwy on wd outside 2f out: styd on strly ins last* **16/1**
0056 **9** *hd* **Intricate Web (IRE)**[14] 5768 8-8-12 **75** .......... WSupple 17 — 77
(EJAlston) *s.s: hdwy 4f out: sn drvn along: one pce fnl 2f* **16/1**
**10** *3 ½* **Darghan (IRE)**[102] 4-9-4 **81** .......... (t) SDrowne 1 — 77
(PDEvans) *in tch: effrt over 3f out: sn chsng ldrs: wknd fnl f* **25/1**
116- **11** *2* **Altay**[222] 389 7-8-11 **77** .......... THamilton(3) 8 — 69
(RAFahey) *chsd ldrs: wknd appr fnl f* **20/1**
661- **12** *1 ½* **Talldark'N'Andsome**[310] 5910 5-8-13 **76** .......... (b) TEDurcan 18 — 65
(NPLittmoden) *bhd: sme hdwy on ins 4f out: nvr a factor* **50/1**
30/0 **13** *1 ¾* **Lewis Island (IRE)**[21] 5607 5-8-12 **75** .......... RLMoore 10 — 61
(BEllison) *s.s: sme hdwy 4f out: nvr a factor* **40/1**
1000 **14** *1* **Love In Seattle (IRE)**[121] 2781 4-8-12 **75** .......... KDarley 2 — 60
(MJohnston) *sn chsng ldrs: led over 3f out: sn hdd: lost pl over 1f out* **25/1**
0400 **15** *5* **Fourth Dimension (IRE)**[33] 5318 5-9-3 **80** .......... ANicholls 4 — 56
(DNicholls) *hld up: a bhd* **25/1**
-050 **16** *3* **Mezuzah**[107] 3212 4-9-0 **77** .......... DaleGibson 14 — 47
(MWEasterby) *chsd ldrs: lost pl over 2f out* **50/1**
1-50 **17** *¾* **Baltic Blazer (IRE)**[23] 5572 4-8-12 **75** .......... (v[1]) JFortune 16 — 44
(PWHarris) *t.k.h: led tl over 3f out: lost pl 2f out* **25/1**
5002 **18** *1 ¼* **Jabaar (USA)**[20] 5650 6-9-7 **84** .......... KFallon 15 — 51
(MWEasterby) *hld up in rr: swtchd to wd outside over 2f out: nvr a factor* **9/2**[2]
2066 **19** *¾* **Czarina Waltz**[41] 5136 5-9-4 **81** .......... RMullen 3 — 46
(CFWall) *mid-div: effrt on ins 4f out: lost pl over 2f out* **20/1**
3100 **20** *1 ½* **Rasid (USA)**[21] 5615 6-9-0 **77** .......... DHolland 6 — 39
(CADwyer) *hld up and a bhd* **33/1**

2m 13.46s (4.02) **Going Correction** +0.45s/f (Yiel) — **20** Ran SP% **124.8**
Speed ratings: **101,99,99,98,98 98,97,96,96,93 92,91,89,88,84 82,81,80,80,79**CSF £290.61 CT £2075.94 TOTE £5.20: £1.70, £20.20, £2.00, £2.70; EX 723.40.
**Owner** Ryedale Partners No 4 **Bred** A G Nicholson **Trained** Great Habton, N Yorks

**FOCUS**
Just a steady gallop until once in line for home, and consequently the winning time was modest for the grade. The form is solid.

**NOTEBOOK**
**Go Tech** looked supremely well but became warm behind the stalls. He came there travelling strongly and made this look a very straight forward task. He is clearly right at the top of his form and will continue to be competitive even from his revised mark.
**Beat The Heat(IRE)**, better known as a handicap hurdler these days, was last seen in action on May Day. Very warm beforehand, he ran out of his skin though in the end firmly put in his place by the winner.
**Stretton(IRE)**, who took this a year ago from a 2lb lower mark, could have done with a stronger early pace. He stayed on well when switched to the outside and in this mood should continue to give a good account of himself.
**Ski Jump(USA)** ran a lot better than of late and is at last being shown some leniency.
**Cripsey Brook**, worst drawn, has slipped to a lenient mark. With just one behind him two out he finished to some purpose and deserves another success before the curtain comes down.
**Trueno(IRE)** looked at his best and travelled very strongly but he does not always find as much as would seem likely when asked a question.
**Petrula** put three below-par efforts behind him and may now be ready for a return to hurdling.
**Ryan's Future(IRE)** gave away ground and then made his effort on the wide outside. He did remarkably well to finish so close.
**Jabaar(USA)** made a sluggish break and seemed to take little interest from start to finish. He has a mind of his own. *Official explanation: jockey said gelding was slow away and never travelling*

## 6044 BETFAIR.COM H'CAP — 7f 205y
**3:15** (3:16) (C1) (0-100,100) 3-Y-O+ — **£13,583** (£5,152; £2,576; £1,171) **Stalls** Low

Form — RPR
5000 **1** **Nashaab (USA)**[6] 5941 7-8-7 **90** .......... (v) KFallon 4 — 100
(PDEvans) *towards rr: pushed along over 3f out: gd hdwy 2f out: rdn and styd on ins last to ld nr fin* **14/1**
1204 **2** *¾* **Adaikali (IRE)**[15] 5755 3-8-1 **87** .......... FNorton 1 — 95
(SirMichaelStoute) *trckd ldng pair: smooth hdwy over 2f out: led wl over 1f out: rdn ins last: hdd and no ex nr fin* **10/1**[3]
4120 **3** *½* **Literatim**[30] 5397 4-8-0 **86** .......... NMackay(3) 15 — 93
(LMCumani) *midfield: gd hdwy over 2f out: rdn and ev ch over 1f out: drvn and hung rt ins last: no ex towards fin* **7/1**[1]
5023 **4** *1* **Penrith (FR)**[27] 5474 3-8-0 **86** .......... RFfrench 14 — 91
(MJohnston) *dwlt and hmpd s: bhd tl hdwy on outer 2f out: rdn over 1f out: styd on ins last: nrst fin* **20/1**
4046 **5** *nk* **Selective**[15] 5755 5-8-5 **88** .......... EAhern 8 — 92
(EFVaughan) *in tch: hdwy to chse ldrs over 2f out: ev ch over 1f out: sn rdn: drvn whn hmpd ins last: nt rcvr* **14/1**
2230 **6** *3* **Vicious Warrior**[6] 5941 5-7-12 **86** .......... BSwarbrick(5) 12 — 83
(RMWhitaker) *in tch: wd st: hdwy over 2f out: sn rdn to chse ldrs over 1f out: drvn and one pce ent last* **11/1**
3011 **7** *¾* **Calcutta**[27] 5462 8-9-3 **100** .......... MHills 16 — 96
(BWHills) *hmpd s: towards rr: hdwy over 2f out: sn rdn and no imp appr last* **10/1**[3]
1240 **8** *shd* **Pango**[12] 5813 5-8-3 **86** .......... RLMoore 7 — 81
(HMorrison) *bhd: rdn along 4f out: hdwy over 2f out: swtchd lft and kpt on ins last: nt rch ldrs* **14/1**
4300 **9** *2 ½* **Mystic Man (FR)**[21] 5603 6-8-5 **88** .......... PFessey 17 — 78
(KARyan) *hmpd s: sn midfield: hdwy over 2f out: rdn to chse ldrs over 1f out: wknd ent last* **16/1**
4043 **10** *2 ½* **Flighty Fellow (IRE)**[12] 5813 4-8-11 **94** .......... (b) GCarter 13 — 78
(TDEasterby) *hmpd s and bhd tl sme late hdwy* **10/1**[3]
3111 **11** *shd* **Dunaskin (IRE)**[51] 4856 4-9-1 **98** .......... KDarley 18 — 82
(DEddy) *hmpd s: sn cl up: led after 1f tl rdn along and hdd 3f out: sn wknd* **8/1**[2]
3005 **12** *1 ¾* **Dark Charm (FR)**[25] 5514 5-8-3 **86** .......... PHanagan 19 — 66
(RAFahey) *bhd tl sme late hdwy* **33/1**
0053 **13** *shd* **Vicious Knight**[42] 5099 6-8-5 **88** .......... ANicholls 3 — 67
(DNicholls) *led 1f: cl up tl led 3f out: rdn 2f out and sn wknd* **14/1**
1201 **14** *nk* **Welcome Stranger**[12] 5813 4-8-12 **98** 6ex .......... LFletcher(3) 11 — 77
(JMPEustace) *hmpd s: a rr* **7/1**[1]
2-06 **15** *1 ¼* **Miss Ivanhoe (IRE)**[153] 1964 4-9-3 **100** .......... DHolland 9 — 76
(GWragg) *chsd ldrs: rdn along 3f out: sn wknd* **25/1**
6660 **16** *1 ½* **Kelucia (IRE)**[27] 5474 3-8-4 **90** .......... CCatlin 2 — 62
(JSGoldie) *a rr* **40/1**
2300 **17** *18* **Crafty Fancy (IRE)**[114] 2971 3-7-12 **87** .......... JFMcDonald(3) 5 — 18
(DJSFrenchDavis) *midfield: effrt and hdwy 3f out: rdn and wknd 2f out* **66/1**
/0-0 **18** *nk* **Northern Desert (IRE)**[14] 5769 5-8-7 **90** .......... DarrenWilliams 6 — 20
(PWHiatt) *chsd ldrs: effrt 3f out: rdn and wknd fnl 2f* **100/1**
3122 **U** **Mrs Moh (IRE)**[19] 5673 3-8-0 **86** .......... DaleGibson 10 — —
(TDEasterby) *stmbld and uns rdr s* **20/1**

1m 39.59s (1.85) **Going Correction** +0.45s/f (Yiel)
**WFA** 3 from 4yo+ 3lb — **19** Ran SP% **125.5**
Speed ratings: **108,107,106,105,105 102,101,101,99,96 96,94,94,94,93 91,73,73,—**CSF £139.40 CT £1112.60 TOTE £14.60: £3.60, £2.60, £2.50, £5.10; EX 98.40 Trifecta £1329.20 Part won. Pool £1,872.12 - 0.50 winning units..
**Owner** M W Lawrence **Bred** Shadwell Farm Inc **Trained** Pandy, Gwent
■ Stewards Enquiry : F Norton one-day ban: careless riding (Oct 19)

**FOCUS**
A strong pace and solid form, although the loose horse caused havoc to those drawn on her outside after the start and there was argy bargy between the second, third and Selective inside the last.

**NOTEBOOK**
**Nashaab(USA)**, a real character, was suited by the strong pace and had the right man to lift him to the front near the line.
**Adaikali(IRE)**, dropping back in trip, travelled strongly but came off a straight line inside the last and was just edged out near the line.
**Literatim**, another taking a drop back in trip, came there to have every chance but with the runner-up rather getting in his way, he could find no extra near the line.
**Penrith(FR)**, one of those taken wide early on by the loose horse, finished with quite a flourish and certainly has the ability to find another race this backend from this mark. *Official explanation: jockey said colt was hampered by a loose horse at the start*
**Selective** has slipped to a handy mark and ran his best race for some time, keeping on strongly until running out of racing room inside the last.
**Vicious Warrior** keeps giving a good account of himself but has not tasted success for over two years.
**Calcutta** was on the back foot after being knocked over soon after the start.
**Dunaskin(IRE)** was the worst sufferer in the melee caused by the loose horse and from his wide draw had to work too hard early on to take the lead. It left him with nothing in reserve fully three furlongs out.
**Vicious Knight** *Official explanation: jockey said gelding ran too keen early on*
**Welcome Stranger**, another knocked sideways soon after the start, never recovered.

## 6045 BETFAIR.COM EBF MAIDEN STKS — 6f
**3:50** (3:50) (D3) 2-Y-O — **£5,489** (£1,689; £844; £422) **Stalls** Centre

Form — RPR
**1** **Mafaheem** 2-9-0 .......... RHills 3 — 84
(MJohnston) *wl grwn: trckd ldrs: ld over 1f out: hld on wl* **10/1**
33 **2** *1* **Pivotal's Princess (IRE)**[13] 5800 2-8-9 .......... DHolland 8 — 76
(BAMcmahon) *led tl over 1f out: no ex ins last* **5/2**[1]
06 **3** *5* **Knot In Wood (IRE)**[15] 5752 2-8-11 .......... THamilton(3) 10 — 66
(RAFahey) *chsd ldrs: outpcd appr fnl f* **50/1**
**4** *½* **Real Cool Cat (USA)** 2-8-9 .......... KDarley 4 — 60
(MJohnston) *lenghy: unf: scope: dwlt: soon chsng ldrs: outpcd fnl 2f* **11/4**[2]
**5** *1* **Lake Carezza (USA)** 2-9-0 .......... EAhern 5 — 62
(JNoseda) *gd sort: hld up in tch: shkn up over 1f out: r.o steadily ins last: improve* **5/1**[3]
0 **6** *1 ¾* **Golden Square**[14] 5772 2-9-0 .......... JFortune 9 — 56
(BJMeehan) *trckd ldrs: effrt over 2f out: kpt on same pce* **12/1**
0 **7** *1* **Ruman (IRE)**[14] 5772 2-9-0 .......... NCallan 1 — 53
(MJAttwater) *rangy: unf: in tch: effrt over 2f out: wknd over 1f out* **66/1**
**8** *shd* **Xebec (IRE)** 2-8-9 .......... NDeSouza(5) 12 — 53
(PFICole) *wl grwn: swvd rt s: sn chsng ldrs: wknd over 1f out* **10/1**
**9** *1 ¼* **Telegram Sam (IRE)** 2-9-0 .......... PHanagan 11 — 49
(RAFahey) *cmpt: s.i.s: sn outpcd and bhd* **16/1**
**10** *½* **Lobengula (IRE)** 2-9-0 .......... CCatlin 7 — 48
(HAlexander) *leggy: unf: s.s: a bhd* **100/1**
000 **11** *6* **Love From Russia**[20] 5633 2-9-0 .......... FLynch 2 — 30
(ABerry) *w ldrs: wknd qckly over 1f out* **100/1**
**12** *21* **Russiannightingale** 2-8-7 .......... JDO'Reilly(7) 13 — —
(JO'Reilly) *cmpt: swvd rt s: sn wl bhd* **66/1**

13 28 **Moonlight Appeal (IRE)** 2-8-6 ........................................ TEaves(3) 6 —
(JSWainwright) *leggy: unf: s.i.s: sn wl bhd* **66/1**

1m 14.12s (1.55) **Going Correction** +0.30s/f (Good) **13** Ran SP% **112.1**
Speed ratings: **101,99,93,92,91 88,87,87,85,84 76,48,11**CSF £32.79 TOTE £8.60: £2.40, £1.40, £10.50; EX 30.90.
**Owner** Hamdan Al Maktoum **Bred** J H And J M Wall **Trained** Middleham Moor, N Yorks

**FOCUS**
An ordinary maiden by York standards with a fair amount of dead wood, but the winner looks promising and the fourth and fifth will improve on their debut efforts. Not an easy race to rate.

**NOTEBOOK**
**Mafaheem**, a February foal, is bred for speed. Standing over plenty of ground and nosiy in the paddock, he will improve a good deal for the outing and leave this bare form behind.
**Pivotal's Princess(IRE)**, bidding to make it third time lucky, took them along and never flinched under a very hard ride. She will remember this but deserves to find a race.
**Knot In Wood(IRE)**, who stands over a fair bit of ground, showed a moderate action and ran a lot better than on his first two starts, clearly appreciating the much easier ground.
**Real Cool Cat(USA)**, a February foal, looked far from the finished article and did not impress at all going to post. The outing will have taught her plenty but she will not be at her best until next year.
**Lake Carezza(USA)** ◆, an April foal, is a deep-bodied, useful-looking colt. He travelled strongly and was given no more than an educational outing on his debut. This will have done him a power of good.
**Golden Square**, a tall individual, showed a fair bit more than on his debut in heavy ground two weeks earlier.

## 6046 PARSONAGE COUNTRY HOUSE HOTEL H'CAP 5f
**4:25** (4:25) (E3) (0-70,74) 3-Y-0+ **£6,037** (£1,857; £928; £464) **Stalls** Centre

Form RPR
1312 **1** **Playful Dane (IRE)**[6] 5949 7-9-6 **74** 6ex........................ DTudhope(5) 18 89+
(WSCunningham) *cl up: led after 1f: rdn clr over 1f out: jst hld on* **5/1**[2]
0053 **2** *nk* **Prince Of Gold**[13] 5798 4-9-0 **63**..........................................(p) KFallon 14 73+
(RHollinshead) *dwlt: gd hdwy 2f out: rdn over 1f out: styd on strly ins last* **8/1**[2]
3404 **3** *nk* **Byo (IRE)**[16] 5734 6-9-5 **68**........................................................ FNorton 8 77
(MQuinn) *cl up: rdn and ev ch 2f out: edgd rt and kpt on ins last* **16/1**
0240 **4** *1* **Kings College Boy**[21] 5605 4-9-5 **68**..............................(v) DaleGibson 4 73
(RAFahey) *towards rr and rdn along 1/2-way: styd on wl u.p appr last: nrst fin* **12/1**
011 **5** *nk* **Oeuf A La Neige**[4] 6001 4-9-11 **74** 6ex................................. OUrbina 16 78+
(GCHChung) *bhd and pushed along 1/2-way: hdwy: nt clr run and swtchd lft 2f out: styd on wl fnl f: nrst fin* **8/1**[2]
4430 **6** *hd* **Winthorpe (IRE)**[13] 5798 4-9-4 **67**......................................(p) RWinston 6 71
(JJQuinn) *in tch: effrt 2f out: sn rdn and kpt on appr last* **11/1**[3]
1000 **7** *2 ½* **Parkside Pursuit**[18] 5704 6-9-7 **70**.................................... RLMoore 7 65
(JMBradley) *behind and pushed along 1/2-way: rdn and hdwy over 1f out: kpt on ins last: nrst fin* **16/1**
5200 **8** *hd* **Prince Cyrano**[18] 5704 5-9-7 **70**........................................ RMullen 9 64
(WJMusson) *dwlt and bhd tl styd on fnl 2f: nvr a factor* **25/1**
4100 **9** *nk* **Roman Mistress (IRE)**[22] 5579 4-9-3 **66**.............................(b) DAllan 12 59
(TDEasterby) *led 1f: cl up tl rdn 2f out and grad wknd* **33/1**
00 **10** *1* **Calypso Dancer (FR)**[15] 5754 4-8-13 **62**.......................(v1) KDarley 10 51
(TDBarron) *trckd ldrs: effrt 2f out: sn rdn and edgd rt: wknd ent last* **33/1**
0013 **11** *½* **Blue Maeve**[9] 5862 4-8-13 **62**............................................... SRighton 2 49
(JHetherton) *s.i.s: bhd tl sme late hdwy* **14/1**
02U0 **12** *½* **Harrison's Flyer (IRE)**[23] 5562 3-9-1 **64**.........................(p) PHanagan 1 50
(RAFahey) *in tch on outer: rdn along 2f out: wknd appr last* **25/1**
0240 **13** *nk* **Cerulean Rose**[4] 6001 5-9-6 **69**........................................... JFortune 15 54
(AWCarroll) *dwlt and bhd: hdwy 2f out: rdn and nt clr run over 1f out: nvr a factor* **16/1**
2450 **14** *shd* **Sharp Hat**[13] 5798 10-8-13 **62**............................................. ACulhane 19 46
(DWChapman) *chsd ldrs to 1/2-way: sn btn* **33/1**
0520 **15** *1* **Aahgowangowan (IRE)**[22] 5579 5-8-9 **63**...........................(t) PMakin(5) 3 44
(MDods) *chsd ldrs: rdn along over 2f out: sn wknd* **18/1**
0530 **16** *nk* **College Queen**[21] 5618 6-8-12 **61**......................................... ANicholls 17 40
(SGollings) *in tch: rdn along over 2f out: sn btn* **28/1**
6000 **17** *3 ½* **Tally (IRE)**[1] 6026 4-8-11 **63** ow2.......................................... LFletcher(3) 20 30
(MJPolglase) *in tch: rdn along 1/2-way: sn wknd* **40/1**
0005 **18** *1* **Izmail (IRE)**[27] 5458 5-9-4 **67**.............................................(v) SDrowne 13 30
(PDEvans) *chsd ldrs: rdn and hung rt 2f out: sn wknd* **25/1**
0210 **19** *9* **Demolition Molly**[156] 1883 3-9-7 **70**....................................(tp) PMcCabe 5 1
(RFMarvin) *prom: rdn along 1/2-way: sn wknd* **50/1**

60.16 secs (0.88) **Going Correction** +0.30s/f (Good) **19** Ran SP% **124.6**
Speed ratings: **104,103,103,101,100 100,96,96,95,94 93,92,92,92,90 89,84,82,68**CSF £17.99 CT £286.96 TOTE £3.70: £1.40, £1.90, £3.90, £2.80; EX 26.60.
**Owner** Ann And David Bell **Bred** Omicida Syndicate **Trained** Hutton Rudby, N Yorks

**FOCUS**
A competitive handicap run in a fast time for the grade, so solid form. Playful Dane is in the form of his life and should continue to perform well.

**NOTEBOOK**
**Playful Dane(IRE)** has been in cracking form in recent weeks and the 6lb higher mark he was racing off here proved no obstacle to him recording his fourth win of the campaign. He raced clear inside the final furlong before getting a little tired in the closing stages and was value for more than the official winning margin.
**Prince Of Gold** has come right back to form the last twice since being dropped in trip and if he continues to progress, will be back in the winner's enclosure before long.
**Byo(IRE)** ran his race and was going on at the line. He is a reliable sort who should continue to pay his way.
**Kings College Boy** showed his last running to be all wrong with a staying-on fourth and may be worth another try at six furlongs.
**Oeuf A La Neige** was probably unlucky not to get fourth, as he did not get the clearest run through and, like Kings College Boy, was finishing fast. This was a good effort under the penalty.
**Winthorpe(IRE)**, 6lb lower than when last winning, is best at this trip and was edging ever nearer at the line.
**Parkside Pursuit** ◆ came right back to form and is on a very winnable mark, so may be worth watching out for in the coming weeks.
**Prince Cyrano** was going on at the end but is a tricky customer.
**Cerulean Rose** never really had a chance to get involved.
**Sharp Hat** *Official explanation: jockey said gelding hung left*

## 6047 GREEN HOWARDS CUP (APPRENTICE H'CAP) 1m 3f 198y
**5:00** (5:02) (E3) (0-70,70) 3-Y-0+ **£4,781** (£1,471; £735; £367) **Stalls** Low

Form RPR
0314 **1** **Scott**[7] 5914 3-8-4 **60**.......................................................... DFox 3 69
(JJay) *trckd ldrs: led over 2f out: edgd rt fnl f: hld on wl* **12/1**
5145 **2** *1* **Night Sight (USA)**[6] 5950 7-9-4 **70**................................ DTudhope(3) 16 77
(MrsSLamyman) *trckd ldrs: chal over 1f out: no ex ins last* **11/1**[3]
066 **3** *¾* **Stallone**[6] 5950 7-9-0 **66**.............................................. PPMathers(3) 4 72
(NWilson) *swvd bdly rt s: bhd: hdwy and nt much room over 2f out: styd on wl fnl f* **12/1**
1242 **4** *hd* **Dance To My Tune**[22] 5584 3-8-8 **67**.................................. DFentiman(3) 13 73
(MWEasterby) *hld up in mid-div: hdwy 3f out: ev ch over 1f out: no ex ins last* **13/2**[1]
5520 **5** *2* **Calatagan (IRE)**[22] 5584 5-9-6 **69**............................................ MSavage 14 71
(JMJefferson) *trckd ldrs: led over 3f out tl over 2f out: one pce appr fnl f* **16/1**
4130 **6** *2 ½* **Smart John**[14] 5764 4-9-7 **70**.................................................. BSwarbrick 5 68
(WMBrisbourne) *hld up in mid-div: effrt 3f out: kpt on same pce* **7/1**[2]
5000 **7** *1* **Archie Babe (IRE)**[14] 5773 8-8-13 **62**.......................................... PMakin 8 59
(JJQuinn) *trckd ldrs: one pce fnl 2f* **16/1**
4506 **8** *hd* **Charmatic (IRE)**[17] 5715 3-8-4 **63**...................................... RoryMoore(3) 11 60
(JAGlover) *t.k.h in rr: hdwy over 3f out: styd on fnl f* **16/1**
1023 **9** *½* **Pont Neuf (IRE)**[56] 4698 4-9-1 **67**........................(t) NataliaGemelova(3) 15 63
(PDEvans) *mid-div: hdwy over 4f out: sn chsng ldrs: wknd over 1f out* **13/2**[1]
1560 **10** *½* **Middlethorpe**[37] 5229 7-9-2 **65**..............................................(b) NDeSouza 7 60
(MWEasterby) *trckd ldrs: rdn and wandered over 2f out: nvr rchd ldrs* **7/1**[2]
-000 **11** *shd* **Dramatic Quest**[37] 5229 7-8-13 **65**..................................(p) AMullen(3) 10 60
(IanWilliams) *rr-div: hdwy on ins to chse ldrs 4f out: lost pl 2f out* **16/1**
4641 **12** *¾* **Broughton Knows**[7] 5914 7-8-4 **58** 6ex...................................(b) AKirby(5) 1 52
(MissGayKelleway) *s.i.s: bhd: hdwy on ins 3f out: nvr on terms* **7/1**[2]
0000 **13** *1 ¾* **Dark Day Blues (IRE)**[9] 5859 3-7-11 **56**.................................... MHalford(3) 6 47
(MDHammond) *mid-div: hdwy over 4f out: sn chsng ldrs: wknd fnl 2f* **50/1**
2033 **14** *½* **Jidiya (IRE)**[22] 5591 5-9-3 **66**................................................ NChalmers 2 56
(SGollings) *trckd ldrs: lost pl 3f out* **33/1**
1600 **15** *1 ¾* **Melodian**[32] 5344 9-8-12 **64**...............................................(b) MLawson(3) 9 51
(MBrittain) *led: qcknd over 4f out: hdd over 3f out: lost pl over 2f out* **25/1**
4500 **16** *14* **Disabuse**[46] 5002 4-8-2 **56** oh7.........................................(p) StaceyRenwick(5) 12 21
(DShaw) *bhd: t.o 2f out* **66/1**

2m 36.19s (7.33) **Going Correction** +0.45s/f (Yiel)
**WFA** 3 from 4yo+ 7lb **16** Ran SP% **121.7**
Speed ratings: **93,92,91,91,90 88,88,87,87,87 87,86,85,85,84 74**CSF £134.22 CT £1636.29 TOTE £17.20: £3.20, £2.70, £2.90, £1.70; EX 254.50 Place 6 £180.89, Place 5 £48.34.
**Owner** Keith Wills **Bred** Keith Wills **Trained** Newmarket, Suffolk
■ Stewards Enquiry : A Mullen one-day ban: careless riding (Oct 20)
D Fox one-day ban: careless riding (Oct 19)

**FOCUS**
A modest handicap run in a moderate time, but the form looks solid. Scott is lightly-raced and progressive and can probably win again.

**NOTEBOOK**
**Scott**, behind Broughton Knows at Lingfield most recently, was worse off at the weights here but had little trouble reversing the form and ran out a game winner. He is relatively lightly raced and open to further improvement, particularly back on sand.
**Night Sight(USA)** is a tough sort who takes his racing well and he ran another sound race. He is still on a winnable mark and it would come as no surprise to see him win again.
**Stallone** is without a win in over a year but was a little unlucky not to finish closer. He would not have won, but this did at least offer encouragement for the future.
**Dance To My Tune** has been in good heart this season and, despite being 7lb higher than when last winning, was still able to run a big race.
**Calatagan(IRE)** ran his race without proving good enough. He needs a drop in the weights.
**Smart John** made only a little late headway and ran only slightly better than last time.
**Pont Neuf(IRE)** looks high enough in the weights at the minute and ran disappointingly.
**Broughton Knows** did not run his race and never got involved, having been held up.
T/Jkpt: Not won. T/Plt: £112.60 to a £1 stake. Pool: £95,241.70. 617.30 winning tickets. T/Qpdt: £23.70 to a £1 stake. Pool: £8,623.45. 268.90 winning tickets. JR

# 5869 SALISBURY (R-H)
Saturday, October 9
**6048 Meeting Abandoned** - waterlogged
Meeting switched from Ascot.

# 5653 WARWICK (L-H)
Saturday, October 9
**OFFICIAL GOING: Good to soft (good in places)**
Wind: Slight across Weather: Fine

## 6055 HANNAH'S LATE BIRTHDAY BASH MAIDEN CLAIMING STKS 1m 4f 134y
**11:25** (11:27) (H5) 3-Y-0+ **£1,498** (£428; £214) **Stalls** Low

Form RPR
600 **1** **Richie Boy**[40] 5176 3-8-13 58.......................................... DaneO'Neill 10 58
(VSmith) *mde all: rdn over 1f out: styd on wl* **11/2**
2224 **2** *1* **Zuleta**[10] 5863 3-8-3 47..................................................(v) BSwarbrick(5) 5 51
(JGMO'Shea) *a.p: chsd wnr over 3f out: ev ch fr over 1f out: hrd rdn ins fnl f: nt run on* **10/3**[1]
3003 **3** *¾* **Calomeria**[21] 5634 3-8-5 50.............................................. NChalmers(3) 4 50
(RMBeckett) *chsd wnr over 8f: rdn over 1f out: styd on same pce* **11/2**
00/6 **4** *¾* **Dark Society**[12] 5830 6-9-7 52................................................. PDoe 3 54
(AWCarroll) *s.i.s: hld up: hdwy 1/2-way: rdn over 1f out: styd on same pce* **9/2**[3]
0056 **5** *8* **Maid The Cut**[14] 5791 3-8-8 45............................................ NPollard 6 37
(ADSmith) *prom: rdn over 2f out: wknd over 1f out* **22/1**
2405 **6** *hd* **Black Legend (IRE)**[36] 5257 5-9-3 45.................................... JFEgan 12 37
(RLee) *hld up in tch: rdn over 3f out: wknd over 1f out* **4/1**[2]
6450 **7** *1 ¾* **Port Sodrick**[12] 5843 3-8-3 55................................... AshleighHorton(7) 2 36
(MDIUsher) *hld up: nvr nrr* **16/1**
6644 **8** *9* **Cloudingswell**[18] 3681 3-8-3 48........................................ NDeSouza(5) 13 20
(DLWilliams) *chsd ldrs: rdn and wknd over 2f out* **20/1**
000/ **9** *1 ¾* **Circle Of Wolves**[147] 3813 6-9-7 45................................... SWhitworth 11 23
(HJManners) *s.i.s: a in rr* **20/1**
000 **10** *dist* **Observation**[12] 5828 3-8-8 ................................................ ADaly 9 —
(MrsJCandlish) *slwoly into stride: hld up: a in rr: wknd 1/2-way* **100/1**
00/ **11** *18* **Diwan (IRE)**[1446] 5157 6-9-2 ........................................... MLawson(5) 8 —
(JParkes) *hld up: a in rr: wknd 1/2-way* **80/1**

000 **12** *23* **Jimmy Hay**[12] 5843 3-8-7 ........ ANicholls 7 —
(JCFox) *hld up: rdn 1/2-way: sn wknd* **100/1**

2m 51.42s (8.12) **Going Correction** +0.575s/f (Yiel)
**WFA** 3 from 5yo+ 8lb **12** Ran SP% **115.0**
Speed ratings: **98,97,96,96,91 91,90,84,83,—** —,— CT £7.50 TOTE £2.80: £1.20, £2.40, £; EX23.60 1.Calomeria was claimed by D. McCain for £5000. Richie Boy was claimed by P. A. Blockley for £5000. Zuleta was claimed by
**Owner** Tony Stafford **Bred** Eurostrait Ltd **Trained** Exning, Suffolk
■ Stewards Enquiry : B Swarbrick four-day ban: used whip with excessive frequency and force (Oct 20-23)

**FOCUS**
The standard to be expected from a race of this type. The front four finished clear of the remainder.

**NOTEBOOK**
**Richie Boy**, who has shown very little in his two most recent starts, was making his debut for the stable and, under a positive ride, was able to get off the mark. Stepping up in trip, he showed improved form and off a mark of only 58 should be able to get competitive in handicaps if building at all on this.
**Zuleta** was never far off the lead and had her chance, but did not look overkeen to go by and had to settle for second.
**Calomeria**, who had the blinkers left off, was unable to reverse Catterick form with Zuleta and will definitely benefit for a return to further.
**Dark Society** built on his seasonal reappearance over a mile at Bath and was suited to this trip. There is more to come from him being a lightly raced individual.

## 6056 ASCOTT TRI-BANDED STKS 1m 22y
11:55 (11:58) (H5) 3-Y-O £1,522 (£435; £217) Stalls Low

Form RPR
0055 **1** **Backlash**[173] 1495 3-8-9 40 ........ SWKelly 9 49
(AWCarroll) *hld up: hdwy over 2f out: rdn to ld ins fnl f: r.o* **11/2**[2]
0000 **2** *1 3/4* **Livia (IRE)**[10] 5863 3-9-0 45 ........ (v) CCatlin 8 50
(JGPortman) *outpcd: hdwy 2f out: r.o* **66/1**
2421 **3** *hd* **Elsinora**[7] 5926 3-9-0 45 ........ (v) DaneO'Neill 10 50
(AGJuckes) *trckd ldr: rdn to ld over 2f out: hung rt over 1f out: nt run on and hdd ins fnl f* **3/1**[1]
0650 **4** *2 1/2* **Jaolins**[35] 5284 3-8-9 40 ........ DKinsella 14 40
(PGMurphy) *mid-div: nt clr run over 2f out: styd on appr fnl f: nrst fin* **25/1**
0542 **5** *3/4* **Nina Fontenail (FR)**[49] 4941 3-9-0 45 ........ RHavlin 13 43
(BRMillman) *mid-div: outpcd 1/2-way: styd on appr fnl f* **14/1**
4005 **6** *shd* **Roving Vixen (IRE)**[7] 5926 3-8-6 40 ........ (b) RMiles(3) 1 38
(JLSpearing) *s.s: bhd: hdwy over 1f out: r.o* **25/1**
3630 **7** *1 1/2* **Speed Racer**[11] 5851 3-9-0 45 ........ KimTinkler 15 40
(DonEnricoIncisa) *sn outpcd: edgd lft over 1f out: nt clr run ins fnl f: r.o: nrst fin* **33/1**
0300 **8** *hd* **Pappy (IRE)**[14] 5794 3-8-4 40 ........ BSwarbrick(5) 3 34
(AWCarroll) *prom: rdn over 2f out: wknd fnl f* **9/1**
04 **9** *1/2* **Primatech (IRE)**[28] 5451 3-8-9 45 ........ (p) PMakin(5) 7 38
(KAMorgan) *chsd ldrs: rdn over 2f out: wknd fnl f* **33/1**
3432 **10** *nk* **Roman The Park (IRE)**[28] 5451 3-9-0 45 ........ PMQuinn 2 38
(TDEasterby) *hld up: hdwy over 3f out: n.m.r over 1f out: wknd fnl f* **7/1**[3]
3005 **11** *hd* **La Calera (GER)**[12] 5843 3-9-0 45 ........ (b) OUrbina 5 37
(GCHChung) *sn drvn along to ld: hdd over 2f out: wknd fnl f* **8/1**
5000 **12** *1 1/4* **Noble Desert (FR)**[7] 5929 3-8-9 40 ........ JFEgan 12 33+
(RGuest) *mid-div: hdwy over 3f out: rdn and wknd over 1f out* **22/1**
0000 **13** *1 1/2* **Moscow Mary**[35] 5282 3-8-9 40 ........ SWhitworth 4 29+
(AGNewcombe) *sn pushed along: a in rr* **25/1**
6065 **14** *3* **Fabuloso**[14] 5794 3-8-9 40 ........ IMongan 16 20
(VSmith) *mid-div: hdwy 1/2-way: wknd 2f out* **8/1**
0630 **15** *15* **Suitcase Murphy (IRE)**[14] 5793 3-8-11 45 ........ NChalmers(3) 11 —
(MsDeborahJEvans) *prom over 5f* **16/1**
000- **16** *5* **Reckless Moment**[330] 5997 3-9-0 45 ........ LEnstone 6 —
(JaneSouthcombe) *chsd ldrs: lost pl over 5f out: bhd fnl 3f* **100/1**
0006 **17** *9* **Seven Shirt**[19] 5691 3-9-0 45 ........ PDoe 17 —
(EGBevan) *prom over 4f* **18/1**

1m 44.79s (5.49) **Going Correction** +0.575s/f (Yiel) **17** Ran SP% **127.2**
Speed ratings: **95,93,93,90,89 89,88,88,87,87 87,85,84,81,66 61,52**CSF £358.70 TOTE £8.70: £1.90, £19.70, £1.90; EX 227.90.
**Owner** One Under Par Racing **Bred** J T Powell-Tuck **Trained** Wixford, Warwicks

**FOCUS**
Pretty poor stuff, and quite what the form is worth with a 66/1 second and the favourite not looking keen to go and win is open to debate.

**NOTEBOOK**
**Backlash** ran disappointingly dropped down to this grade last time but bounced back to form with a cosy win. In rear early, she made some good headway through the field before staying on strongly. There may be more to come from her.
**Livia(IRE)** ran way above herself in second at odds of 66/1. She could not manage to go with them early and was being niggled for some way, but picked up strongly in the closing stages to just get second.
**Elsinora**, easy winner of a banded maiden claimer at Brighton earlier in the month, did not look happy under pressure and threw away any chance she had of winning. She is evidently not one to rely on.
**Jaolins** was unlucky not to finish closer but the likelihood is she would only have managed fourth anyhow.
**Nina Fontenail(FR)**, back down in trip, was doing her best work late - as to be expected - and is worth wtching out for back up in trip.
**Roving Vixen(IRE)** *Official explanation: jockey said filly ran too free*
**Speed Racer** ran better than her finishing position suggests and could sneak a race of similar quality if improving a little.
**Pappy(IRE)** *Official explanation: jockey said filly hung left in the home straight*
**Roman The Park(IRE)** *Official explanation: jockey said filly was "tied up" post race*
**Reckless Moment** *Official explanation: jockey said filly was unsuited by good to soft (good in places) ground*
**Seven Shirt** *Official explanation: jockey said gelding was hanging throughout*

## 6057 WORLD CARGO BANDED STKS 1m 22y
12:25 (12:28) (H5) 3-Y-O+ £1,505 (£430; £215) Stalls Low

Form RPR
0002 **1** **Ballare (IRE)**[6] 5642 5-9-2 45 ........ (v) TWilliams 7 55
(BobJones) *chsd ldrs: rdn to ld and edgd rt over 1f out: r.o* **11/4**[1]
0535 **2** *nk* **Encounter**[7] 5927 8-8-13 45 ........ LPKeniry(3) 13 54
(JHetherton) *hld up: hdwy over 1f out: r.o* **6/1**[3]
0400 **3** *nk* **Vizulize**[7] 5929 5-8-13 40 ........ DNolan(3) 14 54
(AWCarroll) *chsd ldrs: led over 2f out: edgd rt and hdd over 1f out: styd on* **18/1**
0500 **4** *2 1/2* **Printsmith (IRE)**[147] 2128 7-9-2 45 ........ JBramhill 8 48
(JRNorton) *sn pushed along in rr: hdwy over 1f out: edgd lft: r.o* **14/1**
5300 **5** *4* **Happy Camper (IRE)**[112] 3088 4-9-2 45 ........ SWhitworth 6 40
(MRHoad) *hld up: plld hrd: r.o ins fnl f: nvr nrr* **28/1**
0055 **6** *1/2* **The Loose Screw (IRE)**[15] 5770 6-9-2 45 ........ (p) SWKelly 10 39
(GMMoore) *w ldr tl led over 6f out: hdd over 2f out: hung lft over 1f out: wknd ins fnl f* **7/1**
6000 **7** *1/2* **Sinjaree**[52] 4852 6-8-13 40 ........ RThomas(3) 4 38
(MrsSLamyman) *mid-div: outpcd 1/2-way: styd on ins fnl f* **9/2**[2]
0340 **8** *hd* **Rocky Reppin**[75] 4190 4-8-9 45 ........ KPierrepont(7) 16 38
(JBalding) *hld up: effrt over 3f out: wknd over 1f out* **33/1**
0600 **9** *1 3/4* **King Of Meze (IRE)**[114] 3026 3-8-10 40 ........ (t) ABeech(3) 17 34
(GProdromou) *hld up in tch: rdn over 2f out: wknd over 1f out* **22/1**
0500 **10** *3* **Muraqeb**[172] 1534 4-9-2 45 ........ (b) RHavlin 2 28
(MrsBarbaraWaring) *hld up: rdn 1/2-way: wknd over 2f out* **50/1**
0306 **11** *2 1/2* **Pererin**[7] 5927 3-8-13 45 ........ (v[1]) GGibbons 1 22
(IAWood) *plld hrd and prom: rdn and wknd 2f out* **12/1**
0-00 **12** *hd* **St Jude**[41] 5146 4-9-2 45 ........ JEdmunds 5 22
(JBalding) *led: hdd over 6f out: wknd 3f out* **33/1**
4040 **13** *2 1/2* **Jamestown**[50] 4925 7-8-13 45 ........ LFletcher(3) 15 17
(MJPolglase) *prom 5f* **20/1**
550- **14** *12* **Green Ginger**[355] 5672 8-9-2 45 ........ CCatlin 11 —
(CNKellett) *hld up: wknd over 3f out* **33/1**
0-00 **15** *17* **Friday's Takings**[261] 582 5-9-2 40 ........ (b) PaulEddery 3 —
(BSmart) *s.s: outpcd* **16/1**
0000 **16** *2 1/2* **Big Tom (IRE)**[25] 5547 3-8-8 40 ........ (b[1]) DTudhope(5) 9 —
(DCarroll) *hld up in tch: wknd over 3f out* **20/1**

1m 44.34s (5.04) **Going Correction** +0.575s/f (Yiel)
**WFA** 3 from 4yo+ 3lb **16** Ran SP% **125.2**
Speed ratings: **97,96,96,93,89 89,88,88,86,83 81,81,78,66,49 47**CSF £16.82 TOTE £4.50: £1.70, £3.00, £8.90; EX 19.10.
**Owner** The Ballare Partnership **Bred** Oyster Farm **Trained** Wickhambrook, Suffolk

**FOCUS**
A tight finish that went the way of Ballare who was returning to something like his best. The form is a shade above average for this grade without looking all that solid.

**NOTEBOOK**
**Ballare(IRE)** came back to form when second on the All-Weather last time and was able to build on that with a narrow victory. Well served by the return to this trip, he has more to offer and can win again.
**Encounter** continues to knock at the door and it is only a matter of time before he gets his head back in front again.
**Vizulize** had gone right off the boil the last twice and this was a much more respectable effort. If going on from this a poor race is hers for the taking.
**Printsmith(IRE)** was another to bounce back to some sort of form and she will be of interest next time if found a suitable opportunity.
**Happy Camper(IRE)** did himself no favours by pulling in the early stages, and he did well to see the race out as well as he did.

## 6058 NASH MCDERMOTT BANDED STKS 7f 26y
12:55 (12:57) (H5) 3-Y-O+ £1,575 (£450; £225) Stalls Low

Form RPR
6402 **1** **Zhitomir**[19] 5691 6-9-7 50 ........ SWKelly 7 67
(MDods) *hld up: hdwy 1/2-way: hung lft and led 1f out: rdn clr: eased nr fin* **5/2**[1]
0020 **2** *2 1/2* **The Old Soldier**[33] 5346 6-9-4 50 ........ ABeech(3) 1 60
(ADickman) *led over 5f out: rdn and hdd 1f out: styd on same pce* **11/2**[3]
0012 **3** *2* **Caerphilly Gal**[7] 5927 4-9-2 50 ........ DFox(5) 14 55
(PLGilligan) *chsd ldrs: rdn over 2f out: styd on same pce appr fnl f* **9/2**[2]
00 **4** *3 1/2* **Chantelle (IRE)**[17] 5736 4-9-7 50 ........ JFEgan 11 46
(SKirk) *mid-div: nt clr run and lost pl over 3f out: n.d after* **12/1**
6000 **5** *1* **Millfields Dreams**[17] 5736 5-9-4 50 ........ (p) DNolan(3) 13 43
(RBrotherton) *sn led: hdd over 5f out: rdn and wknd over 1f out* **10/1**
0500 **6** *nk* **Elliot's Choice (IRE)**[17] 5736 3-9-2 50 ........ LPKeniry(3) 2 43
(RMStronge) *chsd ldrs: nt clr run and lost pl 1/2-way: n.d after* **11/1**
-660 **7** *4* **Tictactoe**[67] 4414 3-8-12 50 ........ (v[1]) MHalford(7) 8 32
(DJDaly) *s.i.s: in rr: rn wd over 3f out: n.d* **33/1**
0052 **8** *1/2* **Saintly Place**[25] 5552 3-9-5 50 ........ RFitzpatrick 12 31
(CSmith) *prom over 4f* **14/1**
0040 **9** *1/2* **Redoubtable (USA)**[33] 5346 13-9-6 49 ........ ANicholls 5 29
(DWChapman) *chsd ldrs: rdn over 2f out: wknd over 1f out* **12/1**
2505 **10** *3* **Go Free**[51] 4879 3-8-13 49 ........ PMakin(5) 3 21
(AMHales) *bhd fnl 4f* **22/1**
0500 **11** *nk* **Ink In Gold (IRE)**[19] 5693 3-9-5 50 ........ GParkin 10 21
(PABlockley) *s.s: outpcd* **33/1**
3304 **12** *nk* **Sophrano (IRE)**[28] 5448 4-9-7 50 ........ PBradley 9 20
(PABlockley) *hld up: bhd fr 1/2-way* **16/1**
0-00 **13** *20* **Romantic Drama (IRE)**[26] 5510 3-9-4 49 ........ (t) SRighton 6 —
(MrsALMKing) *s.s: a in rr: wknd 4f out* **50/1**

1m 27.05s (2.15) **Going Correction** +0.225s/f (Good)
**WFA** 3 from 4yo+ 2lb **13** Ran SP% **119.7**
Speed ratings: **96,93,90,86,85 85,80,80,79,76 75,75,52**CSF £14.98 TOTE £3.50: £1.50, £2.70, £2.20; EX 22.40.
**Owner** M J K Dods **Bred** Serpentine Bloodstock Et Al **Trained** Piercebridge, Co Durham

**FOCUS**
The field finished pretty strung out for a seven-furlong event. A tidy display from the winner, who can most definitely win again, and the form looks a cut above the usual standard for this grade.

**NOTEBOOK**
**Zhitomir** ran out an emphatic winner - being eased across the line - and found this slight drop in grade right up his alley. Clearly on a high at present, it would come as no surprise to see him follow up back in a better grade.
**The Old Soldier** ran his race and was unfortunate to bump into such an in-form horse. He will find easier opportunities.
**Caerphilly Gal** could never get on terms with the front pair once the race for the line began and had to settle for third.
**Chantelle(IRE)** was trying to get involved when short of room and that halted her progress. She is better than this and deserves another chance.
**Millfields Dreams** did not put up much of a show and was readily held.
**Romantic Drama(IRE)** *Official explanation: jockey said filly had a breathing problem*

## 6059 SHIPSTON BANDED STKS 5f
1:25 (1:25) (H5) 3-Y-O+ £1,484 (£424; £212) Stalls Low

Form RPR
0026 **1** **Joyce's Choice**[67] 4422 5-8-9 45 ........ (v[1]) PPMathers(5) 11 53
(JSWainwright) *a.p: rdn and hung lft 1f out: sn edgd rt: r.o to ld wl ins fnl f* **12/1**
0000 **2** *nk* **Fairgame Man**[55] 4782 6-9-0 45 ........ (p) GParkin 13 52
(JSWainwright) *chsd ldrs: rdn and ev ch whn hmpd 1f out: r.o* **8/1**
-000 **3** *nk* **Whinhill House**[55] 4782 4-9-0 45 ........ LEnstone 5 51
(DWBarker) *chsd ldrs: rdn to ld over 1f out: hdd wl ins fnl f* **50/1**
0166 **4** *shd* **Little Flute**[35] 5282 3-8-11 45 ........ J-PGuillambert(3) 10 51
(TKeddy) *outpcd: hdwy over 1f out: edgd rt ins fnl f: r.o* **10/1**

0030 **5** 3/4 **Flapdoodle**[7] 5930 6-9-0 45 ....(b) DaneO'Neill 4 48
(AWCarroll) *mde most over 3f: unable qck ins fnl f* **8/1**

0500 **6** 1 **Red Leicester**[52] 4854 4-9-0 45 ....(v) SWKelly 12 44
(JAGlover) *w ldrs: rdn and ev ch whn bmpd 1f out: no ex ins fnl f* **22/1**

0003 **7** nk **Chatshow (USA)**[7] 5930 3-8-11 45 .... DNolan(3) 1 43
(AWCarroll) *chsd ldrs: rdn and ev ch over 1f out: styd on same pce* **5/1**[1]

6240 **8** shd **Diamond Ring**[36] 5261 5-9-0 45 .... IMongan 7 43
(MrsJCandlish) *outpcd: hdwy over 1f out: nt trble ldrs* **11/2**[2]

0000 **9** 1 1/4 **Playful Spirit**[106] 3277 5-9-0 45 ....(v) JEdmunds 6 39
(JBalding) *chsd ldrs: rdn over 1f out: no ex* **20/1**

0300 **10** shd **Chorus**[36] 5261 7-9-0 45 ....(b) RHavlin 9 38
(BRMillman) *mid-div: nt clr run and lost pl 1/2-way: n.d after* **16/1**

0000 **11** nk **Radlett Lady**[105] 3322 3-8-7 45 .... MHoward(7) 8 37
(DKIvory) *chsd ldrs over 3f* **40/1**

0430 **12** 1/2 **Mystery Pips**[23] 5579 4-9-0 45 ....(v) KimTinkler 3 36
(NTinkler) *chsd ldrs: rdn 1/2-way: styd on same pce appr fnl f* **7/1**[3]

0000 **13** 4 **John O'Groats (IRE)**[28] 5452 6-8-11 45 ....(b) LPKeniry(3) 16 22
(DWChapman) *chsd ldrs over 3f* **20/1**

0000 **14** shd **Lakelands Lady (IRE)**[55] 4782 4-8-9 45 .... PMakin(5) 15 21
(JBalding) *chsd ldrs over 3f* **28/1**

0640 **15** 7 **Levelled**[51] 4881 10-9-0 45 .... ANicholls 14 —
(DWChapman) *chsd ldrs: rdn 1/2-way: wknd 2f out* **25/1**

-500 **16** 1 1/4 **Rellim**[201] 1075 5-8-11 45 .... LFletcher(3) 2 —
(JBalding) *rrd stalls: dwlt: hdwy over 1f out: sn wknd* **16/1**

63.09 secs (2.89) **Going Correction** +0.525s/f (Yiel) **16 Ran SP% 120.9**
Speed ratings: **97,96,96,95,94 93,92,92,90,90 89,89,82,82,71 69**CSF £94.68 TOTE £7.90: £3.00, £2.70, £9.00; EX 65.30.
**Owner** Mrs Jean Neilson **Bred** Mrs J M Berry **Trained** Kennythorpe, N Yorks
■ Stewards Enquiry : P P Mathers two-day ban: used whip with excessive frequency and force (Oct 20-21)

**FOCUS**
A competitive heat with a few hard-luck stories in behind. They finished well bunched and this is average form for the grade, if solid enough.

**NOTEBOOK**
**Joyce's Choice**, sporting the first-time visor, has never been the most consistent but the headgear seemed to work the oracle and he came with a strong late run to get up close home. He still looked an awkward ride though, hanging under pressure, and would not be one to bank on to repeat the form.
**Fairgame Man** was possibly a little unlucky as he was interfered with a furlong out when still holding every chance and just got nailed in the closing stages. He is on a very winnable mark and can win next time if running to this level.
**Whinhill House**, 9lb lower than when last winning, looked set to cause something of a shock when coming through to take it up over a furlong out but was run out of it late on. Still a creditable effort, he is evidently back to some sort of form but needs to prove this was no flash in the pan.
**Little Flute**, back down to five furlongs, could not go the early gallop and was doing his best work at the death. He has been in fair form and a return to further should see him in a better light.
**Flapdoodle** showed up well early but was readily brushed aside by the principals.
**Red Leicester** lost her chance when hampered and was unlucky not to finish closer.
**Chatshow(USA)** was not beaten far but still has to go down as disappointing.
**Rellim** *Official explanation: trainer said mare hit her head on stalls*

## 6060 RHT 40TH ANNIVERSARY MEDIAN AUCTION MAIDEN STKS 7f 26y
**1:55** (1:56) (H5) 2-Y-O £1,536 (£439; £219) **Stalls** Low

Form RPR

24 **1** **Moon Forest (IRE)**[23] 5578 2-9-0 .... PaulEddery 6 75
(PWChapple-Hyam) *mde virtually all: rdn and edgd rt over 1f out: edgd lft ins fnl f: r.o* **8/11**[1]

0 **2** 2 **Lady Doris Watts**[7] 5943 2-8-9 .... CCatlin 11 65
(MRChannon) *chsd wnr: chal 2f out: styd on same pce fnl f* **7/2**[2]

6 **3** shd **Valiant Act (IRE)**[19] 5688 2-8-6 .... LPKeniry(3) 4 65
(DMSimcock) *chsd ldrs: rdn over 2f out: styd on* **10/1**[3]

0 **4** 3 1/2 **Just Cliff**[8] 5911 2-9-0 .... JFEgan 1 61
(WRMuir) *hld up in tch: racd keenly: rdn over 2f out: styd on same pce* **66/1**

00 **5** 7 **Honour High**[10] 5871 2-9-0 .... DaneO'Neill 7 44
(LadyHerries) *prom over 4f* **14/1**

0 **6** 3/4 **Glads Image**[17] 5846 2-8-9 .... SWKelly 12 37
(DJDaly) *mid-div: rdn 1/2-way: wknd over 2f out* **50/1**

**7** shd **Piper General (IRE)** 2-8-7 .... DerekNolan(7) 5 41
(JSMoore) *s.s: nvr nrr* **40/1**

00 **8** 1/2 **A Qui Le Tour**[70] 4334 2-9-0 .... SWhitworth 3 40
(MRHoad) *sn pushed along in rr: sme hdwy 3f out: sn wknd* **100/1**

**9** 1 1/4 **Brumaire (IRE)** 2-9-0 .... IMongan 2 37
(JLDunlop) *s.s: nvr nr to chal* **12/1**

**10** 1 1/4 **So Elegant (IRE)** 2-8-9 .... OUrbina 13 29
(JJay) *mid-div: rdn 1/2-way: sn wknd* **33/1**

**11** 3 1/2 **Paddy Oliver (IRE)** 2-9-0 .... ANicholls 14 25
(BPalling) *prom over 4f* **28/1**

00 **12** 5 **Davala**[123] 2761 2-9-0 .... NPollard 8 13
(ADSmith) *a bhd* **80/1**

0 **13** 5 **Witchy Vibes**[15] 5771 2-8-9 .... SRighton 9 —
(MAppleby) *bhd fr 1/2-way* **100/1**

1m 28.39s (3.49) **Going Correction** +0.225s/f (Good) **13 Ran SP% 119.1**
Speed ratings: **89,86,86,82,74 73,73,73,71,70 66,60,54**CSF £3.00 TOTE £1.70: £1.10, £1.10, £2.80; EX 3.70 Place 6 £55.98, Place 5 £32.36.
**Owner** Collins Deal Harrison-Allan Chapple-Hyam **Bred** P Conlon And Paul Clarke **Trained** Newmarket, Suffolk

**FOCUS**
A straightforward first win for Moon Forest, who had things his own way in front and came home with something to spare. The race could potentially rate a bit higher than this.

**NOTEBOOK**
**Moon Forest(IRE)** set a high standard on the form of his two previous runs and led throughout for a smooth success. This was not a strong race, but he is going the right way and should not get too stiff a mark, so can get competitive in handicaps.
**Lady Doris Watts** did not shape without promise on her debut at Newmarket and was well suited by this extra furlong. She is going the right way and can win an ordinary affair.
**Valiant Act(IRE)**, who faded late on her debut in heavy ground, saw the race out well on this better surface and is going the right way. There is more to come from her but she is probably more of a handicap type.
**Just Cliff**raced enthusiastically in rear and saw his race out surprisingly well given how sharply he stopped on his debut earlier in the month.
**Honour High** is more of a long-term prospect and will be seen to much better effect in handicaps at three.
T/Plt: £29.60 to a £1 stake. Pool: £25,149.00. 620.00 winning tickets. T/Qpdt: £9.10 to a £1 stake. Pool: £1,742.40. 141.10 winning tickets. CR

# 6020 WOLVERHAMPTON (A.W) (L-H)
Saturday, October 9

**OFFICIAL GOING: Standard**
Wind: mod against Weather: dry

## 6061 ZONGALERO MAIDEN H'CAP 1m 141y(P)
**7:00** (7:01) (F4) (0-55,55) 3-Y-O+ **£3,015** (£861; £430) **Stalls** Low

Form RPR

**1** **Rebel Raider (IRE)**[451] 5587 5-8-9 **50** .... LisaJones 7 59
(BNPollock) *a.p: rdn over 2f out: led 1f out: kpt on wl* **25/1**

4650 **2** 1 3/4 **Irusan (IRE)**[50] 4905 4-8-13 **54** ....(b[1]) IMongan 1 60
(JeddO'Keeffe) *led: rdn 2f out: hdd 1f out: kpt on one pce* **14/1**

0020 **3** 3/4 **Semelle De Vent (USA)**[54] 4798 3-8-10 **55** ....(v) DaneO'Neill 9 59
(JHMGosden) *hld up in tch: hdwy 6f out: chal over 1f out: one pce ins fnl f* **6/1**[3]

6050 **4** 1 1/2 **Mrs Brown**[61] 4604 3-8-9 **54** .... JMackay 13 55+
(SirMarkPrescott) *hld up: rdn over 3f out: hdwy on ins over 2f out: styd on: nvr nr to chal* **9/1**

3004 **5** 1/2 **Musical Top (USA)**[12] 5830 4-8-11 **55** .... LFletcher(3) 11 55
(HMorrison) *prom: rdn 3f out: outpcd fnl 2f* **10/3**[2]

4000 **6** 3 1/2 **Orchestration (IRE)**[65] 4489 3-8-9 **54** .... SWKelly 2 46
(JWUnett) *in tch tl hmpd on bnd after 2f: nvr a danger after* **25/1**

4023 **7** 2 **Queen Lucia (IRE)**[43] 5072 3-8-10 **55** .... KFallon 6 43
(JGGiven) *in tch: rdn 3f out: no prog after* **3/1**[1]

0000 **8** 1 1/4 **Carlburg (IRE)**[38] 5222 3-8-7 **55** ....(b[1]) J-PGuillambert(3) 5 41
(CEBrittain) *s.i.s: rdn over 6f out: nvr got into r* **33/1**

0000 **9** 1 **Dance Party (IRE)**[18] 5714 4-9-0 **55** ....(b[1]) GGibbons 10 39
(MWEasterby) *mid-div: effrt over 2f out: sn btn* **12/1**

006 **10** 9 **Ceylon Round (FR)**[68] 4402 3-8-7 **55** .... DCorby(3) 3 20
(MJWallace) *chsd ldr tl wknd over 3f out* **16/1**

6-40 **11** 3 **Smirfys Dance Hall (IRE)**[21] 5635 4-8-7 **53** .... BSwarbrick(5) 4 11
(WMBrisbourne) *sn pushed along: lost tch 1/2-way* **12/1**

0000 **12** 10 **Saharan Song (IRE)**[22] 5622 3-8-10 **55** .... ACulhane 12 —
(BWHills) *hld up towards rr: sme hdwy over 4f out: sn btn* **12/1**

**13** dist **Any News**[6] 4509 7-9-0 **55** ....(t) SRighton 8 —
(MissMERowland) *sn bhd: rdn 1/2-way: virtually p.u ins fnl f: t.o* **100/1**

1m 50.98s
**WFA** 3 from 4yo+ 4lb **13 Ran SP% 119.6**
Speed ratings: CSF £332.44 CT £2459.95 TOTE £24.30: £8.20, £4.20, £2.00; EX 1003.30.
**Owner** S G B Morrison **Bred** Ivan And Mrs Eileen Heanen **Trained** Medbourne, Leics

**FOCUS**
A poor handicap and this form is very limited.

**NOTEBOOK**
**Rebel Raider(IRE)** showed ability in Ireland in his younger days and was in good form over hurdles when last in action in the summer of last year. Well treated for this return to the Flat, he scored a shade readily despite edging to his right when in front.
**Irusan(IRE)**, tried in blinkers, attempted to make all, something no horse has achieved yet on the new surface at Dunstall Park. This was a decent effort on his first start over this trip.
**Semelle De Vent(USA)** returned to form back on the Polytrack, but gave the impression this trip was on the sharp side.
**Mrs Brown** made late progress from off the pace. Although she never threatened the leaders, this was a more encouraging effort and she will be suited by a step back up in trip.
**Musical Top(USA)**, who has slipped in the weights this season, was having her first run on an artificial surface.
**Orchestration(IRE)**, with the blinkers left off, did well to finish as close as he did after meeting trouble early on. On this evidence he is worth another try at this trip.
**Queen Lucia(IRE)** had also been below-par on her one previous attempt on Polytrack.

## 6062 STARS IN THEIR EYES NIGHT CLAIMING STKS 7f 32y(P)
**7:30** (7:31) (F3) 3-Y-O+ **£4,221** (£1,299; £649; £324) **Stalls** High

Form RPR

0000 **1** **Camp Commander (IRE)**[21] 5650 5-9-9 89 ....(t) LDettori 7 95
(CEBrittain) *hld up in rr: stdy hdwy fr 1/2-way: rdn over 1f out: responded wl to ld nr fin* **2/1**[1]

0005 **2** 3/4 **Gallery Breeze**[3] 6014 5-8-3 65 ....(b) LisaJones 4 73
(JLSpearing) *chsd ldr:: led 3f out: pushed along over 1f out: kpt on but hdd nr fin* **7/1**

040 **3** hd **Point Of Dispute**[32] 5379 9-9-3 76 ....(v) DSweeney 11 86
(PJMakin) *hld up in tch: hdwy to chse ldr over 2f out: ev ch ins fnl f: nt qckn cl home* **9/2**[3]

1601 **4** 7 **Samuel Charles**[7] 5952 6-9-1 75 .... BSwarbrick(5) 8 71
(WMBrisbourne) *chsd ldrs: rdn over 2f out: nt qckn and wknd ins fnl f* **3/1**[2]

2460 **5** 1 1/4 **Smith N Allan Oils**[67] 4425 5-9-3 65 ....(p) SWKelly 3 65
(MDods) *hld up in tch: rdn 1/2-way: no hdwy fr 2f out* **11/1**

3005 **6** 1/2 **Ile Michel**[7] 5952 7-9-2 67 .... DFentiman(7) 6 70
(JGMO'Shea) *hld up: rdn 3f out: nvr on terms* **25/1**

0050 **7** shd **Commander Bond**[21] 5656 3-8-12 67 .... DMcGaffin 2 60
(BSmart) *led tl hdd 3f out: rdn and wknd wl over 1f out* **33/1**

6000 **8** 5 **Risk Free**[51] 4877 7-8-8 65 ....(b) IMongan 12 41
(PDEvans) *in tch: rdn 1/2-way: sn outpcd* **25/1**

0-0 **9** 6 **Bobering**[37] 5237 4-8-9 .... PPMathers(5) 10 32
(BPJBaugh) *a outpcd in rr* **100/1**

0000 **10** 3 1/2 **Ronnie From Donny (IRE)**[2] 6026 4-9-6 66 .... DaneO'Neill 5 29
(BEllison) *prom tl rdn 1/2-way: sn bhd* **14/1**

0 **11** 9 **Marburyanna**[15] 5770 4-8-3 .... SRighton 1 —
(MMullineaux) *slowly away: outpcd in rr thrght* **100/1**

6000 **12** 2 **Oakley Rambo**[52] 4846 5-9-6 66 .... RLMoore 9 —
(RHannon) *sn reminders in rr: a wl bhd* **11/1**

1m 29.19s
**WFA** 3 from 4yo+ 2lb **12 Ran SP% 125.0**
Speed ratings: CSF £17.36 TOTE £3.30: £1.70, £2.90, £2.50; EX 27.60.The winner was claimed by Andrew Page for £11,000. Gallery Breeze was claimed by Nigel Shields for £6,000.
**Owner** A J Richards & S A Richards **Bred** Kildaragh Stud **Trained** Newmarket, Suffolk

**FOCUS**
A fair claimer, run at a decent pace. The winner was 10lb below his AW best but the form looks sound enough.

**NOTEBOOK**
**Camp Commander(IRE)**, a high-class handicapper who won last year's Victoria Cup, had 7lb in hand on official figures on this drop in class. He was left with a bit to do after missing the kick, but cut down the leaders to get on top close home.
**Gallery Breeze**, backed down from 20/1, just failed to land a gamble. She had been beaten in a seller earlier in the week but, benefiting from the drop in trip, looked like holding on until collared near the line.



The Form Book, Raceform Ltd, Compton, RG20 6NL

**Point Of Dispute** gave chase to the leader up the home straight, showing his markedly high head carriage, but could not quite get past. His losing run has now reached 18 races stretching back to November 2001.
**Samuel Charles** was close enough turning for home, but it looked like hard work and he was left trailing by the principals in the final furlong.
**Smith N Allan Oils** faced a stiff task on these terms.
**Ile Michel** again shaped as if in need of a longer trip.

## 6063 HOLIDAY INN GARDEN COURT NOVICE AUCTION STKS 1m 141y(P)
8:00 (8:00) (F3) 2-Y-O £3,380 (£1,040; £520; £260) Stalls Low

Form RPR
4221 **1** **Watchmyeyes (IRE)**$^{2}$ 6020 2-9-1 **77**......(p) KFallon 2 82
(NPLittmoden) *trckd ldrs: strly rdn appr fnl f: r.o to ld nr fin* **7/4**$^{1}$
134 **2** *hd* **Le Corvee (IRE)**$^{31}$ 5395 2-9-6 **94**...... JDSmith 7 87
(AKing) *hld up towards rr: hdwy 4f out: wnt 2nd over 2f out: led over 1f out: rdn and hdd nr fin* **9/4**$^{2}$
3362 **3** *2* **Tumbleweed Galore (IRE)**$^{17}$ 5738 2-8-12 **76**......(b$^{1}$) LDettori 8 74
(BJMeehan) *hld up in rr: hdwy 4f out: rdn over 1f out but nt pce to chal first 2 ins fnl f* **5/2**$^{3}$
1060 **4** *4* **Heres The Plan (IRE)**$^{66}$ 4445 2-8-10 **79**...... RLMoore 5 64
(MGQuinlan) *trckd ldr: led over 3f out: rdn and hdd over 1f out: wknd ins fnl f* **12/1**
3000 **5** *2* **Three Pennies**$^{19}$ 5701 2-8-13 **64**...... SWKelly 6 63
(MDods) *hld up: rdn 3f out: no hdwy ins fnl 2f* **50/1**
6202 **6** *3½* **Ragged Glory (IRE)**$^{17}$ 5741 2-8-12 **77**......(v) DaneO'Neill 3 54
(RHannon) *led tl hdd over 3f out: wknd 2f out* **11/1**
0000 **7** *9* **Sherbourne**$^{23}$ 5593 2-8-3 **45** ow1...... PaulEddery 1 27
(MGQuinlan) *hld up towards rr: lost tch over 2f out* **100/1**
0040 **8** *1¾* **The Keep**$^{19}$ 5701 2-8-2 **54**...... RSmith 4 22
(RHannon) *prom tl lost pl over 3f out: sn bhd* **100/1**

1m 51.78s **8** Ran SP% **115.7**
Speed ratings: CSF £6.06 TOTE £2.50: £1.10, £1.40, £1.60; EX 9.40.
**Owner** V And J Properties **Bred** Sea Syndicate **Trained** Newmarket, Suffolk

**FOCUS**
A steadily-run race. There was little between Watchmyeyes and Le Corvee at the weights,and they fought out a close finish.

**NOTEBOOK**
**Watchmyeyes(IRE)** adopted different tactics than he had earlier in the week and proved more amenable in the cheekpieces. He travelled well, suggesting that a stronger pace would have suited, and was given a good ride from Fallon who produced him to lead in the last half-furlong. He looks to be on the upgrade, but his future is now in the hands of the Handicapper.
**Le Corvee(IRE)**, dropped in class, looked set to score when going on, but appeared to prick his ears at some people on the inside of the track when in front, costing him a little momentum, and was just denied. The return to a mile will suit.
**Tumbleweed Galore(IRE)**, tried in blinkers for the first time, was under pressure some way out and the return to a mile will not pose him any problems.
**Heres The Plan(IRE)**, under a positive ride again, appeared to be caught out by the extra furlong.
**Three Pennies** ran a slightly better race over this longer trip but is not going the right way.
**Ragged Glory(IRE)**, who set only a modest pace, was taken on for the lead and was one of the first beaten.

## 6064 SUE CLEARY 50TH BIRTHDAY H'CAP 7f 32y(P)
8:30 (8:31) (E3) (0-70,70) 3-Y-O £4,570 (£1,406; £703; £351) Stalls High

Form RPR
0000 **1** **Stormy Nature (IRE)**$^{22}$ 5618 3-9-3 **66**...... SCarson 9 74
(PWHarris) *sn trckd ldr: led wl over 2f out: rdn out fnl f* **16/1**
0600 **2** *¾* **Russian Symphony (USA)**$^{14}$ 5801 3-9-4 **67**......(b) ACulhane 8 73
(CREgerton) *hld up in tch: hdwy 3f out: wnt 2nd over 2f out: kpt on but no imp ins fnl f* **25/1**
-020 **3** *1¼* **Charlie Bear**$^{12}$ 5841 3-9-5 **68**...... EAhern 4 71
(EALDunlop) *a.p: rdn over 1f out: kpt on one pce fnl f* **11/2**$^{3}$
4164 **4** *nk* **Hazewind**$^{7}$ 5955 3-9-7 **70**......(vt) KFallon 2 72
(PDEvans) *mid-div: rdn and lost pl 1/2-way: styd on ins fnl 2f but nvr nr to chal* **11/4**$^{1}$
4-44 **5** *shd* **Five Years On (IRE)**$^{12}$ 5829 3-9-4 **67**...... SWKelly 5 69
(WJHaggas) *hld up in rr: rdn and hdwy over 1f out: kpt on one pce* **3/1**$^{2}$
3010 **6** *2½* **Moon Legend (USA)**$^{17}$ 5737 3-9-0 **66**...... HayleyTurner$^{(3)}$ 12 61
(WJarvis) *v.s.a: in rr tl kpt on past btn horses appr and ins fnl f* **25/1**
5-23 **7** *nk* **Bluebok**$^{14}$ 5803 3-9-4 **67**......(t) LDettori 1 61
(DRLoder) *bhd: rdn and effrt over 1f out: sn btn* **7/1**
3562 **8** *2* **Here To Me**$^{21}$ 5657 3-9-7 **70**...... RLMoore 10 59
(RHannon) *prom: rdn 2f out: wknd ent fnl f* **13/2**
0-05 **9** *1* **Three Ships**$^{116}$ 2962 3-9-3 **69**...... BReilly$^{(3)}$ 3 56
(MissJFeilden) *led tl hdd wl over 2f out: wknd over 1f out* **40/1**
5310 **10** *½* **Oh Golly Gosh**$^{34}$ 5316 3-9-0 **66**......(p) J-PGuillambert$^{(3)}$ 6 51
(NPLittmoden) *pushed along in rr early: sn mid-div: wknd wl over 1f out* **16/1**
1402 **11** *1* **Go Yellow**$^{48}$ 4969 3-9-4 **67**...... NCallan 7 50
(PDEvans) *hld up: rdn and c wd over 2f out: sn btn* **14/1**
0000 **12** *3½* **Global Achiever**$^{4}$ 6007 3-9-4 **67**......(t) OUrbina 11 41
(GCHChung) *in tch on outside tl wknd wl over 1f out* **20/1**

1m 28.8s **12** Ran SP% **126.2**
Speed ratings: CSF £380.07 CT £2527.57 TOTE £20.10: £4.40, £8.80, £2.90; EX 1088.60.
**Owner** The Herts Desire **Bred** Terence McDonald **Trained** Ringshall, Bucks
■ Stewards Enquiry : S Carson two-day ban: careless riding (Oct 20-21)

**FOCUS**
They went a good pace and it paid to be prominent. Ordinary form.

**NOTEBOOK**
**Stormy Nature(IRE)** was having her first race on Polytrack, but like all her trainer's horses she works on the surface. Tackling this trip for the first time, she secured the inside rail in the home straight and was always going to hold on.
**Russian Symphony(USA)**, back up in trip, chased the winner hard up the straight without getting to her. This was an encouraging effort on his first run on sand.
**Charlie Bear** ran a sound race on his first try on an artificial surface. He has been running over a mile and a return to that trip could pay off.
**Hazewind** made late progress over a trip on the sharp side for him. He is high enough in the weights at present.
**Five Years On(IRE)**, racing from a 3lb higher mark, was again well backed. After being set plenty to do, he could never quite land a blow but was going on at the finish. The return to a mile should pay dividends.
**Moon Legend(USA)**, on his All-Weather bow, forfeited a lot of ground at the start, not for the first time, but did make some notable late headway.
**Bluebok** *Official explanation: jockey said colt hung right-handed throughout*

## 6065 HOTEL AND CONFERENCING AT DUNSTALL PARK (S) H'CAP 1m 4f 50y(P)
9:00 (9:00) (G4) (0-55,54) 3-5-Y-O £2,595 (£741; £370) Stalls Low

Form RPR
5401 **1** **Romeo's Day**$^{7}$ 5928 3-7-12 **50** ow5...... TO'Brien$^{(7)}$ 10 61
(MRChannon) *hld up: hdwy whn edgd lft 4f out: squeezed through to chal 2f out: sn led: edgd rt ins fnl f: all out* **9/1**
5040 **2** *nk* **Lord Lahar**$^{21}$ 5638 5-8-7 **45**...... CCatlin 6 56
(MRChannon) *slowly away: in rr tl gd hdwy over 3f out: led 2f out: sn hdd: rallied and kpt on wl ins fnl f* **16/1**
0000 **3** *2½* **Brooklands Lodge (USA)**$^{25}$ 5549 3-8-7 **52**...... GGibbons 8 59
(MJAttwater) *in tch: hdwy over 5f out: ev ch 2f out: kpt on one pce fnl f* **50/1**
1020 **4** *2* **Diamond Orchid (IRE)**$^{20}$ 5456 4-8-9 **47**......(p) KFallon 1 54+
(PDEvans) *s.i.s: hdwy whn hmpd on ins 4f out: switched rt and hdwy on outside over 2f out: kpt on one pce fnl f* **5/4**$^{1}$
0604 **5** *8* **King Halling**$^{36}$ 5267 5-9-2 **54**......(p) VSlattery 2 46
(RFord) *led: rdn 4f out: hdd 2f out: wknd over 1f out* **14/1**
0640 **6** *6* **Coolfore Jade (IRE)**$^{7}$ 5928 4-8-4 **45**...... LPKeniry$^{(3)}$ 7 28
(NEBerry) *sn trckd ldr: rdn and wknd over 2f out* **14/1**
0400 **7** *¾* **Spes Bona (USA)**$^{18}$ 5715 3-8-9 **54**...... ACulhane 9 36
(WJHaggas) *hdwy to trck ldrs 7f out: rdn and wknd over 2f out* **9/2**$^{2}$
0610 **8** *½* **Defana**$^{12}$ 5843 3-8-5 **50** ow1...... SWKelly 12 31
(MDods) *hld up: effrt over 4f out: wknd wl over 2f out* **7/1**$^{3}$
0000 **9** *25* **Banners Flying (IRE)**$^{23}$ 5585 4-8-7 **45** oh5......(b$^{1}$) ANicholls 3 —
(DWChapman) *chsd ldrs tl rdn and wknd over 5f out* **50/1**
12-0 **10** *3½* **Queensberry**$^{38}$ 5221 5-8-12 **50**...... IMongan 4 —
(MrsLJMongan) *in tch tl rdn and lost pl 7f out: wl bhd over 4f out* **10/1**
00-0 **11** *9* **Damask Dancer (IRE)**$^{21}$ 5643 5-8-7 **45**......(b) RLMoore 11 —
(JASupple) *hld up in tch tl rdn and wknd wl over 3f out* **25/1**

2m 41.45s
**WFA** 3 from 4yo+ 7lb **11** Ran SP% **121.2**
Speed ratings: CSF £144.77 CT £6652.71 TOTE £8.30: £2.00, £4.20, £20.80; EX 72.70.Diamond Orchid was claimed by Tony Forbes for £6,000.
**Owner** Heart Of The South Racing **Bred** Michael Ng **Trained** West Ilsley, Berks

**FOCUS**
A bad race in which the first two, stablemates in Mick Channon's yard, came from off the pace.

**NOTEBOOK**
**Romeo's Day** followed up his win in banded company, despite drifting badly across the track when in front. In good heart at present, he was visored at Brighton and could need the headgear back on again.
**Lord Lahar**, left with a lot on his plate after a slow start, kept trying but was carried across the track by his stable companion. An inconsistent gelding, this was the first placing of his career.
**Brooklands Lodge(USA)**, minus the cheekpieces, was tackling the full twelve furlongs for the first time and appeared to stay well enough.
**Diamond Orchid(IRE)** was slow to leave the stalls and was then squeezed up on the first bend. She encountered further trouble in the back straight and although she stayed on once in line for home, the leaders were beyond recall. She is less than straightforward but things did not go her way on this occasion.
**King Halling**, tried in cheekpieces rather than blinkers, had no answers once headed.
**Coolfore Jade(IRE)** is a better filly on Fibresand.
**Spes Bona(USA)**, a keen sort, was taking a big step up in trip on this All-Weather bow and failed to stay.

## 6066 DINE IN STYLE H'CAP 5f 216y(P)
9:30 (9:31) (E3) (0-70,70) 3-Y-O+ £3,485 (£1,072; £536; £268) Stalls Low

Form RPR
0023 **1** **Silent Storm**$^{2}$ 6026 4-8-13 **67**...... CCatlin 5 78
(HJCyzer) *hld up in rr: rdn and hdwy on ins 2f out: str run fnl f to ld nr fin* **15/2**$^{3}$
0400 **2** *½* **Willhewiz**$^{24}$ 5564 4-8-13 **70**...... LPKeniry$^{(3)}$ 1 79
(RMStronge) *trckd ldr: rdn and led jst ins fnl f: r.o but hdd nr fin* **33/1**
0106 **3** *1¼* **Sewmuch Character**$^{26}$ 5512 5-9-0 **68**...... KFallon 13 73
(MBlanshard) *a in tch: rdn over 1f out to go 3rd ins fnl f: kpt on* **16/1**
5051 **4** *hd* **Mandarin Spirit (IRE)**$^{30}$ 5425 4-8-12 **66**......(b) OUrbina 10 71
(GCHChung) *mid-div: effrt 2f out: r.o ins fnl f: nvr nrr* **8/1**
1623 **5** *nk* **Larky's Lob**$^{86}$ 3864 5-8-5 **66** ow3...... JDO'Reilly$^{(7)}$ 7 70
(JO'Reilly) *led tl rdn and hdd jst ins fnl f: no ex* **14/1**
2052 **6** *shd* **Bob's Buzz**$^{2}$ 6026 4-9-2 **70**...... LDettori 2 73+
(SCWilliams) *outpcd in rr: swtchd rt over 1f out: r.o ins fnl f* **11/8**$^{1}$
4505 **7** *2* **Obe One**$^{16}$ 5754 4-8-11 **65**......(b$^{1}$) ACulhane 11 62
(ABerry) *hld up in rr: hdwy on outside over 2f out: wknd ins fnl f* **4/1**$^{2}$
1250 **8** *1* **Mr Pertemps**$^{36}$ 5261 6-8-9 **63**......(p) EAhern 3 57
(JJQuinn) *chsd ldrs on ins tl outpcd over 2f out* **14/1**
6000 **9** *¾* **Full Spate**$^{5}$ 6001 9-9-1 **69**...... RLMoore 4 61
(JMBradley) *s.i.s and outpcd in rr: effrt on outside over 2f out: nvr on terms* **16/1**
0001 **10** *1½* **Blueberry Rhyme**$^{23}$ 5579 5-8-11 **65**......(v) NCallan 8 53
(PABlockley) *chsd ldrs: rdn over 2f out: wknd qckly ent fnl f* **20/1**
0050 **11** *4* **Crewes Miss Isle**$^{50}$ 4923 3-8-10 **65**...... SWhitworth 12 41
(AGNewcombe) *racd wd: a in rr* **66/1**
-000 **12** *shd* **Phrenologist**$^{2}$ 6026 4-8-11 **65**......(b$^{1}$) ANicholls 6 40
(AndrewReid) *mid-div: rdn 1/2-way: wknd wl over 1f out* **66/1**
0544 **13** *2½* **Willheconquertoo**$^{2}$ 6026 4-9-1 **69**......(tp) GGibbons 9 37
(AndrewReid) *slowly away and a bhd* **20/1**

1m 15.36s
**WFA** 3 from 4yo+ 1lb **13** Ran SP% **125.5**
Speed ratings: CSF £249.46 CT £3940.65 TOTE £11.70: £2.50, £6.70, £4.00; EX 282.30 Place 6 £2,811.08, Place 5 £529.51.
**Owner** Mrs Charles Cyzer **Bred** Middle Park Stud Ltd **Trained** Newmarket, Suffolk

**FOCUS**
Quite a competitive race of its type and the form looks sound. The winner is progressive and was providing a boost to the race (6026) won by Blythe Spirit here two days earlier.

**NOTEBOOK**
**Silent Storm**, who ran well here two days earlier, had just one behind him turning in but a good run opened up on the rail and he snatched the race close home. He is relatively lightly raced and looks on the upgrade.
**Willhewiz**, without the visor, was always in the first two, but after striking the front he was just worn down.
**Sewmuch Character**, drawn widest of all, was having his first run on sand and this decent effort opens up new opportunities for him.
**Mandarin Spirit(IRE)** ran well, but needs a return to seven furlongs.
**Larky's Lob** ◆, 13lb higher than when scoring here in June, showed excellent pace but faded in the final furlong. Likely to be sharper for this first run for three months, he will be interesting dropped back to the minimum trip.
**Bob's Buzz**, who caught a tartar in Blythe Spirit here two days earlier, could never quite reach a challenging position and could need a return to seven furlongs.

**Obe One**, blinkered for the first time, was well supported for this All-Weather bow. He made progress down the centre of the track before the effort petered out in the final furlong.
T/Plt: £2,954.60 to a £1 stake. Pool: £48,367.00. 11.95 winning tickets. T/Qpdt: £372.80 to a £1 stake. Pool: £2,267.20. 4.50 winning tickets. JS

## $^{6042}$YORK (L-H)
### Saturday, October 9

**OFFICIAL GOING: Good**
After a dry night the going was still reckoned to be ' on the soft side of good and very chewed up on the bends'.
Wind: Moderate 1/2 behind. Weather: Overcast and cool.

### 6067 SYMPHONY GROUP MEDIAN AUCTION MAIDEN STKS (DIV I) — 7f 205y
**1:35** (1:36) (E3) 2-Y-O — **£5,346** (£1,645; £822; £411) **Stalls** Low

Form — RPR
4 **1** **Maidanni (USA)**$^{18}$ [5716] 2-9-0 ........ LDettori 3 82
(SaeedBinSuroor) *mde virtually all: drvn along over 3f out: hld on towards fin* **4/5$^{1}$**
**2** 1/2 **Aylmer Road (IRE)** 2-9-0 ........ KFallon 1 81
(PFICole) *rangy: chsd ldrs: wnt 2nd 2f out: styd on ins last* **6/1$^{2}$**
**3** 1 1/2 **Ticki Tori (IRE)** 2-8-9 ........ NCallan 11 73
(JulianPoulton) *lengthy: unf: hld up towards rr: hdwy over 3f out: styd on fnl f* **33/1**
00 **4** 2 **Selika (IRE)**$^{24}$ [5570] 2-9-0 ........(b$^{1}$) PRobinson 5 73
(MHTompkins) *s.i.s: t.k.h: sn trcking ldrs: kpt on same pce fnl 2f* **25/1**
00 **5** 1 3/4 **Indonesia**$^{26}$ [5522] 2-9-0 ........ KDarley 16 69
(MJohnston) *sn w wnr: chal 4f out: one pce fnl 2f* **28/1**
0 **6** 7 **Penny Wedding (IRE)**$^{18}$ [5716] 2-8-9 ........ WRyan 14 48
(JRFanshawe) *hdwy to chse ldrs 6f out: outpcd over 3f out: wknd over 1f out* **14/1**
**7** *nk* **Virgin's Tears** 2-8-9 ........ AMcCarthy 12 48
(PWChapple-Hyam) *rangy: unf: sn chsng ldrs: wknd over 1f out* **20/1**
**8** 1 3/4 **Woodford Consult** 2-8-6 ........ PMulrennan$^{(3)}$ 7 44
(MWEasterby) *lengthy: unf: rr-div: sme hdwy over 3f out: nvr a factor* **100/1**
0 **9** *hd* **Miss Bear (IRE)**$^{35}$ [5307] 2-8-9 ........ DMcGaffin 13 43
(BSmart) *trckd ldrs: t.k.h: lost pl 2f out* **40/1**
**10** *nk* **Naval Attache** 2-9-0 ........ TPQueally 10 48
(NPLittmoden) *wl grwn: rangy: mid-div: effrt over 3f out: sn btn* **40/1**
000 **11** 1 1/4 **Lightening Fire (IRE)**$^{35}$ [5302] 2-9-0 ........ TEDurcan 15 45
(TJEtherington) *bhd and sn drvn along: nvr on terms* **100/1**
0 **12** 1 1/2 **Sake (IRE)**$^{10}$ [5858] 2-9-0 ........ DaleGibson 8 41
(NTinkler) *chsd ldrs: lost pl 3f out* **100/1**
0004 **13** 3/4 **Our Kes (IRE)**$^{12}$ [5838] 2-8-9 65........ ACulhane 9 35
(PHowling) *a in rr* **7/1$^{3}$**
**14** 2 1/2 **Misters Sister** 2-8-9 ........ MFenton 2 29
(JGGiven) *rangy: scope: bkwd: s.i.s: sn drvn along and a bhd* **33/1**
**15** *nk* **Madame Fatale (IRE)** 2-8-9 ........ PHanagan 4 28
(JeddO'Keeffe) *unf: s.i.s: a bhd* **66/1**
0500 **16** *10* **Hamburg Springer (IRE)**$^{14}$ [5797] 2-9-0 45........ JQuinn 6 11
(MJPolglase) *mid-div: lost pl over 3f out: sn bhd* **100/1**

1m 41.75s (4.01) **Going Correction** +0.425s/f (Yiel) **16** Ran SP% **117.3**
Speed ratings: **96,95,94,92,90 83,82,81,81,80 79,77,77,74,74 64**CSF £4.26 TOTE £1.80: £1.10, £2.00, £9.50; EX 5.40.
**Owner** Godolphin **Bred** Petelain Stable **Trained** Newmarket, Suffolk

**FOCUS**
The pace was not strong and the form is probably just fair. The fourth and fifth were a bit too close for comfort, but the race has provisionally been rated positively. The winner should prove useful at least at three, and there were promising debuts from the second and third.

**NOTEBOOK**
**Maidanni(USA)**, quite a big type, had his own way in front but he still has something to learn and at the line there was nothing to spare. He should leave this form behind over middle distances at three.
**Aylmer Road(IRE)**, who stands over a fair amount of ground, was green to post. He went in pursuit of the winner and though in the end it was quite a close run thing, in truth he never looked like coming out on top.
**Ticki Tori(IRE)**, a May foal, has not yet grown to her frame. Happy to sit off the pace, she stayed on in good style late on and should do even better next year.
**Selika(IRE)**, keen in first-time blinkers, was left short of room on the home turn. He made his effort on the inner but never looked a threat.
**Indonesia**, who has a long stride, ran his best race yet on his third start and there should be better to come over further next year.
**Hamburg Springer(IRE)** *Official explanation: jockey said gelding ran very green around bend*

### 6068 NEWTON INVESTMENT MANAGEMENT ROCKINGHAM STKS (LISTED RACE) — 6f
**2:05** (2:07) (A1) 2-Y-O — **£16,250** (£5,000; £2,500; £1,250) **Stalls** Centre

Form — RPR
0314 **1** **Moth Ball**$^{7}$ [5947] 2-8-11 92........ DHolland 2 111
(JAOsborne) *wnt rt s: sn chsng ldr: hdwy 2f out: rdn to led 1f out edgd rt and styd on wl* **15/2**
0013 **2** 1 1/4 **Nufoos**$^{21}$ [5626] 2-8-6 98........ RHills 8 102
(MJohnston) *in tch: hdwy 2f out: rdn over 1f out: drvn: edgd lft and styd on wl fnl f* **6/1$^{3}$**
1 **3** 2 1/2 **Woodcote (IRE)**$^{47}$ [5003] 2-8-11 93........ LDettori 4 100
(CGCox) *hld up in tch: hdwy 2f out: rdn over 1f out: kpt on same pce ins last* **10/1**
11 **4** 1/2 **Joseph Henry**$^{162}$ [1751] 2-8-11 100........ KDarley 3 98
(MJohnston) *hmpd s: sn chsng ldrs: effrt 2f out: rdn and ev ch over 1f out: sn drvn and one pce* **9/1**
2111 **5** 1/2 **Yajbill (IRE)**$^{10}$ [5873] 2-8-11 95........(v) KFallon 10 97
(MRChannon) *keen: set str pce: rdn along 2f out: drvn and hdd 1f out: grad wknd* **11/4$^{1}$**
1123 **6** 5 **The Crooked Ring**$^{53}$ [4836] 2-8-11 94........ RWinston 9 82
(PDEvans) *s.i.s and bhd: hdwy 2f out: sn rdn and kpt on ins last: nrst fin* **25/1**
21 **7** 1 **Newsround**$^{22}$ [5609] 2-8-11 96........ PRobinson 5 79
(MAJarvis) *hld up in tch: effrt over 2f out: sn rdn: edgd lft and btn* **3/1$^{2}$**
1300 **8** 1 1/2 **Sentiero Rosso (USA)**$^{7}$ [5947] 2-8-11 96........ TEaves 1 74
(BEllison) *sn outpcd and a towards rr* **100/1**
1520 **9** 3 **Madame Topflight**$^{21}$ [5626] 2-8-6 93........ NMackay 6 60
(MrsGSRees) *a rr* **66/1**
1216 **10** 8 **Sundance (IRE)**$^{22}$ [5602] 2-8-11 97........ JQuinn 7 41
(HJCollingridge) *towards rr: effrt and sme hdwy 1/2-way: sn rdn and wknd* **25/1**
3504 **11** 2 1/2 **Next Time Around (IRE)**$^{22}$ [5602] 2-8-11 98........ MFenton 11 34
(MrsLStubbs) *wnt rt s: effrt and sme hdwy 1/2-way: sn rdn and wknd* **40/1**

1m 11.8s (-0.77) **Going Correction** 0.0s/f (Good) **11** Ran SP% **109.4**
Speed ratings: **105,103,100,99,98 92,90,88,84,74 70**CSF £46.01 TOTE £9.50: £3.00, £2.20, £2.20; EX 56.90.
**Owner** Mountgrange Stud **Bred** Stratford Place Stud **Trained** Upper Lambourn, Berks

**FOCUS**
A most competitive Listed race, run at a very strong pace in a faster time than the valuable sprint handicap, and the form is sure to stand up well. The winner gets better and better, the runner-up ran right up to her Ayr form, and the third and fourth showed improved form despite meeting their first defeats.

**NOTEBOOK**
**Moth Ball**, who looked very fit indeed, was as usual restless in the stalls. He kept tabs on the leader and in the end ran out a decisive winner, confirming his improved effort at Redcar was no flash in the pan. Having worked his way through the ranks, he now looks capable of winning at Group level.
**Nufoos**, placed in a Group 3 on her previous start, ran really well but simply met a colt just too good for her on the day.
**Woodcote(IRE)**, on the back of a debut maiden win six weeks earlier, is a really nice type. He ran out of his skin against much more experiencd rivals, but this will have blown a potentially favourable handicap mark out of the water.
**Joseph Henry**, off the track since winning his first two races in the spring and injured himself in the saddling boxes at Beverley in June, was noisy in the paddock. Rather marooned towards the middle, he was still roaring his head off after the race. The potential is there is only it can be channeled in the right direction. He is clearly not easy.
**Yajbill(IRE)**, very keen to post, set off like a bat out of hell and there was never a chance he would last it out. He might be interesting dropped to five furlongs.
**Newsround** looked good when dominating at Newbury, but that was not an option here. He was disappointing, but can leave the form behind next year.
**Madame Topflight** *Official explanation: jockey said filly was unsuited by good ground*

### 6069 DAVIS LANGDON H'CAP — 1m 208y
**2:35** (2:39) (D2) (0-85,84) 3-Y-O+ — **£12,148** (£3,738; £1,869; £934) **Stalls** Low

Form — RPR
2111 **1** **The Prince**$^{23}$ [5581] 10-8-13 **79**........ LDettori 7 97
(IanWilliams) *hld up in rr: hdwy over 3f out: led over 1f out: forged clr* **6/1$^{1}$**
0120 **2** 5 **Khanjar (USA)**$^{21}$ [5631] 4-8-7 **76**........ HayleyTurner$^{(3)}$ 12 84
(KRBurke) *chsd ldrs: led over 2f out tl over 1f out: kpt on same pce* **33/1**
1454 **3** *hd* **Freeloader (IRE)**$^{24}$ [5568] 4-8-12 **78**........ RHills 8 86
(JWHills) *bhd: hdwy on wd outside over 3f out: styd on same pce appr fnl f* **12/1**
0146 **4** 1/2 **Pagan Prince**$^{19}$ [5698] 7-8-11 **77**........ LisaJones 14 84
(JARToller) *mid-div: hdwy 4f out: edgd lft and one pce fnl f* **9/1$^{3}$**
1045 **5** *nk* **Rondelet (IRE)**$^{29}$ [5446] 3-8-10 **80**........ NCallan 16 86
(RMBeckett) *bhd: hdwy over 2f out: styd on wl fnl f* **33/1**
1203 **6** 1 3/4 **Anna Pallida**$^{23}$ [5590] 3-8-11 **81**........(v$^{1}$) MartinDwyer 3 84
(PWHarris) *dwlt: bhd: hdwy over 3f out: styd on fnl f* **11/1**
3261 **7** 1 1/4 **Goodbye Mr Bond**$^{36}$ [5265] 4-8-11 **77**........ DAllan 11 77
(EJAlston) *mid-div: hdwy to join ldrs over 2f out: kpt on same pce* **8/1$^{2}$**
4016 **8** 1 3/4 **Blonde Streak (USA)**$^{12}$ [5835] 4-8-12 **78**........ DHolland 13 75
(TDBarron) *w ldrs: led over 3f out tl over 2f out: one pce* **16/1**
1050 **9** *nk* **Danelor (IRE)**$^{30}$ [5423] 6-9-4 **84**........ PHanagan 18 80
(RAFahey) *trckd ldrs: one pce fnl 2f* **20/1**
1241 **10** 1 1/2 **Compton Drake**$^{17}$ [5739] 5-8-13 **79**........ EAhern 4 72
(GAButler) *trckd ldrs: rdn over 3f out: outpcd fnl 2f* **6/1$^{1}$**
21 **11** 1/2 **Cesare**$^{170}$ [1557] 3-8-10 **80**........ KDarley 2 72
(JRFanshawe) *trckd ldrs: upsides over 2f out: wknd over 1f out* **12/1**
3040 **12** 2 **Tedstale (USA)**$^{26}$ [5514] 6-8-11 **77**........(b) TEDurcan 1 65
(TDEasterby) *rr-div: rdn over 3f out: nvr a factor* **22/1**
3160 **13** *shd* **Best Before (IRE)**$^{47}$ [5004] 4-8-13 **79**........ KFallon 15 67
(PDEvans) *mid-div: sn drvn along: nvr on terms* **14/1**
5030 **14** 2 **Harry Potter (GER)**$^{21}$ [5627] 5-8-11 **77**........(v) DarrenWilliams 6 61
(KRBurke) *bhd: hdwy over 3f out: sn rdn and hung lft: nvr on terms* **33/1**
0220 **15** 1/2 **Ultimata**$^{46}$ [5025] 4-9-1 **81**........ WRyan 5 64
(JRFanshawe) *chsd ldrs: lost pl over 2f out* **25/1**
0401 **16** 1 **Huxley (IRE)**$^{25}$ [5544] 5-8-12 **78**........(t) RLMoore 10 59
(MGQuinlan) *a in rr* **10/1**
6050 **17** *nk* **Tony Tie**$^{12}$ [5835] 8-8-8 **77**........ TEaves$^{(3)}$ 17 57
(JSGoldie) *chsd ldrs: lost pl 3f out* **33/1**
-160 **18** 5 **Maganda (IRE)**$^{126}$ [2692] 3-8-10 **80**........ PRobinson 19 50
(MAJarvis) *dwlt: a in rr* **50/1**
1466 **19** 5 **Hills Of Gold**$^{21}$ [5631] 5-8-10 **76**........ DaleGibson 20 36
(MWEasterby) *mid-div: lost pl over 3f out* **33/1**
3310 **20** 9 **Threezedzz**$^{30}$ [5419] 6-9-1 **81**........(t) RWinston 9 23
(PDEvans) *restless in stalls: led tl over 3f out: lost pl and eased 2f out* **33/1**

1m 52.25s (2.29) **Going Correction** +0.425s/f (Yiel)
**WFA** 3 from 4yo+ 4lb **20** Ran SP% **127.6**
Speed ratings: **106,101,101,100,100 99,98,96,96,94 94,92,92,90,90 89,89,84,80,72**CSF £216.89 CT £2348.03 TOTE £5.90: £2.10, £7.90, £2.70, £2.80; EX 420.80 Trifecta £1156.30 Part won. Pool: £1,628.70. 0.10 winning units..
**Owner** Patrick Kelly **Bred** Bottisham Heath Stud **Trained** Portway, Warwicks

**FOCUS**
Probably just ordinary handicap form, but an emphatic win for The Prince on this switch from claiming company.

**NOTEBOOK**
**The Prince**, successful on six of his last seven starts in claiming company, was able to race off a mark 6lb lower than when last running in a handicap and ran out an emphatic winner. Unless turned out under a penalty, his immediate future would appear to lie in the hands of the handicapper, but he is rated just 80 on the All-Weather and would be hard to beat if that mark goes unchanged.
**Khanjar(USA)**, runner-up in claiming company just two starts previously, proved no match for the winner, but this was still a good effort and, lightly raced, he is the type to keep improving.
**Freeloader(IRE)** continues in good heart, but the winner was clear by the time he really got going. His winning record would suggest he is at his best on fast ground.
**Pagan Prince**, successful in this race last year off a 10lb lower mark, ran his race but looks high enough in the weights.
**Rondelet(IRE)** ran a solid race but may just be better over another furlong.
**Anna Pallida** seemed to take well enough to a first-time visor, but she shaped as though a return to ten furlongs would suit.
**Goodbye Mr Bond** was not quite at his best off a career-high mark, but is not one to write off just yet.

**Compton Drake**, beaten in a handicap off a mark of 72 two starts previously, had to race off a mark 7lb higher thanks to a win on Polytrack and was well held. *Official explanation: jockey said gelding was unsuited by good ground*

## 6070 FOUR HIGH PETERGATE HOTEL AND SAWFISH SOFTWARE STKS (H'CAP) 6f 217y

**3:05** (3:09) (D2) (0-85,89) 3-Y-0+ **£11,475** (£3,531; £1,765; £882) **Stalls** Low

Form RPR

0335 **1** **Marshman (IRE)**[21] 5631 5-8-12 **79** ... RHills 16 98
(MHTompkins) *hld up in rr: smooth hdwy over 2f out: rdn to ld over 1f out: sn clr* **14/1**

3560 **2** *5* **Cd Flyer (IRE)**[22] 5603 7-9-0 **84** ... PMulrennan(3) 9 90+
(BEllison) *hld up towards rr: hdwy over 2f out: nt clr run and swtchd lft over 1f out: sn rdn and styd wl towards fin* **20/1**

4112 **3** *shd* **Hartshead**[13] 5818 5-8-12 **79** ... KFallon 3 85
(GASwinbank) *in tch: hdwy 3f out: rdn to ld briefly over 1f out: sn drvn and one pce* **9/2**[1]

2264 **4** *hd* **Kingscross**[10] 5874 6-8-13 **80** ... DSweeney 17 88+
(MBlanshard) *hld up towards rr: hdwy over 2f out: rdn and styd on wl fnl f: nrst fin* **16/1**

0010 **5** *½* **Armagnac**[22] 5614 6-9-2 **83** ... ACulhane 5 87
(MABuckley) *in tch: effrt and hdwy 2f out: rdn and n.m.r over 1f out: drvn and one pce ent last* **20/1**

2010 **6** *1* **Harrison Point (USA)**[30] 5419 4-9-3 **84** ... AMcCarthy 12 85
(PWChapple-Hyam) *wnt lft s: midfield: hdwy 3f out: rdn along to chse ldrs 2f out: sn drvn and kpt on same pce appr last* **7/1**[2]

1500 **7** *1* **Soyuz (IRE)**[92] 3698 4-9-2 **83** ... PRobinson 10 82
(MAJarvis) *chsd ldrs: rdn along over 2f out: sn drvn and one pce* **25/1**

0363 **8** *1* **Johnston's Diamond (IRE)**[12] 5832 6-9-8 **89** ... KDarley 15 85
(EJAlston) *cl up: wd st: rdn along wl over 2f out: grad wknd* **25/1**

1620 **9** *¾* **Arctic Desert**[22] 5614 4-8-11 **78** ... MartinDwyer 1 72
(AMBalding) *keen: trckd ldrs: hdwy over 2f out: rdn and ev ch over 1f out: sn drvn and wknd ent last* **12/1**

3010 **10** *hd* **Presumptive (IRE)**[21] 5631 4-9-1 **82** ... LDettori 20 76
(RCharlton) *racd wd: bhd tl sme late hdwy* **9/1**[3]

0233 **11** *shd* **Watching**[21] 5631 7-9-2 **83** ... PHanagan 7 76
(RAFahey) *towards rr: pushed along 1/2-way: rdn over 2f out: nvr rch ldrs* **10/1**

0610 **12** *1* **Jath**[15] 5766 3-8-11 **80** ... NCallan 11 77+
(JulianPoulton) *s.i.s and bhd: hdwy 1/2-way: rdn to chse ldrs over 2f out: sn drvn and wknd* **25/1**

0000 **13** *½* **Grizedale (IRE)**[14] 5781 5-9-4 **85** ... (t) DHolland 18 74
(JAkehurst) *chsd ldrs: wd st: rdn along over 2f out and sn wknd* **25/1**

6303 **14** *hd* **Primo Way**[21] 5652 3-9-0 **83** ... MHills 13 72
(BWHills) *dwlt: a rr* **14/1**

0004 **15** *nk* **Master Robbie**[8] 5921 5-9-3 **84** ... SHitchcott 14 72
(MRChannon) *midfield: rdn along halfway: sn wknd* **10/1**

3015 **16** *shd* **Young Mr Grace (IRE)**[15] 5769 4-9-4 **85** ... DAllan 6 73
(TDEasterby) *chsd ldr: wd st: rdn over 2f out and grad wknd* **25/1**

0150 **17** *2* **King Harson**[21] 5631 5-9-4 **85** ... (v) TPQueally 4 68
(JDBethell) *led: rdn along over 2f out: sn drvn: hdd & wknd over 1f out* **50/1**

02B2 **18** *6* **Manaar (IRE)**[7] 5937 4-9-2 **83** ... (b[1]) EAhern 19 50
(JNoseda) *chsd ldrs: wd st: rdn long 3f out and sn wknd* **12/1**

1m 24.62s (1.31) **Going Correction** +0.425s/f (Yiel)
**WFA** 3 from 4yo+ 2lb **18** Ran SP% **124.2**
Speed ratings: **109,103,103,102,102 101,100,98,98,97 97,96,96,95,95 95,93,86**CSF £274.64 CT £1518.01 TOTE £19.50: £5.00, £6.00, £1.20, £3.50; EX 415.30 TRIFECTA Not won..
**Owner** J H Ellis **Bred** E Moloney **Trained** Newmarket, Suffolk

**FOCUS**

A strongly-run handicap which suited those held up for a late run. Fair form.

**NOTEBOOK**

**Marshman(IRE)**, 3lb lower than when last successful, had the race run to suit and burst back to form in style. Connections will surely be keen to turn him out under a penalty while he is in this form.

**Cd Flyer(IRE)** has never won over this far but he seemed to see the trip out alright. He goes well with some cut in the ground, had the race run to suit, and continues to hold his form.

**Hartshead** ran well considering he raced near the pace. The race was run at a strong pace, which suited those who came from behind, so this was a solid effort in the circumstances.

**Kingscross** was another suited by the way the race was run but he remains on a stiff mark.

**Armagnac** ran his usual solid race.

**Harrison Point(USA)** kept on without threatening the leaders. He looks a better horse on the sand.

**Johnston's Diamond(IRE)** was not sure to stay and racing up with the strong pace did not help him in that regard.

**Jath** *Official explanation: jockey said filly was denied a clear run*

**Grizedale(IRE)** *Official explanation: jockey said gelding hung left*

**Manaar(IRE)** *Official explanation: jockey said gelding was unsuited by good ground*

## 6071 CORAL SPRINT TROPHY (H'CAP) 6f

**3:40** (3:41) (C1) (0-100,100) 3-Y-0+ **£19,500** (£6,000; £3,000; £1,500) **Stalls** Centre

Form RPR

0013 **1** **Jonny Ebeneezer**[8] 5921 5-9-0 **96** ... (be) LDettori 14 106+
(DFlood) *hld up: hdwy and nt clr run over 1f out: swtchd rt: r.o wl to ld nr fin* **13/2**[2]

0220 **2** *½* **Talbot Avenue**[21] 5647 6-9-4 **100** ... KFallon 1 108
(MMullineaux) *racd far side: chsd ldr: led overall over 2f out: hdd nr fin* **16/1**

0026 **3** *½* **Fantasy Believer**[14] 5799 6-8-13 **98** ... THamilton(3) 3 105
(JJQuinn) *hld up in tch far side: effrt 2f out: kpt on wl ins last* **16/1**

0000 **4** *1 ¼* **Connect**[21] 5628 7-8-8 **90** ... (b) PRobinson 2 93
(MHTompkins) *racd far side: chsd ldrs: nt qckn fnl f* **66/1**

1004 **5** *1 ¼* **River Falcon**[14] 5787 4-8-5 **87** ... WSupple 16 86
(JSGoldie) *chsd ldrs: kpt on wl fnl f* **25/1**

0005 **6** *nk* **Bonus (IRE)**[18] 5712 4-8-11 **93** ... RLMoore 13 91
(WJHaggas) *chsd ldrs: kpt on same pce appr fnl f* **14/1**

0046 **7** *hd* **Danzig River (IRE)**[14] 5786 3-8-6 **89** ow1 ... MHills 9 87
(BWHills) *racd far side: bhd: hdwy 2f out: styd on wl ins last* **25/1**

0350 **8** *shd* **Tom Tun**[21] 5628 9-9-1 **97** ... (b) TLucas 12 94
(JBalding) *chsd ldrs: nt qckn fnl 2f* **25/1**

0001 **9** *¾* **Pic Up Sticks**[14] 5799 5-9-1 **97** ... ACulhane 19 92
(MRChannon) *hld up and bhd: hdwy 2f out: kpt on: nvr nr ldrs* **10/1**

0514 **10** *½* **Partners In Jazz (USA)**[14] 5786 3-8-5 **88** ... KDarley 5 81
(TDBarron) *led far side gp tl over 2f out: wknd over 1f out* **20/1**

2222 **11** *hd* **Compton's Eleven**[15] 5762 3-8-13 **96** ... SHitchcott 7 89
(MRChannon) *racd far side: chsd ldrs: wknd over 1f out* **12/1**

0014 **12** *1* **Mine Behind**[19] 5704 4-8-6 **88** ... MartinDwyer 11 83+
(JRBest) *chsd ldrs: drvn along over 2f out: one pce* **12/1**

2005 **13** *hd* **Valjarv (IRE)**[9] 5898 3-8-8 **91** ... DHolland 4 80
(NPLittmoden) *racd far side: sn outpcd and in rr* **25/1**

0020 **14** *nk* **Marsad (IRE)**[14] 5799 10-8-1 **86** ... FPFerris(3) 10 74
(JAkehurst) *rrd s: nvr on terms* **20/1**

1000 **15** *1* **Cardinal Venture (IRE)**[21] 5628 6-8-10 **92** ... NCallan 17 77
(KARyan) *led stands' side: wknd over 1f out* **22/1**

4005 **16** *2* **Philharmonic**[12] 5832 3-8-12 **95** ... PHanagan 6 74
(RAFahey) *trckd ldrs far side: lost pl over 1f out* **16/1**

0000 **17** *2 ½* **Pomfret Lad**[8] 5921 6-8-5 **87** ... JQuinn 15 59
(DNicholls) *sn in rr* **25/1**

0003 **18** *nk* **Smart Hostess**[14] 5799 5-8-10 **92** ... RWinston 8 63
(JJQuinn) *chsd ldrs: lost pl over 1f out* **8/1**[3]

0204 **19** *4* **Mutawaqed (IRE)**[21] 5628 6-8-6 **88** ... (t) EAhern 18 47
(MAMagnusson) *swtg: dwlt: hdwy stands' side rail 2f out: lost plcd and heavily eased ins last* **6/1**[1]

1000 **20** *1 ¾* **Zilch**[21] 5628 6-8-13 **95** ... RMullen 20 49
(MLWBell) *sn bhd: eased ins last* **20/1**

1m 11.92s (-0.65) **Going Correction** 0.0s/f (Good)
**WFA** 3 from 4yo+ 1lb **20** Ran SP% **126.9**
Speed ratings: **104,103,102,101,99 98,98,98,97,96 96,95,95,94,93 90,87,86,81,79**CSF £91.37 CT £1664.99 TOTE £6.10: £1.90, £3.20, £5.20, £16.60; EX 103.90 Trifecta £3527.10 Part won. Pool: £4,967.85. 0.80 winning units..
**Owner** Mrs Ruth M Serrell **Bred** John Purcell **Trained** Upper Lambourn, Berks

**FOCUS**

A competitive renewal of the Coral Sprint Trophy and a career-best effort from Jonny Ebeneezer, who overcame an apparent bias to those drawn low. The second, third and fourth home were all drawn in the bottom three stalls and raced far side. Decent form, held down slightly by the time which was not great.

**NOTEBOOK**

**Jonny Ebeneezer**, 7lb higher than when winning over five furlongs at Haydock, showed he is still improving with a career-best effort. Given a confident ride by Frankie Dettori, he had plenty to do inside the final two furlongs but responded well to pressure to get the better of those towards the far side. His trainer is keen to give him a long break off the back of this busy campaign and feels he could progress further next year and, on this evidence, he could well be Pattern class.

**Talbot Avenue**, dropped in grade, was 15lb higher than when last winning in July 2003 but ran a cracker, only just failing to hold off the improving winner.

**Fantasy Believer**, 3lb higher than when runner-up in the Ayr Gold Cup two starts previously, ran another good race and appears to still be improving.

**Connect** had never won over this trip on turf and has been running below his best recently, but this represented an encouraging return to form.

**River Falcon**, 8lb better off with today's winner for a four-length beating at Haydock on his previous start, can have no real excuses.

**Bonus(IRE)**, having just his second start for William Haggas, did not run badly and is one to keep on the right side of.

**Pic Up Sticks**, off a 4lb higher mark, did not run to the form he showed to win at Ripon on his previous start.

**Philharmonic** *Official explanation: jockey said gelding lost its action*

**Smart Hostess** was disappointing, even allowing for the ground not being as fast as she would have liked.

**Mutawaqed(IRE)**, in good heart in similar events recently, was a long way below form and may just have had enough for the time being. *Official explanation: trainer said gelding bled from nose*

## 6072 SYMPHONY GROUP MEDIAN AUCTION MAIDEN STKS (DIV II) 7f 205y

**4:15** (4:17) (C1) 2-Y-O **£5,323** (£1,638; £819; £409) **Stalls** Low

Form RPR

2303 **1** **Mister Genepi**[9] 5895 2-9-0 100 ... MartinDwyer 12 88+
(WRMuir) *hld up: smooth hdwy 3f out: chal 2f out and sn led: qcknd clr over 1f out* **8/13**[1]

6452 **2** *5* **William Tell (IRE)**[25] 5539 2-9-0 78 ... ACulhane 3 77
(MRChannon) *chsd ldrs: rdn along 3f out and sn outpcd: drvn and styd on again appr last: no ch w wnr* **7/1**[2]

0 **3** *1* **Mineral Star (IRE)**[18] 5718 2-9-0 ... PRobinson 10 75
(MHTompkins) *trckd ldrs: smooth hdwy 3f out: chal over 2f out and ev ch tl rdn and one pce over 1f out* **50/1**

06 **4** *2 ½* **Truckle**[35] 5302 2-9-0 ... KDarley 7 69
(MJohnston) *chsd ldr: rdn along over 3f out: drvn and one pce fnl 2f* **20/1**[3]

005 **5** *¾* **Katana**[17] 5735 2-8-9 62 ... TPQueally 5 62
(IAWood) *led: rdn along over 3f out: hdd 2f out and sn wknd* **40/1**

03 **6** *nk* **Orpendonna (IRE)**[11] 5846 2-8-9 ... NCallan 8 62
(KARyan) *trckd ldrs: hdwy over 3f out: rdn 2f out and sn one pce* **7/1**[2]

0 **7** *nk* **Royal Sailor (IRE)**[18] 5716 2-9-0 ... JTate 11 66
(JMPEustace) *in tch: rdn along over 3f out: no hdwy* **40/1**

03 **8** *1* **Moonfleet (IRE)**[7] 5925 2-8-9 ... SHitchcott 14 59
(MFHarris) *a rr* **50/1**

25 **9** *nk* **Alani (IRE)**[20] 5669 2-8-9 ... PHanagan 9 58
(JeddO'Keeffe) *chsd ldrs: rdn along over 3f out: sn wknd* **25/1**

**10** *hd* **Queen Nefitari** 2-8-9 ... DaleGibson 1 58
(MWEasterby) *leggy: unf: scope: a rr* **100/1**

0 **11** *5* **Nobbler**[30] 5407 2-9-0 ... MHills 6 51
(JWHills) *a rr* **20/1**[3]

B **12** *nk* **Baileys Honour**[16] 5752 2-8-9 ... RFrench 13 46
(MJohnston) *rangy: unf: a rr* **40/1**

0 **13** *2* **Mount Butler (IRE)**[119] 2898 2-9-0 ... MFenton 2 46+
(JGGiven) *a rr* **50/1**

**14** *2 ½* **Another Plan (IRE)** 2-9-0 ... RLMoore 16 41
(MGQuinlan) *lengthy: dwlt: a bhd* **25/1**

0 **15** *6* **Avizandum (IRE)**[25] 5542 2-9-0 ... TEDurcan 15 27
(TJEtherington) *dwlt: a bhd* **100/1**

1m 41.8s (4.06) **Going Correction** +0.425s/f (Yiel) **15** Ran SP% **119.3**
Speed ratings: **96,91,90,87,86 86,86,85,84,84 79,79,77,74,68**CSF £3.78 TOTE £1.70: £1.10, £1.60, £13.50; EX 4.90.
**Owner** Mike Caddy & Brian Moss **Bred** Whitsbury Manor Stud **Trained** Lambourn, Berks

**FOCUS**

No strength in depth here, and Mister Genepi did not need to be anywhere near his best to record an overdue first success.

**NOTEBOOK**

**Mister Genepi**, a bonny, active colt, looked to have been found a simple task to gain an overdue first win and he made it look easy. This will have done his confidence a power of good.

**William Tell(IRE)**, rated 78, stayed on to secure second spot but the winner, rated a stone and a half better than him, was in a different class.

**Mineral Star(IRE)** ran a lot better than on his debut, but after looking likely to extend the winner at one stage he was firmly put in his place. *Official explanation: jockey said colt ran too keen early on*

**Truckle**, whose three runs have been well spaced out, is the type to do better in handicap company next year.

**Katana**, rated just 62, took them along but once the dash for home began in earnest she was soon put in her place.

**Orpendonna(IRE)**, long in the back, raced down the stands' side in the home straight and did not reproduce her Nottingham running. She should come into her own next year.

## 6073 SHIRLEY HEIGHTS E B F MAIDEN STKS — 7f 205y

**4:45** (4:49) (D3) 2-Y-O — **£5,414** (£1,666; £833; £416) **Stalls** Low

Form — RPR

1 **Daring Ransom (USA)** 2-9-0 .......... EAhern 11 83+
(JNoseda) *leggy: unf: s.s: hdwy to trck ldrs over 5f out: styd on wl fnl 2f: led ins last: r.o wl* **25/1**

2 1 1/4 **Tarraman (USA)** 2-9-0 .......... KDarley 1 80+
(MJohnston) *leggy: scope: hdwy on ins to chse ldrs over 4f out: wnt 2nd over 3f out: ev ch whn rdn and wnt lft ins last: no ex* **7/2**[2]

2 3 1 **Noble Duty (USA)**[22] 5612 2-9-0 .......... LDettori 6 78
(SaeedBinSuroor) *led: qcknd over 3f out: hdd ins last: fdd* **8/13**[1]

4 4 **Blue Train (IRE)** 2-9-0 .......... KFallon 9 69+
(SirMichaelStoute) *tal: unf: in rr tl kpt on fnl 2f: nvr a threat* **6/1**[3]

5 hd **Perfect Tone (USA)** 2-8-9 .......... PHanagan 4 64
(MAMagnusson) *lenghy: unf: sn chsng ldrs: outpcd over 3f out: kpt on fnl 2f* **25/1**

0 6 5 **Palace Walk (FR)**[10] 5870 2-9-0 .......... MartinDwyer 12 57
(AMBalding) *swtchd lft after s: hld up in rr: effrt over 3f out: nvr on terms* **100/1**

06 7 hd **Tiamo**[28] 5467 2-9-0 .......... PRobinson 10 57
(MHTompkins) *chsd ldrs: outpcd over 3f out: sn btn* **50/1**

0 8 1 **Lillas Forest**[25] 5543 2-9-0 .......... GFaulkner 2 55
(PCHaslam) *chsd ldrs: wknd over 2f out* **100/1**

9 1 1/4 **Ellerslie Tom** 2-9-0 .......... JQuinn 7 52
(OBrennan) *rangy: unf: s.s: t.k.h in rr: wandered and lost pl 3f out* **66/1**

10 1 1/2 **Mahmjra** 2-9-0 .......... TEDurcan 8 49
(MRChannon) *wl grwn: chsd ldrs: drvn along 4f out: lost pl 3f out* **50/1**

000 11 2 1/2 **High Treason (USA)**[8] 5915 2-9-0 .......... ACulhane 3 43
(JGGiven) *a towards rr* **66/1**

1m 42.27s (4.53) **Going Correction** +0.425s/f (Yiel) — **11** Ran SP% **115.0**
Speed ratings: **94,92,91,87,87 82,82,81,80,78 76**CSF £106.21 TOTE £26.00: £3.60, £1.30, £1.10; EX 136.20.
**Owner** R Bates Newton **Bred** Vinery Llc And Westwood Thoroughbreds **Trained** Newmarket, Suffolk

**FOCUS**
An interesting maiden run at just a steady pace. The form is not outstanding by York standards, but it was a taking debut from the winner.

**NOTEBOOK**
**Daring Ransom(USA)**, very much on the leg, knew his job much better than the runner-up and in the end that proved decisive. He looks promising.
**Tarraman(USA)** ◆, on the leg, made his effort on the inner. Upsides inside the last he then basically threw it away going left-handed. He came here with quite a reputation and looks a bright prospect.
**Noble Duty(USA)**, a tall type, failed to confirm his Newbury promise. He had his own way in front but after quickening up the pace at the halfway mark was simply not good enough and was beaten by two newcomers.
**Blue Train(IRE)**, an April foal, is up in the air and was very noisy and green beforehand. He will have learnt a fair bit but will not be ready to do himself justice until next year.
**Perfect Tone(USA)**, a March foal, looks as though she still needs time but she did show some ability on her debut.

## 6074 COLDSTREAM GUARDS ASSOCIATION H'CAP — 1m 5f 197y

**5:20** (5:22) (D3) (0-70,70) 3-Y-O+ — **£5,432** (£1,671; £835; £417) **Stalls** Low

Form — RPR

1334 1 **Treason Trial**[36] 5274 3-7-13 **58** .......... NMackay(3) 11 69+
(MrsStefLiddiard) *hld up and bhd. smooth hdwy 4f out: shkn up over 1f out: styd on to ld last 50yds* **14/1**

4055 2 1/2 **Northern Nymph**[12] 5826 5-9-1 **62** .......... WSupple 3 72
(RHollinshead) *trckd ldrs: led over 3f out: hdd and no ex wl ins last* **16/1**

1334 3 3/4 **Hearthstead Dream**[24] 5560 3-8-13 **69** .......... TQuinn 6 78
(JDBethell) *chsd ldrs: chal over 1f out: nt qckn ins last* **10/1**[3]

3334 4 5 **Skye's Folly (USA)**[22] 5619 4-9-9 **70** .......... (b) MFenton 1 72
(JGGiven) *mid-div: hdwy 5f out: sn chsng ldrs: one pce fnl 2f* **10/1**[3]

-500 5 2 1/2 **Salamba**[64] 4512 3-8-10 **66** .......... PRobinson 12 65
(MHTompkins) *t.k.h in rr: hdwy on ins 4f out: edgd rt: kpt on: nvr rchd ldrs* **33/1**

0604 6 1 3/4 **Gargoyle Girl**[17] 5519 7-8-6 **56** .......... TEaves(3) 13 52
(JSGoldie) *mid-div: hdwy 4f out: styd on same pce fnl 2f* **20/1**

0042 7 3 **Isa'Af (IRE)**[9] 5889 5-9-1 **67** .......... PMakin(5) 8 59
(PWHiatt) *w ldrs: led over 7f out tl over 4f: wknd fnl 2f* **7/1**[2]

2115 8 1/2 **Inchnadamph**[77] 4155 4-9-1 **62** .......... (t) KFallon 14 53
(TJFitzgerald) *stdd s: hdwy 8f out: drvn along over 3f out: nvr nr ldrs* **5/2**[1]

2000 9 1 3/4 **Royal Distant (USA)**[24] 5560 3-8-4 **63** .......... PMulrennan(3) 5 52
(MWEasterby) *bhd: hdwy over 3f out: kpt on: nvr nrr* **25/1**

200 10 hd **Claradotnet**[12] 5826 4-8-12 **59** .......... TEDurcan 15 47
(MRChannon) *rr-div: kpt on fnl 3f: nvr on terms* **25/1**

0000 11 1 **Sovereign Dreamer (USA)**[21] 5635 4-9-7 **68** .......... (t) PHanagan 4 55
(PFICole) *bhd: sme hdwy on ins 4f out: nvr on terms* **40/1**

5633 12 3 **Welkino's Boy**[40] 5190 3-8-6 **62** .......... DaleGibson 20 45
(JMackie) *t.k.h: w ldrs: wknd over 2f out* **14/1**

1000 13 2 **It's Blue Chip**[59] 4630 3-8-3 **59** .......... (e) JFEgan 2 39
(PWD'Arcy) *mid-div: effrt 3f out: nvr on terms* **33/1**

4100 14 5 **Zan Lo (IRE)**[5] 5993 4-8-9 **56** oh7 .......... RFitzpatrick 16 29
(BSRothwell) *in tch: effrt over 3f out: sn btn* **50/1**

0230 15 7 **Pont Neuf (IRE)**[1] 6047 4-9-6 **67** .......... (t) NCallan 10 30
(PDEvans) *bhd: sme hdwy over 3f out: nvr a factor* **12/1**

0002 16 3 **Perfect Punch**[10] 5875 5-9-7 **68** .......... EAhern 7 27
(CFWall) *w ldrs: led over 4f out: hdd over 3f out: lost pl over 2f out* **11/1**

0430 17 11 **Distant Cousin**[7] 5951 7-8-9 **56** oh2 .......... (b[1]) ACulhane 17 —
(MABuckley) *in tch: jnd ldrs 6f out: lost pl over 3f out* **33/1**

0006 18 10 **Bold Blade**[21] 5634 3-8-0 **56** oh6 .......... JQuinn 18 —
(MJPolglase) *led tl over 7f out: lost pl 4f out: sn bhd* **66/1**

10-0 19 2 1/2 **Kaluana Court**[12] 5826 8-9-5 **66** .......... MartinDwyer 19 —
(RJPrice) *chsd ldrs: lost pl over 4f out: sn bhd* **16/1**

0000 20 dist **Dr Cool**[26] 5523 7-8-6 **56** oh4 .......... FPFerris(3) 9 —
(JAkehurst) *virtually ref to r: a wl t.o* **33/1**

3m 1.04s (4.64) **Going Correction** +0.425s/f (Yiel)
**WFA** 3 from 4yo+ 9lb — **20** Ran SP% **130.5**
Speed ratings: **103,102,102,99,98 97,95,95,94,93 93,91,90,87,83 81,75,69,68,—**CSF £210.28 CT £2374.63 TOTE £18.70: £3.70, £3.90, £2.50, £3.20; EX 361.40 Place 6 £172.85, Place 5 £134.81.
**Owner** Simon Mapletoft Racing I **Bred** A Pereira, Arnstein Stud **Trained** Great Shefford, Berks

**FOCUS**
A 0-70 handicap run at just a steady pace until once in line for home. The form looks sound enough but does not rate too highly despite the gap back to the fourth.

**NOTEBOOK**
**Treason Trial**, much improved in his new yard, travelled supremely well, and under a confident ride was always going to get there.
**Northern Nymph**, who has slipped to a career low-mark, did his level best to record his first win since his two-year-old days but in the end the winner was simply a fraction better.
**Hearthstead Dream**, with the blinkers again left off, ran right up to his best and this 'split' distance seemed ideal.
**Skye's Folly(USA)**, 2lb lower, still seems to be fighting a losing battle with the Handicapper.
**Salamba**, having his first run for two months, was never in the contest.
**Inchnadamph**, absent for eleven weeks, was off the bridle early in the straight and never looked like giving the champion a poignant success - he was apprenticed to Jimmy FitzGerald who died three days earlier.
**Perfect Punch** *Official explanation: jockey said gelding had no more to give*
**Distant Cousin** *Official explanation: jockey said gelding had no more to give*
**Dr Cool** *Official explanation: jockey said gelding refused to jump out of stalls*
T/Jkpt: Not won. T/Plt: £130.80 to a £1 stake. Pool: £115,651.95. 645.30 winning tickets. T/Qpdt: £27.60 to a £1 stake. Pool: £8,311.95. 222.75 winning tickets. WG

# 5976 LONGCHAMP (R-H)

Saturday, October 9

**OFFICIAL GOING: Soft**

## 6075a PRIX DU RANELAGH (LISTED) — 1m

**1:15** (1:15) 3-Y-O+ — **£15,845** (£6,338; £4,754; £3,169)

RPR

1 **Night Chapter**[21] 5668 3-8-11 .......... SPasquier 8 105
(MmeCHead-Maarek, France)

2 2 1/2 **Tiganello (GER)**[41] 5169 3-9-1 .......... OPeslier 7 104
(FHead, France)

3 1 1/2 **Advice**[60] 4623 3-9-1 .......... CSoumillon 3 101
(AFabre, France)

4 shd **Reine De Vati (FR)**[62] 5-8-11 .......... MCherel 6 94
(YDeNicolay, France)

5 1 1/2 **Excelsius (IRE)**[15] 5769 4-9-0 .......... (b) DBonilla 4 94
(JLDunlop) *raced in 2nd, pushed along straight, outpaced 1 1/2fout, no extra*

6 1 1/2 **Ballast (IRE)**[17] 3-8-11 .......... C-PLemaire 1 91
(MZilber, France)

7 5 **Activo (FR)**[69] 4384 3-8-11 .......... ABoschert 9 81
(PRau, Germany)

1m 38.6s
**WFA** 3 from 4yo+ 3lb — **7** Ran
Speed ratings:
**Owner** K Abdulla **Bred** Juddmonte Farms **Trained** France

**NOTEBOOK**
**Excelsius(IRE)** has had a disappointing season and, although he had conditions in his favour, he once again failed to deliver.

## 6076a PRIX DE LA FORET (GROUP 1) — 7f

**3:00** (3:01) 3-Y-O+ — **£80,479** (£32,197; £16,099; £8,042)

RPR

1 **Somnus**[35] 5289 4-9-2 .......... MJKinane 6 123
(TDEasterby) *hld up, 6th st, pushed along & hdwy in centre from 2f out, driven to chal over 1f out, led cl home, pushed out* **26/10**[1]

2 3/4 **Denebola (USA)**[34] 5332 3-8-11 .......... C-PLemaire 3 119
(PBary, France) *raced in 4th, 3rd straight, ran on from over 1 1/2f out, ridden and went 2nd inside final furlong, not pace of winner* **41/10**[3]

3 1 **Le Vie Dei Colori**[34] 5332 4-9-2 .......... CSoumillon 7 119
(LMCumani) *raced in 3rd, 5th and pushed along straight, stayed on steadily under pressure to retake 3rd from over 1f out* **64/10**

4 nk **Monsieur Bond (IRE)**[35] 5289 4-9-2 .......... (b) FLynch 1 118
(BSmart) *racd in 2nd, led halfway, shaken up and ran on str, 3l clr 1 1/2f out, ran on til hdd and no ex cl home* **165/10**

5 1 **Pastoral Pursuits**[30] 5414 3-9-0 .......... SDrowne 5 116
(HMorrison) *held up, 4th straight, never in contention* **41/10**[3]

6 3 **Nayyir**[14] 5782 6-9-2 .......... JFortune 2 108
(GAButler) *held up, last shaken up straight, never dangerous* **39/10**[2]

7 6 **Charming Groom (FR)**[62] 4595 5-9-2 .......... OPeslier 4 93
(FHead, France) *led to half-way, weakened from well over 1 1/2f out* **56/10**

1m 22.3s **Going Correction** +0.35s/f (Good)
**WFA** 3 from 4yo+ 2lb — **7** Ran SP% **121.8**
Speed ratings: **117,116,115,114,113 110,103.**
**Owner** Legard Sidebottom & Sykes **Bred** Lady Legard **Trained** Great Habton, N Yorks

**NOTEBOOK**
**Somnus**, given a very professional ride, just adored the cut in the ground. He was virtually last early on and then came with a beautifully timed late run up the centre of the track. He joined the leaders running into the final furlong and won with a bit in hand. When conditions are right he is a top-class gelding, and the four year old will now be rested until next season when he will have a similar sort of programme.
**Denebola(USA)**, given every possible chance, settled on the rail in third place and then moved up smoothly to lead at the furlong marker. She kept up the good work but had nothing in hand to hold off the winner, and the filly now runs in the Matriarch Stakes at Hollywood Park. She looks back to her very best.
**Le Vie Dei Colori**, in fifth position soon after the start, started his run with the winner but could not go with him as the race came to an end. He ran on gamely to hold third place, which was a good effort given that the colt was unsuited by the ground, which had become very testing by the time the race was run. There are no plans for the moment.
**Monsieur Bond(IRE)**, smartly into his stride, tried to lead from pillar to post. He built up a lead of several lengths at the two furlong marker but, although he battled gamely all the way to the line, he dropped out of the places.
**Pastoral Pursuits**, in fourth position at the entrance to the straight, quickened from a furlong and a half out and was then one-paced as the race drew to a close. There was little doubt that he was not at home on the testing ground.
**Nayyir**, not too lucky at the start, was sixth entering the straight and never made any further progress. The horse has had a fairly hard season and was probably feeling the effects of it, so this outing is probably best ignored.

# [5825]BATH (L-H)

Sunday, October 10

**OFFICIAL GOING: Good to soft (good in places)**

Wind: str bhd Weather: dry and bright

## 6077 107.9 BATH FM MAIDEN STKS (DIV I) 1m 5y

2:10 (2:15) (D3) 2-Y-O £3,965 (£1,220; £610; £305) Stalls Low

Form RPR

3 **1** **Mayadeen (IRE)**[57] 4747 2-9-0 RHills 4 68
(MPTregoning) *a.p: led approching fnl f: kpt up to work but styd on wl* **1/1**[1]

6U0 **2** 3/4 **Tranquilizer**[15] 5792 2-8-6 (t) HayleyTurner(3) 14 62
(DJCoakley) *a.p: styd on to chse wnr fnl f* **66/1**

**3** 1 1/4 **Skyscape** 2-8-9 MartinDwyer 8 59
(MrsAJPerrett) *a in tch: outpcd over 2f out: rdn over 1f out: styd on fnl f* **10/1**[3]

50 **4** nk **Napapijri (FR)**[15] 5789 2-8-9 DSweeney 9 58
(DPKeane) *trckd ldr: led over 2f out: rdn and hdd appr fnl f: one pce after* **100/1**

06 **5** shd **Cost Analysis (IRE)**[19] 5718 2-9-0 PRobinson 1 63
(MAJarvis) *led tl hdd over 2f out: rdn and one pce ent fnl f* **12/1**

**6** 1 **Key Of Solomon (IRE)** 2-9-0 (t) SDrowne 10 66+
(HMorrison) *mid-div: rdn over 2f out: kpt on one pce* **33/1**

000 **7** 3 1/2 **Volitio**[31] 5407 2-8-11 LPKeniry(3) 12 53
(SKirk) *in tch tl rdn and wknd over 1f out* **100/1**

50 **8** 2 **Loch Quest (IRE)**[18] 5729 2-9-0 IMongan 5 49
(MrsAJPerrett) *in tch: riddever 3f out: sn struggling in rr* **14/1**

0 **9** 1/2 **Legally Fast (USA)**[58] 4728 2-9-0 JFEgan 16 48
(PFICole) *a bhd* **66/1**

**10** 3 1/2 **Ancient Egypt** 2-9-0 FNorton 11 51+
(JHMGosden) *mid-div tl lost tch and bhd fnl 2f* **14/1**

**11** 1 3/4 **Alfred The Great (IRE)** 2-9-0 RFfrench 2 36
(MJohnston) *slowly away: a towards rr* **12/1**

00 **12** 28 **Reference (IRE)**[62] 4611 2-9-0 MHills 6 —
(RHannon) *a bhd: t.o fnl 3f* **100/1**

5 **U** **Court Ruler**[20] 5703 2-8-11 RThomas(3) 15 —
(RJPrice) *bhd whn uns rdr after 2f* **100/1**

1m 47.41s (6.41) **Going Correction** +0.40s/f (Good) 13 Ran SP% 116.9
Speed ratings: **83,82,81,80,80 79,76,74,73,70 68,40,**—CSF £76.10 TOTE £1.60: £1.10, £7.10, £1.80; EX 55.40.
**Owner** Hamdan Al Maktoum **Bred** Shadwell Estate Company Limited **Trained** Lambourn, Berks

**FOCUS**
A very slow time, 2.63 seconds slower than the second division, and weak maiden form as it stands. However there were still several interesting performances and the race is certain to produce winners.

**NOTEBOOK**
**Mayadeen(IRE)**, who made a highly promising debut when third at Newbury in a race that has worked out well - runner-up Titian Time subsequently went on to finish placed at Group One level - faced a much easier task here and with his stable having come back into a little bit of form in recent weeks, looked a strong favourite. Never far off the pace, he was driven into the lead around a furlong out and was never going to be pegged back. There is more to come from this colt and he deserves a step up in class.
**Tranquilizer** stepped up massively on previous form and very nearly caused a shock. She does little for the form, but she does not know that and is a filly going the right way.
**Skyscape**, whose stable have the occasional juvenile winner at the course, hit a flat spot just as the race began to heat up and could not get to the front pair in time. Sure to come on for the run, a faster surface is going to suit this daughter of Zafonic and she can win her maiden.
**Napapijri(FR)**, a most promising fifth behind Playful Act on her debut, did not confirm that initial promise when only eighth next time, but this was much more like it. She is now qualified for nurseries.
**Cost Analysis(IRE)** is gradually progressing and can be expected to make up into a fair handicapper next season.
**Key Of Solomon(IRE)** made a promising debut and this son of Machiavellian should come on for the experience.
**Volitio** is now eligible for nurseries and that will be more his bag.
**Loch Quest(IRE)** will make up into a fair middle-distance handicapper next season.
**Ancient Egypt** did not look fully wound up for this and appreciable improvement can be expected. *Official explanation: jockey said colt lost its action; vet said colt was struck into left hind cannon*
**Alfred The Great(IRE)** shaped like a typical backward Mark Johnston-trained two-year-old - being unable to go the early gallop after a sluggish start and not knowing enough to show his form. He will improve considerably for the run and will make a much better three-year-old.

## 6078 107.9 BATH FM MAIDEN STKS (DIV II) 1m 5y

2:45 (2:47) (D3) 2-Y-O £3,955 (£1,217; £608; £304) Stalls Low

Form RPR

02 **1** **Notability (IRE)**[25] 5570 2-9-0 PRobinson 11 80
(MAJarvis) *led tl over 6f out: styd trcking ldr tl drvn to ld wl over 1f out: pushed clr ins last: readily* **4/1**[3]

30 **2** 1 1/2 **Rain Stops Play (IRE)**[22] 5646 2-9-0 SHitchcott 6 77
(MRChannon) *led over 6f out: rdn 3f out: hdd wl over 1f out: kpt on but nt pce of wnr ins last* **16/1**

0 **3** 1 1/4 **Natalie Jane (IRE)**[12] 5846 2-8-9 JFortune 8 69+
(GAButler) *bhd: pushed along and hdwy over 4f out: rdn and styd on fnl 2f: nt pce to rch ldrs ins last* **20/1**

4 **4** 1 **Rightful Ruler**[27] 5508 2-9-0 MHills 16 72
(BWHills) *in tch: chsd ldrs 3f out: rdn 2f out: outpcd fnl f* **10/1**

3 **5** 3 **Alfie Noakes**[22] 5646 2-9-0 SDrowne 1 65+
(MrsAJPerrett) *s.i.s: sn rcvrd and in tch: rdn and outpcd over 2f out: n.d after* **9/4**[1]

000 **6** 2 **Montjeu Baby (IRE)**[31] 5406 2-8-9 RSmith 14 56
(RHannon) *chsd ldrs: rdn 3f out: wknd wl over 1f out* **100/1**

4 **7** 1 1/4 **Pittsburgh**[23] 5612 2-9-0 MartinDwyer 2 58
(AMBalding) *chsd ldrs: rdn 3f out: wknd fr 2f out* **7/2**[2]

5 **8** 3 1/2 **Shiny Thing (USA)**[20] 5694 2-8-9 DKinsella 15 46
(AKing) *in tch: rdn to chse ldrs 3f out: wknd qckly 2f out* **33/1**

30 **9** 2 **Red River Rock (IRE)**[23] 5620 2-8-11 JFMcDonald(3) 9 46
(CTinkler) *bhd most of way* **33/1**

00U **10** 1 1/2 **Sea Map**[63] 4579 2-9-0 JFEgan 3 43
(SKirk) *rdn over 3f out: a bhd* **50/1**

**11** nk **French Gold** 2-8-9 IMongan 12 37
(PFICole) *slowly away: bhd: rdn and styd on fnl 3f: nvr a danger* **50/1**

62 **12** 1 **Hawridge Star (IRE)**[26] 5534 2-8-11 LPKeniry(3) 4 40
(WSKittow) *in tch: rdn 3f out: sn wknd* **15/2**

**13** 6 **Tiger Dawn (IRE)** 2-9-0 (b[1]) RHills 5 27
(WJHaggas) *a in rr* **33/1**

6 **14** 14 **Silver Court**[20] 5703 2-8-11 RThomas(3) 10 —
(RJPrice) *chsd ldrs: wknd qckly 3f out* **100/1**

0 **15** 13 **Solar Falcon**[13] 5838 2-8-6 FPFerris(3) 7 —
(AGNewcombe) *in tch 3f: bhd fr 1/2-way* **100/1**

0 **16** dist **Speedy Spirit**[23] 5609 2-8-9 ADaly 13 —
(MSalaman) *sddle slipped: a bhd: t.o* **100/1**

1m 44.78s (3.78) **Going Correction** +0.40s/f (Good) 16 Ran SP% 121.2
Speed ratings: **97,95,94,93,90 88,87,83,81,80 79,78,72,58,45** —CSF £61.43 TOTE £6.00: £2.10, £3.70, £3.40; EX 98.90.
**Owner** Sheikh Mohammed **Bred** Darley **Trained** Newmarket, Suffolk

**FOCUS**
Only an ordinary time for the grade, despite being 2.63 seconds faster than the first division, but the race is still likely to work out well. It paid to race near the pace.

**NOTEBOOK**
**Notability(IRE)**showed improved form when second to the very highly regarded Home Affairs in a Yarmouth maiden most recently and, under a typically well-judged ride from Philip Robinson, went on at the right point and settled the matter quickly. This was a decent performance and he is worth chancing in a higher grade.
**Rain Stops Play(IRE)**, who made a promising debut on his debut in a decent Kempton conditions event, failed to confirm that promise last time, but this was much more like his form and he is now qualified for a handicap mark.
**Natalie Jane(IRE)**, who made a pleasing debut at Nottingham, showed the benefit of experience and, under a patient ride, stayed on well in the final quarter mile to take third. She is a winner waiting to happen.
**Rightful Ruler** is going to appreciate middle-distances next season and will need a stiffer test than this if he is to win as a juvenile.
**Alfie Noakes** failed to confirm Newbury form with the second and may appreciate better ground. He is worth another chance.
**Montjeu Baby(IRE)** is now qualified for a handicap mark and will do better in that sphere.
**Pittsburgh** was disappointing and may have been flattered by his debut run in a Newbury conditions event. He may do better at three.

## 6079 OVAL MOTOR GROUP CLAIMING STKS 5f 161y

3:20 (3:20) (F4) 3-Y-O £3,066 (£876; £438) Stalls Low

Form RPR

0300 **1** **Innstyle**[18] 5737 3-8-4 61 LisaJones 10 67
(JLSpearing) *s.i.s: hdwy over 2f out: rdn to ld appr fnl f: drvn out* **16/1**

1045 **2** 1 **La Vie Est Belle**[4] 6016 3-8-9 63 JFortune 19 69
(BRMillman) *slowly away: hdwy over 2f out: chal appr fnl f: kpt on but nt qckn* **11/2**[2]

0504 **3** 1 **Called Up**[13] 5844 3-8-7 65 DSweeney 4 64
(HCandy) *towards rr: rdn and hdwy over 1f out: r.o wl fnl f: nvr nrr* **20/1**

1350 **4** nk **Trick Cyclist**[30] 5440 3-9-3 71 MartinDwyer 14 73
(AMBalding) *trckd ldr: led 2f out: hrd rdn and hdd appr fnl f: nt qckn* **11/2**[2]

0665 **5** hd **Shielaligh**[44] 5101 3-8-8 66 (p) IMongan 5 63
(MissGayKelleway) *slowly away: rdn 1/2-way: swtchd lft appr fnl f: kpt on one pce* **12/1**

0000 **6** 3/4 **Desert Daisy (IRE)**[121] 2833 3-7-11 47 JFMcDonald(3) 9 54+
(IAWood) *bhd: hdwy whn short of room appr fnl f: kpt on one pce ins* **66/1**

1000 **7** nk **Miss Judgement (IRE)**[23] 5618 3-8-2 62 RFfrench 12 54
(WRMuir) *chsd ldrs: rdn 2f out: nt qckn appr fnl f* **14/1**

0105 **8** 3/4 **Red Sovereign**[10] 5893 3-8-10 81 RMullen 6 59
(IAWood) *in tch: rdn 2f out: no imp fnl f* **3/1**[1]

5260 **9** nk **Ever Cheerful**[4] 6016 3-8-4 66 (p) SHaddon(7) 17 59
(WGMTurner) *in rr: hung rt and c wd into st: effrt over 2f out: nvr nr to chal* **40/1**

0000 **10** 3 **Bella Tutrice (IRE)**[4] 6016 3-7-13 64 (p) FPFerris(3) 1 41
(IAWood) *prom: rdn 3f out: wknd 2f out* **25/1**

0500 **11** 1/2 **Iltravitore (IRE)**[18] 5737 3-8-4 57 JFEgan 11 41
(DRCElsworth) *s.i.s: sn mid-div: nvr nr to chal* **25/1**

0604 **12** 1 3/4 **Melody King**[20] 5702 3-8-6 55 ow1 (b) SDrowne 3 38
(PDEvans) *mid-div: outpcd fr 1/2-way* **8/1**[3]

0640 **13** 3/4 **Black Sabbeth**[39] 5219 3-8-5 59 RSmith 7 34
(PJMakin) *a towards rr* **50/1**

0 **14** 1 1/4 **Java Gold**[61] 4617 3-7-6 CHaddon(7) 13 24
(WGMTurner) *led tl rdn and hdd 2f out: wknd qckly* **100/1**

2000 **15** nk **He's A Rocket (IRE)**[18] 5736 3-8-6 52 (b) HayleyTurner(3) 16 33
(KRBurke) *prom on outside: rdn 3f out: wknd over 2f out* **16/1**

0246 **16** 9 **Arfinnit (IRE)**[43] 5117 3-8-10 55 (v) SHitchcott 8 6
(MRChannon) *s.i.s: sn rdn: a bhd* **12/1**

00 **17** nk **Master Rat**[25] 5564 3-8-9 DKinsella 15 4
(RJHodges) *outpcd and a bhd* **100/1**

1m 11.62s (0.48) **Going Correction** 0.0s/f (Good) 17 Ran SP% 121.0
Speed ratings: **96,94,93,92,92 91,91,90,89,85 85,82,81,80,79 67,67**CSF £94.36 TOTE £17.50: £4.40, £2.90, £4.10; EX 192.80.
**Owner** The Square Milers **Bred** Mrs H B Raw **Trained** Kinnersley, Worcs

**FOCUS**
A modest claimer won by Innstyle, who was getting off the mark at the 19th attempt. The form looks solid for the grade.

**NOTEBOOK**
**Innstyle**, still a maiden after 18 starts coming into the race, finally got off the mark and did not have to fight too hard to do so. This will do her confidence good but she is not one to bank on to repeat the effort.
**La Vie Est Belle** did herself no favours with a slow start and she would have been much closer had she got away on terms. She should continue to pay her way.
**Called Up** was doing his best work late and seemed well served by the drop into this grade.
**Trick Cyclist** was a little disappointing on this drop in grade and failed to run to his capabilities.
**Shielaligh** was another who was slowly away and she was never getting there in time. *Official explanation: jockey said filly clipped heels soon after start*
**Desert Daisy(IRE)**, who showed a good level of form as a two-year-old, has gone completely the wrong way this season but this was a much improved effort and if going on from this she can win in the grade.
**Red Sovereign**, fifth behind Nights Cross in Listed company last month, ran way below par on her first crack at claiming level and the only excuse can be the ground as her two wins have both come on a fast surface.
**Iltravitore(IRE)** *Official explanation: jockey said gelding was never travelling*
**Master Rat** *Official explanation: jockey said gelding hung right handed*

## 6080 GROSVENOR CASINOS NURSERY 5f 11y

3:55 (3:55) (E3) (0-75,72) 2-Y-O £4,930 (£1,517; £758; £379) Stalls Low

Form RPR

1003 **1** **Chilly Cracker**[15] 5797 2-8-13 64 DSweeney 13 71
(RHollinshead) *mde virtually all: rdn 2f out: kpt on strly fnl f* **12/1**

2022 **2** *1 1/2* **Starduster**[8] 5932 2-9-2 **67** .......... GBaker 16 69
(BRMillman) *chsd ldrs: wnt 2nd 3f out: rdn over 1f out: kpt on fnl f but no imp on wnr* **3/1[1]**

555 **3** *shd* **Auwitesweetheart**[26] 5536 2-9-3 **68** .......... SDrowne 18 70
(BRMillman) *bhd: hdwy over 2f out: styd on but hung bdly lft ins fnl f: fin wl to press for 2nd but nt rch wnr* **14/1**

6350 **4** *1 3/4* **Il Pranzo**[27] 5507 2-9-5 **70** .......... JFEgan 12 66
(SKirk) *in tch: drvn and hdwy to chse ldrs over 2f out: kpt on same pce appr fnl f* **7/1[3]**

2010 **5** *3/4* **Lucky Emerald (IRE)**[34] 5351 2-9-7 **72** ..........(t) SHitchcott 14 65
(BPalling) *bhd: gd hdwy fr 2f out: chsng ldrs whn hmpd ins last: nt revover* **25/1**

4240 **6** *2* **Majestical (IRE)**[13] 5839 2-8-5 **59** .......... LPKeniry(3) 6 45
(WRMuir) *chsd ldrs: rdn over 2f out: wknd appr fnl f* **11/1**

5000 **7** *1 1/2* **Cross My Shadow (IRE)**[16] 5767 2-7-13 **57** ..........(bt[1]) CHaddon(7) 11 38
(MFHarris) *chsd ldrs: rdn over 2f out: wknd over 1f out* **50/1**

3604 **8** *1/2* **Robmantra**[20] 5690 2-8-5 **59** ..........(p) DCorby(3) 10 38
(BJLlewellyn) *bhd and sn pushed along: kpt on fr over 1f out but nvr gng pce to rch ldrs* **16/1**

4200 **9** *1/2* **Agent Kensington**[22] 5648 2-9-2 **67** .......... JFortune 3 44
(RHannon) *in tch: rdn fr 1/2-way and nvr gng pce to trble ldrs* **10/1**

6533 **10** *1/2* **Concert Time**[65] 4516 2-7-9 **49** oh2 .......... HayleyTurner(3) 19 24
(CRDore) *chsd ldrs: rdn rdn 3f out: wknd over 1f out* **33/1**

0000 **11** *hd* **Before The Dawn**[36] 5281 2-7-13 **50** .......... DKinsella 9 25
(AGNewcombe) *chsd ldrs: rdn 1/2-way: wknd fr 2f out* **20/1**

4264 **12** *2* **Little Biscuit (IRE)**[85] 3924 2-8-9 **60** .......... RFfrench 4 28
(KRBurke) *s.i.s: sn rdn in mid-div: wknd qckly 2f out* **14/1**

5400 **13** *1* **Ruby's Dream**[13] 5839 2-8-13 **64** .......... PFitzsimons 1 28
(JMBradley) *chsd ldrs early: wknd 1/2-way* **33/1**

3600 **14** *hd* **Mister Bell**[27] 5509 2-8-0 **54** .......... JFMcDonald(3) 17 18
(JGMO'Shea) *aloly into stride: n.m.r fr 2f out: a bhd* **33/1**

4203 **15** *nk* **Knock Bridge (IRE)**[20] 5690 2-9-0 **65** .......... JDekeyser 8 27
(PDEvans) *s.i.s: a bhd* **6/1[2]**

5660 **16** *1 1/2* **Town End Tom**[38] 5240 2-8-7 **58** ..........(b[1]) MartinDwyer 7 15
(DMSimcock) *chsng ldrs whn n.m.r and stmbld after 1f: bhd fr 1/2-way* **33/1**

4064 **17** *1* **Waterline Lover**[48] 5005 2-8-1 **57** ..........(v[1]) NataliaGemelova(5) 20 11
(PDEvans) *racd wd: chsd ldrs to 1/2-way* **33/1**

0600 **18** *2* **Ms Polly Garter**[59] 4670 2-7-13 **49** oh4 ow4 .......... RThomas(3) 5 —
(JMBradley) *chsd ldrs to 1/2-way* **66/1**

0136 **19** *25* **Little Wizzy**[146] 2180 2-9-4 **72** .......... FPFerris(3) 15 —
(PDEvans) *bhd: sddled slipped: virtually p.u fnl 2f* **20/1**

62.76 secs (0.26) **Going Correction** 0.0s/f (Good) **19** Ran SP% **127.6**
Speed ratings: **97,94,94,91,90 87,84,84,83,82 82,78,77,77,76 74,72,69,29**CSF £43.97 CT £543.96 TOTE £17.20: £3.50, £1.90, £2.70, £2.30; EX 84.00.
**Owner** John L Marriott **Bred** Henry And Mrs Rosemary Moszkowicz **Trained** Upper Longdon, Staffs

**FOCUS**

A good performance that saw Chilly Cracker return to winning ways. Solid if unspectacular form from those in behind.

**NOTEBOOK**

**Chilly Cracker** came right back to form when third at a big price at Ripon and was able to build on that run with an all-the-way success. She will get further than this and should continue to pay her way.
**Starduster** has now finished second on the last three occasions and must be beginning to frustrate connections. She does not lack for want of trying and will get her turn eventually.
**Auwitesweetheart** would have been second but for hanging under pressure - she did so on her only other start here - and will be better off back on a more conventional track. She has a race in her. *Official explanation: jockey said filly hung badly left handed*
**Il Pranzo** has been struggling since moving into nurseries and, although this was a slightly better effort, needs to drop further in the weights before he is winning. *Official explanation: jockey said he was hampered shortly after start*
**Lucky Emerald(IRE)** was staying on when hampered in the final furlong and that ended her chance of reaching the frame.
**Majestical(IRE)** ran well for most of the way but ideally needs a drop in grade.
**Concert Time** *Official explanation: jockey said filly hung both ways*
**Town End Tom** *Official explanation: jockey said gelding ran too freely in first time blinkers*
**Little Wizzy** *Official explanation: jockey said saddle slipped*

## 6081 BET365 CALL 08000 322365 H'CAP 1m 5y

**4:30** (4:31) (E3) (0-70,70) 3-Y-O+ **£4,729** (£1,455; £727; £363) **Stalls** Low

Form RPR

4303 **1** **Parnassian**[26] 5540 4-9-1 **70** .......... RThomas(3) 13 81
(GBBalding) *s.i.s: hld up and sn pushed along: hdwy over 2f out: led appr fnl f: drvn out* **8/1**

5032 **2** *nk* **Welcome Signal**[33] 5370 4-9-1 **67** ..........(p) MHills 6 77
(JRFanshawe) *hld up: hdwy on outside 2f out: r.o to press wnr fnl f* **5/1[1]**

5401 **3** *2* **Tagula Blue (IRE)**[22] 5657 4-9-4 **70** ..........(t) DKinsella 8 76
(JAGlover) *v.s.a: hld up in rr: hdwy on outside over 2f out: r.o: nvr nrr* **6/1[2]**

0005 **4** *1 3/4* **Lockstock (IRE)**[13] 5841 6-9-1 **70** ..........(p) NMackay(3) 7 72
(MSSaunders) *a.p: led wl over 1f out: rdn and hdd appr fnl f: one pce after* **7/1[3]**

4050 **5** *2* **Nearly A Fool**[19] 5713 6-9-1 **67** ..........(v) NPollard 2 65
(GGMargarson) *mid-div: hrd rdn over 1f out: kpt on: n.d* **28/1**

650 **6** *nk* **J R Stevenson (USA)**[77] 4164 8-9-3 **69** .......... IMongan 1 66
(MWigham) *hld up in mid-div: rdn over 2f out: no hdwy appr fnl f* **12/1**

3010 **7** *1 1/2* **Danifah (IRE)**[18] 5737 3-8-11 **69** .......... FPFerris(3) 4 63
(PDEvans) *led tl hdd wl over 1f out: no ex after* **16/1**

323 **8** *1* **Premier Rouge**[20] 5693 3-8-12 **67** .......... PRobinson 15 59
(EFVaughan) *trckd ldr to over 2f out: wknd appr fnl f* **10/1**

0126 **9** *nk* **Smoothly Does It**[6] 5998 3-9-0 **69** .......... JFEgan 5 61
(MrsAJBowlby) *towards rr: rdn over 2f out: nvr on terms* **8/1**

0064 **10** *1/2* **Lakota Brave**[26] 5540 10-9-3 **69** .......... SDrowne 11 60
(MrsStefLiddiard) *mid-div: rdn over 2f out: sn btn* **25/1**

5100 **11** *1* **Dark Raider (IRE)**[74] 4230 3-8-12 **70** .......... DCorby(3) 16 58
(APJones) *orininet: chsd ldr over 3f out tl over 3f out: wknd wl over 1f out* **50/1**

5010 **12** *1* **Del Mar Sunset**[173] 1522 5-8-13 **65** .......... RHills 10 51
(WJHaggas) *towards rr: rdn over 2f out: nvr on terms* **14/1**

6020 **13** *5* **Travelling Band (IRE)**[24] 5581 6-9-1 **70** ..........(b[1]) LPKeniry(3) 9 46
(AMBalding) *in rr: rdn over 2f out: nvr on terms* **16/1**

640 **14** *3 1/2* **Priors Dale**[38] 5252 4-8-13 **65** ..........(t) MartinDwyer 12 34
(KBell) *a in rr* **40/1**

0443 **15** *4* **Hunter's Valley**[4] 6015 3-8-10 **65** .......... JFortune 3 25
(RHannon) *prom tl rdn over 3f out: sn wknd* **20/1**

4430 **16** *2 1/2* **Fen Gypsy**[35] 5317 6-8-13 **70** .......... NataliaGemelova(5) 14 25
(PDEvans) *mid-div tl wknd over 2f out* **20/1**

1m 42.7s (1.70) **Going Correction** +0.40s/f (Good)
**WFA** 3 from 4yo+ 3lb **16** Ran SP% **122.1**
Speed ratings: **107,106,104,102,100 100,99,98,97,97 96,95,90,86,82 80**CSF £43.55 CT £276.06 TOTE £9.40: £2.50, £1.90, £1.80, £3.10; EX 42.90.
**Owner** Miss B Swire **Bred** Miss B Swire **Trained** Kimpton,Hants

**FOCUS**

A good finish to this fair handicap that saw Parnassian record his fourth win of the campaign. The form looks sound.

**NOTEBOOK**

**Parnassian** has had a profitable season and was recording his fourth win of the year. Ideally served by this sort of ground, he came with a strong run in the final furlong and a half and was always just holding Welcome Signal. He was racing off a 14lb higher mark than his first win back May and will go up again, but seems to be improving enough to keep on defying the rise.
**Welcome Signal**could not quite get there in time and remains a maiden after 13 starts. He is in good spirits at present though and it is only a matter of time before he wins a race of this nature.
**Tagula Blue(IRE)**, a horse full of ability, has more than his fare share of temperamental problems and displayed them again in being reluctant to leave the stalls. He finished well having been held up, but lost his race at the start and remains one to be wary of.
**Lockstock(IRE)** ran his race but is still 5lb higher than when last winning and needs a drop in the weights.
**Nearly A Fool** was keeping on towards the finish and is only 2lb higher than when last winning, so is probably worth keeping an eye on.
**Smoothly Does It** made some modest late headway but was never in the race.

## 6082 COAST SPAS MAIDEN STKS 1m 2f 46y

**5:05** (5:05) (D3) 3-Y-O+ **£3,688** (£1,135; £567; £283) **Stalls** Low

Form RPR

**1** **Marias Magic**[126] 2709 3-8-7 .......... MartinDwyer 10 73+
(JohnMOxx, Ire) *led 1f: styd trcking ldrs: led ins fnl 2f: pushed along and hld on wl fnl f* **5/2[1]**

3550 **2** *1 1/2* **Safirah**[16] 5768 3-8-7 69 .......... PRobinson 7 70
(MAJarvis) *in tch: chsd ldrs 3f out: rdn over 2f out: swtchd lft and styd on u.p fnl f: no imp on wnr* **9/2[3]**

**3** *hd* **Swift Sailor** 3-8-12 .......... RFfrench 2 75+
(MJohnston) *sn w ldrs: chal fr over 6f out tl slt ld 4f out: sn rdn: 3f out: hdd ins fnl 2f: one pce ins last* **16/1**

0 **4** *1 3/4* **Dovedale**[16] 5770 4-8-12 .......... VSlattery 9 66
(MrsMaryHambro) *in ouch: hdwy to chse ldrs 5f out: rdn and styd on to dispute 2nd 2f out: outpcd ins last* **80/1**

022 **5** *1 1/2* **Star Magnitude (USA)**[145] 2195 3-8-12 75 .......... JFortune 15 69
(JHMGosden) *sn chsng ldrs: rdn 3f out: wknd fnl f* **9/2[3]**

0 **6** *2 1/2* **Rambo Blue**[11] 5867 4-9-3 .......... DSweeney 12 64
(AWCarroll) *hld up in rr: kpt on steadily fnl 2f: nt trble ldrs* **100/1**

6 **7** *1/2* **Jonanaud**[9] 5913 5-9-0 .......... FPFerris(3) 13 63
(HJManners) *sn in tch: hrd drvn over 3f out: styd on u.p fr over 1f out: nvr gng pce to rch ldrs* **16/1**

2233 **8** *1* **News Sky (USA)**[8] 5936 3-8-12 75 ..........(p) MHills 6 62
(BWHills) *sn chsng ldrs: rdn 3f out: wknd fr 2f out* **4/1[2]**

000 **9** *1* **Mrs Philip**[6] 5999 5-8-12 .......... SDrowne 19 55
(PJHobbs) *bhd: rdn over 3f out: kpt on fnl 2f but nvr a danger* **66/1**

**10** *2* **Isleofhopeantears (IRE)**[68] 4428 5-9-3 .......... DKinsella 16 56
(AEJones) *slowly away: bhd: hdwy to chse ldrs over 3f out:wknd qckly over 2f out* **50/1**

0 **11** *1 1/4* **Alghaazy (IRE)**[16] 5770 3-8-9 .......... NMackay(3) 3 54+
(LMCumani) *chsd ldrs tl wknd over 2f out* **20/1**

0000 **12** *1 1/4* **Gentle Raindrop (IRE)**[51] 4916 3-8-7 58 .......... JFEgan 5 47
(SKirk) *bhd most of way* **40/1**

**13** *3* **Woolstone Boy (USA)** 3-8-12 .......... GBaker 17 46
(JJay) *s.i.s: a in rr* **50/1**

3-4 **14** *5* **Tyup Pompey (IRE)**[28] 5495 3-8-9 .......... LPKeniry(3) 4 37
(DRCElsworth) *led after 1f: hdd 4f out: styd pressing ldrs: wknd qckly 2f out* **20/1**

0043 **15** *hd* **Princess Bankes**[17] 5751 3-8-7 45 .......... IMongan 11 32
(MissGayKelleway) *sn in tch: chsd ldrs 6f out: wknd u.p 3f out* **40/1**

00 **16** *3/4* **Favourable**[13] 5828 3-8-7 .......... RHills 18 31
(AWCarroll) *s.i.s: a in rr* **100/1**

-006 **17** *3/4* **Bijou Dancer**[122] 2813 4-9-0 46 .......... HayleyTurner(3) 1 34
(MRBosley) *in tch tl wknd 3f out* **50/1**

0-00 **18** *shd* **Deewaar (IRE)**[81] 2537 4-9-3 45 .......... PFitzsimons 14 34
(JCFox) *s.i.s: a in rr* **80/1**

2m 13.27s (2.27) **Going Correction** +0.40s/f (Good)
**WFA** 3 from 4yo+ 5lb **18** Ran SP% **122.9**
Speed ratings: **106,104,104,103,102 100,99,98,98,96 95,94,92,88,87 87,86,86**CSF £12.10 TOTE £3.20: £1.70, £2.20, £3.50; EX 23.70.
**Owner** Newsells Park Stud **Bred** Newsells Park Stud Limited **Trained** Currabeg, Co Kildare

**FOCUS**

A pretty uncompetitive maiden producing muddling form which should not be taken literally, but there were a couple of promising performances for the future.

**NOTEBOOK**

**Marias Magic**, a rare runner at one of the lesser British tracks for John Oxx, is a big, scopey filly and had relatively little trouble dealing with some ordinary maidens. She will stay further and should progress again, so can probably do well in handicaps back in Ireland.
**Safirah**, well held on her handicap debut at Haydock - in heavy ground - ran much better back on this better surface and was doing her best work late. She can win back in handicaps, possibly at a mile and a half.
**Swift Sailor ◆**, a half-brother to useful staying handicapper Stunning Force, made a highly pleasing debut, staying on well all the way to the line having been passed, and he will relish an additional couple of furlongs.
**Dovedale** improved on her debut effort and although not doing a great deal for the form, can be expected to improve further and is the type to do well in handicaps.
**Star Magnitude(USA)**, having his first start since May, ran a long way below form and appeared not to stay the distance.
**News Sky(USA)** is going the wrong way and cheekpieces did little for him.
**Isleofhopeantears(IRE)** *Official explanation: jockey said gelding was unsettled in the stalls and lost ground at start*
**Bijou Dancer** *Official explanation: trainer said gelding was struck into*

## 6083 BIFFA WASTE SERVICES H'CAP 1m 3f 144y

**5:40** (5:40) (E3) (0-70,74) 3-Y-O+ **£4,568** (£1,405; £702; £351) **Stalls** Low

Form RPR

3211 **1** **Dont Call Me Derek**[3] 6025 3-9-11 **74** 6ex .......... MartinDwyer 18 84+
(SCWilliams) *trckd ldrs: led wl over 2f out: pushed out fnl f: comf* **5/4[1]**

1030 **2** *1* **Mount Benger**[24] 5584 4-9-2 **61** ..........(v[1]) FPFerris(3) 15 69
(RMBeckett) *hld up: gd hdwy on outside to chse wnr ins fnl f* **33/1**

3040 **3** *nk* **Carriacou**[45] 5057 3-8-12 **61** .......... JFEgan 16 69
(PWD'Arcy) *hld up: hdwy on ouside 3f out: rdn and styd on wl fnl fnl f* **25/1**

3064 **4** *nk* **Critical Stage (IRE)**[11] 5869 5-8-12 **61** .......... MHalford(7) 7 68
(JDFrost) *in tch: chsd wnr over 1f out tl nt qckn ins fnl f* **20/1**

203 **5** *2* **Miss Inkha**[16] 5773 3-8-10 **62** .......... NMackay(3) 11 66
(RGuest) *hld up: rdn 2f out: styd on: nvr nrr* **22/1**

0045 **6** *hd* **Gold Guest**[35] 5320 5-9-6 **62** .......... JDekeyser 6 66
(PDEvans) *mid-div: rdn 2f out: nt pce to chal after* **33/1**

1403 **7** *1* **Milk And Sultana**[8] 5956 4-9-4 **60** .......... ADaly 3 62
(GAHam) *mid-div: rdn 2f out: nvr nr to chal* **14/1**

6335 **8** *1* **Champion Lion (IRE)**[12] 5853 5-9-11 **67** .......... SHitchcott 1 68
(MRChannon) *in tch: hrd rdn 2f out: wknd appr fnl f* **5/1**[2]

/0-0 **9** *1 1/2* **Chivite (IRE)**[15] 2787 5-9-8 **67** .......... RThomas(3) 17 66
(PJHobbs) *in tch: rdn over 3f out: wknd over 1f out* **22/1**

0046 **10** *nk* **Onward To Glory (USA)**[16] 5773 4-9-7 **63** .......... SDrowne 4 61
(JLDunlop) *prom tl rdn and wknd over 1f out* **28/1**

6000 **11** *3* **Zaffeu**[26] 5549 3-8-11 **60** .......... VSlattery 13 54
(NPLittmoden) *in tch tl rdn and wknd 2f out* **25/1**

4000 **12** *nk* **Gallant Boy (IRE)**[4] 6013 5-9-7 **63** .......... (vt) IMongan 10 56
(PDEvans) *in tch: rdn 3f out: sn btn* **25/1**

3566 **13** *1 1/4* **Mustang Ali (IRE)**[31] 5410 3-8-11 **63** .......... LPKeniry(3) 9 54
(SKirk) *mid-div tl rdn and wknd 3f out* **16/1**

0010 **14** *9* **Swift Alchemist**[33] 5374 4-9-0 **56** .......... (p) GBaker 8 34
(MrsHSweeting) *s.i.s: a bhd* **33/1**

0506 **15** *3 1/2* **Competitor**[11] 5869 3-9-0 **63** .......... DSweeney 2 36
(JAkehurst) *a in rr* **50/1**

2043 **16** *nk* **Theatre Tinka (IRE)**[10] 5546 5-9-0 **56** .......... (p) RFfrench 20 28
(RHollinshead) *led tl hdd wl over 2f out: wknd qckly* **14/1**

0000 **17** *1 3/4* **Billy Bathwick (IRE)**[4] 6013 7-9-1 **57** .......... PFitzsimons 19 26
(JMBradley) *prom tl rdn and wknd 3f out* **33/1**

0000 **18** *15* **Western (IRE)**[11] 5875 4-9-0 **56** .......... (p) NPollard 5 3
(JAkehurst) *prom: rdn over 3f out: sn btn* **50/1**

0061 **19** *5* **Polish Spirit**[42] 5153 9-9-7 **63** .......... JFortune 12 2
(BRMillman) *prom on outside tl wknd 5f out* **6/1**[3]

2m 34.69s (4.39) **Going Correction** +0.40s/f (Good)
**WFA** 3 from 4yo+ 7lb **19** Ran SP% **138.7**
Speed ratings: **101,100,100,99,98 98,97,97,96,95 93,93,92,86,84 84,83,73,69**CSF £67.46 CT £874.28 TOTE £2.40: £1.30, £5.00, £7.90, £3.50; EX 119.30 Place 6 £131.91, Place 5 £94.30.
**Owner** The Chummy Northerners **Bred** Whitsbury Manor Stud **Trained** Newmarket, Suffolk

**FOCUS**
Another smooth success for the well-in Dont Call Me Derek, who is red hot at present. The form of those behind is solid.

**NOTEBOOK**
**Dont Call Me Derek** has been in cracking form of late and had little trouble defying his 6lb penalty. Always going well, he came through to take it up over quarter of a mile out and merely had to be pushed out to score cosily. He was racing off a 16lb higher mark here than when first winning five runs back and will go up again, although is improving enough to defy a further rise.
**Mount Benger** has struggled a bit since winning at Haydock in July, but this was a much better effort and he is only 1lb higher than when last winning.
**Carriacou** finished well to claim third, but remains winless in 16 starts and can not be relied upon to repeat the effort.
**Critical Stage(IRE)** is currently 16lb higher than when last successful on turf and generally performs better on the Fibresand at Southwell.
**Miss Inkha** was keeping on without posing a major threat and has a similar race in her.
**Champion Lion(IRE)** is without a win in over two years and has never been the most consistent.
**Competitor** *Official explanation: jockey said colt had a breathing problem*
**Polish Spirit** ran too bad to be true and deserves a chance to show this running to be all wrong. *Official explanation: jockey said gelding lost its action; vet said gelding was lame*
T/Plt: £252.00 to a £1 stake. Pool: £42,290.35. 122.50 winning tickets. T/Qpdt: £35.70 to a £1 stake. Pool: £3,356.20. 69.50 winning tickets. JS

## 5885 GOODWOOD (R-H)
### Sunday, October 10

**OFFICIAL GOING: Good to soft**

## 6084 UCELLO II AND UBU III TROPHY STKS (H'CAP) (FOR NATIONAL HUNT JOCKEYS) 2m
**2:00** (2:02) (E3) (0-70,78) 3-Y-O+ **£3,513** (£1,081; £540; £270) **Stalls** High

Form RPR

2000 **1** **San Hernando**[11] 5875 4-11-9 **65** .......... RYoung 3 75
(DRCElsworth) *hld up: prog to ld over 10f out: mde rest: rdn and hrd pressed 1f out: kpt on wl* **11/1**

P526 **2** *1 1/2* **Madiba**[5] 6005 5-10-12 **54** .......... MAFitzgerald 10 62
(PHowling) *hld up midfield: stdy prog over 3f out: chsd wnr 2f out: plld out to chal 1f out: fnd nil* **16/1**

5040 **3** *shd* **Rossall Point**[41] 5205 3-10-8 **61** .......... TScudamore 9 69
(JLDunlop) *b: hld up wl in rr: prog over 2f out: drvn and r.o to chse ldng pair ent fnl f: one pce* **16/1**

0640 **4** *5* **Snow's Ride**[11] 5875 4-11-2 **58** .......... JMMaguire 8 60
(WRMuir) *lw: trckd ldrs: pushed along over 3f out: effrt over 2f out: wknd jst over 1f out* **11/1**

0321 **5** *2 1/2* **Irish Blade (IRE)**[11] 5875 3-11-11 **78** .......... RJohnson 4 77
(HCandy) *b.hind: prom: chsd wnr over 4f out to 2f out: wknd* **2/1**[1]

-301 **6** *3/4* **Tommy Carson**[15] 4603 9-10-11 **53** oh13 .......... SCurran 16 51
(JamiePoulton) *led at slow pce to over 10f out: outpcd over 4f out: one pce after* **33/1**

6600 **7** *6* **Moon Emperor**[37] 5274 7-11-11 **67** .......... RHughes 15 58
(JRJenkins) *hld up rr: sme prog over 3f out: no imp 2f out: wknd* **11/1**

2335 **8** *3* **Sungio**[172] 1547 6-10-11 **53** oh8 .......... CStudd 12 40
(BGPowell) *racd midfield: rdn and struggling 3f out: n.d after* **33/1**

4520 **9** *shd* **Heart Springs**[34] 5354 4-10-11 **53** oh8 .......... AThornton 2 40
(DrJRJNaylor) *dwlt: hld up wl in rr: effrt on inner over 3f out: no imp over 2f out: wknd over 1f out* **50/1**

0030 **10** *1 1/2* **Redspin (IRE)**[29] 5456 4-11-3 **59** .......... SDurack 14 44
(JSMoore) *prom: chsd wnr over 6f out: to over 4f out: wknd fr 3f out* **14/1**

2620 **11** *2 1/2* **Pipssalio (SPA)**[122] 2816 7-10-11 **53** oh8 .......... (t) MBatchelor 6 35
(JamiePoulton) *b: a in rr: last and struggling 6f out: no ch after* **33/1**

0500 **12** *2* **Sun Hill**[16] 5773 4-11-9 **65** .......... CLlewellyn 13 45
(MBlanshard) *chsd ldr to over 10f out: lost pl and struggling over 5f out: sn no ch* **10/1**[3]

0204 **13** *1 1/4* **Henry Island (IRE)**[13] 5826 11-10-13 **55** .......... LFletcher 7 34
(MrsAJBowlby) *swtg: hld up midfield: rdn and struggling over 4f out: wknd* **9/1**[2]

50-0 **14** *1 1/4* **Kaparolo (USA)**[155] 1958 5-11-10 **66** .......... JCrowley 11 43
(MrsAJPerrett) *lw: prom tl wknd rapidly over 3f out* **14/1**

60-2 **15** *7* **Mister Putt (USA)**[160] 1520 6-11-4 **60** .......... (b) LAspell 1 29
(MrsNSmith) *hld up: a in rr: last and wkng over 3f out* **20/1**

3m 42.33s (11.67) **Going Correction** +0.55s/f (Yiel)
**WFA** 3 from 4yo+ 11lb **15** Ran SP% **124.0**
Speed ratings: **92,91,91,88,87 87,84,82,82,81 80,79,78,78,74**CSF £161.66 CT £2796.31 TOTE £13.60: £3.80, £5.30, £6.00; EX 151.20.
**Owner** The Madding Crowd **Bred** The National Stud Owner Breeders Club Ltd **Trained** Whitsbury, Hants

**FOCUS**
A moderate handicap confined to National Hunt jockeys that was run at a very steady early gallop. The first three came clear but the form is unlikely to work out too well.

**NOTEBOOK**
**San Hernando** took the race by the scruff of the neck just before halfway and proved game when the challengers emerged in the straight to score his first win of the current campaign. He has been very frustrating to follow this year, and is far from certain to follow up on this, but he is talented on his day and a spell over hurdles this winter could bring about improvement. *Official explanation: trainer said, regarding the improved form shown, gelding is inconsistent and the race was run to suit today*
**Madiba** held every chance, but looked none too willing to go past the winner late on. This was an improvement on his previous effort just five days previously, but he is fiendishly hard to win with and his proximity at the death sums up the form.
**Rossall Point** made good headway from well off the pace two out, but he could not quicken when it mattered and will get closer to a first success when eased slightly in trip.
**Snow's Ride** had his chance, but failed to find a change of gear under pressure. Although he has plummeted in the weights on the turf this season, he shows little sign of capitalising, and connections will be hoping a return to the sand brings about some improvement.
**Irish Blade(IRE)** , an impressive winner at Salisbury 11 days previously, was totally found out by his 9lb rise in the weights.

## 6085 ROYAL NAVY CLAIMING STKS 1m 3f
**2:35** (2:35) (E3) 3-Y-O **£6,841** (£2,105; £1,052; £526) **Stalls** Low

Form RPR

423 **1** **St Barchan (IRE)**[42] 5146 3-9-3 72 .......... TQuinn 7 72+
(WJarvis) *trckd ldr 2f: restrained into 3rd: wnt 2nd again 3f out and gng easily: delayed effrt tl led last 150yds: pushed out* **5/1**[3]

5544 **2** *1 1/2* **Zuma (IRE)**[39] 5217 3-9-5 72 .......... RHughes 5 72
(RHannon) *hld up rr: prog 3f out: chsd ldng pair and rdn 2f out: styd on to take 2nd nr fin* **10/1**

4043 **3** *1/2* **Maria Bonita (IRE)**[26] 5549 3-8-12 60 .......... SWhitworth 3 64+
(MrsStefLiddiard) *hld up last: nt clr run 3f out: prog 2f out: styd on fnl f: tk 3rd on line* **12/1**

0035 **4** *shd* **Keepers Knight (IRE)**[58] 4711 3-8-9 62 .......... NDeSouza(5) 9 66
(PFICole) *hld up: prog over 3f out: swtchd lft and rdn over 1f out: styd on same pce* **20/1**

6001 **5** *nk* **Soviet Sceptre (IRE)**[13] 5843 3-8-7 66 .......... RMiles(3) 2 62
(MissDMountain) *trckd ldr after 2f: led over 4f out and kicked on: hrd rdn fnl 2f: hdd and btn last 150yds* **9/2**[2]

0456 **6** *3* **Pangloss (IRE)**[26] 5538 3-9-0 60 .......... (b) RLMoore 4 61
(GLMoore) *hld up midfield: rdn over 3f out: hanging rt and no imp fnl 2f* **7/1**

2401 **7** *5* **Fizzy Lady**[11] 5863 3-8-4 52 .......... CCatlin 6 43
(NEBerry) *b.hind: trckd ldrs: rdn 4f out: wknd wl over 1f out* **10/1**

0033 **8** *5* **Polar Dancer**[10] 5891 3-9-0 63 .......... WSupple 8 45
(MrsAJPerrett) *trckd ldrs: rdn wl over 3f out: wkng and no ch whn squeezed out over 1f out* **6/1**

24-3 **9** *18* **Kabis Booie (IRE)**[33] 5371 3-8-9 70 .......... WRyan 1 11
(HRACecil) *lw: led to over 4f out: sn drvn: wknd rapidly fnl 2f: t.o* **4/1**[1]

2m 32.16s (6.05) **Going Correction** +0.55s/f (Yiel) **9** Ran SP% **112.3**
Speed ratings: **100,98,98,98,98 96,92,88,75**CSF £51.76 TOTE £5.60: £2.00, £2.40, £3.90; EX 51.90.The winner was claimed by John O'Shea for £18,000
**Owner** The Phantom House Partnership **Bred** Tom Darcy And Vincent McCarthy **Trained** Newmarket, Suffolk
■ Stewards Enquiry : S Whitworth caution: careless riding

**FOCUS**
Fair form for the class, even though it featured largely disappointing three-year-olds.

**NOTEBOOK**
**St Barchan(IRE)** , who had hit the frame in three maidens previously, won with authority on this drop in class. This step up in trip suited, and he should have more to offer, but it has to be considered disappointing that he was dropped to this level in order to score on only his fourth outing.
**Zuma(IRE)** was again doing all of his best work too late in the day. He is a very tricky ride and remains a maiden after ten outings, but could find a race if kept to this lowly level.
**Maria Bonita(IRE)** stayed on well inside the final furlong and would have been closer but for meeting trouble three out. She is running out of excuses, but this is clearly her level and she could find a weaker race.
**Keepers Knight(IRE)** again failed to find much off the bridle and has badly gone the wrong way this season.
**Soviet Sceptre(IRE)** failed to quicken over this longer trip and on this softer ground. He ran well enough in the circumstances and can do better when reverting in trip.
**Kabis Booie(IRE)** ran well below par and failed to stay this trip under a positive ride. He looks one to avoid on this evidence.

## 6086 GORDON'S OF YIEWSLEY STKS (H'CAP) 1m
**3:10** (3:11) (C2) (0-85,82) 3-Y-O **£6,743** (£2,075; £1,037; £518) **Stalls** High

Form RPR

0403 **1** **Lord Links (IRE)**[8] 5934 3-8-11 **77** .......... RLMoore 8 84
(RHannon) *chsd ldr: rdn to ld over 2f out: hrd pressed over 1f out: drvn and hld on wl* **3/1**[2]

3034 **2** *nk* **Master Theo (USA)**[4] 6017 3-8-7 **73** .......... TQuinn 7 79
(HJCollingridge) *trckd ldrs: pressed wnr over 2f out: upsides fnl f: fnd little and hld nr fin* **12/1**

5400 **3** *2* **Cartronageeraghlad (IRE)**[42] 5151 3-8-8 **74** .......... (b) DaneO'Neill 9 76
(JAOsborne) *t.k.h: trckd ldrs: effrt over 2f out: chsd ldng pair over 1f out: no imp* **20/1**

0560 **4** *1/2* **Mrs Pankhurst**[25] 5566 3-8-3 **69** .......... JQuinn 4 70
(BWHills) *t.k.h: hld up in rr: nt clr run 2f out: plld out over 1f out: r.o fnl f: nvr nrr* **12/1**

0405 **5** *1 1/4* **Tranquil Sky**[14] 5818 3-9-0 **80** .......... WSupple 2 78
(NACallaghan) *hld up in last pair: rdn over 2f out: styd on fr over 1f out: nvr able to chal* **13/2**[3]

0 **6** *nk* **Lady's View (USA)**[25] 5572 3-9-2 **82** .......... TEDurcan 6 80
(DJDaly) *s.i.s: hld up midfield: effrt over 2f out: no imp ldrs over 1f out: fdd* **25/1**

4046 **7** *hd* **Enford Princess**[10] 5886 3-9-0 **80** .......... RHughes 5 77
(RHannon) *trckd ldrs: rdn and effrt over 2f out: no imp over 1f out: fdd* **8/1**

2234 **8** 1 ½ **Border Music**[16] 5766 3-8-11 **80** ...................................... NChalmers(3) 1 74
(AMBalding) *lw: racd wd: towards rr: effrt over 2f out: nt qckn over 1f out: wknd fnl f* **5/2**[1]

6000 **9** 3 ½ **Freak Occurence (IRE)**[22] 5652 3-8-8 **74** ................................ RHavlin 3 61
(MissECLavelle) *hld up in rr: effrt and pushed along whn hmpd 2f out: no ch after* **12/1**

2535 **10** 1 ½ **Fleet Anchor**[20] 5693 3-8-2 **68** oh13 ...................................... CCatlin 10 52
(JMBradley) *a in rr: rdn and struggling over 3f out* **50/1**

0000 **11** 25 **Overdrawn (IRE)**[16] 5766 3-8-9 **75** ...................................(b) SWKelly 11 6
(JAOsborne) *dwlt: pushed up to ld and rn freely: clr 5f out: hdd over 2f out: wkng whn hmpd sn after: t.o* **20/1**

1m 40.97s (0.70) **Going Correction** +0.225s/f (Good) **11** Ran SP% **116.4**
Speed ratings: **105,104,102,102,100 100,100,98,95,93 68**CSF £36.12 CT £615.22 TOTE £3.90: £1.50, £2.60, £4.30; EX 49.40 Trifecta £1029.00 Pool £14,783.82, 10.20 w/u.
**Owner** Coriolan Links Partnership VI **Bred** Thomas Doherty **Trained** East Everleigh, Wilts

**FOCUS**
Not a strong handicap, but it was competitive and was run at a sound pace. The form looks sound enough for the grade.

**NOTEBOOK**
**Lord Links(IRE)** , who hinted at a return to form off this mark at Epsom last time, produced a tenacious display to score all-out. He handled this ground and could go in again, providing the handicapper does not overreact to this first success since his debut in 2003.
**Master Theo(USA)** had every chance, but could not pass the winner, try as he might. This was another solid display, and he was clear of the rest, so deserves to find a race in which to get off the mark.
**Cartronageeraghlad(IRE)** , well beaten in a claimer latest, posted a much-improved effort. He is still a touch high in the weights, but a repeat of this effort could see him find a race this season.
**Mrs Pankhurst** , despite running freely and meeting trouble in the straight, ran on well enough when in the clear and turned in a more encouraging effort. She could build on this.
**Border Music** , whose recent placed efforts gave him every chance in this, failed to get competitive from his wide draw and can do better. He is in danger of becoming frustrating, however.
**Overdrawn(IRE)** *Official explanation: jockey said gelding ran too free early on*

## 6087 EUROPEAN BREEDERS FUND RACING UK ON SKY 432 FILLIES' STKS (H'CAP) 1m 4f
**3:45** (3:46) (C1) (0-100,94) 3-Y-0+ **£13,279** (£4,086; £2,043; £1,021) **Stalls** Low

Form RPR

-150 **1** **Nuzooa (USA)**[32] 5401 3-9-3 **90** ................................................ WSupple 3 100
(MPTregoning) *hld up: rdn to chse ldr over 2f out: led over 1f out: edgd lft but kpt on u.p* **6/1**

1203 **2** 3 ½ **Sand And Stars (IRE)**[32] 5402 3-8-9 **82** ............................... JMackay 1 87
(MHTompkins) *rn in snatches: lost pl and rdn 5f out: kpt on u.p to take 2nd ins fnl f* **2/1**[1]

1156 **3** ½ **Light Wind**[15] 5788 3-8-13 **86** ............................................... RLMoore 6 90
(MrsAJPerrett) *lw: led for 4f: lost pl 1/2-way: effrt to chse ldr 4f out to over 2f out: one pce u.p* **7/2**[3]

3142 **4** 2 ½ **Blaze Of Colour**[37] 5273 3-8-5 **78** ......................................(v) JQuinn 7 78
(SirMichaelStoute) *t.k.h: led after 4f: 3l clr and gng easily 3f out: drvn and hdd over 1f out: wknd* **3/1**[2]

3630 **5** 5 **Carini**[47] 5025 3-9-7 **94** ................................................ DaneO'Neill 2 87
(HCandy) *dwlt: in tch: rdn and struggling over 4f out: no ch fnl 2f* **11/1**

4606 **6** dist **Quickstyx**[5] 6006 3-7-7 **73** oh8 ..............................................(v[1]) TDean(7) 4 —
(MRChannon) *free to post: plld hrd: chsd ldr 7f out to 4f out: wknd rapidly: t.o* **20/1**

2m 42.88s (3.95) **Going Correction** +0.55s/f (Yiel) **6** Ran SP% **107.9**
Speed ratings: **108,105,105,103,100** —CSF £17.01 TOTE £6.60: £2.80, £1.70; EX 18.90.
**Owner** Hamdan Al Maktoum **Bred** Shadwell Farm Llc **Trained** Lambourn, Berks

**FOCUS**
A decent fillies' handicap run at a solid pace.

**NOTEBOOK**
**Nuzooa(USA)** , with the blinkers left off this time, responded gamely to pressure from two out and ran on strongly to win going away in the end. She is tricky, but her stable has not been firing as normal this season and she could have more to offer if her paddocks career is delayed.
**Sand And Stars(IRE)** turned in yet another sound effort, but was firmly put in her place by the winner. She can win off this mark and may be worth another chance over further on decent ground.
**Light Wind** had her chance, but could not quicken with the principals. This now looks to be her best trip and she can improve again when reverting to a faster surface.
**Blaze Of Colour** looked to be travelling best of all turning for home, but not for the first time found less than looked likely under pressure, and folded tamely when headed. She can do better when consenting to settle, but looks exposed.

## 6088 AUTUMN EXTENDED MAIDEN STKS 1m 6f
**4:20** (4:22) (D3) 3-Y-0 **£3,474** (£1,069; £534; £267) **Stalls** High

Form RPR

3206 **1** **Turnstile**[36] 5300 3-9-0 73 ............................................. RLMoore 7 80
(RHannon) *lw: hld up midfield: prog 4f out: led over 2f out: sn jnd: battled on wl fnl f: jst hld on* **3/1**[2]

043 **2** shd **Niobe's Way**[59] 4693 3-8-9 66 ................................................ WRyan 6 75
(PRChamings) *hld up last pair: stdy prog fr 4f out: jnd wnr 2f out: upsides after: jst pipped nr fin* **14/1**

-333 **3** 9 **Market Leader**[31] 5409 3-8-9 67 ........................................ DaneO'Neill 4 63
(MrsAJPerrett) *trckd ldrs: cl up over 2f out: sn fnd little u.p and btn: tk 3rd nr fin* **9/1**

342 **4** nk **Tashreefat (IRE)**[34] 5339 3-8-9 68 ......................................(t) WSupple 2 63
(EFVaughan) *lw: prom: led over 3f out to over 2f out: sn hrd rdn and btn: wknd fnl f* **8/1**

0-3 **5** ½ **Day One**[64] 4554 3-9-0 ....................................................... TQuinn 5 67
(GWragg) *racd midfield: rdn over 4f out: cose enough 3f out: wknd 2f out* **9/4**[1]

04 **6** ¾ **Helm (IRE)**[9] 5913 3-9-0 ....................................................... PDoe 12 66
(RRowe) *hld up rr: rdn and outpcd over 4f out: plodded on fnl 2f* **33/1**

0 **7** 8 **Fender**[11] 5867 3-9-0 ...............................................(b) RHughes 11 56
(HRACecil) *t.k.h: prom: led over 4f out to over 3f out: sn wknd* **14/1**

44 **8** 4 **All Blue (IRE)**[11] 5867 3-9-0 ..........................................(t) TEDurcan 13 51
(SaeedBinSuroor) *trckd ldrs: cl enough whn nt clr run 3f out: sn rdn and wknd* **7/1**[3]

4000 **9** ¾ **Verasi**[9] 5913 3-9-0 60 .............................................(b) SWKelly 9 50
(GLMoore) *a in rr: drvn bef 1/2-way: struggling over 4f out* **66/1**

035 **10** 3 ½ **Ruggtah**[9] 5913 3-8-9 65 ................................................ CCatlin 10 40
(MRChannon) *chsd ldrs: rdn over 4f out: sn wknd* **16/1**

05 **11** dist **Silken John (IRE)**[26] 5538 3-8-11 ........................................ RMiles(3) 3 —
(JGPortman) *led: clr after 4f: hdd over 4f out: wknd rapidly: t.o* **50/1**

3m 7.66s (3.91) **Going Correction** +0.55s/f (Yiel) **11** Ran SP% **115.0**
Speed ratings: **110,109,104,104,104 103,99,97,96,94** —CSF £43.08 TOTE £4.70: £2.00, £2.60, £2.50; EX 52.50.
**Owner** The Queen **Bred** The Queen **Trained** East Everleigh, Wilts

**FOCUS**
Average maiden form, but the first two came well clear, and it was a decent winning time for the type of race given the conditions.

**NOTEBOOK**
**Turnstile** gamely held on close home to register his first success at the ninth time of asking. This was his best effort to date and, although the form is nothing special, this versatile individual could progress again now he seems to have found an optimum trip.
**Niobe's Way ◆** , who had progressed in each of her previous three outings this year, again improved for this much longer trip and went down fighting. Her pedigree suggests she will be best suited by a real stamina test, and this effort proves that point, so a reproduction of this form should see her land a similar race. Her current rating also looks there to be expoited in handicaps but she faces a rise for this.
**Market Leader**, with the blinkers left off, was again found wanting for pace when it mattered and ran up to her recent form. She is the benchmark for this form, but will most likely struggle to win in this grade on the Flat.
**Tashreefat(IRE)**, racing with a tongue tie for the first time, dropped away tamely having been handy from the off and failed to improve over this longer distance on this easier ground. She may be capable of better, but could be going the wrong way, unless a switch to handicaps can bring about improvement. *Official explanation: jockey said filly had a breathing problem*
**Day One**, who did not look 100% fit in the paddock, ran well below the form of his recent form with the winner over this longer trip. It's fair to say he failed to stay this far and he is now eligible for handicaps, so is not one to write off when reverting to shorter in that sphere. *Official explanation: jockey said colt was never travelling*
**All Blue(IRE)**, taking a big step up in trip, can be rated slightly better than the bare form, but again looked one-paced and connections will be praying that a switch to handicaps musters some improvement.

## 6089 COCKED HAT MAIDEN STKS 6f
**4:55** (4:58) (D3) 3-Y-0+ **£3,454** (£1,063; £531; £265) **Stalls** Low

Form RPR

0340 **1** **Dr Synn**[6] 6001 3-9-0 66 ................................................ MTebbutt 6 76
(JAkehurst) *lw: cl up: led over 2f out: drvn and hrd pressed fnl f: hld on wl* **5/1**[2]

0032 **2** hd **Great Exhibition (USA)**[33] 5378 3-9-0 77 ...........................(t) TEDurcan 10 75
(SaeedBinSuroor) *taken steadily to post: trckd ldrs: rdn 2f out: effrt to chal ins fnl f: w wnr last 100yds: nt go by* **2/1**[1]

**3** 2 **Russian Cafe (IRE)** 3-8-9 ..............................................(t) DaneO'Neill 11 64+
(MAMagnusson) *w'like: b.bkwd: racd on outer: in tch: prog over 2f out: chsd wnr briefly 1f out: eased whn hld nr fin* **14/1**

0205 **4** 5 **Imtalkinggibberish**[13] 5845 3-9-0 75 ........................................ WRyan 8 54
(JRJenkins) *hld up midfield: effrt over 2f out: chsd ldrs over 1f out: wknd fnl f* **8/1**[3]

00 **5** ½ **Rabbit**[12] 5851 3-8-9 ....................................................... SRighton 4 48
(MrsALMKing) *led to over 2f out: wknd over 1f out* **33/1**

0000 **6** 1 ¼ **Diaphanous**[13] 5844 6-8-10 30 ............................................ SCarson 9 44
(EAWheeler) *t.k.h: hld up last pair: rdn and effrt over 2f out: wknd over 1f out* **66/1**

0024 **7** 1 **Bee Minor**[58] 4717 3-8-9 70 ............................................ RLMoore 2 41
(RHannon) *dwlt: sn trckd ldrs: rdn and fnd nil over 2f out: hanging and btn over 1f out* **2/1**[1]

5506 **8** 1 **Top Place**[113] 3106 3-8-9 35 ............................................. WSupple 1 38
(BAPearce) *racd midfield: rdn and no prog wl over 1f out: wknd rapidly fnl f* **33/1**

002- **9** nk **Lady Korrianda**[309] 6129 3-8-6 60 ........................................ RMiles(3) 5 37
(LadyHerries) *w ldr to 1/2-way: sn wknd* **20/1**

0000 **10** 3 **Lady Franpalm (IRE)**[51] 4926 4-8-10 40 .................................... JQuinn 7 28
(MJHaynes) *b: a last pair: nvr a factor* **100/1**

6450 **11** 28 **Victoriana**[12] 5849 3-8-9 54 ................................................ TQuinn 3 —
(HJCollingridge) *spd over 2f: wknd: t.o and eased fnl f* **20/1**

1m 12.69s (-0.15) **Going Correction** 0.0s/f (Good)
**WFA** 3 from 4yo+ 1lb **11** Ran SP% **119.0**
Speed ratings: **101,100,98,91,90 89,87,86,86,82 44**CSF £14.65 TOTE £5.60: £1.60, £1.10, £3.30; EX 21.60.
**Owner** Canisbay Bloodstock **Bred** Collin Stud **Trained** Epsom, Surrey

**FOCUS**
A modest maiden featuring plenty of exposed performers. The form looks solid enough for the grade.

**NOTEBOOK**
**Dr Synn**, who produced a poor effort at Windsor six days previously when missing the break, was always just holding the runner-up close home and got off the mark at the 12th time of asking. This was much like his true form, plus he does look on a favourable mark for handicaps, but he is not consistent and is far from one to lump on for a follow-up bid. *Official explanation: trainer had no explanation for the improved form shown*
**Great Exhibition(USA)**, who has had plenty of chances for his powerful stable, again threw in a moody effort. He was coming back at the winner late on, but does struggle to finish his races, and although the drop back to this trip suited he will always be one to oppose.
**Russian Cafe(IRE) ◆**, a 50,000gns purchase, is certainly the horse to take from the race with a view to the future. She raced distinctly green on this belated debut and should improve plenty, so can find a similar race over this trip en route to better things.
**Imtalkinggibberish** could not find the necessary turn of foot to trouble the principals in this ground and was well held. He has now failed to build on his encouraging effort at Newmarket in August in three subsequent outings on this softer ground, and does look flattered by his current rating.
**Rabbit** improved a touch for this shorter trip and now qualifies for handicaps.
**Bee Minor** ran well below her best form and remains a maiden after 15 outings. *Official explanation: jockey said filly was never travelling*
**Lady Franpalm(IRE)** *Official explanation: jockey said filly missed the break*

## 6090 FINALE NURSERY STKS (H'CAP) 7f
**5:30** (5:31) (D2) (0-85,85) 2-Y-0 **£7,231** (£2,225; £1,112; £556) **Stalls** Low

Form RPR

4520 **1** **Enforcer**[35] 5314 2-8-11 **78** .............................................. RMiles(3) 5 81+
(WRMuir) *hld up in last: detached fr remainder 3f out: taken to nr side and rapid prog over 1f out: storming run to ld last stride* **16/1**

621 **2** shd **King Marju (IRE)**[19] 5720 2-9-7 **85** ........................................ JQuinn 7 88+
(PWChapple-Hyam) *lw: t.k.h: trckd ldrs: effrt to ld jst over 1f out: hrd rdn fnl f: hdd last stride* **9/4**[1]

0320 **3** 1 **Wavertree Warrior (IRE)**[21] 5681 2-8-10 **77** ........... J-PGuillambert(3) 6 78
(NPLittmoden) *racd midfield: drvn 3f out: prog u.p over 1f out: r.o fnl f: nrst fin* **20/1**

426 **4** ½ **Coup D'Etat**[58] 4730 2-9-6 **84** ................................................ TQuinn 13 83
(JLDunlop) *lw: dwlt: hld up towards rr: rdn 3f out: hanging but prog over 1f out: r.o fnl f: nrst fin* **9/1**

050 **5** shd **River Biscuit (USA)**[51] 4913 2-8-6 **70** ..................................... RLMoore 18 69
(RHannon) *racd midfield: rdn over 2f out: styd on fr over 1f out: unable to chal* **25/1**

1504 **6** *shd* **Keep Backckinhit (IRE)**[19] 5721 2-8-9 **78**............................ AQuinn(5) 16 77
(GLMoore) *trckd ldrs: styd far side in st: styd on same pce fnl 2f: nvr able to chal* **10/1**

0526 **7** *1/2* **Brooklime (IRE)**[14] 5810 2-9-2 **80**.................................... SWKelly 12 78
(JAOsborne) *chsd ldr: rdn over 2f out: cl up and ch 1f out: wknd last 100yds* **9/1**

4522 **8** *nk* **Aberdeen Park**[9] 5909 2-8-5 **69**........................................ PDoe 9 66
(MrsHSweeting) *chsd ldr: rdn to chal 2f out: w ldr 1f out: wknd last 100yds* **7/1[2]**

15 **9** *3/4* **Ratukidul (FR)**[17] 5753 2-9-2 **80**...................................... DaneO'Neill 11 75
(SirMichaelStoute) *racd midfield: shkn up 2f out: one pce and nvr rchd ldrs* **8/1[3]**

0635 **10** *hd* **Penny Island (IRE)**[19] 5719 2-8-8 **72**................................ JDSmith 17 66
(AKing) *led: rdn and hdd jst over 1f out: wknd last 100yds* **12/1**

5210 **11** *1 1/2* **Briannsta (IRE)**[26] 5539 2-8-12 **76**.................................... TEDurcan 4 67
(MRChannon) *settled wl in rr: shkn up over 2f out: edgd rt but kpt on fr over 1f out: nvr nr ldrs* **20/1**

6000 **12** *2* **Benedict Bay**[26] 5539 2-8-2 **66** ow1...................................(v[1]) SCarson 14 52
(GBBalding) *dwlt: racd in last trio: u.p and struggling over 3f out* **100/1**

5010 **13** *2 1/2* **Simplify**[31] 5421 2-8-13 **77**...............................................(b) RHughes 1 56
(DRLoder) *stdd s: hld up in rr: brief effrt over 2f out: sn no prog* **16/1**

1440 **14** *1* **Cusoon**[14] 5810 2-8-12 **76**.......................................... SWhitworth 15 53
(GLMoore) *a towards rr: u.p and struggling 3f out* **25/1**

422 **15** *1 1/2* **Maneki Neko (IRE)**[27] 5516 2-8-11 **75**................................ JMackay 8 48
(MHTompkins) *hanging thrght: chsd ldrs: rdn 3f out: wknd* **14/1**

5400 **16** *2* **Ellens Princess (IRE)**[20] 5701 2-8-1 **65**.............................. CCatlin 10 33
(RHannon) *chsd ldrs to 1/2-way: sn wknd* **25/1**

1m 29.44s (1.41) **Going Correction** +0.225s/f (Good) **16** Ran SP% **131.6**
Speed ratings: **100,99,98,98,98 97,97,97,96,95 94,91,89,87,86 83**CSF £51.74 CT £645.86 TOTE £22.50: £4.40, £1.50, £2.90, £2.50; EX 43.40 Place 6 £691.51, Place 5 £88.47.
**Owner** D G Clarke & C L A Edginton **Bred** Mrs H B Raw **Trained** Lambourn, Berks

**FOCUS**
A fair nursery that was run at a sound gallop. The first two both produced decent efforts and should remain competitive when re-assessed.

**NOTEBOOK**
**Enforcer** came from out of the clouds to collar the runner-up on the line and win his first race at the fifth attempt. He was last turning in and really picked up with style after coming down the hill, so should have more to offer next year, and should make a nice handicapper at up to a mile.
**King Marju(IRE)**, very well backed to follow up his Newmarket maiden success, took a fierce hold through the first two furlongs, but still looked all over the winner until he was grabbed on the line. This was a solid effort in the circumstances, he proved he handles this ground and he is certainly capable of making amends when consenting to settle.
**Wavertree Warrior(IRE)**, outclassed at the Curragh latest, was keeping on under a patient ride and showed his true colours. He stayed this trip, handled the ground and should pick up a race before the year is out.
**Coup D'Etat** was staying on well enough on this handicap debut and may be better served by a more conventional track. He will do better next year. *Official explanation: jockey said colt missed break*
**River Biscuit(USA)** was doing all of his best work all too late, but improved for this switch to a handicap and looks on a fair mark.
**Ratukidul(FR)** is starting to look fairly exposed now, but is the type who could improve as a three-year-old.
**Simplify** *Official explanation: jockey said colt hung left throughout*
T/Jkpt: Not won. T/Plt: £574.50 to a £1 stake. Pool: £48,051.80. 61.05 winning tickets. T/Qpdt: £31.90 to a £1 stake. Pool: £4,437.40. 102.85 winning tickets. JN

## 5855 NEWCASTLE (L-H)
### Sunday, October 10

**OFFICIAL GOING: Good (good to firm in places)**
The riders reported the going was 'very nearly perfect, just a shade on the quick side'.
Wind: Fresh 1/2 behind. Weather: Overcast and cool.

## 6091 NPOWER MAIDEN AUCTION STKS (DIV I) 7f
**1:50** (1:52) (E3) 2-Y-O **£3,542** (£1,090; £545; £272) **Stalls** High

Form RPR

00 **1** **Azahara**[43] 5128 2-8-4 ........................................ DaleGibson 6 67
(KGReveley) *bhd: gd hdwy on ins over 1f out: styd on strly to ld cl home* **100/1**

0 **2** *nk* **Wester Lodge (IRE)**[33] 5373 2-8-13 ................................ JTate 12 75
(JMPEustace) *prom: effrt over 2f out: led ins fnl f: hung rt: hdd cl home* **14/1**

62 **3** *3/4* **Hannah's Dream (IRE)**[25] 5559 2-8-5 ............................ KDarley 13 66
(MJohnston) *mde most to over 1f out: rallied: hung lft ins last: one pce whn n.m.r cl home* **10/3[2]**

4 **4** *2 1/2* **Scripted**[9] 5911 2-8-13 .............................................. SSanders 9 67
(SirMarkPrescott) *cl up: rdn and disp ld fr over 2f out: nt qckn ins fnl f* **6/4[1]**

0000 **5** *2 1/2* **Artic Fox**[11] 5858 2-8-12 55.................................................(b) DAllan 10 60
(TDEasterby) *w ldrs tl rdn and nt qckn over 1f out* **66/1**

**6** *2 1/2* **Damburger Xpress** 2-8-11 .......................................... MFenton 11 53
(DMSimcock) *leggy: scope: hld up: hdwy over 1f out: nvr rchd ldrs* **33/1**

4200 **7** *1 1/2* **Invertiel (USA)**[21] 5670 2-8-11 75........................................ RWinston 14 49
(ISemple) *hmpd s: sn prom: effrt over 2f out: hung lft and wknd over 1f out* **8/1[3]**

0 **8** *5* **Mink Mitten**[72] 4292 2-8-4 ...............................................(t) PHanagan 8 30
(DJDaly) *dwlt: hld up in tch: rdn and wknd over 1f out* **12/1**

06 **9** *shd* **Pacific Pirate (IRE)**[19] 5720 2-8-11 .............................. GFaulkner 2 36
(MGQuinlan) *keen: hld up in tch: rdn 2f out: sn btn* **14/1**

**10** *1 1/4* **Villa Chigi (IRE)** 2-8-10 ............................................. DMcGaffin 5 32
(BSmart) *cmpt: in tch: lost pl 4f out: n.d after* **50/1**

5 **11** *1 3/4* **Boschette**[39] 5227 2-8-5 ............................................ TPQueally 1 23
(JDBethell) *prom on outside: rdn over 3f out: sn outpcd* **9/1**

50 **12** *17* **Emerald Destiny (IRE)**[6] 5988 2-8-5 ow1.......................... DTudhope(5) 7 —
(DCarroll) *keen: cl up 3f: sn lost pl* **100/1**

1m 26.15s (-1.87) **Going Correction** -0.40s/f (Firm) **12** Ran SP% **113.6**
Speed ratings: **94,93,92,89,87 84,82,76,76,75 73,53**CSF £1110.92 TOTE £104.80: £13.20, £3.00, £1.10; EX 1407.00.
**Owner** J Stevenson **Bred** Barton Stud **Trained** Lingdale, N Yorks
■ Stewards Enquiry : J Tate seven-day ban: used whip with excessive force, on an inexperienced 2yo, marking colt in the wrong place (Oct 21-23,25-28)

**FOCUS**
The field converged on the stands' side. This is modest form, and the winning time was 0.44 seconds slower than the second division.

**NOTEBOOK**
**Azahara** had been unsighted on her first two runs but she appreciated the faster underfoot conditions here. Coming from last to first with a strong run against the rail, she will stay a bit farther than this on breeding.
**Wester Lodge(IRE)**, who went off at 100/1 on his debut, showed more this time, but having got to the front inside the last he could not withstand the winner's late burst.
**Hannah's Dream(IRE)** , who had a couple of subsequent scorers behind her when runner-up at Beverley, hung to the left when trying to rally, allowing the winner through against the rail.
**Scripted**, having his first run on turf, did not look entirely suited by the extra furlong and might need easier ground.
**Artic Fox**, down in trip and with blinkers refitted, ran a better race than of late.
**Damburger Xpress**, whose unraced dam is a half-sister to high-class sprinter Up And At 'Em, shaped with a bit of promise on his debut.
**Invertiel(USA)** *Official explanation: jockey said colt hung left from two out*

## 6092 NPOWER MAIDEN AUCTION STKS (DIV II) 7f
**2:20** (2:21) (E3) 2-Y-O **£3,542** (£1,090; £545; £272) **Stalls** High

Form RPR

2 **1** **Real Quality (USA)**[24] 5578 2-8-13 ................................ RWinston 9 86+
(ISemple) *hld up: hdwy to ld 2f out: hld on wl towards fin* **6/4[1]**

3 **2** *3/4* **Three Degrees (IRE)**[23] 5616 2-8-6 ............................ MFenton 14 77+
(RMBeckett) *chsd ldr: ev ch over 1f out: no ex wl ins last* **11/4[2]**

**3** *9* **Le Chiffre (IRE)** 2-8-13 ................................................ TPQueally 3 62
(DRLoder) *tall: bmpd s: hld up: effrt over 2f out: kpt on fnl f* **7/1[3]**

62 **4** *1 1/4* **Nepal (IRE)**[11] 5856 2-8-3 ............................................ PFessey 12 48
(TDBarron) *hld up: hdwy over 2f out: sn rdn and kpt on same pce* **10/1**

5006 **5** *1 3/4* **Aza Wish (IRE)**[11] 5856 2-7-12 58.................................. RoryMoore(5) 10 48
(MsDeborahJEvans) *led tl 2f out: wknd over 1f out* **50/1**

0 **6** *nk* **Kudbeme**[121] 2860 2-8-2 ............................................. JBramhill 1 43
(NBycroft) *swtchd rt after 1f: hld up: hdwy over 2f out: nvr nr ldrs* **100/1**

**7** *6* **Hayraan (IRE)** 2-8-9 ..................................................... JCarroll 4 49
(GCBravery) *lengthy: scope: sn chsng ldrs: hung lft thrght: lost pl over 1f out* **14/1**

00 **8** *1 1/2* **Haenertsburg (IRE)**[24] 5578 2-8-3 ................................ GGibbons 2 28
(ABerry) *swvd rt s: chsd ldrs: lost pl over 1f out* **28/1**

0 **9** *3/4* **Victor Buckwell**[23] 5604 2-8-9 .................................... TEaves(3) 13 34
(BEllison) *dwlt: nvr on terms* **25/1**

00 **10** *hd* **Woodford Wonder (IRE)**[15] 5800 2-8-4 ow5............ PMulrennan(3) 6 27
(MWEasterby) *sn in rr: nvr a factor* **100/1**

000 **11** *3* **Cala Fons (IRE)**[37] 5264 2-8-4 ...................................... KimTinkler 8 23
(NTinkler) *chsd ldrs: lost pl 3f out: sn bhd* **100/1**

50 **12** *1 1/2* **Mary Gray**[73] 4272 2-8-4 ................................................. SChin 5 16
(MJohnston) *chsd ldrs: hung bdly lft over 2f out: sn lost pl and bhd* **14/1**

0 **13** *7* **Stanley Arthur**[24] 5578 2-8-10 ...................................... ANicholls 11 18
(DNicholls) *s.i.s: a bhd* **66/1**

1m 25.71s (-2.31) **Going Correction** -0.40s/f (Firm) **13** Ran SP% **115.3**
Speed ratings: **97,96,85,84,84 82,82,75,73,72 72,69,67**CSF £4.87 TOTE £2.50: £1.10, £1.80, £3.80; EX 4.80.
**Owner** David McKenzie **Bred** Woodsfield Farm **Trained** Carluke, S Lanarks

**FOCUS**
The time was 0.44 seconds faster than the first division. The field tended to race on the near side, but not as markedly as division one. It developed into a two-horse race and the first two are nice prospects.

**NOTEBOOK**
**Real Quality(USA)** duly improved for his debut experience over this extra furlong, running on strongly in a sprint to the line which saw the first two quickly draw well clear. Unlikely to run again this term, he should go on to better things.
**Three Degrees(IRE)**, upped in trip after a promising debut effort, lost little in defeat and finished a long way ahead of the remainder. Her turn will come.
**Le Chiffre(IRE)**, a half-brother to three winners, was very noisy in the paddock. He merely finished best of the rest this time but should be capable of improvement.
**Nepal(IRE)** was keeping on reasonably well against the near rail, but this was still a step down from his debut effort.
**Aza Wish(IRE)** is a limited performer but this was a slightly more encouraging effort.
**Kudbeme**, having her first run since June, shaped as if in need of farther.
**Hayraan(IRE)**, well backed at long odds, was on one rein throughout. He should improve given time and experience. *Official explanation: jockey said colt hung left throughout*

## 6093 SAINT GOBAIN PIPELINES (S) NURSERY 6f
**2:55** (2:58) (F4) (0-65,62) 2-Y-O **£2,688** (£768; £384) **Stalls** High

Form RPR

0002 **1** **Hows That**[41] 5192 2-8-12 **53**.................................... DarrenWilliams 2 60+
(KRBurke) *chsd far side ldrs: rdn to ld that gp appr fnl f: kpt on wl* **6/1[1]**

5600 **2** *1 1/2* **Strathtay**[22] 5636 2-9-0 **55**.......................................................(v[1]) KDarley 5 55
(PCHaslam) *s.i.s: outpcd far side: gd hdwy over 1f out: kpt on: nt rch wnr* **10/1[3]**

0010 **3** *nk* **Wiltshire (IRE)**[9] 5910 2-9-4 **59**...................................... JCarroll 7 58
(MRChannon) *sn niggled towards rr far side: hdwy over 1f out: kpt on fnl f* **9/1[2]**

0006 **4** *1/2* **Mercari**[11] 5865 2-9-3 **61**................................................... TEaves(3) 8 59
(GMMoore) *in tch far side: effrt over 2f out: kpt on fnl f: no imp* **16/1**

060 **5** *nk* **Dancing Deano (IRE)**[26] 5543 2-8-11 **52**.............................(v[1]) VHalliday 16 49
(RMWhitaker) *cl up stands side: led that gp over 2f out: kpt on fnl f: no ch w far side* **16/1**

0000 **6** *nk* **Desert Buzz (IRE)**[25] 5556 2-8-12 **53**.................................(p) TPQueally 1 49
(JHetherton) *cl up far side: led that gp 1/2-way to appr fnl f: outpcd ins last* **16/1**

6000 **7** *3/4* **Sweet Marguerite**[15] 5800 2-9-0 **55**.................................. DAllan 10 49
(TDEasterby) *trckd far side ldrs: rdn over 2f out: one pce fnl f* **10/1[3]**

6100 **8** *1 1/2* **Lakesdale (IRE)**[24] 5593 2-8-10 **56**.................................. PMakin(5) 15 45
(MissDMountain) *hld up in tch stands side: effrt over 2f out: kpt on fnl f: no imp* **14/1**

3005 **9** *shd* **Singhalongtasveer**[29] 5447 2-9-4 **59**................................ JBramhill 4 48
(WStorey) *bhd far side: rdn and hdwy over 1f out: no imp whn n.m.r ins last* **20/1**

0656 **10** *1* **Ms Three**[14] 5816 2-9-0 **55**.............................................. PHanagan 11 41
(RFord) *prom stands side: rdn 1/2-way: no ex over 1f out* **10/1[3]**

0520 **11** *1* **Chicago Nights (IRE)**[33] 5369 2-8-10 **51**........................ GFaulkner 20 34
(PCHaslam) *led stands side tl hdd and no ex over 2f out* **12/1**

0540 **12** *3/4* **Tit For Tat**[24] 5596 2-9-1 **56**.................................................(b[1]) MFenton 13 37
(JGGiven) *s.i.s: bhd stands side: sme late hdwy: nvr on terms* **16/1**

306 **13** *1/2* **Alzarma**[55] 4816 2-9-7 **62**................................................ RWinston 14 41
(ABailey) *in tch stands side: rdn and egded lft over 2f out: sn outpcd* **12/1**

1000 **14** *2* **Apetite**[6] 5989 2-8-12 **60**................................................ AReilly(7) 18 33
(NBycroft) *s.s: bhd stands side: sme late hdwy: nvr on terms* **16/1**

5606 **15** *1/2* **Satin Rose**[25] 5561 2-8-13 **54**......................................... GGibbons 17 26
(TDEasterby) *cl up stands side to 2f out: sn btn* **14/1**

050 **16** *1* **Lady Vee (IRE)**[15] 5792 2-8-11 **55** THamilton(3) 9 24
(PDNiven) *s.i.s: a bhd far side* **14/1**

0020 **17** *19* **Mas O Menos (IRE)**[15] 5797 2-9-7 **62** ANicholls 6 —
(MsDeborahJEvans) *led far side to 1/2-way: sn wknd* **20/1**

3400 **18** *20* **Shatin Leader**[24] 5578 2-8-11 **52** PFessey 12 —
(MissLAPerratt) *unruly in stalls: hld up stands side: rdn and wknd fr 1/2-way* **20/1**

1m 14.39s (-0.65) **Going Correction** -0.40s/f (Firm) **18** Ran SP% **130.6**
Speed ratings: **88,86,85,84,84 84,83,81,81,79 78,77,76,74,73 72,46,20**CSF £392.47 CT £7.00 TOTE £1.60: £5.20, £2.10, £5.80, £; EX50.50 1.There was no bid for the winner. Wiltshire was claimed by D J Flood for £6,000. Strathtay was claimed by Mr E Nisbet for

**Owner** D Wigglesworth & J Harthen **Bred** Mrs F Denniff **Trained** Middleham Moor, N Yorks

■ Stewards Enquiry : P Makin two-day ban: careless riding (Oct 21,22)

**FOCUS**

A poor race. The field split into two groups and the far side emerged on top.

**NOTEBOOK**

**Hows That**, well drawn as it turned out in stall 2, ran out a comfortable winner in the end, comprehensively turning round Ripon form with Apetite. She is on the upgrade, albeit starting from a low base.

**Strathtay**, in a first-time visor, was staying on late in the day and will be suited by a return to farther. She changed hands after the race.

**Wiltshire(IRE)**, back in the bottom grade, was doing his best work towards the finish.

**Mercari**, dropped into the bottom grade, was also making her handicap bow.

**Dancing Deano(IRE)**, sharpened up by the first-time visor, came out on top in the stands'-side group.

**Desert Buzz(IRE)**, down in trip, showed up prominently in the far-side bunch before fading inside the last.

**Sweet Marguerite** had been badly drawn on her previous start but could not claim that on this occasion.

**Lakesdale(IRE)**, back at six furlongs, finished second best on the unfavoured stands' side.

**Mas O Menos(IRE)** *Official explanation: jockey said gelding hung right throughout*

**Shatin Leader** *Official explanation: trainer said gelding had a breathing problem; jockey said gelding became upset in stalls*

## 6094 NORTHUMBRIAN WATER H'CAP 7f

**3:30** (3:31) (E3) (0-70,69) 3-Y-O+ **£5,426** (£1,669; £834; £417) **Stalls** High

Form RPR

0005 **1** **Seneschal**[22] 5652 3-8-5 **67** TO'Brien(7) 16 80
(MRChannon) *racd stands' side: hdwy and edgd lft over 2f out to r centre: styd on wl to ld overall last 150yds* **12/1**[3]

5054 **2** *1 3/4* **No Grouse**[19] 5713 4-8-10 **63** (p) PHanagan 14 71
(RAFahey) *racd stands' side: in tch: hdwy to ld that side 1f out: kpt on wl* **7/1**[1]

3601 **3** *nk* **Yorker (USA)**[13] 5833 6-8-9 **62** (b) SSanders 20 69
(MsDeborahJEvans) *led stands' side tl 1f out: no ex* **12/1**[3]

4604 **4** *3/4* **Ballyhurry (USA)**[14] 5818 7-8-11 **67** TEaves(3) 17 72
(JSGoldie) *racd stands' side: sn pushed along: hdwy over 2f out: styd on fnl f* **7/1**[1]

2010 **5** *3/4* **Mount Hillaby (IRE)**[19] 5713 4-8-10 **63** TLucas 15 66
(MWEasterby) *racd stands' side: chsd ldrs: kpt on same pce appr fnl f* **16/1**

1306 **6** *1/2* **Menai Straights**[11] 5861 3-8-8 **63** RWinston 18 65
(RFFisher) *racd stands' side: chsd ldrs: one pce fnl 2f* **25/1**

1210 **7** *3/4* **Jubilee Street (IRE)**[19] 5713 5-8-6 **62** ABeech(3) 1 62
(MrsADuffield) *racd far side: chsd ldrs: styd on to ld that side ins last* **12/1**[3]

6505 **8** *1 3/4* **Blue Patrick**[26] 5540 4-9-0 **67** JTate 8 63
(JMPEustace) *s.i.s: racd far side: hrd rdn and hdwy 2f out: nvr nr ldrs* **20/1**

0600 **9** *1/2* **Mister Sweets**[8] 5945 5-8-6 **66** (t) DTudhope(5) 19 60
(DCarroll) *s.i.s: racd stands' side: bhd tl kpt on fnl 2f* **8/1**[2]

6134 **10** *1 1/2* **Landucci**[18] 5737 3-8-10 **65** (t) TPQueally 4 55
(JWHills) *racd far side: trckd ldrs: effrt 2f out: fdd appr fnl f* **8/1**[2]

0056 **11** *shd* **Queen Charlotte (IRE)**[26] 5544 5-8-9 **62** DaleGibson 9 52
(MrsKWalton) *led on far side tl hdd & wknd ins last* **16/1**

000 **12** *nk* **Aswan (IRE)**[86] 3921 6-8-4 **62** ow2 (t) PMakin(5) 11 51
(SRBowring) *racd stands' side: chsd ldrs: wknd appr fnl f* **33/1**

0000 **13** *2* **Vademecum**[21] 5674 3-8-10 **65** DMcGaffin 3 49
(BSmart) *racd far side: nvr rchd ldrs* **25/1**

1305 **14** *2 1/2* **Kingsmaite**[19] 5715 3-8-11 **66** (b) JBramhill 2 44
(SRBowring) *racd far side: w ldr: wknd over 1f out* **16/1**

6200 **15** *1* **Fair Shake (IRE)**[13] 5833 4-9-1 **68** (p) KDarley 6 43
(DEddy) *racd far side: in rr and sn pushed along: sme hdwy over 2f out: sn lost pl* **12/1**[3]

0050 **16** *hd* **Grey Cossack**[80] 4047 7-9-1 **68** RFitzpatrick 10 42
(NWilson) *swtchd rt and racd stands' side: hld up: hdwy over 2f out: sn wknd* **28/1**

0265 **17** *2* **Downland (IRE)**[24] 5583 8-8-11 **64** KimTinkler 7 33
(NTinkler) *racd far side: sn pushed along: bhd fnl 2f* **20/1**

0000 **18** *4* **Cashneem (IRE)**[8] 5945 6-8-6 **59** DAllan 13 18
(WMBrisbourne) *racd stands' side: in tch: lost pl over 2f out: sn bhd* **25/1**

0400 **19** *hd* **Dara Mac**[8] 5945 5-8-5 **61** THamilton(3) 12 19
(NBycroft) *racd stands' side: a in rr: bhd fnl 2f* **25/1**

1m 25.39s (-2.63) **Going Correction** -0.40s/f (Firm)
**WFA** 3 from 4yo+ 2lb **19** Ran SP% **126.9**
Speed ratings: **99,97,96,95,94 94,93,91,90,89 89,88,86,83,82 82,79,75,75**CSF £84.20 CT £1062.41 TOTE £16.60: £3.30, £2.30, £2.00, £2.10; EX 100.70.

**Owner** Peter Taplin **Bred** Michael E Broughton **Trained** West Ilsley, Berks

**FOCUS**

An ordinary handicap in which the field split into two groups again. This time the stands' side held sway, although the winner ended up racing near the centre after drifting away from the whip.

**NOTEBOOK**

**Seneschal**, whose yard is in good form at the moment, began the season on a 27lb higher mark. After racing in the stands'-side group, he drifted into the centre of the course as his rider persisted in using the whip in his right hand but still ran out a clear-cut winner.

**No Grouse** is running consistently well at present. He is on a long losing run, but is 13lb lower than when last winning and is capable of picking up a race soon.

**Yorker(USA)**, 5lb higher than at Hamilton, showed plenty of pace to lead against the near rail but was found out by the extra furlong.

**Ballyhurry(USA)** was keeping on well in the latter stages and is capable of finding a race before the end of the season provided the ground remains on the fast side.

**Mount Hillaby(IRE)** was 3lb higher than when scoring at York over a furlong more.

**Jubilee Street(IRE)**, a consistent individual over this trip, emerged on top of the eight-strong group which raced on the unfavoured side.

**Kingsmaite** *Official explanation: jockey said gelding had a breathing problem*

## 6095 ORANGE MAIDEN FILLIES' STKS 1m 2f 32y

**4:05** (4:09) (D3) 3-Y-O+ **£3,740** (£1,151; £575; £287) **Stalls** Centre

Form RPR

334 **1** **Into The Shadows**[149] 2077 4-9-0 72 TEaves(3) 1 66+
(KGReveley) *trckd ldrs: smooth hdwy to ld appr fnl f: shkn up and r.o strly* **11/4**[2]

3262 **2** *3* **Bubbling Fun**[13] 5836 3-8-12 66 SSanders 6 61
(EALDunlop) *in tch: hdwy to ld briefly over 1f out: kpt on same pce fnl f* **2/1**[1]

0 **3** *3/4* **Lady Karr**[38] 5239 3-8-12 KDarley 5 60
(MJohnston) *midfield: rdn and outpcd over 3f out: r.o fnl f: no imp* **12/1**

4660 **4** *3/4* **Rosie Mac**[39] 5223 3-8-5 54 AReilly(7) 4 58
(NBycroft) *disp ld to over 1f out: nt qckn* **33/1**

330 **5** *shd* **Red Sail**[30] 5445 3-8-12 76 RWinston 9 58
(JRFanshawe) *sn prom: effrt over 2f out: nt qckn fr over 1f out* **11/4**[2]

**6** *1/2* **Bottomless Wallet** 3-8-9 THamilton(3) 7 57
(FWatson) *hld up: hdwy ins 2f out: no imp fnl f* **40/1**

**7** *3* **Awaken** 3-8-12 PHanagan 3 52
(GASwinbank) *chsd ldrs to 3f out: sn outpcd* **8/1**[3]

5000 **8** *5* **Gaiety Girl (USA)**[34] 5346 3-8-12 46 DAllan 8 43
(TDEasterby) *mde most to over 1f out: sn btn* **28/1**

0-0 **9** *2* **Dorisima (FR)**[15] 5803 3-8-9 PMulrennan(3) 10 39
(MWEasterby) *hld up: rdn over 3f out: sn btn* **66/1**

2m 15.06s (3.46) **Going Correction** -0.05s/f (Good)
**WFA** 3 from 4yo 5lb **9** Ran SP% **115.8**
Speed ratings: **84,81,81,80,80 79,77,73,71**CSF £8.48 TOTE £4.10: £1.40, £1.30, £3.60; EX 10.20.

**Owner** R C Mayall **Bred** Mrs Linda Corbett And Mrs Mary Mayall **Trained** Lingdale, N Yorks

**FOCUS**

A pedestrian gallop for much of the way and the contest basically developed into a three-furlong sprint. The winning time was very slow as a result, 4.52 seconds slower than the following handicap. Only a modest maiden, but the winner looks improved.

**NOTEBOOK**

**Into The Shadows**, last seen in May, seems to have improved in the meantime and was very well backed to get off the mark. She travelled supremely well just behind the leaders, and when asked to go and win her race completely left her rivals for dead. She has a decent turn of foot and still has scope for further improvement, but if she does go over hurdles she may need an easy track in order to get the trip.

**Bubbling Fun** came with her effort on the outside to hit the front over a furlong from home, but when the winner clicked into gear she was left standing. She probably ran into a progressive sort here, but has come up too short too often to be supported with any confidence.

**Lady Karr** was probably not suited by the way the race was run as she only got going when it was too late. She has only had two races in her life and should be seen to better effect in a truly-run race.

**Rosie Mac** appeared to perform better than her official mark entitled her to under a positive ride, but given the way the race was run she did not really prove her stamina for this trip.

**Red Sail** disappointed for the second time and is going to struggle to justify her official mark.

## 6096 LUMSDEN AND CARROLL CONSTRUCTION H'CAP 1m 2f 32y

**4:40** (4:42) (E3) (0-70,70) 3-Y-O+ **£4,058** (£1,248; £624; £312) **Stalls** Centre

Form RPR

3241 **1** **Mambina (USA)**[8] 5936 3-8-12 **66** DAllan 3 74+
(MRChannon) *mid-div: nt clr run over 2f out: squeezed through and str run to ld last 50yds* **5/1**[2]

0141 **2** *1/2* **Lucayan Dancer**[17] 5757 4-8-12 **61** SSanders 13 68
(DNicholls) *in tch: hdwy 4f out: chal ins last: no ex nr fin* **3/1**[1]

3134 **3** *3/4* **Easibet Dot Net**[27] 5517 4-9-3 **69** (p) TEaves(3) 4 75
(ISemple) *trckd ldrs: hung lft and led over 2f out: hdd and no ex wl ins last* **12/1**

0460 **4** *shd* **Sahaat**[12] 5853 6-9-1 **64** DarrenWilliams 8 69
(CRDore) *s.i.s: hld up and bhd: stdy hdwy on ins over 2f out: ev ch ins last: no ex* **20/1**

0225 **5** *1 1/4* **Colway Ritz**[8] 5951 10-8-12 **61** JBramhill 14 64
(WStorey) *hld up and bhd: hdwy on ins over 2f out: n.m.r 1f out: kpt on same pce* **12/1**

5100 **6** *shd* **Market Avenue**[12] 5853 5-9-0 **63** (p) PHanagan 6 66
(RAFahey) *s.i.s: hdwy 3f out: chal 1f out: wknd towards fin* **9/1**[3]

350 **7** *7* **Medalla (FR)**[34] 5345 4-9-2 **70** MLawson(5) 7 60
(MBrittain) *hld up: stmbld 6f out: sme hdwy 2f out: nvr on terms* **50/1**

3420 **8** *2* **Futoo (IRE)**[34] 5344 3-9-2 **70** KDarley 9 57
(GMMoore) *led 1f: chsd ldrs: lost pl over 1f out* **20/1**

5230 **9** *2 1/2* **Super King**[16] 5773 3-8-6 **65** PMakin(5) 15 47
(NBycroft) *mid-div: effrt over 3f out: lost pl over 1f out* **28/1**

4100 **10** *2* **Jake Black (IRE)**[23] 5622 4-9-0 **63** RWinston 5 42
(JJQuinn) *trckd ldrs: effrt and nt clr run over 2f out: wknd over 1f out* **33/1**

4120 **11** *1/2* **Havetoavit (USA)**[29] 5459 3-8-11 **65** TPQueally 2 43
(JDBethell) *led after 1f tl over 2f out: sn wknd* **11/1**

0 **12** *8* **Inchdura**[26] 5544 6-9-1 **64** KimTinkler 17 27
(NTinkler) *bhd: sme hdwy over 2f out: nvr a factor* **25/1**

0 **13** *2 1/2* **Kaymich Perfecto**[11] 5868 4-8-11 **60** VHalliday 1 19
(RMWhitaker) *in tch: effrt 3f out: lost pl over 1f out* **66/1**

2000 **14** *7* **Santiburi Lad (IRE)**[16] 5768 7-8-13 **65** THamilton(3) 12 11
(NWilson) *prom eraly: lost pl 5f out* **14/1**

0020 **15** *7* **Bond Millennium**[11] 5859 6-8-13 **62** DMcGaffin 16 —
(BSmart) *in tch: effrt on outer over 3f out: lost pl over 2f out: sn bhd* **12/1**

5453 **16** *6* **Dream Easy**[38] 5237 3-8-13 **67** (b[1]) RPrice 10 —
(PLGilligan) *chsd ldrs: lost pl over 3f out: sn bhd* **25/1**

-000 **17** *7* **Silvertown**[15] 3199 9-9-0 **66** PMulrennan(3) 11 —
(LLungo) *chsd ldrs: drvn along and lost pl over 4f out: sn bhd and eased* **12/1**

2m 10.54s (-1.06) **Going Correction** -0.05s/f (Good)
**WFA** 3 from 4yo+ 5lb **17** Ran SP% **124.5**
Speed ratings: **102,101,101,100,99 99,94,92,90,89 88,82,80,74,69 64,58**CSF £18.33 CT £179.67 TOTE £6.20: £1.70, £1.50, £3.20, £4.80; EX 14.90.

**Owner** R A Scarborough **Bred** Michael And Joility And Robert Scarborough **Trained** West Ilsley, Berks

■ Stewards Enquiry : P Hanagan caution: careless riding

**FOCUS**

Just a fair gallop and a group of six finished in a heap at the front, though they did finish a long way clear of the others. Only an ordinary time for the grade, despite being 4.52 seconds faster than the preceding maiden, and this is pretty modest form.

**NOTEBOOK**

**Mambina(USA)**, raised 3lb for her Epsom victory, had to switch positions in order to get a clear run in the straight and threatened to get squeezed out at a vital stage, but she held her ground and forced her way through to get up near the line. She is at the top of her game just now and can complete the hat-trick, but would probably not want the ground any faster than this.

**Lucayan Dancer**, whose only previous win in a handicap came in an amateur riders' event off a 6lb lower mark, did little wrong and delivered her challenge at just the right time, but the winner was that much more determined.
**Easibet Dot Net** is not always the most straightforward, but did not do much wrong and was just done for foot where it mattered over this shorter trip.
**Sahaat** looked the likely winner for much of the home straight, so well was he travelling, but when he came off the bridle he did not find as much as had looked likely, though he did keep staying on. He is proving so hard to win with despite his handicap mark being in freefall.
**Colway Ritz** was making his effort when getting hampered against the inside rail inside the last furlong, but it is hard to say it made that much difference to the result. He is still 7lb higher than for his last win in a handicap, despite that being two years ago.
**Market Avenue** came to win his race a furlong from home, but then hung badly to his left and was completely run out of the placings.

## 6097 CONOR SADLER UTS CLASSIFIED STKS — 1m 3y(S)
5:15 (5:18) (F3) 3-Y-0+ — £3,503 (£1,078; £539; £269) Stalls High

Form — RPR

5200 **1** **Tedsdale Mac**[8] 5945 5-8-12 57 ........ PMakin(5) 15 68
(NBycroft) *hld up stands side: hdwy 3f out: led ins fnl f: pushed out* **8/1**[3]

6604 **2** 3/4 **Night Frolic**[20] 5693 3-8-11 58 ........ TPQueally 20 63
(JWHills) *hld up midfield stands side: smooth hdwy to ld over 2f out: hdd ins fnl f: r.o* **12/1**

0603 **3** 1 **Regent's Secret (USA)**[8] 5945 4-9-3 56 ........ (p) SSanders 14 64
(JSGoldie) *dwlt: hld up stands side: rdn 3f out: r.o fnl f* **11/2**[2]

0403 **4** 5 **Wrenlane**[15] 5622 3-9-0 60 ........ PHanagan 16 52
(RAFahey) *in tch stands side: effrt and rdn 3f out: outpcd over 1f out* **10/1**

2400 **5** 1/2 **Legal Set (IRE)**[17] 5757 8-9-3 60 ........ (t) AnnStokell 18 51
(MissAStokell) *cl up stands side: ev ch over 2f out: wknd over 1f out* **25/1**

0066 **6** 3 **Every Note Counts**[28] 3265 4-9-3 60 ........ RWinston 5 44+
(JJQuinn) *swtchd to stands side after 2f: hld up: hdwy 2f out: sn no imp* **28/1**

0314 **7** 3 **Newcorp Lad**[8] 5945 4-9-3 69 ........ (p) JCarroll 12 38
(MrsGSRees) *led stands side to over 2f out: wknd over 1f out* **11/10**[1]

0200 **8** 3 1/2 **Always Flying (USA)**[19] 5715 3-8-11 57 ........ THamilton(3) 13 29
(NWilson) *cl up stands side tl wknd over 2f out* **40/1**

3000 **9** 4 **Pagan Storm (USA)**[31] 5411 4-8-10 52 ........ KristinStubbs(7) 11 20
(MrsLStubbs) *towards rr stands side: rdn 1/2-way: nvr rchd ldrs* **50/1**

3000 **10** 1 3/4 **Shardda**[34] 5345 4-8-11 55 ........ PMulrennan(3) 17 13
(FWatson) *bhd stands side: rdn 1/2-way: n.d* **33/1**

-500 **11** 1 **New Wish (IRE)**[35] 5316 4-9-3 57 ........ DaleGibson 6 14+
(MWEasterby) *swtchd to stands side after 1f: hld up: n.d* **16/1**

4400 **12** nk **Lord Baskerville**[8] 5945 3-8-9 52 ........ MLawson(5) 8 13
(WStorey) *prom: rdn 1/2-way: wknd fr 3f out* **100/1**

4002 **13** 3 **Aliba (IRE)**[48] 5001 3-9-0 60 ........ DMcGaffin 10 6
(BSmart) *midfield: rdn over 3f out: sn btn* **66/1**

0616 **14** shd **Jordans Spark**[34] 5344 3-9-0 57 ........ (p) DAllan 7 6
(ISemple) *prom centre: rdn and edgd rt over 2f out: sn btn* **16/1**

3015 **15** 2 **Miskina**[51] 4902 3-8-6 58 ........ BSwarbrick(5) 3 —
(WMBrisbourne) *cl up centre tl outpcd fr over 2f out* **40/1**

5-00 **16** 3 1/2 **Glencairn Star**[24] 5582 3-8-11 60 ........ TEaves(3) 9 —
(JSGoldie) *chsd centre ldrs: rdn over 3f out: wknd over 2f out* **100/1**

5454 **17** 15 **Danettie**[22] 5637 3-8-11 60 ........ MFenton 1 —
(WMBrisbourne) *spd centre tl wknd over 3f out* **40/1**

0000 **18** 18 **Bonsai (IRE)**[22] 5657 3-8-11 60 ........ (t) KDarley 4 —
(RTPhillips) *s.i.s: sn wl bhd centre* **50/1**

1m 39.33s (-1.87) **Going Correction** -0.40s/f (Firm)
**WFA** 3 from 4yo+ 3lb — **18** Ran SP% **127.6**
Speed ratings: **93,92,91,86,85 82,79,76,72,70 69,69,66,66,64 60,45,27**CSF £96.52 TOTE £9.70: £2.50, £3.20, £2.00; EX 119.40 Place 6 £55.08, Place 5 £12.85.
**Owner** Barrie Abbott **Bred** N Bycroft **Trained** Brandsby, N Yorks

**FOCUS**
A modest classified contest in which those drawn high dominated. The field split into two early, though those who raced towards the far side thinned out to a group of five within the first couple of furlongs and never figured after that. The front three pulled well clear of the others. The winning time was moderate for the grade.

**NOTEBOOK**
**Tedsdale Mac** looks best suited by this sort of trip these days and was brought with a well-timed run to score and end a losing run stretching back two and a half years. A rise in the weights will leave him in trouble and his profile does not suggest a follow up is likely. *Official explanation: trainer said, regarding the improved form shown, the easier ground had suited on this occasion*
**Night Frolic** ran a fine race on ground that would have been faster than ideal. Given easier conditions she should be winning before long.
**Regent's Secret(USA)** again ran with credit and picked up yet more prize money, but is now a maiden after 30 attempts.
**Wrenlane**, back on the level after a spin over hurdles, was well beaten by the front three and is still a maiden after 10 starts on the Flat.
**Legal Set(IRE)** still seems to find this trip too far and appears to have gone off the boil for the time being.
**Newcorp Lad**, who would have been upwards of 6lb worse in with his rivals in a handicap, started plenty short enough, almost certainly on account of his easy win here last month, but he dropped out very tamely after making much of the running.
**Aliba(IRE)** *Official explanation: jockey said gelding was never travelling*
**Jordans Spark** *Official explanation: trainer said gelding overreached and lost its action*
**Miskina** *Official explanation: jockey said filly hung right handed*
**Bonsai(IRE)** *Official explanation: jockey said filly lost her action*
T/Plt: £10.50 to a £1 stake. Pool: £39,609.60. 2,741.85 winning tickets. T/Qpdt: £6.20 to a £1 stake. Pool: £3,348.80. 397.20 winning tickets. RY

6098 - 6099a (Foreign Racing) - See Raceform Interactive

# 5958 CURRAGH (R-H)
Sunday, October 10

**OFFICIAL GOING: Round course - good to yielding; straight course - yielding to soft**

## 6100a JUDDMONTE BERESFORD STKS (GROUP 2) — 1m
3:00 (3:00) 2-Y-0 — £59,507 (£17,394; £8,239; £2,746)

RPR

**1** **Albert Hall**[21] 5675 2-9-0 ........ JPSpencer 2 106
(APO'Brien, Ire) *led: hdd 2f out: rdn to regain ld under 1f out: edgd lft: kpt on wl* **4/5**[1]

**2** 1/2 **Merger (USA)**[10] 5900 2-9-0 ........ PJSmullen 3 105
(DKWeld, Ire) *trckd ldr in 2nd: led and edgd rt 2f out: hdd under 1f out: sltly hmpd cl home: kpt on wl* **9/2**[3]

**3** 4 1/2 **Sant Jordi**[11] 5872 2-9-0 ........ MJKinane 5 95
(BJMeehan) *chsd ldrs in 3rd: drvn along fr bef 1/2-way: 4ht 2f out: kpt on same pce* **16/1**

**4** 1 1/2 **Indesatchel (IRE)**[21] 5680 2-9-0 107 ........ JPMurtagh 1 92
(DavidWachman, Ire) *hld up in rr: prog ent st: 3rd 2f out: sn rdn and no imp: wknd ins fnl f* **11/4**[2]

**5** 2 **Falstaff (IRE)**[45] 5065 2-9-0 88 ........ (b[1]) JAHeffernan 4 87
(APO'Brien, Ire) *settled 4th: last and no imp fr over 2f out* **14/1**

1m 43.8s **Going Correction** +0.325s/f (Good) — **5** Ran SP% **113.0**
Speed ratings: **108,107,103,101,99**CSF £5.10 TOTE £1.70: £1.10, £2.60; DF 4.00.
**Owner** Mrs John Magnier **Bred** Bjorn E Nielsen **Trained** Ballydoyle, Co Tipperary

**FOCUS**
By no means a vintage renewal of a long-established race, but the front two are promising staying performers in the making.

**NOTEBOOK**
**Albert Hall** showed improvement on his second in a maiden here three weeks ago but he was still very green and hung out from the rail continually after being headed over a furlong and a half out. He regained the advantage inside the last and stayed on without being asked too much. He was allowed to keep the race after a Stewards' enquiry. The Racing Post Trophy has been mentioned but a lot more is required.
**Merger(USA)** was a wide-margin winner of a Thurles maiden ten days previously and certainly justified his trainer's decision to run here. He got by the winner with over a furlong and a half to race but was palpably inconvenienced by Albert Hall's tendency to hang left into him. He too was running a bit green and Smullen could not draw his whip hand. He was undoubtedly unlucky, but it is hard to visualise him turning the form around in future.
**Sant Jordi** kept on at the same pace despite being under pressure from halfway.
**Indesatchel(IRE)** moved third with two furlongs to race but was done with in a matter of strides. This was his seventh start of the season and his most disappointing. On this evidence he does not get a mile, although his maiden win in June was over seven furlongs.
**Falstaff(IRE)**, beaten off 85 in a Tralee nursery last time, and wearing first-time blinkers, did not count over the last quarter.

## 6101a FLAME OF TARA EUROPEAN BREEDERS FUND STKS (LISTED RACE) (FILLIES) — 6f
3:30 (3:32) 2-Y-0 — £34,383 (£10,088; £4,806; £1,637)

RPR

**1** **Bibury Flyer**[11] 5878 2-8-11 ........ ACulhane 12 96
(MRChannon) *hld up in tch: 6th 2f out: impr into 2nd over 1f out: led ins fnl f: kpt on wl* **12/1**

**2** 1/2 **Virginia Waters (USA)**[8] 5961 2-8-11 99 ........ (t) JPSpencer 3 95
(APO'Brien, Ire) *trckd ldrs: 6th 1/2-way: hdwy 2f out: led under 1 1/2f out: hdd ins fnl f: kpt on wl* **9/4**[2]

**3** 4 1/2 **Gouache (IRE)**[11] 5876 2-8-11 76 ........ DPMcDonogh 6 81
(KevinPrendergast, Ire) *hld up: 7th and rdn 1 1/2f out: kpt on to go mod 3rd ins fnl f* **20/1**

**4** nk **Pout (IRE)**[11] 5876 2-8-11 79 ........ DMGrant 9 80
(JohnJosephMurphy, Ire) *prom on outer: 3rd 1/2-way: 5th 1 1/2f out: kpt on same pce* **20/1**

**5** 1 1/2 **National Swagger (IRE)**[48] 5009 2-8-11 101 ........ KJManning 11 76
(JSBolger, Ire) *chsd ldrs: 4th and rdn 2f out: one pce fr 2f out* **8/1**[3]

**6** 1 1/2 **Lightwood Lady (IRE)**[22] 5659 2-8-11 ........ TPO'Shea 4 71
(MHalford, Ire) *hld up: towards rr 1/2-way: sme late prog* **11/1**

**7** hd **All Night Dancer (IRE)**[21] 5681 2-8-11 81 ........ WMLordan 8 71
(DavidWachman, Ire) *prom: 2nd 2f out: sn rdn and no imp: wknd fnl f* **12/1**

**8** nk **Rare Cross (IRE)**[7] 5971 2-8-11 90 ........ JAHeffernan 1 70
(JosephGMurphy, Ire) *sn led: hdd under 1 1/2f out: no ex fnl f* **20/1**

**9** 4 1/2 **Mount Eliza (IRE)**[20] 5707 2-8-11 87 ........ NGMcCullagh 2 56
(CharlesO'Brien, Ire) *sn bhd and outpcd: rdn and no imp fr 1/2-way* **14/1**

**10** 20 **Russian Waltz (IRE)**[8] 5958 2-8-11 ........ PJSmullen 7 —
(DKWeld, Ire) *broke wl and led early: wknd bef 1/2-way* **10/1**

1m 17.3s **Going Correction** +0.45s/f (Yiel) — **10** Ran SP% **132.0**
Speed ratings: **100,99,93,92,90 88,88,88,82,55**CSF £23.12 TOTE £14.30: £3.20, £1.30, £4.50; DF 27.00.
**Owner** Ridgeway Downs Racing **Bred** Baydon House Stud **Trained** West Ilsley, Berks

**NOTEBOOK**
**Bibury Flyer** created something of a surprise on her nineteenth outing of the season, getting on top inside the final furlong and running on strongly.
**Virginia Waters(USA)** led a furlong and a half out but immediately looked vulnerable to the winner's challenge.
**Gouache(IRE)** is basically a nursery performer.
**Pout(IRE)** won a Fairyhouse nursery off 74 last time.
**National Swagger(IRE)**, a 101-rated maiden, ran nowhere near that mark here on her sixth outing to date.

## 6102a RATHBARRY STUD'S BARATHEA FINALE STKS (LISTED RACE) — 1m 4f
4:00 (4:00) 3-Y-0+ — £25,214 (£7,397; £3,524; £1,200)

RPR

**1** **Tipperary All Star (FR)**[8] 5962 4-9-5 106 ........ JPMurtagh 8 104
(MHalford, Ire) *trckd ldrs in 4th: qcknd into ld 5f out: clr bef st: styd on wl u.p fr 2f out: all out* **12/1**

**2** 1/2 **Starrystarrynight (IRE)**[72] 4312 3-8-9 ........ WMLordan 9 100
(APO'Brien, Ire) *settled 3rd: outpcd 4f out: 6th 2f out: styd on wl u.p fr over 1f out* **12/1**

**3** 1/2 **Tarakala (IRE)**[32] 5394 3-8-12 101 ........ (b) MJKinane 13 103
(JohnMOxx, Ire) *trckd ldrs in 6th: 3rd and hdwy 2f out: 2nd 1f out: kpt on u.p* **5/2**[1]

**4** nk **Cairdeas (IRE)**[140] 2333 3-8-12 101 ........ PJSmullen 6 102
(DKWeld, Ire) *hld up: 8th 4f out: 5th and hdwy 2f out: 3rd over 1f out: kpt on* **5/2**[1]

**5** 1 **Zarafsha (IRE)**[149] 2102 3-8-9 92 ........ FMBerry 10 98
(JohnMOxx, Ire) *hld up in rr: styd on fr 2f out: nvr nrr* **14/1**

**6** 1 1/2 **Marinnette (IRE)**[47] 5031 3-8-9 90 ........ JAHeffernan 4 95
(MPSunderland, Ire) *chsd ldrs in 5th: 3rd bef st: no ex fr 2f out* **14/1**

**7** 3/4 **Emmas Princess (IRE)**[8] 5962 4-9-2 93 ........ NGMcCullagh 2 94
(EdwardLynam, Ire) *towards rr: effrt early st: 7th under 2f out: kpt on same pce* **16/1**

**8** 2 **Because (IRE)**[10] 5902 3-8-9 ........ CO'Donoghue 12 91?
(APO'Brien, Ire) *nvr a factor: kpt on one pce st* **20/1**

**9** nk **Akarem**[18] 5742 3-8-12 92 ........ DPMcDonogh 11 94
(KevinPrendergast, Ire) *mid-div: 8th 1/2-way: no imp fr 4f out* **10/1**[3]

**10** 3 1/2 **Royal Devotion (IRE)**[34] 5357 4-9-5 98 ........ (p) TPO'Shea 1 88
(MHalford, Ire) *s.i.s: settled in 7th: rdn bef st: sn no ex* **10/1**[3]

**11** 4 **Lord Admiral (USA)**[29] 5481 3-8-12 105 ........ EAhern 5 82
(CharlesO'Brien, Ire) *led: hdd and outpcd briefly 5f out: rdn ent st: wknd fr under 2f out* **7/1**[2]

12 *8* **Queen (IRE)**[11] [5882] 3-8-9 ........................ JPSpencer 3 67
(APO'Brien, Ire) *cl up in 2nd: rdn and outpcd 4f out: wknd fr 2f out: eased* **10/1**[3]

2m 39.0s **Going Correction** +0.325s/f (Good)
**WFA** 3 from 4yo 7lb **12 Ran SP% 136.3**
Speed ratings: **113,112,112,112,111 110,109,108,108,106 103,98**CSF £169.67 TOTE £13.50: £2.30, £7.70, £1.50; DF 236.90.
**Owner** Cathal M Ryan **Bred** M Victor Resk Horsinvest Corpo **Trained** the Curragh, Co Kildare

**NOTEBOOK**
**Tipperary All Star(FR)** bounced back to winning form after taking the initiative and going on with over a half mile to race. He never looked like being caught although he was just holding on at the finish. A novice hurdling career beckons.
**Starrystarrynight(IRE)** finished well after being outpaced with over two furlongs to run.
**Tarakala(IRE)** stayed on in third place over the last quarter mile to be nearest at the finish.
**Cairdeas(IRE)** only got going inside the last two furlongs
**Zarafsha(IRE)** was another strong late finisher.
**Lord Admiral(USA)** led until headed by the winner and dropped right away in the last quarter mile.

## 6104a LEINSTER LEADER WATERFORD TESTIMONIAL STKS (LISTED RACE) 6f

**5:00** (5:03) 3-Y-0+ **£25,214** (£7,397; £3,524; £1,200)

RPR

1 **Striking Ambition**[42] [5171] 4-9-1 ........................ JPMurtagh 4 114
(RCharlton) *mde all: drew clr travelling wl fr 1/2-way: rdn and r.o wl fnl f: easily* **4/1**[1]

2 *3 1/2* **Grand Reward (USA)**[7] [5977] 3-9-0 106 ........................ (bt) JPSpencer 5 103
(APO'Brien, Ire) *in tch: 5th appr 1/2-way: 3rd and rdn 2f out: 2nd and kpt on fnl f: no ch w wnr* **5/1**[2]

3 *1/2* **Senor Benny (USA)**[8] [5960] 5-9-1 87 ........................ EAhern 2 102
(MMcdonagh, Ire) *trckd ldrs: 2nd 1/2-way: sn rdn and outpcd: kpt on u.p* **14/1**

4 *4* **Glocca Morra (IRE)**[22] [5661] 6-9-1 106 ........................ KJManning 8 90
(WTFarrell, Ire) *hld up: prog into 6th 2f out: kpt on u.p* **11/2**[3]

5 *2* **Dangle (IRE)**[7] [5972] 3-8-11 101 ........................ (b[1]) FMBerry 13 81
(EdwardLynam, Ire) *hld up: 9th and rdn 1 1/2f out: kpt on fnl f* **10/1**

6 *2* **Lupine (IRE)**[22] [5660] 5-8-12 85 ........................ CatherineGannon 9 75
(GWRobinson, Ire) *hld up: kpt on fr 2f out* **25/1**

7 *nk* **Ulfah (USA)**[22] [5661] 3-9-1 104 ........................ DPMcDonogh 1 78
(KevinPrendergast, Ire) *prom: 3rd 1/2-way: 5th and no ex fr over 1f out* **7/1**

8 *shd* **Palace Star (IRE)**[56] [4787] 3-8-11 96 ........................ JAHeffernan 12 73
(PeterCasey, Ire) *chsd ldrs early: outpcd 1/2-way: kpt on fr 2f out* **16/1**

9 *3 1/2* **Millybaa (USA)**[10] [5893] 4-8-12 ........................ (b[1]) MJKinane 17 63
(RGuest) *hld up on outer: 6th over 1f out: sn no ex and eased* **12/1**

10 *nk* **One Won One (USA)**[29] [5482] 10-9-1 100 ........................ PShanahan 10 65
(MsJoannaMorgan, Ire) *nvr a factor: sme late prog* **14/1**

11 *1 1/2* **Jacks Estate (IRE)**[22] [5660] 9-9-1 100 ........................ WMLordan 14 60
(AdrianMcguinness, Ire) *cl up early: outpcd 1/2-way: no imp fr 2f out* **12/1**

12 *2* **Southern Bound (IRE)**[149] [2101] 3-8-11 93 ........................ NGMcCullagh 3 51
(JGBurns, Ire) *nvr a factor* **20/1**

13 *nk* **Blue Dream (IRE)**[14] [5811] 4-8-12 95 ........................ (tp) PCosgrave 15 51
(THogan, Ire) *chsd ldrs on outer: rdn and wknd fr 2 1/2f out* **16/1**

14 *1* **Nights Cross (IRE)**[10] [5893] 3-9-4 ........................ (b) ACulhane 7 55
(MRChannon) *prom: 3rd 1/2-way: sn wknd* **6/1**

15 *3 1/2* **Cepangie (IRE)**[90] [3813] 7-8-12 46 ........................ DMGrant 6 37
(PatrickJFlynn, Ire) *a bhd* **66/1**

16 *3 1/2* **Miss Serendipity (IRE)**[158] [1893] 3-8-11 91 ........................ TPO'Shea 16 27
(MHalford, Ire) *chsd ldrs to 1/2-way: sn wknd and eased* **14/1**

17 *1* **Favourite Nation (IRE)**[29] [5482] 3-9-0 96 ........................ PJSmullen 11 27
(DKWeld, Ire) *chsd ldrs: wknd 1/2-way: bhd and eased fr 1 1/2f out* **12/1**

1m 15.1s **Going Correction** +0.45s/f (Yiel)
**WFA** 3 from 4yo+ 1lb **17 Ran SP% 152.9**
Speed ratings: **115,110,109,104,101 99,98,98,93,93 91,88,88,87,82 77,76**CSF £28.79 TOTE £5.30: £1.60, £2.00, £1.80, £1.70; DF 33.70.
**Owner** Peter Webb **Bred** Lord Huntingdon **Trained** Beckhampton, Wilts

**NOTEBOOK**
**Striking Ambition**, who returned to form when third at Deauville most recently, loves getting his toe in and routed the opposition on this drop in grade. He is still open to improvement and deserves his chance back in stronger company.
**Grand Reward(USA)** has not been placed to the best effect this season - faced a hopeless task in the Prix L'Abbaye latest - and this was more his grade. He ran well enough without winning, but is not one to rely and should continue to be avoided.
**Senor Benny(USA)** is an admirable performer who continues to improve. He rarely runs a bad race and pulled far enough clear of the fourth to suggest he can win in this grade.
**Millybaa(USA)** was a little disappointing, failing to make up any ground having been in rear early.
**Nights Cross(IRE)** failed to run his race and it is safe to assume he is better than this. Knowing what a tough character he is, he looks sure to bounce back. *Official explanation: jockey said colt lost its action and was eased from 3f out*

6103 - 6105a (Foreign Racing) - See Raceform Interactive

# [4183] DUSSELDORF (R-H)
Sunday, October 10

**OFFICIAL GOING: Soft**

## 6106a GROSSER PREIS DER LANDESHAUPTSTADT DUSSELDORF (GROUP 3) 1m 110y

**3:05** (3:18) 3-Y-0+ **£22,535** (£9,155; £4,577; £2,465)

RPR

1 **Peppercorn (GER)**[15] [5809] 7-9-0 ........................ PHeugl 2 113
(UOstmann, Germany) *held up towards rear, improved to 4th straight, strong run from 2f out to lead inside final f, comfortably*

2 *1 3/4* **Glad Lion (GER)**[357] [5660] 3-8-9 ........................ IFerguson 1 109
(UOstmann, Germany) *soon led, headed inside final f, unable to quicken*[1]

3 *1/2* **Putra Pekan**[15] [5809] 6-9-0 ........................ NCallan 7 109
(MAJarvis) *always close up, 2nd straight, every chance distance, kept on but always just outpaced* 3

4 *3/4* **Fight Club (GER)**[21] [5683] 3-8-11 ........................ NRichter 4 108
(ASchutz, Germany) *raced in 3rd, every chance 1 1/2f out, one pace final stages* 2

5 *7* **Madresal (GER)**[106] [3335] 5-9-0 ........................ JBojko 3 94
(PSchiergen, Germany) *mid-division, 6th straight, kept on one pace*

6 *2 1/2* **Blomquist (GER)**[112] [3134] 5-9-0 ........................ AGoritz 5 89
(ASchutz, Germany) *prominent, 5th & weakening straight*

7 *4* **Attilia (GER)**[102] [3434] 3-8-5 ow1 ........................ ASuborics 6 77
(PSchiergen, Germany) *always behind*

8 *5* **Seraphine (GER)**[81] [4039] 4-8-10 ........................ GBenoist 8 68
(WHimmel, Germany) *slowly away & last throughout*

1m 45.21s
**WFA** 3 from 4yo+ 3lb **8 Ran SP% 134.4**
Speed ratings: .
**Owner** Stall Biovita **Bred** P A Battel Et Al **Trained** Germany

**NOTEBOOK**
**Peppercorn(GER)** reversed earlier season form with Putra Pekan and in the process landed this race for the third time.
**Putra Pekan** came with every chance approaching the final furlong, but was always just held.

# [5683] FRANKFURT (L-H)
Sunday, October 10

**OFFICIAL GOING: Soft**

## 6107a FRANKFURTER STUTENPREIS DER MEHL-MUHLENS-STIFTUNG (GROUP 3) (F&M) 1m 2f 165y

**3:30** (3:40) 3-Y-0+ **£21,127** (£7,746; £4,225; £2,113)

RPR

1 **Give Me Five (GER)**[68] [4430] 3-8-10 ........................ J-PCarvalho 8 103
(FrauEMader, Germany) *chased leader til went on over 3f out, soon well clear, unchallenged* 2

2 *5* **Mity Dancer (GER)**[29] [5489] 4-9-4 ........................ THellier 4 96
(DKRichardson, Germany) *mid-division, 6th straight, ran on strongly from 1 1/2f out but never threatened winner* 3

3 *3/4* **Golden Rose (GER)**[84] [3973] 4-9-4 ........................ ADeVries 1 95
(HHesse, Germany) *always leading group, 5th straight, kept on well to line*

4 *1* **Anna Victoria (GER)**[7] [5975] 4-9-4 ........................ DVSmith 7 93
(GSybrecht, Germany) *raced in 3rd, went 2nd 3f out, weakened inside final f*

5 *1 1/2* **Norina**[84] 3-8-10 ........................ DBoeuf 5 88
(H-APantall, France) *held up, last at half-way, ran on well from 2f out, nearest at finish*

6 *1/2* **Lysuna (GER)**[21] [5683] 4-9-4 ........................ ABoschert 11 89
(ATrybuhl, Germany) *in rear early, improved quickly at half-way, 4th straight, no extra*

7 *1* **Iduna (GER)**[100] [3504] 3-8-10 ........................ CCzachary 3 86
(WHickst, Germany) *towards rear, 7th straight, stayed on at one pace*

8 *1 3/4* **Silver Swan (USA)** 4-9-4 ........................ PRoberts 10 85
(CVonDerRecke, Germany) *mid-division, 9th straight, one pace*

9 *nk* **Kitara (GER)** 4-9-4 ........................ GBocskai 12 84
(PVovcenko, Germany) *never dangerous*

10 *1 3/4* **Morbidezza (GER)**[21] [5683] 4-9-4 ........................ LHammer-Hansen 6 81
(MTrinker, Germany) *always towards rear* 1

11 *3 1/2* **Esposita (GER)**[357] 4-9-4 ........................ JPalik 9 75
(PRau, Germany) *always behind*

12 *14* **Aliette (FR)**[22] 4-9-4 ........................ ASchikora 2 50
(PRau, Germany) *led until headed over 3f out, weakened quickly*

2m 17.99s
**WFA** 3 from 4yo 6lb **12 Ran SP% 131.4**
Speed ratings: .
**Owner** Stall Capricorn **Bred** Gestut Karlshof **Trained** Germany

# [5970] SAN SIRO (R-H)
Sunday, October 10

**OFFICIAL GOING: Good**

## 6108a PREMIO DORMELLO (GROUP 3) (FILLIES) 1m

**3:50** (4:02) 2-Y-0 **£58,363** (£27,399; £15,449; £7,724)

RPR

1 **Nouvelle Noblesse (GER)** 2-8-11 ........................ EBotti 9 100
(MarioHofer, Germany) *held up, 6th straight, headway over 1f out, ran on well to lead 50 yards out SP 3.41-1* 2

2 *2 1/2* **Gold Marie (IRE)**[77] [4184] 2-8-11 ........................ MDemuro 1 94
(BGrizzetti, Italy) *hld up, cl 7th str, hdwy 2f out, chal appr fnl f, tk narrow ld 100yds out, hdd 50yds out, no extra*

3 *shd* **Umniya (IRE)**[8] [5939] 2-8-11 ........................ (v) DHolland 6 94
(MRChannon) *hld up, hdwy on ins & 5th str, nt clr run fr wl over 1f out, switched outside jst ins fnl f, ran on 7 just missed 2nd* 1

4 *hd* **Novarra (IRE)** 2-8-11 ........................ WMongil 2 94
(ASchutz, Germany) *led over 1f, 2nd straight, headway to lead 2f out to 100 yards out, kept on one pace* 3

5 *1* **Lasika**[35] [5330] 2-8-11 ........................ DVargiu 8 91
(BGrizzetti, Italy) *always prominent, 4th straight, every chance 1f out, one pace*

6 *2* **Pagnottella (IRE)**[102] [3436] 2-8-11 ........................ LDettori 7 87
(BGrizzetti, Italy) *held up, 8th straight, moved outside, one pace final furlong* 2

7 *9* **Sofia's Stream (ITY)** 2-8-11 ........................ PAgus 3 67
(FContu, Italy) *last but well in touvh straight, beaten 2f out*

8 *1 1/2* **Aischa** 2-8-11 ........................ MPasquale 4 64
(LBrogi, Italy) *tracked leaders, 3rd straight, weakend 2f out* 2

9 *9* **Matipapi** 2-8-11 ........................ GBietolini 5 44
(LauraGrizzetti, Italy) *led over 6f out to 2f out, soon weakened*

1m 40.9s **9 Ran SP% 129.1**
Speed ratings: .
**Owner** E Sauren **Bred** F W Holtkotter & Dr N Poth **Trained** Germany

**NOTEBOOK**
**Nouvelle Noblesse(GER)** has a stamina-laden pedigree and middle distances look certain to suit next year.
**Umniya(IRE)** sent off favourite, did not enjoy the run of the race and can be considered unfortunate not to have taken second place.

## 6109a PREMIO VITTORIO DI CAPUA (GROUP 1) — 1m
4:20 (4:40) 3-Y-O+ £129,085 (£64,067; £37,077; £18,539)

RPR

1 **Ancient World (USA)**[43] 5134 4-8-13 ........ LDettori 4 120
(SaeedBinSuroor) *soon led, pushed out, ran on well SP 1.09-1* **6/4**[1]

2 1 1/4 **Majestic Desert**[8] 5940 3-8-6 ........ DHolland 3 113
(MRChannon) *hld up, 6th str, hdwy on outside over 2f out, qcknd to chase wnr fr over 1f out, hard rdn and no imp last 150 yards* **7/1**

3 1 1/2 **Hurricane Alan (IRE)**[8] 5967 4-8-13 ........ PDobbs 7 114
(RHannon) *raced in 4th to straight, 6th to over 1f out, ran on under pressure to take 3rd well inside final furlong* **7/2**[3]

4 snk **Scabiun (IRE)**[1485] 4568 6-8-13 ........ EBotti 2 114
(ABotti, Italy) *5th straight, went 3rd approaching final furlong, ridden and one pace inside last, lost 3rd* **20/1**

5 4 **Horeion Directa (GER)**[40] 5215 5-8-13 ........ GBietolini 8 106
(AndreasLowe, Germany) *first to show, tracked winner to over 2f out* **33/1**

6 1 **Marbye (IRE)**[70] 4383 4-8-10 ........ MDemuro 1 101
(BGrizzetti, Italy) *raced in 3rd to straight, weakened 1f out* **3/1**[2]

7 shd **Ryono (USA)**[15] 5809 5-8-13 ........ TCastanheira 6 104
(PLautner, Germany) *always behind* **14/1**

1m 37.8s
**WFA** 3 from 4yo+ 3lb **7 Ran SP% 114.1**
Speed ratings: .
**Owner** Godolphin **Bred** Darley Stud Management, L L C **Trained** Newmarket, Suffolk

**NOTEBOOK**
**Ancient World(USA)** completed his progression from good handicapper to Group One winner with this front-running performance. He will not run again this year, but remains in training in 2005.
**Majestic Desert** could not peg back the winner with her effort in the final stages. She is another who will be back in 2005 and should profit from the increased opportunites for older fillies.
**Hurricane Alan(IRE)** turned in a consistent performance again and should continue to pay his way at this level.

# 5626 AYR (L-H)
## Monday, October 11

**OFFICIAL GOING: Soft (good to soft in places)**
Wind: mod, hlf bhd Weather: overcast

## 6110 RACING UK ON SKY 432 H'CAP — 1m 7f
2:00 (2:01) (E3) (0-70,70) 3-Y-O+ £3,406 (£1,048; £524; £262) Stalls Low

Form RPR

3050 1 **Habitual Dancer**[41] 5214 3-7-13 **57** ........ PHanagan 3 65
(JeddO'Keeffe) *chsd ldrs: rdn over 3f out: led 2f out: hung lft: kpt on wl* **7/1**

6366 2 1 1/4 **Winslow Boy (USA)**[8] 5817 3-7-5 **56** ........ DFentiman(7) 10 62+
(PMonteith) *hld up and bhd: hdwy 3f out: n.m.r over 1f out: r.o wl fnl f* **10/1**

5216 3 6 **Spring Breeze**[12] 5860 3-8-1 **59** ........(v) PFessey 7 58
(MDods) *led after 1f to 2f out: sn outpcd* **11/2**[3]

1330 4 1 1/4 **Little Tobias (IRE)**[7] 5991 5-8-6 **56** oh3 ........ ANicholls 1 54
(AndrewTurnell) *bhd and sn pushed along: effrt 3f out: no imp fr 2f out* **12/1**

0-60 5 1 1/4 **Alam (USA)**[3] 5834 5-9-8 **70** ........ RWinston 5 66
(PMonteith) *cl up: rdn over 3f out: ev ch 2f out: sn outpcd* **9/2**[2]

2510 6 3 1/2 **Platinum Charmer (IRE)**[59] 4698 4-8-3 **56** oh3 ........(p) RoryMoore(5) 8 48
(KRBurke) *hld up in tch: hdwy 4f out: wknd 2f out* **8/1**

0-04 7 5 **Flame Of Zara**[177] 1463 5-8-5 **56** oh3 ........ TEaves(3) 11 42
(JamesMoffatt) *hld up: rdn 6f out: btn over 2f out* **14/1**

405 8 6 **Pilgrims Progress (IRE)**[15] 5820 4-9-8 **70** ........ TWilliams 4 49
(DWThompson) *keen in tch: rdn over 4f out: wknd fr 3f out* **25/1**

0320 9 3/4 **Crackleando**[7] 5991 3-8-1 **59** ........ JBramhill 9 37
(NPLittmoden) *chsd ldrs: rdn 1/2-way: wknd over 3f out* **4/1**[1]

0000 10 12 **Gran Dana (IRE)**[35] 5344 4-9-4 **66** ........ RFfrench 6 29
(MJohnston) *prom: lost pl 6f out: n.d after* **20/1**

-500 11 18 **Flight Commander (IRE)**[17] 5773 4-9-0 **62** ........ DAllan 2 4
(ISemple) *hld up: rdn over 5f out: sn btn* **66/1**

3m 28.9s (6.43) **Going Correction** +0.575s/f (Yiel)
**WFA** 3 from 4yo+ 10lb **11 Ran SP% 110.7**
Speed ratings: **105,104,101,100,99 97,95,92,91,85 75**CSF £68.70 CT £394.14 TOTE £7.30: £3.10, £3.60, £2.70; EX 117.90.
**Owner** The Country Stayers **Bred** Mrs A Yearley **Trained** Middleham Moor, N Yorks

**FOCUS**
A moderate handicap, but they went a good pace and the form looks reliable.

**NOTEBOOK**
**Habitual Dancer** has not always had things go his way this season but the decent pace suited and he got an ideal trip. He is only modest and needs things to go his way.
**Winslow Boy(USA)**, returned to the Flat after an unsuccessful spin over hurdles, finished well having been very patiently ridden and pulled clear of all bar the winner. He should find a similar race over a staying trip.
**Spring Breeze** had to be encouraged to get to the front, but very much had the run of the race once there and can have no excuses.
**Little Tobias(IRE)** did not really travel that enthusiastically and, although this was an improvement on his previous run, it was still a little disappointing and this ground may have been soft enough.
**Alam(USA)**, an emphatic winner of a handicap hurdle at Carlisle on his previous start, was well held returned to the Flat.
**Platinum Charmer(IRE)** seemed to have every chance but did not appear to stay.
**Crackleando** looked to have conditions to suit and appeared on a fair mark, but he dropped out very tamely. *Official explanation: jockey said gelding was never travelling*

## 6111 EUROPEAN BREEDERS FUND LINFERN MAIDEN FILLIES' STKS — 1m
2:30 (2:30) (D2) 2-Y-O £5,470 (£1,683; £841; £420) Stalls Low

Form RPR

3 1 **Russian Revolution**[20] 5717 2-8-11 ........(t) KMcEvoy 4 80
(SaeedBinSuroor) *chsd ldr: led 2f out: jst hld on* **8/13**[1]

63 2 shd **Squaw Dance**[17] 5771 2-8-11 ........ PHanagan 1 80
(WJHaggas) *keen: prom: effrt over 2f out: r.o wl fnl f: jst hld* **16/1**

3202 3 1 **Consider This**[24] 5604 2-8-11 **79** ........ SWKelly 5 78
(WMBrisbourne) *led to 2f out: kpt on ins fnl f* **12/1**

220 4 1 1/4 **Inca Wood (UAE)**[19] 5729 2-8-11 **74** ........ RFfrench 2 75
(MJohnston) *towards rr: outpcd 3f out: styd on wl fnl f: no imp* **33/1**

642 5 2 1/2 **Zayn Zen**[13] 5846 2-8-11 **80** ........ PRobinson 6 70
(MAJarvis) *trckd ldrs: effrt over 2f out: one pce over 1f out* **9/2**[2]

2 6 5 **Mintlaw**[65] 4532 2-8-11 ........ RWinston 9 60
(ISemple) *keen: hld up: hdwy over 2f out: hung lft and sn no imp* **16/1**

044 7 5 **Globe Trekker (USA)**[12] 5858 2-8-11 **71** ........ JCarroll 7 50
(JamesMoffatt) *bhd: struggling 3f out: nvr on terms* **50/1**

8 7 **Whirling** 2-8-11 ........ NCallan 3 36
(JGGiven) *chsd ldrs: rdn 1/2-way: struggling 3f out* **100/1**

3 9 dist **Limit (IRE)**[16] 5789 2-8-11 ........ ACulhane 8 —
(MRChannon) *in tch: rdn 3f out: edgd lft and sn btn* **10/1**[3]

1m 47.96s (4.84) **Going Correction** +0.575s/f (Yiel) **9 Ran SP% 114.5**
Speed ratings: **98,97,96,95,93 88,83,76,—**CSF £12.80 TOTE £1.70: £1.02, £2.50, £3.20; EX 10.70.
**Owner** Godolphin **Bred** Gainsborough Stud Management Ltd **Trained** Newmarket, Suffolk

**FOCUS**
Hard to know quite what to make of this maiden but the bare form looks fair. Russian Revolution did not really impress in getting off the mark, the third Consider This is pretty exposed but consistent and the 80-rated Zayn Zen did not run to form.

**NOTEBOOK**
**Russian Revolution**, third in a good Newmarket maiden on her debut, made hard work of this and was somewhat disappointing in getting off the mark. She will need to improve significantly to get competitive in a higher grade.
**Squaw Dance**, who showed promise in two runs over six furlongs, improved for this step up to a mile and only just failed. She should find a similar race.
**Consider This**, racing over a mile for the first time, ran respectably but again found a couple too good for her and this trip appeared to stretch her stamina.
**Inca Wood(UAE)** never really landed a serious blow and gives the impression that more positive tactics will suit - it seems to work for so many of her stablemates.
**Zayn Zen** offered plenty of promise on her three previous starts, including when shaping as though this sort of ground would suit on her previous outing. However, having appeared to be going well enough, she lacked a change of pace and did not run to her mark of 80.
**Mintlaw ◆**, runner-up on her debut over six furlongs, was unable to sustain a promising-looking effort and gave the impression she will be seen to much better effect back over shorter, possibly on better ground. One to keep an eye on.
**Limit(IRE)** *Official explanation: trainer's representative was unable to offer any explanation for poor form shown*

## 6112 DAILY RECORD PUNTER "PREMIER" CLAIMING STKS — 1m 2f
3:00 (3:00) (D3) 3-Y-O £5,397 (£1,660; £830; £415) Stalls Low

Form RPR

1 **Trickstep**[60] 4695 3-9-1 **47** ........ DarrenWilliams 1 65
(ISemple) *trckd ldrs: rdn to ld over 2f out: hdd briefly nr fin: all out* **16/1**

0040 2 shd **Charlie Tango (IRE)**[9] 5955 3-8-12 **63** ........ RWinston 3 61
(NTinkler) *hld up: hdwy to chse ldrs over 2f out: effrt over 1f out: led briefly nr fin: jst hld* **6/1**[3]

4011 3 6 **Platinum Pirate**[21] 5705 3-8-10 **65** ........(b) RoryMoore(5) 7 54
(KRBurke) *hld up in tch: hdwy to chse wnr 2f out: edgd rt and outpcd over 1f out* **11/4**[2]

5302 4 3/4 **Campbells Lad**[30] 5449 3-8-8 **45** ........ PHanagan 5 46
(ABerry) *keen: in tch: effrt over 2f out: wknd appr fnl f* **25/1**

460 5 4 **Bijou Dan**[14] 5836 3-8-9 **58** ........ TEaves(3) 8 43
(ISemple) *cl up tl rdn and wknd 2f out* **40/1**

-222 6 nk **Zakfree (IRE)**[7] 5999 3-9-1 **66** ........(b) JBramhill 9 46
(NPLittmoden) *hld up: effrt over 2f out: nt pce to chal* **11/4**[2]

0005 7 3 **Great Scott**[7] 5992 3-9-1 **74** ........(p) RFfrench 2 41
(MJohnston) *led to over 2f out: sn rdn and wknd* **5/2**[1]

0005 P **Fifth Column (USA)**[27] 5545 3-8-5 **53** ........ TWilliams 6 —
(DWThompson) *chsd ldrs tl wknd over 3f out: p.u and dismntd over 2f out* **66/1**

2m 18.58s (6.39) **Going Correction** +0.575s/f (Yiel) **8 Ran SP% 109.9**
Speed ratings: **97,96,92,91,88 88,85,—**CSF £98.39 TOTE £15.70: £5.50, £1.80, £1.70; EX 57.80.
**Owner** Market Avenue Racing Club Ltd **Bred** P Onslow **Trained** Carluke, S Lanarks

**FOCUS**
Just a moderate claimer and, as they went steady early, the winning time was modest for the grade.

**NOTEBOOK**
**Trickstep**, formally trained in Ireland, had the blinkers left off for this first start in 60 days and made a winning debut for his new connections despite having it all to do at the weights - he had 19lb to find with the runner-up alone. Likely to take a sharp rise in the handicap for this, he would have to be of interest if turned out under a penalty.
**Charlie Tango(IRE)**, below form on the Polytrack at Wolverhampton on his previous start, ran better returned to turf and dropped in grade, pulling clear of all bar the improved winner.
**Platinum Pirate**, in good form in similar company recently, winning his last two starts, had blinkers replacing a visor for some reason and that is the only obvious explanation for this below-par effort.
**Campbells Lad**, still a maiden, had never previously raced on ground this soft and did not get home having appeared to be going very well.
**Zakfree(IRE)** had been in good form under similar conditions in maidens recently, but this was most disappointing. *Official explanation: jockey said gelding was unsuited by slow early pace*
**Great Scott** was the best in on official figures, but is regressing and this was a poor effort.
**Fifth Column(USA)** *Official explanation: jockey said gelding lost its action*

## 6113 RACINGUK.TV JOE CARR MEMORIAL NURSERY — 6f
3:30 (3:32) (D2) (0-85,85) 2-Y-O £5,574 (£1,715; £857; £428) Stalls High

Form RPR

0040 1 **Paris Bell**[28] 5520 2-7-12 **62** ........ PMQuinn 7 65+
(TDEasterby) *in tch: rdn over 2f out: led ins fnl f: kpt on wl* **33/1**

1244 2 nk **Zomerlust**[11] 5896 2-9-1 **79** ........ RWinston 11 83+
(JJQuinn) *hld up: nt clr run fr 1/2-way tl swtchd over 1f out: r.o fnl f: hld towards fin* **9/4**[1]

0000 3 1/2 **Selkirk Storm (IRE)**[17] 5767 2-8-1 **65** ........ DaleGibson 4 66
(MWEasterby) *cl up: led over 2f out to ins fnl f: kpt on* **16/1**

3134 4 1/2 **Propellor (IRE)**[58] 4757 2-9-6 **84** ........ DAllan 12 85+
(ADickman) *bhd tl hdwy over 1f out: kpt on wl fnl f* **11/1**

331 5 shd **Tsaroxy (IRE)**[44] 5125 2-8-11 **78** ........ PMulrennan(3) 9 77
(JHowardJohnson) *cl up gng wl: ev ch 2f out: rdn and one pce ins fnl f* **5/1**[2]

4435 6 3 **Dispol Isle (IRE)**[6] 6003 2-8-1 **65** ........ PFessey 14 55
(TDBarron) *prom: n.m.r over 2f out: sn rdn and nt qckn* **7/1**[3]

2530 7 1/2 **Nasseem Dubai (USA)**[5] 6012 2-9-0 **78** ........ ACulhane 15 66
(MrsADuffield) *led to over 2f out: wknd over 1f out* **12/1**

2044 8 1 1/4 **Catwalk Cleric (IRE)**[23] 5630 2-9-7 **85** ........ NCallan 5 69
(MJWallace) *prom: rdn over 2f out: sn one pce* **10/1**

6050 9 2 **Society Music (IRE)**[19] 5738 2-8-10 **74** ........(b) SWKelly 8 52
(MDods) *in tch: lost pl over 2f out: n.d after* **20/1**

0500 10 7 **Sydneyroughdiamond**[17] 5767 2-8-6 **70** ........ SRighton 6 27
(MMullineaux) *bhd: effrt wd over 2f out: btn over 1f out* **66/1**

3060 11 3 1/2 **African Gift**[46] 5060 2-8-2 **66** ........ PHanagan 3 13
(JGGiven) *bhd: hdwy wd over 2f out: hung lft and wknd over 1f out* **33/1**

066 **12** *shd* **Compton Classic**[25] 5578 2-7-13 **63** oh6 ow1 ...................... RFfrench 2 10
(JSGoldie) *bhd: effrt centre over 2f out: sn btn* **40/1**

0000 **13** *1 3/4* **Romantic Gift**[58] 4753 2-8-0 **64** ...................... ANicholls 13 5
(JMPEustace) *trckd ldrs tl wknd over 2f out* **14/1**

160 **14** *4* **Striking Endeavour**[31] 5434 2-8-12 **76** ...................... JBramhill 1 5
(NPLittmoden) *bhd: effrt centre over 2f out: sn rdn and btn* **20/1**

1m 14.98s (1.26) **Going Correction** +0.125s/f (Good) **14** Ran SP% **116.9**
Speed ratings: **96,95,94,94,94 90,89,87,85,75 71,71,68,63**CSF £98.64 CT £1328.28 TOTE £33.40: £6.20, £2.00, £3.20; EX 208.50.
**Owner** Ryedale Partners No 8 **Bred** M H Easterby **Trained** Great Habton, N Yorks
■ Stewards Enquiry : N Callan one-day ban: failed to keep straight from stalls (Oct 22)

**FOCUS**
Fairly strong nursery form. The pace was good which played into the hands of the hold-up performers.

**NOTEBOOK**
**Paris Bell** had not gone on from a promising debut on his last five starts, but this was more like it and he ran by far his best race to date to get off the mark. He has not looked the most trustworthy in the past and one could not confidently predict a follow up, but this will have boosted his confidence and he could well go on from this.
**Zomerlust**, in good form in similar company over six and seven furlongs since winning his maiden, did not get the clearest of runs and had to be switched wide for his run, but he was not an unlucky loser. There is a similar race in him.
**Selkirk Storm(IRE)** ◆ started his nursery career off an estimated mark of 86 but has dropped to a very reasonable rating off the back of some below-par efforts. Faring best of those to race on the pace, this represented a return to form and he should be placed to effect in similar company before the season is out, especially if getting his favoured soft ground.
**Propellor(IRE)**, returned to nursery company, was last of all at about halfway but finished to good effect and clearly appreciated the good pace.
**Tsaroxy(IRE)**, off the mark at Redcar on his previous start, ran creditably in this tougher heat and there should yet be more to come.
**Dispol Isle(IRE)** did not get the clearest of runs and is a little better than the form would suggest.
**African Gift** *Official explanation: jockey said filly hung left*
**Romantic Gift** *Official explanation: jockey said filly was never travelling*
**Striking Endeavour** *Official explanation: jockey said colt lost a front shoe*

## 6114 DOCTOR BILL MORRIS H'CAP — 5f
**4:00** (4:01) (E3) (0-70,71) 3-Y-O **£3,399** (£1,046; £523; £261) **Stalls** High

Form RPR

0201 **1** **Westborough (IRE)**[6] 6009 3-8-10 **58** 6ex ...................... (t) KimTinkler 11 68
(NTinkler) *cl up: led 1/2-way: styd on strly* **20/1**

6022 **2** *1* **Sir Loin**[30] 5473 3-8-12 **60** ...................... (v) ACulhane 10 67
(NTinkler) *led to 1/2-way: rallied: kpt on same pce fnl f* **8/1**[3]

240 **3** *3/4* **Short Chorus**[30] 5473 3-8-7 **55** ...................... (p) DAllan 1 59+
(JBalding) *prom: rdn 1/2-way: kpt on u.p fnl f* **14/1**

1042 **4** *1/2* **Trojan Flight**[18] 5754 3-9-7 **69** ...................... RWinston 12 72
(MrsJRRamsden) *hld up: hdwy over 1f out: kpt on fnl f: no imp* **2/1**[1]

6000 **5** *nk* **George The Best (IRE)**[42] 5193 3-9-0 **62** ...................... PHanagan 3 64
(MDHammond) *hld up in tch: swtchd to far side 1/2-way: kpt on fnl f: no imp* **25/1**

0300 **6** *1 1/4* **Sweet Cando (IRE)**[22] 5674 3-8-10 **58** ...................... (p) RFfrench 5 55
(MissLAPerratt) *in tch: effrt over 2f out: no imp over 1f out* **16/1**

-000 **7** *1* **O'l Lucy Broon**[30] 5452 3-8-7 **55** oh10 ...................... PFessey 7 49
(JSGoldie) *bhd: rdn 1/2-way: kpt on fnl f: n.d* **66/1**

2104 **8** *hd* **Musiotal**[52] 4902 3-8-4 **55** oh1 ...................... TEaves(3) 9 48
(JSGoldie) *bhd tl sme late hdwy: n.d* **16/1**

061 **9** *1/2* **Sessay**[6] 6004 3-9-4 **71** 6ex ...................... PMakin(5) 6 63
(DNicholls) *in tch: rdn 1/2-way: sn no imp* **8/1**[3]

0-66 **10** *1 1/2* **Juniper Banks**[16] 5803 3-8-4 **57** ...................... PPMathers(5) 8 44
(MissAStokell) *bhd: rdn 1/2-way: nvr rchd ldrs* **50/1**

00 **11** *3* **Madra Rua (IRE)**[140] 2353 3-8-5 **55** ow1 ...................... PMulrennan(3) 2 32
(MissLAPerratt) *in tch: rdn 1/2-way: sn outpcd* **50/1**

0004 **12** *1/2* **Fyodor (IRE)**[9] 5949 3-9-7 **69** ...................... SWKelly 14 44
(WJHaggas) *in tch: rdn 1/2-way: sn btn* **4/1**[2]

2020 **13** *hd* **Blue Power (IRE)**[25] 5579 3-8-12 **60** ...................... DarrenWilliams 4 34
(KRBurke) *in tch to 1/2-way: sn rdn and btn* **14/1**

4100 **14** *3 1/2* **Troodos Jet**[22] 5674 3-8-11 **59** ...................... NCallan 13 21
(ABerry) *prom: rdn over 2f out: sn btn* **40/1**

0600 **15** *13* **Mrs Spence**[13] 5849 3-8-7 **55** oh3 ...................... (b[1]) TLucas 15 —
(MWEasterby) *cl up to 1/2-way: wknd qckly* **33/1**

60.90 secs (0.47) **Going Correction** +0.125s/f (Good) **15** Ran SP% **120.1**
Speed ratings: **101,99,98,97,96 94,93,93,92,89 85,84,83,78,57**CSF £164.07 CT £2380.98 TOTE £29.00: £5.30, £3.40, £4.80; EX 49.30.
**Owner** Mr Venning, Mr Parks & Mr Raybould **Bred** Ballyhane Stud **Trained** Langton, N Yorks

**FOCUS**
A moderate sprint handicap but the form seems solid enough. Nothing could get into it from off the pace. Fifth-placed George The Best raced alone far side.

**NOTEBOOK**
**Westborough(IRE)** had looked pretty exposed, even when winning a moderate maiden at Catterick on his previous start but, in defying a 6lb penalty, this was a career-best effort and he is clearly improving.
**Sir Loin**, stablemate of the winner, continues in good form without quite managing to win. He has the ability to find a race, but appeals as one to take on.
**Short Chorus**, 8lb higher than when last successful, would not have minded this ground and ran creditably.
**Trojan Flight** has not been much of a price lately and was being sent off favourite for the eighth race in succession, but he ran well against a bias towards those on the pace.
**George The Best(IRE)**, below par in recent outings, returned to form with a good effort on his own against the far side. He could not get over as soon as he would have liked as there were horses on his outside and he lost a lot of ground when finally doing so, but it is impossible to say just how it affected his chances.
**O'l Lucy Broon** *Official explanation: jockey said filly ran flat*
**Sessay**, off the mark when dead-heating in a weak maiden over six furlongs at Catterick on his previous start, would have found this tougher but was not at his best in any case.
**Fyodor(IRE)** was most disappointing, even allowing for this trip being on the short side.
**Mrs Spence** *Official explanation: jockey said filly lost its action*

## 6115 SUBSCRIBE TO RACING UK ON 08700 860432 LOCHRANZA H'CAP — 1m 2f
**4:30** (4:31) (D2) (0-85,80) 3-Y-O+ **£6,830** (£2,101; £1,050; £525) **Stalls** Low

Form RPR

1112 **1** **Artistic Style**[17] 5773 4-9-4 **80** ...................... TEaves(3) 1 101+
(BEllison) *in tch: smooth hdwy to ld over 1f out: sn clr* **4/1**[1]

1 **2** *9* **Reem One (IRE)**[14] 5836 3-8-9 **73** ...................... PRobinson 5 80+
(MAJarvis) *keen: cl up: effrt over 2f out: kpt on: no ch w wnr* **9/2**[2]

**3** *2 1/2* **Karelian**[107] 3-8-9 **73** ...................... (b) NCallan 8 73
(KARyan) *led to over 2f out: kpt on same pce* **9/1**

3133 **4** *shd* **Millagros (IRE)**[15] 5821 4-9-0 **73** ...................... (p) DAllan 6 73
(ISemple) *prom: rdn to ld over 2f out: hdd over 1f out: sn outpcd* **25/1**

1423 **5** *shd* **Trouble Mountain (USA)**[17] 5768 7-8-13 **75** ...................... PMulrennan(3) 14 74
(MWEasterby) *bhd: rdn over 3f out: styd on fnl f: n.d* **11/2**[3]

2223 **6** *2* **Charnock Bates One (IRE)**[16] 5788 3-8-8 **72** ...................... GGibbons 9 68
(TDEasterby) *s.i.s: hld up: effrt over 2f out: no imp over 1f out* **6/1**

5100 **7** *1/2* **Rotuma (IRE)**[24] 5607 5-9-2 **75** ...................... (b) SWKelly 10 70
(MDods) *chsd ldrs tl rdn and outpcd over 2f out* **20/1**

5450 **8** *3/4* **York Cliff**[25] 5581 6-9-3 **76** ...................... ACulhane 7 70
(WMBrisbourne) *hld up: effrt outside 3f out: nvr rchd ldrs* **33/1**

0100 **9** *2 1/2* **Little Bob**[24] 5607 3-8-8 **72** ...................... KMcEvoy 2 62
(JDBethell) *keen: hld up: rdn over 3f out: n.d* **25/1**

0500 **10** *1 3/4* **Dower House**[17] 5768 9-9-1 **74** ...................... (t) RFfrench 3 61
(AndrewTurnell) *hld up: rdn whn n.m.r over 2f out: nvr on terms* **33/1**

1103 **11** *1 3/4* **Double Vodka (IRE)**[7] 5990 3-8-9 **73** ...................... PHanagan 4 57
(MrsJRRamsden) *in tch: effrt over 2f out: sn rdn and btn* **8/1**

4401 **12** *19* **Lauro**[22] 5672 4-9-1 **74** ...................... RWinston 13 25
(MissJACamacho) *hld up: rdn over 3f out: sn btn* **14/1**

4315 **13** *5* **Tytheknot**[25] 5582 3-8-9 **73** ...................... (p) DarrenWilliams 11 16
(JeddO'Keeffe) *cl up tl wknd over 3f out* **33/1**

210 **14** *10* **Lyford Lass**[157] 1931 3-8-6 **70** ...................... PFessey 15 —
(ISemple) *s.i.s: hdwy and cl up 1/2-way: rdn and wknd fr 3f out* **66/1**

2m 17.07s (4.88) **Going Correction** +0.575s/f (Yiel)
**WFA** 3 from 4yo+ 5lb **14** Ran SP% **118.4**
Speed ratings: **103,95,93,93,93 92,91,91,89,87 86,71,67,59**CSF £19.33 CT £154.76 TOTE £7.20: £2.40, £1.80, £2.30; EX 28.60.
**Owner** Mr & Mrs D A Gamble **Bred** Juddmonte Farms **Trained** Norton, N Yorks

**FOCUS**
A fair handicap won very impressively by the improving Artistic Style. The pace was just ordinary.

**NOTEBOOK**
**Artistic Style** ◆, 6lb higher than when runner-up in a competitive Haydock handicap on his previous start, stepped up on that form with a career-best effort, settling and travelling really well before picking up impressively for pressure. The winner of five of his last seven starts, easy ground is the key to him and he is improving all the time. He should win if turned out under a penalty, but will remain worth following even when reassessed and the November Handicap is a possible target.
**Reem One(IRE)**, off the mark on her debut in similar ground over nine furlongs at Hamilton, ran respectably in this tougher heat but was left behind by the impressive winner. She is capable of improving, but is nothing special.
**Karelian** ◆, a winner over a mile three on good ground when trained in France by Andre Fabre, attracted support on his debut for Kevin Ryan and first start in 107 days and showed enough to suggest he can make his mark in this country.
**Millagros(IRE)** ran respectably over a trip she has still to totally prove herself over, but did not shape like a winner waiting to happen.
**Trouble Mountain(USA)** had conditions to suit and he had been in good form lately, but he was not quite at his best and looks high enough in the weights.
**Charnock Bates One(IRE)** probably would have preferred a stronger pace after missing the break.
**Lauro** *Official explanation: jockey said filly had no more to give*

## 6116 DAWN CONSTRUCTION CONDITIONS STKS — 1m
**5:00** (5:01) (C2) 3-Y-O **£5,997** (£2,274; £1,137; £517) **Stalls** Low

Form RPR

16-0 **1** **Sabbeeh (USA)**[24] 5610 3-8-9 110 ...................... (t) KMcEvoy 5 101+
(SaeedBinSuroor) *keen: led and sn clr: rdn over 1f out: jst hld on* **5/4**[1]

4524 **2** *shd* **Jazz Scene (IRE)**[10] 5920 3-8-9 93 ...................... (v[1]) ACulhane 3 101
(MRChannon) *chsd wnr after 2f: rdn and outpcd 3f out: rallied over 1f out: kpt on wl fnl f: jst hld* **6/4**[2]

1406 **3** *18* **Banana Grove (IRE)**[22] 5672 3-8-7 66 ...................... PPMathers(5) 1 68
(ABerry) *in tch: outpcd 3f out: sn btn* **100/1**

1-14 **4** *6* **Divine Gift**[184] 1330 3-9-5 102 ...................... PRobinson 4 63
(MAJarvis) *chsd wnr 2f: struggling fr 1/2-way* **7/2**[3]

**5** *23* **Katie Kai** 3-8-4 ow3 ...................... TEaves(3) 2 5
(MissSEForster) *sn wl bhd* **200/1**

1m 46.91s (3.79) **Going Correction** +0.575s/f (Yiel) **5** Ran SP% **108.2**
Speed ratings: **104,103,85,79,56**CSF £3.28 TOTE £1.90: £1.70, £1.10; EX 3.70 Place 6 £201.59, Place 5 £63.65.
**Owner** Godolphin **Bred** W R Barnett **Trained** Newmarket, Suffolk

**FOCUS**
A race to treat with caution. Only three mattered on form and one of those, Divine Gift, was a long way below his best. Of the other two, Sabbeeh did not have to run to his mark to win having built up a big enough advantage over Jazz Scene to last home despite not finding much off the bridle.

**NOTEBOOK**
**Sabbeeh(USA)**, a pretty smart juvenile for Michael Jarvis, was disappointing on his reappearance in a Newbury Listed race and did not run near his mark of 110 in getting off the mark for the season. He was quite free early on, but Kerrin McEvoy sensibly let him bowl along rather than try and restrain him and he had built up enough of a lead over the runner-up to enable him to hold on despite finding little off the bridle. He still has quite a bit to prove, but may be capable of better back in a more conventional race.
**Jazz Scene(IRE)**, racing in a visor for the first time, had 17lb to find with the eventual winner at the weights. He took plenty of stoking up to try and peg that one back and may well have beaten him had he not allowed him to get so far clear early on.
**Banana Grove(IRE)** had next to no chance on the form and was outclassed.
**Divine Gift**, not seen since finishing a respectable but well-beaten fourth in the Easter Stakes 184 days previously, was never going and something was surely amiss.
**Katie Kai**, a half-sister to a dual hurdles winner, was in the wrong grade for her debut.
T/Plt: £332.40 to a £1 stake. Pool: £34,227.70. 75.15 winning tickets. T/Qpdt: £69.30 to a £1 stake. Pool: £2,790.90. 29.80 winning tickets. RY

# 5701 LEICESTER (R-H)
## Monday, October 11

**OFFICIAL GOING: Good (good to soft in places)**
The riders reported the ground was 'near perfect, no soft places'.
Wind: Fresh 1/2 against. Weather: Fine but cool and windy.

## 6117 SHELDUCK FILLIES' H'CAP — 5f 218y
**2:10** (2:14) (E3) (0-70,70) 3-Y-O+ **£3,612** (£1,111; £555; £277) **Stalls** Low

Form RPR

0400 **1** **Indian Maiden (IRE)**[65] 4542 4-8-8 **62** ...................... SWhitworth 10 73
(MSSaunders) *dwlt: hld up: hdwy over 1f out: r.o to ld post* **25/1**

0005 **2** *hd* **Emerald Fire**[27] 5541 5-8-3 **57** ...................... MartinDwyer 15 67
(AMBalding) *a.p: led and hung lft over 1f out: hdd post* **7/1**[3]

4306 **3** *1* **Indian Steppes (FR)**[80] 4090 5-8-12 **66** ...................... IMongan 1 73
(JulianPoulton) *hld up in tch: rdn over 1f out: r.o* **20/1**

0-43 **4** *1 1/2* **Riquewihr**[24] 5618 4-8-8 **62** ...................... LDettori 9 65
(DRLoder) *chsd ldrs: rdn over 1f out: styd on same pce ins fnl f* **9/2**[1]

1015 **5** ½ **Bint Royal (IRE)**[16] 5798 6-8-5 **59** ow1 .................... JFEgan 13 60
(MissVHaigh) *mid-div: hdwy over 1f out: styd on same pce ins fnl f* **12/1**

5435 **6** 1¼ **Asbo**[24] 5618 4-8-0 **57** .................... RThomas(3) 8 55
(DrJDScargill) *chsd ldrs: rdn and hung lft over 1f out: eased whn btn ins fnl f* **14/1**

0030 **7** nk **Favour**[12] 5862 4-8-12 **66** .................... KFallon 5 63
(MrsJRRamsden) *hld up: hdwy u.p over 1f out: nt rch ldrs* **5/1**[2]

5064 **8** nk **Missus Links (USA)**[7] 6001 3-9-1 **70** .................... RHughes 18 66
(RHannon) *prom: rdn over 2f out: wknd over 1f out* **11/1**

4551 **9** 1 **Fair Compton**[51] 4937 3-8-3 **58** .................... RSmith 12 51
(RHannon) *prom: rdn over 2f out: wknd over 1f out* **14/1**

0005 **10** hd **Karminskey Park**[44] 5126 5-8-4 **58** .................... WSupple 17 50
(TJEtherington) *chsd ldrs: rdn and ev ch over 1f out: wknd fnl f* **20/1**

4003 **11** ½ **Sharoura**[25] 5583 8-8-7 **64** .................... THamilton(3) 11 55
(RAFahey) *prom over 4f* **12/1**

2464 **12** 1¾ **Pink Sapphire (IRE)**[79] 4148 3-9-1 **70** .................... (b¹) KDarley 20 56
(DRCElsworth) *chsd ldrs over 4f* **20/1**

6061 **13** ½ **Cyfrwys (IRE)**[6] 6004 3-8-8 **66** 6ex .................... (vt¹) FPFerris(3) 4 50
(BPalling) *chsd ldrs: rdn over 2f out: wknd over 1f out* **14/1**

6604 **14** 1¾ **Marabar**[45] 5101 6-8-2 **56** .................... JQuinn 16 35
(DWChapman) *outpcd: nvr nrr* **20/1**

1200 **15** 2½ **Innclassic (IRE)**[62] 4622 3-8-0 **60** .................... (b) BSwarbrick(5) 19 31
(JaneSouthcombe) *led: hung rt and hdd over 1f out: sn wknd* **66/1**

1003 **16** 1 **Somewhere My Love**[154] 2005 3-8-9 **64** .................... RHills 7 32
(TGMills) *prom: rdn over 2f out: sn wknd* **33/1**

0-0P **17** 6 **Red Galaxy (IRE)**[166] 1708 4-9-2 **70** .................... JPMurtagh 2 20
(DWPArbuthnot) *bhd fr 1/2-way* **50/1**

3330 **18** 2 **Emsam Ballou (IRE)**[43] 5155 3-8-9 **64** .................... SSanders 6 8
(VSmith) *hld up: effrt 1/2-way: sn wknd* **14/1**

1m 12.77s (-0.63) **Going Correction** +0.10s/f (Good)
**WFA** 3 from 4yo+ 1lb **18** Ran SP% **127.0**
Speed ratings: **108,107,106,104,103 102,101,101,99,99 99,96,96,93,90 89,81,78**CSF £181.56 CT £3721.89 TOTE £45.30: £8.20, £2.30, £4.70, £1.80; EX 499.10.
**Owner** Chris Scott & Peter Hall **Bred** Shadwell Estate Company Limited **Trained** Haydon, Somerset

**FOCUS**
A modest handicap, but the form looks sound for the grade. It was a very smart winning time for the type of race.

**NOTEBOOK**
**Indian Maiden(IRE)**, returning from a 65-day break, found a rare turn of foot to collar the runner-up close home and win her first race since April 2003. She has dropped 10lb in the weights this season and may be capable of going in again, providing she does not go up too much for this success.
**Emerald Fire** , very well backed throughout the day for this return to six furlongs, was handy throughout and had every chance, but had no more to offer when the winner challenged her at the line. This was by far her best effort for some time and she can certainly make amends off this sort of mark now she looks to have hit form.
**Indian Steppes(FR)**, not disgraced last time off this mark in a much better race, ran another sound race and is one to keep an eye on when reverting to the All-Weather.
**Riquewihr** had her chance, but failed to quicken where it mattered. She ran close to the form of her previous race with Abso, and although this look about as good as she is, she can find a race.
**Bint Royal(IRE)**, who ran a solid race from a bad draw at Ripon latest, again turned in a sound effort, but could not quicken and looks in the Handicapper's grip at present.
**Asbo** did not aid her cause by hanging under pressure, but still ran up to the form of her previous outing at Nottingham.
**Favour** was given a fair bit to do and never looked like getting to the principals. She needs things to fall right in her races and has become frustrating.
**Karminskey Park** was holding every chance until her stamina gave way inside the final furlong. She is best kept to the minimum trip.
**Marabar** *Official explanation: trainer said mare was in season*
**Innclassic(IRE)** *Official explanation: jockey said filly hung right in final furlong*
**Emsam Ballou(IRE)** *Official explanation: jockey said filly was never travelling*

## 6118 EBF HARE MAIDEN FILLIES' STKS (DIV I) — 7f 9y
**2:40** (2:44) (D2) 2-Y-O **£5,707** (£1,756; £878; £439) **Stalls** Low

Form RPR

**1** **Corcoran (USA)** 2-8-11 .................... RHughes 16 76+
(MrsAJPerrett) *lengthy: scope: dwlt: sn trcking ldrs: styd on to ld last 100yds: edgd rt and hld on towards fin* **16/1**

0 **2** nk **Kahira (IRE)**[25] 5592 2-8-11 .................... MHills 11 75
(MLWBell) *bhd: hdwy on outside over 2f out: styd on wl ins last* **66/1**

**3** nk **Tempestad (IRE)** 2-8-11 .................... WRyan 8 74
(HRACecil) *tall: unf: prom: hdwy over 1f out: styd on wl ins last* **11/4**[2]

**4** ½ **Tajaathub (USA)** 2-8-11 .................... RHills 15 74+
(EFVaughan) *rangy: chsd ldrs: led over 1f out: hdd ins last: no ex whn n.m.r nr fin* **14/1**

**5** 3 **Arian** 2-8-11 .................... RSmith 1 70+
(CGCox) *w'like: leggy: scope: dwlt: hdwy in mid-field on ins whn n.m.r over 3f out: nt clr run and swtchd rt 2f out: edgd lft and k* **66/1**

**6** 2 **Hashimiya (USA)** 2-8-11 .................... LDettori 19 60
(SaeedBinSuroor) *rangy: scope: dwlt: sn chsng ldrs: wknd over 1f out* **15/8**[1]

0 **7** 1¾ **Tarabut**[35] 5348 2-8-11 .................... WSupple 13 56
(EALDunlop) *chsd ldrs: n.m.r 2f out: sn wknd* **66/1**

04 **8** nk **Shamrock Bay**[26] 5559 2-8-11 .................... MFenton 12 55
(JGGiven) *led tl hdd & wknd over 1f out* **20/1**

**9** 1 **Toque** 2-8-11 .................... SDrowne 20 53
(HMorrison) *lengthy: unf: unruly ss: mid-div: effrt over 2f out: nvr nr ldrs* **50/1**

000 **10** 1¾ **Ruby Murray**[9] 5943 2-8-11 .................... SWhitworth 3 48
(BJMeehan) *bhd: sme hdwy over 2f out: nvr a factor* **66/1**

0 **11** shd **Queen Tomyra (IRE)**[20] 5717 2-8-8 .................... NMackay(3) 2 48
(LMCumani) *s.i.s: bhd tl sme hdwy fnl 2f* **50/1**

**12** hd **Hoh Hedsor** 2-8-11 .................... JFEgan 17 48
(SKirk) *cmpt: mid-divsion: effrt over 2f out: nvr a factor* **100/1**

04 **13** nk **Romanova (IRE)**[35] 5348 2-8-11 .................... SSanders 14 47
(DRLoder) *chsd ldrs: wandered and wknd 2f out* **10/1**

0 **14** nk **Ti Adora (IRE)**[21] 5694 2-8-11 .................... KFallon 7 54+
(PWChapple-Hyam) *chsd ldrs: wkng whn hmpd over 1f out* **9/1**[3]

00 **15** 1 **Maggie Tulliver (IRE)**[39] 5247 2-8-11 .................... TEDurcan 4 44
(PWHarris) *a in rr* **25/1**

**16** shd **Missella (IRE)** 2-8-11 .................... KDarley 9 48+
(MJohnston) *rangy: unf: dwlt: a in rr* **28/1**

**17** 2½ **Creek Dancer** 2-8-11 .................... JQuinn 5 37
(RGuest) *lengthy: unf: sn bhd* **100/1**

0 **18** nk **Fantasia's Forest (IRE)**[108] 3259 2-8-11 .................... IMongan 10 36
(JLDunlop) *s.i.s: a in rr* **100/1**

0 **19** 3½ **Roma Valley (FR)**[21] 5695 2-8-11 .................... MartinDwyer 18 28
(RGuest) *mid-div: bhd fnl 3f* **100/1**

1m 27.77s (1.67) **Going Correction** +0.10s/f (Good) **19** Ran SP% **119.0**
Speed ratings: **94,93,93,92,89 87,85,84,83,81 81,81,80,80,79 79,76,76,72**CSF £821.64 TOTE £17.50: £4.30, £17.20, £1.40; EX 506.20.
**Owner** K Abdulla **Bred** Juddmonte Farms Inc **Trained** Pulborough, W Sussex
■ Stewards Enquiry : R Hughes caution: careless riding

**FOCUS**
Probably just an ordinary backend maiden run at just a steady pace.

**NOTEBOOK**
**Corcoran(USA)** is long in the back and showed quite a knee action going down. In front she tended to edge right, but did just enough in the end and should make an even better three-year-old.
**Kahira(IRE)**, well beaten on her debut three weeks earlier, stayed on strongly from way off the pace and looks to be crying out for a mile at least.
**Tempestad(IRE)**, a 240,000gns yearling, is up in the air and needs time to furnish. She was putting in all her best work at the finish and looks sure to improve for this and make her mark, but will not be seen at her best until next year.
**Tajaathub(USA)**, a half-sister to useful handicapper Nashaab, stands over plenty of ground. After showing ahead she could find no more when left short of room by the winner well inside the last. This might be as far as she wants to go at two.
**Arian**, a May foal, showed ability on this debut despite a slow start and then meeting trouble when trying to improve towards the inner. She will improve plenty for this.
**Hashimiya(USA)**, a sister to world record-setting miler Elusive Quality, stands over plenty of ground. Bred in the purple, she cost $3.8m as a yearling, but she looks far from the finished article yet and connections will be hoping for a much better return for their money at three.
**Ruby Murray** *Official explanation: jockey said filly ran too freely in early stages and hung right-handed*

## 6119 DORMOUSE MAIDEN STKS — 7f 9y
**3:10** (3:10) (D3) 3-Y-O **£3,601** (£1,108; £554; £277) **Stalls** Low

Form RPR

5554 **1** **Star Pupil**[23] 5652 3-9-0 73 .................... (b¹) MartinDwyer 6 76
(AMBalding) *chsd ldrs: led 5f out: clr 1/2-way: rdn over 1f out: hung lft ins fnl f: all out* **5/2**[2]

4203 **2** 1½ **Barons Spy (IRE)**[14] 5829 3-9-0 65 .................... SSanders 7 72
(AWCarroll) *hld up: hdwy 1/2-way: chsd wnr fnl 2f: styd on* **14/1**

4354 **3** shd **Tenny's Gold (IRE)**[17] 5770 3-8-9 66 .................... MHills 3 67
(BWHills) *chsd ldrs: rdn 1/2-way: styd on ins fnl f* **9/1**

0263 **4** 1¼ **Antigua Bay (IRE)**[27] 5551 3-8-9 66 .................... LisaJones 9 63
(JARToller) *s.i.s: hdwy 1/2-way: nt trble ldrs* **11/1**

22 **5** 3½ **Woodland Glade**[27] 5537 3-8-9 .................... RHughes 2 54
(RHannon) *s.i.s: hld up: hdwy over 2f out: rdn and wknd over 1f out* **13/8**[1]

000 **6** nk **Electras Dream (IRE)**[88] 3882 3-8-9 .................... IMongan 8 54
(MrsCADunnett) *s.i.s: hld up: hdwy u.p over 2f out: wknd over 1f out* **100/1**

4200 **7** 2½ **Scriptorium**[14] 5829 3-8-11 61 .................... (v¹) NMackay(3) 1 52
(LMCumani) *led 2f: remaied handy tl wknd over 2f out* **20/1**

5 **8** 5 **Eshaadeh (USA)**[28] 5525 3-8-9 .................... (t) LDettori 5 34
(SaeedBinSuroor) *chsd ldrs over 4f* **8/1**[3]

-0 **9** 19 **Baba (IRE)**[196] 1174 3-9-0 .................... JQuinn 4 —
(TPTate) *plld hrd and prom: wknd 3f out: eased over 1f out* **40/1**

1m 27.07s (0.97) **Going Correction** +0.10s/f (Good) **9** Ran SP% **111.0**
Speed ratings: **98,96,96,94,90 90,87,81,60**CSF £34.09 TOTE £3.80: £1.20, £4.60, £4.10; EX 32.00.
**Owner** J C Smith **Bred** Littleton Stud **Trained** Kingsclere, Hants

**FOCUS**
No strength in depth to this maiden. It was an ordinary time for the grade and 1.27 seconds slower than the second division.

**NOTEBOOK**
**Star Pupil**, racing in first-time blinkers, won well under a positive ride and did not have to run up to his best to score. This was his first success at the 11th time of asking, and he is far from straightforward, but has ability and his confidence will be high after this.
**Barons Spy(IRE)**, who would have been in reciept of 8lb from the winner in a handicap, ran a solid race at the weights. He was staying on as though a return to a mile would be best and can be placed to find a similarly weak maiden before the season is out.
**Tenny's Gold(IRE)** improved on her recent efforts, but lacked the pace to get serious over this shorter trip. *Official explanation: trainer's representative said filly bled from nose*
**Antigua Bay(IRE)** lost it at the start. She is bred to get much further.
**Woodland Glade** did not help her chances with a sluggish start, but still ran too badly to be true and has not built on the promise of her debut at Newbury in August. She has a lot to prove now, but is eligible for handicaps after this and could show more in that sphere.
**Eshaadeh(USA)** *Official explanation: trainer's representative said filly bled from nose*
**Baba(IRE)** *Official explanation: jockey said gelding ran too freely and tongue was found to be over the bit*

## 6120 STOAT (S) STKS — 1m 1f 218y
**3:40** (3:40) (G4) 3-Y-O **£2,982** (£852; £426) **Stalls** High

Form RPR

0403 **1** **Yashin (IRE)**[27] 5552 3-8-11 53 .................... LDettori 14 69+
(MHTompkins) *trckd ldrs gng wl: led on bit over 1f out: sn shkn up and qcknd wl clr: v easily* **11/2**[2]

0602 **2** 8 **Smart Boy Prince (IRE)**[12] 5863 3-9-2 54 .................... KFallon 1 58
(MJAttwater) *swtchd rt after s: led tl over 1f out: kpt on: no ch w wnr* **7/1**[3]

0353 **3** ½ **Red Rocky**[21] 5702 3-8-1 45 .................... (p) StephanieHollinshead(5) 9 47
(RHollinshead) *trckd ldrs: t.k.h: styd on fnl f* **16/1**

004 **4** shd **Bertocelli**[14] 5843 3-8-11 50 .................... SSanders 17 52
(GGMargarson) *mid-div: hdwy over 2f out: styd on fnl f* **7/1**[3]

5006 **5** hd **Vittorioso (IRE)**[14] 5843 3-8-8 45 .................... BReilly(3) 7 52
(MissGayKelleway) *mid-div: hdwy over 2f out: kpt on fnl f* **50/1**

62P5 **6** 1¼ **Auroville**[27] 5549 3-8-11 55 .................... MartinDwyer 2 49
(MLWBell) *chsd ldrs: one pce fnl 2f* **9/2**[1]

3653 **7** 1¼ **Anisette**[9] 5928 3-7-13 40 .................... MHalford(7) 4 42+
(JulianPoulton) *s.i.s: hdwy on ins whn hmpd over 2f out: nvr nr ldrs* **11/1**

6001 **8** shd **Richie Boy**[2] 6055 3-9-2 58 .................... IMongan 3 52
(PABlockley) *s.i.s: hdwy over 2f out: nt clr run and swtchd lft over 1f out: nvr nr ldrs* **8/1**

0030 **9** 3 **Venetian Romance (IRE)**[44] 5130 3-8-3 35 .................... (v¹) NMackay(3) 8 36
(APJones) *bhd: hdwy over 5f out: nvr nr ldrs* **50/1**

0605 **10** nk **Chiqitita (IRE)**[15] 5451 3-8-1 40 .................... BSwarbrick(5) 13 36
(MissMERowland) *in tch: effrt over 2f out: sn outpcd* **66/1**

0045 **11** 3½ **Valiant Air (IRE)**[12] 5863 3-8-11 40 .................... (b) JQuinn 11 35
(JRWeymes) *bhd: sme hdwy on wd outside over 2f out: nvr on terms* **33/1**

0450 **12** 1¾ **Keltic Rainbow (IRE)**[38] 5257 3-8-6 35 .................... (v) JFEgan 5 26
(DHaydnJones) *mid-divsion: effrt 3f out: nvr a factor* **33/1**

5000 **13** shd **Kalishka (IRE)**[20] 5715 3-8-11 55 .................... KDarley 16 31
(AndrewTurnell) *s.i.s: sme hdwy 3f out: nvr a factor* **7/1**[3]

2000 **14** *nk* **Cayman Calypso (IRE)**[12] 5868 3-8-8 58........ THamilton(3) 6 31
(JMJefferson) *a in rr* **16/1**
6050 **15** *1 ¾* **Mr Moon**[28] 5524 3-8-7 30 ow1........ MLawson(5) 15 29
(JParkes) *chsd ldrs: wknd 2f out* **50/1**
4500 **16** *7* **Ses Seline**[44] 5130 3-8-3 40........ (b[1]) FPFerris(3) 18 10
(JohnAHarris) *mid-div: lost pl over 2f out* **100/1**
6400 **17** *3* **Weaver Spell**[23] 5634 3-8-4 35........ (v) AMullen(7) 12 10
(JRNorton) *mid-div: lost pl 3f out* **66/1**
0000 **18** *14* **Brother Cadfael**[37] 5284 3-8-11 35........ SWhitworth 10 —
(JohnAHarris) *a bhd: lost tch 2f out* **100/1**

2m 8.04s (-0.36) **Going Correction** -0.10s/f (Good) **18** Ran SP% **119.0**
Speed ratings: **97,90,90,90,89 88,87,87,85,85 82,81,80,80,79 73,71,60**CSF £40.11 TOTE £6.80: £2.70, £2.50, £2.90; EX 21.10.The winner was sold to Nigel Shields for 12,000gns. Smart Boy Prince was claimed by Trevor Sleath for £6,000.
**Owner** Roalco Limited **Bred** Wickfield Farm Partnership **Trained** Newmarket, Suffolk

**FOCUS**
A one-sided contest. The winner, who produced a decent effort for the grade, attracted plenty of interest at the auction, and the runner-up was claimed.

**NOTEBOOK**
**Yashin(IRE)**, a fair sort for a plater, went to post early and was walked down. He travelled supremely well and a shake of the reins was sufficient for him to leave this lot for dead. Not surprisingly he was the subject of a spirited auction and he will be interesting in low-grade events from his new quarters.
**Smart Boy Prince(IRE)**, drawn one, soon showed in front hard against the running rail. He tried hard but it was clear some way out that the winner was simply toying with him. He was claimed and is expected to join Charles Smith's yard.
**Red Rocky**, quite keen, stayed on surprisingly well and stamina was not a problem over this extended trip.
**Bertocelli**, restless in the stalls, continues to under-achieve.
**Vittorioso(IRE)**, a maiden after 13 previous starts, had a lot to find and certainly appreciated the extended trip this time.
**Auroville** had a better chance than the winner on official figures but it did not work out that way and he disappointed for the third time in a row.
**Richie Boy** *Official explanation: jockey said colt missed break*

## 6121 TOTEPLACEPOT H'CAP — 1m 3f 183y
**4:10** (4:13) (C1) (0-100,98) 3-Y-O **£13,916** (£4,282; £2,141; £1,070) **Stalls** High

Form RPR
0105 **1** **Massif Centrale**[11] 5892 3-9-8 **96**........ JFEgan 9 106
(DRCElsworth) *chsd ldrs tl led over 2f out: rdn clr over 1f out: styd on* **28/1**
2501 **2** *1 ¼* **Zeitgeist (IRE)**[14] 5834 3-8-13 **90**........ NMackay(3) 3 98+
(LMCumani) *s.i.s: hld up: hdwy over 3f out: nt clr run wl over 1f out: r.o ins fnl f: nt rch wnr* **12/1**
112 **3** *½* **Carte Diamond (USA)**[11] 5892 3-9-8 **96**........ KDarley 8 103
(MJohnston) *chsd ldrs: rdn and ev ch over 2f out: hung lft over 1f out: styd on* **9/4**[1]
1152 **4** *nk* **Lets Roll**[23] 5632 3-8-10 **84**........ MartinDwyer 7 91
(CWThornton) *hld up: rdn over 1f out: r.o ins fnl f: nrst fin* **14/1**
1040 **5** *hd* **Odiham**[40] 5226 3-8-13 **87**........ SDrowne 13 94
(HMorrison) *hld up: r.o fnl f: nrst fin* **16/1**
001 **6** *¾* **Dune Raider (USA)**[32] 5409 3-8-3 **84** oh2........ AMullen(7) 14 89+
(KARyan) *chsd ldrs: nt clr run and lost pl over 2f out: styd on ins fnl f* **50/1**
5012 **7** *shd* **Qudraat (IRE)**[19] 5732 3-9-0 **88**........ RHills 6 93
(EFVaughan) *a.p: rdn over 2f out: styd on same pce fnl f* **10/1**
3000 **8** *½* **Thyolo (IRE)**[23] 5650 3-9-9 **97**........ RSmith 4 102
(CGCox) *hld up: hdwy over 3f out: rdn over 1f out: styd on same pce* **66/1**
1200 **9** *1 ¼* **Motive (FR)**[9] 5942 3-9-2 **90**........ KFallon 2 93
(SirMichaelStoute) *hld up: hdwy over 2f out: rdn over 1f out: wknd ins fnl f* **9/2**[2]
2521 **10** *5* **Camrose**[21] 5699 3-9-6 **94**........ LDettori 5 89
(JLDunlop) *chsd ldrs: rdn and hung rt fr over 2f out: wknd fnl f* **12/1**
1220 **11** *1 ¼* **Secretary General (IRE)**[21] 5699 3-9-6 **94**........ SSanders 10 87
(PFICole) *s.i.s: hld up: hdwy over 3f out: wknd wl over 1f out* **40/1**
1211 **12** *1 ½* **Nordwind (IRE)**[19] 5732 3-9-5 **93**........ IMongan 1 83
(PWHarris) *w ldr tl led over 7f out: rdn and hdd over 2f out: wknd over 1f out* **14/1**
3-12 **13** *1 ¾* **Corsican Native (USA)**[9] 5942 3-9-5 **93**........ RHughes 11 80
(MrsAJPerrett) *led over 4f: rdn and ev ch over 2f out: sn wknd* **7/1**[3]
3140 **14** *13* **Haadef**[100] 3521 3-9-10 **98**........ (b[1]) WSupple 15 65
(JHMGosden) *slwly into stride: hld up: effrt over 3f out: sn wknd* **33/1**
3010 **15** *13* **Settlement Craic (IRE)**[75] 4229 3-9-2 **90**........ JPMurtagh 12 36
(TGMills) *s.i.s: hld up: a bhd: lost tch fnl 5f* **66/1**

2m 31.01s (-3.67) **Going Correction** -0.10s/f (Good) **15** Ran SP% **118.9**
Speed ratings: **108,107,106,106,106 106,105,105,104,101 100,99,98,89,81**CSF £319.49 CT £1072.08 TOTE £42.20: £10.60, £5.30, £1.20; EX 569.30 Trifecta £820.30 Pool: £1,155.48. 1.00 winning unit..
**Owner** Raymond Tooth **Bred** Cliveden Stud Ltd **Trained** Whitsbury, Hants

**FOCUS**
A strong three-year-old handicap run at a true gallop and the form is solid for the class.

**NOTEBOOK**
**Massif Centrale ◆**, 11th of 14 in the Epsom Derby, produced his best display to date and won with authority, despite still looking a touch green. He reversed his recent Listed form with the third horse and can be rated better than the bare form. He is a most imposing sort who is likely to do much better as a four-year-old, and connections are resisting the opportunity to go jumping, in order to give him a Flat campaign next year.
**Zeitgeist(IRE) ◆** picked up really well when in the clear entering the final furlong and has to be considered a little unlucky. He would not have won, but can be rated better than the bare form and should be found other opportunities at this level to get his head back in front.
**Carte Diamond(USA)** again hung left under pressure and failed to confirm his recent Listed form with the winner over this shorter trip. This was slightly disappointing, but he may be capable of much better when back up in trip and with further experience under his belt.
**Lets Roll** was staying on well at the death and enjoyed coming off the decent gallop. He will stay further and on this evidence has not been weighted out of winning just yet.
**Odiham** got going all too late, but turned in a much-improved effort and showed his previous form to be all wrong. He needs cut to be seen at his best and may be worth trying over a little further. *Official explanation: jockey said gelding hung left*
**Dune Raider(USA)**, winner of an average maiden last time on his debut for current connections, confirmed his current well-being and was not at all disgraced.
**Qudraat(IRE)**
**Thyolo(IRE)** failed to stay this trip on the ground, but was travelling sweetly before stamina became an issue and may be about to hit form once again.
**Motive(FR)**, well backed to improve on recent efforts over this longer trip, looked to be in with a chance two out, but found less than looked likely when asked for an effort. He has a fair bit to prove now.
**Camrose** *Official explanation: jockey said colt hung right and lost his action*
**Nordwind(IRE)**, who won his fourth race of the season last time at Goodwood, was found out by his 10lb rise in the weights and may struggle at this level now.
**Corsican Native(USA)**, stepping up in trip, paid for helping set the strong early gallop and dropped out tamely from two out. He can do better.
**Haadef** *Official explanation: jockey said colt lost his action*

## 6122 RACECOURSE VIDEO SERVICES CONDITIONS STKS — 1m 1f 218y
**4:40** (4:41) (C2) 2-Y-O **£6,078** (£2,305; £1,152; £524) **Stalls** High

Form RPR
21 **1** **Sunday Symphony**[37] 5302 2-9-1 83........ LDettori 7 89
(SaeedBinSuroor) *sn trcking ldrs: shkn up over 2f out: styd on to ld last 100yds: hld on nr fin* **11/10**[1]
41 **2** *½* **Bayeux De Moi (IRE)**[52] 4913 2-9-1 81........ JPMurtagh 1 88
(MrsAJPerrett) *trckd ldr: led 3f out tl over 1f out: kpt on wl: no ex wl ins last* **10/3**[2]
601 **3** *shd* **Pevensey (IRE)**[11] 5897 2-9-1 87........ (b) KDarley 2 88
(JHMGosden) *sn trcking ldrs: chal 4f out: led over 1f out tl ins last: no ex* **14/1**
3421 **4** *½* **Haatmey**[14] 5827 2-9-1 87........ TEDurcan 5 87
(MRChannon) *trckd ldrs: effrt 3f out: hung bdly lft over 1f out: styd on ins last* **5/1**[3]
00 **5** *6* **Swords**[11] 5897 2-8-11........ SWhitworth 6 72
(DJDaly) *rrd s: in tch in rr: outpcd fnl 2f* **100/1**
341 **6** *1 ½* **Saadigg (IRE)**[38] 5264 2-8-13 87........ KFallon 3 72
(MAJarvis) *led tl 3f out: sn lost pl over 1f out* **7/1**
1530 **7** *15* **Fenrir**[15] 5819 2-8-13 83........ JQuinn 4 45
(JRWeymes) *in rr: drvn along over 3f out: sn lost pl and bhd* **50/1**

2m 9.04s (0.64) **Going Correction** -0.10s/f (Good) **7** Ran SP% **109.5**
Speed ratings: **93,92,92,92,87 86,74**CSF £4.41 TOTE £1.90: £1.10, £2.60; EX 4.70.
**Owner** Godolphin **Bred** Darley **Trained** Newmarket, Suffolk

**FOCUS**
No gallop to past halfway and as a result a moderate time for the class, exactly a second slower than the seller for older horses.

**NOTEBOOK**
**Sunday Symphony**, who has plenty of size and scope, is a good walker. Caught in a pocket and tapped for toe when the dash for the line started, he buckled down well and was always going to get there. A stiffer test will be in his favour and he should make an even better three-year-old.
**Bayeux De Moi(IRE)** went on and stepped up the pace. He battled back when headed and regain second spot near the line. An even stiffer test will be very much in his favour and he is progressing well.
**Pevensey(IRE)**, who has turned over a new leaf since being gelded and fitted with blinkers, did nothing at all wrong but was just held in the end. He looks to have more stamina than raw speed.
**Haatmey** could have done with a much stronger gallop. He hung violently, only straightened by the running rail, but to his credit stayed on all the way to the line. A left-handed track may be more in his favour.
**Swords**, well beaten on his first two starts, picked up £262 just for turning up.
**Saadigg(IRE)** had the best chance on official ratings, but after setting his own pace dropped right away with no apparent excuse.

## 6123 EBF HARE MAIDEN FILLIES' STKS (DIV II) — 7f 9y
**5:10** (5:10) (D2) 2-Y-O **£5,694** (£1,752; £876; £438) **Stalls** Low

Form RPR
**1** **Saywaan (USA)** 2-8-11........ LDettori 8 83+
(SaeedBinSuroor) *lengthy: unf: scope: hld up: hdwy over 2f out: led over 1f out: r.o wl* **7/4**[1]
0 **2** *3 ½* **Queen Of Iceni**[10] 5915 2-8-11........ IMongan 12 74
(JLDunlop) *s.i.s: sn prom: led wl over 1f out: sn hdd and outpcd* **125/1**
**3** *hd* **Art Eyes (USA)** 2-8-11........ SSanders 1 74+
(DRCElsworth) *cmpt: s.s: hld up: nt clr run over 1f out: swtchd rt and r.o wl ins fnl f* **8/1**[3]
262 **4** *shd* **Rubies**[14] 5825 2-8-8 77........ NMackay(3) 6 74
(RFJohnsonHoughton) *chsd ldrs: rdn over 1f out: styd on same pce ins fnl f* **25/1**
**5** *1 ½* **Always Mine** 2-8-11........ MartinDwyer 10 70+
(MrsAJPerrett) *rangy: unf: s.i.s: hld up: hdwy 2f out: styd on* **40/1**
62 **6** *¾* **Abide (FR)**[21] 5694 2-8-11........ RHughes 11 74+
(RHannon) *trckd ldrs: hmpd and lost pl over 1f out: r.o ins fnl f* **12/1**
34 **7** *shd* **Nice Tune**[30] 5469 2-8-11........ MHills 2 68
(CEBrittain) *chsd ldrs: rdn over 1f out: no ex fnl f* **3/1**[2]
0 **8** *shd* **Royal Jelly**[21] 5694 2-8-11........ RHavlin 17 67
(JHMGosden) *chsd ldrs: led over 2f out: hdd wl over 1f out: wknd fnl f* **66/1**
**9** *2 ½* **Alsharq (IRE)** 2-8-11........ RHills 18 61
(MPTregoning) *leggy: unf: chsd ldrs: rdn and ev ch over 2f out: wknd fnl f* **16/1**
54 **10** *shd* **Blueberry Tart (IRE)**[45] 5088 2-8-11........ SDrowne 13 61
(BJMeehan) *chsd ldrs: rdn over 2f out: wkng whn n.m.r ins fnl f* **14/1**
**11** *1* **Desert Glory (IRE)** 2-8-11........ WSupple 7 58
(DRLoder) *leggy: unf: hld up: hdwy 2f out: wkng whn hmpd ins fnl f* **66/1**
**12** *hd* **Kathryn Janeway (IRE)** 2-8-11........ JFEgan 9 58
(WRMuir) *rangy: unf: hld up: hdwy and hmpd over 2f out: wknd fnl f* **80/1**
**13** *hd* **Figgy's Brew** 2-8-11........ RSmith 5 57
(CGCox) *cmpt: prom: rdn over 2f out: wknd over 1f out* **125/1**
**14** *10* **Mambo's Melody** 2-8-11........ JQuinn 14 32
(PWChapple-Hyam) *leggy: unf: prom 5f* **40/1**
0 **15** *1 ¼* **Moonside**[14] 5825 2-8-8........ RThomas(3) 19 29
(GBBalding) *s.i.s: outpcd* **125/1**
**16** *nk* **Fantastic Night (DEN)** 2-8-11........ KDarley 16 29
(RGuest) *leggy: unf: hld up in tch: wknd 2f out* **125/1**
0 **17** *10* **Make It Snappy**[45] 5088 2-8-11........ TEDurcan 3 —
(PWHarris) *s.i.s: a in rr: bhd whn hmpd over 1f out* **66/1**
40 **18** *26* **Bowled Out (GER)**[36] 5319 2-8-11........ MFenton 15 —
(PJMcbride) *led over 4f: wkng whn hmpd over 1f out* **80/1**
**U** **Maritima** 2-8-11........ KFallon 4 68+
(SirMichaelStoute) *rangy: scope: s.s: hdwy 4f out: rdn whn hmpd and uns rdr over 1f out* **8/1**[3]

1m 26.5s (0.40) **Going Correction** +0.10s/f (Good) **19** Ran SP% **122.7**
Speed ratings: **101,97,96,96,94 94,93,93,91,90 89,89,89,77,76 76,64,34,—**CSF £331.76 TOTE £3.40: £1.10, £43.10, £2.20; EX 312.80.
**Owner** Godolphin **Bred** The Thoroughbred Corporation **Trained** Newmarket, Suffolk

**FOCUS**
This was the stronger of the two maidens and it produced a smart time for the grade, 1.27 seconds faster than the first division.

**NOTEBOOK**

**Saywaan(USA)** ◆, a $1,500,000 purchase whose dam is a half-sister to the top-class middle-distance winner Royal Anthem, produced a taking display to win on her debut. She showed a decent turn of foot to go clear late on and is value for more than the official winning margin. A Derby entrant, she unlikely to race again this term, but looks to have a very bright future and will easily get further next year.

**Queen Of Iceni** , a half-sister to her yard's smart stayer Give Notice among others, stepped up markedly on the form of her recent Newmarket debut and belied her odds of 125/1. She did well to overcome a sluggish start, and despite holding no chance with the winner, did more than enough to suggest she can win a race this year. However, she will not come into her own until tackling much further next year.

**Art Eyes(USA)** ◆, a 48,000gns yearling whose dam is from the same family as High Chaparral, made a pleasing debut. She ran green early on, but picked up well when switched for a run late in the day and finished best of all behind the winner. She is bred to appreciate further and will not come into her own until next year, but can win a race while her yard remains in great form.

**Rubies** ran another sound race, but could not quicken over this longer trip and may be best kept to slightly shorter for now. A switch to handicaps could bring about more improvement.

**Always Mine**, a half-sister to five winners, stayed on under a sympathetic ride after missing the break. She will stay much further in time.

**Abide(FR)** was done no favours when hampered entering the final furlong and can be rated better than the bare form. She will improve when going handicapping, but can find a small maiden.

**Nice Tune**, not disgraced in Listed company last time, ran below par and was disappointing. She qualifies for nurseries after this, but has it all to prove now.

**Maritima**, half-sister to the top-class juvenile Armiger amongst others, was just starting to mount her challenge when clipping heels with Abide.

## 6124 TELETEXT RACING "HANDS AND HEELS" APPRENTICE SERIES H'CAP 7f 9y

**5:40** (6:07) (E3) (0-70,70) 3-Y-O+ **£3,620** (£1,114; £557; £278) **Stalls** Low

Form RPR

3406 **1** **Snow Bunting**[28] 5526 6-8-4 **59** TBlock(3) 6 70
(JeddO'Keeffe) *dwlt: hdwy to go 2nd over 2f out: led 1f out: kpt on wl* **9/1**

0526 **2** *1 1/4* **Bob's Buzz**[2] 6066 4-8-11 **66** SO'Hara(3) 19 74
(SCWilliams) *s.i.s: hedadway over 3f out: styd on to go 2nd jst ins last: no imp* **5/1**[2]

4200 **3** *hd* **Ask The Clerk (IRE)**[9] 5934 3-9-2 **70** StevenHarrison 17 77
(VSmith) *hld up: hdwy 3f out: styd on wl fnl f* **20/1**

1004 **4** *1 1/2* **Little Englander**[12] 5868 4-8-0 **57** JDoyle(5) 12 60
(HCandy) *dwlt: bhd: hdwy over 2f out: styd on wl fnl f* **10/1**

5461 **5** *nk* **Fearby Cross (IRE)**[27] 5541 8-8-11 **66** LauraPike(3) 11 69
(WJMusson) *hld up in mid-div: effrt over 2f out: styd on ins last* **8/1**[3]

0200 **6** *1 1/2* **Hand Chime**[47] 5039 7-8-8 **65** DanielleDeverson(5) 8 64
(WJHaggas) *sn chsng ldrs: one pce whn hung rt over 1f out* **20/1**

0000 **7** *nk* **Out For A Stroll**[54] 4852 5-8-13 **70** JBrennan(5) 13 68
(SCWilliams) *mid-div: styd on fnl 2f: nvr trbld ldrs* **10/1**

1050 **8** *1/2* **Arran**[38] 5260 4-8-1 **56** oh4 KMay(3) 5 53
(VSmith) *rr div: hdwy 2f out: kpt on: nvr nr ldrs* **12/1**

5604 **9** *shd* **Oases**[44] 5108 5-8-1 **56** oh5 (p) StaceyRenwick(3) 4 52
(DShaw) *reluctant to go to s: s.s: kpt on fnl 2f: nvr nr ldrs* **20/1**

0003 **10** *hd* **Colemanstown**[19] 5733 4-8-1 **56** oh3 DonnaCaldwell(3) 7 52
(BEllison) *chsd ldrs: one pce fnl 2f* **8/1**[3]

2000 **11** *1 1/2* **Fiveoclock Express (IRE)**[21] 5706 4-9-0 **69** (p) AKirby(3) 16 61
(MissGayKelleway) *hld up in rr: sme hdwy over 2f out: nvr a factor* **22/1**

0405 **12** *1 1/2* **Craic Sa Ceili (IRE)**[38] 5259 4-8-3 **58** KirstyMilczarek(3) 15 46
(MSSaunders) *racd wd: led after 2f: clr over 2f out: hung rt: hdd & wknd 1f out* **14/1**

0030 **13** *1* **Pheckless**[147] 2178 5-8-2 **57** LiamJones(3) 1 42
(JMBradley) *trckd ldrs: outpcd fnl 2f* **50/1**

0130 **14** *1* **Book Matched**[40] 5223 3-8-1 **58** MStainton(3) 10 41
(BSmart) *chsd ldrs: wknd fnl 2f* **40/1**

2000 **15** *1* **Morag**[29] 5493 3-8-1 **58** RKeogh(3) 14 38
(IAWood) *a towards rr* **50/1**

1400 **16** *3/4* **Simply The Guest (IRE)**[28] 5526 5-7-13 **56** oh2...(t) JaniceWebster(5) 2 34
(DonEnricoIncisa) *a in rr* **100/1**

0100 **17** *2 1/2* **Danifah (IRE)**[1] 6081 3-8-12 **69** RJKilloran(3) 3 41
(PDEvans) *led 2f: chsd ldr: lost pl over 2f out* **14/1**

2000 **18** *nk* **Pick Of The Crop**[23] 5652 3-8-12 **69** AHamblett(3) 9 40
(JRJenkins) *in tch: effrt over 2f out: sn lost pl* **100/1**

3-52 **19** *3 1/2* **Young Alex (IRE)**[27] 5541 6-9-2 **68** (v) HPoulton 20 30
(MCPipe) *racd wd: sn bhd* **4/1**[1]

1400 **20** *7* **Shamrock Tea**[13] 5849 3-7-12 **57** NLawes(5) 18 1
(RAFahey) *mid-div: effrt on outer over 3f out: lost pl 2f out* **40/1**

1m 26.58s (0.48) **Going Correction** +0.10s/f (Good)
**WFA** 3 from 4yo+ 2lb **20** Ran SP% **137.5**
Speed ratings: **101,99,99,97,97 95,95,94,94,94 92,90,89,88,87 86,83,83,79,71**CSF £53.93 CT £951.67 TOTE £12.30: £2.90, £2.40, £4.60, £3.20; EX 102.70 Place 6 £160.08, Place 5 £49.45.

**Owner** W R B Racing 49 (wrbracing.com) **Bred** The Queen **Trained** Middleham Moor, N Yorks

■ Due to Fallon's fall in the previous event the race was 27 minutes late off while a replacement ambulance arrived on the track.

**FOCUS**

An ordinary handicap for inexperienced apprentices. The form seems to tie up.

**NOTEBOOK**

**Snow Bunting**, suited by the strong gallop, recorded his first win for over two years. He was value for a little further as he was eased near the line.

**Bob's Buzz**, who is being kept busy, settled much better as a result of the strong gallop and he stayed on to snatch second spot inside the last without ever looking like troubling the winner.

**Ask The Clerk(IRE)**, who had won just once from 30 previous starts, bounced back after two below-par efforts.

**Little Englander**, suited by the less-firm ground, stayed on strongly from off the pace and really needs at least a mile.

**Fearby Cross(IRE)**, with the blinkers left off, was never competitive, simply staying on in his own time from off the pace. He needs more forceful handling and the headgear back on.

**Hand Chime**, who hasn't won for over two years, is these days just a schoolmaster for the stable's least experienced apprentices.

**Young Alex(IRE)**, runner-up to Fearby Cross at Salisbury, walked round the paddock during the lengthy delay with his ears pinned right back. Drawn wide, he seemed to take no interest from start to finish.

T/Jkpt: Not won. T/Plt: £345.20 to a £1 stake. Pool: £42,682.25. 90.25 winning tickets. T/Qpdt: £17.70 to a £1 stake. Pool: £3,645.40. 151.80 winning tickets. CR

# 5995 WINDSOR (R-H)

Monday, October 11

**OFFICIAL GOING: Good (good to firm in places)**

Wind: light against Weather: fine, becoming cloudy

## 6125 DAVIES COLLISON EBF MAIDEN STKS (DIV I) 6f

**1:50** (1:53) (D3) 2-Y-O **£5,278** (£1,624; £812; £406) **Stalls** High

Form RPR

2 **1** **Nota Bene**[61] 4637 2-8-11 LPKeniry(3) 12 81+
(DRCElsworth) *mde all: rdn over 1f out: styd on to assert fnl 150yds* **7/4**[1]

4 **2** *1* **Gimasha**[13] 5848 2-8-9 SHitchcott 9 73
(MRChannon) *pressed wnr thrght: hanging lft over 1f out: one pce last 150yds* **6/1**[2]

34 **3** *1 1/4* **Inka Dancer (IRE)**[14] 5825 2-8-9 JFortune 2 69
(BPalling) *chsd ldng pair: pushed along 1/2-way: styd on same pce fr over 1f out* **10/1**

36 **4** *nk* **Great Belief (IRE)**[77] 4191 2-9-0 TQuinn 14 74+
(TDMccarthy) *chsd ldng pair: plld out and effrt over 1f out: one pce fnl f* **18/1**

**5** *1* **Peace Lily** 2-8-9 SCarson 8 65+
(RFJohnsonHoughton) *s.s: last trio tl pushed along and prog 2f out: styd on wl fnl f: nvr nrr* **33/1**

6 **6** *2 1/2* **Babe Maccool (IRE)**[7] 5996 2-8-9 AMedeiros(5) 13 63
(BWHills) *racd midfield: outpcd bef 1/2-way: pushed along and one pce fnl 2f* **12/1**

406 **7** *3/4* **Tiggers Touch**[27] 5534 2-8-9 73 DaneO'Neill 10 55
(BRMillman) *chsd ldng quartet: outpcd over 2f out: shuffled along and no imp after* **12/1**

0042 **8** *1 1/2* **Archie Glenn**[21] 5689 2-9-0 79 PMcCabe 7 56
(MSSaunders) *towards rr: outpcd bef 1/2-way: rdn and no imp 2f out* **8/1**

0355 **9** *nk* **Aviation**[12] 5872 2-9-0 76 RLMoore 4 55
(RHannon) *sn pushed along in rr: n.d* **13/2**[3]

05 **10** *1 3/4* **Nodina**[10] 5908 2-9-0 EAhern 3 50
(SCWilliams) *dwlt: a struggling in rr* **25/1**

0 **11** *2 1/2* **Sorceress**[28] 5521 2-8-9 DSweeney 11 37
(JGallagher) *nvr beyond midfield: shkn up and btn over 2f out* **100/1**

**12** *2 1/2* **Athboy Nights (IRE)** 2-8-9 AMcCarthy 5 30
(MJWallace) *dwlt: a in last trio: rdn and no prog over 2f out* **33/1**

**13** *3 1/2* **Mad Marty Wildcard** 2-8-11 DNolan(3) 6 24
(RBrotherton) *sn pushed along in rr: n.d: wknd over 1f out* **66/1**

1m 15.18s (1.31) **Going Correction** +0.15s/f (Good) **13** Ran SP% **117.0**
Speed ratings: **97,95,94,93,92 88,87,85,85,83 79,76,71**CSF £10.90 TOTE £2.00: £1.10, £2.60, £3.20; EX 14.30.

**Owner** W V & Mrs E S Robins **Bred** Usk Valley Stud **Trained** Whitsbury, Hants

**FOCUS**

An average maiden, although the quicker of the two divisions by 1.26sec.

**NOTEBOOK**

**Nota Bene**, off the track for a couple of months since his promising debut due to a muscular problem, had a good draw and made every yard. He did it well enough for his in-form stable and could have a run in a nursery before the season is out.

**Gimasha** looked the main danger to the winner based on her debut effort, and she kept the favourite honest. She looks capable of winning a maiden against her own sex.

**Inka Dancer(IRE)** had a difficult draw to overcome and was not disgraced in the circumstances. She is now eligible to run in nurseries.

**Great Belief(IRE)** had looked likely to appreciate the step up to six furlongs, and he probably ran his best race to date. Handicaps are now open to him as well.

**Peace Lily**, a half-sister to Gimcrack winner Bannister and useful juvenile sprinter Roo, was not fancied in the market but she ran a promising race on her debut. Staying on well from the rear, she shaped as though she would come on for the run and appreciate seven furlongs.

**Babe Maccool(IRE)** is bred to do better as a three-year-old over farther.

**Archie Glenn** *Official explanation: trainer had no explanation for the poor form shown*

## 6126 DAVIES COLLISON EBF MAIDEN STKS (DIV II) 6f

**2:20** (2:23) (D3) 2-Y-O **£5,278** (£1,624; £812; £406) **Stalls** High

Form RPR

0 **1** **Tractor Boy**[49] 5003 2-9-0 TQuinn 2 80
(WJHaggas) *racd midfield: prog 2f out: hrd rdn and styd on to ld ins fnl f* **33/1**

20 **2** *1/2* **Holly Springs**[23] 5648 2-8-9 JFortune 10 74
(JHMGosden) *dwlt: trckd ldng pair: led wl over 1f out: sn hanging bdly lft and hrd rdn: hdd and nt qckn ins fnl f* **5/6**[1]

0 **3** *1* **Miss Tolerance (USA)**[21] 5694 2-8-9 SCarson 14 71
(SirMichaelStoute) *trckd ldng pair: rdn wl over 1f out: styd on u.p ins fnl f* **25/1**

55 **4** *4* **Dart Along (USA)**[10] 5915 2-9-0 RLMoore 13 64
(RHannon) *mde most to wl over 1f out: wknd fnl f* **4/1**[2]

652 **5** *3/4* **Entertaining**[13] 5847 2-8-9 70 DaneO'Neill 9 56
(HCandy) *w ldr to wl over 1f out: wknd fnl f* **8/1**

**6** *2* **High Rhythm** 2-8-9 NPollard 3 50
(SCWilliams) *dwlt: outpcd in rr: kpt on same pce fnl 2f: n.d* **33/1**

0 **7** *1 3/4* **Rosie Muir**[28] 5507 2-8-9 SHitchcott 11 45
(MrsALMKing) *wnt lft s: racd midfield: rdn 2f out: grad fdd* **100/1**

0 **8** *nk* **Flying Heart**[11] 5890 2-8-9 CCatlin 7 44
(MRChannon) *racd midfield: rdn over 2f out: fdd* **20/1**

5 **9** *shd* **Eidsfoss (IRE)**[18] 5746 2-9-0 JMackay 1 49
(TTClement) *restless stalls: dwlt: wl in rr: effrt u.p on outer over 2f out: wknd over 1f out* **50/1**

**10** *1 1/2* **Kitchen Sink (IRE)** 2-9-0 DSweeney 8 44
(PJMakin) *s.v.s: sn in tch in rr: nudged along and lost grnd fnl 2f* **25/1**

**11** *1/2* **Tycheros** 2-8-9 DFox(5) 12 43
(SCWilliams) *racd midfield: u.p wl over 2f out: wknd* **33/1**

**12** *nk* **Sol Rojo** 2-9-0 TPQueally 4 42
(JAOsborne) *dwlt: a struggling and wl in rr* **40/1**

000 **13** *2 1/2* **Waterfront Dancer**[4] 6023 2-9-0 GBaker 6 34
(JRBest) *a wl in rr* **80/1**

1m 16.44s (2.57) **Going Correction** +0.15s/f (Good) **13** Ran SP% **126.9**
Speed ratings: **88,87,86,80,79 77,74,74,74,72 71,71,67**CSF £50.55 TOTE £9.50: £1.80, £1.10, £6.20; EX 39.90.

**Owner** Simon and Holly Turner **Bred** Bearstone Stud **Trained** Newmarket, Suffolk

**FOCUS**

Probably the weaker of the two divisions, run in a time 1.26sec slower than the first race on the card. The race could be rated higher than it has been but the time governs the level for now.

**NOTEBOOK**

**Tractor Boy** was always behind after fluffing the start on his debut here, but he had clearly learnt plenty from that experience and was far more professional on this occasion. Staying on well from his poor draw to take it up inside the last, he shapes as though he will be suited by seven furlongs, although his pedigree suggests sprinting will be his game.

**Holly Springs** looked to hold a strong chance on what she had done to date and she was given every chance. She threw the race away by hanging to her left though, and while easier ground would probably have suited her better, she may just be one to have reservations about. *Official explanation: jockey said filly had been hanging left*

**Miss Tolerance(USA)**, who had shown some speed on her debut, appeared to appreciate the drop back to six furlongs.

**Dart Along(USA)** showed pace again, making most of the running from his good draw, but once again failed to see it out. He is now eligible for nurseries.

**Entertaining** looks worth dropping back to five furlongs.

## 6127 HAINES WATTS CHARTERED ACCOUNTANTS (S) STKS — 1m 67y

**2:50** (2:51) (F3) 2-Y-O — **£3,445** (£1,060; £530; £265) **Stalls** High

Form — RPR

650 **1** — **Missie Baileys**[21] 5695 2-8-7 70 — TQuinn 2 — 63
(DRCElsworth) *prog to chse ldr after 1f: rdn to ld 2f out: in command fnl f* — **5/1**[3]

000 **2** *1 ¾* **Ferrara Flame (IRE)**[40] 5218 2-8-7 — TPQueally 5 — 59
(JAOsborne) *racd midfield: rdn and prog over 2f out: chsd wnr and hung lft fr jst over 1f out: no imp* — **25/1**

000 **3** *2* **Picot De Say**[38] 5268 2-8-11 ow2 — LFletcher(3) 12 — 62
(JohnBerry) *settled towards rr: rdn wl over 2f out: prog over 1f out: nt clr run jst over 1f out and ins fnl f: styd on* — **33/1**

2606 **4** *1 ½* **Lateral Thinker (IRE)**[10] 5910 2-8-13 65 — JFortune 6 — 57
(JAOsborne) *settled midfield: rdn wl over 2f out: styd on fnl f: no ch w ldrs* — **7/2**[1]

0410 **5** *1* **Lorna Dune**[13] 5852 2-8-13 66 — (v) DSweeney 13 — 55
(JGMO'Shea) *trckd ldrs: lost pl 2f out and nt clr run: swtchd lft and one pce over 1f out* — **9/2**[2]

160 **6** *¾* **Pon My Soul (IRE)**[25] 5596 2-9-4 60 — RLMoore 10 — 59
(MGQuinlan) *trckd ldrs: rdn to dispute 2nd pl 2f out: wknd fnl f* — **8/1**

0 **7** *1 ½* **Edith Bankes**[28] 5508 2-8-0 — CHaddon(7) 3 — 44
(WGMTurner) *wl in rr: drvn 3f out: plugged on fnl 2f: no ch* — **66/1**

4305 **8** *4* **Pennestamp (IRE)**[10] 5910 2-8-12 62 — NPollard 14 — 41
(MrsPNDutfield) *led to 2f out: wknd over 1f out* — **9/2**[2]

**9** *1* **Raven (IRE)** 2-8-7 — EAhern 7 — 44+
(JAOsborne) *t.k.h: hld up midfield: prog to press ldrs 3f out: wknd rapidly and eased over 1f out* — **10/1**

6000 **10** *¾* **High Chart**[14] 5839 2-8-13 62 — (t) AMcCarthy 1 — 38
(GGMargarson) *midfield whn rn wd bnd 5f out: struggling in rr after* — **7/1**

00 **11** *3 ½* **Berham Maldu (IRE)**[186] 1307 2-8-4 — HayleyTurner(3) 4 — 24
(MJWallace) *t.k.h: hld up bhd ldrs: rdn and wknd over 2f out* — **66/1**

0 **12** *11* **Stunning Spark**[14] 5840 2-8-7 — PDoe 11 — —
(TDMccarthy) *s.s: sn wl t.o: kpt on same pce fnl 3f* — **66/1**

0 **13** *21* **Jules Lee**[61] 4638 2-8-7 — (p) AQuinn(5) 9 — —
(WGMTurner) *pressed ldrs tl wknd rapidly over 3f out: t.o* — **100/1**

0 **14** *5* **Charlieslastchance**[16] 5792 2-8-7 — CCatlin 8 — —
(JJBridger) *sn bhd: t.o fr 1/2-way* — **66/1**

1m 48.55s (2.95) **Going Correction** +0.15s/f (Good) — **14** Ran SP% **121.7**

Speed ratings: **91,89,87,85,84 84,82,78,77,76 73,62,41,36** CT £4.80 TOTE £1.40: £5.60, £14.50, £; EX275.10 1.The winner was bought in for 10,400gns.Ferrara Flame was claimed by Roy Brotherton for £6,000. Raven was claimed by M. Sowersby for £6,

**Owner** Mrs J Wotherspoon **Bred** Mrs J Wotherspoon **Trained** Whitsbury, Hants

**FOCUS**

Probably a fair seller. The winner did not need to run at her best to account for a couple of improvers.

**NOTEBOOK**

**Missie Baileys**, representing an in-form stable, had the highest official rating of those to have run often enough to qualify for one and was receiving weight from many of her rivals. She appreciated the step up to a mile and drop in grade, ran out a clear winner, and shapes as though she will stay even farther as a three-year-old. Connections clearly think there is better to come as they went to 10,400gns to retain her.

**Ferrara Flame(IRE)** had been readily held over sprint distances, including in this grade, but she improved on that form on her first attempt over a mile. She was later claimed for £6,000.

**Picot De Say** ran a decent race down in grade, staying on from the rear without quite being in a position to land a blow on the winner.

**Lateral Thinker(IRE)**, one of the more experienced runners in the line-up, ran a solid race on her first attempt over a mile. She is likely to be kept busy on the All-Weather over the winter.

**Lorna Dune**, another with plenty of experience, had her chance at the weights and was slightly disappointing.

**Pon My Soul(IRE)** looked up against it conceding weight all round, and so it proved.

## 6128 TOTEEXACTA H'CAP — 1m 2f 7y

**3:20** (3:20) (D2) (0-85,85) 3-Y-O+ — **£7,221** (£2,222; £1,111; £555) **Stalls** Low

Form — RPR

5400 **1** — **Best Be Going (IRE)**[37] 5297 4-8-9 73 — (v1) TQuinn 18 — 85
(PWHarris) *trckd ldrs: effrt 2f out: drvn and styd on to ld last 100yds* — **14/1**

14 **2** *nk* **Diego Cao (IRE)**[7] 5998 3-9-1 84 — RLMoore 2 — 95
(GLMoore) *racd midfield: prog over 2f out: led wl over 1f out: hdd and hld last 100yds* — **8/1**[3]

1000 **3** *3* **Burning Moon**[24] 5607 3-8-12 81 — (v) EAhern 8 — 87
(JNoseda) *trckd ldrs: effrt over 2f out: rdn and kpt on same pce fr over 1f out* — **20/1**

3544 **4** *shd* **Street Life (IRE)**[37] 5297 6-8-8 72 — DaneO'Neill 15 — 78
(WJMusson) *dwlt: wl in rr: prog on outer fr over 2f out: styd on same pce fnl f* — **9/2**[1]

1050 **5** *shd* **Sangiovese**[37] 5297 5-8-11 75 — PDobbs 12 — 81
(HMorrison) *prom in chsng gp: chsd ldr 4f out: led over 2f out to wl over 1f out: outpcd sn after* — **11/1**

2102 **6** *1 ¼* **Patterdale**[7] 5992 3-8-5 74 — TPQueally 10 — 77
(WJHaggas) *prom in chsng gp: effrt to dispute ld jst over 2f out: fdd over 1f out* — **9/1**

0030 **7** *1* **Maystock**[19] 5728 4-8-5 72 — (v) HayleyTurner(3) 17 — 74
(GAButler) *dwlt: wl in rr: nt clr run on inner 4f out: effrt u.p over 2f out: kpt on one pce* — **12/1**

3250 **8** *2 ½* **Arry Dash**[15] 5821 4-8-9 73 — (v) SHitchcott 20 — 70
(MRChannon) *dwlt: sn prom in chsng gp: cl up 2f out: hanging lft and wknd jst over 1f out* — **8/1**[3]

0000 **9** *hd* **Border Edge**[11] 5887 6-8-10 74 — (v) GBaker 6 — 71
(JJBridger) *towards rr: rdn wl over 2f out: one pce and no ch w ldrs* — **33/1**

0-60 **10** *¾* **Brooklyn's Gold (USA)**[17] 5768 9-8-11 75 — CCatlin 1 — 70
(IanWilliams) *towards rr: rdn and effrt on outer over 2f out: sn no prog and btn* — **6/1**[2]

1630 **11** *hd* **Desert Island Disc**[38] 5273 7-8-7 74 — ABeech(3) 19 — 69
(JJBridger) *chsd clr ldng pair to 4f out: u.p and losing pl over 2f out* — **14/1**

0060 **12** *½* **Taminoula (IRE)**[17] 5766 3-8-5 74 — SCarson 9 — 68
(MrsAJPerrett) *dwlt: wl in rr: rdn and stl at rr of main gp whn nt clr run 2f out: no prog after* — **16/1**

4400 **13** *7* **Golden Grace**[67] 4490 3-9-2 85 — JFortune 3 — 67
(EALDunlop) *a towards rr: rdn and struggling over 3f out* — **20/1**

341- **14** *3* **Space Cowboy (IRE)**[169] 5173 4-8-9 78 — AQuinn(5) 4 — 54
(GLMoore) *hld up in rr: shkn up and no prog over 3f out: no ch after* — **25/1**

3100 **15** *2 ½* **Threezedzz**[2] 6069 6-9-0 81 — (t) LPKeniry(3) 7 — 53
(PDEvans) *disp ld at furious pce: clr 4f out to 3f out: hdd & wknd jst over 2f out: eased* — **20/1**

3-00 **16** *nk* **Camille Pissarro (USA)**[9] 5941 4-9-0 85 — FrancesPickard(7) 13 — 56
(DJWintle) *racd midfield: lost pl and btn 3f out: sn bhd* — **33/1**

1500 **17** *dist* **A One (IRE)**[44] 5134 5-8-12 83 — DerekNolan(7) 14 — —
(HJManners) *disp ld at furious pce to 4f out: wknd rapidly and sn t.o* **14/1**

2m 7.60s (-0.70) **Going Correction** +0.15s/f (Good)

**WFA** 3 from 4yo+ 5lb — **17** Ran SP% **130.6**

Speed ratings: **108,107,105,105,105 104,103,101,101,100 100,100,94,92,90 89,**—CSF £117.88 CT £2285.03 TOTE £17.90: £3.60, £2.30, £4.30, £1.90; EX 251.00.

**Owner** Mrs P W Harris **Bred** Michael Normanly **Trained** Ringshall, Bucks

**FOCUS**

The front two pulled three lengths clear of the remainder in what was an ordianry handicap. The pace was strong and the form looks sound.

**NOTEBOOK**

**Best Be Going(IRE)**, sporting the first-time visor, had not quite got it together this season, but the headgear did the trick and he came with a strong challenge down the straight to edge ahead in the final half-furlong. He is on a reasonable mark and if the visor continues to have the same effect, can probably win again.

**Diego Cao(IRE)** has created a good impression since coming over from France and, having won on his British debut at Sandown, performed creditably to finish fourth here earlier in the month off a 6lb higher mark. Back on this sounder surface, he was able to improve again and finished far enough clear of the third to suggest he will still be on a winnable mark after this - he looks highly likely to go up.

**Burning Moon**, who is ideally suited by getting his toe in, ran much his best race since winning at Newcastle and may improve for stepping up to a mile and a half.

**Street Life(IRE)** is without a win in well over two years and, not for the first time, he was doing his best work after the race was all over.

**Sangiovese**, 2lb higher than when last winning, had been starting to lose his form, but this was a much more respectable effort.

**Taminoula(IRE)**, not for the first time this season, received no luck in running and deserves another chance.

## 6129 QUALITY HEATING SERVICES NURSERY — 1m 67y

**3:50** (3:51) (D2) (0-85,82) 2-Y-O — **£7,221** (£2,222; £1,111; £555) **Stalls** High

Form — RPR

2402 **1** — **Alright My Son (IRE)**[20] 5719 2-9-6 81 — RLMoore 11 — 89
(RHannon) *chsd ldrs: prog to ld 2f out: drvn and in command fnl f* — **9/2**[2]

4154 **2** *2* **Im Spartacus**[15] 5810 2-8-13 74 — (p) PDoe 9 — 78
(IAWood) *racd midfield: rdn and prog over 2f out: chsd wnr over 1f out: kpt on but no imp* — **16/1**

622 **3** *1 ¼* **Mystery Lot (IRE)**[21] 5687 2-8-13 74 — JDSmith 10 — 75
(AKing) *hld up last trio: prog on outer over 2f out: styd on ins fnl f: unable to chal* — **14/1**

056 **4** *hd* **Tuvalu (GER)**[42] 5198 2-8-4 68 — NChalmers(3) 14 — 69
(AMBalding) *dwlt: sn midfield: gng wl enough over 2f out: shkn up and one pce over 1f out* — **16/1**

0003 **5** *2* **Darko Karim**[7] 5995 2-8-13 74 — TPQueally 7 — 70
(DRLoder) *hld up towards rr: rdn and effrt over 2f out: one pce and no imp over 1f out* — **12/1**

0313 **6** *1* **Catch A Star**[9] 5938 2-9-3 81 — LPKeniry(3) 5 — 75
(NACallaghan) *t.k.h: hld up midfield: shkn up 2f out: kpt on ins fnl f: n.d* — **4/1**[1]

031 **7** *1* **Speightstown**[14] 5838 2-9-7 82 — TQuinn 1 — 74
(PFICole) *w ldr: led 4f out to 2f out: sn btn* — **7/1**

6243 **8** *5* **Sign Writer (USA)**[43] 5154 2-9-2 77 — EAhern 6 — 58
(JNoseda) *t.k.h: chsd ldrs: rdn over 2f out: wknd over 1f out* — **13/2**[3]

0040 **9** *1 ½* **Fair Along (GER)**[45] 5090 2-8-11 72 — MTebbutt 3 — 49
(WJarvis) *t.k.h: prom: hrd rdn over 2f out: wknd over 1f out* — **33/1**

4100 **10** *shd* **Emerald Penang (IRE)**[45] 5090 2-9-0 75 — JFortune 4 — 52
(PWChapple-Hyam) *led to 4f out: styd w ldr tl wknd 2f out* — **25/1**

453 **11** *1* **Bertrose**[19] 5729 2-9-3 78 — DaneO'Neill 2 — 53
(JLDunlop) *a wl in rr: rdn and struggling 3f out* — **14/1**

024 **12** *1 ¾* **Krasivi's Boy (USA)**[19] 5735 2-8-9 70 — PDobbs 13 — 41
(GLMoore) *chsd ldrs: lost pl and rdn 3f out: sn btn* — **50/1**

0341 **13** *1 ½* **Come On Jonny (IRE)**[7] 5995 2-9-3 78 6ex — JMackay 8 — 46
(RMBeckett) *plld hrd: hld up rr: rdn and no prog over 2f out: wknd and eased fnl f* — **13/2**[3]

1m 46.23s (0.63) **Going Correction** +0.15s/f (Good) — **13** Ran SP% **118.9**

Speed ratings: **102,100,98,98,96 95,94,89,88,87 86,85,83**CSF £72.97 CT £678.46 TOTE £4.80: £2.10, £5.70, £4.20; EX 47.70.

**Owner** James Crickmore **Bred** Calley House Syndicate **Trained** East Everleigh, Wilts

**FOCUS**

A decent time for the type of race, exactly the same time as the following maiden for older horses.

**NOTEBOOK**

**Alright My Son(IRE)**, headed on the line when second at Newmarket most recently, scored a deserved first win. He always held a good position from his double-figure stall and stayed on strongly to run out an emphatic winner. He may be capable of following up under a penalty.

**Im Spartacus**, having his 13th start of the season, takes his racing extremely well and ran another solid race. He should continue to pay his way.

**Mystery Lot(IRE)** is steadily progressing and kept on well without ever posing a serious threat to the front pair. This trip suits and she will be winning before long.

**Tuvalu(GER)** ◆ was unable to take advantage of his good draw and had done all his running by the time he reached a challenging position. He is on a very good mark and will not be long in winning.

**Darko Karim** has run better the last twice and is steadily progressing, but his current mark is a very stiff one for what he has achieved.

**Catch A Star** had run well in a much better race at Newmarket last time and was disappointing. Being held up at this course is never an advantage and she deserves another chance.

**Speightstown** was slightly disappointing, not finding as much as one may have hoped under pressure.

**Come On Jonny(IRE)**, successful in a similar race at the course most recently, pulled too hard to do himself justice and faded out of it.



The Form Book, Raceform Ltd, Compton, RG20 6NL

## 6130 WINDSOR FIREWORKS EXTRAVAGANZA SAT 6TH NOVEMBER MAIDEN STKS (DIV I) 1m 67y

**4:20** (4:20) (D3) 3-Y-O+ **£4,147** (£1,276; £638; £319) **Stalls** High

Form RPR

0222 **1** **Thistle**[13] 5851 3-9-0 76 .......... JFortune 3 70+
(JHMGosden) *mde all: drew clr fnl 2f: easily* **4/9**[1]

0506 **2** *5* **Mac's Elan**[7] 5999 4-9-3 35 .......... EAhern 8 51
(ABCoogan) *hld up midfield: prog over 2f out: shkn up to take 2nd ins fnl f: no ch w wnr* **33/1**

0403 **3** *1 ¾* **Catch The Fox**[9] 5926 4-9-3 40 .......... GBaker 9 47
(JJBridger) *chsd ldrs: rdn over 2f out: kpt on one pce to take 3rd ins fnl f* **33/1**

3243 **4** *¾* **Zwadi (IRE)**[23] 5637 3-8-9 70 .......... DaneO'Neill 1 40
(HCandy) *t.k.h: chsd wnr: rdn and no imp 2f out: fdd and lost 2 pls ins fnl f* **6/1**[2]

4550 **5** *6* **Rood Boy (IRE)**[133] 2517 3-8-11 55 .......... HayleyTurner(3) 10 31
(JSKing) *plld hrd early: chsd ldrs: wknd 2f out* **14/1**

0-2 **6** *1 ¾* **Just Dance Me (FR)**[109] 3222 3-8-9 .......... DSweeney 2 22
(RCharlton) *chsd ldrs: effrt over 3f out: carried hd high and wknd 2f out* **10/1**[3]

6-00 **7** *nk* **Chain Of Hope (IRE)**[15] 5184 3-8-11 49 .......... ABeech(3) 11 27
(DECantillon) *prom: rdn 3f out: wknd 2f out* **50/1**

036 **8** *½* **Shaamit's All Over**[9] 5926 5-8-12 30 .......... DKinsella 7 21
(BAPearce) *s.i.s: a wl in rr* **100/1**

**9** *1* **Caspian Lake (IRE)** 3-9-0 .......... VSlattery 6 23
(MrsLCJewell) *a wl in rr: rdn and struggling 3f out* **100/1**

00-0 **10** *6* **Zorn**[7] 5999 5-9-3 35 .......... JMackay 5 9
(PHowling) *plld hrd: hld up in rr: effrt on outer 3f out: sn no prog: wknd fnl f* **100/1**

0 **11** *6* **Sandokan (GER)**[50] 4972 3-9-0 .......... TPQueally 4 —
(BJCurley) *hld up: rn wd bnds over 5f out and over 4f out: lost tch 3f out* **33/1**

1m 46.23s (0.63) **Going Correction** +0.15s/f (Good)
**WFA** 3 from 4yo+ 3lb **11** Ran SP% **113.0**
Speed ratings: **102,97,95,94,88 86,86,85,84,78 72**CSF £26.79 TOTE £1.50: £1.02, £6.60, £4.30; EX 32.30.
**Owner** Duke Of Devonshire **Bred** Side Hill Stud **Trained** Manton, Wilts

**FOCUS**
A very modest maiden and an ordinary time for the class, the same time as the preceding nursery and 0.54 seconds slower than the second division.

**NOTEBOOK**
**Thistle** had shown the last three times that he had the ability to win a race of this nature and, with credible opposition thin on the ground, made light work of this. This victory taught us little we did not already know.
**Mac's Elan** improved on his placing in another maiden here last week, although this looked an even weaker event. Connections still did well to capture the £1,276 prize money for finishing runner-up with this 35-rated gelding, however.
**Catch The Fox** is only plating class and has had plenty of chances. Connections must be praised for picking up some prize money with this moderate gelding, though.
**Zwadi(IRE)**, who looked the only serious danger to the winner on form, ran badly and looks one to leave well alone.
**Rood Boy(IRE)** will be of more interest back in handicap company on Fibresand.

## 6131 NATIONAL HUNT RACING RETURNS TO WINDSOR H'CAP 6f

**4:50** (4:52) (E3) (0-70,74) 3-Y-O+ **£3,786** (£1,165; £582; £291) **Stalls** High

Form RPR

2562 **1** **Yomalo (IRE)**[24] 5618 4-9-1 **67** .......... CCatlin 12 81
(RGuest) *racd in detached last: swtchd to wd outside and rapid prog fr 2f out: led last 150yds: drvn clr* **12/1**

0322 **2** *1 ½* **Roman Quintet (IRE)**[7] 6001 4-8-10 **62** ..........(p) TQuinn 18 71
(DWPArbuthnot) *hld up bhd ldrs: got through 2f out: cruised up to chal jst over 1f out: outpcd by wnr last 150yds* **7/2**[1]

0503 **3** *1 ¼* **Flaran**[19] 5734 4-8-6 **58** .......... EAhern 4 63
(EFVaughan) *prom: led over 2f out and kicked on: hdd and outpcd last 150yds* **12/1**

0000 **4** *nk* **Full Spate**[2] 6066 9-9-3 **69** .......... RLMoore 9 73
(JMBradley) *hld up midfield: effrt 2f out: styd on fr over 1f out: nvr able to chal* **12/1**

0404 **5** *2 ½* **Majik**[27] 5541 5-8-3 **58** .......... JFMcDonald(3) 10 55
(DJSFfrenchDavis) *rrd s: wl in rr: prog on outer 2f out: kpt on same pce* **14/1**

3022 **6** *hd* **I Wish**[51] 4937 6-8-2 **57** .......... NChalmers(3) 7 53
(MMadgwick) *racd towards rr: effrt on outer 2f out: one pce over 1f out* **16/1**

4303 **7** *hd* **Branston Tiger**[7] 6001 5-8-8 **63** ..........(v) LPKeniry(3) 15 59
(PDEvans) *hld up midfield: rdn 2f out: no prog over 1f out* **8/1**[3]

115 **8** *½* **Oeuf A La Neige**[3] 6046 4-9-8 **74** 6ex .......... OUrbina 8 68
(GCHChung) *s.s: hld up wl in rr: nt clr run 2f out: styng on but no ch whn bmpd 1f out* **7/1**[2]

0010 **9** *hd* **Kew The Music**[18] 5754 4-8-5 **57** ow1 ..........(v) SHitchcott 3 51
(MRChannon) *hld up wl in rr: nt clr run 2f out: sme prog whn nt clr run over 1f out: swtchd lft: nt clr run again fnl f* **20/1**

0050 **10** *2* **Sundried Tomato**[7] 6001 5-8-11 **66** .......... LFletcher(3) 13 54
(PWHiatt) *mde most to over 2f out: wknd over 1f out* **14/1**

0150 **11** *½* **Mimic**[28] 5526 4-9-1 **67** .......... PDoe 14 53
(RGuest) *hld up rr: nt clr run fr 2f out: no ch* **33/1**

0066 **12** *nk* **Extremely Rare (IRE)**[7] 6001 3-8-11 **64** .......... ADaly 16 49
(MSSaunders) *prom: chsd ldr 2f out to over 1f out: wknd* **28/1**

5600 **13** *nk* **Generous Gesture (IRE)**[24] 5618 3-8-8 **61** .......... JMackay 19 45
(MLWBell) *s.s: hld up rr: nt clr run 2f out: styng on but no ch whn nt clr run over 1f out* **20/1**

2400 **14** *½* **High Ridge**[7] 6001 5-9-4 **70** ..........(p) DaneO'Neill 20 53
(JMBradley) *racd midfield: rdn and no ch whn hmpd over 1f out* **12/1**

4-1 **15** *3* **Elvina**[68] 4440 3-8-4 **57** .......... DKinsella 2 31
(AGNewcombe) *wnt lft s: racd on wd outside and in tch: wkng whn bmpd over 1f out* **20/1**

4030 **16** *1* **Dandouce**[5] 6016 3-8-12 **65** .......... JFortune 11 36
(PWChapple-Hyam) *chsd ldrs: wkng whn n.m.r wl over 1f out* **14/1**

6230 **17** *2* **Joy And Pain**[120] 2915 3-8-13 **66** .......... TPQueally 6 31
(GLMoore) *wnt rt s: sn chsd ldrs: wknd 2f out* **33/1**

0100 **18** *6* **Blakeshall Quest**[136] 2455 4-8-5 **57** ..........(v) SCarson 5 4
(RBrotherton) *w ldr to over 2f out: wkng whn bmpd abt after* **33/1**

2602 **19** *2* **Knead The Dough**[6] 6009 3-7-12 **56** oh1 .......... DFox(5) 17 —
(DECantillon) *chsd ldrs to 1/2-way: wknd and hmpd sn after* **25/1**

1m 13.98s (0.11) **Going Correction** +0.15s/f (Good)
**WFA** 3 from 4yo+ 1lb **19** Ran SP% **132.9**
Speed ratings: **105,103,101,100,97 97,97,96,96,93 92,92,92,91,87 86,83,75,72**CSF £51.08 CT £556.93 TOTE £12.00: £2.40, £1.80, £4.30, £4.10; EX 60.80.
**Owner** F Nowell **Bred** Ballyhane Stud **Trained** Newmarket, Suffolk

**FOCUS**
Not a clean race, with plenty of horses finding trouble in running. An ordinary handicap, although the form looks sound.

**NOTEBOOK**
**Yomalo(IRE)** appears to be at her best in the autumn, and having signalled a return to form at Nottingham last time, went one better, finishing well down the outside and avoiding the trouble in running many of her rivals suffered in the process. She should continue to run well for the remainder of the turf season.
**Roman Quintet(IRE)**, who had the cheekpieces back on, finally looked likely to break his string of runner-up places, but he found less than had looked likely under pressure and is clearly not easy to win with.
**Flaran** had few excuses, bar his low draw, as he was clear of the trouble and was still not good enough.
**Full Spate** usually runs well here but he remains a shade high in the weights.
**Majik**, who has performed well here in the past, ran with credit considering he gave up a lot of ground when rearing up at the start.
**Oeuf A La Neige**, in good form of late, is the type who needs to be brought with a late run, and those tactics sometimes mean he will suffer trouble in running. He got no luck this time. *Official explanation: jockey said gelding missed the break*
**Kew The Music** is another who is at his best held up off the pace. He enjoyed little luck in running and can be rated better than his finishing position. He is, however, currently racing off a mark 8lb higher than when last successful.

## 6132 WINDSOR FIREWORKS EXTRAVAGANZA SAT 6TH NOVEMBER MAIDEN STKS (DIV II) 1m 67y

**5:20** (5:23) (D3) 3-Y-O+ **£4,134** (£1,272; £636; £318) **Stalls** High

Form RPR

**1** **Sleeping Indian** 3-9-0 .......... JFortune 4 89+
(JHMGosden) *hld up midfield and off the pce: stdy prog to ld wl over 1f out : sn clr: easily* **1/1**[1]

2-00 **2** *6* **Lasanga**[37] 5297 5-9-3 75 .......... TPQueally 3 68
(LadyHerries) *led after 2f: carried hd high and hdd wl over 1f out: no ch w wnr* **9/2**[3]

00- **3** *4* **Mister Right (IRE)**[353] 5733 3-9-0 .......... CCatlin 6 59
(KBell) *dwlt: wl off the pce in rr: styd on fr over 2f out to take 3rd nr fin* **25/1**

03- **4** *1 ¼* **Bluefield (IRE)**[352] 5757 3-9-0 .......... SCarson 1 56
(RFJohnsonHoughton) *reluctant to enter stalls: chsd ldrs: hung bdly lft bnd over 5f out : drvn and effrt 3f out: looked reluctant and one pce f* **4/1**[2]

004 **5** *hd* **Russian Applause**[42] 5204 4-9-3 65 .......... SHitchcott 9 56
(PRChamings) *chsd ldr over 5f out: rdn to chal over 2f out: wknd over 1f out* **10/1**

2000 **6** *1 ½* **Kindness**[14] 5830 4-8-12 49 .......... DaneO'Neill 2 47
(ADWPinder) *chsd ldrs: rn wd bnd over 5f out: rdn 3f out: sn struggling* **16/1**

000 **7** *5* **King's Minstrel (IRE)**[11] 5891 3-9-0 .......... PDoe 10 41
(RRowe) *s.v.s: wl bhd: effrt 3f out: no ch* **20/1**

**8** *2* **Sustainable Style (FR)**[190] 3-8-9 .......... VSlattery 7 31
(LADace) *s.i.s: a wl off the pce in rr* **33/1**

0-00 **9** *18* **Kwai Baby (USA)**[11] 5891 3-8-6 35 .......... HayleyTurner(3) 11 —
(JJBridger) *s.i.s: a wl in rr: hrd rdn and wknd 4f out: t.o* **50/1**

00 **10** *8* **Czech Summer (IRE)**[10] 5913 3-9-0 ..........(b) ADaly 5 —
(RMFlower) *s.v.s: a t.o* **50/1**

0400 **11** *28* **Unprecedented (IRE)**[27] 5545 3-9-0 48 ..........(v) JMackay 8 —
(TTClement) *led for 2f: wknd rapidly 5f out: t.o* **33/1**

1m 45.69s (0.09) **Going Correction** +0.15s/f (Good)
**WFA** 3 from 4yo+ 3lb **11** Ran SP% **121.6**
Speed ratings: **105,99,95,93,93 92,87,85,67,59 31**CSF £5.41 TOTE £2.00: £1.20, £1.80, £5.90; EX 8.00 Place 6 £216.70, Place 5 £140.57 .
**Owner** George Strawbridge **Bred** George Strawbridge **Trained** Manton, Wilts

**FOCUS**
The sort of time you would expect for the class and 0.54 seconds faster than the first division. The winner impressed but the race is not easy to rate.

**NOTEBOOK**
**Sleeping Indian**, a half-brother to ten-furlong winner and Listed placed Jalisco, to high-class ten-furlong filly Felicity, and to mile winner Spanish Star, ran out a clear winner on his debut. He did not beat much but the style of his success suggests he should pay his way in handicap company.
**Lasanga** had the highest official rating of those to have qualified for one, and he ran a solid race, despite carrying his head high, but he had no chance with the easy winner.
**Mister Right(IRE)**, returning from a year's absence, appreciated the step up to a mile and stayed on well for the minor placing. He is now eligible for handicaps.
**Bluefield(IRE)**, another returning from a year's absence and qualifying for a mark, would have finished closer had he not lost ground when running wide on the bottom bend.
**Russian Applause** probably ran as well as could be expected.
T/Plt: £30.60 to a £1 stake. Pool: £34,046.30. 812.15 winning tickets. T/Qpdt: £23.80 to a £1 stake. Pool: £2,354.90. 73.00 winning tickets. JN

6136 - (Foreign Racing) - See Raceform Interactive

# 5884 MAISONS-LAFFITTE (R-H)

Monday, October 11

**OFFICIAL GOING: Soft**

## 6137a PRIX SCARAMOUCHE (LISTED RACE) 1m 7f 110y

**2:50** (2:50) 3-Y-O+ **£15,845** (£6,338; £4,754; £3,169)

RPR

**1** **Frosted Aclaim (IRE)**[137] 4-9-4 .......... ELegrix 1 106
(BSecly, France)

**2** *¾* **Superman (FR)**[115] 5-9-4 .......... MCherel 5 106
(YDeNicolay, France)

**3** *nk* **Top World (FR)**[347] 5843 5-9-7 .......... ASanglard 8 108
(MCesandri, France)

**4** *2* **Clety (FR)**[29] 5503 8-9-4 ..........(b) TThulliez 7 103
(FDoumen, France)

**5** *nk* **Dusky Warbler**[116] 2998 5-9-7 .......... DBonilla 10 106
(MLWBell) *soon led, pushed along straight, headed 2f out, kept on til weakened final 100 yards*

6 3 **Affirmative Action (IRE)**[29] 5503 4-9-7 ............ TGillet 2 103
(JEPease, France)
7 4 **Soreze (FR)**[51] 6-9-4 ............ (b) OPeslier 4 96
(DSepulchre, France)
8 1 1/2 **Violet Moon (FR)**[29] 5-9-1 ............ YGourraud 9 92
(JBertranDeBalanda, France)
9 nk **Darkara (IRE)**[28] 5533 3-8-8 ............ CSoumillon 3 95
(ADeRoyer-Dupre, France)
10 snk **Epopee (IRE)**[29] 5503 4-9-1 ............ (b) J-BEyquem 11 91
(FRohaut, France)

3m 21.1s
**WFA** 3 from 4yo+ 10lb **10** Ran
Speed ratings: .
**Owner** Marquesa De Moratalla **Bred** George Strawbridge **Trained** France

**NOTEBOOK**
**Dusky Warbler** did not waste much time before taking the advantage and set a reasonable pace throughout. Kicked on early in the straight, he battled on gamely and only lost fourth place in the dying stages. Unusually the ground was less testing than usual at this Parisian track, and he had not run for some time so this race will have done him good. He now goes into the horses in training sale at Newmarket later in the month.

## 6110 AYR (L-H)
Tuesday, October 12

**OFFICIAL GOING: Good to soft (soft in places)**
Wind: lt, hlf bhd Weather: overcast

### 6138 RACINGUK.TV H'CAP — 7f 50y
**2:00** (2:05) (E3) (0-70,73) 3-Y-0+ £3,606 (£1,109; £554; £277) **Stalls** Low

Form RPR
5/0- 1 **Wizard Of Us**[526] 1408 4-8-5 **55** oh5 ............ SRighton 14 63
(MMullineaux) *cl up: rdn over 2f out: edgd rt and lft ins last: kpt on to ld towards fin* **100/1**
5312 2 3/4 **Locombe Hill (IRE)**[15] 5833 8-9-0 **69** ............ DTudhope(5) 15 75
(NWilson) *led: rdn over 2f out: hdd and no ex towards fin* **9/2**[1]
0063 3 1/2 **Able Mind**[40] 5236 4-8-7 **57** ............ PFessey 4 62
(ACWhillans) *in tch: rdn over 2f out: r.o fnl f* **16/1**
0433 4 1/2 **Cherished Number**[15] 5835 5-9-4 **68** ............ (b) RWinston 18 71
(ISemple) *bhd tl gd hdwy over 1f out: r.o wl fnl f* **10/1**[2]
0300 5 nk **Fair Spin**[45] 5127 4-8-10 **60** ............ KDarley 9 65+
(MDHammond) *hld up: rdn over 3f out: hdwy over 1f out: keeping on whn n.m.r towards fin* **12/1**[3]
0051 6 hd **Seneschal**[2] 6094 3-9-0 **73** 6ex ............ TO'Brien(7) 6 75
(MRChannon) *in tch: effrt over 2f out: edgd lft: one pce fnl f* **9/2**[1]
1420 7 2 **Scotland The Brave**[26] 5583 4-9-5 **69** ............ (p) KMcEvoy 7 66
(JDBethell) *trckd ldrs: effrt over 2f out: no ex ins fnl f* **10/1**[2]
6-01 8 3 **Insubordinate**[153] 2036 3-8-6 **61** ............ TEaves(3) 2 50
(JSGoldie) *hld up: effrt and shkn up over 2f out: n.d* **16/1**
0340 9 nk **Rare Coincidence**[26] 5583 3-8-8 **60** ............ (p) PHanagan 12 48
(RFFisher) *cl up tl rdn and wknd over 1f out* **16/1**
4000 10 shd **Francis Flute**[19] 4333 6-8-5 **55** oh6 ............ RFfrench 11 43
(BMactaggart) *in tch: effrt over 3f out: wknd over 1f out* **25/1**
2100 11 1/2 **Parisian Playboy**[45] 5127 4-7-12 **55** oh6 ............ LeanneKershaw(7) 8 42
(JeddO'Keeffe) *midfield: rdn 3f out: sn one pce* **12/1**[3]
0000 12 1/2 **Pop Up Again**[98] 3606 4-9-4 **68** ............ WSupple 17 53
(GASwinbank) *hld up: rdn over 2f out: edgd lft: sn n.d* **50/1**
0500 13 nk **Pawan (IRE)**[66] 4558 4-9-3 **67** ............ AnnStokell 10 52
(MissAStokell) *hld up towards rr: rdn over 2f out: n.d* **40/1**
1040 14 1/2 **Musiotal**[1] 6114 3-8-3 **55** oh1 ............ CCatlin 3 38
(JSGoldie) *hld up: rdn 3f out: n.d* **14/1**
300 15 2 **Washbrook**[13] 5859 3-8-3 **55** ............ (t) ANicholls 1 33
(AndrewTurnell) *a bhd* **50/1**
0020 16 1/2 **Showtime Annie**[13] 5859 3-9-0 **66** ............ MFenton 16 43
(ABailey) *midfield: rdn 3f out: sn btn* **20/1**
5105 17 1 **Headland (USA)**[14] 5849 6-8-7 **57** ............ (be) ACulhane 13 31
(DWChapman) *dwlt: a bhd* **25/1**

1m 34.92s (2.45) **Going Correction** +0.55s/f (Yiel)
**WFA** 3 from 4yo+ 2lb **17** Ran **SP% 114.0**
Speed ratings: **108,107,106,106,105 105,103,99,99,99 98,98,97,97,94 94,93** CSF £465.38 CT £7769.74 TOTE £114.10: £27.80, £1.60, £4.40, £1.60; EX 1671.20.
**Owner** P Currey **Bred** S Mellor **Trained** Alpraham, Cheshire

**FOCUS**
A shock winner, but no apparent fluke in the result and the time was good. An ordinary handicap.

**NOTEBOOK**
**Wizard Of Us**, returning from 526 days off, was a clear winner after being settled close to the pace. He had never indicated a win was due but having had treatment on his teeth, and a good rest, he showed much improved form. He appears to be a nervous type on the racecourse, but if this has not left its mark on him he could be able to follow up in a similarly low grade.
**Locombe Hill(IRE)** has been in fine form recently and again ran a solid race. He managed to take up the running from his moderate draw and was only collared inside the final furlong. His form figures suggests he runs well at this time of the year and another win cannot be ruled out before the end of this season under similar ground conditions.
**Able Mind**, who has a lot of placed efforts in his form, added another third. He has form at up to a mile and unsurprisingly stayed on well towards the line. It would be a bit unfair to call him a tricky ride, given his form figures, but he did appear to waver a touch inside the final furlong. If everything goes right for him he should be able to pick up a similar contest.
**Cherished Number** was going nowhere fast entering the straight but finished to good effect on the outside. He was dropped in trip from nine furlongs recently and understandably stayed on well without ever looking likely to win. He almost certainly wants a bit further, and is well handicapped at this moment, but does not win very often and will probably pop up when least expected.
**Fair Spin** has looked a difficult ride on occasions and again dropped towards the rear early on. He has been running over a mile recently so it was no surprise to see him weave through weakening horses and finish fairly well. He has not won since his debut in Italy and, although the ability is probably there, he is clearly not easy to win with. *Official explanation: jockey said gelding ran out of room in closing stages*
**Seneschal**, who had won two days previously, was always thereabouts and stayed on without ever looking threatening. His win had come on faster ground at Newcastle so perhaps he does not want it as soft as it was on this occasion.
**Scotland The Brave** is very slowly coming down in the handicap and was running a fair race until meeting minor interference in the final stages. However this did not affect his eventual placing.

### 6139 EUROPEAN BREEDERS FUND KIRKOSWALD MAIDEN STKS — 7f 50y
**2:30** (2:35) (D2) 2-Y-0 £5,605 (£1,724; £862; £431) **Stalls** Low

Form RPR
42 1 **Kames Park (IRE)**[23] 5669 2-9-0 ............ RWinston 4 80
(ISemple) *keen: chsd ldr: effrt over 2f out: led and hung lft ins fnl f: r.o* **16/1**
4 2 1 **Alrafidain (IRE)**[12] 5897 2-9-0 ............ WSupple 8 78
(MJohnston) *led: pushed along 2f out: hdd ins fnl f: one pce* **4/5**[1]
3 3 3 1/2 **Onyergo (IRE)**[43] 5186 2-8-11 ............ PMulrennan(3) 2 69
(JRWeymes) *prom: rdn over 2f out: kpt on fnl f: no imp* **33/1**
3 4 4 **Il Colosseo (IRE)**[45] 5128 2-9-0 ............ DAllan 9 59
(MrsLStubbs) *in tch: outpcd over 2f out: n.d after* **12/1**[3]
5 1 3/4 **Scriptwriter (IRE)** 2-9-0 ............ KMcEvoy 3 55
(SaeedBinSuroor) *s.i.s: sn niggled along in rr: styd alone far side ent st: rdn and flashed tail over 2f out: no imp* **5/2**[2]
0436 6 1 3/4 **Lake Wakatipu**[17] 5789 2-8-9 **57** ............ SRighton 7 46
(MMullineaux) *chsd ldrs tl rdn and wknd over 2f out* **66/1**
6 7 1 1/4 **Blue Bajan (IRE)**[13] 5858 2-9-0 ............ CCatlin 6 48
(AndrewTurnell) *hld up in tch: pushed along 3f out: sn btn* **25/1**
0 8 9 **Showtime Faye**[13] 5855 2-8-9 ............ PHanagan 5 21
(ABailey) *in tch to over 3f out: sn btn* **150/1**
006 9 5 **Ansells Legacy (IRE)**[31] 5476 2-9-0 **53** ............ ACulhane 1 13
(ABerry) *hld up: lost tch fr over 3f out* **150/1**

1m 37.36s (4.89) **Going Correction** +0.55s/f (Yiel) **9** Ran **SP% 107.3**
Speed ratings: **94,92,88,84,82 80,78,68,62** CSF £26.32 TOTE £8.10: £2.20, £1.02, £5.90; EX 55.80.
**Owner** Mrs June Delaney **Bred** Pat Beirne **Trained** Carluke, S Lanarks
■ Stewards Enquiry : S Righton one-day ban: used whip when filly was showing no response (Oct 25)

**FOCUS**
This form looks solid although the time doesn't back this up. The first two dominated.

**NOTEBOOK**
**Kames Park(IRE)**, dropped back a furlong since his last run, stayed on really well to the line to overhaul the long-time leader in the final furlong. He is a nice big type and will probably improve with age, and connections even muted he may make a nice hurdler in time.
**Alrafidain(IRE)**, dropped back a furlong from his last run, set out to make all and looked to have plenty on the stretch inside the last two furlongs. However he tired inside the final furlong and probably found his early exertions taking their toll in the end. He is worth another chance on this evidence and a quicker surface.
**Onyergo(IRE)** could never land a blow on the two protagonists, but stayed on nicely to beat the rest the field in fair style. His relations include staying types so he is probably going to be seen to better effect next year over middle distances, although he does appear to have enough ability as a two-year-old to could pick up a mile plus maiden in the right grade.
**Il Colosseo(IRE)** had shown a modicum of promise on his debut and continued in that vain by staying on towards the end. He will need a less competitive maiden to have a chance of winning though on this evidence
**Scriptwriter(IRE)**, who was not overly fancied for such a well-bred Godolphin newcomer, showed as much temperament as ability in the race. He completely missed the break and stayed away from the rest of the field on the far-side- rail. To be fair to the horse he never got totaly left behind but, did flash his tail a few times when given a few taps with the tip and looks to be a tricky customer on this evidence. *Official explanation: jockey said colt ran green*
**Lake Wakatipu** was reluctant to go in the stalls and was never a factor.
**Blue Bajan(IRE)** again showed a modicum of ability and will make a better three-year-old.

### 6140 DAILY RECORD GARY OWEN NURSERY — 1m
**3:00** (3:02) (D2) (0-85,82) 2-Y-0 £5,616 (£1,728; £864; £432) **Stalls** Low

Form RPR
2221 1 **King's Account (USA)**[27] 5561 2-9-7 **82** ............ KDarley 4 87
(MJohnston) *cl up: led over 2f out: sn hrd pressed: hld on gamely fnl f* **9/2**[2]
002 2 nk **Stancomb Wills (IRE)**[27] 5561 2-9-0 **75** ............ NCallan 5 80
(MHTompkins) *trckd ldrs: rdn 3f out: kpt on wl fnl f* **10/1**
6653 3 nk **Guinea A Minute (IRE)**[28] 5539 2-7-12 **62** ............ HayleyTurner(3) 6 66
(MLWBell) *keen: cl up: effrt and disp ld over 2f out: one pce wl ins fnl f* **5/1**[3]
004 4 2 1/2 **Last Pioneer (IRE)**[15] 5831 2-8-4 **65** ............ RFfrench 3 64
(TPTate) *hld up: effrt and rdn over 3f out: no imp fnl f* **40/1**
0312 5 1 **Lady Misha**[43] 5188 2-8-12 **73** ............ PHanagan 10 69
(JeddO'Keeffe) *hld up in tch: effrt 3f out: nt clr run over 1f out: kpt on fnl f: no imp* **4/1**[1]
6004 6 shd **Along The Nile**[24] 5636 2-8-9 **70** ............ ACulhane 11 66
(MrsJRRamsden) *hld up: rdn 3f out: kpt on fnl f: nvr rchd ldrs* **7/1**
0326 7 2 **Robinzal**[38] 5307 2-8-8 **69** ............ DAllan 7 61
(TDEasterby) *keen in midfield: effrt over 2f out: btn fnl f* **25/1**
0320 8 1 1/4 **Velveteen Rabbit**[28] 5548 2-8-11 **72** ............ KMcEvoy 2 61
(SaeedBinSuroor) *prom: effrt over 2f out: btn fnl f* **16/1**
0001 9 1/2 **Bronze Dancer (IRE)**[13] 5856 2-8-9 **70** ............ RWinston 8 58
(GASwinbank) *in tch: effrt over 2f out: hung lft and wknd over 1f out* **14/1**
0006 10 6 **Shujune Al Hawaa (IRE)**[12] 5885 2-8-2 **63** ............ (v) CCatlin 12 38
(MRChannon) *sn bhd: outpcd fr over 3f out* **16/1**
5600 11 1 1/4 **Three Aces (IRE)**[20] 5738 2-7-12 **59** oh3 ............ (b) JMackay 9 31
(RMBeckett) *s.i.s: nvr on terms* **50/1**
003 12 12 **Blushing Russian (IRE)**[38] 5301 2-7-6 **60** ............ DFentiman(7) 1 5
(PCHaslam) *led to over 2f out: sn btn* **10/1**

1m 47.66s (4.54) **Going Correction** +0.55s/f (Yiel) **12** Ran **SP% 112.2**
Speed ratings: **99,98,98,95,94 94,92,91,91,85 83,71** CSF £45.39 CT £230.07 TOTE £5.30: £1.60, £4.60, £2.70; EX 31.00.
**Owner** Brian Yeardley Continental Ltd **Bred** Barnett Enterprises **Trained** Middleham Moor, N Yorks

**FOCUS**
A competitive nursery on paper with a good finish. The form looks pretty solid and should work out well.

**NOTEBOOK**
**King's Account(USA)**, who confirmed positions with the second on 7lb worse terms, stayed on really well to the line, looking to appreciate the step back up in trip. He has form on the going and looks to be improving, but his future will be governed by what the Handicapper does with him now.
**Stancomb Wills(IRE)** was better off with the winner but never looked like using that advantage. He was settled in midfield and had his chance in the home straight but could never get on terms. He has the ability to win a race on this evidence at this trip.
**Guinea A Minute(IRE)** has been running well of late since being stepped up in trip, and ran another solid race although receiving a lot of weight. She does have a tendency to hang under pressure but did not appear to do so this time, and has the ability to run well in a similar contest.
**Last Pioneer(IRE)** still looked a bit green on this nursery debut, but stayed on well from a midfield position. He can pick up a weak nursery somewhere before the end of the season, probably at a stiffer track.

**Lady Misha**, who has risen over 10lb in the weights since her nursery win, was staying on fairly well when getting hampered inside the last two furlongs. She stays a mile well but the incident happened a bit too late to know how much effect it had on the final result. She is probably still more than capable off this mark though. *Official explanation: jockey said filly hung left handed throughout*
**Along The Nile** always seems to run the same kind of race. Held up at the back, he took an age to pick up until finding his stride late on. He will probably be a hard horse to win with.
**Bronze Dancer(IRE)** *Official explanation: jockey said gelding was unsuited by good to soft, soft in places ground*
**Blushing Russian(IRE)** went off exceptional quickly in the conditions but stayed competitive for at least six furlongs. He surely needs to revert to sprinting on this evidence.

## 6141 SUBSCRIBE TO RACING UK ON 08700 860432 MAIDEN STKS 1m 2f
**3:30** (3:32) (E3) 3-Y-0+ **£5,491** (£1,689; £844; £422) **Stalls** Low

| Form | | | | | RPR |
|---|---|---|---|---|---|
| 4325 | **1** | | **Ouninpohja (IRE)**[38] 5297 3-9-0 72 | RWinston 9 | 76+ |
| | | | (GASwinbank) *hld up: hdwy over 2f out: hung lft: led over 1f out: sn clr* | **10/11**[1] | |
| 2263 | **2** | *4* | **Young Rooney**[10] 5950 4-9-5 70 | KDarley 7 | 64 |
| | | | (MMullineaux) *led and sn clr: hdd over 1f out: no ch w wnr* | **3/1**[2] | |
| 0240 | **3** | *2* | **Loaded Gun**[26] 5584 4-9-5 53 | SWKelly 11 | 60 |
| | | | (WMBrisbourne) *hld up in tch: hdwy 3f out: no imp over 1f out* | **12/1** | |
| 30-2 | **4** | *6* | **Shares (IRE)**[197] 1172 4-9-5 60 | RFfrench 10 | 49 |
| | | | (PMonteith) *hld up: rdn over 3f out: no imp fr 2f out* | **9/1**[3] | |
| 00 | **5** | *5* | **Stravonian**[50] 4987 4-9-0 | PPMathers(5) 2 | 40 |
| | | | (DANolan) *midfield: effrt over 3f out: wknd fr 2f out* | **150/1** | |
| 4330 | **6** | *14* | **Kyber**[13] 5860 3-9-0 60 | PHanagan 1 | 15 |
| | | | (RFFisher) *chsd ldrs to 3f out: sn wknd* | **40/1** | |
| 0 | **7** | *3* | **Bodfari Dream**[18] 5770 3-8-9 | SRighton 5 | 5 |
| | | | (MMullineaux) *dwlt: a bhd* | **100/1** | |
| 5-25 | **8** | *½* | **Queen's Echo**[36] 5345 3-8-9 57 | LEnstone 4 | 4 |
| | | | (MDods) *prom tl wknd over 2f out* | **33/1** | |
| 0/0- | **9** | *3½* | **Spectrum Star**[43] 1308 4-9-2 40 | PMulrennan(3) 13 | 2 |
| | | | (FPMurtagh) *a bhd* | **100/1** | |
| P5 | **10** | *2* | **Rhum**[43] 5189 4-9-2 | TEaves(3) 3 | — |
| | | | (ISemple) *prom tl wknd over 3f out* | **66/1** | |
| 4-30 | **11** | *14* | **Arran Scout (IRE)**[122] 2900 3-9-0 74 | (b[1]) NCallan 6 | — |
| | | | (KARyan) *chsd clr ldr: rdn over 3f out: sn wknd* | **12/1** | |
| 5- | **12** | *dist* | **Ocotillo**[619] 432 4-9-5 | KMcEvoy 8 | — |
| | | | (MrsLBNormile) *dwlt: a bhd* | **50/1** | |
| 400 | **P** | | **Perrywinkle Boy**[46] 5086 3-9-0 40 | (t) MFenton 12 | — |
| | | | (MDHammond) *bhd: rdn and struggling 4f out: p.u over 1f out* | **100/1** | |

2m 16.03s (3.84) **Going Correction** +0.55s/f (Yiel) **13 Ran SP% 115.2**
**WFA** 3 from 4yo 5lb
Speed ratings: **106,102,101,96,92 81,78,78,75,74 62,—,—**CSF £3.18 TOTE £2.20: £1.10, £1.40, £2.80; EX 4.70.
**Owner** Am No Havin That **Bred** Gerard Hayes **Trained** Melsonby, N Yorks

**FOCUS**
A modest maiden, with the third the most obvious guide to the form at this stage.

**NOTEBOOK**
**Ouninpohja(IRE)** returned to better form in this weak event. Sat in behind the fast early pace, he picked up inside the last two furlongs to collar the weakening front-runner and win easily. This race took very little winning so what relevance this form will have in the future is debatable, but connections suggest better ground will suit him and he can progress. He may go hurdling this coming season.
**Young Rooney** has always blazed a trail in front and took a while to be caught. He has the ability to win a race but keeps finding one decent opponent every time he makes the racecourse. A sharper track is always likely to suit him rather than a big galloping one. He deserves to win a race soon.
**Loaded Gun** was not well weighted here on official figures and won the race for third place. He is fairly well exposed and ran as well as he was entitled to, without showing he is a winner about to happen.
**Shares(IRE)**, a winning hurdler, was running for the first time since March and stayed on up the centre of the track. This possibly was a prelude to going back over hurdles.
**Stravonian** has not shown much on the course but stayed on from a long way back without indicating he is about to win.
**Arran Scout(IRE)** pulled fairly hard in the first-time blinkers and found nothing in the home straight. *Official explanation: jockey said gelding was unsuited by good to soft, soft in places ground*
**Ocotillo** *Official explanation: trainer said gelding had mucus in his lungs post race*
**Perrywinkle Boy** *Official explanation: vet said gelding lost a shoe and was lame behind*

## 6142 FAMILY DAY AT AYR ON 7TH NOVEMBER (S) STKS 1m 1f 20y
**4:00** (4:01) (F3) 3-Y-0+ **£4,251** (£1,308; £654; £327) **Stalls** Low

| Form | | | | | RPR |
|---|---|---|---|---|---|
| 6000 | **1** | | **Fiddlers Creek (IRE)**[11] 1341 5-8-13 54 | (p) DTudhope(5) 11 | 47 |
| | | | (RAllan) *hld up in tch: effrt over 2f out: led ins fnl f: all out* | **9/2**[2] | |
| 0103 | **2** | *hd* | **Reversionary**[78] 4190 3-9-5 48 | (b) RWinston 6 | 52 |
| | | | (MWEasterby) *cl up: led over 3f out to ins fnl f: rallied: jst failed* | **14/1** | |
| 0612 | **3** | *½* | **Rymer's Rascal**[26] 5587 12-9-9 49 | DAllan 4 | 51 |
| | | | (EJAlston) *keen in tch: effrt over 2f out: kpt on fnl f: hld cl home* | **9/2**[2] | |
| 5 | **4** | *2½* | **King Summerland**[23] 5673 7-9-4 50 | RFfrench 12 | 41 |
| | | | (BMactaggart) *chsd ldrs: effrt over 2f out: one pce ins fnl f* | **10/1** | |
| 000 | **5** | *hd* | **The Spook**[66] 4535 4-9-4 35 | MFenton 8 | 41 |
| | | | (MissLAPerratt) *missed break: bhd: hdwy and flashed tail 2f out: kpt on fnl f* | **100/1** | |
| 21/ | **6** | *8* | **Dubai Lightning (USA)**[607] 4-9-4 80 | (p) DSweeney 7 | 25 |
| | | | (JGMO'Shea) *keen in tch: effrt over 2f out: rdn and wknd appr fnl f* | **5/2**[1] | |
| 2200 | **7** | *1¼* | **Prince Prospect**[178] 1479 8-9-2 40 | KristinStubbs(7) 1 | 27 |
| | | | (MrsLStubbs) *bhd: rdn over 3f out: nvr rchd ldrs* | **50/1** | |
| U436 | **8** | *3* | **Merlins Profit**[10] 5928 4-9-4 40 | (b[1]) SWKelly 2 | 16 |
| | | | (MDods) *led to over 3f out: wknd 2f out* | **16/1** | |
| 0/42 | **9** | *¾* | **Ash Bold (IRE)**[43] 5187 7-9-1 45 | TEaves(3) 3 | 15 |
| | | | (BEllison) *cl up tl rdn and wknd over 2f out* | **10/1** | |
| 5500 | **10** | *9* | **Open Handed (IRE)**[46] 5080 4-9-9 47 | PHanagan 5 | — |
| | | | (BEllison) *in tch: rdn over 3f out: hung lft and sn btn* | **6/1**[3] | |
| 0 | **11** | *dist* | **Blackpool Jack**[71] 4387 3-8-11 | PMulrennan(3) 9 | — |
| | | | (FPMurtagh) *cl up 2f: qckly lost pl: virtually p.u in st* | **100/1** | |

2m 5.54s (9.00) **Going Correction** +0.55s/f (Yiel) **11 Ran SP% 113.9**
**WFA** 3 from 4yo+ 4lb
Speed ratings: **82,81,81,79,78 71,70,68,67,59** —CSF £63.18 TOTE £6.30: £1.60, £3.80, £2.60; EX 78.40.There was no bid for the winner. Dubai Lightning (USA) was claimed by J. G. M. O'Shea for £6,000 (friendly).
**Owner** I Flannigan, R Allan & A Grant **Bred** Mrs Belinda Strudwick **Trained** Cornhill-on-Tweed, Northumberland

**FOCUS**
This was as bad as a seller gets and the time was pedestrian.

**NOTEBOOK**
**Fiddlers Creek(IRE)**, running over a significantly shorter trip than is usual for him, stayed on from the back of the field to land this. He has a fair record in these very low-grade events and is well handicapped on his best form. However this was a very weak event and the form has to be questionable.
**Reversionary** was always close to the pace and just kept plugging away to the line. This appears to be his grade and he may be at his best at a stiffer course.
**Rymer's Rascal** still continues to run his race at the age of 12. He tended to pull a bit hard early, but had every chance inside the last furlong before getting a little squeezed for room close home. He is running to form recently and looks to be still enjoying himself.
**King Summerland** has not shown much for a long time. He ran a touch better here without suggesting he is about to win.
**The Spook** missed the break badly, which is usual with him, but made stealthy headway up the straight to finish fairly well. He clearly has a few ideas of his own as he was flashing his tail under pressure, but if he can ever get away on terms he may trouble the judge at big odds. Perhaps a stiffer course might help in the future.
**Dubai Lightning(USA)**, off the track since running in the UAE 2,000 Guineas in February last year, was the gamble of the race, presumably due to his previous connections. Wearing front bandages for this race, he ran with plenty of zest early on before the going and time off the track probably told. He is clearly not as good as his current handicap mark suggests, but an All-Weather seller may be within his range if he is kept sound.
**Merlins Profit** made the early running in first-time blinkers but faded badly at the business end of the race.
**Open Handed(IRE)** *Official explanation: jockey said gelding hung left handed throughout*
**Blackpool Jack** *Official explanation: jockey said gelding hung right handed throughout*

## 6143 RACING UK ON SKY 432 STKS (H'CAP) 1m 5f 13y
**4:30** (4:30) (D2) (0-85,81) 3-Y-0+ **£8,184** (£2,518; £1,259; £629) **Stalls** Low

| Form | | | | | RPR |
|---|---|---|---|---|---|
| 15 | **1** | | **Winged D'Argent (IRE)**[172] 1588 3-8-10 76 | KDarley 9 | 89 |
| | | | (MJohnston) *in tch: rdn and outpcd over 4f out: rallied 2f out: hung lft and styd on wl to ld ins fnl f: r.o wl* | **7/1**[3] | |
| 2114 | **2** | *1* | **Circassian (IRE)**[18] 5773 3-8-11 77 | JMackay 5 | 89 |
| | | | (SirMarkPrescott) *cl up: led 3f out: hung lft over 1f out: hdd ins fnl f: r.o* | **2/1**[1] | |
| 2106 | **3** | *5* | **Shredded (USA)**[60] 4715 4-9-6 78 | (t) WSupple 6 | 83 |
| | | | (JHMGosden) *in tch: smooth hdwy and ev ch 2f out: rdn and hung lft: outpcd ins last* | **14/1** | |
| 5510 | **4** | *3½* | **Patrixprial**[26] 5595 3-8-10 76 | NCallan 7 | 76 |
| | | | (MHTompkins) *chsd ldrs: rdn 3f out: outpcd fr 2f out* | **9/1** | |
| 1004 | **5** | *2½* | **First Centurion**[67] 4520 3-9-0 80 | SWhitworth 4 | 77 |
| | | | (JWHills) *hld up: rdn 5f out: rallied over 2f out: n.d* | **25/1** | |
| 3123 | **6** | *2* | **Charlotte Vale**[62] 4636 3-8-8 74 | MFenton 3 | 68 |
| | | | (MDHammond) *chsd ldrs tl wknd fr 2f out* | **16/1** | |
| 0102 | **7** | *16* | **Fort Churchill (IRE)**[10] 5944 3-8-12 78 | (b) PHanagan 1 | 49 |
| | | | (BEllison) *keen: led to 3f out: wknd 2f out* | **10/3**[2] | |
| 0214 | **8** | *3* | **Master Wells (IRE)**[25] 5608 3-9-1 81 | KMcEvoy 2 | 48 |
| | | | (JDBethell) *in tch: rdn over 6f out: outpcd fr over 2f out* | **7/1**[3] | |
| /21- | **9** | *dist* | **Cake It Easy (IRE)**[153] 1788 4-9-3 75 | ACulhane 8 | — |
| | | | (KGReveley) *hld up in tch: rdn over 6f out: sn wknd* | **33/1** | |

3m 2.16s (6.31) **Going Correction** +0.55s/f (Yiel) **9 Ran SP% 110.7**
**WFA** 3 from 4yo 8lb
Speed ratings: **102,101,98,96,94 93,83,81,—**CSF £20.02 CT £180.88 TOTE £8.20: £2.40, £1.50, £2.10; EX 13.80 Trifecta £174.10 Pool of £882.92 - 3.60 winning tickets.
**Owner** Daniel A Couper **Bred** Daniel A Couper And George Hosie **Trained** Middleham Moor, N Yorks

**FOCUS**
A fair staying handicap won by an improving three-year-old. The form will probably prove reliable.

**NOTEBOOK**
**Winged D'Argent(IRE)** had been absent from the track for 172 days but enjoyed the step up in trip to win going away. His relations include Mana D'Argent so is entitled to appreciate this trip, and as he was unraced at two he can continue to improve. He took a long time to find his stride and looks to need at least this far. He looks promising.
**Circassian(IRE)** was stepped up in trip again and got to the lead over two furlongs out. He stayed on dourly up the home straight and, although wandering in front, stayed on really well. Two miles looks within his capabilities and he is a typically progressive horse for the stable.
**Shredded(USA)** looked to be absolutely cruising approaching the last two furlongs until finding very little. He stays this trip well so the reason for this effort is difficult to fathom.
**Patrixprial**, dropped in trip since his last run, was being pushed along entering the home straight but stayed on well to the line. He looks like he wants at least this far on this evidence
**First Centurion** was well behind until running on for pressure up the straight. He may want another step up in trip.
**Fort Churchill(IRE)** ensured this was a good test from the front. When he came under pressure in the home straight he found very little, and probably went a bit too fast in front in these conditions. *Official explanation: trainer said gelding had mucus in its lungs post race*

## 6144 SERENDIPITY INTERATIVE TICKETING H'CAP 6f
**5:00** (5:03) (E3) (0-70,70) 3-Y-0+ **£4,228** (£1,301; £650; £325) **Stalls** High

| Form | | | | | RPR |
|---|---|---|---|---|---|
| 4242 | **1** | | **Northern Games**[26] 5583 5-9-0 65 | (b) NCallan 14 | 85 |
| | | | (KARyan) *cl up: led over 1f out: pushed clr: readily* | **4/1**[1] | |
| 5201 | **2** | *5* | **On The Trail**[7] 6007 7-8-5 56 oh2 | RFfrench 12 | 61 |
| | | | (DWChapman) *led to over 1f out: kpt on: no ch w wnr* | **7/1**[3] | |
| 0300 | **3** | *nk* | **Midnight Parkes**[19] 5754 5-9-4 69 | DAllan 19 | 73 |
| | | | (EJAlston) *prom: outpcd 2f out: swtchd lft and kpt on fnl f* | **22/1** | |
| 3026 | **4** | *½* | **Highland Warrior**[25] 5605 5-9-5 70 | WSupple 8 | 73+ |
| | | | (JSGoldie) *hld up: nt clr run over 2f out: effrt and rdn over 1f out: one pce fnl f* | **12/1** | |
| 0400 | **5** | *1¼* | **Ulysees (IRE)**[15] 5833 5-9-3 68 | PHanagan 18 | 67 |
| | | | (ISemple) *in tch: outpcd 1/2-way: rallied over 1f out: no imp fnl f* | **14/1** | |
| 2440 | **6** | *nk* | **Online Investor**[19] 5754 5-8-10 61 | ANicholls 16 | 59 |
| | | | (DNicholls) *plld hrd: hld up: hdwy and prom over 1f out: edgd lft: one pce fnl f* | **14/1** | |
| 0424 | **7** | *¾* | **Trojan Flight**[1] 6114 3-9-3 69 | RWinston 5 | 65+ |
| | | | (MrsJRRamsden) *swtchd to stands side sn after s: hld up: hdwy over 1f out: no imp fnl f* | **5/1**[2] | |
| 2000 | **8** | *1½* | **Pays D'Amour (IRE)**[15] 5833 7-8-4 58 oh5 ow2 | TEaves(3) 6 | 49+ |
| | | | (MissLAPerratt) *bhd tl kpt on fnl f: nvr on terms* | **50/1** | |
| 4500 | **9** | *1¾* | **Sharp Hat**[4] 6046 10-8-11 62 | ACulhane 21 | 48+ |
| | | | (DWChapman) *hld up: nt clr run fr 1/2-way: n.d* | **16/1** | |
| 000 | **10** | *1¼* | **Indian Shores**[66] 4542 5-8-5 56 oh11 | SRighton 9 | 38 |
| | | | (MMullineaux) *bhd: rdn 1/2-way: n.d* | **100/1** | |
| 0044 | **11** | *shd* | **Flying Edge (IRE)**[15] 5833 4-8-0 56 oh2 | NataliaGemelova(5) 13 | 38 |
| | | | (EJAlston) *prom to 2f out: sn rdn and btn* | **10/1** | |
| 200 | **12** | *nk* | **Haulage Man**[29] 5526 6-8-3 57 | (p) THamilton(3) 11 | 38 |
| | | | (DEddy) *prom: sn rdn along: outpcd over 2f out: n.d after* | **20/1** | |

5050 **13** *hd* **Robwillcall**[26] 5579 4-8-0 **56** oh10.................................(p) PMathers(5) 15 36
(ABerry) *chsd ldrs: ev ch over 2f out: sn rdn and btn* **50/1**

504 **14** *3½* **Zoom Zoom**[13] 5861 4-9-4 **69**.................................... MFenton 4 39+
(MrsLStubbs) *prom centre: outpcd fr 1/2-way* **16/1**

3006 **15** *1¼* **College Maid (IRE)**[13] 5862 7-7-12 **56** oh2.........................(b) JCurrie(7) 3 22+
(JSGoldie) *prom centre to 1/2-way: sn btn* **25/1**

04-3 **16** *2½* **Foxies Future (IRE)**[280] 458 3-7-11 **56**........................ DFentiman(7) 1 15+
(JRWeymes) *racd centre: outpcd fr 1/2-way* **66/1**

0620 **17** *2* **Strawberry Patch (IRE)**[19] 5754 5-8-9 **60**........................(p) JMackay 20 13
(MissLAPerratt) *chsd ldrs to 2f out: sn btn* **14/1**

5402 **18** *4* **Thornaby Green**[23] 5674 3-8-6 **63**.................................... PMakin(5) 2 4+
(TDBarron) *racd centre: struggling fr 1/2-way* **16/1**

0000 **19** *13* **Speedfit Free (IRE)**[94] 3735 7-7-12 **56** oh16...................(v) TO'Brien(7) 7 —+
(MissAStokell) *racd centre: lost tch fr 1/2-way* **100/1**

1m 13.51s (-0.21) **Going Correction** +0.05s/f (Good)
**WFA** 3 from 4yo+ 1lb **19** Ran SP% **123.9**
Speed ratings: **103,96,95,95,93 93,92,90,87,86 86,85,85,80,79 75,73,67,50**CSF £28.45 CT £565.35 TOTE £6.80: £2.10, £2.20, £5.80, £4.00; EX 30.50 Place 6 £43.01, Place 5 £14.64.
**Owner** R E Robinson **Bred** Mrs Wendy Robinson **Trained** Hambleton, N Yorks

**FOCUS**

A typically ultra-competitive sprint won with ease by Northern Games, producing a career-best performance so far.

**NOTEBOOK**

**Northern Games** has been running over seven furlongs recently but enjoyed the drop down to six. The manner of the win suggests he is in good heart at the moment and he could easily follow up this success in the near future.

**On The Trail** made use of a fair draw by blazing the trail, as is usual for him. He appears in good heart at the moment but will always be vulnerable to a horse that finishes well.

**Midnight Parkes** was always slightly pushed along in the early stages, but finshed well from out of the pack. He is on a winning mark but probably wants a stiffer course than this.

**Highland Warrior**, who was the winner of this race last season off a 16lb lower mark, was settled in midfield and found the inevitable trouble that goes with this kind of race. He has run well enough off this higher mark but would never have bothered the very easy winner.

**Ulysees(IRE)**, who had the visor taken off this time, showed much more on this occasion than he had done on recent runs. He looks to have been battling with the handicapper this year, but is now down to a handicap mark he can go close off in this company.

**Online Investor** still has no win since May 2001 but probably ran one of his better recent races. He remains very difficult to win with and is never easy to catch right.

**Trojan Flight**, who for once was not favourite, was switched from his poor draw shortly after leaving the stalls. He had his chance and almost certainly wants a break on the evidence of this run.

**Sharp Hat** met lots of trouble in running and this run is best forgotten. *Official explanation: jockey said gelding was continually denied a clear run*

T/Plt: £12.10 to a £1 stake. Pool: £38,173.30. 2,289.95 winning tickets. T/Qpdt: £4.50 to a £1 stake. Pool: £2,694.50. 437.40 winning tickets. RY

## 6117 LEICESTER (R-H)

### Tuesday, October 12

**OFFICIAL GOING: Good (good to soft in places)**

The going had eased slightly overnight and was described as 'on the easy side of good', easing further late on.

Wind: Slight 1/2 against. Weather: Overcast and cool, drizzle at first then rain last 2.

### 6145 E B F LADBROKES.COM REFERENCE POINT MAIDEN STKS (C&G) 7f 9y

1:50 (1:51) (D2) 2-Y-O **£5,980** (£1,840; £920; £460) **Stalls** Low

Form RPR

33 **1** **Eqdaam (USA)**[73] 4315 2-8-11 .................................... RHavlin 7 82
(JHMGosden) *led tl over 1f out: rallied to ld last 50yds* **11/1**[3]

**2** *½* **Flag Lieutenant** 2-8-11 .................................... MartinDwyer 11 81
(SirMichaelStoute) *leggy: scope: trckd ldrs: edgd lft over 1f out: r.o strly ins last* **12/1**

**3** *hd* **Tragedian (USA)** 2-8-11 .................................... JFortune 5 80
(JHMGosden) *lengthy: unf: trckd ldrs: styd on wl ins last* **16/1**

46 **4** *shd* **World Report (USA)**[33] 5406 2-8-11 .................................... RLMoore 14 80
(RHannon) *w ldrs: led over 1f out: hdd and no ex wl ins last* **40/1**

0 **5** *1¼* **Mostashaar (FR)**[65] 4567 2-8-11 .................................... RHills 20 77
(SirMichaelStoute) *w ldrs: styd on same pce ins last* **6/1**[2]

**6** *2* **Firesong** 2-8-11 .................................... DHolland 3 72
(SKirk) *rangy: s.s: bhd: hdwy and edgd lft over 1f out: styd on ins last* **40/1**

0 **7** *nk* **Lake Chini (IRE)**[6] 6010 2-8-11 .................................... PRobinson 9 71
(MAJarvis) *w ldrs: outpcd 2f out: styd on ins last* **66/1**

**8** *nk* **Jabraan (USA)** 2-8-11 .................................... LDettori 17 70
(SaeedBinSuroor) *lengthy: unf: trckd ldrs: effrt over 2f out: fdd appr fnl f* **4/5**[1]

30 **9** *¾* **Croix Rouge (USA)**[15] 5838 2-8-11 .................................... RHughes 10 72+
(MrsAJPerrett) *w ldrs: wknd fnl f* **40/1**

02 **10** *hd* **Atacama Star**[11] 5910 2-8-11 .................................... TEDurcan 6 68
(BGPowell) *dwlt: hdwy over 2f out: hmpd and swtchd rt 1f out: nvr rchd ldrs* **33/1**

**11** *shd* **Prince Vector** 2-8-11 .................................... JDSmith 2 71+
(AKing) *rangy: unf: bhd: sme hdwy over 2f out: nvr nr ldrs* **100/1**

**12** *hd* **Neutrino** 2-8-8 .................................... NMackay(3) 19 67
(LMCumani) *rangy: unf: mid-didivsion: outpcd fnl 2f* **66/1**

**13** *1¾* **Shortbread** 2-8-11 .................................... IMongan 12 63
(JLDunlop) *rangy: unf: sn outpcd and in rr: sme hdwy 2f out: nvr on terms* **100/1**

**14** *½* **Seattle Robber** 2-8-11 .................................... JFEgan 1 62
(SKirk) *lengthy: mid-divsion: outpcd fnl 3f* **33/1**

0 **15** *¾* **Reaching Out (IRE)**[106] 3377 2-8-11 .................................... SDrowne 18 60
(HJCollingridge) *hld up: nvr on terms* **100/1**

0 **16** *hd* **Interwoven (IRE)**[45] 5125 2-8-11 .................................... SChin 16 59
(MJohnston) *hmpd s: sn chsng ldrs: drvn along over 2f out: sn wknd* **100/1**

00 **17** *3½* **Will The Till**[15] 5825 2-8-11 .................................... PFitzsimons 4 51
(JMBradley) *w ldrs: drvn along over 3f out: sn lost pl* **200/1**

54 **18** *6* **Spanish Ridge (IRE)**[21] 5718 2-8-11 .................................... TQuinn 15 36
(JLDunlop) *swvd rt s: sn chsng ldrs: lost pl 2f out* **14/1**

**19** *25* **Valet** 2-8-8 .................................... LPKeniry(3) 13 —
(JGMO'Shea) *unf: s.s: bhd: hung lft over 3f out: sn lost tch* **150/1**

1m 26.56s (0.46) **Going Correction** +0.05s/f (Good) **19** Ran SP% **119.7**
Speed ratings: **99,98,98,98,96 94,94,93,92,92 92,92,90,89,88 88,84,77,49**CSF £126.27 TOTE £13.10: £3.80, £5.70, £3.60; EX 96.40.
**Owner** Hamdan Al Maktoum **Bred** Shadwell Farm Llc **Trained** Manton, Wilts

**FOCUS**

A good Leicester maiden with plenty of the top connections represented. The race is sure to throw up plenty of future winners.

**NOTEBOOK**

**Eqdaam(USA)**, who did not quite live up to expectations earlier in the season, was put away to strengthen up and clearly benefited greatly from the time off. Sporting his owners second colours, this strong galloper was up there throughout and rallied gamnely to regain the lead in the final half furlong. There is more to come from him over a mile and he should make up into a decent three-year-old.

**Flag Lieutenant**, on his toes and noisy in the paddock, was seemingly the lesser-fancied Stoute runner, but fared best of the pair, flashing home to snatch second on the line. He was outpaced at the vital stage of the race and, like the winner, will be suited by a mile next season.

**Tragedian(USA)**, a stablemate of the winner, may ideally have preferred the ground a bit faster, but he still shaped with plenty of promise. Having travelled well for much of the way, he showed signs of inexperience, but still proved good enough to get up for third. A run-of-the-mill maiden should be his for the taking, with improvement expected.

**World Report(USA)** appreciated being able to get his toe in - he was unsuited by the fast ground when a disappointing favourite at Chepstow most recently - and ran much better than his odds entitled him to. Now eligible for nurseries, he can win in that sphere while the soft ground is about.

**Mostashaar(FR)**, seemingly the better fancied of the Stoute pair, looked in need of the outing when only seventh here on his debut back in early August, but had been given time off to strengthen. He posed a threat around two furlongs out, but could not quicken under pressure and a mile will bring about considerable improvement.

**Firesong** is well regarded by connections, but blew his chances of winning with a slow start. He should improve for this and will find easier opportunities.

**Lake Chini(IRE)** ran better than he had done at Lingfield last week and is going the right way.

**Jabraan(USA)**, evidently well regarded judging by the price he went off, was soon on the heels of the leaders, but looked in a bit of trouble with two to run and weakened out of it. His rider reported after the race that the colt had breathing difficulties, and he deserves another chance if returning in a tongue tie.

### 6146 LADBROKES.COM (S) H'CAP 7f 9y

2:20 (2:21) (G4) (0-55,55) 3-4-Y-O **£3,018** (£862; £431) **Stalls** Low

Form RPR

2340 **1** **Armentieres**[20] 5733 3-8-9 **52**.............................................(b) SDrowne 20 59
(JLSpearing) *hld up: hdwy over 2f out: r.o u.p to ld nr fin* **13/2**[2]

0000 **2** *½* **Disco Diva**[68] 4489 3-8-9 **52**.................................... FNorton 17 58
(MBlanshard) *s.i.s: hld up: hdwy over 2f out: rdn to ld wl ins fnl f: hdd nr fin* **33/1**

5020 **3** *½* **Calusa Lady (IRE)**[66] 4542 4-8-11 **52**.................................... SCarson 12 56
(GBBalding) *chsd ldrs: led over 1f out: hdd wl ins fnl f* **14/1**

0500 **4** *nk* **Cayman Breeze**[29] 5512 4-9-0 **55**.................................... RLMoore 7 59
(JMBradley) *hld up: hdwy over 2f out: r.o* **16/1**

-000 **5** *nk* **Light The Dawn (IRE)**[113] 3154 4-8-1 **47**.................... BSwarbrick(5) 14 50
(WMBrisbourne) *hld up: plld hrd: hdwy over 2f out: nt clr run and lost pl over 1f out: r.o ins fnl f* **16/1**

0000 **6** *1½* **Cross Ash (IRE)**[7] 6007 4-8-5 **53**.................................... HFellows(7) 13 52
(RHollinshead) *hld up: hdwy over 2f out: rdn and ev ch over 1f out: hung lft and no ex ins fnl f* **40/1**

5004 **7** *1¾* **Certa Cito**[20] 5736 4-8-12 **53**.................................... LDettori 19 47
(DFlood) *chsd ldrs tl led 1/2-way: hdd wl over 1f out: wknd ins fnl f* **10/3**[1]

2010 **8** *hd* **Naughty Girl (IRE)**[26] 5587 4-8-4 **48**.............................(vt) FPFerris(3) 11 42
(PDEvans) *plld hrd and prom: rdn over 1f out: wknd ins fnl f* **9/1**

4004 **9** *shd* **Man Crazy (IRE)**[27] 5564 3-8-7 **50**.................................... JFEgan 1 44
(CADwyer) *plld hrd and prom: lost pl 4f out: rallied over 1f out: wknd ins fnl f* **11/1**

06R3 **10** *hd* **Chandelier**[6] 6014 4-8-4 **48** ow1.................................... LPKeniry(3) 18 41
(MSSaunders) *chsd ldrs: led wl over 1f out: sn hdd: wknd ins fnl f* **7/1**[3]

001 **11** *½* **Zalebe**[28] 5552 3-8-12 **55**.................................... JQuinn 3 47
(JPearce) *sn outpcd: sme hdwy over 1f out: n.d* **9/1**

660 **12** *1¾* **Ollijay**[43] 5204 3-8-7 **50**.................................... GGibbons 10 37
(MrsHDalton) *chsd ldrs: rdn 1/2-way: wknd over 1f out* **50/1**

5050 **13** *nk* **Go Free**[3] 6058 3-8-6 **49**.................................... TPQueally 9 35
(AMHales) *prom: rdn 1/2-way: wknd 2f out* **25/1**

4010 **14** *½* **Inescapable (USA)**[10] 5927 3-8-10 **53**.................................... MartinDwyer 4 38
(WRMuir) *wnt rt s: prom: rdn 3f out: sn wknd* **16/1**

1100 **15** *1¼* **Iamback**[137] 2456 4-8-12 **53**.............................................(p) DHolland 2 35
(MissGayKelleway) *chsd ldrs: lost pl over 4f out: n.d after* **22/1**

6200 **16** *2* **Blunham**[64] 4605 4-8-2 **46**.................................... BReilly(3) 8 23
(MCChapman) *led to 1/2-way: wknd over 1f out* **20/1**

3600 **17** *4* **Palvic Moon**[58] 4782 3-8-7 **50**.............................................(p) RFitzpatrick 5 16
(CSmith) *hmpd s: sn bhd* **50/1**

1m 26.57s (0.47) **Going Correction** +0.05s/f (Good)
**WFA** 3 from 4yo 2lb **17** Ran SP% **123.8**
Speed ratings: **99,98,97,97,97 95,93,93,93,92 92,90,89,89,87 85,81**CSF £217.73 CT £2909.04 TOTE £7.10: £1.80, £8.80, £3.70, £2.20; EX 158.10.The winner was bought in for 4,000gns.
**Owner** J Spearing **Bred** White Horse Bloodstock Ltd **Trained** Kinnersley, Worcs

**FOCUS**

A competitive, albeit modest seller.

**NOTEBOOK**

**Armentieres** has been running consistently of late and, challenging on the wide outside, came to grab the spoils inside the final half-furlong. She is only moderate but she does seem ideally suited by a big field, as her record in fields of 16 runners or more now reads 69133471.

**Disco Diva** had shown little earlier this season, but a drop in grade on her return from a two-month break resulted in a much-improved effort. *Official explanation: jockey said filly lost a front shoe and lugged left*

**Calusa Lady(IRE)**, another returning from a two-month absence, remains a maiden but has shown on more than one occasion that she is capable of winning a race of this nature.

**Cayman Breeze** ran a fair race under top weight and, as a winner on Polytrack, is likely to be kept busy on the All-Weather over the winter.

**Light The Dawn(IRE)** was returning from a four-month absence and dropping into selling grade after four fruitless outings in maiden company. She flashed her tail under pressure but ran on quite well considering she had pulled hard in the early stages.

**Certa Cito** was stepping up to seven furlongs for the first time and appeared not to get home.

**Palvic Moon** *Official explanation: trainer said filly was struck into*

### 6147 LADBROKES.COM WREAKE FILLIES' CONDITIONS STKS 1m 9y

2:50 (2:50) (C2) 3-Y-O **£6,095** (£2,312; £1,156; £525) **Stalls** High

Form RPR

1-33 **1** **Mansfield Park**[17] 5783 3-8-9 102.................................... LDettori 5 87+
(SaeedBinSuroor) *led: edgd rt after 1f: shkn up and qcknd over 2f out: sn clr: eased last 100yds* **4/9**[1]

1-23 **2** *5* **Coqueteria (USA)**[156] 1983 3-8-9 102.................................... SDrowne 3 75+
(GWragg) *trckd ldrs: effrt on ins 2f out: styd on to take 2nd last 75yds* **15/2**[3]

2030 **3** *1* **Marinaite**[40] 5244 3-8-13 73 ........ JBramhill 8 77
(SRBowring) *chsd wnr: sltly hmpd after 1f: edgd rt and lost 2nd wl ins last* **80/1**

6444 **4** *2 ½* **Silk Fan (IRE)**[27] 5573 3-8-9 95 ........ MartinDwyer 1 67
(PWHarris) *restless in stalls: dwlt: sn trcking ldrs: effrt over 2f out: wknd over 1f out* **7/2[2]**

011- **5** *4* **Milly Waters**[353] 5751 3-8-9 85 ........ SSanders 2 58
(WMBrisbourne) *hld up in tch: effrt over 2f out: sn outpcd and lost pl* **25/1**

0630 **6** *3* **Summerise**[158] 1946 3-8-9 51 ........ PRobinson 7 51
(HJCollingridge) *sn detached in last: sme hdwy over 2f out: nvr on terms* **200/1**

0030 **7** *1 ½* **Primeshade Promise**[22] 5693 3-8-9 53 ........ JTate 6 48
(DBurchell) *chsd ldrs: outpcd over 2f out: sn lost pl* **150/1**

0400 **8** *½* **Flame Queen**[10] 5945 3-8-9 57 ........ TPQueally 4 46
(MrsCADunnett) *t.k.h: in tch: effrt over 2f out: sn lost pl* **150/1**

1m 41.46s (-1.14) **Going Correction** 0.0s/f (Good) **8** Ran SP% **110.1**
Speed ratings: **105,100,99,96,92 89,88,87**CSF £4.08 TOTE £1.50: £1.02, £1.30, £13.00; EX 3.70.
**Owner** Godolphin **Bred** Darley **Trained** Newmarket, Suffolk

**FOCUS**
This was a three-horse race on official ratings, and it was the strongly-supported favourite Mansfield Park who ran out an emphatic winner. Despite the 73-rated Marinaite finishing third and doing little for the form, the front pair are worth following.

**NOTEBOOK**
**Mansfield Park**, strongly supported on the exchanges throughout the day, had the makings of an improving filly having finished third in Listed company on her most recent start. This represented by far her easiest task of the season so far and Dettori is lethal if allowed to dominate. She had them all in trouble with two to run and, once asked to stretch out, she came right away before being eased down. She looks worthy of a place back in Listed company.
**Coqueteria(USA)**, last seen finishing third in the German 1000 Guineas back in May, took a long time to find her stride and ran as though the run would bring her on. She finished well and, although she only beat the 73-rated Marinaite a length, deserves to be stepped back up in grade.
**Marinaite** ran way above herself in third and was evidently flattered. The Handicapper will not take kindly to this effort and her best chance of winning in future will be back on the All-Weather.
**Silk Fan(IRE)**, who got a little upset in the stalls, did not run her race and may have had enough for the time being.

## 6148 EBF LADBROKES.COM SOAR MAIDEN STKS (DIV I) 1m 9y
**3:20** (3:22) (D2) 2-Y-O **£5,668** (£1,744; £872; £436) **Stalls** High

Form RPR

43 **1** **Luis Melendez (USA)**[27] 5567 2-9-0 ........ RLMoore 3 82
(PFICole) *mde all: rdn out* **5/2[1]**

60 **2** *¾* **Barbary Coast (FR)**[11] 5915 2-9-0 ........ MartinDwyer 1 81
(WRMuir) *a.p: rdn to chse wnr 2f out: r.o* **16/1**

4 **3** *1 ¼* **Kong (IRE)**[17] 5790 2-9-0 ........ TQuinn 7 78
(JLDunlop) *chsd ldrs: rdn over 2f out: styd on* **14/1**

**4** *2* **Groomsman** 2-8-11 ........ LFletcher(3) 4 74
(HMorrison) *rangy: unf: scope: mid-div: hdwy over 3f out: styd on same pce fnl f* **16/1**

02 **5** *nk* **Phi (USA)**[15] 5840 2-9-0 ........ SSanders 9 73
(SirMichaelStoute) *disp ld over 2f: chsd wnr to 2f out: no ex fnl f* **3/1[2]**

0 **6** *3 ½* **Mont Saint Michel (IRE)**[27] 5570 2-9-0 ........ DHolland 13 65
(GWragg) *hld up: hdwy 1/2-way: wknd over 1f out* **66/1**

0 **7** *1 ¾* **Groundcover**[31] 5467 2-9-0 ........ RHughes 8 61
(MrsAJPerrett) *unruly stalls: s.s: outpcd: nvr nrr* **33/1**

**8** *nk* **Tilt** 2-9-0 ........ JPMurtagh 11 61
(JRFanshawe) *lengthy: unf: hld up in tch: rdn over 3f out: wknd 2f out* **16/1**

**9** *½* **Kabis Amigos** 2-9-0 ........ (t) WRyan 6 60
(HRACecil) *leggy: unf: dwlt and hmpd s: outpcd* **20/1**

**10** *1 ½* **Seeking An Alibi (USA)** 2-9-0 ........ LDettori 12 56
(SaeedBinSuroor) *neat: unf: s.s: hdwy over 2f out: wknd wl over 1f out* **5/1[3]**

40 **11** *2* **My Portfolio (IRE)**[39] 5268 2-9-0 ........ SDrowne 5 52
(RCharlton) *a in rr* **16/1**

0 **12** *5* **Danita Dancer (IRE)**[14] 5846 2-8-6 ........ FPFerris(3) 2 36
(BPalling) *hld up: hdwy over 3f out: wknd over 2f out* **125/1**

**13** *5* **Hiddensee (USA)** 2-9-0 ........ SChin 14 30
(MJohnston) *lengthy: unf: scope: sn pushed along and prom: lost pl over 5f out: sn bhd* **40/1**

4 **P** **Travel Tip (USA)**[19] 5756 2-9-0 ........ JFortune 10 —
(JHMGosden) *mid-div: rdn over 3f out: wknd over 2f out: p.u ins fnl f: lame* **16/1**

1m 42.41s (-0.19) **Going Correction** 0.0s/f (Good) **14** Ran SP% **118.7**
Speed ratings: **100,99,98,96,95 92,90,90,89,88 86,81,76,—**CSF £42.53 TOTE £3.60: £1.20, £5.10, £3.00; EX 46.50.
**Owner** Richard Green (fine Paintings) **Bred** Bloomsbury Stud **Trained** Whatcombe, Oxon

**FOCUS**
Without doubt the better of the two divisions, with the form of those who finished in the frame looking superior. The time was 0.82 seconds faster than the second division to boot and the race will produce plenty of future winners.

**NOTEBOOK**
**Luis Melendez(USA)**, who had shown plenty of promise on both his previous starts, progressed again with a battling success under a fine ride from Ryan Moore, the pair appearing determined not to let anything pass. He is expected to improve again by connections as he still shows signs of greenness, and it is hoped he will make up into a useful three-year-old handicapper.
**Barbary Coast(FR)** was arguably taking a drop in class having run behind the smart Rob Roy at Newmarket last time and he ran his best race to date, staying on well for second without being able to get by the winner. He has now qualified for a handicap mark, which is likely to be pretty stiff, and trying his luck in another maiden may be the best option for now.
**Kong(IRE)** ◆ is bred, and shapes like a middle distance performer, so connections can take encouragement from his two promising efforts to date over inadequate trips. A big, rangy sort, he can win his maiden this season if found an opening where stamina is at a premium. *Official explanation: jockey said colt hung left*
**Groomsman** ◆, who was mounted in the saddling boxes before unseating his rider coming out on to the course, made plenty of noise in the paddock and looked badly in need of the experience both mentally and physically. It is to his credit that he managed to run so well and he looked a real threat when tacking on to the heels of the leaders over two furlongs out. Lack of experience told in the closing stages though, and he had to settle for fourth. This was a most promising initial effort, and he is another who will relish middle distances. Great improvement can be expected.
**Phi(USA)** was a little disappointing, but this ground would have done him no favours and he can be expected to continue his progress back on a fast surface, although at this time of year he is far from certain to get it.
**Mont Saint Michel(IRE)** showed his debut running to be all wrong, when he reportedly lost his action, and shaped much better this time. One more run will see him eligible for nurseries and he can do better in that sphere.
**Groundcover** looks to be steadily progressing and, like Mont Saint Michel, is very much a handicap type.
**Tilt** ran a little better than her finishing positions suggests and should improve.
**Seeking An Alibi(USA)** comes from a stable who have had a blinding season with their juveniles, but on this evidence he is one of the lesser lights. He can still win races nonetheless.
**My Portfolio(IRE)** seems to be going the wrong way, but is likely to get a decent mark as a result and would be interesting in a handicap if coming back to something like the form of his debut run.
**Hiddensee(USA)** looked a typical Mark Johnston juvenile, in that he was too green and inexperienced to do himself justice, and there will be much better to come next season.
**Travel Tip(USA)** pulled up lame and this run should be ignored.

## 6149 EBF LADBROKES.COM SOAR MAIDEN STKS (DIV II) 1m 9y
**3:50** (3:52) (D2) 2-Y-O **£5,668** (£1,744; £872; £436) **Stalls** High

Form RPR

5 **1** **River Alhaarth (IRE)**[36] 5347 2-9-0 ........ MHills 9 72
(PWChapple-Hyam) *trckd ldr: led over 2f out tl over 1f out: rallied to ld nr fin* **6/1[3]**

5 **2** *¾* **Registrar**[21] 5718 2-9-0 ........ SSanders 10 70
(MrsAJPerrett) *dwlt: sn trcking ldrs: led on ins over 1f out: edgd lft: hdd towards fin* **6/1[3]**

0 **3** *2* **Hawkes Bay**[21] 5720 2-9-0 ........ RHills 2 66
(MHTompkins) *stdd s: hld up in rr: hdwy on outer over 2f out: styd on wl ins last* **25/1**

0 **4** *shd* **Bulwark (IRE)**[24] 5646 2-9-0 ........ JPMurtagh 6 65
(MrsAJPerrett) *trckd ldrs: effrt and carried hd high over 2f out: kpt on same pce* **12/1**

0 **5** *½* **One Good Thing (USA)**[64] 4611 2-9-0 ........ LDettori 14 64
(SaeedBinSuroor) *led tl over 2f out: styd on same pce appr fnl f* **5/1[2]**

6 **6** *1 ½* **Mt Desert**[13] 5870 2-9-0 ........ JFortune 4 67+
(JHMGosden) *bhd and drvn along after 2f: hdwy 2f out: edgd rt and styd on fnl f* **7/1**

**7** *½* **Hawk Arrow (IRE)** 2-9-0 ........ SDrowne 1 60
(HMorrison) *rangy: unf: dwlt: sn chsng ldrs: outpcd fnl 2f* **33/1**

0 **8** *3* **Ampelio (IRE)**[39] 5268 2-9-0 ........ MartinDwyer 3 53
(SirMichaelStoute) *rr-div: drvn along 3f out: nvr nr ldrs* **12/1**

5 **9** *6* **Cave Of The Giant (IRE)**[27] 5567 2-9-0 ........ TQuinn 7 40
(TDMccarthy) *hld up towards rr: effrt over 2f out: nvr on terms* **4/1[1]**

0 **10** *½* **Zaville**[22] 5694 2-8-9 ........ PRobinson 11 34
(MAJarvis) *chsd ldrs: lost pl over 1f out* **25/1**

**11** *4* **Finnegans Rainbow** 2-9-0 ........ RLMoore 5 30
(PFICole) *wl grwn: in tch: effrt over 2f out: sn btn* **16/1**

0 **12** *hd* **Pebble Mill (IRE)**[13] 5857 2-9-0 ........ DHolland 13 30
(MJohnston) *mid-div: drvn along over 3f out: nvr a factor* **25/1**

5 **13** *5* **Turnover**[22] 5687 2-8-9 ........ TEDurcan 12 14
(MJWallace) *sn bhd and drvn along* **33/1**

0 **14** *9* **Fantastic Luck (IRE)**[21] 5716 2-9-0 ........ IMongan 8 11+
(JLDunlop) *s.s: a bhd* **66/1**

1m 43.23s (0.63) **Going Correction** 0.0s/f (Good) **14** Ran SP% **117.9**
Speed ratings: **96,95,93,93,92 91,90,87,81,81 77,76,71,62**CSF £37.77 TOTE £8.50: £3.10, £1.90, £6.30; EX 49.70.
**Owner** R J Arculli **Bred** J F Tuthill **Trained** Newmarket, Suffolk

**FOCUS**
The weaker of the two divisions with the form not looking as strong and the time being 0.82 seconds slower than the first division. The race should still produce winners, but in the main the majority of runners are not going to be seen at their best until next season.

**NOTEBOOK**
**River Alhaarth(IRE)**, who shaped with promise on his debut at Warwick, battled back gamely to regain the lead from Registrar in the closing stages, having been passed just over a furlong out. Connections believe he will make up into a decent handicapper next season, and he may have one more run before the year is out, probably in a nursery.
**Registrar**, a bit tardy coming out of the stalls, was soon tracking the leaders and looked set to score when going on just over a furlong out. However, he started to look around and ended up being re-claimed by River Alhaarth. He is going the right way and still has some learning to do, so can be expected to improve again.
**Hawkes Bay** did not get going until late, but finished strongly for third and improved on his initial effort. Despite being bred for speed, he saw this trip out extremely well and, like the second, should progress again.
**Bulwark(IRE)**, who looked too inexperienced to do himself justice on his debut, carried his head high for most of the straight and never really let himself down. Finishing fourth was a decent effort considering, and if whatever was bothering him can be sorted out, assuming it was not a temperament problem, he will win races.
**One Good Thing(USA)** is evidently no star, but is in the right hands to win races and will probably improve for match practice.
**Mt Desert** is a middle-distance handicapper in the making and will not be seen at his best until next season.
**Hawk Arrow(IRE)** did not shape without promise and will do better next season.
**Ampelio(IRE)** still looks too inexperienced to win as a juvenile and is another three-year-old handicapper in the making.
**Cave Of The Giant(IRE)** finished lame and deserves another chance to build on his promising debut run. *Official explanation: jockey said colt finished lame*
**Zaville**, one of only two fillies in the race, is a long-term prospect and simply lacks the pace to win at this stage of her career.

## 6150 LADBROKES.COM CLAIMING STKS 1m 3f 183y
**4:20** (4:20) (E3) 3-4-Y-O **£3,542** (£1,090; £545; £272) **Stalls** High

Form RPR

430 **1** **Sovietta (IRE)**[36] 5339 3-7-11 65 ........ NMackay(3) 4 66
(RMBeckett) *hld up: hdwy over 4f out: led 1f out: edgd rt and r.o wl* **14/1**

0500 **2** *3 ½* **Secret Jewel (FR)**[13] 5869 4-8-9 65 ........ (b[1]) RLMoore 5 62
(LadyHerries) *hld up: rdn over 3f out: r.o ins fnl f: nt trble wnr* **16/1**

4600 **3** *½* **Weet A Head (IRE)**[22] 5706 3-9-5 72 ........ RHughes 3 78
(RHollinshead) *hld up: hdwy over 4f out: led over 1f out: sn hdd and outpcd* **10/1**

0000 **4** *1 ½* **Silver City**[20] 5728 4-9-12 70 ........ LDettori 2 76
(MrsAJPerrett) *hld up: hdwy over 6f out: led over 2f out: rdn and hdd over 1f out: styd on same pce* **11/2[2]**

44 **5** *5* **Chestall**[35] 5367 3-8-4 ........ RKennemore(7) 6 60
(RHollinshead) *prom: rdn over 3f out: wknd over 1f out* **66/1**

0320 **6** *1 ¼* **Go Green**[5] 6006 3-8-1 54 ........ (t) FPFerris(3) 1 51
(PDEvans) *s.i.s: sn chsng ldrs: rdn over 2f out: wknd over 1f out* **14/1**

3540 **7** *1* **Hinode (IRE)**[13] 5875 3-8-4 57 ........ JQuinn 12 49
(JARToller) *prom: chsd ldr over 5f out: led 4f out: rdn and hdd over 2f out: wknd over 1f out* **25/1**

-400 **8** *1 ¾* **Crociera (IRE)**[7] 6006 3-8-11 63 ........ (b[1]) PRobinson 11 53
(MHTompkins) *hld up: sme hdwy over 1f out: nvr trbld ldrs* **33/1**

3000 **9** *3* **Wodhill Hope**[24] 5654 4-8-11 40 ........ MTebbutt 14 42
(DMorris) *s.s: hdwy over 6f out: rdn over 3f out: wknd over 1f out* **80/1**

1065 **10** *2 ½* **Arresting**[115] [3095] 4-9-12 84 .......... JPMurtagh 16 53
(JRFanshawe) *prom: rdn over 3f out: wknd 2f out* **6/5**[1]
6300 **11** *3* **Zazous**[15] [5829] 3-9-5 58 .......... JDSmith 7 48
(AKing) *hld up: rdn over 3f out: sn wknd* **80/1**
204 **12** *½* **Killing Me Softly**[24] [5658] 3-9-0 51 .......... RFitzpatrick 9 42
(JGallagher) *led 1f: remained handy tl rdn and wknd over 2f out* **33/1**
6450 **13** *26* **Airedale Lad (IRE)**[91] [3822] 3-8-5 30 .......... JBramhill 10 —
(JRNorton) *hld up: rdn over 4f out: sn wknd* **100/1**
6600 **14** *1* **Lawrence Of Arabia (IRE)**[29] [5523] 4-8-13 56 .......... SSanders 8 —
(SirMarkPrescott) *led after 1f: rdn and hdd 4f out: wknd and eased 3f out* **7/1**[3]
000- **15** *dist* **Torzal**[308] [6153] 4-8-13 45 .......... LFletcher(3) 15 —
(MissMERowland) *hld up: rdn 7f out: wknd over 5f out* **125/1**

2m 34.08s (-0.60) **Going Correction** 0.0s/f (Good)
**WFA** 3 from 4yo 7lb **15** Ran SP% **117.1**
Speed ratings: **102,99,99,98,95 94,93,92,90,88 86,86,69,68,—**CSF £203.26 TOTE £15.20: £5.10, £3.50, £4.30; EX 88.50.The winner was claimed by T Newcombe for £6,000.
**Owner** J H Richmond-Watson **Bred** Lawn Stud **Trained** Lambourn, Berks

**FOCUS**
An ordinary claimer. The market favoured Arresting over Sovietta and Secret Jewel, despite there being little between the three on official adjusted ratings.

**NOTEBOOK**
**Sovietta(IRE)**, unexposed after just three outings in maiden company, had reportedly been unsuited by the firm ground when running badly at Bath last time and found these easier conditions far more suitable. She came home strongly off her light weight and provided her in-form stable with its third winner from its last 11 runners.
**Secret Jewel(FR)**, whose form had appeared to be regressive, found the application of blinkers bringing about an improved display. She was never nearer than at the finish.
**Weet A Head(IRE)**, over whom there was a big stamina doubt, appeared to see out this longer trip alright, albeit not as well as the winner.
**Silver City** had a bit to find with the front three at the weights and in the circumstances did not run badly, although his stamina appeared to give out in the ground.
**Chestall**, the most inexperienced runner in the field, ran his best race to date, although he had no more to give inside the final quarter-mile.
**Arresting** was dropping into a claimer for the first time on his return from a four-month break and, with the ground as he likes it, looked to have plenty in his favour. He was given every chance and had no excuse.
**Airedale Lad(IRE)** *Official explanation: jockey said gelding lost his action*

## 6151 LADBROKES.COM CONDITIONS STKS 7f 9y
4:50 (4:50) (C2) 2-Y-O £6,148 (£2,332; £1,166) Stalls Low

Form RPR
322 **1** **Foxhaven**[20] [5729] 2-8-10 88 .......... MartinDwyer 3 93+
(PRChamings) *mde all: rdn over 1f out: r.o* **6/1**[3]
136 **2** *1 ½* **Red Peony**[33] [5413] 2-8-10 99 .......... SSanders 1 89+
(SirMarkPrescott) *chsd wnr: rdn over 2f out: styd on same pce ins fnl f* **10/11**[1]
32 **3** *1* **Silent Jo (JPN)**[35] [5373] 2-8-10 .......... LDettori 2 87+
(SaeedBinSuroor) *hld up in tch: swtchd rt 3f out: rdn over 1f out: no ex ins fnl f* **6/4**[2]

1m 30.69s (4.59) **Going Correction** +0.05s/f (Good) **3** Ran SP% **106.7**
Speed ratings: **75,73,72**CSF £11.62 TOTE £8.00; EX 21.10.
**Owner** Mrs Ann Jenkins **Bred** Highclere Stud Ltd **Trained** Baughurst, Hants

**FOCUS**
They went a modest gallop in the early part of the race and that resulted in a slow time. Although probably flattered a little, Foxhaven is progressive and did the job well from the front.

**NOTEBOOK**
**Foxhaven**, who is fully effective on the ground and stays a mile well, was always going to be dangerous if allowed his own way out in front and, having took them along at a modest gallop, kicked again and stayed on strongly with the rail to run against. Everything went his way so he may have been flattered, but he had been progressive and deserves a chance to show this win to be no fluke.
**Red Peony**, officially rated 11lb superior to the winner, went off way too fast when disappointing in the May Hill at Doncaster most recently and could have done with a truer gallop on this drop in grade. She is better than this and will no doubt step back up in grade now.
**Silent Jo(JPN)**, bred to appreciate middle distances on his dam's side, was least favoured by the way the race was run as he was held up last and could not quicken when switched to deliver his challenge. Back on faster ground over a mile, he can win his maiden.

## 6152 LADBROKES.COM H'CAP 1m 1f 218y
5:20 (5:20) (E3) (0-70,69) 3-Y-O+ £5,129 (£1,578; £789; £394) Stalls High

Form RPR
4000 **1** **Duelling Banjos**[15] [5841] 5-8-11 61 .......... SSanders 4 71
(JAkehurst) *hld up: hdwy over 3f out: rdn over 1f out: r.o u.p to ld nr fin* **5/1**[2]
0032 **2** *hd* **Planters Punch (IRE)**[14] [5853] 3-9-0 69 .......... RHughes 1 79
(RHannon) *a.p: chsd ldr 1/2-way: rdn to ld over 1f out: hdd nr fin* **12/1**
1350 **3** *¾* **Fuel Cell (IRE)**[38] [5297] 3-9-0 69 .......... (b) RLMoore 7 77
(RHannon) *chsd ldrs: rdn and ev ch fr over 1f out: styd on* **25/1**
0660 **4** *1 ¼* **Blazing The Trail (IRE)**[13] [5869] 4-8-11 61 .......... RHills 5 67+
(JWHills) *hld up: hdwy and nt clr run over 1f out: r.o: nt rch ldrs* **20/1**
0000 **5** *½* **Garden Society (IRE)**[13] [5868] 7-8-10 60 .......... FNorton 8 65
(WAO'Gorman) *hld up: hdwy over 3f out: rdn and ev ch over 1f out: styd on same pce ins fnl f* **9/1**[3]
0245 **6** *hd* **Elidore**[24] [5657] 4-9-2 66 .......... LDettori 2 71
(BPalling) *led 7f: sn rdn: styd on same pce fnl f* **12/1**
0210 **7** *2 ½* **Adorata (GER)**[41] [5223] 3-8-12 67 .......... MTebbutt 12 67
(JJay) *hld up: hdwy over 3f out: rdn over 1f out: styd on same pce* **25/1**
4400 **8** *2* **Kylkenny**[18] [5764] 9-9-0 67 .......... (t) LFletcher(3) 16 64
(HMorrison) *chsd ldr to 1/2-way: led 3f out: rdn and hdd over 1f out: wknd ins fnl f* **16/1**
5303 **9** *¾* **Zonic Boom (FR)**[13] [5867] 4-8-12 62 .......... JPMurtagh 3 57
(JRFanshawe) *chsd ldrs over 8f* **9/1**[3]
5420 **10** *1* **Iberus (GER)**[18] [5764] 6-9-3 67 .......... DHolland 18 61
(SGollings) *hld up: hdwy over 3f out: rdn and ev ch over 1f out: wknd ins fnl f* **20/1**
6430 **11** *1* **Miss Monica (IRE)**[39] [5265] 3-8-12 67 .......... WRyan 17 59
(HRACecil) *hld up: hdwy over 3f out: wknd over 1f out* **50/1**
0056 **12** *hd* **Kabeer**[15] [5841] 6-8-9 62 .......... LPKeniry(3) 10 53
(PSMcentee) *mid-div: hdwy over 3f out: rdn and wknd over 1f out* **22/1**
0112 **13** *½* **Stephano**[33] [5410] 3-9-0 69 .......... MHills 9 59
(BWHills) *hld up: sme hdwy over 2f out: wknd over 1f out* **9/4**[1]
5320 **14** *1 ½* **General**[18] [5773] 7-9-2 66 .......... JBramhill 13 54
(CRDore) *s.s: hld up: rdn over 2f out: a in rr* **16/1**
0300 **15** *1 ½* **Waziri (IRE)**[22] [5693] 3-8-13 68 .......... (v[1]) SDrowne 6 53
(HMorrison) *mid-div: plld hrd: lost pl over 4f out: sn bhd* **50/1**
340- **16** *5* **Sharp Rigging (IRE)**[183] [5279] 4-9-5 69 .......... TPQueally 19 45
(AMHales) *chsd ldrs over 7f* **40/1**
0306 **17** *9* **Reap**[147] [2218] 6-9-1 65 .......... JQuinn 11 25
(JPearce) *chsd ldrs over 7f* **40/1**

2m 7.95s (-0.45) **Going Correction** 0.0s/f (Good)
**WFA** 3 from 4yo+ 5lb **17** Ran SP% **124.9**
Speed ratings: **101,100,100,99,98 98,96,95,94,93 92,92,92,91,89 85,78**CSF £56.66 CT £1396.64 TOTE £7.70: £1.90, £2.40, £4.30, £6.20; EX 55.70 Place 6 £1,481.56, Place 5 £257.26.
**Owner** E & S Racing III **Bred** L T And M Foster **Trained** Epsom, Surrey

**FOCUS**
A modest handicap to round off with, but it was competitive and produced an exciting finish.

**NOTEBOOK**
**Duelling Banjos** was always travelling strongly and made good headway to close in on the leaders over two furlongs out. Having hit a flat spot, he came with a strong late run under a strong ride from Seb Sanders to claim Planters Punch and will be of interest if turned out quickly under a penalty as he is on a good mark.
**Planters Punch(IRE)**, who has been in fair form of late without winning, ran well but again found one too good. He continues to sneak up the weights without getting his head in front, but will get his turn eventually.
**Fuel Cell(IRE)**, returning from a short break, ran well and will appreciate returning to a faster surface.
**Blazing The Trail(IRE)** showed his poor showing at Salisbury to be all wrong and was doing his best work late.
**Garden Society(IRE)** has been running reasonably well since returning this season and improved slightly for the step back up in trip.
**Elidore** kept battling away after being passed and may require a stiffer test.
**Stephano**, who has been enjoying a purple patch, ran most disappointingly and may be in need of a short break. He now has something to prove. *Official explanation: jockey said gelding moved badly throughout*

T/Jkpt: Not won. T/Plt: £1,157.40 to a £1 stake. Pool: £40,193.55. 25.35 winning tickets. T/Qpdt: £42.80 to a £1 stake. Pool: £3,580.30. 61.80 winning tickets. CR

# 6010 LINGFIELD (L-H)
Wednesday, October 13

**OFFICIAL GOING: Standard**
Wind: almost nil Weather: persistent rain from race one

## 6153 BET DIRECT AT LINGFIELD PARK MAIDEN STKS (DIV I) 7f (P)
1:15 (1:18) (D3) 2-Y-O £4,238 (£1,304; £652; £326) Stalls Low

Form RPR
**1** **Happy As Larry (USA)** 2-9-0 .......... (t) LDettori 3 87+
(SaeedBinSuroor) *lenghty: lw: dwlt: wl in rr: gd prog fr 1/2-way: sustained run to ld over 1f out: sn clr: promising* **5/1**[2]
**2** *2 ½* **Karen's Caper (USA)** 2-8-9 .......... JFortune 14 73+
(JHMGosden) *legy: lw: s.v.s: bhd: gd prog on outer fr over 2f out: r.o to take 2nd last 50yds: improve* **7/1**[3]
44 **3** *½* **King's Kama**[37] [5347] 2-9-0 .......... MartinDwyer 7 77
(SirMichaelStoute) *sn chsd ldr: rdn over 1f out: kpt on same pce* **13/8**[1]
5 **4** *3 ½* **Three Deuces (USA)**[51] [5003] 2-8-9 .......... DHolland 10 63
(BJMeehan) *racd freely: led: rdn and hdd over 1f out: sn btn* **5/1**[2]
00 **5** *1 ¼* **Overjoy Way**[16] [5838] 2-8-9 .......... TPQueally 4 60
(PRChamings) *t.k.h early: trckd ldng pair: rdn over 2f out: fdd over 1f out* **20/1**
06 **6** *1* **Bold Diktator**[34] [5420] 2-9-0 .......... SDrowne 8 63
(WRMuir) *lw: chsd ldng pair: rdn 1/2-way: fdd fnl 2f* **50/1**
000 **7** *3 ½* **My Rascal (IRE)**[37] [5347] 2-9-0 .......... AMcCarthy 2 54
(MJWallace) *chsd ldrs: rdn over 2f out: wknd wl over 1f out* **100/1**
0005 **8** *nk* **In Dream'S (IRE)**[9] [5996] 2-9-0 .......... FNorton 6 53
(BGubby) *racd midfield: rdn and outpcd wl over 2f out: grad wknd* **33/1**
**9** *¾* **Lekka Ding (IRE)** 2-8-9 .......... JQuinn 12 46
(CFWall) *leggy: bkwd: scope: s.i.s: rn green and a towards rr: shkn up and no prog over 2f out* **50/1**
**10** *shd* **Gallantian (IRE)** 2-9-0 .......... PHanagan 13 51
(GAButler) *str: bkwd: s.s and hmpd: rn green: a wl in rr* **25/1**
00 **11** *¾* **Belle Chanson**[13] [5890] 2-8-9 .......... TQuinn 5 44
(JRBoyle) *chsd ldrs: pushed along over 4f out: wknd wl over 2f out* **50/1**
**12** *1 ¼* **Oblique (IRE)** 2-8-9 .......... SSanders 1 41
(SirMarkPrescott) *small: narrow: bkwd: dwlt: v green and a wl in rr on outer* **14/1**
**13** *1 ¾* **Petticoat Hill (UAE)** 2-8-9 .......... RHavlin 9 37
(JHMGosden) *rangy: lw: s.i.s: rn green and a bhd* **20/1**
0 **14** *2 ½* **La Cygne Blanche (IRE)**[15] [5847] 2-8-2 .......... CHaddon(7) 11 30
(MrsNMacauley) *racd midfield: wknd over 3f out* **100/1**

1m 25.2s (-0.74) **Going Correction** -0.05s/f (Stan) **14** Ran SP% **114.8**
Speed ratings: **102,99,98,94,93 92,88,87,86,86 85,84,82,79**CSF £33.96 TOTE £3.90: £2.20, £3.40, £1.10; EX 32.70.
**Owner** Godolphin **Bred** C H Kitchen And Jeffrey Cook **Trained** Newmarket, Suffolk

**FOCUS**
A race dominated by those with American pedigrees. The race was hand-timed and the resulting time was smart, 2.7 seconds faster than the second division.

**NOTEBOOK**
**Happy As Larry(USA)** was slightly slowly away but warmed to his task through the race. Once reaching the head of affairs he stretched away nicely and is yet another nice looking prospect from a stable full of juvenile talent.
**Karen's Caper(USA)**, who was very slowly away, made steady progress on the outside of the field to run a race full of promise. She never threatened to win but beat the rest of the field nicely.
**King's Kama** set a fair standard coming into the race and again ran well in defeat. He stayed close to the early pace and had every chance in the home straight. This may have been a warm maiden again and he should win in due course.
**Three Deuces(USA)** managed to get the inside draw from his wide position and set off at a quick pace. She stayed prominent until approaching the last furlong where he faded quite quickly. *Official explanation: jockey said filly ran too free to post*
**Overjoy Way**, who had excuses for his last run, sat just behind the pace and ran a fair race. She is now eligible for nurseries.
**Bold Diktator** continues to show bits of promise, and did so again. He would be interesting in a nursery if given a sensible handicap mark.
**Oblique(IRE)** ran extremely green and the experience will not be lost on her.

## 6154 BET DIRECT "RED TO BET" ON ITV CLASSIFIED STKS 1m (P)
1:45 (1:46) (F4) 4-Y-O+ £2,912 (£832; £416) Stalls High

Form RPR
1310 **1** **Fantasy Crusader**[6] [6024] 5-8-12 55 .......... (p) DaneO'Neill 12 65
(JAGilbert) *racd on outer in rr: pushed along 3f out: prog over 1f out: drvn to ld last 50yds* **14/1**

0425 **2** ½ **Oh So Rosie (IRE)**[31] 5496 4-8-9 54 (p) MartinDwyer 5 61
(JSMoore) *settled in last pair: stl in last pair over 1f out: angled to outer and r.o fnl f to take 2nd nr fin* **8/1**[3]

0561 **3** *nk* **Ryan's Bliss (IRE)**[25] 5643 4-8-11 57 CCatlin 3 62
(TDMccarthy) *trckd ldrs: effrt over 1f out: squeezed through to ld jst ins fnl f: hdd u.p last 50yds* **20/1**

-160 **4** *nk* **Hollywood Henry (IRE)**[77] 4238 4-8-12 55 (p) JQuinn 6 62
(JAkehurst) *settled in rr: nt clr run and swtchd rt 1f out: styd on: unable to chal* **20/1**

2460 **5** ¾ **Galloway Mac**[181] 1427 4-9-0 57 DHolland 8 63
(WAO'Gorman) *a.p: rdn to chal over 2f out: upsides ent fnl f: one pce* **25/1**

2220 **6** ½ **Pepper Road**[14] 5859 5-8-12 54 RFfrench 4 60
(RBastiman) *trckd ldrs: nt clr run over 1f out to ins fnl f: kpt on same pce* **11/2**[2]

3600 **7** ¾ **Sister Sophia (USA)**[25] 5657 4-8-9 55 (t) RMullen 2 55
(WJMusson) *lw: rrd and s.s: racd in last pair: nowhere to go over 1f out: r.o last 100yds: no ch* **33/1**

2011 **8** *shd* **Nautical**[6] 6024 6-9-4 55 LDettori 10 64
(AWCarroll) *hld up: prog 3f out: poised to chal over 1f out: fnd nil: wknd last 150yds* **1/1**[1]

0000 **9** *3* **Muyassir (IRE)**[94] 3771 9-8-12 54 SSanders 1 51
(MissBSanders) *bit bkwd: racd towards rr: pushed along over 2f out: one pce fr over 1f out* **16/1**

**10** *hd* **Darling River (FR)**[352] 5-9-0 60 TQuinn 11 52
(SDow) *led for 1f: restrained: led again wl over 2f out: gng easily over 1f out: hdd jst ins fnl f: wkng whn hmpd sn after* **66/1**

4602 **11** 1½ **Ziet D'Alsace (FR)**[6] 6024 4-8-9 53 JFortune 9 44
(AWCarroll) *cl up: led over 5f out: hdd wl over 2f out: wknd fnl f* **9/1**

0006 **12** 1¼ **Its Ecco Boy**[7] 6014 6-8-12 53 LisaJones 7 44
(PHowling) *t.k.h: led after 1f to over 5f out: lost pl on inner over 2f out: n.m.r 1f out: wknd* **66/1**

1m 39.59s (0.04) **Going Correction** -0.05s/f (Stan) **12** Ran SP% **118.3**
Speed ratings: **97,96,96,95,95 94,93,93,90,90 89,87**CSF £111.39 TOTE £21.40: £4.80, £2.10, £4.50; EX 170.30.
**Owner** The Fantasy Fellowship **Bred** J R C And Mrs Wren **Trained** Hargrave, Suffolk
■ Stewards Enquiry : R Ffrench caution: careless riding
C Catlin caution: careless riding

**FOCUS**
A tight classified stakes with a close finish, but the favourite was disappointing.

**NOTEBOOK**
**Fantasy Crusader**, who has a fair record on the Lingfield turf course, gained his first win on the All-Weather surface after being driven along for quite a long way. He stays further than this trip so may have a few more options than most in the field as far as future races are concerned. The trainer reported he did not handle Wolverhampton's new surface last time out. *Official explanation: trainer said, regarding the improved form shown, gelding was better suited by today's change in tactics and faster track*
**Oh So Rosie(IRE)** ran her usual race from way off the pace. She finished very well on the outside and looks to be in reasonable form at the moment.
**Ryan's Bliss(IRE)** found the gap he was looking for entering the last furlong and had every chance. He stays further than this and might appreciate a step back up to ten furlongs again.
**Hollywood Henry(IRE)** does not have a consistent profile but ran fairly well. He looked to be travelling really well for a long way before meeting a little trouble in running. He can pick up a similar event on this evidence.
**Galloway Mac** was always close to the pace and weakened late on. He may need to return to Southwell to recapture his winning form.
**Pepper Road** pulled hard early on and had a few traffic problems at the business end of the race. He is better than this.
**Sister Sophia(USA)** was travelling well for most of the race and found all the gaps closing on her at important times of the race. She looked an unlucky loser but still remains a maiden.
**Nautical** was very impressive at Wolverhampton last week but failed to repeat that form here. He moved into contention in the home straight and found very little. The early pace did not appear that strong and perhaps that affected his chance.

## 6155 BET DIRECT AT LINGFIELD PARK MAIDEN STKS (DIV II) 7f (P)
**2:15** (2:17) (F4) 2-Y-0 **£4,238** (£1,304; £652; £326) **Stalls** Low

Form RPR

000 **1** **Meditation**[7] 6010 2-8-9 NCallan 6 65
(IAWood) *mde virtually all: set slow pce tl kicked on over 2f out: edgd rt fnl f: jst hld on* **10/1**

0 **2** *shd* **King's Majesty (IRE)**[22] 5718 2-9-0 DHolland 2 72+
(SirMichaelStoute) *lw: s.i.s: sn midfield: outpcd over 2f out: hanging lft over 1f out: r.o strly fnl f: jst failed: too much to do* **11/10**[1]

**3** 1¼ **Bodhi Tree (USA)** 2-8-9 JFortune 12 61
(JHMGosden) *leegy: scope: dwlt: sn rcvrd and pressed wnr: clr of remainder 2f out: kpt on same pce fnl f* **7/1**[3]

**4** *1* **Missatacama (IRE)** 2-8-9 RFfrench 3 59
(DJDaly) *w'like: racd midfield: prog to chse clr ldng pair wl over 1f out: kpt on same pce* **33/1**

**5** 3½ **Contented (IRE)** 2-9-0 RMullen 14 55
(EALDunlop) *tall: b.: s.i.s: racd wd and hld up: outpcd over 2f out: shuffled along and kpt on fr over 1f out* **33/1**

0 **6** *4* **Song Sparrow**[7] 6011 2-8-9 PHanagan 11 40
(GAButler) *racd midfield: outpcd over 2f out: n.d after* **50/1**

**7** *nk* **Cape Enterprise (USA)** 2-9-0 MHills 13 44
(JWHills) *str: bkwd: s.i.s: rn green in rr: nvr a factor* **16/1**

000 **8** 1¼ **Red Opera**[7] 6010 2-9-0 SSanders 10 41
(SirMarkPrescott) *racd midfield: outpcd over 2f out: no ch after* **33/1**

0 **9** 2½ **Lambriggan Lad**[30] 5508 2-9-0 VSlattery 7 35
(MissVictoriaRoberts) *t.k.h: prom to 3f out: wknd* **100/1**

00 **10** *1* **Aramat**[7] 6010 2-8-9 TQuinn 5 27
(JRBoyle) *chsd ldrs tl wknd rapidly over 2f out* **100/1**

**11** *5* **Livvies Lady (IRE)** 2-8-9 MartinDwyer 9 15
(DKIvory) *tall: unf: s.s: rn green and a bhd* **33/1**

**12** *3* **Mon Plaisir** 2-8-9 JQuinn 1 7
(CFWall) *scope: s.s: rn v green and a bhd* **33/1**

**13** ½ **Hugo The Boss (IRE)** 2-9-0 DaneO'Neill 4 11
(JRBoyle) *s.s: rn green and a bhd* **50/1**

06 **U** **Mel's Moment (USA)**[13] 5897 2-9-0 SDrowne 8 —
(MrsAJPerrett) *stmbld and uns rdr s* **4/1**[2]

1m 27.9s (1.96) **Going Correction** -0.05s/f (Stan) **14** Ran SP% **115.7**
Speed ratings: **86,85,84,83,79 74,74,72,70,68 63,59,59,—**CSF £19.36 TOTE £19.00: £4.00, £1.10, £2.40; EX 60.30.
**Owner** Paddy Barrett **Bred** P E Barrett **Trained** Upper Lambourn, Berks

**FOCUS**
Like the first division, this race was hand-timed and a slow pace resulted in a time 2.7 seconds slower.

**NOTEBOOK**
**Meditation** may be slightly flattered by the bare result but won on merit. There have been a couple of excuses for her three previous runs and connections believe she is a fair animal so success was not completely out of the blue. Her future will depend on what the Handicapper does.
**King's Majesty(IRE)** would almost certainly have got up with a less troubled path. He got into some traffic problems on the home turn but, once straightened out, flew up the home straight. A similar maiden should be picked up on this evidence.
**Bodhi Tree(USA)** managed to get a decent position from her wide draw despite missing the break. She had to switch back inside the winner in the last furlong but stayed on nicely to the line. This was a good effort and she should be able to pick up a similar event of this evidence.
**Missatacama(IRE)** was always close up and stayed on in pleasing style. She was swept past in the last furlong but still shaped with some promise. She should stay further than this.
**Contented(IRE)** ran fairly green on this debut and ran on for pressure. He will have learnt plenty from this.
**Aramat** *Official explanation: jockey said filly hung left in the straight*
**Mon Plaisir** *Official explanation: jockey said filly missed the break and ran very green*
**Mel's Moment(USA)** unseated his rider leaving the stalls.

## 6156 BET DIRECT ON SUPER LEAGUE GRAND FINAL H'CAP 1m (P)
**2:50** (2:52) (E3) (0-70,73) 3-Y-0+ **£3,523** (£1,084; £542; £271) **Stalls** High

Form RPR

0012 **1** **Omaha City (IRE)**[7] 6014 10-9-3 **70** FNorton 9 79
(BGubby) *t.k.h early: hld up midfield: prog wl over 1f out: drvn and styd on gamely to ld last 75yds* **5/1**[2]

5401 **2** ¾ **Analyze (FR)**[7] 6014 6-9-6 **73** 6ex JFortune 6 80
(BGPowell) *trckd ldng pair: effrt 2f out: rdn to ld ent fnl f: hdd and hld last 75yds* **14/1**

0042 **3** *nk* **Concer Eto**[13] 5887 5-9-3 **70** (p) LDettori 11 77
(SCWilliams) *hld up last pair: prog over 2f out: clsd on ldrs ent fnl f: fnd little last 100yds* **5/2**[1]

0050 **4** *nk* **Lilli Marlane**[21] 5740 4-9-2 **69** JFEgan 8 78+
(NACallaghan) *hld up midfield: lost pl over 2f out: prog over 1f out: clsng on ldrs whn nowhere to go ins fnl f: nt rcvr* **16/1**

2465 **5** 1¼ **Pure Mischief (IRE)**[45] 5158 5-9-0 **70** RThomas(3) 2 73
(CRDore) *dwlt: hld up last pair: on wd outside and stl last pair over 1f out: rdn and r.o fnl f: hopeless task* **25/1**

0030 **6** *nk* **Kindlelight Debut**[11] 5948 4-9-1 **68** DHolland 1 70
(DKIvory) *trckd ldr: rdn to ld over 1f out: hdd & wknd ent fnl f* **16/1**

1541 **7** 1¾ **Riska King**[11] 5955 4-9-1 **68** PHanagan 12 66
(RAFahey) *settled in rr: rdn 2f out: one pce and no imp ldrs* **5/1**[2]

4030 **8** *nk* **Voice Mail**[39] 5297 5-9-0 **70** (v) LPKeniry(3) 4 68
(AMBalding) *trckd ldng pair: rdn 2f out: wknd fnl f* **6/1**[3]

3410 **9** ½ **Liberty Royal**[25] 5657 5-9-1 **68** (p) SSanders 7 64
(PJMakin) *dwlt: wl in rr: rdn and prog to chse ldrs over 2f out: wknd fnl f* **8/1**

0-00 **10** *nk* **Blackmail (USA)**[11] 5935 6-9-3 **70** (b) SCarson 5 66
(MissBSanders) *a towards rr: rdn and no prog wl over 1f out* **50/1**

-000 **11** ½ **Electrique (IRE)**[21] 5739 4-9-3 **70** (b[1]) MartinDwyer 3 65
(JAOsborne) *lw: trckd ldrs on inner: cl up over 1f out: hanging and looked reluctant whn nt clr run sn after* **16/1**

/00- **12** *3* **Harry The Hoover (IRE)**[319] 6099 4-9-0 **70** BReilly(3) 10 58
(MJGingell) *led to over 1f out: wknd rapidly* **50/1**

1m 39.12s (-0.43) **Going Correction** -0.05s/f (Stan) **12** Ran SP% **119.4**
Speed ratings: **100,99,98,98,97 97,95,95,94,94 93,90**CSF £72.54 CT £218.86 TOTE £6.30: £1.90, £2.90, £1.90; EX 40.10.
**Owner** Brian Gubby Ltd **Bred** Brownstown Stud Farm **Trained** Bagshot, Surrey

**FOCUS**
An ordinary but competitive handicap on official figures with a close finish.

**NOTEBOOK**
**Omaha City(IRE)** took advantage of an 8lb turnaround with the second and a change in tactics to continue his purple patch. He has been in good form in the last month and timed his run to get there at the death. He seems to be enjoying himself and should keep running well in similar races.
**Analyze(FR)** just failed to confirm positions with Omaha City on 8lb worse terms, and looks to be running well at the moment. He took it up with a furlong to go and looked likely to win until pounced on late on. He can continue to run well in a similar grade.
**Concer Eto** was held up at the rear of the field before working his way slowly into contention. He had his chance but did not find as much as looked likely close to home. He has looked tricky in the past and may become more difficult to win with.
**Lilli Marlane** may have been slightly unlucky not to finish closer. She travelled well during the race but ran into every closed gap going at the business end of the race. Given her style of running she will always need luck, but she can win if she gets it. *Official explanation: jockey said filly was denied a clear run*
**Pure Mischief(IRE)** was held up at the back of the field and had a lot to do from the turn. He finished well after being pulled out wide, and will appreciate a step back up in trip.
**Riska King** was only 3lb higher than when winning on Wolverhampton's new surface recently, but showed nothing like that form on this occasion.
**Voice Mail** is fully effective off his mark but did not appear to run to it.
**Electrique(IRE)** travelled really well into the straight before finding a wall of horses in front of him. He is worth another chance and hopefully he will get the breaks next time.

## 6157 BETDIRECT.CO.UK CLAIMING STKS 7f (P)
**3:25** (3:28) (F4) 3-Y-0+ **£3,080** (£880; £440) **Stalls** Low

Form RPR

5550 **1** **Linning Wine (IRE)**[11] 5952 8-9-6 93 TQuinn 12 83
(BGPowell) *lw: hld up in rr: smooth prog 3f out: hanging lft 1f out: r.o wl fnl f to ld last 75yds* **7/1**

5000 **2** 1½ **Western Roots**[11] 5955 3-8-10 67 JQuinn 9 71
(KAMorgan) *chsd ldrs: rdn and effrt 2f out: styd on to join ldrs ins fnl f: outpcd by wnr last 75yds* **25/1**

5600 **3** 1¼ **Blonde En Blonde (IRE)**[21] 5740 4-9-1 64 (b) NCallan 10 71
(NPLittmoden) *trckd ldrs: rdn to chse ldr over 1f out: upsides ins fnl f: one pce* **16/1**

0350 **4** *shd* **Takes Tutu (USA)**[35] 5403 5-9-10 76 (v) SWhitworth 3 80
(KRBurke) *hld up wl in rr: sme prog over 2f out: hanging over 1f out: styd on ins fnl f: n.d* **5/1**[3]

5360 **5** ½ **Ammenayr (IRE)**[26] 5614 4-9-10 67 JFortune 11 78
(TGMills) *lw: w ldr: led 1/2-way: drvn and hdd last 75yds: wknd* **13/2**

1636 **6** *nk* **Pertemps Magus**[27] 5583 4-8-3 62 (v[1]) PHanagan 7 57
(RAFahey) *t.k.h: trckd ldng pair: stl cl up over 1f out: hanging bdly lft and reluctant after* **7/2**[2]

4000 **7** *3* **Cheese 'n Biscuits**[26] 5603 4-9-0 75 AQuinn(5) 6 65
(GLMoore) *hld up towards rr: effrt over 2f out: nt pce to rch ldrs* **12/1**

05-0 **8** *nk* **Wall Street Runner**[26] 5618 3-8-4 62 DFox(5) 1 56
(CADwyer) *lw: chsd ldrs: rdn over 2f out: wknd jst over 1f out* **50/1**

5000 **9** 1½ **Golden Dixie (USA)**[14] 5874 5-9-10 75 MartinDwyer 2 65
(AMBalding) *b.front: w ldrs: drvn over 2f out: wknd over 1f out* **3/1**[1]

6400 **10** *3* **Multiple Choice (IRE)**[7] 6016 3-9-0 64..........(bt) TEDurcan 8 49
(NPLittmoden) *a towards rr: u.p and struggling over 2f out* **25/1**

000 **11** *16* **Green Ridge**[23] 5693 3-8-10 62.......... HayleyTurner(3) 4 7
(MissAMNewton-Smith) *led to 1/2-way: sn wknd u.p: t.o* **50/1**

2500 **12** *1 3/4* **Superchief**[39] 5282 9-9-2 64..........(bt) SSanders 13 3
(MissBSanders) *s.i.s: a bhd: t.o fnl 2f* **16/1**

0-00 **13** *5* **Mannyman (IRE)**[29] 5552 3-8-3 .......... CCatlin 5 —
(WJarvis) *a bhd: t.o fnl 2f* **50/1**

040- **14** *7* **Sahara Scirocco (IRE)**[351] 5816 3-8-4 61.......... TPQueally 14 —
(IAWood) *chsd ldrs: rdn over 4f out: sn wknd: t.o* **66/1**

1m 25.1s (-0.84) **Going Correction** -0.05s/f (Stan)
**WFA** 3 from 4yo+ 2lb **14** Ran SP% **124.2**
Speed ratings: **102,100,98,98,98 97,94,94,92,88 70,68,62,54**CSF £183.00 TOTE £7.10: £2.10, £9.10, £2.90; EX 151.20.Lining Wine was claimed by Nigel Shields for £12,000
**Owner** Favourites Racing **Bred** His Highness The Aga Khan's Studs S C **Trained** Morestead, Hants

**FOCUS**
Hand-timed. Not a bad claimer strictly based on the official ratings of those competing, but many of the field arrived here out of form.

**NOTEBOOK**
**Linning Wine(IRE)** came with a sustained run down the middle of the course to pick up the leaders. He was really well in here on official figures and stays much further than this seven furlongs, so he should have a few options available to him in a similar grade.
**Western Roots** has not been running particularly well recently but had a chance on official figures. He came with a run at the same time as the winner but did not get home as well. He does not look easy to place.
**Blonde En Blonde(IRE)**, back over a more suitable trip, ran a solid race. She had the upper hand on those who sat close to the early pace inside the final furlong, but got swamped by the late runs of the two on the outside. She can run well in a similar event.
**Takes Tutu(USA)** finished fairly well from off the pace. He remains very hard to place and will need everything to go right for him to regain the winning thread.
**Ammenayr(IRE)** managed to get a good position from his moderate draw and stay prominent until close to home. He was not particularly well in with a lot of his rivals in this event and will need to be set an easier task than this to win.
**Pertemps Magus**, running in a first-time visor, was travelling well just in behind the pace until finding nowhere to go at a crucial point of the race. She appeared to handle the surface and would be interesting if able to enjoy a better passage next time. Her rider reported that she hung left inside the final furlong. *Official explanation: jockey said filly had hung left in the final furlong*
**Golden Dixie(USA)**, who has an American pedigree, was well supported before the off but showed very little during it. The jockey reported that the gelding hung throughout the race. *Official explanation: jockey said gelding hung right throughout*

## 6158 BET DIRECT 1/4 FIRST FIVE AT NEWMARKET CONDITIONS STKS 6f (P)
**4:00** (4:01) (C2) 2-Y-O **£5,476** (£1,685; £842; £421) **Stalls** Low

Form RPR

351 **1** **Emerald Lodge**[12] 5911 2-9-4 79..........(v) LDettori 4 88
(JNoseda) *lw: mde all: rdn fnl f: styd on wl* **11/8**[1]

20 **2** *1 1/4* **Middle Earth (USA)**[56] 4844 2-8-11 ..........(t) MartinDwyer 1 77
(AMBalding) *lw: trckd ldng pair: rdn to chse wnr over 1f out: kpt on wl but a hld* **3/1**[2]

03 **3** *1 1/2* **Vague Star (ITY)**[14] 5865 2-8-11 .......... NDay 5 73
(RIngram) *racd midfield: rdn and hanging over 1f out: styd on ins fnl f: nvr able to chal* **12/1**

6500 **4** *2 1/2* **Lowestoft Playboy**[11] 5947 2-8-8 62.......... HayleyTurner(3) 8 65
(MrsCADunnett) *chsd ldng pair: rdn wl over 2f out: one pce fnl 2f* **25/1**

2530 **5** *shd* **Kwame**[23] 5701 2-8-9 77..........(v) JFortune 9 63
(MissECLavelle) *hld up: plenty to do whn rdn over 1f out: no imp ldrs* **5/1**[3]

2001 **6** *2 1/2* **On The Waterline (IRE)**[9] 6000 2-8-13 72..........(v) NCallan 6 59
(PDEvans) *chsd wnr: rdn to chal 2f out: wknd over 1f out* **6/1**

**7** *6* **Definitely Royal (IRE)** 2-8-4 .......... PHanagan 3 32
(RMHCowell) *leggy: bkwd: dwlt: a detached in last pair* **66/1**

**8** *3* **Pride Of Poona (IRE)** 2-8-4 .......... TPQueally 7 23
(RMHCowell) *w'like: bkwd: dwlt: a detached in last pair* **40/1**

1m 12.2s (-0.72) **Going Correction** -0.05s/f (Stan) **8** Ran SP% **113.5**
Speed ratings: **102,100,98,95,94 91,83,79**CSF £5.45 TOTE £2.00: £1.40, £1.20, £1.60; EX 9.10.
**Owner** Hesmonds Stud **Bred** M P B Bloodstock Ltd **Trained** Newmarket, Suffolk

**FOCUS**
Hand-timed. A decent pace for this conditions event and the form should work out.

**NOTEBOOK**
**Emerald Lodge**, over the same course and distance as for his recent win, was again given a positive ride and soon bagged the inside rail in front. He did not enjoy an uncontested lead, but still found plenty when asked and is beginning to look a useful sprint prospect.
**Middle Earth(USA)** ◆, given a short break since his disappointing performance in soft ground at Kempton, appreciated the return to a sounder surface and this was much more like it. Travelling well just behind the leaders, he put in a determined effort once in line for home but the winner proved too classy. He should find a race on this surface.
**Vague Star(ITY)** ran a strange race. Asked for his effort on straightening up, he carried his head at a funny angle and looked reluctant, but then found his stride and stayed on strongly to the line. The ability is certainly there, but so are one or two question marks.
**Lowestoft Playboy**, totally outclassed in Listed company last time, ran a creditable race using official ratings as a guide and may be worth considering for a low-grade nursery off his proper mark.
**Kwame** was disappointing considering she had the form to do better, and the inference must be that she did not take to the surface.
**On The Waterline(IRE)**, who made all to win on soft ground at Windsor last time, could not adopt the same tactics on this occasion thanks to the favourite, and her efforts to keep tabs on him eventually took their toll.

## 6159 LITTLEWOODS BET DIRECT H'CAP 2m (P)
**4:35** (4:35) (F4) (0-55,55) 3-Y-0+ **£2,926** (£836; £418) **Stalls** Low

Form RPR

3400 **1** **Vandenberghe**[18] 5796 5-8-8 50.......... RKeogh(7) 7 58
(JAOsborne) *sn midfield: effrt over 2f out: pushed into ld last 150yds: styd on wl* **10/1**

2032 **2** *1 1/2* **Peak Park (USA)**[42] 5221 4-8-13 48..........(v) JFEgan 6 54
(JARToller) *hld up in rr: prog over 3f out: rdn to ld 1f out: hdd and one pce last 150yds* **7/2**[1]

5005 **3** *1 1/4* **Private Benjamin**[24] 4736 4-9-4 53.......... PDoe 2 58
(JamiePoulton) *settled in rr: prog 3f out: rdn and nt qckn over 1f out: styd on* **18/1**

F **4** *1 1/4* **Cambo (FR)**[8] 6006 3-8-9 55.......... PHanagan 14 58
(RFord) *hld up in last pair: prog on outer over 2f out: outpcd wl over 1f out: styd on ins fnl f* **50/1**

0000 **5** *1/2* **Surface To Air**[36] 5371 3-8-7 53 ow1.......... RHavlin 12 56
(MrsPNDutfield) *racd midfield: rdn over 4f out: prog u.p over 2f out: one pce over 1f out* **100/1**

5110 **6** *shd* **Lazzaz**[9] 5993 6-9-0 54.......... PMakin(5) 10 56
(PWHiatt) *lw: led to 3f out: styd chsng ldrs to over 1f out: wknd fnl f* **12/1**

3005 **7** *shd* **Galandora**[25] 5645 4-8-13 48.......... ADaly 13 50
(DrJRJNaylor) *trckd ldrs: prog to ld 3f out: hdd & wknd 1f out* **20/1**

0500 **8** *1/2* **Another Con (IRE)**[16] 5843 3-8-9 55.......... LisaJones 9 57
(PHowling) *trckd ldrs: rdn over 2f out: cl up over 1f out: wknd* **33/1**

3010 **9** *2* **Most-Saucy**[16] 5826 8-9-6 55.......... LDettori 1 54
(IAWood) *b.fr: hld up towards rr: effrt over 2f out: no prog and btn over 1f out* **4/1**[2]

4012 **10** *nk* **Indian Chase**[25] 5645 7-8-8 46.......... RThomas(3) 4 45
(DrJRJNaylor) *hld up in last: outpcd over 2f out: one pce and no ch after* **10/1**

0256 **11** *1 1/4* **Muslin**[29] 5546 3-8-7 53.......... DaneO'Neill 3 51
(JRFanshawe) *hld up midfield: no room on inner 3f out and lost pl: nt clr run again over 2f out: no ch after* **7/1**[3]

2030 **12** *11* **Montosari**[18] 5796 5-9-6 55.......... DHolland 11 39
(PMitchell) *lw: trckd ldrs: lost pl 3f out: wkng whn hmpd over 2f out* **7/1**[3]

0003 **13** *7* **Medica Boba**[13] 5889 3-8-9 55 ow1.......... JFortune 8 31
(HMorrison) *chsd ldr to 3f out: wkng whn bmpd over 2f out* **14/1**

0454 **14** *2* **Bakhtyar**[55] 4870 3-8-9 55..........(b) SSanders 5 29
(RCharlton) *chsd ldng pair: pushed along over 4f out: wkng whn bmpd over 2f out* **12/1**

3m 27.28s (-1.30) **Going Correction** -0.05s/f (Stan)
**WFA** 3 from 4yo+ 11lb **14** Ran SP% **123.4**
Speed ratings: **101,100,99,99,98 98,98,98,97,97 96,91,87,86**CSF £44.89 CT £648.25 TOTE £13.70: £3.00, £2.50, £4.10; EX 81.90.
**Owner** D Marks **Bred** Douglas Marks **Trained** Upper Lambourn, Berks
■ Stewards Enquiry : R Keogh three-day ban: careless riding (Oct 25-27)

**FOCUS**
A routine modest Polytrack staying handicap, contested by several horses that have met each other before and will do so again. With only about eight lengths covering the first 11 home and trouble on the home bend, the form is probably moderate.

**NOTEBOOK**
**Vandenberghe** wins in his turn and was brought with a well-timed effort to reverse the form with the three who finished in front of him here last month under a more patient ride. He does not strike as the sort to follow up though.
**Peak Park(USA)**, well backed, hit the front at just the right time and did nothing wrong, but again found one to come and do him. The fact that he is still a maiden is not down to lack of application.
**Private Benjamin**, trying this trip for the first time on the level, had every chance, and lack of finishing pace rather than lack of stamina proved his downfall.
**Cambo(FR)**, none the worse for his unfortunate experience at Catterick on his British debut, was doing his best work late and looks to need an even greater test of stamina. He could be an interesting sort for staying novice hurdles.
**Surface To Air**, whose previous outings had all been over ten furlongs, ran a fair handicap debut over this much longer trip, but what he actually achieved is hard to gauge.
**Lazzaz** set the pace as he likes to do but, when it came down to a test of finishing speed over the final couple of furlongs, he was found wanting.
**Most-Saucy**, just 2lb higher than when she had a lot of these behind her over course and distance last month, never managed to land a blow this time.
**Montosari** already looked beaten when running into trouble approaching the final bend. *Official explanation: trainer said gelding lost its action*

## 6160 BET DIRECT ON 0800 329393 H'CAP 1m 2f (P)
**5:10** (5:12) (E3) (0-70,69) 3-Y-O **£3,542** (£1,090; £545; £272) **Stalls** Low

Form RPR

2224 **1** **Revenir (IRE)**[11] 5936 3-9-3 68.......... DaneO'Neill 4 76
(EFVaughan) *lw: dwlt: hld up last trio: gd prog on wd outside fr 3f out: drvn to ld last 75yds* **8/1**

0050 **2** *nk* **The Violin Player (USA)**[35] 5402 3-9-1 66.......... DHolland 5 73
(HJCollingridge) *pressed ldr: hrd rdn to chal 2f out: upsides ins fnl f: kpt on* **9/2**[2]

2062 **3** *1/2* **Almond Willow (IRE)**[11] 5955 3-9-4 69.......... LDettori 6 75
(JNoseda) *led: shkn up 2f out: flashed tail u.p fnl f: hdd last 75yds* **11/4**[1]

6000 **4** *nk* **Ali Deo**[11] 5955 3-9-1 66.......... TPQueally 13 71
(WJHaggas) *b.hind: hld up last trio: plenty to do whn prog on outer 2f out: r.o wl fnl f: nvr nrr* **20/1**

5060 **5** *hd* **Competitor**[3] 6083 3-9-3 68..........(p) TQuinn 8 73
(JAkehurst) *trckd ldrs: rdn and effrt 2f out: styng on but hld whn squeezed out ins fnl f* **20/1**

004 **6** *nk* **Ground Patrol**[20] 5749 3-9-1 66..........(t) JFortune 2 71
(GLMoore) *racd midfield: effrt 2f out: rdn and styd on fnl f: nt pce to chal* **16/1**

0006 **7** *3/4* **Off Beat (USA)**[20] 5748 3-9-4 69.......... SCarson 11 72
(RFJohnsonHoughton) *hld up midfield: lost pl sltly over 2f out: drvn and styd on fr over 1f out: nt rch ldrs* **33/1**

6003 **8** *hd* **Chigorin**[42] 5223 3-9-0 65.......... TEDurcan 9 68
(JMPEustace) *lw: chsd ldrs: lost pl u.p 3f out: renewed effrt 2f out: keeping on whn nt clr run ins fnl f* **7/1**[3]

1205 **9** *2 1/2* **The Fun Merchant**[16] 5829 3-9-2 67.......... JQuinn 12 65
(JPearce) *settled in rr: plenty to do whn effrt 2f out: nt clr run sn after: no ch: kpt on* **10/1**

4035 **10** *1 1/2* **Jomus**[26] 5622 3-9-1 66.......... AMcCarthy 1 61
(LMontagueHall) *settled towards rr on inner: no prog 2f out: swtchd wd over 1f out: no imp* **20/1**

5440 **11** *1 1/4* **Port 'n Starboard**[11] 5956 3-9-0 65..........(v[1]) CCatlin 10 58
(CACyzer) *hld up in rr: effrt on outer 3f out: no prog and btn 2f out* **50/1**

6326 **12** *4* **Paintbox**[16] 5828 3-9-3 68.......... SSanders 3 53
(MrsAJPerrett) *trckd ldrs: gng wl enough over 2f out: wknd rapidly over 1f out* **10/1**

0360 **13** *1 1/4* **Come What July (IRE)**[55] 4882 3-8-12 68..........(b) PMakin(5) 7 51
(MrsNMacauley) *b.hind: trckd ldrs tl wknd rapidly 2f out* **14/1**

6100 **14** *2 1/2* **Belisco (USA)**[36] 5381 3-8-13 69.......... DFox(5) 14 47
(CADwyer) *lw: reluctant to enter stalls: dwlt: hld up in last trio: wl bhd fnl 2f* **20/1**

2m 7.20s (-0.65) **Going Correction** -0.05s/f (Stan) **14** Ran SP% **123.1**
Speed ratings: **100,99,99,99,98 98,98,97,95,94 93,90,89,87**CSF £40.46 CT £128.65 TOTE £9.60: £2.60, £1.80, £2.00; EX 72.90 Place 6 £165.99, Place 5 £121.51.
**Owner** M A Whelton **Bred** Jerry O'Brien **Trained** Newmarket, Suffolk
■ Stewards Enquiry : Dane O'Neill two-day ban: careless riding (Oct 25,26)

**FOCUS**
Hand-timed. An ordinary but competitive little handicap run at a fair pace, and one or two traffic problems in the closing stages.

**NOTEBOOK**
**Revenir(IRE)**, given a patient ride, made giant strides on the wide outside racing down the false straight, but had to battle hard to force his way to the front in the dying strides. He seems to like this surface, but gives the impression this is as far as he wants.

**The Violin Player(USA)** ◆ appreciated the drop in trip and positive ride and was only just denied. He is becoming well handicapped and can certainly win off this sort of mark.
**Almond Willow(IRE)**, who has looked a character in the past, was certainly ridden as though there were no stamina doubts over this trip, but once her rider was eventually forced to go for the whip, the tail went once again and she was run out of it. She looks one to treat with caution.
**Ali Deo** ◆, out of form since the spring, ran with credit from his draw and was finishing with a flourish. He looks worth another go under the same conditions when hopefully the draw will be kinder.
**Competitor** ◆, runner-up in a similar contest over course and distance at the start of the year on his last visit, was fighting for a place in the frame when squeezed out in the closing stages. He looks capable of gaining compensation.
**Ground Patrol** did not run badly on his return to this surface and his trainer is likely to find the right opportunity for him here this winter.
**Off Beat(USA)**, a winner here last winter, was already beaten when messed about in the very closing stages.
**Chigorin**, a maiden stepping up in trip and on sand for the first time, may have been a length or two closer had he not had to take evasive action well inside the last furlong.
**Belisco(USA)** *Official explanation: jockey said gelding was never travelling*
T/Plt: £116.40 to a £1 stake. Pool: £35,436.65. 222.20 winning tickets. T/Qpdt: £12.20 to a £1 stake. Pool: £3,219.20. 194.60 winning tickets. JN

# BORDEAUX LE BOUSCAT (R-H)

Wednesday, October 13

**OFFICIAL GOING: Soft**

## 6169a GRAND CRITERIUM DE BORDEAUX (LISTED RACE) 1m

**1:20** (1:23) 2-Y-O **£15,845** (£6,338; £4,754; £3,169)

RPR

1 **Witten (USA)**[59] 2-8-8 ........ OPeslier 6 104
(J-CRouget, France)
2 2 **Medigating (FR)**[22] 2-8-11 ........ TGillet 3 103
(MRoussel, France)
3 3 **Olaya (USA)**[34] 2-8-8 ........ IMendizabal 4 94
(J-CRouget, France)
4 1 **Riverbride (USA)**[39] 5313 2-8-8 ........ C-PLemaire 7 92
(NClement, France)
5 3/4 **Thunderwing (IRE)**[27] 5580 2-8-11 ........ DWilliams 5 93
(KRBurke) *in touch, tk clsr order appr str, 2nd and pushed along str, rdn and one pace fr 1 1/2f out*
6 1 1/2 **Fol Parade (ARG)**[149] 2-8-11 ........ MBlancpain 2 90
(MDelcher-Sanchez, Spain)
7 5 **Songoku (IRE)**[22] 2-8-11 ........ PSogorb 8 80
(RMartin-Sanchez, Spain)
8 10 **Benta Berri (FR)** 2-8-11 ........(b) CNora 1 60
(RMartin-Sanchez, Spain)

1m 41.2s **8** Ran
Speed ratings: .
**Owner** N Radwan **Bred** Mr & Mrs S H Rogers **Trained** France

**NOTEBOOK**
**Thunderwing(IRE)** has looked progressive and was chasing a four-timer on his first crack at Pattern company. In the end he was found out by the step up in grade.

## 6170a PRIX ANDRE BABOIN (GRAND PRIX DES PROVINCES) (GROUP 3) 1m 1f 110y

**2:20** (2:31) 3-Y-O+ **£25,704** (£10,282; £7,711; £5,141)

RPR

1 **Valentino (FR)**[11] 5968 5-8-10 ........ IMendizabal 9 113
(ADeRoyer-Dupre, France) *in touch, 4th straight, driven to challenge 1 1/2f out, ridden to lead 150 yards out, went clear close home, readily* 1
2 3 **Marshall (FR)**[22] 5727 4-9-0 ........ MBlancpain 10 112
(CLaffon-Parias, France) *mid-div, disp 5th straight, headway over 1 1/2f out, ridden and ran on final furlong to take 2nd 100 yards out* 2
3 nk **Tunduru (IRE)** 3-8-6 ........ OTrigodet 14 108
(RMartin-Sanchez, Spain) *towards rear, 11th straight, stayed on well on outside final furlong to take 3rd, nearest at finish*
4 3/4 **Pont D'Or (IRE)**[60] 4766 5-8-10 ........ OPeslier 1 106
(DSepulchre, France) *slowly into stride, disputing 7th on outside straight, stayed on steadily final furlong to take 4th final strides*
5 hd **Weightless**[11] 5968 4-8-10 ........ TThulliez 8 106
(PBary, France) *raced in close 2nd, led over 3f out, ridden and ran on from over 1f out, headed and no extra 150 yards out* 3
6 nk **Allez Olive (IRE)**[11] 6-8-10 ........ JBesse 4 105
(J-PDespeyroux, France) *mid-division, stayed on final furlong but never in contention*
7 1/2 **King Of Cry (FR)**[129] 2722 3-8-6 ........ CNora 7 105
(RMartin-Sanchez, Spain) *mid-division, disputing 5th straight, ridden over 1f out, syaed on to line*
8 2 **Wunderwood (USA)**[32] 5465 5-8-10 ........ J-BEyquem 2 101
(LadyHerries) *held up, some late headway but never a factor*
9 2 1/2 **Prends Ton Temps (FR)**[37] 5361 7-8-10 ........ DBoeuf 12 97
(DSmaga, France) *prominent early, disputing 7th straight, ridden 1 1/2f out, one pace*
10 5 **Matin De Tempete (FR)**[45] 5169 4-8-7 ........ TJarnet 11 85
(SMorineau, France) *prominent, disputing 2nd straight, ridden and one pace from 1 1/2f out*
11 1 **Jersey Bounce (IRE)**[53] 3-8-6 ........ C-PLemaire 6 87
(FRohaut, France) *prominent, disputing 2nd and pushed along to chase leader straight, soon weakened*
12 6 **Secret De Famille (FR)**[21] 5-8-10 ........ ELegrix 3 76
(MDelzangles, France) *mid-division, never dangerous*
13 5 **Invasian (IRE)**[46] 5106 3-8-6 ........ WRyan 13 68
(HRACecil) *led narrowly to over 3f out, disputing 7th and weakening straight*
14 2 **Colisay**[21] 5731 5-8-10 ........ TGillet 5 63
(EFVaughan) *behind, pushed along well before half-way, never a factor*

2m 5.00s
**WFA** 3 from 4yo+ 4lb **14** Ran SP% **122.4**
Speed ratings: .
**Owner** E Fierro **Bred** Mme Gilles Forien & Gilles Forien **Trained** France

**NOTEBOOK**
**Valentino(FR)** ran out an impressive winner of this Group Three contest, and seemed well suited by the drop in grade. He should continue to run well.
**Wunderwood(USA)**, who is much better over greater distances than this, is at his best when racing prominently and was not given the best of rides, being held up right off the pace. He is better than this and deserves another chance.
**Invasian(IRE)** was up there throughout, but simply fell short of the required standard.
**Colisay** was another not up to the task.

# 5938 NEWMARKET (R-H)

Thursday, October 14

**OFFICIAL GOING: Soft**
Heavy rain forced the official going to be changed to soft, although times suggest it was no worse than good to soft.
Wind: Slight half-behind Weather: Early mist and rain giving way to sunshine.

## 6171 ROBERT SANGSTER MEMORIAL EBF MAIDEN STKS 6f

**1:40** (1:42) (D2) 2-Y-O **£7,072** (£2,176; £1,088; £544) **Stalls** High

Form RPR

1 **Tomoohat (USA)** 2-8-9 ........ WSupple 18 89+
(SirMichaelStoute) *w'like: scope: a.p: rdn to ld ins fnl f: r.o* **12/1**
4 2 1 1/4 **Kenmore**[23] 5720 2-9-0 ........ MHills 2 90+
(BWHills) *chsd ldrs: led 1/2-way: rdn and hdd ins fnl f: unable qck* **4/1**[2]
3 3 3/4 **River Royale**[47] 5118 2-9-0 ........ JFortune 3 88+
(PWChapple-Hyam) *a.p: rdn over 1f out: edgd rt: styd on* **7/2**[1]
4 1 1/2 **Teeba (USA)** 2-8-9 ........ RHills 11 84+
(JLDunlop) *leggy: scope: s.s: hdwy and hmpd 1/2-way: sn lost pl: r.o ins fnl f: nt rch ldrs* **16/1**
5 2 1/2 **Poker Player (IRE)** 2-9-0 ........ DHolland 1 76+
(BJMeehan) *w'like: scope: s.s: hdwy over 2f out: styd on: nt trble ldrs* **20/1**
2 6 hd **Desert Chief**[15] 5857 2-9-0 ........ LDettori 16 75
(SaeedBinSuroor) *sn led: hdd 1/2-way: rdn and ev ch over 1f out: wknd ins fnl f* **4/1**[2]
0 7 shd **Waatheb (IRE)**[126] 2804 2-9-0 ........ DaneO'Neill 24 75
(RHannon) *prom: rdn over 1f out: styd on same pce* **50/1**
8 3 **Tucker** 2-9-0 ........ TQuinn 15 66
(DRCElsworth) *w'like: scope: mid-div: rdn 1/2-way: styd on ins fnl f: nvr trbld ldrs* **16/1**
0 9 1 1/4 **Red Finesse**[73] 4399 2-8-9 ........ PRobinson 7 57
(MAJarvis) *b.hind: chsd ldrs: edgd rt and wknd over 1f out* **20/1**
F 10 1 1/4 **Matsunosuke**[21] 5752 2-9-0 ........ TWilliams 22 59
(ABCoogan) *prom over 4f* **100/1**
11 1/2 **Shareb (USA)** 2-9-0 ........ ACulhane 20 57
(BWHills) *gd sort: b.hind: dwlt: outpcd: nvr nrr* **50/1**
12 1/2 **Munsef** 2-9-0 ........ TEDurcan 12 56+
(JLDunlop) *w'like: s.i.s: outpcd: nvr nrr* **50/1**
13 1 3/4 **Chief Exec** 2-9-0 ........ NCallan 21 50
(CACyzer) *leggy: scope: lw: slowly into stride: hdwy over 2f out: edgd rt and wknd wl over 1f out* **66/1**
0 14 1/2 **Latin Express (IRE)**[31] 5507 2-9-0 ........ SDrowne 17 49
(WRMuir) *prom over 4f* **50/1**
15 2 1/2 **Banjo Patterson** 2-9-0 ........ SSanders 8 41
(GAHuffer) *w'like: scope: chsd ldrs: hung rt and wknd over 1f out* **20/1**
16 1 1/4 **Diamond Dan (IRE)** 2-9-1 ow1 ........ JDekeyser 9 39
(JohnBerry) *neat: s.s: bhd fr 1/2-way* **100/1**
17 nk **Petite Spectre** 2-8-9 ........ RLMoore 23 32
(RHannon) *w'like: mid-div: wknd 1/2-way* **25/1**
0 18 nk **Pagan Quest**[27] 5609 2-9-0 ........ LisaJones 5 36
(JARToller) *chsd ldrs 4f* **25/1**
19 nk **Woolfall Joanna** 2-8-9 ........ AMcCarthy 19 30
(GGMargarson) *neat: sn outpcd* **100/1**
20 1/2 **Horningsheath** 2-8-9 ........ RMullen 6 28
(CFWall) *lt-f: leggy: mid-div: hdwy 1/2-way: wknd 2f out* **66/1**
21 2 1/2 **Krullind (IRE)** 2-9-0 ........ JQuinn 10 26
(PWChapple-Hyam) *leggy: scope: s.s: outpcd* **50/1**
003 22 shd **Montecito**[15] 5873 2-8-9 82........ PDobbs 13 21
(RHannon) *prom to 1/2-way* **9/1**[3]
23 14 **Whispering Death** 2-9-0 ........ SWKelly 4 —
(WJHaggas) *w'like: scope: s.s: outpcd* **25/1**

1m 13.1s (0.01) **Going Correction** +0.225s/f (Good) **23** Ran SP% **133.3**
Speed ratings: **108,106,105,103,100 99,99,95,93,92 91,90,88,87,84 82,82,82,81,81 77,77,58**CSF £54.60 TOTE £15.90: £4.00, £2.00, £2.30; EX 110.10.
**Owner** Hamdan Al Maktoum **Bred** Monticule Llc **Trained** Newmarket, Suffolk

**FOCUS**
A decent maiden run in a very smart time which should produce its share of winners next year.

**NOTEBOOK**
**Tomoohat(USA)**, a $650,000 purchase whose dam is a half-sister to Mubtaker, wore her owner's second colours. Tracking the pace for much of the race, she picked up well when asked to go and win her race and, with the placed horses giving the form a solid look, she looks the type to progress into Pattern company next year. A mile should suit on breeding.
**Kenmore**, who ran a promising race here on his debut, did little wrong in defeat. He is more of a sprinting type than the winner.
**River Royale** was staying on well at the finish, giving the impression that, as his pedigree suggests, he will be suited by another furlong.
**Teeba(USA)** ◆ carried the owner's first colours and is well bred, being a half-sister to several stakes performers, including Bint Shadayid, Alshadiyah and Imtiyaz. She ran well considering that she was slowly away and had to be switched mid-race when encountering traffic problems, and nothing was finishing better in the closing stages. She looks capable of a lot better next year.
**Poker Player(IRE)**, a half-brother to dual-purpose winner Nonchalant, was a fairly cheap purchase in the context of this race and is already a gelding. He shaped with plenty of promise though, and will appreciate a bit farther next year.
**Desert Chief**, as a son of Green Desert, was not sure to appreciate these softer conditions, and for that reason it is probably worth excusing his modest effort.
**Waatheb(IRE)** improved enormously on his anonymous debut effort and looks a three-year-old handicapper in the making.
**Tucker** came in for some market support and ran a pleasing race on his debut, sticking on well without quite threatening the principlals. He is a half-brother to six winners and looks sure to do better over farther next year.
**Red Finesse** showed pace for a long way before weakening entering the dip.
**Shareb(USA)**, whose dam was a smart miler and is a half-sister to Ramooz, looked to need the race experience-wise, and he will do better in time.
**Munsef** is bred to need a good deal farther than this next year.
**Banjo Patterson**, who showed up well for four furlongs, is another son of Green Desert who may not have been totally at ease on the ground.

## 6172 RHT 40TH ANNIVERSARY H'CAP 1m 4f
2:15 (2:18) (C1) (0-100,98) 3-Y-O+ £12,532 (£4,753; £2,376; £1,080) Stalls High

Form RPR
3211 1 **Flamboyant Lad**[12] 5942 3-8-1 **84** PHanagan 22 92
(BWHills) *hld up in tch: rdn to ld ins fnl f: styd on* **13/2**[3]
3562 2 *hd* **Big Moment**[19] 5785 6-9-6 **96** SWKelly 17 104+
(MrsAJPerrett) *hld up: hdwy over 2f out: r.o wl ins fnl f* **8/1**
-210 3 *2* **Soulacroix**[56] 4888 3-8-7 **90** SSanders 11 95
(MrsAJPerrett) *lw: a.p: chsd ldr 3f out: sn rdn: ev ch over 1f out: styd on same pce ins fnl f* **12/1**
/002 4 *½* **Manorson (IRE)**[13] 5919 5-8-13 **89** (t) DaneO'Neill 20 94
(MAMagnusson) *b: b.hind: sn led: rdn over 1f out: hdd and no ex ins fnl f* **11/2**[1]
0600 5 *5* **Swagger Stick (USA)**[26] 5650 3-8-3 **86** (b) JQuinn 18 84
(JLDunlop) *hld up: hdwy over 4f out: rdn over 2f out: styd on same pce appr fnl f* **14/1**
0035 6 *shd* **Enhancer**[33] 5472 6-8-4 **83** oh13 JFMcDonald(3) 7 80?
(MrsLCJewell) *b.hind: prom: rdn over 3f out: hung rt over 1f out: styd on same pce* **66/1**
2013 7 *3½* **Solo Flight**[13] 5919 7-8-12 **88** RLMoore 12 80
(HMorrison) *hld up: hdwy over 4f out: wknd fnl f* **12/1**
0505 8 *1¼* **Bendarshaan**[19] 5785 4-8-9 **85** KDarley 23 76
(MJohnston) *hld up: hdwy and nt clr run over 2f out: styd on: nt trble ldrs* **33/1**
0110 9 *7* **Tawny Way**[18] 5814 4-9-1 **91** TQuinn 13 72
(WJarvis) *chsd ldrs: rdn over 2f out: wknd over 1f out* **16/1**
1650 10 *11* **Flotta**[18] 5814 5-8-0 **83** oh2 TO'Brien(7) 3 49
(MRChannon) *s.i.s: hdwy 10f out: wknd over 3f out* **33/1**
00-0 11 *nk* **Sharmy (IRE)**[20] 5761 8-9-0 **90** CCatlin 19 55
(IanWilliams) *hld up: n.d* **50/1**
1333 12 *6* **Credit (IRE)**[24] 5699 3-8-8 **91** ow1 DHolland 8 48
(RHannon) *lw: chsd ldrs: rdn over 3f out: wknd over 2f out* **16/1**
1624 13 *1½* **Gold Ring**[17] 5834 4-9-7 **97** SCarson 6 52
(GBBalding) *lw: chsd ldrs: hmpd over 10f out: rdn and wknd 3f out* **14/1**
0540 14 *6* **Perfect Storm**[110] 3325 5-9-1 **91** FNorton 2 37
(MBlanshard) *lw: hld up: sme hdwy over 4f out: sn wknd* **25/1**
1266 15 *23* **Star Member (IRE)**[34] 5435 5-9-6 **96** NCallan 9 10
(APJarvis) *hld up: rdr over 4f out: sn wknd* **20/1**
2122 16 *1* **Elmustanser**[24] 5699 3-9-1 **98** (t) LDettori 14 11
(SaeedBinSuroor) *b: b.hind: hld up: wknd over 4f out* **6/1**[2]
50-0 17 *15* **Mac**[19] 5784 4-8-9 **85** MartinDwyer 15 —
(MPTregoning) *sn drvn to chse ldr: hung lft over 10f out: wknd over 4f out* **25/1**
0-36 18 *dist* **Corton (IRE)**[19] 5784 5-8-7 **83** oh2 ACulhane 5 —
(PFICole) *prom to 1/2-way* **40/1**
0050 19 *6* **Muhareb (USA)**[13] 5919 5-9-0 **90** KMcEvoy 16 —
(CEBrittain) *prom: lost pl 10f out: sn rdn: bhd fr 1/2-way* **50/1**

2m 32.75s (-0.71) **Going Correction** +0.225s/f (Good)
**WFA** 3 from 4yo+ 7lb **19** Ran SP% **120.8**
Speed ratings: **111,110,109,109,105 105,103,102,97,90 90,86,85,81,66 65,55,—,—**CSF £50.02 CT £620.94 TOTE £7.80: £2.80, £2.40, £3.30, £2.10; EX 73.70 Trifecta £1345.60 Part won. Pool: £1,894.95. 0.40 winning tickets..
**Owner** Maktoum Al Maktoum **Bred** Gainsborough Stud Management Ltd **Trained** Lambourn, Berks

**FOCUS**
A competitive handicap run at a decent pace, resulting in a fair time for the class. The form however, may not be as strong as at first sight.

**NOTEBOOK**
**Flamboyant Lad** had looked likely to appreciate this longer trip and, proven in the ground, notched up the hat-trick in good style. He was all out to hold on at the finish, but is a progressive type and could well have a decent handicap in him next year.
**Big Moment** stays a lot farther than this of course, but the ground was in his favour and the good pace in this big-field handicap ensured that he travelled well throughout and, staying on strongly, he almost got up. He is a consistent sort.
**Soulacroix**, given a break since disappointing in the Melrose, bounced back to his best off a mark 5lb higher than for his last win. He goes well with some cut in the ground.
**Manorson(IRE)**, like last time, made most of the running. He kept on well but had no response when the first three swept past. It might be worth dropping him back to his winning distance of ten furlongs.
**Swagger Stick(USA)** has yet to recapture his promising early-season form, but this was more encouraging. Give in the ground is essential to him.
**Enhancer** ran an excellent race given that he was racing from 13lb out of the handicap and, if a race can be found for him in the next few days off his correct mark, he could be one to on.
**Solo Flight**, who travelled well, ran his usual sort of race.
**Bendarshaan**, who stays farther than this, was doing his best work at the finish.
**Credit(IRE)** *Official explanation: jockey said gelding suffered interference turning for home*
**Elmustanser** ran way below his best and the ground must be considered the likeliest reason. *Official explanation: jockey said colt was unsuited by the soft ground*
**Muhareb(USA)** *Official explanation: jockey said gelding was unsuited by the soft ground*

## 6173 LANWADES STUD SEVERALS STKS (LISTED RACE) (F&M) 1m 2f
2:50 (2:51) (A1) 3-Y-O+ £17,400 (£6,600; £3,300; £1,500) Stalls High

Form RPR
2-26 1 **Sundrop (JPN)**[132] 2640 3-8-9 115 LDettori 11 97+
(SaeedBinSuroor) *h.d.w: hld up in rr: nt clr run 2f out: swtchd outside and gd hdwy over 1f out: rdn and ducked lft ins last: kpt on to ld c* **11/8**[1]
0 2 *½* **I Had A Dream**[56] 4899 3-8-9 92 PRobinson 4 96
(MAJarvis) *lw: reluctant to load: trckd ldr: t.k.h: upsides ins last: no ex nr fin* **10/1**
6021 3 *½* **La Sylphide**[19] 5788 7-9-0 85 SWKelly 2 95
(GMMoore) *led: qcknd over 5f out: styd on gamely: hdd nr fin* **9/1**
12 4 *1½* **Tahtheeb (IRE)**[64] 4640 3-8-9 100 RHills 5 92
(MPTregoning) *dwlt: hld up in mid-div: effrt over 2f out: styd on fnl f* **3/1**[2]
5200 5 *2½* **Blue Oasis (IRE)**[12] 5969 3-8-9 92 TQuinn 1 88
(RGuest) *stdd s: hld up in rr: effrt over 2f out: kpt on fnl f* **20/1**
2402 6 *1¼* **Shamara (IRE)**[29] 5573 4-9-0 92 KDarley 9 86
(CFWall) *hld up in mid-div: effrt over 2f out: kpt on same pce* **13/2**[3]
6051 7 *hd* **Honorine (IRE)**[15] 5866 4-9-0 80 JFEgan 8 86
(JWPayne) *hld up in rr: effrt and nt clr run over 2f out: sn rdn: kpt on fnl f* **25/1**
0500 8 *½* **Weecandoo (IRE)**[18] 5814 6-9-0 82 GCarter 13 85
(CNAllen) *lw: chsd ldrs: drvn along 5f out: one pce fnl 2f* **50/1**
-000 9 *5* **Star Of Normandie (USA)**[15] 5866 5-9-0 78 AMcCarthy 7 76
(GGMargarson) *chsd ldrs: drvn along over 4f out: wknd 2f out* **50/1**
3410 10 *8* **Tata Naka**[21] 5757 4-9-0 68 HayleyTurner 6 63
(MrsCADunnett) *trckd ldrs on outer: effrt over 3f out: lost pl 2f out* **66/1**

2m 7.92s (2.23) **Going Correction** +0.225s/f (Good)
**WFA** 3 from 4yo+ 5lb **10** Ran SP% **113.6**
Speed ratings: **100,99,99,98,96 95,94,94,90,84**CSF £15.09 TOTE £2.30: £1.40, £2.10, £2.00; EX 15.30.
**Owner** Godolphin **Bred** Y Hosakawa **Trained** Newmarket, Suffolk
■ Stewards Enquiry : L Dettori caution: careless riding

**FOCUS**
A below-average Listed event and not much pace on, which resulted in a very moderate time for a race of its type.

**NOTEBOOK**
**Sundrop(JPN)**, who had over a stone in hand of her nearest rival on official ratings, was ridden with plenty of confidence. She made hard work of it though, only getting up close home after hanging in behind the eventual runner-up, and the race did not show her at her best. She is now Dubai-bound.
**I Had A Dream**, having her first outing for her new stable, goes well in soft ground, benefited from racing up with the pace off a slow gallop and earned some valuable black type.
**La Sylphide** had plenty to find with a number of her rivals on official ratings, but she had conditions to suit and enjoyed the run of the race in a steadily-run affair. Connections will no doubt be over the moon to have secured some black type.
**Tahtheeb(IRE)**, for whom this easier ground was an unknown, could not match the change of pace of the winner, but she kept on well enough. A stronger pace would have suited her.
**Blue Oasis(IRE)** was held up in a steadily-run affair and, although the winner proved good enough to overcome that handicap, she could not.
**Shamara(IRE)**, who does not mind some cut in the ground and whose form entitled her to finish closer, was another unsuited by the way the race was run.
**Honorine(IRE)**, for whom the ground was a worry beforehand, merely stayed on without getting into contention.

## 6174 £100000 TATTERSALLS AUTUMN AUCTION STKS 6f
3:25 (3:27) (B1) 2-Y-O £70,300 (£28,120; £14,060; £8,436) Stalls High

Form RPR
2 1 **Cape Columbine**[14] 5890 2-8-8 TQuinn 17 98+
(DRCElsworth) *b.hind: racd centre: bhd: hdwy and hung lft over 1f out: r.o to ld wl ins fnl f* **5/1**[1]
311 2 *2* **Obe Gold**[12] 5947 2-9-5 (v) ACulhane 12 103
(MRChannon) *lw: racd centre: swtchd to r stands' side over 4f out: chsd ldrs: led that gp over 1f out: hdd wl ins fnl f* **5/1**[1]
5020 3 *shd* **Gifted Gamble**[12] 5947 2-8-9 NCallan 26 93
(KARyan) *racd far side: hld up in tch: rdn to ld that gp 1f out: r.o* **14/1**
3512 4 *hd* **Arabian Dancer**[26] 5648 2-8-0 CCatlin 24 83
(MRChannon) *racd far side: hld up: hdwy 2f out: r.o* **7/1**[2]
4560 5 *nk* **Alta Petens**[12] 5939 2-8-2 JMackay 8 84
(MLWBell) *racd stands' side: chsd ldrs: rdn over 2f out: styd on* **12/1**
3410 6 *shd* **Diamonds And Dust**[18] 5810 2-8-9 PRobinson 20 91
(MHTompkins) *racd far side: chsd ldrs: outpcd 2f out: r.o ins fnl f* **33/1**
1202 7 *1* **Mary Read**[27] 5602 2-8-10 FLynch 27 89
(BSmart) *b.hind: racd far side: led: hdd over 4f out: led again wl over 1f out: hdd 1f out: no ex whn n.m.r towards fin* **9/1**[3]
3203 8 *2½* **Highland Cascade**[24] 5701 2-8-0 JTate 6 71
(JMPEustace) *racd stands' side: sn led: rdn and hdd over 1f out: no ex* **16/1**
1150 9 *1* **Pitch Up (IRE)**[33] 5464 2-9-1 GCarter 30 83
(TGMills) *racd far side: chsd ldrs: rdn over 1f out: no ex* **25/1**
2641 10 *1* **Polar Dawn**[45] 5200 2-8-0 LisaJones 7 65
(BRMillman) *racd stands' side: hld up: effrt over 2f out: styd on ins fnl f: nvr trbld ldrs* **25/1**
0031 10 *dht* **Louphole**[12] 5932 2-8-7 SSanders 13 72
(PJMakin) *lw: racd centre: swtchd stands' side over 4f out: chsd ldrs: rdn over 2f out: wknd fnl f* **16/1**
1204 12 *hd* **Whatatodo**[30] 5548 2-8-2 JQuinn 28 67
(MLWBell) *racd far side: chsd ldrs over 4f* **100/1**
1500 13 *hd* **Jane Jubilee (IRE)**[12] 5939 2-8-4 KDarley 3 68
(MJohnston) *racd stands' side: chsd ldrs: rdn over 2f out: wknd over 1f out* **25/1**
2100 14 *1¼* **Polly Alexander (IRE)**[67] 4597 2-8-10 RLMoore 23 70
(MJWallace) *lw: racd far side: chsd ldrs: rdn and hung lft over 2f out: wknd over 1f out* **25/1**
1301 15 *hd* **Rockburst**[15] 5864 2-8-2 ANicholls 14 62
(KRBurke) *racd centre: swtchd to r stands' side over 4f out: prom: rdn and hung rt over 2f out: wknd over 1f out* **14/1**
5140 16 *shd* **Treat Me Wild (IRE)**[33] 5466 2-8-0 RSmith 21 60
(RHannon) *racd far side: hld up: n.d* **66/1**
3500 17 *hd* **Madhavi**[26] 5648 2-8-8 (b) DaneO'Neill 22 67
(RHannon) *racd far side: hld up: rdn 1/2-way: n.d* **66/1**
0031 18 *1* **Safendonseabiscuit**[10] 5989 2-8-11 DHolland 15 67
(SKirk) *led centre over 4f: sn wknd* **33/1**
4014 19 *2* **Fong Shui**[26] 5655 2-8-9 (v[1]) MartinDwyer 19 59
(PJMakin) *racd far side: hld up: rdn over 2f out: sn wknd* **40/1**
2260 20 *2½* **Persian Carpet**[26] 5648 2-8-0 FNorton 18 42
(IAWood) *racd centre: chsd ldr 4f* **100/1**
6 21 *¾* **Tapa**[14] 5890 2-8-2 RMullen 11 42
(AMBalding) *racd stands' side: mid-div: rdn 1/2-way: wknd 2f out* **66/1**
3301 22 *nk* **Angelofthenorth**[19] 5800 2-8-2 TPQueally 10 41
(JDBethell) *s.i.s: racd stands' side: hdwy 4f out: rdn and wknd over 1f out* **100/1**
606 23 *1½* **Purple Door**[37] 5376 2-8-2 NMackay 9 37
(RMBeckett) *racd stands' side: hmpd s: n.d* **100/1**
043 24 *¾* **Rudaki**[15] 5856 2-8-9 RWinston 4 42
(MGQuinlan) *lw: racd stands' side: s.i.s: a in rr* **66/1**
024 25 *¾* **Avertigo**[12] 5925 2-8-7 (b[1]) SDrowne 1 37
(WRMuir) *racd stands' side: chsd ldrs over 4f* **100/1**
004 26 *1¼* **Killena Boy (IRE)**[29] 5561 2-8-9 JFortune 29 36
(WJarvis) *racd far side: led over 4f out: hdd & wknd wl over 1f out* **100/1**
1040 27 *1* **Time For You**[49] 5052 2-8-0 FPFerris 2 24
(JMBradley) *racd stands' side: bhd: rdn over 2f out: sn wknd* **100/1**
041 28 *¾* **Raffish**[22] 5741 2-8-9 TEDurcan 5 30
(JMPEustace) *lw: racd stands' side: hld up: rdn and wknd over 2f out* **100/1**
0 29 *6* **Dizzy Future**[17] 5838 2-8-9 WRyan 16 12
(WJarvis) *racd centre: s.i.s: swtchd stands' side over 4f out: a bhd* **100/1**

1m 13.76s (0.67) **Going Correction** +0.225s/f (Good) **29** Ran SP% **127.2**
Speed ratings: **104,101,101,100,100 100,99,95,94,93 93,92,92,90,90 90,90,88,86,82 81,81,79,78,77 75,74,73,65**CSF £22.87 TOTE £6.10: £2.70, £3.20, £5.10; EX 32.20.
**Owner** Mrs R F Lowe **Bred** Templeton Stud **Trained** Whitsbury, Hants

**FOCUS**
The field split into three groups, with the smallest up the centre, which included the winner, eventually joining the stands'-side group. The form looks solid with the four immediately behind the winner close to pre-race marks.

**NOTEBOOK**
**Cape Columbine ◆**, who put up such a promising effort on her debut, did well to overcome both her inexperience and the handicap of racing in the smallest of the three groups, to come with a fabulous late run to win. She looks to have plenty of speed, but her connections are keen to see whether she will get a mile next year, and the likely starting point will be a Classic Trial next spring.
**Obe Gold**, a winner in Listed company last time, had to give weight all round and ran well in the circumstances, beating the rest of his stands'-side companions well. He clearly takes his racing well but looks the type who might be difficult to place next season.
**Gifted Gamble** was 16lb better off with Obe Gold compared to Redcar and that weight difference brought them a lot closer. He won his race on the far side and clearly has no fear of soft ground. *Official explanation: jockey said colt hung left*
**Arabian Dancer** ran another sound race in defeat despite probably being ideally suited by a quicker surface.
**Alta Petens** has been running over farther of late but showed she has the pace for sprinting, at least when the ground is on the slow side.
**Diamonds And Dust** was dropping back from seven furlongs and looked to find this shorter trip too sharp. *Official explanation: jockey said colt hung left*
**Mary Read** showed plenty of pace on the far side but it would be harsh to suggest she did not stay the extra furlong.
**Polly Alexander(IRE)** *Official explanation: jockey said filly hung left*
**Safendonseabiscuit** *Official explanation: jockey said colt was unsuited by the soft ground*

## 6175 E B F CHRISTO PHILIPSON BOADICEA FILLIES' STKS (LISTED RACE) 6f

**4:00** (4:01) (A1) 3-Y-O+ **£20,300** (£7,700; £3,850; £1,750) **Stalls High**

Form RPR

2320 **1** **Ruby Rocket (IRE)**[26] 5661 3-8-11 105 SDrowne 4 110
(HMorrison) *lw: swtchd lft after 1f and racd stands' side. chsd ldrs: led that gp over 1f out: styd on wl to ld overall ins last* **6/1**[3]

1100 **2** *1 ½* **Ringmoor Down**[11] 5977 5-9-3 108 TQuinn 1 110
(DWPArbuthnot) *b.hind: dwlt: racd stands' side: hdwy 2f out: wnt 2nd that side over 1f out: no ex ins last* **7/1**

2101 **3** *2 ½* **Paradise Isle**[14] 5898 3-8-11 105 KDarley 12 98
(CFWall) *led far side: clr that gp 2f out: hdd overall ins last* **6/1**[3]

0050 **4** *1 ¾* **Valjarv (IRE)**[5] 6071 3-8-11 91 NCallan 8 92
(NPLittmoden) *racd far side: chsd ldrs: outpcd over 2f out: hdwy over 1f out: styd on ins last* **33/1**

0355 **5** *½* **Fanny's Fancy**[42] 5249 4-8-12 87 SSanders 11 91
(CFWall) *sn drvn along: sn chsng ldrs on far side: outpcd over 2f out: styd on fnl f* **16/1**

1216 **6** *½* **Delphie Queen (IRE)**[18] 5811 3-8-11 102 JFEgan 9 89
(SKirk) *lw: racd far side: chsd ldrs: hung rt and outpcd over 2f out: kpt on wl fnl f* **5/1**[1]

0400 **7** *nk* **Tychy**[33] 5454 5-8-12 95 MartinDwyer 3 88
(SCWilliams) *lw: b: led stands' side tl over 1f out: fdd fnl f* **16/1**

45-0 **8** *1* **Voile (IRE)**[18] 5811 3-8-11 100 RLMoore 14 85
(RHannon) *racd far side: chsd ldrs: lost pl over 2f out: kpt on wl fnl f* **33/1**

0545 **9** *¾* **Dangle (IRE)**[4] 6104 3-8-11 (v[1]) FMBerry 5 83
(EdwardLynam, Ire) *w'like: swtchd lft after 1f and racd stands side: nvr trbld ldrs* **20/1**

0001 **10** *hd* **Dowager**[30] 5553 3-8-11 90 DaneO'Neill 16 83
(RHannon) *lw: racd far side: chsd ldr: wknd over 1f out* **20/1**

0136 **11** *hd* **Fiddle Me Blue**[30] 5550 3-8-11 76 (v) JFortune 2 82
(HMorrison) *racd stands' side: chsd ldrs: wknd over 1f out* **50/1**

01-5 **12** *3 ½* **Thaminah (USA)**[18] 5811 3-8-11 89 RHills 7 71
(MPTregoning) *lw: swtchd lft after 1f and racd stands' side: chsd ldrs: wknd 2f out* **8/1**

6- **13** *3* **Imshy (IRE)**[31] 3-8-11 DHolland 6 62
(RPritchard-Gordon, France) *w'like: swtchd lft after 1f and racd stands side: nvr nr ldrs* **33/1**

2-32 **14** *¾* **Pearl Grey**[18] 5811 3-8-11 100 (t) LDettori 10 60
(SaeedBinSuroor) *racd far side: chsd ldrs: effrt and n.m.r over 2f out: sn lost pl* **11/2**[2]

0040 **15** *13* **Enchanted**[25] 5671 5-8-12 94 FNorton 13 21
(NACallaghan) *lw: racd far side: lost pl 3f out: sn wl bhd* **40/1**

1m 13.46s (0.37) **Going Correction** +0.225s/f (Good)
**WFA** 3 from 4yo+ 1lb **15** Ran SP% **118.7**
Speed ratings: **106,104,100,98,97 97,96,95,94,94 93,89,85,84,66**CSF £42.80 TOTE £8.10: £2.10, £2.90, £2.70; EX 46.70.
**Owner** Thurloe Thoroughbreds IX **Bred** Roger And Henry O'Callaghan **Trained** East Ilsley, Berks

**FOCUS**
An average Listed race in which the field split into two and once again the mid-track to stands'-side group had the edge. An ordinary time for the type of race but fair form for the grade.

**NOTEBOOK**
**Ruby Rocket(IRE)**, who had chased home subsequent Group One winners Var and Tante Rose earlier in the season, deserved to win a prize of this nature and finally got off the mark for the year. She seems to go on most gound and is very consistent.
**Ringmoor Down**, who did not enjoy much luck in running in the Abbaye, has done her winning this year over five furlongs, but she gets six well. She ran a solid race and probably would not have wanted the ground any softer.
**Paradise Isle**, a progressive filly this year on quicker ground, pulled clear of her group on the far side but found the two on the stands' side just too strong. She has the ability to win in this grade.
**Valjarv(IRE)** has been finding it difficult in handicap company and is not really good enough to win at Listed level. This was not a bad effort but she remains a twilight horse.
**Fanny's Fancy** is another who has run one or two decent races this season, but essentially she remains difficult to place. She may get her chance to win a race back on the Polytrack, on which she is unbeaten, as she is not badly handicapped on the All-Weather.
**Delphie Queen(IRE)** found the drop back to six against her and is happier over seven these days. *Official explanation: jockey said filly was hampered*
**Tychy** showed plenty of speed but did not get home in the ground.
**Pearl Grey** *Official explanation: jockey said filly was unsuited by the soft ground*

## 6176 NGK SPARK PLUGS NURSERY 1m

**4:35** (4:35) (C2) (0-95,87) 2-Y-O **£7,046** (£2,168; £1,084; £542) **Stalls High**

Form RPR

2001 **1** **Danehill Willy (IRE)**[26] 5655 2-8-12 78 DHolland 10 86
(NACallaghan) *lw: broke wl: sn outpcd: hdwy over 1f out: r.o to ld nr fin* **15/2**

01 **2** *hd* **Atlantic Story (USA)**[45] 5179 2-9-4 84 LDettori 9 92
(SaeedBinSuroor) *led: clr over 1f out: wknd: edgd rt and hdd nr fin* **9/2**[2]

0054 **3** *½* **Halla San**[30] 5543 2-8-4 70 CCatlin 6 77
(MrsJRRamsden) *sn outpcd: hdwy over 1f out: r.o* **20/1**

2350 **4** *½* **Sea Hunter**[35] 5417 2-9-4 84 TEDurcan 4 90
(MRChannon) *lw: chsd ldrs: rdn over 1f out: styd on* **16/1**

3331 **5** *9* **Caly Dancer (IRE)**[55] 4914 2-9-6 86 JFortune 11 76
(DRCElsworth) *hld up: hdwy over 2f out: wknd over 1f out* **14/1**

51 **6** *1 ¾* **Thakafaat (IRE)**[48] 5088 2-9-7 87 WSupple 13 73
(JLDunlop) *chsd ldrs over 6f* **11/1**

321 **7** *hd* **Red Affleck (USA)**[26] 5653 2-9-3 83 AMcCarthy 12 69
(PWChapple-Hyam) *lw: prom: rdn 1/2-way: wkng whn n.m.r over 1f out* **13/2**[3]

3024 **8** *¾* **Langston Boy**[33] 5453 2-8-7 73 RMullen 7 58
(MLWBell) *chsd ldrs: rdn over 2f out: wknd over 1f out* **50/1**

5523 **9** *1 ¾* **Mobarhen (USA)**[28] 5596 2-8-10 76 RHills 8 58
(SirMichaelStoute) *lw: slipped s: hld up: hdwy u.p over 2f out: wknd over 1f out* **7/2**[1]

210 **10** *1* **Market Trend**[9] 6003 2-9-2 82 KDarley 2 62
(MJohnston) *prom: rdn to chse ldr over 2f out: edgd rt and wknd over 1f out* **7/1**

5056 **11** *7* **Rosapenna (IRE)**[24] 5694 2-8-4 70 JQuinn 3 37
(CFWall) *hld up in tch: rdn and wknd over 2f out* **20/1**

4026 **12** *7* **Scarlet Invader (IRE)**[30] 5539 2-9-0 80 SSanders 5 35
(JLDunlop) *lw: hld up: wknd 3f out* **50/1**

1m 41.39s (1.99) **Going Correction** +0.225s/f (Good) **12** Ran SP% **112.3**
Speed ratings: **99,98,98,97,88 87,86,86,84,83 76,69**CSF £37.23 CT £642.10 TOTE £9.30: £2.40, £2.00, £5.60; EX 55.30.
**Owner** T Mohan **Bred** Patrick J Farrington **Trained** Newmarket, Suffolk

**FOCUS**
A decent nursery that proved quite a stamina test for these juveniles and the first four finished well clear. The race could be rated higher but is held down by a number failing to give their running.

**NOTEBOOK**
**Danehill Willy(IRE)** looked to be going nowhere two furlongs out, but he found his stride hitting the rising ground and came home in good style. He shapes as though he will appreciate middle distances next year and connections are convinced he is happier on faster ground.
**Atlantic Story(USA)** ran well from the front but he just did not quite get home in the ground. He is clearly on a mark which can be exploited when he gets a quicker surface to race on.
**Halla San**, who has been stepped up in trip on each of his last three starts, ran his best race to date with stamina at a premium. He looks capable of winning a similar race and a likely type for middle-distance handicaps next year.
**Sea Hunter** put a disappointing effort at Doncaster on fast ground behind him and bounced back to his best on this easier surface, finishing well clear of the rest.
**Caly Dancer(IRE)** looked to be found out by his 9lb rise in the handicap for winning at Salisbury.
**Thakafaat(IRE)**, whose stable is out of form, looked to have plenty on her plate giving weight all round on her handicap debut.
**Mobarhen(USA)** never got competitive but he did have an excuse as the saddle slipped. *Official explanation: jockey said colt stumbled on leaving the stalls*
**Scarlet Invader(IRE)** *Official explanation: jockey said colt was never travelling*

## 6177 THOROUGHBRED BREEDERS H'CAP 5f

**5:10** (5:10) (B1) (0-110,106) 3-Y-O+ **£12,040** (£4,567; £2,283; £1,038) **Stalls High**

Form RPR

5032 **1** **Corridor Creeper (FR)**[12] 5933 7-8-11 96 (p) RLMoore 11 104
(JMBradley) *chsd ldr: rdn to ld 1f out: r.o* **7/1**[3]

0002 **2** *½* **If Paradise**[23] 5712 3-8-13 98 DaneO'Neill 13 105
(RHannon) *led: rdn and hdd 1f out: r.o* **20/1**

2540 **3** *nk* **Fruit Of Glory**[14] 5898 5-8-7 92 WRyan 10 98
(JRJenkins) *lw: chsd ldrs: rdn and ev ch ins fnl f: styd on* **9/1**

0304 **4** *hd* **Caribbean Coral**[12] 5933 5-8-12 97 RWinston 9 102+
(JJQuinn) *s.i.s: hld up: nt clr run over 1f out: running on whn hmpd wl ins fnl f: nvr able to chal* **5/1**[1]

1663 **5** *hd* **Forever Phoenix**[14] 5898 4-8-9 99 AQuinn[(5)] 5 103
(RMHCowell) *lw: s.i.s: hld up: hdwy 2f out: rdn and edgd rt fr over 1f out: r.o* **8/1**

4042 **6** *½* **Whistler**[19] 5787 7-8-7 92 oh1 (p) PFitzsimons 3 95
(JMBradley) *hld up: hdwy over 1f out: unable qck towards fin* **8/1**

5650 **7** *1* **Bishops Court**[19] 5787 10-8-12 97 PHanagan 6 97
(MrsJRRamsden) *hld up in tch: rdn over 1f out: no ex ins fnl f: broke blood vesell* **11/1**

04 **8** *1* **Lydgate (USA)**[33] 5471 4-9-7 106 (t) LDettori 2 103
(SaeedBinSuroor) *b: hld up: rdn 1/2-way: r.o ins fnl f: nt trble ldrs* **6/1**[2]

1003 **9** *½* **Dragon Flyer (IRE)**[12] 5933 5-8-13 98 JFEgan 4 93
(MQuinn) *lw: chsd ldrs: rdn over 1f out: hld whn n.m.r ins fnl f* **16/1**

0066 **10** *1 ¾* **Fromsong (IRE)**[37] 5372 6-8-7 92 oh2 SDrowne 8 82
(BRMillman) *chsd ldrs over 3f* **5/1**[1]

60.85 secs (0.44) **Going Correction** +0.225s/f (Good) **10** Ran SP% **111.3**
Speed ratings: **105,104,103,103,103 102,100,99,98,95**CSF £128.92 CT £868.16 TOTE £8.80: £2.40, £4.40, £4.10; EX 116.30 Place 6 £55.30, Place 5 £34.05 .
**Owner** G & L Johnson **Bred** J Byng **Trained** Sedbury, Gloucs

**FOCUS**
A good sprint handicap, but they did not go a mad gallop and very few got into it, the first two being in those positions throughout, which means the form is not as strong as it could have been.

**NOTEBOOK**
**Corridor Creeper(FR)** had gone up 6lb in the handicap this season despite being winless and deserved this change of fortune. He is a consistent individual and, racing close to the pace in a race run at a sensible gallop, was in the right positon to pounce as they hit the rising ground.
**If Paradise** enjoyed the run of the race in front, setting a sensible gallop and only finding one too good. He goes well with cut in the ground.
**Fruit Of Glory** was never far off the pace and kept on well for the minor placing. Although successful over farther earlier in her career, the minimum trip looks to suit her nowadays.
**Caribbean Coral** did not enjoy a clear run and would certainly have placed at least had things panned out in his favour. His style of running means that there is always a risk of this happening, however.
**Forever Phoenix** was never quite able to get into a challenging position after her slow start.
**Whistler**, another 2lb higher, is plenty high enough in the weights at present, being 8lb higher than for his last win in the summer.
**Bishops Court** *Official explanation: vet said gelding bled from the nose*
**Lydgate(USA)** has run his best races on quicker ground and probably found this slower surface against him.
**Dragon Flyer(IRE)** *Official explanation: jockey said mare hung left*
**Fromsong(IRE)**, who was supported in the market despite running from 2lb out of the handicap, has a poor strike-rate and failed his backers.
T/Jkpt: Not won. T/Plt: £63.40 to a £1 stake. Pool: £65,452.05. 753.50 winning tickets. T/Qpdt: £12.30 to a £1 stake. Pool: £4,137.40. 248.90 winning tickets. CR

6178 - 6180a (Foreign Racing) - See Raceform Interactive

# 5925 BRIGHTON (L-H)

Friday, October 15

**OFFICIAL GOING: Soft**

Wind: Moderate half behind, almost nil by race 5 Weather: Showers

## 6181 BBI INSURANCE E B F MEDIAN AUCTION MAIDEN STKS — 7f 214y

2:25 (2:32) (F3) 2-Y-O — £4,260 (£1,311; £655; £327) Stalls Low

Form — RPR

203 **1** **Oligarch (IRE)**[29] 5592 2-9-0 86 ........ OUrbina 9 71+
(NACallaghan) *mde virtually all: slt ld to 1/2-way: drew 3l clr 3f out: rdn to hold on fnl f: pushed out* **11/10**[1]

000 **2** ¾ **Shingle Street (IRE)**[44] 5227 2-9-0 ........ PDoe 3 70
(MHTompkins) *prom in chsng gp: wnt 2nd 3f out: drvn and hung lft over 1f out: a hld* **16/1**

0 **3** 3½ **Sole Agent (IRE)**[34] 5467 2-8-9 ........ AQuinn(5) 6 63
(GLMoore) *towards rr: hdwy and hrd rdn 3f out: kpt on: nt pce to chal* **33/1**

5 **4** 2 **Maxamillion (IRE)**[25] 5688 2-9-0 ........ MFenton 7 59+
(SKirk) *stdd s: plld hrd towards rr: hdwy 3f out: wknd 1f out* **4/1**[2]

0 **5** shd **Empangeni**[27] 5653 2-9-0 ........ DaneO'Neill 5 58
(JLDunlop) *hdwy 5f out: styd on same pce fnl 2f* **33/1**

00 **6** hd **Best Game**[31] 5534 2-9-0 ........ SWhitworth 12 58
(GAButler) *sn pushed along towards rr: styd on fnl 2f: nvr nrr* **25/1**

**7** 1½ **Tangible** 2-8-9 ........ JMackay 11 50
(SirMarkPrescott) *missed break and lost 10l: wl bhd tl r.o fnl 2f: improve* **10/1**[3]

0 **8** hd **Mahmjra**[6] 6073 2-9-0 ........ CCatlin 1 55
(MRChannon) *towards rr: rdn over 3f out: nvr trbld ldrs* **25/1**

0060 **9** 1½ **Wembury Point (IRE)**[23] 5738 2-8-11 56 ........ LPKeniry(3) 2 52
(BGPowell) *prom in chsng gp: hrd rdn 3f out: sn wknd* **40/1**

6 **10** 1¾ **Indian Dove (IRE)**[23] 5735 2-8-9 ........ SChin 4 43
(GAButler) *towards rr: rdn and lost tch 1/2-way: sme hdwy 2f out: no imp* **20/1**

0000 **11** 1¾ **Gogetter Girl**[13] 5947 2-8-6 60 ........ (p) FPFerris(3) 13 40
(JGallagher) *prom in chsng gp 5f* **25/1**

005 **12** 1½ **Piran (IRE)**[18] 5838 2-8-11 70 ........ JFMcDonald(3) 8 42
(BJMeehan) *bhd fnl 3f* **10/1**[3]

000 **13** 15 **Brego (IRE)**[25] 5688 2-9-0 ........ (b) PDobbs 10 12
(JHMGosden) *pressed wnr to 1/2-way: wknd 3f out* **33/1**

1m 40.93s (5.93) **Going Correction** +0.625s/f (Yiel) **13** Ran SP% **119.2**

Speed ratings: **95,94,90,88,88 88,86,86,85,83 81,80,65**CSF £18.63 TOTE £1.90: £1.30, £3.20, £8.70; EX 24.70.

**Owner** Team Havana **Bred** Liam Brennan **Trained** Newmarket, Suffolk

**FOCUS**

A modest maiden and the time confirmed that the ground was soft. As they usually do when conditions are testing here, the whole field came over to the stands' rail on straightening up for home. Difficult form to rate with confidence, but the winner plainly did not need to run to anywhere near his best.

**NOTEBOOK**

**Oligarch(IRE)** had by far the best previous form on show. He had failed to justify significant market support on a couple of occasions, but was able to bag the crucial position against the stands's rail and made no mistake under a positive ride. He never looked like getting caught and may be worth a try in an end-of-season nursery now that connections know he can handle testing conditions.

**Shingle Street(IRE)** did his best to get on terms with the favourite in the closing stages, but was inclined to hang under pressure. This was still his best effort so far, on his first attempt on soft ground, and there may be a small race in him under similar conditions.

**Sole Agent(IRE)** ran much better than on his Goodwood fast-ground debut and is bred to be even better suited by further.

**Maxamillion(IRE)** ran creditably until getting tired in the closing stages and may have been at a disadvantage in racing more towards the centre of the track than his rivals.

**Empangeni** was never in the contest until it was all over, but is likely to come into his own over middle distances next season once handicapped.

**Best Game** showed a little ability and can now be handicapped.

**Tangible**, out of a 12-furlong winner and the only newcomer in the field, was weak in the market and had little chance after badly missing the break. She should improve with experience and is also likely to show more over further next season.

## 6182 32RED ONLINE CASINO MAIDEN STKS — 1m 3f 196y

3:00 (3:02) (D3) 3-Y-O — £5,504 (£1,693; £846; £423) Stalls High

Form — RPR

3022 **1** **Magnetic Pole**[29] 5591 3-9-0 77 ........ DaneO'Neill 5 88+
(SirMichaelStoute) *mde all: pushed clr 3f out: 12 l ahd whn hrd rdn over 1f out: eased fnl 100 yds* **10/3**[2]

00 **2** 21 **River Of Diamonds**[11] 5999 3-9-0 ........ MFenton 2 54
(RGuest) *towards rr: rdn to go mod 4th ent st: styd on to take remote 2nd 1f out* **8/1**[3]

3062 **3** 3 **Seeking A Way (USA)**[14] 5913 3-8-9 70 ........ PDobbs 8 44
(JHMGosden) *pressed wnr tl outpcd 3f out* **10/3**[2]

0-20 **4** ¾ **Chaplin**[133] 2653 3-9-0 84 ........ (p) CCatlin 4 48
(BWHills) *in tch: hrd rdn and outpcd 4f out: sn btn* **2/1**[1]

66 **5** 7 **Sarenne**[43] 5237 3-8-9 ........ SChin 1 34
(MJohnston) *wnt rt s: chsd ldrs 8f* **10/1**

60 **6** 9 **Mariday**[14] 5913 3-9-0 ........ PaulEddery 3 26
(LadyHerries) *dwlt: a bhd: rdn 7f out: sn lost tch* **20/1**

005 **7** 28 **Mr Dinglawi (IRE)**[210] 1050 3-9-0 70 ........ (t) MTebbutt 7 —
(DBFeek) *dwlt: a bhd: rdn 7f out: no ch fnl 5f* **50/1**

0 **8** dist **Pacific Run (USA)**[11] 5999 3-8-11 ........ JFMcDonald(3) 6 —
(BJMeehan) *prom to 1/2-way: rdn and wknd qckly: t.o fnl 4f* **25/1**

2m 38.2s (6.10) **Going Correction** +0.625s/f (Yiel) **8** Ran SP% **110.3**

Speed ratings: **104,90,88,87,82 76,58,—**CSF £27.07 TOTE £3.60: £1.30, £2.70, £1.30; EX 35.00.

**Owner** The Queen **Bred** The Queen **Trained** Newmarket, Suffolk

**FOCUS**

Not a strong maiden and the conditions took their toll, with the field finishing spread out all over the Sussex Downs. Considering the ground, the time was creditable, although it does not suggest the winner has improved much.

**NOTEBOOK**

**Magnetic Pole** had put up his worst effort so far in his only previous try on soft ground, but it proved a different story here as he was allowed to stride on in the testing conditions and gradually pulled further and further clear to record a winning margin more associated with National Hunt racing. The conditions exaggerated the beaten distances though, and therefore the form may not be as spectacular as the winning margin would suggest.

**River Of Diamonds**, up again in trip, ran on through beaten horses to finish a remote second. He probably did not achieve a great deal, but at least can now be handicapped.

**Seeking A Way(USA)** kept the winner company for much of the journey, but eventually got very tired in the conditions. She is only moderate, but obviously needs a sounder surface.

**Chaplin** was racing for the first time since June. He ran nowhere near the form of his second place behind Percussionist earlier in the season and seems to have gone the wrong way.

**Sarenne** patently failed to see out this longer trip in the conditions.

## 6183 32RED.COM H'CAP — 1m 3f 196y

3:35 (3:35) (E3) (0-70,68) 3-Y-O+ — £4,830 (£1,486; £743; £371) Stalls High

Form — RPR

-420 **1** **Precious Mystery (IRE)**[9] 6013 4-9-1 60 ........ AQuinn(5) 10 70
(AKing) *prom: rdn over 2f out: led ins fnl f: drvn out* **8/1**

3141 **2** hd **Scott**[7] 6047 3-8-6 58 ........ DFox(5) 5 68
(JJay) *hdwy 4f out: led 2f out tl ins fnl f: hrd rdn: r.o* **9/4**[1]

-002 **3** 5 **Rumbling Bridge**[51] 5037 3-8-6 53 ........ PDoe 1 56
(JLDunlop) *s.s: gd hdwy 1/2-way: led 3f out tl 2f out: one pce* **20/1**

5562 **4** 1¾ **Make My Hay**[20] 5796 5-8-4 47 oh1 ........ LPKeniry(3) 2 48
(JGallagher) *hld up in midfield: drvn to chse ldrs 3f out: one pce fnl 2f* **6/1**[3]

0151 **5** 2½ **Nounou**[13] 5935 3-9-0 68 ........ MHalford(7) 8 65
(DJDaly) *hld up in rr: rdn and hdwy 3f out: no imp fnl 2f* **4/1**[2]

0031 **6** 5 **Cotton Easter**[25] 5692 3-8-5 55 ........ RThomas(3) 3 45
(MrsAJBowlby) *s.s: hld up in rr: hdwy over 2f out: hung lft and wknd over 1f out* **7/1**

20-0 **7** 3½ **Shush**[16] 5875 6-9-4 58 ........ DaneO'Neill 6 43
(CEBrittain) *chsd ldrs tl hung lft and wknd over 1f out* **25/1**

5660 **8** 13 **Mustang Ali (IRE)**[5] 6083 3-9-2 63 ........ SWhitworth 12 30
(SKirk) *mid-div: rdn 3f out: sn wknd* **22/1**

025 **9** 3 **Alexei**[14] 5907 3-9-2 63 ........ OUrbina 9 26
(JRFanshawe) *towards rr: mod effrt and hrd rdn over 2f out: sn outpcd: eased whn no ch fnl f* **20/1**

0060 **10** 5 **Midshipman Easy (USA)**[72] 4443 3-9-4 65 ........ MFenton 4 21
(PWHarris) *led tl 3f out: wknd 2f out* **20/1**

0054 **11** 3½ **Danze Romance**[15] 5891 3-9-1 62 ........ CCatlin 11 13
(JLDunlop) *prom 7f* **16/1**

0006 **12** 7 **Charing Cross (IRE)**[15] 5891 3-8-7 54 ........ (b[1]) RBrisland 7 —
(GLMoore) *in tch tl wknd 5f out* **33/1**

2m 39.3s (7.20) **Going Correction** +0.625s/f (Yiel)

**WFA** 3 from 4yo+ 7lb **12** Ran SP% **120.0**

Speed ratings: **101,100,97,96,94 91,89,80,78,75 72,68**CSF £23.81 CT £362.31 TOTE £11.00: £3.10, £1.30, £3.70; EX 36.40.

**Owner** The Dunnkirk Partnership **Bred** Miss Wendy Fox **Trained** Barbury Castle, Wilts

**FOCUS**

A fairly competitive, if low-grade handicap, and again the testing conditions took their toll. The runner-up's York run set a decent standard and the form looks sound.

**NOTEBOOK**

**Precious Mystery(IRE)** had run well on soft ground over course and distance in her last turf start and went one better in a driving finish, having bagged the crucial stands' rail in the battle to the line. She won over hurdles last season and is now likely to go back over timber.

**Scott**, who avoided a penalty for his victory in a York apprentice handicap last week, was only just denied in a driving finish. He now goes up 6lb which will make things more difficult, but he has already shown an aptitude for Fibresand and he could do well if campaigned on that surface through the winter.

**Rumbling Bridge**, who split a couple of subsequent winners in a slowly-run race here last time, arguably improved on that, though he tended to hang as he started to tire in the latter stages.

**Make My Hay**, a winner once from 32 starts before this, ran his race from 1lb out of the handicap.

**Nounou**, who showed he could handle undulating tracks when winning at Epsom last time, could never get competitive off a 5lb higher mark.

**Cotton Easter** was close enough on the outside of the field over a furlong from home, but ruined her chance by hanging to her left under pressure and was soon beaten.

## 6184 MICHAEL TONKS FAMILY & FRIENDS MEMORIAL H'CAP — 7f 214y

4:10 (4:11) (F4) (0-55,54) 3-Y-O — £3,367 (£962; £481) Stalls Low

Form — RPR

0040 **1** **Clare Galway**[111] 3304 3-8-9 49 ........ MFenton 7 54
(SKirk) *in rr: pushed along 5f out: hdwy on outside rail 2f out: edgd lft: styd on to ld fnl 100 yds* **20/1**

0000 **2** nk **Doringo**[18] 5830 3-8-3 50 ........ RJKilloran(7) 5 54
(JLSpearing) *prom: led over 2f out tl ins fnl f: kpt on* **14/1**

0604 **3** shd **Beauty Of Dreams**[22] 5748 3-9-0 54 ........ (v[1]) CCatlin 10 58
(MRChannon) *prom: squeezed and swtchd lft over 2f out: drvn to chal fnl f: kpt on* **11/2**[2]

4601 **4** 8 **Sylva Royal (IRE)**[27] 5642 3-9-0 54 ........ DaneO'Neill 8 42
(CEBrittain) *dwlt: plld hrd early: hdwy 3f out: rdn to press ldrs 2f out: wknd 1f out* **8/1**

0504 **5** nk **Mrs Brown**[6] 6061 3-9-0 54 ........ JMackay 1 41
(SirMarkPrescott) *t.k.h: prom: rdn whn n.m.r wl over 1f out: sn btn* **6/1**[3]

-000 **6** 1 **Passion Fruit**[11] 5992 3-8-10 50 ........ PDoe 13 35
(CWFairhurst) *dwlt: sn in midfield: clsd on ldrs 3f out: wknd over 1f out* **8/1**

605 **7** 1¾ **Just One Look**[42] 5260 3-8-10 53 ........ RThomas(3) 4 35
(MBlanshard) *sn pushed along in rr: hdwy into midfield 3f out: no imp fnl 2f: eased whn no ch fnl f* **7/1**

4541 **8** 2 **Magic Verse**[13] 5927 3-8-11 54 ........ JFMcDonald(3) 12 32
(RGuest) *dwlt: nvr trbld ldrs* **7/2**[1]

0-06 **9** 8 **Melinda's Girl**[22] 5750 3-8-4 47 ........ (v[1]) LPKeniry(3) 6 9
(APJarvis) *led tl 3f out: wknd 2f out: wl btn whn n.m.r 1f out* **33/1**

-005 **10** 1¾ **Mr Lewin**[13] 5957 3-8-10 53 ........ THamilton(3) 11 11
(RAFahey) *mid-div: rdn 3f out: sn wknd* **7/1**

0-60 **11** 4 **Monash Girl (IRE)**[81] 4195 3-8-2 45 oh15 ........ NChalmers(3) 9 —
(BRJohnson) *dwlt: a bhd* **50/1**

4606 **12** 7 **The Nibbler**[31] 5545 3-8-9 49 ........ OUrbina 3 —
(GCHChung) *chsd ldrs 3f: bhd fnl 3f* **20/1**

1m 40.79s (5.79) **Going Correction** +0.625s/f (Yiel) **12** Ran SP% **120.2**

Speed ratings: **96,95,95,87,87 86,84,82,74,72 68,61**CSF £268.20 CT £1782.72 TOTE £31.90: £7.00, £7.00, £2.10; EX 329.30.

**Owner** Mrs M Devine **Bred** Whitsbury Manor Stud And Mrs K C Hansberry **Trained** Upper Lambourn, Berks

■ Stewards Enquiry : C Catlin caution: careless riding

**FOCUS**

The first three pulled a long way clear, but this form is little better than selling class. The winner has been rated up to the pick of her Polytrack form and the second as having improved slightly on the best of his weak maiden form.

**NOTEBOOK**

**Clare Galway**, making her debut for the yard and racing for the first time since June, had shown glimpses of form in her previous outings, all but one of them on Polytrack. This was her first try on soft ground and she battled on to emerge best in a three-way photo. Again she was the one racing closest to the stands' rail, which was a help, but now that she has hit the target she may be able to find another small contest.

**Doringo** had not been beaten far at Bath last time, despite only finishing eighth of 16, but this was still a big improvement on his previous efforts and he was only just denied. There may be a small race in him under similar conditions.

**Beauty Of Dreams** was very free in the first-time visor and probably did well to only go down narrowly given that she was also racing widest of the front three in the run to the line. She has slipped a long way in the handicap this year and is running well enough to take advantage at a modest level.

**Sylva Royal(IRE)**, who made her effort on the wide outside, was encountering these conditions for the first time and a combination of the ground and longer trip appeared to find her out.

**Mrs Brown** again appeared to find this trip an inadequate test of stamina, even in these conditions.

**Passion Fruit** was the subject of a gamble which looked as if it might be landed inside the last quarter-mile, only for the petrol to run out soon after.

## 6185 WKD BUILDERS & DECORATORS IN ESSEX CLASSIFIED STKS 1m 1f 209y

**4:45** (4:47) (E3) 3-Y-O+ **£4,182** (£1,287; £643; £321) **Stalls** High

| Form | | | | | RPR |
|---|---|---|---|---|---|
| 2500 | **1** | | **Arry Dash**[4] 6128 4-9-3 73 *(MRChannon) hld up in rr: nt clr run on outside rail 3f out: eased towards centre: hdwy 2f out: led jst ins fnl f: rdn clr* **5/2**[1] | CCatlin 3 | 83 |
| 0000 | **2** | *2 ½* | **Quartino**[17] 5850 3-8-9 70 *(JHMGosden) hld up: hdwy 3f out: led over 1f out tl jst ins fnl f: nt qckn* **16/1** | PDobbs 2 | 76 |
| 6300 | **3** | *2* | **Desert Island Disc**[4] 6128 7-8-12 74 *(JJBridger) sn prom: rdn and lost pl 2f out: rallied to chse ldng pair ins fnl f* **7/2**[2] | ABeech(3) 6 | 73 |
| 5405 | **4** | *2 ½* | **Mad Carew (USA)**[23] 5728 5-9-3 73 (b) *(GLMoore) hdwy 5f out: led 3f out tl over 1f out: btn whn hung lft fnl f* **8/1** | SWhitworth 4 | 70 |
| 34-5 | **5** | *1 ¾* | **Strathspey**[9] 6013 5-8-8 69 *(PJMcbride) hld up in tch: clsd on ldrs 3f out: wknd 1f out* **10/1** | LPKeniry(3) 5 | 61 |
| -165 | **6** | *1* | **Payola (USA)**[37] 5402 3-8-6 70 *(CEBrittain) sn prom: pushed along 3f out: hrd rdn whn n.m.r over 1f out: wknd* **6/1**[3] | DaneO'Neill 1 | 59 |
| 1000 | **7** | *shd* | **Prairie Wolf**[36] 5423 8-9-3 73 *(MLWBell) early reminders: sn led: hdd 3f out: rdn whn n.m.r over 1f out: wknd qckly* **10/1** | MFenton 7 | 65 |
| 016 | **8** | *1* | **Tadawul (USA)**[25] 5706 3-8-8 72 *(EFVaughan) plld hrd: prom: rdn and lost pl over 4f out: btn whn hung lft fnl 2f* **7/1** | JMackay 8 | 59 |

2m 9.32s (6.78) **Going Correction** +0.625s/f (Yiel) 8 Ran SP% **112.8**

**WFA** 3 from 4yo+ 5lb

Speed ratings: **97,95,93,91,90 89,89,88**CSF £42.46 TOTE £2.70: £1.20, £5.40, £1.90; EX 47.70.

**Owner** Mike & Denise Dawes **Bred** Miletrian P L C **Trained** West Ilsley, Berks

**FOCUS**

A tight little classified stakes with just 3lb covering the eight runners on adjusted official ratings, but a modest winning time for the class and the form is not particularly strong. By this stage it did look as though the middle of the track was becoming more favoured as the stands' side was becoming more chewed up.

**NOTEBOOK**

**Arry Dash**, who had the visor left off, had gone 18 months without a win, but was proven in soft ground and saw his race out in good style after having to switch left in order to get a run. It remains to be seen if he can reproduce this form back in regular handicap company.

**Quartino**, dropping back from two miles and with the blinkers dispensed with, ran his best race since making a belated seasonal reappearance and may be able to find a similar contest.

**Desert Island Disc**, looking for her third course win of the season, was not disgraced on her 16th start of the year, but could probably do with a break now.

**Mad Carew(USA)** would have preferred faster ground, but ran well nonetheless and this should put him spot-on for a winter campaign on the Polytrack.

**Strathspey** was reappearing quickly after her return from a year off and probably found this ground softer than ideal.

**Tadawul(USA)** was disappointing and perhaps the testing ground was responsible.

## 6186 32REDPOKER.COM H'CAP 5f 59y

**5:15** (5:16) (E3) (0-70,70) 3-Y-O+ **£4,044** (£1,244; £622; £311) **Stalls** Low

| Form | | | | | RPR |
|---|---|---|---|---|---|
| 2U00 | **1** | | **Harrison's Flyer (IRE)**[7] 6046 3-8-12 **64** (p) *(RAFahey) chsd ldrs: rdn 3f out: edgd lft 2f out: led 1f out: sn clr* **16/1** | GParkin 4 | 76 |
| 0606 | **2** | *2 ½* | **Madrasee**[23] 5734 6-8-8 **60** *(LMontagueHall) chsd ldr: led 2f out tl 1f out: nt pce of wnr* **9/2**[3] | DaneO'Neill 2 | 63 |
| 6052 | **3** | *½* | **Pulse**[23] 5736 6-8-4 **56** (p) *(JMBradley) chsd ldrs: effrt and edgd lft 2f out: one pce fnl f* **9/2**[3] | PFitzsimons 8 | 58 |
| 5000 | **4** | *¾* | **Smart Starprincess (IRE)**[76] 4320 3-8-1 **56** oh2 (p) *(MJAttwater) led tl 2f out: hrd rdn: one pce* **25/1** | FPFerris(3) 3 | 55 |
| 1020 | **5** | *½* | **Taboor (IRE)**[32] 5512 6-8-7 **59** (bt) *(JWPayne) sn outpcd: hdwy 2f out: no imp fnl f* **10/1** | MFenton 1 | 56 |
| 3110 | **6** | *½* | **White Ledger (IRE)**[47] 5157 5-8-3 **58** (v) *(RAFahey) s.i.s: outpcd: nvr nrr* **7/2**[2] | THamilton(3) 6 | 54 |
| -011 | **7** | *1* | **Spinetail Rufous (IRE)**[13] 5930 6-8-4 **56** oh1 (b) *(DFlood) spd over 3f* **11/4**[1] | PDoe 7 | 48 |
| 0000 | **8** | *18* | **Parkside Pursuit**[7] 6046 6-9-4 **70** *(JMBradley) outpcd: sn bhd* **14/1** | CCatlin 5 | 1 |

64.51 secs (2.24) **Going Correction** +0.625s/f (Yiel) 8 Ran SP% **110.7**

Speed ratings: **107,103,102,101,100 99,97,69**CSF £80.89 CT £370.20 TOTE £19.40: £3.70, £2.00, £1.80; EX 86.30 Place 6 £107.72, Place 5 £59.99.

**Owner** P D Smith Holdings Ltd **Bred** Geoff Mulcahy **Trained** Musley Bank, N Yorks

**FOCUS**

A fair winning time for the grade. The winner made his effort down the centre of the track and by now that was definitely the place to be.

**NOTEBOOK**

**Harrison's Flyer(IRE)**, the stable's second string according to the market, made his effort down the centre of the track and pulled right away from his rivals to get off the mark at the 11th attempt. He had shown some ability behind a useful sort on soft ground at Beverley earlier in the season, so these conditions were probably ideal.

**Madrasee**, racing more towards the stands' side, ran well on a track she likes. She has dropped to a winning mark.

**Pulse** ran another sound race, but continues on a lengthy losing run.

**Smart Starprincess(IRE)**, racing for the first time since July, showed bags of early speed and did not fold completely once headed. This was her best effort on turf so far this year and it should put her right for a winter campaign on sand.

**White Ledger(IRE)** never got into the race despite the reapplication of the visor.

**Spinetail Rufous(IRE)** probably found this tougher after two recent wins in banded company.

T/Plt: £101.30 to a £1 stake. Pool: £42,384.75. 305.20 winning tickets. T/Qpdt: £47.00 to a £1 stake. Pool: £3,466.10. 54.50 winning tickets. LM

# 6171 NEWMARKET (R-H)

Friday, October 15

**OFFICIAL GOING: Soft**

Wind: Fresh behind Weather: Raining

## 6187 FEDERATION OF BLOODSTOCK AGENTS MAIDEN STKS 1m

**1:10** (1:13) (D2) 2-Y-O **£7,163** (£2,204; £1,102; £551) **Stalls** High

| Form | | | | | RPR |
|---|---|---|---|---|---|
| | **1** | | **Proclamation (IRE)** 2-9-0 *(JNoseda) leggy: scope: a.p: led over 2f out: hung lft over 1f out: rdn out* **12/1** | EAhern 13 | 90+ |
| 6 | **2** | *3 ½* | **Unfurled (IRE)**[25] 5696 2-9-0 *(JLDunlop) a.p: chsd wnr over 1f out: styd on same pce ins fnl f* **20/1** | TQuinn 9 | 83 |
| | **3** | *1* | **Muraabet** 2-9-0 *(JLDunlop) gd sort: lw: a.p: led over 3f out: hdd over 2f out: no ex fnl f* **25/1** | JFortune 8 | 81+ |
| | **4** | *3 ½* | **Echo Of Light** 2-9-0 (t) *(SaeedBinSuroor) nice colt: bit bkwd: hld up: hdwy 1/2-way: rdn and hung lft fr over 1f out: wknd fnl f* **7/2**[1] | LDettori 23 | 74+ |
| | **5** | *1 ¾* | **Hard Top (IRE)** 2-9-0 *(SirMichaelStoute) gd sort: leggy: dwlt: hld up: hdwy over 2f out: nt rch ldrs* **20/1** | MHills 22 | 71 |
| | **6** | *½* | **Well Established (IRE)** 2-9-0 *(MAJarvis) gd sort: bit bkwd: s.i.s: hdwy over 6f out: wknd over 1f out* **16/1** | PRobinson 10 | 70 |
| | **7** | *nk* | **Azizam** 2-8-9 *(PWChapple-Hyam) neat: prom: rdn over 3f out: wknd over 1f out* **66/1** | AMcCarthy 5 | 64 |
| 640 | **8** | *hd* | **Ocean Gift**[27] 5649 2-9-0 88 *(DRCElsworth) lw: led: hdd over 6f out: remained handy tl wknd over 1f out* **15/2** | RHughes 19 | 69 |
| 0 | **9** | *1 ¼* | **Basserah (IRE)**[24] 5717 2-8-9 *(BWHills) chsd ldrs: rdn over 2f out: wknd over 1f out* **11/2**[2] | WSupple 3 | 61 |
| 0 | **10** | *2* | **Blue Hedges**[9] 6011 2-9-0 *(HJCollingridge) b: b.hind: chsd ldrs over 6f* **100/1** | JQuinn 17 | 62 |
| | **11** | *1 ¼* | **Polish Eagle** 2-9-0 *(EALDunlop) w'like: mid-div: hdwy over 3f out: wknd wl over 1f out* **25/1** | RLMoore 21 | 60 |
| | **12** | *1 ¼* | **Bold Eagle (IRE)** 2-9-0 *(SirMichaelStoute) gd sort: leggy: scope: s.s: outpcd: styd on ins fnl f: nvr nrr* **7/1**[3] | KFallon 16 | 57 |
| | **13** | *½* | **Cash On (IRE)** 2-9-0 *(MPTregoning) wl grwn: hld up: hdwy 3f out: wknd over 1f out* **20/1** | MartinDwyer 25 | 56 |
| | **14** | *½* | **Tawqeet (USA)** 2-9-0 *(JLDunlop) leggy: scope: sn outpcd and bhd* **50/1** | TEDurcan 6 | 55 |
| | **15** | *1 ½* | **Trew Style** 2-9-0 *(MHTompkins) leggy: unf: mid-div: effrt over 2f out: sn wknd* **66/1** | KDarley 14 | 52 |
| 0 | **16** | *3* | **Gold Gun (USA)**[15] 5897 2-8-11 *(MAJarvis) lw: prom over 5f* **100/1** | NMackay(3) 24 | 46 |
| | **17** | *1 ¾* | **Liberty Run (IRE)** 2-9-0 *(NACallaghan) cmpt: scope: s.s: a in rr* **14/1** | DHolland 1 | 43 |
| 06 | **18** | *7* | **Imperioli**[26] 5669 2-9-0 *(PABlockley) led over 6f out: hdd over 3f out: wknd over 2f out* **100/1** | PBradley 4 | 29 |
| | **19** | *16* | **Trew Flight (USA)** 2-9-0 *(MHTompkins) w'like: scope: mid-div: wknd over 2f out* **66/1** | NCallan 15 | — |
| | **20** | *1 ¼* | **Westfield Boy** 2-9-0 *(NPLittmoden) wl grwn: dwlt: bhd fnl 3f* **100/1** | GGibbons 2 | — |
| | **21** | *1 ¾* | **Obezyana (USA)** 2-9-0 *(GAHuffer) w'like: scope: bhd fnl 3f* **33/1** | SSanders 20 | — |

1m 41.78s (2.38) **Going Correction** +0.35s/f (Good) 21 Ran SP% **117.4**

Speed ratings: **102,98,97,94,92 91,91,91,90,88 86,85,85,84,83 80,78,71,55,54 52**CSF £230.68 TOTE £14.00: £3.20, £3.90, £6.70; EX 440.20.

**Owner** Abdullah Saeed Belhab **Bred** Cathal M Ryan **Trained** Newmarket, Suffolk

**FOCUS**

A decent time for the type of race, faster than both the juvenile conditions event and the 0-100 handicap for older horses. They raced down the centre of the track. This is a strong maiden and should produce plenty of winners, but just where to pitch the level of the form is difficult to know given that most of these were unraced and that the ground would have been against a number of them.

**NOTEBOOK**

**Proclamation(IRE)**, a half-brother to middle-distance stayer No Refuge, obviously goes well in soft ground, like a number of King's Best's progeny. Backed down from 20/1, he travelled well and scored in decisive fashion. He looks a nice prospect for middle distances next year.

**Unfurled(IRE)** stepped up on his debut effort and it was only inside the final furlong that he gave best to the winner. He should have no problem winning a maiden.

**Muraabet ♦**, a half-brother to four winners at between six and eight furlongs, notably Shibl, is a stablemate of the runner-up. Showing a knee action which suggested this ground suited him fine, he made a promising debut and will improve for the experience.

**Echo Of Light**, a 1.2 million euro son of Dubai Millennium, out of a useful sister to Salsabil and half-sister to Marju, came with quite a home reputation. Equipped with a crossed noseband for this debut, he was easy to back, and after racing close enough to the pace on the outside of the pack he was unable to pick up when brought under pressure. Eased off inside the final furlong when he started to hang, he should leave this behind. *Official explanation: jockey said colt hung left*

**Hard Top(IRE)**, who holds a Derby entry, is a half-brother to three middle-distance winners. He was slowly away and being niggled along from quite an early stage, but stayed on well in the final quarter-mile. He will do better over further next year.

**Well Established(IRE)**, a bit slow to stride, raced a little away from his rivals on the near-side of the bunch. A half-brother to useful French performers Okabango and Shigeru Summit, he is the sort to make a decent middle-distance handicapper next year.

**Azizam**, one of only two fillies in the field, is out of a half-sister to Derby winner High-Rise. She showed promise on this debut and should be up to winning a maiden against her own sex.

**Ocean Gift**, well supported on this return to maiden company, showed up prominently until fading going to the final furlong. The ground, rather than the longer trip, could have been to blame.

**Basserah(IRE)** was unable to build on her promising debut effort in these very different conditions.

**Blue Hedges**, sent off at 100/1 again on his first run on turf, showed more than he had at Lingfield.

**Bold Eagle(IRE)** is a half-brother to high-class German middle-distance performers Borgia (third in the Arc) and Boreal (Coronation Cup winner). He effectively lost his chance at the start, but was staying on when it was all over and should come into his own when tackling a mile and a half next year.

## 6188 PRESTIGE NURSERY 6f
**1:40** (1:44) (C2) (0-95,88) 2-Y-O **£8,190** (£2,520; £1,260; £630) **Stalls** High

Form RPR

0411 **1** **Ingleton**[7] 6042 2-9-3 **84** 7ex.......... GGibbons 9 97
(BAMcmahon) *a.p: rdn to ld ins fnl f: edgd lft: r.o* **15/8**[1]

0321 **2** *nk* **Our Fugitive (IRE)**[46] 5174 2-9-0 **81**.......... DHolland 6 93
(AWCarroll) *led: rdn and hdd ins fnl f: carried lft: no ex nr fin* **12/1**

4053 **3** *5* **Prince Samos (IRE)**[50] 5054 2-8-13 **80**.......... KFallon 10 78
(RHannon) *bhd: swtchd lft 3f out: hdwy over 1f out: r.o* **16/1**

10 **4** *3/4* **Ghurra (USA)**[43] 5250 2-9-6 **87**.......... WSupple 13 83
(EALDunlop) *hld up in tch: rdn over 2f out: one pce* **16/1**

022 **5** *2 1/2* **Elgin Marbles**[15] 5896 2-9-3 **84**.......... RLMoore 3 73
(RHannon) *chsd ldrs: rdn over 2f out: wknd ins fnl f* **6/1**[2]

4600 **6** *shd* **Empire's Ghodha**[18] 5839 2-9-1 **82**..........(b) JFortune 15 71
(BJMeehan) *bhd tl hdwy 2f out: no further prog fnl f* **25/1**

0016 **7** *5* **On The Waterline (IRE)**[2] 6158 2-8-12 **79** 7ex..........(v) SDrowne 5 54
(PDEvans) *lw: prom: rdn over 2f out: wknd over 1f out* **20/1**

0330 **8** *2* **Orpen Wide (IRE)**[15] 5897 2-8-1 **71**.......... NMackay(3) 4 41
(MCChapman) *lw: prom: rdn over 2f out: wknd wl over 1f out* **40/1**

14 **9** *2 1/2* **Personify**[34] 5457 2-9-5 **86**..........(vt[1]) LDettori 1 49
(SaeedBinSuroor) *chsd ldrs: rdn over 2f out: sn wknd* **8/1**[3]

1344 **10** *hd* **Generous Option**[28] 5606 2-9-2 **83**.......... KDarley 12 46
(MJohnston) *pushed along and sn in mid-div: bhd fnl 2f* **14/1**

0100 **11** *2* **Doctor's Cave**[27] 5649 2-9-7 **88**.......... SSanders 11 45
(CEBrittain) *lw: prom tl wknd wl over 1f out* **40/1**

033 **12** *4* **My Gacho (IRE)**[35] 5434 2-8-13 **80**.......... RHavlin 14 26
(MrsPNDutfield) *a towards rr* **20/1**

0610 **13** *1/2* **Press Express (IRE)**[15] 5885 2-8-11 **78**.......... ACulhane 8 23
(MRChannon) *a bhd* **20/1**

224 **14** *1 1/4* **Drum Dance (IRE)**[31] 5536 2-8-13 **80**.......... SCarson 7 21
(RFJohnsonHoughton) *lw: s.i.s: hld up and bhd: rdn over 2f out: no rspnse* **18/1**

1m 14.2s (1.11) **Going Correction** +0.35s/f (Good) **14** Ran SP% **114.6**
Speed ratings: **106,105,98,97,94 94,87,85,81,81 78,73,72,71**CSF £20.48 CT £272.04 TOTE £2.80: £1.40, £3.00, £2.70; EX 24.60.
**Owner** J C Fretwell **Bred** Thomas Trafford **Trained** Hopwas, Staffs

**FOCUS**
A very smart time for a race of its type and this is smart nursery form. The field raced centre-to-near side, although the low numbers appeared at first to be heading for the stands' rail before changing their minds. Not many got into it, the first two coming clear.

**NOTEBOOK**
**Ingleton**, who was 3lb well in under his penalty, completed the hat-trick, although it was only inside the last that he got the better of the runner-up. He has been progressing well, but the handicapper might have him now. He heads for the sales next week.
**Our Fugitive(IRE)** ◆ bowled along in front and only gave best well inside the last, with Holland not going for his whip on this slightly quirky sort. He obviously handles this ground and could prove hard to beat if turned out before he is reassessed. A return to five furlongs is unlikely to inconvenience him.
**Prince Samos(IRE)**, making his nursery debut, proved his effectiveness on soft ground and stayed on well from off the pace. He will be seen to better effect over an extra furlong or two.
**Ghurra(USA)**, who lost third spot close home, handled the conditions but again shaped as if she would benefit from a step up in trip.
**Elgin Marbles**, who was raised 4lb after finishing runner-up here to subsequent Redcar Two-Year-Old Trophy winner Obe Gold, faded after chasing the pace for a long way.
**Empire's Ghodha**, who is edging down the weights, handles this sort of ground but is probably more effective on a sound surface.
**On The Waterline(IRE)** is likely to struggle from her revised mark.
**Personify**, back down in trip and visored for the first time, did not pick up when asked for his effort. To give him the benefit of the doubt the ground could have been to blame.
**My Gacho(IRE)** *Official explanation: trainer said colt was not suited by soft ground; jockey said colt hung left during race*

## 6189 HEATHAVON STUD HOUGHTON CONDITIONS STKS 1m
**2:15** (2:15) (C1) 2-Y-O **£9,013** (£3,418; £1,709; £777) **Stalls** High

Form RPR

0011 **1** **Something Exciting**[15] 5885 2-9-3 87.......... TQuinn 5 106
(DRCElsworth) *hld up: pushed along 5f out: hdwy to ld over 1f out: styd on wl* **8/1**

1622 **2** *3* **Embossed (IRE)**[37] 5395 2-9-3 100.......... RLMoore 1 100
(RHannon) *lw: hld up: pushed along 1/2-way: hdwy over 2f out: rdn and ev ch over 1f out: no ex ins fnl f* **11/4**[1]

0122 **3** *5* **Skidrow**[49] 5082 2-8-12 89.......... SSanders 9 85
(MLWBell) *lw: led: hdd over 6f out: remained handy: rdn and n.m.r over 1f out: sn outpcd* **25/1**

1 **4** *nk* **Xtra Torrential (USA)**[44] 5227 2-9-1.......... NCallan 7 87
(DMSimcock) *lw: s.i.s and wnt lft s: sn prom: rdn over 2f out: wknd fnl f* **12/1**

2241 **5** *1* **Love Palace (IRE)**[26] 5669 2-9-3 95.......... KDarley 3 87
(MJohnston) *lw: w ldrs: rdn to ld wl over 1f out: sn hdd: wknd fnl f* **9/2**[2]

0002 **6** *hd* **Hallowed Dream (IRE)**[24] 5717 2-8-7 80.......... KFallon 8 77
(CEBrittain) *led over 6f out: rdn and hdd wl over 1f out: wknd fnl f* **25/1**

41 **7** *6* **Night Hour (IRE)**[16] 5871 2-9-3 88.......... MartinDwyer 2 85+
(MPTregoning) *lw: prom: rdn over 2f out: wknd and eased over 1f out* **11/2**[3]

3122 **8** *20* **Hallhoo (IRE)**[27] 5630 2-9-3 89.......... TEDurcan 4 35+
(MRChannon) *prom: rdn over 2f out: sn wknd: eased fnl f* **7/1**

12 **9** *1 3/4* **Sun Kissed (JPN)**[43] 5246 2-9-3 93.......... LDettori 6 32+
(SaeedBinSuroor) *s.i.s and hmpd s: hld up: effrt over 2f out: sn wknd and eased* **15/2**

1m 41.99s (2.59) **Going Correction** +0.35s/f (Good) **9** Ran SP% **111.0**
Speed ratings: **101,98,93,92,91 91,85,65,63**CSF £28.53 TOTE £8.10: £2.30, £1.70, £4.40; EX 29.70.
**Owner** Setsquare Recruitment **Bred** R E Crutchley **Trained** Whitsbury, Hants

**FOCUS**
A decent field, but the conditions obviously played a part and they finished well strung out. The winner revelled in the ground and is improving fast. The runner-up has been rated just below his best.

**NOTEBOOK**
**Something Exciting**, shouldering the maximum 10lb penalty, showed much improved form again to complete the hat-trick. After being pushed along in rear and seemingly going nowhere, she suddenly picked up and swept down the outside to lead. Kept up to her work and never going to be caught, she is really progressive and there will be more to come from her over ten furlongs granted some easy ground.
**Embossed(IRE)**, runner-up to useful colts on his last two starts, was tackling a mile for the first time. After coming from off the pace to deliver his challenge, he was put in his place by the filly but finished clear of the remainder.
**Skidrow** had lost his pitch and was only sixth passing the furlong pole but stayed on to finish a fairly remote third. He stays well and does handle testing ground.
**Xtra Torrential(USA)**, the least experienced member of the field, was slowly away as he had been on his debut. Rather keen in the first part of the race, he had his chance but was unable to pick up in the conditions.
**Love Palace(IRE)** had won his maiden in soft ground but was found out by this rise in class.
**Hallowed Dream(IRE)**, runner-up to subsequent Prix Marcel Boussac second Titian Time on her latest start, was allowed to stride on in front but faded after being headed.
**Night Hour(IRE)** was found wanting in this better grade. *Official explanation: jockey said colt was unsuited by soft ground*
**Hallhoo(IRE)** *Official explanation: jockey said colt was unsuited by soft ground*
**Sun Kissed(JPN)** was always trailing after being hampered by the eventual fourth leaving the stalls. *Official explanation: jockey said colt was unsuited by soft ground*

## 6190 IGLOOS BENTINCK STKS (GROUP 3) 6f
**2:50** (2:51) (A1) 3-Y-O+ **£29,000** (£11,000; £5,500; £2,500) **Stalls** High

Form RPR

0413 **1** **Royal Millennium (IRE)**[12] 5977 6-9-2 111.......... TEDurcan 4 121
(MRChannon) *racd towards stands' side: chsd ldr: rdn over 2f out: led wl ins fnl f: r.o* **7/2**[1]

1002 **2** *shd* **Moss Vale (IRE)**[27] 5661 3-8-11 110.......... MHills 1 117
(BWHills) *lw: racd towards stands' side: led: rdn over 1f out: hdd wl ins fnl f: r.o* **9/2**[2]

5165 **3** *2* **Quito (IRE)**[27] 5628 7-8-12 105..........(b) ACulhane 12 111+
(DWChapman) *hld up in rr: rdn over 2f out: gd hdwy fnl f: r.o* **8/1**[3]

0025 **4** *1 1/2* **Country Reel (USA)**[20] 5780 4-8-12 105..........(t) LDettori 9 107
(SaeedBinSuroor) *lw: led far side tl jst over 2f out: r.o one pce fnl f* **11/1**

3613 **5** *3/4* **Baltic King**[15] 5893 4-8-12 106..........(t) SDrowne 15 104
(HMorrison) *b.hind: a.p: led far side wl over 1f out tl no ex ins fnl f* **12/1**

0131 **6** *1* **Jonny Ebeneezer**[6] 6071 5-8-12 96..........(be) RLMoore 2 101
(DFlood) *b: racd towards stands' side: prom: rdn and one pce fnl 2f* **11/1**

6010 **7** *hd* **Halmahera (IRE)**[15] 5893 9-8-12 101.......... NCallan 8 101
(KARyan) *b.hind: prom: rdn over 2f out: wknd ins fnl f* **25/1**

5052 **8** *hd* **Twilight Blues (IRE)**[13] 5948 5-8-12 103.......... EAhern 18 100
(JNoseda) *lw: prom: rdn over 2f out: wknd ins fnl f* **20/1**

5415 **9** *1 1/4* **Goldeva**[34] 5454 5-8-9 104.......... RHughes 11 95+
(RHollinshead) *s.i.s: hld up: short-lived effrt over 1f out* **16/1**

5340 **10** *1* **Colonel Cotton (IRE)**[15] 5893 5-8-12 95.......... JFortune 6 93
(NACallaghan) *in rr towards stands' side: struggling fnl 2f* **33/1**

2400 **11** *1/2* **Ashdown Express (IRE)**[12] 5982 5-8-12 116.......... SSanders 14 96+
(CFWall) *b: hld up and bhd: hdwy over 1f out: wknd ins fnl f* **10/1**

0006 **12** *4* **Capricho (IRE)**[20] 5780 7-8-12 96.......... TQuinn 13 80
(JAkehurst) *b.hind: hld up in mid-div: bhd fnl f* **20/1**

5602 **13** *shd* **Ellens Academy (IRE)**[20] 5799 9-8-12 86.......... FNorton 17 80
(EJAlston) *hld up in mid-div: bhd fnl f* **66/1**

3024 **14** *2 1/2* **Petardias Magic (IRE)**[145] 2335 3-8-11 88.......... KFallon 16 72
(CADwyer) *prom: led far side jst over 2f out tl wl over 1f out: sn wknd* **20/1**

1m 13.71s (0.62) **Going Correction** +0.35s/f (Good)
**WFA** 3 from 4yo+ 1lb **14** Ran SP% **113.4**
Speed ratings: **109,108,106,104,103 101,101,101,99,98 97,92,92,88**CSF £14.98 TOTE £4.00: £1.70, £1.90, £2.50; EX 15.30.
**Owner** Jackie & George Smith **Bred** Mrs G Smith **Trained** West Ilsley, Berks
■ Stewards Enquiry : T E Durcan caution: used whip without giving gelding time to respond

**FOCUS**
A good renewal but the winning time was modest for a Group Three. Ten raced in a bunch centre-to-far side, with the other four racing nearer the stands' side. The near-side quartet held the call, with the other group at around a two-length disadvantage.

**NOTEBOOK**
**Royal Millennium(IRE)**, runner-up in this event twelve months ago, was conceding 4lb or more all round due to his Group Three penalty. Back over six furlongs after his fine third in the Abbaye, he tracked the leader in the near-side quartet and got on top inside the last, although he pricked his ears on the line as if he thought he had done enough. He is better than ever at present.
**Moss Vale(IRE)** made the running in the near-side quartet but was just denied by old rival Royal Millennium, who had beaten him half a length at the Curragh on effectively the same terms. Verstaile when it comes to ground conditions, he is certainly up to winning a race of this type.
**Quito(IRE)** had no luck in the Ayr Gold Cup and it was a similar story here as he came out best of the ten to race towards the far side but that group was at a disadvantage with the near-side quartet.
**Country Reel(USA)** has produced a couple of decent efforts since the visor was dispensed with but remains difficult to place.
**Baltic King** ran a decent race considering the ground was against him and that a stiff five furlongs is ideal.
**Jonny Ebeneezer**, one of the success stories of the season, was third of the four to race on the favoured near side but ran a thoroughly respectable race on this first crack at pattern company, especially as he is a horse who is ideally suited by more cover.
**Ashdown Express(IRE)** won this event a year ago, but that was on fast ground.
**Petardias Magic(IRE)** *Official explanation: trainer was unable to offer any explanation for poor form shown*

## 6191 BELLWINCH HOMES H'CAP 7f
**3:25** (3:26) (C1) (0-100,100) 3-Y-O+ **£12,486** (£4,736; £2,368; £1,076) **Stalls** High

Form RPR

514 **1** **Stream Of Gold (IRE)**[35] 5443 3-8-3 **87**.......... FNorton 7 106+
(SirMichaelStoute) *a.p: rdn to ld over 1f out: edgd rt: r.o wl* **8/1**[3]

4150 **2** *3 1/2* **King's Caprice**[27] 5628 3-8-4 **88**.......... SCarson 15 97
(GBBalding) *lw: chsd ldr: rdn and ev ch over 1f out: no ex ins fnl f* **16/1**

5300 **3** *4* **Bayeux (USA)**[34] 5462 3-9-0 **98**..........(vt[1]) LDettori 5 97
(SaeedBinSuroor) *hld up: racd keenly: hdwy over 1f out: nt trble ldrs* **12/1**

1016 **4** *nk* **Ettrick Water**[20] 5781 5-9-1 **100**..........(v) NMackay(3) 6 98
(LMCumani) *chsd ldrs: rdn 1/2-way: wknd over 1f out* **12/1**

3351 **5** *shd* **Marshman (IRE)**[6] 6070 5-8-4 **85** 6ex.......... PRobinson 16 84
(MHTompkins) *hld up: hdwy over 1f out: nvr trbld ldrs* **7/2**[1]

**6** *2* **Empirical Power (IRE)**[34] 5482 3-8-11 **95**.......... DPMcDonogh 20 88
(EdwardLynam, Ire) *led: rdn and hdd over 1f out: wknd ins fnl f* **16/1**

2205 **7** *nk* **Digital**[14] 5921 7-8-5 **87**.......... TQuinn 8 79
(MRChannon) *hld up: plld hrd: hdwy over 1f out: nvr trbld ldrs* **7/1**[2]

4000 **8** *1 1/4* **Starbeck (IRE)**[19] 5811 6-8-4 **86** oh9.......... AMcCarthy 2 75
(PHowling) *b: b.hind: s.i.s: hld up: pushed along 1/2-way: styd on ins fnl f: n.d* **66/1**

2055 **9** *3/4* **Oasis Star (IRE)**[21] 5762 3-8-8 **92**.......... MartinDwyer 11 79
(PWHarris) *mid-div: rdn 1/2-way: outpcd over 2f out: n.d after* **11/1**

504 **10** *nk* **Taranaki**[15] 5887 6-7-13 **86** oh2.......... NDeSouza(5) 19 73
(PDCundell) *stmbld s: plld hrd and sn prom: rdn over 2f out: wknd over 1f out* **33/1**

5551 **11** *3 1/2* **Wizard Of Noz**[14] 5921 4-9-1 **97**..........(b) EAhern 21 75
(JNoseda) *prom: rdn over 2f out: wknd over 1f out* **9/1**



The Form Book, Raceform Ltd, Compton, RG20 6NL

0100 **12** *1* **Golden Chalice (IRE)**[99] 3673 5-8-8 **90** DHolland 12 65
(AMBalding) *hld up: rdn whn hmpd over 1f out: n.d* **14/1**

2100 **13** *1 1/4* **Apex**[21] 5762 3-8-3 **87** WSupple 18 59
(EALDunlop) *hld up: plld hrd: hdwy 1/2-way: wknd over 1f out* **14/1**

3104 **14** *1/2* **Moayed**[125] 2891 5-8-4 **86** oh1 (bt) GGibbons 17 57
(NPLittmoden) *s.i.s: sn pushed along in rr: wknd over 1f out* **20/1**

1400 **15** *2 1/2* **Always Esteemed (IRE)**[34] 5462 4-9-0 **96** (b) TEDurcan 13 61
(GWragg) *prom over 5f* **33/1**

0630 **16** *2 1/2* **Oro Verde**[118] 3092 3-8-3 **87** ow1 RLMoore 14 45
(RHannon) *lw: prom: rdn 1/2-way: wknd 2f out* **40/1**

1m 27.25s (0.78) **Going Correction** +0.35s/f (Good)
**WFA** 3 from 4yo+ 2lb **16 Ran SP% 119.2**
Speed ratings: **109,105,100,100,99 97,97,95,95,94 90,89,88,87,84 81**CSF £120.32 CT £1591.03 TOTE £8.90: £2.60, £3.60, £3.00, £3.60; EX 175.90 Trifecta £2369.70 Part won. Pool: £3,337.68. 0.50 winning units..
**Owner** Ballymacoll Stud **Bred** Ballymacoll Stud Farm Ltd **Trained** Newmarket, Suffolk

**FOCUS**
A decent handicap and sound form, although it was advantageous to be up with the pace. The winner looked a big improver, and the runner-up was right back to his best.

**NOTEBOOK**
**Stream Of Gold(IRE)** stays a mile but is probably better suited to this trip and showed much improved form. A progressive type, he looks sure to add to his tally before the season is out.
**King's Caprice** had his favoured soft surface, and probably turned in his best effort to date, despite being beaten.
**Bayeux(USA)**, sharpened up by the first-time visor, was staying on when the race was all but over. However, even allowing for the ground being softer than ideal, he is a disappointing type.
**Ettrick Water**, on ground softer than ideal didn't have things go his way but, still turned in a sound enough effort off this career high mark.
**Marshman(IRE)**, who was officially 3lb well in, didn't run too badly considering the race favoured those to race close to the pace, and that he had to switch wide to launch his challenge. However, he won't find things easy now off a revised mark.
**Empirical Power(IRE)** had a progressive profile coming into this but wasn't as effective on this soft surface.
**Digital** did himself no favours by refusing to settle. *Official explanation: jockey said he was hampered early on in race*
**Starbeck(IRE)** *Official explanation: jockey said mare was unsuited by soft ground*
**Wizard Of Noz** didn't appear to handle the testing conditions.

## 6192 SPORTING INDEX "PREMIER" CLAIMING STKS 1m 4f
**4:00** (4:01) (D2) 3-5-Y-O **£6,838** (£2,104; £1,052; £526) **Stalls** High

Form RPR

1604 **1** **Always Waining (IRE)**[44] 5226 3-8-10 93 JFanning 1 86+
(MJohnston) *w ldr: led 3f out: clr over 1f out: easily* **11/10**[1]

056 **2** *4* **Harrycat (IRE)**[11] 5994 3-8-5 JQuinn 5 69?
(VSmith) *hld up: hdwy over 8f out: rdn and one pce fnl 2f* **50/1**

4500 **3** *1/2* **Prins Willem (IRE)**[14] 5919 5-9-4 85 LDettori 8 74
(JRFanshawe) *a.p: rdn and one pce fnl 2f* **11/4**[2]

1210 **4** *5* **Top Spec (IRE)**[21] 5761 3-8-12 82 RHughes 4 68
(RHannon) *lw: hld up: rdn over 3f out: hdwy over 2f out: sn swtchd rt: wknd over 1f out* **6/1**[3]

0240 **5** *2 1/2* **Patrixtoo (FR)**[30] 5560 3-8-5 58 PRobinson 9 58
(MHTompkins) *led: hung rt and hdd 3f out: wknd 2f out* **25/1**

5442 **6** *2 1/2* **Zuma (IRE)**[5] 6085 3-8-10 72 RLMoore 6 59
(RHannon) *hld up: rdn and hdwy on outside 3f out: sn wknd* **14/1**

6 **7** *14* **Sweetwater (GER)**[8] 6025 4-8-9 70 SDrowne 3 32
(MrsStefLiddiard) *bhd fnl 3f* **33/1**

0000 **8** *1/2* **Gallant Boy (IRE)**[5] 6083 5-8-10 63 (bt[1]) JFortune 2 32
(PDEvans) *b: rdn over 4f out: a bhd* **25/1**

3060 **9** *3 1/2* **Indian Solitaire (IRE)**[77] 3166 5-8-10 72 (p) EAhern 7 27
(BPJBaugh) *lw: bhd fnl 3f* **33/1**

226 **10** *21* **Woolly Back (IRE)**[133] 2653 3-8-9 80 WSupple 10 —
(RHollinshead) *lw: t.k.h: prom tl wknd over 3f out: t.o* **20/1**

2m 37.3s (3.84) **Going Correction** +0.35s/f (Good)
**WFA** 3 from 4yo+ 7lb **10 Ran SP% 115.5**
Speed ratings: **101,98,98,94,93 91,82,81,79,65**CSF £87.80 TOTE £2.10: £1.10, £7.40, £1.60; EX 138.30.Always Waining was claimed by Mr P. Clinton for £30,000. Harrycat was subject to a friendly claim.
**Owner** The Always Trying Partnership **Bred** Barouche Stud Ireland Ltd **Trained** Middleham Moor, N Yorks

**FOCUS**
A mixed bag contested this claimer, in which they crossed over to race close to the stands' rail. The fifth holds the race down, so the winner, third and fourth have all been rated below form, and the runner-up did not improve anything like as much as the bare figures suggest.

**NOTEBOOK**
**Always Waining(IRE)** had been a good fourth off 95 in a York handicap on his previous start and proved different class in this lower grade and did not need to run anywhere near his best. He was value for double the winning margin.
**Harrycat(IRE)**, who was stepping up in trip, left his maiden form behind but did not run as well as first impressions might suggest. He could struggle when reassessed, although there will be opportunities on the All-Weather surfaces this winter.
**Prins Willem(IRE)** has struggled this year and it was no different here, although, the ground would have been softer than ideal.
**Top Spec(IRE)** found the soft ground, on this step up in trip, too much.
**Patrixtoo(FR)** *Official explanation: jockey said colt hung right*
**Gallant Boy(IRE)** *Official explanation: jockey said gelding spread a plate on way to start*
**Indian Solitaire(IRE)** *Official explanation: jockey said gelding was unsuited by soft ground*

## 6193 GEORGE WINSOR LIFETIME IN RACING H'CAP 1m
**4:35** (4:37) (C1) (0-100,100) 3-Y-0+ **£14,019** (£4,313; £2,156; £1,078) **Stalls** High

Form RPR

1211 **1** **Kamanda Laugh**[113] 3230 3-8-1 **83** MartinDwyer 7 90
(BWHills) *b.off hind: w ldr tl led over 5f out: rdn and hdd over 1f out: rallied to ld wl ins fnl f* **10/1**

1443 **2** *nk* **Boule D'Or (IRE)**[13] 5942 3-8-8 **90** NDay 23 96
(RIngram) *chsd ldrs: rdn to ld ins fnl f: sn edgd rt and hdd: styd on* **16/1**

-420 **3** *1/2* **Blaise Castle (USA)**[132] 2685 4-8-11 **90** EAhern 14 95
(GAButler) *lw: chsd ldrs: led over 1f out: rdn and hdd ins fnl f: kpt on* **50/1**

0000 **4** *1* **Finished Article (IRE)**[56] 4920 7-8-6 **85** TQuinn 12 88
(DRCElsworth) *hld up: r.o ins fnl f: nt rch ldrs* **16/1**

0465 **5** *1/2* **Selective**[7] 6044 5-8-9 **88** (p) DHolland 17 90
(EFVaughan) *lw: hld up: hdwy over 1f out: hung lft ins fnl f: styd on same pce* **16/1**

2610 **6** *1 1/4* **Goodbye Mr Bond**[6] 6069 4-8-4 **83** oh6 GGibbons 13 83
(EJAlston) *chsd ldrs: rdn over 2f out: styd on same pce fnl f* **33/1**

0545 **7** *1/2* **Unshakable (IRE)**[13] 5941 5-9-1 **94** FNorton 8 93
(BobJones) *b.hind: hld up: hdwy over 1f out: nt trble ldrs* **13/2**[2]

0-00 **8** *1 1/4* **Mombassa (IRE)**[5] 6098 4-8-10 **92** DJCondon(3) 2 88+
(EdwardLynam, Ire) *s.i.s: hld up: hdwy and nt clr run over 1f out: n.d* **11/2**[1]

10 **9** *shd* **Dafore**[128] 2789 3-8-2 **84** RLMoore 10 80
(RHannon) *mid-div: rdn 1/2-way: hdwy over 1f out: r.o* **50/1**

1031 **10** *shd* **Aperitif**[18] 5835 3-8-4 **86** JQuinn 21 82+
(WJHaggas) *b: dwlt: hld up: running on whn nt clr run ins fnl f: eased* **7/1**[3]

0005 **11** *shd* **Barbajuan (IRE)**[13] 5942 3-8-1 **86** NMackay(3) 16 81
(NACallaghan) *hld up: swtchd rt over 2f out: hdwy over 1f out: nvr trbld ldrs* **20/1**

0600 **12** *1 1/4* **Putra Kuantan**[13] 5941 4-9-4 **97** PRobinson 1 90
(MAJarvis) *lw: led: hdd over 5f out: wknd fnl f* **20/1**

0234 **13** *shd* **Penrith (FR)**[7] 6044 3-8-4 **86** JFanning 20 79
(MJohnston) *prom: rdn over 2f out: wknd fnl f* **16/1**

0001 **14** *1 1/4* **Nashaab (USA)**[7] 6044 7-9-2 **95** 6ex (v) NCallan 19 88+
(PDEvans) *hld up: n.d* **33/1**

5242 **15** *2 1/2* **Jazz Scene (IRE)**[4] 6116 3-8-11 **93** (v) ACulhane 4 78
(MRChannon) *chsd ldrs over 6f* **16/1**

1003 **16** *nk* **Ace Of Hearts**[14] 5920 5-8-11 **90** SSanders 25 75
(CFWall) *hld up: hdwy over 3f out: wknd over 1f out* **20/1**

-102 **17** *1 1/4* **Thajja (IRE)**[19] 5813 3-9-4 **100** WSupple 18 82
(JLDunlop) *hld up: hdwy over 2f out: wknd over 1f out* **14/1**

1-04 **18** *1* **Oman Gulf (USA)**[141] 2420 3-7-8 **83** KMay(7) 6 63
(BWHills) *lw: hld up: effrt over 2f out: hmpd over 1f out: n.d* **66/1**

0-00 **19** *1 1/2* **Fremen (USA)**[14] 5921 4-8-13 **92** KFallon 26 69
(SirMichaelStoute) *lw: hld up in tch: rdn over 2f out: wknd over 1f out* **14/1**

020- **20** *hd* **Faithful Warrior (USA)**[421] 4324 6-8-7 **91** AMedeiros(5) 3 68
(BWHills) *b: chsd ldrs over 5f* **66/1**

5402 **21** *hd* **Leoballero**[14] 5921 4-8-9 **88** (t) JFEgan 5 64
(DJDaly) *lw: hld up: rdn over 2f out: btn whn nt clr run over 1f out* **33/1**

6600 **22** *2* **Lago D'Orta (IRE)**[28] 5610 4-9-4 **97** LDettori 15 69
(CGCox) *lw: b: hld up: effrt over 2f out: sn wknd* **20/1**

1m 42.36s (2.96) **Going Correction** +0.35s/f (Good)
**WFA** 3 from 4yo+ 3lb **22 Ran SP% 127.8**
Speed ratings: **99,98,98,97,96 95,94,93,93,93 93,92,92,90,88 88,86,85,84,84 83,81**CSF £142.33 CT £7587.43 TOTE £13.00: £3.20, £4.20, £10.50, £4.70; EX 420.30.
**Owner** John Sillett **Bred** Miss K Rausing **Trained** Lambourn, Berks

**FOCUS**
The stalls were on the far side, but the field came over to the stands' side and this was another race in which it paid to be up with the pace. The winning time was moderate for the grade and slower than both of the earlier juvenile events over the same trip.

**NOTEBOOK**
**Kamanda Laugh** certainly knows how to win and is a difficult horse for the Handicapper to get hold of, for he again did just enough.
**Boule D'Or(IRE)**, as it turned out didn't have the best of draws, with the field switching to the stands' side. However, although he isn't the easiest of rides, looked to have done everything just right until coming off a true line and getting mugged near the finish.
**Blaise Castle(USA)**, given a break since doing too much in the first-time blinkers at Haydock back in June, had the headgear left off here and looked much happier. She clearly goes well fresh, and with give underfoot.
**Finished Article(IRE)** could have done with a stronger pace, for he got going far too late here.
**Selective** shaped a little better than of late in the first-time cheekpieces, on ground which could well have been soft enough for him.
**Goodbye Mr Bond** turned in a solid effort from out of the handicap, and clearly remains in good form.
**Unshakable(IRE)** was another who could have done with a stronger pace, and although he has only hit the target once this year, there is still time for him to put matters right.
**Mombassa(IRE)** came into this in good form, having won earlier in the week in his native country, but he was denied a run up the rails as Putra Kuantan stopped in front of him.
**Dafore** lacked the experience of his rivals, and although he only finished midfield, didn't shape at all badly on this return to action.
**Aperitif** ◆ found himself with plenty to do having missed the break and been dropped across the back of the field to the stands' rail, but he would certainly have finished a good deal closer with a clear run. He is one to keep an eye on in the closing weeks.
**Fremen(USA)** can be forgiven this for he failed to handle the ground.
**Leoballero** *Official explanation: jockey said gelding had breathing problems*
**Lago D'Orta(IRE)** *Official explanation: jockey said colt lost his action*

## 6194 NEWMARKET CHALLENGE WHIP (A H'CAP) 1m 2f
**5:05** (5:06) (G4) (0-85,81) 3-Y-0+ **£0Stalls** High

Form RPR

2200 **1** **Ultimata**[6] 6069 4-9-0 81 LDettori 1 88
(JRFanshawe) *mde all: rdn over 1f out: styd on* **11/4**[3]

5043 **2** *1 1/4* **Vamp**[18] 5842 3-8-0 75 NMackay(3) 2 80
(RMBeckett) *trckd wnr: chal 4f out: sn rdn: unable qck ins fnl f* **2/1**[2]

4330 **3** *5* **Impersonator**[30] 5568 4-8-9 76 TQuinn 3 72
(JLDunlop) *racd keenly and prom: rdn over 1f out: wknd ins fnl f* **11/10**[1]

2m 10.83s (5.14) **Going Correction** +0.35s/f (Good)
**WFA** 3 from 4yo 5lb **3 Ran SP% 107.6**
Speed ratings: **93,92,88**CSF £7.71 TOTE £2.40; EX 6.00 Place 6 £189.02, Place 5 £18.68.
**Owner** J H Richmond-Watson **Bred** Lawn Stud **Trained** Newmarket, Suffolk

**FOCUS**
This historic event was run on handicap terms for the first time and with the entry qualifications relaxed slightly, but the turnout was pathetic again. The pace was steady and the time moderate.

**NOTEBOOK**
**Ultimata** had a soft lead, and as you would expect a daughter of Unfuwain, relished the give underfoot.
**Vamp** did her best to make a race of it, but she didn't handle the conditions as well as the winner.
**Impersonator** continues to disappoint, even though the ground was in his favour here.
T/Jkpt: Not won. T/Plt: £517.40 to a £1 stake. Pool: £62,266.25. 87.85 winning tickets. T/Qpdt: £16.50 to a £1 stake. Pool: £6,129.90. 274.70 winning tickets. CR

## 5945 REDCAR (L-H)

Friday, October 15

**OFFICIAL GOING: Good changing to good to soft after race 2 (2.00)**

The ground was described as 'good to soft' after the first race but it deteriorated as the afternoon wore on.

Wind: Slight 1/2 against. Weather: Persistent rain.

### 6195 "BECOME A REDCAR ANNUAL MEMBER 2005!" CLAIMING STKS 7f

1:30 (1:36) (F4) 2-Y-O £3,556 (£1,016; £508) **Stalls** Centre

Form RPR

3050 **1** **Exit Smiling**[34] 5477 2-8-13 67 ........ RFfrench 7 70
(MJohnston) *mde virtually all: qcknd 3f out: sn clr: drvn out* **11/2**[3]

0006 **2** *4* **Bella Plunkett (IRE)**[32] 5516 2-8-3 51 ow3 ........ RMullen 2 50
(WMBrisbourne) *chsd ldrs: outpcd 3f out: styd on to go 2nd ins last* **33/1**

0000 **3** *1/2* **Ifit (IRE)**[38] 5368 2-8-4 58 ........ SHitchcott 14 50
(MRChannon) *mid-div: rdn and outpcd 3f out: styd on wl fnl f* **10/1**

440 **4** *1* **Bond Finesse (IRE)**[8] 6022 2-8-12 ........ FLynch 10 55
(BSmart) *s.i.s: hld up: stdy hdwy on ins 3f out: styd on same pce fnl f* **10/1**

0 **5** *1* **After The Snow (IRE)**[14] 5910 2-7-12 ........ DKinsella 4 39
(IAWood) *trckd ldrs: effrt 3f out: kpt on same pce* **40/1**

6300 **6** *nk* **Pro Tempore**[11] 5989 2-8-12 64 ........ PHanagan 6 52
(MrsJRRamsden) *trckd ldrs: effrt 3f out: kpt on same pce* **9/2**[1]

000 **7** *2* **Filey Buoy**[49] 5097 2-7-12 ........ (v[1]) BSwarbrick(5) 1 38
(RMWhitaker) *chsd ldrs: one pce fnl 3f* **40/1**

50 **8** *1* **Sweet Potato (IRE)**[13] 5946 2-8-3 ........ PMakin(5) 5 41
(TDBarron) *swtg: mid-div: drvn along over 3f out: edgd lft: one pce* **5/1**[2]

0050 **9** *1 1/4* **Singhalongtasveer**[5] 6093 2-8-5 59 ........ JBramhill 8 34
(WStorey) *sn outpcd: kpt on fnl 2f: nvr a factor* **16/1**

0530 **10** *3 1/2* **Muestra (IRE)**[65] 4638 2-7-7 45 ow2 ........ AmyBaker(7) 11 21
(MrsPNDutfield) *reluctant to go to s: mid-div: effrt over 2f out: edgd lft: wknd fnl f* **66/1**

**11** *1 1/4* **Queens Hand (IRE)** 2-8-8 ........ RWinston 20 26
(GASwinbank) *leggy: unf: uns rdr and rn loose befhand: swvd lft s: sn chsng ldrs: hung lft over 2f out: sn lost pl* **16/1**

4250 **12** *4* **Riverweld**[30] 5556 2-8-5 55 ........ PMQuinn 15 13
(GMMoore) *chsd ldrs: lost pl 2f out* **20/1**

340 **13** *shd* **Branston Lily**[16] 5857 2-8-12 63 ........ KMcEvoy 17 19
(MrsJRRamsden) *mid-field: outpcd and lost pl 3f out* **6/1**

0 **14** *hd* **Ekaterina**[27] 5633 2-7-13 ow1 ........ DaleGibson 9 6
(WStorey) *sn in rr* **50/1**

0240 **15** *shd* **Countrywide Sun**[29] 5596 2-9-3 56 ........ (p) TPQueally 16 24
(NPLittmoden) *chsd ldrs: lost pl and hmpd 2f out* **14/1**

0040 **16** *6* **Northern Revoque (IRE)**[56] 4907 2-8-0 45 ........ SRighton 3 —
(ABerry) *w ldr early: rdn and lost pl over 3f out: sn bhd* **66/1**

0005 **17** *1/2* **Pips Pearl (IRE)**[44] 5218 2-7-7 45 ........ (vt) DFentiman(7) 19 —
(MrsPNDutfield) *s.v.s: a wl bhd* **33/1**

1m 28.14s (3.24) **Going Correction** +0.45s/f (Yiel) **17** Ran SP% **129.3**

Speed ratings: **99,94,93,92,91 91,88,87,86,82 80,76,76,76,75 69,68**CSF £188.40 TOTE £5.50: £2.10, £6.00, £3.60; EX 85.00.The winner was claimed by David Nicholls for £10,000.

**Owner** Kennet Valley Thoroughbreds VI **Bred** Mrs D O Joly **Trained** Middleham Moor, N Yorks

**FOCUS**

A decent time for a juvenile claimer, fractionally faster than the later three-year-old handicap over the same trip, though that was run on ground made ever softer by the persistent rain. The winner is a cut above claiming class at his best.

**NOTEBOOK**

**Exit Smiling**, who has struggled in nursery company over further, looked a cut above in the paddock and so it proved in the race itself. David Nicholls was soon on the phone to claim him.

**Bella Plunkett(IRE)**, suited by the straight track, achieved her first placing on her fifth start.

**Ifit(IRE)**, who looked very fit indeed, stayed on strongly after struggling to go the pace and a return to further will be in her favour.

**Bond Finesse(IRE)**, back on turf, travelled strongly but tended to hang one way then the other off the bridle. *Official explanation: jockey said filly hung both ways*

**After The Snow(IRE)**, who is only small, showed a lot more than on her debut two weeks earlier.

**Pro Tempore**, a keen type, was always tending to do just too much and did not see out the final furlong as well as others.

**Sweet Potato(IRE)** was awash with sweat at the start on a cold, wet day.

**Branston Lily**, having her second outing for this yard, was again very disappointing.

**Pips Pearl(IRE)** *Official explanation: jockey said filly missed break*

### 6196 EUROPEAN BREEDERS FUND MAIDEN FILLIES' STKS 6f

2:00 (2:06) (D3) 2-Y-O £4,810 (£1,480; £740; £370) **Stalls** Centre

Form RPR

033 **1** **Desert Imp**[30] 5569 2-8-11 78 ........ RWinston 6 80+
(BWHills) *trckd ldrs: hdwy 1/2-way: led wl over 1f out: sn rdn and kpt on* **9/2**[3]

5 **2** *1 1/2* **Fashion House (USA)**[30] 5569 2-8-11 ........ JCarroll 9 73
(SaeedBinSuroor) *led: pushed along over 2f out: rdn and hdd wl over 1f out: drvn and one pce* **9/1**

633 **3** *nk* **Miss Trial**[22] 5747 2-8-11 71 ........ RMullen 1 72
(MAJarvis) *stdd s and hld up in rr: hdwy and pushed along 1/2-way: swtchd lft and rdn over 1f out: kpt on ins last: nrst fin* **4/1**[2]

**4** *1/2* **Gildas Fortuna** 2-8-11 ........ GFaulkner 7 70
(PCHaslam) *tall: unf: dwlt: sn in midfield: hdwy to chse ldrs over 2f out: sn rdn and kpt on same pce appr last* **50/1**

**5** *2 1/2* **Westlake Bond (IRE)** 2-8-11 ........ FLynch 14 63
(BSmart) *cmpt: in tch on wd outside: hdwy over 2f out: sn rdn and no imp appr last* **28/1**

**6** *1* **La Viola** 2-8-11 ........ DarrenWilliams 12 60
(KRBurke) *lengthy: unf: dwlt: sn in midfield: hdwy to chse ldrs 1/2-way: rdn over 2f out and grad wknd* **40/1**

02 **7** *shd* **Lady Doris Watts**[6] 6060 2-8-11 ........ SHitchcott 13 59
(MRChannon) *chsd ldr: pushed along 1/2-way: rdn 2f out and grad wknd* **11/1**

000 **8** *3* **Shekan Star**[62] 4761 2-8-11 ........ DaleGibson 15 50
(KGReveley) *a midfield* **100/1**

5 **9** *2* **Archeology (USA)**[13] 5943 2-8-11 ........ KMcEvoy 10 44
(SaeedBinSuroor) *chsd ldrs: pushed along 1/2-way: sn rdn and wknd 2f out* **13/8**[1]

50 **10** *6* **Some Night (IRE)**[49] 5070 2-8-11 ........ NPollard 11 26
(JHMGosden) *chsd ldrs: rdn along 1/2-way: sn wknd* **33/1**

**11** *1 1/4* **Celtic Carisma** 2-8-11 ........ PHanagan 5 23
(KGReveley) *unf: scope: bkwd: s.i.s: a rr* **50/1**

06 **12** *2 1/2* **Rainbow Treasure (IRE)**[28] 5604 2-8-8 ........ TEaves(3) 2 15
(JSGoldie) *in tch: rdn along 1/2-way: sn wknd* **80/1**

**13** *1/2* **Madame Guillotine** 2-8-11 ........ JEdmunds 8 14
(JBalding) *rangy: scope: bhd fr 1/2-way* **66/1**

**14** *9* **Gifted Lass** 2-8-11 ........ DAllan 3 —
(JBalding) *bkwd: s.i.s: a rr* **50/1**

1m 14.78s (3.08) **Going Correction** +0.45s/f (Yiel) **14** Ran SP% **113.0**

Speed ratings: **97,95,94,93,90 89,89,85,82,74 72,69,68,56**CSF £38.69 TOTE £5.30: £1.30, £2.40, £1.80; EX 25.50.

**Owner** Maktoum Al Maktoum **Bred** Gainsborough Stud Management Ltd **Trained** Lambourn, Berks

**FOCUS**

A fair maiden by Redcar standards. The form looks solid.

**NOTEBOOK**

**Desert Imp**, warm beforehand, had to dig deep but was right on top at the finish. This was a fair maiden and she appeared to improve again.

**Fashion House(USA)**, led to the start this time, made the running and fought back well after looking likely to be swamped by the winner. She can win a similar race.

**Miss Trial**, who continually swished her tail in the paddock, will be suited by a return to seven furlongs.

**Gildas Fortuna**, a February foal, is very much up in the air. She gave a good account of herself on her debut and will be a stronger filly next year.

**Westlake Bond(IRE)**, a February foal, lacks size and scope but made a highly satisfactory debut.

**La Viola**, an April foal, showed ability first time but she looks more of a prospect for next year.

**Archeology(USA)**, a tall filly, was in trouble at halfway and wanted to do nothing but hang right-handed. *Official explanation: jockey said filly hung right*

### 6197 REDCARRACING.CO.UK MEDIAN AUCTION MAIDEN STKS 1m

2:35 (2:37) (F4) 2-Y-O £3,318 (£948; £474) **Stalls** Centre

Form RPR

033 **1** **Duroob**[25] 5688 2-9-0 72 ........ PHanagan 12 72
(EALDunlop) *w ldrs: slt ld over 1f out: styd on wl towards fin* **3/1**[2]

4522 **2** *1/2* **William Tell (IRE)**[6] 6072 2-9-0 78 ........ SHitchcott 6 71
(MRChannon) *led after 2f: rdn and hung lft 2f out: sn hdd: no ex wl ins last* **7/4**[1]

**3** *3 1/2* **Three Wrens (IRE)** 2-8-9 ........ SWKelly 7 58
(DJDaly) *rangy: unf: prom early: sn outpcd: hdwy over 3f out: kpt on same pce* **9/1**

66 **4** *nk* **Wood Spirit (IRE)**[31] 5536 2-8-9 ........ NPollard 10 58
(MrsPNDutfield) *s.i.s: hdwy over 2f out: kpt on: nvr nr to chal* **25/1**

**5** *1* **Woodbury Lane (USA)** 2-8-9 ........ KMcEvoy 5 55
(SaeedBinSuroor) *big: tall: swvd lft s: sn chsng ldrs: rdn over 2f out: kpt on same pce* **9/2**[3]

4060 **6** *1* **Our Choice (IRE)**[49] 5090 2-9-0 59 ........ TPQueally 3 58
(NPLittmoden) *chsd ldrs: one pce fnl 2f* **20/1**

04 **7** *1 3/4* **Hoh My Darling**[18] 5840 2-8-9 ........ RMullen 8 49
(MLWBell) *chsd ldrs: outpcd fnl 2f* **8/1**

6400 **8** *10* **Paris Heights**[11] 5989 2-8-9 63 ........ (v[1]) BSwarbrick(5) 11 32
(RMWhitaker) *led 2f: w ldrs: rdn and lost pl over 2f out* **25/1**

00 **9** *8* **Be Bop**[32] 5522 2-9-0 ........ KimTinkler 9 15
(NTinkler) *chsd ldrs: drvn along 4f out: sn lost pl* **50/1**

0 **10** *3 1/2* **Cliffie (IRE)**[22] 5752 2-9-0 ........ SRighton 4 7
(JHetherton) *hmpd s: a bhd* **100/1**

0 **11** *1 3/4* **Maynooth Prince (IRE)**[16] 5855 2-9-0 ........ JCarroll 1 3
(HAlexander) *mid-div: lost pl over 3f out: sn bhd* **100/1**

0 **12** *11* **Judge Damuss (IRE)**[62] 4761 2-9-0 ........ LEnstone 2 —
(ACrook) *in tch: lost pl over 3f out: sn bhd* **100/1**

1m 43.13s (5.43) **Going Correction** +0.45s/f (Yiel) **12** Ran SP% **118.0**

Speed ratings: **90,89,86,85,84 83,81,71,63,60 58,47**CSF £8.12 TOTE £4.40: £1.50, £1.10, £2.70; EX 8.20.

**Owner** Hamdan Al Maktoum **Bred** Shadwell Estate Company Limited **Trained** Newmarket, Suffolk

**FOCUS**

The two market leaders pulled clear, but this looks no more than a fair maiden. The favourite appeared to run below form, and the race has been rated through the fourth.

**NOTEBOOK**

**Duroob**, up a furlong in trip, settled nicely and saw the mile out very well, getting off the mark with a hard-fought success. He would be interesting if turned out in a nursery under a penalty, and should not be underestimated when reassessed.

**William Tell(IRE)**, second to decent sorts in Something Exciting and Mister Genepi on his previous two starts, did not have anything of their calibre to contend with but was still just held. There is a similar race in him, but he is clearly vulnerable to anything useful.

**Three Wrens(IRE)**, a 26,000gns half-sister to a smart ten-furlong performer in France, a mile winner and a five-furlong juvenile scorer, made a satisfactory debut. She looks the type to progress and might be up to winning in similar company with normal improvement.

**Wood Spirit(IRE)**, stepped up two furlongs in trip, never really threatened the principals but still showed ability. She is going the right way and is now qualified for a handicap mark.

**Woodbury Lane(USA)**, out of an unraced half-sister to a US sprint winner, proved easy to back and was well held. She should come on quite a bit for the experience and faster ground will probably suit, but she will need to improve.

**Our Choice(IRE)** ran his best race yet but is always likely to struggle in maidens.

**Maynooth Prince(IRE)** *Official explanation: jockey said gelding hit its head in stalls*

**Judge Damuss(IRE)** *Official explanation: jockey said colt lost his action two furlongs out*

### 6198 WEATHERBYS INSURANCE SERVICES H'CAP 1m 6f 19y

3:10 (3:11) (E3) (0-70,69) 3-Y-O+ £7,787 (£2,396; £1,198; £599) **Stalls** Low

Form RPR

2322 **1** **Most Definitely (IRE)**[13] 5951 4-9-5 65 ........ DAllan 9 77
(TDEasterby) *hld up and bhd: smooth hdwy over 3f out: effrt to ld and hung rt wl over 1f out: sn rdn clr and styed on* **8/1**

0431 **2** *3/4* **Wing Collar**[30] 5560 3-9-0 69 ........ FLynch 3 81+
(TDEasterby) *hld up in tch: shuffled bk on bnd 6f out: gd hdwy 3f out: nt clr run over 1f out: rdn and styd on ins last: nt rch wnr* **9/1**

2302 **3** *2 1/2* **Danebank (IRE)**[11] 5993 4-8-9 55 oh3 ........ (p) DaleGibson 15 63
(JMackie) *trckd ldrs: hdwy over 3f out: sn rdn: drvn and edgd lft over 1f out: kpt on* **15/2**

0000 **4** *1* **Silvertown**[5] 6096 9-9-3 66 ........ PMulrennan(3) 12 72
(LLungo) *midfield: gd hdwy 3f out: nt clr run and swtchd rt 2f out: rdn and swtchd lft over 1f out: kpt on u.p ins last* **20/1**

5015 **5** *hd* **Ivy League Star (IRE)**[13] 5956 3-9-0 69 ........ RWinston 4 75
(BWHills) *trckd ldrs: hdwy 4f out: rdn along and ch whn sltly hmpd wl over 1f out: sn drvn and one pce* **5/1**[1]

0336 **6** *1* **Macaroni Gold (IRE)**[42] 5274 4-8-7 58 ........ DTudhope(5) 10 62
(WJarvis) *hld up in rr: hdwy on outer 5f out: rdn along over 2f out: kpt on same pce* **7/1**[3]

5005 **7** *3* **Salamba**[6] 6074 3-8-11 66 ........ SHitchcott 1 66
(MHTompkins) *chsd ldrs: hdwy to ld 3f out: sn rdn: drvn and hdd wl over 1f out: sn wknd* **7/1**[3]

3343 **8** ½ **Hearthstead Dream**[6] 6074 3-9-0 **69**.....(b) TPQueally 14 69
(JDBethell) *hld up in midfield: gd hdwy 5f out: rdn to chal 3f out and ev ch tl drvn and wknd fnl 2f* **6/1**[2]

5240 **9** 3 **East Cape**[32] 5523 7-8-9 **55** oh10..... KimTinkler 8 50
(DonEnricoIncisa) *hld up and bhd: sme hdwy 3f out: sn rdn and nvr a factor* **33/1**

6253 **10** 1 ¼ **Majestic Vision**[16] 5875 3-8-13 **68**..... KMcEvoy 5 62
(PWHarris) *led: rdn along 4f out: hdd 3f out and sn wknd* **6/1**[2]

1000 **11** 2 **Zan Lo (IRE)**[6] 6074 4-8-6 **55** oh6..... TEaves(3) 6 46
(BSRothwell) *chsd ldrs: rdn along 4f out: sn wknd* **33/1**

6560 **12** 5 **Weet For Me**[28] 5619 8-9-9 **69**..... RFrench 7 53
(RHollinshead) *chsd ldr: wd st: rdn along 4f out and sn wknd* **20/1**

3m 10.37s (5.37) **Going Correction** +0.45s/f (Yiel)
**WFA** 3 from 4yo+ 9lb **12** Ran SP% **118.5**
Speed ratings: **102,101,100,99,99 98,97,96,95,94 93,90**CSF £74.06 CT £563.84 TOTE £8.50: £3.10, £4.10, £3.10; EX 33.90.
**Owner** B Batey **Bred** Gay O'Callaghan **Trained** Great Habton, N Yorks

**FOCUS**
A modest handicap in which the pace was reasonable given the conditions (the first two came from well off the gallop), although some of these still raced keenly. The race has been rated around the consistent third, and the first two both improved a little.

**NOTEBOOK**
**Most Definitely(IRE)** ◆ was a maiden after 20 starts going into this and had not always found that much under pressure but, under a patient ride, he picked up when well in the clear and always looked like holding off the fast-finishing runner-up. Now he has got his head in front, he is just the type to follow up.
**Wing Collar**, 4lb higher than when off the mark over a mile and a half on fast ground at Beverley on his previous start, was a little unlucky as he had to wait for a gap and be switched at a crucial point. He could go hurdling, but should continue to go well if kept to the Flat.
**Danebank(IRE)**, back to form when runner-up at Pontefract on his previous start, was racing over his furthest trip to date on the Flat and proved no match for the front two. He handles this sort of ground, but may just be better on a fast surface.
**Silvertown** has been very disappointing this year, including over hurdles, but this was much better and he would have been even closer with a clearer run.
**Ivy League Star(IRE)** looked the type that might run up a sequence when getting off the mark at Haydock two starts previously, but so far it would appear the Handicapper already has her measure.
**Hearthstead Dream** has won in blinkers three times, but failed to perform with them back on and this trip appeared to stretch him.
**Majestic Vision** shaped well when third under similar conditions at Salisbury on his previous start, so this was disappointing.

## 6199 "BOOK YOUR WEDDING RECEPTION AT REDCAR RACECOURSE!" H'CAP 7f
**3:45** (3:46) (E3) (0-70,73) 3-Y-O **£5,213** (£1,604; £802; £401) **Stalls** Centre

Form RPR

3060 **1** **Scientist**[16] 5868 3-9-0 **66**..... KMcEvoy 12 77
(JHMGosden) *led after 2f: qcknd clr over 3f out: styd on: unchal* **7/1**[2]

0516 **2** 1 ½ **Seneschal**[3] 6138 3-9-0 **73** 6ex..... TO'Brien(7) 11 80
(MRChannon) *bhd: hdwy over 2f out: hung lft fnl f: kpt on: no real imp* **2/1**[1]

2060 **3** nk **Uhuru Peak**[31] 5547 3-8-4 **56** oh6.....(b) DaleGibson 4 62
(MWEasterby) *s.i.s: sn trcking ldrs: edgd rt over 3f out: kpt on wl fnl f* **20/1**

0000 **4** ½ **Cheverak Forest (IRE)**[11] 5992 3-8-4 **56** oh1.....(t) KimTinkler 13 61
(DonEnricoIncisa) *dwlt: bhd: hdwy over 2f out: kpt on same pce appr fnl f* **40/1**

0000 **5** 1 **Mind Alert**[16] 5862 3-8-8 **60**..... DAllan 1 62
(MissJACamacho) *trckd ldrs far side: kpt on same pce fnl 2f* **25/1**

4020 **6** 1 **Go Yellow**[6] 6064 3-8-12 **67**..... DNolan(3) 6 67
(PDEvans) *trckd ldrs: outpcd over 2f out: kpt on appr fnl f* **9/1**

3066 **7** shd **Menai Straights**[5] 6094 3-8-11 **63**..... RFrench 9 62
(RFFisher) *led 2f: chsd ldrs: wknd over 1f out* **11/1**

6444 **8** 1 ¼ **Fossgate**[45] 5210 3-8-9 **68**.....(p) JCavanagh(7) 14 64
(JDBethell) *racd stands' side: chsd ldrs: outpcd fnl 2f* **8/1**[3]

6000 **9** 3 **Rene Barbier (IRE)**[17] 5849 3-8-6 **58** ow2..... SHitchcott 3 46
(JAGlover) *racd far side: chsd ldrs: fdd over 1f out* **16/1**

0050 **10** 1 **Sweet Reply**[37] 5399 3-9-2 **68**.....(p) TPQueally 10 54
(IAWood) *bhd: effrt 3f out: hung rt: lost pl 2f out* **14/1**

1600 **11** 1 **Neon Blue**[29] 5582 3-9-4 **70**..... SWKelly 5 53
(RMWhitaker) *chsd ldrs: outpcd over 2f out: sn btn* **8/1**[3]

6060 **12** ¾ **Fitzwarren**[17] 5849 3-7-11 **56** oh4..... AReilly(7) 8 37
(NBycroft) *s.v.s: t.k.h: hdwy after 2f: sn chsng ldrs: lost pl over 2f out* **20/1**

0500 **13** 1 **Alice Blackthorn**[79] 4248 3-8-4 **56** oh2..... RMullen 7 35
(BSmart) *hld up: hdwy over 3f out: rdn and lost pl over 2f out* **20/1**

6050 **14** ½ **Compton Micky**[58] 4853 3-8-4 **56** oh3.....(p) JEdmunds 2 33
(JBalding) *t.k.h: racd far side: trckd ldrs: lost pl over 1f out* **33/1**

1m 28.18s (3.28) **Going Correction** +0.45s/f (Yiel) **14** Ran SP% **122.4**
Speed ratings: **99,97,96,96,95 94,93,92,89,87 86,85,84,84**CSF £19.51 CT £289.51 TOTE £7.50: £2.40, £1.10, £6.50; EX 27.90.
**Owner** Highclere Thoroughbred Racing XII **Bred** Tarworth Bloodstock Investments Ltd **Trained** Manton, Wilts

**FOCUS**
A modest handicap, but the form makes sense.

**NOTEBOOK**
**Scientist**, below form on his last three starts, clearly appreciated both the drop in trip and switch to easy ground, getting off the mark in determined fashion. However, he is probably one to oppose next time.
**Seneschal**, racing for the third time in six days, appeared to run his race and had no real excuse.
**Uhuru Peak**, back up a furlong in trip, probably appreciated this switch to easy ground. He was 6lb out of the proper handicap and ran better than of late.
**Cheverak Forest(IRE)** has shown very little all year, including when second last in a claimer on his previous start, but this was most encouraging and he could be running into form.
**Mind Alert**, making his debut for a new trainer, seemed to run better for the removal of blinkers and step back up in trip.

## 6200 ANNE WEBSTER - LIFETIME IN RACING MAIDEN STKS 6f
**4:20** (4:21) (D3) 3-Y-O+ **£3,802** (£1,170; £585; £292) **Stalls** Centre

Form RPR

6606 **1** **Ligne D'Eau**[25] 5693 3-8-11 53.....(b¹) DNolan(3) 19 65
(PDEvans) *cl up: led after 1f: rdn and wandered over 1f out: drvn and edgd lft ent last: drvn and kpt on* **16/1**

3 **2** nk **Russian Cafe (IRE)**[5] 6089 3-8-9.....(t) RWinston 10 59+
(MAMagnusson) *hld up: pushed along over 2f out: hdwy whn hmpd and swtchd over 1f out: drvn and n.m.r ent last: styd on wl nr fin* **6/5**[1]

4003 **3** ½ **Kamenka**[10] 6009 3-8-9 65.....(v¹) PHanagan 20 58
(RAFahey) *cl up: rdn to chal over 1f out and ev ch tl drvn and nt qckn ins last* **4/1**[2]

0000 **4** nk **Dark Champion**[49] 5081 4-8-10 50..... BSwarbrick(5) 11 62
(REBarr) *chsd ldrs: hdwy 2f out: rdn and ch over 1f out: drvn and nt qckn ins last* **22/1**

**5** nk **Come On** 5-9-1..... JDekeyser 9 61
(JHetherton) *in tch: hdwy centre to chse ldrs 2f out: sn rdn and ev ch over 1f out: drvn and nt qckn ins last* **66/1**

**6** hd **Young Kate** 3-8-9..... TPQueally 16 55
(JRBest) *s.i.s: hdwy to chse ldrs 1/2-way: rdn 2f out: kpt on u.p fnl f* **11/1**

0 **7** 3 **Poetry 'n Passion**[55] 4954 3-8-9..... RFrench 17 46
(CACyzer) *chsd ldrs: rdn over 2f out: drvn and wknd over 1f out* **20/1**

0035 **8** nk **New York (IRE)**[22] 5748 3-8-9 55.....(b¹) SWKelly 2 45
(WJHaggas) *racd alone far side: a prom: rdn wl over 1f out: wknd fnl f* **8/1**[3]

0-02 **9** 1 ½ **Forrest Gump**[20] 5801 4-8-12 52..... TEaves(3) 13 46
(CJTeague) *midfield tl styd on fnl 2f: n.d* **25/1**

00-4 **10** ½ **Rose Of York (IRE)**[20] 5803 4-8-7 53..... PMulrennan(3) 18 39
(TDWalford) *chsd ldrs: rdn along 1/2-way: grad wknd* **33/1**

04/0 **11** 2 **Never Forget Bowie**[53] 4985 8-8-10 40..... DTudhope(5) 15 38
(RAllan) *chsd ldrs: rdn along 1/2-way and sn wknd* **80/1**

-660 **12** ½ **Juniper Banks**[4] 6114 3-8-12 57 ow1..... LFletcher(3) 7 38
(MissAStokell) *chsd ldrs: rdn along 1/2-way and sn wknd* **50/1**

0006 **13** 1 ¼ **Svenson**[10] 6004 3-9-0 30..... DAllan 14 33
(JSWainwright) *led 1f: prom tl rdn along 1/2-way and grad wknd* **100/1**

5245 **14** 1 ½ **M For Magic**[20] 5801 5-8-8 45.....(b) KPierrepont(7) 5 29
(CWFairhurst) *bhd fr 1/2-way* **40/1**

0056 **15** ½ **Pay Time**[20] 5801 5-8-6 40 ow1..... MLawson(5) 6 23
(REBarr) *s.i.s: a rr* **66/1**

0035 **16** 2 ½ **Yorke's Folly (USA)**[31] 5547 3-8-9 45.....(v) LEnstone 8 15
(CWFairhurst) *bhd fr 1/2-way* **25/1**

6000 **17** 3 ½ **Lord Wishingwell (IRE)**[13] 5926 3-9-0 30.....(p) PMQuinn 3 9
(JSWainwright) *midfield: rdn along 1/2-way: sn bhd* **40/1**

**18** 2 **Carmarthen Belle** 4-8-10..... TWilliams 1 —
(MissLCSiddall) *v s.i.s: a wl bhd* **66/1**

**19** 17 **Merlin's City** 4-8-10..... DaleGibson 12 —
(MissLCSiddall) *s.i.s: a wl bhd* **66/1**

1m 14.0s (2.30) **Going Correction** +0.45s/f (Yiel)
**WFA** 3 from 4yo+ 1lb **19** Ran SP% **125.6**
Speed ratings: **102,101,100,100,100 99,95,95,93,92 90,89,87,85,85 81,77,74,51**CSF £32.30 TOTE £18.30: £5.10, £1.10, £1.60; EX 86.10.
**Owner** M W Lawrence **Bred** M W Lawrence **Trained** Pandy, Gwent

**FOCUS**
A very moderate maiden. Hand-timed.

**NOTEBOOK**
**Ligne D'Eau**, dropped back from a mile and with blinkers on for the first time, got off the mark at the 11th attempt under a positive ride. He is likely to find things tougher in future, especially if he goes up in the weights for this, and could be one to take on next time.
**Russian Cafe(IRE)**, third in a better maiden than this first time out, ran well below that form but would have won with a clearer run. On this evidence she is just modest.
**Kamenka** was the highest rated of those with official figures, but again found a couple too good and was well below her summer form. The visor did not appear to help significantly.
**Dark Champion** ran better than of late, but has had 32 attempts.
**Come On** is out of a middle-distance/staying winner, so it was a surprise to see him show so much pace. This was a promising debut and he should improve.
**Young Kate**, a half-sister to the high-class seven-furlong/miler Young Ern, showed signs of inexperience but offered some promise.
**Pay Time** *Official explanation: trainer said mare lost a fore shoe and was lame following morning*

## 6201 REDCAR RACECOURSE CONFERENCE CENTRE H'CAP 1m 1f
**4:55** (4:57) (F4) (0-55,55) 3-Y-O+ **£3,961** (£1,219; £609; £304) **Stalls** Low

Form RPR

0025 **1** **Time To Regret**[24] 5714 4-8-10 **51**..... PHanagan 3 64+
(JSWainwright) *in tch: poised whn nt clr run over 2f out: led over 1f out: sn rdn clr* **8/1**[3]

402 **2** 5 **Explode**[70] 4511 7-8-11 **52**..... TWilliams 10 55
(MissLCSiddall) *hld up in mid-div: smooth hdwy on wd outside 4f out: led over 2f out: hdd over 1f out: kpt on same pce* **12/1**

0000 **3** ½ **The Wizard Mul**[39] 5346 4-8-10 **51**..... JBramhill 11 53
(WStorey) *hld up and bhd: hdwy over 3f out: styd on same pce fnl f* **33/1**

0000 **4** hd **Sedge (USA)**[30] 5557 4-8-11 **52**..... LEnstone 12 54
(PTMidgley) *chsd ldrs: effrt over 3f out: one pce fnl 2f* **16/1**

5505 **5** hd **Apache Point (IRE)**[16] 5859 7-8-10 **51**..... KimTinkler 5 52
(NTinkler) *hld up towards rr: effrt and edgd lft over 3f out: styd on fnl 2f: nvr nr to chal* **3/1**[1]

0134 **6** 3 **Calculaite**[13] 5957 3-8-10 **55**..... KMcEvoy 4 50
(MrsGSRees) *trckd ldrs: nt clr run on inner 3f out: swtchd outside 2f out: styd on fnl f* **8/1**[3]

0000 **7** 1 ¼ **Arawan (IRE)**[87] 4008 4-8-12 **53**..... DaleGibson 2 46
(MWEasterby) *lost pl and wl bhd after 2f: styd on fnl 2f: nvr on terms* **16/1**

1060 **8** hd **Westcourt Dream**[31] 5546 4-8-5 **49**..... PMulrennan(3) 16 41
(MWEasterby) *chsd ldrs: drvn along over 3f out: outpcd fnl 2f* **20/1**

0032 **9** nk **Graceful Air (IRE)**[18] 5830 3-8-1 **53**.....(p) DFentiman(7) 1 45
(JRWeymes) *mid-div: drvn along and hmpd over 4f out: outpcd fnl 3f* **14/1**

0030 **10** 5 **Golden Spectrum (IRE)**[13] 5945 5-8-7 **51**..... TEaves(3) 7 33
(DNicholls) *hld up and bhd: effrt 4f out: lost pl 2f out* **20/1**

0031 **11** 4 **Penwell Hill (USA)**[34] 5450 5-8-5 **51**..... PMakin(5) 14 25
(TDBarron) *trckd ldr: led 3f out: sn hdd & wknd* **6/1**[2]

3030 **12** 3 **Senor Eduardo**[11] 5993 7-9-0 **55**..... NPollard 15 23
(SGollings) *trckd ldrs: drvn along 5f out: lost pl over 2f out* **16/1**

1006 **13** 7 **Rocinante (IRE)**[81] 4190 4-8-12 **53**..... RWinston 8 7
(JJQuinn) *in tch: effrt 3f out: sn btn* **20/1**

0400 **14** 6 **Iftikhar (USA)**[16] 5867 5-8-11 **52**.....(b¹) SWKelly 6 —
(WMBrisbourne) *trckd ldrs: lost pl 2f out: sn bhd and eased: b.b.v* **25/1**

0016 **15** 1 **Royal Racer (FR)**[24] 5714 6-8-11 **52**.....(b) TPQueally 13 —
(JRBest) *led tl 3f out: hrd rdn and hung lft: sn lost pl: eased* **10/1**

1m 56.0s (2.60) **Going Correction** +0.45s/f (Yiel)
**WFA** 3 from 4yo+ 4lb **15** Ran SP% **123.7**
Speed ratings: **106,101,101,100,100 98,96,96,96,92 88,85,79,74,73**CSF £94.25 CT £3075.60 TOTE £12.70: £3.50, £5.90, £8.90; EX 89.90 Place 6 £125.58, Place 5 £30.14.
**Owner** Denison Arms **Bred** Speedlith Group **Trained** Kennythorpe, N Yorks

**FOCUS**
Just a moderate handicap but a decent time for the type of contest and the form looks sound. The winner was impressive and looked better than ever.

**NOTEBOOK**
**Time To Regret** did not have things go his way at Beverley on his previous start, but there were few problems this time around and he ran out an emphatic winner. This is career-best form and he would be hard to beat if turned out under a penalty.
**Explode** ran another solid race without posing a serious threat to the winner. He has clearly found his level.
**The Wizard Mul**, with the blinkers left off, had never previously been this far but had ground conditions in his favour and ran creditably.
**Sedge(USA)** travelled well but was one paced when in the clear and this ground was probably soft enough.
**Apache Point(IRE)**, without a win since July 2003, came from an unpromising position to take fifth without landing a serious blow.
**Calculaite** *Official explanation: jockey said gelding was denied a clear run*
**Westcourt Dream** *Official explanation: jockey said filly lost her action*
**Penwell Hill(USA)** gained his only previous turf win on fast ground and did not get home after racing keenly.
**Iftikhar(USA)** *Official explanation: jockey said gelding bled from nose*
T/Plt: £32.50 to a £1 stake. Pool: £30,789.10. 691.25 winning tickets. T/Qpdt: £4.90 to a £1 stake. Pool: £2,785.90. 412.40 winning tickets. JR

# 6137 MAISONS-LAFFITTE (R-H)
Friday, October 15

**OFFICIAL GOING: Very soft changing to holding after race 1 (12:50)**

## 6202a CRITERIUM DE VITESSE (LISTED RACE) 5f
1:50 (1:53) 2-Y-O £15,845 (£6,338; £4,754; £3,169)

RPR
1 **Centifolia (FR)**[17] 2-8-8 .......... IMendizabal 5 111+
(RobertCollet, France)
2 4 **Salut Thomas (FR)**[14] 5922 2-9-2 ..........(b) CSoumillon 1 109
(RobertCollet, France)
3 4 **Key Secret**[28] 5602 2-8-8 .......... HayleyTurner 7 90
(MLWBell) *racd in 2nd on outside, relegated to 3rd 2f out, outpcd by first two but styd on gamely under pressure to hld 3rd fnl f*
4 snk **Semarang**[24] 5726 2-8-11 .......... TGillet 3 93
(JEPease, France)
5 3/4 **Princesse Jasmine (FR)**[14] 5922 2-8-8 .......... C-PLemaire 2 88
(YDeNicolay, France)
6 1 1/2 **Great Blood (FR)**[37] 5404 2-8-12 .......... OPeslier 6 88
(XThomas-Demeaulte, France)
7 4 **Azzuri (GER)** 2-8-8 .......... J-PCarvalho 4 74
(MarioHofer, Germany)
59.50 secs 7 Ran
Speed ratings: .
**Owner** S Berland **Bred** Sca De La Perrigne **Trained** France

**NOTEBOOK**
**Key Secret** was always going to face an uphill task as her form was not good enough to win at this sort of level and although finishing third, was well held. She got some black type though and it was job done for connections.

## 6203a PRIX DE SAINT-CYR (LISTED RACE) (FILLIES) 7f (S)
2:50 (2:55) 3-Y-O £15,845 (£6,338; £4,754; £3,169)

RPR
1 **Dalna (FR)**[37] 5405 3-8-12 .......... SPasquier 8 105
(MmeCHead-Maarek, France)
2 1/2 **Dolma (FR)**[37] 5405 3-9-2 .......... C-PLemaire 9 107
(NClement, France)
3 3 **Coupe De Champe (FR)**[37] 5405 3-9-2 .......... GBenoist 2 100
(PTual, France)
4 hd **Risque De Verglas (FR)**[17] 3-8-12 .......... TGillet 3 95
(MmeR-WAllen, France)
5 2 1/2 **Madhya (USA)**[94] 3-8-12 .......... IMendizabal 7 89
(ADeRoyer-Dupre, France)
6 shd **Malaica (FR)**[73] 3-8-12 .......... TJarnet 5 89
(RPritchard-Gordon, France)
7 1 **River Of Babylon**[23] 5740 3-8-12 .......... HayleyTurner 1 86
(MLWBell) *close up on inside racing keenly, led briefly 2 1/2f out, soon headed, ridden and weakened*
8 1 1/2 **Via Milano (FR)**[73] 4430 3-8-12 .......... TThulliez 4 83
(MmeJLaurent-JoyeRossi, France)
9 3 **Rekindled Applause**[167] 1778 3-8-12 .......... DPorcu 6 75
(MGuarnieri, Italy)
10 3/4 **Indian Beauty (IRE)**[23] 3-8-12 .......... JCrocquevieille 11 73
(PVanDePoele, France)
0 **Marching West (USA)**[119] 3-8-12 .......... CSoumillon 15 —
(AFabre, France)
0 **Glad Lady (GER)**[378] 5353 3-8-12 ..........(b) J-PCarvalho 13 —
(EKurdu, Germany)
0 **Silent Flight (FR)**[14] 5923 3-8-12 .......... DBoeuf 14 —
(MlleHVanZuylen, France)
0 **Landerneau (IRE)**[44] 5255 3-8-12 .......... OPeslier 10 —
(RobertCollet, France)
0 **Casigris (USA)**[187] 1349 3-8-12 .......... MBlancpain 12 —
(CLaffon-Parias, France)
1m 28.3s 15 Ran
Speed ratings: .
**Owner** Mme A Head **Bred** Alec & Mme Ghislaine Head **Trained** France

**NOTEBOOK**
**River Of Babylon**, successful the last twice in lesser company, had her chance and was not up to the task.

# 6002 CATTERICK (L-H)
Saturday, October 16

**OFFICIAL GOING: Good to soft changing to soft after race 5 (4.10)**
The ground was reckoned almost soft after race one and it became ever more testing.
Wind: Moderate 1/2 against. Weather: Persistent rain.

## 6204 RACING UK LIVE ON 432 E B F NOVICE STKS 5f
1:50 (1:51) (D4) 2-Y-O £3,460 (£1,064; £532; £266) Stalls Low

Form RPR
316 1 **Regina**[44] 5250 2-9-0 88 .......... RWinston 5 89
(SirMichaelStoute) *mde all: rdn and edgd lft fr 2f out: hld on wl* **15/8**[1]
2501 2 1 **Bond City (IRE)**[9] 6023 2-9-9 91 .......... FLynch 7 94
(BSmart) *in tch: hdwy to chse wnr over 2f out: rdn and kpt on ins fnl f* **2/1**[2]
252 3 10 **Born For Dancing (IRE)**[15] 5908 2-8-7 73 .......... ACulhane 6 43
(BWHills) *chsd ldrs tl outpcd fr 1/2-way* **7/2**[3]
0400 4 1 3/4 **World At My Feet**[14] 5947 2-9-0 81 ..........(b[1]) NCallan 2 44
(NBycroft) *prom to 1/2-way: sn outpcd* **17/2**
4023 5 1 1/2 **Thornber Court (IRE)**[11] 6002 2-8-2 64 .......... PPMathers[(5)] 1 32
(ABerry) *s.i.s: nvr on terms* **12/1**
060 6 7 **Cilla's Smile**[14] 5947 2-8-7 55 .......... DaleGibson 3 7
(MABuckley) *prom: hung lft thrght: wknd fr 1/2-way* **50/1**
00 7 2 **Miss Jellybean (IRE)**[33] 5513 2-8-4 .......... PMulrennan[(3)] 4 —
(NTinkler) *chsd ldrs to 1/2-way: sn rdn and btn* **66/1**
61.86 secs (1.26) **Going Correction** +0.20s/f (Good) **7 Ran SP% 112.0**
Speed ratings: **97,95,79,76,74 63,59**CSF £5.66 TOTE £2.30: £1.30, £2.10; EX 7.50.
**Owner** Cheveley Park Stud **Bred** Cheveley Park Stud Ltd **Trained** Newmarket, Suffolk

**FOCUS**
A decent novice event with the first two dominating and finishing some way clear, the form could prove slightly better.

**NOTEBOOK**
**Regina**, taken to post early, always looked to be holding the whiphand though in the end she had to dig deep. The easy ground was no problem and this is probably as far as she wants to go at this stage.
**Bond City(IRE)** went in pursuit of the winner but conceding 9lb was always going to finish second best. The plan is to winter him in Dubai.
**Born For Dancing(IRE)**, who looked very fit, had the headgear left off and she was left toiling by the first two from the halfway mark.
**World At My Feet**, in first-time blinkers, was well below her best. On official ratings she ought to have finished on the heels of the runner-up.
**Thornber Court(IRE)**, very edgy beforehand, found this a whole lot tougher.
**Cilla's Smile** gave her rider problems hanging violently left throughout. *Official explanation: jockey said filly hung left throughout*

## 6205 TOTESCOOP6 CATTERICK DASH (A H'CAP) 5f
2:25 (2:26) (D2) (0-92,86) 3-Y-O+ £13,942 (£4,290; £2,145; £1,072) Stalls Low

Form RPR
6106 1 **Malapropism**[14] 5933 4-9-7 82 .......... ACulhane 3 93
(MRChannon) *in tch far side: rdn to ld that gp 1f out: kpt on wl* **14/1**
5035 2 1/2 **Further Outlook (USA)**[21] 5787 10-9-7 82 ..........(p) NCallan 14 91
(DKIvory) *led stands side: rdn 2f out: kpt on wl: jst hld by far side wnr* **6/1**[2]
2003 3 1 **Dancing Mystery**[26] 5704 10-9-4 79 ..........(b) SCarson 15 84
(EAWheeler) *cl up gng wl stands side: effrt over 1f out: r.o fnl f* **8/1**[3]
5640 4 3/4 **Sir Desmond**[29] 5603 6-9-1 76 ..........(p) TPQueally 4 79
(RGuest) *in tch far side: effrt 2f out: kpt on fnl f: no imp* **12/1**
0004 5 1 1/4 **Artie**[21] 5799 5-9-10 85 .......... RWinston 10 83
(TDEasterby) *prom stands side: effrt over 2f out: one pce appr fnl f* **11/2**[1]
5001 6 hd **Jadan (IRE)**[19] 5837 3-9-3 78 .......... DAllan 13 75
(EJAlston) *hld up stands side: hdwy 2f out: kpt on: no imp* **6/1**[2]
6030 7 1 **Handsome Cross (IRE)**[31] 5563 3-9-1 79 .......... LFletcher[(3)] 9 73
(HMorrison) *prom on outside of stands side gp: rdn 1/2-way: one pce over 1f out* **16/1**
0040 8 nk **Bond Boy**[28] 5628 7-9-11 86 .......... FLynch 2 79
(BSmart) *cl up far side tl rdn and no ex over 1f out* **11/1**
0050 9 1 **Sierra Vista**[29] 5603 4-9-2 77 .......... LEnstone 5 66
(DWBarker) *cl up far side: led that gp briefly over 1f out: one pce* **14/1**
3000 10 nk **Baron Rhodes**[27] 5671 3-9-2 80 .......... TEaves[(3)] 12 68
(JSWainwright) *prom stands side: rdn over 2f out: outpcd over 1f out* **14/1**
1450 11 1/2 **Currency**[17] 5874 7-8-10 76 .......... DTudhope[(5)] 11 62
(JMBradley) *bhd stands side: rdn 1/2-way: n.d* **25/1**
5132 12 1 **Tag Team (IRE)**[108] 3420 3-9-1 76 .......... DaneO'Neill 1 59
(AMBalding) *led far side to over 1f out: sn btn* **12/1**
0000 13 2 **Pax**[29] 5605 7-9-3 78 .......... ANicholls 7 54
(DNicholls) *dwlt: bhd: effrt on outside of stands side gp over 1f out: n.d* **33/1**
0040 14 2 **Snow Wolf**[31] 5563 3-9-3 78 .......... DaleGibson 8 46
(JMBradley) *hld up stands side: rdn 1/2-way: sn btn* **33/1**
2010 15 1/2 **Awake**[70] 4538 7-9-9 84 .......... SWKelly 16 51
(DNicholls) *trckd stands side ldrs: rdn over 2f out: wknd over 1f out* **16/1**
61.68 secs (1.08) **Going Correction** +0.35s/f (Good) **15 Ran SP% 120.3**
Speed ratings: **105,104,102,101,99 99,97,97,95,94 94,92,89,86,85**CSF £93.29 CT £743.93 TOTE £14.70: £5.80, £2.40, £2.60; EX 131.70.
**Owner** Michael A Foy **Bred** Michael A Foy **Trained** West Ilsley, Berks

**FOCUS**
The most valuable event run on the Flat at this track and a fair handicap providing a solid level of form. They split into two groups with the first two on opposite wings.

**NOTEBOOK**
**Malapropism**, one of five to race on the far side, responded to a vigorous ride to record his sixth career success but his first on soft ground.
**Further Outlook(USA)**, in first-time cheekpieces, had ground conditions to suit and, after fighting off his one sole serious challenger on the stands' side, at the line he was only second best with the winner on the opposite wing.
**Dancing Mystery** continues in good form but he looks rated to the limit at present.
**Sir Desmond** ran a lot better than Ayr and finished second best on the far side.
**Artie** could never summon the pace to land a blow and five furlongs, even on this ground, is too sharp for him especially on a downhill track such as this.
**Jadan(IRE)**, raised 4lb for his Hamilton success, found this company a good deal tougher.



The Form Book, Raceform Ltd, Compton, RG20 6NL

## 6206 CATTERICKBRIDGE.CO.UK NURSERY 7f
3:00 (3:04) (D2) (0-85,83) 2-Y-O £7,182 (£2,210; £1,105; £552) Stalls Low

Form RPR

2030 **1** **Knock Bridge (IRE)**$^{6}$ [6080] 2-8-3 **65** ................ TPQueally 2 72
(PDEvans) *prom: swtchd to outside of stands side gp over 1f out: led ins last: r.o wl* **14/1**

4030 **2** *nk* **Game Lad**$^{12}$ [5989] 2-8-11 **73** ................ DAllan 15 79
(TDEasterby) *cl up: swtchd to stands side over 2f out: led over 1f out to ins last: r.o* **9/1**

2622 **3** *1 ½* **Forfeiter (USA)**$^{117}$ [3145] 2-9-0 **76** ................ NCallan 14 78
(TDBarron) *pressed ldr: c stands side and led over 2f out: hdd over 1f out: rallied: kpt on* **50/1**

5005 **4** *nk* **Wayward Shot (IRE)**$^{28}$ [5636] 2-7-12 **60** oh2 ................ DaleGibson 8 62
(MWEasterby) *midfield: rdn and c stands side over 2f out: kpt on strly fnl f* **22/1**

531 **5** *1 ¼* **Leslingtaylor (IRE)**$^{28}$ [5633] 2-8-13 **75** ................ RWinston 1 74+
(JJQuinn) *hld up: hdwy centre and prom over 2f out: kpt on fnl f: no imp* **12/1**

5260 **6** *shd* **Brooklime (IRE)**$^{6}$ [6090] 2-9-4 **80** ................ SWKelly 13 78
(JAOsborne) *led to over 2f out: swtchd to outside of stands side gp over 1f out: one pce* **11/1**

3106 **7** *shd* **Breaking Shadow (IRE)**$^{16}$ [5896] 2-8-12 **77** ................ THamilton$^{(3)}$ 9 75
(RAFahey) *sn rdn towards rr: c stands side over 2f out: kpt on fnl f: no imp* **8/1**$^{3}$

6140 **8** *nk* **Pauline's Prince**$^{12}$ [5989] 2-7-12 **65** ................ StephanieHollinshead$^{(5)}$ 6 62
(RHollinshead) *trckd ldrs: effrt and c stands side over 2f out: one pce over 1f out* **40/1**

464 **9** *½* **Boo**$^{27}$ [5669] 2-8-6 **68** ................ LEnstone 10 64
(KRBurke) *trckd ldrs: effrt stands side over 2f out: outpcd over 1f out* **25/1**

3120 **10** *1 ¼* **Following Flow (USA)**$^{37}$ [5417] 2-9-7 **83** ................ FLynch 4 77+
(WJarvis) *bhd: effrt centre over 2f out: n.d* **16/1**

5635 **11** *1 ¼* **Eltizaam (USA)**$^{15}$ [5909] 2-8-12 **74** ................ OUrbina 16 64
(EALDunlop) *trckd ldrs: effrt stands side over 2f out: wknd over 1f out* **9/1**

621 **12** *2 ½* **Hadrian (IRE)**$^{32}$ [5543] 2-9-7 **83** ................ SChin 7 72+
(MJohnston) *sn outpcd in rr: c centre st: n.d* **7/2**$^{1}$

4030 **13** *nk* **Shivaree**$^{25}$ [5719] 2-9-7 **83** ................ ACulhane 5 72+
(MRChannon) *in tch: effrt centre over 2f out: wknd over 1f out* **16/1**

0553 **14** *2* **My Princess (IRE)**$^{11}$ [6003] 2-8-9 **78** ................ AMullen$^{(7)}$ 3 62+
(NACallaghan) *bhd and outpcd: c centre st: hung lft: nvr on terms* **5/1**$^{2}$

1m 32.17s (4.67) **Going Correction** +0.65s/f (Yiel) **14** Ran SP% **117.1**
Speed ratings: **99,98,96,96,95 95,94,94,94,92 91,88,87,85**CSF £126.37 CT £6168.83 TOTE £26.20: £6.00, £2.90, £8.50; EX 238.20.
**Owner** Diamond Racing Ltd **Bred** Peter McCutcheon **Trained** Pandy, Gwent

**FOCUS**
A competitive nursery run at a strong pace but those who stayed towards the far side in the home straight were at a severe disadvantage. Despite that the form looks pretty reliable, with the runner-up providing the level.

**NOTEBOOK**
**Knock Bridge(IRE)**, who is only a pony, proved well suited by the step up in trip and in the past she has proved soft ground holds no terrors for her.
**Game Lad**, quite a big type, was edged out near the line and will make a better three-year-old.
**Forfeiter(USA)**, with the blinkers left off, was reappearing after four months on the sidelines. Encountering soft ground for the first time, he went down fighting.
**Wayward Shot(IRE)**, 2lb out of the handicap, was putting in all his best work at the finish and will appreciate a step up to a mile.
**Leslingtaylor(IRE)**, up in trip on his handicap bow, seemed to struggle slightly in the ground and never really got competitive.
**Brooklime(IRE)**, a keen type, again ran well but he receives no mercy.
**Following Flow(USA)** *Official explanation: jockey said colt hung right throughout*
**Hadrian(IRE)**, who accounted for three susbsequent winners at Thirsk, is not very big and seemed to struggle from the off in the soft ground. *Official explanation: jockey said colt was never travelling*
**My Princess(IRE)** proved unsuited by the soft ground and would not go forward in a straight line. *Official explanation: jockey said filly was unsuited by good to soft ground*

## 6207 GORACING.CO.UK MEDIAN AUCTION MAIDEN STKS (DIV I) 7f
3:35 (3:37) (E4) 2-Y-O £2,976 (£850; £425) Stalls Low

Form RPR

2025 **1** **Kanad**$^{25}$ [5720] 2-9-0 75 ................ (bt$^{1}$) NCallan 1 74
(BHanbury) *trckd ldrs: led over 1f out: styd on* **9/2**$^{3}$

03 **2** *2 ½* **Foxy Gwynne**$^{40}$ [5348] 2-8-9 ................ DaneO'Neill 2 63
(AMBalding) *led tl over 1f out: kpt on same pce* **5/2**$^{1}$

6300 **3** *½* **Chicken Soup**$^{24}$ [5738] 2-9-0 73 ................ SWKelly 6 67
(JAOsborne) *hld up: hdwy and styd far side in home st: kpt on same pce fnl f* **11/2**

0 **4** *9* **Peter Roughley (IRE)**$^{27}$ [5669] 2-9-0 ................ PBradley 10 44
(ABerry) *sn chsng ldrs: wknd over 1f out* **66/1**

4606 **5** *hd* **Zantero**$^{28}$ [5636] 2-8-11 57 ................ THamilton$^{(3)}$ 3 44
(RPElliott) *chsd ldrs: wkng whn sltly hmpd over 1f out* **9/1**

0 **6** *2 ½* **Stevmarie Star**$^{22}$ [5771] 2-8-9 ................ RWinston 9 32
(JAGlover) *chsd ldrs: rdn and lost pl over 2f out* **14/1**

06 **7** *4* **Jeffslottery**$^{19}$ [5831] 2-8-11 ................ PMulrennan$^{(3)}$ 7 27
(JRWeymes) *chsd ldrs: lost pl over 2f out* **100/1**

0 **8** *4* **Franela**$^{26}$ [5695] 2-8-9 ................ TPQueally 5 12
(DRLoder) *sn in rr and drvn along: nvr a factor* **11/1**

**9** *20* **Waterloo Corner** 2-8-11 ................ TEaves$^{(3)}$ 8 —
(RCraggs) *cmpt: s.s: sn wl bhd: t.o 4f out* **80/1**

054 **10** *dist* **Brandexe (IRE)**$^{29}$ [5604] 2-8-9 69 ................ ACulhane 4 —
(BWHills) *sn bhd and drvn along: t.o 4f out: virtually p.u 2f out* **3/1**$^{2}$

1m 33.3s (5.80) **Going Correction** +0.65s/f (Yiel) **10** Ran SP% **115.9**
Speed ratings: **92,89,88,78,78 75,70,66,43,**—CSF £16.05 TOTE £5.90: £1.80, £2.00, £2.00; EX 20.80.
**Owner** Ibrahim Belselah **Bred** Joseph Hogan **Trained** Newmarket, Suffolk

**FOCUS**
A modest maiden but won by the 75-rated Kanad and the form looks reasonable for the grade.

**NOTEBOOK**
**Kanad**, in first-time blinkers, appreciated the step up to seven and in the end ran out a decisive winner.
**Foxy Gwynne**, a very narrow filly, had things her own way in front and this is probably as good as she is.
**Chicken Soup** has not built on his debut effort. He stayed in glorious isolation on the far side and finished well clear of the others.
**Peter Roughley(IRE)** had finished tailed off last on his debut a month earlier.
**Zantero** was nicely backed at long odds, even though he had over a stone to find on official ratings.
**Stevmarie Star** had started slowly when well beaten on her debut three weeks earlier.
**Brandexe(IRE)** ran apallingly and was soon detached in the rear. This was simply too bad to be true. *Official explanation: trainer's representative was unable to offer any explanation for poor form shown*

## 6208 MOULTON APPRENTICE CLAIMING STKS 1m 3f 214y
4:10 (4:10) (F4) 3-Y-O+ £3,043 (£869; £434) Stalls Low

Form RPR

1041 **1** **Yenaled**$^{20}$ [5817] 7-9-2 70 ................ DonnaCaldwell$^{(7)}$ 12 79
(NWilson) *keen: hld up: hdwy 1/2-way: effrt 2f out: led ins fnl f: sn clr* **10/3**$^{3}$

0456 **2** *5* **Gold Guest**$^{6}$ [6083] 5-8-13 62 ................ TPQueally 3 62
(PDEvans) *trckd ldrs: led over 4f out: sn clr: rdn over 1f out: hdd and no ex ins fnl f* **11/4**$^{1}$

5340 **3** *17* **Peter's Imp (IRE)**$^{28}$ [5638] 9-8-8 45 ................ PPMathers$^{(5)}$ 2 38
(ABerry) *hld up and bhd: hdwy over 2f out: kpt on fnl f: n.d* **9/1**

3-30 **4** *2 ½* **Newtonian (USA)**$^{259}$ [651] 5-8-8 69 ................ MLawson$^{(5)}$ 9 35
(JParkes) *keen: hld up: outpcd over 4f out: rallied over 2f out: wandered and sn no imp* **14/1**

5000 **5** *1* **Silver Rhythm**$^{57}$ [4927] 3-7-10 46 ................ AElliott$^{(7)}$ 11 30
(KRBurke) *in tch tl wknd fr over 2f out* **20/1**

210/ **6** *9* **King's Welcome**$^{787}$ [4056] 6-9-9 92 ................ PMulrennan 10 31
(CWFairhurst) *cl up tl wknd fr over 2f out* **3/1**$^{2}$

0450 **7** *7* **Valiant Air (IRE)**$^{5}$ [6120] 3-8-4 40 ow1 ................ TEaves 7 9
(JRWeymes) *cl up tl wknd over 3f out* **25/1**

0-00 **8** *6* **Adjawar (IRE)**$^{22}$ [5768] 6-9-9 75 ................ THamilton 6 13
(JJQuinn) *trckd ldrs to over 4f out: sn btn* **12/1**

000 **9** *16* **Shameless**$^{25}$ [5710] 7-8-5 ow2 ................ (t) RKeogh$^{(7)}$ 4 —
(HAlexander) *mde most to over 4f out: sn wknd* **80/1**

0 **10** *2 ½* **Modulor (FR)**$^{25}$ [5710] 12-8-12 ow2 ................ LFletcher 8 —
(LRJames) *sn bhd: lost tch fr 1/2-way* **100/1**

/P0- **11** *dist* **Zamir**$^{8}$ [383] 5-8-5 30 ................ (v$^{1}$) DTudhope$^{(5)}$ 5 —
(WStorey) *bhd: t.o fr 1/2-way* **50/1**

2m 48.2s (9.20) **Going Correction** +0.90s/f (Soft)
**WFA** 3 from 5yo+ 7lb **11** Ran SP% **111.9**
Speed ratings: **105,101,90,88,88 82,77,73,62,61** —CSF £11.63 TOTE £3.40: £1.50, £1.40, £2.00; EX 12.20.
**Owner** Watson Wilson McKinnon **Bred** R S A Urquhart **Trained** Malton, N Yorks

**FOCUS**
A modest claimer and not many ran to form.

**NOTEBOOK**
**Yenaled**, ridden with bags of confidence, saw it out much the better recording his fifth win this year, his second under this rider, who has a cool head.
**Gold Guest**, a negative on the exchanges, went for home in most determined style but he had been asked to do too much too soon and in the end was readily picked off.
**Peter's Imp(IRE)**, a winner twice over hurdles in August, was given a patient ride and in the end did just enough to secure a remote third spot.
**Newtonian(USA)**, absent since January, was very fresh. This will put him right for an All-Weather campaign.
**King's Welcome**, who had 22lb in hand of the winner on official ratings, went well for a long way on his first outing since finishing lame when last seen over two years ago. *Official explanation: jockey said gelding lost its action*

## 6209 COURSE WITH CHARACTER CLASSIFIED STKS 1m 5f 175y
4:45 (4:46) (F3) 3-Y-O+ £3,435 (£1,057; £528; £264) Stalls Low

Form RPR

0412 **1** **Ego Trip**$^{11}$ [6006] 3-8-9 65 ................ (b) DaleGibson 7 71
(MWEasterby) *chsd ldr: c stands' side in home st: led over 1f out: drvn out* **11/4**$^{1}$

6404 **2** *2 ½* **Snow's Ride**$^{6}$ [6084] 4-9-4 58 ................ TPQueally 5 67
(WRMuir) *sn trcking ldrs: led over 3f out: edgd rt 2f out: sn hdd: kpt on fnl f* **7/2**$^{2}$

4540 **3** *6* **Capitole (IRE)**$^{25}$ [5715] 3-8-9 60 ................ DaneO'Neill 6 59
(EFVaughan) *hld up: hdwy 4f out: sn chsng ldrs: brought wd home st: one pce fnl 2f* **16/1**

4652 **4** *9* **Scurra**$^{44}$ [5238] 5-8-13 58 ................ DTudhope$^{(5)}$ 1 46
(ACWhillans) *chsd ldrs: edgd rt over 2f out: wknd fnl f* **13/2**

5106 **5** *8* **Platinum Charmer (IRE)**$^{5}$ [6110] 4-9-4 53 ................ (p) DarrenWilliams 8 35
(KRBurke) *sn chsng ldrs: outpcd over 3f out: sn btn* **12/1**

063 **6** *½* **Key In**$^{15}$ [5907] 3-8-6 60 ................ ACulhane 4 31
(BWHills) *chsd ldrs: drvn along and lost pl 7f out: bhd tl kpt on fnl f* **11/2**

4325 **7** *21* **Vivre Sa Vie**$^{236}$ [863] 3-8-6 60 ................ NCallan 2 2
(SirMarkPrescott) *led: rn v wd paddock bnd after 5f: hdd over 3f out: wknd over 2f out* **5/1**$^{3}$

000/ **8** *5* **Sir Edward Burrow (IRE)**$^{520}$ [5383] 6-9-4 35 ................ JBramhill 3 —
(WStorey) *chsd ldrs: lost pl over 7f out: sn bhd* **66/1**

0300 **9** *2 ½* **Colonnade**$^{23}$ [5751] 5-8-10 45 ................ PPMathers$^{(5)}$ 10 —
(NWilson) *hld up: lost pl 7f out: sn bhd* **66/1**

0000 **10** *5* **Abbeygate**$^{11}$ [6006] 3-8-9 55 ................ (t) OUrbina 11 —
(TKeddy) *hld up in tch: rdn 5f out: sn lost pl and bhd* **40/1**

-500 **11** *10* **Tioga Gold (IRE)**$^{58}$ [4883] 5-9-4 30 ................ TWilliams 9 —
(LRJames) *sn pushed along in rr: lost pl over 7f out: t.o 5f out* **100/1**

3m 17.85s (13.35) **Going Correction** +0.90s/f (Soft)
**WFA** 3 from 4yo+ 9lb **11** Ran SP% **114.3**
Speed ratings: **97,95,92,87,82 82,70,67,65,63 57**CSF £11.76 TOTE £3.50: £2.20, £1.20, £4.50; EX 24.50.
**Owner** K Hodgson & Mrs J Hodgson **Bred** K And Mrs Hodgson **Trained** Sheriff Hutton, N Yorks

**FOCUS**
An ordinary event in which the runner-up sets the standard, but not particularly solid form.

**NOTEBOOK**
**Ego Trip**, hoisted 7lb in the ratings after his bold effort here last time which has been well advertised since, found the soft ground and extended trip no problem. He has done nothing but improve since being fitted with blinkers.
**Snow's Ride**, whose stamina is proven, stays further than this but had 7lb to find to overcome the winner on official ratings.
**Capitole(IRE)**, with the headgear left off, was taking a big step up in trip and did not see it out anywhere near as well as the first two.
**Scurra**, who has managed just one success in 30 previous starts, did not improve for the extra yardage.
**Platinum Charmer(IRE)** usually runs well here but is much more effective in claiming or selling company. A slightly shorter trip and less soft ground suit him better too.
**Key In** seemed to drop everything setting out on to the final circuit and only her rider's persistence enabled her to finish so close.
**Vivre Sa Vie**, having her first outing on grass, almost ran out when in front on the paddock bend.

## 6210 TOTE BIG SCREEN IS HERE H'CAP — 7f
5:20 (5:21) (E3) (0-77,75) 3-Y-O+ £3,581 (£1,102; £551; £275) Stalls Low

| Form | | | | RPR |
|---|---|---|---|---|
| 2421 | 1 | | **Northern Games**[4] 6144 5-8-12 71 6ex..........(b) AMullen(7) 14<br>(KARyan) *w ldr: led after 2f: r.o wl: readily* 7/2[1] | 83 |
| 4005 | 2 | 3 | **Legal Set (IRE)**[6] 6097 8-8-8 60..........(t) TPQueally 6<br>(MissAStokell) *chsd ldrs: kpt on wl appr fnl f: no imp* 50/1 | 64 |
| 3110 | 3 | 3 | **Bond Playboy**[29] 5603 4-9-0 66.......... FLynch 8<br>(BSmart) *led 2f: w ldrs: styd far side in home st: fdd ins last* 20/1 | 63 |
| 0062 | 4 | nk | **Strong Hand**[19] 5835 4-9-3 72.......... PMulrennan(3) 15<br>(MWEasterby) *chsd ldrs: one pce fnl 2f* 8/1[3] | 68 |
| 0542 | 5 | 2 | **No Grouse**[6] 6094 4-8-8 63..........(p) THamilton(3) 18<br>(RAFahey) *in tch: hdwy on wd outside over 2f out: nvr rchd ldrs* 12/1 | 54 |
| 5162 | 6 | 1 1/4 | **Seneschal**[1] 6199 3-8-12 73 6ex.......... TO'Brien(7) 1<br>(MRChannon) *hld up: hdwy into mid-field whn hmpd over 3f out: styd centre: nvr rchd ldrs* 10/1 | 61 |
| 43-1 | 7 | 1 1/4 | **Plum**[52] 5039 4-9-4 70.......... DaneO'Neill 4<br>(EFVaughan) *hld up in tch: effrt over 2f out: styd on same pce* 4/1[2] | 55 |
| 6305 | 8 | 1 | **Qualitair Wings**[19] 5835 5-9-4 70.......... NCallan 7<br>(JHetherton) *bhd: kpt on fnl 2f: nvr a factor* 12/1 | 52 |
| 0532 | 9 | 2 1/2 | **Prince Of Gold**[8] 6046 4-8-13 65..........(p) ACulhane 11<br>(RHollinshead) *mid-div: n.m.r and lost pl after 1f: sme hdwy 2f out: nvr a factor* 8/1[3] | 41 |
| 0500 | 10 | 1/2 | **Mezuzah**[8] 6043 4-9-8 74.......... DaleGibson 12<br>(MWEasterby) *sn in rr: sme hdwy 2f out: nvr on terms* 40/1 | 49 |
| 4604 | 11 | 2 1/2 | **Sarraaf (IRE)**[17] 5859 8-8-6 61.......... TEaves(3) 2<br>(ISemple) *s.i.s: bhd whn stumbed after 1f: nvr on terms* 20/1 | 29 |
| 4660 | 12 | 1/2 | **Hills Of Gold**[7] 6069 5-9-9 75.......... PFessey 13<br>(MWEasterby) *sn bhd and drvn along: sme late hdwy* 25/1 | 42 |
| 1000 | 13 | 1/2 | **Semenovskii**[24] 5730 4-9-4 70.......... DarrenWilliams 10<br>(RBastiman) *mid-divsion: sn drvn along: lost pl over 2f out* 33/1 | 36 |
| 0303 | 14 | nk | **Marinaite**[4] 6147 3-9-5 73.......... JBramhill 3<br>(SRBowring) *chsd ldrs: lost pl over 1f out* 16/1 | 38 |
| 0000 | 15 | 1/2 | **Aventura (IRE)**[133] 2673 4-9-3 72.......... LFletcher(3) 5<br>(SRBowring) *s.i.s: a in rr* 50/1 | 36 |
| 2100 | 16 | 1 1/4 | **Jubilee Street (IRE)**[6] 6094 5-8-10 62.......... DAllan 9<br>(MrsADuffield) *bhd: sn drvn along: nvr a factor* 12/1 | 23 |

1m 32.07s (4.57) **Going Correction** +0.90s/f (Soft)
**WFA** 3 from 4yo+ 2lb **16** Ran SP% **125.2**
Speed ratings: **109,105,102,101,99 98,96,95,92,92 89,88,88,87,87 85**CSF £205.01 CT £3240.89 TOTE £5.80: £1.80, £7.90, £4.40, £2.00; EX 253.40.
**Owner** R E Robinson **Bred** Mrs Wendy Robinson **Trained** Hambleton, N Yorks

**FOCUS**
A modest handicap run at a very strong pace resulting in a decent time for the grade given the conditions.

**NOTEBOOK**
**Northern Games** is right at the top of his game at present and, grabbing the favoured stands'-side rail, ran out a most convincing winner.
**Legal Set(IRE)** has not shone in four outings since finishing runner-up here last month. He finished clear second best behind an in-form winner.
**Bond Playboy** elected to stay alone on the far side in the straight, but seemed to be bang in contention until his stamina appeared to give out inside the final furlong.
**Strong Hand** again ran well but she is slightly better over the extra furlong.
**No Grouse** has not tasted success for a year and a half and he was always likely to struggle from the outside draw.
**Seneschal**, having his second outing in two days and his fourth in just a week, elected to stay up the middle in the home straight. Rather isolated in no-man's land he never posed a threat.
**Plum**, having just her second start this time and just her fifth in all, was racing from a 3lb higher mark but she never got competitive after turning in on the heels of the leaders seemingly travelling well within herself.

## 6211 GORACING.CO.UK MEDIAN AUCTION MAIDEN STKS (DIV II) — 7f
5:50 (5:52) (E3) 2-Y-O £2,976 (£850; £425) Stalls Low

| Form | | | | RPR |
|---|---|---|---|---|
| 500 | 1 | | **Qawaafil (USA)**[18] 5847 2-8-9 64.......... OUrbina 5<br>(EALDunlop) *chsd ldrs: styd on to ld ins last* 5/1 | 68 |
| 623 | 2 | 3/4 | **Fine Lady**[19] 5831 2-8-9 69.......... SChin 6<br>(MJohnston) *led tl hdd and no ex ins last* 2/1[1] | 66 |
| 60 | 3 | 8 | **Ponente**[40] 5348 2-8-9.......... ACulhane 8<br>(BWHills) *trckd ldrs: effrt over 2f out: kpt on same pce* 9/2[3] | 46 |
| | 4 | 3 1/2 | **Bond Cat (IRE)** 2-8-10 ow1.......... FLynch 2<br>(BSmart) *leggy: unf: s.i.s: hdwy over 3f out: wknd appr fnl f* 11/1 | 38 |
| 0 | 5 | 2 | **Champagne Lujain**[17] 5857 2-8-11.......... PMulrennan(3) 4<br>(MWEasterby) *sn trcking ldrs: lost pl over 1f out* 50/1 | 37 |
| 55 | 6 | 5 | **Beauchamp Turbo**[39] 5376 2-9-0.......... NCallan 9<br>(GABulter) *in tch: pushed along over 3f out: lost pl over 1f out* 10/3[2] | 25 |
| 000 | 7 | 8 | **Italian Touch (IRE)**[17] 5865 2-9-0.......... DaneO'Neill 10<br>(JAGlover) *w ldrs: lost pl 4f out: sn in rr* 7/1 | — |
| 0 | 8 | 16 | **Just Elizabeth**[22] 5771 2-8-6.......... TEaves(3) 7<br>(MESowersby) *w ldrs: lost pl over 3f out: sn bhd* 50/1 | — |
| 0 | 9 | 6 | **Russiannightingale**[8] 6045 2-8-7.......... JDO'Reilly(7) 1<br>(JO'Reilly) *s.i.s: lost pl over 3f out: sn wl bhd* 80/1 | — |

1m 36.13s (8.63) **Going Correction** +0.90s/f (Soft) **9** Ran SP% **117.2**
Speed ratings: **86,85,76,72,69 64,54,36,29**CSF £15.65 TOTE £7.10: £2.40, £1.50, £1.60; EX 26.00 Place 6 £115.34, Place 5 £93.37.
**Owner** Hamdan Al Maktoum **Bred** Shadwell Farm Llc **Trained** Newmarket, Suffolk

**FOCUS**
Much the weaker division and a very slow time for the grade, even allowing for the conditions. The front two were well clear but the form is best treated with caution.

**NOTEBOOK**
**Qawaafil(USA)**, easily the pick of the paddock, relished the extra furlong and the soft ground but it was a weak event with the first two well clear of dead wood.
**Fine Lady**, who carried not one ounce of surplus flesh, tried hard in front but the winner always looked likely to nail her.
**Ponente**, unsuited by the quick going last time, is only small and unlikely to progress.
**Bond Cat(IRE)**, a February foal, is up in the air and narrow but she did show some ability first time and was by no means knocked about. She should be capable of better, especially next year when she will hopefully be a bit stronger.
**Champagne Lujain**, a tall individual, showed a bit more than on his debut two weeks earlier but he has a lot more to find if he is to make any impression this time, even at the lowest level.
**Beauchamp Turbo** was in trouble at the halfway mark and in the end he dropped out completely.
**Italian Touch(IRE)**, stepping up in trip on his fourth start, was a springer in the market but he was on the retreat starting the home turn.

T/Plt: £113.20 to a £1 stake. Pool: £31,749.40. 204.60 winning tickets. T/Qpdt: £23.60 to a £1 stake. Pool: £1,820.40. 56.90 winning tickets. WG

# 6187 NEWMARKET (R-H)
Saturday, October 16

**OFFICIAL GOING: Soft (heavy in places)**
There was a bias towards those who bagged the nearside rail and the winners of the six races on the straight track either set or raced close to the pace.
Wind: Moderate half behind Weather: Fair

## 6212 CORNWALLIS STKS (GROUP 3) — 5f
1:05 (1:05) (A1) 2-Y-O £17,400 (£6,600; £3,300; £1,500) Stalls Low

| Form | | | | RPR |
|---|---|---|---|---|
| 2522 | 1 | | **Castelletto**[28] 5626 2-8-9 98.......... GGibbons 6<br>(BAMcmahon) *led 1f: pressed ldr after: led over 1f out: rdn to hold on fnl f* 15/2 | 104 |
| 112 | 2 | 3/4 | **Cornus**[171] 1707 2-8-12 95.......... RLMoore 3<br>(RHannon) *towards rr: hdwy over 1f out: clsd on wnr fnl f: jst hld* 12/1 | 104 |
| 2451 | 3 | 1 1/4 | **Kay Two (IRE)**[13] 5971 2-9-1.......... MJKinane 9<br>(MsFMCrowley, Ire) *gd sort: lw: prom: chal 2f out: nt qckn fnl f* 5/1[3] | 103 |
| 114 | 4 | hd | **Joseph Henry**[7] 6068 2-8-12 100.......... KDarley 5<br>(MJohnston) *dwlt: hdwy to ld after 1f: hdd over 1f out: one pce* 9/2[2] | 99 |
| 0610 | 5 | 1 | **Prince Charming**[15] 5918 2-9-1 100.......... LDettori 14<br>(JHMGosden) *mid-div on outside: rdn to chse ldrs 2f out: one pce fnl f* 10/3[1] | 99 |
| 3252 | 6 | 1 | **Tournedos (IRE)**[13] 5971 2-9-3 100.......... TEDurcan 4<br>(MRChannon) *lw: in tch: sn pushed along: styd on same pce fnl 2f* 9/1 | 97 |
| 3440 | 7 | nk | **Bunditten (IRE)**[35] 5464 2-8-9 93.......... JFEgan 13<br>(AndrewReid) *spd 3f* 50/1 | 88 |
| 116 | 8 | 1 1/4 | **Sumora (IRE)**[35] 5464 2-8-12 100.......... JFortune 11<br>(GAButler) *dwlt: bhd: sme hdwy and hrd rdn over 1f out: no imp* 8/1 | 87 |
| 2540 | 9 | 1 1/2 | **Amazin**[14] 5947 2-8-12 99.......... RHughes 2<br>(RHannon) *s.s: bhd: rdn 1/2-way: nvr trbld ldrs* 33/1 | 82 |
| 2530 | 10 | 3/4 | **Right Answer**[38] 5392 2-8-9 97.......... KFallon 8<br>(APJarvis) *dwlt: sn in tch: pressed ldrs fr 1/2-way: hrd rdn and wknd over 1f out* 20/1 | 76 |
| 1500 | 11 | nk | **Pitch Up (IRE)**[2] 6174 2-8-12 87.......... GCarter 10<br>(TGMills) *lw: in tch to 1/2-way* 50/1 | 78 |

61.79 secs (1.38) **Going Correction** +0.525s/f (Yiel) **11** Ran SP% **110.1**
Speed ratings: **109,107,105,105,103 102,101,99,97,96 95**CSF £83.67 TOTE £9.20: £2.30, £2.90, £1.60; EX 106.00.
**Owner** J C Fretwell **Bred** Capt J H Wilson **Trained** Hopwas, Staffs
■ This race was transferred here following Salisbury's loss the previous weekend, having originally been switched from Ascot.

**FOCUS**
There appeared to be an advantage in racing close to the stands' rail and three of the first four home took that route. This did not look a strong renewal but, considering the testing ground, the winning time was very creditable for a juvenile Group Three.

**NOTEBOOK**
**Castelletto**, given a positive ride on this drop back to the minimum trip, was able to bag a position close to the stands' rail and battled on very gamely to give her rider his first Group victory. Testing ground obviously does not bother her and, after several near-misses in Pattern company, she deserved this.
**Cornus ◆**, not seen since April due to injury, followed the winner up the stands' rail and put in a stirring finish, but found the filly just too determined. He has not had a hard juvenile campaign and that just might help him next season.
**Kay Two(IRE)**, proven in the ground, ran very well under a positive ride and did best of those that raced furthest from the stands' rail.
**Joseph Henry** was soon racing up with the pace and kept trying all the way to the line. He still has scope having missed so much of the season, but may need an extra furlong now.
**Prince Charming** had no ground worries, but he was rather marooned on the outside of the track and ran better than the bare result suggests.
**Tournedos(IRE)** has had a very hard juvenile campaign, including racing all over Europe, so under the circumstances this was not a bad effort.
**Bunditten(IRE)**, winner of the very first two-year-old contest of the season on the Lingfield Polytrack in March, was far from disgraced from her wide draw in conditions that would not have suited.
**Sumora(IRE)**, who had beaten the winner at Newbury in August, could not confirm the form in these much more testing conditions.

## 6213 OWEN BROWN ROCKFEL STKS (GROUP 2) (FILLIES) — 7f
1:35 (1:35) (A1) 2-Y-O £40,600 (£15,400; £7,700; £3,500) Stalls Low

| Form | | | | RPR |
|---|---|---|---|---|
| 2132 | 1 | | **Maids Causeway (IRE)**[21] 5779 2-8-12 100.......... MHills 1<br>(BWHills) *lw: chsd ldr: led over 2f out: hdd wl ins fnl f: rallied to ld on line* 3/1[1] | 109 |
| 0131 | 2 | shd | **Penkenna Princess (IRE)**[14] 5939 2-8-9 100.......... SSanders 10<br>(RMBeckett) *hld up in tch: effrt over 2f out: drvn to slt ld wl ins fnl f: hdd on line* 7/1 | 106 |
| 1452 | 3 | 3/4 | **Favourita**[14] 5939 2-8-9 100.......... TQuinn 7<br>(CEBrittain) *lw: trckd ldng pair: effrt over 2f out: styd on wl nr fin* 7/1 | 104 |
| 2451 | 4 | 3 1/2 | **Bibury Flyer**[6] 6101 2-8-9 89.......... TEDurcan 3<br>(MRChannon) *hld up in tch: rdn and hung rt fnl 2f: styd on same pce* 12/1 | 96 |
| 1 | 5 | 2 | **Cherokee (USA)**[41] 5322 2-8-12.......... JPSpencer 4<br>(APO'Brien, Ire) *gd sort: lw: hld up in tch: effrt over 2f out: hrd rdn and no ex over 1f out* 4/1[3] | 94 |
| 2150 | 6 | 2 1/2 | **Justaquestion**[28] 5648 2-8-9 93.......... JFortune 5<br>(IAWood) *dwlt: bhd: rdn over 2f out: nvr trbld ldrs* 16/1 | 86 |
| 031 | 7 | 4 | **She's My Outsider**[37] 5407 2-8-9 82.......... FNorton 9<br>(IAWood) *t.k.h towards rr: rdn and lost tch 3f out* 40/1 | 76 |
| 1 | 8 | 9 | **Fen Shui (UAE)**[26] 5694 2-8-9.......... LDettori 8<br>(SaeedBinSuroor) *led tl over 2f out: sn wknd* 7/2[2] | 56 |

1m 28.93s (2.46) **Going Correction** +0.525s/f (Yiel) **8** Ran SP% **108.2**
Speed ratings: **106,105,105,101,98 95,91,81**CSF £21.62 TOTE £4.10: £1.40, £1.90, £2.00; EX 27.30.
**Owner** Martin S Schwartz **Bred** The Vallee Des Reves Syndicate **Trained** Lambourn, Berks

**FOCUS**
Although weakened by some notable withdrawals, this was a decent renewal and the form looks up to scratch. The testing conditions took their toll and the field finished well spread out. Racing close to the stands' rail seemed an advantage again, and the time was creditable for a race of its type.

**NOTEBOOK**

**Maids Causeway(IRE)**, as consistent as they come, was always up with the pace and held an ideal position close to the stands' rail. The fact that she has already shown top-class form over a mile was a big help to her too, as her stamina enabled her to battle back after being headed and snatch the race on the line. Provided she trains on, there should be more Pattern races to be won with her next season.

**Penkenna Princess(IRE)** put up a cracking effort in defeat on her first encounter with soft ground, especially as she was forced to race further away from the stands' rail than most. She appeared to have the measure of the favourite after taking over in front inside the last furlong, but had the race snatched from her on the nod. It would be harsh to say she did not see the trip out in the conditions and she gives her trainer something to go to war with next season.

**Favourita** ◆ finished only marginally further behind Penkenna Princess than she did here a fortnight ago and got significantly closer to Maids Causeway than she did in the May Hill, despite being 3lb worse off. She looks much more the finished article now and the way she was coming back at the front pair at the line suggests a return to a mile is going to prove ideal.

**Bibury Flyer** was not disgraced on this step up in grade, but the front trio were far too classy. She has been kept very busy and must have an iron constitution, but she will not be easy to place next season.

**Cherokee(USA)**, winner of a Group Three on her only previous start, found these very different conditions against her and was beaten some way out. She still has the scope to be a decent filly at three and will presumably avoid this sort of ground in the future. *Official explanation: jockey said filly was unsuited by Soft (Heavy in places) ground*

**Justaquestion** was always at the back and never offered a threat.

**Fen Shui(UAE)**, so impressive on her debut, took the field along for half a mile, but was all at sea on this much softer ground and dropped away tamely. She should be given the benefit of the doubt. *Official explanation: jockey said filly lost her action*

## 6214 VICTOR CHANDLER CHALLENGE STKS (GROUP 2) 7f

**2:05** (2:05) (A1) 3-Y-O+ **£58,000** (£22,000; £11,000; £5,000) **Stalls** Low

Form RPR

-142 **1** **Firebreak**[37] 5414 5-9-4 116 (t) LDettori 9 123
(SaeedBinSuroor) *mde all: drvn along over 1f out: rdn out fnl 50 yds* **11/2**[2]

/245 **2** *1* **Keltos (FR)**[14] 5967 6-9-0 OPeslier 13 117
(CLaffon-Parias, France) *hld up in midfield: effrt 2f out: pressed wnr fnl f: hrd rdn: nt qckn fnl 50 yds* **6/1**[3]

0110 **3** *nk* **Polar Bear**[14] 5967 4-9-0 108 KFallon 7 116
(WJHaggas) *lw: hld up in midfield: rdn over 2f out: hdwy over 1f out: styd on fnl f* **5/1**[1]

2013 **4** *2 1/2* **Polar Way**[16] 5888 5-9-0 114 RHughes 14 110
(MrsAJPerrett) *trckd ldrs gng wl: rdn wl over 1f out: no ex fnl f* **11/1**

-320 **5** *1 3/4* **Balmont (USA)**[58] 4886 3-8-12 112 JPSpencer 8 105
(JNoseda) *hld up and bhd: swtchd outside and hdwy over 1f out: hrd rdn: no imp fnl f* **6/1**[3]

1 **6** *1/2* **Caradak (IRE)**[27] 5676 3-8-12 MJKinane 2 104
(JohnMOxx, Ire) *w'like: prom: edgd rt and hrd rdn 2f out: wknd over 1f out* **20/1**

0332 **7** *3 1/2* **Vanderlin**[16] 5888 5-9-0 105 MartinDwyer 1 95
(AMBalding) *hld up in midfield: effrt over 2f out: no imp* **20/1**

23-1 **8** *3 1/2* **Badminton**[20] 5811 3-8-9 107 (t) KMcEvoy 4 83
(SaeedBinSuroor) *chsd wnr tl hrd rdn and wknd 2f out* **10/1**

2201 **9** *shd* **Polar Ben**[15] 5917 5-9-0 111 JPMurtagh 10 86
(JRFanshawe) *lw: hld up towards rr: gng wl whn nt clr run over 2f out: swtchd lft: rdn and no rspnse: eased whn wl btn fnl f* **11/2**[2]

510- **10** *1 1/2* **Cape Fear**[364] 5640 3-8-12 110 JFortune 5 82
(BJMeehan) *s.i.s: sn in midfield: rdn and wknd 2f out* **33/1**

0540 **11** *18* **Golden Nun**[21] 5780 4-8-11 104 (b) TQuinn 6 34
(TDEasterby) *prom 4f* **25/1**

0003 **12** *8* **Tahirah**[20] 5811 4-8-11 85 SSanders 3 14
(RGuest) *a bhd* **66/1**

1m 27.22s (0.75) **Going Correction** +0.525s/f (Yiel)
**WFA** 3 from 4yo+ 2lb **12** Ran SP% **111.2**
Speed ratings: **116,114,114,111,109 109,105,101,100,99 78,69**CSF £33.12 TOTE £5.00: £2.50, £1.90, £2.10; EX 36.40 Trifecta £134.50 Pool £2,671.30. 14.10 winning units.
**Owner** Godolphin **Bred** R P Williams **Trained** Newmarket, Suffolk

**FOCUS**

A difference of opinion early, with a smaller group of five racing close to the stands' rail whilst the rest raced wider, though the two groups merged at halfway. The conditions resulted in the field finishing well spread out, but the time was as you would expect for a race like this in the ground, despite being slightly slower than the Dewhurst.

**NOTEBOOK**

**Firebreak**, runner-up in this two years ago, had shown he could handle testing conditions as a juvenile and, given a positive ride down the centre of the track, held off all comers for a deserved success. Although just below the Godolphin superstars, he has more than paid his way. He could return to Hong Kong in December.

**Keltos(FR)** has just been missing in Group company since returning from stud and did so again. Proven in these conditions, he tried his best and battled right to the line, but found the winner too determined. He is probably better suited by a mile.

**Polar Bear** ◆, with the ground in his favour, arguably put up his best-ever performance and was still going forward at the line. He finished well clear of the others and there is certainly a very decent prize in him.

**Polar Way** travelled well for a long way, but did not find much when asked. He has won on soft ground, but that was on his racecourse debut and he probably needs it faster.

**Balmont(USA)** tried to put in an effort down the outside over a furlong from home, but it came to little. He has not confirmed the promise of his reappearance in the July Cup and is yet to convince over this trip.

**Caradak(IRE)** seemed to be found out by these more testing conditions on this step up in class.

**Polar Ben** may his been flattered by his victory here a fortnight ago and was disappointing, even though he did not have much room to play with at one stage.

**Golden Nun** *Official explanation: jockey said filly lost her action*

## 6215 TOTESPORT CESAREWITCH (HERITAGE H'CAP) 2m 2f

**2:45** (2:47) (B1) 3-Y-O+ **£75,400** (£28,600; £14,300; £6,500) **Stalls** High

Form RPR

6-64 **1** **Contact Dancer (IRE)**[56] 4934 5-8-2 **83** RFfrench 18 93
(MJohnston) *prom: led over 2f out: edged rt fnl f: hld on gamely* **16/1**[3]

2212 **2** *1/2* **Mr Ed (IRE)**[29] 5619 6-7-13 **80** (p) JQuinn 12 89
(PBowen) *lw: t.k.h in midfield: hdwy 3f out: jnd wnr over 1f out: kpt on wl* **10/1**[1]

6051 **3** *hd* **High Point (IRE)**[30] 5595 6-7-12 **78** 3ex oh1 SWhitworth 32 88
(GPEnright) *lw: hld up towards rr: stdy hdwy 6f out: drvn to chal over 2f out: kpt on* **50/1**

1100 **4** *1/2* **Quedex**[14] 5956 8-7-5 **79** oh5 CHaddon(7) 19 88
(RJPrice) *mid-div: hdwy 4f out: hard ridden over 1f out: edged rt and one pce fnl f* **33/1**

0021 **5** *1* **Escayola (IRE)**[21] 5784 4-8-9 **90** 5ex (v) JFEgan 35 98
(WJHaggas) *hld up and bhd: styd on u.p fnl 2f: nvr nrr* **20/1**

5413 **6** *1/2* **Land 'n Stars**[30] 5595 4-8-2 **83** 3ex ow1 PDoe 20 90
(JamiePoulton) *hld up in midfield: rdn and r.o fnl 2f: nrst fin* **33/1**

4/31 **7** *1/2* **Mirjan (IRE)**[112] 3310 8-8-12 **93** (b) PHanagan 29 99
(LLungo) *hld up in tch: promising effrt 3f out: rdn and one pce fnl 2f* **14/1**[2]

2003 **8** *nk* **Distant Prospect (IRE)**[80] 4226 7-8-11 **92** LDettori 3 98
(AMBalding) *hld up in tch: effrt over 2f out: one pce* **10/1**[1]

0003 **9** *1* **Trance (IRE)**[21] 5785 4-8-2 **88** ow1 PMakin(5) 16 93
(TDBarron) *towards rr: rdn and r.o fnl 2f: nt rch ldrs* **50/1**

0302 **10** *hd* **Kristensen**[20] 5820 5-7-10 **80** oh2 ow1 (p) JFMcDonald(3) 26 85
(DEddy) *prom tl hrd rdn and wknd over 1f out* **33/1**

26/1 **11** *1 1/4* **The Last Cast**[167] 1801 5-7-9 **79** oh3 FPFerris(3) 7 82
(HMorrison) *prom: led 10f out tl over 2f out: sn wknd* **16/1**[3]

0-00 **12** *nk* **Halland**[30] 5595 6-7-12 **82** NMackay(3) 10 85
(NPLittmoden) *hld up towards rr: slightly hampered over 4f out, stayed on final 2f* **66/1**

0000 **13** *1 1/4* **Theatre (USA)**[21] 5784 5-7-12 **79** oh2 AMcCarthy 5 81
(JamiePoulton) *chsd ldrs: chal 3f out: ridden and beaten well over 1f out* **66/1**

000- **14** *2* **Dubai Seven Stars**[198] 5639 6-7-7 **79** oh9 DFox(5) 36 79
(MCPipe) *hld up in midfield: hdwy 5f out: hard rdn and wknd 2f out* **66/1**

403 **15** *1 3/4* **Historic Place (USA)**[29] 5608 4-7-10 **80** RThomas(3) 31 78
(GBBalding) *bhd tl styd on fnl 2f* **20/1**

61/3 **16** *2 1/2* **Monolith**[119] 3078 6-7-12 **84** ow4 NDeSouza(5) 33 79
(LLungo) *hdwy 7f out: wknd over 2f out* **14/1**[2]

0430 **17** *2 1/2* **Almizan (IRE)**[35] 5472 4-8-1 **82** (v) CCatlin 30 74
(MRChannon) *towards rr: rdn 4f out: nt pce to chal* **33/1**

2-31 **18** *nk* **No Refuge (IRE)**[21] 5808 4-9-12 **107** 7ex (b) SSanders 9 99
(SirMarkPrescott) *chsd ldrs tl wknd over 2f out* **16/1**[3]

600 **19** *4* **Laggan Bay (IRE)**[50] 5093 4-7-5 **79** oh7 (v) DFentiman(7) 34 66
(JSMoore) *in rr: drvn along 4f out: n.d* **100/1**

4/35 **20** *2 1/2* **Penny Pictures (IRE)**[55] 4529 5-8-6 **87** RLMoore 21 72
(MCPipe) *rrd s and lost 15 l: hdwy and switched left 4f out: edged left: wknd over 2f out* **16/1**[3]

1021 **21** *5* **Astyanax (IRE)**[20] 5820 4-7-12 **79** 3ex JMackay 13 58
(SirMarkPrescott) *prom tl wknd 5f out* **33/1**

6000 **22** *1/2* **Nakwa (IRE)**[30] 5584 6-8-1 **82** oh14 ow3 ADaly 11 61
(EJAlston) *plld hrd in midfield on outside: wknd 5f out* **100/1**

-203 **23** *1 1/2* **Midas Way**[21] 5784 4-9-0 **95** JPMurtagh 4 72
(PRChamings) *hld up in tch: wknd 6f out* **20/1**

3-00 **24** *14* **King Eider**[15] 5919 5-8-5 **86** TEDurcan 23 48
(BEllison) *held up in midfield: not much room over 5f out: soon ridden and beaten* **16/1**[3]

200- **25** *16* **It's Definite (IRE)**[13] 5639 5-7-13 **80** oh4 ow1 (p) FNorton 24 24
(PBowen) *prom tl wknd 5f out* **33/1**

-020 **26** *1 3/4* **Stance**[21] 5784 5-7-5 **79** (p) JJones(7) 2 21
(GLMoore) *hdwy to join ldrs after 6f: wknd 5f out* **50/1**

635/ **27** *3* **Mujalina (IRE)**[1064] 6-7-13 **80** DKinsella 22 19
(MCPipe) *prom tl wknd over 4f out* **40/1**

1321 **28** *nk* **Tungsten Strike (USA)**[16] 5892 3-8-1 **93** 7ex MartinDwyer 14 31
(MrsAJPerrett) *hld up in midfield: wknd 5f out* **14/1**[2]

1031 **29** *1 3/4* **Glory Quest (USA)**[112] 3300 7-7-11 **81** oh2 ow2 BReilly(3) 17 17
(MissGayKelleway) *a bhd* **100/1**

0150 **30** *10* **Mana D'Argent (IRE)**[21] 5784 7-8-7 **88** JFanning 6 13
(MJohnston) *lw: prom tl wknd 6f out* **50/1**

-505 **31** *11* **Tempsford (USA)**[21] 5784 4-8-5 **86** DHolland 27 —
(SirMarkPrescott) *t.k.h: in tch till wknd qckly 5f out: wl bhd fnl 3f* **20/1**

-404 **32** *7* **It's The Limit (USA)**[21] 5784 5-8-11 **92** MJKinane 8 —
(MrsAJPerrett) *lw: a bhd: no chance final 3f* **25/1**

0-00 **33** *dist* **Kaluana Court**[7] 6074 8-7-7 **79** oh11 NataliaGemelova(5) 28 —
(RJPrice) *t.k.h: in tch: tk clsr order after 5f: wknd qckly 5f out: t.o fnl 3f* **100/1**

-025 **34** *22* **Pushkin (IRE)**[19] 5834 6-9-10 **105** KDarley 25 —
(MJohnston) *led tl 10f out: wknd 5f out: bhd whn virtually p.u over 3f out* **50/1**

3m 58.52s (5.90) **Going Correction** +0.525s/f (Yiel)
**WFA** 3 from 4yo+ 11lb **34** Ran SP% **128.8**
Speed ratings: **107,106,106,106,106 105,105,105,105,104 104,104,103,102,102 100,99,99,97,96 94,94,93,87,80 79**CSF £125.37 CT £7674.78 TOTE £13.70: £3.00, £2.40, £15.30, £7.80; EX 117.50 Trifecta £6134.40 Part won. Pool £8,640.03. 0.20 winning units..
**Owner** Michael H Watt **Bred** Baroda And Baronrath Studs **Trained** Middleham Moor, N Yorks
■ Stewards Enquiry : C Haddon three-day ban: used whip with excessive frequency (Oct 27,28, Nov 11)

**FOCUS**

The pace was solid without being breakneck, resulting in a time that was no more than ordinary for the grade and a bunch finish. The field came over to the centre of the track after turning for home and, not for the first time in this race, it paid to be drawn middle to high. This is solid staying form, but nothing special.

**NOTEBOOK**

**Contact Dancer(IRE)**, a proven stayer who likes this ground, came into this fresher than most having only had two starts this season for his new yard. Always up with the pace, he took over in front over a quarter of a mile out and put his head down and battled right to the line. This was a cracking effort off a 16lb higher mark than for his last handicap win.

**Mr Ed(IRE)**, buried away in the pack, was brought with his effort at just the right time and was just unfortunate to run into an equally determined rival. He hardly deserved to lose and must be one of the most consistent horses in training, having now finished first or second in 11 starts on the Flat and over hurdles within the past 13 months.

**High Point(IRE)**, carrying a 3lb penalty for winning at Yarmouth last month, ran his socks off and was only just held in the closing stages. This was by far his best effort to date and as a proven performer on Polytrack he may be kept going for a while yet.

**Quedex**, backed at long odds, ran a blinder on ground he likes from 5lb out of the handicap and deservedly made the frame. He was in good form over hurdles in the spring and is in good heart if returning to timber now.

**Escayola(IRE)**, carrying a 5lb penalty for his Ascot win, stays all day and utilised his stamina to finish as close as he did. An end-to-end gallop would probably have suited him better, and he could also have done without the rain.

**Land 'n Stars** was off the bridle some way out, but got stronger as the race progressed and nothing was finishing better. This was a good effort considering all his best previous form has been on fast ground.

**Mirjan(IRE)** had not been seen since winning the Northumberland Plate in June and was off a 7lb higher mark. He was travelling well enough three furlongs from home, but did not quite appear to get home.

**Distant Prospect(IRE)**, winner of this in 2001, could never quite land a telling blow. The ground was in his favour, but the draw was not and his only consolation was that he did best of those drawn in single figures.

**Trance(IRE)** did not run at all badly and should be able to find another race at a more realistic level.

**Monolith**, unexposed on the Flat, would have preferred faster ground, but should now be fit and well for a return to hurdles.
**Penny Pictures(IRE)** *Official explanation: jockey said gelding reared as Stalls opened and missed break*
**Tungsten Strike(USA)**, the only three-year-old in the field, had a 7lb penalty to carry for his victory in Listed company here last month and had a question mark over him with regard to the ground. He was one of the first beaten and probably found this too demanding at this stage of his career.
**Tempsford(USA)** *Official explanation: jockey said colt ran too free*

## 6216 EMIRATES AIRLINE CHAMPION STKS (GROUP 1) 1m 2f

**3:25** (3:26) (A1) 3-Y-0+ **£215,064** (£81,576; £40,788; £18,540) **Stalls** Low

Form RPR

1140 **1** **Haafhd**[80] [4228] 3-8-11 122 RHills 9 129+
(BWHills) *lw: chsd ldrs: wnt 2nd 3f out: led over 1f out: rdn out* **12/1**

1133 **2** 2 ½ **Chorist**[55] [4982] 5-8-13 112 KFallon 4 121
(WJHaggas) *led 2f: led over 3f out tl over 1f out: nt qckn* **20/1**

3211 **3** 1 **Azamour (IRE)**[35] [5483] 3-8-11 MJKinane 10 122
(JohnMOxx, Ire) *lw: hld up in rr: hdwy 3f out: styd on same pce fnl 2f* **6/1**

1220 **4** 6 **Norse Dancer (IRE)**[21] [5782] 4-9-2 121 JFEgan 7 112
(DRCElsworth) *lw: hld up in rr: effrt 4f out: styd on fnl f: nvr rchd ldrs* **12/1**

1103 **5** ½ **Refuse To Bend (IRE)**[21] [5782] 4-9-2 121 (t) KMcEvoy 8 111
(SaeedBinSuroor) *mid-div: rdn over 2f out: no imp* **7/1**

5232 **6** nk **Salselon**[15] [5917] 5-9-2 116 (b) JPMurtagh 2 111
(LMCumani) *lw: stdd s: hld up and bhd: effrt and veered bdly rt 2f out: nvr nr to chal* **16/1**

2110 **7** 1 ¾ **Doyen (IRE)**[35] [5483] 4-9-2 127 LDettori 5 108
(SaeedBinSuroor) *hld up in rr: rdn and sme hdwy 3f out: no imp fnl 2f* **3/1**[1]

14-3 **8** 6 **Mingun (USA)**[14] [5962] 4-9-2 JPSpencer 11 98
(APO'Brien, Ire) *gd sort: prom tl hrd rdn and wknd 2f out* **33/1**

-202 **9** dist **Lucky Story (USA)**[21] [5782] 3-8-11 123 DHolland 3 —
(MJohnston) *mid-div: rdn 1/2-way: sn wknd* **9/2**[2]

5015 **10** dist **Naheef (IRE)**[24] [5731] 5-9-2 (vt) TEDurcan 1 —
(SaeedBinSuroor) *missed break: hdwy to ld after 2f: hdd & wknd over 3f out* **100/1**

1111 **P** **Mister Monet (IRE)**[56] [4965] 3-8-11 117 KDarley 6 —
(MJohnston) *chsd ldrs tl broke down and p.u over 6f out: dead* **5/1**[3]

2m 6.90s (1.21) **Going Correction** +0.525s/f (Yiel)
**WFA** 3 from 4yo+ 5lb **11** Ran SP% **116.6**
Speed ratings: **116,114,113,108,108 107,106,101,—,— —**CSF £224.67 TOTE £13.40: £3.90, £4.20, £2.50; EX 352.60 Trifecta £2023.70 Part won. Pool £2,850.40. 0.70 winning units..
**Owner** Hamdan Al Maktoum **Bred** Shadwell Estate Company Limited **Trained** Lambourn, Berks

**FOCUS**
No fewer than seven of these had the form to win an average renewal, but there were question marks over several of them and it turned out a messy contest, with runners taking several different positions and some wide margins separating them at the finish. The ground certainly had an effect, though the time was more or less as you would expect for a race of this calibre in the conditions.

**NOTEBOOK**
**Haafhd** again demonstrated his liking for a straight track, especially this one, and put his Royal Ascot and Goodwood disappointments well behind him with an effort which puts him behind only Bago and Cherry Mix among the three-year-old colts. Freshened up after a break, he was always travelling well and once he got over to the stands' rail in front the race was over. The extra two furlongs and testing ground were no problem at all and next season will be enhanced no end should he be kept in training.
**Chorist** likes to dominate from the front, so the Godolphin pacemaker was not particularly helpful, but she nonetheless eventually managed to see him off and only the winner was able to get past her. This confirms she has developed into a top-class performer, were there any doubt before, and connections are now tempted to postpone her retirement and race on next year.
**Azamour(IRE)**, tied at one-all with Haafhd on previous meetings, had a big question mark over him on account of the ground and it was only his class that enabled him to get as close as he did. He may return next year, when connections are likely to avoid this sort of ground. All being well, he will be tried at a mile and a half in the King George.
**Norse Dancer(IRE)** seems to reserve his best for galloping tracks and stayed on past beaten horses to snatch fourth. Because of the conditions though, it is hard to quantify what he actually achieved.
**Refuse To Bend(IRE)** reversed Ascot form with Lucky Story, but never looked like winning. He has never been that consistent but retires to stud the winner of four Group One races, including last year's 2,000 Guineas and this year's Eclipse. *Official explanation: trainer said colt was unsuited by Soft (Heavy in places) ground*
**Salselon**, switched right off out the back, was asked to take closer order entering the last couple of furlongs, but only succeeded in hanging so badly right that he almost ended up on the July Course. He cannot be trusted.
**Doyen(IRE)**, bidding to restore his reputation after his tame effort at Leopardstown, did no better here. Connections were inclined to blame the going and he certainly looked nothing like the same horse that was so dominant on fast ground in the summer. This may well have been the wrong race, over the wrong trip, in the wrong conditions, but connections will have to go back to square one now while he winters in Dubai before next year's return. *Official explanation: trainer said colt was unsuited by Soft (Heavy in places) ground*
**Mingun(USA)** has already looked held at this level and was again outclassed.
**Lucky Story(USA)** has won with cut in the ground, but ran a wretched race in these conditions over this longer trip. He is better than this.
**Naheef(IRE)** did not do a great job of pacemaking after missing the break, and with Chorist in the race his presence was not required anyway.
**Mister Monet(IRE)** tragically sustained a triple fracture of the near-hind pastern after three furlongs and could not be saved.

## 6217 DARLEY DEWHURST STKS (GROUP 1) (ENTIRE COLTS & FILLIES) 7f

**4:00** (4:01) (A1) 2-Y-0 **£152,772** (£57,948; £28,974; £13,170) **Stalls** Low

Form RPR

11 **1** **Shamardal (USA)**[80] [4227] 2-9-0 KDarley 4 125
(MJohnston) *lw: mde all: rdn and r.o wl fnl 2f* **9/2**[2]

1211 **2** 2 ½ **Oratorio (IRE)**[13] [5980] 2-9-0 JPSpencer 10 119
(APO'Brien, Ire) *gd sort: prom: rdn over 2f out: nt qckn appr fnl f* **15/2**

114 **3** nk **Montgomery's Arch (USA)**[13] [5980] 2-9-0 100 MJKinane 1 118
(PWChapple-Hyam) *lw: towards rr: pushed along 1/2-way: hdwy 2f out: hrd rdn over 1f out: kpt on fnl f* **10/1**

1123 **4** ½ **Iceman**[15] [5918] 2-9-0 100 JFortune 11 117
(JHMGosden) *prom: rdn over 2f out: styd on same pce* **7/1**[3]

11 **5** ¾ **Librettist (USA)**[38] [5395] 2-9-0 100 KMcEvoy 9 115
(SaeedBinSuroor) *lw: prom: rdn over 2f out: wknd 1f out* **10/1**

2141 **6** 8 **Tremar**[15] [5922] 2-9-0 GCarter 5 97
(TGMills) *lw: prom 5f* **33/1**

1211 **7** 4 **Perfectperformance (USA)**[21] [5778] 2-9-0 100 LDettori 8 88
(SaeedBinSuroor) *in tch tl rdn and wknd over 2f out* **8/1**

11 **8** 4 **Etlaala**[36] [5437] 2-9-0 100 RHills 6 79
(BWHills) *dwlt: hld up in rr: hdwy 3f out: hrd rdn and wknd 2f out* **9/4**[1]

51 **9** 1 ¼ **Home Affairs**[31] [5570] 2-9-0 88 KFallon 7 76
(SirMichaelStoute) *dwlt: hdwy 5f out: rdn and wknd over 2f out* **12/1**

1m 27.16s (0.69) **Going Correction** +0.525s/f (Yiel) **9** Ran SP% **113.1**
Speed ratings: **117,114,113,113,112 103,98,94,92**CSF £37.21 TOTE £5.30: £2.10, £2.40, £2.10; EX 39.30 Trifecta £273.10 Pool £1,692.60. 4.40 winning units.
**Owner** Gainsborough Stud **Bred** Brilliant Stable **Trained** Middleham Moor, N Yorks

**FOCUS**
This looked a fine renewal of the Dewhurst and the winning time was outstanding for the type of race, fractionally faster than the five-year-old Firebreak took to win the Challenge Stakes. The field split into two early, with the larger group of five racing away from the nearside rail whilst four stayed close to it. Significantly the winner stuck close to the rail the whole way.

**NOTEBOOK**
**Shamardal(USA)** ◆, not seen since Glorious Goodwood, justified his trainer's high opinion of him with a sparkling front-running performance and he had this field shot to pieces from some way out. Bagging the stands' rail may have exaggerated the margin a little, but he nonetheless looks the best two-year-old colt around and the winning time suggests he is the one they will all have to beat back here next May provided all goes well in the meantime.
**Oratorio(IRE)**, bidding for back-to-back Group One victories after his Longchamp success, was always near the front of the group who raced furthest from the stands' rail and emerged best on that side, but was beaten pointless by the winner. He is going the right way still and should make his mark in top company at three, but it is hard to see him coping with Shamardal if both make normal progress through the winter.
**Montgomery's Arch(USA)** ◆ finished in good style against the stands' rail and significantly narrowed the gap between himself and Oratorio compared to their meeting on faster ground at Longchamp. He still appears to be improving and could go a long way next season.
**Iceman** put up a most commendable effort considering he was racing on ground that connections were worried about and was towards the wide outside, seeing plenty of daylight.
**Librettist(USA)** ran with credit under a positive ride in the centre-field group, but could not cope with the winner and did not seem to get home in the conditions.
**Tremar**, winner of a Group Three at Chantilly last time, was found out in this company.
**Perfectperformance(USA)** was struggling from a long way out and did not appear to handle the conditions at all. *Official explanation: jockey said colt lost his action*
**Etlaala** ran a shocker as his Doncaster running with Iceman should have put him in the frame at least. The ground seems the most likely reason. *Official explanation: jockey said colt was unsuited by Soft (Heavy in places) ground*
**Home Affairs** found the rise in class and testing ground all too much for him. *Official explanation: jockey said colt was unsuited by Soft (Heavy in places) ground*

## 6218 PERSIAN PUNCH JOCKEY CLUB CUP (GROUP 3) 2m

**4:35** (4:37) (A1) 3-Y-0+ **£34,800** (£13,200; £6,600; £3,000) **Stalls** High

Form RPR

3131 **1** **Millenary**[37] [5415] 7-9-5 119 (b) TQuinn 6 121
(JLDunlop) *lw: t.k.h towards rr: patiently rdn: hdwy on bit 2f out: led ins fnl f: rdn out* **7/2**[1]

4066 **2** 1 ¼ **Franklins Gardens**[20] [5812] 4-9-0 105 DHolland 9 115
(MHTompkins) *chsd ldr: led 6f out tl ins fnl f: kpt on: no ch w wnr* **20/1**

1/ **3** 4 **True Lover (GER)**[168] 7-9-0 SDrowne 14 110
(JWMullins) *chsd ldrs: rdn 3f out: one pce fnl 2f* **66/1**

2234 **4** 1 **Dancing Bay**[13] [5976] 7-9-0 116 WRyan 3 109
(NJHenderson) *hld up in rr: rdn and hdwy over 2f out: styd on same pce* **7/2**[1]

0415 **5** 1 **Gold Medallist**[34] [5503] 4-9-5 112 RHughes 4 112
(DRCElsworth) *led tl 6f out: no ex fnl 2f* **12/1**

0411 **6** 5 **Defining**[20] [5815] 5-9-0 107 JPMurtagh 5 101
(JRFanshawe) *mid-div: effrt over 2f out: no imp appr fnl f* **9/1**

1300 **7** 5 **Anak Pekan**[13] [5976] 4-9-0 105 PRobinson 15 95
(MAJarvis) *lw: prom: rdn 3f out: wknd over 1f out* **8/1**[3]

1132 **8** 5 **Mkuzi**[55] [4977] 5-9-3 MJKinane 8 92
(JohnMOxx, Ire) *trckd ldrs: rdn over 2f out: wknd wl over 1f out: eased whn btn fnl f* **10/1**

-0P3 **9** 6 **Shanty Star (IRE)**[15] [5916] 4-9-0 104 KDarley 10 82
(MJohnston) *s.s: bhd: mod effrt 4f out: n.d fnl 2f* **12/1**

306- **10** 1 ¾ **Pole Star**[401] [4842] 6-9-0 115 MHills 12 80
(JRFanshawe) *lw: stdd s: t.k.h in rr: wknd 3f out* **16/1**

03-1 **11** 5 **Kasthari (IRE)**[37] [5415] 5-9-5 116 PHanagan 1 79
(JHowardJohnson) *s.s: hdwy to chse ldrs after 6f: wknd 3f out* **7/1**[2]

3m 32.1s (5.58) **Going Correction** +0.525s/f (Yiel) **11** Ran SP% **114.7**
Speed ratings: **107,106,104,103,103 100,98,95,92,92 89**CSF £80.47 TOTE £3.90: £1.90, £4.90, £8.70; EX 97.80.
**Owner** L Neil Jones **Bred** Abergwaun Farms **Trained** Arundel, W Sussex

**FOCUS**
Despite an unusually big field, the pace was not great and things did not pick up until half a mile from home, resulting in a modest time for a Group Three. As in the Cesarewitch, the field came wide in the home straight, though on this occasion much closer to the stands' rail.

**NOTEBOOK**
**Millenary** was very much suited by the modest pace, as it enabled him to travel on the bridle for that much longer and to keep enough in reserve for when he had to go and win his race. He would still be one to take on in a truly-run race beyond 14 furlongs, but in the meantime contests like this will still do very nicely when his career record is totted up.
**Franklins Gardens** ◆, racing beyond 12 furlongs for the first time, ran an absolute corker and although he could do nothing about the winner running all over him, he still pulled well clear of the others. This removed any doubts over his stamina or his ability to act in soft ground and he could be an interesting candidate for the better staying contests next season.
**True Lover(GER)**, better known as a hurdler, was racing on the Flat for the first time in this country and put in a huge effort. He had been successful on soft ground on the level in Scandinavia, so at least conditions were suitable, and it will be fascinating to see of he can translate this improvement back to hurdles.
**Dancing Bay** had the ground in his favour, but would probably have benefited from a stronger gallop as he was never getting there quickly enough. He is now likely to return to hurdles.
**Gold Medallist**, carrying the Persian Punch colours, set only an ordinary pace for the first ten furlongs and stayed in touch until done for toe over the last quarter-mile.
**Defining** has shown all his best form on faster ground and could never land a blow in these more testing conditions in this better contest.
**Anak Pekan** raced prominently for a long way, but is yet to really make his mark in Pattern company.
**Kasthari(IRE)** was a very long way below the form of his Doncaster Cup effort and the ground cannot really be used as an excuse. *Official explanation: jockey said gelding was unsuited by Soft (Heavy in places) ground*

## 6219 ROLLS-ROYCE MOTOR CARS LONDON DARLEY STKS (GROUP 3) 1m 1f

**5:10** (5:10) (A1) 3-Y-0+ **£34,800** (£13,200; £6,600; £3,000) **Stalls** Low

Form RPR

0615 **1** **Autumn Glory (IRE)**[28] [5668] 4-9-4 106 SDrowne 7 117
(GWragg) *mde all: rdn and r.o wl fnl 2f* **9/2**[1]

-110 **2** *2* **Sights On Gold (IRE)**[14] 5968 5-9-4 114..........(t) LDettori 3 113
(SaeedBinSuroor) *trckd ldrs: wnt 2nd ins fnl 2f: nt qckn fnl f* **6/1**[2]
5464 **3** *1 3/4* **Babodana**[45] 5225 4-9-0 107.......... DHolland 4 105
(MHTompkins) *lw: a.p: one pce fnl 2f* **9/1**
1034 **4** *1 1/2* **Fruhlingssturm**[13] 5975 4-9-0 112.......... PRobinson 20 102
(MAJarvis) *prom: hrd rdn over 1f out: no ex fnl f* **8/1**
0223 **5** *hd* **Battle Chant (USA)**[24] 5731 4-9-0 106.......... RLMoore 18 102
(MrsAJPerrett) *in tch: drvn to chse ldrs 2f out: one pce* **20/1**
-306 **5** *dht* **Orcadian**[14] 5948 3-8-10 99.......... JFEgan 16 102
(JMPEustace) *prom: rdn and outpcd over 2f out: kpt on fnl f* **100/1**
16-4 **7** *1 3/4* **Imperial Stride**[184] 1410 3-8-10 113.......... KFallon 9 99
(SirMichaelStoute) *t.k.h: prom tl wknd over 1f out* **7/1**[3]
1460 **8** *nk* **Pawn Broker**[14] 5941 7-9-0 108.......... RHughes 13 98
(DRCElsworth) *stdd s: hld up in rr: effrt 2f out: nvr rchd ldrs* **25/1**
3643 **9** *nk* **Bonecrusher**[28] 5629 5-9-0 103..........(v) SSanders 17 97
(DRLoder) *dwlt: in rr tl styd on u.p fnl 2f* **20/1**
16-1 **10** *2 1/2* **Almuraad (IRE)**[148] 2276 3-8-10 105.......... RHills 6 92
(SirMichaelStoute) *lw: hld up towards rr: rdn 3f out: n.d* **16/1**
5150 **11** *1* **Gatwick (IRE)**[14] 5941 3-8-10 108.......... TQuinn 12 90
(MRChannon) *mid-div: rdn 3f out: sn outpcd* **9/2**[1]
3404 **12** *3/4* **Soldera (USA)**[21] 5783 4-8-11 103.......... WRyan 2 86
(JRFanshawe) *towards rr: rdn over 2f out: nvr trbld ldrs* **25/1**
4610 **13** *2* **Brindisi**[21] 5783 3-8-7 98.......... MHills 19 82
(BWHills) *a towards rr* **50/1**
-250 **14** *1 3/4* **Mutahayya (IRE)**[121] 3000 3-8-10 102.......... WSupple 10 81
(JLDunlop) *mid-div: hrd rdn and btn 2f out* **66/1**
142- **15** *3* **Etesaal (USA)**[462] 3222 4-9-0 106.......... KMcEvoy 11 75
(SaeedBinSuroor) *w wnr tl over 2f out: sn wknd* **20/1**
000- **16** *dist* **Dandoun**[378] 5385 6-9-0 111.......... IMongan 14 —
(JLDunlop) *hld up towards rr: hrd rdn and btn 2f out: bhd whn virtually p.u 1f out* **20/1**

1m 54.96s (3.05) **Going Correction** +0.525s/f (Yiel)
**WFA** 3 from 4yo+ 4lb **16** Ran SP% **121.3**
Speed ratings: **107,105,103,102,102 102,100,100,100,97 96,96,94,92,90** —CSF £26.17 TOTE £6.00: £2.30, £3.00, £3.50; EX 33.00 Place 6 £934.56, Place 5 £278.84.
**Owner** Mollers Racing **Bred** Margaret Conlon **Trained** Newmarket, Suffolk

**FOCUS**
Only an ordinary pace and the field raced down the centre of the track. As with the previous contest, a modest winning time for the grade. The winner enjoyed ideal conditions and the run of the race, and the form overall is held down by Orcadian.

**NOTEBOOK**
**Autumn Glory(IRE)**, who had already proved his liking for this sort of ground, gained an uncontested lead and therefore set his own steady pace. That meant he was able to keep enough in reserve for the business end, and when asked to go and win his race, he found plenty. He has come a long way since failing to make the cut in the Lincoln and could be even better as a five-year-old granted suitable conditions.
**Sights On Gold(IRE)** came through to hold a chance a quarter of a mile out, but could never quite get to the winner and probably needs a bit further.
**Babodana**, on ground he likes, saw the trip out well enough considering the conditions, but the front pair were that much better. The Listed contest over a mile at the next meeting here, a race he won last year, looks a good option.
**Fruhlingssturm** racing further away from the nearside rail than most, ran with credit but just seems to come up short in domestic Pattern company.
**Orcadian**, encountering his softest ground to date, appeared to run well. Perhaps he improved for the easier conditions, but equally the modest pace does raise a doubt over interpreting the form literally.
**Battle Chant(USA)** was never far away and ran his race, but looks held at this level.
**Imperial Stride**, on soft ground for the first time, showed up for a long way on this first outing since April.
**Gatwick(IRE)** may not have wanted conditions quite so testing, but he has had a hard season and that might now be telling.
T/Jkpt: Not won. T/Plt: £620.20 to a £1 stake. Pool: £115,722.10. 136.20 winning tickets. T/Qpdt: £145.90 to a £1 stake. Pool: £8,657.10. 43.90 winning tickets. LM

## 6061 WOLVERHAMPTON (A.W) (L-H)
### Saturday, October 16

**OFFICIAL GOING: Standard**
Wind: almost nil Weather: occasional lt rain

### 6220 LADBROKESCASINO.COM H'CAP — 7f 32y(P)
7:00 (7:00) (F4) (0-62,63) 3-Y-O+ — £3,038 (£868; £434) Stalls High

Form — RPR
6502 **1** **Irusan (IRE)**[7] 6061 4-9-0 55..........(b) MFenton 3 67
(JeddO'Keeffe) *a.p: wnt 2nd over 2f out: strly rdn over 1f out: r.o to ld post* **12/1**
0110 **2** *shd* **Nautical**[3] 6154 6-9-8 63.......... LDettori 4 75
(AWCarroll) *hld up in rr: stdy hdwy on ins fr over 2f out: led 1f out: rdn and hdd post* **11/4**[1]
5006 **3** *3 1/2* **Best Desert (IRE)**[14] 5945 3-9-3 60.......... JQuinn 6 63
(JRBest) *hld up in rr: rdn and hdwy wl over 1f out: styd on: nvr nrr* **8/1**
2012 **4** *nk* **On The Trail**[4] 6144 7-8-10 56.......... PMakin(5) 2 58
(DWChapman) *led tl hdd 1f out: fdd fnl f and lost 3rd cl home* **9/2**[2]
0000 **5** *3* **Smokin Joe**[24] 5736 3-9-1 58..........(b) GBaker 1 52
(JRBest) *chsd ldrs: rdn 3f out: no ex and fdd fnl f* **25/1**
4021 **6** *3 1/2* **Zhitomir**[7] 6058 6-9-0 55.......... SWKelly 9 40
(MDods) *s.i.s: and outpcd early: prog to go mid-div: effrt 3f out: one pce after* **6/1**[3]
0100 **7** *1 1/4* **Siraj**[12] 6001 5-8-11 59..........(t) JBrennan(7) 10 41
(PSMcentee) *mid-div: rdn over 2f out: wknd appr fnl f* **20/1**
5000 **8** *nk* **Pawan (IRE)**[4] 6138 4-9-4 59.......... AnnStokell 5 40
(MissAStokell) *slowly away: a outpcd* **33/1**
0304 **9** *nk* **Emaradia**[21] 5794 3-8-11 57.......... DNolan(3) 7 37
(AWCarroll) *chsd ldr for 3f: sn rdn and wknd 2f out* **25/1**
6013 **10** *1 1/2* **Yorker (USA)**[6] 6094 6-9-2 62..........(b) BSwarbrick(5) 8 39
(MsDeborahJEvans) *prom: chsd ldr 4f out tl wknd over 2f out* **9/1**
3010 **11** *10* **Saros (IRE)**[39] 5364 3-9-4 61.......... DMcGaffin 12 12
(BSmart) *outpcd and a bhd* **8/1**
0000 **12** *5* **Warlingham (IRE)**[30] 5597 6-9-5 60.......... RWinston 11 —
(PHowling) *mid-div: rdn over 2f out: wknd wl over 1f out* **25/1**

1m 29.14s
**WFA** 3 from 4yo+ 2lb **12** Ran SP% **118.3**
Speed ratings: CSF £41.93 CT £290.76 TOTE £3.90: £3.00, £2.10, £2.70; EX 48.50.
**Owner** Highbeck Racing **Bred** E Kopica And M Rosenfeld **Trained** Middleham Moor, N Yorks

**FOCUS**
An ordinary handicap, but fair efforts from the first two to pull clear.

**NOTEBOOK**
**Irusan(IRE)** ran well from the front in first-time blinkers here a week ago. He was unable to lead over this shorter trip, but responded to pressure to put his head in front right on the line.
**Nautical** was 8lb higher than when winning over the extended mile here two starts back. After travelling well off the pace, he came through to lead at the furlong pole, but did not do a great deal in front and was just pipped. He handles this new track well and can find further opportunities.
**Best Desert(IRE)**, well suited by seven furlongs on a sound surface on turf, was running on strongly up the far rail in the straight to show that he acts on Polytrack.
**On The Trail**, well drawn for a front-runner in stall 2, drifted right once in line for home and faded after being headed at the furlong pole.
**Smokin Joe** showed a little more promise than of late without shaping as if ready to take advantage of a falling handicap mark.
**Zhitomir**, successful in a fair banded race a week earlier, never reached a challenging position after a slightly slow start.

### 6221 LADBROKES.COM (S) STKS — 7f 32y(P)
7:30 (7:32) (G4) 2-Y-O — £2,660 (£760; £380) Stalls High

Form — RPR
0 **1** **Tiger Dawn (IRE)**[6] 6078 2-8-11.......... SWKelly 8 64+
(WJHaggas) *trckd ldrs: led on bit appr fnl f: sn clr* **7/2**[1]
0 **2** *3* **Branston Penny**[25] 5720 2-8-6.......... MFenton 12 47
(JGGiven) *mid-div: sn pushed along: styd on ins fnl 2f to chse easy wnr ins fnl f* **5/1**[2]
000 **3** *3 1/2* **Tiger Hunter**[21] 5792 2-8-11.......... RWinston 2 43
(PHowling) *led after 1f: rdn and hdd appr fnl f: wknd ins* **12/1**
**4** *2 1/2* **Prospect Point** 2-8-1.......... DFox(5) 6 32
(CADwyer) *slowly away and in rr: rdn over 2f out: styd on past btn horses fnl f* **10/1**
000 **5** *5* **Grand Girl**[26] 5688 2-8-6.......... ADaly 10 19
(BWDuke) *outpcd: rdn 3f out: nvr on terms* **7/2**[1]
**6** *5* **Love Attack (IRE)** 2-8-6.......... YolandaHouben 7 7
(DCarroll) *slowly away: effrt on ins 2f out: sn btn* **10/1**
00 **7** *nk* **Rooks Bridge (IRE)**[28] 5640 2-8-11.......... JQuinn 9 11
(GAHam) *in tch: rdn over 2f out: wknd wl over 1f out* **25/1**
00 **8** *9* **Randalls Touch**[14] 5953 2-8-6.......... BSwarbrick(5) 5 —
(BDLeavy) *mid-div: rdn 1/2-way: wknd over 1f out* **50/1**
00 **9** *1* **Fraambuoyant (IRE)**[17] 5855 2-8-6.......... RFfrench 1 —
(CWFairhurst) *prom for 3f: rdn and sn wknd* **12/1**
000 **10** *1 1/2* **Independent Spirit**[14] 5954 2-8-11.......... PHanagan 3 —
(RPElliott) *led for 1f: rdn and wknd 3f out* **13/2**[3]
0 **11** *9* **Chestminster Girl**[37] 5407 2-8-6..........(p) ANicholls 11 —
(APJones) *outpcd and a wl bhd* **33/1**

1m 32.17s **11** Ran SP% **116.8**
Speed ratings: CSF £20.14 TOTE £4.40: £1.50, £2.30, £4.80; EX 18.70.The winner was bought in for 9,500gns.
**Owner** M S Bloodstock Ltd **Bred** London Thoroughbred S'Ces Ltd & West Blagdon Stud **Trained** Newmarket, Suffolk

**FOCUS**
Tiger Dawn ran out a very easy winner, but this is a difficult race to rate as none of the principals had any previous form to speak of. The time was poor and calculating the level requires some guesswork.

**NOTEBOOK**
**Tiger Dawn(IRE)**, blinkered when down the field in a maiden on his debut, was a very easy winner on this drop into the bottom grade. He obviously goes well on this surface but his future will be governed by the sort of handicap mark he gets.
**Branston Penny**, whose dam was a useful two-year-old, is a half-sister to winning sprinter Falcon Hill. Sticking on under pressure to go second inside the final furlong, she is only moderate but is probably capable of a bit better in time.
**Tiger Hunter**, who showed very little in three runs on turf, shaped more promisingly on this All-Weather bow, but the winner was cantering over him turning into the straight and he faded as if failing to stay.
**Prospect Point** gave away quite a bit of ground when dwelling in the stalls and did well to finish where she did, although she was merely running through beaten horses.
**Grand Girl** found everything happening too quickly for her on this Polytrack debut, even in this lowly company.
**Love Attack(IRE)**, whose jockey has never ridden in this country before, is a half-sister to a juvenile winner in Ireland. After missing the break she made modest late progress.
**Randalls Touch** *Official explanation: jockey said colt lost its action*
**Independent Spirit** *Official explanation: jockey said gelding lost its action*

### 6222 LADBROKES.COM H'CAP — 5f 216y(P)
8:00 (8:02) (E3) (0-77,77) 3-Y-O — £3,409 (£1,049; £524; £262) Stalls Low

Form — RPR
6000 **1** **Burley Flame**[14] 5934 3-10-0 77.......... MFenton 8 86
(JGGiven) *in tch: rdn 1/2-way: led over 1f out: strly pressed fnl f: all out* **20/1**
3500 **2** *nk* **Cherokee Nation**[26] 5697 3-9-3 66.......... JFEgan 12 74
(PWD'Arcy) *a.p: strly rdn to press wnr fnl f: jst failed* **20/1**
4041 **3** *2* **Flying Bantam (IRE)**[21] 5803 3-9-10 73.......... PHanagan 9 75
(RAFahey) *towards rr: hdwy 2f out: hrd rdn over 1f out: kpt on to go 3rd ins fnl f* **6/1**[2]
1002 **4** *3/4* **Jilly Why (IRE)**[19] 5837 3-9-9 72.......... ANicholls 13 72
(MsDeborahJEvans) *trckd ldrs: led over 2f out: hdd over 1f out: fdd ins fnl f* **12/1**
1002 **5** *1 3/4* **Saviours Spirit**[10] 6016 3-9-9 72.......... KFallon 11 67
(TGMills) *mid-div: rdn 1/2-way: no hdwy ins fnl 2f* **2/1**[1]
1500 **6** *2 1/2* **Bridgewater Boys**[15] 5912 3-9-10 73..........(b) RFfrench 4 60
(KARyan) *outpcd in rr: rdn over 3f out: effrt 2f out: no further hdwy* **11/1**
0006 **7** *1* **Beejay**[31] 5563 3-9-9 72.......... LDettori 2 56
(PFICole) *in rr: rdn over 2f out: nvr on terms* **6/1**[2]
-000 **8** *1 3/4* **Soliniki**[28] 5652 3-9-7 70..........(b[1]) SWKelly 5 49
(JAOsborne) *a towards rr* **50/1**
3001 **9** *1* **Innstyle**[6] 6079 3-9-4 67 6ex.......... LisaJones 6 43
(JLSpearing) *bhd and hld up in rr: effrt on outside over 2f out: sn btn* **16/1**
0555 **10** *hd* **Borzoi Maestro**[9] 6026 3-9-0 66..........(p) DNolan(3) 1 41
(JLSpearing) *led for 1f: prom tl wknd wl over 1f out* **10/1**
1000 **11** *3 1/2* **Midnight Ballard (USA)**[15] 5912 3-9-10 73..........(b) SCarson 10 38
(RFJohnsonHoughton) *led after 1f: hdd over 2f out: wknd qckly* **50/1**
0340 **12** *2* **Marysienka**[31] 5563 3-9-5 68.......... JEdmunds 7 27
(JBalding) *in tch to 1/2-way: sn bhd* **50/1**
3500 **13** *7* **Mister Marmaduke**[20] 5818 3-9-13 76.......... RWinston 3 14
(ISemple) *mid-div: effrt over 2f out: wknd wl over 1f out: eased* **7/1**[3]

1m 15.43s **13** Ran SP% **120.8**
Speed ratings: CSF £355.34 CT £2685.96 TOTE £35.10: £10.70, £2.90, £1.50; EX 393.80.
**Owner** Burley Appliances Ltd **Bred** Miss D Fleming **Trained** Willoughton, Lincs

**FOCUS**
An ordinary handicap run at a sound pace.

**NOTEBOOK**

**Burley Flame** had never run over this trip and was making his debut on an artificial surface, so this was a commendable efort under topweight. Only getting on top in the final 50 yards, he will not be inconvenienced by the return to seven furlongs.

**Cherokee Nation** was ridden more prominently than usual and returned to form. Running on down the centre in the straight, he might even have nosed ahead for a stride or two but was edged out close home by a bigger opponent.

**Flying Bantam(IRE)**, who went up 5lb for winning an ordinary Ripon maiden, was keeping on strongly close home but was not going to reach the first two. This was a good effort on his first run on sand.

**Jilly Why(IRE)** took up the running off the home turn but was gunned down going to the final furlong. She is in good form this autumn.

**Saviours Spirit**, from a 2lb higher mark, was never able to get to the leaders, which was a surprise as he has shown plenty of dash on the Lingfield Polytrack. This was his first run at Dunstall Park and he is probably woth another chance.

**Bridgewater Boys**, racing on the same mark as when successful at Ripon in June, has been well held since although he did show a bit more on this occasion.

**Soliniki** *Official explanation: jockey said gelding suffered interference leaving stalls*

**Mister Marmaduke** *Official explanation: jockey said gelding tired rapidly in closing stages*

## 6223 LADBROKES.COM MAIDEN STKS — 1m 141y(P)

8:30 (8:31) (D3) 2-Y-O — £4,270 (£1,314; £657; £328) Stalls Low

Form — RPR

44 **1** **Jazrawy**[77] 4335 2-8-11 ........ NMackay(3) 5 — 70+
(LMCumani) *trckd ldr: led over 4f out: pushed out fnl f: comf* **10/3**[2]

00 **2** 2 **Planet (IRE)**[10] 6011 2-9-0 ........ KFallon 13 — 66
(SirMichaelStoute) *a.p: wnt 3rd 3f out: and 2nd over 1f out: styd on one pce* **3/1**[1]

20 **3** 2 **Spectait**[14] 5953 2-9-0 ........ SSanders 3 — 62
(SirMarkPrescott) *rdn along fr s to keep in tch: pushed along 2f out: wnt 3rd ins fnl f: nt enthusiastic* **3/1**[1]

00 **4** 3/4 **Irish Ballad**[29] 5620 2-9-0 ........ MFenton 10 — 60
(PWHarris) *in tch in mid-div: rdn over 2f out: ntpce to chal after* **25/1**

0 **5** 1/2 **Sandy's Legend (USA)**[16] 5897 2-9-0 ........ LDettori 1 — 59
(JHMGosden) *led to over 4f out: wknd appr fnl f* **5/1**[3]

0 **6** hd **High Card**[10] 6010 2-9-0 ........ JFEgan 6 — 59
(JMPEustace) *in tch: rdn 3f out: wknd 2f out* **12/1**

0 **7** 6 **Millquista D'Or**[21] 5792 2-8-9 ........ ADaly 8 — 41
(GAHam) *a in rr* **80/1**

60 **8** 5 **Figaro's Quest (IRE)**[43] 5269 2-8-9 ........ NDeSouza(5) 9 — 35
(PFICole) *prom: rdn over 3f out: wknd over 2f out* **25/1**

6 **9** 3 1/2 **War Pennant**[19] 5840 2-9-0 ........ JQuinn 7 — 28
(MRChannon) *a bhd* **12/1**

000 **10** 3 **Backstreet Lad**[17] 5870 2-9-0 ........ GBaker 2 — 22
(BRMillman) *a bhd* **66/1**

0 **11** 4 **Patrician Dealer**[26] 5687 2-9-0 ........ VSlattery 4 — 13
(MSSaunders) *a in rr* **66/1**

**12** 10 **Soumillon** 2-8-9 ........ ANicholls 11 — —
(MsDeborahJEvans) *sn prom on outside: rdn 3f out: wknd qckly sn after* **50/1**

1m 51.44s — **12** Ran SP% **119.0**

Speed ratings: CSF £13.23 TOTE £5.00: £1.60, £2.90, £2.10; EX 17.30.

**Owner** Sheikh Mohammed Obaid Al Maktoum **Bred** Scuderia Antonella S R L **Trained** Newmarket, Suffolk

**FOCUS**

Only an ordinary maiden, but the majority of runners are handicappers in the making, too weak and inexperienced to do themselves justice at this stage of their career, meaning the bare form is modest.

**NOTEBOOK**

**Jazrawy**, who has been shaping as though a step up to this sort of trip would suit, was given a positive ride and took it up at just past halfway. He galloped on strongly to score with a bit in hand and will be of interest in a nursery.

**Planet(IRE)** ran on well, but was always being held by the winner. This was his best effort to date and, like the winner, can pay his way in nurseries.

**Spectait**, a disappointment at odds on most recently - reported to have banged his head in the stalls - was never really going and had to be driven for most of the way. He kept on, but never threatened the front pair and will be better off in handicaps next season.

**Irish Ballad** ◆ is going to make up into a much better three-year-old, but this was an improved effort and he will be of interest in a nursery when stamina is at a premium.

**Sandy's Legend(USA)** improved on his debut performance and is steadily progressing. He will progress further at three.

**Figaro's Quest(IRE)** is now qualified for a handicap mark and being a big, unfurnished sort, will not be seen at his best until next season.

## 6224 LADBROKESPOKER.COM MAIDEN H'CAP — 1m 141y(P)

9:00 (9:00) (E3) (0-77,69) 3-Y-0+ — £3,433 (£1,056; £528; £264) Stalls Low

Form — RPR

2000 **1** **Blue Mariner**[17] 5868 4-9-5 **63** ........ MFenton 12 — 69
(PWHarris) *a in tch on outside: wnt 2nd 3f out: led ins fnl f: all out* **14/1**

0350 **2** nk **Truman**[28] 5652 3-9-5 **67** ........ SSanders 11 — 72
(JARToller) *hld up in rr: rdn 3f out: outpcd 2f out: hdwy over 1f out: kpt on u.str.p to go 2nd cl home* **10/1**

3424 **3** hd **Mrs Shilling**[12] 5994 3-9-5 **67** ........ LDettori 13 — 72
(JRFanshawe) *hld up in rr: hdwy on outside 3f out: rdn to go 2nd briefly ins fnl f: nt qckn cl home* **3/1**[1]

0230 **4** 1 **Jarvo**[34] 5496 3-8-12 **60** ........ KFallon 4 — 62
(NPLittmoden) *trckd ldr: led 6f out: rdn and hdd ins fnl f: no ex after* **7/1**[3]

-256 **5** 1 1/2 **Grand Apollo**[24] 5740 3-9-6 **68** ........ RHavlin 5 — 67
(JHMGosden) *towards rr and sn pushed along: mde sme late hdwy: nvr nr to chal* **7/1**[3]

340 **6** nk **Play Bouzouki**[19] 5828 3-9-4 **69** ........ NMackay(3) 3 — 68
(LMCumani) *prom: rdn over 2f out: wknd appr fnl f* **10/1**

3526 **7** 3 1/2 **The Number**[17] 5859 3-9-1 **63** ........(p) RWinston 2 — 54
(ISemple) *in tch tl rdn and wknd appr 2f out* **9/2**[2]

0002 **8** 4 **Mutassem (FR)**[30] 5597 3-8-7 **58** ........ BReilly(3) 7 — 41
(TKeddy) *prom: rdn 3f out: wknd 2f out* **14/1**

4000 **9** 1/2 **Supamach (IRE)**[32] 5537 3-9-6 **68** ........(p) PHanagan 9 — 50
(PFICole) *mid-div on outside: rdn and wknd over 2f out* **20/1**

0000 **10** 22 **Gentle Raindrop (IRE)**[6] 6082 3-8-10 **58** ........(b) JFEgan 6 — —
(SKirk) *prom tl wknd over 3f out* **33/1**

40-0 **11** 11 **Sahara Scirocco (IRE)**[3] 6157 3-8-13 **61** ........ ADaly 1 — —
(IAWood) *led tl hdd 6f out: wknd over 4f out* **100/1**

5023 **P** **Foolish Groom**[12] 5992 3-9-6 **68** ........ JQuinn 8 — —
(RHollinshead) *in tch: lost pl over 4f out: t.o whn p.u over 1f out* **8/1**

1m 51.29s

**WFA** 3 from 4yo 4lb — **12** Ran SP% **119.5**

Speed ratings: CSF £145.80 CT £442.21 TOTE £18.80: £4.40, £3.80, £1.90; EX 261.80.

**Owner** Graham & Lynn Knight **Bred** Mrs M F Taylor And James F Taylor **Trained** Ringshall, Bucks

**FOCUS**

Not much of a race and the form is notparticularly strong, but a thrilling finish that saw Blue Mariner just edge it.

**NOTEBOOK**

**Blue Mariner** has run several good races without winning this season and he deserved to finally get his head in front. There was nothing wrong with his attitude and he held on well under a strong ride from Fenton. He is still relatively lightly raced and may have have some improvement in him off a mark in the 60s.

**Truman** was doing his best work in the latter stages and just got up for second. This trip is about right for him and he may benefit from a more positive ride.

**Mrs Shilling** held her chance, but proved unable to get past Blue Mariner and was collared for second close home. She is nothing special, but will find a small race eventually.

**Jarvo** has had plenty of chances and did nothing to suggest he will be winning anytime soon.

**Grand Apollo** was never really going that well in rear, but stayed on well down the stretch and will improve again for another increase in distance.

**The Number** failed to improve for the first-time cheekpieces and faded out of it disappointingly.

**Foolish Groom** ran a shocker and something was presumably amiss. *Official explanation: jockey said gelding lost its action and pulled up but trotted back sound*

## 6225 LADBROKESGAMES.COM H'CAP — 1m 4f 50y(P)

9:30 (9:32) (F4) (0-62,62) 3-Y-0+ — £2,991 (£854; £427) Stalls Low

Form — RPR

4511 **1** **Heathyards Pride**[12] 5993 4-9-5 **58** ........ KFallon 7 — 72+
(RHollinshead) *hld up in rr: hdwy on outside 2f out: strly rdn to ld nr fin: cleverly* **5/4**[1]

2004 **2** 1/2 **Field Spark**[12] 5993 4-9-1 **54** ........(p) PHanagan 6 — 62
(JAGlover) *hldd up in rr: hdwy over 2f out: hrd rdn over 1f out and str run on ins to go 2nd nr fin* **6/1**[3]

4000 **3** 1/2 **Uncle John**[26] 5692 3-9-0 **60** ........(b[1]) JFEgan 1 — 67
(SKirk) *trckd ldrs: led 3f out: rdn and hdd wl ins fnl f: no ex cl home* **33/1**

0450 **4** 1 3/4 **Kernel Dowery (IRE)**[17] 5869 4-9-7 **60** ........(e) MFenton 12 — 65
(PWHarris) *hld up in rr: hdwy over 2f out: styd on one pce fnl f* **16/1**

2406 **5** shd **Midshipman**[24] 5733 6-9-4 **57** ........(vt) SWKelly 4 — 61
(AWCarroll) *trckd ldrs: wnt 2nd 2f out tl rdn and fdd ins fnl f* **6/1**[3]

3030 **6** 3 1/2 **Zonic Boom (FR)**[4] 6152 4-9-9 **62** ........ LDettori 5 — 61
(JRFanshawe) *mid-div: rdn 2f out: one pce after* **11/2**[2]

1000 **7** 6 **Trusted Mole (IRE)**[28] 5635 6-8-10 **54** ........ BSwarbrick(5) 10 — 44
(WMBrisbourne) *hld up: hdwy to trck ldrs 6f out: rdn over 2f out: sn wknd* **16/1**

5000 **8** 2 **Lampos (USA)**[163] 1668 4-9-1 **54** ........(p) RWinston 9 — 41
(MissJACamacho) *a in rr* **33/1**

4510 **9** 1 1/2 **Habitual (IRE)**[17] 5860 3-9-0 **60** ........ SSanders 3 — 45
(SirMarkPrescott) *trckd ldrs tl rdn and wknd over 2f out* **10/1**

1506 **10** 1 1/4 **Danger Bird (IRE)**[9] 6024 4-8-8 **54** ........ RKennemore(7) 8 — 37
(RHollinshead) *plld hrd: led tl hdd 3f out: wknd qckly* **25/1**

5000 **11** 13 **Fit To Fly (IRE)**[19] 5829 3-8-13 **62** ........ BReilly(3) 2 — 26
(MrsJCandlish) *t.k.h: w ldr tl rdn and wknd qckly over 3f out* **20/1**

2m 43.14s

**WFA** 3 from 4yo+ 7lb — **11** Ran SP% **123.7**

Speed ratings: CSF £9.12 CT £173.84 TOTE £2.50: £1.50, £2.00, £3.50; EX 13.80 Place 6 £68.95, Place 5 £34.78.

**Owner** L A Morgan **Bred** L A Morgan **Trained** Upper Longdon, Staffs

**FOCUS**

The winning run of the in-form Heathyards Pride continued with his third win on the bounce.

**NOTEBOOK**

**Heathyards Pride** has been in blinding form of late and, off a 6lb higher mark than when winning at Pontefract, had little trouble completing the hat-trick. If turned out again under a penalty he can make it four.

**Field Spark** stayed on to take second, but was never going to get to the winner. He is on a winning mark, but not one to totally rely on. has been in blinding form of late and, off a 6lb higher mark than when winning at Pontefract, had little trouble completing the hat-trick. If turned out again under a penalty he can make it four.

**Uncle John** returned to something like his form in the first-time blinkers and, back at a mile two, can probably land a small race. has been in blinding form of late and, off a 6lb higher mark than when winning at Pontefract, had little trouble completing the hat-trick. If turned out again under a penalty he can make it four.

**Kernel Dowery(IRE)** has not been in the best of form and this was a better effort.

**Midshipman** continues to run reasonably in defeat without doing enough to suggest he is about score.

**Habitual(IRE)** is not as progressive as many of his stable's three-year-olds and is too inconsistent to follow.

T/Plt: £80.20 to a £1 stake. Pool: £40,684.20. 370.10 winning tickets. T/Qpdt: £22.50 to a £1 stake. Pool: £1,973.40. 64.75 winning tickets. JS

# 5592 YARMOUTH (L-H)

Saturday, October 16

**OFFICIAL GOING: Good to soft**

Wind: Slight across Weather: Fine and sunny

## 6226 CUSTOM KITCHENS MAIDEN AUCTION STKS — 1m 3y

11:15 (11:18) (H5) 2-Y-O — £1,498 (£428; £214) Stalls High

Form — RPR

3305 **1** **Cava Bien**[18] 5852 2-8-8 70 ........ MFenton 1 — 63
(JGGiven) *mde virtually all: rdn and hung lft ins fnl f: edgd rt towards fin: all out* **8/1**[2]

5005 **2** nk **Sunny Times (IRE)**[21] 5792 2-8-5 57 ........ FNorton 9 — 59
(JWPayne) *hld up: hdwy over 1f out: r.o wl* **16/1**[3]

3 **3** 1 1/4 **Tharua (IRE)**[15] 5915 2-8-6 ........ KFallon 15 — 58
(EALDunlop) *trckd ldr: chal over 2f out: rdn and hung rt over 1f out: no ex ins fnl f* **1/3**[1]

0600 **4** 3 1/2 **Sirce (IRE)**[40] 5335 2-8-5 45 ........ JQuinn 5 — 49
(DJCoakley) *dwlt: sn pushed along in rr: r.o ins fnl f: nvr nrr* **100/1**

0255 **5** hd **Slite**[39] 5369 2-8-4 54 ow4 ........ PMakin(5) 12 — 52
(MissDMountain) *prom: rdn over 2f out: wknd fnl f* **33/1**

04 **6** 1/2 **Mister Elegant**[17] 5870 2-8-9 ........ SWhitworth 6 — 51
(JLSpearing) *chsd ldrs: rdn over 2f out: wknd fnl f* **25/1**

06 **7** 3/4 **Arch Folly**[43] 5256 2-8-6 ........ ABeech(3) 14 — 50
(JGPortman) *chsd ldrs: rdn 1/2-way: wknd over 1f out: hmpd ins fnl f* **25/1**

5064 **8** shd **Tip Toes (IRE)**[30] 5593 2-8-3 45 ........ CCatlin 16 — 43
(MRChannon) *prom over 5f* **33/1**

**9** 3 **Rose Bien** 2-8-2 ........ RMullen 8 — 36
(PJMcbride) *a in rr* **100/1**

0 **10** 5 **Miss Hermione**[15] 5911 2-8-0 ........ HayleyTurner(3) 7 — 26
(MrsCADunnett) *mid-div: rdn 1/2-way: wknd 3f out* **100/1**

05 **11** *3 1/2* **Precious Sammi**[10] 6011 2-8-8 LisaJones 11 23
(JulianPoulton) *unruly stalls: hld up: rdn and wknd over 2f out* **20/1**

**12** *26* **Sign Of Promise** 2-8-5 AMcCarthy 10 —
(SCWilliams) *sn outpcd* **25/1**

050 **13** *1* **Yankey**[31] 5561 2-8-10 SHitchcott 3 —
(CEBrittain) *sn outpcd* **100/1**

**14** *11* **Mishap** 2-8-6 PDoe 13 —
(WJarvis) *s.s: outpcd* **16/1**[3]

1m 42.0s (2.30) **Going Correction** +0.15s/f (Good) **14** Ran SP% **124.0**
Speed ratings: **94,93,92,88,88 88,87,87,84,79 75,49,48,37**CSF £117.46 TOTE £8.70: £1.80, £2.60, £1.02; EX 127.50.
**Owner** Lovely Bubbly Racing **Bred** Mrs Deborah O'Brien **Trained** Willoughton, Lincs

**FOCUS**
A weak, modest maiden, although slightly better than the bare form would suggest as the 57-rated runner-up showed improved form and overall it is unconvincing. They raced middle to stands' side and the favourite ended up right against the rail.

**NOTEBOOK**
**Cava Bien**, dropped back from ten furlongs and switched from nursery company back into a maiden, coped well with the ground (the softest he has encountered to date) and did enough to get off the mark. The runner-up is rated just 57 but has improved, so he is better than the bare form, but things are likely to be tougher in future.
**Sunny Times(IRE)** ◆ showed signs of improvement at Kempton on her previous start and confirmed that with her best effort to date. There is a race in her and she would be very hard to beat if turned out off her current mark in a nursery.
**Tharua(IRE)**, a very promising third behind the potentially smart Rob Roy on her debut in a 23-runner Newmarket maiden, was the form pick by a mile but ran a stinker. She was stepping up a furlong in trip, but that should not have been a problem and the only obvious excuse is the ground, as she did not appear to go through it and drifted under pressure.
**Sirce(IRE)** got an RPR of just 3 on her previous start, so this was quite an improvement. If she managed to get in a nursery, she could go well off her current rating.
**Slite** shaped as though a drop back to six furlongs may suit when fifth in a seller over seven on her previous start, and did not get home over this mile.
**Yankey** *Official explanation: jockey said colt had a breathing problem*

## 6227 SALTWELL SIGNS BANDED STKS 1m 3y
11:45 (11:50) (H5) 3-Y-0+ **£1,568** (£448; £224) **Stalls High**

Form RPR

0123 **1** **Caerphilly Gal**[7] 6058 4-9-0 50 DFox(5) 5 60
(PLGilligan) *a.p: led and hung rt over 1f out: rdn clr: eased nr fin* **5/1**[2]

4001 **2** *2* **Dante's Devine (IRE)**[21] 5794 3-8-12 46 VSlattery 20 52
(ABailey) *hld up in tch: rdn over 1f out: styd on* **7/1**

0400 **3** *1/2* **Wood Fern (UAE)**[14] 5927 4-9-0 45 SHitchcott 1 50
(MRChannon) *a.p: rdn over 2f out: styd on* **12/1**

0053 **4** *nk* **Magari**[19] 5830 3-9-2 50 MFenton 18 54
(JGGiven) *chsd ldrs: rdn over 3f out: styd on same pce fnl f* **20/1**

00 **5** *1* **Flying Spud**[44] 5236 3-8-11 48 DNolan(3) 11 50
(JLSpearing) *led: hdd over 5f out: rdn over 2f out: styd on same pce fnl f* **12/1**

3000 **6** *shd* **Blakeseven**[14] 5926 4-9-0 45 (p) SWhitworth 12 47
(WJMusson) *s.i.s: hld up: hdwy and nt clr run over 1f out: nt rch ldrs* **16/1**

5600 **7** *1/2* **City General (IRE)**[21] 5795 3-8-6 47 (p) DerekNolan(7) 15 48
(JSMoore) *w ldr tl led over 5f out: rdn and hdd over 1f out: no ex* **9/1**

501 **8** *1 1/4* **Delcienne**[14] 5929 3-8-12 49 ABeech(3) 6 47
(GGMargarson) *hld up: hdwy u.p over 1f out: no ex fnl f* **13/2**[3]

0004 **9** *3/4* **Pirouettes (IRE)**[28] 5642 4-8-11 45 DCorby(3) 16 42
(EROertel) *prom: rdn over 2f out: wknd fnl f* **40/1**

5435 **10** *hd* **Tokewanna**[21] 5795 4-9-3 48 (t) WSupple 8 44
(WMBrisbourne) *hld up: plld hrd: n.d* **12/1**

3400 **11** *1* **Rocky Reppin**[7] 6057 4-9-0 40 JEdmunds 7 39
(JBalding) *mid-div: rdn over 3f out: wknd over 1f out* **33/1**

1050 **12** *1* **Lucefer (IRE)**[24] 5733 6-9-2 50 NChalmers(3) 9 42
(GCHChung) *hld up: sme hdwy over 2f out: sn hung lft and btn* **9/2**[1]

6663 **13** *2 1/2* **Sonderborg**[21] 5795 3-9-1 49 (b) LisaJones 10 36
(MissAMNewton-Smith) *hld up: n.d* **20/1**

5352 **14** *3* **Encounter**[7] 6057 8-8-11 45 LPKeniry(3) 3 25
(JHetherton) *prom over 6f* **5/1**[2]

0000 **15** *2 1/2* **Hold Up**[19] 5830 3-8-13 50 BReilly(3) 17 25
(MissJFeilden) *mid-div: rdn over 3f out: wknd and eased over 1f out* **20/1**

-660 **16** *6* **Muqarrar (IRE)**[110] 3380 5-9-0 45 (t) AMcCarthy 2 8
(TJFitzgerald) *mid-div: rdn 1/2-way: wknd over 2f out* **40/1**

4150 **17** *1* **Brandywine Bay (IRE)**[42] 5283 4-8-11 40 (p) HayleyTurner(3) 14 5
(APJones) *mid-div: rdn over 2f out: sn wknd* **20/1**

000 **18** *1 1/2* **Sunset Dreamer (USA)**[21] 5791 3-8-13 47 IMongan 4 4
(PMitchell) *dwlt: hdwy 1/2-way: wknd over 1f out* **40/1**

0500 **19** *10* **Beltane**[14] 5927 6-9-0 45 PDoe 13 —
(WDeBest-Turner) *s.s: a bhd* **50/1**

1m 41.71s (2.01) **Going Correction** +0.15s/f (Good) **19** Ran SP% **147.6**
**WFA** 3 from 4yo+ 3lb
Speed ratings: **95,93,92,92,91 91,90,89,88,88 87,86,83,80,78 72,71,69,59**CSF £43.17 TOTE £10.70: £2.40, £7.20, £6.10; EX 67.20.
**Owner** T Williams **Bred** D J And Mrs Deer **Trained** Newmarket, Suffolk

**FOCUS**
Simply an ordinary banded race but solid enough form for the grade; they raced middle to stands' side.

**NOTEBOOK**
**Caerphilly Gal** was well suited by this step back up in trip and ran out an emphatic winner. She could be forced out of banded company now, but is at least in good heart.
**Dante's Devine(IRE)**, off the mark in a similar race over seven furlongs on fast ground at Kempton on his previous start, coped well with the easy surface and saw the trip out well, but he was never a threat to the winner.
**Wood Fern(UAE)** appreciated the return to easy ground and got closer to the winner than on his last two starts.
**Magari**, third in a maiden handicap at Bath on her previous start, was unable to reproduce that on easier ground.
**Flying Spud** had conditions to suit but was well held.
**Lucefer(IRE)** was a long way below his best, hanging and finding very little under pressure.
**Encounter** was runner-up in a similar event at Warwick on his previous start and looked capable of finding a similar race, so this represented a big step back.
**Brandywine Bay(IRE)** *Official explanation: jockey said filly was lame*
**Sunset Dreamer(USA)** *Official explanation: jockey said filly was unsuited by good to soft ground*

## 6228 FUTTERS BOOKMAKERS MANAGER OF THE YEAR AWARD TRI-BANDED STKS 7f 3y
12:15 (12:22) (H5) 3-Y-0 **£1,498** (£428; £214) **Stalls High**

Form RPR

4213 **1** **Elsinora**[7] 6056 3-9-0 45 (v) CCatlin 2 51
(AGJuckes) *hld up: hdwy over 2f out: led ins fnl f: rdn out* **11/4**[1]

0663 **2** *1/2* **David's Girl**[21] 5794 3-8-6 40 BReilly(3) 10 45
(DMorris) *hld up: hdwy over 2f out: rdn over 1f out: r.o* **8/1**[3]

040 **3** *1 1/2* **Primatech (IRE)**[7] 6056 3-8-9 40 (p) PFitzsimons 19 41
(KAMorgan) *chsd ldrs: ev ch fr over 2f out tl no ex ins fnl f* **25/1**

0050 **4** *1/2* **La Calera (GER)**[7] 6056 3-8-7 45 (b) DeanWilliams(7) 20 45
(GCHChung) *chsd ldrs tl led 1/2-way: hdd and no ex ins fnl f* **16/1**

0056 **5** *1 1/4* **Roving Vixen (IRE)**[7] 6056 3-8-9 40 SHitchcott 5 37
(JLSpearing) *led to 1/2-way: rdn and ev ch 1f out: no ex ins fnl f* **12/1**

3300 **6** *2* **Tsarbuck**[32] 5547 3-9-0 45 (p) GFaulkner 4 36
(RMHCowell) *chsd ldrs: rdn over 1f out: styd on same pce* **9/1**

0060 **7** *3/4* **Tardis**[32] 5552 3-8-9 40 (v[1]) JQuinn 11 29
(MLWBell) *w ldrs: rdn and ev ch 1f out: wknd ins fnl f* **14/1**

3060 **8** *nk* **Pererin**[7] 6057 3-8-9 40 (v) MFenton 15 29
(IAWood) *mid-div: rdn over 2f out: styd on same pce appr fnl f* **8/1**[3]

0000 **9** *2* **Cellino**[35] 5451 3-8-1 35 NChalmers(3) 17 18
(AndrewTurnell) *mid-div: rdn 1/2-way: no imp fnl 2f* **33/1**

2060 **10** *1 1/2* **Zonnebeke**[31] 5575 3-8-11 45 HayleyTurner(3) 7 25
(MrsCADunnett) *hld up: hdwy u.p over 2f out: wknd over 1f out* **6/1**[2]

0000 **11** *3 1/2* **Joans Jewel**[21] 5794 3-8-9 40 (p) JTate 3 10
(GGMargarson) *racd alone far side: w ldrs tl wknd fnl f* **50/1**

0556 **12** *1* **Bookiesindexdotcom**[108] 3425 3-8-9 40 (v) WSupple 12 8
(JRJenkins) *hld up: hdwy over 2f out: wknd over 1f out* **25/1**

00-0 **13** *1 3/4* **Boppys Babe**[49] 5110 3-8-4 30 PDoe 18 —
(RAFahey) *s.s: a in rr* **66/1**

0000 **14** *nk* **Military Two Step (IRE)**[14] 5926 3-9-0 45 (p) IMongan 13 7
(KRBurke) *chsd ldrs: rdn 1/2-way: wknd 2f out* **16/1**

0006 **15** *1 3/4* **Silver Island**[21] 5794 3-8-9 40 (t) RMullen 6 —
(RMHCowell) *hld up: rdn 1/2-way: sn wknd* **16/1**

0036 **16** *nk* **Petrion**[117] 3146 3-8-11 45 DCorby(3) 16 —
(RGuest) *hld up: rdn 1/2-way: sn wknd* **33/1**

0000 **17** *2 1/2* **Shebaan**[50] 5092 3-8-2 40 JBrennan(7) 9 —
(PSMcentee) *hld up: wknd 1/2-way* **66/1**

6000 **18** *2* **Pardon Moi**[21] 5793 3-8-9 40 LisaJones 14 —
(MrsCADunnett) *chsd ldrs 4f* **14/1**

0503 **19** *5* **La Fonteyne**[50] 5086 3-9-0 45 SWhitworth 1 —
(CBBBooth) *swtchd rt sn after s: a bhd* **20/1**

0000 **20** *1/2* **Miss St Albans**[20] 2729 3-8-2 40 AKirby(7) 8 —
(MWigham) *a in rr* **100/1**

1m 28.36s (1.86) **Going Correction** +0.15s/f (Good) **20** Ran SP% **136.1**
Speed ratings: **95,94,92,92,90 88,87,87,84,83 79,78,76,75,73 73,70,68,62,61**CSF £23.96 TOTE £3.80: £1.30, £1.90, £17.40; EX 16.30.
**Owner** R T Juckes **Bred** J Goddard And J Steel **Trained** Abberley, Worcs

**FOCUS**
A competitive enough banded contest in which all bar Joans Jewel raced middle to stands' side. The form is average for the grade but sound.

**NOTEBOOK**
**Elsinora** looked one to be wary of when throwing away a winning chance in a similar event over a mile at Warwick on her previous start, but she has got the ability and did what was required this time.
**David's Girl**, third behind today's winner at Kempton on her previous start, managed to get closer but shaped as though well worth another try over a mile.
**Primatech(IRE)**, racing over a trip short enough for her, acquitted herself with credit and may find one of these moderate events.
**La Calera(GER)**, dropped back in trip, ran better than of late and has found her level.
**Roving Vixen(IRE)**, dropped a furlong in trip and with the blinkers left off, shaped as though worth a try over shorter.
**Tardis** *Official explanation: jockey said filly hung right in final 2f*
**Zonnebeke** was below form and may not have appreciated this ground. *Official explanation: jockey said saddle slipped*

## 6229 CUSTOM KITCHENS BANDED STKS 6f 3y
12:45 (12:47) (H5) 3-Y-0+ **£1,512** (£432; £216) **Stalls High**

Form RPR

0605 **1** **Tappit (IRE)**[14] 5930 5-9-0 45 RMullen 9 55
(NEBerry) *chsd ldrs: led 2f out: hung rt ins fnl f: rdn out* **25/1**

5040 **2** *1 1/2* **Polar Haze**[128] 2823 7-9-0 40 (v) MFenton 8 50
(JPearce) *chsd ldrs: rdn and ev ch fr over 1f out: nt run on towards fin* **14/1**

5500 **3** *2* **Indian Warrior**[144] 2387 8-8-7 40 (b) LiamJones(7) 11 44
(JJay) *s.s: hld up: hdwy over 1f out: r.o* **25/1**

0000 **4** *hd* **Lakelands Lady (IRE)**[7] 6059 4-8-9 45 PMakin(5) 12 43
(JBalding) *chsd ldrs: rdn over 2f out: styd on same pce fnl f* **25/1**

1664 **5** *1 1/4* **Little Flute**[7] 6059 3-8-13 45 SWhitworth 2 40
(TKeddy) *mid-div: hdwy u.p over 2f out: styd on* **8/1**[2]

0200 **6** *hd* **Avit (IRE)**[21] 5793 4-9-0 40 SHitchcott 18 39
(PLGilligan) *chsd ldrs: rdn and ev ch over 1f out: no ex* **20/1**

2004 **7** *shd* **Danakim**[21] 5793 7-9-0 40 IMongan 5 39
(JRWeymes) *chsd ldrs: rdn over 2f out: hung rt and wknd ins fnl f* **6/1**[1]

0002 **8** *nk* **Wodhill Be**[14] 5926 4-9-0 40 PaulEddery 19 38
(DMorris) *s.s: outpcd: hdwy and nt clr run 1f out: nt rch ldrs* **8/1**[2]

0033 **9** *1/2* **Angel Isa (IRE)**[21] 5793 4-9-0 40 (v) GParkin 3 36
(RAFahey) *chsd ldrs: outpcd and swtchd rt over 2f out: r.o ins fnl f* **6/1**[1]

000- **10** *1* **Tom From Bounty**[355] 5787 4-9-0 45 PDoe 1 33
(WDeBest-Turner) *outpcd: styd on ins fnl f: nvr nrr* **66/1**

0453 **11** *3* **Royal Nite Owl**[75] 4391 3-8-13 40 WSupple 13 24
(JBalding) *mde most 4f: wknd fnl f* **11/1**

0003 **12** *hd* **Whinhill House**[7] 6059 4-9-0 45 NPollard 16 24
(DWBarker) *chsd ldrs over 4f* **8/1**[2]

0000 **13** *1/2* **Playful Spirit**[7] 6059 5-9-0 45 (v) JEdmunds 4 22
(JBalding) *chsd ldrs 4f* **10/1**[3]

0650 **14** *nk* **Bank Games**[48] 5141 3-8-13 40 (b[1]) TLucas 14 21
(MWEasterby) *chsd ldrs: rdn over 2f out: wknd over 1f out* **25/1**

0400 **15** *1 3/4* **Scarlett Breeze**[14] 5930 3-8-13 45 MTebbutt 10 16
(JWHills) *trckd ldrs: rdn over 2f out: wknd over 1f out* **20/1**

0000 **16** *1/2* **Hi Darl**[21] 5794 3-8-8 40 RoryMoore(5) 20 15
(WMBrisbourne) *outpcd* **25/1**

0500 **17** *3/4* **Tamarella (IRE)**[42] 5282 4-8-11 45 (b) ABeech(3) 6 12
(GGMargarson) *chsd ldrs over 4f* **20/1**

0000 **18** *6* **Caribbean Blue**[21] 5801 3-8-10 40 (b[1]) HayleyTurner(3) 15 —
(RMWhitaker) *s.s: outpcd* **33/1**

0000 **19** *shd* **Queen Of Bulgaria (IRE)**[14] 5930 3-8-13 40 PMcCabe 17 —
(JPearce) *chsd ldrs 4f* **25/1**

5100 **20** *nk* **Sotonian (HOL)**[21] 5793 11-9-0 40 ........ LisaJones 7 —
(PSFelgate) *bhd fr 1/2-way* **25/1**

1m 15.07s (1.47) **Going Correction** +0.15s/f (Good)
**WFA** 3 from 4yo+ 1lb **20** Ran SP% **131.6**
Speed ratings: **96,94,91,91,89 89,89,88,87,86 82,82,81,81,78 78,77,69,69,68**CSF £308.08 TOTE £22.00: £7.00, £5.00, £7.80; EX 251.90.
**Owner** Mrs Jan Adams **Bred** Larry Ryan **Trained** Earlswood, Monmouths

**FOCUS**
A moderate sprint even in the context of this lowly grade and little solid form to go on. They raced middle to stands' side.

**NOTEBOOK**
**Tappit(IRE)** had gained both his previous wins on really fast ground, but he handles an easy surface and gained his first win in well over a year. He could go in again in similar company.
**Polar Haze** has gained all of his wins on Southwell's Fibresand, but there was little wrong with this effort, especially considering it was his first start in 128 days.
**Indian Warrior**, racing for the first time in 144 days, ran most encouragingly over trip just on the short side and should be able to find a similar event.
**Lakelands Lady(IRE)** is nowhere near as good as she was, but this was a respectable effort and she could make her mark at this level.
**Little Flute** should have appreciated this step back up in trip but he was not at his best.
**Danakim**, who raced right down the middle of the track, would have found this ground too soft.
**Angel Isa(IRE)** is another who may have found this ground soft enough.

## 6230 ADVISION ADVERTISING SERVICES BANDED STKS — 1m 2f 21y
**1:15** (1:15) (H5) 3-Y-O+ **£1,526** (£436; £218) **Stalls** Low

Form RPR
0000 **1** **Ellovamul**[12] 5993 4-8-10 46 ........ (b) BSwarbrick(5) 4 55
(WMBrisbourne) *hld up: hdwy over 2f out: rdn to ld wl ins fnl f: r.o* **14/1**
2132 **2** *2* **Lenwade**[14] 5928 3-8-6 45 ........ ABeech(3) 7 50
(GGMargarson) *chsd ldrs: rdn and ev ch ins fnl f: unable qck* **13/2**
3306 **3** *1 1/2* **Miss Glory Be**[42] 5285 6-9-0 45 ........ (p) LisaJones 6 47
(EROertel) *chsd ldrs: led over 2f out: hdd and no ex wl ins fnl f* **16/1**
0650 **4** *6* **Larad (IRE)**[17] 5863 3-8-3 45 ow1 ........ (b) DerekNolan(7) 12 38
(JSMoore) *chsd ldrs: rdn over 2f out: wknd fnl f* **20/1**
6044 **5** *1 3/4* **Tasneef (USA)**[21] 5796 5-9-3 48 ........ SHitchcott 13 36
(TDMccarthy) *led over 7f: wknd fnl f* **4/1**[1]
6412 **6** *nk* **Dancing Tilly**[21] 5791 6-9-1 46 ........ (p) GParkin 5 34
(RAFahey) *hld up: hdwy over 3f out: rdn and wknd over 1f out* **6/1**[3]
0430 **7** *1* **Princess Bankes**[6] 6082 3-8-2 45 ........ AKirby(7) 14 31
(MissGayKelleway) *hld up: hdwy over 2f out: sn wknd* **50/1**
4 **8** *2* **Idle Journey (IRE)**[21] 5795 3-8-12 48 ........ VSlattery 9 30
(MScudamore) *s.s: hld up: hdwy over 3f out: hung lft and wknd over 1f out* **10/1**
3660 **9** *3 1/2* **No Chance To Dance (IRE)**[60] 4826 4-9-0 45 ........ (t) WSupple 15 21
(HJCollingridge) *hld up: rdn and hung lft fr over 3f out: nt run on* **13/2**
0600 **10** *1 1/4* **Fairland (IRE)**[21] 5791 5-8-8 46 ........ LSmith(7) 1 20
(SDow) *hld up: a in rr* **33/1**
0/03 **11** *nk* **Dee Pee Tee Cee (IRE)**[44] 5238 10-9-0 45 ........ TLucas 3 18
(MWEasterby) *hld up: hdwy over 2f out: sn wknd* **10/1**
0000 **12** *11* **Raheel (IRE)**[10] 6013 4-9-5 50 ........ (t) IMongan 10 4
(PMitchell) *hld up: rdn over 3f out: sn wknd* **20/1**
0033 **13** *1* **Confuzed**[40] 5336 4-9-0 45 ........ (e) RMullen 8 —
(DFlood) *plld hrd and prom: wknd 2f out* **5/1**[2]
646 **14** *4* **Mount Cottage**[48] 5146 3-8-12 48 ........ MFenton 11 —
(JGGiven) *prom over 6f* **33/1**
0003 **15** *18* **Zarneeta**[12] 5999 3-8-9 45 ........ MTebbutt 16 —
(WDeBest-Turner) *dwlt: a bhd* **50/1**

2m 11.81s (3.84) **Going Correction** +0.35s/f (Good)
**WFA** 3 from 4yo+ 5lb **15** Ran SP% **127.7**
Speed ratings: **98,96,95,90,89 88,87,86,83,82 82,73,72,69,55**CSF £100.87 TOTE £16.00: £5.70, £1.70, £5.80; EX 145.40.
**Owner** Clayfields Racing **Bred** Joseph Hogan **Trained** Great Ness, Shropshire

**FOCUS**
One of the better contests on the card and they went a strong pace. The winner goes well here and is above average for the grade.

**NOTEBOOK**
**Ellovamul** had not been in great form in recent outings but, dropped into banded company for the first time and with the blinkers back on, this was more like it. The strong pace enabled her to put her stamina to good use and she was well on top at the finish. There could be more to come, especially back over further, and she can win again.
**Lenwade**, an unlucky loser when beaten just a short-head into second at Brighton on her previous start, again found one too good but did not appear to have any real excuses this time.
**Miss Glory Be** did not last home and this would appear to be the limit of her stamina. This was still a respectable effort, however.
**Larad(IRE)** was beaten quite a way and this ground was probably softer than ideal.
**Tasneef(USA)** was unable to sustain the decent gallop he set and looks better on fast ground.
**Confuzed**, racing over his furthest trip to date, did not stay after racing keenly. *Official explanation: jockey said gelding was too keen early*

## 6231 DESIRA MOTORS BANDED STKS — 1m 6f 17y
**1:45** (1:45) (H5) 3-Y-O+ **£1,505** (£430; £215) **Stalls** Low

Form RPR
3254 **1** **Banningham Blaze**[11] 6005 4-9-5 46 ........ (b) DNolan(3) 2 54
(AWCarroll) *hld up: hdwy over 2f out: led ins fnl f: r.o* **7/2**[2]
0-00 **2** *nk* **Touch Of Ebony (IRE)**[14] 5935 5-9-2 45 ........ (p) AMedeiros(5) 6 53
(CRoberts) *chsd ldrs: led over 1f out: hdd ins fnl f: kpt on* **25/1**
0412 **3** *3* **Annakita**[48] 5159 4-9-7 45 ........ LisaJones 3 49
(WJMusson) *hld up: hdwy over 3f out: rdn over 1f out: styd on same pce* **3/1**[1]
0100 **4** *2 1/2* **Regency Red (IRE)**[11] 6005 6-9-3 46 ........ BSwarbrick(5) 7 46
(WMBrisbourne) *prom: led over 2f out: rdn and hdd over 1f out: wknd ins fnl f* **8/1**[3]
0045 **5** *5* **Ribbons And Bows (IRE)**[28] 5658 4-9-12 50 ........ (v[1]) IMongan 1 44
(CACyzer) *chsd ldrs tl led over 3f out: hdd over 2f out: wknd over 1f out* **8/1**[3]
0402 **6** *6* **Lord Lahar**[7] 6065 5-9-11 49 ........ SHitchcott 16 35
(MRChannon) *stasrted slowly: hld up: effrt over 2f out: n.d* **8/1**[3]
5643 **7** *2 1/2* **Smarter Charter**[28] 5644 11-9-0 35 ........ KristinStubbs(7) 13 28
(MrsLStubbs) *hld up: effrt over 2f out: no ch whn hmpd over 1f out* **16/1**
0300 **8** *1/2* **Venetian Romance (IRE)**[5] 6120 3-8-5 35 ........ MHalford(7) 5 27
(APJones) *hld up: effrt over 3f out: sn wknd* **25/1**
/00- **9** *11* **Who Cares Wins**[158] 392 8-9-7 45 ........ PMcCabe 8 13
(JRJenkins) *hld up: rdn over 3f out: sn wknd* **12/1**
2354 **10** *4* **Little Richard (IRE)**[164] 1887 5-9-7 45 ........ (p) VSlattery 4 8
(MWellings) *chsd ldrs over 10f* **25/1**
0006 **11** *5* **Vanbrugh (FR)**[40] 5354 4-9-7 40 ........ (vt) MFenton 14 1
(MissDAMchale) *chsd ldr tl led over 6f out: hdd & wknd over 3f out* **11/1**
404- **12** *3 1/2* **Ren's Magic**[364] 4486 6-9-7 35 ........ WSupple 11 —
(JRJenkins) *hld up: plld hrd: wknd 4f out* **33/1**
036- **13** *2* **Yaheska (IRE)**[426] 4216 7-9-7 35 ........ RMullen 10 —
(NEBerry) *hld up: bhd fnl 4f* **20/1**
6000 **14** *18* **Jazil**[85] 4082 9-9-7 45 ........ (vt) PFitzsimons 9 —
(KAMorgan) *led: hdd over 6f out: wknd 4f out* **25/1**

3m 11.69s (6.49) **Going Correction** +0.35s/f (Good)
**WFA** 3 from 4yo+ 9lb **14** Ran SP% **125.6**
Speed ratings: **95,94,93,91,88 85,83,83,77,75 72,70,69,58**CSF £101.11 TOTE £5.00: £2.10, £10.10, £1.90; EX 164.60.
**Owner** Dennis Deacon **Bred** D J And Mrs Deer **Trained** Wixford, Warwicks

**FOCUS**
A reasonable enough race for the grade and the pace was decent, with the third setting the standard.

**NOTEBOOK**
**Banningham Blaze**, dropped into banded company and with blinkers re-fitted, gained her third success of the campaign under a very good waiting from Nolan, who produced her as late as possible and eventually won a shade cosily.
**Touch Of Ebony(IRE)**, dropped in grade with the cheekpieces back on, ran a game race in defeat, pulling clear of all bar the winner. He looks up to winning a similar event, but has had 29 chances.
**Annakita** had been in good form in better grades than this lately and looked the one to beat dropped in class, but she proved very one paced in the closing stages and is of limited ability.
**Regency Red(IRE)** travelled strongly but did not last home and may have found this ground softer than ideal.
**Ribbons And Bows(IRE)**, racing in a visor for the first time, had shaped as though well worth a try over this sort of trip on her last couple of outings, but she did not appear to stay. *Official explanation: jockey said filly did not get trip*
**Lord Lahar** *Official explanation: jockey said gelding hung right*
T/Plt: £587.40 to a £1 stake. Pool: £18,308.05. 22.75 winning tickets. T/Qpdt: £345.00 to a £1 stake. Pool: £1,538.60. 3.30 winning tickets. CR

6232 - 6239a (Foreign Racing) - See Raceform Interactive

# 5816 MUSSELBURGH (R-H)
### Sunday, October 17

**OFFICIAL GOING: Good to soft (soft in places in home straight) changing to soft after race 2 (3.00pm)**

## 6240 EUROPEAN BREEDERS FUND MAIDEN STKS — 1m 1f
**2:30** (2:32) (E3) 2-Y-O **£5,463** (£1,681; £840; £420) **Stalls** Low

Form RPR
54 **1** **Kindling**[15] 5946 2-8-9 ........ JFanning 4 80+
(MJohnston) *cl up: led after 2f: rdn clr 2f out: styd on wl* **7/2**[2]
00 **2** *3 1/2* **Caribbean Dancer (USA)**[24] 5756 2-8-9 ........ RFfrench 3 71
(MJohnston) *led 2f: cl up: rdn over 2f out: kpt on same pce* **40/1**
052 **3** *1* **Desperation (IRE)**[10] 6021 2-9-0 75 ........ LEnstone 1 74
(KRBurke) *trckd ldrs: hdwy 3f out: ch over 2f out: sn rdn and kpt on same pce* **10/1**[3]
422 **4** *5* **Master Cobbler (IRE)**[20] 5827 2-9-0 84 ........ LDettori 5 70+
(GAButler) *hld up in tch: swtchd lft and hdwy 3f out: rdn: put hd in air and wandered over 2f out: sn btn* **1/2**[1]
0065 **5** *4* **Aza Wish (IRE)**[7] 6092 2-8-4 58 ........ RoryMoore(5) 7 51
(MsDeborahJEvans) *in tch: rdn along 3f out: swtchd lft and drvn 2f out: nvr a factor* **66/1**
4036 **6** *2 1/2* **Blackcomb Mountain (USA)**[24] 5753 2-8-9 66 ........ ANicholls 6 46
(MFHarris) *prom: pushed along 1/2-way: rdn over 3f out and sn wknd* **20/1**
0004 **7** *1* **The Terminator (IRE)**[36] 5455 2-9-0 50 ........ FLynch 8 49
(ABerry) *a rr* **100/1**
0300 **8** *2 1/2* **Cois Na Tine Eile**[13] 5988 2-8-9 51 ........ SHitchcott 2 39
(MsDeborahJEvans) *dwlt and towards rr: hdwy to chse ldrs 3f out: sn rdn and wknd* **100/1**

1m 58.45s **Going Correction** +0.30s/f (Good) **8** Ran SP% **108.7**
Speed ratings: **95,91,91,86,83 80,79,77**CSF £100.31 TOTE £4.00: £1.70, £8.40, £2.50; EX 74.60.
**Owner** The Duchess Of Roxburghe **Bred** Floors Farming And Christopher J Heath **Trained** Middleham Moor, N Yorks

**FOCUS**
A one-two for Mark Johnston, who typically does well with his staying juveniles, and the winner showed improved form in just a fair contest.

**NOTEBOOK**
**Kindling**, who had shaped with promise in two previous starts over six and seven furlongs, relished every yard of this trip and, having sat on the shoulder of her stable companion Caribbean Dancer for most of the way, she went into the lead before staying on strongly for a comfortable win. Evidently going the right way, she will follow up if being found a suitable opportunity.
**Caribbean Dancer(USA)** had run better than it looked in two previous tries and this was an improved effort. She led for the early part of the race before being overtaken by her stable companion, but kept battling away and will be winning before long.
**Desperation(IRE)** continues to go the right way and will find life easier in nurseries.
**Master Cobbler(IRE)** was very disappointing as his previous form entitled him to win. He made little ground having been held up and did not look over enthusiastic under pressure. He now has something to prove.
**Blackcomb Mountain(USA)** is not really going the right way and needs a drop into selling/claiming company before she gets her head in front again.

## 6241 WEATHERBYS BANK SPRINT CONDITIONS STKS — 5f
**3:00** (3:01) (C1) 2-Y-O **£12,017** (£4,558; £2,279; £1,036) **Stalls** Low

Form RPR
4330 **1** **Bigalos Bandit**[39] 5392 2-9-4 95 ........ RWinston 6 94+
(JJQuinn) *trckd ldrs gng wl: smooth hdwy 2f out: led ent last and sn clr* **6/4**[1]
4321 **2** *2 1/2* **Alexia Rose (IRE)**[23] 5771 2-8-13 78 ........ FLynch 3 77+
(ABerry) *cl up: led wl over 1f out: sn rdn: drvn and hdd ent last: nt qckn* **9/2**[3]
5640 **3** *5* **Handsome Lady**[30] 5602 2-8-7 75 ........ PHanagan 4 54
(ISemple) *cl up: rdn along 2f out: sn one pce* **10/1**
0410 **4** *1 3/4* **Talcen Gwyn (IRE)**[15] 5932 2-8-12 81 ........ ANicholls 2 53
(MFHarris) *sn led: rdn along over 2f out: hdd wl over 1f out and sn wknd* **8/1**
5000 **5** *3/4* **Steal The Thunder**[47] 5213 2-8-7 54 ........ PPMathers(5) 5 50
(ABerry) *dwlt: a rr* **200/1**
1023 **6** *4* **Smiddy Hill**[15] 5932 2-8-11 84 ........ RFfrench 7 35
(RBastiman) *cl up: rdn along 2f out: sn wknd* **5/2**[2]

61.93 secs (1.53) **Going Correction** +0.30s/f (Good) **6** Ran SP% **107.5**
Speed ratings: **99,95,87,84,83 76**CSF £7.84 TOTE £2.50: £1.60, £2.40; EX 6.70.
**Owner** Ian Buckley **Bred** David John Boughton **Trained** Settrington, N Yorks

**FOCUS**
Bigalos Bandit returned to winning ways on this first start after a break. The form is reasonable but held down by the fifth.

**NOTEBOOK**
**Bigalos Bandit**, freshened up by a break, had the best form on offer and came away in the final furlong having travelled well just off the leaders throughout. He will not be easy to place as a three-year-old and needs to improve to win back in a better grade.
**Alexia Rose(IRE)**, off the mark at Haydock most recently, is well served by some cut in the ground and ran well in defeat, pulling clear of the third.
**Handsome Lady** ran a bit better than expected and kept on for third.
**Talcen Gwyn(IRE)** tried to make most of the running, but was readily brushed aside.
**Smiddy Hill** ran a shocker and there was presumably something not quite right.

## 6242 EAST LOTHIAN NEWS (S) STKS — 7f 30y
3:30 (3:40) (E3) 2-Y-O — £6,916 (£2,128; £1,064; £532) Stalls Low

Form — RPR

6002 **1** **Strathtay**$^{7}$ [6093] 2-8-6 55 (v) FNorton 9 — 59
(ABerry) *trckd ldrs on inner: hdwy 3f out: rdn to ld over 1f out: sn drvn and hld on wl* **14/1**

065 **2** ½ **Mossmann Gorge**$^{18}$ [5857] 2-8-11 62 FLynch 7 — 63
(GASwinbank) *keen: trckd ldrs: hmpd after 11/2f: hdwy 3f out: chal ent last: ev ch tl drvn:edgd rt and no ex last 50 yd* **6/1**$^{3}$

3050 **3** 2½ **Mytton's Bell (IRE)**$^{31}$ [5578] 2-8-6 65 DAllan 10 — 52
(ABailey) *led: clr whn rn wd home turn: riidcden over 2f out: drvn and hdd over 1f out: kpt on same pce* **16/1**

0006 **4** 1½ **Beauchamp Twist**$^{78}$ [4335] 2-8-3 61 (b) NMackay$^{(3)}$ 3 — 48
(GAButler) *prom whn hmpd after 11/2f: hdwy to chse ldr over 3f out: rdn over 2f out: sn drvn and one pce* **20/1**

400 **5** hd **Veneer (IRE)**$^{136}$ [2609] 2-8-11 55 RLMoore 2 — 53
(RHannon) *chsd ldrs on outer whn hung bdly rt after 11/2f: prom tl rdn over 2f out and grad wknd* **5/1**$^{2}$

2000 **6** ½ **Invertiel (USA)**$^{7}$ [6091] 2-8-11 75 (v$^{1}$) PHanagan 13 — 51
(ISemple) *bhd: hdwy over 2f out: styd on: nrst fin* **12/1**

0300 **7** 1½ **Street Ballad (IRE)**$^{12}$ [6003] 2-8-6 62 JFanning 14 — 43
(MrsJRRamsden) *in tch on inner: rdn along over 2f out and sn btn* **8/1**

1420 **8** 1¾ **Mount Ephram (IRE)**$^{21}$ [5819] 2-8-13 70 (b) DNolan$^{(3)}$ 6 — 49
(RFFisher) *s.i.s: a rr* **33/1**

1052 **9** 1½ **Corniche Dancer**$^{10}$ [6022] 2-8-11 68 LDettori 12 — 52+
(MRChannon) *midfield: hmpd and swtchd lft after 11/2f: carried wd bnd after 3f and bhd: hdwy on outer 3f out: rdn: edgd lft and btn 2fo* **9/4**$^{1}$

0 **10** ½ **River Card**$^{31}$ [5592] 2-8-6 PRobinson 11 — 34
(MHTompkins) *towards rr whn rn wd bnd after 3f: bhd after* **10/1**

3240 **11** 4 **Spinnakers Girl**$^{59}$ [4878] 2-8-6 69 RWinston 8 — 24
(JRWeymes) *bhd fr 1/2-way* **10/1**

**12** dist **Davids Choice** 2-8-6 PPMathers$^{(5)}$ 5 — —
(ABerry) *s.i.s: a wl bhd* **100/1**

1m 32.41s (2.88) **Going Correction** +0.30s/f (Good) — **12** Ran SP% **119.9**
Speed ratings: **95,94,91,89,89 89,87,85,83,83 78,**—CSF £95.59 TOTE £19.90: £4.00, £2.90, £5.60; EX 140.30.The winner was bought in for 7,200gns. Mossmann Gorge was claimed by D J Flood for £15,000
**Owner** E Nisbet **Bred** Broughton Bloodstock **Trained** Cockerham, Lancs
■ Stewards Enquiry : R L Moore two-day ban: careless riding (Oct 28,29)

**FOCUS**
A fair selling race that looks sure to produce its share of future winners at this sort of level, although it seemed an advantage to race prominently.

**NOTEBOOK**
**Strathtay** has been taking her racing well and built on her recent second to record her first-ever win. The visor has helped the last twice and this seven furlong trip did her no harm, so there may be further improvement to come.
**Mossmann Gorge** ◆ has been running well in maidens and this drop in grade nearly bought about his first win. He may be able to improve again and will be winning before long.
**Mytton's Bell(IRE)** did herself no favours by running wide on the home bend - held the lead at the time - and ran well considering. She kept plugging away and has a bad race in her.
**Beauchamp Twist** ran well on this drop in grade and the blinkers seem to have made a difference the last twice.
**Veneer(IRE)** was all over the place in the early stages and never looked happy.
**Corniche Dancer** did not run her race and may have been unnerved by getting hampered early on. Her best form is on a faster surface to boot and she is worth another chance. *Official explanation: jockey said filly was unsuited by soft ground*
**River Cardh**

## 6243 RACING UK CHANNEL 432 H'CAP — 5f
4:00 (4:01) (C1) (0-107,102) 3-Y-O+ — £12,082 (£4,583; £2,291; £1,041) Stalls Low

Form — RPR

1061 **1** **Malapropism**$^{1}$ [6205] 4-8-12 88 6ex DAllan 10 — 98
(MRChannon) *a.p: effrt to chal 2f out: rdn to ld and edgd lft ins last: styd on wl* **8/1**$^{3}$

0321 **2** 1¾ **Corridor Creeper (FR)**$^{3}$ [6177] 7-9-12 102 6ex (p) RLMoore 9 — 106
(JMBradley) *cl up: led over 1f out: sn rdn: hdd and swtchd rt ins last: kpt on* **5/1**$^{2}$

5400 **3** ½ **Whitbarrow (IRE)**$^{15}$ [5933] 5-8-11 87 FNorton 15 — 89
(JMBradley) *in tch on outer: hdwy 2f out: rdn over 1f out: kpt on ins last* **20/1**

0352 **4** nk **Further Outlook (USA)**$^{1}$ [6205] 10-8-7 83 oh1 (p) JFanning 5 — 84
(DKIvory) *led: rdn along 2f out: sn hdd and one pce ent last* **9/1**

0426 **5** ½ **Whistler**$^{3}$ [6177] 7-9-1 91 (p) PFitzsimons 7 — 91
(JMBradley) *in rr: hdwy on outer 2f out: rdn over 1f out: kpt on ins last: nrst fin* **9/1**

0004 **6** nk **Connect**$^{8}$ [6071] 7-8-13 89 (b) PRobinson 12 — 88
(MHTompkins) *hld up in rr: hdwy 2f out: nt clr run ent and ins last: kpt on* **12/1**

0010 **7** nk **Pic Up Sticks**$^{8}$ [6071] 5-9-7 97 SHitchcott 13 — 95+
(MRChannon) *hld up in rr: hdwy and nt clr run over 1f out: swtchd wd and styd on ins last: nrst fin* **11/1**

1450 **8** ¾ **Rydal (USA)**$^{23}$ [5762] 3-8-10 86 (v) SSanders 1 — 81
(GAButler) *chsd ldrs on inner: rdn over 1f out: wknd ent last* **10/1**

0430 **9** nk **Frascati**$^{15}$ [5933] 4-8-2 83 oh3 PPMathers$^{(5)}$ 11 — 77
(ABerry) *chsd ldrs: rdn along over 1f out: wknd ins last* **20/1**

0045 **10** 1¼ **River Falcon**$^{8}$ [6071] 4-8-9 85 RWinston 2 — 75
(JSGoldie) *trckd ldrs: effrt over 1f out: nt clr run ent last: no imp* **4/1**$^{1}$

330 **11** 3 **Ptarmigan Ridge**$^{22}$ [5787] 8-8-8 87 NMackay$^{(3)}$ 4 — 67
(MissLAPerratt) *in tch: hdwy to chse ldrs 2f out: sn rdn and wknd appr last* **9/1**

0000 **12** 1½ **Henry Hall (IRE)**$^{15}$ [5933] 8-8-7 83 KimTinkler 3 — 57
(NTinkler) *chsd ldrs: rdn along 2f out: sn wknd* **16/1**

0-04 **13** 28 **Alfie Lee (IRE)**$^{80}$ [4279] 7-8-7 83 oh38 (bt) PHanagan 16 — —
(DANolan) *s.i.s: a bhd* **200/1**

60.79 secs (0.39) **Going Correction** +0.30s/f (Good) — **13** Ran SP% **118.8**
Speed ratings: **108,105,104,103,103 102,102,100,100,98 93,91,46**CSF £46.51 CT £784.91 TOTE £7.60: £3.40, £2.50, £5.20; EX 39.70 Trifecta £1516.50 Pool: £26,699.02. 12.50 winning units..
**Owner** Michael A Foy **Bred** Michael A Foy **Trained** West Ilsley, Berks

**FOCUS**
A decent handicap in which two bang in-form sprinters dominated the finish, although neither looked well treated beforehand suggesting the form may not be as strong as it appears at first sight.

**NOTEBOOK**
**Malapropism**, who has always been at his best on a fast surface in the past, handled the soft ground surprisingly well when winning at Catterick in a better race the previous day and again went through it with the minimum of fuss under a 6lb penalty. Clearly on the up, now he has proven his effectiveness on this sort of ground there is no reason why he cannot complete the hat-trick.
**Corridor Creeper(FR)**, who scored for the first time in a while at Newmarket on Thursday, stuck on well without being able to get to the winner and performed creditably under his penalty.
**Whitbarrow(IRE)** is a very inconsistent performer and this was one of his better efforts. Unfortunately he cannot be relied upon to repeat the form.
**Further Outlook(USA)** has been in good form this season and, despite looking to have had a tough race when second to Malapropism the previous day, again ran well. He will continue to pay his way while the ground is in his favour.
**Whistler** is another to have had a good season and he continues to run well without winning at the moment.
**Connect** was doing his best work late and would have been closer with a clearer run.
**Pic Up Sticks** was going on strongly at the death and, like Connect, should have been closer. *Official explanation: jockey said gelding was denied a clear run*
**River Falcon** loves to get his toe in and it was slightly disappointing that he could not get closer, although in fairness he did not get the clearest of runs.
**Ptarmigan Ridge** was another who should have run better on ground he loves.
**Alfie Lee(IRE)** *Official explanation: jockey said gelding lost its action*

## 6244 FAMOUS GROUSE H'CAP — 7f 30y
4:30 (4:30) (D2) (0-92,86) 3-Y-O+ — £7,112 (£2,188; £1,094; £547) Stalls Low

Form — RPR

651- **1** **Go Padero (IRE)**$^{349}$ [5905] 3-9-4 83 JFanning 7 — 91
(MJohnston) *a.p: effrt to chal over 1f out: rdn to ld ins last: drvn and edgd rt: then hung lft last 75 yds:jst hld on* **16/1**

0201 **2** shd **Azreme**$^{29}$ [5631] 4-8-13 76 LDettori 2 — 84
(DKIvory) *hld up in rr: hdwy and pushed along over 2f out:s witched lft and rdn over 1f out: drvn and styd on strly ins last: jst fai* **4/1**$^{1}$

6060 **3** 1 **Les Arcs (USA)**$^{20}$ [5835] 4-8-9 72 (t) FNorton 8 — 80+
(RCGuest) *hld up in rr: hdwy on inner wl over 1f out: nt clr run and swtchd lft ins last: styng on wl whn hmpd nr fin* **40/1**

3010 **4** shd **Doctorate**$^{16}$ [5921] 3-9-7 86 SSanders 14 — 91
(EALDunlop) *stmbld s and bhd: hdwy on inner over 2f out: styng on whn n.m.r ins last: nt qckn* **5/1**$^{3}$

2603 **5** ¾ **Kirkby's Treasure**$^{21}$ [5818] 6-8-13 76 FLynch 5 — 79
(ABerry) *hld up and bhd: hdwy on wd outside 2f out: rdn and ch over 1f out: edgd lft and nt qckn ins last* **9/2**$^{2}$

0040 **6** shd **Namroud (USA)**$^{29}$ [5631] 5-8-9 72 PHanagan 11 — 75
(RAFahey) *chsd ldrs: hdwy over 2f out: rdn and ch over 1f out: drvn and nt qckn ins last: hld whn sltly hmpd ins last* **12/1**

0001 **7** 1½ **Dizzy In The Head**$^{48}$ 5-9-1 78 (b) ANicholls 3 — 77
(PaulJohnson) *led: rdn along 3f out: drvn over 1f out: hdd & wknd ins last* **16/1**

3021 **8** hd **Sea Storm (IRE)**$^{21}$ [5818] 6-9-4 81 RWinston 13 — 84+
(DRMacleod) *chsd ldrs: rdn along 2f out: ch over 1f out tl drvn and nt qckn ins last: hld whn hmpd nr fin* **4/1**$^{1}$

0205 **9** 1½ **Abbajabba**$^{45}$ [5244] 8-8-9 72 PRobinson 9 — 67
(CWFairhurst) *midfield: effrt over 2f out: sn rdn along and wknd over 1f out* **10/1**

0500 **10** 3 **Tony Tie**$^{8}$ [6069] 8-8-9 75 NMackay$^{(3)}$ 1 — 63
(JSGoldie) *hld up: wd st to r alone stand rail: rdn over 2f out and n.d* **20/1**

1406 **11** shd **Brief Goodbye**$^{15}$ [5937] 4-8-13 76 RLMoore 4 — 63
(JohnBerry) *chsd ldr: rdn along over 2f out: sn wknd* **16/1**

1m 31.34s (1.81) **Going Correction** +0.30s/f (Good)
**WFA** 3 from 4yo+ 2lb — **11** Ran SP% **116.5**
Speed ratings: **101,100,99,99,98 98,96,96,95,91 91**CSF £78.33 CT £2586.19 TOTE £18.00: £5.20, £2.00, £11.00; EX 102.00.
**Owner** Pagodero Partnership **Bred** Lisieux Stud **Trained** Middleham Moor, N Yorks

**FOCUS**
A fair handicap and a good performance from seasonal debutant Go Padero. The form is a bit messy with the time being unexceptional, although the winner can rate higher.

**NOTEBOOK**
**Go Padero(IRE)**, not seen since winning his maiden at the third attempt as a juvenile - back in November - was clearly ready to get the job done first time back and he showed no signs of being in need of the run in the closing stages, battling on doggedly to hold Arzeme. He was probably value for a little more than the official margin as he ran around close home - hanging to his left - and there is more to come from him if avoiding the 'bounce' factor next time.
**Azreme**, back to winning ways at Ayr last month, flashed home having steadily made headway through the field and narrowly failed to get there. He has never been the easiest to win with, but is clearly in great spirits at the moment.
**Les Arcs(USA)** ran a huge race for one of his price and was a bit unlucky - not getting the clearest of runs and being impeded close home. He cannot be relied upon to repeat the effort, but deserves a chance to prove it was no flash in the pan.
**Doctorate** was just run out of a place, and was a bit unfortunate as he could never get into a decent position after stumbling coming out of the stalls.
**Kirkby's Treasure** ran another reasonable race, but probably needs a drop in the weights.
**Namroud(USA)** was there if good enough, but he lacked a finishing kick.
**Sea Storm(IRE)** was beaten at the time of getting hampered and had every chance.
**Brief Goodbye** *Official explanation: trainer said gelding had been unsuited by the soft ground*

## 6245 MUSSELBURGH NEWS MAIDEN STKS — 1m 4f
5:00 (5:00) (D3) 3-Y-O+ — £4,849 (£1,492; £746; £373) Stalls High

Form — RPR

3 **1** **Swift Sailor**$^{7}$ [6082] 3-9-0 JFanning 10 — 66+
(MJohnston) *cl up: led 3f out: riddeen clr 2f out: styd on strly* **13/8**$^{1}$

0-35 **2** 7 **Day One**$^{7}$ [6088] 3-9-0 SSanders 5 — 51
(GWragg) *trckd ldrs: hdwy 3f out: rdn 2f out: sn drvn and kpt on same pce* **3/1**$^{3}$

242 **3** 5 **Newnham (IRE)**$^{38}$ [5409] 3-8-11 80 NMackay$^{(3)}$ 7 — 44
(LMCumani) *trckd ldng pair: hdwy 3f out: rdn to chse wnr 2f out: sn drvn and wknd wl over 1f out* **15/8**$^{2}$

3306 **4** ½ **Kyber**$^{5}$ [6141] 3-8-11 60 DNolan$^{(3)}$ 2 — 43
(RFFisher) *led: rdn along and hdd 3f out: grad wknd* **50/1**

0403 **5** *shd* **Sandy Bay (IRE)**[16] 5817 5-9-7 30 ........ PFessey 9 43?
(ARDicken) *midfield: hdwy over 4f out: rdn along 3f out and nvr rch ldrs* **50/1**

005 **6** *12* **Stravonian**[5] 6141 4-9-2 ........ PPMathers(5) 1 26
(DANolan) *s.i.s: a rr* **100/1**

0 **7** *17* **Awaken**[7] 6095 3-8-9 ........ RWinston 4 —
(GASwinbank) *in tch: rdn along over 5f out and so0on wknd* **16/1**

20-0 **8** *1 1/4* **Eyes Dont Lie (IRE)**[189] 1344 6-9-7 35 ........ (p) DAllan 3 1
(DANolan) *a bhd* **200/1**

0-06 **9** *18* **Taili**[14] 5367 3-8-6 30 ........ (b[1]) TEaves(3) 6 —
(DANolan) *bhd fr 1/2-way* **200/1**

**10** *22* **Throwmeupsomething (IRE)** 3-9-0 ........ PBradley 8 —
(ABerry) *s.i.s: a bhd* **66/1**

2m 43.16s **Going Correction** +0.30s/f (Good)
**WFA** 3 from 4yo+ 7lb **10** Ran SP% **111.2**
Speed ratings: **105,100,97,96,96 88,77,76,64,49**CSF £6.41 TOTE £2.40: £1.50, £1.40, £1.10; EX 10.80.
**Owner** Maktoum Al Maktoum **Bred** Gainsborough Stud Management Ltd **Trained** Middleham Moor, N Yorks

**FOCUS**
The field finished well strung out in what was a modest maiden that is not easy to rate, but an emphatic winner who did not need to repeat previous form to score.

**NOTEBOOK**
**Swift Sailor**, a highly-promising third on his debut at Bath last Sunday, faced a weaker class of opposition and ran out an emphatic winner. Always going well, he powered away under pressure and is the type to do well in staying handicaps if not being given too high a mark, as he has plenty of scope for improvement and is just the sort connections excel with.
**Day One**, in need of the run when having his first start for a while at Goodwood most recently, ran better, but was no match for the winner. He was clear of the third and can probably pick up a similar race.
**Newnham(IRE)** ran no more than respectably and is becoming a bit disappointing.
**Kyber** took them along for a fair way before tiring and improved on previous form.
**Sandy Bay(IRE)** looks a staying handicapper in the making.

## 6246 LIVE RACING ON RACING UK CHANNEL 432 CLASSIFIED STKS 5f
**5:30** (5:30) (G4) 3-Y-0+ **£2,996** (£856; £428) **Stalls** Low

Form RPR

1334 **1** **Molotov**[31] 5597 4-8-7 50 ........ NataliaGemelova(5) 13 63
(IWMcinnes) *cl up: led 1/2-way: clr over 1f out: rdn ins last and kpt on* **5/1**[1]

0050 **2** *1* **Coranglais**[25] 5736 4-9-0 52 ........ (b) RLMoore 9 62
(JMBradley) *towards rr: hdwy on outer over 1f out: sn rdn and styd on wl fnl f* **12/1**

2033 **3** *2* **Valiant Romeo**[25] 5736 4-9-2 54 ........ (v) RFfrench 16 57
(RBastiman) *trckd ldrs: rdn to chse wnr whn edgd lft over 1f out: sn drvn and one pce* **8/1**[3]

2460 **4** *hd* **Arfinnit (IRE)**[7] 6079 3-9-3 55 ........ SHitchcott 14 58
(MRChannon) *in tch: hdwy 2f out: sn rdn and kpt on same pce ent last* **16/1**

0202 **5** *1/2* **The Old Soldier**[8] 6058 6-8-12 50 ........ RWinston 10 51
(ADickman) *towards rr: hdwy 2f out: sn rdn and kpt on same pce appr last* **5/1**[1]

2500 **6** *3/4* **Mr Pertemps**[8] 6066 6-9-0 52 ........ DAllan 2 50
(JJQuinn) *chsd ldrs: rdn along 2f out: kpt on same pce appr last* **16/1**

0500 **7** *1 1/4* **Robwillcall**[5] 6144 4-8-4 46 ........ (p) PPMathers(5) 11 41
(ABerry) *towards rr: hdwy wl over 1f out: swtchd rt and styd on ins last: nrst fin* **16/1**

0050 **8** *1 1/2* **Telepathic (IRE)**[63] 4782 4-9-0 52 ........ FLynch 8 41
(ABerry) *bhd tl sme late hdwy* **33/1**

6235 **9** *2 1/2* **Larky's Lob**[8] 6066 5-8-6 47 ow1 ........ JDO'Reilly(7) 7 31
(JO'Reilly) *cl up: rdn 2f out and grad wknd* **7/1**[2]

0500 **10** *2 1/2* **Tomthevic**[31] 5597 6-8-12 48 ........ PFitzsimons 17 22
(JMBradley) *led: rdn along 1/2-way: sn hdd: drvn and wknd over 1f out* **20/1**

0000 **11** *hd* **Fenwicks Pride (IRE)**[45] 5235 6-8-12 50 ........ (v) PHanagan 4 21
(RAFahey) *a rr* **14/1**

0004 **12** *1 3/4* **Smart Starprincess (IRE)**[2] 6186 3-8-13 54 ........ (p) ANicholls 1 16
(MJAttwater) *chsd ldng trio: rdn along over 2f out and sn wknd* **7/1**[2]

0000 **13** *hd* **Regal Song (IRE)**[31] 5579 8-8-13 51 ........ JFanning 6 16
(TJEtherington) *in tch: rdn along 1/2-way: sn wknd* **9/1**

61.92 secs (1.52) **Going Correction** +0.30s/f (Good) **13** Ran SP% **119.2**
Speed ratings: **99,97,94,93,93 91,89,87,83,79 79,76,76**CSF £65.76 TOTE £5.80: £2.20, £5.50, £3.80; EX 92.10 Place 6 £221.64, Place 5 £68.91.
**Owner** Cloak And Dagger Racing Club **Bred** Guy Reed And Mrs A H Daniels **Trained** Catwick, E Yorks

**FOCUS**
An ordinary event with the runner-up the best guide to the value of the form.

**NOTEBOOK**
**Molotov** could be called the winner a long way from home and was always going powerfully. He stayed strongly to the line to hold the fast-finishing Coranglais and will be interesting if turned out under a penalty.
**Coranglais** ran his usual race - being scrubbed along in rear early until finishing well - and seems to appreciate being able to get his toe. This was a better effort and he is worth watching out for next time.
**Valiant Romeo** continues to run well without winning and is creeping up the weights as a consequence.
**Arfinnit(IRE)** ran better than he has been and was staying on towards the finish.
**The Old Soldier** was disappointing and could only keep on at the one pace.
T/Jkpt: Not won. T/Plt: £654.30 to a £1 stake. Pool: £51,764.65. 57.75 winning tickets. T/Qpdt: £108.00 to a £1 stake. Pool: £4,116.70. 28.20 winning tickets. JR

6250 - 6253a (Foreign Racing) - See Raceform Interactive

# KEENELAND (L-H)
Saturday, October 16

**OFFICIAL GOING: Good**

## 6254a QUEEN ELIZABETH II CHALLENGE CUP (GRADE 1) (FILLIES) 1m 1f (T)
**9:45** (9:45) 3-Y-0 **£173,184** (£55,866; £27,933; £13,966)

RPR

**1** **Ticker Tape**[28] 3-8-9 ........ KDesormeaux 5 111
(JCassidy, U.S.A) **17/10**[1]

**2** *1/2* **Barancella (FR)**[34] 5530 3-8-9 ........ EPrado 3 110
(RJFrankel, U.S.A) **23/10**[2]

**3** *1/2* **River Belle**[34] 3-8-9 ........ RBejarano 2 109
(TPletcher, U.S.A) **136/10**

**4** *1* **Phantom Wind (USA)**[35] 5484 3-8-9 ........ JDBailey 6 107
(JHMGosden) *always well in touch, 4th straight on outside, every chance approaching final furlong, one pace* **39/10**[3]

**5** *4 1/2* **Mambo Slew (USA)**[34] 5530 3-8-9 ........ TFarina 1 99
(PLBiancone, U.S.A) **11/1**

**6** *4 1/2* **Humorous Miss (USA)** 3-8-9 ........ (b) JamesGraham 7 90
(FSpringer, U.S.A) **38/1**

**7** *3* **Island Sand (USA)**[112] 3-8-9 ........ (b) PDay 4 84
(LJones, U.S.A) **6/1**

1m 51.35s **7** Ran SP% **119.8**
Speed ratings: .
**Owner** Jim Ford inc, D Pearson and J Sweesy **Bred** Car Colston Hall Stud **Trained** USA

**NOTEBOOK**
**Phantom Wind(USA)** posted a solid US debut. Always in touch on the outside, she kept plugging away up the straight without ever looking like taking a hand in the finish and will be capable of better in future.

# 5822 COLOGNE (R-H)
Sunday, October 17

**OFFICIAL GOING: Soft**

## 6255a OPPENHEIM PRAMERICA AKTIENFONDS-STUTENPREIS (LISTED) (F&M) 1m
**2:35** (2:46) 3-Y-0+ **£9,155** (£2,817; £1,408; £704)

RPR

**1** **Kastalia (GER)** 4-9-2 ........ WMongil 14 101
(PSchiergen, Germany)

**2** *2* **Lotosmaid (GER)** 3-8-12 ........ J-LSilverio 9 96
(NSauer, Germany)

**3** *3/4* **Chrisiida (GER)**[21] 5823 3-8-12 ........ NRichter 5 94
(ASchutz, Germany)

**4** *3* **Nostrana (GER)**[21] 5823 5-9-2 ........ THellier 11 89
(PRau, Germany)

**5** *1/2* **New Princess (GER)**[21] 5823 5-9-2 ........ J-PCarvalho 12 88
(MarioHofer, Germany)

**6** *3/4* **Munaawashat (IRE)**[43] 5304 3-8-12 ........ PRoberts 13 86
(KRBurke) *always prominent, 2nd straight, led 2 1/2f out to 2f out, weakened final f (24/1)*

**7** *2* **Imperialistic (IRE)**[23] 5769 3-8-12 ........ DarrenWilliams 2 82
(KRBurke) *towards rear til some late progress, never nearer (46/10)*

**8** *3* **Maramara** 3-8-12 ........ EPedroza 6 76
(PSchiergen, Germany)

**9** *hd* **Ripley (GER)**[21] 5823 4-9-2 ........ (b) PHeugl 7 76
(MarioHofer, Germany)

**10** *1 1/2* **Ticina (GER)**[25] 4-9-2 ........ LHammer-Hansen 3 73
(GSybrecht, Germany)

**11** *3/4* **Starla (GER)**[476] 4-9-2 ........ ABoschert 10 72
(PRau, Germany)

**12** *3/4* **Free And Easy**[210] 5-9-2 ........ (b) ADeVries 1 70
(EKurdu, Germany)

**13** *1 1/4* **Momou Sy (GER)**[147] 2335 3-8-12 ........ JPalik 4 67
(AndreasLowe, Germany)

**14** *1* **Nicolaia (GER)**[21] 5823 4-9-2 ........ JBojko 15 66
(HSteinmetz, Germany)

**15** *3* **Zarazienne (FR)** 3-8-12 ........ IFerguson 8 59
(FReuterskiold, Sweden)

1m 39.41s
**WFA** 3 from 4yo+ 3lb **15** Ran
Speed ratings: .
**Owner** Gestut Karlshof **Bred** Gestut Schlenderhan **Trained** Germany

**NOTEBOOK**
**Munaawashat(IRE)** chased the leader until taking it up turning for home. Headed passing the two furlong pole, she had shot her bolt soon after.
**Imperialistic(IRE)** never got into the race but did make some late headway.

## 6256a OPPENHEIM PRAMERICA-PREIS DES WINTERFAVORITEN (GROUP 3) 1m
**3:45** (4:02) 2-Y-0 **£59,859** (£21,831; £14,437; £7,254)

RPR

**1** **Manduro (GER)** 2-9-2 ........ THellier 11 —
(PSchiergen, Germany) *always close up, disputed lead entering straight til led over 2f out, soon clear, impressive* 1

**2** *5* **Kahn (GER)** 2-9-2 ........ (b) ABoschert 3 —
(UOstmann, Germany) *held up in rear, 10th straight, good headway on outside to go 2nd 1 1/2f out, kept on but no chance with winner* 2

**3** *3 1/2* **Early Wings (GER)** 2-9-2 ........ EPedroza 8 —
(AWohler, Germany) *led til headed over 2f out, one pace* 3

**4** *3/4* **Prinz Of Australia (GER)** 2-9-2 ........ IFerguson 10 —
(WBaltromei, Germany) *mid division, 4th straight, unable to quicken from 2f out*

**5** *nk* **Fabioso (FR)** 2-9-2 ........ WMongil 7 —
(HBlume, Germany) *held up, 9th straight, never nearer*

**6** *1/2* **Arrow (GER)** 2-9-2 ........ JBojko 9 —
(HSteinmetz, Germany) *close up, 3rd straight, soon ridden and one pace*

**7** *1 3/4* **Kartago (GER)** 2-9-2 ........ JPalik 4 —
(RSuerland, Germany) *raced in 5th, beaten 2f out*

**8** *1/2* **Federstar (GER)** 2-9-2 ........ PRoberts 6 —
(CVonDerRecke, Germany) *always in rear*

**9** *13* **Purus (IRE)** 2-9-2 ........ LHammer-Hansen 1 —
(DKRichardson, Germany) *6th straight, soon weakened*

**10** *12* **Loreo (GER)** 2-9-2 ........ (b) NRichter 2 —
(UOstmann, Germany) *prominent to halfway*

**11** *3* **Esposito**[15] 2-9-2 ........ ADeVries 5 —
(CVonDerRecke, Germany) *always behind*

1m 40.19s **11** Ran SP% **131.1**
Speed ratings: .
**Owner** Baron G Von Ullmann **Bred** Rolf Brunner **Trained** Germany

**NOTEBOOK**
**Manduro(GER)** could hardly have been more impressive and, according to his trainer (who also notched a 1-2 in the juvenile Group 1 in Milan) is the best two-year-old in his yard.



The Form Book, Raceform Ltd, Compton, RG20 6NL

## 4385 MUNICH (L-H)

Sunday, October 17

**OFFICIAL GOING: Soft**

### 6257a GROSSER MKT PREIS - NEREIDE-RENNEN (LISTED) (F&M) — 1m 2f

4:35 (4:48) 3-Y-0+ **£8,451** (£3,099; £1,690; £845)

RPR

1 **Spatzolita (GER)**[753] 5-8-13 .......... JHillis 5 93
(DKRichardson, Germany)

2 *3* **La Hermana**[67] 4640 3-9-0 .......... KKerekes 9 94
(AWohler, Germany)

3 *½* **Mocca (IRE)**[23] 5761 3-8-7 .......... DHolland 1 86
(DJCoakley) *a cl up, chal on ins 2f out, briefly tk narrow ld 1 1/2f out, one pace fnl f & lost 2nd cl home (19-10F)*

4 *4* **Russian Samba (IRE)**[112] 3357 5-8-13 .......... MTimpelan 6 80
(HJGroschel, Germany)

5 *4* **Walerie (GER)** 3-8-7 .......... CCzachary 4 72
(ErichPils, Germany)

6 *1* **Kastoria (GER)**[56] 4980 5-8-13 .......... MO'Reilly 3 71
(AWohler, Germany)

7 *1 ½* **Estefania (GER)**[133] 2723 3-8-7 .......... WPanov 2 68
(PRau, Germany)

8 *3* **Aguilera (GER)**[155] 2138 4-8-13 .......... (b) AngelaKull-Hohn 8 63
(RSuerland, Germany)

9 *hd* **Top Call (GER)**[21] 5822 3-8-10 .......... AGoritz 10 65
(ASchutz, Germany)

2m 21.07s
**WFA** 3 from 4yo+ 5lb — **9** Ran
Speed ratings: .
**Owner** Stall Touchdown **Bred** Gestut Karlshof **Trained** Germany

**NOTEBOOK**
**Mocca(IRE)** failed to justify favouritism. Having looked the likely winner when taking the lead a furlong and a half out, she failed to pick up as expected and was run out of second in the closing stages. Both trainer and jockey were inclined to blame the defeat on the soft ground.

## 6108 SAN SIRO (R-H)

Sunday, October 17

**OFFICIAL GOING: Soft**

### 6258a PREMIO SERGIO CUMANI (GROUP 3) (F&M) — 1m

2:20 (2:28) 3-Y-0+ **£37,852** (£17,474; £9,771; £4,886)

RPR

1 **Snow Goose**[21] 5823 3-8-9 .......... JFortune 1 102
(JLDunlop) *soon led, headed 2f out, rallied to lead again inside final f, ran on well* 3

2 *¾* **Kitcat (GER)**[21] 5823 3-8-9 .......... ASuborics 2 100
(PSchiergen, Germany) *held up in 5th, headway on inside to lead narrowly 2f out, headed inside final f, no extra*

3 *½* **Secret Melody (FR)**[21] 5823 3-8-12 .......... MBlancpain 8 102
(H-APantall, France) *broke well, raced in 2nd, every chance on outside 2f out, stayed on at same pace* 2

4 *1 ½* **Rose Shift (IRE)**[364] 5667 4-8-11 .......... MDemuro 9 95
(BGrizzetti, Italy) *in touch, 4th straight, effort over 2f out, unable to quicken* 1

5 *1 ¼* **Jalys (ITY)**[169] 1778 3-8-9 .......... EBotti 5 94
(ABotti, Italy) *held up in rear, 6th straight, ridden 2f out, stayed on one pace*

6 *1 ¼* **Mysterix (IRE)**[109] 3434 4-8-11 .......... TGillet 3 90
(ASchutz, Germany) *close up in 3rd, pushed along 3f out, soon one pace*

7 *1 ¾* **Shoko**[75] 4430 3-8-9 .......... SMulas 4 88
(BGrizzetti, Italy) *held up in last, never a factor*

8 *3 ½* **Ianina (IRE)**[36] 5488 4-8-11 .......... IRossi 7 80
(RRohne, Germany) *close up early, dropped back to 7th straight, beaten over 2f out*

1m 40.8s
**WFA** 3 from 4yo 3lb — **8** Ran SP% **117.9**
Speed ratings: .
**Owner** Sir Thomas Pilkington **Bred** Sir Thomas Pilkington **Trained** Arundel, W Sussex

**FOCUS**
It was a warm day and the ground, which was sticky to begin with, was drying out all the time.

**NOTEBOOK**
**Snow Goose** set a fair pace and, headed two furlongs from home, showed a willing attitude to battle her way back to the front. She may well now be retired.

### 6259a GRAN CRITERIUM (GROUP 1) (C&F) — 1m

3:00 (3:02) 2-Y-O **£130,880** (£65,414; £37,975; £18,988)

RPR

1 **Konigstiger (GER)** 2-8-11 .......... FilipMinarik 2 105
(PSchiergen, Germany) *held up on inside, 7th straight, 3rd 1f out, ran on well on inside in final f to lead close home* **12/1**

2 *hd* **Idealist (GER)** 2-8-11 .......... ASuborics 3 105
(PSchiergen, Germany) *always close up, ridden to lead inside final f, headed and no extra close home* **9/1**

3 *¾* **Hearthstead Wings**[36] 5469 2-8-11 .......... KDarley 10 103
(MJohnston) *held up, headway to chase leader over 3f out, led over 2f out, soon ridden, headed inside final f, one pace* **7/2**[1]

4 *½* **Merchant (IRE)**[30] 5612 2-8-11 .......... RMullen 7 102
(MLWBell) *close up on outside early, 8th 3f out, stayed on steadily down outside final 2f* **9/2**[2]

5 *1 ½* **Berkhamsted (IRE)**[22] 5778 2-8-11 .......... MartinDwyer 4 99
(JAOsborne) *mid-division, stayed on at same pace under pressure final 2f* **7/1**

6 *½* **Umniya (IRE)**[7] 6108 2-8-8 .......... (v) ACulhane 5 95
(MRChannon) *held up, headway to track leaders 2f out, soon ridden & unable to quicken* **11/2**[3]

7 *3 ½* **Shannon Springs (IRE)**[39] 5396 2-8-11 .......... MHills 8 91
(BWHills) *never a factor* **11/2**[3]

8 *10* **Becrux (ITY)** 2-8-11 .......... EBotti 6 71
(GBotti, Italy) *in touch til weakened 2f out* **13/2**

9 *2* **Timaviet (IRE)** 2-8-11 .......... DVargiu 9 67
(LD'Auria, Italy) *always in rear* **33/1**

10 *9* **Kerlis** 2-8-11 .......... MDemuro 1 49
(BGrizzetti, Italy) *led to over 2f out, weakened quickly* **16/1**

1m 42.3s — **10** Ran SP% **123.5**
Speed ratings: .
**Owner** Gestut Schlenderhan **Bred** Gestut Schlenderhan **Trained** Germany

**FOCUS**
Little more than three lengths covered the first six and this is unlikely to represent genuine Group 1 form.

**NOTEBOOK**
**Hearthstead Wings** making up ground from the rear to track the leader early in the long home straight, he was one of the first off the bridle but ran on gamely to take the lead and only surrendered it inside the finalfurlong.
**Merchant(IRE)** lost a good early pitch before keeping on steadily in the closing stages.
**Berkhamsted(IRE)** was in the midfield throughout and kept on willingly without threatening the leaders.
**Umniya(IRE)** moved up easily to track the leaders two furlongs out but did not find much for pressure.
**Shannon Springs(IRE)** was always among the backmarkers.

### 6260a GRAN PREMIO DEL JOCKEY CLUB (GROUP 1) — 1m 4f

4:10 (4:21) 3-Y-0+ **£151,056** (£80,546; £48,063; £24,032)

RPR

1 **Shirocco (GER)**[42] 5329 3-8-13 .......... ASuborics 3 120
(ASchutz, Germany) *led after 2f, ridden 2f out, just held on* **11/4**[1]

2 *nse* **Electrocutionist (USA)**[193] 1306 3-8-13 .......... EBotti 6 120
(VValiani, Italy) *always in touch, 6th straight, headway to challenge 2f out, hard driven inside final f, just failed* **10/1**

3 *1 ¼* **Sweet Stream (ITY)**[35] 5501 4-9-1 .......... TGillet 5 112
(JEHammond, France) *broke wl, sn hld up in rr, last str, hdwy on ins 3f out, rdn 2f out, kpt on at one pace, fin 4th, placed 3rd* **9/1**

4 *½* **Fair Mix (IRE)**[26] 5727 6-9-4 .......... SPasquier 4 115
(MRolland, France) *led 2f, 3rd str, bhd wnr & switched lft over 2f out, sn under pressure, staying on whn hmpd ins fnl f, fin 5, pl 4* **6/1**[3]

5 *5* **Imperial Dancer**[14] 5981 6-9-4 .......... TEDurcan 2 108
(MRChannon) *hld up, 8th str, hdwy on outside over 2f out, rdn over 1f out, hung rt ins fnl f, kpt on same pce, fin 3, disq, pl 5* **14/1**

6 *shd* **Percussionist (IRE)**[15] 5965 3-8-13 .......... JFortune 1 109
(JHMGosden) *s.i.s, sn prom, 5th & pushed along str, hdwy under pressure wl over 1f out, nrst at fin* **10/1**

7 *nk* **Without Connexion (IRE)**[15] 5970 5-9-4 .......... DVargiu 7 107
(MGuarnieri, Italy) *held up in touch, 7th straight, 4th & under pressure 2f out, beaten when not much room inside final f* **20/1**

8 *5* **Dubai Success**[29] 5662 4-9-4 .......... MHills 9 99
(BWHills) *4th straight, weakened well over 1f out* **6/1**[3]

9 *3* **Bandari (IRE)**[21] 5812 5-9-4 .......... WSupple 8 95
(MJohnston) *soon tracking winner, 2nd straight, weakened well over 2f out* **10/3**[2]

2m 31.6s
**WFA** 3 from 4yo+ 7lb — **9** Ran SP% **117.9**
Speed ratings: .
**Owner** Baron G Von Ullmann **Bred** Baron G Von Ullmann **Trained** Germany
■ Stewards Enquiry : T E Durcan two-day ban: careless riding (Oct 26,27)

**FOCUS**
A good performance by high-class German performer Shirocco, who gained some compensation for having to miss the Arc because of fast ground.

**NOTEBOOK**
**Shirocco(GER)** justified his connections' decision to miss the Arc because of the fast ground and supplement him for this instead. Forced to make his own running, he found that he had a real fight on his hooves when the runner-up loomed up passing the quarter mile pole and he was all out to hold on by the narrowest of margins. He is a very high-class performer and stays in training but some give underfoot is essential for him.
**Electrocutionist(USA)** tasted defeat for the first time but emerged from the race with a huge amount of credit and it would be no surprise if he followed the recent examples of Falbrav and Rakti as a horse to spend his formative years in Italy and go on to become a real force on the world stage. Patiently ridden, he looked the likely winner through much of the final two furlongs. But his inexperience counted against him and he was just outbattled by the winner.
**Imperial Dancer** had just one behind him turning in and, after making up ground down the outside, hung across those fighting it out for a modest third inside the final furlong. His disqualification was justified but he remains in good form and an attempt to repeat last year's Premio Roma triumph must be a possibility.
**Percussionist(IRE)** is a hard ride. Off the bridle half a mile out, he plugged on but all too slowly.
**Dubai Success** was in touch until dropping out soon after the two furlong marker.
**Bandari(IRE)**, in cracking form earlier in the season, coming right back to his top three-year-old form to win four times, has not looked the same horse since returning from a break and this was another disappointing effort. He has had enough for the season now and should return to winning ways next season if given a nice break.

### 6261a PREMIO OMENONI (GROUP 3) — 5f

4:40 (4:59) 2-Y-0+ **£33,655** (£15,417; £8,588; £4,294)

RPR

1 **Raffelberger (GER)**[14] 5977 3-9-4 .......... ASuborics 2 107
(MarioHofer, Germany) *always close up, led over 1f out, ran on well, comfortably* 2

2 *½* **Krisman (IRE)**[98] 3816 5-9-4 .......... SMulas 5 106
(MCiciarelli, Italy) *in touch, headway 2f out, stayed on final f but never threatened winner*

3 *nk* **Regina Saura**[98] 3816 6-9-1 .......... LManiezzi 7 102
(MCiciarelli, Italy) *in touch, headway to chase leaders 1f out, kept on*

4 *1 ¼* **Toupie**[39] 5404 2-8-0 .......... MartinDwyer 3 101
(FRohaut, France) *held up in rear, stayed on from over 1f out, nearets at finish* 1

5 *2* **Cocktail**[140] 2511 3-9-1 .......... DPorcu 4 92
(MInnocenti, Italy) *led after 2f to over 1f out, one pace* 3

6 *3 ½* **Sopran Foldan (IRE)**[140] 2511 6-9-4 .......... MDemuro 6 85
(BGrizzetti, Italy) *led 2f, remained prominent til weakening 1 1/2f out*

7 *1 ½* **Dasami**[98] 3816 5-9-4 .......... EBotti 1 80
(GPucciatti, Italy) *raced on stands rail, never a factor*

58.50 secs — **7** Ran SP% **117.8**
Speed ratings: .
**Owner** Stall Jenny **Bred** Gestut Rheinberg **Trained** Germany

# 6075 LONGCHAMP (R-H)

Sunday, October 17

**OFFICIAL GOING: Heavy**

## 6262a PRIX DE CONDE (GROUP 3) 1m 1f

1:10 (1:10) 2-Y-O £25,704 (£10,282; £7,711; £5,141)

RPR

1 **Musketier (GER)**[29] 5666 2-8-11 ...... C-PLemaire 3 107
(PBary, France) *tracked leader, led 2f out, ridden clear 1f out, pushed out, comfortably* 1

2 6 **Doctor Dino (FR)**[16] 2-8-11 ...... TJarnet 4 98
(RGibson, France) *hld up in rr but a cl up, last str, switched outside, joined wnr 2f out, hard rdn over 1f out, sn btn* 2

3 4 **Wingman (IRE)**[25] 5729 2-8-11 ...... CSoumillon 1 92
(JWHills) *raced in 3rd to straight, ridden & outpaced 2f out, took 3rd approaching final f, no chance with first two*

4 5 **Fixateur**[25] 2-8-11 ...... OPeslier 2 85
(FHead, France) *led to 2f out, soon weakened* 3

1m 59.6s **Going Correction** -0.15s/f (Firm) 4 Ran SP% **122.5**
Speed ratings: **105,99,96,91.**
**Owner** Ecurie J-L Bouchard **Bred** Gestut Gorlsdorf **Trained** France

**NOTEBOOK**
**Musketier(GER)**, settled behind the leader, was always going well within himself. He was headed by the runner-up early in the straight before surging clear from one and a half out. This was a very impressive performance and he is already being talked about as a Jockey-Club runner next year. If he comes out of the race well he will be allowed to take his chance in the Criterium de Saint-Cloud.
**Doctor Dino(FR)**, waited with in the early part of the race, made rapid progress to lead early in the straight before staying on at one pace.
**Wingman(IRE)** was third virtually throughout. Asked for an effort two furlongs out, he stayed on bravely but never threatened the front pair. His jockey felt that the testing ground was a disadvantage.
**Fixateur** tried to make all the running, but was a beaten force early in the straight and just plodded on in the final two furlongs.

## 6263a PRIX DU CONSEIL DE PARIS (GROUP 2) 1m 4f

2:15 (2:18) 3-Y-O+ £42,148 (£16,268; £7,764; £5,176)

RPR

1 **Pride (FR)**[14] 5981 4-9-1 ...... DBonilla 2 113
(ADeRoyer-Dupre, France) *held up in rear, last straight, headway over 2f out, quickened to lead approaching final f, soon clear, comfortably* 3

2 5 **Simplex (FR)**[19] 5854 3-8-9 ...... OPeslier 6 108
(CLaffon-Parias, France) *held up, 7th straight, stayed on from 2f out, ridden approaching final f to take 2nd last strides* 2

3 hd **Geordieland (FR)**[19] 5854 3-8-9 ...... C-PLemaire 3 108?
(J-MBeguigne, France) *led over 1m out, headed approaching final f, one pace*

4 2 **El Hurano (ARG)**[57] 4-9-1 ...... TJarnet 5 104
(RGibson, France) *always close up, tracked leader from 1m out, hard ridden & every chance 2f out, soon weakened*

5 3 **Apsis**[29] 5667 3-8-9 ...... CSoumillon 4 101
(AFabre, France) *always in touch, 5th straight, beaten well over 1f out* 1

6 5 **Martaline**[26] 5727 5-9-2 ...... ELegrix 1 95
(AFabre, France) *led over 3f, 3rd straight, weakened 2f out* 1

7 5 **Frank Sonata**[36] 5463 3-8-9 ...... DBoeuf 8 89
(MGQuinlan) *6th on outside & ridden approaching straight, beaten well over 1f out*

8 15 **Mohandas (FR)**[42] 5329 3-8-9 ...... TThulliez 7 70
(WHefter, Germany) *4th straight, soon weakened*

2m 39.1s **Going Correction** +0.775s/f (Yiel)
**WFA** 3 from 4yo+ 7lb 8 Ran SP% **170.1**
Speed ratings: **115,111,111,110,108 104,101,91.**
**Owner** Np Bloodstock Ltd **Bred** Np Bloodstock Ltd **Trained** France

**NOTEBOOK**
**Pride(FR)** simply outclassed her rivals. Never under the slightest pressure, she cantered at the tail of the field and was last on entering the straight. She started a forward move two out and quickened well to have the race wrapped up by the furlong marker and passed the post on her own. She had been unlucky in the Vermeille and the Arc and this was her just reward. There is a strong possibility she will stay in training next year.
**Simplex(FR)**, held up for a late run, was completely outpaced early in the straight and second place still looked a hopeless task one and a half furlongs out, but he dug deep and grabbed the runner-up spot in the final few strides. He will stay in training next year and should make his presence felt at the highest level.
**Geordieland(FR)**, smartly away, was a little free early on and took the lead with a mile left to run. He quickened up two furlongs out, but was headed at the distance and was caught for second place close home.
**El Hurano(ARG)**an ex-Argentine colt, ran well. He was always well placed and challenged for the lead early in the straight before staying on at one pace. He will certainly make his presence felt next year.
**Frank Sonata** raced on the outside for much of the way, but was being ridden coming into the straight and just plodded on to the line. His jockey rather gave up during the final furlong and a half.

# 5988 PONTEFRACT (L-H)

Monday, October 18

**OFFICIAL GOING: Good (good to soft in places)**
The ground was reckoned by the riders to be on the easy side of good.
Wind: Slight 1/2 behind. Weather: Fine and sunny but cool.

## 6265 TREVOR WOODS MEMORIAL NURSERY 1m 4y

2:20 (2:24) (E3) (0-75,75) 2-Y-O £4,319 (£1,329; £664; £332) Stalls Low

Form RPR

0211 1 **Toldo (IRE)**[52] 5083 2-8-13 **67** ...... LDettori 16 72+
(GMMoore) *midfield: pushed along 1/2-way: gd hdwy on outer to chse ldr 2f out: led wl over 1f out: sn rdn and styd on wl* 9/1[3]

5034 2 2 **Lord Of Dreams (IRE)**[14] 5995 2-8-13 **67** ...... SWKelly 18 67+
(DWPArbuthnot) *midfield: hdwy 3f out: rdn to chse wnr and wandered over 1f out and ins last: kpt on same pce* 14/1

055 3 ½ **Royal Mougins**[19] 5870 2-9-0 **68** ...... DHolland 2 69+
(GWragg) *trckd ldrs on inner: nt clr run fr over 2f out tl ent last styd on strly towards fin* 15/2[1]

0001 4 ¾ **Lola Sapola (IRE)**[25] 5747 2-9-0 **75** ...... AMullen(7) 19 72
(NACallaghan) *bhd: hdwy 3f out: rdn 2f out and kpt on ins last: nrst fin* 18/1

503 5 2½ **Scent**[28] 5687 2-8-12 **66** ...... SSanders 13 58
(JLDunlop) *bhd: hdwy on outer whn pushed wd home turn: styd on wl fnl f: nrst fin* 16/1

0630 6 hd **You Found Me**[20] 5852 2-8-11 **65** ...... CCatlin 17 56
(CTinkler) *chsd ldrs: rdn along over 2f out: kpt on same pce* 50/1

2300 7 1¼ **Brace Of Doves**[30] 5636 2-8-9 **68** ...... PMakin(5) 20 57
(TDBarron) *stdd s and bhd: hdwy 2f out: rdn and kpt on appr last: nrst fin* 28/1

004 8 hd **Selika (IRE)**[9] 6067 2-9-5 **73** ......(b) PRobinson 10 61
(MHTompkins) *s.i.s and bhd: hdwy whn hung rt home turn: sn drvn and kpt on same pce* 10/1

0004 9 ½ **Dover Street**[14] 5988 2-8-11 **65** ...... ACulhane 5 52
(PWD'Arcy) *stdd s and bhd: hdwy 3f out: rdn 2f out and kpt on: nt rch ldrs* 28/1

410 10 2½ **Torrens (IRE)**[34] 5539 2-9-7 **75** ...... JFanning 15 65+
(MJohnston) *cl up: led over 3f out: rdn clr over 2f out: hdd wl over 1f out and sn wknd* 10/1

004 11 1¾ **Hidden Chance**[20] 5852 2-8-13 **67** ...... RLMoore 3 45
(RHannon) *bhd tl sme late hdwy* 10/1

5120 12 nk **Easy Mover (IRE)**[22] 5810 2-9-4 **75** ...... NMackay(3) 6 52
(RGuest) *hld up in rr: hdwy on outer whn hmpd and pushed wd home turn: sn wknd* 8/1[2]

300 13 1 **Road To Heaven (USA)**[41] 5373 2-8-11 **65** ......(t) WSupple 14 40
(EALDunlop) *s.i.s: a rr* 28/1

6003 14 5 **Tamora**[11] 6021 2-8-11 **65** ...... KDarley 4 39+
(APJarvis) *chsd ldrs: rdn along 3f out: sn wknd* 25/1

16 15 ¾ **El Rey Royale**[65] 4757 2-9-4 **75** ...... TEaves(3) 12 37
(MDHammond) *midfield: hdwy to chse ldrs 3f out: sn rdn and wknd* 40/1

4000 16 2½ **English Fellow**[43] 5314 2-8-11 **65** ...... GGibbons 8 22
(BAMcmahon) *in tch: rdn along 3f out: wknd: sn wknd* 28/1

3242 17 8 **Geisha Lady (IRE)**[49] 5200 2-9-3 **71** ...... PHanagan 7 10
(RMBeckett) *midfield: pushed along 1/2-way: sn wknd* 20/1

6040 18 11 **Rich Albi**[62] 4836 2-9-2 **70** ...... DAllan 11 —
(TDEasterby) *bhd fr 1/2-way* 50/1

4335 19 10 **Young Thomas (IRE)**[30] 5630 2-9-1 **69** ...... RWinston 1 —
(MLWBell) *led: rdn along and hdd over 3f out: sn wknd* 16/1

1m 49.24s (3.64) **Going Correction** +0.275s/f (Good) 19 Ran SP% **112.6**
Speed ratings: **92,90,89,88,86 86,84,84,84,81 79,79,78,73,72 70,62,51,41**CSF £91.97 CT £754.49 TOTE £8.50: £2.70, £3.40, £2.40, £6.20; EX 271.20.
**Owner** J W Armstrong **Bred** Mrs C A Moore **Trained** Middleham Moor, N Yorks

**FOCUS**
A fair nursery run at a solid gallop. The field finished well strung out and the form is solid if unspectacular.

**NOTEBOOK**
**Toldo(IRE)**, last seen winning back-to-back events in plating company in August, showed he is progressing well with a tidy display to score on this debut for new connections. He could have been called the winner some way out, he took this step up in class in his stride and there is no reason why he cannot go in again while in this vein of form.
**Lord Of Dreams(IRE)** was forced to race wide from his draw and deserves extra credit. He will go up again in the weights for this, but certainly has the ability to get off the mark in this division, and would be interesting if reverting to the All-Weather over this trip.
**Royal Mougins** ◆, making his handicap debut, was unlucky not to have finished closer. He can win in this grade and looked well suited by the underfoot conditions. *Official explanation: jockey said colt was denied a clear run*
**Lola Sapola(IRE)** was not disgraced on her handicap debut and would appreciate a return to a sound surface, but may have to switch to the All-Weather in order to do so before the season is out. She seemed to stay this extra furlong well enough.
**Scent** was unlucky to have been forced wide turning for home and was doing all of her best work late on. This was a respectable nursery debut and she got the trip well, but will most likely do better next year.
**Selika(IRE)** *Official explanation: jockey said colt its action*
**Easy Mover(IRE)** was not done any favours approaching the home turn and can be rated slightly better than the bare form would suggest. She is better on a faster surface.
**Tamora** *Official explanation: jockey said filly lost its action*

## 6266 SPONSOR A RACE AT PONTEFRACT H'CAP 1m 2f 6y

2:50 (2:52) (E3) (0-77,75) 3-Y-O+ £4,354 (£1,339; £669; £334) Stalls Low

Form RPR

4604 1 **Sahaat**[8] 6096 6-9-1 **64** ...... RWinston 16 75
(CRDore) *hldup in rr: hdwy on outer 2f out: styd on wl to ld last 50yds* 16/1

0322 2 1¼ **Planters Punch (IRE)**[6] 6152 3-9-1 **69** ...... RLMoore 9 78
(RHannon) *trckd ldrs: wnt clr 2nd over 2f out: hung lft and led appr fnl f: hdd and no ex wl ins last* 11/2[1]

2255 3 ½ **Colway Ritz**[8] 6096 10-8-12 **61** ...... JBramhill 4 69
(WStorey) *bhd: hdwy over 2f out: styd on same pce fnl f* 20/1

4352 4 nk **Little Jimbob**[14] 5990 3-9-7 **75** ...... PHanagan 15 82
(RAFahey) *led: hdd and hmpd appr fnl f: kpt on same pce* 16/1

5604 5 3½ **Mrs Pankhurst**[8] 6086 3-9-1 **69** ...... MHills 2 71+
(BWHills) *in tch: effrt on ins and n.m.r over 2f out: kpt on fnl f: nvr rchd ldrs* 10/1

2411 6 1½ **Mambina (USA)**[8] 6096 3-9-4 **72** 6ex ...... ACulhane 8 70
(MRChannon) *mid-div: effrt on outside 3f out: kpt on: nvr rchd ldrs* 6/1[2]

0001 7 5 **Duelling Banjos**[6] 6152 5-9-4 **67** 6ex ...... SSanders 6 56+
(JAkehurst) *mid-div: effrt and edgd lft over 2f out: nvr on terms* 15/2[3]

2001 8 ¾ **Tedsdale Mac**[8] 6097 5-8-9 **63** 6ex ...... PMakin(5) 3 51
(NBycroft) *hld up and bhd: hdwy and edgd lft over 1f out: nvr on terms* 16/1

0005 9 1 **Northside Lodge (IRE)**[44] 5303 6-9-6 **69** ...... SWKelly 13 55
(PWHarris) *chsd ldrs: wknd over 1f out* 9/1

0004 10 nk **Rarefied (IRE)**[16] 5950 3-9-5 **73** ...... DAllan 18 59
(TDEasterby) *bhd: swtchd lft after 1f: sme hdwy on ins 2f out: nvr on terms* 25/1

4022 11 5 **Rani Two**[19] 5869 5-9-6 **69** ...... LDettori 7 46
(WRMuir) *prom early: lost pl bnd 6f out: sn bhd and pushed along: no threat after* 6/1[2]

5000 12 nk **Internationalguest (IRE)**[26] 5739 5-9-3 **66** ......(p) JFanning 14 42
(GGMargarson) *chsd ldrs: lost pl over 2f out* 40/1

0505 13 1½ **Slalom (IRE)**[67] 4678 4-9-7 **70** ...... GFaulkner 11 44
(JulianPoulton) *mid-div: effrt and nt clr run over 2f out: hmpd over 1f out: nvr nr ldrs* 25/1

3105 14 5 **Bluegrass Boy**[19] 5869 4-8-11 **63** ...... RThomas(3) 12 28
(GBBalding) *sn in rr and pushed along* 25/1



The Form Book, Raceform Ltd, Compton, RG20 6NL

0015 **15** *7* **Secluded**[37] 5459 4-9-5 **68**............(b) DHolland 5 20
(EFVaughan) *w ldrs: lost pl over 1f out* **16/1**

1604 **16** *3/4* **Giunchiglio**[11] 6025 5-9-2 **65**............ KDarley 19 16
(WMBrisbourne) *mid-div: drvn along over 3f out: sn lost pl* **50/1**

0000 **17** *4* **Crathorne (IRE)**[16] 5956 4-9-2 **65**............(p) WSupple 10 8
(JDBethell) *mid-div: effrt over 3f out: sn wknd* **33/1**

-000 **18** *1 3/4* **Humid Climate**[19] 5866 4-9-8 **74**............ TEaves(3) 17 14
(RAFahey) *hld up: a in rr* **66/1**

21-0 **19** *8* **Lord Eurolink (IRE)**[33] 5568 10-9-7 **70**............ PRobinson 1 —
(MHTompkins) *chsd ldrs: wkng whn hmpd on inner over 2f out: sn bhd* **50/1**

2m 15.78s (1.87) **Going Correction** +0.275s/f (Good)
**WFA** 3 from 4yo+ 5lb **19** Ran **SP% 125.4**
Speed ratings: **103,102,101,101,98 97,93,92,91,91 87,87,86,82,76 76,72,71,65**CSF £92.89 CT £1820.09 TOTE £23.60: £4.00, £1.60, £4.10, £2.90; EX 137.40.
**Owner** G D J Linder **Bred** Shadwell Estate Company Limited **Trained** West Pinchbeck, Lincs
■ Stewards Enquiry : R L Moore two-day ban: careless riding (Oct 30-31)

**FOCUS**
A fair handicap run at a strong early pace, but the form looks particularly solid.

**NOTEBOOK**
**Sahaat**, who is blind in his right eye, improved from the rear down the outside. He ended a losing run stretching back over two years.
**Planters Punch(IRE)** hung when hitting the front then seemed to be almost waiting for something to go past. This must go down as an opportunity given away.
**Colway Ritz**, the last to make the cut, ran much better than on his two most recent starts but an 11th career win is proving elsuive.
**Little Jimbob**, drawn five from the outside, was soon in front near the running rail. Hampered when headed, he kept on in gallant style all the way to the line.
**Mrs Pankhurst**, ridden to get the trip, was tightened up going into the final turn otherwise she would have finished on the heels of the first four.
**Mambina(USA)**, under her penalty, elected to race on the outer and could never take a hand.
**Rani Two** *Official explanation: jockey said mare had lost her action*

## 6267 PACKSADDLE H'CAP 5f
**3:20** (3:22) (D2) (0-92,88) 3-Y-0+ **£7,182** (£2,210; £1,105; £552) **Stalls** Low

Form RPR

123 **1** **Ok Pal**[19] 5874 4-8-11 **82**............ GCarter 12 91
(TGMills) *chsd ldrs: led 1f out: hld on towards fin* **10/1**

0005 **2** *1/2* **Corps De Ballet (IRE)**[16] 5933 3-8-12 **83**............ JQuinn 13 90
(JLDunlop) *mid-div: hdwy on outer over 1f out: no ex wl ins last* **25/1**

0000 **3** *nk* **Baron Rhodes**[2] 6205 3-8-6 **80**............ TEaves(3) 16 86+
(JSWainwright) *bhd: gd hdwy on wd outside over 1f out: styd on ins last* **28/1**

0140 **4** *hd* **Mine Behind**[9] 6071 4-9-3 **88**............ LDettori 4 93
(JRBest) *sn bhd: gd hdwy on inner 2f out: qckned to chal ins last: no ex* **5/1**[1]

0204 **5** *2 1/2* **Domirati**[38] 5442 4-8-11 **82**............ RLMoore 5 82+
(RCharlton) *s.i.s: hdwy 2f out: nt clr run jst ins last: styd on towards fin* **8/1**

1131 **6** *nk* **Hout Bay**[31] 5605 7-8-4 **75**............ PHanagan 18 70
(RAFahey) *bhd: hdwy on outside over 1f out: nvr rchd ldrs* **6/1**[2]

1100 **7** *shd* **True Magic**[38] 5440 3-7-12 **72**............ NMackay(3) 6 67
(JDBethell) *mid-div: kpt on fnl 2f: nvr rchd ldrs* **33/1**

3000 **8** *1/2* **Bathwick Bill (USA)**[19] 5874 3-8-6 **77**............ RWinston 9 70
(BRMillman) *mid-div: hdwy 2f out: nvr rchd ldrs* **20/1**

0000 **9** *3/4* **Brave Burt (IRE)**[31] 5605 7-8-5 **76**............ ANicholls 14 66
(DNicholls) *led tl 1f out: fdd* **16/1**

0500 **10** *shd* **Matty Tun**[38] 5440 5-8-10 **81**............ WSupple 11 71
(JBalding) *mid-div: kpt on wl fnl f* **7/1**[3]

0024 **11** *1/2* **Jilly Why (IRE)**[2] 6222 3-7-11 **73** ow1............ BSwarbrick(5) 7 61
(MsDeborahJEvans) *rr-div: hdwy 2f out: styd on whn hmpd jst ins last* **16/1**

6122 **12** *3/4* **Catch The Wind**[67] 4688 3-8-12 **83**............(p) SSanders 1 69
(IAWood) *chsd ldrs: lost pl over 1f out* **12/1**

5000 **13** *nk* **Treasure House (IRE)**[28] 5704 3-7-13 **75**............ DFox(5) 15 60
(JJay) *s.i.s: hdwy whn nt clr run over 1f out: hmpd jst ins last: nvr on terms* **33/1**

0100 **14** *1/2* **Awake**[2] 6205 7-8-13 **84**............(v) KDarley 10 67
(DNicholls) *mid-div: effrt 2f out: nvr on terms* **16/1**

2055 **15** *1* **Foley Millennium (IRE)**[16] 5949 6-8-0 **71**............ CCatlin 3 50
(MQuinn) *chsd ldrs: lost pl over 1f out* **25/1**

4405 **16** *2* **Celtic Thunder**[33] 5563 3-8-11 **82**............ DHolland 8 54
(TJEtherington) *a in rr* **25/1**

6200 **17** *3* **Beyond The Clouds (IRE)**[27] 5712 8-7-13 **75**............(p) PPMathers(5) 2 36
(JSWainwright) *s.i.s: hdwy over 2f out: sn chsng ldrs: lost pl over 1f out: eased* **16/1**

0000 **18** *7* **Pomfret Lad**[9] 6071 6-8-12 **83**............(b) JFanning 17 19
(DNicholls) *chsd ldrs: lost pl over 1f out: sn bhd and eased* **25/1**

64.11 secs (0.31) **Going Correction** +0.275s/f (Good) **18** Ran **SP% 124.4**
Speed ratings: **108,107,106,106,102 101,101,100,99,99 98,97,97,96,94 91,86,75**CSF £247.70 CT £6617.16 TOTE £13.50: £3.50, £5.60, £6.80, £2.10; EX 264.10 Trifecta £669.20 Part won. Pool: £942.85 - 0.10 winning units..
**Owner** Sherwoods Transport Ltd **Bred** Sherwoods Transport Ltd **Trained** Headley, Surrey

**FOCUS**
A typical sprint for the grade and the form is sound if not outstanding, with the first three running to form.

**NOTEBOOK**
**Ok Pal** produced a neat turn of foot to seal the race at the furlong pole and was always holding the runner-up close home. This confirmed him in rude health, and he was winning this off a 10lb higher mark than when taking a claimer at Sandown in September, so should continue to pay his way at this level.
**Corps De Ballet(IRE)** again advertised her liking for some give in the ground and ran her best race in a handicap to date. She is in good form and can be placed to advantage, but may need a slightly stiffer test to be seen at her best.
**Baron Rhodes** had to come wide to make her challenge and deserves credit for keeping on as she did. This was her best effort for some time, on ground soft enough, and she looks to be coming back to form.
**Mine Behind** turned in another solid effort, but was keeping on all too late in the day. He can strike again off this mark, but does need things to fall right in his races.
**Domirati** was done no favours by missing the break and then had to suffer trouble in running when challenging late on. He can be rated better than the bare form and deserves to get back to winning ways.
**Hout Bay**, up 5lb for his latest success, was never really in it from off the pace and is capable of better.
**Catch The Wind** was always being niggled to go the early pace and looked to be all at sea on this ground. She can do better.
**Celtic Thunder** *Official explanation: jockey said gelding was unsuited by the good, good to soft in places ground*

## 6268 TOTESPORT SILVER TANKARD STKS (LISTED RACE) 1m 4y
**3:50** (3:50) (A1) 2-Y-O **£20,300** (£7,700; £3,850; £1,750) **Stalls** Low

Form RPR

4111 **1** **Comic Strip**[16] 5931 2-8-11 **100**............ SSanders 3 104+
(SirMarkPrescott) *hld up in tch: hdwy over 2f out: effrt to ld over 1f out: sn rdn: wandered and clr ins last* **4/5**[1]

3331 **2** *3 1/2* **Wise Dennis**[22] 5810 2-8-11 **89**............ KDarley 7 96
(APJarvis) *dwlt: gd hdwy over 3f out: rdn to ld briefly over 1f out: sn hdd and hmpd: swtchd lft and kpt on ins last* **14/1**

412 **3** *4* **Haunting Memories (IRE)**[28] 5703 2-8-11 **97**............ PRobinson 2 87
(MAJarvis) *cl up: led after 11/2f: pushed along and hdd over 3f out: rdn 2f out: sn drvn and kpt on same pce appr last* **10/1**[3]

3241 **4** *3/4* **Little Miss Gracie**[25] 5756 2-8-6 **85**............ RLMoore 1 81
(ABHaynes) *trckd ldrs: hdwy to ld over 3f out: rdn along 2f out: sn hdd and one pce* **14/1**

01 **5** *1 1/2* **Fantasy Ride**[55] 5023 2-8-11 **94**............ JQuinn 4 82
(JPearce) *hld up: hdwy on inner 3f out: rdn over 2f out and sn one pce* **16/1**

1152 **6** *1 3/4* **Claret And Amber**[19] 5873 2-8-11 **97**............ PHanagan 10 78
(RAFahey) *in rr: rdn along 3f out: nvr nr ldrs* **10/1**[3]

1243 **7** *2* **Fiefdom (IRE)**[16] 5931 2-8-11 **95**............ JFanning 8 74
(MJohnston) *led 11/2f: cl up tl rdn along 3f out and sn btn* **25/1**

4313 **8** *2 1/2* **Profit's Reality (IRE)**[29] 5670 2-8-11 **84**............ GGibbons 5 69
(PABlockley) *chsd ldrs: rdn along over 3f out: sn wknd* **66/1**

51 **9** *13* **Humourous (IRE)**[45] 5269 2-8-11 **92**............(t) LDettori 9 40
(SaeedBinSuroor) *trckd ldrs on outer: rdn along over 3f out: sn wknd* **4/1**[2]

1m 46.45s (0.85) **Going Correction** +0.275s/f (Good) **9** Ran **SP% 118.3**
Speed ratings: **106,102,98,97,96 94,92,90,77**CSF £15.19 TOTE £1.90: £1.10, £3.20, £3.00; EX 16.10.
**Owner** Neil Greig - Osborne House **Bred** Floors Farming And Side Hill Stud **Trained** Newmarket, Suffolk

**FOCUS**
A fair time for a juvenile Listed contest in the conditions and all nine runners were previous winners, giving the race a solid appearance.

**NOTEBOOK**
**Comic Strip**, keen to find cover, quickened up in fine style but in front ducked one way then the other. A gelding, he will have one more outing in France before retiring to winter quarters.
**Wise Dennis**, who had 11lb to find with the winner on official figures, is progressing fast and finished clear second best.
**Haunting Memories(IRE)** proved more amenable this time but in the end was firmly put in his place.
**Little Miss Gracie**, quite a big filly, had something to find and is the type to make an even better three-year-old.
**Fantasy Ride** stands over plenty of ground, but he looks very much on the weak side at present and will leave this form behind next year.
**Claret And Amber** never really figured.
**Humourous(IRE)**, long in the back, was the first to come under pressure and, on the retreat long before the home turn, was in the end allowed to complete in his own time. The ground could surely not be the sole reason for this abject display. *Official explanation: jockey said colt was unsuited by the good, good to soft in places ground*

## 6269 BLUFF COVE H'CAP 2m 1f 216y
**4:20** (4:20) (E3) (0-77,73) 3-Y-0+ **£4,120** (£1,267; £633; £316) **Stalls** Low

Form RPR

1031 **1** **Moonshine Beach**[14] 5991 6-9-8 **73**............ PMakin(5) 10 84
(PWHiatt) *mde most: rdn over 2f out: styd on strly* **11/2**[2]

2311 **2** *1 1/2* **Princess Kiotto**[19] 5860 3-8-9 **66**............ DAllan 2 75
(TDEasterby) *trckd ldrs: hdwy 3f out: rdn along 2f out: drvn ent last: kpt on* **7/4**[1]

0464 **3** *nk* **Riyadh**[14] 5991 6-9-4 **64**............ KDarley 11 73
(MJohnston) *trckd ldrs: hdwy 3f out: rdn to chse wnr wl over 1f out: sn drvn and kpt on same pce fnl f* **6/1**[3]

0420 **4** *2* **Isa'Af (IRE)**[9] 6074 5-9-6 **66**............ RLMoore 8 73
(PWHiatt) *hld up in rr: stdy hdwy over 4f out: rdn to chse ldrs wl over 1f out: sn drvn and kpt on same pce* **20/1**

1043 **5** *1* **Best Port (IRE)**[16] 5951 8-8-11 **62**............ MLawson(5) 5 68
(JParkes) *hld up towards rr: hdwy 4f out: rdn along over 2f out and kpt on same pce* **14/1**

2000 **6** *3/4* **Claradotnet**[9] 6074 4-8-10 **56**............ ACulhane 9 61
(MRChannon) *trckd ldrs: effrt over 3f out: sn rdn along and no imp fnl 2f* **20/1**

0050 **7** *1 1/4* **Salamba**[3] 6198 3-8-8 **65**............ PRobinson 6 69
(MHTompkins) *trckd wnr: hdwy to dispute ld 6f out: rdn along 3f out: sn drvn and wknd 2f out* **10/1**

514/ **8** *3/4* **Robbo**[178] 5383 10-8-7 **56**............ TEaves(3) 1 59
(KGReveley) *a rr* **16/1**

3233 **9** *5* **Vicars Destiny**[14] 5991 6-9-4 **64**............ RWinston 4 61
(MrsSLamyman) *hld up towards rr: stdy hdwy on inner 4f out: rdn along over 2f out and sn wknd* **7/1**

6040 **10** *dist* **Toni Alcala**[14] 5991 5-9-6 **66**............ SSanders 7 —
(RFFisher) *in tch: rdn along over 5f out: sn wknd* **16/1**

4m 10.82s (7.82) **Going Correction** +0.275s/f (Good)
**WFA** 3 from 4yo+ 11lb **10** Ran **SP% 115.6**
Speed ratings: **93,92,92,91,90 90,89,89,87,—**CSF £15.31 CT £58.06 TOTE £7.40: £2.10, £1.30, £1.80; EX 16.50.
**Owner** Ken Read and Jill Harmsworth **Bred** Lawrence Shepherd **Trained** Hook Norton, Oxon

**FOCUS**
A modest handicap and it produced a very ordinary time for the grade. The form is reasonable for the level, rated through the third.

**NOTEBOOK**
**Moonshine Beach** produced a brave display of front-running to win with a bit in hand, defying a 3lb rise in the weights for scoring last time. He has seriously improved this season, and this effort confirms he can go on any ground, so should remain hard to pass in similar events while in this form.
**Princess Kiotto**, who came into this looking for the hat-trick, turned in a solid effort off this 4lb higher mark. She had no excuses however, and the Handicapper looks to be getting to grips with her now.
**Riyadh** had his chance, but again looked none-too-willing when it mattered. This enigmatic character is well treated on his previous best efforts, but remains a tricky ride, and will most likely only pop-up when least expected.
**Isa'Af(IRE)** turned in an improved effort, but did not convince as a stayer over this much longer trip. He would get a sharp two miles, and could be worth another chance when reverting to that sort of trip, as he may have more to offer from this mark.
**Vicars Destiny** has had a very consistent, if unsuccessful season, but looked as though she was feeling the effects on this occasion.

**Toni Alcala** *Official explanation: jockey said gelding was unsuited by the good, good to soft in places ground*

## 6270 THANKS TO CHERYL HIBBERT AND ANDREA HALL MAIDEN AUCTION STKS (DIV I) 6f

**4:50** (4:51) (F3) 2-Y-O **£3,445** (£1,060; £530; £265) **Stalls** Low

| Form | | | | | RPR |
|---|---|---|---|---|---|
| 0460 | **1** | | **Grand Option**[26] 5738 2-8-10 63 | ADaly 2 | 70 |
| | | | (BWDuke) *chsd ldrs: hdwy over 2f out: styd on to ld last 75yds* | **11/2**[3] | |
| 3654 | **2** | *½* | **Skiddaw Wolf**[23] 5797 2-8-3 63 | CCatlin 3 | 62 |
| | | | (BSmart) *chsd ldrs: led 2f out: hdd and no ex ins last* | **4/1**[2] | |
| 066 | **3** | *6* | **Daisys Girl**[17] 5908 2-7-12 55 | CHaddon(7) 4 | 46 |
| | | | (BHanbury) *hmpd s: sn outpcd and bhd: hdwy 2f out: kpt on fnl f* | **10/1** | |
| 2620 | **4** | *2* | **Hymn Of Victory (IRE)**[23] 5797 2-8-9 61 | DHolland 9 | 44 |
| | | | (TJEtherington) *swtchd rt s and racd v wd: w ldrs: one pce appr fnl f* | **6/1** | |
| 0540 | **5** | *nk* | **Ashes (IRE)**[23] 5800 2-8-5 64 ow4 | TEaves(3) 6 | 42 |
| | | | (KRBurke) *hmpd s: sn trcking ldrs: one pce appr fnl f* | **20/1** | |
| 4600 | **6** | *2* | **Zendaro**[46] 5234 2-8-10 54 | SWKelly 5 | 38 |
| | | | (WMBrisbourne) *hmpd s: sn chsng ldrs: weaakened over 1f out* | **33/1** | |
| 004 | **7** | *5* | **Archie Wright**[40] 5398 2-8-9 56 | RLMoore 11 | 22 |
| | | | (RHannon) *racd wd: outpcd and struggling over 3f out* | **12/1** | |
| 5500 | **8** | *1 ¼* | **Turks Wood (IRE)**[30] 5630 2-8-11 68 | PRobinson 10 | 35+ |
| | | | (MHTompkins) *hmpd s: nvr nr ldrs: hmpd jst ins last* | **3/1**[1] | |
| 00 | **9** | *1 ¼* | **Mountain Breeze**[11] 6020 2-8-4 | DAllan 1 | 9 |
| | | | (DShaw) *sn outpcd and bhd* | **100/1** | |
| 6000 | **10** | *16* | **Peopleton Brook**[17] 5909 2-8-11 63 | (b[1]) LDettori 7 | — |
| | | | (DWPArbuthnot) *swvd lft s: led tl 2f out: hung rt and sn lost pl: eased ins last* | **11/1** | |
| 0 | **11** | *3 ½* | **Time For Mee**[23] 5800 2-8-3 | PHanagan 12 | — |
| | | | (RAFahey) *sn wl outpcd and bhd: t.o 3f out* | **66/1** | |
| | **12** | *½* | **Scarborough Flyer** 2-8-12 | JEdmunds 8 | — |
| | | | (JBalding) *unf: bkwd: sn wl outpcd and bhd: t.o 3f out* | **40/1** | |

1m 19.87s (2.57) **Going Correction** +0.275s/f (Good) **12** Ran SP% **112.4**
Speed ratings: **93,92,84,81,81 78,71,70,68,47 42,41**CSF £25.10 TOTE £8.60: £2.80, £1.70, £3.80; EX 43.50.
**Owner** The G S M Group **Bred** Whitsbury Manor Stud **Trained** Lambourn, Berks

**FOCUS**
An umcompetitive race run in a time 0.38 seconds faster than the second division and bang on par for the type of race in the conditions. The first two are at the top of their form and give it

**NOTEBOOK**
**Grand Option**, with the blinkers left off, broke his duck at the 12th attempt but it was a weak heat lacking any strength in depth.
**Skiddaw Wolf**, rated 7lb ahead of the winner on official figures, took what looked a decisive lead but she did not see the trip out anywhere near as well as the winner.
**Daisys Girl**, knocked out of her stride at the start, did just enough to secure a remote third spot with the blinkers left off.
**Hymn Of Victory(IRE)**, taken to race wide, was going up and down on the spot in the closing stages and may be better suited by the minimum trip.
**Ashes(IRE)**, with the blinkers discarded, met trouble leaving the gates but she is basically a keen type who is not progressing.
**Zendaro**, quite a big type, was having his second outing in six weeks after a break. He will not reach his full strength until next year.
**Turks Wood(IRE)**, dropping back in trip and with the blinkers left off, took a bump at the start and never figured on ground that possibly counted against him.
**Peopleton Brook**, warm beforehand, wore blinkers for the first time. He dived left leaving the stalls and did far too much in front to give himself any hope of seeing out the trip on the ground. *Official explanation: jockey said colt ran too free*

## 6271 SUBSCRIBE TO RACING UK ON 08700 860432 CLASSIFIED STKS 1m 4y

**5:20** (5:21) (F3) 3-Y-O **£3,484** (£1,072; £536; £268) **Stalls** Low

| Form | | | | | RPR |
|---|---|---|---|---|---|
| 4034 | **1** | | **Wrenlane**[8] 6097 3-8-12 60 | PHanagan 13 | 70 |
| | | | (RAFahey) *in tch on outer: hdwy 3f out: rdn to ld over 1f out: hung lft ins last: drvn and hld on wl* | **12/1** | |
| 6402 | **2** | *nk* | **Intavac Boy**[19] 5859 3-8-12 57 | GFaulkner 12 | 69 |
| | | | (CWThornton) *prom: hdwy to ld over 2f out: sn rdn: hdd over 1f out: rallied wl and carried lft ins last: kpt on gamely* | **16/1** | |
| 6041 | **3** | *4* | **Sachin**[21] 5829 3-9-3 65 | KDarley 5 | 65 |
| | | | (JRBoyle) *in rr: pushed along 1/2-way: hdwy on inner 2f out: rdn and kpt on appr last: nrst fin* | **16/1** | |
| 0101 | **4** | *1* | **Pella**[27] 5715 3-9-0 65 | LDettori 4 | 60 |
| | | | (MBlanshard) *towards rr: pushed along and hdwy or 2f out: sn rdn and kpt on same pce fr over 1f out* | **4/1**[1] | |
| 0325 | **5** | *3* | **Deign To Dance (IRE)**[61] 4848 3-8-11 62 | RLMoore 9 | 54+ |
| | | | (JGPortman) *in rr: hdwy over 2f out: sn rdn and no imp appr last* | **12/1** | |
| 0003 | **6** | *¾* | **Motu (IRE)**[30] 5657 3-9-1 63 | (b) SSanders 8 | 52 |
| | | | (JLDunlop) *towards rr: hdwy on outer 3f out: sn rdn along and no imp fr wl over 1f out* | **11/2**[2] | |
| 0160 | **7** | *nk* | **Bowling Along**[20] 5849 3-8-6 58 | TEaves(3) 2 | 45 |
| | | | (MESowersby) *towards rr: rdn along 3f out: kpt on u.p fnl 2f: nt rch ldrs* | **50/1** | |
| 4005 | **8** | *2 ½* | **Alchera**[16] 5945 3-8-12 58 | SCarson 1 | 42 |
| | | | (RFJohnsonHoughton) *chsd ldrs: effrt over 2f out: sn rdn and wknd wl over 1f out* | **14/1** | |
| 0000 | **9** | *1 ¾* | **Sion Hill (IRE)**[27] 5715 3-8-9 64 | JDO'Reilly(7) 3 | 42 |
| | | | (JO'Reilly) *cl up: effrt and ev ch 3f out tl rdn and wknd fnl 2f* | **25/1** | |
| 0-34 | **10** | *4* | **Lake Diva**[21] 5836 3-8-10 61 | ACulhane 7 | 27+ |
| | | | (JGGiven) *hld up in tch: hdwy whn n.m.r and hmpd 2f out: no ch after* | **50/1** | |
| 6624 | **11** | *½* | **Cottingham (IRE)**[13] 6006 3-8-12 58 | DHolland 11 | 28 |
| | | | (MCChapman) *prom: rdn along 3f out: hmpd over 2f out and sn wknd* | **11/2**[2] | |
| 2101 | **12** | *1* | **Otago (IRE)**[25] 5748 3-9-2 64 | WSupple 10 | 30 |
| | | | (JRBest) *trckd ldrs: effrt 3f out: sn rdn and wknd fnl 2f* | **7/1** | |
| 2315 | **13** | *3* | **Willhego**[17] 5914 3-8-12 59 | JFanning 6 | 19 |
| | | | (JRBest) *led: rdn along 3f out: sn hdd & wknd 2f out* | **13/2**[3] | |

1m 48.05s (2.45) **Going Correction** +0.275s/f (Good) **13** Ran SP% **118.2**
Speed ratings: **98,97,93,92,89 88,88,86,84,80 79,78,75**CSF £185.62 TOTE £14.50: £4.20, £4.90, £4.70; EX 249.80.
**Owner** Keith Taylor **Bred** M P Bishop **Trained** Musley Bank, N Yorks

**FOCUS**
A modest three-year-old handicap run at a decent clip. The first two came clear and the form appears reliable.

**NOTEBOOK**
**Wrenlane** proved game late on and registered his first success at the 12th time of asking. He is a fairly consistent sort who clearly appreciates some cut, and there may be more to come while his yard remain in such grand form.
**Intavac Boy** ◆ went down all guns blazing and confirmed the promise of his recent improved effort at Newcastle. He was well clear in second, handled this softer ground and will most likely be placed to go one better before long.
**Sachin** struggled to go the early pace and never threatened to follow-up his recent Bath success. He is capable of better, but has a bit to prove now.
**Pella** ran her race, but looks high enough in the weights now.
**Deign To Dance(IRE)** was not helped by the recent ease in the ground and ran a fair race in the circumstances.
**Motu(IRE)**, whose previous effort in the first-time blinkers gave him a decent chance in this, failed to sparkle from off the pace. This has to go down as a disappointing effort, with the headgear not having the same effect.
**Cottingham(IRE)** was the subject of support in the market, but weakened out of it after meeting trouble at a crucial stage.

## 6272 THANKS TO CHERYL HIBBERT AND ANDREA HALL MAIDEN AUCTION STKS (DIV II) 6f

**5:50** (5:50) (F3) 2-Y-O **£3,445** (£1,060; £530; £265) **Stalls** Low

| Form | | | | | RPR |
|---|---|---|---|---|---|
| 003 | **1** | | **Doitforreel (IRE)**[42] 5334 2-8-4 68 | WSupple 12 | 64+ |
| | | | (IAWood) *hld up: hdwy over 2f out: rdn to ld over 1f out: kpt on wl* | **6/4**[1] | |
| 05 | **2** | *2* | **Primarily**[24] 5772 2-8-10 | RWinston 3 | 61 |
| | | | (ABerry) *chsd ldrs: drvn along over 2f out: styd on to take 2nd ins last: no imp* | **12/1** | |
| 5605 | **3** | *1* | **Ming Vase**[14] 5989 2-8-5 57 | DTudhope(5) 8 | 58 |
| | | | (DCarroll) *chsd ldrs: outpcd over 2f out: hdwy and swtchd outside over 1f out: hung lft and kpt on same pce* | **6/1**[3] | |
| 0550 | **4** | *½* | **Lady Hopeful (IRE)**[13] 6003 2-8-5 59 | (b[1]) JFanning 7 | 52 |
| | | | (RPElliott) *w ldr: led over 2f out: hung lft and hdd over 1f out: wknd ins last* | **14/1** | |
| 60 | **5** | *7* | **Boppys Dream**[23] 5800 2-8-3 | PHanagan 2 | 29 |
| | | | (RAFahey) *hld up: kpt on fnl 2f: nvr nr ldrs* | **16/1** | |
| 00 | **6** | *¾* | **Silver Swing**[14] 6000 2-8-9 | SWKelly 5 | 32 |
| | | | (WJHaggas) *chsd ldrs: sn drvn along: outpcd over 2f out: lost pl over 1f out* | **20/1** | |
| 2 | **7** | *nk* | **Monkey Madge**[34] 5542 2-8-5 | CCatlin 10 | 27 |
| | | | (BSmart) *chsd ldrs: outpcd and lost pl after 2f: n.d after* | **11/4**[2] | |
| | **8** | *8* | **Iroquois Princess** 2-7-11 | StaceyRenwick(7) 9 | — |
| | | | (DShaw) *lengthy: unf: s.i.s: sn detached in last* | **66/1** | |
| 0060 | **9** | *3* | **Mill By The Stream**[14] 5989 2-8-12 52 | (v[1]) KDarley 6 | — |
| | | | (APJarvis) *led tl over 2f out: lost pl over 1f out: sn bhd and eased* | **16/1** | |

1m 20.25s (2.95) **Going Correction** +0.275s/f (Good) **9** Ran SP% **113.3**
Speed ratings: **91,88,87,86,77 76,75,64,60**CSF £21.13 TOTE £2.60: £1.30, £2.70, £1.90; EX 25.30 Place 6 £66.48, Place 5 £26.59.
**Owner** Jim Browne **Bred** Patrick H Dillon **Trained** Upper Lambourn, Berks

**FOCUS**
A modest maiden with a winning time 0.38 seconds slower than the first division and slightly below par for the grade.

**NOTEBOOK**
**Doitforreel(IRE)**, who behaved herself at the start this time, was dropped in and, though she had to work hard to gain the upper hand, she was right on top at the finish. She is only small but her heart is in the right place.
**Primarily**, keen to post, stayed on to take second spot and will be suited by a step up to seven.
**Ming Vase**, having his seventh start, is starting to look fully exposed and, rated just 57, is the measure of the overall value of the form.
**Lady Hopeful(IRE)**, tried in blinkers this time, went on but even over this furlong shorter trip her finishing effort was very weak.
**Boppys Dream**, having her third outing, was by no means knocked about and should show her true colours in modest handicap company at three.
**Silver Swing**, a narrow type, had shown little in two previous outings and his rider was soon hard at work.
**Monkey Madge**, who has gone in her coat, ran poorly but should bounce back next year.
T/Jkpt: Not won. T/Plt: £117.00 to a £1 stake. Pool: £53,064.35. 331.00 winning tickets. T/Qpdt: £21.00 to a £1 stake. Pool: £3,945.60. 138.70 winning tickets. JR

# 6220 WOLVERHAMPTON (A.W) (L-H)

### Monday, October 18

**OFFICIAL GOING: Standard**
Several horses with proven form on Lingfield's Polytrack were noticeably below form on this surface.
Wind: Slight half-behind Weather: Cloudy

## 6273 BET DIRECT ON ITV PAGE 367 CLASSIFIED STKS 5f 216y(P)

**2:00** (2:01) (F4) 3-Y-O+ **£2,989** (£854; £427) **Stalls** Low

| Form | | | | | RPR |
|---|---|---|---|---|---|
| 5320 | **1** | | **Prince Of Gold**[2] 6210 4-9-1 57 | (p) DSweeney 12 | 73+ |
| | | | (RHollinshead) *hld up: hdwy and nt clr run over 1f out: rdn to ld ins fnl f: r.o* | **5/1**[2] | |
| 4106 | **2** | *1* | **Woodbury**[31] 5618 5-8-12 57 | GBaker 7 | 66 |
| | | | (MrsHSweeting) *led1f: led again over 3f out: rdn and hdd ins fnl f: unable qck* | **5/1**[2] | |
| 4356 | **3** | *1* | **Asbo**[7] 6117 4-8-12 57 | SDrowne 6 | 63 |
| | | | (DrJDScargill) *hld up: hdwy and nt clr run over 1f out: swtchd rt ins fnl f: r.o* | **14/1** | |
| 1000 | **4** | *1 ¼* | **Siraj**[2] 6220 5-9-3 59 | DaneO'Neill 5 | 64 |
| | | | (PSMcentee) *a.p: rdn over 2f out: no ex fnl f* | **25/1** | |
| 0052 | **5** | *2* | **Legal Set (IRE)**[2] 6210 8-9-1 60 | (t) LFletcher(3) 10 | 59 |
| | | | (MissAStokell) *hld up: hdwy 1/2-way: hmpd and lost pl over 2f out: r.o ins fnl f* | **11/1** | |
| 2000 | **6** | *1* | **Zagala**[89] 4026 4-8-12 60 | (t) LPKeniry(3) 9 | 53 |
| | | | (SLKeightley) *chsd ldrs: rdn over 2f out: hung lft over 1f out: wknd fnl f* | **16/1** | |
| 0500 | **7** | *½* | **Kallista's Pride**[20] 5849 4-8-11 56 | (v) TQuinn 2 | 48 |
| | | | (JRBest) *prom: rdn over 1f out: wknd fnl f* | **16/1** | |
| 5401 | **8** | *nk* | **Roman Empire**[42] 5346 4-9-2 58 | (b) NCallan 13 | 52 |
| | | | (KARyan) *chsd ldrs: rdn over 2f out: wknd over 1f out* | **7/2**[1] | |
| 0502 | **9** | *1 ¼* | **Abelard (IRE)**[19] 5862 3-8-11 57 | (v) THamilton(3) 1 | 47 |
| | | | (RAFahey) *chsd ldrs: rdn over 1f out: wknd fnl f* | **6/1**[3] | |
| 0000 | **10** | *2 ½* | **Full Pitch**[49] 5201 8-9-2 58 | VSlattery 3 | 41 |
| | | | (WJenks) *s.s: hdwy 2f out: sn rdn and wknd* | **33/1** | |
| 1035 | **11** | *7* | **Boisdale (IRE)**[50] 5157 6-9-1 57 | RFitzpatrick 8 | 19 |
| | | | (SLKeightley) *led 5f out: hdd over 3f out: wknd over 2f out* | **20/1** | |



The Form Book, Raceform Ltd, Compton, RG20 6NL

0000 **12** *5* **Silver Chime**[31] 5618 4-9-1 60 MFenton 11 4
(DMSimcock) *sn pushed along and prom: wknd over 2f out* **25/1**

1m 15.73s **12** Ran SP% **112.0**
**WFA** 3 from 4yo+ 1lb
Speed ratings: CSF £26.75 TOTE £5.20: £1.80, £2.90, £4.80; EX 32.80.
**Owner** Horne, Hollinshead, Johnson **Bred** Longdon Stud Ltd **Trained** Upper Longdon, Staffs

**FOCUS**
Just a moderate sprint, but a tight race on the figures with just 3lb separating the entire field on adjusted official ratings. With several horses keen to be handy, the pace was strong and the form looks solid.

**NOTEBOOK**
**Prince Of Gold** provided a perfect example of jockeys being able to 'ride a race' on this new Polytrack surface. Held up off the decent pace, he was always travelling noticeably well and found plenty under pressure to confirm he is much better than he was able to show when unlucky on the turf at Catterick just two days previously. He has developed into a sprinter and is worth keeping on the right side of, especially round here.
**Woodbury**, a winner on Polytrack at Lingfield, ran creditably in defeat, faring best of those to race up with the pace.
**Asbo** made an encouraging Polytrack debut and could well make her mark in similar company, possibly over another furlong.
**Siraj**, well beaten over seven furlongs here two days previously, ran better over this shorter trip and can have no excuses, he simply lacked a change of pace.
**Legal Set(IRE)** ran a little better than the bare form would suggest, as despite being upsides the eventual winner on the final turn, he did not get as much luck in running as that one.
**Roman Empire**, with the blinkers back for this return to sand, can be forgiven this as he was stuck widest of all from the highest stall and things did not go his way.
**Abelard(IRE)** returned to form when runner-up over five furlongs at Newcastle on his previous start, but was below that level switched to sand and stepped up in trip.
**Silver Chime** *Official explanation: trainer said filly finished distressed*

## 6274 HOLIDAY INN GARDEN COURT, DUNSTALL PARK H'CAP 5f 20y(P)
**2:30** (2:31) (F4) (0-62,66) 3-Y-O+ **£2,989** (£854; £427) **Stalls** Low

Form RPR
U001 **1** **Harrison's Flyer (IRE)**[3] 6186 3-9-11 **66** 6ex (p) GParkin 9 81
(RAFahey) *chsd ldrs: hung lft and led over 1f out: rdn out* **9/2**[2]
1106 **2** *½* **White Ledger (IRE)**[3] 6186 5-9-0 **58** (v) THamilton(3) 6 71
(RAFahey) *mid-div: rdn 1/2-way: hdwy and nt clr run over 1f out: r.o* **6/1**[3]
6600 **3** *1 ¾* **Juniper Banks**[3] 6200 3-8-13 **57** LFletcher(3) 3 64
(MissAStokell) *prom: rdn 1/2-way: nt clr run over 1f out: styd on u.p* **40/1**
5000 **4** *½* **Sharp Hat**[6] 6144 10-8-13 **59** AQuinn(5) 11 64
(DWChapman) *hld up: r.o ins fnl f: nt trble ldrs* **13/2**
0022 **5** *1* **Desert Light (IRE)**[164] 1934 3-9-0 **55** (v) LisaJones 2 56
(DShaw) *chsd ldrs: rdn and ev ch whn hung lft over 1f out: no ex ins fnl f* **16/1**
4030 **6** *nk* **King Egbert (FR)**[26] 5734 3-9-0 **55** MFenton 8 55
(AWCarroll) *s.i.s: rdn over 1f out: r.o ins fnl f: nvr nrr* **4/1**[1]
2000 **7** *shd* **Innclassic (IRE)**[7] 6117 3-9-4 **59** (b) LEnstone 10 59
(JaneSouthcombe) *chsd ldrs: rdn 1/2-way: hung lft over 1f out: styd on same pce* **20/1**
0000 **8** *hd* **Lady Pekan**[116] 3227 5-9-3 **58** (b) IMongan 13 57
(PSMcentee) *edgd lft s: chsd ldrs: rdn 1/2-way: no imp appr fnl f* **14/1**
0006 **9** *1* **Multahab**[55] 5016 5-9-0 **55** (t) NCallan 5 51
(PSMcentee) *chsd ldrs: nt clr run fr over 1f out: nt rcvr* **20/1**
3303 **10** *nk* **Shaymee's Girl**[13] 6004 3-8-12 **56** NChalmers(3) 1 50
(MsDeborahJEvans) *led over 3f: sn wknd* **25/1**
4120 **11** *3* **Davids Mark**[39] 5412 4-9-0 **55** WRyan 4 39
(JRJenkins) *chsd ldrs over 3f* **6/1**[3]
6000 **12** *½* **Beau Jazz**[154] 2165 3-9-5 **60** PDoe 7 42
(WDeBest-Turner) *a in rr* **66/1**
1003 **13** *2 ½* **Malahide Express (IRE)**[33] 5562 4-8-12 **60** JDO'Reilly(7) 12 33
(EJAlston) *hmpd s: a bhd* **9/1**

63.38 secs **13** Ran SP% **119.9**
Speed ratings: CSF £29.71 CT £1005.75 TOTE £4.90: £2.20, £2.20, £19.30; EX 23.70.
**Owner** P D Smith Holdings Ltd **Bred** Geoff Mulcahy **Trained** Musley Bank, N Yorks

**FOCUS**
A moderate sprint handicap and a one-two for the in-form Richard Fahey. With little recent form to go on, the form may not prove that solid.

**NOTEBOOK**
**Harrison's Flyer(IRE)**, racing under a 6lb penalty for his success on the soft at Brighton on his previous start, followed up on his debut on an All-Weather surface, keeping on well to deny his stablemate having shown good early pace. Things will be tougher when he is reassessed, but he is in the form of his life and could well complete the hat-trick.
**White Ledger(IRE)** returned to form in the summer with a couple of wins, but had been slightly below-par on his last couple of starts, including when behind today's winner on his previous outing. Switched to sand (he has won on Fibresand), he produced a solid effort and gave the impression he will get another furlong.
**Juniper Banks** is still a maiden but ran much better than of late on his sand debut and could be up to winning a minor event.
**Sharp Hat** was unable to hold a position from his high stall and got badly outpaced in the middle of the contest, but he stayed on as well as anything to take fourth.
**Desert Light(IRE)** gained his only previous win on Lingfield's Polytrack and did not run badly, although he did not help his chance by hanging.
**King Egbert(FR)** had been shaping as though there was a small race in him and was backed accordingly but, having his first run on sand, he got behind early on and was disappointing.
**Davids Mark** was disappointing at Chepstow on his previous start and again failed to deliver, despite having winning form on Lingfield's Polytrack.

## 6275 GORDON HODGETTS "LIFETIME IN RACING" MEDIAN AUCTION MAIDEN STKS (DIV I) 5f 216y(P)
**3:00** (3:02) (F4) 3-Y-O **£2,919** (£834; £417) **Stalls** Low

Form RPR
43 **1** **Future Deal**[21] 5845 3-8-9 TQuinn 3 57
(CAHorgan) *hld up: hdwy over 1f out: rdn to ld ins fnl f: r.o* **9/4**[1]
2054 **2** *1* **Imtalkinggibberish**[8] 6089 3-9-0 75 WRyan 12 59
(JRJenkins) *s.i.s: hld up: hdwy over 2f out: edgd lft wl over 1f out: sn rdn: r.o* **5/1**[3]
504 **3** *shd* **Heavens Walk**[50] 5147 3-9-0 50 DSweeney 5 59
(PJMakin) *hld up: hdwy to ld 2f out: hdd and unable qck ins fnl f* **8/1**
0000 **4** *5* **Star Fern**[32] 5597 3-9-0 47 EAhern 2 44
(RMHCowell) *s.i.s: styd on appr fnl f: nvr nrr* **33/1**
304- **5** *2* **Saffron River**[311] 6165 3-9-0 56 DaneO'Neill 1 38
(RHollinshead) *s.i.s: outpcd: rn wd over 2f out: nvr nrr* **16/1**
0033 **6** *3* **Kamenka**[3] 6200 3-8-6 62 (v) THamilton(3) 13 24
(RAFahey) *chsd ldrs: ev ch 2f out: sn rdn and wknd* **4/1**[2]
2300 **7** *2 ½* **Sokoke**[42] 5338 3-9-0 58 MFenton 8 22
(RMBeckett) *chsd ldrs tl led 1/2-way: hdd 2f out: sn rdn and wknd* **10/1**
0 **8** *nk* **Miss Prim**[13] 6009 3-8-6 HayleyTurner(3) 10 16
(GPKelly) *led to 1/2-way: ev ch 2f out: sn rdn and wknd* **100/1**
040 **9** *1* **Raetihi**[42] 5342 3-8-9 40 NCallan 6 13
(ASenior) *chsd ldrs: rdn 1/2-way: sn wknd* **100/1**
2 **10** *2 ½* **Frabrofen**[175] 1664 3-8-9 RFfrench 4 5
(JamesMoffatt) *chsd ldrs to 1/2-way* **13/2**
0400 **11** *nk* **Designer City (IRE)**[23] 5801 3-8-9 35 TEDurcan 11 4
(ABerry) *s.s: outpcd* **66/1**
0505 **12** *5* **Dane Rhapsody (IRE)**[42] 5338 3-8-9 45 SHitchcott 7 —
(BPalling) *chsd ldrs: rdn 1/2-way: wkng whn hmpd wl over 1f out* **16/1**

1m 16.2s **12** Ran SP% **119.1**
Speed ratings: CSF £13.37 TOTE £2.50: £1.20, £2.60, £3.70; EX 19.30.
**Owner** Mohammed Al-Gaoud **Bred** Mrs B Woodford **Trained** Ogbourne Maisey, Wilts

**FOCUS**
A weak sprint maiden that is not easy to rate, but at least the pace was decent.

**NOTEBOOK**
**Future Deal** showed ability in two runs on turf over six and seven furlongs and was able to confirm that promise switched to sand. She did not have the pace to go with some of these early on, but was ridden accordingly and picked up well in the straight. Progressing, she should prove just as effective if not better back over another furlong and her future is in the hands of the Handicapper.
**Imtalkinggibberish**, behind today's winner at Windsor two starts back, had every chance and can have no excuses. Once again, he did not justify his current rating.
**Heavens Walk** had shown pretty moderate form on his three previous starts but, switched to sand for the first time, this represented improvement. He managed to get first run on the eventual winner, but looked to make his challenge a little too soon in doing so and had come right round the outside to get to the front.
**Star Fern** showed promise in his early starts, but has mainly been running to a pretty low level this year. This was a little better, but he still needs to improve.
**Saffron River**, racing for the first time in 311 days, was hampered and taken very wide on the home turn so can be rated better than the bare form.
**Kamenka** folded very tamely in the straight and continues to run quite a bit below her best.
**Frabrofen** shaped well on her debut over five furlongs on soft ground, but had not been seen since April and showed little under these different conditions.
**Dane Rhapsody(IRE)** would have been closer had she not been hampered.

## 6276 WOLVERHAMPTON-RACECOURSE.CO.UK (S) STKS 7f 32y(P)
**3:30** (3:32) (G4) 2-Y-O **£2,709** (£774; £387) **Stalls** High

Form RPR
6064 **1** **Lateral Thinker (IRE)**[7] 6127 2-8-12 68 EAhern 8 62
(JAOsborne) *w ldr tl led over 5f out: styd on u.p* **9/4**[1]
5505 **2** *nk* **Mitchelland**[16] 5954 2-8-12 60 RFfrench 5 61
(JamesMoffatt) *a.p: rdn over 1f out: ev ch ins fnl f: r.o* **10/1**[3]
0400 **3** *hd* **Norcroft**[27] 5719 2-9-3 69 JFEgan 9 66
(NACallaghan) *trckd ldrs: racd keenly: rdn and hung lft over 1f out: styd on* **9/4**[1]
006 **4** *2* **White Star Magic**[42] 5341 2-8-11 69 IMongan 7 55
(JRWeymes) *rr: hdwy over 2f out: nt rch ldrs* **14/1**
5506 **5** *5* **Worth A Grand (IRE)**[28] 5690 2-8-11 62 PDoe 3 42
(JWMullins) *led: hdd over 5f out: rdn and ev ch 2f out: wknd fnl f* **14/1**
060 **6** *nk* **Alzarma**[8] 6093 2-8-13 62 ow2 JDekeyser 12 44
(ABailey) *chsd ldrs over 5f* **16/1**
00 **7** *3* **Mount Kellet (IRE)**[16] 5954 2-8-11 MFenton 2 34
(JGGiven) *chsd ldrs over 4f* **33/1**
**8** *2 ½* **Chicks Babe** 2-8-7 ow1 SHitchcott 4 24
(BPalling) *s.i.s: hdwy over 5f out: wknd over 3f out* **40/1**
1000 **9** *nk* **Good Wee Girl (IRE)**[32] 5596 2-8-9 68 HayleyTurner(3) 1 28
(PSMcentee) *s.i.s: outpcd* **13/2**[2]
000 **10** *11* **Assured (IRE)**[20] 5846 2-8-7 ow1 (b[1]) NCallan 10 —
(PWD'Arcy) *s.i.s: sn prom: lost pl wl over 5f out: wknd over 2f out* **33/1**
00 **11** *3* **La Providence**[53] 5059 2-8-6 (be) PMQuinn 11 —
(DWChapman) *prom to 1/2-way* **100/1**
0006 **P** **Chek Oi**[36] 5494 2-8-11 60 (b[1]) SDrowne 6 —
(WRMuir) *prom tl broke leg and p.u wl over 5f out* **14/1**

1m 32.22s **12** Ran SP% **119.2**
Speed ratings: CSF £27.23 TOTE £2.40: £1.20, £3.30, £1.40; EX 22.10.The winner was bought in for 4,250gns. Norcroft was claimed by Phil McEntee for £6,000
**Owner** Colin G R Booth And Patricia Hughes **Bred** Joe Rogers **Trained** Upper Lambourn, Berks

**FOCUS**
Quite an interesting seller featuring a few horses who were capable of competing at a much higher level earlier in the season, suggesting the form is average or better for the grade.

**NOTEBOOK**
**Lateral Thinker(IRE)**, successful in a nursery off an estimated mark of 66 earlier in the season, had run well enough when dropped into this grade over a mile at Windsor on her previous start, and was able to confirm that switched to a surface she ran well on in much better races at Lingfield earlier in the season. A tough sort, she should continue to pay her way in similar company and is probably one for the forthcoming All-Weather season.
**Mitchelland** showed some pretty useful form earlier in the season, including when fourth in the Brocklesby before a five-length beating of Bibury Flyer, but this is her level now and she only just failed. This trip suited much better than the five furlongs she ran over here on her previous start, and she looks capable of winning a similar race.
**Norcroft** looks regressive and had been a long way below form on his last couple of outings, but there was money for him on this drop in grade. He looked to have every chance but simply found two stronger.
**White Star Magic** was no match for the front three but will find easier sellers than this one and is up to winning a race.
**Worth A Grand(IRE)**, dropped in grade, back up in trip and switched to sand, was well held.
**Good Wee Girl(IRE)** has not gone on since being claimed for £15,000 after winning at Chester earlier in the season and ran a stinker in the lowest-grade event she has contested to date. *Official explanation: jockey said filly would not face the kickback*

## 6277 LADBROKES.COM H'CAP 7f 32y(P)
**4:00** (4:03) (D2) (0-92,84) 3-Y-O+ **£7,147** (£2,199; £1,099; £549) **Stalls** High

Form RPR
6134 **1** **Jay Gee's Choice**[16] 5937 4-9-4 **84** TEDurcan 2 98
(MRChannon) *trckd ldrs: led over 1f out: rdn out* **6/1**
3003 **2** *1 ½* **Miss George**[41] 5379 6-9-3 **83** DaneO'Neill 1 93
(DKIvory) *hld up: ehadway over 1f out: chsd wnr fnl f: no imp* **16/1**
0340 **3** *1* **Flur Na H Alba**[30] 5631 5-8-11 **80** (p) THamilton(3) 9 87
(ISemple) *chsd ldrs: led 2f out: rdn and hdd over 1f out: styd on same pce fnl f* **33/1**
6601 **4** *shd* **Chateau Nicol**[31] 5614 5-9-3 **83** TQuinn 7 90+
(BGPowell) *hld up: hdwy over 2f out: rdn over 1f out: styd on* **9/2**[2]
5000 **5** *hd* **Soyuz (IRE)**[9] 6070 4-9-2 **82** NCallan 12 89
(MAJarvis) *hld up: hdwy over 2f out: rdn over 1f out: styd on* **11/1**
202 **6** *1 ¼* **Eccentric**[47] 5220 3-9-2 **84** JFEgan 8 87
(AndrewReid) *chsd ldrs: outpcd 1/2-way: rallied 2f out: sn ev ch: no ex fnl f* **10/1**

3030 **7** ½ **Primo Way**[9] 6070 3-8-7 **82**..........(p) KMay(7) 5 84
(BWHills) *chsd ldrs: outpcd 1/2-way: styd on ins fnl f* **12/1**

0225 **8** 3 **Flint River**[40] 5403 6-9-0 **83**.......... LFletcher(3) 10 77
(HMorrison) *hld up: hdwy 1/2-way: wknd over 1f out* **5/1**[3]

6000 **9** ½ **Vindication**[17] 5921 4-8-11 **82**..........(t) AQuinn(5) 11 75
(RMHCowell) *hld up: nvr trbld ldrs* **16/1**

0020 **10** hd **Winning Venture**[31] 5614 7-9-0 **80**.......... MFenton 6 72
(AWCarroll) *chsd ldrs: led over 5f out: rdn and hdd 2f out: wknd fnl f* **11/1**

0211 **11** 1 **Idle Power (IRE)**[18] 5887 6-9-2 **82**..........(p) EAhern 3 72
(JRBoyle) *sn led: hdd over 5f out: rdn and ev ch over 1f out: sn wknd and eased* **4/1**[1]

0100 **12** 3 **Just A Glimmer**[18] 5887 4-9-3 **83**.......... SDrowne 4 65
(LGCottrell) *w ldrs: rdn over 2f out: wknd over 1f out* **20/1**

1m 29.72s
**WFA** 3 from 4yo+ 2lb **12 Ran SP% 122.1**
Speed ratings: CSF £101.10 CT £2978.84 TOTE £6.00: £1.80, £2.40, £11.00; EX 59.10.
**Owner** John Guest **Bred** The Lavington Stud **Trained** West Ilsley, Berks

**FOCUS**
A really competitive handicap run at a decent pace and this form should prove pretty reliable for similar events round here.

**NOTEBOOK**
**Jay Gee's Choice** was thought good enough to contest the 2000 Guineas last season and had started this campaign rated 93 but, despite running better than the bare form would suggest at Epsom on his previous start, he had looked in the grip of the Handicapper. However, switched to a sand surface for the first time, he justified significant market confidence with a clear-cut success. On this evidence, he could be capable of better still but was reported to be heading to the Sales.
**Miss George** benefits from being held up off a strong pace but, as a result, she relies quite heavily on luck-in-running and got none of it on this occasion. With a clearer passage she may well have won and must always be respected in this type of event.
**Flur Na H Alba** was well beaten on soft ground at Ayr on his previous start but, switched to sand for the first time, he ran well and clearly took a liking to the surface.
**Chateau Nicol** has a very good record on Lingfield's Polytrack and won round here on Fibresand, but this was a little disappointing. He had to wait for a gap but was pretty one paced in the closing stages. *Official explanation: jockey said gelding lost a fore shoe*
**Soyuz(IRE)** just seemed to lack the pace of some of these and may benefit from a step back up to a mile.
**Eccentric** gained both his previous wins when dominating on Lingfield's Polytrack, but he was unable to get to the front and never really seemed to be going that well.
**Flint River** loved racing on Fibresand round here, but was below form on this new surface.
**Idle Power(IRE)** travelled well into the straight, but weakened tamely in the closing stages and was not given a hard time when beaten. *Official explanation: jockey said gelding ran flat*

## 6278 TIE THE KNOT AT DUNSTALL PARK H'CAP — 1m 5f 194y(P)

4:30 (4:31) (E3) (0-77,70) 3-Y-O+ **£3,458** (£1,064; £532; £266) **Stalls** Low

Form RPR

2503 **1** **Albavilla**[14] 5997 4-9-7 **70**.......... EAhern 10 85
(PWHarris) *a.p: led 5f out: rdn over 2f out: all out* **5/1**[1]

3344 **2** shd **Skye's Folly (USA)**[9] 6074 4-9-6 **69**..........(b) MFenton 7 84
(JGGiven) *hld up: hdwy over 3f out: nt clr run over 2f out: rdn and ev ch ins fnl f: styd on* **5/1**[1]

0066 **3** 10 **Jadeeron**[12] 6013 5-8-11 **60**..........(p) LisaJones 2 61
(MissDAMchale) *mid-div: hdwy over 5f out: rdn over 2f out: wknd fnl f* **11/1**[3]

0342 **4** hd **Dovedon Hero**[11] 6025 4-9-4 **70**..........(b) LPKeniry(3) 12 71
(PJMcbride) *s.i.s: hld up: hdwy over 4f out: nt clr run over 2f out : rdn and wknd over 1f out* **5/1**[1]

**5** 3½ **Indalo Grey (IRE)**[43] 4792 8-9-4 **67**.......... RHavlin 13 63
(MrsStefLiddiard) *s.i.s: hld up: hdwy over 5f out: rdn over 2f out: edgd lft and wknd over 1f out* **33/1**

3424 **6** nk **Regal Gallery (IRE)**[12] 6013 6-9-7 **70**.......... PaulEddery 6 65
(CAHorgan) *hld up: hdwy over 5f out: rdn over 2f out: edgd lft and wknd over 1f out: eased* **11/2**[2]

0000 **7** nk **Once (FR)**[20] 5853 4-8-13 **62**.......... DaneO'Neill 5 57
(JAOsborne) *chsd ldrs: rdn and wknd over 2f out* **14/1**

4030 **8** 21 **Milk And Sultana**[8] 6083 4-9-1 **64**.......... SDrowne 9 29
(GAHam) *hld up: hdwy 6f out: wknd over 2f out* **12/1**

0000 **9** 8 **Zeis (IRE)**[11] 6025 4-8-11 **63** ow3..........(t) LFletcher(3) 11 17
(AndrewReid) *sn pushed along in rr: wknd over 4f out* **40/1**

131- **10** 11 **Hefin**[327] 6079 7-9-1 **64**.......... TQuinn 3 —
(BGPowell) *chsd ldrs over 8f* **5/1**[1]

0000 **11** 10 **Vin Du Pays**[11] 6025 4-8-11 **60**.......... NCallan 1 —
(MBlanshard) *chsd ldrs over 9f* **33/1**

0060 **12** 5 **Vanbrugh (FR)**[2] 6231 4-9-2 **65**..........(v) IMongan 8 —
(MissDAMchale) *led: clr 9f out: hdd & wknd 5f out* **33/1**

3m 4.25s **12 Ran SP% 116.0**
Speed ratings: CSF £28.00 CT £263.38 TOTE £5.00: £2.70, £2.10, £3.30; EX 34.60.
**Owner** Mrs P W Harris **Bred** Pendley Farm **Trained** Ringshall, Bucks
■ The first race ever to be run over this trip at Wolverhampton on either Polytrack or the old Fibresand surface.

**FOCUS**
Just a modest staying handicap, but they went a good pace for much of the way and this form looks reasonable and should be quite reliable in similar events.

**NOTEBOOK**
**Albavilla** went into this a maiden and seemed pretty exposed but, racing over her furthest trip to date and making her debut on sand, she ran out a game winner. The front two were clear of the remainder and she could win again over this sort of trip.
**Skye's Folly(USA)** has been in good form in similar events recently and continued that switched back to Polytrack. He was short of room on the home turn, but had long enough in the straight to pass the eventual winner if good enough.
**Jadeeron** did not run badly, but was no match for the front two and appeared to finish pretty tired. He has only won once from 44 starts.
**Dovedon Hero** showed his ability to handle this surface when runner-up over a mile and a half on his previous start, and is probably a little better than the bare form as he clipped heels and lost a couple of lengths entering the back straight and was short of room on the home turn.
**Indalo Grey(IRE)** ◆ was better known as a hurdler when trained in Ireland, but has joined a stable that does very well with other trainers' cast-offs - especially round here - and shaped very well on his debut in this country. He should improve and is the one to take from the race.
**Regal Gallery(IRE)** goes very well on Lingfield's Polytrack, but was not at her best switched to Wolverhampton.
**Hefin**, racing for the first time in 327 days and making its debut for a new trainer, had winning form on Lingfield's Polytrack but dropped out very tamely down the back straight and has it to prove.

## 6279 SPONSOR A RACE AT DUNSTALL PARK H'CAP — 1m 1f 103y(P)

5:00 (5:01) (E3) (0-77,75) 3-Y-O **£3,857** (£1,187; £593; £296) **Stalls** Low

Form RPR

41 **1** **Gentleman's Deal (IRE)**[60] 4869 3-9-9 **75**.......... EAhern 5 88+
(EALDunlop) *trckd ldrs: led over 2f out: sn hung rt: r.o wl* **7/4**[1]

61 **2** 3 **Miss Polaris**[14] 5994 3-9-8 **74**.......... MFenton 4 81
(PWHarris) *hld up: hdwy over 1f out: styd on same pce fnl f* **7/1**[3]

1644 **3** ¾ **Hazewind**[9] 6064 3-9-4 **70**..........(vt) SDrowne 2 76
(PDEvans) *chsd ldrs: rdn and carried rt wl over 1f out: no ex ins fnl f* **11/2**[2]

0004 **4** nk **Ali Deo**[5] 6160 3-9-0 **66**.......... JFEgan 1 71
(WJHaggas) *hld up: plld hrd: nt clr run wl over 1f out: r.o ins fnl f: nt trble ldrs* **10/1**

0052 **5** shd **St Savarin (FR)**[16] 5950 3-9-7 **73**.......... TQuinn 12 78
(JRBest) *hld up: hdwy over 2f out: rdn and edgd lft over 1f out: styd on* **15/2**

4003 **6** nk **Cartronageeraghlad (IRE)**[8] 6086 3-9-4 **70**..........(b) DaneO'Neill 3 75
(JAOsborne) *prom: rdn over 3f out: no ex fnl f* **14/1**

2050 **7** 1½ **The Fun Merchant**[5] 6160 3-9-1 **67**.......... NCallan 6 69
(JPearce) *chsd ldrs: rdn over 2f out: no ex fnl f* **20/1**

0600 **8** 1½ **Taminoula (IRE)**[7] 6128 3-9-8 **74**..........(b[1]) IMongan 10 73
(MrsAJPerrett) *hld up: effrt over 2f out: nt trble ldrs* **16/1**

1200 **9** 3½ **Cherubim (JPN)**[32] 5595 3-9-8 **74**.......... TPQueally 8 66
(DRLoder) *led: hdd 5f out: rdn over 3f out: wknd over 1f out* **20/1**

4035 **10** 1½ **Jackie Kiely**[16] 5934 3-8-6 **65**..........(t) JBrennan(7) 11 54
(PSMcentee) *s.i.s: hld up: hdwy 4f out: wknd over 2f out* **16/1**

0000 **11** 7 **Benny The Ball (USA)**[17] 5912 3-9-4 **70**.......... TEDurcan 13 46
(NPLittmoden) *s.i.s: sn prom: wkng whn n.m.r wl over 1f out* **22/1**

0015 **12** ¾ **Soviet Sceptre (IRE)**[8] 6085 3-9-0 **66**.......... SHitchcott 9 41
(MissDMountain) *chsd ldr tl led 5f out: rdn and hdd over 2f out: sn wknd* **25/1**

0504 **13** 1¼ **Iskander**[14] 5992 3-9-3 **69**..........(b) JCarroll 7 41
(KARyan) *s.i.s: hdwy 1/2-way: wknd over 2f out* **16/1**

2m 1.39s **13 Ran SP% 127.1**
Speed ratings: CSF £13.94 CT £62.85 TOTE £2.60: £1.50, £1.80, £2.40; EX 10.80.
**Owner** khalifa Sultan and Mohammed Jaber **Bred** C H Wacker Iii **Trained** Newmarket, Suffolk

**FOCUS**
A fair handicap in which they appeared to go a reasonable enough pace. the first two are unexposed and the next three home give the form a solid and reliable look.

**NOTEBOOK**
**Gentleman's Deal(IRE)**, off the mark in a weak maiden at Chepstow on his previous start, coped well with this tougher opposition, following up in good style under his big weight. He will be put away for the year now, but is a very progressive type and appeals as one to keep in mind for next season.
**Miss Polaris** found this harder work than the Pontefract maiden she won on her previous outing, but acquitted herself with credit after getting a really good run towards the inside of the track as the pace was increasing. She is up to winning a similar event, but has clearly not got much in hand.
**Hazewind** has never managed to win beyond a mile and was one paced in the closing stages after getting carried a little wide at the top of the straight, but this was still a decent effort and he acts well on this new surface.
**Ali Deo** had shaped as though returning to form when fourth at Lingfield on his previous start and confirmed that with quite an unlucky run. He was travelling well towards the rear on the final turn, but did have clear passage and was never a serious danger.
**St Savarin(FR)** is on a winning mark, but came pretty wide in the straight and was well held.

## 6280 GORDON HODGETTS "LIFETIME IN RACING" MEDIAN AUCTION MAIDEN STKS (DIV II) — 5f 216y(P)

5:30 (5:31) (F4) 3-Y-O **£2,912** (£832; £416) **Stalls** Low

Form RPR

3522 **1** **Deuxieme (IRE)**[23] 5803 3-8-9 67.......... SDrowne 11 60
(RCharlton) *trckd ldrs: hung lft and led ins fnl f: drvn out* **8/11**[1]

6-P0 **2** 2 **Beresford Boy**[21] 5845 3-9-0 49.......... DSweeney 3 59
(DKIvory) *chsd ldrs: rdn over 1f out: r.o* **80/1**

5620 **3** 1½ **Lakeside Guy (IRE)**[57] 4968 3-9-0 54.......... NCallan 5 55
(PSMcentee) *a.p: rdn to ld over 1f out: hdd and no ex ins fnl f* **14/1**

-020 **4** 2 **Song Koi**[26] 5736 3-8-9 50.......... MFenton 4 44
(JGGiven) *chsd ldrs: outpcd over 3f out: rallied 2f out: styd on same pce fnl f* **9/1**[3]

6020 **5** ½ **Knead The Dough**[7] 6131 3-9-0 55..........(p) JFEgan 12 47
(DECantillon) *trckd ldr: led wl over 1f out: sn hdd and edgd lft: wknd ins fnl f* **4/1**[2]

4600 **6** ¾ **Eight Ellington (IRE)**[60] 4868 3-9-0 55.......... IMongan 8 45
(MissGayKelleway) *sn outpcd: styd on ins fnl f: nvr nrr* **14/1**

60 **7** shd **Onyx**[164] 1942 3-9-0.......... PDoe 1 44
(WDeBest-Turner) *sn outpcd: sme hdwy over 1f out: n.d* **66/1**

0000 **8** 3 **Indian Edge**[45] 5259 3-9-0 51.......... SHitchcott 2 35
(BPalling) *chsd ldrs: outpcd over 3f out: bhd whn hmpd wl over 1f out* **12/1**

000 **9** shd **Tanne Blixen**[21] 5845 3-8-6.......... LPKeniry(3) 13 30
(PSFelgate) *hld up: sme hdwy over 1f out: n.d* **100/1**

-005 **10** 2 **Faites Vos Jeux**[13] 6004 3-8-2 45.......... MHalford(7) 6 24
(CNKellett) *chsd ldrs: rdn to ld over 2f out: hdd wl over 1f out: sn wknd* **66/1**

000 **11** 6 **Miss Chancelot**[13] 6004 3-8-9.......... SWhitworth 7 6
(SPGriffiths) *outpcd* **100/1**

6500 **12** 6 **Velvet Touch**[124] 2986 3-8-9 46.......... WRyan 9 —
(JRJenkins) *led over 3f: wknd over 1f out* **16/1**

1m 15.96s **12 Ran SP% 121.0**
Speed ratings: CSF £112.78 TOTE £1.50: £1.10, £17.10, £4.10; EX 62.10 Place 6 £214.05, Place 5 £87.02.
**Owner** Beckhampton Stables Ltd **Bred** Roger Charlton And Floors Farming **Trained** Beckhampton, Wilts

**FOCUS**
Like the first division, a pretty weak affair, and the winner did not need to run to her best to score. The overall form looks moderate.

**NOTEBOOK**
**Deuxieme(IRE)** has her quirks and has not always found that much off the bridle but, after travelling best, did just enough to come clear and always looked like getting home despite hanging to her left in the closing stages. However, even in victory she did not entirely convince and appeals as one to take on in a better contest.
**Beresford Boy** had run to a very moderate level of ability on his previous starts and had even been pulled up two outings ago, so this was by far his best effort. Rated just 49, he is likely to go up for this and would therefore be of some interest if turned out in banded or minor handicap company before he is reassessed.
**Lakeside Guy(IRE)**, returned to sand, ran respectably but is proving hard to win with.

**Song Koi** did not run badly but does not seem as good as she was at two and may do better in low-grade handicaps or even banded races.
**Knead The Dough** was last in a handicap at Windsor on his previous start and was again well beaten despite switching to sand (he has run well on Lingfield's Polytrack) and having cheekpieces fitted. Five furlongs may suit better, but he is by no means one to follow.
T/Plt: £811.20 to a £1 stake. Pool: £31,950.15. 28.75 winning tickets. T/Qpdt: £44.80 to a £1 stake. Pool: £3,266.10. 53.90 winning tickets. CR

# 6077 BATH (L-H)

## Tuesday, October 19

**OFFICIAL GOING: Soft**

## 6281 TRIANGLECASINO.CO.UK/E.B.F. MAIDEN STKS — 5f 11y

**2:00** (2:00) (D3) 2-Y-O — **£4,238** (£1,304; £652; £326) **Stalls** Low

Form — RPR

054 **1** **Cesar Manrique (IRE)**[33] 5586 2-9-0 75 ........ MHills 8 — 79
(BWHills) *in tch: hdwy over 2f out: drvn to ld over 1f out: styd on strly fnl f* **6/1**[3]

5553 **2** 1 ½ **Auwitesweetheart**[9] 6080 2-8-9 68 ........ SDrowne 5 — 69
(BRMillman) *chsd ldrs: rdn 1/2-way: edgd lft and styd on fr over 1f out: chsd wnr wl ins last but no imp* **3/1**[2]

54 **3** 1 ½ **Malaika**[20] 5865 2-8-4 ........ StephanieHollinshead(5) 2 — 64
(RHollinshead) *s.i.s: sn rcvrd to chse ldrs: led over 2f out: sn shkn up: hdd over 1f out: outpcd ins last* **11/1**

**4** 1 ¼ **Keep Me Warm** 2-8-7 ........ CHaddon(7) 7 — 64
(WGMTurner) *s.i.s: bhd and sn rdn: chsd ldrs 2f out: styd on same pce ins last* **66/1**

0 **5** 1 ½ **Three Strikes (IRE)**[141] 2522 2-8-9 ........ MartinDwyer 6 — 54
(SCWilliams) *chsd ldrs: rdn over 2f out: outpcd over 1f out* **14/1**

**6** 2 **Jennverse** 2-8-9 ........ TQuinn 12 — 47
(DKIvory) *s.i.s: bhd: rdn and sme hdwy over 2f out: n.d and wknd over 1f out* **33/1**

050 **7** nk **Swift Dame (IRE)**[21] 5848 2-8-9 63 ........ RLMoore 1 — 46
(RHannon) *chsd ldrs: rdn 1/2-way: wknd over 1f out* **25/1**

**8** ¾ **Befitting** 2-9-0 ........ TPQueally 10 — 51+
(JAOsborne) *bhd: mod hdwy fr over 1f out* **16/1**

2206 **9** nk **African Storm (IRE)**[53] 5078 2-9-0 71 ........ JFEgan 3 — 47
(SKirk) *chsd ldrs: drvn to chal over 2f out: wknd qckly over 1f out* **14/1**

0 **10** ½ **Kitchen Sink (IRE)**[8] 6126 2-9-0 ........ DSweeney 11 — 46
(PJMakin) *outpcd most of way* **25/1**

00 **11** 1 ½ **Forest Delight (IRE)**[18] 5908 2-8-9 ........ EAhern 9 — 35
(CTinkler) *chsd ldrs to 1/2-way* **33/1**

42 **12** shd **Gimasha**[8] 6125 2-8-9 ........ TEDurcan 4 — 35
(MRChannon) *led tl hdd over 2f out: wknd wl over 1f out* **15/8**[1]

65.25 secs (2.75) **Going Correction** +0.525s/f (Yiel) — **12** Ran SP% **116.7**
Speed ratings: **99,96,94,92,89 86,86,84,84,83 81,81**CSF £22.66 TOTE £6.50: £2.40, £1.90, £3.50; EX 27.40.
**Owner** Philip G Harvey **Bred** Philip Graham Harvey **Trained** Lambourn, Berks
■ Stewards Enquiry : C Haddon two-day ban: excessive use of the whip (Oct 30-31)

**FOCUS**
Probably only a modest maiden run in pretty soft conditions, but fairly solid form for the level.

**NOTEBOOK**
**Cesar Manrique(IRE)**, who often takes a keen hold, ran fairly well behind a well-regarded type last time. Ridden with restraint, he took up the running with a furlong to go and had enough in reserve to hold the late challenge. He is to be put away now for a three-year-old campaign.
**Auwitesweetheart**, who has form on soft ground and may have gone close in a nursery over course and distance previously but for hanging badly, stayed on nicely to gain the runner-up spot. She did not appear to hang on this occasion but could never get to grips with the winner.
**Malaika**, who had run in some fair maidens previously, again appeared to perform well. Always to the fore after missing the break a touch, she only weakened close home and can now be handicapped.
**Keep Me Warm** missed the break and was given a forceful ride to get into contention, for which the jockey received a ban. As this was his debut he is entitled to improve, but it would be no surprise if he did not repeat this effort next time.
**Three Strikes(IRE)**, who was having her first run for the stable, did not show an awful lot on her debut but at least finished within hailing distance of the leaders this time. She is fairly well related, and to horses who acted with cut, and can improve with age.
**Jennverse**, whose dam had won on her two-year-old debut, ran with a little promise before weakening late on.
**Gimasha**, by a sire who enjoys cut, had run two promising races coming into this but weakened very quickly in the straight. Connections reported she finished distressed. *Official explanation: vet said filly finished distressed*

## 6282 EUROPEAN BREEDERS FUND MAIDEN STKS (DIV I) — 1m 5y

**2:30** (2:31) (D3) 2-Y-O — **£4,537** (£1,396; £698; £349) **Stalls** Low

Form — RPR

5022 **1** **Wotchalike (IRE)**[20] 5870 2-9-0 82 ........ TQuinn 8 — 77+
(DRCElsworth) *led after 1f: shkn up 2f out: qcknd fnl f: comf* **1/2**[1]

000 **2** 1 ½ **Wujood**[43] 5347 2-9-0 ........ RHills 10 — 74
(JLDunlop) *bhd: hdwy over 5f out: drvn to chse wnr wl over 1f out: swtchd lft and kpt on ins last but no imp* **10/1**[3]

0050 **3** 7 **Byron Bay**[18] 5909 2-9-0 64 ........ TPQueally 3 — 60
(JJBridger) *in tch: rdn fr 3f out: styd on same pce u.p to hold mod 3rd ins fnl f* **33/1**

**4** ¾ **Grasp** 2-8-11 ........ (t) NChalmers(3) 11 — 59
(RMBeckett) *s.i.s: bhd: drvn over 3f out: hdwy fr 2f out: hung lft and green over 1f out: styd on wl fnl f: nt a danger* **33/1**

0 **5** 1 ½ **Daybreaking (IRE)**[13] 6011 2-9-0 ........ SCarson 6 — 56
(RFJohnsonHoughton) *led 1f: styd disputing 2nd tl over 2f out: wknd over 1f out* **25/1**

**6** ½ **Alamiyan (IRE)** 2-9-0 ........ DHolland 4 — 57+
(SirMichaelStoute) *s.i.s: sn in tch: drvn along fr 6f out:chsd ldrs 3f out: wnt 2nd over 2f out: nvr a danger and wknd over 1f out* **6/1**[2]

00 **7** 1 ¼ **Mothecombe Dream (IRE)**[29] 5696 2-8-11 ........ LPKeniry(3) 7 — 52
(BJMeehan) *chsd ldrs early: rdn and outpcd 4f out: n.d after* **66/1**

000 **8** 3 ½ **Stolen**[12] 6021 2-9-0 ........ SDrowne 13 — 45
(WRMuir) *rdn over 3f out: a in rr* **66/1**

000 **9** 9 **Over Tipsy**[31] 5646 2-9-0 ........ RLMoore 1 — 27
(RHannon) *chsd ldrs: rdn and wknd over 3f out* **20/1**

0605 **10** 1 ¼ **Pussy Cat**[26] 5747 2-8-9 50 ........ DaneO'Neill 2 — 20
(KOCunningham-Brown) *a in rr: no ch fr 1/2-way* **66/1**

0 **11** nk **Xebec (IRE)**[11] 6045 2-9-0 ........ JFortune 12 — 24
(PFICole) *disp 2nd: rdn over 3f out: wknd qckly 2f out* **20/1**

0 **U** **Dream Along**[19] 5897 2-9-0 ........ MartinDwyer 9 — —
(MrsAJPerrett) *unruly stalls: rdr out of sddle whn stalls opened* **25/1**

1m 48.56s (7.56) **Going Correction** +0.775s/f (Yiel) — **12** Ran SP% **117.6**
Speed ratings: **93,91,84,83,82 81,80,77,68,66 66,—**CSF £4.76 TOTE £1.40: £1.10, £2.30, £6.30; EX 4.90.
**Owner** D R C Elsworth **Bred** M Hosokawa **Trained** Whitsbury, Hants

**FOCUS**
A modest winning time for the grade and 1.31 seconds slower than the second division. Howeve, the form appears reliable enough.

**NOTEBOOK**
**Wotchalike(IRE)**, who had run really well in his last two races behind a couple of decent prospects when there was cut in the ground, took up the running early and ran away from them. He was always travelling well in front, dictating the pace, and is probably a bit better than this form.
**Wujood**had shown bits of promise on much firmer ground in three previous efforts, and ran another solid race to be placed. This may not have been the best maiden however, and his future lies over middle distances next season.
**Byron Bay**, who was not beaten far in a nursery last time although only 12th, plugged on for third and probably lets the overall form down a touch.
**Grasp**, sporting a tongue tie on his debut, showed some promise in what might have been a slightly weak maiden. Having missed the break, he stayed on in the straight and weaved his way through tiring rivals. He should get further in time and can improve from this effort.
**Daybreaking(IRE)**, making his turf debut after having his first run on the Polytrack, was prominent until weakening two out.
**Alamiyan(IRE)**, who comes from a fair Aga Khan family, came to have every chance entering the home straight. He did not find much from that point but should progress from this run.
**Mothecombe Dream(IRE)** *Official explanation: jockey said colt hung left*
**Dream Along** had shown nothing on his debut and this time left the stalls while Martin Dwyer was waiting to get back on him, after he started playing up. This goes down as an error by the starter.

## 6283 EUROPEAN BREEDERS FUND MAIDEN STKS (DIV II) — 1m 5y

**3:00** (3:00) (D3) 2-Y-O — **£4,524** (£1,392; £696; £348) **Stalls** Low

Form — RPR

302 **1** **Rain Stops Play (IRE)**[9] 6078 2-9-0 ........ SHitchcott 12 — 81+
(MRChannon) *bhd: stdy hdwy over 3f out: styd on strly to chal jst ins fnl f: drvn to ld fnl 75yds* **3/1**[3]

40 **2** hd **Jaamid**[53] 5096 2-9-0 ........ JFanning 8 — 79
(MJohnston) *led 1f: hung rt and led again bnd 5f out: narrowly hdd 2f out: slt ld again 1f out: hdd fnl 75yds but kpt on wl cl home* **14/1**

6 **3** ¾ **Key Of Solomon (IRE)**[9] 6077 2-9-0 ........ (t) SDrowne 7 — 77
(HMorrison) *bhd: drvn along over 5f out: styd on wl fr over 2f out: str chal appr fnl f tl outpcd fnl 75yds* **20/1**

642 **4** 2 ½ **Tamatave (IRE)**[20] 5858 2-9-0 85 ........ (t) LDettori 11 — 72
(SaeedBinSuroor) *led after 1f: carried rt and hdd bnd 5f out: styd w ld tl slt ld 2f out: sn rdn: hdd 1f out: wknd ins last* **2/1**[1]

**5** 1 ¼ **Undergraduate (IRE)** 2-9-0 ........ JFortune 4 — 70
(SirMichaelStoute) *s.i.s: bhd: rdn 5f out: sme hdwy over 2f out:styd on but nvr gng pce to trble ldrs* **10/1**

0 **6** shd **King Gabriel (IRE)**[31] 5646 2-9-0 ........ DaneO'Neill 13 — 69
(DJSFrenchDavis) *s.i.s: sn rcvrd to chse ldrs: rdn over 2f out: wknd over 1f out* **50/1**

0 **7** 8 **Harlestone Linn**[18] 5915 2-9-0 ........ PaulEddery 2 — 53
(JLDunlop) *bhd: pushed along over 3f out: mod prog fnl 2f* **40/1**

0 **8** 3 **French Gold**[9] 6078 2-8-9 ........ TQuinn 10 — 42
(PFICole) *broke wl: sn bhd: n.d after* **66/1**

4462 **9** 2 ½ **Madam Caversfield**[50] 5172 2-8-9 70 ........ RLMoore 5 — 37
(RHannon) *in tch early: sn bhd: rdn and sme hdwy over 3f out: nvr daangerous and sn wknd* **16/1**

00 **10** shd **Secret Affair**[42] 5373 2-9-0 ........ JDSmith 1 — 42
(AKing) *chsd ldrs: rdn 3f out: wknd qckly over 2f out* **25/1**

602 **11** 1 ½ **Barbary Coast (FR)**[7] 6148 2-9-0 ........ MartinDwyer 3 — 39
(WRMuir) *chsd ldrs: rdn 3f out: wknd qckly over 2f out* **11/4**[2]

1m 47.25s (6.25) **Going Correction** +0.775s/f (Yiel) — **11** Ran SP% **121.1**
Speed ratings: **99,98,98,95,94 94,86,83,80,80 79**CSF £42.78 TOTE £4.20: £1.30, £3.40, £4.30; EX 44.40.
**Owner** John Livock Bloodstock Limited **Bred** Lucayan Stud Ltd **Trained** West Ilsley, Berks

**FOCUS**
A creditable time for the grade, 1.31 seconds faster than the first division and the form looks pretty solid for the grade.

**NOTEBOOK**
**Rain Stops Play(IRE)** had run with promise on all his previous starts, once behind Barbary Coast, and landed a mini-gamble when getting up close to home. He looked to be in a bit of trouble two furlongs out, but responded well to that pressure to stay on to the line. He may stay slightly further than this on better ground.
**Jaamid**, who had run moderately on a softer surface last time after a promising debut, held a prominent position during the race and challenged all the way to the line. He is bound to improve with time, given his big frame, and should stay further on this evidence.
**Key Of Solomon(IRE)**had not achieved much on his debut over course and distance, but showed the benefit of that run to finish close up. His pedigree looks more of a fast ground one so, although he acts with cut, he may find life easier on quicker ground.
**Tamatave(IRE)** was probably the form horse coming into the race after his good second to a well-regarded Michael Bell horse last time. However, these were entirely different conditions and, although unplaced, to his credit stuck to his task well after cutting out a lot of the running. He would not appear to be in the top echelons of the Godolphin camp but should break his maiden sooner rather than later.
**Undergraduate(IRE)**, who hails from a one of Her Majesty's successful breeding lines, missed the break quite badly, but stayed on pleasingly without ever looking a danger. He will probably be seen to better effect over middle distances next season.
**Harlestone Linn**, who is related to some useful stayers, is shaping as though he is in that mould to.
**Barbary Coast(FR)** has run in some decent maidens, including a close second last time out, but appeared to find conditions too soft this time, weakening badly about two furlongs out. *Official explanation: jockey said colt was unsuited by soft ground*

## 6284 WEATHERBYS INSURANCE SERVICES H'CAP — 1m 5y

**3:30** (3:32) (D2) (0-92,86) 3-Y-0+ — **£6,965** (£2,143; £1,071; £535) **Stalls** Low

Form — RPR

0423 **1** **Cello**[25] 5766 3-8-10 78 ........ (t) RHughes 15 — 88
(RHannon) *stdy hdwy on outside 5f out:qcknd to take slt ld 2f out:sn rdn and continually carried hd high: in command ins fnl f* **7/1**[3]

0024 **2** 2 **Alfonso**[33] 5582 3-8-9 77 ........ MHills 13 — 83
(BWHills) *bhd: stdy hdwy on outside fr 5f out: qcknd to chal on stands rail 2f out: styd pressing wnr tl outpcd ins last* **6/1**[2]

2301 **3** nk **Desert Cristal (IRE)**[19] 5886 3-9-2 84 ........ LDettori 7 — 89
(JRBoyle) *led after 1f: rdn 3f out: narrowly hdd 2f out: kpt on same pce u.p fnl f* **6/1**[2]

0310 **4** *hd* **Aperitif**[4] 6193 3-9-4 **86** ... MartinDwyer 10 91
(WJHaggas) *bhd: hdwy fr 3f out: styd on u.p to chse ldrs over 1f out: no imp ins last* **2/1**[1]

1464 **5** *3* **Pagan Prince**[10] 6069 7-8-12 **77** ... EAhern 11 76
(JARToller) *chsd ldrs: rdn over 2f out: wknd ins fnl f* **7/1**[3]

4540 **6** *1 ½* **Giocoso (USA)**[29] 5698 4-8-13 **78** ... TQuinn 16 74
(BPalling) *chsd ldrs: rdn 3f out: wknd over 1f out* **20/1**

0100 **7** *4* **Zweibrucken (IRE)**[25] 5766 3-9-0 **82** ... JFEgan 4 70
(SKirk) *broke wl: sn bhd: rdn and mod hdwy fnl 2f* **25/1**

1606 **8** *10* **Davorin (JPN)**[17] 5934 3-8-10 **78** ... TPQueally 6 46
(DRLoder) *chsd ldrs: rdn 4f out: wknd: wknd 3f out* **66/1**

516 **9** *nk* **Pass The Port**[101] 3728 3-8-10 **78** ... DHolland 9 45
(JRFanshawe) *chsd ldrs tl wknd 3f out* **16/1**

2110 **10** *½* **Zameyla (IRE)**[22] 5835 3-9-1 **83** ... PRobinson 1 49
(MAJarvis) *chsd ldrs: sn pushed along: wknd 4f out* **20/1**

2314 **11** *½* **Backgammon**[15] 5990 3-8-8 **76** ... NPollard 5 41
(DRLoder) *chsd ldrs tl wknd 3f out* **16/1**

0060 **12** *1* **Convent Girl (IRE)**[24] 5783 4-9-4 **83** ... RHavlin 8 46
(MrsPNDutfield) *a in rr* **20/1**

1000 **13** *2* **Threezedzz**[8] 6128 6-8-12 **80** ... (t) LPKeniry(3) 2 39
(PDEvans) *led 1f: wknd over 3f out* **20/1**

1m 46.11s (5.11) **Going Correction** +0.775s/f (Yiel)
**WFA** 3 from 4yo+ 3lb **13** Ran SP% **123.1**
Speed ratings: **105,103,102,102,99 98,94,84,83,83 82,81,79**CSF £44.96 CT £283.45 TOTE £10.70: £2.80, £3.40, £2.10; EX 44.10 Trifecta £583.80 Pool of £2,302.44 - 2.80 winning units.
**Owner** Louis Stalder **Bred** Normandy Developments Ltd **Trained** East Everleigh, Wilts

**FOCUS**
A fair handicap largely dominated by those who had soft ground form and the form looks sound for the grade.

**NOTEBOOK**
**Cello**, who handles soft ground well, ran away from his pursuers in the last furlong. He has not always looked the easiest of rides, but you can hardly fault his consistency. He was better off with the third, even though he had beaten him earlier in the season at Epsom, and now heads to the sales at Newmarket. Connections have stated they will be more than happy to retain him if he does not get sold.
**Alfonso** handles these soft conditions and ran really well in defeat. He is still entitled to improve, and will be interesting on this kind of ground until the end of the season.
**Desert Cristal(IRE)**, who has not raced on anything as soft as this before and had been raised 6lb for her recent easy success, was always close to the pace but came under pressure some way out. She was not well in with the winner on their early-season Epsom form, but this defeat owed more to the ground than her handicap mark.
**Aperitif**, who revels in soft conditions, was making a quick reappearance after running at Newmarket last week. He often has a flat spot in his races and stayed on at the one pace in the closing stages. He set a decent standard for the race, but is probably in the Handicapper's grip at the moment.
**Pagan Prince** is still a bit high in the handicap compared with his last win and probably should have run a bit better. He looks to be struggling with the Handicapper at the moment.
**Giocoso(USA)**, who likes to make the running and has acted with a bit of cut in the past, was to the fore for most of the way until weakening in the closing stages. Perhaps a drop in trip would suit him in these conditions.
**Zameyla(IRE)**, who has run well in soft previously, was behind Aperitif last time out but was much better off with him, but ran absolutely no race at all with no obvious reason. *Official explanation: jockey said filly was never travelling*
**Convent Girl(IRE)** *Official explanation: jockey said filly was unsuited by soft ground*

## 6285 M.J. CHURCH PLANT MAIDEN FILLIES' STKS — 1m 2f 46y
**4:00** (4:00) (D3) 3-Y-O+ **£3,562** (£1,096; £548; £274) **Stalls** Low

Form RPR

0-0 **1** **Radish (IRE)**[95] 3916 3-8-11 ... TEDurcan 14 65+
(EFVaughan) *trckd ldrs: rdn 3f out: drvn to ld jst ins fnl f: pushed out* **9/1**

2003 **2** *5* **Santa Caterina (IRE)**[25] 5770 3-8-11 66 ... LDettori 13 56
(JLDunlop) *led after 1f:rdn 2f out: hdd jst ins fnl f: kpt on same pce* **3/1**[2]

**3** *2* **Whirly Bird** 3-8-11 ... RLMoore 12 53
(MrsAJPerrett) *bhd: hdwy 4f out: styd on and edgd rt to stands side rail over 1f out: kpt on but no imp on ldrs* **9/1**

0P06 **4** *4* **Dances With Angels (IRE)**[25] 5770 4-9-2 35 ... PMQuinn 6 46?
(JWUnett) *bhd: rdn 5f out: hdwy fr 4f out: styd on fnl 2f but nvr gng pce to rch ldrs* **100/1**

06 **5** *3 ½* **Cirrious**[21] 5851 3-8-11 ... DSweeney 4 40
(BPalling) *mid-div: rdn 4f out: styd on same pce and n.d* **25/1**

3535 **6** *5* **Elusive Kitty (USA)**[17] 5936 3-8-11 66 ... DHolland 2 32
(GAButler) *chsd ldrs: rdn over 3f out: wknd over 2f out* **8/1**[3]

53 **7** *2 ½* **Neath**[39] 5445 3-8-11 ... RHughes 7 27
(MrsAJPerrett) *chsd ldrs: rdn 3f out: sn wknd* **2/1**[1]

40 **8** *12* **Angry Bark (USA)**[13] 6015 3-8-11 ... DaneO'Neill 1 7
(HSHowe) *chsd ldrs over 6f* **33/1**

00 **9** *4* **Singitta**[130] 2832 3-8-11 ... PDoe 5 —
(BPalling) *a in rr* **100/1**

060 **10** *3 ½* **Blaze The Trail**[92] 3994 3-8-11 35 ... (b[1]) MartinDwyer 15 —
(Jean-ReneAuvray) *chsd ldrs early:bhd fnl 5f* **100/1**

3600 **11** *4* **Tree Tops**[15] 5999 3-8-11 65 ... JFortune 11 —
(JHMGosden) *led 1f: styd chsng ldr to 3f out: sn wknd: eased whn no ch fnl f* **9/1**

5300 **12** *4* **Gwen John (USA)**[82] 4258 3-8-11 70 ... SDrowne 16 —
(HMorrison) *bhd: sme hdwy 5f out: wknd 3f out* **14/1**

**13** *dist* **Starjestic** 3-8-8 ... LPKeniry(3) 8 —
(MSSaunders) *slowly away: a bhd: t.o* **50/1**

2m 16.64s (5.64) **Going Correction** +0.775s/f (Yiel)
**WFA** 3 from 4yo 5lb **13** Ran SP% **117.8**
Speed ratings: **108,104,102,99,96 92,90,80,77,74 71,68,—**CSF £34.78 TOTE £11.50: £3.50, £1.80, £2.20; EX 62.00.
**Owner** de La Warr Racing **Bred** Denis McDonnell **Trained** Newmarket, Suffolk

**FOCUS**
A very smart winning time for the type of race in the conditions, although several disappointed.

**NOTEBOOK**
**Radish(IRE)**, hailing from a stable in good form but having shown little in maidens previously, powered away in these conditions to win fairly well. A combination of the step up in trip and going must have made a big difference. Given the ratings of those behind she may not be harshly handicapped, and would be interesting if turned out again fairly soon.
**Santa Caterina(IRE)** was stepping back up in trip after her third last time out and attempted to make all. She got swallowed up about a furlong out, after having quite a few in trouble entering the straight, and stayed on to the line. Another step-up in trip could be on the cards.
**Whirly Bird**, a Nashwan filly, made an encouraging debut in these conditions, staying on nicely after settling well off the pace. Connections will be keen to get a win into her for her paddock value.
**Dances With Angels(IRE)** is rated on only 35 and makes this form look distinctly ordinary, although fairly well beaten.
**Cirrious** has been well beaten at big prices in maidens beforehand, and did not show a lot her either.
**Elusive Kitty(USA)** had not shown a lot when last trying conditions this soft, and again looked to struggle.
**Neath** had run well enough in some fair maidens but appeared to hate the ground.
**Blaze The Trail** *Official explanation: jockey said filly kept stumbling*
**Tree Tops** had not shown much since July and appears to be going backwards.
**Gwen John(USA)**, who had not been seen since finishing well behind Masafi in the summer, had never run on anything this soft and showed nothing on it.

## 6286 LEVY BOARD H'CAP — 1m 3f 144y
**4:30** (4:31) (D2) (0-92,82) 3-Y-O+ **£7,014** (£2,158; £1,079; £539) **Stalls** Low

Form RPR

221 **1** **Autumn Wealth (IRE)**[51] 5146 3-8-6 **74** ... MartinDwyer 3 83
(MrsAJPerrett) *chsd ldrs:wnt to far rail and rdn to chal 2f out: led jst ins last: drvn and hld on wl* **5/1**[2]

1551 **2** *1 ½* **Skylarker (USA)**[25] 5764 6-9-2 **77** ... LDettori 6 84
(WSKittow) *chsd ldrs: rdn to take narrow ld 2f out: styd in centre crse: hdd jst ins last kpt on same pce* **5/1**[2]

0156 **3** *1* **Silver Prophet (IRE)**[20] 5875 5-8-2 **66** oh1 ... HayleyTurner(3) 1 72
(MRBosley) *chsd ldrs: drvn to chal fr 2f out: edgd to far side and outpcd ins last* **12/1**

-000 **4** *nk* **Montecristo**[15] 5997 11-8-9 **70** ... RLMoore 4 75
(RGuest) *bhd: hdwy fr 3f out: styd on in centre crse fnl 2f: fin wl but nt rch ldrs* **20/1**

3551 **5** *5* **Merrymaker**[17] 5956 4-8-10 **71** ... JFEgan 5 69
(WMBrisbourne) *bhd: hdwy 5f out: styd on to chse ldrs over 2f out but sn no imp* **10/1**

432- **6** *5* **Fame**[379] 5426 4-9-5 **80** ... PDoe 13 71
(PJHobbs) *led and racd wd: rdn 3f out: hdd 2f out and wknd qckly* **7/1**[3]

1063 **7** *¾* **First Dynasty (USA)**[10] 4808 4-8-8 **72** ... (p) JFMcDonald(3) 12 62
(MissSJWilton) *bhd: rdn 3f out: kpt on fnl 2f but nvr a danger* **33/1**

3346 **8** *1 ½* **Royal Bathwick (IRE)**[15] 5997 4-8-9 **70** ... SDrowne 7 58
(BRMillman) *in tch: rdn 3f out: sn wknd* **14/1**

1124 **9** *9* **Hezaam (USA)**[24] 5785 3-9-0 **82** ... RHills 14 57
(JLDunlop) *in tch tl wknd 5f out* **11/4**[1]

0060 **10** *1 ½* **Over The Rainbow (IRE)**[15] 5998 3-8-10 **78** ... (t) MHills 10 51
(BWHills) *chsd ldrs tl rdn and wknd 3f out* **20/1**

0300 **11** *9* **Maystock**[8] 6128 4-8-11 **72** ... (v) JFortune 11 33
(GAButler) *in tch: hdwy 5f out: wknd qckly 3f out* **12/1**

330- **12** *9* **Parachute**[474] 2923 5-9-4 **79** ... EAhern 2 27
(JABOld) *a in rr* **33/1**

246- **13** *20* **Not Amused (UAE)**[381] 5368 4-8-13 **77** ... RThomas(3) 9 —
(IanWilliams) *chsd ldrs tl wknd 5f out* **16/1**

2m 38.2s (7.90) **Going Correction** +0.775s/f (Yiel)
**WFA** 3 from 4yo+ 7lb **13** Ran SP% **124.9**
Speed ratings: **104,103,102,102,98 95,94,93,87,86 80,74,61**CSF £30.25 CT £293.30 TOTE £5.50: £1.40, £2.50, £4.50; EX 24.40.
**Owner** D J Burke **Bred** Ennistown Stud **Trained** Pulborough, W Sussex

**FOCUS**
A decent handicap but only ordinary form for the grade, although the winner can rate higher.

**NOTEBOOK**
**Autumn Wealth(IRE)**, who had won nicely over slightly shorter in similar conditions, enjoyed the step up in trip to score well. She hung slightly towards the far-side rail, but ran all the way to the line. She has the profile of an improving filly.
**Skylarker(USA)** has shown all his best form on much faster conditions, and was 3lb higher than for his win last time, but came to have every chance in the closing stages. This was a good effort for a horse who handles much faster ground and is probably still in pretty good form.
**Silver Prophet(IRE)** handles soft ground well and was close to his winning mark at Kempton. He came to have every chance from two furlongs out and stayed on to the line. He clearly enjoys these conditions and is on a fair mark.
**Montecristo**was down to a competitive mark and stayed on well all the way to the line. He was in second a few strides past the post and, even though he is advanced in years, he still has the ability to be competitive in this kind of race.
**Merrymaker**, who won on Wolverhampton's new surface last time, found conditions vastly different and did not appear to get home.
**Fame**, having his first run for the stable, looked big and well and took the field along for a long way. He should come on for this and will be interesting next time. This was his first effort in soft ground and he appears to prefer quicker conditions.
**Royal Bathwick(IRE)** was disappointing on this ground last time, her two wins were on much faster going, and she again showed no aptitude for going this soft.
**Hezaam(USA)**, who had no excuses for his last run, looked a progressive sort previously but does not appear to be in that form any more. He never got competitive and was eased from some way out. *Official explanation: trainer was unable to offer any explanation for poor form shown*
**Parachute**, having his first run for Jim Old, has the distinction of winning on all of the All-Weather tracks before Wolverhampton was re-laid. This was his first run for well over a year, and he did not show much.

## 6287 BETFRED.COM NOW ON LINE H'CAP — 2m 1f 34y
**5:00** (5:00) (E3) (0-77,75) 3-Y-O **£3,419** (£1,052; £526; £263) **Stalls** Low

Form RPR

2213 **1** **Sharadi (IRE)**[17] 5944 3-9-7 **70** ... DHolland 5 79+
(VSmith) *sn trcking ldr: led over 4f out: drvn clr over 2f out: wl clr whn wandered ins last* **11/8**[1]

4500 **2** *6* **Port Sodrick**[10] 6055 3-8-0 **56** oh6 ... AshleighHorton(7) 4 58
(MDIUsher) *prom early: dropped rr 1/2-way: stl wl bhd 3f out: styd on fr 2f out: kpt on to take 2nd ins last but no ch w wnr* **50/1**

0403 **3** *5* **Rossall Point**[9] 6084 3-8-12 **61** ... TQuinn 2 58
(JLDunlop) *prom: chsd wnr fr 4f out: sn rdn: no ch fr over 2f out: wknd and lost 2nd ins last* **4/1**[3]

135 **4** *9* **Strangely Brown (IRE)**[17] 5944 3-9-12 **75** ... LDettori 1 62
(SCWilliams) *in tch: rdn and hdwy to chse ldrs 5f out: wknd fr 3f out* **7/2**[2]

F4 **5** *7* **Cambo (FR)**[6] 6159 3-8-7 **56** oh1 ... EAhern 8 35
(RFord) *hld up in rr: hdwy to chse ldrs 5f out: wknd over 3f out* **11/1**

0432 **6** *9* **Niobe's Way**[9] 6088 3-9-3 **66** ... RLMoore 3 35
(PRChamings) *hld up in rr: hdwy 7f out: chsd ldrs 5f out: wknd over 3f out* **4/1**[3]

0 **7** *dist* **Explosive Fox (IRE)**[18] 5907 3-9-2 **65** ... MTebbutt 6 —
(VSmith) *sn led: hdd over 4f out and sn wknd: t.o* **40/1**

-000 **8** *26* **Kwai Baby (USA)**[8] 6132 3-8-4 **56** oh21 ... HayleyTurner(3) 7 —
(JJBridger) *bhd: sme hdwy 1/2-way: sn wknd: t.o* **100/1**

4m 5.33s (15.73) **Going Correction** +0.775s/f (Yiel) **8** Ran SP% **118.1**
Speed ratings: **93,90,87,83,80 76,—,—**CSF £83.03 CT £244.02 TOTE £2.30: £1.10, £17.80, £1.60; EX 101.00.
**Owner** R J Baines **Bred** His Highness The Aga Khan's Studs S C **Trained** Exning, Suffolk

**FOCUS**
A real stamina test and a very moderate time for the class, although the winner is progressive.

**NOTEBOOK**

**Sharadi(IRE)** has enjoyed himself since being stepped up in trip and ran out a very clear winner in these conditions. This Aga Khan cast-off has held his form really well and could easily be still improving, given his pedigree, and will be an interesting prospect next season.

**Port Sodrick** has been beaten in a seller and is almost certainly flattered by finishing second.

**Rossall Point**, probably ran his best race last time out when there was cut, sat close to the pace but never looked likely to win at any stage. This was disappointing even given conditions.

**Strangely Brown(IRE)**, who is still a shade higher than his last winning mark, sat just off the leaders but could never get competitive. His summer improvement looks to have levelled out.

**Cambo(FR)** showed he is not without some talent last time when staying on steadily in a two-mile event on the All-Weather. However, he found conditions very different this time and was struggling a long way out. A return to the All-Weather off his lowly mark will make him of some interest. *Official explanation: jockey said gelding was unsuited by soft ground*

**Niobe's Way** had shown some promise with cut in the ground and was extremely disappointing. Her rider reported she got very tired in the ground. *Official explanation: jockey said filly was tired*

## 6288 WICK APPRENTICE H'CAP 5f 161y

**5:30** (5:30) (F4) (0-62,58) 3-Y-0+ **£2,706** (£773; £386) **Stalls** Low

Form RPR

0030 **1** **Chatshow (USA)**$^{10}$ 6059 3-8-4 **46** oh1 DFentiman 16 59
(AWCarroll) *hld up mid-div: gd hdwy fr 2f out: rdn and qcknd to ld nr fin: drvn out* **25/1**

0502 **2** 1 ¼ **Coranglais**$^{2}$ 6246 4-8-11 **52** (b) RoryMoore 6 61
(JMBradley) *hld up in tch: drvn to ld jst ins fnl 2 fs: hdd and outpcd nr fin* **3/1**$^{1}$

4045 **3** 1 ½ **Majik**$^{8}$ 6131 5-8-12 **58** LiamJones(5) 4 63
(DJSFfrenchDavis) *bhd: hdwy over 2f out: rdn and kpt on u.p cl home* **5/1**$^{2}$

0203 **4** nk **Calusa Lady (IRE)**$^{7}$ 6146 4-8-6 **52** TBlock(5) 11 56
(GBBalding) *chsd ldrs: drvn to chal wl over 1f out: kpt on same pce ins last* **8/1**

6051 **5** hd **Tappit (IRE)**$^{3}$ 6229 5-8-10 **51** 6ex ThomasYeung 5 54
(NEBerry) *chsd ldrs: drievn to ld over 2f out: hdd ins fnl 2f: wknd ins last* **7/1**$^{3}$

0006 **6** ¾ **Desert Daisy (IRE)**$^{9}$ 6079 3-8-0 **47** DonnaCaldwell(5) 14 48
(IAWood) *bhd: hdwy on outaide fr 2f out: kpt on ins last: nt rch ldrs* **16/1**

0110 **7** nk **Spinetail Rufous (IRE)**$^{4}$ 6186 6-8-7 **55** (b) JDoyle(7) 12 55
(DFlood) *chsd ldrs: rdn over 2f out: outpcd fnl f* **15/2**

5600 **8** 1 ½ **A Teen**$^{43}$ 5346 6-8-7 **48** KristinStubbs 1 43
(PHowling) *s.i.s: bhd: hdwy fr 2f out: kpt on fnl f: nvr gng pce to rch ldrs* **25/1**

2665 **9** 1 ¼ **Harbour House**$^{55}$ 5039 5-8-5 **46** oh1 CHaddon 3 38
(JJBridger) *in tch: rdn and styd on fnl 2f: nvr gng pce to rch ldrs* **16/1**

0056 **10** nk **Yorkies Boy**$^{14}$ 6007 9-8-8 **54** (p) JemmaMarshall(5) 2 45
(NEBerry) *stdd s: bhd: kpt on fr over 1f out: gng on cl home but n.d* **14/1**

0006 **11** shd **Appolonious**$^{22}$ 5845 3-8-8 **55** TDean(5) 13 45
(DRCElsworth) *mid-div most of way* **20/1**

0053 **12** 1 ¾ **Ela Figura**$^{53}$ 5101 4-8-5 **46** (p) NataliaGemelova 9 31
(AWCarroll) *led tl hdd over 2f out: wknd over 1f out* **12/1**

1040 **13** 1 **Italian Mist (FR)**$^{144}$ 2455 5-8-8 **49** (e) MHalford 18 31
(JulianPoulton) *chsd ldrs over 3f* **14/1**

4000 **14** 3 **Otylia**$^{17}$ 5930 4-8-5 **46** oh1 (v) DeanWilliams 10 19
(RMHCowell) *chsd ldrs: wkng on rails whn hmpd over 2f out* **33/1**

0000 **15** 1 ¼ **Ninah**$^{22}$ 5830 3-8-1 **48** SO'Hara(5) 19 17
(JMBradley) *spd to 1/2-way* **50/1**

0000 **16** nk **Among Friends (IRE)**$^{46}$ 5258 4-8-4 **52** JoanneThomas(7) 15 21
(BPalling) *s.i.s: a bhd* **40/1**

00-6 **17** ½ **Clearing Sky (IRE)**$^{22}$ 5844 3-8-10 **52** StephanieHollinshead 17 19
(JRBoyle) *chsd ldrs tl wknd qckly over 2f out* **40/1**

560 **18** 1 **Silver Reign**$^{51}$ 5147 3-8-2 **48** ow1 RJKilloran(5) 7 13
(GBBalding) *chsd ldrs over 3f* **40/1**

0000 **19** hd **Cloudless (USA)**$^{74}$ 4509 4-8-5 **46** oh6 LeanneKershaw 8 9
(JWUnett) *bhd fr 1/2-way* **50/1**

1m 14.57s (3.43) **Going Correction** +0.525s/f (Yiel) **19** Ran SP% **136.5**
**WFA** 3 from 4yo+ 1lb
Speed ratings: **98,96,94,93,93 92,92,90,88,88 88,85,84,80,78 78,77,76,76**CSF £101.23 CT £484.92 TOTE £33.10: £7.10, £1.70, £2.00, £1.90; EX 257.80 Place 6 £89.38, Place 5 £45.67.

**Owner** Dennis Deacon **Bred** Juddmonte Farms Inc **Trained** Wixford, Warwicks

■ Stewards Enquiry : Natalia Gemelova two-day ban: careless riding (Oct 30+1)

**FOCUS**

A modest handicap but the form looks sound enough with those in the frame behind the winner close to their marks.

**NOTEBOOK**

**Chatshow(USA)**, from a stable in good form, had been beaten in a banded race last time but finished fairly well against his elders to break his duck. He will find things very difficult, given his level of ability, as he may be rated out of banded events now.

**Coranglais** ran fairly well in similar ground, only two days previously at Musselborough, and ran extremely well from a moderate draw. He looked likely to win inside the final furlong before idling and giving the winner his chance. He is in fair form for his level of ability, and can win again if delivered later.

**Majik**is a better horse generally on the All-Weather and ran with some credit from a moderate draw. He is still rated higher than his last turf win, way back in 2002, and is probably being set up for another winter campaign on the sand.

**Calusa Lady(IRE)**, who handles the soft ground, ran fairly well just behind the placed horses. She is still a maiden and appears to find it difficult to finish her races.

**Tappit(IRE)** has plummeted in the handicap, but struggled to carry the 6lb penalty he picked up for winning last time. He may not have enjoyed underfoot conditions.

**Desert Daisy(IRE)** missed the break and never reached the leaders.

**Spinetail Rufous(IRE)**, who is 15lb higher than when winning his first banded event at Kempton, has form on soft but probably prefers a quicker surface.

**A Teen** missed the break and never got competitive.

T/Jkpt: £45,698.70 to a £1 stake. Pool: £64,364.50. 0.50 winning tickets. T/Plt: £160.90 to a £1 stake. Pool: £43,918.35. 199.25 winning tickets. T/Qpdt: £50.70 to a £1 stake. Pool: £3,042.00. 44.40 winning tickets. ST

# 6273 WOLVERHAMPTON (A.W) (L-H)

Tuesday, October 19

**OFFICIAL GOING: Standard**

Wind: almost nil Weather: overcast, lt rain early

## 6289 DINE IN STYLE AT DUNSTALL PARK EBF MEDIAN AUCTION MAIDEN STKS (DIV I) 5f 216y(P)

**1:50** (1:52) (F4) 2-Y-O **£3,346** (£956; £478) **Stalls** Low

Form RPR

033 **1** **Captain Johnno (IRE)**$^{18}$ 5908 2-9-0 76 (v) WSupple 13 82
(DRLoder) *reluctant to go into stalls: rdn and hdwy on outside over 2f out: hung lft bef led ins fnl f: drvn out* **9/4**$^{1}$

0000 **2** 2 ½ **Mambazo**$^{22}$ 5838 2-9-0 54 SWKelly 3 74
(SCWilliams) *s.i.s but rdn and sn in tch: rdn and r.o to go 2nd ins fnl f* **25/1**

3 **3** ¾ **Revien (IRE)**$^{14}$ 6008 2-9-0 IMongan 5 72
(GAHuffer) *led after 1f: hung lft and hdd ins fnl f: no ex* **9/2**$^{3}$

06 **4** ½ **Joyeaux**$^{25}$ 5771 2-8-9 NCallan 6 65
(SLKeightley) *a.p: ev ch 2f out: rdn and nt qckn ent fnl f* **25/1**

0 **5** 1 ½ **Small Stakes (IRE)**$^{39}$ 5441 2-9-0 JQuinn 7 66
(PJMakin) *mid-div: rdn and short of room appr fnl f: one pce after* **3/1**$^{2}$

4206 **6** ½ **Mulberry Lad (IRE)**$^{13}$ 6012 2-9-0 64 (b) DKinsella 2 64
(WRMuir) *in tch: hrd rdn over 1f out: no further hdwy* **14/1**

603 **7** 1 ½ **All A Dream**$^{42}$ 5375 2-8-9 71 CCatlin 8 55
(RGuest) *towards rr: effrt over 1f out but nt pce to chal* **14/1**

2335 **8** 3 **Bond Babe**$^{36}$ 5520 2-8-9 66 FLynch 12 45
(BSmart) *chsd ldrs tl rdn over 1f out: sn wknd* **10/1**

6200 **9** 2 ½ **Haroldini (IRE)**$^{32}$ 5617 2-9-0 73 (p) JEdmunds 4 42
(JBalding) *led for 1f: wknd over 2f out* **10/1**

0520 **10** 3 **Hiamovi (IRE)**$^{18}$ 5910 2-9-0 60 MHenry 9 33
(RMHCowell) *bahind and a outpcd* **50/1**

**11** 1 **Annibale Caro** 2-9-0 SSanders 10 36+
(SirMarkPrescott) *s.i.s: outpcd and hung rt thrght* **12/1**

50 **12** 3 **Belle Largesse**$^{147}$ 2382 2-8-9 RWinston 1 23+
(CBBBooth) *outpcd after 2f and sn wl bhd* **66/1**

1m 15.64s **12** Ran SP% **124.3**
Speed ratings: CSF £71.65 TOTE £3.10: £1.10, £24.90, £1.20; EX 131.40.

**Owner** The Valais Boys **Bred** Paul Cashman **Trained** Newmarket, Suffolk

**FOCUS**

A modest auction maiden run in a second and a half faster time than the second division and the form looks reasonable for the grade.

**NOTEBOOK**

**Captain Johnno(IRE)**, switched to sand and back up a furlong in trip, found this one of his easiest tasks to date and got off the mark in clear-cut fashion. Given the runner-up went into this rated just 54, more will be required next time.

**Mambazo**, dropped two furlongs in trip and returned to sand for the first time, ran his best race date. He showed enough pace for this sort of trip, but may just prove better over another furlong.

**Revien(IRE)**, up a furlong in trip, improved on his debut running but shaped as though a return to the minimum trip could suit.

**Joyeaux** ran respectably to confirm the improvement she showed on her previous start and could progress again now she is qualified for a handicap, possibly over five furlongs.

**Small Stakes(IRE)**, who had Group race entries earlier in the season but disappointed on his debut, again failed to deliver and could be best watched for the time being.

**Annibale Caro** is not bred to go this sort of trip - his sire was a middle-distance performer and his dam never raced over shorter than a mile or won over shorter than ten furlongs - so it was hardly surprising he was never seen with a chance. He is the type that will earn a modest handicap mark and exploit it when stepped up to a trip his breeding suggests is more appropriate.

## 6290 COME FLOODLIGHT RACING AT DUNSTALL PARK (S) STKS 7f 32y(P)

**2:20** (2:20) (G4) 3-Y-O **£2,590** (£740; £370) **Stalls** High

Form RPR

3315 **1** **Two Of Clubs**$^{51}$ 5141 3-9-5 62 (p) GFaulkner 3 73
(PCHaslam) *chsd ldrs: wnt 2nd over 2f out: led wl over 1f out: rdn out* **9/2**$^{2}$

6000 **2** 1 ¾ **La Puce**$^{75}$ 4483 3-9-0 71 IMongan 6 63
(MissGayKelleway) *slowly away: wl bhd tl gd hdwy over 1f out: hung lft but kpt on to go 2nd ins fnl f* **7/1**$^{3}$

3040 **3** 2 **Emaradia**$^{3}$ 6220 3-8-11 57 (b) DNolan(3) 11 58
(AWCarroll) *led tl hdd wl voer 1f out: rdn and fdd ins fnl f* **10/1**

1050 **4** 1 ¼ **Vonadaisy**$^{17}$ 5955 3-9-0 68 SWKelly 2 55
(WJHaggas) *towards rr tl hdwy 2f out: rdn and kpt on one pce fnl f* **5/2**$^{1}$

0010 **5** 2 ½ **Megabond**$^{26}$ 5748 3-9-5 60 (p) NCallan 10 54
(CADwyer) *bhd tl hdwy on outside over 2f out: nvr nr to chal* **14/1**

1060 **6** 1 ½ **Faith Healer (IRE)**$^{24}$ 5795 3-9-0 57 (b) JQuinn 8 45
(VSmith) *prom on outside: rdn 1/2-way: wknd ent fnl f* **12/1**

0500 **7** nk **Crewes Miss Isle**$^{10}$ 6066 3-9-0 60 SWhitworth 12 44
(AGNewcombe) *in tch: rdn 2f out: one pce appr fnl f* **18/1**

1200 **8** 2 ½ **Diamond Shannon (IRE)**$^{32}$ 5618 3-8-9 58 DTudhope(5) 5 37
(DCarroll) *s.i.s: a bhd* **10/1**

0020 **9** 6 **Aliba (IRE)**$^{9}$ 6097 3-9-0 61 DMcGaffin 1 22
(BSmart) *s.i.s: a struggling in rr* **20/1**

0000 **10** ½ **Morag**$^{8}$ 6124 3-8-9 58 MFenton 7 15
(IAWood) *slowly away: a bhd* **7/1**$^{3}$

6400 **11** 1 ¼ **Black Sabbeth**$^{9}$ 6079 3-9-0 59 (v$^{1}$) SSanders 4 17
(PJMakin) *sn trckd ldr: rdn and wknd qckly over 2f out* **16/1**

1m 31.23s **11** Ran SP% **120.2**
Speed ratings: CSF £37.05 TOTE £7.30: £2.10, £2.70, £3.10; EX 27.60.The winner was sold to John Pointon for 6,750gns. La Puce was claimed by M Attwater for £6,000.

**Owner** Blue Lion Racing II **Bred** P B T Group **Trained** Middleham Moor, N Yorks

**FOCUS**

A pretty moderate seller run at a furious pace, although the form is not bad for the level.

**NOTEBOOK**

**Two Of Clubs**, whose last success came four starts previously on the Fibresand round here, showed his ability to handle this new surface just as well. This grade looks ideal for him.

**La Puce** was three from four round here on the old Fibresand surface, but had been below that level on her only previous run on Polytrack and badly out of sorts on the turf recently. Dropped in grade and returned to sand, she ran better than of late but still not up to her mark, and hardly impressed in getting badly outpaced early on before hanging left-handed in the straight.

**Emaradia** got a few of these beat at an early stage by setting such a strong pace, but was simply unable to hold off the front two.

**Vonadaisy**, with the blinkers left off and dropped in grade and trip, was disappointing and failed to justify her current rating.

**Megabond** was simply unable to go the furious early pace.

**Morag** was never going the pace.

## 6291 ENJOY THEMED RACE NIGHTS MAIDEN AUCTION STKS 7f 32y(P)
2:50 (2:52) (F4) 2-Y-0 £3,101 (£886; £443) Stalls High

Form RPR

1 **Major Faux Pas (IRE)** 2-8-13 ........ SWKelly 11 84+
(JAOsborne) *chsd ldrs: rdn wl over 1f out: r.o to ld ins fnl f* **12/1**

6426 2 1 3/4 **Belly Dancer (IRE)**[17] 5938 2-8-9 75 ow1 ........ SSanders 1 76
(PFICole) *trckd ldr: led 3f out: rdn and hdd ins fnl f: no ex* **5/4**[1]

00 3 2 **Queen Tomyra (IRE)**[8] 6118 2-8-5 ........ NMackay(3) 12 70+
(LMCumani) *s.i.s: sn mid-div: hrd rdn and edgd lft appr fnl f: squeezed through to go 3rd ins* **25/1**

06U 4 1 3/4 **Mel's Moment (USA)**[6] 6155 2-8-13 ........ IMongan 9 71
(MrsAJPerrett) *s.i.s and outpcd early: rdn and hdd 1/2-way: styd on appr fnl f: nvr nr to chal* **7/1**[3]

5036 5 2 1/2 **Chutney Mary (IRE)**[14] 6003 2-8-7 71 ow1 ........ NCallan 6 59
(JGPortman) *led tl hdd 3f out: rdn and wknd appr fnl f* **15/2**

0 6 3/4 **Crown Of Medina**[18] 5915 2-8-9 ........ WSupple 5 62+
(PWHarris) *mid-div: rdn 3f out: nvr a danger after* **12/1**

540 7 3/4 **Blueberry Tart (IRE)**[8] 6123 2-8-6 ........ RWinston 8 54
(BJMeehan) *trckd ldrs tl rdn and wknd over 1f out* **4/1**[2]

64 8 nk **Sand Iron (IRE)**[25] 5771 2-8-3 ow1 ........ RFitzpatrick 4 53+
(SLKeightley) *chsd ldrs: rdn and hld whn hmpd over 1f out* **12/1**

0 9 nk **Sol Rojo**[8] 6126 2-8-2 ........ RKeogh(7) 10 56
(JAOsborne) *hld up in mid-div: rdn bef wknd wl over 1f out* **33/1**

0 10 1 1/4 **Woodford Consult**[10] 6067 2-8-2 ........ DaleGibson 2 45
(MWEasterby) *a bhd* **66/1**

0 11 5 **Formidable Will (FR)**[15] 5996 2-8-11 ........ RSmith 3 42
(CGCox) *bhd fr 1/2-way* **50/1**

00 12 8 **Magdelaine**[12] 6021 2-8-8 ........ CCatlin 7 20
(PMPhelan) *a in rr* **66/1**

1m 30.47s **12 Ran SP% 123.5**

Speed ratings: CSF £27.93 TOTE £21.50: £5.90, £1.10, £11.70; EX 74.00.

**Owner** Martin Collins **Bred** Rathbarry Stud **Trained** Upper Lambourn, Berks

■ Stewards Enquiry : N Mackay one-day ban: careless riding (Oct 30)

**FOCUS**

A fair maiden but reasonably solid form that should produce some winners at this level.

**NOTEBOOK**

**Major Faux Pas(IRE)**, a 35,000euros half-brother to the seven-furlong two-year-old winner, later very useful miler Seihaldi, was easy enough to back but proved good enough to make a winning debut. Always in a good position just off the leaders, he found plenty for pressure and was well on top at the finish. He knew his job, but his trainer expects him to improve and may put him away for the year.

**Belly Dancer(IRE)**, a disappointing favourite on her only previous try on a sand surface (Fibresand), handled Polytrack much better but was simply beaten by a better horse.

**Queen Tomyra(IRE)** ◆ showed improved form without being given a hard time and was a real eye-catcher. She should a get a reasonable mark and is one to follow in handicap company.

**Mel's Moment(USA)**, who unseated his rider at the start on his previous outing, was not quite at his best and looked to find this trip on the short side. He is, however, qualified for a mark.

**Chutney Mary(IRE)** did not run to her mark and was disappointing.

**Crown Of Medina** would have found this easier than the Newmarket maiden he contested on his debut and ran creditably.

**Blueberry Tart(IRE)**, switched to sand, was not at her best with no obvious excuse.

**Sol Rojo** hinted at ability and is worth keeping an eye on when he is handicapped.

## 6292 ZONGALERO RESTAURANT H'CAP 1m 4f 50y(P)
3:20 (3:20) (F4) (0-62,62) 3-Y-0+ £3,088 (£882; £441) Stalls Low

Form RPR

4026 1 **Lord Lahar**[3] 6231 5-8-8 49 ........ CCatlin 1 58
(MRChannon) *hld up in rr: hdwy over 4f out: klept on u.str riding fnl f to ld cl home* **8/1**

2323 2 hd **Captain Marryat**[40] 5410 3-8-12 60 ........ WSupple 8 69
(PWHarris) *in tch: hdwy to ld 2f out: wandered in front appr fnl hung rt ins fnl f u.p: hdd cl home* **9/2**[1]

6220 3 2 1/2 **Traveller's Tale**[53] 5073 5-8-6 54 ........ DerekNolan(7) 9 59
(PGMurphy) *hld up: hdwy over 2f out on outside: styd on to go 3rd ins fnl f* **14/1**

4031 4 5 **Yashin (IRE)**[8] 6120 3-8-11 59 6ex ........ NCallan 12 57
(PABlockley) *prom: rdn 3f out: hmpd but hld appr fnl f* **15/2**

6200 5 nk **Bravely Does It (USA)**[15] 5993 4-8-11 52 ........ SWKelly 3 49
(WMBrisbourne) *prom: led over 5f out: hdd 3f out: wknd over 1f out* **33/1**

4540 6 1 **Head To Kerry (IRE)**[38] 5459 4-9-0 55 ........ SSanders 6 51
(DJSFfrenchDavis) *t.k.h: mid-div: swtchd lft over 1f out: sn wknd* **5/1**[2]

2242 7 2 **Heathers Girl**[57] 4998 5-8-9 50 ........ SWhitworth 5 43
(DHaydnJones) *prom: ld 3f out: hdd 2f out: wknd appr fnl f* **10/1**

0003 8 1 **Factual Lad**[21] 5853 6-9-7 62 ........ GBaker 7 53
(BRMillman) *led tl hdd over 5f out: wknd 2f out* **10/1**

2300 9 2 1/2 **Pont Neuf (IRE)**[10] 6074 4-8-12 56 ........ (t) DNolan(3) 10 44
(PDEvans) *hld up in rr: nvr on terms* **7/1**

0403 10 9 **Carriacou**[9] 6083 3-8-12 60 ........ MFenton 4 34
(PWD'Arcy) *hld up: a bhd* **6/1**[3]

0-06 11 7 **Mythical King (IRE)**[157] 2121 7-8-6 52 ........ BSwarbrick(5) 11 16
(RLee) *a in rr: rdn on outside 5f out and sn lost tch* **10/1**

2m 42.79s

**WFA** 3 from 4yo+ 7lb **11 Ran SP% 121.4**

Speed ratings: CSF £45.40 CT £510.65 TOTE £8.90: £2.10, £1.60, £2.60; EX 94.10.

**Owner** Barry Walters Catering **Bred** B Walters **Trained** West Ilsley, Berks

**FOCUS**

A moderate handicap run at a steady pace until Bravely Does It was sent on down the back straight. The form, rated through the runner-up, is not particularly strong.

**NOTEBOOK**

**Lord Lahar** showed his ability to handle this surface when runner-up in a seller over course and distance two starts previously and, returned to Polytrack, got off the mark in what was a tougher heat. He is only moderate, but could win again at this sort of level.

**Captain Marryat** continues to run his race without managing to win. He did nothing wrong and is likely to find a race before too much longer.

**Traveller's Tale** took well to this surface, posting a good effort without having the pace to trouble the front two. He should prove effective at up to two miles.

**Yashin(IRE)**, a facile winner of a Leicester seller over ten furlongs on his final start for Mark Tompkins, did not get home after racing keenly over his furthest trip to date.

**Bravely Does It(USA)** was unable to sustain his effort after being sent to the front and may do better back over further.

**Head To Kerry(IRE)** continues to find a few too good.

## 6293 RACING WELFARE H'CAP 5f 216y(P)
3:50 (3:51) (E3) (0-77,77) 3-Y-0+ £3,836 (£1,180; £590; £295) Stalls Low

Form RPR

6611 1 **Blythe Spirit**[12] 6026 5-9-10 76 ........ (p) PHanagan 8 87+
(RAFahey) *a in tch: rdn to ld over 1f out: edgd lft ins fnl f: jst hld on* **9/4**[1]

1221 2 nk **Mistral Sky**[67] 4727 5-9-6 72 ........ (v) IMongan 10 82
(MrsStefLiddiard) *outpcd in rr: rdn on outside 2f out: str run appr fnl f: r.o wl to press wnr cl home* **6/1**

1500 3 1/2 **Mimic**[8] 6131 4-9-1 67 ........ CCatlin 2 76
(RGuest) *chsd ldrs: ev ch appr fnl f: r.o one pce after* **20/1**

3200 4 1 1/4 **Another Glimpse**[42] 5379 6-9-11 77 ........ (t) NCallan 7 82
(MissBSanders) *hld up: hdwy whn nt clr run over 2f out: styd on one pce fnl f* **11/1**

0303 5 nk **Musical Fair**[35] 5550 4-9-9 75 ........ RWinston 9 79
(JAGlover) *in tch: tl rdn and one pce appr fnl f* **10/1**

3605 6 2 **Ammenayr (IRE)**[6] 6157 4-8-8 67 ........ AMullen(7) 11 65
(TGMills) *in rr: sme hdwy 2f out: nvr nr to chal* **11/2**[3]

5262 7 1/2 **Bob's Buzz**[8] 6124 4-9-7 73 ........ SSanders 13 69
(SCWilliams) *in tch on outside: hdwy over 2f out: wknd fnl f* **5/1**[2]

4100 8 3 **If By Chance**[143] 2490 6-9-0 69 ........ TEaves(3) 4 56
(RCraggs) *in tch tl lost pl over 3f out: n.d after* **25/1**

3000 9 2 **Playtime Blue**[65] 4774 4-9-5 71 ........ GBaker 5 52
(MrsHSweeting) *led tl rdn and hdd over 1f out: wknd fnl f* **25/1**

1000 10 nk **Blakeshall Quest**[8] 6131 4-9-2 71 ........ (v) DNolan(3) 6 51
(RBrotherton) *prom tl rdn and wqeakened over 1f out* **40/1**

0000 11 nk **Parkside Pursuit**[4] 6186 6-9-2 68 ........ PFitzsimons 12 48
(JMBradley) *prom: ev ch appr fnl f: wknd qckly* **25/1**

6204 12 1 1/2 **Blue Knight (IRE)**[75] 4495 5-9-6 72 ........ SWKelly 1 47
(PHowling) *prom tl lost pl over 2f out: sn bhd* **20/1**

2100 13 3 1/2 **Demolition Molly**[11] 6046 3-9-0 70 ........ (tp) LFletcher(3) 3 35
(RFMarvin) *v.s.a: a bhd* **50/1**

1m 16.01s

**WFA** 3 from 4yo+ 1lb **13 Ran SP% 120.0**

Speed ratings: CSF £13.87 CT £229.60 TOTE £2.20: £1.10, £3.20, £4.80; EX 13.70.

**Owner** The Matthewman Partnership **Bred** W Haggas And W Jarvis **Trained** Musley Bank, N Yorks

**FOCUS**

A fairly competitive sprint handicap in which the vast majority of the field were still close enough if good enough turning for home. The placed horses give the form a solid look, and the result rather backed up the theory that previous form on this new surface is the best guide.

**NOTEBOOK**

**Blythe Spirit** maintained his unbeaten record over course and distance on this new surface off a 7lb higher mark, but unlike last time where he got up on the line, on this occasion he hit the front much sooner and only just held on. He could win again here if his effort is delayed a bit longer.

**Mistral Sky** ◆, off the same mark as when successful on turf on his last outing two months ago, took a while to find his feet, but finished strongly down the outside and would have got there in a few more strides. He has won twice at Lingfield and can win here either over this trip or over an extra furlong.

**Mimic** ◆, placed on her only previous try on Polytrack at Lingfield two years ago, travelled like a dream on the inside but the limited evidence so far suggests that racing tight against the inside rail might be a disadvantage. To be fair, such an inviting gap opened up in front of her turning for home that she was forced to make her effort there and deserves great credit for finishing so close. She looks likely to win here before long.

**Another Glimpse**, held up off the pace, travelled very well and looked sure to figure in the finish once finding room, but in truth he did not find as much off the bridle as had looked likely.

**Musical Fair**, making her sand debut, ran with credit and had every chance but did not convince one way or the other over the suitability of this surface.

**Ammenayr(IRE)**, yet to make the frame on sand, stayed on without ever looking like getting on terms. He has become very well handicapped, but is probably better over seven.

**Bob's Buzz**, beaten despite being well supported in two recent outings here, had still been put up 3lb for that yet finished much further behind Blythe Spirit than he did three starts go, despite being 4lb better off.

## 6294 DINE IN STYLE AT DUNSTALL PARK EBF MEDIAN AUCTION MAIDEN STKS (DIV II) 5f 216y(P)
4:20 (4:20) (E3) 2-Y-0 £3,339 (£954; £477) Stalls Low

Form RPR

4004 1 **Heartsonfire (IRE)**[20] 5864 2-8-9 63 ........ MFenton 8 64
(PWD'Arcy) *towards rr tl hdwy voer 2f out: edgd lft but kpt on u.p to ld wl ins fnl f* **15/2**

4002 2 1/2 **Gaudalpin (IRE)**[14] 6002 2-8-9 64 ........ AMcCarthy 7 62
(MJAttwater) *trckd ldr: led over 3f out: rdn clr: no ex and hdd wl ins fnl f* **7/1**[3]

3 hd **Sweet Namibia (IRE)** 2-8-9 ........ SWhitworth 4 62
(JWHills) *hld up in tch: rdn over 1f out: kpt on fnl f* **10/1**

04 4 nk **Chief Dipper**[12] 6022 2-9-0 ........ JQuinn 9 66
(PJMcbride) *bhd and outpcd: hdwy appr fnl f: r.o: nvr nrr* **25/1**

045 5 shd **Mangrove Cay (IRE)**[17] 5953 2-9-0 67 ........ (v[1]) SSanders 2 66
(DRLoder) *in tch: hrd rdn 2f out: one pce and no ex ins fnl f* **7/1**[3]

00 6 5 **La Cygne Blanche (IRE)**[6] 6153 2-8-4 ........ PMakin(5) 12 45
(MrsNMacauley) *outpcd and wl in rr: plugged on past btn horses ins fnl 2f* **66/1**

6602 7 shd **Llamadas**[17] 5954 2-9-0 64 ........ (v) IMongan 1 50
(MrsStefLiddiard) *slowly away and wl bhd: mde sme late hdwy* **5/1**[2]

2065 8 1/2 **Rainbow Iris**[11] 6042 2-8-9 68 ........ FLynch 10 44
(BSmart) *chsd ldrs tl rdn and wknd 2f out* **5/2**[1]

0006 9 5 **Little Indy**[29] 5687 2-8-11 60 ........ DNolan(3) 11 33
(RBrotherton) *in tch tl wknd over 2f out* **33/1**

04 10 1 3/4 **Crystal Mystic (IRE)**[29] 5687 2-8-11 ........ (b) FPFerris(3) 3 28
(BPalling) *led tl hdd over 3f out: wknd wl over 1f out* **20/1**

00 11 1 1/2 **Elms Schoolboy**[20] 5865 2-8-11 ........ LFletcher(3) 13 23
(JMPEustace) *prom on outside: rdn over 3f out: sn wknd* **25/1**

4000 12 2 1/2 **Ruby's Dream**[9] 6080 2-8-9 64 ........ PFitzsimons 6 11
(JMBradley) *chsd ldrs tl wknd 2f out* **12/1**

0 13 2 **Aggravation**[13] 6010 2-9-0 ........ GGibbons 5 10
(AndrewReid) *plld hrd: in tch tl wknd over 2f out* **16/1**

1m 17.15s **13 Ran SP% 121.6**

Speed ratings: CSF £56.71 TOTE £11.70: £1.90, £3.40, £2.80; EX 60.30.

**Owner** Mrs Jean Mitchell **Bred** Gordon Patterson **Trained** Newmarket, Suffolk

**FOCUS**

This looked inferior to the first division and the form, rated through the runner-up, is modest. The fact the front five were separated by only a length and the time was about a second and a half slower, rather backs that up.



The Form Book, Raceform Ltd, Compton, RG20 6NL

**NOTEBOOK**

**Heartsonfire(IRE)**, whose form in turf maidens is modest, at last found a race she could win. She appeared to have a lot to do turning in, but managed to gain impetus down the centre of the track once in line for home and got up well inside the last furlong. Her handicap mark should not go up by much, but this looked a bad race and she will do well to find many more opportunities.

**Gaudalpin(IRE)** went to the front just before halfway and looked like she may have stolen it when sent several lengths clear turning in. She started to tire and was caught by the winner well inside the last furlong, but the fact she still only went down narrowly and only one rival managed to get past her is as much down to the quality of her opponents as gameness on her part.

**Sweet Namibia(IRE)**, a 130,000gns half-sister to five winners including Macaroon and Bakewell Tart, stayed on nicely down the straight and may have finished a bit closer had she not had to be snatched up for a stride in the closing stages. The form is not great, but she is entitled to have come on for this and is likely to turn out the best of these in time.

**Chief Dipper** stayed on down the wide outside in the home straight and was probably finishing best of all. He can now be handicapped.

**Mangrove Cay(IRE)**, visored for the first time, had every chance on the inside of the track down the home straight but had nothing more to offer in the closing stages.

**Llamadas**, claimed after finishing runner-up in a seller here earlier this month, missed the break and was soon detached. He did pick off a few in the second half of the contest, but was never going to figure and will probably need to return to plating company. *Official explanation: jockey said gelding would not face the kickback*

**Rainbow Iris**, trying sand for the first time, ran a long way below her turf form.

## 6295 WOLVERHAMPTON-RACECOURSE.CO.UK H'CAP 1m 141y(P)

**4:50** (4:51) (F4) (0-62,62) 3-Y-O+ **£3,032** (£866; £433) **Stalls** Low

Form RPR

0606 **1** **King Nicholas (USA)**[52] 5108 5-8-9 **55**........................(tp) MLawson(5) 8 65
(JParkes) *mid-div: nt clr run 3f out: rdn and hdwy over 1f out to ld wl ins fnl f* **7/1**

6600 **2** *1* **La Landonne**[51] 5156 3-8-13 **58**.................................... CCatlin 12 66
(PMPhelan) *in tch on outside: led over 2f out: hdd briefly appr fnl f: kpt on on u.p: hdd wl ins last* **16/1**

3006 **3** *hd* **My Pension (IRE)**[17] 5936 3-9-1 **60**...................................... RWinston 5 67
(PHowling) *a.p: rdn 2f out: r.o one pce fnl f* **14/1**

0200 **4** *hd* **Bond Millennium**[9] 6096 6-9-6 **61**........................................... FLynch 7 68
(BSmart) *hld up in rr: hdwy over 1f out: r.o: nvr nrr* **13/2**[3]

6020 **5** *shd* **Ziet D'Alsace (FR)**[6] 6154 4-8-11 **55**.................................... DNolan(3) 3 62
(AWCarroll) *s.i.s: dropped out in rr: hmpd over 2f out and swtchd rt sn after: r.o wl fnl f* **5/1**[2]

500 **6** *½* **Easter Ogil (IRE)**[140] 2559 9-9-4 **59**.................................... LEnstone 4 65
(JaneSouthcombe) *mid-div: hdwy on ins to ld brieflyappr fnl f: wknd ins last* **11/1**

5-00 **7** *2* **Wall Street Runner**[6] 6157 3-9-3 **62**........................................ JQuinn 11 64
(CADwyer) *towards rr tl gd hdwy on outside over 2f out: sn rdn and wknd appr fnl f* **33/1**

0252 **8** *hd* **Blue Java**[48] 5222 3-8-11 **59**........................................... LFletcher(3) 13 60
(HMorrison) *in tch: rdn over 3f out: wknd over 1f out* **3/1**[1]

0610 **9** *1 ¼* **Mon Secret (IRE)**[34] 5557 6-9-4 **59**.................................... DMcGaffin 10 58
(BSmart) *in rr tl rdn and hdwy on outside over 2f out: wknd over 1f out* **13/2**[3]

0000 **10** *4* **Pawan (IRE)**[3] 6220 4-9-4 **59**............................................ AnnStokell 6 49
(MissAStokell) *in tch tl n.m.r over 2f out: sn btn* **16/1**

0000 **11** *1* **Meelup (IRE)**[27] 5733 4-9-1 **56**.......................................(p) VSlattery 2 44
(JaneSouthcombe) *sn led: hdd over 2f out: wknd qckly* **20/1**

1000 **12** *8* **Iamback**[7] 6146 4-8-12 **53**...............................................(p) IMongan 1 24
(MissGayKelleway) *w ldr: rdn over 3f out: wknd over 2f out* **14/1**

6025 **13** *18* **Penel (IRE)**[22] 5844 3-9-3 **62**...........................................(b) GBaker 9 —
(BRMillman) *prom tl wknd over 2f out: eased appr fnl f* **16/1**

1m 51.9s

**WFA** 3 from 4yo+ 4lb **13** Ran SP% **127.9**

Speed ratings: CSF £122.21 CT £1610.97 TOTE £8.20: £4.00, £12.30, £5.50; EX 271.10.

**Owner** M Wormald **Bred** Calumet Farm **Trained** Upper Helmsley, N Yorks

**FOCUS**

A modest contest and again they finished in a heap, which suggests the form is ordinary and very limited.

**NOTEBOOK**

**King Nicholas(USA)**, returning to this longer trip for the first time since his seasonal reappearance, was given a patient ride before being delivered with his effort down what looked to be the favoured middle of the track. He has also won on the Lingfield Polytrack and on the Southwell Fibresand, so there should be plenty of other opportunities for him on sand should connections decide to persevere.

**La Landonne**, a winner on the Lingfield Polytrack, was always up with the pace and took over turning in, but was ultimately just run out of it. She does not have the most attractive head carriage and her sole win came over shorter, but she was not beaten through lack of stamina.

**My Pension(IRE)**, a maiden making his sand debut, ran well under a positive ride and has dropped to a realistic mark.

**Bond Millennium**, switched off out the back early, travelled very well and gradually weaved his way through the field as the race progressed. He was close enough on the inside of the track starting up the home straight, but those finishing down the centre had the greater impetus. He is on a lengthy losing run, but seems to get little respite from the Handicapper even so.

**Ziet D'Alsace(FR)** ◆, who has already run well on this new surface, deserves extra credit for finishing where she did as she ran into some serious trouble on the home bend when trying to make progress from the rear and dropped back to last. However, she found her stride down the outside in the straight and only just failed to make the frame. She can certainly win on this surface.

**Easter Ogil(IRE)**, reappearing after a three-month break, has faced some impossible tasks on turf this season, but ran better on this return to sand and may even have been a bit closer had he not made his effort right against the inside rail.

**Blue Java** was disappointing and there seemed no obvious excuse, except that it seems as though a decent effort on the Lingfield Polytrack does not guarantee a similar scenario here.

## 6296 BET DIRECT ON 0800 32 93 93 CLASSIFIED STKS 1m 141y(P)

**5:20** (5:20) (G4) 3-Y-O+ **£2,996** (£856; £428) **Stalls** Low

Form RPR

6503 **1** **Temper Tantrum**[12] 6024 6-9-6 54.......................................(p) WSupple 7 66
(JRBest) *hld up in rr: hdwy over 2f out: r.o u.p to ld post* **11/4**[1]

0000 **2** *shd* **Atlantic Ace**[17] 5945 7-9-7 55...............................................(p) FLynch 4 67
(BSmart) *towards rr: hdwy over 2f out: led over 1f out: hung rt ins fnl f: hdd post* **10/1**

050 **3** *1 ¼* **Just One Look**[4] 6184 3-8-12 53........................................... NCallan 10 59
(MBlanshard) *hld up in mid-div: hdwy whn n.m.r over 1f out: styd on fnl f* **20/1**

0000 **4** *2* **Qobtaan (USA)**[74] 4511 5-9-3 51............................................ GBaker 5 56
(MRBosley) *hld up in rr: hdwy whn short of room 2f out: styd on fnl f: nvr nrr* **16/1**

1120 **5** *hd* **Smart Scot**[187] 1427 5-8-13 52.......................................... MSavage(5) 2 57
(BPJBaugh) *chsd ldrs: led over 2f out: rdn and hdd over 1f out: no ex fnl f* **20/1**

4006 **6** *¾* **Cryfield**[28] 5713 7-9-4 52...............................................(v) KimTinkler 1 55
(NTinkler) *trckd ldrs: rdn over 2f out: wknd ent fnl f* **6/1**

0000 **7** *nk* **Muyassir (IRE)**[6] 6154 9-9-6 54............................................ SSanders 6 57
(MissBSanders) *towards rr: rdn and effrt over 2f out: wknd over 1f out* **11/1**

6043 **8** *1 ¼* **Beauty Of Dreams**[4] 6184 3-8-13 54....................................(v) CCatlin 11 51
(MRChannon) *sn chsd ldr: rdn over 2f out: wknd sn after* **7/2**[2]

1 **9** *¾* **Rebel Raider (IRE)**[10] 6061 5-9-7 55.................................... LisaJones 3 53
(BNPollock) *prom whn bmpd and nrly lost rdr after 1f: nvr a factor after* **11/2**[3]

4223 **10** *shd* **Bundaberg**[187] 1425 4-9-2 55............................................ PMakin(5) 9 53
(PWHiatt) *hld up: a bhd* **16/1**

-040 **11** *1* **Sir Alfred**[30] 4616 5-9-4 52...............................................(v) ANicholls 12 48
(AKing) *led: hdd over 2f out: wknd ent fnl f* **20/1**

2440 **12** *3* **Filliemou (IRE)**[40] 5411 3-8-9 53........................................ FPFerris(3) 8 40
(AWCarroll) *chsd ldrs: rdn over 3f out: wknd sn after* **16/1**

0500 **13** *8* **Lady Blade (IRE)**[48] 5222 3-9-0 55...................................... AMcCarthy 13 25
(BHanbury) *slowly away: sn mid-div: bhd fnl 3f* **33/1**

1m 51.82s

**WFA** 3 from 4yo+ 4lb **13** Ran SP% **130.9**

Speed ratings: CSF £33.18 TOTE £5.70: £1.80, £3.00, £5.20; EX 72.50 Place 6 £164.73, Place 5 £83.46.

**Owner** The Little House Partnership **Bred** A S Reid **Trained** Hucking, Kent

**FOCUS**

A dramatic contest and the winning time was marginally faster than the preceding handicap, making the form look fair and sound for the grade.

**NOTEBOOK**

**Temper Tantrum**, another that has already run well under these conditions, had a niggling doubt over him at this trip and if the instructions were to ride him to get it, then they could not have been carried out with better precision. The feeling is that he is better suited by seven.

**Atlantic Ace**, who has tumbled down the handicap over the last couple of seasons, ran his best race for some time and looked to have stolen it soon after turning for home, but he was inclined to hang into the whip in the last furlong and had the race snatched from him on the line. He can make amends.

**Just One Look** ◆, who has failed to make the frame in nine previous starts this season, has dropped 20lb in the handicap as a result. She was just getting into the race when running out of room over a furlong from home and deserves credit for finishing as close as she did. There is a small race to be won with her on this surface.

**Qobtaan(USA)**, who is back on a winning mark, stayed on in the closing stages without ever offering a threat. All his best form is on Fibresand and he will be suited by a return to that surface.

**Smart Scot**, a multiple winner in banded company on Fibresand at the start of the year, was returning from a six-month break. Given a positive ride on this different surface, he hugged the inside rail which was probably not in his favour and he was swamped down the home straight. Under the circumstances he can still be said to have performed with credit.

**Beauty Of Dreams** did not improve for the switch to sand.

**Rebel Raider(IRE)**, reappearing quickly after his course-and-distance victory ten days ago following a long layoff, ran into real trouble after a furlong and his rider was sent into orbit. Fortunately she landed back in the saddle, but this effort can be safely ignored.

T/Plt: £69.40 to a £1 stake. Pool: £31,503.05. 331.10 winning tickets. T/Qpdt: £43.60 to a £1 stake. Pool: £2,226.10. 37.70 winning tickets. JS

# 5169 DEAUVILLE (R-H)

Tuesday, October 19

**OFFICIAL GOING: Soft**

## 6297a PRIX DES RESERVOIRS (GROUP 3) (FILLIES) (ROUND COURSE) 1m (R)

**1:50** (1:51) 2-Y-O **£25,704** (£10,282; £7,711; £5,141)

RPR

**1** **Songerie**[17] 5961 2-8-9 .......................................... J-BEyquem 5 102
(SirMarkPrescott) *racd in 4th on outside, 3rd str, wnt 2nd over 1 1/2f out, rdn over 1f out, hard driven to ld 50y out, ran on wl*

**2** *½* **Soignee (GER)** 2-8-9 .......................................... ASuborics 2 101
(AWohler, Germany) *led, set good pace, ridden approaching final f, headed and no extra final 50 yards* 1

**3** *shd* **Ysoldina (FR)**[28] 2-8-9 .......................................... TJarnet 9 100
(ADeRoyer-Dupre, France) *held up in 7th, headway on outside to go 3rd over 1f out, stayed on under pressure final f* 2

**4** *2* **Pretty Soon (FR)**[36] 5532 2-8-9 .......................................... IMendizabal 6 96
(J-CRouget, France) *raced in 5th, headway to dispute 3rd briefly 1 1/2f out, soon ridden and one pace*

**5** *2 ½* **Glazed Frost (FR)**[45] 5313 2-8-9 .......................................... TThulliez 3 91
(PBary, France) *held up in 8th, stayed on from over 1f out but never near leaders*

**6** *¾* **Birthplace (USA)**[18] 2-8-9 .......................................... C-PLemaire 4 89
(MZilber, France) *tracked leader in 3rd, 4th straight, outpaced from 1 1/2f out* 3

**7** *2* **American Touch (FR)**[45] 5313 2-8-9 .......................................... CSoumillon 8 84
(GDoleuze, France) *held up in last, never a factor*

**8** *¾* **La Reine Mambo (USA)**[27] 2-8-9 .......................................... OPeslier 7 83
(ELellouche, France) *raced in 2nd til weakened over 1 1/2f out*

**9** *¾* **Green Girl (FR)**[10] 2-8-9 .......................................... SPasquier 1 81
(PDemercastel, France) *raced in 6th, outpaced final 1 1/2f*

1m 44.4s **9** Ran SP% **121.3**

Speed ratings: .

**Owner** Miss K Rausing **Bred** Miss K Rausing **Trained** Newmarket, Suffolk

**NOTEBOOK**

**Songerie** made steady progress rounding the final turn and took on the long-time leader early in the straight. She appeared to hesitate a little a furlong out but ran on again bravely and was going away from the others at the finish. She loved the testing ground and this victory proved that she failed to run her race in Ireland last time. She will probably come back to France early next year for a Listed race.

**Soignee(GER)**, a well-backed favourite following two easy victories, tried to make all the running. She was tackled by the winner two out but kept pulling out a little more in the final stages. She was unable to hold her place in the final 20 yards but looks to have a bright future.

**Ysoldina(FR)** still had plenty to do in the straight. She made progress from a furlong and a half out but faltered slightly close home.

**Pretty Soon(FR)** was given every chance but was rather one-paced in the straight and was possibly unsuited by the testing ground.

## [6091]NEWCASTLE (L-H)

Wednesday, October 20

**6298 Meeting Abandoned** - Waterlogged

## [5863]NOTTINGHAM (L-H)

Wednesday, October 20

**OFFICIAL GOING: Heavy**

The first race was run on the normal track, but those on the round course were on the inside track. They tended to come centre to stands' side in the straight.

### 6305 IBETX.COM SPORTS BETTING EXCHANGE NOVICE AUCTION STKS 6f 15y

**2:15** (2:16) (F4) 2-Y-O **£3,248** (£928; £464) **Stalls** Low

Form RPR

0034 **1** **Island Swing (IRE)**[19] 5910 2-9-0 78 SDrowne 9 80+
(JLSpearing) *hld up: hdwy over 2f out: str run to ld over 1f out: sn clr* **10/3**[1]

3300 **2** *5* **Orpen Wide (IRE)**[5] 6188 2-8-6 71 ABeech(3) 1 62
(MCChapman) *led: rdn along over 2f out: drvn and hdd over 1f out: sn one pce* **9/2**[2]

01 **3** *1 1/2* **Manic**[18] 5953 2-8-7 70 JFEgan 8 55
(AndrewReid) *hld up in rr: swtchd rt and hdwy 2f out: sn chsng ldrs: rdn ent last and kpt on same pce* **9/2**[2]

1414 **4** *shd* **Tipsy Lillie**[65] 4816 2-8-8 59 KFallon 6 56
(JulianPoulton) *prom: rdn along over 2f out: drvn and one pce over 1f out* **10/1**

00 **5** *6* **Diamond Heritage**[26] 5772 2-8-11 FNorton 2 43
(JAGlover) *hld up in tch: hdwy to chal 2f out: sn rdn and grad wknd* **33/1**

0606 **6** *8* **Faithisflying**[142] 2523 2-8-4 50 DFox(5) 10 19
(CADwyer) *chsd ldrs: rdn along over 2f out: sn wknd* **66/1**

0201 **7** *1/2* **Beau Marche**[18] 5925 2-8-8 73 IMongan 5 17
(IAWood) *cl up: rdn along over 2f out and sn wknd* **11/2**[3]

500 **8** *3* **Muddy (IRE)**[35] 5570 2-8-10 65 JQuinn 3 11
(GAHuffer) *in tch: rdn along 1/2-way: sn wknd* **11/2**[3]

0320 **9** *1 1/2* **Stan's Girl**[16] 6000 2-8-6 56 WSupple 7 3
(IAWood) *dwlt and keen in rr: effrt and sme hdwy 1/2-way: sn wknd* **20/1**

1m 20.66s (5.86) **Going Correction** +0.825s/f (Soft) **9** Ran SP% **108.5**
Speed ratings: **93,86,84,84,76 65,64,60,58**CSF £16.19 TOTE £5.10: £1.70, £1.20, £2.10; EX 17.60.

**Owner** J Spearing **Bred** Tomaju Investments **Trained** Kinnersley, Worcs

**FOCUS**

The race lost some of its interest with the late withdrawal of the odds-on favourite, but in the testing conditions Island Swing simply powered away from some probably modest rivals. There is little to enthuse about form-wise behind the winner.

**NOTEBOOK**

**Island Swing(IRE)** had the form in the book to win this, and duly did with the minimum of fuss. She did not appear to quite get home in a claimer last time out over this distance, but had no such problems in this field. Although her form says she has won only on much quicker ground previously, the trainer believed that at Haydock there had been cut in the ground.

**Orpen Wide(IRE)**, who had run in a couple of fair Newmarket races prior to this, appreciated this easier task and ran much more in keeping with his earlier form. He has a lot of pace and was the winner's only serious challenger in the race. A return to a less-demanding surface will almost certainly aid his cause.

**Manic** was quite a way behind in the early stages and only came out of the pack late on to grab third. These were vastly different conditions to last time, and she is entitled to keep on improving with time and possibly distance.

**Tipsy Lillie** had won a couple of sellers on much quicker conditions and, although she ran all the way to the line, she almost certainly would have liked quicker ground.

**Diamond Heritage** had not shown a great deal previously, including in heavy ground, and again did not show a lot. He has yet to race on a much sounder surface, so that may bring out some improvement.

**Beau Marche**, who had been put up fully 12lb for winning a banded event last time, could not build on his previous win in ground that was an unknown.

**Muddy(IRE)** had shown a modicum of ability in some fair maidens, but never got competitive in this ground.

### 6306 EVERSHEDS ROYAL STANDARD NOVICE STKS 1m 54y

**2:50** (2:53) (D3) 2-Y-O **£4,595** (£1,414; £707; £353) **Stalls** High

Form RPR

**1** **Public Forum** 2-8-8 KFallon 1 76+
(SirMichaelStoute) *dwlt: sn prom: effrt over 2f out: rdn to ld ent last: edgd rt and kpt on* **9/4**[2]

4100 **2** *nk* **Miss L'Augeval**[18] 5939 2-9-0 81 DHolland 4 81
(GWragg) *led 1f: cl up: pushed along over 4f out: led over 3f out: rdn 2f out: drvn and hdd ent last: edgd rt: kpt on* **11/8**[1]

6 **3** *8* **Numero Due**[16] 5988 2-8-12 PMQuinn 5 63
(GMMoore) *hld up in rr: hdwy over 2f out: sn rdn along and styd on fnl f: nvr a factor* **14/1**

6 **4** *3/4* **Molem**[46] 5298 2-8-12 RHills 2 62
(SirMichaelStoute) *trckd ldrs: hdwy on outer over 3f out: rdn and hung lft wl over 1f out: sn wknd* **11/4**[3]

0 **5** *18* **Ellerslie Tom**[11] 6073 2-8-12 ACulhane 3 26
(OBrennan) *s.i.s: t.k.h and led after 1f: rn wd home turn: pushed along and hdd over 3f out: sn wknd* **25/1**

1m 53.13s (6.73) **Going Correction** +0.975s/f (Soft) **5** Ran SP% **110.1**
Speed ratings: **105,104,96,95,77**CSF £5.75 TOTE £3.30: £1.20, £1.20; EX 6.70.

**Owner** K Abdulla **Bred** Juddmonte Farms **Trained** Newmarket, Suffolk

**FOCUS**

A moderate event that became a two-horse race from a long way out. The winning time was decent for such a contest given the conditions, and with little to go on the runner-up is the best guide to the level.

**NOTEBOOK**

**Public Forum** followed the example set by his sire and dam by winning at the first time of asking. On pedigree he was the one mostly likely to appreciate the underfoot conditions, and so it proved as he powered up the centre of the track to hold off the favourite. He should stay middle distances next season, so will probably be put away until then.

**Miss L'Augeval** has been racing at a fair level since winning at Goodwood, and gave the winner his only scare from some way out. She was conceding 6lb to the winner and, while that was a good effort, the winner is much more likely to make further progress than she is. Being a daughter of Zilzal, the ground may have been a bit soft for her.

**Numero Due** was well behind until running on late on. He basically passed a horse that did not handle the ground late on, and the run probably is not as good as it looks. He should stay at least 12 furlongs next season.

**Molem** looked all at sea on this ground. He is more likely to be seen to better advantage on quicker ground, and was eased when his chance was gone.

**Ellerslie Tom** got extremely upset in the stalls prior to the race, and after missing the break ran through the field to take up the running. He had a problem negotiating the turn and weakened right out of contention up the straight.

### 6307 BROWNE JACOBSON STKS (H'CAP) 1m 1f 213y

**3:25** (3:25) (C1) (0-107,98) 3-Y-O **£13,795** (£4,244; £2,122; £1,061) **Stalls** Low

Form RPR

-114 **1** **Exterior (USA)**[39] 5470 3-8-9 **91** RHughes 5 106+
(MrsAJPerrett) *trckd ldr: hdwy 3f out: rdn along and styd on to ld over 1f out: sn drvn clr* **2/1**[1]

1400 **2** *6* **Haadef**[9] 6121 3-9-2 **98** (b) WSupple 3 103
(JHMGosden) *led after 1f: rdn along 2f out: hdd over 1f out and kpt on same pce* **20/1**

1004 **3** *3* **Nunki (USA)**[21] 5866 3-8-3 **85** (v) JQuinn 2 85
(HRACecil) *trckd ldrs: effrt over 3f out: sn rdn along and wknd 2f out* **12/1**

4602 **4** *7* **Sew'N'So Character (IRE)**[26] 5768 3-8-5 **87** FNorton 6 75
(MBlanshard) *hld up in tch: effrt 4f out: sn rdn along and btn 3f out* **7/2**[2]

4060 **5** *1 1/2* **Dancing Lyra**[18] 5942 3-8-4 **86** TPQueally 1 71
(JWHills) *trckd ldrs on inner: pushed along over 4f out: sn rdn and wknd* **8/1**

3006 **6** *11* **Etmaam**[49] 5226 3-8-8 **90** RHills 8 57
(MJohnston) *prom on outer: rdn along 4f out: sn wknd* **6/1**[3]

-366 **7** *20* **Have Faith (IRE)**[81] 4318 3-8-2 **84** oh3 PHanagan 7 17
(BWHills) *rdn along in rr 1/2-way: a bhd* **33/1**

6530 **8** *26* **Roehampton**[24] 5814 3-9-0 **96** (b[1]) KFallon 4 —
(SirMichaelStoute) *chsd ldrs: rdn along 4f out: sn wknd* **13/2**

2m 17.48s (7.98) **Going Correction** +0.975s/f (Soft) **8** Ran SP% **109.7**
Speed ratings: **107,102,99,94,93 84,68,47**CSF £40.99 CT £349.05 TOTE £2.30: £1.80, £5.40, £3.10; EX 38.70.

**Owner** K Abdulla **Bred** Juddmonte Farms Inc **Trained** Pulborough, W Sussex

**FOCUS**

A decent contest and an impressive display by a confirmed soft-ground performer. It is difficult to be confident of the level of the form, although the winner looks potentially better than a handicapper.

**NOTEBOOK**

**Exterior(USA)** made his challenge about two furlongs out and ran away from his rivals. He has some good form in soft ground, and looked to outclass his rivals under these conditions. He has proved capable of handling the All-Weather surface at Lingfield so has the potential to act on most surfaces, and will be an interesting type next season.

**Haadef** took a fair grip in front, but looked likely to win up the straight when travelling really well. However, his earlier exertions seem to take their toll late on, and he weakened when challenged by the winner. He looks to enjoy conditions on the soft side and could pick up another race before the end of the season. Connections believed he would stay two miles earlier in the season, but a drop to a mile could suit on this showing.

**Nunki(USA)** was always close to the pace and ran fairly well. He may stay a bit further on this evidence.

**Sew'N'So Character(IRE)** handles soft ground well, but pulled fairly hard in the early stages and probably did not get home. He does stay ten furlongs, but may be better at closer to a mile.

**Dancing Lyra**'s form seems to have tailed off since the summer, as he was entitled to run better in these soft conditions. He may be a bit high in the handicap at the moment.

**Etmaam** was struggling from a long way out and did not look like he enjoyed ground this heavy.

**Have Faith(IRE)**, returning from an 81-day break, had never raced on anything this soft before, and did not appear to handle them. Her pedigree, and best form, suggests that faster conditions should suit. *Official explanation: jockey said filly was unsuited by the heavy ground*

**Roehampton**, who had first-time blinkers on, was being niggled from a long way out and lost touch up the straight. He may not be an easy ride.

### 6308 DAVID ASHLEY CONSTRUCTION LIMITED MAIDEN STKS (DIV I) 1m 1f 213y

**4:00** (4:01) (D3) 2-Y-O **£4,615** (£1,420; £710; £355) **Stalls** Low

Form RPR

5400 **1** **Louise Rayner**[72] 4601 2-8-9 56 DHolland 6 67
(MLWBell) *prom: effrt to ld 3f out: rdn 2f out: drvn and kpt on wl fnl f* **28/1**

03 **2** *1* **Sand Repeal (IRE)**[57] 5023 2-8-11 BReilly(3) 10 70
(MissJFeilden) *keen: trckd ldrs on outer: hdwy 3f out: rdn wl over 1f out: styd on ent last: drvn and no ex last 100 yds* **14/1**

6 **3** *1 1/2* **Gabanna (USA)**[23] 5838 2-9-0 LDettori 9 68
(SaeedBinSuroor) *always prom: effrt 3f out: rdn 2f out and ev ch tl drvn and no ex ins last* **11/4**[2]

000 **4** *5* **Kristalchen**[43] 5368 2-8-9 SChin 7 55
(JGGiven) *sn led: rdn along and hdd over 3f out: drvn along over 2f out: wknd over 1f out* **12/1**

362 **5** *1/2* **Royal Jet**[16] 5988 2-9-0 83 (v) ACulhane 8 59
(MRChannon) *trckd ldrs: hdwy 3f out: rdn and ev ch 2f out: sn drvn and wknd* **10/11**[1]

0 **6** *4* **Celtic Promise (IRE)**[14] 6011 2-8-9 SDrowne 4 47
(MrsAJPerrett) *in tch: rdn along 4f out: sn wknd* **33/1**

20 **7** *21* **Amazing Valour (IRE)**[16] 5988 2-9-0 KDarley 2 19
(MJohnston) *dwlt and sn rdn along in rr: bhd fr 1/2-way* **10/1**[3]

00 **8** *1 1/4* **Lambriggan Lad**[7] 6155 2-9-0 VSlattery 3 17
(MissVictoriaRoberts) *chsd ldrs: cl up 1/2-way: rdn along 4f out and sn wknd* **200/1**

00 **9** *9* **Sergeant Shinko (IRE)**[13] 6021 2-9-0 (b) JFEgan 5 —
(MDods) *s.i.s: a bhd* **200/1**

5U **10** *7* **Court Ruler**[10] 6077 2-8-11 RThomas(3) 1 —
(RJPrice) *s.i.s: a bhd* **150/1**

2m 22.39s (12.89) **Going Correction** +0.975s/f (Soft) **10** Ran SP% **110.5**
Speed ratings: **87,86,85,81,80 77,60,59,52,46**CSF £339.90 TOTE £30.40: £4.60, £2.50, £2.00; EX 341.20.

**Owner** Richard Green (fine Paintings) **Bred** Richard Green And New England Stud **Trained** Newmarket, Suffolk

**FOCUS**

A real slog for these youngsters over this trip in such testing ground. This was a very poor maiden and the time was very slow even allowing for the conditions, 1.23 seconds slower than the second division. However, on paper the form makes sense rated through the placed horses.

**NOTEBOOK**

**Louise Rayner**, yet to make the first three in four previous starts and beaten in selling company on one occasion, managed to grind out a dour victory and basically outstayed her rivals in the ground. Her official rating of 56 shows what a bad race this was, made even more uncompetitive by the testing conditions, and she will do well to find another opportunity like this.

**Sand Repeal(IRE)** has already shown that he can handle this sort of ground and battled on to the line. He may not have achieved much in finishing second, but should get a modest handicap mark using the winner as a guide.

**Gabanna(USA)** ran marginally better than on his debut over this longer trip in more testing conditions, but had every chance and was still not good enough. This is one very expensive purchase that seems to have gone wrong.

**Kristalchen**, unplaced in three previous starts, was given a positive ride but did not see out this longer trip in the conditions.

**Royal Jet**, who has already run well over this trip but on much faster ground, was nothing like so effective in these conditions and proved very disappointing. He is worth a chance to redeem himself back on a sound surface.

## 6309 DAVID ASHLEY CONSTRUCTION LIMITED MAIDEN STKS (DIV II) 1m 1f 213y

**4:35** (4:36) (D3) 2-Y-O **£4,595** (£1,414; £707; £353) **Stalls** Low

Form RPR

03 **1** **Natalie Jane (IRE)**[10] 6078 2-8-9 .......... DHolland 3 76
(GAButler) *cl up: led 6f out: rdn along over 2f out: drvn and styd on gamely ins last* **9/4**[2]

33 **2** *2 ½* **Solarias Quest**[25] 5790 2-9-0 .......... JDSmith 9 77
(AKing) *cl up on outer: effrt to dispute ld 3f out and ev ch tl rdn along over 1f out and no ex ins last* **5/1**[3]

0000 **3** *12* **Voir Dire**[21] 5871 2-9-0 63 .......... RHavlin 4 58
(MrsPNDutfield) *s.i.s: hdwy to chse ldrs 1/2-way: rdn along over 3f out: drvn and plugged on same pce fnl 2f* **33/1**

2 **4** *3* **Aylmer Road (IRE)**[11] 6067 2-9-0 .......... KFallon 5 53
(PFICole) *prom: effrt to dispute ld over 4f out: rdn along 3f out and sn wknd* **11/10**[1]

44U0 **5** *½* **Sharp N Frosty**[34] 5596 2-9-0 57 .......... SWKelly 2 52
(WMBrisbourne) *hld up: effrt and rdn along 4f out: drvn and hung lft over 2f out: sn wknd* **20/1**

00 **6** *8* **Mount Butler (IRE)**[11] 6072 2-9-0 .......... ACulhane 1 39
(JGGiven) *in tch on inner: rdn along over 4f out: sn wknd* **66/1**

0 **7** *11* **Misters Sister**[11] 6067 2-8-9 .......... MFenton 6 17
(JGGiven) *s.i.s: a bhd* **50/1**

**8** *12* **Senior Whim** 2-9-0 .......... DaneO'Neill 7 3
(PRWebber) *led 4f: cl up tl rdn along 4f out and sn wknd* **33/1**

60 **9** *11* **Silver Court**[10] 6078 2-8-11 .......... RThomas(3) 8 —
(RJPrice) *s.i.s: hdwy on outer and in tch 4f out: sn rdn and wknd* **200/1**

2m 21.16s (11.66) **Going Correction** +0.975s/f (Soft) **9** Ran SP% **109.7**

Speed ratings: **92,90,80,78,77 71,62,52,44**CSF £11.91 TOTE £3.60: £1.20, £1.10, £4.90; EX 9.50.

**Owner** Woodcote Stud Ltd **Bred** Woodcote Stud Ltd **Trained** Blewbury, Oxon

**FOCUS**

The stronger of the two divisions, at least as far as the front pair are concerned, and the time was 1.23 seconds faster than the first division which is still modest for the grade.

**NOTEBOOK**

**Natalie Jane(IRE)** had suggested in her most recent outing that she would appreciate a greater test of stamina and so it proved. She and the runner-up had the race to themselves from a long way out and she saw her race out just the better. She may now go for the Listed contest over this trip at Newmarket next week and, though she will have to improve again, she is guaranteed to stay.

**Solarias Quest** came right away with the winner in the final couple of furlongs, but was just outstayed in the closing stages. He looks one for staying handicaps next season.

**Voir Dire**, unplaced in four previous starts, plodded on to finish a remote third but probably did not achieve much.

**Aylmer Road(IRE)** was close enough turning in, but patently failed to see out this longer trip in the conditions. He is much better than this.

**Sharp N Frosty** has shown what form he has on faster ground than this and found it all too much. There may still be a small race in him off his proper mark back on a sounder surface.

## 6310 FREETH CARTWRIGHT LLP MAIDEN STKS 1m 1f 213y

**5:10** (5:11) (D3) 3-Y-O **£4,927** (£1,516; £758; £379) **Stalls** Low

Form RPR

-300 **1** **Lomapamar**[19] 5913 3-8-9 70 .......... SDrowne 2 73
(MrsAJPerrett) *midfield: rdn along 4f out: styd on u.p fr over 1f out to ld last 50 yds* **9/1**

**2** *¾* **Stage Left** 3-8-9 .......... RHughes 9 72+
(HRACecil) *a.p: cl up 4f out: sn rdn: much room over 2f out: drvn to ld and edgd lft ins last: hdd and no ex last 50 yds* **4/1**[2]

0 **3** *2 ½* **Indian's Landing (IRE)**[30] 5705 3-9-0 .......... PFitzsimons 6 72?
(KAMorgan) *s.i.s: sn chsng ldrs: hdwy 3f out: rdn and ev ch over 1f out: drvn and one pce ins last* **150/1**

**4** *1 ¾* **Design (FR)** 3-9-0 .......... KFallon 1 70+
(SirMichaelStoute) *dwlt: sn cl up: led 1/2-way: rdn along 3f out: drvn and hdd 1f out: sn wknd* **7/2**[1]

0 **5** *1* **Woolstone Boy (USA)**[10] 6082 3-9-0 .......... GBaker 4 68?
(JJay) *trckd ldrs: hdwy and cl up 3f out: rdn to ld briefly 1f out: sn drvn: hdd & wknd* **33/1**

**6** *3 ½* **I'Ll Do It Today** 3-9-0 .......... IMongan 5 62
(JMJefferson) *s.i.s and bhd: rdn along 4f out: styd on appr last: nrst fin* **25/1**

00 **7** *1 ¾* **Sandokan (GER)**[9] 6130 3-9-0 .......... TPQueally 3 59
(BJCurley) *bhd tl sme late hdwy* **25/1**

440 **8** *½* **All Blue (IRE)**[10] 6088 3-9-0 .......... (vt[1]) LDettori 7 58
(SaeedBinSuroor) *chsd ldrs: rdn along over 3f out: sn wknd* **9/2**[3]

**9** *6* **High Charter** 3-9-0 .......... DaneO'Neill 12 48
(JRFanshawe) *chsd ldrs: rdn along over 3f out: wknd over 2f out* **5/1**

0 **10** *21* **Mtilly**[16] 5994 3-8-9 .......... KDarley 11 7
(MJohnston) *plld hrd: cl up tl lost pl 6f out: sn bhd* **6/1**

000 **11** *2 ½* **Judda**[132] 2815 3-9-0 .......... (tp) JQuinn 8 8
(RFMarvin) *led to 1/2-way: sn rdn along and wknd: bhd fnl 3f* **150/1**

000 **12** *2 ½* **Apron (IRE)**[129] 2911 3-8-9 .......... MTebbutt 10 —
(MJRyan) *chsd ldrs tl lost pl after 3f: bhd fr 1/2-way* **50/1**

2m 23.06s (13.56) **Going Correction** +0.975s/f (Soft) **12** Ran SP% **115.3**

Speed ratings: **84,83,81,80,79 76,75,74,69,53 51,49**CSF £41.87 TOTE £10.10: £3.50, £1.40, £22.30; EX 53.40.

**Owner** Wickham Stud **Bred** Sir Eric Parker **Trained** Pulborough, W Sussex

**FOCUS**

A poor end-of-season maiden and the slowest of the four races run over the trip, slower even than both divisions of the two-year-old maiden. The leaders went off far too fast, which may have contributed to the moderate final time. The form looks distinctly ordinary, being held down by the presence of the third and fifth.

**NOTEBOOK**

**Lomapamar**, who has shown a bit of form on an easy surface, has been tried over as far as 13 furlongs so the fact this became a war of attrition in the latter stages probably helped her and she was able to utilise her stamina to snatch the race in the dying strides. The form is poor, but with her pedigree in mind a victory of any sort is all that matters.

**Stage Left**, a half-sister to a couple of winners including Short Pause, was always up with the pace and deserves credit as she kept on coming back after looking likely to drop away, but the last challenger to arrive proved just too much. These were difficult conditions in which to make her belated debut and she looks to have some ability.

**Indian's Landing(IRE)**, beaten at least 27 lengths in each of his four previous outings, found a huge amount of improvement from somewhere. The conditions may have made it more of a level playing field for horses of varying ability, but his proximity does rather drag the form down.

**Design(FR)**, a 220,000euros gelding out of a Listed winner in France, had his chance but did not see out the trip in the conditions. He may do better on a sounder surface, perhaps even on Polytrack, but is going to have to improve in order to justify his price tag.

**Woolstone Boy(USA)** looked like he might cause an upset when moving up on the stands' rail halfway up the straight, but then his stamina ran out. This appeared to be an improved effort from his debut, but he may not have achieved that much.

**All Blue(IRE)** looks one of the Godolphin outfit's more modest inmates and even the application of a visor made little difference.

**High Charter**, a 78,000gns half-brother to several winners including the high-class First Charter, found this testing ground all too much on this debut. Given the nature of the conditions and his breeding, it may be wise to give him another chance.

**Mtilly**, very well backed on this second outing, became lit up by the presence of the outsider Judda in the early stages and had run her race before reaching halfway.

## 6311 BACK OR LAY WITH IBETX.COM APPRENTICE H'CAP 1m 54y

**5:45** (5:45) (E3) (0-77,76) 3-Y-O+ **£3,955** (£1,217; £608; £304) **Stalls** High

Form RPR

0010 **1** **Richie Boy**[9] 6120 3-8-2 **60** ow2 .......... RJKilloran(3) 5 71
(PABlockley) *bmpd s: sn midfield: hdwy on inner over 2f out: rdn over 1f out: styd on to ld wl ins last* **50/1**

3313 **2** *½* **Mobane Flyer**[21] 5859 4-8-3 **63** .......... NLawes(8) 11 73
(RAFahey) *cl up: riden to ld over 1f out: hdd and no ex wl ins last* **6/1**[2]

1306 **3** *2 ½* **Didnt Tell My Wife**[32] 5657 5-8-5 **65** .......... RebeccaBird(8) 4 70
(CFWall) *keen: hld up in rr: hdwy over 2f out: rdn over 1f out: kpt on ins last: nrst fin* **11/1**

4200 **4** *¾* **Iberus (GER)**[8] 6152 6-8-12 **67** .......... KirstyMilczarek(3) 9 71
(SGollings) *chsd ldrs: rdn along over 2f out: kpt on same pce ent last* **22/1**

0044 **5** *1 ½* **Little Englander**[9] 6124 4-8-0 **57** .......... JDoyle(5) 6 58
(HCandy) *hld up and bhd: hdwy over 2f out: swtchd lft and rdn over 1f out: kpt on ins last: nrst fin* **9/2**[1]

0510 **6** *hd* **Band**[48] 5236 4-8-5 **57** .......... StevenHarrison 8 57
(BAMcmahon) *trckd ldrs: hdwy to ld over 3f out: rdn 2f out: hdd over 1f out: wknd ins last* **9/1**

4655 **7** *3* **Pure Mischief (IRE)**[7] 6156 5-9-4 **70** .......... HPoulton 3 64
(CRDore) *s.i.s: hld up in rr: hdwy over 3f out: rdn to chse ldrs 2f out: kpt on same pce appr last* **9/1**

2601 **8** *shd* **Spirit's Awakening**[21] 5868 5-8-7 **62** .......... MCoumbe(3) 13 56
(JAkehurst) *trckd ldrs: hdwy 4f out: rdn over 2f out: grad wknd* **15/2**

3005 **9** *2* **Fair Spin**[8] 6138 4-8-8 **60** .......... TBlock 17 50
(MDHammond) *midfield: rdn along over 3f out: no hdwy* **13/2**[3]

3613 **10** *¾* **Princess Galadriel**[29] 5715 3-8-3 **61** .......... TO'Brien(3) 2 49
(JRBest) *hld up in rr: effrt and hdwy 3f out: rdn and no imp fnl 2f* **9/1**

2100 **11** *nk* **Adorata (GER)**[8] 6152 3-8-9 **67** .......... LiamJones(3) 18 55
(JJay) *midfield: hdwy on outer to chse ldrs 1/2-way: sn rdn and wknd over 2f out* **18/1**

4500 **12** *2* **York Cliff**[9] 6115 6-9-7 **76** .......... TDean(3) 15 60
(WMBrisbourne) *chsd ldrs: rdn along over 4f out and sn wknd* **16/1**

23-0 **13** *25* **English Rocket (IRE)**[16] 5998 3-8-12 **70** .......... AHindley(3) 14 4
(DJSFrenchDavis) *midfield: rdn along and lost pl 1/2-way: sn bhd* **66/1**

0/0- **14** *5* **Dollar Law**[578] 360 8-8-8 **60** .......... (t) WHogg 1 —
(RJPrice) *sn led: rdn along and hdd over 3f out: wknd qckly* **50/1**

1520 **15** *1 ¾* **Amnesty**[154] 2226 5-8-4 **62** .......... (be) JemmaMarshall(6) 12 —
(GLMoore) *s.i.s: a rr* **25/1**

1m 52.4s (6.00) **Going Correction** +0.975s/f (Soft)

**WFA** 3 from 4yo+ 3lb **15** Ran SP% **120.7**

Speed ratings: **109,108,106,105,103 103,100,100,98,97 97,95,70,65,63**CSF £321.86 CT £3584.10 TOTE £52.20: £13.50, £3.60, £4.20; EX 694.30 Place 6 £84.03, Place 5 £59.99.

**Owner** Clive Whiting **Bred** Eurostrait Ltd **Trained** Southwell, Notts

**FOCUS**

Not the classiest contest of the day, but certainly the most competitive. The pace was decent given the conditions and the time was good for the grade, giving the form a sound appearance.

**NOTEBOOK**

**Richie Boy**, whose only victory earlier this month came over an extended 12 furlongs with cut in the ground, was suited by the decent pace and his guaranteed stamina was a valuable asset at the business end. He will avoid a penalty for this and would be interesting if turned out again quickly under similar conditions.

**Mobane Flyer**, who has been running consistently well in recent months and goes in the ground, ran a decent race considering he was close to the pace the whole way and was only just denied.

**Didnt Tell My Wife** likes this ground and was staying on well over the last couple of furlongs, but could never get there and may need a bit further these days.

**Iberus(GER)**, a dual winner in heavy ground in his native Germany, ran his race but looked short of toe where it mattered, even in these conditions, and may find this trip on the sharp side for him now.

**Little Englander**, whose only win came over course and distance on easy ground in the summer, was switched off out the back and was ridden with a lot of confidence, possibly too much. Stone last turning for home, his effort prove far too little too late.

**Band** had every chance, but did not seem to get home in the conditions. He has run well on this sort of ground in his younger days, but his sole victory came on fast ground and a strongly-run race over this trip on that ground is probably what he needs.

T/Plt: £102.80 to a £1 stake. Pool: £47,389.90. 336.20 winning tickets. T/Qpdt: £86.90 to a £1 stake. Pool: £2,549.90. 21.70 winning tickets. JR

6315 - 6319a (Foreign Racing) - See Raceform Interactive

# 6297 DEAUVILLE (R-H)

Wednesday, October 20

**OFFICIAL GOING: Turf course - very soft; all-weather - standard**

## 6320a PRIX HEROD (LISTED) 6f 110y(S)

**2:05** (2:04) 2-Y-O **£15,845** (£6,338; £4,754; £3,169)

RPR

**1** **Campo Bueno (FR)**[13] 6035 2-9-2 .......... GBenoist 5 102
(XNakkachdji, France)

2 1½ **Silent Name (JPN)**[22] 2-9-2 .................... OPeslier 8 98
(MmeCHead-Maarek, France)
3 ¾ **Josh**[19] 5918 2-9-2 .................... PRobinson 7 96
(MAJarvis) *settled towards rr on outside, hdwy 2f out, pushed along and pressing ldrs 1f out, ev ch 150y out, no ex cl hme*
4 3 **Mathematician (IRE)**[37] 2-9-2 .................... CSoumillon 1 89
(AFabre, France)
5 ¾ **Ascot Dream (IRE)**[18] 2-8-13 ....................(b) YBarberot 6 84
(SWattel, France)
6 2½ **Royal Mistress**[73] 4597 2-8-13 ....................(b) SPasquier 4 78
(RGibson, France)
7 1½ **Lonesome Me (FR)**[37] 5532 2-8-13 .................... C-PLemaire 2 74
(PBary, France)
8 10 **Molto Bello (USA)**[19] 2-9-2 .................... IMendizabal 3 52
(YDeNicolay, France)

1m 19.9s **8** Ran
Speed ratings: .
**Owner** B W Hughes **Bred** Thierry De La Heronniere **Trained** France

**NOTEBOOK**
**Josh** challenged for the lead at the furlong marker but was one-paced during the final 100 yards. He possibly did not get home over this trip on testing ground and his jockey thought he might have been just a little over the top.

# [6181] BRIGHTON (L-H)
Thursday, October 21

**OFFICIAL GOING: Soft (heavy in places) (abandoned after race 1 due to high winds)**
Wind: Strong half against Weather: Fair

## 6322 SOLSTONE PLUS MEDIAN AUCTION MAIDEN STKS 6f 209y
**2:20** (2:20) (E3) 2-Y-O **£4,702** (£1,447; £723; £361) **Stalls** Low

Form RPR
54 1 **Maxamillion (IRE)**[6] 6181 2-9-0 .................... JFEgan 16 80
(SKirk) *in tch: effrt over 2f out: drvn to ld ins fnl f: sn clr* **12/1**
4 2 3½ **Marhoon (USA)**[17] 6000 2-9-0 ....................(t) TEDurcan 15 73
(EFVaughan) *in tch: led over 2f out tl jst ins fnl f: nt qckn* **8/1**
4264 3 ½ **Coup D'Etat**[11] 6090 2-9-0 84 .................... TQuinn 2 72
(JLDunlop) *prom: disp ld over 1f out tl outpcd by wnr ins fnl f* **11/10**[1]
60 4 2 **Secret Cavern (USA)**[47] 5301 2-9-0 .................... EAhern 3 68
(JAOsborne) *chsd ldrs: hrd rdn 2f out: one pce* **20/1**
0002 5 9 **Shingle Street (IRE)**[6] 6181 2-9-0 .................... NCallan 14 50
(MHTompkins) *chsd ldrs tl wknd 2f out* **7/1**[3]
0 6 nk **Goose Chase**[20] 5915 2-9-0 .................... DHolland 10 49
(MLWBell) *led tl over 2f out: sn wknd* **5/1**[2]
00 7 5 **Rock Fever (IRE)**[19] 5943 2-8-9 .................... KFallon 13 34
(MJWallace) *chsd ldrs 4f* **25/1**
0 8 2½ **Gallantian (IRE)**[8] 6153 2-9-0 .................... JFortune 17 34
(GAButler) *dwlt: outpcd in midfield: n.d fr 1/2-way* **33/1**
00 9 ¾ **Mister Troubridge**[22] 5872 2-9-0 .................... SDrowne 8 33
(GBBalding) *sn outpcd in midfield: n.d fr 1/2-way* **100/1**
03 10 hd **Sole Agent (IRE)**[6] 6181 2-8-9 .................... AQuinn(5) 5 33
(GLMoore) *outpcd: a bhd* **25/1**
0 11 nk **Brumaire (IRE)**[12] 6060 2-9-0 .................... IMongan 7 32
(JLDunlop) *dwlt: outpcd: nvr nr ldrs* **66/1**
12 8 **Generous Measure** 2-8-11 .................... LFletcher(3) 4 16
(JMPEustace) *dwlt: sn in midfield: rdn and n.d fr 1/2-way* **66/1**
13 1¼ **Dont Call Me Babe** 2-9-0 .................... PDoe 9 13
(RRowe) *s.s: a wl bhd* **33/1**
00 14 3 **Fantasia's Forest (IRE)**[10] 6118 2-8-9 .................... GCarter 1 —
(JLDunlop) *pushed along in midfield: mod hdwy 2f out: n.d: eased 1f out* **80/1**
15 20 **Al's Glennmay** 2-8-9 .................... ADaly 12 —
(MSSaunders) *dwlt: bhd tl mod hdwy into midfield 1/2-way: wknd and no ch fnl 3f* **66/1**

1m 29.55s (6.95) **Going Correction** +0.875s/f (Soft) **15** Ran **SP% 120.6**
Speed ratings: **95,91,90,88,77 77,71,68,68,67 67,58,56,53,30**CSF £96.46 TOTE £15.40: £3.30, £2.60, £1.10; EX 85.80 Place 6 £1.25.
**Owner** Nicholas Hartery **Bred** Mrs C Hartery **Trained** Upper Lambourn, Berks

**FOCUS**
The ground was barely raceable and, coupled with a strong pace, the race proved quite a test for these juveniles.

**NOTEBOOK**
**Maxamillion(IRE)** had run two good races in bad ground already and was not as inconvenienced as many by the desperate conditions. The ground no doubt flattered him and he may struggle in handicap company if the assessor takes this form literally.
**Marhoon(USA)**, another who had shown ability in soft ground previously, grabbed the favoured stands'-side rail but could not respond when the winner came to challenge. He has shown enough to suggest he can win his maiden.
**Coup D'Etat**, for whom this ground was a worry, was sent off a very short price given the conditions. He did not run badly in the circumstances and will find a race in time.
**Secret Cavern(USA)** had a hard race to finish fourth, well clear of the rest. He is now eligible for handicaps but may well be the type to win a maiden on the All-Weather this winter.
**Shingle Street(IRE)** ran well in soft ground here last time but failed to get home in the testing conditions on this occasion.
**Goose Chase**, a half-brother to seven winners, notably Snow Goose, Dusky Warbler and Merry Merlin, set a strong pace given the conditions and paid for the effort in the closing stages. There should be better to come in time.
**Fantasia's Forest(IRE)** is bred to do better as a three-year-old over middle distances.

## 6323 32RED.COM NURSERY 6f 209y
() (E3) (0-75,) 2-Y-O £

## 6324 EUROPEAN BREEDERS FUND MAIDEN STKS 7f 214y
() (D3) 2-Y-O £

## 6325 WEATHERBYS BANK STKS (H'CAP) 5f 213y
() (D2) (0-92,) 3-Y-O+ £

## 6326 BRITISH OPEN SNOOKER (S) H'CAP 1m 1f 209y
() (G4) (0-55,) 3-Y-O+ £

## 6327 32REDPOKER.COM CLASSIFIED STKS 7f 214y
() (E3) 3-Y-O+ £

## 6328 VIACOM BRAND SOLUTIONS APPRENTICE H'CAP 1m 3f 196y
() (E3) (0-62,) 3-Y-O+ £

T/Jkpt: £114.30 to a £1 stake. Pool £41,698.75. 259.00 winning tickets T/Plt: £1.01 to a £1 stake. Pool £41,175.70. 52,896.90 winning tickets LM

# [5460] DONCASTER (L-H)
Friday, October 22

**OFFICIAL GOING: Soft (heavy in places on round course)**

## 6330 DRANSFIELD NOVELTY COMPANY EBF OCTOBER MAIDEN STKS (DIV I) 7f
**1:05** (1:10) (D3) 2-Y-O **£3,542** (£1,090; £545; £272) **Stalls** High

Form RPR
1 **Ballinteni** 2-9-0 ....................(t) LDettori 10 85+
(SaeedBinSuroor) *sn trcking ldrs: qcknd to ld jst ins fnl f: r.o wl* **5/1**[2]
2 2½ **Full Of Zest** 2-8-9 .................... ACulhane 3 74+
(MrsAJPerrett) *mde most tl hdd over 1f out: styd on u.p to chse wnr ins fnl f: no imp* **8/1**
3 2½ **Cashier** 2-9-0 .................... RHughes 6 73+
(JHMGosden) *hung lft: w ldr tl led over 1f out: rdn and hdd jst ins fnl f: sn btn* **6/1**[3]
0 4 ½ **Neutrino**[10] 6145 2-9-0 .................... NMackay 14 72+
(LMCumani) *hld up: hdwy 3f out: drvn along over 1f out: styd on fnl f: nrst fin* **14/1**
0553 5 1 **Royal Mougins**[4] 6265 2-9-0 68 .................... DHolland 2 69
(GWragg) *cl up: ev ch and rdn over 2f out: fdd* **4/1**[1]
0 6 1¾ **Cavan Gael (FR)**[22] 5897 2-9-0 .................... RWinston 12 65
(PHowling) *keen: trckd ldrs: effrt wl over 1f out: sn drvn along and btn* **33/1**
7 3½ **Kingdom Of Dreams (IRE)** 2-9-0 .................... RHills 5 56
(SirMichaelStoute) *midfield: drvn along and hdwy over 2f out: wknd over 1f out* **6/1**[3]
8 4 **Greatcoat** 2-9-0 .................... WSupple 8 46
(JGGiven) *nvr bttr than mid-div* **50/1**
9 shd **Dinner Date** 2-9-0 .................... KFallon 4 54+
(SirMichaelStoute) *pushed along towards rr 1/2-way: n.d* **13/2**
10 9 **Pitcairn Island** 2-8-9 .................... RFfrench 13 18
(MJohnston) *prom 4f: sn drvn along and wknd* **20/1**
0 11 hd **Whispering Death**[8] 6171 2-9-0 .................... SWKelly 7 23
(WJHaggas) *towards rr most of way* **33/1**
0 12 5 **Beacon Star (USA)**[177] 1709 2-9-0 .................... KDarley 1 10
(MJohnston) *slowly away: drvn along in midfield 1/2-way: wknd over 2f out* **33/1**
13 3½ **Cream Of Esteem** 2-9-0 ....................(t) KimTinkler 11 1
(NTinkler) *slowly away: keen early: a bhd* **100/1**

1m 31.69s (3.88) **Going Correction** +0.575s/f (Yiel) **13** Ran **SP% 112.9**
Speed ratings: **100,97,94,93,92 90,86,82,81,71 71,65,61**CSF £39.00 TOTE £3.90: £2.30, £3.20, £2.20; EX 32.80.
**Owner** Godolphin **Bred** Gainsborough Stud Management Ltd **Trained** Newmarket, Suffolk

**FOCUS**
A decent looking maiden, full of backward juveniles, and it should throw up its share of winners in due course. The first three all made promising starts in a race that has been rated through the fifth

**NOTEBOOK**
**Ballinteni**, half-brother to high-class juvenile Touch Of The Blues, made a winning debut in good style. He responded well to pressure when asked to win his race and looks another nice prospect for his powerful stable. He should stay further next year and could be better suited to a sound surface.
**Full Of Zest** , a 40,000gns April foal, clearly knew her job ahead of this debut and only tired late in the day. She looks to have a future and will be well suited by a mile next year.
**Cashier** , a 360,000gns half-brother to Azarole and Macadamia amongst others, showed ability on this debut, although he did hang badly left under pressure. He should do better as a three-year-old and will have no trouble getting further in time.
**Neutrino** was doing all of his best work at the finish and improved markedly on his recent debut. He enjoyed this softer ground and can improve again with further experience.
**Royal Mougins** had his chance and can have no excuses. He sets the standard for the form and should find a race, but looks exposed now.
**Kingdom Of Dreams(IRE)** , a 300,000gns purchase and whose dam is half-sister to top-class performer Kings Theatre, ran very much as though this experience was needed. He will have to improve plenty if he is to justify his price tag.
**Dinner Date**, a half-brother to his stable's smart Lord Major, showed just modest ability on this debut and may need better ground.

## 6331 DRANSFIELD NOVELTY COMPANY EBF OCTOBER MAIDEN STKS (DIV II) 7f
**1:35** (1:41) (D3) 2-Y-O **£3,542** (£1,090; £545; £272) **Stalls** High

Form RPR
1 **Tasdeed** 2-9-0 .................... TEDurcan 13 85+
(EFVaughan) *hld up: gd hdwy over 1f out: r.o strly u.p to ld ins fnl f: sn clr* **12/1**
223 2 2½ **Daniel Thomas (IRE)**[65] 4844 2-9-0 92 .................... ACulhane 2 79
(MrsAJPerrett) *chsd ldrs: pushed along over 2f out: rdn to ld over 1f out: hdd ins fnl f: styd on: no ch w wnr* **15/8**[1]
3 1 **Golden Feather** 2-9-0 .................... LDettori 14 77
(JHMGosden) *trckd ldrs: effrt 2f out: sn rdn: styd on fnl f* **3/1**[2]
4 nk **Sharp Reply (USA)** 2-9-0 .................... RHughes 5 76+
(SirMichaelStoute) *hld up in rr: hdwy 3f out: in tch and rdn over 1f out: styd on ins fnl f* **12/1**

5 3/4 **Woolsack (USA)** 2-9-0 .......... DHolland 12 74
(HMorrison) *mde most tl rdn and hdd over 1f out: no ex* **18/1**

6 3/4 **Gamble Of The Day (USA)** 2-9-0 .......... KFallon 8 72+
(SirMichaelStoute) *midfield: drvn along 3f out: styd on fnl f: n.d* **9/1**

7 2 **Keon (IRE)** 2-9-0 .......... DSweeney 4 68
(RHollinshead) *hld up: hdwy 1/2-way: ch 2f out: sn rdn and btn* **100/1**

0 8 1/2 **Lekka Ding (IRE)**[9] 6153 2-8-9 .......... JQuinn 11 65+
(CFWall) *hld up in rr: effrt 3f out: styd on fr over 1f out: n.d* **100/1**

9 3/4 **Royal Sapphire (USA)** 2-9-0 .......... RFfrench 3 65
(MJohnston) *sn racd alone far side: in tch: rdn 2f out: no imp on ldrs fnl f* **20/1**

4 10 1 **Real Cool Cat (USA)**[14] 6045 2-8-9 .......... KDarley 9 57
(MJohnston) *w ldr tl rdn and wknd 2f out* **13/2**[3]

00 11 3 1/2 **Spence Appeal (IRE)**[78] 4498 2-9-0 .......... PFessey 6 54
(KARyan) *hld up: rdn 1/2-way* **100/1**

12 6 **Vettorious** 2-9-0 .......... MFenton 10 40
(JGGiven) *in tch: drvn along 1/2-way: sn btn* **40/1**

065 13 2 1/2 **Cost Analysis (IRE)**[12] 6077 2-9-0 .......... PRobinson 7 34
(MAJarvis) *prom to 1/2-way: sn wknd* **14/1**

1m 32.34s (4.53) **Going Correction** +0.575s/f (Yiel) **13** Ran SP% **120.6**
Speed ratings: **97,94,93,92,91 90,88,88,87,86 82,75,72**CSF £34.45 TOTE £19.90: £4.10, £1.40, £1.70; EX 35.40.
**Owner** Sheikh Ahmed Al Maktoum **Bred** Stratford Place Stud **Trained** Newmarket, Suffolk

**FOCUS**

Slower than the first division, and hard to be confident about the exact level of the form, but probably above-average nevertheless and an impressive winner.

**NOTEBOOK**

**Tasdeed ◆**, a 100,000gns half-brother to the ten-furlong winner Day To Remember, made an impressive winning debut. He quickened up neatly when asked to win his race, and did look distinctly green, so should have plenty of improvement in him. He looks potentially useful.

**Daniel Thomas(IRE)** ran another sound race, but could not go with the winner when it mattered. He is in danger of becoming frustrating, but did little wrong this time and gives this form a sound look.

**Golden Feather ◆**, first foal of a dam who is half-sister to the high-class older performer Riyadian, posted a pleasing debut display and looks sure to improve plenty for this experience. He was well backed for this and should have no trouble in losing his maiden tag if found another opportunity this year.

**Sharp Reply(USA)**, a half-brother to Common Request (a ten furlong winner on his debut), shaped with promise and made a pleasing enough debut. He gradually got the hang of things and should know more next time.

**Gamble Of The Day(USA)** , a $260,000 half-brother to smart US performer Najecam, was staying on nicely towards the finish and should do much better next year.

**Real Cool Cat(USA)** dropped out disappointingly towards the business end of the race and failed to build on the promise of her recent York debut over this extra furlong. She would be best kept to six furlongs for the immediate future.

## 6332 PERSIMMON HOMES H'CAP 1m 2f 60y

2:10 (2:10) (D2) (0-92,83) 3-Y-O **£7,295** (£2,244; £1,122; £561) **Stalls** Low

Form RPR

1 1 **Double Deputy (IRE)**[22] 5891 3-9-4 **80** .......... (t) LDettori 13 88
(SaeedBinSuroor) *mde all: rdn 2f out: drvn ent last: hld on gamely* **6/1**[2]

4162 2 nk **Another Choice (IRE)**[18] 5998 3-9-4 **80** .......... (t) TEDurcan 5 89+
(NPLittmoden) *hld up and bhd: effrt and nt clr run 2f out: switched outside and rdn wl over 1f out: styd on strly ins last: jst failed* **16/1**

3100 3 1 1/4 **Iktitaf (IRE)**[20] 5942 3-9-7 **83** .......... RHills 16 88
(JHMGosden) *trckd ldrs: smooth hdwy to chal over 2f out: sn rdn and ev ch tl drvn and one pce ent last* **25/1**

0052 4 hd **Woody Valentine (USA)**[22] 5886 3-9-6 **82** .......... SChin 7 87
(MJohnston) *in tch: effrt and nt clr run 2f out: swtchd ins and rdn: styd on fnl f* **13/2**[3]

3020 5 4 **Sunisa (IRE)**[48] 5297 3-9-6 **82** .......... DHolland 2 80
(BWHills) *trckd ldrs: effrt 3f out: rdn along 2f out: drvn and wknd appr last* **50/1**

4116 6 2 **Mambina (USA)**[4] 6266 3-8-3 **72** 6ex .......... TO'Brien(7) 1 66
(MRChannon) *towards rr: hdwy on inner and nt much roon over 2f out: sn rdn and styd on same pce appr last* **12/1**

2104 7 2 1/2 **Top Spec (IRE)**[7] 6192 3-9-6 **82** .......... PDobbs 9 72
(RHannon) *s.i.s and bhd: hdwy over 3f out: n.m.r and swtchd rt 2f out: sn rdn and kpt on: nrst fin* **33/1**

3143 8 1/2 **Cellarmaster (IRE)**[35] 5615 3-9-3 **79** .......... KDarley 11 68
(EFVaughan) *midfield: hdwy on outer to chse ldrs 4f out: rdn along 3f out and sn one pce* **7/1**

4640 9 1/2 **Slavonic (USA)**[18] 5994 3-8-8 **70** .......... PFessey 4 58
(KARyan) *midfield: rdn along and n.m.r 3f out: kpt on u.p fnl 2f: nvr nr ldrs* **40/1**

0605 10 nk **Alekhine (IRE)**[28] 5766 3-9-6 **82** .......... (e) MFenton 18 70
(PWHarris) *stdd s and bhd: hdwy 3f out: swtchd ins and rdn 2f out: nvr nr ldrs* **12/1**

1060 11 1 **Bright Sun (IRE)**[20] 5934 3-8-10 **72** .......... (t) KimTinkler 10 58
(NTinkler) *n.m.r and checked after 150 yds: keen and in rr tl effrt and sme hdwy over 2f out: nvr a factor* **66/1**

2236 12 3/4 **Charnock Bates One (IRE)**[11] 6115 3-8-10 **72** .......... GGibbons 6 57
(TDEasterby) *chsd ldrs: rdn along and lost pl over 4f out* **20/1**

0313 13 1 1/2 **Ghantoot**[98] 3917 3-8-11 **73** .......... (v) NMackay 3 55
(LMCumani) *chsd ldrs: effrt 3f out: sn rdn along and wknd* **18/1**

440 14 5 **Kings Empire**[28] 5768 3-8-13 **80** .......... (t) DTudhope(5) 14 54
(DCarroll) *cl up: rdn along 4f out: sn wknd* **40/1**

3150 15 1 1/4 **Tytheknot**[11] 6115 3-8-11 **73** .......... PHanagan 8 45
(JeddO'Keeffe) *midfield: hdwy over 3f out: rdn along and wknd over 2f out* **33/1**

1153 16 18 **Flying Adored**[18] 5998 3-9-4 **80** .......... KFallon 19 21
(JLDunlop) *stdd s and bhd: hdwy on outer 4f out: rdn along wl over 2f out and sn wknd* **10/1**

3116 17 1 **New Order**[28] 5766 3-9-2 **78** .......... RHughes 12 17
(BWHills) *in tch: effrt over 3f out: rdn along and wknd 2f out* **9/2**[1]

2005 18 1 1/4 **Saffron Fox**[18] 5990 3-9-0 **76** .......... (p) ACulhane 15 13
(JGPortman) *hld up: hdwy on outer 4f out: rdn along 3f out and sn wknd* **20/1**

1460 19 29 **On Every Street**[33] 5672 3-8-13 **75** .......... RFfrench 17 —
(RBastiman) *a rr: lost touch and wl bhd fnl 3f* **100/1**

2m 16.6s (4.84) **Going Correction** +0.70s/f (Yiel) **19** Ran SP% **122.5**
Speed ratings: **108,107,106,106,103 101,99,99,99,98 97,97,96,92,91 76,75,74,51**CSF £87.15 CT £2257.79 TOTE £4.90: £2.00, £3.50, £4.40, £1.80; EX 56.80.
**Owner** Godolphin **Bred** Gainsborough Stud Management Ltd **Trained** Newmarket, Suffolk

**FOCUS**

A fair handicap, and solid form, but they did not go a strong pace

**NOTEBOOK**

**Double Deputy(IRE)** enjoyed the run of the race and saw off the challenge of the top-weight well before having just enough in reserve to hold the fast-finishing runner-up. This softer ground was no problem to this unexposed son of Sadler's Wells and he can improve again.

**Another Choice(IRE)**, who likes to get his toe in, did not enjoy much luck in running and ran well off a career-high mark, finishing fast and only narrowly failing to get up. He could have done with a stronger pace.

**Iktitaf(IRE)** had clearly come on for his recent reappearance from a four-month absence and appreciated the softer ground. His maiden win at Chester came with cut in the ground and he clearly needs it to show his best.

**Woody Valentine(USA)**, who goes well with cut in the ground, posted another good effort, confirming his return to form.

**Sunisa(IRE)** had an excuse for her poor run last time and this was a lot more like her true form.

**Mambina(USA)**, who was carrying a 6lb penalty, was 3lb badly in at the weights.

**New Order** was disappointing even allowing for the step up in trip being a question mark. *Official explanation: vet said filly finished lame*

## 6333 DBS OCTOBER YEARLING STKS 6f

2:45 (2:49) (B1) 2-Y-O **£22,340** (£8,936; £4,468; £2,234) **Stalls** High

Form RPR

5416 1 **Pivotal Flame**[20] 5947 2-8-11 .......... GCarter 10 88+
(BAMcmahon) *racd far side: hld up: hdwy 2f out: r.o wl u.p to ld cl home* **6/4**[1]

0660 2 hd **Hidden Jewel**[48] 5307 2-8-11 .......... GGibbons 13 87?
(BAMcmahon) *racd far side: cl up: led wl over 2f out: r.o u.p fnl f: hdd cl home* **100/1**

4356 3 1 1/2 **Dispol Isle (IRE)**[11] 6113 2-8-6 .......... KDarley 3 78?
(TDBarron) *racd far side: prom: wnt 2nd 2f out: kpt on u.p: no imp on ldr* **50/1**

1 4 shd **Seamus Shindig**[36] 5586 2-8-11 .......... DSweeney 4 83
(HCandy) *racd far side: hld up: hdwy u.p over 1f out: no imp on ldrs ins fnl f* **12/1**

1236 5 hd **The Crooked Ring**[13] 6068 2-8-11 81 .......... LDettori 8 82
(PDEvans) *racd far side: hld up: hdwy 2f out: kpt on u.p fnl f: nvr able to chal* **11/2**[3]

55 6 5 **Oceancookie (IRE)**[34] 5640 2-8-7 ow1 .......... DHolland 1 63
(AMBalding) *racd far side: chsd ldrs: rdn 2f out: wknd ins fnl f* **66/1**

050 7 1 1/2 **Piddies Pride (IRE)**[15] 6022 2-8-6 70 .......... HayleyTurner 18 58
(PSMcentee) *racd stands side: trckd ldrs: r.o u.p to ld grp ins fnl f: nt trble far side ldrs* **100/1**

004 8 nk **Flaxby**[23] 5857 2-8-11 .......... PRobinson 15 62
(JDBethell) *led stands side grp: drvn along 2f out: lost grp ld ins fnl f: no ex* **100/1**

6001 9 2 **Coconut Squeak**[21] 5910 2-8-6 .......... FNorton 16 51
(MrsStefLiddiard) *racd stands side: chsd ldrs: rdn 2f out: kpt on same pce* **66/1**

2130 10 1 1/2 **Melalchrist**[66] 4836 2-8-11 94 .......... PHanagan 19 51
(JJQuinn) *racd stands side: in tch: rdn 2f out: sn btn* **25/1**

1250 11 3/4 **Graze On**[14] 6042 2-8-11 .......... RWinston 21 49
(JJQuinn) *racd stands side: towards rr: styd on fr over 1f out: n.d* **20/1**

3311 12 3/4 **Space Shuttle**[53] 5195 2-9-3 85 .......... KFallon 7 53
(TDEasterby) *racd far side: dwlt: towards rr early: hdwy into midfield 2f out: wknd fnl f* **7/2**[2]

1110 13 2 **Coleorton Dancer**[22] 5896 2-8-11 65 .......... PFessey 2 41
(KARyan) *racd far side: hood late off and s.v.s: gd hdwy into midfield 1/2-way: no further prog* **11/1**

0003 14 1/2 **Selkirk Storm (IRE)**[11] 6113 2-8-11 81 .......... PMulrennan 22 39
(MWEasterby) *racd stands side: n.d* **25/1**

5601 15 1 1/4 **Davy Crockett**[23] 5855 2-8-11 .......... DMcGaffin 17 35
(BSmart) *racd stands side: prom: rdn over 2f out: wknd appr fnl f* **100/1**

4004 16 5 **World At My Feet**[6] 6204 2-8-6 85 .......... JQuinn 14 15
(NBycroft) *racd stands side: n.d* **80/1**

005 17 3/4 **Little Warning**[23] 5865 2-8-6 .......... NMackay 6 13
(RMBeckett) *racd far side: towards rr most of way* **100/1**

0020 18 1 **Tartatartufata**[54] 5143 2-8-6 .......... RPCleary 12 10
(DShaw) *racd alone centre: no ch fnl 2f* **100/1**

5000 19 3/4 **Forest Viking (IRE)**[20] 5947 2-8-11 .......... GParkin 9 13
(JSWainwright) *racd far side: led tl hdd wl over 2f out: sn wknd* **150/1**

0000 20 9 **Slate Grey**[36] 5578 2-8-11 .......... (v) DarrenWilliams 11 —
(KRBurke) *racd far side: s.i.s: sn midfield: wknd over 2f out* **200/1**

1010 21 5 **Marcela Zabala**[35] 5617 2-8-6 55 .......... MFenton 5 —
(JGGiven) *racd far side: chsd ldrs to 1/2-way: sn wknd* **100/1**

1m 17.92s (3.64) **Going Correction** +0.575s/f (Yiel) **21** Ran SP% **120.4**
Speed ratings: **98,97,95,95,95 88,86,86,83,81 80,79,76,76,74 67,66,65,64,52 45**CSF £248.46 TOTE £2.60: £1.50, £27.10, £11.00; EX 265.00.
**Owner** R L Bedding **Bred** Cheveley Park Stud Ltd **Trained** Hopwas, Staffs

**FOCUS**

The field split into two and those who raced far side dominated the finish. The form is arguably the trickiest to rate of the entire season, for even if the winner is assessed as running 12lb below his best, the runner-up has to be raised 38lb and the third by 11lb.

**NOTEBOOK**

**Pivotal Flame** had the ground back in his favour and looked a strong favourite for this event. In the end he only got home narrowly from his much lower rated stablemate, and the form presents a real puzzle. He looks to have run well below his best.

**Hidden Jewel** provided trainer Bryan McMahon with a one-two, showing vastly improved form on this first start on soft ground. He is clearly a better animal when he can get his toe in and might be able to find a maiden before too long.

**Dispol Isle(IRE)**, who is still a maiden, had plenty to find on the book but ran much better than her form entitled her to. She seems suited by some ease in the ground.

**Seamus Shindig** won his maiden on firm ground, and while that surface was thought to be too fast for him really, these conditions provided an altogether different test. A drifter in the market, he did not run badly in fourth.

**The Crooked Ring**, who has been on the go for a long time now, has shown his best form on a faster surface.

**Oceancookie(IRE)** did not run badly over a trip on the short side for her.

**Piddies Pride(IRE)** came home first on the stands' side but was well held by the far-side group.

**Space Shuttle**, returning from a two-month break, ran below form. It is possible that, although happy enough in good to soft ground, these conditions proved just too much for him.

**Coleorton Dancer** *Official explanation: jockey said he was unable to remove blind from gelding prior to stalls opening*

## 6334 RACING POST £1 MILLION TOTETENTOFOLLOW NURSERY 1m (R)

3:20 (3:23) (C2) (0-90,88) 2-Y-O **£10,686** (£3,288; £1,644; £822) **Stalls** High

Form RPR

001 1 **Alpine Gold (IRE)**[53] 5172 2-8-8 **75** .......... IMongan 3 81
(JLDunlop) *in tch: hdwy 3f out: rdn to chal over 1f out: drvn to ld wl ins last: styd on* **14/1**

442 **2** *hd* **Mokaraba**[43] [5407] 2-8-13 **80** ........ RHills 10 86
(JLDunlop) *hld up in rr: gd hdwy on outer 3f out: rdn to ld 1f out: sn drvn: hdd and no ex wl ins last* **16/1**

0112 **3** *½* **Secret Pact (IRE)**[22] [5885] 2-9-3 **84** ........ KDarley 12 89
(MJohnston) *led: rdn along over 2f out: drvn and hdd 1f out: rallied and ev ch ins last tl no ex nr fin* **10/1**[3]

012 **4** *¾* **I'm So Lucky**[26] [5819] 2-9-6 **87** ........ RFfrench 7 91
(MJohnston) *towards rr and pushed along 1/2-way: hdwy 3f out: swtchd outside and rdn wl over 1f out: styd on ins last: nrst fin* **10/1**[3]

1542 **5** *1¼* **Im Spartacus**[11] [6129] 2-8-0 **74** ........ (p) CHaddon(7) 8 75
(IAWood) *trckd ldrs: effrt and n.m.r 2f out: sn rdn and kpt on same pce* **8/1**[2]

4021 **6** *6* **Alright My Son (IRE)**[11] [6129] 2-9-6 **87** 6ex ........ RHughes 4 76
(RHannon) *cl up: effrt and ev ch 2f out tl rdn and wknd appr last* **9/2**[1]

4110 **7** *½* **Night Of Joy (IRE)**[48] [5292] 2-9-7 **88** ........ PRobinson 6 76
(MAJarvis) *towards rr: hdwy on inner 3f out: rdn along 2f out and sn no imp* **10/1**[3]

41 **8** *1¼* **Maidanni (USA)**[13] [6067] 2-9-3 **84** ........ LDettori 5 72+
(SaeedBinSuroor) *trckd ldrs: hdwy over 3f out and sn ev ch: rdn over 2f out and sn wknd* **9/2**[1]

3203 **9** *9* **Wavertree Warrior (IRE)**[12] [6090] 2-8-7 **77** ........ (p) J-PGuillambert(3) 9 45
(NPLittmoden) *cl up: rdn along 3f out: grad wknd* **14/1**

015 **10** *nk* **Just Waz (USA)**[26] [5819] 2-8-1 **68** ........ FNorton 13 35
(RMWhitaker) *bhd: effrt and sme hdwy over 2f out: nvr a factor* **25/1**

3125 **11** *2* **Lady Misha**[10] [6140] 2-8-6 **73** ........ JMackay 2 36
(JeddO'Keeffe) *chsd ldrs: rdn along 3f out: sn wknd* **14/1**

0000 **12** *½* **John Forbes**[14] [6042] 2-8-5 **75** ........ (b) PMulrennan(3) 1 37
(BEllison) *keen: hld up in midfield: effrt 4f out: rdn along over 3f out and sn wknd* **66/1**

0035 **13** *hd* **Darko Karim**[11] [6129] 2-8-6 **73** ........ WSupple 11 35
(DRLoder) *a rr* **25/1**

014 **14** *10* **Bathwick Finesse (IRE)**[38] [5539] 2-8-13 **80** ........ SWKelly 14 22
(BRMillman) *hld up towards rr: effrt and sme hdwy on outer over 3f out: rdn along over 2f out: sn wknd and eased* **10/1**[3]

1m 45.19s (4.64) **Going Correction** +0.70s/f (Yiel) **14** Ran SP% **118.9**
Speed ratings: **104,103,103,102,101 95,94,93,84,84 82,81,81,71**CSF £214.64 CT £2402.37 TOTE £18.40: £4.70, £4.30, £3.70; EX 82.70.
**Owner** Windflower Overseas Holdings Inc **Bred** Windflower Overseas Holdings Inc **Trained** Arundel, W Sussex

**FOCUS**
This was run at a sound gallop and represents strong nursery form. The first first two are improvers from a resurgent yard, and they were followed home by three horses with strong pre-race credentials. The form should work out well.

**NOTEBOOK**
**Alpine Gold(IRE)**, absent since her Chepstow maiden win, was hard at work three furlongs from home but stayed on in resolute fashion to gain the upper hand near the line. She will improve again over middle distances at three.
**Mokaraba** travelled strongly towards the outside but after forcing her head in front, she just lost out to her stablemate. Like her she will do better over longer trips at three.
**Secret Pact(IRE)**, 5lb higher, handled the totally different ground with disdain and after striking for home, he was only edged out in the closing stages.
**I'm So Lucky**, badly tapped for toe three furlongs out, made his way to the outer and finished best of all. He richly deserves another success. *Official explanation: jockey said colt suffered interference at the start*
**Im Spartacus**, who in the past has proved she can handle soft ground, edged left under pressure and never really threatened to land a blow.
**Alright My Son(IRE)**, awash with sweat at the start, had the leader covered, but after looking to be travelling the better folded in a big way.
**Maidanni(USA)**, unable to dominate, was hard at work fully three furlongs from home and dropped right away in the final furlong. He will be much more the finished article at three. *Official explanation: jockey said colt was unsuited by the going*
**Just Waz(USA)** *Official explanation: jockey said colt hung left*
**Bathwick Finesse(IRE)** *Official explanation: jockey said filly hung right*

## 6335 RACING POST/SIS BETTING SHOP MANAGER OF THE YEAR H'CAP 1m 6f 132y
**3:50** (3:51) (D2) (0-92,90) 3-Y-0+ **£7,178** (£2,208; £1,104; £552) **Stalls** Low

Form RPR

151 **1** **Winged D'Argent (IRE)**[10] [6143] 3-8-13 **82** 6ex ........ KDarley 10 97+
(MJohnston) *racd on outside to 1/2-way: cl up and pushed along 4f out: led 2f out: drvn clr appr fnl f* **9/4**[1]

2101 **2** *8* **Jeepstar**[39] [5517] 4-9-6 **80** ........ MFenton 2 85
(TDEasterby) *led tl rdn and hdd 2f out: kpt on same pce* **20/1**

1211 **3** *hd* **Belle Rouge**[18] [5997] 6-9-6 **80** ........ LDettori 5 84
(CAHorgan) *racd on outside after 1f to 1/2-way: hld up: hdwy over 2f out: rdn to chse first 2 over 1f out: styd on: clsng on runner-up* **5/1**[3]

221 **4** *1¾* **Mandatum**[76] [4554] 3-8-10 **79** ........ KFallon 8 82+
(LMCumani) *hld up: drvn along whn nt clr run over 2f out: styd on u.p fnl f: nvr able to chal* **11/2**

2212 **5** *¾* **Quarrymount**[18] [5997] 3-8-12 **81** ........ JMackay 3 82
(SirMarkPrescott) *hld up: drvn along and outpcd over 2f out: styd on u.p fnl f: n.d* **3/1**[2]

1120 **6** *¾* **Peak Of Perfection (IRE)**[27] [5784] 3-9-7 **90** ........ PRobinson 1 90
(MAJarvis) *racd on outside to 1/2-way: trckd ldrs after: effrt 3f out: sn rdn and btn* **10/1**

3161 **7** *5* **Red Forest (IRE)**[20] [5951] 5-8-12 **72** ........ (t) DaleGibson 9 66
(JMackie) *trckd ldrs: effrt 3f out: sn rdn and wknd* **20/1**

0/00 **8** *dist* **Gracilis (IRE)**[162] [1880] 7-9-1 **75** ........ RWinston 7 —
(GASwinbank) *in tch to 1/2-way: sn bhd and rdn: lost tch fnl 5f: t.o* **66/1**

3m 18.95s (9.21) **Going Correction** +0.70s/f (Yiel)
**WFA** 3 from 4yo+ 9lb **8** Ran SP% **107.9**
Speed ratings: **103,98,98,97,97 96,94,**—CSF £44.91 CT £175.64 TOTE £3.00: £1.90, £2.70, £1.60; EX 49.30.
**Owner** Daniel A Couper **Bred** Daniel A Couper And George Hosie **Trained** Middleham Moor, N Yorks

**FOCUS**
A steady pace and a slow time, with the winner one of three to take the by-pass route. He looks a real stayer and, as this was only his fourth career start, there should be even better to come.

**NOTEBOOK**
**Winged D'Argent(IRE)** ◆, a deep-bodied colt, raced wide until joining the main body of the field on the turn in. He made hard work of it but came right away and should make a smart stayer at four.
**Jeepstar**, 3lb higher, set his own pace but in the end the winner saw it out a whole lot better on this ground.
**Belle Rouge**, 8lb higher than on her last venture into handicap company, was taken wide after the first furlongs or so. She is all heart and would have snatched second spot with a bit further to go. At her own level she must rank as one of the success stories on the Flat this year.
**Mandatum**, on his handicap bow, was left short of room at one stage. Staying on in his own time at the death, he will do better with another year on his head.
**Quarrymount** travelled strongly but he is now rated 22lb higher than for his initial handicap success at Lingfield in July.
**Peak Of Perfection(IRE)**, drawn one, was dropped in leaving the stalls and made his way to the wide outside. He travelled strongly but was on the retreat with almost three furlongs left to run. He looks to have gone off the boil.

## 6336 AUKER RHODES PLUE PARROT EBF MAIDEN FILLIES' STKS 1m (R)
**4:25** (4:31) (D3) 2-Y-O **£4,379** (£1,347; £673; £336) **Stalls** High

Form RPR

2 **1** **Her Own Kind (JPN)**[20] [5946] 2-8-11 ........ LDettori 10 82+
(SaeedBinSuroor) *racd wd: a.p: led on bit 3f out: clr fnl 2f: v easily* **4/5**[1]

0 **2** *3* **Twyla Tharp (IRE)**[65] [4851] 2-8-11 ........ RHughes 2 66+
(JHMGosden) *cl up: ev ch 3f out tl rdn and one pce wl over 1f out* **5/1**[2]

**3** *nk* **Asawer (IRE)** 2-8-11 ........ RHills 8 67+
(SirMichaelStoute) *dwlt: sn in tch: hdwy over 2f out: rdn and kpt on same pce fr wl over 1f out* **13/2**[3]

0 **4** *8* **Missella (IRE)**[11] [6118] 2-8-11 ........ KDarley 1 49
(MJohnston) *cl up on inner: rdn along and outpcd fr wl over 2f out* **33/1**

**5** *1½* **Enamoured** 2-8-11 ........ ACulhane 9 46
(MrsAJPerrett) *dwelt and in rr: hdwy to chse ldrs 3f out: sn rdn and wknd fnl 2f* **14/1**

0 **6** *5* **Kathryn Janeway (IRE)**[11] [6123] 2-8-11 ........ KFallon 6 36
(WRMuir) *hld up in tch: hdwy and cl up 3f out: sn rdn along and wknd 2f out* **10/1**

**7** *3½* **Minnesinger** 2-8-11 ........ PHanagan 3 29
(RMBeckett) *a rr* **80/1**

0655 **8** *3½* **Aza Wish (IRE)**[5] [6240] 2-8-8 58 ........ TEaves(3) 7 22
(MsDeborahJEvans) *led: rdn along 4f out: hdd 3f out and sn wknd* **100/1**

**9** *nk* **Wood Sprite** 2-8-11 ........ MFenton 4 22
(JGGiven) *a bhd* **40/1**

**10** *12* **Anissati** 2-8-11 ........ DHolland 5 —
(CEBrittain) *dwlt: hdwy and in tch 1/2-way: rdn along and wknd 3f out* **25/1**

00 **11** *19* **Whoopsie**[24] [5846] 2-8-11 ........ RWinston 11 —
(JAGlover) *s.i.s: a bhd* **100/1**

1m 47.4s (6.85) **Going Correction** +0.70s/f (Yiel) **11** Ran SP% **113.8**
Speed ratings: **93,90,89,81,80 75,71,68,67,55 36**CSF £4.39 TOTE £1.90: £1.10, £1.40, £2.20; EX 5.10.
**Owner** Godolphin **Bred** Darley Stud Management, L L C **Trained** Newmarket, Suffolk

**FOCUS**
Just a steady pace in a maiden lacking any strength in depth. The form is nothing special, but Her Own Kind was in another league and has been rated 10lb better than the bare result.

**NOTEBOOK**
**Her Own Kind(JPN)** ◆, who raced wide to the turn, travelled supremely well and came clear without any apparent effort, value fully 10 lengths. At this stage she is no better than many others in the stable, but she is a big filly who will hopefully thrive over the winter in Dubai, and she looks a smart prospect for next year.
**Twyla Tharp(IRE)**, absent since making her debut two months earlier, is bred in the purple but lacks scope and is only lightly-made. That said she is sure to win at least a maiden next year.
**Asawer(IRE)** ◆, who stands over a fair amount of ground, looks on the weak side. After a tardy start she kept on in her own time and will leave this behind over further next year.
**Missella(IRE)** showed a bit more than on her debut 11 days earlier but she looks far from the finished article yet.
**Enamoured**, a tall, narrow filly, was on edge at the start and looks immature mentally as yet.
**Kathryn Janeway(IRE)**, well backed at long odds, has size and scope but she looks a somewhat nervous individual at this stage of her development.

## 6337 WEATHERBYS BANK EUROPEAN ASSOCIATION OF RACING SCHOOLS APPRENTICE STKS (H'CAP) 1m 2f 60y
**5:00** (5:00) (E3) (0-77,76) 3-Y-0+ **£7,342** (£2,259; £1,129; £564) **Stalls** Low

Form RPR

0135 **1** **Wellington Hall (GER)**[38] [5554] 6-8-13 **66** ........ AMullen(5) 3 72
(PWChapple-Hyam) *trckd ldrs: hdwy 3f out: rdn to ld over 1f out: edgd lft ins last: styd on* **9/2**[1]

3132 **2** *3½* **Mobane Flyer**[2] [6311] 4-8-12 **63** ........ ABaroni(3) 9 64+
(RAFahey) *hld up in tch: hdwy on inner 3f out: effrt 2f out and ev ch tl drvn and one pce ins last* **9/2**[1]

1412 **3** *2* **Lucayan Dancer**[12] [6096] 4-8-10 **61** ........ SBreux(3) 7 58
(DNicholls) *hld up towards rr: hdwy on outer over 2f out: rdn over 1f out: stayed on ins last: nrst fin* **9/2**[1]

0010 **4** *1½* **Tedsdale Mac**[4] [6266] 5-9-1 **63** 6ex ........ ABonnefoy 1 57
(NBycroft) *led: rdn along 2f out: drvn and hdd over 1f out: grad wknd* **14/1**[3]

0354 **5** *¾* **Keepers Knight (IRE)**[12] [6085] 3-8-9 **62** ........ HayleyTurner 6 55
(PFICole) *hld up towards rr: hdwy 3f out: rdn along 2f out: kpt on ins last: nrst fin* **16/1**

5000 **6** *1* **Muraqeb**[13] [6057] 4-7-13 **52** oh12 ........ CDHayes(5) 8 43
(MrsBarbaraWaring) *in tch: rdn along over 3f out: wknd over 2f out* **100/1**

1405 **7** *¾* **Zandeed (IRE)**[36] [5584] 6-8-6 **57** ........ ASanna(3) 5 47
(MissLAPerratt) *trckd ldr: hdwy 4f out: rdn and hung rt wl over 2f out: sn wknd* **12/1**[2]

0005 **8** *¾* **Garden Society (IRE)**[10] [6152] 7-8-7 **60** ........ PBBeggy(5) 2 49
(WAO'Gorman) *hld up in rr: wd st: rdn along wl over 2f out and no imp* **9/2**[1]

0163 **9** *3* **Snowed Under**[29] [5757] 3-8-5 **58** ........ RFradet 11 41
(JDBethell) *chsd ldrs: rdn along over 3f out: wknd wl over 2f out* **12/1**[2]

2241 **10** *9* **Revenir (IRE)**[9] [6160] 3-9-6 **76** 6ex ........ JMO'Dwyer(3) 10 44
(EFVaughan) *hld up: wd st and hdwy 4f out: rdn along 3f out and sn wknd* **14/1**[3]

2m 19.07s (7.31) **Going Correction** +0.70s/f (Yiel)
**WFA** 3 from 4yo+ 5lb **10** Ran SP% **108.3**
Speed ratings: **98,95,93,92,91 91,90,89,87,80**CSF £20.81 CT £83.17 TOTE £5.70: £1.80, £2.40, £1.70; EX 25.80 Place 6 £241.99, Place 5 £108.09.
**Owner** Allan Darke & Tom Matthews **Bred** Baron G Von Ullmann **Trained** Newmarket, Suffolk

**FOCUS**
An apprentice handicap with an international flavour. They went a sound gallop in the ground and spread all over the track in the home straight, with the first two sticking to the far side. The form could be rated a fair bit higher, but the proximity of the sixth is a concern.

**NOTEBOOK**
**Wellington Hall(GER)**, who looked very fit indeed, had proved in his native Germany that he handles soft ground. Well ridden, he ran out a most decisive winner.
**Mobane Flyer**, having his second outing in three days, never left the inner but on this ground the winner proved much the stronger. His Italian apprentice looked very stylish.
**Lucayan Dancer** for some reason made his effort from off the pace towards the outside. He drifted left under pressure and had given the first two far too much rope.

**Tedsdale Mac** took them along and went for gold half a mile out, but in the end he was simply not good enough under his penalty.
**Keepers Knight(IRE)**, happy to sit off the pace, stayed on in his own own time and never got competitive.
**Muraqeb** did well considering he was 12lb out of the handicap, but the fact remains he has yet to finish in a place after 10 starts now.
**Garden Society(IRE)**came ridiculously wide in the home straight and could never get on terms.
T/Plt: £168.90 to a £1 stake. Pool: £42,965.65. 185.70 winning tickets. T/Qpdt: £55.00 to a £1 stake. Pool: £3,989.40. 53.60 winning tickets. JF

## 5646 NEWBURY (L-H)

Friday, October 22

**OFFICIAL GOING: Soft (heavy in places)**

### 6338 CANTORODDS.COM NURSERY — 7f (S)

**1:15** (1:19) (D3) (0-85,85) 2-Y-O **£5,388** (£1,658; £829; £414) **Stalls** Centre

Form / RPR

241 **1** **Moon Forest (IRE)**$^{13}$ 6060 2-8-7 **76** ThomasYeung$^{(5)}$ 8 — 81
(PWChapple-Hyam) *lw: mde all: rdn fr 2f out: edgd lft u.p ins last: hld on all out* **6/1**$^{2}$

2143 **2** *hd* **Looks Could Kill (USA)**$^{34}$ 5630 2-9-7 **85** JFortune 9 — 90
(GAButler) *lw: trckd ldrs: wnt 2nd over 2f out: sn pushed along to chal: upsides whn carried lft ins last: kpt on wl: jst failed* **9/2**$^{1}$

5102 **3** *½* **Secret History (USA)**$^{18}$ 5995 2-8-11 **75** JFanning 11 — 79
(MJohnston) *lw: chsd ldrs: rdn to chal fr over 2f out: kpt on ins last tl outpcd last half f* **6/1**$^{2}$

336 **4** *2* **Fairmile**$^{23}$ 5872 2-9-1 **79** TQuinn 3 — 78
(PWHarris) *hld up in rr: hdwy over 2f out: rdn to chse ldrs and flashed tail appr last: kpt on same pce* **11/1**

3623 **5** *1½* **Tumbleweed Galore (IRE)**$^{13}$ 6063 2-8-9 **76** JFMcDonald$^{(3)}$ 6 — 72
(BJMeehan) *chsd ldrs: rdn over 2f out: wknd fnl f* **14/1**

3604 **6** *½* **Fasylitator (IRE)**$^{16}$ 6012 2-8-5 **69** SHitchcott 12 — 63
(JAOsborne) *in tch: rdn fr over 3f out: styd on fr over 1f out but nvr gng pce to rch ldrs* **10/1**$^{3}$

5506 **7** *1* **Oasis Way (GR)**$^{18}$ 5995 2-8-6 **70** TPQueally 5 — 62
(PRChamings) *bhd: rdn over 3f out: styd on fr over 1f out but nvr a danger* **50/1**

5156 **8** *5* **Dry Ice (IRE)**$^{41}$ 5466 2-9-4 **82** DaneO'Neill 4 — 62
(HCandy) *in tch: rdn 3f out: wknd fr 2f out* **14/1**

006 **9** *5* **Water Pistol**$^{30}$ 5729 2-8-8 **72** MartinDwyer 7 — 41
(MrsAJPerrett) *sn rdn in rr: a bhd* **20/1**

5201 **10** *2½* **Enforcer**$^{12}$ 6090 2-9-5 **83** 7ex SDrowne 13 — 46
(WRMuir) *lw: sn rdn: a bhd* **6/1**$^{2}$

2250 **11** *1½* **Tom Forest**$^{64}$ 4890 2-8-13 **77** EAhern 1 — 36
(JRFanshawe) *racd on outside: nvr bttr than mid-div: bhd fnl 3f* **14/1**

2023 **12** *shd* **Group Captain**$^{49}$ 5256 2-9-2 **80** RLMoore 2 — 39
(SKirk) *a in rr* **11/1**

0430 **13** *nk* **Naval Force**$^{55}$ 5119 2-8-13 **77** (t) JFEgan 10 — 35
(HMorrison) *chsd ldrs over 4f* **50/1**

0503 **14** *1* **Byron Bay**$^{3}$ 6282 2-8-0 **64** CCatlin 14 — 20
(JJBridger) *chsd ldrs over 4f* **25/1**

1m 30.65s (3.43) **Going Correction** +0.475s/f (Yiel) **14** Ran SP% **119.3**
Speed ratings: **99,98,98,95,94 93,92,86,81,78 76,76,76,74**CSF £31.56 CT £171.11 TOTE £8.00: £3.10, £1.90, £2.20; EX 40.70.
**Owner** Collins Deal Harrison-Allan Chapple-Hyam **Bred** P Conlon And Paul Clarke **Trained** Newmarket, Suffolk

**FOCUS**
A decent nursery, though the ground was testing, and some clearly could not cope. Nothing got into the race from off the pace.

**NOTEBOOK**
**Moon Forest(IRE)** did not look badly treated for his handicap debut and, up there from the start, battled on gamely to hold off his pursuers. He had won his maiden on good to soft and is clearly suited by some give in the ground.
**Looks Could Kill(USA)** failed only narrowly and clearly revels in soft ground. He was not helped by the winner edging left towards him, but given the way he had travelled it was a bit disappointing that he could not get past him and win.
**Secret History(USA)**, whose slightly disappointing runs this season came on fast ground, is clearly at her best when she can get her toe in. She stays farther than this and was gaining on the front pair at the finish.
**Fairmile** has yet to race on anything faster than good to soft in his four outings to date. He kept on well enough but did flash his tail under pressure.
**Tumbleweed Galore(IRE)**, more exposed than some of his rivals, is always likely to be vulnerable to those with a bit more potential.
**Fasylitator(IRE)** saw the trip out well enough but he never got into a position to throw down a challenge to the principals.

### 6339 SODEXHO PRESTIGE H'CAP — 2m

**1:45** (1:46) (D2) (0-92,79) 3-Y-0+ **£7,559** (£2,326; £1,163; £581) **Stalls** High

Form / RPR

1410 **1** **Stoop To Conquer**$^{41}$ 5472 4-9-8 **76** TQuinn 11 — 84+
(JLDunlop) *lw: trckd ldrs: wnt 2nd over 7f out: led over 2f out: drvn and styd on wl fnl f* **6/1**$^{2}$

0000 **2** *3½* **Teresa**$^{35}$ 5619 4-9-2 **70** RLMoore 13 — 74
(JLDunlop) *bhd: hdwy 1/2-way: chsd ldrs 7f out: rdn fr over 2f out: styd on to take 2nd nr fin but no imp on wnr* **20/1**

0140 **3** *½* **Bill Bennett (FR)**$^{20}$ 5944 3-9-0 **78** GBaker 9 — 81
(JJay) *in tch: hdwy 5f out: drvn to chse ldrs over 3f out: kpt on to dispute 2nd ins last but no imp on wnr* **16/1**

2000 **4** *shd* **Linens Flame**$^{30}$ 5728 5-9-3 **71** PJSmullen 5 — 74
(BGPowell) *led: rdn and hdd over 2f out: styd chsng wnr but no imp: wknd and lost 2nd nr fin* **14/1**

6343 **5** *18* **Marine City (JPN)**$^{24}$ 5850 3-8-7 **71** (p) MHenry 3 — 52
(MAJarvis) *lw: bhd: rdn and sme hdwy 5f out: sn no imp: kpt on for poor 5th fnl 2f* **12/1**

3215 **6** *8* **Irish Blade (IRE)**$^{12}$ 6084 3-8-13 **77** DaneO'Neill 1 — 49
(HCandy) *lw: b.hind: chsd ldr to 7f out: rdn and wknd fr 3f out* **9/1**

6111 **7** *15* **Trilemma**$^{24}$ 5850 3-9-1 **79** SSanders 6 — 33
(SirMarkPrescott) *lw: hld up in rr: hdwy 6f out: rdn 5f out: wknd ins fnl 4f* **7/4**$^{1}$

2443 **8** *2½* **Dr Cerullo**$^{30}$ 5728 3-8-9 **73** JFortune 2 — 24
(CTinkler) *in tch: pushed along 7f out: wknd 3f out* **7/1**$^{3}$

3003 **9** *2½* **Desert Island Disc**$^{7}$ 6185 7-9-6 **74** TPQueally 12 — 22
(JJBridger) *b.front: sn bhd* **33/1**

0-50 **10** *10* **Seeyaaj**$^{35}$ 5615 4-9-9 **77** SHitchcott 7 — 13
(JonjoO'Neill) *bhd: rdn and effrt 5f out: sn wknd* **25/1**

43-2 **11** *11* **Tomina**$^{188}$ 1457 4-9-7 **75** SDrowne 8 — —
(MissECLavelle) *bkwd: mid-div: wknd 5f* **9/1**

225 **12** *dist* **Jayer Gilles**$^{76}$ 4554 4-9-10 **78** CCatlin 10 — —
(HCandy) *b.hind: pressed ldrs tl wknd over 7f out: t.o* **50/1**

5000 **13** *7* **Sun Hill**$^{12}$ 6084 4-8-11 **65** RHavlin 4 — —
(MBlanshard) *mid-div: wknd 7f out: t.o* **40/1**

3m 44.91s (9.48) **Going Correction** +0.70s/f (Yiel)
**WFA** 3 from 4yo+ 10lb **13** Ran SP% **119.3**
Speed ratings: **104,102,102,101,92 88,81,80,78,73 68,—,—**CSF £126.75 CT £1832.74 TOTE £5.10: £2.20, £7.40, £5.00; EX 124.20 Trifecta £1052.20 Pool £1,482.76. 1 winning unit.
**Owner** I H Stewart-Brown & M J Meacock **Bred** I Stewart-Brown And M Meacock **Trained** Arundel, W Sussex

**FOCUS**
A thorough test of stamina and very few got into it. With the favourite failing to run her race and only four horses running their races, the form is not strong.

**NOTEBOOK**
**Stoop To Conquer** has plenty of stamina in his pedigree and these conditions brought out the best in him. Successful three times from seven starts this season, he now goes to the sales.
**Teresa** stayed on well to finish runner-up and returned to her spring form. She is well handicapped based on those efforts and could well find a race before the season is out. *Official explanation: jockey said filly hung right throughout*
**Bill Bennett(FR)** is not that badly handicapped at present and ran his race in conditions he loves. His record on good to soft ground or worse now reads 31127143.
**Linens Flame**, below form on quicker ground over shorter of late, is another who revels in the mud. He returned to form but remains a touch high in the weights.
**Marine City(JPN)**, who won her maiden on soft ground, could never reach the leaders having been held up off the pace. She plodded on for a clear fifth.
**Trilemma** was under pressure a fair way out and just could not pick up the leaders in the straight. She was nursed home in the end and the ground must be the likeliest cause of her defeat, although there is also the chance that she has just had enough for the season.
**Sun Hill** *Official explanation: jockey said gelding was unsuited by the soft, heavy in places ground*

### 6340 STAN JAMES HORRIS HILL STKS (GROUP 3) (C&G) — 7f (S)

**2:20** (2:25) (A1) 2-Y-O **£23,200** (£8,800; £4,400; £2,000) **Stalls** Centre

Form / RPR

1113 **1** **Cupid's Glory**$^{33}$ 5680 2-8-9 100 SSanders 8 — 107+
(SirMarkPrescott) *lw: sn in tch: hdwy over 2f out: led over 1f out: pushed clr ins last: forged clr last half f: easily* **2/1**$^{1}$

1101 **2** *4* **Johnny Jumpup (IRE)**$^{41}$ 5457 2-8-9 96 JFEgan 7 — 97
(RMBeckett) *trckd ldrs: rdn to ld ins fnl 2f: hdd over 1f out: kpt on wl fnl f to hold clr 2nd but no ch w wnr* **12/1**

6212 **3** *2½* **King Marju (IRE)**$^{12}$ 6090 2-8-9 85 TQuinn 13 — 91
(PWChapple-Hyam) *s.i.s: plld hrd: hdwy 1/2-way: rdn to chse ldrs over 1f out: styd on same pce ins last* **11/1**

1214 **4** *2* **Brecon Beacon**$^{70}$ 4716 2-8-9 100 SDrowne 10 — 86
(PFICole) *bhd: rdn and styd on fr over 2f out: swtchd lft 1f out: styd on same pce fnl f* **10/1**

222 **5** *½* **Woodsley House (IRE)**$^{51}$ 5227 2-8-9 88 RHavlin 11 — 85
(MrsPNDutfield) *bhd: rdn fr 3f out: styd on ins fnl f but nvr gng pce to rch ldrs* **66/1**

3221 **6** *3* **Foxhaven**$^{10}$ 6151 2-8-9 88 MartinDwyer 12 — 78
(PRChamings) *sn pressing ldrs: rdn and edgd lft over 1f out: wknd ins last* **20/1**

4101 **7** *½* **Sudden Dismissal (IRE)**$^{23}$ 5872 2-8-9 95 EAhern 5 — 77
(GAButler) *lw: chsd ldrs: rdn over 2f out: wknd over 1f out* **16/1**

144 **8** *1¼* **St Andrews Storm (USA)**$^{98}$ 3907 2-8-9 100 DaneO'Neill 9 — 74
(RHannon) *bhd: hdwy 3f out: nvr gng pce to rch ldrs: edgd lft and wknd over 1f out* **25/1**

21 **9** *¾* **Dhaular Dhar (IRE)**$^{41}$ 5455 2-8-9 90 MHills 6 — 72
(BWHills) *chsd ldr: led over 2f out: hdd ins fnl 2f: sn wknd* **11/2**$^{3}$

6222 **10** *1¾* **Embossed (IRE)**$^{7}$ 6189 2-8-9 100 RLMoore 2 — 68
(RHannon) *wnt rt s: sn chsng ldrs: rdn 3f out: wknd 2f out* **9/2**$^{2}$

21 **11** *½* **Russian Consort (IRE)**$^{76}$ 4544 2-8-9 88 JDSmith 3 — 67
(AKing) *bmpd and s.i.s: sn in tch: rdn 3f out: wknd 2f out* **33/1**

311 **12** *9* **The Pheasant Flyer**$^{31}$ 5721 2-8-9 88 JFortune 4 — 45
(BJMeehan) *lw: led tl hdd over 2f out: sn wknd* **20/1**

1 **13** *20* **Zohar (USA)**$^{48}$ 5290 2-8-9 PJSmullen 1 — —
(BJMeehan) *in tch to 1/2-way: sn bhd* **22/1**

1m 28.95s (1.73) **Going Correction** +0.475s/f (Yiel) **13** Ran SP% **120.1**
Speed ratings: **109,104,101,99,98 95,94,93,92,90 89,79,56**CSF £25.31 TOTE £3.40: £1.80, £3.70, £3.40; EX 31.20.
**Owner** Hesmonds Stud **Bred** Cheveley Park Stud Ltd **Trained** Newmarket, Suffolk
■ Stewards Enquiry : E Ahern one-day ban: careless riding (Nov 2)

**FOCUS**
There was a decent pace on here and they finished well strung out. In a race that lacked strength in depth, Cupid's Glory looked some way ahead of the rest on his Irish form and showed only marginal improvement, while leaving the impression there is more to come.

**NOTEBOOK**
**Cupid's Glory** had the form in the book and did not need to improve much to win like this, but he was nevertheless impressive, finding a nice turn of foot in the testing conditions and quickly putting distance between himself and his rivals in the closing stages. He clearly appreciates this sort of ground and so his trainer is keen to run him again (in France) before the season is out. He looks a likely type for one of the Guineas on the continent next year.
**Johnny Jumpup(IRE)** hit the front inside the final two furlongs but the winner soon came by him. This was a good performance and clearly his poor effort in the Solario Stakes was a one off, as he has looked very progressive otherwise.
**King Marju(IRE)** did his chances, especially in this ground, no good by failing to settle. His rider could not get him any cover and in the circumstances he ran well to finish third.
**Brecon Beacon**, off the track for ten weeks following his disappointing effort when sent off favourite for a Listed contest here back in August, ran a respectable race from off the pace on a day when it proved an advantage to race prominently.
**Woodsley House(IRE)** had led on his previous three starts, but on this big step up in grade he found himself out the back for most of the way. Conditions did not favour horses who were held up off the pace and in the circumstances he ran well. He will be suited by a return to a mile.
**Foxhaven** did not get his own way in front this time and had softer ground to contend with too.
**Embossed(IRE)** failed to run his race in these testing conditions.
**The Pheasant Flyer** *Official explanation: jockey said gelding ran flat*
**Zohar(USA)** *Official explanation: jockey said colt was unsuited by the soft, heavy in places ground*

### 6341 Q ASSOCIATES H'CAP — 6f 8y

**2:55** (2:58) (C1) (0-107,98) 3-Y-0+ **£12,550** (£4,760; £2,380; £1,081) **Stalls** Centre

Form / RPR

0146 **1** **Onlytime Will Tell**$^{34}$ 5628 6-8-11 **90** JFanning 3 — 102
(DNicholls) *lw: b.front: trckd ldrs: led appr fnl 2f: drvn and hld on wl fnl f* **5/1**$^{2}$

0460 **2** ¾ **Danzig River (IRE)**[13] 6071 3-8-6 **86** ........ MHills 6 96
(BWHills) *t.k.h: trckd ldrs: n.m.r over 2f out: drvn and hdwy over 1f out: styd on to chse wnr ins last: no imp cl home* **9/1**

6014 **3** 1¼ **Chateau Nicol**[4] 6277 5-8-4 **83** ........ (b) TQuinn 10 90
(BGPowell) *lw: chsd ldrs: rdn to chal fr over 1f out: stl upsides jst ins last: outpcd last half f* **6/1**[3]

0200 **4** 1½ **Marsad (IRE)**[13] 6071 10-8-5 **84** ........ PDoe 8 86
(JAkehurst) *bhd: swtchd lft and hdwy fr 2f out: styd on ins fnl f: nt rch ldrs* **10/1**

0100 **5** shd **Pic Up Sticks**[5] 6243 5-9-4 **97** ........ SHitchcott 2 99
(MRChannon) *t.k.h: hld up in rr: hdwy and n.m.r ins fnl 2f: rdn and one pce fr over 1f out* **10/1**

0000 **6** shd **Grizedale (IRE)**[13] 6070 5-8-4 **83** oh1 ........ (t) SWhitworth 12 88+
(JAkehurst) *hld up in rr: effrt and hmpd 2f out: stl n.m.r 1f out: swtchd lft and r.o last half f: gng on cl home* **25/1**

1502 **7** nk **King's Caprice**[7] 6191 3-8-8 **88** ........ SCarson 9 89
(GBBalding) *pressed ldrs: rdn over 2f out: styd on same pce fnl f* **10/3**[1]

0022 **8** 5 **If Paradise**[6] 6177 3-9-4 **98** ........ DaneO'Neill 4 85
(RHannon) *lw: chsd ldrs: rdn over 2f out: wknd over 1f out* **12/1**

5106 **9** 6 **Saristar**[22] 5898 3-8-8 **88** ........ SDrowne 7 59
(PFICole) *chsd ldrs: rdn 1/2-way: wknd over 2f out* **20/1**

0002 **10** hd **Totally Yours (IRE)**[23] 5874 3-8-3 **83** ........ RLMoore 5 53
(WRMuir) *led tl hdd & wknd over 2f out* **14/1**

1200 **11** 1¾ **Mr Lambros**[20] 5937 3-8-4 **84** ........ MartinDwyer 11 49
(AMBalding) *lw: chsd ldrs tl wknd qckly over 2f out* **10/1**

3050 **12** 2½ **Mazepa (IRE)**[21] 5921 4-8-11 **90** ........ JFEgan 1 49
(NACallaghan) *rdn 1/2-way: a bhd* **33/1**

1m 16.53s (2.16) **Going Correction** +0.475s/f (Yiel)
**WFA** 3 from 4yo+ 1lb **12** Ran SP% **117.2**
Speed ratings: **104,103,101,99,99 98,98,92,84,83 81,78**CSF £47.70 CT £281.44 TOTE £5.30: £2.30, £3.00, £2.10; EX 72.50.
**Owner** D Faulkner & J Hair **Bred** L C And Mrs A E Sigsworth **Trained** Sessay, N Yorks

**FOCUS**

A competitive handicap and once again it proved an advantage to race up with the pace. Straightforward form to rate, with the first three all running to their recent best.

**NOTEBOOK**

**Onlytime Will Tell**, who ran well in the Ayr Gold Cup on his last start and acts well in the soft, was 1lb lower here and, racing up with the pace throughout, held on well from his persistent challengers.

**Danzig River(IRE)**, who has had a disappointing season following a promising juvenile campaign, kept on well for second and has dropped to a reasonable mark. He seems to go on any ground.

**Chateau Nicol**, 2lb higher than when a narrow winner here last month, is probably at his best over seven furlongs but he is clearly perfectly capable over this shorter trip, especially when there is an emphasis on stamina.

**Marsad(IRE)** is on a long losing run but his handicap mark has not benefited greatly. He ran a fair race from off the pace.

**Pic Up Sticks**, who needs to be covered up and have everything fall just right, could not pick up when asked to challenge. He is a little high in the handicap now.

**Grizedale(IRE)** ◆ ideally needs farther than this and, following a disappointing season, this luckless run hinted at a return to form. He is well handicapped now and could be one to look out for during the closing weeks of the turf season.

**King's Caprice** is due to go up another 4lb in the handicap and this performance suggests the assessor may have his measure for the time being.

## 6342 JAMES & COWPER MAIDEN STKS 6f 8y

**3:30** (3:33) (D2) 2-Y-O **£5,980** (£1,840; £920; £460) **Stalls** Centre

Form RPR

00 **1** **Bailey Gate**[49] 5271 2-8-9 ........ RLMoore 13 82+
(RHannon) *bhd: hdwy over 3f out: led ins fnl 2f: pushed clr ins last: readily* **13/2**[3]

**2** 3½ **Westland (USA)** 2-9-0 ........ SSanders 8 79+
(MrsAJPerrett) *tall: wl grwn: scope: bwkd: s.i.s: bhd: stdy hdwy 1/2-way: trcking ldrs whn n.m.r 2f out: drvn to chse wnr 1f out: kpt on s* **7/1**

**3** 2½ **Holiday Camp (USA)** 2-9-0 ........ MHills 7 71
(BWHills) *rangy: str: scope: bkwd: s.i.s: sn rcvrd to chse ldrs: drvn to chal 2f out: wknd fnl f* **11/4**[1]

00 **4** 2½ **Final Promise**[23] 5872 2-9-0 ........ SCarson 14 64+
(GBBalding) *broke wl: stdd rr: hld up: hdwy fr 2f out: styd on fnl f but n.d* **33/1**

464 **5** 4 **World Report (USA)**[10] 6145 2-9-0 ........ DaneO'Neill 6 53
(RHannon) *chsd ldrs: rdn over 2f out: wknd over 1f out* **3/1**[2]

**6** 3 **Darsharp** 2-8-6 ........ BReilly[(3)] 9 39
(MissGayKelleway) *leggy: chsd ldrs: drvn to chal over 2f out: wknd and edgd lft over 1f out* **33/1**

**7** ½ **Prime Contender** 2-9-0 ........ JFortune 1 43+
(BWHills) *leggy: scope: bit bkwd: slowly away: wl bhd 1/2-way: styd on wl fr over 1f out but n.d* **16/1**

00 **8** 1¼ **Flying Heart**[11] 6126 2-8-9 ........ CCatlin 5 35
(MRChannon) *in tch: rdn to chse ldrs over 2f out: sn wknd* **25/1**

**9** 1 **Physical (IRE)** 2-9-0 ........ MartinDwyer 10 37
(MrsAJPerrett) *tall: str: scope: bkwd: s.i.s: bhd: sme hdwy into mid-div: 3f out: sn rdn: wknd 2f out* **11/1**

0 **10** 5 **Virgin's Tears**[13] 6067 2-8-9 ........ AMcCarthy 12 18
(PWChapple-Hyam) *lw: chsd ldrs: led ins fnl 3f: hdd ins fnl 2f: sn wknd* **8/1**

00 **11** ¾ **Speedy Spirit**[12] 6078 2-8-9 ........ SWhitworth 2 16
(MSalaman) *chsd ldrs tl wknd qckly over 2f out* **100/1**

**12** ½ **Young Valentino** 2-9-0 ........ TPQueally 4 20
(AWCarroll) *leggy: scope: bit bkwd: in tch: rdn 3f out: sn wknd* **50/1**

0 **13** 3 **Mad Marty Wildcard**[11] 6125 2-8-11 ........ DNolan[(3)] 3 11
(RBrotherton) *bkwd: sn outpcd* **100/1**

6 **14** ½ **Clipper Hoy**[171] 1871 2-9-0 ........ GBaker 11 10
(MrsHSweeting) *bkwd: led tl hdd ins fnl 3f: sn wknd* **100/1**

1m 18.25s (3.88) **Going Correction** +0.475s/f (Yiel) **14** Ran SP% **117.5**
Speed ratings: **93,88,85,81,76 72,71,70,68,62 61,60,56,55**CSF £48.38 TOTE £8.40: £2.50, £2.20, £1.90; EX 51.00.
**Owner** Timothy N Chick **Bred** Pigeon House Stud **Trained** East Everleigh, Wilts

**FOCUS**

A modest maiden for the track. The winner had experience on her side and coped well with the conditions.

**NOTEBOOK**

**Bailey Gate** had shown promise on her debut but disappointed on fast ground last time. She reportedly had a dirty nose following that outing, too, so clearly all was not well. Back on an easier surface, she beat an ordinary field in good style.

**Westland(USA)**, a $180,000 buy, is out of a mare who won three times on turf in the US. Staying on well from off the pace following a slow start, he looks sure to improve a good deal for the run, as do most of his stable's juveniles.

**Holiday Camp(USA)**, whose stable had won this race four times in the previous nine years, was supported in the ring. A half-brother to several winners in France and the US, over sprint and middle-distances, he looks likely to appreciate farther next year.

**Final Promise** ran his best race to date, staying on well towards the finish. He is now eligible for handicaps.

**World Report(USA)** looked to have a solid chance given that he had the benefit of previous racing experience over many of his rivals, but he was weak in the market and was soon beaten when he came under pressure.

**Darsharp** showed up well for a long way and could be one to follow for the All-Weather over the winter.

**Virgin's Tears** was weak in the market and failed to shine in the ground, despite her breeding.

## 6343 JACK COLLING POLAR JEST APPRENTICE H'CAP 1m 1f

**4:00** (4:02) (E3) (0-77,73) 3-Y-O+ **£4,032** (£1,240; £620; £310) **Stalls** Centre

Form RPR

105 **1** **Mcqueen (IRE)**[28] 5768 4-9-0 **65** ........ NChalmers 3 81
(MrsHDalton) *bhd: hdwy over 3f out: led over 2f out: drvn out fnl f* **13/2**[3]

6432 **2** 1½ **Cormorant Wharf (IRE)**[40] 5493 4-8-9 **65** ........ JemmaMarshall[(5)] 17 78
(TEPowell) *bhd: hdwy fr 3f out: styd on to chse wnr 1f out but no imp ins last* **25/1**

0000 **3** 4 **Count Boris**[46] 5352 3-7-12 **58** ........ TDean[(5)] 1 64
(GBBalding) *bhd: rdn 4f out: styd on u.p fnl 2f: kpt on wl to chse ldrs ins last but n.d* **33/1**

2403 **4** 2½ **Loaded Gun**[10] 6141 4-7-13 **55** oh2 ........ LiamJones[(5)] 12 56
(WMBrisbourne) *bhd: rdn and hdwy 3f out: styd on same pce fr over 1f out* **14/1**

21-6 **5** 5 **Pequenita**[165] 2000 4-8-13 **69** ........ (b) JJones[(5)] 11 61
(GLMoore) *lw: in tch: chsd ldrs 4f out: rdn and grad brought to stands side fr over 2f out but n.d after* **40/1**

3200 **6** 3½ **General**[10] 6152 7-9-1 **66** ........ MSavage 16 52
(CRDore) *in tch: hdwy 5f out: chsd ldrs 4f out: wknd 2f out* **12/1**

6-02 **7** nk **Cornish Gold**[49] 5258 3-8-8 **63** ........ NDeSouza 13 48
(NJHenderson) *lw: bhd: hdwy 4f out: chsd ldrs fr 3f out: wknd 2f out* **16/1**

3063 **8** ¾ **Didnt Tell My Wife**[2] 6311 5-8-9 **65** ........ SO'Hara[(5)] 4 49
(CFWall) *hld up in rr: hdwy to chse ldrs 3f out: sn rdn: wknd fr 2f out* **7/2**[2]

1000 **9** 1¾ **Dark Raider (IRE)**[12] 6081 3-9-1 **70** ........ WJLee 5 51
(APJones) *chsd ldrs: rdn 4f out: wknd fr 3f out* **66/1**

5505 **10** 2 **Rood Boy (IRE)**[11] 6130 3-7-13 **61** ow6 ........ RKingscote[(7)] 9 38
(JSKing) *chsd ldr tl led 4f out: hdd & wknd over 2f out* **66/1**

1300 **11** 10 **Sienna Sunset (IRE)**[35] 5622 5-8-4 **58** ........ RoryMoore[(3)] 6 17
(WMBrisbourne) *b.hind: in tch: rdn over 3f out: sn btn* **20/1**

0220 **12** 2 **Mythical Charm**[27] 5795 5-8-1 **55** ........ (t) MHalford[(3)] 2 11
(JJBridger) *chsd ldrs: rdn over 3f out: sn wknd* **33/1**

2051 **13** 1½ **American Duke (USA)**[23] 5869 3-9-4 **73** ........ DFox 10 26
(BJMeehan) *chsd ldrs over 5f* **7/1**

2456 **14** nk **Elidore**[10] 6152 4-9-1 **66** ........ AQuinn 7 19
(BPalling) *led to 4f out: wknd 3f out* **33/1**

2040 **15** 3 **Mr Belvedere**[29] 5750 3-7-7 **55** oh5 ........ JDoyle[(7)] 8 2
(AJLidderdale) *bhd most of way* **66/1**

**16** 10 **Matouraka (FR)**[61] 3-8-11 **69** ........ ThomasYeung[(3)] 14 —
(PWChapple-Hyam) *lw: chsd ldrs tl wknd qckly fr 3f out: fin lame* **9/4**[1]

4033 **17** 9 **Catch The Fox**[11] 6130 4-8-1 **55** oh15 ........ StephanieHollinshead[(3)] 15 —
(JJBridger) *b.front: chsd ldrs: hung rt and wnt wd bnd 5f out: n.d* **66/1**

1m 59.74s (5.39) **Going Correction** +0.70s/f (Yiel)
**WFA** 3 from 4yo+ 4lb **17** Ran SP% **124.9**
Speed ratings: **104,102,99,96,92 89,89,88,86,85 76,74,73,72,70 61,53**CSF £167.69 CT £5070.73 TOTE £8.40: £2.00, £4.90, £7.20, £2.60; EX 187.50 Place 6 £280.36, Place 5 £156.26.

**Owner** R Edwards And W J Swinnerton **Bred** Philip Newton **Trained** Shifnal, Shropshire

**FOCUS**

Inevitably they finished well strung out in this finale.

**NOTEBOOK**

**Mcqueen(IRE)** goes well in soft ground and has been in cracking form in the second half of this season. He only had the runner-up to worry about inside the final quarter mile and could well win again if turned out quickly without a penalty.

**Cormorant Wharf(IRE)** coped well with these very different conditions, emphasizing his return to form. He is clearly handicapped to win a race at present.

**Count Boris**, who stayed on from off the pace, ran his best race to date on his handicap debut and did best of the three-year-olds.

**Loaded Gun**, who is still a maiden, is due to race off a 5lb higher mark in future and looks likely to struggle off his revised mark.

**Pequenita** is suited by soft ground but looks held off her current mark.

**Didnt Tell My Wife** looked to have plenty in his favour but ran surprisingly disappointingly.

**Matouraka(FR)**, twice a winner on the All-Weather at Deauville for her previous trainer, was well supported on her first run in this country. This was can be forgotten, as she finished lame, and she may well be one to keep an eye on if appearing on the sand over the winter. *Official explanation: trainer said filly finished lame*

**Catch The Fox** *Official explanation: jockey said gelding was hanging badly right-handed*

T/Jkpt: Not won. T/Plt: £852.20 to a £1 stake. Pool: £58,843.65. 50.40 winning tickets. T/Qpdt: £65.20 to a £1 stake. Pool: £6,003.50. 68.10 winning tickets. ST

# 6330 DONCASTER (L-H)

Saturday, October 23

**OFFICIAL GOING: Soft (heavy in places on round course)**

With just 1" rain between Tuesday and Thursday and dry since the riders reckoned the ground was more testing than the previous day, 'soft and sticky'.

Wind: Slight 1/2 against. Weather: Overcast with drizzle, rain last 3 races.

## 6344 "JOCK MURRAY MEMORIAL" NURSERY 7f

**1:50** (1:52) (C1) (0-95,89) 2-Y-O **£14,443** (£4,444; £2,222; £1,111) **Stalls** High

Form RPR

21 **1** **Crosspeace (IRE)**[24] 5857 2-9-2 **84** ........ RFfrench 1 91+
(MJohnston) *led after 1f: rdn along 2f out: styd on wl* **5/1**[2]

443 **2** ¾ **Top The Charts**[24] 5871 2-9-1 **83** ........ RLMoore 3 88
(RHannon) *dwlt: sn trcking ldrs on outer: hdwy over 2f out: rdn and ev ch over 1f out: drvn and one pce ins last* **11/1**

1241 **3** 2 **Hansomelle (IRE)**[18] 6003 2-8-9 **77** ........ DaleGibson 12 78
(BMactaggart) *trckd ldrs on stands rail: hdwy 2f out: sn rdn and kpt on same pce ent last* **14/1**

3210 **4** 1 **Red Affleck (USA)**[9] 6176 2-9-1 **83** ........ AMcCarthy 11 81
(PWChapple-Hyam) *chsd ldrs: hdwy over 2f out: sn rdn and ev ch tl drvn and wknd ent last* **14/1**

4351 **5** 5 **Taras Treasure (IRE)**[39] 5542 2-8-4 **72** ........ PHanagan 9 58
(JJQuinn) *wnt rt s: towards rr: hdwy over 2f out: sn rdn and no imp fr over 1f out* **25/1**

0251 **6** *1 ¾* **Cool Panic (IRE)**[56] 5128 2-9-1 **83** KFallon 14 65
(MLWBell) *prom: rdn along wl over 2f out: grad wknd* **15/2**[3]

6100 **7** *nk* **Press Express (IRE)**[8] 6188 2-8-7 **75** ACulhane 6 57
(MRChannon) *sn outpcd and bhd: hdwy 2f out: styd on appr last: nrst fin* **40/1**

01 **8** *1 ½* **Entailment**[57] 5096 2-8-8 **76** PRobinson 13 54
(MrsJRRamsden) *hld up towards rr: effrt and sme hdwy 2f out: nvr a factor* **16/1**

412 **9** *1 ½* **Daldini**[15] 6042 2-9-0 **82** SSanders 5 57
(JAOsborne) *towards rr and rdn along on outer 1/2-way: sme hdwy over 2f out: sn drvn and btn* **4/1**[1]

0501 **10** *shd* **Exit Smiling**[8] 6195 2-8-4 **72** ANicholls 2 46
(DNicholls) *led and swtchd rt after 100 yds: sn hdd and cl up tl rdn along and wknd wl over 2f out* **33/1**

2111 **11** *2 ½* **Toldo (IRE)**[5] 6265 2-8-5 **73** 6ex JMackay 4 41
(GMMoore) *prom: effrt to chal and ev ch over 2f out: sn rdn and wknd wl over 1f out* **9/1**

232 **12** *1 ¼* **Sam's Secret**[24] 5864 2-8-4 **72** FNorton 10 38
(JAGlover) *chsd ldrs: rdn along over 2f out: sn wknd* **9/1**

3000 **13** *½* **Sentiero Rosso (USA)**[14] 6068 2-9-1 **86** TEaves(3) 7 50
(BEllison) *in tch: rdn along 3f out: sn wknd* **25/1**

120 **14** *1 ½* **Buddy Brown**[44] 5417 2-9-7 **89** RWinston 8 50
(JHowardJohnson) *a rr* **12/1**

1m 30.89s (3.08) **Going Correction** +0.35s/f (Good) **14** Ran SP% **116.7**
Speed ratings: **96,95,92,91,86 84,83,81,80,80 77,75,75,73**CSF £54.80 CT £741.65 TOTE £6.50: £2.80, £4.20, £4.50; EX 81.70.
**Owner** Favourites Racing **Bred** Patrick Jones **Trained** Middleham Moor, N Yorks

**FOCUS**
A decent nursery not run at a strong pace early on and could be rated slightly higher, with the third and fourth the guide to the level.

**NOTEBOOK**
**Crosspeace(IRE)** ◆, on a potentially lenient mark on his nursery bow, always looked in control over this extra furlong and is clearly going the right away.
**Top The Charts** kept straight this time and made the winner knuckle down all the way to the line. A return to a mile will be in his favour.
**Hansomelle(IRE)**, who had luck on her side at Catterick, was racing from a 2lb higher mark. She is as game as a pebble.
**Red Affleck(USA)**, a keen type, again did not get home even though he was dropping back in trip.
**Taras Treasure(IRE)**, quite a big filly, was encountering soft ground for the first time. She will make an even better three-year-old.
**Cool Panic(IRE)**, encountering soft ground for the first time, wanted to do nothing but hang right. He will do much better at three, as he has plenty of size and scope. *Official explanation: jockey said colt hung right*
**Press Express(IRE)**, soon detached in last, put in some eye-catching late work. He has slipped to a handy mark and a return to a mile will suit.
**Daldini** was most disappointing, never going a yard.

## 6345 RACING POST WEEKENDER CONDITIONS STKS 7f
**2:25** (2:25) (B2) 3-Y-O+ **£7,523** (£2,853; £1,426; £648) **Stalls** High

Form RPR

1-02 **1** **Meshaheer (USA)**[36] 5610 5-8-9 105 (t) WSupple 2 107+
(SaeedBinSuroor) *bmpd s: t.k.h: trckd ldrs: smooth hdwy 2f out: qcknd to ld ins last: styd on* **10/3**[2]

0305 **2** *2* **Millennium Force**[20] 5972 6-8-9 104 KFallon 7 102
(MRChannon) *trckd ldr: hdwy 2f out: rdn to ld over 1f out: hdd and nt qckn ins last* **3/1**[1]

1653 **3** *nk* **Quito (IRE)**[8] 6190 7-9-2 105 (b) ACulhane 1 109
(DWChapman) *sltly hmpd s: hld up in rr: hdwy 2f out: rdn over 1f out: kpt on ins last: nrst fin* **10/3**[2]

10-0 **4** *nk* **Mutawaffer**[164] 2043 3-8-7 99 KDarley 9 101
(BWHills) *led: rdn along over 2f out: hdd over 1f out: sn drvn and one pce* **14/1**

-060 **5** *hd* **Cairns (UAE)**[127] 3033 3-8-8 107 TEDurcan 5 101
(SaeedBinSuroor) *trckd ldrs: hdwy over 2f out: rdn wl over 1f out and kpt on same pce* **9/1**

3004 **6** *5* **Traytonic**[28] 5781 3-9-0 101 RWinston 4 96
(JRFanshawe) *wnt lft s: hld up in rr: swtchd outside and hdwy over 2f out: sn rdn and no further prog* **8/1**[3]

-144 **7** *5* **Divine Gift**[12] 6116 3-9-0 102 PRobinson 6 84
(MAJarvis) *prom: rdn along 3f out: sn wknd* **33/1**

0552 **8** *5* **Membership (USA)**[226] 1006 4-8-9 RLMoore 8 65
(CEBrittain) *trckd ldrs: rdn along over 2f out: sn wknd* **12/1**

502/ **9** *18* **Typhoon Ginger (IRE)**[1106] 5265 9-8-4 60 PHanagan 10 18
(GWoodward) *wnt lft s and rdr lost iron: keen and in tch tl rdn along and outpcd wl over 2f out* **200/1**

1m 29.53s (1.72) **Going Correction** +0.35s/f (Good)
**WFA** 3 from 4yo+ 2lb **9** Ran SP% **110.1**
Speed ratings: **104,101,101,101,100 95,89,83,63**CSF £12.66 TOTE £4.80: £1.70, £1.60, £1.50; EX 17.60.
**Owner** Godolphin **Bred** Calogo Bloodstock And Bob Scarborough **Trained** Newmarket, Suffolk

**FOCUS**
A decent conditions event and, although no great pace for the first half mile, in the end quite an impressive winner, although the overall form is not totally solid.

**NOTEBOOK**
**Meshaheer(USA)**, edgy beforehand, travelled supremely well and, given a good lead, quickened up in good style and saw the trip out really well. He should hold his own in better company at six.
**Millennium Force**, who took this in similar ground two years ago, extended his losing sequence to 18 but basically he does little wrong.
**Quito(IRE)**, who has never looked in better shape, did not have the strong, end-to-end gallop he needs. He wriggled through a narrow gap and would have snatched second place with a bit further to go. A winner of 13 races, he looks sure to add to his record at eight.
**Mutawaffer**, who looked very fit indeed, was gifted a soft lead. He wound up the gallop but, on his first run since the Dante at York in May, was readily outspeeded.
**Cairns(UAE)**, absent since Royal Ascot, looked very fit but always looked to be struggling slightly on this ground though in the end far from disgraced.
**Traytonic**found this company too tough. He will now be gelded and hopefully will land a valuable handicap at four.
**Membership(USA)**, having his first outing here this year and his first since March, has yet to show he can handle ground as soft as this.
**Typhoon Ginger(IRE)** *Official explanation: jockey said he lost an iron coming out of the stalls*

## 6346 RACING POST £1 MILLION TOTETENTOFOLLOW H'CAP 1m 4f
**2:55** (2:55) (C1) (0-107,90) 3-Y-O+ **£14,099** (£4,338; £2,169; £1,084) **Stalls** Low

Form RPR

5050 **1** **Tempsford (USA)**[7] 6215 4-9-3 **86** SSanders 3 96
(SirMarkPrescott) *mde all: rdn over 2f out: drvn ent last and styd on wl* **10/1**

5450 **2** *1 ¼* **Millville**[22] 5919 4-9-2 **85** PRobinson 12 93
(MAJarvis) *racd wd to 1/2-way: trckd ldrs: hdwy 3f out: rdn to chse wnr wl over 1f out and ch tl drvn and one pce ins last* **9/1**

5050 **3** *½* **Bendarshaan**[9] 6172 4-9-0 **83** KDarley 2 90
(MJohnston) *trckd wnr: hdwy over 2f out: rdn wl over 1f out: drvn and kpt on ins last* **20/1**

0405 **4** *2 ½* **Odiham**[12] 6121 3-8-11 **87** RLMoore 8 93+
(HMorrison) *racd wd to 1/2-way: hld up and bhd: swtchd outside and hdwy over 2f out: sn rdn and styd on appr last: nrst fin* **11/2**[3]

0024 **5** *5* **Cruise Director**[29] 5768 4-9-2 **85** KFallon 7 86+
(WJMusson) *racd wd to 1/2-way: hld up in rr: hdwy 3f out: rdn along 2f out and sn no imp* **5/1**[2]

6500 **6** *¾* **Flotta**[9] 6172 5-8-12 **81** TEDurcan 6 79+
(MRChannon) *racd wd to 1/2-way: hld up towards rr: hdwy over 3f out: rdn over 2f out and sn no imp* **40/1**

6216 **7** *1 ½* **Countrywide Luck**[21] 5942 3-8-7 **86** J-PGuillambert(3) 11 80
(NPLittmoden) *racd wd to 1/2-way: hld up and bhd: swtchd outside and effrt 3f out: rdn and hung lft 2f out: nvr nr ldrs* **10/1**

4000 **8** *1 ½* **Santando**[43] 5435 4-9-5 **88** SCarson 9 80
(CEBrittain) *racd wd to 1/2-way: trckd ldrs: hdwy to chse wnr 4f out: rdn along wl over 2f out and sn wknd* **40/1**

4003 **9** *2 ½* **Protective**[26] 5834 3-8-10 **86** DAllen 1 74
(JGGiven) *trckd ldrs: rdn along over 3f out: grad wknd* **14/1**

2103 **10** *2 ½* **Soulacroix**[9] 6172 3-9-0 **90** ACulhane 10 75
(MrsAJPerrett) *racd wd and led that gp to 1/2-way: chsd wnr 5f out: rdn along over 3f out and sn wknd* **9/2**[1]

0020 **11** *1 ½* **Jabaar (USA)**[15] 6043 6-9-1 **84** RWinston 4 66
(MWEasterby) *racd wd to 1/2-way: chsd ldrs: rdn along over 4f out and sn wknd* **20/1**

0120 **12** *14* **Qudraat (IRE)**[12] 6121 3-8-11 **87** WSupple 13 50
(EFVaughan) *racd wd to 1/2-way: in tch: rdn along over 3f out: sn btn* **9/1**

1240 **13** *1 ½* **Cold Turkey**[45] 5401 4-9-7 **90** SWhitworth 5 51
(GLMoore) *chsd ldrs: rdn along over 4f out and sn wknd* **9/1**

2m 40.89s (5.19) **Going Correction** +0.625s/f (Yiel)
**WFA** 3 from 4yo+ 7lb **13** Ran SP% **119.5**
Speed ratings: **107,106,105,104,100 100,99,98,96,95 94,84,83**CSF £92.81 CT £1768.37 TOTE £13.50: £4.60, £3.30, £6.00; EX 126.10 TRIFECTA Not won..
**Owner** Syndicate 2001 **Bred** Richard S Trontz, Et Al **Trained** Newmarket, Suffolk

**FOCUS**
The ground on the round course looked even more testing. Four stuck to the inside route including the winner in what was in effect a 0-90 handicap. Although the race was slightly messy, the placed horses give the form a solid appearance.

**NOTEBOOK**
**Tempsford(USA)**, who pulled very hard in the Cesarewitch, settled well in front this time and basically galloped them into the ground. The jumping boys will have their eyes on him.
**Millville**, who for some reason never shines at Newmarket, unlike the winner was taken wide until the home turn. He stuck on well but could never get in a serious blow. The trip and the ground were clearly no problem.
**Bendarshaan**, back on a winning mark, looked on the lean side but this marked a return to form after some lacklustre efforts of late.
**Odiham**, a positive on the betting front, became very upset beforehand. Forced to pull wide halfway up the straight, he stayed on all the way to the line despite a marked tendency to hang left, but he was never going to enter the argument. *Official explanation: jockey said gelding hung left*
**Cruise Director**, who could have done with an even stronger gallop, had the ground to suit but never threatened.
**Flotta**, just 1lb higher than his last success, has never shone on ground as testing as this.
**Soulacroix**, running off the same mark, had the ground to suit but this was a very poor effort.
**Qudraat(IRE)** *Official explanation: jockey said colt was unsuited by the soft ground*

## 6347 RACING POST TROPHY (GROUP 1) (ENTIRE COLTS & FILLIES) 1m (S)
**3:30** (3:32) (A1) 2-Y-O **£120,000** (£46,000; £23,000; £11,000) **Stalls** Low

Form RPR

1 **1** **Motivator**[71] 4728 2-9-0 KFallon 5 118+
(MLWBell) *trckd ldrs: smooth hdwy to ld 21/2f out: rdn and edgd rt over 1f out: styd on strly* **6/4**[1]

1 **2** *2 ½* **Albert Hall**[13] 6100 2-9-0 JPSpencer 7 111
(APO'Brien, Ire) *rangy: angular: hld up in rr: smooth hdwy 3f out: rdn to chse ldrs 2f out: sn drvn and wandered over 1f out: kpt on ins las* **5/2**[2]

12 **3** *1* **Henrik**[107] 3672 2-9-0 TEDurcan 2 109
(MRChannon) *hld up in tch: smooth hdwy to chse wnr 2f out: rdn and ch over 1f out: drvn and one pce ins last* **12/1**

**4** *8* **Hills Of Aran**[46] 5384 2-9-0 CO'Donoghue 1 93
(APO'Brien, Ire) *rangy: unf: led: hdd over 4f out: rdn along 3f out: drvn and outpcd fr over 2f out* **11/1**

6215 **5** *6* **Beaver Patrol (IRE)**[21] 5947 2-9-0 100 SCarson 6 82
(RFJohnsonHoughton) *trckd ldrs on outer: hdwy and prom 1/2-way: rdn along 3f out and sn outpcd* **25/1**

5105 **6** *6* **Berkhamsted (IRE)**[6] 6259 2-9-0 100 RLMoore 4 70
(JAOsborne) *chsd ldrs: rdn along wl over 3f out: sn outpcd* **20/1**

1164 **7** *17* **Elliots World (IRE)**[28] 5778 2-9-0 100 KDarley 3 36
(MJohnston) *cl up: led over 4f out: rdn along and hdd 2f out: sn wknd* **13/2**[3]

235 **8** *shd* **Frith (IRE)**[28] 5778 2-9-0 100 SSanders 8 36
(BWHills) *prom on outer: rdn along 1/2-way: sn wknd* **18/1**

1m 41.62s (0.02) **Going Correction** +0.35s/f (Good) **8** Ran SP% **111.8**
Speed ratings: **113,110,109,101,95 89,72,72**CSF £4.97 TOTE £2.50: £1.50, £1.50, £1.90; EX 6.10 Trifecta £38.40 Pool £1,493.50, 27.60 winning units.
**Owner** The Royal Ascot Racing Club **Bred** Deerfield Farm **Trained** Newmarket, Suffolk

**FOCUS**
Not a vintage renewal but a strong pace and an unbeaten winner of real potential. The stalls were on the far side and for the first three furlongs they raced on virgin ground.

**NOTEBOOK**
**Motivator**, long in the back and under-developed as yet, has a choppy action. Tackling a Group One on the back of his maiden win at Newmarket, he came there full of running to take charge and, despite edging right, ran out a most decisive winner. He is on the edge of the Classic picture for next year but how he will cope with fast ground must be a real concern.
**Albert Hall**, taken down quietly and last, was inclined to get a bit warm. When sent in pursuit of the leading pair he seemed to be galloping at an angle and was never going to get near the winner. He will be more mature and stronger at three, but whether he can make an impact at the top level remains to be seen.
**Henrik**, a tall type, travelled supremely well but when asked to match strides with the winner he seemed to flounder in the ground. He should make a smart three-year-old but a mile might be the limit of his stamina.
**Hills Of Aran**, winner of a Galway maiden, lacks any real substance and has a very short stride. He was simply not up to this task.
**Beaver Patrol(IRE)**, who has a very choppy action, was basically out of his depth.

**Berkhamsted(IRE)**, winner of a Listed race at Deauville, has struggled to make a real impact at a higher level.
**Elliots World(IRE)**, isolated beforehand to keep him cool and calm, became warm down at the start and after showing ahead he dropped right away. His temperament is becoming a cause for concern and he has not progressed since winning on his first two starts.
**Frith(IRE)**, who stands over plenty of ground, has a long flowing stride and underfoot conditions counted heavily against him.

## 6348 AT THE RACES RED BUTTON BETTING DONCASTER STKS (LISTED RACE) 6f

4:05 (4:06) (A1) 2-Y-O £16,250 (£5,000; £2,500; £1,250) Stalls High

Form RPR
120 **1** **Andronikos**[35] 5649 2-8-9 100.....................(t) KFallon 2 104
(PFICole) *trckd ldrs: hdwy 2f out: rdn to ld 1f out: styd on wl* **10/3**[1]
1520 **2** *2* **Harvest Warrior**[21] 5947 2-8-9 97..................... DAllan 7 99
(TDEasterby) *squeezed out and bhd after 1f: pushed along 1/2-way: swtchd lft and hdwy wl over 1f out: swtchd rt and styd on wl fnl f* **10/1**[3]
144 **3** *1 1/4* **Joseph Henry**[7] 6212 2-8-9 100..................... KDarley 4 95
(MJohnston) *led: rdn along 2f out: drvn and hdd 1f out: grad wknd* **4/1**[2]
0203 **4** *3/4* **Gifted Gamble**[9] 6174 2-8-9 84..................... RWinston 1 93
(KARyan) *trckd ldrs: hdwy on outer over 2f out: rdn and ev ch over 1f out: sn drvn and wknd ent last* **16/1**
1105 **5** *9* **Lady Filly**[113] 3481 2-8-4 94..................... ADaly 5 63
(WGMTurner) *chsd ldr: rdn along wl over 2f out and sn wknd* **25/1**
061 **6** *nk* **Ecologically Right**[25] 5847 2-8-4 75..................... WSupple 6 62
(MrsJRRamsden) *squeezed out s: a rr* **25/1**
1122 **7** *9* **Cornus**[7] 6212 2-8-9 95..................... RLMoore 8 43
(RHannon) *chsd ldrs: rdn along wl over 2f out: sn wknd* **10/3**[1]
310 **8** *15* **Dramaticus**[22] 5918 2-8-9 100..................... SSanders 9 1
(DRLoder) *trckd ldrs: effrt over 2f out: sn rdn and wknd* **10/3**[1]

1m 15.82s (1.54) **Going Correction** +0.35s/f (Good) **8** Ran SP% **111.9**
Speed ratings: **103,100,98,97,85 85,73,53**CSF £35.66 TOTE £4.40: £1.60, £3.20, £1.70; EX 43.10.
**Owner** C Shiacolas **Bred** Mrs R D Peacock **Trained** Whatcombe, Oxon

**FOCUS**
A strongly-run Listed race and an improved performance by the winner who was wearing a tongue strap for the first time.

**NOTEBOOK**
**Andronikos**, fitted with a tongue strap, travelled strongly and this big type took this Listed race in most decisive fashion. He has the scope to do well at three.
**Harvest Warrior**, a tall type, did not have the run of the race and in the circumstances did very well but he was only second best anyway.
**Joseph Henry** is settling down with racing. He set a very strong pace and should make a very useful sprinter at three.
**Gifted Gamble**, suited by the soft, ran easily his best race yet on his 13th start. On the other side of the account his handicap rating will shoot up as a result.
**Lady Filly**, absent since finishing lame at Sandown, showed bags of toe but five furlongs may be as far as she wants to go.
**Ecologically Right**, a handful to load, lost her chance at the start. It may prove a blessing in disguise at three, because a prominent showing would have blown her potentially lenient handicap mark out of the water.
**Cornus**, having his second outing in a week after an enforced lay-off, seemed to lose his action altogether and in the end struggled to reach the finishing line. *Official explanation: jockey said colt lost its action*
**Dramaticus**, who wore a cross noseband, dropped out in a matter of strides and floundered badly. This was simply too bad to be true. *Official explanation: jockey said colt lost its action*

## 6349 RECTANGLE GROUP H'CAP 5f

4:40 (4:40) (C1) (0-107,99) 3-Y-O+ £12,101 (£4,590; £2,295; £1,043) Stalls High

Form RPR
5000 **1** **Matty Tun**[5] 6267 5-8-7 85 oh4..................... WSupple 13 99
(JBalding) *keen: hld up: gd hdwy 2f out: rdn and qcknd to ld ins* **16/1**
4003 **2** *3/4* **Whitbarrow (IRE)**[6] 6243 5-8-9 87..................... FNorton 6 99
(JMBradley) *prom: rdn to ld over 1f out: drvn and hdd ins last: kpt on* **12/1**
3500 **3** *1 1/4* **Tom Tun**[14] 6071 9-9-2 94..................... (b) TLucas 4 102
(JBalding) *in tch: hdwy on outer to chse ldrs wl over 1f out: sn rdn and kpt on same pce ent last* **11/1**
0400 **4** *1/2* **Bond Boy**[7] 6205 7-8-7 85 oh1..................... KDarley 11 91
(BSmart) *in rr: hdwy 2f out: sn rdn and kpt on ins last: nrst fin* **12/1**
3212 **5** *1/2* **Corridor Creeper (FR)**[6] 6243 7-9-7 99..................... (p) RLMoore 9 103
(JMBradley) *prom: rdn along and ch wl over 1f out: sn drvn and one pce ent last* **5/1**[2]
6500 **6** *1 1/4* **Bishops Court**[9] 6177 10-9-3 95..................... SSanders 5 95
(MrsJRRamsden) *trckd ldrs: effrt 2f out: sn rdn and kpt on same pce appr last* **20/1**
3524 **7** *1 1/4* **Further Outlook (USA)**[6] 6243 10-8-7 85..................... (p) NCallan 3 81
(DKIvory) *led: rdn along 2f out: drvn and hdd over 1f out: sn wknd* **12/1**
0300 **8** *nk* **Native Title**[36] 5603 6-8-8 86..................... ANicholls 2 81
(DNicholls) *towards rr: hdwy on outer to chse ldrs 2f out: sn rdn and wknd over 1f out* **14/1**
3044 **9** *3/4* **Caribbean Coral**[9] 6177 5-9-5 97..................... RWinston 12 90
(JJQuinn) *hld up: effrt and sme hdwy 2f out: sn rdn and btn* **9/2**[1]
0611 **10** *3/4* **Malapropism**[6] 6243 4-9-3 95 6ex..................... ACulhane 1 85
(MRChannon) *chsd ldrs on outer: rdn along 2f out: sn wknd* **11/2**[3]
0240 **11** *nk* **Petardias Magic (IRE)**[8] 6190 3-8-7 85..................... KFallon 8 74
(CADwyer) *midfield: rdn along 2f out: no hdwy* **8/1**
0030 **12** *1/2* **Dazzling Bay**[28] 5799 4-9-6 98..................... (e[1]) DAllan 7 86
(TDEasterby) *a towards rr* **50/1**
0030 **13** *hd* **Smart Hostess**[14] 6071 5-8-11 92..................... TEaves[(3)] 10 79
(JJQuinn) *chsd ldrs: rdn aloong 1/2-way: sn wknd* **16/1**

61.51 secs (0.09) **Going Correction** +0.35s/f (Good) **13** Ran SP% **117.9**
Speed ratings: **113,111,109,109,108 106,104,103,102,101 100,100,99**CSF £193.24 CT £2272.68 TOTE £21.40: £4.50, £3.60, £3.90; EX 248.30.
**Owner** Mrs O Tunstall **Bred** T Tunstall **Trained** Scrooby, Notts

**FOCUS**
A 0-99 handicap run at a fast and furious pace and the form looks very sound.

**NOTEBOOK**
**Matty Tun**, who looked outstandingly well, was 4lb out of the handicap. He seemed to revel in the ground and, after travelling very strongly, was always going to do enough to record his sixth career success. He will shoot back up the ratings as a result though. *Official explanation: trainer said, regarding the improved form shown, gelding was unsuited by the dead ground and stiffer track at Pontefract last time*
**Whitbarrow(IRE)**, who has a mind of his own, unusually for him managed to string two good efforts in succession together.
**Tom Tun**, a half-brother to the winner, loves the mud and this 18-times winner was making a rare foray over the minimum trip.
**Bond Boy**, whose last success was this race two years ago from a 5lb higher mark, was last of all at halfway. He finished best of all and will be suited by a return to six furlongs.
**Corridor Creeper(FR)**, 3lb higher than his Newmarket win two outings ago, continues in top form.
**Bishops Court**, who broke a blood-vessel on his previous start just nine days earlier, is on the decline and this winner of 11 races is surely nearing the end of the line.
**Further Outlook(USA)** had to do a lot of running early on to get the stands' rail from his outside draw and not surprisingly, he failed to see it out.
**Caribbean Coral**, out of luck at Newmarket, never fired for some reason or other.
**Malapropism**, 13lb higher than Catterick and 7lb higher than Musselburgh, had the worst of the draw and there will be easier opportunities over the closing two weeks of the turf Flat season.

## 6350 TELETEXT RACING "HANDS AND HEELS" APPRENTICE SERIES FINAL H'CAP 7f

5:15 (5:15) (E2) (0-92,86) 3-Y-O £6,839 (£2,104; £1,052; £526) Stalls High

Form RPR
1626 **1** **Seneschal**[7] 6210 3-8-2 72..................... TO'Brien[(3)] 9 90
(MRChannon) *dwlt: sn trcking ldrs: smooth hdwy to ld 2f out and sn clr* **9/2**[1]
-300 **2** *11* **Arran Scout (IRE)**[11] 6141 3-8-2 72..................... DonnaCaldwell[(3)] 2 64
(KARyan) *in tch: hdwy 2f out: kpt on appr last: no ch w wnr* **50/1**
2003 **3** *1 1/4* **Ask The Clerk (IRE)**[12] 6124 3-8-1 71 oh1..................... MStainton[(3)] 6 60
(VSmith) *sltly hmpd s: hld up towards rr: hdwy 2f out: kpt on ins last* **11/2**[2]
122U **4** *3/4* **Mrs Moh (IRE)**[15] 6044 3-9-5 86..................... JDO'Reilly 5 73
(TDEasterby) *s.i.s: sn prom: pushed along to dispute ld 3f out: wknd wl over 1f out* **8/1**
0102 **5** *3/4* **Morse (IRE)**[21] 5952 3-8-11 81..................... RKeogh[(3)] 3 67
(JAOsborne) *cl up: led 3f out: sn pushed along: rdr dropped reins and hdd 2f out: grad wknd* **13/2**
2164 **6** *1/2* **Kali**[22] 5912 3-8-3 75..................... RKingscote[(5)] 11 60
(RCharlton) *led: pushed along and hdd 3f out: grad wknd* **6/1**[3]
1300 **7** *1* **Citrine Spirit (IRE)**[38] 5566 3-8-1 71..................... RJKilloran[(3)] 10 53
(JHMGosden) *cl up: pushed along wl over 2f out and sn wknd* **8/1**
1440 **8** *1* **Keyaki (IRE)**[35] 5652 3-8-6 78..................... NatalieJankiewicz[(5)] 1 58
(CFWall) *s.i.s: a rr* **20/1**
3123 **9** *8* **Muy Bien**[178] 1702 3-8-8 78..................... TBlock[(3)] 7 39
(JRJenkins) *bhd fr 1/2-way* **12/1**
1000 **10** *2* **Molcon (IRE)**[33] 5698 3-9-1 82..................... WHogg 8 38
(NACallaghan) *in tch: pushed along 1/2-way: sn wknd* **11/1**
4530 **11** *shd* **Parkview Love (USA)**[21] 5942 3-8-13 85..................... (b[1]) AElliott[(5)] 4 41
(MJohnston) *s.i.s: a bhd* **9/1**

1m 30.17s (2.36) **Going Correction** +0.35s/f (Good) **11** Ran SP% **116.2**
Speed ratings: **100,87,86,85,84 83,82,81,72,70 69**CSF £221.97 CT £1287.59 TOTE £6.10: £2.00, £14.50, £2.10; EX 191.50 Place 6 £423.47, Place 5 £126.86.
**Owner** Peter Taplin **Bred** Michael E Broughton **Trained** West Ilsley, Berks

**FOCUS**
A 0-86 apprentices' handicap run in detiorating underfoot conditions after over an hour of steady rain.

**NOTEBOOK**
**Seneschal**, warm beforehand, is standing up really well to a busy schedule and he came right away for an emphatic success.
**Arran Scout(IRE)**, with the blinkers left off on his handicap bow, seemed to revel in the ground despite connections reporting that he was unsuited by the good to soft last time, his first start for this yard.
**Ask The Clerk(IRE)** travelled strongly but his strike rate, just one from 32 starts now, tells it all.
**Mrs Moh(IRE)**, awkward at the start, is weighted to the limit and ground as soft as this is not in her favour.
**Morse(IRE)** has slipped to a lenient mark, but he had already been overtaken when his young rider dropped his reins.
**Kali**, who has presumably had problems with the stalls, took them along at a sound gallop but the ground had turned against her.
T/Plt: £720.60 to a £1 stake. Pool: £82,039.40. 83.10 winning tickets. T/Qpdt: £125.70 to a £1 stake. Pool: £5,453.10. 32.10 winning tickets. JR

# 6338 NEWBURY (L-H)

Saturday, October 23

**OFFICIAL GOING: Heavy**
Incessant rain in the morning, plus a strong crosswind, meant conditions were extremely testing. The form should be treated with great caution.

## 6351 CANTORODDS.COM EBF MAIDEN STKS (DIV I) 1m (S)

1:00 (1:01) (D2) 2-Y-O £6,734 (£2,072; £1,036; £518) Stalls Centre

Form RPR
44 **1** **Spear Thistle**[31] 5729 2-9-0..................... JFortune 2 85
(JHMGosden) *lw: mde virtually all: drvn and hld on wl thrght fnl f* **11/4**[1]
**2** *nk* **General Jumbo** 2-9-0..................... DHolland 6 84
(BJMeehan) *rangy: str: scope: bkwd: sn in tch: chsd ldrs 1/2-way:drvn and styd on to chse wnr ins fnl f: kpt on wl but no imp cl home* **16/1**
06 **3** *3 1/2* **Tanzanite (IRE)**[24] 5864 2-8-9..................... DSweeney 11 72
(DWPArbuthnot) *t.k.h: trckd ldrs: chsd wnr over 2f out: rdn:outpcd and lost 2nd ins last: wknd nr fin* **66/1**
**4** *4* **Bayard (USA)** 2-9-0..................... TQuinn 8 69
(DRCElsworth) *leggy: bhd: rdn and hdwy 3f out: styd on fnl 2f but nvr gng pce to rch ldrs* **8/1**
04 **5** *2* **Bulwark (IRE)**[11] 6149 2-9-0..................... SWKelly 14 65
(MrsAJPerrett) *lw: racd stands side and chsd that ldr tl led that gp over 2f out: no ch w wnr in centre crse fr wl over 1f out* **7/1**[3]
**6** *5* **Cross Time (USA)** 2-9-0..................... CCatlin 12 55
(MRChannon) *leggy: bit bkwd: bhd: drvn along 1/2-way: kpt on fnl 2f but n.d* **16/1**
**7** *1/2* **Tritonville Lodge (IRE)** 2-8-11..................... LPKeniry[(3)] 10 54
(MissECLavelle) *leggy: scope: slowly away: bhd: hdwy 5f out: chsd ldrs but no imp over 2f out: n.d after* **50/1**
0 **8** *2* **Shortbread**[11] 6145 2-9-0..................... IMongan 5 50
(JLDunlop) *bhd: pushed along 1/2-way: sme hdwy fnl 2f* **16/1**
0 **9** *3* **Kabis Amigos**[11] 6148 2-9-0..................... (t) WRyan 16 44
(HRACecil) *racd stand side: bhd fnl 3f* **16/1**
00 **10** *shd* **Oakley Absolute**[24] 5870 2-9-0..................... PDobbs 13 44
(RHannon) *led stands side nd w wnr in centre crse 5f: wknd 2f out* **40/1**
4 **11** *1* **Groomsman**[11] 6148 2-8-11..................... LFletcher[(3)] 1 42
(HMorrison) *b.hind: chsd wnr: rdn over 2f out: sn btn* **8/1**
0 **12** *1* **Hoh Hedsor**[12] 6118 2-8-9..................... JFEgan 7 35
(SKirk) *chsd ldrs: rdn 3f out: sn wknd* **33/1**

13 2 ½ **Intrepid Jack** 2-9-0 ........ SDrowne 9 35
(HMorrison) *a in rr* **25/1**

0 14 *shd* **Mpenzi**[22] [5915] 2-8-9 ........ DaneO'Neill 4 30
(JLDunlop) *lw: s.i.s: sn in tch: bhd fnl 3f* **7/2**[2]

06 15 3 **Palace Walk (FR)**[14] [6073] 2-9-0 ........ MartinDwyer 3 29
(AMBalding) *chsd ldrs over 5f* **33/1**

0 16 *dist* **City Trader**[46] [5373] 2-9-0 ........ MHills 15 —
(CEBrittain) *bit bkwd: s.i.s: racd stands side and a bhd: hung lft to centre over 3f out: sn t.o* **50/1**

1m 49.58s (8.75) **Going Correction** +1.05s/f (Soft) **16** Ran SP% **124.7**
Speed ratings: **98,97,94,90,88 83,82,80,77,77 76,75,73,73,70** —CSF £48.26 TOTE £3.90: £1.80, £6.70, £16.70; EX 92.10.
**Owner** Duke Of Devonshire **Bred** Side Hill Stud **Trained** Manton, Wilts

**FOCUS**
A group of four raced on the stands' side, but the main action took place up the centre of the track. A fair maiden formwise, rated through the fifth.

**NOTEBOOK**
**Spear Thistle** was not at home on Goodwood's undulations last time. His stamina proven, he made just about all the running down the centre of the track and showed a gritty attitude to hold on in bad conditions.
**General Jumbo**, out of an unraced half-sister to Compton Bolter, is a half-brother to several winners including middle-distance perfomer Azhar. Just unable to force his head in front, this sizeable individual should make the grade next year.
**Tanzanite(IRE)**, whose dam was a winner over two miles, stepped up on two previous runs over six furlongs. She was one of the few to travel well in the ground but just got tired in the last half-furlong.
**Bayard(USA)**, whose dam won the Prix Royal-Oak over 15 furlongs, is a half-brother to useful French middle-distance performer Martien. He will appreciate ten furlongs plus next year.
**Bulwark(IRE)** came out on top of the small group that raced up the stands' side, again showing a noticeably high head carriage. A half-brother to smart performers Claxon and Bull Run, he is capable of making a name for himself but does not look straightforward.
**Cross Time(USA)**, a half-brother to several winners notably useful two-year-old Al Nufooth, ran well despite not looking at home in the ground.
**Tritonville Lodge(IRE)**, a half-brother to a number of middle-distance winners, should improve given time and a longer trip.
**Shortbread** *Official explanation: jockey said colt was unsuited by the soft, heavy in places ground*
**Groomsman** failed to get home in this ground after racing prominently.
**Mpenzi** was found out by the conditions.
**City Trader** *Official explanation: jockey said gelding was weak and immature and got tired in the ground*

## 6352 CANTORODDS.COM EBF MAIDEN STKS (DIV II) 1m (S)
**1:35** (1:38) (D2) 2-Y-0 **£6,734** (£2,072; £1,036; £518) **Stalls** Centre

Form RPR

1 **Descartes** 2-9-0 ........ LDettori 14 86+
(SaeedBinSuroor) *str: well grown: lw: s.i.s: hld up in rr: stdy hdwy on stands side fr 1/2-way: qcknd to ld appr fnl 2f: comf* **1/1**[1]

06 2 1 ¼ **High Card**[7] [6223] 2-9-0 ........ SWKelly 4 77
(JMPEustace) *chsd ldrs: rdn over 2f out: chsd wnr 1f out and kpt on wl but no imp ins last* **33/1**

3 4 **Los Organos (IRE)** 2-8-9 ........ RHavlin 9 65
(PWChapple-Hyam) *lt-fr: scope: lw: chsd ldrs tl slt advantage ins fnl 3f: hdd appr fnl 2f: wknd fnl f* **9/1**[2]

4 3 **Gifted Musician** 2-9-0 ........ DaneO'Neill 7 64
(JLDunlop) *tall: scope: bit bkwd: bhd: hdwy fr 2f out: swtchd rt to stands rail 1f out:fin wl but nvr gng pce to rch ldrs* **10/1**[3]

0 5 *nk* **Queen's Dancer**[32] [5717] 2-8-9 ........ CCatlin 2 58
(MRChannon) *bhd: hdwy over 2f out: styd on u.p fnl f but nvr gng pce to rch ldrs* **100/1**

0 6 *hd* **Kiama**[25] [5846] 2-8-9 ........ MartinDwyer 6 58
(HMorrison) *mde most tl hdd ins fnl 3f: sn rdn: wknd over 1f out* **14/1**

0 7 9 **Eloquent Knight (USA)**[32] [5716] 2-9-0 ........ SDrowne 1 46
(WRMuir) *prom: outpcd 1/2-way and sn rdn: n.d after* **16/1**

00 8 2 ½ **Victor Buckwell**[13] [6092] 2-9-0 ........ JFanning 3 41
(BEllison) *mid-div: hdwy 1/2-way: chsd ldrs and rdn 3f out: wknd over 2f out* **33/1**

6 9 9 **Dream Tonic**[135] [2804] 2-9-0 ........ SHitchcott 12 24
(MRChannon) *bhd: rdn and sme hdwy on stands rail 3f out: sn wknd* **12/1**

10 14 **Ophistrolie (IRE)** 2-9-0 ........ JFEgan 10 —
(SKirk) *legy: bkwd: chsd ldrs to 1/2-way: sn wknd* **33/1**

11 1 ¼ **Top Mark** 2-8-11 ........ LFletcher(3) 13 —
(HMorrison) *leggy: w ldr tl swtchd rt to stands rail 3f out: sn wknd* **50/1**

12 1 ¾ **Climate Change (USA)** 2-9-0 ........ RHughes 8 —
(JHMGosden) *tall: rangy: str: scope: s.i.s: sn rcvrd: in tch 1/2-way: sn pushed along: wknd 3f out* **10/1**[3]

13 10 **Christom** 2-9-0 ........ DHolland 11 —
(GAButler) *str: bkwd: chsd ldrs over 5f* **16/1**

14 1 ½ **Along Came Molly** 2-8-9 ........ JFortune 5 —
(BJMeehan) *b.hind: leggy: scope: bit bkwd: slowly away: a wl bhd* **20/1**

15 3 **Princess Links** 2-8-9 ........ PDobbs 15 —
(RHannon) *str: bwkd: chsd ldrs to 1/2-way* **25/1**

1m 50.11s (9.28) **Going Correction** +1.05s/f (Soft) **15** Ran SP% **124.7**
Speed ratings: **95,93,89,86,86 86,77,74,65,51 50,48,38,37,34**CSF £54.58 TOTE £2.10: £1.40, £12.40, £2.80; EX 55.80.
**Owner** Godolphin **Bred** Darley **Trained** Newmarket, Suffolk

**FOCUS**
They bet 9/1 bar one, and the winner apart this looked a modest maiden, so it is rated cautiously for now. The field raced up the centre of the track.

**NOTEBOOK**
**Descartes**, whose dam was a middle-distance winner, is a half-brother to French filly Goldamix, who won the Group One Crierium de Saint-Cloud as a juvenile in heavy ground. A comfortable winner, although asked to do no more than was necessary to win his race, he looks a bright prospect but holds no fancy entries at this stage.
**High Card**, whose two previous runs were on Polytrack, stayed on well in the final furlong to cut the gap but was flattered by his proximity to the winner. He looks the sort for middle-distance handicaps next year.
**Los Organos(IRE)** is by a noted soft-ground sire out of a mare who won on a sound surace. Well backed for her debut, she showed up well until fading in the final furlong.
**Gifted Musician**, whose dam was a Listed winner at two in Ireland, was staying on to some purpose late in the day and there are races to be won with him.
**Queen's Dancer** showed more than she had on her debut at Newmarket. Out of a winning stayer/hurdler, she stayed on in the latter stages, showing an action suited to soft ground.
**Kiama**, whose debut had been on fast ground, only faded going to the final furlong and finished well clear of the rest.
**Top Mark** *Official explanation: jockey said colt hung right-handed*

## 6353 STANJAMESUK.COM RADLEY STKS (LISTED RACE) 7f (S)
**2:10** (2:10) (A1) 2-Y-0 **£14,500** (£5,500; £2,750; £1,250) **Stalls** Centre

Form RPR

4514 1 **Bibury Flyer**[7] [6213] 2-8-11 89 ........ SHitchcott 6 93
(MRChannon) *lw: hld up in rr: stdy hdwy over 2f out to ld over 1f out: wandered lft and rt u.p ins last: styd on strly* **3/1**[1]

3141 2 2 **Wedding Party**[21] [5938] 2-8-8 83 ........ SDrowne 4 86
(MrsAJPerrett) *chsd ldrs: drvn to chal over 1f out: kpt on to chse wnr ins last but no imp* **3/1**[1]

31 3 2 **Sheboygan (IRE)**[21] [5946] 2-8-8 84 ........ LDettori 7 82
(JGGiven) *trckd ldrs tl led jst ins fnl 2f: hdd over 1f out: wknd last half f* **7/2**[2]

1 4 ¾ **Brecon**[39] [5534] 2-8-8 ........ TQuinn 2 80
(DRCElsworth) *h.d.w: lw: stdd s: t.k.h in rr: shkn up and one pce 2f out: kpt on u.p fnl f: fin wl and gng on cl home* **6/1**[3]

340 5 3 **Nice Tune**[12] [6123] 2-8-8 ........ DHolland 3 73
(CEBrittain) *chsd ldr tl wknd fr 2f out* **16/1**

2102 6 7 **Sharp As A Tack (IRE)**[36] [5613] 2-8-8 88 ........ (b) JFortune 5 58
(BJMeehan) *led tl hdd & wknd jst ins fnl 2f* **16/1**

6 7 8 **Clara Bow (IRE)**[33] [5695] 2-8-8 ........ MHills 1 40
(BWHills) *lw: a bhd: lost tch fnl 3f* **8/1**

1m 35.94s (8.72) **Going Correction** +1.05s/f (Soft) **7** Ran SP% **109.4**
Speed ratings: **92,89,87,86,83 75,66**CSF £11.03 TOTE £4.00: £2.10, £2.20; EX 13.70.
**Owner** Ridgeway Downs Racing **Bred** Baydon House Stud **Trained** West Ilsley, Berks

**FOCUS**
The fillies raced down the centre of the track. The early pace was surprisingly fast given the conditions and it turned into a slog, but the placed horses ran to their marks and the form looks reliable.

**NOTEBOOK**
**Bibury Flyer** was having her 21st race of the season, and her experience proved invaluable in these conditions as she seemed to find it hard work in the ground. Set to go to the sales now, while she has shown improved form lately the likelihood is that she will be hard to place at three, although she is admirably tough..
**Wedding Party**, winner of a competitive nursery last time, handles cut in the ground but these conditions were a different matter. This was a commendable effort in the circumstances.
**Sheboygan(IRE)** won a fast-ground Redcar maiden which has been working out well. She ran a good race until running out of steam in the last 100 yards and will appreciate a return to a sounder surface.
**Brecon** failed to pick up when first coming under pressure, having been keen in rear, but she finished quite strongly to close the gap on the front three. She looks a nice middle-distance prospect for next year.
**Nice Tune**, back up in grade, was not disgraced given she did not handle the conditions.
**Sharp As A Tack(IRE)** went plenty fast enough in this ground and did not last much more than five furlongs.

## 6354 STAN JAMES 08000 383384 H'CAP 1m 2f 6y
**2:40** (2:40) (C1) (0-107,103) 3-Y-O+ **£13,305** (£5,046; £2,523; £1,147) **Stalls** Centre

Form RPR

0042 1 **Tiger Tiger (FR)**[83] [4379] 3-7-10 86 oh3 ........ JFMcDonald(3) 1 99
(JamiePoulton) *lw: trckd ldrs: drvn to ld 1f out: drvn and kpt on strly fnl f* **5/1**[1]

0000 2 2 **Turbo (IRE)**[35] [5650] 5-8-4 89 ........ (p) RThomas(3) 2 99
(GBBalding) *lw: hld up in rr: stdy hdwy on ins over 3f out to take slt ld over 2f out: rdn and hdd 1f out: kpt on same pce u.p* **10/1**[3]

0645 3 1 ¼ **Pagan Sky (IRE)**[22] [5919] 5-8-4 86 oh3 ........ LisaJones 14 94
(JARToller) *lw: chsd ldrs: rdn to chal over 2f out: styd on same pce fnl f* **12/1**

30/5 4 2 **Torcello (IRE)**[30] [5755] 6-8-6 87 ow1 ........ SDrowne 3 93
(GWragg) *lw: in tch: rdn and hdwy over 2f out: chsd ldrs over 1f out and sn one pce* **16/1**

0006 5 7 **Blythe Knight (IRE)**[21] [5941] 4-9-7 103 ........ (p) LDettori 8 97
(EALDunlop) *t.k.h: hld up in rr: stdy hdwy on outside over 3f out: effrt to chse leaaders fr 2f out: no imp and wknd over 1f out* **11/2**[2]

3333 6 1 ¼ **Shahzan House (IRE)**[66] [4856] 5-9-1 97 ........ (p) DHolland 12 89
(MAJarvis) *chsd ldrs: rdn over 2f out: sn btn* **5/1**[1]

1424 7 2 ½ **Namroc (IRE)**[21] [5942] 3-8-0 87 ........ MartinDwyer 11 75
(EFVaughan) *prom: rdn to chse ldrs fr 3f out: wknd ins fnl 2f* **5/1**[1]

0000 8 2 ½ **Bourgainville**[90] [4163] 6-8-5 90 ........ LPKeniry(3) 6 74
(AMBalding) *hld up in rr: rdn over 2f out and no rspnse* **25/1**

0550 9 ¾ **Tizzy May (FR)**[33] [5699] 4-8-8 90 ........ DaneO'Neill 13 72
(RHannon) *sn pressing ldr: slt ld over 3f out: hdd over 2f out and sn wknd* **25/1**

5400 10 1 ¾ **Perfect Storm**[9] [6172] 5-8-8 90 ........ DSweeney 9 70
(MBlanshard) *chsd ldrs: rdn over 2f out: wknd qckly wl over 1f out* **10/1**[3]

41 11 *dist* **Solor**[179] [1683] 3-8-2 89 ........ PDoe 10 —
(DJCoakley) *broke wl: sn bhd: hung bdly rt 4f out: t.o* **20/1**

-600 12 3 **Millafonic**[113] [3482] 4-8-11 93 ........ NMackay 7 —
(LMCumani) *bit bkwd: a bhd: t.o* **16/1**

33-6 13 9 **Carte Sauvage (USA)**[261] [691] 3-9-0 101 ........ JFanning 5 —
(MJohnston) *sn led: hdd over 3f out: sn wknd: t.o* **25/1**

0204 14 11 **Prime Powered (IRE)**[31] [5732] 3-7-13 86 oh1 ........ (b[1]) CCatlin 4 —
(GLMoore) *a bhd: rdn 5f out: t.o* **16/1**

2m 22.73s (14.02) **Going Correction** +1.675s/f (Heav)
**WFA** 3 from 4yo+ 5lb **14** Ran SP% **125.2**
Speed ratings: **110,108,107,105,100 99,97,95,94,93** —,—,—,—CSF £54.39 CT £573.54 TOTE £4.90: £1.80, £3.40, £4.10; EX 69.80 Trifecta £942.70 Part won. Pool: £1,327.80. 0.30 winning tickets..
**Owner** R W Huggins **Bred** Pierre Talvard And Jean-Claude Seroul **Trained** Telscombe, E Sussex

**FOCUS**
A solid enough pace was set in the conditions and the form looks strong and can prove a sound guide to similar handicaps before the end of the season. The field came up the centre in the home straight and the first four finished clear.

**NOTEBOOK**
**Tiger Tiger(FR)**, having his first run since early August, had winning form in soft ground earlier in the year and landed a bit of a gamble. He is a versatile sort in terms of trip and there should be more to come from him next year.
**Turbo(IRE)** was runner-up to Pagan Sky in this a year ago before going on to land the November Handicap off this mark. This will have put him just right for another crack at the Doncaster race, when he will be bidding to give Toby Balding a big winner on his last day as a trainer.
**Pagan Sky(IRE)**, who won this event 12 months ago on fast ground, was 5lb lower here and is due to be dropped a further 3lb. This was a respectable effort on ground that did not really suit him.
**Torcello(IRE)**, having his second run back after a long absence, showed that he retains ability. Currently rated 20lb lower than at his peak, he has won on soft ground in the past but has always looked better on a sound surface.
**Blythe Knight(IRE)** travelled well enough but not for the first time failed to produce much when let down, although the ground was a valid excuse on this occasion.

**Shahzan House(IRE)** has had a frustrating season, without a win but having been placed on each of his previous six runs, and edging up 3lb in the weights in the process. He has also proved costly to follow, having been at the the head of the market on four of his last five outings.
**Namroc(IRE)**, whose win came on fast ground, failed to get home in the conditions.
**Solor** *Official explanation: jockey said colt finished lame*

## 6355 STAN JAMES ST SIMON STKS (GROUP 3) 1m 4f 5y
**3:10** (3:11) (A1) 3-Y-0+ **£29,000** (£11,000; £5,500; £2,500) **Stalls** Centre

Form RPR
3065 **1** **Orcadian**[7] 6219 3-8-7 99 MartinDwyer 8 108
(JMPEustace) *lw: mde all: forged clr fr 2f out: drvn wl clr fnl f* **33/1**
1100 **2** *15* **Frank Sonata**[6] 6263 3-8-7 105 SDrowne 4 89
(MGQuinlan) *hld up in rr: styd on fnl 3f to chse wnr ins fnl 2f but nvr any ch* **12/1**
6552 **3** *8* **Self Defense**[27] 5812 7-9-0 112 LDettori 6 78
(PRChamings) *hld up in rr:hdwy fr 5f out to dispute 2nd ins fnl 3f: nvr gng pce to rch wnr: wknd and dropped to 3rd over 1f out* **5/2**[1]
0215 **4** *2* **The Whistling Teal**[119] 3333 8-9-0 112 JFEgan 5 76
(GWragg) *bit bkwd: disp 2nd tl chsd wnr over 6f out: rdn 3f out: wknd 2f out* **7/2**[3]
4301 **5** *dist* **Collier Hill**[41] 5506 6-9-3 106 JFortune 7 —
(GASwinbank) *a bhd: no ch fr over 3f out: t.o* **8/1**
1051 **6** *27* **Massif Centrale**[12] 6121 3-8-7 101 DaneO'Neill 2 —
(DRCElsworth) *lw: disp 2nd tl wknd qckly 4f out: t.o* **7/1**
/21- **7** *dist* **Asian Heights**[534] 1449 6-9-0 DHolland 1 —
(GWragg) *bkwd: chsd wnr tl wknd over 6f out: t.o* **10/3**[2]
3200 **P** **Top Seed (IRE)**[27] 5814 3-8-7 98 SHitchcott 3 —
(MRChannon) *a bhd: t.o whn p.u ins fnl 2f and dismntd* **16/1**
2m 53.11s (16.82) **Going Correction** +1.675s/f (Heav)
**WFA** 3 from 6yo+ 7lb **8** Ran **SP% 114.0**
Speed ratings: **110,100,94,93,— —,—,—**CSF £367.94 TOTE £46.80: £6.10, £2.40, £1.60; EX 194.80 Trifecta £267.70 Pool £1,131.30. 3.00 winning units.
**Owner** J C Smith **Bred** Littleton Stud **Trained** Newmarket, Suffolk

**FOCUS**
A weak Group Three in which the field finished at long intervals. This form is likely to have little bearing on the future and therefore is rated cautiously.

**NOTEBOOK**
**Orcadian**, who ran well on his first encounter with soft ground at Newmarket, is a half-brother to Rapscallion who relished testing conditions. Tackling further than nine furlongs for the first time, he belied any stamina doubts, making all the running, although the pre-race plan had been to hold him up, and keeping up the gallop to rout the opposition.
**Frank Sonata**, down in class, battled bravely to move past a couple of rivals into second place but the winner was out of sight.
**Self Defense**, who has some high-class form in heavy ground to his name over hurdles, ran respectably but had no more to give in the final furlong and a half. He is likely to return to Emma Lavelle now for a hurdling campaign.
**The Whistling Teal**, winner of this race two years ago in soft ground, was having his first run since June. After looking a possible danger turning into the straight, he began to struggle with two furlongs left to run.
**Collier Hill** was rerouted here after the plan to send him to the Canadian International had to be ditched after a problem with flights. Facing a stiff task under his Group Three penalty, he was always trailing.
**Asian Heights** had been off the track with leg problems since winning the Ormonde Stakes at Chester in May last year. This ground should have suited him more than most but he did not last beyond halfway.
**Top Seed(IRE)** *Official explanation: jockey said colt had a breathing problem*

## 6356 SIR GERALD WHENT MEMORIAL NURSERY 6f 8y
**3:45** (3:48) (D2) (0-85,85) 2-Y-0 **£7,299** (£2,246; £1,123; £561) **Stalls** Centre

Form RPR
0401 **1** **Paris Bell**[12] 6113 2-8-3 65 PMQuinn 8 81+
(TDEasterby) *hld up in rr: stdy hdwy 3f out: drvn to ld appr fnl f: r.o strly* **9/1**
6600 **2** *3 ½* **Go Mo (IRE)**[19] 5995 2-8-6 68 JFEgan 14 75
(SKirk) *lw: chsd ldr tl led 3f out: kpt slt ld tl hdd appr fnl f: kpt on but outstyd by wnr ins last* **40/1**
5220 **3** *3 ½* **Aberdeen Park**[13] 6090 2-8-6 68 PDoe 10 66
(MrsHSweeting) *s.i.s: sn rcvrd: chsd ldrs 3f out: sn rdn: styd on same pce fr over 1f out* **12/1**
4216 **4** *10* **Little Dalham**[63] 4953 2-9-6 82 DHolland 9 55
(PWChapple-Hyam) *mid-div: rdn 3f out: kpt on fnl 2f to take moderate 4th ins last* **15/2**[3]
2314 **5** *hd* **Cree**[21] 5932 2-8-2 64 MartinDwyer 13 37
(WRMuir) *led 3f: styd pressing ldr tl over 2f out: wknd wl over 1f out* **7/1**[2]
550 **6** *2 ½* **Crocodile Kiss (IRE)**[63] 4936 2-8-8 70 LDettori 4 37
(JAOsborne) *in tch: rdn and one pce fnl 3f* **16/1**
630 **7** *¾* **Red Rudy**[38] 5561 2-8-6 68 TPQueally 11 33
(RMBeckett) *chsd ldrs:rdn 3f out: wknd qckly 2f out* **14/1**
0520 **8** *1* **Corniche Dancer**[6] 6242 2-8-6 68 SHitchcott 12 30
(MRChannon) *chsd ldrs: rdn over 3f out: wknd over 2f out* **33/1**
3040 **9** *1 ½* **Celtic Spa (IRE)**[29] 5767 2-9-7 83 RHavlin 16 41
(MrsPNDutfield) *chsd ldrs tl wknd over 2f out* **20/1**
2500 **10** *11* **Adoration**[49] 5292 2-8-11 73 JFanning 15 —
(MJohnston) *n.d* **20/1**
6440 **11** *2 ½* **Alexander Capetown (IRE)**[33] 5701 2-8-6 68 MHills 20 —
(BWHills) *sn bhd: no ch fr over 2f out* **12/1**
003 **12** *¾* **Midnight Lace**[25] 5847 2-8-1 63 DKinsella 17 —
(RHannon) *early pce: bhd fr 1/2-way* **14/1**
3054 **13** *2* **Azuree (IRE)**[19] 5989 2-7-13 64 (b) JFMcDonald(3) 3 —
(RHannon) *chsd ldrs tl wknd qckly over 2f out* **25/1**
4050 **14** *2 ½* **Monsieur Mirasol**[21] 5947 2-8-11 73 TQuinn 7 —
(KARyan) *bhd most of way* **13/2**[1]
0341 **15** *5* **Island Swing (IRE)**[3] 6305 2-9-9 85 7ex SDrowne 5 —
(JLSpearing) *chsd ldrs: rdn 3f out: wknd qckly over 2f out* **7/1**[2]
2606 **16** *3* **Brooklime (IRE)**[7] 6206 2-9-2 78 SWKelly 6 —
(JAOsborne) *lw: in tch: rdn 3f out: sn wknd* **8/1**
0030 **17** *2 ½* **Guyana (IRE)**[22] 5909 2-8-3 65 CCatlin 19 —
(SKirk) *lw: bhd fr 1/2-way* **33/1**
1360 **18** *nk* **Little Wizzy**[13] 6080 2-8-1 66 FPFerris(3) 18 —
(PDEvans) *s.i.s: a bhd* **50/1**
405 **19** *5* **Methodical**[36] 5609 2-8-4 67 ow2 LPKeniry(3) 1 —
(IAWood) *chsd ldrs tl wknd over 2f out* **33/1**
4015 **20** *12* **Missed A Beat**[29] 5767 2-8-13 75 DSweeney 2 —
(MBlanshard) *in tch over 3f* **25/1**
1m 20.88s (6.51) **Going Correction** +1.05s/f (Soft) **20** Ran **SP% 136.2**
Speed ratings: **98,93,88,75,75 71,70,69,67,52 49,48,45,42,35 31,28,28,21,5**CSF £359.08 CT £4373.94 TOTE £9.80: £2.70, £8.70, £4.10, £2.90; EX 467.20.
**Owner** Ryedale Partners No 8 **Bred** M H Easterby **Trained** Great Habton, N Yorks

**FOCUS**
Few got into this nursery and more than half the field were allowed to come home in their own time. The first three finished well clear. A group of five raced initially on the stands' side, but the main action took place in the centre.

**NOTEBOOK**
**Paris Bell** was proven in soft ground and he ran out a decisive winner. Likely to stay further next year, he is not straightforward but is improving.
**Go Mo(IRE)**, dropped in trip, handled the ground unlike most of these but the winner was too good on the day.
**Aberdeen Park** soon recovered after giving away quite a bit of ground when standing still as the stalls opened. One of a handful to be seen with a chance, she finished a long way clear of the remainder.
**Little Dalham** stayed on for a fairly remote fourth over this shorter trip, and it would appear that the ground was probably not the reason for his lacklustre run at Sandown.
**Cree**, a heavy-ground winner at Chepstow, showed pace before understandably fading.
**Monsieur Mirasol**, without the blinkers this time, showed nothing on ground he had promised to handle. *Official explanation: jockey said gelding was never travelling*

## 6357 MIKE LESTER & FRIENDS - BULLDOG TAKES THE BISCUIT MAIDEN STKS 1m 2f 6y
**4:20** (4:21) (D3) 3-Y-0 **£5,687** (£1,750; £875; £437) **Stalls** Centre

Form RPR
2506 **1** **Jolizero**[22] 5914 3-9-0 58 RHavlin 9 68
(PWChapple-Hyam) *lw: mde virtually all: rdn clr fr 2f out: drvn out ins last* **6/1**
025 **2** *17* **Nietzsche (IRE)**[152] 2374 3-9-0 85 SWKelly 3 43
(JNoseda) *trckd wnr 4f: drvn to chal over 3f out: outstyd as wnr wnt clr fr 2f out: hld on wl for mod 2nd* **3/1**[2]
2-46 **3** *3* **Maid To Treasure (IRE)**[122] 3204 3-8-9 76 LDettori 8 33
(JLDunlop) *lw: chaed ldrs: wnt 2nd 6f out tl over 3f out: sn rdn and lost pl: styd on again for mod 3rd fnl f* **2/1**[1]
**4** *2* **Sheshalan (IRE)** 3-9-0 JFortune 4 35
(SirMichaelStoute) *str: bkwd: chsd ldrs: rdn over 3f out and sn no ch: mod prog again fnl f* **9/2**[3]
3-40 **5** *9* **Tyup Pompey (IRE)**[13] 6082 3-8-11 60 LPKeniry(3) 5 22
(DRCElsworth) *bhd: rdn and effrt 3f out: sn wknd* **25/1**
**6** *2 ½* **Fuss** 3-8-9 TQuinn 6 13
(WJarvis) *w'like: bkwd: slowly into stride: a bhd* **9/1**
**7** *12* **Majestic Star** 3-8-9 RPrice 2 —
(MJRyan) *well grown: bkwd: chsd ldrs: rdn 5f out: wknd 4f out* **20/1**
05 **8** *3 ½* **Polish Rose**[30] 5749 3-8-9 DaneO'Neill 1 —
(EFVaughan) *chsd ldrs tl wknd over 3f out* **16/1**
2m 27.4s (18.69) **Going Correction** +1.95s/f (Heav) **8** Ran **SP% 115.3**
Speed ratings: **103,89,87,85,78 76,66,63**CSF £24.59 TOTE £8.20: £1.90, £1.50, £1.30; EX 31.90.
**Owner** Norcroft Park Stud **Bred** Norcroft Park Stud **Trained** Newmarket, Suffolk
■ Stewards Enquiry : R Havlin one-day ban: excessive use of the whip (Nov 3)

**FOCUS**
A weak maiden in which the winner set a fair pace and had seen off his rivals with two furlongs to run. It is hard to know what he achieved formwise given the conditions.

**NOTEBOOK**
**Jolizero** was one of the few horses on the card to look at home in the conditions. Setting a decent pace, he initially took the centre-track route in the straight but edged over to the stands' rail with more than two furlongs to run and was driven right out to pulverise the opposition. Officially rated only 58, he had previously seemed fully exposed and this form should certainly not be read literally.
**Nietzsche(IRE)** was having his first run since May. He had 27lb in hand of the eventual winner on BHB ratings, but that counted for nothing in these extreme conditions.
**Maid To Treasure(IRE)**, who had been off the track since June, was in trouble when coming off the bridle but did keep on again late in the day.
**Sheshalan(IRE)**, whose dam won at up to 15 furlongs in France, did not show a great deal on this belated debut. It would be no surprise to see him sold as a hurdles prospect.
**Fuss**, a half-sister to middle-distance winners Rolling Stone and First Impression, showed nothing on this racecourse bow.

## 6358 MENTOR LADY JOCKEYS' CHAMPIONSHIP H'CAP 1m (S)
**4:55** (4:55) (D2) (0-92,85) 3-Y-0+ **£7,233** (£2,225; £1,112; £556) **Stalls** Centre

Form RPR
0505 **1** **Sangiovese**[12] 6128 5-10-3 74 MrsSBosley 6 84
(HMorrison) *bhd: hdwy 3f out: taken to far rail and rdn to ld appr fnl f: hld on all out* **6/1**[1]
6311 **2** *shd* **Mr Velocity (IRE)**[27] 5821 4-10-2 76 MissJoannaRees(3) 1 86
(EFVaughan) *sn led: rdn: hung lft and hdd appr fnl f: rallied u.p ins last: kpt on cl home: jst failed* **8/1**[3]
5142 **3** *5* **Desert Reign**[21] 5934 3-9-7 72 MissKellyBurke(5) 10 73
(APJarvis) *in tch: hdwy over 2f out: styd on fnl f but no imp on ldrs* **8/1**[3]
3004 **4** *shd* **Tidy (IRE)**[91] 4134 4-10-7 78 MissEJJones 8 79
(MDHammond) *lw: bhd: hdwy over 2f out: styd on same pce fr over 1f out* **6/1**[1]
0 **5** *2 ½* **Darghan (IRE)**[15] 6043 4-10-0 78 (t) MissABevan(7) 3 74
(PDEvans) *chsd ldrs: rdn 3f out: styd on same pce fnl 2f* **33/1**
1026 **6** *6* **Patterdale**[12] 6128 3-9-13 73 MsCWilliams 2 59
(WJHaggas) *lw: chsd ldrs tl rdn and lost position ins fnl 3f: n.d after* **12/1**
0530 **7** *2* **Vicious Knight**[15] 6044 6-10-11 85 MissKellyHarrison(3) 5 67
(DNicholls) *bhd: hdwy 3f out: rdn: hung rt and wknd over 1f out* **11/1**
3031 **8** *2* **Parnassian**[13] 6081 4-9-10 74 MissJHannaford(7) 9 52
(GBBalding) *b.hind: in tch: rdn and sme hdwy over 2f out: nvr rchd ldrs and sn wknd* **6/1**[1]
3122 **9** *13* **Locombe Hill (IRE)**[11] 6138 8-9-11 71 oh1 MrsNWilson(3) 11 26
(NWilson) *chsd ldrs tl wknd over 2f out* **7/1**[2]
0321 **10** *2 ½* **Ridge Boy (IRE)**[21] 5934 3-9-13 76 MrsSMoore(3) 7 26
(RHannon) *in tch 5f* **10/1**
3212 **11** *8* **Johannian**[38] 5574 6-9-9 71 MissFayeBramley(5) 13 7
(JMBradley) *in tch over 5f* **10/1**
1600 **12** *6* **Best Before (IRE)**[14] 6069 4-10-2 76 MissEFolkes(3) 4 1
(PDEvans) *prom over 3f* **20/1**
10 **13** *8* **Nimello (USA)**[66] 4852 8-10-7 78 MissCHannaford 12 —
(AGNewcombe) *sn bhd* **8/1**[3]
-000 **14** *6* **Camille Pissarro (USA)**[12] 6128 4-10-2 80 MissHMLewis(7) 14 —
(DJWintle) *prom 4f* **66/1**
1m 57.73s (16.90) **Going Correction** +2.25s/f (Heav)
**WFA** 3 from 4yo+ 3lb **14** Ran **SP% 132.1**
Speed ratings: **105,104,99,99,97 91,89,87,74,71 63,57,49,43**CSF £57.91 CT £418.54 TOTE £8.10: £3.60, £3.30, £3.60; EX 87.80 Place 6 £131.75, Place 5 £44.89.
**Owner** Kentisbeare Quartet **Bred** Jeremy Green And Sons **Trained** East Ilsley, Berks

**FOCUS**
A very open betting race for this ordinary ladies' handicap, which took place on terrible ground. A group of four raced apart from the others on the stands' side until halfway, when the field fanned out across the track.
**NOTEBOOK**
**Sangiovese** was only a pound higher than when scoring at Kempton in June. Switched to the far rail in the straight, where the ground had not been raced on during the day, he made steady progress to strike the front and responded to some hard driving to see off a persistent rival. The drop in trip was not a problem in the conditions.
**Mr Velocity(IRE)** came very close to landing the hat-trick. Up there from the off, he was collared going to the final furlong but rallied gamely. This was a brave effort in defeat.
**Desert Reign** led a quartet which initially raced apart from the main body of the field up the stands' side. This was only his eighth race and his first try on anything like testing ground.
**Tidy(IRE)**, who has form in soft ground and was well backed, ran his race and probably saw out this longer trip.
**Darghan(IRE)**, a winner in Ireland for John Oxx last year, was having only his second run for this yard having had a spell racing in the States.
T/Plt: £263.80 to a £1 stake. Pool: £61,111.30. 169.10 winning tickets. T/Qpdt: £70.60 to a £1 stake. Pool: £5,109.80. 53.50 winning tickets. ST

## 6289 WOLVERHAMPTON (A.W) (L-H)
Saturday, October 23

**OFFICIAL GOING: Standard**
Riders reported that the surface was riding on the slow side.
Wind: Slight behind Weather: Cloud giving way to rain after the third race.

### 6359 DUNSTALL PARK MAIDEN AUCTION STKS 5f 20y(P)
11:15 (11:20) (H5) 2-Y-O £1,477 (£422; £211) Stalls Low

| Form | | | | RPR |
|---|---|---|---|---|
| 3504 | 1 | | **Il Pranzo**13 6080 2-8-10 68 MFenton 5 (SKirk) *chsd ldrs: led over 1f out: edgd rt ins fnl f: drvn out* 11/4[1] | 68 |
| 0034 | 2 | ½ | **Depressed**16 6023 2-8-5 64 ow1 GGibbons 8 (AndrewReid) *chsd ldrs: ev ch over 1f out: styd on* 10/3[2] | 61 |
| 53 | 3 | 1 | **Our Little Secret (IRE)**21 5954 2-8-4 FNorton 7 (ABerry) *led: hung rt and hdd over 1f out: styd on same pce ins fnl f* 25/1 | 57 |
| 322 | 4 | ¾ | **Pinafore**21 5925 2-8-3 65 ow1 TPQueally 9 (HMorrison) *chsd ldrs: rdn over 1f out: styd on same pce* 10/3[2] | 53 |
| 5004 | 5 | nk | **Lowestoft Playboy**10 6158 2-8-8 68 HayleyTurner(3) 11 (MrsCADunnett) *prom: rdn and hung lft over 1f out: styd on same pce* 9/1 | 60 |
| 4445 | 6 | 1 | **Beverley Beau**27 5816 2-8-9 67 SWhitworth 6 (MrsLStubbs) *mid-div: sn pushed along: hmpd over 3f out: hdwy 1/2-way: no imp appr fnl f* 20/1 | 54 |
| 06 | 7 | nk | **Navigation (IRE)**24 5857 2-8-4 KristinStubbs(7) 2 (TJEtherington) *s.i.s: outpcd: r.o ins fnl f: nt rch ldrs* 14/1 | 65+ |
| 6004 | 8 | 3 | **Ducal Diva**21 5954 2-7-10 54 (p) DFentiman(7) 13 (JRWeymes) *mid-div: rdn 1/2-way: n.d* 40/1 | 37 |
| 000 | 9 | 1 ½ | **Rooks Bridge (IRE)**7 6221 2-8-7 JQuinn 3 (GAHam) *hld up: rdn over 1f out: n.d* 100/1 | 36 |
| 0022 | 10 | ¾ | **Gaudalpin (IRE)**4 6294 2-8-4 64 AMcCarthy 12 (MJAttwater) *chsd ldrs 3f* 5/1[3] | 30 |
| 000 | 11 | 6 | **Mochaccino (IRE)**25 5847 2-8-7 ow2 (v1) DarrenWilliams 1 (DShaw) *sn outpcd* 66/1 | 12 |
| 6560 | 12 | ½ | **Ms Three**13 6093 2-8-5 55 JoannaBadger 4 (RFord) *dwlt: outpcd* 50/1 | 8 |
| 00 | 13 | ½ | **Isle Dream**30 5752 2-8-5 JEdmunds 10 (JBalding) *s.i.s: sn prom: wknd 1/2-way* 100/1 | 6 |

64.91 secs 13 Ran SP% 122.6
Speed ratings: CSF £11.73 TOTE £4.10: £2.20, £1.70, £4.00; EX 24.50.
**Owner** David P Moss **Bred** Mrs F A Veasey **Trained** Upper Lambourn, Berks
**FOCUS**
A modest maiden with the runner-up providing the best line to the form, which is just fair for the grade.
**NOTEBOOK**
**Il Pranzo** had shown enough on turf to suggest that a race of this nature was within his ability, and when it came down to a battle, he showed more determination than the runner-up.
**Depressed** was travelling best of all turning into the straight but, when it came to finding under pressure, the winner pulled out more. She has the ability to win a similar race, though.
**Our Little Secret(IRE)**, who hung right, was beaten in a seller last time but she was one of the least experienced runners in the field and ran a solid race from the front. She is now eligible for a mark. *Official explanation: jockey said filly had hung right-handed*
**Pinafore** once again ran a solid race and certainly did not lack for pace on this drop in trip.
**Lowestoft Playboy** ran a fair race in a conditions event last time and this represented an easier task. He shaped as though he would appreciate a return to six. *Official explanation: jockey said gelding became upset at the start*
**Navigation(IRE)** could not go the early pace but was putting in some good work at the finish. He needed this for a mark and should not be too harshly treated on what he has done to date. He will be suited by a step up in trip.

### 6360 WOLVERHAMPTON-RACECOURSE.CO.UK BANDED STKS 1m 4f 50y(P)
11:45 (11:49) (H5) 3-Y-O+ £1,459 (£417; £208) Stalls Low

| Form | | | | RPR |
|---|---|---|---|---|
| 2000 | 1 | | **Melograno (IRE)**109 3604 4-8-13 40 DNolan(3) 6 (MarkCampion) *hld up: hdwy to chse ldr over 4f out: led over 2f out: rdn clr: eased nr fin* 7/1 | 51 |
| 5000 | 2 | 5 | **Bretton**35 5645 3-8-9 40 (p) TPQueally 8 (BAPearce) *hld up: hdwy over 4f out: rdn to chse wnr over 1f out: no imp* 5/1[3] | 44 |
| 4500 | 3 | 3 ½ | **Valiant Air (IRE)**7 6208 3-8-6 40 (b) PMulrennan(3) 3 (JRWeymes) *hld up in tch: led over 5f out: rdn and hdd over 2f out: wknd over 1f out* 14/1 | 38 |
| 0000 | 4 | 1 ¾ | **Spanish Star**89 4189 7-8-9 40 SarahSayer(7) 7 (MrsNMacauley) *dwlt: hld up: hdwy over 2f out: n.d* 10/1 | 36+ |
| 5535 | 5 | 19 | **Vitelucy**9 1572 5-8-11 40 (v) AQuinn(5) 2 (MissSJWilton) *chsd ldrs: rdn 8f out: wknd 4f out* 11/4[1] | 7 |
| 605 | 6 | 6 | **Ben's Revenge**72 4673 4-9-2 40 VSlattery 9 (MWellings) *hld up: hdwy 6f out: wknd over 3f out* 50/1 | — |
| 2020 | 7 | 2 | **Ben Kenobi**106 3695 6-8-9 40 DeanWilliams(7) 11 (MrsPFord) *s.s: hld up: plld hrd: effrt over 3f out: sn wknd* 10/1 | — |
| | 8 | ½ | **Green Master (POL)**48 4-8-13 40 NChalmers(3) 5 (ASadik) *mid-div: rdn 7f out: wknd 5f out* 18/1 | — |
| 6060 | 9 | shd | **Ricky Martan**28 5796 3-8-9 40 SWhitworth 10 (GCBravery) *plld hrd and prom: wknd 3f out* 12/1 | — |
| 0600 | 10 | 2 ½ | **Mary Carleton**68 4798 3-8-9 40 MHenry 12 (RMHCowell) *s.i.s: hdwy to ld 9f out: hdd over 5f out: wknd over 3f out* 25/1 | — |
| 0000 | 11 | 25 | **Caper**35 5638 4-8-11 40 StephanieHollinshead(5) 4 (RHollinshead) *led 3f: wknd 5 out* 16/1 | — |
| 600- | 12 | 3 ½ | **Brios Boy**306 6234 4-9-2 40 DarrenWilliams 1 (KRBurke) *hld up in tch: wknd 4f out* 9/2[2] | — |

2m 45.13s
**WFA** 3 from 4yo+ 7lb 12 Ran SP% 123.5
Speed ratings: CSF £43.78 TOTE £14.90: £2.70, £3.10, £8.60; EX 64.90.
**Owner** Faulkner West **Bred** David John Brown **Trained** Whitewall, N Yorks
**FOCUS**
A poor event made up of inconsistent types, but the first four finished well clear of the rest.
**NOTEBOOK**
**Melograno(IRE)**, who travelled well throughout, picked up in good style in the straight to win easily. Generally inconsistent, he was winning for the first time in 18 starts.
**Bretton** has now gone 22 races without a win but has finished runner-up three times. He appreciated the return to this trip having failed to get home over two miles last time.
**Valiant Air(IRE)** has plenty of form over this trip but on this occasion he did not see it out as well as the first two.
**Spanish Star**, returning from a break, is an eight-time winner on Fibresand and it remains to be seen how he adapts to this different surface.
**Vitelucy**, returning to the Flat having been successful over hurdles during the summer, has winning form on Polytrack, but she was a disappointing favourite on this occasion.
**Brios Boy** came in for market support on his first start in ten months, but he dropped out tamely with half a mile to run.

### 6361 HOLIDAY INN GARDEN COURT TRI-BANDED STKS 1m 1f 103y(P)
12:15 (12:15) (H5) 3-Y-O £1,473 (£421; £210) Stalls Low

| Form | | | | RPR |
|---|---|---|---|---|
| 6504 | 1 | | **Larad (IRE)**7 6230 3-8-3 40 ow1 (b) DerekNolan(7) 6 (JSMoore) *s.i.s: hld up: hdwy 3f out: led over 1f out: rdn clr: eased nr fin* 3/1[1] | 46 |
| 0040 | 2 | 1 ¾ | **Knight Of Hearts (IRE)**54 5178 3-8-9 45 MLawson(5) 12 (PABlockley) *hld up in tch: racd keenly: rdn to ld over 2f out: hdd over 1f out: styd on same pce fnl f* 8/1 | 47 |
| 3024 | 3 | ¾ | **Campbells Lad**12 6112 3-8-9 45 PPMathers(5) 1 (ABerry) *a.p: rdn over 2f out: styd on same pce fnl f* 7/1[3] | 45 |
| 5000 | 4 | 1 ¾ | **Ink In Gold (IRE)**14 6058 3-9-0 45 VSlattery 3 (PABlockley) *s.i.s: hld up: hdwy over 2f out: nt clr run over 1f out : nt rch ldrs* 33/1 | 42 |
| 005 | 5 | ¾ | **Flying Spud**7 6227 3-8-12 45 ow1 DNolan(3) 9 (JLSpearing) *hld up: hdwy over 2f out: styd on* 9/2[2] | 42 |
| 0030 | 6 | 1 | **Sixtilsix (IRE)**37 5585 3-9-0 45 JCarroll 7 (HAlexander) *led 7f: wknd fnl f* 16/1 | 39 |
| 2413 | 7 | 1 ¾ | **Secret Bloom**165 2016 3-9-0 45 (v) DarrenWilliams 2 (JRNorton) *prom 7f* 8/1 | 36 |
| 3533 | 8 | ½ | **Red Rocky**12 6120 3-8-9 45 (p) StephanieHollinshead(5) 4 (RHollinshead) *trckd ldrs: plld hrd: rdn and wknd over 1f out* 15/2 | 35 |
| 0656 | 9 | 3 | **Acca Larentia (IRE)**24 5863 3-8-11 45 HayleyTurner(3) 10 (RMWhitaker) *prom 7f* 14/1 | 29 |
| 5000 | 10 | 2 | **Lady Predominant**28 5793 3-8-7 45 FrancesPickard(7) 11 (GFBridgwater) *hld up: hdwy 5f out: wknd over 3f out* 33/1 | 25 |
| -500 | 11 | 3 ½ | **Warif (USA)**27 2485 3-8-11 45 THamilton(3) 5 (MESowersby) *hld up: rdn 1/2-way: a bhd* 66/1 | 19 |
| 0602 | 12 | 7 | **Game Flora**55 5141 3-8-11 45 PMulrennan(3) 8 (MESowersby) *plld hrd: trckd ldr: rdn and ev ch over 2f out: wknd over 1f out* 9/1 | 6 |

2m 7.21s 12 Ran SP% 119.6
Speed ratings: CSF £27.33 TOTE £5.00: £1.70, £3.40, £2.60; EX 35.80.
**Owner** A P Crook **Bred** Mrs E Thompson **Trained** East Garston, Berks
**FOCUS**
The pace was not that strong in this fair banded event.
**NOTEBOOK**
**Larad(IRE)** found the return to Poytrack bringing about an improved display. He picked up well in the straight to win with ease, and he has now been successful three times in banded grade.
**Knight Of Hearts(IRE)**, returning from a two-month break, failed to stay two miles last time and appreciated the drop back in trip. He was running in banded company for the first time and has clearly found his level.
**Campbells Lad**, who was trying Polytrack for the first time, kept on well enough in the straight, but his best trip remains a mystery.
**Ink In Gold(IRE)** ran his best race on turf over seven furlongs in heavy ground. This was a fair effort on his All-Weather debut given that he fluffed the start.
**Flying Spud** stayed on fairly well from off the pace, and did not look to fail through lack of stamina.

### 6362 ANDREW HIGGINBOTTOM 40TH BIRTHDAY BANDED STKS 7f 32y(P)
12:45 (12:46) (H5) 3-Y-O+ £1,501 (£429; £214) Stalls High

| Form | | | | RPR |
|---|---|---|---|---|
| 4350 | 1 | | **Tokewanna**7 6227 4-8-11 45 (t) PPMathers(5) 6 (WMBrisbourne) *hld up in tch: hmpd and lost pl over 2f out: swtchd rt and hdwy over 1f out: str run to ld wl ins fnl f* 9/2[2] | 57+ |
| 5050 | 2 | 1 | **Ace-Ma-Vahra**37 5587 6-9-2 45 (b) JBramhill 11 (SRBowring) *hld up in tch: rdn over 2f out: ev ch ins fnl f: styd on* 12/1 | 48 |
| 3600 | 3 | 1 | **Dexileos (IRE)**33 5691 5-8-13 45 (t) NChalmers(3) 12 (ADWPinder) *chsd ldrs: rdn to ld 1f out: hdd wl ins fnl f* 10/1 | 46 |
| 0010 | 4 | 1 ½ | **Savernake Brave (IRE)**28 5794 3-9-0 45 GBaker 8 (MrsHSweeting) *s.s: hdwy over 2f out: rdn and edgd lft over 1f out: styd on same pce fnl f* 9/2[2] | 42 |
| 55-0 | 5 | ½ | **Eastern Scarlet (IRE)**75 4605 4-9-2 45 (p) JQuinn 7 (VSmith) *s.s: hdwy over 5f out: styd on same pce appr fnl f* 11/2[3] | 41 |
| 0000 | 6 | 1 ¼ | **Pagan Storm (USA)**13 6097 4-8-9 45 KristinStubbs(7) 10 (MrsLStubbs) *plld hrd: led 6f out: hdd & wknd 1f out* 7/2[1] | 38 |
| 3606 | 7 | 1 ½ | **Spring Dancer**35 5639 3-8-11 45 (t) PMulrennan(3) 9 (TJFitzgerald) *prom over 5f* 7/1 | 34 |
| 0040 | 8 | shd | **Gemini Lady**28 5795 4-9-2 45 (b) JCarroll 4 (MrsGSRees) *hld up: hdwy 3f out: wknd 2f out* 10/1 | 34 |
| 6050 | 9 | 9 | **Balmacara**49 5283 5-9-2 45 TPQueally 3 (MissKBBoutflower) *chsd ldrs over 4f* 20/1 | 12 |
| 4000 | 10 | nk | **Bahama Belle**78 4517 3-9-0 45 OUrbina 2 (MrsLCJewell) *prom to 1/2-way* 25/1 | 11 |
| 0600 | 11 | 11 | **Sonearsofar (IRE)**56 5110 4-9-2 45 GGibbons 1 (JParkes) *led 1f: remained handy tl wknd over 2f out* 40/1 | — |

1m 32.8s
**WFA** 3 from 4yo+ 2lb 11 Ran SP% 123.4
Speed ratings: CSF £59.08 TOTE £5.70: £2.40, £4.10, £3.80; EX 57.10.
**Owner** Merryland Properties Ltd **Bred** Brook Stud Ltd **Trained** Great Ness, Shropshire
■ Stewards Enquiry : P P Mathers caution: careless riding
**FOCUS**
A very modest race but the form appears solid, although the whole field combined could boast just five wins from 221 starts.

**NOTEBOOK**
**Tokewanna** suffered a desperate run on the final bend and, having lost ground, was forced to challenge widest of all. She finished very strongly though, and although she took 24 runs to get off the mark, she looks capable of winning again on this surface in this grade.
**Ace-Ma-Vahra** finally got the measure of Dexileos, only to get mugged by the winner close home. She ran well but could be of more interest in this grade on the Southwell Fibresand.
**Dexileos(IRE)** ran a fair race on his Polytrack debut but his losing run now extends to 25 starts.
**Savernake Brave(IRE)** lost his race at the start. He was successful in this grade at Folkestone last month and has the ability to win a similar race if getting away on terms. *Official explanation: jockey said gelding missed the break*
**Eastern Scarlet(IRE)** is another who does his chances no good by often starting slowly.
**Pagan Storm(USA)** failed to settle on his first outing in banded company.
**Balmacara** *Official explanation: trainer said filly was unsuited by the loose surface*
**Bahama Belle** *Official explanation: jockey said filly was hanging*

## 6363 CIVIL WEDDINGS AT DUNSTALL PARK BANDED STKS 5f 216y(P)
1:15 (1:17) (H5) 3-Y-O+ £1,494 (£427; £213) Stalls Low

Form RPR
0000 1 **Regal Song (IRE)**[6] 6246 8-9-5 49 (b) OUrbina 4 64+
(TJEtherington) *trckd ldrs: rdn to ld over 1f out: r.o* **16/1**
3000 2 2 ½ **Chorus**[14] 6059 7-9-0 49 (v) AQuinn(5) 12 56
(BRMillman) *prom: hmpd and lost pl 5f out: hdwy over 1f out: r.o: nt rch wnr* **12/1**
450 3 2 **Breezit (USA)**[124] 3155 3-8-12 48 PMakin(5) 13 49
(SRBowring) *hld up: rdn over 2f out: hung lft and r.o ins fnl f: nt rch ldrs* **20/1**
0000 4 ¾ **Long Weekend (IRE)**[85] 4291 6-9-6 50 DarrenWilliams 3 49
(DShaw) *s.s: hdwy and nt clr run over 1f out: nt trble ldrs* **10/1**
0000 5 nk **O'l Lucy Broon**[12] 6114 3-9-4 49 PFessey 9 47
(JSGoldie) *outpcd: r.o ins fnl f: nvr nrr* **10/1**
0515 6 shd **Tappit (IRE)**[4] 6288 5-8-13 48 MSavage(5) 7 46
(NEBerry) *led 5f out to 4f: rdn over 1f out: wknd fnl f* **4/1**[1]
1200 7 1 ¼ **Baytown Flyer**[37] 5597 4-9-6 50 TPQueally 5 44
(PSMcentee) *led 1f: remained w ldrs: rdn to ld wl over 1f out: sn hdd : wknd ins fnl f* **6/1**[3]
20-0 8 2 ½ **Amber Legend**[224] 1008 3-9-5 50 SChin 10 36
(MsDeborahJEvans) *hld up: rdn over 2f out: n.d* **33/1**
0200 9 ½ **Scary Night (IRE)**[65] 4881 4-9-6 50 (p) JEdmunds 2 35
(JBalding) *w ldrs: led 4f out: rdn and hdd wl over 1f out: sn wknd* **10/1**
0310 10 3 **Rehia**[31] 5736 3-9-4 49 RSmith 11 25
(JWHills) *chsd ldrs 4f* **20/1**
5430 11 ½ **Linden's Lady**[35] 5639 4-8-12 49 (b) DFentiman(7) 6 23
(JRWeymes) *hld up in tch: plld hrd: rdn and wknd 2f out* **6/1**[3]
-100 12 1 ½ **Strike Lucky**[98] 3935 4-9-5 49 JQuinn 8 19
(PJMakin) *chsd ldrs: hmpd and lost pl over 3f out: n.d after* **5/1**[2]
4000 13 dist **Sounds Lucky**[112] 3533 8-9-6 50 (b) GGibbons 1 —
(AndrewReid) *s.s: a t.o* **20/1**

1m 18.23s
**WFA** 3 from 4yo+ 1lb 13 Ran SP% **123.3**
Speed ratings: CSF £190.69 TOTE £21.50: £7.10, £4.70, £7.50; EX 201.60.
**Owner** J Brierley **Bred** Humphrey Okeke **Trained** Norton, N Yorks

**FOCUS**
A fair banded event won by a horse who was rated much higher at the start of the season.

**NOTEBOOK**
**Regal Song(IRE)** has had a poor season but has dropped in the handicap as a result. Having his first start in banded company, he got this six furlongs well, despite having done all his previous winning over the minimum trip.
**Chorus** used to be suited by the Fibresand surface here, and on this evidence she has adapted well to the new Polytrack surface.
**Breezit(USA)**, running in banded grade for the first time, stays farther than this and was keeping on well at the end of the race.
**Long Weekend(IRE)** was chopped for room early in the straight and in the circumstances he was not disgraced. His slow starts always put him at a disadvantage, though.
**O'l Lucy Broon** looks worth trying over another furlong.
**Tappit(IRE)** showed plenty of pace but he was backpeddling entering the straight.
**Strike Lucky** *Official explanation: jockey said gelding was hampered on the bend*
**Sounds Lucky** *Official explanation: jockey said gelding was unruly and missed the break*

## 6364 RINGSIDE BANDED STKS 1m 141y(P)
1:45 (1:45) (H5) 4-Y-O+ £1,480 (£423; £211) Stalls Low

Form RPR
0000 1 **Adobe**[24] 5868 9-9-0 50 MSavage(5) 2 59+
(WMBrisbourne) *trckd ldrs: racd keenly: led over 1f out: r.o wl* **13/2**[3]
1160 2 1 ¾ **Extemporise (IRE)**[44] 5411 4-9-5 50 GBaker 13 56
(TTClement) *hld up: hdwy over 2f out: n.m.r over 1f out: r.o* **25/1**
0006 3 1 ¼ **Cross Ash (IRE)**[11] 6146 4-9-0 50 PMakin(5) 3 53
(RHollinshead) *hld up: r.o ins fnl f: nt rch ldrs* **28/1**
0006 4 ½ **Kindness**[12] 6132 4-9-4 49 JQuinn 10 51
(ADWPinder) *plld hrd and prom: led 6f out: hung lft and hdd over 1f out: no ex ins fnl f* **25/1**
0500 5 nk **Lucefer (IRE)**[7] 6227 6-9-3 48 OUrbina 11 49
(GCHChung) *hld up: hdwy over 2f out: nt trble ldrs* **10/1**
0251 6 1 **Time To Regret**[8] 6201 4-9-3 51 THamilton(3) 8 50
(JSWainwright) *plld hrd: led: hdd 6f out: remained handy: rdn over 2f out: styd on same pce appr fnl f* **10/3**[1]
1231 7 1 ½ **Caerphilly Gal**[7] 6227 4-8-12 48 (e[1]) DFox(5) 4 44
(PLGilligan) *hld up: hdwy over 1f out: nvr trbld ldrs* **9/2**[2]
5000 8 shd **Disabuse**[15] 6047 4-9-3 48 (v[1]) DarrenWilliams 12 44
(DShaw) *dwlt: hld up: n.d* **20/1**
5030 9 ¾ **Scarrotoo**[38] 5575 6-9-3 48 (be) EstherRemmerswaal 6 43
(SCWilliams) *s.i.s: hld up: n.d* **11/1**
0021 10 1 ¼ **Ballare (IRE)**[14] 6057 5-9-5 50 (v) TWilliams 5 42
(BobJones) *w ldrs: racd keenly: rdn 1/2-way: wknd over 1f out* **13/2**[3]
4050 11 2 **Sorbiesharry (IRE)**[61] 5002 5-9-3 48 (p) PMcCabe 1 36
(MrsNMacauley) *plld hrd and prom: wknd over 1f out* **12/1**
0050 12 1 ¼ **Lasser Light (IRE)**[30] 5751 4-9-2 50 DNolan(3) 7 36
(DGBridgwater) *hld up: wknd over 3f out: wknd over 2f out* **50/1**
/0-1 13 nk **Wizard Of Us**[11] 6138 4-9-13 58 SRighton 9 43
(MMullineaux) *plld hrd and prom: wknd over 2f out* **12/1**

1m 53.66s 13 Ran SP% **118.6**
Speed ratings: CSF £166.40 TOTE £5.50: £1.90, £6.40, £4.30; EX 177.50 Place 6 £3,241.59, Place 5 £1,757.15.
**Owner** P R Kirk **Bred** Sheikh Mohammed Bin Rashid Al Maktoum **Trained** Great Ness, Shropshire

**FOCUS**
A fair event and strong form for the grade.

**NOTEBOOK**
**Adobe** has been struggling off marks in the 60s on turf this season but found this lower grade of racing far easier. He got first run on the runner-up and could go in again at a similar level while in this mood.
**Extemporise(IRE)** had to wait for a gap on the inside and in the meantime the winner got first run. Twice a winner earlier in the year, he looks sure to go one better in this grade before long.
**Cross Ash(IRE)** stayed this longer trip well on his first start on Polytrack.
**Kindness**, still a maiden after 29 starts, did not settle in front and was there to be shot at.
**Lucefer(IRE)**, a disappointing favourite at Yarmouth last time, never got himself into a competitive position.
**Time To Regret** lost his chance by pulling too hard in front.
T/Plt: £4,194.30 to a £1 stake. Pool: £22,982.50. 4.00 winning tickets. T/Qpdt: £550.60 to a £1 stake. Pool: £2,306.70. 3.10 winning tickets. CR

6365 - 6366a (Foreign Racing) - See Raceform Interactive

# 6098 CURRAGH (R-H)
Saturday, October 23

**OFFICIAL GOING: Soft (soft to heavy in straight)**

## 6367a GERRARDSTOWN HOUSE STUD SILKEN GLIDER STKS (LISTED RACE) (FILLIES) 1m
3:00 (3:01) 2-Y-O £25,214 (£7,397; £3,524; £1,200)

RPR
1 **Allexina**[24] 5878 2-8-11 FMBerry 9 100+
(JohnMOxx, Ire) *mde virtually all: rdn early st: styd on wl fr over 1f out* **14/1**
2 2 **Adaala (USA)**[21] 5961 2-8-11 96 DPMcDonogh 12 96+
(KevinPrendergast, Ire) *a.p: 4th travelling wl ent st: impr into 2nd 2f out: no imp fr over 1f out: kpt on wl* **9/2**[1]
3 3 ½ **Alexander Icequeen (IRE)**[76] 4592 2-8-11 101 PJSmullen 13 89
(DKWeld, Ire) *hld up towards rr: 7th and hdwy early st: mod 3rd and kpt on fr over 1f out* **6/1**[2]
4 1 ½ **Laurannah**[13] 6105 2-8-11 76 NGMcCullagh 1 86
(AndrewOliver, Ire) *chsd ldrs on outer: 3rd and rdn ent st: kpt on same pce fr 2f out* **14/1**
5 1 **Queen Titi (IRE)**[10] 6164 2-8-11 PCosgrave 6 84
(JosephCrowley, Ire) *hld up towards rr: prog on outer ent st: 6th 1 1/2f out: no imp fnl f* **6/1**[2]
6 ½ **Sweet Gypsy Rose (IRE)**[76] 4592 2-8-11 95 WMLordan 11 83
(DavidWachman, Ire) *towards rr: prog on inner early st: styd on fr 2f out* **12/1**
7 2 **Briolette (IRE)**[10] 6164 2-8-11 JAHeffernan 4 79
(APO'Brien, Ire) *settled 2nd: rdn early st: no ex fr 1 1/2f out* **12/1**
8 ½ **Pout (IRE)**[13] 6101 2-8-11 81 DMGrant 8 78
(JohnJosephMurphy, Ire) *chsd ldrs: 7th appr st: no imp fr 2f out* **16/1**
9 1 ½ **Showbiz (IRE)**[93] 4071 2-8-11 KJManning 5 75
(DavidWachman, Ire) *mid-div: 5th appr st: no ex fr over 2f out* **6/1**[2]
10 nk **Waldblume (GER)**[37] 5599 2-8-11 MJKinane 10 74
(JohnMOxx, Ire) *mid-div: 6th 1/2-way: rdn and wknd fr 2f out* **9/2**[1]
11 shd **Bonita Rock (IRE)**[13] 6105 2-8-11 RMBurke 7 74
(RJOsborne, Ire) *hld up in tch: wknd early st* **10/1**[3]
12 9 **Secret Crypt (USA)**[119] 3329 2-8-11 TPO'Shea 2 56
(WTFarrell, Ire) *a towards rr* **50/1**
13 shd **Fuerta Ventura (IRE)**[21] 5961 2-8-11 82 PShanahan 3 56
(KJCondon, Ire) *towards rr: wknd st* **33/1**

1m 48.5s 13 Ran SP% **127.8**
Speed ratings: CSF £81.23 TOTE £38.40: £8.70, £1.70, £2.00; DF 240.60.
**Owner** J Higgins **Bred** Gerrardstown House Stud **Trained** Currabeg, Co Kildare

**NOTEBOOK**
**Allexina** was a short-head winner of her maiden at Limerick but paid tribute to her subsequent sixth behind Gaff at Fairyhouse with a fairly comprehensive all-the-way win here. She set an ordinary enough pace but was stretching them early in the straight and her stamina shone through.
**Adaala(USA)** looked a possibility turning into the straight but, in second place over the last two furlongs, could never get in an effective blow.
**Alexander Icequeen(IRE)** is flattered by her rating. She looked very one-paced in third from over a furlong out.
**Laurannah** is only rated 76 and has rather blown her chance of a nursery success with this improved display.
**Queen Titi(IRE)**, third in a Navan maiden ten days earlier, was another to show improved form.
**Waldblume(GER)**, a better-fancied stable companion of the winner with a Tipperary maiden success behind here, did not experience much luck in running and was done with over a quarter mile out.

6374 - 6376a (Foreign Racing) - See Raceform Interactive

# 5329 BADEN-BADEN (L-H)
Sunday, October 24

**OFFICIAL GOING: Soft**

## 6377a PREIS DES WINTERKONIGIN (GROUP 3) (FILLIES) 1m
1:15 (1:17) 2-Y-O £42,254 (£16,197; £7,746; £4,225)

RPR
1 **Sorrent (GER)** 2-8-11 THellier 2 106+
(ASchutz, Germany) *raced in 6th, stayed on inside & went 3rd straight, led just over 2f out, soon 2l clear, driven out*
2 4 **Gonbarda (GER)** 2-8-11 ABoschert 6 98
(UOstmann, Germany) *outpaced early & in rear, good headway well over 1f out, ran on to take 2nd close home* 2
3 ½ **Kahlua (GER)** 2-8-11 ASuborics 7 97
(MarioHofer, Germany) *always in touch, 4th straight, headway to reach 2nd approaching final f, kept on one pace & lost 2nd close home* 1
4 2 **Wings Of Glory (GER)** 2-8-11 WMongil 5 93
(HBlume, Germany) *always prominent, went 2nd 3f out, ridden & outpaced by winner over 1f out, no extra final f* 3
5 nk **Free Dreams (GER)**[51] 5280 2-8-11 FilipMinarik 11 92
(MarioHofer, Germany) *held up, 8th straight, good headway 2f out, ran on same pace final f*
6 shd **Mandahush (GER)** 2-8-11 J-PCarvalho 1 92
(MarioHofer, Germany) *mid-division, 7th straight, soon one pace*
7 6 **Glenaka (GER)** 2-8-11 IFerguson 3 80
(CVonDerRecke, Germany) *mid-division, 6th straight, soon beaten*
8 hd **Alpenrot (IRE)** 2-8-11 NRichter 9 79
(PRau, Germany) *raced keenly, led to just over 2f out, weakened quickly*

**9** *3* **Fighting Lady (GER)** 2-8-11 ................................ LHammer-Hansen 10 73
(DKRichardson, Germany) *always behind*

**10** *½* **Wonderful Day (GER)** 2-8-11 ................................ JPalik 12 72
(MTrinker, Germany) *tracked leaders, 5th straight, soon beaten*

**11** *4 ½* **Fantastic Fleur (GER)** 2-8-11 ................................ JQuinn 8 63
(CVonDerRecke, Germany) *chased leader to 3f out, soon weakened*

1m 43.86s **11** Ran SP% **112.1**
Speed ratings: .
**Owner** Frau M Herbert **Bred** Dr K Schulte **Trained** Germany

## 6378a BADEN-WURTTEMBERG TROPHY (GROUP 3) 1m 3f
**2:35** (2:39) 3-Y-0+ **£26,761** (£10,563; £5,634; £3,169)

RPR

**1** **Deva (GER)**[28] 5824 5-9-0 ................................ ASuborics 6 101
(DRonge, Germany) *mid-division, 5th on inside straight, switched to outside 2f out, ran on to lead 100y out, driven out*

**2** *½* **Champion's Day (GER)** 3-8-7 ................................ FilipMinarik 5 99
(MRulec, Germany) *chsd ldr, led 3f out, hdd 1 1/2f out, every chance inside final f, swished tail & hung under pressure but ran on well*

**3** *nk* **Mity Dancer (GER)**[14] 6107 4-8-10 ................................ LHammer-Hansen 7 96
(DKRichardson, Germany) *disputed 3rd, 2nd straight, quickened to take narrow lead 1 1/2f out, headed 100y out, just outpaced final stages*

**4** *½* **Longridge (GER)**[28] 5824 6-9-2 ................................ J-PCarvalho 1 101
(MarioHofer, Germany) *always close up, 3rd straight, every chance from 1 1/2f out, no extra closing stages & slightly hampered last strides* 3

**5** *½* **Fight Club (GER)**[14] 6106 3-8-12 ................................ NRichter 4 102
(ASchutz, Germany) *held up, 2nd last to 3f out, kept on final 2f but never reached first four* 1

**6** *2 ½* **Near Honor (GER)**[21] 5975 6-9-0 ................................ WMongil 10 94
(PVovcenko, Germany) *mid-division, 7th straight, never able to challenge*

**7** *1* **Royal Experiment (USA)**[42] 5506 5-9-0 ................................ THellier 3 93
(WidoNeuroth, Norway) *prominent, 6th straight, one pace*

**8** *1* **Standby Dancer (GER)**[182] 1655 8-9-2 ................................ JQuinn 9 93
(DrABolte, Germany) *always towards rear*

**9** *½* **Mambembe (ARG)** 6-9-0 ................................ YvonneDurant 8 90
(RoyArneKvisla, Sweden) *led to 3f out, 4th straight, weakened quickly*

**10** *3 ½* **Dalicia (GER)**[36] 5667 3-8-6 ow1 ................................ ABoschert 11 83
(PRau, Germany) *last to straight, always behind* 2

**11** *7* **Santiago Matias (CHI)**[42] 5506 5-9-0 ................................ (b) IFerguson 2 74
(FCastro, Sweden) *always towards rear*

2m 28.13s
**WFA** 3 from 4yo+ 6lb **11** Ran SP% **131.0**
Speed ratings: .
**Owner** Gestut Park Wiedingen **Bred** H Von Finck **Trained** Germany

## 6379a WETTARENA BADEN SPRINT-CUP (GROUP 3) 7f
**3:55** (4:01) 3-Y-0+ **£27,761** (£10,563; £5,634; £3,169)

RPR

**1** **Areias (GER)**[53] 5255 6-8-13 ................................ THellier 4 111
(ASchutz, Germany) *always close up, 3rd & not much room 1 1/2f out, switched right & quickened to lead 100y out, ran on well*

**2** *½* **Key To Pleasure (GER)**[53] 5255 4-8-13 ................................ J-PCarvalho 7 110
(MarioHofer, Germany) *led or disputed lead til gained definite advantage 1 1/2f out, headed 100y out, kept on* 1

**3** *2 ½* **Lindholm (GER)**[43] 5488 5-8-13 ................................ KKerekes 13 104
(WernerGlanz, Germany) *always close up, 4th straight, stayed on under pressure final 2f*

**4** *hd* **Glad To Be Fast (IRE)**[53] 5255 4-8-13 ................................ JQuinn 3 103
(MarioHofer, Germany) *mid-division, 7th straight, staye don well from over 1f out*

**5** *nk* **Felicity (GER)**[53] 5255 3-8-7 ................................ ABoschert 14 99
(PRau, Germany) *disputed lead to 1 1/2f out, one pace* 2

**6** *1* **Forever Free (GER)**[84] 4378 4-8-13 ................................ NRichter 1 100
(DKRichardson, Germany) *held up, stayed on steadily final 2f*

**7** *2 ½* **Musadif (USA)**[42] 5505 6-9-1 ................................ YvonneDurant 16 96
(RoyArneKvisla, Sweden) *raced in 5th, one pace final 2f*

**8** *1 ¼* **Shinko's Best (IRE)** 3-8-7 ................................ IFerguson 12 87
(AWohler, Germany) *raced in 6th, one pace final 2f* 3

**9** *1* **Apple Green (DEN)**[43] 6-8-11 ................................ LHammer-Hansen 6 86
(SJensen, Denmark) *always mid-division*

**10** *nk* **Gold Type (IRE)**[53] 5255 5-8-11 ................................ ADeVries 15 85
(KWoodburn) *always mid-division*

**11** *1 ¼* **Toylsome**[77] 4596 5-8-13 ................................ ASuborics 8 84
(PSchiergen, Germany) *always towards rear* 3

**12** *½* **Blaise Castle (USA)**[9] 6193 4-8-8 ow2 ................................ RWinston 11 78
(GAButler) *missed break, never a factor*

**13** *½* **Night Set (GER)**[75] 5-8-11 ................................ FilipMinarik 2 80
(MWeber, Germany) *never a factor*

**14** *2* **Barrichello (GER)**[77] 4596 4-8-11 ................................ (b) WMongil 5 75
(PSchiergen, Germany) *always in rear*

**15** *¾* **Chagall**[441] 4037 7-8-11 ................................ (b) AngelaKull-Hohn 10 73
(BruceHellier, Germany) *always behind*

**16** *nse* **Austrian (GER)**[189] 3-8-10 ................................ JPalik 9 74
(MSowa, Germany) *always behind*

**WFA** 3 from 4yo+ 2lb **16** Ran SP% **129.6**
Speed ratings: .
**Owner** S Glink **Bred** Gestut Graditz **Trained** Germany

**NOTEBOOK**
**Blaise Castle(USA)** missed the break, which was always going to make things difficult from her double-figure draw, and did not get the clearest of runs when trying to make up ground on the home bend.

# 5330 CAPANNELLE (R-H)
Sunday, October 24

**OFFICIAL GOING: Good to soft**

## 6380a PREMIO GUIDO BERARDELLI (GROUP 3) 1m 1f
**2:30** (2:45) 2-Y-0 **£38,222** (£17,751; £9,956; £4,978)

RPR

**1** *1 ½* **Le Giare (IRE)** 2-8-11 ................................ OFrancera 5 98
(RBrogi, Italy) *mid-division, headway over 3f out, went 2nd 1 1/2f out, kept on, finished 2nd, awarded race* 3

**2** *1 ½* **Tedo (GER)** 2-8-11 ................................ MDemuro 7 92
(BGrizzetti, Italy) *racd in 4th, hdwy to press ldrs whn bmpd and lost pl over 1 1/2f out, rallied to tk 3rd clsng stages, fin 3rd, plcd 2nd* 1

**3** **Bernard (FR)** 2-8-11 ................................ TQuinn 13 92
(PSchiergen, Germany) *raced in 3rd, led 2f out, soon ridden and hung left, ridden out, ran on well, finished first, disqualified, placed 3rd* 2

**4** *1 ½* **Stick At Nothing (IRE)** 2-8-11 ................................ GTemperini 6 89
(IBugattella, Italy) *held up towards rear, headway to go 3rd over 1f out, lost 3rd close home*

**5** *nse* **Montalegre (IRE)** 2-8-11 ................................ EBotti 14 89
(GBotti, Italy) *raced in 5th, stayed on at same pace under pressure final 2f*

**6** *1 ½* **Jane's Park (IRE)** 2-8-11 ................................ GMarcelli 8 86
(LDiDio, Italy) *raced in 8th, stayed on at one pace final 2 f*

**7** *nk* **For Pub (ITY)** 2-8-11 ................................ PAgus 2 85
(LRiccardi, Italy) *led til headed over 2f out, weakened*

**8** *1 ½* **Ballycotton Bay (IRE)** 2-8-11 ................................ DVargiu 4 82
(LD'Auria, Italy) *held up in rear, never a factor*

**9** *hd* **Mister Fasliyev (IRE)**[142] 2669 2-8-11 ................................ GCossu 12 82
(GColella, Italy) *raced in 2nd til led over 2f out, soon headed and weakened*

**10** *3 ½* **Peppone (ITY)**[142] 2669 2-8-11 ................................ (b) CFiocchi 9 75
(RMenichetti, Italy) *always in rear*

**11** *2* **Urgente** 2-8-11 ................................ MBelli 15 71
(LBrogi, Italy) *always in rear*

**12** *4* **Jayat** 2-8-11 ................................ MPasquale 11 63
(LRiccardi, Italy) *spread plate and reshod before start, raced in 7th, weakened 3f out*

**13** *2 ½* **Green Chapel (ITY)** 2-8-11 ................................ LSorrentino 3 58
(FOliverio, Italy) *raced in 6th, weakened over 3f out*

1m 53.7s **13** Ran SP% **133.7**
Speed ratings: .
**Owner** Scuderia Elena **Bred** Mountvilla Pertnership **Trained** Italy
■ Stewards Enquiry : T Quinn five-day ban: careless riding

## 6381a PREMIO LYDIA TESIO DARLEY (GROUP 1) (3YO+ FILLIES & MARES) 1m 2f
**3:30** (3:51) 3-Y-0+ **£136,690** (£69,771; £40,880; £20,440)

RPR

**1** **Lune D'Or (FR)**[42] 5501 3-8-10 ................................ TJarnet 4 112
(RGibson, France) *held up, 8th straight, smooth headway to lead well over 1f out, driven out* **758/100**

**2** *2* **Walkamia (FR)**[21] 5978 4-8-13 ................................ ELegrix 12 106
(AFabre, France) *always prominent, hard ridden & every chance well over 1f out, kept on same pace final f* **5/2**[2]

**3** *½* **Super Bobbina (IRE)**[85] 4356 3-8-10 ................................ DVargiu 1 108
(IBugattella, Italy) *broke well, held up, 7th straight, headway over 2f out, every chance well over 1f out, kept on same pace final f* **107/10**

**4** *2* **Royal Fantasy (GER)**[22] 5966 4-8-13 ................................ GBietolini 11 102
(HSteinmetz, Germany) *rear early, headway & 5th on outside straight, brought wide, kept on one pace final f* **163/10**

**5** *1 ½* **Landinium (ITY)**[22] 5970 5-8-13 ................................ CColombi 7 99
(VValiani, Italy) *held up in rear, still last 2f out, finished well* **54/1**

**6** *1 ½* **Mazuna (IRE)**[30] 5763 3-8-10 ................................ RMoore 14 99
(CEBrittain) *towards rear to straight, headway over 2f out, kept on, never near to challenge* **103/10**

**7** *nse* **Windy Britain**[39] 5576 5-8-13 ................................ PAgus 5 96
(VValiani, Italy) *mid-division on outside straight, brought wide, some progress under pressure final 2f, never a threat* **176/10**

**8** *1* **Saldentigerin (GER)**[28] 5824 3-8-10 ................................ TQuinn 9 97
(PSchiergen, Germany) *soon led, set strong pace, 3l clear straight, headed well over 1f out, gradually weakened* **22/10**[1]

**9** *2* **Step Danzer (IRE)**[122] 3258 3-8-10 ................................ MMonteriso 10 93
(ABotti, Italy) *held up, kept on under pressure final 2f, never nearer* **38/1**

**10** *3* **Holy Moon (IRE)**[39] 5576 4-8-13 ................................ EBotti 8 86
(ABotti, Italy) *headway over 2f out, 6th over 1f out, hard ridden & weakened quickly from distance* **62/1**

**11** *4* **Monturani (IRE)**[35] 5679 5-8-13 ................................ TEDurcan 16 78
(GWragg) *raced in 2nd to turn, 3rd straight, ridden well over 2f out, soon weakened* **82/10**

**12** *3* **Quetena (GER)**[63] 4980 4-8-13 ................................ IRossi 3 73
(PRau, Germany) *held up, headway on inside over 3f out to press leaders, ridden & beaten 2f out* **80/1**

**13** *2* **Marbye (IRE)**[14] 6109 4-8-13 ................................ MDemuro 6 69
(BGrizzetti, Italy) *held up in rear til headway on inside entering straight, close up & hard ridden over 2f out, soon beaten & eased* **44/10**[3]

**14** *dist* **Bond Deal (IRE)**[154] 2341 3-8-10 ................................ PAragoni 13 —
(LRiccardi, Italy) *prominent, 2nd straight, weakened over 2f out* **216/1**

2m 2.40s
**WFA** 3 from 4yo+ 5lb **14** Ran SP% **137.1**
Speed ratings: .
**Owner** Mme P De Moussac **Bred** Haras De Mezeray S A **Trained** France

**NOTEBOOK**
**Mazuna(IRE)** kept on steadily from the rear without threatening to take a hand in the finish.
**Monturani(IRE)** was bang there on the outside with three furlongs to run but then dropped away tamely.

## 6329 LONGCHAMP (R-H)

Sunday, October 24

**OFFICIAL GOING: Heavy**

### 6382a PRIX ROYAL-OAK (GROUP 1) 1m 7f 110y

**2:20** (2:21) 3-Y-0+ **£80,479** (£32,197; £16,099; £8,042)

RPR

**1** **Westerner**[21] 5976 5-9-4 ........ SPasquier 4 119
(ELellouche, France) *held up, 5th straight, led just under 2f out, ran on well, easily* **2/5**[1]

**2** 2 1/2 **Behkara (IRE)**[22] 5966 4-9-1 ........ CSoumillon 3 114
(ADeRoyer-Dupre, France) *racd keenly in 3rd early, cl 5th str, rdn 2f out, soon switched to outside, styd on fnl f to take 2nd cl hme* **48/10**[2]

**3** 1/2 **Alcazar (IRE)**[36] 5662 9-9-4 ........ MFenton 6 116
(HMorrison) *racd in 4th, wnt 3rd over 4f out, disp ld briefly 2f out, sn rdn and outpaced by wnr, lost 2nd cl hme* **21/1**

**4** 2 **Le Carre (USA)**[21] 5976 6-9-4 ........ DBoeuf 5 114
(ADeRoyer-Dupre, France) *hld up in last, outpcd and pushed along 4f out, 6th str, stayed on under pressure fnl 2f to tk 4th last 150yds* **63/10**[3]

**5** 5 **Percussionist (IRE)**[7] 6260 3-8-9 ........(b) JFortune 9 110
(JHMGosden) *led til headed 4f out, 2nd straight, soon weakened* **27/1**

**6** 2 **Franklins Gardens**[8] 6218 4-9-4 ........ DHolland 1 107
(MHTompkins) *raced in 2nd til led 4f out, headed 2f out, weakened* **25/1**

**7** 6 **Holy Orders (IRE)**[21] 5976 7-9-4 ........(b) DJCondon 2 101
(WPMullins, Ire) *held up, outpaced and dropped back to last over 4f out, never a factor* **39/1**

**8** 10 **Double Green (IRE)**[45] 5433 3-8-6 ........ OPeslier 8 89
(FHead, France) *held up, outpaced from 4f out* **156/10**

3m 28.9s (3.40) **Going Correction** +0.325s/f (Good)
**WFA** 3 from 4yo+ 9lb **8** Ran SP% **122.9**
Speed ratings: **104,102,102,101,99 98,95,90.**
**Owner** Ecurie Wildenstein **Bred** Dayton Investments Ltd **Trained** France

**FOCUS**
Another top-class performance by the brilliant Westerner.

**NOTEBOOK**
**Westerner**, the top stayer in Europe, had nothing more than a training canter, and this classy horse could not have been more impressive. He was cantering throughout and moved smoothly into the lead a furlong and a half out. A couple of strides later the race for first place was over. He appears to be getting better with age, and happily the five-year-old stays in training next year when one of his main targets will be the Gold Cup at York, a race he already looks set to take all the beating in if staying in one piece.
**Behkara(IRE)** had no chance with the winner but still ran a very sound race. Settled in behind the leaders, she was outpaced early in the straight before running on again at the end. She is still a fresh filly and connections are hoping for an invitation to the Hong Kong Vase.
**Alcazar(IRE)** put up a very decent performance. Fourth early on, he quickened early in the straight and looked to have second place wrapped up at the furlong marker, but was passed well inside the final furlong and had to settle for third position. Despite his age he is still keen and capable. He is finished for the year and, all being well, will remain in training next season.
**Le Carre(USA)**, dropped out last, was being niggled along running down the hill. He made a forward move early in the straight and quickened well without really threatening the third. This soft-ground specialist should visit the winner's enclosure again in the not-too-distant future.
**Percussionist(IRE)**, smartly into his stride, tried to make all the running at a good pace. He lasted in front until just before the straight and then stayed on at the one pace inside the final two furlongs. The colt was wearing blinkers for the first time and was felt by the jockey to be feeling the effects of a fairly long and hard season.
**Franklins Gardens** settled in second place and appeared to be going well within himself when taking the lead just before the straight. He kept up the good work until the furlong marker but then dropped out of contention. It was his second run in a staying race in eight days. He remains in training next season.
**Holy Orders(IRE)** was never going the pace to get involved.

## 5686 WOODBINE (R-H)

Sunday, October 24

**OFFICIAL GOING: Good**

### 6383a E P TAYLOR STKS (GRADE 1) (F&M) 1m 2f (T)

**8:26** (8:28) 3-Y-0+ **£194,805** (£64,935; £35,714; £19,481)

RPR

**1** **Commercante (FR)**[22] 5983 4-8-11 ........ JRVelazquez 115
(RJFrankel, U.S.A) **51/20**[2]

**2** 1/2 **Punctilious**[67] 4859 3-8-6 ........ LDettori 114
(SaeedBinSuroor) *raced in 5th, led briefly just inside final f, soon headed and one pace* **11/10**[1]

**3** nk **Classic Stamp (CAN)**[35] 4-8-11 ........ PHusbands 114
(CHopmansJr, Canada) **105/10**

**4** 2 1/4 **Samando (FR)**[22] 5966 4-8-11 ........ BBlanc 110
(FDoumen, France) **17/2**

**5** nse **Mona Rose (CAN)**[99] 4-8-11 ........ ERosaDaSilva 110
(REBarnett) **30/1**

**6** 1 **Asti (IRE)**[22] 5967 3-8-6 ........ RMigliore 108
(ELellouche, France) **147/10**

**7** 2 1/4 **Ometsz (IRE)**[49] 5331 3-8-6 ........ EPrado 104
(RodCollet, France) **6/1**[3]

**8** 1/2 **Heyahohowdy (CAN)**[35] 5-8-11 ........ RSabourin 103
(AKatryan, Canada) **58/1**

2m 4.02s
**WFA** 3 from 4yo+ 5lb **8** Ran SP% **120.6**
Speed ratings: .
**Owner** A Falourd, H Guy & R Trussel **Bred** Haras De Bernesq & S C Ecurie Ouaki Fabien **Trained** USA

**NOTEBOOK**
**Punctilious** ran a sound race although she did wander around a bit when coming through to challenge approaching the furlong pole. After leading for a few strides, she was just outpaced by the winner but kept sticking her neck out to hold second.

### 6384a PATTISON CANADIAN INTERNATIONAL (GRADE 1) 1m 4f (T)

**10:07** (10:07) 3-Y-0+ **£389,610** (£129,870; £71,429; £38,961)

RPR

**1** **Sulamani (IRE)**[68] 4834 5-9-0 ........ LDettori 3 124
(SaeedBinSuroor) *hld up towards rr on inside, angled out 3f out, 6th str, hdwy on outside to ld just ins fnl f, ran on strongly* **17/20**[1]

**2** 1 1/2 **Simonas (IRE)**[49] 5329 5-9-0 ........ KFallon 10 122
(AWohler, Germany) *held up towards rear, headway on outside to go 5th straight, led over 1 1/2f out, headed just inside final f, no extra* **214/10**

**3** 2 **Brian Boru**[36] 5662 4-9-0 ........ JPSpencer 5 119
(APO'Brien, Ire) *held up in last, stayed on final 2f to take 3rd close home* **49/10**[2]

**4** 3/4 **Mubtaker (USA)**[49] 5329 7-9-0 ........ RHills 1 118
(MPTregoning) *missed break, soon recovered to race in 6th on outside, 4th straight, went 3rd over 1f out, lost 3rd close home* **11/2**[3]

**5** 4 1/4 **King's Drama (IRE)**[43] 4-9-0 ........ JRVelazquez 2 112
(RJFrankel, U.S.A) **11/1**

**6** 3 3/4 **Senor Swinger (USA)**[36] 4-9-0 ........ EPrado 6 106
(BBaffert, U.S.A) **92/10**

**7** 7 1/4 **Burst Of Fire (CAN)**[99] 3-8-7 ........(b) SCallaghan 9 95
(MFrostad, Canada) **35/1**

**8** 2 1/2 **Colorful Judgement (CAN)**[22] 4-9-0 ........ TKabel 7 91
(MFrostad, Canada) **32/1**

**9** 1 **Sabiango (GER)**[29] 6-9-0 ........ BBlanc 11 90
(TimYakteen, U.S.A) **22/1**

**10** 1 **Lenny The Lender (CAN)**[22] 8-9-0 ........(b) ChantalSutherland 4 88
(RichardHJukosky, Canada) **38/1**

2m 28.64s
**WFA** 3 from 4yo+ 7lb **10** Ran SP% **121.7**
Speed ratings: .
**Owner** Godolphin **Bred** The Niarchos Family **Trained** Newmarket, Suffolk

**NOTEBOOK**
**Sulamani(IRE)** retires to stud after this, his sixth victory at the top level in four different countries and three different continents. Taken to the outside on the final turn, he was the only one to respond when Fallon kicked for home aboard Simonas and, leading 200 yards out, won with a little in hand.
**Simonas(IRE)** produced a career best effort, circling the field on the home turn then exhibiting a good turn of foot to have all but the winner in trouble.
**Brian Boru** was devoid of early pace and was last of all until staying on steadily in the last quarter mile to fill the same position as he had in this race in 2003.
**Mubtaker(USA)** missed the break quite badly as he was watching the handlers standing up in the stalls. Hills had to push him along for a few strides to regain contact with the field, and, although he was in close touch in fourth entering the straight, those early exertions may have taken their toll.

## 6145 LEICESTER (R-H)

Monday, October 25

**6385 Meeting Abandoned** - Waterlogged

## 6153 LINGFIELD (L-H)

Monday, October 25

**OFFICIAL GOING: Standard**

Wind: str bhd races 1-3, str agst race 4, remainder almost nil Weather: mainly sunny, heavy shower race 4

### 6392 BET DIRECT ON 0800 329393 MAIDEN AUCTION STKS (DIV I) 1m (P)

**1:40** (1:43) (E3) 2-Y-0 **£4,186** (£1,288; £644; £322) **Stalls** High

Form RPR

3050 **1** **Gryskirk**[39] 5596 2-8-8 62........ TQuinn 2 67
(PWD'Arcy) *sn trckd ldrs and a gng wl: effrt over 1f out: led ins fnl f: pushed out* **10/1**[3]

0306 **2** 3/4 **Kandidate**[30] 5778 2-8-11 95........ RLMoore 4 68
(CEBrittain) *w ldr: led jst over 2f out: hrd rdn over 1f out: hdd and one pce ins fnl f* **8/15**[1]

5 **3** 3 **Contented (IRE)**[12] 6155 2-8-8 ........ JQuinn 8 59
(EALDunlop) *n.m.r after 2f and lost pl: effrt on wd outside 2f out: styd on fnl f to take 3rd last stride* **14/1**

**4** shd **Cross The Line (IRE)** 2-8-12 ........ DHolland 9 63
(APJarvis) *rn green and racd wd: chsd ldrs: rdn over 1f out: kpt on same pce fnl f* **11/2**[2]

0600 **5** 1 1/4 **Wembury Point (IRE)**[10] 6181 2-8-10 56........(v[1]) RWinston 1 58
(BGPowell) *hld up towards rr: effrt on inner over 2f out: hanging and one pce over 1f out* **100/1**

4600 **6** 4 **Kempsey**[21] 5996 2-8-7 59........ MartinDwyer 7 46
(JJBridger) *w ldrs: stl upsides 2f out: wknd over 1f out* **33/1**

0 **7** 3/4 **Christom**[2] 6352 2-8-12 ........ JFortune 11 49
(GAButler) *settled in last pair: shkn up over 2f out: sme prog fnl f: n.d* **33/1**

0304 **8** 3/4 **Starlight River (IRE)**[24] 5909 2-8-7 62 ow1........ SDrowne 5 43
(WRMuir) *t.k.h: trckd ldrs: cl up 2f out: sn wknd* **14/1**

0040 **9** 1 1/4 **Our Kes (IRE)**[16] 6067 2-8-6 62 ow2........ SWKelly 3 39
(PHowling) *mde most to jst over 2f out: wknd rapidly jst over 1f out* **40/1**

B0 **10** 4 **Baileys Honour**[16] 6072 2-8-3 ........ RFrench 6 27
(MJohnston) *hmpd and snatched up over 6f out: racd in last pair after: rdn and struggling over 2f out* **50/1**

00 **11** 1 1/2 **Soft Focus (IRE)**[18] 6020 2-8-2 ........ CCatlin 10 23
(JAOsborne) *dwlt: in tch: lost pl and rdn over 2f out: wknd* **33/1**

1m 39.88s (0.33) **Going Correction** -0.05s/f (Stan) **11** Ran SP% **117.3**
Speed ratings: **96,95,92,92,90 86,86,85,84,80 78**CSF £15.29 TOTE £17.60: £2.20, £1.20, £1.50; EX 25.60.
**Owner** Charnwood Boy Partnership & Mrs J Harris **Bred** Plantation Stud **Trained** Newmarket, Suffolk

**FOCUS**
Not an easy race to assess with Kandidate failing to run anywhere near the form he showed to finish sixth in the Royal Lodge and earn a rating of 95. It looks jsut modest, but should produce winners.

**NOTEBOOK**

**Gryskirk** had 30lb to find with the eventual runner-up at the weights and looked pretty exposed but, returned to maiden company and switched back to the sand, he proved good enough to get off the mark. This represents improved form and he would be probably be well-in if turned out before he is reassessed.

**Kandidate** has been quite highly tried since finishing last on his debut in a Newmarket maiden, but justifiably so given he was sixth in the Royal Lodge at Ascot on his previous start. However, returned to maiden company, he was not at his best despite appearing to have every chance.

**Contented(IRE)**, fifth in a seven-furlong maiden on his debut, was short of room early on and lost his position. At the business end, he got going too late and could not get to the front two, but he is going the right way and should find a race.

**Cross The Line(IRE)**, a 34,000gns first foal, out of a seven-furlong three-year-old winner, was quite well supported and made a respectable debut. The experience should bring him on. *Official explanation: jockey said colt hung left in the straight*

**Wembury Point(IRE)** ran creditably in the first-time visor, but is more of a handicap type.

## 6393 BET DIRECT ON 0800 329393 MAIDEN AUCTION STKS (DIV II) 1m (P)

**2:10** (2:13) (E3) 2-Y-O **£4,173** (£1,284; £642; £321) **Stalls** High

Form RPR

2043 **1** **Musical Day**[18] 6020 2-8-5 75 ....(b[1]) RLMoore 11 68
(BJMeehan) *prom: trckd ldr over 4f out: rdn to ld over 1f out: drvn out* **7/2[2]**

30 **2** 3/4 **Limit (IRE)**[14] 6111 2-8-6 .... CCatlin 8 67
(MRChannon) *t.k.h: hld up in rr: prog over 2f out: drvn to chse wnr on inner ins fnl f: a hld* **12/1**

35 **3** 1 1/4 **Alfie Noakes**[15] 6078 2-8-12 .... SDrowne 1 71
(MrsAJPerrett) *dwlt: sn trckd ldrs: lost pl over 3f out: nt clr run over 2f out: r.o fnl f: nt rch ldng pair* **11/10[1]**

00 **4** 1/2 **Blue Hedges**[10] 6187 2-8-10 .... JQuinn 10 68
(HJCollingridge) *t.k.h: hld up in rr: smooth prog on outer 3f out: trckd ldrs over 1f out: rdn and fnd little after: one pce* **33/1**

5550 **5** 1/2 **Silver Visage (IRE)**[39] 5596 2-8-1 60 ....(p) DeanWilliams[(7)] 7 64
(MissJFeilden) *mde most to over 1f out: wknd ins fnl f* **33/1**

**6** 1 **Persian Khanoom (IRE)** 2-8-1 .... JFMcDonald[(3)] 6 62+
(JAOsborne) *hld up in last trio: gng wl enough over 2f out: styng on whn nt clr run over 1f out: n.d: bttr for experience* **33/1**

00 **7** hd **Sol Rojo**[6] 6291 2-8-8 .... SWKelly 5 62
(JAOsborne) *dwlt: racd in last trio: pushed along over 4f out: sme prog 2f out: no imp ldrs* **66/1**

00 **8** 1 **Waatheb (IRE)**[11] 6171 2-8-12 .... PDobbs 9 64
(RHannon) *prom: hrd rdn 2f out: wknd rapidly fnl f* **7/1[3]**

0 **9** nk **Cash On (IRE)**[10] 6187 2-8-10 .... MartinDwyer 2 61
(MPTregoning) *dwlt: a in rr: rdn over 2f out: one pce* **15/2**

6 **10** 8 **Kergolay (IRE)**[18] 6020 2-8-8 .... JFEgan 4 41
(WRMuir) *t.k.h: trckd ldrs: rdn over 3f out: wknd over 2f out* **25/1**

5004 **11** 9 **Tahlal (IRE)**[26] 5856 2-8-8 61 ....(p) RFfrench 3 22
(MrsADuffield) *plld hrd: chsd ldr to over 4f out: wknd 3f out: t.o* **33/1**

1m 39.78s (0.23) **Going Correction** -0.05s/f (Stan) **11** Ran SP% **118.9**
Speed ratings: **96,95,94,93,93 92,91,90,90,82 73**CSF £40.81 TOTE £4.00: £1.50, £2.50, £1.10; EX 36.30.
**Owner** T G Holdcroft **Bred** Bearstone Stud **Trained** Upper Lambourn, Berks

**FOCUS**

The form of this maiden is nothing special, but the race should produce winners.

**NOTEBOOK**

**Musical Day** had appeared to find this trip on the short side at Wolverhampton on her previous start but, fitted with blinkers for the first time, she had sufficient speed and made no mistake. She is not one to underestimate in handicaps.

**Limit(IRE)**, last in a nine-runner maiden at Ayr on her previous start, left that form behind and showed enough to suggest she can find a similar race.

**Alfie Noakes**, disappointing when a beaten favourite on easy ground at Bath on his previous start, ran better switched to sand but simply took too long to pick up. There is a race in him, but he is not one to take too short a price about.

**Blue Hedges** is progressing with every run and ran another solid race. He is qualified for a handicap mark, but could yet find a maiden.

**Silver Visage(IRE)**, with cheekpieces on instead of blinkers, ran creditably and should be competitive off his current sort of mark in handicaps.

**Persian Khanoom(IRE)**, a 15,000gns half-sister to a juvenile placed over seven furlongs, out of an 11-furlong three-year-old winner, made a promising debut. She met some trouble and, not given too hard a time, was never going to get to the principals. She should improve.

**Sol Rojo** again showed something and is one run away from a handicap mark.

**Waatheb(IRE)** had appeared to be progressing, but he did not run to the form he showed at Newmarket on his previous start. He needs one run for a handicap mark.

**Cash On(IRE)** should have found this easier than the Newmarket maiden he made his debut in, but was well held.

## 6394 LITTLEWOODS BET DIRECT NOVICE STKS 6f (P)

**2:40** (2:42) (D3) 2-Y-O **£5,096** (£1,568; £784; £392) **Stalls** Low

Form RPR

5 **1** **Postgraduate (IRE)**[19] 6010 2-8-12 .... SDrowne 9 79+
(HMorrison) *racd midfield: pushed along 1/2-way: effrt on outer over 2f out: picked up wl fnl f and r.o to ld last 50yds* **6/1[3]**

**2** 3/4 **Excusez Moi (USA)** 2-8-9 ow1 .... SSanders 8 74
(CEBrittain) *dwlt: hld up: prog on wd outside over 2f out: rdn to ld ent fnl f: hdd last 50yds* **12/1**

0646 **3** 1 **Bold Marc (IRE)**[17] 6042 2-9-4 83 .... DarrenWilliams 4 80
(KRBurke) *prom: trckd ldr wl over 2f out: rdn to ld wl over 1f out : hdd and one pce ent fnl f* **12/1**

63 **4** 3/4 **John Robie (USA)**[50] 5319 2-8-12 .... JFortune 7 75+
(GAButler) *dwlt: hld up in last trio: outpcd and plenty to do 2f out: plld out and r.o wl fnl f: too much to do* **3/1[2]**

0225 **5** shd **Elgin Marbles**[10] 6188 2-9-0 83 .... RLMoore 5 77+
(RHannon) *trckd ldrs: pushed along and lost pl over 2f out: hrd rdn and hanging lft over 1f out: styd on ins fnl f* **15/8[1]**

54 **6** 1/2 **Three Deuces (USA)**[12] 6153 2-8-7 .... DHolland 2 65
(BJMeehan) *led to wl over 1f out: fdd ins fnl f* **8/1**

03 **7** 1 1/4 **Miss Tolerance (USA)**[14] 6126 2-8-7 .... RWinston 3 61
(SirMichaelStoute) *hld up: n.m.r on inner over 4f out: last and no ch over 2f out : shkn up and kpt on fnl f* **8/1**

0 **8** 1 **Perfect Solution (IRE)**[34] 5720 2-8-7 .... JFEgan 1 58
(JARToller) *dwlt: a towards rr: rdn and one pce fnl 2f* **40/1**

0105 **9** 6 **Lucky Emerald (IRE)**[15] 6080 2-8-8 70 ....(t) FPFerris[(3)] 6 44
(BPalling) *chsd ldr to wl over 2f out: wknd wl over 1f out* **25/1**

1m 12.74s (-0.18) **Going Correction** -0.05s/f (Stan) **9** Ran SP% **118.0**
Speed ratings: **99,98,96,95,95 94,93,91,83**CSF £76.29 TOTE £9.90: £2.70, £2.30, £2.00; EX 99.30.
**Owner** Thurloe Thoroughbreds XII **Bred** Austin Lyons **Trained** East Ilsley, Berks
■ Stewards Enquiry : S Drowne two-day ban: careless riding (Nov 5,6)

**FOCUS**

Not a bad novice event and the form looks solid enough, rated through the third.

**NOTEBOOK**

**Postgraduate(IRE)** showed promise on his debut round here over seven furlongs and improved on that dropped a furlong in trip. He should be just as effective back up in distance and, progressing, will be worthy of respect in better company.

**Excusez Moi(USA)** ♦, $410,000 first foal, out of a juvenile placed over six furlongs, created a big impression on his racecourse debut. After a slow start, he had to brought widest of all with his challenge round a sharp enough bend for a newcomer, but made up the ground in taking fashion and only gave way in the closing stages. He would not need to improve to win a race, but is the type to really progress and must be followed.

**Bold Marc(IRE)** had yet to really convince over this trip but he seemed to just about get it and ran well under his big weight.

**John Robie(USA)** has shown promise in a couple of starts in maidens and again ran creditably switched to Polytrack. He took a while to really get going, but is likely to be sharper for this first run in 50 days and can find a race before too much longer.

**Elgin Marbles** may not have been quite at his best but, rated 83, he still gives a reasonable guide to the strength of the form.

**Three Deuces(USA)** was unable to sustain the gallop and may do better in slightly lesser company, possibly back over five furlongs.

**Miss Tolerance(USA)** was short of room and lost her position early on. She is better than this.

## 6395 BET DIRECT PREDICTOR.COM H'CAP 1m (P)

**3:10** (3:11) (E3) (0-77,76) 3-Y-0+ **£3,517** (£1,082; £541; £270) **Stalls** High

Form RPR

5114 **1** **Sharp Needle**[51] 5304 3-9-4 **73** .... SWKelly 12 84+
(JNoseda) *hld up midfield: prog over 2f out: chsd ldr over 1f out: hrd rdn and styd on to ld last 75yds* **8/1**

5050 **2** 1/2 **Slalom (IRE)**[7] 6266 4-9-2 **68** .... GFaulkner 11 77
(JulianPoulton) *trckd ldrs: prog on outer 3f out: led 2f out: hrd rdn fnl f: hdd last 75yds* **25/1**

6550 **3** 1 1/2 **Pure Mischief (IRE)**[5] 6311 5-9-1 **70** .... RThomas[(3)] 7 76
(CRDore) *dwlt: hld up wl in rr: stl in last trio over 2f out: prog over 1f out: hrd rdn and r.o fnl f: tk 3rd last stride* **16/1**

4012 **4** shd **Analyze (FR)**[12] 6156 6-9-8 **74** .... TQuinn 8 80
(BGPowell) *hld up in rr: effrt over 2f out: drvn and hanging lft over 1f out: styd on: nvr able to chal* **11/2[3]**

6023 **5** 1 1/2 **Island Rapture**[23] 5955 4-9-3 **69** .... SSanders 10 71
(JARToller) *dwlt: prog fr rr 1/2-way: chsd ldrs 2f out: no ex over 1f out: fdd* **9/2[2]**

1530 **6** 1/2 **Franksalot (IRE)**[35] 5698 4-9-10 **76** .... SDrowne 1 77
(MissBSanders) *s.i.s: sn trckd ldng pair: lost pl and rdn over 2f out: kpt on one pce and no imp after* **13/2**

0662 **7** 5 **Greenwood**[150] 2441 6-9-7 **73** .... DKinsella 6 63
(PGMurphy) *t.k.h: prom: led wl over 2f out to 2f out: wknd fnl f* **16/1**

0504 **8** 10 **Lilli Marlane**[12] 6156 4-9-3 **69** .... JFEgan 5 36
(NACallaghan) *nvr gng particularly wl in rr: no prog and btn over 2f out: eased fnl f* **7/2[1]**

0000 **9** 3/4 **Electrique (IRE)**[12] 6156 4-9-4 **70** ....(b) MartinDwyer 3 35
(JAOsborne) *w ldr at fast pce to 3f out: sn wknd* **11/1**

1030 **10** 1 1/4 **Corky (IRE)**[38] 5614 3-9-7 **76** .... RLMoore 4 38
(RHannon) *a in rr: dropped to last and rdn 1/2-way: struggling after* **14/1**

0050 **11** 1 1/2 **Gems Bond**[26] 5866 4-8-13 **72** .... DerekNolan[(7)] 9 31
(JSMoore) *a towards rr: wknd over 2f out* **33/1**

0000 **12** 16 **Cheese 'n Biscuits**[12] 6157 4-8-13 **70** .... AQuinn[(5)] 2 —
(GLMoore) *led at furious pce to wl over 2f out: wknd rapidly: t.o* **16/1**

1m 38.36s (-1.19) **Going Correction** -0.05s/f (Stan)
**WFA** 3 from 4yo+ 3lb **12** Ran SP% **119.7**
Speed ratings: **103,102,101,100,99 98,93,83,83,81 80,64**CSF £191.76 CT £3155.90 TOTE £10.00: £3.30, £10.70, £6.10; EX 353.60.
**Owner** Arashan Ali **Bred** Sentinel Bloodstock And Arashan Ali **Trained** Newmarket, Suffolk
■ Stewards Enquiry : R L Moore one-day ban: careless riding (Nov 5)

**FOCUS**

A modest handicap and the form looks pretty ordinary.

**NOTEBOOK**

**Sharp Needle** had no excuses when beaten into fourth at Thirsk on her previous start but, switched to sand, she stepped up on that form. Clearly progressing, she could well defy another rise in the weights.

**Slalom(IRE)**, mainly below form since winning his maiden at Wolverhampton (Fibresand) earlier in the year, posted one of his better efforts and was just held.

**Pure Mischief(IRE)** ran a cracker over a trip just short of his best and could well find a similar race at around ten furlongs.

**Analyze(FR)** has been running well since being switched to Polytrack, but he looks high enough in the weights now.

**Island Rapture** may do better over slightly further under a patient ride.

**Lilli Marlane** failed to confirm or build on the form she showed when fourth over course and distance on her previous start. *Official explanation: jockey said filly suffered interference in running and was never travelling thereafter*

## 6396 LADBROKES.COM H'CAP 1m 4f (P)

**3:40** (3:40) (D2) (0-92,88) 3-Y-O **£6,854** (£2,109; £1,054; £527) **Stalls** Low

Form RPR

0036 **1** **Winners Delight**[23] 5944 3-9-0 **78** .... RWinston 6 88
(APJarvis) *dwlt: hld up in last: prog on wd outside 3f out: drvn to chse ldng over 1f out and hanging: forced ahd nr fin* **16/1**

1040 **2** nk **King Of Diamonds**[40] 5574 3-8-12 **76** .... MartinDwyer 9 86
(JRBest) *t.k.h: hld up in rr: prog over 3f out: led jst over 2f out : drvn fnl f: hdd nr fin* **25/1**

0540 **3** 2 **Pagan Magic (USA)**[33] 5728 3-8-10 **74** .... LisaJones 7 81
(JARToller) *t.k.h: hld up in rr: effrt but nt handling bnd over 2f out: r.o to take 3rd ins fnl f: gaining at fin* **10/1**

6605 **4** 3 1/2 **Graham Island**[28] 5842 3-9-5 **83** .... DHolland 5 84
(GWragg) *trckd ldrs: cl up 3f out: lost pl over 2f out and n.m.r sn after: one pce fr over 1f out* **12/1**

1142 **5** 1/2 **Circassian (IRE)**[13] 6143 3-9-3 **81** .... SSanders 8 82
(SirMarkPrescott) *prom: led 4f out: rdn 3f out: hdd jst over 2f out: wknd fnl f* **1/1[1]**

2144 **6** 1 **Sunny Lady (FR)**[28] 5842 3-8-13 **77** .... JFortune 10 76
(EALDunlop) *trckd ldrs: gng wl 3f out: n.m.r briefly 2f out: rdn and fnd nil over 1f out* **16/1**

521 **7** 2 1/2 **Barathea Blue**[26] 5867 3-8-11 **75** .... TQuinn 4 70
(PWHarris) *t.k.h: pressed ldr: led over 6f out to 4f out: wknd 2f out* **13/2[3]**

142 **8** 6 **Diego Cao (IRE)**[14] 6128 3-9-10 **88** .... RLMoore 1 74
(GLMoore) *hld up in tch: rdn 3f out: no imp: eased whn btn over 1f out* **11/2[2]**

0045 **9** 5 **First Centurion**[13] 6143 3-9-0 **78** .... MHills 2 57
(JWHills) *drvn to chse ldrs: lost pl 5f out: wknd 3f out* **16/1**

4320 **10** *dist* **Principessa**[20] 6006 3-8-5 **72**................................................ FPFerris(3) 3 —
(BPalling) *led to over 6f out: sn drvn: wknd over 4f out: t.o* **33/1**

2m 32.27s (-1.97) **Going Correction** -0.05s/f (Stan) **10** Ran SP% **119.9**
Speed ratings: **104,103,102,100,99 99,97,93,90,**—CSF £359.43 CT £4159.17 TOTE £16.60: £4.20, £3.60, £2.70; EX 160.70 Trifecta £778.00 Part won. Pool: £1,095.86 - 0.10 winning units..

**Owner** Breckland Bingo **Bred** Peter Barclay **Trained** Twyford, Bucks

**FOCUS**
There was a decent pace on here and those who were held up ended up contesting the victory. A fair handicap and the form looks sound.

**NOTEBOOK**
**Winners Delight**, held on turf this year off this sort of mark, appreciated the switch to the Polytrack. The strong pace played into his hands and he came from last to first. He is a tricky ride, but hopefully this will have done his confidence some good.
**King Of Diamonds** appreciated the step up from a mile and came through from the rear to look the winner, only to be headed close home. He is a keen sort and will always need a good pace to be seen at his best.
**Pagan Magic(USA)**, despite not looking at home on the track, ran on well from the rear to finish third. He is difficult to catch right.
**Graham Island**, who was making his Polytrack debut, failed to get a clear run when the race began to hot up and could never make up the ground afterwards. He is a bit better than this bare form suggests.
**Circassian(IRE)** paid for racing prominently off the strong pace.
**Sunny Lady(FR)** failed to pick up when it mattered.

## 6397 BET DIRECT ON THE BREEDERS CUP MAIDEN STKS 7f (P)
**4:10** (4:15) (D3) 3-Y-0+ **£3,877** (£1,193; £596; £298) **Stalls** Low

Form RPR

06 **1** **Mister Muja (IRE)**[56] 5204 3-9-5 ........................................(t) RLMoore 5 69
(PWHarris) *racd midfield: effrt and nt clr run briefly over 2f out: drvn and r.o fr over 1f out: led nr fin* **20/1**

35/ **2** *¾* **Grand Ideas**[720] 5630 5-9-7 ............................................ DaleGibson 7 67
(JulianPoulton) *mostly chsd ldr: rdn over 2f out: no imp tl styd on fnl f: jst outpcd by wnr* **66/1**

0 **3** *nk* **Pearl Farm**[68] 4845 3-9-0 ................................................ DHolland 8 61
(CAHorgan) *hld up wl in rr: nt clr run over 2f out: gd prog on inner over 1f out: styd on fnl f: jst hld* **50/1**

3223 **4** *shd* **Kauri Forest (USA)**[19] 6017 3-9-5 77....................................(t) MHills 14 66
(JRFanshawe) *led: kicked on over 2f out: looked in command ent fnl f: wknd and hdd nr fin* **3/1[1]**

**5** *1* **Katavi (USA)** 3-9-0 ................................................ SWKelly 4 58+
(JNoseda) *trckd ldrs: c wd bnd 2f out: shkn up briefly over 1f out: r.o nr fin: nvr nrr: bttr for experience* **3/1[1]**

000 **6** *1 ¼* **Mad**[19] 6015 3-9-0 ................................................ JFEgan 13 55
(AndrewReid) *racd towards rr: c wdst of all bnd 2f out: styd on fnl f: nrst fin* **100/1**

0/0 **7** *1 ½* **King At Last**[19] 6015 5-9-7 ............................................ DRMcCabe 1 56
(KBell) *prom: rdn over 2f out: stl w chsng gp ent fnl f: wknd* **66/1**

24-5 **8** *½* **Authority (IRE)**[19] 6017 4-9-7 70.......................................... SSanders 9 55
(LadyHerries) *trckd ldrs: shuffled along briefly 3f out: lost pl over 2f out: nvr nr ldrs after: do bttr* **7/2[2]**

0 **9** *3* **Shamdian (IRE)**[23] 1460 4-9-7 83........................................(t) TQuinn 3 47
(NJHenderson) *racd midfield: pushed along 1/2-way: prog 2f out: keeping on whn hmpd jst over 1f out: wknd* **4/1[3]**

00 **10** *3 ½* **Poetry 'n Passion**[10] 6200 3-9-0 ........................................ RFfrench 11 33
(CACyzer) *racd wd: prom: c wd bnd 2f out: wknd over 1f out* **33/1**

**11** *6* **Red Lantern** 3-9-5 ................................................ MHenry 6 22
(RMHCowell) *s.s: a wl in rr: rdn 3f out: wknd 2f out* **100/1**

6 **12** *shd* **Young Kate**[10] 6200 3-9-0 ............................................ MartinDwyer 2 17
(JRBest) *hld up wl in rr: gng wl enough whn hmpd on inner over 2f out: eased* **12/1**

4045 **13** *2* **Moonshaft (USA)**[23] 5955 3-9-5 66........................................(v[1]) SDrowne 10 17
(EALDunlop) *pressed ldrs tl wknd rapidly 2f out* **10/1**

60 **14** *nk* **Terenure Girl**[28] 5844 3-9-0 ............................................ LisaJones 12 11
(PSFelgate) *a wl bhd* **100/1**

1m 26.01s (0.07) **Going Correction** -0.05s/f (Stan)
**WFA** 3 from 4yo+ 2lb **14** Ran SP% **124.6**
Speed ratings: **97,96,95,95,94 93,91,90,87,83 76,76,74,73**CSF £935.16 TOTE £19.80: £3.90, £8.20, £22.00; EX 696.90.

**Owner** The Mint **Bred** J F Tuthill **Trained** Ringshall, Bucks

**FOCUS**
A modest maiden, and the form looks difficult to assess.

**NOTEBOOK**
**Mister Muja(IRE)**, who broke a blood-vessel when sixth on his previous start, came with a late challenge to get up close home. This was not a great maiden but he should not be too harshly treated by the Handicapper as a result.
**Grand Ideas**, off the track for almost two years, had made his previous two starts over middle distances on turf. His performance does not do a lot for the value of the form. *Official explanation: jockey said gelding hung right*
**Pearl Farm**, who is a half-sister to middle-distance winner Ocean Avenue, appreciated the step up in trip and improved a great deal on her debut effort. She will be suited by even farther.
**Kauri Forest(USA)** confirmed the impression of his previous outing here and is one to be wary of, as he looked to have the race won only to give it away close home.
**Katavi(USA)**, who cost $230,000, is a half-sister to several winners. Clearly in need of the experience, she will come on a good deal for the run and should be placed to advantage before long.
**Authority(IRE)** may be seen to better effect on the Southwell Fibresand. *Official explanation: jockey said gelding hung left*
**Shamdian(IRE)** *Official explanation: jockey said gelding was squeezed 1 1/2f out*
**Poetry 'n Passion** *Official explanation: jockey said filly hung badly throughout*
**Young Kate** *Official explanation: jockey said filly moved badly and lost her action on the final bend*
**Moonshaft(USA)** *Official explanation: jockey said colt moved badly and eased*

## 6398 BET DIRECT "RED TO BET" ON ITV APPRENTICE H'CAP 6f (P)
**4:40** (4:42) (F4) (0-62,61) 3-Y-0+ **£2,994** (£855; £427) **Stalls** Low

Form RPR

0000 **1** **Party Princess (IRE)**[38] 5618 3-9-1 **57**.................................... AMullen 6 68
(JAGlover) *led to over 3f out: styd prom: led over 1f out: pushed clr: comf* **14/1**

0205 **2** *2* **Taboor (IRE)**[10] 6186 6-9-6 **61**..........................................(bt) RoryMoore 9 66
(JWPayne) *hld up: prog on outer over 2f out: rdn and nt qckn over 1f out: styd on to take 2nd last 75yds* **10/1**

1200 **3** *¾* **Davids Mark**[7] 6274 4-8-9 **55**.......................................... RJKilloran(5) 7 58
(JRJenkins) *racd midfield: prog to ld 2f out: hdd over 1f out: no ch w wnr after* **10/1**

3006 **4** *¾* **Tsarbuck**[9] 6228 3-8-10 **59**..........................................(p) GBartley(7) 2 60
(RMHCowell) *prom: lost pl over 3f out: rdn and renewed effrt over 2f out: styd on same pce* **20/1**

1062 **5** *nk* **Woodbury**[7] 6273 5-9-2 **57**.......................................... DTudhope 12 57
(MrsHSweeting) *racd wd: in tch: effrt 2f out: kpt on one pce over 1f out* **5/2[1]**

3000 **6** *½* **Ben Lomand**[41] 5541 4-8-9 **55**.......................................... AKirby(5) 11 53
(BWDuke) *dwlt: hld up: prog over 2f out: c v wd bnd 2f out: styd on again fnl f* **16/1**

0000 **7** *1* **Warlingham (IRE)**[9] 6220 6-9-3 **58**.......................................... DerekNolan 3 53
(PHowling) *towards rr: rdn 2f out: n.m.r sn after: one pce and nt rch ldrs* **14/1**

0100 **8** *¾* **Kew The Music**[14] 6131 4-8-10 **56**..........................................(v) TO'Brien(5) 5 49
(MRChannon) *dwlt: racd in detached last: effrt 2f out: n.m.r but kpt on fnl f: no ch* **3/1[2]**

6012 **9** *nk* **Stamford Blue**[203] 1270 3-8-11 **58**.......................................... LauraReynolds(5) 1 50
(JSMoore) *pressed ldrs: rdn and steadily lost pl fnl 2f* **12/1**

0060 **10** *1* **Multahab**[7] 6274 5-9-0 **55**..........................................(t) MHalford 4 44
(PSMcentee) *racd midfield: no prog over 2f out: lost pl fr over 1f out* **8/1[3]**

0000 **11** *2* **Goodwood Prince**[125] 3174 4-8-7 **55**..........................................(v) LSmith(7) 10 38
(SDow) *racd freely: prom: led over 3f out to 2f out: wknd rapidly* **33/1**

0006 **12** *2 ½* **Cheeky Chi (IRE)**[61] 5040 3-9-0 **56**.......................................... DeanWilliams 8 31
(PSMcentee) *prom tl wknd over 2f out* **25/1**

1m 12.98s (0.06) **Going Correction** -0.05s/f (Stan)
**WFA** 3 from 4yo+ 1lb **12** Ran SP% **121.3**
Speed ratings: **97,94,93,92,91 91,89,88,88,87 84,81**CSF £146.81 CT £1481.81 TOTE £18.80: £4.10, £3.40, £4.10; EX 225.30.

**Owner** Derrick Bloy **Bred** Hardys Of Kilkeel Ltd **Trained** Carburton, Notts

**FOCUS**
A weak handicap made up of many out-of-form performers, although the form looks sound enough.

**NOTEBOOK**
**Party Princess(IRE)** has been running poorly on turf of late but, back down to her last winning mark, found this lesser contest much more to her liking. She won easily and would be interesting if turned out quickly as she would not have to shoulder a penalty.
**Taboor(IRE)** remains high enough in the weights and this effort will not do him much good on that front. He saw the trip out well enough though, despite his best form being over five.
**Davids Mark** was disappointing on the new surface at Wolverhampton last time but bounced back at a track where he has been successful in the past.
**Tsarbuck** was making his Polytrack debut and did not run too badly, although he may be at his best on Fibresand.
**Woodbury** likes to make the running but she was never going to get to the front from her wide stall position.

## 6399 BET DIRECT AT LINGFIELD PARK CLASSIFIED STKS 1m (P)
**5:10** (5:11) (F4) 3-Y-O **£2,905** (£830; £415) **Stalls** High

Form RPR

0063 **1** **My Pension (IRE)**[6] 6295 3-9-3 60.......................................... RWinston 6 66
(PHowling) *hld up midfield: prog to chse ldr 2f out: hrd rdn and kpt on to ld last 50yds* **8/1**

006 **2** *1* **King Of Music (USA)**[57] 5156 3-8-12 52.......................................... OUrbina 1 59
(GProdromou) *chsd ldng pair: prog to ld over 2f out: hrd rdn over 1f out: hdd last 50yds* **12/1**

6014 **3** *½* **Sylva Royal (IRE)**[10] 6184 3-8-9 54.......................................... RLMoore 8 55
(CEBrittain) *hld up in rr: prog over 2f out: hrd rdn and styd on to take 3rd ins fnl f: unable to chal* **7/2[1]**

0063 **4** *nk* **Best Desert (IRE)**[9] 6220 3-9-2 59.......................................... JQuinn 5 61
(JRBest) *hld up midfield: rdn and effrt 2f out: kpt on same pce fr over 1f out* **7/2[1]**

004 **5** *2* **Hana Dee**[32] 5750 3-8-9 47.......................................... SHitchcott 9 49
(MRChannon) *hld up in rr: prog 3f out: unable qck 2f out: one pce after* **33/1**

0051 **6** *1 ½* **Blake Hall Lad (IRE)**[28] 5830 3-8-8 58.......................... DeanWilliams(7) 7 52
(MissJFeilden) *hld up in rr: effrt over 2f out: no imp on ldrs over 1f out* **8/1**

2634 **7** *2* **Antigua Bay (IRE)**[14] 6119 3-9-0 60.......................................... JFEgan 4 46
(JARToller) *chsd ldrs: rdn 3f out: lost pl over 2f out: swtchd rt over 1f out: no prog* **6/1[3]**

0430 **8** *3* **Beauty Of Dreams**[6] 6296 3-8-9 54..........................................(v) CCatlin 3 34
(MRChannon) *mounted on crse: led at fast pce: hdd & wknd over 2f out* **12/1**

-655 **9** *5* **Kinbrace**[42] 5510 3-8-11 57.......................................... MartinDwyer 2 25
(MPTregoning) *chsd ldr to wl over 2f out: nt run on: last whn hung bdly over 1f out* **4/1[2]**

1m 39.34s (-0.21) **Going Correction** -0.05s/f (Stan) **9** Ran SP% **119.3**
Speed ratings: **99,98,97,97,95 93,91,88,83**CSF £101.49 TOTE £7.90: £2.00, £4.40, £2.10; EX 145.40 Place 6 £19,501.52, Place 5 £15,527.85.

**Owner** David Andrew Brown **Bred** E O'Leary **Trained** Newmarket, Suffolk

**FOCUS**
There was a fast pace to this modest heat.

**NOTEBOOK**
**My Pension(IRE)**, who had run with promise on his Polytrack debut at Wolverhampton last time, showed the right attitude and reversed turf form with the runner-up from two months earlier.
**King Of Music(USA)** had finished a long way in front of the winner on his previous start in soft ground, but the change of venue suited his rival better, and perhaps this run was needed after eight weeks off.
**Sylva Royal(IRE)**, who can take a keen hold, was suited by the way the race was run and stayed on well for third. She got the trip well and is handicapped to win a race. *Official explanation: jockey said filly hung left*
**Best Desert(IRE)** had conditions to suit and proved slightly disappointing. He is, however, a difficult horse to catch right, having won just one race in his career to date, and that by the narrowest of margins.
**Kinbrace** would have probably been better off being held up. She blew her chance by chasing the strong pace set by the filly who finished one place in front of her.

T/Jkpt: Not won. T/Plt: £32,995.50 to a £1 stake. Pool: £45,199.35. 0.90 winning tickets. T/Qpdt: Not won. JN

# $^{6359}$WOLVERHAMPTON (A.W) (L-H)

Monday, October 25

**OFFICIAL GOING: Standard**

Wind: Fresh behind Weather: Cloudy

## 6400 RINGSIDE MAIDEN AUCTION STKS 7f 32y(P)

2:20 (2:23) (H5) 2-Y-0 £1,477 (£422; £211) Stalls High

Form RPR

4 1 **Bird Over**$^{37}$ [5640] 2-8-2 NMackay 6 58+
(RMBeckett) *plld hrd and prom: led over 1f out: sn edgd lft: rdn clr: edgd rt nr fin* **11/10**$^{1}$

2 2 **Fullandby (IRE)** 2-8-11 JFanning 2 62+
(TJEtherington) *s.s: hdwy 4f out: rdn over 1f out: styd on* **9/1**

50 3 shd **Paparaazi (IRE)**$^{26}$ [5856] 2-8-9 PHanagan 5 60
(RAFahey) *trckd ldrs: rdn over 1f out: styd on same pce ins fnl f* **7/1**$^{3}$

04 4 3 **Just Cliff**$^{16}$ [6060] 2-8-11 FNorton 12 54
(WRMuir) *hld up in tch: rdn over 2f out: wknd ins fnl f* **3/1**$^{2}$

0 5 5 **So Elegant (IRE)**$^{16}$ [6060] 2-7-13 DFox$^{(5)}$ 11 35
(JJay) *hld up: edgd lft over 1f out: styd on ins fnl f: nvr nrr* **16/1**

6 6 ¾ **Love Attack (IRE)**$^{9}$ [6221] 2-8-5 DAllan 8 34
(DCarroll) *mid-div: sn rdn along: outpcd over 2f out: n.d after* **25/1**

7 ½ **Highest Regard** 2-8-9 RPrice 4 37
(PLGilligan) *chsd ldr tl led 1/2-way: hdd & wknd over 1f out* **14/1**

00 8 11 **Showtime Faye**$^{13}$ [6139] 2-8-3 JMackay 7 3
(ABailey) *dwlt: outpcd* **80/1**

0 9 4 **Iroquois Princess**$^{7}$ [6272] 2-8-5 SWhitworth 9 —
(DShaw) *a in rr* **100/1**

0 10 3½ **Gifted Lass**$^{10}$ [6196] 2-8-6 JEdmunds 10 —
(JBalding) *plld hrd and prom: rdn and wknd wl over 1f out* **100/1**

00 11 28 **Autumn Daze**$^{33}$ [5741] 2-8-2 ANicholls 3 —
(MJRyan) *led to 1/2-way: wknd over 2f out* **80/1**

1m 32.37s **11** Ran SP% **116.0**

Speed ratings: CSF £12.07 TOTE £1.70: £1.10, £2.60, £2.10; EX 8.30.

**Owner** Mrs Robert Langton **Bred** Mrs Robert Langton **Trained** Lambourn, Berks

**FOCUS**

A poor All-Weather maiden and the future already looks bleak for some of the also-rans.

**NOTEBOOK**

**Bird Over**, despite taking a keen hold through the early stages, confirmed the promise of her recent Lingfield debut and won with a little in hand. She is due to be put away for a three-year-old campaign now, will be well suited by a mile in due course and clearly likes this surface.

**Fullandby(IRE)**, whose dam was a four-times winner in Italy, made a pleasing debut and was doing all of his best work at the finish. He has the scope to improve and find a race on this surface during the winter.

**Paparaazi(IRE)**, who had been awkward from the gates on his previous two outings, turned in a creditable performance and is going the right way. He was very easy in the market for this, but now qualifies for nurseries and could be capable of better.

**Just Cliff** looked a threat on entering the straight, but could not sustain his effort and finished well held. He is now eligible for nurseries.

## 6401 ZONGALERO BANDED STKS (DIV I) 7f 32y(P)

2:50 (2:52) (H5) 3-Y-0+ £1,473 (£421; £210) Stalls High

Form RPR

0500 1 **Compton Micky**$^{10}$ [6199] 3-9-2 49 (p) JEdmunds 8 59
(JBalding) *plld hrd and prom: led over 1f out: edgd rt ins fnl f: rdn out* **50/1**

2025 2 ¾ **The Old Soldier**$^{8}$ [6246] 6-9-2 50 ABeech$^{(3)}$ 9 58
(ADickman) *hld up in tch: rdn and ev ch ins fnl f: nt run on nr fin* **11/4**$^{1}$

343 3 5 **Now And Again**$^{221}$ [639] 5-8-12 48 NataliaGemelova$^{(5)}$ 2 43
(IWMcinnes) *s.i.s: sn prom: outpcd over 2f out: styd on ins fnl f* **25/1**

0440 4 shd **Flying Edge (IRE)**$^{13}$ [6144] 4-9-5 50 DAllan 7 45
(EJAlston) *led 6f out: rdn and hdd over 1f out: wknd ins fnl f* **5/1**$^{2}$

2000 5 3 **Baytown Flyer**$^{2}$ [6363] 4-9-2 50 HayleyTurner$^{(3)}$ 5 37
(PSMcentee) *chsd ldrs: rdn over 1f out: wknd fnl f* **10/1**

0060 6 shd **Its Ecco Boy**$^{12}$ [6154] 6-9-4 49 JFanning 6 36
(PHowling) *led 1f: remained handy tl wknd over 1f out* **16/1**

004 7 1¼ **Chantelle (IRE)**$^{16}$ [6058] 4-9-3 48 ACulhane 12 31
(SKirk) *hld up: sme hdwy over 2f out: nvr nr to chal* **8/1**$^{3}$

0050 8 ½ **Mr Lewin**$^{10}$ [6184] 3-9-3 50 PHanagan 4 32
(RAFahey) *hld up: rdn over 2f out: n.d* **5/1**$^{2}$

0520 9 1½ **Saintly Place**$^{16}$ [6058] 3-9-1 48 RFitzpatrick 3 26
(CSmith) *s.i.s: a in rr* **10/1**

60P0 10 2½ **Unintentional**$^{35}$ [5692] 3-8-12 48 (b$^{1}$) DNolan$^{(3)}$ 11 20
(RBrotherton) *dwlt: outpcd* **66/1**

1044 11 nk **Bulawayo**$^{66}$ [4925] 7-9-0 50 (b) BSwarbrick$^{(5)}$ 10 21
(AndrewReid) *sn outpcd* **5/1**$^{2}$

0060 12 14 **Ceylon Round (FR)**$^{16}$ [6061] 3-9-0 50 DCorby$^{(3)}$ 1 —
(MJWallace) *chsd ldrs 4f* **16/1**

1m 31.88s

**WFA** 3 from 4yo+ 2lb **12** Ran SP% **125.0**

Speed ratings: CSF £193.38 TOTE £20.20: £6.00, £2.00, £5.10; EX 314.60.

**Owner** J M Lacey **Bred** J M Lacey **Trained** Scrooby, Notts

**FOCUS**

Fair form for the grade with the first two clear.

**NOTEBOOK**

**Compton Micky** ran very keen through the early parts, but still had enough in reserve to keep finding more and repel the runner-up close home on this All-Weather bow. This was by far his best form to date, and although this was a poor event, he may have more to offer now he has got his head in front.

**The Old Soldier**, making his All-Weather debut, had his chance yet could not get past the winner inside the final furlong. He looked a little reluctant in the finish, but he was clear in second and can find a similarly weak event at this level in a bid to go one better.

**Now And Again**, having his first run for new connections and making his Polytrack debut, would have been a lot closer but for blowing the start. He spent too much energy in trying to recover and should be capable of improving on this return from a 269-day break from the Flat.

**Flying Edge(IRE)** had the run of the race in front, but tired out of contention on this Polytrack debut and was disappointing. He is worth another chance on this surface with more patient tactics.

**Baytown Flyer**, who made hay in this grade during the spring, again shaped as though this run would bring her on.

**Mr Lewin**

**Saintly Place** was popular in the market for this All-Weather bow, but blew the start and was never a threat.

**Bulawayo** was disappointing. Although he was at home on the Fibresand, this was just his second run on Polytrack, and both have been tame efforts.

## 6402 HOLIDAY INN GARDEN COURT MAIDEN CLAIMING STKS 1m 141y(P)

3:20 (3:20) (H5) 3-Y-0+ £1,487 (£425; £212) Stalls Low

Form RPR

2/0- 1 **Tyneham**$^{353}$ 4-8-9 59 (p) CHaddon$^{(7)}$ 4 61
(WGMTurner) *trckd ldrs tl led 1/2-way: rdn over 1f out: all out* **16/1**

000 2 shd **Charlie Masters**$^{19}$ [6017] 3-8-12 JFanning 10 61
(PHowling) *a.p: jnd wnr over 2f out: rdn over 1f out: styd on* **14/1**

/420 3 2 **Ash Bold (IRE)**$^{13}$ [6142] 7-8-7 45 TEaves$^{(3)}$ 12 51
(BEllison) *hld up: hdwy over 3f out: outpcd over 2f out: styd on ins fnl f* **3/1**$^{2}$

0002 4 2½ **Livia (IRE)**$^{16}$ [6056] 3-8-7 50 (v) ACulhane 5 46
(JGPortman) *chsd ldrs tl led over 5f out: hdd over 3f out: sn rdn: hung lft and wknd fnl f* **11/8**$^{1}$

0060 5 3 **Prince Renesis**$^{26}$ [5863] 3-8-9 45 PMulrennan$^{(3)}$ 2 45
(IWMcinnes) *mid-div: rdn 1/2-way: outpcd over 3f out: styd on ins fnl f* **33/1**

-000 6 1¼ **Bold Ridge (IRE)**$^{141}$ [2705] 4-8-10 53 (b) PHanagan 8 36
(BGPowell) *chsd ldrs: rdn over 3f out: wknd wl over 1f out* **9/1**

6440 7 5 **Cloudingswell**$^{16}$ [6055] 3-8-2 45 NDeSouza$^{(5)}$ 3 27
(DLWilliams) *led 3f: wknd 3f out* **8/1**$^{3}$

6400 8 ¾ **Dual Purpose (IRE)**$^{25}$ [5258] 9-9-2 55 (b$^{1}$) SWhitworth 9 30
(CRoberts) *chsd ldrs 6f* **20/1**

00/0 9 5 **Diwan (IRE)**$^{16}$ [6055] 6-8-11 MLawson$^{(5)}$ 13 20
(JParkes) *outpcd* **33/1**

0 10 ¾ **Nippy Nipper**$^{35}$ [5702] 3-8-3 (t) JMackay 11 9
(MissJFeilden) *hld up: plld hrd: hdwy 1/2-way: wknd 3f out* **66/1**

000 11 3½ **Pico Alto**$^{19}$ [6014] 3-8-2 ow1 ANicholls 7 —
(BPalling) *s.i.s: outpcd* **66/1**

12 8 **A Double Ewe Bee** 3-8-3 ow1 PMakin$^{(5)}$ 1 —
(WGMTurner) *hld up: wknd over 3f out* **12/1**

1m 54.85s

**WFA** 3 from 4yo+ 4lb **12** Ran SP% **122.1**

Speed ratings: CSF £215.43 TOTE £19.00: £6.60, £4.50, £2.20; EX 328.10.

**Owner** T Lightbowne **Bred** K J Mercer **Trained** Sigwells, Somerset

**FOCUS**

A modest event that produced a thrilling finish. They were well strung out behind the first two.

**NOTEBOOK**

**Tyneham**, whose career has been plagued by lameness to date, responded positively to the first-time cheekpieces and got up in a bobbing finish to score on this debut for new connections. It is hard to imagine he will follow up, but he may have more to offer at this level.

**Charlie Masters** produced his best display to date on this drop back in class and only just failed. He is clearly limited, but is only lightly raced and looked to enjoy this surface, so could be placed to find a race at this level in order to go one better.

**Ash Bold(IRE)**, whose narrow defeat in a claimer at Newcastle in August gave him every chance in this, hit a flat spot turning for home and was staying on again all too late. He is a very tricky customer.

**Livia(IRE)**, best in at the weights according to official figures, has to go down as disappointing on this drop back in grade. She is a moody filly and remains a maiden after 13 starts.

## 6403 WOLVERHAMPTON-RACECOURSE.CO.UK BANDED STKS 5f 20y(P)

3:50 (3:52) (H5) 3-Y-0+ £1,452 (£415; £207) Stalls Low

Form RPR

2002 1 **Cargo**$^{23}$ [5930] 5-9-0 45 (bt) PDoe 3 53
(BAPearce) *fly j. s: hld up: hdwy 1/2-way: hung rt and led over 1f out: rdn out* **7/2**$^{2}$

0301 2 1 **Chatshow (USA)**$^{6}$ [6288] 3-8-7 45 DFentiman$^{(7)}$ 10 49
(AWCarroll) *hld up: hdwy over 1f out: r.o wl* **3/1**$^{1}$

5006 3 nk **Red Leicester**$^{16}$ [6059] 4-9-0 45 (v) FNorton 13 48
(JAGlover) *hld up: hdwy 2f out: rdn and ev ch over 1f out: styd on* **12/1**

0060 4 1 **Estoille**$^{59}$ [5101] 3-9-0 45 (t) TPQueally 2 45
(MrsSLamyman) *chsd ldrs: rdn and ev ch over 1f out: hung lft and no ex ins fnl f* **25/1**

0050 5 1½ **Hagley Park**$^{37}$ [5642] 5-9-0 45 JFanning 11 39
(MissKMGeorge) *chsd ldrs: rdn 1/2-way: styd on same pce fnl f* **16/1**

4026 6 ¾ **Travelling Times**$^{63}$ [5000] 5-9-0 45 (v) DAllan 7 37
(JSWainwright) *outpcd: r.o ins fnl f: nt trble ldrs* **4/1**$^{3}$

0160 7 ¾ **Pleasure Time**$^{141}$ [2707] 11-9-0 45 (v) RFitzpatrick 4 34
(CSmith) *chsd ldr: rdn and hung rt over 1f out: wknd ins fnl f* **50/1**

0305 8 3 **Flapdoodle**$^{16}$ [6059] 6-9-0 45 (b) NCallan 8 23
(AWCarroll) *chsd ldrs: rdn 1/2-way: wknd 2f out* **8/1**

5503 9 nk **The Leather Wedge (IRE)**$^{67}$ [4881] 5-9-0 45 PBradley 1 22
(ABerry) *led: hung rt and hdd over 1f out: wknd ins fnl f* **8/1**

0550 10 nk **Run On**$^{23}$ [5930] 6-8-12 45 ow1 DNolan$^{(3)}$ 6 22
(DGBridgwater) *mid-div: sn pushed along: wknd 2f out* **33/1**

5000 11 1¼ **Tamarella (IRE)**$^{9}$ [6229] 4-8-11 45 (v) ABeech$^{(3)}$ 5 16
(GGMargarson) *prom 3f* **25/1**

4300 12 1 **Mystery Pips**$^{16}$ [6059] 4-9-0 45 (v) KimTinkler 12 13
(NTinkler) *hld up: rdn 3f out: sn wknd* **20/1**

5000 13 10 **Rellim**$^{16}$ [6059] 5-9-0 45 JEdmunds 9 —
(JBalding) *chsd ldrs 3f* **16/1**

63.00 secs **13** Ran SP% **126.3**

Speed ratings: CSF £14.40 TOTE £3.60: £1.50, £2.50, £2.50; EX 15.00.

**Owner** Noel Lawless **Bred** Mrs Henry Keswick **Trained** Newchapel, Surrey

**FOCUS**

Sound form for the grade and it was run at a decent gallop. The race was hand-timed.

**NOTEBOOK**

**Cargo**, despite fly-jumping at the start, came wide off the home bend full of running and then sustained his gallop to score his first success since 2002. He has been consistent at this sort of level, and this goes down as a deserved success, but he would not be an obvious candidate to follow up.

**Chatshow(USA)** got going too late and may have got up with a little further to go. He was behind the winner at Brighton in this grade three starts previously, and does not look quite as good on the All-Weather, but with a more positive ride he would have claims of reversing this form in the future.

**Red Leicester** had her chance and posted another sound effort. She looks to be running into form and may be worth another try back over six furlongs now.

**Estoille** ran with credit, although she did hang under pressure, and has now shown her best form in two starts on the All-Weather.

**Hagley Park** improved on her most recent effort, and may be capable of getting her head back in front around this track during the winter, but this now looks her level.

**Travelling Times** found this drop back to five furlongs against him, even allowing for the decent gallop throughout. He can do better in this grade when reverting to six furlongs.

## 6404 HOSPITALITY AT DUNSTALL PARK BANDED STKS 1m 141y(P)
4:20 (4:21) (H5) 3-Y-0+ £1,494 (£427; £213) Stalls Low

Form RPR
3501 1 **Tokewanna**[2] 6362 4-9-1 45................(t) PPMathers(5) 5 61
(WMBrisbourne) *trckd ldrs: led over 1f out: r.o* 3/1[1]
6052 2 1 1/4 **Labelled With Love**[23] 5929 4-9-0 45................(t) ACulhane 2 52
(JRBoyle) *s.i.s: hld up: hmpd over 3f out: hdwy over 2f out: rdn hung lft and ev ch fr over 1f out: nt run on* 14/1
0004 3 2 **Ink In Gold (IRE)**[2] 6361 3-8-10 45................ VSlattery 1 48
(PABlockley) *s.i.s: sn chsng ldrs: rdn over 2f out: styd on same pce fnl f* 6/1[3]
5-05 4 nk **Eastern Scarlet (IRE)**[2] 6362 4-9-0 45................(v[1]) SCarson 12 47
(VSmith) *hld up: hdwy 4f out: ev ch 2f out: styd on same pce fnl f* 20/1
3000 5 3/4 **Nuzzle**[30] 5791 4-9-0 45................(v) FNorton 6 46
(MQuinn) *chsd ldr tl led 1/2-way: edgd rt and hdd over 1f out: styd on same pce* 12/1
0000 6 1/2 **Pas De Surprise**[39] 5581 6-9-0 45................ NCallan 7 45
(PDEvans) *chsd ldrs: rdn over 2f out: no ex fnl f* 4/1[2]
6124 7 3 1/2 **Levantine (IRE)**[23] 5927 7-8-7 45................ KirstyMilczarek(7) 10 37
(MissJFeilden) *chsd ldrs: ev ch 2f out: n.m.r over 1f out: eased whn btn ins fnl f* 4/1[2]
0502 8 5 **Ace-Ma-Vahra**[2] 6362 6-9-0 45................(b) JBramhill 13 27
(SRBowring) *hld up in tch: rdn and ev ch over 2f out: wknd over 1f out* 10/1
060 9 11 **Dine 'N' Dash**[49] 5338 3-8-10 45................ SWhitworth 8 4
(AGNewcombe) *hld up: wknd 4f out* 50/1
6100 10 1 1/2 **Haithem (IRE)**[215] 1102 7-9-0 45................(t) PHanagan 9 —
(DShaw) *s.i.s: a bhd* 22/1
5550 11 2 1/2 **Dancing King (IRE)**[19] 6014 8-8-9 45................ PMakin(5) 3 —
(PWHiatt) *led to 1/2-way: wknd over 2f out* 16/1
6000 12 1 1/2 **Susiedil (IRE)**[23] 5927 3-8-10 45................ PDoe 4 —
(PWHarris) *hld up: a bhd* 33/1
6400 13 25 **Single Track Mind**[116] 3441 6-8-9 45................(p) NDeSouza(5) 11 —
(JRBoyle) *s.i.s: a bhd* 33/1

1m 52.49s
**WFA** 3 from 4yo+ 4lb 13 Ran SP% **125.6**
Speed ratings: CSF £47.63 TOTE £4.50: £1.40, £4.50, £3.50; EX 52.70.
**Owner** Merryland Properties Ltd **Bred** Brook Stud Ltd **Trained** Great Ness, Shropshire

**FOCUS**
A poor event, but it is fair form for the grade.

**NOTEBOOK**
**Tokewanna** readily followed up her win in this grade two days previously over this longer trip. She has struck a rich vein of form, looked well-suited by this step up in distance and it is hard to rule out the hat-trick if she is found another opportunity at this venue.
**Labelled With Love** loomed up as a live threat to the winner two out, despite dwelling at the start and meeting trouble approaching the home turn, but could not sustain his gallop and looked reluctant under pressure. This goes down as another good run in this grade, and he may prefer a return to shorter, but he has a few questions to answer now regarding his attitude.
**Ink In Gold(IRE)** , very well backed throughout the day, again missed a beat at the start and paid for it in the straight. He clearly has the ability to score in this grade, but must learn to break better from the gates before he does.
**Eastern Scarlet(IRE)** , despite a visor replacing the cheekpieces and the return to this more suitable trip, could not quicken when it mattered and ran very much up to the form of his effort behind the winner at this track two days previously.
**Pas De Surprise** ran his race with no excuses.
**Levantine(IRE)** was not given a hard time when his winning chance evaporated in the straight and may be going the wrong way. He is often at his best when fresh. *Official explanation: jockey said gelding was hanging left-handed in the home straight*

## 6405 ZONGALERO BANDED STKS (DIV II) 7f 32y(P)
4:50 (4:51) (H5) 3-Y-0+ £1,473 (£421; £210) Stalls High

Form RPR
4030 1 **Molinia**[41] 5552 3-9-3 50................(t) TPQueally 6 62
(RMBeckett) *prom: hmpd and lost pl 6f out: hdwy over 2f out: led over 1f out: rdn out* 20/1
5000 2 2 **Lily Of The Guild (IRE)**[51] 5282 5-9-3 48................(p) FNorton 8 55
(WSKittow) *hld up: hdwy 2f out: sn hung lft: chsd wnr fnl f: styd on* 10/1
0004 3 1 **Long Weekend (IRE)**[2] 6363 6-9-5 50................ SWhitworth 12 54
(DShaw) *s.i.s: hld up: hdwy 2f out: styd on* 10/1
5000 4 5 **Fulvio (USA)**[61] 5035 4-9-5 50................ NCallan 4 41
(PDEvans) *chsd ldrs: led over 2f out: rdn and hdd over 1f out: wknd ins fnl f* 9/2[2]
0300 5 3/4 **Scarrottoo**[2] 6364 6-9-3 48................ DAllan 1 37
(SCWilliams) *chsd ldrs: pushed along 1/2-way: wknd over 1f out* 7/2[1]
0060 6 1/2 **Dubai Dreams**[39] 5585 4-9-0 50................ PMakin(5) 11 38
(SRBowring) *prom: rdn over 2f out: wknd over 1f out* 10/1
2131 7 shd **Elsinora**[9] 6228 3-9-2 49................(v) DSweeney 10 37
(AGJuckes) *s.i.s: hld up: effrt over 1f out: n.d* 7/2[1]
0401 8 1 1/4 **Clare Galway**[10] 6184 3-9-3 50................ ACulhane 5 35
(SKirk) *prom: lost pl over 5f out: nt clr run over 1f out and ins fnl f: n.d* 7/1[3]
0045 9 2 **Farnborough (USA)**[35] 5692 3-9-1 48................ AMcCarthy 7 27
(RJPrice) *prom: rdn 1/2-way: wknd wl over 1f out* 20/1
0600 10 1/2 **Doctor Dennis (IRE)**[23] 5930 7-9-5 50................(v) NPollard 3 28
(JPearce) *led over 4f: wknd fnl f* 16/1
5006 11 3/4 **Elliot's Choice (IRE)**[16] 6058 3-8-12 48................ LPKeniry(3) 9 24
(RMStronge) *trckd ldrs: ev ch 2f out: sn rdn and wknd* 16/1
-000 12 nk **Phoenix Eye**[138] 2777 3-9-3 50................ LEnstone 2 25
(MMullineaux) *prom: rdn 1/2-way: wknd over 2f out* 33/1

1m 30.99s
**WFA** 3 from 4yo+ 2lb 12 Ran SP% **126.6**
Speed ratings: CSF £216.10 TOTE £18.90: £4.90, £4.10, £5.00; EX 161.60.
**Owner** Larksborough Stud Limited **Bred** Larksborough Stud Limited **Trained** Lambourn, Berks

**FOCUS**
The second division of this contest and the form is marginally better than the first. It looks sound enough.

**NOTEBOOK**
**Molinia** improved markedly on her latest effort in a seller and ran out a cosy winner on this All-Weather bow. This was her first success in 12 attempts and she may have a little more to offer on this surface now her confidence will have been boosted.
**Lily Of The Guild(IRE)** hung left when asked to win her race in the straight, but stayed on well enough to the line, albeit at the one pace. This was a much-improved effort, the cheekpieces had the desired effect and this showed the benefit of her recent return from a break.
**Long Weekend(IRE)** was easy to back and was always up against it after another sluggish start.
**Fulvio(USA)** managed to improve a touch for this drop in class, but weakened quickly in the straight and looks regressive.
**Scarrottoo** would have excellent claims of winning in this grade on his turf expoits, but does not look in the same class on sand.
**Elsinora** was a decent winner in this grade at Yarmouth nine days previously but spoilt her chance of following up with a slow start. She has now disappointed in two starts on the Polytrack.

## 6406 CIVIL WEDDINGS AT DUNSTALL PARK BANDED STKS 1m 1f 103y(P)
5:20 (5:21) (H5) 4-Y-0+ £1,487 (£425; £212) Stalls Low

Form RPR
1 **Montara (IRE)**[118] 3405 5-9-0 45................(p) ACulhane 4 55
(LindsayWoods, Ire) *hld up: hdwy over 1f out: rdn to ld ins fnl f: r.o* 8/1[3]
300- 2 1 1/2 **Vrubel (IRE)**[481] 2889 5-9-0 45................(vt[1]) MTebbutt 10 52
(VSmith) *chsd ldrs: rdn over 2f out: styd on* 7/1[2]
6000 3 nk **Lahob**[37] 5654 4-9-0 45................ FNorton 12 52
(PHowling) *led after 1f: rdn over 1f out: hdd and unable qck ins fnl f* 12/1
0000 4 shd **Sinjaree**[16] 6057 6-9-0 45................ TPQueally 3 51
(MrsSLamyman) *led 1f: remained handy: rdn and ev ch 1f out: styd on same pce ins fnl f* 12/1
4126 5 1 1/4 **Dancing Tilly**[9] 6230 6-9-0 45................(p) PHanagan 1 49
(RAFahey) *trckd ldrs: rdn over 1f out: styd on same pce* 9/4[1]
4044 6 1/2 **Ela Re**[91] 4189 5-9-0 45................ JBramhill 13 48
(CRDore) *hld up: hdwy 1/2-way: outpcd over 2f out: styd on ins fnl f* 9/4[1]
00-0 7 1 **Summer Stock (USA)**[22] 554 6-9-0 45................(tp) NPollard 9 46
(JASupple) *chsd ldrs: rdn over 1f out: no ex fnl f* 33/1
1455 8 nk **Misty Man (USA)**[159] 2228 6-9-0 45................(b) SWhitworth 2 46
(MissJFeilden) *hld up: nt clr run over 2f out: hdwy over 1f out: no ex ins fnl f* 33/1
0460 9 2 1/2 **Little Task**[9] 4210 6-8-11 45................ TEaves(3) 6 41
(JSWainwright) *sn pushed along in rr: n.d* 25/1
000- 10 2 1/2 **Rescind (IRE)**[337] 3733 4-9-0 45................ JFanning 7 36
(JeddO'Keeffe) *hld up: a in rr* 14/1
113P 11 3 1/2 **Eurolink Artemis**[137] 2816 7-9-0 45................(p) NCallan 11 29
(JulianPoulton) *hld up: effrt over 2f out: hung lft and wknd over 1f out* 11/1
3-00 12 8 **Sheer Focus (IRE)**[23] 5927 6-8-9 45................ NataliaGemelova(5) 8 14
(IWMcinnes) *w ldr 7f: wknd over 1f out* 16/1

2m 5.01s 12 Ran SP% **131.1**
Speed ratings: CSF £68.97 TOTE £11.50: £4.00, £4.50, £4.80; EX 89.60 Place 6 £370.98, Place 5 £254.80.
**Owner** White Heather Syndicate **Bred** Seamus F Mullan **Trained** Strabane, Co Tyrone

**FOCUS**
A race that took little winning, but the pace was sound throughout.

**NOTEBOOK**
**Montara(IRE)**, whose form in Ireland during the summer was strong in the context of this event, found a fair turn of foot to collar his rivals late in the straight and get off the mark on this first run in Britain. He looked suited by this surface and is entitled to improve after this first run for four months.
**Vrubel(IRE)** made a pleasing return from his 481-day layoff and responded positively to the first-time tongue tie and visor. He can build on this first outing for new connections and is one to keep an eye on at this level.
**Lahob** had the run of the race as he prefers in front, but found little when challenged and can have no excuses.
**Sinjaree** held every chance if good enough and looked very one-paced at the business end of the race. This was still an improvement on her most recent displays, however.
**Dancing Tilly** found less than had looked likley off the bridle approaching the last furlong, having travelled sweetly to that point. She has been in good form at this level of late on turf, but does not look quite as good on the sand.
**Ela Re** was well backed, but got markedly outpaced at a crucial stage and was never a serious threat. He was fourth on the All-Weather prior to his success over hurdles at Cheltenham in January and this will have sharpened him nicely for his return to that sphere. *Official explanation: jockey said gelding had no more to give*
T/Plt: £554.90 to a £1 stake. Pool: £43,331.95. 57.00 winning tickets. T/Qpdt: £179.90 to a £1 stake. Pool: £3,428.20. 14.10 winning tickets. CR

6407 - (Foreign Racing) - See Raceform Interactive

# 5480 LEOPARDSTOWN (L-H)
Monday, October 25

**OFFICIAL GOING: Soft**

## 6408a KILAVULLAN STKS (GROUP 3) 7f
2:30 (2:34) 2-Y-O £32,091 (£9,415; £4,485; £1,528)

RPR
1 **Footstepsinthesand**[8] 6247 2-9-0................ JPSpencer 6 112+
(APO'Brien, Ire) *trckd ldr in 2nd: qcknd into ld ent st: styd on wl fr 1 1/2f out: comf* 4/5[1]
2 2 **Gaff (USA)**[26] 5878 2-9-0................ PJSmullen 3 107
(DKWeld, Ire) *trckd ldrs: 4th 3f out: 2nd 2f out: edgd rt: drifted lft and no imp fnl f: kpt on wl* 10/3[2]
3 7 **Clash Of The Ash (USA)**[138] 2792 2-9-0 94................ KJManning 7 91
(JSBolger, Ire) *chsd ldrs: 3rd 3f out: outpcd early st: kpt on fnl f* 12/1
4 nk **Crystal View (IRE)**[8] 6250 2-8-11 95................ DPMcDonogh 5 87
(KevinPrendergast, Ire) *s.i.s: hld up in tch: 5th and rdn early st: kpt on fnl f* 9/1[3]
5 9 **Night Prayers (IRE)**[36] 5675 2-9-0................ NGMcCullagh 1 69
(JCHayden, Ire) *led: rdn and hdd ent st: sn no ex: wknd fnl f* 16/1
6 7 **Tatamagouche (IRE)**[95] 4071 2-8-11................ MJKinane 2 50
(JohnMOxx, Ire) *hld up in tch: effrt and no imp early st: eased fnl f* 14/1

1m 32.9s **Going Correction** +0.625s/f (Yiel) 6 Ran SP% **108.9**
Speed ratings: **115,112,104,104,94 94**CSF £3.34 TOTE £1.50: £1.20, £1.80; DF 3.30.
**Owner** Michael Tabor **Bred** Hascombe And Valiant Studs **Trained** Ballydoyle, Co Tipperary

**NOTEBOOK**
**Footstepsinthesand** confirmed the good impression he had made when winning his maiden at Naas earlier in the month. He led off the last bend and was not troubled afterwards although he was not extending his margin.
**Gaff(USA)** has a big home reputation but could not go with the winner. He edged right early in the straight, possibly in search of the better ground, nothing went with him and he drifted left inside the last. He found only the one pace but the winner was not getting away from him. He will be interesting on better ground.
**Clash Of The Ash(USA)** was left struggling early in the straight.
**Crystal View(IRE)** consistency in nurseries was not enough to see this busy filly make much impression here after a slow start
**Night Prayers(IRE)** *Official explanation: trainer said colt lost a hind shoe in running*

6409 - 6415a (Foreign Racing) - See Raceform Interactive

## 6204 CATTERICK (L-H)
Tuesday, October 26
**6416 Meeting Abandoned** - Waterlogged

## 6305 NOTTINGHAM (L-H)
Tuesday, October 26
**6423 Meeting Abandoned** - Waterlogged

6434 - 6436a (Foreign Racing) - See Raceform Interactive

## 6035 SAINT-CLOUD (L-H)
Tuesday, October 26

**OFFICIAL GOING: Soft**

### 6437a PRIX DE FLORE (GROUP 3) (F&M) 1m 2f 110y
2:20 (2:20) 3-Y-O+ £25,704 (£10,282; £7,711; £5,141)

RPR

1 **Australie (IRE)**24 5966 3-8-7 .......... TJarnet 11 103
(RGibson, France) *held up in rear, headway on outside from 3f out, 9th straight, ridden to lead just inside final furlong, ran on well*

2 ½ **Elopa (GER)** 3-8-7 .......... IMendizabal 7 102
(ASchutz, Germany) *midfield, 8th on ins str, switched rt and hdwy 1 1/2f out, hard drvn to press wnr ins fnl f, no imp cl hme* 2

3 ¾ **Dream Play (IRE)**51 5331 3-8-7 .......... MSautjeau 12 101
(AFabre, France) *hld up in rr, hdwy on outside over 3f out, 7th str, pressing ldr over 2f out, rdn 1 1/2f out, led briefly 1f out, one pace*

4 2 **Russian Hill**24 5966 4-8-11 .......... CSoumillon 13 96
(AFabre, France) *close up, 4th straight, led narrowly just under 2f out, ridden 1 1/2f out, headed 1f out, weakened* 1

5 ¾ **Reverie Solitaire (IRE)**24 5966 3-8-7 .......... MBlancpain 10 96
(CLaffon-Parias, France) *midfield, 10th straight, stayed on steadily under pressure from over 1 1/2f out*

6 ½ **Anabaa Republic (FR)**24 5966 3-8-7 .......... (b) ELegrix 9 95
(FDoumen, France) *held up, 11th straight, ridden 2f out, stayed on at one pace to take 6th close home*

7 shd **Flip Flop (FR)**24 5969 3-8-7 .......... SPasquier 8 95
(DProd'Homme, France) *close up, 6th and bumped rival entering straight, ridden to go 4th 1 1/2f out, one pace*

8 4 **Anna Victoria (GER)**16 6107 4-8-11 .......... SMaillot 2 86
(GSybrecht, Germany) *held up in rear, last straight, ridden on outside over 2f out, kept on but never threatened leaders*

9 5 **Petite Speciale (USA)**65 4982 5-8-11 .......... OPlacais 5 77
(ELecoiffier, France) *in touch, 3rd straight, pressing leader on inside 2 1/2f out, soon weakened*

10 ¾ **Lilla Creek (USA)**19 4-8-11 .......... TGillet 1 76
(JEPease, France) *held up in rear, 12th straight, never a factor* 3

11 **Prairie Flower (IRE)**24 5965 3-8-7 .......... OPeslier 4 78
(ELellouche, France) *prominent, 2nd straight, led briefly 2 1/2f out, weakened*

12 **Buoyant (IRE)**24 5966 3-8-7 .......... DBonilla 3 78
(FHead, France) *in touch, 5th when bumped entering straight, soon weakened* 3

13 **Trinity Joy**38 5667 3-8-7 .......... (b) TThulliez 6 78
(RGibson, France) *led to 2 1/2f out, weakened*

2m 16.4s
**WFA** 3 from 4yo+ 5lb **13** Ran SP% **125.8**
Speed ratings: .
**Owner** H De Burgh **Bred** Swettenham Stud & Ben Sangster **Trained** France

**NOTEBOOK**

**Australie(IRE)** has done really well. Dropped out early on, she was second last into the straight before being brought with a storming late run. She was given a reminder a furlong out and then quickened to win with something in hand. She loves cut in the ground and is improving, and her trainer hopes she will remain in training next year.

**Elopa(GER)** put up an excellent effort on only her second ever start. She still had plenty to do in the straight and had to wait a little before she could start her run, but came home well. This half-sister to the Singapore Cup winner Epalo certainly looks to have a bright future.

**Dream Play(IRE)** was held up early on and began a forward move at the entrance to the straight. She held a narrow lead one out but was then one-paced in the final stages.

**Russian Hill**, settled in mid-division early on, joined the leaders at the two-furlong marker. She battled on well to the line but could not quicken as well as those in front and may have made her effort a little early.

## 6226 YARMOUTH (L-H)
Wednesday, October 27

**OFFICIAL GOING: Soft (good to soft in places)**
Wind: Fresh half against Weather: Cloudy

### 6438 WEATHERILL BROTHERS MARQUEES (S) STKS 1m 6f 17y
1:10 (1:10) (G4) 3-4-Y-O £2,506 (£716; £358) Stalls High

Form RPR

00-0 1 **Ensemble**22 6005 4-9-5 40 .......... NCallan 5 53
(DMSimcock) *a.p: chsd ldr 9f out: led 4f out: hung lft ins fnl f: drvn out* **33/1**

5002 2 3 **Secret Jewel (FR)**15 6150 4-9-0 60 .......... (b) RLMoore 6 44
(LadyHerries) *bhd: pushed along 1/2-way: hdwy u.p to chse wnr and hung lft fr over 2f out: nt clr run ins fnl f: nt run on* **8/15**1

1053 3 10 **Mister Completely (IRE)**28 5863 3-9-2 47 .......... TPQueally 3 42
(JRBest) *hld up: effrt over 2f out: sn wknd* **11/2**2

0000 4 6 **Purr**15 5286 3-8-7 49 .......... HayleyTurner(3) 2 28
(TTClement) *led 1f: remained handy tl rdn and wknd over 2f out* **20/1**

5 hd **Katie Mernagh (IRE)**416 4758 4-9-0 .......... (b1) SWKelly 1 23
(PSMcentee) *s.s: rdn to ld after 1f: hdd 4f out: wknd over 2f out* **28/1**

0004 6 1¼ **Signora Panettiera (FR)**39 5634 3-8-6 40 ow1 .......... SHitchcott 4 22
(MRChannon) *prom: rdn 5f out: wknd over 2f out* **6/1**3

3m 16.32s (11.12) **Going Correction** +0.575s/f (Yiel)
**WFA** 3 from 4yo 9lb **6** Ran SP% **106.1**
Speed ratings: **91,89,83,80,80 79**CSF £47.02 TOTE £30.60: £8.00, £1.10; EX 44.40.There was no bid for the winner.
**Owner** David Sugars & Bob Parker **Bred** Cheveley Park Stud Ltd **Trained** Newmarket, Suffolk

**FOCUS**
A poor event run in testing conditions. The form is basically worthless.

**NOTEBOOK**

**Ensemble** was difficult to fancy on what he had achieved to date, but this was the first time he had run on soft ground and it clearly made a huge difference.

**Secret Jewel(FR)** had run well in a claimer last time but had yet to prove that she handled this sort of ground. She hung in behind the winner and did not look at all resolute.

**Mister Completely(IRE)** had both his stamina and ability to handle this soft ground to prove. Either way, he failed to get home.

**Purr**, returning from an unsuccessful spell over hurdles, was beating a retreat with over a quarter mile to run.

**Signora Panettiera(FR)** *Official explanation: jockey said filly hung right*

### 6439 E.B.F./POTTERS LEISURE RESORT MAIDEN STKS (DIV I) 7f 3y
1:40 (1:44) (D3) 2-Y-O £4,192 (£1,290; £645; £322) Stalls High

Form RPR

1 **Zalongo** 2-9-0 .......... RWinston 7 86+
(SirMichaelStoute) *hld up: hdwy over 1f out: rdn to ld towards fin* **20/1**

2 ½ **Paradise Mill (USA)** 2-8-9 .......... JFortune 15 80
(JHMGosden) *s.i.s: hld up: hdwy 1/2-way: led over 1f out: sn rdn: hdd towards fin* **17/2**2

3 3 hd **Ticki Tori (IRE)**18 6067 2-8-9 .......... NCallan 6 80
(JulianPoulton) *chsd ldrs: rdn over 1f out: r.o* **12/1**3

4 3 **Red Racketeer (USA)** 2-9-0 .......... RLMoore 4 78
(EALDunlop) *hld up: hdwy over 2f out: rdn over 1f out: no ex fnl f* **16/1**

5504 5 1½ **Dante's Diamond (IRE)**39 5653 2-9-0 75 .......... GBaker 9 74
(FJordan) *sn led: hdd over 1f out: wknd ins fnl f* **20/1**

3 6 2 **Muraabet**12 6187 2-9-0 .......... RHills 8 69
(JLDunlop) *chsd ldr: rdn and edgd lft over 1f out: sn wknd* **4/6**1

00 7 ¾ **Gallantian (IRE)**6 6322 2-9-0 .......... DHolland 13 68
(GAButler) *hld up: styd on ins fnl f: nvr nr to chal* **66/1**

8 1 **Barcardero (USA)** 2-9-0 .......... KDarley 10 65
(MJohnston) *prom: lost pl and n.m.r 4f out: styd on ins fnl f* **14/1**

06 9 2 **Goose Chase**6 6322 2-9-0 .......... JMackay 3 60
(MLWBell) *chsd ldrs 5f* **25/1**

0 10 nk **Horningsheath**13 6171 2-8-9 .......... JQuinn 11 55
(CFWall) *plld hrd and prom: wknd over 2f out* **100/1**

05 11 1 **Born For Diamonds (IRE)**29 5847 2-8-9 .......... MHills 14 52
(BWHills) *sn prom: wknd over 2f out* **20/1**

12 5 **Taxman (IRE)** 2-9-0 .......... SSanders 1 46
(CEBrittain) *s.i.s: sn outpcd* **28/1**

13 2½ **Forehand (IRE)** 2-8-9 .......... DaneO'Neill 2 35
(EFVaughan) *dwlt: outpcd* **25/1**

14 9 **Angel River** 2-8-9 .......... RPrice 12 14
(MJRyan) *hld up: rdn 1/2-way: sn wknd* **100/1**

1m 29.77s (3.27) **Going Correction** +0.475s/f (Yiel) **14** Ran SP% **119.7**
Speed ratings: **100,99,99,95,94 91,90,89,87,87 86,80,77,67**CSF £164.98 TOTE £21.90: £4.20, £2.70, £2.30; EX 210.10.
**Owner** Athos Christodoulou **Bred** A Christodoulou **Trained** Newmarket, Suffolk

**FOCUS**
The slower of the two divisions, but nevertheless a fair maiden, won by a well-bred sort, and a race likely to throw up a few winners. The fifth is a good guide to the form.

**NOTEBOOK**

**Zalongo**, a half-brother to eight winners, most notably top-class middle-distance performer Posidonas, betrayed his inexperience by running green, but he picked up well when finally getting the hang of things and won in the style of a colt who will appreciate farther next season.

**Paradise Mill(USA)**, who is out of a ten-furlong winner, came with a good-looking run to take up the running inside the final two furlongs but was nailed close home. This was a promising start to her career and she is another who will be seen to better effect next year.

**Ticki Tori(IRE)** ran another solid race in defeat, finishing clear of the rest. She has the ability to win a maiden but only needs one more run before she will be eligible for handicaps. As things stand she does not look likely to be generously handicapped, though.

**Red Racketeer(USA)**, a half-brother to Group Two-winning miler China Visit, finished his race well and, with this experience behind him, looks sure to do better next year.

**Dante's Diamond(IRE)**, who is fairly exposed as a mid-70s performer, is probably a good guide to the level of the form.

**Muraabet** had run with plenty of promise on his debut at Newmarket and was all the rage in the market for this seemingly easier race. He failed to give his true running, though, weakening out of contention in the closing stages. Perhaps the race came too soon.

**Gallantian(IRE)** looks the type who will do better next year in handicap company.

### 6440 E.B.F./POTTERS LEISURE RESORT MAIDEN STKS (DIV II) 7f 3y
2:15 (2:18) (D3) 2-Y-O £4,192 (£1,290; £645; £322) Stalls High

Form RPR

3 1 **Plea Bargain**28 5870 2-9-0 .......... JFortune 4 90+
(JHMGosden) *w ldr tl led over 2f out: rdn clr fnl f: eased nr fin* **2/1**1

0 2 5 **Polish Eagle**12 6187 2-9-0 .......... SSanders 6 78
(EALDunlop) *a.p: rdn over 2f out: chsd wnr over 1f out: styd on same pce* **14/1**

0 3 3 **Munsef**13 6171 2-9-0 .......... RHills 8 70
(JLDunlop) *hld up: hdwy over 1f out: nt rch ldrs* **7/1**3

4 1¼ **Vip** 2-9-0 .......... DHolland 14 67
(SaeedBinSuroor) *mde most over 4f: wknd fnl f* **11/2**2

5 ¾ **Diamond Circle** 2-8-9 .......... MHills 11 60
(BWHills) *s.s: hld up: hdwy 3f out: hung lft and wknd over 1f out* **14/1**

6 2½ **Arturius (IRE)** 2-9-0 .......... RLMoore 12 59
(SirMichaelStoute) *dwlt: hdwy over 1f out: n.d* **7/1**3

0 7 1¼ **Hayraan (IRE)**17 6092 2-9-0 .......... PRobinson 7 56
(GCBravery) *prom: sn pushed along: wknd over 2f out* **40/1**

02 8 1 **Wester Lodge (IRE)**17 6091 2-9-0 .......... SWKelly 15 53
(JMPEustace) *chsd ldrs: rdn 1/2-way: wknd 2f out* **8/1**

00 9 3 **Aggravation**8 6294 2-9-0 .......... JFEgan 13 46
(AndrewReid) *hld up in tch: plld hrd: wknd 3f out* **100/1**

0 10 2½ **Mon Plaisir**14 6155 2-8-9 .......... JQuinn 3 34
(CFWall) *plld hrd and prom: rdn 1/2-way: wknd over 2f out* **100/1**

00 11 1 **Whispering Death**5 6330 2-9-0 .......... ACulhane 5 37
(WJHaggas) *s.i.s: outpcd* **40/1**

05 12 4 **Come To Daddy (IRE)**60 5131 2-9-0 .......... GBaker 2 27
(FJordan) *chsd ldrs 4f* **100/1**

000 **13** *7* **Rockys Girl**[37] [5694] 2-8-9 ........ MHenry 10 4
(MJRyan) *s.i.s: outpcd* **150/1**

**14** *20* **Fallujah** 2-8-9 ........ JFanning 1 —
(MJohnston) *chsd ldrs to 1/2-way* **14/1**

1m 29.24s (2.74) **Going Correction** +0.475s/f (Yiel) **14 Ran SP% 113.3**
Speed ratings: **103,97,93,92,91 88,87,86,82,79 78,74,66,43**CSF £30.86 TOTE £2.50: £1.40, £4.50, £2.20; EX 44.60.

**Owner** Sheikh Mohammed **Bred** W And R Barnett Ltd **Trained** Manton, Wilts

**FOCUS**

A decent maiden which should produce plenty of future winners, mostly over farther. It was run in a time 0.53sec faster than the first division.

**NOTEBOOK**

**Plea Bargain** had clearly come on for his debut outing and ran out an impressive winner. The ground proved no problem to him and on this evidence he could be running in Pattern company next year. He should stay a mile and a quarter in time.

**Polish Eagle** was another who improved for his debut run, coming home a clear second. He appreciated the drop back in trip and looks fully capable of winning his maiden.

**Munsef** was doing his best work at the finish and appreciated the step up in trip. His dam won over a mile and a half and he looks likely to be suited by middle-distances next season.

**Vip**, whose dam was a Grade One winner in the US, was fairly weak in the market on his debut. He made the running for a long way but was firmly put in his place inside the final quarter mile. Nevertheless, there is a race to be won with him.

**Diamond Circle**, a half-sister to Hawajiss, who was placed in both the English and Irish Oaks, ran with promise. As her breeding suggests, the best of her will not be seen until she tackles middle-distances next season.

**Arturius(IRE)**, who cost 230,000gns, is out of a mare who won twice in France. He ran as though in need of the experience, was not knocked about, and the run should do him good.

## 6441 GREAT YARMOUTH AND CAISTER GOLF CLUB MAIDEN STKS 1m 3y

2:50 (2:51) (D3) 2-Y-O £3,594 (£1,106; £553; £276) Stalls High

Form RPR

**1** **Very Wise** 2-9-0 ........ ACulhane 3 77
(WJHaggas) *s.i.s: hld up: hdwy over 2f out: edgd rt ins fnl f: r.o to ld nr fin* **50/1**

5 **2** *hd* **Scriptwriter (IRE)**[15] [6139] 2-9-0 ........ TPQueally 19 77
(SaeedBinSuroor) *chsd ldrs: led and hung lft over 1f out: swvd lft ins fnl f: hdd nr fin* **16/1**

**3** *hd* **Forgery (IRE)** 2-9-0 ........ RWinston 4 76
(GAButler) *hld up: hdwy over 2f out: r.o* **16/1**

**4** *6* **Princelet (IRE)** 2-9-0 ........ PRobinson 1 64
(MAJarvis) *hld up: swtchd rt and hdwy over 2f out: nt trble ldrs* **14/1**

**5** *1 1/2* **Quizzene (USA)** 2-9-0 ........ KDarley 10 61
(MJohnston) *sn outpcd: styd on ins fnl f: nvr nrr* **33/1**

4 **6** *nk* **Bureaucrat**[28] [5871] 2-9-0 ........ JFortune 14 61
(JHMGosden) *chsd ldr: led over 2f out: hdd and hmpd over 1f out: wknd ins fnl f* **9/4**[1]

**7** *hd* **Dooie Dancer** 2-9-0 ........ WRyan 20 60
(HRACecil) *hld up in tch: rdn and wknd over 1f out* **20/1**

**8** *3* **Breamore** 2-9-0 ........ SSanders 8 54
(MrsAJPerrett) *hld up: hdwy over 2f out: wknd over 1f out* **25/1**

**9** *shd* **Sun And Showers (IRE)** 2-9-0 ........ RHavlin 15 54
(JHMGosden) *s.s: outpcd: styd on ins fnl f: nvr nrr* **33/1**

00 **10** *3* **Fantastic Luck (IRE)**[15] [6149] 2-9-0 ........ GCarter 9 48+
(JLDunlop) *sn pushed along in rr: n.d* **100/1**

**11** *1/2* **Silber Mond** 2-9-0 ........ DaneO'Neill 18 47
(MLWBell) *s.s: nvr nrr* **40/1**

05 **12** *nk* **One Good Thing (USA)**[15] [6149] 2-9-0 ........ DHolland 2 46
(SaeedBinSuroor) *mid-div: rdn 1/2-way: wknd 2f out* **10/1**[3]

00 **13** *1 3/4* **Neferura**[25] [5946] 2-8-9 ........ SWKelly 12 38
(WJHaggas) *prom over 4f* **66/1**

44 **14** *1 1/2* **Rightful Ruler**[17] [6078] 2-9-0 ........ MHills 6 40
(BWHills) *prom 5f* **10/1**[3]

42 **15** *3* **Kerashan (IRE)**[37] [5696] 2-9-0 ........ RLMoore 7 34
(SirMichaelStoute) *chsd ldrs: rdn over 3f out: wknd wl over 1f out* **10/3**[2]

**16** *5* **Golden Gate (IRE)** 2-9-0 ........ JMackay 16 24
(MLWBell) *dwlt: outpcd* **22/1**

0 **17** *5* **Naval Attache**[18] [6067] 2-8-11 ........ J-PGuillambert(3) 13 14
(NPLittmoden) *chsd ldrs over 5f* **66/1**

**18** *1 1/2* **First Fought (IRE)** 2-9-0 ........ JFanning 11 11
(MJohnston) *chsd ldrs over 4f* **33/1**

**19** *3 1/2* **Colour Blind (IRE)** 2-9-0 ........ PFitzsimons 17 4
(MLWBell) *sn outpcd* **50/1**

**20** *18* **Love And Honour** 2-8-9 ........ NCallan 5 —
(JulianPoulton) *mid-div: rdn 1/2-way: sn wknd* **100/1**

1m 44.5s (4.80) **Going Correction** +0.475s/f (Yiel) **20 Ran SP% 123.6**
Speed ratings: **95,94,94,88,87 86,86,83,83,80 80,79,77,76,73 68,63,61,58,40**CSF £663.13 TOTE £100.80: £14.90, £4.50, £5.20; EX 826.50.

**Owner** J M Greetham **Bred** J M Greetham **Trained** Newmarket, Suffolk

**FOCUS**

A shock result but there was no fluke about it. The race is difficult to rate, however.

**NOTEBOOK**

**Very Wise**, a half-brother to very useful sprinter Forever Phoenix, was slowly away, but he travelled strongly in the race itself and picked up well to get up close home. He looked in need of this outing beforehand and will come on for the run.

**Scriptwriter(IRE)**, who did not look straightforward on his debut, once again failed to impress. Hanging violently when he hit the front, he gave up plenty of ground by wandering all over the place, and was eventually caught close home. He clearly has ability, but he might just be a nutcase.

**Forgery(IRE)**, a brother to Listed-race winner Dr Greenfield, came through to finish a close third, clear of the rest. He certainly has the ability to win a similar maiden and will get middle-distances next year.

**Princelet(IRE)**, whose dam won twice in Listed grade, ended up racing next to the stands'-side rail despite being drawn one. He kept on well to finish fourth and will improve for this outing. *Official explanation: jockey said colt hung right*

**Quizzene(USA)**, a half-brother to mile winner Itemise, struggled to go the early pace but stayed on well towards the end of the race.

**Bureaucrat** was not done any favours by the runner-up, who hung into him, but he was under pressure at the time and soon beat a retreat.

**Kerashan(IRE)** failed to run up to his previous form on this softer ground. He is now eligible for handicaps. *Official explanation: jockey said colt was never travelling*

**Love And Honour** *Official explanation: jockey said filly was unsuited by today's soft, good to soft in places ground*

## 6442 HALLS GROUP NURSERY 5f 43y

3:25 (3:26) (D2) (0-85,81) 2-Y-O £6,708 (£2,064; £1,032; £516) Stalls High

Form RPR

1250 **1** **Russian Rocket (IRE)**[25] [5947] 2-9-2 **79** ........ HayleyTurner(3) 2 81
(MrsCADunnett) *a.p: led over 1f out: r.o* **11/2**[3]

0500 **2** *1 1/2* **Piddies Pride (IRE)**[5] [6333] 2-8-6 **66** ........ SWKelly 7 65+
(PSMcentee) *sn pushed along and prom: swtchd lft and n.m.r over 1f out: r.o* **4/1**[2]

5041 **3** *nk* **Il Pranzo**[4] [6359] 2-9-1 **75** 7ex ........ JFEgan 3 71
(SKirk) *chsd ldrs: rdn over 1f out: styd on same pce ins fnl f* **3/1**[1]

6050 **4** *1/2* **Hits Only Cash**[33] [5772] 2-8-3 **63** ........ JQuinn 4 57
(PABlockley) *plld hrd and prom: rdn and nt clr run ins fnl f: swtchd rt: r.o* **4/1**[2]

0660 **5** *hd* **Asharon**[36] [5719] 2-8-10 **70** ........ SSanders 6 64
(CEBrittain) *dwlt: hdwy u.p over 1f out: styd on* **11/1**

2210 **6** *3/4* **Paris Tapis**[20] [6023] 2-7-11 **60** ........ FPFerris(3) 1 51
(PSMcentee) *led 1f: remained handy: rdn over 1f out: no ex ins fnl f* **10/1**

4104 **7** *3 1/2* **Talcen Gwyn (IRE)**[10] [6241] 2-9-7 **81** ........ ANicholls 8 60
(MFHarris) *led 4f out: rdn and hdd over 1f out: wknd ins fnl f* **10/1**

1600 **8** *nk* **Piper Lily**[19] [6042] 2-8-13 **73** ........ DSweeney 5 51
(MBlanshard) *chsd ldrs: rdn 1/2-way: wknd over 1f out* **10/1**

66.20 secs (3.50) **Going Correction** +0.475s/f (Yiel) **8 Ran SP% 116.0**
Speed ratings: **91,88,88,87,87 85,80,79**CSF £28.19 CT £78.90 TOTE £6.20: £2.00, £1.20, £2.00; EX 25.30.

**Owner** Mrs Christine Dunnett **Bred** Tally-Ho Stud **Trained** Hingham, Norfolk

**FOCUS**

An ordinary nursery. The winner was running right up to his best.

**NOTEBOOK**

**Russian Rocket(IRE)**, outclassed in Listed company last time, found the return to handicap company far more to his liking. He had not run particularly well in testing ground on his debut, but he handled the conditions better than his rivals on this occasion.

**Piddies Pride(IRE)**, first home on the wrong side at Doncaster last time, ran another solid race in defeat. She takes her racing well.

**Il Pranzo** did not achieve a great deal when winning his maiden on the All-Weather last time, and his penalty meant he was effectively 4lb badly in at the weights.

**Hits Only Cash** failed to settle and did not appear to find the drop back in trip in his favour.

**Asharon**, whose four previous starts had been over a mile, found the drop back to the minimum trip too severe.

**Piper Lily** *Official explanation: jockey said filly lost her action*

## 6443 TOTEEXACTA LADY GODIVA FILLIES' STKS (LISTED RACE) 1m 6f 17y

4:00 (4:00) (A1) 3-Y-O+ £17,400 (£6,600; £3,300; £1,500) Stalls High

Form RPR

2065 **1** **Modesta (IRE)**[49] [5394] 3-8-5 95 ........ WRyan 3 97
(HRACecil) *chsd ldrs: led over 1f out: rdn out* **3/1**[2]

0 **2** *1 1/2* **Corrine (IRE)**[48] 5-9-3 ........ ACulhane 10 99
(S-ELilja, Norway) *a.p: led 2f out: sn rdn and hdd: styd on same pce ins fnl f* **25/1**

2233 **3** *1 3/4* **Bowstring (IRE)**[49] [5394] 3-8-5 97 ........ PRobinson 6 93
(JHMGosden) *chsd ldrs tl led over 3f out: rdn and hdd 2f out: no ex fnl f* **2/1**[1]

3144 **4** *3/4* **Goslar**[69] [4884] 3-8-5 90 ........ DSweeney 8 92
(HCandy) *a.p: rdn over 3f out: no ex fnl f* **8/1**[3]

5224 **5** *2 1/2* **Fling**[32] [5788] 3-8-5 83 ........ RWinston 7 89
(JRFanshawe) *s.i.s: hld up: hung lft and styd on ins fnl f: nvr nrr* **10/1**

1563 **6** *shd* **Light Wind**[17] [6087] 3-8-5 85 ........ RLMoore 12 89
(MrsAJPerrett) *trckd ldrs tl led 11f out: rdn and hdd over 3f out: wknd over 1f out* **11/1**

4243 **7** *14* **Samaria (GER)**[26] [5913] 3-8-5 70 ........ JQuinn 4 71
(CFWall) *hld up: wknd over 4f out* **66/1**

5031 **8** *4* **Albavilla**[9] [6278] 4-9-0 70 ........ JFortune 2 65
(PWHarris) *led 3f: remained w ldr tl rdn and wknd over 3f out* **14/1**

0341 **9** *3 1/2* **Shastye (IRE)**[26] [5907] 3-8-6 73 ow1 ........ RHavlin 5 62
(JHMGosden) *s.i.s: hld up: rdn and wknd over 4f out* **20/1**

3-60 **10** *3/4* **Opera Comique (FR)**[49] [5394] 3-8-5 ........ (t) DHolland 1 60
(SaeedBinSuroor) *prom over 9f* **11/1**

5P13 **11** *19* **Trullitti (IRE)**[31] [5822] 3-8-5 84 ........ (b) KDarley 11 35
(JLDunlop) *hld up: hung rt fnl 9f: wknd 5f out* **33/1**

000 **12** *7* **Moon Spinner**[25] [5952] 7-9-0 ........ JFEgan 9 26
(AndrewReid) *hld up: rdn and wknd 5f out* **300/1**

3m 10.5s (5.30) **Going Correction** +0.575s/f (Yiel)
**WFA** 3 from 4yo+ 9lb **12 Ran SP% 115.2**
Speed ratings: **107,106,105,104,103 103,95,92,90,90 79,75**CSF £83.07 TOTE £4.40: £1.40, £3.80, £1.40; EX 104.40.

**Owner** K Abdulla **Bred** Juddmonte Farms **Trained** Newmarket, Suffolk

**FOCUS**

An ordinary Listed race as not one of the runners could boast an official rating in three figures, and not strong form for the grade.

**NOTEBOOK**

**Modesta(IRE)** boosted her paddocks value with a gutsy win in this fairly uncompetitive Listed contest. She had struggled to a large degree since winning her maiden here in the spring, but ran a fair race in the Park Hill Stakes, and that effort gave her every chance in this lesser contest.

**Corrine(IRE)**, three times a winner over a mile and a half in Norway this year, including once in Listed grade, ran a great race under her 3lb penalty, justifying her trainer's decision to bring her over. Her performance does, however, show up the home-trained fillies as nothing special.

**Bowstring(IRE)**, who ought to have been suited by the softer ground, looked to have plenty in her favour having had the winner behind her in the Park Hill last time. She failed to see it out as well as the first two, though, and is still hunting for that elusive second victory.

**Goslar**, one of the more lightly-raced fillies in the field, ran well but perhaps found this trip stretching her stamina at this stage in her career.

**Fling** came from a long way back to finish fifth. She had a bit to find with the principals on official ratings and ran as well as could be expected in the circumstances.

**Light Wind**, another who had plenty on her plate, did her winning in the summer on quick ground.

**Shastye(IRE)** *Official explanation: jockey said filly was unsuited by today's soft, good to soft in places ground*

**Trullitti(IRE)** *Official explanation: jockey said filly hung right throughout*

## 6444 WEATHERBYS INSURANCE CLASSIFIED STKS 1m 2f 21y

4:35 (4:35) (C2) 3-Y-O+ £6,812 (£2,096; £1,048; £524) Stalls Low

Form RPR

2503 **1** **Ofaraby**[60] [5122] 4-9-5 88 ........ PRobinson 3 95
(MAJarvis) *edgd rt s: chsd ldrs: rdn to ld ins fnl f: sn hung lft: styd on* **7/2**[2]

-501 **2** *3/4* **Wiggy Smith**[58] [5183] 5-9-2 85 ........ DaneO'Neill 4 91
(HCandy) *hmpd s: hld up: hdwy over 3f out: rdn over 1f out: styd on* **9/2**[3]

1-20 **3** 1 **Tip The Dip (USA)**[26] 5919 4-9-2 85..............(t) JFortune 6 89
(JHMGosden) *chsd ldrs: led over 2f out: rdn and hung lft over 1f out: hdd ins fnl f: styng on same pce whn n.m.r sn after* **9/2**[3]

0421 **4** shd **Tiger Tiger (FR)**[4] 6354 3-9-3 83.............. JFEgan 8 95
(JamiePoulton) *hld up: hdwy over 3f out: rdn and edgd lft over 1f out: styd on same pce* **5/2**[1]

0400 **5** 3 **Silent Hawk (IRE)**[49] 5397 3-8-11 85..............(vt) TPQueally 2 84
(SaeedBinSuroor) *hld up: hdwy over 3f out: sn rdn: styd on same pce appr fnl f* **16/1**

2001 **6** 3½ **Ultimata**[12] 6194 4-8-13 82.............. RWinston 5 75
(JRFanshawe) *chsd ldr tl led over 3f out: hdd over 2f out: wknd over 1f out* **14/1**

6120 **7** 3½ **Barking Mad (USA)**[25] 5950 6-9-2 84.............. DHolland 7 72
(MLWBell) *sn led: hdd over 3f out: wknd wl over 1f out* **18/1**

30-0 **8** 6 **Bayadere (GER)**[35] 5731 4-8-13 85.............. MHenry 12 59
(VSmith) *prom over 7f* **50/1**

3300 **9** nk **Dream Magic**[25] 5950 6-8-9 77..............(v[1]) MHalford[(7)] 10 61
(MJRyan) *dwlt: hld up: hdwy over 4f out: hung rt and wknd over 2f out* **25/1**

10/6 **10** dist **King's Welcome**[11] 6208 6-9-2 85.............. ACulhane 1 —
(CWFairhurst) *hld up: bhd fr 1/2-way* **50/1**

2m 13.97s (6.00) **Going Correction** +0.575s/f (Yiel)
**WFA** 3 from 4yo+ 5lb **10** Ran SP% **112.7**
Speed ratings: **99,98,97,97,95 92,89,84,84,—**CSF £18.65 TOTE £5.40: £1.90, £2.40, £1.70; EX 18.30.
**Owner** T G Warner **Bred** Red House Stud **Trained** Newmarket, Suffolk

**FOCUS**
A competitive classified event. Decent form for the grade, and solid enough.

**NOTEBOOK**
**Ofaraby** travelled well and, when the gap came, took his chance. He did not do a lot in front but won with a bit more in hand than the official margin would suggest. These are his ideal conditions.
**Wiggy Smith**, lightly raced over the last two seasons, was racing off a mark 5lb higher than at Epsom. He acts well in this sort of ground and ran another good race, only finding one too good.
**Tip The Dip(USA)** had to prove his ability in these testing conditions and in the event coped with them well. The first-time tongue tie might have helped.
**Tiger Tiger(FR)** loves this sort of ground and ran well considering he had had a hard race four days earlier in heavy ground.
**Silent Hawk(IRE)**, who has not progressed since winning his maiden, is unlikely to remain in the Godolphin colours for another year on this evidence.
**Ultimata** enjoyed the run of the race last time but did not have things falling into her lap this time.

## 6445 EVENTGUARD H'CAP 7f 3y
**5:10** (5:11) (E3) (0-77,76) 3-Y-O+ **£4,317** (£1,328; £664; £332) **Stalls** High

Form RPR

0033 **1** **Ask The Clerk (IRE)**[4] 6350 3-9-0 **70**.............. DHolland 9 81
(VSmith) *racd centre: hld up: hdwy and nt clr run over 1f out: r.o to ld nr fin* **6/1**[1]

0042 **2** ½ **Outer Hebrides**[26] 5912 3-9-6 **76**..............(t) RLMoore 4 86
(DRLoder) *racd centre: hld up: hdwy over 2f out: led 1f out: hdd nr fin* **8/1**[2]

0514 **3** 3½ **Mandarin Spirit (IRE)**[18] 6066 4-8-12 **66**..............(b) OUrbina 7 67
(GCHChung) *racd centre: chsd ldrs: led over 1f out: sn hdd and no ex* **14/1**

0303 **4** 2½ **Grandma Lily (IRE)**[29] 5849 6-8-5 **59**.............. JQuinn 10 54
(DCarroll) *racd centre: chsd ldrs: rdn and ev ch over 1f out: no ex* **9/1**[3]

0000 **5** shd **Semenovskii**[11] 6210 4-9-0 **68**.............. RFfrench 2 63
(RBastiman) *racd centre: bhd: hdwy over 1f out: nt rch ldrs* **33/1**

1220 **6** 1¾ **Mugeba**[77] 4650 3-7-12 **61**.............. AKirby[(7)] 8 51
(MissGayKelleway) *racd centre: hld up: hdwy over 2f out: wknd fnl f* **33/1**

4252 **7** ½ **Oh So Rosie (IRE)**[14] 6154 4-8-3 **57**..............(p) JFEgan 12 46
(JSMoore) *racd centre: chsd ldrs: rdn over 2f out: wknd fnl f* **8/1**[2]

4615 **8** 2½ **Fearby Cross (IRE)**[16] 6124 8-8-12 **66**..............(b) JFortune 17 49
(WJMusson) *racd stands' side: hld up: hdwy to ld that gp over 2f out: styd on: no ch w centre* **8/1**[2]

0406 **9** hd **Namroud (USA)**[10] 6244 5-9-1 **72**.............. THamilton[(3)] 6 54
(RAFahey) *racd centre: chsd ldrs over 5f* **10/1**

0000 **10** 3 **Lizarazu (GER)**[60] 5135 5-8-9 **63**.............. ACulhane 5 38
(FJordan) *racd centre: hld up: nvr trbld ldrs* **28/1**

2006 **11** 2½ **Hand Chime**[16] 6124 7-8-2 **63**.............. DanielleDeverson[(7)] 1 31
(WJHaggas) *racd centre: hld up: effrt over 2f out: wknd over 1f out* **12/1**

1002 **12** nk **Warden Warren**[77] 4652 6-9-3 **74**..............(b) HayleyTurner[(3)] 11 42
(MrsCADunnett) *led centre over 5f: sn wknd* **16/1**

5405 **13** 3 **Topton (IRE)**[76] 4672 10-9-6 **74**..............(b) RWinston 13 34
(PHowling) *racd stands' side: hld up: hdwy 1/2-way: wknd 2f out* **14/1**

6010 **14** nk **Spirit's Awakening**[7] 6311 5-8-5 **62**.............. FPFerris[(3)] 19 21
(JAkehurst) *racd stands' side: chsd ldrs over 4f* **9/1**[3]

0200 **15** 2½ **After The Show**[23] 6001 3-8-11 **67**.............. WRyan 18 20
(JRJenkins) *racd stands' side: hld up: plld hrd: n.d* **33/1**

2300 **16** 2½ **Joy And Pain**[16] 6131 3-8-7 **63**.............. TPQueally 15 10
(GLMoore) *racd stands' side: chsd ldr: rdn whn hmpd over 2f out: sn wknd* **40/1**

3401 **17** 3 **Dr Synn**[17] 6089 3-9-0 **70**.............. MTebbutt 14 9
(JAkehurst) *racd stands' side: chsd ldrs over 4f* **14/1**

0-00 **18** 9 **Buzz Buzz**[23] 5998 3-8-10 **66**.............. SSanders 20 —
(CEBrittain) *racd stands' side: prom 4f* **33/1**

0040 **19** 5 **Fyodor (IRE)**[16] 6114 3-8-11 **67**.............. SWKelly 16 —
(WJHaggas) *led stands' side: hung lft: hdd & wknd over 2f out* **25/1**

6000 **20** 1¾ **Mister Sweets**[17] 6094 5-8-3 **64**..............(t) MHalford[(7)] 3 —
(DCarroll) *stmbld bdly s: racd centre: a bhd* **20/1**

1m 29.72s (3.22) **Going Correction** +0.475s/f (Yiel)
**WFA** 3 from 4yo+ 2lb **20** Ran SP% **136.5**
Speed ratings: **100,99,95,92,92 90,89,87,86,83 80,80,76,76,73 70,67,56,51,49**CSF £51.38 CT £686.28 TOTE £7.50: £2.00, £2.00, £4.20, £2.70; EX 57.80 Place 6 £389.35, Place 5 £283.88.
**Owner** R J Baines **Bred** M A Begley And Mrs T Stack **Trained** Exning, Suffolk

**FOCUS**
An ordinary but competitive handicap. The field split into two groups and those who raced towards the centre held the call over those who raced stands' side.

**NOTEBOOK**
**Ask The Clerk(IRE)**, who has been largely consistent this term, notched his second success of the campaign in good style, his rider bringing him with a well-timed run to get up close home.
**Outer Hebrides** ran his best race of the campaign on his first outing on soft ground, only being caught close home and finishing clear of the rest.
**Mandarin Spirit(IRE)** had never previously run on ground as soft as this and had done his winning on a quick surface. He coped well with the conditions, though.
**Grandma Lily(IRE)** is worth noting for when she returns to the Fibresand as she is back down to her last winning mark on the All-Weather.
**Semenovskii** did not run badly given that he looks happiest over six furlongs on a faster surface.
**Mugeba**, who won a firm-ground seller over the course and distance in the summer, found conditions very different on this occasion.
**Oh So Rosie(IRE)** *Official explanation: jockey said colt hung right*
**After The Show** *Official explanation: jockey said colt hung left*
**Mister Sweets** *Official explanation: jockey said gelding missed the break*
T/Plt: £329.00 to a £1 stake. Pool: £27,697.80. 61.45 winning tickets. T/Qpdt: £53.60 to a £1 stake. Pool: £3,495.80. 48.20 winning tickets. CR

# 6392 LINGFIELD (L-H)
### Thursday, October 28

**OFFICIAL GOING: Standard**
Wind: lt bhd Weather: mostly fine

## 6446 SHIRLEY OAKS EBF MAIDEN FILLIES' STKS (DIV I) 7f (P)
**1:50** (1:55) (D3) 2-Y-O **£5,265** (£1,620; £810; £405) **Stalls** Low

Form RPR

00 **1** **Royal Jelly**[17] 6123 2-8-11 .............. JFortune 10 74+
(JHMGosden) *t.k.h early: cl up: rdn to chse ldr 2f out: drvn and styd on wl to ld last 100yds* **7/2**[1]

50 **2** ¾ **Archeology (USA)**[13] 6196 2-8-11 .............. EAhern 5 72+
(SaeedBinSuroor) *lw: prom: led 1/2-way: kicked on 2f out: hdd last 100yds: kpt on* **7/2**[1]

00 **3** 5 **Make It Snappy**[17] 6123 2-8-11 .............. TQuinn 6 60+
(PWHarris) *trckd ldrs: rdn and outpcd over 2f out: styd on fnl f to take 3rd nr fin* **20/1**

3 **4** nk **Hashima (USA)**[76] 4706 2-8-11 .............. MHills 14 59
(CEBrittain) *t.k.h: prom: outpcd by ldng pair wl over 1f out: fdd fnl f* **4/1**[2]

0 **5** 2 **Tangible**[13] 6181 2-8-11 .............. SSanders 1 64+
(SirMarkPrescott) *lw: dwlt: settled in midfield: shuffled along and outpcd over 2f out: kpt on steadily fr over 1f out: improve* **7/1**[3]

0 **6** ¾ **Shades Of Green**[37] 5717 2-8-11 .............. JFEgan 7 52
(NACallaghan) *hld up towards rr: outpcd wl over 2f out: shuffled along and styd on steadily over 1f out: do bttr* **16/1**

0 **7** ¾ **Girlsweekend**[27] 5911 2-8-11 .............. IMongan 2 50
(MrsLJMongan) *led to 1/2-way: chsd ldr to 2f out: wknd over 1f out* **50/1**

0 **8** 6 **Pride Of Poona (IRE)**[15] 6158 2-8-11 .............. MHenry 9 35
(RMHCowell) *t.k.h: trckd ldrs tl wknd over 2f out* **33/1**

**9** hd **Xaara Doon (IRE)** 2-8-11 .............. SRighton 12 35
(MJAttwater) *w'like: angular: s.i.s: detached in last: wl bhd over 2f out: no ch* **25/1**

00 **10** hd **Just Beware**[127] 3202 2-8-8 .............. NChalmers[(3)] 4 34
(MissZCDavison) *dwlt: a wl in rr: wl bhd over 2f out* **100/1**

**11** ¾ **Bella Miranda** 2-8-11 .............. TPQueally 11 32
(DRLoder) *leggy: a wl in rr: wl bhd over 2f out* **10/1**

00 **12** 3½ **Eforetta (GER)**[24] 5996 2-8-4 .............. FrancesPickard[(7)] 8 24
(DJWintle) *dwlt: a wl in rr: wl bhd over 2f out* **100/1**

33 **13** ¾ **Georgie Belle (USA)**[197] 1390 2-8-11 .............. CCatlin 13 22
(CTinkler) *bit bkwd: t.k.h: pressed ldrs to 3f out: wknd rapidly: hanging over 1f out* **10/1**

0 **14** 12 **Livvies Lady (IRE)**[15] 6155 2-8-11 .............. DaneO'Neill 3 —
(DKIvory) *s.s: rchd midfield 4f out: wknd rapidly 3f out: t.o* **40/1**

1m 26.1s (0.16) **Going Correction** -0.05s/f (Stan) **14** Ran SP% **118.9**
Speed ratings: **97,96,90,90,87 86,86,79,79,78 77,73,73,59**CSF £14.34 TOTE £5.70: £2.00, £1.80, £4.30; EX 22.70.
**Owner** Cliveden Stud **Bred** Cliveden Stud Ltd **Trained** Manton, Wilts

**FOCUS**
Probably just modest maiden form and not that solid, but it was run in a faster time than the second division and the first two came clear.

**NOTEBOOK**
**Royal Jelly** stepped up markedly on the fom of her previous two outings with a gritty display to score on this All-Weather debut. She is entitled to come on again for this, but her future looks to lie with the Handicapper.
**Archeology(USA)**, who failed to run up to her debut form when a disappointing favourite last time, duly improved for this quicker surface and went down fighting. She is far from one of her powerful stable's leading lights, but was clear in second and should be able to win a similar race.
**Make It Snappy** broke much better than on both of her previous starts and duly improved as a result. She was keeping on as though she will want further next year and now qualifies for handicaps.
**Hashima(USA)** did not aid her cause by refusing to settle early on and then having to race wide for most of the way. She already looks in need of a mile and is capable of better.
**Tangible**, as on her debut, was very slow to break and ran distinctly green through the first half of the contest. She was keeping on late however, and is the type her trainer excels with over further as a three-year-old.
**Shades Of Green** duly improved a touch on her debut effort, and was keeping on with promise in the straight, over what will surely turn out to be an inadequate trip.

## 6447 SHIRLEY OAKS EBF MAIDEN FILLIES' STKS (DIV II) 7f (P)
**2:20** (2:25) (D3) 2-Y-O **£5,265** (£1,620; £810; £405) **Stalls** Low

Form RPR

05 **1** **Allied Cause**[43] 5570 2-8-11 .............. NMackay 4 70+
(LMCumani) *lw: led for 1f: trckd ldng pair after: effrt to ld again ins fnl f: drvn and jst hld on* **5/1**[3]

23 **2** nk **Celtique**[51] 5368 2-8-11 .............. RWinston 11 69+
(SirMichaelStoute) *trckd ldrs: rdn over 2f out: unable qck over 1f out: styd on ins fnl f: jst failed* **2/1**[1]

50 **3** nk **Orlar (IRE)**[33] 5789 2-8-11 .............. SWKelly 1 69+
(JAOsborne) *hld up midfield: cl up whn nt clr run briefly over 1f out: shkn up and r.o fnl f: nrst fin: do bttr* **11/1**

0 **4** shd **Sign Of Luck (IRE)**[38] 5695 2-8-11 .............. MHills 6 68+
(CEBrittain) *settled in rr: stl in last trio wl over 1f out: rdn and r.o wl fnl f: gaining at fin* **40/1**

4 **5** 1 **Angel Rays**[22] 6010 2-8-11 .............. DHolland 13 66
(GAButler) *lw: racd freely: led after 1f: hdd & wknd ins fnl f* **4/1**[2]

**6** shd **Irreversible** 2-8-11 .............. JFortune 3 68+
(JHMGosden) *unf: s.i.s: wl in rr but in tch: prog on inner 2f out: chsd ldrs ins fnl f: no ex* **10/1**

**7** ¾ **Elle Nino** 2-8-11 .............. SDrowne 7 66+
(GWragg) *unf: scope: hld up midfield: pushed along and kpt on one pce fr over 1f out: bttr for experience* **12/1**

0 **8** 1¼ **Petite Spectre**[14] 6171 2-8-11 .............. DaneO'Neill 8 61
(RHannon) *racd midfield on outer: effrt to chse ldrs 2f out: wknd fnl f* **50/1**

**9** nk **Arrivato** 2-8-11 .............. MartinDwyer 9 65+
(AMBalding) *w'like: bit bkwd: s.s: racd in last pair: sme prog whn nt clr run over 1f out: styd on: bttr for experience* **28/1**

0 **10** *nk* **Flaunt N Flirt**[28] 5890 2-8-11 ........ TQuinn 2 59
(MPTregoning) *chsd ldrs: cl enough 2f out: pushed along and wknd fnl f* **50/1**

0 **11** *½* **Oblique (IRE)**[15] 6153 2-8-11 ........ SSanders 12 63+
(SirMarkPrescott) *pushed along in rr: prog on wd outside 3f out: outpcd 2f out: kpt on again fnl f* **50/1**

**12** *4* **Suturia** 2-8-11 ........ EAhern 14 48
(NoelTChance) *w'like: bit bkwd: racd freely: chsd ldr over 5f out to over 1f out: wknd rapidly* **25/1**

0 **13** *1* **Creme De La Creme (IRE)**[71] 4851 2-8-11 ........ TPQueally 5 50+
(DRLoder) *chsd ldrs: rdn and lost pl 1/2-way: nvr on terms after* **14/1**

**14** *2 ½* **Rosablanca (IRE)** 2-8-11 ........ ACulhane 10 39
(JGGiven) *leggy: snatched up after 1f: wl in rr: detached in last 3f out* **50/1**

1m 27.19s (1.25) **Going Correction** -0.05s/f (Stan) **14** Ran SP% **119.4**
Speed ratings: **90,89,89,89,88 87,87,85,85,84 84,79,78,75**CSF £14.38 TOTE £7.40: £2.50, £1.30, £3.00; EX 20.40.
**Owner** Helena Springfield Ltd **Bred** Meon Valley Stud **Trained** Newmarket, Suffolk
■ Stewards Enquiry : D Holland two-day ban: careless riding (Nov 8,9)

**FOCUS**
This looked marginally the weaker of the two divsions, an opinion backed up by the slower time. The first four home finished in a heap giving the form a messy appearance.

**NOTEBOOK**
**Allied Cause** , who had shown ability in two fairly decent maidens previously, put up her best display to date and got off the mark in tenacious style. She is choicely-bred and could make up into a useful filly next year, with a mile sure to pose no problems.
**Celtique** again failed to quicken all that well at the business end of the race and was just denied. She certainly has the form, and now qualifies for handicaps, but is becoming frustrating to follow.
**Orlar(IRE)** ◆, who can be made fitter still, stepped up on her previous two efforts and left the impression she will prefer the step up to a mile. This quicker surface was much more to her liking and it would be a surprise were her trainer not find an opportunity on the All-Weather in which to gain compensation.
**Sign Of Luck(IRE)** was motoring at the finish and improved markedly on her debut effort at Kempton. She should come into her own next year over further.
**Angel Rays** had the run of the race in front, but did not settle all that well early on and paid for it when challenged in the straight. Bred to to be better over further next year, she could well be placed to find a race on this surface during the winter.
**Irreversible** , half-sister to dual two-year-old winner Go Bananas, shaped with promise and is sure to better in due course with this experience under her belt.
**Arrivato** *Official explanation: jockey said filly suffered interference in running*

## 6448 NICHOLAS HALL EBF MAIDEN STKS (C&G) (DIV I) 7f (P)
**2:50** (2:50) (D3) 2-Y-O **£5,148** (£1,584; £792; £396) **Stalls** Low

Form RPR

2232 **1** **Daniel Thomas (IRE)**[6] 6331 2-8-11 92 ........ ACulhane 3 79+
(MrsAJPerrett) *trckd ldr over 4f out: led 2f out: shkn up over 1f out: pushed out fnl f* **4/6**[1]

0 **2** *2 ½* **Chief Exec**[14] 6171 2-8-11 ........ DSweeney 4 73+
(CACyzer) *led to over 5f out: settled bhd ldrs: effrt to chse wnr over 1f out: kpt on but no imp* **20/1**

0 **3** *2 ½* **Liberty Run (IRE)**[13] 6187 2-8-11 ........ JFEgan 2 67
(NACallaghan) *lw: racd midfield: rdn fr 4f out: styd on u.p fnl 2f: no ch w ldng pair* **7/2**[2]

554 **4** *2* **Dart Along (USA)**[17] 6126 2-8-11 78 ........ DaneO'Neill 9 62
(RHannon) *trckd ldrs: cl up 2f out: wknd over 1f out* **15/2**[3]

0 **5** *2 ½* **Annibale Caro**[9] 6289 2-8-11 ........ SSanders 10 62+
(SirMarkPrescott) *rn green: hld up in rr: outpcd fr 3f out: shuffled along and styd on over 1f out: do bttr* **20/1**

0 **6** *5* **Expeditious (USA)**[27] 5915 2-8-11 ........(bt[1]) EAhern 5 43
(SaeedBinSuroor) *led over 5f out to 2f out: wknd rapidly over 1f out* **12/1**

**7** *6* **Ready Teddy Go** 2-8-11 ........ ANicholls 8 28
(DKIvory) *w'like: dwlt: a in rr: wl bhd over 2f out: modest late prog* **66/1**

0 **8** *1 ¾* **Hugo The Boss (IRE)**[15] 6155 2-8-11 ........ MartinDwyer 7 23
(JRBoyle) *chsd ldrs tl wknd 3f out* **66/1**

**9** *½* **Canadian Danehill (IRE)** 2-8-11 ........ MHenry 6 22
(RMHCowell) *w'like: s.s: a wl bhd* **33/1**

00 **10** *11* **Chiracahua (IRE)**[27] 5911 2-8-11 ........ RWinston 1 —
(BJMeehan) *racd midfield: wknd 2f out: heavily eased fr wl over 1f out* **33/1**

1m 25.89s (-0.05) **Going Correction** -0.05s/f (Stan) **10** Ran SP% **120.1**
Speed ratings: **98,95,92,90,87 81,74,72,72,59**CSF £23.51 TOTE £1.60: £1.40, £5.10, £1.20; EX 24.10.
**Owner** J H Richmond-Watson **Bred** Lawn Stud **Trained** Pulborough, W Sussex

**FOCUS**
A modest maiden which was run at a sound pace and the field came home strung out. It was run in a much slower time than the second division, and the winner did not need to run to its best to score.

**NOTEBOOK**
**Daniel Thomas(IRE)** got off the mark at the fifth time of asking with a fairly straightforward success. He has shown a decent level of form in all of his starts to date, and appreciated this surface, but will not be that easy to place off his mark now unless he makes further improvement.
**Chief Exec** stepped up markedly on his recent debut effort at Newmarket, really appreciating this better surface. A similar performance can see him go one better.
**Liberty Run(IRE)** ◆ , well backed to improve on his recent Newmarket debut, did just that, but got going all too late and never looked like landing the gamble. He was green again this time, so clearly has further improvement in him and will be of definite interest when handicapped over a longer distance.
**Dart Along(USA)** ran his race with no excuses. He now looks fully exposed.
**Annibale Caro** , as on his recent Wolverhampton debut, struggled to go the early gallop and ran distinctly green throughout. He was keeping on late however, and will no doubt only come into his own when handicapped next year.
**Expeditious(USA)** *Official explanation: jockey said colt lost its action*
**Chiracahua(IRE)** *Official explanation: jockey said gelding lost its action*

## 6449 ELEANOR HARRINGTON CONDITIONS STKS 5f (P)
**3:20** (3:20) (C2) 2-Y-O **£4,872** (£1,848; £924; £420) **Stalls** High

Form RPR

5012 **1** **Bond City (IRE)**[12] 6204 2-9-5 94 ........ FLynch 5 94
(BSmart) *chsd ldr: rdn to ld jst over 1f out: sn clr: drvn out* **11/4**[3]

113 **2** *1 ¼* **Cyclical**[28] 5896 2-9-2 93 ........ JFortune 2 87+
(GAButler) *lw: settled in 4th: rdn and outpcd wl over 1f out: r.o to take 2nd last 100yds: nt rch wnr* **7/4**[2]

131 **3** *3 ½* **Sharplaw Star**[37] 5711 2-9-2 100 ........ MHills 4 73
(WJHaggas) *b.hind: chsd ldng pair: rdn 2f out: outpcd and btn over 1f out* **6/4**[1]

**4** *shd* **Cashel House (IRE)**[46] 5497 2-8-11 ........ ACulhane 3 68
(DanielMarkLoughnane, Ire) *w'like: led: qcknd 1/2-way: hdd & wknd jst over 1f out* **25/1**

0 **5** *6* **Snowdrift**[30] 5847 2-8-6 ........(b[1]) SWKelly 6 41
(DJDaly) *s.i.s: hld up in last: wknd wl over 1f out* **50/1**

59.70 secs (-0.08) **Going Correction** -0.05s/f (Stan) **5** Ran SP% **108.8**
Speed ratings: **98,96,90,90,80**CSF £7.79 TOTE £3.60: £1.70, £1.40; EX 7.90.
**Owner** R C Bond **Bred** David Ryan **Trained** Hambleton, N Yorks

**FOCUS**
An interesting condtions stakes that saw the first two come clear. The pace was sound and the winner is the best guide to the level of the form.

**NOTEBOOK**
**Bond City(IRE)** won with plenty in hand under a positive ride and has now won both of his outings on the Polytrack. He looks another very useful sprinter in the making for his connections, and will be worth another shot back over six furlongs on this evidence.
**Cyclical** took his time to hit full stride and was making up ground hand over fist in the last furlong, but never really looked like getting there in time. This drop back to the minimum trip was against him and he certainly remains of promise.
**Sharplaw Star**, whose only defeat to date was at the hands of Damson in the Queen Mary, ran well below her best on this All-Weather bow. On form she should have been a lot closer, and it is worrying that she was easy to back this time, so could be going the wrong way.
**Cashel House(IRE)** , who had shown just modest form in four previous starts in Ireland, was far from disgraced having made most of the running until the final furlong on this British debut.

## 6450 BARCLAYCARD BUSINESS H'CAP 1m 4f (P)
**3:50** (3:50) (E3) (0-77,74) 3-Y-O+ **£3,515** (£1,081; £540; £270) **Stalls** Low

Form RPR

011 **1** **Mith Hill**[22] 6013 3-9-0 70 ........ EAhern 13 81+
(EALDunlop) *trckd ldrs: prog over 2f out: rdn to ld over 1f out: styd on strly* **5/2**[1]

3424 **2** *2 ½* **Dovedon Hero**[10] 6278 4-9-7 70 ........(b) SSanders 2 77
(PJMcbride) *lw: hld up in midfield: prog 2f out: drvn and stdy on to take 2nd wl ins fnl f: no ch w wnr* **11/2**[2]

-150 **3** *¾* **Gingko**[159] 820 7-9-5 68 ........ DaneO'Neill 7 74
(PRWebber) *racd wd in midfield: prog 4f out: chalng whn rn wd bnd 2f out: hrd rdn to chse wnr 1f out: one pce* **25/1**

0/00 **4** *½* **Lewis Island (IRE)**[20] 6043 5-9-7 70 ........ JFEgan 12 75
(BEllison) *s.s: hld up in last trio: shkn up 2f out: r.o wl fnl f: nvr nrr* **16/1**

-000 **5** *nk* **Blackmail (USA)**[15] 6156 6-9-4 67 ........(b) SCarson 11 72
(MissBSanders) *racd midfield: effrt 3f out: rdn to chse ldrs 2f out: kpt on same pce* **25/1**

5262 **6** *shd* **Madiba**[18] 6084 5-9-0 63 ........ RWinston 9 68
(PHowling) *t.k.h: hld up in rr: rdn 3f out: styd on fr over 1f out: nvr able to chal* **14/1**

320 **7** *½* **Champagne Shadow (IRE)**[28] 5889 3-9-0 70 ........(b) JFortune 10 74
(GLMoore) *chsd ldr 9f out: rdn and upsides 2f out: wknd fnl f* **10/1**

6232 **8** *½* **Eastborough (IRE)**[109] 3773 5-9-2 65 ........ JFanning 3 68
(BGPowell) *hld up towards rr: prog on inner 2f out: clsd on ldrs 1f out: nt clr run sn after and eased* **16/1**

2605 **9** *¾* **Aoninch**[29] 5875 4-8-11 60 ........ SWhitworth 8 62
(MrsPNDutfield) *hld up in detached last: shuffled along over 2f out: styd on fr over 1f out: do bttr* **14/1**

0000 **10** *shd* **Western (IRE)**[18] 6083 4-9-2 65 ........(p) TQuinn 5 67
(JAkehurst) *dwlt: hld up wl in rr: stl in last trio on wd outside over 2f out : swtchd to inner over 1f out: nt clr run last 150yds: ho* **12/1**

2-25 **11** *¾* **Atlantic City**[133] 3015 3-8-12 68 ........(e[1]) NCallan 16 68
(MrsLRichards) *prom: effrt on inner and cl up over 1f out: wknd fnl f* **33/1**

1000 **12** *½* **Rasid (USA)**[20] 6043 6-9-11 74 ........ DHolland 14 74
(CADwyer) *b. nr hind: led after 1f to over 1f out: wknd* **16/1**

4246 **13** *1 ¼* **Regal Gallery (IRE)**[10] 6278 6-9-7 70 ........ PaulEddery 1 68
(CAHorgan) *racd midfield: rdn to chse ldrs over 2f out: no imp over 1f out: losing pl whn n.m.r ins fnl f and eased* **7/1**[3]

44-0 **14** *7* **Scalloway (IRE)**[14] 5657 4-9-2 65 ........ VSlattery 15 51
(DJWintle) *prom tl lost pl u.p over 3f out: no ch after* **40/1**

0020 **15** *5* **Sewmore Character**[22] 6013 4-9-4 67 ........ DSweeney 6 45
(MBlanshard) *lw: racd midfield: wknd 2f out* **20/1**

/5-0 **16** *3* **Red Rackham (IRE)**[27] 5907 4-9-0 63 ........ MTebbutt 4 37
(JNicol) *led for 1f: wknd u.p over 2f out* **20/1**

2m 33.43s (-0.81) **Going Correction** -0.05s/f (Stan)
**WFA** 3 from 4yo+ 7lb **16** Ran SP% **126.8**
Speed ratings: **100,98,97,97,97 97,96,96,96,96 95,95,94,89,86 84**CSF £13.74 CT £299.05 TOTE £3.20: £1.20, £1.30, £5.80, £4.50; EX 18.20.
**Owner** Mohammed Jaber **Bred** Floors Farming, Hmh Management Ltd And John Warren **Trained** Newmarket, Suffolk

**FOCUS**
A modest handicap that was run at a fair gallop. The winner looks capable of improving further on this surface, but the proximity of the fifth and sixth holds the form down somewhat.

**NOTEBOOK**
**Mith Hill** landed the hat-trick in grand style, outstaying his rivals in the straight. He is evidently a rapidly-improving handicapper and can go in again, providing the Handicapper does not hammer him for this authoritive display.
**Dovedon Hero** ran another sound race, but could was not a serious threat to the winner. He is reliable and deserves to end his long losing run, but his habit of finding one or two too good will always temper confidence.
**Gingko** , last seen pulling up over hurdles 159 days previously, posted a decent return to action and only tired late on. He is entitled to come on for this, although he is high enough in the weights at present.
**Lewis Island(IRE)** , now better known for his exploits over hurdles, ran a promising race on this All-Weather bow. He was forced to bide his time, having missed the break, and stayed on with effect in the straight, leaving the impression he can pick up another race off his declining mark.
*Official explanation: jockey said gelding pulled hard early on*
**Atlantic City** , sporting a first-time eyeshield, showed up well for a long way before weakening rapidly on this first run for 133 days. He showed ability for William Haggas as a juvenile and may have more to offer at this level for his new yard, providing he remains sound.

## 6451 LADBROKES.COM STKS (H'CAP) 7f (P)
**4:20** (4:20) (C1) (0-107,102) 3-Y-O+ **£13,520** (£4,160; £2,080; £1,040) **Stalls** Low

Form RPR

2001 **1** **Goodenough Mover**[29] 5874 8-8-1 86 ........ HayleyTurner(3) 10 97
(JSKing) *ldng trio: rdn 2f out: led jst over 1f out: hld on wl nr fin* **20/1**

3601 **2** *hd* **Khabfair**[34] 5762 3-9-1 99 ........ DaneO'Neill 8 110
(MrsAJPerrett) *lw: hld up midfield: prog over 1f out: drvn and r.o fnl f: jst hld* **7/1**[2]

6605 **3** *nk* **Greenslades**[27] 5921 5-8-8 90 ........ DSweeney 3 100
(PJMakin) *lw: trckd ldng trio: effrt on inner over 1f out: pressed wnr ins fnl f: hld nr fin* **15/2**[3]

014 **4** *1 ¼* **Dame De Noche**[28] 5898 4-8-4 **86** EAhern 7 93
(JGGiven) *pressed ldr: ev ch jst over 1f out: one pce ins fnl f* **14/1**

046 **5** *nk* **Lygeton Lad**[78] 4652 6-9-6 **102** (t) SDrowne 4 108
(MissGayKelleway) *b: b.hind: trckd ldrs: rdn over 2f out: kpt on u.p: nvr able to chal* **8/1**

3515 **6** *nk* **Marshman (IRE)**[13] 6191 5-8-7 **89** PRobinson 13 94
(MHTompkins) *lw: hld up wl in rr: effrt on wd outside over 1f out: styd on fnl f: nvr nrr* **7/1**[2]

0164 **7** *nk* **Ettrick Water**[13] 6191 5-9-4 **100** (v) NMackay 11 104
(LMCumani) *lw: chsd ldrs: rdn 2f out: kpt on same pce fr over 1f out* **6/1**[1]

5403 **8** *¾* **Fruit Of Glory**[14] 6177 5-8-10 **92** DHolland 1 94
(JRJenkins) *lw: racd midfield: effrt on inner over 1f out: one pce fnl f* **16/1**

3000 **9** *shd* **Uhoomagoo**[33] 5781 6-8-4 **86** oh1 (b) PHanagan 9 88
(KARyan) *sn pushed along in last: no prog tl styd on fnl f: no ch* **10/1**

0300 **10** *½* **High Reach**[28] 5893 4-8-12 **94** GCarter 5 95
(TGMills) *led to jst over 1f out: wknd* **10/1**

316- **11** *1 ¼* **Little Good Bay**[397] 5210 4-9-2 **98** (v) JFortune 2 96
(JHMGosden) *s.s: hld up in rr: effrt 2f out: fdd over 1f out* **8/1**

0000 **12** *shd* **Te Quiero**[75] 4751 6-9-4 **100** (t) ACulhane 6 97
(MissGayKelleway) *b: b.hind: hld up midfield: rdn 2f out: sn outpcd and btn* **40/1**

0000 **13** *2* **Massey**[47] 5452 8-8-8 **95** PMakin(5) 12 87
(TDBarron) *a towards rr: under presssure and struggling 3f out* **50/1**

2-53 **14** *2 ½* **Hanzano (IRE)**[9] 6-9-4 **100** CCatlin 14 86
(AreHyldmo, Norway) *racd wd in midfield: rdn 1/2-way: sn btn* **33/1**

1m 24.19s (-1.75) **Going Correction** -0.05s/f (Stan)
**WFA** 3 from 4yo+ 2lb **14** Ran SP% **116.1**
Speed ratings: **108,107,107,106,105 105,104,104,104,103 102,101,99,96**CSF £145.40 CT £1189.55 TOTE £25.00: £6.80, £2.60, £2.20; EX 164.70 Trifecta £811.50 Pool: £1,142.98. 0.20 winning tickets..
**Owner** D Goodenough Removals & Transport **Bred** G Foster **Trained** Broad Hinton, Wilts

**FOCUS**
A good handicap and solid All-Weather form and it should throw up its share of winners. The pace was strong throughout.

**NOTEBOOK**
**Goodenough Mover** followed-up his recent success at Salisbury with a brave display on this return to the All-Weather. He was winning this off a 6lb higher mark and is clearly in rude health at present, but can expect yet another rise in the weights for this, which may scupper the hat-trick bid.
**Khabfair**, who showed ability on this surface as a juvenile, proved he gets the trip and was only just denied. This now opens up further opportunites for connections and he is still open to more improvement.
**Greenslades**, making his All-Weather debut, tried his best to get on top close home yet was just denied. This was another sound effort, and he seemed to enjoy this track, so could find another race on this surface in which to gain compensation.
**Dame De Noche**, having her first outing on the All-Weather, had her chance, but could not quicken where it mattered over this extra furlong. She looks best over shorter these days and was not at all disgraced.
**Lygeton Lad**, returning from a 78-day break, ran with credit under his big weight and should come on for the run.
**Marshman(IRE)** was not helped by having to come wide to challenge, but still got going all too late.
**Ettrick Water**, another making his All-Weather debut, had his chance but found little off the bridle and was a little disappointing. He looks high enough in the weights now and has a bit to prove.

## 6452 FORMARK SCAFFOLDING CLASSIFIED STKS 7f (P)
**4:50** (4:53) (F3) 3-Y-0+ **£3,542** (£1,090; £545; £272) **Stalls** Low

Form RPR

0505 **1** **Nearly A Fool**[18] 6081 6-9-0 60 (v) NPollard 14 76
(GGMargarson) *hld up in last: prog on outer fr 3f out: drvn and r.o fr over 1f out: led last strides* **7/1**[3]

3222 **2** *1 ¼* **Roman Quintet (IRE)**[17] 6131 4-9-0 60 TQuinn 8 73
(DWPArbuthnot) *led: gng easily over 1f out: shkn up ent fnl f: wknd and hdd last strides* **3/1**[1]

0015 **3** *1 ½* **Torquemada (IRE)**[36] 5737 3-8-12 60 PDoe 12 69
(WJarvis) *racd midfield: rdn and prog to chse ldr wl over 1f out: cl up 1f out: no ex last 100yds* **7/2**[2]

0226 **4** *1* **I Wish**[17] 6131 6-8-11 59 GBaker 5 63
(MMadgwick) *t.k.h: hld up towards rr: effrt and nt clr run 2f out: styd on fr over 1f out: n.d* **8/1**

1220 **5** *1* **Jazzy Millennium**[30] 5849 7-9-0 59 (b) SDrowne 6 64
(BRMillman) *trckd ldrs: rdn 2f out: one pce and no imp over 1f out* **12/1**

0560 **6** *shd* **Kabeer**[16] 6152 6-9-0 59 (t) DRMcCabe 7 63
(PSMcentee) *sn restrained in rr: stl in last pair wl over 1f out: swtchd to inner and shuffled along: r.o wl: nvr nr ldrs* **16/1**

0525 **7** *1* **Legal Set (IRE)**[10] 6273 8-9-0 60 (t) TPQueally 13 61
(MissAStokell) *b.hind: trckd ldrs: rdn and nt qckn 2f out: one pce* **12/1**

0600 **8** *1* **Lord Of The Sea (IRE)**[22] 6017 3-8-12 59 (b[1]) JFEgan 9 58
(JamiePoulton) *hld up in rr: n.m.r briefly over 2f out: no prog over 1f out* **14/1**

0105 **9** *2* **Megabond**[9] 6290 3-8-12 60 (v[1]) FLynch 11 53
(CADwyer) *settled in rr and r on outer: rdn over 2f out: one pce and no imp* **50/1**

-000 **10** *nk* **Wall Street Runner**[9] 6295 3-8-4 59 DFox(5) 3 49
(CADwyer) *prom: rdn 3f out: losing pl whn n.m.r briefly over 2f out: wknd* **25/1**

0000 **11** *2* **Chairman Bobby**[21] 6026 6-9-0 60 DHolland 4 47
(BAMcmahon) *t.k.h: hld up midfield: n.m.r over 2f out: wknd over 1f out* **10/1**

040 **12** *5* **Superfling**[31] 5844 3-8-12 60 DaneO'Neill 2 34
(RHannon) *a in rr: struggling in last pair over 2f out* **33/1**

3300 **13** *½* **Emsam Ballou (IRE)**[17] 6117 3-8-9 60 NCallan 1 30
(VSmith) *prom: snatched up over 5f out: wkng whn n.m.r on inner over 2f out* **20/1**

0 **14** *3* **Darling River (FR)**[15] 6154 5-8-11 58 JMackay 10 22
(SDow) *mostly chsd ldr to 2f out: wknd rapidly* **25/1**

1m 24.95s (-0.99) **Going Correction** -0.05s/f (Stan)
**WFA** 3 from 4yo+ 2lb **14** Ran SP% **125.2**
Speed ratings: **103,101,99,98,97 97,96,95,92,92 90,84,83,80**CSF £27.66 TOTE £8.50: £2.30, £1.60, £2.20; EX 39.90.
**Owner** J Burns **Bred** Mrs S Shaw **Trained** Newmarket, Suffolk
■ Stewards Enquiry : J Mackay caution: careless riding

**FOCUS**
A moderate, but competitive classified event. Very few, however, managed to get into it due to the strong pace, but the form appears solid enough for the level.

**NOTEBOOK**
**Nearly A Fool** ◆, rated 7lb lower on this surface than on turf, produced a neat turn of foot to get up late on and win going away. He enjoyed racing off this fast gallop and does look go well on this surface, so could have more to offer still.
**Roman Quintet(IRE)** set the brisk pace and looked the most likely winner one out, but found less than expected off the bridle and had no answer to the winner late on. He has now found one too good on his last four outings, but did little wrong this time and does deserve to go one better.
**Torquemada(IRE)**, unlucky in running on turf at this venue last time, could not go with the winner in the straight and faded over this extra furlong. He is not the easiest of rides, but clearly remains on a fair mark.
**I Wish** did not help her cause by taking a fierce pull early on and so did not run a bad race in the circumstances.
**Jazzy Millennium** could not quicken when it mattered and may be feeling the effects of a busy season now.

## 6453 NICHOLAS HALL EBF MAIDEN STKS (C&G) (DIV II) 7f (P)
**5:20** (5:24) (D3) 2-Y-O **£5,135** (£1,580; £790; £395) **Stalls** Low

Form RPR

02 **1** **King's Majesty (IRE)**[15] 6155 2-8-11 DHolland 7 84+
(SirMichaelStoute) *trckd ldrs: rdn and hanging over 1f out: drvn to ld ins fnl f: styd on wl* **13/8**[1]

**2** *1 ½* **Dubai Dreamer (USA)** 2-8-11 EAhern 5 80+
(SaeedBinSuroor) *w'like: scope: sn trckd ldrs: prog on outer to ld wl over 1f out: rdn and hdd ins fnl f: one pce* **7/2**[3]

**3** *hd* **Macaulay (IRE)** 2-8-11 SDrowne 6 79+
(RCharlton) *w'like: scope: settled at rr of main gp: shkn up wl over 1f out: r.o wl fnl f: promising* **33/1**

52 **4** *½* **Optimus (USA)**[22] 6010 2-8-11 JFortune 11 78
(GAButler) *lw: trckd ldrs: effrt to join ldr wl over 1f out: hrd rdn and upsides ent fnl f: one pce* **2/1**[2]

**5** *5* **Don Pasquale** 2-8-11 SSanders 3 66
(DRLoder) *w'like: in tch in rr: outpcd 2f out: kpt on steadily fnl f* **25/1**

**6** *2 ½* **Croon** 2-8-11 NMackay 2 59
(LMCumani) *leggy: w'like: bit bkwd: racd in last pair of main gp: outpcd over 2f out: no ch after: kpt on* **33/1**

00 **7** *1 ¼* **Royal Sailor (IRE)**[19] 6072 2-8-11 SWKelly 10 56
(JMPEustace) *pressed ldr to 2f out: wkng whn n.m.r sn after* **40/1**

033 **8** *1 ¼* **Vague Star (ITY)**[15] 6158 2-8-11 74 NDay 8 53
(RIngram) *led to wl over 1f out: wknd* **12/1**

050 **9** *7* **Precious Sammi**[12] 6226 2-8-11 60 NCallan 4 36
(JulianPoulton) *t.k.h: prom tl wknd rapidly over 2f out* **66/1**

**10** *hd* **Follow The Game** 2-8-11 TQuinn 1 35
(PWHarris) *leggy: s.v.s: a t.o* **20/1**

1m 25.04s (-0.90) **Going Correction** -0.05s/f (Stan) **10** Ran SP% **119.8**
Speed ratings: **103,101,101,100,94 91,90,89,81,80**CSF £7.37 TOTE £2.50: £1.20, £1.50, £7.20; EX 10.40 Place 6 £40.81, Place 5 £21.95.
**Owner** Saeed Suhail **Bred** Mrs T V Ryan **Trained** Newmarket, Suffolk

**FOCUS**
A fairly decent maiden run at a sound pace and the first four were clear. It should throw up its share of winners. The time was markedly faster than the first division and the form should prove at least this good.

**NOTEBOOK**
**King's Majesty(IRE)**, who looked unlucky over course and distance last time, outstayed his rivals close home and got off the mark at the third time of asking. He is choicely bred, has scope and looks sure to do better over further as a three-year-old.
**Dubai Dreamer(USA)** ◆, who cost $3,100,000 and has a decent US pedigree, was a little one paced late on yet still posted a pleasing debut. He was well backed for this and should have no trouble in going one better if his powerful connections can find him another opportunity on this surface.
**Macaulay(IRE)**, a 60,000gns purchase whose dam won over this trip as a three-year-old, registered a pleasing debut effort. He was doing all of his best work at the finish and should improve a fair bit with this run under his belt.
**Optimus(USA)**, a fast finishing runner-up over course and distance last time, had every chance yet failed to see out his race all that well. This was no disgrace, however, and he now qualifies for handicaps.
**Don Pasquale**, a 90,000gns purchase whose dam was a dual winner over this trip, was not given a hard time of it on this debut. He kept on as though he will get a mile in time and could be capable of better.
**Croon** unseated his rider in the paddock.
T/Jkpt: £25,660.00 to a £1 stake. Pool: £72,281.75. 2.00 winning tickets. T/Plt: £32.90 to a £1 stake. Pool: £47,027.85. 1,042.30 winning tickets. T/Qpdt: £10.80 to a £1 stake. Pool: £2,714.60. 185.40 winning tickets. JN

# 6212 NEWMARKET (R-H)
### Friday, October 29

**OFFICIAL GOING: Soft**
With 10mm of rain overnight and quite a fresh wind in the faces of the runners, conditions were quite testing. Most of the races unfolded up the centre.
Wind: Fresh half-against. Weather: Cloud giving way to sunshine.

## 6454 EBF GEORGE COLLING MAIDEN STKS (DIV I) 6f
**1:00** (1:01) (D3) 2-Y-O **£4,754** (£1,463; £731; £365) **Stalls** High

Form RPR

0 **1** **Tucker**[15] 6171 2-9-0 TQuinn 3 85+
(DRCElsworth) *lw: hld up: hdwy over 2f out: led over 1f out: sn hung lft: r.o* **5/2**[1]

00 **2** *1 ¾* **Lake Chini (IRE)**[17] 6145 2-9-0 PRobinson 4 80
(MAJarvis) *chsd ldrs: rdn over 1f out: edgd rt: styd on* **9/1**

02 **3** *1 ¼* **Bolodenka (IRE)**[28] 5911 2-9-0 CCatlin 6 76
(WJMusson) *lw: trckd ldrs: rdn over 1f out: styd on same pce* **7/2**[2]

**4** *1* **Jessiaume** 2-8-9 DaneO'Neill 1 68
(HCandy) *w'like: hld up in tch: rdn rdn over 2f out: edgd rt over 1f out: styd on same pce* **14/1**

4 **5** *hd* **Grand Show**[36] 5752 2-9-0 MartinDwyer 7 73
(PWHarris) *w ldr over 4f: wknd ins fnl f* **7/1**

3 **6** *3 ½* **Diamond Josh**[137] 2947 2-9-0 LisaJones 9 62
(JohnBerry) *unf: mde most over 4f: wknd fnl f* **9/1**

**7** *1 ¼* **Helen House** 2-8-9 NCallan 2 53
(MHTompkins) *w'like: s.s: hdwy over 2f out: edgd rt and wknd over 1f out* **40/1**

05 **8** *2* **Love Me Tender**[63] 5088 2-8-9 WRyan 10 47
(HRACecil) *neat: chsd ldrs over 4f* **13/2**[3]

00 **9** *nk* **Cup Of Love (USA)**[38] 5717 2-8-9 SSanders 8 47
(RGuest) *hld up: effrt over 2f out: sn wknd* **40/1**

10 1 3/4 **Binty** 2-8-6 ........................................ LPKeniry(3) 11 41
(JLSpearing) *neat: s.s: hdwy 1/2-way: wknd over 1f out* **25/1**

11 8 **Cara Sposa (IRE)** 2-9-0 ........................................ FNorton 5 22
(MrsStefLiddiard) *w'like: s.s: outpcd* **40/1**

1m 16.88s (3.79) **Going Correction** +0.675s/f (Yiel) **11** Ran SP% **115.6**
Speed ratings: **101,98,97,95,95 90,89,86,86,83 73**CSF £24.57 TOTE £3.50: £1.40, £3.10, £1.80; EX 34.50.

**Owner** Ray Richards **Bred** Berkshire Equestrian Services Ltd **Trained** Whitsbury, Hants

**FOCUS**
This didn't look the strongest of maidens, although the winner looks a nice prospect and the form has provisionally been assessed positively.

**NOTEBOOK**
**Tucker ◆** had clearly learnt from his debut, and although this may not have taken that much winning, he left the impression he would have found more had it been required. He looks quite promising and will do better next year over 7f or more.
**Lake Chini(IRE)** handled this softer ground well, and will have more options open to him now in handicaps.
**Bolodenka(IRE)** travelled well for much of the trip, but didn't find as much as he looked like doing. Better ground will suit, and now he is qualified for handicaps, he should find plenty of openings.
**Jessiaume** shaped really well over a trip that will surely prove to be too sharp for her, as she is out of a mare that stayed 15 furlongs and is from the same family as the useful stayer Tioman Island.
**Grand Show**, a likeable sort, didn't look that happy on the surface and may appreciate quicker ground.
**Diamond Josh** ran well enough, considering he looked like a hairy goat in the paddock.

## 6455 EBF GEORGE COLLING MAIDEN STKS (DIV II) 6f
**1:30** (1:31) (D3) 2-Y-O **£4,745** (£1,460; £730; £365) **Stalls** High

Form RPR

1 **Maggie Jordan (USA)** 2-8-9 ........................................ JFortune 5 82+
(BJMeehan) *leggy: scope: hld up in tch: rdn to ld and hung lft ins fnl f: r.o* **7/2[3]**

2 2 2 **Puya**[25] 5996 2-8-9 ........................................ DaneO'Neill 4 76
(HCandy) *a.p: jnd ldr 1/2-way: rdn to ld over 1f out: edgd lft and hdd ins fnl f: unable qck* **5/2[2]**

3 3 **Topatoo** 2-8-9 ........................................ PRobinson 1 67
(MHTompkins) *lt-f: leggy: unf: s.s: hld up: hdwy and hung rt over 1f out: styd on same pce ins fnl f* **50/1**

4 1 3/4 **Sound Breeze** 2-9-0 ........................................ JFanning 2 67
(MJohnston) *neat: lw: chsd ldrs: rdn over 1f out: wknd ins fnl f* **12/1**

04 5 4 **Guildenstern (IRE)**[25] 5996 2-9-0 ........................................ RHughes 9 55
(HMorrison) *lw: prom over 4f: hung lft ins fnl f* **12/1**

2 6 shd **Oranmore Castle (IRE)**[42] 5609 2-9-0 ........................................ MHills 7 54
(BWHills) *lw: led over 4f: wknd fnl f* **6/4[1]**

7 5 **Quatre Saisons** 2-9-0 ........................................ PFitzsimons 8 39
(JMBradley) *tall: scope: s.s: a bhd* **66/1**

000 8 nk **Elms Schoolboy**[10] 6294 2-8-11 ........................................ LFletcher(3) 3 39
(JMPEustace) *w ldr 2f: rdn 1/2-way: wknd 2f out* **66/1**

9 1/2 **Tito Gofirst** 2-9-0 ........................................ JQuinn 6 37
(JPearce) *cmpt: bit bkwd: dwlt: hld up: wknd over 2f out* **40/1**

0 10 11 **Fantastic Night (DEN)**[18] 6123 2-8-9 ........................................ KDarley 10 —
(RGuest) *hld up: wknd over 2f out* **100/1**

1m 17.61s (4.52) **Going Correction** +0.675s/f (Yiel) **10** Ran SP% **114.6**
Speed ratings: **96,93,89,87,81 81,74,74,73,59**CSF £12.30 TOTE £4.90: £1.40, £1.30, £9.60; EX 13.50.

**Owner** Andy J Smith **Bred** Strategy Bloodstock **Trained** Upper Lambourn, Berks

**FOCUS**
On paper this looked the stronger division of the maiden, but the time was .73 seconds slower and the form is of a broadly similar level. The winner looks very promising, but it would be hard to rate her any higher on the bare form.

**NOTEBOOK**
**Maggie Jordan(USA)** came with a big reputation and didn't disappoint. She won with something to spare and could well make up into a Listed performer next year.
**Puya** did nothing wrong and just met one too good on the day. There will be other opportunities for her.
**Topatoo**, a half-sister to miler Toparudi, was very green and is sure to have learnt plenty from the experience. Her dam stayed 11 furlongs, so with improvement to come as she steps up in trip, she should have no trouble paying her way.
**Sound Breeze**, a half-brother to five winners, shaped with plenty of promise over what will prove to be an inadequate trip.
**Guildenstern(IRE)** will have more options open to him now in handicaps.
**Oranmore Castle(IRE)** was disappointing, and connections reported that he failed to handle the ground. *Official explanation: jockey said colt was unsuited by today's soft ground*

## 6456 EBF BOSRA SHAM FILLIES' STKS (LISTED RACE) 6f
**2:05** (2:05) (A1) 2-Y-O **£17,400** (£6,600; £3,300; £1,500) **Stalls** High

Form RPR

410 1 **Bahia Breeze**[27] 5947 2-8-8 86 ........................................ CCatlin 2 96
(RGuest) *hld up: hdwy over 1f out: rdn to ld wl ins fnl f: r.o: edgd rt nr fin* **11/1**

2 2 hd **Nanabanana (IRE)**[61] 5149 2-8-8 ........................................ KDarley 8 95
(MmeCHead-Maarek, France) *lw: trckd ldrs: rdn and edgd lft over 1f out: ev ch ins fnl f: r.o* **4/5[1]**

1040 3 3/4 **Siena Gold**[51] 5404 2-8-8 93 ........................................ JFortune 1 93
(BJMeehan) *lw: w ldr tl led over 1f out: sn rdn: edgd lft and hdd wl ins fnl f* **11/1**

1550 4 1 3/4 **All For Laura**[27] 5939 2-8-8 95 ........................................ SSanders 6 88
(DRLoder) *hld up: rdn over 2f out: hdwy over 1f out: styd on same pce ins fnl f* **17/2[3]**

0031 5 2 **Doitforreel (IRE)**[11] 6272 2-8-8 68 ........................................ WSupple 3 82?
(IAWood) *hld up: hdwy over 1f out: edgd lft and no ex ins fnl f* **50/1**

4400 6 1 **Banditten (IRE)**[13] 6212 2-8-8 90 ........................................ JFEgan 9 79
(AndrewReid) *trckd ldrs: plld hrd: rdn whn hmpd and lost pl over 1f out: n.d after* **33/1**

3212 7 2 1/2 **Alexia Rose (IRE)**[12] 6241 2-8-8 78 ........................................ JFanning 5 71
(ABerry) *led over 4f: wknd fnl f* **25/1**

5141 8 nk **Bibury Flyer**[6] 6353 2-8-11 94 ........................................ EAhern 7 73
(JNoseda) *lw: hld up: hdwy over 2f out: ev ch over 1f out: wkng whn hmpd ins fnl f* **4/1[2]**

1m 16.41s (3.32) **Going Correction** +0.675s/f (Yiel) **8** Ran SP% **111.5**
Speed ratings: **104,103,102,100,97 96,93,92**CSF £19.39 TOTE £13.40: £2.20, £1.10, £2.30; EX 21.70.

**Owner** F Nowell **Bred** P And Mrs Venner **Trained** Newmarket, Suffolk

**FOCUS**
This was the quickest of the races to be run over this trip, but it looked weak by Listed standards and both the third and the fifth hold the form down.

**NOTEBOOK**
**Bahia Breeze**, the least experienced in the field, showed fine battling qualities to gain some valuable black type.
**Nanabanana(IRE)** proved well suited by this drop in trip, but she had been in a battle from some way out and that may have just cost her.
**Siena Gold**, for whom this ground may well have been soft enough, had no trouble lasting out this trip.
**All For Laura** had already been found out at this level, and it was no different here. She will not be easy to place off her current mark.
**Doitforreel(IRE)**
**Banditten(IRE)**, who was led to post, did herself no favours in the race by taking a fierce grip.
**Bibury Flyer**, who changed hands for 75,000 gns earlier in the week, turned in a rare moderate effort. However, she has had a busy season this being her 22nd outing, and may have had enough for the time being.

## 6457 TNT EXPRESS EBF FILLIES' H'CAP 1m 4f
**2:40** (2:40) (D2) (0-92,90) 3-Y-O+ **£8,381** (£3,179; £1,589; £722) **Stalls** Centre

Form RPR

3341 1 **Into The Shadows**[19] 6095 4-8-5 **72** ........................................ TEaves(3) 5 78
(KGReveley) *lw: hld up: hdwy over 2f out: rdn to ld ins fnl f: r.o* **4/1[3]**

12 2 1/2 **Reem One (IRE)**[18] 6115 3-8-4 **75** ........................................ PRobinson 6 80
(MAJarvis) *lw: trckd ldrs: led 3f out: rdn and edgd lft over 1f out: hdd ins fnl f: r.o* **15/8[1]**

1-00 3 nk **Miss Langkawi**[186] 1672 3-8-0 **71** ........................................ FNorton 3 76
(GWragg) *led 1f: remained handy: outpcd over 2f out: r.o ins fnl f* **12/1**

4200 4 hd **Big Bertha**[31] 5853 6-8-5 **69** oh3 ........................................ JFEgan 8 74
(JohnBerry) *hld up and bhd: hdwy over 3f out: rdn and ev ch fr over 1f out: styd on* **16/1**

31 5 3/4 **Batik (IRE)**[46] 5511 3-8-6 **77** ........................................ NMackay 2 81
(LMCumani) *lw: hld up in tch: outpcd over 2f out: edgd lft over 1f out: r.o* **5/2[2]**

1563 6 1/2 **Goodwood Finesse (IRE)**[37] 5732 3-8-3 **74** ........................................ JQuinn 7 77
(JLDunlop) *chsd ldrs: led over 3f out: sn hdd: rdn over 1f out: styd on* **8/1**

-000 7 dist **Kaluana Court**[13] 6215 8-8-2 **69** oh5 ........................................ RThomas(3) 1 —
(RJPrice) *led after 1f: hdd over 3f out: sn wknd* **25/1**

2m 40.54s (7.08) **Going Correction** +0.675s/f (Yiel)
**WFA** 3 from 4yo+ 7lb **7** Ran SP% **111.9**
Speed ratings: **103,102,102,102,101 101,**—CSF £11.40 CT £78.07 TOTE £4.60: £2.30, £2.00; EX 11.70.

**Owner** R C Mayall **Bred** Mrs Linda Corbett And Mrs Mary Mayall **Trained** Lingdale, N Yorks

**FOCUS**
A fair contest, but there was no early pace and they finished in a heap after it turned into a three-furlong sprint.

**NOTEBOOK**
**Into The Shadows** is a progressive filly and, although a narrow winner, left the impression she could have found more.
**Reem One(IRE)** lacks experience and didn't have the race run to suit, but she showed the right attitude and remains progressive.
**Miss Langkawi** shaped with plenty of promise on this return to action, and gave the impression an even stiffer test would suit better still.
**Big Bertha** ran well enough considering she was racing from out the handicap. A winner on the Polytrack, this effort should put her spot on for the coming weeks.
**Batik(IRE)** wasn't suited to the lack of a decent gallop, and only got going when the race was all but over.

## 6458 JAMES SEYMOUR STKS (LISTED RACE) 1m 2f
**3:15** (3:15) (A1) 3-Y-O+ **£17,400** (£6,600; £3,300; £1,500) **Stalls** High

Form RPR

501 1 **Spanish Don**[27] 5941 6-9-0 100 ........................................ LPKeniry 1 109
(DRCElsworth) *chsd ldr tl led over 7f out: rdn and edgd lft over 1f out: r.o* **4/1[2]**

512- 2 3/4 **Menokee (USA)**[384] 5478 3-8-9 95 ........................................ KDarley 2 108
(SirMichaelStoute) *h.d.w: hld up: plld hrd: hdwy over 2f out: rdn over 1f out: styd on* **13/2[3]**

6430 3 1 **Bonecrusher**[13] 6219 5-9-0 103 ........................................(v) SSanders 6 106
(DRLoder) *lw: trckd ldrs: plld hrd: hrd rdn fnl f: nt run on* **9/4[1]**

3-60 4 2 1/2 **Carte Sauvage (USA)**[6] 6354 3-8-9 101 ........................................ JFanning 4 102
(MJohnston) *led: hdd over 7f out: n.m.r and lost pl 4f out: rallied over 1f out: no ex ins fnl f* **12/1**

1 5 8 **Iktibas**[45] 5545 3-8-9 ........................................(t) RHills 5 88
(SaeedBinSuroor) *b.hind: hld up in tch: rdn and wknd 2f out* **9/4[1]**

5000 6 hd **Weecandoo (IRE)**[15] 6173 6-8-9 82 ........................................ GCarter 3 83
(CNAllen) *lw: hld up: hdwy over 3f out: wknd over 1f out* **16/1**

2m 12.05s (6.36) **Going Correction** +0.675s/f (Yiel)
**WFA** 3 from 5yo+ 5lb **6** Ran SP% **108.4**
Speed ratings: **101,100,99,97,91 91**CSF £26.88 TOTE £5.10: £1.90, £2.30; EX 29.00.

**Owner** Richard J Cohen **Bred** Juddmonte Farms **Trained** Whitsbury, Hants

■ Stewards Enquiry : L P Keniry four-day ban: used whip with excessive frequency (Nov 9-10,12-13)
S Sanders one-day ban: used whip with excessive frequency (Nov 9)

**FOCUS**
A moderate pace resulted in an ordinary time for a Listed race, and the form does not look that solid.

**NOTEBOOK**
**Spanish Don**, who was forced to make his own running, continues to progress and was winning at this level for the first time. His trainer is hoping he has done enough to get an invitation to go to Hong Kong in December.
**Menokee(USA)**, returning from a lengthy break, was a bit too fresh for his own good, but nevertheless stepped up significantly on his juvenile form.
**Bonecrusher** not for the first time, didn't look to try too hard and is one to have reservations about.
**Carte Sauvage(USA)** shaped better than he had at Newbury, despite the ground being softer than ideal.
**Iktibas** was beaten some way out, but whether that was down to the ground, or step up in class is hard to say. *Official explanation: jockey said colt was unsuited by today's soft ground*

## 6459 BURWELL CONDITIONS STKS 6f
**3:50** (3:52) (C1) 2-3-Y-O **£12,110** (£4,593; £2,296; £1,044) **Stalls** High

Form RPR

21 1 **Nota Bene**[18] 6125 2-8-4 84 ow1 ........................................ LPKeniry(3) 10 95
(DRCElsworth) *chsd ldrs: rdn to ld and hung rt 1f out: r.o* **7/1[3]**

0503 2 nk **Word Perfect**[21] 6042 2-8-1 86 ........................................ DaleGibson 8 88
(MWEasterby) *lw: w ldr tl led 2f out: rdn edgd lft and hdd 1f out: r.o* **4/1[2]**

0003 3 1 1/2 **Baron Rhodes**[11] 6267 3-9-0 78 ........................................ TEaves(3) 2 81
(JSWainwright) *hld up in tch: outpcd over 1f out: hung rt and r.o ins fnl f* **14/1**

0504 4 1/2 **Valjarv (IRE)**[15] 6175 3-9-6 90 ........................................ NCallan 6 82
(NPLittmoden) *s.s: hdwy over 2f out: rdn over 1f out: no ex ins fnl f* **4/1[2]**

443 **5** *hd* **Joseph Henry**$^{6}$ [6348] 2-8-6 100 JFanning 9 87
(MJohnston) *led 4f: sn rdn: styd on same pce fnl f* **9/4**$^{1}$

21-0 **6** *2 ½* **Great Fox (IRE)**$^{30}$ [5874] 3-9-8 73 RPrice 12 76
(PLGilligan) *lw: w ldrs over 3f: hung lft over 1f out: wknd ins fnl f* **33/1**

3660 **7** *1 ½* **Golden Anthem (USA)**$^{27}$ [5939] 2-7-12 90 JQuinn 11 67
(JPearce) *hld up: rdn over 2f out: nvr trbld ldrs* **10/1**

3450 **8** *3 ½* **Fools Entire**$^{52}$ [5370] 3-9-8 55 (e) DaneO'Neill 5 61
(JAGilbert) *prom 4f* **100/1**

0020 **9** *shd* **Totally Yours (IRE)**$^{7}$ [6341] 3-9-3 83 (p) MartinDwyer 4 56
(WRMuir) *mid-div: hdwy 1/2-way: wknd over 1f out* **16/1**

3102 **10** *¾* **Fission**$^{37}$ [5737] 3-9-3 71 FNorton 7 53
(MrsStefLiddiard) *dwlt: hld up: wknd 2f out* **33/1**

0040 **11** *nk* **Man Crazy (IRE)**$^{17}$ [6146] 3-9-3 48 JFEgan 3 53
(CADwyer) *prom: lost pl 4f out: wknd over 2f out* **150/1**

1m 16.55s (3.46) **Going Correction** +0.675s/f (Yiel) **11** Ran SP% **112.4**
Speed ratings: **103,102,100,99,99 96,94,89,89,88 88**CSF £33.07 TOTE £6.70: £2.10, £1.50, £3.30; EX 29.40.
**Owner** W V & Mrs E S Robins **Bred** Usk Valley Stud **Trained** Whitsbury, Hants

**FOCUS**
There didn't look much strength in depth in this rare clash between two-year-olds and their elders. The race has been assessed through the runner-up's most solid bit of previous form.

**NOTEBOOK**
**Nota Bene** didn't look entirely happy on the ground but posted his best effort yet. He is a progressive performer, who should continue to give a good account.
**Word Perfect** is a tough filly and stuck to her task well, having been up in the firing line throughout.
**Baron Rhodes** didn't come down the hill at all well, but she came home in good style and proved that she does stay this far.
**Valjarv(IRE)** did herself no favours by falling out of the stalls, but deserves credit for finishing as close as she did.
**Joseph Henry** was disappointing.Even though he has done most of his racing on a soft surface, he may prefer better ground.

## 6460 SUBSCRIBE TO RACING UK ON 08700 860432 H'CAP — 2m
**4:25** (4:28) (D2) (0-92,85) 3-Y-0+ **£6,078** (£2,305; £1,152; £524) **Stalls** Centre

Form RPR

3312 **1** **Race The Ace**$^{31}$ [5850] 3-8-6 **79** TQuinn 6 101+
(JLDunlop) *hld up in tch: led over 2f out: drvn clr fnl f* **3/1**$^{1}$

000 **2** *7* **Laggan Bay (IRE)**$^{13}$ [6215] 4-8-8 **71** oh1 (b) MartinDwyer 2 79
(JSMoore) *lw: hld up: hdwy 3f out: hung lft and ev ch over 1f out: no ex* **33/1**

0001 **3** *¾* **San Hernando**$^{19}$ [6084] 4-8-8 **71** oh3 JFEgan 5 78
(DRCElsworth) *hld up: hdwy 3f out: sn rdn: hung rt and wknd over 1f out* **10/1**

0610 **4** *10* **Dr Sharp (IRE)**$^{55}$ [5288] 4-9-4 **81** PHanagan 3 76
(TPTate) *lw: trckd ldrs: plld hrd: led over 6f out: rdn: hung rt and hdd over 2f out: wknd over 1f out* **9/2**$^{2}$

4136 **5** *3 ½* **Land 'n Stars**$^{13}$ [6215] 4-9-8 **85** PDoe 8 76
(JamiePoulton) *hld up: hdwy 5f out: rdn and wknd over 2f out* **9/2**$^{2}$

5104 **6** *3* **Patrixprial**$^{17}$ [6143] 3-8-2 **75** JFanning 4 62
(MHTompkins) *lw: chsd ldr over 9f: wknd 2f out* **12/1**

1403 **7** *3* **Bill Bennett (FR)**$^{7}$ [6339] 3-8-0 **78** DFox$^{(5)}$ 10 62
(JJay) *chsd ldrs: rdn 5f out: wknd over 3f out* **14/1**

000 **8** *nk* **Bid For Fame (USA)**$^{137}$ [2935] 7-8-13 **76** PRobinson 1 59
(CGCox) *hld up in tch: hung rt and wknd over 4f out* **28/1**

0002 **9** *nk* **Teresa**$^{7}$ [6339] 4-8-8 **71** oh1 JQuinn 7 54
(JLDunlop) *hld up: hdwy over 5f out: wknd 2f out* **10/1**

0004 **10** *2* **Linens Flame**$^{7}$ [6339] 5-8-8 **71** DHolland 9 52
(BGPowell) *led over 9f: wknd over 2f out* **8/1**$^{3}$

0002 **11** *24* **Mamcazma**$^{34}$ [5784] 6-9-4 **81** TEDurcan 11 33
(DMorris) *lw: prom over 10f* **12/1**

3m 35.1s (8.58) **Going Correction** +0.675s/f (Yiel)
**WFA** 3 from 4yo+ 10lb **11** Ran SP% **119.1**
Speed ratings: **105,101,101,96,94 92,91,91,91,90 78**CSF £113.84 CT £901.33 TOTE £3.70: £1.50, £5.90, £3.70; EX 123.50.
**Owner** I H Stewart-Brown & M J Meacock **Bred** I Stewart-Brown And M Meacock **Trained** Arundel, W Sussex

**FOCUS**
A fair handicap and an impressive performance from Race The Ace, who could be named the winner some way out. Third-placed San Hernando is probably the best guide to the form.

**NOTEBOOK**
**Race The Ace** goes from strength to strength and is developing into a useful stayer, particularly when there is give underfoot. He was most impressive here and looks to have a nice staying prize in him.
**Laggan Bay(IRE)** was unproven under the conditions but turned in a sound enough effort over the trip, though ultimately outstayed by a progressive performer. He has slipped to a fair mark.
**San Hernando** came into this in good form and probably didn't run too bad off this higher mark, but he has lacked consistency in the past and can't be relied on.
**Dr Sharp(IRE)** did himself no favours by refusing to settle, and it was no surprise when he failed to get home.
**Land 'n Stars** had quite a hard race in the Cesarewitch and may have found this coming too soon.
**Mamcazma** *Official explanation: jockey said gelding was unsuited by today's soft ground*

## 6461 ELLA & WHITE LIMITED APPRENTICE H'CAP — 1m
**5:00** (5:02) (E3) (0-77,70) 3-Y-0 **£3,441** (£1,058; £529; £264) **Stalls** High

Form RPR

0002 **1** **La Puce**$^{10}$ [6290] 3-8-1 **56** CHaddon$^{(3)}$ 19 67
(MJAttwater) *lw: hld up: hdwy over 1f out: ev ch ins fnl f: r.o to ld post* **25/1**

6130 **2** *nk* **Princess Galadriel**$^{9}$ [6311] 3-8-6 **61** ThomasYeung$^{(3)}$ 16 71
(JRBest) *lw: hld up: hdwy to ld 1f out: hdd post* **14/1**

0500 **3** *3 ½* **The Fun Merchant**$^{11}$ [6279] 3-9-0 **66** (p) MLawson 18 69
(JPearce) *plld hrd and prom: rdn and ev ch whn hung lft over 1f out: no ex ins fnl f* **16/1**

0402 **4** *nk* **Charlie Tango (IRE)**$^{18}$ [6112] 3-8-8 **60** (t) NDeSouza 14 62
(NTinkler) *s.i.s: hld up: hdwy 1/2-way: rdn over 1f out: styd on same pce* **7/1**$^{3}$

6042 **5** *1* **Night Frolic**$^{19}$ [6097] 3-8-3 **58** DerekNolan$^{(3)}$ 20 58
(JWHills) *chsd ldr tl led 6f out: rdn and hdd 1f out: no ex* **6/1**$^{1}$

1000 **6** *nk* **Adorata (GER)**$^{9}$ [6311] 3-8-13 **65** DFox 12 65
(JJay) *hld up: hmpd 6f out: hdwy over 2f out: edgd rt over 1f out: one pce* **10/1**

3516 **7** *¾* **Cantarna (IRE)**$^{25}$ [5990] 3-9-4 **70** BSwarbrick 17 68
(JMackie) *plld hrd and prom: rdn over 2f out: styd on same pce fnl f* **10/1**

0413 **8** *3* **Sachin**$^{11}$ [6271] 3-8-13 **65** PMakin 13 57
(JRBoyle) *b.hind: prom: rdn over 3f out: edgd rt and wknd over 1f out* **10/1**

0205 **9** *1* **True (IRE)**$^{25}$ [5994] 3-8-1 **56** AMullen$^{(3)}$ 1 46
(MrsSLamyman) *b.hind: s.s: hld up: rdn over 3f out: sme hdwy over 1f out: n.d* **16/1**

0653 **10** *1 ¾* **Gay Romance**$^{30}$ [5868] 3-8-7 **64** KMay$^{(5)}$ 10 51
(BWHills) *led 2f: remained handy tl wknd over 1f out* **13/2**$^{2}$

5350 **11** *nk* **Fleet Anchor**$^{19}$ [6086] 3-8-1 **56** oh1 RoryMoore$^{(3)}$ 6 42
(JMBradley) *hld up: plld hrd: hdwy 1/2-way: wknd over 2f out* **33/1**

0220 **12** *2* **Heversham (IRE)**$^{27}$ [5945] 3-8-11 **66** DTudhope$^{(3)}$ 11 48
(JHetherton) *rrd s: hld up: plld hrd: rdn over 2f out: n.d* **14/1**

0516 **13** *5* **Blake Hall Lad (IRE)**$^{4}$ [6399] 3-8-3 **58** DeanWilliams$^{(3)}$ 2 30
(MissJFeilden) *hmpd s: hld up: rdn over 2f out: n.d* **20/1**

5045 **14** *2 ½* **Mrs Brown**$^{14}$ [6184] 3-8-1 **56** oh5 StephanieHollinshead$^{(3)}$ 7 23
(SirMarkPrescott) *plld hrd and prom: rdn over 3f out: hung rt and wknd 2f out* **14/1**

4400 **15** *5* **Filliemou (IRE)**$^{10}$ [6296] 3-8-1 **56** oh3 (v$^{1}$) DFentiman$^{(3)}$ 5 13
(AWCarroll) *hld up: hdwy 3f out: wknd wl over 1f out* **33/1**

0002 **16** *2* **Western Roots**$^{16}$ [6157] 3-8-13 **65** PPMathers 3 18
(KAMorgan) *wnt lft s: hld up: hdwy 1/2-way: wknd over 2f out* **14/1**

4530 **17** *11* **Dream Easy**$^{19}$ [6096] 3-8-8 **63** NicolPolli$^{(3)}$ 8 —
(PLGilligan) *lw: hld up: plld hrd: wknd 3f out* **40/1**

32-0 **18** *5* **Chariot (IRE)**$^{229}$ [1022] 3-8-9 **64** MHalford$^{(3)}$ 9 —
(MRBosley) *plld hrd and prom: wknd over 3f out* **50/1**

1m 44.3s (4.90) **Going Correction** +0.675s/f (Yiel) **18** Ran SP% **124.7**
Speed ratings: **102,101,98,97,96 96,95,92,91,90 89,87,82,80,75 73,62,57**CSF £328.98 CT £3066.57 TOTE £35.20: £6.40, £3.10, £5.10, £2.40; EX 388.70 Place 6 £73.37, Place 5 £47.26.
**Owner** Brooklands Racing **Bred** R P Williams **Trained** Wysall, Notts

**FOCUS**
A high draw was beneficial in ths moderate contest, in which the leaders appeared to go off too fast.

**NOTEBOOK**
**La Puce** took advantage of her 14lb lower turf mark to gain that elusive first success on grass.
**Princess Galadriel**, like the winner came from a some way back, and looked like holding on until getting mugged on the line. This trip cleary suits her, although, she could probably do with better ground.
**The Fun Merchant** didn't run too badly, considering he was a bit keen early on in the first-time cheekpieces.
**Charlie Tango(IRE)** didn't have the best of breaks, but that can hardly be used as an excuse.
**Night Frolic** had her favoured soft ground, but paid late on for having helped set too strong a gallop.
**Adorata(GER)** didn't run too badly considering she got into a bumping match early on. A winner on the Fibresand, she should be capable of scoring again when returned to that surface.
**True(IRE)** *Official explanation: jockey said filly hung left*
T/Jkpt: Not won. T/Plt: £149.80 to a £1 stake. Pool: £44,528.25. 216.85 winning tickets. T/Qpdt: £22.40 to a £1 stake. Pool: £4,052.40. 133.40 winning tickets. CR

# 6202 MAISONS-LAFFITTE (R-H)
Friday, October 29

**OFFICIAL GOING: Very soft**

## 6462a CRITERIUM DE MAISONS-LAFFITTE (GROUP 2) — 6f (S)
**1:50** (1:51) 2-Y-0 **£76,268** (£29,437; £14,049; £9,366)

RPR

**1** **Centifolia (FR)**$^{14}$ [6202] 2-8-11 IMendizabal 1 114
(RobertCollet, France) *mde all against stands' rail: rdn ins fnl f: r.o wl* $^{1}$

**2** *2* **Salut Thomas (FR)**$^{14}$ [6202] 2-9-0 (b) SMaillot 5 112
(RobertCollet, France) *mid-div: rdn to go 2nd over 1f out: no imp on wnr but kpt on gamely to hold 2nd* $^{1}$

**3** *hd* **Campo Bueno (FR)**$^{9}$ [6320] 2-9-0 GBenoist 7 111
(XNakkachdji, France) *hld up on outside: hrd rdn to chal for 2nd ins fnl f: kpt on*

**4** *2 ½* **Prince Charming**$^{13}$ [6212] 2-9-0 RHavlin 2 105
(JHMGosden) *cl up on ins rail: chsd wnr over 2f out: lost 2nd over 1f out: one pce*

**5** *1* **Obe Gold**$^{15}$ [6174] 2-9-0 (v) ACulhane 3 103
(MRChannon) *towards rr and sn niggled along: rdn over 2f out: styd on u.p to take 5th fnl 50yds* $^{2}$

**6** *¾* **Nipping (IRE)**$^{28}$ [5922] 2-8-11 TJarnet 4 98
(RobertCollet, France) *cl up tl outpcd fnl 1 1/2f* $^{1}$

**7** *2* **Istan (USA)**$^{21}$ 2-9-0 MBlancpain 6 96
(CLaffon-Parias, France) *hld up in rr: hdwy 1/2-way: btn over 1f out: nt pushed clsng stages*

**8** *6* **Kay Two (IRE)**$^{13}$ [6212] 2-9-0 DPMcDonogh 9 81
(MsFMCrowley, Ire) *prom early on outside: rdn sn after 1/2-way: wknd fr over 2f out*

**9** *nk* **Tony James (IRE)**$^{26}$ [5980] 2-9-0 DBoeuf 8 80
(CEBrittain) *a in rr* $^{3}$

1m 12.0s **Going Correction** +0.05s/f (Good) **9** Ran SP% **210.5**
Speed ratings: **117,114,114,110,109 108,105,97,97.**
**Owner** S Berland **Bred** Sca De La Perrigne **Trained** France

**NOTEBOOK**
**Prince Charming** has had a long season, but continues to run reasonably well.
**Obe Gold** found himself struggling to go the early gallop before running on through beaten horses to claim fifth. He has had a profitable season.
**Tony James(IRE)** was never going the gallop and was disappointing.

## 6463a PRIX DE SEINE-ET-OISE (GROUP 3) — 6f (S)
**2:50** (2:55) 3-Y-0+ **£25,704** (£10,282; £7,711; £5,141)

RPR

**1** **Miss Emma (IRE)**$^{28}$ [5923] 4-8-9 FSpanu 11 113
(JEHammond, France) *mde virtually all: r.o wl fnl f: pushed out*

**2** *½* **Striking Ambition**$^{19}$ [6104] 4-8-13 TThulliez 10 115
(RCharlton) *prom: disputing 3rd 1/2-way: 2nd appr fnl f: rdn and ev ch ins fnl f: no ex u.p fnl 100yds*

**3** *1* **Patavellian (IRE)**$^{26}$ [5977] 6-8-13 (b) SDrowne 3 112
(RCharlton) *prom: disputing 3rd 1/2-way: pushed along to chse ldr 1 1/2f out: rdn and r.o u.p ins fnl f tl no ex cl home* $^{1}$

**4** *2* **Dalna (FR)**$^{14}$ [6203] 3-8-8 SPasquier 1 102
(MmeCHead-Maarek, France) *mid-div on rail: rdn 1 1/2f out: styd on u.p to take 4th*

**5** *1 ½* **Swedish Shave (FR)**$^{28}$ [5923] 6-8-13 TJarnet 5 102
(RGibson, France) *mid-div: shkn up 2f out: nvr in chalng position*

**6** *1* **Chineur (FR)**$^{28}$ [5923] 3-8-12 ELegrix 6 99
(MDelzangles, France) *towards rr: styd on at one pce in centre fnl stages*$^{3}$

7 *shd* **Ratio**[26] 5977 6-8-13 TGillet 8 98
(JEHammond, France) *bhd: nvr a factor*

8 *5* **Welsh Emperor (IRE)**[32] 5832 5-8-13 (b) RWinston 4 83
(TPTate) *broke wl: racd in 2nd: pushed along 1/2-way: rdn and wknd 2f out*

9 *nk* **Star Valley (FR)**[61] 5171 4-9-1 IMendizabal 9 84
(J-CRouget, France) *bhd: nvr a factor* 2

10 *1 1/2* **Autumn Pearl**[40] 5671 3-8-8 DBoeuf 2 74
(MAJarvis) *mid-div: pushed along 2f out: wknd*

11 *1* **Blanche (FR)**[28] 5923 5-8-9 DBonilla 7 71
(JRossi, France) *a towards rr*

1m 12.1s **Going Correction** +0.05s/f (Good)
**WFA** 3 from 4yo+ 1lb **11** Ran SP% **121.3**
Speed ratings: **116,115,114,111,109 108,107,101,100,98 97**.
**Owner** T Wada **Bred** Derek Iceton **Trained** France

**NOTEBOOK**

**Miss Emma(IRE)**, an ex-Irish performer, has been running well in defeat and proved good enough to gain her first win of the season in very determined fashion.
**Striking Ambition ◆**, successful four times in Listed company, very nearly made the step up to Group company. He travelled as well as anything and looked the most likely winner, but he could not quite get there. He is going the right way and could be a sprinter to follow next year.
**Patavellian(IRE)**, a beaten favourite in the Abbaye on his previous start, ran respectably but simply found two too strong.
**Welsh Emperor(IRE)** had conditions to suit but was not at his best.
**Autumn Pearl** found this tougher than the Listed race she contested on her previous start, but was not at her best in any case.

# 6138 AYR (L-H)

Saturday, October 30

**OFFICIAL GOING: Soft (heavy in places)**

## 6464 RACING UK ON SKY 432 MEDIAN AUCTION MAIDEN STKS 1m

11:00 (11:02) (H5) 2-Y-O £1,449 (£414; £207) **Stalls** Low

Form RPR

3 **1** **Three Wrens (IRE)**[15] 6197 2-8-9 SWKelly 2 51
(DJDaly) *keen: cl up: led over 1f out: edgd rt: rdn and hld on wl* **6/4[1]**

060 **2** *nk* **Jeffslottery**[14] 6207 2-9-0 45 (b[1]) RWinston 6 55
(JRWeymes) *s.i.s: hld up in tch: hdwy to press wnr over 1f out: kpt on fnl f: jst hld* **25/1**

00 **3** *2 1/2* **Woodford Consult**[11] 6291 2-8-9 TLucas 4 45
(MWEasterby) *hld up: hdwy and hung lft fr 2f out: kpt on fnl f: no imp* **25/1**

2400 **4** *1 1/2* **Spinnakers Girl**[13] 6242 2-8-6 64 PMulrennan(3) 5 42
(JRWeymes) *led 2f: cl up tl rdn and no ex fr 2f out* **5/1[2]**

05 **5** *hd* **Danzatrice**[36] 5771 2-8-6 TEaves(3) 3 42
(CWThornton) *prom: rdn over 3f out: no imp fr 2f out* **6/4[1]**

00 **6** *2 1/2* **Ekaterina**[15] 6195 2-8-9 JBramhill 7 37
(WStorey) *led after 2f to over 1f out: hung lft and sn btn* **33/1**

0400 **7** *9* **Northern Revoque (IRE)**[15] 6195 2-8-4 45 PPMathers(5) 8 19
(ABerry) *trckd ldrs: effrt over 2f out: sn btn* **20/1[3]**

00 **8** *9* **Casalese**[33] 5831 2-9-0 DarrenWilliams 1 —
(MDHammond) *hld up in tch: rdn over 3f out: lost tch fnl 2f* **33/1**

1m 57.48s (14.36) **Going Correction** +1.375s/f (Soft) **8** Ran SP% **110.8**
Speed ratings: **83,82,80,78,78 76,67,58**CSF £45.03 TOTE £2.50: £1.10, £4.20, £4.70; EX 27.10.
**Owner** Mrs James Wigan **Bred** Mrs James Wigan **Trained** Newmarket, Suffolk

**FOCUS**

An uncompetitive race and, with Danzatrice failing to find the anticipated improvement over this trip, this race took even less winning than had seemed likely.

**NOTEBOOK**

**Three Wrens(IRE)** did not have to improve to win this and will find life tougher in handicap company from now on. Given she should not be rated too highly though, she may well be capable of better.
**Jeffslottery**, tried in blinkers, turned in an improved effort back over this trip but it remains to be seen whether the headgear will have the desired effect next time.
**Woodford Consult**, down in grade, confirmed she has a little ability but, although she did not look the easiest of rides, may well be suited by a stiffer test of stamina.
**Spinnakers Girl** was again a big disappointment and is likely to continue to struggle in this type of event or from her current mark of 64 in handicaps.
**Danzatrice**, a full-sister to middle-distance/stayer Lets Roll, could have reasonably been expected to improve for the step up to this trip on this ground, but she was a big disappointment and is one to tread carefully with.
**Ekaterina**, who had the run of this modest event, looked less than an easy ride and again achieved precious little.

## 6465 SIMPSON AND SHAW MAIDEN CLAIMING STKS 7f 50y

11:30 (11:30) (H5) 3-Y-O+ £1,473 (£421; £210) **Stalls** Low

Form RPR

0006 **1** **Passion Fruit**[15] 6184 3-8-4 47 (b[1]) PMulrennan(3) 7 57
(CWFairhurst) *prom: outpcd 3f out: rallied to ld ins fnl f: styd on wl* **5/1[2]**

0556 **2** *5* **The Loose Screw (IRE)**[21] 6057 6-9-0 40 (p) NPollard 3 50
(GMMoore) *led: hung lft over 1f out: hdd and no ex ins fnl f* **11/4[1]**

0000 **3** *2 1/2* **Blade's Edge**[88] 4419 3-8-12 40 RWinston 2 43
(ABailey) *hld up: hdwy centre 2f out: kpt on fnl f: no imp* **14/1**

5030 **4** *6* **La Fonteyne**[14] 6228 3-8-8 45 ow1 GParkin 4 24
(CBBBooth) *hld up: rdn and effrt over 2f out: nvr rchd ldrs* **8/1**

4/00 **5** *5* **Never Forget Bowie**[15] 6200 8-8-7 40 PPMathers(5) 14 14
(RAllan) *missed break: hld up: hdwy over 2f out: sn no imp* **7/1[3]**

5000 **6** *1 1/2* **Canlis**[47] 5524 5-8-8 40 TWilliams 9 6
(DWThompson) *prom: effrt 3f out: wknd over 1f out* **5/1[2]**

400P **7** *5* **Perrywinkle Boy**[18] 6141 3-8-12 40 (t) DarrenWilliams 8 —
(MDHammond) *cl up tl rdn and wknd fr 2f out* **33/1**

4050 **8** *2* **Lady Of The Links (IRE)**[155] 2457 3-8-7 45 (t) KimTinkler 10 —
(NTinkler) *in tch on outside: rdn and wknd over 2f out* **7/1[3]**

5/0- **9** *nk* **Lady Tilly**[453] 3835 7-8-9 30 (t) JMcAuley 5 —
(DANolan) *s.i.s: a bhd* **50/1**

000/ **10** *17* **Golden Shell**[21] 2939 5-8-6 35 ow4 DTudhope(5) 13 —
(ACWhillans) *prom tl edgd lft and wknd fr over 2f out* **16/1**

00 **11** *14* **Blackpool Jack**[18] 6142 3-8-6 ow3 TEaves(3) 6 —
(FPMurtagh) *a bhd* **50/1**

040 **12** *2 1/2* **Transkei**[58] 5237 3-8-5 35 DAllan 12 —
(MrsLStubbs) *keen: cl up to 3f out: sn rdn and btn* **33/1**

1m 41.87s (9.40) **Going Correction** +1.375s/f (Soft)
**WFA** 3 from 5yo+ 2lb **12** Ran SP% **118.5**
Speed ratings: **101,95,92,85,79 78,72,70,69,50 34,31**CSF £18.63 TOTE £5.60: £2.00, £1.70, £4.20; EX 22.70.
**Owner** G H & S Leggott **Bred** G H And Simon Leggott **Trained** Middleham Moor, N Yorks

**FOCUS**

A poor race but, although the pace was sound, there was very little to take out of this contest for the future.

**NOTEBOOK**

**Passion Fruit**, an inconsistent sort who failed to justify market support on her previous start, ran up to her best in the first-time blinkers. She should prove equally effective over a mile but would be no certainty to reproduce this next time.
**The Loose Screw(IRE)** set a decent pace in the conditions and ran up to his recent best. However, he is not the easiest of rides and a record of no wins from 31 starts does not inspire confidence.
**Blade's Edge**, on soft ground for the first time, fared the best of those that came from off the pace so may be a bit better than the bare form. However, his overall record means he remains one to tread carefully with.
**La Fonteyne** has form in testing conditions but was again below her best and did not show anywhere near enough to suggest she is about to open her account.
**Never Forget Bowie** was again soundly beaten this year and is of little interest for the future.
**Canlis** attracted support but was soundly beaten on this first run in very testing conditions. Better ground will help but he is another with which to take a cautious approach.

## 6466 FERGUSON MEDIA BANDED STKS 1m

12:00 (12:01) (H5) 3-Y-O+ £1,470 (£420; £210) **Stalls** Low

Form RPR

6600 **1** **Muqarrar (IRE)**[14] 6227 5-8-11 40 (vt[1]) PMulrennan(3) 9 51
(TJFitzgerald) *hld up: smooth hdwy and ev ch over 2f out: rdn over 1f out: kpt on to ld towards fin* **20/1**

0243 **2** *nk* **Campbells Lad**[7] 6361 3-8-6 45 PPMathers(5) 5 50
(ABerry) *trckd ldrs: rdn to ld over 1f out: kpt on: hdd towards fin* **4/1[2]**

3520 **3** *3 1/2* **Encounter**[14] 6227 8-9-0 45 DAllan 4 43
(JHetherton) *hld up: rdn 3f out: hdwy over 1f out: no imp* **7/2[1]**

6506 **4** *8* **Desert Fury**[42] 5641 7-9-0 40 (t) RWinston 13 27
(RBastiman) *in tch: hdwy to ld over 2f out: hdd over 1f out: sn btn* **5/1[3]**

656/ **5** *6* **The Count (FR)**[38] 5117 5-8-11 40 TEaves(3) 10 15
(FPMurtagh) *in tch: outpcd over 2f out: n.d after* **33/1**

000 **6** *5* **Dispol Verity**[44] 5587 4-9-0 35 SWKelly 8 5
(WMBrisbourne) *hld up: rdn over 3f out: nvr rchd ldrs* **25/1**

0352 **7** *3* **Mexican (USA)**[63] 3804 5-9-0 40 (t) DarrenWilliams 11 —
(MDHammond) *cl up: led over 3f to over 2f out: sn btn* **6/1**

60-6 **8** *1/2* **Never Promise (FR)**[13] 5449 6-8-9 40 (v) AMedeiros(5) 7 —
(CRoberts) *bhd: rdn centre 3f out: n.d* **16/1**

0005 **9** *3 1/2* **Cezzaro (IRE)**[88] 4423 6-9-0 40 (p) DaleGibson 3 —
(TAKCuthbert) *led to over 3f out: wknd over 2f out* **12/1**

2450 **10** *6* **Zahunda (IRE)**[71] 4905 5-8-9 40 BSwarbrick(5) 12 —
(WMBrisbourne) *cl up tl hung lft and wknd over 2f out* **7/1**

0005 **11** *5* **Andreyev (IRE)**[134] 3040 10-8-7 40 JCurrie(7) 2 —
(JSGoldie) *cl up: ev ch over 2f out: sn rdn and wknd* **10/1**

00-0 **12** *3/4* **Second Wind**[33] 5832 9-8-9 40 (t) DTudhope(5) 6 —
(DANolan) *trckd ldrs tl wknd over 2f out* **50/1**

0200 **13** *23* **Tiz Wiz**[62] 5141 3-8-11 40 JBramhill 1 —
(WStorey) *in tch to 1/2-way: sn rdn and btn* **25/1**

1m 53.14s (10.02) **Going Correction** +1.375s/f (Soft)
**WFA** 3 from 4yo+ 3lb **13** Ran SP% **125.7**
Speed ratings: **104,103,100,92,86 81,78,77,74,68 63,62,39**CSF £98.94 TOTE £32.90: £8.60, £1.40, £2.00; EX 315.50.
**Owner** Kramo Racing **Bred** Shadwell Estate Company Limited **Trained** Norton, N Yorks

**FOCUS**

A weak race in which the gallop was fair but the form is poor.

**NOTEBOOK**

**Muqarrar(IRE)** is an unreliable type but turned in an improved effort on this first start on soft ground and in the first-time visor. Although he outbattled the runner-up, his record suggests he will be one to take on next time.
**Campbells Lad** is consistent at a low level and looks a good guide to the level of this form. He did not do a lot wrong this time and may be able to pick up a similar event.
**Encounter** is a very tricky ride but, although he has the ability to win a race of this nature he was again below his best and is one to tread very carefully with.
**Desert Fury**, who has not won for over three years, may be best suited by a sounder surface but he is an unreliable sort who again folded tamely in the first time tongue-tie.
**The Count(FR)**, a low grade and temperamental hurdler, achieved little on this first Flat start for over two years.
**Dispol Verity** is a poor performer these days and she offered no immediate promise.
**Tiz Wiz** *Official explanation: jockey said filly boiled over at the start*

## 6467 DAILY RECORD GOOD MORNING BANDED STKS 1m 2f

12:30 (12:32) (H5) 3-Y-O+ £1,508 (£431; £215) **Stalls** Low

Form RPR

022 **1** **Top Style (IRE)**[194] 1493 6-8-11 40 PMulrennan(3) 13 52
(JHowardJohnson) *prom: niggled 1/2-way: rdn and hdwy 2f out: led ins fnl f: hung bdly lft: kpt on wl* **4/1[2]**

1032 **2** *3* **Reversionary**[18] 6142 3-9-0 50 (b) RWinston 9 52
(MWEasterby) *trckd ldrs gng wl: rdn to ld over 1f out: hung lft and hdd ins fnl f: r.o* **3/1[1]**

2400 **3** *1 3/4* **East Cape**[15] 6198 7-9-0 45 KimTinkler 3 44
(DonEnricoIncisa) *bhd and niggled along: hdwy 2f out: r.o fnl f* **8/1**

2456 **4** *1 3/4* **Spree Vision**[38] 5581 8-8-9 47 (v) DFentiman(7) 2 43
(PMonteith) *dwlt: hld up: hdwy and prom wl over 1f out: sn one pce* **6/1[3]**

0003 **5** *5* **The Wizard Mul**[15] 6201 4-9-5 50 JBramhill 7 38
(WStorey) *hld up: hdwy and in tch 2f out: sn rdn and outpcd* **8/1**

0550 **6** *1/2* **Kyle Of Lochalsh**[86] 4485 4-8-11 45 TEaves(3) 5 32
(JSGoldie) *midfield: effrt over 2f out: wknd over 1f out* **16/1**

4026 **7** *1/2* **Danefonique (IRE)**[58] 5238 3-8-9 50 DTudhope(5) 8 36
(DCarroll) *bhd: outpcd over 3f out: sme late hdwy: nvr on terms* **10/1**

0005 **8** *3/4* **Koodoo**[68] 4989 3-8-9 45 GParkin 4 30
(KARyan) *prom tl wknd over 2f out* **8/1**

0000 **9** *1/2* **Five Gold (IRE)**[42] 5656 3-9-0 50 NPollard 1 34
(ACWhillans) *led to over 1f out: sn btn* **20/1**

2505 **10** *7* **Aston Lad**[33] 5836 3-9-0 50 DarrenWilliams 12 22
(MDHammond) *in tch on outside: rdn over 3f out: btn over 2f out* **8/1**

0000 **11** *1* **Myannabanana (IRE)**[31] 5863 3-8-9 40 (b) DAllan 11 15
(JRWeymes) *keen: trckd ldrs tl wknd over 2f out* **33/1**

4000 **12** *3/4* **Iftikhar (USA)**[15] 6201 5-9-7 52 SWKelly 6 21
(WMBrisbourne) *a bhd* **16/1**

6000 **13** *21* **Devine Light (IRE)**$^{34}$ [5821] 4-9-0 45 ........ PFessey 10 —
(BMactaggart) *prom tl wknd fr 4f out* **50/1**

2m 26.35s (14.16) **Going Correction** +1.375s/f (Soft)
**WFA** 3 from 4yo+ 5lb **13** Ran SP% **134.2**
Speed ratings: **98,95,94,92,88 88,88,87,87,81 80,80,63**CSF £18.41 TOTE £4.60: £1.90, £1.50, £2.80; EX 14.40.
**Owner** Thomas Harty **Bred** Jordan Fogarty **Trained** Crook, Co Durham

**FOCUS**
A low-grade event in which the gallop was only fair and suited those racing prominently. The runner-up gives the guide to the form.

**NOTEBOOK**
**Top Style(IRE)** did not look the easiest ride but turned in an improved effort on this first run since April and for new connections. A stronger gallop may have suited and he may well be capable of better on the Flat or if tried over hurdles.
**Reversionary** is a decent guide to the level of this form and seemed to run his race, but he once again looked a very tricky ride when put under pressure and would not be one to place any great faith in.
**East Cape** had conditions to suit and fared the best of those that came from off the pace. A stronger gallop and a bit further would have suited but his win record is anything but inspiring.
**Spree Vision**, who returned to winning ways over hurdles on his previous start, was not totally disgraced having attempted to make ground from off the pace.
**The Wizard Mul**, upped further in trip, failed to get home. The return to shorter trips should suit but his inconsistency means he is not one to place much faith in.
**Kyle Of Lochalsh** is a poor and inconsistent sort who was soundly beaten on this first run on soft ground on this first start for his current stable.

## 6468 AFRICAN DANCER BANDED STKS 1m 5f 13y
1:00 (1:02) (H5) 3-Y-O+ **£1,466** (£419; £209) **Stalls** Low

Form RPR

5546 **1** **Boris The Spider**$^{61}$ [5197] 3-9-2 48 ........ DarrenWilliams 5 49
(MDHammond) *keen: cl up: effrt over 2f out: led over 1f out: styd on wl* **11/2**$^{3}$

00/0 **2** *2* **Sir Edward Burrow (IRE)**$^{14}$ [6209] 6-9-7 30 ........ JBramhill 6 43
(WStorey) *led: hung lft over 2f out: hdd over 1f out: one pce ins fnl f* **20/1**

-002 **3** *8* **Touch Of Ebony (IRE)**$^{6}$ [6231] 5-9-3 46 ........ AMedeiros$^{(5)}$ 3 33
(CRoberts) *plld hrd: hld up: hdwy to chse ldrs over 4f out: outpcd over 2f out: no imp fnl f* **6/4**$^{1}$

5332 **4** *2* **Staff Nurse (IRE)**$^{39}$ [5710] 4-9-7 35 ........ KimTinkler 4 29
(DonEnricoIncisa) *in tch: outpcd over 4f out: rallied 2f out: no imp* **11/2**$^{3}$

6430 **5** *1 ½* **Smarter Charter**$^{14}$ [6231] 11-9-0 35 ........ KristinStubbs$^{(7)}$ 1 27
(MrsLStubbs) *bhd: effrt over 3f out: sn btn* **10/1**

0030 **6** *5* **Dancer King (USA)**$^{63}$ [5110] 3-9-4 50 ........ RWinston 9 25
(TPTate) *cl up: effrt over 3f out: edgd lft and wknd wl over 1f out* **4/1**$^{2}$

/0-0 **7** *1* **Spectrum Star**$^{18}$ [6141] 4-9-4 35 ........ TEaves$^{(3)}$ 8 19
(FPMurtagh) *cl up tl rdn and wknd over 2f out* **33/1**

0054 **8** *26* **Howards Dream (IRE)**$^{42}$ [5629] 6-9-7 30 ........ (t) DAllan 10 —
(DANolan) *hld up in tch: rdn over 4f out: sn btn* **10/1**

-000 **9** *3* **Maravedi (IRE)**$^{164}$ [2230] 4-9-7 35 ........ SWKelly 2 —
(WMBrisbourne) *in tch tl rdn and wknd over 3f out* **16/1**

3m 17.57s (21.72) **Going Correction** +1.375s/f (Soft)
**WFA** 3 from 4yo+ 8lb **9** Ran SP% **122.5**
Speed ratings: **88,86,81,80,79 76,76,60,58**CSF £112.14 TOTE £7.80: £2.10, £5.90, £1.20; EX 127.10.
**Owner** The Adbrokes Partnership **Bred** David Smeaton **Trained** Middleham, N Yorks

**FOCUS**
Another low-grade event in which the pace was on the steady side and the form is very weak.

**NOTEBOOK**
**Boris The Spider** has stamina on the dam's side of his pedigree and ran up to his best on this first start over further than a mile and a quarter. He showed the right attitude, but the proximity of the runner-up shows this form amounts to little.
**Sir Edward Burrow(IRE)**, a longstanding maiden, seemed to run well in the face of a stiff task and pulled clear of the remainder. Given his inconsistency and the fact he had the rub of things, he would be no certainty to reproduce this next time.
**Touch Of Ebony(IRE)** looked to have solid claims on these terms and came here having run well in a similar event at Yarmouth, but pulled far too hard to do himself justice in this steadily run race. He is worth another chance.
**Staff Nurse(IRE)** was not totally disgraced and may have been suited by a stiffer test, but is on a losing run of over two years and is too inconsistent to be of any interest in the near future.
**Smarter Charter** is a poor performer who, although not really getting the race run to suit under less than ideal conditions, remains one to be wary of.
**Dancer King(USA)** handles soft ground and looked to have decent claims on these terms, but failed to get home upped markedly in trip. The return to a mile in similar company may enable him to get off the mark.

## 6469 LAUGHING ZEBRA AT AFRICAN INTERIORS BANDED STKS 6f
1:35 (1:35) (H5) 3-Y-O+ **£1,477** (£422; £211) **Stalls** High

Form RPR

0000 **1** **John O'Groats (IRE)**$^{21}$ [6059] 6-9-0 45 ........ JMcAuley 9 52
(BMactaggart) *mde all: clr whn hung lft over 1f out: hld on wl* **9/1**

1000 **2** *nk* **Stellite**$^{71}$ [4905] 4-8-11 45 ........ TEaves$^{(3)}$ 6 51
(JSGoldie) *sn prom: effrt and chsd wnr over 1f out: edgd lft: kpt on ins last* **5/2**$^{1}$

0040 **3** *3* **Danakim**$^{14}$ [6229] 7-8-7 40 ........ DFentiman$^{(7)}$ 2 42
(JRWeymes) *chsd wnr: rdn over 2f out: one pce over 1f out* **11/2**

-200 **4** *¾* **Hebenus**$^{89}$ [4386] 5-9-0 45 ........ DaleGibson 7 40
(TAKCuthbert) *prom: outpcd over 2f out: kpt on same pce fnl f* **6/1**

0000 **5** *nk* **Hi Darl**$^{14}$ [6229] 3-8-13 35 ........ NPollard 10 39
(WMBrisbourne) *hld up: rdn over 2f out: no imp over 1f out* **20/1**

0-00 **6** *2* **Procreate (IRE)**$^{37}$ [4464] 4-9-0 45 ........ RWinston 8 33
(MissLAPerratt) *hld up: rdn 2f out: nvr able to chal* **14/1**

0500 **7** *2* **Be My Alibi (IRE)**$^{124}$ [3368] 3-8-8 35 ........ BSwarbrick$^{(5)}$ 4 27
(WMBrisbourne) *bhd: rdn 1/2-way: n.d* **20/1**

0000 **8** *2* **Miss Wizz**$^{42}$ [5639] 4-8-9 45 ........ (p) RoryMoore$^{(5)}$ 5 21
(WStorey) *hld up in tch: rdn over 2f out: sn btn* **4/1**$^{2}$

-000 **9** *7* **Las Ramblas (IRE)**$^{33}$ [5832] 7-9-0 45 ........ (tp) DAllan 1 —
(DANolan) *chsd ldrs to 1/2-way: sn wknd* **28/1**

0650 **10** *6* **Indian Music**$^{33}$ [5833] 7-8-9 45 ........ PPMathers$^{(5)}$ 3 —
(ABerry) *hld up on outside: rdn 1/2-way: btn wl over 1f out* **9/2**$^{3}$

1m 18.55s (4.83) **Going Correction** +0.75s/f (Yiel)
**WFA** 3 from 4yo+ 1lb **10** Ran SP% **126.1**
Speed ratings: **97,96,92,91,91 88,85,83,73,65**CSF £33.70 TOTE £9.20: £2.50, £1.50, £1.90; EX 45.50 Place 6 £25.39, Place 5 £11.41.
**Owner** Miss E Johnston **Bred** Paul Traynor **Trained** Hawick, Borders

**FOCUS**
An uncompetitive event but a decent gallop and a return to winning ways from John O'Groats with the form average for the grade. As is usually the case in sprints here, those racing close to the pace held the edge.

**NOTEBOOK**
**John O'Groats(IRE)**, with the headgear left off, showed he retains ability and made a winning debut for his new stable and may be a bit better than the bare form. Whether this is reproduced next time remains to be seen, though.
**Stellite** down to the grade that saw him get off the mark at this course over seven furlongs in April, ran creditably despite not looking the easiest of rides and shaped as though the return to that trip would suit.
**Danakim** was not disgraced on ground that would have been plenty soft enough, but is likely to continue to look vulnerable in this grade on this evidence.
**Hebenus** handled the conditions well enough on this first run for three months, but left the impression that the step up to seven furlongs will be in his favour.
**Hi Darl**, who had a stiff task at the weights, fared the best of those to come from off the pace on this first run on soft ground. The return to seven furlongs may suit but her record suggests she is one to tread carefully with.
**Procreate(IRE)**, having his first run for his new stable, did not show enough to suggest he would be of any interest in the near future.
T/Plt: £48.90 to a £1 stake. Pool: £16,969.70. 253.20 winning tickets. T/Qpdt: £12.60 to a £1 stake. Pool: £1,727.30. 101.00 winning tickets. RY

# 6454 NEWMARKET (R-H)
Saturday, October 30

**OFFICIAL GOING: Good to soft (soft in places)**
The large fields tended to split into two groups, but there didn't appear to be any advantage to either group.
Wind: Slight across. Weather: Cloud with sunny periods, giving way to rain for the last race.

## 6470 EUROPEAN BREEDERS FUND MAIDEN FILLIES' STKS (DIV I) 7f
1:00 (1:01) (D3) 2-Y-O **£4,881** (£1,502; £751; £375) **Stalls** Low

Form RPR

**1** **Read Federica** 2-8-11 ........ DHolland 11 82
(SirMichaelStoute) *w'like: scope: str: racd centre: sn pushed along in mid-div: outpcd 1/2-way: hdwy over 1f out: r.o to ld nr fin* **14/1**

300 **2** *nk* **Sharaby (IRE)**$^{63}$ [5109] 2-8-11 70 ........ EAhern 5 81
(EALDunlop) *led centre: rdn over 1f out: hdd nr fin* **25/1**

**3** *¾* **My Dubai (IRE)** 2-8-11 ........ (t) TEDurcan 1 79
(SaeedBinSuroor) *neat: leggy: racd stands' side: chsd ldrs: led that gp over 1f out: r.o* **6/1**$^{2}$

**4** *1* **Gulchina (USA)** 2-8-11 ........ TQuinn 13 77
(DRCElsworth) *w'like: leggy: racd centre: prom: outpcd 1/2-way: hdwy over 1f out: r.o* **15/2**

**5** *hd* **Nawaaem (USA)** 2-8-11 ........ RHills 3 76
(BWHills) *w'like: racd stands' side: chsd ldr tl led that gp 1/2-way: hdd over 1f out: styd on* **8/1**

**6** *½* **Antoinette (USA)** 2-8-11 ........ KDarley 18 75
(SirMichaelStoute) *leggy: scope: racd centre: chsd ldrs: rdn over 2f out: styd on* **14/1**

**7** *½* **Heart Stopping (USA)** 2-8-11 ........ MHills 8 74
(BWHills) *unf: scope: racd centre: chsd ldr over 5f: styd on same pce fnl f* **16/1**

**8** *shd* **Mineko** 2-8-11 ........ SSanders 10 73
(EFVaughan) *w'like: bit bkwd: dwlt: racd centre: sn prom: outpcd over 2f out: styd on ins fnl f* **33/1**

**9** *½* **Cameron Orchid (IRE)** 2-8-11 ........ PRobinson 4 72
(MAJarvis) *w'like: bit bkwd: led stands' side to 1/2-way: rdn and hung rt over 1f out: styd on same pce* **10/1**

02 **10** *2 ½* **Queen Of Iceni**$^{19}$ [6123] 2-8-11 ........ IMongan 7 66
(JLDunlop) *racd stands' side: chsd ldrs: rdn 1/2-way: styd on same pce fnl 2f* **11/2**$^{1}$

**11** *1 ¼* **Swallow Senora (IRE)** 2-8-11 ........ JQuinn 14 63
(PWChapple-Hyam) *unf: leggy: racd centre: hld up: hdwy 1/2-way: wknd over 1f out* **33/1**

**12** *2 ½* **Let Slip** 2-8-11 ........ MartinDwyer 12 57
(WJarvis) *unf: s.i.s: racd centre: hld up: hdwy over 2f out: wknd over 1f out* **33/1**

**13** *1* **Savoie** 2-8-11 ........ WRyan 19 54
(HRACecil) *leggy: bit bkwd: racd centre: chsd ldrs 5f* **9/1**

00 **14** *9* **Moonside**$^{19}$ [6123] 2-8-8 ........ (v$^{1}$) RThomas$^{(3)}$ 9 32
(GBBalding) *racd centre: prom over 4f* **100/1**

**15** *6* **Prakara (IRE)** 2-8-4 ........ AHamblett$^{(7)}$ 16 17
(LMCumani) *w'like: scope: bit bkwd: s.i.s: racd centre: hld up: wknd over 2f out* **66/1**

**16** *2 ½* **Mrs Chippy (IRE)** 2-8-11 ........ NCallan 6 10
(MHTompkins) *w'like: bit bkwd: s.s: racd centre: a bhd* **66/1**

0 **17** *5* **Causeway Girl (IRE)**$^{29}$ [5915] 2-8-11 ........ SWhitworth 15 —
(DMSimcock) *dwlt: racd centre: hld up: hdwy 1/2-way: wknd over 2f out* **50/1**

0 **18** *4* **Cayuse**$^{78}$ [4730] 2-8-11 ........ MTebbutt 2 —
(TTClement) *racd stands' side: s.i.s: bhd fr 1/2-way* **100/1**

**19** *5* **Sunny Nature** 2-8-11 ........ RHughes 17 —
(JHMGosden) *w'like: s.s: racd centre: a bhd: eased 1/2-way* **7/1**$^{3}$

1m 31.39s (4.92) **Going Correction** +0.60s/f (Yiel) **19** Ran SP% **122.9**
Speed ratings: **95,94,93,92,92 91,91,91,90,87 86,83,82,72,65 62,56,52,46**CSF £341.65 TOTE £21.20: £5.10, £8.80, £2.20; EX 353.00.
**Owner** Mrs R J Jacobs **Bred** Newsells Park Stud Limited **Trained** Newmarket, Suffolk

**FOCUS**
Difficult to know what to make of this, especially as the winner looked clueless, yet was still more than good enough. It has been rated using the time as a guide.

**NOTEBOOK**
**Read Federica** ◆, a $140,000 first foal, is out of a mare that won a Listed sprint in the USA. She looked clueless for much of the trip, but clearly has her fair share of ability and should improve no end for the experience.
**Sharaby(IRE)**, given a break since disappointing last time, showed her true colours, although she did have something of a soft lead.
**My Dubai(IRE)**, a half-sister to several winners including seven-furlong Group Three winner Kareymah, may have been a shade unlucky for she won her race on the stands' side, only for the first two to race up the centre of the track.
**Gulchina(USA)** ◆, a $75,000 first foal, took a while to grasp what was required, but came home in good style and looks sure to improve for the experience.
**Nawaaem(USA)**, who is from the same family as the high-class Shadayid, did not shape at all badly and can do better still next term when stepping up in trip.
**Antoinette(USA)**, a $200,000 yearling, is quite stoutly bred and will appreciate middle-distances next year.

**Heart Stopping(USA)**, an early foal, is out of the useful maiden Clog Dance. She showed up well for much of the trip, on ground which could well have been soft enough for her.
**Mineko**, a half-sister to Mameyuki, did not shape at all badly over a trip which will prove to be on the sharp side for her.
**Queen Of Iceni** had no excuses other than the ground may have been softer than ideal.

## 6471 EUROPEAN BREEDERS FUND MAIDEN FILLIES' STKS (DIV II) 7f

**1:30** (1:37) (D3) 2-Y-O **£4,881** (£1,502; £751; £375) **Stalls** Low

| Form | Pos | Dist | Horse | Jockey | RPR |
|---|---|---|---|---|---|
| | **1** | | **Song Thrush (USA)** 2-8-11 (PFICole) *leggy: scope: racd alone stands' side: mde virtually all: rdn out* **20/1** | SSanders 1 | 89+ |
| | **2** | 2 ½ | **Ladeena (IRE)** 2-8-11 (JLDunlop) *unf: scope: racd centre: trckd ldrs: rdn to ld that gp over 1f out: r.o* **12/1** | WSupple 10 | 83 |
| | **3** | 1 | **Shared Dreams** 2-8-11 (LMCumani) *unf: scope: racd centre: hld up: hdwy over 1f out: r.o* **16/1** | DaneO'Neill 7 | 80 |
| 2 | **4** | ½ | **Lysandra (IRE)**$^{54}$ [5348] 2-8-11 (SirMichaelStoute) *racd centre: led that gp over 5f out: edgd lft and hdd over 1f out : styd on same pce* **5/1**$^{2}$ | KDarley 14 | 79 |
| | **5** | 2 | **Villarosi (IRE)** 2-8-11 (PWChapple-Hyam) *unf: bit bkwd: racd centre: mid-div: hdwy 1/2-way: rdn over 1f out: no ex* **16/1** | AMcCarthy 15 | 74 |
| | **6** | hd | **Linnet (GER)** 2-8-11 (MrsAJPerrett) *leggy: scope: racd centre: s.i.s: hdwy 1/2-way: edgd rt over 1f out: styd on same pce* **14/1** | DHolland 3 | 74 |
| | **7** | 1 ½ | **Prithee** 2-8-11 (JHMGosden) *w'like: scope: bit bkwd: racd centre: hld up: hdwy 2f out: no ex fnl f* **8/1** | RHughes 4 | 70 |
| 0 | **8** | 1 | **Alsharq (IRE)**$^{19}$ [6123] 2-8-11 (MPTregoning) *racd centre: w ldrs: rdn over 2f out: wknd fnl f* **11/2**$^{3}$ | RHills 12 | 67 |
| 5 | **9** | 1 ¼ | **Peace Lily**$^{19}$ [6125] 2-8-11 (RFJohnsonHoughton) *racd centre: led: hdd over 5f out: wknd over 1f out* **8/1** | SCarson 8 | 64 |
| 06 | **10** | 2 ½ | **Magic Flo**$^{24}$ [6011] 2-8-11 (GCBravery) *mid-div: effrt over 2f out: wknd over 1f out* **100/1** | SWhitworth 18 | 58 |
| | **11** | 1 | **Helen Sharp** 2-8-11 (MAJarvis) *leggy: scope: racd centre:c hased ldrs 5f* **7/1** | PRobinson 2 | 55 |
| | **12** | 3 | **La Bella Grande (IRE)** 2-8-11 (RCharlton) *w'like: scope: s.i.s: racd centre: rdn 1/2-way: wknd over 2f out* **16/1** | SDrowne 17 | 48 |
| | **13** | 5 | **Ciel Bleu** 2-8-11 (BWHills) *w'like: bit bkwd: s.s: racd centre: a bhd* **20/1** | MHills 9 | 35 |
| 0 | **14** | 4 | **Woolfall Joanna**$^{16}$ [6171] 2-8-11 (GGMargarson) *racd centre: prom 5f* **66/1** | JMackay 16 | 25 |
| | **15** | 3 ½ | **Katy Jem** 2-8-8 (DMSimcock) *w'like: bit bkwd: s.s: racd centre: a bheind: hung lft 1/2-way* **33/1** | LPKeniry$^{(3)}$ 13 | 17 |
| | **16** | ½ | **Snow Lynx (USA)** 2-8-11 (SaeedBinSuroor) *unf: scope: racd centre: prom to 1/2-way* **8/1** | TEDurcan 5 | 15 |

1m 30.74s (4.27) **Going Correction** +0.60s/f (Yiel) **16** Ran SP% **124.8**
Speed ratings: **99,96,95,94,92 91,90,89,87,84 83,80,74,69,65 65**CSF £239.74 TOTE £35.00: £7.50, £4.20, £7.70; EX 181.80.
**Owner** The Hon Mrs J M Corbett & C Wright **Bred** Joseph Stavola And William Stavola, Inc **Trained** Whatcombe, Oxon

**FOCUS**
The winner deserves plenty of credit for racing alone, albeit with the help of the stands'-side rail. Another race difficult to evaluate, but there were plenty of well-regarded types on show and it was 0.65 seconds quicker than the first division and the form may prove decent.

**NOTEBOOK**
**Song Thrush(USA)** ◆, who is related to several winners in the USA, did things the hard way, racing alone and making all of the running. She looks a nice prospect for next year.
**Ladeena(IRE)** ◆ has a lot to live up to for she comes from a high-class family. However, there was plenty to like about this first effort, winning the race up the centre, and she looks sure to pay her way in due course.
**Shared Dreams** is quite stoutly bred and should come into her own when stepping up in trip next year.
**Lysandra(IRE)** stepped up on her debut and time may tell this was not a bad efffort.
**Villarosi(IRE)**, who is a half-sister to a top-class three-year-old in Brazil, shaped quite nicely considering she looks the sort to do better next year over middle distances.
**Linnet(GER)**, a half-sister to a couple of winners in Germany, did not shape at all badly and improvement can be expected over middle distances next term.
**Snow Lynx(USA)** was reported to have been unsuited by the ground. *Official explanation: jockey said filly was unsuited by the good to soft (soft in places) ground*

## 6472 WILLIAM CLARIDGE MEMORIAL ZETLAND STKS (LISTED RACE) 1m 2f

**2:05** (2:07) (A1) 2-Y-O **£14,500** (£5,500; £2,750; £1,250) **Stalls** Low

| Form | Pos | Dist | Horse | Jockey | RPR |
|---|---|---|---|---|---|
| 51 | **1** | | **Ayam Zaman (IRE)**$^{26}$ [5988] 2-8-6 86 (MAJarvis) *trckd ldrs: led over 2f out: rdn clr fnl f: eased nr fin* **3/1**$^{2}$ | PRobinson 1 | 98+ |
| 015 | **2** | 5 | **Fantasy Ride**$^{12}$ [6268] 2-8-11 94 (JPearce) *lw: s.s: hld up: swtchd rt and hdwy over 1f out: no ch w wnr* **16/1** | JQuinn 5 | 90 |
| 031 | **3** | 2 | **Natalie Jane (IRE)**$^{10}$ [6309] 2-8-6 (GAButler) *trckd ldrs: rdn over 2f out: styd on same pce appr fnl f* **12/1** | PHanagan 3 | 82 |
| 14 | **4** | shd | **Brecon**$^{7}$ [6353] 2-8-6 (DRCElsworth) *hld up: racd keenly: hdwy over 2f out: sn hung lft and rdn: styd on same pce appr fnl f* **6/1**$^{3}$ | TQuinn 4 | 81 |
| 211 | **5** | 1 ¼ | **Sunday Symphony**$^{19}$ [6122] 2-8-11 89 (SaeedBinSuroor) *hld up in tch: hung lft and chsd wnr over 2f out: wknd fnl f* **9/4**$^{1}$ | TEDurcan 8 | 84 |
| 0221 | **6** | 5 | **Wotchalike (IRE)**$^{11}$ [6282] 2-8-11 82 (RJPrice) *lw: s.i.s: sn prom: rdn over 3f out: wknd over 1f out* **22/1** | AMcCarthy 9 | 76 |
| 0011 | **7** | 3 | **Danehill Willy (IRE)**$^{16}$ [6176] 2-8-11 81 (NACallaghan) *lw: chsd ldr: rdn 1/2-way: led over 3f out: hdd and hmpd over 2f out: sn wknd* **6/1**$^{3}$ | DHolland 6 | 71 |
| 212 | **8** | dist | **Active Asset (IRE)**$^{80}$ [4645] 2-8-11 89 (MRChannon) *chsd ldrs: hmpd over 2f out: sn wknd* **12/1** | ACulhane 7 | — |
| 4003 | **9** | 13 | **Norcroft**$^{12}$ [6276] 2-8-11 69 (PSMcentee) *led over 6f: wknd over 2f out* **100/1** | HayleyTurner 2 | — |

2m 10.53s (4.84) **Going Correction** +0.60s/f (Yiel) **9** Ran SP% **110.9**
Speed ratings: **103,99,97,97,96 92,89,—,—**CSF £46.48 TOTE £3.40: £1.60, £3.40, £2.70; EX 46.50.
**Owner** Saif Ali **Bred** Dr T A Ryan **Trained** Newmarket, Suffolk
■ Stewards Enquiry : T E Durcan two-day ban: careless riding (Nov 10,12); further caution: careless riding

**FOCUS**
This did not look a strong Listed race, but the winner is clearly progressive and could turn out to be a major player in the fillies' middle-distance races next term.

**NOTEBOOK**
**Ayam Zaman(IRE)** ◆ handled this easier surface well enough and won with a ton in hand. While this probably did not take much winning, she is clearly on the upgrade and should be capable of holding her own in some better-class fillies' races next year.
**Fantasy Ride** came out best of the rest, but in all honesty was only playing for places anyway.
**Natalie Jane(IRE)** was not disgraced on this step up in class, and while she may well be difficult to place from now on, has at least got some black type next to her name now.
**Brecon** travelled well for much of the race, but left the impression that this trip was far enough for her.
**Sunday Symphony** tried to mix it with the winner, but folded tamely up the hilll and was reported not to have handled the softer ground. *Official explanation: jockey said colt was unsuited by the good to soft (soft in places) ground*

## 6473 BEST BET JOHN 0800 587 7086 EBF MONTROSE FILLIES' STKS (LISTED RACE) 1m

**2:35** (2:35) (A1) 2-Y-O **£14,500** (£5,500; £2,750; £1,250) **Stalls** Low

| Form | Pos | Dist | Horse | Jockey | RPR |
|---|---|---|---|---|---|
| 632 | **1** | | **Squaw Dance**$^{19}$ [6111] 2-8-8 81 (WJHaggas) *mde all: qcknd over 2f out: rdn out* **16/1** | PHanagan 8 | 102 |
| 0111 | **2** | 1 ½ | **Something Exciting**$^{15}$ [6189] 2-8-8 100 (DRCElsworth) *hld up: rdn over 3f out: hdwy over 1f out: hung rt ins fnl f: styd on* **1/1**$^{1}$ | TQuinn 7 | 98 |
| 1403 | **3** | 2 ½ | **Borthwick Girl (IRE)**$^{28}$ [5939] 2-8-8 98 (BJMeehan) *lw: chsd wnr: rdn and ev ch over 2f out: edgd rt over 1f out : styd on same pce* **13/2**$^{2}$ | JFortune 2 | 93 |
| 1506 | **4** | hd | **Justaquestion**$^{14}$ [6213] 2-8-8 93 (IAWood) *trckd ldrs: rdn over 2f out: styd on same pce fnl f* **14/1** | NCallan 1 | 92 |
| 3 | **5** | 1 ½ | **Tempestad (IRE)**$^{19}$ [6118] 2-8-8 (HRACecil) *lw: chsd ldrs: rdn over 2f out: no ex fnl f* **15/2** | WRyan 3 | 89 |
| 5 | **6** | nk | **Always Mine**$^{19}$ [6123] 2-8-8 (MrsAJPerrett) *hld up: outpcd over 2f out: styd on ins fnl f* **22/1** | MartinDwyer 5 | 88 |
| 0011 | **7** | nk | **Alpine Gold (IRE)**$^{8}$ [6334] 2-8-8 75 (JLDunlop) *lw: trckd ldrs: racd keenly: rdn over 2f out: wknd ins fnl f* **7/1**$^{3}$ | IMongan 6 | 88 |
| 3 | **8** | ½ | **Los Organos (IRE)**$^{7}$ [6352] 2-8-8 (PWChapple-Hyam) *hld up: rdn over 2f out: wknd over 1f out* **25/1** | RHavlin 4 | 87 |

1m 45.55s (6.15) **Going Correction** +0.60s/f (Yiel) **8** Ran SP% **108.3**
Speed ratings: **90,88,86,85,84 84,83,83**CSF £29.30 TOTE £12.80: £2.90, £1.10, £2.10; EX 34.00.
**Owner** Tony Hirschfeld **Bred** M L Page **Trained** Newmarket, Suffolk

**FOCUS**
Ann ordinary Listed contest distinguished by a fine front-running ride from Hanagan who soon made his way across to the stands' side rail. The form does not appear that strong, however.

**NOTEBOOK**
**Squaw Dance** had something of a soft lead and, with the rails to help, never looked like being pegged back.
**Something Exciting** did not have the strong pace she needs, so in the circumstances did not run too badly.
**Borthwick Girl(IRE)** always had the winner in her sights, but failed to pick up as she might have done on a faster surface.
**Justaquestion** appeared to run her race, but she has been found out at this level before.
**Tempestad(IRE)**, who is quite stoutly bred, would not have been suited to the lack of pace.
**Always Mine** looks the sort to do better over middle distances next term.

## 6474 BEST BET JOHN 0800 587 7086 BEN MARSHALL STKS (LISTED RACE) 1m

**3:10** (3:10) (A1) 3-Y-O+ **£17,400** (£6,600; £3,300; £1,500) **Stalls** Low

| Form | Pos | Dist | Horse | Jockey | RPR |
|---|---|---|---|---|---|
| 1 | **1** | shd | **Sleeping Indian**$^{19}$ [6132] 3-8-10 (JHMGosden) *lw: trckd ldrs: nt clr run over 1f out: swtchd rt and r.o ins fnl f: carried rt: jst failed: fin 2nd: plcd 1st* **5/1**$^{2}$ | JFortune 1 | 112+ |
| 4643 | **2** | | **Babodana**$^{14}$ [6219] 4-8-13 107 (MHTompkins) *hld up in tch: nt clr run over 1f out: rdn to ld and hung rt ins fnl f: all out: fin 1st: disq: plcd 2nd* **9/2**$^{1}$ | DHolland 3 | 110 |
| 1222 | **3** | 1 | **Take A Bow**$^{28}$ [5941] 3-8-10 102 (PRChamings) *chsd ldr: rdn over 3f out: ev ch over 1f out: edgd rt ins fnl f: styd on* **5/1**$^{2}$ | JQuinn 4 | 108 |
| 0604 | **4** | 1 | **Tout Seul (IRE)**$^{29}$ [5917] 4-9-2 105 (RFJohnsonHoughton) *hld up: hdwy over 1f out: sn rdn: styd on same pce ins fnl f* **12/1** | SCarson 9 | 109 |
| 6533 | **5** | 1 ½ | **Quito (IRE)**$^{7}$ [6345] 7-8-13 104 (DWChapman) *hld up: styd on ins fnl f: nt trble ldrs* **11/2**$^{3}$ | (b) ACulhane 6 | 103 |
| 0-23 | **6** | ½ | **Funfair**$^{29}$ [5917] 5-8-13 106 (MrsAJPerrett) *hld up: hdwy over 1f out: styng on whn hmpd ins fnl f : nt rcvr* **15/2** | SSanders 7 | 102 |
| 10-0 | **7** | ½ | **Cape Fear**$^{14}$ [6214] 3-8-10 107 (BJMeehan) *lw: chsd ldrs: led over 2f out: rdn over 1f out: hdd & wknd ins fnl f* **33/1** | EAhern 10 | 101 |
| 0023 | **8** | 1 ½ | **Putra Pekan**$^{20}$ [6106] 6-9-2 109 (MAJarvis) *lw: led over 5f: hmpd and wknd over 1f out* **10/1** | (b) PRobinson 2 | 101 |
| 6-40 | **9** | ½ | **Imperial Stride**$^{14}$ [6219] 3-8-10 109 (SirMichaelStoute) *chsd ldrs: rdn over 1f out: wknd ins fnl f* **8/1** | KDarley 11 | 97 |
| 6130 | **10** | 1 ¼ | **Audience**$^{28}$ [5941] 4-8-13 105 (JAkehurst) *hld up: hdwy over 2f out: wknd over 1f out* **20/1** | (p) MTebbutt 8 | 95 |
| 412- | **11** | 8 | **Josephus (IRE)**$^{372}$ [5731] 3-8-10 104 (RCharlton) *hld up: wknd over 2f out* **33/1** | SDrowne 5 | 79 |

1m 41.32s (1.92) **Going Correction** +0.60s/f (Yiel)
**WFA** 3 from 4yo+ 3lb **11** Ran SP% **117.2**
Speed ratings: **110,111,109,108,107 106,106,104,104,103 95**CSF £27.06 TOTE £6.80: £2.60, £2.10, £2.20; EX 40.00.
**Owner** George Strawbridge **Bred** George Strawbridge **Trained** Manton, Wilts
■ Stewards Enquiry : D Holland two-day ban: careless riding (Nov 10,12)
J Fortune two-day ban: careless riding (Nov 10,12)

**FOCUS**
A controversial end to a decent contest. Babodana's connections' appeal against the decision to demote him was unsuccessful. The form is just fair for the grade but appears sound.

**NOTEBOOK**
**Sleeping Indian** would have been a most unlucky loser, having got into all sorts of trouble in the dip. However, switched to get a run inside the final furlong, hampering Funfair in the process, he picked up in good style and despite tending to go right handed anyway, was intimidated by Babodona in the latter stages and given the race in the Stewards' room. A highly progressive colt, he looks destined for further honours.

**Babodana**, the winner of this last year, was unlucky not to follow up, as he was somewhat harshly thrown out after passing the post a narrow winner. There is no doubt he drifted across the track, intimidating his rival rather than carrying him, but the pair never touched and Fortune never had to stop riding on Sleeping Indian.
**Take A Bow** confirmed himself a progressive performer, and certainly looks capable of making his mark at this level. His rider later reported that the colt had been struck into. *Official explanation: jockey said colt had been struck into*
**Tout Seul(IRE)** looks to be travelling as well as anything going into the dip, but not for the first time did not quite see this trip out.
**Quito(IRE)** was always going to be struggling for a run from his position.
**Funfair** was just about to get into the action when all but knocked over by Sleeping Indian.

## 6475 BEST BET JOHN 0800 587 7086 MILE H'CAP 1m
**3:45** (3:45) (C1) (0-107,94) 3-Y-0+ **£17,400** (£6,600; £3,300; £1,500) **Stalls** Low

Form RPR
0022 **1** **Zero Tolerance (IRE)**[63] 5122 4-9-7 **94** PHanagan 9 103
(TDBarron) *mde all: qcknd over 2f out: rdn over 1f out: r.o* **9/1**
130 **2** ¾ **Impeller (IRE)**[28] 5941 5-9-5 **92** SDrowne 3 100+
(WRMuir) *hld up: nt clr run over 1f out: r.o wl ins fnl f: nt rch wnr* **20/1**
1111 **3** 1¼ **The Prince**[21] 6069 10-8-8 **88** AMullen(7) 6 93
(IanWilliams) *s.s: hld up: nt clr run over 1f out: r.o wl ins fnl f: nt rch ldrs* **6/1**[2]
51-1 **4** 1½ **Go Padero (IRE)**[13] 6244 3-8-9 **85** JFanning 12 87
(MJohnston) *lw: chsd wnr: rdn and edgd lft over 1f out: styd on same pce* **6/1**[2]
2111 **5** *nk* **Kamanda Laugh**[15] 6193 3-8-11 **87** MHills 10 88
(BWHills) *b.off hind: chsd ldrs: rdn over 2f out: styd on same pce fnl f* **7/2**[1]
160 **6** 1¾ **Wake (USA)**[163] 2241 4-9-3 **90** RHughes 7 88
(MLWBell) *swtg: a.p: rdn over 1f out: wknd ins fnl f* **50/1**
4000 **7** ½ **Perfect Storm**[7] 6354 5-9-0 **87** DSweeney 11 84
(MBlanshard) *prom: rdn over 2f out: wknd ins fnl f* **16/1**
0004 **8** ½ **Finished Article (IRE)**[15] 6193 7-8-7 **85** PMakin(5) 2 81
(WJMusson) *hld up: swtchd rt over 2f out: rdn and hmpd over 1f out: edgd lft and wknd ins fnl f* **6/1**[2]
0030 **9** 1 **Ace Of Hearts**[15] 6193 5-9-3 **90** SSanders 13 84
(CFWall) *hld up: rdn over 3f out: edgd rt and wknd over 1f out* **22/1**
100 **10** ½ **Dafore**[15] 6193 3-8-3 **82** JFMcDonald(3) 1 75
(RHannon) *hld up: hdwy over 3f out: wknd over 1f out* **16/1**
0310 **11** 2½ **Norton (IRE)**[34] 5813 7-9-7 **94** JFortune 8 82
(TGMills) *trckd ldrs: hmpd over 1f out: nt rcvr* **20/1**
5450 **12** 3½ **Unshakable (IRE)**[15] 6193 5-9-6 **93** FNorton 4 74
(BobJones) *b.hind: hld up: a in rr* **15/2**[3]
5150 **13** 3 **Krugerrand (USA)**[28] 5941 5-8-9 **89** LauraPike(7) 5 64
(WJMusson) *s.s: a bhd* **40/1**

1m 42.02s (2.62) **Going Correction** +0.60s/f (Yiel)
**WFA** 3 from 4yo+ 3lb **13** Ran SP% **116.9**
Speed ratings: **107,106,105,103,103 101,100,100,99,98 96,92,89**CSF £180.44 CT £1204.18 TOTE £11.00: £2.50, £5.80, £2.30; EX 181.80 Trifecta £300.70 Pool £1,906.24, 4.50 winning tickets.
**Owner** The Hornsey Warriors Racing Syndicate **Bred** Cliveden Stud Ltd **Trained** Maunby, N Yorks

**FOCUS**
A decent handicap, but the winner had the run of the race and may be slightly flattered and the form has a messy look.

**NOTEBOOK**
**Zero Tolerance(IRE)** quickly made his way across to the favoured stands' side rail, a tactic which his rider employed successfully earlier on. While on paper this will go down as a career-best effort, he may be slightly flattered by the result, as several of his rivals suffered trouble in running.
**Impeller(IRE)** looked to turn in a career-best effort, even though he did not have the best of runs and, the ground would have been easier than ideal. He is clearly at the top of his game at present, but he does need things to fall his way.
**The Prince** ◆ looked a most unlucky loser, for he gave away more ground at the start than he was beaten, and then he had to sit and wait for the gaps to appear, and when they did, the race was all but over.
**Go Padero(IRE)** may have found this coming too soon after his effort at Musselburgh on his belated seasonal debut.
**Kamanda Laugh** has been on the go since March, and has been wonderfully consistent, but while he probably ran close to his best, it is possible that his schedule has caught up with him.
**Wake(USA)** has clearly had his problems, but there is no doubt he does have ability, for he travelled like a good horse for much of the trip. *Official explanation: jockey said colt suffered interference in running*

## 6476 EUROPEAN BREEDERS FUND MAIDEN STKS (C&G) 7f
**4:20** (4:21) (D3) 2-Y-0 **£4,998** (£1,538; £769; £384) **Stalls** Low

Form RPR
**1** **Centaurus** 2-8-11 TEDurcan 14 96+
(SaeedBinSuroor) *leggy: scope: a.p: chsd ldr over 2f out: led 1f out: r.o* **3/1**[2]
**2** 1¼ **Master Of The Race** 2-8-11 DHolland 20 93+
(SirMichaelStoute) *leggy: scope: bit bkwd: a.p: rdn over 2f out: r.o* **7/1**[3]
33 **3** 2 **River Royale**[16] 6171 2-8-11 AMcCarthy 12 88
(PWChapple-Hyam) *trckd ldrs: plld hrd: swtchd lft and led 1/2-way: rdn and hdd 1f out: no ex* **11/4**[1]
0 **4** 5 **Trew Style**[15] 6187 2-8-11 DaneO'Neill 17 76
(MHTompkins) *hld up: hdwy over 2f out: nt trble ldrs* **25/1**
**5** 1¼ **Zadalrakib** 2-8-11 MHills 1 72
(SirMichaelStoute) *leggy: bit bkwd: s.i.s: sn prom: rdn over 2f out: wknd over 1f out* **12/1**
0 **6** 3½ **Krullind (IRE)**[16] 6171 2-8-6 ThomasYeung(5) 9 64
(PWChapple-Hyam) *led to 1/2-way: hung lft and wknd over 1f out* **66/1**
4 **7** 4 **Bonfire**[36] 5765 2-8-11 JFanning 11 54
(MJohnston) *chsd ldrs over 5f* **14/1**
**8** 1¼ **Pagan Sword** 2-8-11 SSanders 15 51
(MrsAJPerrett) *w'like: bit bkwd: dwlt: hdwy 1/2-way: wknd over 1f out* **16/1**
**9** ½ **Goodbye Ben** 2-8-11 JFortune 2 49
(JHMGosden) *w'like: scope: bit bkwd: chsd ldrs over 4f* **12/1**
0 **10** 1 **Bachelor Affair**[29] 5915 2-8-11 MartinDwyer 4 47
(WJarvis) *plld hrd and prom: wknd over 1f out* **50/1**
**11** *hd* **National Trust** 2-8-11 KDarley 13 46
(SirMichaelStoute) *gd sort: w'like: scope: bit bkwd: mid-div: sn pushed along: n.d* **12/1**
**12** ½ **Raison Detre** 2-8-11 JQuinn 6 45
(JPearce) *leggy: s.s: bhd tl sme late hdwy* **66/1**
**13** *nk* **Taakeed** 2-8-11 PRobinson 8 44
(MAJarvis) *w'like: bity bkwd: chsd ldrs over 4f* **20/1**
**14** 3 **New Realm (USA)** 2-8-11 SDrowne 18 37
(EFVaughan) *w'like: s.s: a in rr* **33/1**
**15** ½ **Ben Bacchus (IRE)** 2-8-11 PDoe 5 36
(MHTompkins) *w'like: bit bkwd: s.i.s: a in rr* **66/1**
**16** 7 **Last Chapter (IRE)** 2-8-11 VSlattery 10 18
(JohnBerry) *w'like: bit bkwd: s.s: a in rr* **66/1**
**17** 2 **Blood Money** 2-8-11 JFEgan 7 13
(NACallaghan) *leggy: dwlt: a in rr* **20/1**
**18** 2 **Bullseye** 2-8-11 TQuinn 19 8
(PWD'Arcy) *str: bit bkwd: s.i.s: hdwy 1/2-way: wknd over 2f out* **50/1**
**19** 13 **Johnny Chi (IRE)** 2-8-11 ACulhane 3 —
(PWD'Arcy) *w'like: bit bkwd: dwlt: a bhd* **33/1**

1m 29.61s (3.14) **Going Correction** +0.60s/f (Yiel) **19** Ran SP% **128.9**
Speed ratings: **106,104,102,96,95 91,86,85,84,83 83,82,82,78,78 70,68,65,50**CSF £22.80 TOTE £4.20: £1.60, £3.00, £2.00; EX 37.00.
**Owner** Godolphin **Bred** Newgate Stud Co **Trained** Newmarket, Suffolk

**FOCUS**
This looked a warm maiden with the third having already shown a decent level of form in two prior runs, and he provides the guide to the level of the form.

**NOTEBOOK**
**Centaurus** ◆, an early foal, is out of a mare that won as a juvenile. He is a scopey sort, who should do better with another year on his back.
**Master Of The Race** ◆ still looked a little green, but shaped with plenty of promise for the future and will certainly stay middle-distances next term.
**River Royale**, who had shown a fair level of form coming into this, did himself no favours by racing too keenly through the first half of the race. While he was soundly beaten here, time may tell he was tackling two above-average colts.
**Trew Style** is still learning and showed enough to suggest he can make his mark next year in middle-distance handicaps.
**Zadalrakib**, who is out of a mare that won over a mile, is a brother to Group Two winner Titus Livius. He showed enough to suggest he can pay his way next year.

## 6477 RACING UK ON SKY 432 H'CAP 7f
**4:55** (4:56) (D2) (0-92,89) 3-Y-0+ **£6,988** (£2,150; £1,075; £537) **Stalls** Low

Form RPR
0242 **1** **Alfonso**[11] 6284 3-8-11 **77** MHills 18 91+
(BWHills) *racd centre: chsd ldrs: led over 2f out: rdn out* **5/1**[2]
6200 **2** 2½ **Arctic Desert**[21] 6070 4-8-13 **77** PHanagan 17 84
(AMBalding) *b: racd centre: hld up: hdwy to chse wnr over 1f out: styd on* **25/1**
0005 **3** ½ **Queens Rhapsody**[43] 5603 4-9-2 **80** JFortune 14 86
(ABailey) *racd centre: chsd ldrs: rdn over 2f out: styd on* **14/1**
0000 **4** ½ **Cardinal Venture (IRE)**[21] 6071 6-9-4 **89** AMullen(7) 1 94
(KARyan) *racd stands' side: led that gp: rdn over 1f out: r.o: no ch w centre* **16/1**
0044 **5** 2 **Tidy (IRE)**[7] 6358 4-8-13 **77** TEDurcan 19 77
(MDHammond) *racd centre: hdwy over 2f out: sn rdn: styd on* **14/1**
2050 **6** ½ **Digital**[15] 6191 7-9-7 **85** SHitchcott 6 84
(MRChannon) *racd stands' side: hld up: r.o ins fnl f: nvr nrr* **10/1**
2-10 **7** ¾ **Sydney Star**[147] 2692 3-9-4 **84** MartinDwyer 16 81
(BWHills) *led centre over 4f: wknd fnl f* **33/1**
6-13 **8** *hd* **Mutamared (USA)**[43] 5614 4-9-5 **83** RHills 4 79
(MPTregoning) *racd stands' side: ev ch that gp over 2f out: wknd fnl f* **7/2**[1]
0143 **9** ½ **Chateau Nicol**[8] 6341 5-9-5 **83** (b) TQuinn 9 78
(BGPowell) *racd stands' side: hld up: hdwy 2f out: wknd fnl f* **12/1**
0410 **10** ½ **Crail**[40] 5706 4-8-10 **74** LisaJones 20 68
(CFWall) *racd centre: hld up: effrt over 2f out: n.d* **50/1**
3400 **11** ½ **Surf The Net**[42] 5652 3-8-13 **79** (v) RHughes 8 71
(RHannon) *chsd ldr stands' side over 4f: wknd over 1f out* **50/1**
2012 **12** 2½ **Azreme**[13] 6244 4-8-13 **77** ACulhane 3 63
(DKIvory) *b.hind: racd stands' side hld up in tch: rdn and wknd over 1f out* **7/1**[3]
5000 **13** ½ **Camberwell**[57] 5275 3-8-12 **78** GCarter 13 63
(TGMills) *racd centre: prom over 4f* **66/1**
3521 **14** ¾ **Middleton Grey**[77] 4751 6-8-4 **71** (b) LPKeniry(3) 10 54
(AGNewcombe) *racd stands' side: hld up: hdwy over 2f out: wknd fnl f* **20/1**
210 **15** 1¾ **Serre Chevalier (IRE)**[50] 5444 3-8-12 **78** DHolland 12 57
(PWHarris) *racd centre: hld up: rdn over 2f out: n.d* **33/1**
0300 **16** 1¼ **Tregarron**[40] 5697 3-8-5 **71** FNorton 15 47
(RHannon) *racd centre: prom over 4f* **66/1**
3-10 **17** 1¾ **Kodiac**[36] 5766 3-9-2 **82** PRobinson 2 53
(JLDunlop) *racd stands' side: chsd ldrs 5f* **12/1**
0200 **18** 3½ **Winning Venture**[12] 6277 7-9-1 **79** WSupple 5 41
(AWCarroll) *racd stands' side: hld up: rdn over 2f out: sn wknd* **25/1**
5441 **19** *nk* **Vienna's Boy (IRE)**[64] 5092 3-8-13 **79** DaneO'Neill 11 41
(WJMusson) *lw: unruly in stalls: racd centre: hld up: hdwy 1/2-way: wknd over 2f out* **25/1**
2644 **20** 3½ **Kingscross**[21] 6070 6-9-2 **80** DSweeney 7 33
(MBlanshard) *lw: racd stands' side: prom over 4f* **12/1**

1m 30.91s (4.44) **Going Correction** +0.60s/f (Yiel)
**WFA** 3 from 4yo+ 2lb **20** Ran SP% **131.9**
Speed ratings: **98,95,94,94,91 91,90,90,89,88 88,85,84,84,82 80,78,74,74,70**CSF £137.52 CT £1704.61 TOTE £6.50: £2.10, £6.10, £3.90, £5.50; EX 239.30 Place 6 £657.55, Place 5 £150.46.
**Owner** Guy Reed **Bred** G Reed **Trained** Lambourn, Berks

**FOCUS**
A competitive handicap in which the field split into two, and the first three home raced up the centre of the course. Despite this the form looks sound for the grade.

**NOTEBOOK**
**Alfonso** ◆ had his favoured easy surface, and never looked in any danger after striking the front. He has a similar profile to his brother Pablo, who won last year's Lincoln, in that he too was highly progressive as a three-year-old and actually won at this meeting on his final start that year. Although you need luck with the draw at Doncaster, he would certainly have to be on the short list for that cavalry charge.
**Arctic Desert** put behind him a couple of below-par efforts with a solid display, but he lacks consistency and cannot be relied upon to reproduce this.
**Queens Rhapsody** has struggled with the Handicapper since winning back-to-back races on the All-Weather last year, but he is now back down to a realistic mark on turf, although it may be too late this year to take advantage.
**Cardinal Venture(IRE)**, a bit keen to post, did best of those to race on the stands' side. He has struggled off higher marks since scoring at Haydock back in June, but there was a little more promise in this effort than of late.
**Tidy(IRE)**, at his best of soft ground, was doing his best work in the latter stages and may be worth another try at a mile.
**Digital** again hinted that his turn isn't far away.

**Mutamared(USA)** travelled well on the stands' side, but could not pick up from the run into the dip and was comfortably held by those at the head of his group.
T/Plt: £1,986.40 to a £1 stake. Pool: £56,328.95. 20.70 winning tickets. T/Qpdt: £20.30 to a £1 stake. Pool: £5,288.50. 192.50 winning tickets. CR

# 6400 WOLVERHAMPTON (A.W) (L-H)
Saturday, October 30

**OFFICIAL GOING: Standard**
Wind: nil Weather: dry

## 6478 LADBROKES.COM MEDIAN AUCTION MAIDEN STKS — 5f 216y(P)
7:00 (7:04) (F3) 2-Y-O — £3,464 (£1,066; £533; £266) Stalls Low

| Form | | | Horse | | RPR |
|---|---|---|---|---|---|
| 03 | 1 | | **Pamir (IRE)**[26] 6000 2-9-0 — SDrowne 10<br>(LMCumani) *a.p: rdn to ld 1f out: kpt up to work* **7/2**[1] | | 75+ |
| 4 | 2 | ½ | **Keep Me Warm**[11] 6281 2-8-9 — PMakin(5) 1<br>(WGMTurner) *trckd ldr: led 2f out: hdd wl over 1f out: rallied ins fnl f* **5/1**[2] | | 71 |
| 3 | 3 | 1½ | **Sweet Namibia (IRE)**[11] 6294 2-8-9 — SSanders 4<br>(JWHills) *s.i.s: sn in tch on ins: led wl over 1f out: rdn and hdd 1f out: one pce after* **7/2**[1] | | 61 |
| | 4 | nk | **Dash Of Lime** 2-8-9 — JFEgan 5<br>(SKirk) *slowly away: hld up: rdn and hdwy over 2f out: styd on: nvr nrr* **7/1**[3] | | 60 |
| 5 | 5 | nk | **Seamless**[120] 3476 2-9-0 — SWKelly 9<br>(WJHaggas) *hld up in tch: rdn over 2f out: nt qckn fnl f* **5/1**[2] | | 64 |
| | 6 | 7 | **Rossin Gold (IRE)** 2-9-0 — (b[1]) VSlattery 6<br>(PABlockley) *v.s.a: hdwy after 2f: wknd appr fnl f* **20/1** | | 43 |
| 0 | 7 | ½ | **Queens Hand (IRE)**[15] 6195 2-8-6 — THamilton(3) 12<br>(GASwinbank) *outpcd and nvr on terms* **33/1** | | 37 |
| 4 | 8 | 2½ | **Prospect Point**[14] 6221 2-8-4 — (p) DFox(5) 11<br>(CADwyer) *in tch on outside tl wknd over 2f out* **14/1** | | 29 |
| 0 | 9 | 3 | **Lugana Point**[45] 5555 2-9-0 — CCatlin 7<br>(JBalding) *sn led: hdd 2f out: wknd ent fnl f* **25/1** | | 25 |
| 0 | 10 | 6 | **Scarborough Flyer**[12] 6270 2-9-0 — DAllan 8<br>(JBalding) *s.i.s: sn in tch: wknd over 2f out* **66/1** | | 7 |
| | 11 | 1¾ | **Compton Spark** 2-8-11 — TEaves(3) 3<br>(JSGoldie) *slowly away: outpcd thrght* **28/1** | | 2 |
| 06 | 12 | 2 | **Stevmarie Star**[14] 6207 2-8-9 — JQuinn 13<br>(JAGlover) *outpcd and a bhd* **66/1** | | — |
| 0 | 13 | 23 | **Madame Guillotine**[15] 6196 2-8-9 — JEdmunds 2<br>(JBalding) *chsd ldrs tl wknd over 3f out: t.o* **50/1** | | — |

1m 17.41s — 13 Ran SP% **116.0**
Speed ratings: CSF £18.79 TOTE £3.60: £2.00, £1.70, £2.10; EX 24.10.
**Owner** Mrs E H Vestey **Bred** James Kavanagh **Trained** Newmarket, Suffolk

**FOCUS**
An ordinary sprint maiden that is rated through first and third.

**NOTEBOOK**
**Pamir(IRE)** had shown enough on turf to suggest that a race such as this was within his capability, and with Drowne replacing the apprentices who had ridden him in his previous starts, he made it third time lucky. The Handicapper should not go overboard about this.
**Keep Me Warm** had looked likely to appreciate the step up to six furlongs on his debut. He ran a solid race, and it was good to see him rally after being headed.
**Sweet Namibia(IRE)**, like the winner, by Namid, had the advantage of previous course experience, but she still found two too good.
**Dash Of Lime**, a half-sister to high-class sprinter Sampower Star and multiple sprint winners Absent Friends and Fire Up The Band, was not particularly strong in the market and ran as though in need of the experience. She can be expected to improve for racing.
**Seamless** is bred to do better over farther, but he had run a promising race over this trip on his debut at Haydock and in the circumstances this was slightly disappointing.
**Rossin Gold(IRE)**, blinkered on his debut, ran as though in need of both the run and experience.

## 6479 LADBROKESCASINO.COM MAIDEN AUCTION STKS — 1m 141y(P)
7:30 (7:32) (E3) 2-Y-O — £3,412 (£1,050; £525; £262) Stalls Low

| Form | | | Horse | | RPR |
|---|---|---|---|---|---|
| 54 | 1 | | **Kangrina**[23] 6020 2-8-8 — SSanders 5<br>(SirMarkPrescott) *in tch whn hmpd on ins after 2f: hdwy on outside over 2f out: rdn and styd on to ld wl ins fnl f* **5/1**[3] | | 79+ |
| 02 | 2 | ¾ | **Linda's Colin (IRE)**[23] 6020 2-8-10 — NCallan 7<br>(PWD'Arcy) *sn prom: rdn over 1f out: led briefly ins fnl f: kpt on* **2/1**[1] | | 77 |
| 6U02 | 3 | ½ | **Tranquilizer**[20] 6077 2-8-2 69 — (t) JQuinn 4<br>(DJCoakley) *a.p: short of room and swtchd lft over 1f out: ev ch ins fnl f: no ex nr fin* **9/1** | | 69+ |
| 300 | 4 | hd | **Red River Rock (IRE)**[20] 6078 2-8-13 75 — CCatlin 1<br>(CTinkler) *led tl hdd and no ex ins fnl f* **10/1** | | 79 |
| 000 | 5 | 1 | **Sol Rojo**[5] 6393 2-8-10 — VSlattery 6<br>(JAOsborne) *mid-div: outpcd 3f out: rllied and making hdwy whn short of room ins fnl f: no ex* **20/1** | | 74 |
| 06U4 | 6 | 2½ | **Mel's Moment (USA)**[11] 6291 2-8-13 74 — SWKelly 8<br>(MrsAJPerrett) *trckd ldr: ev ch 2f out tl hrd rdn wknd ins fnl f* **7/2**[2] | | 71 |
| | 7 | 1¾ | **Innpursuit** 2-8-10 — SDrowne 2<br>(JMPEustace) *mid-div: rdn over 3f out: no hdwy fnl 2f* **14/1** | | 65 |
| | 8 | 5 | **Inn For The Dancer** 2-8-7 — JFEgan 12<br>(JAGlover) *s.i.s: sn rdn: a towards rr* **40/1** | | 52 |
| 0 | 9 | ½ | **Definitely Royal (IRE)**[17] 6158 2-8-8 — MHenry 3<br>(RMHCowell) *s.i.s: hld up: a bhd* **50/1** | | 52 |
| 0 | 10 | 3 | **Madame Fatale (IRE)**[21] 6067 2-8-3 ow1 — TPQueally 11<br>(JeddO'Keeffe) *in tch: rdn 1/2-way: wknd 3f out* **50/1** | | 40 |
| 0 | 11 | 6 | **Whirling**[19] 6111 2-8-2 — JMackay 10<br>(JGGiven) *prom early on outside: sn bhd* **66/1** | | 27 |
| 05 | 12 | 5 | **Sadie's Star (IRE)**[31] 5856 2-8-5 — LisaJones 9<br>(MDods) *prom tl wknd 3f out* **20/1** | | 20 |
| | 13 | 28 | **Suncliff** 2-8-7 — (b[1]) DAllan 13<br>(MrsADuffield) *bhd and sn rdn: t.o* **66/1** | | — |

1m 53.61s — 13 Ran SP% **116.8**
Speed ratings: CSF £14.08 TOTE £5.20: £2.50, £2.10, £2.30; EX 9.50.
**Owner** Faisal Salman **Bred** Gestut Fahrhof **Trained** Newmarket, Suffolk

**FOCUS**
An average maiden but fairly decent for the track. The winner is progressing and can rate higher.

**NOTEBOOK**
**Kangrina** had finished two and a half lengths behind Linda's Colin on identical terms on her previous start, but her trainer was clearly not worried about taking him on again. Brought with a decisive late challenge, she looks to be improving with racing and shapes as though she will get farther in handicap company.
**Linda's Colin(IRE)** looked to have been found an ideal opening but, having finally got to the lead inside the last, he soon relinquished it to the winner, whom he had beaten by two and a half lengths on his previous start. He has the ability to win a similar race but is vulnerable to something with a bit more potential.
**Tranquilizer**, having her fifth start, looked to be flattered at Bath last time and was unable to take advantage of this lesser opposition.
**Red River Rock(IRE)** tried to make all the running, which has proved very difficult at this track since the new Polytrack surface was put down.
**Sol Rojo** shapes as though he will be suited by farther in handicap company.
**Mel's Moment(USA)** had looked likely to appreciate the step up in trip, but he appeared to find this extra furlong and a half too far.

## 6480 LADBROKES.COM H'CAP — 7f 32y(P)
8:00 (8:00) (E3) (0-77,75) 3-Y-O+ — £3,432 (£1,056; £528; £264) Stalls High

| Form | | | Horse | | RPR |
|---|---|---|---|---|---|
| 0050 | 1 | | **Up Tempo (IRE)**[140] 2899 6-9-4 72 — (b) NCallan 1<br>(KARyan) *mid-div on ins: rdn 3f out and sn mde hdwy: led wl ins fnl f: drvn out* **11/2**[2] | | 84 |
| 0001 | 2 | 1½ | **Stormy Nature (IRE)**[21] 6064 3-9-0 70 — SSanders 12<br>(PWHarris) *hld up in rr: hdwy on outside over 2f out: r.o u.p to go 2nd post* **9/2**[1] | | 78 |
| 6014 | 3 | shd | **Samuel Charles**[21] 6062 6-9-2 75 — BSwarbrick(5) 9<br>(WMBrisbourne) *in tch: led 2f out: hrd rdn and hdd wl ins fnl f: no ex and lost 2nd post* **7/1** | | 83 |
| 2140 | 4 | 2½ | **Templet (USA)**[36] 5768 4-9-2 70 — (b) PHanagan 11<br>(ISemple) *s.i.s and outpcd: wl in rr tl hdwy on outside wl over 1f out: styd on: nvr nrr* **10/1** | | 72 |
| -150 | 5 | 2 | **West Highland Way (IRE)**[44] 5582 3-9-2 75 — TEaves(3) 3<br>(ISemple) *bhd: rdn over 2f out: styd on fnl 2f: nvr nr to chal* **20/1** | | 71 |
| 6503 | 6 | 1¼ | **H Harrison (IRE)**[28] 5937 4-9-6 74 — (p) LVickers 10<br>(IWMcinnes) *hld up in touc: wnt 2nd 2f out: edgd lft and wknd fnl f* **13/2**[3] | | 67 |
| 4450 | 7 | 3 | **Musical Gift**[172] 1275 4-9-1 69 — TPQueally 8<br>(GAHuffer) *bhd: rdn and c wd into st: nvr nr to chal* **14/1** | | 54 |
| 2040 | 8 | 1¾ | **Blue Knight (IRE)**[11] 6293 5-9-2 70 — SWKelly 2<br>(PHowling) *hld up towards rr: rdn over 2f out: nvr on terms* **33/1** | | 51 |
| 0000 | 9 | 1¾ | **Zariano**[33] 5841 4-9-2 70 — SDrowne 5<br>(RMStronge) *led after 1f: hdd 5f out: wknd over 2f out* **25/1** | | 46 |
| 1063 | 10 | 1¼ | **Sewmuch Character**[21] 6066 5-9-0 68 — DSweeney 6<br>(MBlanshard) *sn trckd ldr: led 5f out: rdn over 2f out and sn hdd: wknd qckly* **8/1** | | 41 |
| 0000 | 11 | 8 | **Aventura (IRE)**[14] 6210 4-8-9 68 — PMakin(5) 4<br>(SRBowring) *led for 1f: wknd wl over 2f out* **10/1** | | 20 |
| 3105 | 12 | 5 | **Zanjeer**[71] 4903 4-8-12 69 — THamilton(3) 7<br>(NWilson) *trckd ldr after 2f: wknd rapidly 2f out* **9/1** | | 8 |

1m 31.0s
**WFA** 3 from 4yo+ 2lb — 12 Ran SP% **116.9**
Speed ratings: CSF £29.21 CT £179.16 TOTE £7.80: £2.60, £2.40, £2.50; EX 36.80.
**Owner** Yorkshire Racing Club & Derek Blackhurst **Bred** T Burns **Trained** Hambleton, N Yorks
■ The first time Neil Callan has reached 100 winners in a season.

**FOCUS**
A fair handicap but a good pace on and most of the principals came from off the pace. The third indicates the level of the form.

**NOTEBOOK**
**Up Tempo(IRE)** appreciates a decent pace off which to challenge and he had that here. Returning from a three and a half-month absence, he was racing off an 11lb higher mark than when last seen on the All-Weather, but he does run well on sand, having now won three times and finished placed four times from ten starts.
**Stormy Nature(IRE)** usually races prominently but, from her wide draw, she was held up on this occasion. That proved a blessing given that the leaders all hit the wall, and she came with a good late run to claim second.
**Samuel Charles** is in good form at present and did best of those who raced up with the decent pace. *Official explanation: jockey said gelding lugged to the right in the closing stages, in behind the eventual winner, making it impossible for him to continue pushing with the same degree of vigour*
**Templet(USA)**, a winner over nine furlongs in the summer, found this trip on the short side.
**West Highland Way(IRE)**, making his All-Weather debut, never got into a position to challenge and will appreciate a return to a mile.
**H Harrison(IRE)** was slightly disappointing as he is currently fairly handicapped and had conditions to suit.

## 6481 LADBROKES.COM MAIDEN STKS — 1m 1f 103y(P)
8:30 (8:32) (D3) 3-Y-O+ — £3,432 (£1,056; £528; £264) Stalls Low

| Form | | | Horse | | RPR |
|---|---|---|---|---|---|
| 3 | 1 | | **Whirly Bird**[11] 6285 3-8-9 — SSanders 6<br>(MrsAJPerrett) *s.i.s: hld up towards rr: swtchd rt and hdwy over 2f out: rdn and r.o to ld ins fnl f: won gng away* **1/1**[1] | | 65+ |
| 56 | 2 | 2 | **Tromp**[127] 3261 3-9-0 — TPQueally 13<br>(DJCoakley) *hld up in tch: hdwy on outside 3f out: led 2f out: rdn and hdd ins fnl f: no ex* **12/1** | | 66 |
| 00 | 3 | 5 | **Irish Playwright (IRE)**[29] 5907 4-9-1 — (b[1]) DNolan(3) 10<br>(DGBridgwater) *trckd ldr: led after 2f: hdd 2f out: wknd fnl f* **25/1** | | 56 |
| 000 | 4 | 1½ | **Miss Merenda**[145] 2729 3-8-9 — JFEgan 9<br>(DECantillon) *bhd: rdn over 3f out: hdwy on outside wl over 1f out: sn edgd lft and nvr nr to chal* **10/1** | | 48 |
| 04 | 5 | 1¼ | **Dovedale**[20] 6082 4-8-13 — VSlattery 11<br>(MrsMaryHambro) *s.i.s and bhd: hdwy whn short of room appr fnl f: styd on ins: nvr nrr* **6/1**[3] | | 46 |
| 50 | 6 | 3½ | **Nopleazinu**[32] 5851 4-8-13 — GGibbons 2<br>(MrsNMacauley) *in tch tl wknd wl over 1f out* **33/1** | | 39 |
| | 7 | nk | **Boldini (USA)**[16] 3-9-0 — SDrowne 5<br>(MrsStefLiddiard) *in tch tl wknd over 2f out* **5/1**[2] | | 43 |
| 0 | 8 | 1¼ | **Caspian Lake (IRE)**[19] 6130 3-8-11 — LPKeniry(3) 7<br>(MrsLCJewell) *trckd ldrs: wnt 2nd 3f out: wknd appr fnl f* **66/1** | | 40 |
| | 9 | nk | **Won Of A Few** 4-8-11 — AKirby(7) 4<br>(MWigham) *slowly away and in rr tl sme over 3f out: sn wknd* **33/1** | | 40 |
| 06 | 10 | nk | **Rambo Blue**[20] 6082 4-9-4 — JQuinn 8<br>(AWCarroll) *mid-div on outside: hdwy 4f out: wknd over 2f out* **12/1** | | 39 |
| / | 11 | ¾ | **Celtic Tanner (IRE)**[30] 5-9-4 — SHitchcott 12<br>(DJWintle) *led for 2f: wknd 3f out* **40/1** | | 38 |
| 0 | 12 | 20 | **Delta Star**[36] 5770 4-8-13 — NCallan 1<br>(KARyan) *trckd ldrs: rdn over 3f out: sn bhd* **20/1** | | — |
| | 13 | 3½ | **Archie Clarke (GER)** 4-9-4 — DSweeney 3<br>(JGallagher) *hld up towards: rr: rdn over 3f out: sn btn* **33/1** | | — |

2m 5.17s
**WFA** 3 from 4yo+ 4lb — 13 Ran SP% **126.8**
Speed ratings: CSF £15.13 TOTE £2.20: £1.20, £2.50, £6.90; EX 19.70.
**Owner** Woodcote Stud Ltd **Bred** Woodcote Stud Ltd **Trained** Pulborough, W Sussex

**FOCUS**
A really modest maiden and an ideal opportunity for well-bred Whirly Bird to get off the mark. The third and fourth proved the line to the level of the form, but it may be slightly high.

**NOTEBOOK**
**Whirly Bird**, a half-sister to 2003 Oaks fourth Inchberry, took a while to get into top gear but she put the matter beyond doubt inside the final furlong, winning going away. She looks likely to progress with racing and, in time, will appreciate a step up in trip.
**Tromp** made his bid for glory turning into the straight and had all but the winner in trouble. He was eventually run out of it but the step up in trip suited and he looks capable of winning a similar race.
**Irish Playwright(IRE)** raced far more prominently than he had in his first two starts and the blinkers appeared to have a positive effect.
**Miss Merenda** ran her best race to date on her All-Weather debut and handicaps could provide her with better opportunities.
**Dovedale** needs farther than this on the Flat and is now eligible for handicaps.
**Boldini(USA)**, whose last three starts were over hurdles, wore a visor over timber, but has been without the headgear in his starts on the Flat.

## 6482 LADBROKESPOKER.COM H'CAP — 5f 216y(P)
9:00 (9:01) (E3) (0-77,74) 3-Y-0+ — £3,443 (£1,059; £529; £264) Stalls Low

Form — RPR
0413 **1** **Flying Bantam (IRE)**[14] 6222 3-9-6 **73** ... PHanagan 3 — 89
(RAFahey) *mid-div in tch on ins: rdn over 3f out: r.o to ld wl ins fnl f: drvn out* — **5/1**[2]
3050 **2** *nk* **Kingsmaite**[20] 6094 3-9-0 **72** ...(b) PMakin(5) 5 — 87
(SRBowring) *a in tch: led appr fnl f: rdn and hdd wl ins: kpt on* — **16/1**
5006 **3** *3 1/2* **Bridgewater Boys**[14] 6222 3-9-3 **70** ...(b) NCallan 8 — 75
(KARyan) *hmpd and swtchd rt after 2f: rdn 1/2-way: hdwy 2f out: kpt on fnl f: nvr nrr* — **7/1**
5002 **4** *1 1/4* **Cherokee Nation**[14] 6222 3-9-2 **69** ... JFEgan 1 — 70
(PWD'Arcy) *trckd ldr: led 2f out: hdd appr fnl f: wknd ins* — **11/2**[3]
0240 **5** *1/2* **Jilly Why (IRE)**[12] 6267 3-8-12 **70** ... BSwarbrick(5) 9 — 69
(MsDeborahJEvans) *a abt same position: one pce ins fnl 2f* — **10/1**
4000 **6** *1/2* **Hilites (IRE)**[43] 5603 3-9-4 **71** ...(p) SWhitworth 12 — 69
(JSMoore) *outpcd and in rr: styd on fnl f: nvr nrr* — **22/1**
0000 **7** *nk* **Blakeshall Quest**[11] 6293 4-9-0 **69** ...(v) DNolan(3) 2 — 66
(RBrotherton) *hld up in rr: nvr on terms* — **28/1**
0020 **8** *1* **Smirfys Systems**[42] 5631 5-9-7 **73** ... SWKelly 13 — 67
(WMBrisbourne) *trckd ldrs: ev ch 2f out: wknd ent fnl f* — **10/1**
4002 **9** *shd* **Willhewiz**[21] 6066 4-9-4 **73** ... LPKeniry(3) 11 — 67
(RMStronge) *led tl hdd 2f out: rdn and wknd 1f out* — **8/1**
6000 **10** *3 1/2* **Cashel Mead**[28] 5952 4-9-4 **70** ... LisaJones 7 — 53
(JLSpearing) *in tch to 1/2-way: eased whn btn ins fnl f* — **18/1**
0060 **11** *nk* **Beejay**[14] 6222 3-8-13 **71** ... NDeSouza(5) 4 — 53
(PFICole) *in tch tl hmpd after 2f: sn bhd* — **16/1**
2212 **12** *9* **Mistral Sky**[11] 6293 5-9-8 **74** ...(v) SDrowne 6 — 29
(MrsStefLiddiard) *sn lost pl and wl bhd fr 1/2-way: eased whn btn wl over 1f out* — **3/1**[1]

1m 15.81s
**WFA** 3 from 4yo+ 1lb — **12** Ran SP% **123.7**
Speed ratings: CSF £86.30 CT £584.04 TOTE £7.20: £1.80, £6.40, £2.90; EX 138.40.
**Owner** The Matthewman Partnership **Bred** Robinski Bloodstock Limited **Trained** Musley Bank, N Yorks
■ Stewards Enquiry : L P Keniry seven-day ban: careless riding (Nov 15-17, 19-20, 22-23)

**FOCUS**
An ordinary handicap in which there was some trouble early on as Willhewiz crossed over to lead from his wide draw and caused interference to a number of horses. Despite this the race should work out overall.

**NOTEBOOK**
**Flying Bantam(IRE)** had two lengths to find with Cherokee Nation on their last meeting, but he was 3lb better off at the weights and turned the form around comprehensively. Whether he can cope with a rise in the handicap though, remains to be seen.
**Kingsmaite** stays farther than this but is perfectly effective at this trip. He finished clear of the rest and can win a similar race off this sort of mark.
**Bridgewater Boys**, who was one of those done no favours by the manoeuvre of Willhewiz, has won off a higher mark than this on turf, but he does not look quite as good on the All-Weather.
**Cherokee Nation** had finished in front of the winner last time and really should have got closer to that rival on just 3lb worse terms.
**Jilly Why(IRE)** may be beginning to feel the effects of a busy time of it over the last two months.
**Willhewiz** got to the front from his wide draw but caused a concertina effect of interference in the process. That manoeuvre cost his rider a seven-day ban.
**Mistral Sky** was one of the worst sufferers of the interference caused by Willhewiz's attempt to get to the front from his wide draw. *Official explanation: jockey said gelding suffered interference shortly after the start*

## 6483 LADBROKESGAMES.COM H'CAP — 1m 1f 103y(P)
9:30 (9:30) (F4) (0-62,64) 3-Y-0+ — £3,022 (£863; £431) Stalls Low

Form — RPR
6033 **1** **Regent's Secret (USA)**[20] 6097 4-9-0 **58** ... TEaves(3) 8 — 69
(JSGoldie) *hld up in rr: hdwy 2f out: str run to ld ins fnl f: r.o wl* — **9/2**[2]
5060 **2** *1 3/4* **Charmatic (IRE)**[22] 6047 3-9-3 **62** ... JQuinn 1 — 70
(JAGlover) *hld up in tch: hdwy and ev ch 1f out: nt pce of wnr* — **8/1**
0341 **3** *1* **Wrenlane**[12] 6271 3-9-5 **64** ... PHanagan 12 — 70
(RAFahey) *in tch: led 2f out: edgd lft and hdd jst ins fnl f: kpt on one pce* — **4/1**[1]
2000 **4** *nk* **Zawrak (IRE)**[39] 5713 5-8-13 **57** ...(p) JFMcDonald(3) 4 — 62
(IWMcinnes) *hld up and wl in rr: rdn over 2f out: gd hdwy on ins fnl f: nvr nrr* — **22/1**
00 **5** *3/4* **Inchdura**[20] 6096 6-9-6 **61** ... KimTinkler 3 — 64
(NTinkler) *a in tch: one pce fnl f* — **22/1**
006 **6** *1/2* **Easter Ogil (IRE)**[11] 6295 9-9-3 **58** ... LEnstone 13 — 60
(JaneSouthcombe) *bhd: rdn and hdwy over 1f out: edgd lft: r.o: nvr nr to chal* — **9/1**
2004 **7** *3/4* **Bond Millennium**[11] 6295 6-9-6 **61** ... FLynch 5 — 62
(BSmart) *hld up: hdwy on outside 2f out: nt qckn appr fnl f* — **11/2**[3]
0343 **8** *1/2* **Efrhina (IRE)**[23] 6025 4-9-5 **60** ... SDrowne 11 — 60
(MrsStefLiddiard) *mid-div: hdwy 2f out: rdn and nt qckn fnl f* — **9/1**
6040 **9** *hd* **Sarraaf (IRE)**[14] 6210 8-9-4 **59** ... SWKelly 7 — 59
(ISemple) *hld up in rr: hdwy whn swtchd rt over 1f out: carried lft and no ch after* — **7/1**
0000 **10** *hd* **Surdoue**[24] 6013 4-9-5 **60** ... NPollard 2 — 59
(PHowling) *led for 1f: in tch tl rdn and wknd appr fnl f* — **22/1**
0130 **11** *2* **Yorker (USA)**[14] 6220 6-9-5 **60** ...(b) NCallan 10 — 55
(MsDeborahJEvans) *hld up: hdwy 3f wknd 1f out* — **14/1**
6000 **12** *3 1/2* **Quintoto**[42] 5657 4-8-13 **57** ... THamilton(3) 6 — 45
(RAFahey) *led after 1f: hdd 2f out: sn wknd* — **33/1**
000 **13** *27* **Dave (IRE)**[49] 5473 3-9-2 **61** ... GBaker 9 — —
(JRBest) *t.k.h: prom tl rdn and wknd wl over 1f out: eased: t.o* — **20/1**

2m 4.47s
**WFA** 3 from 4yo+ 4lb — **13** Ran SP% **124.6**
Speed ratings: CSF £38.86 CT £161.58 TOTE £7.30: £2.80, £2.10, £2.10; EX 82.60 Place 6 £25.95, Place 5 £18.94..
**Owner** Mrs M Craig **Bred** Adena Springs **Trained** Uplawmoor, E Renfrews

**FOCUS**
A moderate race and, although the form is not strong, it looks sound.

**NOTEBOOK**
**Regent's Secret(USA)** had not managed to get his head in front in 30 previous starts, but he had been placed in numerous races and deserved this first win. This longer trip suited and he appears suited by the Polytrack surface, having previously run well at Lingfield.
**Charmatic(IRE)**, back down to the mark off which she won at Beverley in the spring, ran a solid race in defeat. She looks sure to pay her way on the surface over the winter.
**Wrenlane** made his bid for glory turning for home but in the end had to settle for third. He was 4lb higher for his classified race win and seemed to run his race with no excuse.
**Zawrak(IRE)**, who has been in the doldrums recently, bounced back to form on her return to the Polytrack with cheekpieces fitted for the first time.
**Inchdura** has dropped 11lb in the handicap this term but still looks too high in the weights.
**Easter Ogil(IRE)** is fairly handicapped at the moment but is struggling to find his best form.
**Dave(IRE)** *Official explanation: jockey said gelding ran free early on*
T/Plt: £25.50 to a £1 stake. Pool £36,224.55. 1,036.10 winning tickets. T/Qpdt: £26.40 to a £1 stake. Pool £1,604.30. 44.80 winning tickets. JS

# LONE STAR PARK
Saturday, October 30

**OFFICIAL GOING: Dirt course - fast; turf course - yielding**
The pace bias on the dirt track favoured those who raced prominently and it proved impossible to successfully challenge from way off the gallop.

## 6484a BREEDERS' CUP DISTAFF (GRADE 1) (F&M) (DIRT) — 1m 1f
6:20 (6:21) 3-Y-0+ — £581,006 (£223,464; £122,905; £63,687)

RPR
**1** **Ashado (USA)**[28] 3-8-7 ... JRVelazquez 1 — 117
(TPletcher, U.S.A) *wl grwn, str, lw, prom in 4th on rail, 3rd str, pushed along to chal over 1f out, rdn to ld fnl f, rdn clr fnl 100yds, drvn* — **3/1**[1]
**2** *1 1/4* **Storm Flag Flying (USA)**[21] 4-8-11 ... JDBailey 7 — 114
(CMcgaugheyIii, U.S.A) *lw, towards rr, tk clsr order fr halfway, 6th str, rdn over 1f out, fin strongly fnl 100 yds to take 2nd cl hme* — **4/1**[2]
**3** *nk* **Stellar Jayne (USA)**[29] 3-8-7 ...(b) RAlbarado 11 — 113
(DWayneLukas, U.S.A) *last, gd hdwy fr 4f out to be 4th and chal str, rdn and ran on fr over 1f out, went 2nd 150yds out til lost 2nd fnl strides* — **10/1**
**4** *1 1/2* **Tamweel (USA)**[20] 4-8-11 ... RDouglas 3 — 110
(WCatalano, U.S.A) *led, pressed entering straight, ran on til headed final furlong, kept on* — **14/1**
**5** *1 3/4* **Island Fashion (USA)**[27] 4-8-11 ...(b) KJohn 10 — 107
(MPolanco, U.S.A) *mid-div, gd hdwy on outside 2 1/2f out to press ldr str, stayed on at one pace til no extra close home* — **5/1**
**6** *3 3/4* **Indy Groove (USA)**[32] 4-8-11 ... MGuidry 8 — 99
(TProctor, U.S.A) *raced in close 3rd, pushed along approaching straight, hampered and 5th straight, no extra* — **50/1**
**7** *1* **Elloluv (USA)**[27] 4-8-11 ...(b) CNakatani 2 — 97
(CraigDollase, U.S.A) *mid-division, 7th straight, unable to quicken from over 1f out* — **16/1**
**8** *nk* **Nebraska Tornado (USA)**[28] 5940 4-8-11 ... EPrado 5 — 97
(AFabre, France) *reluctant to load, raced in 2nd, lost place over 2 1/2f out, soon weakened* — **6/1**
**9** *nk* **Society Selection (USA)**[21] 3-8-7 ... CVelasquez 4 — 96
(HAJerkens, U.S.A) *mid-division, 9th and weakening straight* — **9/2**[3]
**10** *1/2* **Hollywood Story (USA)**[119] 3-8-7 ...(b) TBaze 6 — 95
(JShirreffs, U.S.A) *lw, towards rear, dropped to last and outpaced 3 1/2f out* — **33/1**
**11** *1 3/4* **Bare Necessities (USA)**[56] 5-8-11 ... JValdiviaJr 9 — 92
(FrankJKirby, U.S.A) *towards rear, weakened from 4f out* — **40/1**

1m 48.26s
**WFA** 3 from 4yo+ 4lb — **11** Ran SP% **123.1**
Speed ratings: .
**Owner** Starlight Stables & P Saylor & J Martin **Bred** Aaron U Jones & Marie D Jones **Trained** USA

**FOCUS**
A strong, but open renewal of this filly and mares' event that was run at a furious pace. The winner smashed the track record and was crowned the champion three-year-old filly.

**NOTEBOOK**
**Ashado(USA)** , runner-up in the Juvenile Fillies' event at this meeting last year, was always in the perfect postion under Velazquez and when the gaps appeared in the straight she really flew home to score with plenty in hand. Breaking the track record, this was her ninth success from 14 outings to date and her third Grade One victory of the current campaign. She ends the season as the Champion three-year-old filly and may well stay in training next year.
**Storm Flag Flying(USA)** , winner of the Juvenile Fillies' event at this meeting in 2002, stayed on all too late in the straight and never really looked a serious threat to the winner. Granted she was given a fair bit to do, but this was still a very solid effort and she again left the impression that this trip does stretch her stamina. This was her last race and she will be very valuable for breeding purposes.
**Stellar Jayne(USA)** , a dual Grade One winner over this trip at Belmont Park this year, ran her heart out and was well suited by the strong pace.
**Tamweel(USA)** , who came into this with some solid form yet had not scored in Graded company previously, turned in a valiant effort and did best of those to force the pace.
**Nebraska Tornado(USA)** played up at the gates and ran too keenly throught the early stages. She had no more to give in the straight and has to go down as disappointing. This was probably her last run and she is due to remain stateside for breeding purposes.

## 6485a BREEDERS' CUP JUVENILE FILLIES (GRADE 1) (FILLIES) (DIRT) — 1m 110y
6:55 (6:56) 2-Y-0 — £290,503 (£111,732; £61,453; £31,844)

RPR
**1** **Sweet Catomine (USA)**[28] 2-8-7 ...(b) CNakatani 10 — 119+
(JCanani, U.S.A) *str, lengthy, scope, lw, disp 6th, nt clr run & stumbled over 2f out, sn rcvrd, 4th str, led jst ins fnl f, ran on strongly* — **2/1**[1]
**2** *3 3/4* **Balletto (UAE)**[21] 2-8-7 ... JDBailey 1 — 111
(TAlbertrani, U.S.A) *str, lw, raced in 3rd, 2nd & ridden straight, ran on one pace under pressure final furlong* — **5/1**[3]
**3** *1 1/4* **Runway Model (USA)**[22] 2-8-7 ... RBejarano 4 — 109
(BFlint, U.S.A) *lw, mid-division, stayed on inside & 3rd straight, boxed in on rail from distance, switched out 100yds out, ran on* — **12/1**

4 ¾ **Sis City (USA)**[21] 2-8-7 ............ JRVelazquez 7 107
(RDutrowJr, U.S.A) *pressed leader, led 4f out to just inside final f, one pace* **18/1**

5 nk **Dance Away Capote (USA)**[22] 2-8-7 ............ RADominguez 6 106
(HGMotion, U.S.A) *towards rear early, headway on inside 4f out, 10th straight, 5th 1f out, kept on under pressure* **14/1**

6 1 ¼ **Sharp Lisa (USA)**[22] 2-8-7 ............ LDettori 12 104
(DougO'Neill, U.S.A) *always in touch, close 5th on outside straight, soon one pace* **10/1**

7 2 ¼ **Culinary (USA)**[41] 2-8-7 ............ CHMarquezJr 5 99
(MStidham, U.S.A) *raced in 4th to over 2f out, 6th straight, soon beaten* **8/1**

8 hd **Play With Fire (USA)**[21] 2-8-7 ............ PDay 13 99
(MHennig, U.S.A) *always outpaced* **33/1**

9 3 **Sense Of Style (USA)**[22] 2-8-7 ............ EPrado 9 93
(PLBiancone, U.S.A) *slowly into stride, always in rear* **4/1**[2]

10 1 **Culture Clash (USA)**[28] 2-8-7 ............(b) KJohn 11 91
(MPolanco, U.S.A) *always towards rear* **50/1**

11 5 ¼ **Mona Lisa**[35] 5779 2-8-7 ............ JPSpencer 8 81
(APO'Brien, Ire) *slowly into stride, always in rear* **16/1**

12 2 ¼ **Higher World (USA)**[27] 2-8-7 ............ PHusbands 2 76
(MCasse, Canada) *led to 4f out, weakened over 2f out* **33/1**

1m 41.65s **12** Ran SP% **123.5**
Speed ratings: .
**Owner** Mr & Mrs Martin J Wygod **Bred** Mr & Mrs Martin J Wygod **Trained** USA

■ Sweet Catomine recorded the fastest time in the history of this race, and posted a quicker time that the colts later on the card.

**FOCUS**
A cracking renewal of this event with a brilliant winner in Sweet Catomine.

**NOTEBOOK**
**Sweet Catomine(USA)**, a Californian-based filly, had little trouble collecting the Del Mar Debutante and Oak Leaf Stakes at Santa Anita en route to this - the same path taken by last year's winner Halfbridled. She worked the house down at Santa in her preparation - recording the second-fastest gallop figure of 130 the previous weekend. Rightly made favourite, she took a perfect sit in behind the pace and managed to overcome being squeezed out as she was making ground to power clear, putting up the fastest time in the race's history. A sizeable filly, she has the potential to be a household name stateside and her trainer, who has a remarkable record at the Breeders' Cup, is strongly considering taking the Kentucky Derby path, as opposed to the traditional Oaks route. It is not hard to see why considering her time was faster than that set by the colts in the Juvenile and she has the physical capacity to match the colts.
**Balletto(UAE)**, whose only defeat prior to this came when a slightly unlucky second behind Sense Of Style at Belmont in September, got back on track in the Frizette last time and would have run out a good winner of this any other year, but she appeared to run into something special. She stuck on well down the stretch without proving a match for the winner, but this improving filly is bred to stay further and she will be a realistic Kentucky Oaks candidate if doing well from two to three.
**Runway Model(USA)** was the most experienced filly in the line-up, with eight previous runs under her belt, and she acquitted herself well considering she was boxed on the rail when trying to come with a run. She lacks the scope of the front two and is more of a Grade Two filly.
**Sis City(USA)**, whose two victories had come at a lower level, finished behind Balletto in the Frizette and ran pretty much to form with that rival. Like the third, she will be more at home in a slightly lower grade, but she continues to improve.
**Dance Away Capote(USA)** had a bit to find with some of these on Keeneland form, but she stays this trip well and ran on past tiring rivals down the stretch to claim a creditable fifth. She wants further and there will be improvement to come next season, so may be the type to surprise a few in the Oaks.
**Sharp Lisa(USA)**, an impressive winner when waltzing home to win by six lengths on her debut over five and a half furlongs, was subsequently sold and handled the extra three furlongs well when caught close home behind Runaway Model at Keeneland most recently. She ran well enough in defeat without suggesting she is a Grade One filly and she will find easier opportunities, possibly back in distance.
**Culinary(USA)**, who beat Runway Model when scoring at Arlington last month, seemingly ran below form and will make up into a better three-year-old once she has had time to grow into herself.
**Sense Of Style(USA)**, below par when only fifth at Keeneland most recently, again failed to run to form and was never in the hunt.
**Mona Lisa**, a maiden coming into the race, was a little unlucky when fourth in the Fillies' Mile at Ascot last time, but was out of her depth here and never had any chance after a slow start.

## 6486a NETJETS BREEDERS' CUP MILE (GRADE 1) (TURF) 1m
7:35 (7:37) 3-Y-O+ **£488,045** (£187,709; £103,240; £53,479)

RPR

1 **Singletary (USA)**[21] 4-9-0 ............ DFlores 10 123
(DChatlosJr, U.S.A) *tall, str, lw, racd in 5th, hdwy and disp 2nd str, drvn to ld app fnl f, rdn and ran on strongly fnl f, driven out* **16/1**

2 ½ **Antonius Pius (USA)**[35] 5782 3-8-10 ............ JPSpencer 7 121
(APO'Brien, Ire) *lw, towards rr, drvn & hdwy app str, disp 4th str, rdn to chal 1f out, fin strongly & ev ch 100y out, no extra* **16/1**

3 1 ½ **Six Perfections (FR)**[76] 4795 4-8-11 ............ JDBailey 11 116+
(PBary, France) *mid-division, disputing 8th straight, ridden and ran on 1f out in centre to take 3rd on line* **9/2**[1]

4 nk **Soaring Free (CAN)**[41] 5686 5-9-0 ............ TKabel 4 118
(MFrostad, Canada) *led, headed approaching final furlong, ran on but lost 3rd on line* **16/1**

5 ¾ **Silver Tree (USA)**[21] 4-9-0 ............ EPrado 2 116
(WMott, U.S.A) *in touch disputing 6th, disputing 4th straight, ridden 1f out, ran on steadily to line* **25/1**

6 nk **Musical Chimes (USA)**[21] 4-8-11 ............ KDesormeaux 9 112
(NDrysdale, U.S.A) *mid-division, 11th straight, soon driven, never in challenging position* **16/1**

7 nk **Blackdoun (FR)**[54] 3-8-10 ............(b) CNakatani 13 114
(JCanani, U.S.A) *raced in last, pushed along approaching straight, stayed on steadily final furlong* **12/1**

8 nk **Diamond Green (FR)**[35] 5782 3-8-10 ............ LDettori 8 113
(AFabre, France) *held up in 13th, 10th straight, never dangerous* **12/1**

9 1 **Mr O'Brien (IRE)**[21] 5-9-0 ............ ECoa 14 112
(RobinLGraham, U.S.A) *in touch disputing 6th, driven and disputing 4th straight, one pace from over 1f out* **20/1**

10 nse **Whipper (USA)**[55] 5332 3-8-10 ............ CSoumillon 1 111
(RobertCollet, France) *lw, prominent in 4th on rail, driven and disputing 2nd entering straight, hard ridden final furlong, no extra* **6/1**[2]

11 nse **Nothing To Lose (USA)**[21] 4-9-0 ............(b) JRVelazquez 12 112
(RJFrankel, U.S.A) *held up in 11th, 12th and driven straight, never a threat* **6/1**[2]

12 ½ **Artie Schiller (USA)**[34] 3-8-10 ............ RMigliore 6 109+
(JJerkens, U.S.A) *towards rear, pushed along over 2 1/2f out, never in contention* **9/2**[1]

13 3 ¾ **Special Ring (USA)**[97] 7-9-0 ............(b) VEspinoza 3 102
(JCanani, U.S.A) *raced in close 3rd, pushed along 3f out and lost place, weakened* **9/1**[3]

14 3 ½ **Domestic Dispute (USA)**[28] 5986 4-9-0 ............ KJohn 5 94
(PGallagher, U.S.A) *racd in 2nd, pushed along and lost place over 2f out, hmpd appr str whn looking beaten, no danger after* **40/1**

1m 36.9s
**WFA** 3 from 4yo+ 3lb **14** Ran SP% **124.9**
Speed ratings: .
**Owner** Little Red Feather Racing **Bred** Disler Farms Ltd **Trained** USA

**FOCUS**
A typically competitive renewal of the Breeders' Cup Mile, but the pace was just ordinary and there were plenty of hard-luck stories, not least Antonius Pius and Six Perfections. Those two help to give the race a solid look but, given that Singletary was winning for the first time at this level, it does leave some doubts as to how good the form actually is.

**NOTEBOOK**
**Singletary(USA)**, at the age of four, finally made his mark in Grade One company and managed to do so at the expense of three of the best milers Europe had to offer. Although clearly raising his game for the big occasion, he still has to go down as a somewhat fortunate winner as both the second and third home enjoyed anything but trouble-free runs. He stays in training and could yet run again this season in Hollywood Park's Citation Handicap, while next year's campaign will be geared towards a follow-up bid in this race at Belmont Park.
**Antonius Pius(USA)**, below form in the Queen Elizabeth II Stakes at Ascot on his previous outing, came right back to form and probably should have gained his first success at the highest level. Everything went well for him in the early stages and he was ideally placed to make his challenge but, under a strong drive with the whip in Jamie Spencer's right hand, he hung to his left and then lugged in behind the eventual winner. It would be a little harsh to blame the jockey, but he admits himself things may have been different had he not hit the horse a third time, while had he switched whip hands the horse may not have been so inclined to hang. Whatever the case, the colt has an attitude problem, but some serious ability to go with it and, if persevered with, he can surely make his mark at this level.
**Six Perfections(FR)**, last year's winner, had been trained for a follow-up bid but has gone winless all season in the process. She ran a good race, but did not get a clear passage and simply had too short a straight to get to the front two. She has been retired.
**Soaring Free(CAN)** has won ten of his last 11 starts in Canada, yet he had been unplaced on four of his previous five starts on a US track. Despite getting his own way up front at reasonable fractions, he was simply unable to sustain his effort and again just failed to make the frame.
**Silver Tree(USA)** met a little bit of trouble but was just not good enough.
**Musical Chimes(USA)** was very unlucky and may well have been in the frame with a clearer run.
**Blackdoun(FR)** ran much better than his finishing positions suggests as he was short of room on the final turn and had to come widest of all with his challenge.
**Diamond Green(FR)** found himself with a lot to do when the pace increased and did not get a clear run. He is better than this and is likely to stay in training.
**Mr O'Brien(IRE)** could not maintain his challenge in the straight.
**Whipper(USA)**, a beaten favourite and about a length behind Antonius Pius in the Prix du Moulin at Longchamp on his previous start, had since been trained for this race, but failed to deliver. He was in a lovely position for much of the way, but found very little when asked to make his challenge up the rail and put in a lacklustre display. Interestingly, he has shown all of his best form on a straight course. He is finished for the season and is not certain to stay in training next year.
**Nothing To Lose(USA)** could offer little in the straight; only Blackdoun came wider on the final turn.
**Artie Schiller(USA)** lost his winning chance when snatched up on the final bend and was by no means given a hard time when not getting much of a run in the straight.
**Special Ring(USA)** did not run his race and had to be snatched up when beaten.
**Domestic Dispute(USA)** was having just his second race on turf and this was asking too much of him.

## 6487a BREEDERS' CUP SPRINT (GRADE 1) (DIRT) 6f
8:10 (8:13) 3-Y-O+ **£307,933** (£118,436; £65,140; £33,754)

RPR

1 **Speightstown (USA)**[28] 5984 6-9-0 ............ JRVelazquez 2 126
(TPletcher, U.S.A) *lw, str, scope, prominent on inside in 4th, slipped through on rail to lead 1 1/2f out, ran on well* **4/1**[2]

2 1 ¼ **Kela (USA)**[76] 6-9-0 ............(b) JDBailey 5 122
(MMitchell, U.S.A) *towards rear, 10th on outside straight, stayed on well down outside to take 2nd final 50 yards* **7/2**[1]

3 ¾ **My Cousin Matt (USA)**[30] 5-9-0 ............ RADominguez 12 120
(JeffMullins, U.S.A) *9th early, headway on inside to go 4th straight, hard ridden to chase winner 110 yards out, lost 2nd final 50 yards* **40/1**

4 ½ **Bwana Charlie (USA)**[28] 3-8-11 ............ RMigliore 1 117
(SAsmussen, U.S.A) *gd sort, str, scope, lw, missed break, in rear, 11th straight on wide outside, stayed on final 1 1/2f, nearest finish* **25/1**

5 ¾ **Cajun Beat (USA)**[28] 5984 4-9-0 ............(b) CVelasquez 11 116
(RJFrankel, U.S.A) *in touch in 5th or 6th, 5th straight on outside, stayed on at same pace final 1 1/2f* **10/1**

6 hd **Clock Stopper (USA)**[22] 4-9-0 ............(b) PDay 7 116
(DStewart, U.S.A) *started slowly, last til headway 1 1/2f out, stayed on* **8/1**

7 hd **Champali (USA)**[22] 4-9-0 ............ RBejarano 3 115
(GregoryDFoley, U.S.A) *8th halfway, 7th straight, soon ridden and one pace* **13/2**

8 nk **Pt's Grey Eagle (USA)**[20] 3-8-11 ............(b) CNakatani 8 112
(CraigDollase, U.S.A) *missed break, outpaced in 12th, some late headway* **22/1**

9 nk **Gold Storm (USA)**[22] 4-9-0 ............(b) LTaylor 9 113
(CWBubbaCascio, U.S.A) *raced in 2nd, close 3rd on outside entering straight, went 2nd 1 1/2f out, lost 2nd 110 yards out, weakened* **16/1**

10 1 ½ **Midas Eyes (USA)**[56] 4-9-0 ............ EPrado 13 109
(RJFrankel, U.S.A) *7th halfway, 9th straight, never a factor* **5/1**[3]

11 3 ½ **Abbondanza (USA)**[28] 3-8-11 ............ ECoa 6 96
(TTullock, U.S.A) *led to 1 1/2f out, weakened* **33/1**

12 1 ¼ **Our New Recruit (USA)**[54] 5-9-0 ............ TBaze 4 95
(JWSadler, U.S.A) *prom but soon pushed along, disp 5th halfway, 7th whn hmpd and carried lft entering str, no danger after* **8/1**

13 8 ½ **Cuvee (USA)**[42] 3-8-11 ............ RAlbarado 10 67
(SAsmussen, U.S.A) *raced in 3rd, 6th straight, soon weakened* **33/1**

68.11 secs
**WFA** 3 from 4yo+ 1lb **13** Ran SP% **125.9**
Speed ratings: .
**Owner** Eugene & Laura Melnyk **Bred** Aaron U & Marie Jones **Trained** USA

**FOCUS**
Once again those held up a long way off the pace found it difficult to get involved.

**NOTEBOOK**
**Speightstown(USA)**, who in the absence of Pico Central set the standard, bagged a good position on the inside tracking the pace, before making his bid for glory at the entrance of the straight. Getting a gap on the field, he was able to hold off his rivals with a bit to spare, and although the track favoured his style of running, this was still a good performance.

**Kela(USA)** has done most of his racing over seven furlongs and a mile, so it was always likely that he would struggle to go the early pace. His style of racing, to be held up for a late run, also put him at a disadvantage on this pace-favouring track, so in the circumstances he ran really well.
**My Cousin Matt(USA)** recaptured some of his best form from a couple of years ago to finish in the frame. He stayed on well but was never going to threaten the winner.
**Bwana Charlie(USA)**, who had a lot to find at this level, came from a long way back after missing the break. Pushed very wide on the turn into the straight, he stayed on well past beaten horses.
**Cajun Beat(USA)**, off the track for six months following his below-par run in the Dubai Golden Shaheen, had looked in need of his reappearance outing four weeks earlier and ran much better this time. It was always going to be difficult for him to lead from his wide draw, though.
**Clock Stopper(USA)** merely stayed on past beaten horses.

## 6488a ALBERTO VO5 BREEDERS' CUP FILLY & MARE TURF (GRADE 1) (F&M) 1m 3f

**8:45** (8:48) 3-Y-0+ **£409,609** (£157,542; £86,648; £44,899)

RPR

1 **Ouija Board**[27] 5981 3-8-6 ........ KFallon 5 121
(EALDunlop) *lw, racd in tch, 4th halfway, hdwy 3f out, 3rd and gng wl str, ran on strongly to ld over 1f out, pushed out* **10/11**[1]

2 *1 ½* **Film Maker (USA)**[28] 5983 4-8-11 ........ (b) JRVelazquez 3 117
(HGMotion, U.S.A) *raced in 2nd, pushed along 1 1/2f out, ridden over 1f out, ran on but no chance with winner* **20/1**

3 *nk* **Wonder Again (USA)**[28] 5983 5-8-11 ........ EPrado 12 117
(JamesJToner, U.S.A) *held up, disputing 5th straight, stayed on steadily to take 3rd but never challenged leaders* **12/1**

4 *2 ¾* **Moscow Burning (USA)**[28] 5983 4-8-11 ........ JValdiviaJr 4 113
(JCassidy, U.S.A) *lw, led, 4 lengths clear after 3f, pushed along approaching straight, ran on til headed over 1f out, kept on at one pace* **20/1**

5 *1 ¼* **Yesterday (IRE)**[27] 5978 4-8-11 ........ (v) JPSpencer 11 111
(APO'Brien, Ire) *lw, mid-division, driven and headway 2 1/2f out, 4th straight, unable to quicken under pressure* **8/1**[3]

6 *1* **Shaconage (USA)**[20] 4-8-11 ........ RBejarano 6 109
(MShirota, U.S.A) *raced in last, disputing 7th straight, stayed on final furlong but never a threat* **50/1**

7 *¾* **Light Jig**[28] 5987 4-8-11 ........ RDouglas 7 108
(RJFrankel, U.S.A) *held up, disputing 7th straight, ridden and no impression from over 1f out* **5/1**[2]

8 *½* **Riskaverse (USA)**[28] 5983 5-8-11 ........ CVelasquez 9 107
(PatrickJKelly, U.S.A) *in touch, disputing 5th straight, ridden over 1f out, unable to quicken* **12/1**

9 *1* **Super Brand (SAF)**[20] 5-8-10 ........ PDay 1 104
(KMclaughlin, U.S.A) *in touch til lost place over 2f out, one pace in straight* **33/1**

10 *5 ½* **Katdogawn**[28] 5987 4-8-11 ........ KDesormeaux 2 97
(JCassidy, U.S.A) *held up, driven entering straight, never a factor* **40/1**

11 *1* **Megahertz**[152] 5-8-11 ........ CNakatani 10 95
(RJFrankel, U.S.A) *mid-division, never a threat* **11/1**

12 *nk* **Aubonne (GER)**[28] 5983 4-8-11 ........ JDBailey 8 95
(ELibaud, France) *raced in 3rd til lost place 3f out, weakened* **18/1**

2m 18.25s
**WFA** 3 from 4yo+ 6lb **12** Ran SP% **126.0**
Speed ratings: .
**Owner** Lord Derby **Bred** Stanley Estate And Stud Co **Trained** Newmarket, Suffolk

**FOCUS**
A slow gallop saw few get into the argument from off the pace. It still rates as an excellent effort by Ouija Board, who could not have been more impressive on ground slower then ideal.

**NOTEBOOK**
**Ouija Board** , a slightly unlucky yet highly-respectable third in the Arc de Triomphe last time, was soon handy from her favourable draw. She was always travelling with ease before being brought wide off the home turn and quickening impressively in the straight for a cosy success on ground slower than ideal. This stamped her among the best fillies in the world, and the best at her distance, so the decision to swerve the Turf and take up this challenge was a smart move by connections. Set to stay in training, she could hit even greater heights as a four-year-old, and looks set to bid for the Summer Triple Crown and another tilt at the Arc en route to a return to this meeting, possibly for a crack at the boys in the Turf.
**Film Maker(USA)** , slightly unlucky when fourth in the Grade One Flower Bowl last time, was always handy and had every chance, but could not muster the speed to trouble Ouija Bourd when it mattered in the straight. This was a career-best effort however, and she is better suited to a more galloping track and faster ground.
**Wonder Again(USA)** , a dual Grade One winner, finished strongly from off the pace and ran a very solid race. She did by far the best of those drawn in double figures.
**Moscow Burning(USA)** , who just failed to make all in the Grade One Flower Bowl last time, again made a bold bid from the front yet was a sitting duck for the finishers in the straight. This was another solid effort, however.
**Yesterday(IRE)** , third in this race last year and sporting the first-time visor, was not disgraced from her wide draw. She would have been closer with a stronger gallop, but has not looked quite the same filly this year in a limited campaign.
**Light Jig** , an impressive winner of the Grade One Yellow Ribbon last time and largely considered the best Turf filly in the US, failed to show her usual turn of foot when asked to improve from off the pace and has to go down as disappointing.

## 6489a BESSEMER TRUST BREEDERS' CUP JUVENILE (GRADE 1) (C&G) (DIRT) 1m 110y

**9:20** (9:24) 2-Y-0 **£435,754** (£167,598; £92,179; £47,765)

RPR

1 **Wilko (USA)**[35] 5778 2-8-10 ........ LDettori 8 120
(JNoseda) *cl up on outside, 4th and pushed along over 2 1/2f out, rdn 2f out, styd on dourly down outside to ld 100y out, drvn out* **20/1**

2 *¾* **Afleet Alex (USA)**[21] 2-8-10 ........ JRose 3 119
(TFRitchey, U.S.A) *in rr, hdwy on outside to press ldrs 3f out, rdn ent str, ev ch on outside 1 1/2f out to 100 yards out, kept on* **10/3**[3]

3 *nk* **Sun King (USA)**[21] 2-8-10 ........ EPrado 1 118
(NZito, U.S.A) *lw, scope, towards rr, hdwy on ins after 3f, hdwy on rail to ld narrowly under 3f out, pressed til hdd 100y out, one pace* **15/2**

4 *1 ¼* **Consolidator (USA)**[21] 2-8-10 ........ RBejarano 4 115
(DWayneLukas, U.S.A) *raced in 2nd til led briefly 3f out, remained prominent between rivals and still every chance til weakened 120 yards out* **9/1**

5 *1 ½* **Roman Ruler (USA)**[27] 2-8-10 ........ CNakatani 2 112
(BBaffert, U.S.A) *str, lengthy, lw, hld up in rr, hdwy on ins to chase ldrs in 5th ent str, rdn and switched rt over 1f out, unable to quicke* **2/1**[1]

6 *1 ¼* **Proud Accolade (USA)**[21] 2-8-10 ........ JRVelazquez 6 110
(TPletcher, U.S.A) *in touch in 4th or 5th, 6th straight, soon ridden and unable to quicken* **11/4**[2]

7 *9 ¾* **Twice Unbridled (USA)**[27] 2-8-10 ........ (b) VEspinoza 7 89
(DJensen, U.S.A) *led til headed and squeezed up 3f out, in rear from 2 1/2f out* **66/1**

8 *1 ¼* **Scandinavia (USA)**[35] 5778 2-8-10 ........ JPSpencer 5 87
(APO'Brien, Ire) *missed break, recovered to race in 5th on outside on first turn, relegated to last 4f out, no factor final 3f* **12/1**

1m 42.09s **8** Ran SP% **118.8**
Speed ratings: .
**Owner** J Paul Reddam & Susan Roy **Bred** Ro Parra **Trained** Newmarket, Suffolk
■ With just two runners, this was Britain's smallest ever Breeders' Cup team, but both were victorious.

**FOCUS**
A shock British success but there looked no fluke about it.

**NOTEBOOK**
**Wilko(USA)**, a smart juvenile on turf back home, had nevertheless been beaten on each occasion he had set foot in Pattern company. He is, however, bred for dirt and was far more battle-hardened than his rivals, having already had ten starts. Jumping off well, he got into a good early position and, when it came down to stamina in the straight, he was not found wanting. He will remain in the US now and be trained by Craig Dollase in California, and the Kentucky Derby will be the aim.
**Afleet Alex(USA)** was popular in the market but he missed the break and that probably cost him. He made steady progress down the back straight before being brought with what looked a well-timed run entering the straight, but could not see off his two rivals on his inside and could do little to repel the late challenge of the winner.
**Sun King(USA)**, who had finished a length and a quarter behind Afleet Alex in the Champagne Stakes last time, got a little closer to that rival, and turned the tables on their conqueror that day Proud Accolade.
**Consolidator(USA)**, the most experienced American runner in the race, had won a relatively weak Grade One race last time. He ran a solid race.
**Roman Ruler(USA)**, who entered the race with a tall reputation, was a disappointing favourite. His chance was not helped by the fact that he took a keen hold in rear though, and although travelling well enough entering the straight, he found little when asked for his effort.
**Proud Accolade(USA)** had finished in front of the eventual runner-up and third when successful in the Champagne Stakes last time, so this has to go down as a disappointing effort.
**Scandinavia(USA)** had finished one place in front of Wilko when runner-up in the Royal Lodge last time and, being by Fusaichi Pegasus, was equally well bred for the dirt. However, while his European rival broke well, he fluffed the start and was always struggling thereafter.

## 6490a JOHN DEERE BREEDERS' CUP TURF (GRADE 1) 1m 4f

**9:55** (9:59) 3-Y-0+ **£581,006** (£223,464; £122,905; £63,687)

RPR

1 **Better Talk Now (USA)**[49] 5-9-0 ........ RADominguez 5 124
(HGMotion, U.S.A) *racd in 7th, hdwy over 3f out, disp 2nd str, hung lft and crossed Magistretti over 1f out, rdn to ld jst ins fin f, ran on* **33/1**

2 *1 ¾* **Kitten's Joy (USA)**[28] 5985 3-8-9 ........ JRVelazquez 4 123+
(DaleRomans, U.S.A) *w'like, lw, racd in 3rd, disp 2nd str, hmpd by wnr over 1f out, rdn and stayed on fnl f, tk 2nd cl home* **4/5**[1]

3 *1* **Powerscourt**[49] 5483 4-9-0 ........ (v) JPSpencer 1 119+
(APO'Brien, Ire) *lw, missed break, racd in 6th, gd hdwy to ld over 3f out, drvn over 1 1/2f out, ran on til hdd jst ins fnl f, no ex cl home* **11/4**[2]

4 *2 ¼* **Magistretti (USA)**[28] 5985 4-9-0 ........ EPrado 6 118+
(PLBiancone, U.S.A) *lw, disputed 4th early, 4th halfway, driven entering straight, crossed by winner over 1f out, no extra final f* **6/1**[3]

5 *2 ¾* **Mustanfar (USA)**[21] 3-8-9 ........ (b) JSantos 8 114
(KMclaughlin, U.S.A) *held up in last, ridden 2f out, disputing 5th straight, stayed on at one pace but never dangerous* **22/1**

6 *nk* **Request For Parole (USA)**[28] 5985 5-9-0 ........ PDay 2 111
(SHough, U.S.A) *disputed 4th early, last straight, never a threat* **33/1**

7 *4* **Strut The Stage (USA)**[28] 6-9-0 ........ (b) CNakatani 3 105
(MFrostad, Canada) *raced in 2nd til lost place over 2 1/2f out* **33/1**

8 *3 ¾* **Star Over The Bay (USA)**[27] 6-9-0 ........ TBaze 7 100
(MMitchell, U.S.A) *clear leader til headed over 3f out, weakened* **10/1**

2m 29.7s
**WFA** 3 from 4yo+ 7lb **8** Ran SP% **118.8**
Speed ratings: .
**Owner** Bushwood Stables **Bred** Wimborne Farm Inc **Trained** USA

**FOCUS**
A below-par renewal of this famous race with the two fancied runners both being unable to hold the late charge of outsider Better Talk Now, who had not looked good enough to win a race of this nature in previous outings. He caused interference in the straight, but it made no difference to the outcome and the result rightly stood.

**NOTEBOOK**
**Better Talk Now(USA)**, who had looked a little short of this company in recent starts, caused quite a shock in upsetting Kitten's Joy and Powerscourt and did so in fairly controversial circumstances as he crossed Magistretti when coming with his winning challenge - not dissimilar to the manouevre that saw Powerscourt thrown out of the Arlington Million. He was the best horse on the day though and deserved his victory, but in all honesty, it was one of the weaker renewals of this race and he will not go down as an American turf great.
**Kitten's Joy(USA)**, fully expected to win by his trainer and much of the American public, had been on the go since February - winning six of his seven races - and had had several hard races along the way. He was never far off the pace and was just starting to get going when slightly hampered by the winner as that one went on, but it made no difference to the result. Given he is only a three-year-old, he could probably do with a break and he remains one of America's top turf horses.
**Powerscourt**, representing Aidan O'Brien, who has an excellent record in this event - a second and two wins in the last three years - had the right profile to win this race and, in many Europeans' view, had to be held up until as late as possible before unleashing his turn of foot to prevail. However, having missed the break, he was for some reason sent on just under half a mile out and had run his race by the furlong pole. This is not the first time this season Spencer has gone for glory too soon on the colt - did so in the Irish Champion Stakes - and he is better than he showed.
**Magistretti(USA)**, who has done well since being trained in America, ran a good race and would have been closer but for the winner causing interference, although fourth was still the best he could have hoped for.
**Mustanfar(USA)** kept on without ever threatening to play a serious part in the finish and ran as well as could have been expected.
**Request For Parole(USA)** kept on past a couple of tiring rivals to claim sixth.
**Strut The Stage(USA)** appeared to do a bit too much too early and dropped out in the latter stages.
**Star Over The Bay(USA)**, on a roll coming into the race under aggressive tactics, again took a clear early lead, but he did a bit too much and acted nowhere near as well on this yielding ground. He is better than this but, approaching his seventh birthday, may not have that much improvement left in him.

## 6491a BREEDERS' CUP CLASSIC - POWERED BY DODGE (GRADE 1) (DIRT) 1m 2f

**10:35** (10:42) 3-Y-0+ **£1,162,011** (£446,927; £245,810; £127,374)

RPR

1 **Ghostzapper (USA)**[49] 4-9-0 ........ (b) JCastellano 1 133
(RJFrankel, U.S.A) *made all, driven clear over 1f out, ran on well* **4/1**[2]

2 3 **Roses In May (USA)**[42] 4-9-0 ........ JRVelazquez 6 128
(DaleRomans, U.S.A) *str, lw, pressed winner, 2nd straight, ridden and not quicken over 1f out* **7/1**

3 4 **Pleasantly Perfect (USA)**[69] [5014] 6-9-0 ........(b) JDBailey 12 121+
(RichardEMandella, U.S.A) *lw, hld up towards rr, gd hdwy on outside fr 3f out, rdn whn carried wd and 6th str, stayed on same pace* **2/1**[1]

4 ¾ **Perfect Drift (USA)**[28] 5-9-0 ........ KDesormeaux 4 121+
(MurrayWJohnson, U.S.A) *mid division, headway well over 2f out, 5th and carried wide straight, reached 3rd 1f out, no extra last 100y* **14/1**

5 2 **Azeri (USA)**[20] 6-8-11 ........ PDay 3 113
(DWayneLukas, U.S.A) *tracked leader, 3rd on inside straight, one pace* **12/1**

6 2 **Personal Rush (USA)**[40] 3-8-9 ........ LDettori 8 112
(KYamauchi, Japan) *outpaced and pushed along early to race in touch, 8th straight, kept on at one pace* **25/1**

7 ¾ **Birdstone (USA)**[63] 3-8-9 ........ EPrado 7 111
(NZito, U.S.A) *never a factor* **6/1**[3]

8 nk **Dynever (USA)**[22] 4-9-0 ........ CNakatani 13 110
(ChristopheClement, U.S.A) *good headway on outside over 3f out, 3rd over 2f out, hung right approaching straight, soon weakened* **14/1**

9 ¾ **Fantasticat (USA)**[35] 3-8-9 ........(b) GMelancon 5 109
(BBarnett, U.S.A) *always outpaced* **66/1**

10 ¾ **Funny Cide (USA)**[28] [5986] 4-9-0 ........ JSantos 9 108
(BTagg, U.S.A) *lw, prominent, closed up well over 2f out to dispute 3rd, 4th straight, soon weakened* **8/1**

11 nk **Bowman's Band (USA)**[28] [5986] 6-9-0 ........ CVelasquez 11 107
(HAJerkens, U.S.A) *always towards rear* **66/1**

12 3 **Newfoundland (USA)**[28] [5986] 4-9-0 ........(b) ECoa 10 102
(TPletcher, U.S.A) *tracked leaders to 3f out, soon weakened* **40/1**

13 6 **Freefourinternet (USA)**[28] 6-9-0 ........ GretaKuntzweiller 2 91
(MichaelJMaker, U.S.A) *broke with field, soon dropped back, tailed off after 2f* **50/1**

1m 59.02s
**WFA** 3 from 4yo+ 5lb **13** Ran SP% **123.5**
Speed ratings: .
**Owner** Stronach Stables **Bred** Adena Springs **Trained** USA

**FOCUS**
A truly world-class renewal of the Breeders' Cup Classic featuring the likes of last year's winner and this season's Dubai World Cup scorer Pleasantly Perfect, recent Japanese Grade One victor Personal Rush, leading US mare Azeri and most notably the new star of American racing, Ghostzapper. That one produced a quite outstanding performance and could become one of the greatest dirt performers of all time. They did not exactly go flat to the boards early on and the first two home were in the first two throughout

**NOTEBOOK**
**Ghostzapper(USA)** ◆ started his career as a sprinter, but had proven his ability to stay as far as nine furlongs when winning a Grade Three at Monmouth Park and most recently the Woodward Stakes at Belmont Park. In the latter race, he got very tired late on and only scraped home, but this distance proved no problem and he ran out a mightily impressive winner to emulate his sire Awesome Again, who won in 1998. Always well placed from his inside draw, he was a touch keen early on but still travelled with ease all the way into the straight before drawing away from a truly world-class field. He stays in training in 2005 and it is hardly an exaggeration to suggest he could go on to become one of the greatest dirt performers of all time. Connections have stated he will race solely in the US next season, ruling out trips to Dubai and Japan, but there are still plenty of options for him. He is likely to start off in the Metropolitan Handicap at Belmont Park, while the Jockey Club Gold Cup would fit nicely into a schedule that will surely include repeat bids in both the Woodward and Classic.
**Roses In May(USA)** appeared to come into this off a good preparation and had every chance in the race itself; he simply bumped into a superstar. It is hard to see him ever reversing placings with the winner and, if he is kept in training, connections will probably hope to avoid Ghostzapper.
**Pleasantly Perfect(USA)**, despite winning this race last year and the Dubai World Cup this season, had not convinced everyone that he was up there with the best dirt performers of recent years. Faced with his toughest task yet, he was well held. Things did not go his way and he may have preferred a stronger pace, but he probably would not have been good enough whatever the case. He has been retired.
**Perfect Drift(USA)** finds it very difficult to win these days, but this was a fine effort in defeat.
**Azeri(USA)** had been well beaten on her only previous run against the colts/gelding and had never won beyond nine furlongs, so the decision to switch to this race from the Distaff (she would have gone off favourite) was a bold one, but it did not pay off. Despite winning three times this season, she has not convinced she is as good as in previous years and was beaten at the top of the straight. She may have a couple more runs, but her long-term future is as a broodmare and it should not be forgotten just how good she was.
**Personal Rush(USA)**, a Grade One winner in his native Japan, acquitted himself creditably in this very competitive heat.
**Birdstone(USA)** turned over Smarty Jones when winning the Belmont Stakes earlier in the season, and has since added the Travers Stakes to his collection, but he has never shown his best in a big field and did not perform. He has been retired from racing due to an ankle injury.
**Funny Cide(USA)** came back to form to win the Jockey Gold Cup at Belmont on his previous start, but this was much tougher and he did not run to his mark.

## 6446 LINGFIELD (L-H)
### Sunday, October 31

**OFFICIAL GOING: Standard**
Wind: nil Weather: mostly overcast

## 6492 TESTERS OF EDENBRIDGE ALL NEW DISCOVERY 3 MAIDEN STKS (DIV I) 1m (P)
12:25 (12:27) (D3) 2-Y-O £4,329 (£1,332; £666; £333) **Stalls** High

Form RPR

2 1 **Karen's Caper (USA)**[18] [6153] 2-8-9 ........ JFortune 4 85+
(JHMGosden) *pressed ldr: led 2f out: pushed clr jst over 1f out: comf* **4/5**[1]

0 2 5 **Obezyana (USA)**[16] [6187] 2-9-0 ........ NCallan 6 79
(GAHuffer) *t.k.h: hld up bhd ldrs: n.m.r briefly 2f out: rdn and r.o fnl f to take 2nd last strides* **50/1**

3 3 nk **Kinrande (IRE)**[34] [5840] 2-9-0 ........ DSweeney 9 78
(PJMakin) *trckd ldng pair: rdn 2f out: kpt on same pce fr over 1f out* **16/1**

2 4 hd **Mr Aitch (IRE)**[34] [5838] 2-9-0 ........ DaneO'Neill 5 78
(JAOsborne) *t.k.h hld up midfield: n.m.r briefly 2f out: swtchd rt ent fnl f: styd on: nvr nrr* **9/1**

4 5 ¾ **Missatacama (IRE)**[18] [6155] 2-8-9 ........ SWKelly 8 71
(DJDaly) *racd wd: in tch: rdn over 2f out: sn outpcd: styd on u.p fnl f* **20/1**

0 6 ¾ **Nanton (USA)**[171] [2058] 2-9-0 ........ TQuinn 2 75
(PFICole) *led to 2f out: wknd fnl f* **6/1**[3]

52 7 1 ¾ **Registrar**[19] [6149] 2-9-0 ........ SDrowne 1 71
(MrsAJPerrett) *dwlt: sn chsd ldng pair: rdn over 2f out: wknd fnl f* **9/2**[2]

0 8 1 ¼ **Seeking An Alibi (USA)**[19] [6148] 2-9-0 ........(t) TEDurcan 11 68
(SaeedBinSuroor) *chsd ldrs: rdn over 2f out: wknd over 1f out* **16/1**

9 nk **Zabadani** 2-9-0 ........ MartinDwyer 7 62
(MrsAJPerrett) *dwlt: rn green in rr: n.d fr over 2f out: kpt on nr fin* **33/1**

05 10 2 ½ **Empangeni**[16] [6181] 2-9-0 ........ TPQueally 12 62
(JLDunlop) *a towards rr: rdn over 3f out: struggling after* **33/1**

00 11 10 **Mahmjra**[16] [6181] 2-9-0 ........ CCatlin 10 40
(MRChannon) *sn in rr: rdn and struggling over 3f out: t.o* **66/1**

0 12 3 ½ **Another Plan (IRE)**[22] [6072] 2-9-0 ........ GBaker 3 32
(MGQuinlan) *dwlt: a in rr: t.o* **100/1**

1m 38.22s (-1.33) **Going Correction** -0.125s/f (Stan) **12** Ran SP% **124.9**
Speed ratings: **101,96,95,95,94 94,92,91,90,88 78,74**CSF £81.35 TOTE £1.80: £1.30, £18.70, £3.70; EX 99.70.
**Owner** Stoneside Stables Llc **Bred** Stoneside Stable **Trained** Manton, Wilts

**FOCUS**
Probably a fair maiden, with many of the top stables represented, and run in a decent time. The winner looks a smart prospect and the form is rated with cautious optimism.

**NOTEBOOK**
**Karen's Caper(USA)**, a highly promising second at the course on her debut - when she blew her chance with a very slow start before finishing well - made no mistake this time and quickened away to win impressively. Reportedly well regarded, she should improve from two to three and is probably capable of winning at Pattern level next summer when the fast ground will help. It would come as no surprise to see her sold to race in America however, as she has the ideal pedigree.
**Obezyana(USA)**, last of 21 when evidently not running his race onhis debut, showed greatly improved form and was unlucky to run into a "good one". He will find easier opportunities and can be placed to winning effect by his shrewd connections.
**Kinrande(IRE)**, a promising third on his deut at Windsor, again ran well and probably showed a slight improvement in form. He will win an ordinary heat if holding his form.
**Mr Aitch(IRE)** momentarily found himself short of running room and is a little better than the form indicates. He, like the third placed horse, can win his maiden if holding his form.
**Missatacama(IRE)** confirmed the promise of her initial effort and is a fair handicap prospect for next season.
**Nanton(USA)**, who would have found the five-furlong trip he made his debut over back in May too short, went about his business from the front but did not last home on this step up in trip. He is more of a handicap sort, but it remains to be seen what his trip is.
**Registrar** was disappointing and failed to go on from his decent second last time. This was his third run in a maiden though, so there may be more to come in handicaps next season.
**Seeking An Alibi(USA)**, evidently one of his stable's lesser juveniles, can probably be placed to win a small race, but does not appeal as one to follow until showing more.
**Zabadani**, related to several middle-distance performers, did not know his job well enough to do himself justice and will make a much better three-year-old.
**Empangeni**, whose stable are renowned for prospering with their backward juveniles when they are sent handicapping at three, looks just the type to win a race ot two in handicap company next term.
**Mahmjra** is more of a handicap prospect for next season.

## 6493 BET DIRECT "RED TO BET" ON ITV CLASSIFIED STKS 7f (P)
12:55 (12:57) (F4) 3-Y-O+ £2,954 (£844; £422) **Stalls** Low

Form RPR

0 1 **Mac's Talisman (IRE)**[62] [5201] 4-9-1 56........(tp) DHolland 8 69
(VSmith) *settled midfield: prog wl over 2f out: led wl over 1f out: pushed out* **5/2**[1]

5051 2 1 **Nearly A Fool**[3] [6452] 6-9-11 60........(v) NPollard 3 76
(GGMargarson) *wl plcd: effrt to chse wnr over 1f out: styd on but no imp* **5/2**[1]

0005 3 ¾ **Smokin Joe**[15] [6220] 3-8-12 55........(b) GBaker 13 63
(JRBest) *hld up in rr: prog on wd outside over 2f out: rdn and styd on to take 3rd ins fnl f: nt look keen* **16/1**

3563 4 2 **Asbo**[13] [6273] 4-8-11 55........ SDrowne 5 55
(DrJDScargill) *hld up towards rr: sme prog over 2f out: rdn and kpt on same pce fr over 1f out* **6/1**[2]

6000 5 shd **Kinsman (IRE)**[85] [4546] 7-8-11 55........(b) J-PGuillambert(3) 9 58
(TDMcCarthy) *s.s: wl in rr: sme prog 2f out: styd on fnl f : no ch* **33/1**

3160 6 1 ½ **Adantino**[77] [4774] 5-9-2 57........(b) JFortune 6 56
(BRMillman) *hld up in rr: prog on outer 3f out: chsd ldrs 2f out: fdd fnl f* **10/1**[3]

0020 7 2 **Mutassem (FR)**[15] [6224] 3-8-12 55........ MHenry 2 48
(TKeddy) *hld up midfield: nt clr run on inner over 2f out and wl over 1f out: one pce after* **16/1**

0500 8 hd **Glendale**[36] [5791] 3-9-0 57........ DaneO'Neill 12 50
(DKIvory) *trckd ldrs: prog to ld over 2f out: hdd & wknd wl over 1f out* **33/1**

02-0 9 3 **Lady Korrianda**[21] [6089] 3-8-11 57........ TPQueally 7 39
(LadyHerries) *racd midfield: rdn and no prog over 2f out: wknd* **20/1**

0000 10 ½ **Margalita (IRE)**[39] [5734] 4-8-11 55........(bt) LisaJones 14 36
(PMitchell) *plld hrd: mde most to over 2f out: wknd: sddle slipped* **33/1**

0300 11 shd **Phecklesss**[20] [6124] 5-9-5 60........ PFitzsimons 11 44
(JMBradley) *s.s: a wl in rr: no ch over 2f out* **20/1**

0030 12 1 ¾ **Noble Mount**[114] [3708] 3-8-5 55........ DerekNolan(7) 4 34
(ABHaynes) *racd midfield: wknd over 2f out* **33/1**

060 13 ¾ **Arogant Prince**[111] [3800] 7-9-0 55........ TQuinn 10 32
(JPearce) *pressed ldr to wl over 2f out: wknd* **40/1**

0050 14 3 **Captain Darling (IRE)**[146] [2735] 4-9-0 60........(p) AQuinn(5) 1 29
(RMHCowell) *prom tl wknd wl over 2f out* **12/1**

1m 24.78s (-1.16) **Going Correction** -0.125s/f (Stan)
**WFA** 3 from 4yo+ 2lb **14** Ran SP% **123.7**
Speed ratings: **101,99,99,96,96 94,92,92,88,88 88,86,85,81**CSF £7.05 TOTE £3.90: £2.20, £1.80, £3.00; EX 12.50.
**Owner** V Smith **Bred** Miss C A Green And R Haim **Trained** Exning, Suffolk

**FOCUS**
Only an ordinary race, a shade above average for the grade, but it should produce the odd winner at a similar level.

**NOTEBOOK**
**Mac's Talisman(IRE)**, whose sole win prior to today was back in January of 2003, came with a perfectly-timed run to score with a bit in hand and he evidently appreciated the return to the All-Weather. He is only a moderate performer, but seven furlongs is his trip and he can probably win again against a similar calibre of horse.
**Nearly A Fool**, bidding to follow up his success in a similar event at the course earlier in the week, ran well without ever looking set to get to the winner and he should continue to pay his way.
**Smokin Joe** remains to have just a sole victory to his name in 18 starts and, although third, does not look set to be adding to that win anytime soon.
**Asbo** seemed a bit better suited to this trip - she has been running over six - and he may benefit further from a more positive ride.
**Kinsman(IRE)** has not been running very well on turf and appreciated the return to this surface. He may soon be winning a small race.
**Adantino** *Official explanation: jockey said gelding had run too free*

## 6494 TESTERS OF EDENBRIDGE ALL NEW DISCOVERY 3 MAIDEN STKS (DIV II) 1m (P)
1:25 (1:32) (F4) 2-Y-0 £4,316 (£1,328; £664; £332) Stalls High

Form RPR
42 **1** **Marhoon (USA)**[10] 6322 2-9-0 ............(t) TEDurcan 3 85
(EFVaughan) *cl up: chsd ldr wl over 1f out: rdn to ld jst ins fnl f: sn clr* **11/4**[1]
**2** *3* **Rollerbird** 2-8-9 ............ MartinDwyer 8 73
(AMBalding) *cl up: led over 2f out: rdn and rn green over 1f out: hdd and no ex jst ins fnl f* **11/4**[1]
**3** *3* **Maria Delfina (IRE)** 2-8-9 ............ JFortune 11 67+
(JHMGosden) *dwlt: hld up in last: taken to outer over 3f out: nudged along and styd on steadily fnl 2f: tk 3rd nr fin: improve* **4/1**[2]
**4** *nk* **The Geezer** 2-8-11 ............ LPKeniry(3) 10 71
(DRCElsworth) *racd towards rr and rn green: pushed along fr 1/2-way: styd on fnl 2f: nrst fin* **13/2**[3]
**5** *1/2* **Chocolate Caramel (USA)** 2-9-0 ............ SWKelly 9 70
(MrsAJPerrett) *racd midfield: lost pl and in rr over 4f out: hrd rdn over 2f out : kpt on one pce* **16/1**
04 **6** *nk* **Busaco**[88] 4432 2-9-0 ............ TQuinn 4 69
(JLDunlop) *chsd ldrs: effrt over 2f out: hanging lft over 1f out: no imp* **20/1**
0 **7** *3* **Mr Mayfair (IRE)**[43] 5653 2-9-0 ............ PFitzsimons 6 63
(JAOsborne) *chsd ldrs: rdn wl over 2f out: wknd over 1f out* **16/1**
**8** *3 1/2* **Ma'Am (USA)** 2-8-9 ............ NCallan 7 50
(IAWood) *s.i.s: sn pushed along and green in rr: nvr a factor* **66/1**
0 **9** *3/4* **Toque**[20] 6118 2-8-9 ............ SDrowne 5 48
(HMorrison) *a towards rr: u.p and struggling wl over 2f out* **14/1**
00 **10** *4* **Hugo The Boss (IRE)**[3] 6448 2-9-0 ............ DaneO'Neill 12 45
(JRBoyle) *hld up: racd wd: brief effrt 3f out: sn wknd* **66/1**
0 **11** *hd* **Wiz In**[30] 5911 2-9-0 ............ MHenry 2 44
(TKeddy) *uns rdr and bolted bef s: led to over 2f out: wknd v rapidly* **66/1**
0 **12** *14* **La Musique**[40] 5716 2-9-0 ............ SWhitworth 1 13
(PJMcbride) *dwlt: sn w ldr: wknd v rapidly 3f out: t.o* **100/1**

1m 38.72s (-0.83) **Going Correction** -0.125s/f (Stan) **12** Ran SP% **115.3**
Speed ratings: **99,96,93,92,92 91,88,85,84,80 80,66**CSF £9.33 TOTE £3.20: £1.50, £2.30, £1.80; EX 13.10.
**Owner** Sheikh Ahmed Al Maktoum **Bred** Darley **Trained** Newmarket, Suffolk

**FOCUS**
The weaker of the two divisions, with little to go on, but although confidence in not strong, the race should still produce winners.

**NOTEBOOK**
**Marhoon(USA)**, who set the standard on soft ground turf form, had little trouble handling this surface and finished strongly in the final furlong to win going away. His stable have been doing well with their juveniles of late and this fellow can probably win again if found a novice event somewhere.
**Rollerbird**, by dual Derby and Arc winning sire Sinndar, made a pleasing start to his career and would have given the winner more to think about had he not run green. There is more to come from this scopey sort and he is in the right hands to win races.
**Maria Delfina(IRE)**, representing the winning jockey/trainer combination of the first division, was given a considerate ride and will improve greatly for the experience. She should be up to winning an ordinary maiden before going on to better things.
**The Geezer**, whose stable's juveniles have had a rich time of it in the second half of the season, was too inexperienced to do himself justice and, like the third placed horse, will improve greatly for the outing.
**Chocolate Caramel(USA)** is bred to be effective on this sort of surface and is another who will have learned a lot from this debut experience.
**Busaco** is now qualified for handicaps and will do better in that sphere.
**Mr Mayfair(IRE)** *Official explanation: jockey said gelding stumbled on leaving the stalls*
**Ma'Am(USA)** showed a little bit of hope for the future and should improve with the run under her belt.

## 6495 CHRIS DAVIES CLASSIFIED STKS 1m 4f (P)
2:00 (2:02) (F3) 3-Y-0+ £3,571 (£1,099; £549; £274) Stalls Low

Form RPR
60-6 **1** **Stormy Day**[55] 5339 4-9-1 60............(e[1]) SDrowne 9 66
(MrsAJPerrett) *hld up in last: stl in last trio over 2f out: prog and wd bnd 2f out: drvn and r.o to ld last 75yds* **16/1**
0003 **2** *1* **Uncle John**[15] 6225 3-8-11 60............(b) JFEgan 8 67
(SKirk) *cl up: effrt over 2f out: rdn to ld ins fnl f: hdd and outpcd last 75yds* **14/1**
6010 **3** *1 1/2* **Smoothie (IRE)**[32] 5869 6-9-4 60............(p) LEnstone 6 65
(IanWilliams) *settled in rr: shkn up 4f out: prog over 2f out: drvn and r.o fnl f: nrst fin* **16/1**
0042 **4** *nk* **King Of Knight (IRE)**[30] 5914 3-8-8 60............ ABeech(3) 13 64
(GProdromou) *t.k.h: trckd ldrs: effrt to ld over 2f out: hdd & wknd ins fnl f* **9/2**[1]
1003 **5** *3/4* **Ellina**[26] 6006 3-8-8 60............ TQuinn 16 60
(JPearce) *settled wl in rr: stl in last trio over 2f out: shkn up and prog over 1f out: styd on fnl f: nvr nrr* **12/1**
0053 **6** *1/2* **King Flyer (IRE)**[30] 5914 8-9-1 58............ BReilly(3) 15 62
(MissJFeilden) *hld up in rr: reminder 4f out: prog 3f out: chsd ldrs 2f out: one pce after* **9/1**
6055 **7** *nk* **Saida Lenasera (FR)**[26] 6006 3-8-8 60............ TEDurcan 12 59
(MrsPSly) *t.k.h early: pressed ldr: lost pl 4f out: hmpd sn after and dropped towards rr: kpt on again fr over 1f out* **25/1**
3150 **8** *shd* **Willhego**[13] 6271 3-8-11 58............ MartinDwyer 5 62
(JRBest) *plld hrd early: restrained bhd ldrs: effrt 3f out: w ldr 2f out tl wknd ent fnl f* **16/1**
0000 **9** *2 1/2* **Airgusta (IRE)**[44] 5622 3-8-11 57............ ADaly 10 58
(CPMorlock) *t.k.h: trckd ldrs: rdn over 2f out: fdd over 1f out* **66/1**
3101 **10** *nk* **Fantasy Crusader**[18] 6154 5-9-4 58............(p) DaneO'Neill 7 58
(JAGilbert) *t.k.h: hld up wl in rr: prog on outer over 2f out: fdd over 1f out* **10/1**
0030 **11** *1 1/4* **Desert Island Disc**[9] 6339 7-9-1 59............ GBaker 14 53
(JJBridger) *hld up wl in rr: effrt over 2f out: sn no prog and btn* **10/1**
-050 **12** *2 1/2* **Sunshine On Me**[30] 5907 3-8-8 60............ TPQueally 2 49
(CFWall) *cl up tl wknd u.p over 2f out* **11/2**[2]
0550 **13** *4* **Anyhow (IRE)**[34] 5826 7-8-12 60............ DNolan(3) 11 43
(MissKMGeorge) *hld up: prog on outer 1/2-way: led 4f out to over 2f out: wknd* **10/1**
4504 **14** *5* **Kernel Dowery (IRE)**[15] 6225 4-9-4 59............(e) DHolland 1 39
(PWHarris) *led to 4f out: wknd over 2f out* **15/2**[3]
4200 **15** *2 1/2* **Disparity (USA)**[25] 6013 3-8-8 60............(t) PHanagan 3 32
(JRFanshawe) *racd midfield: rdn and wknd over 3f out: wl bhd over 2f out* **25/1**
3000 **16** *1/2* **Red Skelton (IRE)**[26] 6005 3-8-11 60............ NCallan 4 34
(MsDeborahJEvans) *racd midfield: n.m.r 4f out: wknd over 2f out: eased over 1f out* **25/1**

2m 34.58s (0.34) **Going Correction** -0.125s/f (Stan)
**WFA** 3 from 4yo+ 7lb **16** Ran SP% **127.6**
Speed ratings: **93,92,91,91,90 90,90,90,88,88 87,85,83,79,78 77**CSF £226.26 TOTE £21.60: £6.70, £2.90, £6.30; EX 377.40.
**Owner** Sir Eric Parker **Bred** Sir Eric Parker **Trained** Pulborough, W Sussex

**FOCUS**
Only ordinary form, but those in the frame were close to their marks giving the form a sound enough appearance, and the lightly-raced Stormy Day has improvement to come.

**NOTEBOOK**
**Stormy Day**, who had gone the wrong way in maidens, was making her handicap debut in the first-time eyeshield and it seemed to do the trick as she came through late on to land the spoils, winning with a bit in hand. If the headgear continues to have the effect, this unexposed filly should continue to run well.
**Uncle John** showed his run last week in blinkers to be no fluke and, if continuing to hold this level of form, will get his head in front eventually.
**Smoothie(IRE)** made some good late headway, but was never going get there in time and had to settle for third.
**King Of Knight(IRE)** made some good late headway, but was never going get there in time and had to settle for third.
**Ellina** was doing her best work all too late, but is due a bad run as she has performed well the last twice and is none too consistent.
**King Flyer(IRE)** had his chance and failed to run up to the form of his second last time.
**Saida Lenasera(FR)** lost her pitch with around half a mile to run and could never make the ground back up. It was a fair effort considering.

## 6496 LADBROKES.COM STKS (H'CAP) 6f (P)
2:35 (2:36) (D2) (0-92,94) 3-Y-0+ £7,034 (£2,164; £1,082; £541) Stalls Low

Form RPR
1040 **1** **Moayed**[16] 6191 5-8-12 **84**............(bt) J-PGuillambert(3) 7 100
(NPLittmoden) *dwlt: hld up in last: rapid prog on wd outside over 2f out: edgd lft but led ins fnl f: pushed out* **8/1**
5500 **2** *1 3/4* **Quiet Times (IRE)**[176] 1974 5-9-5 **88**............(b) NCallan 4 99
(KARyan) *prom: rdn to ld 2f out: hdd and one pce ins fnl f* **25/1**
6111 **3** *1* **Blythe Spirit**[12] 6293 5-8-11 **80**............(p) PHanagan 12 88
(RAFahey) *chsd ldrs: rdn and effrt over 2f out: styd on same pce u.p fnl f* **6/1**[3]
035 **4** *shd* **Aversham**[36] 5799 4-8-11 **80**............ SDrowne 9 88
(RCharlton) *racd midfield: effrt over 2f out: hmpd over 1f out: drvn and r.o fnl f: nrst fin* **5/1**[1]
0022 **5** *1* **Just Fly**[34] 5841 4-8-13 **82**............ JFortune 5 87
(SKirk) *settled in last quartet: effrt 2f out: styd on ins fnl f: no ch w ldrs* **8/1**
2501 **6** *1 3/4* **Jayanjay**[29] 5933 5-8-10 **82**............ RThomas(3) 11 81
(MissBSanders) *hld up in last quartet: effrt and n.m.r 2f out: kpt on same pce* **11/1**
1211 **7** *1 1/4* **Who's Winning (IRE)**[41] 5697 3-8-11 **81**............ TQuinn 8 77
(BGPowell) *pressed ldrs: poised to chal 2f out: hanging and wknd tamely over 1f out: no ch whn hmpd nr fin* **11/2**[2]
0052 **8** *1/2* **Corps De Ballet (IRE)**[13] 6267 3-9-1 **85**............ TPQueally 2 79
(JLDunlop) *racd midfield: effrt to chse ldrs 2f out: wknd jst over 1f out* **11/1**
2110 **9** *1 1/4* **Idle Power (IRE)**[13] 6277 6-8-13 **82**............(p) DSweeney 3 72
(JRBoyle) *racd on inner: led to 2f out: wknd fnl f* **9/1**
6110 **10** *2 1/2* **Malapropism**[8] 6349 4-9-4 **94**............ TO'Brien(7) 6 77
(MRChannon) *chsd ldrs: rdn and losing pl over 2f out: wknd over 1f out* **14/1**
0000 **11** *2* **Law Breaker (IRE)**[32] 5874 6-9-3 **89**............ BReilly(3) 1 66
(JAGilbert) *racd midfield: rdn whn n.m.r on inner 2f out: wknd* **14/1**
**12** *11* **Auentraum (GER)**[91] 4-8-6 **80**............ PMakin(5) 10 24
(DFlood) *a in rr: t.o fnl 2f* **25/1**

1m 10.9s (-2.02) **Going Correction** -0.125s/f (Stan)
**WFA** 3 from 4yo+ 1lb **12** Ran SP% **116.3**
Speed ratings: **108,105,104,104,102 100,98,98,96,93 90,75**CSF £186.41 CT £1291.70 TOTE £8.30: £2.40, £6.10, £2.60; EX 147.40 Trifecta £488.60 Part won. Pool: £688.18 - 0.30 winning units..
**Owner** Nigel Shields **Bred** Sentinal Bloodstock And Wong Chung Mat **Trained** Newmarket, Suffolk

**FOCUS**
A competitive sprint handicap and strong form for the time of year, that went the way of Moayed, who won going away.

**NOTEBOOK**
**Moayed** bounced right back to form with the combination of the return to artificial surfaces and dropping back to six furlongs making the difference. He made some stealthy headway at the halfway stage and saw his race out strongly to win going away. He will need to improve again if he is to defy a higher mark, but that is not out of the question. *Official explanation: jockey said gelding was hanging left*
**Quiet Times(IRE)** has been out of sorts on the turf and was another who appreciated the return to All-Weather. He ran his race, but the winner simply had too much speed for him in the latter stages of the race.
**Blythe Spirit**, who has been in blinding form of late - completing a hat-trick with a narrow success at Wolverhampton most recently - was up in grade and in the weights and ran well on this different surface. The Handicapper may have a grip on him for the time being.
**Aversham** would have been third but for being hampered and ran well. He has not won for over two years and continues to find at least one too good.
**Just Fly**, who was strongly fancied to win last time when a neck second to Omaha City at Windsor, found this drop in trip against him, and may be able to win again when stepped back up in distance.
**Jayanjay** never really threatened and does not seem as good on Polytrack as he is on turf.
**Who's Winning(IRE)** looked very awkward under pressure and stopped quickly.
**Law Breaker(IRE)** *Official explanation: jockey said gelding had hung right*

## 6497 LITTLEWOODS BET DIRECT EBF FLEUR DE LYS FILLIES' STKS (LISTED RACE) 1m (P)
3:10 (3:12) (A1) 3-Y-0+ £17,400 (£6,600; £3,300; £1,500) Stalls High

Form RPR
0032 **1** **Miss George**[13] 6277 6-8-13 83............ DaneO'Neill 10 92
(DKIvory) *dwlt: hld up in rr: plld out over 1f out: qcknd ent fnl f: led last 75yds* **16/1**
0030 **2** *1* **Tahirah**[15] 6214 4-8-13 92............ MartinDwyer 5 90
(RGuest) *racd in last trio: effrt on outer over 1f out: r.o wl fnl f: tk 2nd on line* **20/1**
0310 **3** *shd* **Zietory**[59] 5249 4-9-2 95............ TQuinn 9 92
(PFICole) *trckd ldr after 2f: effrt 2f out: drvn to ld jst over 1f out: hdd and outpcd last 75yds* **8/1**[3]

1113 **4** *shd* **Peeress**[94] 4268 3-8-10 96 ........ DHolland 1 89+
(SirMichaelStoute) *dwlt: wl in rr: nt clr run fr over 2f out: stl nowhere to go over 1f out: r.o strly fnl f: nt rcvr* **5/6**[1]

11-5 **5** *1 ½* **Milly Waters**[19] 6147 3-8-10 83 ........ SWKelly 4 86
(WMBrisbourne) *trckd ldrs: effrt 2f out: rdn and styd on same pce fr over 1f out* **50/1**

0100 **6** *nk* **Aricia (IRE)**[92] 4356 3-8-10 94 ........ JFortune 8 85
(JHMGosden) *led for 1f: styd cl up: rdn and one pce fnl 2f* **12/1**

5650 **7** *hd* **Najaaba (USA)**[31] 5886 4-8-13 80 ........ BReilly 6 85
(MissJFeilden) *racd in rr: prog on wd outside to chse ldrs 2f out: no ex over 1f out* **33/1**

0000 **8** *hd* **Star Of Normandie (USA)**[17] 6173 5-8-13 82 ........ AMcCarthy 12 84
(GGMargarson) *racd midfield: effrt 2f out: one pce fr over 1f out* **40/1**

5-00 **9** *1 ½* **Voile (IRE)**[17] 6175 3-8-10 95 ........ FNorton 3 81
(RHannon) *racd midfield on inner: pushed along over 2f out: fdd over 1f out* **16/1**

-232 **10** *½* **Coqueteria (USA)**[19] 6147 3-8-10 100 ........ SDrowne 7 80
(GWragg) *t.k.h: prom: rdn and cl up over 1f out: wknd* **5/1**[2]

0421 **11** *nk* **Zerlina (USA)**[27] 5990 3-8-10 80 ........ CCatlin 11 79
(WJMusson) *led after 1f: kicked on over 2f out: hdd & wknd jst over 1f out* **18/1**

5044 **12** *¾* **Valjarv (IRE)**[2] 6459 3-8-10 90 ........ NCallan 2 77
(NPLittmoden) *detached in last tl jnd rr of main gp 5f out: wknd wl over 1f out* **14/1**

1m 38.1s (-1.45) **Going Correction** -0.125s/f (Stan)
**WFA** 3 from 4yo+ 3lb **12** Ran SP% **125.8**
Speed ratings: **102,101,100,100,99 99,98,98,97,96 96,95**CSF £310.93 TOTE £16.00: £3.60, £5.70, £2.30; EX 316.70.
**Owner** Mrs A Shone **Bred** Mrs C S Knowles **Trained** Radlett, Herts
■ Stewards Enquiry : Martin Dwyer one-day ban: careless riding (Nov 12)

**FOCUS**
An ordinary Listed race and moderate form for the grade with the winner having been running in Class D handicaps, but there are one or two to take for the future.

**NOTEBOOK**
**Miss George**, who has been running well in some tough handicaps of late, relished every yard of this trip and caused something of a surprise. She has evidently been successfully transformed into a miler from a sprinter and this will do her paddock value no end of good. She quickened smartly to win going away and there may be more to come from her.
**Tahirah** showed her running at Newmarket last time to be all wrong - with soft ground a valid excuse - and bounced right back to her best. She has not won for around a year and life will remain difficult off her current rating.
**Zietory** has shown a liking for soft ground in the past - winning three of her four races in it - and was unable to pick up quite as well on this surface.
**Peeress**, who had been progressive earlier in the season - winning three of her four races - was last seen finishing third in a competitive handicap at Goodwood and was rightly made favourite on this first venture into Listed company. She was always going well, but did not get a clear run in the straight and it cost her at least a place. She remains progressive and is up to winning at at least this level.
**Milly Waters** improved on her seasonal debut effort and was sticking on well enough at the end, suggesting she is worthy of her rating.
**Aricia(IRE)** was tapped for pace early in the straight and could only keep on at the one pace.
**Coqueteria(USA)**, who had yet to run a bad race this season, would not have been suited by this speed-reliant test and ran disappointingly. She is much better than this and over a mile plus on soft ground, will return to form.

## 6498 BET DIRECT ON ITV PAGE 367 H'CAP 1m 2f (P)
3:45 (3:46) (E3) (0-77,76) 3-Y-O £3,526 (£1,085; £542; £271) Stalls Low

Form RPR

0502 **1** **The Violin Player (USA)**[18] 6160 3-9-3 66 ........ DHolland 5 77
(HJCollingridge) *prom: trckd ldr over 6f out: led over 2f out: drvn and edgd rt fnl f: styd on wl* **11/2**[3]

0402 **2** *1 ¾* **King Of Diamonds**[6] 6396 3-9-13 76 ........ MartinDwyer 14 84
(JRBest) *t.k.h: wl plcd: effrt to join wnr 2f out: sn rdn and fnd nthing: hld fnl f* **7/2**[1]

3255 **3** *3* **Deign To Dance (IRE)**[13] 6271 3-9-2 65 ........ CCatlin 3 68
(JGPortman) *settled wl in rr: plenty to do over 2f out: n.m.r briefly over 1f out: styd on fnl f to snatch 3rd nr fin* **25/1**

046 **4** *nk* **Ground Patrol**[18] 6160 3-9-2 65 ........(t) TPQueally 11 67
(GLMoore) *racd in rr: pushed along 4f out: effrt u.p over 2f out: kpt on same pce* **14/1**

1014 **5** *shd* **Pella**[13] 6271 3-9-2 65 ........ DSweeney 13 67
(MBlanshard) *hld up towards rr: prog on outer to chse ldrs 2f out: one pce over 1f out* **14/1**

1600 **6** *1 ¾* **Habanero**[37] 5766 3-9-13 76 ........ FNorton 9 75
(RHannon) *t.k.h: chsd ldr to over 6f out: rdn over 2f out: fdd over 1f out* **25/1**

2116 **7** *hd* **Science Academy (USA)**[68] 5019 3-8-13 67 ........ NDeSouza(5) 6 65
(PFICole) *racd midfield: rdn and no prog over 2f out: one pce after* **14/1**

3524 **8** *3 ½* **Little Jimbob**[13] 6266 3-9-12 75 ........ PHanagan 8 67
(RAFahey) *led to over 2f out: wknd* **9/2**[2]

0605 **9** *1 ½* **Competitor**[18] 6160 3-9-5 68 ........(p) TQuinn 2 57
(JAkehurst) *chsd ldrs but nvr gng wl: wknd u.p wl over 1f out* **10/1**

5343 **10** *1 ½* **Tetcott (IRE)**[43] 5656 3-9-2 68 ........ LPKeniry(3) 12 55
(AGNewcombe) *reluctant on way to post: s.i.s: hld up in last: prog on outer over 3f out: wknd over 2f out* **33/1**

0500 **11** *1 ¼* **Sweet Reply**[16] 6199 3-9-2 65 ........ NCallan 10 49
(IAWood) *wl in rr: rdn over 4f out: struggling and no prog over 2f out* **50/1**

6045 **12** *shd* **Mrs Pankhurst**[13] 6266 3-9-4 67 ........ SDrowne 1 51
(BWHills) *racd on inner in midfield: lost pl and in rr 3f out: sn btn* **8/1**

2565 **13** *5* **Grand Apollo**[15] 6224 3-9-3 66 ........ JFortune 4 41
(JHMGosden) *chsd ldrs tl wknd over 2f out* **8/1**

2m 5.20s (-2.65) **Going Correction** -0.125s/f (Stan) **13** Ran SP% **119.7**
Speed ratings: **105,103,101,100,100 99,99,96,95,94 93,93,89**CSF £24.13 CT £453.72 TOTE £7.20: £2.10, £1.70, £6.00; EX 27.20.
**Owner** Peter Webb **Bred** Stephen D Peskoff **Trained** Exning, Suffolk

**FOCUS**
Modest stuff, but the runner-up sets a decent standard for the grade and the winner can leave the form behind in time.

**NOTEBOOK**
**The Violin Player(USA)** has been tumbling down the ratings after a disappointing season - having mainly been running on ground that is too soft or over to stiffer trip - but he has been performing better since joining his current stable and this comfy win signalled a return to his best. It will be most disappointing if he cannot defy a penalty.
**King Of Diamonds**, although not appearing to put up much of a fight, was never going to beat the winner and ran as well as could have been expected back in second.
**Deign To Dance(IRE)** was flying at the death and should have been closer, but would not have improved on her position of third. Her turf form is inconsistent, but she has a decent record on the All-Weather and may be worth bearing in mind for a slightly lesser race in future.
**Ground Patrol** ran slightly below par on a form line with the winner, but it was still a fair effort. He remains a maiden. *Official explanation: trainer said gelding had lost a shoe*
**Pella** lacked the necessary kick to make a winning challenge and may be better at a strongly run mile.
**Habanero** ran well to a point, but is not the most reliable of characters.
**Competitor** *Official explanation: trainer said colt had a breathing problem*
**Mrs Pankhurst** was disappointing and will be better back in a strongly-run mile.

## 6499 JOHN WHITTINGTON 65TH BIRTHDAY & RETIREMENT APPRENTICE H'CAP 7f (P)
4:20 (4:22) (F4) (0-62,62) 3-Y-O+ £3,022 (£863; £431) Stalls Low

Form RPR

0005 **1** **Mind Alert**[16] 6199 3-8-13 57 ........ DAllan 8 66
(MissJACamacho) *trckd ldr after 2f: rdn to ld wl over 1f out: sn clr* **10/1**

0660 **2** *2 ½* **Menai Straights**[16] 6199 3-8-12 56 ........ DNolan 11 59
(RFFisher) *cl up: rdn over 2f out: chsd wnr 1f out: no imp* **10/1**

1100 **3** *nk* **Frank's Quest (IRE)**[116] 3626 4-9-4 60 ........ SHitchcott 7 62
(ABHaynes) *wl in rr: pushed along fr 1/2-way: c wd in st: styd on wl fnl f: nrst fin* **25/1**

6366 **4** *shd* **Pertemps Magus**[18] 6157 4-9-2 58 ........(v) THamilton 2 59
(RAFahey) *t.k.h: hld up bhd ldrs: n.m.r 2f out: styd on u.p fnl f* **7/2**[1]

4026 **5** *1* **Iced Diamond (IRE)**[52] 5411 5-8-12 57 ........ BSwarbrick(3) 12 56
(WMBrisbourne) *t.k.h: racd on outer: trckd ldrs: effrt 2f out: carried hd high and fnd nil over 1f out* **5/1**[2]

000 **6** *shd* **Calypso Dancer (FR)**[23] 6046 4-8-12 57 ........ PMakin(3) 3 56
(TDBarron) *dwlt: hld up towards rr: nt clr run 2f out: kpt on same pce over 1f out* **16/1**

0000 **7** *nk* **Warlingham (IRE)**[6] 6398 6-9-2 58 ........ J-PGuillambert 6 56
(PHowling) *plld hrd: cl up: rdn over 2f out: hanging and btn over 1f out* **11/1**

5250 **8** *nk* **Legal Set (IRE)**[3] 6452 8-9-0 56 ........(t) TPQueally 13 53
(MissAStokell) *t.k.h: led after 2f: hdd wl over 1f out: wknd fnl f* **8/1**[3]

0004 **9** *shd* **Siraj**[13] 6273 5-9-0 56 ........ LPKeniry 1 53
(PSMcentee) *hld up in rr: effrt on inner over 2f out: no prog wl over 1f out* **14/1**

5000 **10** *¾* **Superchief**[18] 6157 9-9-6 62 ........(bt) BReilly 10 57
(MissBSanders) *dwlt: wl in rr: drvn and prog over 2f out: wknd over 1f out* **16/1**

6402 **11** *hd* **Feast Of Romance**[46] 5575 7-8-5 54 ........(b) RJKilloran(7) 4 48
(GAHuffer) *chsd ldrs: rdn wl over 2f out: wknd over 1f out* **9/1**

0030 **12** *hd* **Sharoura**[20] 6117 8-8-9 58 ........(p) NLawes(7) 9 52
(RAFahey) *t.k.h: racd v wd: nvr on terms* **9/1**

3300 **13** *2 ½* **Scarlett Rose**[54] 5370 3-9-1 62 ........ MSavage(3) 5 49
(DrJDScargill) *led for 2f: lost pl u.p 3f out* **25/1**

4000 **14** *12* **Ashstanza**[139] 2932 3-9-4 62 ........ RThomas 14 18
(MrsLRichards) *a last: t.o fr 1/2-way* **50/1**

1m 25.46s (-0.48) **Going Correction** -0.125s/f (Stan)
**WFA** 3 from 4yo+ 2lb **14** Ran SP% **124.6**
Speed ratings: **97,94,93,93,92 92,92,91,91,90 90,90,87,73**CSF £108.32 CT £2459.47 TOTE £13.20: £4.20, £4.30, £4.90; EX 101.30 Place 6 £349.13, Place 5 £201.44.
**Owner** David W Armstrong **Bred** P T Tellwright **Trained** Norton, N Yorks

**FOCUS**
Another moderate affair, with the third to sixth setting the standard, but the winner did it well and used to be better than this.

**NOTEBOOK**
**Mind Alert** ran out an emphatic winner in taking his first race for over a year. He has not been in the best of form, but this first crack at All-Weather seemed to improve him and he can probably win again off his lowly rating.
**Menai Straights**, 3lb lower than when last successful, ran well without proving a match for the winner.
**Frank's Quest(IRE)** was doing his best work late and would have been second in a few more strides. He is entitled to improve for the outing.
**Pertemps Magus**, although not beaten far, was a little disappointing and is best on a slower surface.
**Iced Diamond(IRE)** looked far from enthusiastic under pressure and is not one to to make a habit of backing.
**Calypso Dancer(FR)** made a little late headway, but was never getting there in time.
**Ashstanza** *Official explanation: trainer said gelding was found to be suffering from colic after the race*

T/Jkpt: Not won. T/Plt: £839.10 to a £1 stake. Pool: £35,809.30. 31.15 winning tickets. T/Qpdt: £522.50 to a £1 stake. Pool: £2,754.20. 3.90 winning tickets. JN

6500 - 6502a (Foreign Racing) - See Raceform Interactive

# 6407 LEOPARDSTOWN (L-H)
Sunday, October 31

**OFFICIAL GOING: Soft to heavy (heavy in places)**

## 6503a EYREFIELD STKS (LISTED RACE) 1m 1f
2:15 (2:17) 2-Y-O £22,922 (£6,725; £3,204; £1,091) Stalls Far side

RPR

**1** **Yehudi (IRE)**[18] 6165 2-9-0 ........ JPSpencer 8 101
(APO'Brien, Ire) *disp ld: sent on appr st: clr fnl f: eased cl home* **7/4**[1]

**2** *3* **Imperial Brief (IRE)**[7] 6374 2-9-0 97 ........ DPMcDonogh 3 96
(KevinPrendergast, Ire) *hld up towards rr: 6th and hdwy appr st: 2nd and rdn over 1f out: no imp: kpt on* **7/4**[1]

**3** *2 ½* **In The Ribbons**[41] 5709 2-8-11 61 ........ DMGrant 6 88?
(JohnJosephMurphy, Ire) *hld up towards rr: 8th and rdn ent st: mod 4th 1f out: kpt on u.p* **33/1**

**4** *¾* **Clash Of The Ash (USA)**[6] 6408 2-9-0 94 ........ KJManning 2 90
(JSBolger, Ire) *disp ld: hdd appr st: 3rd and no ex over 1f out* **8/1**[2]

**5** *1* **Mister Hight (FR)**[40] 5725 2-9-0 ........ DJCondon 4 88
(WPMullins, Ire) *hld up in rr: kpt on fr 2f out* **8/1**[2]

**6** *¾* **Vallee Blanche (IRE)**[32] 5877 2-8-11 ........ NGMcCullagh 1 84
(MJGrassick, Ire) *chsd ldrs on inner: 5th 1/2-way: no ex appr st* **14/1**

**7** *1 ½* **Sweet Gypsy Rose (IRE)**[8] 6367 2-8-11 95 ........ MJKinane 7 81
(DavidWachman, Ire) *in tch: 6th 1/2-way: no imp st* **12/1**

**8** *3 ½* **Piano Man**[18] 6165 2-9-0 77 ........ FMBerry 9 78
(ThomasCarmody, Ire) *chsd ldrs in 4th: wknd early st* **25/1**

9 *8* **Mermaid Island (IRE)**[31] 5899 2-8-11 ....................(b[1]) PShanahan 5 60
(DKWeld, Ire) *sn cl up in 3rd: wknd ent st* **9/1**[3]

2m 2.20s **Going Correction** +0.60s/f (Yiel) **9** Ran SP% **126.1**
Speed ratings: **105,102,100,99,98 98,98,98,98**CSF £5.05 TOTE £2.90: £1.60, £1.20, £15.60; DF 5.00.
**Owner** Mrs John Magnier **Bred** Barronstown Stud & Orpendale **Trained** Ballydoyle, Co Tipperary

**NOTEBOOK**
**Yehudi(IRE)** ◆, who overcame greenness to beat a better-fancied stablemate when winning on his debut over a mile at Navan, showed the benefit of that run to win nicely on this step up in grade and trip. It is hard to tell where he ranks among the Ballydoyle juveniles, but he is a really likeable colt who should keep improving and is well worth having on your side next season. He was quoted at 25/1 for the Derby.
**Imperial Brief(IRE)**, held up to utilise his turn of foot, went second inside the last but could not get in any sort of an effective blow.
**In The Ribbons**, a 61 rated nursery performer, ran above herself here, coming with a sustained run up the outer to be nearest at the finish.
**Clash Of The Ash(USA)** went with the winner until being outpaced coming off the last bend. He only relinquished third spot close home.
**Mister Hight(FR)** stayed on in the straight without threatening.

6504 - 6507a (Foreign Racing) - See Raceform Interactive

## 4980 BREMEN
Sunday, October 31

**OFFICIAL GOING: Soft**

### 6508a GROSSER PREIS DER FREIEN HANSESTADT BREMEN (GROUP 3) 1m
**2:45** (3:01) 3-Y-0+ **£21,127** (£7,746; £4,225; £2,113)

RPR

1 **Tiberius Caesar (FR)** 4-9-2 .................... ASuborics 14 111
(PSchiergen, Germany) *prominent til rushed into lead after 3f, soon 8 lengths clear, unchallenged*

2 *11* **Madresal (GER)**[21] 6106 5-9-2 .................... WPanov 7 94
(PSchiergen, Germany) *held up, finished well down wide outside to take 2nd closing stages*

3 *1* **So Royal (GER)**[394] 5-8-11 .................... APietsch 13 88
(SWegner, Germany) *led 3f, 4th straight, stayed on at one pace final 2f*

4 *shd* **Salon Turtle (GER)** 5-9-0 .................... EPedroza 12 90
(AWohler, Germany) *chased clear leader from halfway til lost 2nd and weakened closing stages* 2

5 *3* **Apeiron (GER)**[42] 5683 3-8-12 .................... J-PCarvalho 5 87
(MarioHofer, Germany) *held up, stayed on at one pace from over 2f out* 3

6 *nk* **Open Offer**[63] 5169 4-8-11 .................... THuet 10 82
(MmeCBoqueho-Vergne, France) *held up towards rear, kept on steadily final 2f* 1

7 *3* **Kastalia (GER)**[14] 6255 4-8-11 .................... LHammer-Hansen 9 78
(PSchiergen, Germany) *held up in rear, modest late headway*

8 *3 1/2* **Freedom (GER)**[35] 5823 3-8-6 .................... NRichter 8 71
(ASchutz, Germany) *always behind*

9 *1 1/4* **Glad Lion (GER)**[21] 6106 3-8-10 .................... IFerguson 11 73
(UOstmann, Germany) *raced in 4th, 5th straight, soon beaten* 1

10 *5* **Peppercorn (GER)**[21] 6106 7-9-4 .................... PHeugl 6 70
(UOstmann, Germany) *always behind*

11 *8* **Blueberry Forest (IRE)**[137] 6-9-0 .................... MO'Reilly 2 54
(PHirschberger, Germany) *never a factor*

12 *3* **Capital Secret (USA)**[77] 7-9-0 .................... MTimpelan 1 50
(MarioHofer, Germany) *prominent to halfway*

13 *9* **Bodyguard Of Spain (GER)**[77] 5-9-2 .......... HelenaHryniewiecka 3 38
(CZschache, Germany) *3rd halfway, weakened*

1m 37.96s
**WFA** 3 from 4yo+ 3lb **13** Ran SP% **131.2**
Speed ratings: .
**Owner** Gestut Schlenderhan **Bred** Gestut Eberstein & Scea Haras Du Logis **Trained** Germany

## 1779 MULHEIM (R-H)
Sunday, October 31

**OFFICIAL GOING: Soft**

### 6509a SILVERNES BAND DER RUHR (LISTED) 2m 1f
**2:30** (2:35) 3-Y-0+ **£8,451** (£3,099; £1,690; £845)

RPR

1 **Lamantan (GER)**[371] 5-9-0 .................... AGoritz 3 102
(DAustmeyer, Germany) 3

2 *hd* **Altamirano (GER)**[36] 5808 5-9-0 .................... THellier 1 102
(WBaltromei, Germany)

3 *1 1/4* **Bailamos (GER)**[36] 5808 4-9-7 .................... FilipMinarik 5 108
(PSchiergen, Germany) 1

4 *20* **Stargate (GER)**[351] 5-9-0 .................... ADeVries 4 81
(THorwart, Germany)

5 *24* **Mana D'Argent (IRE)**[15] 6215 7-9-7 .................... JFanning 7 64
(MJohnston) *raced in 4th, went 3rd halfway, ridden and beaten 3f out* 2

6 *dist* **Classic Law**[259] 785 5-9-0 .................... ABest 2 —
(HPRosport, Germany)

7 *dist* **Westfalenkrone (GER)** 3-8-3 ow2.................... J-LSilverio 6 —
(TimGibson, Germany)

4m 7.36s
**WFA** 3 from 4yo+ 10lb **7** Ran SP% **132.3**
Speed ratings: .
**Owner** D Austmeyer **Bred** Stiftung Gestut Fahrhof **Trained** Germany

**NOTEBOOK**
**Mana D'Argent(IRE)** dropped out quickly three furlongs from home and probably needs a break.

## 6437 SAINT-CLOUD (L-H)
Sunday, October 31

**OFFICIAL GOING: Very soft**

### 6510a CRITERIUM INTERNATIONAL (GROUP 1) (C&F) 1m
**2:25** (2:27) 2-Y-0 **£100,599** (£40,246; £20,123; £10,053)

RPR

1 **Helios Quercus (FR)**[43] 5666 2-9-0 .................... ARoussel 1 112
(CDiard, France) *led 1f, 3rd straight, led over 1f out, driven out* **51/10**

2 *1 1/2* **Dubai Surprise (IRE)**[36] 5779 2-8-11 .................... TJarnet 3 107
(DRLoder) *6th straight, headway 2f out, ran on under pressure to take 2nd well inside final f* **26/1**

3 *snk* **Walk In The Park (IRE)**[9] 2-9-0 .................... TGillet 2 109
(JEHammond, France) *held up in rear & pulling hard early, 7th straight, stayed on steadily from over 1f out* **41/10**[3]

4 *3/4* **Cupid's Glory**[9] 6340 2-9-0 .................... SSanders 6 108
(SirMarkPrescott) *always in touch, 4th straight, hard ridden & every chance over 1f out, one pace final f* **89/10**

5 *2 1/2* **Stop Making Sense**[24] 6035 2-9-0 .................... CSoumillon 5 104
(AFabre, France) *always in touch, 5th straight, ridden over 1f out, kept on one pace* **46/10**

6 *2 1/2* **Early March**[28] 5980 2-9-0 .................... RHughes 4 99
(MmeCHead-Maarek, France) *led after 1f, headed over 1f out, weakened quickly* **11/10**[1]

7 *2 1/2* **Merchant (IRE)**[14] 6259 2-9-0 .................... KDarley 8 95
(MLWBell) *soon tracking leader, 2nd straight, every chance well over 1f out, soon weakened* **19/10**[2]

8 *3* **Umniya (IRE)**[14] 6259 2-8-11 ....................(v) ACulhane 7 86
(MRChannon) *last straight, always in rear* **50/1**

1m 45.3s **Going Correction** -0.275s/f (Firm) **8** Ran SP% **151.7**
Speed ratings: **107,105,105,104,102 99,97,94.**
**Owner** T Maudet **Bred** D Chassagneux **Trained** France

**NOTEBOOK**
**Helios Quercus(FR)** took the step up in class in his stride, gradually pulling clear of his opposition to win in decent style. He is not sure to stay much further but will now be let down and be prepared for next seasons Prix du Jockey Club.
**Dubai Surprise(IRE)** arrived on the scene a furlong out and battled on gamely to take second place well inside the final furlong. Her jockey feels she will stay ten furlongs next season.
**Walk In The Park(IRE)** came with a promising run up the centre of the track from one and a half out but was not able to continue his effort to the bitter end. His keenness early on might have cost him second place.
**Cupid's Glory** came with a progressive run from two out and held the lead for a short time just before the furlong marker, but he was one paced thereafter.
**Merchant(IRE)** was soon sharing the lead and under strong pressure when hampered one and a half out. He could play no further part from that point and dropped out of contention. A disappointing effort and he was probably feeling the effects of a long and hard season.
**Umniya(IRE)** was always struggling in last position and never really at the races.

### 6511a PRIX PERTH (GROUP 3) 1m
**3:30** (3:35) 3-Y-0+ **£25,704** (£10,282; £7,711; £5,141)

RPR

1 **Valentino (FR)**[18] 6170 5-9-4 .................... IMendizabal 6 113
(ADeRoyer-Dupre, France) *held up, 7th straight towards inside, edged right and headway 2f out, led 60 yards out, driven out* 2

2 *nk* **Svedov (FR)**[14] 6264 3-8-11 .................... TThulliez 8 108
(ELellouche, France) *held up in rear, 8th straight, ridden & headway on outside from over 1f out, every chance 100 yards out, ran on but not pac*[3]

3 *nk* **Keltos (FR)**[15] 6214 6-9-1 .................... MBlancpain 2 109
(CLaffon-Parias, France) *in touch, 4th straight, led narrowly approaching final f til headed and no extra last 70 yards* 1

4 *1* **Night Chapter**[22] 6075 3-8-11 .................... RHughes 1 106
(MmeCHead-Maarek, France) *prominent, 2nd straight, ridden & every chance 2f out til no extra final 100 yards*

5 *nk* **Tiganello (GER)**[22] 6075 3-8-11 .................... DBonilla 4 105
(FHead, France) *got loose before start, in rear, 9th straight, hard ridden on outside over 1f out, stayed on under strong driving final f,*

6 *1/2* **Grandes Illusions (FR)**[29] 5967 3-8-8 .................... DBoeuf 3 101
(DSmaga, France) *close up, 5th straight, effort and one pace from over 1f out*

7 *1/2* **Cattiva Generosa**[29] 5969 3-8-8 .................... TJarnet 7 100
(RGibson, France) *prominent, 3rd straight, no room tracking leaders 2f out, to over 1f out, ridden and unable to quicken final f*

8 *1/2* **Maxwell (FR)**[29] 5968 4-9-1 ....................(b) CSoumillon 9 103
(MmeCHead-Maarek, France) *led, ridden 2 1/2f out, headed approaching final f, weakened*

9 *3/4* **Askant (GER)**[127] 3335 7-9-1 .................... JBojko 10 102
(HFanelsa, Germany) *held up, 6th straight, ridden 2f out, soon one pace*

10 *6* **Reine De Vati (FR)**[22] 6075 5-8-11 .................... MCherel 5 86
(YDeNicolay, France) *held up in rear, last straight, lost touch 1 1/2f out*

1m 45.4s **Going Correction** -0.275s/f (Firm)
**WFA** 3 from 4yo+ 3lb **10** Ran SP% **122.0**
Speed ratings: **107,106,106,105,105 104,104,103,102,96.**
**Owner** E Fierro **Bred** Mme Gilles Forien & Gilles Forien **Trained** France

**NOTEBOOK**
**Valentino(FR)** is going from strength to strength and gained back-to-back wins in Group Three company. He followed the favorite throughout and, bought with a finely timed late run, he battled on gamely. Next year races like the Prix du Muguet and Lockinge Stakes will be looked at and a trip to Dubai has not been completely ruled out.
**Svedov(FR)** still had plenty to do when entering the straight and, brought with a late run up the centre of the track, he stayed on well. He remains in training next year and may well make his presence felt at this level.
**Keltos(FR)** looked the likely winner when quickening one and a half out but was just run out of things inside the final furlong.
**Night Chapter** was asked for an effort two out and kept on bravely throughout the final stages, but he just lacked a little finishing speed as the race came to an end.

# 6258 SAN SIRO (R-H)

Sunday, October 31

**OFFICIAL GOING: Heavy**

## 6512a ST LEGER ITALIANO (LISTED) 1m 6f

**2:20** (2:25) 3-Y-O+ **£24,648** (£10,845; £5,915; £2,958)

RPR

1 **Liquido (GER)**[36] 5808 5-9-5 ............ EBotti 6 114
(HSteinmetz, Germany)

2 1¾ **Fiepes Winged (GER)**[28] 5974 3-8-9 ............(b) FJovine 1 111
(MarioHofer, Germany)

3 5 **Kasus (GER)**[36] 5808 6-9-3 ............(b) IRossi 5 105
(PVovcenko, Germany)

4 1½ **Quartier Latin (USA)**[28] 5974 3-8-11 ............ MDemuro 3 106
(ASchutz, Germany)

5 1 **Bussoni (GER)**[189] 3-8-9 ............ WMongil 4 103
(HBlume, Germany)

6 7 **Andre Chenier (IRE)** 3-8-9 ............ DPorcu 9 96
(FrauJMayer, Germany)

7 1 **Le Royal (GER)**[36] 5808 4-9-3 ............ DVargiu 2 94
(HJGroschel, Germany)

8 1¼ **Zeitgeist (IRE)**[20] 6121 3-8-9 ............ NMackay 11 94
(LMCumani) *prominent to 2f out*

9 7 **One Little David (GER)**[29] 5970 4-9-3 ............ ABoschert 12 86
(HSteinmetz, Germany)

10 nk **Wildest Dream (IRE)**[154] 2509 5-9-3 ............ MMonteriso 8 86
(EBorromeo, Italy)

11 19 **Sept Clefs**[746] 5332 4-9-5 ............ WGambarota 10 69
(SIbido, Italy)

12 14 **Isoplu (IRE)** 4-9-3 ............ GBietolini 7 53
(RNatale, Italy)

3m 13.0s
**WFA** 3 from 4yo+ 9lb **12 Ran**
Speed ratings: .
**Owner** G Engel **Bred** Gestut Evershorst **Trained** Germany

**NOTEBOOK**
**Zeitgeist(IRE)** began backpeddaling with over two furlongs to run. He has shown a preference for soft ground but had never experienced anything as soft as this.

## 6513a PREMIO CHIUSURA (GROUP 3) 7f

**2:50** (3:00) 2-Y-O+ **£34,859** (£16,320; £9,190; £4,595)

RPR

1 **Horeion Directa (GER)**[21] 6109 5-9-8 ............ GBietolini 9 111
(AndreasLowe, Germany) *made virtually all, went clear from 2f out, ridden out*

2 3½ **Arc Bleu (GER)** 3-9-7 ............ EBotti 2 103
(FrauJMayer, Germany) *always in touch, kept on final f but no threat to winner*

3 snk **Glad To Be Fast (IRE)**[7] 6379 4-9-8 ............ WMongil 5 102
(MarioHofer, Germany) *mid-division, stayed on under pressure final f, just missed 2nd*

4 ½ **Roxagu (GER)**[133] 3134 3-9-7 ............ ABoschert 4 102
(UStoltefuss, Germany) *mid-division, stayed on final f, nearest at finish*

5 shd **Fisich**[728] 5-9-8 ............(b) IRossi 7 101
(ABotti, Italy) *in touch, headway when not much room & lost place 2f out, stayed on again final f, nearest at finish*

6 2½ **Krisman (IRE)**[14] 6261 5-9-8 ............ SMulas 11 94
(MCiciarelli, Italy) *pressed winner to 2f out, one pace*

7 6 **Dream Impact (USA)** 3-9-7 ............ PAragoni 3 80
(LRiccardi, Italy) *close up to 2f out*

8 4 **Arrears (USA)**[189] 4-9-8 ............ LManiezzi 1 69
(RMenichetti, Italy) *raced in 3rd til weakening 2f out*

9 1½ **Honey Bunny**[151] 2608 4-9-8 ............ MEsposito 8 66
(VCaruso, Italy) *always behind*

10 1½ **Rose Shift (IRE)**[14] 6258 4-9-5 ............ MDemuro 6 59
(BGrizzetti, Italy) *prominent to half-way*

11 15 **Armagh (IRE)** 3-9-4 ............ DVargiu 10 22
(RBrogi, Italy) *raced wide, always towards rear, tailed off from well over 1f out*

12 nk **Rekindled Applause**[16] 6203 3-9-4 ............ DPorcu 12 22
(MGuarnieri, Italy) *raced wide, beaten 2f out, tailed off*

1m 27.4s
**WFA** 3 from 4yo+ 2lb **12 Ran**
Speed ratings: .
**Owner** Rennstall Directa **Bred** H Kahrs **Trained** Germany

# 6195 REDCAR (L-H)

Monday, November 1

**OFFICIAL GOING: Soft (heavy in places)**

## 6514 MANNY BERNSTEIN FREEPHONE 0800 821 821 EBF MAIDEN STKS 7f

**1:00** (1:02) (D3) 2-Y-O **£4,728** (£1,455; £727; £363) **Stalls** Centre

Form RPR

0302 1 **Game Lad**[16] 6206 2-9-0 76 ............ DAllan 4 73
(TDEasterby) *led after 2f: mde rest: edgd rt and rdn 2f out: styd on wl fnl f* **5/4**[1]

2 2 **Restoration (FR)** 2-9-0 ............ JFortune 5 68
(JHMGosden) *led 2f: remained cl up: drvn along over 2f out: no imp on wnr fnl f* **9/2**[2]

3 hd **Blue Opal** 2-8-9 ............ RFfrench 9 63
(MissSEHall) *sn disputing ld: drvn along 3f out: kpt on wl u.p fnl f* **25/1**

54 4 2½ **E Bride (USA)**[34] 5847 2-8-9 ............ ACulhane 3 57
(JGGiven) *dwlt: sn trcking ldrs: drvn along 1/2-way: styd on fnl f* **12/1**

0 5 ½ **Lobengula (IRE)**[24] 6045 2-9-0 ............ FNorton 7 61
(HAlexander) *prom: drvn along and outpcd 3f out: styd on fnl f* **66/1**

60 6 1½ **Katie's Biscuit**[30] 5946 2-8-9 ............ NPollard 1 52
(IanEmmerson) *rr div: hdwy over 2f out: kpt on u.p fnl f: n.d* **50/1**

0 7 3½ **Calfraz**[51] 5447 2-9-0 ............ DarrenWilliams 13 49
(MDHammond) *midfield: rdn 1/2-way: no hdwy* **66/1**

00 8 nk **Blacknyello Bonnet (USA)**[33] 5856 2-8-9 ............ KDarley 2 43
(MJohnston) *chsd ldrs: drvn along 1/2-way: sn btn* **16/1**

9 nk **Brut Force (IRE)** 2-9-0 ............ JFEgan 14 48
(MissVHaigh) *dwlt: rr div: kpt on u.p fnl 2f: n.d* **33/1**

0 10 3 **Celtic Carisma**[17] 6196 2-8-6 ............ TEaves[(3)] 6 36
(KGReveley) *dwlt: sn chsng ldrs: rdn 1/2-way: fdd* **16/1**

0 11 3 **Telegram Sam (IRE)**[24] 6045 2-9-0 ............ PHanagan 8 34
(RAFahey) *trckd ldrs: drvn along and lost pl 1/2-way* **10/1**[3]

05 12 1¾ **Champagne Lujain**[16] 6211 2-8-11 ............ PMulrennan[(3)] 11 29
(MWEasterby) *dwlt: towards rr most of way* **20/1**

13 nk **Cascade Lakes** 2-8-9 ............ SWKelly 10 24
(WMBrisbourne) *dwlt: towards rr: hdwy into midfield 1/2-way: rdn and wknd over 2f out* **25/1**

00 14 5 **Cliffie (IRE)**[17] 6197 2-9-0 ............ SRighton 12 17
(JHetherton) *midfield tl rdn and lost pl 1/2-way* **200/1**

1m 31.28s (6.38) **Going Correction** +0.625s/f (Yiel) **14 Ran SP% 112.0**
Speed ratings: **88,85,85,82,82 80,76,76,75,72 68,66,66,60**CSF £4.96 TOTE £2.20: £1.20, £2.20, £7.00; EX 6.30.
**Owner** Mrs J B Mountifield **Bred** M H Easterby **Trained** Great Habton, N Yorks

**FOCUS**
A pretty ordinary maiden and very few got into it, although the winner did not need to run to his best to score. They came down the middle of the track.

**NOTEBOOK**
**Game Lad** had been in good form without winning and did enough to get off the mark at the seventh attempt. He is likely to find things tougher in future, but should make the grade at three.
**Restoration(FR)**, a 110,000euros half-brother to a six-furlong juvenile scorer and a winner at up to ten furlongs, has been given a Derby entry. Always up with the pace, he found the winner too strong in the closing stages but kept on to the line and should be able to find a similar race.
**Blue Opal**, a first foal out of a 12-furlong four-year-old winner, made a pleasing debut and should improve with time.
**E Bride(USA)** again showed ability and would appear to be going the right way. She is now qualified for a handicap mark.
**Lobengula(IRE)** made his debut in a much better maiden than this, but this was still improved form.

## 6515 MANNY BERNSTEIN 1ST FOR TELEPHONE BETTING NURSERY 1m

**1:30** (1:32) (E3) (0-75,75) 2-Y-O **£5,102** (£1,570; £785; £392) **Stalls** Centre

Form RPR

012 1 **The Pen**[60] 5240 2-8-4 58 ............ NPollard 8 64
(PCHaslam) *a.p: effrt 2f out: rdn to ld over 1f out: kpt on wl u.p fnl f* **9/1**[3]

0003 2 1¾ **Picot De Say**[21] 6127 2-8-6 60 ............ KDarley 18 63+
(JohnBerry) *in tch towards stands side: effrta nd pushed along over 2f out: sn rdn and styd on ins last: nrst fin* **16/1**

4100 3 hd **Torrens (IRE)**[14] 6265 2-9-3 71 ............ ANicholls 13 73
(SPGriffiths) *cl up: led over 2f out: rdn and hdd over 1f out: drvn and one pce ins last* **25/1**

0021 4 ½ **Strathtay**[15] 6242 2-8-5 59 ............(v) FNorton 20 59
(ABerry) *in tch towards stands side: hdwy over 2f out: rdn and ch over 1f out: drvn and one pce ins last* **7/1**[2]

503 5 1¼ **Majestic Movement (USA)**[28] 5988 2-9-0 68 ............ JFortune 15 66
(JHMGosden) *cl up: rdn along over 2f out: drvn over 1f out and wknd ent last* **7/1**[2]

0042 6 ¾ **Herencia (IRE)**[55] 5369 2-8-0 54 ............(p) SRighton 17 50
(PABlockley) *hld up towards rr: hdwy 2f out: sn rdn and kpt on ins last: nrst fin* **12/1**

6000 7 2 **Three Aces (IRE)**[20] 6140 2-7-13 53 ............(b) JQuinn 11 45
(RMBeckett) *dwlt: hdwy into midfield 1/2-way: pushed along over 2f out: sn rdn and kpt on same pce appr last* **33/1**

1060 8 2 **Breaking Shadow (IRE)**[16] 6206 2-9-7 75 ............ PHanagan 1 62
(RAFahey) *tracked ldrs: rdn along 2f out: drvn and btn over 1f out* **5/1**[1]

500 9 1 **Mary Gray**[22] 6092 2-8-10 64 ............ JFanning 19 49
(MJohnston) *prom: rdn along over 3f out: grad wknd* **33/1**

0440 10 4 **Mister Buzz**[60] 5234 2-8-3 57 ............ NMackay 12 33
(MDHammond) *in tch: effrt over 2f out: sn rdn along and no imp* **50/1**

001 11 ½ **Azahara**[22] 6091 2-9-4 72 ............ DaleGibson 16 47
(KGReveley) *towards rr: effrt and sme hdwy over 3f out: nvr a factor* **14/1**

0022 12 2 **Grand Welcome (IRE)**[33] 5855 2-8-12 66 ............(b) CCatlin 2 37
(CTinkler) *led: rdn along and hdd over 2f out: sn wknd* **11/1**

4000 13 ¾ **Vision Victory (GER)**[51] 5466 2-8-1 55 ............ RFfrench 3 24
(TPTate) *chsd ldrs on outer: rdn along 1/2-way and sn wknd* **50/1**

006 14 hd **Best Game**[17] 6181 2-8-8 62 ............ DHolland 9 31
(GAButler) *prom: rdn along 1/2-way: sn wknd* **10/1**

2340 15 2½ **Algorithm**[27] 6003 2-8-4 58 ow1 ............ DAllan 6 21
(TDEasterby) *wnt lft s: hdwy 1/2-way: effrt to chse ldrs over 2f out: sn rdn and wknd* **12/1**

040 16 1½ **King Zafeen (IRE)**[46] 5592 2-8-10 67 ............ PMulrennan[(3)] 7 27
(MWEasterby) *dwlt: a rr* **20/1**

4200 17 2½ **Mount Ephram (IRE)**[15] 6242 2-8-8 62 ............ RWinston 5 16
(RFFisher) *midfield: hdwy over 2f out: sn swtchd lft: rdn along and wknd* **50/1**

4636 18 7 **Patxaran (IRE)**[34] 5852 2-8-12 66 ............ GFaulkner 4 5
(PCHaslam) *bmpd s: a rr* **20/1**

030 19 6 **Moonfleet (IRE)**[23] 6072 2-8-4 61 ow2 ............ TEaves[(3)] 10 —
(MFHarris) *midfield: rdn along and wknd after 3f: sn bhd* **33/1**

1m 43.98s (6.28) **Going Correction** +0.625s/f (Yiel) **19 Ran SP% 125.1**
Speed ratings: **93,91,91,90,89 88,86,84,83,79 79,77,76,76,73 72,69,62,56**CSF £130.57 CT £3535.09 TOTE £8.60: £2.30, £4.20, £6.10, £2.20; EX 188.60.
**Owner** Middleham Park Racing XXVIII **Bred** Mrs R D Peacock **Trained** Middleham Moor, N Yorks

**FOCUS**
A pretty modest nursery with the first, second and fourth all boasting selling form, but the form is solid enough for the level. The came middle to stands' side and, of the first seven finishers, six were drawn in double-figure stalls.

**NOTEBOOK**
**The Pen** seems to have taken a liking to this course. She landed a seller here two starts previously over six furlongs and was then second, again at Redcar, in a nursery when last seen 60 days ago. Returned from her short break, she was as good as ever and saw the mile out really well. This was a good effort considering the next six home were drawn in double figures, and there are more races to be won with her.
**Picot De Say**, third in a seller at Windsor on his previous start, did well to come from off the pace given the first and third home were always on the speed, but he never really looked like winning and could benefit from more positive tactics.
**Torrens(IRE)**, having his first start for new connections having been sold out of Mark Johnston's yard for £14,000, ran his race and did not appear to have any excuses.
**Strathtay**, off the mark in a seven-furlong seller at Musselburgh on her previous start, just lacked a change of pace over this extra furlong in better company.

**Majestic Movement(USA)**, 11½-length third to subsequent Zetland Stakes winner Ayam Zaman in a Pontefract maiden on his previous start, did not offer a great deal dropped in trip and switched to handicap company.
**Breaking Shadow(IRE)** did not have a great draw, given that six of the first seven home came from double-figure stalls and he was well held.
**Grand Welcome(IRE)** *Official explanation: jockey said gelding hung right throughout*

## 6516 MANNY BERNSTEIN FREE £20 BET NEW ACCOUNTS (S) STKS 1m 2f
2:00 (2:00) (G4) 3-5-Y-O £3,122 (£892; £446) Stalls Low

Form RPR
0101 1 **Richie Boy**[12] 6311 3-9-3 63 NCallan 8 52+
(PABlockley) *sn trcking ldr: led 4f out: clr 2f out: pushed out* 4/7[1]
2600 2 3 **Miss Fleurie**[103] 4015 4-8-10 30 RWinston 7 36
(RCraggs) *prom: wnt 2nd over 2f out: styd on u.p: no real imp on wnr* 33/1
-000 3 4 **Golden Fields (IRE)**[41] 5710 4-8-10 40 (b) SHitchcott 9 29
(MrsJCandlish) *rr div: drvn along over 4f out: styd on u.p fnl 3f: wnt 3rd wl ins fnl f: nvr able to chal* 20/1
2000 4 ½ **Always Flying (USA)**[22] 6097 3-9-0 54 THamilton(3) 10 39
(NWilson) *led tl hdd 4f out: kpt on same pce* 13/2[2]
0000 5 1½ **Shardda**[22] 6097 4-8-10 50 (t) PRobinson 11 26
(FWatson) *in tch: drvn along over 3f out: kpt on same pce* 14/1[3]
0050 6 7 **Turftanzer (GER)**[39] 5757 5-9-1 30 (t) KimTinkler 2 19
(DonEnricoIncisa) *midfield: rdn over 3f out: no hdwy* 28/1
005 7 4 **The Spook**[20] 6142 4-9-1 40 JFanning 4 12
(MissLAPerratt) *dwlt: hld up: hdwy into midfield 3f out: wknd 2f out* 20/1
-350 8 1 **Bien Good**[27] 6005 3-8-4 45 ow1 TEaves(3) 1 6
(KGReveley) *dwlt: towards rr: rdn over 4f out: no hdwy* 25/1
6055 9 3 **Indi Ano Star (IRE)**[137] 3007 3-8-6 52 DTudhope(5) 6 5
(DCarroll) *dwlt: rr: rdn over 4f out: no hdwy* 14/1[3]
0 10 8 **Merlin's City**[17] 6200 4-8-10 TWilliams 3 —
(MissLCSiddall) *dwlt: sn midfield: drvn along 1/2-way: rdn and wknd 3f out* 200/1
00-0 11 3½ **Queen Louisa**[245] 941 4-8-7 PMulrennan(3) 5 —
(FWatson) *in tch: drvn along over 3f out: wknd 2f out* 200/1

2m 15.02s (8.22) **Going Correction** +0.725s/f (Yiel)
**WFA** 3 from 4yo+ 4lb 11 Ran SP% 111.1
Speed ratings: **96,93,90,90,88 83,80,79,76,70 67**CSF £30.63 TOTE £1.50: £1.10, £5.30, £4.00; EX 24.50.The winner was bought in for 12,500gns.
**Owner** Clive Whiting **Bred** Eurostrait Ltd **Trained** Southwell, Notts

**FOCUS**
A very weak seller; the winner had plenty in hand but the runner-up was rated just 30.

**NOTEBOOK**
**Richie Boy**, claimed after winning over a mile and a half at Warwick four starts previously, got off the mark for his new connections over a mile at Nottingham on his previous start and, dropped in grade and back up in trip, was able to follow up. Clearly quite versatile, there could yet be more races to be won with him and he was bought in for 12,500gns.
**Miss Fleurie**, dropped in grade, had 30lb to find with the winner at the weights and ran very well to finish clear in second. On this evidence, she would have to go well back in banded company.
**Golden Fields(IRE)** gained her only previous win in this grade, but she was well held and is another who would probably be better off in banded company.
**Always Flying(USA)** had half a chance at the weights, but had never previously raced on ground this soft and was well held.
**Shardda** ran a little better than of late and the step up in trip and drop in grade clearly suited.

## 6517 MANNY BERNSTEIN DON'T BE DISQUALIFIED AGAIN H'CAP 6f
2:30 (2:30) (D2) (0-92,89) 3-Y-O+ £10,816 (£3,328; £1,664; £832) Stalls Centre

Form RPR
6404 1 **Sir Desmond**[16] 6205 6-8-12 76 (p) CCatlin 14 86
(RGuest) *hld up towards rr stands side: hdwy 2f out: swtchd lft and rdn over 1f out: styd on wl fnl f to ld last 50 yds* 14/1
4131 2 nk **Flying Bantam (IRE)**[2] 6482 3-9-1 79 6ex PHanagan 6 88+
(RAFahey) *in tch: hdwy over 2f out: rdn and nt clr run ent last: swtchd rt and styd on wl towards fin* 12/1
3630 3 nk **Johnston's Diamond (IRE)**[23] 6070 6-9-10 88 DAllan 11 96
(EJAlston) *cl up stands side: led wl over 1f out: sn rdn: drvn ent last: hdd and no ex last 50 yds* 12/1
3413 4 nk **Imperial Echo (USA)**[37] 5786 3-9-6 84 PFessey 12 91
(TDBarron) *tracked ldrs stand side: effrt 2f out: rdn and ev ch over 1f out tl driv en and no ex wl ins last* 25/1
0045 5 shd **Artie**[16] 6205 5-9-6 84 RWinston 13 91
(TDEasterby) *overall ldr stands rail: rdn along and hdd wl over 1f out: sn drvn and no ex wl ins last* 12/1
2050 6 1½ **Abbajabba**[15] 6244 8-8-7 71 oh1 JFanning 16 74
(CWFairhurst) *trckd ldrs stands rail: effrt 2f out: sn rdn and kpt on same pce ent last* 14/1
0000 7 2 **Freak Occurence (IRE)**[22] 6086 3-8-7 71 oh1 NCallan 4 68
(MissECLavelle) *cl up centre: rdn along over 2f out: drvn over 1f out and grad wknd* 16/1
0001 8 1 **Burley Flame**[16] 6222 3-9-4 82 ACulhane 15 76
(JGGiven) *towards rr stands side and pushed along 1/2-way: styd on appr last: nt rch ldrs* 25/1
6000 9 ½ **Indian Spark**[30] 5949 10-8-4 71 oh3 TEaves(3) 9 63
(JSGoldie) *bhd tl sme late hdwy* 16/1
0041 10 5 **Marker**[66] 5075 4-8-11 78 RThomas(3) 5 55
(GBBalding) *in tch centre: effrt 2f out: sn rdn and wknd over 1f out* 4/1[1]
4004 11 nk **Circuit Dancer (IRE)**[35] 5832 4-9-11 89 FLynch 2 65
(ABerry) *in tch centre: hdwy on outer 2f out: rdn over 1f out and sn btn* 33/1
5602 12 2½ **Cd Flyer (IRE)**[23] 6070 7-9-3 84 PMulrennan(3) 1 53
(BEllison) *in tch centre: effrt 2f out: sn rdn and btn* 9/1[3]
3030 13 1 **Marinaite**[16] 6210 3-8-4 73 PMakin(5) 10 39
(SRBowring) *chsd ldrs stands side: rdn along over 2f out: sn wknd* 100/1
0450 14 1¾ **River Falcon**[15] 6243 4-9-5 83 NMackay 3 43
(JSGoldie) *in tch centre: hdwy over 2f out: rdn wl over 1f out and sn wknd* 12/1
4211 15 1 **Northern Games**[16] 6210 5-8-8 79 (b) AMullen(7) 7 36
(KARyan) *s.i.s: a rr* 9/2[2]
1150 16 1½ **Oeuf A La Neige**[21] 6131 4-8-9 73 OUrbina 8 26
(GCHChung) *dwlt: a rr* 11/1

1m 13.69s (1.99) **Going Correction** +0.625s/f (Yiel) 16 Ran SP% 124.0
Speed ratings: **111,110,110,109,109 107,105,103,103,96 95,92,91,88,87 85**CSF £170.31 CT £2180.25 TOTE £13.70: £3.00, £1.90, £4.30, £5.50; EX 360.60 TRIFECTA Not won..
**Owner** A P Davies **Bred** M G T Stokes **Trained** Newmarket, Suffolk

**FOCUS**
A strongly-run, competitive sprint handicap and the form looks solid. They raced middle to stands' side; those that stayed towards the middle were well beaten and, as a result, the higher stalls were favoured.

**NOTEBOOK**
**Sir Desmond**, 1lb lower than when last winning in July 2003, had been promising all season to get his head in front once again and finally managed to deliver, appreciating the strong pace to get on top in the closing stages. This should have boosted his confidence and he acts on sand, so he could well follow up.
**Flying Bantam(IRE)**, in great form lately, was racing under a 6lb penalty for his success at Wolverhampton just two days previously and only just failed to follow up from a unfavourable low draw. He is another who acts on sand and must be kept on the right side of whilst in this form.
**Johnston's Diamond(IRE)** appreciated the drop back from seven furlongs and ran a cracker under a positive ride. His ability to handle the sand will provide him with more opportunities before the year is out, not least because he is 10lb lower on that surface.
**Imperial Echo(USA)**, off the track for 37 days, returned from that short break with a decent effort in defeat.
**Artie** had conditions in his favour and ran well, especially considering he helped force the strong pace.
**Abbajabba** had conditions to suit but is very hard to win with.
**Freak Occurence(IRE)** fared best of those to race up the middle of the track.
**Marker**, 5lb higher than when winning at Goodwood under similar conditions on his previous start, did not run anywhere near that form from an unfavourably low draw.
**Cd Flyer(IRE)** had to race down the centre of the track from the worst draw of all and was not at his best.
**Northern Games** has been in really good form lately and seemed to have conditions to suit, but he never got in a blow after missing the break. *Official explanation: jockey said gelding missed break*

## 6518 MANNY BERNSTEIN STABLE STAFF APPRECIATION CLASSIFIED STKS 5f
3:00 (3:00) (E3) 3-Y-O+ £7,215 (£2,220; £1,110; £555) Stalls Centre

Form RPR
-000 1 **Little Ridge (IRE)**[31] 5912 3-8-11 72 LFletcher(3) 11 83
(HMorrison) *led stands side: edgd lft u.p over 1f out: carried rt and overall ldr ins fnl f: all out* 12/1
0264 2 1¾ **Highland Warrior**[20] 6144 5-8-12 69 NMackay 8 76
(JSGoldie) *dwlt: racd stands side: hld up: n.m.r over 1f out: r.o strly ins fnl f: nt rch wnr* 9/2[2]
0010 3 ½ **Prime Recreation**[48] 5550 7-8-12 70 LisaJones 2 75
(PSFelgate) *racd far side: led: drifted over to stands side and rdn over 1f out: hdd ins fnl f: no ex* 16/1
1000 4 ½ **If By Chance**[13] 6293 6-8-12 73 (b) TEaves(3) 7 76
(RCraggs) *racd stands side: chsd wnr: rdn appr fnl f: no imp* 20/1
3045 5 ½ **Paddywack (IRE)**[42] 5704 7-9-0 72 (b) ACulhane 3 74
(DWChapman) *racd stands side: sn rr and pushed along: hdwy appr fnl f: r.o wl towards fin: nvr nrr* 5/1[3]
0530 6 1 **Lets Get It On (IRE)**[42] 5704 3-8-10 71 RWinston 6 67
(JJQuinn) *hld up stands side: n.m.r over 1f out: swtchd lft appr fnl f: r.o: n.d* 20/1
1316 7 1 **Hout Bay**[14] 6267 7-9-3 75 PHanagan 10 71
(RAFahey) *racd stands side: dwlt: sn pushed along in rr: sme hdwy whn nt clr run appr fnl f: n.d* 5/2[1]
2404 8 nk **Kings College Boy**[24] 6046 4-8-12 68 (v) DaleGibson 5 65
(RAFahey) *racd stands side: midfield: rdn 2f out: no hdwy* 11/2
0500 9 1 **Mynd**[37] 5798 4-8-12 57 VHalliday 9 62
(RMWhitaker) *prom: rdn wl over 1f out: sn btn* 33/1
0400 10 1¼ **Hello Roberto**[47] 5564 3-8-9 69 KimTinkler 4 55
(NTinkler) *racd stands side: towards rr most of way* 25/1
5200 11 1½ **Strensall**[41] 5712 7-8-12 75 PPMathers(5) 12 58
(REBarr) *chsd ldrs stands side: rdn 1/2-way: wknd over 1f out* 16/1
0400 12 11 **A Little Bit Yarie**[128] 3293 3-9-1 73 (v) DarrenWilliams 1 23
(KRBurke) *racd far side: chsd ldr: rdn 1/2-way: sn btn: lost tch fnl f* 20/1

61.09 secs (2.39) **Going Correction** +0.625s/f (Yiel) 12 Ran SP% 119.3
Speed ratings: **105,102,101,100,99 98,96,96,94,92 90,72**CSF £60.60 TOTE £17.90: £4.10, £1.70, £4.20; EX 115.50.
**Owner** Lady Margadale **Bred** M P B Bloodstock Ltd **Trained** East Ilsley, Berks

**FOCUS**
A fair, competitive sprint and the form is ordinary but sound. Two horses raced alone far side in the early stages and Prime Recreation fared best in third.

**NOTEBOOK**
**Little Ridge(IRE)** is 11lb lower than at the start of the season and, returned to trip he last won over, came right back to form under a positive ride. Clearly not badly handicapped, he could well add to this. *Official explanation: trainer's representative said, regarding the improved form shown, gelding appeared better suited by the return to 5f and had previously shown winning form at this time of year*
**Highland Warrior** has never won over a trip this short but it proved no problem, he simply bumped into a better-handicapped rival.
**Prime Recreation** boldly raced with just one other horse on the far side of the track in the early stages and still held every chance when hanging towards the centre to join the eventual winner. This was a good effort in the circumstances.
**If By Chance** has gained all of his wins over six furlongs.
**Paddywack(IRE)** is holding his form quite well without managing to win.
**Lets Get It On(IRE)** has just a maiden debut won to her name, but would have been closer with better luck.
**Hout Bay** got little luck in running and was unable to pose a threat as a result. *Official explanation: jockey said gelding was never travelling*
**Kings College Boy** appeared to have every chance.

## 6519 MANNY BERNSTEIN HEDGING FOR BOOKMAKERS MAIDEN STKS 1m 2f
3:30 (3:30) (D3) 3-Y-O £3,526 (£1,085; £542; £271) Stalls Low

Form RPR
5502 1 **Safirah**[22] 6082 3-8-9 69 PRobinson 2 65
(MAJarvis) *cl up: led over 1f out: styd on u.p* 15/8[2]
4260 2 1½ **Turtle Patriarch (IRE)**[31] 5914 3-9-0 58 DHolland 1 67
(MrsAJPerrett) *in tch: keen early: effrt over 2f out: rdn to chse wnr appr fnl f: hung lft ins last: no imp* 7/2[3]
0562 3 1½ **Harrycat (IRE)**[17] 6192 3-9-0 70 JQuinn 7 65
(VSmith) *sn cl up: led wl over 2f out: rdn and hdd over 1f out: no ex* 13/8[1]
6 4 8 **Bottomless Wallet**[22] 6095 3-8-6 THamilton(3) 5 46
(FWatson) *hld up: pushed along over 3f out: styd on fnl f: n.d* 33/1
03 5 1 **Indian's Landing (IRE)**[12] 6310 3-9-0 KDarley 8 50
(KAMorgan) *in tch: ch and drvn along over 2f out: wknd over 1f out* 12/1
6600 6 ½ **Inmom (IRE)**[65] 5110 3-8-4 52 PMakin(5) 4 44
(SRBowring) *led tl rdn and hdd wl over 2f out: wknd wl over 1f out* 33/1
6 7 3 **I'Ll Do It Today**[12] 6310 3-9-0 PHanagan 3 44
(JMJefferson) *hld up: keen early: effrt over 3f out: sn btn* 16/1

0-6 **8** *dist* **Whitkirk Star (IRE)**[81] [4679] 3-9-0 ........................ ANicholls 6 —
(SPGriffiths) *wl bhd and rdn 1/2-way: t.o* **200/1**

2m 14.57s (7.77) **Going Correction** +0.725s/f (Yiel) **8** Ran SP% **113.2**
Speed ratings: **97,95,94,88,87 87,84,**—CSF £8.70 TOTE £2.10: £1.10, £1.20, £1.80; EX 9.70.
**Owner** Sheikh Ahmed Al Maktoum **Bred** Darley **Trained** Newmarket, Suffolk

**FOCUS**
Safirah did not have to be at her best to win a poor maiden, and the runner-up provides the guide to the level of the form.

**NOTEBOOK**
**Safirah** would had to have worked harder if the runner-up managed to get clearer passage, and she did not have to be at her best to gain a paddock-value boosting victory.
**Turtle Patriarch(IRE)** had 16lb to find with the winner, but would have finished even closer had he been able to get one continuous run. It did not look like Holland's finest hour, but he may have been a difficult ride.
**Harrycat(IRE)** shaped well when runner-up in a mile and a half claimer on his previous start and had just 4lb to find with the winner at the weights, but he was not at his best and was well held.
**Bottomless Wallet** should have more options when handicapped.

## 6520 MANNY BERNSTEIN 1ST FOR PRICES DAILY H'CAP — 1m 2f
**4:00** (4:01) (E3) (0-77,73) 3-Y-O+ **£5,380** (£1,655; £827; £413) **Stalls** Low

Form — RPR

051 **1** **Mcqueen (IRE)**[10] [6343] 4-9-8 **71** ........................ JFEgan 5 82
(MrsHDalton) *s.i.s and sn pushed along in rr: hdwy 1/2-way: rdn 3f out: led 2f out: drvn appr last and styd on wl* **9/4**[1]

0500 **2** *1 3/4* **Maritime Blues**[25] [6025] 4-8-11 **60** ........................ ACulhane 4 68
(JGGiven) *in tch: effrt over 3f out: sn rdn: drvn to chse wnr ent last: kpt on* **25/1**

0050 **3** *1/2* **Fair Spin**[12] [6311] 4-8-9 **58** ........................ KDarley 12 65
(MDHammond) *midfield: hdwy 3f out: rdn 2f out: styd on appr last: nrst fin* **12/1**

4123 **4** *3/4* **Lucayan Dancer**[10] [6337] 4-8-13 **62** ........................ DHolland 3 68
(DNicholls) *in tch: hdwy to chse ldrs 4f out: rdn wl over 2f out and kpt on same pce* **3/1**[2]

0140 **5** *1* **Creskeld (IRE)**[35] [5835] 5-9-5 **68** ........................ FLynch 11 72
(BSmart) *hld up and bhd: hdwy over 3f out: rdn along over 2f out: styd on appr last: nrst fin* **25/1**

2632 **6** *1 1/2* **Young Rooney**[20] [6141] 4-9-7 **70** ........................ TPQueally 2 72
(MMullineaux) *led: rdn along 3f out: drvn and hdd 2f out: wknd appr last* **9/1**

0660 **7** *3/4* **Phone Tapping**[88] [4493] 3-8-3 **56** oh1 ........................ PRobinson 8 56
(MHTompkins) *midfield: lost position and bhd 1/2-way: hdwy on outer 3f out: rdn 2f out: edgd lft and kpt on: nrst fin* **7/1**[3]

1000 **8** *shd* **Rotuma (IRE)**[21] [6115] 5-9-10 **73** ........................ SWKelly 6 73
(MDods) *chsd ldrs: rdn along and n.m.r 3f out: kpt on same pce fnl 2f* **20/1**

0000 **9** *3 1/2* **Royal Distant (USA)**[23] [6074] 3-8-4 **56** ow2 ........................ PMulrennan(3) 17 54
(MWEasterby) *bhd tl sme late hdwy* **25/1**

6000 **10** *1* **Melodian**[24] [6047] 9-8-11 **60** ........................(b) TWilliams 16 53
(MBrittain) *chsd ldrs: rdn along 4f out: wknd wl over 2f out* **14/1**

-060 **11** *1/2* **Mister Arjay (USA)**[25] [6025] 4-9-4 **70** ........................ TEaves(3) 15 62
(BEllison) *midfield: effrt over 3f out: sn rdn along and no hdwy* **25/1**

2100 **12** *8* **Lyford Lass**[21] [6115] 3-9-1 **68** ........................ RWinston 9 46
(ISemple) *a rr* **33/1**

5000 **13** *nk* **Mezuzah**[16] [6210] 4-9-7 **70** ........................ DaleGibson 14 48
(MWEasterby) *chsd ldr: rdn along over 4f out: sn wknd* **25/1**

0000 **14** *11* **Ace Coming**[33] [5859] 3-8-8 **61** ........................(b) JQuinn 1 20
(DEddy) *chsd ldrs: rdn along 4f out: sn wknd* **33/1**

4600 **15** *11* **On Every Street**[10] [6332] 3-9-3 **70** ........................ RFfrench 13 10
(RBastiman) *a rr* **100/1**

0-05 **16** *hd* **Eva Jean**[34] [5851] 3-8-7 **60** ........................ JFanning 7 —
(HMorrison) *chsd ldrs: rdn along 1/2-way: sn wknd* **25/1**

0430 **17** *8* **Captain Saif**[41] [5713] 4-8-12 **64** ........................ THamilton(3) 10 —
(NWilson) *a rr* **50/1**

2m 13.18s (6.38) **Going Correction** +0.725s/f (Yiel)
**WFA** 3 from 4yo+ 4lb **17** Ran SP% **129.3**
Speed ratings: **103,101,101,100,99 98,98,97,95,94 93,87,87,78,69 69,63**CSF £71.56 CT £611.36 TOTE £4.00: £1.30, £4.00, £3.00, £1.70; EX 72.80 Place 6 £108.35, Place 5 £81.14.
**Owner** R Edwards And W J Swinnerton **Bred** Philip Newton **Trained** Shifnal, Shropshire
■ Stewards Enquiry : J F Egan caution: careless riding

**FOCUS**
A modest handicap run at what seemed to be a very decent pace. The form is sound with the runner-up and fourth setting the standard.

**NOTEBOOK**
**Mcqueen(IRE)**, 6lb higher than when scoring at Newbury on his previous start, overcame a slow start and came from off the decent pace to follow up in determined fashion. The winner of four of his last six races, he is in cracking form and may not be finished with just yet, especially as he acts on the All-Weather.
**Maritime Blues**, back on a winning mark and with conditions to suit, ran his race and can have few excuses.
**Fair Spin** has just a six-furlong success on heavy ground in Italy to his name but, stepped up to ten furlongs for the first time, this was a very encouraging effort.
**Lucayan Dancer** was a touch disappointing, as he seemed to go from very travelling really well to just staying on at the one pace in the space of seconds.
**Creskeld(IRE)** was racing over his furthest trip to date on pretty testing ground, but was doing his best work at the finish.
**Young Rooney** seems so game and really does deserve to hang on one of these days.
T/Jkpt: Not won. T/Plt: £91.10 to a £1 stake. Pool: £38,649.35. 309.45 winning tickets. T/Qpdt: £20.80 to a £1 stake. Pool: £2,664.50. 94.60 winning tickets. JF

# 6204 CATTERICK (L-H)
Tuesday, November 2

**OFFICIAL GOING: Soft (heavy in places)**

## 6521 ROBIN HOOD'S BAY MAIDEN AUCTION STKS (DIV I) — 7f
**1:00** (1:00) (E4) 2-Y-O **£2,926** (£836; £418) **Stalls** Low

Form — RPR

0025 **1** **Mceldowney**[44] [5670] 2-8-11 **76** ........................ JFanning 1 73
(MJohnston) *mde all: pushed out: styd on wl* **7/2**[2]

0033 **2** *3* **Outrageous Flirt (IRE)**[48] [5556] 2-8-4 **47** ........................ JMackay 6 59
(ADickman) *keen: trckd ldrs: drvn to go 2nd 2f out: rdn appr fnl f: styd on: no imp on wnr* **14/1**

4036 **3** *3* **Plenty Cried Wolf**[26] [6021] 2-8-9 **69** ........................ PHanagan 9 57
(RAFahey) *chsd ldrs: rdn wl over 1f out: kpt on same pce* **10/1**[3]

2023 **4** *1* **Consider This**[22] [6111] 2-8-2 **79** ........................ DAllan 2 48
(WMBrisbourne) *cl up: rdn 2f out: sn btn* **4/7**[1]

0 **5** *5* **Trew Flight (USA)**[18] [6187] 2-9-0 ........................ PRobinson 8 48
(MHTompkins) *dwlt: rr div: hdwy into midfield and pushed along 1/2-way: in tch and rdn 2f out: sn btn* **12/1**

0005 **6** *7* **Steal The Thunder**[16] [6241] 2-8-2 **54** ........................ PPMathers(5) 10 24
(ABerry) *midfield: outpcd 1/2-way: n.d* **66/1**

**7** *5* **With Honours** 2-8-2 ........................ ANicholls 7 8
(TJFitzgerald) *dwlt: sn wl bhd* **50/1**

00 **8** *5* **Sooyou Sir (IRE)**[29] [5988] 2-8-7 ........................ ACulhane 4 1
(MrsADuffield) *sn pushed along in rr: lost tch over 2f out* **66/1**

**9** *2 1/2* **Grass Widow (IRE)** 2-8-4 ........................ RFfrench 3 —
(JJQuinn) *dwlt: towards rr: lost tch over 2f out* **20/1**

1m 34.82s (7.32) **Going Correction** +0.975s/f (Soft) **9** Ran SP% **119.0**
Speed ratings: **97,93,90,89,83 75,69,63,61**CSF £49.14 TOTE £5.90: £1.70, £2.60, £2.90; EX 45.50.
**Owner** C G Maybury **Bred** St Clare Hall Stud **Trained** Middleham Moor, N Yorks

**FOCUS**
A modest maiden run in bad ground and the form, although it could be rated higher, is not that solid.

**NOTEBOOK**
**Mceldowney** had the second highest official rating of those eligible for one and made every yard in these testing conditions. This was a modest maiden and, with the favourite running poorly, took little winning.
**Outrageous Flirt(IRE)**, beaten in selling company on her last two starts, had little hope with a few of these on official ratings, but she handled the ground better than most and ran her best race to date.
**Plenty Cried Wolf**, who had made the running in his last two starts, was happy to track the pace on this occasion. He ran alright and this does look his best trip.
**Consider This** was a long way clear on adjusted official ratings and proven in the ground, but he completely failed to run to his best. *Official explanation: jockey said filly was unsuited by track*
**Trew Flight(USA)**, whose dam is from the top-class family of Darshaan and Daliapour, looks more of a handicap type.

## 6522 ROBIN HOOD'S BAY MAIDEN AUCTION STKS (DIV II) — 7f
**1:30** (1:30) (E4) 2-Y-O **£2,919** (£834; £417) **Stalls** Low

Form — RPR

0503 **1** **Mytton's Bell (IRE)**[16] [6242] 2-7-11 **58** ........................ DFox(5) 8 64
(ABailey) *broke smartly: mde all: rdn clr over 1f out: 6 l ahd ins fnl f: eased fnl 75yds* **10/3**[1]

04 **2** *4* **Peter Roughley (IRE)**[17] [6207] 2-8-7 ........................ PBradley 7 59
(ABerry) *trckd wnr: effrt over 2f out: sn rdn: kpt on: no imp* **16/1**

052 **3** *shd* **Primarily**[15] [6272] 2-8-9 **68** ........................ RWinston 5 61
(ABerry) *chsd ldrs: drvn along 3f out: kpt on u.p fnl 2f* **7/2**[2]

30 **4** *2 1/2* **Bold Haze**[58] [5319] 2-8-2 ........................ LeanneKershaw(7) 1 55
(MissSEHall) *s.i.s: bhd: gd hdwy u.p 2f out: kpt on fnl f: n.d* **9/2**[3]

0005 **5** *7* **Artic Fox**[23] [6091] 2-8-11 **60** ........................(b) DAllan 2 39
(TDEasterby) *chsd ldrs: drvn along 3f out: wknd 2f out* **11/2**

000 **6** *1 1/2* **Fraambuoyant (IRE)**[17] [6221] 2-8-2 ........................($v^1$) RFfrench 6 27
(CWFairhurst) *in tch to 1/2-way: sn outpcd* **50/1**

0 **7** *1/2* **Breeder's Folly**[112] [3818] 2-8-6 ........................ PHanagan 10 29
(TJFitzgerald) *s.i.s: a bhd* **20/1**

4004 **8** *1* **Spinnakers Girl**[3] [6464] 2-8-2 **64** ........................($b^1$) CCatlin 9 23
(JRWeymes) *prom to 1/2-way: sn wknd* **9/1**

0 **9** *16* **Taragan**[39] [5771] 2-7-12 ow1 ........................ KGhunowa(7) 3 —
(JJQuinn) *s.i.s: a wl bhd* **8/1**

0 **10** *3 1/2* **Demolition Frank**[52] [5447] 2-8-7 ........................ PMQuinn 4 —
(MDHammond) *s.i.s: sn rdn and wl bhd* **33/1**

1m 34.44s (6.94) **Going Correction** +0.975s/f (Soft) **10** Ran SP% **115.5**
Speed ratings: **99,94,94,91,83 81,81,80,61,57**CSF £54.70 TOTE £4.40: £1.80, £7.50, £1.30; EX 76.00.
**Owner** Gordon Mytton **Bred** Michael Fitzpatrick **Trained** Little Budworth, Cheshire

**FOCUS**
Marginally the faster of the two divisions, but a weak event with little strengths behind the winner.

**NOTEBOOK**
**Mytton's Bell(IRE)** had been beaten in selling grade twice in her last three starts but she was proven in the ground and, making all, scored easily. She looks a likely type for the All-Weather this winter.
**Peter Roughley(IRE)** is improving with racing and is now eligible for a mark.
**Primarily** looked likely to appreciate the step up to seven, but the winner was always beyond reach.
**Bold Haze**, like the winner by Bold Edge, had run well in soft ground on his debut. He lost his chance at the start but is now eligible for a mark.
**Artic Fox** appeared to have less to do in this company, but he failed to take advantage of the weaker opposition.
**Spinnakers Girl** *Official explanation: jockey said filly was unsuited by the going - soft, heavy in places*

## 6523 THOMAS DARLEY NURSERY — 5f 212y
**2:00** (2:00) (D2) (0-85,79) 2-Y-O **£6,831** (£2,102; £1,051; £525) **Stalls** Low

Form — RPR

4011 **1** **Paris Bell**[10] [6356] 2-9-3 **75** ........................ PMQuinn 2 82
(TDEasterby) *missed break: bhd: gd hdwy and in tch 1/2-way: styd on wl u.p to ld wl ins fnl f: all out* **3/1**[2]

6002 **2** *shd* **Go Mo (IRE)**[10] [6356] 2-8-12 **70** ........................ JFEgan 9 77
(SKirk) *towards rr but in tch: hdwy over 2f out: led wl over 1f out: rdn and hdd wl ins fnl f: styd on* **11/2**[3]

5334 **3** *2 1/2* **Monash Lad (IRE)**[106] [3975] 2-9-2 **74** ........................ PRobinson 7 73
(MHTompkins) *towards rr but in tch: hdwy u.p 2f out: styd on fnl f: nvr able to chal* **11/1**

0650 **4** *3 1/2* **Rainbow Iris**[14] [6294] 2-8-10 **68** ........................ FLynch 4 57
(BSmart) *prom: ev ch 2f out: sn rdn: no ex* **16/1**

3002 **5** *3* **Orpen Wide (IRE)**[13] [6305] 2-8-6 **64** ........................ LisaJones 1 44
(MCChapman) *prom: ev ch and rdn 2f out: fdd* **16/1**

020 **6** *1/2* **Lady Doris Watts**[18] [6196] 2-8-6 **64** ........................ CCatlin 3 42
(MRChannon) *prom: drvn along and ev ch 2f out: fdd* **11/1**

0000 **7** *1/2* **John Forbes**[11] [6334] 2-8-9 **70** ........................ TEaves(3) 5 47
(BEllison) *s.i.s: bhd: styd on fnl 2f: n.d* **25/1**

0431 **8** *5* **Harrys House**[28] [6002] 2-9-5 **77** ........................ RWinston 6 39
(JJQuinn) *midfield: effrt 2f out: hung lft and sn btn* **8/1**

0060 **9** *3* **Dorn Dancer (IRE)**[28] [6003] 2-9-7 **79** ........................ LEnstone 10 32
(DWBarker) *sn towards rr: bhd whn faltered and stmbld 2f out* **28/1**

3315 **10** *1 1/4* **Tsaroxy (IRE)**[22] [6113] 2-9-3 **78** (b[1]) PMulrennan(3) 8 27
(JHowardJohnson) *led: 4 l clr 1/2-way: hdd wl over 1f out: wknd qckly* **2/1**[1]

1m 20.28s (6.28) **Going Correction** +0.975s/f (Soft) **10** Ran SP% **120.6**
Speed ratings: **97,96,93,88,84 84,83,76,72,71**CSF £20.87 CT £167.38 TOTE £4.10: £1.70, £2.30, £2.80; EX 23.60.
**Owner** Ryedale Partners No 8 **Bred** M H Easterby **Trained** Great Habton, N Yorks

**FOCUS**
An ordinary nursery but the form of the winner's Newbury victory was upheld, with the runner-up following him home again.

**NOTEBOOK**
**Paris Bell** has improved a great deal this autumn - he was running off a mark 13lb higher than when securing the first of his three wins - and loves this soft ground. He stayed on well to lead close home and gives the impression that he will stay farther.
**Go Mo(IRE)**, 8lb better off with the winner for a beating of three and a half lengths at Newbury, closed that gap to almost nothing. He clearly has the ability to win a race of this nature off this sort of mark, but time is running out this turf season.
**Monash Lad(IRE)**, dropped 6lb, had less to do in this company. He had never previously run on soft ground but appeared to handle conditions well enough.
**Rainbow Iris**, a beaten favourite on the Polytrack last time, looks held in handicap company off his current mark.
**Orpen Wide(IRE)** failed to build on the promise of his Nottingham effort despite being dropped 7lb since that run.
**Dorn Dancer(IRE)** *Official explanation: jockey said filly stumbled badly approximately two furlongs out*
**Tsaroxy(IRE)** was too keen in the first-time blinkers and hit the wall inside the final quarter mile. *Official explanation: trainer's representative was unable to offer any explanation for poor form shown*

## 6524 HAMBLETON MAIDEN STKS — 1m 3f 214y
**2:30** (2:31) (D3) 3-Y-O+ **£3,513** (£1,081; £540; £270) **Stalls** Low

Form RPR
03 **1** **Lady Karr**[23] [6095] 3-8-9 JFanning 6 69+
(MJohnston) *mde all: edgd lft and drew clr over 1f out: in total command fnl f: unchal* **4/1**[3]
5062 **2** *6* **Mac's Elan**[22] [6130] 4-9-6 46 ACulhane 8 57
(ABCoogan) *in tch: hdwy 4f out: wnt 2nd 3f out: styd on u.p: no ch w wnr* **16/1**
-002 **3** *1 3/4* **Classic Event (IRE)**[102] [4103] 3-9-0 62 DAllan 2 55
(TDEasterby) *s.s: bhd: drvn along and hdwy 4f out: wnt 3rd 2f out: styd on u.p: nvr able to chal* **9/1**
3/5 **4** *7* **Selkirk Grace**[43] [5705] 4-9-6 PHanagan 4 45
(KAMorgan) *midfield: drvn along over 3f out: no imp on ldrs* **5/1**
P064 **5** *5* **Dances With Angels (IRE)**[14] [6285] 4-9-1 40 PMQuinn 7 33
(JWUnett) *chsd wnr tl wknd 3f out* **25/1**
4030 **6** *7* **Carriacou**[14] [6292] 3-8-9 61 JFEgan 5 23
(PWD'Arcy) *hld up: effrt over 3f out: sn rdn and btn* **7/2**[2]
00-0 **7** *3 1/2* **Calcar (IRE)**[302] [440] 4-9-6 45 LVickers 3 23
(MrsSLamyman) *chsd ldrs tl rdn and wknd over 3f out* **100/1**
000 **8** *23* **Sandokan (GER)**[13] [6310] 3-9-0 TPQueally 11 —
(BJCurley) *midfield tl outpcd and lost tch 4f out: t.o* **20/1**
4605 **9** *5* **Bijou Dan**[22] [6112] 3-9-0 54 RWinston 1 —
(ISemple) *chsd ldrs: drvn along 1/2-way: wknd 4f out: t.o* **50/1**
**10** *10* **Express Lily**[361] 5-9-1 DarrenWilliams 12 —
(KRBurke) *towards rr: lost tch 4f out: t.o* **33/1**
0-00 **11** *5* **Red Mountain**[90] [4444] 3-8-11 TEaves(3) 9 —
(DWBarker) *towards rr: lost tch 4f out: t.o* **100/1**
-463 **12** *3* **Maid To Treasure (IRE)**[10] [6357] 3-8-9 75 KDarley 10 —
(JLDunlop) *trckd ldrs: drvn along 4f out: wknd 3f out: wl bhd whn eased fnl f: t.o* **3/1**[1]

2m 49.97s (10.97) **Going Correction** +0.975s/f (Soft) **12** Ran SP% **115.3**
**WFA** 3 from 4yo+ 6lb
Speed ratings: **102,98,96,92,88 84,81,66,63,56 53,51**CSF £58.30 TOTE £4.60: £2.00, £3.60, £2.20; EX 75.70.
**Owner** Iona Equine **Bred** The Old Suffolk Stud **Trained** Middleham Moor, N Yorks

**FOCUS**
A modest maiden but won in decisive fashion, and although it is difficult to be totally convinced about the form, the winner should be interesting in handicaps if the Handicapper does not overreact.

**NOTEBOOK**
**Lady Karr** proved suited by the step up in trip and won easily on her first try on soft ground. The race did not take much winning, the Handicapper should not overreact, and she is clearly going the right way.
**Mac's Elan**, stepping up in trip from a mile, kept on well to pick up some more runner-up prize-money. He is only moderate but is paying his way well.
**Classic Event(IRE)** stayed on but could never quite reach the first two. He shapes as though he will be suited by a step up to staying trips.
**Selkirk Grace** had run a promising race on his reappearance so it was slightly disappointing that he failed to make more of an impact in this modest contest. *Official explanation: jockey said gelding hung left throughout*
**Dances With Angels(IRE)**, beaten in banded company on a number of occasions, is a poor performer.
**Carriacou** *Official explanation: jockey said filly became unbalanced in final two furlongs*
**Maid To Treasure(IRE)**, now a beaten favourite on her last three starts, failed to run her race. *Official explanation: jockey said filly lost both front shoes and was never travelling*

## 6525 TOTEPLACEPOT STKS (H'CAP) — 7f
**3:00** (3:01) (D2) (0-92,85) 3-Y-O+ **£6,983** (£2,148; £1,074; £537) **Stalls** Low

Form RPR
1-14 **1** **Go Padero (IRE)**[3] [6475] 3-9-3 **85** JFanning 1 96+
(MJohnston) *prom: styd on u.p to ld ins fnl f: all out* **9/4**[1]
1500 **2** *3/4* **King Harson**[24] [6070] 5-9-1 **82** (v) PRobinson 8 88
(JDBethell) *led tl rdn and hdd ins fnl f: no ex* **16/1**
6035 **3** *hd* **Kirkby's Treasure**[16] [6244] 6-8-9 **76** ow1 FLynch 11 82
(ABerry) *bhd: gd hdwy 2f out: ch and rdn ins fnl f: no ex clsng stages* **8/1**
0506 **4** *2 1/2* **Digital**[3] [6477] 7-9-4 **85** ACulhane 5 84
(MRChannon) *chsd ldrs: ch and rdn 2f out: kpt on same pce* **9/2**[2]
0150 **5** *1 1/2* **Young Mr Grace (IRE)**[24] [6070] 4-9-3 **84** DAllan 9 80
(TDEasterby) *prom: ev ch and rdn 2f out: fdd* **20/1**
1000 **6** *5* **Nevada Desert (IRE)**[36] [5835] 4-7-13 **71** (p) BSwarbrick(5) 4 54
(RMWhitaker) *midfield: effrt 3f out: no hdwy* **20/1**
0120 **7** *3/4* **Azreme**[3] [6477] 4-8-10 **77** RFfrench 2 58
(DKIvory) *midfield: hmpd and lost pl over 4f out: pushed along and sme hdwy over 2f out: sn btn* **11/2**[3]
4005 **8** *1* **Ulysees (IRE)**[21] [6144] 5-8-4 **71** oh5 PHanagan 7 50
(ISemple) *rr div fr 1/2-way* **16/1**
1450 **9** *1* **Raymond's Pride**[38] [5799] 4-8-13 **80** (b) NCallan 6 56
(KARyan) *towards rr: effrt and sme hdwy over 2f out: sn btn* **11/1**
6100 **10** *10* **Jath**[24] [6070] 3-8-10 **78** KDarley 3 29
(JulianPoulton) *s.i.s: sn midfield: chsng ldrs and rdn 2f out: wknd qckly* **8/1**

1m 33.82s (6.32) **Going Correction** +0.975s/f (Soft) **10** Ran SP% **116.2**
**WFA** 3 from 4yo+ 1lb
Speed ratings: **102,101,100,98,96 90,89,88,87,76**CSF £42.16 CT £248.19 TOTE £3.20: £1.90, £4.00, £2.00; EX 34.80 Trifecta £432.50 Pool of £4,142.25 - 6.80 winning tickets.
**Owner** Pagodero Partnership **Bred** Lisieux Stud **Trained** Middleham Moor, N Yorks

**FOCUS**
A decent little handicap for the track and solid form, with the winner looking capable of better.

**NOTEBOOK**
**Go Padero(IRE)**, back down to his optimum trip, found plenty for pressure to record his second win of this year's brief campaign. Provided he can be kept sound, he could make up into a very useful handicapper next year.
**King Harson**, back down to his last winning mark, bounced back to his best under his ideal conditions.
**Kirkby's Treasure** has run a number of good races this term off this sort of mark but gives the impression that he needs a little leniency to be winning again.
**Digital** has dropped 8lb during the course of the year and is 5lb lower than his last winning mark, but he continues to find a few too good.
**Young Mr Grace(IRE)** is another who looks high enough in the weights for the moment.
**Azreme**, who had conditions to suit, was hampered on the turn and his chance went there.
**Jath** *Official explanation: jockey said filly was unsuited by the going - soft, heavy in places*

## 6526 BOROUGHBRIDGE CLAIMING STKS — 5f
**3:30** (3:30) (F4) 3-Y-O+ **£3,024** (£864; £432) **Stalls** Low

Form RPR
0005 **1** **Trinculo (IRE)**[46] [5605] 7-9-10 75 ANicholls 14 91+
(DNicholls) *mde most: drvn wl clr appr fnl f: eased fnl 100yds* **4/1**[2]
5000 **2** *8* **Robwillcall**[16] [6246] 4-8-1 45 (p) PHanagan 8 44
(ABerry) *midfield: hdwy u.p over 1f out: wnt 2nd ins fnl f: no ch w wnr* **14/1**
4012 **3** *2 1/2* **Loughlorien (IRE)**[28] [6007] 5-8-3 56 DTudhope(5) 11 44
(REBarr) *sn bhd: hdwy u.p over 1f out: r.o fnl f: nvr able to chal* **9/2**[3]
5030 **4** *nk* **The Leather Wedge (IRE)**[8] [6403] 5-8-0 40 ow1 PPMathers(5) 10 40
(ABerry) *w ldrs: rdn wl over 1f out: no ex* **25/1**
20-0 **5** *2* **Bond Romeo (IRE)**[122] [3511] 3-8-8 67 DMcGaffin 2 37
(BSmart) *w ldrs: rdn wl over 1f out: wknd ins fnl f* **20/1**
0005 **6** *1 1/4* **George The Best (IRE)**[22] [6114] 3-8-12 62 ACulhane 1 37
(MDHammond) *slowly away: racd alone far rail: n.d* **8/1**
0020 **7** *nk* **Torrent**[38] [5798] 9-8-4 56 (b) LisaJones 13 28
(DWChapman) *chsd ldrs: rdn over 1f out: sn btn* **9/1**
0560 **8** *hd* **Pay Time**[18] [6200] 5-8-0 40 ow1 CCatlin 6 24
(REBarr) *chsd ldrs: rdn 2f out: no hdwy* **66/1**
20 **9** *9* **Frabrofen**[15] [6275] 3-8-13 RFfrench 9 10
(JamesMoffatt) *sn towards rr* **25/1**
0300 **10** *1* **Brigadier Monty (IRE)**[28] [6007] 6-8-12 52 RWinston 12 6
(MrsSLamyman) *sn towards rr* **7/1**
0000 **11** *8* **Miss Ceylon**[31] [5949] 4-8-5 35 DAllan 15 —
(SPGriffiths) *sn towards rr* **80/1**
-00 **12** *2 1/2* **Baba (IRE)**[22] [6119] 3-8-12 KDarley 5 —
(TPTate) *midfield to 1/2-way: sn wknd* **28/1**
113 **13** *3* **Beauvrai**[52] [5458] 4-9-4 77 (b) OUrbina 4 —
(GCHChung) *in tch to 1/2-way: bhd whn eased appr fnl f* **7/2**[1]

62.35 secs (1.75) **Going Correction** +0.375s/f (Good) **13** Ran SP% **119.3**
Speed ratings: **101,88,84,83,80 78,78,77,63,61 48,44,40**CSF £53.51 TOTE £5.20: £2.00, £4.20, £2.40; EX 87.90.The winner was retained by a friendly claim.
**Owner** D Nicholls **Bred** Humphrey Okeke **Trained** Sessay, N Yorks

**FOCUS**
A decisive win for the dropped-in-grade winner, who looks capable of a better for his new stable, but the form behind is banded class.

**NOTEBOOK**
**Trinculo(IRE)**, who had the headgear left off for the first time in a long time, hacked up from a modest field. He was the second highest rated on official ratings, was making his debut for his new stable and was of course taking on much lesser opposition than he has been tackling for most of the season. He could be interesting back on the All-Weather this winter.
**Robwillcall**, who won a worse claimer than this in the summer, handles this ground and probably ran up to his recent best in second.
**Loughlorien(IRE)**, whose record at this track now reads 014154033423, clearly likes it here, but he is only modest and is vulnerable to a horse like the winner who is dropping in grade.
**The Leather Wedge(IRE)** had plenty to find with most of these at the weights and was not disgraced in the circumstances. He is more effective on Fibresand.
**Bond Romeo(IRE)** looks badly handicapped on his recent efforts. *Official explanation: jockey said gelding finished distressed*
**Beauvrai** has been in good form of late but struggled on this occasion from his low draw. *Official explanation: jockey said gelding finished distressed.*

## 6527 OLIVER CROMWELL H'CAP — 1m 5f 175y
**4:00** (4:00) (E3) (0-77,70) 3-Y-O+ **£3,548** (£1,091; £545; £272) **Stalls** Low

Form RPR
0460 **1** **Onward To Glory (USA)**[23] [6083] 4-9-0 **60** WRyan 3 70
(JLDunlop) *hld up in rr: stdy hdwy fr over 3f out: led over 1f out: drvn out* **13/2**
1150 **2** *1* **Inchnadamph**[24] [6074] 4-9-1 **61** (t) KDarley 5 70
(TJFitzgerald) *hld up in tch: tk clsr order 6f out: led over 3f out: rdn and hdd over 1f out: styd on* **7/1**
1412 **3** *3 1/2* **Scott**[18] [6183] 3-8-10 **64** GBaker 2 68
(JJay) *hld up: hdwy to trck ldrs over 3f out: ch 2f out: sn chsng first 2: rdn appr fnl f: no imp* **10/3**[1]
0004 **4** *1 1/4* **Montecristo**[14] [6286] 11-9-10 **70** CCatlin 8 72
(RGuest) *hld up: drvn along and hdwy 3f out: styd on u.p fr over 1f out: nvr able to chal* **9/2**[3]
3064 **5** *10* **Kyber**[16] [6245] 3-8-2 **56** oh1 RFfrench 4 44
(RFFisher) *led tl hdd over 3f out: wknd 2f out* **25/1**
4201 **6** *1* **Precious Mystery (IRE)**[18] [6183] 4-9-2 **67** AQuinn(5) 1 54
(AKing) *midfield: outpcd 4f out: n.d after* **4/1**[2]
-400 **7** *4* **The Fairy Flag (IRE)**[47] [5584] 6-8-5 **56** oh1 (p) DFox(5) 9 37
(ABailey) *chsd ldrs: drvn along 4f out: in tch and rdn 2f out: sn wknd* **16/1**
4050 **8** *10* **Pilgrims Progress (IRE)**[22] [6110] 4-9-5 **65** (p) TWilliams 6 32
(DWThompson) *cl up: slt ld over 3f out: sn hdd and rdn: wknd over 2f out* **25/1**
0000 **9** *19* **Archie Babe (IRE)**[25] [6047] 8-9-0 **60** RWinston 7 1
(JJQuinn) *prom tl wknd 4f out: t.o* **13/2**

100- 10 *dist* **Win Alot**[20] [3664] 6-8-10 **56** oh11 ........................ LisaJones 10 —
(MCChapman) *towards rr: lost tch 4f out: t.o fnl 2f* **66/1**

3m 17.64s (13.14) **Going Correction** +0.975s/f (Soft)
**WFA** 3 from 4yo+ 8lb **10** Ran SP% **115.5**
Speed ratings: **101,100,98,97,92 91,89,83,72,**—CSF £49.91 CT £178.43 TOTE £9.20: £2.70, £2.90, £1.50; EX 101.90 Place 6 £134.40, Place 5 £44.36.
**Owner** Michael H Watt **Bred** Ron Dufficy **Trained** Arundel, W Sussex

**FOCUS**
An ordinary handicap and only modest form although, with the placed horses setting the standard, it appears sound enough for the level.

**NOTEBOOK**
**Onward To Glory(USA)** had dropped 13lb in the handicap since the beginning of the season and found this step up in trip playing to his strengths. A test of stamina is clearly what he wants.
**Inchnadamph** coped with this softer ground well but was just outstayed. He has had a good season and could be the type to enjoy some success over hurdles this winter.
**Scott**, 6lb higher, had his stamina to prove over this longer trip. Although he saw it out well enough, the impression is that he is high enough in the weights for the time being.
**Montecristo** looked likely to run well over this longer trip with his official rating back down to his last handicap winning mark but, despite pulling clear of the majority of the field, he could never quite get to the prinicpals.
**Kyber** enjoyed the run of the race but did not get home.
**Precious Mystery(IRE)** *Official explanation: jockey said filly hung right in straight*
T/Plt: £68.00 to a £1 stake. Pool: £30,539.50. 327.80 winning tickets. T/Qpdt: £22.50 to a £1 stake. Pool: £3,699.30. 121.20 winning tickets. JF

# FLEMINGTON (R-H)
## Tuesday, November 2

**OFFICIAL GOING: Good to soft**

## 6528a EMIRATES MELBOURNE CUP (GROUP 1) (H'CAP) 2m
**4:10** (4:10) 3-Y-0+ **£1,176,471** (£306,723; £140,756; £71,429)

RPR

1 **Makybe Diva**[17] 7-8-11 ........................ GBoss 7 123
(LeeFreedman, Australia) *racd in 14th, 16th 4f out, prog on ins to go 8th bhd ldrs str, hdwy on ins to ld jst over 1f out, ran on strongly* **26/10**[1]

2 1 1/4 **Vinnie Roe (IRE)**[45] [5662] 6-9-2 ........................(b) PJSmullen 10 126
(DKWeld, Ire) *racd in 12th, 10th str on outside, rdn to ld briefly appr fnl f, ran on under pressure but not pace of wnr* **5/1**[2]

3 2 1/2 **Zazzman (AUS)**[3] 6-8-4 ........................(b) NRyan 6 111
(TVasil, Australia) *led 7f, 3rd halfway, 2nd straight, led 2f out to approaching final f, one pace* **100/1**

4 1 1/2 **Elvstroem (AUS)**[10] [6373] 4-8-13 ........................ NRawiller 3 118
(TVasil, Australia) *always close up, 7th straight, headway to go 2nd briefly 1 1/2f out, one pace* **15/1**

5 *nk* **Hugs Dancer (FR)**[17] 7-8-4 ........................ GChilds 4 109
(TMcevoy, Australia) *in touch lost place 4f out, 17th straight, stayed on strongly down outside from over 1f out* **16/1**

6 1 3/4 **Distinction (IRE)**[53] [5438] 5-8-7 ........................ DBeadman 12 110
(SirMichaelStoute) *raced in 18th, edging towards outside and not much room 4f out to 3f out, 12th straight, kept on* **12/1**[3]

7 *shd* **Mamool (IRE)**[30] [5981] 5-9-0 ........................ LDettori 21 117
(SaeedBinSuroor) *raced in 10th, short of room 4f out, 13th straight towards outside, headway to go 5th 1f out, one pace* **25/1**

8 *nk* **Catchmeifyoucan (NZ)**[3] 5-7-10 ........................(b) BShinn 1 98
(MMoroney, Australia) *raced in 6th, 3rd straight, 2nd just under 2f out to 1 1/2f out, one pace* **20/1**

9 *nk* **Razkalla (USA)**[32] [5916] 6-8-10 ........................ KMcEvoy 16 112
(SaeedBinSuroor) *raced in 8th, 9th straight, stayed on at one pace final 2f* **40/1**

10 1 1/4 **Strasbourg (AUS)**[3] 5-8-3 ........................(b) MDuPlessis 22 103
(JBCummings, Australia) *in rear, 23rd over 4f out, 19th straight, stayed on down outside final 2f* **40/1**

11 *nk* **On A Jeune (AUS)**[13] 4-8-0 ........................(b) JBowditch 18 100
(PMontgomerie, Australia) *in rear, headway 4f out, 6th straight towards outside, weakened 1 1/2f out* **60/1**

12 *nk* **Media Puzzle (USA)**[45] [5662] 7-8-11 ........................(b) DMOliver 11 111
(DKWeld, Ire) *racd in 19th, hdwy towards outside in tight quarters fr over 4f out, 14th str on wd outside, sn rdn and one pace* **20/1**

13 2 **Grey Song (AUS)**[17] 6-8-3 ........................ DBeasley 24 100
(TJHughesJnr, Australia) *raced in 17th, 15th on inside straight, never a factor* **20/1**

14 1 1/4 **Roman Arch (AUS)**[3] 5-8-4 ........................ LCurrie 5 100
(MWhittle, Australia) *raced in 13th, 16th straight, never a factor* **100/1**

15 3 **Upsetthym (NZ)**[17] 5-8-1 ........................ RMcLeod 23 93
(KarenFursdon, New Zealand) *raced in 23rd, 18th straight on outside, never a factor* **70/1**

16 1 1/2 **Another Warrior (AUS)**[10] 6-8-1 ........................(b) JimByrne 13 91
(AlanBailey, Australia) *in rear, last 4f out, 23rd straight, always behind* **40/1**

17 1 1/4 **Winning Belle (NZ)**[3] 4-7-11 ........................ CMunce 17 86
(MrsGaiWaterhouse, Australia) *close up, 11th straight, soon weakened* **40/1**

18 5 **Lashed (AUS)**[3] 5-8-3 ........................(b) JimCassidy 20 86
(GRogerson, Australia) *last to beyond halfway, 20th straight, always behind* **80/1**

19 1 3/4 **Mummify (AUS)**[17] 5-8-12 ........................ DNikolic 15 93
(LeeFreedman, Australia) *prominent, 4th straight, weakened quickly from over 2f out* **30/1**

20 4 **Don Raphael (AUS)**[3] 5-8-0 ........................ SSeamer 19 76
(KParker, Australia) *led after 7f, headed 3 1/2f out, 5th straight, weakened quickly* **60/1**

21 1 1/4 **Pacific Dancer (NZ)**[13] 4-8-2 ........................ GGrylls 8 76
(ShaunDwyer, Australia) *raced in 16th, 21st straight, always behind* **17/1**

22 1 1/2 **Hard To Get (AUS)**[10] 4-8-1 ........................ LNolen 14 74
(MKavanagh, Australia) *close up til went 2nd halfway, led 3 1/2f out to 2f out, weakened quickly* **100/1**

23 25 **Delzao (AUS)**[10] [6373] 4-8-7 ........................(b) StevenKing 2 50
(GKavanagh, Australia) *raced in 11th, weakened 3f out* **40/1**

24 15 **She's Archie (AUS)**[31] 5-8-2 ........................(b) CoreyBrown 9 27
(DWeir, Australia) *towards rear til weakened 4f out, tailed off from over 2f out, finished lame* **14/1**

3m 28.55s **24** Ran SP% **118.9**
Speed ratings: .
**Owner** Emily Krstina Pty Ltd Syndicate **Bred** Emily Kristina (aust) Pty Ltd **Trained** Australia
■ The winner set a new weight-carrying record for mares in the race.

**FOCUS**
A cracking renewal of this historic race that went to Makybe Diva for a second consecutive year. Frankie Dettori received a one-month careless riding ban, harsh to say the least, for causing interference to Distinction who was in turn pushed out on to Media Puzzle.

**NOTEBOOK**
**Makybe Diva** set a new weight-carrying record for mares with her second successive win in Australia's greatest race. She benefited from a very daring ride (Boss ghosted up the inside and approaching the home turn she squeezed through the narrowest of gaps on the rail) but she won with such authority that she would surely have prevailed whatever route her pilot chose. She has little more to prove Down Under and trainer Lee Freedman mooted a tilt at next year's Arc in Paris.
**Vinnie Roe(IRE)** was suited by the rain that fell before and during the race and lost no caste in defeat. Sensibly brought around the outside, given that the local jockeys were hardly going to do Smullen any favours, he was travelling noticeably well on the heels of the leaders early in the straight but had to give best to an outstanding champion.
**Hugs Dancer(FR)** was ninth in this last year when trained by James Given.
**Distinction(IRE)** was given an odd ride for a horse who stays so well but lacks a turn of foot. Jumped off among the backmarkers, he was forced to begin a long surge for home over three furlongs out. Denied a passage to the outside by Media Puzzle, he kept on grinding it out without ever threatening the lead. He needed to be ridden more prominently.
**Mamool(IRE)** engaged in a relatively minor bout of jostling three furlongs out which the Stewards deemed worthy of a one-month ban for Dettori. Thanks to his jockey's determination, he got as close as fifth a furlong out but his stamina seemed to give out in the closing stages.
**Razkalla(USA)** was in much the same position throughout, saving ground towards the inside, and was simply not good enough.
**Media Puzzle(USA)** , having only his third run since winning this race in 2002, needs firm ground. Forced to circle the field around the outside, he was close enough entering the home straight but then flattened out.

# 6462 MAISONS-LAFFITTE (R-H)
## Tuesday, November 2

**OFFICIAL GOING: Heavy**

## 6529a PRIX MIESQUE (GROUP 3) (FILLIES) (STRAIGHT) 7f (S)
**1:20** (1:19) 2-Y-0 **£25,704** (£10,282; £7,711; £5,141)

RPR

1 **Stella Blue (FR)**[50] 2-8-11 ........................ TThulliez 3 106
(PBary, France) *made all, pushed out, ran on well*

2 2 **Mirabilis (USA)**[30] [5979] 2-8-12 ........................ CSoumillon 4 102
(AFabre, France) *held up, headway well over 1f out, reached 2nd 1f out, ridden & kept on same pace, no threat to winner* **1**

3 *nk* **Arabian Spell (IRE)**[18] 2-8-12 ........................ TJarnet 2 102
(RGibson, France) *raced in 3rd behind winner, ridden over 1f out, kept on under pressure*

4 *nk* **Cours De La Reine (IRE)**[30] [5979] 2-9-1 ........................ IMendizabal 6 104
(PWChapple-Hyam) *pressed winner, racing wide to half-way, ridden over 1f out, kept on one pace final f* **3**

5 2 1/2 **Princesse Jasmine (FR)**[18] [6202] 2-8-12 ........................(b) SPasquier 5 95
(YDeNicolay, France) *disputed 3rd, effort 2f out, weakened approaching final f*

6 2 **Novarra (IRE)**[23] [6108] 2-8-11 ........................ C-PLemaire 1 89
(ASchutz, Germany) *held up, never in contention*

7 1 1/2 **Beirut (GER)**[60] [5280] 2-8-11 ........................ WMongil 7 86
(PSchiergen, Germany) *always in rear* **2**

1m 30.6s **7** Ran SP% **122.6**
Speed ratings: .
**Owner** Ecurie Stella Maris **Bred** Snc Stella Maris **Trained** France

**NOTEBOOK**
**Stella Blue(FR)**, hugging the rail throughout, made virtually every yard of the running and was not over extended in the final furlong. She is likely to come back to this course and distance next April for the Prix Imprudence and will be entered in both the 1,000 Guineas and the Pouliches - she should stay a mile.
**Mirabilis(USA)** settled behind the leaders early on before making a forward move one and a half out. She looked dangerous at the furlong pole, but could only find the one pace.
**Arabian Spell(IRE)** was outpaced when things warmed up one and a half out before staying on really well, only missed second place by a neck. A promising effort from this maiden.
**Cours De La Reine(IRE)** had to give weight to the rest of the field so this was a decent effort in the circumstances. She loves cut in the ground and is expected to stay further than a mile in the future.

# 6240 MUSSELBURGH (R-H)
## Wednesday, November 3

**OFFICIAL GOING: Good to soft (good in places)**
Wind: Slight 1/2 behind. Weather: Overcast.

## 6530 TOTEPLACEPOT E B F MEDIAN AUCTION MAIDEN STKS 7f 30y
**1:30** (1:31) (E3) 2-Y-0 **£4,221** (£1,299; £649; £324) **Stalls** Low

Form RPR

26 1 **Mintlaw**[23] [6111] 2-8-9 ........................ RWinston 7 76+
(ISemple) *trckd ldrs: hdwy on ins to ld 1f out: hung bdly lft and sn clr* **5/1**[3]

0234 2 3 1/2 **Consider This**[1] [6521] 2-8-4 79 ........................ PPMathers(5) 11 65
(WMBrisbourne) *mde most: hdd 1f out: keeping on same pce whn swtchd rt wl ins last* **4/1**[2]

3 3/4 **Piccolomini** 2-9-0 ........................ KDarley 3 69
(MJohnston) *rangy: scope: mid-div: hdwy over 2f out: styng on wl whn n.m.r wl ins last* **12/1**

0 4 1/2 **Halcyon Express (IRE)**[30] [6000] 2-9-0 ........................(t) MartinDwyer 4 67
(PFICole) *w ldr: styd on same pce fnl f* **10/1**

6 5 1 3/4 **La Viola**[19] [6196] 2-8-9 ........................ DarrenWilliams 2 58
(KRBurke) *trckd ldrs: effrt 2f out: kpt on one pce* **10/1**

5 6 1 1/2 **Woolsack (USA)**[12] [6331] 2-9-0 ........................ SDrowne 1 59
(HMorrison) *trckd ldrs: chal over 2f out: wknd jst ins last* **10/3**[1]

0 7 3 1/2 **Ammirare**[29] [6008] 2-8-6 ........................ PMulrennan(3) 5 46
(CWThornton) *s.i.s: hdwy and swtchd lft over 2f out: nvr nr ldrs* **66/1**

0 8 1/2 **Linzis Lad**[60] [5301] 2-8-7 ........................ AMullen(7) 13 50
(KARyan) *mid-div: effrt 3f out: wknd over 1f out* **66/1**

00 9 *shd* **Hannah's Tribe (IRE)**[86] [4606] 2-8-9 ........................ FLynch 14 44
(BSmart) *a in rr* **50/1**

10 *nk* **Port D'Argent (IRE)** 2-8-9 ........................ JFanning 10 54+
(MJohnston) *rangy: chsd ldrs: edgd lft over 2f out: sn lost pl* **10/1**

11 ½ **Brads House (IRE)** 2-8-11 .................... TEaves(3) 8 47
(JGMO'Shea) *rangy: unf: s.s: a bhd* **66/1**

00 12 *nk* **Christom**[9] [6392] 2-9-0 .................... PHanagan 6 47
(GAButler) *s.s: bhd: hdwy u.p on ins 3f out: nvr on terms* **16/1**

13 ¾ **Bold Pursuit (IRE)** 2-9-0 .................... DAllan 12 45
(MrsADuffield) *lengthy: scope: bkwd: a in rr* **50/1**

00 14 *11* **Tyrone Sam**[62] [5241] 2-9-0 .................... GParkin 9 18
(KARyan) *sn bhd: t.o* **66/1**

1m 32.57s (3.04) **Going Correction** +0.375s/f (Good) **14** Ran SP% **110.5**
Speed ratings: **97,93,92,91,89 87,83,83,83,82 82,81,81,68**CSF £22.43 TOTE £6.40: £1.70, £1.70, £3.00; EX 35.80.
**Owner** Evelyn Duchess Of Sutherland **Bred** The Duchess Of Sutherland **Trained** Carluke, S Lanarks

**FOCUS**
A fair maiden but whether the 79-rated runner-up ran to that mark is open to question.

**NOTEBOOK**
**Mintlaw** had suggested that a drop back in trip was required last time and ran out a clear winner on her first start over seven furlongs. She may not receive a very favourable mark considering she beat an exposed 79-rated performer into second, however.
**Consider This** has run numerous good races this season in defeat and once again appeared to run her race, although whether the she ran to her mark is open to question. She is proving expensive to follow.
**Piccolomini**, a half-brother to two winners, including Godolphin Mile winner Conflict, made a promising start to his career. He should do a lot better next year and this experience will not be lost on him.
**Halcyon Express(IRE)**, tounge tied for the first time, improved on his debut effort and looks the type to progress with racing.
**La Viola** could be one for All-Weather handicaps after one more run.
**Woolsack(USA)**, a half-brother to a sprint winner in the US, was slightly disappointing. He may do better over six furlongs in the short term.

## 6531 TOTESPORT 0800 221 221 E B F MAIDEN STKS 1m
**2:00** (2:00) (D2) 2-Y-O **£5,486** (£1,688; £844; £422) **Stalls** Low

Form RPR

60 **1** **Dream Tonic**[11] [6352] 2-9-0 .................... SHitchcott 5 82
(MRChannon) *chsd ldrs: led 2f out: styd on wl fnl f* **20/1**

63 **2** *1 ¾* **Key Of Solomon (IRE)**[15] [6283] 2-9-0 .................... SDrowne 2 78
(HMorrison) *mid-div: effrt over 2f out: chsd wnr fnl f: no real imp* **7/2**[2]

33 **3** *3 ½* **Onyergo (IRE)**[22] [6139] 2-9-0 .................... RWinston 10 70
(JRWeymes) *swvd rt s: chsd ldrs: edgd rt 1f out: kpt on same pce* **14/1**

544 **4** *1* **Cordage (IRE)**[56] [5400] 2-9-0 80 .................... PHanagan 4 68
(GAButler) *trckd ldrs: effrt on inner over 2f out: keeping on same pce whn n.m.r and swtchd lft 1f out* **9/2**[3]

402 **5** *5* **Love Beauty (USA)**[39] [5790] 2-9-0 79 .................... JFanning 6 59+
(MJohnston) *w ldrs: hmpd over 2f out: sn btn* **2/1**[1]

4 **6** *nk* **Bond Cat (IRE)**[18] [6211] 2-8-9 .................... FLynch 9 53+
(BSmart) *led: edgd lft 3f out: hdd 2f out: sn wknd* **25/1**

0 **7** *1* **Arthurs Dream (IRE)**[103] [4081] 2-8-11 .................... TEaves(3) 3 54
(JGMO'Shea) *s.i.s: bhd tl sme late hdwy* **66/1**

4 **8** *1* **Bayard (USA)**[11] [6351] 2-8-11 .................... LPKeniry(3) 1 52
(DRCElsworth) *in rr: drvn along over 4f out: nvr a factor* **5/1**

0 **9** *16* **Valet**[22] [6145] 2-8-11 .................... PMulrennan(3) 7 17
(JGMO'Shea) *s.i.s: a bhd: t.o* **66/1**

1m 44.48s (1.78) **Going Correction** +0.375s/f (Good) **9** Ran SP% **108.7**
Speed ratings: **106,104,100,99,94 94,93,92,76**CSF £80.72 TOTE £20.60: £3.10, £2.10, £1.90; EX 120.90.
**Owner** The National Stud Owner-Breeders' Club **Bred** The National Stud Owner Breeders Club Ltd **Trained** West Ilsley, Berks

**FOCUS**
A fair maiden with 80-rated Cordage and 79-rated Love Beauty setting a fair standard.

**NOTEBOOK**
**Dream Tonic** had run with promise on his debut but had been found out by the testing conditions on his last start. He saw the mile out well and there could be more to come from him in handicap company.
**Key Of Solomon(IRE)** appeared to run his race and finished clear of the rest. Quicker ground will suit on breeding and he is now eligible for handicaps, although he has the ability to win a maiden.
**Onyergo(IRE)** ran a decent race in what was probably a fair heat. He is now eligible for a mark and hopefully the Handicapper will not overburden him.
**Cordage(IRE)**, stepping up from six furlongs, did not get the best of runs but did not exactly pick up when finally getting racing room.
**Love Beauty(USA)**, whose stable won this race in 1999, 2000 and 2001, was a disappointing favourite, even allowing for the fact that he was hampered.
**Bayard(USA)** is going to be suited by a test of stamina on a galloping track next season.

## 6532 TOTEQUADPOT H'CAP 5f
**2:35** (2:35) (D2) (0-92,84) 3-Y-0+ **£6,799** (£2,092; £1,046; £523) **Stalls** Low

Form RPR

0011 **1** **Harrison's Flyer (IRE)**[16] [6274] 3-8-9 72 .................... PHanagan 7 86+
(RAFahey) *lw: trckd ldrs: led jst ins fnl f: r.o wl* **7/1**[3]

1360 **2** *1 ¼* **Fiddle Me Blue**[20] [6175] 3-8-13 76 .................... SDrowne 9 83
(HMorrison) *sn chsng ldrs: kpt on wl fnl f: no imp* **12/1**

1-06 **3** *1* **Great Fox (IRE)**[5] [6459] 3-8-10 73 .................... KDarley 2 77
(PLGilligan) *mde most tl 1f out: no ex* **7/1**[3]

4004 **4** *nk* **Bond Boy**[11] [6349] 7-9-7 84 .................... FLynch 11 86+
(BSmart) *sn in rr: hdwy and nt clr run over 1f out: swtchd rt: kpt on wl* **7/1**[3]

4134 **5** *½* **Imperial Echo (USA)**[2] [6517] 3-9-7 84 .................... PFessey 6 85
(TDBarron) *chsd ldrs: styd on same pce appr fnl f* **5/1**[2]

2642 **6** *2 ½* **Highland Warrior**[2] [6518] 5-8-7 70 oh1 .................... RWinston 4 62
(JSGoldie) *s.i.s: hdwy on ins 2f out: nvr rchd ldrs* **4/1**[1]

0035 **7** *1 ¾* **Kathology (IRE)**[94] [4366] 7-8-12 78 .................... LPKeniry(3) 5 64
(DRCElsworth) *w ldrs: wknd 1f out* **8/1**

3504 **8** *1 ¼* **Trick Cyclist**[24] [6079] 3-8-8 71 .................... DaleGibson 8 52
(MWEasterby) *mid-div: outpaced fnl 2f* **16/1**

0033 **9** *2 ½* **Baron Rhodes**[5] [6459] 3-9-1 81 .................... (p) TEaves(3) 3 54
(JSWainwright) *w ldr: disp ld after 2f tl over 1f out: sn lost pl* **9/1**

2000 **10** *nk* **Strensall**[2] [6518] 7-8-7 75 .................... PPMathers(5) 12 47
(REBarr) *s.i.s: hdwy on wd outside 3f out: lost pl over 1f out* **25/1**

5550 **11** *1 ¼* **Tribute (IRE)**[47] [5614] 3-8-1 71 .................... AMullen(7) 10 38
(KARyan) *s.i.s: a in rr* **33/1**

61.77 secs (1.37) **Going Correction** +0.40s/f (Good) **11** Ran SP% **115.6**
Speed ratings: **105,103,101,100,100 96,93,91,87,86 84**CSF £86.40 CT £622.19 TOTE £7.30: £2.10, £5.00, £2.90; EX 116.90 Trifecta £914.10 Pool: £1,287.54. 0.60 winning tickets..
**Owner** P D Smith Holdings Ltd **Bred** Geoff Mulcahy **Trained** Musley Bank, N Yorks

**FOCUS**
A fair handicap won by a progressive winner, and the form should prove solid.

**NOTEBOOK**
**Harrison's Flyer(IRE)**, 8lb higher than for the first of his wins, finds these conditions perfect and racked up the hat-trick in good style. He is in fine form at present and would not be one to right off if attempting the four-timer back on the Polytrack.
**Fiddle Me Blue** has shown a preference for fast ground so this was a fine performance in the circumstances.
**Great Fox(IRE)** appreciated the return to the minimum trip having failed to see out six furlongs recently.
**Bond Boy**, 9lb lower than at the beginning of the season, is still struggling to recapture his best form.
**Imperial Echo(USA)** found the drop back to the minimum trip on this sharp track putting too much emphasis on speed.
**Highland Warrior** was a strange favourite given that his best form is over six furlongs and his tendency to start slowly promised to put him at a disadvantage over this sharp five.

## 6533 TOTEPOOL H'CAP 1m 4f
**3:05** (3:06) (E3) (0-77,77) 3-Y-0+ **£3,485** (£1,072; £536; £268) **Stalls** High

Form RPR

2411 **1** **Shape Up (IRE)**[148] [2753] 4-8-9 58 .................... (b) RWinston 10 66
(RCraggs) *hld up in mid-div: stdy hdwy 3f out: rdn to ld over 1f out: hld on wl* **12/1**

1343 **2** *1* **Easibet Dot Net**[24] [6096] 4-9-3 69 .................... (p) TEaves(3) 2 76
(ISemple) *sn trcking ldrs: led over 3f out: hung lft and carried hd high: led over 1f out: kpt on* **10/1**

16-0 **3** *1* **Altay**[26] [6043] 7-10-0 77 .................... PHanagan 6 83
(RAFahey) *mid-div: hdwy over 2f out: styd on wl fnl f* **5/1**[2]

0001 **4** *1* **Fiddlers Creek (IRE)**[22] [6142] 5-8-2 56 oh4 .................... (p) PPMathers(5) 7 60
(RAllan) *bhd: hdwy over 3f out: kpt on wl fnl f* **14/1**

0663 **5** *nk* **Stallone**[26] [6047] 7-9-0 66 .................... THamilton(3) 5 70
(NWilson) *mid-divsion: effrt over 2f out: kpt on: nvr rchd ldrs* **10/1**

4121 **6** *3* **Ego Trip**[18] [6209] 3-8-10 65 .................... (b) DaleGibson 12 65
(MWEasterby) *plld hrd: mde most for 3f: trckd ldrs: drvn along over 4f out: wknd over 1f out* **7/2**[1]

6524 **7** *1 ¾* **Scurra**[18] [6209] 5-8-3 57 .................... DTudhope(5) 1 54
(ACWhillans) *hdwy on outside to chse ldrs after 3f: lost pl over 2f out* **16/1**

0060 **8** *nk* **Off Beat (USA)**[21] [6160] 3-8-1 56 .................... PFessey 11 53
(TDBarron) *bhd: sme hdwy 3f out: nvr a factor* **20/1**

0541 **9** *½* **Minivet**[39] [5479] 9-8-5 57 .................... PMulrennan(3) 9 53
(RAllan) *w ldr: led after 3f tl over 3f out: wknd 2f out* **6/1**[3]

2300 **10** *nk* **Lucky Arthur (IRE)**[29] [6006] 3-8-1 56 oh2 .................... (v[1]) RFfrench 4 52
(JGMO'Shea) *s.i.s: sme hdwy on outer 3f out: nvr a factor* **33/1**

6400 **11** *1 ½* **Slavonic (USA)**[12] [6332] 3-8-12 67 .................... (p) GParkin 3 60
(KARyan) *chsd ldrs: lost pl 3f out* **25/1**

5000 **12** *1 ¼* **Flight Commander (IRE)**[23] [6110] 4-8-9 58 .................... (v[1]) DAllan 13 50
(ISemple) *chsd ldrs: lost pl over 3f out* **50/1**

5-60 **13** *dist* **Beacon Blue (IRE)**[35] [5859] 3-8-7 62 .................... KDarley 8 —
(MJohnston) *a towards rera: lost pl over 3f out: sn bhd and eased* **12/1**

2m 42.06s (4.06) **Going Correction** +0.375s/f (Good)
**WFA** 3 from 4yo+ 6lb **13** Ran SP% **112.8**
Speed ratings: **101,100,99,99,98 96,95,95,95,94 93,93,—**CSF £114.55 CT £678.70 TOTE £7.80: £3.00, £2.90, £2.20; EX 153.00.
**Owner** Ray Craggs **Bred** Gainsborough Stud Management Ltd **Trained** Sedgefield, Co Durham
■ Robert Winston's maiden century.

**FOCUS**
A modest handicap run at a sound gallop. The field were strung out at the finish and the form looks just ordinary.

**NOTEBOOK**
**Shape Up(IRE)**, last seen completing back-to-back wins in amateur events 148 days previously, bagged the hat-trick in good style on this debut for his new connections. He could have been called the winner halfway up the straight and is value for further than the winning margin, as he hit the front plenty soon enough and tended to idle. Clearly progressing, he was rated 69 last season so could be one to follow on the All-Weather this winter.
**Easibet Dot Net** ran another sound race, although he hit the front plenty soon enough this time and again threw his head about when in the lead. He had no chance with the winner, but remains in fair form.
**Altay** improved on his recent seasonal debut at York and turned in a sound effort under top weight. He should come on again for this and he has the option of reverting to hurdles or the Polytrack, a surface he goes well on.
**Fiddlers Creek(IRE)**, all out to win a seller at Ayr last time, ran respectably back over this more suitable longer trip. He lacked the turn of foot to get to the principals, but remains in good heart at present and could enjoy a return to the All-Weather.
**Stallone** looked to find this ground soft enough and did not run badly in the circumstances. He has slipped to a favourable mark.
**Ego Trip** ran far too keen early and blew all chance of landing the hat-trick. He is well worthy of another chance.
**Minivet** dropped right away having helped set the pace for most of the way. He can do better back on a faster surface over further.
**Beacon Blue(IRE)** *Official explanation: jockey said filly lost its action*

## 6534 TOTESPORT WILLIE PARK STKS (LISTED RACE) 2m
**3:40** (3:40) (A1) 3-Y-0+ **£23,200** (£8,800; £4,400; £2,000) **Stalls** Low

Form RPR

2053 **1** **Alcazar (IRE)**[10] [6382] 9-9-6 113 .................... SDrowne 3 112+
(HMorrison) *trckd ldrs: wnt 2nd 9f out: led 3f out: shkn up and qckned over 1f out: styd on strly: eased nr fin* **11/8**[1]

1511 **2** *5* **Winged D'Argent (IRE)**[12] [6335] 3-8-7 96 .................... KDarley 6 102+
(MJohnston) *lw: chsd ldr: drvn along 8f out: wnt 2nd over 2f out: kpt on: no ch w wnr* **13/8**[2]

2245 **3** *7* **Fling**[7] [6443] 3-8-2 83 .................... PHanagan 1 89
(JRFanshawe) *t.k.h: trckd ldrs: effrt 3f out: edgd rt: one pce* **8/1**

4150 **4** *3* **Holy Orders (IRE)**[10] [6382] 7-9-6 .................... (b) DJCondon 4 94
(WPMullins, Ire) *s.i.s: in rr: hdwy 4f out: kpt on: nvr nr ldrs* **5/1**[3]

1304 **5** *16* **Tudor Bell (IRE)**[36] [5850] 3-8-7 79 .................... RWinston 2 71
(JGMO'Shea) *led tl 3f out: sn lost pl: eased clsng stages* **66/1**

6046 **6** *8* **Gargoyle Girl**[4] [6074] 7-8-11 55 .................... TEaves 5 57
(JSGoldie) *s.i.s: sn trcking ldrs: outpcd 7f out: bhd fnl 4f* **150/1**

3m 36.75s (3.05) **Going Correction** +0.375s/f (Good)
**WFA** 3 from 7yo+ 9lb **6** Ran SP% **110.1**
Speed ratings: **107,104,101,99,91 87**CSF £3.70 TOTE £2.30: £1.50, £1.30; EX 4.40.
**Owner** J Repard,F Melrose,O Pawle,M Stokes,R Black **Bred** J Repard **Trained** East Ilsley, Berks

**FOCUS**
A decent Listed race that was run at a true gallop in the testing ground. The form looks solid, although the winner did not need to run to his best to score.

**NOTEBOOK**

**Alcazar(IRE)** , a gallant third to Westerner in a Group One in France ten days previously, posted a deserved win in decisive fashion and can be rated value for further than the winning margin. He has run well in many of the top staying events this term, without quite being good enough to score, but is a hard horse to beat at this level and should go well again next year with a similar campaign likely.

**Winged D'Argent(IRE)** ◆ , who has looked most progressive in his last two starts, ran a solid race and did well to trouble the winner at these weights. He looks well up to winning off this sort of mark, should prove even better as a four-year-old and got this trip well.

**Fling** ran too keen and ruined her chances of seeing out this longer trip. She stuck to her guns however, and faced a very tough task at the weights, so was not disgraced and now earns some valuable black type to enhance her paddock value.

**Holy Orders(IRE)** , beaten around 15 lengths behind Alcazar in France last time, did not help his cause at the start and ran another moody race.

## 6535 TOTESPORT.COM STKS (H'CAP) 2m

**4:10** (4:11) (D2) (0-92,85) 3-Y-0+ **£8,411** (£2,588; £1,294; £647) **Stalls** Low

Form RPR

1113 **1** **Sendintank**[60] 5288 4-9-9 **85** MartinDwyer 10 101+
(SCWilliams) *hld up: stdy hdwy over 3f out: led over 1f out: shkn up and qcknd ins last: readily* **6/5**[1]

3221 **2** *2* **Most Definitely (IRE)**[19] 6198 4-8-10 **72** DAllan 2 85
(TDEasterby) *rrd s: hld up in rr: smooth hdwy to ld over 2f out: hdd over 1f out: kpt on same pce ins last* **8/1**[3]

3020 **3** *6* **Kristensen**[18] 6215 5-9-0 **76** (p) PFessey 7 82
(DEddy) *mid-div: hdwy to ld over 3f out: hdd over 2f out: styd on same pce* **7/1**[2]

0004 **4** *2* **Ski Jump (USA)**[26] 6043 4-9-2 **78** (v) PHanagan 5 82
(RAFahey) *hld up in rr: hdwy over 4f out: one pce fnl 2f* **12/1**

4300 **5** *4* **Almizan (IRE)**[18] 6215 4-9-4 **80** SHitchcott 8 79
(MRChannon) *a in tch: effrt over 3f out: one pce* **10/1**

3 **6** *3* **Karelian**[23] 6115 3-8-1 **72** RFfrench 9 67
(KARyan) *led 2f: chsd ldrs: lost pl 2f out* **10/1**

3216 **7** *hd* **Typhoon Tilly**[48] 5595 7-8-11 **73** KDarley 1 68
(CREgerton) *t.k.h in rr: gd hdwy to chse ldrs after 5f: wknd over 2f out* **14/1**

456 **8** *10* **Kid'Z'Play (IRE)**[26] 5584 8-8-6 **71** oh8 TEaves(3) 3 54
(JSGoldie) *w ldrs: led 4f out: c wd and sn hdd: lost pl 3f out* **33/1**

-360 **9** *25* **Corton (IRE)**[20] 6172 5-9-4 **80** (p) JFanning 6 33
(PFICole) *led after 2f tl 4f out: edgd lft and sn lost pl: bhd and eased fnl 2f* **20/1**

304- **10** *6* **Marble Arch**[350] 3112 8-9-8 **84** SDrowne 11 30
(HMorrison) *lost pl after 5f: sn last: t.o fnl 5f* **25/1**

-160 **11** *dist* **Acceleration (IRE)**[18] 1661 4-8-6 **71** oh9 (p) PMulrennan(3) 4 —
(RAllan) *chsd ldrs: drvn along 6f out: lost pl over 3f out: sn bhd and eased: t.o* **50/1**

3m 37.97s (4.27) **Going Correction** +0.375s/f (Good)
**WFA** 3 from 4yo+ 9lb **11** Ran SP% **115.1**
Speed ratings: **104,103,100,99,97 95,95,90,77,74** —CSF £10.10 CT £48.75 TOTE £2.40: £1.10, £2.00, £2.10; EX 8.00 Place 6 £75.03, Place 5 £41.08.
**Owner** Steve Jones And Phil McGovern **Bred** K G Powter **Trained** Newmarket, Suffolk

**FOCUS**
A fair staying handicap that was run at a sound pace. The first two came clear and the form is not that easy to rate, but looks sound enough.

**NOTEBOOK**

**Sendintank** got back to winning ways with a decisive success. This was his ninth win of the year, off a 35lb higher mark than when first successful at Wolverhampton in January, and he is clearly still ahead of the Handicapper. He takes his racing very well and is just as effective at shorter, so could make up into an even better performer next year.

**Most Definitely(IRE)** , raised 7lb for losing his maiden tag at the 21st attempt last time, took up the running going as well as any two out, but could not match the winner when it mattered. He is a model of consistency and this goes down as yet another improved display, but the suspicion is that he may be better over slightly shorter.

**Kristensen** , who turned in a respectable display in the Cesarewitch last time, ran his race with no excuses. He is reliable enough at this level, but very hard to win with.

**Ski Jump(USA)** , held up to get the trip, ran well enough on ground that looked too testing. It is hard to know whether he fully gets this trip, but he would have much better claims of staying on his preferred faster going.

T/Jkpt: Not won. T/Plt: £161.20 to a £1 stake. Pool: £41,102.70. 186.05 winning tickets. T/Qpdt: £25.70 to a £1 stake. Pool: £3,098.80. 89.00 winning tickets. WG

# 6478 WOLVERHAMPTON (A.W) (L-H)

## Wednesday, November 3

**OFFICIAL GOING: Standard**

Not as much kickback as there had been at recent meetings and no apparent draw bias. First of a series of early-evening cards put on at short notice.
Wind: Slight behind Weather: Cloudy

## 6536 LITTLEWOODS BET DIRECT MAIDEN STKS 7f 32y(P)

**4:15** (4:18) (D3) 2-Y-0 **£3,614** (£1,112; £556; £278) **Stalls** High

Form RPR

34 **1** **Il Colosseo (IRE)**[22] 6139 2-9-0 DaneO'Neill 3 78+
(MrsLStubbs) *mde all: qcknd clr over 2f out: eased nr fin* **7/1**[3]

00 **2** *5* **Flaunt N Flirt**[6] 6447 2-8-4 NDeSouza(5) 7 59
(MPTregoning) *chsd ldrs: hmpd 6f out: outpcd over 2f out: rdn and hung lft appr fnl f: styd on* **14/1**

0 **3** *1 1/4* **Cape Enterprise (USA)**[21] 6155 2-9-0 MHills 8 61
(JWHills) *hld up in tch: rdn over 2f out: styd on same pce appr fnl f* **14/1**

04 **4** *nk* **Neutrino**[12] 6330 2-9-0 NMackay 10 60
(LMCumani) *hld up: styd on fnl 2f: nvr trbld ldrs* **13/8**[1]

**5** *1* **Blue Azure (USA)** 2-8-9 DHolland 6 53
(GAButler) *s.i.s: outpcd: hdwy over 1f out: nrst fin* **12/1**

302 **6** *1 1/4* **Limit (IRE)**[9] 6393 2-8-9 ACulhane 12 49
(MRChannon) *prom: chsd wnr over 2f out: rdn and hung lft over 1f out: wknd fnl f* **9/2**[2]

000 **7** *2 1/2* **Aggravation**[7] 6440 2-9-0 JFEgan 1 48
(AndrewReid) *prom: hmpd 6f out: rdn over 2f out: wknd over 1f out* **40/1**

05 **8** *3* **Annibale Caro**[6] 6448 2-9-0 SSanders 4 41
(SirMarkPrescott) *s.i.s: outpcd: nvr nrr* **7/1**[3]

**9** *2* **Sea Lark** 2-9-0 SWKelly 5 36
(WJHaggas) *dwlt: outpcd* **20/1**

**10** *7* **Sweet Sioux** 2-8-9 EAhern 2 14
(PWHarris) *s.i.s: outpcd* **10/1**

0 **11** *5* **Degree Of Honor (FR)**[47] 5604 2-8-9 KFallon 9 2
(JGGiven) *chsd ldr: rdn 1/2-way: wkng whn hmpd over 2f out: eased* **14/1**

12 *4* **Blue Otis (IRE)** 2-8-9 GBaker 11 —
(MrsHSweeting) *hld up: rdn 1/2-way: sn wknd* **40/1**

1m 32.04s **12** Ran SP% **127.7**
Speed ratings: CSF £106.79 TOTE £9.60: £1.60, £5.30, £6.10; EX 188.90.
**Owner** Des Thurlby **Bred** Miss Audrey F Thompson **Trained** Malton, N. Yorks

**FOCUS**
A messy contest in which the winner won with plenty in hand, although he did have the run of the race and the standard in behind is modest.

**NOTEBOOK**

**Il Colosseo(IRE)**, even allowing for him having the run of the race, was still pretty impressive and value for more than the winning margin.

**Flaunt N Flirt** did not have the best of luck in running, but showed enough to suggest she can find a little race when going handicapping.

**Cape Enterprise(USA)** is still learning and can do better when facing a stiffer test.

**Neutrino**, who is bred to be suited by middle-distances, would not have been suited to the steady early pace. He will have more options open to him now in handicaps.

**Blue Azure(USA)**, a half-sister to a middle-distance winner in the USA, was far too green to do herself justice, but will have learnt plenty from the experience.

**Limit(IRE)** was a shade disappointing, and may have done better had she been made a bit more use of.

**Annibale Caro** will have plenty of options open to him now he can go handicapping, and will certainly appreciate a step up in trip.

**Degree Of Honor(FR)** *Official explanation: jockey said he suffered interference turning into home straight*

## 6537 BET DIRECT ON ITV PAGE 367 CLASSIFIED STKS 7f 32y(P)

**4:40** (4:40) (F3) 3-Y-0 **£3,497** (£1,076; £538; £269) **Stalls** High

Form RPR

3543 **1** **Tenny's Gold (IRE)**[23] 6119 3-8-9 60 MHills 3 68
(BWHills) *hld up: hdwy over 2f out: rdn to ld ins fnl f: r.o* **7/2**[3]

1340 **2** *2* **Landucci**[24] 6094 3-9-3 65 (t) KFallon 11 71
(JWHills) *hld up in tch: chsd ldr over 2f out: sn rdn: led and edgd lft ins fnl f: sn hdd and unable qck* **5/2**[1]

6456 **3** *nk* **Double Dagger Lady (USA)**[66] 5155 3-8-9 60 EAhern 6 62
(JNoseda) *chsd ldrs: led over 2f out: rdn over 1f out: hdd and no ex ins fnl f* **3/1**[2]

0150 **4** *nk* **Miskina**[24] 6097 3-8-4 58 BSwarbrick(5) 4 64+
(WMBrisbourne) *prom: n.m.r and lost pl 1/2-way: hdwy over 2f out: sn rdn: nt clr run and hmpd ins fnl f: styd on* **12/1**

6250 **5** *1 1/4* **The Job**[177] 1997 3-8-12 59 ACulhane 8 61
(ADSmith) *hld up: hdwy and nt clr run over 2f out: sn rdn: r.o ins fnl f: nt rch ldrs* **10/1**

6004 **6** *1* **Extra Cover (IRE)**[28] 6014 3-9-1 63 (b) DSweeney 10 61
(MsDeborahJEvans) *hld up: hdwy over 1f out: nvr trbld ldrs* **16/1**

0000 **7** *1/2* **Sion Hill (IRE)**[16] 6271 3-8-5 60 JDO'Reilly(7) 9 57
(JO'Reilly) *hld up: hdwy over 2f out: sn rdn: styd on same pce appr fnl f* **12/1**

0000 **8** *1 1/2* **Wall Street Runner**[6] 6452 3-8-9 59 JQuinn 2 50
(CADwyer) *outpcd: nvr nrr* **33/1**

0000 **9** *4* **Fit To Fly (IRE)**[18] 6225 3-8-12 58 (p) ANicholls 1 43
(MrsJCandlish) *chsd ldr 3f: wknd 3f out* **33/1**

0064 **10** *1/2* **Tsarbuck**[9] 6398 3-8-12 59 (p) GFaulkner 7 41
(RMHCowell) *chsd ldrs: rdn: hung lft and wknd over 2f out* **11/1**

0000 **11** *3* **Vademecum**[24] 6094 3-8-12 60 DMcGaffin 5 34
(BSmart) *sn led: hdd over 2f out: rdn and wknd over 1f out* **14/1**

0340 **12** *hd* **Wings Of Morning (IRE)**[50] 5552 3-8-5 60 DanielleMcCreery(7) 12 33
(DCarroll) *s.i.s: hdwy over 5f out: wknd 4f out* **33/1**

1m 32.23s **12** Ran SP% **130.0**
Speed ratings: CSF £13.88 TOTE £5.60: £2.20, £1.40, £1.80; EX 16.30.
**Owner** Rick Barnes **Bred** Barouche Stud (ire) Ltd **Trained** Lambourn, Berks

**FOCUS**
Not a strong contest in which the winner did not have to improve any to win, and the form, rated through the fifth, is ordinary.

**NOTEBOOK**

**Tenny's Gold(IRE)**, who reportedly bled last time, faced her easiest task to date and did not have to improve any to get off the mark.

**Landucci**, who was beaten by the draw last time, had no such excuses and remains a frustrating animal.

**Double Dagger Lady(USA)**, as you would expect of her pedigree, proved well suited to this surface. While she is nothing out of the ordinary, it would be a surprise if there wasn't a little handicap in her somewhere.

**Miskina** would have pushed the winner close had she any luck at all in running.

**The Job** turned in a solid effort on this return to action, over a trip which is on the sharp side for him.

**Extra Cover(IRE)** does have ability, but is none too reliable.

## 6538 BET DIRECT ON AT THE RACES H'CAP 5f 20y(P)

**5:05** (5:07) (E3) (0-77,78) 3-Y-0 **£3,437** (£1,057; £528; £264) **Stalls** Low

Form RPR

0000 **1** **Global Achiever**[25] 6064 3-8-12 64 OUrbina 13 74
(GCHChung) *s.i.s: hld up: hdwy over 1f out: led wl ins fnl f: r.o* **25/1**

4104 **2** *hd* **Kostar**[44] 5697 3-9-8 74 RSmith 7 83
(CGCox) *s.i.s: sn prom: chsd ldr 1/2-way: nt clr run ins fnl f: sn ev ch: r.o: edgd lft nr fin* **12/1**

0001 **3** *3* **Little Ridge (IRE)**[2] 6518 3-9-9 78 6ex LFletcher(3) 6 76
(HMorrison) *led 4f out: clr 2f out: rdn: hung rt and hdd wl ins fnl f: no ex* **11/4**[1]

0530 **4** *shd* **Only If I Laugh**[95] 4320 3-8-10 67 MLawson(5) 3 65
(PABlockley) *chsd ldrs: rdn 1/2-way: styd on ins fnl f* **20/1**

4200 **5** *3/4* **Maluti**[53] 5473 3-8-4 56 oh1 CCatlin 11 51
(RGuest) *hld up: hdwy over 1f out: nt rch ldrs* **9/1**

2405 **6** *2 1/2* **Jilly Why (IRE)**[4] 6482 3-9-4 70 ANicholls 9 56
(MsDeborahJEvans) *chsd ldrs: rdn 1/2-way: styd on same pce fnl 2f* **8/1**

3400 **7** *1/2* **Skyharbor**[42] 5730 3-9-8 74 KFallon 12 59
(AMBalding) *sn pushed along in rr: nvr nrr* **11/2**[3]

1603 **8** *3/4* **Nanna (IRE)**[32] 5949 3-8-7 59 ACulhane 4 41
(RHollinshead) *chsd ldrs: rdn whn hmpd 2f out: sn wknd* **9/2**[2]

0000 **9** *1 3/4* **Inclassic (IRE)**[16] 6274 3-8-4 56 oh1 (b) LisaJones 2 25
(JaneSouthcombe) *chsd ldrs over 3f* **16/1**

0400 **9** *dht* **Snow Wolf**[18] 6205 3-9-10 76 DaneO'Neill 8 45
(JMBradley) *led 1f: wknd 2f out* **33/1**

6200 **11** *7* **Laconia (IRE)**[129] 3344 3-8-5 64 DerekNolan(7) 1 8
(JSMoore) *hld up in tch: hmpd 3f out: wknd 2f out* **25/1**

6003 **12** *2 1/2* **Juniper Banks**[16] 6274 3-8-0 57 DFox(5) 5 —
(MissAStokell) *in rr whn hmpd 3f out: sn wknd* **20/1**

63.66 secs **12** Ran SP% **115.1**
Speed ratings: CSF £242.67 CT £845.09 TOTE £46.20: £9.90, £3.20, £1.80; EX 306.40.

**Owner** Dr Johnny Hon **Bred** Limestone Stud **Trained** Newmarket, Suffolk

**FOCUS**

An ordinary contest, but it appeared to be soundly run and the front pair finished nicely clear, despite which there are doubts over the form.

**NOTEBOOK**

**Global Achiever**, having only his second try at the minmum, showed a smart turn of foot to score. Just as effective over an extra furlong, he should be capable of scoring again.

**Kostar**, having his first outing on this surface, stuck to his task well despite not having the clearest of runs. He shouldn't be too difficult to place through the winter.

**Little Ridge(IRE)** wasn't disgraced under his penalty, but he probably did a little too much, too soon.

**Only If I Laugh** isn't one to trust, but there is no doubt he does have ability if he cares to use it.

**Maluti** found things happening too quickly for him, and may be worth another try at six on this surface.

**Innclassic(IRE)** *Official explanation: trainer said filly was struck into*

**Juniper Banks** *Official explanation: jockey said gelding suffered interference leaving back straight*

## 6539 BET DIRECT ON SKY ACTIVE CLASSIFIED STKS 5f 216y(P)

5:30 (5:30) (F3) 3-Y-O+ £3,510 (£1,080; £540; £270) Stalls Low

| Form | | | | RPR |
|---|---|---|---|---|
| 4200 | 1 | | **Merdiff**$^{35}$ [5868] 5-9-1 63 ........ KFallon 4<br>(WMBrisbourne) *sn pushed along and prom: rdn to ld wl over 1f out: sn hung lft: styd on* 11/2$^{2}$ | 73 |
| 3201 | 2 | nk | **Prince Of Gold**$^{16}$ [6273] 4-9-1 63 ........ (p) DSweeney 2<br>(RHollinshead) *hld up in tch: rdn and nt clr run ins fnl f: swtchd rt: r.o* 13/8$^{1}$ | 72+ |
| 2420 | 3 | ¾ | **Roman Maze**$^{48}$ [5583] 4-9-3 65 ........ SWKelly 9<br>(WMBrisbourne) *s.i.s: hdwy over 1f out: sn nt clr run: rdr dropped whip ins fnl f: r.o* 7/1$^{3}$ | 72+ |
| 5440 | 4 | 2 | **Willheconquertoo**$^{25}$ [6066] 4-9-3 65 ........ (tp) JFEgan 7<br>(AndrewReid) *hld up: hdwy over 2f out: rdn and ev ch whn hung lft over 1f out: no ex ins fnl f* 20/1 | 66 |
| 2616 | 5 | 1 ¾ | **Kensington (IRE)**$^{28}$ [6016] 3-9-0 62 ........ SSanders 3<br>(RGuest) *mid-div: outpcd and rn wd over 2f out: hung lft and styd on ins fnl f* 8/1 | 58 |
| 4600 | 6 | ½ | **Val De Maal (IRE)**$^{27}$ [6026] 4-9-1 63 ........ (p) OUrbina 10<br>(GCHChung) *chsd ldrs: ev ch 2f out: styd on same pce appr fnl f* 14/1 | 57 |
| 531 | 7 | 1 ¼ | **Tayif**$^{152}$ [2656] 8-9-3 65 ........ (t) SCarson 12<br>(AndrewReid) *stdd s: sn swtchd lft: hdwy over 1f out: no imp fnl f* 9/1 | 55 |
| 0040 | 8 | ¾ | **Obe Bold (IRE)**$^{45}$ [5674] 3-8-13 64 ........ FNorton 13<br>(ABerry) *hld up: n.d* 20/1 | 49 |
| 3030 | 9 | 1 | **Branston Tiger**$^{23}$ [6131] 5-8-12 63 ........ (b) DNolan$^{(3)}$ 6<br>(PDEvans) *mid-div: rdn 1/2-way: wknd over 1f out* 12/1 | 48 |
| /50- | 10 | ½ | **Bragadino**$^{55}$ [5430] 5-9-3 65 ........ (vt$^{1}$) ACulhane 11<br>(LindsayWoods, Ire) *sn outpcd* 20/1 | 49 |
| -020 | 11 | 3 ½ | **Sholto**$^{136}$ [3126] 6-8-8 63 ........ (b) JDO'Reilly$^{(7)}$ 8<br>(JO'Reilly) *led early: remained handy: rdn and ev ch 2f out: sn wknd* 25/1 | 36 |
| 2223 | 12 | 1 ¼ | **Mount Royale (IRE)**$^{179}$ [1971] 6-9-2 64 ........ (vt) KimTinkler 5<br>(NTinkler) *chsd ldrs over 3f* 20/1 | 33 |
| 51P0 | 13 | 7 | **Weet Watchers**$^{57}$ [5364] 4-9-2 64 ........ GGibbons 1<br>(PABlockley) *led over 5f out: hdd wl over 1f out: sn wknd* 20/1 | 12 |

1m 16.91s **13** Ran SP% **129.1**

Speed ratings: CSF £14.21 TOTE £9.20: £3.50, £1.10, £1.90; EX 28.30.

**Owner** Team Racing **Bred** Sheikh Ahmed Bin Rashid Al Maktoum **Trained** Great Ness, Shropshire

**FOCUS**

Another ordinary contest, but the pace looked fair and the form looks above average for the grade and solid enough.

**NOTEBOOK**

**Merdiff** was never on the bridle over this shorter trip, but he responded gamely enough, despite drifting to his left.

**Prince Of Gold**, done no favours as the winner drifted across him, is clearly on good terms with himself at present.

**Roman Maze** was doing his best work late on, despite his rider losing his whip inside the final furlong. Better over an extra furlong, it will be a surprise if his handler can't place him to advantage in the coming weeks.

**Willheconquertoo**, who has yet to win on the All-Weather surfaces, didn't impress with his attitude down the straight.

**Kensington(IRE)** didn't appear to handle the track that well, and never looked likely to get into the argument.

**Weet Watchers** *Official explanation: jockey said gelding tired very rapidly*

## 6540 BETDIRECT.CO.UK H'CAP 1m 4f 50y(P)

5:55 (5:55) (F4) (0-62,60) 4-Y-O+ £2,609 (£745; £372) Stalls Low

| Form | | | | RPR |
|---|---|---|---|---|
| 6043 | 1 | | **Greenwich Meantime**$^{46}$ [5635] 4-9-3 58 ........ LGoncalves 4<br>(MrsJRRamsden) *led 2f: remained handy: led wl over 1f out: rdn clr* 4/1$^{2}$ | 79 |
| 10 | 2 | 8 | **Rebel Raider (IRE)**$^{15}$ [6296] 5-9-0 55 ........ JQuinn 7<br>(BNPollock) *chsd ldr 10f out: led over 2f out: rdn and hdd wl over 1f out: sn outpcd* 14/1 | 64 |
| 0042 | 3 | 1 ¼ | **Field Spark**$^{18}$ [6225] 4-9-0 55 ........ (p) DHolland 5<br>(JAGlover) *hld up: hdwy over 3f out: rdn over 2f out: styd on same pce* 3/1$^{1}$ | 62 |
| 2203 | 4 | nk | **Traveller's Tale**$^{15}$ [6292] 5-8-6 54 ........ DerekNolan$^{(7)}$ 10<br>(PGMurphy) *s.i.s: hld up: hdwy over 2f out: rdn and hung lft ins fnl f: nvr trbld ldrs* 11/1 | 61 |
| 6040 | 5 | 1 ½ | **Our Destiny**$^{46}$ [5658] 6-8-9 55 ........ PMakin$^{(5)}$ 9<br>(AWCarroll) *hld up: hdwy 5f out: hmpd and nt clr run wl over 1f out: styd on same pce* 16/1 | 59 |
| 3430 | 6 | ¾ | **Efrhina (IRE)**$^{4}$ [6483] 4-9-5 60 ........ FNorton 1<br>(MrsStefLiddiard) *hld up: hdwy over 3f out: rdn over 2f out: styd on same pce* 16/1 | 63 |
| 2541 | 7 | 2 ½ | **Banningham Blaze**$^{18}$ [6231] 4-9-1 59 ........ (v) DNolan$^{(3)}$ 2<br>(AWCarroll) *hld up: effrt over 3f out: nt clr run over 1f out: nvr trbld ldrs* 10/1 | 58 |
| 1106 | 8 | 3 | **Lazzaz**$^{21}$ [6159] 6-8-12 53 ........ JoannaBadger 12<br>(PWHiatt) *led after 2f: rdn and hdd over 2f out: wknd over 1f out* 15/2 | 48 |
| 2505 | 9 | 2 ½ | **Tropical Son**$^{248}$ [931] 5-8-6 47 ........ (be$^{1}$) SWhitworth 6<br>(DShaw) *s.i.s: hld up: n.d* 25/1 | 38 |
| 0261 | 10 | 19 | **Lord Lahar**$^{15}$ [6292] 5-8-13 54 ........ CCatlin 11<br>(MABuckley) *hld up: plld hrd: hdwy 4f out: wknd over 2f out* 11/2$^{3}$ | 17 |
| 3000 | 11 | 2 | **Pont Neuf (IRE)**$^{15}$ [6292] 4-9-0 55 ........ (t) KFallon 3<br>(PDEvans) *chsd ldrs: rdn over 3f out: wknd over 2f out* 11/1 | 15 |
| | P | | **Alaipour (IRE)**$^{21}$ [6163] 5-8-12 53 ........ ACulhane 8<br>(LindsayWoods, Ire) *prom: lost pl 6f out: sn p.u* 20/1 | — |

2m 43.25s **12** Ran SP% **124.9**

Speed ratings: CSF £62.88 CT £198.06 TOTE £7.50: £3.20, £3.40, £1.70; EX 232.10.

**Owner** J D Martin **Bred** Juddmonte Farms **Trained** Sandhutton, N Yorks

**FOCUS**

An ordinary handicap, but a much-improved performance from the winner than of late on this Polytrack debut, and should rate higher.

**NOTEBOOK**

**Greenwich Meantime**, who was tackling this surface for the first time, took advantage of his tumbling mark and absolutely dotted up. Always travelling well, he showed a nice turn of foot to go clear, despite some fairly vigorous tail swishing, and won with plenty in hand. While he is sure to suffer for this, it would be no surprise to see out again quickly under a penalty.

**Rebel Raider(IRE)** appeared to stay this longer trip well enough, but just met one better treated on the day.

**Field Spark** had no excuses and was made to look very one paced.

**Traveller's Tale** was not doing much to help his rider but, while he may be worth a try over further, he may not be one to rely on.

**Lord Lahar** *Official explanation: jockey said gelding was hanging*

**Pont Neuf(IRE)** *Official explanation: jockey said filly failed to travel during latter stages of race*

**Alaipour(IRE)** *Official explanation: jockey said horse lost its action*

## 6541 BET DIRECT FOOTBALL CASHBACKS CLASSIFIED STKS 1m 141y(P)

6:20 (6:20) (G4) 3-Y-O £2,716 (£776; £388) Stalls Low

| Form | | | | RPR |
|---|---|---|---|---|
| 5000 | 1 | | **Fisby**$^{41}$ [5748] 3-9-3 55 ........ JFEgan 6<br>(SKirk) *s.i.s: hld up: hdwy u.p over 2f out: edgd lft over 1f out: styd on to ld wl ins fnl f* 16/1 | 66 |
| 0002 | 2 | 1 ½ | **Disco Diva**$^{22}$ [6146] 3-8-12 53 ........ FNorton 9<br>(MBlanshard) *hld up: hdwy over 2f out: rdn and ev ch ins fnl f: styd on same pce* 12/1 | 58 |
| 1346 | 3 | nk | **Calculaite**$^{19}$ [6201] 3-9-2 54 ........ SSanders 3<br>(MrsGSRees) *led: rdn over 1f out: edgd lft: hdd wl ins fnl f* 15/8$^{1}$ | 61 |
| 4300 | 4 | 2 | **Beauty Of Dreams**$^{9}$ [6399] 3-8-9 50 ........ ACulhane 2<br>(MRChannon) *trckd ldr: plld hrd: chal over 2f out tl no ex ins fnl f* 11/2$^{2}$ | 50 |
| 5001 | 5 | 1 ¼ | **Compton Micky**$^{9}$ [6401] 3-9-4 49 ........ (p) JEdmunds 8<br>(JBalding) *plld hrd and prom: rdn over 2f out: no ex fnl f* 10/1 | 56 |
| 5360 | 6 | nk | **Trois Etoiles (IRE)**$^{32}$ [5957] 3-8-13 54 ........ MHills 7<br>(JWHills) *prom: rdn over 2f out: no ex fnl f* 7/1$^{3}$ | 51 |
| 0006 | 7 | 3 | **Orchestration (IRE)**$^{25}$ [6061] 3-8-13 51 ........ SWhitworth 10<br>(JWUnett) *chsd ldrs: rdn over 2f out: wknd fnl f* 20/1 | 44 |
| 010 | 8 | 1 | **Delcienne**$^{18}$ [6227] 3-8-9 50 ........ AMcCarthy 4<br>(GGMargarson) *chsd ldrs: rdn over 3f out: wknd 2f out* 8/1 | 38 |
| -250 | 9 | 1 | **Queen's Echo**$^{22}$ [6141] 3-9-0 55 ........ SWKelly 12<br>(MDods) *stmbld s: hld up: rdn over 3f out: a in rr* 20/1 | 41 |
| 1000 | 10 | nk | **Dial Square**$^{50}$ [5546] 3-9-2 54 ........ KFallon 5<br>(PHowling) *hld up: rdn over 2f out: n.d* 7/1$^{3}$ | 43 |
| 0024 | 11 | ¾ | **Livia (IRE)**$^{9}$ [6402] 3-8-9 50 ........ (v) CCatlin 1<br>(JGPortman) *prom: rdn and lost pl over 3f out: sn wknd* 14/1 | 34 |
| -003 | 12 | 9 | **Weet An Haul**$^{103}$ [4102] 3-9-0 52 ........ (v) GGibbons 13<br>(PABlockley) *hld up: plld hrd: hdwy 1/2-way: wknd over 2f out* 16/1 | 20 |

1m 53.14s **12** Ran SP% **131.0**

Speed ratings: CSF £214.62 TOTE £24.40: £3.50, £3.50, £1.20; EX 212.90 Place 6 £57.38, Place 5 £8.92.

**Owner** Peter Valentine **Bred** Helshaw Grange Stud Ltd **Trained** Upper Lambourn, Berks

**FOCUS**

A moderate contest run at a steady pace and the form may not be that sound.

**NOTEBOOK**

**Fisby**, unlike most of his rivals was open to a little improvement. However, this took little winning and he will need to find more if he is to follow up.

**Disco Diva**, who showed a return to form last time, seemed to stay this longer trip well enough.

**Calculaite** had an easy lead, so it was disappointing he could make more use of it.

**Beauty Of Dreams** did herself no favours by refusing to settle.

**Compton Micky**, the winner of a banded race here last week, found it tough going in this slightly better contest.

**Queen's Echo** *Official explanation: jockey said filly stumbled leaving stalls and was never travelling thereafter*

T/Plt: £234.00 to a £1 stake. Pool £32,931.10. 102.70 winning units T/Qpdt: £9.90 to a £1 stake. Pool £4,660.50. 346.40 winning units CR

# 6512 SAN SIRO (R-H)

Wednesday, November 3

**OFFICIAL GOING: Heavy**

## 6542a PREMIO CANTALUPO (MAIDEN) (C&G) 1m

4:40 (4:40) 2-Y-O £7,042 (£3,099; £1,690; £845)

| | | | RPR |
|---|---|---|---|
| 1 | | **Famcapii (IRE)** 2-8-11 ........ EBotti 10<br>(LMCumani) *raced in 6th or 7th, headway entering straight, led 1f out, ran on well to hold challenge of 2nd SP 2.34-1* | — |
| 2 | shd | **Harar (GER)** 2-8-11 ........ DPorcu 12<br>(AndreasLowe, Germany) | — |
| 3 | 4 | **E Adesso Basta (GER)** 2-9-0 ........ GBietolini 7<br>(RFeligioni, Italy) | — |
| 4 | 2 ½ | **Ambohitra (ITY)** 2-9-0 ........ MTellini 5<br>(PPaciello, Italy) | — |
| 5 | 6 | **Ugo Capeto** 2-8-11 ........ SMulas 3<br>(BGrizzetti, Italy) | — |
| 6 | hd | **Fuego (GER)** 2-8-11 ........ GBatistic 2<br>(WGulcher, Germany) | — |
| 7 | ½ | **Piergaudenzio (ITY)** 2-9-0 ........ PConvertino 9<br>(VRamaioli, Italy) | — |
| 8 | 2 | **Ulisse (IRE)** 2-9-0 ........ MDemuro 4<br>(BGrizzetti, Italy) | — |
| 9 | 2 ½ | **Gio (ITY)** 2-9-0 ........ PAgus 11<br>(LBatzella, Italy) | — |
| 10 | 5 | **Tabor King (IRE)** 2-8-11 ........ IRossi 8<br>(A&GBotti, Italy) | — |
| 11 | 1 ½ | **Terenzium (IRE)** 2-8-11 ........ MMonteriso 1<br>(LMCumani) *missed break, mid-divison, effort entering straight, no impression* | — |
| 12 | 3 | **Mount Etna (IRE)** 2-8-10 ........ MEsposito 6<br>(MWeiss, Switzerland) | — |
| 13 | dist | **Rainbow Majestic (IRE)** 2-8-11 ........ APitzalis 13<br>(MCiciarelli, Italy) | — |

1m 49.3s **13** Ran

Speed ratings: .

**Owner** Scuderia Rencati **Bred** Azienda Agricola Francesca **Trained** Newmarket, Suffolk

**NOTEBOOK**
**Famcapii(IRE)**, out of a useful sprinter/miler in Italy, by the top middle-distance performer Montjeu, has been given a Derby entry and proved good enough to make a successful debut. The front two were clear and he is a promising sort.
**Terenzium(IRE)**, whose dam was placed over seven and a half furlongs in Italy, is a stablemate of the English-trained winner but was never a threat. He should improve for the experience.

## 6305 NOTTINGHAM (L-H)
### Thursday, November 4
**OFFICIAL GOING: Heavy (soft in places)**

## 6543 CITY LIFE MAGAZINE MAIDEN STKS — 6f 15y
1:25 (1:26) (D3) 2-Y-O — £6,175 (£1,900; £950; £475) Stalls Low

Form — RPR

| Form | Pos | Dist | Horse / Comment | Jockey | RPR |
|---|---|---|---|---|---|
| | 1 | | **Starchy** 2-8-9 — *(MJohnston) midfield: hdwy over 2f out: styd on to ld ent last: sn clr* **12/1**[3] | JFanning 5 | 79+ |
| | 2 | 6 | **Allegretto (FR)** 2-9-0 — *(SKirk) towards rr: hdwy over 2f out: rdn and styd on wl fnl f: nrst fin* **20/1** | JFEgan 14 | 69+ |
| 6602 | 3 | nk | **Hidden Jewel**[13] 6333 2-9-0 82 — *(BAMcmahon) led: rdn 2f out and sn clr: hdd & wknd qckly ent last* **5/4**[1] | GGibbons 1 | 68 |
| 00 | 4 | 6 | **Oblique (IRE)**[7] 6447 2-8-9 — *(SirMarkPrescott) s.i.s and bhd: swtchd rt and hdwy 1/2-way: styd on appr last: nrst fin* **16/1** | SSanders 7 | 48 |
| 000 | 5 | nk | **Street Dancer (IRE)**[51] 5542 2-9-0 — *(JJQuinn) midfield: pushed along 1/2-way: yeon u.p fnl 2f* **50/1** | RWinston 8 | 52 |
| 6026 | 6 | hd | **Layed Back Rocky**[40] 5790 2-9-0 60 — *(MMullineaux) bhd tl styd on fnl 2f: nrst fin* **40/1** | CCatlin 9 | 52 |
| | 7 | shd | **Miracle Baby** 2-8-9 — *(GBBalding) bhd tl styd on fnl 2f: nrst fin* **40/1** | SCarson 3 | 46 |
| 00 | 8 | 6 | **Komreyev Star**[36] 5857 2-8-7 — *(RAFahey) a rr* **50/1** | NLawes(7) 10 | 36 |
| 00 | 9 | 2 ½ | **Iroquois Princess**[10] 6400 2-8-9 — *(DShaw) a rr* **125/1** | SWhitworth 13 | 25 |
| 0 | 10 | 4 | **Passionately Royal**[30] 6002 2-9-0 — *(RAFahey) bhd fr 1/2-way* **25/1** | PHanagan 4 | 20 |
| 040 | 11 | ¾ | **Crystal Mystic (IRE)**[16] 6294 2-8-11 60 — *(BPalling) prom: rdn along 1/2-way: sn wknd* **50/1** | FPFerris(3) 11 | 18 |
| 000 | 12 | nk | **Soft Focus (IRE)**[10] 6392 2-8-9 — *(JAOsborne) bhd fr 1/2-way* **80/1** | SWKelly 2 | 12 |
| 5543 | 13 | 3 ½ | **Xeeran**[31] 5989 2-8-9 61 — *(MAJarvis) cl up: rdn along 1/2-way: wknd qckly over 2f out* **2/1**[2] | PRobinson 6 | — |
| 0 | 14 | hd | **Athboy Nights (IRE)**[24] 6125 2-8-9 — *(MJWallace) cl up: rdn over 2f out and sn wknd* **16/1** | KFallon 12 | — |

1m 21.1s (6.30) **Going Correction** +0.825s/f (Soft) **14** Ran SP% **117.9**
Speed ratings: **91,83,82,74,74 73,73,65,62,57 56,55,51,50**CSF £225.47 TOTE £10.70: £2.50, £4.10, £1.10; EX 129.50.
**Owner** Maktoum Al Maktoum **Bred** Gainsborough Stud Management Ltd **Trained** Middleham Moor, N Yorks

**FOCUS**
An uncompetitive maiden run on testing ground in which few could be seriously fancied. The winner could not have won any easier, though, and although the race is hard to gauge the sixth sets the level.

**NOTEBOOK**
**Starchy**, a half-sister to high-class Group Two and Group Three sprint winner Land Of Dreams, coped with the testing ground better than anything else. The market suggested that not too much was expected first time, but she won easily and looks interesting for next year.
**Allegretto(FR)**, whose dam is a half-sister to Oaks winner Shahtoush, shaped with promise over a trip plenty short enough. The testing conditions brought his stamina into play and he has the makings of a decent middle-distance handicapper next season.
**Hidden Jewel** excelled himself when finishing runner-up in a sales race last time. His rating had shot up from 48 to 82 on the back of that effort, and that may flatter him now.
**Oblique(IRE)**, who is a half-sister to One Off, who stayed two miles, and Optimal, who won over ten furlongs, is out of a mare who won seven races between a mile and a half and two miles. She was running on well at the end of this sprint trip and looks the type to run up a sequence in handicap company next season when stepped up to a more suitable distance.
**Street Dancer(IRE)** did not run badly although he has yet to suggest he is any better than plating class.
**Iroquois Princess** *Official explanation: jockey said filly hung left-handed*
**Soft Focus(IRE)** *Official explanation: jockey said filly was unsuited by heavy ground*
**Xeeran** *Official explanation: jockey said filly was unsuited by heavy ground*
**Athboy Nights(IRE)** *Official explanation: jockey said filly was unsuited by heavy ground*

## 6544 BHB/RCA SEASON FINALE LUNCH NURSERY — 5f 13y
1:55 (1:55) (E3) (0-75,74) 2-Y-O — £4,192 (£1,290; £645; £322) Stalls Low

| Form | Pos | Dist | Horse / Comment | Jockey | RPR |
|---|---|---|---|---|---|
| 600 | 1 | | **Penang Sapphire**[58] 5376 2-8-1 54 — *(GAButler) bhd: gd hdwy on outer 2f out: rdn and str run ent last: led last 100 yds* **40/1** | CCatlin 12 | 61 |
| 3145 | 2 | ½ | **Cree**[12] 6356 2-8-11 64 — *(WRMuir) in tch: hdwy 2f out: rdn to ld briefly ins last: drvn and hdd last 100 yds* **4/1**[2] | MartinDwyer 6 | 69 |
| 0315 | 3 | 1 | **Doitforreel (IRE)**[6] 6456 2-9-1 68 — *(IAWood) s.i.s and bhd: gd hdwy over 2f out: effrt whn n.m.r over 1f out: sn rdn and kpt on ins last* **9/2**[3] | SSanders 2 | 70 |
| 5550 | 4 | 1 ½ | **Task's Muppet (IRE)**[52] 5509 2-8-1 57 — *(JAOsborne) midfield: hdwy wl over 2f out: rdn over 1f out: styd on ins last* **66/1** | JFMcDonald(3) 14 | 55 |
| 0504 | 5 | shd | **Hits Only Cash**[8] 6442 2-8-10 63 — *(PABlockley) chsd ldrs: rdn along over 2f out: drvn over 1f out and kpt on same pce* **5/2**[1] | KFallon 8 | 60 |
| 5405 | 6 | ¾ | **Ashes (IRE)**[17] 6270 2-8-4 57 — *(KRBurke) towards rr: hdwy over 2f out: rdn to chse ldrs over 1f out: swtchd lft and kpt on ins last* **33/1** | PHanagan 3 | 52 |
| 6040 | 7 | shd | **Robmantra**[25] 6080 2-8-5 58 — *(BJLlewellyn) bhd: hdwy 2f out: rdn and kpt on fnl f: nrst fin* **33/1** | (p) SWhitworth 11 | 53 |
| 2640 | 8 | 2 ½ | **Little Biscuit (IRE)**[25] 6080 2-8-6 59 ow1 — *(KRBurke) in tch: hdwy to chse ldrs 2f out: sn rdn and ev ch tl drvn and wknd appr last* **66/1** | VHalliday 15 | 46 |
| 6542 | 9 | 2 | **Skiddaw Wolf**[17] 6270 2-8-10 63 — *(BSmart) cl up: rdn along 2f out: grad wknd* **14/1** | FLynch 10 | 44 |
| 5031 | 10 | nk | **Mytton's Bell (IRE)**[2] 6522 2-8-7 65 7ex — *(ABailey) prom: led wl over 1f out: sn rdn: hdd & wknd ins last* **8/1** | DFox(5) 16 | 45 |
| 0031 | 11 | 1 ¾ | **Chilly Cracker**[25] 6080 2-9-3 70 — *(RHollinshead) led: rdn over 2f out: hdd & wknd wl over 1f out* **12/1** | DSweeney 17 | 45 |
| 5002 | 12 | 1 ¼ | **Piddies Pride (IRE)**[8] 6442 2-8-10 66 — *(PSMcentee) chsd ldrs: swtchd lft 2f out: sn rdn and wknd over 1f out* **14/1** | FPFerris(3) 4 | 37 |
| 3100 | 13 | 5 | **Roko**[45] 5690 2-8-1 54 — *(DShaw) a rr* **40/1** | (v) LisaJones 7 | 10 |
| 5504 | 14 | 2 ½ | **Lady Hopeful (IRE)**[17] 6272 2-8-6 59 — *(RPElliott) cl up: rdn along over 2f out: sn wknd* **20/1** | (b) JFanning 9 | 8 |
| 5000 | 15 | 5 | **Kristikhab (IRE)**[46] 5670 2-8-0 53 — *(ABerry) s.i.s: a rr* **66/1** | PFessey 5 | — |
| 2240 | 16 | 5 | **Wizardmicktee (IRE)**[70] 5060 2-9-7 74 — *(ABailey) a rr* **33/1** | RWinston 1 | — |

65.65 secs (3.85) **Going Correction** +0.825s/f (Soft) **16** Ran SP% **121.8**
Speed ratings: **102,101,99,97,97 95,95,91,88,88 85,83,75,71,63 55**CSF £185.27 CT £930.22 TOTE £51.00: £13.60, £1.90, £1.80, £14.70; EX 323.40.
**Owner** Mrs A K H Ooi **Bred** Mrs A K H Ooi **Trained** Blewbury, Oxon

**FOCUS**
An ordinary nursery, producing a shock result, but several of those close up appear to have run to their marks, suggesting the form is sound enough.

**NOTEBOOK**
**Penang Sapphire** is bred to need a mile plus next year and it was his stamina in these testing conditions which saw him record a shock victory on his handicap debut.
**Cree**, a consistent performer who goes well in testing ground, ran his race with no excuse.
**Doitforreel(IRE)**, fifth in a Listed race last time, was 12lb well in compared with her revised rating. She did not break well though, and although she stayed on well through the pack, she was never quite doing enough. She looks likely to struggle off her revised mark.
**Task's Muppet(IRE)** had not run on ground as bad as this before but she coped admirably and ran her best race to date.
**Hits Only Cash** had not enjoyed much luck at Yarmouth last time and was favoured in the market on this occasion. He was a little disappointing though, merely keeping on under pressure without troubling the principals. *Official explanation: jockey said colt was unsuited by heavy ground*
**Ashes(IRE)** did not appear to appreciate the drop back to the minimum trip.
**Skiddaw Wolf** *Official explanation: jockey said filly was denied clear run*
**Wizardmicktee(IRE)** *Official explanation: jockey said colt moved badly throughout*

## 6545 FASTEST GROWING BETTING EXCHANGE IBETX.COM MAIDEN STKS — 1m 54y
2:25 (2:25) (D3) 2-Y-O — £6,389 (£1,966; £983; £491) Stalls High

| Form | Pos | Dist | Horse / Comment | Jockey | RPR |
|---|---|---|---|---|---|
| 0 | 1 | | **Tawqeet (USA)**[20] 6187 2-9-0 — *(JLDunlop) midfield: hdwy to trck ldrs 1/2-way: chal 3f out: rdn to ld wl over 1f out: kpt on* **11/2**[3] | RHills 14 | 72 |
| 05 | 2 | 1 | **Queen's Dancer**[12] 6352 2-8-9 — *(MRChannon) in tch: hdwy to chse ldrs 3f out: rdn and kpt on appr last* **4/1**[2] | CCatlin 4 | 65 |
| | 3 | ¾ | **Consular** 2-9-0 — *(MAJarvis) trckd ldrs: hdwy 3f out: rdn 2f out: kpt on fnl f* **6/1** | PRobinson 2 | 69 |
| | 4 | ½ | **Crete (IRE)** 2-9-0 — *(WJHaggas) trckd ldrs: hdwy to ld 3f out: shkn up and hdd wl over 1f out: wknd ins last* **3/1**[1] | ACulhane 13 | 68 |
| | 5 | 5 | **Roman Army (IRE)** 2-9-0 — *(AMBalding) s.i.s and bhd: hdwy 3f out: styd on appr last: nrst fin* **16/1** | MartinDwyer 11 | 58 |
| 0U0 | 6 | 2 ½ | **Sea Map**[25] 6078 2-9-0 — *(SKirk) towards rr: hdwy 3f out: sn rdn and kpt on appr last* **33/1** | JFEgan 12 | 53 |
| 5 | 7 | 1 ½ | **Enamoured**[13] 6336 2-8-9 — *(MGQuinlan) bhd: hdwy on i9nner 3f out: rdn along 2f out: kpt on: nt rch ldrs* **14/1** | DRMcCabe 8 | 45 |
| 00 | 8 | 1 ½ | **Back To Reality**[38] 5827 2-8-11 — *(BPalling) mde most tl rdn and hdd 3f out: grad wknd* **50/1** | FPFerris(3) 10 | 47 |
| 040 | 9 | ½ | **Allizam**[81] 4776 2-9-0 53 — *(BAMcmahon) bhd: hdwy on outer 3f out: rdn over 2f out and sn btn* **22/1** | SSanders 6 | 46 |
| | 10 | 5 | **Michaels Pride (IRE)** 2-8-9 — *(MJohnston) s.i.s: rapid prog and sn prom: rdn along over 3f out and grad wknd* **12/1** | JFanning 1 | 31 |
| 000 | 11 | 4 | **Royal Sailor (IRE)**[7] 6453 2-9-0 — *(JMPEustace) prom: hdwy to ld 4f out: rdn and hdd 3f out: sn wknd* **10/1** | KDarley 5 | 28 |
| | 12 | 5 | **Briar Ghyll** 2-8-4 — *(IAWood) a rr* **66/1** | DFox(5) 3 | 13 |
| 0 | 13 | 3 | **Golden Gate (IRE)**[8] 6441 2-9-0 — *(MLWBell) s.i.s: a bhd* **28/1** | JMackay 15 | 12 |
| 00 | 14 | 1 ½ | **Chestminster Girl**[19] 6221 2-8-6 — *(APJones) cl up: rdn along over 4f out: sn wknd* **100/1** | (p) DCorby(3) 7 | — |
| 0 | 15 | 3 | **Colour Blind (IRE)**[8] 6441 2-9-0 — *(MLWBell) sn outpcd and bhd* **66/1** | PFitzsimons 9 | — |

1m 54.84s (8.44) **Going Correction** +0.975s/f (Soft) **15** Ran SP% **120.7**
Speed ratings: **96,95,94,93,88 86,84,83,82,77 73,68,65,64,61**CSF £26.30 TOTE £6.80: £2.70, £1.70, £2.00; EX 31.00.
**Owner** Hamdan Al Maktoum **Bred** 6 C Stallions Limited **Trained** Arundel, W Sussex

**FOCUS**
Probably only a fair maiden and several with modest form set the level, although the first four, who came clear, are all expected to do better as three-year-olds.

**NOTEBOOK**
**Tawqeet(USA)**, whose dam won over 11 furlongs, had clearly come on for his debut in a Newmarket maiden and found the competition here much less demanding. He picked up well when asked to go and win his race, and should get ten furlongs next year.
**Queen's Dancer** confirmed her liking for soft ground and appears to be improving with racing. She is now eligible for a handicap mark.
**Consular**, a half-brother to Tregarron out of a half-sister to Tomba and Prix du Jockey-Club winner Holding Court, made a promising start to his career. He should be up to winning races as a three-year-old.
**Crete(IRE)**, whose dam was a multiple winner in Italy, including in Listed company, was sent off favourite for his debut. He ran well but looked in need of the experience and looks the type to improve with a winter over his head.
**Roman Army(IRE)**, a half-brother to a winner over a mile in Italy, should not want much farther than this on breeding, but he was running on towards the end of the race.
**Sea Map** ran a bit better, perhaps as a result of the heavy ground.

## 6546 BETTING WITH IBETX.COM H'CAP — 1m 1f 213y
3:00 (3:00) (E3) (0-77,77) 3-Y-O+ — £4,462 (£1,373; £686; £343) Stalls Low

| Form | Pos | Dist | Horse / Comment | Jockey | RPR |
|---|---|---|---|---|---|
| 0450 | 1 | | **Ryan's Future (IRE)**[27] 6043 4-9-7 73 — *(JAkehurst) in tch: hdwy 3f out: led wl over 1f out: rdn clr ent last styd on wl* **15/2**[3] | SSanders 6 | 87 |
| 0511 | 2 | 4 | **Mcqueen (IRE)**[3] 6520 4-9-11 77 6ex — *(MrsHDalton) midfield: hdwy on outer 3f out and sn pushed along: rdn over 2f out drvn and kpt on same pce ins ent last* **9/4**[1] | JFEgan 14 | 84 |

1166 **3** *1 ¾* **Mambina (USA)**[13] 6332 3-8-12 **68** ........ SHitchcott 7 72
(MRChannon) *led: rdn along and hdd 3 out: drvn and rallied over 1f out: kpt on ins last* **11/1**

5106 **4** *¾* **Band**[15] 6311 4-8-4 **56** ........ GGibbons 8 59
(BAMcmahon) *hld up towards rr: hdwy 1/2-way: swtchd rt and effrt 2f out: sn rdn and edgd lft over 1f out: kpt on* **16/1**

4013 **5** *1 ¼* **Tagula Blue (IRE)**[25] 6081 4-9-4 **70** ........(t) JCrowley 3 71
(JAGlover) *stdd s and bhd: hdwy over 3f out: rdn 2f out: kpt on ins last: nrst fin* **11/1**

1322 **6** *hd* **Mobane Flyer**[13] 6337 4-8-12 **64** ........ PHanagan 15 64
(RAFahey) *prom: led 3f out: sn rdn: hdd wl over 1f out and sn wknd* **4/1**[2]

0032 **7** *hd* **Santa Caterina (IRE)**[16] 6285 3-8-7 **63** ........ KDarley 4 63
(JLDunlop) *trckd ldrs: hdwy 3f out: rdn 2f out: wkng whn n.m.r over 1f out* **10/1**

3545 **8** *2* **Keepers Knight (IRE)**[13] 6337 3-8-6 **62** ........(t) JFanning 13 59
(PFICole) *midfield: effrt 3f out: rdn along and no imp fnl 2f* **33/1**

0-00 **9** *3 ½* **Mr Lear (USA)**[159] 2471 5-8-9 **68** ........ NLawes(7) 10 59
(RAFahey) *cl up: effrt 3f out and ev ch tl rdn 2f out and sn wknd* **100/1**

0113 **10** *3 ½* **Platinum Pirate**[24] 6112 3-8-5 **64** ........(b) TEaves(3) 11 49
(KRBurke) *a towards rr* **28/1**

0000 **11** *1 ½* **Rasid (USA)**[7] 6450 6-9-9 **75** ........ KFallon 1 57
(CADwyer) *chsd ldrs: rdn along over 3f out: sn wknd* **14/1**

5200 **12** *1 ¾* **Amnesty**[15] 6311 5-8-8 **60** ........(be) EAhern 12 39
(GLMoore) *chsd ldrs: rdn along 1/2-way: sn wknd* **28/1**

0540 **13** *2* **Danze Romance**[20] 6183 3-8-4 **60** ........ MartinDwyer 16 36
(JLDunlop) *a rr* **50/1**

0000 **14** *10* **Camille Pissarro (USA)**[12] 6358 4-9-4 **70** ........ MTebbutt 5 29
(DJWintle) *in tch: hdwy to chse ldrs 4f out: rdn along 3f out and sn wknd* **100/1**

342- **15** *20* **Irie Rasta (IRE)**[489] 2973 5-9-0 **66** ........ SWhitworth 9 —
(SKirk) *a rr: t.o fnl 4f* **33/1**

0600 **16** *1 ¾* **Bold Phoenix (IRE)**[47] 5657 3-8-9 **65** ........ TPQueally 2 —
(BJCurley) *a rr: t.o fnl 4f* **50/1**

2m 19.36s (9.86) **Going Correction** +0.975s/f (Soft)
**WFA** 3 from 4yo+ 4lb **16** Ran SP% **119.5**
Speed ratings: **99,95,94,93,92 92,92,90,88,85 84,82,81,73,57 55**CSF £22.69 CT £191.32 TOTE £9.10: £2.30, £1.60, £3.40, £3.50; EX 40.70 Trifecta £406.20 Pool £2,059.85, 3.60 w/u.
**Owner** Vimal Khosla **Bred** A F O'Callaghan **Trained** Epsom, Surrey

**FOCUS**
Just a fair handicap run at a sensible pace, but the form, rated through the placed horses, looks sound for the grade.

**NOTEBOOK**
**Ryan's Future(IRE)**, back down to a mark just 1lb higher than when last successful on turf, coped well with the testing conditions and had the race won entering the final furlong. A consistent individual, he won on the Polytrack off a mark of 75 last December so could yet taste more success this winter.
**Mcqueen(IRE)**, who has been in such good form, was making a quick reappearance under a penalty and racing off a mark 27lb higher than he ran off when notching the first of his four wins this season. He once again ran his race, but just found one too good at the weights this time.
**Mambina(USA)** ran well from the front and rallied well to get back up for third. The Handicapper still looks to just have her measure, however.
**Band** usually finds two or three too good and, although he ran well, it was a similar story again.
**Tagula Blue(IRE)**, whose style of running is to be held up at the rear for a late run, could have done with a stronger pace.
**Mobane Flyer**, who has had a busy time of it over the last three months but has held his form well, may have found this one race too many.

## 6547 IBETX.COM - THE PUNTERS CHOICE CONDITIONS STKS 1m 54y
3:35 (3:36) (C2) 3-Y-0+ **£12,087** (£4,584; £2,292; £1,042) **Stalls** High

Form RPR

5010 **1** **St Andrews (IRE)**[33] 5941 4-8-10 104 ........ PRobinson 2 107
(MAJarvis) *trckd ldrs: smooth hdwy to ld wl over 3f out: styd on wl appr last* **10/11**[1]

4223 **2** *3 ½* **Fine Silver (IRE)**[33] 5941 3-9-2 98 ........ KFallon 4 108
(PFICole) *trckd ldrs: hdwy to chse wnr 2f out: sn rdn and kpt on same pce* **10/3**[2]

00-0 **3** *3* **Dandoun**[19] 6219 6-8-10 105 ........ SSanders 7 94
(JLDunlop) *hld up: hdwy over 3f out: rdn 2f out: kpt on same pce* **7/1**

0506 **4** *3* **Duck Row (USA)**[68] 5134 9-8-10 102 ........ EAhern 8 88
(JARToller) *hld up: hdwy 3f out: rdn 2f out and sn btn* **6/1**[3]

4560 **5** *7* **Elidore**[13] 6343 4-8-0 63 ........ DFox(5) 5 69?
(BPalling) *cl up: rdn along over 3f out: sn wknd* **100/1**

5500 **6** *3* **Dancing King (IRE)**[10] 6404 8-8-8 45 ........ PMakin(5) 1 71?
(PWHiatt) *led: rdn along and hdd over wl over 3f out: sn wknd* **300/1**

4-00 **7** *4* **Legacy (JPN)**[130] 3349 4-8-10 103 ........ MTebbutt 3 60
(TTClement) *dwlt: a rr* **100/1**

0601 **8** *27* **Scientist**[20] 6199 3-8-8 69 ........ KDarley 6 6
(DBurchell) *chsd ldrs: rdn along 1/2-way: wknd 3f out* **40/1**

1m 52.54s (6.14) **Going Correction** +0.975s/f (Soft)
**WFA** 3 from 4yo+ 2lb **8** Ran SP% **107.0**
Speed ratings: **108,104,101,98,91 88,84,57**CSF £3.43 TOTE £1.80: £1.10, £1.10, £2.30; EX 5.00.
**Owner** Team Havana **Bred** P D Savill **Trained** Newmarket, Suffolk

**FOCUS**
They finished pretty strung out in this decent little contest, but the third and fourth look to be running below their current ratings, and the fifth and sixth restrict the form.

**NOTEBOOK**
**St Andrews(IRE)**, who was 13lb better off with Fine Silver for a beating of about seven lengths in the Cambridgeshire, had conditions to suit and reversed the form in good style, galloping on strongly to record his second win of the season. Clearly soft ground suits him well and connections are apparently now considering a trip to Saint-Cloud for a Listed race before the end of the month.
**Fine Silver(IRE)** did not run at all badly given that his best form is on much quicker ground, and he was 13lb worse off with the winner compared to when they met in the Cambridgeshire.
**Dandoun**, who has clearly had his problems, has been very lightly raced this season. He ran much better than he had at Newmarket, but this was still some way short of his best.
**Duck Row(USA)** comfortably held this season, looks to be regressing.
**Elidore** did best of the outsiders but was still outclassed.

## 6548 BACK OR LAY WITH IBETX.COM H'CAP 1m 54y
4:05 (4:05) (F4) (0-62,62) 3-Y-0+ **£3,561** (£1,017; £508) **Stalls** High

Form RPR

1151 **1** **Boppys Princess**[33] 5957 3-8-13 **59** ........ PHanagan 15 75
(RAFahey) *hld up: wd st: gd hdwy 3f out: rdn to ld over 1f out: styd on wl* **5/1**[2]

0-10 **2** *3 ½* **Wizard Of Us**[12] 6364 4-8-7 **58** ........ LiamJones(7) 4 67
(MMullineaux) *led after 1f: pushed along and hdd 3f out: rdn and ev ch over 1f out: kpt on same pce ins last* **25/1**

1465 **3** *hd* **Commitment Lecture**[28] 6024 4-8-8 **52** ........(t) KDarley 13 61
(MDods) *hld up: wd st: hdwy and nt clr run on stands rail over 3f out: swtchd lft and hdwy 2f out: rdn and kpt on fnl f* **5/1**[2]

2516 **4** *7* **Time To Regret**[12] 6364 4-9-1 **59** ........ KFallon 3 54
(JSWainwright) *prom: hdwy to ld 3f out: sn rdn and hung lft: drvn and hdd over 1f out: wknd ent last* **7/2**[1]

40/0 **5** *5* **Ca'D'Oro**[77] 4871 11-8-8 **55** ........ RThomas(3) 11 40
(GBBalding) *hld up towards rr: hdwy 3f out: rdn 2f out and plugged on same pce* **20/1**

6204 **6** *3 ½* **Acorazado (IRE)**[195] 1595 5-8-9 **53** ........(b) SSanders 16 31
(GLMoore) *in tch: wd st: gd hdwy and ev ch 3f out: rdn and edgd lft 2f out: sn btn* **15/2**[3]

3401 **7** *2* **Armentieres**[4] 6146 3-8-9 **55** ........(b) EAhern 12 29
(JLSpearing) *prom: wd st and ev ch 3f out: sn rdn and wknd 2f out* **9/1**

2310 **8** *2 ½* **Caerphilly Gal**[12] 6364 4-8-6 **55** ........ DFox(5) 5 24
(PLGilligan) *led 1f: chsd ldrs tl rdn wl over 2f out and grad wknd* **16/1**

0060 **9** *2* **Rocinante (IRE)**[20] 6201 4-8-7 **51** ........ RFfrench 17 16
(JJQuinn) *cl up on outer: wd st: rdn along over 3f out and sn wknd* **11/1**

022 **10** *5* **Explode**[20] 6201 7-8-8 **52** ........ TWilliams 6 7
(MissLCSiddall) *prom: rdn along 1/2-way: sn wknd* **14/1**

6640 **11** *2* **Albee (IRE)**[187] 1770 4-8-10 **54** ........ PFitzsimons 10 5
(MissGayKelleway) *bhd fr 1/2-way* **50/1**

2230 **12** *1* **Bundaberg**[16] 6296 4-8-6 **55** ........ PMakin(5) 7 4
(PWHiatt) *bhd fr 1/2-way* **33/1**

4002 **13** *1 ¾* **Jakeal (IRE)**[125] 3471 5-8-9 **53** ........ VHalliday 1 —
(RMWhitaker) *prom: rdn along 4f out: sn wknd* **33/1**

1300 **14** *hd* **Yorker (USA)**[5] 6483 6-8-13 **62** ........(b) NataliaGemelova(5) 14 7
(MsDeborahJEvans) *prom: rdn along 4f out: sn wknd* **33/1**

3260 **15** *5* **Pride Of Kinloch**[52] 5526 4-8-11 **55** ........ MTebbutt 8 —
(JHetherton) *s.i.s: a bhd* **40/1**

0200 **16** *6* **Mutarafaa (USA)**[216] 1233 5-8-7 **51** ........(v) LisaJones 9 —
(DShaw) *s.i.s: a bhd* **50/1**

1m 53.37s (6.97) **Going Correction** +0.975s/f (Soft)
**WFA** 3 from 4yo+ 2lb **16** Ran SP% **122.0**
Speed ratings: **104,100,100,93,88 84,82,80,78,73 71,70,68,68,63 57**CSF £133.23 CT £688.95 TOTE £5.30: £2.20, £8.00, £1.40, £1.60; EX 176.70 Place 6 £17.14, Place 5 £9.61.
**Owner** Mrs S Bond **Bred** Mrs Sylvia Bond **Trained** Musley Bank, N Yorks

**FOCUS**
A moderate handicap, but the time of the race compared favourably with the conditions race earlier on the card, being only 0.83sec slower.

**NOTEBOOK**
**Boppys Princess** was winning for the fifth time from seven starts this season, off a mark 21lb higher than for the first of those victories. Indeed, she may not have finished winning yet, as she is clearly effective on Polytrack and has the potential to progress even further this winter.
**Wizard Of Us**, a free-running sort who was a shock winner over seven furlongs at Ayr last month, ran well over a trip which probably stretches his stamina.
**Commitment Lecture** had the ground in her favour and finished well from off the pace. She is fairly handicapped at present, but time has run out for this season and she may have to look for success on the All-Weather.
**Time To Regret** went up 8lb for his wide-margin Redcar win and, although this ground may have been more testing than ideal, he now looks in the Handicapper's grip.
**Ca'D'Oro** ran well enough considering this was only his second start back after a four-year absence.
**Acorazado(IRE)** has not won on turf for three years and seems happier on the artificial surfaces.
*Official explanation: jockey said gelding had no more to give*
T/Jkpt: Not won. T/Plt: £18.60 to a £1 stake. Pool £41,403. 1,617.25 winning units T/Qpdt: £6.60 to a £1 stake. Pool £2,333. 257.90 winning units JR

# 6536 WOLVERHAMPTON (A.W) (L-H)
Thursday, November 4

**OFFICIAL GOING: Standard**
As yesterday there appeared to be no draw bias.
Wind: Slight behind Weather: Cloudy

## 6549 BET DIRECT AT DUNSTALL PARK CLASSIFIED STKS 1m 141y(P)
4:10 (4:11) (F3) 3-Y-0 **£3,562** (£1,096; £548; £274) **Stalls** Low

Form RPR

3413 **1** **Wrenlane**[5] 6483 3-8-13 64 ........ THamilton(3) 5 71
(RAFahey) *a.p: chsd ldr 6f out: led 2f out: shkn up nr fin: jst hld on* **3/1**[1]

**2** *hd* **Lytham (IRE)**[15] 6317 3-9-3 65 ........ SDrowne 2 72
(MJWallace) *chsd ldrs: rdn over 1f out: r.o* **12/1**

0100 **3** *1 ¾* **Saros (IRE)**[19] 6220 3-8-12 58 ........ FLynch 10 63
(BSmart) *led over 6f: styd on same pce ins fnl f* **16/1**

5040 **4** *¾* **Infidelity (IRE)**[33] 5957 3-8-9 52 ........ JQuinn 6 58
(ABailey) *chsd ldrs: rdn 1/2-way: styd on* **25/1**

1010 **5** *nk* **Otago (IRE)**[17] 6271 3-9-2 64 ........ GBaker 8 65
(JRBest) *hld up: hdwy over 1f out: nt rch ldrs* **12/1**

0350 **6** *½* **Jomus**[22] 6160 3-8-13 61 ........ RWinston 13 61
(LMontagueHall) *hld up: hdwy over 2f out: styd on: nt trble ldrs* **8/1**

4130 **7** *2 ½* **Sachin**[8] 6461 3-9-3 65 ........ DaneO'Neill 4 59
(JRBoyle) *hld up in tch: rdn over 3f out: staaeyad on same pce appr fnl f* **12/1**

0413 **8** *¾* **Iffy**[92] 4443 3-9-1 63 ........ RHavlin 11 56
(PDCundell) *s.i.s: hld up: nvr trbld ldrs* **9/2**[2]

0060 **9** *2* **Amwell Brave**[45] 5692 3-9-0 62 ........ WRyan 12 51
(JRJenkins) *chsd ldrs over 6f* **33/1**

2010 **10** *2 ½* **Son Of Thunder (IRE)**[70] 5063 3-8-13 61 ........ SWKelly 9 44
(MDods) *hld up: a in rr* **16/1**

2003 **11** *½* **Noble Mind**[77] 4880 3-9-2 64 ........ DKinsella 3 46
(PGMurphy) *s.s: hit rails over 3f out: a bhd* **25/1**

1302 **12** *nk* **Princess Galadriel**[6] 6461 3-8-5 61 ........ ThomasYeung(5) 7 40
(JRBest) *hld up in tch: lost pl over 6f out: bhd fnl 4f: hung lft over 1f out* **5/1**[3]

1230 **13** *¾* **One Upmanship**[33] 5381 3-9-3 65 ........ DSweeney 1 45
(JGPortman) *chsd ldrs 6f* **20/1**

1m 53.1s **13** Ran SP% **121.2**
Speed ratings: CSF £39.35 TOTE £3.80: £1.10, £7.90, £12.60; EX 61.40.
**Owner** Keith Taylor **Bred** M P Bishop **Trained** Musley Bank, N Yorks

**FOCUS**
The time was slightly quicker than the following race, and comparable with the previous day's contest over the trip, but the form is not particularly strong.

**NOTEBOOK**

**Wrenlane** proved better suited to this shorter trip, and although a narow winner, his jockey was intent on giving him as easy a time as possible.
**Lytham(IRE)**, who had shown bits of form in Ireland, turned in a sound-enough effort on this All-Weather debut and left the impression he will appreciate a bit further.
**Saros(IRE)** found this more his level, but this extended mile just appeared to stretch him.
**Infidelity(IRE)** is not the most consistent of animals, but he stuck to his task well enough.
**Otago(IRE)** took a while to get the hang of this surface, but was closing faster than any at the line.
**Princess Galadriel**, who lost a good early pitch before entering the back straight, was reported by her rider to have never been travelling. *Official explanation: jockey said filly was never travelling*

## 6550 BET DIRECT "RED TO BET" ON ITV CLASSIFIED STKS — 1m 141y(P)
4:35 (4:35) (G4) 4-Y-0+ — £2,625 (£750; £375) Stalls Low

Form — RPR
0004 **1** **Qobtaan (USA)**[16] 6296 5-8-13 51 GBaker 13 63
(MRBosley) *s.i.s: hld up: hdwy over 2f out: led over 1f out: hung lft ins fnl f: rdn out* **9/1**
0432 **2** 1 3/4 **Mobo-Baco**[43] 5733 7-9-1 53 SDrowne 4 61
(RJHodges) *chsd ldr: led wl over 1f out: sn hdd: styng on same pce whn hmpd ins fnl f* **7/2**[1]
0205 **3** nk **Ziet D'Alsace (FR)**[16] 6295 4-8-11 55 DNolan(3) 9 59
(AWCarroll) *hld up: hdwy over 3f out: rdn and ev ch over 1f out: styng on same pce whn hmpd ins fnl f* **9/2**[3]
2000 **4** 2 1/2 **Middleham Park (IRE)**[53] 4015 4-8-9 54 GBartley(7) 2 56
(PCHaslam) *hld up: hmpd over 2f out: r.o appr fnl f: nrst fin* **25/1**
0001 **5** 1 1/2 **Adobe**[12] 6364 9-8-11 54 MSavage(5) 6 53
(WMBrisbourne) *chsd ldrs: rdn over 2f out: styd on same pce appr fnl f* **4/1**[2]
0000 **6** 3/4 **Time To Remember (IRE)**[30] 6007 6-8-11 52 THamilton(3) 7 49
(RAFahey) *hld up in tch: led over 2f out: hdd wl over 1f out: wknd ins fnl f* **14/1**
0-05 **7** 3/4 **Mister Benji**[273] 686 5-9-3 55 ACulhane 5 51
(BPJBaugh) *prom: outpcd over 3f out: styd on ins fnl f* **20/1**
0066 **8** 1 1/2 **Cryfield**[16] 6296 7-8-13 51 (v) KimTinkler 12 44
(NTinkler) *hld up: hdwy 1/2-way: wknd 2f out* **16/1**
2520 **9** 8 **Oh So Rosie (IRE)**[8] 6445 4-8-6 54 (p) DerekNolan(7) 1 27
(JSMoore) *hld up: hmpd over 2f out: n.d* **4/1**[2]
1000 **10** 2 **Burnt Copper (IRE)**[40] 4485 4-9-0 52 NPollard 3 24
(JRBest) *s.s: hdwy over 2f out: sn wknd* **25/1**
0000 **11** 2 1/2 **Pawan (IRE)**[16] 6295 4-9-2 54 AnnStokell 11 20
(MissAStokell) *chsd ldrs: wkng whn hung lft over 2f out* **33/1**
-000 **12** 27 **Friday's Takings**[26] 6057 5-8-12 50 (b) FLynch 10 —
(BSmart) *sn rdn to ld: hdd & wknd over 2f out: eased* **33/1**

1m 53.12s — **12** Ran SP% **121.3**
Speed ratings: CSF £38.92 TOTE £9.60: £2.40, £2.20, £1.80; EX 56.40.
**Owner** Inca Financial Services **Bred** Darley Stud Management, L L C **Trained** Kingston Lisle, Oxon

**FOCUS**
Another weak heat, but the time was only fractionally slower than the first.

**NOTEBOOK**
**Qobtaan(USA)**, like so many at this level, lacks consistency, but he had the decent pace he needs and, despite hanging across his rivals, never looked like getting caught.
**Mobo-Baco**, one of the more reliable ones, again ran his race without quite being good enough.
**Ziet D'Alsace(FR)** had her chance, but she does need things to fall just right her.
**Middleham Park(IRE)** looked to find this an insufficient test, for he took an age to pick up.
**Adobe**, a prolific winner in the past, looks to have his own ideas about the game now.
**Time To Remember(IRE)** failed to stay this longer trip.
**Friday's Takings** *Official explanation: trainer's representative said gelding had a breathing problem*

## 6551 BET DIRECT ON ITV PAGE 367 CLASSIFIED STKS — 1m 1f 103y(P)
5:00 (5:01) (F4) 4-Y-0+ — £2,618 (£748; £374) Stalls Low

Form — RPR
0455 **1** **Ribbons And Bows (IRE)**[19] 6231 4-8-9 48 (v) DSweeney 12 64
(CACyzer) *chsd ldrs: led 3f out: rdn clr over 1f out: hung rt ins fnl f: r.o* **16/1**
0030 **2** 4 **Factual Lad**[16] 6292 6-9-3 60 GBaker 5 64
(BRMillman) *chsd ldrs: outpcd over 2f out: styd on ins fnl f* **4/1**[2]
3000 **3** nk **Sienna Sunset (IRE)**[13] 6343 5-8-5 56 BSwarbrick(5) 13 56
(WMBrisbourne) *hld up: hdwy 1/2-way: rdn to chse wnr over 2f out: no ex fnl f* **8/1**
1604 **4** 4 **Hollywood Henry (IRE)**[22] 6154 4-8-12 55 (p) JQuinn 4 51
(JAkehurst) *hld up: hdwy u.p over 1f out: nvr nrr* **11/2**[3]
1 **5** 1 **Montara (IRE)**[10] 6406 5-9-4 45 (p) ACulhane 1 55
(LindsayWoods, Ire) *mid-div: hdwy 3f out: sn rdn: wknd wl over 1f out* **2/1**[1]
6100 **6** shd **Mon Secret (IRE)**[16] 6295 6-9-0 57 DMcGaffin 6 51
(BSmart) *hld up: hdwy 3f out: rdn and wknd wl over 1f out* **12/1**
0001 **7** 1 3/4 **Ellovamul**[19] 6230 4-8-4 50 PPMathers(5) 9 42
(WMBrisbourne) *hld up: rdn over 3f out: n.d* **9/1**
1500 **8** 1/2 **Zarin (IRE)**[33] 5945 6-9-2 59 ANicholls 10 48
(DWChapman) *hld up: hdwy over 2f out: hung lft over 1f out: n.d* **14/1**
5060 **9** 4 **Danger Bird (IRE)**[19] 6225 4-8-9 50 WRyan 8 34
(RHollinshead) *chsd ldr tl led over 3f out: sn hdd: wknd wl over 1f out* **12/1**
0005 **10** 5 **Kumakawa**[33] 5929 6-8-8 47 ow1 AQuinn(5) 7 28
(DKIvory) *hld up: hdwy 1/2-way: wknd 3f out* **40/1**
0006 **11** hd **Pas De Surprise**[10] 6404 6-8-9 45 (p) DNolan(3) 11 27
(PDEvans) *chsd ldrs 7f* **12/1**
414- **12** 1 1/4 **Mujkari (IRE)**[461] 3761 8-8-12 46 (b) FNorton 2 25
(JMBradley) *hld up in tch: plld hrd: lost pl 1/2-way: sn bhd* **16/1**
0000 **13** 5 **Quintoto**[5] 6483 4-8-11 57 (p) THamilton(3) 3 17
(RAFahey) *led 6f: wknd over 2f out* **20/1**

2m 3.51s — **13** Ran SP% **138.5**
Speed ratings: CSF £91.53 TOTE £18.80: £7.60, £2.30, £3.40; EX 99.00.
**Owner** Mrs Charles Cyzer **Bred** Denis McDonnell **Trained** Maplehurst, W Sussex

**FOCUS**
This was not that competitive a classified contest and the form does not appear that solid.

**NOTEBOOK**
**Ribbons And Bows(IRE)** proved well suited by the drop in trip and was never in any danger after going for home. However, whether she will reproduce this is anyone's guess.
**Factual Lad** was another to be suited by the drop in trip having failed to stay last time, but he let the winner get first run and could never get back into it.
**Sienna Sunset(IRE)** showed a bit more than of late and may be running back into form.
**Hollywood Henry(IRE)** was left with plenty to do and deserves credit for finishing as close as he did.
**Montara(IRE)** was a shade disappointing having been well backed, but that should not have been too much of a surprise given his record in Ireland.
**Mujkari(IRE)** *Official explanation: jockey said gelding ran too freely*

## 6552 BET DIRECT FOOTBALL CASHBACKS H'CAP — 1m 4f 50y(P)
5:30 (5:30) (F4) (0-62,62) 3-Y-O — £2,662 (£760; £380) Stalls Low

Form — RPR
5000 **1** **Another Con (IRE)**[22] 6159 3-8-13 54 RWinston 3 63
(PHowling) *mde all: rdn clr over 2f out: unchal* **10/1**
0010 **2** 4 **Papeete (GER)**[62] 5274 3-9-1 56 SDrowne 12 59
(MissBSanders) *a.p: rdn to chse wnr over 1f out: no imp* **11/2**[2]
0433 **3** 5 **Maria Bonita (IRE)**[25] 6085 3-9-6 61 SWhitworth 9 57
(MrsStefLiddiard) *hld up: hdwy u.p over 1f out: nt rch ldrs* **13/2**
3011 **4** 1 **Daydream Dancer**[42] 5750 3-8-13 54 (b) RSmith 6 48
(CGCox) *prom: rdn over 3f out: sn outpcd* **6/1**[3]
1 **5** 2 **Trickstep**[24] 6112 3-9-3 58 (b) DarrenWilliams 5 49
(ISemple) *chsd ldrs: rdn over 2f out: wknd over 1f out* **8/1**
2106 **6** 1 1/2 **Turks And Caicos (IRE)**[33] 5957 3-8-7 55 GBartley(7) 10 44
(PCHaslam) *hld up: hdwy over 4f out: wknd 2f out* **7/1**
0000 **7** 5 **It's Blue Chip**[26] 6074 3-9-0 55 SWKelly 4 36
(PWD'Arcy) *s.s: effrt over 2f out: nvr nr to chal* **10/3**[1]
5500 **8** 3/4 **Chara**[50] 5560 3-9-4 59 FLynch 11 39
(JRJenkins) *s.i.s: effrt over 2f out: n.d* **22/1**
4315 **9** 7 **On Cloud Nine**[39] 5817 3-9-4 59 RHavlin 8 29
(JGMO'Shea) *s.i.s: rdn 3f out: a in rr* **20/1**
060 **10** 1 3/4 **Pins 'n Needles (IRE)**[38] 5828 3-9-3 58 DSweeney 2 25
(CACyzer) *prom: rdn over 3f out: wknd over 2f out* **33/1**
0000 **11** 4 **Red Skelton (IRE)**[4] 6495 3-9-5 60 ANicholls 7 21
(MsDeborahJEvans) *chsd ldrs: rdn over 4f out: wknd over 2f out* **25/1**
5356 **12** 2 1/2 **Elusive Kitty (USA)**[16] 6285 3-9-2 62 (b1) ThomasYeung(5) 1 19
(GAButler) *hld up in tch: rdn and wknd over 2f out* **16/1**

2m 43.69s — **12** Ran SP% **120.6**
Speed ratings: CSF £62.15 CT £394.51 TOTE £10.30: £3.10, £2.60, £3.00; EX 87.90.
**Owner** D C Patrick **Bred** Matthew Tynan **Trained** Newmarket, Suffolk

**FOCUS**
Another uncompetitive event, with the field strung out like three-mile chasers, and not a race to take much from.

**NOTEBOOK**
**Another Con(IRE)** was much happier over this trip and allowed a soft lead, had this won turning for home.
**Papeete(GER)** turned in a sound enough effort on this All-Weather debut, and should be up to winning a similar contest off her current mark.
**Maria Bonita(IRE)** did well to finish as close as she did, for she was stone last turning for home. This trip was not a problem for her, and her shrewd handler should be able to find a race for her on this surface.
**Daydream Dancer**, who had given the impression at Brighton that this trip ought to suit, was a shade disappointing. However, there was not much of a gallop and she is certainly worth another chance.
**It's Blue Chip**, as he had done in the past, ruined his chance by not getting out of the stalls. *Official explanation: jockey said gelding was reluctant to leave stalls*
**Chara** *Official explanation: jockey said filly hung left when she came under pressure*
**Red Skelton(IRE)** *Official explanation: jockey said gelding had no more to give*

## 6553 BET DIRECT ON SKY ACTIVE CLASSIFIED STKS — 7f 32y(P)
5:55 (5:57) (E3) 3-Y-O+ — £3,523 (£1,084; £542; £271) Stalls High

Form — RPR
040 **1** **Zoom Zoom**[23] 6144 4-9-0 66 RWinston 4 79
(MrsLStubbs) *racd keenly: sn led: rdn clr over 1f out: styd on* **4/1**[1]
6000 **2** 1 1/4 **How's Things**[66] 5176 4-9-1 67 RHavlin 10 77
(DHaydnJones) *s.i.s: hld up: hdwy over 2f out: r.o* **25/1**
6443 **3** nk **Hazewind**[17] 6279 3-8-13 69 (vt) DNolan(3) 12 78
(PDEvans) *a.p: chsd wnr over 2f out: styd on* **4/1**[1]
3034 **4** 1 1/2 **Grandma Lily (IRE)**[8] 6445 6-8-7 67 DTudhope(5) 3 69
(DCarroll) *hld up in tch: lost pl over 5f out: nt clr run over 2f out: hdwy over 1f out: nt rch ldrs* **8/1**
6044 **5** 5 **Ballyhurry (USA)**[25] 6094 7-9-0 66 NMackay 7 58
(JSGoldie) *chsd ldrs: rdn 1/2-way: wknd fnl f* **5/1**[2]
-002 **6** 1/2 **Lasanga**[24] 6132 5-9-4 70 TPQueally 9 61
(LadyHerries) *s.s: hld up: rdn over 2f out: nvr nrr* **8/1**
**7** shd **Kalani Star (IRE)**[56] 5430 4-9-1 70 TEaves(3) 11 61
(ISemple) *hld up: rdn over 2f out: n.d* **16/1**
-010 **8** 1 **Constable Burton**[49] 5583 3-9-2 69 DAllan 2 57
(MrsADuffield) *chsd ldrs: rdn 1/2-way: wknd over 1f out* **20/1**
0056 **9** 1/2 **Ile Michel**[26] 6062 7-9-1 67 DSweeney 6 54
(JGMO'Shea) *hld up: a in rr* **25/1**
0400 **10** nk **Blue Knight (IRE)**[5] 6480 5-9-4 70 SWKelly 8 56
(PHowling) *hld up: a in rr* **20/1**
0306 **11** hd **Kindlelight Debut**[22] 6156 4-8-12 67 DaneO'Neill 5 50
(DKIvory) *chsd ldrs: rdn over 2f out: wknd over 1f out* **6/1**[3]
0506 **12** 3 1/2 **Abbajabba**[3] 6517 8-9-4 70 JFanning 1 46
(CWFairhurst) *led early: remained handy tl wknd 2f out* **9/1**

1m 30.71s
**WFA** 3 from 4yo+ 1lb — **12** Ran SP% **126.3**
Speed ratings: CSF £118.90 TOTE £6.30: £2.10, £7.60, £1.30; EX 408.00.
**Owner** H Conlon **Bred** Simon Curtis **Trained** Malton, N. Yorks

**FOCUS**
A fair contest with the first four finishing nicely clear and the form seems reliable.

**NOTEBOOK**
**Zoom Zoom** was plenty keen enough through the early stages, but still had enough left to repell the finishers at the business end, landing something of a touch for connections. Just as effective over six, he looks capable of scoring again.
**How's Things** looked to find this trip on the sharp side, especially as there was not much of a gallop early on. Twice a winner this time last year, he could well be running into form
**Hazewind**, who stays further than this, would have preferred a stronger pace. A tough and consistent animal, he will find other opportunities through the winter.
**Grandma Lily(IRE)** did not have the best of luck in running, but she is clearly on good terms with herself at present.

## 6554 BETDIRECT.CO.UK H'CAP — 5f 20y(P)
6:20 (6:21) (E3) (0-77,77) 4-Y-O+ — £3,429 (£1,055; £527; £263) Stalls Low

Form — RPR
1224 **1** **Jagged (IRE)**[52] 5512 4-8-11 63 (v) FLynch 4 72
(JRJenkins) *led 1f: chsd ldr: rdn 1/2-way: led ins fnl f: jst hld on* **7/2**[1]
4043 **2** shd **Byo (IRE)**[27] 6046 6-8-11 63 FNorton 10 72
(MQuinn) *chsd ldrs: rdn 1/2-way: ev ch ins fnl f: r.o* **5/1**[2]
2004 **3** 1/2 **Another Glimpse**[16] 6293 6-9-11 77 (t) SDrowne 3 84
(MissBSanders) *hld up: nt clr run 1/2-way: hdwy over 1f out: rdn and ev ch ins fnl f: r.o* **8/1**
1430 **4** nk **Savile's Delight (IRE)**[61] 5299 5-9-1 67 (b) CCatlin 2 73
(RBrotherton) *hld up: hdwy over 1f out: r.o* **14/1**

0000 **5** 1 3/4 **Parkside Pursuit**[16] 6293 6-8-11 63 PFitzsimons 11 63
(JMBradley) *mid-div: rdn 1/2-way: r.o ins fnl f: nt trble ldrs* **20/1**
4500 **6** *shd* **Currency**[19] 6205 7-9-4 70 JFEgan 8 69
(JMBradley) *s.i.s: r.o ins fnl f: nrst fin* **10/1**
0601 **7** *nk* **Polish Emperor (USA)**[33] 5949 4-9-11 77 (e) JFanning 13 75
(PWHarris) *s.i.s: sn chsng ldrs: rdn and hung lft over 1f out: styd on same pce: sdle slipped* **11/2**[3]
2350 **8** 3/4 **Larky's Lob**[18] 6246 5-8-6 65 JDO'Reilly(7) 12 61
(JO'Reilly) *led 4f out: clr 2f out: hdd and no ex ins fnl f* **14/1**
0000 **9** 2 **Playtime Blue**[16] 6293 4-9-3 69 GBaker 7 57
(MrsHSweeting) *chsd ldrs: rdn 1/2-way: wknd fnl f* **16/1**
0050 **10** *nk* **Izmail (IRE)**[27] 6046 5-8-10 65 (b[1]) DNolan(3) 5 52
(PDEvans) *chsd ldrs: rdn 1/2-way: wknd fnl f* **10/1**
50-0 **11** 5 **Bragadino**[1] 6539 5-8-13 65 (vt[1]) ACulhane 6 34
(LindsayWoods, Ire) *stasrted slowly: outpcd* **20/1**
035 **12** 1 3/4 **Musical Fair**[16] 6293 4-9-8 74 RWinston 1 37
(JAGlover) *chsd ldrs: rdn 1/2-way: wknd over 1f out* **8/1**
0040 **P** **Seven No Trumps**[69] 5071 7-9-8 74 SWKelly 9 —
(JMBradley) *s.i.s: hld up: hung rt and p.u 1/2-way* **16/1**

63.14 secs **13 Ran SP% 129.3**

Speed ratings: CSF £21.87 CT £140.88 TOTE £5.20: £2.00, £1.50, £3.30; EX 32.00 Place 6 £195.60, Place 5 £70.74.

**Owner** The Jagged Partnership **Bred** Ellesmere Bloodstock Ltd **Trained** Royston, Herts

**FOCUS**

A competitive contest which should throw up its fair share of winners this winter.

**NOTEBOOK**

**Jagged(IRE)** lost out on the battle for the early lead, but showed plenty of resolution in the latter stages to gain the day. While he stays six, he is more effective over the minimum.

**Byo(IRE)** has yet to strike on the All-Weather surfaces, but he stuck to his task well enough and looks capable of picking up one of these sprint handicaps this winter, especially now he is getting some respite from the Handicapper.

**Another Glimpse** confirmed himself in good form and, had he got out when he wanted, may well have prevailed.

**Savile's Delight(IRE)**, who enjoyed a good summer on turf, is 8lb higher than when last seen on the All-Weather. However, he is still competitive and he will win again in his turn.

**Parkside Pursuit** left the impression this trip around here was too sharp for him. He is well treated on this surface compared to his turf mark, and can be found another opening when tackling an extra furlong.

**Polish Emperor(USA)** *Official explanation: jockey said saddle slipped round*

**Larky's Lob** did too much too soon from his wide draw, and did not quite get home. A pacey individual, he will find other opportunities when blessed with a better stall.

**Musical Fair** *Official explanation: jockey said filly hung right up straight*

**Seven No Trumps** *Official explanation: jockey said gelding was hanging badly right and was distressed*

T/Plt: £168.10 to a £1 stake. Pool: £35,292.05. 153.20 winning tickets. T/Qpdt: £34.20 to a £1 stake. Pool: £4,458.50. 96.20 winning tickets. CR

# 6549 WOLVERHAMPTON (A.W) (L-H)

## Friday, November 5

**OFFICIAL GOING: Standard**

Wind: mod breeze ahd Weather: dry

## 6555 BET DIRECT ON 0800 32 93 93 MAIDEN STKS — 1m 141y(P)

4:15 (4:15) (D3) 2-Y-O — £3,620 (£1,114; £557; £278) Stalls Low

Form — RPR

000 **1** **Maggie Tulliver (IRE)**[25] 6118 2-8-9 SWKelly 2 67+
(PWHarris) *pushed along to chse ldr after 3f: led over 2f out: sn clr: pushed out: easily* **11/4**[2]
05 **2** 5 **Sandy's Legend (USA)**[20] 6223 2-9-0 (v[1]) RHavlin 7 62
(JHMGosden) *sn led: hdd over 2f out: kpt on but nt pce of wnr* **8/1**
**3** *nk* **Novelina (IRE)** 2-8-9 ACulhane 10 56
(WJHaggas) *mid-div: hdwy 3f out: kpt on ins fnl 2f: nvr nrr* **9/1**
0 **4** *shd* **Taxman (IRE)**[9] 6439 2-9-0 SCarson 3 61
(CEBrittain) *chsd ldr for 3f: styd in tch but outpcd ins fnl 2f* **25/1**
**5** 3/4 **Bridegroom** 2-9-0 PHanagan 8 59
(EALDunlop) *in tch: outpcd 1/2-way: kpt on one pce ins fnl 2f* **13/2**[3]
0000 **6** 3/4 **Gogetter Girl**[21] 6181 2-8-9 55 (p) NCallan 11 53
(JGallagher) *in tch: rdn 3f out: wknd appr fnl f* **25/1**
**7** *shd* **Rustler** 2-9-0 DSweeney 4 57
(RCharlton) *a mid-div: sme late hdwy but nvr nr to chal* **10/1**
**8** 5 **Ramsgill (USA)** 2-9-0 LisaJones 1 47
(JARToller) *a towards rr* **14/1**
4360 **9** 1 3/4 **Zolash (IRE)**[50] 5593 2-8-7 59 DerekNolan(7) 9 43
(JSMoore) *a towards rr* **25/1**
05 **10** 3/4 **Tangible**[8] 6446 2-8-9 SSanders 13 37
(SirMarkPrescott) *s.i.s: a on outside: nvr on terms* **2/1**[1]
0002 **11** 5 **Ferrara Flame (IRE)**[25] 6127 2-8-10 58 ow4 DNolan(3) 12 30
(RBrotherton) *towards rr: rdn 1/2-way: btn over 2f out* **25/1**
**12** 9 **Germanicus** 2-8-7 RKingscote(7) 6 12
(RCharlton) *slowly away: a toiling in rr* **33/1**
0 **13** 5 **Canadian Danehill (IRE)**[8] 6448 2-9-0 PDoe 5 2
(RMHCowell) *prom on outside tl ridden and wknd wl over 2f out* **66/1**

1m 53.83s **13 Ran SP% 130.0**

Speed ratings: CSF £25.70 TOTE £2.90: £1.10, £2.80, £9.30; EX 41.70.

**Owner** Mrs P W Harris **Bred** Pendley Farm **Trained** Ringshall, Bucks

■ A winner with his final runner for Peter Harris, who now hands over the licence to his son-in-law Walter Swinburn.

**FOCUS**

A run-of-the-mill maiden run at an ordinary gallop and those that raced up with the pace had the edge. The winner was quite impressive, but there was little strength in depth.

**NOTEBOOK**

**Maggie Tulliver(IRE)** turned in a much-improved effort on her All-Weather debut and her first start over this trip. She should stay further but may not be easy to place after reassessment.

**Sandy's Legend(USA)**, tried in a visor, ran creditably. He is likely to continue to look vulnerable to anything progressive in this grade, but may be the type to fare better in ordinary handicaps. He should stay a mile and a quarter.

**Novelina(IRE)**, out of a dam who won over a mile in France, showed enough on this racecourse debut to suggest a small race can be found in due course.

**Taxman(IRE)** bettered his debut effort in this ordinary event on this All-Weather debut, but left the impression that modest handicaps and a further step up in trip would suit.

**Bridegroom**, a half-brother to multiple winner up to a mile Gilded Dancer, was not disgraced on this racecourse debut and looks another that may do better in handicaps, granted a stiffer test, in due course.

**Gogetter Girl**'s proximity confirms that the form behind the winner is modest at best.

**Tangible** attracted support but could never land a blow in a race in which it paid to race prominently. She should be suited by further next year and would not be one to write off just yet. *Official explanation: jockey had no explanation for the poor form shown*

## 6556 BET DIRECT AT DUNSTALL PARK CLASSIFIED STKS — 1m 141y(P)

4:40 (4:40) (F4) 3-Y-O — £2,653 (£758; £379) Stalls Low

Form — RPR

-340 **1** **Lake Diva**[18] 6271 3-8-11 57 ACulhane 12 58
(JGGiven) *hld up: hdwy 1/2-way: led 1f out: rdn out* **12/1**
0631 **2** 2 **My Pension (IRE)**[11] 6399 3-9-9 60 RWinston 5 66
(PHowling) *a.p: wnt 2nd over 3f out: led 2f out: hdd 2f out: kpt on but nt pce of wnr* **7/4**[1]
0503 **3** 1/2 **Just One Look**[17] 6296 3-8-9 51 NCallan 8 51
(MBlanshard) *hld up in rr: hdwy over 3f out: hrd rdn 2f out: kpt on but nt pce to chal* **3/1**[2]
6050 **4** 1/2 **Petite Colleen (IRE)**[63] 5258 3-8-11 57 (v[1]) DKinsella 6 52
(DHaydnJones) *sn rdn and wl in rr: mde late hdwy appr fnl f: r.o: nvr nrr* **8/1**
4503 **5** 1/2 **Breezit (USA)**[13] 6363 3-8-4 47 PMakin(5) 11 49
(SRBowring) *in tch: rdn 3f out: no real hdwy ins fnl 2f* **14/1**
6160 **6** 3 **Jordans Spark**[26] 6097 3-8-11 57 (b[1]) TEaves(3) 4 47
(ISemple) *led for 1f: led again over 3f out: hdd 2f out: fdd ent fnl f* **9/1**
0045 **7** 1 **Hana Dee**[11] 6399 3-8-2 47 TO'Brien(7) 9 40
(MRChannon) *a towards rr* **11/2**[3]
0000 **8** 7 **Ninah**[17] 6288 3-8-9 45 SWKelly 3 26
(JMBradley) *chsd ldrs for 3f: sn outpcd* **50/1**
0060 **9** 2 **Devious Ayers (IRE)**[59] 5381 3-8-12 58 LFletcher(3) 10 27
(JMBradley) *in tch tl wknd wl over 2f out* **25/1**
040 **10** 6 **Killing Me Softly**[24] 6150 3-8-12 48 RFitzpatrick 1 12
(JGallagher) *led after 1f: hdd over 3f out: rdn and sn wknd* **25/1**
0000 **11** 3/4 **Cloud Catcher (IRE)**[82] 4775 3-8-9 30 (t) SRighton 7 7
(MAppleby) *a struggling in rr* **100/1**

1m 52.9s **11 Ran SP% 122.9**

Speed ratings: CSF £34.21 TOTE £16.10: £5.40, £1.10, £1.10; EX 57.00.

**Owner** P B Doyle **Bred** Jeremy Gompertz **Trained** Willoughton, Lincs

**FOCUS**

A low-grade event, but one run at a sound pace throughout and the form should prove reliable at a similar level.

**NOTEBOOK**

**Lake Diva** has not proved entirely reliable but turned in an improved effort to win on only this second start on sand. Although this was not much of a race, she may be capable of better and should stay further.

**My Pension(IRE)** looked to have fair claims on his recent form on Polytrack and he again gave it his best shot. He looks a good guide to the level of this form and should continue to give a good account at a similar level.

**Just One Look** again ran creditably and again left the impression that the step up to a mile and a quarter would be in her favour. She looks capable of winning a similar event.

**Petite Colleen(IRE)**, an unreliable maiden, was not disgraced in the first-time visor but, although a return to further will suit, would be no certainty to put it all in next time.

**Breezit(USA)**, back up in trip, was not disgraced but is struggling to find her ideal trip and did not really shape like a winner waiting to happen.

**Jordans Spark**, with first-time blinkers replacing the cheekpieces, was not totally disgraced on this All-Weather debut but is likely to continue to look vulnerable in this type of event.

**Killing Me Softly** *Official explanation: jockey said gelding had hung to the right*

## 6557 BETDIRECT.CO.UK CLASSIFIED STKS — 7f 32y(P)

5:05 (5:05) (E3) 3-Y-O — £3,415 (£1,051; £525; £262) Stalls High

Form — RPR

3360 **1** **Night Storm**[182] 1939 3-8-9 65 SSanders 9 70
(SDow) *hld up on outside: hdwy 3f out: rdn and r.o to ld fnl 50yds* **14/1**
0314 **2** *nk* **Yashin (IRE)**[17] 6292 3-8-12 64 DSweeney 7 72+
(PABlockley) *hld up: rdn and hdwy on ins 2f out: r.o u.p to go 2nd nr fin* **10/1**[3]
4321 **3** 1/2 **Indiana Blues**[39] 5845 3-8-6 63 NChalmers(3) 4 68
(AMBalding) *led: clr over 2f out: rdn appr fnl f: no ex and hdd fnl 50yds* **9/2**[2]
0100 **4** 4 **Constable Burton**[1] 6553 3-9-2 69 DAllan 3 64
(MrsADuffield) *sn rdn: hdwy to go 2nd 1/2-way: one pce appr fnl f* **22/1**
0000 **5** *shd* **Overdrawn (IRE)**[26] 6086 3-9-3 70 (b) SWKelly 1 65
(JAOsborne) *prom: rdn over 2f out: one pce after* **9/2**[2]
1505 **6** 1 **Stevedore (IRE)**[36] 5887 3-9-3 70 GBaker 2 62
(BRMillman) *slowly away and outpcd: mde sme late hdwy past btn horses* **3/1**[1]
050 **7** 1 1/4 **Certifiable**[128] 3419 3-8-12 70 BSwarbrick(5) 5 59
(AndrewReid) *in tch tl wknd wl over 1f out* **25/1**
0063 **8** 3/4 **Bridgewater Boys**[6] 6482 3-9-3 70 (b) NCallan 6 57
(KARyan) *mid-div: rdn 1/2-way: nvr on terms* **3/1**[1]
1000 **9** 5 **Danifah (IRE)**[25] 6124 3-8-8 67 DNolan(3) 10 38
(PDEvans) *chsd ldr to 1/2-way: wknd over 2f out* **10/1**[3]
0010 **10** *nk* **Innstyle**[20] 6222 3-8-9 63 LisaJones 11 35
(JLSpearing) *in tch on outside to 1/2-way* **25/1**
6020 **L** **Love Of Life**[34] 5927 3-8-9 47 (v[1]) GFaulkner 8 —
(JulianPoulton) *ref to leave stalls* **66/1**

1m 31.36s **11 Ran SP% 124.7**

Speed ratings: CSF £148.30 TOTE £15.00: £6.40, £2.80, £1.90; EX 145.00.

**Owner** Anderson, Connolly and Thornton **Bred** The Lavington Stud **Trained** Epsom, Surrey

**FOCUS**

An ordinary event, but run at a strong gallop, which played into the hands of those coming from off the pace. The form is fair and appears sound.

**NOTEBOOK**

**Night Storm**, off the course since May with back problems, elected to put her best foot forward. A consistent Polytrack performer, she will prove equally effective back over a mile and should continue to give a good account.

**Yashin(IRE)** ◆, dropped markedly in trip, showed more than enough to suggest he can win a similar event at least, especially when returned to a mile.

**Indiana Blues** fared the best of those that raced up with the decent gallop and extended her run of consistent efforts back on sand. She may be a bit better than the bare form, but it is also worth remembering that she did not look the easiest of rides.

**Constable Burton** fared better than at this course the previous day but it may have to come down a bit in the weights if he is to return to winning ways in handicap company.

**Overdrawn(IRE)**, down markedly in grade for this Polytrack debut, was again a fair way below his best and does not look the most straightforward. *Official explanation: jockey said gelding had a breathing problem*

**Stevedore(IRE)** attracted plenty of support for this Polytrack debut but did not travel with any fluency and did not show enough to suggest he is going to be of interest in the near future.

## 6558 BET DIRECT ON AT THE RACES CLASSIFIED STKS 7f 32y(P)
5:30 (5:31) (G4) 3-Y-0+ £2,625 (£750; £375) Stalls High

Form RPR
0304 **1** **Charlottebutterfly**[39] 5845 4-8-12 52 GBaker 4 59
(TTClement) *in rr tl hdwy over 2f out: led over 1f out: rdn out* **16/1**
0216 **2** 3/4 **Zhitomir**[20] 6220 6-9-1 52 SWKelly 5 60
(MDods) *s.i.s: hdwy over 2f out: chsd wnr over 1f out: no imp fnl 100yds* **6/1**[3]
0006 **3** 1 1/2 **Head Boy**[48] 5656 3-9-1 53 SSanders 3 57
(SDow) *mid-div on ins: swtchd rt 2f out: hrd rdn and r.o fnl f: nvr nrr* **8/1**
0004 **4** 5 **Lakelands Lady (IRE)**[20] 6229 4-9-0 54 JEdmunds 7 42
(JBalding) *trckd ldrs rdn over 1f out: fdd ins fnl f* **20/1**
6040 **5** 1 **Oases**[25] 6124 5-9-0 51 (p) PHanagan 2 40
(DShaw) *s.i.s: racd on outside: r.o fnl f: nvr nr to chal* **4/1**[1]
6000 **6** nk **A Teen**[17] 6288 6-9-1 52 RWinston 1 40
(PHowling) *mid-div: effrt over 1f out: sn btn* **9/1**
0403 **7** 2 **Emaradia**[17] 6290 3-8-12 53 ow3 (v) DNolan(3) 12 36
(AWCarroll) *led tl hdd over 1f out: wknd qckly* **11/1**
6040 **8** 1 3/4 **Marabar**[25] 6117 6-9-0 54 (be) ACulhane 6 29
(DWChapman) *a towards rr* **10/1**
2206 **9** 1 1/4 **Pepper Road**[23] 6154 5-9-3 54 RFfrench 8 29
(RBastiman) *prom: rdn and ev ch 2f out: wknd over 1f out* **5/1**[2]
4540 **10** 6 **Danettie**[26] 6097 3-9-0 55 NPollard 11 11
(WMBrisbourne) *trckd ldr tl wknd over 2f out* **25/1**
1205 **11** 3 **Smart Scot**[17] 6296 5-9-1 52 DarrenWilliams 9 3
(BPJBaugh) *prom on outside to 1/2-way: wknd over 2f out* **8/1**
5004 **12** 1 **Cayman Breeze**[24] 6146 4-9-0 51 PDoe 10 —
(JMBradley) *trckd ldrs tl wknd over 2f out* **12/1**

1m 31.17s
**WFA** 3 from 4yo+ 1lb **12** Ran SP% **122.8**
Speed ratings: CSF £113.04 TOTE £20.90: £7.20, £3.10, £5.00; EX 112.80.
**Owner** Future Electrical Services Ltd **Bred** J T O'Neill **Trained** Newmarket, Suffolk

**FOCUS**
Another ordinary event, but the gallop was fair and the form looks sound for the grade.

**NOTEBOOK**
**Charlottebutterfly**, mainly a reliable sort, ran right up to her best to get off the mark at the 16th attempt. She should continue to give a good account but this race does not appeal as one that will be throwing up too many winners.
**Zhitomir** has had a good year, with three wins over this trip, and ran right up to his best. Whether he will reproduce this next time is open to debate, though.
**Head Boy**, who has only won once in 19 starts, looks a bit better than the bare form, as he did not get room at a crucial stage. However, given his record, he may not be one to place too much faith in.
**Lakelands Lady(IRE)**, having only her second start on Polytrack, was again below her best and she does not look one to place maximum faith in.
**Oases**, an infrequent winner, was well supported and was not totally disgraced on this return to sand, but he will have to better this effort to return to winning ways in the near future.
**A Teen** shaped as though the return to six furlongs would be in his favour, but he is not really one to be placing too much faith in.

## 6559 LITTLEWOODS BET DIRECT CLASSIFIED STKS 5f 216y(P)
5:55 (5:55) (G4) 3-Y-0+ £2,660 (£760; £380) Stalls Low

Form RPR
0111 **1** **Inch By Inch**[38] 5849 5-8-9 55 (b) AQuinn(5) 5 68+
(PJMakin) *hld up: hdwy over 2f out: led 1f out: r.o wl* **9/4**[1]
3606 **2** 1 3/4 **Chickado (IRE)**[84] 4717 3-9-0 55 RHavlin 4 62+
(DHaydnJones) *in toch on ins: hdwy 2f out: rdn and r.o to go 2nd cl home* **11/1**
0124 **3** shd **On The Trail**[20] 6220 7-9-3 55 ACulhane 12 65
(DWChapman) *led tl hdd 1f out: kpt on but lost 2nd cl home* **4/1**[2]
0640 **4** 3/4 **Mr Bountiful (IRE)**[94] 4425 6-9-3 55 (t) SWKelly 2 63+
(MDods) *bhd tl hdwy over 1f out: r.o: nvr nrr* **16/1**
0000 **5** 3/4 **St Austell**[38] 5849 4-9-2 54 SSanders 8 60
(JARToller) *s.i.s: rdn 2f out: kpt on ins fnl 2f but nvr nr to chal* **9/1**[3]
0050 **6** 2 1/2 **Karminskey Park**[25] 6117 5-9-0 55 GBaker 6 50
(TJEtherington) *nvr bttr than mid-div: b.b.v* **10/1**
0523 **7** 1/2 **Pulse**[21] 6186 6-9-1 53 (p) PFitzsimons 1 50
(JMBradley) *prom on ins: rdn 2f out: wknd appr fnl f* **11/1**
0000 **8** 1/2 **Margalita (IRE)**[5] 6493 4-9-0 55 (bt) GGibbons 3 47
(PMitchell) *towards rr: rdn 2f out: nt improve position* **40/1**
U440 **9** 1 1/2 **Park Star**[132] 3301 4-9-0 55 RWinston 9 43
(DShaw) *a struggling in rr* **20/1**
0000 **10** 1 1/4 **Goodwood Prince**[11] 6398 4-9-3 55 (v) LisaJones 7 42
(SDow) *mid-div: rdn 1/2-way: sn bhd* **40/1**
6500 **11** 1/2 **Stagnite**[43] 5754 4-9-0 55 (p) NChalmers(3) 10 40
(MrsHSweeting) *prom tl rdn and wknd wl over 1f out* **20/1**
0333 **12** 1 **Valiant Romeo**[19] 6246 4-9-1 53 (v) RFfrench 11 35
(RBastiman) *in tch: hdwy on outside 1/2-way: nt qckn u.p 2f out: sn btn* **10/1**
0600 **13** 9 **Arogant Prince**[5] 6493 7-9-3 55 (b) NCallan 13 10
(JPearce) *chsd ldr tl wknd qckly 2f out* **25/1**

1m 16.27s **13** Ran SP% **119.7**
Speed ratings: CSF £26.23 TOTE £2.60: £1.60, £4.20, £1.10; EX 23.00.
**Owner** Mrs Anna L Sanders **Bred** Mrs Anna L Sanders **Trained** Ogbourne Maisey, Wilts

**FOCUS**
An ordinary event but a decent gallop and the winner won with more in hand than the official margin suggests. The third sets the standard and the form could work out.

**NOTEBOOK**
**Inch By Inch** ◆, off a lower mark on sand than turf, won with more in hand than the official margin suggests on this return to an artificial surface and appeals strongly as the type to win again in similar company over this trip in the coming weeks.
**Chickado(IRE)** is vulnerable to progressive or well-treated rivals in this type of event and was unlucky to meet one that fell into both of those categories. She looks capable of winning a small event around this trip on sand this winter.
**On The Trail**, down in trip, had the run of the race after his break and ran creditably once again. This reliable sort, looks a good guide to the level of this form.
**Mr Bountiful(IRE)** is a quirky peformer who left the impression that the return to seven furlongs would be in his favour but he is not really one to be taking a short price about.
**St Austell** was not disgraced on this All-Weather debut, but is inconsistent and would be no certainty to reproduce this next time.
**Karminskey Park**, a Polytrack winner at Lingfield early last year, was not totally disgraced, especially as it transpired that she broke a blood-vessel, but she has never been one to place maximum faith in. *Official explanation: jockey said mare had bled from the nose*

## 6560 BET DIRECT FOOTBALL CASHBACKS CLASSIFIED STKS 1m 1f 103y(P)
6:20 (6:20) (F4) 3-Y-0 £2,597 (£742; £371) Stalls Low

Form RPR
0203 **1** **Semelle De Vent (USA)**[27] 6061 3-8-9 55 (v) RHavlin 5 61+
(JHMGosden) *chsd ldr: led over 3f out: kpt up to work ins fnl f: eased cl home* **11/2**[3]
0052 **2** 3/4 **Velocitas**[34] 5957 3-9-0 57 (v[1]) PHanagan 1 63
(HJCollingridge) *in tch: chsd wnr 3f out: kpt on fnl f but nvr threatened to chal* **3/1**[2]
4633 **3** 3 1/2 **Mr Midasman (IRE)**[55] 5459 3-8-13 56 DSweeney 8 55
(RHollinshead) *chsd ldr to 3f out: kpt on but nvr pce to chal after* **3/1**[2]
0340 **4** 11 **Dancing Bear**[35] 5914 3-8-12 55 (b) NCallan 9 33
(JulianPoulton) *led tl hdd over 3f out: wknd over 1f out* **9/1**
0000 **5** 3 1/2 **Alianna (FR)**[132] 3305 3-8-9 35 LisaJones 2 24
(SDow) *a towards rr: lost tch over 4f out* **40/1**
0030 **6** 5 **Zarneeta**[20] 6230 3-8-9 35 PDoe 3 14
(WDeBest-Turner) *totally outpcd thrght* **33/1**
6600 **7** nk **Ollijay**[24] 6146 3-8-12 47 GGibbons 4 17
(MrsHDalton) *in tch tl hrd rdn 1/2-way: sn btn* **16/1**
0634 **8** nk **Best Desert (IRE)**[11] 6399 3-9-2 59 SSanders 7 20
(JRBest) *prom on ouside tl rdn 4f out: sn wknd* **9/4**[1]
6R0L **P** **Princess Ismene**[57] 5408 3-8-9 48 (v[1]) SRighton 6 —
(MAppleby) *v.s.a: ref to r* **40/1**

2m 2.99s **9** Ran SP% **119.9**
Speed ratings: CSF £23.07 TOTE £5.50: £2.30, £1.10, £1.40; EX 29.70 Place 6 £106.28, Place 5 £45.81.
**Owner** Skara Glen Stables **Bred** Skara Glen Stables **Trained** Manton, Wilts

**FOCUS**
An ordinary contest in which the pace was just fair and the form is only modest.

**NOTEBOOK**
**Semelle De Vent(USA)** had showed enough on sand this year to suggest she had solid claims in this company, and she ran right up to her best back over this longer trip. She should continue to give a good account.
**Velocitas**, whose latest form at this course had been franked by the winner earlier in the week, again shaped well with the first-time visor and looks capable of winning a similar event when things drop right.
**Mr Midasman(IRE)** was not disgraced back on sand but left the impression that a stiffer test of stamina would have been in his favour.
**Dancing Bear**, dropped in trip, had the run of the race but did not show enough to suggest he will be of interest in a similar grade in the near future.
**Alianna(FR)**, dropped in trip, again achieved little.
**Best Desert(IRE)** looked to have fair claims in this company, but was beaten before stamina became an issue and he looks one to tread carefully with. *Official explanation: jockey had no explanation for the poor form shown*
T/Plt: £92.40 to a £1 stake. Pool: £36,374.00. 287.30 winning tickets. T/Qpdt: £18.40 to a £1 stake. Pool: £5,068.00. 203.80 winning tickets. JS

# 6438 YARMOUTH (L-H)
Friday, November 5

**OFFICIAL GOING: Soft (good to soft in places)**
As has been the norm this season, most of the action on the straight course took place up the centre of the track.
Wind: Fresh across. Weather: Cloudy with sunny spells.

## 6561 SHARP MINDS BETFAIR CLAIMING STKS 1m 3y
1:00 (1:02) (F4) 3-Y-0+ £3,108 (£888; £444) Stalls Low

Form RPR
506 **1** **J R Stevenson (USA)**[26] 6081 8-8-13 67 KFallon 4 68
(MWigham) *hld up: hdwy 3f out: rdn to ld over 1f out: hung rt ins fnl f: styd on* **15/8**[1]
0640 **2** 1/2 **Lakota Brave**[26] 6081 10-9-1 66 EAhern 12 69
(MrsStefLiddiard) *a.p: rdn to chse wnr and rdr dropped reins ins fnl f: r.o* **9/1**[3]
0600 **3** 5 **Pererin**[20] 6228 3-8-2 40 (v) JFMcDonald(3) 3 51
(IAWood) *led over 6f out: wandered and hdd over 1f out: wknd ins fnl f* **50/1**
4-55 **4** 3/4 **Strathspey**[21] 6185 5-8-9 66 LPKeniry(3) 13 54
(PJMcbride) *chsd ldrs: rdn over 2f out: wknd ins fnl f* **7/1**[2]
5524 **5** 1 **Esperance (IRE)**[53] 5524 4-8-9 46 (p) JQuinn 2 49
(JAkehurst) *s.s: hdwy over 2f out: rdn over 1f out: wknd ins fnl f* **14/1**
0004 **6** hd **Sinjaree**[11] 6406 6-8-10 40 FPFerris(3) 5 53
(MrsSLamyman) *chsd ldrs: rdn over 3f out: wknd fnl f* **40/1**
0301 **7** 2 **Eastern Hope (IRE)**[67] 5187 5-8-10 59 KristinStubbs(7) 9 53
(MrsLStubbs) *s.s: hdwy over 2f out: wknd fnl f* **11/1**
4100 **8** 1 **Grand Rapide**[34] 5957 3-8-2 53 SWhitworth 8 38
(JLSpearing) *prom: lost pl 5f out: nt clr run over 2f out: n.d after* **10/1**
0 **9** 3 **A Double Ewe Bee**[11] 6402 3-7-11 DFox(5) 7 32
(WGMTurner) *led: hdd over 6f out: wkng whn n.m.r over 2f out* **100/1**
5410 **10** 3/4 **Magic Verse**[21] 6184 3-8-6 53 CCatlin 18 35
(RGuest) *hld up: rdn 1/2-way: n.d* **11/1**
/0-1 **11** 4 **Tyneham**[11] 6402 4-8-4 59 (p) CHaddon(5) 1 28
(WGMTurner) *prom over 4f* **11/1**
6 **12** 1 **Claranete Princess (IRE)**[286] 597 3-9-3 DCorby(3) 17 39
(MJWallace) *s.i.s: a in rr* **25/1**
0040 **13** 1 1/2 **Eight (IRE)**[84] 4698 8-8-9 45 KDarley 15 23
(JMPEustace) *hld up: wknd over 3f out* **20/1**
00 **14** 8 **Nippy Nipper**[11] 6402 3-7-9 (t) MHalford(7) 10 2
(MissJFeilden) *plld hrd and prom: wknd over 2f out* **80/1**
4010 **15** 3/4 **Alafzar (IRE)**[30] 6014 6-8-9 57 (vt) TPQueally 14 5
(PDEvans) *mid-div: rdn 1/2-way: wknd over 2f out* **14/1**
0 **16** 11 **Sustainable Style (FR)**[25] 6132 3-9-0 SHitchcott 6 —
(LADace) *unruly in stalls: dwlt: a bhd* **66/1**
0 **17** 3/4 **Carmarthen Belle**[21] 6200 4-9-2 JFanning 16 —
(MissLCSiddall) *dwlt: outpcd* **100/1**

1m 41.19s (1.49) **Going Correction** +0.30s/f (Good)
**WFA** 3 from 4yo+ 2lb **17** Ran SP% **122.4**
Speed ratings: **104,103,98,97,96 96,94,93,90,89 85,84,83,75,74 63,62** CSF £17.38 TOTE £2.40: £1.60, £3.50, £10.60; EX 21.30. The winner was claimed by E Oertel for £8,000
**Owner** Claret & Blue Army **Bred** Mike Jones **Trained** Newmarket, Suffolk

**FOCUS**
Not much strength in depth in this claimer, with the banded-class third and sixth setting the standard.

**NOTEBOOK**
**J R Stevenson(USA)** took advantage of the drop in class, but he had been in front plenty long enough for him and he was pulling himself up near the finish.
**Lakota Brave** stuck to his task bravely, despite his rider dropping his reins in the latter stages. He clearly retains his enthusiasm and, while he has yet to win this term, should be capable of putting that right when returning to the All-Weather surfaces.
**Pererin** had something to find on these terms, but probably did not run too badly, on ground which could well have been soft enough for him.
**Strathspey** not for the first time did not find as much as she might have, but in her defence the ground may have been softer than than ideal.
**Esperance(IRE)** is not straightforward and again gave himself plenty to do after falling out of the stalls.
**Nippy Nipper** *Official explanation: jockey said filly hung right*

## 6562 SHARP MINDS WINNERS WELCOME NURSERY 1m 3y
1:30 (1:33) (E3) (0-75,75) 2-Y-O £4,140 (£1,274; £637; £318) Stalls Low

Form RPR
400 1 **Bowled Out (GER)**[25] 6123 2-8-6 **60** TPQueally 13 65
(PJMcbride) *s.i.s and hmpd s: hdwy 1/2-way: led over 1f out: rdn out* **25/1**
005 2 1 1/4 **Akraan**[68] 5142 2-8-10 **64** RHills 10 67
(EALDunlop) *chsd ldrs: led 2f out: rdn and hdd over 1f out: styd on* **16/1**
406 3 nk **Baddam**[67] 5200 2-8-11 **65** KDarley 17 67
(JLDunlop) *hld up: outpcd over 3f out: hdwy over 1f out: r.o* **10/1**
0064 4 1/2 **Union Jack Jackson (IRE)**[50] 5596 2-8-8 **62** PRobinson 18 63
(JGGiven) *hld up in tch: rdn to chse wnr and edgd lft over 1f out: styd on same pce ins fnl f* **16/1**
0032 5 hd **Picot De Say**[4] 6515 2-8-6 **60** NMackay 1 61
(JohnBerry) *hld up: hdwy and swtchd rt over 2f out: r.o: nt rch ldrs* **8/1**[3]
3005 6 1/2 **Uncle Bulgaria (IRE)**[50] 5596 2-8-7 **61** SWhitworth 3 61
(GCBravery) *chsd ldrs: riden over 2f out: styd on same pce ins fnl f* **25/1**
0014 7 3/4 **Lola Sapola (IRE)**[18] 6265 2-9-7 **75** DHolland 2 73
(NACallaghan) *chsd ldrs: outpcd over 3f out: r.o ins fnl f* **7/1**[1]
0052 8 1 3/4 **Sunny Times (IRE)**[20] 6226 2-8-9 **63** PCosgrave 16 58
(JWPayne) *hld up: rdn and nt clr run over 1f out: r.o ins fnl f: nt rch ldrs* **16/1**
013 9 1/2 **Manic**[16] 6305 2-8-10 **64** JFEgan 20 58
(AndrewReid) *hld up: hdwy over 2f out: sn rdn: edgd lft over 1f out: no etxra fnl f* **25/1**
0000 10 1/2 **Volitio**[26] 6077 2-8-6 **60** EAhern 14 53
(SKirk) *chsd ldrs: rdn and ev ch over 1f out: wknd ins fnl f* **33/1**
3000 11 3/4 **Flag Point (IRE)**[36] 5885 2-9-3 **71** DaneO'Neill 9 62
(JLDunlop) *chsd ldrs: rdn over 2f out: wknd fnl f* **25/1**
5003 12 1 **Captain Margaret**[35] 5909 2-8-8 **62** (t) JQuinn 8 51
(JPearce) *chsd ldrs: rdn over 2f out: wknd fnl f* **14/1**
002 13 nk **Caribbean Dancer (USA)**[19] 6240 2-9-4 **72** JFanning 5 61
(MJohnston) *chsd ldr: led over 5f out: rdn and hdd 2f out: wknd fnl f* **14/1**
310 14 1/2 **Daisy Bucket**[31] 6003 2-8-11 **65** CCatlin 11 53
(DMSimcock) *hld up: rdn over 3f out: n.d* **20/1**
005 15 1 **Swords**[25] 6122 2-9-4 **72** KFallon 12 58
(DJDaly) *s.i.s: hdwy 5f out: rdn over 2f out: wknd and eased fnl f* **8/1**[3]
2500 16 1 1/4 **Bongoali**[38] 5852 2-7-11 **58** TDean(7) 7 41
(MRChannon) *s.s: hdwy over 4f out: rdn and wknd over 1f out* **14/1**
5003 17 3/4 **Tybalt**[44] 5738 2-8-10 **64** (v) MartinDwyer 15 46
(PWHarris) *plld hrd and prom: rdn and wknd over 1f out* **12/1**
6533 18 1 1/4 **Guinea A Minute (IRE)**[24] 6140 2-8-10 **64** JFortune 6 43
(PDEvans) *chsd ldrs over 5f* **15/2**[2]
0600 19 shd **Yardstick**[32] 5988 2-8-6 **60** OUrbina 19 39
(SKirk) *hld up: rdn 1/2-way: a in rr* **33/1**
0045 20 1 1/4 **Lowestoft Playboy**[13] 6359 2-8-4 **65** LeanneKershaw(7) 4 41
(MrsCADunnett) *plld hrd: hdd over 5f out: wknd wl over 1f out* **20/1**

1m 42.5s (2.80) **Going Correction** +0.30s/f (Good) **20** Ran **SP% 131.7**
Speed ratings: **98,96,96,95,95 95,94,92,92,91 91,90,89,89,88 86,86,84,84,83**CSF £369.95 CT £4334.74 TOTE £34.80: £6.20, £3.00, £2.70, £5.20; EX 814.50.
**Owner** The Silver-Lining Cricketers Syndicate **Bred** Graf And Grafin Von Stauffenberg **Trained** Newmarket, Suffolk

**FOCUS**
Several unexposed types in this modest handicap, with the first three places filled by those making their handicap debut, but sound-enough form.

**NOTEBOOK**
**Bowled Out(GER)** confirmed the promise shown on her debut, and won with a little more in hand than the verdict suggested. She should have no trouble scoring again.
**Akraan** handled conditions well enough and stuck to her task bravely. She is bred to appreciate middle distances next year and should certainly have no trouble getting off the mark.
**Baddam** got the hang of things all too late, and will certainly appreciate a stiffer test next year.
**Union Jack Jackson(IRE)** turned in a solid-enough effort, but just came up against three unexposed types.
**Picot De Say** none the worse for his effort earlier in the week, travelled well through the race and really ought to have done better. Maybe having a bit more use of him will make the difference.
**Lola Sapola(IRE)** tended to run her race in snatches, but was still far from disgraced under her big weight.
**Sunny Times(IRE)** appeared to handle this softer ground well enough, but she had no luck in running and can be rated a bit better than her finishing position.

## 6563 EUROPEAN BREEDERS FUND SHARP MINDS AT BETFAIR MAIDEN STKS 6f 3y
2:00 (2:02) (D3) 2-Y-O £4,949 (£1,523; £761; £380) Stalls Low

Form RPR
2 1 **Westland (USA)**[14] 6342 2-9-0 KFallon 6 79+
(MrsAJPerrett) *w ldrs tl led 2f out: sn rdn: r.o* **11/10**[1]
2 3 **Stage School (USA)** 2-8-9 JFanning 8 65
(MJohnston) *chsd ldrs: ev ch 2f out: styd on same pce fnl f* **10/1**[3]
0 3 shd **Helen House**[7] 6454 2-8-9 PRobinson 12 65
(MHTompkins) *led: hdd over 4f out: rdn and ev ch over 1f out: no ex fnl f* **12/1**
4 2 **Legal Belle** 2-8-9 SHitchcott 18 59
(JLSpearing) *hld up: hdwy u.p over 1f out: styd on same pce ins fnl f* **50/1**
00 5 nk **Miss Hermione**[20] 6226 2-8-9 DaneO'Neill 9 58
(MrsCADunnett) *racd keenly: led over 4f out: hdd 2f out: styd on same pce appr fnl f* **80/1**
06 6 1 1/2 **Krullind (IRE)**[6] 6476 2-9-0 AMcCarthy 1 58
(PWChapple-Hyam) *dwlt: hld up: hdwy over 1f out: nvr nr to chal* **12/1**
0 7 1/2 **Highest Regard**[11] 6400 2-8-9 DFox(5) 14 57
(PLGilligan) *mid-div: rdn over 2f out: nvr trbld ldrs* **33/1**
0 8 hd **Physical (IRE)**[14] 6342 2-8-9 DHolland 13 56
(MrsAJPerrett) *w ldrs over 3f: styd on same pce fnl 2f* **14/1**
5 9 1 1/2 **Lake Carezza (USA)**[28] 6045 2-9-0 EAhern 5 52
(JNoseda) *hld up: rdn over 1f out: nvr trbld ldrs* **7/2**[2]
0 10 nk **Angel River**[9] 6439 2-8-9 MartinDwyer 15 46
(MJRyan) *hld up in tch: wknd over 2f out* **100/1**
0 11 3/4 **Binty**[7] 6454 2-8-6 LPKeniry(3) 3 44
(JLSpearing) *chsd ldrs over 4f* **20/1**
12 1 1/4 **Suivez Moi (IRE)** 2-9-0 JQuinn 10 45
(PWChapple-Hyam) *s.s: rn green in rr: n.m.r over 1f out: nvr nr to chal* **18/1**
0 13 1 3/4 **Red Apache (IRE)**[59] 5373 2-9-0 JFEgan 7 40
(HJCollingridge) *s.s: a in rr* **40/1**
000 14 1/2 **Rock Fever (IRE)**[15] 6322 2-8-6 DCorby(3) 11 33
(MJWallace) *chsd ldrs over 3f* **25/1**
0000 15 5 **Rockys Girl**[9] 6440 2-8-9 SWhitworth 2 18
(MJRyan) *in rr: effrt over 2f out: sn wknd* **66/1**
16 5 **Chillin Out** 2-9-0 MTebbutt 17 8
(WJarvis) *s.s: plld hrd: hdwy 4f out: wknd over 2f out* **40/1**
000 17 1 3/4 **Autumn Daze**[11] 6400 2-8-9 MHenry 16 —
(MJRyan) *w ldrs to 1/2-way: sn rdn and wknd* **100/1**

1m 15.98s (2.38) **Going Correction** +0.30s/f (Good) **17** Ran **SP% 129.3**
Speed ratings: **96,92,91,89,88 86,86,85,83,83 82,80,78,77,71 64,62**CSF £13.39 TOTE £2.00: £1.10, £3.20, £3.60; EX 18.00.
**Owner** Mr & Mrs R Scott **Bred** Bruce Hundley **Trained** Pulborough, W Sussex

**FOCUS**
Probably an ordinary maiden and not a strong contest, but the winner was nicely on top and is capable of better.

**NOTEBOOK**
**Westland(USA)** confirmed the promise of his debut and ran right away from his rivals. Out of a mare that stayed a mile, he should improve further as he steps up in trip.
**Stage School(USA)**, a half-sister to the high-class pair Arazi and Noverre, has plenty to live up to. She may never reach those heights, but certainly showed enough to suggest she can win a race.
**Helen House** certainly knew more this time, but her future looks to lie in handicaps.
**Legal Belle**, who is a half-sister to 2002 Lincoln winner Zucchero, shaped well enough to suggest she should pay her way in due course.
**Miss Hermione** was too keen for her own good on the ground, and did not get home. She should find easier pickings on the All-Weather.
**Krullind(IRE)** can be guaranteed to be found an opening by shrewd connections, now he is qualified for handicaps.
**Lake Carezza(USA)** looked all at sea on the soft ground, and is certainly capable of better than he showed.
**Suivez Moi(IRE)** is a really late foal, and was very green on this racecourse debut. Not knocked around, there is plenty of improvement to come.
**Chillin Out** *Official explanation: jockey said colt stumbled*

## 6564 SHARP MINDS BETFAIR: BEST ODDS (S) STKS 1m 3f 101y
2:30 (2:30) (G4) 3-Y-O £2,590 (£740; £370) Stalls Low

Form RPR
002 1 **River Of Diamonds**[21] 6182 3-8-12 60 KFallon 5 55
(RGuest) *a.p: rdn over 2f out: styd on u.p to ld ins fnl f: jst hld on* **11/4**[1]
0000 2 shd **Zaffeu**[26] 6083 3-9-5 55 PCosgrave 4 62
(NPLittmoden) *hld up: hdwy over 3f out: sn rdn: r.o wl: jst failed* **11/2**[3]
0-60 3 3/4 **Hat Trick Man**[86] 4648 3-8-12 70 JQuinn 2 54
(JAkehurst) *chsd ldrs: led 2f out: rdn and hdd ins fnl f: unable qck* **3/1**[2]
3206 4 3/4 **Go Green**[24] 6150 3-9-0 50 (t) JFortune 3 55
(PDEvans) *s.s: hld up: hdwy over 3f out: edgd rt over 1f out: styd on u.p* **11/4**[1]
000 5 1 1/4 **Poetry 'n Passion**[11] 6397 3-8-7 JFEgan 7 46
(CACyzer) *chsd ldr 8f out: led over 3f out: rdn and hdd 2f out: edgd lft and no ex fnl f* **14/1**
00-0 6 13 **Bebopskiddly**[30] 6015 3-8-12 55 EAhern 1 33
(BGPowell) *led: hdd 10f out: remained handy tl wknd over 2f out* **14/1**
0000 7 2 1/2 **Apron (IRE)**[16] 6310 3-8-7 50 MartinDwyer 6 24
(MJRyan) *racd keenly: led 10f out: rdn and hdd over 3f out: wknd over 2f out* **25/1**

2m 36.67s (9.27) **Going Correction** +0.725s/f (Yiel) **7** Ran **SP% 110.9**
Speed ratings: **95,94,94,93,92 83,81**CSF £17.07 TOTE £2.80: £1.70, £2.80; EX 19.10.Hat Trick Man was sold to R. E. R. Williams for £6,000
**Owner** J J May **Bred** J J May, Esterdale Stud **Trained** Newmarket, Suffolk

**FOCUS**
A weak affair run at a steady pace and the winner did not need to repeat previous form to score.

**NOTEBOOK**
**River Of Diamonds** took advantage of the easier task, but it was a close call, as he was all out to hold on. While it will be difficult for him to follow up, there are some similar weak heats on the All-Weather.
**Zaffeu**, another taking a drop in grade, showed a bit more than of late. He was not disgraced on these terms and should be able to find another opening on the sand.
**Hat Trick Man** came there looking the likely winner, but for one reason or another did not appear to go through with his effort. He is clearly flattered by his current mark.
**Go Green** took an age to get going and would have appreciated a stronger pace.

## 6565 SHARP MINDS BETFAIR: BACK AND LAY MAIDEN STKS 1m 2f 21y
3:00 (3:06) (D3) 2-Y-O £3,464 (£1,066; £533; £266) Stalls Low

Form RPR
5 1 **Quizzene (USA)**[9] 6441 2-9-0 KDarley 6 71
(MJohnston) *a.p: chsd ldr over 1f out: r.o u.p to ld post* **9/2**[3]
5444 2 shd **Cordage (IRE)**[2] 6531 2-9-0 80 (p) JFortune 4 71
(GAButler) *led over 8f out: rdn clr over 1f out: hdd post* **11/2**
0 3 3/4 **Subtle Affair (IRE)**[58] 5396 2-8-9 TPQueally 13 65
(MGQuinlan) *s.s: hld up: hdwy over 3f out: rdn over 1f out: r.o* **20/1**
4 4 1 1/4 **Rosecliff**[84] 4728 2-9-0 MartinDwyer 2 68
(AMBalding) *hld up: hdwy over 3f out: edgd lft over 2f out: styd on same pce ins fnl f* **15/8**[1]
06 5 nk **Celtic Promise (IRE)**[16] 6308 2-8-9 PRobinson 8 62
(MrsAJPerrett) *led: hdd over 8f out: remained handy: chsd ldr over 2f out to over 1f out: no ex ins fnl f* **66/1**
00 6 3 **Nobbler**[27] 6072 2-9-0 SWhitworth 10 62
(JWHills) *hld up in tch: rdn over 2f out: styd on same pce appr fnl f* **33/1**
7 1 **Self Respect (USA)** 2-9-0 EAhern 5 60
(JNoseda) *s.s: hld up: hdwy 1/2-way: rdn over 3f out: styd on same pce fnl 2f* **3/1**[2]
00 8 3 **Ti Adora (IRE)**[25] 6118 2-8-9 AMcCarthy 9 50
(PWChapple-Hyam) *hld up: effrt over 3f out: nvr trbld ldrs* **50/1**
000 9 1 1/2 **Christom**[2] 6530 2-9-0 JFEgan 14 53
(GAButler) *hld up: nvr nrr* **66/1**
0 10 3/4 **Silber Mond**[9] 6441 2-9-0 KFallon 12 51
(MLWBell) *unruly at s: s.i.s: sn prom: rdn over 2f out: wknd over 1f out* **20/1**

00 **11** ¾ **Silver Song**[37] 5870 2-9-0 .......... DaneO'Neill 7 50
(JLDunlop) *prom: chsd ldr over 4f out to over 2f out: wknd over 1f out* **66/1**
0 **12** 2½ **Westfield Boy**[21] 6187 2-8-7 .......... StevenHarrison(7) 3 46
(NPLittmoden) *plld hrd and prom: hmpd and wknd over 2f out* **100/1**
00 **13** hd **Misters Sister**[16] 6309 2-8-9 .......... (b¹) JMackay 1 41
(JGGiven) *s.i.s: a bhd* **100/1**
4 **14** 15 **Grasp**[17] 6282 2-9-0 .......... (t) DHolland 11 20
(RMBeckett) *s.s: sn pushed along: a in rr* **16/1**
00 **15** 16 **Winter Mist**[60] 5349 2-8-9 .......... PCosgrave 16 —
(NPLittmoden) *hld up: rdn over 3f out: sn wknd* **100/1**
00 **16** 2 **City Trader**[13] 6351 2-9-0 .......... (b¹) JQuinn 15 —
(CEBrittain) *mid-div: rdn over 4f out: wkng whn stmbld over 2f out* **100/1**

2m 15.61s (7.64) **Going Correction** +0.725s/f (Yiel) **16** Ran SP% **122.1**
Speed ratings: **98,97,97,96,96 93,92,90,89,88 88,86,85,73,61 59**CSF £27.60 TOTE £5.70: £1.60, £2.20, £5.80; EX 44.40.
**Owner** Favourites Racing **Bred** Moreton Binn Racing,Breeding And Sales Llc **Trained** Middleham Moor, N Yorks

**FOCUS**
This did not look a bad maiden with some well-regarded types on show. However, it was only steadily run and the proximity of the runner-up suggests the form is only fair.

**NOTEBOOK**
**Quizzene(USA)** still looked a little green, but he knuckled down well to nail the winner on the post. There will be plenty of improvement to come from him over middle-distances next term.
**Cordage(IRE)** set a fair standard and had this won everywhere bar the post. The cheekpieces and the step up in trip clearly suited, and an ordinary maiden should be his for the taking.
**Subtle Affair(IRE)** appreciated the step up in trip and showed enough to suggest he can make his mark in due course.
**Rosecliff** still looked a little green at the start, for he was continually looking behind him. He did not appear to do much wrong in the race itself and can be found an opening somewhere.
**Celtic Promise(IRE)** looks to be going the right way and should do better now he is qualified for handicaps.
**Nobbler** is another who left his previous form behind on this step up in trip, and will be seen to better effect when going handicapping.
**Self Respect(USA)**, a January foal, wore a rug for stalls entry. He attracted plenty of support, so he must have been giving the right signs at home and, although well beaten, is worth another chance on better ground.
**City Trader** *Official explanation: jockey said colt lost its action*

## 6566 SHARP MINDS BETFAIR H'CAP 1m 2f 21y
**3:30** (3:32) (E3) (0-77,75) 3-Y-0+ **£3,982** (£1,225; £612; £306) **Stalls** Low

Form RPR
5444 **1** **Street Life (IRE)**[25] 6128 6-8-10 **71** .......... ARutter(7) 8 83+
(WJMusson) *hld up: hdwy and nt clr run fr over 2f out: r.o to ld wl ins fnl f: comf* **3/1²**
0003 **2** 1¼ **Count Boris**[14] 6343 3-8-0 **58** .......... MartinDwyer 1 65
(GBBalding) *s.s: hld up: rdn over 4f out: hdwy over 1f out: r.o* **10/1**
1503 **3** shd **Gingko**[8] 6450 7-8-9 **63** .......... DaneO'Neill 5 70
(PRWebber) *chsd ldrs: rdn over 4f out: led over 1f out: edgd lft and hdd wl ins fnl f* **7/1**
3060 **4** hd **Reap**[24] 6152 6-8-8 **62** .......... JQuinn 6 69
(JPearce) *chsd ldrs: nt clr run over 2f out: swtchd rt over 1f out: styd on* **33/1**
6216 **5** 2½ **Double Ransom**[80] 4826 5-8-11 **65** .......... (b) KFallon 10 67
(MrsLStubbs) *hld up: rdn over 4f out: hdwy and hung lft over 1f out: styd on same pce ins fnl f* **5/1³**
4026 **6** ½ **Kind Emperor**[38] 5853 7-8-8 **62** .......... AMackay 11 64
(PLGilligan) *led: clr 1/2-way: hdd over 1f out: btn whn hmpd ins fnl f* **12/1**
040 **7** 6 **Rajayoga**[90] 4556 3-7-13 **57** .......... MHenry 9 48
(MHTompkins) *chsd ldrs: rdn over 2f out: wknd over 1f out* **40/1**
4100 **8** 1 **Tata Naka**[22] 6173 4-9-0 **68** .......... JoannaBadger 7 58
(MrsCADunnett) *plld hrd and prom: rdn over 2f out: wkng whn hmpd over 1f out* **25/1**
1 **9** 1¾ **Marias Magic**[26] 6082 3-9-3 **75** .......... JFanning 2 62
(MJohnston) *chsd ldr: rdn and edgd lft over 2f out: wknd over 1f out* **7/4¹**
00-3 **10** 1¼ **Mister Right (IRE)**[25] 6132 3-8-5 **63** .......... CCatlin 3 48
(KBell) *hld up: plld hrd: rdn over 4f out: wknd over 2f out* **25/1**
6000 **11** 2½ **Tiber Tiger (IRE)**[39] 5841 4-8-13 **67** .......... PCosgrave 4 47
(NPLittmoden) *hld up: rdn over 2f out: sn wknd* **16/1**

2m 13.79s (5.82) **Going Correction** +0.725s/f (Yiel)
**WFA** 3 from 4yo+ 4lb **11** Ran SP% **126.3**
Speed ratings: **105,104,103,103,101 101,96,95,94,93 91**CSF £34.63 CT £205.92 TOTE £4.60: £1.60, £2.60, £2.50; EX 45.80 Trifecta £636.20 Pool £1,523.48, 1.70 w/u.
**Owner** W J Musson **Bred** Derek Veitch **Trained** Newmarket, Suffolk
■ Stewards Enquiry : A Rutter three-day ban: careless riding (Nov 16,17,19)

**FOCUS**
A competitive contest run at a sound pace in the conditions, with those in the frame giving a fair guide to the level.

**NOTEBOOK**
**Street Life(IRE)** is not the easiest of rides as he needs producing late, but his young rider rode him with plenty of confidence and the horse won without really knowing he had been in a race.
**Count Boris** left the impression a step up in trip would be of benefit.
**Gingko**, one of the first off the bridle, kept responding to pressure. This trip would be the bare minimum for him.
**Reap**, who has struggled to find his form this term, shaped much better here. He has started to slip in the weights and is one to keep in mind for a return to the All-Weather.
**Double Ransom** took a fair bit of stoking up and did not do much to help his rider.
**Kind Emperor** turned in a solid effort on ground softer than ideal, but was fading when squeezed out late on.
**Marias Magic**, who was having her first outing for current connections, may have found the ground on the soft side.

## 6567 SHARP MINDS PHONE 0870 90 80 121 H'CAP 6f 3y
**4:00** (4:00) (F4) (0-62,58) 3-Y-0 **£3,340** (£954; £477) **Stalls** Low

Form RPR
0604 **1** **Estoille**[11] 6403 3-8-2 **46** oh6 .......... (t) FPFerris(3) 9 55
(MrsSLamyman) *w ldrs: led over 2f out: rdn out* **20/1**
3012 **2** ½ **Chatshow (USA)**[11] 6403 3-8-4 **52** .......... DFentiman(7) 7 59
(AWCarroll) *hld up: hdwy over 2f out: rdn to chse wnr over 1f out: r.o* **7/2¹**
**3** nk **Margaret's Dream (IRE)**[16] 6313 3-8-6 **47** .......... EAhern 16 53
(MsCarolineHutchinson, Ire) *outpcd: hdwy and hung lft over 1f out: r.o* **7/1²**
0400 **4** 2 **Man Crazy (IRE)**[7] 6459 3-8-7 **48** .......... PCosgrave 14 48
(CADwyer) *plld hrd and prom: rdn over 2f out: styd on same pce fnl f* **14/1**
0306 **5** shd **King Egbert (FR)**[18] 6274 3-8-7 **55** .......... TDean(7) 12 55
(AWCarroll) *hld up: hdwy over 1f out: nt rch ldrs* **15/2³**
6336 **6** 2 **Vendors Mistake (IRE)**[148] 2800 3-8-6 **47** .......... JFEgan 18 41
(AndrewReid) *hld up: hdwy over 1f out: sn edgd lft: styd on same pce fnl f* **25/1**
0040 **7** nk **Bold Wolf**[48] 5642 3-8-5 **46** oh1 .......... SWhitworth 5 39
(JLSpearing) *prom: rdn over 2f out: no ex fnl f* **25/1**
0200 **8** shd **Mutassem (FR)**[5] 6493 3-9-3 **58** .......... DHolland 2 51
(TKeddy) *hld up: hdwy over 2f out: one pce fnl f* **8/1**
6000 **9** nk **Generous Gesture (IRE)**[25] 6131 3-9-3 **58** .......... JMackay 10 50
(MLWBell) *s.s: hdwy 1/2-way: outpcd over 2f out: styd on ins fnl f* **9/1**
6040 **10** 1 **Melody King**[26] 6079 3-8-12 **53** .......... (b) JFortune 15 42
(PDEvans) *prom: rdn over 2f out: wknd fnl f* **16/1**
0002 **11** nk **Absolutely Soaked (IRE)**[46] 5702 3-8-6 **47** .......... (b) NMackay 11 35
(DrJDScargill) *hld up: effrt over 2f out: nvr trbld ldrs* **10/1**
6004 **12** 1½ **Shifty Night (IRE)**[77] 4926 3-8-5 **46** oh1 .......... AMcCarthy 6 29
(MrsCADunnett) *disp ld tl led 1/2-way: sn hdd: wknd fnl f* **25/1**
0060 **13** nk **Cheeky Chi (IRE)**[11] 6398 3-8-8 **56** .......... JBrennan(7) 8 38
(PSMcentee) *unruly in stalls: hld up: wknd over 1f out* **66/1**
5000 **14** 2½ **Velvet Touch**[18] 6280 3-8-11 **52** .......... TPQueally 17 27
(JRJenkins) *mde most to 1/2-way: wkng whn nt much over 1f out* **40/1**
0600 **15** 2½ **Zonnebeke**[20] 6228 3-8-5 **46** oh1 .......... CCatlin 4 13
(MrsCADunnett) *outpcd* **20/1**
1030 **16** 1¾ **Sam The Sorcerer**[70] 5081 3-8-5 **46** oh1 .......... JQuinn 13 8
(JRNorton) *hld up in tch: plld hrd: wknd over 1f out* **20/1**
4500 **17** nk **Fools Entire**[7] 6459 3-9-0 **55** .......... (e) DaneO'Neill 1 16
(JAGilbert) *chsd ldrs over 4f* **14/1**
0066 **18** 2½ **Desert Daisy (IRE)**[17] 6288 3-8-3 **47** .......... JFMcDonald(3) 3 1
(IAWood) *w ldrs to 1/2-way: wknd 2f out* **11/1**

1m 16.29s (2.69) **Going Correction** +0.30s/f (Good) **18** Ran SP% **134.0**
Speed ratings: **94,93,92,90,90 87,87,86,86,85 84,82,82,79,75 73,73,69**CSF £88.33 CT £597.22 TOTE £38.90: £5.30, £1.60, £2.20, £7.80; EX 260.60 Place 6 £274.95, Place 5 £123.00.

**Owner** B C S Kemp **Bred** B And Mrs H Kemp **Trained** Louth, Lincs
■ Trainer Jim Gilbert sadly suffered a fatal heart attack moments before his horse Fools Entire ran in this race.

**FOCUS**
This was no better than a seller, although the winner improved on previous efforts.

**NOTEBOOK**
**Estoille**, who had looked moderate in her efforts to date, was closely matched with Chatshow on their running last time, and probably did not have to improve to win.
**Chatshow(USA)**, who had the winner behind last time, looked to run somewhere near to that form on these revised terms.
**Margaret's Dream(IRE)**, a poor maiden in Ireland, did not shape too badly on this British debut. Although she is clearly nothing special, there ought to be a small race in her on this showing.
**Man Crazy(IRE)** did herself no favours by pulling too hard.
**King Egbert(FR)**, tackling his softest surface to date, may be worth another try at this trip on better ground.
T/Jkpt: £75,612.50 to a £1 stake. Pool: £212,993.00. 2.00 winning tickets. T/Plt: £264.50 to a £1 stake. Pool: £46,601.05. 128.60 winning tickets. T/Qpdt: £13.10 to a £1 stake. Pool: £2,981.80. 167.45 winning tickets. CR

# 6344 DONCASTER (L-H)
Saturday, November 6

**OFFICIAL GOING: Round course - soft; straight course - good to soft (good in places) changing to good to soft on straight course after race 2 (12.45)**
There had been just 3mm of rain over the previous week yet the going was still described as 'genuine soft, very tiring and hard work'.
Wind: Moderate 1/2 against. Weather: Overcast.

## 6568 ROBIN HASTINGS MEMORIAL FUND APPRENTICE STKS (H'CAP) 7f
**12:15** (12:19) (D2) (0-92,84) 3-Y-0+ **£7,088** (£2,181; £1,090; £545) **Stalls** High

Form RPR
0005 **1** **Soyuz (IRE)**[19] 6277 4-8-10 **81** .......... AMullen(5) 16 96
(KARyan) *chsd ldr: led over 3f out: clr over 1f out: unchal* **8/1³**
0353 **2** 3 **Kirkby's Treasure**[4] 6525 6-8-6 **75** .......... PPMathers(3) 17 82
(ABerry) *bhd: hdwy over 2f out: styd on fnl f: no ch w wnr* **10/1**
0053 **3** nk **Queens Rhapsody**[7] 6477 4-9-0 **80** .......... SHitchcott 11 86
(ABailey) *mid-div: hdwy over 2f out: kpt on wl fnl f* **6/1²**
50-0 **4** 1¼ **Diamond Max (IRE)**[35] 5941 6-9-1 **81** .......... LisaJones 18 84
(JohnBerry) *bhd: hdwy over 2f out: styd on fnl f* **11/1**
0050 **5** 1½ **Barathea Dreams (IRE)**[43] 5766 3-8-7 **79** .......... DerekNolan(5) 14 78
(JSMoore) *w ldrs: fdd fnl f* **14/1**
3112 **6** 2½ **Mr Velocity (IRE)**[14] 6358 4-8-13 **79** .......... TPQueally 2 72
(EFVaughan) *racd far side: chsd ldrs: led that gp 1f out: no ch w stands' side* **5/1¹**
5320 **7** 3½ **St Pancras (IRE)**[70] 5122 4-8-13 **82** .......... PMakin(3) 21 66
(DWChapman) *s.i.s: styd on fnl 2f: nvr rchd ldrs* **12/1**
-040 **8** hd **Oman Gulf (USA)**[22] 6193 3-8-4 **78** .......... KMay(7) 6 62
(JGGiven) *led far side tl over 2f out: one pce* **33/1**
1630 **9** shd **Climate (IRE)**[99] 4308 5-8-4 **77** .......... DonnaCaldwell(7) 19 61
(KARyan) *in tch: edgd lft and kpt on fnl 2f* **33/1**
5036 **10** 1¾ **H Harrison (IRE)**[7] 6480 4-8-6 **77** .......... NataliaGemelova(5) 4 56
(IWMcinnes) *racd far side: w ldrs: led that gp over 2f out tl 1f out: no ex* **25/1**
0000 **11** ½ **Retirement**[68] 5194 5-8-10 **76** .......... BReilly 9 54
(MHTompkins) *in tch: effrt over 2f out: no hdwy* **14/1**
0-00 **12** ¾ **Northern Desert (IRE)**[29] 6044 5-9-2 **82** .......... LPKeniry 12 58
(PWHiatt) *chsd ldrs: one pce fnl 2f* **66/1**
05 **13** 3½ **Darghan (IRE)**[14] 6358 4-8-3 **76** .......... (t) AmyMyatt(7) 1 43
(PDEvans) *swtchd lft and racd far side: sn outpcd* **33/1**
6020 **14** 1¼ **Cd Flyer (IRE)**[5] 6517 7-9-4 **84** .......... PMulrennan 15 48
(BEllison) *a in rr* **14/1**
3-40 **15** 1 **Romaric (USA)**[33] 5992 3-8-13 **80** .......... (v) THamilton 7 42
(JRNorton) *racd far side: chsd ldrs: lost pl over 2f out* **66/1**
0445 **16** 1 **Tidy (IRE)**[7] 6477 4-8-10 **76** .......... NMackay 10 35
(MDHammond) *mid-div: effrt over 2f out: sn lost pl* **9/1**
6000 **17** 1¾ **Best Before (IRE)**[14] 6358 4-8-11 **77** ow1 .......... DNolan 8 32
(PDEvans) *chsd ldrs: lost pl over 2f out* **50/1**
0020 **18** nk **Warden Warren**[10] 6445 6-8-4 **73** .......... (p) BSwarbrick(3) 22 27
(MrsCADunnett) *led stands'side tl over 3f out: sn lost pl* **25/1**
-440 **19** 5 **Marcus Eile (IRE)**[264] 798 3-8-13 **80** .......... LEnstone 20 22
(KRBurke) *a in rr* **66/1**

0000 **20** 12 **Vindication**[19] 6277 4-9-0 **83** .......... AQuinn(3) 5 —
(RMHCowell) *s.i.s: racd far side: bhd fnl 3f* **33/1**

1m 31.18s (3.37) **Going Correction** +0.825s/f (Soft)
**WFA** 3 from 4yo+ 1lb **20** Ran SP% **123.1**
Speed ratings: **106,102,102,100,99 96,92,92,91,89 89,88,84,83,81 80,78,78,72,58**CSF £77.32 CT £521.92 TOTE £10.00: £2.80, £2.10, £2.30, £2.30; EX 120.40.
**Owner** The Fishermen **Bred** Mount Coote Stud **Trained** Hambleton, N Yorks
■ Stewards Enquiry : P P Mathers two-day ban: careless riding (Nov 17,19)

**FOCUS**
The field split into two and the larger group on the stands' side dominated.

**NOTEBOOK**
**Soyuz(IRE)** had done his previous winning in soft ground and, with the ground riding more testing than the official description suggested, ran out a clear winner on his debut for his new stable. He will go up quite a bit for this but could be a Lincoln possible next year.
**Kirkby's Treasure** continues to run well but once again ran into one too good at the weights.
**Queens Rhapsody**, rated 9lb higher on the All-Weather, is showing himself to be in good form prior to the switch back to the artificial surfaces.
**Diamond Max(IRE)** made the early running in the Cambridgeshire but was ridden with a lot more restraint on this occasion.
**Barathea Dreams(IRE)** looked progressive on easy ground in the spring but his form tailed off on a quicker surface during the summer. This was more like it, and clearly he reserves his best for when he can get his toe in.
**Mr Velocity(IRE)** has been in terrific form of late and seems to go on any ground. He won his race on the far side but found himself well beaten by the stands'-side runners.
**St Pancras(IRE)** ◆ finished runner-up in the Group Two Champagne Stakes as a two-year-old, but he has been something of an under-achiever since. He has moved stable however, and his new trainer, who has been so successful with the owner's Quito, looks just the man to recapture the colt's latent talent.
**Oman Gulf(USA)** made the running and finished second on the far side. This was his first sign of form since his debut win as a two-year-old.

## 6569 EUROPEAN BREEDERS FUND FREECLAIM IDC MAIDEN STKS 6f
**12:45** (12:50) (D3) 2-Y-O **£4,473** (£1,376; £688; £344) **Stalls** High

Form RPR
**1** **Bow Wave** 2-9-0 .......... DaneO'Neill 7 72+
(HCandy) *w'like: dwlt: gd hdwy on outside 2f out: r.o wl to ld last 100yds* **11/1**
5 **2** 1 3/4 **Westlake Bond (IRE)**[22] 6196 2-8-10 ow1 .......... FLynch 16 63
(BSmart) *w ldr: led over 3f out tl ins last: no ex* **10/1**[3]
**3** nk **Oatcake** 2-8-9 .......... DHolland 19 61
(GAButler) *leggy: unf: scope: sn chsng ldrs: ran green end edgd lft 1f out: kpt on wl ins last* **10/1**[3]
55 **4** shd **Chinalea (IRE)**[40] 5825 2-9-0 .......... RSmith 22 66
(CGCox) *unruly in stalls: led tl over 3f out: edgd lft and styd on same pce fnl f* **13/2**[1]
0 **5** hd **Prime Contender**[15] 6342 2-9-0 .......... MHills 14 65+
(BWHills) *bhd: hdwy 2f out: styd on wl ins last* **11/1**
0 **6** nk **Raven (IRE)**[26] 6127 2-8-6 .......... PMulrennan(3) 6 59
(MESowersby) *w ldrs: kpt on same pce fnl f* **66/1**
**7** 2 **Dabbers Ridge (IRE)** 2-9-0 .......... MartinDwyer 15 58
(BWHills) *lengthy: scope: mid-divsion: hdwy 2f out: kpt on fnl f* **33/1**
06 **8** 1/2 **Cavan Gael (FR)**[15] 6330 2-9-0 .......... RWinston 1 57
(PHowling) *in tch: effrt over 2f out: kpt on same pce* **16/1**
**9** 1 1/4 **Over The Limit (IRE)** 2-8-9 .......... SSanders 17 48
(MrsAJPerrett) *lengthy: unf: scope: chsd ldrs: one pce fnl 2f* **12/1**
**10** shd **Atriffic Story** 2-8-11 .......... BReilly(3) 4 53
(MissGayKelleway) *w'like: lengthy: mid-div: hdwy over 2f out: one pce fnl f* **33/1**
**11** 1 1/2 **In The Know** 2-9-0 .......... JFortune 20 48
(JHMGosden) *tall: unf: s.s: bhd: hung lft and styd on wl fnl 2f: nt rch ldrs* **13/2**[1]
0 **12** nk **Pitcairn Island**[15] 6330 2-8-9 .......... RFfrench 18 42
(MJohnston) *chsd ldrs: one pce fnl 2f* **25/1**
0 **13** 3/4 **Cream Of Esteem**[15] 6330 2-9-0 ..........(t) KimTinkler 3 45
(NTinkler) *s.i.s: bhd tl kpt on wl appr fnl f* **100/1**
**14** hd **Grande Roche (IRE)** 2-9-0 .......... RHills 11 44
(BWHills) *wl grwn: bit bkwd: rr-div: sn drvn along: kpt on fnl 2f: nvr on terms* **18/1**
**15** 3 **Nellie Gwyn** 2-8-9 .......... KFallon 21 30
(JGGiven) *w'like: s.s: bhd tl kpt on fnl 2f* **12/1**
0 **16** shd **Guadiaro (USA)**[64] 5262 2-9-0 .......... KDarley 5 35
(BWHills) *in tch: hung lft and eased over 1f out* **20/1**
**17** nk **It's Peggy Speech** 2-8-9 .......... RFitzpatrick 8 29
(SLKeightley) *leggy: unf: chsd ldrs: lost pl 2f out* **66/1**
66 **18** shd **Love Attack (IRE)**[12] 6400 2-9-1 ow6 .......... JDekeyser 9 35
(DCarroll) *w ldrs: lost pl 2f out* **66/1**
6 **19** hd **Darsharp**[15] 6342 2-8-9 .......... ACulhane 2 28
(MissGayKelleway) *mid-div: lost pl 2f out* **33/1**
**20** 6 **Manrique (USA)** 2-9-0 .......... JFanning 12 15
(MJohnston) *lengthy: unf: scope: in tch: hung lft and lost pl over 2f out: sn bhd* **8/1**[2]
00 **21** 8 **Just Elizabeth**[21] 6211 2-8-6 .......... TEaves(3) 13 —
(MESowersby) *chsd ldrs: lost pl over 2f out: sn bhd* **100/1**

1m 20.43s (6.15) **Going Correction** +0.825s/f (Soft) **21** Ran SP% **123.0**
Speed ratings: **92,89,89,89,88 88,85,85,83,83 81,80,79,79,75 75,75,75,74,66 56**CSF £106.26 TOTE £11.20: £3.50, £3.70, £3.80; EX 260.90.
**Owner** Henry Candy & Partners **Bred** T P Young And D Hanson **Trained** Wantage, Oxon

**FOCUS**
A modest maiden, highlighted by the performance of the sixth.

**NOTEBOOK**
**Bow Wave**, whose stable has had a good strike-rate this year with its juveniles first time out, finished well from off the pace to enhance that record. He overcame the disadvantage of a low draw and looks the type to do better with a winter on his back.
**Westlake Bond(IRE)** had the benefit of previous racecourse experience and put that to good use, racing prominently throughout and fighting off the attention of the eventual fourth.
**Oatcake**, a half-sister to several winners, kept on well despite betraying obvious greenness. She looks likely to benefit a great deal from the experience.
**Chinalea(IRE)** set just a modest standard. He played up in the stalls beforehand but it did not seem to affect his running for he had every chance.
**Prime Contender** gives the impression that he will do better when racing over farther in handicap company next season.
**Raven(IRE)**, beaten a fair way in a seller on her debut, was making her debut for her new connections. Her performance puts the form of the race into context.
**In The Know** is a half-brother to middle-distance winners in France and looks the type to do better over farther in time.

## 6570 CIU SERLBY STKS (LISTED RACE) 1m 4f
**1:20** (1:20) (A1) 3-Y-O+ **£19,500** (£6,000; £3,000; £1,500) **Stalls** Low

Form RPR
5622 **1** **Big Moment**[7] 6172 6-8-13 99 .......... SWKelly 5 93+
(MrsAJPerrett) *s.i.s: pushed along to take clsr order 1/2-way: hdwy on bit to chal 2f out: shkn up to ld ins last: qcknd clr* **2/1**[2]
5112 **2** 5 **Foreign Affairs**[55] 5506 6-9-4 109 .......... SSanders 2 83
(SirMarkPrescott) *trckd ldng pair: chsd ldr fr 1/2-way: rdn to ld over 2f out: hrd drvn over 1f out: hdd ins last and one pce* **11/10**[1]
6326 **3** 2 1/2 **Young Rooney**[5] 6520 4-8-13 70 .......... DHolland 1 74
(MMullineaux) *led: rdn along over 3f out: hdd over 2f out: kpt on u.p fnl f* **50/1**
0213 **4** 6 **La Sylphide**[23] 6173 7-8-8 90 .......... KFallon 6 61
(GMMoore) *trckd ldrs: pushed along over 4f out: rdn 3f out and sn btn* **5/1**[3]
500 **5** 9 **Crystal (IRE)**[52] 5573 3-8-2 90 ..........(b[1]) JFMcDonald 4 48
(BJMeehan) *chsd ldr: pushed along 1/2-way: rdn along over 4f out and sn wknd* **25/1**
200P **P** **Top Seed (IRE)**[14] 6355 3-8-7 98 ..........(t) ACulhane 3 —
(MRChannon) *sn pushed along in rr: losr tch after 4f and bhd whn p.u over 5f out* **14/1**

2m 43.2s (7.50) **Going Correction** +0.825s/f (Soft)
**WFA** 3 from 4yo+ 6lb **6** Ran SP% **110.1**
Speed ratings: **108,104,103,99,93** —CSF £4.35 TOTE £3.10: £1.70, £1.30; EX 4.30.
**Owner** R Doel,A Black,Dr J Howells,R & P Scott **Bred** Juddmonte Farms **Trained** Pulborough, W Sussex

**FOCUS**
An uncompetitive Listed race.

**NOTEBOOK**
**Big Moment** only had to be shaken up to go clear in the closing stages and won with much more in hand than the official margin suggests. The testing conditions proved ideal but, for a horse with plenty of stamina, he is not short of speed. His trainer suggested that the gelding would have a couple of runs over hurdles this winter before being aimed once more at the Chester Cup.
**Foreign Affairs** was favoured by the race conditions but not by the ground conditions. Although he has won with give in the past, his best form is on a sound surface, and he had no answer to the winner when he loomed upsides.
**Young Rooney** ran a terrific race at the weights but it is probably wise not to read too much into his performance. He is fairly exposed but really does deserve to break his duck.
**La Sylphide** runs her best races from the front but she was unable to dominate on this occasion.
**Crystal(IRE)**, who began the season in promising fashion, has gone backwards since, and the application of blinkers this time had little positive impact.
**Top Seed(IRE)** *Official explanation: jockey said colt finished distressed*

## 6571 EBF GILLIES FILLIES' STKS (LISTED RACE) 1m 2f 60y
**1:50** (1:51) (A1) 3-Y-O+ **£19,500** (£6,000; £3,000; £1,500) **Stalls** Low

Form RPR
2420 **1** **Mango Mischief (IRE)**[43] 5761 3-8-10 90 .......... DaneO'Neill 6 95
(JLDunlop) *hld up towards rr: hdwy on inner over 4f out: swtchd rt 3f out: rdn to ld wl over 1f out: drvn clr ins last: styd on* **12/1**
0000 **2** 3 1/2 **Star Of Normandie (USA)**[6] 6497 5-9-0 78 .......... AMcCarthy 8 89
(GGMargarson) *bhd: hdwy 3f out: rdn wl over 1f out: styd on wl fnl f: nrst fin* **100/1**
2211 **3** shd **Autumn Wealth (IRE)**[18] 6286 3-8-10 79 .......... MartinDwyer 1 89
(MrsAJPerrett) *chsd ldrs on inner: hdwy 4f out: rdn and ev ch over 2f out: drvn and outpcd wl over 1f out: styd on ins last* **6/1**[2]
220P **4** 1/2 **Glen Innes (IRE)**[35] 5969 3-8-10 101 .......... SSanders 5 88
(DRLoder) *midfield: smooth hdwy 4f out: chal on bit over 2f out and ev ch tl shkn up over 1f out and kpt on same pce* **12/1**
6263 **5** 3 **Mocca (IRE)**[20] 6257 3-8-10 88 .......... KDarley 12 83
(DJCoakley) *trckd ldrs: hdwy 4f out: rdn to ld over 2f out: sn drvn: hdd and grad wknd* **14/1**
5530 **6** 1/2 **Imperialistic (IRE)**[20] 6255 3-8-10 91 .......... DarrenWilliams 7 82
(KRBurke) *hld up and bhd: gd hdwy 3f out: rdn to chse ldrs wl over 1f out: wknd appr last* **16/1**
02 **7** 5 **I Had A Dream**[23] 6173 3-8-10 92 .......... PRobinson 13 74
(MAJarvis) *trckd ldrs: hdwy 4f out: led over 3f out: rdn and hdd over 2f out: sn drvn and wknd* **9/2**[1]
0510 **8** 2 **Honorine (IRE)**[23] 6173 4-9-0 80 .......... JFEgan 9 70
(JWPayne) *hld up and bhd: hdwy 3f out: rdn along 2f out and sn no imp* **25/1**
2333 **9** 8 **Bowstring (IRE)**[10] 6443 3-8-10 97 ..........(b[1]) JFortune 10 57
(JHMGosden) *keen: trckd ldr tl led after 3f: rdn along and hdd over 3f out: sn wknd* **9/2**[1]
2005 **10** 3 1/2 **Blue Oasis (IRE)**[23] 6173 3-8-10 92 .......... KFallon 11 51
(RGuest) *a rr* **11/1**[3]
2-21 **11** 14 **Baboosh (IRE)**[39] 5851 3-8-10 76 .......... RWinston 14 27
(JRFanshawe) *chsd ldrs: rdn along wl over 2f out: sn wknd* **14/1**
-003 **12** 1 1/2 **Miss Langkawi**[8] 6457 3-8-10 71 .......... DHolland 4 24
(GWragg) *led 3f: prom tl rdn along 4f out and sn wknd* **20/1**
2/1- **13** 6 **Tawoos (FR)**[27] 5-9-3 ..........(b) ACulhane 2 17
(ALund, Norway) *midfield: effrt 4f out: sn riddne along and btn* **11/1**[3]
56 **14** 7 **Marinnette (IRE)**[27] 6102 3-8-10 .......... TPQueally 3 —
(MPSunderland, Ire) *midfield: pushed along 5f out: sn wknd* **20/1**

2m 18.16s (6.40) **Going Correction** +0.825s/f (Soft)
**WFA** 3 from 4yo+ 4lb **14** Ran SP% **116.3**
Speed ratings: **107,104,104,103,101 100,96,95,88,86 74,73,68,63**CSF £903.07 TOTE £14.80: £4.50, £15.10, £2.70; EX 524.70.
**Owner** Antoniades Family **Bred** A G Antoniades **Trained** Arundel, W Sussex

**FOCUS**
A competitive Listed race run at a decent pace.

**NOTEBOOK**
**Mango Mischief(IRE)** had not run on ground as soft as this before and had done her winning on a much quicker surface. She handled conditions well though, and won in decisive fashion. She has not had that many starts and there might be better still to come.
**Star Of Normandie(USA)** had not cut much ice in Listed grade on her last two starts, but she finished with a rare flourish to grab some valuable black type.
**Autumn Wealth(IRE)** has been in good form lately in lower grade and she translated that form to this tougher contest, running on well at the finish. Clearly progressive, she goes well in soft ground.
**Glen Innes(IRE)** did not find as much off the bridle as had looked likely, and in the end she did not see the trip out as well as her main rivals, losing two places close home.
**Mocca(IRE)**, whose connections blamed the soft ground when she was beaten into third in a Listed race in Germany last time, once again found conditions against her.
**Imperialistic(IRE)**, stepping up in distance from a mile, failed to see the trip out.
**I Had A Dream** looked to have plenty in her favour but, for one reason or another, failed to run to her best form.

**Bowstring(IRE)**, who was blinkered for the first time, raced keenly and expended too much energy in the first half of the race.
**Baboosh(IRE)** *Official explanation: jockey said filly had no more to give*

## 6572 TOTESCOOP6 WENTWORTH STKS (LISTED RACE) 6f
**2:20** (2:22) (A1) 3-Y-0+ **£19,500** (£6,000; £3,000; £1,500) **Stalls** High

Form RPR

5335 **1** **Quito (IRE)**$^{7}$ 6474 7-8-11 104 (b) ACulhane 5 112
(DWChapman) *lw: towards rr: hdwy over 2f out: qckd ent last: led last 50 yds sn clr* **7/2**$^{2}$

3052 **2** *1 1/4* **Millennium Force**$^{14}$ 6345 6-8-11 103 KFallon 10 108
(MRChannon) *dwlt:towards rr: gd hdwy 2f out: rdn over 1f out: styd on strly ins last* **13/2**$^{3}$

3201 **3** *shd* **Ruby Rocket (IRE)**$^{23}$ 6175 3-8-9 105 JFortune 3 106
(HMorrison) *trckd ldrs: hdwy 2f out: rdn to ld over 1f out: drvn ins last: hdd and nt qckn ins last* **3/1**$^{1}$

0100 **4** *3/4* **Royal Storm (IRE)**$^{37}$ 5888 5-9-0 105 DHolland 8 108
(MrsAJPerrett) *lw: led to 1/2-way: cl up and ev ch over 1f out: sn rdn and one pce ins last* **14/1**

0-00 **5** *2* **Cape Fear**$^{7}$ 6474 3-8-11 107 EAhern 2 99
(BJMeehan) *cl up centre: led 1/2-way: rdn 2f out: hdd over 1f out and sn wknd* **9/1**

4150 **6** *2 1/2* **Goldeva**$^{22}$ 6190 5-8-9 103 WRyan 7 90
(RHollinshead) *s.i.s and bhd tl styd fnl 2f: nrst fin* **10/1**

5003 **7** *1* **Tom Tun**$^{14}$ 6349 9-8-11 94 (b) TLucas 4 89
(JBalding) *trckd ldrs: effrt 2f out and ev ch tl rdn and wknd over 1f out* **16/1**

1461 **8** *2* **Onlytime Will Tell**$^{15}$ 6341 6-8-11 95 JFanning 11 83
(DNicholls) *cl up: rdn along 2f out: wknd over 1f out* **12/1**

0100 **9** *1 1/4* **Halmahera (IRE)**$^{22}$ 6190 9-8-11 100 NCallan 9 79
(KARyan) *in tch: hdwy over 2f out: sn rdn and wknd over 1f out* **14/1**

4000 **10** *16* **Millybaa (USA)**$^{27}$ 6104 4-8-6 90 CCatlin 1 26
(RGuest) *in tch: effrt over 2f out: sn rdn along and wknd* **50/1**

2144 **11** *2* **Texas Gold**$^{37}$ 5893 6-8-11 104 MartinDwyer 6 25
(WRMuir) *keen: chsd ldrs: rdn along over 2f out and sn wknd* **14/1**

2053 **12** *5* **Romany Nights (IRE)**$^{96}$ 4394 4-8-11 79 (b) SSanders 12 10
(MissGayKelleway) *chsd ldrs: rdn along 1/2-way: sn wknd* **100/1**

1m 16.64s (2.36) **Going Correction** +0.825s/f (Soft) **12** Ran SP% **116.2**
Speed ratings: **110,108,108,107,104 101,99,97,95,74 71,64**CSF £26.06 TOTE £5.00: £1.90, £2.40, £1.60; EX 25.60.
**Owner** Michael Hill **Bred** Sheikh Mohammed Bin Rashid Al Maktoum **Trained** Stillington, N Yorks
■ Goldeva was Willie Ryan's final ride before retirement.

**FOCUS**
A decent Listed race run at a good pace. The form is fair for the grade and looks sound, and could rate slightly higher.

**NOTEBOOK**
**Quito(IRE)** appreciated the drop back to sprinting and came with his trademark late burst to lead close home. A tough performer, he takes his racing particularly well and deserved this first Pattern success. He is apparently going to be kept on the go on the All-Weather over the winter, although given his rating opportunities will be few.
**Millennium Force** had the race run to suit and ran well, but he really needs seven furlongs to show his best.
**Ruby Rocket(IRE)**, successful in a similar race at Newmarket last time, looked to have been brought with a winning run until the first two, who had been held up at the rear, came with their storming late charges.
**Royal Storm(IRE)**, another who is happier over seven, did not run at all badly given that the ground was not really in his favour. *Official explanation: jockey said horse hung left in the final 2f*
**Cape Fear**, who has had three starts in the space of four weeks since returning from a year's absence, was expected to appreciate the drop back to sprinting. Racing towards the centre of the track while most of his rivals congregated more towards the stands' side, he was joined by them in the latter stages and run out of the places.
**Goldeva** has won four races in her career but three of those wins came against her own sex.
**Texas Gold** *Official explanation: jockey said gelding had no more to give*
**Romany Nights(IRE)** *Official explanation: jockey said gelding was unsuited by the good to soft ground*

## 6573 ENTER THE £1 MILLION TOTETENTOFOLLOW NOVEMBER STKS (HERITAGE H'CAP) 1m 4f
**2:55** (2:55) (B1) (0-110,97) 3-Y-0+ **£35,425** (£10,900; £5,450; £2,725) **Stalls** Low

Form RPR

1123 **1** **Carte Diamond (USA)**$^{26}$ 6121 3-9-6 97 KFallon 3 108
(BEllison) *in tch on inner: smooth hdwy 3f out: led over 2f out: rdn clr over 1f out: styd on* **12/1**

0030 **2** *2 1/2* **Distant Prospect (IRE)**$^{21}$ 6215 7-9-7 92 LDettori 6 99
(AMBalding) *bhd: gd hdwy on inner over 3f out: rdn wl over 1f out: styd on to chse wnr ins last: kpt on* **20/1**

0503 **3** *3* **Bendarshaan**$^{14}$ 6346 4-8-13 84 (b$^{1}$) JFanning 1 87
(MJohnston) *trckd ldrs: effrt and n.m.r on inner 2f out: swtchd rt and rdn to chse wnr wl over 1f out: drvn and one pce inslast* **20/1**

1012 **4** *1 1/4* **Jeepstar**$^{15}$ 6335 4-8-9 80 GGibbons 4 81
(TDEasterby) *keen: led: rdn along 3f out: hdd over 2f out: kpt on u.p fnl f* **28/1**

0245 **5** *hd* **Cruise Director**$^{14}$ 6346 4-8-8 84 PMakin$^{(5)}$ 7 85
(WJMusson) *hld up towards rr: hdwy over 3f out: rdn 2f out and kpt on appr last: nrst fin* **20/1**

1121 **6** *6* **Artistic Style**$^{26}$ 6115 4-9-7 95 TEaves$^{(3)}$ 21 87
(BEllison) *hld up towards rr: hdwy over 3f out: swtchd rt 2f out and sn rdn: no imp* **14/1**

1622 **7** *3* **Another Choice (IRE)**$^{15}$ 6332 3-8-5 82 (t) PCosgrave 2 70
(NPLittmoden) *hld up towards rr: hdwy 4f out: rdn over 2f out and sn no imp* **14/1**

2113 **8** *1 3/4* **Tender Falcon**$^{43}$ 5764 4-8-11 82 PHanagan 9 68
(RJHodges) *in tch: rdn along over 3f out: grad wknd* **12/1**

6453 **9** *3 1/2* **Pagan Sky (IRE)**$^{14}$ 6354 5-9-0 85 LisaJones 24 66
(JARToller) *stdd s and swtchd towards inner: bhd tl hdwy on inner 3f out: sn rdn along and no prog fnl 2f* **25/1**

4502 **10** *3/4* **Millville**$^{14}$ 6346 4-9-2 87 PRobinson 19 67
(MAJarvis) *hld up towards rr: swtchd outside and hdwy over 3f out: sn rdn along and nvr a factor* **12/1**

0200 **11** *2 1/2* **Jabaar (USA)**$^{14}$ 6346 6-8-10 81 (v) TPQueally 12 57
(MWEasterby) *a rr* **33/1**

0002 **12** *5* **Turbo (IRE)**$^{14}$ 6354 5-9-5 90 (p) SCarson 20 59
(GBBalding) *hld up and bhd: swtchd oustdie and hdwy over 3f out: sn rdn along and nvr a factor* **4/1**$^{1}$

0501 **13** *3 1/2* **Tempsford (USA)**$^{14}$ 6346 4-9-7 92 SSanders 14 56
(SirMarkPrescott) *trckd ldr: effrt over 3f out and ev ch tl rdn over 2f out and sn wknd* **8/1**$^{2}$

1063 **14** *6* **Shredded (USA)**$^{25}$ 6143 4-8-7 78 (t) KDarley 17 34
(JHMGosden) *in tch: effrt over 3f out: sn rdn along and wknd* **22/1**

61-0 **15** *1 1/4* **Talldark'N'Andsome**$^{11}$ 6043 5-8-5 76 (b) NMackay 13 30
(NPLittmoden) *a rr* **66/1**

0030 **16** *4* **Protective**$^{14}$ 6346 3-8-8 85 EAhern 11 34
(JGGiven) *midfield: hdwy on outer over 3f out: sn rdn along and wknd* **66/1**

0111 **17** *1/2* **Mith Hill**$^{9}$ 6450 3-7-12 78 JFMcDonald$^{(3)}$ 15 26
(EALDunlop) *trckd ldrs: rdn along 3f out: sn wknd* **9/1**$^{3}$

2111 **18** *shd* **Go Tech**$^{29}$ 6043 4-9-5 90 DAllan 18 38
(TDEasterby) *a rr* **20/1**

1403 **19** *3 1/2* **Bessemer (JPN)**$^{48}$ 5673 3-8-7 84 (t) PFessey 5 27
(ISemple) *trckd ldrs: rdn along 4f out: wknd 3f out* **50/1**

0-00 **20** *nk* **Bayadere (GER)**$^{10}$ 6444 4-8-6 77 (v$^{1}$) MHenry 22 19
(VSmith) *a rr* **100/1**

0016 **21** *5* **Dune Raider (USA)**$^{26}$ 6121 3-8-6 83 NCallan 23 18
(KARyan) *bhd fr 1/2-way* **33/1**

4002 **22** *1* **Albanov (IRE)**$^{40}$ 5834 4-9-9 94 (b) DHolland 16 28
(MJohnston) *chsd ldrs: rdn along over 4f out: sn wknd* **33/1**

-203 **23** *dist* **Tip The Dip (USA)**$^{10}$ 6444 4-9-0 85 (t) JFortune 8 —
(JHMGosden) *a rr: t.o and virtually p.u fnl 3f* **14/1**

6041 **24** *nk* **Always Waining (IRE)**$^{22}$ 6192 3-9-2 93 ACulhane 10 —
(PLClinton) *a rr: t.o and virtually p.u fnl 3f* **33/1**

2m 43.16s (7.46) **Going Correction** +0.825s/f (Soft)
**WFA** 3 from 4yo+ 6lb **24** Ran SP% **132.6**
Speed ratings: **108,106,104,103,103 99,97,96,93,93 91,88,86,82,81 78,78,78,75,75 72,71,—,—**CSF £239.82 CT £4758.76 TOTE £14.40: £2.90, £4.20, £5.80, £5.30; EX 173.50 Trifecta £2504.60 Pool of £3,880.40 - 1.10 winning tickets.
**Owner** Ashley Carr **Bred** The Thoroughbred Corporation **Trained** Norton, N Yorks

**FOCUS**
A big field for what is always a competitive handicap, but six of the first seven home came from the lowest seven stalls. The conditions have prompted a cautios rating, with the runner-up the key to the form.

**NOTEBOOK**
**Carte Diamond(USA)**, previously with Mark Johnston, was bought by his current connections for 105,000gns at the Newmarket Sales, and they got a third of that purchase price back on his first outing for them. He was one of the most lightly-raced runners in the field and his trainer had been worried whether the colt would handle the testing ground, but he need not have been as the son of Theatrical relished the conditions. He is to go hurdling now, but the Ebor was mentioned as a possible target for next season.
**Distant Prospect(IRE)**, eighth in the Cesarewitch last time, ran well over a trip short of his optimum. He stayed on well to finish a clear second.
**Bendarshaan** came out best of those who ran in the Racing Post £1 Million totetentofollow Handicap over course and distance two weeks earlier. In the process he reversed form with Tempsford and Millville, and clearly the first-time blinkers did him some good.
**Jeepstar** made a bold bid from the front, but he was probably a bit too keen for his own good.
**Cruise Director** remains in the grip of the Handicapper but ran a fair race, staying on from the rear.
**Artistic Style** did well to finish where he did given his wide draw in 21. He was the only horse to finish in the first eight from a double-figure draw and this progressive colt, who was running off a 15lb higher mark than when successful at Ayr last time, ran well over a trip which probably stretches his stamina.
**Another Choice(IRE)** has shown his best form over ten furlongs.
**Turbo(IRE)**, who won this race last year off a 1lb lower mark, was at the back of the field for much of the way and never looked like landing a sentimental public punt for his soon-to-be retired trainer. *Official explanation: jockey said gelding was unsuited by the soft ground*
**Tempsford(USA)** made every yard over course and distance two weeks earlier but he was 6lb higher here, was not as well drawn, and had tougher rivals to take on.
**Mith Hill**, successful on Polytrack on his last two starts, looked to find conditions too testing back on turf.
**Tip The Dip(USA)** *Official explanation: jockey said colt weakened quickly and no more to give*
**Always Waining(IRE)** *Official explanation: jockey said colt was unsuited by the soft ground*

## 6574 TOTESPORT.COM NURSERY 7f
**3:25** (3:31) (D2) (0-85,85) 2-Y-0 **£7,202** (£2,216; £1,108; £554) **Stalls** High

Form RPR

0600 **1** **Breaking Shadow (IRE)**$^{5}$ 6515 2-8-11 75 (p) PHanagan 5 81
(RAFahey) *in tch: effrt over 2f out: styd on to ld last 75yds* **16/1**

3025 **2** *1/2* **Royal Orissa**$^{37}$ 5896 2-9-1 79 (t) LDettori 9 84
(DHaydnJones) *trckd ldrs gng wl: smooth hdwy to ld over 1f out: hdd and no ex ins last* **5/1**$^{1}$

2442 **3** *1/2* **Zomerlust**$^{26}$ 6113 2-9-3 81 RWinston 7 85
(JJQuinn) *rr-div: hdwy over 2f out: styd on wl fnl f* **8/1**$^{2}$

3021 **4** *1 3/4* **Game Lad**$^{5}$ 6514 2-9-5 83 7ex DAllan 18 83
(TDEasterby) *racd stands' side: chsd ldrs: edgd lft over 1f out: styd on same pce ins last* **14/1**

0000 **5** *shd* **John Forbes**$^{4}$ 6523 2-8-6 70 JFanning 4 69
(BEllison) *in tch: effrt over 2f out: kpt on wl fnl f* **50/1**

541 **6** *2 1/2* **Maxamillion (IRE)**$^{16}$ 6322 2-9-3 81 JFEgan 12 75
(SKirk) *in tch: effrt over 2f out: kpt on same pce* **11/1**

2031 **7** *1* **Oligarch (IRE)**$^{22}$ 6181 2-9-7 85 DHolland 6 76
(NACallaghan) *led tl over 1f out: sn wekened* **9/1**$^{3}$

2104 **8** *shd* **Red Affleck (USA)**$^{14}$ 6344 2-9-4 82 AMcCarthy 13 73
(PWChapple-Hyam) *trckd ldrs: chal 2f out: sn rdn and wknd* **12/1**

0046 **9** *1 1/4* **Along The Nile**$^{25}$ 6140 2-8-5 69 LGoncalves 19 57
(MrsJRRamsden) *racd stands' side: chsd ldrs: edgd lft 2f out: sn btn* **33/1**

5045 **10** *hd* **Dante's Diamond (IRE)**$^{10}$ 6439 2-8-11 75 GBaker 2 63
(FJordan) *chsd ldrs: outpcd fnl 2f* **50/1**

5315 **11** *shd* **Leslingtaylor (IRE)**$^{21}$ 6206 2-8-6 73 THamilton$^{(3)}$ 10 60
(JJQuinn) *rr div: hdwy over 2f out: n.m.r and eased wl ins last* **20/1**

0301 **12** *3 1/2* **Knock Bridge (IRE)**$^{21}$ 6206 2-8-5 69 TPQueally 3 48
(PDEvans) *w ldrs: wknd appr fnl f* **12/1**

556 **13** *10* **Beauchamp Turbo**$^{21}$ 6211 2-8-1 65 NMackay 14 21
(GAButler) *in tch: effrt over 2f out: sn btn* **33/1**

1003 **14** *1 1/2* **Torrens (IRE)**$^{5}$ 6515 2-8-7 71 (t) DaleGibson 11 23
(SPGriffiths) *bhd: hdwy over 3f out: lost pl over 2f out* **33/1**

5001 **15** *2 1/2* **Qawaafil (USA)**$^{21}$ 6211 2-8-7 71 RHills 22 17
(EALDunlop) *racd stands' side: w ldrs: lost pl over 2f out: sn bhd* **14/1**

2305 **16** *hd* **Shosolosa (IRE)**$^{35}$ 5938 2-8-3 70 JFMcDonald$^{(3)}$ 20 16
(BJMeehan) *racd stands' side: chsd ldrs: lost pl 3f out* **14/1**

6605 **17** *1 3/4* **Asharon**$^{10}$ 6442 2-8-4 68 SCarson 1 10
(CEBrittain) *s.i.s: alway bhd* **20/1**

0060 **18** *nk* **Superstitious (IRE)**$^{57}$ 5434 2-8-1 65 CCatlin 15 6
(BAMcmahon) *s.i.s: a in rr* **33/1**

6223 **19** *shd* **Forfeiter (USA)**$^{21}$ 6206 2-8-12 76 (v$^{1}$) KDarley 16 17
(TDBarron) *rr-div: effrt 3f out: nvr a factor* **16/1**

0001 **20** *3* **Meditation**[24] 6155 2-8-7 **71**........ KFallon 17 5
(IAWood) *chsd ldrs: lost pl over 2f out: sn bhd* **10/1**

1m 33.29s (5.48) **Going Correction** +0.825s/f (Soft) **20** Ran SP% **127.6**
Speed ratings: **101,100,99,97,97 94,93,93,92,91 91,87,76,74,71 71,69,69,69,65**CSF £87.79 CT £715.56 TOTE £21.80: £4.40, £1.90, £2.50, £4.10; EX 195.40.
**Owner** G Morrill **Bred** Christoph Amerian **Trained** Musley Bank, N Yorks

**FOCUS**
A competitive nursery with those who raced in the bigger centre group coming out on top over the smaller stands'-side group. The form is solid for the level and should stand up.

**NOTEBOOK**
**Breaking Shadow(IRE)**, who had finished behind Royal Orissa over six furlongs on a couple of occasions this season, saw this longer trip out better than that rival this time. Seven furlongs seems to suit him better than a mile for the time being.
**Royal Orissa** came to the front travelling well, but in the end he failed to see out the trip in these testing conditions as well as the winner. He can win over this trip on quicker ground.
**Zomerlust** has not finished outside the first four in seven starts this season and ran another solid race in defeat.
**Game Lad** was the first home from the small group which raced next to the stands'-side rail. He acts well in soft ground but his 7lb penalty may just have found him out.
**John Forbes**, who has looked regressive this backend, posted a more encouraging effort.
**Maxamillion(IRE)** had shown at Brighton that he excels in testing conditions, and this was a solid effort on his handicap debut. He will get a mile next year.

## 6575 MERLIN™ NEW DISCOVERY 3" H'CAP 2m 110y
4:00 (4:00) (C1) (0-107,91) 3-Y-O+ £13,436 (£4,134; £2,067; £1,033) Stalls Low

Form RPR
1131 **1** **Sendintank**[3] 6535 4-9-9 **91** 6ex........ MartinDwyer 5 104
(SCWilliams) *trckd ldrs: t.k.h: effrt over 3f out: r.o to ld last 75yds: hld on towards fin* **10/11**[1]
6104 **2** *½* **Dr Sharp (IRE)**[8] 6460 4-8-12 **80**........ RWinston 2 92
(TPTate) *lw: led: qcknd 7f out: hdd ins last: r.o* **14/1**
-641 **3** *8* **Contact Dancer (IRE)**[21] 6215 5-9-7 **89**........ RFfrench 7 93
(MJohnston) *swtg: trckd ldr: drvn along over 4f out: edgd rt and outpcd appr fnl f* **4/1**[2]
2453 **4** *9* **Fling**[3] 6534 3-8-10 **87**........ KFallon 3 82
(JRFanshawe) *swtg: trckd ldrs: t.k.h: lost pl 4f out: n.d after* **7/1**[3]
0030 **5** *3* **Trance (IRE)**[21] 6215 4-8-12 **85**........ PMakin(5) 6 77
(TDBarron) *hld up: hdwy on outside over 5f out: wknd 2f out* **14/1**
030 **6** *5* **Historic Place (USA)**[21] 6215 4-8-11 **79**........ SSanders 4 66
(GBBalding) *hld up: drvn along and outpcd over 4f out: sn lost pl* **8/1**
2140 **7** *4* **Master Wells (IRE)**[25] 6143 3-8-3 **80**........ CCatlin 1 63
(JDBethell) *hld up: effrt 4f out: sn rdn and lost pl* **25/1**

3m 56.95s (14.99) **Going Correction** +0.825s/f (Soft)
**WFA** 3 from 4yo+ 9lb **7** Ran SP% **113.2**
Speed ratings: **97,96,93,88,87 85,83**CSF £15.45 TOTE £2.00: £1.50, £3.70; EX 12.70 Place 6 £317.44, Place 5 £148.89.
**Owner** Steve Jones And Phil McGovern **Bred** K G Powter **Trained** Newmarket, Suffolk
■ Historic Place was the last ever runner for Toby Balding, who began his training career in 1957.

**FOCUS**
The pace was not that strong for this staying handicap and, although the form is only fair, the winner continued his improvement, gaining his tenth victory of the year.

**NOTEBOOK**
**Sendintank** raced a bit keenly off the steady gallop and took a while to pick up, but he ran on well to lead close home, notching his tenth handicap win of the year. The first of those successes came on the All-Weather off a mark of 50, and he was winning here off a mark of 91.
**Dr Sharp(IRE)** had conditions to suit and did not look badly handicapped on a mark just 1lb higher than for his last win. He set a steady pace and his rider's brave attempt to steal the race from the front almost paid off.
**Contact Dancer(IRE)**, 6lb higher for his Cesarewitch win, would have preferred a stronger pace over this shorter trip.
**Fling** raced too keenly again and she is another who would have been suited by a stronger pace.
**Trance(IRE)**, 9lb better off at the weights with Contact Dancer compared to Newmarket, really should have done better.
T/Jkpt: Not won. T/Plt: £555.40 to a £1 stake. Pool: £69,547.90. 91.40 winning tickets. T/Qpdt: £48.90 to a £1 stake. Pool: £5,773.10. 87.20 winning tickets. JR

# 6555 WOLVERHAMPTON (A.W) (L-H)
Saturday, November 6

**OFFICIAL GOING: Standard**
Wind: almost nil Weather: drizzle

## 6576 BET DIRECT FOOTBALL CASHBACKS H'CAP 1m 1f 103y(P)
4:30 (4:30) (F4) (0-62,64) 3-Y-O+ £3,068 (£876; £438) Stalls Low

Form RPR
4065 **1** **Midshipman**[21] 6225 6-9-5 **56**........(vt) SWKelly 7 66
(AWCarroll) *hld up and bhd: rdn over 3f out: hdwy wl over 1f out: edgd lft and r.o wl to ld wl ins fnl f* **9/2**[3]
0602 **2** *2* **Charmatic (IRE)**[7] 6483 3-9-10 **64**........ JQuinn 9 70
(JAGlover) *t.k.h: led 7f out: rdn clr wl over 1f out: hdd and no ex wl ins fnl f* **4/1**[2]
0405 **3** *1* **Our Destiny**[3] 6540 6-8-11 **55**........ DFentiman(7) 2 59
(AWCarroll) *hld up: hdwy whn nt clr run jst over 1f out: swtchd rt ins fnl f: kpt on wl towards fin* **16/1**
0333 **4** *shd* **My Maite (IRE)**[42] 5791 5-8-9 **53**........(vt) JLoveridge(7) 6 57
(RIngram) *a.p: rdn over 3f out: one pce fnl 2f* **16/1**
5000 **5** *1 ½* **Glendale**[6] 6493 3-9-3 **57**........ ANicholls 1 58
(DKIvory) *led over 1f: chsd ldr tl over 4f out: rdn over 3f out: one pce fnl 2f* **50/1**
1006 **6** *1 ¾* **Market Avenue**[27] 6096 5-9-11 **62**........(p) DarrenWilliams 5 60
(RAFahey) *plld hrd in mid-div: hdwy on ins over 2f out: swtchd lft over 1f out: wknd ins fnl f* **9/1**
0004 **7** *hd* **Zawrak (IRE)**[7] 6483 5-9-2 **56**........(p) LFletcher(3) 8 53
(IWMcinnes) *hld up: rdn and hdwy 5f out: btn whn bmpd jst ins fnl f* **12/1**
4551 **8** *½* **Ribbons And Bows (IRE)**[2] 6551 4-9-3 **54** 6ex........(v) DSweeney 4 50
(CACyzer) *a.p: wnt 2nd over 4f out: rdn 3f out: wknd ins fnl f* **9/4**[1]
0000 **9** *½* **Burnt Copper (IRE)**[2] 6550 4-9-1 **52**........ NPollard 10 47
(JRBest) *s.i.s: bhd: short-lived effrt on outside over 1f out* **20/1**
4660 **10** *3* **Orion Express**[24] 5223 3-8-12 **55**........ PMulrennan(3) 3 45
(MWEasterby) *prom tl wknd over 4f out* **25/1**
4546 **11** *3 ½* **My Michelle**[38] 5867 3-8-12 **55**........ FPFerris(3) 11 38
(BPalling) *hld up in mid-div: hdwy over 4f out: rdn over 3f out: wknd wl over 1f out* **25/1**
0000 **12** *3* **Herodotus**[65] 5251 6-9-1 **55**........ LPKeniry(3) 12 32
(KOCunningham-Brown) *a bhd* **20/1**
4034 **13** *½* **Loaded Gun**[15] 6343 4-8-13 **55**........ BSwarbrick(5) 13 31
(WMBrisbourne) *hld up and bhd: hdwy over 5f out: rdn 4f out: sn wknd* **15/2**

2m 2.75s
**WFA** 3 from 4yo+ 3lb **13** Ran SP% **129.3**
Speed ratings: CSF £23.28 CT £282.84 TOTE £7.70: £2.20, £1.10, £5.20; EX 19.30.
**Owner** Langwood Racing **Bred** Frank Sheridan **Trained** Wixford, Warwicks

**FOCUS**
A moderate handicap run at a strong early pace. The runner-up sets the standard and the form appears sound.

**NOTEBOOK**
**Midshipman**, reverting to a shorter trip, ended a long losing run having been rated 85 for his last victory which came here on Boxing Day 2001.
**Charmatic(IRE)**, raised 2lb after an encouraging All-Weather debut here a week ago, produced another sound performance especially considering she ran too freely.
**Our Destiny**, a stable companion of the winner, had run over a mile and a half here earlier in the week. He did not get the best of passages in the home straight over this shorter distance.
**My Maite(IRE)**, a ten-furlong winner on the Polytrack at Lingfield, has plenty of experience on this surface.
**Glendale**, who landed a weak mile maiden at Lingfield back in February, was 5lb lower when last in a handicap on sand.
**Market Avenue** eventually paid the penalty for refusing to accept restraint on this sand debut.
**Ribbons And Bows(IRE)** may have found this coming too soon after winning over course and distance only two days ago.

## 6577 BET DIRECT "RED TO BET" ON ITV CLAIMING STKS 5f 20y(P)
5:00 (5:00) (F4) 3-Y-O+ £3,038 (£868; £434) Stalls Low

Form RPR
0400 **1** **Panjandrum**[170] 2246 6-8-10 61........ MSavage(5) 5 73
(NEBerry) *mde all: hung rt fr over 2f out: rdn over 1f out: drifted to stands' side: drvn out* **14/1**
4404 **2** *1 ½* **Willheconquertoo**[3] 6539 4-9-0 65........(tp) BSwarbrick(5) 7 72
(AndrewReid) *hld up: rdn 3f out: hdwy 2f out: r.o ins fnl f: nt rch wnr* **6/1**
0000 **3** *1 ½* **St Ivian**[98] 4336 4-8-12 61........ LFletcher(3) 3 62
(MrsNMacauley) *hld up: hdwy whn n.m.r over 2f out: kpt on u.p ins fnl f* **25/1**
-006 **4** *nk* **Dvinsky (USA)**[35] 5952 3-8-5 78........(t) EAhern 8 51
(GAButler) *hld up: hdwy over 2f out: one pce fnl f* **7/2**[1]
0100 **5** *1* **Canterloupe (IRE)**[45] 5730 6-8-9 81........ DFox(5) 11 57
(CADwyer) *s.i.s: hdwy on ins over 1f out: r.o* **11/2**[3]
2000 **6** *2* **Diamond Shannon (IRE)**[18] 6290 3-8-5 58........ DTudhope(5) 10 45
(DCarroll) *dwlt: hdwy fnl f: nvr nr to chal* **25/1**
1050 **7** *nk* **Red Sovereign**[27] 6079 3-8-10 79........ JQuinn 6 44
(IAWood) *a.p: rdn 3f out: no hdwy fnl 2f* **11/2**[3]
0-05 **8** *shd* **Bond Romeo (IRE)**[4] 6526 3-8-9 67........ DMcGaffin 4 43
(BSmart) *prom: rdn over 2f out: btn whn sltly hmpd jst over 1f out* **25/1**
0000 **9** *1 ½* **Brave Burt (IRE)**[19] 6267 7-9-5 72........ ANicholls 9 47
(DNicholls) *prom: rdn 3f out: wnt 2nd briefly 2f out: edgd lft jst over 1f out: wknd ins fnl f* **9/2**[2]
00 **10** *1 ½* **Java Gold**[27] 6079 3-7-9........ CHaddon(5) 1 23
(WGMTurner) *chsd wnr: rdn over 1f out: wknd ins fnl f* **50/1**
5000 **11** *¾* **A One (IRE)**[26] 6128 5-8-12 70........ FPFerris(3) 12 35
(HJManners) *outpcd* **11/1**
0500 **12** *2* **Izmail (IRE)**[2] 6554 5-8-8 65........ J-PGuillambert(3) 13 24
(PDEvans) *bhd fnl 3f* **16/1**

62.46 secs **12** Ran SP% **119.8**
Speed ratings: CSF £93.26 TOTE £14.90: £4.70, £2.20, £7.40; EX 55.40.Dvinsky (USA) was claimed by A.W. Carroll for £5,000.
**Owner** Leeway Group Limited **Bred** John And Susan Davis **Trained** Earlswood, Monmouths

**FOCUS**
A fair claimer but several of these found this distance on the short side and the form is not the most reliable.

**NOTEBOOK**
**Panjandrum** was returning after a five-month absence due to a fractured cannon-bone. His trainer was left wondering if he was still feeling the injury given his antics in the home straight.
**Willheconquertoo**, who ran over six here three days ago, should appreciate a return to that trip on this evidence.
**St Ivian** shaped well on his first outing since the end of July over a distance short of his best.
**Dvinsky(USA)**, dropping back to the minimum trip, was fitted with a tongue strap after his breathing problems last time.
**Canterloupe(IRE)** ◆, who changed hands recently for 7,000gns, was not helped by a tardy start and will appreciate a return to six.
**Diamond Shannon(IRE)** ◆, a winner over seven on the Fibresand at Southwell, caught the eye late on after missing the break over this inadequate distance.

## 6578 BET DIRECT ON 0800 32 93 93 MAIDEN STKS 5f 20y(P)
5:25 (5:28) (D3) 3-Y-O+ £3,435 (£1,057; £528; £264) Stalls Low

Form RPR
5 **1** **Dutch Key Card (IRE)**[78] 4929 3-9-0 61........ EAhern 5 75
(GAButler) *a.p: rdn wl over 1f out: led wl ins fnl f: r.o wl* **7/2**[1]
3030 **2** *2 ½* **Shaymee's Girl**[19] 6274 3-8-6 52........ NChalmers(3) 1 61
(MsDeborahJEvans) *led: rdn wl over 1f out: hdd wl ins fnl f: no ex* **20/1**
5020 **3** *1 ½* **Abelard (IRE)**[19] 6273 3-9-0 54........ DaleGibson 7 61
(RAFahey) *mid-div: rdn over 3f out: hrd rdn and hdwy over 1f out: kpt on ins fnl f* **9/2**[2]
6203 **4** *1 ¼* **Lakeside Guy (IRE)**[19] 6280 3-9-0 55........ SWKelly 2 56
(PSMcentee) *chsd ldr: rdn over 2f out: wknd ins fnl f* **11/1**
5 **5** *¾* **Come On**[22] 6200 5-9-0........ MTebbutt 3 53
(JHetherton) *a chsng ldrs: no real prog fnl 2f* **8/1**[3]
0030 **6** *2 ½* **Juniper Banks**[3] 6538 3-9-0 57........ AnnStokell 8 44
(MissAStokell) *chsd ldrs: no hdwy fnl 2f* **20/1**
0 **7** *2 ½* **Won Of A Few**[7] 6481 4-8-7........ AKirby(7) 4 35
(MWigham) *nvr nr ldrs* **66/1**
60 **8** *1 ¼* **Young Kate**[12] 6397 3-8-9........ JQuinn 11 26
(JRBest) *outpcd* **12/1**
**9** *¾* **Big Mystery (IRE)** 3-8-9........ NPollard 10 23
(JRBest) *s.v.s: outpcd* **11/1**
00 **10** *5* **Radmore Spirit**[157] 2586 4-8-9........ SWhitworth 12 5
(JWUnett) *s.s: outpcd* **100/1**

63.27 secs **10** Ran SP% **87.9**
Speed ratings: CSF £41.23 TOTE £3.70: £1.20, £3.30, £1.70; EX 78.20.
**Owner** M Berger **Bred** G Berger **Trained** Blewbury, Oxon

**FOCUS**
They were soon strung out in this poor maiden which was made even weaker by the withdrawal of the favourite at the start. Despite that the form looks solid at a low level.

**NOTEBOOK**

**Dutch Key Card(IRE)** won going away and again gave the impression he will not be inconvenienced by a step back up in trip.

**Shaymee's Girl** adopted her usual tactics but had no answer to the winner in the closing stages after setting a strong pace.

**Abelard(IRE)** struggled to go the pace after failing to get home over six here last time.

**Lakeside Guy(IRE)** eventually paid the price for trying to keep tabs on the tearaway leader.

**Come On** should do better when reverting to a longer distance.

## 6579 LITTLEWOODS BET DIRECT FILLIES' H'CAP — 1m 141y(P)

**5:55** (5:57) (E3) (0-77,77) 3-Y-O+ **£4,159** (£1,279; £639; £319) **Stalls** Low

Form RPR

0105 **1** **Mount Hillaby (IRE)**[27] 6094 4-8-10 **62** PMulrennan(3) 2 71
(MWEasterby) *hld up in tch: hrd rdn to ld cl home* **9/2**[2]

1646 **2** *shd* **Kali**[14] 6350 3-9-8 **74** DSweeney 5 83
(RCharlton) *chsd ldr 2f: remained prom: rdn to ld and egded lft jst over 1f out: hdd cl home* **9/1**

0456 **3** *nk* **Cloud Dancer**[41] 5818 5-9-4 **74** AMullen(7) 4 82
(KARyan) *hld up: hdwy over 2f out: rdn and ev ch ins fnl f: r.o* **6/1**[3]

5605 **4** *1 ¼* **Elidore**[2] 6547 4-8-11 **63** FPFerris(3) 13 69
(BPalling) *led: rdn and hdd 2f out: no ex ins fnl f* **33/1**

4010 **5** *¾* **Lauro**[26] 6115 4-9-9 **72** RWinston 7 76
(MissJACamacho) *hld up and bhd: hdwy awl over 1f out: r.o one pce fnl f* **9/1**

0160 **6** *1* **Blonde Streak (USA)**[28] 6069 4-9-9 **77** PMakin(5) 6 79
(TDBarron) *a.p: wnt 2nd over 6f out: led 2f out: rdn and hdd jst over 1f out: wknd ins fnl f* **7/1**

5431 **7** *1 ¼* **Tenny's Gold (IRE)**[3] 6537 3-9-0 **66** 6ex MHills 10 65
(BWHills) *hld up: hdwy on outside over 2f out: no further prog* **7/2**[1]

4060 **8** *hd* **And Toto Too**[45] 5740 4-9-4 **70** (b) DNolan(3) 3 69
(PDEvans) *hld up: hdwy over 1f out: n.d* **14/1**

1334 **9** *½* **Millagros (IRE)**[26] 6115 4-9-9 **72** (p) PHanagan 1 70
(ISemple) *hld up in tch: rdn 3f out: wknd over 1f out* **11/1**

0150 **10** *5* **Farriers Charm**[38] 5869 3-9-2 **68** EAhern 12 55
(DJCoakley) *hld up in tch: wknd over 1f out* **14/1**

2520 **11** *¾* **Summer Shades**[35] 5955 6-8-9 **63** BSwarbrick(5) 9 49
(WMBrisbourne) *a bhd* **10/1**

0600 **12** *7* **Cuddles (FR)**[45] 5740 5-8-13 **65** (b) LPKeniry(3) 8 36
(KOCunningham-Brown) *s.s: hld up and bhd: rdn over 3f out: no rspnse* **20/1**

-0P0 **13** *9* **Red Galaxy (IRE)**[26] 6117 4-9-0 **63** (e[1]) SWKelly 11 15
(DWPArbuthnot) *hld up and bhd: hdwy over 4f out: rdn over 3f out: sn wknd* **50/1**

1m 51.26s

**WFA** 3 from 4yo+ 3lb **13** Ran SP% **127.6**

Speed ratings: CSF £47.49 CT £213.71 TOTE £4.80: £2.00, £5.10, £3.50; EX 112.00.

**Owner** The Woodford Group Limited **Bred** Lodge Park Stud **Trained** Sheriff Hutton, N Yorks

■ Stewards Enquiry : P Mulrennan four-day ban: used whip with excessive frequency (Nov 17,19,20,22)

**FOCUS**

A wide-open handicap which produced an exciting finish and the form, rated through those in the frame, looks sound.

**NOTEBOOK**

**Mount Hillaby(IRE)**, a winner on good to firm at York in September, had no problem with this surface and just prevailed in a driving finish.

**Kali**, whose last five starts have been over seven furlongs, was only just touched off on this step back up in distance.

**Cloud Dancer**, another reverting to a longer distance, lost no caste in defeat.

**Elidore** did not cave in once headed on her Polytrack debut.

**Lauro** may require a bit further these days on a surface as quick as this.

**Blonde Streak(USA)** had no obvious excuses on her All-Weather debut.

**Tenny's Gold(IRE)** was trying to defy a penalty for her win over seven here earlier in the week.

## 6580 BET AT THE RACES ON 0800 083 83 83 H'CAP — 1m 141y(P)

**6:20** (6:21) (F4) (0-62,62) 3-Y-O+ **£3,178** (£908; £454) **Stalls** Low

Form RPR

01 **1** **Mac's Talisman (IRE)**[6] 6493 4-9-10 **62** 6ex (tp) NCallan 12 75
(VSmith) *hld up in mid-div: hdwy over 3f out: rdn over 2f out: led ins fnl f: r.o* **2/1**[1]

0002 **2** *nk* **Atlantic Ace**[18] 6296 7-9-6 **58** (p) FLynch 4 70
(BSmart) *hld up and bhd: stdy hdwy over 2f out: hrd rdn and ev ch ins fnl f: kpt on* **15/2**[3]

5031 **3** *1 ¾* **Temper Tantrum**[18] 6296 6-9-6 **58** (p) EAhern 9 66
(JRBest) *hld up and bhd: hdwy over 3f out: rdn over 1f out: ev ch ins fnl f: nt qckn* **7/1**[2]

6061 **4** *½* **King Nicholas (USA)**[18] 6295 5-9-0 **57** (tp) MLawson(5) 13 64
(JParkes) *hld up: hdwy over 5f out: rdn over 2f out: ev ch 1f out: nt qckn* **8/1**

0051 **5** *1 ½* **Mind Alert**[6] 6499 3-9-2 **57** DAllan 5 61
(MissJACamacho) *plld hrd: prom: led over 5f out tl over 4f out: led over 3f out: rdn and edgd rt 1f out: sn hdd: no ex* **7/1**[2]

0400 **6** *3* **Sarraaf (IRE)**[7] 6483 8-9-5 **57** RWinston 8 55
(ISemple) *hld up towards rr: hdwy over 3f out: rdn over 2f out: wknd over 1f out* **7/1**[2]

1300 **7** *nk* **Wind Chime (IRE)**[55] 5493 7-8-10 **51** LPKeniry(3) 10 48
(AGNewcombe) *prom: lost pl over 3f out: n.d after* **12/1**

-123 **8** *1* **Rock Concert**[288] 590 6-9-5 **62** NataliaGemelova(5) 1 57
(IWMcinnes) *prom: lost pl over 5f out: n.d after* **14/1**

0000 **9** *3* **Dial Square**[3] 6541 3-8-13 **54** SWKelly 6 43
(PHowling) *bhd fnl 3f* **25/1**

5011 **10** *5* **Tokewanna**[12] 6404 4-8-10 **53** (t) PPMathers(5) 11 31
(WMBrisbourne) *plld hrd: sddle sn slipped: hdwy over 5f out: led over 4f out tl over 3f out: wknd wl over 1f out: eased* **15/2**[3]

3000 **11** *2 ½* **Eager Angel (IRE)**[131] 3376 6-8-13 **54** LFletcher(3) 7 27
(RFMarvin) *hld up and bhd: short-lived effrt over 2f out* **50/1**

-000 **12** *1 ¼* **Indian Call**[208] 1366 3-9-0 **55** GGibbons 3 25
(BAMcmahon) *prom: rdn 6f out: wknd over 4f out* **33/1**

0500 **13** *4* **Hsi Wang Mu (IRE)**[136] 3190 3-9-4 **62** DNolan(3) 2 24
(RBrotherton) *led: hdd over 5f out: rdn over 4f out: wknd over 2f out* **66/1**

1m 52.22s

**WFA** 3 from 4yo+ 3lb **13** Ran SP% **130.1**

Speed ratings: CSF £18.80 CT £101.65 TOTE £5.30: £1.70, £2.40, £2.10; EX 46.30.

**Owner** V Smith **Bred** Miss C A Green And R Haim **Trained** Exning, Suffolk

**FOCUS**

Another competitive handicap with five of the runners in with a chance in the home straight. The form is fair for the grade and solid.

**NOTEBOOK**

**Mac's Talisman(IRE)** held on well to defy his penalty over a longer trip and he is clearly in good heart at the moment.

**Atlantic Ace** was given a lot to do and found the winner would not be denied when challenging in the closing stages.

**Temper Tantrum** could not confirm his short head defeat of Atlantic Ace over course and distance last month on a pound worse terms.

**King Nicholas(USA)** failed to over come a 2lb rise in the weights for winning a similar event here last month.

**Mind Alert** did well to finish so close given how hard he pulled on this step up from seven.

**Sarraaf(IRE)** has dropped to a career-low mark.

**Tokewanna**, 6lb higher than when last in a handicap, this run on her hat-trick bid is best ignored as her saddle slipped forward early.

## 6581 BET DIRECT ON AT THE RACES H'CAP — 2m 119y(P)

**6:50** (6:50) (F4) (0-62,60) 4-Y-O+ **£2,917** (£833; £416) **Stalls** Low

Form RPR

3350 **1** **Sungio**[27] 6084 6-9-1 **52** (b) DaleGibson 2 59
(BGPowell) *s.i.s: hdwy over 5f out: led jst over 1f out: edgd lft ins fnl f: drvn out* **12/1**

0435 **2** *¾* **Best Port (IRE)**[19] 6269 8-9-0 **51** DAllan 12 57
(JParkes) *hld up and bhd: stdy hdwy over 3f out: rdn over 1f out: ev ch whn carried lft ins fnl f: nt qckn* **4/1**[2]

0322 **3** *1 ¾* **Peak Park (USA)**[24] 6159 4-8-13 **50** (v) PHanagan 6 54
(JARToller) *hld up in mid-div: hdwy 5f out: rdn 3f out: styd on one pce fnl f* **7/2**[1]

000/ **4** *2 ½* **Ellway Prospect**[202] 5385 4-8-12 **52** NChalmers(3) 3 53
(MissIECraig) *hld up: rdn 6f out: outpcd over 4f out: hdwy over 1f out: edgd lft ins fnl f: styd on* **33/1**

2005 **5** *shd* **Bravely Does It (USA)**[18] 6292 4-8-8 **50** BSwarbrick(5) 11 51
(WMBrisbourne) *hld up in mid-div: hdwy over 5f out: led over 3f out: rdn and hdd jst over 1f out: sn btn* **12/1**

6600 **6** *shd* **Simon's Seat (USA)**[36] 5907 5-9-7 **58** SWKelly 9 59
(PHowling) *s.i.s: hld up: hdwy over 5f out: nt clr run over 5f out: swtchd rt over 2f out: sn rdn: styd on fnl f* **16/1**

0000 **7** *3 ½* **Lampos (USA)**[21] 6225 4-9-0 **51** RWinston 8 48
(MissJACamacho) *bhd: rdn and hdwy on ins over 1f out: eased whn nt imp ins fnl f* **8/1**[3]

60 **8** *1 ½* **Sweetwater (GER)**[22] 6192 4-9-9 **60** DSweeney 1 55
(MrsStefLiddiard) *hld up in tch: lost pl over 3f out: sn rdn: n.d after* **25/1**

0-01 **9** *14* **Ensemble**[10] 6438 4-8-13 **50** NCallan 10 28
(DMSimcock) *prom: led over 4f out tl over 3f out: wknd 2f out* **12/1**

2515 **10** *8* **Bojangles (IRE)**[35] 5935 5-9-4 **58** DNolan(3) 7 26
(RBrotherton) *prom: rdn over 5f out: sn wknd* **9/1**

0600 **11** *2* **Vanbrugh (FR)**[19] 6278 4-9-4 **55** (vt) FLynch 5 21
(MissDAMchale) *w ldr tl 5f out: wknd qckly* **25/1**

1060 **12** *3 ½* **Lazzaz**[3] 6540 6-8-11 **53** PMakin(5) 4 15
(PWHiatt) *led: hdd over 4f out: rdn over 3f out: sn wknd* **4/1**[2]

**13** *28* **Tania Di Sceptre (ITY)**[37] 5905 4-9-0 **51** (p) EAhern 13 —
(MsCarolineHutchinson, Ire) *hld up in tch: rdn 7f out: wknd 5f out: t.o* **10/1**

3m 43.51s **13** Ran SP% **132.0**

Speed ratings: CSF £64.75 CT £217.48 TOTE £11.20: £4.10, £2.20, £1.80; EX 53.00 Place 6 £186.38, Place 5 £72.08.

**Owner** Mrs Rachel A Powell **Bred** Baldernock Bloodstock Ltd **Trained** Morestead, Hants

**FOCUS**

They went no pace in this ordinary stayers' handicap, and although the form is not strong it appears sound enough.

**NOTEBOOK**

**Sungio** had a pipe-opener without the blinkers in the National Hunt jockeys' race at Goodwood last month. He has now been ridden by Gibson for all four of his wins on the Flat.

**Best Port(IRE)**, three times a winner of turf this year, found this a totally different kettle of fish to the Fibresand surface he had previously tried.

**Peak Park(USA)** had twice been raised 2lb for finishing second over two miles on this surface at Lingfield.

**Ellway Prospect**, last seen over hurdles in April, was not disgraced on her first outing on the level for two years.

**Bravely Does It(USA)** may have found this extended two miles stretching his stamina to the limit.

**Simon's Seat(USA)** has never been the most consistent of performers but did not get the run of the race on this occasion.

T/Plt: £110.60 to a £1 stake. Pool: £41,836.40. 276.05 winning tickets. T/Qpdt: £7.90 to a £1 stake. Pool: £4,788.10. 445.90 winning tickets. KH

# 6528 FLEMINGTON (R-H)

Saturday, November 6

**OFFICIAL GOING: Heavy**

## 6582a QUEEN ELIZABETH STKS (H'CAP) (GROUP 2) — 1m 4f 110y

**5:30** (5:30) 4-Y-O+ **£68,908** (£21,008; £9,454; £4,202)

RPR

**1** **Fantastic Love (USA)**[36] 5916 4-8-11 (b) KMcEvoy —
(SaeedBinSuroor) *soon tracking leader, pulling & led 9f out, went 2l up well over 1f out, all out (9-2)* 2

**2** *snk* **Manawa King (NZ)**[35] 5-8-5 (b) RMcLeod —
(JConlan, Australia) *34-10F* 1

**3** *hd* **Di Capo (AUS)** 5-8-2 SallyWynne —
(LouiseBonella, Australia) *8-1*

**4** *1* **Pantani (NZ)**[173] 5-8-5 KForrester —
(RLaing, Australia) *11-2* 3

**5** *nk* **Dancing Daggers (NZ)**[28] 3-8-4 BShinn —
(GBegg, Australia)

**7** *2 ½* **Tomorrow's Party (NZ)**[145] 5-8-2 (b) MWalker —
(MMoroney, Australia)

2m 44.8s

**WFA** 3 from 4yo+ 6lb **7** Ran SP% **67.4**

Speed ratings:

**Owner** Godolphin **Bred** A W I **Trained** Newmarket, Suffolk

**NOTEBOOK**

**Fantastic Love(USA)** did not settle properly until allowed to bowl along in front from over a mile out. Sticking to the inside rail in the straight, he showed real tenacity to hold off two challengers under strong driving. The ground was probably against him here, which makes his performance even more creditable. The Melbourne Cup, for which he just missed the cut this year, is his target for 2005.



The Form Book, Raceform Ltd, Compton, RG20 6NL

# 6510 SAINT-CLOUD (L-H)

Saturday, November 6

**OFFICIAL GOING: Very soft**

**6583a** **CRITERIUM DE SAINT-CLOUD (GROUP 1) (C&F)** **1m 2f**
**2:20** (2:20) 2-Y-O **£80,479** (£32,197; £16,099; £8,042)

RPR

1 **Paita** 2-8-11 ........................................ ASuborics 2 109
(MarioHofer, Germany) *held up, close 6th straight, switched right 2f out, ridden 1f out, ran on to lead 100y out, well in command close home* **198/10**

2 3/4 **Yehudi (IRE)**[6] 6503 2-9-0 ........................................ JPSpencer 3 111
(APO'Brien, Ire) *led after 1f to 7f out, racd outside ldr to str, led narrowly 1 1/2f out, hard rdn 1f out, hdd 100y out, kpt on under press* **27/10**[2]

3 1 **Laverock (IRE)**[30] 2-9-0 ........................................ MBlancpain 5 109
(CLaffon-Parias, France) *disputed 3rd, close 4th straight, ridden 1f out, kept on same pace* **38/10**[3]

4 2 **Grand Bahama (IRE)**[28] 2-9-0 ........................................ CSoumillon 8 106
(AFabre, France) *disputed 3rd, 3rd straight, one pace final 2f* **58/10**

5 nk **Musketier (GER)**[20] 6262 2-9-0 ........................................ C-PLemaire 7 106
(PBary, France) *broke well, settled in 5th, last but well in touch straight, stayed on inside final f but never a threat* **11/10**[1]

6 1/2 **Eligibilis (FR)** 2-9-0 ........................................ SLeloup 1 105
(J-PGallorini, France) *led 1f, narrow leader from 7f out to 1 1/2f out, hard ridden & every chance 1f out, weakened close home* **34/1**

7 5 **Kappelmann (FR)**[15] 2-9-0 ........................................ IMendizabal 6 97
(RobertCollet, France) *held up in rear, 5th straight, slipped through on inside to be 3rd over 2f out, weakened over 1f out* **24/1**

2m 19.0s **7** Ran SP% **121.9**

Speed ratings: .

**Owner** M Hofer & Stall Steigenberger **Bred** Gestut Fahrhof **Trained** Germany

**NOTEBOOK**

**Paita** looked in great shape in the paddock and was waited with early on in the race. Still last in the straight, she had to bide her time before moving out to challenge one and a half out. After a couple of reminders she quickened and took the lead well inside the final furlong. This was a pretty impressive effort considering she has only won a small race in Italy when making her debut. She can only improve and her trainer is already talking about next years Prix de Diane.

**Yehudi(IRE)**, given every possible chance, was always one of the leaders and he took control of the race halfway up the straight. The colt ran on bravely but he just could not pull out quite enough to hold off the winner as the race drew to an end. He Looks a very progressive sort and should not be long before making it at Group level.

**Laverock(IRE)**, mid-division early on, he looked extremely dangerous when making a challenge for the lead at the furlong marker. He was then one-paced during the final stages. He is quite a cold individual and maybe an even longer trip would be an advantage.

**Grand Bahama(IRE)** raced in third place early on he was caught for speed when things quickened up in the straight. The colt was one-paced but staying on at the finish. An even longer trip will certainly be to his benefit.

# INDEX TO MEETINGS FLAT 2004



† Abandoned
* All-Weather
(M) Mixed meeting

# INDEX TO FLAT RACING

Horses are shown in alphabetical order; the trainer's name follows the name of the horse. The figures to the right are current master ratings for all-weather and turf; the all-weather rating is preceded by the letter 'a'.Underneath the horse's name is its age, colour and sex in abbreviated format e.g. 6 b g indicates the horse is six-years-old, bay in colour, and a gelding.The descriptive details are followed by the race numbers of the races in which it has taken part in chronological order; a superscript figure indicates its finishing position in that race (brackets indicate it was the winner of the race).

## A

**Aahgowangowan (IRE)** 5 b m Tagula (IRE) -Cabcharge Princess (IRE) (Rambo Dancer (CAN)) 1421[12] 1525[7] 2784[5] 3225[2] (3399) 3795[5] 4133[9] 4828[5] 5101[2]5579[11] 6046[15] **>54a 71f<**

**Aastral Magic** 2 b f Magic Ring (IRE) -Robanna (Robellino (USA)) (2300) (3343) 4581[4] 5068[6] **>83f<**

**Abbajabba** 8 b g Barrys Gamble-Bo Babbity (Strong Gale) 1007[10] 1106[10] 1354[11] 1500[13] 4635[2] 4759[8] 5244[5] 6244[9]6517[6] 6553[12] **>46a 78f<**

**Abbeygate** 3 b c Unfuwain (USA) -Ayunli (Chief Singer) 3746[10] 4628[11] 4939[10] 6006[11] 6209[10] **>59a 49f<**

**Abbeylara (USA)** 2 b f Stravinsky (USA) -Parish Manor (USA) (Waquoit (USA)) 3859a[9] **>85f<**

**Abbiejo (IRE)** 7 b m Blues Traveller (IRE) -Chesham Lady (IRE) (Fayruz) 1075[6] 1176[5] 1444[6] 1515[6] 1591[7] 1856[14] **>37a 38f<**

**Abbondanza (USA)** 3 ch c Alphabet Soup (USA) -Katie McLaury (USA) (Centrust (USA)) 6487a[11] **>96a<**

**Abdulbey (IRE)** 4 b c Eagle Eyed (USA) -Honesty (IRE) (Tenby) 5488a[15] ><

**A Beetoo (IRE)** 4 b f Bahhare (USA) -Sonya s Pearl (IRE) (Conquering Hero (USA)) 623[9] **>66da<**

**Abelard (IRE)** 3 b g Fasliyev (USA) -Half-Hitch (USA) (Diesis) 2650[6] 2877[5] 4051[10] 4576[5] 5562[15] 5862[2] 6273[9] 6578[3] **>61a 65f<**

**Aberdeen (IRE)** 2 b c Xaar-Olivia Jane (IRE) (Ela-Mana-Mou) 5051[6] 5494[2] 5931[4] **>68a 82f<**

**Aberdeen Park** 2 gr f Environment Friend-Michelee (Merdon Melody) 1853[5] 2111[10] 2884[8] 3192[4] 5655[5] 5701[2] 5909[2] 6090[8]6356[3] **>70f<**

**Aberdovey** 2 b f Mister Baileys-Annapurna (IRE) (Brief Truce (USA)) 2275[5] (2550) 3634[3] 5391[5] 5938[10] **>76f<**

**Abide (FR)** 2 ch f Pivotal-Ariadne (GER) (King s Lake (USA)) 5247[6] 5694[2] 6123[6] **>74+f<**

**A Bid In Time (IRE)** 3 b f Danetime (IRE) -Bidni (IRE) (Maelstrom Lake) 524[8] 747[8] 1517[2] 1689[9] 1934[6] 2778[6] 3234[6] 3624[8] **>36a 44f<**

**Abigail Adams** 3 ch f Kris-Rose Vibert (Caerleon (USA)) 4954[8] 5371[10] **>42f<**

**Abington Angel** 3 ch f Machiavellian (USA) -Band (USA) (Northern Dancer) 2112[15] 2587[13] 4848[8] (5217 ) 5728[14] **>65a 76df<**

**A Bit Of Fun** 3 ch g Unfuwain (USA) -Horseshoe Reef (Mill Reef (USA)) 730[5] 945[2] 1407[7] (2016) 2349[8] 3822[11] **>47a 33f<**

**Ablaj (IRE)** 3 ch g Horse Chestnut (SAF) -Passe Passe (USA) (Lear Fan (USA)) 1613[8] 2660[4] 2931[4] 3305[5] **>50a 57f<**

**Able Baker Charlie (IRE)** 5 b g Sri Pekan (USA) -Lavezzola (IRE) (Salmon Leap (USA)) 2201[4] 2969[2] 3937[8] 5941[16] **>83 a 102f<**

**Able Charlie (GER)** 2 ch g Lomitas-Alula (GER) (Monsun (GER)) 4048[2] 4606[6] 5542[7] **>75f<**

**Able Mind** 4 b g Mind Games-Chlo-Jo (Belmez (USA)) 2779[12] 3265[10] 3779[6] 5236[3] 6138[3] **>51a 62f<**

**Aboustar** 4 b g Abou Zouz (USA) -Three Star Rated (IRE) (Pips Pride) 567[5] 934[8] 1191[5] 5342[5] **>39a 39f<**

**Above Board** 9 b g Night Shift (USA) -Bundled Up (USA) (Sharpen Up) 470[5] 502[8] 612[2] 680[8] 728[3] 936[14] (1092) 1262[14]1423[6] 1941[14] 1994[11] **>53a 24f<**

**Abracadabjar** 6 b g Royal Abjar (USA) -Celt Song (IRE) (Unfuwain (USA)) 456[8] **>32a 32f<**

**Abraxas** 6 b g Emperor Jones (USA) -Snipe Hall (Crofthall) 543[5] 560[9] 898[7] 1131[16] 1518[7] 1988[9] **>57da 45f<**

**Abraxas Antelope (IRE)** 2 b c Imperial Ballet (IRE) -Lypharden (IRE) (Lyphard s Special (USA)) (2780) (3865) 4857[3] 5195[2] **>102f<**

**Abrogate (IRE)** 3 b g Revoque (IRE) -Czarina s Sister (Soviet Lad (USA)) 521[12] 615[2] 802[4] 2176[5] 4102[9] **>51a 49f<**

**Absent Friends** 7 b g Rock City-Green Supreme (Primo Dominie) 1955[8] 2293[6] 2488[13] 3480[6] 3713[10] 5105[10] 5287[8] 5372[9]5550[4] 5712[7] 5787[11] **>50a 95f<**

**Absinther** 7 b g Presidium-Heavenly Queen (Scottish Reel) 2728[8] 3263[2] (3393) 4196[4] 4416[3] 4616[3] 5021[12] 5286[8] **>47a 56f<**

**Absolut Edge** 2 ch g Atraf-Sparkling Edge (Beveled (USA)) 3491[11] 3709[6] ><

**Absolutely Fab (IRE)** 3 ch f Entrepreneur-Hamama (USA) (Majestic Light (USA)) 2596[14] 3305[14] 3707[10] **>17a 27f<**

**Absolutely Soaked (IRE)** 3 b f Alhaarth (IRE) -Vasilopoula (IRE) (Kenmare (FR)) 1224[5] 1712[6] 1998[8] 4201[9] 4655[10] 5702[2] 6567[11] **>59f<**

**Absolutelythebest (IRE)** 3 b c Anabaa (USA) -Recherchee (Rainbow Quest (USA)) (492) 1416[2] 2070[2] 2397[6] 2910[4] 3806[5] 4692[8] 5732[9] **>75a 87f<**

**Absolute Utopia (USA)** 11 b g Mr Prospector (USA) -Magic Gleam (USA) (Danzig (USA)) 495[7] 664[2] 894[2] 964[3] 1088[4] (1168) (1687) 2262[P] **>70a 63 f<**

**Absolut Power (GER)** 3 ch c Acatenango (GER) -All Our Dreams (Caerleon (USA)) 4377a[3] 5974a[7] **>95f<**

**Abstract Folly (IRE)** 2 b g Rossini (USA) -Cochiti (Kris) 5301[4] 5855[4] **>65f<**

**Abuelos** 5 b g Sabrehill (USA) -Miss Oasis (Green Desert (USA)) 536[3] 659[4] 791[10] 1279[12] 4421[5] 4825[10] 4985[6] 5305[6]5449[5] **>44 a 44 f<**

**Abunawwas (IRE)** 4 b c In The Wings-Copper Creek (Habitat) 1254a[7] (1893a) (2603a) 3967a[9] 5972a[9] **>112f<**

**Academy (IRE)** 9 ch g Archway (IRE) -Dream Academy (Town And Country) 2249[2] 2731[11] 4352[9] 5354[2] 5638[P] **>52a 68f<**

**Acca Larentia (IRE)** 3 gr f Titus Livius (FR) -Daisy Grey (Nordance (USA)) 2390[14] 2757[10] 3252[3] 3817[10] 4451[9] 5366[6] 5524[5] 5863[6]6361[9] **>29a 42f<**

**Acceleration (IRE)** 4 b g Groom Dancer (USA) -Overdrive (Shirley Heights) (1173) 1316[6] 1661[13] 6535[11] **>50a 69f<**

**Accendere** 3 b g Machiavellian (USA) -Littlewick (IRE) (Green Desert (USA)) 816[12] 1052[14] 1366[5] 1844[7] (2766) 3636[7] 5411[3] **>30a 60f<**

**Accepting** 7 b g Mtoto-D Azy (Persian Bold) 1287[5] 1501[13] 3108[2] 3363[4] 5991[10] **>62 f<**

**Acciacatura (USA)** 3 gr f Stravinsky (USA) -Lady In Waiting (USA) (Woodman (USA)) 1983a[12] **>98f<**

**Ace (IRE)** 3 b c Danehill (USA) -Tea House (Sassafras (FR)) (4786a) 5782[5] **>118+f<**

**Ace Club** 3 ch g Indian Rocket-Presently (Cadeaux Genereux) 1881[5] 2269[9] 3420[7] 4434[4] 5040[2] 5219[11] 5737[12] 6001[16] **>65a 72f<**

**Ace Coming** 3 b g First Trump-Tarry (Salse (USA)) 1108[12] 1363[3] (1667) (1932) 2078[13] 3903[8] 4490[10] 4826[16] 5859[14] 6520[14] **>71f<**

**Ace In The Hole** 4 br f So Factual (USA) -Timely Raise (USA) (Raise A Man (USA)) 1369[20] 2387[17] **>15a 51f<**

**Ace-Ma-Vahra** 6 b m Savahra Sound-Asmarina (Ascendant) 717[6] 737[7] 782[6] (823) 878[6] 1233[13] 1941[12] 2350[10]2451[5] 2778[9] 2875[3] 3169[14] 3381[6] 3616[3] 3804[3]4350[5] 4605[14] 5000[5] 5587[14] 6362[2] 6404[8] **>51a 46f<**

**Ace Of Hearts** 5 b g Magic Ring (IRE) -Lonely Heart (Midyan (USA)) 1114[14] 1273[5] 1623[15] 2196[2] (2504) (2905) (3119) 3539[9] 5194[13] 5920[3] 6193[16]6475[9] **>80a 98+f<**

**Achilles Rainbow** 5 ch g Deploy-Naughty Pistol (USA) (Big Pistol (USA)) 663[4] 788[12] 894[6] 947[F] **>45a 45f<**

**Acola (FR)** 4 ch f Acatenango (GER) -Wardara (Sharpo) 1560[8] 1940[10] 2594[13] 4066[10] **>41a 58f<**

**Acomb** 4 b g Shaamit (IRE) -Aurora Bay (IRE) (Night Shift (USA)) 1199[12] 1452[6] 1757[9] (2368) (2560) 2781[7] 3872[8] 4543[6] 5861[9] **>85+f<**

**Acorazado (IRE)** 5 b g Petorius-Jaldi (IRE) (Nordico (USA)) 491[7] 624[2] 701[7] (745) 870[6] 1055[2] 1373[7] 1595[4]6548[6] **>69a 55f<**

**Acropolis (IRE)** 3 b c Sadler s Wells (USA) -Dedicated Lady (IRE) (Pennine Walk) (5481a) 5981a[4] **>123f<**

**Action Fighter (GER)** 4 ch g Big Shuffle (USA) -Action Art (IRE) (Bustino) 485[3] 544[14] **>94a 88f<**

**Action This Day (USA)** 3 b c Kris S (USA) -Najecam (USA) (Trempolino (USA)) 1781a[6] **>113a<**

**Active Account (USA)** 7 bb g Unaccounted For (USA) -Ameritop (USA) (Topsider (USA)) 970[2] 1141[2] 1598[5] 1757[6] 2938[6] 3534[3] 3781[9] 4240[8]5374[14] 5757[6] **>74a 77f<**

**Active Asset (IRE)** 2 ch c Sinndar (IRE) -Sacristy (Godswalk (USA)) 2095[2] (4198) 4645[2] 6472[8] **>87f<**

**Activo (FR)** 3 b c Trempolino (USA) -Acerbis (GER) (Rainbow Quest (USA)) 6075a[7] **>96f<**

**Act Of The Pace (IRE)** 4 b f King s Theatre (IRE) -Lady In Pace (Burslem) 1662[4] (2983) 3443[2] 3902[6] 5093[3] **>86f<**

**Actrice (IRE)** 4 b f Danehill (USA) -Ange Bleu (USA) (Alleged (USA)) 1952a[6] (2543a) 2967[4] 5332a[11] 5978a[5] **>109f<**

**Acuzio** 3 b c Mon Tresor-Veni Vici (IRE) (Namaqualand (USA)) 1761[6] 2270[6] 2654[8] 3004[4] 3780[8] 4338[8] 4680[5] 5692[8] **>59f<**

**Adaala (USA)** 2 b f Sahm (USA) -Alshoowg (USA) (Riverman (USA)) 5961a[4] 6367a[2] **>96+f<**

**Adaikali (IRE)** 3 b c Green Desert (USA) -Adaiyka (IRE) (Doyoun) 1771[7] 2270[2] (2732) 4061[2] 4343[9] 5755[4] 6044[2] **>60a 96+f<**

**Adalar (IRE)** 4 br g Grand Lodge (USA) -Adalya (IRE) (Darshaan) 600[9] 768[9] 872[11] 887[11] 1088[6] 2121[10] 2210[7]2753[10] 3459[4] 3771[7] 4479[2] 4802[2] 5259[9] **>73a 68f<**

**Adalpour (IRE)** 6 b g Kahyasi-Adalya (IRE) (Darshaan) 483[7] 594[8] ><

**Adantino** 5 b g Glory Of Dancer-Sweet Whisper (Petong) 465[6] 541[3] 639[4] (660) 738[3] 928[3] 2483[6] 2823[3](3935) 4403[6] 4774[8] 6493[6] **>64a 64f<**

**Adaptable** 3 b f Groom Dancer (USA) -Adeptation (USA) (Exceller (USA)) 2182[8] 2611[9] **>66f<**

**Adeeba (IRE)** 3 b f Alhaarth (IRE) -Nedaarah (Reference Point) 1628[6] 2484[13] **>40a 50f<**

**Adees Dancer** 3 b f Danehill Dancer (IRE) -Note (GER) (Reliance Ii) 1557[10] 2198[11] 3473[5] 3984[8] 4307[16] **>61f<**

**Adiemus** 6 b g Green Desert (USA) -Anodyne (Dominion) 687a[4] 832a[3] (922a) 1003a[P] **>111a 103f<**

**Adjawar (IRE)** 6 b g Ashkalani (IRE) -Adjriyna (Top Ville) 4754[8] 5768[18] 6208[8] **>83a 91+f<**

**Adjiram (IRE)** 8 b g Be My Guest (USA) -Adjriyna (Top Ville) 793[3] 857[5] 945[4] (1861) 2055[2] 3263[12] **>39a 38f<**

**Admiral (IRE)** 3 b c Alhaarth (IRE) -Coast Is Clear (IRE) (Rainbow Quest (USA)) 1461[9] (2397) 2683[3] (2999) 4229[11] **>94f<**

**Admiral Compton** 3 ch c Compton Place-Sunfleet (Red Sunset) 2842[2] 3487[2] 5851[3] (6015) **>72a 76f<**

**Admire Don (JPN)** 5 b h Timber Country (USA) -Vega (JPN) (Tony Bin) 1147a[8] **>114a<**

**Admittance (USA)** 2 bb f Red Ransom (USA) -Quittance (USA) (Riverman (USA)) 4048[8] 4487[8] 4761[11] 5095[11] 5556[10] **>51f<**

**Adobe** 9 b g Green Desert (USA) -Shamshir (Kris) 1845[15] 2410[7] 2945[3] 3127[4] 3191[4] 3771[2] 4008[9] 4142[7]4349[4] 4569[8] 4802[5] 5317[10] 5544[7] 5657[11] 5868[13] (6364) 6550[5] **>69a 68f<**

**Adopted Hero (IRE)** 4 b g Sadler s Wells (USA) -Lady Liberty (NZ) (Noble Bijou (USA)) (2163a) **>84+a 103f<**

**Adorata (GER)** 3 b f Tannenkonig (IRE) -Adora (GER) (Danehill (USA)) 956[10] 1243[11] 1749[7] 2211[3] 2756[2] 3180[12] 3517[2] 3708[3]3875[9] 4726[2] (4880) 5223[12] 6152[7] 6311[11] 6461[6] **>66a 74f<**

**Adoration** 2 b c Royal Applause-Unconditional Love (IRE) (Polish Patriot (USA)) 2024[3] 2470[2] 2677[5] 3677[12] 5292[8] 6356[10] **>75 f<**

**A Double Ewe Bee** 3 b f Kingsinger (IRE) -Some Dream (Vitiges (FR)) 6402[12] 6561[9] **>32f<**

**Adriatic Adventure (IRE)** 3 ch f Foxhound (USA) -Theda (Mummy s Pet) 591[10] 662[12] **>15a 34f<**

**Ad Valorem (USA)** 2 b c Danzig (USA) -Classy Women (USA) (Relaunch (USA)) (5680a) (5918) **>121f<**

**Advice** 3 b c Seeking The Gold (USA) -Anna Palariva (IRE) (Caerleon (USA)) 2072a[6] 6075a[3] **>101f<**

**Aegean Mist** 4 ch f Prince Sabo-Dizzydaisy (Sharpo) 5801[4] **>41a 43f<**

**Aesculus (USA)** 3 b f Horse Chestnut (SAF) -Crafty Buzz (USA) (Crafty Prospector (USA)) 1613[12] 2097[5] 2428[3] 2790[20] 3473[3] 4066[2] (4435) **>66a 79f<**

**Aetheling (USA)** 3 b f Swain (IRE) -Etheldreda (USA) (Diesis) 5216[9] ><

**Affirmative Action (IRE)** 4 b c Rainbow Quest (USA) -Bombazine (IRE) (Generous (IRE)) 5503a[8] 6137a[6] **>108f<**

**Afghan (USA)** 6 ch g Hennessy (USA) -Affirm The Gold (USA) (Golden Act (USA)) 687a[3] 757a[3] 832a[4] **>91a<**

**Afleet Alex (USA)** 2 b c Northern Afleet (USA) -Maggy Hawk (USA) (Hawkster (USA)) 6489a[2] **>119a<**

**Afrashad (USA)** 2 ch c Smoke Glacken (USA) -Flo White (USA) (Whitesburg (USA)) (3847) **>98+a<**

**African Breeze** 2 b f Atraf-Luanshya (First Trump) 2129[7] 2568[4] (3055) 3445[4] 4348[5] 5391[11] 5606[8] **>78f<**

**African Dawn** 6 b g Spectrum (IRE) -Lamu Lady (IRE) (Lomond (USA)) 2767[6] 3263[14] 3682[9] 4098[4] **>70a 57f<**

**African Dream** 3 b g Mark Of Esteem (IRE) -Fleet Hill (IRE) (Warrshan (USA)) 766[3] (845) (1134) (1437) (1586) (1924) 3540[10] 3863a[4] 4685[7] **>81a 115f<**

**African Emperor (FR)** 2 gr g Highest Honor (FR) -Land Of Ivory (USA) (The Minstrel (CAN)) 3424[6] 5735[9] 6022[8] **>44a<**

**African Gift** 2 b f Cadeaux Genereux-African Light (Kalaglow) 2651[3] 3693[7] 4560[6] 5060[7] 6113[11] **>64f<**

**African Sahara (USA)** 5 br h El Gran Senor (USA) -Able Money (USA) (Distinctive (USA)) 643[6] (768) 915[11] (961) 1066[6] 1114[8] 1273[6] 1460[15] 1623[17]3299[6] 3597[9] 3869[3] 4164[4] 4293[3] (4558) 4920[4] 5135[2] 5265[2] **>88a 93f<**

**African Spur (IRE)** 4 b g Flying Spur (AUS) -African Bloom (African Sky) 515[9] 586[7] 670[2] 938[2] 1175[15] 1358[10] 1526[14] 1665[19]1868[13] 1974[16] 2130[19] 2823[6] 3148[5] 3277[10] 3579[10] 3637[11]4014[7] 4154[4] 4350[6] 4557[16] **>70a 54f<**

**African Star** 3 b c Mtoto-Pass The Rose (IRE) (Thatching) 415[6] 3107[5] 3461[6] 4128[4] 5153[11] 5750[9] **>63a 56f<**

**African Storm (IRE)** 2 b c Fasliyev (USA) -Out Of Africa (IRE) (Common Grounds) 2846[5] 3302[2] 3413[2] 4637[7] 5078[6] 6281[9] **>47f<**

**African Sunset (IRE)** 4 b g Danehill Dancer (IRE) -Nizamiya (Darshaan) 2257[3] 2856[5] **>52f<**

**After All (IRE)** 3 gr f Desert Story (IRE) -All Ashore (Nureyev (USA)) 414[3] 856[5] **>60a 52f<**

**After Lent (IRE)** 3 b g Desert Style (IRE) -Yashville (Top Ville) 2519[8] 4332[6] 5086[9] **>68f<**

**After The Ball (SAF)** 4 ch f Rocky Marriage (USA) -Aerial Dancer (SAF) (Dancing Champ (USA)) 1002a[7] **>85a 73f<**

**After The Show** 3 b c Royal Applause-Tango Teaser (Shareef Dancer (USA)) 1333[6] 1689[10] 2082[6] 2889[7] 4489[2] 4810[8] 6001[15] 6445[15] **>55a 71f<**

**After The Snow (IRE)** 2 b f Danetime (IRE) -State (Dominion) 5910[16] 6195[5] **>39f<**

**Again Jane** 4 ch f Then Again-Janie-O (Hittite Glory) 825[7] ><

**Agata (FR)** 3 b f Poliglote-Ambri Piotta (FR) (Caerwent) 2338a[3] 2925a[5] **>110f<**

**Agent Kensington** 2 b f Mujahid (USA) -Monawara (IRE) (Namaqualand (USA)) 1670[2] 1905[2] 2786[5] 3532[3] 4058[2] 4474[4] 4621[2] 5334[9]5648[24] 6080[9] **>68f<**

**Age Of Kings (USA)** 2 b c Kingmambo (USA) -Everhope (USA) (Danzig (USA)) 2058[3] 2959[6] **>86f<**

**Aggi Mac** 3 b f Defacto (USA) -Giffoine (Timeless Times (USA)) 828[5] 4309[17] 4925[7] 5451[8] 5637[8] 5770[9] **>32a 32f<**

**Aggravation** 2 b g Sure Blade (USA) -Confection (Formidable (USA)) 6010[9] 6294[13] 6440[9] 6536[7] **>52+a 46f<**

**Agilete** 2 b g Piccolo-Ingerence (FR) (Akarad (FR)) 1853[9] 2263[3] 3104[3] 3805[5] 5351[13] **>75f<**

**Agilis (IRE)** 4 b g Titus Livius (FR) -Green Life (Green Desert (USA)) 647[11] 677[6] 770[11] 1241[9] 1935[9] 2030[12] 2226[10]2325[7] 2441[6] **>82a 54f<**

**Agouti** 3 b f Pennekamp (USA) -La Dama Bonita (USA) (El Gran Senor (USA)) 2182[16] 2950[10] **>28f<**

**Agreat Dayoutwithu** 2 ch f Defacto (USA) -Lonely Lass (Headin Up) 3116[8] 5209[11] 5800[15] **>19+f<**

**Aguila Loco (IRE)** 5 ch g Eagle Eyed (USA) -Go Likecrazy (Dowsing (USA)) 433[3] 470[2] 499[6] 625[2] 717[5] 799[3] (834) 895[4]918[7] 930[6] 1176[2] 1268[10] 1477[3] 1595[7] 2099[3]2178[6] 2404[8] 2703[8] 2803[10] 3616[4] **>63a 63f<**

**Aguilera (GER)** 4 b f Winged Love (IRE) -Adjani (Surumu (GER)) 2138a[6] 6257a[8] **>96f<**

**Aguilera** 3 ch f Wolfhound (USA) -Mockingbird (Sharpo) 1362[7] 2908[8] 3368[10] 3739[4] 3836[13] 4391[9] 4701[12] 5342[8] **>25f<**

**Ahaz** 2 b g Zaha (CAN) -Classic Faster (IRE) (Running Steps (USA)) 1686[14] 2074[6] 3083[12] 3390[5] 4200[4] 4638[6] 5218[16] **>46f<**

**Ahdaaf (USA)** 2 bb f Bahri (USA) -Ashraakat (USA) (Danzig (USA)) 3676[3] 4137[3] 5943[4] **>78f<**

**Ahlefisia** 3 b f Efisio-Ahla (Unfuwain (USA)) 2723a[13] **>68f<**

**Aimee s Delight** 4 b f Robellino (USA) -Lloc (Absalom) 1273[9] 1372[9] 1746[6] 2304[8] 2410[10] 2757[7] 3536[12] 3609[9] **>70a 70f<**

**Ain t Here (AUS)** 4 b g Dehere (USA) -Ain t She A Daisy (USA) (Sabona (USA)) 1657a[11] 2156a[4] **>114f<**

**Aintnecessarilyso** 6 ch g So Factual (USA) -Ovideo (Domynsky) 504[5] 536[5] (626) 748[4] 896[3] 1033[6] 1051[3] 1140[3]1584[3] 1859[2] 2246[2] 2404[2] 2707[3] 2885[6] (3043) (3298) 3606[5] 3775[3]4034[6] 4403[8] 4542[10] **>68a 61f<**

**Airedale Lad (IRE)** 3 b g Charnwood Forest (IRE) -Tamarsiya (USA) (Shahrastani (USA)) 1192[6] 1425[4] 1916[5] 3822[13] 6150[13] **>17a<**

**Aire De Mougins (IRE)** 2 b g Pennekamp (USA) -Colouring (IRE) (Catrail (USA)) 2045[8] 2674[4] 3560[4] 5314[4] 5831[2] **>75f<**

**Airgusta (IRE)** 3 b g Danehill Dancer (IRE) -Ministerial Model (IRE) (Shalford (IRE)) 1202[8] 1755[10] 1998[7] 5622[10] 6495[9] **>59a 55f<**

**Air Mail** 7 b g Night Shift (USA) -Wizardry (Shirley Heights) 643[4] 749[8] 775[9] 1013[12] 1424[4] 1475[6] 1598[8]4096[6] 4928[4] **>83 a 66 f<**

**Air Of Esteem** 8 b g Forzando-Shadow Bird (Martinmas) 442[5] 700[5] 800[6] 939[7] 1444[2] 1915[4] 2813[5]3804[9] **>51a 40f<**

**Air Of Supremacy (IRE)** 3 gr c Royal Applause-Lap Of Luxury (Sharrood (USA)) 597[7] 890[6] 1104[7] **>56a 70f<**

**Airwave** 4 b f Air Express (IRE) -Kangra Valley (Indian Ridge) 2021[6] 3073[6] 3674[9] (3976) 4886[6] 5289[11] 5647[3] 5780[2] **>108 f<**

**Aischa** 2 b f Giant s Causeway (USA) -Al Hasnaa (Zafonic (USA)) 6108a[8] **>64f<**

**Aitana** 4 b f Slip Anchor-Tsungani (Cure The Blues (USA)) 449[6] 729[4] 763[9] **>32a 60f<**

**Ajeel (IRE)** 5 b g Green Desert (USA) -Samheh (USA) (Private Account (USA)) 3052[8] **>63f<**

**Ajvazovsky (IRE)** 2 b c Lahib (USA) -Noci (USA) (Lypheor) (5389a) ><

**Akarem** 3 b c Kingmambo (USA) -Spirit Of Tara (IRE) (Sadler s Wells (USA)) 2796a[8] 6102a[9] **>94f<**

**Akash (IRE)** 4 b g Dr Devious (IRE) -Akilara (IRE) (Kahyasi) (1286) 1655a[2] 1762[12] 4530[10] 5211[11] 5768[17] **>99f<**

**Akimbo (USA)** 3 b c Kingmambo (USA) -All At Sea (USA) (Riverman (USA)) 1461$^3$ **>94+f<**
**Akindayim (IRE)** 5 b h Hamas (IRE) -Snoozy Time (Cavo Doro) 5488a$^6$ ><
**Akiramenai (USA)** 4 br f Salt Lake (USA) -Bold Wench (USA) (Bold Forbes (USA)) 708$^9$ 1991$^4$ 2367$^{10}$ 3096$^6$ 3512$^7$ 3935$^{14}$ 4708$^{10}$ 5643$^{13}$ **>57f<**
**Akraan** 2 ch f Erhaab (USA) -Nafhaat (USA) (Roberto (USA)) 4292$^9$ 4706$^7$ 5142$^5$ 5662$^2$ **>67f<**
**Akritas** 3 b c Polish Precedent (USA) -Dazzling Heights (Shirley Heights) 1899$^4$ 2397$^4$ 2683$^5$ 4075$^3$ **>93f<**
**Akshar (IRE)** 5 b g Danehill (USA) -Akilara (IRE) (Kahyasi) 1156a$^7$ 1849a$^3$ 3034$^{11}$ **>114f<**
**Alaared (USA)** 4 b g King Of Kings (IRE) -Celtic Loot (USA) (Irish River (FR)) 4799$^3$ **>86f<**
**Alafdal (USA)** 4 b g Gone West (USA) -Aqaarid (USA) (Nashwan (USA)) 2287$^8$ **>29 f<**
**Alafzar (IRE)** 6 b g Green Desert (USA) -Alasana (IRE) (Darshaan) 469$^4$ 738$^7$ (815) 888$^3$ (918) 2325$^3$ 2459$^{14}$ 2703$^4$ 2834$^9$ 4276$^4$ 4549$^4$ 5017$^{10}$ (5408) 6014$^8$ 6561$^{15}$ **>69a 62f<**
**Alaipour (IRE)** 5 b h Kahyasi-Alaiyda (USA) (Shahrastani (USA)) 6540$^P$ **>73f<**
**Alaloof (USA)** 3 b f Swain (IRE) -Alattrah (USA) (Shadeed (USA)) 1688$^6$ 2146$^6$ 3421$^8$ **>70f<**
**Alam (USA)** 5 b g Silver Hawk (USA) -Ghashtah (USA) (Nijinsky (CAN)) 5608$^6$ 5834$^7$ 6110$^5$ **>74+f<**
**Alamiyan (IRE)** 2 b c King s Best (USA) -Alasana (IRE) (Darshaan) 6282$^6$ **>57f<**
**Alani (IRE)** 2 b f Benny The Dip (USA) -Toi Toi (IRE) (In The Wings) 5186$^2$ 5669$^5$ 6072$^9$ **>63f<**
**Al Ash Hab (USA)** 5 ch h Dixieland Band (USA) -Meteor Cap (USA) (Capote (USA)) 688a$^7$ 757a$^7$ **>68a<**
**Alastair Smellie** 8 ch g Sabrehill (USA) -Reel Foyle (USA) (Irish River (FR)) 876$^{10}$ 1021$^8$ 1283$^2$ 1510$^2$ (1724) 2123$^{15}$ 3277$^{12}$ 3616$^{10}$ 4701$^{15}$ **>46a 52f<**
**Al Azhar** 10 b g Alzao (USA) -Upend (Main Reef) 3022$^6$ 3165$^3$ 3835$^3$ **>44a 44f<**
**Albadi** 3 b g Green Desert (USA) -Lyrist (Cozzene (USA)) 2046$^{11}$ 2286$^9$ 2693$^7$ (2931) 3321$^{17}$ 4199$^{12}$ 5795$^{19}$ **>54f<**
**Albanov (IRE)** 4 b g Sadler s Wells (USA) -Love For Ever (IRE) (Darshaan) 4226$^{15}$ 4529$^8$ 4932$^4$ 5288$^{19}$ 5465$^8$ 5834$^2$ 6573$^{22}$ **>102f<**
**Albanova** 5 gr m Alzao (USA) -Alouette (Darshaan) (4183a) (4794a) (5824a) **>112 f<**
**Albaran (GER)** 11 b h Sure Blade (USA) -Araqueen (GER) (Konigsstuhl (GER)) 4380a$^9$ **>107f<**
**Albashoosh** 6 b g Cadeaux Genereux-Annona (USA) (Diesis) 1929$^6$ 2291$^5$ 2492$^6$ (2735) 2936$^8$ 3400$^3$ 4291$^4$ 4534$^3$ 4727$^2$ 5631$^{15}$ **>80 f<**
**Albavilla** 4 b f Spectrum (IRE) -Lydia Maria (Dancing Brave (USA)) 1684$^3$ 4572$^2$ 5273$^5$ 5728$^8$ 5997$^3$ (6278) 6443$^8$ **>85a 81f<**
**Albee (IRE)** 4 b g Grand Lodge (USA) -Wolf Cleugh (IRE) (Last Tycoon) 639$^6$ 697$^6$ 1138$^4$ 1770$^7$ 6548$^{11}$ **>51a 29f<**
**Al Beedaa (USA)** 3 ch f Swain (IRE) -Histoire (FR) (Riverman (USA)) 1521$^4$ 1823$^3$ 2323$^3$ 2840$^{10}$ **>76f<**
**Albert Hall** 2 b c Danehill (USA) -Al Theraab (USA) (Roberto (USA)) (6100a) 6347$^2$ **>111f<**
**Albertine** 4 b f Bahhare (USA) -Rosa Royale (Arazi (USA)) 3085$^9$ 3427$^8$ 3846$^8$ **>16a 31f<**
**Albinus** 3 gr c Selkirk (USA) -Alouette (Darshaan) 1461$^{10}$ 2169$^2$ (2394) (3210) 3927$^3$ 5611$^5$ **>67a 111f<**
**Albury Heath** 4 b g Mistertopogigo (IRE) -Walsham Witch (Music Maestro) 791$^{12}$ 860$^{11}$ **>28a 28f<**
**Alcaidesa** 3 b g Charnwood Forest (IRE) -Calachuchi (Martinmas) 1528$^4$ 1820$^{11}$ **>66f<**
**Alcazar (IRE)** 9 b g Alzao (USA) -Sahara Breeze (Ela-Mana-Mou) (1212) 2067$^2$ 2998$^{13}$ 5662a$^5$ 6382a$^3$ (6534) **>117f<**
**Alcharinga (IRE)** 2 b g Ashkalani (IRE) -Bird In Blue (IRE) (Bluebird (USA)) 2173$^5$ 2522$^9$ 3011$^4$ **>63f<**
**Alchemist Master** 5 b g Machiavellian (USA) -Gussy Marlowe (Final Straw) 2368$^6$ 2776$^2$ 2965$^2$ 3058$^2$ (3409) (3586) 3714$^4$ 3884$^6$ 4349$^3$ 5194$^{10}$ 5379$^7$ 5713$^3$ 5818$^P$ **>88 a 79+f<**
**Alchera** 3 b g Mind Games-Kind Of Shy (Kind Of Hush) 1333$^{13}$ 1702$^{13}$ 2181$^6$ 2610$^4$ 3201$^4$ 3628$^{10}$ 4817$^4$ 5135$^7$ 5496$^7$ 5945$^5$ 6271$^8$ **>70f<**
**Alcinos (FR)** 3 ro c Highest Honor (FR) -Alshazam (IRE) (Petong) 1350a$^9$ 2159a$^5$ **>88f<**
**Aldente** 2 gr f Green Desert (USA) -Alruccaba (Crystal Palace (FR)) 4560$^2$ 4930$^P$ **>72f<**
**Alderney Race (USA)** 3 ch c Seeking The Gold (USA) -Oyster Catcher (IRE) (Bluebird (USA)) 1124$^5$ 1796$^2$ (2211) 2897$^4$ (3598) 4531$^2$ (4750) **>57a 108f<**
**Aleida (IRE)** 3 ch f Diesis-Pump (USA) (Forli (ARG)) 3328a$^{11}$ 4159a$^8$ **>82f<**
**Alekhine (IRE)** 3 b g Soviet Star (USA) -Alriyaah (Shareef Dancer (USA)) 2135$^2$ 2448$^3$ 2676$^{16}$ 3477$^8$ 3915$^6$ 4319$^9$ 5766$^5$ 6332$^{10}$ **>92f<**
**Alenushka** 3 b f Soviet Star (USA) -National Portrait (IRE) (Royal Academy (USA)) 2805$^9$ 3592$^6$ 4195$^4$ 4644$^2$ **>69f<**
**Aleron (IRE)** 6 b g Sadler s Wells (USA) -High Hawk (Shirley Heights) 1928$^2$ (2039) 2393$^2$ 3199$^{10}$ 3563$^4$ 3731$^3$ 3953$^5$ 4363$^2$ 4777$^8$ **>67a 80f<**
**Aleshanee** 2 b f Bold Edge-Nesyred (IRE) (Paris House) 3583$^{10}$ 4704$^7$ 4936$^{18}$ 5376$^{17}$ ><
**Alethea Gee** 6 b m Sure Blade (USA) -Star Flower (Star Appeal) 3587$^{11}$ 3896$^8$ 4396$^6$ **>33f<**
**Aleutian** 4 gr g Zafonic (USA) -Baked Alaska (Green Desert (USA)) (574) (770) (1011) 1242$^6$ 1610$^{11}$ 5224$^{13}$ **>105a 78f<**
**Alexander Ambition (IRE)** 3 b f Entrepreneur-Lady Alexander (IRE) (Night Shift (USA)) 492$^4$ 585$^3$ 702$^4$ 959$^2$ (1086) **>70+a 68f<**
**Alexander Capetown (IRE)** 2 b f Fasliyev (USA) -Hawas (Mujtahid (USA)) 1839$^2$ 2071$^5$ 3904$^6$ 5119$^4$ 5351$^4$ 5701$^8$ 6365$^{11}$ **>71f<**
**Alexander Duchess (IRE)** 3 b f Desert Prince (IRE) -Lionne (Darshaan) 1485a$^6$ 1879$^7$ 3328a$^2$ 3959a$^6$ 4893a$^{10}$ **>103f<**
**Alexander Goldrun (IRE)** 3 b f Gold Away (IRE) -Renashaan (FR) (Darshaan) (1070a) (1980a) 2330a$^2$ 2925a$^4$ 3331a$^2$ (5978a) **>118f<**
**Alexander Icequeen (IRE)** 2 b f Soviet Star (USA) -Regal Revolution (Hamas (IRE)) 3859a$^2$ 4592a$^5$ 6367a$^3$ **>98f<**
**Alexei** 3 ch g Ashkalani (IRE) -Sherkova (USA) (State Dinner (USA)) 1304$^7$ 5382$^2$ 5907$^5$ 6183$^9$ **>68a 26f<**
**Alexia Rose (IRE)** 2 b f Mujadil (USA) -Meursault (IRE) (Salt Dome (USA)) 2780$^6$ 3196$^{13}$ 4776$^4$ 5441$^3$ 5586$^2$ (5771) 6241$^2$ 6456$^7$ **>82f<**
**Aleyah** 2 ch f Bachir (IRE) -Silver Peak (FR) (Sillery (USA)) 5271$^{13}$ ><
**Alfelma (IRE)** 4 gr f Case Law-Billie Grey (Chilibang) 2236$^9$ 2383$^{15}$ 2778$^{18}$ **>43f<**
**Alfhala (IRE)** 3 b f Acatenango (GER) -Maid Of Kashmir (IRE) (Dancing Brave (USA)) 3916$^{18}$ **>45f<**
**Alfie Lee (IRE)** 7 ch g Case Law-Nordic Living (IRE) (Nordico (USA)) 4247$^7$ 4279$^4$ 6243$^{13}$ **>48f<**
**Alfie Noakes** 2 b c Groom Dancer (USA) -Crimson Rosella (Polar Falcon (USA)) 5646$^3$ 6078$^5$ 6393$^3$ **>71a 83f<**
**Alfonso** 3 ch g Efisio-Winnebago (Kris) (760) 1418$^7$ 1795$^{12}$ 5120$^2$ 5582$^4$ 6284$^2$ (6477) **>81+a 91+f<**
**Alfred The Great (IRE)** 2 b c King s Best (USA) -Aigue (High Top) 6077$^{11}$ **>36f<**
**Alfridini** 3 ch g Selkirk (USA) -Vivre En Paix (Nureyev (USA)) 447$^{11}$ 597$^8$ 816$^2$ 927$^2$ (985) 1120$^4$ 1509$^{12}$ (2915) 3213$^3$ 3750$^5$ 4056$^5$ **>72a 81f<**
**Al Garhoud Bridge** 2 b c Josr Algarhoud (IRE) -Pluck (Never So Bold) 2111$^5$ 2609$^7$ (3406) 4326$^4$ **>87+f<**
**Alghaazy (IRE)** 3 b g Mark Of Esteem (IRE) -Kentmere (FR) (Galetto (FR)) 5770$^{10}$ 6082$^{11}$ **>54f<**
**Algorithm** 2 b f Danehill Dancer (IRE) -Dominelle (Domynsky) 3950$^8$ 4099$^6$ 4347$^5$ 5240$^6$ 5314$^2$ 5636$^3$ 5819$^4$ 6003$^9$ 6515$^{15}$ **>59f<**
**Alhaadh (USA)** 2 b f Diesis-Wishah (USA) (Red Ransom (USA)) 5943$^9$ **>62+f<**
**Aliabad (IRE)** 9 bb g Doyoun-Alannya (FR) (Relko) 528$^5$ **>12 a 36df<**
**Alianna (FR)** 3 b f Anabaa (USA) -Ambassadrice (FR) (Be My Guest (USA)) 982$^{12}$ 1059$^{11}$ 1189$^9$ 2562$^{14}$ 3305$^{11}$ 6560$^5$ **>34a 34f<**
**Aliba (IRE)** 3 ch g Ali-Royal (IRE) -Kiba (IRE) (Tirol) 1597$^4$ 2217$^{10}$ 2815$^{11}$ 5001$^2$ 6097$^{13}$ 6290$^9$ **>65a 57f<**
**Alibongo (CZE)** 3 ch g Dara Monarch-Alvilde (Alzao (USA)) 728$^{13}$ 751$^9$ **>10a 33f<**
**Ali Bruce** 4 b g Cadeaux Genereux-Actualite (Polish Precedent (USA)) 2520$^5$ 3002$^2$ (3376) 4602$^3$ 6557$^4$ **>68a 70f<**
**Alice Blackthorn** 3 b f Forzando-Owdbetts (IRE) (High Estate) 1464$^{15}$ 1775$^7$ 2937$^5$ 3623$^{10}$ 4248$^8$ 6199$^{13}$ **>67f<**
**Alice King (IRE)** 2 b f Key Of Luck (USA) -Java Jive (Hotfoot) 1468$^4$ 1666$^4$ 2194$^9$ 2405$^2$ 2593$^5$ 4516$^7$ **>49a 26f<**
**Ali Deo** 3 ch g Ali-Royal (IRE) -Lady In Colour (IRE) (Cadeaux Genereux) (2195) 2516$^3$ 3312$^{11}$ 4079$^6$ 4817$^{12}$ 5510$^7$ 5955$^7$ 6160$^4$ 6279$^4$ **>71a 78f<**
**Alien (ITY)** 2 gr f Morigi-Alin (ITY) (Brook (USA)) 3436a$^5$ ><
**Aliette (FR)** 4 b f Lando (GER) -Acerbis (GER) (Rainbow Quest (USA)) 6107a$^{12}$ **>50f<**
**Alimiste (IRE)** 4 b f Ali-Royal (IRE) -Miss Senate (IRE) (Alzao (USA)) 555$^9$ 664$^9$ 871$^9$ 1101$^8$ 1281$^{10}$ 1581$^8$ **>40a<**
**Alinda (IRE)** 3 b f Revoque (IRE) -Gratclo (Belfort (FR)) (3525) (4084) **>67a 84f<**
**Ali Pasha** 5 b g Ali-Royal (IRE) -Edge Of Darkness (Vaigly Great) 1511$^6$ **>50da 52df<**
**Alisa (IRE)** 4 b f Slip Anchor-Ariadne (GER) (King s Lake (USA)) 520$^8$ 651$^3$ 818$^5$ 962$^5$ 1940$^6$ 2375$^{11}$ **>59a 30f<**
**Alisar (IRE)** 4 b c Entrepreneur-Aliya (IRE) (Darshaan) 2163a$^{12}$ **>92+f<**
**A Little Bit Yarie** 3 b g Paris House-Slipperose (Persepolis (FR)) 1473$^3$ 1602$^7$ 1659$^4$ 2075$^7$ 3293$^{11}$ 6518$^{12}$ **>81f<**
**Alizar (IRE)** 3 b f Rahy (USA) -Capua (USA) (Private Terms (USA)) 420$^9$ 496$^2$ 591$^3$ (620) 721$^4$ 868$^2$ 891$^3$ 2033$^6$ 2326$^7$ 2518$^6$ 2741$^{18}$ (2932) 3175$^{11}$ 3849$^9$ 4267$^9$ 4937$^7$ 5219$^{19}$ 5564$^{11}$ **>61a 61f<**
**Aljaareh (USA)** 3 bb c Storm Cat (USA) -Muhbubh (USA) (Blushing Groom (FR)) 2113$^{12}$ **>58f<**
**Al Jadeed (USA)** 4 b c Coronado s Quest (USA) -Aljawza (USA) (Riverman (USA)) 1006a$^9$ **>111f<**
**Aljafliyah** 3 ch f Halling (USA) -Arruhan (IRE) (Mujtahid (USA)) 3094$^U$ 3759$^8$ 3948$^7$ 4718$^9$ 5123$^{15}$ **>43f<**
**Aljomar** 5 b g College Chapel-Running For You (FR) (Pampabird) 428$^9$ 500$^6$ 875$^{10}$ 940$^{12}$ **>30a 47f<**
**Alkaadhem** 4 b c Green Desert (USA) -Balalaika (Sadler s Wells (USA)) 1125$^5$ 1456$^4$ (2241) 2957$^{11}$ 3484$^4$ 4285$^3$ (5492) (5731) **>118f<**
**Alkaased (USA)** 4 b c Kingmambo (USA) -Chesa Plana (Niniski (USA)) 2691$^2$ (3521) (4285) 5296$^2$ **>118f<**
**Alke (USA)** 4 b c Grand Slam (USA) -Pasampsi (USA) (Crow (FR)) 1145a$^2$ **>115a<**
**All A Dream** 2 br f Desert Story (IRE) -Alioli (Nishapour (FR)) 4187$^6$ 4924$^{10}$ 5375$^3$ 6289$^7$ **>62a<**
**All Blade (GER)** 10 ch g Sure Blade (USA) -Anzille (USA) (Plugged Nickle (USA)) 786a$^2$ ><
**All Bleevable** 7 b g Presidium-Eve s Treasure (Bustino) 3608$^6$ 4397$^6$ 5546$^7$ **>48f<**
**All Blue (IRE)** 3 b g Green Desert (USA) -Talented (Bustino) 5621$^4$ 5867$^4$ 6088$^8$ 6310$^8$ **>74f<**
**Allegretto (FR)** 2 b c Anabaa (USA) -Aimores (IRE) (Persian Heights) 6543$^2$ **>69+f<**
**Allerton Boy** 5 ch g Beveled (USA) -Darakah (Doulab (USA)) 411$^4$ 470$^7$ 637$^6$ 792$^8$ **>40a 62f<**
**Allexina** 2 ch f Barathea (IRE) -Grecian Bride (IRE) (Groom Dancer (USA)) 5878a$^6$ (6367a) **>100+f<**
**Allez Mousson** 6 b g Hernando (FR) -Rynechra (Blakeney) 1112$^{11}$ 1287$^{13}$ 3928$^9$ 4448$^7$ 4778$^9$ **>15a 42f<**
**Allez Olive (IRE)** 6 b g Spectrum (IRE) -Mondsee (Caerleon (USA)) 6170a$^6$ **>108f<**
**All For Laura** 2 ch f Cadeaux Genereux-Lighthouse (Warning) 2690$^4$ (4298) 4744$^5$ 5250$^5$ 5939$^8$ 6456$^4$ **>92f<**
**Allied Cause** 2 ch f Giant s Causeway (USA) -Alligram (USA) (Alysheba (USA)) 4753$^8$ 5570$^5$ (6447) **>70a 63f<**
**Allied Victory (USA)** 4 b c Red Ransom (USA) -Coral Dance (FR) (Green Dancer (USA)) (459) 564$^{11}$ 671$^9$ 3475$^2$ 3781$^8$ 4634$^3$ 5144$^7$ 5266$^4$ **>64a 81f<**
**Allizam** 2 b c Tragic Role (USA) -Mazilla (Mazilier (USA)) 3925$^{12}$ 4239$^4$ 4776$^{18}$ 6545$^9$ **>50f<**
**All Night Dancer (IRE)** 2 b f Danehill Dancer (IRE) -Nocturnal (FR) (Night Shift (USA)) 2745a$^5$ 3445$^2$ 3859a$^{10}$ 5681a$^2$ 6101a$^7$ **>83f<**
**Allodarlin (IRE)** 3 b f Cape Cross (IRE) -Sharp Circle (IRE) (Sure Blade (USA)) 3990$^8$ 4499$^{12}$ 4802$^{11}$ **>42a 55df<**
**All On My Own (USA)** 9 ch g Unbridled (USA) -Someforall (USA) (One For All (USA)) 426$^8$ 532$^4$ 730$^2$ 793$^4$ 940$^8$ 1167$^{12}$ 1513$^5$ 1592$^3$ 1987$^4$ 2345$^9$ **>38a 41f<**
**All Quiet** 3 b f Piccolo-War Shanty (Warrshan (USA)) 2029$^3$ 2223$^2$ 2425$^3$ 2808$^5$ 4916$^5$ 5378$^5$ 5845$^7$ **>81f<**
**Allspice (USA)** 4 b f Coronado s Quest (USA) -Music House (USA) (Sadler s Wells (USA)) 4735a$^4$ ><
**Allstar Princess** 2 b f Environment Friend-Turf Moor (IRE) (Mac s Imp (USA)) 3197$^7$ 3760$^{11}$ 4131$^7$ 5098$^{12}$ **>47f<**
**All Too Beautiful (IRE)** 3 b f Sadler s Wells (USA) -Urban Sea (USA) (Miswaki (USA)) (1634a) 2640$^2$ 3968a$^4$ 5679a$^3$ **>113f<**
**Ally Boy (IRE)** 2 b c Fasliyev (USA) -Annie Girl (IRE) (Danehill (USA)) (3435a) ><
**Ally Makbul** 4 b f Makbul-Clarice Orsini (Common Grounds) (442) 487$^4$ 594$^4$ 695$^8$ (810) **>65a 54f<**
**Al Maali (IRE)** 5 b h Polar Falcon (USA) -Amwag (USA) (El Gran Senor (USA)) 635a$^{10}$ 754a$^7$ 1001a$^4$ **>89a 101f<**
**Al Mabrook (IRE)** 9 b g Rainbows For Life (CAN) -Sky Lover (Ela-Mana-Mou) 2987$^7$ **>45a<**
**Almah (SAF)** 6 b m Al Mufti (USA) -Jazz Champion (SAF) (Dancing Champ (USA)) 3725$^{14}$ 4218$^{12}$ 4529$^6$ 5288$^{17}$ 5784$^9$ **>92f<**
**Almanac (IRE)** 3 b c Desert Style (IRE) -Share The Vision (Vision (USA)) 683$^7$ 890$^{11}$ 4880$^{10}$ 5352$^{10}$ **>46a 13f<**
**Almanshood (USA)** 2 bb c Bahri (USA) -Lahan (Unfuwain (USA)) 3483$^5$ 4913$^3$ **>71f<**
**Almansoora (USA)** 2 b f Bahri (USA) -Bashayer (USA) (Mr Prospector (USA)) 3676$^2$ (5248) **>84f<**
**Almara** 4 b f Wolfhound (USA) -Alacrity (Alzao (USA)) 536$^{15}$ 718$^4$ 780$^{11}$ 1694$^5$ **>23a 23f<**
**Almaty Express** 2 b g Almaty (IRE) -Express Girl (Sylvan Express) 1523$^3$ 2035$^8$ 2352$^7$ 3144$^3$ 3577$^4$ (3620) **>65f<**
**Almaviva (IRE)** 4 b f Grand Lodge (USA) -Kafayef (USA) (Secreto (USA)) 1332$^7$ 1762$^{15}$ **>93f<**
**Almendrados (IRE)** 2 b f Desert Prince (IRE) -Sevi s Choice (USA) (Sir Ivor (USA)) 2690$^3$ **>86f<**
**Almizan (IRE)** 4 b g Darshaan-Bint Albaadiya (USA) (Woodman (USA)) 1880$^{10}$ 2240$^9$ 2613$^4$ 2958$^8$ 4226$^4$ 4934$^3$ 5472$^{10}$ 6215$^{17}$ 6535$^5$ **>91f<**
**Almnadia (IRE)** 5 b m Alhaarth (IRE) -Mnaafa (IRE) (Darshaan) 1173$^9$ 2249$^5$ 2531$^6$ **>55a 63f<**
**Almond Beach** 4 ch g Hector Protector (USA) -Dancing Spirit (IRE) (Ahonoora) 423$^7$ 468$^{10}$ **>30a 73df<**
**Almond Mousse (FR)** 5 b m Exit To Nowhere (USA) -Missy Dancer (Shareef Dancer (USA)) 1163a$^4$ 1780a$^6$ 2923a$^5$ 3791a$^6$ 5169a$^7$ 5668a$^8$ **>110f<**
**Almond Willow (IRE)** 3 b f Alhaarth (IRE) -Miss Willow Bend (USA) (Willow Hour (USA)) 3387$^9$ 3780$^2$ 4680$^7$ 5223$^6$ 5955$^2$ 6160$^3$ **>77a 70f<**
**Almost Perfect (IRE)** 2 ch f Priolo (USA) -Talbiya (IRE) (Mujtahid (USA)) 1735$^6$ 2617$^3$ **>17a 66f<**
**Almost Welcome** 3 b g First Trump-Choral Sundown (Night Shift (USA)) 702$^{10}$ 788$^9$ 871$^3$ 1017$^5$ 1356$^7$ 3572$^{10}$ 4941$^{10}$ **>59a 51f<**
**Al Moulatham** 5 b h Rainbow Quest (USA) -High Standard (Kris) 692a$^7$ 922a$^{11}$ **>105+f<**
**Almuraad (IRE)** 3 b c Machiavellian (USA) -Wellspring (IRE) (Caerleon (USA)) (2276) 6219$^{10}$ **>109f<**
**Alnaja (USA)** 5 b g Woodman (USA) -Cursory Look (USA) (Nijinsky (CAN)) 1245$^P$ 1520$^9$ **>76f<**
**Alnitak (USA)** 3 br c Nureyev (USA) -Very True (USA) (Proud Truth (USA)) 2721a$^8$ 3360a$^3$ 5500a$^8$ **>103?f<**
**Along Came Molly** 2 ch f Dr Fong (USA) -Torrid Tango (USA) (Green Dancer (USA)) 6352$^{14}$ ><
**Along The Nile** 2 b g Desert Prince (IRE) -Golden Fortune (Forzando) 3918$^7$ 4454$^3$ 4761$^6$ 5212$^9$ 5466$^{10}$ 5636$^4$ 6140$^6$ 6574$^9$ **>70f<**
**Alopecurus (IRE)** 3 b f Sri Pekan (USA) -All Away (IRE) (Glow (USA)) 1778a$^{16}$ **>79f<**
**Alpaga Le Jomage (IRE)** 2 b c Orpen (USA) -Miss Bagatelle (Mummy s Pet) 1412$^3$ 1707$^3$ 1884$^2$ 2532$^4$ 2627$^5$ 2959$^8$ 3176$^5$ (3577) 3938$^4$ 4288$^7$ **>88f<**
**Alpenrot (IRE)** 2 b f Barathea (IRE) -Adlona (USA) (Trempolino (USA)) 6377a$^8$ **>79f<**
**Alph** 7 b g Alflora (IRE) -Royal Birthday (St Paddy) 4939$^4$ **>73a<**
**Alpha Echo (USA)** 5 bb h Spinning World (USA) -Add (USA) (Spectacular Bid (USA)) 1138$^7$ **>27a<**
**Alpha Juliet (IRE)** 3 b f Victory Note (USA) -Zara s Birthday (IRE) (Waajib) 3251$^6$ 4573$^6$ 5196$^6$ **>46f<**
**Alpha Zeta** 3 b g Primo Dominie-Preening (Persian Bold) 2621$^{10}$ 3269$^9$ 3511$^{10}$ 4102$^{10}$ 4259$^9$ 5524$^{13}$ **>32f<**
**Alphecca (USA)** 3 b c Kingmambo (USA) -Limbo (USA) (A.P. Indy (USA)) (3422) 4163$^3$ 5180$^6$ **>103+f<**
**Alpine Gold (IRE)** 2 b f Montjeu (IRE) -Ski For Gold (Shirley Heights) 4234$^{12}$ 4753$^7$ (5172) (6334) 6473$^7$ **>88f<**
**Alpine Hideaway (IRE)** 11 b g Tirol-Arbour (USA) (Graustark) 2473$^{14}$ 3471$^6$ 4605$^{10}$ (4624) 5587$^7$ 5714$^7$ **>53f<**
**Alpine Special (IRE)** 3 gr g Orpen (USA) -Halomix (Linamix (FR)) 1129$^6$ 2732$^{10}$ 3614$^4$ 4678$^2$ 4830$^2$ 5058$^{12}$ 5956$^7$ **>72a 76f<**
**Alpino Chileno (ARG)** 5 gr h Alpino Fitz (ARG) -Fairyland (ARG) (Lode (USA)) 4380a$^6$ 4984a$^4$ 5506a$^4$ 5812$^8$ **>101f<**
**Alqaahir (USA)** 2 b c Swain (IRE) -Crafty Example (USA) (Crafty Prospector (USA)) 5570$^3$ **>75f<**
**Al Qudra (IRE)** 2 b c Cape Cross (IRE) -Alvilda (IRE) (Caerleon (USA)) 1686$^5$ (2852) 3672$^{12}$ 3907$^5$ 4581$^2$ 5810$^{10}$ 6042$^{15}$ **>83a 89f<**
**Alqwah (IRE)** 3 b f Danehill (USA) -Delage (Bellypha) (3209) **>79f<**
**Alrafid (IRE)** 5 ch g Halling (USA) -Ginger Tree (USA) (Dayjur (USA)) 1460$^{14}$ 1762$^5$ 2201$^6$ 2637$^2$ 3212$^7$ 4214$^{12}$ 5470$^6$ 5813$^7$ **>93a 93f<**
**Alrafidain (IRE)** 2 b c Monsun (GER) -Demeter (USA) (Diesis) 5897$^4$ 6139$^2$ **>84 f<**
**Alrida (IRE)** 5 b g Ali-Royal (IRE) -Ride Bold (USA) (J O Tobin (USA)) 3236$^4$ (4226) **>75 f<**
**Alright My Son (IRE)** 2 b c Pennekamp (USA) -Pink Stone (FR) (Bigstone (IRE)) 1853$^8$ 1996$^2$ 2439$^4$ 4089$^5$ 4524$^2$ 5090$^4$ 5417$^7$ 5719$^2$(6129) 6334$^6$ **>89f<**
**Al s Glennmay** 2 b f High Estate-Payvashooz (Ballacashtal (CAN)) 6322$^{15}$ ><
**Alsharq (IRE)** 2 b f Machiavellian (USA) -Balaabel (USA) (Sadler s Wells (USA)) 6123$^9$ 6471$^8$ **>67f<**
**Alshawameq (IRE)** 3 b g Green Desert (USA) -Azdihaar (USA) (Mr Prospector (USA)) 2135$^3$ (2692) 3001$^7$ 3671$^5$ 4171$^3$ 4780$^2$ **>94f<**
**Al Shuua** 3 b f Lomitas-Sephala (USA) (Mr Prospector (USA)) 2243$^2$ 2732$^{12}$ 3392$^4$ 5057$^{13}$ 5828$^{10}$ **>82f<**
**Al Sifaat** 3 ch f Unfuwain (USA) -Almurooj (Zafonic (USA)) 2221$^7$ 3053$^4$ **>79f<**
**Alsu (IRE)** 2 b f Fasliyev (USA) -Pourquoi Pas (IRE) (Nordico (USA)) 1686$^3$ (2074) 3286a$^{10}$ 3727$^6$ 4017$^3$ 4508$^3$ 4918$^6$ **>71f<**
**Altamirano (GER)** 5 b g Law Society (USA) -Azul (GER) (Konigsstuhl (GER)) 5808a$^6$ 6509a$^2$ **>102f<**
**Alta Petens** 2 b f Mujadil (USA) -Be Exciting (IRE) (Be My Guest (USA)) 1498$^4$ (2096) 3031$^{10}$ 3938$^{12}$ 4365$^4$ 5469$^5$ 5648$^6$ 5939$^7$ 6174$^5$ **>88f<**
**Altares** 3 b c Alhaarth (IRE) -Reach The Wind (USA) (Relaunch (USA)) 416$^{10}$ 787$^9$ 1080$^{13}$ 2395$^9$ 3809$^9$ **>38a 38df<**
**Altay** 7 b g Erin s Isle-Aliuska (IRE) (Fijar Tango (FR)) 6043$^{11}$ 6533$^3$ **>83+a 83f<**
**Altieri** 6 ch h Selkirk (USA) -Minya (USA) (Blushing Groom (FR)) (2155a) 3136a$^4$ **>117f<**
**Altinordu (TUR)** 3 b c Bold Bid-Busecik (Anshan) 5489a$^{11}$ ><
**Altitude Dancer (IRE)** 4 b g Sadler s Wells (USA) -Height Of Passion (Shirley Heights) 616$^3$ 666$^2$ (684) 899$^4$ 1112$^8$ 1173$^{11}$ **>69a 72f<**
**Alula** 2 ch f In The Wings-Aryaf (CAN) (Vice Regent (CAN)) 4712$^{10}$ 5368$^9$ 5846$^{13}$ **>54f<**
**Alunissage (USA)** 6 b h Rainbow Quest (USA) -Moonshell (IRE) (Sadler s Wells (USA)) 850a$^8$ **>113f<**
**Alvarinho Lady** 2 b f Royal Applause-Jugendliebe (IRE) (Persian Bold) (1208) 1707$^5$ 3242$^4$ 4612$^4$ 5202$^{13}$ 5391$^{19}$ **>70f<**
**Always Believe (USA)** 8 b g Carr De Naskra (USA) -Wonder Mar (USA) (Fire Dancer (USA)) 642$^9$ 989$^9$ **>57a 42f<**
**Always Daring** 5 b m Atraf-Steamy Windows (Dominion) 3148$^{14}$ 3800$^{11}$ 4257$^9$ **>11 f<**
**Always Esteemed (IRE)** 4 b g Mark Of Esteem (IRE) -Always Far (USA) (Alydar (USA)) 1623$^2$ 2066$^7$

2527$^{14}$ 3119$^{4}$ (3850) 4341$^{4}$ 4887$^{13}$ 5462$^{13}$ 6191$^{15}$ >104a 104f<

**Always First** 3 b c Barathea (IRE) -Pink Cristal (Dilum (USA)) 3323$^{8}$ 3878$^{2}$ 4229$^{3}$ 4833$^{4}$ 5611$^{8}$ >113f<

**Always Flying (USA)** 3 ch g Fly So Free (USA) -Dubiously (USA) (Jolie Jo (USA)) (563) 704$^{5}$ 1108$^{2}$ 1932$^{6}$ 2390$^{6}$ 3102$^{8}$ 3367$^{2}$ 3817$^{7}$ 5715$^{17}$6097$^{8}$ 6516$^{4}$ >67a 70f<

**Always King (FR)** 3 b c Desert King (IRE) -Always On Time (Lead On Time (USA)) 1289a$^{3}$ >100f<

**Always Mine** 2 ch f Daylami (IRE) -Mamoura (IRE) (Lomond (USA)) 6123$^{5}$ 6473$^{6}$ >88f<

**Always Rainbows (IRE)** 6 b g Rainbows For Life (CAN) -Maura s Guest (IRE) (Be My Guest (USA)) 1615$^{16}$ 1928$^{8}$ >55f<

**Always Waining (IRE)** 3 b c Unfuwain (USA) -Glenarff (USA) (Irish River (FR)) 2145$^{3}$ 2298$^{3}$ (2513) 3474$^{5}$ 3678$^{3}$ (4123) 4229$^{6}$ 4888$^{9}$ 5226$^{4}$ (6192) 6573$^{24}$ >102+f<

**Alyousufeya (IRE)** 3 ch f Kingmambo (USA) -Musicale (USA) (The Minstrel (CAN)) 1310$^{4}$ >68f<

**Alzarma** 2 b g Alzao (USA) -Skimra (Hernando (FR)) 2609$^{11}$ 3444$^{3}$ 3818$^{7}$ 4816$^{6}$ 6093$^{13}$ 6276$^{6}$ >44a 62f<

**Amalfi Coast** 5 b g Emperor Jones (USA) -Legend s Daughter (USA) (Alleged (USA)) 5110$^{8}$ 5546$^{11}$ 5714$^{17}$ 6005$^{16}$ >58f<

**Amalgam (IRE)** 2 ch f Namid-Carhue Gold (IRE) (Bob Back (USA)) 1853$^{14}$ 2300$^{16}$ 3679$^{11}$ 3883$^{5}$ 4095$^{7}$ 5825$^{10}$ >19a 45f<

**Amalie (IRE)** 2 b f Fasliyev (USA) -Princess Amalie (USA) (Rahy (USA)) 5248$^{7}$ (5521) >88+f<

**Amanda s Lad (IRE)** 4 b g Danetime (IRE) -Art Duo (Artaius (USA)) 473$^{6}$ 612$^{3}$ 681$^{4}$ 721$^{9}$ 805$^{6}$ 824$^{4}$ 954$^{6}$1025$^{6}$ 1200$^{3}$ 1453$^{5}$ 1820$^{5}$ 2130$^{10}$ 2236$^{4}$ 2658$^{2}$ 2899$^{7}$3019$^{3}$ 3249$^{5}$ 3407$^{4}$ 3512$^{5}$ 4011$^{6}$ 4105$^{3}$ 4309$^{3}$ 4422$^{9}$6007$^{4}$ >50a 61f<

**Amanderica (IRE)** 2 b f Indian Lodge (IRE) -Striking Gold (USA) (Strike The Gold (USA)) 2129$^{10}$ 3164$^{10}$ 3506$^{14}$ 4498$^{10}$ ><

**Amandus (USA)** 4 b g Danehill (USA) -Affection Affirmed (USA) (Affirmed (USA)) 1286$^{9}$ 1623$^{7}$ 2201$^{2}$ 2969$^{4}$ 3673$^{7}$ 4287$^{12}$ >83a 104f<

**Amankila (IRE)** 3 b f Revoque (IRE) -Steel Habit (Habitat) 1224$^{9}$ 1532$^{3}$ (1912) 2665$^{6}$ 2973$^{4}$ 3312$^{13}$ >46a 71f<

**Amanpuri (GER)** 6 b g Fairy King (USA) -Aratika (FR) (Zino) 491$^{12}$ 652$^{4}$ 814$^{9}$ 945$^{6}$ 1593$^{2}$ 1721$^{7}$ >37a 48f<

**Amar (CZE)** 3 ch g Beccari (USA) -Autumn (FR) (Rainbow Quest (USA)) 7131$^{4}$ 746$^{7}$ 5634$^{11}$ >9a<

**Amarette (GER)** 3 b f Monsun (GER) -Avocette (GER) (Kings Lake (USA)) (2157a) (2723a) >98f<

**Amaretto Express (IRE)** 5 b g Blues Traveller (IRE) -Cappuchino (IRE) (Roi Danzig (USA)) 5524$^{14}$ >31f<

**Amarula Ridge (IRE)** 3 b c Indian Ridge-Mail Boat (Formidable (USA)) 1256a$^{3}$ 1487a$^{3}$ 2315a$^{7}$ >98f<

**Amathia (IRE)** 5 b m Darshaan-Zivania (IRE) (Shernazar) 1952a$^{6}$ >105f<

**Amazin** 2 b c Primo Dominie-Aegean Blue (Warning) 3157$^{2}$ (3414) 3703$^{2}$ 4288$^{5}$ 5464$^{4}$ 5947$^{16}$ 6212$^{9}$ >96f<

**Amazing Grace Mary** 2 b f Dancing Spree (USA) -Frisky Miss (IRE) (Fayruz) 5555$^{12}$ 5848$^{8}$ >26f<

**Amazing Valour (IRE)** 2 b c Sinndar (IRE) -Flabbergasted (IRE) (Sadler s Wells (USA)) 5756$^{2}$ 5988$^{8}$ 6308$^{7}$ >75f<

**Amazonic** 3 b f First Trump-Mystic Beauty (IRE) (Alzao (USA)) 2486$^{13}$ ><

**Amber Fox (IRE)** 3 b f Foxhound (USA) -Paradable (IRE) (Elbio) 2290$^{5}$ 2620$^{6}$ 3019$^{5}$ 4619$^{10}$ 5691$^{3}$ 5794$^{7}$ >52f<

**Amber Legend** 3 b f Fraam-Abstone Queen (Presidium) 1008$^{9}$ 6363$^{8}$ >49 a 42f<

**Ambersong** 6 ch g Hernando (FR) -Stygian (USA) (Irish River (FR)) 467$^{3}$ 505$^{3}$ 603$^{8}$ 724$^{6}$ 1630$^{4}$ 2728$^{3}$ 3429$^{3}$3774$^{11}$ (3996) 4476$^{4}$ 5056$^{3}$ 5350$^{6}$ 5796$^{14}$ >58a 59f<

**Ambohitra (ITY)** 2 b c Roi Danzig (USA) -Annonay (IRE) (Rousillon (USA)) 6542a$^{4}$ ><

**Ambushed (IRE)** 8 b g Indian Ridge-Surprise Move (IRE) (Simply Great (FR)) 3040$^{6}$ 3367$^{4}$ 3796$^{8}$ 5514$^{10}$ >44f<

**Ameeq (USA)** 2 bb c Silver Hawk (USA) -Haniya (IRE) (Caerleon (USA)) 4743$^{3}$ 5268$^{3}$ 5696$^{9}$ >83f<

**Amelia (IRE)** 6 b m General Monash (USA) -Rose Tint (IRE) (Salse (USA)) 407$^{5}$ 510$^{2}$ 626$^{5}$ 1082$^{5}$ 1178$^{5}$ 1229$^{3}$ 1477$^{10}$(1750) 1855$^{3}$ 2875$^{2}$ 3178$^{5}$ 3680$^{3}$ 4104$^{3}$ 4331$^{8}$ >57a 67f<

**American Cousin** 9 b g Distant Relative-Zelda (USA) (Sharpen Up) (1171) 1283$^{17}$ (2175) 2461$^{16}$ 2582$^{2}$ 2975$^{5}$ 3269$^{8}$ 3894$^{14}$ 4105$^{6}$ 4247$^{6}$4509$^{5}$ 4701$^{7}$ >47a 52 f<

**American Duke (USA)** 3 b g Cryptoclearance (USA) -Prologue (USA) (Theatrical) 2790$^{14}$ 3543$^{8}$ 4443$^{2}$ 4582$^{7}$ 5293$^{5}$ (5869) 6343$^{13}$ >79+f<

**American Post** 3 br c Bering-Wells Fargo (Sadler s Wells (USA)) (1218a) (1653a) (2161a) 2680$^{6}$ 5332a$^{10}$ >117 f<

**American Touch (FR)** 2 b f Perugino (USA) -Victoire Classique (Rainbow Quest (USA)) 5313a$^{11}$ 6297a$^{7}$ >93f<

**Amethyst Rock** 6 b g Rock Hopper-Kind Lady (Kind Of Hush) 1164$^{11}$ 1511$^{3}$ (1697) 1918$^{6}$ 2185$^{2}$ 2689$^{9}$ 4190$^{16}$ >44a 39f<

**Ameyrah (IRE)** 3 b f In The Wings-Alfaaselah (GER) (Dancing Brave (USA)) 916$^{7}$ 1221$^{7}$ 1529$^{11}$ >55a 52f<

**Amiata** 4 b f Pennekamp (USA) -Star And Garter (Soviet Star (USA)) 5660a$^{12}$ >83f<

**Amica** 2 b f Averti (IRE) -Friend For Life (Lahib (USA)) 4399$^{2}$ 4670$^{2}$ (5400) 5864$^{5}$ >78f<

**Amid The Chaos (IRE)** 4 ch c Nashwan (USA) -Celebrity Style (USA) (Seeking The Gold (USA)) 2958$^{16}$ >94f<

**Amie De Mix (FR)** 3 gr f Linamix (FR) -Amen (USA) (Alydar (USA)) 4899a$^{8}$ >105f<

**Amigra (IRE)** 2 b f Grand Lodge (USA) -Beaming (Mtoto) 4936$^{16}$ 5281$^{12}$ 5741$^{4}$ >63a 28f<

**Amir Zaman** 6 ch g Salse (USA) -Colorvista (Shirley Heights) (513) 735$^{6}$ >84a 68f<

**Ammenayr (IRE)** 4 b g Entrepreneur-Katiyfa (Auction Ring (USA)) 494$^{9}$ 1132$^{8}$ 1225$^{3}$ 1294$^{5}$ 4652$^{3}$ 4917$^{6}$ 5614$^{15}$ 6157$^{5}$6293$^{6}$ >78a 83f<

**Ammirare** 2 b f Diktat-Mathaayl (USA) (Shadeed (USA)) 6008$^{8}$ 6530$^{7}$ >46f<

**Amnesty** 5 ch g Salse (USA) -Amaranthus (Shirley Heights) 449$^{8}$ 602$^{4}$ 676$^{5}$ 874$^{8}$ 966$^{11}$ 1207$^{6}$ (1274) (1522) 1675$^{5}$1857$^{2}$ 2226$^{13}$ 6311$^{15}$ 6546$^{12}$ >61a 75f<

**Among Dreams** 3 ch f Among Men (USA) -Russell Creek (Sandy Creek) 462$^{15}$ 1841$^{15}$ 2371$^{13}$ >60a 53f<

**Among Equals** 7 b g Sadler s Wells (USA) -Epicure s Garden (USA) (Affirmed (USA)) 1308$^{18}$ >83f<

**Among Friends (IRE)** 4 b g Among Men (USA) -Anita s Contessa (IRE) (Anita s Prince) 1294$^{6}$ 2091$^{9}$ 2724$^{8}$ 3141$^{7}$ 3536$^{11}$ 5258$^{14}$ 6288$^{16}$ >73a 72df<

**A Monk Swimming (IRE)** 3 br g Among Men (USA) -Sea Magic (IRE) (Distinctly North (USA)) 3146$^{4}$ 4055$^{3}$ 4499$^{7}$ >38f<

**Amourallis (IRE)** 3 b f Dushyantor (USA) -Motley (Rainbow Quest (USA)) 3328a$^{9}$ (4371a) 4893a$^{3}$ 5162a$^{9}$ >99f<

**Ampelio (IRE)** 2 ch c Grand Lodge (USA) -Bordighera (USA) (Alysheba (USA)) 5268$^{13}$ 6149$^{8}$ >53f<

**Amphitheatre (IRE)** 2 b g Titus Livius (FR) -Crimson Ring (Persian Bold) 2268$^{5}$ 2609$^{16}$ 2858$^{3}$ 3677$^{11}$ 4094$^{3}$ 4521$^{3}$ 4878$^{11}$ (5369) >60a 65f<

**Amsterdam (IRE)** 2 b c Danehill (USA) -Dathiyna (IRE) (Kris) 2045$^{5}$ 4158a$^{3}$ >97f<

**Amusement** 8 ch g Mystiko (USA) -Jolies Eaux (Shirley Heights) 2662$^{4}$ 3087$^{6}$ 3637$^{12}$ 4098$^{3}$ >49a<

**Amwell Brave** 3 b g Pyramus (USA) -Passage Creeping (IRE) (Persian Bold) 450$^{2}$ 522$^{2}$ 598$^{3}$ 739$^{3}$ 916$^{5}$ 1104$^{10}$ 1532$^{5}$1755$^{8}$ 1997$^{8}$ 2665$^{7}$ 5057$^{6}$ 5692$^{7}$ 6549$^{9}$ >59a 59f<

**Anabaa Republic (FR)** 3 b f Anabaa (USA) -Gigawatt (FR) (Double Bed (FR)) 5033a$^{3}$ 5501a$^{11}$ 5966a$^{8}$ 6437a$^{6}$ >100f<

**Anacapri** 4 b f Barathea (IRE) -Dancerette (Groom Dancer (USA)) 585$^{8}$ 668$^{6}$ 783$^{11}$ 1722$^{7}$ >20a 6f<

**Anak Pekan** 4 ch g In The Wings-Trefoil (FR) (Blakeney) (1329) (1880) 3310$^{3}$ 4270$^{8}$ 5976a$^{7}$ 6218$^{7}$ >108f<

**Analyze (FR)** 6 b g Anabaa (USA) -Bramosia (Forzando) 2030$^{2}$ 2304$^{3}$ 3127$^{5}$ 3239$^{4}$ 3872$^{11}$ (6014) 6156$^{2}$ 6395$^{4}$ >80a 81f<

**Anani (USA)** 4 ch c Miswaki (USA) -Mystery Rays (USA) (Nijinsky (CAN)) 756a$^{7}$ 922a$^{3}$ 979a$^{4}$ 1062$^{2}$ 1455$^{13}$ 2241$^{6}$ 3034$^{7}$ 4214$^{4}$4887$^{15}$ >113a 108f<

**Anatolian Queen (USA)** 3 b f Woodman (USA) -Imia (USA) (Riverman (USA)) 1830$^{3}$ 3161$^{4}$ (3759) >77f<

**Anatom** 3 ch f Komaite (USA) -Zamarra (Clantime) 865$^{7}$ 1725$^{5}$ 1985$^{4}$ 2187$^{9}$ >28a 26f<

**Anbari** 7 b g Muhtarram (USA) -Mashair (USA) (Diesis) 2163a$^{17}$ ><

**Anchor Date** 2 b c Zafonic (USA) -Fame At Last (USA) (Quest For Fame) 5536$^{2}$ 6000$^{7}$ >75 f<

**Ancient Egypt** 2 b c Singspiel (IRE) -Nekhbet (Artaius (USA)) 6077$^{10}$ >51+f<

**Ancient World (USA)** 4 bb g Spinning World (USA) -Headline (Machiavellian (USA)) 1999$^{2}$ 2588$^{2}$ (4287) 4685$^{8}$ (5134) (6109a) >120f<

**Andaad** 4 b f Alzao (USA) -Ghazwat (USA) (Riverman (USA)) 555$^{5}$ 797$^{4}$ 914$^{7}$ >53a 45f<

**Andaluza (IRE)** 3 b f Mujadil (USA) -Hierarchy (Sabrehill (USA)) 1243$^{4}$ (1597) 2112$^{3}$ 2536$^{8}$ >64a 76f<

**Andean** 3 b c Singspiel (IRE) -Anna Matrushka (Mill Reef (USA)) (1371) 2043$^{5}$ >101 f<

**Andre Chenier (IRE)** 3 b c Perugino (USA) -Almada (GER) (Lombard (GER)) 6512a$^{6}$ >96f<

**Andreyev (IRE)** 10 ch g Presidium-Missish (Mummy s Pet) 1719$^{6}$ 1929$^{11}$ 1994$^{10}$ 2260$^{14}$ 3040$^{5}$ 6466$^{11}$ >35f<

**Andronikos** 2 ch c Dr Fong (USA) -Arctic Air (Polar Falcon (USA)) (3900) 4857$^{2}$ 5649$^{7}$ (6348) >104f<

**And Toto Too** 4 br f Averti (IRE) -Divina Mia (Dowsing (USA)) 677$^{11}$ 742$^{6}$ 917$^{2}$ 960$^{4}$ 1229$^{4}$ 2064$^{2}$ 2483$^{4}$2521$^{8}$ 2788$^{2}$ 3086$^{10}$ 3457$^{4}$ 3910$^{4}$ 4067$^{2}$ (4148) 4652$^{4}$ 4773$^{7}$5454$^{6}$ 5740$^{9}$ 6579$^{8}$ >77a 88?f<

**Anduril** 3 ch c Kris-Attribute (Warning) 1120$^{6}$ 1392$^{7}$ 1641$^{3}$ 1997$^{6}$ 2361$^{4}$ 2949$^{10}$ 4443$^{8}$ 4680$^{4}$5057$^{8}$ 5773$^{17}$ >66a 70f<

**Andy Mal** 2 b f Mark Of Esteem (IRE) -Sunflower Seed (Mummy s Pet) 4606$^{8}$ 5095$^{6}$ 5301$^{8}$ >47f<

**Anfield Dream** 2 b c Lujain (USA) -Fifth Emerald (Formidable (USA)) 2574$^{6}$ 3491$^{3}$ 5865$^{12}$ >71f<

**Ange Gardien (IRE)** 3 b c King s Theatre (IRE) -Settler (Darshaan) 2722a$^{5}$ >112f<

**Angela s Girl** 2 gr f Baryshnikov (AUS) -Filly Bergere (IRE) (Sadler s Wells (USA)) 2702$^{7}$ 3140$^{9}$ 5015$^{10}$ >23f<

**Angelica Garnett** 4 ch f Desert Story (IRE) -Vanessa Bell (IRE) (Lahib (USA)) 469$^{10}$ 520$^{6}$ 815$^{10}$ 933$^{10}$ (995) 1297$^{10}$ 1858$^{17}$ >53a 39f<

**Angel Isa (IRE)** 4 b f Fayruz-Isa (Dance In Time (CAN)) 2936$^{14}$ 3428$^{11}$ 3457$^{12}$ 4004$^{7}$ 4257$^{3}$ 5793$^{3}$ 6229$^{9}$ >55a 46f<

**Angel Maid** 3 b f Forzando-Esilam (Frimley Park) 4440$^{9}$ >34f<

**Angelofthenorth** 2 b f Tomba-Dark Kristal (IRE) (Gorytus (USA)) 1616$^{3}$ 2933$^{4}$ 3408$^{3}$ 3898$^{3}$ 4700$^{3}$ 4875$^{10}$ (5800) 6174$^{22}$ >67f<

**Angelo s Pride** 3 ch c Young Ern-Considerable Charm (Charmer) 424$^{3}$ 529$^{7}$ 811$^{2}$ 877$^{3}$ 1022$^{3}$ 1078$^{3}$ (1600) 1740$^{5}$ >59a<

**Angel Rays** 2 ch f Unfuwain (USA) -Success Story (Sharrood (USA)) 6010$^{4}$ 6447$^{5}$ >66a<

**Angel River** 2 ch f Bold Edge-Riviere Rouge (Forzando) 6439$^{14}$ 6563$^{10}$ >46f<

**Angel Sprints** 2 b f Piccolo-Runs In The Family (Distant Relative) 2057$^{3}$ 2427$^{3}$ 3208$^{6}$ (3992) (5131) 5873$^{4}$ >85f<

**Angels Venture** 8 ch g Unfuwain (USA) -City Of Angels (Woodman (USA)) 919$^{11}$ >57a 57f<

**Angiolini (USA)** 7 ch g Woodman (USA) -Danse Royale (IRE) (Caerleon (USA)) 812$^{11}$ >50f<

**Anglo Saxon (USA)** 4 b c Seeking The Gold (USA) -Anna Palariva (IRE) (Caerleon (USA)) 1273$^{11}$ 2142$^{9}$ 2612$^{3}$ 3005$^{6}$ >87f<

**Angry Bark (USA)** 3 ch f Woodman (USA) -Polemic (USA) (Roberto (USA)) 5828$^{4}$ 6015$^{7}$ 6285$^{8}$ >42a 62f<

**Anicaflash** 3 b f Cayman Kai (IRE) -Sharp Top (Sharpo) 1174$^{14}$ 1420$^{8}$ >31f<

**Anisette** 3 b f Abou Zouz (USA) -Natural Gold (USA) (Gold Meridian (USA)) 444$^{3}$ 506$^{7}$ 1676$^{6}$ 2098$^{16}$ 2667$^{6}$ 2822$^{4}$ 3529$^{9}$ 3932$^{8}$3990$^{6}$ 4460$^{3}$ 5080$^{6}$ 5284$^{5}$ 5928$^{3}$ 6120$^{7}$ >43a 45f<

**Anissati** 2 ch f Machiavellian (USA) -Inchacooley (IRE) (Rhoman Rule (USA)) 6336$^{10}$ ><

**Anna Frid (GER)** 4 ch f Big Shuffle (USA) -Aerleona (IRE) (Caerleon (USA)) 1893a$^{8}$ 2744a$^{9}$ 2903a$^{8}$ 4159a$^{5}$ 5327a$^{7}$ 5661a$^{11}$ >102f<

**Anna Gayle** 3 ch f Dr Fong (USA) -Urban Dancer (IRE) (Generous (IRE)) 3843$^{12}$ 4195$^{14}$ 4775$^{5}$ 5284$^{11}$ 5643$^{9}$ >24a 40f<

**Annakita** 4 b f Unfuwain (USA) -Cuban Reef (Dowsing (USA)) 1282$^{9}$ 1693$^{7}$ 2385$^{10}$ 3429$^{4}$ (4202) 5159$^{2}$ 6231$^{3}$ >39a 49f<

**Annals** 2 b f Lujain (USA) -Anna Of Brunswick (Rainbow Quest (USA)) (5115) 5613$^{4}$ >80f<

**Annambo** 4 ch g In The Wings-Anna Matrushka (Mill Reef (USA)) 1401$^{11}$ 2365$^{8}$ >91f<

**Anna Pallida** 3 b f Sadler s Wells (USA) -Masskana (IRE) (Darshaan) 1461$^{18}$ 2060$^{2}$ 2280$^{2}$ 2653$^{3}$ (3630) 4173$^{2}$ 4906$^{8}$ 5590$^{3}$ 6069$^{6}$ >91+f<

**Anna Panna** 3 b f Piccolo-Miss Laetitia (IRE) (Entitled) 3209$^{6}$ 3486$^{2}$ 4144$^{5}$ 4580$^{5}$ 4954$^{2}$ 5136$^{8}$ >48a 76f<

**Annatalia** 2 ch f Pivotal-See You Later (Emarati (USA)) 2846$^{4}$ 3286a$^{6}$ (3570) 3938$^{21}$ 5515$^{8}$ 5797$^{8}$ 6023$^{8}$ >45a 85 f<

**Anna Umbra** 2 b f Spectrum (IRE) -Slip Lass (ITY) (Slip Anchor) 5390a$^{5}$ ><

**Anna Victoria (GER)** 4 b f Royal Solo (IRE) -A Priori (GER) (Prince Ippi (GER)) 3504a$^{13}$ 4980a$^{11}$ 5975a$^{2}$ 6107a$^{4}$ 6437a$^{8}$ >104f<

**Anna Walhaan (IRE)** 5 b g Green Desert (USA) -Queens Music (USA) (Dixieland Band (USA)) 1845$^{14}$ 2304$^{7}$ 2560$^{2}$ 2878$^{5}$ 5657$^{12}$ >7a 78f<

**Annibale Caro** 2 b c Mtoto-Isabella Gonzaga (Rock Hopper) 6289$^{11}$ 6448$^{5}$ 6536$^{8}$ >62+a<

**Annie Harvey** 3 ch f Fleetwood (IRE) -Resemblance (State Diplomacy (USA)) 1464$^{20}$ 1992$^{8}$ 2988$^{2}$ 3507$^{5}$ >75a 69f<

**Annie Miller (IRE)** 3 b f Night Shift (USA) -Lost Dream (Niniski (USA)) 3530$^{9}$ 4496$^{7}$ >29a 60f<

**Annijaz** 7 b m Alhijaz-Figment (Posse (USA)) 1855$^{2}$ 1992$^{2}$ 2215$^{4}$ 2428$^{7}$ 2886$^{14}$ 3047$^{4}$ 3301$^{6}$ 3457$^{7}$3698$^{7}$ 4083$^{14}$ 4477$^{8}$ 4771$^{14}$ 5260$^{16}$ >55a 68 f<

**Annishirani** 4 b f Shaamit (IRE) -Silent Miracle (IRE) (Night Shift (USA)) 494$^{12}$ 599$^{6}$ >83+a 68f<

**Anniversary Guest (IRE)** 5 bb m Desert King (IRE) -Polynesian Goddess (IRE) (Salmon Leap (USA)) 789$^{8}$ 1164$^{3}$ 1593$^{4}$ 1693$^{3}$ 1728$^{7}$ 2167$^{9}$ 2385$^{5}$ 2659$^{7}$ >42a 44f<

**Anolitas (GER)** 4 b c Lomitas-Auengrafin (GER) (Big Shuffle (USA)) 3134a$^{2}$ 3972a$^{2}$ 5683a$^{5}$ >108f<

**Another Bottle (IRE)** 3 b g Cape Cross (IRE) -Aster Aweke (IRE) (Alzao (USA)) 1129$^{8}$ (2419) (3452) 3797$^{3}$ (5194) >92+f<

**Another Choice (IRE)** 3 ch c Be My Guest (USA) -Gipsy Rose Lee (IRE) (Marju (IRE)) 1214$^{3}$ (1559) (1688) 2107$^{10}$ 3678$^{10}$ 3915$^{11}$ 4921$^{4}$ (5158) 5568$^{6}$ 5998$^{2}$ 6332$^{2}$6573$^{7}$ >89 f<

**Another Con (IRE)** 3 b f Lake Coniston (IRE) -Sweet Unison (USA) (One For All (USA)) 598$^{4}$ (822) 985$^{4}$ 1100$^{5}$ 1365$^{11}$ 1688$^{12}$ 2485$^{2}$ 2740$^{8}$4600$^{5}$ 4940$^{8}$ 5843$^{12}$ 6159$^{8}$ (6552) >69a 48f<

**Another Deal (FR)** 5 ch g Barathea (IRE) -Mill Rainbow (FR) (Rainbow Quest (USA)) 3988$^{9}$ 4871$^{9}$ 5175$^{11}$ >69f<

**Another Expletive** 3 b f Wizard King-French Project (IRE) (Project Manager) 529$^{8}$ 790$^{6}$ >23a 28f<

**Another Faux Pas (IRE)** 3 b f Slip Anchor-Pirie (USA) (Green Dancer (USA)) (2223) 2557$^{11}$ >82f<

**Another Glimpse** 6 b g Rudimentary (USA) -Running Glimpse (IRE) (Runnett) 912$^{4}$ (1057) 1230$^{9}$ 1537$^{9}$ 1909$^{2}$ 1937$^{3}$ 2455$^{2}$ 3326$^{9}$5379$^{8}$ 6293$^{4}$ 6554$^{3}$ >90a 78f<

**Another Legend (IRE)** 3 ch c Mark Of Esteem (IRE) -Elrayahin (Riverman (USA)) 753a$^{4}$ ><

**Another Plan (IRE)** 2 b g Entrepreneur-Tammany Hall (IRE) (Petorius) 6072$^{14}$ 6492$^{12}$ >32a 41f<

**Another Secret** 6 b m Efisio-Secrets Of Honour (Belmez (USA)) 672$^{3}$ 874$^{5}$ 914$^{4}$ >53a 57 f<

**Another Victim** 10 ch g Beveled (USA) -Ragtime Rose (Ragstone) 3307$^{6}$ 3810$^{15}$ >39a 62f<

**Another Warrior (AUS)** 6 ch h Brave Warrior (AUS) -Kate Be Good (AUS) (Semipalatinsk (USA)) 6528a$^{16}$ >105f<

**Anousa (IRE)** 3 b c Intikhab (USA) -Annaletta (Belmez (USA)) 1357$^{12}$ (1831) 2070$^{11}$ 2558$^{8}$ 2999$^{7}$ 3292$^{3}$ (3639) 3927$^{7}$ 4274$^{4}$ 5093$^{17}$5892$^{7}$ >103+f<

**Ansells Legacy (IRE)** 2 b g Charnwood Forest (IRE) -Hanzala (FR) (Akarad (FR)) 3336$^{8}$ 4930$^{12}$ 5476$^{6}$ 6139$^{9}$ >51f<

**Answer Do** 4 b f Groom Dancer (USA) -Be My Lass (IRE) (Be My Guest (USA)) 2290$^{6}$ >10f<

**Answered Promise (FR)** 5 ro g Highest Honor (FR) -Answered Prayer (Green Desert (USA)) 525$^{9}$ 605$^{7}$ 623$^{6}$ 672$^{2}$ 3127$^{3}$ 3426$^{3}$ 3771$^{8}$ >52a 64+f<

**Antananarivo (FR)** 3 b c Anabaa (USA) -Star Aline (Shardari) 4965a$^{9}$ >85f<

**Antediluvian** 3 b f Air Express (IRE) -Divina Mia (Dowsing (USA)) (3223) (3541) >104f<

**Anthemion (IRE)** 7 ch g Night Shift (USA) -New Sensitive (Wattlefield) 1345$^{10}$ 1783$^{2}$ 2078$^{11}$ 2580$^{10}$ 3039$^{9}$ 3401$^{10}$ 3797$^{5}$ 3879$^{3}$(3903) 4008$^{3}$ 4333$^{2}$ 4826$^{15}$ 5518$^{9}$ 5583$^{7}$ 5821$^{8}$ 5945$^{14}$ >71?f<

**Anthos (GER)** 3 b f Big Shuffle (USA) -Anemoni (GER) (Motley (USA)) 3275$^{5}$ 3914$^{8}$ >89f<

**Anticipating** 4 b g Polish Precedent (USA) -D Azy (Persian Bold) 1054$^{9}$ 2681$^{4}$ 3075$^{7}$ 3590$^{2}$ 4218$^{14}$ 4729$^{7}$ 5182$^{8}$ 5615$^{12}$ >84a 95f<

**Antigiotto (IRE)** 3 ch g Desert Story (IRE) -Rofool (IRE) (Fool s Holme (USA)) 1226$^{8}$ 1771$^{11}$ 2001$^{11}$ 2729$^{4}$ 3213$^{2}$ 3882$^{2}$ 4416$^{8}$ 5446$^{10}$5836$^{3}$ >47a 74f<

**Antigua Bay (IRE)** 3 b f Turtle Island (IRE) -Vilanika (FR) (Top Ville) 1400$^{11}$ 2311$^{8}$ 4653$^{2}$ 5001$^{6}$ 5551$^{3}$ 6119$^{4}$ 6399$^{7}$ >46a 76+f<

**Antioche (FR)** 2 b c Gold Away (IRE) -Tamarouna (FR) (Pampabird) 3388a$^{7}$ 5313a$^{9}$ >81f<

**Antique Rose (GER)** 4 ch f Desert King (IRE) -Alte Kunst (IRE) (Royal Academy (USA)) 2138a$^{11}$ 3973a$^{3}$ 4980a$^{10}$ 5822a$^{9}$ >95f<

**Antley Court (IRE)** 2 ch g Tagula (IRE) -Changed Around (IRE) (Doulab (USA)) 2352$^{13}$ ><

**Antoinette (USA)** 2 b f Silver Hawk (USA) -Excellentadventure (USA) (Slew City Slew (USA)) 6470$^{6}$ >75f<

**Antonio Canova** 8 ch g Komaite (USA) -Joan s Venture (Beldale Flutter (USA)) 1185$^{9}$ 1500$^{10}$ (2091) 3298$^{11}$ 4090$^{7}$ 4652$^{5}$ 5008$^{15}$ 5124$^{11}$ >86f<

**Antonio Stradivari (IRE)** 2 bb c Stravinsky (USA) -Dearest (USA) (Riverman (USA)) 4117$^{7}$ 5051$^{7}$ 5341$^{5}$ >66a 64f<

**Antonius Pius (USA)** 3 b c Danzig (USA) -Catchascatchcan (Pursuit Of Love) 1653a$^{4}$ 2161a$^{5}$ 2956$^{3}$ 3674$^{7}$ 4228$^{5}$ 5332a$^{3}$ 5782$^{9}$ 6486a$^{2}$ >121f<

**Antony Ebeneezer** 5 ch h Hurricane Sky (AUS) -Captivating (IRE) (Wolfhound (USA)) 500$^{5}$ 583$^{3}$ 724$^{9}$ 919$^{10}$ (1042) 1164$^{5}$ 1281$^{11}$ 3423$^{12}$4189$^{2}$ 5524$^{6}$ >47a 47f<

**Anuvasteel** 3 gr g Vettori (IRE) -Mrs Gray (Red Sunset) 1134$^{6}$ 1795$^{8}$ 2224$^{9}$ 5444$^{6}$ 5887$^{12}$ >83 a 79f<

**Anyhow (IRE)** 7 b m Distant Relative-Fast Chick (Henbit (USA)) 602$^{9}$ 618$^{11}$ 767$^{2}$ (962) 1053$^{4}$ 1122$^{5}$ 1684$^{4}$ 1940$^{2}$(2167) 2514$^{5}$ 2767$^{3}$ 2914$^{2}$ (3181) 3638$^{8}$ 4196$^{5}$ 4642$^{5}$ 5826$^{8}$ 6495$^{13}$ >71a 75f<

**Any News** 7 ch g Karinga Bay-D Egliere (FR) (Port Etienne (FR)) 6061$^{13}$ >71f<

**Aolus (GER)** 5 b h Winged Love (IRE) -Asuma (GER) (Surumu (GER)) 3357a$^{3}$ >110f<

**A One (IRE)** 5 b g Alzao (USA) -Anita s Contessa (IRE) (Anita s Prince) 1692$^{4}$ 2379$^{3}$ (2833) (3347) (3591) 3698$^{8}$ (4029) (4192) 4401$^{5}$ 4772$^{10}$ 5134$^{7}$ 6128$^{17}$6577$^{11}$ >53a 89 f<

**Aoninch** 4 ch f Inchinor-Willowbank (Gay Fandango (USA)) 962$^{6}$ 1135$^{11}$ 1297$^{5}$ 2167$^{8}$ 2537$^{6}$ 2767$^{8}$ 3752$^{2}$ 4019$^{6}$4642$^{2}$ 4849$^{6}$ 5203$^{10}$ 5875$^{5}$ 6450$^{9}$ >63a 71f<

**Apache Point (IRE)** 7 ch g Indian Ridge-Ausherra (USA) (Diesis) 1247$^{10}$ 1502$^{8}$ 2120$^{5}$ 2551$^{4}$ 3058$^{5}$ 3520$^{5}$ 3738$^{2}$ 4005$^{3}$4511$^{5}$ 4826$^{5}$ 5085$^{5}$ 5235$^{5}$ 5557$^{9}$ 5859$^{5}$ 6201$^{5}$ >9a 73f<

**A P Adventure (USA)** 3 b f A.P. Indy (USA) -Nataliano (USA) (Fappiano (USA)) $^{6}$ >106a<

**Apeiron (GER)** 3 b c Devil River Peek (USA) -Asuma (GER) (Surumu (GER)) (1656a) 2510a$^{10}$ 3565a$^{9}$ 4284a$^{3}$ 4965a$^{4}$ 5683a$^{7}$ 6508a$^{5}$ >109f<

**Aperitif** 3 ch g Pivotal-Art Deco Lady (Master Willie) 2069$^{7}$ 2847$^{4}$ 3671$^{3}$ 3896$^{3}$ (4679) 5265$^{7}$ 5607$^{3}$ (5835) 6193$^{10}$ 6284$^{4}$ >72a 98+f<

**Apetite** 2 ch g Timeless Times (USA) -Petite Elite (Anfield) 4175$^{10}$ 4559$^{9}$ 4776$^{10}$ 5097$^{2}$ (5192) 5314$^{10}$ 5630$^{10}$ 5989$^{11}$ 6093$^{14}$ >64f<

**Apex** 3 ch c Efisio-Royal Loft (Homing) (1841) 2306$^{5}$ 2692$^{12}$ 3750$^{3}$ 4126$^{2}$ (4717) 5224$^{11}$ 5762$^{10}$

6191$^{13}$ >**93f**<

**Apokalypse (GER)** **3** b f Lomitas-Allure (Bustino) 1983a$^{11}$ >**79f**<

**Apollo Gee (IRE)** **3** b g Spectrum (IRE) -Suspiria (IRE) (Glenstal (USA)) *1422$^{13}$ 1478$^{8}$* >**14a 60f**<

**Apologies** **2** b c Robellino (USA) -Mistook (USA) (Phone Trick (USA)) 1128$^{7}$ (1324) 1819$^{4}$ 3677$^{13}$ 3924$^{6}$ 4508$^{10}$ 5143$^{3}$ 5363$^{6}$ 5617$^{3}$*6022$^{3}$* >**77a 70f**<

**Appalachian Trail (IRE)** **3** b g Indian Ridge-Karinski (USA) (Palace Music (USA)) 1104$^{3}$ (1420) 1585$^{2}$ 1900$^{14}$ 2295$^{4}$ (3053) 3542$^{6}$ 3943$^{6}$ 4570$^{5}$ 5920$^{5}$ >**96f**<

**Appetina** **3** b f Perugino (USA) -Tina Heights (Shirley Heights) 2243$^{5}$ 2729$^{5}$ 3261$^{4}$ 4049$^{4}$ 4698$^{14}$ 5156$^{10}$ 5547$^{14}$ >**66f**<

**Apple Green (DEN)** **6** ch g Perceive Arrogance (USA) -Ellen James (USA) (Plugged Nickle (USA)) 6379a$^{9}$ >**86f**<

**Apple Of My Eye** **2** b f Fraam-Fresh Fruit Daily (Reprimand) 2884$^{10}$ 3992$^{4}$ (4399) 4914$^{10}$ 5391$^{18}$ >**80f**<

**Appolonious** **3** b g Case Law-Supreme Thought (Emarati (USA)) *1015$^{7}$ 1226$^{7}$* 4811$^{7}$ 5378$^{9}$ 5845$^{6}$ 6288$^{11}$ >**53a 55f**<

**April Ace** **8** ch g First Trump-Champ D Avril (Northfields (USA)) *539$^{7}$* >**4a 27f**<

**April Shannon** **2** b f Tipsy Creek (USA) -Westering (Auction Ring (USA)) 5376$^{16}$ 5872$^{11}$ >**9f**<

**Apron (IRE)** **3** b f Grand Lodge (USA) -Sultana (Unfuwain (USA)) 1440$^{9}$ 2059$^{9}$ 2911$^{11}$ 6310$^{12}$ 6564$^{7}$ >**63f**<

**Apsara** **3** br f Groom Dancer (USA) -Ayodhya (IRE) (Astronef) 3204$^{2}$ (3607) 4368$^{4}$ >**85f**<

**Apsis** **3** b c Barathea (IRE) -Apogee (Shirley Heights) 5667a$^{2}$ 6263a$^{5}$ >**109+f**<

**Aqribaa (IRE)** **6** b g Pennekamp (USA) -Karayb (IRE) (Last Tycoon) 5557$^{13}$ 5714$^{15}$ >**64?f**<

**Aqualung** **3** b c Desert King (IRE) -Aquarelle (Kenmare (FR)) 1683$^{12}$ (2144) 2896$^{8}$ 5462$^{15}$ >**90f**<

**Aqua Pura (GER)** **5** b g Acatenango (GER) -Actraphane (Shareef Dancer (USA)) *750$^{8}$* >**18a**<

**A Qui Le Tour** **2** b g Pyramus (USA) -Dolphin Beech (IRE) (Dolphin Street (FR)) 3805$^{10}$ *4334$^{8}$* 6060$^{8}$ >**40f**<

**Arabian Ana (IRE)** **2** b c Night Shift (USA) -Al Shaqrah (USA) (Sir Ivor (USA)) 3876$^{6}$ (4135) 4907$^{4}$ 5188$^{4}$ >**74f**<

**Arabian Dancer** **2** b f Dansili-Hymne (FR) (Saumarez) 2550$^{2}$ 3031$^{6}$ 3599$^{5}$ 4498$^{3}$ 4866$^{5}$ (5334) 5648$^{2}$ 6174$^{4}$ >**83f**<

**Arabian Knight (IRE)** **4** ch g Fayruz-Cheerful Knight (IRE) (Mac s Imp (USA)) *987$^{12}$ 1180$^{8}$* 1313$^{7}$ 1504$^{9}$ 1909$^{8}$ 2166$^{13}$ 5411$^{20}$ >**65 a 65f**<

**Arabian Moon (IRE)** **8** ch g Barathea (IRE) -Excellent Alibi (USA) (Exceller (USA)) (4799) 5074$^{8}$ 5456$^{7}$ *6025$^{9}$* >**62a 73f**<

**Arabian Spell (IRE)** **2** ch f Desert Prince (IRE) -Truly Bewitched (USA) (Affirmed (USA)) 6529a$^{3}$ >**102f**<

**Arabie** **6** b g Polish Precedent (USA) -Always Friendly (High Line) 692a$^{11}$ *757a$^{12}$* 922a$^{12}$ 1328$^{17}$ 3871$^{4}$ *4093$^{11}$* >**21a 111f**<

**Aragon Dancer** **3** b g Aragon-Jambo (Rambo Dancer (CAN)) *452$^{8}$* >**2a 12f**<

**Aragon s Boy** **4** ch g Aragon-Fancier Bit (Lion Cavern (USA)) 2084$^{17}$ 2776$^{11}$ (3171) 3555$^{7}$ 4142$^{4}$ 4435$^{11}$ 5364$^{7}$ 5859$^{13}$ >**73f**<

**Arakan (USA)** **4** br c Nureyev (USA) -Far Across (Common Grounds) (1409) 2021$^{3}$ 2316a$^{2}$ 2957$^{12}$ (3318) >**119 f**<

**Aramat** **2** b f Cigar-Winze Kible (Baldhu Cavalier) 5003$^{14}$ *6010$^{14}$ 6155$^{10}$* >**27a**<

**Aramram (USA)** **5** b h Danzig (USA) -Felawnah (USA) (Mr Prospector (USA)) *689a$^{6}$* >**93a 111f**<

**Aravis (FR)** **7** b g Subotica (FR) -Annee De La Femme (IRE) (Common Grounds) 633a$^{6}$ >**94f**<

**Arawan (IRE)** **4** b g Entrepreneur-Asmara (USA) (Lear Fan (USA)) 1604$^{10}$ 1821$^{20}$ 2142$^{19}$ 2551$^{14}$ 2982$^{8}$ 3470$^{10}$ 4008$^{10}$ 6201$^{7}$ >**55f**<

**Arbella** **2** ch f Primo Dominie-Kristal Bridge (Kris) 3627$^{2}$ 4234$^{4}$ 4552$^{4}$ 5373$^{3}$ >**95f**<

**Arbors Little Girl** **2** b f Paris House-Arbor Ealis (IRE) (Woods Of Windsor (USA)) (4620) (5509) 5617$^{5}$ 5910$^{3}$ >**66f**<

**Arcalis** **4** gr g Lear Fan (USA) -Aristocratique (Cadeaux Genereux) (2258) (3756) >**110f**<

**Arc Bleu (GER)** **3** ch c Monsagem (USA) -Antala (FR) (Antheus (USA)) 6513a$^{2}$ >**103f**<

**Arc El Ciel (ARG)** **6** b g Fitzcarraldo (ARG) -Ardoise (USA) (Diamond Prospect (USA)) *(488) 564$^{3}$ 641$^{5}$ 677$^{9}$ 775$^{7}$ 862$^{3}$ 961$^{11}$ 1013$^{6}$* >**87a 55f**<

**Arc En Ciel** **6** b g Rainbow Quest (USA) -Nadia Nerina (CAN) (Northern Dancer) *413$^{4}$ 645$^{8}$* >**53a 79f**<

**Archduke Ferdinand (FR)** **6** ch g Dernier Empereur (USA) -Lady Norcliffe (USA) (Norcliffe (CAN)) 1880$^{13}$ 2240$^{2}$ 2684$^{14}$ >**93f**<

**Archenko** **4** b g Weldnaas (USA) -Silverdale Rose (Nomination) 1344$^{8}$ 1662$^{7}$ 1786$^{6}$ 2348$^{5}$ >**41f**<

**Archeology (USA)** **2** bb f Seeking The Gold (USA) -Caress (USA) (Storm Cat (USA)) 5943$^{5}$ 6196$^{9}$ *6446$^{2}$* >**72+a 72f**<

**Archerfield (IRE)** **3** ch f Docksider (USA) -Willow River (CAN) (Vice Regent (CAN)) *580$^{2}$ 741$^{2}$ 890$^{3}$* 1309$^{11}$ 2577$^{17}$ 3171$^{2}$ 3441$^{3}$ 3875$^{3}$4264$^{4}$ 5259$^{4}$ 5748$^{9}$ >**75 a 64f**<

**Arch Folly** **2** b g Silver Patriarch (IRE) -Folly Fox (Alhijaz) 4584$^{7}$ 5256$^{6}$ 6226$^{7}$ >**61f**<

**Archias (GER)** **5** b g Darshaan-Arionette (Lombard (GER)) 5343$^{7}$ >**65f**<

**Archie Babe (IRE)** **8** ch g Archway (IRE) -Frensham Manor (Le Johnstan) 1103$^{10}$ (1245) 1282$^{5}$ 2121$^{13}$ 5229$^{11}$ 5773$^{15}$ 6047$^{7}$ 6527$^{9}$ >**55a 75f**<

**Archie Clarke (GER)** **4** b g Taishan (GER) -Anthela (GER) (Orfano (GER)) *6481$^{13}$* ><

**Archie Glenn** **2** b c Lake Coniston (IRE) -La Ballerine (Lafontaine (USA)) 2370$^{7}$ 2736$^{15}$ 5494$^{4}$ 5689$^{2}$ 6125$^{8}$ >**77f**<

**Archie Wright** **2** ch c Lake Coniston (IRE) -Roisin Clover (Faustus (USA)) 4730$^{17}$ 5198$^{7}$ 5398$^{4}$ 6270$^{7}$ >**48 f**<

**Archirondel** **6** b g Bin Ajwaad (IRE) -Penang Rose (NZ) (Kingdom Bay (NZ)) *464$^{6}$ 874$^{10}$* 1103$^{U}$ 1245$^{14}$ 1393$^{8}$ 1993$^{2}$ (2551) 2879$^{10}$ 3149$^{2}$(3369) 3881$^{5}$ 4397$^{5}$ >**59a 72f**<

**Arch Rebel (USA)** **3** b c Arch (USA) -Sheba s Step (USA) (Alysheba (USA)) 5357a$^{3}$ >**101f**<

**Arc Of Light (IRE)** **2** b c Spectrum (IRE) -Siwaayib (Green Desert (USA)) 2310$^{5}$ 3808$^{7}$ 4567$^{11}$ >**63f**<

**Arc Royal (GER)** **7** ch h Big Shuffle (USA) -Alepha (Celestial Storm (USA)) 5255a$^{12}$ >**96f**<

**Arctic Blue** **4** b g Polar Prince (IRE) -Miss Sarajane (Skyliner) 3461$^{9}$ *4129$^{10}$* >**51a 67f**<

**Arctic Burst (USA)** **4** bb g Royal Academy (USA) -Polar Bird (Thatching) 1391$^{12}$ 1500$^{15}$ 1765$^{30}$ *2404$^{12}$* 3010$^{18}$ 3623$^{11}$ 4085$^{14}$ 4181$^{12}$4782$^{12}$ >**37a 37f**<

**Arctic Cove** **3** b g Vettori (IRE) -Sundae Girl (USA) (Green Dancer (USA)) 5123$^{17}$ ><

**Arctic Desert** **4** b g Desert Prince (IRE) -Thamud (IRE) (Lahib (USA)) *1065$^{13}$* 1385$^{18}$ 3036$^{28}$ 3324$^{14}$ 3698$^{18}$ 4122$^{11}$ *4602$^{6}$* (4969)5135$^{6}$ 5419$^{2}$ 5614$^{9}$ 6070$^{9}$ 6477$^{2}$ >**68a 85 f**<

**Arctic Silk** **3** ch f Selkirk (USA) -Cape Verdi (IRE) (Caerleon (USA)) 3204$^{10}$ 3916$^{3}$ 4168$^{2}$ 4691$^{9}$ >**82f**<

**Ardasnails (IRE)** **2** b g Spectrum (IRE) -Fey Lady (IRE) (Fairy King (USA)) 3259$^{12}$ 4638$^{12}$ >**27f**<

**Ardbeg (IRE)** **5** b g Lake Coniston (IRE) -Belle De Cadix (IRE) (Law Society (USA)) *1953a$^{9}$* ><

**Ardere (USA)** **3** ch f El Prado (IRE) -Flaming Torch (Rousillon (USA)) 5445$^{7}$ >**36f**<

**Ardkeel Lass (IRE)** **3** ch f Fumo Di Londra (IRE) -Wot-A-Noise (IRE) (Petorius) 2610$^{9}$ 3084$^{14}$ 3344$^{2}$ 3772$^{4}$ 5040$^{5}$ 5337$^{12}$ 5412$^{6}$ >**62f**<

**Areias (GER)** **6** b h Second Set (IRE) -Appena La (IRE) (Tirol) 2466a$^{5}$ 3552a$^{3}$ 4596a$^{4}$ 5255a$^{10}$ (6379a) >**111f**<

**Are You There** **3** b f Presidium-Scoffera (Scottish Reel) *587$^{9}$ 744$^{6}$ 828$^{4}$ 845$^{9}$* >**38a 36f**<

**Arfinnit (IRE)** **3** b g College Chapel-Tidal Reach (USA) (Kris S (USA)) 1129$^{19}$ 1270$^{3}$ 1841$^{12}$ 2061$^{6}$ 2266$^{5}$ (2389) 2657$^{6}$ 2839$^{6}$ (3037) 3338$^{6}$3558$^{4}$ 3772$^{8}$ 4052$^{8}$ 4489$^{7}$ 4617$^{2}$ 5040$^{4}$ 5117$^{6}$ 6079$^{16}$6246$^{4}$ >**67f**<

**Argent** **3** b g Barathea (IRE) -Red Tiara (USA) (Mr Prospector (USA)) *1179$^{P}$* 1201$^{8}$ 1959$^{2}$ 2176$^{7}$ 3002$^{15}$ 4008$^{8}$ 4332$^{2}$ 4989$^{3}$ >**44a 50f**<

**Argentum** **3** b g Sillery (USA) -Frustration (Salse (USA)) 3161$^{10}$ 3666$^{5}$ (4853) 5560$^{2}$ 5875$^{8}$ >**62f**<

**Argonaut** **4** b g Rainbow Quest (USA) -Chief Bee (Chief s Crown (USA)) 1286$^{6}$ 4123$^{3}$ 4345$^{7}$ 5093$^{4}$ >**96f**<

**Arian** **2** b f Josr Algarhoud (IRE) -Hope Chest (Kris) 6118$^{5}$ >**70+f**<

**Ariane Star (IRE)** **2** b f Marju (IRE) -Northgate Raver (Absalom) 3157$^{9}$ 3532$^{11}$ 4197$^{5}$ 4521$^{11}$ >**53f**<

**Arian s Lad** **3** b g Prince Sabo-Arian Da (Superlative) 2165$^{8}$ 2586$^{12}$ *2815$^{7}$* 4869$^{3}$ >**21a 52f**<

**Aricia (IRE)** **3** b f Nashwan (USA) -Rahaam (USA) (Secreto (USA)) 1400$^{8}$ (2505) 3033$^{10}$ 4356a$^{11}$ *6497$^{6}$* >**85a 94f**<

**Aries (GER)** **4** ch f Big Shuffle (USA) -Auenlust (GER) (Surumu (GER)) 2368$^{9}$ *2881$^{14}$* >**43a 80f**<

**Ariesanne (IRE)** **3** ch f Primo Dominie-Living Legend (ITY) (Archway (IRE)) 4758$^{3}$ 5104$^{7}$ 5306$^{6}$ >**33f**<

**Ariodante** **2** b g Groom Dancer (USA) -Maestrale (Top Ville) 3157$^{3}$ (3633) 4166$^{4}$ 4890$^{12}$ >**77f**<

**Aristaios (GER)** **3** b c Alkalde (GER) -Aerleona (IRE) (Caerleon (USA)) 2335a$^{7}$ 3552a$^{9}$ >**89f**<

**Arjay** **6** b g Shaamit (IRE) -Jenny s Call (Petong) *1097$^{12}$* 1620$^{15}$ *2007$^{3}$ 2456$^{5}$* 2551$^{3}$ *2816$^{12}$* 3929$^{10}$ >**48a 52f**<

**Ark Admiral** **5** b g Inchinor-Kelimutu (Top Ville) 3412$^{12}$ 3747$^{10}$ 4479$^{11}$ >**78df**<

**Arkando (GER)** **3** ch c Kornado-Advantage (GER) (Glow (USA)) 2926a$^{6}$ >**89f**<

**Arkholme** **3** b g Robellino (USA) -Free Spirit (IRE) (Caerleon (USA)) 1799$^{4}$ 2683$^{13}$ 3271$^{2}$ (3689) 4237$^{2}$ 4648$^{9}$ 5004$^{3}$ (5275) 5698$^{4}$ 5886$^{4}$ >**88f**<

**Arlecchina (GER)** **4** b f Mtoto-Arctic Appeal (IRE) (Ahonoora) 1776a$^{3}$ 2138a$^{7}$ 2336a$^{6}$ 3434a$^{3}$ 3792a$^{4}$ 4378a$^{9}$ 4984a$^{9}$ 5488a$^{9}$ >**101f**<

**Arlekinada (IRE)** **5** ch m Lycius (USA) -Arctic Appeal (IRE) (Ahonoora) 3434a$^{6}$ >**92f**<

**Armagh (IRE)** **3** b f Entrepreneur-Aunt Hester (IRE) (Caerleon (USA)) 6513a$^{11}$ >**22f**<

**Armagnac** **6** b g Young Ern-Arianna Aldini (Habitat) 1106$^{19}$ 1354$^{7}$ 1825$^{8}$ 2094$^{3}$ 2261$^{6}$ 2391$^{8}$ 3298$^{10}$ 3691$^{2}$3941$^{3}$ 4047$^{2}$ 4553$^{3}$ 4742$^{7}$ 5299$^{11}$ (5444) 5614$^{7}$ 6070$^{5}$ >**78a 89f**<

**Armand (GER)** **3** b c Winged Love (IRE) -Arpista (GER) (Chief Singer) 1656a$^{7}$ 2926a$^{8}$ >**88f**<

**Armatore (USA)** **4** b g Gone West (USA) -Awesome Account (USA) (Lyphard (USA)) 4028$^{11}$ 5459$^{13}$ >**64?f**<

**Armentieres** **3** b f Robellino (USA) -Perfect Poppy (Shareef Dancer (USA)) *416$^{6}$* 3989$^{8}$ 4628$^{7}$ 4853$^{6}$ 5036$^{2}$ 5260$^{3}$ 5411$^{4}$ 5733$^{7}$(6146) 6548$^{7}$ >**50a 59f**<

**Arms Acrossthesea** **5** b g Namaqualand (USA) -Zolica (Beveled (USA)) 1867$^{2}$ (2214) *(2456)* 2547$^{4}$ 3128$^{10}$ *4096$^{7}$* (4458) 4655$^{6}$ 5374$^{17}$ 5622$^{13}$ >**66a 61f**<

**Army Of Angels (IRE)** **2** ch c King s Best (USA) -Angelic Sounds (IRE) (The Noble Player (USA)) 3643$^{2}$ (4239) 5594$^{2}$ >**94 f**<

**Arogant Prince** **7** ch g Aragon-Versaillesprincess (Legend Of France (USA)) *423$^{4}$ 509$^{4}$ 608$^{7}$ 642$^{6}$ 654$^{3}$ (762) 799$^{10}$ (904) 968$^{7}$* 1131$^{8}$ *1180$^{7}$* (1516) *1738$^{11}$* 2246$^{17}$ 3260$^{6}$ *3800$^{12}$6493$^{13}$ 6559$^{13}$* >**67a 67f**<

**Around Alone** **7** b h Rudimentary (USA) -Mistress Thames (Sharpo) 2340a$^{2}$ >**109f**<

**Arous (FR)** **2** br f Desert King (IRE) -Moneefa (Darshaan) 5848$^{7}$ >**59+f**<

**Arran** **4** ch g Selkirk (USA) -Humble Pie (Known Fact (USA)) 2596$^{9}$ 3049$^{3}$ 3626$^{9}$ *4096$^{2}$ (4190) 4602$^{9}$* 4852$^{5}$ 5260$^{13}$6124$^{8}$ >**70a 59f**<

**Arran Scout (IRE)** **3** b g Piccolo-Evie Hone (IRE) (Royal Academy (USA)) 1972$^{3}$ 2900$^{10}$ 6141$^{11}$ 6350$^{2}$ >**78f**<

**Arrears (USA)** **4** br c Barkerville (USA) -Granny Goodrich (USA) (Pool Court (USA)) 6513a$^{8}$ >**69f**<

**Arresting** **4** b g Hector Protector (USA) -Misbelief (Shirley Heights) (1221) 1832$^{11}$ 2691$^{6}$ 3095$^{5}$ 6150$^{10}$ >**91f**<

**Arrgatt (IRE)** **3** gr c Intikhab (USA) -Nuit Chaud (USA) (Woodman (USA)) 2311$^{3}$ 2555$^{2}$ 3057$^{2}$ (3899) 4582$^{4}$ >**83f**<

**Arrivato** **2** b f Efisio-Beloved Visitor (USA) (Miswaki (USA)) *6447$^{9}$* >**65+a**<

**Arrjook** **3** b c Intikhab (USA) -Chief Ornament (USA) (Chief s Crown (USA)) 3094$^{4}$ >**69f**<

**Arrow** **5** b g Pivotal-Cremets (Mummy s Pet) *966$^{9}$* >**46a 56f**<

**Arrow (GER)** **2** b c Dashing Blade-Anemoni (GER) (Motley (USA)) 6256a$^{6}$ ><

**Arry Dash** **4** b g Fraam-Miletrian Cares (IRE) (Hamas (IRE)) *915$^{4}$* 1114$^{9}$ 1321$^{2}$ 1540$^{13}$ 2474$^{7}$ 2789$^{3}$ 3097$^{7}$ 3442$^{6}$3842$^{11}$ 4301$^{6}$ 4719$^{2}$ 4903$^{3}$ 5153$^{2}$ 5297$^{3}$ 5423$^{2}$ 5568$^{5}$5821$^{7}$ 6128$^{8}$ (6185) >**87a 83f**<

**Artadi** **2** b f Bien Bien (USA) -Gibaltarik (IRE) (Jareer (USA)) 1299$^{7}$ 1905$^{3}$ 3986$^{5}$ 4482$^{6}$ *4999$^{5}$* 5218$^{4}$ 5369$^{6}$ 5593$^{6}$ >**28a 49f**<

**Art Affair (GER)** **3** b f Germany (USA) -A Real Work Of Art (IRE) (Keen) 5168a$^{9}$ >**64f**<

**Arte Et Labore (IRE)** **4** b f Raphane (USA) -Bouffant (High Top) *652$^{8}$* >**9a 9 f**<

**Art Elegant** **2** b c Desert Prince (IRE) -Elegant (IRE) (Marju (IRE)) 4290$^{10}$ 5269$^{5}$ 5729$^{7}$ >**71 f**<

**Art Expert (FR)** **6** b g Pursuit Of Love-Celtic Wing (Midyan (USA)) *3281$^{7}$* >**24a**<

**Art Eyes (USA)** **2** ch f Halling (USA) -Careyes (IRE) (Sadler s Wells (USA)) 6123$^{3}$ >**74+f**<

**Arthurs Dream (IRE)** **2** b c Desert Prince (IRE) -Blueprint (USA) (Shadeed (USA)) 4081$^{13}$ 6531$^{7}$ >**54f**<

**Arthur Wardle (USA)** **2** b g Stravinsky (USA) -Avanti Sassa (GER) (Sassafras (FR)) 2780$^{2}$ 3228$^{5}$ 3588$^{13}$ 4235$^{6}$ 5377$^{13}$ >**69f**<

**Artic Fox** **2** b g Robellino (USA) -Lets Be Fair (Efisio) 3233$^{5}$ 3758$^{12}$ 4761$^{13}$ 5227$^{9}$ 5858$^{8}$ 6091$^{5}$ 6522$^{5}$ >**60f**<

**Articulation** **3** b c Machiavellian (USA) -Stiletta (Dancing Brave (USA)) 3603$^{4}$ 4087$^{2}$ (4492) >**88f**<

**Artie** **5** b g Whittingham (IRE) -Calamanco (Clantime) 1106$^{13}$ 1361$^{7}$ 1774$^{2}$ (1956) 2041$^{18}$ 3509$^{15}$ (3713) 4324$^{7}$ 4538$^{16}$ 4759$^{7}$4837$^{14}$ 5605$^{7}$ 5799$^{4}$ 6205$^{5}$ 6517$^{5}$ >**95f**<

**Artie Schiller (USA)** **3** b c El Prado (IRE) -Hidden Light (USA) (Majestic Light (USA)) 6486a$^{12}$ >**110f**<

**Artie s Lad (IRE)** **3** ch g Danehill Dancer (IRE) -Bold Avril (IRE) (Persian Bold) 1530$^{5}$ >**59f**<

**Artiste Royal (IRE)** **3** b c Danehill (USA) -Agathe (USA) (Manila (USA)) 4965a$^{8}$ 5667a$^{6}$ >**102f**<

**Artisticimpression (IRE)** **3** b c Rainbow Quest (USA) -Entice (FR) (Selkirk (USA)) *1015$^{10}$* 1360$^{11}$ >**29a 63f**<

**Artistic Lad** **4** ch c Peintre Celebre (USA) -Maid For The Hills (Indian Ridge) 5436$^{5}$ >**89+f**<

**Artistic Style** **4** b c Anabaa (USA) -Fine Detail (IRE) (Shirley Heights) 1711$^{8}$ 1972$^{6}$ 2122$^{8}$ 2218$^{7}$ (3579) 4327$^{3}$ (4808) (5085) (5584) 5773$^{2}$ (6115) 6573$^{6}$ >**99+f**<

**Artist Rifle (IRE)** **3** b g Orpen (USA) -Rosy Scintilla (IRE) (Thatching) 3094$^{12}$ >**21f**<

**Artistry** **4** b f Night Shift (USA) -Arriving (Most Welcome) *(1229)* 1372$^{5}$ 1531$^{10}$ 3841$^{10}$ 4199$^{5}$ *4602$^{2}$* >**69a 63f**<

**Artists Retreat** **5** ch m Halling (USA) -Jumairah Sunset (Be My Guest (USA)) 4476$^{11}$ 5145$^{10}$ >**40f**<

**Art Legend** **2** b g Indian Ridge-Solo Performance (IRE) (Sadler s Wells (USA)) 1331$^{4}$ 2111$^{12}$ 4689$^{10}$ >**54f**<

**Art Master (USA)** **3** b c Royal Academy (USA) -True Flare (USA) (Capote (USA)) (3163a) >**109f**<

**Art Moderne (USA)** **4** ch c Woodman (USA) -Action Francaise (USA) (Nureyev (USA)) 1163a$^{2}$ 2923a$^{10}$ 3769a$^{8}$ >**111f**<

**Art Royal (USA)** **2** b c Royal Academy (USA) -Chelsea Green (USA) (Key To The Mint (USA)) 5373$^{5}$ 5915$^{18}$ >**77f**<

**Art Trader (USA)** **3** b c Arch (USA) -Math (USA) (Devil s Bag (USA)) 3915$^{2}$ (4271) >**108+f**<

**Arturius (IRE)** **2** b c Anabaa (USA) -Steeple (Selkirk (USA)) 6440$^{6}$ >**59f**<

**Artzola (IRE)** **4** b f Alzao (USA) -Polistatic (Free State) *1102$^{9}$ 4339$^{12}$ 4517$^{7}$* 5791$^{7}$ >**43a 54f**<

**Asaateel (IRE)** **2** br c Unfuwain (USA) -Alabaq (USA) (Riverman (USA)) 3931$^{10}$ 4689$^{8}$ 5173$^{4}$ 5655$^{9}$ >**65f**<

**Asadara** **2** ch f Timeless Times (USA) -Julie s Gift (Presidium) 4175$^{6}$ >**47f**<

**Asaleeb** **3** b f Alhaarth (IRE) -Gharam (USA) (Green Dancer (USA)) 2805$^{2}$ (3460) (4642) 5303$^{15}$ >**91 f**<

**Asawer (IRE)** **2** b f Darshaan-Sassy Bird (USA) (Storm Bird (CAN)) 6336$^{3}$ >**67+f**<

**Asbo** **4** b f Abou Zouz (USA) -Star (Most Welcome) 3887$^{5}$ 4459$^{4}$ 5147$^{3}$ 5618$^{5}$ 6117$^{6}$ *6273$^{3}$ 6493$^{4}$* >**63a 66f**<

**Ascertain (IRE)** **3** ch g Intikhab (USA) -Self Assured (IRE) (Ahonoora) *(522) 704$^{2}$ (913) 1143a$^{5}$* >**103a 23f**<

**Ascetic Silver (FR)** **4** ch c Kendor (FR) -Snowdrop Ii (FR) (Niniski (USA)) 980a$^{10}$ ><

**Ascot Dream (IRE)** **2** b f Pennekamp (USA) -Kafayef (USA) (Secreto (USA)) 3790a$^{5}$ 4964a$^{6}$ 5313a$^{7}$ 6320a$^{5}$ >**84f**<

**As Des As (FR)** **5** b g Homme De Loi (IRE) -Asania (FR) (Ace Of Aces (USA)) 911a$^{10}$ ><

**Ashado (USA)** **3** b f Saint Ballado (CAN) -Goulash (USA) (Mari s Brook (USA)) *( ) (6484a)* >**120a**<

**As Handsome Does** **2** ch g Handsome Ridge-Fast To Light (Pharly (FR)) 3444$^{2}$ 3758$^{13}$ 4446$^{13}$ 5240$^{7}$ >**66df**<

**Asharon** **2** b c Efisio-Arriving (Most Welcome) 4807$^{7}$ 5023$^{6}$ 5396$^{6}$ 5719$^{13}$ 6442$^{5}$ 6574$^{17}$ >**73f**<

**Ash Bold (IRE)** **7** ch g Persian Bold-Pasadena Lady (Captain James) 4624$^{4}$ 5187$^{2}$ 6142$^{9}$ *6402$^{3}$* >**51a 48f**<

**Ashdown Express (IRE)** **5** ch g Ashkalani (IRE) -Indian Express (Indian Ridge) 1409$^{3}$ 2021$^{12}$ 2373$^{2}$ 3073$^{7}$ 3674$^{2}$ 4595a$^{4}$ 5289$^{9}$ 5982a$^{13}$6190$^{11}$ >**121f**<

**Ashes (IRE)** **2** b f General Monash (USA) -Wakayi (Persian Bold) 1670$^{11}$ 2023$^{5}$ 2388$^{4}$ 5800$^{10}$ 6270$^{5}$ 6544$^{6}$ >**61f**<

**Ash Hab (USA)** **6** b g A.P. Indy (USA) -Histoire (FR) (Riverman (USA)) 4146$^{10}$ *5221$^{11}$ 5645$^{14}$* >**42f**<

**Ashkal Way (IRE)** **2** ch c Ashkalani (IRE) -Golden Way (IRE) (Cadeaux Genereux) 5696$^{5}$ >**78f**<

**Ashkawar (IRE)** **5** ch h Rudimentary (USA) -Ashkara (IRE) (Chief Singer) 5668a$^{6}$ >**101f**<

**Ash Laddie (IRE)** **4** ch g Ashkalani (IRE) -Lady Ellen (Horage) 1820$^{20}$ 2551$^{11}$ 2943$^{12}$ *3804$^{13}$* 5450$^{16}$ >**28a 37f**<

**Ashstanza** **3** gr g Ashkalani (IRE) -Poetry In Motion (IRE) (Ballad Rock) *447$^{4}$ 752$^{3}$ 957$^{4}$* 1222$^{13}$ 2688$^{10}$ 2932$^{9}$ *6499$^{14}$* >**64a 39f**<

**Ashtaroute (USA)** **4** b f Holy Bull (USA) -Beating The Buzz (IRE) (Bluebird (USA)) *432$^{6}$* 2133$^{9}$ 3508$^{5}$ >**35a 61f**<

**Ashtree Belle** **5** b m Up And At Em-Paris Babe (Teenoso (USA)) *410$^{2}$* >**84a 76f**<

**Ashwaaq (USA)** **3** b f Gone West (USA) -Wasnah (USA) (Nijinsky (CAN)) (1419) 5652$^{15}$ 5990$^{7}$ >**77f**<

**Asian Heights** **6** b h Hernando (FR) -Miss Rinjani (Shirley Heights) 6355$^{7}$ >**119f**<

**Asian Tiger (IRE)** **2** b c Rossini (USA) -Dry Lightning (Shareef Dancer (USA)) 2024$^{2}$ 2205$^{2}$ 2370$^{5}$ 3242$^{3}$ 3677$^{5}$ *4022$^{8}$* (4797) >**65a 82f**<

**Asiatic** **3** ch c Lomitas-Potri Pe (ARG) (Potrillazo (ARG)) 1899$^{2}$ 2070$^{13}$ 2999$^{10}$ 3590$^{4}$ >**95f**<

**Asia Winds (IRE)** **3** ch f Machiavellian (USA) -Ascot Cyclone (USA) (Rahy (USA)) 2020$^{5}$ 2295$^{9}$ 5249$^{12}$ 5921$^{11}$ >**93f**<

**Askant (GER)** **7** b g Goofalik (USA) -Askura (GER) (Cagliostro (GER)) 3335a$^{6}$ 6511a$^{9}$ >**102f**<

**Ask For Rain** **2** gr f Green Desert (USA) -Requesting (Rainbow Quest (USA)) 5247$^{12}$ 5609$^{3}$ >**65f**<

**Ask For The Moon (FR)** **3** b f Dr Fong (USA) -Lune Rouge (IRE) (Unfuwain (USA)) (1320a) (2338a) 2925a$^{7}$ >**110f**<

**Ask The Clerk (IRE)** **3** b g Turtle Island (IRE) -Some Fun (Wolverlife) *462$^{12}$ 606$^{3}$ 708$^{5}$ 747$^{11}$* (1184) 1388$^{13}$ 1702$^{2}$ 2091$^{8}$2444$^{3}$ 2726$^{4}$ 3089$^{6}$ 3384$^{4}$ 3949$^{3}$ 4267$^{3}$ 4456$^{7}$ 4717$^{5}$5219$^{4}$ 5399$^{2}$ 5652$^{20}$ 5934$^{10}$ 6124$^{3}$ 6350$^{3}$ (6445) >**65a 81f**<

**Ask The Driver** **3** b g Ashkalani (IRE) -Tithcar (Cadeaux Genereux) 1467$^{2}$ 1667$^{4}$ *2484$^{3}$* 3246$^{3}$ 3556$^{7}$ *4128$^{13}$* 5830$^{5}$ >**57a 57f**<

**Askwith (IRE)** **2** b g Marju (IRE) -Hayward (Indian Ridge) 4135$^{5}$ 5098$^{3}$ 5561$^{8}$ >**66f**<

**Aspen Ridge (IRE)** **2** ch f Namid-Longueville Lady (IRE) (Hamas (IRE)) 1670$^{9}$ 2177$^{7}$ *4599$^{7}$* 4866$^{10}$ 5701$^{5}$ >**53a 58f**<

**Aspired (IRE)** **3** b f Mark Of Esteem (IRE) -Dreams (Rainbow Quest (USA)) 3994$^{7}$ 4629$^{P}$ >**63+f**<

**Assigh Lady (IRE)** **6** b m Great Commotion (USA) -Tumble On (Tumble Wind) 3961a$^{11}$ 4371a$^{9}$ 5660a$^{14}$ >**87f**<

**Assiun (GER)** **3** b c Monsun (GER) -Assia (IRE) (Royal Academy (USA)) 2158a$^{3}$ 3792a$^{2}$ 5215a$^{3}$ 5809a$^{3}$ >**109f**<

**Assoon** **5** b g Ezzoud (IRE) -Handy Dancer (Green God) 4125$^{7}$ 4870$^{3}$ >**65f**<

**Assured (IRE)** **2** ch f Shinko Forest (IRE) -Errazuriz (IRE) (Classic Music (USA)) 4292$^{16}$ 5569$^{17}$ 5846$^{14}$ *6276$^{10}$* >**40f**<

**Asteem** 2 b g Mark Of Esteem (IRE) -Amidst (Midyan (USA)) 3157[14] 3659[5] 4866[8] 5406[10] 5745[8] **>53f<**

**Asti (IRE)** 3 b f Sadler s Wells (USA) -Astorg (USA) (Lear Fan (USA)) 1803a[2] 2338a[2] 2925a[9] 4430a[6] 5967a[4] 6383a[6] **>109f<**

**Aston Lad** 3 b c Bijou D Inde-Fishki (Niniski (USA)) 2250[4] 3015[6] 3625[6] 3955[2] 4628[5] 5130[8] 5836[5] 6467[10] **>63f<**

**Astrac (IRE)** 13 b g Nordico (USA) -Shirleen (Daring Display (USA)) 1368[5] 1625[9] 1941[17] 2834[2] 3416[4] 3884[9] 4336[8] 5337[7]5452[4] 5930[9] **>52a 52f<**

**Astral Prince** 6 ch g Efisio-Val D Erica (Ashmore (FR)) 1710[5] 1867[6] **>48a 51f<**

**Astrocharm (IRE)** 5 b m Charnwood Forest (IRE) -Charm The Stars (Roi Danzig (USA)) 1746[5] (2277) 2471[7] 3091[5] (3443) 3678[2] (4176) (4321) 5394[7] 5763[5] **>70a 102f<**

**Astromancer (USA)** 4 bb f Silver Hawk (USA) -Colour Dance (Rainbow Quest (USA)) 618[10] 889[4] 1463[5] 1866[8] 2287[7] 2462[3] (3099) 3429[7] 5205[3]6005[15] **>56a 56f<**

**Astronomic** 4 b g Zafonic (USA) -Sky Love (USA) (Nijinsky (CAN)) 3716[13] **>99f<**

**Astronomical (IRE)** 2 b c Mister Baileys-Charm The Stars (Roi Danzig (USA)) 5534[3] 5897[7] **>75f<**

**Astyanax (IRE)** 4 b c Hector Protector (USA) -Craigmill (Slip Anchor) 2116[18] 3821[5] 4075[9] (4457) 4934[8] 5595[2] (5820) 6215[21] **>79+a 87f<**

**Aswan (IRE)** 6 ch g Ashkalani (IRE) -Ghariba (Final Straw) 2591[5] 3012[3] 3470[12] 3779[9] 3921[18] 6094[12] **>63a 75f<**

**Atacama Star** 2 ch g Desert King (IRE) -Aunty (FR) (Riverman (USA)) 5646[15] 5910[2] 6145[10] **>77f<**

**Atahuelpa** 4 b g Hernando (FR) -Certain Story (Known Fact (USA)) 785a[9] 911a[7] 1066[10] 4145[3] 4518[3] **>79a 88f<**

**Atavus** 7 b h Distant Relative-Elysian (Northfields (USA)) 2044[12] 2283[6] 3036[22] 3337[5] 3673[15] 4553[18] 5121[2] 5471[6]5888[11] **>98f<**

**A Teen** 6 ch h Presidium-Very Good (Noalto) 465[5] 576[2] 674[7] (896) 1082[6] 1504[6] 2094[13] 2399[16]3298[6] 3593[10] 3887[10] 4130[10] 4727[5] 4923[6] 5261[7] 5346[18]6288[8] 6558[6] **>58a 69f<**

**Athboy** 3 ch c Entrepreneur-Glorious (Nashwan (USA)) 598[11] (741) (885) 959[9] 3419[8] 5693[13] **>68a<**

**Athboy Nights (IRE)** 2 b f Night Shift (USA) -Missing Love (IRE) (Thatching) 6125[12] 6543[14] **>30f<**

**Athollbrose (USA)** 3 b g Mister Baileys-Knightly Cut Up (USA) (Gold Crest (USA)) 1360[4] 1559[2] 1843[4] 2197[5] 2571[4] 3060[10] 3822[12] 5524[3] **>47a 57f<**

**Atlantic Ace** 7 b g First Trump-Risalah (Marju (IRE)) 1114[18] 1773[11] 2237[7] 2493[6] 3470[8] 3869[9] 4220[11] 5544[12]5713[15] 5945[8] 6296[2] 6580[2] **>70a 71f<**

**Atlantic Breeze** 3 br f Deploy-Atlantic Air (Air Trooper) 566[7] 752[7] 955[9] 1267[7] 1529[7] 1740[3] 1946[9] **>44a 42f<**

**Atlantic City** 3 ch g First Trump-Pleasuring (Good Times (ITY)) 2250[2] 3015[5] 6450[11] **>68a 72f<**

**Atlantic Quest (USA)** 5 b g Woodman (USA) -Pleasant Pat (USA) (Pleasant Colony (USA)) 1199[14] 1772[5] 1821[7] 2215[12] (2366) 2905[5] 3597[16] 4006[B] 4209[10]4558[4] **>86a 91f<**

**Atlantic Story (USA)** 2 bb c Stormy Atlantic (USA) -Story Book Girl (USA) (Siberian Express (USA)) 4730[8] (5179) 6176[2] **>92f<**

**Atlantic Tern** 3 b c Atraf-Great Tern (Simply Great (FR)) 492[6] 916[11] 1116[10] **>55a 36f<**

**Atlantic Viking (IRE)** 9 b g Danehill (USA) -Hi Bettina (Henbit (USA)) 2293[13] 2679[10] 2859[4] 3266[8] 4165[16] (4617) 4811[4] (5181) 5393[17] **>100f<**

**Atlantic Waltz** 4 b g Singspiel (IRE) -Fascination Waltz (Shy Groom (USA)) 1612[15] **><**

**At Once (GER)** 3 b f Kendor (FR) -Aberdeen (GER) (Polish Precedent (USA)) 2335a[3] **>95f<**

**A Touch Of Frost** 9 gr m Distant Relative-Pharland (FR) (Bellypha) 690a[15] 831a[3] 921a[5] **>97f<**

**Atriffic Story** 2 ch c Atraf-Composition (Wolfhound (USA)) 6569[10] **>53f<**

**Atsos (IRE)** 2 b g Imperial Ballet (IRE) -Victim Of Love (Damister (USA)) 1826[6] 2058[6] 2761[13] 4770[5] 5509[6] 5738[17] **>61f<**

**Attacca** 3 b g Piccolo-Jubilee Place (IRE) (Prince Sabo) 1418[6] 1760[10] 2075[11] 4574[7] 5193[16] 5798[18] **>72f<**

**Attache** 6 ch g Wolfhound (USA) -Royal Passion (Ahonoora) 634a[8] 852a[8] 1006a[10] **>77a 116f<**

**Attack Minded** 3 ch g Timeless Times (USA) -French Ginger (Most Welcome) 5545[8] **>18f<**

**Attila The Hun** 5 b g Piccolo-Katya (IRE) (Dancing Dissident (USA)) 944[4] 2175[6] 2350[11] 2620[5] **>29a 29 f<**

**Attilia (GER)** 3 b f Tiger Hill (IRE) -Akasma (GER) (Windwurf (GER)) 1983a[9] 3434a[9] 6106a[7] **>82f<**

**Attishoe** 2 b f Atraf-Royal Shoe (Hotfoot) 5003[8] 5376[11] **>48f<**

**Attorney** 6 ch g Wolfhound (USA) -Princess Sadie (Shavian) 421[3] 509[7] (530) 573[10] 625[7] 654[4] 796[7] 897[11]938[6] 990[5] 1018[3] 1092[9] 1206[7] (1443) (1497) 1584[2] 1738[8] 2166[3] 2399[6] 2626[6] 2885[5] 3151[16] 3378[9] 3616[8]3663[6] 3864[11] 4291[13] 4881[15] **>39a 49f<**

**Attraction** 3 b f Efisio-Flirtation (Pursuit Of Love) (1791) (2330a) (3033) 3600[2] 4795a[10] 5484a[2] (5940) **>123f<**

**Attune** 3 br f Singspiel (IRE) -Arriving (Most Welcome) 1400[4] 1704[10] (2135) 2557[13] 4140[8] (4340) (5249) (5416) 5917[10] **>105f<**

**At Your Request** 3 gr g Bering-Requesting (Rainbow Quest (USA)) 1285[3] 1561[3] 3138[3] **>75f<**

**Aubonne (GER)** 4 ch f Monsun (GER) -Anna Maria (GER) (Night Shift (USA)) 1952a[4] (3030a) 4767a[6] 6488a[12] **>113f<**

**Aud (USA)** 4 br f Wild Again (USA) -Gail s Brush (USA) (Broad Brush (USA)) 4767a[7] **>108f<**

**Audience** 4 b g Zilzal (USA) -Only Yours (Aragon) 1107[10] 1385[12] 1828[7] 2283[7] 2969[8] 3597[2] 3937[4] 4287[6](4887) 5291[3] 5941[23] 6474[10] **>106f<**

**Auditorium** 3 b c Royal Applause-Degree (Warning) 2308[4] 2966[12] 4322[8] **>112f<**

**Auenteufel (GER)** 5 ch h Lomitas-Auenqueen (GER) (Big Shuffle (USA)) 785a[6] 1655a[10] **>108f<**

**Auentraum (GER)** 4 br c Big Shuffle (USA) -Auenglocke (GER) (Surumu (GER)) 6496[12] **>24a<**

**Aunt Doris** 7 b m Distant Relative-Nevis (Connaught) 470[10] 497[11] **>44a 44f<**

**Aunt Julia** 2 b f In The Wings-Original (Caerleon (USA)) 5695[3] **>72f<**

**Aunty Euro (IRE)** 2 br f Cape Cross (IRE) -Alexander Goddess (IRE) (Alzao (USA)) 1117[4] 1299[3] 2256[3] 2852[2] 3987[9] 4186[6] **>58a 58f<**

**Aurelia** 3 b f Rainbow Quest (USA) -Fern (Shirley Heights) 4389[3] 5472[8] **>80f<**

**Auroville** 3 b c Cadeaux Genereux-Silent Tribute (IRE) (Lion Cavern (USA)) 1392[8] 1755[4] 2134[7] 2571[5] 2949[7] 3746[7] 4103[6] 4654[2]4940[P] 5549[5] 6120[6] **>67f<**

**Australian** 2 b c Danzero (AUS) -Auspicious (Shirley Heights) (5696) **>80+f<**

**Australie (IRE)** 3 b f Sadler s Wells (USA) -Asnieres (USA) (Spend A Buck (USA)) 2338a[6] 5966a[6] (6437a) **>106f<**

**Austrian (GER)** 3 br c Second Set (IRE) -Autriche (IRE) (Acatenango (GER)) 6379a[16] **>74f<**

**Authenticate** 2 b f Dansili-Exact Replica (Darshaan) 3741[4] 4851[6] 5247[10] 5648[18] **>69f<**

**Authority (IRE)** 4 b g Bluebird (USA) -Persian Tapestry (Tap On Wood) 6017[5] 6397[6] **>59a 74f<**

**Autumn Daze** 2 b f Danzig Connection (USA) -Autumn Stone (IRE) (Bigstone (IRE)) 4599[10] 5741[11] 6400[11] 6563[17] **>10a<**

**Autumn Fantasy (USA)** 5 b h Lear Fan (USA) -Autumn Glory (USA) (Graustark) 1744[4] 1973[12] 2249[7] 2409[8] **>47a 61 f<**

**Autumn Flyer (IRE)** 3 ch g Salse (USA) -Autumn Fall (USA) (Sanglamore (USA)) 2168[9] 2949[9] 3852[8] 4618[5] 5751[10] **>59a 61f<**

**Autumn Glory (IRE)** 4 b c Charnwood Forest (IRE) -Archipova (IRE) (Ela-Mana-Mou) (1114) (2044) 2969[28] 4120[16] 4685[6] (5169a) 5668a[5] (6219) **>117f<**

**Autumn Melody (FR)** 2 b f Kingmambo (USA) -Dance Of Leaves (Sadler s Wells (USA)) 3627[5] 4234[6] 4560[5] **>70f<**

**Autumn Pearl** 3 b f Orpen (USA) -Cyclone Flyer (College Chapel) (1829) 2636[2] 3092[3] 3976[6] 4269[13] 5671[2] 6463a[10] **>79a 103f<**

**Autumn Wealth (IRE)** 3 ch f Cadeaux Genereux-Prickwillow (USA) (Nureyev (USA)) 3630[2] 4141[2] (5146) (6286) 6571[3] **>89f<**

**Auwitesweetheart** 2 b f Josr Algarhoud (IRE) -Miss Kirsty (USA) (Miswaki (USA)) 2837[5] 5070[5] 5536[5] 6080[3] 6281[2] **>70f<**

**Avas (GER)** 2 b c Monsun (GER) -Averna (Heraldiste (USA)) 5389a[7] **><**

**Avec Plaisir (GER)** 5 br m Acatenango (GER) -Aminata (GER) (Local Suitor (USA)) 2711a[10] **>94f<**

**Aveiro (IRE)** 8 b g Darshaan-Avila (Ajdal (USA)) 440[2] (570) 629[3] 825[3] 973[3] 1016[2] (1041) 1136[2]1501[8] 1668[10] 2525[7] 2662[5] 2978[8] **>70a 47f<**

**Avening** 4 br g Averti (IRE) -Dependable (Formidable (USA)) 5874[17] **>86 f<**

**Avenir Rubra (GER)** 4 ch f Lomitas-Adorea (GER) (Dashing Blade) 3434a[11] 5823a[6] **>109f<**

**Aventura (IRE)** 4 b g Sri Pekan (USA) -La Belle Katherine (USA) (Lyphard (USA)) 768[14] 837[9] 961[4] 1114[19] 1321[10] 1765[9] 1840[7] 2673[7]6210[15] 6480[11] **>88a 79f<**

**Averami** 3 bb f Averti (IRE) -Friend For Life (Lahib (USA)) 817[9] 965[5] 1184[11] 3636[13] 4025[6] 4309[10] 4708[11] 5642[6] **>40a 40f<**

**Averlline** 3 b f Averti (IRE) -Spring Sunrise (Robellino (USA)) 2444[7] 2839[8] 4414[8] 4937[10] **>69f<**

**Aversham** 4 b c Averti (IRE) -Vavona (Ballad Rock) 755a[11] 5299[3] 5799[5] 6496[4] **>88a 95f<**

**Avertaine** 3 b f Averti (IRE) -Roufontaine (Rousillon (USA)) 982[9] 1052[12] 1186[5] 1529[2] 2199[7] 2484[6] 3193[5] 3697[8] **>48a 53f<**

**Avertigo** 2 b c Averti (IRE) -Green Run (USA) (Green Dancer (USA)) 3632[5] 3823[3] 4239[2] 4914[11] 5281[2] 5925[4] 6174[25] **>75f<**

**Averting** 2 br c Averti (IRE) -Sweet Compliance (Safawan) 3570[5] 4481[2] 4739[7] 5351[7] 5617[19] 5839[17] **>63f<**

**Avesomeofthat (IRE)** 3 b g Lahib (USA) -Lacinia (Groom Dancer (USA)) 2168[6] 2578[9] **>69f<**

**Avessia** 3 b f Averti (IRE) -Alessia (Caerleon (USA)) 4144[4] **>69f<**

**Aviane (GER)** 3 b f Winged Love (IRE) -Averna (Heraldiste (USA)) (5822a) **>80f<**

**Aviation** 2 b c Averti (IRE) -Roufontaine (Rousillon (USA)) 4844[7] 5290[3] 5494[5] 5872[5] 6125[9] **>76f<**

**Aviation Falcon (USA)** 3 ch c King Of Kings (IRE) -Alisidora (IRE) (Nashwan (USA)) 848a[7] **>62a<**

**Avit (IRE)** 4 ch f General Monash (USA) -Breakfast Boogie (Sizzling Melody) 708[8] 791[11] 1000[2] 1546[3] 1859[9] 2183[6] 2227[8](2800) 3084[4] 4085[5] 4400[11] 4622[2] 5734[15] 5793[7] 6229[6] **>48a 42f<**

**Avizandum (IRE)** 2 b g Daggers Drawn (USA) -Miss Dilletante (Primo Dominie) 5542[12] 6072[15] **>27f<**

**Avonbridge** 4 b c Averti (IRE) -Alessia (Caerleon (USA)) 1763[2] (2719a) 3073[5] 4269[4] 4886[4] 5977a[5] **>119f<**

**Avorado (IRE)** 6 b g Royal Academy (USA) -Voronova (IRE) (Sadler s Wells (USA)) 1254a[11] 1849a[7] 2793a[6] 3967a[8] **>110f<**

**Awaaser (USA)** 2 ch f Diesis-Forest Storm (USA) (Woodman (USA)) 5609[4] **>62f<**

**Awake** 7 ch g First Trump-Pluvial (Habat) 1113[12] 1500[6] 1537[5] 1956[11] (2754) 3249[6] 3645[2] 3920[9] (4133) 4538[13]6205[15] 6267[14] **>93f<**

**Awaken** 3 b f Zafonic (USA) -Dawna (Polish Precedent (USA)) 6095[7] 6245[7] **>52f<**

**Awarding** 4 ch g Mark Of Esteem (IRE) -Monaiya (Shareef Dancer (USA)) 515[5] 912[8] 1051[14] 2132[17] 2612[8] 4145[7] 4687[15] **>79a 79f<**

**Awesome Love (USA)** 3 br c Awesome Again (CAN) -Circus Toons (USA) (Wild Again (USA)) 2286[3] 2487[2] 2777[2] 3168[2] 3610[6] 4008[12] 4829[5] **>80f<**

**A Woman In Love** 5 gr m Muhtarram (USA) -Ma Lumiere (FR) (Niniski (USA)) 1229[6] (2325) (2703) (2929) (3086) 3690[4] 4164[7] 4435[15] **>69a 86f<**

**Awwal Marra (USA)** 4 ch f King Of Kings (IRE) -Secretariat Lass (USA) (Secretariat (USA)) 2133[7] 3899[3] 4213[14] 5110[9] 5546[16] **>65+f<**

**Axford Lord** 4 gr g Petong-Bellyphax (Bellypha) 4136[6] 4635[8] 4905[15] 5581[16] **>36a 36f<**

**Ayam Zaman (IRE)** 2 b f Montjeu (IRE) -Kardashina (FR) (Darshaan) 5717[5] (5988) (6472) **>98+f<**

**Aylmer Road (IRE)** 2 b c Groom Dancer (USA) -Pekan s Pride (Sri Pekan (USA)) 6067[2] 6309[4] **>81f<**

**Aynsley** 2 ch f Tomba-Eggy (Risk Me (FR)) 5262[4] 5586[5] 5954[8] **>29a 59f<**

**Azahara** 2 b f Vettori (IRE) -Branston Express (Bay Express) 4446[16] 5128[7] (6091) 6515[11] **>67f<**

**Azamour (IRE)** 3 b c Night Shift (USA) -Asmara (USA) (Lear Fan (USA)) 1764[3] 2315a[2] (2956) (5483a) 6216[3] **>126f<**

**Azarole (IRE)** 3 b g Alzao (USA) -Cashew (Sharrood (USA)) 1396[5] 2476[4] 5610[4] **>106f<**

**Aza Wish (IRE)** 2 b f Mujadil (USA) -Kilcsem Eile (IRE) (Commanche Run) 1743[7] 1882[5] 2141[16] 2550[8] 5856[6] 6092[5] 6240[5] 6336[8] **>51f<**

**Azeri (USA)** 6 ch m Jade Hunter (USA) -Zodiac Miss (AUS) (Ahonoora) 6491a[5] **>127a<**

**Azizam** 2 ch f Singspiel (IRE) -Perdicula (IRE) (Persian Heights) 6187[7] **>64f<**

**Azreme** 4 ch c Unfuwain (USA) -Mariette (Blushing Scribe (USA)) (1877) 2119[5] 2483[7] 2989[4] 3025[5] 3386[4] 3690[3] 3910[12] 4846[2]4969[7] (5631) 6244[2] 6477[12] 6525[7] **>69a 84f<**

**Azuni (IRE)** 3 b c Second Empire (IRE) -Zanic (IRE) (Ezzoud (IRE)) 1306a[12] **><**

**Azuree (IRE)** 2 b f Almutawakel-Cappella (IRE) (College Chapel) 1798[2] 2023[6] 2876[3] 3208[8] 3840[4] 4432[3] 4752[13] 5548[5]5989[4] 6356[13] **>64f<**

**Azzuri (GER)** 2 br c Big Shuffle (USA) -Atlantic City (GER) (Medicus (GER)) 6202a[7] **>74f<**

## B

**Baaridd** 6 b h Halling (USA) -Millstream (USA) (Dayjur (USA)) 755a[5] 850a[3] 1001a[8] **>102f<**

**Baawrah** 3 ch g Cadeaux Genereux-Kronengold (USA) (Golden Act (USA)) 492[2] (598) 704[4] 1108[13] 3543[6] 6006[14] **>74a 66f<**

**Baba (IRE)** 3 ch g Indian Ridge-Theory Of Law (Generous (IRE)) 1174[8] 6119[9] 6526[12] **>48f<**

**Babe Maccool (IRE)** 2 ch c Giant s Causeway (USA) -Kotama (USA) (Shahrastani (USA)) 5996[6] 6125[6] **>63f<**

**Babodana** 4 ch c Bahamian Bounty-Daanat Nawal (Machiavellian (USA)) (1125) 1621[6] 1758[3] 3323[5] 3724[5] 4745[4] 4889[6] 5225[4] 6219[3]6474[2] **>91a 118f<**

**Baboosh (IRE)** 3 b f Marju (IRE) -Slipper (Suave Dancer (USA)) 4781[2] (5851) 6571[11] **>74f<**

**Baboushka (IRE)** 3 b f Soviet Star (USA) -Kabayil (Dancing Brave (USA)) 1250[8] 1559[12] **>54f<**

**Baby Barry** 7 b g Komaite (USA) -Malcesine (IRE) (Auction Ring (USA)) 2524[11] 2931[3] 3380[11] 3734[3] 4083[10] 4425[2] 4702[8] 5450[2](5733) 6024[8] **>55a 56f<**

**Baccino (USA)** 6 ch g Twining (USA) -Bering Down (USA) (Bering) 5103a[0] **><**

**Bachelor Affair** 2 b c Bachir (IRE) -Profit Alert (IRE) (Alzao (USA)) 5915[14] 6476[10] **>50f<**

**Bachelor Duke (USA)** 3 b c Miswaki (USA) -Gossamer (USA) (Seattle Slew (USA)) 1764[7] (2315a) 2956[7] **>121f<**

**Back At De Front (IRE)** 3 b f Cape Cross (IRE) -Bold Fashion (FR) (Nashwan (USA)) (547) 591[5] 747[5] 891[4] 1008[5] 1047[6] 1121[13] 1464[18]2359[11] 2664[8] 2986[6] **>57a 66f<**

**Backgammon** 3 b c Sadler s Wells (USA) -Game Plan (Darshaan) 1713[2] 2077[3] (5345) 5990[4] 6284[11] **>84f<**

**Back In Action** 4 b g Hector Protector (USA) -Lucca (Sure Blade (USA)) 2945[7] 3678[14] **>75a 83f<**

**Back In Fashion** 3 b f Puissance-Spring Collection (Tina s Pet) 3229[16] **><**

**Back In Spirit** 4 ch g Primo Dominie-Pusey Street Girl (Gildoran) 510[10] 626[10] 2183[10] 3381[7] 3742[2] 4881[4] 5691[14] **>39 a 48f<**

**Backlash** 3 b f Fraam-Mezza Luna (Distant Relative) 489[8] 574[13] 731[7] 1300[5] 1495[5] (6056) **>44a 49f<**

**Backstreet Lad** 2 b c Fraam-Forest Fantasy (Rambo Dancer (CAN)) 4681[15] 5535[9] 5870[10] 6223[10] **>22a 57f<**

**Back To Reality** 2 ch g Magic Ring (IRE) -Arian Da (Superlative) 5406[13] 5827[8] 6545[8] **>47f<**

**Ba Clubman (IRE)** 4 b g Royal Abjar (USA) -Ah Ya Zein (Artaius (USA)) 1612[14] 1912[5] 2273[9] **>12f<**

**Baddam** 2 b c Mujahid (USA) -Aude La Belle (FR) (Ela-Mana-Mou) 3150[4] 4567[8] 5200[6] 6562[3] **>67f<**

**Bad Intentions (IRE)** 4 b f Victory Note (USA) -Fallacy (Selkirk (USA)) 3195[6] 3428[14] 3680[10] 4265[6] 5155[10] **>39f<**

**Badminton** 3 b f Zieten (USA) -Badawi (USA) (Diesis) (5811) 6214[8] **>104+f<**

**Badou** 4 b g Averti (IRE) -Bint Albadou (IRE) (Green Desert (USA)) 535[6] (658) 788[4] (859) 930[7] 946[7] 1098[12] 1497[2]1988[4] 2803[9] 2885[10] 5283[13] 5793[12] **>53a 30f<**

**Badr (USA)** 3 b c Theatrical-Bejat (USA) (Mr Prospector (USA)) 1747[6] 2197[7] 2529[5] 3231[17] 3738[7] **>69 f<**

**Baffle** 3 b f Selkirk (USA) -Elude (Slip Anchor) (1325) 1831[5] 3478[7] 4490[6] 5265[13] **>76f<**

**Bagan (FR)** 5 bb h Rainbow Quest (USA) -Maid Of Erin (USA) (Irish River (FR)) 1401[4] 1768[4] 2066[4] 4831[18] 5465[4] 5919[15] **>96f<**

**Bago (FR)** 3 b c Nashwan (USA) -Moonlight s Box (USA) (Nureyev (USA)) (2721a) (3360a) 4834[3] 5500a[3] (5981a) **>129f<**

**Bahama Belle** 3 b f Bahamian Bounty-Barque Bleue (USA) (Steinlen) 2063[13] 2765[4] 3530[12] 4043[7] 4517[14] 6362[10] **>11a 58f<**

**Bahama Reef (IRE)** 3 b g Sri Pekan (USA) -Caribbean Dancer (Shareef Dancer (USA)) 1096[8] 2204[9] 2404[5] 2931[2] 3554[8] 3988[3] 4338[3] 4546[3]5378[11] **>59a 70f<**

**Bahamian Bay** 2 b f Bahamian Bounty-Moly (Inchinor) 3718[8] 4149[13] 5800[8] **>36f<**

**Bahamian Belle** 4 b f Bahamian Bounty-Marjorie s Memory (IRE) (Fairy King (USA)) 1057[6] 1169[9] 1421[4] 1855[7] 2118[15] 2246[18] 2482[13] 2800[8]3175[9] 3668[5] 3991[7] 5793[13] 5926[4] **>37a 36f<**

**Bahamian Breeze** 3 b g Piccolo-Norgabie (Northfields (USA)) 1673[9] 2181[12] **>78+f<**

**Bahamian Magic** 2 b c Royal Applause-Out Like Magic (Magic Ring (IRE)) 3758[4] 4334[3] (5507) 5896[12] 6012[2] **>85a 78f<**

**Bahamian Pirate (USA)** 9 ch g Housebuster (USA) -Shining Through (USA) (Deputy Minister (CAN)) (1211) 1409[4] 1610[4] 1759[2] (1955) 2021[10] 2955[7] 3073[8] 3308[10] 3674[17](4091) 4269[6] (4886) 5289[12] 5977a[9] **>118f<**

**Bahamian Spring (IRE)** 2 b c Danehill Dancer (IRE) -Siana Springs (IRE) (Emarati (USA)) 5091[12] **><**

**Bahia Breeze** 2 b f Mister Baileys-Ring Of Love (Magic Ring (IRE)) 4844[4] (5281) 5947[8] (6456) **>96f<**

**Bahiano (IRE)** 3 ch c Barathea (IRE) -Trystero (Shareef Dancer (USA)) 593[2] (869) 913[2] 1063[3] 1459[6] 2019[7] 2295[17] 2966[4]4120[19] 4322[9] 5610[12] 5781[8] **>101a 106f<**

**B A Highflyer** 4 b g Compton Place-Primulette (Mummy s Pet) 1230[13] 1531[5] 1857[9] 2399[12] 2703[13] 4403[5] 4687[4] 4774[B] **>68a 69f<**

**Bahja (USA)** 2 ch f Seeking The Gold (USA) -Valentine Waltz (IRE) (Be My Guest (USA)) 4753[4] 5248[3] **>82f<**

**Bailador (IRE)** 4 b c Alzao (USA) -Alymatrice (USA) (Alysheba (USA)) 3030a[6] (4039a) 5170a[3] 5727a[4] **>110f<**

**Bailamos (GER)** 4 b c Lomitas-Bandeira (GER) (Law Society (USA)) 1182a[5] 1779a[3] 2320a[2] 4832[8] 5808a[5] 6509a[3] **>108f<**

**Bailaora (IRE)** 3 bb c Shinko Forest (IRE) -Tart (FR) (Warning) 1830[6] 2113[8] 2378[6] 3535[3] 4056[7] 4170[5] 4618[12] 4972[4] **>78f<**

**Bailey Gate** 2 b f Mister Baileys-Floppie (FR) (Law Society (USA)) 4714[7] 5271[9] (6342) **>82+f<**

**Baileys Applause** 2 b f Royal Applause-Thicket (Wolfhound (USA)) 1670[5] 2002[3] 2275[6] 3930[12] 4612[12] 4752[6] 5746[4] **>45a 62f<**

**Baileys Dancer** 3 b f Groom Dancer (USA) -Darshay (FR) (Darshaan) 1585[8] 2089[4] 2281[9] 2587[12] 3274[2] 3953[10] (4389) 4729[9] 5517[8] **>82f<**

**Baileys Honour** 2 b f Mark Of Esteem (IRE) -Kanz (USA) (The Minstrel (CAN)) 5752[B] 6072[12] 6392[10] **>27a 46f<**

**Bailieborough (IRE)** 5 b g Charnwood Forest (IRE) -Sherannda (USA) (Trempolino (USA)) 1199[10] 1358[6] 1451[7] 1868[3] 2078[4] 2218[8] (2445) 2776[3] 3023[8](3367) 3796[6] 4132[5] (4276) (4535) 4985[3] 5061[2] 5317[9] **>59a 75f<**

**Baker Of Oz** 3 b c Pursuit Of Love-Moorish Idol (Aragon) 890[2] 1012[6] 1294[4] (2737) 3525[7] 4327[9] 4726[7] 5656[9] **>72a 81f<**

**Bakhtyar** 3 gr g Daylami (IRE) -Gentilesse (Generous (IRE)) 1509[8] 1998[12] 3160[4] 4129[5] 4870[4] 6159[14] **>57a 61f<**

**Bakira (GER)** 2 b f Chato (USA) -Bundheimerin (GER) (Ordos) 3436a[7] **><**

**Bakiri (IRE)** 6 b g Doyoun-Bakiya (USA) (Trempolino (USA)) 1275[13] 1520[4] 1928[12] 2116[5] 2584[2] 2659[3] 2964[2] 3128[4]3450[7] 4196[9] (4616) **>68f<**

**Bakke** 2 b g Danehill (USA) -Valagalore (Generous

(IRE)) 2111[9] 3451[14] >**63f**<

**Balakiref** 5 b g Royal Applause-Pluck (Never So Bold) (1268) 1361[9] 1531[2] 1663[2] 1877[2] 2673[U] (3079) 3309[10] 3755[9] 4134[8]4677[5] (4904) 5124[3] 5603[4] >**71a 81f**<

**Balalaika Tune (IRE)** 5 b m Lure (USA) -Bohemienne (USA) (Polish Navy (USA)) *428[8] 567[7] 783[9] 1026[6]* 1527[15] 1721[4] 1866[7] 2408[10]2759[4] 3099[6] 3518[13] 3578[3] 3835[2] 4423[6] >**35a 38f**<

**Balashova** 2 b f Imperial Ballet (IRE) -Almasi (IRE) (Petorius) 1616[5] 1666[U] >**38f**<

**Balavista (USA)** 3 br c Distant View (USA) -Balabina (USA) (Nijinsky (CAN)) (3447) 4490[9] >**83+f**<

**Balearic Star (IRE)** 3 b c Night Shift (USA) -La Menorquina (USA) (Woodman (USA)) 1214[6] 1831[7] (2371) 2887[7] 3543[14] 4147[6] (4852) >**78f**<

**Balerno** 5 b g Machiavellian (USA) -Balabina (USA) (Nijinsky (CAN)) *(533) 815[3] 888[11] 933 [4] 988[5] 1020[8] 1098[5]* 1373[2]1748[3] 2597[7] 2886[4] 3127[7] 3321[2] (3841) 4199[2] 4438[5] 4846[11]5425[6] >**56a 71f**<

**Balgarth (USA)** 2 b g Zamindar (USA) -Vaguely Regal (IRE) (Sadler s Wells (USA)) 4446[11] >**54f**<

**Balimaya (IRE)** 3 b f Barathea (IRE) -Banque Privee (USA) (Private Account (USA)) 1395[8] 1926[6] >**65f**<

**Bali Royal** 6 b m King s Signet (USA) -Baligay (Balidar) 2475[6] 2913[4] 3162a[8] 3537[12] 3976[9] 4526[10] >**70a 111f**<

**Bali-Star** 9 b g Alnasr Alwasheek-Baligay (Balidar) *411[10] 499[2] 792[4] 1000[7]* 1368[17] *1546[4]* (1584) 1941[16]2166[9] >**41a 56f**<

**Balkan Knight** 4 b c Selkirk (USA) -Crown Of Light (Mtoto) 1460[6] (2022) 3521[12] 3947[3] >**91f**<

**Balkan Leader (USA)** 2 b c Stravinsky (USA) -Baydon Belle (USA) (Al Nasr (FR)) 5633[4] *6011[2]* >**69a 51f**<

**Ballare (IRE)** 5 b g Barathea (IRE) -Raindancing (IRE) (Tirol) *537[9] 788[3] 929[4] 1020[6] (1278)* 1373[10] 1531[4] 2597[14]4083[9] 5285[11] *5642[2]* (6057) *6364[10]* >**56a 55f**<

**Ballast (IRE)** 3 ch c Desert Prince (IRE) -Suedoise (Kris) 6075a[6] ><

**Ball Boy** 2 b g Xaar-Tanz (IRE) (Sadler s Wells (USA)) 3451[7] 3870[5] 4208[2] 4633[5] >**73f**<

**Ballerina Suprema (IRE)** 4 b f Sadler s Wells (USA) -Gravieres (FR) (Saint Estephe (FR)) 3327[5] 4321[7] >**84f**<

**Ballet Ballon (USA)** 2 b f Rahy (USA) -Bella Ballerina (Sadler s Wells (USA)) 5695[11] >**45f**<

**Balletomaine (IRE)** 2 b f Sadler s Wells (USA) -Ivy (USA) (Sir Ivor (USA)) 4234[8] 4625[7] *5380[8]* >**39a 62f**<

**Ballet Ruse** 3 ch f Rainbow Quest (USA) -El Opera (IRE) (Sadler s Wells (USA)) 4195[16] 4306[11] 5178[7] >**28f**<

**Balletto** 2 b f Robellino (USA) -Denial (Sadler s Wells (USA)) 3123[3] 4074[7] >**65f**<

**Balletto (UAE)** 2 ch f Timber Country (USA) -Destiny Dance (USA) (Nijinsky (CAN)) *6485a[2]* >**111a**<

**Ballinger Express** 4 ch f Air Express (IRE) -Branston Ridge (Indian Ridge) *846[8] 1059[5] 1227[3]* 2217[2] 2670[9] 2836[15] 4194[2] 4400[9]4622[10] 5618[13] 5844[3] >**64a 68f**<

**Ballinger Ridge** 5 b g Sabrehill (USA) -Branston Ridge (Indian Ridge) *520[2] 660[3] 790[2] 948[2] (997) 1055[6]* >**61a 61f**<

**Ballin Rouge** 3 ch f Dr Fong (USA) -Bogus John (CAN) (Blushing John (USA)) 2195[10] 3582[7] 5451[6] >**27f**<

**Ballinteni** 2 b c Machiavellian (USA) -Silabteni (USA) (Nureyev (USA)) (6330) >**85f**<

**Ballyboro (IRE)** 3 b f Entrepreneur-Tathkara (USA) (Alydar (USA)) 1904[6] 2367[11] 2822[9] >**53f**<

**Ballybunion (IRE)** 5 ch g Entrepreneur-Clarentia (Ballad Rock) 1787[10] 2130[15] 2490[11] 2899[11] 3010[5] 3169[3] 3249[9] 3446[10]3820[9] 3864[9] 4013[5] (4181) 4291[7] 4774[3] 5346[2] 5579[13] 5754[4]5862[4] >**51 a 65f**<

**Ballycotton Bay (IRE)** 2 b c Orpen (USA) -Flicker Of Hope (IRE) (Baillamont (USA)) 6380a[8] >**82f**<

**Ballycroy Girl (IRE)** 2 ch f Pennekamp (USA) -Hulm (IRE) (Mujtahid (USA)) 2256[6] 3081[2] 3718[5] (3974) 4089[8] 5314[6] 5630[7] >**72f**<

**Ballygriffin Kid** 4 gr g Komaite (USA) -Ballygriffin Belle (Another Realm) *946[8] 1280[3] 1443[4] (2051)* 2387[10] >**43a 58df**<

**Bally Hall (IRE)** 4 b g Saddlers Hall (IRE) -Sally Rose (Sallust) *820[11]* >**69a 79 f**<

**Ballyhurry (USA)** 7 b g Rubiano (USA) -Balakhna (FR) (Tyrant (USA)) 1345[11] 2291[6] 2492[4] 3079[6] 3977[8] 5818[4] 6094[4] *6553[5]* >**58a 81f**<

**Ballyliffin (IRE)** 3 b g Daggers Drawn (USA) -Blues Quartet (Cure The Blues (USA)) 1683[18] 1912[2] >**57f**<

**Ballyrush (IRE)** 4 ch g Titus Livius (FR) -Mandoline (IRE) (Suave Dancer (USA)) *643[8] 862[5] 907[4] 1031[5]* 1274[6] 1617[5] *2015[2](2231)* 2387[12] >**50a 33f**<

**Balmacara** 5 b m Lake Coniston (IRE) -Diabaig (Precocious) *520[7] 815[9]* 2943[6] 3609[12] 4066[5] 5283[10] *6362[9]* >**53a 46f**<

**Balmont (USA)** 3 b c Stravinsky (USA) -Aldebaran Light (USA) (Seattle Slew (USA)) 3674[3] 4091[2] 4886[7] 6214[5] >**117f**<

**Balthasar** 2 b c Lujain (USA) -Anatase (Danehill (USA)) 2522[15] 4633[6] 4824[7] 5192[6] >**58f**<

**Baltic Blazer (IRE)** 4 b g Polish Precedent (USA) -Pine Needle (Kris) 2624[5] 5572[9] 6043[17] >**74f**<

**Baltic Dip (IRE)** 2 b f Benny The Dip (USA) -Drei (USA) (Lyphard (USA)) (2245) 3316[4] 5648[8] 5939[4] >**96f**<

**Baltic King** 4 b c Danetime (IRE) -Lindfield Belle (IRE) (Fairy King (USA)) 1763[6] 2373[8] (4165) 5105[3] 5418[6] (5712) 5893[3] 6190[5] >**116+f**<

**Baltic Wave** 3 b g Polish Precedent (USA) -Flourish (Selkirk (USA)) 2907[6] 3295[4] 3598[11] >**89f**<

**Balwearie (IRE)** 3 b g Sesaro (USA) -Eight Mile Rock (Dominion) 1659[6] 2259[9] 2530[6] >**62f**<

**Bamboozled** 2 b f Mujadil (USA) -Tintinara (Selkirk (USA)) *1060[6]* 1984[9] *2405[7]* 2725[5] >**41a 9f**<

**Bamford Castle (IRE)** 9 b g Scenic-Allorette (Ballymore) *579[9]* >**16a 84f**<

**Bamzooki** 2 b f Zilzal (USA) -Cavernista (Lion Cavern (USA)) 3632[4] 4936[5] >**60f**<

**Banana Grove (IRE)** 3 b g Sesaro (USA) -Megan s Dream (IRE) (Fayruz) 3878[3] 4180[7] 4491[P] (4573) 4989[4] 5210[7] 5672[6] 6116[3] >**68f**<

**Banchieri** 2 b c Dubai Millennium-Belle Et Deluree (USA) (The Minstrel (CAN)) 4567[3] 5228[3] 5620[2] >**82f**<

**Band** 4 b g Band On The Run-Little Tich (Great Nephew) 1708[12] 2271[12] *3023[12]* 3387[10] 3781[4] 3929[8] 4493[5] (4818) 5236[7]6311[6] 6546[4] >**35a 62f**<

**Bandari (IRE)** 5 b h Alhaarth (IRE) -Miss Audimar (USA) (Mr. Leader (USA)) 1455[11] (1767) (1902) (2559) 2968[9] (3642) 4121[7] 5296[3] 5812[3] 6260a[9] >**124f**<

**Bandbox (IRE)** 9 ch g Imperial Frontier (USA) -Dublah (USA) (Private Account (USA)) *2854[8] 3024[5] 3376[7]* 4469[3] >**43a 49 f**<

**Bandiera (GER)** 2 b f Eden Rock (GER) -Barrocal (GER) (Navarino (GER)) 5577a[12] ><

**Bandit Queen** 4 b f Desert Prince (IRE) -Wildwood Flower (Distant Relative) 2143[3] 2506[4] 2750[2] 3691[9] >**16a 95f**<

**Bandos** 4 ch g Cayman Kai (IRE) -Lekuti (Le Coq D Or) 2553[3] 3079[13] 3235[18] 5631[4] 5861[5] >**43a 82f**<

**Banjo Bay (IRE)** 6 b g Common Grounds-Thirlmere (Cadeaux Genereux) 1927[8] 2132[14] 2467[3] 2682[11] 3036[18] 3399[6] 4047[8] 4577[8]5016[10] 5316[7] 5526[5] 5798[14] >**70 f**<

**Banjo Patterson** 2 b c Green Desert (USA) -Rumpipumpy (Shirley Heights) 6171[15] >**41f**<

**Banjo s Spirit (IRE)** 3 b c Fumo Di Londra (IRE) -Flash Donna (USA) (Well Decorated (USA)) 4357a[12] >**95f**<

**Bank Games** 3 b g Mind Games-Piggy Bank (Emarati (USA)) 2984[8] *3279[8] 4097[6]* 4393[5] 5141[11] 6229[14] >**45a 34f**<

**Banknote** 2 b c Zafonic (USA) -Brand (Shareef Dancer (USA)) 2478[4] 3197[4] (4208) 5417[13] >**75f**<

**Bank On Him** 9 b g Elmaamul (USA) -Feather Flower (Relkino) *(495) 554[6] (623) 745[2] 820[2] 882[2] 1232[2] 1475[5]*(2034) *2381[3]* 2643[4] *2881[3]* >**69a 58f**<

**Banners Flying (IRE)** 4 ch g Zafonic (USA) -Banafsajee (USA) (Pleasant Colony (USA)) *1424[8] 2454[13] 2851[4]* 3060[11] *3799[4] 4189[13]* 4609[9]5243[12] 5585[10] *6065[9]* >**28a 28f**<

**Banningham Blaze** 4 b f Averti (IRE) -Ma Pavlova (USA) (Irish River (FR)) *671[11]* 1198[9] 1644[4] (2031) 2363[2] 2443[2] 3128[3] 3393[6] 3885[5]3989[3] (4139) 4433[3] 4467[2] 4799[2] 5257[2] 5354[3] 5654[2] 5796[5]6005[4] (6231) *6540[7]* >**69 a 56f**<

**Bannister** 6 ch g Inchinor-Shall We Run (Hotfoot) *884[3] 968[9]* 1531[3] 1675[14] >**61a 70f**<

**Bansha Bru (IRE)** 4 b g Fumo Di Londra (IRE) -Pride Of Duneane (IRE) (Anita s Prince) *1476[3]* 1912[S] >**58a**<

**Baqah (IRE)** 3 ch f Bahhare (USA) -Filfilah (Cadeaux Genereux) (2193a) (2720a) 3600[3] 4795a[7] 5967a[9] >**111f**<

**Barabella (IRE)** 3 gr f Barathea (IRE) -Thatchabella (IRE) (Thatching) 1309[12] 1689[5] 1855[14] 2266[4] 3211[5] 3772[13] 3988[4] 4434[5]4868[12] 5261[15] 5691[11] >**61f**<

**Baradore (IRE)** 2 ch f Barathea (IRE) -High Flying Adored (IRE) (In The Wings) 3913[2] (4498) >**87f**<

**Baraka (IRE)** 3 b f Danehill (USA) -Cocotte (Troy) (1963) 5679a[9] >**107+f**<

**Barakana (IRE)** 6 b g Barathea (IRE) -Safkana (IRE) (Doyoun) *1166[10]* >**22a 16f**<

**Barancella (FR)** 3 ch f Acatenango (GER) -Baranciaga (USA) (Bering) 2028a[3] 2925a[6] 5033a[5] 5530a[2] 6254a[2] >**110f**<

**Baranook (IRE)** 3 b c Barathea (IRE) -Gull Nook (Mill Reef (USA)) 2950[13] 3922[7] 4492[5] *6013[3]* >**74+a 66f**<

**Baranquilla** 3 ch f Acatenango (GER) -Carnival Spirit (Kris) 4566a[11] >**84f**<

**Barathea Blue** 3 ch c Barathea (IRE) -Empty Purse (Pennine Walk) 3922[5] 5445[2] (5867) *6396[7]* >**70a 75f**<

**Barathea Dreams (IRE)** 3 b c Barathea (IRE) -Deyaajeer (USA) (Dayjur (USA)) *(871) (1017) 1100[4]* (1585) 2069[3] 3000[10] 3452[7] 5443[5] 5766[14] 6568[5] >**65a 91f**<

**Barati (IRE)** 3 b g Sadler s Wells (USA) -Oriane (Nashwan (USA)) 1979a[4] 2333a[3] 3032[3] >**103f**<

**Barbajuan (IRE)** 3 b c Danehill Dancer (IRE) -Courtier (Saddlers Hall (IRE)) 1330[5] 1764[12] 2043[8] 2476[7] 3598[13] 3943[10] 5468[13] 5942[5]6193[11] >**109f**<

**Barbary Coast (FR)** 2 b c Anabaa (USA) -Viking s Cove (USA) (Miswaki (USA)) 5646[6] 5915[8] 6148[2] 6283[11] >**81f**<

**Barbilyrifle (IRE)** 3 b g Indian Rocket-Age Of Elegance (Troy) *868[9] 1047[11]* 1220[3] 1854[9] >**41a 58f**<

**Barbirolli** 2 b c Machiavellian (USA) -Blushing Barada (USA) (Blushing Groom (FR)) 5870[12] >**39f**<

**Barcardero (USA)** 2 b c Danzig (USA) -Very Confidential (USA) (Fappiano (USA)) 6439[8] >**65f**<

**Barcelona** 7 b g Barathea (IRE) -Pipitina (Bustino) 3695[9] >**72f**<

**Bare Necessities (USA)** 5 rg m Silver Deputy (CAN) -Shrewd Vixen (USA) (Spectacular Bid (USA)) *6484a[11]* >**112a**<

**Bargain Hunt (IRE)** 3 b g Foxhound (USA) -Atisayin (USA) (Al Nasr (FR)) 1360[10] 1784[2] 2146[7] 2760[7] 3513[3] 3581[6] 3836[10] 4004[11]4102[4] 5451[3] >**45f**<

**Barholm Charlie** 3 b g Atraf-Lady-H (Never So Bold) 2236[19] 2586[14] 3681[8] >**11f**<

**Barking Mad (USA)** 6 bb g Dayjur (USA) -Avian Assembly (USA) (General Assembly (USA)) 1671[6] 2278[4] 2738[3] 3385[2] (3705) 4173[6] 4533[2] 4754[6] (5006) 5514[2]5950[7] 6444[7] >**80a 89f**<

**Barmad Di San Jore (ITY)** 3 b f Masad (IRE) -Basaroa (ITY) (Roakarad) 5576a[4] ><

**Barman (USA)** 5 ch g Atticus (USA) -Blue Tip (FR) (Tip Moss (FR)) 2671[10] 4772[7] (5318) >**92a 89f**<

**Barnbrook Empire (IRE)** 2 b f Second Empire (IRE) -Home Comforts (Most Welcome) 2609[14] 3164[5] 4081[3] 4621[7] >**60f**<

**Bar Of Silver (IRE)** 4 ch g Bahhare (USA) -Shaping Up (USA) (Storm Bird (CAN)) *412[9] 788[5] 941[11] 1544[5]* >**42a 42f**<

**Barolo** 5 b g Danehill (USA) -Lydia Maria (Dancing Brave (USA)) 1455[12] (2240) 3310[17] (3862a) (5251) >**118f**<

**Baron Rhodes** 3 b f Presidium-Superstream (Superpower) 1473[2] 1788[2] 2369[2] 2650[3] (2889) 3077[3] 3372[7] 3777[5] (4331) 4608[3]4862[13] 5105[8] 5671[7] 6205[10] 6267[3] 6459[3] 6532[9] >**36a 86f**<

**Baron s Pit** 4 b c Night Shift (USA) -Incendio (Siberian Express (USA)) (1353) >**120f**<

**Barons Spy (IRE)** 3 b c Danzero (AUS) -Princess Accord (USA) (D Accord (USA)) 2505[4] 2941[2] 3452[10] 5829[3] 6119[2] >**72f**<

**Baroque** 3 b c Merdon Melody-Dubitable (Formidable (USA)) *1022[10]* 1221[8] 1466[13] 1959[6] 2554[14] 3371[10] ><

**Barrantes** 7 b m Distant Relative-Try The Duchess (Try My Best (USA)) 4090[9] 4401[7] 4526[9] 4772[14] 5275[13] >**82a 90f**<

**Barras (IRE)** 3 b g Raphane (USA) -Lady Fleetsin (IRE) (Double Schwartz) *547[8] 610[8] 731[3] 958[5] 1008[4] 2850[7]* 3636[11]4393[3] >**57?a 50f**<

**Barrichello (GER)** 4 ch c Waky Nao-Bandira (GER) (Nityo (USA)) 4596a[5] 6379a[14] >**96f**<

**Barrissimo (IRE)** 4 b g Night Shift (USA) -Belle De Cadix (IRE) (Law Society (USA)) 1762[18] 2066[11] >**104f**<

**Barry Island** 5 b g Turtle Island (IRE) -Pine Ridge (High Top) *(554) 600[5] 706[2] 872[4] 1232[4]* 1460[3] 1762[10] 2084[9]2305[3] 2537[8] 3692[6] 4029[4] (4343) 4950[14] >**85a 84f**<

**Barton Flower** 3 br f Danzero (AUS) -Iota (Niniski (USA)) 1250[7] 1528[8] 3008[9] 3837[11] 3984[14] 5130[7] >**36f**<

**Barton Sands (IRE)** 7 b g Tenby-Hetty Green (Bay Express) (1590) (4655) 5056[2] 5493[4] 5853[4] >**73f**<

**Barzak (IRE)** 4 b g Barathea (IRE) -Zakuska (Zafonic (USA)) *488[8] 582[5] 681[3]* 1225[10] 1620[8] 2172[8] 2776[15] >**75a 56f**<

**Basic System (USA)** 2 b c Belong To Me (USA) -Foible (USA) (Riverman (USA)) 3946[8] 4263[5] >**70f**<

**Basic Woman** 3 b f Piccolo-Brush Away (Ahonoora) 1778a[18] >**38f**<

**Basinet** 6 b g Alzao (USA) -Valiancy (Grundy) 1620[12] 2078[12] 2551[8] 3559[4] 3921[8] 4333[6] 4871[4] 5374[8]5557[8] >**68a 71f**<

**Basserah (IRE)** 2 b f Unfuwain (USA) -Blueberry Walk (Green Desert (USA)) 5717[7] 6187[9] >**73f**<

**Bastikiya (SAF)** 3 b f Fort Wood (USA) -Clair Anne (SAF) (Gallic League) *1005a[8]* >**53a**<

**Batchworth Beau** 3 ch g Bluegrass Prince (IRE) -Batchworth Belle (Interrex (CAN)) 1796[11] 2113[16] 2785[9] 3179[10] >**44f**<

**Batchworth Breeze** 6 ch m Beveled (USA) -Batchworth Dancer (Ballacashtal (CAN)) *470[9]* >**13a 35f**<

**Bathwick Bill (USA)** 3 ch g Stravinsky (USA) -Special Park (USA) (Trempolino (USA)) 1333[9] 1797[6] 2264[2] 3384[3] 3845[8] 5697[11] 5874[11] 6267[8] >**85f**<

**Bathwick Bruce (IRE)** 6 b g College Chapel-Naivity (IRE) (Auction Ring (USA)) 5176[7] 5657[7] >**85a 81f**<

**Bathwick Dream** 7 b m Tragic Role (USA) -Trina (Malaspina) *661[12]* >**19a 39f**<

**Bathwick Finesse (IRE)** 2 b f Namid-Lace Flower (Old Vic) 4866[7] (5256) 5539[4] 6334[14] >**80f**<

**Batik (IRE)** 3 gr f Peintre Celebre (USA) -Dali s Grey (Linamix (FR)) 4644[3] (5511) 6457[5] >**81f**<

**Battle Back (BEL)** 3 b f Pursuit Of Love-Batalya (BEL) (Boulou) *415[12] 532[9]* >**32a 22f**<

**Battle Chant (USA)** 4 b g Coronado s Quest (USA) -Appointed One (USA) (Danzig (USA)) 3937[3] 4287[18] 5180[2] 5492[2] 5731[3] 6219[5] >**110f**<

**Battledress (IRE)** 2 b g In The Wings-Chaturanga (Night Shift (USA)) 5091[8] 5508[3] 5827[4] >**77f**<

**Battle Games (IRE)** 3 b c Docksider (USA) -Chancel (USA) (Al Nasr (FR)) 4588a[11] >**90f**<

**Bawsian** 9 b g Persian Bold-Bawaeth (USA) (Blushing Groom (FR)) *2163a[6]* >**90a 90f**<

**Bayadere (GER)** 4 br f Lavirco (GER) -Brangane (IRE) (Anita s Prince) 5731[8] 6444[8] 6573[20] >**91f**<

**Bayard (USA)** 2 gr c Lord Avie (USA) -Mersey (Crystal Palace (FR)) 6351[4] 6531[8] >**69f**<

**Bayberry (UAE)** 4 ch f Bering-Baya (USA) (Nureyev (USA)) 4640[5] 4948[2] 5436[3] >**109f**<

**Baychevelle (IRE)** 3 ch f Bahamian Bounty-Phantom Ring (Magic Ring (IRE)) 1749[12] >**50f**<

**Bayeux (USA)** 3 b c Red Ransom (USA) -Elizabeth Bay (USA) (Mr Prospector (USA)) 1766[5] 2276[3] 2672[7] 5462[10] 6191[3] >**101f**<

**Bayeux De Moi (IRE)** 2 b c Barathea (IRE) -Rivana (Green Desert (USA)) 4078[4] (4913) 6122[2] >**88f**<

**Bay Hawk** 2 b c Alhaarth (IRE) -Fleeting Vision (IRE) (Vision (USA)) 3749[3] >**74f**<

**Bayhirr** 3 b c Selkirk (USA) -Pass The Peace (Alzao (USA)) 1224[3] (1612) 2018[5] 3347[2] 3943[11] >**91f**<

**Baylaw Star** 3 b g Case Law-Caisson (Shaadi (USA)) 1473[6] 1659[3] 2549[7] 2650[4] 2889[9] 3077[10] 4608[6] 5193[15]5473[11] 5674[6] >**74f**<

**Baymist** 2 b f Mind Games-Millisecent (Primo Dominie) 3583[5] 3818[6] (3980) 4330[4] (4508) 5143[6] 5797[7] >**67f**<

**Bayonet** 8 b m Then Again-Lambay (Lorenzaccio) 4148[8] 4937[8] >**45f**<

**Bayou Princess** 3 ch f Bluegrass Prince (IRE) -Josifina (Master Willie) 1911[7] 2513[7] 3882[5] 4673[3] 5116[6] >**54f**<

**Bayreuth** 2 ch f Halling (USA) -South Shore (Caerleon (USA)) 4851[13] >**41f**<

**Bay Solitaire** 3 b g Charnwood Forest (IRE) -Golden Wings (USA) (Devil s Bag (USA)) 2555[6] 3837[8] 5130[9] >**39f**<

**Baytown Flyer** 4 ch f Whittingham (IRE) -The Fernhill Flyer (IRE) (Red Sunset) *1094[2] 1167[2] 1191[10] (1403) (1510) (1544) 1573[2]* (1591) *(1692) 1724[2]2123[14]* 5597[15] *6363[7] 6401[5]* >**58a 57f**<

**Bay Tree (IRE)** 3 b f Daylami (IRE) -My Branch (Distant Relative) 1398[6] 2020[3] 2971[11] 4430a[8] >**98f**<

**Bazelle** 2 ch f Ashkalani (IRE) -Dona Royale (IRE) (Darshaan) 2786[16] 3664[4] 5368[2] 5717[6] >**78f**<

**Beach Party (IRE)** 3 b f Danzero (AUS) -Shore Lark (USA) (Storm Bird (CAN)) *1226[3] 1627[9]* >**64a 53f**<

**Beacon Blue (IRE)** 3 ch f Peintre Celebre (USA) -Catch The Blues (IRE) (Bluebird (USA)) 2774[6] 5859[7] 6533[13] >**62f**<

**Beacon Star (USA)** 2 ch c Stravinsky (USA) -Careless Kitten (USA) (Caro) 1709[8] 6330[12] >**10f**<

**Beady (IRE)** 5 b g Eagle Eyed (USA) -Tales Of Wisdom (Rousillon (USA)) 5129[6] >**70a 70f**<

**Beamish Prince** 5 ch g Bijou D Inde-Unconditional Love (IRE) (Polish Patriot (USA)) 4449[7] 5518[7] >**69 f**<

**Beamsley Beacon** 3 ch g Wolfhound (USA) -Petindia (Petong) 1360[12] 1667[9] 2351[4] 2528[11] *2849[6] 2986[4] 4880[4]* 5141[8]5637[5] >**53a 48f**<

**Bear King (GER)** 7 b h Mujtahid (USA) -Bearall (IRE) (Al Hareb (USA)) (2336a) 3792a[6] 4378a[5] 5215a[4] >**112f**<

**Beat The Heat (IRE)** 6 b g Salse (USA) -Summer Trysting (USA) (Alleged (USA)) 6043[2] >**88a 91f**<

**Beau Cadeau (IRE)** 3 b c Monsun (GER) -Bela-M (IRE) (Ela-Mana-Mou) 2926a[5] >**92f**<

**Beauchamp Pilot** 6 ch g Inchinor-Beauchamp Image (Midyan (USA)) 2678[6] 2957[16] 3323[4] >**106 a 109f**<

**Beauchamp Ribbon** 4 b f Vettori (IRE) -Beauchamp Kate (Petoski) 3383[7] 4080[19] 4262[9] >**64a 72f**<

**Beauchamp Star** 3 ch f Pharly (FR) -Beauchamp Cactus (Niniski (USA)) 1295[9] 1370[3] 1842[2] 2400[8] 2906[4] 3129[2] >**77f**<

**Beauchamp Trump** 2 b g Pharly (FR) -Beauchamp Kate (Petoski) *5054[7]* 5179[10] 5420[4] >**63a 64f**<

**Beauchamp Turbo** 2 ch g Pharly (FR) -Compton Astoria (USA) (Lion Cavern (USA)) *5053[5]* 5376[5] 6211[6] 6574[13] >**65a 60f**<

**Beauchamp Twist** 2 b f Pharly (FR) -Beauchamp Cactus (Niniski (USA)) 3176[8] 3491[10] *4022[12]* 4335[6] 6242[4] >**31a 56f**<

**Beau Cheval (IRE)** 5 b m Spectrum (IRE) -Feminine Wiles (IRE) (Ahonoora) 2603a[10] >**85f**<

**Beau Jazz** 3 br c Merdon Melody-Ichor (Primo Dominie) *764[5] 868[3] 986[7]* 1223[6] 1313[13] 1689[14] 2165[14] *6274[12]* >**67a 64?f**<

**Beau Marche** 2 b g My Best Valentine-Beau Dada (IRE) (Pine Circle (USA)) 4239[5] 4770[8] 4936[13] 5218[2] 5792[11] (5925) 6305[7] >**69f**<

**Beaumont Girl (IRE)** 2 ch f Trans Island-Persian Danser (IRE) (Persian Bold) 4675[7] (5097) 5593[15] 5636[16] >**53f**<

**Beaune** 2 b c Desert Prince (IRE) -Tipsy (Kris) 5262[3] 5616[6] *6022[10]* >**51a 75f**<

**Beauteous (IRE)** 5 ch g Tagula (IRE) -Beauty Appeal (USA) (Shadeed (USA)) *503[8] 655[8] 934[6]* 1345[4] *1403[4] (1445) (1513) (1548) (1573)* 1783[4] >**69a 71f**<

**Beautifix (GER)** 2 b f Bering-Beautimix (FR) (Linamix (FR)) 4382a[7] (4962a) >**94f**<

**Beautifulballerina (USA)** 4 b f Nureyev (USA) -Khulasah (USA) (Affirmed (USA)) 5162a[15] >**88f**<

**Beautiful Maria (IRE)** 2 b f Sri Pekan (USA) -Puteri Wentworth (Sadler s Wells (USA)) 1399[7] >**33f**<

**Beautiful Mover (USA)** 2 ch f Spinning World (USA) -Dancer s Glamour (USA) (Danzig Connection (USA)) 2275[2] 2758[3] 3382[8] *5054[4]* 5839[18] >**72a 73f**<

**Beautiful Noise** 3 b f Piccolo-Mrs Moonlight (Ajdal (USA)) 1755$^{14}$ 2207$^{6}$ 2790$^{5}$ 3636$^{5}$ 4496$^{5}$ 4650$^{5}$ 5621$^{5}$ 5748$^{2}$5994$^{9}$ >**67?f**<

**Beauty Of Dreams** 3 b f Russian Revival (USA) -Giggleswick Girl (Full Extent (USA)) 3478$^{9}$ 3926$^{10}$ 4020$^{7}$ 4483$^{5}$ 4771$^{3}$ 5020$^{12}$ 5141$^{6}$ 5510$^{8}$5748$^{4}$ 6184$^{3}$ *6296$^{8}$ 6399$^{8}$ 6541$^{4}$* >**51a 69f**<

**Beauvrai** 4 b g Bahamian Bounty-Lets Be Fair (Efisio) *486$^{12}$ 703$^{9}$* 1765$^{8}$ 2303$^{11}$ 2724$^{5}$ 3090$^{3}$ 3645$^{13}$ 3945$^{12}$4294$^{2}$ 4472$^{3}$ (5026) (5184) 5458$^{3}$ 6526$^{13}$ >**93a 85f**<

**Beaver Diva** 3 b f Bishop Of Cashel-Beaver Skin Hunter (Ballacashtal (CAN)) 1524$^{4}$ 1784$^{7}$ *2232$^{7}$* 3037$^{2}$ 3364$^{2}$ 3954$^{16}$ 4387$^{9}$ 5793$^{17}$ >**45f**<

**Beaver Patrol (IRE)** 2 ch c Tagula (IRE) -Erne Project (IRE) (Project Manager) (1505) 1878$^{3}$ 2180$^{2}$ (2478) 2954$^{11}$ 3907$^{6}$ 4527$^{2}$ (4958a) 5947$^{5}$ 6347$^{5}$ >**105f**<

**Bebek Cafe (TUR)** 4 b f Distant Relative-Cihanyandi Lutfiye (TUR) (Kilicaslan (TUR)) 5488a$^{13}$ ><

**Be Bop** 2 ch g Groom Dancer (USA) -Norpella (Northfields (USA)) 5302$^{11}$ 5522$^{9}$ 6197$^{9}$ >**49f**<

**Be Bop Aloha** 2 b f Most Welcome-Just Julia (Natroun (FR)) 1670$^{15}$ 2095$^{6}$ *2985$^{3}$* 3553$^{5}$ 4198$^{11}$ 4584$^{8}$ 5369$^{18}$ 5556$^{14}$ >**43a 50f**<

**Bebopskiddly** 3 b c Robellino (USA) -Adarama (IRE) (Persian Bold) *6015$^{10}$* 6564$^{6}$ >**36a 61f**<

**Because (IRE)** 3 b f Sadler s Wells (USA) -Jude (Darshaan) 6102a$^{8}$ >**91?f**<

**Beckermet (IRE)** 2 b g Second Empire (IRE) -Razida (IRE) (Last Tycoon) 1782$^{3}$ (2268) (2655) 2980$^{2}$ (3290) (3703) 4217$^{9}$ 4860$^{4}$ 5464$^{11}$ 5602$^{5}$ >**93f**<

**Becrux (ITY)** 2 b c Glen Jordan-Rebecca Parisi (IRE) (Persian Heights) 6259a$^{8}$ >**71f**<

**Bedamix (FR)** 2 gr c Double Bed (FR) -Hesse (FR) (Linamix (FR)) 4963a$^{6}$ >**80f**<

**Bedanken (USA)** 5 rg m Geri (USA) -Danka (USA) (Strawberry Road (AUS)) 4767a$^{5}$ >**110f**<

**Bedtime Blues** 2 b f Cyrano De Bergerac-Boomerang Blade (Sure Blade (USA)) 1128$^{9}$ 1390$^{8}$ >**48f**<

**Beeches Theatre (IRE)** 2 b f King s Theatre (IRE) -Sandpiper (Green Desert (USA)) 2585$^{11}$ 2884$^{11}$ >**14f**<

**Beechy Bank (IRE)** 6 b m Shareef Dancer (USA) -Neptunalia (Slip Anchor) *467$^{8}$* 2167$^{7}$ 3181$^{5}$ 3683$^{3}$ 4075$^{5}$ 5274$^{9}$ >**65a 76f**<

**Bee Dees Legacy** 3 b g Atraf-Bee Dee Dancer (Ballacashtal (CAN)) *2486$^{8}$ 2882$^{10}$* 3044$^{8}$ 3669$^{9}$ >**52a 32f**<

**Beejay** 3 b f Piccolo-Letluce (Aragon) (1464) 2112$^{20}$ 2518$^{12}$ 4717$^{8}$ 5563$^{6}$ *6222$^{7}$ 6482$^{11}$* >**56a 79f**<

**Beekeeper** 6 b h Rainbow Quest (USA) -Chief Bee (Chief s Crown (USA)) 1767$^{8}$ >**116f**<

**Bee Minor** 3 b f Barathea (IRE) -Bee Off (IRE) (Wolfhound (USA)) 2694$^{8}$ 3178$^{2}$ 3455$^{8}$ 3941$^{16}$ 4144$^{2}$ 4717$^{4}$ 6089$^{7}$ >**75f**<

**Beenaboutabit** 6 b m Komaite (USA) -Tassagh Bridge (IRE) (Double Schwartz) *665$^{9}$ 1121$^{15}$* 3175$^{5}$ 3227$^{16}$ >**20a 28f**<

**Bee Stinger** 2 b c Almaty (IRE) -Nest Egg (Prince Sabo) 2761$^{10}$ 3083$^{3}$ 3633$^{2}$ 4131$^{2}$ 4488$^{4}$ >**73f**<

**Befitting** 2 b g Inchinor-Ellebanna (Tina s Pet) 6281$^{8}$ >**51+f**<

**Before The Dawn** 2 b f Lugana Beach-Chayanee s Arena (IRE) (High Estate) 3532$^{7}$ 4081$^{8}$ 4936$^{12}$ 5281$^{9}$ 6080$^{11}$ >**50f**<

**Behan** 5 ch g Rainbows For Life (CAN) -With Finesse (Be My Guest (USA)) *430$^{9}$ 571$^{5}$ 699$^{7}$* >**34 a 34f**<

**Behkara (IRE)** 4 b f Kris-Behera (Mill Reef (USA)) 4983a$^{6}$ 5966a$^{3}$ 6382a$^{2}$ >**114f**<

**Beirut (GER)** 2 br f Turtle Island (IRE) -Bajonette (IRE) (Lomond (USA)) 5280a$^{2}$ 6529a$^{7}$ >**98f**<

**Belenus (IRE)** 2 ch c Dubai Millennium-Ajhiba (IRE) (Barathea (IRE)) (3601) >**86+f**<

**Belisco (USA)** 3 b g Royal Academy (USA) -A Mean Fit (USA) (Fit To Fight (USA)) 1683$^{7}$ 4170$^{7}$ 4738$^{6}$ *(4940)* 5245$^{13}$ *5381$^{8}$ 6160$^{14}$* >**67+a 66f**<

**Bella Beguine** 5 b m Komaite (USA) -On The Record (Record Token) *612$^{5}$ 646$^{14}$ 1680$^{2}$* 2172$^{14}$ 3006$^{4}$ 3820$^{4}$ 4105$^{5}$ 4702$^{12}$4782$^{11}$ >**78a 65f**<

**Bella Boy Zee (IRE)** 3 b f Anita s Prince-Waikiki (GER) (Zampano (GER)) *610$^{3}$ 731$^{2}$ 865$^{5}$* (4320) 4576$^{8}$ 4608$^{14}$ >**53a 63f**<

**Bella Estella (GER)** 3 gr f Sternkoenig (IRE) -Bankula (GER) (Local Suitor (USA)) 5962a$^{14}$ >**44f**<

**Bellalou** 2 b f Vettori (IRE) -Spinning Mouse (Bustino) 3051$^{8}$ 3259$^{7}$ 3824$^{3}$ *4601$^{11}$* >**19a 48f**<

**Bella Miranda** 2 ch f Sinndar (IRE) -Bella Lambada (Lammtarra (USA)) *6446$^{11}$* >**32a**<

**Bellamont Forest (USA)** 8 b h Hermitage (USA) -Teresa s Spirit (USA) (Master Derby (USA)) 4984a$^{12}$ ><

**Bella Pavlina** 6 ch m Sure Blade (USA) -Pab s Choice (Telsmoss) *(532) 583$^{2}$ (653) (715) 777$^{4}$ (825) 908$^{5}$ (1030)* 1103$^{17}$ *1203$^{3}$* >**79a 50f**<

**Bella Plunkett (IRE)** 2 ch f Daggers Drawn (USA) -Amazona (IRE) (Tirol) 4487$^{12}$ 4876$^{7}$ 5200$^{7}$ 5516$^{6}$ 6195$^{2}$ >**55f**<

**Bella Tutrice (IRE)** 3 b f Woodborough (USA) -Institutrice (IRE) (College Chapel) 2877$^{15}$ 3122$^{3}$ 3307$^{4}$ *3420$^{10}$ 3849$^{3}$* 4052$^{9}$ 4740$^{12}$ 5737$^{17}$*6016$^{10}$* 6079$^{10}$ >**67a 67f**<

**Belle Ange (FR)** 3 b f Ganges (USA) -Wait And See One (FR) (The Wonder (FR)) 4899a$^{2}$ >**103f**<

**Belle Artiste (IRE)** 2 b f Namid-Beltisaal (FR) (Belmez (USA)) 3859a$^{6}$ 5325a$^{5}$ 5680a$^{4}$ >**102f**<

**Belle Chanson** 2 b f Kingsinger (IRE) -Tallulah Belle (Crowning Honors (CAN)) 5536$^{7}$ 5890$^{8}$ *6153$^{11}$* >**44a 52f**<

**Belleinga (IRE)** 3 b f Orpen (USA) -Bellissi (IRE) (Bluebird (USA)) 5660a$^{4}$ >**81f**<

**Belle Largesse** 2 b f Largesse-Palmstead Belle (IRE) (Wolfhound (USA)) 1666$^{5}$ 2382$^{13}$ *6289$^{12}$* >**23 a 23f**<

**Belle Rouge** 6 b m Celtic Swing-Gunner s Belle (Gunner B) *931$^{2}$* 1135$^{2}$ (1297) 3851$^{2}$ *(4129)* 4647$^{2}$ (5073) 5274$^{2}$ (5728) (5997) 6335$^{3}$ >**70a 87f**<

**Bells Beach (IRE)** 6 b m General Monash (USA) -Clifton Beach (Auction Ring (USA)) *572$^{6}$ 654$^{2}$ 728$^{8}$ (791) 859$^{9}$ (884) 930$^{5}$ 987$^{6}$(1206)* 1516$^{9}$ *1739$^{4}$* 2178$^{4}$ *(2404)* 2843$^{5}$ 3533$^{10}$ *4517$^{8}$ 4879$^{7}$*4937$^{9}$ >**59a 55f**<

**Bells Boy s** 5 b g Mind Games-Millie s Lady (IRE) (Common Grounds) *499$^{3}$ 572$^{3}$ 813$^{5}$ 936$^{15}$ 1092$^{4}$ 1191$^{12}$ 2183$^{3}$*2384$^{3}$ 2556$^{14}$ 4309$^{14}$ 4350$^{15}$ >**41a 39f**<

**Belly Dancer (IRE)** 2 gr f Danehill Dancer (IRE) -Persian Mistress (IRE) (Persian Bold) 2522$^{6}$ *3021$^{4}$* 5653$^{2}$ 5938$^{6}$ *6291$^{2}$* >**76a 76f**<

**Belshazzar (USA)** 3 b c King Of Kings (IRE) -Bayou Bidder (USA) (Premiership (USA)) 2144$^{9}$ 2412$^{4}$ 3168$^{7}$ 3780$^{5}$ 4493$^{13}$ >**69f**<

**Beltane** 6 b g Magic Ring (IRE) -Sally s Trust (IRE) (Classic Secret (USA)) *705$^{10}$ 842$^{11}$ (860) 1095$^{2}$* 1373$^{12}$ 3386$^{13}$ 4558$^{15}$ 4574$^{5}$5259$^{7}$ 5927$^{9}$ 6227$^{19}$ >**51a 53?f**<

**Belton** 2 b c Lujain (USA) -Efficacious (IRE) (Efisio) 2234$^{13}$ 2470$^{8}$ 4699$^{7}$ 5083$^{8}$ 5369$^{17}$ (5556) >**56f**<

**Be My Alibi (IRE)** 3 ch f Daggers Drawn (USA) -Join The Party (Be My Guest (USA)) 1908$^{7}$ *2187$^{5}$* 2620$^{10}$ 3368$^{11}$ 6469$^{7}$ >**31a 31f**<

**Ben Bacchus (IRE)** 2 b c Bahhare (USA) -Bodfaridistinction (IRE) (Distinctly North (USA)) 6476$^{15}$ >**36f**<

**Benbaun (IRE)** 3 b g Stravinsky (USA) -Escape To Victory (Salse (USA)) (1760) 1881$^{8}$ (2131) 2744a$^{2}$ (2892) 3816a$^{3}$ 5327a$^{2}$ >**107f**<

**Benbyas** 7 b g Rambo Dancer (CAN) -Light The Way (Nicholas Bill) 1103$^{6}$ (1282) (1326) 1669$^{5}$ >**83f**<

**Ben Casey** 2 b c Whittingham (IRE) -Hot Ice (IRE) (Petardia) 2860$^{18}$ 4804$^{6}$ 5241$^{3}$ 5555$^{3}$ 6008$^{5}$ >**65f**<

**Bendarshaan** 4 b c Darshaan-Calypso Run (Lycius (USA)) 3276$^{4}$ (3608) (3947) 4176$^{2}$ 4218$^{9}$ 4715$^{5}$ 5288$^{18}$ 5785$^{5}$ 6172$^{8}$ 6346$^{3}$6573$^{3}$ >**92f**<

**Benedict** 2 b c Benny The Dip (USA) -Abbey Strand (USA) (Shadeed (USA)) 4809$^{7}$ 5179$^{8}$ >**57f**<

**Benedict Bay** 2 b c In The Wings-Persia (IRE) (Persian Bold) 3241$^{6}$ 3749$^{10}$ 4166$^{7}$ 5539$^{12}$ 6090$^{12}$ >**65f**<

**Beneking** 4 bb g Wizard King-Gagajulu (Al Hareb (USA)) 1876$^{9}$ 2473$^{3}$ 2834$^{8}$ 3151$^{6}$ 3734$^{13}$ 4213$^{5}$ 5110$^{10}$ 5320$^{8}$5714$^{14}$ 5993$^{14}$ >**44a 56f**<

**Beneventa** 4 b f Most Welcome-Dara Dee (Dara Monarch) (1332) (1790) 2042$^{2}$ 2967$^{8}$ (3944) 4566a$^{10}$ 5763$^{7}$ >**114f**<

**Ben Hur** 5 b g Zafonic (USA) -Gayane (Nureyev (USA)) 1393$^{18}$ (2362) 2776$^{13}$ 2938$^{2}$ (3040) (3291) 3441$^{5}$ 3705$^{4}$ 4363$^{5}$ 4691$^{6}$ 5006$^{3}$5151$^{9}$ 5581$^{14}$ >**73a 80f**<

**Benjamin (IRE)** 6 b g Night Shift (USA) -Best Academy (USA) (Roberto (USA)) *1407$^{2}$ 1494$^{2}$ 2052$^{5}$* 2387$^{11}$ 3489$^{14}$ 3774$^{15}$ 4419$^{5}$ >**42a 55 f**<

**Ben Kenobi** 6 ch g Accondy (IRE) -Nour El Sahar (USA) (Sagace (FR)) *1889$^{5}$ 2017$^{2}$ 2184$^{2}$* 2939$^{7}$ 3342$^{2}$ 3695$^{8}$ *6360$^{7}$* >**36a 50f**<

**Ben Lomand** 4 ch g Inchinor-Benjarong (Sharpo) 1185$^{12}$ 2399$^{13}$ 4727$^{3}$ 4846$^{9}$ 5201$^{9}$ 5541$^{10}$ *6398$^{6}$* >**53a 83f**<

**Bennanabaa** 5 b g Anabaa (USA) -Arc Empress Jane (IRE) (Rainbow Quest (USA)) *463$^{13}$ 644$^{5}$ 869$^{7}$* 1310$^{9}$ *2128$^{12}$* 2834$^{11}$ 3575$^{8}$ 4044$^{5}$4617$^{13}$ 4687$^{8}$ 5081$^{8}$ 5253$^{13}$ >**60a 54f**<

**Benny Bathwick (IRE)** 3 b g Midyan (USA) -Sweet Pavlova (USA) (Zilzal (USA)) 2765$^{7}$ 3161$^{12}$ >**50f**<

**Benny The Ball (USA)** 3 bb g Benny The Dip (USA) -Heloise (USA) (Forty Niner (USA)) 1408$^{15}$ 2295$^{11}$ 2549$^{9}$ *5912$^{10}$ 6279$^{11}$* >**81a 82f**<

**Benny The Bus** 2 b g Komaite (USA) -Amy Leigh (IRE) (Imperial Frontier (USA)) 4359$^{11}$ 4507$^{10}$ 4824$^{11}$ 6008$^{2}$ >**63f**<

**Ben s Revenge** 4 b g Emperor Jones (USA) -Bumble Boogie (IRE) (Bluebird (USA)) 3885$^{6}$ 4492$^{11}$ 4673$^{5}$ *6360$^{6}$* >**41f**<

**Benta Berri (FR)** 2 ch c Priolo (USA) -Masslama (FR) (No Pass No Sale) 6169a$^{8}$ >**60f**<

**Bentley s Ball (USA)** 3 bb g Stravinsky (USA) -Slide By (Aragon) 1388$^{6}$ 3001$^{13}$ 3542$^{8}$ 4031$^{3}$ 4750$^{4}$ 5762$^{4}$ >**93f**<

**Bentley s Bush (IRE)** 2 ch f Barathea (IRE) -Veiled Threat (IRE) (Be My Guest (USA)) 2083$^{5}$ 2690$^{2}$ (3045) 3727$^{3}$ 4060$^{3}$ >**91f**<

**Benvolio** 7 br g Cidrax (FR) -Miss Capulet (Commanche Run) 5710$^{11}$ >**9a 17f**<

**Benwilt Breeze (IRE)** 2 b c Mujadil (USA) -Image Of Truce (IRE) (Brief Truce (USA)) 3286a$^{11}$ >**86 f**<

**Berber (GER)** 6 gr h Dashing Blade-Bergwelt (GER) (Solarstern (FR)) 4378a$^{10}$ >**101f**<

**Berenson (IRE)** 2 b c Entrepreneur-On Air (FR) (Chief Singer) 5678a$^{2}$ >**114f**<

**Beresford Boy** 3 b g Easycall-Devils Dirge (Song) 5338$^{P}$ 5845$^{10}$ *6280$^{2}$* >**59a 37f**<

**Bergamo** 8 b g Robellino (USA) -Pretty Thing (Star Appeal) *716$^{7}$ 1023$^{7}$* >**57a 57 f**<

**Berham Maldu (IRE)** 2 b f Fraam-Corniche Quest (IRE) (Salt Dome (USA)) 1105$^{15}$ 1307$^{10}$ 6127$^{11}$ >**24f**<

**Berkeley Heights** 4 b f Hector Protector (USA) -Dancing Heights (IRE) (High Estate) *446$^{4}$ 570$^{10}$ 1023$^{6}$ 1193$^{2}$ 1512$^{3}$ 1698$^{4}$ (2230)* 3108$^{9}$3576$^{12}$ >**46a 46 f**<

**Berkhamsted (IRE)** 2 b c Desert Sun-Accounting (Sillery (USA)) (1219) 2954$^{6}$ 3726$^{2}$ 4227$^{5}$ (4963a) 5778$^{8}$ 6259a$^{5}$ 6347$^{6}$ >**99f**<

**Bernard (FR)** 2 ch c Trempolino (USA) -Belmoda (GER) (Jalmood (USA)) 6380a$^{3}$ >**92f**<

**Berry Racer (IRE)** 3 ch f Titus Livius (FR) -Opening Day (Day Is Done) 2942$^{11}$ >**48f**<

**Berrywhite (IRE)** 6 ch g Barathea (IRE) -Berryville (USA) (Hatchet Man (USA)) *1042$^{7}$* 1527$^{8}$ 1668$^{3}$ 2249$^{3}$ 2759$^{5}$ >**28a 44f**<

**Bertocelli** 3 ch c Vettori (IRE) -Dame Jude (Dilum (USA)) 2063$^{14}$ 2378$^{14}$ 2727$^{3}$ 3155$^{4}$ 3525$^{8}$ 4092$^{7}$ 4483$^{6}$ 4738$^{8}$5245$^{7}$ 5733$^{10}$ 5843$^{4}$ 6120$^{4}$ >**74f**<

**Bertrose** 2 ch c Machiavellian (USA) -Tularosa (In The Wings) 4747$^{4}$ 5268$^{5}$ 5729$^{3}$ 6129$^{11}$ >**78 f**<

**Beseeka Runnin Fox** 3 b f Hi Nod-Windsor Fox (IRE) (Mandalus) 3121$^{7}$ ><

**Bespoke** 2 ch g Pivotal-Immaculate (Mark Of Esteem (IRE)) 4003$^{5}$ 4172$^{6}$ 4454$^{9}$ 5539$^{8}$ >**47f**<

**Bessemer (JPN)** 3 b g Carnegie (IRE) -Chalna (IRE) (Darshaan) 1745$^{5}$ 3053$^{3}$ 3365$^{6}$ (4533) 4906$^{4}$ 5607$^{19}$ 5673$^{3}$ 6573$^{19}$ >**92+f**<

**Best About** 2 ch f King s Best (USA) -Up And About (Barathea (IRE)) 5694$^{7}$ >**57f**<

**Best Before (IRE)** 4 b g Mujadil (USA) -Miss Margate (IRE) (Don t Forget Me) *596$^{7}$ 846$^{7}$ (932)* 1675$^{2}$ 1845$^{2}$ 2226$^{16}$ 2643$^{2}$ (2945) 3048$^{3}$3177$^{3}$ 3631$^{3}$ (3911) 4164$^{6}$ 5004$^{9}$ 6069$^{13}$ 6358$^{12}$ 6568$^{17}$ >**66a 87f**<

**Best Be Going (IRE)** 4 b g Danehill (USA) -Bye Bold Aileen (IRE) (Warning) 1460$^{17}$ 2537$^{7}$ 3415$^{5}$ 4019$^{4}$ 4831$^{14}$ 5297$^{16}$ (6128) >**85f**<

**Bestbyfar (IRE)** 2 b c King s Best (USA) -Pippas Song (Reference Point) 5604$^{7}$ >**56f**<

**Best Desert (IRE)** 3 b g Desert Style (IRE) -La Alla Wa Asa (IRE) (Alzao (USA)) 2097$^{4}$ 2377$^{2}$ 3180$^{14}$ 3750$^{8}$ 4126$^{5}$ (4390) 4756$^{5}$ 5156$^{12}$ 5674$^{7}$5945$^{6}$ *6220$^{3}$ 6399$^{4}$ 6560$^{8}$* >**63a 68f**<

**Best Flight** 4 gr g Sheikh Albadou-Bustling Nelly (Bustino) 1821$^{11}$ 2084$^{15}$ 3591$^{4}$ 4075$^{11}$ 4971$^{9}$ 5203$^{9}$ >**78+a 69f**<

**Best Force** 3 b f Compton Place-Bestemor (Selkirk (USA)) 1689$^{4}$ 1907$^{7}$ >**56f**<

**Best Game** 2 b g Mister Baileys-Bestemor (Selkirk (USA)) 5376$^{12}$ 5534$^{7}$ 6181$^{6}$ 6515$^{14}$ >**58f**<

**Best Horse (FR)** 2 b c Xaar-Poplife (FR) (Zino) 5313a$^{4}$ >**92f**<

**Best Lead** 5 b g Distant Relative-Bestemor (Selkirk (USA)) *(411) 540$^{9}$ 608$^{4}$ 796$^{4}$ 1474$^{3}$* 1870$^{4}$ 2175$^{3}$ 2582$^{3}$2975$^{3}$ 3269$^{3}$ 3735$^{8}$ >**56a 61f**<

**Best Port (IRE)** 8 b g Be My Guest (USA) -Portree (Slip Anchor) 1198$^{10}$ (1463) *2126$^{11}$* (2531) 3236$^{6}$ (4352) 5318$^{9}$ 5523$^{4}$ 5951$^{3}$ 6269$^{5}$*6581$^{2}$* >**57a 71f**<

**Bestseller** 4 ch f Selkirk (USA) -Top Shop (Nashwan (USA)) *484$^{4}$ 722$^{3}$ 838$^{5}$* >**51a 31f**<

**Best Smiling (GER)** 4 br f Big Shuffle (USA) -Bergwelt (GER) (Solarstern (FR)) 2466a$^{10}$ >**8f**<

**Betfred** 3 b g Pursuit Of Love-Shamaka (Kris) 4332$^{8}$ ><

**Bethanys Boy (IRE)** 3 ch g Docksider (USA) -Daymoon (USA) (Dayjur (USA)) 1108$^{14}$ 1418$^{10}$ 2119$^{8}$ >**75a 71f**<

**Bettalatethannever (IRE)** 3 ch g Titus Livius (FR) -Shambodia (IRE) (Petardia) *(493) 1063$^{4}$* 1408$^{20}$ 2642$^{12}$ 3053$^{2}$ *3850$^{6}$* 4268$^{7}$ 4646$^{8}$(5937) >**98a 103f**<

**Better Off** 6 ch g Bettergeton-Miami Pride (Miami Springs) *423$^{5}$ 694$^{8}$ 1035$^{6}$ 1479$^{13}$ 2013$^{5}$* >**47a 41f**<

**Better Pal** 5 ch g Prince Sabo-Rattle Along (Tap On Wood) *472$^{14}$* >**29a 66 f**<

**Better Talk Now (USA)** 5 b g Talkin Man (CAN) -Bendita (USA) (Baldski (USA)) (6490a) >**124f**<

**Betterthedeviluno** 5 b g Hector Protector (USA) -Aquaglow (Caerleon (USA)) *1090$^{12}$* >**51f**<

**Betterware Boy** 4 ch g Barathea (IRE) -Crystal Drop (Cadeaux Genereux) *4129$^{7}$* 4398$^{11}$ >**67a 71f**<

**Bettys Pride** 5 b m Lion Cavern (USA) -Final Verdict (IRE) (Law Society (USA)) 2252$^{9}$ 2369$^{4}$ 2656$^{16}$ 2909$^{6}$ 3680$^{6}$ 3894$^{13}$ (4247) 4331$^{7}$ 5562$^{6}$(5736) 5862$^{12}$ >**62f**<

**Betty Stogs (IRE)** 3 b f Perugino (USA) -Marabela (IRE) (Shernazar) 1327$^{9}$ 4684$^{5}$ 5249$^{14}$ 5887$^{16}$ >**78f**<

**Bettys Valentine** 4 b f My Best Valentine-Fairy Ballerina (Fairy King (USA)) *935$^{4}$* 1528$^{10}$ 1718$^{8}$ 2346$^{12}$ 2975$^{9}$ 3269$^{13}$ >**15a 30f**<

**Beverley Beau** 2 b c Inchinor-Oriel Girl (Beveled (USA)) 1314$^{5}$ 1717$^{5}$ 2523$^{4}$ 5362$^{4}$ 5558$^{4}$ 5816$^{5}$ *6359$^{6}$* >**54a 66f**<

**Bevier** 10 b g Nashwan (USA) -Bevel (USA) (Mr Prospector (USA)) *652$^{5}$ 812$^{3}$ 903$^{4}$ 989$^{2}$* 1282$^{8}$ *1572$^{4}$ 1888$^{7}$*5175$^{12}$ 5449$^{15}$ >**15a 15f**<

**Be Wise Girl** 3 ch f Fleetwood (IRE) -Zabelina (USA) (Diesis) *1192$^{3}$* (1465) 5658$^{14}$ *5957$^{8}$* >**49a 56f**<

**Beyond Calculation (USA)** 10 ch g Geiger Counter (USA) -Placer Queen (Habitat) 1774$^{18}$ 2118$^{16}$ 2274$^{7}$ 2440$^{10}$ 3043$^{4}$ 3269$^{7}$ 3533$^{4}$ 3742$^{4}$4014$^{5}$ 4350$^{11}$ 5184$^{8}$ >**57a 58f**<

**Beyond The Clouds (IRE)** 8 b g Midhish-Tongabezi (IRE) (Shernazar) 1343$^{12}$ 1774$^{12}$ 3016$^{12}$ 3399$^{2}$ 3509$^{9}$ 3713$^{9}$ 4133$^{3}$ 4626$^{7}$5062$^{15}$ 5107$^{6}$ 5440$^{2}$ 5704$^{7}$ 5712$^{10}$ 6267$^{17}$ >**97f**<

**Beyond The Pole (USA)** 6 b g Ghazi (USA) -North Of Sunset (USA) (Northern Baby (CAN)) *(740) 867$^{12}$ (931)* >**62a 47f**<

**Bhutan (IRE)** 9 b g Polish Patriot (USA) -Bustinetta (Bustino) 2689$^{10}$ 3827$^{2}$ 4398$^{8}$ >**17a 51f**<

**Bianconi (SAF)** 4 b c Rambo Dancer (CAN) -Coconut Ice (SAF) (Jungle Cove (USA)) 1006a$^{8}$ >**69f**<

**Bibi Helen** 2 b f Robellino (USA) -Tarry (Salse (USA)) 2478$^{6}$ 3319$^{11}$ 4728$^{11}$ >**57f**<

**Bibury Flyer** 2 br f Zafonic (USA) -Affair Of State (IRE) (Tate Gallery (USA)) 1130$^{2}$ 1248$^{2}$ 2655$^{3}$ 2868$^{3}$ 3208$^{5}$ 3408$^{2}$ 3868$^{2}$ 3938$^{6}$(4046) 4325$^{2}$ 4575$^{9}$ 4914$^{7}$ 5078$^{3}$ 5174$^{3}$ 5391$^{3}$ 5548$^{2}$ 5648$^{4}$5878a$^{5}$ (6101a) 6213$^{4}$ (6353) 6456$^{8}$ >**96f**<

**Bid For Fame (USA)** 7 bb g Quest For Fame-Shroud (USA) (Vaguely Noble) 1329$^{15}$ 1457$^{13}$ 2047$^{14}$ 2935$^{10}$ 6460$^{8}$ >**59 a 59f**<

**Bid Spotter (IRE)** 5 b g Eagle Eyed (USA) -Bebe Auction (IRE) (Auction Ring (USA)) *1077$^{4}$ 1238$^{13}$* 3461$^{13}$ >**54 a 62df**<

**Bien Good** 3 b f Bien Bien (USA) -Southern Sky (Comedy Star (USA)) 3625$^{3}$ 3955$^{5}$ 6005$^{20}$ 6516$^{8}$ >**43f**<

**Bienheureux** 3 b g Bien Bien (USA) -Rochea (Rock City) *683$^{9}$ 808$^{8}$ 946$^{13}$* 2915$^{11}$ 3371$^{2}$ (4055) 4302$^{5}$ >**41a 51f**<

**Bienvenue** 3 ch f Bien Bien (USA) -Mossy Rose (King Of Spain) 2848$^{4}$ (3348) 3806$^{2}$ 4062$^{6}$ 4618$^{8}$ 5402$^{6}$ >**66a 78f**<

**Bigalos Bandit** 2 ch c Compton Place-Move Darling (Rock City) (1359) 1819$^{2}$ 2570$^{4}$ 3703$^{8}$ 4217$^{4}$ 4860$^{3}$ 5213$^{3}$ 5392$^{15}$ (6241) >**95f**<

**Big Bad Bob (IRE)** 4 br c Bob Back (USA) -Fantasy Girl (IRE) (Marju (IRE)) 2241$^{3}$ 3030a$^{4}$ 4160a$^{5}$ (5436) >**118 f**<

**Big Bad Burt** 3 ch g Efisio-Mountain Bluebird (USA) (Clever Trick (USA)) *580$^{4}$ 675$^{2}$ 891$^{2}$ 965$^{3}$* 1874$^{7}$ 2122$^{3}$ 2377$^{4}$ 2973$^{6}$*3613$^{9}$* 4065$^{9}$ 4458$^{4}$ 4911$^{7}$ 5018$^{4}$ >**65a 69f**<

**Big Bambo (IRE)** 2 ch c Monashee Mountain (USA) -Bamboo (IRE) (Thatching) 1269$^{8}$ 2300$^{17}$ >**21f**<

**Big Bertha** 6 ch m Dancing Spree (USA) -Bertrade (Homeboy) *467$^{4}$ 549$^{2}$ 618$^{8}$* 5853$^{15}$ 6457$^{4}$ >**74a 74f**<

**Big Bradford** 3 b g Tamure (IRE) -Heather Honey (Insan (USA)) 2309$^{2}$ 2897$^{12}$ 3598$^{16}$ 5120$^{12}$ *5379$^{6}$* 5697$^{14}$ 5874$^{18}$ >**84a 93f**<

**Big Hassle (IRE)** 2 b c Namid-Night After Night (Night Shift (USA)) 3196$^{5}$ 3514$^{2}$ (3818) 4857$^{9}$ >**87 f**<

**Big Hoo Hah** 2 ch f Halling (USA) -Gentilesse (Generous (IRE)) 3627$^{16}$ 4705$^{6}$ 5172$^{4}$ 5596$^{7}$ >**65f**<

**Big Hurry (USA)** 3 b f Red Ransom (USA) -Call Me Fleet (USA) (Afleet (CAN)) 4369$^{11}$ >**47f**<

**Big Moment** 6 ch g Be My Guest (USA) -Petralona (USA) (Alleged (USA)) 1880$^{3}$ 3076$^{5}$ 4218$^{6}$ 5785$^{2}$ 6172$^{2}$ (6570) >**104f**<

**Big Mystery (IRE)** 3 b f Grand Lodge (USA) -Mysterious Plans (IRE) (Last Tycoon) *6578$^{9}$* >**23a**<

**Big Smoke (IRE)** 4 gr g Perugino (USA) -Lightning Bug (Prince Bee) 2781$^{11}$ *3022$^{4}$ 3281$^{5}$* 3892$^{3}$ >**53a 53f**<

**Big Tom (IRE)** 3 ch c Cadeaux Genereux-Zilayah (USA) (Zilzal (USA)) 4491$^{9}$ *4929$^{11}$* 5104$^{10}$ 5547$^{19}$ 6057$^{16}$ >**6a 66f**<

**Bijan (IRE)** 6 b m Mukaddamah (USA) -Alkariyh (USA) (Alydar (USA)) *407$^{8}$ 429$^{4}$ 503$^{9}$* >**42a 39f**<

**Bijou Dan** 3 ch g Bijou D Inde-Cal Norma s Lady (IRE) (Lyphard s Special (USA)) 3899$^{4}$ 5371$^{6}$ 5836$^{7}$ 6112$^{5}$ 6524$^{9}$ >**54f**<

**Bijou Dancer** 4 ch g Bijou D Inde-Dancing Diana (Raga Navarro (ITY)) 1675$^{12}$ 2362$^{7}$ *2813$^{6}$* 6082$^{17}$ >**35a 58f**<

**Bill Bennett (FR)** 3 b g Bishop Of Cashel-Concert (Polar Falcon (USA)) *450$^{6}$ 566$^{9}$ 829$^{6}$* 1201$^{5}$ (1365) (1843) 1947$^{2}$ 2397$^{5}$ 2561$^{7}$(3160) 3396$^{4}$ 5944$^{8}$ 6339$^{3}$ 6460$^{7}$ >**61a 86f**<

**Billet (IRE)** 2 b f Danehill (USA) -Tathkara (USA) (Alydar (USA)) 4589a$^{4}$ >**92df**<

**Billy Bathwick (IRE)** 7 ch g Fayruz-Cut It Fine (USA) (Big Spruce (USA)) 2302$^{9}$ 2430$^{8}$ 2835$^{3}$ 3143$^{3}$ (3459) 3773$^{7}$ 5258$^{5}$ 5493$^{8}$ 5554$^{12}$5869$^{7}$ *6013$^{14}$* 6083$^{17}$ >**51a 64f**<

**Billy One Punch** 2 b c Mark Of Esteem (IRE) -Polytess (IRE) (Polish Patriot (USA)) 5091$^{7}$ >**68f**<

**Billy The Kid (IRE)** 6 b g Danehill (USA) -Bleu Cerise (Sadler s Wells (USA)) 1110a$^{4}$ 1435a$^{11}$ >**105f**<

**Billy Two Rivers (IRE)** 5 ch g Woodborough (USA) -Good Visibility (IRE) (Electric) 3576$^{5}$ >**56f**<

**Billy Whistler** 3 ch c Dancing Spree (USA) -Polar Refrain (Polar Falcon (USA)) *1022$^{12}$* ><

**Binanti** 4 b g Bin Ajwaad (IRE) -Princess Rosananti (IRE) (Shareef Dancer (USA)) 2534$^{13}$ 2891$^{6}$ 3337$^{6}$ *3850$^{9}$* 4120$^{17}$ 4690$^{5}$ *5055$^{5}$* 5444$^{3}$5886$^{7}$ >**86 a 97f**<

**Binary File (USA)** 6 b h Nureyev (USA) -Binary (Rainbow Quest (USA)) 4380a$^{7}$ 4984a$^{3}$ 5727a$^{5}$ 5968a$^{10}$ >**114f**<

**Binary Vision (USA)** 3 ch c Distant View (USA) -Binary (Rainbow Quest (USA)) (2900) 3323$^{6}$ >**105f**<

**Binnion Bay (IRE)** 3 b g Fasliyev (USA) -Literary (Woodman (USA)) 2576$^{8}$ 3527$^{11}$ 3689$^{9}$ 3988$^{6}$ 4619$^{7}$ >**71a 76f**<

**Bint Il Sultan (IRE)** 2 b f Xaar-Knight s Place (IRE) (Hamas (IRE)) 2837$^{3}$ 3438$^{7}$ 3840$^{12}$ *4601$^{8}$* >**50+a 60f**<

**Bint Royal (IRE)** 6 ch m Royal Abjar (USA) -Living Legend (USA) (Septieme Ciel (USA)) *1625$^{5}$* 2238$^{5}$

2473[12] 2506[3] 2598[4] 2670[7] 2875[4] 3047[3] 3372[8] 3457[9] 3779[5] 3867[8] 4066[8] 4122[19] 4248[2] (4260) 5411[13] (5639) 5798[5] 6117[5] >**74a 63f**<

**Binty** 2 b f Prince Sabo-Mistral s Dancer (Shareef Dancer (USA)) 6454[10] 6563[11] >**44f**<

**Biographie** 4 b f Mtoto-Biosphere (Pharly (FR)) 2138a[14] >**82f**<

**Bi Polar** 4 b g Polar Falcon (USA) -Doctor Bid (USA) (Spectacular Bid (USA)) 1765[23] 2064[19] 2727[2] 3626[2] 3910[13] 4846[3] 5419[6] 5887[3] >**66a 81f**<

**Bipop (ITY)** 3 b c Love The Groom (USA) -Twin Skin (FR) (Double Bed (FR)) 3135a[2] >**82f**<

**Birchall (IRE)** 5 b g Priolo (USA) -Ballycuirke (Taufan (USA)) 3917[14] >**58f**<

**Bird Key** 3 b f Cadeaux Genereux-Portelet (Night Shift (USA)) 4555[8] >**25f**<

**Bird Over** 2 b f Bold Edge-High Bird (IRE) (Polar Falcon (USA)) 5640[4] (6400) >**58a**<

**Birdstone (USA)** 3 b c Grindstone (USA) -Dear Birdie (USA) (Storm Bird (CAN)) 1781a[8] (2701a) 6491a[7] >**125a**<

**Birikina** 3 b f Atraf-Fizzy Fiona (Efisio) 435[6] 547[7] >**48a 45f**<

**Biriyani (IRE)** 2 b f Danehill (USA) -Breyani (Commanche Run) 5270[4] >**74f**<

**Birthday Star (IRE)** 2 b c Desert King (IRE) -White Paper (IRE) (Marignan (USA)) 5319[14] >**49f**<

**Birthday Suit (IRE)** 3 ch f Daylami (IRE) -Wanton (Kris) 1417[3] 1822[3] >**96f**<

**Birth Of The Blues** 8 ch g Efisio-Great Steps (Vaigly Great) 495[8] 661[8] 838[6] 1101[3] (1281) 1492[4] 1644[6] 2031[6] >**45a 45f**<

**Birthplace (USA)** 2 b f King Of Kings (IRE) -Berceau (USA) (Alleged (USA)) 6297a[6] >**89f**<

**Birthstone** 2 ch f Machiavellian (USA) -Baya (USA) (Nureyev (USA)) (5532a) >**104+f**<

**Biscar Two (IRE)** 3 b g Daggers Drawn (USA) -Thoughtful Kate (Rock Hopper) 615[4] 804[6] 1363[2] 1667[2] 2088[2] 2390[8] (3582) 4853[9] >**40a 55f**<

**Bischoff s Boy (GER)** 3 b c Alkalde (GER) -Bischoffsgorl (Elegant Air) 2158a[6] >**101f**<

**Bish Bash Bosh (IRE)** 3 b f Bien Bien (USA) -Eurolink Virago (Charmer) 591[9] 751[8] >**32a 30f**<

**Bishopric** 4 b g Bishop Of Cashel-Nisha (Nishapour (FR)) 1821[19] (2687) 3477[14] 4856[10] >**105f**<

**Bishops Bounce** 3 b g Bishop Of Cashel-Heights Of Love (Persian Heights) 3002[14] 4257[8] >**46a 59f**<

**Bishops Court** 10 ch g Clantime-Indigo (Primo Dominie) (1438) 1955[2] 2041[7] 2636[3] 3162a[3] 3732[7] 4269[10] 4805[2] 5105[5] 5181[6] 5418[5] 5787[8] 6177[7] 6349[6] >**107f**<

**Bishopstone Man** 7 b g Piccolo-Auntie Gladys (Great Nephew) 1275[18] 1624[7] 2170[4] 3191[8] 3771[6] 4083[2] >**63a 80f**<

**Bishop To Actress** 3 ch f Paris House-Chess Mistress (USA) (Run The Gantlet (USA)) 438[13] 876[15] >**41a 43f**<

**Bits Of Paradise (FR)** 3 b f Desert Prince (IRE) -Don t Worry Me (IRE) (Dancing Dissident (USA)) 2193a[4] 4356a[12] >**100f**<

**Blackburn Meadows** 7 b m Flying Tyke-Hatshepsut (Ardross) 3251[12] ><

**Blackchurch Mist (IRE)** 7 b m Erin s Isle-Diandra (Shardari) 3076[11] >**35f**<

**Black Combe Lady (IRE)** 2 br f Indian Danehill (IRE) -Florinda (CAN) (Vice Regent (CAN)) 2352[12] 2972[7] 3366[7] 4010[13] 4095[11] >**2f**<

**Blackcomb Mountain (USA)** 2 bb f Royal Anthem (USA) -Ski Racer (FR) (Ski Chief (USA)) 3679[5] 3983[3] 4277[4] 4601[4] 4890[9] 5516[3] 5753[6] 6240[6] >**67a 61f**<

**Blackdoun (FR)** 3 rg c Verglas (IRE) -Rade (FR) (Kaldoun (FR)) 1218a[3] 1653a[2] 6486a[7] >**114f**<

**Black Draft** 2 bb g Josr Algarhoud (IRE) -Tilia (Primo Dominie) 2057[9] 2376[8] >**63f**<

**Blackheath (IRE)** 8 ch g Common Grounds-Queen Caroline (USA) (Chief s Crown (USA)) 1106[14] 1454[4] 1673[4] 2461[13] 2682[6] 2899[2] 3098[2] 3509[6] 3713[4] (3901) 4076[4] 4165[5] 4324[23] 4538[12] 5287[13] 5603[26] >**96f**<

**Black Legend (IRE)** 5 b g Marju (IRE) -Lamping (Warning) 4669[2] 4883[4] 5175[9] 5257[5] 6055[6] >**43a 55f**<

**Blackmail (USA)** 6 b g Twining (USA) -Black Penny (USA) (Private Account (USA)) 5379[13] 5935[14] 6156[10] 6450[5] >**90a 66 f**<

**Blacknyello Bonnet (USA)** 2 bb f Seeking The Gold (USA) -Salt It (USA) (Salt Lake (USA)) 5578[9] 5856[8] 6514[8] >**43f**<

**Black Oval** 3 b f Royal Applause-Corniche Quest (IRE) (Salt Dome (USA)) 1119[4] 1196[4] 1312[5] 1464[11] 1517[3] 2380[8] 2577[12] 2800[5] 3211[8] 4267[8] 4548[11] 5564[9] >**60a 56f**<

**Blackpool Jack** 3 b g Mtoto-Endearing Val (Entitled) 4387[11] 6142[11] 6465[11] ><

**Black Sabbeth** 3 br g Desert Story (IRE) -Black Orchid (IRE) (Persian Bold) 1830[11] 2808[11] 3487[10] 4144[6] 4484[4] 5219[18] 6079[13] 6290[11] >**17a 68f**<

**Black Swan (IRE)** 4 b g Nashwan (USA) -Sea Spray (IRE) (Royal Academy (USA)) 4080[13] 4513[5] 4870[8] 5354[13] >**43?f**<

**Blackthorn** 5 ch g Deploy-Balliasta (USA) (Lyphard (USA)) 1103[4] 1754[12] 2449[3] 2584[3] 4352[6] >**67f**<

**Black Velvet** 2 br g Inchinor-Three Owls (IRE) (Warning) (2058) 3907[2] 4227[8] >**100f**<

**Blade Of Gold (IRE)** 2 ch f Daggers Drawn (USA) -Be Prepared (IRE) (Be My Guest (USA)) 5353[10] >**48f**<

**Blade Runner (IRE)** 2 ch f Daggers Drawn (USA) -Leitrim Lodge (IRE) (Classic Music (USA)) 1364[10] 4866[14] 5825[13] >**19f**<

**Blades Boy** 2 ch g Paris House-Banningham Blade (Sure Blade (USA)) 5125[8] 5362[9] (5513) >**61f**<

**Blade s Daughter** 3 gr f Paris House-Banningham Blade (Sure Blade (USA)) 1288[6] 1676[11] 1742[7] 2012[6] >**19a 28f**<

**Blade s Edge** 3 b c Daggers Drawn (USA) -Hayhurst (Sandhurst Prince) 675[12] 819[5] 1127[3] 1196[9] 3004[8] 3533[18] 3734[12] 4004[12] 4350[18] 4419[10] 6465[3] >**36a 43f**<

**Blaeberry** 3 b f Kirkwall-Top Berry (High Top) 1104[11] 1466[7] 2218[5] 2820[5] 3156[4] (3636) 4020[5] (4338) 4574[2] 5370[10] 5945[12] >**69f**<

**Blaina** 4 ch f Compton Place-Miss Silca Key (Welsh Saint) 2517[5] 2788[8] >**6a 83f**<

**Blaise Castle (USA)** 4 b f Irish River (FR) -Castellina (USA) (Danzig Connection (USA)) 1964[4] 2282[2] 2685[11] 6193[3] 6379a[12] >**74 a 95f**<

**Blaise Hollow (USA)** 2 b c Woodman (USA) -Castellina (USA) (Danzig Connection (USA)) 3476[8] 3931[5] (4579) 4807[5] >**83f**<

**Blaise Wood (USA)** 3 b g Woodman (USA) -Castellina (USA) (Danzig Connection (USA)) 2204[10] 2632[6] 2931[8] 3391[2] 3991[11] 4419[7] 4604[11] >**16a 61f**<

**Blake Hall Lad (IRE)** 3 b g Cape Cross (IRE) -Queen Of Art (IRE) (Royal Academy (USA)) 1386[9] 1939[14] 5092[5] (5830) 6399[6] 6461[13] >**52a 61f**<

**Blakeset** 9 ch g Midyan (USA) -Penset (Red Sunset) (410) 544[16] (612) (733) 748[2] 886[3] 1013[11] 1140[5] 1423[3] 1739[2] >**84a 71f**<

**Blakeseven** 4 b g Forzando-Up And Going (FR) (Never So Bold) 512[3] 686[2] 824[2] 918[3] 1020[7] 5575[7] 5926[7] 6227[6] >**56a 56f**<

**Blakeshall Girl** 4 ch f Piccolo-Giggleswick Girl (Full Extent (USA)) 608[12] 773[8] >**9a 57f**<

**Blakeshall Hope** 2 ch g Piccolo-Elite Hope (USA) (Moment Of Hope (USA)) 3150[3] 3802[8] 4474[7] 4620[4] >**38a 57f**<

**Blakeshall Quest** 4 b f Piccolo-Corniche Quest (IRE) (Salt Dome (USA)) 480[9] 515[4] 680[4] 803[4] 834[5] (1178) 1368[9] (1625) 1750[14] 2455[8] 6131[18] 6293[10] 6482[7] >**77a 62f**<

**Blanche (FR)** 5 b m Loup Solitaire (USA) -Polomia (FR) (General Assembly (USA)) 2438a[8] 3769a[5] 4357a[3] 5171a[5] 6463a[11] >**111f**<

**Bla Shak (IRE)** 2 b c Alhaarth (IRE) -Really Gifted (IRE) (Cadeaux Genereux) 2111[P] ><

**Blatant** 5 ch h Machiavellian (USA) -Negligent (Ahonoora) 635a[8] 756a[5] 5782[11] >**93a 117f**<

**Blau Grau (GER)** 7 gr g Neshad (USA) -Belle Orfana (GER) (Orfano (GER)) 5826[15] 5928[10] >**55a 40f**<

**Blaze Of Colour** 3 ch f Rainbow Quest (USA) -Hawait Al Barr (Green Desert (USA)) 1713[3] 2513[4] 3160[2] 3383[3] (3989) 4416[4] 5273[2] 6087[4] >**83+f**<

**Blaze The Trail** 3 b f Classic Cliche (IRE) -Explorer (Krisinsky (USA)) 3161[11] 3454[6] 3994[14] 6285[10] >**21f**<

**Blazing Saddles (IRE)** 5 b g Sadler s Wells (USA) -Dalawara (IRE) (Top Ville) 781[6] >**25a 47f**<

**Blazing The Trail (IRE)** 4 ch g Indian Ridge-Divine Pursuit (Kris) 463[4] 555[8] 765[2] 882[5] (1097) 1298[3] 1944[2] 2302[3] 2537[10] 3274[6] 5554[6] 5869[11] 6152[4] >**68a 74f**<

**Blazing View (USA)** 2 b f Bahri (USA) -Dixie Eyes Blazing (USA) (Gone West (USA)) 3588[5] 4399[9] 5270[13] >**63f**<

**Blessed Place** 4 ch g Compton Place-Cathedra (So Blessed) 560[8] 796[11] 896[13] 1937[12] 2663[8] 2943[16] 3126[3] 3151[3] 3524[5] 3575[4] (3810) 4181[5] 4232[12] 4400[7] 4774[6] >**40a 60f**<

**Blessingindisguise** 11 b g Kala Shikari-Blowing Bubbles (Native Admiral (USA)) 2407[9] 3169[8] 3524[17] >**24a 56f**<

**Blissphilly** 2 b f Primo Dominie-Majalis (Mujadil (USA)) 4212[9] 4559[6] 5059[11] >**31f**<

**Blizz Bless (ARG)** 7 ch g Lode (USA) -Bless The Bride (USA) (Blushing Groom (FR)) 2156a[12] >**94f**<

**Blofeld** 3 b g Royal Applause-Bliss (IRE) (Statoblest) (458) 547[6] >**75a 50f**<

**Blomquist (GER)** 5 br h Kondor (GER) -Blue Devil (Batshoof) 3134a[9] 6106a[6] >**89f**<

**Blonde En Blonde (IRE)** 4 ch f Hamas (IRE) -Hulm (IRE) (Mujtahid (USA)) 410[6] 488[6] 599[8] (624) 698[2] 742[13] 917[3] 960[3] 1055[10] 2875[12] 3006[3] 3680[9] 4260[5] 4414[6] 4549[7] 5740[12] 6157[3] >**74a 61f**<

**Blonde Streak (USA)** 4 ch f Dumaani (USA) -Katiba (USA) (Gulch (USA)) 2410[4] 2521[4] 3198[7] (3714) 5835[6] 6069[8] 6579[6] >**79a 87f**<

**Blood Money** 2 b g Dracula (AUS) -Guinea (Sillery (USA)) 6476[17] >**13f**<

**Blue Azure (USA)** 2 bb f American Chance (USA) -Kibitzing (USA) (Wild Again (USA)) 6536[5] >**53a**<

**Blue Bajan (IRE)** 2 b g Montjeu (IRE) -Gentle Thoughts (Darshaan) 5858[6] 6139[7] >**66f**<

**Blue Banner (IRE)** 3 b f Grand Lodge (USA) -Banariya (USA) (Lear Fan (USA)) 4893a[8] >**83f**<

**Blueberry Forest (IRE)** 6 br h Charnwood Forest (IRE) -Abstraction (Rainbow Quest (USA)) 6508a[11] >**54f**<

**Blueberry Jim** 3 ch g First Trump-Short And Sharp (Sharpen Up) 3291[8] 3448[11] >**35f**<

**Blueberry Rhyme** 5 b g Alhijaz-Irenic (Mummy s Pet) 479[2] 708[2] (898) 1033[8] (1180) 1929[5] 2423[8] 4105[14] 4542[20] (5579) 6066[10] >**72a 73f**<

**Blueberry Tart (IRE)** 2 b f Bluebird (USA) -Tart (FR) (Warning) 4714[5] 5088[4] 6123[10] 6291[7] >**54a 76f**<

**Blue Bijou** 4 b g Bijou D Inde-Jucea (Bluebird (USA)) 642[12] 935[5] 1718[10] ><

**Bluebok** 3 ch c Indian Ridge-Blue Sirocco (Bluebird (USA)) 5204[2] 5803[3] 6064[7] >**61a 70f**<

**Blue Canari (FR)** 3 ch c Acatenango (GER) -Delicieuse Lady (Trempolino (USA)) 1654a[4] (2722a) 5500a[5] 5981a[12] >**118f**<

**Blue Circle** 4 b c Whittingham (IRE) -Reshift (Night Shift (USA)) 422[11] 502[9] ><

**Blue Corrig (IRE)** 4 gr g Darnay-Myristica (IRE) (Doyoun) 4977a[10] 5357a[5] 5662a[10] 5962a[13] >**102f**<

**Blue Crush (IRE)** 3 ch f Entrepreneur-Prosaic Star (IRE) (Common Grounds) 1379a[7] 2316a[9] 2744a[13] 3976[10] 4862[10] 5062[10] 5712[6] 5933[7] >**99 f**<

**Blue Dakota (IRE)** 2 b c Namid-Touraya (Tap On Wood) (1412) (1996) (2180) (2996) 4288[6] >**106f**<

**Blue Daze** 3 b f Danzero (AUS) -Sparkling (Kris) 2112[14] 2694[12] 2887[5] 3478[5] 3684[5] 4020[11] 4848[7] 5541[7] 5702[6] >**69f**<

**Blue Dream (IRE)** 4 b f Cadeaux Genereux-Hawait Al Barr (Green Desert (USA)) 4159a[4] 4893a[4] 5454[2] 5811[8] 6104a[13] >**100f**<

**Blue Emperor (IRE)** 3 b g Groom Dancer (USA) -Bague Bleue (IRE) (Last Tycoon) 956[14] 1266[7] 1425[5] 1478[7] 2908[11] 3039[11] 3299[12] >**49a 52f**<

**Blue Empire (IRE)** 3 b g Second Empire (IRE) -Paleria (USA) (Zilzal (USA)) 466[4] 493[5] (696) 769[4] 845[2] 955[6] 2202[15] 2571[8] >**80 a 60f**<

**Bluefield (IRE)** 3 b c Second Empire (IRE) -Imco Reverie (IRE) (Grand Lodge (USA)) 6132[4] >**70f**<

**Bluegrass Boy** 4 b g Bluegrass Prince (IRE) -Honey Mill (Milford) 1308[3] 2302[11] 2810[8] 3450[8] 4029[3] (4641) 5374[7] 5869[5] 6266[14] >**70a 71f**<

**Blue Hedges** 2 b c Polish Precedent (USA) -Palagene (Generous (IRE)) 6011[13] 6187[10] 6393[4] >**68a 62f**<

**Blue Hills** 3 br g Vettori (IRE) -Slow Jazz (USA) (Chief s Crown (USA)) 1509[11] 1786[5] 2561[11] 5116[11] 5875[16] >**71f**<

**Blue Java** 3 ch g Bluegrass Prince (IRE) -Java Bay (Statoblest) 2790[9] 3180[8] 3875[12] 4241[2] 4882[5] 5222[2] 6295[8] >**64a 63f**<

**Blue Kandora (IRE)** 2 b c Cape Cross (IRE) -Party Dress (Lahib (USA)) 2024[4] 3093[7] >**70f**<

**Blue Knight (IRE)** 5 ch g Bluebird (USA) -Fer De Lance (IRE) (Diesis) 801[2] 968[4] 1057[7] 1537[6] 2303[2] 2399[11] 4495[4] 6293[12] 6480[8] 6553[10] >**60a 60f**<

**Blue Leader (IRE)** 5 b g Cadeaux Genereux-Blue Duster (USA) (Danzig (USA)) 600[15] >**86df**<

**Blue Line** 2 gr f Bluegrass Prince (IRE) -Out Line (Beveled (USA)) 2177[17] 2702[5] 4468[8] >**59f**<

**Blue Maeve** 4 b g Blue Ocean (USA) -Louisville Belle (IRE) (Ahonoora) 441[4] 730[11] 809[4] 875[13] 2734[8] 3016[4] 3314[2] 3511[4] 4181[2] (4422) 4626[5] 4935[12] 5242[15] (5754) 5862[3] 6046[11] >**34a 73f**<

**Blue Marble** 2 b g Fraam-Fizzy Fiona (Efisio) 2396[4] 2677[6] 3157[16] (3531) 3753[7] 4325[9] >**73f**<

**Blue Mariner** 4 b g Marju (IRE) -Mazarine Blue (Bellypha) 1972[9] 2367[3] 2878[2] 3239[2] 3631[14] 4301[9] 5868[15] (6224) >**69a 74f**<

**Blue Moon Hitman (IRE)** 3 ch g Blue Ocean (USA) -Miss Kookaburra (IRE) (Namaqualand (USA)) 2265[3] 2836[7] 3344[3] 3635[3] 4585[8] 4868[13] >**47a 62f**<

**Blue Nun** 3 b f Bishop Of Cashel-Matisse (Shareef Dancer (USA)) 1524[5] 2144[8] 2392[10] 4396[5] 4444[8] 5141[9] 5305[14] >**28f**<

**Blue Oasis (IRE)** 3 b f Sadler s Wells (USA) -Humble Eight (USA) (Seattle Battle (USA)) (1972) 2641[5] 3311[2] 5162a[13] 5969a[9] 6173[5] 6571[10] >**95f**<

**Blue Opal** 2 b f Bold Edge-Second Affair (IRE) (Pursuit Of Love) 6514[3] >**63f**<

**Blue Otis (IRE)** 2 ch f Docksider (USA) -Minstrel s Gift (The Minstrel (CAN)) 6536[12] ><

**Blue Patrick** 4 gr g Wizard King-Great Intent (Aragon) 600[10] 1903[11] 2237[14] 2735[2] 2948[11] 3455[6] 4846[5] 5275[12] 5540[5] 6094[8] >**93a 84f**<

**Blue Power (IRE)** 3 b c Zieten (USA) -La Miserable (USA) (Miswaki (USA)) 610[10] 678[9] 1236[3] 1517[5] 2353[3] (2850) 3077[8] 3270[2] 4701[16] 4929[2] 5579[12] 6114[13] >**69a 69f**<

**Blue Prince (USA)** 2 ch c Dixieland Band (USA) -Tussle (USA) (Kris S (USA)) 3983[2] >**69f**<

**Blue Quiver (IRE)** 4 b g Bluebird (USA) -Paradise Forum (Prince Sabo) 871[6] 988[2] 2614[9] 5175[15] 5733[11] >**61a 50f**<

**Blue Reema (IRE)** 4 ch f Bluebird (USA) -Princess Reema (USA) (Affirmed (USA)) 1070a[2] 1634a[6] 3969a[9] 5162a[16] 5679a[11] 5962a[12] >**92f**<

**Blue Rondo (IRE)** 4 b g Hernando (FR) -Blueberry Walk (Green Desert (USA)) 950[7] >**66a 28f**<

**Blues And Royals (USA)** 2 b c Honour And Glory (USA) -Dixieland Blues (USA) (Dixieland Band (USA)) (2898) 3939[2] 4645[4] >**96f**<

**Blue Savanna** 4 ch g Bluegrass Prince (IRE) -Dusk In Daytona (Beveled (USA)) 579[6] 656[4] 997[2] (1101) 1263[12] 2740[5] 3303[6] 3809[4] 3996[4] 4433[2] 4600[6] >**51a 51f**<

**Blue Sky Thinking (IRE)** 5 b g Danehill Dancer (IRE) -Lauretta Blue (IRE) (Bluebird (USA)) (649) 842[5] 1062[6] 1125[13] 2258[3] 3717[4] 4887[6] 5099[2] 5461[7] >**108a 100f**<

**Blues Over (IRE)** 3 b f Sri Pekan (USA) -Crystal Blue (IRE) (Bluebird (USA)) 416[8] >**1a**<

**Blue Spectrum (IRE)** 2 b g Spectrum (IRE) -Storm River (USA) (Riverman (USA)) 3931[12] 4335[9] 4521[10] 5792[14] >**52f**<

**Blue Spinnaker (IRE)** 5 b g Bluebird (USA) -Suedoise (Kris) 1125[7] (1773) 2044[4] (2527) 3756[10] 4856[4] 5462[6] 5650[3] 5941[4] >**114+f**<

**Blues Princess** 4 b f Bluebird (USA) -Queen Shirley (IRE) (Fairy King (USA)) 2252[13] 2778[14] 3524[12] 4350[14] >**37f**<

**Blue Stitch** 5 ch g Selkirk (USA) -Possessive Artiste (Shareef Dancer (USA)) 1657a[9] >**112f**<

**Blue Streak (IRE)** 7 ch g Bluebird (USA) -Fleet Amour (USA) (Afleet (CAN)) 3088[10] 4433[5] 5056[5] >**50a 57f**<

**Blue Tomato** 3 b c Orpen (USA) -Ocean Grove (IRE) (Fairy King (USA)) 1396[9] >**101 f**<

**Bluetoria** 3 b f Vettori (IRE) -Blue Birds Fly (Rainbow Quest (USA)) 2392[4] 3154[7] 5245[5] 5374[13] >**72f**<

**Blue Torpedo (USA)** 2 ch c Rahy (USA) -Societe Royale (Milford) 5653[8] (6010) >**78a 54f**<

**Blue Track (IRE)** 3 b c Woodborough (USA) -Aryaah (Green Desert (USA)) 3882[8] 4087[7] 4545[8] >**35f**<

**Blue Train (IRE)** 2 b c Sadler s Wells (USA) -Igreja (ARG) (Southern Halo (USA)) 6073[4] >**69+f**<

**Blue Trojan (IRE)** 4 b g Inzar (USA) -Roman Heights (IRE) (Head For Heights) 419[2] 559[2] 1708[7] 2226[15] (2271) 2534[4] 2637[12] 3036[15] 3597[4] 3698[2] 3937[11] 4690[7] 5004[8] 5614[2] (5698) 5941[8] >**77a 98f**<

**Blue Venture (IRE)** 4 ch g Alhaarth (IRE) -September Tide (IRE) (Thatching) 952[8] 1962[9] 2356[9] 2408[4] 3411[13] 3518[14] 4015[3] >**35a 53f**<

**Blue Viking (IRE)** 3 b g Danetime (IRE) -Jenny Spinner (IRE) (Bluebird (USA)) 2412[8] 2853[5] 3379[10] 5957[11] >**44a 6f**<

**Blue Water** 4 b f Shaamit (IRE) -November Song (Scorpio (FR)) 943[10] >**45a 45?f**<

**Blu Fasliyeva (IRE)** 3 b f Fasliyev (USA) -Peaceful Raider (USA) (Hold Your Peace (USA)) 2607a[4] ><

**Blu For Life (IRE)** 7 ch h Rainbows For Life (CAN) -Tinte Blu (IRE) (The Noble Player (USA)) 2155a[7] >**95f**<

**Blunham** 4 b g Danzig Connection (USA) -Relatively Sharp (Sharpen Up) 499[4] 572[5] 612[9] 1197[14] 3167[6] 3586[2] 4425[17] 4605[16] 6146[16] >**39a 63df**<

**Blushing Prince (IRE)** 6 b g Priolo (USA) -Eliade (IRE) (Flash Of Steel) 1037[5] >**73a 65f**<

**Blushing Russian (IRE)** 2 b g Fasliyev (USA) -Ange Rouge (Priolo (USA)) 4149[8] 4804[9] 5301[3] 6140[12] >**58f**<

**Bluvet (IRE)** 2 b c Vettori (IRE) -Blue Guard (IRE) (Bluebird (USA)) 3435a[4] ><

**Blythe Knight (IRE)** 4 ch c Selkirk (USA) -Blushing Barada (USA) (Blushing Groom (FR)) 1328[4] (1540) 1762[4] 2638[6] 3034[3] 3756[15] 4214[13] 4856[8] 5941[6] 6354[5] >**109f**<

**Blythe Spirit** 5 b g Bahamian Bounty-Lithe Spirit (IRE) (Dancing Dissident (USA)) 2391[5] 2899[13] 3098[9] 3606[12] 4280[6] 5370[6] (5798) (6026) (6293) 6496[3] >**88a 76+f**<

**Boanerges (IRE)** 7 br g Caerleon (USA) -Sea Siren (Slip Anchor) 1368[18] 1872[5] 2274[6] 2707[2] 3016[4] 3084[7] 3249[12] 3558[5] 3575[11] 3864[15] 4336[15] 4800 4923[10] 5184[9] >**56f**<

**Boavista (IRE)** 4 b f Fayruz-Florissa (FR) (Persepolis (FR)) 674[9] 733[3] 803[2] 869[4] 893[5] 1044[3] 1268[4] 1368[4] 1625[2] 2165[2] (2428) 2482[10] 2875[9] 3141[8] 3680[2] 3772[2] 4011[8] 4211[3] 4299[3] 4622[6] >**66a 68f**<

**Bob Baileys** 2 b g Mister Baileys-Bob s Princess (Bob s Return (IRE)) 4599[4] 5198[10] >**63a 38f**<

**Bobbie Love** 2 ch g Fraam-Enlisted (IRE) (Sadler s Wells (USA)) 3093[6] 3438[8] >**58f**<

**Bobby Charles** 3 ch g Polish Precedent (USA) -Dina Line (USA) (Diesis) 5621[9] >**64f**<

**Bobering** 4 b g Bob s Return (IRE) -Ring The Rafters (Batshoof) 5237[9] 6062[9] >**32a 7f**<

**Bo Bid (USA)** 4 ch c Helmsman (USA) -I m Italian (USA) (Alleged (USA)) 923a[3] >**83a**<

**Bob s Buzz** 4 ch g Zilzal (USA) -Aethra (USA) (Trempolino (USA)) 1608[11] 3428[5] 4067[3] 4462[5] 4549[2] 5316[14] 5370[5] 6026[2] 6066[6] 6124[2] 6293[7] >**76a 74f**<

**Bob s Flyer** 2 br f Lujain (USA) -Gymcrak Flyer (Aragon) 4936[15] 5209[4] 5334[8] 5475[2] 5513[4] 5800[4] (5954) >**64a 64f**<

**Bobsleigh** 5 b g Robellino (USA) -Do Run Run (Commanche Run) 1112[6] 1329[13] 3947[4] 4226[6] 4457[3] >**85f**<

**Bodden Bay** 2 b g Cayman Kai (IRE) -Badger Bay (IRE) (Salt Dome (USA)) 5302[9] 5447[8] 5910[10] 6022[13] >**15a 48f**<

**Bodfari Dream** 3 ch f Environment Friend-Al Reet (IRE) (Alzao (USA)) 5770[11] 6141[7] >**23f**<

**Bodhi Tree (USA)** 2 b f Southern Halo (USA) -Dharma (USA) (Zilzal (USA)) 6155[3] >**61a**<

**Bodyguard Of Spain (GER)** 5 b h Surako (GER) -Belgica (Valiyar (IRE)) 3552a[6] 4596a[11] 6508a[13] >**69f**<

**Bogaz (IRE)** 2 b c Rossini (USA) -Fastnet (Forzando) 1936[2] 2522[8] 4598[7] 5421[14] 5954[9] >**59a 60f**<

**Bohola Flyer (IRE)** 3 b f Barathea (IRE) -Sharp Catch (IRE) (Common Grounds) (1243) 1333[4] 1702[6] 1907[4] (2741) (3158) 3523[4] 3914[5] 3995[2] 4194[11] 5442[5] 5697[6] >**67a 81f**<

**Boing Boing (IRE)** 4 b g King s Theatre (IRE) -Limerick Princess (IRE) (Polish Patriot (USA)) 2473[15] 3682[6] 5267[5] >**51a 51f**<

**Boisdale (IRE) 6** b g Common Grounds-Alstomeria (Petoski) *1625[6] (1913) 2404[6] 2663[5]* 3227[19] *(3381) 3616[9]* 4702[3]5157[5] *6273[11]* >**63a 63 f**<

**Bojangles (IRE) 5** b g Danehill (USA) -Itching (IRE) (Thatching) *838[7]* 1305[8] (1582) 1875[3] 2943[10] 3103[3] *3282[4]* 3412[5] 3682[3]4473[4] (4713) 5175[2] 5354[5] (5658) 5935[5] *6581[10]* >**50a 63f**<

**Bold Blade 3** b g Sure Blade (USA) -Golden Ciel (USA) (Septieme Ciel (USA)) *566[2] 595[5]* 1392[16] 1613[14] *(2452)* 3292[8] *4096[10]* 4421[2]4636[4] 5058[9] 5205[9] 5365[7] 5634[6] 6074[18] >**72a 57 f**<

**Bold Bunny 3** b f Piccolo-Bold And Beautiful (Bold Lad (IRE)) 2908[3] 4337[3] 4845[7] >**56f**<

**Bold Counsel (IRE) 2** b c Titus Livius (FR) -Daisy Dobson (Gorytus (USA)) 4432[5] 5301[2] *5640[6]* (5792) >**61a 66f**<

**Bold Demand 10** b h Rainbow Quest (USA) -Dafrah (USA) (Danzig (USA)) *(634a) 754a[4] 923a[5]* >**98a**<

**Bold Diktator 2** b c Diktat-Madam Bold (Never So Bold) 4743[10] 5420[6] *6153[6]* >**63a 53f**<

**Bold Eagle (IRE) 2** ch c Rainbow Quest (USA) -Britannia (GER) (Tarim) 6187[12] >**57f**<

**Bold Effort (FR) 12** b g Bold Arrangement-Malham Tarn (Riverman (USA)) *441[9] 990[10]* >**13a 13f**<

**Bold Enough 11** ch m Bold Arrangement-Sweet Enough (Caerleon (USA)) 2344a[2] ><

**Bold Haze 2** ch g Bold Edge-Melody Park (Music Boy) 4761[3] 5319[16] 6522[4] >**60f**<

**Boldini (USA) 3** ch g Atticus (USA) -Bold Bold (IRE) (Sadler s Wells (USA)) *6481[7]* >**46a**<

**Bold Maggie 2** ch f Bold Edge-Vera s First (IRE) (Exodal (USA)) 4643[6] >**50f**<

**Bold Marc (IRE) 2** b g Bold Fact (USA) -Zara s Birthday (IRE) (Waajib) 1170[4] (1314) 1769[2] (2526) 2959[11] 3975[6] 5711[4] 6042[6] *6394[3]* >**80a 86 f**<

**Bold Minstrel (IRE) 2** br c Bold Fact (USA) -Ponda Rosa (IRE) (Case Law) 2268[7] 2872[3] 3491[2] (3729) 4041[2] 4803[4] 5068[2] 5421[5] 5711[5]5932[6] *6023[2]* >**84a 83f**<

**Bold Phoenix (IRE) 3** b c Dr Fong (USA) -Subya (Night Shift (USA)) 2311[10] 2888[8] 3603[6] 4610[8] 5657[10] 6546[16] >**65f**<

**Bold Pursuit (IRE) 2** br c Bold Fact (USA) -Lyphard Belle (Noble Patriarch) 6530[13] >**45f**<

**Bold Ridge (IRE) 4** b g Indian Ridge-Cutting Ground (IRE) (Common Grounds) 1311[10] 2029[8] 2705[11] *6402[6]* >**55a 41f**<

**Bold Terms (USA) 2** b c Outflanker (USA) -Bantry Fair (USA) (Private Terms (USA)) 2669a[4] >**60f**<

**Bold Trump 3** b g First Trump-Blue Nile (IRE) (Bluebird (USA)) *660[4]* 1796[12] 4674[15] 5338[10] >**49a 44f**<

**Bold Wolf 3** b g Wolfhound (USA) -Rambold (Rambo Dancer (CAN)) *1083[4]* 1300[4] *1676[4]* 2380[14] 2836[18] 3991[9] 4548[8] *5000[4]5642[10]* 6567[7] >**52a 50f**<

**Boleyn Castle (USA) 7** ch g River Special (USA) -Dance Skirt (CAN) (Caucasus (USA)) 2475[10] 3074[28] 4091[7] 4294[4] 4614[9] 5372[10] 5553[6] 5933[11] >**79a 90f**<

**Bollin Annabel 3** b f King s Theatre (IRE) -Bollin Magdalene (Teenoso (USA)) 1450[2] 1713[5] 2199[10] 2554[4] 3479[9] 3984[12] >**55f**<

**Bollin Archie 3** b c First Trump-Bollin Joanne (Damister (USA)) 1127[5] 1453[11] 1711[4] >**55f**<

**Bollin Edward 5** b g Timeless Times (USA) -Bollin Harriet (Lochnager) 2461[6] 2735[5] 2965[3] 3298[2] 3606[7] 4305[2] 4577[7] 5126[2]5316[11] 5583[4] >**71f**<

**Bollin Janet 4** b f Sheikh Albadou-Bollin Emily (Lochnager) 1500[11] 2143[15] 3016[10] 3446[12] 3744[9] >**81f**<

**Bollin Ruth 2** gr f Silver Patriarch (IRE) -Bollin Roberta (Bob s Return (IRE)) 2961[8] >**38f**<

**Bollin Thomas 6** b g Alhijaz-Bollin Magdalene (Teenoso (USA)) 5785[7] >**88f**<

**Bollucoiton Bay (IRE) 2** b c Orpen (USA) -Flicker Of Hope (IRE) (Baillamont (USA)) 5389a[3] ><

**Bolodenka (IRE) 2** b c Soviet Star (USA) -My-Lorraine (IRE) (Mac s Imp (USA)) 4611[8] *5911[2]* 6454[3] >**73a 76f**<

**Bolshevik (IRE) 3** b g Fasliyev (USA) -Cheviot Amble (IRE) (Pennine Walk) 1711[11] 2356[10] 2657[11] >**31f**<

**Bolshoi Ballet 6** b g Dancing Spree (USA) -Broom Isle (Damister (USA)) 1198[11] 3300[6] >**74 a 67f**<

**Bolton Hall (IRE) 2** b g Imperial Ballet (IRE) -Muneera (USA) (Green Dancer (USA)) (2570) 3071[6] 4836[5] 5119[6] 5453[5] 5797[11] 6042[7] >**83 f**<

**Boltraffio (FR) 3** ch c Baryshnikov (AUS) -Bessie Bennett (IRE) (Be My Guest (USA)) 1306a[5] ><

**Bo McGinty (IRE) 3** ch g Fayruz-Georges Park Lady (IRE) (Tirol) 1881[7] (2075) 2981[2] 3122[7] 4152[8] 4394[4] 5287[5] (5563) 5786[5] >**92f**<

**Bond Babe 2** b f Forzando-Lindfield Belle (IRE) (Fairy King (USA)) 4245[4] 4388[2] 4986[3] 5209[3] 5520[5] *6289[8]* >**45a 69f**<

**Bond Boy 7** b g Piccolo-Arabellajill (Aragon) *486[4] 669[7] 761[8] 1007[4]* 1113[7] 1391[6] 1789[8] 3509[3]3754[8] 4759[11] 5075[10] 5287[4] 5628[14] 6205[8] 6349[4] 6532[4] >**86a 101f**<

**Bond Cat (IRE) 2** ch f Raise A Grand (IRE) -Merrily (Sharrood (USA)) 6211[4] 6531[6] >**53+f**<

**Bond City (IRE) 2** b g Trans Island-Where s Charlotte (Sure Blade (USA)) 2234[8] (3196) 3468[3] 3938[3] 4860[5] 5213[2] 5464[5] 5947[10] *(6023)* 6204[2]*(6449)* >**94a 94f**<

**Bond Deal (IRE) 3** ch f Pivotal-Prima (Primo Dominie) 1778a[5] 2341a[11] 6381a[14] >**90f**<

**Bond Domingo 5** b g Mind Games-Antonia s Folly (Music Boy) *936[11] 1075[12] 1190[3] 1445[6] 1568[4]* >**51a 57f**<

**Bond Finesse (IRE) 2** b f Danehill Dancer (IRE) -Funny Cut (IRE) (Sure Blade (USA)) 1717[4] 1960[4] *6022[7]* 6195[4] >**46a 55f**<

**Bond May Day 4** b f Among Men (USA) -State Romance (Free State) 2142[18] 2964[7] 3342[4] 3510[4] 4045[8] 5635[13] >**63a 77f**<

**Bond Millennium 6** ch g Piccolo-Farmer s Pet (Sharrood (USA)) *667[10]* 5344[11] 5518[2] 5859[8] 6096[15] *6295[4] 6483[7]* >**70a 71f**<

**Bond Moonlight 3** ch g Danehill Dancer (IRE) -Interregnum (Interrex (CAN)) *808[2] 969[2] 1012[3] 1179[2]* 1360[9] 1995[8] >**65a 39f**<

**Bond Playboy 4** b g Piccolo-Highest Ever (FR) (Highest Honor (FR)) *486[5] 586[6] 761[7] 1007[6]* 1131[10] 1361[16] 1500[8] 2215[17]3167[14] 4447[3] (4827) (5126) 5603[19] 6210[3] >**96a 88f**<

**Bond Puccini 2** b g Piccolo-Baileys By Name (Nomination) 3577[7] 5209[2] 5475[7] 5989[15] >**63f**<

**Bond Romeo (IRE) 3** ch g Titus Livius (FR) -At Amal (IRE) (Astronef) 3511[9] 6526[5] *6577[8]* >**43a 63f**<

**Bond Royale 4** ch f Piccolo-Passiflora (Night Shift (USA)) *515[2] 607[13] 836[8]* >**83a 85f**<

**Bond Shakira 3** ch f Daggers Drawn (USA) -Cinnamon Lady (Emarati (USA)) 1362[3] 1530[14] 2778[4] *2850[8]* 3169[16] *3801[4] 4185[5]* 4701[11] >**45a 54f**<

**Bonecrusher 5** b g Revoque (IRE) -Eurolink Mischief (Be My Chief (USA)) 636a[6] *842[4] 1009[8]* 1328[5] 1540[2] 2076[9] 3034[5] 3661[5]4214[3] 4540[6] 5461[4] 5629[3] 6219[9] 6458[3] >**105a 114f**<

**Bonfire 2** b c Machiavellian (USA) -Forest Express (AUS) (Kaaptive Edition (NZ)) 5765[4] 6476[7] >**65f**<

**Bongoali 2** b f Fraam-Stride Home (Absalom) 4053[4] 4468[5] 5083[2] 5335[5] 5596[17] 5852[8] 6562[16] >**67f**<

**Bonita Rock (IRE) 2** b f Orpen (USA) -Olympic Rock (IRE) (Ballad Rock) 6367a[11] >**83f**<

**Bonjour Bond (IRE) 3** ro g Portrait Gallery (IRE) -Musical Essence (Song) *1192[4]* 1532[7] 1843[11] 1959[3] 2199[11] 3582[3] 3822[10] 4207[5]4825[8] 5634[5] >**7a 50 f**<

**Bonnabee (IRE) 2** b f Benny The Dip (USA) -Samhat Mtoto (Mtoto) 4966[11] *5640[7]* 5792[6] >**42a 52f**<

**Bonne De Fleur 3** b f Whittingham (IRE) -L Estable Fleurie (IRE) (Common Grounds) (1417) 2897[10] 3523[13] 4394[5] 4862[7] 5263[9] >**92f**<

**Bonnetts (IRE) 3** ch f Night Shift (USA) -Brief Lullaby (IRE) (Brief Truce (USA)) 2223[11] 3916[17] 4718[8] 5123[10] >**53f**<

**Bon Nuit (IRE) 2** b f Night Shift (USA) -Pray (IRE) (Priolo (USA)) (5848) >**81f**<

**Bonsai (IRE) 3** b f Woodman (USA) -Karakia (IRE) (Sadler s Wells (USA)) 2182[7] 2562[9] 4369[10] 5657[14] 6097[18] >**65f**<

**Bontadini 5** b g Emarati (USA) -Kintail (Kris) *554[5] 705[11] 776[7]* 2801[3] 3173[7] 5928[17] >**54 a 42f**<

**Bonus (IRE) 4** b g Cadeaux Genereux-Khamseh (Thatching) 1409[6] 2021[11] 2373[9] 3324[9] 5712[5] 6071[6] >**114 f**<

**Bonus Points (IRE) 3** b c Ali-Royal (IRE) -Asta Madera (IRE) (Toca Madera) *4880[9] 5381[6] 5643[10]* 5843[3] >**59a 56f**<

**Boo 2** b c Namaqualand (USA) -Violet (IRE) (Mukaddamah (USA)) 4761[4] 5319[6] 5669[4] 6206[9] >**74f**<

**Boogie Magic 4** b f Wizard King-Dalby Dancer (Bustiki) 2596[10] 3460[2] 3809[3] 4201[13] *4600[4]* >**45a 65f**<

**Boogie Street 3** b c Compton Place-Tart And A Half (Distant Relative) 1763[3] 2294[2] (2475) 2955[6] 3537[4] 4269[2] 5647[10] >**115f**<

**Bookiesindexdotcom 3** b f Great Dane (IRE) -Fifth Emerald (Formidable (USA)) *640[9] 760[3] 840[7] 958[6] 1046[6]* 1844[8] *2232[5]2849[5]* 3425[6] 6228[12] >**57a 55f**<

**Book Matched 3** b g Efisio-Princess Latifa (Wolfhound (USA)) *798[3] (907) 1029[4]* 1214[18] *2814[6]* 3102[10] *(4093) 4882[3]*5223[19] 6124[14] >**74a 51f**<

**Book Of Kings (USA) 3** b c Kingmambo (USA) -Honfleur (IRE) (Sadler s Wells (USA)) 3353a[6] >**115f**<

**Boom Or Bust (IRE) 5** ch g Entrepreneur-Classic Affair (USA) (Trempolino (USA)) *663[8] 857[7] 3637[13]* >**42a 42f**<

**Boot n Toot 3** b f Mtoto-Raspberry Sauce (Niniski (USA)) 1186[9] (4583) 5446[9] 5573[6] >**84?f**<

**Boozy Douz 4** ch f Abou Zouz (USA) -Ackcontent (USA) (Key To Content (USA)) 1541[8] *2017[6]* 2386[8] >**17a 44f**<

**Boppys Babe 3** ch f Clan Of Roses-Joara (FR) (Radetzky) 5110[11] 6228[13] >**30df**<

**Boppys Dream 2** ch f Clan Of Roses-Laurel Queen (IRE) (Viking (USA)) 5555[6] 5800[11] 6272[5] >**29f**<

**Boppys Princess 3** b f Wizard King-Laurel Queen (IRE) (Viking (USA)) (3822) 4259[2] (4680) (4902) 5557[5] *(5957)* (6548) >**63a 75f**<

**Boracay Beauty 2** b f Tipsy Creek (USA) -Grandads Dream (Never So Bold) 1468[10] 1970[9] 2364[11] 3144[8] >**16f**<

**Boracay Dream (IRE) 2** ch c Grand Lodge (USA) -Mild Intrigue (USA) (Sir Ivor (USA)) 4681[8] >**50f**<

**Border Artist 5** ch g Selkirk (USA) -Aunt Tate (Tate Gallery (USA)) 1175[11] 1451[11] (2172) 2368[7] 2781[9] 2965[4] 3167[3] 3555[4] 3895[5]4154[5] >**56a 71f**<

**Border Castle 3** b c Grand Lodge (USA) -Tempting Prospect (Shirley Heights) (5122) 5761[7] >**95+f**<

**Border Edge 6** b g Beveled (USA) -Seymour Ann (Krayyan) *648[11] 770[10]* 5004[10] 5275[9] 5614[16] 5887[8] 6128[9] >**88a 95f**<

**Borderlescott 2** b c Compton Place-Jeewan (Touching Wood (USA)) 2860[6] 3196[10] 3818[3] (4330) >**67f**<

**Border Music 3** b g Selkirk (USA) -Mara River (Efisio) *1056[7]* 1437[8] 4490[3] 4738[2] 5275[2] 5446[3] 5766[4] 6086[8] >**83a 84+f**<

**Border Saint 3** b g Selkirk (USA) -Caramba (Belmez (USA)) *1050[3] 1235[7]* 1387[4] 2070[14] >**66a 79f**<

**Border Subject 7** b g Selkirk (USA) -Topicality (USA) (Topsider (USA)) 1789[6] 2475[9] 4152[15] >**118f**<

**Border Tale 4** b g Selkirk (USA) -Likely Story (IRE) (Night Shift (USA)) *523[8] (795) 971[7]* >**85a 85f**<

**Border Terrier (IRE) 6** b g Balnibarbi-Ring Side (IRE) (Alzao (USA)) 1527[16] 2174[8] 2649[9] 3041[3] 3411[12] 3794[4] 4139[4] 5238[12] >**44f**<

**Boris The Spider 3** b g Makbul-Try Vickers (USA) (Fuzzbuster (USA)) 1711[2] 1975[9] 2351[8] 2880[5] 3060[5] 3822[4] 5197[6] (6468) >**61f**<

**Born For Dancing (IRE) 2** b f Fasliyev (USA) -Fancy Boots (IRE) (Salt Dome (USA)) 2940[2] 5334[5] 5908[2] 6204[3] >**72f**<

**Born For Diamonds (IRE) 2** b f Night Shift (USA) -Kirri (IRE) (Lycius (USA)) 5720[7] 5847[5] 6439[11] >**58 f**<

**Borodinsky 3** b g Magic Ring (IRE) -Valldemosa (Music Boy) 2530[5] 2962[7] 3234[4] 3517[7] 4101[2] 4573[4] 5086[8] 5525[2] >**48f**<

**Borrego (USA) 3** ch c El Prado (IRE) -Sweet As Honey (USA) (Strike The Gold (USA)) *1781a[10] 2139a[7]* >**103a**<

**Borrego (IRE) 4** br c Green Desert (USA) -Pripet (USA) (Alleged (USA)) 2673[2] 2891[8] 3426[6] 3477[11] 4435[14] 5244[4] (5419) 5698[8] 5861[8] >**81f**<

**Borsato (GER) 7** ch h Monsun (GER) -Boccia (Priamos (GER)) 1655a[8] ><

**Borthwick Girl (IRE) 2** b f Cape Cross (IRE) -Shannon Dore (IRE) (Turtle Island (IRE)) (3272) 4060[4] 5325a[9] 5939[3] 6473[3] >**97f**<

**Borzoi Maestro 3** ch g Wolfhound (USA) -Ashkernazy (IRE) (Salt Dome (USA)) 1854[2] 2181[3] (2444) 2552[9] 2889[4] 3845[3] 4059[8] 4585[5] 4717[12]4810[6] 5184[7] 5564[5] 5734[5] *6026[5] 6222[10]* >**74a 79f**<

**Boschette 2** b f Dansili-Secret Dance (Sadler s Wells (USA)) 5227[5] 6091[11] >**52f**<

**Bosco (IRE) 3** br c Petardia-Classic Goddess (IRE) (Classic Secret (USA)) 1509[9] 1672[10] 2302[13] (2801) 3529[6] 3809[8] 3917[13] >**58f**<

**Bosphorus 5** b g Polish Precedent (USA) -Ancara (Dancing Brave (USA)) *1492[3] (1572)* >**51a 53f**<

**Boston Lodge 4** ch g Grand Lodge (USA) -Ffestiniog (IRE) (Efisio) 690a[3] 755a[2] 924a[3] 1004a[2] 2636[4] 2679[13] 3074[9] 3539[8]4273[3] 5468[2] 5781[11] >**94a 104f**<

**Botanical (USA) 3** b c Seeking The Gold (USA) -Satin Flower (USA) (Shadeed (USA)) 2080[5] 2642[15] 4750[8] >**97f**<

**Bottomless Wallet 3** ch f Titus Livius (FR) -Furry Dance (USA) (Nureyev (USA)) 6095[6] 6519[4] >**57f**<

**Bought Direct 5** b h Muhtarram (USA) -Muhybh (USA) (Dayjur (USA)) *643[12] 667[11] 952[6] 1479[5] 1681[4]* 2614[6] 3520[8] >**54a 68f**<

**Boule D Or (IRE) 3** b c Croco Rouge (IRE) -Saffron Crocus (Shareef Dancer (USA)) 2207[4] (2400) 2809[4] 3543[2] 3728[9] (4754) 5401[4] 5761[4] 5942[3] 6193[2] >**96f**<

**Boumahou (IRE) 4** b c Desert Story (IRE) -Kilbride Lass (IRE) (Lahib (USA)) *603[3] 676[3] (743)* 1135[7] >**82a 60f**<

**Boundless Prospect (USA) 5** b g Boundary (USA) -Cape (USA) (Mr Prospector (USA)) *494[7] 647[10]* 2304[11] 2806[10] 3101[2] 3455[3] (3910) 4293[6] 4742[11]5275[8] >**74a 83f**<

**Bound To Please 9** b g Warrshan (USA) -Hong Kong Girl (Petong) 1591[10] *1739[6] 2013[7]* >**67a 50f**<

**Bountiful 2** gr f Pivotal-Kinsaile (Robellino (USA)) 3904[7] >**62f**<

**Bounty Quest 2** b c Fasliyev (USA) -Just Dreams (Salse (USA)) 3176[3] 3476[4] 4263[3] >**78f**<

**Bourgainville 6** b g Pivotal-Petonica (IRE) (Petoski) *842[8] 1062[4]* 1622[5] 1902[5] 2220[14] 2527[13] 3756[17] 4163[7]6354[8] >**107a 107f**<

**Bourgeois 7** ch g Sanglamore (USA) -Bourbon Girl (Ile De Bourbon (USA)) 1286[2] 2076[3] (2365) 3521[10] 3757[12] 4856[9] 5435[12] >**104f**<

**Bowing 4** b g Desert Prince (IRE) -Introducing (Mtoto) *564[13] 651[5] 964[13]* 1272[17] 2430[12] *3281[9]* >**58a 58f**<

**Bowland Bride (IRE) 2** b f Raise A Grand (IRE) -Red Riding Hood (FR) (Mummy s Pet) 1468[5] 1970[10] 2140[4] 2288[4] (2364) 2622[7] *3278[7]* 3620[5] *4095[10]* >**3a 48f**<

**Bowled Out (GER) 2** b f Dansili-Braissim (Dancing Brave (USA)) 5089[4] 5319[12] 6123[18] (6562) >**65f**<

**Bowlegs Billy 4** gr g Raphane (USA) -Swallow Bay (Penmarric (USA)) 3169[12] 3511[8] 4425[10] 4818[16] >**24a 45f**<

**Bowling Along 3** b f The West (USA) -Bystrouska (Gorytus (USA)) 1750[5] 2238[8] 2457[8] 3372[9] 3622[4] 3887[3] 4391[2] 4557[14]5063[10] (5526) 5798[6] 5849[10] 6271[7] >**66f**<

**Bowman (USA) 5** b h Irish River (FR) -Cherokee Rose (IRE) (Dancing Brave (USA)) 710a[5] 978a[7] >**116f**<

**Bowman s Band (USA) 6** ch h Dixieland Band (USA) -Hometown Queen (USA) (Pleasant Colony (USA)) *6491a[11]* >**116a**<

**Bowman s Crossing (IRE) 5** b g Dolphin Street (FR) -Biraya (Valiyar) 1657a[4] 2156a[3] 2957[7] 3724[6] >**121f**<

**Bowsprit 4** ch g Fleetwood (IRE) -Longwood Lady (Rudimentary (USA)) *449[9]* >**58a 63f**<

**Bow Strada 7** ch g Rainbow Quest (USA) -La Strada (Niniski (USA)) 3851[3] >**82f**<

**Bowstring (IRE) 3** b f Sadler s Wells (USA) -Cantanta (Top Ville) (1189) 1538[2] 1963[2] 5025[3] 5394[3] 6443[3] 6571[9] >**103f**<

**Bow Wave 2** b c Danzero (AUS) -Moxby (Efisio) (6569) >**72+f**<

**Box Builder 7** ch g Fraam-Ena Olley (Le Moss) *(750) 827[2]* >**73a 70 f**<

**Boxgrove (FR) 3** ro g Trempolino (USA) -Little Emily (Zafonic (USA)) *466[7] 595[6]* >**77a**<

**Boxhall (IRE) 2** b c Grand Lodge (USA) -March Hare (Groom Dancer (USA)) 5087[6] 5570[10] >**70f**<

**Boysun (IRE) 3** ch c Ashkalani (IRE) -Babalu (IRE) (Doyoun) 2510a[12] >**98f**<

**Brace Of Doves 2** b g Bahamian Bounty-Overcome (Belmez (USA)) 1390[14] *2812[5]* 3233[2] 3605[3] 4012[3] 4278[2] 4445[3] 5477[10]5636[7] 6265[7] >**40a 69f**<

**Bradamante 3** b f Sadler s Wells (USA) -Balisada (Kris) 1803a[5] >**99f**<

**Brads House (IRE) 2** b c Rossini (USA) -Gold Stamp (Golden Act (USA)) 6530[11] >**47f**<

**Brag (IRE) 2** b f Mujadil (USA) -Boast (Most Welcome) 2058[2] 2427[4] 3208[7] (4017) 4348[3] 4752[9] >**83 f**<

**Bragadino 5** b h Zilzal (USA) -Graecia Magna (USA) (Private Account (USA)) *6539[10] 6554[11]* >**49a 92f**<

**Brahminy Kite (USA) 2** b c Silver Hawk (USA) -Cope s Light (USA) (Copelan (USA)) 4625[2] (4919) >**92+f**<

**Brahy (USA) 3** ch c Rahy (USA) -Bint Pasha (USA) (Affirmed (USA)) 5168a[10] >**64f**<

**Brain Storm (IRE) 4** b f Sri Pekan (USA) -Kelmscot (Le Fabuleux (FR)) 5576a[6] ><

**Brain Washed 3** b f Mind Games-Bollin Dorothy (Rambo Dancer (CAN)) 2621[16] 3096[4] 3267[2] 3839[5] 5104[3] 5801[3] 6009[6] >**66f**<

**Bramantino (IRE) 4** b g Perugino (USA) -Headrest (Habitat) *667[5] 800[3] (902) 962[12]* 1245[2] 2299[5] 2449[7] 3782[5]4698[5] (5144) (5229) 5374[3] 5773[5] >**62a 69f**<

**Brandexe (IRE) 2** b f Xaar-Tintara (IRE) (Caerleon (USA)) 5248[11] 5406[5] 5604[4] 6207[10] >**66f**<

**Brandy Cove 7** b g Lugana Beach-Tender Moment (IRE) (Caerleon (USA)) *512[4] 1427[13] 3023[5] 3282[5] 4096[5]* >**72+a 36f**<

**Brandywine Bay (IRE) 4** b f Mujadil (USA) -Ned s Contessa (IRE) (Persian Heights) *1278[8] 2052[4]* (4419) 4708[5] 5283[9] 6227[17] >**46a 46f**<

**Branston Lily 2** ch f Cadeaux Genereux-Indefinite Article (IRE) (Indian Ridge) 4532[3] 5521[4] 5857[9] 6195[13] >**65df**<

**Branston Nell 5** b m Classic Cliche (IRE) -Indefinite Article (IRE) (Indian Ridge) *777[12] 950[5]* >**30a 27f**<

**Branston Penny 2** ch f Pennekamp (USA) -Branston Jewel (IRE) (Prince Sabo) 5720[13] *6221[2]* >**47a 11f**<

**Branston Tiger 5** b g Mark Of Esteem (IRE) -Tuxford Hideaway (Cawston s Clown) *1013[5]* 1106[11] 1361[14] 1608[8] 1825[6] 2215[5] 3321[15] 3779[7]*(4185)* 5124[4] 5201[3] 5583[8] 6001[3] 6131[7] *6539[9]* >**73a 73f**<

**Brantwood (IRE) 4** b g Lake Coniston (IRE) -Angelic Sounds (IRE) (The Noble Player (USA)) 1313[14] 1368[16] 1872[9] 2118[4] 2524[3] *3025[2]* 3446[3] 3884[10]4308[6] 4542[18] 5107[5] 5579[8] >**64a 66f**<

**Brave Burt (IRE) 7** ch g Pips Pride-Friendly Song (Song) 2679[18] 3293[10] 3645[14] 4748[2] 4837[17] 4935[11] 5181[11] 5605[10]6267[9] *6577[9]* >**47a 92 f**<

**Brave Chief 3** ch c Komaite (USA) -Victoria Sioux (Ron s Victory (USA)) *438[7]* 2166[17] *2664[5] 2850[6] 3378[15] 3801[5]* >**52a 23f**<

**Brave Dane (IRE) 6** b g Danehill (USA) -Nuriva (USA) (Woodman (USA)) *(672) (765) 872[5] 964[6]* (1109) *1935[2] 2881[10]* 4122[10] 4437[2]4814[7] >**82a 79+f**<

**Brave Knight 7** b g Presidium-Agnes Jane (Sweet Monday) 4630[8] >**47f**<

**Bravely Does It (USA) 4** gr g Holy Bull (USA) -Vigors Destiny (USA) (Vigors (USA)) 2653[9] 3297[10] 3607[6] 4261[2] 4934[12] 5993[17] *6292[5] 6581[5]* >**51a 62f**<

**Bravemore (USA) 2** b c Diesis-Private Indy (USA) (A.P. Indy (USA)) 5915[6] >**74+f**<

**Brave Tara (IRE) 2** b f Brave Act-Gone With The Wind (IRE) (Common Grounds) 5095[14] 5447[12] 5800[12] >**11f**<

**Bravo Maestro (USA) 3** b c Stravinsky (USA) -Amaranthus (USA) (Kingmambo (USA)) *1063[6] 1239[7]* 2224[5] 5762[9] 5920[9] >**97+a 94f**<

**Bravo Tazio (IRE) 3** b c Sri Pekan (USA) -Exemina (USA) (Slip Anchor) 1777a[2] 2510a[5] >**106f**<

**Brazilian Sun (IRE) 3** b f Barathea (IRE) -Braziliz (USA) (Kingmambo (USA)) 1485a[7] >**80f**<

**Brazilian Terrace 4** ch f Zilzal (USA) -Elaine s Honor (USA) (Chief s Crown (USA)) *961[3] 1055[4]* 1372[10] (2119) (2871) 3191[3] *3419[9]* 4142[2] 4771[2]5136[9] 5574[3] >**82a 83f**<

**Brazil Nut 3** b g Deploy-Garota De Ipanema (FR) (Al Nasr (FR)) 4082[15] ><

**Bread Of Heaven 3** b f Machiavellian (USA) -Khubza (Green Desert (USA)) 1829[7] 4084[6] >**75f**<

**Breaking Shadow (IRE) 2** br g Danehill Dancer

(IRE) -Crimbourne (Mummy s Pet) 3818[2] 4388[3] 4804[3] (5212) 5434[10] 5896[6] 6206[7] 6515[8] (6574) >**81 f**<

**Breaking The Rule (IRE) 3** ch f King Of Kings (IRE) -Thirtysomething (USA) (Thirty Six Red (USA)) *2486[10]* 3194[6] 4141[5] 4853[15] 5750[10] >**44a 47f**<

**Breamore 2** b c Dansili-Maze Garden (USA) (Riverman (USA)) 6441[8] >**51f**<

**Breathing Fire 2** b c Pivotal-Pearl Venture (Salse (USA)) 5118[5] 5772[3] >**76f**<

**Breathing Sun (IRE) 3** b g Bahhare (USA) -Zapata (IRE) (Thatching) 1414[14] 2069[10] 3543[9] 4582[3] 4950[12] >**42a 79f**<

**Brecon 2** ch f Unfuwain (USA) -Welsh Valley (USA) (Irish River (FR)) (5534) 6353[4] 6472[4] >**81f**<

**Brecon Beacon 2** b c Spectrum (IRE) -Ffestiniog (IRE) (Efisio) (2024) (2321) 3071[2] (4295) 4716[4] 6340[4] >**101f**<

**Breeder s Folly 2** b f Mujahid (USA) -Wynona (IRE) (Cyrano De Bergerac) 3818[11] 6522[7] >**30f**<

**Breezer 4** b g Forzando-Lady Lacey (Kampala) 1687[7] 4912[12] 5069[3] >**42f**<

**Breezit (USA) 3** b f Stravinsky (USA) -Sharka (Shareef Dancer (USA)) 1467[4] 2176[4] 2942[5] 3155[12] *6363[3] 6556[5]* >**49a 55f**<

**Bregaglia 2** ch f Zaha (CAN) -Strath Kitten (Scottish Reel) 3259[14] 4292[15] 4753[14] *4999[3]* 5218[13] >**29a 24f**<

**Brego (IRE) 2** b g Monashee Mountain (USA) -White-Wash (Final Straw) 5269[14] 5407[8] 5688[11] 6181[13] >**57f**<

**Breid (IRE) 5** b h Green Desert (USA) -Ardassine (Ahonoora) 3816a[6] ><

**Bressbee (USA) 6** ch g Twining (USA) -Bressay (USA) (Nureyev (USA)) *564[8] 671[2] 735[4] 887[8] (1037) 1118[12]* 1298[P] >**77a 66f**<

**Bretton 3** b g Polar Prince (IRE) -Understudy (In The Wings) *482[2] 566[6] 1040[6]* 1499[4] *1736[4]* 1959[4] *2014[3]2231[7] 3637[2]* 3990[5] *4940[9]* 5284[13] *5645[9] 6360[2]* >**44a 41f**<

**Brevity 9** b g Tenby-Rive (USA) (Riverman (USA)) 2975[10] 3697[16] >**61 a 72f**<

**Brian Boru 4** b c Sadler s Wells (USA) -Eva Luna (USA) (Alleged (USA)) (1156a) 1849a[5] 2639[5] 2998[5] 4183a[5] 4983a[2] 5662a[2] 6384a[3] >**121 f**<

**Briannie (IRE) 2** b f Xaar-Annieirwin (IRE) (Perugino (USA)) 5400[6] 5653[6] 5996[7] >**59f**<

**Briannsta (IRE) 2** b c Bluebird (USA) -Nacote (IRE) (Mtoto) 4048[6] 4584[5] 4966[2] (5198) 5539[10] 6090[11] >**75f**<

**Briar (CZE) 5** b h House Rules (USA) -Bright Angel (AUT) (Antuco (GER)) *459[6]* >**22a**<

**Briareus 4** ch g Halling (USA) -Lower The Tone (IRE) (Phone Trick (USA)) *418[10] 523[10]* 1460[10] 1821[2] 2084[7] 2624[3] 3075[6] 3692[7]3909[6] >**83a 86f**<

**Briar Ghyll 2** ch f Zaha (CAN) -Charlotte Penny (High Kicker (USA)) 6545[12] >**13f**<

**Bridegroom 2** b c Groom Dancer (USA) -La Piaf (FR) (Fabulous Dancer (USA)) *6555[5]* >**59a**<

**Bridewell (USA) 5** b g Woodman (USA) -La Alleged (USA) (Alleged (USA)) *1026[15]* 1341[8] 1722[6] *2055[8]* >**9a 29f**<

**Bridge Pal 4** ch f First Trump-White Domino (Sharpen Up) 4328[6] 5479[9] >**62a 66f**<

**Bridge Place 2** b c Polar Falcon (USA) -Dark Eyed Lady (IRE) (Exhibitioner) 1130[7] 2321[3] 2736[2] (3009) >**72f**<

**Bridge T The Stars 2** b f Josr Algarhoud (IRE) -Petra s Star (Rock City) (3770) 4541[5] *5052[10]* >**54a 71f**<

**Bridgewater Boys 3** b g Atraf-Dunloe (IRE) (Shaadi (USA)) *458[4] (640) 758[3]* (2063) (2269) 2457[2] (2981) 3737[5] 5193[9] *5912[8] 6222[6]6482[3] 6557[8]* >**75a 85f**<

**Brief Goodbye 4** b g Slip Anchor-Queen Of Silk (IRE) (Brief Truce (USA)) (1315) 1821[4] 2493[8] (2789) 3797[4] 5265[10] 5937[6] 6244[11] >**86f**<

**Briery Mec 9** b g Ron s Victory (USA) -Briery Fille (Sayyaf) *456[7] 539[6]* 3827[15] >**25a 19f**<

**Brigadier Du Pin (FR) 6** b h Dear Doctor (FR) -Naskra s Trick (USA) (Star De Naskra (USA)) 785a[11] 1655a[11] ><

**Brigadier Monty (IRE) 6** b g College Chapel-Miss St Cyr (Brigadier Gerard) 1265[11] 1872[6] 2656[7] 3010[9] 3407[2] 3509[5] 3810[5] 4181[10]5107[3] 5562[10] 6007[9] 6526[10] >**60f**<

**Brigadore 5** b g Magic Ring (IRE) -Music Mistress (IRE) (Classic Music (USA)) 1774[6] 2130[3] 2423[6] 2490[12] >**79f**<

**Bright Abundance (USA) 3** b f Quiet American (USA) -Quality Gift (Last Tycoon) 2720a[7] 3258a[4] 4356a[10] 4899a[5] 5969a[3] >**104f**<

**Bright Fire (IRE) 3** b f Daggers Drawn (USA) -Jarmar Moon (Unfuwain (USA)) *906[5]* 4092[4] 4443[6] 4853[2] >**15a 54f**<

**Bright Mist 5** b m Anita s Prince-Out On Her Own (Superlative) 1584[12] *2183[4] 2811[7] 3381[16]* >**31a 26f**<

**Bright Moll 2** b f Mind Games-Molly Brown (Rudimentary (USA)) (1183) 1943[2] 2129[2] 2970[5] (3445) >**87f**<

**Bright Sky (IRE) 5** ch m Wolfhound (USA) -Bright Moon (USA) (Alysheba (USA)) 980a[2] 1146a[7] >**121 f**<

**Bright Sun (IRE) 3** b c Desert Sun-Kealbra Lady (Petong) 1614[8] 1900[10] 2019[10] 2589[4] 3059[3] 3585[7] 4050[3] 4340[4](4726) 5120[8] 5582[6] 5934[8] 6332[11] >**81f**<

**Brilliant Red 11** b g Royal Academy (USA) -Red Comes Up (USA) (Blushing Groom (FR)) *418[16] 649[9] 743[6] 844[4] 1054[7] 1232[5]* 1768[15] >**96a 98 f**<

**Brilliantrio 6** ch m Selkirk (USA) -Loucoum (FR) (Iron Duke (FR)) *428[2] 474[4] 567[9] 686[6] 719[U] 1021[3] 1191[6]*2597[2] (2757) >**39a 63f**<

**Brilliant Waters 4** ch g Mark Of Esteem (IRE) -Faraway Waters (Pharly (FR)) *1098[15]* >**48a 58f**<

**Brillyant Dancer 6** b m Environment Friend-Brillyant Glen (IRE) (Glenstal (USA)) *807[6] 934[11]* >**5a 45f**<

**Brindisi 3** b f Dr Fong (USA) -Genoa (Zafonic (USA)) 1311[3] 1793[4] (2270) 2971[4] 3541[4] 4077[6] (4773) 5783[7] 6219[13] >**99f**<

**Briolette (IRE) 2** b f Sadler s Wells (USA) -Cocotte (Troy) 6367a[7] >**79f**<

**Brios Boy 4** ch g My Best Valentine-Rose Elegance (Bairn (USA)) *6360[12]* >**43f**<

**Brioso (IRE) 4** b g Victory Note (USA) -Presently (Cadeaux Genereux) *626[7]* >**30a 24f**<

**Briviesca 3** ch f Peintre Celebre (USA) -Kimono (IRE) (Machiavellian (USA)) 5033a[6] >**88f**<

**Broadway Score (USA) 6** b g Theatrical-Brocaro (USA) (Mr Prospector (USA)) 1284[7] 1604[9] 1821[9] 2142[13] 2775[9] 3097[10] 3470[11] 3952[8] >**58a 58 f**<

**Bronwen (IRE) 2** b f King s Best (USA) -Tegwen (USA) (Nijinsky (CAN)) 5089[6] >**55f**<

**Bronx Bomber 6** ch g Prince Sabo-Super Yankee (IRE) (Superlative) *(2056) (2229) 2854[7]* 3887[13] >**51a 40f**<

**Bronze Dancer (IRE) 2** b g Entrepreneur-Scrimshaw (Selkirk (USA)) 5059[12] 5302[8] 5543[7] (5856) 6140[9] >**68+f**<

**Brooklands Lodge (USA) 3** ch f Grand Lodge (USA) -Princess Dixieland (USA) (Dixieland Band (USA)) 3049[6] 3536[9] 4138[9] 4518[8] 5374[19] 5549[10] *6065[3]* >**57a 64f**<

**Brooklands Time (IRE) 3** b f Danetime (IRE) -Lute And Lyre (IRE) (The Noble Player (USA)) *805[7] 906[7] 1044[11] 1165[12]* 1197[16] >**58da 63f**<

**Brooklime (IRE) 2** b c Namid-Wildflower (Namaqualand (USA)) *4599[6]* 4809[4] (4866) 5119[10] 5212[5] 5655[2] 5810[6] 6090[7] 6206[6]6356[16] >**61a 80f**<

**Brooklyn s Gold (USA) 9** b g Seeking The Gold (USA) -Brooklyn s Dance (FR) (Shirley Heights) *768[6]* 5768[8] 6128[10] >**83a 83f**<

**Brother Cadfael 3** ch g So Factual (USA) -High Habit (Slip Anchor) *508[3] 611[8] 802[3]* 1296[2] 1467[6] 1594[6] 1864[6] 2088[7]*3707[7]* 4497[7] 5284[10] 6120[18] >**32a 32f**<

**Brother s Valcour (FR) 6** b h River Mist (USA) -Lady De Valcour (FR) (Labus (FR)) 785a[4] 1655a[9] ><

**Brough Supreme 3** b g Sayaarr (USA) -Loriner s Lady (Saddlers Hall (IRE)) 1674[5] 2090[4] 3340[6] 3743[8] *4545[3]* >**65a 69f**<

**Broughton Bounty 3** b f Bahamian Bounty-Sleave Silk (IRE) (Unfuwain (USA)) 4092[12] >**62f**<

**Broughton Knows 7** b g Most Welcome-Broughtons Pet (IRE) (Cyrano De Bergerac) *(440) (539) (781) (878) 937[2] 1238[4]* 1668[6] 5546[4] *(5914)* 6047[12] >**66a 57f**<

**Broughton Melody 5** ch m Alhijaz-Broughton Singer (IRE) (Common Grounds) *501[3] 724[8] 973[4] 2987[4] 3803[5]* >**40a 46f**<

**Broughtons Flush 6** b g First Trump-Glowing Reference (Reference Point) *889[7] 1238[8] 1698[5] (2987)* >**50a 44f**<

**Broughtons Mill 9** gr g Ron s Victory (USA) -Sandra s Desire (Grey Desire) *664[5] 857[6] 947[6] 994[8] 1543[6]* >**31a 31f**<

**Brown Dragon 3** ch g Primo Dominie-Cole Slaw (Absalom) *606[6] 774[2] 1038[2]* 1530[12] 3322[10] *3708[6]* >**65a 40f**<

**Brumaire (IRE) 2** b c Second Empire (IRE) -Ar Hyd Y Knos (Alzao (USA)) 6060[9] 6322[11] >**37f**<

**Brunel (IRE) 3** b c Marju (IRE) -Castlerahan (IRE) (Thatching) (1396) (2158a) 2956[5] 4595a[11] 5113[6] >**115f**<

**Brut 2** b g Mind Games-Champenoise (Forzando) 1128[10] 1314[6] 3003[2] 3233[17] 3924[5] 4150[5] >**57f**<

**Brut Force (IRE) 2** b g Desert Style (IRE) -La Foscarina (Rudimentary (USA)) 6514[9] >**48f**<

**Bruzella 5** b m Hernando (FR) -Hills Presidium (Presidium) *601[9] 984[11]* >**31a**<

**Bubbling Fun 3** b f Marju (IRE) -Blushing Barada (USA) (Blushing Groom (FR)) 1619[4] 2059[7] 2442[4] 3156[3] 3421[3] 3989[2] 4562[6] 5836[2]6095[2] >**72f**<

**Buchanan Street (IRE) 3** b c Barathea (IRE) -Please Believe Me (Try My Best (USA)) 2426[16] 2928[6] 3193[6] 3582[2] 4082[5] 4867[7] 5863[15] >**38a 49 f**<

**Buckenham Stone 5** ch m Wing Park-Walk That Walk (Hadeer) 1519[11] 2520[9] *2990[7] 3637[7]* 4065[8] *4600[9]* >**29a 34f**<

**Buckeye Wonder (USA) 3** b c Silver Hawk (USA) -Ameriflora (USA) (Danzig (USA)) 1382[2] (2632) 3000[13] >**90f**<

**Bucks 7** b g Slip Anchor-Alligram (USA) (Alysheba (USA)) *618[14]* 1272[3] 1539[11] 1801[2] (2116) (2689) 3199[2] 3629[5] 4123[8] 4450[2]4772[2] 4911[5] 5619[6] 5764[8] >**82a 87f**<

**Buddy Brown 2** b c Lujain (USA) -Rose Bay (Shareef Dancer (USA)) (3081) 4632[2] 5417[17] 6344[14] >**88+f**<

**Budelli (IRE) 7** b g Elbio-Eves Temptation (IRE) (Glenstal (USA)) 3961a[8] 5660a[6] >**100f**<

**Buffalo Boy (IRE) 6** gr g Distinctly North (USA) -Eclipse Bid (Rusticaro (FR)) *1954a[10]* ><

**Bugle Call 4** b g Zamindar (USA) -Petillante (Petong) *727[10] 886[7] 967[8] 994[13]* >**46a**<

**Bukit Fraser (IRE) 3** b g Sri Pekan (USA) -London Pride (USA) (Lear Fan (USA)) (1356) 2107[4] 2578[7] 3210[9] 4062[9] 4441[5] 5093[10] 5728[12] >**87f**<

**Bulawayo 7** b g Prince Sabo-Ra Ra Girl (Shack (USA)) *439[5] 565[3] 642[7] 810[3] 910[8] 1043[6] (1176) 2123[7]*2379[6] *2666[4] 3024[2] (3612) 3804[8] 4190[4] 4925[4] 6401[11]* >**57a 54f**<

**Bulberry Hill 3** b g Makbul-Hurtleberry (IRE) (Tirol) *907[8] 1022[5]* 5552[5] 5702[8] 5863[10] >**26a 43f**<

**Bulgaria Moon 4** ch g Groom Dancer (USA) -Gai Bulga (Kris) 1668[7] 2462[9] 2759[7] 3518[8] >**36f**<

**Bullish Luck (USA) 5** b g Royal Academy (USA) -Wild Vintage (USA) (Alysheba (USA)) 1657a[10] >**108f**<

**Bull Run (IRE) 3** gr c Daylami (IRE) -Bulaxie (Bustino) (1271) (1538) >**115+f**<

**Bullseye 2** b c Polish Precedent (USA) -Native Flair (Be My Native (USA)) 6476[18] >**8f**<

**Bulwark (IRE) 2** b c Montjeu (IRE) -Bulaxie (Bustino) 5646[10] 6149[4] 6351[5] >**65f**<

**Bumptious 3** b c Mister Baileys-Gleam Of Light (IRE) (Danehill (USA)) 1222[3] 1416[3] (1786) 2561[4] 3035[4] 3639[3] 5093[14] >**91f**<

**Bundaberg 4** b g Komaite (USA) -Lizzy Cantle (Homing) *628[4] 779[2] 1078[2] 1425[3] 6296[10]* 6548[12] >**53a 32f**<

**Bunditten (IRE) 2** gr f Soviet Star (USA) -Felicita (IRE) (Catrail (USA)) *(1060)* 2532[3] 2970[4] 3481[4] 5464[8] 6212[7] 6456[6] >**73a 91f**<

**Bundy 8** b g Ezzoud (IRE) -Sanctuary Cove (Habitat) 1452[8] 1665[13] 1877[10] 2779[2] 2976[2] 3226[3] 3400[2] 3606[8]3735[4] 3923[4] 5583[11] 5833[7] >**73f**<

**Bunino Ven 3** gr g Silver Patriarch (IRE) -Plaything (High Top) *1084[8]* 1375[4] 1499[7] 1862[5] *2014[4]* >**31a**<

**Bunkhouse 4** ch g Wolfhound (USA) -Maid Welcome (Mummy s Pet) 2621[8] 3085[7] 3487[13] *3848[8]* 4419[8] 4669[14] >**24a 45f**<

**Bunny Rabbit (USA) 2** b c Cherokee Run (USA) -Jane s The Name (USA) (Trempolino (USA)) 3373[3] 4295[5] *5051[4]* 5417[8] (5719) >**81a 94f**<

**Bunyah (IRE) 3** ch f Distant View (USA) -Miss Mistletoes (IRE) (The Minstrel (CAN)) *1096[9]* >**37a 55f**<

**Buoyant (IRE) 3** b f Peintre Celebre (USA) -Wavey (Kris) 3566a[2] 4430a[11] 5966a[10] 6437a[12] >**97f**<

**Bureaucrat 2** b c Machiavellian (USA) -Lajna (Be My Guest (USA)) 5871[4] 6441[6] >**82f**<

**Burgundian (USA) 2** b c Red Ransom (USA) -Prospectora (USA) (Mr Prospector (USA)) 5570[4] >**73f**<

**Burgundy 7** b g Lycius (USA) -Decant (Rousillon (USA)) *559[6] 745[3] 932[4] 1088[2]* 1369[7] 2034[9] 2324[8] 2594[3]2810[6] (3441) *(3637) (3934)* 4262[2] (4438) 4571[2] 5183[5] 5496[4] 5935[6] >**70+a 72f**<

**Burkees Graw (IRE) 3** ch g Fayruz-Dancing Willma (IRE) (Dancing Dissident (USA)) *685[7] 762[7] 1089[9]* 2207[14] 2661[2] 3820[17] 4393[2] *4929[10]* >**29a 49f**<

**Burley Firebrand 4** b g Bahamian Bounty-Vallauris (Faustus (USA)) 1369[19] 2121[8] 3041[15] >**65a 65f**<

**Burley Flame 3** b g Marju (IRE) -Tarsa (Ballad Rock) 1370[4] 1771[3] 2134[3] (2569) 3001[22] 3527[3] (3819) 4140[6] 4646[7] 5120[7]5934[11] *(6222)* 6517[8] >**86a 83f**<

**Burlington Place 3** b g Compton Place-Wandering Stranger (Petong) 3180[10] *3849[7]* 4242[2] 4418[8] 5259[18] >**64a 63f**<

**Burn 3** ch f Selkirk (USA) -River Cara (USA) (Irish River (FR)) 2805[7] 3222[3] 3592[11] 3993[12] >**60f**<

**Burning Moon 3** b c Bering-Triple Green (Green Desert (USA)) 1325[5] (3238) 3678[15] 5106[11] 5607[10] 6128[3] >**94f**<

**Burning Truth (USA) 10** ch g Known Fact (USA) -Galega (Sure Blade (USA)) 4139[9] >**69a 69f**<

**Burnley Al (IRE) 2** ch g Desert King (IRE) -Bold Meadows (Persian Bold) 4861[5] 5319[10] >**62f**<

**Burnt Copper (IRE) 4** b g College Chapel-Try My Rosie (Try My Best (USA)) 3263[10] (3604) 3774[8] 4080[9] 4485[9] *6550[10] 6576[9]* >**64a 62f**<

**Burnt Ember (USA) 5** ch h Smoke Glacken (USA) -Castle Gardens (IRE) (Common Grounds) *634a[5] (754a) 974a[4]* >**104a**<

**Burst Of Fire (CAN) 3** b g Smart Strike (CAN) -Quiet Cheer (USA) (No Louder (USA)) 6384a[7] >**95f**<

**Burton Ash 2** bb f Diktat-Incendio (Siberian Express (USA)) 2071[7] 2550[4] 3741[3] 4524[4] 5240[9] 5753[9] >**70f**<

**Busaco 2** b c Mister Baileys-War Shanty (Warrshan (USA)) 3157[15] 4432[4] *6494[6]* >**69a 62f**<

**Buscador (USA) 5** ch g Crafty Prospector (USA) -Fairway Flag (USA) (Fairway Phantom (USA)) *507[8]* 1715[9] 2120[13] 2551[9] 3082[9] 3705[8] >**79+a 59f**<

**Bushido (IRE) 5** br g Brief Truce (USA) -Pheopotstown (Henbit (USA)) 3782[6] 4698[8] 5638[2] 5991[8] >**65f**<

**Business Matters (IRE) 4** b f Desert Style (IRE) -Hear Me (Simply Great (FR)) *767[11]* 1527[10] 1993[12] 5239[5] 5581[15] >**19a 67?f**<

**Business Traveller (IRE) 4** ch g Titus Livius (FR) -Dancing Venus (Pursuit Of Love) 5205[15] >**49f**<

**Bussoni (GER) 3** br c Goofalik (USA) -Blumme (CHI) (Jadar (CHI)) 6512a[5] >**103f**<

**Bust (IRE) 2** b c Fraam-Purse (Pursuit Of Love) 2860[13] 3366[6] >**44f**<

**Bustan (IRE) 5** b h Darshaan-Dazzlingly Radiant (Try My Best (USA)) *1062[3]* 1355[2] 1622[9] 3661[4] >**110a 112f**<

**Bustling Rio (IRE) 8** b g Up And At Em-Une Venitienne (FR) (Green Dancer (USA)) *483[4] 603[7] (666)* 1287[8] >**73a 73f**<

**Buthaina (IRE) 4** b f Bahhare (USA) -Haddeyah (USA) (Dayjur (USA)) 1757[12] 1992[9] 2368[15] 2687[10] 3291[9] 3520[11] 4509[10] >**50f**<

**Buying A Dream (IRE) 7** ch g Prince Of Birds (USA) -Cartagena Lady (IRE) (Prince Rupert (FR)) *943[5] 1026[13] (1543) 1700[3] (2055)* >**43a 43f**<

**Buy On The Red 3** b c Komaite (USA) -Red Rosein (Red Sunset) *1169[2]* 1472[2] (2029) (2309) 3845[7] 4059[2] 4289[12] 4874[12] >**75a 91+f**<

**Buz Kiri (USA) 6** b g Gulch (USA) -Whitecorners (USA) (Caro) *539[3] 661[2] (727) 783[2] 880[2] (943) 992[2] 1077[2]1136[6]* 1581[2] (1862) >**53a 44f**<

**Buzz Buzz 3** b f Mtoto-Abuzz (Absalom) 2971[13] 5998[8] 6445[18] >**63f**<

**Buzz Maite 2** b g Komaite (USA) -Scotland Bay (Then Again) 2644[5] ><

**Bwana Charlie (USA) 3** b c Indian Charlie (USA) -Shahalo (USA) (Halo (CAN)) *6487a[4]* >**117a**<

**By Definition (IRE) 6** gr m Definite Article-Miss Goodbody (Castle Keep) *532[8] 875[15] 932[9]* >**28 f**<

**Bygone Days 3** ch g Desert King (IRE) -May Light (Midyan (USA)) (1133) 2019[3] 2309[4] 3309[5] (4394) 4862[3] >**98f**<

**Byinchka 4** br g Inchinor-Bystrouska (Gorytus (USA)) *472[9]* >**38a 49f**<

**Byo (IRE) 6** gr g Paris House-Navan Royal (IRE) (Dominion Royale) *454[7]* 1131[6] 1518[2] 1937[10] (2274) 2440[7] 2873[6] 3125[6] 3195[7]3775[12] (4044) 4415[3] 4617[4] 5253[8] 5734[4] 6046[3] *6554[2]* >**76a 77f**<

**Byrd Island 3** b f Turtle Island (IRE) -Arusha (IRE) (Dance Of Life (USA)) 1104[14] 1371[17] 2092[10] >**12f**<

**Byron 3** b c Green Desert (USA) -Gay Gallanta (USA) (Woodman (USA)) 2161a[3] 2956[8] (4216) 4795a[9] >**117f**<

**Byron Bay 2** b c My Best Valentine-Candarela (Damister (USA)) 4739[9] 5269[9] 5535[5] 5909[12] 6282[3] 6338[14] >**64f**<

## C

**Cabin Fever 2** b f Averti (IRE) -Julietta Mia (USA) (Woodman (USA)) 3904[8] 4621[5] 4936[7] 5218[8] 5792[3] >**59f**<

**Cabopino Lad (USA) 2** b g Comic Strip (USA) -Roxanne (USA) (Woodman (USA)) 5522[10] >**42f**<

**Cabriac 7** bb h Machiavellian (USA) -Chief Bee (Chief s Crown (USA)) *1954a[8]* ><

**Cache Creek (IRE) 6** b m Marju (IRE) -Tongue River (USA) (Riverman (USA)) 2102a[2] 2711a[5] 2796a[4] 4160a[3] (5162a) 5679a[12] >**106f**<

**Cacique (IRE) 3** b c Danehill (USA) -Hasili (IRE) (Kahyasi) 2721a[2] 3360a[2] (4284a) 4834[4] (5967a) >**117f**<

**Cadeaux Rouge (IRE) 3** ch f Croco Rouge (IRE) -Gift Of Glory (FR) (Niniski (USA)) 1509[4] 1947[7] 2546[15] 4213[19] >**60f**<

**Cadogen Square 2** ch f Takhlid (USA) -Mount Park (IRE) (Colonel Collins (USA)) 3469[12] 3865[7] 4137[10] 4559[4] 5363[8] 5520[10] 5556[7] >**43f**<

**Ca D Oro 11** ch g Cadeaux Genereux-Palace Street (USA) (Secreto (USA)) 4871[12] 6548[5] >**40f**<

**Cadwallader (USA) 4** ch g Kingmambo (USA) -Light On Your Feet (USA) (Nijinsky (CAN)) *879[4] 1016[6] 1492[5] 1693[U]* 2171[8] 2385[13] >**40a 56f**<

**Caerphilly Gal 4** b f Averti (IRE) -Noble Lustre (USA) (Lyphard s Wish (FR)) 2098[9] 2614[13] 3321[9] 5411[9] (5795) 5927[2] 6058[3] (6227) *6364[7]* 6548[8] >**45a 60f**<

**Caesar Beware (IRE) 2** b g Daggers Drawn (USA) -Red Shareef (Marju (IRE)) (2609) (4581) (5392) 5947[2] >**112 f**<

**Caesarion (IRE) 5** b h Danehill (USA) -Carelaine (USA) (Woodman (USA)) 2923a[6] >**112f**<

**Cafe Americano 4** b g Labeeb-Coffee Ice (Primo Dominie) 2322[7] 3151[5] 3828[9] 4801[2] 4869[2] 5147[7] 5733[12] >**41a 56f**<

**Cafe Bostonian (USA) 5** b h Boston Harbor (USA) -Libby Lee (USA) (Sutter s Prospect (USA)) 5982a[15] >**83f**<

**Caiman (USA) 3** b c Malibu Moon (USA) -Storming Up (USA) (Storm Bird (CAN)) *2701a[8]* >**78a**<

**Cairdeas (IRE) 3** b c Darshaan-Sabaah (USA) (Nureyev (USA)) 2333a[2] 6102a[4] >**103f**<

**Cairns (UAE) 3** b f Cadeaux Genereux-Tanami (Green Desert (USA)) 1791[10] 2160a[6] 3033[9] 6345[5] >**106f**<

**Caitlin (IRE) 2** ch f Intikhab (USA) -Esteraad (IRE) (Cadeaux Genereux) 1709[6] *2812[2] 3802[4] (4186) 4878[3]* (5240) 5636[2] 5819[3] 5938[P] >**71a 79f**<

**Cajun Beat (USA) 4** bb g Grand Slam (USA) -Beckys Shirt (USA) (Cure The Blues (USA)) *1145a[4] 6487a[5]* >**116a**<

**Cake It Easy (IRE) 4** ch f Kendor (FR) -Diese Memory (USA) (Diesis) 6143[9] >**70a 77f**<

**Cala Fons (IRE) 2** b f Alhaarth (IRE) -Lemon Tree (USA) (Zilzal (USA)) 4048[16] 5098[10] 5264[7] 6092[11] >**38f**<

**Calamari (IRE) 2** ch f Desert King (IRE) -Mrs Fisher (IRE) (Salmon Leap (USA)) 4099[10] 5109[4] 5846[15] >**59f**<

**Calamintha 4** b f Mtoto-Calendula (Be My Guest (USA)) 1754[2] 2167[6] (2613) 3153[3] 5205[5] >**40+a 72f**<

**Calara Hills 3** ch f Bluegrass Prince (IRE) -Atlantic Line (Capricorn Line) 1465[11] 1843[3] 2199[12] >**43a 50f**<

**Calatagan (IRE) 5** ch g Danzig Connection (USA) -

Calachuchi (Martinmas) 1198[3] (1393) 1661[5] 2121[5] 5229[2] 5584[18] 6047[5] >71f<

**Calcar (IRE)** 4 b g Flying Spur (AUS) -Poscimur (IRE) (Prince Rupert (FR)) *440[9]* 6524[7] >47a 47f<

**Calculaite** 3 b g Komaite (USA) -Miss Calculate (Mummy s Game) 2270[9] 3624[6] 3877[6] 4489[4] 4827[5] *5000[7]* (5451) *5642[3] 5957[4]*6201[6] *6541[3]* >61a 67+f<

**Calcutta** 8 b h Indian Ridge-Echoing (Formidable (USA)) 1385[10] 2044[13] 2283[10] 2534[8] 2969[19] 3119[2] 3539[12] 4178[3]4528[9] (5315) (5462) 6044[7] >107f<

**Calderini (FR)** 2 b f Fasliyev (USA) -Sopran Dandy (IRE) (Doyoun) 3436a[8] ><

**Caldy Dancer (IRE)** 3 ch f Soviet Star (USA) -Smile Awhile (USA) (Woodman (USA)) 3969a[11] 4773[11] >104f<

**Caledonian (IRE)** 3 b g Soviet Star (USA) -Supercal (Environment Friend) 5614[22] 5886[9] >78 a 68f<

**Calendar Girl (IRE)** 4 b f Revoque (IRE) -March Fourteenth (USA) (Tricky Creek (USA)) *443[10] 792[6]* >40a 53f<

**Calfraz** 2 bb g Tamure (IRE) -Pas De Chat (Relko) 5447[9] 6514[7] >49f<

**Caliban (IRE)** 6 ch g Rainbows For Life (CAN) -Amour Toujours (IRE) (Law Society (USA)) *2004[7]* 2590[10] 3108[3] 5205[10] 5654[8] >52a 55f<

**Calibre (USA)** 4 b c Lear Fan (USA) -Carya (USA) (Northern Dancer) 3315[6] 3757[14] >98f<

**Called Up** 3 b g Easycall-Clued Up (Beveled (USA)) 1749[4] 2211[7] 2765[9] 3322[5] *4024[11]* 5844[4] 6079[3] >6a 67f<

**Call Me Big (GER)** 6 ch h Big Shuffle (USA) -Call Me Alice (Alzao (USA)) 2466a[8] 5255a[16] >87f<

**Call Me Max** 2 b g Vettori (IRE) -Always Vigilant (USA) (Lear Fan (USA)) 4198[4] 4584[3] 4967[5] 5264[3] >81f<

**Call Me Sunshine** 4 b f Robellino (USA) -Kirana (Niniski (USA)) *(697) 795[7] 1045[5]* 1282[17] 2174[3] 2531[7] >64a 67f<

**Call Of The Wild** 4 ch g Wolfhound (USA) -Biba (IRE) (Superlative) *546[8] 903[3] 1043[3] 1181[3]* 1305[6] *2007[4] 2128[4]2456[2]* 2938[12] *3380[12]* >57a 66f<

**Cal Mac** 5 b g Botanic (USA) -Shifting Mist (Night Shift (USA)) 2201[18] *2454[11]* 2928[7] 3173[2] 3662[7] *3934[10]* >53a 53f<

**Calomeria** 3 b f Groom Dancer (USA) -Calendula (Be My Guest (USA)) 1224[11] 1440[8] 2146[14] 3250[4] 3743[10] 3928[3] 4448[8] 4870[7]5634[3] 6055[3] >29a 65f<

**Calonnog (IRE)** 4 ch f Peintre Celebre (USA) -Meadow Spirit (USA) (Chief s Crown (USA)) 1770[2] 2198[9] >67f<

**Calstone Light O (JPN)** 6 b h Warning-Oshima Lucia (JPN) (Crystal Glitters) (5982a) >126?f<

**Caluki** 7 b h Kris-Chevisaunce (Fabulous Dancer (USA)) *(1062) 1954a[9]* 2608a[7] >114a 95f<

**Calusa Lady (IRE)** 4 ch f Titus Livius (FR) -Solas Abu (IRE) (Red Sunset) 1855[5] 2788[9] 3747[2] 4542[17] 6146[3] 6288[4] >57a 65f<

**Calvados (USA)** 5 b g Seattle Slew (USA) -A Votre Sante (USA) (Irish River (FR)) *863[2]* >44a 53f<

**Caly Dancer (IRE)** 2 ch g Entrepreneur-Mountain Dancer (IRE) (Rainbow Quest (USA)) 1505[9] 2058[5] 2627[3] 2761[3] 4365[3] (4914) 6176[5] >90f<

**Calypso Dancer (FR)** 4 b f Celtic Swing-Calypso Grant (IRE) (Danehill (USA)) 5440[19] 5754[14] 6046[10] *6499[6]* >56a 54f<

**Camacho** 2 b c Danehill (USA) -Arabesque (Zafonic (USA)) (3946) 5395[3] >93f<

**Camberley (IRE)** 7 b g Sri Pekan (USA) -Nsx (Roi Danzig (USA)) 1132[2] 1385[5] 1765[26] >98f<

**Camberwell** 3 b g Royal Applause-Into Orbit (Safawan) (2765) 3751[5] 4031[9] 4646[9] 5275[14] 6477[13] >87f<

**Cambo (FR)** 3 bb g Mansonnien (FR) -Royal Lie (FR) (Garde Royale) 6006[F] *6159[4]* 6287[5] >58a 35f<

**Camelot** 5 br g Machiavellian (USA) -Bombazine (IRE) (Generous (IRE)) *687a[6] 757a[6]* 922a[6] >82a 98f<

**Cameraman (FR)** 8 b g Exit To Nowhere (USA) -Calvina (FR) (Kaldoun (FR)) 785a[13] ><

**Cameron Orchid (IRE)** 2 b f Sri Pekan (USA) -London Pride (USA) (Lear Fan (USA)) 6470[9] >72f<

**Camille Pissarro (USA)** 4 b g Red Ransom (USA) -Serenity (Selkirk (USA)) 5769[9] 5941[29] 6128[16] 6358[14] 6546[14] >95 a 98f<

**Cammies Future** 2 gr c Efisio-Impulsive Decision (IRE) (Nomination) 1324[3] (4048) 4962a[2] 5392[6] >94f<

**Camouflage (FR)** 2 gr c Verglas (IRE) -Calithea (IRE) (Marju (IRE)) 4589a[5] >76f<

**Campbells Lad** 3 b c Mind Games-T O O Mamma S (IRE) (Classic Secret (USA)) *1596[5] 2232[4]* 2688[8] 3060[12] 3513[5] 4207[3] 5110[14] 5449[2]6112[4] *6361[3]* 6466[2] >45a 50f<

**Campbell s Tale (IRE)** 5 gr g Lake Coniston (IRE) -Fair Tale (USA) (Groovy (USA)) *585[11] 654[12]* ><

**Camp Commander (IRE)** 5 gr h Pennekamp (USA) -Khalatara (IRE) (Kalaglow) 1968[9] 2283[4] 2969[5] 3539[7] 3937[17] 4528[8] 5112[7] 5650[18](6062) >102a 105f<

**Campeon (IRE)** 2 b g Monashee Mountain (USA) -Arcticlead (USA) (Arctic Tern (USA)) 1128[12] 1383[5] 1743[9] 2947[5] 3553[2] 3823[4] 4149[3] 4508[5]4816[2] *4997[4]* 5132[2] >51a 73df<

**Campo Bueno (FR)** 2 b c Septieme Ciel (USA) -Herba Buena (FR) (Fabulous Dancer (USA)) 6035a[4] (6320a) 6462a[3] >111f<

**Camrose** 3 ch c Zafonic (USA) -Tularosa (In The Wings) 1588[4] 2244[3] 2764[2] 3325[5] 5183[2] (5699) 6121[10] >98f<

**Canadian Danehill (IRE)** 2 b c Indian Danehill (IRE) -San Jovita (CAN) (St Jovite (USA)) *6448[9] 6555[13]* >24a<

**Canadian Storm** 3 gr c With Approval (CAN) -Sheer Gold (USA) (Cutlass (USA)) 1869[5] 2097[7] 2546[4] 2930[5] (3529) >43a 69f<

**Canary Dancer** 2 b f Groom Dancer (USA) -Bird Of Time (IRE) (Persian Bold) 2213[11] 2616[4] 2730[2] 4012[8] 4909[9] 5097[7] >59f<

**Canatrice (IRE)** 4 gr f Brief Truce (USA) -Cantata (IRE) (Saddlers Hall (IRE)) 1858[15] >45a 51f<

**Can Can Flyer (IRE)** 3 ch c In The Wings-Can Can Lady (Anshan) (4628) 5144[2] 5365[2] 5773[7] 6006[7] >38a 76f<

**Candleriggs (IRE)** 8 ch g Indian Ridge-Ridge Pool (IRE) (Bluebird (USA)) 1956[13] 2130[13] 2936[7] 4011[13] >61 f<

**Candy Anchor (FR)** 5 b m Slip Anchor-Kandavu (Safawan) *1277[2] 1545[7] 3710[7]* >44a 48f<

**Canlis** 5 b g Halling (USA) -Fajjoura (IRE) (Fairy King (USA)) 2658[7] 2879[2] 3471[12] 4246[12] 4423[7] 4605[5] 5238[7] 5305[9]5524[8] 6465[6] >32a 42f<

**Canni Thinkaar (IRE)** 3 b g Alhaarth (IRE) -Cannikin (IRE) (Lahib (USA)) 1640[6] 2146[15] 2821[7] 3746[4] 4138[10] *4940[3]* 5493[12] >51a 65f<

**Cantarna (IRE)** 3 ch f Ashkalani (IRE) -Lancea (IRE) (Generous (IRE)) 2654[2] 3142[3] 3607[5] (5621) 5990[6] 6461[7] >75f<

**Cantemerle (IRE)** 4 b f Bluebird (USA) -Legally Delicious (Law Society (USA)) 2038[2] 2363[7] 3250[7] 3443[6] 3928[7] 5238[9] >42a 61f<

**Canterloupe (IRE)** 6 b m Wolfhound (USA) -Missed Again (High Top) *486[8]* 2477[10] 3416[7] 3941[7] (4740) 5075[8] 5730[8] *6577[5]* >88a 84 f<

**Canton (IRE)** 2 b c Desert Style (IRE) -Thirlmere (Cadeaux Genereux) 1130[6] *(1240)* 1878[4] 3727[4] 3938[5] *4514[3]* 4752[3] 5131[3] 5392[13] >87a 96f<

**Cantoris** 4 b g Unfuwain (USA) -Choir Mistress (Chief Singer) 2874[12] >70f<

**Cantrip** 4 b f Celtic Swing-Circe (Main Reef) *413[8] 867[14]* 2032[7] 2375[17] (2728) 2893[3] 4441[9] *4603[12]*5286[5] *5645[11]* 5889[5] >43a 58f<

**Caona (USA)** 2 b f Miswaki (USA) -Hawzah (Green Desert (USA)) 4074[8] 4399[5] 4714[10] >66f<

**Capable Guest (IRE)** 2 bb c Cape Cross (IRE) -Alexander Confranc (IRE) (Magical Wonder (USA)) 2045[3] 2310[3] 2954[3] 4078[2] (4567) 4835[4] 5469[3] 5666a[4] >106f<

**Cape Canaveral (IRE)** 5 b g Sadler s Wells (USA) -Emmaline (USA) (Affirmed (USA)) *818[7]* >38a 74f<

**Cape Columbine** 2 b f Diktat-Cape Merino (Clantime) 5890[2] (6174) >98+f<

**Cape Enterprise (USA)** 2 b c Cape Canaveral (USA) -Principessa (USA) (Alydeed (CAN)) *6155[7] 6536[3]* >61a<

**Cape Fear** 3 b c Cape Cross (IRE) -Only In Dreams (Polar Falcon (USA)) 6214[10] 6474[7] 6572[5] >108+f<

**Cape Greko** 2 ro c Loup Sauvage (USA) -Onefortheditch (USA) (With Approval (CAN)) 3240[2] (3726) >93+f<

**Cape Of Good Hope** 6 ch g Inchinor-Cape Merino (Clantime) 2955[2] 3073[3] 3674[4] 5982a[3] >124f<

**Cape Quest** 2 b c Piccolo-Belle Vue (Petong) 3601[10] 4193[3] (4637) 5466[8] >85f<

**Caper** 4 b g Salse (USA) -Spinning Mouse (Bustino) 4261[9] *4883[15]* 5238[11] 5638[14] *6360[11]* >54f<

**Cape Royal** 4 b g Prince Sabo-Indigo (Primo Dominie) 1113[9] 1343[6] (1537) 1923[7] 2041[6] 2679[11] 3293[2] 3713[8] 3945[3]4366[2] 4538[17] >97f<

**Capestar (IRE)** 3 b f Cape Cross (IRE) -Sedulous (Tap On Wood) 1400[6] 2046[2] (2479) 3306[4] >78f<

**Cape St Vincent** 4 gr g Paris House-Cape Merino (Clantime) 2091[10] *(2455)* 3339[2] 3439[7] 4090[8] >88a 81f<

**Capetown Girl** 3 b f Danzero (AUS) -Cavernista (Lion Cavern (USA)) (1288) 1606[12] 2239[8] 3006[7] 3517[10] 4104[12] 4905[13] 5702[11] >42a 55 f<

**Cape Vincent** 3 b c Cape Cross (IRE) -Samhat Mtoto (Mtoto) (4683) 5076[5] >91+f<

**Capital Secret (USA)** 7 br g Capote (USA) -Proflare (USA) (Mr Prospector (USA)) *1954a[12]* 2336a[7] 6508a[12] >104f<

**Capitole (IRE)** 3 b g Imperial Ballet (IRE) -Blue Glass (Ardkinglass) 3094[11] 3607[4] 4781[5] 5510[4] 5715[11] 6209[3] >66f<

**Capped For Victory (USA)** 3 b c Red Ransom (USA) -Nazoo (IRE) (Nijinsky (CAN)) 1972[2] 2295[7] 4122[12] >91f<

**Capricho (IRE)** 7 gr g Lake Coniston (IRE) -Star Spectacle (Spectacular Bid (USA)) 1126[17] 2466a[4] 4120[11] 4553[10] 4889[11] 5289[16] 5628[9] 5780[6]6190[12] >105f<

**Captain Clipper** 4 b g Royal Applause-Collide (High Line) 1172[3] (1470) 2022[17] >82f<

**Captain Cloudy** 4 b g Whittingham (IRE) -Money Supply (Brigadier Gerard) *491[5] 745[6] 895[6]* 1642[14] 4044[10] 4419[3] 4802[12] 5261[4]5411[7] 5733[4] >58a 68f<

**Captain Crusoe** 6 b g Selkirk (USA) -Desert Girl (Green Desert (USA)) *1031[3] 1101[10]* >77a 77f<

**Captain Darling (IRE)** 4 b g Pennekamp (USA) -Gale Warning (IRE) (Last Tycoon) *834[6] 1088[7]* 1265[2] 1451[9] 2030[7] 2483[5] 2735[7] *6493[14]* >69a 66f<

**Captain Fearless** 3 ch g Defacto (USA) -Madam Poppy (Risk Me (FR)) *683[13] 769[8]* 1375[6] >1f<

**Captain Hurricane** 2 b c Desert Style (IRE) -Ravine (Indian Ridge) 2817[2] 3242[2] (3640) 4981a[4] 5392[16] >107f<

**Captain Johnno (IRE)** 2 b g Tagula (IRE) -Thornby Park (Unfuwain (USA)) 4682[7] 5578[3] 5908[3] *(6289)* >82a 75f<

**Captain Margaret** 2 b f Royal Applause-Go For Red (IRE) (Thatching) 3675[10] 4198[5] 5200[10] 5596[12] 5909[3] 6562[12] >63+f<

**Captain Marryat** 3 ch g Inchinor-Finlaggan (Be My Chief (USA)) 1310[2] 1827[11] 2915[2] 3155[2] 3386[3] 5293[2] 5410[3] *6292[2]* >69a 69+f<

**Captain Miller** 8 b g Batshoof-Miller s Gait (Mill Reef (USA)) 2047[2] 2305[2] 5093[15] >79f<

**Captain Saif** 4 b c Compton Place-Bahawir Pour (USA) (Green Dancer (USA)) 2201[14] 2283[16] 3212[11] 3441[4] 3871[3] 5713[14] 6520[17] >85 f<

**Cara Bella** 3 ch f Seeking The Gold (USA) -Cherokee Rose (IRE) (Dancing Brave (USA)) 1400[7] 1842[5] 2694[3] 3457[6] >77f<

**Caracara (IRE)** 3 ch f Nashwan (USA) -Vividimagination (USA) (Raise A Man (USA)) 2018[13] >77 f<

**Caradak (IRE)** 3 b c Desert Style (IRE) -Caraiyma (IRE) (Shahrastani (USA)) (4405a) 6214[6] >112f<

**Cara Fantasy (IRE)** 4 b f Sadler s Wells (USA) -Gay Fantasy (Troy) 1326[4] 2240[7] 3947[2] >86f<

**Cara Sposa (IRE)** 2 b c Lend A Hand-Charlton Spring (IRE) (Masterclass (USA)) 6454[11] >22f<

**Cardinal Venture (IRE)** 6 b g Bishop Of Cashel-Phoenix Venture (IRE) (Thatching) *1011[2]* 1114[11] 1772[7] 1927[15] (2626) 3074[8] 3673[16] 5628[15] 6071[15]6477[4] >103a 96f<

**Cargo** 5 b g Emarati (USA) -Portvasco (Sharpo) *465[11] 674[4] 859[2] 884[11] 1692[2] 1913[3]* 2379[2]3103[8] 3533[7] 3988[2] 4469[2] 4802[9] 5282[9] 5930[2] *(6403)* >53a 52f<

**Caribbean Blue** 3 b f First Trump-Something Blue (Petong) 2411[5] 2660[8] 3234[9] 4309[19] 5801[7] 6229[18] >45 f<

**Caribbean Coral** 5 ch g Brief Truce (USA) -Caribbean Star (Soviet Star (USA)) 1113[8] 1391[2] (2679) (3266) 4324[13] 5105[11] 5418[3] 5647[11] 5933[4] 6177[4]6349[9] >109f<

**Caribbean Dancer (USA)** 2 b f Theatrical-Enticed (USA) (Stage Door Johnny (USA)) 5109[10] 5756[8] 6240[2] 6562[13] >71f<

**Caribbean Diamond (IRE)** 2 b f Imperial Ballet (IRE) -Bebe Auction (IRE) (Auction Ring (USA)) 4498[9] >24f<

**Caribe (FR)** 5 b g Octagonal (NZ) -Caring Society (Caerleon (USA)) 1469[6] 2291[12] 2779[10] *3025[8] 3800[10]* >36a 36f<

**Carini** 3 b f Vettori (IRE) -Secret Waters (Pharly (FR)) 2221[3] 3912[6] 4525[3] 5025[8] 6087[5] >95f<

**Cark** 6 b g Farfelu-Precious Girl (Precious Metal) *443[6] (460) 538[2] 794[8] 938[7] 1262[13]* 1872[14] >56a 56f<

**Carla Moon** 3 b f Desert Prince (IRE) -Khambani (IRE) (Royal Academy (USA)) 2097[11] 3530[19] 4201[12] 4496[10] >65f<

**Carlburg (IRE)** 3 b g Barathea (IRE) -Ichnusa (Bay Express) 2244[10] 3949[11] 4338[12] *5222[12] 6061[8]* >41a 68f<

**Carlo Bank (IRE)** 8 b h Lahib (USA) -Lagrion (USA) (Diesis) 2340a[7] >67f<

**Carlton (IRE)** 10 ch g Thatching-Hooray Lady (Ahonoora) *701[8] 771[4] 833[4] 1087[10]* 1268[2] 1373[4] *1424[15]*1526[2] 1665[2] 1873[2] 1969[7] *2666[8]* 3982[5] 4447[9] 4827[9]5108[10] >64a 66f<

**Carlys Quest** 10 ch g Primo Dominie-Tuppy (USA) (Sharpen Up) 2958[27] >15f<

**Carmania (IRE)** 2 b g Desert Sun-Scatter Brain (Risk Me (FR)) 3444[16] 3729[5] 4675[9] 5363[13] 5520[12] >53f<

**Carmarthen Belle** 4 b f Merdon Melody-Woodland Steps (Bold Owl) 6200[18] 6561[17] ><

**Carnegie Hall (IRE)** 2 b c Danehill (USA) -Bolshaya (Cadeaux Genereux) 4959a[4] >102f<

**Carnivore** 2 ch c Zafonic (USA) -Ermine (IRE) (Cadeaux Genereux) 4347[2] >71f<

**Carnt Spell** 3 b g Wizard King-Forever Shineing (Glint Of Gold) 5770[13] >24f<

**Carols Choice** 7 ch m Emarati (USA) -Lucky Song (Lucky Wednesday) *421[6] 443[5] 499[10]* >39a 33f<

**Caronte (IRE)** 4 b g Sesaro (USA) -Go Likecrazy (Dowsing (USA)) *474[10] 499[12] 626[12] 713[13] 998[10] (1089) 1445[8] 1699[8]*2175[7] >41a 18f<

**Caroubier (IRE)** 4 ch g Woodborough (USA) -Patsy Grimes (Beveled (USA)) *507[5] 605[2] (720) 862[2] 1066[9]* (1275) 1671[9] 2226[9] 2474[14]3198[15] *3614[6]* 5203[12] 5853[14] >80a 86f<

**Carrara (ITY)** 2 b f Shantou (USA) -Cara Marialetizia (IRE) (Be My Guest (USA)) 5390a[7] ><

**Carriacou** 3 b f Mark Of Esteem (IRE) -Cockatoo Island (High Top) 1357[6] *1627[4]* 1969[5] 3230[9] 3949[5] 4201[3] 4655[7] 4848[4]5057[7] 6083[3] *6292[10]* 6524[6] >66a 69f<

**Carrizo Creek (IRE)** 3 b c Charnwood Forest (IRE) -Violet Spring (IRE) (Exactly Sharp (USA)) 1396[7] 4745[7] >106f<

**Carrowdore (IRE)** 4 b c Danehill (USA) -Euromill (Shirley Heights) *984[2]* 2471[4] 2787[3] 3095[4] 3459[2] 4518[2] 5374[4] 5554[3]5935[4] >82a 82f<

**Carry On Doc** 3 b c Dr Devious (IRE) -Florentynna Bay (Aragon) *1597[3]* 2267[6] (3554) 4151[5] 4437[3] (5185) 5403[11] 5934[7] >65a 87f<

**Carry On Katie (USA)** 3 br f Fasliyev (USA) -Dinka Raja (USA) (Woodman (USA)) 1791[6] 2160a[9] >109f<

**Carte Diamond (USA)** 3 ch c Theatrical-Liteup My Life (USA) (Green Dancer (USA)) (3057) (3716) 5892[2] 6121[3] (6573) >108f<

**Carte Noire** 3 b f Revoque (IRE) -Coffee Cream (Common Grounds) 1309[5] (2658) *2989[8]* 3589[11] 5370[11] 5748[7] >37a 63f<

**Carte Royale** 2 ch g Loup Sauvage (USA) -Noble One (Primo Dominie) (2352) 2868[2] 3224[6] >87 f<

**Carte Sauvage (USA)** 3 rg c Kris S (USA) -See You (USA) (Gulch (USA)) *691a[6]* 6354[13] 6458[4] >85a 102f<

**Cartography (IRE)** 3 b c Zafonic (USA) -Sans Escale (USA) (Diesis) 2308[3] 2966[3] 3940[2] 5289[18] 5832[2] >111f<

**Cartronageeraghlad (IRE)** 3 b g Mujadil (USA) -Night Scent (IRE) (Scenic) 1129[10] 1333[12] 1841[9] 2304[9] 2400[2] 2591[4] 2887[4] 3543[5]3610[4] 4443[12] 5151[8] 6086[3] *6279[6]* >75a 82f<

**Casalese** 2 ch g Wolfhound (USA) -Little Redwing (Be My Chief (USA)) 5447[13] 5831[7] 6464[8] >36f<

**Casantella** 3 b f Atraf-Ramajana (USA) (Shadeed (USA)) *473[8] 514[4] 585[5] 611[7] 736[5] 808[10] 965[8]1017[9]* >44a 43f<

**Cascade Lakes** 2 ch f Fraam-Spring Flyer (IRE) (Waajib) 6514[13] >24f<

**Casey s House** 4 gr f Paris House-Case Dismissed (IRE) (Case Law) 1342[12] 2040[8] 3096[10] *4879[11]* >24f<

**Cash** 6 b g Bishop Of Cashel-Ballad Island (Ballad Rock) *681[7] (794) 905[3] 1027[5]* 1421[18] 1525[11] 1665[14] (1870) 2130[18]4701[13] >69a 65f<

**Cashbar** 3 b f Bishop Of Cashel-Barford Sovereign (Unfuwain (USA)) *3848[2]* (4303) 4756[8] >64+a 81+f<

**Cashel House (IRE)** 2 b c Bishop Of Cashel-Forest Treasure (USA) (Green Forest (USA)) *6449[4]* >68a 67f<

**Cashel Mead** 4 b f Bishop Of Cashel-Island Mead (Pharly (FR)) *417[5] 511[9] 770[8]* 1185[6] 1608[15] 2091[12] *5952[7] 6482[10]* >84a 84f<

**Cashema (IRE)** 3 b f Cape Cross (IRE) -Miss Shema (USA) (Gulch (USA)) 1507[8] 1946[16] 2545[8] 3160[16] >50f<

**Cashier** 2 gr c Alhaarth (IRE) -Cashew (Sharrood (USA)) 6330[3] >73f<

**Cashneem (IRE)** 6 b g Case Law-Haanem (Mtoto) 1877[4] 2215[6] (2598) 2673[4] 3058[7] 3559[9] 3698[14] 5945[24] 6094[18] >69f<

**Cash On (IRE)** 2 ch c Spectrum (IRE) -Lady Lucre (IRE) (Last Tycoon) 6187[13] *6393[9]* >61a 56f<

**Cash Time** 2 ch f Timeless Times (USA) -Cashmirie (Domynsky) 2622[6] 3444[14] 3620[4] 4699[12] >34f<

**Casigris (USA)** 3 gr f Cozzene (USA) -Laluche (USA) (Alleged (USA)) 6203a[0] >93f<

**Caspian Dusk** 3 b g Up And At Em-Caspian Morn (Lugana Beach) *1022[2] 1084[3] (1192) 1736[2] (2127) 2452[3] 3022[7]* >70a 42f<

**Caspian Lake (IRE)** 3 ch g Lake Coniston (IRE) -Hardtimes (IRE) (Distinctly North (USA)) 6130[9] *6481[8]* >43a 23f<

**Cassanos (IRE)** 3 b g Ali-Royal (IRE) -I m Your Girl (Shavian) *482[3] 808[6]* >45a 54f<

**Cassydora** 2 b f Darshaan-Claxon (Caerleon (USA)) 3905[6] (4753) 5413[4] >97f<

**Castagna (USA)** 3 ch f Horse Chestnut (SAF) -Thrilling Day (Groom Dancer (USA)) 3630[4] (4141) 4884[7] 5763[8] >83f<

**Castaigne (FR)** 5 ch m Pivotal-Storm Warning (Tumble Wind) *464[7] 623[13]* 2302[6] 2430[7] 3490[4] 3670[4] 3827[11] >64a 66f<

**Castanet** 5 b m Pennekamp (USA) -Addaya (IRE) (Persian Bold) 1534[5] 2514[9] >52a 70f<

**Castaway Queen (IRE)** 5 ch m Selkirk (USA) -Surfing (Grundy) 1308[2] *1940[13]* 2302[8] 2929[3] 3699[9] >52a 69f<

**Castelletto** 2 b f Komaite (USA) -Malcesine (IRE) (Auction Ring (USA)) 1943[3] 2585[2] 2970[16] 3382[2] (3583) 4744[2] 4885[5] 5250[2] 5626[3](6212) >104f<

**Casterossa** 2 ch f Rossini (USA) -First Musical (First Trump) 2837[6] 4137[4] 4399[4] 5202[6] 5648[19] >71f<

**Castledale (IRE)** 3 b c Peintre Celebre (USA) -Louju (USA) (Silver Hawk (USA)) *1781a[14]* >121a 98f<

**Castleshane (IRE)** 7 b g Kris-Ahbab (IRE) (Ajdal (USA)) 2527[11] >94f<

**Castleton** 3 b c Cape Cross (IRE) -Craigmill (Slip Anchor) 1939[2] 2307[3] (2693) 2956[6] >115?f<

**Casual Attitude (USA)** 4 br f Formal Gold (CAN) -Cooleemee (USA) (Foolish Pleasure (USA)) *4735a[2]* ><

**Casual Glance** 2 b f Sinndar (IRE) -Spurned (USA) (Robellino (USA)) 4272[13] 4913[9] >53f<

**Catalini** 3 ch g Seeking The Gold (USA) -Calando (USA) (Storm Cat (USA)) *1015[2] 1120[5]* 2704[5] 3397[6] >75a 75f<

**Cat Belling (IRE)** 4 br f Catrail (USA) -Lute And Lyre (IRE) (The Noble Player (USA)) 636a[5] 690a[8] 710a[9] 831a[6] (850a) (921a) 978a[6] 1002a[4] >72a 102f<

**Catcando (IRE)** 6 ch g Catrail (USA) -Tongabezi (IRE) (Shernazar) (2343a) >38a 64f<

**Catch A Star** 2 ch f Giant s Causeway (USA) -Amy Hunter (USA) (Jade Hunter (USA)) 2275[3] 2690[5] 3319[8] 3675[3] (5620) 5938[3] 6129[6] >84f<

**Catchmeifyoucan (NZ)** 5 b g Senor Pete (USA) -Glamis (NZ) (Oak Ridge (FR)) 6528a[8] >98f<

**Catchthebatch** 8 b g Beveled (USA) -Batchworth Dancer (Ballacashtal (CAN)) *560[4] 762[3] 1027[11]* 3084[11]

3378$^{11}$ 4400$^{16}$ 4811$^{10}$5253$^{15}$ >**55a 55f**<

**Catch The Cat (IRE)** **5** b g Catrail (USA) -Tongabezi (IRE) (Shernazar) 1421$^{3}$ 1665$^{7}$ 1956$^{2}$ 2118$^{8}$ (2490) 2859$^{6}$ 3326$^{5}$ 3509$^{7}$ 3713$^{7}$3920$^{10}$ (4279) 4452$^{8}$ 4855$^{8}$ 5062$^{14}$ 5949$^{14}$ >**53a 79f**<

**Catch The Fox** **4** b g Fraam-Versaillesprincess (Legend Of France (USA)) 1352$^{12}$ 1582$^{2}$ 1986$^{7}$ 2302$^{10}$ 2573$^{4}$ 3631$^{12}$ 4438$^{9}$ 4713$^{10}$5080$^{4}$ 5641$^{7}$ 5926$^{3}$ 6130$^{3}$ 6343$^{17}$ >**30a 49f**<

**Catch The Wind** **3** b f Bahamian Bounty-Tinkerbird (Music Boy) 1881$^{13}$ 2264$^{5}$ 3420$^{5}$ 3777$^{6}$ (4043) 4299$^{2}$ 4688$^{2}$ 6267$^{12}$ >**74a 86f**<

**Caterham Common** **5** b g Common Grounds-Pennine Pink (IRE) (Pennine Walk) 582$^{11}$ 713$^{6}$ 875$^{8}$ 994$^{10}$ 1094$^{5}$ >**33a 34f**<

**Catherine Howard** **3** b f Kingmambo (USA) -Darling Flame (USA) (Capote (USA)) 1418$^{4}$ 2134$^{9}$ 2587$^{4}$ 3012$^{5}$ >**74f**<

**Catherine Wheel** **3** b f Primo Dominie-Prancing (Prince Sabo) 1453$^{2}$ (2468) (3178) (3849) >**82+a 82+f**<

**Catstar (USA)** **3** bb f Storm Cat (USA) -Advancing Star (USA) (Soviet Star (USA)) (711a) 2629$^{5}$ 3105$^{5}$ >**108a 104 f**<

**Catstone (FR)** **2** b c Grindstone (USA) -Catskill Mountain (USA) (Mountain Cat (USA)) 5432a$^{6}$ >**88f**<

**Cat s Whiskers** **5** b g Catrail (USA) -Haut Volee (Top Ville) 1321$^{7}$ 1773$^{3}$ 3299$^{4}$ 3731$^{15}$ 5127$^{2}$ 5211$^{7}$ 5581$^{5}$ >**86f**<

**Cattiva Generosa** **3** b f Cadeaux Genereux-Signorina Cattiva (USA) (El Gran Senor (USA)) 2160a$^{8}$ 3258a$^{2}$ 4383a$^{6}$ 5969a$^{4}$ 6511a$^{7}$ >**109f**<

**Ca Turtle (GER)** **3** b c Turtle Island (IRE) -Ca Alors (FR) (Highest Honor (FR)) 1306a$^{4}$ ><

**Catwalk Cleric (IRE)** **2** b c Orpen (USA) -Ministerial Model (IRE) (Shalford (IRE)) 1505$^{4}$ (1882) 2669a$^{2}$ 2954$^{13}$ 5202$^{4}$ 5630$^{4}$ 6113$^{8}$ >**88f**<

**Cause Celebre (IRE)** **3** gr f Peintre Celebre (USA) -Madame Belga (USA) (Al Nasr (FR)) (2168) 2683$^{10}$ (3340) 3908$^{6}$ 5615$^{13}$ 5950$^{8}$ >**83f**<

**Causeway Girl (IRE)** **2** br f Giant s Causeway (USA) -Darbela (IRE) (Doyoun) 5915$^{17}$ 6470$^{17}$ >**42f**<

**Caustic Wit (IRE)** **6** b g Cadeaux Genereux-Baldemosa (FR) (Lead On Time (USA)) (509) 1477$^{13}$ (1909) (2524) (2763) (2948) 3324$^{2}$ 3453$^{2}$ 3941$^{9}$ 4614$^{12}$ 4951$^{4}$ 5263$^{6}$5874$^{6}$ >**60a 95f**<

**Cava Bien** **2** b g Bien Bien (USA) -Bebe De Cham (Tragic Role (USA)) 2961$^{7}$ 3366$^{3}$ 4277$^{3}$ 5227$^{7}$ 5852$^{5}$ (6226) >**68f**<

**Cavalarra** **2** b c Green Desert (USA) -Ya Tarra (Unbridled (USA)) 5262$^{8}$ 5616$^{5}$ >**59f**<

**Cavan Gael (FR)** **2** b c Dansili-Time Will Show (FR) (Exit To Nowhere (USA)) 5897$^{9}$ 6330$^{6}$ 6569$^{8}$ >**65f**<

**Cavaradossi** **2** gr c Lake Coniston (IRE) -Floria Tosca (Petong) 3588$^{P}$ 4809$^{15}$ ><

**Cave Of The Giant (IRE)** **2** b c Giant s Causeway (USA) -Maroussie (FR) (Saumarez) 5567$^{5}$ 6149$^{9}$ >**73f**<

**Caveral** **3** ch f Ashkalani (IRE) -Melting Gold (USA) (Cadeaux Genereux) 1704$^{8}$ 2200$^{7}$ (2372) 2685$^{10}$ 4526$^{3}$ 5249$^{10}$ 5416$^{6}$ 5811$^{11}$ >**101f**<

**Cavorting** **2** ch g Polar Falcon (USA) -Prancing (Prince Sabo) 1412$^{4}$ 6002$^{7}$ >**73f**<

**Cayenne (GER)** **2** ch f Efisio-Carola Rouge (Arazi (USA)) 4704$^{5}$ 5301$^{5}$ >**52f**<

**Cayman Breeze** **4** b g Danzig (USA) -Lady Thynn (FR) (Crystal Glitters (USA)) 448$^{12}$ 723$^{5}$ 791$^{4}$ (858) 2528$^{8}$ 4617$^{5}$ 5408$^{9}$ 5512$^{10}$6146$^{4}$ 6558$^{12}$ >**57a 60f**<

**Cayman Calypso (IRE)** **3** ro g Danehill Dancer (IRE) -Warthill Whispers (Grey Desire) 2311$^{9}$ 2808$^{8}$ 3487$^{6}$ 3852$^{7}$ 4092$^{6}$ 4491$^{2}$ 4624$^{2}$ 5197$^{12}$5715$^{12}$ 5868$^{17}$ 6120$^{14}$ >**63f**<

**Cayman King** **2** b g Cayman Kai (IRE) -Distinctly Laura (IRE) (Distinctly North (USA)) 5857$^{14}$ ><

**Cayman Mischief** **4** b f Cayman Kai (IRE) -Tribal Mischief (Be My Chief (USA)) 424$^{7}$ 3269$^{14}$ 4257$^{6}$ 4701$^{8}$ >**31f**<

**Caymans Gift** **4** ch g Cayman Kai (IRE) -Gymcrak Cyrano (IRE) (Cyrano De Bergerac) 1786$^{4}$ 2077$^{5}$ 2487$^{6}$ 3042$^{3}$ 3369$^{10}$ >**60f**<

**Cayman Sunrise (IRE)** **4** gr f Peintre Celebre (USA) -Sum (USA) (Spectacular Bid (USA)) 552$^{8}$ >**61a 70f**<

**Cayman Venture (IRE)** **4** b c Entrepreneur-Saninka (IRE) (Doyoun) 5506a$^{9}$ >**75a 77f**<

**Cayuse** **2** b f Double Trigger (IRE) -Suile Mor (Satin Wood) 4730$^{18}$ 6470$^{18}$ >**1f**<

**Cazenove** **3** b g Royal Applause-Celestina (IRE) (Priolo (USA)) 1306a$^{10}$ 3666$^{4}$ 3948$^{6}$ 4478$^{7}$ 4817$^{13}$ >**61f**<

**Cazisa Star (USA)** **3** ch f Mister Baileys-Placer Queen (Habitat) 2848$^{11}$ 3459$^{8}$ 4055$^{9}$ >**57f**<

**Cd Europe (IRE)** **6** ch g Royal Academy (USA) -Woodland Orchid (IRE) (Woodman (USA)) 2132$^{8}$ 3074$^{25}$ 3309$^{17}$ 3755$^{10}$ 3901$^{6}$ 4324$^{10}$ 4759$^{10}$ 5491$^{2}$5603$^{2}$ >**74a 100f**<

**Cd Flyer (IRE)** **7** ch g Grand Lodge (USA) -Pretext (Polish Precedent (USA)) 1106$^{5}$ 1500$^{2}$ 1765$^{19}$ 2065$^{7}$ 2626$^{4}$ (3098) 3309$^{13}$ 3755$^{4}$ 4179$^{3}$4759$^{5}$ 5075$^{6}$ 5603$^{18}$ 6070$^{2}$ 6517$^{12}$ 6568$^{14}$ >**79a 95f**<

**Ceasar (IRE)** **3** b g Orpen (USA) -Fen Princess (IRE) (Trojan Fen) 611$^{2}$ (752) 957$^{10}$ (1499) 2199$^{3}$ 2821$^{9}$ >**52a 61f**<

**Cedar Master (IRE)** **7** b g Soviet Lad (USA) -Samriah (IRE) (Wassl) 2893$^{10}$ 3851$^{7}$ >**73a 78f**<

**Cedric Coverwell** **4** ch g Charmer-Marsara (Never So Bold) 1169$^{4}$ 1352$^{17}$ 1796$^{13}$ 2586$^{11}$ 3175$^{12}$ 3533$^{16}$ 3635$^{5}$ 4548$^{9}$ >**35a 41f**<

**Cefira (USA)** **3** b f Distant View (USA) -Bold Jessie (Never So Bold) 1288$^{3}$ 1413$^{8}$ (2290) 5618$^{7}$ 6001$^{17}$ >**66f**<

**Ceiriog Valley** **2** b f In The Wings-Bodfari Quarry (Efisio) 4272$^{8}$ (4930) 5292$^{11}$ >**83+f**<

**Celadon (IRE)** **3** b g Fasliyev (USA) -Dancing Drop (Green Desert (USA)) 764$^{2}$ >**56a 70 f**<

**Celebre Citation (IRE)** **3** ch g Peintre Celebre (USA) -Kotama (USA) (Shahrastani (USA)) 1371$^{12}$ 4402$^{5}$ 5123$^{12}$ 5773$^{18}$ >**62f**<

**Celestial Arc (USA)** **2** b c Southern Halo (USA) -Perfect Arc (USA) (Brown Arc (USA)) 3241$^{3}$ 3749$^{11}$ 4143$^{7}$ 5417$^{12}$ 5852$^{7}$ >**71f**<

**Cellarmaster (IRE)** **3** ch g Alhaarth (IRE) -Cheeky Weeky (Cadeaux Genereux) 3160$^{3}$ (3746) 4754$^{4}$ 5615$^{3}$ 6332$^{8}$ >**69a 87f**<

**Cellino** **3** b f Robellino (USA) -Celandine (Warning) 1027$^{12}$ 2661$^{4}$ 4105$^{10}$ 4309$^{7}$ 4868$^{10}$ 5451$^{10}$ 6228$^{9}$ >**25f**<

**Cello** **3** gr c Pivotal-Raffelina (USA) (Carson City (USA)) 1366$^{2}$ (1541) 1900$^{6}$ 2642$^{9}$ 3001$^{25}$ 4691$^{4}$ 5076$^{2}$ 5766$^{3}$ (6284) >**52a 88f**<

**Celtic Blaze (IRE)** **5** b m Charente River (IRE) -Firdaunt (Tanfirion) 3821$^{3}$ 4352$^{8}$ 5214$^{7}$ 5343$^{5}$ >**58a 65f**<

**Celtic Carisma** **2** b f Celtic Swing-Kathryn s Pet (Blakeney) 6196$^{11}$ 6514$^{10}$ >**36f**<

**Celtic Heroine (IRE)** **3** ch f Hernando (FR) -Celtic Fling (Lion Cavern (USA)) 1357$^{2}$ (1931) 2420$^{2}$ (2971) 3223$^{2}$ 3641$^{5}$ 4077$^{2}$ 4899a$^{6}$ >**80+a 109f**<

**Celtic Mill** **6** b g Celtic Swing-Madam Millie (Milford) (607) 761$^{4}$ 1765$^{15}$ (2132) (2373) 3308$^{9}$ 4269$^{7}$ 5121$^{6}$ (5418) 5647$^{8}$ 5780$^{4}$ >**94a 113f**<

**Celtic Promise (IRE)** **2** b f Celtic Swing-Tainted Halo (USA) (Halo (USA)) 6011$^{14}$ 6308$^{6}$ 6565$^{5}$ >**28a 62f**<

**Celtic Romance** **5** b m Celtic Swing-Southern Sky (Comedy Star (USA)) 1247$^{14}$ 1358$^{8}$ 1606$^{8}$ 1992$^{5}$ 2757$^{8}$ 3006$^{6}$ 3471$^{7}$ 3835$^{4}$ >**39a 39f**<

**Celtic Solitude (IRE)** **3** b f Celtic Swing-Smart n Noble (USA) (Smarten (USA)) 2144$^{12}$ 2554$^{13}$ >**28a 34+f**<

**Celtic Spa (IRE)** **2** gr f Celtic Swing-Allegorica (IRE) (Alzao (USA)) 1670$^{7}$ (1943) 2532$^{7}$ 2959$^{5}$ 3346$^{3}$ 3938$^{13}$ 4958a$^{4}$ 5767$^{7}$ 6356$^{9}$ >**83f**<

**Celtic Star (IRE)** **6** b g Celtic Swing-Recherchee (Rainbow Quest (USA)) 3128$^{11}$ 3573$^{6}$ 4192$^{15}$ >**70 f**<

**Celtic Tanner (IRE)** **5** b g Royal Abjar (USA) -Mills Pride (IRE) (Posen (USA)) 6481$^{11}$ >**41a**<

**Celtic Thatcher** **6** b g Celtic Swing-Native Thatch (IRE) (Thatching) 2454$^{2}$ >**56a**<

**Celtic Thunder** **3** b g Mind Games-Lake Mistassiu (Tina s Pet) 1659$^{2}$ 2131$^{9}$ 2552$^{5}$ 2877$^{8}$ 3203$^{2}$ 3523$^{7}$ 3845$^{4}$ 4576$^{4}$5299$^{18}$ 5563$^{5}$ 6267$^{16}$ >**85f**<

**Celtic Vision (IRE)** **8** b g Be My Native (USA) -Dream Run (Deep Run) 1212$^{6}$ 1249$^{6}$ 1367$^{10}$ 1615$^{14}$ 1866$^{4}$ 2004$^{6}$ 3129$^{5}$ >**34f**<

**Celtique** **2** b f Celtic Swing-Heart s Harmony (Blushing Groom (FR)) 5088$^{2}$ 5368$^{3}$ 6447$^{2}$ >**69a 81f**<

**Cemgraft** **3** b f In The Wings-Soviet Maid (IRE) (Soviet Star (USA)) 4028$^{5}$ 4554$^{9}$ 5537$^{6}$ 6013$^{16}$ >**47a 64f**<

**Centaurus** **2** gr c Daylami (IRE) -Dandanna (IRE) (Linamix (FR)) (6476) >**96+f**<

**Centifolia (FR)** **2** gr f Kendor (FR) -Djayapura (FR) (Fabulous Dancer (USA)) 4597a$^{10}$ (6202a) (6462a) >**114f**<

**Cepangie (IRE)** **7** b m Hamas (IRE) -Zina (IRE) (Taufan (USA)) 6104a$^{15}$ >**57+f**<

**Ceprin (IRE)** **3** b c Desert Prince (IRE) -Black Wood (USA) (Woodman (USA)) 1777a$^{3}$ 2510a$^{13}$ >**104f**<

**Cerebus** **2** b f Wolfhound (USA) -Bring On The Choir (Chief Singer) 3676$^{6}$ 4099$^{4}$ 4243$^{2}$ 5240$^{3}$ 5466$^{3}$ 5701$^{6}$ 5938$^{14}$ >**77f**<

**Certa Cito** **4** b f Mind Games-Bollin Dorothy (Rambo Dancer (CAN)) 1175$^{10}$ 1361$^{13}$ 2219$^{5}$ 2670$^{13}$ 3524$^{10}$ 5736$^{4}$ 6146$^{7}$ >**36a 61f**<

**Certain Justice (USA)** **6** gr g Lit De Justice (USA) -Pure Misk (Rainbow Quest (USA)) 1623$^{8}$ 1840$^{6}$ 2516$^{5}$ 3419$^{10}$ 3871$^{5}$ 4093$^{7}$ >**86a 82f**<

**Certifiable** **3** b g Deploy-Gentle Irony (Mazilier (USA)) 811$^{4}$ (890) (1120) 1585$^{5}$ 2069$^{12}$ 2906$^{5}$ 3419$^{11}$ 6557$^{7}$ >**76a 70f**<

**Cerulean Rose** **5** ch m Bluegrass Prince (IRE) -Elegant Rose (Noalto) 1937$^{4}$ 2246$^{9}$ 2909$^{2}$ 3178$^{8}$ 4085$^{3}$ 4232$^{15}$ 4854$^{2}$ 5094$^{4}$6001$^{20}$ 6046$^{13}$ >**78f**<

**Cesare** **3** b g Machiavellian (USA) -Tromond (Lomond (USA)) 1301$^{2}$ (1557) 6069$^{11}$ >**73+f**<

**Cesar Manrique (IRE)** **2** ch c Vettori (IRE) -Norbella (Nordico (USA)) 5003$^{9}$ 5441$^{5}$ 5586$^{4}$ (6281) >**79f**<

**Ceylon Round (FR)** **3** b f Royal Applause-Tea Colony (USA) (Pleasant Colony (USA)) 3554$^{7}$ 4195$^{7}$ 4402$^{6}$ 6061$^{10}$ 6401$^{12}$ >**20a 58 f**<

**Cezzaro (IRE)** **6** ch g Ashkalani (IRE) -Sept Roses (USA) (Septieme Ciel (USA)) 1444$^{5}$ 1697$^{6}$ 2347$^{11}$ 3056$^{2}$ 3165$^{2}$ 3247$^{12}$ 4015$^{15}$ 4189$^{9}$4423$^{5}$ 6466$^{9}$ >**42a 53f**<

**Chagall** **7** ch h Fraam-Pooka (Dominion) 6379a$^{15}$ >**96f**<

**Chain Of Hope (IRE)** **3** ch g Shinko Forest (IRE) -Fleeting Smile (IRE) (Bluebird (USA)) 4868$^{16}$ 5184$^{10}$ 6130$^{7}$ >**52f**<

**Chairman Bobby** **6** ch g Clantime-Formidable Liz (Formidable (USA)) 1343$^{5}$ 1774$^{7}$ 1974$^{19}$ 2079$^{3}$ 2407$^{2}$ 2461$^{19}$ 2784$^{2}$ 2976$^{5}$3407$^{8}$ 3606$^{11}$ 4011$^{9}$ 5107$^{17}$ 5242$^{10}$ 6026$^{8}$ 6452$^{11}$ >**71a 77f**<

**Chairman Rick (IRE)** **2** b c Danehill Dancer (IRE) -Come Together (Mtoto) 3664$^{7}$ 3847$^{6}$ 4064$^{4}$ 4439$^{7}$ 5234$^{7}$ >**51a 62f**<

**Chakra** **10** gr g Mystiko (USA) -Maracuja (USA) (Riverman (USA)) 1406$^{6}$ 1687$^{5}$ 1863$^{3}$ 2017$^{8}$ 2262$^{10}$ >**17a 36f**<

**Chalison (IRE)** **2** b c Anabaa (USA) -Raincloud (Rainbow Quest (USA)) 1505$^{2}$ 2225$^{3}$ 3726$^{5}$ >**80f**<

**Chambray (IRE)** **3** b f Barathea (IRE) -Spurned (USA) (Robellino (USA)) 1311$^{8}$ 2517$^{8}$ 3383$^{5}$ >**56f**<

**Champagne Brandy (IRE)** **2** ch f Spectrum (IRE) -Petite Liqueurelle (IRE) (Shernazar) 1128$^{13}$ 2609$^{13}$ 2736$^{12}$ >**32f**<

**Champagne Cracker** **3** ch f Up And At Em-Kiveton Komet (Precocious) 1991$^{8}$ 2290$^{3}$ (2650) 3077$^{5}$ 3624$^{9}$ 4279$^{9}$ 4904$^{6}$ 5579$^{25}$ >**67f**<

**Champagne In Paris** **2** gr f Paris House-Ashleen (Chilibang) 1364$^{11}$ ><

**Champagne Lujain** **2** b g Lujain (USA) -Brief Glimpse (IRE) (Taufan (USA)) 5857$^{12}$ 6211$^{5}$ 6514$^{12}$ >**40f**<

**Champagne Rider** **8** b g Presidium-Petitesse (Petong) 428$^{3}$ 474$^{5}$ (572) >**46a 33f**<

**Champagne Rossini (IRE)** **2** b g Rossini (USA) -Alpencrocus (IRE) (Waajib) 3805$^{9}$ 4498$^{5}$ 4997$^{6}$ 5593$^{12}$ >**51a 53f**<

**Champagne Shadow (IRE)** **3** b c Kahyasi-Moet (IRE) (Mac s Imp (USA)) 447$^{8}$ 739$^{4}$ 916$^{12}$ 1100$^{2}$ 1672$^{8}$ 2882$^{2}$ 3304$^{3}$5216$^{2}$ 5889$^{9}$ 6450$^{7}$ >**76a 65f**<

**Champain Sands (IRE)** **5** b g Green Desert (USA) -Grecian Bride (IRE) (Groom Dancer (USA)) 1479$^{3}$ 2120$^{4}$ 2424$^{2}$ 2618$^{5}$ 3005$^{7}$ 3952$^{9}$ 5320$^{9}$ 5557$^{6}$ >**54a 55f**<

**Champali (USA)** **4** b c Glitterman (USA) -Radioactivity (USA) (Dixieland Band (USA)) 6487a$^{7}$ >**123a**<

**Champion Lion (IRE)** **5** b g Sadler s Wells (USA) -Honey Bun (Unfuwain (USA)) 1103$^{15}$ 1326$^{10}$ 1539$^{5}$ 1768$^{7}$ 1928$^{6}$ 2120$^{3}$ 5584$^{3}$ 5853$^{5}$6083$^{8}$ >**75+f**<

**Champion s Day (GER)** **3** ch c Valanour (IRE) -Courtly Times (Machiavellian (USA)) 6378a$^{2}$ >**99f**<

**Chance For Romance** **3** ch f Entrepreneur-My First Romance (Danehill (USA)) 2549$^{2}$ 3203$^{6}$ 3995$^{5}$ 4434$^{7}$ 4740$^{10}$ >**74df**<

**Chancellor (IRE)** **6** ch h Halling (USA) -Isticanna (USA) (Far North (CAN)) 1355$^{9}$ (1622) 1804a$^{8}$ 2559$^{9}$ 3540$^{12}$ 4539$^{6}$ >**115f**<

**Chandelier** **4** ch g Sabrehill (USA) -La Noisette (Rock Hopper) 565$^{5}$ 707$^{3}$ 888$^{6}$ 932$^{7}$ 1680$^{3}$ 2006$^{2}$ 2426$^{15}$(3697) 3910$^{6}$ 4479$^{10}$ 4672$^{8}$ 5176$^{6}$ 5336$^{RR}$ 6014$^{3}$ 6146$^{10}$ >**61a 56f**<

**Chandi Dasa (IRE)** **3** b f Sadler s Wells (USA) -Antique Pearl (Darshaan) 5033a$^{9}$ >**96f**<

**Chanfron** **3** ch g Double Trigger (IRE) -Mhargaidh Nua (Thowra (FR)) 2546$^{7}$ 3160$^{5}$ 3683$^{5}$ 4473$^{9}$ 5914$^{14}$ >**28a 61f**<

**Changari (USA)** **3** b f Gulch (USA) -Danzari (Arazi (USA)) 2892$^{5}$ >**84f**<

**Change The Grange (AUS)** **6** gr g Umatilla (NZ) -Je Reviens (AUS) (The Challenge (AUS)) 635a$^{7}$ 757a$^{9}$ >**93a**<

**Channel Four (USA)** **4** b c Gold Fever (USA) -Run To Reign (USA) (Sovereign Dancer (USA)) 757a$^{5}$ >**78a**<

**Chantaco (USA)** **2** b c Bahri (USA) -Dominant Dancer (Primo Dominie) 4016$^{5}$ 4432$^{2}$ (5301) >**74+f**<

**Chantelle (IRE)** **4** b f Lake Coniston (IRE) -Kristabelle (IRE) (Elbio) 5253$^{7}$ 5736$^{12}$ 6058$^{4}$ 6401$^{7}$ >**31a 59f**<

**Chantelle s Dream** **2** ch f Compton Place-Polar Peak (Polar Falcon (USA)) 4514$^{10}$ 4704$^{6}$ >**5f**<

**Chanteloup** **3** ch f Grand Lodge (USA) -Nibbs Point (IRE) (Sure Blade (USA)) 1557$^{2}$ 2020$^{4}$ 3374$^{4}$ 4492$^{3}$ 5266$^{5}$ 5907$^{10}$ >**53a 95f**<

**Chanterelle (IRE)** **3** ch f Indian Ridge-Chantereine (USA) (Trempolino (USA)) 3914$^{6}$ 4731$^{6}$ 5652$^{17}$ >**87f**<

**Chanteuse** **4** b f Rudimentary (USA) -Enchanting Melody (Chief Singer) 407$^{10}$ 444$^{6}$ 658$^{11}$ >**21a 61f**<

**Chantilly Beauty (FR)** **2** b f Josr Algarhoud (IRE) -Lysabelle (FR) (Lesotho (USA)) 3031$^{14}$ >**90f**<

**Chantilly Gold (USA)** **5** ch m Mutakddim (USA) -Bouffant (USA) (Alydar (USA)) 423$^{10}$ 444$^{5}$ 497$^{10}$ >**20a**<

**Chantilly Sunset (IRE)** **3** b f General Monash (USA) -Alpine Sunset (Auction Ring (USA)) 5306$^{8}$ 5552$^{15}$ ><

**Chantress** **4** b f Peintre Celebre (USA) -Up Anchor (IRE) (Slip Anchor) 1790$^{8}$ 2297$^{3}$ 3519$^{7}$ >**98f**<

**Chantry Falls (IRE)** **4** br g Mukaddamah (USA) -Woodie Dancer (USA) (Green Dancer (USA)) 1176$^{8}$ 2007$^{6}$ 2556$^{11}$ 2886$^{12}$ >**33a 49f**<

**Chapelco** **3** b g Robellino (USA) -Lady Kris (IRE) (Kris) 3054$^{6}$ 3454$^{7}$ 4673$^{P}$ >**54f**<

**Chapel Royale (IRE)** **7** gr g College Chapel-Merci Royale (Fairy King (USA)) 605$^{6}$ 759$^{5}$ >**14a 14f**<

**Chaplin** **3** b c Groom Dancer (USA) -Princess Borghese (USA) (Nijinsky (CAN)) 1387$^{2}$ 2653$^{8}$ 6182$^{4}$ >**90 f**<

**Chaplinesque (USA)** **5** ch g Mt. Livermore (USA) -Silent City (USA) (Carson City (USA)) 689a$^{10}$ >**50a**<

**Chappel Cresent (IRE)** **4** ch g College Chapel-Inshad (Indian King (USA)) 641$^{8}$ 761$^{12}$ 1106$^{8}$ 1246$^{5}$ 1385$^{2}$ 1773$^{5}$ (1927) 2065$^{5}$ 3235$^{17}$4837$^{19}$ 5627$^{10}$ >**60a 102f**<

**Chapter (IRE)** **2** ch c Sinndar (IRE) -Web Of Intrigue (Machiavellian (USA)) 2890$^{2}$ 3241$^{2}$ 4689$^{7}$ 5335$^{3}$ 5729$^{5}$ >**75f**<

**Chapter House (USA)** **5** b g Pulpit (USA) -Lilian Bayliss (IRE) (Sadler s Wells (USA)) 3282$^{6}$ 3492$^{7}$ 4698$^{15}$ 5267$^{7}$ >**61a 61f**<

**Chara** **3** ch f Deploy-Subtle One (IRE) (Polish Patriot (USA)) 1186$^{3}$ (1394) 1672$^{7}$ 1963$^{5}$ 4138$^{5}$ 4346$^{5}$ 4692$^{9}$ 5560$^{12}$ 6552$^{8}$ >**60a 67f**<

**Charing Cross (IRE)** **3** ch c Peintre Celebre (USA) -Charlotte Corday (Kris) 4939$^{13}$ 5217$^{7}$ 5538$^{9}$ 5891$^{6}$ 6183$^{12}$ >**40a 38f**<

**Chariot (IRE)** **3** ch g Titus Livius (FR) -Battle Queen (Kind Of Hush) 1022$^{9}$ 6461$^{18}$ >**61a 57f**<

**Charlatan (IRE)** **6** b g Charnwood Forest (IRE) -Taajreh (IRE) (Mtoto) 2556$^{16}$ >**23a 25f**<

**Charleston** **3** ch g Pursuit Of Love-Discomatic (USA) (Roberto (USA)) 1830$^{2}$ 2168$^{2}$ 2611$^{2}$ 2882$^{4}$ 3348$^{11}$ >**69a 76f**<

**Charlie Bear** **3** ch c Bahamian Bounty-Abi (Chief s Crown (USA)) 1365$^{10}$ 2251$^{2}$ 5841$^{8}$ 6064$^{3}$ >**71a 70f**<

**Charlie George** **3** ch g Idris (IRE) -Faithful Beauty (IRE) (Last Tycoon) 3002$^{9}$ 3475$^{6}$ 4631$^{5}$ >**63f**<

**Charlieismydarling** **3** b g Mind Games-Blessed Lass (HOL) (Good Times (ITY)) 2359$^{4}$ 2766$^{8}$ 3193$^{10}$ >**44a 39f**<

**Charlie Masters** **3** b g Polar Falcon (USA) -Bowden Rose (Dashing Blade) 5378$^{13}$ 5843$^{14}$ 6017$^{9}$ 6402$^{2}$ >**61a 34f**<

**Charlie Parkes** **6** ch g Pursuit Of Love-Lucky Parkes (Full Extent (USA)) 2130$^{12}$ 2293$^{11}$ >**74f**<

**Charlieslastchance** **2** b f Sure Blade (USA) -Sea Mist (IRE) (Shalford (IRE)) 5792$^{19}$ 6127$^{14}$ ><

**Charlies Profit** **3** ch f Deploy-Care And Comfort (Most Welcome) 492$^{13}$ ><

**Charlie Tango (IRE)** **3** b g Desert Prince (IRE) -Precedence (IRE) (Polish Precedent (USA)) 985$^{3}$ 1222$^{7}$ 1957$^{10}$ 2169$^{11}$ 2419$^{3}$ 2558$^{9}$ 2915$^{4}$ (3102) 3394$^{3}$3796$^{4}$ 4249$^{3}$ 4536$^{5}$ 4806$^{7}$ 5223$^{9}$ 5510$^{12}$ 5715$^{4}$ 5955$^{8}$6112$^{2}$ 6461$^{4}$ >**75a 72f**<

**Charlottebutterfly** **4** b f Millkom-Tee Gee Jay (Northern Tempest (USA)) 1855$^{11}$ 2524$^{4}$ 3428$^{9}$ 3841$^{8}$ 5008$^{3}$ 5575$^{15}$ 5845$^{4}$ (6558) >**59a 59f**<

**Charlotte Vale** **3** ch f Pivotal-Drying Grass Moon (Be My Chief (USA)) 2069$^{6}$ 2688$^{5}$ 3007$^{2}$ (3250) 3561$^{3}$ (3919) 4389$^{2}$ 4636$^{3}$ 6143$^{6}$ >**79f**<

**Charlottine (IRE)** **3** b f Spectrum (IRE) -Lady Dulcinea (ARG) (General (FR)) 4251a$^{16}$ 5692$^{3}$ >**75f**<

**Charmatic (IRE)** **3** br f Charnwood Forest (IRE) -Instamatic (Night Shift (USA)) 1250$^{5}$ 1502$^{2}$ 1755$^{2}$ (1957) 2587$^{5}$ 2732$^{4}$ 3231$^{5}$ 5145$^{7}$ 5715$^{6}$6047$^{8}$ 6483$^{2}$ 6576$^{2}$ >**70a 70f**<

**Charmed By Fire (USA)** **3** b c Silver Charm (USA) -Mama Dean (USA) (Woodman (USA)) 3843$^{11}$ 4369$^{7}$ 4693$^{5}$ 5007$^{11}$ >**70f**<

**Charmed Forest (IRE)** **3** b f Shinko Forest (IRE) -Charmed Lady (Rainbow Quest (USA)) 2711a$^{8}$ >**90f**<

**Charming Admiral (IRE)** **11** b g Shareef Dancer (USA) -Lilac Charm (Bustino) 1287$^{6}$ 1501$^{2}$ >**56f**<

**Charming Groom (FR)** **5** gr h Kaldoun (FR) -Danagroom (USA) (Groom Dancer (USA)) 1741a$^{6}$ 2438a$^{4}$ 2923a$^{2}$ (3361a) 4595a$^{13}$ 6076a$^{7}$ >**111f**<

**Charmo (FR)** **3** gr c Charnwood Forest (IRE) -Marie De Ken (FR) (Kendor (FR)) 2072a$^{3}$ 2721a$^{4}$ 3163a$^{3}$ 4284a$^{5}$ >**107f**<

**Charnock Bates One (IRE)** **3** b f Desert Sun-Fleetwood Fancy (Taufan (USA)) 1392$^{4}$ 1755$^{6}$ 3312$^{8}$ (3507) 4050$^{2}$ 4318$^{2}$ 4760$^{2}$ 5788$^{3}$ 6115$^{6}$6332$^{12}$ >**79f**<

**Charnwood Pride (IRE)** **3** gr g Charnwood Forest (IRE) -Pride Of Pendle (Grey Desire) 2374$^{12}$ 2632$^{11}$ 3608$^{9}$ >**42f**<

**Charnwood Street (IRE)** **5** b g Charnwood Forest (IRE) -La Vigie (King Of Clubs) 475$^{5}$ 568$^{5}$ >**54a 54df**<

**Chase The Rainbow** **3** gr f Danzig Connection (USA) -Delta Tempo (IRE) (Bluebird (USA)) 1627$^{6}$ 1784$^{6}$ 2259$^{12}$ 2548$^{6}$ 2766$^{11}$ 3193$^{11}$ >**54a 41 f**<

**Chasing The Dream (IRE)** **3** b f Desert Sun-Dream Of Jenny (Caerleon (USA)) (447) 883$^{2}$ 1799$^{6}$ 2400$^{10}$ 2737$^{3}$ 3246$^{4}$ >**77a 73f**<

**Chasm** **2** b c Gulch (USA) -Subito (Darshaan) 5420$^{3}$ 5858$^{5}$ >**72f**<

**Chateau Istana** **2** ch c Grand Lodge (USA) -Miss Queen (USA) (Miswaki (USA)) 1505$^{6}$ (2208) (2959) 3640$^{7}$ (5464) 5918$^{9}$ >**109f**<

**Chateau Nicol** **5** b g Distant Relative-Glensara (Petoski) (417) 556$^{3}$ 648$^{13}$ (742) 1056$^{4}$ (1294) 1500$^{3}$ 1840$^{3}$ 2064$^{3}$ 2575$^{4}$(3205) 3453$^{5}$ 3690$^{6}$ 3941$^{6}$ 4122$^{7}$ (5614) 6277$^{4}$ 6341$^{3}$ 6477$^{9}$ >**90+a 90f**<

**Chater Flair** **7** b g Efisio-Native Flair (Be My Native (USA)) 609$^{12}$ >**25a 25f**<

**Chatshow (USA)** **3** br g Distant View (USA) -Galanty Show (Danehill (USA)) 2211$^{10}$ 2517$^{15}$ 2908$^{4}$ 3428$^{12}$ 3707$^{5}$ 3991$^{8}$ 4548$^{10}$ 5691$^{12}$5930$^{3}$ 6059$^{7}$ (6288) 6403$^{2}$ 6567$^{2}$ >**59a 63f**<

**Checkit (IRE)** **4** br c Mukaddamah (USA) -Collected (IRE) (Taufan (USA)) 853a$^{4}$ 978a$^{3}$ 1001a$^{3}$ 1146a$^{6}$ 1621$^{8}$ 2109$^{7}$ 2339a$^{3}$ 2678$^{4}$2957$^{8}$ 3792a$^{3}$ 3978$^{4}$ 4228$^{8}$ 4539$^{3}$ 4984a$^{6}$ 5215a$^{2}$ 5651$^{2}$5917$^{7}$ >**117f**<

**Cheeky Chi (IRE)** **3** b f Desert Style (IRE) -Grey Patience (IRE) (Common Grounds) 1052$^{4}$ 1096$^{4}$ 1243$^{3}$ (1362) 1737$^{4}$ 1883$^{13}$ 2033$^{7}$ 2181$^{11}$2326$^{8}$ 5040$^{6}$ 6398$^{12}$ 6567$^{13}$ >**60a 61f**<

**Cheese n Biscuits** 4 b f Spectrum (IRE) -Bint Shihama (USA) (Cadeaux Genereux) 1372[11] 1765[20] 1938[2] 2284[8] 2575[11] 3698[15] *4549[11]* 4731[5]4969[4] *5055[12]* 5541[11] 5603[25] *6157[7]* *6395[12]* **>91a 79f<**
**Chek Oi** 2 b c Dr Fong (USA) -Silver Sun (Green Desert (USA)) 2396[8] 3438[9] *3847[7]* 5494[6] *6276[P]* **>49a 55f<**
**Chelsea Rose (IRE)** 2 ch f Desert King (IRE) -Cinnamon Rose (USA) (Trempolino (USA)) 4592a[3] (5325a) **>106f<**
**Chelsea s Diamond** 4 b f Man Among Men (IRE) -Sharp Thistle (Sharpo) 3194[5] 4028[13] 4265[9] **>43f<**
**Chem s Legacy (IRE)** 4 b g Victory Note (USA) -Merlannah (IRE) (Shy Groom (USA)) 3085[12] 4063[4] 4125[8] **>48f<**
**Cherished Number** 5 b g King s Signet (USA) -Pretty Average (Skyliner) 1284[9] 1773[4] 2271[9] 2410[6] 2781[3] 3005[3] 3198[10] 3745[4]3977[4] 4333[7] 4569[5] 4826[3] 4988[7] 5315[4] 5581[3] 5835[3]6138[4] **>77a 81 f<**
**Cherokee (USA)** 2 b f Storm Cat (USA) -Totemic (USA) (Vanlandingham (USA)) (5322a) 6213[5] **>102f<**
**Cherokee Bay** 4 b f Primo Dominie-Me Cherokee (Persian Bold) *4954 6593 7871[2] 8551[2]* **>43a 43f<**
**Cherokee Nation** 3 br c Emperor Jones (USA) -Me Cherokee (Persian Bold) 1465[4] *1600[4]* (2380) 2726[7] 3158[2] (3428) (3585) 3624[10] 4051[3] 4244[5]*4926[9]* 5697[15] *6222[2] 6482[4]* **>74a 74+f<**
**Cherry Mix (FR)** 3 gr c Linamix (FR) -Cherry Moon (USA) (Quiet American (USA)) 1350a[2] 2073a[3] (5170a) 5981a[2] **>128f<**
**Cherry Pickings (USA)** 7 b g Miner s Mark (USA) -Cherry D Or (USA) (Cassaleria (USA)) *(974a) 1142a[8]* **>115a<**
**Chertsey (IRE)** 3 ch f Medaaly-Cerisette (IRE) (Polar Falcon (USA)) 2818[3] 3171[3] 3486[5] 4066[9] 4414[5] 4650[6] *5001[5]* **>35a 60f<**
**Cherubim (JPN)** 3 ch f Sunday Silence (USA) -Curly Angel (JPN) (Judge Angelucci (USA)) 1440[5] 3142[5] (3392) *3933[2]* 5402[10] 5595[12] *6279[9]* **>79a 76f<**
**Chesnut Ripple** 5 ch m Cosmonaut-Shaft Of Sunlight (Sparkler) *4594* **>48a 67f<**
**Chestall** 3 b g Polar Prince (IRE) -Maradata (IRE) (Shardari) 3013[4] 5367[4] 6150[5] **>60f<**
**Chestminster Girl** 2 ch f Tomba-Nannie Annie (Persian Bold) 5407[14] *6221[11]* 6545[14] **><**
**Cheverak Forest (IRE)** 3 ch g Shinko Forest (IRE) -Meranie Girl (IRE) (Mujadil (USA)) 1392[10] 4138[12] 4610[9] 5223[16] 5993[12] 6199[4] **>57a 61f<**
**Chevin** 5 ch m Danzig Connection (USA) -Starr Danias (USA) (Sensitive Prince (USA)) 3369[5] 4015[14] (4424) 5243[7] 5546[9] 5796[8] **>51 f<**
**Chevronne** 4 b g Compton Place-Maria Isabella (FR) (Young Generation) 2000[17] 2762[10] 2833[2] 3412[16] 3698[16] **>75a 64f<**
**Chic** 4 ch f Machiavellian (USA) -Exclusive (Polar Falcon (USA)) 2242[6] 2967[7] 4286[3] (4745) (5113) 5940[2] **>123f<**
**Chica (IRE)** 3 gr f Spectrum (IRE) -Wild Rose Of York (Unfuwain (USA)) *4201[1]* **>22a 34f<**
**Chicago Bond (USA)** 3 b f Real Quiet (USA) -Shariyfa (FR) (Zayyani) 3252[7] 3473[11] 3955[6] 4574[9] **>58f<**
**Chicago Nights (IRE)** 2 ch f Night Shift (USA) -Enclave (USA) (Woodman (USA)) 1616[4] 2489[7] 2617[10] *4094[5]* 5022[2] 5369[14] 6093[11] **>25a 49f<**
**Chica Roca (USA)** 3 ch f Woodman (USA) -Amenixa (FR) (Linamix (FR)) 2113[9] 2577[16] 2785[6] 2984[9] *5222[10]* **>39a 61f<**
**Chickado (IRE)** 3 b f Mujadil (USA) -Arcevia (IRE) (Archway (IRE)) *547[3]* 1266[6] 3887[7] 4717[6] *6559[2]* **>69a 60f<**
**Chickasaw Trail** 6 ch m Be My Chief (USA) -Maraschino (Lycius (USA)) *4279 9451[0] 9949 1037[6]* 1592[5] (1863) 1987[11] 2387[5]2833[15] 2943[14] **>17a 45f<**
**Chicken Soup** 2 br c Dansili-Radiancy (IRE) (Mujtahid (USA)) 4487[6] *5053[3]* 5179[7] 5738[19] 6207[3] **>73a 73f<**
**Chicks Babe** 2 br f Chickawicka (IRE) -Ballasilla (Puissance) *6276[8]* **>24a<**
**Chico Guapo (IRE)** 4 b g Sesaro (USA) -Summer Queen (Robellino (USA)) *841[8] 912[5]* 1113[16] 1537[8] (1774) 2041[17] 2130[5] 2293[9] 2754[11]3126[17] 3407[12] 4626[13] 5062[13] 5458[13] 5754[12] **>76 a 85f<**
**Chief Dipper** 2 b c Benny The Dip (USA) -Cuban Reef (Dowsing (USA)) 5716[15] *6022[4] 6294[4]* **>66a 31f<**
**Chief Exec** 2 b g Zafonic (USA) -Shot At Love (IRE) (Last Tycoon) 6171[13] *6448[2]* **>73a 50f<**
**Chief Scout** 2 br c Tomba-Princess Zara (Reprimand) 3925[7] 4730[4] (5087) 5895[8] **>84f<**
**Chigorin** 3 b g Pivotal-Belle Vue (Petong) 2479[9] 2847[6] 3312[7] 4092[8] 5223[3] *6160[8]* **>68a 72f<**
**Chilali (IRE)** 2 b f Monashee Mountain (USA) -Pam Story (Sallust) 1743[5] *2002[7]* 2489[3] 3003[3] 3469[9] 3729[3] 4046[6] 4347[4]4803[9] *4999[2]* **>46a 58f<**
**Chillin Out** 2 ch c Bahamian Bounty-Steppin Out (First Trump) 6563[16] **>8f<**
**Chilly Cracker** 2 ch f Largesse-Polar Storm (IRE) (Law Society (USA)) 1364[2] 1882[6] *(3021)* 3886[10] 4508[8] 5797[3] (6080) 6544[11] **>66a 71f<**
**Chimali (IRE)** 3 b g Foxhound (USA) -Mari-Ela (IRE) (River Falls) (3512) 3777[4] *4026[3]* (5219) 5697[3] **>73a 77+f<**
**Chimes At Midnight (USA)** 7 b h Danzig (USA) -Surely Georgies (USA) (Alleged (USA)) 2958[24] 2998[11] 3862a[8] 5662a[12] **>63f<**
**Chimes Eight** 3 b f Octagonal (NZ) -Bell Toll (High Line) *563[8]* **>34a<**
**Chinalea (IRE)** 2 b c Danetime (IRE) -Raise-A-Secret (IRE) (Classic Secret (USA)) 5507[5] 5825[5] 6569[4] **>69f<**
**Chin Dancer** 2 ch f Inchinor-Red Hot Dancer (USA) (Seattle Dancer (USA)) 3083[17] 3679[10] *4095[6]* 4638[10] **>23a 23f<**
**Chinese Puzzle** 2 b c Dr Fong (USA) -Verbose (USA) (Storm Bird (CAN)) 3749[6] 4208[6] 4567[9] 5302[3] 5522[3] **>74f<**
**Chineur (FR)** 3 b c Fasliyev (USA) -Wardara (Sharpo) 2162a[4] 2719a[6] (3162a) 5333a[3] 6463a[6] **>108f<**
**Chinkara** 4 ch g Desert Prince (IRE) -You Make Me Real (USA) (Give Me Strength (USA)) 1456[19] 2534[10] 2969[23] 3415[4] 4214[10] 5470[3] 5941[24] **>81a 98+f<**
**Chiqitita (IRE)** 3 b f Saddlers Hall (IRE) -Funny Cut (IRE) (Sure Blade (USA)) *6751[1] 8911[0]* 1464[13] 1907[10] *3710[9]* 4241[7] 4568[6] 5284[8]5451[5] 6120[10] **>34a 36f<**
**Chiracahua (IRE)** 2 ch g Desert Prince (IRE) -Irish Celebrity (USA) (Irish River (FR)) 5646[16] *5911[7] 6448[10]* **>35a<**
**Chisel** 3 ch g Hector Protector (USA) -Not Before Time (IRE) (Polish Precedent (USA)) 2195[8] 2519[10] 2777[6] 3401[8] 3981[10] 4562[8] 4985[5] 5187[11] **>59f<**
**Chiselled (IRE)** 2 b c Rossini (USA) -Con Dancer (Shareef Dancer (USA)) 1324[4] 1743[2] 2208[2] 3938[9] 4607[4] 5233[2] **>85f<**
**Chivalry** 5 b g Mark Of Esteem (IRE) -Gai Bulga (Kris) 1125[18] **>99f<**
**Chivite (IRE)** 5 b g Alhaarth (IRE) -Laura Margaret (Persian Bold) 2787[9] 6083[9] **>69a 79+f<**
**Chocolate Boy (IRE)** 5 b g Dolphin Street (FR) -Kawther (Tap On Wood) *662[5] 788[2] 855[4] 995[4] (1016) 1081[10]* 2031[2] 2443[5]2930[6] *5914[7]* **>57a 66f<**
**Chocolate Caramel (USA)** 2 b c Storm Creek (USA) -Sandhill (BRZ) (Baynoun) *6494[5]* **>70a<**
**Choir Leader** 3 b c Sadler s Wells (USA) -Choir Mistress (Chief Singer) 1612[13] (4180) 4780[3] **>99+f<**
**Chookie Heiton (IRE)** 6 br g Fumo Di Londra (IRE) -Royal Wolff (Prince Tenderfoot (USA)) 1126[4] 1789[5] 3673[14] 3901[11] (5105) 5628[12] **>113f<**
**Chopoulou (FR)** 3 gr c Nombre Premier-Oulouwatou (FR) (Comrade In Arms) 1289a[6] **>95f<**
**Choreographic (IRE)** 2 b c Komaite (USA) -Lambast (Relkino) 3469[7] 4009[3] 4488[10] 5234[8] **>60f<**
**Chorist** 5 ch m Pivotal-Choir Mistress (Chief Singer) (2733) (3331a) 4323[3] 4982a[3] 6216[2] **>119f<**
**Choristar** 3 ch g Inchinor-Star Tulip (Night Shift (USA)) 2880[6] 3636[2] 3935[5] 4127[3] **>60f<**
**Chorus** 7 b m Bandmaster (USA) -Name That Tune (Fayruz) *504[9] 608[3]* 5080[13] 5261[20] 6059[10] *6363[2]* **>64a 42f<**
**Chorus Beauty** 3 b f Royal Applause-Happy Lady (FR) (Cadeaux Genereux) 1464[14] 1874[10] 2377[7] *2883[3] (3615)* **>72a 55f<**
**Chrisiida (GER)** 3 gr f Winged Love (IRE) -Chalkidiki (GER) (Nebos (GER)) 1983a[6] 5823a[4] 6255a[3] **>94f<**
**Christina s Dream** 3 b f Spectrum (IRE) -Christine Daae (Sadler s Wells (USA)) 3622[5] *4024[8]* **>45a 71f<**
**Christmas Truce (IRE)** 5 b g Brief Truce (USA) -Superflash (Superlative) *4551[0] 483[9]* **>80a 79f<**
**Christom** 2 b c Groom Dancer (USA) -Throw Away Line (USA) (Assert) 6352[13] *6392[7]* 6530[12] 6565[9] **>49a 53f<**
**Chronos (IRE)** 6 b h Spectrum (IRE) -Trojan Miss (Troy) 633a[12] **>106f<**
**Chubbes** 3 b g Kris-St Radegund (Green Desert (USA)) 2030[13] 2361[10] 3229[4] 3513[4] 4102[7] (4387) 5021[13] 5336[10] **>50a 55f<**
**Chutney Mary (IRE)** 2 bb f Indian Danehill (IRE) -Grade A Star (IRE) (Alzao (USA)) 1670[12] 2535[6] 3164[2] *3611[2] 4186[5]* 4468[2] 4914[5] 5377[11]5890[3] 6003[6] *6291[5]* **>68a 72f<**
**Ciacole** 3 b f Primo Dominie-Dance On A Cloud (USA) (Capote (USA)) *5991[3] 736[4]* 1394[10] 1499[3] (1959) 2199[13] 3371[8] 3582[5] **>48a 48f<**
**Ciel Bleu** 2 ch f Septieme Ciel (USA) -Valthea (FR) (Antheus (USA)) 6471[13] **>35f<**
**Ciendra Girl (IRE)** 2 ch f Rossini (USA) -Simply Special (IRE) (Petit Loup (USA)) 5349[12] 5508[11] 6000[11] **><**
**Cilla s Smile** 2 b f Lake Coniston (IRE) -Tinkerbird (Music Boy) 1399[8] 5262[6] 5947[18] 6204[6] **>54f<**
**Cimyla (IRE)** 3 b c Lomitas-Coyaima (GER) (Night Shift (USA)) 1134[3] 1414[12] (2089) 2692[10] (2887) **>81a 97+f<**
**Cinnamon Ridge (IRE)** 3 b g Indian Ridge-Savoury (Salse (USA)) 1906[8] 2029[9] 2265[7] **>46f<**
**Circassian (IRE)** 3 b g Groom Dancer (USA) -Daraliya (IRE) (Kahyasi) 4443[9] 4915[2] (5554) (5635) 5773[4] 6143[2] *6396[5]* **>82a 89 f<**
**Circle Of Wolves** 6 ch g Wolfhound (USA) -Misty Halo (High Top) 6055[9] **>46f<**
**Circuit Dancer (IRE)** 4 b g Mujadil (USA) -Trysinger (IRE) (Try My Best (USA)) 1471[3] 1759[4] 2065[14] (2857) 3074[16] 3522[5] 4324[22] 4908[4] 5224[7]5628[13] 5832[4] 6517[11] **>101f<**
**Circumspect (IRE)** 2 b g Spectrum (IRE) -Newala (Royal Academy (USA)) 5752[2] **>70f<**
**Circus Maximus (USA)** 7 b g Pleasant Colony (USA) -Crockadore (USA) (Nijinsky (CAN)) 2299[9] 3099[4] 3667[12] 3776[2] 4202[3] *5221[9]* 5826[11] **>22a 59f<**
**Cirrious** 3 gr f Cloudings (IRE) -Westfield Mist (Scallywag) 5621[8] 5851[6] 6285[5] **>60f<**
**Citrine Spirit (IRE)** 3 gr f Soviet Star (USA) -Casessa (USA) (Caro) 1619[6] (1945) 2284[3] 2587[9] 5566[10] 6350[7] **>79f<**
**Citrus Magic** 7 b g Cosmonaut-Up All Night (Green Desert (USA)) *(426) 568[2] 581[7]* **>51a 45 f<**
**City Affair** 3 b g Inchinor-Aldevonie (Green Desert (USA)) *4961[0] 606[9] 817[4]* 2061[14] **>58a 58f<**
**City General (IRE)** 3 ch g General Monash (USA) -Astra (IRE) (Glenstal (USA)) 1197[3] 1296[3] 2061[4] 2322[3] 2362[5] 2762[7] 3425[2] 3626[7]4018[5] (4497) 4674[14] 4798[5] 5072[6] 5336[7] 5795[7] 6227[7] **>49a 49f<**
**City Lass** 4 b f Rock City-Kilkenny Lass (IRE) (Fayruz) 4781[12] **><**
**City Palace** 3 ch g Grand Lodge (USA) -Ajuga (USA) (The Minstrel (CAN)) (1304) 2018[9] **>76f<**
**City Torque (USA)** 2 ch f Marquetry (USA) -Citiscape (USA) (Citidancer (USA)) 1340[6] 2616[8] **>53f<**
**City Trader** 2 ch c Entrepreneur-Kameez (IRE) (Arazi (USA)) 5373[15] 6351[16] 6565[16] **>29f<**
**Clann A Cougar** 4 ch g Bahamian Bounty-Move Darling (Rock City) *1141[7] 1424[7]* 1857[6] 2078[8] 2762[6] 3471[11] 3774[7] **>41a 60f<**
**Claptrap** 4 b c Royal Applause-Stardyn (Star Appeal) *478[2] 594[5] 699[6]* **>57 a 53f<**
**Clara Bow (IRE)** 2 b f Sadler s Wells (USA) -Brigid (USA) (Irish River (FR)) 5695[6] 6353[7] **>67f<**
**Claradotnet** 4 b f Sri Pekan (USA) -Lypharitissima (FR) (Lightning (FR)) 1272[16] 1684[9] 2062[8] 2299[6] 2619[3] 2935[8] 4146[3] 4578[2]5058[10] 5826[10] 6074[10] 6269[6] **>71f<**
**Claranete Princess (IRE)** 3 b f Princely Heir (IRE) -Sheryl Lynn (Miller s Mate) *597[6]* 6561[12] **>47a 39f<**
**Clare Galway** 3 b f Compton Place-Oublier L Ennui (FR) (Bellman (FR)) *673[9] 890[5] 1064[9]* 2402[10] *2484[4] 3304[9]* (6184) 6405[8] **>54a 54f<**
**Claret And Amber** 2 b g Forzando-Artistic Licence (High Top) 3469[3] 3758[5] 4149[5] (4575) (4909) 5392[5] 5873[2] 6268[6] **>95f<**
**Clarinch Claymore** 8 b g Sabrehill (USA) -Salu (Ardross) 2116[2] 2491[12] 2684[5] 3300[3] (3821) 4627[5] **>67a 80f<**
**Clash Of The Ash (USA)** 2 b c King Of Kings (IRE) -Ceirseach (IRE) (Don t Forget Me) 2792a[3] 6408a[3] 6503a[4] **>91f<**
**Clasp** 2 ch c Singspiel (IRE) -Embrace Me (Nashwan (USA)) 3726[8] 5559[2] **>83f<**
**Class Above (USA)** 3 br f Quiet American (USA) -Rainbow Promise (USA) (Known Fact (USA)) *11* **>87a<**
**Classical Act (IND)** 5 b g Placerville (USA) -Stunning (IND) (Ascot Knight (CAN)) *754a[9]* 849a[3] 1001a[7] **>64a 94f<**
**Classical Dancer** 3 ch f Dr Fong (USA) -Gorgeous Dancer (IRE) (Nordico (USA)) (1507) 2242[2] 2807[3] 3699[8] **>100f<**
**Classical Waltz (IRE)** 6 ch m In The Wings-Fascination Waltz (Shy Groom (USA)) *1885[4] 2184[3]* 2386[9] 2728[7] **>24a 31f<**
**Classic Croco (GER)** 3 gr g Croco Rouge (IRE) -Classic Light (IRE) (Classic Secret (USA)) 3565a[14] **>80f<**
**Classic Event (IRE)** 3 ch g Croco Rouge (IRE) -Delta Town (USA) (Sanglamore (USA)) 1201[7] 2146[10] 4103[2] 6524[3] **>62f<**
**Classic Expression** 3 ch f Classic Cliche (IRE) -Breezy Day (Day Is Done) *3279[6]* 4555[7] *4880[7]* 5770[15] **>26a 34f<**
**Classic Guest** 2 b f Xaar-My Lass (Elmaamul (USA)) 2837[4] 3176[6] 5247[15] 5720[12] **>59f<**
**Classicism (USA)** 2 bb f A.P. Indy (USA) -Colour Chart (USA) (Mr Prospector (USA)) 5247[5] **>79+f<**
**Classic Law** 5 b h Law Society (USA) -Classic Light (IRE) (Classic Secret (USA)) 785a[8] 6509a[6] **>103f<**
**Classic Lease** 3 b g Cyrano De Bergerac-Vado Via (Ardross) 3447[10] 4101[5] 4679[3] 5293[10] **>55f<**
**Classic Lin (FR)** 4 gr f Linamix (FR) -Classic Storm (Belfort (FR)) *969[8]* **><**
**Classic Millennium** 6 b m Midyan (USA) -Classic Colleen (IRE) (Sadler s Wells (USA)) *1081[7] 1426[2] 1630[2]* 2167[5] 2787[7] 3181[4] **>52a 65f<**
**Classic Primrose (IRE)** 3 b f King s Theatre (IRE) -Flower From Heaven (Baptism) 1634a[7] **>55f<**
**Classic Role** 5 b g Tragic Role (USA) -Clare Island (Connaught) *523[4] 6181[2] 679[3] 887[4] (1122)* 1272[2] 1369[2] 1540[10]2084[10] 2738[8] **>79a 82f<**
**Classic Stamp (CAN)** 4 b f Regal Classic (CAN) -Native Rights (USA) (Our Native (USA)) 6383a[3] **>110f<**
**Classic Style (IRE)** 2 b f Desert Style (IRE) -Classic Ring (IRE) (Auction Ring (USA)) *3021[5]* 3233[9] *3611[7]* 4131[5] **>37a 60f<**
**Classic Vision** 4 b f Classic Cliche (IRE) -Orient (Bay Express) *(438) 584[9] 7711[0] 917[4]* 1971[5] 2597[11] (2879) 3117[7] 3386[6]3586[8] 3911[11] 4066[14] **>56a 59f<**
**Clear Impression (IRE)** 2 b f Danehill (USA) -Shining Hour (USA) (Red Ransom (USA)) 4231[2] **>84+f<**
**Clearing Sky (IRE)** 3 gr f Exploit (USA) -Litchfield Hills (USA) (Relaunch (USA)) 5844[6] 6288[17] **>52a 50f<**
**Clear Thinking** 4 b c Rainbow Quest (USA) -Coraline (Sadler s Wells (USA)) 1110a[5] 1435a[3] 2337a[3] 3963a[3] 4983a[7] 5503a[3] 5976a[8] **>111f<**
**Cleaver** 3 ch g Kris-Much Too Risky (Bustino) 1356[5] 2093[9] **>54f<**
**Cleo Collins (IRE)** 2 b f General Monash (USA) -Madrina (Waajib) 1853[13] **><**
**Clety (FR)** 8 b h Sillery (USA) -La Bucaille (FR) (Labus (FR)) 2337a[5] 4983a[5] 5503a[6] 6137a[4] **>110f<**
**Cleveland Way** 4 b g Forzando-Fallal (IRE) (Fayruz) *(421) 429[2] 509[6] 625[5] 748[6] 904[4] 1033[5]* 1268[11] *1445[2] 1696[2] 1915[6] 2183[2] (2227)* 2735[14] 4422[15] 4557[13] **>51a 51f<**
**Clifden (IRE)** 3 ch c Gold Away (IRE) -Romora (FR) (Sillery (USA)) *691a[14] 977a[8]* **>98a 98f<**
**Cliffie (IRE)** 2 ch g Timeless Times (USA) -Suppression (Kind Of Hush) 5752[8] 6197[10] 6514[14] **>17f<**
**Climate (IRE)** 5 ch g Catrail (USA) -Burishki (Chilibang) *1055[5]* 1273[4] 1708[11] 2304[2] *(2406)* 3086[6] 3159[3] 4308[9] 6568[9] **>86a 84f<**
**Climate Change (USA)** 2 ch c Langfuhr (CAN) -Summer Mist (USA) (Miswaki (USA)) 6352[12] **><**
**Clinet (IRE)** 2 b f Docksider (USA) -Oiche Mhaith (Night Shift (USA)) 1670[8] 2096[5] 2396[2] 3532[13] 3727[5] 4089[10] *5052[7]* (5335) 5852[3] **>50a 68f<**
**Clipperdown (IRE)** 3 b g Green Desert (USA) -Maroussie (FR) (Saumarez) 3448[3] 3916[7] (4455) 5866[5] **>80f<**
**Clipper Hoy** 2 ch c Bahamian Bounty-Indian Flag (IRE) (Indian Ridge) 1871[6] 6342[14] **>10f<**
**Cliquey** 5 b g Muhtarram (USA) -Meet Again (Lomond (USA)) *5891[1] 6931[1] 867[9]* **>39a<**
**Cloann (IRE)** 2 b f Danetime (IRE) -Rustic Lawn (Rusticaro (FR)) 2300[5] 2522[11] (2946) **>58f<**
**Clock Stopper (USA)** 4 ch g Gilded Time (USA) -Great Fun (USA) (Farma Way (USA)) *6487a[6]* **>116a<**
**Clod Ber Junior (BRZ)** 6 b h Clod Ber (BRZ) -Idade De Prata (BRZ) (Mogambo (URU)) 924a[7] *974a[9]* **>66a<**
**Clodion (IRE)** 8 b g Nikos-Didia Clara (FR) (Sea Break) 633a[5] 692a[3] 712a[3] 854a[6] 922a[4] 976a[7] 1003a[3] **>101f<**
**Cloon (USA)** 3 b f Lure (USA) -Axe Creek (USA) (Gulch (USA)) 3258a[3] 4430a[3] **>107f<**
**Cloonavery (IRE)** 2 b g Xaar-Hero s Pride (FR) (Hero s Honor (USA)) 5407[4] *(6021)* **>80a 74f<**
**Cloud Catcher (IRE)** 3 br f Charnwood Forest (IRE) -Notley Park (Wolfhound (USA)) 2061[7] *2454[12]* 4583[11] 4775[7] *6556[11]* **>7a 20f<**
**Cloud Dancer** 5 bb m Bishop Of Cashel-Summer Pageant (Chief s Crown (USA)) *599[3] 648[8] 733[2] 861[2]* (2899) 3372[3] 3754[5] 4122[17]4837[4] 5419[5] 5818[6] *6579[3]* **>82a 81f<**
**Cloudingswell** 3 b f Cloudings (IRE) -L Ancressaan (Dalsaan) 1440[10] 1843[6] 2737[6] 3385[4] 3681[4] 6055[8] *6402[7]* **>57a 54f<**
**Cloudless (USA)** 4 bb f Lord Avie (USA) -Summer Retreat (USA) (Gone West (USA)) *6081[1] 773[2] 826[4] 9601[0] 1039[3] 1178[3]* 1606[6]1855[6] 2098[19] *2451[9]* 3227[18] 4509[12] 6288[19] **>66a 48f<**
**Clouds Of Gold (IRE)** 3 b f Goldmark (USA) -Tongabezi (IRE) (Shernazar) 1342[10] 1711[3] 2145[11] 2556[18] **>43f<**
**Cloudy Sky (IRE)** 8 b g Sadler s Wells (USA) -Dancing Shadow (Dancer s Image (USA)) 1801[14] **>70f<**
**Clove (USA)** 2 b f Distant View (USA) -Nidd (USA) (Known Fact (USA)) 3208[4] (4191) 5520[2] 5839[5] **>86 f<**
**Clueless** 2 b c Royal Applause-Pure (Slip Anchor) 5592[4] 5897[3] **>86f<**
**Coalition** 5 b g Polish Precedent (USA) -Selection Board (Welsh Pageant) 2671[9] 3244[2] 4033[2] 4550[3] **>73 a 85f<**
**Coat Of Honour (USA)** 4 gr g Mark Of Esteem (IRE) -Ballymac Girl (Niniski (USA)) 3756[16] (4214) 4540[2] (5312a) **>52a 107f<**
**Cobalt Blue (IRE)** 3 b g Bluebird (USA) -Amy Hunter (USA) (Jade Hunter (USA)) 2251[8] 2688[6] (3146) 3746[5] *4128[5]* 4710[9] 4798[3] 5072[11] 5750[2] **>48a 55f<**
**Cobalt Runner (IRE)** 3 b c Fayruz-Bui-Doi (IRE) (Dance Of Life (USA)) *764[8]* 2675[13] **><**
**Cobra (IRE)** 3 b c Sadler s Wells (USA) -Puck s Castle (Shirley Heights) 2796a[3] 3353a[9] 4977a[9] **>103f<**
**Cocktail** 3 b f Most Welcome-Cockatrice (Petong) 6261a[5] **>92f<**
**Coconut Cookie** 3 ch f Bahamian Bounty-Spicy Manner (USA) (Cryptoclearance (USA)) 2112[18] 2587[11] 2929[7] **>64f<**
**Coconut Moon** 2 b f Bahamian Bounty-Lunar Ridge (Indian Ridge) 4607[6] **>46f<**
**Coconut Penang (IRE)** 4 b c Night Shift (USA) -Play With Fire (FR) (Priolo (USA)) 1126[14] 1391[7] 3074[2] 3673[18] 4324[25] 5121[5] 5471[P] **>103f<**
**Coconut Squeak** 2 b f Bahamian Bounty-Creeking (Persian Bold) 4131[3] 4900[6] 5098[7] 5738[9] (5910) 6333[9] **>65f<**
**Coco Point Breeze** 3 b f Great Dane (IRE) -Flying Colours (IRE) (Fairy King (USA)) *3846[7]* 4306[8] 4644[7] 4972[10] 5449[14] **>29a 32f<**
**Coco Reef** 3 b f Kingsinger (IRE) -Highland Blue (Never So Bold) 3229[6] *3616[12] 4097[5]* 4617[10] **>50a 36f<**
**Code Orange** 2 b f Green Desert (USA) -Warning Belle (Warning) 2876[2] 5271[2] **>82f<**
**Cody** 5 ch g Zilzal (USA) -Ibtihaj (USA) (Raja Baba (USA)) *5645[3]* 5826[14] **>46a 55f<**

**Coeur Courageux (FR)** 2 b c Xaar-Linoise (FR) (Caerwent) 4315[7] >**50f**<
**Cois Na Tine Eile** 2 br f Cois Na Tine (IRE) -Water Pixie (IRE) (Dance Of Life (USA)) 2140[3] *2985[10]* 3506[3] 5792[13] 5988[10] 6240[8] >**4a 52f**<
**Cold Climate** 9 ch g Pursuit Of Love-Sharpthorne (USA) (Sharpen Up) *847[9] 1204[4]* 3428[7] 3841[5] 4336[2] 4522[2] 4727[9] 5425[4] >**73a 64f**<
**Cold Cold Woman** 3 ch f Machiavellian (USA) -Banquise (IRE) (Last Tycoon) 5962a[9] >**90f**<
**Cold Encounter (IRE)** 9 ch g Polar Falcon (USA) -Scene Galante (FR) (Sicyos (USA)) *5645[13]* >**13a**<
**Cold Turkey** 4 bb g Polar Falcon (USA) -South Rock (Rock City) *(523) (600) 706[3] 1054[2]* 1329[4] (1539) 2110[2] 2240[4] 5401[10] 6346[13] >**98+a 98f**<
**Colemanstown** 4 b g Charnwood Forest (IRE) -Arme Fatale (IRE) (Trempolino (USA)) 1246[11] 1452[7] 2461[18] 2581[12] 2779[8] 3235[16] 3440[10] 4122[14] 5108[7] 5733[3] 6124[10] >**67f**<
**Coleorton Dancer** 2 ch g Danehill Dancer (IRE) -Tayovullin (IRE) (Shalford (IRE)) 1462[8] 1865[4] *2125[4]* 3104[4] 3704[7] (4607) (4803) (4875) (5119) 5896[9] 6333[13] >**53a 91f**<
**Coleorton Dane** 2 gr g Danehill Dancer (IRE) -Cloudy Nine (Norton Challenger) 2045[6] 3336[3] 3834[2] (4277) 5212[3] 5417[14] >**78f**<
**Coleorton Prince (IRE)** 3 b g Paris House-Tayovullin (IRE) (Shalford (IRE)) *744[10]* >**29a 32f**<
**Colisay** 5 b g Entrepreneur-La Sorrela (IRE) (Cadeaux Genereux) 2358[3] 3539[6] 4528[4] (5461) 5731[4] 6170a[14] >**109 f**<
**Collada (IRE)** 3 b f Desert Prince (IRE) -Bright Spells (USA) (Alleged (USA)) 1507[18] 2243[12] 2765[6] 4674[16] >**47f**<
**Colledoro** 4 ch c Primo Dominie-Conca Peligna (Persian Bold) 3816a[12] ><
**College Delinquent (IRE)** 5 br g College Chapel-St Cyr Aty (IRE) (Ela-Mana-Mou) *647[3] 1241[4] 1935[6] 2406[7]* >**74a 64f**<
**College Hippie** 5 b m Cosmonaut-Eccentric Dancer (Rambo Dancer (CAN)) 2778[12] 3126[16] 3169[15] 3864[14] >**23a 23 f**<
**College Maid (IRE)** 7 b m College Chapel-Maid Of Mourne (Fairy King (USA)) 1319[4] 1421[13] 1870[6] 2252[7] 2423[7] 2670[2] 2779[4] (3006) 3038[3] 3225[5] 3623[6] 3979[6] 4104[6] 4248[6] 4534[5] 4904[3] 5242[13] 5579[17] 5862[6] 6144[15] >**65f**<
**College Queen** 6 b m Lugana Beach-Eccentric Dancer (Rambo Dancer (CAN)) 2143[11] 2252[6] 2670[5] 2909[4] 3372[5] 3668[2] 4104[11] 4970[7] 5242[5] 5412[3] 5618[15] 6046[16] >**78 f**<
**College Star** 6 b g Lugana Beach-Alis Princess (Sayf El Arab (USA)) *497[8] 685[8]* >**22a 22f**<
**Collier Hill** 6 ch g Dr Devious (IRE) -Polar Queen (Polish Precedent (USA)) 1880[11] (2076) 3310[4] 3757[3] 4858[9] (5506a) 6355[5] >**110f**<
**Colloseum** 3 b g Piccolo-Trig Point (Rudimentary (USA)) 1342[7] 2259[4] 2756[12] 3231[16] 4537[8] 5478[6] >**59f**<
**Colne Valley Amy** 7 b m Mizoram (USA) -Panchellita (USA) (Pancho Villa (USA)) *535[4] 663[2] 778[8] 860[8] 4093[12]* >**49a 54f**<
**Colonel Bilko (IRE)** 2 b g General Monash (USA) -Mari-Ela (IRE) (River Falls) 1183[2] 1462[10] 2439[6] (3886) 4235[10] >**67f**<
**Colonel Cotton (IRE)** 5 b g Royal Applause-Cutpurse Moll (Green Desert (USA)) 1379a[6] 1763[10] 1955[6] 2475[5] 2636[5] 2955[16] 3537[3] 3940[10] 4091[6] 5471[5] 5553[3] 5712[4] 5893[15] 6190[10] >**66a 114df**<
**Colonial Girl (IRE)** 2 b f Desert Style (IRE) -Telemania (IRE) (Mujtahid (USA)) 2129[4] 2585[3] *3021[2]* 3583[4] >**66a 68f**<
**Colonnade** 5 b m Blushing Flame (USA) -White Palace (Shirley Heights) *501[2] 750[7] 1023[3]* 1668[9] 5751[7] 6209[9] >**50a 56f**<
**Colony Band (USA)** 3 b f Dixieland Band (USA) -Hostessante (USA) (Pleasant Colony (USA)) 2925a[14] 5969a[10] >**97f**<
**Colophony (USA)** 4 ch g Distant View (USA) -Private Line (USA) (Private Account (USA)) 1671[12] 2878[4] 3474[7] 4240[6] >**82f**<
**Colorado Falls (IRE)** 6 b g Nashwan (USA) -Ballet Shoes (IRE) (Ela-Mana-Mou) (1785) 2782[5] 3078[4] 3902[8] 4448[4] 4990[3] 5190[4] >**87f**<
**Colorful Judgement (CAN)** 4 ch g Diesis-Colorful Vices (CAN) (Regal Classic (CAN)) 6384a[8] >**91f**<
**Colour Blind (IRE)** 2 b c Spectrum (IRE) -Saroob s Love (USA) (Nureyev (USA)) 6441[19] 6545[15] >**1f**<
**Colour Code (IRE)** 3 b c Spectrum (IRE) -Viendra Nur (USA) (Nureyev (USA)) 1352[14] >**64a 28f**<
**Colourful Lady (USA)** 4 b f Quest For Fame-Special Park (USA) (Trempolino (USA)) *505[5]* >**52a 70f**<
**Colour Wheel** 3 ch c Spectrum (IRE) -Risanda (Kris) 1585[6] 2295[15] 3052[2] 3690[11] 4031[7] 5921[10] >**95f**<
**Columbian Emerald (IRE)** 3 ch g Among Men (USA) -Sarabi (Alzao (USA)) 1747[7] 2257[4] 3013[5] 4536[7] *5221[10]* >**50f**<
**Colway Ritz** 10 b g Rudimentary (USA) -Million Heiress (Auction Ring (USA)) 5144[11] 5320[2] 5635[2] 5951[5] 6096[5] 6266[3] >**69f**<
**Comanche Woman** 4 b f Distinctly North (USA) -Possibility (Robellino (USA)) *426[9]* >**4a 40f**<
**Come Away With Me (IRE)** 4 b f Machiavellian (USA) -Vert Val (USA) (Septieme Ciel (USA)) 2098[2] (3680) >**59a 62f**<
**Come Good** 2 ch g Piccolo-The Frog Lady (IRE) (Al Hareb (USA)) 1996[5] 2263[2] 2736[6] 4325[3] 4671[2] 5015[7] >**69f**<
**Come On** 5 b g Aragon-All On (Dunbeath (USA)) 6200[5] *6578[5]* >**53a 61f**<
**Come On Jonny (IRE)** 2 b c Desert King (IRE) -Idle Fancy (Mujtahid (USA)) 4611[12] 5096[3] 5341[4] (5995) 6129[13] >**77f**<
**Comeraincomeshine (IRE)** 3 ch f Night Shift (USA) -Future Past (USA) (Super Concorde (USA)) *881[3]* 1312[6] 2482[4] 2741[2] 3211[7] 4085[15] (5338) >**57a 68f**<
**Comete (FR)** 5 b m Jeune Homme (USA) -Cocooning (FR) (Galetto (FR)) (5668a) >**108f**<
**Come To Daddy (IRE)** 2 ch g Fayruz-Forgren (IRE) (Thatching) 4454[13] 5131[5] 6440[12] >**48f**<
**Come What July (IRE)** 3 b g Indian Rocket-Persian Sally (IRE) (Persian Bold) *(739) 864[2] 985[5]* 1201[6] 1669[6] 2259[11] *2485[3]* 3681[5] *(3707)* 3981[7] 4213[3] 4628[6] *4882[7] 6160[13]* >**75a 62f**<
**Comfy (USA)** 5 b h Lear Fan (USA) -Souplesse (USA) (Majestic Light (USA)) 2559[5] 2968[7] >**117f**<
**Comical Errors (USA)** 2 b g Distorted Humor (USA) -Fallibility (USA) (Tom Rolfe) 3918[11] 4606[4] 5095[5] 5852[15] >**61f**<
**Comic Genius** 3 b f Comic Strip (USA) -Itsy Bitsy Betsy (USA) (Beau Genius (CAN)) *736[3] 1040[5]* 1529[9] 1579[6] >**39a 35f**<
**Comic Strip** 2 b g Marju (IRE) -Comic (IRE) (Be My Chief (USA)) *(3802)* 3983[4] (5453) (5630) (5931) (6268) >**84+a 104+f**<
**Comic Tales** 3 b g Mind Games-Glorious Aragon (Aragon) 2908[6] 3839[6] 4674[7] 5525[6] 6009[5] >**44f**<
**Comic Times** 4 b f Puissance-Glorious Aragon (Aragon) 2778[19] >**18f**<
**Coming Again (IRE)** 3 b g Rainbow Quest (USA) -Hagwah (USA) (Dancing Brave (USA)) 1382[5] 2374[2] 2680[12] >**86f**<
**Comintrue (IRE)** 2 ch f Namid-Gute (IRE) (Petardia) *1276[7]* 1383[7] 2617[11] 2773[2] 4017[7] 5281[14] >**30a 44f**<
**Commander Bond** 3 b g Piccolo-Lonesome (Night Shift (USA)) 1775[8] 2239[12] *(3280)* 3517[9] *4188[8]* 4456[8] *4928[7]* 5210[5] 5656[11] *6062[7]* >**74a 69f**<
**Commander Flip (IRE)** 4 ch g In Command (IRE) -Boldabsa (Persian Bold) *969[4]* 1282[14] >**45a 61f**<
**Commando Scott (IRE)** 3 b g Danetime (IRE) -Faye (Monsanto (FR)) (1453) 1881[12] 2269[8] 3059[2] 3252[2] 3585[2] 3819[6] (3926) (4051) 4531[5] 4874[8] 5786[7] >**93f**<
**Commemoration Day (IRE)** 3 b g Daylami (IRE) -Bequeath (USA) (Lyphard (USA)) 1972[7] 2449[6] *3379[8]* 3746[15] >**63f**<
**Commendable Coup (USA)** 2 bb c Commendable (USA) -Bird Dance (USA) (Storm Bird (CAN)) 3248[5] 3758[7] 5264[6] >**68f**<
**Commercante (FR)** 4 b f Marchand De Sable (USA) -Deception (FR) (Tropular) 4767a[9] (6383a) >**111f**<
**Commitment Lecture** 4 b f Komaite (USA) -Hurtleberry (IRE) (Tirol) 1247[5] (1606) 1875[4] 5518[6] *6024[5]* 6548[3] >**53a 67f**<
**Common World (USA)** 5 ch h Spinning World (USA) -Spenderella (FR) (Common Grounds) 1982a[9] >**107f**<
**Compassion (IRE)** 3 b f Alhaarth (IRE) -Titania (Fairy King (USA)) *1627[10]* 2029[10] 2545[7] 3002[4] 3222[4] 3396[5] 3581[3] 3798[6] 4387[8] 4535[3] 4825[F] >**16a 56f**<
**Competitor** 3 b c Danzero (AUS) -Ceanothus (IRE) (Bluebird (USA)) *490[2]* 3048[9] 3387[12] 5153[5] 5568[13] 5869[6] 6083[15] *6160[5] 6498[9]* >**73a 67+f**<
**Complication** 4 b f Compton Place-Hard Task (Formidable (USA)) 2094[7] 2506[6] 2763[2] 2948[4] 3372[2] (3606) 5588[7] >**78f**<
**Compton Arrow (IRE)** 8 b g Petardia-Impressive Lady (Mr Fluorocarbon) 1873[10] 2064[15] 2483[14] 2673[11] 3298[18] 4083[15] >**24a 39 f**<
**Compton Aviator** 8 ch g First Trump-Rifada (Ela-Mana-Mou) *1085[6]* 1858[11] *2381[5]* 3774[9] 4070[6] 5350[5] 5733[8] >**67a 55f**<
**Compton Banker (IRE)** 7 br g Distinctly North (USA) -Mary Hinge (Dowsing (USA)) *586[15]* 2834[6] 3125[5] 3395[2] 3663[7] 4044[3] 4614[15] 5337[15] >**92a 79 f**<
**Compton Bay** 4 b g Compton Place-Silver Sun (Green Desert (USA)) *694[11] 936[9] 1191[11] 1446[5]* >**27a 50f**<
**Compton Bolter (IRE)** 7 b g Red Sunset-Milk And Honey (So Blessed) *757a[4]* 976a[10] 1003a[5] 1144a[10] 1925[3] 2241[2] 2638[5] 3034[10] 3484[6] 4285[5] 4746[3] 5133[3] 5438[2] 5611[3] 5812[4] >**107a 116f**<
**Compton Classic** 2 b c Compton Place-Ayr Classic (Local Suitor (USA)) 4003[7] 5513[6] 5578[6] 6113[12] >**55f**<
**Compton Commander** 6 ch g Barathea (IRE) -Triode (USA) (Sharpen Up) *558[11] 971[8]* >**95a 88f**<
**Compton Dragon (USA)** 5 ch g Woodman (USA) -Vilikaia (USA) (Nureyev (USA)) *1056[8]* 1114[12] 1821[5] 2142[12] 2272[5] 2583[2] 2752[2] 2964[5] 3510[2] 3731[12] 4258[6] 4319[10] 4901[4] 5211[10] >**80a 83f**<
**Compton Drake** 5 b g Mark Of Esteem (IRE) -Reprocolor (Jimmy Reppin) 4220[17] 4641[2] (4871) 5185[2] 5615[4] *(5739)* 6069[10] >**87a 82f**<
**Compton Eagle** 4 b g Zafonic (USA) -Gayane (Nureyev (USA)) 1295[11] *2006[6]* >**14a 56f**<
**Compton Eclaire (IRE)** 4 ch f Lycius (USA) -Baylands Sunshine (IRE) (Classic Secret (USA)) *549[3]* 1744[3] *2004[2]* 2167[4] 2514[6] (3128) 3393[2] 3528[4] *4129[2]* 4686[4] *5221[7]* >**62a 66f**<
**Compton Micky** 3 ch c Compton Place-Nunthorpe (Mystiko (USA)) 1111[8] 1453[6] 2411[12] 2660[5] 2756[6] 4051[9] 4610[5] 4853[12] 6199[14] *(6401) 6541[5]* >**59a 57f**<
**Compton Plume** 4 ch g Compton Place-Brockton Flame (Emarati (USA)) 1975[7] 2219[3] 2556[DSQ] 2656[3] 3096[2] (3410) 4013[7] 4452[13] 5107[7] (5562) 5798[9] >**31a 71f**<
**Compton Princess** 4 b f Compton Place-Curlew Calling (IRE) (Pennine Walk) 1283[3] *1696[6]* 1824[10] 2346[14] 2528[9] 3019[8] >**5a 55f**<
**Compton Quay** 2 ch c Compton Place-Roonah Quay (IRE) (Soviet Lad (USA)) 5347[6] 5872[7] *6010[6]* >**64a 68f**<
**Compton s Eleven** 3 gr g Compton Place-Princess Tara (Prince Sabo) 1388[8] 1797[8] 2224[7] 2557[8] 3089[5] 3455[2] (3737) 4268[2] 4510[2] 4874[2] 5762[2] 6071[11] >**102f**<
**Compton Spark** 2 ch g Compton Place-Rhinefield Beauty (IRE) (Shalford (IRE)) *6478[11]* >**2a**<
**Comtesse Lalande (USA)** 2 ch f King Of Kings (IRE) -Beyond The Realm (USA) (Stop The Music (USA)) 3260[6] >**53f**<
**Conceal** 6 b g Cadeaux Genereux-Mystery Play (IRE) (Sadler s Wells (USA)) *632a[3] 689a[4]* 755a[6] *(851a) 977a[5]* 1004a[4] *1145a[9]* >**93a 90f**<
**Concer Eto** 5 ch g Sabrehill (USA) -Drudwen (Sayf El Arab (USA)) *647[12] 847[10] 1118[2] 1935[3]* 2030[4] (4199) 4569[2] 4877[10] 5419[10] 5574[4] 5887[2] *6156[3]* >**78a 84f**<
**Concert Hall (USA)** 3 b f Stravinsky (USA) -Proflare (USA) (Mr Prospector (USA)) 1186[4] 3213[6] >**66f**<
**Concert Time** 2 ch f Timeless Times (USA) -Thalya (Crofthall) 1115[7] 2194[3] 2364[6] *3278[5]* 3526[3] *4516[3]* 6080[10] >**46a 38f**<
**Conchonita** 4 b f Bishop Of Cashel-Cactus Road (FR) (Iron Duke (FR)) *605[9]* >**47a 31f**<
**Concubine (IRE)** 5 b m Danehill (USA) -Bye Bold Aileen (IRE) (Warning) 2441[3] 2703[7] 3047[2] 3178[4] 3440[7] 4127[12] 4740[13] >**54a 59f**<
**Conflict (FR)** 8 b h Warning-La Dama Bonita (USA) (El Gran Senor (USA)) *635a[11] 974a[5] 1142a[7]* >**104a**<
**Confluence (NZ)** 8 b m Paris Opera (AUS) -Tristrams Jewel (NZ) (Sir Tristram) 2156a[P] ><
**Confuzed** 4 b g Pivotal-Times Of Times (IRE) (Distinctly North (USA)) *791[9] 893[3] 946[6] 987[14] 1228[9] 1280[11] 3378[8]* 3991[4] *4185[11]* 4617[9] 5035[3] 5336[3] 6230[13] >**56a 52f**<
**Congo Man** 11 b g Rainbow Quest (USA) -African Dance (USA) (El Gran Senor (USA)) 2978[10] 3928[8] >**13f**<
**Conjuror** 3 b c Efisio-Princess Athena (Ahonoora) 4144[U] (4555) 5263[11] >**79+f**<
**Connect** 7 b g Petong-Natchez Trace (Commanche Run) 2293[2] 2488[4] 2859[10] 3480[4] (3945) 4165[4] 4366[8] 4538[11] 5393[15] 5628[19] 6071[4] 6243[6] >**81a 98f**<
**Connotation** 2 b f Mujahid (USA) -Seven Wonders (USA) (Rahy (USA)) 2927[2] *3418[2]* 4413[3] *5052[13]* (5520) 5721[6] *6023[3]* >**73a 73f**<
**Conquering Love (IRE)** 6 b g Pursuit Of Love-Susquehanna Days (USA) (Chief s Crown (USA)) 3716[11] 4176[RR] 5303[P] ><
**Conroy (USA)** 6 b g Gone West (USA) -Crystal Gazing (USA) (El Gran Senor (USA)) *(977a) 1145a[3]* >**111a**<
**Consensus (IRE)** 5 b m Common Grounds-Kilbride Lass (IRE) (Lahib (USA)) 1106[4] 1956[16] 2143[13] 2238[3] 2461[20] 2670[12] 4452[4] 4626[6] 5107[16] 5588[8] 5862[10] >**33a 83f**<
**Consider This** 2 b f Josr Algarhoud (IRE) -River Of Fortune (IRE) (Lahib (USA)) 3116[2] 3532[5] 4099[3] 4612[2] 5391[7] 5604[2] 6111[3] 6521[4] 6530[2] >**79f**<
**Considine (USA)** 3 b c Romanov (IRE) -Libeccio (NZ) (Danzatore (CAN)) *1422[8]* (1714) 2561[2] (2821) 3236[8] 4062[2] 4692[6] 5300[4] >**55a 76 f**<
**Consignia (IRE)** 5 ch m Definite Article-Coppelia (IRE) (Mac s Imp (USA)) *406[11] 552[9] 562[5]* >**61a 35 f**<
**Consolidator (USA)** 2 ch c Storm Cat (USA) -Good Example (FR) (Crystal Glitters (USA)) *6489a[4]* >**115a**<
**Consonant (IRE)** 7 ch g Barathea (IRE) -Dina Lina (FR) (Top Ville) *(531) (604) (837) (915)* 1903[9] 2534[6] 2894[8] 3212[2] 3477[3] 3756[14] 4887[7] 5470[7] >**97a 100f**<
**Constable Burton** 3 b g Foxhound (USA) -Actress (Known Fact (USA)) 1342[9] *(1425)* 5583[18] *6553[8] 6557[4]* >**66a 46f**<
**Constantine** 4 gr g Linamix (FR) -Speremm (IRE) (Sadler s Wells (USA)) 5764[14] >**84f**<
**Constructor** 3 b g So Factual (USA) -Love And Kisses (Salse (USA)) 4195[10] *4939[7] 5217[9]* 5851[12] >**61a 55 f**<
**Consular** 2 br c Singspiel (IRE) -Language Of Love (Rock City) 6545[3] >**69f**<
**Contact Dancer (IRE)** 5 b g Sadler s Wells (USA) -Rain Queen (Rainbow Quest (USA)) 3821[6] 4934[4] (6215) 6575[3] >**93f**<
**Contented (IRE)** 2 b c Orpen (USA) -Joyfullness (USA) (Dixieland Band (USA)) *6155[5] 6392[3]* >**59a**<
**Continent** 7 ch g Lake Coniston (IRE) -Krisia (Kris) 3522[3] 3674[15] (4805) 5105[7] 5372[5] 5628[3] 5977a[10] >**113f**<
**Continental Flyer (IRE)** 2 b f Piccolo-Sunshine Coast (Posse (USA)) 4606[RR] 5855[8] >**29f**<
**Convent Girl (IRE)** 4 b f Bishop Of Cashel-Right To The Top (Nashwan (USA)) 1125[23] 2044[8] 2534[12] 2637[7] 2969[30] 4287[17] 5249[6] 5783[6] 6284[12] >**95f**<
**Conviction** 3 b g Machiavellian (USA) -Beldarian (IRE) (Last Tycoon) 3054[5] 3297[14] >**54f**<
**Convince (USA)** 3 ch g Mt. Livermore (USA) -Conical (Zafonic (USA)) 1388[9] 2019[8] 2295[13] 3295[5] 4126[6] 4236[5] 4749[12] *5739[11]* >**52a 84 f**<
**Cooden Beach (IRE)** 4 b f Peintre Celebre (USA) -Joyful (IRE) (Green Desert (USA)) *552[11] 996[4] 1278[4]* 2122[4] 2597[20] >**47a 57f**<
**Cool Bart** 4 ch g Cool Jazz-Margaretrose Anna (Handsome Sailor) *502[11]* ><
**Cool Bathwick (IRE)** 5 b g Entrepreneur-Tarafa (Akarad (FR)) *(484) 505[2] 609[6]* 1369[10] 1858[7] 2121[7] 2375[7] 2590[9] 3776[4] 4146[5] >**65a 50f**<
**Cool Clear Water (USA)** 3 b f Seeking The Gold (USA) -Miznah (IRE) (Sadler s Wells (USA)) *1052[11]* 1271[11] 2243[8] 2611[6] >**37a 60f**<
**Cool Conductor (USA)** 3 b c Stravinsky (USA) -Verinha (BRZ) (Baronius (BRZ)) 4769a[5] >**101f**<
**Cool Cristal** 2 ch f Loup Sauvage (USA) -Lyrical Bid (USA) (Lyphard (USA)) 3438[12] 5262[10] 5341[9] >**12f**<
**Coolfore Jade (IRE)** 4 ch f Mukaddamah (USA) -Cashel Princess (IRE) (Fayruz) *464[9] (517) 548[4] (630) 682[4] 734[3] 777[5] 962[8] 984[5] 1042[12] 1136[7]* 2324[19] 2728[6] *2851[3] 3303[6]* 4669[10] 5021[9] 5286[6] 5710[4] 5928[12] *6065[6]* >**61a 48f**<
**Cooling Castle (FR)** 8 ch g Sanglamore (USA) -Syphaly (USA) (Lyphard (USA)) *812[8]* >**16a 20f**<
**Cool Panic (IRE)** 2 b c Brave Act-Geht Schnell (Fairy King (USA)) 2502[7] 4193[2] 4809[5] (5128) 6344[6] >**84f**<
**Cool Sands (IRE)** 2 b c Trans Island-Shalerina (USA) (Shalford (IRE)) 5128[8] 5290[14] *6023[6]* >**51a**<
**Cool Temper** 8 b g Magic Ring (IRE) -Ovideo (Domynsky) 1315[5] 1542[3] 1757[11] 4029[8] 4238[10] 4672[2] 5176[13] >**60a 70f**<
**Coombe Centenary** 2 b f Robellino (USA) -Shining Dancer (Rainbow Quest (USA)) 3632[7] 4193[10] 4967[11] *5375[9]* >**43a 48f**<
**Copperfields Lass** 5 b m Millkom-Salvezza (IRE) (Superpower) *613[9] 809[7]* >**15a 66df**<
**Coppice (IRE)** 3 ch c Rainbow Quest (USA) -Woodwin (IRE) (Woodman (USA)) 1371[6] 4369[4] 4972[5] 5621[3] >**77f**<
**Coppington Flyer (IRE)** 4 ch f Eagle Eyed (USA) -Miss Flite (IRE) (Law Society (USA)) *599[4] 888[8] 929[4] 1019[10] 1102[4]* 3386[12] 3828[17] 5283[4] >**32a 32f**<
**Copplestone (IRE)** 8 b g Second Set (IRE) -Queen Of The Brush (Averof) *471[7]* 1721[6] 3099[9] ><
**Coqueteria (USA)** 3 b f Cozzene (USA) -Miss Waikiki (USA) (Miswaki (USA)) 1327[2] 1983a[3] 6147[2] *6497[10]* >**80a 99f**<
**Coranglais** 4 ch g Piccolo-Antonia s Folly (Music Boy) 1772[16] 2064[13] 2399[8] 2763[8] 3298[9] 3395[4] (3772) 4085[12] 4459[7] 4707[5] 4774[12] 5337[8] 5412[5] 5736[10] 6246[2] 6288[2] >**74f**<
**Corbel (USA)** 4 b f Diesis-Corsini (Machiavellian (USA)) 5123[11] 5541[16] >**80f**<
**Corcoran (USA)** 2 b f Lear Fan (USA) -Corsini (Machiavellian (USA)) (6118) >**76+f**<
**Cordage (IRE)** 2 ch c Dr Fong (USA) -Flagship (Rainbow Quest (USA)) 4739[5] 5015[4] 5400[4] 6531[4] 6565[2] >**76f**<
**Cordier** 2 b c Desert Style (IRE) -Slipper (Suave Dancer (USA)) 4335[10] >**48f**<
**Corker** 2 ch g Grand Lodge (USA) -Immortelle (Arazi (USA)) 3192[6] 3793[5] >**54f**<
**Corky (IRE)** 3 b g Intikhab (USA) -Khamseh (Thatching) 2808[4] 3322[3] (3666) 4646[11] 4938[3] 5614[14] *6395[10]* >**38a 83f**<
**Cormorant Wharf (IRE)** 4 b g Alzao (USA) -Mercy Bien (IRE) (Be My Guest (USA)) *417[7] 494[6] 648[5] 742[8] 961[10] 1051[5] 1230[8]* 3326[7] 3747[6] *4026[4]* 4479[3] 5493[2] 6343[2] >**81a 78 f**<
**Cornelius** 7 b g Barathea (IRE) -Rainbow Mountain (Rainbow Quest (USA)) *1009[12]* 1828[9] 3212[5] >**71a 100f**<
**Corniche Dancer** 2 b f Marju (IRE) -Sellette (IRE) (Selkirk (USA)) 3905[12] 4231[8] 4579[10] *5053[2]* (5362) 5648[26] 5745[5] *6022[2]* 6242[9] 6356[8] >**68a 68 f**<
**Cornish Gold** 3 b f Slip Anchor-Sans Diablo (IRE) (Mac s Imp (USA)) 2949[12] 5258[2] 6343[7] >**45a 67f**<
**Cornus** 2 ch c Inchinor-Demerger (USA) (Distant View (USA)) (1269) (1383) 1707[2] 6212[2] 6348[7] >**104f**<
**Cornwallis** 3 b g Forzando-Up And Going (FR) (Never So Bold) *673[11]* (1854) 2063[2] 3589[14] *4185[7]* >**52a 70f**<
**Coronado Forest (USA)** 5 b g Spinning World (USA) -Desert Jewel (USA) (Caerleon (USA)) *463[2] 555[4] (601) 650[10] 820[14]* 1522[9] 3173[6] *3637[10]* >**25a 25f**<
**Coroner (IRE)** 4 b c Mtoto-Tamnia (Green Desert (USA)) 1261a[7] 4983a[9] >**116f**<
**Corps De Ballet (IRE)** 3 b f Fasliyev (USA) -Dwell (USA) (Habitat) 2264[7] (2589) 3598[19] 4294[10] 5491[9] 5933[5] 6267[2] *6496[8]* >**79a 90f**<
**Corran Ard (IRE)** 3 b g Imperial Ballet (IRE) -Beeper The Great (USA) (Whadjathink (USA)) 1761[4] >**84f**<
**Corrib Eclipse** 5 b g Double Eclipse (IRE) -Last Night s Fun (IRE) (Law Society (USA)) (3076) 3538[6] 4832[6] 5415[6] (5589) 5815[4] >**108f**<
**Corridor Creeper (FR)** 7 ch g Polish Precedent (USA) -Sonia Rose (USA) (Superbity (USA)) 1923[5] 2041[4] 2222[4] 2488[2] 2679[6] 3074[24] 3266[2] 3480[34] 4165[6] 4324[18] 4538[3] 5181[5] 5393[7] 5787[3] 5933[2] (6177) 6243[2] 6349[5] >**106f**<

**Corrine (IRE)** 5 gr m Spectrum (IRE) -La Luna (USA) (Lyphard (USA)) 3504a$^{12}$ 6443$^{2}$ **>99f<**

**Corriolanus (GER)** 4 b c Zamindar (USA) -Caesarea (GER) (Generous (IRE)) *842$^{3}$ 1062$^{11}$* 1355$^{7}$ 1540$^{16}$ 2220$^{6}$ 3034$^{9}$ 4163$^{6}$ (4525) 4984a$^{14}$5488a$^{8}$ 5731$^{7}$ **>103a 105f<**

**Corsario (FR)** 2 b c Zafonic (USA) -Miss Party Line (USA) (Phone Trick (USA)) (4597a) 5432a$^{4}$ **>103f<**

**Corsican Native (USA)** 3 b c Lear Fan (USA) -Corsini (Machiavellian (USA)) (5495) 5942$^{2}$ 6121$^{13}$ **>100f<**

**Corton (IRE)** 5 gr g Definite Article-Limpopo (Green Desert (USA)) 5472$^{3}$ 5784$^{6}$ 6172$^{18}$ 6535$^{9}$ **>88f<**

**Corton Denham** 3 ch g Wolfhound (USA) -Wigit (Safawan) *598$^{12}$* **>19a<**

**Cosi Fan Tutte** 6 b g Inchinor-Bumpkin (Free State) 2740$^{2}$ 3387$^{3}$ 3825$^{7}$ 4192$^{7}$ 4476$^{2}$ *4600$^{2}$* **>56a 63f<**

**Cosmic Case** 9 b m Casteddu-La Fontainova (IRE) (Lafontaine (USA)) (2287) 2615$^{7}$ 2978$^{3}$ 3221$^{5}$ 3578$^{2}$ 3740$^{3}$ 3902$^{7}$ 4007$^{3}$ (4250) 4328$^{2}$5058$^{5}$ 5479$^{8}$ **>53f<**

**Cosmic Destiny (IRE)** 2 b f Soviet Star (USA) -Cruelle (USA) (Irish River (FR)) 5319$^{7}$ **>65f<**

**Cosmic Ranger** 6 b g Magic Ring (IRE) -Lismore (Relkino) *3799$^{9}$* **>40a 52f<**

**Costa Del Sol (IRE)** 3 ch g General Monash (USA) -L Harmonie (USA) (Bering) *452$^{9}$ 536$^{11}$ 702$^{11}$ 790$^{4}$* 2322$^{10}$ 3844$^{16}$ 3991$^{6}$ 4419$^{9}$4968$^{8}$ *5644$^{13}$* **>34 a 34f<**

**Cost Analysis (IRE)** 2 ch c Grand Lodge (USA) -Flower Girl (Pharly (FR)) 5091$^{10}$ 5718$^{6}$ 6077$^{5}$ 6331$^{13}$ **>63f<**

**Cote Quest (USA)** 4 b f Green Desert (USA) -West Brooklyn (USA) (Gone West (USA)) 1332$^{4}$ 1741a$^{11}$ 2044$^{14}$ 2242$^{4}$ 2733$^{4}$ 3311$^{3}$ 3699$^{6}$ 4773$^{12}$5783$^{12}$ **>97f<**

**Cote Soleil** 7 ch g Inchinor-Sunshine Coast (Posse (USA)) *546$^{10}$* 4713$^{8}$ 5080$^{7}$ **>56a 63f<**

**Cotosol** 3 b g Forzando-Emerald Dream (IRE) (Vision (USA)) 1129$^{7}$ (1452) 1841$^{5}$ 2069$^{8}$ *3280$^{3}$* **>80a 82f<**

**Cotrina (GER)** 3 br f Lavirco (GER) -Cocorna (Night Shift (USA)) 2723a$^{9}$ **><**

**Cottage Flower (ITY)** 5 ch m Bahamian Bounty-Jarrwah (Niniski (USA)) 3816a$^{5}$ **>97f<**

**Cottam Grange** 4 b c River Falls-Karminski (Pitskelly) *446$^{10}$* **>42a 56f<**

**Cottam Karminski** 3 b f River Falls-Karminski (Pitskelly) 2346$^{11}$ 2572$^{8}$ 2908$^{13}$ 3511$^{6}$ 3822$^{14}$ 4102$^{14}$ **>35f<**

**Cottingham (IRE)** 3 b c Perugino (USA) -Stately Princess (Robellino (USA)) *(473)* 3252$^{4}$ 3507$^{6}$ 4050$^{6}$ 4305$^{12}$ 4610$^{2}$ 5223$^{15}$ 5245$^{6}$ 5364$^{6}$5622$^{6}$ 5757$^{2}$ 6006$^{4}$ 6271$^{11}$ **>63a 67f<**

**Cotton Easter** 3 b f Robellino (USA) -Pluck (Never So Bold) 1441$^{12}$ 2517$^{9}$ 3142$^{6}$ 3589$^{12}$ 4083$^{12}$ 4853$^{7}$ 5175$^{3}$ (5692) 6183$^{6}$ **>56f<**

**Cougar Cat (USA)** 2 b c Storm Cat (USA) -Excellent Meeting (USA) (General Meeting (USA)) 2996$^{4}$ 3965a$^{2}$ **>106f<**

**Could She Be Magic (IRE)** 3 b f Titus Livius (FR) -Ponteilla (FR) (Arctic Tern (USA)) *631$^{2}$ (758) 955$^{7}$ 1678$^{2}$* 2036$^{8}$ 2389$^{5}$ **>59a 38f<**

**Councellor (FR)** 2 b c Gilded Time (USA) -Sudden Storm Bird (USA) (Storm Bird (CAN)) 2804$^{3}$ 3319$^{4}$ 4219$^{4}$ 5718$^{2}$ **>83f<**

**Council Member (USA)** 2 b c Seattle Slew (USA) -Zoe Montana (USA) (Seeking The Gold (USA)) (2579) 2954$^{2}$ 3640$^{2}$ 4857$^{11}$ 5295$^{2}$ **>107f<**

**Counsel s Opinion (IRE)** 7 ch g Rudimentary (USA) -Fairy Fortune (Rainbow Quest (USA)) 1328$^{3}$ 2638$^{4}$ 3075$^{11}$ 3521$^{9}$ 4163$^{4}$ 4530$^{2}$ 5650$^{17}$ **>91a 113f<**

**Count Boris** 3 b g Groom Dancer (USA) -Bu Hagab (IRE) (Royal Academy (USA)) 2114$^{13}$ 4813$^{7}$ 5007$^{7}$ 5352$^{7}$ 6343$^{3}$ 6566$^{2}$ **>65f<**

**Count Cougar (USA)** 4 b g Sir Cat (USA) -Gold Script (USA) (Seeking The Gold (USA)) *543$^{3}$ 578$^{10}$* 3010$^{17}$ 3407$^{6}$ 4422$^{14}$ 5562$^{17}$ 5949$^{11}$ **>45a 45 f<**

**Countdown** 2 ch c Pivotal-Quiz Time (Efisio) 3900$^{3}$ *4334$^{2}$* (4507) (4918) 5005$^{2}$ 5404a$^{8}$ *6023$^{5}$* **>80a 90+f<**

**Count Dracula** 3 b g Dracula (AUS) -Chipaya (Northern Prospect (USA)) *(1015)* 1357$^{13}$ *2988$^{6}$* 4619$^{12}$ **>67a 55f<**

**Countess Elton (IRE)** 4 ch f Mukaddamah (USA) -Be Prepared (IRE) (Be My Guest (USA)) *434$^{12}$* **><**

**Count Kristo** 2 br c Dr Fong (USA) -Aryadne (Rainbow Quest (USA)) 4743$^{2}$ 5646$^{12}$ **>83f<**

**Count On Us** 4 ch g Danehill Dancer (IRE) -Capricious Lady (IRE) (Capricorn Line) *996$^{13}$* **>42a 49f<**

**Country Rambler (USA)** 2 b c Red Ransom (USA) -Country Garden (Selkirk (USA)) 2470$^{10}$ (3124) 3672$^{7}$ 5457$^{3}$ (5802) **>93f<**

**Country Reel (USA)** 4 b c Danzig (USA) -Country Belle (USA) (Seattle Slew (USA)) 2021$^{8}$ 2373$^{4}$ 3073$^{4}$ 3674$^{11}$ 4745$^{12}$ 5553$^{2}$ 5780$^{5}$ 6190$^{4}$ **>115f<**

**Countrywide Dream (IRE)** 2 ch g Definite Article-Grosvenor Miss (IRE) (Tirol) 2268$^{11}$ 2758$^{14}$ 3009$^{8}$ 3145$^{5}$ **>10f<**

**Countrywide Flyer (IRE)** 3 b g Revoque (IRE) -Unbidden Melody (USA) (Chieftain) *466$^{5}$ (595) 641$^{2}$ 883$^{3}$* **>96a 65f<**

**Countrywide Girl (IRE)** 5 ch m Catrail (USA) -Polish Saga (Polish Patriot (USA)) *421$^{10}$ 497$^{3}$ 527$^{5}$ 809$^{3}$ 875$^{6}$ 1446$^{4}$ 1510$^{3}$1573$^{3}$ 1890$^{2}$ (2017) 2229$^{5}$ 3376$^{3}$ 3612$^{4}$* 4132$^{10}$ 4509$^{11}$ **>46a 4f<**

**Countrywide Luck** 3 b g Inchinor-Thelma (Blakeney) 3916$^{6}$ 4492$^{2}$ (5237) 5942$^{6}$ 6346$^{7}$ **>91f<**

**Countrywide Star (IRE)** 6 ch g Common Grounds-Silver Slipper (Indian Ridge) *814$^{12}$* **>26 a 26 f<**

**Countrywide Sun** 2 b g Benny The Dip (USA) -Sundae Girl (USA) (Green Dancer (USA)) 1412$^{8}$ 2087$^{10}$ 3665$^{7}$ 4304$^{2}$ *4878$^{4}$* 5591$^{8}$ 6195$^{15}$ **>57a 53f<**

**Count Walewski** 4 b g Polish Precedent (USA) -Classic Beauty (IRE) (Fairy King (USA)) 1460$^{20}$ *1935$^{12}$* **>7a 76f<**

**County Clare** 2 ch f Barathea (IRE) -Input (Primo Dominie) 2481$^{10}$ 4364$^{2}$ 4753$^{3}$ 5648$^{15}$ 5943$^{6}$ **>77f<**

**Countykat (IRE)** 4 b g Woodborough (USA) -Kitty Kildare (USA) (Seattle Dancer (USA)) *592$^{6}$ 679$^{13}$* 2039$^{7}$ 2445$^{2}$ *(2989)* 3198$^{2}$ 3347$^{7}$ 3977$^{7}$ **>84+a 89 f<**

**Coup De Chance (IRE)** 4 ch f Ashkalani (IRE) -Tout A Coup (IRE) (Ela-Mana-Mou) *1054$^{11}$* 2210$^{5}$ 4361$^{3}$ 4772$^{13}$ **>69a 93+f<**

**Coup D Etat** 2 b c Diktat-Megdale (IRE) (Waajib) 3051$^{4}$ 3760$^{2}$ 4730$^{6}$ 6090$^{4}$ 6322$^{3}$ **>85f<**

**Coupe De Champe (FR)** 3 b f Take Risks (FR) -Banakill (FR) (Funambule (USA)) 6203a$^{3}$ **>100f<**

**Courageous Duke (USA)** 5 b g Spinning World (USA) -Araadh (USA) (Blushing Groom (FR)) 633a$^{3}$ 712a$^{5}$ 2969$^{20}$ 4118$^{2}$ 4520$^{3}$ 5461$^{2}$ 5761$^{2}$ **>66a 102f<**

**Courageously** 2 b c Aljabr (USA) -Eishin Eleuthera (IRE) (Sadler s Wells (USA)) 2180$^{5}$ **>33f<**

**Courant D Air (IRE)** 3 b g Indian Rocket-Red River Rose (IRE) (Red Sunset) *425$^{7}$ 611$^{3}$ 752$^{6}$ 808$^{5}$* (1594) 5451$^{7}$ **>34a 34 f<**

**Cours De La Reine (IRE)** 2 b f Fasliyev (USA) -Society Queen (IRE) (Law Society (USA)) 2786$^{3}$ 3031$^{13}$ (4964a) 5979a$^{10}$ 6529a$^{4}$ **>105f<**

**Court Chancellor** 3 b g Primo Dominie-Welcome Home (Most Welcome) 2479$^{13}$ 2915$^{12}$ 4337$^{7}$ 5794$^{17}$ 5926$^{10}$ **>35f<**

**Court Emperor** 4 b g Mtoto-Fairfields Cone (Celtic Cone) 1221$^{9}$ 1612$^{9}$ 2090$^{9}$ **>45f<**

**Courtintime** 2 b f Atraf-Royal Girl (Kafu) 2268$^{9}$ 5800$^{13}$ **>6f<**

**Courtledge** 9 b g Unfuwain (USA) -Tremellick (Mummy s Pet) *1404$^{7}$* **>11a<**

**Court Masterpiece** 4 b c Polish Precedent (USA) -Easy Option (IRE) (Prince Sabo) 2200$^{3}$ 2623$^{5}$ 3318$^{4}$ 3673$^{2}$ (4120) 5113$^{4}$ 5414$^{3}$ 5888$^{6}$ **>117f<**

**Court Music (IRE)** 5 bb m Revoque (IRE) -Lute And Lyre (IRE) (The Noble Player (USA)) *429$^{7}$ 502$^{2}$ 780$^{6}$ 941$^{9}$* **>34a 34f<**

**Court Of Appeal** 7 ch g Bering-Hiawatha s Song (USA) (Chief s Crown (USA)) (1198) (1928) 2365$^{3}$ 2895$^{2}$ 4123$^{10}$ 4831$^{2}$ 5629$^{6}$ **>83a 98f<**

**Court One** 6 b g Shareef Dancer (USA) -Fairfields Cone (Celtic Cone) *1042$^{14}$* 1376$^{7}$ (1593) (2385) 2893$^{11}$ 4261$^{7}$ 5205$^{8}$ 5354$^{11}$ **>27a 50f<**

**Court Ruler** 2 b g Kayf Tara-Fairfields Cone (Celtic Cone) 5703$^{5}$ 6077$^{U}$ 6308$^{10}$ **><**

**Coustou (IRE)** 4 b g In Command (IRE) -Carranza (IRE) (Lead On Time (USA)) 1317$^{6}$ 1663$^{10}$ 1974$^{8}$ 2172$^{4}$ 2292$^{3}$ 3738$^{3}$ 3903$^{7}$ **>65 f<**

**Coventina (IRE)** 3 gr f Daylami (IRE) -Lady Of The Lake (Caerleon (USA)) 1108$^{7}$ 1416$^{8}$ 2179$^{2}$ 2910$^{3}$ 4062$^{3}$ (4550) **>95f<**

**Coy (IRE)** 3 b f Danehill (USA) -Demure (Machiavellian (USA)) 2276$^{5}$ 2548$^{2}$ 2971$^{2}$ (4077) **>109f<**

**Crackleando** 3 ch g Forzando-Crackling (Electric) *416$^{3}$ 822$^{9}$* 1714$^{3}$ (1947) 3479$^{16}$ 4561$^{3}$ 4778$^{2}$ 5991$^{7}$ 6110$^{9}$ **>55a 66f<**

**Cracow (IRE)** 7 b g Polish Precedent (USA) -Height Of Secrecy (Shirley Heights) 2525$^{2}$ *2816$^{14}$* 3885$^{4}$ 4139$^{5}$ 4433$^{8}$ 4971$^{11}$ **>51f<**

**Crafty Calling (USA)** 4 b c Crafty Prospector (USA) -Glorious Calling (USA) (Nijinsky (CAN)) 1789$^{9}$ 2283$^{17}$ 3052$^{11}$ 3260$^{4}$ 5177$^{8}$ **>92f<**

**Crafty Fancy (IRE)** 3 ch f Intikhab (USA) -Idle Fancy (Mujtahid (USA)) 1323$^{2}$ 1706$^{3}$ 2080$^{8}$ 2971$^{10}$ 6044$^{17}$ **>91f<**

**Crafty Politician (USA)** 7 ch h Supremo (USA) -Sauve Qui Peut (CAN) (Cerf Volant (CAN)) *782$^{4}$ (1406) 1544$^{2}$* 1639$^{5}$ 1859$^{6}$ 2246$^{13}$ **>51a 49f<**

**Crafty Trust (USA)** 4 b c Crafty Prospector (USA) -Blind Trust (USA) (Bold Ruckus (USA)) *688a$^{11}$* **>46a<**

**Craic Sa Ceili (IRE)** 4 b f Danehill Dancer (IRE) -Fay s Song (IRE) (Fayruz) 1708$^{10}$ 2064$^{17}$ 2521$^{9}$ 3455$^{4}$ 4740$^{8}$ 5259$^{5}$ 6124$^{12}$ **>38a 55 f<**

**Craigmor** 4 br g Polar Falcon (USA) -Western Horizon (USA) (Gone West (USA)) *442$^{8}$ 562$^{8}$* **>5a 4f<**

**Craig s Falcon (FR)** 5 b h Polar Falcon (USA) -Royale Figurine (IRE) (Dominion Royale) 1110a$^{8}$ 1922a$^{7}$ **>111f<**

**Crail** 4 b g Vettori (IRE) -Tendency (Ballad Rock) 1708$^{3}$ 2560$^{7}$ 3177$^{4}$ (4912) 5706$^{10}$ 6477$^{10}$ **>35a 82f<**

**Craiova (IRE)** 5 b h Turtle Island (IRE) -Velvet Appeal (IRE) (Petorius) 1125$^{16}$ 1456$^{22}$ 2575$^{7}$ 3205$^{7}$ 3477$^{9}$ 3690$^{9}$ 4742$^{4}$ 5614$^{12}$ **>65a 88f<**

**Crathes** 3 ch f Zilzal (USA) -Sweet Dreams (Selkirk (USA)) 1288$^{2}$ 1869$^{4}$ *2853$^{6}$* **>33a 55f<**

**Crathorne (IRE)** 4 b g Alzao (USA) -Shirley Blue (IRE) (Shirley Heights) 2022$^{4}$ 2471$^{3}$ 2964$^{4}$ 3678$^{13}$ 4831$^{11}$ 5303$^{13}$ 5581$^{13}$ *5956$^{8}$*6266$^{17}$ **>69a 80f<**

**Crazy Like A Fool (IRE)** 5 b g Charnwood Forest (IRE) -Shanghai Girl (Distant Relative) 3579$^{13}$ **><**

**Cream Of Esteem** 2 b g Mark Of Esteem (IRE) -Chantilly (FR) (Sanglamore (USA)) 6330$^{13}$ 6569$^{13}$ **>45f<**

**Creative Character (USA)** 2 bb c Theatrical-Shannkara (IRE) (Akarad (FR)) 3931$^{4}$ 4689$^{9}$ 5406$^{9}$ **>73f<**

**Credit (IRE)** 3 b c Intikhab (USA) -Tycooness (IRE) (Last Tycoon) 1310$^{3}$ 1794$^{3}$ (2114) 3001$^{10}$ 3671$^{7}$ 4173$^{4}$ (4582) 4749$^{3}$ 5226$^{3}$ 5699$^{3}$6172$^{12}$ **>97+f<**

**Cree** 2 b c Indian Ridge-Nightitude (Night Shift (USA)) 1436$^{8}$ 1686$^{13}$ 4388$^{5}$ 4704$^{2}$ 5005$^{5}$ 5078$^{2}$ 5490$^{3}$ (5690) 5932$^{4}$6356$^{5}$ 6544$^{2}$ **>69f<**

**Creek Dancer** 2 b f Josr Algarhoud (IRE) -Dance Land (IRE) (Nordance (USA)) 6118$^{17}$ **>37f<**

**Creme De La Creme (IRE)** 2 b f Montjeu (IRE) -Pride Of Place (IRE) (Caerleon (USA)) 4851$^{8}$ *6447$^{13}$* **>50+a 63f<**

**Creskeld (IRE)** 5 b g Sri Pekan (USA) -Pizzazz (Unfuwain (USA)) *1009$^{3}$* 1247$^{12}$ 1451$^{14}$ 2078$^{14}$ 3520$^{9}$ 3779$^{8}$ (4826) 5127$^{4}$ 5835$^{14}$6520$^{5}$ **>94a 79f<**

**Cressex Katie** 5 b m Komaite (USA) -Kakisa (Forlorn River) *701$^{13}$* **>52a 82f<**

**Cretan Gift** 13 ch g Cadeaux Genereux-Caro s Niece (USA) (Caro) *410$^{5}$ 519$^{4}$* **>82a 100f<**

**Crete (IRE)** 2 b c Montjeu (IRE) -Paesanella (Seattle Song (USA)) 6545$^{4}$ **>68f<**

**Crewes Miss Isle** 3 b f Makbul-Riviere Rouge (Forzando) *591$^{4}$ 1303$^{6}$ (1626)* 1907$^{5}$ 2181$^{8}$ 2518$^{9}$ *2849$^{7}$* 4052$^{5}$ 4923$^{8}$*6066$^{11}$ 6290$^{7}$* **>44a 44f<**

**Crimson Bow (GER)** 2 ch f Night Shift (USA) -Carma (IRE) (Konigsstuhl (GER)) 4487$^{9}$ **>51f<**

**Crimson Palace (SAF)** 5 b m Elliodor (FR) -Perfect Guest (SAF) (Northern Guest (USA)) (636a) 1146a$^{4}$ (2042) 2967$^{6}$ (4767a) **>113f<**

**Crimson Silk** 4 ch g Forzando-Sylhall (Sharpo) 1126$^{8}$ 1409$^{8}$ 1610$^{10}$ 1968$^{12}$ 2623$^{9}$ 3324$^{3}$ 3940$^{11}$ 4614$^{3}$ **>102f<**

**Crimson Star (IRE)** 3 bb f Soviet Star (USA) -Crimson Shower (Dowsing (USA)) 1945$^{7}$ *2486$^{11}$* 2765$^{12}$ 4195$^{15}$ 4968$^{3}$ 5283$^{2}$ *5641$^{2}$* 5793$^{2}$ **>46a 50+f<**

**Crimson Sun (USA)** 2 b c Danzig (USA) -Crimplene (IRE) (Lion Cavern (USA)) 2045$^{2}$ (2470) (4088) 4857$^{8}$ 5895$^{2}$ **>103f<**

**Cripsey Brook** 6 ch g Lycius (USA) -Duwon (IRE) (Polish Precedent (USA)) 1773$^{6}$ 2066$^{6}$ 2527$^{7}$ 2894$^{7}$ 3097$^{2}$ 3299$^{5}$ 4178$^{6}$ 4540$^{12}$5122$^{7}$ 5303$^{12}$ 6043$^{5}$ **>84f<**

**Crispin House** 4 b f Inchinor-Ayr Classic (Local Suitor (USA)) 4139$^{12}$ **>20f<**

**Cristoforo (IRE)** 7 b g Perugino (USA) -Red Barons Lady (IRE) (Electric) (1305) 1611$^{10}$ (3263) (3437) (4262) (4398) **>62+a 87+f<**

**Critical Stage (IRE)** 5 b g King s Theatre (IRE) -Zandaka (FR) (Doyoun) *507$^{3}$ (735) 829$^{3}$* 4080$^{10}$ 4479$^{6}$ 5869$^{4}$ 6083$^{4}$ **>71a 68f<**

**Crociera (IRE)** 3 b g Croco Rouge (IRE) -Ombry Girl (IRE) (Distinctly North (USA)) 1285$^{4}$ 1843$^{9}$ 6006$^{17}$ 6150$^{8}$ **>60f<**

**Crocodile Dundee (IRE)** 3 b c Croco Rouge (IRE) -Miss Salsa Dancer (Salse (USA)) *1063$^{7}$ 1239$^{6}$* 1766$^{3}$ 2203$^{2}$ 3000$^{2}$ (3484) (4380a) **>96a 113f<**

**Crocodile Kiss (IRE)** 2 b f Rossini (USA) -Pipe Opener (Prince Sabo) 3840$^{5}$ 4256$^{5}$ 4936$^{10}$ 6356$^{6}$ **>70f<**

**Crocolat** 3 ch f Croco Rouge (IRE) -Lamanka Lass (USA) (Woodman (USA)) 1794$^{20}$ 2001$^{9}$ 2818$^{5}$ 3172$^{2}$ *3379$^{4}$ (3799) (4998)* 5274$^{3}$ 5991$^{2}$ **>73+a 74+f<**

**Croix De Guerre (IRE)** 4 gr g Highest Honor (FR) -Esclava (USA) (Nureyev (USA)) 5654$^{3}$ **>36a 56+f<**

**Croix Rouge (USA)** 2 b c Chester House (USA) -Rougeur (USA) (Blushing Groom (FR)) 5347$^{3}$ 5838$^{12}$ 6145$^{9}$ **>73 f<**

**Cromarty Bay** 3 b f Victory Note (USA) -Cromarty (Shareef Dancer (USA)) 3882$^{11}$ **><**

**Cronkyvoddy** 3 b g Groom Dancer (USA) -Miss Pout (Kris) 2596$^{6}$ *2853$^{11}$* 3448$^{6}$ 5189$^{4}$ **>61f<**

**Croon** 2 b c Sinndar (IRE) -Shy Minstrel (USA) (The Minstrel (CAN)) *6453$^{6}$* **>59a<**

**Cross Ash (IRE)** 4 ch g Ashkalani (IRE) -Priorite (IRE) (Kenmare (FR)) 1603$^{7}$ 3525$^{10}$ *4093$^{14}$* 5364$^{17}$ 6007$^{11}$ 6146$^{6}$ *6364$^{3}$* **>53a 52f<**

**Cross My Shadow (IRE)** 2 b g Cape Cross (IRE) -Shadowglow (Shaadi (USA)) 4579$^{7}$ 5034$^{5}$ 5198$^{9}$ 5509$^{7}$ 5767$^{12}$ 6080$^{7}$ **>53f<**

**Crossover** 2 b f Cape Cross (IRE) -Somfas (USA) (What A Pleasure (USA)) 5404a$^{2}$ 5922a$^{2}$ **>100f<**

**Crosspeace (IRE)** 2 b c Cape Cross (IRE) -Announcing Peace (Danehill (USA)) 5341$^{2}$ (5857) (6344) **>91f<**

**Cross The Line (IRE)** 2 b c Cape Cross (IRE) -Baalbek (Barathea (IRE)) *6392$^{4}$* **>63a<**

**Cross Time (USA)** 2 b c Cape Cross (IRE) -Reine Maid (USA) (Mr Prospector (USA)) 6351$^{6}$ **>55f<**

**Crossways** 6 b g Mister Baileys-Miami Dancer (USA) (Seattle Dancer (USA)) *650$^{4}$ (919) 1122$^{9}$* 2116$^{4}$ 2590$^{2}$ 2787$^{2}$ **>70a 76f<**

**Crown Agent (IRE)** 4 b g Mukaddamah (USA) -Supreme Crown (USA) (Chief s Crown (USA)) *818$^{10}$* 1103$^{5}$ 1272$^{8}$ 1801$^{9}$ *2882$^{7}$* **>66a 74f<**

**Crown City (USA)** 4 b f Coronado s Quest (USA) -Trisha Brown (USA) (Theatrical) *823$^{7}$ 894$^{8}$ 1090$^{9}$* 1592$^{10}$ **>26a 56f<**

**Crown Of Medina** 2 ch c Fraam-Medina De Rioseco (Puissance) 5915$^{15}$ *6291$^{6}$* **>62 a 49f<**

**Crow Wood** 5 b g Halling (USA) -Play With Me (IRE) (Alzao (USA)) 1540$^{8}$ 1903$^{3}$ 2527$^{3}$ 3118$^{5}$ 3521$^{2}$ 4858$^{13}$ 5288$^{6}$ 5785$^{6}$ **>79a 103 f<**

**Cruise Director** 4 b g Zilzal (USA) -Briggsmaid (Elegant Air) *418$^{3}$ 600$^{13}$ 795$^{3}$ 1030$^{7}$* (1272) 1401$^{13}$ 1661$^{11}$ 2022$^{25}$5768$^{4}$ 6346$^{5}$ 6573$^{5}$ **>93a 93f<**

**Crunchy (IRE)** 6 ch g Common Grounds-Credit Crunch (IRE) (Caerleon (USA)) 1109$^{13}$ **>74a 55f<**

**Crusoe (IRE)** 7 b g Turtle Island (IRE) -Self Reliance (Never So Bold) *861$^{3}$ 903$^{11}$ 970$^{9}$ 1043$^{4}$* 1109$^{18}$ *1233$^{8}$ 1479$^{4}$1681$^{2}$ 2007$^{7}$* 2649$^{11}$ *2814$^{2}$ 3023$^{9}$ 3282$^{10}$* **>57 a 27f<**

**Crusty Lily** 8 gr m Whittingham (IRE) -Miss Crusty (Belfort (FR)) *2056$^{3}$* 2384$^{13}$ 2823$^{7}$ 5929$^{12}$ **>28a 42f<**

**Crux** 2 b g Pivotal-Penny Dip (Cadeaux Genereux) 5865$^{14}$ **>37f<**

**Cruzspiel** 4 br c Singspiel (IRE) -Allespagne (USA) (Trempolino (USA)) 3333a$^{3}$ 3862a$^{7}$ 5662a$^{9}$ **>111?f<**

**Cryfield** 7 b g Efisio-Ciboure (Norwick (USA)) 1109$^{15}$ 1451$^{8}$ 1620$^{6}$ 2099$^{2}$ 2368$^{4}$ 2776$^{7}$ 3167$^{8}$ (3470) 3714$^{6}$4209$^{4}$ 4537$^{3}$ *5002$^{4}$* 5236$^{9}$ 5622$^{11}$ 5713$^{6}$ *6296$^{6}$ 6550$^{8}$* **>69a 68f<**

**Cry Of The Wolf** 2 ch c Loup Sauvage (USA) -Hopesay (Warning) 2095$^{9}$ 2310$^{8}$ **>48f<**

**Cryptogam** 4 b f Zamindar (USA) -Moss (Alzao (USA)) *581$^{8}$ 684$^{8}$ 824$^{9}$* 2551$^{10}$ 2757$^{11}$ 3411$^{5}$ 3919$^{11}$ 4015$^{16}$ **>44f<**

**Crystal (IRE)** 3 b f Danehill (USA) -Solar Crystal (IRE) (Alzao (USA)) 1440$^{2}$ (1674) 2640$^{5}$ 5025$^{11}$ 5573$^{8}$ 6570$^{5}$ **>94f<**

**Crystal Castle (USA)** 6 b g Gilded Time (USA) -Wayage (USA) (Mr Prospector (USA)) 1741a$^{3}$ 2438a$^{3}$ 3073$^{2}$ 4216$^{5}$ 4595a$^{17}$ **>104a 119f<**

**Crystal Choir** 4 b f Singspiel (IRE) -Crystal Ring (IRE) (Kris) 1224$^{15}$ 2059$^{6}$ 2573$^{13}$ **>60f<**

**Crystal Curling (IRE)** 3 ch f Peintre Celebre (USA) -State Crystal (IRE) (High Estate) 1879$^{3}$ 2081$^{3}$ 2997$^{7}$ 3311$^{5}$ 5180$^{5}$ 5783$^{13}$ **>99f<**

**Crystalline** 2 b f Green Desert (USA) -Crown Of Light (Mtoto) 4344$^{3}$ 4706$^{11}$ **>72f<**

**Crystal Mystic (IRE)** 2 b c Anita s Prince-Out On Her Own (Superlative) 5406$^{11}$ 5687$^{4}$ *6294$^{10}$* 6543$^{11}$ **>28a 58f<**

**Crystal View (IRE)** 2 b f Imperial Ballet (IRE) -Fey Rouge (IRE) (Fayruz) 5878a$^{7}$ 6408a$^{4}$ **>90f<**

**Ctesiphon (USA)** 3 b f Arch (USA) -Beautiful Bedouin (USA) (His Majesty (USA)) 1619$^{8}$ 1946$^{10}$ *2667$^{10}$* **>45a 47f<**

**Cubic Confessions (IRE)** 2 b f Cape Cross (IRE) -Debinnair (FR) (Wolfhound (USA)) *1060$^{4}$ 1240$^{4}$* 4054$^{4}$ **>47a<**

**Cuddles (FR)** 5 b m Anabaa (USA) -Palomelle (FR) (Moulin) *1053$^{7}$* 1187$^{5}$ 1297$^{9}$ 2806$^{4}$ 3206$^{5}$ 3773$^{3}$ 4127$^{8}$ 4640$^{10}$5136$^{7}$ 5258$^{6}$ 5658$^{11}$ *5740$^{7}$ 6579$^{12}$* **>69a 56f<**

**Cugina Nicola** 3 b f Nicolotte-Cugina (Distant Relative) 3843$^{10}$ 4492$^{10}$ 5371$^{9}$ **>55f<**

**Culcabock (IRE)** 4 b g Unfuwain (USA) -Evidently (IRE) (Slip Anchor) 5479$^{7}$ **>38f<**

**Culinary (USA)** 2 rg f El Amante (USA) -Volunteer (ARG) (Ski Champ (USA)) *6485a$^{7}$* **>99a<**

**Culminate** 7 ch g Afzal-Straw Blade (Final Straw) *809$^{11}$* **><**

**Culture Clash (USA)** 2 bb f Petionville (USA) -Antonia Bin (IRE) (Sadler s Wells (USA)) *6485a$^{10}$* **>91a<**

**Cultured** 3 b f Danzero (AUS) -Seek The Pearl (Rainbow Quest (USA)) 2001$^{5}$ 2243$^{6}$ **>58f<**

**Cumbria** 3 b f Singspiel (IRE) -Whitehaven (Top Ville) 1605$^{3}$ 2133$^{4}$ **>69f<**

**Cumbrian Knight (IRE)** 6 b g Presenting-Crashrun (Crash Course) 5867$^{8}$ **>49f<**

**Cumbrian Princess** 7 gr m Mtoto-Cumbrian Melody (Petong) *549$^{4}$ 700$^{10}$ 1080$^{8}$ (1167) (1407) 1494$^{3}$ 2231$^{6}$ 3088$^{3}$4339$^{6}$* 4719$^{6}$ 4912$^{10}$ **>48a 35f<**

**Cummiskey (IRE)** 2 b c Orpen (USA) -Ansariya (USA) (Shahrastani (USA)) 1269$^{5}$ 4040$^{3}$ 4191$^{4}$ 5351$^{2}$ 5490$^{2}$ **>82f<**

**Cumwhitton** 5 b m Jumbo Hirt (USA) -Dominance (Dominion) *783$^{5}$ 1026$^{9}$ (1091) 1914$^{6}$* **>51a 23f<**

**Cunning Pursuit** 3 b g Pursuit Of Love-Mistitled (USA) (Miswaki (USA)) 1371$^{10}$ *1679$^{6}$* 1942$^{5}$ 2349$^{6}$ 2822$^{2}$ 3479$^{10}$ 4302$^{9}$ (5284) 5791$^{4}$ **>32a 49f<**

**Cupid s Glory** 2 b c Pursuit Of Love-Doctor s Glory (USA) (Elmaamul (USA)) *4022$^{6}$ (4598)* (4933) *(5052)* 5680a$^{3}$ (6340) 6510a$^{4}$ **>103a 108f<**

**Cupids Ray (IRE)** 3 b c Fayruz-Cupid Miss (Anita s Prince) 3961a$^{15}$ **>99f<**

**Cup Of Love (USA)** 2 ch f Behrens (USA) -Cup Of Kindness (USA) (Secretariat (USA)) 5271$^{8}$ 5717$^{12}$ 6454$^{9}$ **>54f<**

**Cupola** 3 b c Fasliyev (USA) -Spring Mood (FR) (Nashwan (USA)) *691a$^{12}$ 848a$^{6}$* **>74a 85f<**

**Curate (USA)** 5 ch g Unfuwain (USA) -Carniola (Rainbow Quest (USA)) 2856$^{6}$ **>23a 51f<**

**Curfew** 5 b m Marju (IRE) -Twilight Patrol (Robellino (USA)) 1685$^{4}$ 3732$^{5}$ 3976$^{8}$ 4357a$^{13}$ **>102f<**

**Curragh Gold (IRE)** 4 b f Flying Spur (AUS) -Go Indigo (IRE) (Cyrano De Bergerac) 3997$^{9}$ 4808$^{11}$ *5645$^{12}$* **>29a 29f<**

**Currency** 7 b g Sri Pekan (USA) -On Tiptoes (Shareef Dancer (USA)) *417$^{12}$ 454$^{3}$ 526$^{2}$ 578$^{4}$ 742$^{7}$ 847$^{12}$* 2399$^{14}$2784$^{4}$ 3141$^{9}$ 3416$^{6}$ 3645$^{3}$ 4034$^{9}$ 4291$^{11}$ 4459$^{5}$ 4687$^{2}$(4774) 5440$^{4}$ 5730$^{5}$ 5874$^{13}$ 6205$^{11}$ *6554$^{6}$* **>80a 90f<**

**Curule (USA)** 7 br h Go For Gin (USA) -Reservation (USA) (Cryptoclearance (USA)) *635a$^{6}$ 832a$^{2}$* **>116a<**

**Curzon Lodge (IRE)** 4 ch g Grand Lodge (USA) -Curzon Street (Night Shift (USA)) *463$^{9}$* 2833$^{10}$ 4063$^{P}$ **>42a 38f<**

**Cusco (IRE)** 3 ch f Titus Livius (FR) -John s Ballad (IRE) (Ballad Rock) 1829$^{2}$ 2089$^{6}$ 2971$^{9}$ 3275$^{2}$ 3602$^{9}$ 4731$^{2}$ 5249$^{9}$ 5898$^{9}$ **>96f<**

**Cusoon** 2 b c Dansili-Charming Life (Habitat)

40583 (4413) 50684 54214 581012 609014 **>82 f<**
**Cusp 4** b f Pivotal-Bambolona (Bustino) 16682 **>54f<**
**Cut And Dried 3** ch g Daggers Drawn (USA) -Apple Sauce (Prince Sabo) *(764) (868) 9866 10999* 20335 22654 33446 36284 *38495451511* 45477 547310 **>69a 66f<**
**Cute Cait 3** b f Atraf-Clunk Click (Star Appeal) *302413* 35136 **>8a 48f<**
**Cutlass Gaudy 2** br c Nomination-Cutlass Princess (USA) (Cutlass (USA)) 27494 44547 57112 60025 **>82f<**
**Cut Quartz (FR) 7** b h Johann Quatz (FR) -Cutlass (IRE) (Sure Blade (USA)) 4983a3 5503a2 5976a2 **>114f<**
**Cut Ridge (IRE) 5** b m Indian Ridge-Cutting Ground (IRE) (Common Grounds) 209818 23509 277817 360911 42483 42602 (4546) 47082 4937552357 563913 **>59f<**
**Cut Short (USA) 3** bb f Diesis-Sun And Shade (Ajdal (USA)) 22235 (2647) 46133 **>86+f<**
**Cutthroat 4** ch g Kris-Could Have Been (Nomination) 24127 **>21f<**
**Cutting Crew (USA) 3** ch c Diesis-Poppy Carew (IRE) (Danehill (USA)) 15883 (2070) 22446 36922 (4229) **>78a 107f<**
**Cut To The Chase 2** b g Fraam-Chasetown Cailin (Suave Dancer (USA)) 509614 **>20f<**
**Cuvee (USA) 3** ch c Carson City (USA) -Christmas Star (USA) (Star De Naskra (USA)) *6487a13* **>67a<**
**Cyber Santa 6** b g Celtic Swing-Qualitair Ridge (Indian Ridge) 26896 34728 49112 51448 **>53f<**
**Cyclical 2** b c Pivotal-Entwine (Primo Dominie) (4986) (5490) 58963 *64492* **>87a 95f<**
**Cyclonic Storm 5** b m Catrail (USA) -Wheeler s Wonder (IRE) (Sure Blade (USA)) 29743 32004 360910 **>78f<**
**Cyfrwys (IRE) 3** b f Foxhound (USA) -Divine Elegance (IRE) (College Chapel) 211216 34102 *37112* 40836 471710 57376 (6004) 611713 **>65a 66f<**
**Czarina Waltz 5** b m Emperor Jones (USA) -Ballerina Bay (Myjinski (USA)) 27382 332710 *39336* 51366 604319 **>92a 90f<**
**Czaritza (IRE) 5** b m Spectrum (IRE) -Last Exit (Dominion) 1070a9 **>93f<**
**Czar Wars 9** b g Warrshan (USA) -Dutch Czarina (Prince Sabo) *6088 6706 12377* **>73a 65 f<**
**Czech Summer (IRE) 3** b g Desert Sun-Prague Spring (Salse (USA)) *53828 591312* 613210 **><**

## D

**Dabbers Ridge (IRE) 2** b c Indian Ridge-Much Commended (Most Welcome) 65697 **>58f<**
**Dabiroun (IRE) 3** b g Desert Prince (IRE) -Dabaya (IRE) (In The Wings) 1256a2 1489a2 **>100f<**
**Dabus 9** b g Kris-Licorne (Sadler s Wells (USA)) 44238 **>45f<**
**Di Capo (AUS) 5** ch g 6582a3 **><**
**Dafa 8** b g Deploy-Linpac North Moor (Moorestyle) *(527) (947) 10776 15458 17286 21854* **>49a 26f<**
**Dafina (IRE) 4** b f Mtoto-Dafayna (Habitat) 31294 *36133* **>57a 73f<**
**Dafore 3** b c Dr Fong (USA) -Aquaglow (Caerleon (USA)) (1796) 27897 61939 647510 **>83f<**
**Daggers Canyon 3** ch g Daggers Drawn (USA) -Chipewyas (FR) (Bering) 12672 14679 (2390) **>64a 66f<**
**Dagola (IRE) 3** b g Daggers Drawn (USA) -Diabola (USA) (Devil s Bag (USA)) (1467) 26887 323110 35893 41474 44512 46194 586811 **>72f<**
**Dahjee (USA) 3** b c Seeking The Gold (USA) -Colorado Dancer (Shareef Dancer (USA)) 34174 **>74f<**
**Dahliyev (IRE) 2** b g Fasliyev (USA) -Thaidah (CAN) (Vice Regent (CAN)) 32289 39313 46819 **>72f<**
**Dahman 2** b c Darshaan-Nuriva (USA) (Woodman (USA)) 41694 468911 **>79f<**
**Dahteer (IRE) 2** b g Bachir (IRE) -Reematna (Sabrehill (USA)) 21414 (2439) (2831) 3790a6 422710 49332 54533 57673 60429 **>91f<**
**Daimajin (IRE) 5** b g Dr Devious (IRE) -Arrow Field (USA) (Sunshine Forever (USA)) *(487) 5629 7735 8384 9027* 139312 15039 1875112007821707 34599 374510 392117 40707 42506 4556104818135 44912 *564412* 579315 **>23a 23f<**
**Daintree Affair (IRE) 4** b g Charnwood Forest (IRE) -Madam Loving (Vaigly Great) *8019* **>69a 66f<**
**Daisy Bucket 2** b f Lujain (USA) -Masrora (USA) (Woodman (USA)) 30839 41983 (5034) 600316 656214 **>64f<**
**Daisy Pooter (IRE) 2** b f Charnwood Forest (IRE) -Idrak (Young Generation) 509612 **>50+f<**
**Daisys Girl 2** b f Inchinor-Andbell (Trojan Fen) 527110 58006 59086 60273 **>50f<**
**Daldini 2** b c Josr Algarhoud (IRE) -Arianna Aldini (Habitat) 53764 (5689) 60422 63449 **>86f<**
**Dalicia (GER) 3** b f Acatenango (GER) -Dynamis (IRE) (Dancing Brave (USA)) 2157a8 2723a5 3504a11 5667a4 6378a10 **>102f<**
**Dalida 3** ch f Pursuit Of Love-Debutante Days (Dominion) *628U* 11115 13635 276613 425910 **>35a 48f<**
**Dalisay (IRE) 3** b f Sadler s Wells (USA) -Dabiliya (Vayrann) 28883 33743 *49392 59076* **>74a 72f<**
**Daliya (IRE) 2** b f Giant s Causeway (USA) -Dalara (IRE) (Doyoun) 53496 60002 **>69f<**
**Dalkeys Lass 3** gr f Wolfhound (USA) -Dalkey Sound (Crash Course) 38998 43324 49879 **>20f<**
**Dallaah 3** b f Green Desert (USA) -Saeedah (Bustino) 28926 **>91f<**
**Dallington Brook 5** b g Bluegrass Prince (IRE) -Valetta (Faustus (USA)) 16397 **><**
**Dallool 3** b c Unfuwain (USA) -Sardonic (Kris) 13875 (1605) 20704 26834 (4486) 47298 **>92+f<**
**Dalmarnock (IRE) 3** ch g Grand Lodge (USA) -Lochbelle (Robellino (USA)) 214410 31689 41805 **>58?f<**
**Dalna (FR) 3** b f Anabaa (USA) -Devalois (FR) (Nureyev (USA)) 1652a6 2160a7 4899a7 (6203a) 6463a4 **>106f<**
**Dalon (POL) 5** b g Winds Of Light (USA) -Dikte (POL) (Babant (GER)) 19107 *28166* 366711 **>49a 41f<**
**Dalriath 5** b m Fraam-Alsiba (Northfields (USA)) *541110 6716 8266 9524 16972 (1918) 22312* 275753049 32503 *33805* 40152 421010 43978 *49984* **>44a 44f<**
**Dalyan (IRE) 7** b g Turtle Island (IRE) -Salette (Sallust) 234510 **>29f<**
**Damachida (IRE) 5** ch g Mukaddamah (USA) -Lady Loire (Wolverlife) *1953a2* 5505a11 **>84f<**
**Damask Dancer (IRE) 5** b g Barathea (IRE) -Polish Rhythm (IRE) (Polish Patriot (USA)) *56437 606511* **>40a<**
**Damburger Xpress 2** b c Josr Algarhoud (IRE) -Upping The Tempo (Dunbeath (USA)) 60916 **>53f<**
**Dame De Noche 4** b f Lion Cavern (USA) -Goodnight Kiss (Night Shift (USA)) 13326 192713 22823 27509 307410 345311 39765 4291343949 50627 (5442) 58984 *64514* **>93a 100f<**
**Dame Margaret 4** ch f Elmaamul (USA) -Pomorie (IRE) (Be My Guest (USA)) *7295 85714* **>49a 51f<**
**Dame Nova (IRE) 3** b f Definite Article-Red Note (Rusticaro (FR)) 145313 23556 *302615* 42079 552412 **>50f<**
**Dami (USA) 3** b f Dynaformer (USA) -Trampoli (USA) (Trempolino (USA)) 237115 25955 29292 31392 (3394) (4264) 48065 55735 59427 **>84f<**
**Damson (IRE) 2** b f Entrepreneur-Tadkiyra (IRE) (Darshaan) (2745a) (2970) (4589a) 58943 **>110 f<**
**Danaatt (USA) 2** b f Gulch (USA) -Agama (USA) (Nureyev (USA)) 527015 **>16f<**
**Danakil 9** b g Warning-Danilova (USA) (Lyphard (USA)) *82012 88714* 11039 15399 20322 23054 *(2381)* 2689232072 41554 47296 518211 576413 **>79a 81f<**
**Danakim 7** b g Emarati (USA) -Kangra Valley (Indian Ridge) *6576 (718) 7807 8768 11904 14438 16997* (2383)25245 28852 303810 353313 38369 41057 42474 43502445210 45348 57934 62297 64693 **>38a 47f<**
**Dance Anthem 2** ch c Royal Academy (USA) -Statua (IRE) (Statoblest) (1865) 25922 295410 39248 **>86f<**
**Dance Away 2** ch f Pivotal-Dance On (Caerleon (USA)) 13992 (2071) 474412 56265 **>91 f<**
**Dance Away Capote (USA) 2** rg f Capote (USA) -Ingot s Dance Away (USA) (Gate Dancer (USA)) *6485a5* **>106a<**
**Dance Flower (IRE) 2** b f Cape Cross (IRE) -Ninth Wonder (USA) (Forty Niner (USA)) 36932 40743 43645 53914 57532 593815 **>78 f<**
**Dance In The Sun 4** ch f Halling (USA) -Sunny Davis (USA) (Alydar (USA)) *5586 6004 9152 (1053)* **>95a 81f<**
**Danceinthevalley (IRE) 2** b c Imperial Ballet (IRE) -Dancing Willma (IRE) (Dancing Dissident (USA)) 351410 38939 **>39f<**
**Dance Light (IRE) 5** b m Lycius (USA) -Embracing (Reference Point) *60310* 22498 31085 35083 422619 527410 55195 600514 **>57a 69+f<**
**Dance Night (IRE) 2** b c Danehill Dancer (IRE) -Tiger Wings (IRE) (Thatching) 11052 (1390) (1878) 29966 3965a7 42176 (4860) 539211 56023 **>102f<**
**Dance On The Top 6** ch g Caerleon (USA) -Fern (Shirley Heights) *(494) (677) 10659* 39196 *38505* 44357 518514 569810 **>101a 83 f<**
**Dance Party (IRE) 4** b f Charnwood Forest (IRE) -Society Ball (Law Society (USA)) *7053 7673 88211* 11098 12974 24467 *28817* 33487571412 *60619* **>70a 71f<**
**Dancer King (USA) 3** b g King Of Kings (IRE) -Tigresa (USA) (Tejano (USA)) 32515 35879 41019 46103 51107 64686 **>55f<**
**Dancer s Serenade (IRE) 2** b g Almutawakel-Dance Serenade (IRE) (Marju (IRE)) 30813 35605 41319 585210 **>66f<**
**Dances In Time 4** b f Danetime (IRE) -Yo-Cando (IRE) (Cyrano De Bergerac) *4248 5295 56912 67410 79412 9423 11919* **>50a<**
**Dances With Angels (IRE) 4** b f Mukaddamah (USA) -Lady Of Leisure (USA) (Diesis) *127711 140211* 18623 23479 238512 3490P 382712 5770662854 65245 **>34a 46?f<**
**Dance To My Tune 3** b f Halling (USA) -Stolen Melody (Robellino (USA)) *14226* (2037) 22517 38974 (4806) 51292 52454 55842 60474 **>40a 74f<**
**Dance To The Blues (IRE) 3** br f Danehill Dancer (IRE) -Blue Sioux (Indian Ridge) 21659 25863 (4484) 49708 **>64f<**
**Dance World 4** b g Spectrum (IRE) -Dansara (Dancing Brave (USA)) *(1235)* 140112 18323 26127 *36147* 48085 (4971) 520313 **>69a 79f<**
**Dancing Bay 7** b g Suave Dancer (USA) -Kabayil (Dancing Brave (USA)) (2684) 30762 48322 54153 5976a4 62184 **>119f<**
**Dancing Bear 3** b g Groom Dancer (USA) -Sickle Moon (Shirley Heights) 11164 14669 22503 54094 *591410 65604* **>49a 61f<**
**Dancing Daggers (NZ) 3** ch g Daggers Drawn (USA) -Dancing Doll (NZ) (Dance Floor (USA)) 6582a5 **>106f<**
**Dancing Deano (IRE) 2** b g Second Empire (IRE) -Ultimate Beat (USA) (Go And Go) 21419 51256 554312 60935 **>52f<**
**Dancing Dolphin (IRE) 5** b m Dolphin Street (FR) -Dance Model (Unfuwain (USA)) 15813 *19176* 19876 238612 **>20a 39f<**
**Dancing Duchess (IRE) 2** ch f Danehill Dancer (IRE) -Lady Karam (IRE) (Baba Karam) 5971a3 **>88f<**
**Dancing Forest (IRE) 4** br g Charnwood Forest (IRE) -Fauna (IRE) (Taufan (USA)) *4689 6025* **>74a 68 f<**
**Dancingintheclouds (IRE) 2** b f Rainbow Quest (USA) -Ballerina (IRE) (Dancing Brave (USA)) 57178 **>58+f<**
**Dancing King (IRE) 8** b g Fairy King (USA) -Zariysha (IRE) (Darshaan) *4345 53311 5624 60411 7135 7782 (809) 8753(910) 9525 9704 10198 10398 10766 11772* 1367618752 *20075* 24455 51995 54085 55875 *60149 64041165476* **>45a 71?f<**
**Dancing Lyra 3** b c Alzao (USA) -Badaayer (USA) (Silver Hawk (USA)) *6216 (916)* (1799) 22022 26764 427111 47096 594210 63075 **>71a 96f<**
**Dancing Moonlight (IRE) 2** b f Danehill Dancer (IRE) -Silver Moon (Environment Friend) 25446 *298513* 36329 *43347* 58649 **>21a 20f<**
**Dancing Mystery 10** b g Beveled (USA) -Batchworth Dancer (Ballacashtal (CAN)) *(586) 7033 8415* 111317 153712 19378 27394 (2912) 3339437235 43669 45388 47488 48472 50719 544014 5704362053 **>101a 94f<**
**Dancing Pearl 6** ch m Dancing Spree (USA) -Elegant Rose (Noalto) 122412 13265 31087 35183 **>30a 55f<**
**Dancing Phantom 9** b g Darshaan-Dancing Prize (IRE) (Sadler s Wells (USA)) *4783 6822* **>63a 84f<**
**Dancing Prince (IRE) 3** b g Imperial Ballet (IRE) -Eastern Aura (IRE) (Ahonoora) *6735 8084 9189 98313 10468* **>49a 44f<**
**Dancing Ridge (IRE) 7** b g Ridgewood Ben-May We Dance (IRE) (Dance Of Life (USA)) *9909* 128315 *15685 16996 18867* **>23a 23f<**
**Dancing Rose (IRE) 2** b f Danehill Dancer (IRE) -Shinkoh Rose (FR) (Warning) 38052 44743 (5070) 54345 576711 **>75f<**
**Dancing Shirl 2** b f Dancing Spree (USA) -Shirl (Shirley Heights) 41006 43043 50833 54773 **>58f<**
**Dancing Tilly 6** b m Dancing Spree (USA) -L Ancressaan (Dalsaan) *4274 5002 5454 6636* 53054 (5449) 57912 62306*64065* **>49a 49f<**
**Danclare (USA) 3** ch f Stravinsky (USA) -Beyond Temptation (USA) (Sunny s Halo (CAN)) 139812 27886 29715 33204 **>90f<**
**Dan Di Canio (IRE) 3** b g Bahri (USA) -Khudud (Green Desert (USA)) 25195 31619 34475 40925 524512 58298 **>71f<**
**Dandouce 3** b f Danzero (AUS) -Douce Maison (IRE) (Fool s Holme (USA)) 18416 20973 23714 25779 47073 *601611* 613116 **>69a 73f<**
**Dandoun 6** b h Halling (USA) -Moneefa (Darshaan) 621916 65473 **>117f<**
**Dandygrey Russett (IRE) 3** gr f Singspiel (IRE) -Christian Church (IRE) (Linamix (FR)) 146111 18274 55374 59999 **>63f<**
**Dandy Jim 3** b c Dashing Blade-Madam Trilby (Grundy) *7328 7805 9349 9589 11955* 20376 *2187722328* 234913 **>24a 11f<**
**Danebank (IRE) 4** b g Danehill (USA) -Snow Bank (IRE) (Law Society (USA)) 185611 25475 (3682) 44732 50733 577313 59932 61983 **>48a 63f<**
**Danecare (IRE) 4** b c Danetime (IRE) -Nordic Flavour (IRE) (Nordico (USA)) 1893a9 26254 2744a5 4371aS **>95 f<**
**Danefonique (IRE) 3** b f Danetime (IRE) -Umlaut (Zafonic (USA)) 11168 12673 14652 21992 25465 28216 *33058* 40154462812 51102 52386 64677 **>46a 58f<**
**Danehill Angel 2** ch f Danehill Dancer (IRE) -Ace Girl (Stanford) *17357* 290412 **>10a 45f<**
**Danehill Dazzler (IRE) 2** b f Danehill Dancer (IRE) -Finnegans Dilemma (IRE) (Marktingo) 32024 **>66f<**
**Danehill Fairy (IRE) 2** b f Danehill Dancer (IRE) -Turntable (IRE) (Dolphin Street (FR)) 14987 16662 245815 26166 27733 29603 36203 39512455912 46754 51928 **>41f<**
**Danehill Lad (IRE) 4** b g Danehill (USA) -River Missy (USA) (Riverman (USA)) *467P* **>75a 66f<**
**Danehill Stroller (IRE) 4** b g Danetime (IRE) -Tuft Hill (Grundy) 247713 307417 34539 39414 436612 529910 561418 57301758745 **>81 a 89f<**
**Danehill Willy (IRE) 2** b c Danehill Dancer (IRE) -Lowtown (Camden Town) 40642 42928 50919 (5655) (6176) 64727 **>86f<**
**Danelissima (IRE) 3** br f Danehill (USA) -Zavaleta (IRE) (Kahyasi) 1485a5 2333a4 2711a4 (2993a) 35193 3968a6 48596 **>107f<**
**Danelor (IRE) 6** b g Danehill (USA) -Formulate (Reform) *10094* 11145 26387 28958 31195 37148 (4634) 49888 5122554238 60699 **>89a 93+f<**
**Dane Rhapsody (IRE) 3** bb f Danetime (IRE) -Hil Rhapsody (Anshan) *60610* 25865 332213 44225 46749 53385 *627512* **>26a 50f<**
**Dane s Castle (IRE) 2** b g Danetime (IRE) -Faypool (IRE) (Fayruz) 35883 *38022* 39862 *45983* 48033 (5908) **>73a 79f<**
**Danescourt (IRE) 2** b c Danetime (IRE) -Faye (Monsanto (FR)) *45995 49978* 52183 **>62a 61f<**
**Danesmead (IRE) 3** b c Danehill Dancer (IRE) -Indian Honey (Indian King (USA)) 20196 230911 **>95f<**
**Dane s Rock (IRE) 2** b g Indian Danehill (IRE) -Cutting Ground (IRE) (Common Grounds) *12644* 20957 24896 26222 *40947* 46999 50834 **>46a 50f<**
**Danethorpe Lady (IRE) 2** b f Brave Act-Annie s Travels (IRE) (Mac s Imp (USA)) 52096 55554 58648 **>37f<**
**Danettie 3** b f Danzero (AUS) -Petite Heritiere (Last Tycoon) 18429 43325 46154 49105 56374 609717 *655810* **>11a 59f<**
**Danger Bird (IRE) 4** ch f Eagle Eyed (USA) -Danger Ahead (Mill Reef (USA)) *4062 5523 6058 7632 9094 11814 (1479) 3615540968 60246 622510 65519* **>60a 53f<**
**Dangerous Dave 5** b g Superpower-Lovely Lilly (Arrasas (USA)) 59269 **>39a 21f<**
**Danger Zone 2** b c Danzero (AUS) -Red Tulle (USA) (A.P. Indy (USA)) 380812 43358 46815 537715 *56403* **>68a 68f<**
**Dangle (IRE) 3** b f Desert Style (IRE) -Dawn Chorus (IRE) (Mukaddamah (USA)) 3547a4 4956a9 5661a5 5972a4 6104a5 61759 **>104f<**
**Dan Grey (IRE) 4** gr f Danehill (USA) -Myrtle Beach (IRE) (Kenmare (FR)) 2138a7 3137a9 **>96f<**
**Daniella 2** b f Dansili-Break Point (Reference Point) 591513 **>46f<**
**Danielle s Lad 8** b g Emarati (USA) -Cactus Road (FR) (Iron Duke (FR)) *4884 5642 6249 8664 (967) 11413* 12657 *15983*20647 222617 **>79a 94f<**
**Daniel Thomas (IRE) 2** b c Dansili-Last Look (Rainbow Quest (USA)) 33192 42962 48443 63312 *(6448)* **>79a 86f<**
**Danifah (IRE) 3** b f Perugino (USA) -Afifah (Nashwan (USA)) *108612* 13127 216616 25188 29424 353010 357513 4460444774 46196 (4674) (4968) 52193 537016 (5693) 573713 60817 612417 *65579* **>45a 73f<**
**Dani Ridge (IRE) 6** b m Indian Ridge-Daniella Drive (USA) (Shelter Half (USA)) 26854 29097 33724 37326 394115 **>88a 88f<**
**Danish Monarch 3** b g Great Dane (IRE) -Moly (Inchinor) 161311 220713 28363 318019 408319 48686 52199 542512 **>67 f<**
**Danita Dancer (IRE) 2** b f Barathea (IRE) -Carranita (IRE) (Anita s Prince) 584612 614812 **>44f<**
**D Anjou 7** b g Marju (IRE) -Rose De Thai (USA) (Lear Fan (USA)) (710a) 1006a6 *1142a9* (1982a) 2603a9 3355a6 **>66a 116f<**
**Danny Leahy (FR) 4** b g Danehill (USA) -Paloma Bay (IRE) (Alzao (USA)) *5835* 117310 12879 **>63a 74f<**
**Dano-Mast 8** b h Unfuwain (USA) -Camera Girl (Kalaglow) 4380a4 5329a11 5824a9 **>120f<**
**Danse D Ecole (USA) 3** b f Daylami (IRE) -Dance Of Leaves (Sadler s Wells (USA)) 5822a10 **>52f<**
**Dan s Heir 2** b g Dansili-Million Heiress (Auction Ring (USA)) 22688 27552 34067 40122 *48789* 53697 **>37a 55f<**
**Dantana (AUS) 5** br g Danzero (AUS) -Big Sky Montana (AUS) (Lord Seymour) *689a12 851a3 977a4 1145a12* **>94a 103f<**
**Dante s Battle (IRE) 12** bb g Phardante (FR) -No Battle (Khalkis) *379911* **><**
**Dante s Devine (IRE) 3** b g Ashkalani (IRE) -Basilea (FR) (Frere Basile (FR)) *5686 9066* 13015 21768 *26674 285410* 44899 (5794)62272 **>36a 56f<**
**Dante s Diamond (IRE) 2** b c Orpen (USA) -Flower From Heaven (Baptism) 12082 14152 20865 25225 520211 56534 64395 657410 **>76f<**
**Danum 4** b c Perpendicular-Maid Of Essex (Bustino) *4314 8115 9028* **>49a 53 f<**
**Danzare 2** b f Dansili-Shot Of Redemption (Shirley Heights) 56957 *60214* **>64a 58f<**
**Danzatrice 2** b f Tamure (IRE) -Miss Petronella (Petoski) 52629 57715 64645 **>67f<**
**Danzero Con Te 3** b g Danzero (AUS) -Twilight Patrol (Robellino (USA)) 3135aF **><**
**Danze Romance 3** b f Danzero (AUS) -By Arrangement (IRE) (Bold Arrangement) 39168 436914 48135 58914 618311 654613 **>68f<**
**Danzig River (IRE) 3** b c Green Desert (USA) -Sahara Breeze (Ela-Mana-Mou) 13882 230916 28979 332416 416513 453110 48744 578660717 63412 **>102f<**
**Danzig Star 4** b f Danzig Connection (USA) -Julie s Star (IRE) (Thatching) *6566* **>24f<**
**Danzili Bay 2** b c Dansili-Lady Bankes (IRE) (Alzao (USA)) 35704 47704 (5241) 583911 **>81f<**
**Daphne s Doll (IRE) 9** b m Polish Patriot (USA) -Helietta (Tyrnavos) *116710* **>39a 42f<**
**Darab (POL) 4** ch g Alywar (USA) -Damara (POL) (Pyjama Hunt) 45569 585311 **>52f<**
**Darabanka (IRE) 3** b f In The Wings-Dararita (IRE) (Halo (USA)) 2416a6 **>65f<**
**Dara Girl (IRE) 2** b f Key Of Luck (USA) -Tavildara (IRE) (Kahyasi) 278613 308315 37489 **>47f<**
**Dara Mac 5** b g Presidium-Nishara (Nishapour (FR)) 199314 26602 29656 30583 (3247) 35597 392113 (4605) 48779 51276531714 55444 57137 59459 609419 **>67f<**

**Darasim (IRE) 6** b g Kahyasi-Dararita (IRE) (Halo (USA)) 1703$^{6}$ (2320a) 2998$^{3}$ (4270) 5415$^{5}$ 5976a$^{6}$ >**119f**<

**Darcie Mia 3** ch f Polar Falcon (USA) -Marie La Rose (FR) (Night Shift (USA)) *427$^{12}$* >**24 a 32f**<

**Dareneur (IRE) 4** ch f Entrepreneur-Darayna (IRE) (Shernazar) *1628$^{7}$* 1842$^{8}$ 2198$^{5}$ >**55f**<

**Darghan (IRE) 4** b g Air Express (IRE) -Darsannda (IRE) (Kahyasi) 6043$^{10}$ 6358$^{5}$ 6568$^{13}$ >**77f**<

**Daring Affair 3** b f Bien Bien (USA) -Daring Destiny (Daring March) *435$^{3}$ 569$^{2}$ (779) 955$^{5}$ (1627)* 1874$^{4}$ *(2005)* >**70a 65f**<

**Daring Aim 3** b f Daylami (IRE) -Phantom Gold (Machiavellian (USA)) 3204$^{5}$ (4087) 4321$^{5}$ 5842$^{8}$ >**88f**<

**Daring Games 3** b f Mind Games-Daira (Daring March) 2460$^{5}$ 3374$^{6}$ 3587$^{15}$ >**40f**<

**Daring Love (GER) 2** b f Big Shuffle (USA) -Daring Action (Arazi (USA)) (5280a) >**101f**<

**Daring Ransom (USA) 2** b c Red Ransom (USA) -Young And Daring (USA) (Woodman (USA)) (6073) >**83+f**<

**Dario Gee Gee (IRE) 2** ch c Bold Fact (USA) -Magical Peace (IRE) (Magical Wonder (USA)) (1128) 1383$^{2}$ 2447$^{2}$ 2954$^{8}$ 3865$^{2}$ (4757) 5195$^{5}$ 5392$^{19}$ 5947$^{3}$ >**95f**<

**Darkara (IRE) 3** b f Halling (USA) -Daralbayda (IRE) (Doyoun) 6137a$^{9}$ ><

**Dark Champion 4** b g Abou Zouz (USA) -Hazy Kay (IRE) (Treasure Kay) *444$^{2}$ 698$^{9}$ 805$^{4}$ 856$^{6}$ 1044$^{5}$* 1975$^{3}$ 2219$^{9}$2734$^{13}$ 3019$^{4}$ 3410$^{5}$ 3894$^{12}$ 4309$^{16}$ 4782$^{14}$ 5081$^{10}$ 6200$^{4}$ >**55a 67 f**<

**Dark Charm (FR) 5** b g Anabaa (USA) -Wardara (Sharpo) 1125$^{3}$ 4887$^{12}$ 5315$^{8}$ 5514$^{5}$ 6044$^{12}$ >**96a 97df**<

**Dark Cheetah (USA) 2** b c Storm Cat (USA) -Layounne (USA) (Mt. Livermore (USA)) 2959$^{7}$ >**108+f**<

**Dark Cut (IRE) 4** b g Ali-Royal (IRE) -Prima Nox (Sabrehill (USA)) *765$^{13}$* 1245$^{13}$ 1463$^{17}$ 3221$^{7}$ 3401$^{12}$ 3604$^{9}$ 4386$^{11}$ 4624$^{13}$ >**11a 42f**<

**Dark Day Blues (IRE) 3** ch g Night Shift (USA) -Tavildara (IRE) (Kahyasi) 1418$^{8}$ 1957$^{14}$ 2251$^{11}$ (2756) 3252$^{8}$ 4151$^{6}$ 4280$^{5}$ 4451$^{5}$ 5063$^{13}$5364$^{10}$ 5715$^{9}$ 5859$^{9}$ 6047$^{13}$ >**66f**<

**Dark Dolores 6** bb m Inchinor-Pingin (Corvaro (USA)) *793$^{5}$* >**37a 50f**<

**Dark Empress (IRE) 3** br f Second Empire (IRE) -Good Reference (IRE) (Reference Point) 3105$^{6}$ >**92f**<

**Darko Karim 2** b c Groom Dancer (USA) -Russian Rose (IRE) (Soviet Lad (USA)) 2310$^{4}$ 3071$^{10}$ 4193$^{9}$ 5314$^{11}$ 5995$^{3}$ 6129$^{5}$ 6334$^{13}$ >**75f**<

**Dark Parade (ARG) 3** b c Parade Marshal (USA) -Charming Dart (ARG) (D Accord (USA)) 5378$^{14}$ *5643$^{5}$* 5749$^{7}$ >**37a 23f**<

**Dark Raider (IRE) 3** bg f Definite Article-Lady Shikari (Kala Shikari) 1945$^{2}$ 2267$^{5}$ 2805$^{5}$ (3007) 3908$^{10}$ 4230$^{12}$ 6081$^{11}$ 6343$^{9}$ >**69f**<

**Dark Shah (IRE) 4** b g Night Shift (USA) -Shanjah (Darshaan) *873$^{5}$ 1098$^{11}$* 2426$^{10}$ 3103$^{14}$ >**41a 75f**<

**Dark Society 6** b g Imp Society (USA) -No Candles Tonight (Star Appeal) 5830$^{6}$ 6055$^{4}$ >**69f**<

**Darla (IRE) 3** b f Night Shift (USA) -Darbela (IRE) (Doyoun) 3874$^{8}$ 4194$^{5}$ 4650$^{2}$ 5219$^{6}$ 5618$^{16}$ 5737$^{11}$ *6016$^{3}$* >**71a 73f**<

**Darling River (FR) 5** b m Double Bed (FR) -Oh Lucky Day (Balidar) *6154$^{10}$ 6452$^{14}$* >**52a**<

**Darn Good 3** ch g Bien Bien (USA) -Thimbalina (Salmon Leap (USA)) *492$^{9}$ 871$^{8}$ 1100$^{3}$* 1365$^{14}$ 2546$^{6}$ 2840$^{7}$ (3108) (3488) 3683$^{2}$4441$^{10}$ 4647$^{6}$ 5205$^{6}$ 5456$^{14}$ (5826) 5889$^{4}$ >**58da 76f**<

**Darsalam (IRE) 3** ch c Desert King (IRE) -Moonsilk (Solinus) 5463$^{6}$ 5824a$^{3}$ (5974a) >**116f**<

**Darsharp 2** b f Josr Algarhoud (IRE) -Dizzydaisy (Sharpo) 6342$^{6}$ 6569$^{19}$ >**39f**<

**Dart Along (USA) 2** b c Bahri (USA) -Promptly (IRE) (Lead On Time (USA)) 5765$^{5}$ 5915$^{5}$ 6126$^{4}$ *6448$^{4}$* >**64a 76f**<

**Dartanian 2** b g Jurado (USA) -Blackpool Mamma S (Merdon Melody) 2057$^{7}$ 3124$^{5}$ 3458$^{6}$ 4010$^{3}$ *4601$^{7}$* (4699) 4909$^{7}$ 5314$^{16}$ >**49a 56f**<

**Darvish (FR) 3** b c Kahyasi-Dancing Tide (Pharly (FR)) 1306a$^{8}$ ><

**Dasami 5** b h Prince Sabo-Desacara (Arctic Tern (USA)) 3816a$^{4}$ 6261a$^{7}$ >**80f**<

**Dasar 4** ch f Catrail (USA) -Rising Of The Moon (IRE) (Warning) *428$^{6}$ 625$^{4}$ 725$^{7}$ 1515$^{2}$ 2451$^{3}$ 2854$^{9}$* 3471$^{15}$ >**51a 61f**<

**Dash For Cover (IRE) 4** b g Sesaro (USA) -Raindancing (IRE) (Tirol) 1187$^{2}$ 1308$^{11}$ 1675$^{7}$ 1875$^{10}$ 2030$^{5}$ 2279$^{6}$ 2573$^{9}$ 4912$^{5}$5252$^{13}$ >**64f**<

**Dash For Glory 5** ch g Bluegrass Prince (IRE) -Rekindled Flame (IRE) (King s Lake (USA)) *1281$^{9}$ 1448$^{8}$ 1693$^{8}$* 3490$^{7}$ 4417$^{3}$ 5257$^{11}$ >**60a 55 f**<

**Dashiki (USA) 3** ch f Distant View (USA) -Musicanti (USA) (Nijinsky (CAN)) 1441$^{3}$ >**76f**<

**Dashing Home (IRE) 5** b g Lahib (USA) -Dashing Rose (Mashhor Dancer (USA)) 5962a$^{4}$ >**104f**<

**Dash Of Lime 2** b f Bold Edge-Green Supreme (Primo Dominie) *6478$^{4}$* >**60a**<

**Dash Of Magic 6** b m Magic Ring (IRE) -Praglia (IRE) (Darshaan) *(430) 440$^{6}$ 570$^{2}$ 715$^{5}$ (1026)* 1560$^{11}$ 2347$^{6}$ 2649$^{3}$ *(2816)* 3099$^{5}$ 4698$^{10}$ *4998$^{7}$* >**51a 45f**<

**Dash To The Top 2** b f Montjeu (IRE) -Millennium Dash (Nashwan (USA)) 4851$^{2}$ (5368) 5779$^{3}$ >**110+f**<

**Datahill (IRE) 4** b f Danehill (USA) -Animatrice (USA) (Alleged (USA)) *722$^{5}$* ><

**Daunted (IRE) 8** b g Priolo (USA) -Dauntess (Formidable (USA)) *440$^{3}$ (455) 609$^{10}$ 616$^{8}$ (714) (879) (901) (1028)* >**70a 50f**<

**Davala 2** b c Lake Coniston (IRE) -Velvet Heart (IRE) (Damister (USA)) 2095$^{11}$ 2761$^{11}$ 6060$^{12}$ >**32f**<

**Dave (IRE) 3** b g Danzero (AUS) -Paradise News (Sure Blade (USA)) (4052) 5008$^{16}$ 5020$^{10}$ 5473$^{15}$ *6483$^{13}$* >**67f**<

**David Junior (USA) 2** ch c Pleasant Tap (USA) -Paradise River (USA) (Irish River (FR)) 5543$^{3}$ (5765) >**83+f**<

**Davids Choice 2** b g Wizard King-Welch s Dream (IRE) (Brief Truce (USA)) 6242$^{12}$ ><

**David s Girl 3** b f Royal Applause-Cheer (Efisio) *1695$^{5}$* 2088$^{6}$ 2766$^{6}$ 3229$^{5}$ 3425$^{8}$ 4497$^{8}$ 5092$^{6}$ 5552$^{6}$5794$^{3}$ 6228$^{2}$ >**22a 45f**<

**Davids Mark 4** b g Polar Prince (IRE) -Star Of Flanders (Puissance) *1082$^{10}$* 1516$^{3}$ 2166$^{4}$ *2663$^{4}$* 2885$^{4}$ (4400) 4782$^{2}$ 5412$^{10}$ *6274$^{11}$6398$^{3}$* >**61 a 63f**<

**David s Symphony (IRE) 2** ch g Almutawakel-Habemus (FR) (Bluebird (USA)) 3748$^{11}$ 4016$^{16}$ 4579$^{8}$ 5198$^{17}$ >**39f**<

**Davignon 5** b h Highest Honor (FR) -Dancing Drop (Green Desert (USA)) 3162a$^{0}$ >**98f**<

**Davorin (JPN) 3** br c Warning-Arvola (Sadler s Wells (USA)) (1386) 2135$^{6}$ *5220$^{10}$* 5934$^{6}$ 6284$^{8}$ >**62a 82f**<

**Davy Crockett 2** b g Polar Prince (IRE) -Sing With The Band (Chief Singer) 2579$^{7}$ 3233$^{16}$ 3918$^{5}$ 4256$^{6}$ 5477$^{11}$ (5855) 6333$^{15}$ >**69f**<

**Davyd Sho (FR) 7** b h Cricket Ball (USA) -Sho Biz (FR) (Solicitor (FR)) 1741a$^{9}$ >**102f**<

**Dawn Air (USA) 3** b f Diesis-Midnight Air (USA) (Green Dancer (USA)) 1770$^{3}$ 2133$^{10}$ 3479$^{18}$ 3984$^{15}$ >**60f**<

**Dawn Duel (IRE) 3** b f Daggers Drawn (USA) -Dawn s Folly (IRE) (Bluebird (USA)) 1530$^{9}$ 1869$^{8}$ >**42f**<

**Dawn Invasion (IRE) 5** b h Common Grounds-Princess Of Zurich (IRE) (Law Society (USA)) 1156a$^{3}$ >**109f**<

**Dawn Piper (USA) 4** b g Desert Prince (IRE) -June Moon (IRE) (Sadler s Wells (USA)) *(520) 648$^{7}$ 1056$^{2}$* 1385$^{13}$ 1840$^{2}$ 2196$^{9}$ 2441$^{4}$ >**93a 87f**<

**Dawn Surprise (USA) 3** b f Theatrical-Lignify (ARG) (Confidental Talk (USA)) 2059$^{2}$ (2911) 3602$^{5}$ (4442) (5099) 5920$^{2}$ >**103+f**<

**Dawton (POL) 6** br h Greinton-Da Wega (POL) (Who Knows) 3909$^{10}$ >**49f**<

**Dayano (GER) 3** b c Lomitas-Dawn Side (CAN) (Bold Forbes (USA)) 2510a$^{2}$ 3565a$^{11}$ 4183a$^{2}$ 5489a$^{4}$ >**113f**<

**Daybreaking (IRE) 2** br c Daylami (IRE) -Mawhiba (USA) (Dayjur (USA)) *6011$^{7}$* 6282$^{5}$ >**52a 56f**<

**Day Care 3** gr c Daylami (IRE) -Ancara (Dancing Brave (USA)) 5891$^{2}$ >**70+f**<

**Daydream Dancer 3** gr f Daylami (IRE) -Dancing Wolf (IRE) (Wolfhound (USA)) 1370$^{5}$ *2484$^{12}$* 3156$^{12}$ 3421$^{10}$ 3700$^{3}$ 4479$^{8}$ (4798) (5750) *6552$^{4}$* >**48a 57f**<

**Day Flight 3** b c Sadler s Wells (USA) -Bonash (Rainbow Quest (USA)) (1800) (2068) 2722a$^{4}$ 5611$^{4}$ >**116f**<

**Daygar 2** b c Spectrum (IRE) -Milly Ha Ha (Dancing Brave (USA)) 4016$^{11}$ >**51f**<

**Day Of Reckoning 3** b f Daylami (IRE) -Trying For Gold (USA) (Northern Baby (CAN)) 3994$^{3}$ (5007) >**77+f**<

**Day One 3** ch c Daylami (IRE) -Myself (Nashwan (USA)) 4554$^{3}$ 6088$^{5}$ 6245$^{2}$ >**61a 75f**<

**Day Or Night 3** gr c Daylami (IRE) -Amaryllis (IRE) (Sadler s Wells (USA)) 1654a$^{2}$ 2722a$^{10}$ >**109f**<

**Daytime Girl (IRE) 3** gr f Daylami (IRE) -Snoozeandyoulose (IRE) (Scenic) 1414$^{3}$ 1714$^{5}$ (2751) 3292$^{6}$ >**77f**<

**Daytona (GER) 3** b f Lando (GER) -Daytona Beach (GER) (Konigsstuhl (GER)) 2723a$^{8}$ 3504a$^{10}$ 4980a$^{2}$ >**96f**<

**Day To Remember 3** gr c Daylami (IRE) -Miss Universe (IRE) (Warning) 1352$^{5}$ (4813) 5150$^{3}$ (5998) >**95f**<

**Daze 3** b f Daylami (IRE) -Proud Titania (IRE) (Fairy King (USA)) 2280$^{3}$ (4910) 5615$^{7}$ 5944$^{4}$ >**78f**<

**Dazzling Bay 4** b g Mind Games-Adorable Cherub (USA) (Halo (USA)) 1471$^{6}$ 2065$^{13}$ 2857$^{3}$ 3074$^{5}$ 3522$^{2}$ 4324$^{24}$ 4759$^{14}$ 5712$^{3}$5799$^{14}$ 6349$^{12}$ >**107f**<

**Deal In Facts 5** ch m So Factual (USA) -Timely Raise (USA) (Raise A Man (USA)) *527$^{9}$ 572$^{16}$* >**32a 54f**<

**Deangate (IRE) 3** ch g Vettori (IRE) -Moonlight (IRE) (Night Shift (USA)) 3121$^{P}$ 5448$^{12}$ ><

**Dear Sir (IRE) 4** ch g Among Men (USA) -Deerussa (IRE) (Jareer (USA)) 3851$^{9}$ >**30a 56f**<

**Debbie 5** b m Deploy-Elita (Sharpo) *552$^{7}$ 570$^{9}$ 655$^{4}$* >**48a 65+f**<

**Debs Broughton 2** b f Prince Sabo-Coy Debutante (IRE) (Archway (IRE)) 2382$^{12}$ 2786$^{15}$ 2946$^{2}$ 4612$^{7}$ 5369$^{4}$ 5593$^{5}$ >**55f**<

**De Bullions 2** b g Mujahid (USA) -Stolen Melody (Robellino (USA)) 5290$^{13}$ >**18f**<

**Decelerate 4** ch c Polar Falcon (USA) -Speed To Lead (IRE) (Darshaan) *1097$^{8}$ 1231$^{8}$* >**63a 59f**<

**Decoration 2** b c Mark Of Esteem (IRE) -Forever Shineing (Glint Of Gold) 4747$^{11}$ >**40f**<

**Deeday Bay (IRE) 2** b f Brave Act-Skerries Bell (Taufan (USA)) (3296) 3748$^{4}$ 5131$^{2}$ >**80f**<

**Dee Dee Girl (IRE) 3** b f Primo Dominie-Chapel Lawn (Generous (IRE)) *821$^{11}$* >**5a 50f**<

**Dee En Ay (IRE) 3** ch g Shinko Forest (IRE) -Edwina (IRE) (Caerleon (USA)) 2046$^{12}$ 3587$^{10}$ 4306$^{5}$ 4491$^{6}$ >**51f**<

**Deekazz (IRE) 5** b m Definite Article-Lyric Junction (IRE) (Classic Secret (USA)) 4015$^{11}$ 4213$^{15}$ 4519$^{6}$ >**42a 47f**<

**Dee Pee Tee Cee (IRE) 10** b g Tidaro (USA) -Silver Glimpse (Petingo) 4624$^{7}$ 5238$^{3}$ 6230$^{11}$ >**64f**<

**Deeper In Debt 6** ch g Piccolo-Harold s Girl (FR) (Northfields (USA)) *647$^{2}$ 870$^{4}$ 1118$^{3}$ 1241$^{3}$* 1542$^{5}$ 2030$^{10}$ 3048$^{7}$ 3412$^{18}$3844$^{13}$ >**84a 70f**<

**Deep Purple 3** b g Halling (USA) -Seal Indigo (IRE) (Glenstal (USA)) (3843) 4950$^{4}$ 5615$^{6}$ >**93+f**<

**Deewaar (IRE) 4** b g Ashkalani (IRE) -Chandni (IRE) (Ahonoora) 1856$^{7}$ 2537$^{11}$ 6082$^{18}$ >**57a 57f**<

**Defana 3** b g Defacto (USA) -Thalya (Crofthall) *451$^{5}$* 3371$^{3}$ 3681$^{3}$ 4018$^{11}$ 5130$^{6}$ (5524) 5843$^{7}$ *6065$^{8}$* >**32a 54f**<

**Deferlant (FR) 7** ch g Bering-Sail Storm (USA) (Topsider (USA)) 2305$^{10}$ 2787$^{15}$ 3774$^{12}$ >**54f**<

**Defining 5** b g Definite Article-Gooseberry Pie (Green Desert (USA)) 2110$^{11}$ 2691$^{3}$ 3310$^{7}$ 4858$^{4}$ (5288) (5815) 6218$^{6}$ >**77a 111 f**<

**Definite Guest (IRE) 6** gr g Definite Article-Nicea (IRE) (Dominion) 2637$^{3}$ 2894$^{13}$ 3482$^{9}$ 3937$^{15}$ 4287$^{5}$ 4558$^{10}$ >**75a 90f**<

**Definitely Royal (IRE) 2** b f Desert Prince (IRE) -Specifically (USA) (Sky Classic (CAN)) *6158$^{7}$ 6479$^{9}$* >**52a**<

**Definitely Special (IRE) 6** b m Definite Article-Legit (IRE) (Runnett) *465$^{8}$ 536$^{7}$ 625$^{9}$ 1000$^{10}$ 1279$^{8}$ 1403$^{6}$* 1583$^{4}$1863$^{7}$ >**47a 28f**<

**Degree Of Honor (FR) 2** ch f Highest Honor (FR) -Sheba Dancer (FR) (Fabulous Dancer (USA)) 5604$^{10}$ *6536$^{11}$* >**2a**<

**Deign To Dance (IRE) 3** b f Danetime (IRE) -Lady Montekin (Montekin) *1096$^{5}$* 1464$^{19}$ 2061$^{8}$ 2377$^{5}$ *(2883)* 3700$^{10}$ 3993$^{3}$ 4580$^{2}$ 4848$^{5}$6271$^{5}$ *6498$^{3}$* >**70a 70f**<

**Dejeeje (IRE) 3** ch c Grand Lodge (USA) -Christan (IRE) (Al Hareb (USA)) 5306$^{9}$ 5525$^{7}$ ><

**Delaware Trail 5** b g Catrail (USA) -Dilwara (IRE) (Lashkari) *1444$^{8}$* 1710$^{9}$ >**46f**<

**Delcienne 3** b f Golden Heights-Delciana (IRE) (Danehill (USA)) 1467$^{13}$ 1844$^{11}$ 2349$^{3}$ 2760$^{9}$ 3193$^{2}$ (3391) 3822$^{5}$ 4259$^{7}$ (5929) 6227$^{8}$*6541$^{8}$* >**51a 53f**<

**Delegate 11** ch g Polish Precedent (USA) -Dangora (USA) (Sovereign Dancer (USA)) 2739$^{13}$ 2869$^{7}$ (3195) >**73a 74 f**<

**Delfinia 3** b f Kingsinger (IRE) -Delvecchia (Glint Of Gold) 2562$^{15}$ 2832$^{4}$ 3138$^{6}$ >**37f**<

**Delfos (IRE) 3** ch c Green Tune (USA) -Akhla (USA) (Nashwan (USA)) (1898a) 2722a$^{12}$ 3863a$^{2}$ 4965a$^{2}$ (5667a) >**113f**<

**Delightful Gift 4** b f Cadeaux Genereux-Delightful Chime (IRE) (Alzao (USA)) 2346$^{6}$ *2814$^{14}$* 3471$^{8}$ 5587$^{17}$ >**43f**<

**Delightfully 3** b f Definite Article-Kingpin Delight (Emarati (USA)) 1293$^{7}$ *1679$^{2}$* 2267$^{4}$ *2882$^{6}$* 3107$^{3}$ *(3303)* >**65a 68f**<

**Delightful Sofie (GER) 4** b f Grand Lodge (USA) -Daring Delight (GER) (Robellino (USA)) 3504a$^{9}$ ><

**Dellagio (IRE) 3** b c Fasliyev (USA) -Lady Ounavarra (IRE) (Simply Great (FR)) *1099$^{8}$* 1388$^{19}$ 1702$^{15}$ 2097$^{16}$ 2326$^{4}$ 2889$^{8}$ 3636$^{8}$ (4391) 4817$^{14}$5337$^{10}$ >**56a 57f**<

**Della Roggia (ITY) 2** gr f Distinctly North (USA) -Petite Queen (IRE) (King Of Clubs) 5388a$^{3}$ ><

**Della Salute 2** gr f Dansili-Marie Dora (FR) (Kendor (FR)) 3675$^{6}$ 4263$^{8}$ >**68f**<

**Del Mar Sunset 5** b g Unfuwain (USA) -City Of Angels (Woodman (USA)) *507$^{4}$ 837$^{5}$ 961$^{8}$ (1141)* 1522$^{12}$ 6081$^{12}$ >**88a 76f**<

**Delphie Queen (IRE) 3** ch f Desert Sun-Serious Delight (Lomond (USA)) 2082$^{4}$ 2269$^{3}$ (2694) 2897$^{2}$ (3751) 5811$^{6}$ 6175$^{6}$ >**107f**<

**Delsarte (USA) 4** b c Theatrical-Delauncy (Machiavellian (USA)) 1144a$^{9}$ 2108$^{2}$ 3912$^{5}$ 4932$^{6}$ 5438$^{4}$ >**114f**<

**Delsun (IRE) 3** b c Monsun (GER) -Dunnellon (Shareef Dancer (USA)) 2541a$^{4}$ 3565a$^{13}$ >**97f**<

**Delta 3** ch f Zafonic (USA) -Fleet River (USA) (Riverman (USA)) 2193a$^{9}$ >**89f**<

**Delta Force 5** b g High Kicker (USA) -Maedaley (Charmer) *(432) 456$^{2}$ (581) 671$^{4}$ 724$^{4}$ 734$^{5}$* 1644$^{3}$ 2429$^{2}$ 2935$^{6}$ >**70a 58f**<

**Delta Lady 3** b f River Falls-Compton Lady (USA) (Sovereign Dancer (USA)) 1363$^{16}$ *1916$^{6}$* 2348$^{9}$ 2657$^{5}$ 3229$^{14}$ 4102$^{8}$ 5187$^{12}$ 5451$^{9}$5587$^{6}$ >**27a 34f**<

**Delta Star 4** ch f Abou Zouz (USA) -Lamloum (IRE) (Vacarme (USA)) 5770$^{12}$ *6481$^{12}$* >**21f**<

**Delusion 3** b f Hennessy (USA) -Another Fantasy (IRE) (Danehill (USA)) 2411$^{6}$ 2657$^{3}$ 3002$^{11}$ 4241$^{15}$ 4387$^{7}$ >**58f**<

**Delzao (AUS) 4** b c Encosta De Lago (AUS) -Amanusa (AUS) (Alzao (USA)) 6528a$^{23}$ >**115f**<

**Demesne Man (IRE) 2** b g Bahhare (USA) -Mihnah (IRE) (Lahib (USA)) 4958a$^{10}$ >**68 f**<

**Democratic Deficit (IRE) 2** b c Soviet Star (USA) -Grandiose Idea (IRE) (Danehill (USA)) (3352a) 4959a$^{2}$ 5678a$^{4}$ 5980a$^{5}$ >**110f**<

**Demolition Frank 2** b g Cayman Kai (IRE) -Something Speedy (IRE) (Sayf El Arab (USA)) 5447$^{11}$ 6522$^{10}$ >**32f**<

**Demolition Molly 3** b f Rudimentary (USA) -Persian Fortune (Forzando) *610$^{9}$ 747$^{6}$ 868$^{8}$* 1209$^{2}$ *(1236)* 1883$^{15}$ 6046$^{19}$ *6293$^{13}$* >**71a 71f**<

**Demon Dancer (FR) 7** gr g Kaldoun (FR) -Habidancer (IRE) (Groom Dancer (USA)) 4039a$^{2}$ 4766a$^{2}$ >**112f**<

**Denebola (USA) 3** b f Storm Cat (USA) -Coup De Genie (USA) (Mr Prospector (USA)) 1652a$^{3}$ 4383a$^{7}$ 5332a$^{4}$ 6076a$^{2}$ >**121f**<

**Denise Best (IRE) 6** ch m Goldmark (USA) -Titchwell Lass (Lead On Time (USA)) 3682$^{11}$ 5175$^{5}$ *5641$^{5}$* >**34a 20f**<

**Dennick 2** b g Nicolotte-Branston Dancer (Rudimentary (USA)) 2972$^{4}$ >**55f**<

**Denominado (ARG) 5** b h Victory Speech (USA) -Dama Real (ARG) (Sings (ARG)) *2163a$^{16}$* 5727a$^{8}$ >**90f**<

**Denounce 3** b c Selkirk (USA) -Didicoy (USA) (Danzig (USA)) 1395$^{2}$ 1794$^{8}$ >**89f**<

**Den Perry 2** ch c Tipsy Creek (USA) -Beverley Monkey (IRE) (Fayruz) 2570$^{6}$ 2858$^{10}$ 3373$^{7}$ 3703$^{7}$ 4359$^{8}$ 4757$^{7}$ 4933$^{5}$ 5213$^{8}$ >**48f**<

**Den S-Joy 8** b m Archway (IRE) -Bonvin (Taufan (USA)) 2000$^{19}$ 2084$^{16}$ 2375$^{10}$ 2594$^{11}$ 3049$^{8}$ >**62 a 62f**<

**Denver (IRE) 3** b c Danehill (USA) -Born Beautiful (USA) (Silver Deputy (CAN)) *704$^{7}$ 955$^{2}$ (1029)* >**89a 73f**<

**Deodatus (USA) 6** b h Darshaan-Intrepidity (Sadler s Wells (USA)) *688a$^{3}$ (832a)* >**101a**<

**Deo Gratias (POL) 4** b c Enjoy Plan (USA) -Dea (POL) (Canadian Winter (CAN)) 3776$^{17}$ >**32f**<

**Deploia 2** ch f Deploy-Special Society (IRE) (Imp Society (USA)) 5390a$^{6}$ ><

**Depressed 2** ch f Most Welcome-Sure Care (Caerleon (USA)) *5053$^{7}$* 5569$^{7}$ *5953$^{3}$ 6023$^{4}$ 6359$^{2}$* >**61a 63f**<

**Deputy Of Wood (USA) 2** bb f Deputy Minister (CAN) -Wood Of Binn (USA) (Woodman (USA)) 2071$^{8}$ >**34f**<

**Deraasaat 3** ch f Nashwan (USA) -Nafhaat (USA) (Roberto (USA)) 1879$^{8}$ 2221$^{6}$ 2887$^{12}$ >**88+f**<

**Derwent (USA) 5** bb g Distant View (USA) -Nothing Sweeter (USA) (Darby Creek Road (USA)) 1821$^{16}$ 2365$^{9}$ 2775$^{8}$ 3375$^{4}$ 3985$^{6}$ 4450$^{6}$ 4808$^{9}$ 5344$^{3}$5853$^{13}$ >**69f**<

**Descartes 2** b c Dubai Millennium-Gold s Dance (FR) (Goldneyev (USA)) (6352) >**86+f**<

**Desert Air (JPN) 5** ch g Desert King (IRE) -Greek Air (IRE) (Ela-Mana-Mou) 4616$^{13}$ >**79f**<

**Desert Arc (IRE) 6** b g Spectrum (IRE) -Bint Albadou (IRE) (Green Desert (USA)) 1345$^{12}$ (2556) (2779) 3038$^{6}$ 3079$^{11}$ 3747$^{13}$ 5798$^{10}$ >**72f**<

**Desert Battle (IRE) 3** ch g Desert Sun-Papal (Selkirk (USA)) 1755$^{15}$ 1998$^{19}$ 2688$^{16}$ *2989$^{12}$* >**17a 27f**<

**Desert Buzz (IRE) 2** b c Desert Story (IRE) -Sugar (Hernando (FR)) 1960$^{7}$ 2382$^{6}$ 2758$^{8}$ 3514$^{5}$ 4048$^{9}$ 4607$^{10}$ 5097$^{8}$ 5556$^{8}$6093$^{6}$ >**49f**<

**Desert Chief 2** b c Green Desert (USA) -Oriental Fashion (IRE) (Marju (IRE)) 5857$^{2}$ 6171$^{6}$ >**79+f**<

**Desert City 5** b g Darnay-Oasis (Valiyar) 5773$^{20}$ >**79f**<

**Desert Classic 2** b f Green Desert (USA) -High Standard (Kris) 4523$^{9}$ 5248$^{14}$ >**60f**<

**Desert Commander (IRE) 2** b c Green Desert (USA) -Meadow Pipit (CAN) (Meadowlake (USA)) 3749$^{4}$ 4315$^{6}$ (4649) >**81f**<

**Desert Coral (IRE) 3** ch f Desert Story (IRE) -Sleeping Beauty (Mill Reef (USA)) *2853$^{13}$* ><

**Desert Cristal (IRE) 3** ch f Desert King (IRE) -Damiana (IRE) (Thatching) 1541$^{2}$ 1704$^{6}$ 3728$^{3}$ (4125) 4812$^{3}$ 5024$^{2}$ 5275$^{3}$ 5566$^{9}$ (5886) 6284$^{3}$ >**89f**<

**Desert Daisy (IRE) 3** gr f Desert Prince (IRE) -Pomponette (USA) (Rahy (USA)) 1309$^{9}$ 2146$^{13}$ 2545$^{9}$ 2833$^{12}$ 6079$^{6}$ 6288$^{6}$ 6567$^{18}$ >**54f**<

**Desert Dance (IRE) 4** b g Desert Story (IRE) -Cindy s Star (IRE) (Dancing Dissident (USA)) *1241$^{11}$* >**39a 73f**<

**Desert Deer 6** ch h Cadeaux Genereux-Tuxford Hideaway (Cawston s Clown) 2109$^{14}$ ><

**Desert Demon (IRE) 2** b c Unfuwain (USA) -Baldemosa (FR) (Lead On Time (USA)) 3946$^{5}$ 5536$^{3}$ >**77+f**<

**Desert Destiny 4** b g Desert Prince (IRE) -High Savannah (Rousillon (USA)) 2623$^{7}$ 3318$^{2}$ 3906$^{5}$ 5199$^{2}$ 5422$^{4}$ >**112f**<

**Desert Diplomat (IRE) 3** br g Machiavellian (USA) -Desert Beauty (IRE) (Green Desert (USA)) 1506$^{7}$ 3155$^{14}$ >**67f**<

**Desert Dreamer (IRE) 3** b g Green Desert (USA) -Follow That Dream (Darshaan) 1900$^{5}$ 2202$^{8}$ 2642$^{6}$ 3295$^{7}$ 4268$^{11}$ 5419$^{12}$ 5697$^{12}$ >**83f**<

**Desert Fantasy (IRE) 5** b g Desert King (IRE) -Petite Fantasy (Mansooj) 1254a$^{13}$ 4590a$^{6}$ 4956a$^{2}$ 5972a$^{10}$ >**114f**<

**Desert Fern (IRE) 2** b f Desert Style (IRE) -Lady Fern (Old Vic) *2812$^{4}$ 2985$^{14}$* >**39a**<

**Desert Fury 7** b g Warning-Number One Spot (Reference Point) *1681$^{8}$ 2123$^{10}$* 2597$^{6}$ *4190$^{5}$* 5081$^{12}$ *5641$^{6}$* 6466$^{4}$ >**44a 44f**<

**Desert Glory (IRE) 2** gr f Desert Prince (IRE) -True Love (Robellino (USA)) 6123$^{11}$ >**58f**<

**Desert Glow (IRE) 4** b f Machiavellian (USA) -Alumisiyah (USA) (Danzig (USA)) 831a$^{2}$ 1002a$^{2}$ >**93f**<

**Desert Gold (IRE)** 3 b f Desert Prince (IRE) -Brief Sentiment (IRE) (Brief Truce (USA)) 3328a$^{8}$ **>99f<**
**Desert Hawk** 3 b c Cape Cross (IRE) -Milling (IRE) (In The Wings) 1794$^{13}$ 2114$^{11}$ 2842$^{5}$ 3631$^{4}$ 4079$^{7}$ 4719$^{8}$ 5153$^{6}$ 5510$^{2}$5693$^{10}$ 5829$^{2}$ 5992$^{9}$ **>73f<**
**Desert Heat** 6 b h Green Desert (USA) -Lypharitissima (FR) (Lightning (FR)) 412$^{13}$ 776$^{2}$ (800) 909$^{2}$ 970$^{8}$ 1172$^{14}$ 1629$^{4}$ 1718$^{2}$ **>68a 68 f<**
**Desert Image (IRE)** 3 b c Desert King (IRE) -Identical (IRE) (Machiavellian (USA)) (462) 622$^{2}$ 864$^{6}$ 1222$^{10}$ 1365$^{8}$ 1688$^{3}$ 2169$^{3}$ 2870$^{2}$ 3340$^{4}$4027$^{9}$ 4618$^{7}$ 5459$^{7}$ **>72a 77f<**
**Desert Imp** 2 b f Green Desert (USA) -Devil s Imp (IRE) (Cadeaux Genereux) 4714$^{9}$ 5270$^{3}$ 5569$^{3}$ (6196) **>80f<**
**Desert Island Disc** 7 b m Turtle Island (IRE) -Distant Music (Darshaan) 1308$^{16}$ 1671$^{4}$ 2062$^{4}$ 2474$^{8}$ 2914$^{3}$ 3046$^{8}$ 3415$^{6}$ (3557) 3989$^{5}$(4233) (4416) 4950$^{6}$ 5182$^{3}$ 5273$^{8}$ 6128$^{11}$ 6185$^{3}$ 6339$^{9}$ 6495$^{11}$ **>53a 82f<**
**Desert Leader (IRE)** 3 b c Green Desert (USA) -Za Aamah (USA) (Mr Prospector (USA)) 2270$^{8}$ 2654$^{7}$ 3279$^{2}$ 3780$^{7}$ 5316$^{17}$ 5583$^{17}$ **>64a 65f<**
**Desert Light (IRE)** 3 b c Desert Sun-Nacote (IRE) (Mtoto) (452) 502$^{3}$ 1047$^{7}$ 1209$^{7}$ 1236$^{2}$ 1934$^{2}$ 6274$^{5}$ **>53a 57f<**
**Desert Lightning (IRE)** 2 ch c Desert Prince (IRE) -Saibhreas (IRE) (Last Tycoon) 6011$^{3}$ **>68a<**
**Desert Lord** 4 b c Green Desert (USA) -Red Carnival (USA) (Mr Prospector (USA)) 4294$^{6}$ (4553) **>92+f<**
**Desert Lover (IRE)** 2 b c Desert Prince (IRE) -Crystal Flute (Lycius (USA)) 2310$^{6}$ **>53f<**
**Desert Moonbeam (IRE)** 2 b f Desert Prince (IRE) -Pip s Dream (Glint Of Gold) 4637$^{6}$ 5406$^{14}$ 5872$^{10}$ **>43f<**
**Desert Move (IRE)** 2 b f Desert King (IRE) -Campestral (USA) (Alleged (USA)) (5095) **>75f<**
**Desert Opal** 4 ch c Cadeaux Genereux-Nullarbor (Green Desert (USA)) 1125$^{9}$ 1456$^{8}$ 1828$^{5}$ 2201$^{12}$ 3347$^{6}$ **>87f<**
**Desert Phoenix (IRE)** 2 ch f Desert Story (IRE) -Bird In My Hand (IRE) (Bluebird (USA)) 3583$^{6}$ 4048$^{14}$ **>45f<**
**Desert Plus (IRE)** 5 b g Desert King (IRE) -Welcome Break (Wollow) 1435a$^{10}$ **>94f<**
**Desert Quest (IRE)** 4 b g Rainbow Quest (USA) -Jumilla (USA) (El Gran Senor (USA)) 2076$^{7}$ 2638$^{2}$ 3325$^{4}$ 3756$^{11}$ (4530) 4932$^{5}$ 5650$^{10}$ **>103f<**
**Desert Quill (IRE)** 4 ch f In The Wings-Aljood (Kris) 2662$^{2}$ 3363$^{5}$ 3443$^{7}$ 4082$^{8}$ 4421$^{4}$ **>46a 55f<**
**Desert Reign** 3 ch g Desert King (IRE) -Moondance (Siberian Express (USA)) 1052$^{5}$ (3875) 4443$^{4}$ 5934$^{2}$ 6358$^{3}$ **>58a 76f<**
**Desert Royalty (IRE)** 4 b f Alhaarth (IRE) -Buraida (Balidar) 1671$^{2}$ (2062) 2297$^{2}$ 2993a$^{4}$ 3716$^{4}$ 3944$^{9}$ 4530$^{7}$ 4884$^{3}$ 5394$^{9}$ **>99f<**
**Desert Star** 4 b g Green Desert (USA) -Phantom Gold (Machiavellian (USA)) 5462$^{3}$ 5917$^{13}$ **>106f<**
**Desert Tigress (USA)** 2 b f Storm Cat (USA) -Sky Beauty (USA) (Blushing Groom (FR)) 3859a$^{4}$ 4592a$^{8}$ 5322a$^{7}$ **>85f<**
**Desert Tommy** 3 b g Desert King (IRE) -Flambera (FR) (Akarad (FR)) 492$^{11}$ 6511$^{3}$ **>26a 25f<**
**Design (FR)** 3 ch g Machiavellian (USA) -Vitaba (USA) (Northern Baby (CAN)) 6310$^{4}$ **>70+f<**
**Designer City (IRE)** 3 b f Mujadil (USA) -Carnickian (IRE) (Sri Pekan (USA)) 1288$^{10}$ 2621$^{12}$ 2908$^{10}$ 3096$^{8}$ 3410$^{11}$ 4393$^{4}$ 5104$^{9}$ 5801$^{9}$6275$^{11}$ **>36a 36f<**
**Desiree (IRE)** 3 b f Desert Story (IRE) -Elba (IRE) (Ela-Mana-Mou) 5621$^{13}$ 5999$^{14}$ **>48f<**
**Desires Destiny** 6 b m Grey Desire-Tanoda (Tyrnavos) 472$^{6}$ 570$^{7}$ 730$^{6}$ 1444$^{3}$ 1560$^{9}$ 1918$^{2}$ 2348$^{8}$ **>42a 50f<**
**Desperation (IRE)** 2 b g Desert Style (IRE) -Mauras Pride (IRE) (Cadeaux Genereux) 4924$^{8}$ 5186$^{5}$ 6021$^{2}$ 6240$^{3}$ **>75a 74f<**
**Destinate (IRE)** 2 b c Desert Style (IRE) -Double Eight (IRE) (Common Grounds) 1412$^{7}$ (2310) 3672$^{9}$ 4227$^{4}$ 4527$^{4}$ 4919$^{2}$ 5469$^{2}$ **>100f<**
**Destination Dubai (USA)** 3 bb c Kingmambo (USA) -Mysterial (USA) (Alleged (USA)) (1761) 2397$^{3}$ 2999$^{8}$ 3716$^{7}$ 5397$^{13}$ (5761) **>97f<**
**Detonate** 2 b c Mind Games-Bron Hilda (IRE) (Namaqualand (USA)) 1436$^{6}$ 1707$^{4}$ 2205$^{7}$ 3242$^{6}$ 3704$^{3}$ 4752$^{11}$ **>73f<**
**Detroit Dancer** 2 b c Makbul-First Play (Primo Dominie) 2904$^{15}$ 3818$^{5}$ 4446$^{15}$ **>44f<**
**Deusexmachina** 2 b c Xaar-Moonlight (IRE) (Night Shift (USA)) 3568a$^{3}$ **><**
**Deuxieme (IRE)** 3 b f Second Empire (IRE) -Kardelle (Kalaglow) 2808$^{3}$ 3666$^{3}$ 4718$^{5}$ 5338$^{2}$ 5803$^{2}$ (6280) **>60a 79f<**
**Deva (GER)** 5 ch m Platini (GER) -Diana s Quest (IRE) (Rainbow Quest (USA)) (2138a) 3137a$^{2}$ 4385a$^{5}$ 4980a$^{5}$ 5824a$^{5}$ (6378a) **>104f<**
**Devant (NZ)** 4 b f Zabeel (NZ) -Frenetic (NZ) (Truly Vain (AUS)) 1828$^{11}$ 2237$^{4}$ 2521$^{7}$ 3299$^{2}$ 3597$^{14}$ 4678$^{3}$ 5074$^{5}$ **>85f<**
**Devil s Bite** 3 ch g Dracula (AUS) -Niggle (Night Shift (USA)) 927$^{P}$ 1628$^{P}$ **>75f<**
**Devil s Island** 2 b c Green Desert (USA) -Scandalette (Niniski (USA)) 5689$^{5}$ 5857$^{8}$ 6011$^{11}$ **>42a 61+f<**
**Devine Command** 3 b g In Command (IRE) -Adriya (Vayrann) 447$^{9}$ 598$^{14}$ 660$^{2}$ 790$^{5}$ **>54a<**
**Devine Light (IRE)** 4 b f Spectrum (IRE) -Siskin (IRE) (Royal Academy (USA)) 2258$^{8}$ 3367$^{9}$ 3892$^{6}$ 4260$^{11}$ 5672$^{8}$ 5821$^{12}$ 6467$^{13}$ **>19 a 19f<**
**Devious Ayers (IRE)** 3 br g Dr Devious (IRE) -Yulara (IRE) (Night Shift (USA)) 1679$^{4}$ 1830$^{8}$ 4346$^{14}$ 4989$^{6}$ 5381$^{12}$ 6556$^{9}$ **>61a 47f<**
**Devious Paddy (IRE)** 4 b g Dr Devious (IRE) -Night Arcade (IRE) (Night Shift (USA)) 861$^{12}$ 1031$^{7}$ **>43a 69f<**
**Devise (IRE)** 5 b g Hamas (IRE) -Soreze (IRE) (Gallic League) (1313) 1673$^{6}$ 1765$^{27}$ (2303) 2873$^{5}$ 3243$^{5}$ 3645$^{4}$ 4232$^{7}$ 4538$^{2}$ 4951$^{3}$5071$^{2}$ 5287$^{2}$ 5491$^{8}$ **>33a 95f<**
**Devito (FR)** 3 ch g Trempolino (USA) -Snowy (FR) (Wollow) 2357$^{2}$ 3454$^{5}$ 3984$^{13}$ **>50f<**
**Devon Flame** 5 b g Whittingham (IRE) -Uaeflame (IRE) (Polish Precedent (USA)) 2399$^{2}$ (2739) 2873$^{2}$ 3416$^{2}$ 3691$^{4}$ 3941$^{10}$ 4291$^{19}$ 4774$^{2}$ 5075$^{11}$5704$^{9}$ **>86+f<**
**Devote** 6 b g Pennekamp (USA) -Radiant Bride (USA) (Blushing Groom (FR)) 1687$^{9}$ 3996$^{6}$ 4870$^{9}$ **>40f<**
**Dewin Coch** 2 b g Wizard King-Drudwen (Sayf El Arab (USA)) 5198$^{14}$ 5688$^{7}$ 5925$^{6}$ **>57f<**
**Dexileos (IRE)** 5 b g Danehill (USA) -Theano (IRE) (Thatching) 1308$^{9}$ 1522$^{10}$ 1876$^{10}$ 2122$^{12}$ 2598$^{7}$ 3321$^{12}$ 3871$^{7}$ 3991$^{3}$4811$^{6}$ 5282$^{8}$ 5691$^{9}$ 6362$^{3}$ **>46a 44f<**
**Dexterity (USA)** 6 b h Kingmambo (USA) -Diese (USA) (Diesis) 1741a$^{7}$ 4595a$^{8}$ 5488a$^{12}$ **>107?f<**
**Dhabyan (USA)** 4 ch g Silver Hawk (USA) -Fleur De Nuit (USA) (Woodman (USA)) 2672$^{8}$ **>102 f<**
**Dhaular Dhar (IRE)** 2 b c Indian Ridge-Pescara (IRE) (Common Grounds) 5091$^{2}$ (5455) 6340$^{9}$ **>88+f<**
**Dhefaaf (IRE)** 2 b c Lujain (USA) -Paparazza (IRE) (Arazi (USA)) 2208$^{7}$ **>44f<**
**Dhehdaah** 3 b g Alhaarth (IRE) -Carina Clare (Slip Anchor) 2361$^{7}$ 2774$^{3}$ 3572$^{5}$ **>65f<**
**Diable** 5 b h Big Shuffle (USA) -Diasprina (GER) (Aspros (GER)) 5255a$^{6}$ **>101f<**
**Diagon Alley (IRE)** 4 ro g Petong-Mubadara (IRE) (Lahib (USA)) 989$^{8}$ 2184$^{6}$ **>26a 37f<**
**Dial Square** 3 b g Bluegrass Prince (IRE) -Honey Mill (Milford) 529$^{9}$ (659) 1020$^{3}$ 1165$^{2}$ 1278$^{3}$ (1495) (1695) (1726) 3636$^{10}$4818$^{17}$ 5546$^{17}$ 6541$^{10}$ 6580$^{9}$ **>61+a 34f<**
**Diamond Circle** 2 br f Halling (USA) -Canadian Mill (USA) (Mill Reef (USA)) 6440$^{5}$ **>60f<**
**Diamond Dan (IRE)** 2 b g Foxhound (USA) -Kawther (Tap On Wood) 6171$^{16}$ **>39f<**
**Diamond Dazzler** 6 br g Sula Bula-Dancing Diamond (IRE) (Alzao (USA)) 5458$^{4}$ **><**
**Diamond George (IRE)** 3 b g Sri Pekan (USA) -Golden Choice (Midyan (USA)) 547$^{5}$ 640$^{6}$ 1841$^{11}$ **>54a 54f<**
**Diamond Green (FR)** 3 bb c Green Desert (USA) -Diamonaka (FR) (Akarad (FR)) 1653a$^{3}$ 2161a$^{2}$ 2956$^{2}$ 3791a$^{2}$ 5332a$^{2}$ 5782$^{8}$ 6486a$^{8}$ **>121f<**
**Diamond Heritage** 2 ch c Compton Place-Eccolina (Formidable (USA)) 3818$^{12}$ 5772$^{10}$ 6305$^{5}$ **>43f<**
**Diamond Hombre (USA)** 2 gr c Two Punch (USA) -Flowing (USA) (El Gran Senor (USA)) 2502$^{4}$ 4143$^{6}$ 4514$^{7}$ **>62a 68f<**
**Diamond Josh** 2 ch g Primo Dominie-Exit (Exbourne (USA)) 2947$^{3}$ 6454$^{6}$ **>69f<**
**Diamond Katie (IRE)** 2 b f Night Shift (USA) -Fayrooz (USA) (Gulch (USA)) 5270$^{8}$ 5648$^{7}$ 5943$^{3}$ **>76f<**
**Diamond Lodge** 3 ch f Grand Lodge (USA) -Movieland (USA) (Nureyev (USA)) 1395$^{4}$ (2182) 2557$^{2}$ (3159) (3943) (4230) 4442$^{5}$ 5294$^{2}$ **>100 f<**
**Diamond Max (IRE)** 6 b g Nicolotte-Kawther (Tap On Wood) 5941$^{20}$ 6568$^{4}$ **>90a 97f<**
**Diamond Orchid (IRE)** 4 gr f Victory Note (USA) -Olivia s Pride (IRE) (Digamist (USA)) 472$^{3}$ 715$^{2}$ 812$^{4}$ 995$^{2}$ 1856$^{2}$ (2375) 3088$^{5}$ (3429) 4146$^{12}$4603$^{2}$ 5456$^{12}$ 6065$^{4}$ **>53a 64f<**
**Diamond Racket** 4 b g Cyrano De Bergerac-Reina (Homeboy) 499$^{15}$ 944$^{6}$ 1089$^{11}$ 1190$^{9}$ **>42a 56f<**
**Diamond Ribby (IRE)** 3 br f Desert Sun-Kathleen s Dream (USA) (Last Tycoon) 999$^{9}$ **>18a 11f<**
**Diamond Ring** 5 b m Magic Ring (IRE) -Reticent Bride (IRE) (Shy Groom (USA)) 1584$^{5}$ 2350$^{14}$ 2869$^{3}$ 3227$^{15}$ 3772$^{3}$ 4044$^{6}$ 4557$^{2}$ 4854$^{5}$5261$^{9}$ 6059$^{8}$ **>41a 53f<**
**Diamonds And Dust** 2 b c Mister Baileys-Dusty Shoes (Shareef Dancer (USA)) 3946$^{4}$ 4488$^{3}$ 4967$^{4}$ (5314) 5810$^{7}$ 6174$^{6}$ **>91f<**
**Diamond Shannon (IRE)** 3 b f Petorius-Balgren (IRE) (Ballad Rock) 1127$^{7}$ 1472$^{7}$ 1941$^{5}$ (2811) 2990$^{2}$ 3615$^{14}$ 5618$^{19}$ 6290$^{8}$6577$^{6}$ **>66a 48f<**
**Diamonds Will Do (IRE)** 7 b m Bigstone (IRE) -Clear Ability (IRE) (Be My Guest (USA)) 3695$^{6}$ **>64f<**
**Diamond Tango (FR)** 3 b f Acatenango (GER) -Diamond Dance (FR) (Dancehall (USA)) 2028a$^{5}$ 5033a$^{4}$ 5501a$^{5}$ 5966a$^{4}$ **>109f<**
**Diamond Way (USA)** 3 ch c Boundary (USA) -Discover Silver (USA) (Valid Appeal (USA)) (521) **>67a 57f<**
**Diaphanous** 6 b m Beveled (USA) -Sharp Venita (Sharp Edge) 443$^{8}$ 538$^{7}$ 1000$^{9}$ 3575$^{17}$ 3810$^{14}$ 4440$^{7}$ 4881$^{13}$5408$^{13}$ 5844$^{7}$ 6089$^{6}$ **>46a 47f<**
**Diatonic** 2 b g Deploy-Vic Melody (FR) (Old Vic) 1115$^{9}$ 2405$^{8}$ 2858$^{8}$ 3278$^{2}$ 5477$^{7}$ **>47a 47f<**
**Dickie Deadeye** 7 b g Distant Relative-Accuracy (Gunner B) 1109$^{6}$ 1298$^{5}$ 1503$^{2}$ 1715$^{2}$ 2084$^{3}$ (3695) (3866) 4486$^{3}$ 4814$^{4}$ 5229$^{9}$5869$^{3}$ 5997$^{8}$ **>61a 76f<**
**Dick The Taxi** 10 b g Karlinsky (USA) -Another Galaxy (IRE) (Anita s Prince) 592$^{3}$ 2753$^{3}$ 3018$^{9}$ 3291$^{4}$ **>71f<**
**Diction (IRE)** 2 br f Diktat-Waft (USA) (Topsider (USA)) 2364$^{7}$ 2622$^{5}$ (3278) (4094) 4278$^{5}$ 4878$^{2}$ **>72a 36f<**
**Didnt Tell My Wife** 5 ch g Aragon-Bee Dee Dancer (Ballacashtal (CAN)) 1877$^{6}$ 2406$^{6}$ 2883$^{9}$ 3520$^{4}$ 3911$^{3}$ (4719) 4912$^{3}$ 5317$^{15}$ 5657$^{6}$6311$^{3}$ 6343$^{8}$ **>72a 74f<**
**Didoe** 5 br m Son Pardo-My Diamond Ring (Sparkling Boy) 3103$^{15}$ 3489$^{7}$ 3827$^{9}$ (4042) 4519$^{2}$ (4771) 5017$^{8}$ 5411$^{17}$ 5557$^{10}$ **>35 a 57f<**
**Diego Cao (IRE)** 3 b g Cape Cross (IRE) -Lady Moranbon (USA) (Trempolino (USA)) (5568) 5998$^{4}$ 6128$^{2}$ 6396$^{8}$ **>74a 95f<**
**Diequest (USA)** 3 ch c Diesis-Nuance (IRE) (Rainbow Quest (USA)) 4813$^{8}$ 5007$^{8}$ 5999$^{13}$ **>57f<**
**Different Planet** 3 b c Inchinor-Take Heart (Electric) 2114$^{4}$ 2519$^{4}$ 3161$^{5}$ **>75f<**
**Digger (IRE)** 5 ch g Danzig Connection (USA) -Baliana (Midyan (USA)) (516) 629$^{4}$ 679$^{9}$ 795$^{2}$ 899$^{5}$ 1109$^{17}$ **>78a 71f<**
**Digital** 7 ch g Safawan-Heavenly Goddess (Soviet Star (USA)) 1065$^{10}$ 1132$^{3}$ 1246$^{4}$ 1456$^{16}$ 1828$^{3}$ 1927$^{6}$ 2206$^{8}$ 2575$^{8}$2891$^{5}$ 3079$^{2}$ 3235$^{2}$ 3755$^{2}$ 4120$^{7}$ 4273$^{8}$ 4742$^{8}$ 4908$^{2}$5112$^{2}$ 5468$^{12}$ 5921$^{5}$ 6191$^{7}$ 6477$^{6}$ 6525$^{4}$ **>93a 96f<**
**Diktatit** 2 b f Diktat-Mystique Smile (Music Boy) 2177$^{13}$ 4507$^{5}$ 4620$^{7}$ **>49f<**
**Diktatorial** 2 br c Diktat-Reason To Dance (Damister (USA)) 4295$^{7}$ (4922) (5895) **>104f<**
**Dil** 9 b g Primo Dominie-Swellegant (Midyan (USA)) 612$^{7}$ 807$^{6}$ **>43a 30f<**
**Dilag (IRE)** 2 b f Almutawakel-Terracotta Hut (Habitat) 4962a$^{8}$ **>89f<**
**Dildaar (USA)** 3 ch c Woodman (USA) -Cap Rouge (USA) (Summer Squall (USA)) (753a) **><**
**Diligent Lad** 4 b g Secret Appeal-Mohibbah (USA) (Conquistador Cielo (USA)) 1786$^{9}$ 2408$^{13}$ **>53?f<**
**Diliza** 5 b m Dilum (USA) -Little White Lies (Runnett) 468$^{4}$ 554$^{8}$ 659$^{6}$ **>41a 61df<**
**Dillagi (USA)** 3 bb c Family Calling (USA) -Native Northrop (USA) (Northrop (USA)) 920a$^{5}$ **><**
**Dilys** 5 b m Efisio-Ramajana (USA) (Shadeed (USA)) 536$^{8}$ **>61a 60f<**
**Dine N Dash** 3 ch g Komaite (USA) -Instinction (Never So Bold) 4683$^{11}$ 5147$^{6}$ 5338$^{11}$ 6404$^{9}$ **>4a 27f<**
**Dingley Lass** 4 ch f Fleetwood (IRE) -Riverine (Risk Me (FR)) 4545$^{6}$ 5073$^{10}$ 5354$^{12}$ **>35a 56f<**
**Dinner Date** 2 ch c Groom Dancer (USA) -Misleading Lady (Warning) 6330$^{9}$ **>54+f<**
**Dinyeper** 5 ch h Vettori (IRE) -Early Call (Kind Of Hush) 756a$^{4}$ 979a$^{2}$ 1147a$^{10}$ **>116a<**
**Dipterous (IRE)** 2 b f Mujadil (USA) -Dajarra (IRE) (Blushing Groom (FR)) 3859a$^{11}$ **>80f<**
**Directa Star (GER)** 3 b c Dashing Blade-Directa Germania (IRE) (Priolo (USA)) 2335a$^{2}$ **>97f<**
**Disabuse** 4 ch g Fleetwood (IRE) -Agony Aunt (Formidable (USA)) 541$^{2}$ (588 ) 902$^{3}$ 1042$^{4}$ 1136$^{4}$ 2583$^{5}$ 3536$^{4}$ 3743$^{5}$4189$^{8}$ 5002$^{13}$ 6047$^{16}$ 6364$^{8}$ **>62a 57f<**
**Disco Diva** 3 ch f Spectrum (IRE) -Compact Disc (IRE) (Royal Academy (USA)) 1119$^{7}$ 2063$^{12}$ 2378$^{10}$ 2875$^{15}$ 4489$^{18}$ 6146$^{2}$ 6541$^{2}$ **>58a 66f<**
**Discomania** 2 b c Pursuit Of Love-Discomatic (USA) (Roberto (USA)) 3451$^{12}$ 3870$^{4}$ 4263$^{6}$ 5090$^{12}$ **>69f<**
**Discuss (USA)** 2 b f Danzig (USA) -Private Line (USA) (Private Account (USA)) 5943$^{2}$ **>81+f<**
**Disguise** 2 b c Pursuit Of Love-Nullarbor (Green Desert (USA)) 3808$^{5}$ 4172$^{2}$ 5507$^{4}$ 5865$^{2}$ **>78f<**
**Dishdasha (IRE)** 2 b g Desert Prince (IRE) -Counterplot (IRE) (Last Tycoon) 2234$^{14}$ 2858$^{7}$ 3100$^{3}$ 4186$^{10}$ 4567$^{14}$ 5636$^{12}$ **>45f<**
**Disparity (USA)** 3 b f Distant View (USA) -Eternity (Suave Dancer (USA)) 3204$^{14}$ 3882$^{4}$ 4545$^{2}$ 5382$^{7}$ 6013$^{15}$ 6495$^{15}$ **>60+a 57f<**
**Dispol Charm (IRE)** 2 br f Charnwood Forest (IRE) -Phoenix Venture (IRE) (Thatching) 5209$^{5}$ 5633$^{8}$ **>38f<**
**Dispol Evita** 5 ch m Presidium-She s A Breeze (Crofthall) 767$^{9}$ 892$^{4}$ 962$^{2}$ 3638$^{7}$ 3933$^{4}$ 4416$^{9}$ 4642$^{9}$5585$^{U}$ **>59a 57f<**
**Dispol Foxtrot** 6 ch m Alhijaz-Foxtrot Pie (Shernazar) 1660$^{2}$ 1931$^{3}$ **>40a 77f<**
**Dispol In Mind** 2 b f Mind Games-Sans Diablo (IRE) (Mac s Imp (USA)) 3620$^{2}$ 4124$^{3}$ (4770) **>64f<**
**Dispol Isle (IRE)** 2 gr f Trans Island-Pictina (Petong) 2860$^{4}$ 3514$^{4}$ 4804$^{4}$ 5233$^{4}$ 5606$^{3}$ 6003$^{5}$ 6113$^{6}$ 6333$^{3}$ **>78?f<**
**Dispol Katie** 3 ch f Komaite (USA) -Twilight Time (Aragon) 1774$^{14}$ 2143$^{6}$ 3744$^{3}$ 4331$^{5}$ 4626$^{18}$ 4862$^{2}$ 5440$^{9}$ 5605$^{11}$ **>85f<**
**Dispol Peto** 4 gr g Petong-Plie (Superlative) 686$^{11}$ 733$^{5}$ 772$^{2}$ 833$^{8}$ 1595$^{5}$ 2172$^{9}$ 2813$^{2}$ **>65a 65 f<**
**Dispol Veleta** 3 b f Makbul-Foxtrot Pie (Shernazar) 438$^{3}$ 569$^{7}$ (808) 864$^{4}$ (1214) 1418$^{3}$ 2134$^{13}$ 2390$^{10}$ (2988) 3312$^{12}$3780$^{9}$ 4882$^{11}$ 5223$^{2}$ **>77a 71f<**
**Dispol Verity** 4 b f Averti (IRE) -Fawley Mist (Suave Dancer (USA)) 2663$^{12}$ 3151$^{11}$ 3710$^{11}$ 3954$^{10}$ 5587$^{12}$ 6466$^{6}$ **>11a 26f<**
**Dissident (GER)** 6 b h Polish Precedent (USA) -Diasprina (GER) (Aspros (GER)) 784a$^{U}$ (1231) 1369$^{8}$ 1535$^{2}$ 1611$^{2}$ (1768) 1832$^{4}$ 2471$^{5}$ 2681$^{6}$ 3442$^{5}$5182$^{12}$ **>57a 94?f<**
**Distant Connection (IRE)** 3 b c Cadeaux Genereux-Night Owl (Night Shift (USA)) 1382$^{8}$ 1841$^{10}$ 1900$^{8}$ 2224$^{6}$ (2536) 2790$^{2}$ (3017) 3542$^{5}$ 3755$^{3}$ 4151$^{2}$4268$^{10}$ (5055) 5220$^{3}$ **>103+a 89f<**
**Distant Country (USA)** 5 b g Distant View (USA) -Memsahb (USA) (Restless Native) 1199$^{6}$ 1451$^{6}$ 1772$^{12}$ 2410$^{2}$ 2581$^{5}$ 2905$^{2}$ 4122$^{5}$ 4558$^{13}$4577$^{3}$ 5419$^{8}$ **>78f<**
**Distant Cousin** 7 b g Distant Relative-Tinaca (USA) (Manila (USA)) 1203$^{7}$ 2235$^{5}$ 2394$^{3}$ 2590$^{15}$ 3300$^{8}$ 4297$^{4}$ 5523$^{3}$ 5951$^{8}$6074$^{17}$ **>78 a 69f<**
**Distant King** 11 b g Distant Relative-Lindfield Belle (IRE) (Fairy King (USA)) 4350$^{16}$ **><**
**Distant Prospect (IRE)** 7 b g Namaqualand (USA) -Ukraine s Affair (USA) (The Minstrel (CAN)) 1880$^{4}$ 2684$^{2}$ 3310$^{12}$ 3725$^{12}$ 4226$^{3}$ 6215$^{8}$ 6573$^{2}$ **>99f<**
**Distant Times** 3 b c Orpen (USA) -Simply Times (USA) (Dodge (USA)) 1129$^{5}$ (1303) 1614$^{3}$ 2309$^{13}$ 2981$^{11}$ 3926$^{5}$ (4211) 4626$^{17}$ 4862$^{6}$ 5193$^{11}$ **>84f<**
**Distant Way (USA)** 3 b c Distant View (USA) -Grey Way (USA) (Cozzene (USA)) 2510a$^{4}$ **>106f<**
**Distinction (IRE)** 5 b g Danehill (USA) -Ivy Leaf (IRE) (Nureyev (USA)) 1455$^{14}$ 2108$^{5}$ (3757) (5438) 6528a$^{6}$ **>119f<**
**Distinctive Mind** 2 b g Mind Games-Primum Tempus (Primo Dominie) 5290$^{12}$ 5558$^{8}$ 5865$^{9}$ **>57f<**
**Distinctly Game** 2 b c Mind Games-Distinctly Blu (IRE) (Distinctly North (USA)) 1782$^{2}$ 2141$^{2}$ 2453$^{2}$ (2860) 4508$^{4}$ 4836$^{2}$ 5392$^{2}$ **>75a 103f<**
**Distinctlythebest** 4 b g Distinctly North (USA) -Euphyllia (Superpower) 4444$^{9}$ 4573$^{8}$ 5366$^{8}$ **>7f<**
**Dium Mac** 3 b g Presidium-Efipetite (Efisio) 4101$^{7}$ 4455$^{5}$ **>70f<**
**Diva Dancer** 4 ch f Dr Devious (IRE) -Catina (Nureyev (USA)) 567$^{15}$ 783$^{10}$ 2386$^{10}$ 2759$^{8}$ 3518$^{11}$ **>4a 35f<**
**Divani (IRE)** 2 b f Shinko Forest (IRE) -Supreme Crown (USA) (Chief s Crown (USA)) 2177$^{19}$ **><**
**Diverted** 3 b f Averti (IRE) -Whittle Rock (Rock City) 907$^{9}$ 1052$^{13}$ 1189$^{8}$ 1519$^{10}$ 3193$^{12}$ 4497$^{5}$ 4654$^{10}$ **>30a 30f<**
**Divina** 3 b f King s Theatre (IRE) -Heuston Station (IRE) (Fairy King (USA)) 683$^{11}$ 835$^{8}$ 1050$^{11}$ 1220$^{8}$ 1548$^{4}$ 1736$^{3}$ 1916$^{2}$2054$^{2}$ 2345$^{8}$ 3710$^{10}$ **>42a 19f<**
**Divine Diva** 2 b f Diktat-Maid To Dance (Pyramus (USA)) 3904$^{11}$ 4081$^{4}$ **>60f<**
**Divine Gift** 3 b c Groom Dancer (USA) -Child s Play (USA) (Sharpen Up) (1123) 1330$^{4}$ 6116$^{4}$ 6345$^{7}$ **>102f<**
**Divinely Decadent (IRE)** 2 br f Turtle Island (IRE) -Divine Prospect (IRE) (Namaqualand (USA)) (5569) 5939$^{9}$ **>87f<**
**Divine Proportions (USA)** 2 b f Kingmambo (USA) -Myth To Reality (FR) (Sadler s Wells (USA)) (3388a) (4184a) (4981a) (5979a) **>117+f<**
**Divine Spirit** 3 b g Foxhound (USA) -Vocation (IRE) (Royal Academy (USA)) 1883$^{12}$ 2131$^{12}$ 2309$^{17}$ 2552$^{3}$ 2877$^{6}$ (3077) 3273$^{7}$ 3702$^{3}$ 4059$^{6}$4289$^{13}$ 4688$^{3}$ **>88f<**
**Divine Task (USA)** 6 ch h Irish River (FR) -Set In Motion (USA) (Mr Prospector (USA)) 974a$^{3}$ **>106a 110f<**
**Diwan (IRE)** 6 b g Be My Guest (USA) -Nectarine (IRE) (Darshaan) 6055$^{11}$ 6402$^{9}$ **>20a<**
**Dixieanna** 2 ch f Night Shift (USA) -Dixielake (IRE) (Lake Coniston (IRE)) 5003$^{2}$ **>72f<**
**Dixie Dancing** 5 ch m Greensmith-Daylight Dreams (Indian Ridge) 1229$^{5}$ 3023$^{14}$ 3932$^{4}$ 4517$^{2}$ 4740$^{3}$ **>65a 65f<**
**Dixie Evans** 4 ch f Efisio-Kingpin Delight (Emarati (USA)) 1070a$^{10}$ 1634a$^{8}$ 3328a$^{12}$ 3547a$^{8}$ **>98f<**
**Dixie Queen (IRE)** 2 b f King Of Kings (IRE) -Dixieline City (USA) (Dixieland Band (USA)) 1960$^{5}$ 2617$^{7}$ 3679$^{9}$ 4135$^{3}$ 5227$^{10}$ 6020$^{9}$ **>35a 65f<**
**Dizzy Future** 2 b g Fraam-Kara Sea (USA) (River Special (USA)) 5838$^{7}$ 6172$^{9}$ **>54f<**
**Dizzy In The Head** 5 b g Mind Games-Giddy (Polar Falcon (USA)) 1361$^{19}$ (1994) 2582$^{6}$ 2779$^{3}$ (3010) 3125$^{2}$ (3339) 3501$^{14}$ 3732$^{9}$ 4011$^{12}$ (4635)6244$^{7}$ **>77f<**
**Dizzy Lizzy** 2 gr f Sendawar (IRE) -Black Velvet (FR) (Black Tie Affair) 3438$^{13}$ 3696$^{5}$ 5172$^{9}$ **>11f<**
**Dlinnoukiy (IRE)** 2 b f General Monash (USA) -Phantom Rain (Rainbow Quest (USA)) 3436a$^{11}$ **><**
**Dobby Road (FR)** 5 b h Grape Tree Road-Domino Queen (IRE) (Primo Dominie) 2162a$^{6}$ 2719a$^{5}$ 3162a$^{6}$ 4357a$^{5}$ 5333a$^{5}$ 5668a$^{10}$ **>103f<**
**Docduckout** 4 b g Bluegrass Prince (IRE) -Fayre Holly (IRE) (Fayruz) 510$^{P}$ **>63a 57f<**
**Docklands Blue (IRE)** 3 ch f Cadeaux Genereux-Copious (IRE) (Generous (IRE)) 414$^{2}$ 606$^{8}$ 708$^{7}$ 840$^{3}$ 983$^{6}$ 1086$^{4}$ 1119$^{3}$1300$^{8}$ 2098$^{8}$ **>55a 44f<**
**Docklands Dude (IRE)** 2 ch g Namid-Cheeky Weeky (Cadeaux Genereux) 1115$^{6}$ 1307$^{8}$ **>40f<**
**Docklands Grace (USA)** 2 gr f Honour And Glory (USA) -Afarel (USA) (Runaway Groom (CAN)) 2002$^{5}$ 4124$^{5}$ 4704$^{3}$ **>41a 60f<**
**Doctorate** 3 b c Dr Fong (USA) -Aunt Tate (Tate Gallery (USA)) 1104$^{9}$ (1519) 2569$^{2}$ 3452$^{5}$ 5055$^{3}$ 5265$^{9}$ (5652) 5921$^{8}$ 6244$^{4}$ **>89a 91f<**
**Doctor Dennis (IRE)** 7 b g Last Tycoon-Noble Lustre (USA) (Lyphard s Wish (FR)) 896$^{5}$ (930) 1018$^{6}$ 2325$^{8}$ (2707) 3593$^{14}$ 3828$^{6}$ 5597$^{14}$ 5930$^{10}$6405$^{10}$ **>55a 61f<**
**Doctor Dino (FR)** 2 ch c Muhtathir-Logica (IRE) (Priolo (USA)) 4963a$^{3}$ 6262a$^{2}$ **>98f<**
**Doctored** 3 ch g Dr Devious (IRE) -Polygueza (FR)

(Be My Guest (USA)) *913$^{8}$ 983$^{15}$ 1015$^{4}$ 1084$^{6}$* (1296) *(1736)* 1909$^{10}$ (2426) (3773) (3852) (4170) 4300$^{3}$4443$^{10}$ 4648$^{6}$ 4806$^{8}$ *5739$^{4}$* 5866$^{7}$ 5944$^{10}$ **>76a 83f<**
**Doctor Hilary 2** b c Mujahid (USA) -Agony Aunt (Formidable (USA)) 2087$^{4}$ (2256) 2478$^{2}$ 3290$^{3}$ 3975$^{2}$ 4581$^{5}$ **>93+f<**
**Doctor John 7** ch g Handsome Sailor-Bollin Sophie (Efisio) *539$^{4}$ 750$^{2}$ (839)* 1173$^{6}$ *1512$^{2}$ 1698$^{2}$* 2385$^{8}$ *4098$^{2}$*4609$^{4}$ 5638$^{12}$ 6005$^{2}$ **>49a 53f<**
**Doctor s Cave 2** b c Night Shift (USA) -Periquitum (Dilum (USA)) 2478$^{7}$ 2804$^{8}$ 3319$^{7}$ 3983$^{7}$ (4219) 4981a$^{8}$ 5649$^{9}$ 6188$^{11}$ **>89f<**
**Doctrine 3** b f Barathea (IRE) -Auspicious (Shirley Heights) 1327$^{4}$ 2971$^{8}$ 3699$^{5}$ 4367$^{9}$ **>94f<**
**Doire-Chrinn (IRE) 8** bb m Unblest-Princess Monarch (IRE) (Fairy King (USA)) 3328a$^{16}$ **>83f<**
**Doitforreel (IRE) 2** b f Princely Heir (IRE) -Chehana (Posse (USA)) 4364$^{12}$ 4804$^{8}$ 5334$^{3}$ (6272) 6456$^{5}$ 6544$^{3}$ **>82?f<**
**Doitnow (IRE) 3** b g Princely Heir (IRE) -Tony s Gift (Midyan (USA)) (2984) 3523$^{2}$ 3941$^{2}$ 4531$^{6}$ 5120$^{6}$ 5762$^{11}$ **>97f<**
**Dolce Piccata 3** ch f Piccolo-Highland Rhapsody (IRE) (Kris) 1388$^{15}$ 1829$^{5}$ 2181$^{4}$ 2549$^{5}$ 2981$^{7}$ 3203$^{8}$ 4059$^{9}$ 4289$^{11}$4688$^{7}$ 5473$^{6}$ *6016$^{9}$* **>60a 66f<**
**Dolce Voche (IRE) 3** b f Intikhab (USA) -Lindesberg (Doyoun) 3328a$^{13}$ **>84f<**
**Dollar Law 8** ch g Selkirk (USA) -Western Heights (Shirley Heights) 6311$^{14}$ **>42a 71f<**
**Dolly Peel 2** b f Josr Algarhoud (IRE) -Transylvania (Wolfhound (USA)) 4776$^{17}$ **><**
**Dolly Wotnot (IRE) 3** b f Desert King (IRE) -Riding School (IRE) (Royal Academy (USA)) 1394$^{5}$ 1998$^{16}$ 2442$^{5}$ 2783$^{3}$ **>33a 66f<**
**Dolma (FR) 3** b f Marchand De Sable (USA) -Young Manila (USA) (Manila (USA)) 1290a$^{2}$ 2193a$^{2}$ 2720a$^{3}$ 4595a$^{3}$ 6203a$^{2}$ **>56a 116f<**
**Dolphinelle (IRE) 8** b g Dolphin Street (FR) -Mamie s Joy (Prince Tenderfoot (USA)) *707$^{4}$ 821$^{3}$* **>52a 45f<**
**Dolzago 4** b g Pursuit Of Love-Doctor s Glory (USA) (Elmaamul (USA)) *(676) 919$^{2}$ 1054$^{3}$* 1832$^{13}$ 3181$^{9}$ 3437$^{8}$ **>74a 58f<**
**Domart (POL) 4** gr g Baby Bid (USA) -Dominet (POL) (Dixieland (POL)) 3181$^{10}$ **>54f<**
**Domdemil (IRE) 3** b c Fasliyev (USA) -Ma Bouche (IRE) (Shirley Heights) 2510a$^{11}$ **>98f<**
**Domenico (IRE) 6** b g Sadler s Wells (USA) -Russian Ballet (USA) (Nijinsky (CAN)) 2285$^{12}$ 2689$^{3}$ 2958$^{26}$ *4129$^{6}$* 4778$^{14}$ 5093$^{12}$ **>46a 46f<**
**Domestic Dispute (USA) 4** ch c Unbridled s Song (USA) -Majestical Moment (USA) (Magesterial (USA)) *1147a$^{6}$* 6486a$^{14}$ **>92a 94f<**
**Dominer (IRE) 2** b c Desert Prince (IRE) -Smart (IRE) (Last Tycoon) 2164$^{6}$ 2263$^{6}$ 3570$^{6}$ 5494$^{8}$ **>35f<**
**Domirati 4** b g Emarati (USA) -Julia Domna (Dominion) 2477$^{17}$ 2754$^{4}$ 3243$^{2}$ 3645$^{7}$ 4034$^{2}$ 4366$^{14}$ 5442$^{4}$ 6267$^{5}$ **>79+a 88f<**
**Donald (POL) 4** b g Enjoy Plan (USA) -Dahira (POL) (Dakota) 2429$^{3}$ 2787$^{14}$ 3244$^{6}$ 3776$^{13}$ **>64f<**
**Don Argento 3** gr g Sri Pekan (USA) -Grey Galava (Generous (IRE)) 1366$^{9}$ 2324$^{12}$ 2614$^{14}$ 3684$^{U}$ 3827$^{3}$ 3990$^{10}$ 4798$^{11}$ **>45f<**
**Donastrela (IRE) 3** b f Tagula (USA) -David s Star (Welsh Saint) *1226$^{6}$* 1507$^{11}$ 2402$^{11}$ (3190) 3773$^{4}$ (4045) 4307$^{3}$ 4618$^{3}$ 5300$^{5}$ 5635$^{4}$5935$^{7}$ **>48a 74f<**
**Donatello (GER) 3** b c Auenadler (GER) -Devika (Alzao (USA)) 2335a$^{7}$ **>85f<**
**Donegal Shore (IRE) 5** b h Mujadil (USA) -Distant Shore (IRE) (Jareer (USA)) *433$^{4}$ 498$^{2}$ 782$^{2}$ 910$^{4}$ 1681$^{3}$ 3380$^{7}$* 3742$^{6}$*3804$^{7}$* 4605$^{4}$ *4881$^{8}$* **>53a 45f<**
**Don Fayruz (IRE) 12** b g Fayruz-Gobolino (Don) *554$^{12}$* **>63a 65f<**
**Don Fernando 5** b h Zilzal (USA) -Teulada (USA) (Riverman (USA)) 1302$^{7}$ 2285$^{5}$ 2958$^{10}$ 3076$^{6}$ 3644$^{2}$ **>91f<**
**Donna Francesca 3** ch f Dr Fong (USA) -Grey Angel (Kenmare (FR)) 1805a$^{10}$ **><**
**Donna s Double 9** ch g Weldnaas (USA) -Shadha (Shirley Heights) 3401$^{5}$ 3738$^{6}$ 3903$^{3}$ 4132$^{4}$ 4328$^{3}$ 4826$^{4}$ 5187$^{6}$ 5581$^{2}$5714$^{16}$ 5817$^{2}$ 5993$^{8}$ **>62 f<**
**Donna Vita 3** b f Vettori (IRE) -Soolaimon (IRE) (Shareef Dancer (USA)) 1963$^{4}$ 3541$^{8}$ 4749$^{9}$ 5572$^{13}$ **>71+a 86f<**
**Don Pasquale 2** br c Zafonic (USA) -Bedazzling (IRE) (Darshaan) *6453$^{5}$* **>66a<**
**Don Pele (IRE) 2** b c Monashee Mountain (USA) -Big Fandango (Bigstone (IRE)) 2300$^{15}$ 2609$^{2}$ (3157) (3907) 5392$^{22}$ **>106f<**
**Don Raphael (AUS) 5** b g Runyon (IRE) -Rain Queen (AUS) (Been There (AUS)) 6528a$^{20}$ **>100f<**
**Dont Call Me Babe 2** b g Easycall-Ok Babe (Bold Arrangement) 6322$^{13}$ **>13f<**
**Dont Call Me Derek 3** b g Sri Pekan (USA) -Cultural Role (Night Shift (USA)) *414$^{5}$ 708$^{6}$ 1057$^{8}$* 4327$^{7}$ 4483$^{7}$ 4680$^{2}$ *(4882)* 5156$^{3}$5868$^{2}$ (6006) *(6025)* (6083) **>88a 84+f<**
**Dont Let Go 3** b f Danzero (AUS) -Il Doria (IRE) (Mac s Imp (USA)) 3161$^{14}$ 3261$^{8}$ **>24a<**
**Don t Matter 4** b f Petong-Cool Run (Deep Run) 3383$^{8}$ **>58f<**
**Don t Sioux Me (IRE) 6** b g Sadler s Wells (USA) -Commanche Belle (Shirley Heights) *706$^{10}$* 3590$^{5}$ 5866$^{10}$ **>54a 77f<**
**Don t Tell Mum (IRE) 2** b f Dansili-Zinnia (Zilzal (USA)) (2427) 2970$^{6}$ 3938$^{2}$ **>91f<**
**Don t Tell Rosey 4** b g Barathea (IRE) -Patsy Western (Precocious) *1230$^{7}$* **>64a 76f<**
**Dont Tell Simon 3** ch g Keen-Circumnavigate (Slip Anchor) 2145$^{10}$ 2555$^{7}$ 4781$^{11}$ **>6f<**
**Don t Tell Trigger (IRE) 2** b f Mujadil (USA) -Ordinate (Nashwan (USA)) 2057$^{10}$ 2296$^{6}$ (2515) 3886$^{11}$ 4089$^{7}$ (4521) 4958a$^{8}$ 5335$^{7}$ **>71 f<**
**Dont Worry Bout Me (IRE) 7** b g Brief Truce (USA) -Coggle (Kind Of Hush) *857$^{8}$* **>21a 61f<**
**Donyana 2** b f Mark Of Esteem (IRE) -Albarsha (Mtoto) 4753$^{5}$ (5247) 5719$^{4}$ **>87f<**
**Doohulla (USA) 3** ch f Stravinsky (USA) -Viva Zapata (USA) (Affirmed (USA)) 2897$^{5}$ 3598$^{7}$ **>80a 95f<**
**Dooie Dancer 2** b c Entrepreneur-Vayavaig (Damister (USA)) 6441$^{7}$ **>57f<**
**Dora Corbino 4** b f Superpower-Smartie Lee (Dominion) *697$^{5}$ 935$^{3}$ 991$^{2}$ 1077$^{9}$ 1514$^{6}$* 1593$^{3}$ 1862$^{2}$1989$^{4}$ *2230$^{2}$* 2347$^{3}$ 3341$^{4}$ *3803$^{7}$* **>45a 47f<**
**Dorange (ITY) 2** b c Distinctly North (USA) -Darubena (ITY) (Chief Singer) 3568a$^{4}$ **><**
**Dorchester 7** b g Primo Dominie-Penthouse Lady (Last Tycoon) *866$^{6}$* 1608$^{5}$ 2091$^{7}$ **>84a 86f<**
**Doric (USA) 3** ch c Distant View (USA) -Doree (USA) (Stop The Music (USA)) 1289a$^{4}$ **>90f<**
**Doringo 3** b c Prince Sabo-Mistral s Dancer (Shareef Dancer (USA)) 1366$^{8}$ 1674$^{12}$ 2950$^{11}$ 5830$^{8}$ 6184$^{2}$ **>54f<**
**Dorisima (FR) 3** ch f Mark Of Esteem (IRE) -Suhaad (Unfuwain (USA)) 5803$^{8}$ 6095$^{9}$ **>39f<**
**Doris Souter (IRE) 4** bb f Desert Story (IRE) -Hope And Glory (USA) (Well Decorated (USA)) *892$^{2}$ 1053$^{9}$ 1203$^{5}$* 2062$^{9}$ 2403$^{3}$ 2738$^{10}$ 3327$^{3}$ 3591$^{2}$ **>78a 74f<**
**Dormy Two (IRE) 4** b f Eagle Eyed (USA) -Tartan Lady (IRE) (Taufan (USA)) 1560$^{13}$ 1866$^{3}$ 2171$^{6}$ **>55f<**
**Dorn Dancer (IRE) 2** b f Danehill Dancer (IRE) -Appledorn (Doulab (USA)) 2213$^{9}$ (2749) 3011$^{5}$ 3753$^{8}$ 5391$^{21}$ 5606$^{6}$ 6003$^{15}$ 6523$^{9}$ **>79f<**
**Dorn Hill 2** b f Lujain (USA) -Benedicite (Lomond (USA)) 2164$^{5}$ 2522$^{13}$ **>32f<**
**Dorothy s Friend 4** b g Grand Lodge (USA) -Isle Of Flame (Shirley Heights) 2684$^{10}$ (3095) (3725) 4218$^{8}$ (4529) 4858$^{10}$ **>100+f<**
**Dorr (ITY) 3** b f Stuck (USA) -Donna Vesa (ITY) (Flash Of Steel) 1778a$^{3}$ **>94f<**
**Dorset (USA) 3** b f Deputy Commander (USA) -Draconienne (USA) (Trempolino (USA)) 1395$^{16}$ 2168$^{14}$ 2832$^{6}$ **>29f<**
**Dorubako (IRE) 3** b c Danzig (USA) -Spring Pitch (USA) (Storm Cat (USA)) 3732$^{4}$ 4595a$^{18}$ **>103+f<**
**Dossier 4** b f Octagonal (NZ) -Papering (IRE) (Shaadi (USA)) 1070a$^{5}$ 1254a$^{8}$ **>103f<**
**Double Aspect (IRE) 3** b g Dr Fong (USA) -Spring (Sadler s Wells (USA)) 2085$^{4}$ (3245) 4173$^{5}$ 4777$^{4}$ **>94f<**
**Double Blade 9** b g Kris-Sesame (Derrylin) 2214$^{6}$ 4275$^{8}$ **>60a 53 f<**
**Double Coeur (FR) 3** b f Septieme Ciel (USA) -Chene De Coeur (FR) (Comrade In Arms) 1290a$^{5}$ **>92f<**
**Double Dagger Lady (USA) 3** b f Diesis-Darby Jane (CAN) (Silver Deputy (CAN)) 2374$^{6}$ 2950$^{4}$ 3592$^{5}$ 5155$^{6}$ *6537$^{3}$* **>62a 66f<**
**Double Deputy (IRE) 3** b c Sadler s Wells (USA) -Janaat (Kris) (5891) (6332) **>88f<**
**Double Green (IRE) 3** b f Green Tune (USA) -Green Bend (USA) (Riverman (USA)) 5433a$^{3}$ 6382a$^{8}$ **>102f<**
**Double Honour (FR) 6** gr g Highest Honor (FR) -Silver Cobra (USA) (Silver Hawk (USA)) 3076$^{8}$ **>107f<**
**Double Kudos (FR) 2** gr c Highest Honor (FR) -Black Tulip (FR) (Fabulous Dancer (USA)) 4198$^{2}$ 4966$^{7}$ 5522$^{7}$ **>75f<**
**Double M 7** ch g First Trump-Girton Degree (Balliol) *491$^{4}$ (560) 573$^{3}$ 624$^{7}$ 674$^{2}$ 928$^{4}$ 1057$^{2}$ (1087) 1230$^{11}$* 1368$^{6}$ 2166$^{5}$ 2246$^{5}$ 2399$^{3}$ 2724$^{2}$ (2885) 3084$^{3}$ 3243$^{6}$*4026$^{6}$* (4232) 4400$^{2}$ 4748$^{9}$ 5008$^{7}$ 5253$^{9}$ 5512$^{3}$ 5734$^{7}$ **>68a 74f<**
**Double Obsession 4** b c Sadler s Wells (USA) -Obsessive (USA) (Seeking The Gold (USA)) 2022$^{13}$ 2365$^{7}$ 2684$^{7}$ (2958) 3772$^{5}$ 4270$^{4}$ 4529$^{2}$ 4983a$^{4}$ **>111f<**
**Double Ransom 5** b g Bahamian Bounty-Secrets Of Honour (Belmez (USA)) *525$^{2}$ 623$^{3}$ (933) 988$^{4}$* 1527$^{2}$ (1783) 2120$^{6}$ 3401$^{2}$ (4511) 4826$^{6}$6566$^{5}$ **>63a 73f<**
**Double Spey 5** b g Atraf-Yankee Special (Bold Lad (IRE)) 2649$^{6}$ **>36a 36f<**
**Double Turn 4** ch g Double Trigger (IRE) -Its My Turn (Palm Track) 2273$^{5}$ 2653$^{10}$ 2977$^{6}$ **>70f<**
**Double Vodka (IRE) 3** bb g Russian Revival (USA) -Silius (Junius (USA)) 1755$^{12}$ 2134$^{6}$ 2571$^{2}$ 3312$^{4}$ 3561$^{7}$ (4050) (4395) (4780) 5950$^{11}$ 5990$^{3}$ 6115$^{11}$ **>82+f<**
**Doughty 2** b g Bold Edge-Marquante (IRE) (Brief Truce (USA)) 2749$^{9}$ 3192$^{10}$ 3588$^{19}$ 4040$^{11}$ **>29f<**
**Dove Cottage (IRE) 2** b c Great Commotion (USA) -Pooka (Dominion) 2208$^{6}$ 3104$^{5}$ 3570$^{3}$ (4475) 4890$^{2}$ 5466$^{5}$ 5885$^{4}$ **>67f<**
**Dovedale 4** b f Groom Dancer (USA) -Peetsie (IRE) (Fairy King (USA)) 5770$^{7}$ 6082$^{4}$ *6481$^{5}$* **>49a 66f<**
**Dovedon Hero 4** ch g Millkom-Hot Topic (IRE) (Desse Zenny (USA)) 1401$^{17}$ 1768$^{11}$ 2277$^{2}$ 2671$^{8}$ 2893$^{4}$ 3276$^{6}$ 3678$^{12}$ 4174$^{2}$4550$^{7}$ 5273$^{3}$ 5951$^{4}$ *6025$^{2}$ 6278$^{4}$ 6450$^{2}$* **>81a 77f<**
**Dovedon Lass 3** b f Abou Zouz (USA) -Violette Sabo (Prince Sabo) 2092$^{8}$ **><**
**Dover Street 2** ch g Zafonic (USA) -Seeker (Rainbow Quest (USA)) 2904$^{5}$ 3157$^{8}$ 4048$^{10}$ 5477$^{9}$ 5988$^{4}$ 6265$^{9}$ **>62f<**
**Dovizioso (IRE) 2** b c Sri Pekan (USA) -Piccola Barbara (ITY) (Scouting Miller) 3435a$^{6}$ **><**
**Dowager 3** b f Groom Dancer (USA) -Rose Noble (USA) (Vaguely Noble) 1964$^{5}$ 2903a$^{4}$ 3522$^{6}$ 3940$^{3}$ 4286$^{11}$ 4779$^{7}$ 5121$^{8}$ 5454$^{10}$(5553) 6175$^{10}$ **>107+f<**
**Dower House 9** ch g Groom Dancer (USA) -Rose Noble (USA) (Vaguely Noble) *577$^{4}$ 649$^{6}$ 735$^{5}$ 768$^{4}$ 915$^{10}$ 1066$^{5}$* 1460$^{16}$5768$^{12}$ 6115$^{10}$ **>86a 86f<**
**Downland (IRE) 8** b g Common Grounds-Boldabsa (Persian Bold) 1526$^{8}$ 1994$^{2}$ (2260) 2735$^{6}$ 2965$^{5}$ *(3380) (3800) 4096$^{3}$* 4577$^{13}$ *4928$^{2}$*5316$^{6}$ 5583$^{5}$ 6094$^{17}$ **>81a 67 f<**
**Down To The Woods (USA) 6** ch g Woodman (USA) -Riviera Wonder (USA) (Batonnier (USA)) *1479$^{9}$* 1754$^{14}$ *2053$^{8}$* **>45a 45f<**
**Doyen (IRE) 4** b c Sadler s Wells (USA) -Moon Cactus (Kris) 2639$^{2}$ (3072) (4121) 5483a$^{7}$ 6216$^{7}$ **>131+f<**
**Dragon Flyer (IRE) 5** b m Tagula (IRE) -Noble Rocket (Reprimand) *1061$^{4}$* 1379a$^{2}$ 1685$^{7}$ 2041$^{8}$ 2636$^{11}$ 2955$^{11}$ 3732$^{3}$ 3976$^{4}$4091$^{3}$ 4269$^{11}$ 4805$^{4}$ (5372) 5671$^{11}$ 5893$^{7}$ 5933$^{3}$ 6177$^{9}$ **>88a 103f<**
**Dragon Prince 4** b g Zamindar (USA) -Nawafell (Kris) 3375$^{10}$ 3623$^{12}$ 3895$^{14}$ **>72a 74f<**
**Dragozza (ITY) 2** b f Sikeston (USA) -Mount Badeon (FR) (Scenic) 5577a$^{7}$ **><**
**Dralion 2** ch c Dr Fong (USA) -Rosy Outlook (USA) (Trempolino (USA)) 3424$^{5}$ 4064$^{5}$ 4611$^{15}$ **>60f<**
**Drama (IRE) 2** b f Sadler s Wells (USA) -Inkling (USA) (Seeking The Gold (USA)) 5325a$^{12}$ **>75f<**
**Dramatic Quest 7** b g Zafonic (USA) -Ultra Finesse (USA) (Rahy (USA)) 4086$^{7}$ 4398$^{12}$ 5229$^{10}$ 6047$^{11}$ **>60a 60f<**
**Dramatic Review (IRE) 2** b g Indian Lodge (IRE) -Dramatic Shift (IRE) (Night Shift (USA)) 1390$^{10}$ 2074$^{5}$ *2453$^{7}$* 5083$^{6}$ 5593$^{10}$ **>18a 63f<**
**Dramaticus 2** b c Indian Ridge-Corinium (IRE) (Turtle Island (IRE)) 1871$^{3}$ (5772) 5918$^{7}$ 6348$^{8}$ **>103f<**
**Drax 2** b g Mark Of Esteem (IRE) -Tanasie (Cadeaux Genereux) 2961$^{3}$ 3406$^{8}$ 3601$^{12}$ 5240$^{4}$ **>73f<**
**Dr Cerullo 3** b g Dr Fong (USA) -Precocious Miss (USA) (Diesis) *490$^{3}$ 522$^{3}$* 1688$^{10}$ 3584$^{2}$ 4486$^{4}$ 5203$^{4}$ 5728$^{3}$ 6339$^{8}$ **>77a 82f<**
**Dr Cool 7** b g Ezzoud (IRE) -Vayavaig (Damister (USA)) 4398$^{14}$ 4849$^{15}$ 5152$^{7}$ 5523$^{9}$ 6074$^{20}$ **>80f<**
**Dream Alive 3** b c Unfuwain (USA) -Petite Sonnerie (Persian Bold) 4492$^{8}$ 4813$^{3}$ 5146$^{4}$ 5554$^{14}$ **>64f<**
**Dream Along 2** b c Sinndar (IRE) -Dream Quest (Rainbow Quest (USA)) 5897$^{15}$ 6282$^{U}$ **>54+f<**
**Dream Easy 3** b g Pyramus (USA) -Hush Baby (IRE) (Ballacashtal (CAN)) *2853$^{8}$* 3094$^{5}$ 3948$^{4}$ 4726$^{5}$ 5237$^{3}$ 6096$^{16}$ 6461$^{17}$ **>13a 66f<**
**Dreamer s Lass 2** b f Pyramus (USA) -Qualitair Dream (Dreams To Reality (USA)) 2164$^{2}$ 2382$^{9}$ 3770$^{6}$ 5015$^{9}$ 5509$^{12}$ **>52f<**
**Dream Falcon 4** b g Polar Falcon (USA) -Pip s Dream (Glint Of Gold) 1305$^{16}$ **>53f<**
**Dream For Ever (FR) 7** b g Green Tune (USA) -Yerville (FR) (Luthier) 785a$^{12}$ **><**
**Dream Impact (USA) 3** b c Royal Academy (USA) -One Fit Cat (USA) (Storm Cat (USA)) 6513a$^{7}$ **>86f<**
**Dreaming Of You (IRE) 3** b f Spectrum (IRE) -Gay Hellene (Ela-Mana-Mou) (1842) 2284$^{15}$ 3327$^{7}$ **>78f<**
**Dreaming Waters 3** ch f Groom Dancer (USA) -Faraway Waters (Pharly (FR)) *1940$^{14}$* 2371$^{12}$ 3338$^{5}$ **>36a 54f<**
**Dream Magic 6** b g Magic Ring (IRE) -Pip s Dream (Glint Of Gold) 1460$^{4}$ 1604$^{8}$ 2084$^{5}$ 2537$^{13}$ 3842$^{12}$ 4737$^{3}$ 4814$^{2}$ 4950$^{3}$5183$^{5}$ 5568$^{3}$ 5768$^{14}$ 5950$^{10}$ 6444$^{9}$ **>82a 84f<**
**Dream Of Dubai (IRE) 3** b f Vettori (IRE) -Immortelle (Arazi (USA)) *869$^{8}$* 2377$^{16}$ 3156$^{8}$ 3700$^{12}$ *4517$^{10}$ 4941$^{12}$* 5691$^{15}$ **>61a 53f<**
**Dream Play (IRE) 3** b f In The Wings-Lustre (USA) (Halo (USA)) 3566a$^{3}$ 4566a$^{8}$ 6437a$^{3}$ **>101f<**
**Dream Scene (IRE) 3** b f Sadler s Wells (USA) -Highest Accolade (Shirley Heights) 5239$^{3}$ **>70f<**
**Dreams Come True (FR) 3** b f Zafonic (USA) -Moonlight Dreams (IRE) (Caerleon (USA)) 2925a$^{8}$ **>103f<**
**Dreams Forgotten (IRE) 4** b f Victory Note (USA) -Sevens Are Wild (Petorius) 2446$^{4}$ 4655$^{11}$ 5259$^{17}$ 5993$^{16}$ **>60a 70f<**
**Dreams United 3** br f Dancing Spree (USA) -Kaliala (FR) (Pharly (FR)) *6591$^{1}$* **>1a 35f<**
**Dream Tonic 2** b c Zafonic (USA) -Dream On Deya (IRE) (Dolphin Street (FR)) 2804$^{6}$ 6352$^{9}$ (6531) **>82f<**
**Dream Valley (IRE) 3** b f Sadler s Wells (USA) -Vallee Des Reves (USA) (Kingmambo (USA)) 5007$^{6}$ *5217$^{6}$* 5409$^{5}$ **>43a 63f<**
**Dreemon 2** ch g Tipsy Creek (USA) -Prudence (Grundy) 2736$^{7}$ 3438$^{3}$ 3931$^{8}$ *5052$^{9}$* 5335$^{10}$ 5909$^{9}$ **>53a 72f<**
**Dress Pearl 3** b f Atraf-Dress Design (IRE) (Brief Truce (USA)) *1190$^{7}$ 1571$^{3}$ 2187$^{2}$* **>30a 38f<**
**Dr Fox (IRE) 3** b g Foxhound (USA) -Eleonora D Arborea (Prince Sabo) *1202$^{11}$* 1467$^{11}$ 2040$^{7}$ 2359$^{7}$ 2886$^{16}$ 3229$^{13}$ **>35a 60f<**
**Drizzle 3** ch g Hector Protector (USA) -Rainy Sky (Rainbow Quest (USA)) *959$^{12}$* **>54a 62f<**
**Dr Julian (IRE) 4** b g Sesaro (USA) -Toda (Absalom) *472$^{12}$ 501$^{5}$ 568$^{8}$ 594$^{9}$* **>53a 53f<**
**Droopys Joel 2** b g Primo Dominie-Zaima (IRE) (Green Desert (USA)) *1117$^{9}$* 1324$^{10}$ 2616$^{7}$ **>7f<**
**Dr Raj 5** ch g In The Wings-Tawaaded (IRE) (Nashwan (USA)) *630$^{9}$ 726$^{11}$* **>39f<**
**Dr Sharp (IRE) 4** ch g Dr Devious (IRE) -Stoned Imaculate (IRE) (Durgam (USA)) 1615$^{8}$ (1958) 3300$^{2}$ (3449) 3725$^{9}$ 4512$^{6}$ (4934) 5288$^{14}$ 6460$^{4}$ 6575$^{2}$ **>92 f<**
**Dr Synn 3** br c Danzero (AUS) -Our Shirley (Shirley Heights) 1352$^{8}$ 1749$^{6}$ 2063$^{3}$ 3180$^{6}$ 3384$^{5}$ 3949$^{9}$ 4845$^{2}$ 4938$^{8}$5541$^{3}$ 5798$^{4}$ 6001$^{18}$ (6089) 6445$^{17}$ **>76f<**
**Dr Thong 3** ch c Dr Fong (USA) -Always On My Mind (Distant Relative) 1461$^{4}$ (1820) 2224$^{2}$ 3089$^{4}$ (3527) 3819$^{11}$ 4646$^{4}$ 5150$^{2}$ 5698$^{7}$ 5937$^{5}$ **>87f<**
**Druid 3** b g Magic Ring (IRE) -Country Spirit (Sayf El Arab (USA)) *521$^{9}$ 587$^{6}$* **>47a 26f<**
**Drum Dance (IRE) 2** b c Namid-Socialite (IRE) (Alzao (USA)) 2522$^{2}$ 2846$^{2}$ 5536$^{4}$ 6188$^{14}$ **>84f<**
**Drury Lane (IRE) 4** bb g Royal Applause-Ghost Tree (IRE) (Caerleon (USA)) *719$^{10}$ 799$^{9}$ 1032$^{11}$* 1665$^{18}$ 2219$^{15}$ 2656$^{4}$ 2965$^{11}$ 3098$^{14}$3935$^{4}$ 4013$^{14}$ 4308$^{11}$ 4542$^{8}$ 5346$^{19}$ **>71a 71df<**
**Dry Ice (IRE) 2** b c Desert Sun-Snowspin (Carwhite) 2736$^{5}$ (3336) 3983$^{5}$ 5466$^{6}$ 6338$^{8}$ **>82f<**
**Dry Wit (IRE) 3** b f Desert Prince (IRE) -Nawasib (IRE) (Warning) 2694$^{9}$ 3807$^{6}$ 4201$^{11}$ 4641$^{10}$ 5336$^{6}$ **>63f<**
**Dr Zalo 2** ch g Dr Fong (USA) -Azola (IRE) (Alzao (USA)) 5494$^{3}$ 6000$^{5}$ **>79 f<**
**Dual Purpose (IRE) 9** b g Rainbows For Life (CAN) -Gracieuse Amie (FR) (Gay Mecene (USA)) 4028$^{9}$ 4513$^{6}$ 4869$^{4}$ 5176$^{9}$ 5258$^{12}$ *6402$^{8}$* **>30a 67?f<**
**Dubaian Gift 5** b g Bahamian Bounty-Hot Lavender (CAN) (Shadeed (USA)) 1438$^{10}$ 1763$^{12}$ 2222$^{7}$ 2636$^{8}$ 2955$^{19}$ **>78a 109df<**
**Dubaian Mist 3** b f Docksider (USA) -Robellino Miss (USA) (Robellino (USA)) *597$^{12}$* 2380$^{5}$ 5639$^{2}$ **>42a 59f<**
**Dubai Down Under (NZ) 7** b g Prized (USA) -Skylarking (AUS) (Twig Moss (FR)) *688a$^{9}$ 979a$^{7}$* **>74a<**
**Dubai Dreamer (USA) 2** gr c Stephen Got Even (USA) -Blacktie Bid (USA) (Black Tie Affair) *6453$^{2}$* **>80a<**
**Dubai Dreams 4** b g Marju (IRE) -Arndilly (Robellino (USA)) *513$^{4}$ 588$^{2}$ 643$^{5}$ 671$^{8}$* 3472$^{7}$ 3921$^{10}$ *5002$^{6}$*5585$^{7}$ *6405$^{6}$* **>62a 62f<**
**Dubai Escapade (USA) 2** b f Awesome Again (CAN) -Sassy Pants (USA) (Saratoga Six (USA)) 2585$^{5}$ **>54f<**
**Dubai Honor 5** b h Highest Honor (FR) -Lovely Noor (USA) (Fappiano (USA)) *635a$^{4}$ 979a$^{6}$* 1003a$^{9}$ **>105a 74f<**
**Dubai Lightning (USA) 4** br g Seeking The Gold (USA) -Heraklia (USA) (Irish River (FR)) 6142$^{6}$ **>91+a 86+f<**
**Dubai Seven Stars 6** ch m Suave Dancer (USA) -Her Honour (Teenoso (USA)) 6215$^{14}$ **>79f<**
**Dubai Success 4** b c Sadler s Wells (USA) -Crystal Spray (Beldale Flutter (USA)) (1455) 1792$^{4}$ 2639$^{8}$ 3333a$^{2}$ 4746$^{2}$ 5662a$^{4}$ 6260a$^{8}$ **>119f<**
**Dubai Surprise (IRE) 2** b f King s Best (USA) -Toujours Irish (USA) (Irish River (FR)) 3905$^{3}$ (4560) (5149) 5779$^{8}$ 6510a$^{2}$ **>107f<**
**Dubai Tower (USA) 4** b c Imperial Ballet (IRE) -Multimara (USA) (Arctic Tern (USA)) 786a$^{7}$ **>73+a 76f<**
**Dubai Venture 2** ch c Rainbow Quest (USA) -Bombazine (IRE) (Generous (IRE)) 4523$^{6}$ **>77f<**
**Dubai World (USA) 6** b h Deputy Minister (CAN) -Good Mood (USA) (Devil s Bag (USA)) *757a$^{8}$* 849a$^{8}$ **>65a 84f<**
**Dubawi (IRE) 2** b c Dubai Millennium-Zomaradah (Deploy) (2644) (3672) (5678a) **>122+f<**
**Dubois 3** b c Sadler s Wells (USA) -Dazzle (Gone West (USA)) (2204) 2558$^{10}$ (3728) 3943$^{12}$ **>96f<**
**Dubonai (IRE) 4** ch g Peintre Celebre (USA) -Web Of Intrigue (Machiavellian (USA)) 2038$^{11}$ 2375$^{8}$ 2879$^{3}$ 2943$^{9}$ *4190$^{9}$ (5002)* 5235$^{9}$ *6024$^{4}$* **>66a 60f<**
**Dubrovsky 4** ch g Hector Protector (USA) -Reuval (Sharpen Up) 1623$^{4}$ 3299$^{8}$ 4442$^{6}$ 4754$^{7}$ **>91f<**
**Duca D Atri (IRE) 5** ch h Dr Devious (IRE) -When Lit (Northfields (USA)) 2155a$^{5}$ **>104f<**
**Ducal Diva 2** b f Bahamian Bounty-Lucky Thing (Green Desert (USA)) 3248$^{7}$ 4245$^{2}$ *4924$^{6}$* 5241$^{7}$ 5816$^{7}$ *5954$^{4}$ 6359$^{8}$* **>46a 61f<**
**Duchess Of Ross (IRE) 3** b f Fasliyev (USA) -Annemasse (FR) (Suave Dancer (USA)) 4251a$^{6}$ **>50f<**
**Duck Row (USA) 9** ch g Diesis-Sunny Moment (USA) (Roberto (USA)) 2044$^{2}$ 2678$^{9}$ 3355a$^{5}$ 4745$^{10}$ 5134$^{6}$ 6547$^{4}$ **>116f<**
**Duc s Dream 6** b g Bay Tern (USA) -Kala s Image (Kala Shikari) *984$^{7}$* 1198$^{7}$ (2595) 2787$^{8}$ 3050$^{9}$ 4070$^{5}$ 4196$^{10}$ 5658$^{3}$ 5935$^{3}$5993$^{5}$ **>69a 68f<**
**Dudley Docker (IRE) 2** b c Victory Note (USA) -Nordic Abu (IRE) (Nordico (USA)) 4016$^{15}$ **>43f<**
**Due Diligence (IRE) 5** ch g Entrepreneur-Kerry Project (IRE) (Project Manager) 1748$^{12}$ 2528$^{14}$ **>12a 72 f<**
**Duelling Banjos 5** ch g Most Welcome-Khadino (Relkino) *512$^{8}$* 1675$^{4}$ 2218$^{11}$ 3177$^{11}$ 5841$^{7}$ (6152) 6266$^{7}$ **>71a 75f<**
**Due Respect (IRE) 4** b c Danehill (USA) -Stylish (Anshan) 4371a$^{16}$ **>92f<**

**Due To Me** 4 gr f Compton Place-Always Lucky (Absalom) 702[5] 949[2] 1407[5] (1494) 1986[4] 2053[6] 2703[3] 2803[4] 3828[7] 4912[8] 5285[7] **>47a 40f<**

**Duggan s Dilemma (IRE)** 3 b g Lake Coniston (IRE) -Miss Ironwood (Junius (USA)) 752[8] 865[6] **>42f<**

**Duke Of Modena** 7 ch g Salse (USA) -Palace Street (USA) (Secreto (USA)) 5627[9] 5835[13] **>101 f<**

**Duke Of Venice (USA)** 3 b c Theatrical-Rihan (USA) (Dayjur (USA)) (1822) 2307[2] (3035) 4215[5] 4832[10] **>110 f<**

**Duke s View (IRE)** 3 b g Sadler s Wells (USA) -Igreja (ARG) (Southern Halo (USA)) 1843[10] 3160[13] 3394[5] 3556[5] 4080[18] 4467[6] 5021[10] 5549[6] 5751[12] **>46f<**

**Dulce De Leche** 3 b g Cayman Kai (IRE) -Give Us A Treat (Cree Song) 617[7] 660[6] 732[4] 817[12] 958[10] 1296[7] **>57a 45f<**

**Dulcimer** 3 ch f Piccolo-Superspring (Superlative) 1441[13] 1796[10] 2223[12] 2765[11] **>45f<**

**Dumaran (IRE)** 6 b g Be My Chief (USA) -Pine Needle (Kris) 915[9] 1125[14] 1328[2] 2066[3] 2637[5] 4887[9] 5650[6] 5941[RR] **>96a 101f<**

**Dumfries** 3 ch g Selkirk (USA) -Pat Or Else (Alzao (USA)) 1672[5] 1899[3] 2683[6] 3345[5] **>85f<**

**Dumnoni** 3 b f Titus Livius (FR) -Lamees (USA) (Lomond (USA)) 1063[10] 1225[6] 1506[3] 2400[11] 2694[4] (3089) 3698[3] 4236[2] 4756[2] 5937[9] **>81+a 88f<**

**Dunaskin (IRE)** 4 b g Bahhare (USA) -Mirwara (IRE) (Darshaan) 1114[15] 1821[8] 2022[7] 2982[5] 3716[6] 3953[3] (4136) (4540) (4856) 6044[11] **>105f<**

**Duncanbil (IRE)** 3 b f Turtle Island (IRE) -Saintly Guest (What A Guest) 2451[11] 2854[15] 3625[2] 3984[P] **>38a 49f<**

**Dundonald** 5 ch g Magic Ring (IRE) -Cal Norma s Lady (IRE) (Lyphard s Special (USA)) 776[6] 838[8] 861[8] 940[3] 994[4] 1037[7] 1177[6] 1263[5] 1376[8] 1513[3] 1583[3] 1885[3] 2228[9] 5929[6] **>34a 32f<**

**Dundry** 3 b g Bin Ajwaad (IRE) -China s Pearl (Shirley Heights) 3245[3] 3843[3] 4850[2] 5079[2] (5382) 5842[12] **>85a 81f<**

**Dunedin Rascal** 7 b g Piccolo-Thorner Lane (Tina s Pet) 448[15] 519[8] 575[10] 674[11] **>42a 42f<**

**Dune Raider (USA)** 3 b c Kingmambo (USA) -Glowing Honor (USA) (Seattle Slew (USA)) 2085[7] 3297[11] (5409) 6121[6] 6573[21] **>89+f<**

**Dunhill Star (IRE)** 4 b c Danehill (USA) -Sueboog (IRE) (Darshaan) 1124[2] **>78a 109f<**

**Dunlea (IRE)** 8 b g Common Grounds-No Distractions (Tap On Wood) 5926[16] **>25f<**

**Dunlea Dancer** 3 b g Groom Dancer (USA) -Be My Lass (IRE) (Be My Guest (USA)) 1559[3] 2567[4] 3042[2] (3396) 3479[6] **>70f<**

**Dunlows Minstrel** 2 ch c Opening Verse (USA) -Mary From Dunlow (Nicholas Bill) 5840[10] **>14f<**

**Dunmaglass (USA)** 2 ch g Cat Thief (USA) -Indian Fashion (USA) (General Holme (USA)) 3451[10] 3931[7] **>67f<**

**Dunmidoe** 4 b f Case Law-Rion River (IRE) (Taufan (USA)) 1592[8] 1889[8] **>37a 37f<**

**Dunn Deal (IRE)** 4 b g Revoque (IRE) -Buddy And Soda (IRE) (Imperial Frontier (USA)) 1033[3] 1230[10] (1368) 1738[2] 2118[7] 2274[5] 2423[14] 3524[6] 3810[6] 4299[5] **>69a 69+f<**

**Duo Leoni** 4 ch f Vettori (IRE) -La Dolce Vita (Mazilier (USA)) 928[6] (1039) **>68a 70f<**

**Du Pre** 3 b f Singspiel (IRE) -Child Prodigy (IRE) (Ballad Rock) 3209[7] 3554[2] (3993) 4368[3] 4814[10] **>80+f<**

**Durandal (JPN)** 5 ch h Sunday Silence (USA) -Sawayaka Princess (JPN) (Northern Taste (CAN)) 5982a[2] **>125f<**

**During (USA)** 4 bb c Cherokee Run (USA) -Blading Saddle (USA) (Blade (USA)) 1142a[6] **>115a<**

**Duroob** 2 b c Bahhare (USA) -Amaniy (USA) (Dayjur (USA)) 4598[8] 4866[3] 5688[3] (6197) **>65+a 72f<**

**Dusk Dancer (FR)** 4 b g Groom Dancer (USA) -Nightitude (Night Shift (USA)) 415[4] 559[12] 861[11] **>64a 74+f<**

**Dusky Warbler** 5 br g Ezzoud (IRE) -Bronzewing (Beldale Flutter (USA)) 1212[2] 1703[2] 2320a[8] 2998[12] 6137a[5] **>111f<**

**Dustini (IRE)** 2 ch c Rossini (USA) -Truly Modest (IRE) (Imp Society (USA)) 1292[3] 1638[5] 1853[3] 2095[10] 3418[7] **>19a 55f<**

**Dusty Carpet** 6 ch g Pivotal-Euridice (IRE) (Woodman (USA)) 418[13] 523[12] 618[7] 743[11] 2000[18] 4641[12] 5176[11] **>77a 77f<**

**Dusty Dane (IRE)** 2 b c Indian Danehill (IRE) -Teer On Eer (IRE) (Persian Heights) 1905[5] 3009[6] 3242[5] 3553[3] 4186[9] 4907[6] 5256[4] **>26a 68f<**

**Dusty Dazzler (IRE)** 4 ch f Titus Livius (FR) -Satinette (Shirley Heights) (556) 1061[6] 1685[12] 2094[5] **>102a 92f<**

**Dusty Wugg (IRE)** 5 b m General Monash (USA) -Welsh Berry (USA) (Sir Ivor) 670[5] 1025[3] 1092[7] 1197[5] 1283[7] **>42a 48f<**

**Dutch Gold (USA)** 4 ch c Lahib (USA) -Crimson Conquest (USA) (Diesis) 756a[9] 854a[2] 976a[9] 1455[10] 2067[5] 2678[2] 3484[5] 3724[9] **>77+a 112f<**

**Dutch Key Card (IRE)** 3 b g Key Of Luck (USA) -Fanny Blankers (IRE) (Persian Heights) 4929[5] (6578) **>75a 74f<**

**Duxford** 3 ch g Young Ern-Marsara (Never So Bold) 5844[8] 6015[2] **>63a 47f<**

**Dvinsky (USA)** 3 b c Stravinsky (USA) -Festive Season (USA) (Lypheor) 3702[10] 4268[14] 5952[6] 6577[4] **>62a 88+f<**

**Dynever (USA)** 4 br c Dynaformer (USA) -Flamboyance (USA) (Zilzal (USA)) 6491a[8] **>124a<**

E

**Eachy Peachy (IRE)** 5 ch m Perugino (USA) -Miss Big John (IRE) (Martin John) 5751[5] **>37 a 40 f<**

**E Adesso Basta (GER)** 2 b c Midyan (USA) -Exy Girl (IRE) (Alzao) 6542a[3] **><**

**Eager Angel (IRE)** 6 b m Up And At Em-Seanee Squaw (Indian Ridge) 474[2] 614[4] 686[9] (725) 803[5] (826) 909[10] 1424[3] 1531[9] 1992[13] 3376[9] 6580[11] **>60a 56f<**

**Eagle Feathers** 3 b f Indian Ridge-Flying Squaw (Be My Chief (USA)) 2145[7] **>27f<**

**Eagle Rise (IRE)** 4 b c Danehill (USA) -Evening Breeze (GER) (Surumu (GER)) 2608a[5] 3335a[3] 4378a[2] (5809a) **>113f<**

**Earl Of Links (IRE)** 2 ch c Raise A Grand (IRE) -Metroella (IRE) (Entitled) 1331[3] (1871) 3634[6] 3938[24] 4909[4] 5174[6] **>72f<**

**Earlsfield Raider** 4 ch g Double Trigger (IRE) -Harlequin Walk (IRE) (Pennine Walk) (729) **>56a 65f<**

**Earlston** 4 ch g Fleetwood (IRE) -Mystique Smile (Music Boy) 723[4] 810[7] 833[P] **>46a 73f<**

**Early March** 2 br c Dansili-Emplane (USA) (Irish River (FR)) (5432a) 5980a[2] 6510a[6] **>117f<**

**Early Wings (GER)** 2 b c Winged Love (IRE) -Emy Coasting (USA) (El Gran Senor (USA)) 6256a[3] **><**

**Easibet Dot Net** 4 gr g Atraf-Silvery (Petong) 908[4] 1245[9] 2174[2] 2424[3] 2659[9] 3166[5] 3781[3] (4328) 4830[3] 5517[4] 6096[3] 6533[2] **>56a 76f<**

**Easily Averted (IRE)** 3 b g Averti (IRE) -Altishaan (Darshaan) 524[5] 617[5] 868[10] 891[9] 1131[15] 2033[10] 2322[6] 4546[15] 5040[7] **>44a 44f<**

**Eastborough (IRE)** 5 b g Woodborough (USA) -Easter Girl (Efisio) 418[14] 554[3] (605) 820[7] 870[3] 970[4] 1187[3] 1308[4] 1675[6] 2032[6] 2810[2] 3450[3] 3773[2] 6450[8] **>68a 66f<**

**East Cape** 7 b g Bering-Reine De Danse (USA) (Nureyev (USA)) 440[5] 500[3] 671[7] (880) 1023[8] 1238[11] 1527[11] 2038[6] 3099[3] 3472[5] 4210[2] 5144[4] 5523[7] 6198[9] 6467[3] **>49a 53?f<**

**Eastern Blue (IRE)** 5 ch m Be My Guest (USA) -Stifen (Burslem) 625[6] 674[5] 930[3] **>56a 67f<**

**Eastern Breeze (IRE)** 6 b g Sri Pekan (USA) -Elegant Bloom (IRE) (Be My Guest (USA)) 418[4] (558) 842[2] 1062[7] 1397[5] 3756[13] (3912) 4285[P] **>108a 110?f<**

**Eastern Dagger** 4 b g Kris-Shehana (USA) (The Minstrel (CAN)) 1502[14] 2813[10] 3118[7] 3238[6] 3471[16] **>30 a 60?f<**

**Eastern Hope (IRE)** 5 b g Danehill Dancer (IRE) -Hope And Glory (USA) (Well Decorated (USA)) 1213[12] 1358[7] 2218[3] 2560[11] 2776[9] 3559[3] 3911[16] (5187) 6561[7] **>80f<**

**Eastern Magenta (IRE)** 4 b g Turtle Island (IRE) -Blue Heights (IRE) (Persian Heights) 1213[14] **>84f<**

**Eastern Mandarin** 2 b g Tipsy Creek (USA) -Hotel Street (USA) (Alleged (USA)) 5083[5] 5831[5] **>60f<**

**Eastern Pearl** 3 ch f Wolfhound (USA) -Wild Humour (IRE) (Fayruz) 1473[10] 1602[8] 2850[10] **>51a 70f<**

**Eastern Scarlet (IRE)** 4 b g Woodborough (USA) -Cuddles (IRE) (Taufan (USA)) 4605[11] 6362[5] 6404[4] **>47a 52f<**

**Easter Ogil (IRE)** 9 ch g Pips Pride-Piney Pass (Persian Bold) 419[5] 523[9] 559[3] 618[3] 645[2] 745[4] 765[12] 842[9] 882[12] 967[11] 1187[8] 1298[2] 1355[6] 1522[5] 2076[11] 2559[8] 6295[6] 6483[6] **>65 a 65 f<**

**East Flares** 4 gr g Environment Friend-Ijada Bianca (Absalom) 507[10] 765[11] **>41a 65f<**

**East Of Shannon (IRE)** 2 b f Surako (GER) -Evening Gold (Linamix (FR)) 5577a[6] **><**

**East Riding** 4 b f Gothenberg (IRE) -Bettynouche (Midyan (USA)) 1342[5] 1596[6] 1748[6] 1876[3] 2216[10] 2446[11] 2659[8] 2944[5] 3200[5] 3367[7] 3410[10] **>20a 39f<**

**Eastwell Magic** 2 b f Polish Precedent (USA) -Kinchenjunga (Darshaan) 4022[13] 5269[13] **>29a 21f<**

**Eastwell Violet** 4 b f Danzig Connection (USA) -Kinchenjunga (Darshaan) 3803[10] **>52a 32f<**

**Easy Feeling (IRE)** 2 b f Night Shift (USA) -Talena (Zafonic (USA)) 2296[3] 2544[3] 2686[4] (4325) 4958a[5] 5391[12] **>83f<**

**Easy Mover (IRE)** 2 ch f Bluebird (USA) -Top Brex (FR) (Top Ville) 4172[5] 4797[5] (5307) 5565[2] 5810[9] 6265[12] **>76f<**

**Eau Pure (FR)** 7 b m Epervier Bleu-Eau De Nuit (King s Lake (USA)) 1728[4] **>39a<**

**Ebaziyan (IRE)** 3 gr c Daylami (IRE) -Ebadiyla (IRE) (Sadler s Wells (USA)) 2796a[10] **>84f<**

**Ebinzayd (IRE)** 8 b g Tenby-Sharakawa (IRE) (Darshaan) 2935[9] 3564[7] 5190[5] 5608[5] **>80f<**

**Eboracum (IRE)** 3 b f Alzao (USA) -Fire Of London (Shirley Heights) 2569[8] 2989[9] 3478[2] 4049[2] 4307[11] 4562[4] (4989) (5223) (5582) **>32a 83f<**

**Eboracum Lady (USA)** 4 b f Lure (USA) -Konvincha (USA) (Cormorant (USA)) 3490[6] 3710[5] 4201[10] **>46a 57 f<**

**Eborarry (IRE)** 2 b g Desert Sun-Aztec Princess (Indian King (USA)) 3505[4] 4208[10] 4625[10] **>52f<**

**E Bride (USA)** 2 rg f Runaway Groom (CAN) -Fast Selection (USA) (Talinum (USA)) 3116[5] 5847[4] 6514[4] **>57f<**

**Ebtikaar (IRE)** 2 b c Darshaan-Jawlaat (USA) (Dayjur (USA)) 4523[8] **>74f<**

**Eccentric** 3 ch g Most Welcome-Sure Care (Caerleon (USA)) 845[4] (927) (1119) 1333[11] 3420[4] 3849[2] 4024[2] 4268[13] 5220[2] 6277[6] **>93a 63f<**

**Eccentricity (USA)** 2 ch f Kingmambo (USA) -Shiva (JPN) (Hector Protector (USA)) 3456[6] **>67f<**

**Echelon** 2 b f Danehill (USA) -Exclusive (Polar Falcon (USA)) (5118) 5779[7] **>104+f<**

**Echoes In Eternity (IRE)** 4 b f Spinning World (USA) -Magnificient Style (USA) (Silver Hawk (USA)) 1790[4] 2318a[4] 4323[5] (5394) 5966a[11] **>112f<**

**Echo Of Light** 2 b c Dubai Millennium-Spirit Of Tara (IRE) (Sadler s Wells (USA)) 6187[4] **>74+f<**

**Eclipse West (ARG)** 5 bl h Westbridge (USA) -Legitime (ARG) (Southern Halo (USA)) 5967a[11] **><**

**Ecole D Art (USA)** 3 b c Theatrical-Colour Chart (USA) (Mr Prospector (USA)) 5727a[10] **>97f<**

**Ecologically Right** 2 b f Entrepreneur-Logic (Slip Anchor) 5096[7] 5559[6] (5847) 6348[6] **>77f<**

**Ecology (IRE)** 6 b h Sri Pekan (USA) -Ecco Mi (IRE) (Priolo (USA)) 4984a[10] **>70f<**

**Ecomium (IRE)** 3 b c Sadler s Wells (USA) -Encens (Common Grounds) (1382) 5962a[2] **>115f<**

**Eddies Jewel** 4 b g Presidium-Superstream (Superpower) 2386[2] 3586[5] 3982[4] 4210[5] 4630[11] 5110[6] 5449[4] **>37f<**

**Eddington (USA)** 3 ch c Unbridled (USA) -Fashion Star (USA) (Chief s Crown (USA)) 2139a[3] 2701a[4] **>115a<**

**Eden Star (IRE)** 2 b f Soviet Star (USA) -Gold Prospector (IRE) (Spectrum (IRE)) 4191[10] 4611[18] 5053[11] 5334[11] **>31a 25f<**

**Edged In Gold** 2 ch f Bold Edge-Piccante (Wolfhound (USA)) 4670[6] 5070[9] **>36f<**

**Edge Fund** 2 b c Bold Edge-Truly Madly Deeply (Most Welcome) 1208[3] 1505[3] 2376[3] 2831[2] 3228[3] 3938[22] 4439[3] 4770[9] **>76f<**

**Edgehill (IRE)** 3 b g Ali-Royal (IRE) -Elfin Queen (IRE) (Fairy King (USA)) 3251[4] 4079[2] 5245[8] **>46a 71+f<**

**Edge Of Blue** 2 b c Bold Edge-Blue Goddess (IRE) (Blues Traveller (IRE)) 4117[6] 4643[3] 5003[10] 5400[5] **>69f<**

**Edge Of Italy** 2 ch f Bold Edge-Brera (IRE) (Tate Gallery (USA)) 5054[10] 5507[6] 5953[6] **>50a 60f<**

**Edith Bankes** 2 ch f Woodborough (USA) -Mayday Kitty (Interrex (CAN)) 5508[10] 6127[7] **>44f<**

**Edmo Yewkay (IRE)** 4 bb g Sri Pekan (USA) -Mannequin (IRE) (In The Wings) 1198[12] 1326[11] **>70f<**

**Effective** 4 ch g Bahamian Bounty-Efficacy (Efisio) 596[10] 680[3] 742[14] 1032[5] 1121[9] (1230) 1477[5] 2178[2] 2948[8] (3623) 4154[6] **>69a 73f<**

**Effie Gray** 5 b m Sri Pekan (USA) -Rose Bouquet (General Assembly (USA)) 715[12] 861[7] 972[4] **>41a 59f<**

**Efidium** 6 b g Presidium-Efipetite (Efisio) 1452[2] 1620[9] 1868[4] 2218[2] 2368[3] (2459) 2673[5] 3101[3] 3516[5] 3779[4] (4349) 4558[2] 5244[9] 5419[21] **>55a 83f<**

**Efimac** 4 b f Presidium-Efipetite (Efisio) 1824[11] 2528[10] 2778[7] 2979[4] 3169[10] 4260[7] 4624[12] 5305[3] **>49a 48f<**

**Efistorm** 3 b c Efisio-Abundance (Cadeaux Genereux) 5372[11] 5786[10] **>55f<**

**Eforetta (GER)** 2 ch f Dr Fong (USA) -Erminora (GER) (Highest Honor (FR)) 5616[8] 5996[10] 6446[12] **>24a 43f<**

**Efrhina (IRE)** 4 ch f Woodman (USA) -Eshq Albahr (USA) (Riverman (USA)) 4192[10] 4583[7] 4641[3] 4849[10] 4972[2] 5153[8] 5740[10] 5828[3] 5956[4] 6025[3] 6483[8] 6540[6] **>70a 71f<**

**Egerton (GER)** 3 b c Groom Dancer (USA) -Enrica (GER) (Niniski (USA)) 1656a[5] 2541a[2] 3565a[12] 4385a[9] 5329a[2] 5824a[4] **>118f<**

**Ego Trip** 3 b c Deploy-Boulevard Rouge (USA) (Red Ransom (USA)) 1667[8] (2251) 2760[3] 3837[9] 4389[4] (5546) 6006[2] (6209) 6533[6] **>74f<**

**Egyptian Lady** 2 ch f Bold Edge-Calypso Lady (IRE) (Priolo (USA)) 4930[11] 5233[8] 5307[5] **>64f<**

**Ehab (IRE)** 5 b g Cadeaux Genereux-Dernier Cri (Slip Anchor) 926[6] **>73a 63f<**

**Eidsfoss (IRE)** 2 b g Danehill Dancer (IRE) -Alca Egeria (ITY) (Shareef Dancer (USA)) 5746[5] 6126[9] **>49f<**

**Ei Ei** 9 b g North Briton-Branitska (Mummy s Pet) 2689[7] **>25f<**

**Eight (IRE)** 8 ch g Thatching-Up To You (Sallust) 4080[12] 4213[13] 4457[4] 4698[9] 6561[13] **>46a 56f<**

**Eight Ellington (IRE)** 3 b g Ali-Royal (IRE) -Where s Charlotte (Sure Blade (USA)) 1293[11] 2836[4] 3179[6] 3486[7] 4868[18] 6280[6] **>45a 61df<**

**Eight Woods (IRE)** 6 ch g Woods Of Windsor (USA) -Cd Super Targeting (IRE) (Polish Patriot (USA)) 517[3] 776[4] **>69a 90f<**

**Eijaaz (IRE)** 3 b c Green Desert (USA) -Kismah (Machiavellian (USA)) 2505[8] 3106[7] 3554[4] 5621[11] 6013[10] **>63a 64f<**

**Eisteddfod** 3 ch g Cadeaux Genereux-Ffestiniog (IRE) (Efisio) (1906) 2839[3] 3295[3] (3995) (4917) (5603) (5786) **>112+f<**

**Eizawina Docklands** 3 b g Zilzal (USA) -Sandrella (IRE) (Darshaan) 1794[22] 2113[7] 2311[12] 3002[12] 3271[8] 3529[7] **>47f<**

**Ejay** 5 bb m Emperor Jones (USA) -Lough Erne (Never So Bold) 541[9] 728[6] 813[9] 876[2] 1262[10] 1421[15] 1584[9] 1988[2] 2227[7] **>45a 49f<**

**Ekaterina** 2 b f Merdon Melody-Hsian (Shantung) 5633[9] 6195[14] 6464[6] **>37f<**

**Eklim (IRE)** 4 ch c Mark Of Esteem (IRE) -Tapage Nocturne (USA) (Irish River (FR)) 1982a[4] **>107f<**

**Ektishaaf** 2 b f Mujahid (USA) -Tahnee (Cadeaux Genereux) 3286a[8] **>70f<**

**Ela D Argent (IRE)** 5 b m Ela-Mana-Mou-Petite-D-Argent (Noalto) 549[8] **>32a 71f<**

**Ela Figura** 4 ch f The West (USA) -Chili Bouchier (USA) (Stop The Music (USA)) 1642[6] 1855[12] 2707[8] 2800[3] 2843[6] 3262[5] 3810[8] 4034[13] 4232[14] 4923[5] 5101[3] 6288[12] **>49a 53f<**

**Ela Jay** 5 b m Double Eclipse (IRE) -Papirusa (IRE) (Pennine Walk) 616[5] **>42a 42f<**

**Ela Merici (FR)** 4 b f Beaudelaire (USA) -Eternalsplendor (USA) (Miswaki (USA)) 3162a[0] 5333a[9] **>102f<**

**Ela Paparouna** 3 b f Vettori (IRE) -Pretty Poppy (Song) 1530[3] 2112[8] 2577[6] 3209[3] 4020[2] 4551[3] 5537[3] **>77f<**

**Ela Re** 5 ch g Sabrehill (USA) -Lucia Tarditi (FR) (Crystal Glitters (USA)) 546[4] 724[7] 2816[4] 4189[4] 6406[6] **>51a 57 f<**

**El Chaparral (IRE)** 4 b g Bigstone (IRE) -Low Line (High Line) 1352[7] 1796[6] 2118[10] 2483[12] 3386[2] 3841[11] 4192[2] 4615[10] (4814) 5017[11] 5135[9] 5381[9] **>57a 80f<**

**El Coto** 4 b c Forzando-Thatcherella (Thatching) 1125[17] (1456) 1758[5] 2044[5] 2283[9] 2623[8] 2969[13] 3673[4] 4120[20] 4287[4] 4887[8] 5941[9] **>111f<**

**El Dessert (GER)** 5 b h Green Desert (USA) -Elisha (GER) (Konigsstuhl (GER)) 2508a[8] **>107f<**

**Eleazar (GER)** 3 b c Alkalde (GER) -Eicidora (GER) (Surumu (GER)) 1656a[6] 2541a[5] **>94f<**

**Election Seeker (IRE)** 2 b g Intikhab (USA) -Scottish Eyes (USA) (Green Dancer (USA)) 4290[8] 4730[14] 5114[9] 5535[7] 5885[15] **>62f<**

**Electras Dream (IRE)** 3 ch f Docksider (USA) -Elli Pyrelli (IRE) (Tenby) 2505[16] 3304[11] 3882[9] 6119[6] **>32a 54f<**

**Electrique (IRE)** 4 b g Elmaamul (USA) -Majmu (USA) (Al Nasr (FR)) 4691[8] 5297[18] 5739[9] 6156[11] 6395[9] **>65a 68f<**

**Electrocutionist (USA)** 3 b c Red Ransom (USA) -Elbaaha (Arazi (USA)) (1306a) 6260a[2] **>120f<**

**Elegance Champion (AUS)** 5 b g Fuji Kiseki (JPN) -Carinosa (AUS) (Kenmare (FR)) 632a[4] 851a[2] 977a[7] **>80a<**

**Elegant Fashion (AUS)** 6 ch m Danewin (AUS) -Wily Trick (USA) (Clever Trick (USA)) 1657a[2] **>119f<**

**Elegant Gracie (IRE)** 4 ch f Desert Prince (IRE) -Elegant Fragrant (IRE) (Be My Guest (USA)) 651[2] 818[6] 1031[2] 1194[4] **>64a<**

**Elghani** 7 br h Lahib (USA) -Fawaakeh (USA) (Lyphard (USA)) 687a[2] 832a[11] **>102a<**

**Elgin Marbles** 2 b g Lujain (USA) -Bold Gem (Never So Bold) (1686) 3865[6] 4601[12] 5721[2] 5896[2] 6188[5] 6394[5] **>77+a 87f<**

**El Giza (USA)** 6 ch g Cozzene (USA) -Gazayil (USA) (Irish River (FR)) 659[7] **>27a 51f<**

**El Hamra (IRE)** 6 gr g Royal Abjar (USA) -Cherlinoa (FR) (Crystal Palace (FR)) 1035[5] 1187[9] 3667[14] **>77a 65f<**

**El Hurano (ARG)** 4 b c Octante (ARG) -Lazy Moon (ARG) (Ahmad (ARG)) 6253a[3] **>104f<**

**Elidore** 4 b f Danetime (IRE) -Beveled Edge (Beveled (USA)) 1608[13] 4084[5] 4542[14] 4871[2] 5176[4] 5657[5] 6152[6] 6343[14] 6547[5] 6579[4] **>69a 79+f<**

**Eligibilis (FR)** 2 b c Octagonal (NZ) -Bayaniya (IRE) (Barathea (IRE)) 6583a[6] **><**

**Elisha (IRE)** 2 ch f Raise A Grand (IRE) -Social Butterfly (USA) (Sir Ivor (USA)) 1670[4] 2129[5] (2396) 3290[10] 3930[6] 4326[6] 5421[2] 5745[2] **>70f<**

**Elitista (FR)** 3 gr f Linamix (FR) -Elacata (GER) (Acatenango (GER)) 1844[12] **>48a 27f<**

**Elizabethan Age (FR)** 2 b f King s Best (USA) -Dolydille (IRE) (Dolphin Street (FR)) 4344[2] 5248[2] 5939[12] **>84f<**

**Elizabeth s Choice** 2 b f Unfuwain (USA) -Nur (USA) (Diesis) 3093[8] 3840[10] **>40f<**

**Ellamyte** 4 b f Elmaamul (USA) -Deanta In Eirinn (Red Sunset) 573[12] 652[7] 792[9] 2017[5] 2387[15] **>28a 30f<**

**Ellenare (IRE)** 2 ch f Bahhare (USA) -Lady Ellen-M (IRE) (Ballad Rock) 1709[9] 2453[9] **><**

**Elle Nino** 2 b f Inchinor-Robellino Miss (USA) (Robellino (USA)) 6447[7] **>66+a<**

**Ellen Mooney** 5 ch m Efisio-Budby (Rock City) 457[2] 614[3] 737[4] 1122[10] 1606[9] 1931[13] 2292[8] **>44a 44 f<**

**Ellens Academy (IRE)** 9 b g Royal Academy (USA) -Lady Ellen (Horage) 511[4] 607[6] 669[3] 749[4] 1765[2] 2132[4] 2467[4] 3309[2] 3754[2] 4152[3] 4510[5] 5224[6] 5603[21] 5799[2] 6190[13] **>87a 95f<**

**Ellens Lad (IRE)** 10 b g Polish Patriot (USA) -Lady Ellen (Horage) 543[7] 681[5] 836[9] 1131[11] **>80a 92f<**

**Ellens Princess (IRE)** 2 b f Desert Prince (IRE) -Lady Ellen (Horage) 4272[5] 4705[4] 5270[7] 5701[12] 6090[16] **>74df<**

**Elle Royal (IRE)** 5 br m Ali-Royal (IRE) -Silvretta (IRE) (Tirol) 996[11] 1281[12] 1700[6] **>29a 26f<**

**Ellerslie Tom** 2 br g Octagonal (NZ) -Tetravella (IRE) (Groom Dancer (USA)) 6073[9] 6306[5] **>52f<**

**Elliebow** 2 br f Pharly (FR) -Primo Donna Magna (Primo Dominie) 2550[11] 3444[15] 5192[9] **>55f<**

**Ellina** 3 b f Robellino (USA) -Native Flair (Be My Native (USA)) 1507[10] 2001[4] 2848[6] 3172[4] 3421[7] (4027) 4346[10] 5554[13] 6006[3] 6495[5] **>60a 70f<**

**Elliot s Choice (IRE)** 3 b g Foxhound (USA) -Indian City (Lahib (USA)) 1473[4] 1602[4] 2784[11] 3249[7] 3344[4] 3512[3] 3585[6] 3708[8] 4151[11] 4608[12] 4626[15] 4758[2]

5026$^4$ 5107$^{14}$ 5193$^5$ 5370$^{14}$5736$^8$ 6058$^6$ *6405$^{11}$* **>35a 68f<**

**Elliots World (IRE)** 2 b c King s Best (USA) -Morning Welcome (IRE) (Be My Guest (USA)) (3718) (4835) 5437$^6$ 5778$^4$ 6347$^7$ **>105f<**

**Ellis Cave** 2 gr g Diktat-Cole Slaw (Absalom) 2141$^7$ 2674$^{12}$ *3377$^4$ 3802$^7$ 4094$^{10}$* **>43a 40 f<**

**Elloluv (USA)** 4 b f Gilded Time (USA) -Currency Quest (USA) (Cryptoclearance (USA)) *6484a$^7$* **>111a<**

**Ellovamul** 4 b f Elmaamul (USA) -Multi-Sofft (Northern State (USA)) 2974$^4$ 3461$^8$ 3578$^4$ 4070$^8$ (4201) *4339$^8$* 5019$^7$ 5374$^{11}$ 5714$^{10}$5993$^{13}$ (6230) *6551$^7$* **>58a 58f<**

**Ellway Heights** 7 b g Shirley Heights-Amina (Brigadier Gerard) 2978$^2$ 3369$^2$ 3576$^2$ 3740$^5$ 4250$^3$ 4849$^8$ 5456$^6$ 5710$^7$5993$^{12}$ **>61+f<**

**Ellway Prospect** 4 ch f Pivotal-Littlemisstrouble (USA) (My Gallant (USA)) *6581$^4$* **>53a 58f<**

**El Magnifico** 3 b g Forzando-Princess Poquito (Hard Fought) *521$^6$ 622$^7$* 2402$^8$ 2546$^{11}$ *4600$^8$* **>50a 43f<**

**Elms Schoolboy** 2 ch c Komaite (USA) -Elms Schoolgirl (Emarati (USA)) 5441$^9$ 5865$^{11}$ *6294$^{11}$* 6455$^8$ **>23a 48f<**

**Elmustanser** 3 b c Machiavellian (USA) -Elfaslah (IRE) (Green Desert (USA)) 2562$^2$ (3054) 4520$^2$ 5699$^2$ 6172$^{16}$ **>103f<**

**El Oahid** 8 b g Elmaamul (USA) -Last Request (Dancer s Image (USA)) (786a) **><**

**Elopa (GER)** 3 b f Tiger Hill (IRE) -Evening Kiss (Kris) 6437a$^2$ **>102f<**

**Eloquent Knight (USA)** 2 bb c Aljabr (USA) -Matinee Mimic (USA) (Silent Screen (USA)) 5716$^8$ 6352$^7$ **>61f<**

**El Palmar** 3 b g Case Law-Aybeegirl (Mazilier (USA)) 1664$^3$ 2040$^3$ 2457$^{17}$ (2657) *2849$^2$* 3079$^9$ **>63a 73f<**

**El Pedro** 5 b g Piccolo-Standard Rose (Ile De Bourbon (USA)) *478$^4$ 715$^3$ 1404$^4$ 1698$^7$ 2228$^2$* 2347$^4$ **>50a 50f<**

**El Potro** 2 b c Forzando-Gaelic Air (Ballad Rock) 5209$^7$ 5772$^{12}$ **>38+f<**

**Elrafa Mujahid** 2 b f Mujahid (USA) -Fancier Bit (Lion Cavern (USA)) *4544$^3$* 4851$^7$ *(5640)* **>65a 67f<**

**El Rey Del Mambo (USA)** 2 b c Kingmambo (USA) -Scarab Bracelet (USA) (Riverman (USA)) *5911$^3$* **>67a<**

**El Rey Royale** 2 b g Royal Applause-Spanish Serenade (Nashwan (USA)) (3918) 4757$^6$ 6265$^{15}$ **>73f<**

**Elshadi (IRE)** 3 b c Cape Cross (IRE) -Rispoto (Mtoto) 2680$^{13}$ 3032$^2$ 3936$^6$ 4525$^2$ **>105f<**

**Elsie Hart (IRE)** 2 b f Revoque (IRE) -Family At War (USA) (Explodent (USA)) (1523) 2023$^3$ 2959$^{14}$ **>79f<**

**Elsie Wagg (USA)** 2 bb f Mt. Livermore (USA) -Hoedown Honey (CAN) (Country Light (USA)) 2396$^3$ 2544$^4$ 3950$^5$ 4358$^6$ 5490$^7$ **>64f<**

**Elsinora** 3 b f Great Dane (IRE) -Deanta In Eirinn (Red Sunset) *959$^{11}$* 2325$^9$ 3156$^{10}$ 3513$^2$ 4018$^6$ 4241$^3$ 5035$^5$ 5282$^2$5552$^4$ 5794$^2$ (5926) 6056$^3$ (6228) *6405$^7$* **>46a 51f<**

**Elsundus (USA)** 6 b g Gone West (USA) -Aljawza (USA) (Riverman (USA)) 3879$^6$ **>88f<**

**El Tiger (GER)** 3 b c Tiger Hill (IRE) -Elea (GER) (Dschingis Khan) 3565a$^6$ 4183a$^4$ **>108f<**

**Eltihaab (USA)** 3 bb f Danzig (USA) -Futuh (USA) (Diesis) 3447$^9$ 4351$^3$ 4653$^4$ **>57f<**

**Eltizaam (USA)** 2 b c Bahri (USA) -Saffaanh (USA) (Shareef Dancer (USA)) 4169$^6$ *4544$^5$* 5179$^6$ 5655$^3$ 5909$^5$ 6206$^{11}$ **>64a 74f<**

**Elusive Double (IRE)** 2 ch c Grand Lodge (USA) -Lady Luck (IRE) (Kris) (4158a) 4959a$^3$ 5678a$^6$ **>103f<**

**Elusive Dream** 3 b g Rainbow Quest (USA) -Dance A Dream (Sadler s Wells (USA)) *(3614)* (3669) (3825) (3902) 4888$^3$ (5632) 5814$^2$ **>75++a 99f<**

**Elusive Kitty (USA)** 3 b f Elusive Quality (USA) -Al Fahda (Be My Chief (USA)) *490$^6$* 4351$^{LFT}$ 4580$^3$ 4987$^3$ 5537$^5$ 5749$^3$ 5936$^5$ 6285$^6$*6552$^{12}$* **>67a 76f<**

**Elvina** 3 b f Mark Of Esteem (IRE) -Pharaoh s Joy (Robellino (USA)) (4440) 6131$^{15}$ **>30a 59f<**

**Elvina Hills (IRE)** 2 ch f Bluebird (USA) -Women In Love (IRE) (Danehill (USA)) 1299$^9$ 1839$^7$ 3045$^5$ 3438$^6$ *4022$^{10}$* **>49a 60f<**

**Elvington Boy** 7 ch g Emarati (USA) -Catherines Well (Junius (USA)) 2130$^U$ **>89df<**

**Elvstroem (AUS)** 4 b c Danehill (USA) -Circles Of Gold (AUS) (Marscay (AUS)) 6528a$^4$ **>119f<**

**Elzees** 3 b g Magic Ring (IRE) -White Flash (Sure Blade (USA)) *553$^9$* 5891$^8$ **>45a 16f<**

**Emaradia** 3 ch f Emarati (USA) -Rewardia (IRE) (Petardia) *524$^3$ (591) 640$^2$ 696$^8$ (865) 958$^2$ 1008$^2$ 1178$^6$*4434$^6$ 4622$^8$ *4879$^3$* 5016$^9$ 5794$^4$ *6220$^9$ 6290$^3$ 6558$^7$* **>64a 46f<**

**Emarati s Image** 6 b g Emarati (USA) -Choir s Image (Lochnager) *537$^{12}$ 858$^6$ 951$^4$ 1000$^6$ 1191$^4$ 1886$^6$* **>28a 28 f<**

**Embassy Lord** 3 b g Mind Games-Keen Melody (USA) (Sharpen Up) 1883$^4$ 2294$^8$ 2877$^9$ **>60a 82?f<**

**Embassy Sweets (USA)** 3 b f Affirmed (USA) -Leaveemlaughing (USA) (Dynaformer (USA)) 1541$^4$ 5340$^{11}$ *5914$^{13}$* **>50a 50f<**

**Ember Days** 5 gr m Reprimand-Evening Falls (Beveled (USA)) *4645* 1369$^{17}$ 1857$^3$ 2170$^{10}$ 2573$^2$ 3459$^3$ (3573) 3670$^3$ 3917$^2$4045$^4$ 4192$^{17}$ **>63a 73f<**

**Embossed (IRE)** 2 b c Mark Of Esteem (IRE) -L-Way First (IRE) (Vision (USA)) 3808$^6$ (4030) 4527$^6$ 4949$^2$ 5395$^2$ 6189$^2$ 6340$^{10}$ **>102f<**

**Emerald Bay (IRE)** 2 b c King s Best (USA) -Belle Etoile (FR) (Lead On Time (USA)) 4532$^4$ **>70f<**

**Emerald Dancer** 2 b f Groom Dancer (USA) -Green Bonnet (IRE) (Green Desert (USA)) 5870$^{13}$ **>23f<**

**Emerald Destiny (IRE)** 2 b g Key Of Luck (USA) -Green Belt (FR) (Tirol) 5790$^5$ 5988$^{14}$ 6091$^{12}$ **>51f<**

**Emerald Fire** 5 b m Pivotal-Four-Legged Friend (Aragon) *526$^6$ 5991$^0$* 3747$^{11}$ 5008$^8$ 5541$^5$ 6117$^2$ **>77a 77f<**

**Emerald Lodge** 2 b c Grand Lodge (USA) -Emerald Peace (IRE) (Green Desert (USA)) 4815$^3$ 5262$^5$ *(5911) (6158)* **>88a 63f<**

**Emerald Penang (IRE)** 2 b g Alzao (USA) -Run To Jane (IRE) (Doyoun) 1219$^5$ 2592$^4$ (3438) 4326$^7$ 5090$^{10}$ 6129$^{10}$ **>76f<**

**Emeraude Du Cap** 2 b f Tipsy Creek (USA) -High Typha (Dowsing (USA)) 3157$^{17}$ 3532$^{10}$ 4212$^3$ 5022$^8$ **>49f<**

**Emile Zola** 2 b c Singspiel (IRE) -Ellie Ardensky (Slip Anchor) (5467) 5931$^5$ **>76f<**

**Emilys Dawn** 3 b f Komaite (USA) -Spice And Sugar (Chilibang) *420$^7$ 621$^{11}$* **>44a<**

**Eminence Gift** 2 b f Cadeaux Genereux-Germane (Distant Relative) 2617$^{12}$ 2904$^{14}$ **>20f<**

**Eminent Aura (USA)** 3 ch f Charismatic (USA) -Perfectly Clear (USA) (Woodman (USA)) *1046$^9$* **><**

**E Minor (IRE)** 5 b m Blushing Flame (USA) -Watch The Clock (Mtoto) *549$^5$ 693$^7$ 777$^6$ 1041$^6$ 1630$^7$* **>56 a 56f<**

**Emmas Princess (IRE)** 4 b f Bahhare (USA) -Staff Approved (Teenoso (USA)) 5962a$^7$ 6102a$^7$ **>98f<**

**Emma s Venture** 2 b f Paris House-Emma Amour (Emarati (USA)) 1115$^5$ 1468$^2$ 1666$^6$ 2194$^4$ 2364$^8$ *4999$^4$* **>28a 43f<**

**Emmervale** 5 b m Emarati (USA) -Raintree Venture (Good Times (ITY)) 2098$^5$ 2707$^9$ 2823$^{11}$ *4517$^9$* **>34a 55f<**

**Empangeni** 2 b g Mtoto-Shibui (Shirley Heights) 5653$^{11}$ 6181$^5$ *6492$^{10}$* **>62a 58f<**

**Emperor Cat (IRE)** 3 b g Desert Story (IRE) -Catfoot Lane (Batshoof) *732$^2$ 807$^3$ 958$^{12}$ 1025$^8$* 2426$^{13}$ 3229$^{11}$ *3800$^6$*4968$^6$ 5691$^{16}$ **>56a 42f<**

**Emperor s Well** 5 ch g First Trump-Catherines Well (Junius (USA)) 4213$^{12}$ 5021$^3$ (5557) (5714) **>59a 72f<**

**Empireneyev (USA)** 8 b h Nureyev (USA) -La Pitie (USA) (Devil s Bag (USA)) 786a$^8$ **><**

**Empire s Ghodha** 2 b c Mujadil (USA) -La Caprice (USA) (Housebuster (USA)) 2057$^5$ 2205$^3$ 2370$^2$ 2522$^3$ (2872) 2996$^5$ 3481$^3$ 3753$^4$ 4325$^6$4752$^8$ 5839$^8$ 6188$^6$ **>81f<**

**Empirical Power (IRE)** 3 b c Second Empire (IRE) -Rumuz (IRE) (Marju (IRE)) 6191$^6$ **>99f<**

**Empress Eugenie (FR)** 3 b f Second Empire (IRE) -High Finish (High Line) 1507$^4$ 1713$^6$ 2250$^5$ **>70f<**

**Empress Josephine** 4 b f Emperor Jones (USA) -Valmaranda (USA) (Sir Ivor) *(637) 794$^2$ 905$^5$ 1738$^3$* 2482$^{14}$ 3307$^{11}$ **>64a 50f<**

**Emran (USA)** 4 br c Silver Hawk (USA) -Indihash (USA) (Gulch (USA)) *634a$^{10}$* **>29a 98f<**

**Emsam Ballou (IRE)** 3 ch f Bluebird (USA) -Persian Tapestry (Tap On Wood) *982$^3$ 1059$^3$* 1133$^3$ 5155$^9$ 6117$^{18}$ *6452$^{13}$* **>66a 61f<**

**Emteyaz** 6 b h Mark Of Esteem (IRE) -Najmat Alshemaal (IRE) (Dancing Brave (USA)) *688a$^4$ (757a)* **>98a 89f<**

**Emtilaak** 3 b g Marju (IRE) -Just A Mirage (Green Desert (USA)) *1202$^2$* 1420$^3$ (2450) 2726$^9$ *3420$^9$* 4267$^4$ *4515$^4$* **>77a 82 f<**

**Enamoured** 2 b f Groom Dancer (USA) -Ascendancy (Sadler s Wells (USA)) 6336$^5$ 6545$^7$ **>46f<**

**Enborne Again (IRE)** 2 ch c Fayruz-Sharp Ellie (IRE) (Sharp Victor (USA)) 5125$^7$ 5578$^{14}$ 5857$^{11}$ **>51f<**

**Encanto (IRE)** 2 ch f Bahhare (USA) -Born To Glamour (Ajdal (USA)) 2177$^{11}$ 2609$^6$ 2872$^2$ 3286a$^2$ 3659$^2$ (4137) 4342$^4$ 4612$^5$ 5864$^3$ **>83f<**

**Enchanted** 5 b m Magic Ring (IRE) -Snugfit Annie (Midyan (USA)) (2143) (2282) 2503$^7$ 2903a$^7$ 4286$^7$ 5121$^7$ 5416$^4$ 5671$^8$ 6175$^{15}$ **>99f<**

**Enchanted Ocean (USA)** 5 b m Royal Academy (USA) -Ocean Jewel (USA) (Alleged (USA)) 1224$^{13}$ 2767$^{11}$ 3942$^8$ 4642$^7$ 5073$^{12}$ **>56f<**

**Enchanted Princess** 4 b f Royal Applause-Hawayah (IRE) (Shareef Dancer (USA)) 1275$^{15}$ 1857$^5$ (2284) 2733$^6$ 3320$^7$ **>79f<**

**Enchantment** 3 b f Compton Place-Tharwa (IRE) (Last Tycoon) 1797$^5$ 2143$^2$ (2264) (2552) 2892$^2$ 3702$^4$ (4862) 5105$^4$ 5418$^4$ 5671$^4$ **>109f<**

**Encompass (FR)** 3 b f Sadler s Wells (USA) -Totality (Dancing Brave (USA)) 2632$^9$ 3608$^3$ 4028$^6$ **>68f<**

**Encora Bay** 3 b f Primo Dominie-Brave Revival (Dancing Brave (USA)) 4683$^6$ 5204$^3$ 5378$^{10}$ **>64f<**

**Encore Royale** 4 b f Royal Applause-Verbena (IRE) (Don t Forget Me) *1681$^7$* 1910$^5$ *2456$^6$ 2666$^{12}$* 2879$^{11}$ **>43a 61f<**

**Encounter** 8 br g Primo Dominie-Dancing Spirit (IRE) (Ahonoora) 1393$^{11}$ 1660$^7$ 1993$^3$ 2356$^5$ 2580$^6$ 2879$^8$ 3559$^8$ 3903$^2$4333$^5$ 4511$^9$ 4826$^8$ 5129$^5$ 5587$^3$ 5927$^5$ 6057$^2$ 6227$^{14}$6463$^3$ **>57f<**

**Encouragement** 2 b f Royal Applause-Gentle Persuasion (Bustino) 2585$^8$ 4364$^3$ 5070$^{10}$ 5441$^4$ 5720$^3$ 5943$^7$ **>77f<**

**Endless Peace (IRE)** 3 ch f Russian Revival (USA) -Magical Peace (IRE) (Magical Wonder (USA)) 4251a$^8$ **>61f<**

**Endless Summer** 7 b g Zafonic (USA) -Well Away (IRE) (Sadler s Wells (USA)) 1106$^3$ 1673$^5$ 2366$^5$ 2461$^{10}$ 2843$^4$ 3339$^6$ 3945$^9$ 4935$^2$(5704) (5730) 5874$^7$ **>93f<**

**End Of An Error** 5 b m Charmer-Needwood Poppy (Rolfe (USA)) 3576$^9$ **><**

**Energetic (NZ)** 6 b g Oregon (USA) -Kisumu (NZ) (Khozaam (USA)) *634a$^7$ 851a$^8$* **>62a<**

**Enforcer** 2 b c Efisio-Tarneem (USA) (Zilzal (USA)) 4193$^4$ 4611$^5$ 4936$^2$ 5314$^8$ (6090) 6338$^{10}$ **>81+f<**

**Enford Princess** 3 b f Pivotal-Expectation (IRE) (Night Shift (USA)) 1797$^4$ 3943$^9$ 4684$^3$ 5148$^4$ 5249$^7$ 5566$^4$ 5886$^6$ 6086$^7$ **>86f<**

**English Fellow** 2 b c Robellino (USA) -Q Factor (Tragic Role (USA)) 2087$^3$ 2352$^4$ 2758$^4$ 3886$^{14}$ 4487$^7$ 5314$^{17}$ 6265$^{16}$ **>70df<**

**English Rocket (IRE)** 3 b g Indian Rocket-Golden Charm (IRE) (Common Grounds) 5998$^9$ 6311$^{13}$ **>60a 70f<**

**Enhancer** 6 b g Zafonic (USA) -Ypha (USA) (Lyphard (USA)) 2562$^7$ 4028$^7$ 4819$^3$ 5472$^5$ 6172$^6$ **>80?f<**

**Enjoy The Buzz** 5 b h Prince Of Birds (USA) -Abaklea (IRE) (Doyoun) *421$^4$ 443$^4$ 509$^{11}$ 572$^2$ 658$^3$ (728) 813$^2$ 936$^4$990$^2$* 2885$^{17}$ (3084) *3381$^9$* 3575$^2$ (3668) 3935$^7$ 4336$^3$ 4548$^2$5201$^5$ 5261$^5$ 5597$^9$ 5736$^6$ **>51a 58f<**

**Enna (POL)** 5 ch m Don Corleone-Elba (POL) (Freedom s Choice (USA)) 1533$^4$ 2520$^6$ *2811$^9$* 3489$^8$ 3697$^4$ 3828$^{12}$ *3934$^4$* 4546$^2$4771$^9$ 4871$^6$ 5035$^7$ 5350$^4$ *5641$^3$* (5791) **>43a 52f<**

**Enrapture (USA)** 3 b f Lear Fan (USA) -Cheviot Hills (USA) (Gulch (USA)) (4718) 5148$^3$ 5652$^{18}$ **>82f<**

**Enrika s Gift (IRE)** 3 b f Orpen (USA) -Guana Bay (Cadeaux Genereux) 1778a$^{17}$ **>52f<**

**Ensemble** 4 b g Polish Precedent (USA) -Full Orchestra (Shirley Heights) 6005$^{19}$ (6438) *6581$^9$* **>28a 53f<**

**Entailment** 2 b g Kris-Entail (USA) (Riverman (USA)) 4776$^8$ (5096) 6344$^8$ **>72f<**

**Entertain** 2 b f Royal Applause-Darshay (FR) (Darshaan) 3627$^{12}$ 4053$^{13}$ **>67+f<**

**Entertaining** 2 b f Halling (USA) -Quaver (USA) (The Minstrel (CAN)) 3116$^6$ 4705$^5$ 5847$^2$ 6126$^5$ **>72f<**

**Enticer (FR)** 2 b c Astair (FR) -Feofee (FR) (Solicitor (FR)) 4597a$^4$ 5313a$^5$ **>82f<**

**Entusiasmo (ITY)** 3 ch f Masad (IRE) -Emy Delight (USA) (Aloma s Ruler (USA)) 1805a$^2$ 2340a$^5$ 2607a$^2$ 3569a$^2$ **>95f<**

**Environmentalist** 5 b g Danehill (USA) -Way O Gold (USA) (Slew O Gold (USA)) 1342$^{11}$ 1787$^{11}$ 2260$^{13}$ 3367$^8$ 4276$^9$ 4537$^{12}$ **>29a 29f<**

**Environment Audit** 5 ch g Kris-Bold And Beautiful (Bold Lad (IRE)) *516$^7$ 671$^{10}$* 1188$^7$ 1768$^{12}$ 3387$^{11}$ 5056$^7$ **>57a 59f<**

**Enzed (AUS)** 6 u u (USA) -(USA) (Rainbow Quest (USA)) 6582a$^6$ **><**

**Epalo (GER)** 5 b h Lando (GER) -Evening Kiss (Kris) (2156a) 4377a$^2$ 4768a$^3$ **>120f<**

**Epaminondas (USA)** 3 ch c Miswaki (USA) -Nora Nova (USA) (Green Dancer (USA)) 1702$^7$ 2790$^{17}$ 3089$^{12}$ 3529$^2$ 3689$^8$ 4079$^4$ 5006$^7$ **>68f<**

**Ephesus** 4 b g Efisio-Composition (Wolfhound (USA)) *641$^3$ 749$^7$ 837$^7$ 971$^9$* 1845$^9$ 2064$^6$ (2226) 2646$^4$2891$^2$ 3048$^2$ 3597$^{18}$ *3850$^{10}$* 4220$^{12}$ 4569$^3$ 5210$^6$ 5705$^3$ **>89 a 87f<**

**Epiphany** 2 br f Zafonic (USA) -Galette (Caerleon (USA)) 4074$^2$ (4532) 5701$^7$ 6003$^8$ **>83f<**

**Epitomise** 2 b f Mind Games-Yanomami (USA) (Slew O Gold (USA)) 2884$^6$ 3408$^4$ 3992$^{10}$ 4439$^6$ 5351$^{10}$ **>64f<**

**Epoca (IRE)** 2 b f Grand Lodge (USA) -Monodora (IRE) (Marju (IRE)) 5390a$^3$ **><**

**Epopee (IRE)** 4 b f Sadler s Wells (USA) -Encens (Common Grounds) 5503a$^7$ 6137a$^{10}$ **>102f<**

**Eqdaam (USA)** 2 b c Diesis-Awaamir (Green Desert (USA)) 3319$^3$ 4315$^3$ (6145) **>82f<**

**Equus (IRE)** 3 b g Desert Style (IRE) -Iolanta (IRE) (Danehill (USA)) *2665$^8$ 2987$^{10}$* **>26a 61f<**

**Ermine Grey** 3 gr g Wolfhound (USA) -Impulsive Decision (IRE) (Nomination) 1222$^8$ 1613$^7$ 2688$^3$ *3280$^4$* 4171$^4$ **>84a 74f<**

**Erracht** 6 gr m Emarati (USA) -Port Na Blath (On Your Mark) *794$^7$ 904$^5$* (1642) 2130$^6$ 2246$^{14}$ 2482$^{11}$ 3772$^7$ *4025$^5$*4400$^8$ 4800 5754$^{16}$ **>61 a 75f<**

**Erreur (IRE)** 3 b f Desert King (IRE) -Abergwrle (Absalom) 3328a$^5$ **>82f<**

**Errol** 5 ch g Dancing Spree (USA) -Primo Panache (Primo Dominie) *1193$^9$* **>42a 37f<**

**Ersaal (USA)** 4 ch g Gulch (USA) -Madame Secretary (USA) (Secretariat (USA)) *914$^{10}$ 1077$^3$ 1166$^{11}$ (1514) 1690$^3$* 1989$^{10}$ 3263$^{15}$ **>60a 68f<**

**Ershaad (USA)** 3 b c Kingmambo (USA) -Insight (FR) (Sadler s Wells (USA)) 2161a$^4$ 2721a$^3$ 4284a$^2$ 5169a$^8$ 5667a$^7$ **>108f<**

**Erte** 3 ch g Vettori (IRE) -Cragreen (Green Desert (USA)) 1613$^{13}$ 2545$^6$ 2801$^6$ 3056$^3$ *3305$^2$* 3990$^{11}$ 4207$^7$ **>54a 50f<**

**Erupt** 11 b g Beveled (USA) -Sparklingsovereign (Sparkler) *1885$^5$* 2214$^7$ *2990$^3$* 3579$^9$ 4624$^8$ 4825$^4$ 5187$^3$ 5449$^9$ **>37a 48f<**

**Esatto** 5 b g Puissance-Stoneydale (Tickled Pink) 2948$^{15}$ 3439$^9$ **>64a 85f<**

**Escalade** 7 b g Green Desert (USA) -Sans Escale (USA) (Diesis) *406$^9$* 2121$^4$ 2216$^{12}$ 2659$^5$ 3041$^4$ 3263$^3$ 3450$^4$ 3472$^3$3695$^5$ 4233$^6$ 4519$^8$ **>61a 65f<**

**Escayola (IRE)** 4 b g Revoque (IRE) -First Fling (IRE) (Last Tycoon) 2240$^8$ 2855$^2$ 3310$^{11}$ 3725$^{16}$ 5472$^2$ (5784) 6215$^5$ **>43a 99f<**

**Eshaadeh (USA)** 3 b f Storm Cat (USA) -Sarayir (USA) (Mr Prospector (USA)) 5525$^5$ 6119$^8$ **>34f<**

**Esher Common (IRE)** 6 b g Common Grounds-Alsahah (IRE) (Unfuwain (USA)) 1109$^{19}$ **>53a 82f<**

**Eskdale (IRE)** 2 b g Perugino (USA) -Gilding The Lily (IRE) (High Estate) 2141$^8$ 4175$^9$ 4930$^3$ 5059$^2$ 5186$^6$ 5516$^4$ **>65f<**

**Eskimo s Nest** 2 b f Polar Falcon (USA) -White House (Pursuit Of Love) 5570$^8$ **>57f<**

**Espada (IRE)** 8 b g Mukaddamah (USA) -Folk Song (CAN) (The Minstrel (CAN)) *448$^8$ 575$^7$* 1274$^7$ 1675$^{15}$ 2322$^4$ 2426$^4$ (2886) 2945$^5$ 3489$^8$3626$^4$ 3871$^6$ 4438$^{10}$ 5305$^{13}$ 5411$^{10}$ **>44a 44f<**

**Esperance (IRE)** 4 ch g Bluebird (USA) -Dioscorea (IRE) (Pharly (FR)) *672$^{11}$* 1856$^{13}$ 3386$^5$ 3662$^5$ 4238$^8$ 4460$^5$ *4940$^5$* 5336$^2$5524$^4$ 6561$^5$ **>52a 53f<**

**Esperanto (IRE)** 3 b c Sadler s Wells (USA) -River Missy (USA) (Riverman (USA)) 1654a$^5$ 2159a$^4$ **>104f<**

**Esposita (GER)** 4 ch f Sternkoenig (IRE) -Enrica (GER) (Niniski (USA)) 6107a$^{11}$ **>75f<**

**Esposito** 2 ch c Inchinor-Celebrate (IRE) (Generous (IRE)) 6256a$^{11}$ **>74f<**

**Esquire** 2 b c Dubai Millennium-Esperada (ARG) (Equalize (USA)) 5268$^6$ (5646) **>91+f<**

**Esrar (IRE)** 2 b c Mujadil (USA) -Island Desert (IRE) (Green Desert (USA)) 5653$^9$ **>51f<**

**Essay Baby (FR)** 4 b f Saumarez-Easter Baby (Derrylin) *537$^4$ 931$^4$ 995$^{13}$ 1081$^{13}$* **>58a 63f<**

**Essex Star (IRE)** 3 b f Revoque (IRE) -Touch Of White (Song) 2098$^{10}$ *2811$^3$ 3710$^3$* 4968$^5$ **>50a 56df<**

**Establishment** 7 b g Muhtarram (USA) -Uncharted Waters (Celestial Storm (USA)) 1329$^{11}$ 1768$^8$ 2285$^8$ 2613$^{10}$ 2958$^{14}$ 4075$^8$ 5152$^4$ 5472$^{12}$ **>81a 76f<**

**Esteban** 4 b g Groom Dancer (USA) -Ellie Ardensky (Slip Anchor) 1502$^{12}$ 2658$^4$ 3586$^{11}$ **>49a 49f<**

**Estefania (GER)** 3 b f Acatenango (GER) -Eirehill (IRE) (Danehill (USA)) 2157a$^7$ 2723a$^{12}$ 6257a$^7$ **>80f<**

**Estepona** 3 ch g Polar Falcon (USA) -Kingdom Ruby (IRE) (Bluebird (USA)) 1557$^4$ 1771$^{10}$ 2392$^{12}$ 5293$^8$ 5773$^{11}$ **>67f<**

**Estihlal** 3 b f Green Desert (USA) -Ta Rib (USA) (Mr Prospector (USA)) 1288$^7$ 2063$^4$ (2351) 2839$^2$ 3211$^4$ (3530) 4104$^4$ 4434$^3$ 4740$^5$ **>79 f<**

**Estilo** 4 b g Deploy-Vilcabamba (USA) (Green Dancer (USA)) 2728$^{10}$ **>40a<**

**Estimate** 4 b f Mark Of Esteem (IRE) -Mistle Thrush (USA) (Storm Bird (CAN)) *4847 549$^9$ 614$^8$* (2092) 2446$^{12}$ 3206$^7$ 3609$^2$ 4201$^2$ *4339$^{11}$*4713$^4$ 5145$^8$ **>56a 59f<**

**Estimation** 4 b f Mark Of Esteem (IRE) -Mohican Girl (Dancing Brave (USA)) *457$^3$ 614$^6$ 826$^3$ 1036$^5$ 1229$^{12}$* 1372$^8$ *1935$^7$2406$^{10}$ 3023$^7$* **>75a 75f<**

**Estimraar (USA)** 7 rg g Holy Bull (USA) -Verbasle (USA) (Slewpy (USA)) *974a$^6$ 1142a$^4$* **>113a<**

**Estoille** 3 b f Paris House-Nampara Bay (Emarati (USA)) 2450$^7$ 2675$^{12}$ 3512$^8$ 4351$^7$ *4929$^6$* 5101$^8$ *6403$^4$* (6567) **>45a 55f<**

**Estrella Levante** 4 ch g Abou Zouz (USA) -Star Of Modena (IRE) (Waajib) *664$^7$ 707$^5$ 790$^3$ 888$^{10}$ 933$^6$ 1165$^8$* 3555$^{10}$4519$^{11}$ *4940$^{12}$* 5378$^7$ *5641$^8$* **>29a 26 f<**

**Estuary (USA)** 9 ch g Riverman (USA) -Ocean Ballad (Grundy) *1081$^{11}$* 1263$^{14}$ *2987$^{12}$* **>37a 37f<**

**Etaar** 2 b c Zafonic (USA) -Hawayah (IRE) (Shareef Dancer (USA)) 3913$^4$ 4625$^4$ 5616$^4$ **>80f<**

**Etbash (RUS)** 7 b h Triple Buck (USA) -Emira (SU) (Ivory Tower) 785a$^3$ **><**

**Etching (USA)** 4 b f Groom Dancer (USA) -Eternity (Suave Dancer (USA)) (1684) 1973$^9$ 2590$^{16}$ 5523$^5$ 5826$^{18}$ **>35a 68f<**

**Etendard Indien (FR)** 3 b c Selkirk (USA) -Danseuse Indienne (IRE) (Danehill (USA)) (5433a) 5965a$^7$ **>100f<**

**Eternal Beauty (USA)** 4 b f Zafonic (USA) -Strawberry Roan (IRE) (Sadler s Wells (USA)) *479$^6$* **>45f<**

**Eternal Bloom** 6 b m Reprimand-Forever Roses (Forzando) *(502) 527$^2$ 572$^{13}$ 626$^{13}$ 936$^{12}$ 1445$^3$ 1515$^3$ 1913$^8$*2384$^9$ **>49a 29f<**

**Eternal Dancer (USA)** 3 b g Royal Academy (USA) -Tara Roma (USA) (Lyphard (USA)) *835$^{12}$ 1024$^9$* **>29f<**

**Eternally** 2 ch c Timeless Times (USA) -Nice Spice (IRE) (Common Grounds) 1314$^7$ *1735$^3$ 2125$^5$* 2799$^3$ *(3709)* 4046$^8$ *6023$^9$* **>51a 37f<**

**Eternal Sunshine (IRE)** 2 b f Rossini (USA) -Sweet As A Nut (IRE) (Pips Pride) 2622$^8$ 2960$^{10}$ 3526$^8$ *3709$^3$ 4999$^{10}$* **>23a 20f<**

**Etesaal (USA)** 4 bb c Danzig (USA) -Electric Society (IRE) (Law Society (USA)) 6219$^{15}$ **>93+a 113f<**

**Ethon (IRE)** 2 bb g Alzao (USA) -Crown Brief (IRE) (Brief Truce (USA)) 4958a$^{12}$ **>68f<**

**Etlaala** 2 ch c Selkirk (USA) -Portelet (Night Shift (USA)) (4743) (5437) 6217$^8$ **>117 f<**

**Etmaam** 3 b c Intikhab (USA) -Sudeley (Dancing

Brave (USA)) (1174) 1418[5] (2169) 2472[2] (2896) 2999[3] 4229[15] 4831[17] 5226[6] 6307[6] **>102f<**

**Etoile Russe (IRE)** 2 b g Soviet Star (USA) -To The Skies (USA) (Sky Classic (CAN)) 4149[7] **>60f<**

**Eton (GER)** 8 ch g Suave Dancer (USA) -Ermione (Surumu (GER)) 1109[3] 1282[10] 1867[5] (2856) 3237[2] 3557[3] 3872[5] 4423[2] 5006[9]5320[4] 5374[15] **>72 f<**

**Etroubles (FR)** 3 gr f Indian Ridge-Kamakha (IRE) (Natroun (FR)) 1778a[11] **>78f<**

**Ettrick Water** 5 ch g Selkirk (USA) -Sadly Sober (IRE) (Roi Danzig (USA)) 2271[5] (2575) (3052) 4120[10] (5468) 5781[6] 6191[4] *6451[7]* **>104a 107f<**

**Eugenie** 3 ch f Primo Dominie-Misty Goddess (IRE) (Godswalk (USA)) *489[13] 587[13]* **>25a<**

**Euippe** 3 b f Air Express (IRE) -Myth (Troy) 2390[11] 2821[5] (3479) 3928[4] 4457[7] **>74+f<**

**Eukleia (USA)** 2 ch f Devil His Due (USA) -Good Reputation (USA) (Gran Zar (MEX)) 3248[6] 4137[8] *4924[5]* 5234[17] **>34a 63f<**

**Eunice Choice** 3 b g College Chapel-Aquiletta (Bairn (USA)) *816[15] 2986[9]* **>9a<**

**Eurobound (USA)** 3 b f Southern Halo (USA) -Eurostorm (USA) (Storm Bird (CAN)) 5339[5] **>69f<**

**Eurolink Artemis** 7 b m Common Grounds-Taiga (Northfields (USA)) *425[13] 1166[4] 1277[10] (1511)* (1580) *1888[3] 2816[P] 6406[11]* **>44a 62f<**

**Eurolink Zante (IRE)** 8 b g Turtle Island (IRE) -Lady Eurolink (Kala Shikari) *707[7] 788[6] 855[7]* 5350[11] **>49a 52f<**

**Eva Jean** 3 b f Singspiel (IRE) -Go For Red (IRE) (Thatching) 2182[14] 5851[5] 6520[16] **>54f<**

**Evaluator (IRE)** 3 b c Ela-Mana-Mou-Summerhill (Habitat) 1352[4] 1755[3] 1957[11] 2790[6] (3180) 3527[2] 3750[2] 4220[8] 5004[2]5766[2] **>64a 93f<**

**Evanesce** 2 b f Lujain (USA) -Search Party (Rainbow Quest (USA)) *1117[2] 1240[2]* 1374[4] 1616[2] 2617[2] (2761) 2933[2] 3242[8] 3938[11]4197[4] 4612[10] 5363[12] 6003[13] **>69a 72f<**

**Evangelist (IRE)** 4 b f Namaqualand (USA) -Errazuriz (IRE) (Classic Music (USA)) *498[3] 608[9] (813) 990[7] 1092[6] 1165[14]* **>45a 59f<**

**Eva Peron (IRE)** 4 b f Alzao (USA) -High Flying Adored (IRE) (In The Wings) *1121[10]* 1389[8] 1687[6] 2034[8] 2426[7] **>44 a 44f<**

**Evasive Quality (FR)** 2 b f Highest Honor (FR) -Exocet (USA) (Deposit Ticket (USA)) 3904[10] **>56f<**

**Eva Soneva So Fast (IRE)** 2 ch c In The Wings-Azyaa (Kris) 4681[10] 5091[5] 5467[2] (5840) **>78f<**

**Even Easier** 3 gr f Petong-Comme Ca (Cyrano De Bergerac) *557[8] 741[7] 845[5]* 1309[7] 2324[6] 2766[4] 2929[4] 3246[5]3827[7] 4470[5] 5080[12] **>51a 60f<**

**Even Hotter** 3 b f Desert Style (IRE) -Level Pegging (IRE) (Common Grounds) 2165[12] 2785[5] 3211[11] **>50f<**

**Ever Cheerful** 3 b g Atraf-Big Story (Cadeaux Genereux) *408[2] (489) 557[10] 817[5] 893[2] 1008[6] 6016[8]* 6079[9] **>71 a 71f<**

**Everest (IRE)** 7 ch g Indian Ridge-Reine D Beaute (Caerleon (USA)) 1114[7] 1762[13] 2142[10] 2752[9] 3198[14] (3597) (3937) 4178[7] 5627[4] 5941[3] **>71a 91f<**

**Every Note Counts** 4 b g Bluegrass Prince (IRE) -Miss Mirror (Magic Mirror) 1103[21] 1393[15] 2216[14] 2945[6] 3265[6] 6097[6] **>58a 58f<**

**Eviyrn (IRE)** 8 b g In The Wings-Evrana (USA) (Nureyev (USA)) 1534[12] **>42f<**

**Evolving Tactics (IRE)** 4 b g Machiavellian (USA) -Token Gesture (IRE) (Alzao (USA)) (925a) 1146a[9] 2969[27] **>109f<**

**Evoque** 3 b f Revoque (IRE) -Chimere (FR) (Soviet Lad (USA)) 1413[10] **>59f<**

**Exaggerate (NZ)** 5 b g Zabeel (NZ) -Enhancer (NZ) (Red Tempo (NZ)) 2156a[13] **>91f<**

**Exalted (IRE)** 11 b g High Estate-Heavenward (USA) (Conquistador Cielo (USA)) 1668[5] 2287[5] 2615[8] 3221[6] **>58f<**

**Excalibur (IRE)** 4 b c Danehill (USA) -Sharaniya (USA) (Alleged (USA)) 5357a[6] **>113+f<**

**Exceed And Excel (AUS)** 4 b c Danehill (USA) -Patrona (USA) (Lomond (USA)) 3674[19] **>111f<**

**Excellento (USA)** 4 ch c Rahy (USA) -Golden Opinion (USA) (Slew O Gold (USA)) 2044[17] 2534[9] **>107f<**

**Excelsius (IRE)** 4 ch c Dr Devious (IRE) -Folgore (USA) (Irish River (FR)) 1107[9] 1999[3] 3323[9] 4887[11] 5291[4] 5769[2] 6075a[5] **>103f<**

**Excessivepleasure (USA)** 4 br g In Excess-Pleasing (USA) (Falstaff (USA)) *1142a[3]* **>104a<**

**Exclusive Danielle** 3 ch f Thunder Gulch (USA) -Hasta (USA) (Theatrical) 1619[5] (5367) **>73f<**

**Excusez Moi (USA)** 2 b c Fusaichi Pegasus (USA) -Jiving (Generous (IRE)) *6394[2]* **>74a<**

**Execute (FR)** 7 ch h Suave Dancer (USA) -She s My Lovely (Sharpo) 1261a[2] (1804a) 5981a[11] **>117f<**

**Exit Smiling** 2 ch c Dr Fong (USA) -Away To Me (Exit To Nowhere (USA)) 1658[2] 2074[3] 3938[17] 4326[5] 5477[13] (6195) 6344[10] **>70f<**

**Exit To Heaven** 4 ch f Exit To Nowhere (USA) -Shona (USA) (Lyphard (USA)) *440[7] 484[6] 549[7] 750[9]* **><**

**Ex Mill Lady** 3 br f Bishop Of Cashel-Hickleton Lady (IRE) (Kala Shikari) 1906[4] 2468[2] 3262[2] (3635) **>47a 65f<**

**Exor (ITY)** 2 b c Shantou (USA) -Heil (Star Appeal) 5389a[4] **><**

**Expected Bonus (USA)** 5 bb g Kris S (USA) -Nidd (USA) (Known Fact (USA)) 2573[10] 3166[4] 3604[17] 4246[9] 4818[6] 5285[15] **>45a 45f<**

**Expectedtofli (IRE)** 6 b m Mujadil (USA) -Zurarah (Siberian Express (USA)) *1510[10] 3282[15]* **>37a 41f<**

**Expeditious (USA)** 2 bb c Forestry (USA) -Nonies Dancer Ali (USA) (Danzatore (CAN)) 5915[22] *6448[6]* **>45a 41f<**

**Explicit (IRE)** 3 ch c Definite Article-Queen Canute (IRE) (Ahonoora) *3304[12]* 3922[10] 4813[9] *5001[8] 5641[11]* **>35a 26f<**

**Explode** 7 b g Zafonic (USA) -Didicoy (USA) (Danzig (USA)) 1876[4] 1993[9] 4511[2] 6201[2] 6548[10] **>58f<**

**Explosive Fox (IRE)** 3 ch c Foxhound (USA) -Grise Mine (FR) (Crystal Palace (FR)) *5907[11]* 6287[7] **>57a 67f<**

**Exponential (IRE)** 2 b g Namid-Exponent (USA) (Exbourne (USA)) 3469[13] (4804) **>80f<**

**Express Lily** 5 b m Environment Friend-Jaydeeglen (Bay Express) 6524[10] **><**

**Extemporise (IRE)** 4 ch c Indian Ridge-No Rehearsal (FR) (Baillamont (USA)) *796[8] 990[3] 1039[5]* (1592) (1986) *2854[6]* 5411[15] *6364[2]* **>56a 56f<**

**Exterior (USA)** 3 ch c Distant View (USA) -Alvernia (USA) (Alydar (USA)) *(4545)* (5076) 5470[4] (6307) **>89+a 106+f<**

**Extinguisher** 5 ch g Zamindar (USA) -Xaymara (USA) (Sanglamore (USA)) 1175[18] 2391[9] 2461[9] 2776[8] 3082[5] 3409[14] *5000[11]* **>24a 64f<**

**Extra Cover (IRE)** 3 b g Danehill Dancer (IRE) -Ballycurrane (IRE) (Elbio) *1226[2]* 1508[2] 1911[2] *2853[3] (3711) 4188[6]* 4456[2] *5220[13]*5697[7] *6014[4] 6537[6]* **>63 a 63f<**

**Extra Mark** 2 b g Mark Of Esteem (IRE) -No Comebacks (Last Tycoon) 1930[2] *2125[2]* 2627[4] 5377[20] 5670[14] **>73a 73f<**

**Extreme Beauty (USA)** 2 ch f Rahy (USA) -Mediation (IRE) (Caerleon (USA)) 2481[6] (2730) 3031[7] 3599[3] 4552[10] **>88f<**

**Extremely Rare (IRE)** 3 b f Mark Of Esteem (IRE) -Colourflash (IRE) (College Chapel) 1200[2] 1530[7] (1991) 3301[10] 3562[7] 3585[9] 4952[6] 6001[6] 6131[12] **>66f<**

**Eyeq (IRE)** 4 b f Cadeaux Genereux-Sans Prix (FR) (Caerleon (USA)) (3434a) **><**

**Eyes Dont Lie (IRE)** 6 b g Namaqualand (USA) -Avidal Park (Horage) 1344[9] 6245[8] **>38f<**

**Eyes Only (USA)** 3 b f Distant View (USA) -Yashmak (USA) (Danzig (USA)) (5123) **>82f<**

**Ezz Elkheil** 5 b g Bering-Numidie (FR) (Baillamont (USA)) *603[2] 706[4] 887[3] 1054[10]* 1539[12] 2305[7] 2752[7] **>84a 67f<**

F

**Faasel (IRE)** 3 b c Unfuwain (USA) -Waqood (USA) (Riverman (USA)) 4784a[6] 5357a[4] **>104f<**

**Faayej (IRE)** 4 b g Sadler s Wells (USA) -Russian Ballet (USA) (Nijinsky (CAN)) (2537) 2845[4] 4950[5] 5632[3] **>90f<**

**Fabios (IRE)** 2 b c Fasliyev (USA) -Bios (Lammtarra (USA)) 3362a[6] **>82f<**

**Fabioso (FR)** 2 gr c Medaaly-Formida (FR) (Highest Honor (FR)) 6256a[5] **><**

**Fabranese** 4 b f Dr Devious (IRE) -Babsy Babe (Polish Patriot (USA)) *2882[12]* **>22a 24f<**

**Fabria (PER)** 7 b m Farallon P (USA) -Singer (USA) (Stallion (USA)) *635a[5]* 831a[11] **>99a 47f<**

**Fabrian** 6 b g Danehill (USA) -Dockage (CAN) (Riverman (USA)) *525[8]* **>74a 64f<**

**Fabuleux River (FR)** 4 gr g Myrakalu (FR) -River Sans Retour (FR) (Vacarme (USA)) 911a[3] 1741a[14] 2438a[10] **>80f<**

**Fabuloso** 3 b f Dr Fong (USA) -Shafir (IRE) (Shaadi (USA)) *2231[5]* 4496[6] 4848[10] 5424[6] 5794[5] 6056[14] **>44a 44f<**

**Face The Limelight (IRE)** 5 b g Quest For Fame-Miss Boniface (Tap On Wood) 1393[14] 3056[6] 3835[7] **>42a 42f<**

**Fact And Fiction (IRE)** 2 b c Fasliyev (USA) -Flyleaf (FR) (Persian Bold) 3150[7] **><**

**Factual Lad** 6 b g So Factual (USA) -Surprise Surprise (Robellino (USA)) 2084[13] 2430[10] (2705) 4029[7] 4435[10] 5183[9] 5853[3] *6292[8] 6551[2]* **>64a 75f<**

**Factual Lady** 2 b f Factual (USA) -Shiny Kay (Star Appeal) 5521[11] **><**

**Fadael (IRE)** 2 b f In The Wings-Gift Box (IRE) (Jareer (USA)) 3491[7] 4198[6] 4579[3] 5476[3] 5753[8] *6021[5]* **>61a 63f<**

**Fadeela (IRE)** 3 ch f Desert King (IRE) -Gift Box (IRE) (Jareer (USA)) 1327[5] 1408[8] 2112[13] 2506[7] **>72a 72f<**

**Failed To Hit** 11 b g Warrshan (USA) -Missed Again (High Top) *594[3] 699[4] 950[6]* **>56 a 3f<**

**Faint Heart (IRE)** 2 b f Sadler s Wells (USA) -Never So Fair (Never So Bold) 5532a[3] 5961a[7] **>96f<**

**Fair Along (GER)** 2 b g Alkalde (GER) -Fairy Tango (FR) (Acatenango (GER)) 1505[7] 2096[8] 2382[7] 4584[4] 5090[9] 6129[9] **>70f<**

**Fair Compton** 3 b f Compton Place-Fair Eleanor (Saritamer (USA)) 2029[4] 2444[6] 2610[5] 3530[4] 4125[5] 4547[5] (4937) 6117[9] **>64f<**

**Fair Dream (GER)** 3 b f Dashing Blade-Fairlight (GER) (Big Shuffle (USA)) 5823a[11] **>75f<**

**Fairest Cape (USA)** 2 b f Storm Cat (USA) -Myth (USA) (Ogygian (USA)) 5971a[8] **>62f<**

**Fairgame Man** 6 ch g Clantime-Thalya (Crofthall) 1421[7] 1870[8] 2350[2] 3169[7] 3314[5] (3820) 3894[8] 4181[9] 4626[8]4782[8] 6059[2] **>27a 54+f<**

**Fairland (IRE)** 5 b g Blues Traveller (IRE) -Massive Powder (Caerleon (USA)) *2053[3]* 2324[4] 2939[10] *3088[6]* 5658[18] 5791[14] 6230[10] **>48a 54f<**

**Fairlie** 3 b f Halling (USA) -Fairy Flax (IRE) (Dancing Brave (USA)) 2355[5] 2973[7] 3507[7] (3817) 4449[3] 4760[8] **>66f<**

**Fairly Glorious** 3 b g Tina s Pet-Steamy Windows (Dominion) *591[8] 606[11] 835[9]* **>42a<**

**Fairmile** 2 b c Spectrum (IRE) -Juno Marlowe (IRE) (Danehill (USA)) 3665[3] 4730[3] 5872[6] 6338[4] **>80f<**

**Fair Mix (IRE)** 6 gr h Linamix (FR) -Fairlee Wild (USA) (Wild Again (USA)) (976a) 1144a[6] 1804a[3] 2924a[2] 5170a[6] (5727a) 6260a[4] **>121f<**

**Fairmorning (IRE)** 5 b g Ridgewood Ben-The Bratpack (IRE) (Mister Majestic) *446[2] 483[6] 880[5] 1514[2]* **>45a<**

**Fair Options** 3 gr g Marju (IRE) -Silver Singing (USA) (Topsider (USA)) 1796[17] 2029[7] 2236[3] 2703[16] **>67f<**

**Fair Shake (IRE)** 4 b g Sheikh Albadou-Shamrock Fair (IRE) (Shavian) 1175[7] 1246[10] 1665[3] 3079[5] 3309[15] 4130[2] 4837[6] 5242[2]5583[14] 5833[8] 6094[15] **>65a 75f<**

**Fair Spin** 4 ch g Pivotal-Frankie Fair (IRE) (Red Sunset) 3038[7] 3520[3] 3921[7] 5127[9] 6138[5] 6311[9] 6520[3] **>72f<**

**Fairy Monarch (IRE)** 5 b g Ali-Royal (IRE) -Cookawara (IRE) (Fairy King (USA)) 2408[2] 3041[8] 3411[2] 5546[15] 5714[8] 5796[6] **>48a 55 f<**

**Fairy Pass (IRE)** 3 ch f Houmayoun (FR) -Fairy Express (IRE) (Fayruz) 3328a[6] 5660a[10] **>79f<**

**Fairy Wind (GER)** 7 b h Dashing Blade-Fairy Bluebird (Be My Guest (USA)) *467[12] 715[9] 2186[3]* 2689[8] **>25a 25f<**

**Faites Vos Jeux** 3 b f Foxhound (USA) -Desert Bloom (FR) (Last Tycoon) 5141[13] 5547[15] 6004[5] *6280[10]* **>48a 42f<**

**Faithful Flash** 2 b f Tipsy Creek (USA) -Tudorealm (USA) (Palace Music (USA)) 2819[6] 3506[8] 3824[4] 4304[6] 5022[5] **>43f<**

**Faithfull Girl (IRE)** 2 b f Second Empire (IRE) -Cairde Nua (IRE) (Mukaddamah (USA)) *1276[9] 2405[9]* 2439[8] **>40a<**

**Faithful Warrior (USA)** 6 ch g Diesis-Dabaweyaa (IRE) (Shareef Dancer (USA)) 6193[20] **>98f<**

**Faith Healer (IRE)** 3 br f Key Of Luck (USA) -Cindy s Star (IRE) (Dancing Dissident (USA)) 1755[18] 2284[18] 2546[14] 2820[4] 3156[6] *(3710)* 3949[10] 4470[6] 5795[17]*6290[6]* **>61a 49f<**

**Faithisflying** 2 ch c Wolfhound (USA) -Niggle (Night Shift (USA)) 1589[13] 2096[6] 2382[11] 2523[6] 6305[6] **>37f<**

**Fait Le Jojo (FR)** 7 b g Pistolet Bleu (IRE) -Pretty Davis (USA) (Trempolino (USA)) 4441[12] 5619[11] **>72f<**

**Falcon Goer (USA)** 2 b f Zamindar (USA) -Elizabeth Eliza (USA) (Northern Prospect (USA)) 2213[8] 5096[13] 5341[8] **>43f<**

**Fall In Line** 4 gr g Linamix (FR) -Shortfall (Last Tycoon) *(609) (629) (645) (671) (679) (705)* **>92+a 61f<**

**Fallujah** 2 ch f Dr Fong (USA) -Brilliance (Cadeaux Genereux) 6440[14] **><**

**Falstaff (IRE)** 2 b c Montjeu (IRE) -Dance Of Love (IRE) (Pursuit Of Love) 6100a[5] **>87f<**

**Famcapii (IRE)** 2 b c Montjeu (IRE) -Scostes (Cadeaux Genereux) (6542a) **><**

**Fame** 4 ch g Northern Amethyst-First Sapphire (Simply Great (FR)) 6286[6] **>79f<**

**Familiar Affair** 3 b g Intikhab (USA) -Familiar (USA) (Diesis) 4490[7] 4780[10] (5210) 5672[3] 5992[11] **>81f<**

**Famous Grouse** 4 b g Selkirk (USA) -Shoot Clear (Bay Express) 1762[17] 5180[4] 5461[6] 5919[14] **>104f<**

**Fancy Foxtrot** 3 b c Danehill Dancer (IRE) -Smooth Princess (IRE) (Roi Danzig (USA)) *(1226)* 1795[10] 2202[14] 2642[3] 3598[9] *3850[7]* 4268[9] 4742[16] *5912[6]* **>89a 94f<**

**Fanling Lady** 3 gr f Highest Honor (FR) -Pain Perdu (IRE) (Waajib) 2392[8] 3952[7] 4562[10] **>73f<**

**Fanny s Fancy** 4 b f Groom Dancer (USA) -Fanny s Choice (IRE) (Fairy King (USA)) 1438[7] 2041[10] 3074[15] 3914[3] 4526[5] 5249[5] 6175[5] **>97+a 97f<**

**Fano Adriano (IRE)** 3 br c Wixim (USA) -Carmen The Best (IRE) (Waajib) 2340a[6] **><**

**Fantaisiste** 2 b f Nashwan (USA) -Fantastic Belle (IRE) (Night Shift (USA)) 4053[11] 4468[3] *5054[2] (6012)* **>79+a 68f<**

**Fantasia s Forest (IRE)** 2 b f Shinko Forest (IRE) -Persian Fantasia (Alzao (USA)) 3259[11] 6118[18] 6322[14] **>36f<**

**Fantasticat (USA)** 3 b c Storm Cat (USA) -Lotta Dancing (USA) (Alydar (USA)) *6491a[9]* **>109a 79f<**

**Fantastic Fleur (GER)** 2 f (USA) - (USA) (Baillamont (USA)) 6377a[11] **>63f<**

**Fantastic Horse (ARG)** 5 gr g Equalize (USA) -Farway Oca (ARG) (Egg Toss (USA)) 692a[6] 854a[4] 1003a[8] **>101f<**

**Fantastic Love (USA)** 4 b g Peintre Celebre (USA) -Moon Flower (IRE) (Sadler s Wells (USA)) 4214[8] 4858[7] 5435[3] 5916[2] (6582a) **>109f<**

**Fantastic Luck (IRE)** 2 b c Josr Algarhoud (IRE) -Fantastic Fantasy (IRE) (Lahib (USA)) 5716[16] 6149[14] 6441[10] **>45+f<**

**Fantastic Night (DEN)** 2 ch f Night Shift (USA) -Gaelic s Fantasy (IRE) (Statoblest) 6123[16] 6455[10] **>29f<**

**Fantastico (IRE)** 4 b f Bahhare (USA) -Minatina (IRE) (Ela-Mana-Mou) 2299[4] 2615[9] 4448[3] 4778[12] 5343[6] **>64a 64f<**

**Fantastic Star** 2 b f Lahib (USA) -Fervent Fan (IRE) (Soviet Lad (USA)) 1364[9] 2213[12] *4095[9]* **>12a 22f<**

**Fantastic View (USA)** 3 ch c Distant View (USA) -Promptly (IRE) (Lead On Time (USA)) 1410[5] 5439[4] **>110f<**

**Fantasy Believer** 6 b g Sure Blade (USA) -Delicious (Dominion) 1246[12] 1385[17] 1765[29] 2283[14] 2682[9] 3309[4] (3453) 3691[10] (4130) 4324[2]4837[10] 5393[20] 5628[2] 5799[6] 6071[3] **>105f<**

**Fantasy Crusader** 5 ch g Beveled (USA) -Cranfield Charger (Northern State (USA)) 1373[16] 2034[3] 2324[3] 2594[10] 2705[3] *3088[2]* 3423[9] 3911[17]4436[3] (4519) 4818[3] (5493) *6024[10] (6154) 6495[10]* **>65a 65f<**

**Fantasy Defender (IRE)** 2 b g Fayruz-Mrs Lucky (Royal Match) 1324[9] 1961[8] 2674[8] 3083[11] 4446[9] 4816[5] 5240[13] **>55 f<**

**Fantasy Ride** 2 b c Bahhare (USA) -Grand Splendour (Shirley Heights) 4292[7] (5023) 6268[5] 6472[2] **>90f<**

**Fantorini (USA)** 2 b c Theatrical-Beyrouth (USA) (Alleged (USA)) 4315[8] 5567[4] **>77f<**

**Farabutt (IRE)** 2 ch c Zafonic (USA) -Sonda (IRE) (Dolphin Street (FR)) 5389a[5] **><**

**Faraway Echo** 3 gr f Second Empire (IRE) -Salalah (Lion Cavern (USA)) 1214[15] *1678[6]* 2088[3] 3139[8] 4102[5] (4830) *4998[5]* **>39a 60f<**

**Faraway Look (USA)** 7 br g Distant View (USA) -Summer Trip (USA) (L Emigrant (USA)) *406[4] 512[5] 583[10]* **>57a 57f<**

**Fardaan (KSA)** 6 b h Mirror Black-Flying Mogambo (USA) (Mogambo (USA)) *634a[4]* **>88a<**

**Farewell Gift** 3 b c Cadeaux Genereux-Daring Ditty (Daring March) 1413[4] 1796[3] 2301[2] 2576[3] 2785[2] 3203[3] 4236[3] 4555[3](4845) 5652[7] **>82f<**

**Far For Lulu** 3 ch f Farfelu-Shady Habitat (Sharpo) *587[14] 660[12]* **>23a 32f<**

**Farnborough (USA)** 3 b g Lear Fan (USA) -Gretel (Hansel (USA)) *1015[5] 1202[7]* 2061[9] 2379[7] 3981[13] 4259[17] 5072[4] 5692[5]*6405[9]* **>53a 69f<**

**Farne Isle** 5 ch m Midnight Legend-Biloela (Nicholas Bill) 2653[4] 2983[3] 3587[7] 4155[13] **>65f<**

**Far Note (USA)** 6 ch g Distant View (USA) -Descant (USA) (Nureyev (USA)) *511[6] 543[2] 586[9] 680[9] 806[4] 897[6] (1033)* 1665[12] *(1738)* 1974[4] 2734[4] 3010[7] 3249[4] 3298[8] 3779[10] **>82a 70f<**

**Farouge (FR)** 3 gr c Croco Rouge (IRE) -Fablimixa (FR) (Linamix (FR)) 3565a[8] **>98f<**

**Farriers Charm** 3 b f In Command (IRE) -Carn Maire (Northern Prospect (USA)) *(1678)* 2112[12] 4580[7] (4848) 5136[5] 5869[10] *6579[10]* **>63a 72f<**

**Farthing (IRE)** 2 b f Mujadil (USA) -Neat Shilling (IRE) (Bob Back (USA)) 4197[2] 4643[4] 5334[2] 5816[3] **>75f<**

**Fascination Street (IRE)** 3 b f Mujadil (USA) -Loon (FR) (Kaldoun (FR)) 4351[2] 4801[3] 5352[2] (5637) 5868[6] **>70f<**

**Fashion House (USA)** 2 b f Quiet American (USA) -Polish Style (USA) (Danzig (USA)) 5569[5] 6196[2] **>73f<**

**Fast And Furious (FR)** 3 br c Singspiel (IRE) -Helvellyn (USA) (Gone West (USA)) 1350a[3] 2073a[6] **>107f<**

**Fast Gate (USA)** 5 gr h Gate Dancer (USA) -Myshiphascomin (USA) (Premiership (USA)) *1065[8]* **>93a<**

**Fast Heart** 3 b c Fasliyev (USA) -Heart Of India (IRE) (Try My Best (USA)) 1763[8] 2041[14] 2294[4] 2897[13] **>98f<**

**Fastidia** 3 b f Fasliyev (USA) -Intellectuelle (Caerleon (USA)) 2193a[7] **>92f<**

**Fast Lane (IRE)** 5 ch g Hamas (IRE) -Rainstone (Rainbow Quest (USA)) 1174[13] 1389[17] **><**

**Fasylitator (IRE)** 2 b c Fasliyev (USA) -Obsessed (Storm Bird (CAN)) 44206 48093 50156 537710 *60124* 63386 **>67a 76f<**

**Fatayaat (IRE)** 3 b f Machiavellian (USA) -Maraatib (IRE) (Green Desert (USA)) 242510 **>57f<**

**Fatehalkhair (IRE)** 12 ch g Kris-Midway Lady (USA) (Alleged (USA)) 128211 **>76f<**

**Father Seamus** 6 b g Bin Ajwaad (IRE) -Merry Rous (Rousillon (USA)) *393413* **>52f<**

**Fattaan (IRE)** 4 b g Danehill (USA) -Bintalshaati (Kris) 408213 **>62f<**

**Faussaire (IRE)** 2 br c Fasliyev (USA) -Chalosse (Doyoun) 3790a7 **>82f<**

**Favour** 4 b f Gothenberg (IRE) -Prejudice (Young Generation) 22382 24599 33726 38677 413412 55883 586211 61177 **>80f<**

**Favourable** 3 b f Mark Of Esteem (IRE) -Top Society (High Top) 218217 582811 608216 **>31f<**

**Favourable Terms** 4 b f Selkirk (USA) -Fatefully (USA) (Private Account (USA)) (2967) 36006 (4323) **>115f<**

**Favouring (IRE)** 2 ch c Fayruz-Peace Dividend (IRE) (Alzao (USA)) 13144 196011 42568 47002 49184 56067 59896 **>67 f<**

**Favourita** 2 b f Diktat-Forthwith (Midyan (USA)) (4468) 51494 54135 59392 62133 **>104f<**

**Favourite Nation (IRE)** 3 ch c Cadeaux Genereux-Fernanda (Be My Chief (USA)) 2316a7 29666 3355a7 6104a17 **>97f<**

**Fayr Firenze (IRE)** 3 b g Fayruz-Shillay (Lomond (USA)) 1020$^{9}$ 1078$^{4}$ 1280$^{6}$ 1571$^{2}$ 1594$^{5}$ 1725$^{2}$ 1864$^{2}$2379$^{4}$ >48a 50f<

**Fayr Jag (IRE)** 5 b g Fayruz-Lominda (IRE) (Lomond (USA)) 2021$^{13}$ (3073) 3674$^{13}$ 4886$^{10}$ 5255a$^{9}$ 5982a$^{16}$ >120f<

**Fayrway Rhythm (IRE)** 7 b g Fayruz-The Way She Moves (North Stoke) 432$^{9}$ >14a 44f<

**Fayrz Please (IRE)** 3 ch g Fayruz-Castlelue (IRE) (Tremblant) 569$^{4}$ 747$^{4}$ 956$^{12}$ 1111$^{12}$ 5862$^{13}$ 6004$^{9}$ >57a 24f<

**Feaat** 3 b f Unfuwain (USA) -Trois Heures Apres (Soviet Star (USA)) 2059$^{3}$ (2555) 2997$^{6}$ 3944$^{6}$ 4321$^{4}$ >95f<

**Fearby Cross (IRE)** 8 b g Unblest-Two Magpies (Doulab (USA)) 847$^{6}$ 1204$^{7}$ 1969$^{4}$ 2646$^{5}$ 3205$^{8}$ 3321$^{8}$ 4294$^{5}$ 4727$^{4}$5124$^{6}$ (5541) 6124$^{5}$ 6445$^{8}$ >69a 75f<

**Fearless Flyer (IRE)** 2 bb f Brave Act-Canary Bird (IRE) (Catrail (USA)) 4158a$^{7}$ >84f<

**Fearless Spirit (USA)** 2 ch f Spinning World (USA) -Hot Princess (Hot Spark) 5846$^{5}$ >65+f<

**Fearn Royal (IRE)** 5 b m Ali-Royal (IRE) -Sparrowhawk (IRE) (Doyoun) 2603a$^{3}$ 4893a$^{2}$ 5972a$^{2}$ >108+f<

**Feast Of Romance** 7 b g Pursuit Of Love-June Fayre (Sagaro) 468$^{3}$ 503$^{3}$ (565) 642$^{3}$ 685$^{2}$ 707$^{6}$ 723$^{2}$ (807) 861$^{5}$ 1204$^{12}$ 1373$^{3}$ 1516$^{12}$ 2598$^{6}$ 2823$^{4}$ 3615$^{15}$ 5575$^{2}$6499$^{11}$ >62a 59f<

**Federstar (GER)** 2 b c In A Tiff (IRE) -Federspiel (Konigsstuhl (GER)) 6256a$^{8}$ ><

**Feed The Meter (IRE)** 4 b f Desert King (IRE) -Watch The Clock (Mtoto) 2236$^{16}$ 3008$^{2}$ (3383) 3692$^{11}$ 3917$^{10}$ >58f<

**Feeling Blue** 5 b m Missed Flight-Blues Indigo (Music Boy) 638$^{10}$ 876$^{16}$ >11a 57f<

**Feel The Need** 2 ch c Chocolat De Meguro (USA) -Mary Miller (Sharpo) 4347$^{9}$ ><

**Feet So Fast** 5 ch g Pivotal-Splice (Sharpo) 921a$^{DSQ}$ (1004a) 1145a$^{10}$ >89a 117 f<

**Felicity (GER)** 3 ch f Inchinor-Felina (GER) (Acatenango (GER)) 1983a$^{8}$ (4596a) 5255a$^{4}$ 6379a$^{5}$ >106f<

**Felicity (IRE)** 4 b f Selkirk (USA) -Las Flores (IRE) (Sadler s Wells (USA)) 1790$^{7}$ 2102a$^{3}$ 2297$^{4}$ (3699) 4982a$^{11}$ >102f<

**Felidae (USA)** 4 ch c Storm Cat (USA) -Colcon (USA) (Pleasant Colony (USA)) 446$^{9}$ 695$^{11}$ >45a 46f<

**Fellbeck Fred** 2 gr c Paris House-Wyse Folly (Colmore Row) 2686$^{8}$ 3248$^{13}$ 3526$^{7}$ 3709$^{4}$ >22a 35f<

**Feminist (IRE)** 2 b f Alhaarth (IRE) -Miss Willow Bend (USA) (Willow Hour (USA)) 1798$^{5}$ 2574$^{3}$ 2872$^{7}$ 4621$^{9}$ >67f<

**Fender** 3 b c Rainbow Quest (USA) -Rockfest (USA) (Stage Door Johnny (USA)) 5867$^{7}$ 6088$^{7}$ >58f<

**Fen Game (IRE)** 2 b c Montjeu (IRE) -Hatton Gardens (Auction Ring (USA)) 5620$^{6}$ 5915$^{9}$ >71f<

**Fen Gypsy** 6 b g Nashwan (USA) -Didicoy (USA) (Danzig (USA)) 745$^{5}$ 882$^{4}$ 932$^{10}$ 1055$^{7}$ 1097$^{9}$ 1274$^{2}$ (1533) 1876$^{2}$2560$^{4}$ 2833$^{5}$ (3626) 3734$^{2}$ 3841$^{4}$ (4401) 4438$^{4}$ 4846$^{4}$ 5176$^{3}$ 5317$^{8}$6081$^{16}$ >64a 77f<

**Fenrir** 2 ch c Loup Solitaire (USA) -Whoops (Shernazar) 4208$^{7}$ (4900) 5128$^{5}$ 5580$^{3}$ 5819$^{8}$ 6122$^{7}$ >83f<

**Fen Shui (UAE)** 2 b f Timber Country (USA) -Crystal Gazing (USA) (El Gran Senor (USA)) (5694) 6213$^{8}$ >86 f<

**Fenwicks Pride (IRE)** 6 b g Imperial Frontier (USA) -Stunt Girl (IRE) (Thatching) 1941$^{3}$ 2219$^{8}$ 4782$^{7}$ 4827$^{13}$ 5235$^{14}$ 6246$^{11}$ >12a 60f<

**Fernery** 4 b f Danehill (USA) -Fern (Shirley Heights) 1321$^{4}$ 1671$^{7}$ >81f<

**Fern House (IRE)** 2 b c Xaar-Certain Impression (USA) (Forli (ARG)) 5233$^{12}$ >45f<

**Ferrara Flame (IRE)** 2 b f Titus Livius (FR) -Isolette (Wassl) 4621$^{8}$ 4997$^{9}$ 5218$^{7}$ 6127$^{2}$ 6555$^{11}$ >39a 59f<

**Festive Affair** 6 b g Mujadil (USA) -Christmas Kiss (Taufan (USA)) 460$^{3}$ 625$^{11}$ 1237$^{4}$ >65a 58f<

**Festive Chimes (IRE)** 3 b f Efisio-Delightful Chime (IRE) (Alzao (USA)) 3267$^{7}$ 3839$^{3}$ 4097$^{7}$ 4868$^{8}$ 5448$^{6}$ 5639$^{9}$ >34a 56f<

**Festive Style (SAF)** 3 b f Fort Wood (USA) -Fanciful (ARG) (Ringaro (USA)) 711a$^{3}$ (831a) 1005a$^{2}$ 1143a$^{9}$ >111a 111f<

**Feu Duty (IRE)** 3 b f Fayruz-Fire Reply (IRE) (Royal Academy (USA)) 1742$^{6}$ (2353) 2650$^{9}$ 2784$^{12}$ 3894$^{18}$ 4279$^{13}$ 5242$^{18}$ >21a 68f<

**Ffiffiffer (IRE)** 6 b h Definite Article-Merry Twinkle (Martinmas) 1081$^{4}$ (1136) 1238$^{10}$ 1520$^{8}$ >67a 46f<

**Ffizzamo Go** 3 b g Forzando-Lady Lacey (Kampala) 4087$^{6}$ 4561$^{4}$ 5069$^{6}$ >33f<

**Fiamma Royale (IRE)** 6 b m Fumo Di Londra (IRE) -Ariadne (Bustino) 510$^{4}$ 896$^{12}$ 930$^{12}$ 1855$^{13}$ 3575$^{6}$ 4044$^{7}$ >53a 63f<

**Fictional** 3 b c Fraam-Manon Lescaut (Then Again) (2877) 3384$^{6}$ >91f<

**Fiddle Me Blue** 3 ch f Bluebird (USA) -Fiddle-Dee-Dee (IRE) (Mujtahid (USA)) 1473$^{5}$ 2181$^{9}$ 2741$^{14}$ 4289$^{9}$ (4622) 5442$^{3}$ 5550$^{6}$ 6175$^{11}$ 6532$^{2}$ >83f<

**Fiddlers Creek (IRE)** 5 b g Danehill (USA) -Mythical Creek (USA) (Pleasant Tap (USA)) 516$^{6}$ 679$^{10}$ 1172$^{7}$ 1341$^{7}$ (6142) 6533$^{4}$ >84a 71f<

**Fiddlers Ford (IRE)** 3 b g Sadler s Wells (USA) -Old Domesday Book (High Top) 492$^{3}$ 598$^{2}$ 916$^{2}$ 985$^{6}$ 1050$^{4}$ 1249$^{7}$ 2881$^{4}$3160$^{10}$ (3341) >79a 64f<

**Fiddles Music** 3 b f Fraam-Fiddles Delight (Colmore Row) 1227$^{9}$ (1375) 3190$^{4}$ 3391$^{5}$ 3669$^{6}$ 4467$^{5}$ 4941$^{7}$ (5036) 5284$^{6}$5750$^{7}$ >31a 46f<

**Fiefdom (IRE)** 2 br c Singspiel (IRE) -Chiquita Linda (IRE) (Mujadil (USA)) 1462$^{5}$ 2045$^{4}$ (2904) 3727$^{2}$ 4100$^{4}$ 5931$^{3}$ 6268$^{7}$ >95f<

**Fielding (IRE)** 4 b c Ali-Royal (IRE) -Night Scent (IRE) (Scenic) 5970a$^{7}$ >100f<

**Field Spark** 4 b g Sillery (USA) -On The Top (High Top) 1463$^{6}$ (2212) 2394$^{5}$ 2659$^{2}$ 2964$^{3}$ 3199$^{13}$ 3866$^{2}$ 5144$^{12}$ 5554$^{8}$5993$^{4}$ 6225$^{2}$ 6540$^{3}$ >62a 64 f<

**Fiennes (USA)** 6 bb g Dayjur (USA) -Artic Strech (USA) (Arctic Tern (USA)) 411$^{9}$ 460$^{7}$ 791$^{13}$ >40a 40f<

**Fiepes Shuffle (GER)** 4 br g Big Shuffle (USA) -Fiepe (GDR) (Zigeunersohn (EG)) 2466a$^{9}$ 3552a$^{2}$ 4596a$^{8}$ 5255a$^{14}$ >105f<

**Fiepes Winged (GER)** 3 b c Winged Love (IRE) -Fiepe (GDR) (Zigeunersohn (EG)) 5974a$^{3}$ 6512a$^{2}$ >111f<

**Fiery Angel (IRE)** 3 ch f Machiavellian (USA) -Flaming June (USA) (Storm Bird (CAN)) 4916$^{10}$ >10f<

**Fife And Drum (USA)** 7 bb g Rahy (USA) -Fife (IRE) (Lomond (USA)) 525$^{7}$ 623$^{14}$ 2034$^{6}$ 2324$^{17}$ 2594$^{12}$ 3489$^{13}$ >66a 66f<

**Fifth Column (USA)** 3 b g Allied Forces (USA) -Miff (USA) (Beau Genius (CAN)) 2519$^{7}$ 3168$^{11}$ 4303$^{9}$ 5545$^{5}$ 6112$^{P}$ >69f<

**Figaro s Quest (IRE)** 2 b c Singspiel (IRE) -Seren Quest (Rainbow Quest (USA)) 4689$^{6}$ 5269$^{11}$ 6223$^{8}$ >35a 65f<

**Figgy s Brew** 2 ch f Ashkalani (IRE) -Marabela (IRE) (Shernazar) 6123$^{13}$ >57f<

**Fight Club (GER)** 3 b c Lavirco (GER) -Flaming Song (IRE) (Darshaan) (2541a) 3565a$^{10}$ 5683a$^{2}$ 6106a$^{4}$ 6378a$^{5}$ >110f<

**Fighting Lady (GER)** 2 br f Big Shuffle (USA) -Flatina (GER) (Platini (GER)) 6377a$^{9}$ >73f<

**Fighting Tom Cat (USA)** 2 ch c Storm Cat (USA) -Elizabeth Bay (USA) (Mr Prospector (USA)) 3946$^{11}$ 4649$^{6}$ (5154) >78f<

**Fight The Feeling** 6 ch g Beveled (USA) -Alvecote Lady (Touching Wood (USA)) 505$^{4}$ 581$^{2}$ 693$^{2}$ 777$^{8}$ 962$^{14}$ 1136$^{5}$ 2212$^{11}$2590$^{6}$ 3244$^{10}$ 3300$^{5}$ 5654$^{9}$ >64a 59df<

**Fight Your Corner** 5 b h Muhtarram (USA) -Dame Ashfield (Grundy) 2076$^{8}$ 5251$^{3}$ >113f<

**Figura** 6 b m Rudimentary (USA) -Dream Baby (Master Willie) 559$^{14}$ 650$^{3}$ 767$^{5}$ 892$^{6}$ 1053$^{6}$ 1097$^{6}$ 1940$^{5}$2324$^{16}$ 2594$^{8}$ 2929$^{8}$ 3441$^{8}$ 3934$^{5}$ 4339$^{14}$ >40a 40f<

**Figuresti (IRE)** 3 b f Indian Ridge-Refilee (IRE) (Sadler s Wells (USA)) 1805a$^{9}$ >78f<

**Filey Buoy** 2 b g Factual (USA) -Tugra (FR) (Baby Turk) 3233$^{13}$ 3834$^{7}$ 5097$^{13}$ 6195$^{7}$ >38f<

**Filliemou (IRE)** 3 gr f Goldmark (USA) -St Louis Lady (Absalom) 2112$^{9}$ 2648$^{10}$ 3301$^{8}$ 3700$^{5}$ 3993$^{2}$ 4470$^{4}$ 4580$^{4}$ 5411$^{18}$6296$^{12}$ 6461$^{15}$ >40a 61f<

**Film Maker (USA)** 4 bb f Dynaformer (USA) -Miss Du Bois (USA) (Mr Prospector (USA)) 6488a$^{2}$ >117f<

**Final Dividend (IRE)** 8 b g Second Set (IRE) -Prime Interest (IRE) (King s Lake (USA)) 3018$^{11}$ 3461$^{5}$ 3604$^{6}$ 4080$^{5}$ (4467) 4698$^{6}$ >54a 56f<

**Final Lap** 8 b g Batshoof-Lap Of Honour (Final Straw) 838$^{11}$ 994$^{3}$ 1514$^{7}$ >28a<

**Final Overture (IRE)** 2 b f Rossini (USA) -Two Magpies (Doulab (USA)) 3116$^{7}$ ><

**Final Promise** 2 b c Lujain (USA) -Unerring (Unfuwain (USA)) 5534$^{10}$ 5872$^{8}$ 6342$^{4}$ >64f<

**Financial Future** 4 b g Barathea (IRE) -In Perpetuity (Great Nephew) 1768$^{17}$ 2110$^{15}$ 2681$^{12}$ 3909$^{8}$ 4363$^{7}$ 5303$^{7}$ 5635$^{14}$ >75f<

**Financial Times (USA)** 2 b c Awesome Again (CAN) -Investabull (USA) (Holy Bull (USA)) 2804$^{2}$ >83f<

**Finders Keepers** 3 b g Selkirk (USA) -La Nuit Rose (FR) (Rainbow Quest (USA)) 1052$^{2}$ 1202$^{3}$ (1342) 1702$^{8}$ 2378$^{8}$ 2704$^{8}$ (4515) 5220$^{12}$ 5837$^{8}$ >81a 64f<

**Fine Frenzy (IRE)** 4 b f Great Commotion (USA) -Fine Project (IRE) (Project Manager) 1389$^{7}$ 1680$^{4}$ 2209$^{11}$ >55a 61 f<

**Fine Lady** 2 ch f Selkirk (USA) -Rua D Oro (USA) (El Gran Senor (USA)) 5172$^{6}$ 5406$^{2}$ 5831$^{3}$ 6211$^{2}$ >69f<

**Fine Palette** 4 ch c Peintre Celebre (USA) -Filly Mignonne (IRE) (Nashwan (USA)) (1967) (2210) 2691$^{5}$ 3482$^{5}$ 4118$^{3}$ 4540$^{19}$ >97f<

**Fine Silver (IRE)** 3 gr c Intikhab (USA) -Petula (Petong) 2019$^{4}$ 2306$^{10}$ (2420) 3001$^{4}$ 3943$^{2}$ 4271$^{2}$ 5941$^{3}$ 6547$^{2}$ >108f<

**Finger Of Fate** 4 br g Machiavellian (USA) -La Nuit Rose (FR) (Rainbow Quest (USA)) 546$^{9}$ 604$^{12}$ 684$^{7}$ 765$^{14}$ 897$^{12}$ 1018$^{12}$ 1699$^{2}$1738$^{6}$ 2012$^{4}$ 2227$^{6}$ 2350$^{13}$ 3580$^{8}$ 3801$^{3}$ 4132$^{14}$4568$^{3}$ 4800 5526$^{10}$ 5818$^{12}$ >48a 48f<

**Finished Article (IRE)** 7 b g Indian Ridge-Summer Fashion (Moorestyle) 1456$^{13}$ 2201$^{5}$ 2534$^{3}$ 2969$^{16}$ 3539$^{10}$ 4287$^{19}$ 4920$^{9}$ 6193$^{4}$6475$^{8}$ >99f<

**Finnegans Rainbow** 2 ch c Spectrum (IRE) -Fairy Story (IRE) (Persian Bold) 6149$^{11}$ >30f<

**Finnforest (IRE)** 4 ch g Eagle Eyed (USA) -Stockrose (Horage) 5221$^{12}$ >58f<

**Finningley Connor** 4 b g Cosmonaut-Arroganza (Crofthall) 1032$^{10}$ 1389$^{16}$ 1533$^{11}$ >9a 74df<

**Fiore Di Bosco (IRE)** 3 b f Charnwood Forest (IRE) -Carabine (USA) (Dehere (USA)) 2075$^{5}$ 2391$^{10}$ 2880$^{4}$ 3122$^{4}$ 3515$^{6}$ >75+a 80f<

**Fire At Will** 2 b c Lugana Beach-Kahyasi Moll (IRE) (Brief Truce (USA)) 3140$^{7}$ 3571$^{7}$ 5132$^{8}$ 5508$^{7}$ >40f<

**Firebelly** 3 b f Nicolotte-Desert Delight (IRE) (Green Desert (USA)) 913$^{5}$ 4570$^{7}$ 5898$^{10}$ >65a 86f<

**Firebird** 3 b f Soviet Star (USA) -Al Corniche (IRE) (Bluebird (USA)) 4144$^{3}$ >69f<

**Firebird Rising (USA)** 3 b f Stravinsky (USA) -Capable (USA) (Capote (USA)) 2450$^{5}$ 2675$^{8}$ 2937$^{3}$ 3517$^{6}$ 3954$^{9}$ 4387$^{4}$ 4702$^{7}$ 5141$^{7}$5448$^{3}$ 5639$^{14}$ >47f<

**Firebreak** 5 b h Charnwood Forest (IRE) -Breakaway (Song) (1142a) 2109$^{4}$ 5414$^{2}$ (6214) >118a 121f<

**Firecat** 5 ch g Beveled (USA) -Noble Soul (Sayf El Arab (USA)) 529$^{11}$ 1445$^{7}$ 1584$^{10}$ 1909$^{9}$ 2246$^{11}$ 3262$^{6}$ >53a 53f<

**Firedance (GER)** 3 br f Lomitas-Fraulein Tobin (USA) (J O Tobin (USA)) 1652a$^{8}$ >85f<

**Fire Dome (IRE)** 12 ch g Salt Dome (USA) -Penny Habit (Habitat) 918$^{13}$ >80 f<

**Fire Dragon (IRE)** 3 b g Sadler s Wells (USA) -Cattermole (USA) (Roberto (USA)) 3292$^{5}$ 4692$^{4}$ >82f<

**Fire Finch** 3 ch f Halling (USA) -Fly For Fame (Shaadi (USA)) 1311$^{6}$ 2081$^{6}$ 2425$^{8}$ 2809$^{6}$ 3837$^{14}$ >51f<

**Firenze** 3 ch f Efisio-Juliet Bravo (Glow (USA)) 3179$^{9}$ (4097) >77+a 34f<

**Firesong** 2 b c Dansili-Leaping Flame (USA) (Trempolino (USA)) 6145$^{6}$ >72f<

**Fire Up The Band** 5 b h Prince Sabo-Green Supreme (Primo Dominie) 1061$^{7}$ 1126$^{7}$ 1353$^{3}$ 1471$^{4}$ 3074$^{21}$ (3732) 4269$^{12}$ 4886$^{11}$ 5505a$^{7}$5628$^{21}$ >88a 114f<

**Firewire** 6 b g Blushing Flame (USA) -Bay Risk (Risk Me (FR)) (3386) 3631$^{16}$ >52a 72f<

**Firework** 6 b g Primo Dominie-Prancing (Prince Sabo) 771$^{11}$ 987$^{11}$ 1087$^{12}$ 1909$^{6}$ 2399$^{5}$ 2948$^{9}$ (3260) 3663$^{9}$4403$^{12}$ 5184$^{4}$ 5849$^{4}$ >64a 69f<

**Firozi** 5 b m Forzando-Lambast (Relkino) 4386$^{5}$ >55 f<

**First Candlelight** 3 b f First Trump-No Candles Tonight (Star Appeal) 1704$^{9}$ 2642$^{17}$ 3602$^{7}$ 4646$^{12}$ >79f<

**First Centurion** 3 b c Peintre Celebre (USA) -Valley Of Hope (USA) (Riverman (USA)) (1827) 2281$^{8}$ 2683$^{11}$ 4520$^{4}$ 6143$^{5}$ 6396$^{9}$ >60a 87f<

**First Charter** 5 b h Polish Precedent (USA) -By Charter (Shirley Heights) 1925$^{9}$ (3315) 4285$^{2}$ (4832) 5662a$^{3}$ >119f<

**First Class Girl** 5 b m Charmer-Boulevard Girl (Nicholas Bill) 471$^{4}$ 2520$^{10}$ >1a 36f<

**First Class Lady** 4 ch f Lion Cavern (USA) -Tino-Ella (Bustino) 659$^{5}$ 857$^{12}$ >35a 35f<

**First Counsel** 3 b g Wolfhound (USA) -Supreme Kingdom (Take A Reef) 2270$^{5}$ 2654$^{3}$ >76f<

**First Dawn** 3 ch f Dr Fong (USA) -Delight Of Dawn (Never So Bold) 2286$^{7}$ 2577$^{11}$ 3246$^{8}$ 5259$^{16}$ >66f<

**First Dynasty (USA)** 4 bb c Danzig (USA) -Willow Runner (USA) (Alydar (USA)) (1628) 1845$^{7}$ 4209$^{6}$ 4808$^{3}$ 6286$^{7}$ >80a 87f<

**First Eagle** 5 b g Hector Protector (USA) -Merlin s Fancy (Caerleon (USA)) 406$^{12}$ 5585$^{3}$ >55a 40f<

**First Eclipse (IRE)** 3 b f Fayruz-Naked Poser (IRE) (Night Shift (USA)) 3838$^{9}$ 4320$^{11}$ >47f<

**First Fought (IRE)** 2 b g Germany (USA) -Royal Flame (IRE) (Royal Academy (USA)) 6441$^{18}$ >8f<

**First Maite** 11 b g Komaite (USA) -Marina Plata (Julio Mariner) 437$^{6}$ 485$^{6}$ 627$^{6}$ 825$^{4}$ 2591$^{3}$ 3103$^{2}$ 3282$^{3}$3604$^{5}$ >78a 65f<

**First Of May** 3 b f Halling (USA) -Finger Of Light (Green Desert (USA)) 597$^{3}$ 766$^{4}$ 1095$^{6}$ >53a 52f<

**First Order** 3 b g Primo Dominie-Unconditional Love (IRE) (Polish Patriot (USA)) 3945$^{2}$ 4165$^{22}$ 4805$^{6}$ 5564$^{2}$ >108 f<

**First Rhapsody (IRE)** 2 b f Rossini (USA) -Tinos Island (IRE) (Alzao (USA)) 2458$^{12}$ 2730$^{11}$ 5953$^{4}$ >56a 26f<

**First Row (IRE)** 2 b c Daylami (IRE) -Ballet Society (FR) (Sadler s Wells (USA)) 4030$^{5}$ >76f<

**First Rule** 2 ch c Primo Dominie-Tarsa (Ballad Rock) 1826$^{7}$ 2947$^{4}$ 3302$^{4}$ 3930$^{8}$ 5721$^{8}$ >68f<

**Fisby** 3 ch g Efisio-Trilby (In The Wings) 3846$^{5}$ 4195$^{5}$ 4717$^{14}$ 5252$^{10}$ 5748$^{10}$ (6541) >66a 65 f<

**Fisher s Dream** 3 b g Groom Dancer (USA) -Cremets (Mummy s Pet) 433$^{7}$ >48a 32f<

**Fishlake Flyer (IRE)** 3 b f Desert Style (IRE) -Millitrix (Doyoun) 1362$^{4}$ 2468$^{3}$ 4021$^{4}$ >64f<

**Fisich** 5 ch h Halling (USA) -Sispre (Master Willie) 6513a$^{5}$ >113f<

**Fisio Therapy** 4 b g Efisio-Corn Lily (Aragon) 1456$^{9}$ 1604$^{4}$ 1903$^{P}$ >89+f<

**Fission** 3 ch f Efisio-Area Girl (Jareer (USA)) 591$^{6}$ 696$^{3}$ (817) 965$^{9}$ 5737$^{2}$ 6459$^{10}$ >73a 76f<

**Fitting Guest (IRE)** 3 ch c Grand Lodge (USA) -Sarah-Clare (Reach) 1508$^{6}$ 2197$^{2}$ 2390$^{2}$ (2878) 3001$^{14}$ >78+f<

**Fit To Fly (IRE)** 3 b g Lahib (USA) -Maid Of Mourne (Fairy King (USA)) 906$^{2}$ 982$^{5}$ (1044) 2847$^{5}$ 3280$^{6}$ 3535$^{9}$ 3689$^{5}$ 4493$^{12}$4882$^{8}$ 5829$^{7}$ 6225$^{11}$ 6537$^{9}$ >69a 80f<

**Fitz The Bill (IRE)** 4 b f Mon Tresor-In The Sky (IRE) (Imp Society (USA)) 535$^{8}$ 1164$^{8}$ 1727$^{3}$ 2092$^{3}$ 2520$^{7}$ 4065$^{11}$ 4202$^{9}$ >38a 41f<

**Fitzwarren** 3 b g Presidium-Coney Hills (Beverley Boy) 2457$^{14}$ 3562$^{3}$ 3777$^{10}$ 4320$^{9}$ 4456$^{3}$ 4576$^{6}$ 5242$^{17}$ 5754$^{6}$5849$^{18}$ 6199$^{12}$ >69f<

**Five Dynasties (USA)** 3 b c Danehill (USA) -Star Begonia (Sadler s Wells (USA)) 1966$^{3}$ 2722a$^{8}$ (3032) 3353a$^{8}$ >111f<

**Five Gold (IRE)** 3 b g Desert Prince (IRE) -Ceide Dancer (IRE) (Alzao (USA)) 2614$^{11}$ 2880$^{7}$ 5370$^{16}$ 5656$^{10}$ 6467$^{9}$ >69a 68f<

**Fiveoclock Express (IRE)** 4 gr g Woodborough (USA) -Brooks Masquerade (Absalom) 1065$^{4}$ 1772$^{2}$ 1968$^{13}$ 2366$^{7}$ 2504$^{5}$ 3850$^{2}$ 4122$^{16}$ 4751$^{10}$5706$^{9}$ 6124$^{11}$ >97a 90f<

**Five Years On (IRE)** 3 b g Desert Sun-Snowspin (Carwhite) 5478$^{4}$ 5829$^{4}$ 6064$^{5}$ >69a 70f<

**Fixateur** 2 b c Anabaa (USA) -Fabulous Account (USA) (Private Account (USA)) 6262a$^{4}$ >85f<

**Fizzy Lady** 3 b f Efisio-The Frog Lady (IRE) (Al Hareb (USA)) 553$^{4}$ 606$^{4}$ (751) 2727$^{7}$ 3700$^{11}$ 4241$^{12}$ 5072$^{7}$ 5260$^{14}$5408$^{2}$ 5692$^{4}$ 5791$^{10}$ (5863) 6085$^{7}$ >67a 57f<

**Fizzy Lizzy** 4 b f Cool Jazz-Formidable Liz (Formidable (USA)) 2556$^{12}$ 3381$^{11}$ 3954$^{8}$ (4257) 4879$^{9}$ >34a 43f<

**Fizzy Pop** 5 b m Robellino (USA) -Maria Isabella (FR) (Young Generation) 4351$^{6}$ 4987$^{8}$ >31f<

**Flag Lieutenant** 2 b c Machiavellian (USA) -Fairy Godmother (Fairy King (USA)) 6145$^{2}$ >81f<

**Flag Point (IRE)** 2 b c Indian Danehill (IRE) -Bianca Cappello (IRE) (Glenstal (USA)) 3240$^{3}$ 4335$^{7}$ 4967$^{9}$ 5885$^{11}$ 6562$^{11}$ >76f<

**Flamand (USA)** 2 ch f Miswaki (USA) -Sister Sorrow (USA) (Holy Bull (USA)) 2730$^{5}$ >61f<

**Flambe** 6 b g Whittingham (IRE) -Uaeflame (IRE) (Polish Precedent (USA)) 437$^{4}$ >65a 64f<

**Flambo (GER)** 4 ch c Platini (GER) -Flaming Song (IRE) (Darshaan) 1259a$^{2}$ >108f<

**Flamboyant Lad** 3 ch c Nashwan (USA) -Cheeky Charm (USA) (Nureyev (USA)) 1116$^{3}$ 3603$^{3}$ 4850$^{3}$ 5371$^{2}$ (5591) (5942) (6172) >92f<

**Flamenco Bride** 4 b f Hernando (FR) -Premier Night (Old Vic) 3752$^{7}$ 4075$^{7}$ 4441$^{3}$ 5875$^{11}$ >77f<

**Flame Of Zara** 5 ch m Blushing Flame (USA) -Sierra Madrona (USA) (Woodman (USA)) 1173$^{7}$ 1463$^{4}$ 6110$^{7}$ >59f<

**Flame Princess** 4 ch f Bluegrass Prince (IRE) -Rekindled Flame (IRE) (King s Lake (USA)) 856$^{3}$ 951$^{11}$ 999$^{8}$ 1020$^{14}$ >46a 44f<

**Flame Queen** 3 b f The West (USA) -Red Cloud (IRE) (Taufan (USA)) 3089$^{9}$ 3478$^{11}$ 3993$^{9}$ 4496$^{4}$ 5156$^{8}$ 5371$^{4}$ 5572$^{12}$ 5945$^{7}$6147$^{8}$ >69f<

**Flamingo Palace** 3 ch g Croco Rouge (IRE) -Chantilly (FR) (Sanglamore (USA)) 2312$^{7}$ ><

**Flaming Spirt** 5 b m Blushing Flame (USA) -Fair Test (Fair Season) 4339$^{4}$ 4616$^{4}$ 4713$^{2}$ 5021$^{17}$ >47a 58f<

**Flamjica (USA)** 3 ch f Real Quiet (USA) -Fiamma (IRE) (Irish River (FR)) 2693$^{4}$ 3094$^{2}$ >71f<

**Flapdoodle** 6 b m Superpower-My Concordia (Belfort (FR)) 3084$^{5}$ 3575$^{12}$ 4085$^{11}$ 4400$^{14}$ 4970$^{3}$ 5930$^{11}$ 6059$^{5}$ 6403$^{8}$ >45a 63f<

**Flaran** 4 b g Emarati (USA) -Fragrance (Mtoto) 4034$^{15}$ 4800 5008$^{11}$ 5734$^{3}$ 6131$^{3}$ >69f<

**Flashing Blade** 4 b f Inchinor-Finlaggan (Be My Chief (USA)) 1126$^{15}$ 1453$^{7}$ 1685$^{13}$ 2143$^{12}$ 2506$^{9}$ (3154) 3536$^{7}$ 3867$^{6}$ 4305$^{5}$4779$^{9}$ 5304$^{2}$ >70f<

**Flash Ram** 3 b g Mind Games-Just A Gem (Superlative) 1209$^{6}$ 2217$^{4}$ 3019$^{2}$ 3251$^{2}$ 3410$^{6}$ (3896) 4489$^{6}$ 5063$^{3}$ 5317$^{19}$ >67f<

**Flaunting It (IRE)** 2 ch f Alhaarth (IRE) -Ide Say (IRE) (Grand Lodge (USA)) 4053$^{5}$ 4682$^{8}$ 5115$^{4}$ 5548$^{6}$ >66f<

**Flaunt N Flirt** 2 b f Erhaab (USA) -Lets Fall In Love (USA) (Northern Baby (CAN)) 5890$^{9}$ 6447$^{10}$ 6536$^{2}$ >59a 29f<

**Flaxby** 2 b g Mister Baileys-Harryana (Efisio) 3233$^{14}$ 5362$^{8}$ 5857$^{4}$ 6333$^{8}$ >62f<

**Fleet Anchor** 3 b c Fleetwood (IRE) -Upping The Tempo (Dunbeath (USA)) 3486$^{9}$ 3954$^{7}$ 4309$^{3}$ 4674$^{2}$ 4868$^{5}$ 5510$^{3}$ 5693$^{5}$ 6086$^{10}$6461$^{11}$ >62f<

**Fleetfoot Mac** 3 b g Fleetwood (IRE) -Desert Flower (Green Desert (USA)) (1579) (1998) 2561$^{8}$ 2753$^{14}$ 3379$^{3}$ 3806$^{4}$ 4210$^{9}$ 5205$^{13}$ >68a 70f<

**Fleeting Moon** 4 ch f Fleetwood (IRE) -Aunt Judy (Great Nephew) 449$^{2}$ 676$^{2}$ (935) 981$^{3}$ 2167$^{2}$ 3638$^{4}$ >69a 70f<

**Fleetstreet Dancer (USA)** 6 br g Smart Strike (USA) -Street Ballet (USA) (Nijinsky (CAN)) 1147a$^{7}$ >114a<

**Fleetwood Bay** 4 b g Fleetwood (IRE) -Caviar And Candy (Soviet Star (USA)) 1225$^{16}$ 1504$^{14}$ 1845$^{6}$ 3086$^{3}$ 3440$^{6}$ 3698$^{9}$ 4238$^{2}$ 4438$^{6}$4912$^{7}$ 5201$^{10}$ >85a 80f<

**Fletcher** 10 b g Salse (USA) -Ballet Classique (USA) (Sadler s Wells (USA)) 1081$^{12}$ 1644$^{5}$ (1693) 2385$^{7}$ 2501$^{12}$ 2874$^{10}$ 4261$^{4}$ >49a 47 f<

**Fleurie Domaine** 5 b m Unfuwain (USA) -Craigmill (Slip Anchor) 1259a$^{5}$ 1952a$^{10}$ 3504a$^{8}$ 3973a$^{8}$ >97f<

**Flier s Fantasy (TUR)** 5 b h Lahib (USA) -Fantasy Flyer (USA) (Lear Fan (USA)) 5488a$^{10}$ ><

**Flight Commander (IRE)** 4 b g In The Wings-Lucrezia (IRE) (Machiavellian (USA)) 4987$^{5}$ 5344$^{7}$ 5773$^{16}$ 6110$^{11}$ 6533$^{12}$ >62f<

**Flight Of Esteem** 4 b g Mark Of Esteem (IRE) -Miss Up N Go (Gorytus (USA)) 418$^{2}$ 600$^{2}$ >101a 97f<

**Flighty Fellow (IRE)** 4 ch g Flying Spur (AUS) -Al Theraab (USA) (Roberto (USA)) 1125$^{15}$ 1284$^{6}$ (2196) 2969$^{18}$ 3477$^{6}$ 3717$^{2}$ 4178$^{4}$ 4540$^{16}$ 5462$^{4}$5813$^{3}$ 6044$^{10}$ >102f<

**Fling** 3 b f Pursuit Of Love-Full Orchestra (Shirley

Heights) (1532) 2403[5] 3091[2] 4729[2] 5788[4] 6443[5] 6534[3] 6575[4] >**91f**<

**Flint River** 6 b g Red Ransom (USA) -She s All Class (USA) (Rahy (USA)) *486[2] 607[7] 775[8] 1065[12] (1139)* 1317[2] 1927[4] 2206[10]2575[9] 4435[2] 5017[2] 5403[5] *6277[8]* >**92a 81f**<

**Flipando (IRE)** 3 b g Sri Pekan (USA) -Magic Touch (Fairy King (USA)) 1702[4] 2269[2] 2907[2] (3523) 4750[5] 5120[3] (5474) >**94f**<

**Flip Flop (FR)** 3 b f Zieten (USA) -Flaponny (USA) (Vernon Castle (USA)) (5969a) 6437a[7] >**100f**<

**Flip Flop And Fly (IRE)** 3 b g Woodborough (USA) -Angelus Chimes (Northfields (USA)) 1437[14] 1797[11] (2378) 2642[7] 3750[6] 4031[2] 4646[5] 5294[8] >**87f**<

**Flirting Groom** 3 b c Groom Dancer (USA) -Minstrel s Dance (USA) (Pleasant Colony (USA)) 4379a[5] ><

**Floosie (IRE)** 2 b f Night Shift (USA) -German Lady (Mon Tresor) 4058[9] 4243[10] >**11f**<

**Florenzar (IRE)** 6 b m Inzar (USA) -Nurse Tyra (USA) (Dr Blum (USA)) *589[10] 672[9]* >**21a 60f**<

**Florian** 6 b g Young Ern-Murmuring (Kind Of Hush) *2883[12]* 3386[8] 3841[13] 4418[5] 5035[6] 5337[18] 5597[8] >**71a 70f**<

**Florida Heart** 3 ch f First Trump-Miami Dancer (USA) (Seattle Dancer (USA)) 2284[4] 3206[6] >**74f**<

**Flossytoo** 2 b f Royal Applause-Nite-Owl Dancer (Robellino (USA)) 1105[10] (1601) 2129[9] 2568[12] 4508[9] >**69f**<

**Flotta** 5 ch g Elmaamul (USA) -Heavenly Goddess (Soviet Star (USA)) *1054[4]* 1401[5] 2110[7] 2491[4] 2855[4] 3276[3] 3485[7] (4453) 5182[6]5615[5] 5814[10] 6172[10] 6346[6] >**90a 93f**<

**Flower Bowl (FR)** 2 b f Anabaa (USA) -Lady Vettori (Vettori (IRE)) 4597a[9] >**69f**<

**Flowerdrum (USA)** 4 b f Mister Baileys-Norelands (USA) (Irish River (FR)) 1246[8] (1372) 2271[4] (3212) 4287[14] 4773[5] 5025[10] 5783[5] >**86+a 94f**<

**Flower Hill (FR)** 6 b h Esprit Du Nord (USA) -Fleur Du Cap (IRE) (Deep Run) 785a[2] ><

**Flower Seeker** 2 b f Lujain (USA) -Kingpin Delight (Emarati (USA)) 5198[16] 5688[9] 5871[12] >**22f**<

**Flur Na H Alba** 5 b g Atraf-Tyrian Belle (Enchantment) (2291) 3079[12] 4006[3] 5263[4] 5631[13] *6277[3]* >**87a 91f**<

**Flushing Meadows (USA)** 3 b c Grand Slam (USA) -Sheepish Grin (USA) (Our Native (USA)) 5553[5] >**86f**<

**Flying Adored** 3 b f Polar Falcon (USA) -Shining High (Shirley Heights) 1519[3] 3527[10] (4738) (5150) 5566[5] 5998[3] 6332[16] >**87f**<

**Flying Bantam (IRE)** 3 b g Fayruz-Natural Pearl (Petong) 1975[2] 2530[2] 2908[2] 3410[4] 3877[7] 4456[2] 4855[4] 5193[7]5526[4] (5803) *6222[3] (6482)* 6517[2] >**89a 88+f**<

**Flying Dancer** 2 b f Danzero (AUS) -Alzianah (Alzao (USA)) 4399[3] *5053[4]* 5434[17] 5767[9] >**67a 74f**<

**Flying Edge (IRE)** 4 b g Flying Spur (AUS) -Day Is Dawning (IRE) (Green Forest (USA)) *509[12] 719[2] 772[7]* 1787[5] 2215[14] 2899[6] 2936[5] 3409[16]3516[10] 4305[8] 4542[4] 5833[4] 6144[11] *6401[4]* >**58a 69f**<

**Flying Express** 4 ch c Air Express (IRE) -Royal Loft (Homing) 1385[6] 1623[12] 2469[2] 2750[8] 2891[3] 4360[11] *5055[9]* 5614[23] >**77a 93 f**<

**Flying Faisal (USA)** 6 b h Alydeed (CAN) -Peaceful Silence (USA) (Proper Reality (USA)) *421[8] 465[9] 572[10] 654[6] 665[8] 813[4] 858[15]941[8] 1089[3] 1180[10] 1510[4]* 1584[6] (1639) 1859[8] 2178[10]2322[9] 2383[13] 3151[18] >**38a 51f**<

**Flying Heart** 2 ch f Bahamian Bounty-Flying Wind (Forzando) 5890[7] 6126[8] 6342[8] >**44f**<

**Flying Highest** 2 b f Spectrum (IRE) -Mainly Sunset (Red Sunset) 5689[7] >**17f**<

**Flying Pass** 2 b g Alzao (USA) -Complimentary Pass (Danehill (USA)) 1826[8] 2300[3] 2736[8] 3438[2] *4023[2]* 4524[5] 4914[6] 5335[4]5852[2] 5995[7] >**69a 73f**<

**Flying Patriarch** 3 gr g Silver Patriarch (IRE) -Flying Wind (Forzando) 1674[13] 2840[8] >**38a 35f**<

**Flying Red (IRE)** 3 b f Entrepreneur-Mary Ellen Best (IRE) (Danehill (USA)) 1662[8] ><

**Flying Ridge (IRE)** 2 ch f Indian Ridge-Jarrayan (Machiavellian (USA)) 2786[14] 4488[5] 4876[5] (5233) >**76f**<

**Flying Spirit (IRE)** 5 b g Flying Spur (AUS) -All Laughter (Vision (USA)) (2032) (2798) (3873) 4772[9] 5182[2] >**64a 87f**<

**Flying Spud** 3 ch g Fraam-Lorcanjo (Hallgate) *1038[5] 1478[4]* 1844[5] (2088) 2395[7] *2667[7]* 3489[15] 3822[2]4624[9] 5236[11] 6227[5] *6361[5]* >**48a 54f**<

**Flying Tackle** 6 ch g First Trump-Frighten The Life (King s Lake (USA)) *453[10]* 1171[7] 2582[7] 2735[3] 3169[2] (3575) 3820[15] 3894[9] 4181[17]5346[11] 5452[2] 5736[11] >**43a 57f**<

**Flying Tara** 2 b f Kayf Tara-Arcady (Slip Anchor) 2360[7] ><

**Flying Treaty (USA)** 7 br h You And I (USA) -Cherie s Hope (USA) (Flying Paster (USA)) *486[11] 544[8] 641[9] 795[6]* 1199[8] 1345[7] *3419[5]*3555[6] 3997[8] >**75a 64f**<

**Flying With Eagles** 3 ch g Most Welcome-Super Sol (Rolfe (USA)) 2029[13] 2211[14] 2596[13] *2815[6]* 3984[17] >**21a 35f**<

**Fly Kicker** 7 ch g High Kicker (USA) -Double Birthday (Cavo Doro) 3518[7] 4007[6] >**40f**<

**Fly Me To Dunoon (IRE)** 2 b f Rossini (USA) -Toledana (IRE) (Sure Blade (USA)) 4277[8] 5154[6] *5735[10]* >**39a 37f**<

**Fly More** 7 ch g Lycius (USA) -Double River (USA) (Irish River (FR)) 4687[12] 5107[13] >**87f**<

**Flyoff (IRE)** 7 b g Mtoto-Flyleaf (FR) (Persian Bold) *3087[9]* 3885[10] >**14a 55f**<

**Fly So High** 3 b f Danzero (AUS) -Fly The Flag (NZ) (Sir Tristram) *816[10] 927[7]* 1127[8] 3529[11] >**24a 11f**<

**Fly To Dubai (IRE)** 2 b c Fly To The Stars-Morna s Fan (FR) (Lear Fan (USA)) 2300[11] 3080[6] *4023[13]* >**56f**<

**Focus Group (USA)** 3 b c Kris S (USA) -Interim (Sadler s Wells (USA)) (5239) >**77f**<

**Fokine (USA)** 3 b c Royal Academy (USA) -Polar Bird (Thatching) *1063[2]* 1459[2] (2308) 2966[2] >**105a 115f**<

**Fold Walk** 2 ch f Paris House-Georgia (Missed Flight) 1468[7] 1556[4] 2194[U] 2248[11] 3980[5] *4997[3]* 5097[11] 5556[13] >**46a 34f**<

**Foley Millennium (IRE)** 6 ch g Tagula (IRE) -Inshirah (USA) (Caro) 1518[8] (1988) (2869) (3126) (3524) 3772[12] 3979[2] (4299) 4547[4] 4855[2] 5094[8] 5550[5]5949[5] 6267[15] >**54a 81f**<

**Foley Prince** 3 b g Makbul-Princess Foley (IRE) (Forest Wind (USA)) *965[7] 1121[3] 1139[7]* (1997) 2371[2] 2847[2] 3155[3] 3527[6] >**65a 79f**<

**Folga** 2 b f Atraf-Desert Dawn (Belfort (FR)) 4245[3] 4607[9] (5475) 5839[5] >**71f**<

**Folio (IRE)** 4 b g Perugino (USA) -Bayleaf (Efisio) 4553[6] >**101f**<

**Follow (USA)** 3 b f Seeking The Gold (USA) -Bound (USA) (Nijinsky (CAN)) 2330a[12] 3547a[6] 4159a[7] >**88f**<

**Following Flow (USA)** 2 bb g King Of Kings (IRE) -Sign Here (USA) (Private Terms (USA)) 3601[9] *4022[3]* (4420) 4909[2] 5417[15] 6206[10] >**71a 79f**<

**Follow My Lead** 2 b f Night Shift (USA) -Launch Time (USA) (Relaunch (USA)) 2947[9] 3176[7] 5271[7] >**55f**<

**Follow The Game** 2 b c Mind Games-Play The Game (Mummy s Game) *6453[10]* >**35a**<

**Fol Parade (ARG)** 2 ch c Parade Marshal (USA) -Sadler s Folie (ARG) (Careafolie) 6169a[6] >**90f**<

**Fomalhaut (USA)** 5 b h Spinning World (USA) -Coup De Folie (USA) (Halo (USA)) 4795a[8] >**106f**<

**Fong Shui** 2 ch c Dr Fong (USA) -Manila Selection (USA) (Manila (USA)) 2096[4] *4022[7]* (4967) 5655[4] 6174[19] >**70+a 76f**<

**Fong s Thong (USA)** 3 ch c Dr Fong (USA) -Bacinella (USA) (El Gran Senor (USA)) (3906) (4322) 5414[5] 5782[7] >**114f**<

**Fongtastic** 2 ch c Dr Fong (USA) -Kelso Magic (USA) (Distant View (USA)) 3946[3] (4292) >**85f**<

**Fonthill Road (IRE)** 4 ch g Royal Abjar (USA) -Hannah Huxtable (IRE) (Master Willie) 2976[6] (3400) 3779[3] 4542[2] 4677[2] (4837) (5124) 5603[6] 5874[8] >**77+a 88f**<

**Foodbroker Founder** 4 ch g Groom Dancer (USA) -Nemea (USA) (The Minstrel (CAN)) 2241[7] 3034[6] 3482[6] 4214[15] 5133[6] 5401[8] 5761[12] >**101f**<

**Foolish Groom** 3 ch g Groom Dancer (USA) -Scared (Royal Academy (USA)) 1325[3] 2270[4] 2654[5] 3102[6] 3780[3] 4050[5] 4360[9] 5770[2]5992[3] *6224[P]* >**72f**<

**Foolish Thought (IRE)** 4 b g Green Desert (USA) -Trusted Partner (USA) (Affirmed (USA)) *491[6] 575[5] 605[4] (654) 993[5] 1098[14] 1279[11]* 3533[20] >**57a 13f**<

**Fools Entire** 3 ch g Fraam-Poly Blue (IRE) (Thatching) *462[2] 557[9] 675[3]* 1123[6] 1214[13] 2097[14] 2457[18] *4024[7]4515[9] 4926[3]* 5077[4] 5156[5] 5370[12] 6459[8] 6567[17] >**70a 61f**<

**Football Crazy (IRE)** 5 b g Mujadil (USA) -Schonbein (IRE) (Persian Heights) 1539[13] 2116[10] >**99f**<

**Foot Fault (IRE)** 3 b f Danehill (USA) -Mockery (Nashwan (USA)) *420[15] 1017[4] 1084[4] 1168[4]* >**54a 48f**<

**Footstepsinthesand** 2 b c Giant s Causeway (USA) -Glatisant (Rainbow Quest (USA)) (6408a) >**112+f**<

**Fora Smile** 3 ch c Forzando-Don t Smile (Sizzling Melody) *591[7] 696[10] 817[10] 907[7] 1083[11]* 1296[5] *1405[7]* >**44a 40f**<

**Forbearing (IRE)** 7 b g Bering-For Example (USA) (Northern Baby (CAN)) 3885[3] 4042[2] 5710[6] >**59f**<

**Force Nine (USA)** 2 br c Stormin Fever (USA) -Screener (USA) (Major Impact (USA)) 5592[5] >**68f**<

**Force Of Nature (USA)** 4 b f Sadler s Wells (USA) -Yashmak (USA) (Danzig (USA)) 2059[10] 2460[2] 2983[4] >**76f**<

**Forehand (IRE)** 2 b f Lend A Hand-Set Trail (IRE) (Second Set (IRE)) 6439[13] >**35f**<

**Foreign Affairs** 6 ch h Hernando (FR) -Entente Cordiale (USA) (Affirmed (USA)) (1110a) 1182a[3] 1435a[4] 1802a[5] (4377a) (4784a) 5506a[2] 6570[2] >**110f**<

**Forest Air (IRE)** 4 br f Charnwood Forest (IRE) -Auriga (Belmez (USA)) 1660[9] (1718) 1993[8] 2974[7] 3579[5] 3796[2] 4005[6] 4537[7] >**52f**<

**Forest Delight (IRE)** 2 ch f Shinko Forest (IRE) -Laurel Delight (Presidium) 5003[7] 5908[8] 6281[11] >**52f**<

**Forest Heath (IRE)** 7 gr g Common Grounds-Caroline Lady (JPN) (Caro) *672[10] 995[14]* >**15 a 15 f**<

**Forestier (FR)** 4 ch c Nikos-Forest Hills (FR) (Sicyos (USA)) 1578a[2] (2337a) (3963a) >**111f**<

**Forest Magic (IRE)** 4 b c Charnwood Forest (IRE) -Adultress (IRE) (Ela-Mana-Mou) 1124[4] 1455[9] 1925[5] 2108[7] >**100f**<

**Forest Queen** 7 b m Risk Me (FR) -Grey Cree (Creetown) *994[11] 2185[10]* 2620[13] *3612[9]* ><

**Forest Rail (IRE)** 4 b f Catrail (USA) -Forest Heights (Slip Anchor) 5372[12] 5553[8] >**66a 49f**<

**Forest Tune (IRE)** 6 b g Charnwood Forest (IRE) -Swift Chorus (Music Boy) 1109[14] 1298[10] 2032[8] 2212[6] 2705[9] *2881[11]* 3291[6] 3917[4]4086[5] 4485[3] >**66a 62f**<

**Forest Viking (IRE)** 2 b g Orpen (USA) -Berhala (IRE) (Doyoun) 2447[5] 2904[8] 4149[11] 5947[22] 6333[19] >**55f**<

**Forever Free (GER)** 4 ch c Platini (GER) -Forever Nice (GER) (Greinton) 3335a[8] 4378a[11] 6379a[6] >**100f**<

**Forever My Lord** 6 b g Be My Chief (USA) -In Love Again (IRE) (Prince Rupert (FR)) *672[8] 867[10] 919[9]* 2287[6] >**51a 51 f**<

**Forever Phoenix** 4 b f Shareef Dancer (USA) -With Care (Warning) *544[5] 596[6] (803) (917) 1051[2] (1205)* 1454[3] (1937) 2117[2] 2636[LFT]2857[9] 3976[2] 4165[3] 4526[7] 4805[3] 5105[6] (5287) 5393[6] 5671[6]5898[3] 6177[5] >**96a 106f**<

**Forfeiter (USA)** 2 ch g Petionville (USA) -Picabo (USA) (Wild Again (USA)) 1314[2] 1743[6] 2961[2] 3145[2] 6206[3] 6574[19] >**78f**<

**Forged (IRE)** 3 b c Peintre Celebre (USA) -Imitation (Darshaan) 1683[20] 2513[3] 3297[2] (4103) >**97+f**<

**Forge Lane (IRE)** 3 b g Desert Style (IRE) -March Fourteenth (USA) (Tricky Creek (USA)) *816[9] 890[9]* 1939[9] 2114[12] *3305[10]* 3827[4] 3990[2] 4436[9]4798[8] *4941[8]* 5658[17] >**51a 59f**<

**Forgery (IRE)** 2 ch c Dr Devious (IRE) -Memory Green (USA) (Green Forest (USA)) 6441[3] >**73f**<

**For Life (IRE)** 2 b c Bachir (IRE) -Zest (USA) (Zilzal (USA)) 3760[3] 5392[18] >**87+f**<

**Formalise** 4 b g Forzando-Esilam (Frimley Park) 2303[13] 2763[7] 3141[5] 3416[9] 3747[5] 4403[13] 4774[9] 5253[4]5512[12] 5736[14] >**71f**<

**Formeric** 8 ch g Formidable (USA) -Irish Limerick (Try My Best (USA)) *434[8] 474[9]* 1526[3] 1986[16] 3269[11] 4827[14] >**8a 45f**<

**Formidable Will (FR)** 2 b c Efisio-Shewillifshewants (IRE) (Alzao (USA)) 5996[11] *6291[11]* >**42a**<

**For Nowt** 2 b c Forzando-Angel Chimes (Most Welcome) 3055[6] 3444[12] 4135[9] 4559[10] 4699[13] >**34f**<

**Forpetesake** 2 ch g Primo Dominie-Showcase (Shareef Dancer (USA)) 2579[9] 2960[6] 3506[6] 4208[8] 5128[6] 5831[8] 5988[15] >**54f**<

**For Pub (ITY)** 2 b c Kafhar-Tetjna (IRE) (Marju (IRE)) 6380a[7] >**85f**<

**Forrest Gump** 4 ch g Zilzal (USA) -Mish Mish (Groom Dancer (USA)) 5345[10] 5801[2] 6200[9] >**51f**<

**Fort** 3 ch g Dr Fong (USA) -Chief s Quest (USA) (Chief s Crown (USA)) 2089[3] 2676[11] 3692[3] 4123[2] 4229[10] 5397[5] (5814) 5919[6] >**106f**<

**Fort Churchill (IRE)** 3 b g Barathea (IRE) -Brisighella (IRE) (Al Hareb (USA)) 2093[5] 2595[3] 4170[4] 4698[2] 5203[7] (5538) 5768[9] 5944[2] 6143[7] >**84f**<

**Fort Dignity (USA)** 3 b c Seeking The Gold (USA) -Kitza (IRE) (Danehill (USA)) 1459[4] 2068[4] >**108f**<

**Forthright** 3 b g Cadeaux Genereux-Forthwith (Midyan (USA)) *(450) 691a[8] 848a[4]* 1586[5] 3001[6] 3943[13] 4118[7] 4780[9]*5220[6]* 5766[9] 5992[6] >**89a 96f**<

**Fort Knox (GER)** 11 br h Surumu (GER) -Festival (GER) (Rocket) 786a[4] ><

**Fort McHenry (IRE)** 4 b g Danehill Dancer (IRE) -Griqualand (Connaught) 1185[8] 2976[8] (4495) *4602[12]* >**41a 68f**<

**Fortnum** 2 b c Forzando-Digamist Girl (IRE) (Digamist (USA)) 1826[5] 1936[3] 2736[9] 4365[5] 4914[3] 5909[10] >**60f**<

**Fortuna Mea** 4 b f Mon Tresor-Veni Vici (IRE) (Namaqualand (USA)) 1580[6] *2004[9]* >**52a 43f**<

**Fortunate Dave (USA)** 5 b g Lear Fan (USA) -Lady Ameriflora (USA) (Lord Avie (USA)) *740[11]* >**60a 60f**<

**Fortunate Isle (USA)** 2 ch c Swain (IRE) -Isla Del Rey (USA) (Nureyev (USA)) 5915[2] >**80+f**<

**Fortune Point (IRE)** 6 ch g Cadeaux Genereux-Mountains Of Mist (IRE) (Shirley Heights) *554[4] 695[10] 720[2] (874) 931[3] 1097[2]* 1272[19] 2121[12]*2883[4]* 3177[10] *4093[6]* 4436[2] 5258[9] >**67a 67 f**<

**Fortunes Favourite** 4 ch f Barathea (IRE) -Golden Fortune (Forzando) *461[9] 781[3] 937[4] 1238[12]* (1617) 2038[7] 2214[10] >**36a 50f**<

**Fortune s Princess** 3 b f Desert Prince (IRE) -Golden Fortune (Forzando) 3054[2] 3374[2] (3922) 4240[2] 5297[9] >**81f**<

**Forty Forte** 8 b g Pursuit Of Love-Cominna (Dominion) *412[11] 487[8] 861[9] 1194[3]* 1305[9] *1629[6] (2013) 2454[9]* >**56a 59f**<

**Forward Move (IRE)** 2 ch c Dr Fong (USA) -Kissing Gate (USA) (Easy Goer (USA)) 5269[2] (5716) >**93+f**<

**Forzeen** 2 ch g Forzando-Mazurkanova (Song) *2125[3]* 2872[4] 3104[2] *3418[3]* (3930) 4046[4] 4348[7] 5392[21] (5839)5932[8] *(6022)* >**87a 87f**<

**Forzenuff** 3 b c Mujadil (USA) -Sada (Mujtahid (USA)) *496[5] 619[7] 819[6] 959[8]* 3084[10] 3307[12] 3636[12] 5597[19] >**59a 68f**<

**Fossgate** 3 ch g Halling (USA) -Peryllys (Warning) 1420[2] 1957[16] 2571[3] 3152[6] 4258[4] 4781[4] 5210[4] 6199[8] >**77f**<

**Four Amigos (USA)** 3 b c Southern Halo (USA) -Larentia (Salse (USA)) 1333[5] (1473) 1614[9] 3077[6] 3523[3] 3702[7] 3926[9] 4862[11] 5117[4]5563[9] 5837[7] >**46a 89f**<

**Four Jays (IRE)** 4 b g Alzao (USA) -Paparazzi (IRE) (Shernazar) *448[9] 491[9]* >**86a 92f**<

**Four Kings** 3 b c Forzando-High Cut (Dashing Blade) *1228[5]* 1530[8] 2450[3] 2973[3] 3271[9] 4249[6] 4447[16] 4698[17] >**61a 67f**<

**Four Pence (IRE)** 3 b c Rainbow Quest (USA) -American Queen (FR) (Fairy King (USA)) 2944[4] 3454[2] *5216[6]* >**30a 71f**<

**Four Pleasure** 2 ch f King s Best (USA) -Please (Kris) 5569[16] 5915[23] >**35f**<

**Foursquare (IRE)** 3 b g Fayruz-Waroonga (IRE) (Brief Truce (USA)) (1602) 1883[5] 2293[10] 2877[4] 3523[12] 3795[3] >**93f**<

**Fourswainby (IRE)** 3 b g Foxhound (USA) -Arena (Sallust) 1420[6] 2037[3] >**39f**<

**Fourth Dimension (IRE)** 5 b g Entrepreneur-Isle Of Spice (USA) (Diesis) 3716[10] 4176[4] 4218[7] 5318[7] 6043[15] >**87 f**<

**Fox** 2 b c Diktat-Badawi (USA) (Diesis) 2644[2] (3093) 3672[4] 4227[3] 4949[6] >**100f**<

**Fox Covert (IRE)** 3 b g Foxhound (USA) -Serious Contender (IRE) (Tenby) 1200[7] 1614[14] 2036[11] 2351[2] 2457[3] 3059[5] 3410[8] 3877[4]4181[14] 5193[10] 5342[3] (5547) 5736[13] >**70f**<

**Foxhaven** 2 ch c Unfuwain (USA) -Dancing Mirage (IRE) (Machiavellian (USA)) 4681[3] 5268[2] 5729[2] (6151) 6340[6] >**93f**<

**Fox Hollow (IRE)** 3 b c Foxhound (USA) -Soignee (Night Shift (USA)) *451[7] 620[9] 751[3] 1040[2]* 1296[6] *1600[2] 2127[3]*2740[9] *3026[12] 4128[8]* 5571[10] >**54a 27f**<

**Foxies Future (IRE)** 3 b f General Monash (USA) -Indescent Blue (Bluebird (USA)) *458[3]* 6144[16] >**54a 46f**<

**Foxilla (IRE)** 3 ch f Foxhound (USA) -Lilissa (IRE) (Doyoun) *916[9] 1017[7]* 2949[3] (3156) 3383[4] 4079[3] 4368[2] >**48a 66f**<

**Foxy Gwynne** 2 b f Entrepreneur-Nahlin (Slip Anchor) *5053[10]* 5348[3] 6207[2] >**32a 70f**<

**Foxy Trix** 5 bb m Mind Games-Hill Vixen (Goldhill) *797[7]* ><

**Fraambuoyant (IRE)** 2 b f Fraam-River Maiden (USA) (Riverman (USA)) *2985[11]* 5855[10] *6221[9]* 6522[6] >**2a 27f**<

**Fraamtastic** 7 b m Fraam-Fading (Pharly (FR)) *713[2] 783[4] (875) 953[6] 1020[15] (1080) (1444)* 1583[2] >**53a 44f**<

**Frabrofen** 3 b f Mind Games-Oh My Oh My (Ballacashtal (CAN)) 1664[2] *6275[10]* 6526[9] >**5a 62f**<

**Fragrant Star** 3 gr f Soviet Star (USA) -Norfolk Lavender (CAN) (Ascot Knight (CAN)) 1458[8] 3091[7] 3320[10] 3728[10] 4496[9] >**77f**<

**Fraloga (IRE)** 2 b f Grand Lodge (USA) -Fragrant Hill (Shirley Heights) 5979a[3] >**107f**<

**Frambo (IRE)** 3 b f Fraam-Wings Awarded (Shareef Dancer (USA)) *746[9] 804[7] 1084[5]* 1267[10] 1499[6] *2485[4] 3305[4]*4207[4] 4302[3] 4867[3] 5178[6] >**49a 42f**<

**Frambroise** 2 ch f Diesis-Applaud (USA) (Rahy (USA)) 5569[13] >**32f**<

**Francis Flute** 6 b g Polar Falcon (USA) -Darshay (FR) (Darshaan) 1783[7] 2260[2] 2580[4] 3039[7] 4004[9] 4333[9] 6138[10] >**62f**<

**Franela** 2 b f Dansili-Pernilla (IRE) (Tate Gallery (USA)) 5695[10] 6207[8] >**52f**<

**Frangipani (IRE)** 3 b f Sri Pekan (USA) -Sharkashka (IRE) (Shardari) 2706[3] 3348[12] 4196[14] 4491[7] >**57f**<

**Frankies Wings (IRE)** 3 b g In The Wings-River Fantasy (USA) (Irish River (FR)) 1224[7] 1356[6] 2821[8] 3669[8] 3852[11] >**17a 54f**<

**Franklins Gardens** 4 b c Halling (USA) -Woodbeck (Terimon) 1622[4] 4539[4] 5170a[7] 5438[6] 5812[6] 6218[2] 6382a[6] >**115f**<

**Franksalot (IRE)** 4 ch g Desert Story (IRE) -Rosie s Guest (IRE) (Be My Guest (USA)) 2483[16] (3174) 3440[4] 3555[5] 4437[4] *(4602)* 5185[5] 5403[3] 5698[12] *6395[6]* >**81a 76f**<

**Frankskips** 5 b g Bishop Of Cashel-Kevins Lady (Alzao (USA)) *448[11] 604[5] 701[12] 745[7] 926[3] 1098[3] 1207[8]* >**60a 59f**<

**Frank Sonata** 3 b c Opening Verse (USA) -Megdale (IRE) (Waajib) 1437[6] (2018) 2107[3] (2683) (3927) 5463[9] 6263a[7] 6355[2] >**108f**<

**Frank s Quest (IRE)** 4 b g Mujadil (USA) -Questuary (IRE) (Rainbow Quest (USA)) *498[7] 714[2] 773[3] 874[3] 988[6]* 1389[10] *1598[4]*1710[7] *2007[2] (2454) (2990) 3023[11]* 3626[12] *6499[3]* >**62a 56f**<

**Fransiscan** 2 ch g Fraam-Ordained (Mtoto) 2074[7] 2248[8] 3100[6] 5083[10] 5556[5] >**41f**<

**Frantic** 2 ch f Fraam-Carn Maire (Northern Prospect (USA)) 2585[10] 3116[4] 3531[4] >**58f**<

**Frantoio (ITY)** 2 b c Shantou (USA) -Alfrance (IRE) (Alzao (USA)) 5389a[6] ><

**Frascati** 4 b f Emarati (USA) -Fizzy Fiona (Efisio) *543[8] 586[14] 801[8] 1178[4]* (1319) 1956[17] 2079[2] 2369[3]2490[8] (2909) (3293) 3580[2] 3744[8] 4935[7] 5458[4] 5671[3] 5933[10] 6243[9] >**85a 87f**<

**Fraternity** 7 b g Grand Lodge (USA) -Catawba (Mill Reef (USA)) *427[6] 500[7] 653[9]* >**38a**<

**Freak Occurence (IRE)** 3 b g Stravinsky (USA) -Date Mate (USA) (Thorn Dance (USA)) 1437[7] 1831[3] 2069[4] 2295[6] 2557[3] 2676[14] 5004[6] 5135[8]*5379[12]* 5652[16] 6086[9] 6517[7] >**82a 86f**<

**Freddie Freccles** 3 ch g Komaite (USA) -Leprechaun Lady (Royal Blend) *466[6]* 5715[13] >**59a**

55f<
**Frederick James** 10 b g Efisio-Rare Roberta (USA) (Roberto (USA)) 1969$^{13}$ 2384$^{11}$ 2762$^{12}$ 4871$^{15}$ >23f<
**Fred s First** 3 b g Nomination-Perecapa (IRE) (Archway (IRE)) 2454$^{5}$ 3138$^{8}$ 3799$^{10}$ >30a<
**Free And Easy** 5 b m Bigstone (IRE) -Noble Lustre (USA) (Lyphard s Wish (FR)) 6255a$^{12}$ >70f<
**Freedom (GER)** 3 b f Second Empire (IRE) - Flamanda (Niniski (USA)) 1983a$^{4}$ 2723a$^{10}$ 5823a$^{10}$ 6508a$^{8}$ >98f<
**Freedom Now (IRE)** 6 b g Sadler s Wells (USA) - Free At Last (Shirley Heights) 1615$^{9}$ 2047$^{12}$ 2409$^{6}$ 2935$^{7}$ 4352$^{7}$ >87f<
**Free Dreams (GER)** 2 b f Areion (GER) -Free Pride (GER) (Executive Pride) 5280a$^{4}$ 6377a$^{5}$ >92f<
**Freefourinternet (USA)** 6 b h Tabasco Cat (USA) -Dixie Chimes (USA) (Dixieland Band (USA)) 6491a$^{13}$ >91a 117f<
**Free Lift** 2 ch f Cadeaux Genereux-Step Aloft (Shirley Heights) (3904) 5250$^{10}$ >81 f<
**Freeloader (IRE)** 4 b g Revoque (IRE) -Indian Sand (Indian King (USA)) 1460$^{7}$ 2624$^{4}$ 2878$^{3}$ 3631$^{8}$ (3844) 4220$^{4}$ 5135$^{5}$ 5568$^{4}$ 6069$^{3}$ >68a 86f<
**Free Option (IRE)** 9 ch g Indian Ridge-Saneena (Kris) 494$^{5}$ 564$^{12}$ 873$^{3}$ 894$^{3}$ (1496) 2406$^{5}$ >77a 77f<
**Free Style (GER)** 4 ch f Most Welcome-Furiella (Formidable (USA)) 412$^{6}$ 545$^{3}$ 724$^{12}$ (857) 943$^{4}$ 995$^{5}$ 1081$^{5}$ 1644$^{2}$1858$^{12}$ 2363$^{4}$ 2728$^{5}$ 3429$^{8}$ 3682$^{12}$ >49a 56f<
**Free Trip** 3 ch c Cadeaux Genereux-Well Away (IRE) (Sadler s Wells (USA)) (1129) 1408$^{6}$ 1900$^{13}$ 2378$^{2}$ 2642$^{5}$ 3001$^{5}$ 4268$^{5}$ 4646$^{2}$ (5443) 5781$^{7}$ >101f<
**Free Wheelin (IRE)** 4 b g Polar Falcon (USA) - Farhana (Fayruz) 1354$^{14}$ 1603$^{3}$ 2091$^{13}$ 3025$^{11}$ 4923$^{7}$ 5008$^{13}$ >21a 64f<
**Free Will** 7 ch g Indian Ridge-Free Guest (Be My Guest (USA)) 3411$^{16}$ >29f<
**Fremen (USA)** 4 ch c Rahy (USA) -Northern Trick (USA) (Northern Dancer) 1125$^{12}$ 5921$^{7}$ 6193$^{19}$ >99+f<
**French Gigolo** 4 ch g Pursuit Of Love-French Mist (Mystiko (USA)) 3846$^{4}$ 4940$^{6}$ >53a 77f<
**French Gold** 2 b f Bien Bien (USA) -Shalad Or (Golden Heights) 6078$^{11}$ 6283$^{8}$ >42f<
**French Horn** 7 b g Fraam-Runcina (Runnett) (468) 531$^{4}$ 726$^{3}$ 821$^{5}$ 914$^{3}$ 929$^{P}$ >53a 53f<
**French Kisses** 2 b f Paris House-Clashfern (Smackover) 2730$^{15}$ 4048$^{12}$ 5142$^{10}$ >34f<
**Frenchmans Lodge** 4 b g Piccolo-St Helena (Monsanto (FR)) 1176$^{11}$ 1519$^{13}$ 1859$^{7}$ 1988$^{7}$ 2359$^{2}$ 2556$^{5}$ 2869$^{6}$ 3378$^{6}$ >46a 46f<
**French Risk (IRE)** 4 b g Entrepreneur-Troyes (Troy) 1630$^{8}$ 2594$^{15}$ >51a 55f<
**French School** 2 b f Desert Prince (IRE) -Bint Shihama (USA) (Cadeaux Genereux) 4053$^{15}$ 5375$^{4}$ >59a<
**Fresh Connection** 3 b f Danzig Connection (USA) -Naturally Fresh (Thatching) 553$^{7}$ 620$^{14}$ 1227$^{7}$ 1375$^{5}$ 1695$^{4}$ >48a 38f<
**Friar Tuck** 9 ch g Inchinor-Jay Gee Ell (Vaigly Great) 1526$^{15}$ 1663$^{7}$ 1748$^{8}$ (1787) 2261$^{4}$ 2421$^{6}$ 2581$^{4}$ 2976$^{3}$ 3038$^{8}$3226$^{7}$ 3400$^{4}$ 4130$^{9}$ 4542$^{7}$ >63f<
**Frida** 2 b f Lujain (USA) -Ishona (Selkirk (USA)) 4243$^{11}$ ><
**Friday s Takings** 5 ch g Beveled (USA) -Pretty Pollyanna (General Assembly (USA)) 437$^{9}$ 582$^{8}$ 6057$^{15}$ 6550$^{12}$ >46a 46f<
**Friends Hope** 3 ch f Docksider (USA) -Stygian (USA) (Irish River (FR)) 1201$^{9}$ (1529) 1643$^{5}$ 2937$^{2}$ >59f<
**Friends Lake (USA)** 3 ch c A.P. Indy (USA) - Antespend (USA) (Spend A Buck (USA)) 1781a$^{15}$ >60a<
**Frimley s Matterry** 4 b g Bluegrass Prince (IRE) - Lonely Street (Frimley Park) 779$^{6}$ 877$^{7}$ 1342$^{6}$ 1994$^{6}$ 2556$^{6}$ 3096$^{5}$ 3559$^{16}$ 4350$^{3}$(4557) 4827$^{6}$ 5126$^{6}$ 5346$^{8}$ >20 a 58f<
**Frisby Ridge (IRE)** 2 b f Monashee Mountain (USA) -Suave Lady (FR) (Suave Dancer (USA)) 1390$^{12}$ 1556$^{5}$ 2248$^{10}$ 2364$^{5}$ 2773$^{5}$ 3144$^{4}$ 3506$^{9}$ 4559$^{3}$ >44f<
**Frith (IRE)** 2 b c Benny The Dip (USA) -Melodist (USA) (The Minstrel (CAN)) 3601$^{2}$ 4292$^{3}$ 5778$^{5}$ 6347$^{8}$ >101f<
**Frixos (IRE)** 4 ch g Barathea (IRE) -Local Lass (Local Suitor (USA)) 3637$^{6}$ 4082$^{6}$ 4473$^{10}$ 5408$^{12}$ >77a 56f<
**Frizzante** 5 b m Efisio-Juliet Bravo (Glow (USA)) 1409$^{2}$ (1763) 2955$^{3}$ (3674) 4595a$^{10}$ 5289$^{17}$ >119f<
**Frogs Gift (IRE)** 2 gr f Danehill Dancer (IRE) - Warthill Whispers (Grey Desire) 2141$^{14}$ 3197$^{6}$ 4099$^{8}$ >47f<
**Fromsong (IRE)** 6 b g Fayruz-Lindas Delight (Batshoof) 1211$^{2}$ 1438$^{4}$ 1763$^{4}$ 2372$^{4}$ 2475$^{4}$ 2913$^{7}$ 3537$^{8}$ 3723$^{6}$5372$^{5}$ 6177$^{10}$ >76a 105f<
**From The North (IRE)** 3 ch f Foxhound (USA) - Best Swinger (IRE) (Ela-Mana-Mou) 1975$^{14}$ 2468$^{5}$ 3562$^{13}$ 4391$^{4}$ 5448$^{10}$ 5547$^{7}$ >44f<
**Frontier** 7 b g Indian Ridge-Adatiya (IRE) (Shardari) 2210$^{2}$ (2752) 3143$^{2}$ 3325$^{3}$ >83f<
**Front Stage (IRE)** 2 bb c Grand Lodge (USA) - Dreams (Rainbow Quest (USA)) 4743$^{8}$ 5269$^{3}$ >82f<
**Frosted Aclaim (IRE)** 4 b g Highest Honor (FR) - Snowdip (IRE) (Sadler s Wells (USA)) (6137a) ><
**Frosty Wind (IRE)** 6 ch g Forest Wind (USA) -Feline Special (Lyphard s Special (USA)) 4371a$^{17}$ >100f<
**Fruhlingssturm** 4 b c Unfuwain (USA) - Fruhlingserwachen (USA) (Irish River (FR)) 3315$^{5}$ (3661) 3978$^{7}$ 5134$^{3}$ 5975a$^{4}$ 6219$^{4}$ >114f<
**Fruhtau (GER)** 7 ch h Hero s Honor (USA) - Fainting Spell (FR) (Top Ville) 3357a$^{6}$ 3972a$^{8}$ >108f<
**Fruit Of Glory** 5 b m Glory Of Dancer-Fresh Fruit Daily (Reprimand) 755a$^{9}$ 831a$^{5}$ 921a$^{4}$ 1353$^{4}$ 1537$^{3}$ 1765$^{7}$ 2206$^{4}$ 2372$^{2}$(3744) 3914$^{4}$ 4526$^{2}$ 4779$^{2}$ 4951$^{5}$ 5454$^{4}$ 5898$^{7}$ 6177$^{3}$ 6451$^{8}$ >94a 100f<
**Fubos** 3 b g Atraf-Homebeforemidnight (Fool s Holme (USA)) 415$^{5}$ 580$^{6}$ 2097$^{17}$ >65a 65f<
**Fuego (GER)** 2 ch c Acatenango (GER) -Fireglow (FR) (Glow (USA)) 6542a$^{6}$ ><
**Fuel Cell (IRE)** 3 b c Desert Style (IRE) -Tappen Zee (Sandhurst Prince) 1461$^{8}$ 2113$^{11}$ 2401$^{3}$ 2915$^{3}$ 3589$^{8}$ (4057) 4648$^{3}$ 5057$^{5}$ 5297$^{10}$6152$^{3}$ >77f<
**Fuerta Ventura (IRE)** 2 bb f Desert Sun-Cradle Brief (IRE) (Brief Truce (USA)) 5961a$^{6}$ 6367a$^{13}$ >79f<
**Fu Fighter** 3 b g Unfuwain (USA) -Runelia (Runnett) 2085$^{8}$ 2561$^{5}$ 2840$^{4}$ 3341$^{3}$ 4870$^{11}$ 5116$^{9}$ 5549$^{2}$ >72a 76f<
**Fullandby (IRE)** 2 b c Monashee Mountain (USA) - Ivory Turner (Efisio) 6400$^{2}$ >62a<
**Full Egalite** 8 gr g Ezzoud (IRE) -Milva (Jellaby) 1402$^{4}$ 1492$^{6}$ >42a 37f<
**Full Of Zest** 2 ch f Pivotal-Tangerine (Primo Dominie) 6330$^{2}$ >74f<
**Full Pitch** 8 ch g Cadeaux Genereux-Tricky Note (Song) 669$^{9}$ 836$^{12}$ 1603$^{6}$ (1872) 2118$^{13}$ 2455$^{12}$ 3524$^{8}$ 5201$^{12}$6273$^{10}$ >41a 77f<
**Full Spate** 9 ch g Unfuwain (USA) -Double River (USA) (Irish River (FR)) 1313$^{6}$ 1608$^{7}$ 1873$^{5}$ 2091$^{4}$ 2219$^{6}$ 2399$^{4}$ 2581$^{6}$ 2948$^{3}$3141$^{2}$ 3298$^{7}$ 3887$^{9}$ 4083$^{11}$ 4403$^{2}$ (4542) 4707$^{6}$ 4837$^{9}$ 5201$^{8}$6001$^{12}$ 6066$^{9}$ 6131$^{4}$ >61a 79f<
**Fully Fledged** 4 b f Fraam-Alarming Motown (Warning) 1684$^{10}$ >57f<
**Fulminant (IRE)** 3 b c Big Shuffle (USA) -Flagny (FR) (Kaldoun (FR)) (2335a) >101f<
**Fulvio (USA)** 4 b g Sword Dance-One Tuff Gal (USA) (Lac Ouimet (USA)) 2883$^{11}$ 3626$^{13}$ 3826$^{7}$ 3932$^{5}$ 4602$^{14}$ 4687$^{11}$ 5035$^{9}$ 6405$^{4}$ >55 a 55f<
**Fu Manchu** 2 b c Desert Style (IRE) -Robsart (IRE) (Robellino (USA)) 4169$^{9}$ (4730) >84f<
**Funfair** 5 b g Singspiel (IRE) -Red Carnival (USA) (Mr Prospector (USA)) 5462$^{2}$ 5917$^{3}$ 6474$^{6}$ >111f<
**Funfair Wane** 5 b g Unfuwain (USA) -Ivory Bride (Domynsky) 3052$^{10}$ 3266$^{7}$ 4091$^{4}$ 4165$^{19}$ 4324$^{27}$ 5287$^{6}$ 5393$^{12}$ (5628) 5832$^{6}$ >104f<
**Funny Cide (USA)** 4 ch g Distorted Humor (USA) - Belle s Good Cide (USA) (Slewacide (USA)) 6491a$^{10}$ >112a<
**Fun To Ride** 3 ch f Desert Prince (IRE) -Zafaaf (Kris) (1413) 1881$^{2}$ 2897$^{20}$ 3598$^{14}$ 5393$^{11}$ >98f<
**Funward (FR)** 5 ch g Funambule (USA) - Grundygold (FR) (Grundy) 1655a$^{6}$ ><
**Furioso Directa (GER)** 4 b c Second Set (IRE) - Foudre (GER) (Acatenango (GER)) 3335a$^{7}$ 4596a$^{10}$ >107f<
**Furl Away** 2 b g Squared Away-Miss Pel (Pelder (IRE)) 4169$^{10}$ >61f<
**Furniture Factors (IRE)** 4 b g Magic Ring (IRE) - Make Hay (Nomination) 1715$^{7}$ 2456$^{10}$ >67df<
**Further Outlook (USA)** 10 gr g Zilzal (USA) - Future Bright (USA) (Lyphard s Wish (FR)) (1131) 1230$^{3}$ 1354$^{10}$ 1923$^{11}$ 2222$^{11}$ 2628$^{4}$ 2739$^{2}$ 3243$^{3}$ 3324$^{15}$3945$^{7}$ 4366$^{10}$ 4614$^{6}$ 4748$^{5}$ (4847) 5071$^{5}$ 5181$^{12}$ 5564$^{3}$ 5787$^{5}$6205$^{2}$ 6243$^{4}$ 6349$^{7}$ >80a 92f<
**Fusillade (IRE)** 4 ch g Grand Lodge (USA) -Lili Cup (FR) (Fabulous Dancer (USA)) 3251$^{14}$ 4015$^{19}$ >43f<
**Fuss** 3 b f Unfuwain (USA) -First Sapphire (Simply Great (FR)) 6357$^{6}$ >13f<
**Futoo (IRE)** 3 b g Foxhound (USA) -Nicola Wynn (Nicholas Bill) 1957$^{6}$ 2251$^{5}$ (2688) 3004$^{3}$ 3819$^{7}$ (3981) 4395$^{3}$ 4628$^{4}$ 5197$^{2}$ 5344$^{8}$6096$^{8}$ >73f<
**Future Deal** 3 b f First Trump-Katyushka (IRE) (Soviet Star (USA)) 4718$^{4}$ 5845$^{3}$ (6275) >57a 67f<
**Future To Future (IRE)** 4 gr g Linamix (FR) -Finir En Beaute (FR) (Groom Dancer (USA)) 4849$^{14}$ 5221$^{14}$ >31f<
**Futuristic** 4 b g Magic Ring (IRE) -Corn Futures (Nomination) 695$^{2}$ 909$^{9}$ 1620$^{16}$ >64a 62f<
**Fyodor (IRE)** 3 b g Fasliyev (USA) -Royale Figurine (IRE) (Dominion Royale) 2131$^{13}$ 2549$^{6}$ 2877$^{7}$ 5440$^{20}$ 5730$^{7}$ 5949$^{4}$ 6114$^{12}$ 6445$^{19}$ >85f<

## G

**Gabana (IRE)** 3 br f Polish Precedent (USA) -Out West (USA) (Gone West (USA)) 1129$^{12}$ 1309$^{6}$ 2371$^{9}$ 2820$^{3}$ 3246$^{2}$ 3684$^{3}$ 4066$^{3}$ >57a 74f<
**Gabanna (USA)** 2 b c Kingmambo (USA) -Star Begonia (Sadler s Wells (USA)) 5838$^{6}$ 6308$^{3}$ >68f<
**Gablesea** 10 b g Beveled (USA) -Me Spede (Valiyar) 3929$^{16}$ ><
**Gabor** 5 b g Danzig Connection (USA) -Kiomi (Niniski (USA)) 2032$^{14}$ 2728$^{9}$ 4799$^{5}$ >61a 58f<
**Gaelic Princess** 4 b f Cois Na Tine (IRE) -Berenice (ITY) (Marouble) 761$^{11}$ 1065$^{14}$ 2143$^{6}$ 2477$^{19}$ 2763$^{9}$ 3074$^{12}$ 4122$^{15}$ 4687$^{5}$ >85 a 83f<
**Gaelic Probe (IRE)** 10 b g Roi Danzig (USA) - Scottish Gaelic (USA) (Highland Park (USA)) 426$^{6}$ >26a<
**Gaelic Roulette (IRE)** 4 b f Turtle Island (IRE) - Money Spinner (USA) (Teenoso (USA)) 3528$^{3}$ 4033$^{8}$ 4642$^{10}$ >46a 78f<
**Gaff (USA)** 2 b c Maria s Mon (USA) - Ionlyhaveeyesforu (USA) (Tunerup (USA)) (5878a) 6408a$^{2}$ >107f<
**Gaiety Girl (USA)** 3 b f Swain (IRE) -Knoosh (USA) (Storm Bird (CAN)) 2197$^{9}$ 2732$^{6}$ 3042$^{5}$ 3478$^{8}$ 4260$^{10}$ 5346$^{20}$ 6095$^{8}$ >55f<
**Galandora** 4 b f Bijou D Inde-Jelabna (Jalmood (USA)) 1188$^{5}$ 1297$^{6}$ (1534) 1958$^{11}$ (2171) 2462$^{2}$ 2893$^{8}$ 3667$^{3}$ 3776$^{3}$ 4202$^{7}$5354$^{7}$ 5645$^{5}$ 6159$^{7}$ >50a 58f<
**Gala Sunday (USA)** 4 b g Lear Fan (USA) - Sunday Bazaar (USA) (Nureyev (USA)) 1469$^{7}$ 1762$^{19}$ 2066$^{12}$ 2775$^{7}$ 3097$^{12}$ 3563$^{6}$ 4258$^{7}$ 4574$^{6}$5317$^{16}$ 5713$^{12}$ 5942$^{5}$ >54 f<
**Galaxy Fallon** 6 b m Dancing Spree (USA) -No Comebacks (Last Tycoon) 1031$^{6}$ 1094$^{9}$ 2386$^{6}$ >39?a 29f<
**Galeota (IRE)** 2 b c Mujadil (USA) -Refined (IRE) (Statoblest) 2057$^{4}$ (3808) 4857$^{5}$ 5295$^{5}$ (5460) (5649) >111f<
**Galey River (USA)** 5 ch g Irish River (FR) - Carefree Kate (USA) (Lyphard (USA)) 815$^{8}$ 895$^{10}$ 933$^{5}$ 996$^{7}$ 1166$^{5}$ (1277) 1545$^{6}$ 1888$^{2}$2015$^{3}$ 2053$^{5}$ 2573$^{7}$ 2810$^{4}$ 3450$^{5}$ 3917$^{11}$ 4556$^{6}$ 4604$^{4}$4713$^{5}$ >46a 46 f<
**Gallant Boy (IRE)** 5 ch g Grand Lodge (USA) - Damerela (IRE) (Alzao (USA)) 418$^{9}$ 523$^{13}$ 679$^{4}$ 706$^{9}$ 887$^{13}$ 2752$^{5}$ 3128$^{7}$3591$^{6}$ 3629$^{4}$ 3731$^{8}$ 3947$^{5}$ 4192$^{4}$ 4363$^{4}$ 4772$^{4}$ 4971$^{4}$5456$^{13}$ 5997$^{9}$ 6013$^{8}$ 6083$^{12}$ 6192$^{8}$ >77a 77f<
**Gallantian (IRE)** 2 gr g Turtle Island (IRE) - Galletina (IRE) (Persian Heights) 6153$^{10}$ 6322$^{8}$ 6439$^{7}$ >51a 68f<
**Gallas (IRE)** 3 b c Charnwood Forest (IRE) -Nellie s Away (IRE) (Magical Strike (USA)) 1957$^{15}$ 2900$^{9}$ 3168$^{8}$ 3817$^{2}$ 4092$^{9}$ 4259$^{14}$ 4624$^{16}$ >53f<
**Gallego** 2 br c Danzero (AUS) -Shafir (IRE) (Shaadi (USA)) 3476$^{12}$ 4023$^{11}$ 4675$^{10}$ >14a 5f<
**Galleon Beach** 7 b g Shirley Heights-Music In My Life (IRE) (Law Society (USA)) 3508$^{4}$ 3821$^{8}$ 4226$^{14}$ >48a 73f<
**Gallery Breeze** 5 b m Zamindar (USA) -Wantage Park (Pas De Seul) (3301) 3910$^{11}$ 4549$^{9}$ 5017$^{9}$ 5541$^{9}$ 6014$^{5}$ 6062$^{2}$ >73a 78f<
**Gallery God (FR)** 8 ch g In The Wings-El Fabulous (FR) (Fabulous Dancer (USA)) 1328$^{15}$ 2681$^{9}$ 3076$^{10}$ 4123$^{9}$ 5074$^{7}$ 5423$^{9}$ >76f<
**Galley Law** 4 ch g Most Welcome-Miss Blitz (Formidable (USA)) 653$^{3}$ 727$^{2}$ (783) 875$^{2}$ 943$^{2}$ 1448$^{4}$ >46a 16f<
**Galloway Boy (IRE)** 7 ch g Mujtahid (USA) - Supportive (IRE) (Nashamaa) 3961a$^{13}$ >71f<
**Galloway Mac** 4 ch c Environment Friend- Docklands (On Your Mark) 473$^{3}$ 613$^{3}$ 805$^{12}$ (877) 1032$^{2}$ 1187$^{4}$ 1298$^{6}$ 1427$^{6}$6154$^{5}$ >69a 64f<
**Galvanise (USA)** 3 b c Run Softly (USA) -Shining Bright (Rainbow Quest (USA)) 1104$^{6}$ (3015) 3641$^{7}$ 5211$^{3}$ 5397$^{7}$ >93f<
**Gamble Of The Day (USA)** 2 ch c Cozzene (USA) -Sue Warner (USA) (Forli (ARG)) 6331$^{6}$ >72+f<
**Gambling Spirit** 2 ch f Mister Baileys-Royal Roulette (Risk Me (FR)) 5846$^{11}$ >50f<
**Game Dame** 3 ch f Nashwan (USA) -Gentle Dame (Kris) 2805$^{4}$ (3142) 4395$^{5}$ >80f<
**Game Flora** 3 b f Mind Games-Breakfast Creek (Hallgate) (1711) 1941$^{4}$ 2411$^{9}$ 3624$^{5}$ 4181$^{16}$ 4391$^{6}$ 5000$^{12}$ 5141$^{2}$ 6361$^{12}$ >6a 55f<
**Game Guru** 5 b g First Trump-Scarlett Holly (Red Sunset) 518$^{7}$ (542) 627$^{3}$ (686) 733$^{4}$ 970$^{6}$ (1031) 1369$^{9}$ 1535$^{5}$2127$^{5}$ >74a 71f<
**Game Lad** 2 b c Mind Games-Catch Me (Rudimentary (USA)) 4187$^{3}$ 4446$^{4}$ 5096$^{9}$ 5314$^{3}$ 5989$^{7}$ 6206$^{2}$ (6514) 6574$^{4}$ >55a 83f<
**Gameset N Match** 3 b g Hector Protector (USA) - Tanasie (Cadeaux Genereux) 3441$^{6}$ 4026$^{10}$ 4265$^{4}$ 5184$^{3}$ >38a 64f<
**Gamut (IRE)** 5 b h Spectrum (IRE) -Greektown (Ela-Mana-Mou) 1455$^{2}$ (1792) (3567a) 4121$^{4}$ 5329a$^{5}$ >121f<
**Ganymede** 3 gr c Daylami (IRE) -Germane (Distant Relative) 1224$^{2}$ 1450$^{3}$ 2281$^{2}$ 2645$^{2}$ 3422$^{2}$ 3915$^{8}$ 4554$^{4}$ 5367$^{5}$5728$^{6}$ >76f<
**Garance** 2 b f Zafonic (USA) -Arletty (Rainbow Quest (USA)) 3451$^{11}$ 4334$^{7}$ 5172$^{8}$ 5871$^{14}$ >68f<
**Gardasee (GER)** 2 gr g Dashing Blade-Gladstone Street (IRE) (Waajib) 2812$^{7}$ 3233$^{7}$ 3611$^{6}$ >40a 45f<
**Garden Society (IRE)** 7 ch g Caerleon (USA) - Eurobird (Ela-Mana-Mou) 3090$^{8}$ 4293$^{7}$ 5317$^{11}$ 5868$^{7}$ 6152$^{5}$ 6337$^{8}$ >65f<
**Gargoyle Girl** 7 b m Be My Chief (USA) -May Hills Legacy (IRE) (Be My Guest (USA)) 6931$^{0}$ 1341$^{5}$ (1866) 2038$^{10}$ 2491$^{6}$ 3236$^{11}$ 5519$^{4}$ 6074$^{6}$ 6534$^{6}$ >3a 69f<
**Garhoud** 2 b c Grand Lodge (USA) -Puce (Darshaan) 4728$^{9}$ >50f<
**Garlinote (FR)** 4 b f Poliglote-Garling (FR) (Garde Royale) 1741a$^{10}$ >105f<
**Garmud** 2 b c Spectrum (IRE) -Guntakal (IRE) (Night Shift (USA)) 3435a$^{2}$ ><
**Garnett (IRE)** 3 b g Desert Story (IRE) -In Behind (IRE) (Entitled) 3348$^{4}$ 4087$^{3}$ 4513$^{3}$ 5300$^{9}$ 5382$^{3}$ 5850$^{5}$ >66a 77f<
**Garnock Belle (IRE)** 3 b f Marju (IRE) -Trojan Relation (Trojan Fen) 530$^{11}$ 802$^{12}$ 994$^{5}$ 1080$^{12}$ >27a 38df<
**Garnock Venture (IRE)** 3 b c Mujadil (USA) -Stay Sharpe (USA) (Sharpen Up) 435$^{4}$ 587$^{11}$ 696$^{7}$ (1046) 1676$^{8}$ 1742$^{3}$ 1934$^{7}$ 2457$^{7}$(2849) 3234$^{11}$ 3368$^{7}$ 3708$^{5}$ 4387$^{5}$ 5141$^{12}$ >73a 55f<
**Garrigon** 3 b c Hector Protector (USA) -Queen Of The Keys (Royal Academy (USA)) 557$^{5}$ 675$^{7}$ 741$^{4}$ 817$^{15}$ 885$^{4}$ 965$^{6}$ 1017$^{2}$ >60a 64f<
**Garryurra** 3 gr f Daylami (IRE) -Tropical (Green Desert (USA)) 2060$^{5}$ 2514$^{10}$ >70f<
**Garston Star** 3 ch g Fleetwood (IRE) -Conquista (Aragon) 1643$^{3}$ (2395) 2802$^{2}$ 3658$^{2}$ 4062$^{12}$ 4389$^{5}$ (4736) 4927$^{6}$ 5889$^{6}$ >21a 72f<
**Gasparini (IRE)** 3 ch c Docksider (USA) -Tarjou (Marju (IRE)) 1453$^{12}$ 1820$^{10}$ 2457$^{12}$ 3102$^{4}$ 3517$^{3}$ 3819$^{9}$ 4101$^{3}$ 4309$^{12}$ >60f<
**Gateman** 7 b g Owington-Scandalette (Niniski (USA)) 636a$^{2}$ 710a$^{6}$ 978a$^{8}$ 1107$^{2}$ (1397) 1621$^{2}$ 2109$^{11}$ 2678$^{3}$ (3323) 3724$^{2}$3978$^{2}$ 5134$^{2}$ 5968a$^{2}$ >117f<
**Gatewick (IRE)** 4 b c Sunday Silence (USA) - Greek Air (IRE) (Ela-Mana-Mou) 1435a$^{8}$ >103f<
**Gatwick (IRE)** 3 b c Ali-Royal (IRE) -Airport (Warpath) (1104) 1437$^{3}$ (2202) (2295) 2680$^{10}$ 3000$^{6}$ 4271$^{8}$ 4965a$^{5}$ (5106) 5650$^{5}$ 5941$^{7}$6219$^{11}$ >114+f<
**Gaudalpin (IRE)** 2 b f Danetime (IRE) -Lila Pedigo (IRE) (Classic Secret (USA)) 1276$^{3}$ 1399$^{4}$ 2884$^{7}$ 3532$^{4}$ 3886$^{13}$ 5617$^{7}$ 6002$^{2}$ 6294$^{2}$6359$^{10}$ >62a 62f<
**Gavioli (IRE)** 2 b c Namid-Pamina (IRE) (Perugino (USA)) 2360$^{5}$ 2609$^{18}$ 2831$^{4}$ 3150$^{2}$ 3748$^{10}$ 3886$^{9}$ 4475$^{3}$ 4671$^{5}$ >60f<
**Gavroche (IRE)** 3 b c Docksider (USA) -Regal Revolution (Hamas (IRE)) (566) 595$^{2}$ 864$^{3}$ 957$^{5}$ 1640$^{2}$ 1831$^{2}$ 2070$^{5}$ (2472) (2841) 3345$^{4}$(3706) 4271$^{9}$ 4709$^{8}$ 5106$^{8}$ >73a 91+f<
**Gayle Storm (IRE)** 3 b f Mujadil (USA) -Mercy Bien (IRE) (Be My Guest (USA)) 462$^{6}$ 580$^{8}$ 741$^{8}$ 802$^{5}$ >49a 56f<
**Gay Romance** 3 ch f Singspiel (IRE) -Gaijin (Caerleon (USA)) 3209$^{8}$ 3592$^{10}$ 4369$^{6}$ 5197$^{5}$ 5868$^{3}$ 6461$^{10}$ >70f<
**Gdansk (IRE)** 7 b g Pips Pride-Merry Twinkle (Martinmas) 1500$^{9}$ 1603$^{U}$ 1824$^{8}$ >85f<
**Gee Bee Em** 2 b f Piccolo-Cibenze (Owington) 2837$^{2}$ (3192) 3414$^{4}$ 4041$^{4}$ 4235$^{9}$ 6012$^{11}$ >34a 70f<
**Geespot** 5 b m Pursuit Of Love-My Discovery (IRE) (Imperial Frontier (USA)) 422$^{12}$ 536$^{4}$ 5991$^{2}$ 662$^{7}$ 860$^{9}$ 999$^{3}$ 1020$^{12}$1165$^{7}$ >46a 45f<
**Geisha Lady (IRE)** 2 b f Raise A Grand (IRE) - Mitsubishi Style (Try My Best (USA)) 2627$^{6}$ 3770$^{3}$ 4081$^{2}$ 4475$^{4}$ 5200$^{2}$ 6265$^{17}$ >68f<
**Geller** 3 b g Mind Games-Time To Tango (Timeless Times (USA)) 2611$^{5}$ 2764$^{4}$ 3452$^{8}$ 3875$^{8}$ 4340$^{5}$ >76f<
**Gem Bien (USA)** 6 b g Bien Bien (USA) -Eastern Gem (USA) (Jade Hunter (USA)) 1773$^{17}$ 2789$^{8}$ 4624$^{3}$ 4928$^{8}$ >53a 87df<
**Gemi Bed (FR)** 9 b g Double Bed (FR) -Gemia (FR) (King Of Macedon) 740$^{6}$ (889) 981$^{5}$ 1188$^{4}$ >55a 54f<
**Gemini Diamond (IRE)** 4 bb f Desert King (IRE) - Wakria (IRE) (Sadler s Wells (USA)) 5822a$^{2}$ >89f<
**Gemini Girl (IRE)** 3 b f Petardia-Miss Sabre (Sabrehill (USA)) 1689$^{7}$ 2661$^{9}$ 3147$^{8}$ 3562$^{12}$ 3798$^{7}$ 4102$^{15}$ 4259$^{18}$ 4393$^{8}$ >49f<
**Gemini Lady** 4 b f Emperor Fountain-Raunchy Rita (Brigadier Gerard) 1993$^{15}$ 2387$^{2}$ 2879$^{12}$ 3520$^{13}$ 5450$^{9}$ 5639$^{4}$ 5795$^{13}$ 6362$^{8}$ >34a 52f<
**Gemma** 4 b f Petong-Gem (Most Welcome) 537$^{11}$ 661$^{13}$ >41a 48f<
**Gems Bond** 4 b g Magic Ring (IRE) -Jucinda (Midyan (USA)) 4122$^{21}$ 4672$^{9}$ 5444$^{5}$ 5861$^{14}$ 6395$^{11}$ >31a 89f<
**General** 7 b g Cadeaux Genereux-Bareilly (USA) (Lyphard (USA)) (972) 1030$^{2}$ 1122$^{7}$ 1213$^{5}$ 1539$^{2}$ 1661$^{10}$ 2110$^{12}$ 3199$^{19}$3658$^{5}$ 4093$^{3}$ 5085$^{2}$ 5773$^{10}$ 6152$^{14}$ 6343$^{6}$ >77a 77f<
**General Feeling (IRE)** 3 b g General Monash (USA) -Kamadara (IRE) (Kahyasi) 1906$^{3}$ 2165$^{3}$ 2836$^{11}$ 3158$^{4}$ (4251a) (4470) 5150$^{4}$ 5652$^{14}$ >85+f<
**General Flumpa** 3 b g Vettori (IRE) -Macca Luna (IRE) (Kahyasi) 1370$^{6}$ 1628$^{3}$ 1998$^{3}$ 2665$^{5}$ 3340$^{2}$ 3746$^{6}$ 4655$^{3}$ 5057$^{4}$ >67a 69f<
**General Haigh** 2 b g Mujahid (USA) -Stygian (USA) (Irish River (FR)) 4334$^{6}$ 4704$^{4}$ 4936$^{4}$ 6012$^{9}$ >40a 68f<
**General Jumbo** 2 b c Dansili-Aunt Jemima (Busted) 6351$^{2}$ >84f<
**General Max (IRE)** 2 b c General Monash (USA) - Sawaki (Song) 2422$^{3}$ 4100$^{7}$ 4761$^{12}$ 5314$^{13}$ >55f<
**General Nuisance (IRE)** 2 ch g General Monash (USA) -Baywood (Emarati (USA)) 1115$^{2}$ 1307$^{6}$ 1984$^{4}$ 2523$^{5}$ 2819$^{4}$ 3390$^{3}$ 3824$^{2}$ 4200$^{3}$4475$^{7}$ 4651$^{3}$ 5022$^{9}$ >53f<
**General Smith** 5 b g Greensmith-Second Call (Kind Of Hush) 1502$^{13}$ 1868$^{10}$ 2368$^{16}$ 2656$^{18}$ 4211$^{LFT}$ >57a 42 f<
**Genereux (ARG)** 4 b c French Deputy (USA) - Griffe De Paris (BRZ) (Telescopico (ARG)) 922a$^{10}$ ><
**Generous Gesture (IRE)** 3 b f Fasliyev (USA) - Royal Bounty (IRE) (Generous (IRE)) (956) 1119$^{5}$ 1464$^{6}$ (1737) 2112$^{17}$ 2704$^{6}$ 3280$^{5}$ 4244$^{6}$ 4969$^{8}$5618$^{9}$ 6131$^{13}$ 6567$^{9}$ >84a 74f<
**Generous Measure** 2 b c Largesse-Stormy Heights (Golden Heights) 6322$^{12}$ >16f<
**Generous Option** 2 ch f Cadeaux Genereux-Easy Option (IRE) (Prince Sabo) 3296$^{5}$ (3741) 3975$^{3}$ 5212$^{4}$ 5606$^{4}$ 6188$^{10}$ >87f<
**Generous Share** 4 ch f Cadeaux Genereux-Marl

(Lycius (USA)) *439$^{6}$* **>47a 66df<**

**Generous Spirit (IRE)** 3 ch c Cadeaux Genereux-Miss Rossi (Artaius (USA)) 1295$^{8}$ 1796$^{9}$ 1906$^{7}$ 2029$^{6}$ 4052$^{7}$ **>61f<**

**Genghis (IRE)** 5 br g Persian Bold-Cindys Baby (Bairn (USA)) 3276$^{2}$ 3449$^{5}$ 3909$^{2}$ 4831$^{8}$ 5266$^{3}$ 5619$^{3}$ 5764$^{2}$ **>88f<**

**Genios (GER)** 3 b c Oxalagu (GER) -Glacial Star (Royal Academy (USA)) 1656a$^{4}$ 2541a$^{7}$ 5168a$^{8}$ **>96f<**

**Gennie Bond** 2 b f Pivotal-Miriam (Forzando) 3272$^{4}$ 3693$^{3}$ 3992$^{2}$ 4342$^{11}$ 5391$^{16}$ 5648$^{22}$ **>79f<**

**Genny Lim (IRE)** 4 b f Barathea (IRE) -Atsuko (IRE) (Mtoto) 1070a$^{7}$ **>93f<**

**Gentleman George** 3 b g Kingsinger (IRE) -Miss Bigwig (Distinctly North (USA)) *451$^{8}$ 524$^{9}$* **>40da 4f<**

**Gentleman s Deal (IRE)** 3 b c Danehill (USA) -Sleepytime (IRE) (Royal Academy (USA)) 3916$^{4}$ (4869) *(6279)* **>88+a 79+f<**

**Gentle Raindrop (IRE)** 3 b f College Chapel-Dream Chaser (Record Token) 2114$^{9}$ 2286$^{5}$ 2808$^{10}$ 3700$^{13}$ 4580$^{10}$ 4916$^{7}$ 6082$^{12}$ *6224$^{10}$* **>64f<**

**Gentle Response** 4 b f Puissance-Sweet Whisper (Petong) *465$^{13}$ 538$^{9}$ 884$^{6}$ 951$^{3}$ (998) 1165$^{9}$ 1497$^{5}$ 1692$^{6}$* 5930$^{12}$ **>52+a 61f<**

**Gentle Tiger (GER)** 3 b c Tiger Hill (IRE) -Glorosia (FR) (Bering) 2541a$^{3}$ 3565a$^{5}$ 4385a$^{6}$ **>100f<**

**Gentle Warning** 4 b f Parthian Springs-Manx Princess (Roscoe Blake) 4644$^{8}$ 5146$^{11}$ 5371$^{13}$ **>18f<**

**Genuinely (IRE)** 3 b f Entrepreneur-Fearless (Groom Dancer (USA)) *816$^{11}$* 1507$^{16}$ *3305$^{6}$* 4070$^{3}$ 4302$^{7}$ 5178$^{3}$ **>37a 45f<**

**Geography (IRE)** 4 ch g Definite Article-Classic Ring (IRE) (Auction Ring (USA)) *664$^{P}$ 776$^{8}$ 874$^{6}$ 931$^{11}$* 1564$^{12}$ 5928$^{16}$ **>51a 18f<**

**Geojimali** 2 ch c Compton Place-Harrken Heights (IRE) (Belmez (USA)) 3793$^{6}$ 3974$^{6}$ 4532$^{5}$ **>51f<**

**Geordie Dancer (IRE)** 2 b c Dansili-Awtaar (USA) (Lyphard (USA)) 5233$^{11}$ 5516$^{5}$ 5856$^{7}$ **>55f<**

**Geordieland (FR)** 3 gr c Johann Quatz (FR) -Aerdee (FR) (Highest Honor (FR)) 6263a$^{3}$ **>108?f<**

**George Stubbs (USA)** 6 bb g Affirmed (USA) -Mia Duchessa (USA) (Nijinsky (CAN)) *413$^{7}$ 629$^{6}$ 734$^{2}$ 827$^{3}$ 971$^{6}$ 1030$^{4}$* 1112$^{7}$ 1302$^{3}$ (1615) 1785$^{3}$ 2047$^{5}$ 2409$^{5}$ 3078$^{5}$ 3644$^{11}$ **>79a 79f<**

**George The Best (IRE)** 3 b g Imperial Ballet (IRE) -En Retard (IRE) (Petardia) 1614$^{13}$ 1760$^{6}$ 2075$^{4}$ 3309$^{14}$ 3523$^{6}$ 3819$^{13}$ 3926$^{11}$ 5193$^{20}$ 6114$^{5}$ 6526$^{6}$ **>80 f<**

**Georgie Belle (USA)** 2 ch f Southern Halo (USA) -Saabikah (USA) (Dayjur (USA)) 1219$^{3}$ 1390$^{3}$ *6446$^{13}$* **>22a 61f<**

**Georgina** 2 ch f Polish Precedent (USA) -Rose Bourbon (USA) (Woodman (USA)) 3456$^{8}$ 4053$^{14}$ 4468$^{7}$ **>65f<**

**Germanicus** 2 b c Desert King (IRE) -Simacota (GER) (Acatenango (GER)) *6555$^{12}$* **>12a<**

**Geronimo** 7 b g Efisio-Apache Squaw (Be My Guest (USA)) *476$^{2}$ 509$^{8}$ 772$^{3}$ (909) 967$^{9}$ 1035$^{4}$* **>68a 61f<**

**Get Stuck In (IRE)** 8 b g Up And At Em-Shoka (FR) (Kaldoun (FR)) 1175$^{16}$ 1343$^{14}$ 1525$^{12}$ **>85f<**

**Get To The Point** 3 ch g Daggers Drawn (USA) -Penny Mint (Mummy s Game) *514$^{8}$* 1530$^{2}$ 2029$^{2}$ 2211$^{5}$ 2444$^{9}$ 2589$^{9}$ 2931$^{7}$ 3344$^{5}$ 4817$^{7}$ **>49a 60f<**

**Ghaill Force** 2 b g Piccolo-Coir A Ghaill (Jalmood (USA)) 5792$^{2}$ **>65f<**

**Ghantoot** 3 ch c Inchinor-Shall We Run (Hotfoot) 1419$^{11}$ 1749$^{8}$ 2195$^{7}$ 2392$^{11}$ 3102$^{3}$ (3556) 3917$^{3}$ 6332$^{13}$ **>81+f<**

**Ghasiba (IRE)** 2 gr f Daylami (IRE) -Night Owl (Night Shift (USA)) 4074$^{6}$ 4705$^{2}$ 4885$^{7}$ 5391$^{15}$ 5779$^{9}$ **>78+f<**

**Ghostzapper (USA)** 4 b c Awesome Again (CAN) -Baby Zip (USA) (Relaunch (USA)) *(6491a)* **>133a<**

**Ghurra (USA)** 2 b f War Chant (USA) -Futuh (USA) (Diesis) (4494) 5250$^{7}$ 6188$^{4}$ **>83f<**

**Giant s Rock (IRE)** 2 ch g Giant s Causeway (USA) -En Garde (USA) (Irish River (FR)) 5765$^{3}$ **>66f<**

**Gibraltar Bay (IRE)** 2 b f Cape Cross (IRE) -Secrets Of Honour (Belmez (USA)) 4198$^{12}$ 4579$^{4}$ 4851$^{15}$ **>56f<**

**Gidam Gidam (IRE)** 2 b g King s Best (USA) -Flamands (IRE) (Sadler s Wells (USA)) 5228$^{6}$ 5592$^{6}$ 5827$^{3}$ **>66f<**

**Gifted Flame** 5 b g Revoque (IRE) -Littleladyleah (USA) (Shareef Dancer (USA)) 1393$^{9}$ 2078$^{10}$ 2938$^{4}$ 3586$^{7}$ 3911$^{7}$ 4209$^{3}$ (4386) 4537$^{4}$ 5108$^{5}$ 5236$^{6}$ 5544$^{8}$ (5713) 5945$^{15}$ **>46a 77 f<**

**Gifted Gamble** 2 b c Mind Games-Its Another Gift (Primo Dominie) 1324$^{7}$ 1658$^{3}$ 2268$^{3}$ 2749$^{3}$ 3196$^{2}$ 3900$^{2}$ (4124) 4325$^{5}$ 5515$^{9}$ 5670$^{2}$ 5947$^{11}$ 6174$^{3}$ 6348$^{4}$ **>93f<**

**Gifted Lass** 2 b f Bold Edge-Meeson Times (Enchantment) 6196$^{14}$ *6400$^{10}$* **><**

**Gifted Musician** 2 b c Sadler s Wells (USA) -Photogenic (Midyan (USA)) 6352$^{4}$ **>64f<**

**Gift Horse** 4 ch g Cadeaux Genereux-Careful Dancer (Gorytus (USA)) 2206$^{11}$ 2575$^{2}$ 3205$^{3}$ 3597$^{8}$ 5769$^{4}$ 5941$^{30}$ **>99+f<**

**Gift Voucher (IRE)** 3 ch c Cadeaux Genereux-Highland Gift (IRE) (Generous (IRE)) 2085$^{11}$ 3417$^{3}$ 3922$^{8}$ 4297$^{2}$ (4819) **>86+f<**

**Gig Harbor** 5 b g Efisio-Petonica (IRE) (Petoski) *(418) 600$^{11}$ (706) 915$^{5}$ 1054$^{6}$* 3325$^{11}$ 3631$^{4}$ 3937$^{13}$ 4737$^{8}$ **>102a 84f<**

**Giko** 10 b g Arazi (USA) -Gayane (Nureyev (USA)) *661$^{11}$ 857$^{3}$ 995$^{12}$ 1164$^{6}$ 1402$^{7}$* 2344a$^{6}$ 2767$^{2}$ 3492$^{3}$ 3776$^{11}$ 4686$^{8}$ 5286$^{10}$ 5540$^{2}$ 5796$^{16}$ **>46a 48f<**

**Gildas Fortuna** 2 b f Fort Wood (USA) -Gleaming Sky (SAF) (Badger Land (USA)) 6196$^{4}$ **>70f<**

**Gilded Cove** 4 b c Polar Prince (IRE) -Cloudy Reef (Cragador) *515$^{7}$ 680$^{7}$ 748$^{3}$ 897$^{3}$ 968$^{5}$ (1140) (1474) 2455$^{4}$ 3025$^{4}$* **>70a 50f<**

**Gilly s General (IRE)** 4 ch g General Monash (USA) -Good Aim (IRE) (Priolo (USA)) *779$^{4}$ 946$^{10}$ (1515) 2666$^{6}$* 2833$^{11}$ *3024$^{12}$* 4265$^{10}$ **>49a 46f<**

**Gimasha** 2 b f Cadeaux Genereux-First Waltz (FR) (Green Dancer (USA)) 5848$^{4}$ 6125$^{2}$ 6281$^{12}$ **>73f<**

**Ginger Cookie** 2 ch f Bold Edge-Pretty Pollyanna (General Assembly (USA)) 5319$^{15}$ **>41f<**

**Ginger Ice** 4 ch g Bahamian Bounty-Sharp Top (Sharpo) *534$^{3}$ 663$^{5}$ 789$^{10}$* **><**

**Gingiefly** 2 b c Sinndar (IRE) -Native Ring (FR) (Bering) 5373$^{10}$ 5838$^{3}$ **>64f<**

**Gingko** 7 b g Pursuit Of Love-Arboretum (IRE) (Green Desert (USA)) *(419) 559$^{5}$ 820$^{10}$ 6450$^{3}$* 6566$^{3}$ **>76a 74f<**

**Ginner Morris** 9 b g Emarati (USA) -Just Run (IRE) (Runnett) *497$^{6}$* **>20a 58df<**

**Gin N Fonic (IRE)** 4 ch g Zafonic (USA) -Crepe Ginger (IRE) (Sadler s Wells (USA)) 4084$^{7}$ **>67a 74f<**

**Gio (ITY)** 2 b c Law Society (USA) -Gilda Zanzic (GER) (Esclavo (FR)) 6542a$^{9}$ **><**

**Gioco Pericoloso (IRE)** 3 b g Desert Style (IRE) -Golden Superlative (IRE) (Superlative) 3135a$^{4}$ **><**

**Giocoso (USA)** 4 b c Bahri (USA) -Wing My Chimes (USA) (Flying Paster (USA)) 2646$^{6}$ 3415$^{9}$ 3842$^{9}$ (4569) 4672$^{4}$ 5004$^{5}$ 5177$^{4}$ 5698$^{9}$ 6284$^{6}$ **>90f<**

**Giovane Imperatore** 6 b h Halling (USA) -Siddharta (USA) (Chief s Crown (USA)) 2608a$^{4}$ **>111f<**

**Girl Scoud (BRZ)** 5 b m Mensageiro Alado (BRZ) -Ingradire Sempre (BRZ) (Adjutor (BRZ)) 831a$^{9}$ 1002a$^{10}$ **>53f<**

**Girlsweekend** 2 b f Benny The Dip (USA) -Snoozy (Cadeaux Genereux) *5911$^{10}$ 6446$^{7}$* **>50a<**

**Girl Warrior (USA)** 3 ch f Elusive Quality (USA) -Qhazeenah (Marju (IRE)) 2223$^{6}$ 2425$^{4}$ 2848$^{12}$ **>69f<**

**Gironde** 3 b c Sadler s Wells (USA) -Sarah Georgina (Persian Bold) 1382$^{4}$ 1674$^{3}$ 2999$^{12}$ 3806$^{3}$ (4703) **>93+f<**

**Gitche Manito (IRE)** 2 b c Namid-Chasing Rainbows (Rainbow Quest (USA)) 4682$^{3}$ 5087$^{11}$ 5298$^{5}$ 5747$^{2}$ **>74f<**

**Giunchiglio** 5 ch g Millkom-Daffodil Fields (Try My Best (USA)) *1232$^{3}$ (2302)* 2573$^{12}$ 3291$^{3}$ 3731$^{6}$ 3844$^{10}$ 4571$^{4}$ (4911) 5459$^{6}$ 5584$^{13}$ *6025$^{4}$* 6266$^{16}$ **>68a 73f<**

**Giust In Temp (IRE)** 5 b h Polish Precedent (USA) -Blue Stricks (Bluebird (USA)) *445$^{4}$ 532$^{2}$ 590$^{9}$ 652$^{6}$* 3607$^{9}$ 4042$^{4}$ 4485$^{8}$ 4624$^{10}$ **>38a 46 f<**

**Give Back Calais (IRE)** 6 b g Brief Truce (USA) -Nichodoula (Doulab (USA)) 784a$^{5}$ **>74a 95f<**

**Give Him Credit (USA)** 4 b g Quiet American (USA) -Meniatarra (USA) (Zilzal (USA)) *1423$^{5}$* 2218$^{12}$ 3623$^{8}$ 3836$^{11}$ 4132$^{6}$ **>28a 52f<**

**Give Me Five (GER)** 3 gr f Monsun (GER) -Grey Pearl (GER) (Magic Mirror) 2723a$^{14}$ 3504a$^{3}$ 4430a$^{10}$ (6107a) **>103f<**

**Givemethemoonlight** 5 ch m Woodborough (USA) -Rockin Rosie (Song) *412$^{2}$ 463$^{5}$ 552$^{2}$ (562) 605$^{3}$ 623$^{5}$ 695$^{3}$ 763$^{6}$(772) 800$^{2}$ 866$^{3}$ 909$^{6}$ 970$^{3}$* **>65a 41f<**

**Given A Chance** 3 b g Defacto (USA) -Milly Molly Mango (Mango Express) *434$^{4}$ 611$^{5}$ 713$^{8}$* 1499$^{5}$ 1874$^{3}$ 1946$^{4}$ 2349$^{2}$ 2571$^{6}$ 3375$^{8}$ 3684$^{6}$ 3822$^{3}$ **>25a 51 f<**

**Given A Choice (IRE)** 2 b c Trans Island-Miss Audimar (USA) (Mr. Leader (USA)) 4523$^{4}$ 5620$^{7}$ 5897$^{5}$ **>82+f<**

**Giverand** 5 bb m Royal Applause-Petersford Girl (IRE) (Taufan (USA)) 1969$^{10}$ 3772$^{10}$ 3810$^{13}$ **>28a 39f<**

**Gjovic** 3 br g Singspiel (IRE) -Photo Call (Chief Singer) *1064$^{2}$* 1322$^{5}$ 2069$^{14}$ 2298$^{4}$ 2648$^{3}$ 2809$^{3}$ 3160$^{8}$ 5732$^{6}$ **>79a 75f<**

**Glad Big (GER)** 2 b c Big Shuffle (USA) -Glady Sum (GER) (Surumu (GER)) 5376$^{3}$ 5772$^{8}$ **>72f<**

**Glad Lady (GER)** 3 ch f Big Shuffle (USA) -Glady Sum (GER) (Surumu (GER)) 6203a$^{0}$ **>76f<**

**Glad Lion (GER)** 3 b c Dashing Blade-Glady Beauty (GER) (Big Shuffle (USA)) 6106a$^{2}$ 6508a$^{9}$ **>109f<**

**Glad Master (GER)** 7 b h Big Shuffle (USA) -Glady Star (GER) (Star Appeal) 1004a$^{9}$ **>63f<**

**Glads Image** 2 ch f Handsome Ridge-Secret So And So (So Factual (USA)) 5846$^{18}$ 6060$^{6}$ **>37f<**

**Glad To Be Fast (IRE)** 4 ch g Big Shuffle (USA) -Glad To Be Here (IRE) (Waajib) *(1953a)* 3769a$^{9}$ 5255a$^{15}$ 6379a$^{4}$ 6513a$^{3}$ **>103f<**

**Gladys Aylward** 4 b f Polar Falcon (USA) -Versami (USA) (Riverman (USA)) *630$^{5}$ 682$^{7}$* **>28a 63f<**

**Glanworth (IRE)** 3 ch c Woodman (USA) -Leo Girl (USA) (Seattle Slew (USA)) 2093$^{10}$ 2312$^{6}$ 2693$^{11}$ *2990$^{11}$* **><**

**Glaramara** 3 b g Nicolotte-Digamist Girl (IRE) (Digamist (USA)) *1063$^{11}$* 1384$^{2}$ 1764$^{10}$ 1900$^{3}$ 2897$^{8}$ 2966$^{13}$ 3730$^{4}$ 4531$^{4}$ 4873$^{4}$ 4931$^{8}$ 5628$^{17}$ **>81a 104f<**

**Glasson Lodge** 2 b f Primo Dominie-Petrikov (IRE) (In The Wings) *1234$^{4}$* 1505$^{5}$ 2352$^{6}$ 2515$^{3}$ 2946$^{4}$ 3140$^{2}$ 3571$^{2}$ 3824$^{6}$ 4475$^{8}$ 4651$^{4}$ **>41a 39f<**

**Glavalcour (FR)** 4 b c Glaieul (USA) -Lady De Valcour (FR) (Labus (FR)) 1655a$^{4}$ **><**

**Glazed Frost (FR)** 2 gr f Verglas (IRE) -Vol Sauvage (FR) (Always Fair (USA)) 4963a$^{2}$ 5313a$^{8}$ 6297a$^{5}$ **>92f<**

**Glebe Garden** 3 b f Soviet Star (USA) -Trounce (Barathea (IRE)) 1704$^{5}$ 2089$^{5}$ 3306$^{6}$ 3728$^{11}$ 4032$^{8}$ (4496) 5155$^{2}$ 5399$^{10}$ *5912$^{11}$* **>57a 84f<**

**Glenaka (GER)** 2 b f Turtle Island (IRE) -Giralda (IRE) (Tenby) 6377a$^{7}$ **>80f<**

**Glencairn Star** 3 b c Selkirk (USA) -Bianca Nera (Salse (USA)) 1174$^{11}$ 5582$^{11}$ 6097$^{16}$ **>61f<**

**Glencalvie (IRE)** 3 ch c Grand Lodge (USA) -Top Of The Form (IRE) (Masterclass (USA)) 1794$^{21}$ 3587$^{5}$ 3916$^{15}$ 4338$^{4}$ (4817) (5737) *5912$^{13}$* **>46a 79+f<**

**Glencoe Solas (IRE)** 4 ch f Night Shift (USA) -Boranwood (IRE) (Exhibitioner) 1750$^{6}$ 1909$^{4}$ 2428$^{2}$ 2506$^{2}$ (2670) 2948$^{5}$ 3141$^{3}$ 3663$^{2}$ 3775$^{6}$ 4130$^{12}$ **>81f<**

**Glendale** 3 ch g Opening Verse (USA) -Kayartis (Kaytu) *(790)* 1222$^{11}$ 1414$^{13}$ 1957$^{9}$ 2571$^{7}$ *2988$^{5}$* 3556$^{9}$ 5791$^{12}$ *6493$^{8}$ 6576$^{5}$* **>65a 55f<**

**Glen Ida** 2 ch c Selkirk (USA) -Yanka (USA) (Blushing John (USA)) 4922$^{3}$ 5264$^{2}$ (5858) **>90f<**

**Glen Innes (IRE)** 3 b f Selkirk (USA) -Shinko Hermes (IRE) (Sadler s Wells (USA)) (1250) 1704$^{2}$ 2020$^{2}$ 2641$^{7}$ 5969a$^{P}$ 6571$^{4}$ **>101f<**

**Glen Vale Walk (IRE)** 7 ch g Balla Cove-Winter Harvest (Grundy) 2272$^{6}$ 2525$^{3}$ 2939$^{5}$ **>50a 54f<**

**Glenviews Polly (IRE)** 4 b f Poliglote-Fun Board (FR) (Saumarez) *423$^{6}$ 474$^{8}$ 565$^{11}$* **>32 a 32 f<**

**Glesni** 5 gr m Key Of Luck (USA) -Llwy Bren (Lidhame) *601$^{7}$* **>28a<**

**Glide** 3 ch g In The Wings-Ash Glade (Nashwan (USA)) 1365$^{3}$ 2070$^{12}$ 2840$^{3}$ **>77f<**

**Gliding By** 3 ch f Halling (USA) -Waft (USA) (Topsider (USA)) 3630$^{9}$ 3994$^{13}$ 4433$^{7}$ **>45a 60f<**

**Glimmer Of Light (IRE)** 4 b g Marju (IRE) -Church Light (Caerleon (USA)) 1821$^{6}$ 2738$^{13}$ 3274$^{7}$ 4029$^{9}$ 5258$^{16}$ **>74f<**

**Glinting Desert (IRE)** 2 b f Desert Prince (IRE) -Dazzling Park (IRE) (Warning) 3859a$^{8}$ **>74f<**

**Global Achiever** 3 b g Key Of Luck (USA) -Inflation (Primo Dominie) *593$^{3}$ 668$^{2}$ 760$^{2}$ (906)* 1333$^{16}$ 1742$^{8}$ 2097$^{15}$ *2455$^{7}$* 5526$^{9}$ 6007$^{14}$ *6064$^{12}$ (6538)* **>74a 41f<**

**Global Banker (IRE)** 2 b c Desert Prince (IRE) -Luisa Demon (IRE) (Barathea (IRE)) 3588$^{17}$ *4334$^{5}$* **>37a 32f<**

**Globe Beauty (IRE)** 6 b m Shalford (IRE) -Pen Bal Duchess (Chaparly (FR)) *534$^{6}$ 723$^{7}$* **>17a<**

**Globe Trekker (USA)** 2 gr f Aljabr (USA) -Amazonia (USA) (Deputy Minister (CAN)) 4488$^{11}$ 5227$^{4}$ 5858$^{4}$ 6111$^{7}$ **>73f<**

**Glocca Morra (IRE)** 6 b g Catrail (USA) -Delphinus (Soviet Star (USA)) 2744a$^{3}$ 4956a$^{7}$ 5327a$^{4}$ 5661a$^{4}$ 6104a$^{4}$ **>110f<**

**Gloirez (FR)** 3 b f Saumarez-Glaoutchka (FR) (Glaieul (USA)) 5501a$^{12}$ **><**

**Gloria Nimbus** 2 b f Cloudings (IRE) -Glorious Aragon (Aragon) 1601$^{7}$ 2296$^{9}$ 2749$^{6}$ 3770$^{9}$ 6008$^{9}$ **>40f<**

**Glorious Step (USA)** 2 b f Diesis-Bessie s Chips (USA) (Rakeen (USA)) 3456$^{3}$ (4584) 4964a$^{8}$ (5753) **>87+f<**

**Glory Girl** 4 ch f Factual (USA) -Glory Gold (Hittite Glory) *1913$^{6}$* 1941$^{6}$ **>34a 44f<**

**Glory Quest (USA)** 7 b g Quest For Fame-Sonseri (Prince Tenderfoot (USA)) *513$^{2}$ 592$^{7}$ 666$^{3}$ 827$^{5}$ 971$^{2}$ 1010$^{2}$ (1045)* 1103$^{13}$ 1211$^{6}$ 2365$^{4}$ (2652) 2958$^{20}$ 3244$^{3}$ (3300) 6215$^{29}$ **>78a 81f<**

**Gloved Hand** 2 b f Royal Applause-Fudge (Polar Falcon (USA)) (2585) 2970$^{14}$ 5551$^{10}$ 5711$^{6}$ **>87 f<**

**Go Bananas** 3 b g Primo Dominie-Amsicora (Cadeaux Genereux) 4031$^{6}$ 4570$^{4}$ *5220$^{9}$* 5614$^{17}$ **>67a 87f<**

**Go Between** 3 b f Daggers Drawn (USA) -Pizzicato (Statoblest) 2112$^{2}$ 2694$^{7}$ 3178$^{6}$ 4020$^{6}$ (4248) 4731$^{7}$ 5249$^{13}$ **>89f<**

**Goblin** 3 b g Atraf-Forest Fantasy (Rambo Dancer (CAN)) 1184$^{4}$ *(1422)* 1688$^{5}$ (2197) 2501$^{3}$ 2949$^{5}$ (3107) 3340$^{3}$ **>69a 79f<**

**Go Classic** 4 b f Classic Cliche (IRE) -Edraianthus (Windjammer (USA)) *981$^{7}$* 1135$^{13}$ 2212$^{14}$ **>69a 69f<**

**Godalming (USA)** 4 b g Miswaki (USA) -Diamonds Direct (CAN) (Diamond Sword (USA)) *709a$^{7}$* **><**

**Godsend** 2 b f Royal Applause-Gracious Gift (Cadeaux Genereux) 2177$^{2}$ (3491) 4475$^{2}$ 5351$^{3}$ 5938$^{8}$ **>77f<**

**Go For Gold (IRE)** 3 br c Machiavellian (USA) -Kithanga (IRE) (Darshaan) 2068$^{3}$ 4215$^{2}$ 4833$^{3}$ 5463$^{7}$ **>115f<**

**Go Free** 3 gr g Easycall-Miss Traxdata (Absalom) *2815$^{2}$ 3613$^{5}$* 4018$^{9}$ *4879$^{5}$* 6058$^{10}$ 6146$^{13}$ **>56a 35f<**

**Go Garuda** 3 b g Air Express (IRE) -Free As A Bird (Robellino (USA)) 3447$^{3}$ 4195$^{12}$ **>63+f<**

**Gogetter Girl** 2 b f Wolfhound (USA) -Square Mile Miss (IRE) (Last Tycoon) 1105$^{6}$ 1299$^{2}$ 1383$^{4}$ 1839$^{10}$ 2208$^{4}$ 2458$^{6}$ *5054$^{11}$* 5520$^{9}$ 5617$^{11}$ 5947$^{20}$ 6181$^{11}$ *6555$^{6}$* **>53a 68f<**

**Go Go Girl** 4 ch f Pivotal-Addicted To Love (Touching Wood (USA)) (1855) 6001$^{7}$ **>48a 73f<**

**Go Got (USA)** 6 b h Solid Illusion (USA) -Fab s Melody (USA) (Devil s Bag (USA)) 1922a$^{8}$ **>76f<**

**Go Green** 3 ch f Environment Friend-Sandra Mac (Marju (IRE)) *683$^{8}$* 1325$^{8}$ 1683$^{13}$ 1926$^{7}$ 2426$^{5}$ 3155$^{7}$ 3697$^{2}$ (4476) 4798$^{4}$ 4853$^{3}$ 5021$^{2}$ 5175$^{6}$ 5410$^{13}$ 5538$^{3}$ 5705$^{2}$ 6006$^{13}$ 6150$^{6}$ 6564$^{4}$ **>41a 63f<**

**Gojo (IRE)** 3 b f Danetime (IRE) -Pretonic (Precocious) 1464$^{4}$ 1750$^{2}$ 1855$^{9}$ 2741$^{15}$ 5618$^{12}$ 6001$^{19}$ *6016$^{F}$* **>73f<**

**Golano** 4 gr g Linamix (FR) -Dimakya (USA) (Dayjur (USA)) *2881$^{2}$* 3325$^{10}$ 4950$^{8}$ 5266$^{6}$ 5768$^{13}$ **>83a 84f<**

**Golband** 2 b f Cadeaux Genereux-Hatheethah (IRE) (Machiavellian (USA)) 2780$^{5}$ **>44f<**

**Goldbricker** 4 b g Muhtarram (USA) -Sally Slade (Dowsing (USA)) *518$^{6}$ 695$^{5}$ (811)* **>50a 64f<**

**Gold Card** 3 b g First Trump-Fleuve D Or (IRE) (Last Tycoon) *1192$^{2}$* 1933$^{2}$ 2146$^{5}$ 2584$^{5}$ 3396$^{2}$ (3796) **>42a 67f<**

**Golden Anthem (USA)** 2 ch f Lion Cavern (USA) -Bacinella (USA) (El Gran Senor (USA)) (1984) 3031$^{16}$ 3316$^{3}$ 4060$^{6}$ 5626$^{6}$ 5939$^{14}$ 6459$^{7}$ **>87f<**

**Golden Applause (FR)** 2 b f Royal Applause-Golden Circle (USA) (Theatrical) 4081$^{7}$ **>49f<**

**Golden Asha** 2 ch f Danehill Dancer (IRE) -Snugfit Annie (Midyan (USA)) 5558$^{3}$ 5908$^{7}$ **>65 f<**

**Golden Bankes (IRE)** 3 ch f Foxhound (USA) -Semence D Or (FR) (Kaldoun (FR)) 5378$^{12}$ 6004$^{7}$ **>36f<**

**Golden Boot** 5 ch g Unfuwain (USA) -Sports Delight (Star Appeal) 1661$^{6}$ 1754$^{8}$ 1785$^{9}$ (2443) **>29a 71f<**

**Golden Bounty** 5 b h Bahamian Bounty-Cumbrian Melody (Petong) 1673$^{10}$ 3141$^{6}$ 3416$^{10}$ 4687$^{14}$ 5734$^{10}$ **>61f<**

**Golden Cast (JPN)** 4 b c Taiki Shuttle (USA) -Return Bandam (JPN) (Niniski (USA)) 5982a$^{11}$ **>100f<**

**Golden Chalice (IRE)** 5 ch g Selkirk (USA) -Special Oasis (Green Desert (USA)) *485$^{5}$ 556$^{6}$* 1456$^{12}$ 1772$^{9}$ (1968) 2283$^{19}$ 3673$^{17}$ 6191$^{12}$ **>85a 99f<**

**Golden Chance (IRE)** 7 b g Unfuwain (USA) -Golden Digger (USA) (Mr Prospector (USA)) 3018$^{8}$ (3461) **>45a 58f<**

**Golden Danetime (IRE)** 4 b c Danetime (IRE) -Banco Solo (Distant Relative) 3816a$^{10}$ **>96f<**

**Golden Devious (IRE)** 4 b c Dr Devious (IRE) -Tajarib (IRE) (Last Tycoon) 2608a$^{6}$ **>109f<**

**Golden Dixie (USA)** 5 ch g Dixieland Band (USA) -Beyrouth (USA) (Alleged (USA)) 3453$^{10}$ 3778$^{2}$ 4090$^{5}$ 4837$^{5}$ 5299$^{8}$ 5603$^{24}$ 5874$^{9}$ *6157$^{9}$* **>65a 93f<**

**Golden Drift** 3 ch f Inchinor-Carpet Of Leaves (USA) (Green Forest (USA)) 2182$^{12}$ 2693$^{5}$ 3160$^{7}$ 3852$^{2}$ 4655$^{5}$ 5245$^{11}$ 5560$^{3}$ 5951$^{6}$ **>39a 62f<**

**Golden Dual** 4 b g Danehill (USA) -Golden Digger (USA) (Mr Prospector (USA)) *463$^{7}$ 555$^{10}$ 618$^{6}$ 724$^{13}$ 867$^{7}$ 931$^{9}$ 1081$^{2}$* 1188$^{9}$ 1463$^{16}$ *4600$^{7}$* **>63a 69f<**

**Golden Dynasty** 2 ch c Erhaab (USA) -Ajeebah (IRE) (Mujtahid (USA)) 3240$^{8}$ 4747$^{9}$ 5173$^{6}$ 5696$^{7}$ **>70f<**

**Golden Empire (USA)** 3 br g Red Ransom (USA) -Golden Gorse (USA) (His Majesty (USA)) *1138$^{2}$* 1344$^{2}$ 1605$^{4}$ (1662) 3160$^{14}$ 4027$^{8}$ **>62a 71f<**

**Golden Feather** 2 ch c Dr Fong (USA) -Idolize (Polish Precedent (USA)) 6331$^{3}$ **>77f<**

**Golden Fields (IRE)** 4 b f Definite Article-Quickstep Queen (FR) (Pampabird) 4609$^{10}$ 5350$^{7}$ 5710$^{8}$ 6516$^{3}$ **>47a 46 f<**

**Golden Fury** 2 ch c Cadeaux Genereux-Galaxie Dust (USA) (Blushing Groom (FR)) 2904$^{4}$ 4523$^{3}$ 5246$^{4}$ 5567$^{2}$ 5858$^{3}$ **>86f<**

**Golden Gate (IRE)** 2 b c Giant s Causeway (USA) -Bay Queen (Damister (USA)) 6441$^{16}$ 6545$^{13}$ **>21f<**

**Golden Gift** 6 ch g Cadeaux Genereux-Casting For Gold (IRE) (Hansel (USA)) *5504a$^{9}$* **>71a 95f<**

**Golden Grace** 3 b c Green Desert (USA) -Chief Bee (Chief s Crown (USA)) 1414$^{9}$ 2018$^{4}$ 2281$^{4}$ 2999$^{17}$ 4490$^{12}$ 6128$^{13}$ **>95f<**

**Golden Island (IRE)** 3 ch f Selkirk (USA) -Daftiyna (IRE) (Darshaan) 2243$^{3}$ 2632$^{2}$ (3294) 3694$^{5}$ (4551) 4773$^{9}$ 5249$^{3}$ 5783$^{2}$ **>94f<**

**Golden Key** 3 b g Rainbow Quest (USA) -Keyboogie (USA) (Lyphard (USA)) 2085$^{9}$ 2611$^{10}$ **>55f<**

**Golden Legacy (IRE)** 2 b f Rossini (USA) -Dissidentia (IRE) (Dancing Dissident (USA)) 2758$^{2}$ 3031$^{8}$ (4009) (4358) 4876$^{3}$ (5626) 5894$^{4}$ **>104f<**

**Golden Legend (IRE)** 7 b g Last Tycoon-Adjalisa (IRE) (Darshaan) *2006$^{7}$ 2055$^{7}$* **>10a 10f<**

**Golden Millenium (GER)** 3 br c Monsun (GER) -Gluckskind (GER) (Mister Rock S (GER)) 3565a$^{18}$ 5168a$^{6}$ **>82f<**

**Golden Nun** 4 b f Bishop Of Cashel-Amber Mill (Doulab (USA)) 1126$^{11}$ 1649a$^{2}$ 1964$^{3}$ (2117) 2685$^{3}$ (2903a) 3715$^{7}$ 4286$^{5}$ 4595a$^{7}$ 5255a$^{5}$ 5414$^{4}$ 5780$^{10}$ 6214$^{11}$ **>89a 105f<**

**Golden Oldie (IRE)** 6 b g Old Vic-Misty Gold (Arizona Duke) *999$^{10}$* **><**

**Golden Pivotal** 3 b c Pivotal-Classy Relation (Puissance) 1777a$^{8}$ **>91f<**

**Golden Pyramid (IRE)** 2 ch c Daggers Drawn (USA) -Fashion Scout (IRE) (Thatching) 2669a$^{7}$ (3568a) **>52f<**

**Golden Queen** 3 b f Unfuwain (USA) -Queen Linear (USA) (Polish Navy (USA)) *5381$^{14}$* 5571$^{3}$ 5828$^{14}$ **>15a 37f<**

**Golden Quest** 3 ch g Rainbow Quest (USA) -Souk (IRE) (Ahonoora) *(969) (1100)* 1416$^{7}$ (2561) 2999$^{5}$ **>82+a 91f<**

**Golden Rose (GER)** 4 b f Winged Love (IRE) -Grey Pearl (GER) (Magic Mirror) 3973a$^{4}$ 6107a$^{3}$ **>95f<**

**Golden Sahara (IRE)** 3 b c Green Desert (USA) -Golden Digger (USA) (Mr Prospector (USA)) 1764$^{14}$ 3751$^{3}$ (4273) 5468$^{3}$ 5921$^{14}$ **>105f<**

**Golden Sensation (IRE)** 2 b f Turtle Island (IRE) -

Poly Dancer (Suave Dancer (USA)) 2668a$^{4}$ >**82f**<

**Golden Shell** 5 ch m Hatim (USA) -Sonnenelle (Sonnen Gold) 6465$^{10}$ >**32f**<

**Golden Spectrum (IRE)** 5 ch g Spectrum (IRE) -Plessaya (USA) (Nureyev (USA)) 1787$^{3}$ 2292$^{5}$ 2936$^{10}$ 3921$^{15}$ 4425$^{3}$ 4557$^{12}$ 4702$^{14}$ 5235$^{12}$5557$^{3}$ 5945$^{17}$ 6201$^{10}$ >**65a 65 f**<

**Golden Square** 2 ch g Tomba-Cherish Me (Polar Falcon (USA)) 5772$^{9}$ 6045$^{6}$ >**56f**<

**Golden Squaw** 2 ch f Grand Lodge (USA) -Wig Wam (IRE) (Indian Ridge) 3164$^{6}$ 4048$^{11}$ 5098$^{14}$ 5561$^{9}$ >**44f**<

**Golden Stravinsky (USA)** 2 b c Stravinsky (USA) -Shagadellic (USA) (Devil s Bag (USA)) (2669a) 3362a$^{4}$ >**87f**<

**Golden Wild** 3 b c Desert Sun-Superetta (Superlative) (3135a) >**55f**<

**Goldeva** 5 gr m Makbul-Gold Belt (IRE) (Bellypha) (1126) 2021$^{5}$ 3308$^{11}$ 3715$^{5}$ 4362$^{4}$ (4779) 5454$^{5}$ 6190$^{9}$ 6572$^{6}$ >**104f**<

**Gold Guest** 5 ch g Vettori (IRE) -Cassilis (IRE) (Persian Bold) *(464) 559$^{7}$* 4083$^{7}$ 4736$^{4}$ 5320$^{5}$ 6083$^{6}$ 6208$^{2}$ >**72a 68f**<

**Gold Gun (USA)** 2 b c Seeking The Gold (USA) -Possessive Dancer (Shareef Dancer (USA)) 5897$^{14}$ 6187$^{16}$ >**46f**<

**Goldhill Prince** 2 b c Prince Sabo-Lady Mabel (Inchinor) 1115$^{8}$ 1307$^{4}$ 1686$^{9}$ *2003$^{2}$* (2140) (2288) (2616) (2799) 3170$^{3}$ *4094$^{6}$* 4304$^{5}$4816$^{3}$ 5910$^{9}$ >**56a 56f**<

**Gold History (USA)** 3 b c Seeking The Gold (USA) -Battle Hymn (USA) (Danzig (USA)) 1123$^{2}$ (1411) 1586$^{3}$ 3032$^{5}$ 3937$^{16}$ 4271$^{10}$ 4856$^{6}$ 5106$^{5}$ (5470) 5761$^{8}$ >**106f**<

**Gold Majesty** 2 b f Josr Algarhoud (IRE) -Calcutta Queen (Night Shift (USA)) 3208$^{11}$ 3840$^{8}$ 4040$^{9}$ 5534$^{13}$ 5825$^{8}$ >**48f**<

**Gold Marie (IRE)** 2 b f Green Desert (USA) -Toutzi (FR) (Vettori (IRE)) 3362a$^{5}$ 4184a$^{8}$ 6108a$^{2}$ >**94f**<

**Gold Mask (USA)** 3 bb c Seeking The Gold (USA) -Leo s Gypsy Dancer (USA) (Leo Castelli (USA)) 1386$^{6}$ 2204$^{2}$ (2842) 3001$^{15}$ >**79f**<

**Gold Medallist** 4 ch g Zilzal (USA) -Spot Prize (USA) (Seattle Dancer (USA)) 2108$^{6}$ 3538$^{7}$ 4529$^{4}$ (4983a) 5503a$^{5}$ 6218$^{5}$ >**113f**<

**Gold Quay (IRE)** 2 b f Docksider (USA) -Viaticum (IRE) (Scenic) 2858$^{2}$ 3346$^{4}$ 3703$^{6}$ >**75f**<

**Gold Queen** 2 b f Grand Lodge (USA) -Silver Colours (USA) (Silver Hawk (USA)) 4712$^{3}$ (5109) >**73+f**<

**Gold Relic (USA)** 3 b f Kingmambo (USA) -Gold Bust (Nashwan (USA)) 3592$^{12}$ 5511$^{9}$ >**51f**<

**Gold Ring** 4 ch g Groom Dancer (USA) -Indubitable (Sharpo) 1401$^{7}$ 1661$^{2}$ 2022$^{3}$ 2240$^{6}$ 2855$^{5}$ 3716$^{3}$ (3909) 4345$^{6}$ 4858$^{2}$5834$^{4}$ 6172$^{13}$ >**102f**<

**Gold Storm (USA)** 4 ch c Seeking The Gold (USA) -Storm Teal (USA) (Storm Bird (CAN)) *6487a$^{9}$* >**117a**<

**Gold Type (IRE)** 5 b h Goldmark (USA) -Crimson Crest (Pampapaul) 2466a$^{7}$ 3552a$^{4}$ 4596a$^{3}$ 5255a$^{13}$ 6379a$^{10}$ >**102f**<

**Golfagent** 6 b g Kris-Alusha (Soviet Star (USA)) *1193$^{4}$* 1593$^{6}$ >**36a 43f**<

**Golnessa** 3 b f Pyramus (USA) -My Pretty Niece (Great Nephew) *1022$^{11}$* 1366$^{12}$ 1945$^{6}$ >**19f**<

**Go Mo (IRE)** 2 br c Night Shift (USA) -Quiche (Formidable (USA)) 2804$^{12}$ 4611$^{6}$ *5053$^{6}$* 5909$^{8}$ 5995$^{8}$ 6356$^{2}$ 6523$^{2}$ >**62a 77f**<

**Gonbarda (GER)** 2 b f Lando (GER) -Gonfalon (Slip Anchor) 6377a$^{2}$ >**98f**<

**Gondolin (IRE)** 4 b g Marju (IRE) -Galletina (IRE) (Persian Heights) 4715$^{8}$ 4934$^{10}$ >**81a 91f**<

**Gone Fishing (IRE)** 2 ch f Cadeaux Genereux-Dabbing (USA) (Cure The Blues (USA)) 2481$^{7}$ 3560$^{2}$ 4625$^{3}$ *5380$^{3}$* >**72a 76f**<

**Gone Loco** 3 b f Piccolo-Missed Again (High Top) 3139$^{9}$ >**46f**<

**Gone N Dunnett (IRE)** 5 b g Petardia-Skerries Bell (Taufan (USA)) *454$^{10}$ 480$^{8}$ 801$^{10}$ 904$^{8}$* 1516$^{15}$ 2094$^{10}$ *2455$^{6}$*2707$^{6}$ (2823) 3307$^{7}$ 3428$^{3}$ (3558) 4130$^{8}$ 4415$^{5}$ 4800 5016$^{2}$ 5550$^{11}$5754$^{15}$ 5849$^{11}$ >**59 a 66f**<

**Gone Too Far** 6 b g Reprimand-Blue Nile (IRE) (Bluebird (USA)) (4007) >**57f**<

**Gonfilia (GER)** 4 b f Big Shuffle (USA) -Gonfalon (Slip Anchor) 831a$^{8}$ (1002a) 1964$^{2}$ (2242) (2641) 2967$^{9}$ 4286$^{4}$ 5416$^{2}$ (5948) >**111f**<

**Gonpardo (GER)** 3 br c Big Shuffle (USA) -Gonfalon (Slip Anchor) 2336a$^{8}$ >**97f**<

**Good Article (IRE)** 3 b g Definite Article-Good News (IRE) (Ajraas (USA)) 1508$^{12}$ 1912$^{B}$ 2562$^{16}$ 3002$^{13}$ >**42f**<

**Goodbye Ben** 2 b c Benny The Dip (USA) -Alifandango (IRE) (Alzao (USA)) 6476$^{9}$ >**49f**<

**Goodbye Mr Bond** 4 b g Elmaamul (USA) -Fifth Emerald (Formidable (USA)) *406$^{5}$ 512$^{6}$ 910$^{3}$* 1247$^{4}$ 1620$^{3}$ 1993$^{4}$ (2580) (2781) (3058) (3198) 4164$^{3}$4258$^{2}$ 5194$^{6}$ (5265) 6069$^{7}$ 6193$^{6}$ >**62a 83f**<

**Goodbye Mrs Chips** 5 ch m Zilzal (USA) -Happydrome (Ahonoora) 1720$^{6}$ >**45a 56f**<

**Goodenough Mover** 8 ch g Beveled (USA) -Rekindled Flame (IRE) (King s Lake (USA)) *1230$^{2}$* (2064) 2483$^{2}$ 2614$^{2}$ (2834) (3455) 3698$^{5}$ 4084$^{2}$ 4917$^{7}$ 5444$^{15}$(5874) *(6451)* >**97a 91f**<

**Goodenough Star** 4 b f Stronz (IRE) -Goodenough Girl (Mac s Imp (USA)) *455$^{9}$* >**14a 38f**<

**Good Form (IRE)** 4 b g Danetime (IRE) -Faapette (Runnett) *424$^{5}$ 527$^{6}$ 665$^{12}$* >**26a 26f**<

**Good Investment** 2 b g Silver Patriarch (IRE) -Bundled Up (USA) (Sharpen Up) 3918$^{3}$ 4606$^{5}$ 4900$^{9}$ *6020$^{11}$* >**37a 69f**<

**Good Loser (IRE)** 4 b g Mujadil (USA) -Cockney Star (IRE) (Camden Town) 1389$^{15}$ 2092$^{9}$ >**68f**<

**Goodricke** 2 b c Bahamian Bounty-Star (Most Welcome) 1269$^{2}$ (1607) (2086) 2954$^{9}$ >**89 f**<

**Good Time Bobby** 7 b g Primitive Rising (USA) -Goodreda (Good Times (ITY)) 2445$^{3}$ *2662$^{7}$* 3896$^{4}$ 4422$^{12}$ 4557$^{15}$ 4782$^{16}$ 5450$^{13}$ >**41f**<

**Good Timing** 6 gr g Timeless Times (USA) -Fort Vally (Belfort (FR)) *445$^{2}$ 570$^{15}$ 726$^{7}$* 2346$^{13}$ 3041$^{13}$ >**34a 34f**<

**Good Vibrations** 3 b f Bijou D Inde-Showcase (Shareef Dancer (USA)) *420$^{3}$ 640$^{5}$ 817$^{6}$ 884$^{7}$* >**50a 25f**<

**Good Wee Girl (IRE)** 2 b f Tagula (IRE) -Auriga (Belmez (USA)) 3192$^{7}$ 3532$^{14}$ 3823$^{2}$ (4243) 4475$^{5}$ (4907) 5090$^{8}$ 5377$^{9}$ 5596$^{11}$ *6276$^{9}$* >**28a 71f**<

**Goodwood Finesse (IRE)** 3 b f Revoque (IRE) -Key To Paris (ARG) (Profit Key (USA)) (3044) 3908$^{5}$ 5152$^{6}$ 5732$^{3}$ 6457$^{6}$ >**77f**<

**Goodwood Prince** 4 b g Emperor Jones (USA) -Scarlet Lake (Reprimand) *454$^{5}$ 526$^{12}$* 1608$^{17}$ 2246$^{16}$ 2303$^{12}$ 2707$^{10}$ 3174$^{8}$ *6398$^{11}$6559$^{10}$* >**45a 45f**<

**Goodwood Spirit** 2 b c Fraam-Rechanit (IRE) (Local Suitor (USA)) 3414$^{2}$ 4040$^{2}$ 4739$^{3}$ (5420) 5810$^{5}$ >**80f**<

**Goose Chase** 2 b g Inchinor-Bronzewing (Beldale Flutter (USA)) 5915$^{10}$ 6322$^{6}$ 6439$^{9}$ >**66f**<

**Go Padero (IRE)** 3 ch c Night Shift (USA) -Watch The Clock (Mtoto) (6244) 6475$^{4}$ (6525) >**96+f**<

**Gordy s Joy** 4 b f Cloudings (IRE) -Beatle Song (Song) *2662$^{3}$* 2874$^{14}$ 4082$^{12}$ >**37a 41f**<

**Gorella (FR)** 2 ch f Grape Tree Road-Exciting Times (FR) (Jeune Homme (USA)) 4964a$^{3}$ 5979a$^{7}$ >**105f**<

**Gortumblo** 2 b g Sri Pekan (USA) -Evergreen (IRE) (Lammtarra (USA)) (2205) 2677$^{3}$ 3242$^{10}$ 4325$^{8}$ 5453$^{7}$ 5745$^{9}$ >**89f**<

**Gorylla (BRZ)** 6 b h New Colony (USA) -Steffi (ARG) (Ahmad (ARG)) 1144a$^{13}$ ><

**Goslar** 3 ch f In The Wings-Anna Of Brunswick (Rainbow Quest (USA)) 2060$^{3}$ (2832) 3944$^{4}$ 4884$^{4}$ 6443$^{4}$ >**96f**<

**Go Solo** 3 b c Primo Dominie-Taza (Persian Bold) 1129$^{14}$ 2207$^{3}$ 2847$^{3}$ 3475$^{5}$ 4266$^{3}$ 5185$^{9}$ 5607$^{15}$ 5992$^{8}$ >**83f**<

**Go Supersonic** 3 b f Zafonic (USA) -Shirley Superstar (Shirley Heights) 4954$^{4}$ 5511$^{4}$ >**73+f**<

**Go Tech** 4 b g Gothenberg (IRE) -Bollin Sophie (Efisio) 1114$^{20}$ 1246$^{9}$ 1772$^{6}$ 2215$^{8}$ 2687$^{6}$ 2982$^{2}$ 3238$^{4}$ 3534$^{6}$3714$^{7}$ 4319$^{4}$ 5568$^{2}$ (5755) (5950) (6043) 6573$^{18}$ >**96f**<

**Got One Too (FR)** 7 ch g Green Tune (USA) -Gloria Mundi (FR) (Saint Cyrien (FR)) 2285$^{2}$ 2958$^{12}$ >**81f**<

**Got To Be Cash** 5 ch m Lake Coniston (IRE) -Rasayel (USA) (Bering) *1079$^{4}$* 1560$^{2}$ (1910) 2034$^{10}$ 2446$^{5}$ 3008$^{3}$ 3264$^{11}$ 3929$^{7}$ (4669) 4808$^{4}$5085$^{11}$ 5658$^{10}$ >**49a 59f**<

**Gotya** 4 b f Gothenberg (IRE) -Water Well (Sadler s Wells (USA)) *797$^{8}$* >**5f**<

**Gouache (IRE)** 2 bl f Key Of Luck (USA) -Sketch Pad (Warning) 6101a$^{3}$ >**81f**<

**Government (IRE)** 3 b g Great Dane (IRE) -Hidden Agenda (FR) (Machiavellian (USA)) 2114$^{15}$ 3015$^{4}$ 5366$^{5}$ 6009$^{7}$ >**42f**<

**Go Yellow** 3 b g Overbury (IRE) -Great Lyth Lass (IRE) (Waajib) 1408$^{13}$ 1881$^{11}$ 2457$^{5}$ 2836$^{2}$ 3180$^{4}$ 3525$^{6}$ (4069) 4244$^{4}$ 4646$^{10}$4969$^{2}$ *6064$^{11}$* 6199$^{6}$ >**50a 76f**<

**Grace Darling** 3 b f Botanic (USA) -Light On The Waves (Greensmith) 1579$^{5}$ ><

**Graceful Air (IRE)** 3 b f Danzero (AUS) -Samsung Spirit (Statoblest) *1038$^{4}$* 1288$^{5}$ 1869$^{2}$ 2259$^{2}$ 2572$^{4}$ 2963$^{7}$ 3004$^{5}$ 3609$^{4}$3878$^{4}$ 4248$^{5}$ 5063$^{11}$ 5236$^{10}$ 5478$^{3}$ 5830$^{2}$ 6201$^{9}$ >**50a 63f**<

**Graceful Flight** 2 gr f Cloudings (IRE) -Fantasy Flight (Forzando) 5096$^{16}$ 5521$^{10}$ >**2f**<

**Gracia** 5 gr m Linamix (FR) -Francia (Legend Of France (USA)) 1275$^{11}$ 1372$^{7}$ 1542$^{4}$ >**71a 76f**<

**Gracie s Gift (IRE)** 2 b g Imperial Ballet (IRE) -Settle Petal (IRE) (Roi Danzig (USA)) 2247$^{4}$ 2489$^{4}$ >**46f**<

**Gracilis (IRE)** 7 b g Caerleon (USA) -Grace Note (FR) (Top Ville) *899$^{7}$* 1880$^{15}$ 6335$^{8}$ >**20a 87f**<

**Gracious Air (USA)** 6 b m Bahri (USA) -Simply Bell (USA) (Simply Majestic (USA)) *663$^{10}$ (778) 875$^{5}$ 953$^{3}$ 989$^{3}$ 1024$^{10}$* >**52a 62df**<

**Grady** 5 ch g Bluegrass Prince (IRE) -Lady Sabina (Bairn (USA)) 1582$^{6}$ 2408$^{6}$ 2753$^{12}$ 3041$^{6}$ 3461$^{12}$ 3695$^{7}$ 4423$^{13}$ >**42a 41f**<

**Graft** 5 b g Entrepreneur-Mariakova (USA) (The Minstrel (CAN)) 1172$^{11}$ 1393$^{6}$ 2120$^{2}$ 2501$^{14}$ 3018$^{10}$ (3412) 4122$^{13}$ >**77a 77f**<

**Graham Island** 3 b g Acatenango (GER) -Gryada (Shirley Heights) (1442) 1901$^{6}$ 2203$^{6}$ 3078$^{8}$ 5842$^{5}$ *6396$^{4}$* >**84a 90f**<

**Gralmano (IRE)** 9 b g Scenic-Llangollen (IRE) (Caerleon (USA)) *844$^{7}$* 1880$^{12}$ 2855$^{6}$ 2958$^{13}$ >**82a 90f**<

**Gramada (IRE)** 2 b f Cape Cross (IRE) -Decatur (Deploy) 4399$^{10}$ >**49f**<

**Grampian** 5 b h Selkirk (USA) -Gryada (Shirley Heights) 1618$^{2}$ 2076$^{6}$ 2672$^{2}$ 3521$^{3}$ 4858$^{18}$ 5251$^{2}$ 5814$^{5}$ >**109f**<

**Granary Girl** 2 b f Kingsinger (IRE) -Highland Blue (Never So Bold) 1686$^{8}$ 2609$^{8}$ >**42f**<

**Granato (GER)** 3 b c Cadeaux Genereux-Genevra (IRE) (Danehill (USA)) 1388$^{11}$ 2075$^{8}$ 2692$^{4}$ 4031$^{4}$ >**89f**<

**Gran Clicquot** 9 gr m Gran Alba (USA) -Tina s Beauty (Tina s Pet) *933$^{8}$ 996$^{8}$ 1723$^{2}$* 2324$^{7}$ (2643) 3103$^{13}$ 3412$^{2}$ 4438$^{7}$5285$^{8}$ 5795$^{12}$ >**49a 54f**<

**Grandalea** 3 b f Grand Lodge (USA) -Red Azalea (Shirley Heights) 3159$^{5}$ 3807$^{3}$ *(4024)* 5185$^{6}$ >**88a 80f**<

**Gran Dana (IRE)** 4 b g Grand Lodge (USA) -Olean (Sadler s Wells (USA)) 1221$^{2}$ (1344) 1661$^{9}$ 2047$^{10}$ 2782$^{8}$ 3199$^{17}$ 5344$^{13}$ 6110$^{10}$ >**81df**<

**Grand Apollo** 3 ch f Grand Lodge (USA) -Narva (Nashwan (USA)) 2425$^{2}$ 2911$^{5}$ *5740$^{6}$ 6224$^{5}$ 6498$^{13}$* >**72a 65f**<

**Grand Bahama (IRE)** 2 b c Singspiel (IRE) -Rum Cay (USA) (Our Native (USA)) 6583a$^{4}$ ><

**Grand But One (IRE)** 3 ch c Grand Lodge (USA) -Unscathed (Warning) 1395$^{6}$ 2113$^{2}$ 2392$^{2}$ 3094$^{3}$ (3587) 5813$^{6}$ (5992) >**88f**<

**Grand Desert (FR)** 4 b c Apeldoorn (FR) -Tots Off (NZ) (Young Runaway) *5103a$^{7}$* ><

**Grand Ekinoks (TUR)** 6 b h Barnato (USA) -Violent Girl (TUR) (Aristocrat) 1144a$^{7}$ 5489a$^{8}$ >**117f**<

**Grande Roche (IRE)** 2 b c Grand Lodge (USA) -Arabian Lass (SAF) (Al Mufti (USA)) 6569$^{14}$ >**44f**<

**Grandes Illusions (FR)** 3 ch f Kendor (FR) -Largesse (FR) (Saumarez) 1652a$^{5}$ 2160a$^{12}$ 5169a$^{9}$ 5967a$^{6}$ 6511a$^{6}$ >**107f**<

**Grande Terre (IRE)** 3 b f Grand Lodge (USA) -Savage (IRE) (Polish Patriot (USA)) 1325$^{P}$ 1761$^{7}$ 2259$^{14}$ 4848$^{12}$ 5546$^{12}$ 5860$^{12}$ >**48f**<

**Grand Fromage (IRE)** 6 ch g Grand Lodge (USA) -My First Paige (IRE) (Runnett) 2285$^{13}$ 2613$^{9}$ 3733$^{3}$ >**59f**<

**Grand Girl** 2 b f Mark Of Esteem (IRE) -Ayunli (Chief Singer) 5272$^{7}$ 5535$^{11}$ 5688$^{8}$ *6221$^{5}$* >**19a 49f**<

**Grand Hombre (USA)** 4 br g Grand Slam (USA) -Santona (CHI) (Winning (USA)) *1147a$^{4}$* >**104a**<

**Grand Ideas** 5 br g Grand Lodge (USA) -Afrafa (IRE) (Lashkari) *6397$^{2}$* >**67a 67f**<

**Grand Lass (IRE)** 5 b m Grand Lodge (USA) -Siskin (IRE) (Royal Academy (USA)) *406$^{3}$ 517$^{4}$ (726) 810$^{2}$ 909$^{5}$ 1037$^{4}$* 1263$^{3}$ 1305$^{13}$1535$^{8}$ *1677$^{4}$* >**53a 58f**<

**Grandma Lily (IRE)** 6 b m Bigstone (IRE) -Mrs Fisher (IRE) (Salmon Leap (USA)) *540$^{3}$ 586$^{13}$ 680$^{10}$ 803$^{8}$* 1199$^{17}$ 1421$^{17}$ 1750$^{3}$ 5544$^{14}$5849$^{3}$ 6445$^{4}$ *6553$^{4}$* >**82a 59f**<

**Grand Marque (IRE)** 2 ch c Grand Lodge (USA) -Royal Fizz (IRE) (Royal Academy (USA)) 3093$^{5}$ (3451) (3939) 4639$^{2}$ 5437$^{5}$ 5778$^{7}$ >**102f**<

**Grandma Ryta** 2 br f Cyrano De Bergerac-Tamara (Marju (IRE)) 5558$^{9}$ 6002$^{9}$ >**29f**<

**Grandma s Girl** 2 b f Desert Style (IRE) -Sakura Queen (IRE) (Woodman (USA)) 3808$^{10}$ 4468$^{4}$ 5348$^{5}$ 5719$^{8}$ 5995$^{10}$ >**67 f**<

**Grand Music (IRE)** 4 b g Grand Lodge (USA) -Abury (IRE) (Law Society (USA)) 4554$^{12}$ *5913$^{10}$* >**32a**<

**Grand Option** 2 ch c Compton Place-Follow The Stars (Sparkler) *1060$^{7}$* 1130$^{3}$ 1331$^{2}$ 1462$^{3}$ 2057$^{2}$ 2396$^{5}$ 3938$^{20}$ 4235$^{7}$5198$^{4}$ 5655$^{6}$ 5738$^{16}$ (6270) >**42a 70f**<

**Grandos (IRE)** 2 b c Cadeaux Genereux-No Reservations (IRE) (Commanche Run) 4487$^{11}$ 4930$^{5}$ 5096$^{8}$ >**62f**<

**Grand Passion (IRE)** 4 b g Grand Lodge (USA) -Lovers Parlour (Beldale Flutter (USA)) *558$^{2}$ (842) 1062$^{9}$* 1902$^{9}$ 2398$^{4}$ 2796a$^{2}$ (3355a) 4786a$^{3}$ 5917$^{6}$ >**110a 110f**<

**Grand Place** 2 b g Compton Place-Comme Ca (Cyrano De Bergerac) 3157$^{12}$ 3413$^{4}$ 3938$^{23}$ (4704) 5119$^{15}$ 5434$^{4}$ 5617$^{4}$ 5932$^{5}$ >**79f**<

**Grand Prairie (SWE)** 8 b g Prairie-Platonica (ITY) (Primo Dominie) *645$^{5}$* >**60a 59f**<

**Grand Rapide** 3 ch f Grand Lodge (USA) -Vax Rapide (Sharpo) 2621$^{6}$ 3251$^{10}$ 4195$^{9}$ 4674$^{4}$ (5072) 5714$^{13}$ *5957$^{12}$* 6561$^{8}$ >**24a 60f**<

**Grand Reward (USA)** 3 b c Storm Cat (USA) -Serena s Song (USA) (Rahy (USA)) 1847a$^{2}$ 2315a$^{5}$ 2966$^{15}$ 4590a$^{LFT}$ 4956a$^{3}$ 5327a$^{6}$ 5661a$^{3}$ 5977a$^{15}$6104a$^{2}$ >**110 f**<

**Grand Show** 2 b c Efisio-Christine Daae (Sadler s Wells (USA)) 5752$^{4}$ 6454$^{5}$ >**73f**<

**Grand Stand (NZ)** 7 br g Mi Preferido (USA) -Regal Gazelle (NZ) (Vice Regal (NZ)) *(687a) 832a$^{7}$* >**103a**<

**Grand View** 8 ch g Grand Lodge (USA) -Hemline (Sharpo) *665$^{6}$ 713$^{11}$* 1283$^{4}$ 1591$^{2}$ *(1694)* 1719$^{7}$ 2384$^{7}$ 2886$^{11}$3742$^{19}$ 4350$^{7}$ >**43a 46f**<

**Grand Welcome (IRE)** 2 b g Indian Lodge (IRE) -Chocolate Box (Most Welcome) 1686$^{12}$ 2087$^{7}$ 3083$^{13}$ 5034$^{2}$ 5855$^{2}$ 6515$^{12}$ >**67f**<

**Grand Wizard** 4 b g Grand Lodge (USA) -Shouk (Shirley Heights) *1122$^{4}$* 1801$^{17}$ 2595$^{10}$ 4911$^{9}$ 5705$^{6}$ >**70a 57f**<

**Granita** 2 bb f Machiavellian (USA) -Actualite (Polish Precedent (USA)) 4637$^{10}$ >**30f**<

**Granston (IRE)** 3 gr g Revoque (IRE) -Gracious Gretclo (Common Grounds) 1129$^{3}$ (1418) 1795$^{6}$ 2448$^{6}$ 2907$^{7}$ 4340$^{2}$ 5120$^{5}$ 5419$^{3}$ (5766) >**84f**<

**Grant (IRE)** 4 b g Bahamian Bounty-Verify (IRE) (Polish Precedent (USA)) *866$^{5}$ 912$^{6}$* >**61a 70f**<

**Granuaile O Malley (IRE)** 4 b f Mark Of Esteem (IRE) -Dame Laura (IRE) (Royal Academy (USA)) *4741$^{3}$* >**44a 53f**<

**Grasp** 2 b c Kayf Tara-Circe (Main Reef) 6282$^{4}$ 6565$^{14}$ >**59f**<

**Grasslandik** 8 b g Ardkinglass-Sophisticated Baby (Bairn (USA)) *1262$^{16}$* >**51a 58f**<

**Grass Widow (IRE)** 2 b f Mujadil (USA) -Noble Clare (IRE) (The Noble Player (USA)) 6521$^{9}$ ><

**Gravardlax** 3 ch g Salse (USA) -Rubbiyati (Cadeaux Genereux) 1330$^{7}$ 1683$^{4}$ 2107$^{8}$ 5766$^{10}$ >**87f**<

**Graze On** 2 b g Factual (USA) -Queens Check (Komaite (USA)) 4175$^{2}$ (4776) 5143$^{2}$ 5515$^{5}$ 6042$^{10}$ 6333$^{11}$ >**81f**<

**Great As Gold (IRE)** 5 b g Goldmark (USA) -Great Land (USA) (Friend s Choice (USA)) (1501) 1958$^{2}$ >**64a 69f**<

**Great Belief (IRE)** 2 b c Namid-Fairy Lore (IRE) (Fairy King (USA)) 3805$^{3}$ 4191$^{6}$ 6125$^{4}$ >**74+f**<

**Great Blasket (IRE)** 3 b f Petardia-Alexander Goddess (IRE) (Alzao (USA)) 3993$^{8}$ 5036$^{9}$ 5072$^{8}$ 5524$^{11}$ >**34a 52f**<

**Great Blood (FR)** 2 ch f Great Palm (USA) -Young Blood (FR) (Northern Crystal) 3388a$^{2}$ 4184a$^{4}$ 5404a$^{4}$ 6202a$^{6}$ >**97f**<

**Greatcoat** 2 ch g Erhaab (USA) -Vaula (Henbit (USA)) 6330$^{8}$ >**46f**<

**Greatest By Phar** 3 b g Pharly (FR) -Greatest Friend (IRE) (Mandalus) *621$^{9}$ 739$^{12}$* >**45a**<

**Great Exhibition (USA)** 3 b c Gone West (USA) -Touch Of Greatness (USA) (Hero s Honor (USA)) *1143a$^{8}$* 1827$^{9}$ 2505$^{3}$ 5378$^{2}$ 6089$^{2}$ >**78a 84f**<

**Great Fox (IRE)** 3 b c Foxhound (USA) -Good Enough (IRE) (Simply Great (FR)) 5874$^{14}$ 6459$^{6}$ 6532$^{3}$ >**77f**<

**Great General (IRE)** 2 ch c General Monash (USA) -Racing Brenda (Faustus (USA)) 5154$^{7}$ 5653$^{10}$ >**50f**<

**Great Gidding** 3 b g Classic Cliche (IRE) -Arcady (Slip Anchor) 2090$^{7}$ 2357$^{3}$ 2729$^{8}$ 3479$^{15}$ 3996$^{5}$ 4302$^{14}$ >**47f**<

**Great Opinions (USA)** 2 b f Rahy (USA) -Gracie Lady (IRE) (Generous (IRE)) 2585$^{9}$ 3456$^{2}$ 4234$^{10}$ 4705$^{11}$ >**79df**<

**Great Scott** 3 b g Fasliyev (USA) -Arabis (Arazi (USA)) 3205$^{9}$ 3542$^{10}$ 4061$^{5}$ 4319$^{3}$ 4395$^{4}$ 4906$^{7}$ 5444$^{13}$ 5835$^{12}$5992$^{5}$ 6112$^{7}$ >**88f**<

**Great View (IRE)** 5 b g Great Commotion (USA) -Tara View (IRE) (Wassl) *966$^{8}$ (1081)* 1305$^{2}$ (1644) 1858$^{2}$ 2212$^{4}$ 2501$^{10}$ 3492$^{2}$ 3825$^{3}$4233$^{7}$ 5203$^{2}$ 5554$^{4}$ 5935$^{9}$ >**56a 71f**<

**Greek Star** 3 b g Soviet Star (USA) -Graecia Magna (USA) (Private Account (USA)) 2357$^{4}$ 2888$^{9}$ 4346$^{15}$ 5751$^{6}$ >**45f**<

**Greek Sun (USA)** 3 br c Danzig (USA) -Sunlit Silence (USA) (Trempolino (USA)) 4769a$^{2}$ >**112f**<

**Greenborough (IRE)** 6 b g Dr Devious (IRE) -Port Isaac (USA) (Seattle Song (USA)) *653$^{7}$ 814$^{7}$* >**12a 15f**<

**Green Chapel (ITY)** 2 b c College Chapel-Plytroca (USA) (Lyphard (USA)) 6380a$^{13}$ >**58f**<

**Green Conversion (IRE)** 3 ch g Desert King (IRE) -Blue Bangor (IRE) (Thatching) 4421$^{P}$ ><

**Green Falcon** 3 b c Green Desert (USA) -El Jazirah (Kris) *597$^{13}$ 702$^{3}$ 846$^{3}$* 2097$^{8}$ 2472$^{7}$ 2847$^{13}$ 4818$^{11}$ 5153$^{7}$ >**68a 51f**<

**Green Ginger** 8 ch g Ardkinglass-Bella Maggio (Rakaposhi King) 6057$^{14}$ >**53a 56f**<

**Green Girl (FR)** 2 b f Lord Of Men-Green Sails (IRE) (Slip Anchor) 6297a$^{9}$ >**88f**<

**Green Manalishi** 3 b c Green Desert (USA) -Silca-Cisa (Hallgate) *986$^{4}$ 1099$^{2}$* 1883$^{2}$ (2181) 2488$^{9}$ 2877$^{3}$ (3092) 3324$^{5}$ 3702$^{5}$4165$^{20}$ 4289$^{10}$ 5181$^{10}$ 5893$^{12}$ >**85a 96f**<

**Green Master (POL)** 4 bl g Who Knows-Green Fee (GER) (Windwurf (GER)) *6360$^{8}$* ><

**Green N Gold** 4 b f Cloudings (IRE) -Fishki (Niniski (USA)) (1287) 1501$^{10}$ 2249$^{4}$ 2531$^{8}$ 3120$^{8}$ 3576$^{8}$ 4778$^{10}$ >**52a 61f**<

**Green Noon (FR)** 3 ch f Green Tune (USA) -Terring (FR) (Bering) 5032a$^{4}$ 5667a$^{5}$ 5978a$^{9}$ >**108f**<

**Green Ocean** 4 gr f Environment Friend-Northern Swinger (Northern State (USA)) 1560$^{15}$ 3348$^{14}$ >**53f**<

**Green Pirate** 2 b c Bahamian Bounty-Verdura (Green Desert (USA)) 5718$^{11}$ >**23f**<

**Green Ridge** 3 b f Muhtarram (USA) -Top Of The Morning (Keen) 1991$^{2}$ 3179$^{4}$ 3273$^{11}$ 3524$^{11}$ 5693$^{12}$ *6157$^{11}$* >**64a 65f**<

**Greenslades** 5 ch h Perugino (USA) -Woodfield Rose (Scottish Reel) 1385$^{4}$ 1765$^{4}$ 2283$^{2}$ 3074$^{13}$ 3673$^{3}$ 4120$^{14}$ 4528$^{6}$ 4742$^{6}$5781$^{10}$ 5921$^{5}$ *6451$^{3}$* >**100a 103f**<

**Green Swallow (FR)** 3 b f Green Tune (USA) -Green Sails (IRE) (Slip Anchor) 1803a$^{3}$ 2338a$^{7}$ >**106f**<

**Green Way (FR)** 3 ch f Green Tune (USA) -Pollyana (FR) (Hellios (USA)) 4430a$^{5}$ >**99f**<

**Greenwich Meantime** 4 b g Royal Academy (USA) -Shirley Valentine (Shirley Heights) 1210$^{8}$ 1615$^{3}$ 2047$^{16}$ 2631$^{9}$ 2935$^{3}$ 3199$^{14}$ 3821$^{7}$ 4352$^{5}$4627$^{6}$ 5100$^{7}$ 5343$^{4}$ 5635$^{3}$ *(6540)* >**79a 74 f**<

**Greenwood** 6 ch g Emarati (USA) -Charnwood Queen (Cadeaux Genereux) *511$^{10}$ 648$^{3}$ 742$^{11}$ 1055$^{8}$ 1241$^{6}$* 2206$^{6}$ 2441$^{2}$*6395$^{7}$* >**81a 93f**<

**Gregorian (IRE)** 7 b g Foxhound (USA) -East River (FR) (Arctic Tern (USA)) 2375$^{14}$ >**54a 55f**<

**Grele (USA)** 3 gr f Loup Sauvage (USA) -Fiveblushingroses (USA) (Runaway Groom (CAN))

3251$^7$ 3701$^5$ 4259$^6$ 5237$^4$ 5451$^{11}$ 5863$^{12}$ **>46 f<**
**Gretna** 3 ch f Groom Dancer (USA) -Llia (Shirley Heights) (1186) 1357$^8$ 2281$^{14}$ 3206$^8$ 4749$^{14}$ **>83f<**
**Grey Admiral (USA)** 3 gr g Cozzene (USA) -Remarkable Style (USA) (Danzig (USA)) 3245$^9$ 3695$^{10}$ **>58a 64f<**
**Grey Boy (GER)** 3 gr g Medaaly-Grey Perri (Siberian Express (USA)) 1939$^8$ 2195$^5$ **>50a 64f<**
**Grey Clouds** 4 gr f Cloudings (IRE) -Khalsheva (Shirley Heights) 1393$^4$ 1752$^2$ 2142$^8$ (2446) 2775$^2$ 3091$^3$ 3705$^2$ 4153$^2$ 4634$^5$5572$^{10}$ 5755$^8$ **>87f<**
**Grey Cossack** 7 gr g Kasakov-Royal Rebeka (Grey Desire) 1225$^9$ (1361) 1956$^{12}$ 2261$^{12}$ 2626$^5$ 2899$^{18}$ 2976$^{11}$ 3309$^{11}$ 3778$^5$4047$^{10}$ 6094$^{16}$ **>39a 86 f<**
**Greyfield (IRE)** 8 b g Persian Bold-Noble Dust (USA) (Dust Commander (USA)) 2501$^5$ 2835$^7$ 3942$^6$ 4146$^7$ 4473$^{11}$ **>58f<**
**Grey Fortune** 5 gr m Grey Desire-Mere Melody (Dunphy) 1972$^{12}$ 5086$^4$ 5803$^7$ **>36f<**
**Grey Glitters (FR)** 4 gr c Grey Risk (FR) -Marie Glitters (FR) (Crystal Glitters (USA)) 1182a$^4$ **>104f<**
**Grey Gurkha** 3 gr c Kasakov-Royal Rebeka (Grey Desire) 2040$^6$ 2621$^9$ 3512$^6$ **>39f<**
**Grey Lilas (IRE)** 3 gr f Danehill (USA) -Kenmist (Kenmare (FR)) (1652a) 2160a$^2$ 2925a$^3$ (5032a) (5332a) 5978a$^2$ **>118f<**
**Grey Orchid** 3 gr f Opening Verse (USA) -Marjorie s Orchid (Petong) 1972$^{14}$ 2450$^6$ 2778$^{15}$ 3368$^{13}$ 5110$^{16}$ **>43f<**
**Grey Pearl** 5 gr m Ali-Royal (IRE) -River s Rising (FR) (Mendez (FR)) *488$^5$ (599) (648) 770$^3$ 1056$^6$ 1242$^4$* 1372$^6$ *1953a$^7$*3090$^4$ (3275) 4286$^9$ 5454$^{11}$ 5712$^8$ **>94a 97f<**
**Grey Samurai** 4 gr g Gothenberg (IRE) -Royal Rebeka (Grey Desire) 2460$^6$ 2653$^{12}$ 3056$^8$ 3490$^{12}$ 4139$^8$ **>28f<**
**Grey Song (AUS)** 6 gr g Unbridled s Song (USA) -Tonzazip (NZ) (Kaapstad (NZ)) 6528a$^{13}$ **>115f<**
**Grey Swallow (IRE)** 3 gr c Daylami (IRE) -Style Of Life (USA) (The Minstrel (CAN)) (1487a) 1764$^4$ 2315a$^3$ (3353a) 5483a$^4$ 5981a$^{18}$ **>125f<**
**Grezie** 2 gr f Mark Of Esteem (IRE) -Lozzie (Siberian Express (USA)) 1115$^4$ *1276$^4$* 1607$^3$ 5548$^{12}$ **>42a 42f<**
**Grigorovitch (IRE)** 2 b c Fasliyev (USA) -Hasty Words (IRE) (Polish Patriot (USA)) 4219$^8$ **>41f<**
**Grist Mist (IRE)** 3 gr f Imperial Ballet (IRE) -Ard Dauphine (IRE) (Forest Wind (USA)) 1271$^8$ 1683$^{14}$ 1998$^{17}$ 2395$^6$ 2643$^{15}$ **>47a 47f<**
**Grizebeck (IRE)** 2 b g Trans Island-Premier Amour (Salmon Leap (USA)) 5264$^8$ **>7f<**
**Grizedale (IRE)** 5 ch g Lake Coniston (IRE) -Zabeta (Diesis) 3673$^5$ 4120$^{21}$ 5112$^8$ 5468$^{15}$ 5781$^{13}$ 6070$^{13}$ 6341$^6$ **>101 f<**
**Grooms Affection** 4 b c Groom Dancer (USA) -Love And Affection (USA) (Exclusive Era (USA)) (2845) 3325$^6$ 4123$^7$ 4715$^7$ 5093$^{16}$ **>90f<**
**Groomsman** 2 b g Groom Dancer (USA) -Trois Heures Apres (Soviet Star (USA)) 6148$^4$ 6351$^{11}$ **>74f<**
**Groom Tesse** 3 ch c Groom Dancer (USA) -Vicomtesse Mag (FR) (Highest Honor (FR)) (2510a) 3136a$^7$ **>116f<**
**Grosgrain (USA)** 3 b f Diesis-Green Lady (IRE) (Green Desert (USA)) 3162a$^0$ **>85f<**
**Grosvenor Square (IRE)** 2 b c Dubai Millennium-Embassy (Cadeaux Genereux) 5290$^6$ (5718) **>90+f<**
**Groundcover** 2 b c Zafonic (USA) -Moss (Alzao (USA)) 5467$^{10}$ 6148$^7$ **>61f<**
**Ground Patrol** 3 b g Ashkalani (IRE) -Good Grounds (USA) (Alleged (USA)) *553$^3$ 621$^4$ 822$^3$* 1271$^6$ 2244$^8$ *2988$^7$* 5749$^4$ *6160$^6$6498$^4$* **>72a 66f<**
**Ground Rules (USA)** 2 b c Boundary (USA) -Gombeen (USA) (Private Account (USA)) 3483$^2$ 4290$^9$ **>81f<**
**Group Captain** 2 b c Dr Fong (USA) -Alusha (Soviet Star (USA)) 2651$^5$ 2890$^4$ 3679$^2$ 4166$^2$ 4527$^8$ 4967$^2$ 5256$^3$ 6338$^{12}$ **>81f<**
**Grouville** 3 b g Groom Dancer (USA) -Dance Land (IRE) (Nordance (USA)) *(553) 913$^9$* 1222$^{16}$ **>76a<**
**Growler** 3 ch g Foxhound (USA) -Femme Femme (USA) (Lyphard (USA)) 1613$^{15}$ 2931$^3$ 3875$^{11}$ 4419$^2$ (5147) 5737$^{16}$ 5861$^7$ **>73f<**
**Grub Street** 8 b g Barathea (IRE) -Broadmara (IRE) (Thatching) *713$^3$ 875$^4$ (953) 1026$^7$* **>39a 28f<**
**Gruff** 5 ch g Presidium-Kagram Queen (Prince Ragusa) *718$^{10}$ 780$^{13}$ 1089$^{12}$* 1283$^{12}$ 2384$^8$ *2854$^{13}$* 3742$^{12}$ **>30f<**
**Grumpyintmorning** 5 b g Magic Ring (IRE) -Grecian Belle (Ilium) 1295$^{12}$ 1969$^{11}$ 3103$^P$ 3490$^{11}$ **>57f<**
**Gruntled** 5 b h Blushing Flame (USA) -Decant (Rousillon (USA)) 2156a$^9$ 2923a$^9$ **>109f<**
**Gryskirk** 2 b g Selkirk (USA) -Gryada (Shirley Heights) 1292$^4$ 1412$^6$ 2096$^3$ 2890$^7$ 3677$^8$ 3987$^7$ *4601$^3$ 4878$^{10}$*5377$^5$ 5596$^{10}$ *(6392)* **>67a 62 f<**
**Guadaloup** 2 ch f Loup Sauvage (USA) -Rash (Pursuit Of Love) 5319$^{13}$ **>47f<**
**Guadiaro (USA)** 2 b c El Prado (IRE) -Splendid (IRE) (Mujtahid (USA)) 5262$^7$ 6569$^{16}$ **>58f<**
**Guard** 4 b g Night Shift (USA) -Gaijin (Caerleon (USA)) 4419$^{11}$ *4604$^{13}$* **>58a 5f<**
**Guardian Spirit** 5 b m Hector Protector (USA) -Amongst The Stars (USA) (Proctor (USA)) 2122$^{17}$ *4517$^{13}$* **>13a 54f<**
**Guilded Flyer** 5 b g Emarati (USA) -Mo Ceri (Kampala) 1460$^8$ (1903) 2638$^9$ 3415$^3$ 3842$^8$ **>91a 92f<**
**Guildenstern (IRE)** 2 b c Danetime (IRE) -Lyphard Abu (IRE) (Lyphard s Special (USA)) 4081$^9$ 5996$^4$ 6455$^5$ **>64f<**
**Guillaume Tell (IRE)** 2 ch c Rossini (USA) -Accell (IRE) (Magical Wonder (USA)) 6035a$^2$ **>106f<**
**Guinea A Minute (IRE)** 2 ch f Raise A Grand (IRE) -Repique (USA) (Sharpen Up) 2786$^9$ 3659$^3$ 3992$^6$ 4524$^6$ *4878$^5$* 5539$^3$ 6140$^3$ 6562$^{18}$ **>57a 66f<**
**Gulchina (USA)** 2 b f Gulch (USA) -Harda Arda (USA) (Nureyev (USA)) 6470$^4$ **>77f<**
**Gulf (IRE)** 5 ch g Persian Bold-Broken Romance (IRE) (Ela-Mana-Mou) 1329$^{18}$ 2108$^3$ 3538$^5$ 5251$^5$ **>113f<**
**Gunnerbergkamp** 2 b g Defacto (USA) -Judys Girl (IRE) (Simply Great (FR)) 4304$^{10}$ 4559$^{11}$ 4699$^{14}$ **>19f<**
**Gunnhildr (IRE)** 4 ch f In Command (IRE) -Queen Canute (IRE) (Ahonoora) 2098$^{20}$ **>59a 62f<**
**Gun Salute** 4 b g Mark Of Esteem (IRE) -Affair Of State (IRE) (Tate Gallery (USA)) *596$^8$ (674) 896$^8$ 1051$^4$ 1098$^6$* 1516$^{14}$ 2325$^6$ 2707$^{11}$2885$^{11}$ **>45a 45f<**
**Guns Blazing** 5 b g Puissance-Queen Of Aragon (Aragon) 1642$^{15}$ 1872$^8$ (2118) 2246$^3$ 2440$^6$ 3126$^{10}$ (3307) 3558$^8$ 4034$^7$ 4232$^{12}$ **>35a 76f<**
**Gurrun** 2 b c Dansili-Mashmoon (USA) (Habitat) 3601$^{14}$ 3913$^9$ 4730$^{11}$ 4966$^{15}$ 5745$^6$ **>60f<**
**Gustavo** 3 b g Efisio-Washita (Valiyar) 1386$^{11}$ 1820$^8$ 2046$^9$ 3448$^9$ *5002$^2$* 5658$^2$ **>62a 62f<**
**Guyana (IRE)** 2 b c Lend A Hand-Romora (FR) (Sillery (USA)) 3451$^{15}$ 4030$^9$ *4599$^3$* 5909$^{16}$ 6356$^{17}$ **>71a 62f<**
**Gwazi** 4 b g Pennekamp (USA) -Made Of Pearl (USA) (Nureyev (USA)) *570$^{11}$ 776$^3$* 1389$^{14}$ *2188$^6$* **>37a 40f<**
**Gwen John (USA)** 3 ch f Peintre Celebre (USA) -River Jig (USA) (Irish River (FR)) 2647$^5$ 3044$^3$ 3908$^{11}$ 4258$^8$ 6285$^{12}$ **>69f<**
**Gwyneth** 2 b f Zafonic (USA) -Llyn Gwynant (Persian Bold) 3202$^5$ 4272$^9$ **>68f<**
**Gymera (GER)** 3 ch f Sternkoenig (IRE) -Gyrena (FR) (Esprit Du Nord (USA)) 3973a$^7$ **><**
**Gypsy Fair** 2 b f Compton Place-Marjorie s Memory (IRE) (Fairy King (USA)) 1449$^7$ 1865$^9$ **>31f<**
**Gypsy Johnny** 2 gr c Bachir (IRE) -Gentle Gypsy (Junius (USA)) (3505) 5630$^{11}$ **>74+f<**
**Gypsy Royal (IRE)** 2 b f Desert Prince (IRE) -Menominee (Soviet Star (USA)) 3588$^{11}$ 5349$^9$ 5825$^{11}$ **>46f<**

**H**

**Haadef** 3 b c Sadler s Wells (USA) -Taqreem (IRE) (Nashwan (USA)) 2085$^3$ (2562) 3032$^4$ 3521$^{15}$ 6121$^{14}$ 6307$^2$ **>103f<**
**Haafhd** 3 ch c Alhaarth (IRE) -Al Bahathri (USA) (Blushing Groom (FR)) (1410) (1764) 2956$^4$ 4228$^9$ (6216) **>127+f<**
**Haatmey** 2 b c Josr Algarhoud (IRE) -Raneen Alwatar (Sadler s Wells (USA)) 4480$^3$ 4900$^4$ 5522$^2$ (5827) 6122$^4$ **>87f<**
**Habanero** 3 b c Cadeaux Genereux-Queen Of Dance (IRE) (Sadler s Wells (USA)) 1222$^{15}$ 1588$^9$ 1997$^5$ 2371$^3$ (2847) 3231$^3$ 4032$^3$ (4266) 4756$^6$ 5403$^9$5761$^7$ *6498$^6$* **>77a 84f<**
**Habibti Sara** 4 ch f Bijou D Inde-Cut Velvet (USA) (Northern Dancer) *653$^{12}$* **>32f<**
**Habitual (IRE)** 3 b g Kahyasi-Kick The Habit (Habitat) *1096$^{10}$ 1226$^{10}$* 3984$^4$ 4499$^5$ *(5645)* 5860$^8$ *6225$^9$* **>56+a 49f<**
**Habitual Dancer** 3 b g Groom Dancer (USA) -Pomorie (IRE) (Be My Guest (USA)) 1111$^6$ (1267) 1714$^2$ 3396$^3$ 3479$^{11}$ 4778$^5$ 5214$^8$ (6110) **>65f<**
**Habshan (USA)** 4 ch g Swain (IRE) -Cambara (Dancing Brave (USA)) 1371$^9$ 2279$^4$ 2806$^3$ 3536$^5$ (4293) 4852$^7$ 5252$^3$ **>79f<**
**Hachita (USA)** 2 ch f Gone West (USA) -Choice Spirit (USA) (Danzig (USA)) (4234) 4645$^3$ 5457$^2$ **>85f<**
**Hadrian (IRE)** 2 b c King s Best (USA) -Wanton (Kris) 3313$^6$ 4263$^2$ (5543) 6206$^{12}$ **>83f<**
**Haenertsburg (IRE)** 2 b f Victory Note (USA) -Olivia s Pride (IRE) (Digamist (USA)) 5319$^9$ 5578$^7$ 6092$^8$ **>59f<**
**Hagley Park** 5 b m Petong-Gi La High (Rich Charlie) *411$^2$ 657$^2$ 762$^6$ 876$^5$ 893$^4$ 1075$^3$ 1180$^{11}$1443$^3$ (1886) 2663$^{11}$ 3378$^7$* 3575$^9$ 4194$^9$ 4622$^5$ *5642$^{14}$6403$^5$* **>52a 48f<**
**Haiban** 2 b c Barathea (IRE) -Aquarela (Shirley Heights) 4633$^4$ 4930$^2$ 5669$^3$ **>70f<**
**Hail The Chief** 7 b h Be My Chief (USA) -Jade Pet (Petong) *(485) 641$^4$ 842$^{10}$* 1746$^3$ 1927$^{14}$ 4327$^6$ 4814$^8$ 5185$^8$ 5425$^{11}$5841$^{10}$ **>106a 88f<**
**Haithem (IRE)** 7 b g Mtoto-Wukk (IRE) (Glow (USA)) *434$^6$ 472$^{13}$ 531$^{10}$ 594$^7$ 655$^3$ 726$^{10}$ 778$^6$814$^8$ 860$^5$ 929$^6$ (949) 1085$^8$ 1102$^7$ 6404$^{10}$* **>47a 38f<**
**Hajeer (IRE)** 6 b g Darshaan-Simouna (Ela-Mana-Mou) *461$^5$ 551$^2$* **>62a 48f<**
**Halabaloo (IRE)** 3 b f Intikhab (USA) -Outcry (Caerleon (USA)) 1400$^5$ 1704$^{11}$ 2223$^3$ 4726$^6$ 4954$^6$ **>61a 78f<**
**Halcyon Express (IRE)** 2 b c Mujadil (USA) -Hakkaniyah (Machiavellian (USA)) 6000$^8$ 6530$^4$ **>67f<**
**Halcyon Magic** 6 b g Magic Ring (IRE) -Consistent Queen (Queens Hussar) 1516$^2$ 1941$^9$ 2597$^{15}$ 3049$^2$ 3321$^{14}$ 3626$^6$ 3911$^{12}$ (5575) 5691$^5$ **>38a 60 f<**
**Halesia Carolina (USA)** 3 ch f Diesis-Halo s Charm (USA) (Halo (USA)) 1778a$^{15}$ **>57f<**
**Half A Handful** 3 b g Victory Note (USA) -Enaam (Shirley Heights) *1169$^{10}$* 1293$^{12}$ 1530$^{11}$ 2211$^6$ 3158$^3$ 3410$^3$ 3798$^2$ 4052$^3$4242$^{11}$ **>1a 68f<**
**Half Inch** 4 b f Inchinor-Anhaar (Ela-Mana-Mou) *1097$^{11}$* 1298$^4$ 1560$^{12}$ 3658$^7$ **>50a 70f<**
**Halfsong (SWE)** 4 br f Songline (SWE) -Half And Half (DEN) (Muthhil (IRE)) 633a$^{11}$ 692a$^{10}$ *754a$^{10}$ 977a$^{12}$* **>46a 71f<**
**Halicardia** 3 br f Halling (USA) -Pericardia (Petong) 1327$^3$ (2221) 2807$^2$ **>104f<**
**Hallahoise Hydro (IRE)** 3 ch g Lake Coniston (IRE) -Flo Bear (IRE) (Prince Rupert (FR)) 5193$^{12}$ 5547$^{18}$ **>46f<**
**Halland** 6 ch g Halling (USA) -Northshiel (Northfields (USA)) 4345$^8$ 5595$^{10}$ 6215$^{12}$ **>86f<**
**Halla San** 2 b g Halling (USA) -St Radegund (Green Desert (USA)) 4347$^8$ 4776$^{13}$ 5096$^5$ 5543$^4$ 6176$^3$ **>77f<**
**Halle Bop** 2 b f Dubai Millennium-Napoleon s Sister (IRE) (Alzao (USA)) 4714$^2$ (5270) **>86f<**
**Hallhoo (IRE)** 2 gr c Indian Ridge-Nuit Chaud (USA) (Woodman (USA)) 4117$^3$ (4747) 5292$^2$ 5630$^2$ 6189$^8$ **>90f<**
**Hallings Overture (USA)** 5 b g Halling (USA) -Sonata (Polish Precedent (USA)) *882$^6$ 1085$^7$* 1352$^2$ 5252$^{16}$ **>65a 70f<**
**Hallowed Dream (IRE)** 2 b f Alhaarth (IRE) -Salul (Soviet Star (USA)) 4498$^7$ 5088$^9$ 5368$^8$ 5717$^2$ 6189$^6$ **>81f<**
**Hallucinate** 2 b c Spectrum (IRE) -Swift Spring (FR) (Bluebird (USA)) 2376$^{11}$ 3343$^4$ 4016$^2$ 4482$^3$ 4890$^4$ 5227$^3$ **>78f<**
**Halmahera (IRE)** 9 b g Petardia-Champagne Girl (Robellino (USA)) 1126$^{10}$ 1471$^2$ 1955$^4$ 2065$^6$ 2857$^6$ 3074$^{20}$ 3266$^5$ 3961a$^{12}$4324$^6$ 4759$^9$ (5393) 5893$^9$ 6190$^7$ 6572$^9$ **>107f<**
**Hamaasy** 3 b g Machiavellian (USA) -Sakha (Wolfhound (USA)) 2984$^5$ 3511$^7$ 4320$^7$ 4608$^{15}$ **>59f<**
**Hamairi (IRE)** 3 ch c Spectrum (IRE) -Handaza (IRE) (Be My Guest (USA)) 2793a$^2$ 4786a$^2$ (5972a) **>111f<**
**Hambleden** 7 b g Vettori (IRE) -Dalu (IRE) (Dancing Brave (USA)) 1902$^6$ 2220$^9$ 3075$^4$ 3521$^4$ 4218$^{13}$ 4530$^6$ 4932$^3$ **>106f<**
**Hamburg Springer (IRE)** 2 b g Charnwood Forest (IRE) -Kyra Crown (IRE) (Astronef) 2234$^{12}$ 3370$^5$ 5555$^8$ 5797$^{15}$ 6067$^{16}$ **>32f<**
**Hammer Of The Gods (IRE)** 4 ch g Tagula (IRE) -Bhama (FR) (Habitat) 4462$^3$ 5026$^3$ 5575$^{11}$ **>26a 49f<**
**Hamriya** 3 b c Alzao (USA) -Cravatte Noire (USA) (Black Tie Affair) 1654a$^6$ **>103f<**
**Hanabad (IRE)** 4 ch c Cadeaux Genereux-Handaza (IRE) (Be My Guest (USA)) 2316a$^4$ 3350a$^4$ 4371a$^{10}$ 4590a$^8$ 4956a$^5$ 5661a$^9$ **>115f<**
**Hana Dee** 3 b f Cadeaux Genereux-Jumairah Sun (IRE) (Scenic) *1052$^{10}$* 1309$^{14}$ 2112$^6$ 2306$^{13}$ 2756$^{11}$ 3798$^4$ 4147$^5$ 4451$^3$4619$^9$ 5072$^{12}$ 5750$^4$ *6399$^5$ 6556$^7$* **>49a 62f<**
**Hanami** 4 b f Hernando (FR) -Russian Rose (IRE) (Soviet Lad (USA)) 2318a$^3$ 3331a$^6$ 4982a$^{12}$ **>108 f<**
**Hanazakari** 3 b c Danzero (AUS) -Russian Rose (IRE) (Soviet Lad (USA)) 4819$^9$ *5216$^5$* **>32a 39f<**
**Hand Chime** 7 ch g Clantime-Warning Bell (Bustino) *486$^9$ 544$^{13}$ 770$^5$* 1132$^9$ 1358$^9$ 4462$^2$ 4687$^7$ 5039$^{10}$6124$^6$ 6445$^{11}$ **>91a 95f<**
**Handsome Cross (IRE)** 3 b c Cape Cross (IRE) -Snap Crackle Pop (IRE) (Statoblest) 1840$^5$ 2378$^5$ 2576$^6$ 3455$^{12}$ 4289$^3$ 5563$^8$ 6205$^7$ **>83f<**
**Handsome Lady** 2 ch f Handsome Ridge-Il Doria (IRE) (Mac s Imp (USA)) (1717) 2129$^6$ 2568$^{10}$ 3290$^5$ 4508$^6$ 5060$^4$ 5602$^{11}$ 6241$^3$ **>73f<**
**Hannah s Dream (IRE)** 2 b f King s Best (USA) -Meritxell (IRE) (Thatching) 5362$^6$ 5559$^2$ 6091$^3$ **>66f<**
**Hannah s Tribe (IRE)** 2 b f Daggers Drawn (USA) -Cala-Holme (IRE) (Fool s Holme (USA)) 4256$^9$ 4606$^9$ 6530$^9$ **>50f<**
**Hanseatic League (USA)** 2 b c Red Ransom (USA) -Rhine Valley (USA) (Danzig (USA)) 2388$^2$ 2686$^2$ 4776$^6$ (5996) **>81f<**
**Hansomelle (IRE)** 2 b f Titus Livius (FR) -Handsome Anna (IRE) (Bigstone (IRE)) 3893$^4$ (4329) 5234$^2$ 5670$^4$ (6003) 6344$^3$ **>78f<**
**Hanzano (IRE)** 6 b h Alzao (USA) -Movie Legend (USA) (Affirmed (USA)) *1954a$^5$ 5504a$^3$ 6451$^{14}$* **>86a 68f<**
**Happy As Larry (USA)** 2 bb c Yes It s True (USA) -Don t Be Blue (USA) (Henbane (USA)) *(6153)* **>87+a<**
**Happy At Last** 3 ch f In The Wings-Elevate (Ela-Mana-Mou) 2711a$^9$ **>85f<**
**Happy Banker (IRE)** 2 gr c With Approval (CAN) -Tropical Paradise (USA) (Manila (USA)) 3749$^{14}$ **>28f<**
**Happy Camper (IRE)** 4 b g Pennekamp (USA) -Happy Dancer (USA) (Seattle Dancer (USA)) *519$^{11}$ 1087$^{11}$ 1279$^6$ 1496$^5$* 1986$^3$ 2209$^8$ *3088$^{12}$*6057$^5$ **>43a 43f<**
**Happy Crusader (IRE)** 3 b c Cape Cross (IRE) -Les Hurlants (IRE) (Barathea (IRE)) 1822$^2$ 2203$^4$ 3000$^8$ **>103f<**
**Happy Event** 2 b c Makbul-La Belle Vie (Indian King (USA)) (2736) 3242$^7$ 3938$^{19}$ (5068) 5703$^4$ **>84f<**
**Harambee (IRE)** 4 b f Robellino (USA) -Hymenee (USA) (Chief s Crown (USA)) 2022$^P$ 2775$^U$ 2982$^{11}$ 3443$^8$ **>36f<**
**Harar (GER)** 2 ch c Acatenango (GER) -Hosea (GER) (Lagunas) 6542a$^2$ **><**
**Harbour House** 5 b g Distant Relative-Double Flutter (Beldale Flutter (USA)) *465$^7$ 787$^2$ 895$^8$ 1278$^6$ 1497$^3$* (1859) 1988$^3$ 2707$^{15}$3558$^2$ 4400$^6$ 4548$^6$ 5039$^5$ 6288$^9$ **>51a 52f<**
**Harbour Legend** 2 b f Dansili-English Harbour (Sabrehill (USA)) 2730$^{13}$ 3834$^6$ 4900$^{11}$ **>27f<**
**Harbour Princess** 3 b f Bal Harbour-Gipsy Princess (Prince Daniel (USA)) *438$^9$ 524$^6$ 898$^6$ 1447$^6$ 1544$^3$* 1863$^4$ *2054$^8$* **>36a 22f<**
**Harcourt (USA)** 4 b c Cozzene (USA) -Ballinamallard (USA) (Tom Rolfe) 1540$^{12}$ 2110$^{14}$ **>86+f<**
**Hard Buck (BRZ)** 5 br h Spend A Buck (USA) -Social Secret (Secreto (USA)) 1144a$^2$ 4121$^2$ **>84a 123f<**
**Hard To Catch (IRE)** 6 b g Namaqualand (USA) -Brook s Dilemma (Known Fact (USA)) *526$^7$ 646$^7$ 701$^2$ 742$^4$ (771) 1057$^9$ 1082$^4$ 1204$^5$*1313$^5$ 2091$^6$ 2303$^{10}$ (2440) (2724) 3125$^3$ 3395$^3$ 3778$^{10}$ 4291$^6$ 4522$^3$*5055$^7$* 5299$^{12}$ *5379$^{14}$* **>78a 83f<**
**Hard To Get (AUS)** 4 b g Geiger Counter (USA) -Rarely Caught (NZ) (Danzatore (CAN)) 6528a$^{22}$ **>112f<**
**Hard Top (IRE)** 2 b c Darshaan-Well Head (IRE) (Sadler s Wells (USA)) 6187$^5$ **>71f<**
**Harelda** 4 ch f Hector Protector (USA) -Hen Harrier (Polar Falcon (USA)) *(722) 1045$^6$* 1401$^{18}$ **>71 a 71f<**
**Harford Bridge** 3 ch g Bandmaster (USA) -Double Or Bust (Presidium) *1012$^{10}$* **><**
**Haribini** 4 bb f Groom Dancer (USA) -Mory Kante (USA) (Icecapade (USA)) *1940$^{12}$* 2302$^{16}$ **>52a 52df<**
**Harik** 10 ch g Persian Bold-Yaqut (USA) (Northern Dancer) *413$^6$* 2874$^2$ 3667$^7$ **>85a 55f<**
**Haripur** 5 b h Rainbow Quest (USA) -Jamrat Jumairah (IRE) (Polar Falcon (USA)) *6491$^0$* **>106a 73f<**
**Harlestone Linn** 2 ch g Erhaab (USA) -Harlestone Lake (Riboboy (USA)) 5915$^{12}$ 6283$^7$ **>53f<**
**Harlot** 4 b f Bal Harbour-Queen Of The Quorn (Governor General) *464$^{12}$ 767$^{10}$* **>63a 44f<**
**Haroldini (IRE)** 2 b g Orpen (USA) -Ciubanga (IRE) (Arazi (USA)) 1686$^7$ 2095$^4$ 2523$^2$ 3886$^6$ *4094$^2$* 4521$^7$ 5617$^{17}$ *6289$^9$* **>73a 65f<**
**Harrington Bates** 3 ch g Wolfhound (USA) -Fiddling (Music Boy) 2468$^4$ 2984$^6$ 3251$^8$ 3838$^5$ **>67f<**
**Harrison Point (USA)** 4 br c Nureyev (USA) -Maid s Broom (USA) (Deputy Minister (CAN)) *(847) (1066)* 2279$^2$ 2646$^2$ 3597$^{10}$ *(4549)* 5419$^3$ 6070$^6$ **>93+a 89f<**
**Harrison s Flyer (IRE)** 3 b g Imperial Ballet (IRE) -Smart Pet (Petong) 3410$^7$ 3511$^2$ 3819$^{12}$ 4021$^2$ 4309$^{15}$ 5306$^2$ 5342$^U$ 5562$^{12}$6046$^{12}$ (6186) *(6274)* (6532) **>78a 86+f<**
**Harry Came Home** 3 b g Wizard King-Kirby s Princess (Indian King (USA)) *1050$^{10}$* 1356$^{10}$ 1800$^{12}$ 2267$^{11}$ 2766$^{16}$ *4600$^{11}$* 4912$^{11}$ 5259$^{14}$5843$^{13}$ **>26a 36f<**
**Harrycat (IRE)** 3 b g Bahhare (USA) -Quiver Tree (Lion Cavern (USA)) 5123$^7$ 5478$^5$ 5994$^6$ 6192$^2$ 6519$^3$ **>69f<**
**Harry Lad** 3 ch g Then Again-Silly Sally (Music Boy) *835$^5$ 969$^5$* 1450$^6$ **>44a<**
**Harry Potter (GER)** 5 b g Platini (GER) -Heavenly Storm (USA) (Storm Bird (CAN)) *643$^{11}$ 847$^{14}$ 1055$^3$* 1247$^{11}$ (1451) 1772$^8$ 2271$^6$ 2687$^9$3082$^3$ (4008) (4142) 4349$^5$ 5004$^{13}$ 5315$^3$ 5627$^8$ 6069$^{14}$ **>72a 84f<**
**Harrys House** 2 gr g Paris House-Rum Lass (Distant Relative) 4175$^4$ 4776$^7$ 5186$^4$ 5447$^3$ (6002) 6523$^8$ **>77+f<**
**Harry s Simmie (IRE)** 2 ch f Spectrum (IRE) -Minstrels Folly (USA) (The Minstrel (CAN)) 3406$^{10}$ 4487$^{13}$ *6021$^{10}$* **>29a 32f<**
**Harry The Hoover (IRE)** 4 b g Fayruz-Mitsubishi Style (Try My Best (USA)) *6156$^{12}$* **>58a 78f<**
**Harry Tu** 4 b g Millkom-Risky Tu (Risk Me (FR)) *585$^9$ 793$^9$* **>19a<**
**Harry Up** 3 ch c Piccolo-Faraway Lass (Distant Relative) 1223$^2$ 1323$^3$ 1883$^9$ 2115$^3$ 2552$^4$ 2897$^{16}$ 4289$^{21}$ **>89f<**
**Hartshead** 5 b g Machiavellian (USA) -Zalitzine (USA) (Zilzal (USA)) 1974$^2$ 2407$^8$ 2936$^6$ (3096) (3515) 4047$^4$ (4308) (5244) 5818$^2$ 6070$^3$ **>86f<**
**Harvest Warrior** 2 br g Mujahid (USA) -Lammastide (Martinmas) 1871$^2$ 2749$^2$ (3476) 3865$^5$ 5767$^2$ 5947$^{12}$ 6348$^2$ **>99f<**
**Hasaiyda (IRE)** 3 b f Hector Protector (USA) -Hasainiya (IRE) (Top Ville) (2401) 3694$^4$ (4648) 5402$^8$ 5568$^{12}$ **>91+f<**
**Hasayis** 3 b f Danehill (USA) -Intizaa (USA) (Mr Prospector (USA)) (1301) 2097$^{10}$ 4020$^4$ 4771$^7$ **>69f<**
**Hashid (IRE)** 4 b g Darshaan-Alkaffeyeh (IRE) (Sadler s Wells (USA)) 1221$^6$ 2611$^3$ 3095$^8$ 3752$^{12}$ 4080$^6$ 5073$^5$ **>83f<**
**Hashima (USA)** 2 b f Kingmambo (USA) -Fairy Heights (IRE) (Fairy King (USA)) 4706$^3$ *6446$^4$* **>59a 69f<**
**Hashimiya (USA)** 2 b f Gone West (USA) -Touch Of Greatness (USA) (Hero s Honor (USA)) 6118$^6$ **>60f<**
**Hasilat** 4 b c Piccolo-Fontenoy (USA) (Lyphard s Wish (FR)) 5488a$^{14}$ **><**
**Haskilclara (FR)** 3 ch f Green Tune (USA) -Helvetica (FR) (Cricket Ball (USA)) 1652a$^7$ 2193a$^{10}$ **>98f<**

**Hasty Prince** 6 ch g Halling (USA) -Sister Sophie (USA) (Effervescing (USA)) 5699$^S$ >**97 f**<

**Hatch** 3 ch c Cadeaux Genereux-Footlight Fantasy (USA) (Nureyev (USA)) 696$^2$ 869$^2$ (982) 1223$^3$ (1317) 1745$^3$ 2202$^{13}$ 2844$^4$ 3850$^{11}$4750$^{10}$ >**78a 96f**<

**Hatch A Plan (IRE)** 3 b g Vettori (IRE) -Fast Chick (Henbit (USA)) 1243$^9$ 1613$^U$ 2732$^7$ (3387) 3706$^2$ 4170$^2$ 4572$^4$ 4915$^{10}$ 5568$^{11}$5997$^5$ >**38a 77f**<

**Hathaal (IRE)** 5 b h Alzao (USA) -Ballet Shoes (IRE) (Ela-Mana-Mou) 2163a$^{15}$ >**79f**<

**Hathlen (IRE)** 3 b c Singspiel (IRE) -Kameez (IRE) (Arazi (USA)) 1249$^8$ 1416$^6$ 1714$^6$ 2133$^5$ 2561$^6$ (2840) 4062$^5$ 5100$^6$ 5595$^7$5820$^6$ >**79f**<

**Hathrah (IRE)** 3 gr f Linamix (FR) -Zivania (IRE) (Shernazar) (1327) 1791$^3$ >**112f**<

**Hatif (BRZ)** 4 u u Spend A Buck (USA) - (USA) (Solford (USA)) 4768a$^{13}$ >**87f**<

**Hat Trick Man** 3 gr c Daylami (IRE) -Silver Kristal (Kris) 3994$^6$ 4648$^8$ 6564$^3$ >**58a 70f**<

**Haulage Man** 6 ch g Komaite (USA) -Texita (Young Generation) 2976$^{10}$ 3269$^2$ 3559$^{11}$ 4154$^2$ 4542$^9$ 5526$^8$ 6144$^{12}$ >**75f**<

**Haunting Memories (IRE)** 2 b c Barathea (IRE) -King Of All (IRE) (King Of Clubs) 4296$^4$ (4861) 5703$^2$ 6268$^3$ >**94f**<

**Haunt The Zoo** 9 b m Komaite (USA) -Merryhill Maid (IRE) (M Double M (USA)) 1861$^5$ 2814$^8$ 3023$^3$ 3282$^8$ 3804$^{12}$ >**68a**<

**Haute Ransom (USA)** 2 b c Red Ransom (USA) -Balenciaga (USA) (Gulch (USA)) 5432a$^5$ >**92f**<

**Havana Rose (IRE)** 4 b f Goldmark (USA) -Roses Red (IRE) (Exhibitioner) 875$^{16}$ 944$^8$ >**11a 33f**<

**Havantadoubt (IRE)** 4 ch f Desert King (IRE) -Batiba (USA) (Time For A Change (USA)) 1522$^7$ 2302$^{14}$ 3670$^{13}$ 5285$^5$ 5658$^9$ 5796$^{18}$ >**45f**<

**Have A Heart (IRE)** 3 b f Daggers Drawn (USA) -Sukeena (IRE) (Brief Truce (USA)) 1256a$^7$ >**69 f**<

**Have Faith (IRE)** 3 b f Machiavellian (USA) -Fatefully (USA) (Private Account (USA)) 3017$^3$ 3452$^6$ 4318$^6$ 6307$^7$ >**87f**<

**Have Some Fun** 4 ch g Bering-Hilaris (Arazi (USA)) 520$^3$ 601$^2$ 3177$^{12}$ 3771$^{11}$ 4549$^{13}$ 4602$^{13}$ >**67a 33f**<

**Havetoavit (USA)** 3 b g Theatrical-Summer Crush (USA) (Summer Squall (USA)) 1770$^5$ 2146$^3$ 2567$^2$ 3020$^4$ 3561$^{11}$ 4103$^4$ (4562) 5245$^2$ 5459$^{14}$6096$^{11}$ >**58a 71+f**<

**Havoc** 5 b g Hurricane Sky (AUS) -Padelia (Thatching) 1043$^9$ >**24a 77f**<

**Hawaajes** 3 b g Royal Applause-Aegean Blue (Warning) 1794$^{11}$ 2195$^3$ (2621) 3317$^4$ 3926$^{12}$ >**80f**<

**Hawadeth** 9 ch g Machiavellian (USA) -Ghzaalh (USA) (Northern Dancer) 1329$^5$ 2958$^{17}$ >**86f**<

**Hawk** 6 b g A P Jet (USA) -Miss Enjoleur (USA) (L Enjoleur (CAN)) 417$^{14}$ 519$^7$ 608$^{10}$ 794$^{11}$ 2869$^{11}$ >**30 a 30f**<

**Hawk Arrow (IRE)** 2 ch c In The Wings-Barbizou (FR) (Selkirk (USA)) 6149$^7$ >**60f**<

**Hawkes Bay** 2 b c Vettori (IRE) -Nordico Princess (Nordico (USA)) 5720$^{10}$ 6149$^3$ >**66f**<

**Hawkit (USA)** 3 b g Silver Hawk (USA) -Hey Ghaz (USA) (Ghazi (USA)) 798$^5$ 907$^2$ (1012) 1120$^7$ (1784) 2949$^2$ 3271$^7$ 4749$^{10}$ 4931$^5$ >**67a 80f**<

**Hawks Tor (IRE)** 2 b c Danehill (USA) -Born Beautiful (USA) (Silver Deputy (CAN)) 3081$^6$ >**43f**<

**Hawridge King** 2 b g Erhaab (USA) -Sadaka (USA) (Kingmambo (USA)) 2360$^3$ 3336$^5$ 4579$^6$ 5052$^5$ 5539$^5$ >**62a 67f**<

**Hawridge Prince** 4 b g Polar Falcon (USA) -Zahwa (Cadeaux Genereux) (2084) (3239) 3842$^2$ 4530$^4$ 5133$^2$ 5650$^{16}$ >**112f**<

**Hawridge Sensation** 2 ch g Polish Precedent (USA) -Looks Sensational (USA) (Majestic Light (USA)) 5840$^7$ >**44f**<

**Hawridge Star (IRE)** 2 b c Alzao (USA) -Serenity (Selkirk (USA)) 3240$^6$ 5534$^2$ 6078$^{12}$ >**76f**<

**Hayburn Street (IRE)** 3 ch c Barathea (IRE) -Always Far (USA) (Alydar (USA)) 2315a$^8$ >**92f**<

**Haydn (USA)** 3 b g Stravinsky (USA) -Circular (USA) (What A Pleasure (USA)) 669$^5$ 1333$^{14}$ 1702$^{17}$ 2839$^5$ 3428$^{13}$ 4170$^6$ 4556$^{12}$ 5156$^{14}$ >**87a 78 f**<

**Hayraan (IRE)** 2 b c Bluebird (USA) -Alma Latina (IRE) (Persian Bold) 6092$^7$ 6440$^7$ >**56f**<

**Haystacks (IRE)** 8 b g Contract Law (USA) -Florissa (FR) (Persepolis (FR)) 1721$^3$ 2171$^7$ >**56f**<

**Hazarista (IRE)** 3 b f Barathea (IRE) -Hazaradjat (IRE) (Darshaan) (2102a) 3968a$^3$ 4859$^3$ 5679a$^{10}$ >**113f**<

**Haze Babybear** 4 b f Mujadil (USA) -River s Rising (FR) (Mendez (FR)) 3025$^9$ 3381$^{14}$ 3801$^6$ >**60a 62f**<

**Hazelhatch** 4 b g Mukaddamah (USA) -Stop Out (Rudimentary (USA)) 690a$^9$ (755a) 852a$^4$ 921a$^8$ >**92f**<

**Hazewind** 3 gr g Daylami (IRE) -Fragrant Oasis (USA) (Rahy (USA)) 574$^{11}$ 816$^4$ 885$^2$ (928) 1357$^7$ 1841$^{17}$ 2207$^7$ 2377$^9$2648$^2$ 2835$^5$ (3684) (3949) 4171$^6$ 5120$^4$ (5316) 5540$^6$ 5955$^4$ 6064$^4$6279$^3$ 6553$^3$ >**78a 76f**<

**Hazyview** 3 b c Cape Cross (IRE) -Euridice (IRE) (Woodman (USA)) 1222$^2$ (1414) (1588) (1766) 1966$^2$ (2307) 2680$^8$ 3863a$^3$ 4769a$^6$ >**111f**<

**Head Boy** 3 ch g Forzando-Don t Jump (IRE) (Entitled) 462$^4$ 521$^{10}$ 741$^{12}$ 1270$^5$ 1613$^6$ 1908$^5$ 3874$^4$ 4338$^2$4546$^8$ 5020$^9$ 5259$^8$ 5656$^6$ 6558$^3$ >**57a 61f**<

**Headland (USA)** 6 bb g Distant View (USA) -Fijar Echo (USA) (In Fijar (USA)) 439$^4$ 487$^2$ 584$^7$ 698$^7$ 723$^3$ 799$^{11}$ 1076$^3$3024$^9$ 3376$^6$ 3533$^2$ 4188$^2$ (4305) 4702$^5$ 4926$^5$ (5000) 5364$^{11}$5849$^5$ 6138$^{17}$ >**67a 59f**<

**Head Of State** 3 br g Primo Dominie-Lets Be Fair (Efisio) 496$^8$ 610$^{12}$ (731) 819$^8$ 1047$^3$ 1270$^{10}$ 2850$^9$ 3037$^5$ >**66a 31f**<

**Head To Kerry (IRE)** 4 b g Eagle Eyed (USA) -The Poachers Lady (IRE) (Salmon Leap (USA)) 2116$^{17}$ 2480$^8$ 2893$^9$ 3181$^3$ 3488$^5$ 3942$^3$ 4080$^4$ 4233$^2$4441$^4$ 4849$^5$ 5153$^4$ 5459$^9$ 6292$^6$ >**56a 72f**<

**Healey (IRE)** 6 ch g Dr Devious (IRE) -Bean Siamsa (Solinus) 3604$^8$ 3921$^{12}$ 5021$^7$ >**36a 53f**<

**Heartbeat** 3 b f Pursuit Of Love-Lyrical Bid (USA) (Lyphard (USA)) 574$^4$ 702$^8$ 798$^7$ 1267$^4$ 1389$^4$ 2390$^5$ 2546$^9$ 2822$^7$3193$^3$ >**46a 55f**<

**Heartbreaker (IRE)** 4 b g In Command (IRE) -No Hard Feelings (IRE) (Alzao (USA)) 3712$^8$ >**37f**<

**Hearthstead Dream** 3 ch g Dr Fong (USA) -Robin Lane (Tenby) 2134$^{18}$ 2354$^3$ 2545$^2$ (2783) 2973$^5$ (3237) 3881$^2$ (4397) 4762$^3$ 5214$^3$ 5560$^4$6074$^3$ 6198$^8$ >**78f**<

**Hearthstead Wings** 2 b c In The Wings-Inishdalla (IRE) (Green Desert (USA)) (2141) 3071$^4$ 3672$^6$ (5469) 6259a$^3$ >**103f**<

**Heart Of Eternity (IRE)** 2 b f Namid-Kurfuffle (Bluebird (USA)) 1670$^{14}$ 1936$^4$ 4809$^{12}$ >**47f**<

**Heart s Desire (IRE)** 3 b f Royal Applause-Touch And Love (IRE) (Green Desert (USA)) 2647$^6$ 3701$^2$ 5239$^6$ 5945$^{10}$ >**69f**<

**Heartsonfire (IRE)** 2 bl f Bold Fact (USA) -Jazirah (Main Reef) 4243$^4$ 4804$^{14}$ 5373$^7$ 5864$^4$ (6294) >**64a 67f**<

**Heart Springs** 4 b f Parthian Springs-Metannee (The Brianstan) 2273$^7$ 2950$^8$ 3488$^{10}$ 4129$^4$ 4603$^5$ 4870$^2$ 5354$^{14}$ 6084$^9$ >**52a 46f**<

**Heart Stopping (USA)** 2 b f Chester House (USA) -Clog Dance (Pursuit Of Love) 6470$^7$ >**74f**<

**Heathers Girl** 5 ch m Superlative-Kristis Girl (Ballacashtal (CAN)) 642$^{11}$ (776) 910$^6$ 1037$^2$ 1590$^4$ 2127$^2$ 2816$^2$ 3281$^4$4998$^2$ 6292$^7$ >**58a 50f**<

**Heathwood (IRE)** 2 b c Green Desert (USA) -Woodsia (Woodman (USA)) 6011$^9$ >**47a**<

**Heathyardsblessing (IRE)** 7 b g Unblest-Noble Nadia (Thatching) 576$^8$ 608$^6$ 654$^5$ 799$^{12}$ 938$^3$ 1092$^5$ 1180$^5$ >**40a 40f**<

**Heathyards Joy** 3 ch f Komaite (USA) -Heathyards Lady (USA) (Mining (USA)) 587$^7$ 696$^{12}$ 942$^4$ 1195$^4$ 1594$^2$ 1864$^5$ 1985$^5$ 2187$^6$2346$^8$ 3817$^3$ 4102$^2$ >**31a 39f**<

**Heathyards Pride** 4 b g Polar Prince (IRE) -Heathyards Lady (USA) (Mining (USA)) (424) 1305$^{19}$ 2356$^4$ 3774$^5$ (5350) (5993) (6225) >**72+a 65f**<

**Heat Of The Night** 2 b f Lear Fan (USA) -Hot Thong (BRZ) (Jarraar (USA)) 3627$^4$ 4234$^9$ 5349$^2$ 5946$^5$ >**76f**<

**Heavens Walk** 3 ch c Compton Place-Ghost Dancing (Lion Cavern (USA)) 4440$^5$ 4845$^8$ 5147$^4$ 6275$^3$ >**59a 47f**<

**Hebenus** 5 b g Hamas (IRE) -Stinging Nettle (Sharpen Up) 1720$^2$ 2779$^7$ 4386$^{14}$ 6469$^4$ >**37a 59df**<

**Hedingham Knight (IRE)** 2 b c Fasliyev (USA) -Exclusive Davis (USA) (Our Native (USA)) 2502$^6$ 3051$^9$ >**53f**<

**Hefin** 7 ch g Red Rainbow-Summer Impressions (USA) (Lyphard (USA)) 6278$^{10}$ >**70a 68f**<

**Heidi s Dash (IRE)** 2 b f Green Desert (USA) -Child Prodigy (IRE) (Ballad Rock) 2057$^8$ 2535$^4$ >**59f**<

**Heir To Be** 5 b g Elmaamul (USA) -Princess Genista (Ile De Bourbon (USA)) 1302$^5$ 1457$^{14}$ 1615$^6$ >**88 f**<

**Heisse** 4 b c Darshaan-Hedera (USA) (Woodman (USA)) 1124$^5$ 1329$^{14}$ 1539$^{17}$ 5435$^8$ 5919$^{11}$ >**98f**<

**He Jaa (IRE)** 3 gr f Daylami (IRE) -Calpella (Ajdal (USA)) 1461$^7$ 1793$^P$ >**70f**<

**Hektikos** 4 ch g Hector Protector (USA) -Green Danube (USA) (Irish River (FR)) 818$^{11}$ 1207$^{11}$ 1494$^5$ >**30a 64f**<

**Helderberg (USA)** 4 b f Diesis-Banissa (USA) (Lear Fan (USA)) 2284$^{19}$ 2551$^5$ 3012$^6$ >**77f**<

**Helen House** 2 b f Tipsy Creek (USA) -Tiempo (King Of Spain) 6454$^7$ 6563$^3$ >**65f**<

**Helen Sharp** 2 ch f Pivotal-Sunny Davis (USA) (Alydar (USA)) 6471$^{11}$ >**55f**<

**Helios Quercus (FR)** 2 br c Diableneyev (USA) -Criss Cross (FR) (Crystal Palace (FR)) (5666a) (6510a) >**112f**<

**Helixalot (IRE)** 3 ch g College Chapel-Last Ambition (IRE) (Cadeaux Genereux) 5913$^{14}$ ><

**Hellbent** 5 b g Selkirk (USA) -Loure (USA) (Lyphard (USA)) 504$^8$ 728$^{12}$ 858$^{11}$ 951$^9$ 1167$^5$ 1277$^6$ 1402$^3$1580$^4$ 1885$^6$ 2055$^5$ >**43a 38f**<

**Hello It s Me** 3 ch g Deploy-Evening Charm (IRE) (Bering) 1414$^2$ 2018$^{11}$ 3477$^2$ 4140$^5$ 4343$^4$ 5106$^3$ 5465$^5$ 5942$^{12}$ >**95+f**<

**Hello Roberto** 3 b f Up And At Em-Hello Hobson S (IRE) (Fayruz) 493$^7$ 619$^2$ 669$^8$ 819$^2$ 986$^5$ 3270$^3$ 3562$^9$(3702) 3894$^{10}$ 4289$^{20}$ 4515$^{10}$ 4929$^4$ 5458$^7$ 5564$^7$ 6518$^{10}$ >**80a 75f**<

**Hello Sid** 3 ch g Hello Mister-Moving Up (IRE) (Don t Forget Me) 764$^9$ ><

**Hello Tiger** 3 gr g Terimon-Blue Peru (IRE) (Perugino (USA)) 1192$^8$ 1371$^{19}$ 3613$^{10}$ 4069$^5$ ><

**Helm (IRE)** 3 b g Alhaarth (IRE) -Pipers Pool (IRE) (Mtoto) 1612$^{10}$ 5913$^4$ 6088$^6$ >**70a 66f**<

**Hemaris (IRE)** 2 b f Sri Pekan (USA) -Sovereign Grace (IRE) (Standaan (FR)) 5322a$^9$ >**80f**<

**Heneseys Leg** 4 b f Sure Blade (USA) -Away s Halo (USA) (Sunny s Halo (CAN)) (1845) (2403) (3200) 3933$^5$ 4760$^3$ 5303$^{16}$ >**68a 83f**<

**Henndey (IRE)** 3 b g Indian Ridge-Del Deya (IRE) (Caerleon (USA)) 1174$^2$ 1519$^2$ >**78f**<

**Hennie s Song (USA)** 4 b f Unbridled s Song (USA) -Zama Hummer (USA) (Knights Choice (USA)) 4735a$^6$ ><

**Henrik** 2 b c Primo Dominie-Clincher Club (Polish Patriot (USA)) (2225) 3672$^2$ 6347$^3$ >**109f**<

**Henry Afrika (IRE)** 6 b g Mujadil (USA) -Floralia (Auction Ring (USA)) 564$^7$ 866$^{12}$ >**79a 88f**<

**Henry Hall (IRE)** 8 b h Common Grounds-Sovereign Grace (IRE) (Standaan (FR)) 1211$^3$ 1391$^{10}$ 2041$^3$ 2679$^9$ 2859$^3$ 3480$^{10}$ 3945$^8$ 4538$^{15}$5181$^7$ 5787$^{10}$ 5933$^8$ 6243$^{12}$ >**101f**<

**Henry Island (IRE)** 11 ch g Sharp Victor (USA) -Monterana (Sallust) 1520$^5$ 2429$^7$ 3683$^4$ 4033$^7$ 4647$^{10}$ 5205$^2$ 5456$^{10}$ 5826$^4$6084$^{13}$ >**61a 80f**<

**Henry Tun** 6 b g Chaddleworth (IRE) -B Grade (Lucky Wednesday) 411$^3$ 538$^5$ 638$^7$ 721$^2$ (938) 954$^3$ 1027$^7$ 1262$^2$1584$^7$ 2246$^7$ 2350$^6$ 2869$^8$ 3378$^{13}$ >**64a 52f**<

**Herakles (GER)** 3 b c Lagunas-Haraka (FR) (Kahyasi) 1306a$^2$ ><

**Herencia (IRE)** 2 b c Victory Note (USA) -Originality (Godswalk (USA)) 3248$^{11}$ 4200$^7$ 4607$^8$ 5097$^4$ 5369$^2$ 6515$^6$ >**52f**<

**Heres Harry** 4 b c Most Welcome-Nahla (Wassl) 2178$^{18}$ 2843$^8$ >**4f**<

**Heres The Plan (IRE)** 2 b f Revoque (IRE) -Fanciful (IRE) (Mujtahid (USA)) (2275) 3316$^7$ 4089$^6$ 4445$^{10}$ 6063$^4$ >**64a 77f**<

**Heretic** 6 b g Bishop Of Cashel-Barford Lady (Stanford) (1469) 1705$^4$ 3673$^{19}$ 4889$^{10}$ >**113f**<

**Here To Me** 3 ch f Muhtarram (USA) -Away To Me (Exit To Nowhere (USA)) 2112$^5$ 2377$^3$ 2577$^4$ 2871$^4$ 3180$^2$ (3486) 3874$^3$ 4515$^5$ 5148$^6$5657$^2$ 6064$^8$ >**72a 76f**<

**Heriot** 3 br g Hamas (IRE) -Sure Victory (IRE) (Stalker) 1827$^{10}$ 2842$^9$ 3106$^8$ 4144$^7$ >**65f**<

**Hermitage Court (USA)** 3 ch g Out Of Place (USA) -Russian Act (USA) (Siberian Express (USA)) (3916) 4749$^4$ 5403$^6$ 5766$^{12}$ >**91f**<

**Hernandita** 6 b m Hernando (FR) -Dara Dee (Dara Monarch) 2731$^4$ 2958$^{15}$ 3488$^6$ >**70f**<

**Hernando s Boy** 3 b g Hernando (FR) -Leave At Dawn (Slip Anchor) 1285$^5$ 1559$^9$ 1995$^7$ 3561$^{12}$ 4397$^2$ >**63f**<

**Herne Bay (IRE)** 4 b g Hernando (FR) -Charita (IRE) (Lycius (USA)) (2126) 2590$^{14}$ 3733$^5$ >**66a 64df**<

**Herodotus** 6 b g Zafonic (USA) -Thalestria (FR) (Mill Reef (USA)) 2681$^{13}$ 3325$^{12}$ 3752$^{13}$ 5251$^7$ 6576$^{12}$ >**32a 7f**<

**Heron s Wing** 3 ch g Hernando (FR) -Celtic Wing (Midyan (USA)) 598$^8$ >**56a**<

**Hero s Journey** 5 ch h Halling (USA) -Zahwa (Cadeaux Genereux) 636a$^3$ 690a$^{10}$ 925a$^7$ 1001a$^{10}$ >**53a 104f**<

**Her Own Kind (JPN)** 2 b f Dubai Millennium-The Caretaker (Caerleon (USA)) 5946$^2$ (6336) >**82+f**<

**He s A Diamond** 2 ch g Vettori (IRE) -Azira (Arazi (USA)) 2761$^5$ (3553) 3987$^3$ 4365$^8$ 5377$^{16}$ 5596$^{15}$ >**75f**<

**He s A Rocket (IRE)** 3 b g Indian Rocket-Dellua (IRE) (Suave Dancer (USA)) 452$^6$ 1220$^5$ (1517) (1742) 1934$^3$ 2269$^6$ 2650$^7$ 3562$^{10}$ 4279$^6$ 4585$^9$4701$^2$ 4828$^7$ 5562$^{16}$ 5736$^9$ 6079$^{15}$ >**30a 63f**<

**He s A Star** 2 ch c Mark Of Esteem (IRE) -Sahara Belle (USA) (Sanglamore (USA)) 2609$^9$ 2927$^4$ 3157$^7$ 4365$^6$ 5738$^6$ 5885$^9$ >**61f**<

**Heversham (IRE)** 3 b c Octagonal (NZ) -Saint Ann (USA) (Geiger Counter (USA)) 506$^4$ (766) 843$^2$ 1134$^7$ 2135$^7$ 2448$^9$ 2704$^4$ 3427$^2$ 3610$^5$4050$^7$ 4447$^{17}$ 5223$^7$ 5317$^7$ 5544$^2$ 5715$^2$ 5945$^{23}$ 6461$^{12}$ >**85a 72f**<

**He Who Dares (IRE)** 6 b g Distinctly North (USA) -Sea Clover (IRE) (Ela-Mana-Mou) 464$^2$ 742$^{12}$ 882$^3$ 926$^4$ 1502$^3$ (1969) 2262$^2$ >**65a 69f**<

**Heyahohowdy (CAN)** 5 br m Domasca Dan (CAN) -Executive Diamond (CAN) (Bold Executive (CAN)) 6383a$^8$ >**99f**<

**Heybrook Boy (USA)** 2 ch c Woodman (USA) -Liberada (USA) (Spend A Buck (USA)) 3233$^8$ 3918$^4$ 4277$^2$ >**71f**<

**Hey Presto** 4 b g Piccolo-Upping The Tempo (Dunbeath (USA)) 2477$^{14}$ 2763$^{10}$ 3243$^9$ 3416$^5$ 3887$^6$ (4122) 4553$^{19}$ 4846$^{13}$ 5419$^{18}$5887$^9$ >**78f**<

**Heyward Place** 4 b f Mind Games-Ginny Binny (Ahonoora) 541$^{12}$ 1371$^{18}$ 1911$^{10}$ ><

**Hezaam (USA)** 3 b c Red Ransom (USA) -Ashraakat (USA) (Danzig (USA)) 1408$^{12}$ 2134$^5$ 2648$^8$ (3543) (4762) 5074$^2$ 5785$^4$ 6286$^9$ >**89f**<

**H Harrison (IRE)** 4 b g Eagle Eyed (USA) -Penrose (IRE) (Wolfhound (USA)) 1199$^{18}$ 1345$^6$ 1840$^4$ 1927$^5$ 2366$^4$ (2750) 2899$^{16}$ 3036$^{23}$ 3440$^3$4179$^5$ 4360$^8$ 4931$^{11}$ 5055$^6$ 5574$^5$ 5818$^8$ 5937$^3$ 6480$^6$6568$^{10}$ >**80a 93f**<

**Hiamovi (IRE)** 2 b g Monashee Mountain (USA) -Dunfern (Wolver Hollow) 1462$^{11}$ 3377$^5$ 4997$^2$ 5910$^{12}$ 6289$^{10}$ >**57a 37f**<

**Hiats** 2 b c Lujain (USA) -Naulakha (Bustino) 1105$^{13}$ 1359$^6$ 2579$^{10}$ >**37f**<

**Hiawatha (IRE)** 5 b g Danehill (USA) -Hi Bettina (Henbit (USA)) 516$^4$ (548) 649$^3$ 768$^7$ 961$^7$ (2424) 2738$^7$ 3291$^5$ 4634$^7$5607$^{20}$ >**83 a 80f**<

**Hibernate (IRE)** 10 ch g Lahib (USA) -Ministra (USA) (Deputy Minister (CAN)) 2347$^{12}$ 3149$^6$ 3369$^4$ 3835$^{10}$ 4015$^{13}$ 4250$^5$ >**41a 45 f**<

**Hiccups** 4 b g Polar Prince (IRE) -Simmie s Special (Precocious) 1454$^2$ 1825$^{13}$ 2132$^3$ (2467) 3098$^{10}$ 3606$^6$ 4047$^3$ 4759$^3$ 5062$^9$ >**89f**<

**Hickerthriftcastle** 5 ch g Carlingford Castle-Sun Sprite (Morston (FR)) 2740$^{12}$ ><

**Hi Darl** 3 ch f Wolfhound (USA) -Sugar Token (Record Token) 3478$^{10}$ 4020$^{13}$ 4674$^{13}$ 5452$^8$ 5794$^{16}$ 6229$^{16}$ 6469$^5$ >**20a 39f**<

**Hidden Chance** 2 ch f Hernando (FR) -Catch (USA) (Blushing Groom (FR)) 3627$^7$ (4053) 5090$^{11}$ 5377$^8$ 5852$^4$ 6265$^{11}$ >**69f**<

**Hidden Dragon (USA)** 5 b g Danzig (USA) -Summer Home (USA) (Easy Goer (USA)) 1065$^2$ 1242$^2$ 2283$^{11}$ 2469$^{10}$ 4759$^6$ 5372$^4$ 5628$^7$ 5799$^9$ >**108a 108df**<

**Hidden Hope** 3 ch f Daylami (IRE) -Nuryana (Nureyev (USA)) 1507$^2$ (1879) 2997$^5$ 3519$^4$ 4566a$^2$ 5763$^3$ >**58a 106f**<

**Hidden Jewel** 2 ch c Forzando-Manhattan Diamond (Primo Dominie) 2522$^{18}$ 2812$^6$ 3377$^6$ 5307$^9$ 6333$^2$ 6543$^3$ >**36a 87?f**<

**Hiddensee (USA)** 2 b c Cozzene (USA) -Zarani Sidi Anna (USA) (Danzig (USA)) 6148$^{13}$ >**30f**<

**Hidden Star** 2 br c Lujain (USA) -Inimitable (Polish Precedent (USA)) 3343$^3$ 3918$^6$ >**68+f**<

**Hide And Seek (SWE)** 8 br h Island Reef-Memorabilia (Dominion) 1953a$^3$ >**96a**<

**Higgys Prince** 2 b g Prince Sabo-Themeda (Sure Blade (USA)) 1589$^{10}$ 2574$^7$ >**31f**<

**High Accolade** 4 b c Mark Of Esteem (IRE) -Generous Lady (Generous (IRE)) 2639$^4$ 3072$^2$ 3642$^3$ 4121$^8$ 4794a$^2$ 5415$^4$ (5812) >**123f**<

**High Action (USA)** 4 ch g Theatrical-Secret Imperatrice (USA) (Secretariat (USA)) 1401$^{15}$ 1821$^{15}$ 3725$^8$ (4174) (4361) 5288$^8$ 5435$^5$ >**96 f**<

**Highbury Lass** 2 ch f Entrepreneur-Princess Victoria (Deploy) 2388$^{12}$ 2755$^6$ 4699$^{10}$ >**5f**<

**High Cane (USA)** 4 ch f Diesis-Aerleon Jane (Caerleon (USA)) 871$^{12}$ 1174$^3$ 1451$^{17}$ 1665$^{20}$ 1992$^{12}$ 2814$^{15}$ >**65f**<

**High Card** 2 b g So Factual (USA) -High Cut (Dashing Blade) 6010$^8$ 6223$^6$ 6352$^2$ >**60a 77f**<

**High Chart** 2 b f Robellino (USA) -Bright Spells (Salse (USA)) (1670) 2023$^4$ 2370$^4$ 2970$^{12}$ 4197$^3$ 4342$^8$ 4612$^6$ 5377$^{14}$ 5648$^{25}$5839$^{15}$ 6127$^{10}$ >**45f**<

**High Charter** 3 b g Polish Precedent (USA) -By Charter (Shirley Heights) 6310$^9$ >**48f**<

**High Class Pet** 4 b f Petong-What A Pet (Mummy s Pet) 3587$^{12}$ 4444$^6$ >**21f**<

**High Dawn (IRE)** 2 b g Namid-Highbrook (USA) (Alphabatim (USA)) 1269$^6$ >**45f**<

**High Diva** 5 b m Piccolo-Gifted (Shareef Dancer (USA)) 537$^6$ 583$^4$ 666$^6$ 814$^5$ 860$^U$ 949$^5$ >**44a 44f**<

**High Drama** 7 bb g In The Wings-Maestrale (Top Ville) (2874) 3667$^2$ 4778$^4$ >**48f**<

**High Dyke** 2 b c Mujahid (USA) -Gold Linnet (Nashwan (USA)) 3228$^7$ 3491$^5$ 4016$^6$ 5200$^5$ 5655$^7$ >**71f**<

**Higher Love (IRE)** 2 b f Sadler s Wells (USA) -Dollar Bird (IRE) (Kris) 5368$^6$ 5789$^2$ >**73f**<

**Higher World (USA)** 2 rg f Peaks And Valleys (USA) -Sarah s World (USA) (Holy Bull (USA)) 6485a$^{12}$ >**76a**<

**Highest (IRE)** 5 b h Selkirk (USA) -Pearl Kite (USA) (Silver Hawk (USA)) 2067$^7$ 2998$^7$ >**120f**<

**High Esteem** 8 b g Common Grounds-Whittle Woods Girl (Emarati (USA)) 436$^4$ 612$^8$ 4185$^9$ 4701$^{14}$ >**47a 44f**<

**Highest Regard** 2 b c Mark Of Esteem (IRE) -Free As A Bird (Robellino (USA)) 6400$^7$ 6563$^7$ >**37a 57f**<

**Highest Return (USA)** 2 bb c Theatrical-Hasene (FR) (Akarad (FR)) 3974$^4$ 4290$^{11}$ >**67f**<

**High Finance (IRE)** 4 bb f Entrepreneur-Phylella (Persian Bold) 1317$^5$ 2282$^6$ 5055$^{14}$ >**66a 85f**<

**High Flash (IRE)** 3 ch c Selkirk (USA) -Hint Of Silver (USA) (Alysheba (USA)) 4284a$^3$ >**105f**<

**Highfluting** 3 b f Piccolo-Vilcabamba (USA) (Green Dancer (USA)) 916$^{13}$ 2060$^9$ 2168$^{16}$ 2323$^7$ >**31a 2f**<

**High Frequency (IRE)** 3 ch g Grand Lodge (USA) -Freak Out (FR) (Bering) 1395$^{10}$ 2204$^6$ 2517$^7$ >**66f**<

**High Hope (FR)** 6 ch g Lomitas-Highness Lady (GER) (Cagliostro (GER)) 418$^7$ 5152$^5$ >**91a 71f**<

**Highland Cascade** 2 ch f Tipsy Creek (USA) -Highland Hannah (IRE) (Persian Heights) (2095) 2817$^3$ 3343$^2$ 5391$^8$ 5701$^3$ 6174$^8$ >**75f**<

**Highland Dancer (FR)** 3 ch c Kendor (FR) -Zarzaya (USA) (Caro) 3163a$^5$ >**107f**<

**Highland Diva (IRE)** 2 ch f Selkirk (USA) -Drama Class (IRE) (Caerleon (USA)) 5248$^4$ >**73+f**<

**Highland Games (IRE)** 4 b g Singspiel (IRE) -Highland Gift (IRE) (Generous (IRE)) 1744$^2$ 2047$^{13}$ 2365$^2$ 2691$^4$ 3075$^5$ 4345$^3$ 4529$^3$ 5435$^{13}$5784$^P$ >**95f**<

**Highland Lass** 3 b f Nicolotte-Portvasco (Sharpo) 3322$^8$ 4125$^{10}$ 4718$^6$ 5008$^{10}$ 6007$^{13}$ >**57?f**<

**Highland Reel** 7 ch g Selkirk (USA) -Taj Victory (Final Straw) (2201) 2534$^{11}$ 2969$^{26}$ 3212$^4$ 3937$^9$ 4220$^3$ 4442$^4$ 5151$^4$ >**96f**<

**Highland Warrior** 5 b h Makbul-Highland Rowena (Royben) 1175$^3$ 1345$^3$ 1525$^2$ 1774$^3$ 1929$^4$ (2261) 2490$^6$ 2581$^7$ 2784$^8$3038$^4$ 3309$^6$ 3446$^6$ 3979$^3$ 4130$^{15}$ 4904$^2$ 5605$^6$ 6144$^4$6518$^2$ 6532$^6$ >**79f**<

**Highlight Girl** 3 ch f Forzando-Norska (Northfields (USA)) 2001$^{14}$ 3142$^9$ >**38f**<

**High Minded** 2 b g Mind Games-Pips Way (IRE) (Pips Pride) 2388$^7$ 3003$^6$ >**57f**<

**High Petergate (IRE)** 2 b f Mujadil (USA) -Anamara (IRE) (Fairy King (USA)) 2388[5] 5241[4] 5578[10] 5989[16] **>59f<**

**High Point (IRE)** 6 b g Ela-Mana-Mou-Top Lady (IRE) (Shirley Heights) *418[15] 523[7] 600[7] 743[2]* 1329[3] 2047[3] 2480[3] 3644[6]4075[12] 5093[5] (5595) 6215[3] **>87a 88f<**

**High Policy (IRE)** 8 ch g Machiavellian (USA) -Road To The Top (Shirley Heights) *684[4] 2987[3]* **>72a 61f<**

**High Priestess (IRE)** 5 b m Priolo (USA) -Boss Lady (IRE) (Last Tycoon) 4977a[4] 5357a[7] **>104?f<**

**High Reach** 4 b g Royal Applause-Lady Of Limerick (IRE) (Thatching) 1354[3] 1765[6] 3074[3] 3453[7] 4324[3] 5647[9] 5893[10] *6451[10]* **>95a 103f<**

**High Reserve** 3 b f Dr Fong (USA) -Hyabella (Shirley Heights) 5123[3] (5540) **>74+f<**

**High Rhythm** 2 b f Piccolo-Slave To The Rythm (IRE) (Hamas (IRE)) 6126[6] **>50f<**

**High Ridge** 5 ch g Indian Ridge-Change For A Buck (USA) (Time For A Change (USA)) 1873[9] (2166) 2614[5] (2873) 2948[2] 3339[3] 3775[4] (3923) 4244[2] 4291[2] 4403[4]5730[10] 6001[11] 6131[14] **>80f<**

**High School** 3 b f Sadler s Wells (USA) -High Hawk (Shirley Heights) 1189[2] 1521[6] 2198[4] 3156[2] 3989[6] **>75f<**

**High Treason (USA)** 2 ch c Diesis-Fabula Dancer (USA) (Northern Dancer) 3319[12] 5396[8] 5915[21] 6073[11] **>61f<**

**High View (USA)** 3 ch c Distant View (USA) -Disco Doll (USA) (Diesis) 1827[7] 2085[16] 2374[9] 2654[13] 3669[10] 5080[11] 5654[13] **>47f<**

**High Voltage** 3 ch g Wolfhound (USA) -Real Emotion (USA) (El Prado (IRE)) (1614) 2294[3] 2897[6] 3092[7] 3598[17] 4531[8] (4874) 5393[21] 5786[12] **>103f<**

**Hilarious (IRE)** 4 b f Petorius-Heronwater (IRE) (Ela-Mana-Mou) 1875[5] *2451[4]* 2879[5] *3710[6]* 3997[4] *4339[9]* 4669[6] 5039[8]5286[12] 5928[13] **>36a 36f<**

**Hilbre Island** 4 b c Halling (USA) -Faribole (IRE) (Esprit Du Nord (USA)) 1212[3] 1455[16] 1703[P] 2533[5] 4270[9] **>113f<**

**Hilites (IRE)** 3 ch f Desert King (IRE) -Slayjay (IRE) (Mujtahid (USA)) 1829[3] 2082[11] 2549[3] 2877[10] 3328a[7] 3602[6] 4084[3] 4230[9]4266[4] 4717[9] 5399[8] 5603[14] *6482[6]* **>69a 82f<**

**Hillabilla (IRE)** 2 b f Imperial Ballet (IRE) -London Rose (USA) (Machiavellian (USA)) 4866[15] 5248[16] **>31f<**

**Hill Fairy** 2 ch f Monsun (GER) -Homing Instinct (Arctic Tern (USA)) 2617[6] 4807[4] 5789[5] **>69f<**

**Hillside Heather (IRE)** 2 ch f Tagula (IRE) -Danzig Craft (IRE) (Roi Danzig (USA)) 3055[4] 3370[3] 3583[2] 3950[7] 4212[2] 4575[4] 4875[5] 5143[7]5520[6] (5816) **>70f<**

**Hills Of Aran** 2 b c Sadler s Wells (USA) -Danefair (Danehill (USA)) 6347[4] **>93f<**

**Hills Of Gold** 5 b g Danehill (USA) -Valley Of Gold (FR) (Shirley Heights) 1358[4] (1620) 3235[7] 3714[3] 3869[2] 3985[2] (4877) 4988[4] 5265[6] 5631[6]6069[19] 6210[12] **>86f<**

**Hills Spitfire (IRE)** 3 bb g Kahyasi-Questina (FR) (Rainbow Quest (USA)) 3607[3] **>93f<**

**Hilltime (IRE)** 4 b g Danetime (IRE) -Ceannanas (IRE) (Magical Wonder (USA)) 1974[9] 2656[13] 3314[8] 3559[10] 4301[3] 4577[15] **>53f<**

**Hilltop Rhapsody** 3 b f Bin Ajwaad (IRE) -Saferjel (Elmaamul (USA)) 1395[15] 3297[9] (3592) 5293[14] 5841[4] **>73f<**

**Hilly Be** 3 b f Silver Patriarch (IRE) -Lolita (FR) (Hellios (USA)) 1301[8] **><**

**Hinchley Wood (IRE)** 5 b g Fayruz-Audriano (IRE) (Cyrano De Bergerac) *702[6] 814[10] 858[7] 947[10] 998[5] 1206[5] 1279[4]1406[2] 1497[6]* **>45a<**

**Hinode (IRE)** 3 ch c Vettori (IRE) -Juvenilia (IRE) (Masterclass (USA)) 1395[14] 1794[17] *3707[3]* 5037[5] 5549[4] 5875[18] 6150[7] **>67a 59f<**

**Hip Hop Harry** 4 b c First Trump-Rechanit (IRE) (Local Suitor (USA)) *516[8] 679[2] (872) 887[2]* 1768[18] 2210[14] 4453[5] **>89 a 67+f<**

**Hirayna** 5 b m Doyoun-Himaya (IRE) (Mouktar) 3057[3] 3487[8] 3701[4] 4771[4] 5021[8] 5714[11] 5795[16] **>48f<**

**His Majesty** 2 ch c Case Law-Eternal Triangle (USA) (Barachois (CAN)) *1060[10]* 4054[3] 4651[2] 5022[6] 5369[13] **>51f<**

**Historic Place (USA)** 4 b g Dynaformer (USA) -Captive Island (Northfields (USA)) 2653[2] 3245[4] 3912[8] 5608[3] 6215[15] 6575[6] **>90?f<**

**Hits Only Cash** 2 b c Inchinor-Persian Blue (Persian Bold) 4388[6] 4507[7] 5578[5] 5772[7] 6442[4] 6544[5] **>61f<**

**Hit s Only Money (IRE)** 4 br g Hamas (IRE) -Toordillon (IRE) (Contract Law (USA)) 1367[8] 2201[15] 2469[9] 3235[14] 4179[7] 4510[7] **>110f<**

**Hobart Junction (IRE)** 9 ch g Classic Secret (USA) -Art Duo (Artaius (USA)) 4473[19] **>53a<**

**Hoh Bleu Dee** 3 b g Desert Style (IRE) -Ermine (IRE) (Cadeaux Genereux) 2224[10] 2557[6] 3543[15] 3689[2] (4145) 4435[9] 5092[4] 5538[8] **>87f<**

**Hoh Hedsor** 2 ch f Singspiel (IRE) -Ghassanah (Pas De Seul) 6118[12] 6351[12] **>48f<**

**Hoh Hoh Hoh** 2 ch c Piccolo-Nesting (Thatching) (2263) **>87+f<**

**Hoh My Darling** 2 br f Dansili-Now And Forever (IRE) (Kris) 5088[7] 5840[4] 6197[7] **>60f<**

**Hoh Nelson** 3 b g Halling (USA) -Birsay (Bustino) 1419[3] 2179[9] 3232[8] 4870[6] 5116[4] **>70f<**

**Hoh s Back** 5 b g Royal Applause-Paris Joelle (IRE) (Fairy King (USA)) *512[9] 700[9] 1233[12]* 1451[2] *1598[9]* 1868[6] *2128[10]*2580[7] *2814[5] 2990[10]* 3127[11] 3167[13] 3734[14] 4246[7] 5085[7]5305[8] 5450[5] **>43 a 43f<**

**Holbeck Ghyll (IRE)** 2 ch c Titus Livius (FR) -Crimada (IRE) (Mukaddamah (USA)) 2609[3] 2996[8] 3196[3] **>75f<**

**Holderness Girl** 11 b m Lapierre-Isobel s Choice (Green God) 2445[6] *2990[13]* **><**

**Hold The Line** 3 b g Titus Livius (FR) -Multi-Sofft (Northern State (USA)) *769[6] (1022) 1427[6]* **>64a 53f<**

**Hold Up** 3 ch f Daggers Drawn (USA) -Select Sale (Auction Ring (USA)) 3054[7] 3348[10] 3603[7] 3993[7] 4496[8] 5830[9] 6227[15] **>56?f<**

**Holiday Camp (USA)** 2 b c Chester House (USA) -Arewehavingfunyet (USA) (Sham (USA)) 6342[3] **>71f<**

**Holiday Cocktail** 2 b g Mister Baileys-Bermuda Lily (Dunbeath (USA)) 5555[9] **>22f<**

**Hollingwood Soul** 2 ch f Timeless Times (USA) -Crystal Chandelier (Pivotal) 2194[7] 2364[9] 2773[9] 3506[10] 4010[12] **>32f<**

**Hollow Jo** 4 b g Most Welcome-Sir Hollow (USA) (Sir Ivor (USA)) 1531[15] 1608[9] 2303[4] 2524[9] **>77 f<**

**Holly Rose** 5 b m Charnwood Forest (IRE) -Divina Luna (Dowsing (USA)) 1516[10] 2034[2] 2262[4] 2446[13] 2939[4] 3423[4] 3670[2] 4213[16]*4339[13]* 5021[15] **>54?a 61f<**

**Holly Springs** 2 b f Efisio-Anotheranniversary (Emarati (USA)) 5270[2] 5648[11] 6126[2] **>84f<**

**Holly Walk** 3 ch f Dr Fong (USA) -Holly Blue (Bluebird (USA)) 1363[11] 1561[2] 1947[5] 2199[5] 2760[4] *3026[3] 3379[2]* 3837[13]*4927[3]* **>53a 48 f<**

**Hollywood Critic (USA)** 3 b g Theatrical-Lyphard s Starlite (USA) (Lyphard (USA)) 3002[8] 3475[8] 3899[5] 4829[3] **>62f<**

**Hollywood Henry (IRE)** 4 b g Bahhare (USA) -Takeshi (IRE) (Cadeaux Genereux) (2943) 3660[6] 4238[9] *6154[4] 6551[4]* **>62a 73f<**

**Hollywood Story (USA)** 3 bb f Wild Rush (USA) -Wife For Life (USA) (Dynaformer (USA)) *5 6484a[10]* **>105a 106f<**

**Holy Moon (IRE)** 4 b f Hernando (FR) -Centinela (Caerleon (USA)) 2138a[9] 3137a[5] 5576a[2] 6381a[10] **>96f<**

**Holy Orders (IRE)** 7 b h Unblest-Shadowglow (Shaadi (USA)) 2416a[4] 3076[4] (4977a) 5976a[5] 6382a[7] 6534[4] **>116f<**

**Home Affairs** 2 b c Dansili-Orford Ness (Selkirk (USA)) 3913[5] (5570) 6217[9] **>83 f<**

**Homebred Star** 3 ch g Safawan-Celtic Chimes (Celtic Cone) 3161[7] 3666[7] 4478[10] **>41f<**

**Home By Socks (IRE)** 5 ch m Desert King (IRE) -Propitious (IRE) (Doyoun) 1533[10] 3297[12] **>17a 56f<**

**Home Coming** 6 br g Primo Dominie-Carolside (Music Maestro) *470[6] 527[8]* **>28a 36f<**

**Home Front (IRE)** 3 b g Intikhab (USA) -Felicita (IRE) (Catrail (USA)) 5104[11] **><**

**Homegrown (IRE)** 3 b f Mujadil (USA) -Don t Wary (FR) (Lomond (USA)) 4251a[9] **>30f<**

**Homeric Trojan** 4 ch c Hector Protector (USA) -Housefull (Habitat) *585[6] 902[11]* 1173[12] *1448[6] 1512[6]* **>41a 55f<**

**Homeward (IRE)** 3 ch f Kris-Home Truth (Known Fact (USA)) 4478[5] 5123[13] **>45f<**

**Homme Dangereux** 2 b c Royal Applause-Happy Lady (FR) (Cadeaux Genereux) *2852[3]* 4058[8] *4187[5]* 4953[8] **>54a 33f<**

**Honest Injun** 3 b c Efisio-Sioux (Kris) *(506)* 1506[4] 1831[4] 2134[12] 3714[5] 4050[4] 4780[5] 5092[2] 5706[2]5821[5] **>67a 79f<**

**Honey Bunny** 4 b c Zamindar (USA) -Siddharta (USA) (Chief s Crown (USA)) 2608a[2] 6513a[9] **>103f<**

**Honeymooning** 3 b f Groom Dancer (USA) -Ever Genial (Brigadier Gerard) 2001[7] 2312[4] 3013[3] 3535[8] **>68f<**

**Honey Ryder** 2 b f Compton Place-Urania (Most Welcome) 4099[2] 4815[2] 5890[4] **>81 f<**

**Honey s Gift** 5 b m Terimon-Honeycroft (Crofter (USA)) *947[7]* **>35a 54f<**

**Honeystreet (IRE)** 4 b f Woodborough (USA) -Ring Of Kerry (IRE) (Kenmare (FR)) 2753[13] 3412[13] **>33a 51f<**

**Honeysuckle Player (SWE)** 6 ch h The Noble Player (USA) -Honeysuckle (SWE) (Palace Gold (FR)) *1954a[6]* 4984a[13] 5506a[7] **><**

**Honorine (IRE)** 4 b f Mark Of Esteem (IRE) -Blue Water (USA) (Bering) 2504[6] 4230[10] 5275[5] (5866) 6173[7] 6571[8] **>87f<**

**Honor Rouge (IRE)** 5 ch m Highest Honor (FR) -Ayers Rock (IRE) (In The Wings) 2305[6] 4416[13] **>69 f<**

**Honour High** 2 gr g Cloudings (IRE) -Meant To Be (Morston (FR)) 5467[7] 5871[7] 6060[5] **>53f<**

**Hoops And Blades** 3 gr c Peintre Celebre (USA) -Mare Aux Fees (Kenmare (FR)) 1104[16] 2693[8] 3916[16] 4492[9] 4870[12] **>56f<**

**Hopelessly Devoted** 2 b f Compton Place-Alpi Dora (Valiyar) 3444[10] 3980[6] (4675) *4997[10]* 5234[5] 5520[4] **>31a 55f<**

**Hope Sound (IRE)** 4 b g Turtle Island (IRE) -Lucky Pick (Auction Ring (USA)) 3236[7] 3621[4] **>58f<**

**Horeion Directa (GER)** 5 ch h Big Shuffle (USA) -Hosianna (GER) (Surumu (GER)) 2336a[2] 3361a[5] 4378a[6] 5215a[5] 6109a[5] (6513a) **>113f<**

**Horizontal (USA)** 4 ch g Distant View (USA) -Proud Lou (USA) (Proud Clarion) *574[6] 1228[6]* 1531[8] 1875[12] 2598[5] *3088[13]* **>51a 62f<**

**Hormuz (IRE)** 8 b g Hamas (IRE) -Balqis (USA) (Advocator) 1993[19] 3148[11] 3734[11] 5449[10] **>32 a 32 f<**

**Horner (USA)** 3 b c Rahy (USA) -Dynashore (CAN) (Dynaformer (USA)) 1437[11] 2179[4] 2513[2] (2944) 3210[10] 4176[3] 5402[2] **>88f<**

**Horningsheath** 2 b f Royal Applause-Pacifica (Robellino (USA)) 6171[20] 6439[10] **>55f<**

**Hornpipe** 2 b c Danehill (USA) -Dance Sequence (USA) (Mr Prospector (USA)) 2846[6] (3150) **>79+f<**

**Hors La Loi (FR)** 8 ch g Exit To Nowhere (USA) -Kernia (IRE) (Raise A Cup (USA)) 2210[10] **>65f<**

**Hot Lips Page (FR)** 3 b f Hamas (IRE) -Salt Peanuts (IRE) (Salt Dome (USA)) 2788[5] (3139) 3993[4] 4551[8] 5136[10] **>78+f<**

**Houbara** 3 bb c Octagonal (NZ) -Kissing Cousin (IRE) (Danehill (USA)) *753a[5] 848a[8]* **><**

**Houdini Bay (IRE)** 2 b f Indian Lodge (IRE) -Do The Right Thing (Busted) 1601[8] *2003[8]* 2288[2] **>9a 30f<**

**House Martin** 2 b f Spectrum (IRE) -Guignol (IRE) (Anita s Prince) 4292[4] 5248[10] **>72f<**

**House Of Blues** 3 b g Grand Lodge (USA) -Sartigila (Efisio) 1683[15] *2665[9]* 3529[5] 4421[3] **>58a 51f<**

**House Of Fortune (USA)** 3 br f Free House (USA) -So Fortunate (USA) (Garthorn (USA)) *8* **>93a<**

**Hout Bay** 7 ch g Komaite (USA) -Maiden Pool (Sharpen Up) *(540) 576[3] 680[6]* 4626[2] 4935[4] (5094) (5107) 5579[3] (5605) 6267[6] 6518[7] **>64a 82f<**

**Hov** 4 gr g Petong-Harifa (Local Suitor (USA)) *507[11] 735[8]* 1247[8] 1358[2] 1665[6] 1845[8] 2218[10] **>92a 82f<**

**Hovman (DEN)** 5 ch g Kateb (IRE) -Skee The Feen (Viking (USA)) 4984a[2] *5504a[2]* 5967a[10] **>91f<**

**Howards Dream (IRE)** 6 b g King s Theatre (IRE) -Keiko (Generous (IRE)) 1341[10] 1722[4] 2260[18] 2619[6] 2978[7] 3369[7] 3740[7] 4328[5]5629[4] 6468[8] **>60?f<**

**Howards Princess** 2 gr f Lujain (USA) -Grey Princess (IRE) (Common Grounds) 3445[5] 3950[2] 4986[2] 5475[4] 5797[9] **>69f<**

**Howards Rocket** 3 ch g Opening Verse (USA) -Houston Heiress (USA) (Houston (USA)) 2077[7] 3447[8] 3899[6] 4537[9] 4905[11] **>50f<**

**Hows That** 2 ch f Vettori (IRE) -Royalty (IRE) (Fairy King (USA)) 3918[13] 4292[11] 4761[7] 4967[10] 5192[2] (6093) **>60+f<**

**How s Things** 4 b g Danzig Connection (USA) -Dim Ots (Alhijaz) *862[6]* 3520[14] 4719[7] 5176[10] *6553[2]* **>79a 61f<**

**Hsi Wang Mu (IRE)** 3 ch f Dr Fong (USA) -Oh Hebe (IRE) (Night Shift (USA)) *835[2] 1012[5]* 1222[9] 1529[5] 2425[9] 3190[11] *6580[13]* **>53a 50f<**

**Huboob (FR)** 2 bb g Almutawakel-Atnab (USA) (Riverman (USA)) 5729[11] **>44f<**

**Huggin Mac (IRE)** 3 b f Spectrum (IRE) -Little Love (Warrshan (USA)) 2046[6] 2572[7] **>45f<**

**Hugo The Boss (IRE)** 2 ch g Trans Island-Heartland (Northfields (USA)) *6155[13] 6448[8] 6494[10]* **>45a<**

**Hugs Dancer (FR)** 7 b g Cadeaux Genereux-Embracing (Reference Point) 6528a[5] **>114f<**

**Hugs Destiny (IRE)** 3 b g Victory Note (USA) -Embracing (Reference Point) 2900[5] *3304[2]* **>70a 71f<**

**Hula Ballew** 4 ch f Weldnaas (USA) -Ballon (Persian Bold) 1247[9] 1620[5] 1783[13] 2580[9] 3006[5] 3117[5] 3301[9] (3609) 3921[5]4201[5] 5236[2] 5544[3] 5859[11] **>67f<**

**Hum (IRE)** 3 ch f Cadeaux Genereux-Ensorceleuse (FR) (Fabulous Dancer (USA)) 3609[14] 3875[14] **>58f<**

**Humdinger (IRE)** 4 b f Charnwood Forest (IRE) -High Finish (High Line) *505[11] 952[10] 1016[8]* 4808[12] **>66a 67f<**

**Humid Climate** 4 ch g Desert King (IRE) -Pontoon (Zafonic (USA)) 4908[8] 5590[7] 5866[13] 6266[18] **>85f<**

**Humilis (IRE)** 4 b f Sadler s Wells (USA) -Humble Eight (USA) (Seattle Battle (USA)) 1156a[8] 5162a[14] **>100f<**

**Humility** 3 b f Polar Falcon (USA) -Rich In Love (IRE) (Alzao (USA)) 2165[11] **>39f<**

**Humorous Miss (USA)** 3 b f Distorted Humor (USA) -Starry Miss (USA) (Star De Naskra (USA)) 6254a[6] **>90f<**

**Humourous (IRE)** 2 b c Darshaan-Amusing Time (IRE) (Sadler s Wells (USA)) 4567[5] (5269) 6268[9] **>86f<**

**Hunipot** 2 ch f Aragon-Acinom (Rambo Dancer (CAN)) 1556[7] 1961[9] 2773[11] 3408[8] 3620[6] 4559[13] **>17f<**

**Hunter s Valley** 3 b f Nicolotte-Down The Valley (Kampala) 2479[8] 2765[2] 2911[4] 3320[8] 4813[4] 5223[4] *6015[3]* 6081[15] **>53a 68f<**

**Hunting Lodge (IRE)** 3 ch c Grand Lodge (USA) -Vijaya (USA) (Lear Fan (USA)) 3671[14] **>95f<**

**Hunting Pink** 3 b f Foxhound (USA) -Dancing Bluebell (IRE) (Bluebird (USA)) *587[2] 615[3] 717[4] 828[3]* **>51a 46f<**

**Hurricane Alan (IRE)** 4 b c Mukaddamah (USA) -Bint Al Balad (IRE) (Ahonoora) 1397[3] (1621) 2109[5] 2957[10] 3724[3] 4228[7] 4685[3] 5113[3] 5967a[2]6109a[3] **>119f<**

**Hurricane Coast** 5 b g Hurricane Sky (AUS) -Tread Carefully (Sharpo) *(433) (436) (519) 556[3] (578) 586[3] 607[2] 648[12] 761[9] 841[4](968) 1007[9]* (1531) 1608[6] 1828[6] 3698[4] **>90a 83 f<**

**Hurricane Floyd (IRE)** 6 ch g Pennekamp (USA) -Mood Swings (IRE) (Shirley Heights) 1385[11] 1828[8] 2503[10] 3036[14] 3426[4] 5184[2] 5631[14] *5952[10]* **>40a 86f<**

**Hursley** 2 b f Compton Place-Kilcoy (USA) (Secreto (USA)) 4335[14] 4705[10] **>55f<**

**Husky (POL)** 6 b g Special Power-Hallo Bambina (POL) (Neman (POL)) *446[5] (1404) 1691[3] 2053[13]* 4436[5] 4519[4] **>50 a 55f<**

**Huxley (IRE)** 5 b g Danehill Dancer (IRE) -Biddy Mulligan (Ballad Rock) 1284[12] 1456[20] 1708[9] 2084[18] 3911[4] 4142[8] (5544) 6069[16] **>87f<**

**Hymn Of Love (IRE)** 4 ch f Barathea (IRE) -Perils Of Joy (IRE) (Rainbow Quest (USA)) 2318a[5] **>100f<**

**Hymn Of Victory (IRE)** 2 b c Bluebird (USA) -Vaga Follia (IRE) (Alzao (USA)) 2352[9] 2579[5] 3080[2] 3605[6] 5513[2] 5797[12] 6270[4] **>66f<**

**Hymns And Arias** 3 b f Mtoto-Ewenny (Warrshan (USA)) *810[9] 1031[4]* 1267[14] 1529[10] *1916[7]* 2657[10] **>44a 30f<**

**Hypnotic** 2 ch c Lomitas-Hypnotize (Machiavellian (USA)) *3847[4] (4023) (4601) 5051[3]* (5313a) 5666a[7] **>94a 98f<**

**I**

**Iamback** 4 b f Perugino (USA) -Smouldering (IRE) (Caerleon (USA)) *424[2] 529[6] (656) 903[6] 972[7] 1090[4] 1177[3]* 1582[8]*(1888) (2015) 2053[9] 2456[9]* 6146[15] *6295[12]* **>54a 49f<**

**Iam Foreverblowing** 2 ch f Dr Fong (USA) -Farhana (Fayruz) 1299[5] 1798[4] 2263[5] *2453[10]* 2959[15] 4637[11] 4875[9] **>13f<**

**Ianina (IRE)** 4 b f Eagle Eyed (USA) -Ice Dream (GER) (Mondrian (GER)) 1776a[7] 2242[7] 5488a[5] 6258a[8] **>80f<**

**Ibda Ae (KSA)** 3 b f Namaqualand (USA) -Fantasy Trick (FR) (Clever Trick (USA)) *711a[4] 1005a[6]* **>96a<**

**Iberus (GER)** 6 b g Monsun (GER) -Iberica (GER) (Green Dancer (USA)) 1456[25] 1821[18] 2215[7] 3101[5] 3470[4] 5267[2] 5764[7] 6152[10]6311[4] **>73f<**

**Ibisco (GER)** 4 b c Royal Solo (IRE) -Itza (GER) (Local Suitor (USA)) 4378a[14] **>67f<**

**Icannshift (IRE)** 4 b g Night Shift (USA) -Cannikin (IRE) (Lahib (USA)) *448[10] 554[9] 602[6]* 1298[8] 1522[2] (1611) 1856[3] 2302[12] 2537[3]2573[6] 2810[3] *3088[11]* 3662[3] 3827[10] 4262[4] 5350[2] 5493[6]5733[5] **>58a 62f<**

**Icarus Dream (IRE)** 3 ch g Intikhab (USA) -Nymphs Echo (IRE) (Mujtahid (USA)) 4192[11] 4736[9] 5116[10] **>78f<**

**Ice And Fire** 5 b g Cadeaux Genereux-Tanz (IRE) (Sadler s Wells (USA)) *902[10]* **>4a 57f<**

**Icecap** 4 b f Polar Falcon (USA) -Warning Light (High Top) *3804[16]* (4414) 4771[13] 5260[15] 5425[7] **>62a 65f<**

**Ice Cube (SAF)** 3 ch c Western Winter (USA) -Annie (SAF) (Trigger Finger (USA)) *691a[9] 754a[5]* 850a[6] **>84a 104f<**

**Iced Diamond (IRE)** 5 b g Petardia-Prime Site (IRE) (Burslem) *(694) 772[9]* 2806[7] 3321[7] 3734[7] 3841[9] 4199[4] 4360[4] 4877[7]5235[2] 5411[6] *6499[5]* **>62a 59f<**

**Ice Dragon** 3 b f Polar Falcon (USA) -Qilin (IRE) (Second Set (IRE)) 2596[7] 5020[8] **>62a 57f<**

**Iceman** 2 b c Polar Falcon (USA) -Virtuous (Exit To Nowhere (USA)) 1853[2] (2111) (2954) 5437[2] 5918[3] 6217[4] **>117f<**

**Icenaslice (IRE)** 3 b f Fayruz-Come Dancing (Suave Dancer (USA)) 1934[9] (2661) *2850[4]* (3270) 3838[8] 4289[4] 4862[9] 5837[4] **>52a 74f<**

**Iceni Warrior** 2 b g Lake Coniston (IRE) -Swing Job (Ezzoud (IRE)) *1117[5]* **>57a<**

**Ice Palace** 4 ch f Polar Falcon (USA) -White Palace (Shirley Heights) 2196[3] 2733[2] (3311) 5025[4] 5941[17] **>102f<**

**Ice Planet** 3 b c Polar Falcon (USA) -Preference (Efisio) 1174[15] 1472[3] 1771[5] 3954[14] 4051[5] **>68f<**

**Ice Ruby** 2 b f Polar Prince (IRE) -Simply Style (Bairn (USA)) 1415[9] 1589[9] *2003[7]* **>7a 32f<**

**Icey Run** 4 b g Runnett-Polar Storm (IRE) (Law Society (USA)) 4513[7] *5645[6]* **>42a 34f<**

**Icing** 2 br f Polar Falcon (USA) -Dance Steppe (Rambo Dancer (CAN)) 3741[6] *4598[4] (5380)* 5938[11] **>77a 64f<**

**Idaho Quest** 7 br h Rainbow Quest (USA) -Javandra (USA) (Lyphard (USA)) 1110a[7] 1578a[3] 2337a[6] **>119f<**

**Idealist (GER)** 2 b c Tiger Hill (IRE) -I Go Bye (GER) (Don t Forget Me) 6259a[2] **>105f<**

**Idealistic (IRE)** 3 b f Unfuwain (USA) -L Ideale (USA) (Alysheba (USA)) 1674[10] 2298[2] 2832[2] 4028[2] (4775) **>80f<**

**Idle Journey (IRE)** 3 b g Mujadil (USA) -Camassina (IRE) (Taufan (USA)) 5795[4] 6230[8] **>51f<**

**Idle Power (IRE)** 6 b g Common Grounds-Idle Fancy (Mujtahid (USA)) 1504[8] 1927[10] (2399) (2441) 2682[14] 2838[2] 3691[3] 3941[8] 4291[9] 5077[2]*(5379)* (5887) *6277[11] 6496[9]* **>89+a 89f<**

**Iduna (GER)** 3 b f Waky Nao-Isuma (GER) (Surumu (GER)) 2157a[5] 2723a[6] 3504a[5] 6107a[7] **>86f<**

**If By Chance** 6 ch g Risk Me (FR) -Out Of Harmony (Song) *480[10]* 1175[2] 1361[4] 1665[4] (1974) 2303[8] 2490[15] *6293[8]* 6518[4] **>75a 76f<**

**Iffraaj** 3 b c Zafonic (USA) -Pastorale (Nureyev (USA)) 1408[4] **>94f<**

**Iffy** 3 b g Orpen (USA) -Hopesay (Warning) *675[4]* 3527[7] 3875[4] (4079) 4443[3] *6549[8]* **>59a 66f<**

**Ifit (IRE)** 2 b f Inchinor-Robin (Slip Anchor) 4016[12] 4364[8] 5179[9] 5368[10] 6195[3] **>54f<**

**If Paradise** 3 b c Compton Place-Sunley Stars (Sallust) (1323) 2080[9] 2636[6] 2955[13] 4269[9] 5418[9] 5712[2] 6177[2] 6341[8] **>105f<**

**Ifteradh** 3 b c Bahhare (USA) -Matila (IRE) (Persian Bold) *(1096)* 1408[2] **>77a 96f<**

**Iftikhar (USA)** 5 b g Storm Cat (USA) -Muhbubh

(USA) (Blushing Groom (FR)) 2272[9] 3520[16] 3929[14] 4556[4] 5320[7] 5867[10] 6201[14] 6467[12] >57f<

**Ignition** 2 ch f Rock City-Fire Sprite (Mummy s Game) 4099[5] 4930[4] 5198[3] 5447[4] 5636[10] 6003[10] >58f<

**I Got Rhythm** 6 gr m Lycius (USA) -Eurythmic (Pharly (FR)) 1534[9] 1668[8] >50f<

**I Had A Dream** 3 b f Bering-Dirigeante (FR) (Lead On Time (USA)) 4899a[9] 6173[2] 6571[7] >96f<

**Ikan (IRE)** 4 br f Sri Pekan (USA) -Iktidar (Green Desert (USA)) *1061[10]* 1391[3] 1685[9] 2041[16] >75a 100f<

**Ikhtyar (IRE)** 4 b c Unfuwain (USA) -Sabria (USA) (Miswaki (USA)) 1705[3] 2109[6] 2559[2] 2968[3] 3540[6] 3978[3] >122 f<

**Iktibas** 3 b c Sadler s Wells (USA) -Bint Shadayid (USA) (Nashwan (USA)) (5545) 6458[5] >89+f<

**Iktitaf (IRE)** 3 b c Alhaarth (IRE) -Istibshar (USA) (Mr Prospector (USA)) 1371[8] 1683[3] (1926) 2281[7] 5942[13] 6332[3] >88f<

**Il Bimbo De Oro** 5 ch h Hernando (FR) -Cue The Groom (USA) (Blushing Groom (FR)) 2340a[3] >101f<

**Il Cavaliere** 9 b g Mtoto-Kalmia (Miller s Mate) 1958[5] 2731[8] >68f<

**Il Colosseo (IRE)** 2 b g Spectrum (IRE) -Valley Lights (IRE) (Dance Of Life (USA)) 5128[3] 6139[4] *(6536)* >78+a 78f<

**Ile Facile (IRE)** 3 b c Turtle Island (IRE) -Easy Pop (IRE) (Shernazar) *438[2] 529[4] 597[2] 668[4] (856) 1239[9]* 2732[2] 3231[7]3475[4] (3837) 4027[4] 4300[5] >73a 76f<

**Ile Michel** 7 b g Machiavellian (USA) -Circe s Isle (Be My Guest (USA)) *837[8]* 2206[16] 2612[4] 2856[3] 3159[8] 5698[15] *5952[5] 6062[6]6553[9]* >70a 80f<

**Ile Rousse** 4 gr f Danehill (USA) -Sporades (USA) (Vaguely Noble) 4566a[12] >84f<

**Iles Marquises (IRE)** 3 ch f Unfuwain (USA) -Good To Dance (IRE) (Groom Dancer (USA)) 3258a[7] 5969a[7] >92f<

**I Ll Do It Today** 3 b g Mtoto-Knayton Lass (Presidium) 6310[6] 6519[7] >62f<

**Illeana (GER)** 3 ch f Lomitas-Illyria (IRE) (Nashwan (USA)) 1189[4] 1688[7] 1998[14] (2584) 3421[9] *3638[3]* 4302[11] 5889[8] >63a 62f<

**I Ll Fly** 4 ch g Polar Falcon (USA) -I Ll Try (Try My Best (USA)) 1612[8] >43f<

**Illicium (IRE)** 5 b m Fourstars Allstar (USA) -Sweet Mignonette (Tina s Pet) 1344[6] 1557[9] 1786[7] 2462[P] >34f<

**Illusionist** 6 b g Mujtahid (USA) -Merlin s Fancy (Caerleon (USA)) *685[9] 776[5] 879[5]* >16a<

**Illusive (IRE)** 7 b g Night Shift (USA) -Mirage (Red Sunset) *596[12] 680[15] 771[3] 928[5] 1057[11] 1087[7] 1121[2]1204[2] 1230[6]* 2166[2] *2404[9]* 3010[13] 3428[4] 3606[14] *4026[5]* >67 a 69f<

**Illustrious Duke** 6 b g Dancing Spree (USA) -Killick (Slip Anchor) *576[13] 698[10] 903[10] 1080[11] 1176[6] 1233[11] 1446[2]1625[7]* >45a 40 f<

**Illustrious Miss (USA)** 3 b f Kingmambo (USA) -Our Wildirish Rose (USA) (Irish Tower (USA)) (1441) (1964) 2330a[3] 3600[5] >111+f<

**Iloveturtle (IRE)** 4 b g Turtle Island (IRE) -Gan Ainm (IRE) (Mujadil (USA)) 1103[14] *1698[3]* 2689[5] 4015[U] 4210[6] 4609[6] >42a 54f<

**Il Pranzo** 2 b c Piccolo-St Helena (Monsanto (FR)) *1276[8]* 3805[6] 4064[3] 4474[5] 5507[7] 6080[4] *(6359)* 6442[3] >68a 71f<

**Iltravitore (IRE)** 3 ch g Daggers Drawn (USA) -May Hinton (Main Reef) 2301[7] 2765[8] 4845[5] 5253[14] 5737[14] 6079[11] >59f<

**Ilwadod** 3 b g Cadeaux Genereux-Wedoudah (IRE) (Sadler s Wells (USA)) (1946) 2037[2] 2546[2] 2821[2] 3020[2] 3479[7] >33a 64f<

**I m A Dark Horse** 3 b g Alzao (USA) -Romoosh (Formidable (USA)) 2133[11] 2934[5] 3625[7] >39f<

**I m Aimee** 2 ch f Timeless Times (USA) -Marfen (Lochnager) *1060[2]* 1324[6] 1449[3] 1878[7] 2268[4] 2376[7] 3704[2] 3924[2]4046[2] 4358[2] 4676[3] 4875[7] 5174[4] 5334[4] 5509[5] >71a 69f<

**I m Dancing** 3 b f Polish Precedent (USA) -Dancing Heights (IRE) (High Estate) *1422[7]* 1995[2] >30a 64f<

**Imdina (IRE)** 3 b f Soviet Star (USA) -Stellina (IRE) (Caerleon (USA)) 4588a[9] >75f<

**Imoya (IRE)** 5 b m Desert King (IRE) -Urgent Liaison (IRE) (High Estate) 1634a[3] 2498a[5] >102?f<

**Impaciente Gg (URU)** 4 ch c Gulpha George (USA) -Impudica (URU) (((( (USA)) (USA)) (USA)) ( 692a[9] 854a[8] 922a[8] >85f<

**Impeller (IRE)** 5 ch g Polish Precedent (USA) -Almaaseh (IRE) (Dancing Brave (USA)) 1456[10] 2201[7] 2534[2] 2637[6] 2969[9] 3937[5] 4214[2] 4287[2](5401) 5761[3] 5941[11] 6475[2] >100+f<

**Imperative (USA)** 4 ch g Woodman (USA) -Wandesta (Nashwan (USA)) *651[4] 797[6] 863[3] 969[3]* >64a 58f<

**Imperatrice** 2 b f Emperor Jones (USA) -Fine Honor (FR) (Highest Honor (FR)) *4924[15]* 5218[6] 5746[6] 5910[17] >41f<

**Imperial Brief (IRE)** 2 br g Imperial Ballet (IRE) -Lyphards Goddess (IRE) (Lyphard s Special (USA)) 5681a[8] 6503a[2] >96f<

**Imperial Dancer** 6 b h Primo Dominie-Gorgeous Dancer (IRE) (Nordico (USA)) 1455[3] 2156a[6] 2639[9] 3540[7] 4385a[3] 4834[7] 5225[3] 5483a[6]5611[2] 5981a[14] 6260a[5] >118f<

**Imperial Dragon (USA)** 4 b g Meadowlake (USA) -South Cove (Forli (ARG)) *1059[9]* 1174[4] 1352[10] >44a 56f<

**Imperial Dynasty (USA)** 2 b c Devil s Bag (USA) -Leasears (USA) (Lear Fan (USA)) 3248[9] 4454[5] 4900[10] 5240[11] >60f<

**Imperial Echo (USA)** 3 b g Labeeb-Regal Baby (USA) (Northern Baby (CAN)) 1745[7] 2309[9] 2981[4] 3122[9] 3737[2] 4133[2] 4289[17] 4576[3]4862[4] (5193) 5786[3] 6517[4] 6532[5] >91f<

**Imperialism (USA)** 3 gr c Langfuhr (CAN) -Bodhavista (USA) (Pass The Tab (USA)) *1781a[3] 2139a[5]* >117a<

**Imperialistic (IRE)** 3 b f Imperial Ballet (IRE) -Shefoog (Kefaah (USA)) 1129[4] (1322) (1558) 2641[8] 4948[5] 5194[5] 5769[3] 6255a[7] 6571[6] >76a 102+f<

**Imperial Miss (IRE)** 2 b f Imperial Ballet (IRE) -Miss Flite (IRE) (Law Society (USA)) 2481[11] 3123[6] 3627[8] 4053[6] 4234[11] 5377[17] >65f<

**Imperial Princess (IRE)** 3 b f Imperial Ballet (IRE) -Rose Tint (IRE) (Salse (USA)) *620[13]* >22a 43f<

**Imperial Rose (IRE)** 2 gr f Imperial Ballet (IRE) -Mixwayda (FR) (Linamix (FR)) 4958a[11] >77f<

**Imperial Royale (IRE)** 3 ch g Ali-Royal (IRE) -God Speed Her (Pas De Seul) 2653[5] 3232[9] 3535[6] 3837[10] 4138[8] 4698[13] 5320[10] 5830[12]*5957[7]* >47a 41f<

**Imperial Sound** 2 b c Efisio-Final Trick (Primo Dominie) (3011) 3468[2] 3938[10] (4392) 5392[17] 5515[6] >90f<

**Imperial Stride** 3 b c Indian Ridge-Place De L Opera (Sadler s Wells (USA)) 1410[4] 6219[7] 6474[9] >113+f<

**Imperial Wizard** 3 ch g Magic Ring (IRE) -Paula s Joy (Danehill (USA)) *574[10]* 4440[8] 4845[10] 5338[9] 5794[14] >30a 39f<

**Imperioli** 2 b c Fraam-Jussoli (Don) 4567[13] 5669[6] 6187[18] >39f<

**Imperium** 3 b g Imperial Ballet (IRE) -Partenza (USA) (Red Ransom (USA)) *927[4] 1083[7] 1228[2]* 1313[11] 1689[12] 1854[5] (2033) (2326) 2610[3]2877[12] 3628[7] *3849[10]* 4267[6] 4289[19] 4472[2] 4800 5117[3]5473[14] >73 a 76f<

**Impersonator** 4 b g Zafonic (USA) -Conspiracy (Rudimentary (USA)) 1623[10] 1938[4] 4543[3] 5135[3] 5568[7] 6194[3] >94f<

**Impish Jude** 6 b m Imp Society (USA) -Miss Nanna (Vayrann) 1754[4] >14a 66?f<

**Impressive Flight (IRE)** 5 b m Flying Spur (AUS) -Certain Impression (USA) (Forli (ARG)) 4394[8] 4759[12] 5062[11] 5491[6] 5558[5] 5799[7] 5898[8] >101f<

**Improvise** 2 b f Lend A Hand-Mellow Jazz (Lycius (USA)) 2690[6] *5375[2]* 5720[2] >70+a 78f<

**Impulsive Bid (IRE)** 3 b f Orpen (USA) -Tamburello (IRE) (Roi Danzig (USA)) 1266[4] 1464[12] 2036[2] 3301[15] 3517[5] 3981[9] 4451[11] 5293[9] >51f<

**Imshy (IRE)** 3 ch f Daggers Drawn (USA) -Paganina (FR) (Galetto (FR)) 6175[13] >80f<

**I m So Lucky** 2 b c Zilzal (USA) -City Of Angels (Woodman (USA)) 3080[7] (3679) 5819[2] 6334[4] >91f<

**Im Spartacus** 2 b g Namaqualand (USA) -Captivating (IRE) (Wolfhound (USA)) *1060[8]* 1307[2] (1638) 2086[6] 2478[5] 3242[9] 3677[6] 4166[5] 4482[4](4953) 5292[5] 5810[4] 6129[2] 6334[5] >30a 78f<

**Imtalkinggibberish** 3 b g Pursuit Of Love-Royal Orchid (IRE) (Shalford (IRE)) 1386[7] 2046[5] 2966[8] 4555[2] 4845[11] 5845[5] 6089[4] *6275[2]* >59a 86f<

**Imtihan (IRE)** 5 ch h Unfuwain (USA) -Azyaa (Kris) 1305[7] 2613[11] >44f<

**Imtiyaz (USA)** 5 ro h Woodman (USA) -Shadayid (USA) (Shadeed (USA)) 2398[2] 3661[2] 4525[4] >115f<

**Imtouchingwood** 3 b f Fleetwood (IRE) -Shanuke (IRE) (Contract Law (USA)) 2374[17] ><

**Inagh** 2 b f Tipsy Creek (USA) -Compton Amber (Puissance) 2940[6] 5689[3] *6021[13]* >62f<

**Inamorato (USA)** 4 bb c Tale Of The Cat (USA) -Be My Sweetheart (USA) (No Robbery (USA)) *756a[2] 1142a[5]* >110+a<

**Inca Wood (UAE)** 2 b f Timber Country (USA) -Lady Icarus (Rainbow Quest (USA)) 5023[2] 5398[2] 5729[10] 6111[4] >75f<

**Inch By Inch** 5 b m Inchinor-Maid Welcome (Mummy s Pet) 2875[7] *4025[4]* 4232[18] (5412) (5734) (5849) *(6559)* >68+a 73+f<

**Inchcape Rock** 2 ch c Inchinor-Washm (USA) (Diesis) 2058[8] *4023[9]* 4866[12] 5173[2] 5827[10] >30a 73f<

**Inchconnel** 3 b g Inchinor-Sharanella (Shareef Dancer (USA)) 1116[11] 1387[8] 1946[15] >61f<

**Inchcoonan** 6 b m Emperor Jones (USA) -Miss Ivory Coast (USA) (Sir Ivor) *457[4] 685[4] 941[2] 993[2]* >52a 52f<

**Inchdura** 6 ch g Inchinor-Sunshine Coast (Posse (USA)) 3235[11] 3755[14] 4447[6] 5544[9] 6096[12] *6483[5]* >64a 75 f<

**Incheni (IRE)** 3 b f Nashwan (USA) -Inchmurrin (Lomond (USA)) 1398[2] 1791[14] 2242[3] (2807) 3699[4] 4640[6] >67a 102f<

**Inching** 4 b f Inchinor-Tshusick (Dancing Brave (USA)) *479[4] 896[4] 1018[9] 1178[8]* 2098[14] 2350[17] 2482[2] 2724[6]2800[7] 3084[2] 3147[9] 3307[9] >53a 56f<

**Inchinnan** 7 b m Inchinor-Westering (Auction Ring (USA)) *650[5]* 1660[10] 2038[5] >66a 71f<

**Inchloss (IRE)** 3 b g Imperial Ballet (IRE) -Earth Charter (Slip Anchor) 1111[11] 1325[4] (1749) 2069[2] 2448[10] 2907[10] 3230[6] (3745) 4140[2] 4490[2]5106[4] 5397[12] 5942[16] >88f<

**Inchnadamph** 4 b g Inchinor-Pelf (USA) (Al Nasr (FR)) 1962[6] 2649[2] 3041[2] (3221) (3740) 4155[5] 6074[8] 6527[2] >70+f<

**Inchpast** 3 ch c Inchinor-Victor Ludorum (Rainbow Quest (USA)) 1997[14] 3160[15] 3837[4] (4070) 4346[2] (4630) (5365) (5523) >66a 83+f<

**Incise** 3 ch f Dr Fong (USA) -Pretty Sharp (Interrex (CAN)) 1685[6] 1883[7] 2636[10] 2892[4] 3273[4] 4289[8] 4810[5] >89f<

**Incisor** 3 b g Dracula (AUS) -Last Night s Fun (IRE) (Law Society (USA)) 1465[5] (1643) *(2484) (2667)* 2949[13] >78a 55f<

**Incline (IRE)** 5 b g Danehill (USA) -Shalwar Kameez (IRE) (Sadler s Wells (USA)) *770[6]* >88a 85f<

**Incroyable** 3 gr f Linamix (FR) -Crodelle (IRE) (Formidable (USA)) 5344[2] (5622) 5935[12] >70+f<

**Incursion** 3 b g Inchinor-Morgannwg (IRE) (Simply Great (FR)) (2001) 2281[10] 3152[3] 3806[7] 4915[7] >87f<

**Indalo Grey (IRE)** 8 bb g Toca Madera-Pollyfaster (Polyfoto) *6278[5]* >63a 67f<

**In Deep** 3 b f Deploy-Bobbie Dee (Blakeney) 1108[8] 2676[15] 3160[6] 3908[8] 4806[2] >67 f<

**Independent Spirit** 2 ch g Wolfhound (USA) -Kigema (IRE) (Case Law) 3531[9] 5542[10] *5954[12] 6221[10]* >12a 36f<

**Indesatchel (IRE)** 2 b c Danehill Dancer (IRE) -Floria (IRE) (Petorius) 3965a[3] 4958a[2] 5322a[3] 5680a[2] 6100a[4] >105f<

**Indiana Blues** 3 ch f Indian Ridge-Blue Siren (Bluebird (USA)) 2223[4] 2621[11] 3179[7] 3554[3] 4148[5] 4868[3] 5201[4] 5338[3]5637[2] (5845) *6557[3]* >68a 70f<

**Indian Bazaar (IRE)** 8 ch g Indian Ridge-Bazaar Promise (Native Bazaar) 2246[15] 2724[10] 2885[2] 3084[12] 3126[12] 3307[2] 3593[16] 3772[6]4085[13] 4336[9] 4687[10] 4774[11] 5337[9] 5412[8] 5734[14] >57f<

**Indian Beauty (IRE)** 3 b f Mujadil (USA) -Mary Linda (Grand Lodge (USA)) 6203a[10] >73f<

**Indian Blaze** 10 ch g Indian Ridge-Odile (Green Dancer (USA)) *645[6] 914[2] (929) 966[2] 988[10] 1019[3] 1102[6] 1207[7]*3844[6] *4604[10]* 5795[15] >58a 55 f<

**Indian Call** 3 ch g Classic Cliche (IRE) -Crees Sqaw (Cree Song) 1108[11] 1222[18] 1366[11] *6580[12]* >25a 64f<

**Indian Chase** 7 b g Terimon-Icy Gunner (Gunner B) *1547[2]* 2090[6] 2562[12] 3120[9] 3752[8] 4082[4] *4603[8]* (4870) *5645[2]6159[10]* >48a 54f<

**Indian Dove (IRE)** 2 b f Indian Danehill (IRE) -African Dance (USA) (El Gran Senor (USA)) *5735[6]* 6181[10] >48a 43f<

**Indian Edge** 3 ch g Indian Rocket-Beveled Edge (Beveled (USA)) *1202[9]* 1749[5] 1942[2] 2377[11] 3322[12] 4868[9] 5259[11] *6280[8]* >47a 71f<

**Indian Filly** 3 ch f Indian Ridge-Speremm (IRE) (Sadler s Wells (USA)) 2341a[7] 3569a[6] >81f<

**Indian Haven** 4 ch c Indian Ridge-Madame Dubois (Legend Of France (USA)) 1621[5] 2109[9] 2438a[6] >109f<

**Indian Hope (IRE)** 2 b f Indian Lodge (IRE) -Kingston Cara (USA) (Seattle Slew (USA)) 5330a[7] >36f<

**Indian Lily** 3 ch f Compton Place-Princess Lily (Blakeney) 1293[5] 1519[9] 1906[6] 2942[7] 3530[7] 4708[7] 5575[10] 5791[15] >40f<

**Indian Maiden (IRE)** 4 br f Indian Ridge-Jinsiyah (USA) (Housebuster (USA)) *6461[1]* 3326[4] 3775[11] 4542[11] (6117) >73 a 76f<

**Indian Music** 7 b g Indian Ridge-Dagny Juel (USA) (Danzig (USA)) *810[6] (1191)* 1283[5] *1445[4] 1696[4] 1915[3] 2012[3] 2664[2]3024[4] 3277[6] 3381[2] 3616[7]* 3836[12] *4879[6]* 5081[5]5833[10] 6469[10] >61?a 45f<

**Indiannie Star** 2 b f Fraam-Ajig Dancer (Niniski (USA)) 2083[2] (2376) 2532[6] 2970[13] 3388a[5] (3696) 3907[3] 4552[5] >91f<

**Indian Oak (IRE)** 3 b f Indian Rocket-Marathon Maid (Kalaglow) *678[8] 764[7] 895[13] 965[14]* >26a<

**Indi Ano Star (IRE)** 3 b g Indian Rocket-Audriano (IRE) (Cyrano De Bergerac) 1174[6] 1325[6] 1528[6] 2259[8] 2658[5] 3007[5] 6516[9] >54f<

**Indian Pearl (IRE)** 2 b f Indian Lodge (IRE) -Thatchabella (IRE) (Thatching) 2427[8] ><

**Indian Pipe Dream (IRE)** 2 br c Indian Danehill (IRE) -Build A Dream (USA) (Runaway Groom (CAN)) 5268[9] 5871[6] >63f<

**Indian Shores** 5 b m Forzando-Cottonwood (Teenoso (USA)) *407[9] 510[9] 638[6] 725[8] 876[9] 951[12]* 2473[18]4542[16] 6141[10] >33a 38f<

**Indian s Landing (IRE)** 3 b g Barathea (IRE) -We Ve Just Begun (USA) (Huguenot (USA)) 5705[10] 6310[3] 6519[5] >72?f<

**Indian Smoke** 2 b g Makbul-Indian Flower (Mansingh (USA)) 2522[16] >33f<

**Indian Solitaire (IRE)** 5 b g Bigstone (IRE) -Terrama Sioux (Relkino) 1103[3] 2022[9] 2982[6] 3166[7] 6192[9] >75a 82f<

**Indian Spark** 10 ch g Indian Ridge-Annes Gift (Ballymoss) 1211[4] 1353[7] 2065[4] 2293[4] 2625[6] 3074[11] 3266[11] 3754[10]4152[9] 4394[6] 4837[8] 5603[23] 5949[7] 6517[9] >75f<

**Indian Steppes (FR)** 5 b m Indian Ridge-Ukraine Venture (Slip Anchor) 2117[6] 2473[6] 2670[4] 3326[3] 3914[7] 4090[6] 6117[3] >82a 82 f<

**Indian Trail** 4 ch g Indian Ridge-Take Heart (Electric) 3455[9] (3941) >96f<

**Indian Warrior** 8 b g Be My Chief (USA) -Wanton (Kris) *(441) 536[9] 725[10] 859[4] 990[8] 1445[5] 1692[5]* 1986[15]2387[14] 6229[3] >42a 44f<

**Indian Welcome** 5 ch g Most Welcome-Qualitair Ridge (Indian Ridge) *1118[8]* >84a 70f<

**Indian Well (IRE)** 2 b g Indian Lodge (IRE) -Pride Of Pendle (Grey Desire) 5200[14] >49f<

**Indibar (IRE)** 3 b g Indian Ridge-Barbara Frietchie (IRE) (Try My Best (USA)) 2555[8] >6f<

**Indibraun (IRE)** 2 b g Indian Rocket-The Aspecto Girl (IRE) (Alzao (USA)) 1170[5] (2234) 2447[4] 3145[4] *4186[8]* 4907[3] 5059[4] 5617[12] *6022[6]* >45a 74f<

**Indiena** 2 ch f Indian Ridge-Aliena (IRE) (Grand Lodge (USA)) 3676[4] 3904[5] 4541[2] 4876[4] 5391[2] 5848[3] >76f<

**Individual Talents (USA)** 4 ch f Distant View (USA) -Indigenous (USA) (Lyphard (USA)) 1539[8] 2116[16] 2277[8] >76df<

**Indonesia** 2 ch c Lomitas-Idraak (Kris) 5142[8] 5522[8] 6067[5] >69f<

**Indrani** 3 b f Bijou D Inde-Tea And Scandals (USA) (Key To The Kingdom (USA)) *561[13] 751[6] 958[4] 1047[8] 1236[7] 1571[4] 1725[7]*1985[2] *2187[8]* 3530[5] 3877[9] 4650[8] 4708[9] 5026[2] 5552[13] >45a 46f<

**Indrapura Star (USA)** 4 b g Foxhound (USA) -Royal Recall (USA) (Native Royalty (USA)) *877[6] 997[7]* >28f<

**In Dream S (IRE)** 2 b g Dr Fong (USA) -No Sugar Baby (FR) (Crystal Glitters (USA)) 2205[8] 3588[15] 5467[8] 5996[5] *6153[8]* >53a 59f<

**Indy Groove (USA)** 4 ch f A.P. Indy (USA) -Niner s Home (USA) (Forty Niner (USA)) *6484a[6]* >99a<

**Inescapable (USA)** 3 b c Cape Town (USA) -Danyross (IRE) (Danehill (USA)) 4144[9] 4337[8] 4741[4] 5260[19] (5702) 5927[8] 6146[14] >57f<

**In Every Street (USA)** 3 br f Favorite Trick (USA) -Hit The Bid (USA) (Lear Fan (USA)) *3848[7]* 4141[6] >37+a 47f<

**In Excelsis (USA)** 2 b c Fusaichi Pegasus (USA) -Lakeway (USA) (Seattle Slew (USA)) 3071[5] 5678a[5] >97f<

**Infidelity (IRE)** 3 b f Bluebird (USA) -Madaniyya (USA) (Shahrastani (USA)) *704[6] 822[8]* 1108[10] 1899[8] 2197[6] 2446[10] 2974[6] 3007[3]3443[5] 5374[16] 5459[4] *5957[9] 6549[4]* >58a 61+f<

**Ingleton** 2 b c Komaite (USA) -Dash Cascade (Absalom) 4804[7] 5319[4] (5578) (6042) (6188) >97f<

**Inglewood** 4 ch g Fleetwood (IRE) -Preening (Persian Bold) *426[7]* >12a 42?f<

**Ingrandire (JPN)** 5 b h White Muzzle-Marilyn Momoko (JPN) (Real Shadai (USA)) 2998[9] >120f<

**Inhabitant** 2 ch c Zafonic (USA) -Infringe (Warning) (3790a) 4382a[2] >100f<

**Inistrahull Island (IRE)** 4 b g Flying Spur (AUS) -Dolcezza (FR) (Lichine (USA)) *596[3] 624[6] 745[11]* 2979[6] 3247[15] >65a 60f<

**Inka Dancer (IRE)** 2 ch f Intikhab (USA) -Grannys Reluctance (IRE) (Anita s Prince) 5507[3] 5825[4] 6125[3] >69f<

**Ink In Gold (IRE)** 3 b g Intikhab (USA) -Your Village (IRE) (Be My Guest (USA)) 2517[10] 5086[5] 5196[9] 5693[11] 6058[11] *6361[4] 6404[3]* >48a 55f<

**In Luck** 6 b m In The Wings-Lucca (Sure Blade (USA)) *505[7]* >46a 71f<

**Inmom (IRE)** 3 b f Barathea (IRE) -Zakuska (Zafonic (USA)) 1945[3] 2235[11] *2814[4]* 3231[6] 3473[6] *4190[14]* 5110[18] 6519[6] >57a 63f<

**Innclassic (IRE)** 3 b f Stravinsky (USA) -Kyka (USA) (Blushing John (USA)) 2080[10] 2741[17] *2849[3]* (3338) *3801[2]* 4044[8] 4622[9] 6117[15] *6274[7]6538[9]* >68a 66f<

**Inn For The Dancer** 2 b g Groom Dancer (USA) -Lady Joyce (FR) (Galetto (FR)) *6479[8]* >52a<

**Innocent Rebel (USA)** 3 ch c Swain (IRE) -Cadeaux D Amie (USA) (Lyphard (USA)) 2204[8] *2486[4]* 4972[3] 5875[10] >66a 60f<

**Innocent Splendour** 2 b f Mtoto-Maureena (IRE) (Grand Lodge (USA)) 4234[2] (4966) 5885[7] >79f<

**Innpursuit** 2 b c Inchinor-Quest For The Best (Rainbow Quest (USA)) *6479[7]* >65a<

**Innstyle** 3 b f Daggers Drawn (USA) -Tarneem (USA) (Zilzal (USA)) 3085[6] 3344[10] 5219[7] 5337[3] 5512[8] 5737[15] (6079) *6222[9] 6557[10]* >43a 68f<

**In Rhubarb** 2 ch g Piccolo-Versami (USA) (Riverman (USA)) 4064[6] 5816[8] 6008[7] >45f<

**Insignia (IRE)** 2 b c Royal Applause-Amathea (FR) (Exit To Nowhere (USA)) 2208[5] 4481[5] *5053[6]* >50a 59f<

**Insignificance** 4 b g Bishop Of Cashel-Summer Pageant (Chief s Crown (USA)) *909[7] 929[9]* >41a 49f<

**Insinuation (IRE)** 2 b f Danehill (USA) -Hidden Meaning (USA) (Gulch (USA)) 5272[6] >69f<

**Inspector Blue** 6 ch g Royal Academy (USA) -Blue Siren (Bluebird (USA)) 4499[10] >24f<

**In Spirit (IRE)** 6 b g Distinctly North (USA) -June Goddess (Junius (USA)) *505[9]* >68a 68f<

**Instant Recall (IRE)** 3 ch c Indian Ridge-Happy Memories (IRE) (Thatching) *1052[3] (1202)* 1408[10] 1881[4] 2082[5] 2576[4] 3317[5] *(3420)* 3845[2]4051[4] 4717[7] *5379[11]* >88a 84f<

**Instinct** 3 b g Zafonic (USA) -Gracious Gift (Cadeaux Genereux) *816[5] 982[7]* 1184[3] 1270[9] 2063[10] 2614[12] 4265[3] 4470[3]4868[2] (5551) 6001[14] >52a 65f<

**Instructor** 3 ch g Groom Dancer (USA) -Doctor s Glory (USA) (Elmaamul (USA)) *1096[2] (1227)* 2202[16] 2560[8] 5887[10] >78a 74f<

**Insubordinate** 3 ch g Subordination (USA) -Manila Selection (USA) (Manila (USA)) 1214[16] (2036) 6138[8] >45a 65f<

**Intavac Boy** 3 ch g Emperor Fountain-Altaia (FR) (Sicyos (USA)) 1975[6] 2586[6] 3512[4] 4489[11] 5859[2] 6271[2] >69f<

**Intellibet One** 4 b f Compton Place-Safe House

(Lyphard (USA)) 2656$^{15}$ 3126$^{11}$ 3524$^{3}$ 3593$^{4}$ 3810$^{7}$ 4013$^{9}$ 4232$^{21}$ 4400$^{10}$ >**52 a 65f**<

**Intendant (GER)** 3 b c Lando (GER) -Incenza (GER) (Local Suitor (USA)) 2926a$^{4}$ 3565a$^{16}$ (4385a) >**116f**<

**Intended** 2 b f Singspiel (IRE) -Introducing (Mtoto) 5247$^{11}$ >**65f**<

**Intensity** 8 b g Bigstone (IRE) -Brillante (FR) (Green Dancer (USA)) 867$^{3}$ 902$^{9}$ 1109$^{16}$ 1463$^{2}$ 1644$^{11}$ >**62a 64f**<

**Interceptor** 4 ch c Hector Protector (USA) -Moorish Idol (Aragon) 1762$^{11}$ >**94 f**<

**Interim Payment (USA)** 2 b f Red Ransom (USA) -Interim (Sadler s Wells (USA)) 5368$^{5}$ >**70f**<

**Internationalguest (IRE)** 5 b g Petardia-Banco Solo (Distant Relative) 418$^{11}$ 523$^{2}$ 600$^{14}$ 677$^{8}$ 706$^{7}$ 872$^{2}$ 1114$^{16}$1272$^{10}$ 3238$^{5}$ 3591$^{5}$ 3985$^{5}$ 4616$^{14}$ 5158$^{8}$ 5739$^{13}$ 6266$^{12}$ >**87a 87f**<

**Interstice** 7 b g Never So Bold-Mainmast (Bustino) 455$^{3}$ 581$^{6}$ 800$^{5}$ >**58a 55f**<

**Inter Vision (USA)** 4 b g Cryptoclearance (USA) -Fateful (USA) (Topsider (USA)) 1343$^{11}$ 1500$^{14}$ 2132$^{5}$ 3098$^{11}$ 3778$^{7}$ 4308$^{4}$ 4394$^{2}$ 4577$^{10}$5440$^{7}$ 5799$^{10}$ >**95f**<

**Interwoven (IRE)** 2 b c Woodman (USA) -Woven Silk (USA) (Danzig (USA)) 5125$^{10}$ 6145$^{16}$ >**59f**<

**In The Fan (USA)** 2 b g Lear Fan (USA) -Dippers (USA) (Polish Numbers (USA)) 3093$^{2}$ (3870) 4295$^{3}$ 4807$^{2}$ >**92f**<

**In The Know** 2 b c Desert Prince (IRE) -Evocatrice (Persepolis (FR)) 6569$^{11}$ >**48f**<

**In The Lead (USA)** 2 bb f Bahri (USA) -Air De Noblesse (USA) (Vaguely Noble) 5646$^{7}$ >**59f**<

**In The Pink (IRE)** 4 gr f Indian Ridge-Norfolk Lavender (CAN) (Ascot Knight (CAN)) 1877$^{8}$ 2284$^{17}$ (3047) 3301$^{2}$ 3457$^{10}$ 4148$^{2}$ 4551$^{7}$ 5155$^{4}$ 5614$^{5}$5861$^{3}$ >**79f**<

**In The Ribbons** 2 ch f In The Wings-My Mariam (Salse (USA)) 6503a$^{3}$ >**88?f**<

**In The Shadows** 2 b f Lujain (USA) -Addicted To Love (Touching Wood (USA)) 5068$^{7}$ 5695$^{12}$ 6010$^{13}$ >**22a 36f**<

**In The Stars (IRE)** 6 ch g Definite Article-Astronomer Lady (IRE) (Montekin) 623$^{8}$ >**46a 46f**<

**Intitnice (IRE)** 3 b g Danehill Dancer (IRE) -Gathering Place (USA) (Hawaii) 425$^{12}$ 620$^{11}$ 4147$^{11}$ 4674$^{17}$ >**39a 51f**<

**Into The Breeze (IRE)** 4 b g Alzao (USA) -Catalane (USA) (Septieme Ciel (USA)) 2283$^{20}$ >**83 a 101f**<

**Into The Dark** 3 ch c Rainbow Quest (USA) -Land Of Dreams (Cadeaux Genereux) (3297) (3915) (5226) (5629) >**117f**<

**Into The Shadows** 4 ch f Safawan-Shadows Of Silver (Carwhite) 1528$^{3}$ 1786$^{3}$ 2077$^{4}$ (6095) (6457) >**78f**<

**Intoxicating** 2 b c Mujahid (USA) -Salalah (Lion Cavern (USA)) (3228) 3748$^{3}$ >**84f**<

**Intrepid Jack** 2 b c Compton Place-Maria Theresa (Primo Dominie) 6351$^{13}$ >**35f**<

**Intricate Web (IRE)** 8 b g Warning-In Anticipation (IRE) (Sadler s Wells (USA)) (507) (643) 735$^{2}$ 971$^{4}$ 1321$^{6}$ 1604$^{7}$ (2142) 2271$^{3}$ 2687$^{3}$ 2894$^{12}$(3097) 3477$^{10}$ 4319$^{12}$ 4540$^{15}$ 5590$^{5}$ 5768$^{6}$ 6043$^{9}$ >**93a 88f**<

**Intrigued** 2 gr f Darshaan-Last Second (IRE) (Alzao (USA)) 5109$^{3}$ (5398) 5979a$^{4}$ >**106f**<

**Intriguing Glimpse** 3 bb f Piccolo-Running Glimpse (IRE) (Runnett) 1907$^{3}$ 2181$^{2}$ 2326$^{2}$ 2889$^{2}$ 4267$^{7}$ >**71a 80f**<

**Introduction** 3 b g Opening Verse (USA) -Cartuccia (IRE) (Doyoun) 1019$^{9}$ 2740$^{13}$ 3984$^{10}$ 4867$^{5}$ 5069$^{9}$ >**41a 22f**<

**In Tune** 4 b g Distinctly North (USA) -Lingering (Kind Of Hush) 1308$^{14}$ 1856$^{16}$ 2123$^{13}$ 2833$^{8}$ 3697$^{10}$ 3934$^{11}$ >**61a 29f**<

**Invader** 8 b g Danehill (USA) -Donya (Mill Reef (USA)) 410$^{7}$ 577$^{8}$ 641$^{6}$ 775$^{10}$ 2560$^{9}$ 3086$^{8}$ (3419) 3842$^{10}$4462$^{6}$ 5275$^{6}$ 5403$^{8}$ 5841$^{14}$ >**84a 68f**<

**Invasian (IRE)** 3 ch c Desert Prince (IRE) -Jarrayan (Machiavellian (USA)) (2654) 3017$^{2}$ 3943$^{8}$ 4268$^{15}$ (4709) 5106$^{2}$ 6170a$^{13}$ >**103+f**<

**Inver Gold** 7 ch h Arazi (USA) -Mary Martin (Be My Guest (USA)) 478$^{7}$ >**83a 67f**<

**Invertiel (USA)** 2 br c Royal Academy (USA) -Intriguing (USA) (Deputy Minister (CAN)) 3876$^{4}$ 4329$^{2}$ 4900$^{12}$ 5670$^{10}$ 6091$^{7}$ 6242$^{6}$ >**74f**<

**Investment Affair (IRE)** 4 b g Sesaro (USA) -Superb Investment (IRE) (Hatim (USA)) 5459$^{10}$ >**76 f**<

**Invitation** 6 b g Bin Ajwaad (IRE) -On Request (IRE) (Be My Guest (USA)) 1103$^{11}$ 1272$^{6}$ 1801$^{4}$ 2000$^{2}$ 2084$^{8}$ 2631$^{2}$ 2958$^{28}$ >**78f**<

**Inviting (USA)** 3 b f Exploit (USA) -Raging Apalachee (USA) (Apalachee (USA)) 3916$^{14}$ >**64f**<

**Invogue (FR)** 4 b f Bin Ajwaad (IRE) -Wenda (IRE) (Priolo (USA)) 3799$^{6}$ 4093$^{10}$ >**17a**<

**Io Callisto** 3 br f Hector Protector (USA) -Queen Shirley (IRE) (Fairy King (USA)) 3512$^{9}$ >**39f**<

**Ionian Spring (IRE)** 9 b g Ela-Mana-Mou-Well Head (IRE) (Sadler s Wells (USA)) (1460) 1762$^{9}$ (2624) 3756$^{9}$ 4540$^{18}$ 4856$^{5}$ 5315$^{7}$ >**94a 93f**<

**Iphigenia (IRE)** 3 bb f Orpen (USA) -Silver Explosive (Rock Hopper) 2267$^{7}$ 2425$^{5}$ 2803$^{7}$ 3261$^{2}$ 3684$^{4}$ 3875$^{5}$ 4083$^{3}$ (4483) 4702$^{2}$4969$^{6}$ 5399$^{6}$ >**48a 77f**<

**Ipledgeallegiance (USA)** 8 b g Alleged (USA) -Yafill (USA) (Nureyev (USA)) 471$^{2}$ 545$^{5}$ 571$^{3}$ 630$^{6}$ 727$^{5}$ 943$^{8}$ 995$^{7}$1042$^{10}$ 1194$^{5}$ 1231$^{5}$ 1721$^{8}$ 2386$^{5}$ 2978$^{5}$ 3099$^{2}$ 3411$^{11}$3576$^{3}$ 3803$^{2}$ 4007$^{7}$ 4250$^{7}$ >**41a 41f**<

**Ipsa Loquitur** 4 b f Unfuwain (USA) -Plaything (High Top) 1224$^{10}$ 1611$^{4}$ 2212$^{P}$ >**63a 66f**<

**Iqte Saab (USA)** 3 b c Bahri (USA) -Shuhrah (USA) (Danzig (USA)) (1384) 2308$^{6}$ 3940$^{9}$ 5422$^{5}$ 5948$^{3}$ >**109 f**<

**Iranoo (IRE)** 7 b g Persian Bold-Rose Of Summer (IRE) (Taufan (USA)) 1867$^{7}$ >**23f**<

**Ireland s Eye (IRE)** 9 b g Shareef Dancer (USA) -So Romantic (IRE) (Teenoso (USA)) 475$^{3}$ 528$^{4}$ >**35a**<

**Irie Rasta (IRE)** 5 ch g Desert King (IRE) -Seeds Of Doubt (IRE) (Night Shift (USA)) 6546$^{15}$ >**73 f**<

**Irish Ballad** 2 b c Singspiel (IRE) -Auenlust (GER) (Surumu (GER)) 5023$^{8}$ 5620$^{10}$ 6223$^{4}$ >**60a 44f**<

**Irish Blade (IRE)** 3 b c Kris-Perle D Irlande (FR) (Top Ville) 1508$^{4}$ 1800$^{3}$ 3345$^{10}$ 4486$^{7}$ 4749$^{11}$ 5116$^{3}$ 5456$^{2}$ (5875) 6084$^{5}$6339$^{6}$ >**51a 82f**<

**Irish Chapel (IRE)** 8 b g College Chapel-Heart Of Flame (Top Ville) 2362$^{8}$ 3022$^{9}$ >**27f**<

**Irish Empire (IRE)** 6 b g Tirol-Hazy Image (Ahonoora) 4588a$^{17}$ >**92f**<

**Irish Playwright (IRE)** 4 b g King s Theatre (IRE) -Marino Waltz (Thatching) 4478$^{8}$ 5907$^{13}$ 6481$^{3}$ >**59a 35f**<

**Iron Temptress (IRE)** 3 ch f Piccolo-River Divine (USA) (Irish River (FR)) 4305$^{13}$ 4882$^{10}$ 5365$^{6}$ 5560$^{10}$ 5634$^{8}$ >**42a 48f**<

**Iron Warrior (IRE)** 4 b g Lear Fan (USA) -Robalana (USA) (Wild Again (USA)) 5993$^{15}$ >**64a 32f**<

**Irony (IRE)** 5 gr g Mujadil (USA) -Cidaris (IRE) (Persian Bold) 1132$^{7}$ 1623$^{9}$ 2196$^{4}$ 2637$^{13}$ 3212$^{10}$ >**91f**<

**Iroquois Princess** 2 ch f Polish Precedent (USA) -Chelsea (USA) (Miswaki (USA)) 6272$^{8}$ 6400$^{9}$ 6543$^{9}$ >**25f**<

**Irreversible** 2 b f Diktat-Amsicora (Cadeaux Genereux) 6447$^{6}$ >**68+a**<

**Irusan (IRE)** 4 br g Catrail (USA) -Ostrusa (AUT) (Rustan (HUN)) 1820$^{6}$ 2236$^{8}$ 2621$^{13}$ 3279$^{4}$ 3615$^{6}$ 4188$^{5}$ 4905$^{8}$ 6061$^{2}$(6220) >**67a 62f**<

**Isa Af (IRE)** 5 b g Darshaan-Shauna s Honey (IRE) (Danehill (USA)) (1077) 1238$^{2}$ (1535) (1754) 2449$^{10}$ 2615$^{2}$ 2782$^{4}$ 3232$^{4}$ (3743) 3873$^{6}$ 4698$^{16}$5203$^{8}$ 5456$^{4}$ 5889$^{2}$ 6074$^{7}$ 6269$^{4}$ >**64+a 75f**<

**Isaz** 4 b c Elmaamul (USA) -Pretty Poppy (Song) 1295$^{5}$ 1796$^{5}$ 2236$^{5}$ 3326$^{8}$ 3593$^{12}$ >**68f**<

**I See No Ships** 4 b f Danzig Connection (USA) -Killick (Slip Anchor) 3019$^{7}$ 3774$^{17}$ >**15a 31f**<

**Isidore Bonheur (IRE)** 3 b c Mtoto-Way O Gold (USA) (Slew O Gold (USA)) 1411$^{4}$ 1766$^{4}$ 1901$^{4}$ 3639$^{4}$ 5462$^{12}$ 5942$^{14}$ >**101f**<

**Isitloveyourafter (IRE)** 2 b f Orpen (USA) -Pericolo (IRE) (Kris) 2651$^{9}$ 3003$^{5}$ 4277$^{6}$ 5520$^{14}$ >**44f**<

**Iskander** 3 b g Danzero (AUS) -Amber Mill (Doulab (USA)) 1614$^{6}$ 2019$^{9}$ 2642$^{14}$ 2981$^{10}$ 3523$^{9}$ 3926$^{6}$ 4490$^{4}$ 5275$^{10}$5672$^{5}$ 5821$^{10}$ 5992$^{4}$ 6279$^{13}$ >**41a 87f**<

**Island Fashion (USA)** 4 rg f Petionville (USA) -Danzigs Fashion (USA) (A Native Danzig (USA)) 6484a$^{5}$ >**117a 114f**<

**Island House (IRE)** 8 ch h Grand Lodge (USA) -Fortitude (IRE) (Last Tycoon) 1355$^{3}$ 1622$^{7}$ 2241$^{5}$ 3315$^{3}$ 3912$^{3}$ >**118f**<

**Island Light (USA)** 4 ch g Woodman (USA) -Isla Del Rey (USA) (Nureyev (USA)) 1401$^{20}$ 1821$^{17}$ 2142$^{16}$ 2624$^{9}$ >**69f**<

**Island Rapture** 4 b f Royal Applause-Gersey (Generous (IRE)) 1623$^{11}$ 2279$^{8}$ 2630$^{4}$ 3091$^{10}$ 3419$^{3}$ 3826$^{2}$ 4771$^{6}$ 5185$^{11}$5740$^{2}$ 5955$^{3}$ 6395$^{5}$ >**76a 78f**<

**Island Sand (USA)** 3 br f Tabasco Cat (USA) -Sue s Last Dance (USA) (Forty Niner (USA)) $^{2}$ 6254a$^{7}$ >**116a 84f**<

**Islands Farewell** 4 b g Emarati (USA) -Chief Island (Be My Chief (USA)) 1318$^{7}$ 1993$^{17}$ 3899$^{2}$ 4246$^{5}$ 5002$^{11}$ 5080$^{3}$ 5585$^{2}$ 5751$^{2}$ >**14a 56f**<

**Island Sound** 7 b g Turtle Island (IRE) -Ballet (Sharrood (USA)) 4525$^{6}$ 5180$^{3}$ 5651$^{3}$ >**109f**<

**Island Spell** 3 b f Singspiel (IRE) -Shifty Mouse (Night Shift (USA)) 1904$^{3}$ 2367$^{5}$ 3267$^{3}$ 3562$^{15}$ 3838$^{10}$ 4104$^{9}$ >**58f**<

**Island Star (IRE)** 4 b g Turtle Island (IRE) -Orthorising (Aragon) 468$^{8}$ 519$^{10}$ 575$^{14}$ 1727$^{4}$ 1862$^{6}$ >**69a 12f**<

**Island Swing (IRE)** 2 ch f Trans Island-Farmers Swing (IRE) (River Falls) 2177$^{15}$ (2622) (2858) 4235$^{4}$ 4612$^{11}$ 5202$^{8}$ 5594$^{3}$ 5910$^{4}$ (6305) 6356$^{15}$ >**80f**<

**Isle Dream** 2 ch f Forzando-La Volta (Komaite (USA)) 5241$^{10}$ 5752$^{7}$ 6359$^{13}$ >**6a**<

**Isleofhopeantears (IRE)** 5 b g College Chapel-Fontaine Lodge (IRE) (Lafontaine (USA)) 6082$^{10}$ >**56f**<

**Isle Of Light (IRE)** 2 b f Trans Island-Singled Out (IRE) (Fairy King (USA)) 4243$^{13}$ 4999$^{8}$ >**3a**<

**Islero Noir (FR)** 3 b c Septieme Ciel (USA) -Mioura (FR) (Saumarez) 3359a$^{6}$ 4965a$^{3}$ 5667a$^{9}$ >**110f**<

**Ismahaan** 5 ch m Unfuwain (USA) -River Divine (USA) (Irish River (FR)) 4583$^{6}$ 5196$^{5}$ >**65f**<

**Isoplu (IRE)** 4 b c King s Theatre (IRE) -Lady Isotta (IRE) (Imp Society (USA)) 6512a$^{12}$ >**53f**<

**Issy Blue** 2 b f Inchinor-Mountain Bluebird (USA) (Clever Trick (USA)) 4053$^{9}$ 4488$^{8}$ 4681$^{11}$ >**61f**<

**Istan (USA)** 2 b c Gone West (USA) -Ronda (Bluebird (USA)) 6462a$^{7}$ >**96f**<

**Istithmar (FR)** 4 b c Marju (IRE) -Heartbreak House (FR) (Shavian) 709a$^{6}$ ><

**Italian Counsel (IRE)** 7 b g Leading Counsel (USA) -Mullaghroe (Tarboosh (USA)) 663$^{12}$ 2055$^{4}$ >**31a**<

**Italian Mist (FR)** 5 b g Forzando-Digamist Girl (IRE) (Digamist (USA)) (422) 509$^{3}$ 576$^{5}$ (626) 694$^{2}$ 738$^{9}$ (1027) 1131$^{3}$ (1477) 1516$^{7}$ 1738$^{4}$ 2455$^{10}$ 6288$^{13}$ >**73a 46f**<

**Italian Touch (IRE)** 2 b g Rossini (USA) -Attached (IRE) (Forest Wind (USA)) 5353$^{7}$ 5616$^{9}$ 5865$^{8}$ 6211$^{7}$ >**58f**<

**I T Consultant** 6 b g Rock City-Game Germaine (Mummy s Game) 1525$^{13}$ >**52a 61 f**<

**Ithaca (USA)** 3 ch f Distant View (USA) -Reams Of Verse (USA) (Nureyev (USA)) 1384$^{3}$ 1879$^{6}$ 2081$^{5}$ 3541$^{3}$ 4773$^{4}$ 5416$^{3}$ 5948$^{5}$ >**102f**<

**It Must Be Speech** 3 b g Advise (FR) -Maiden Speech (Pitskelly) 752$^{5}$ 1042$^{2}$ 1235$^{5}$ 5715$^{16}$ 6006$^{15}$ >**71a 54f**<

**It s A Blessing** 3 b f Inchinor-Benedicite (Lomond (USA)) 492$^{12}$ ><

**Itsa Monkey (IRE)** 2 b g Merdon Melody-Gracious Imp (USA) (Imp Society (USA)) 1060$^{9}$ 2799$^{6}$ 3709$^{2}$ 4012$^{12}$ 4304$^{8}$ 4878$^{12}$ 5142$^{7}$ 5447$^{14}$5556$^{11}$ >**35a 35 f**<

**Its A Mystery (IRE)** 5 b m Idris (IRE) -Blue Infanta (Chief Singer) 4499$^{11}$ >**34f**<

**It s Blue Chip** 3 b g Polar Falcon (USA) -Bellateena (Nomination) 563$^{3}$ 739$^{9}$ (1509) 1823$^{4}$ 1998$^{6}$ 2665$^{4}$ (3379) 3806$^{10}$ 4346$^{13}$4630$^{7}$ 6074$^{13}$ 6552$^{7}$ >**67a 69f**<

**It s Definite (IRE)** 5 b g Definite Article-Taoveret (IRE) (Flash Of Steel) 6215$^{25}$ >**84da 81f**<

**Its Ecco Boy** 6 ch g Clantime-Laena (Roman Warrior) 453$^{4}$ 504$^{4}$ (625) 833$^{7}$ 897$^{9}$ 928$^{7}$ 2739$^{12}$ 3090$^{7}$3321$^{13}$ 3887$^{14}$ 4185$^{10}$ 6014$^{6}$ 6154$^{12}$ 6401$^{6}$ >**57a 57 f**<

**Its My Son** 3 b g Sea Raven (IRE) -Fay Eden (IRE) (Fayruz) 4402$^{9}$ ><

**Itsonlyagame** 4 b c Ali-Royal (IRE) -Mena (Blakeney) (534) 602$^{8}$ 645$^{9}$ 914$^{5}$ 1016$^{7}$ 1168$^{2}$ 1858$^{13}$ >**56a 56f**<

**It s Peggy Speech** 2 b f Bishop Of Cashel-Marsara (Never So Bold) 6569$^{17}$ >**29f**<

**It s The Limit (USA)** 5 b g Boundary (USA) -Beside (USA) (Sportin Life (USA)) 4123$^{4}$ 5288$^{13}$ 5784$^{4}$ 6215$^{32}$ >**98f**<

**Ivana Illyich (IRE)** 2 ch f Tipsy Creek (USA) -Tolstoya (Northfields (USA)) 1839$^{5}$ 2177$^{9}$ 2481$^{4}$ 3886$^{8}$ 4612$^{3}$ 4953$^{3}$ 5377$^{7}$ 5738$^{10}$ >**70f**<

**Ivory Coast (IRE)** 3 b f Cape Cross (IRE) -Ivory League (Last Tycoon) 490$^{4}$ (622) 2355$^{2}$ 2949$^{8}$ 3156$^{7}$ 3773$^{11}$ 4458$^{5}$ 4654$^{9}$ (5018)5705$^{9}$ >**56a 64f**<

**Ivory Lace** 3 b f Atraf-Miriam (Forzando) 496$^{5}$ 524$^{2}$ 610$^{11}$ (678) 744$^{3}$ (1312) (1689) 2033$^{4}$ (2610) 4688$^{5}$5563$^{13}$ 5730$^{12}$ 6016$^{4}$ >**71a 79f**<

**Ivory Venture** 4 b f Reprimand-Julietta Mia (USA) (Woodman (USA)) 453$^{13}$ 538$^{8}$ 660$^{9}$ 707$^{12}$ (792) 858$^{13}$ >**45a 20 f**<

**Ivory Wolf** 2 ch g Wolfhound (USA) -Ashkernazy (IRE) (Salt Dome (USA)) 2702$^{8}$ 3104$^{7}$ 3664$^{10}$ >**34f**<

**Ivowen (USA)** 4 bb f Theatrical-Shee Cat (USA) (Storm Cat (USA)) 2498a$^{2}$ 3331a$^{3}$ 3862a$^{4}$ 4977a$^{5}$ >**102f**<

**Ivy House Lad (IRE)** 4 b g Presidium-Nice Spice (IRE) (Common Grounds) 1168$^{5}$ ><

**Ivy League Star (IRE)** 3 b f Sadler s Wells (USA) -Ivy (USA) (Sir Ivor (USA)) 2312$^{5}$ 2665$^{10}$ (5773) 5956$^{5}$ 6198$^{5}$ >**75a 78+f**<

**Ivy Moon** 4 b f Emperor Jones (USA) -Bajan Rose (Dashing Blade) 531$^{3}$ 698$^{6}$ 787$^{7}$ 2178$^{3}$ 2379$^{5}$ 2833$^{3}$ 3489$^{4}$ 3988$^{8}$4477$^{5}$ 5336$^{11}$ >**47a 71f**<

**I Wish** 6 ch m Beveled (USA) -Ballystate (Ballacashtal (CAN)) 599$^{9}$ 960$^{5}$ 1229$^{8}$ 1855$^{4}$ (2178) 2482$^{5}$ 3047$^{5}$ 3178$^{3}$ 4194$^{13}$4414$^{2}$ 4937$^{2}$ 6131$^{6}$ 6452$^{4}$ >**76a 70f**<

**I Wish I Knew** 3 br g Petong-Hoh Dancer (Indian Ridge) 942$^{6}$ 1300$^{11}$ 2380$^{11}$ 2766$^{7}$ 2932$^{11}$ >**59?a 35f**<

**I Won t Dance (IRE)** 3 b c Marju (IRE) -Carnelly (IRE) (Priolo (USA)) 2082$^{8}$ 2704$^{7}$ 3750$^{7}$ 4126$^{4}$ 5220$^{8}$ >**61a 78f**<

**Izmail (IRE)** 5 b g Bluebird (USA) -My-Lorraine (IRE) (Mac s Imp (USA)) 1537$^{13}$ 1774$^{19}$ 2490$^{10}$ 3126$^{7}$ 3558$^{10}$ (3894) 4181$^{18}$ 4935$^{10}$ 5337$^{14}$5412$^{12}$ 5458$^{5}$ 6046$^{18}$ 6554$^{10}$ 6577$^{12}$ >**52a 79f**<

**Izza** 3 br f Wizard King-Nicholas Mistress (Beveled (USA)) 780$^{14}$ >**25f**<

**Izzet Muzzy (FR)** 6 ch g Piccolo-Texanne (BEL) (Efisio) 543$^{9}$ >**62 a 66f**<

## J

**Jaamid** 2 b c Desert Prince (IRE) -Strictly Cool (USA) (Bering) 4420$^{4}$ 5096$^{10}$ 6283$^{2}$ >**79f**<

**Jabaar (USA)** 6 gr g Silver Hawk (USA) -Sierra Madre (FR) (Baillamont (USA)) 1114$^{21}$ 1821$^{3}$ 2066$^{5}$ 2258$^{6}$ 3291$^{2}$ 3756$^{5}$ 4831$^{10}$ 5211$^{8}$5650$^{2}$ 6043$^{18}$ 6346$^{11}$ 6573$^{11}$ >**95f**<

**Jabraan (USA)** 2 b c Aljabr (USA) -Miss Zafonic (FR) (Zafonic (USA)) 6145$^{8}$ >**70f**<

**Jacaranda (IRE)** 4 ch g Bahhare (USA) -Near Miracle (Be My Guest (USA)) 1225$^{11}$ 1452$^{5}$ 2834$^{10}$ 3412$^{9}$ 3662$^{2}$ 3985$^{4}$ (4086) 4571$^{3}$ 4772$^{6}$5568$^{10}$ 5764$^{5}$ 5997$^{10}$ >**66a 84f**<

**Jacira (FR)** 5 b m Sillery (USA) -Vol Sauvage (FR) (Always Fair (USA)) 2138a$^{2}$ >**98f**<

**Jackadandy (USA)** 2 b g Lear Fan (USA) -Chandra (CAN) (Morning Bob (USA)) 3718$^{4}$ 4633$^{3}$ 5302$^{13}$ >**66f**<

**Jack Dawson (IRE)** 7 b g Persian Bold-Dream Of Jenny (Caerleon (USA)) (2491) 4550$^{8}$ >**82f**<

**Jack Durrance (IRE)** 4 b g Polish Precedent (USA) -Atlantic Desire (IRE) (Ela-Mana-Mou) 1308$^{17}$ 1687$^{10}$ 2740$^{4}$ 3492$^{9}$ 3776$^{10}$ 4139$^{10}$ >**47a 47f**<

**Jackie Kiely** 3 ch g Vettori (IRE) -Fudge (Polar Falcon (USA)) 415$^{7}$ 598$^{6}$ 822$^{2}$ 1017$^{8}$ 1509$^{5}$ 1843$^{5}$ 2402$^{4}$ 2801$^{2}$(3026) 3190$^{14}$ (3827) (3917) 4015$^{9}$ 4070$^{10}$ 4556$^{3}$ 4648$^{7}$ 5185$^{4}$ 5374$^{10}$5493$^{3}$ 5934$^{5}$ 6279$^{10}$ >**60a 73+f**<

**Jack Of Trumps (IRE)** 4 b c King s Theatre (IRE) -Queen Caroline (USA) (Chief s Crown (USA)) (463) 577$^{11}$ 1298$^{7}$ 3050$^{4}$ (3752) (4155) (5074) 5517$^{9}$ >**92?a 82f**<

**Jack s Check** 3 b g Factual (USA) -Ski Baby (Petoski) 5770$^{14}$ 5994$^{10}$ >**24f**<

**Jacks Delight** 4 b g Bettergeton-Impromptu Melody (IRE) (Mac s Imp (USA)) 807$^{7}$ 2359$^{14}$ 2664$^{10}$ >**12a**<

**Jacks Estate (IRE)** 9 b g High Estate-Lady Tristram (Miami Springs) 632a$^{8}$ 755a$^{12}$ 830a$^{6}$ 925a$^{5}$ 978a$^{10}$ 3961a$^{2}$ 4371a$^{15}$ (5660a)6104a$^{11}$ >**53a 103f**<

**Jack Sullivan (USA)** 3 ch g Belong To Me (USA) -Provisions (USA) (Devil s Bag (USA)) 691a$^{2}$ 1143a$^{4}$ 2629$^{4}$ 3036$^{9}$ 4322$^{5}$ >**102a 99f**<

**Jack The Giant (IRE)** 2 b c Giant s Causeway (USA) -State Crystal (IRE) (High Estate) 3588$^{8}$ 5087$^{9}$ >**63f**<

**Jacob (IRE)** 3 b g Victory Note (USA) -Persian Mistress (IRE) (Persian Bold) 956$^{5}$ 1022$^{4}$ 1078$^{8}$ >**38a 52f**<

**Jacobin (USA)** 3 b c Tamayaz (CAN) -Simply Follow Me (USA) (Green Dancer (USA)) 2888$^{10}$ 4554$^{10}$ >**33f**<

**Jadan (IRE)** 3 b g Imperial Ballet (IRE) -Sports Post Lady (IRE) (M Double M (USA)) 1473$^{9}$ 1883$^{14}$ 3201$^{3}$ 3270$^{6}$ 3562$^{6}$ (3777) 4059$^{5}$ 4608$^{10}$ 4874$^{9}$(5837) 6205$^{6}$ >**82f**<

**Jadeeron** 5 b g Green Desert (USA) -Rain And Shine (FR) (Rainbow Quest (USA)) 467$^{2}$ 592$^{2}$ 777$^{2}$ 919$^{3}$ 1210$^{4}$ 1341$^{4}$ 1615$^{7}$ 2235$^{10}$5956$^{6}$ 6013$^{6}$ 6278$^{3}$ >**68a 72f**<

**Jade Quest (IRE)** 4 ch c Rainbow Quest (USA) -Jade Jewel (USA) (Mr Prospector (USA)) 1156a$^{4}$ 2416a$^{5}$ 3333a$^{6}$ 3862a$^{6}$ 4977a$^{6}$ 5962a$^{5}$ >**108f**<

**Jade Star (USA)** 4 b f Jade Hunter (USA) -Danzig s Girl (USA) (Danzig (USA)) 581$^{4}$ (763) 914$^{11}$ 1181$^{2}$ 1479$^{6}$ 1560$^{4}$ 3461$^{4}$ 3670$^{14}$4065$^{3}$ 4190$^{15}$ 5791$^{17}$ >**58a 48f**<

**Jagged (IRE)** 4 b g Sesaro (USA) -Latin Mass (Music Boy) 1082$^{13}$ 1873$^{8}$ 2166$^{8}$ 3277$^{2}$ 3935$^{3}$ 4336$^{6}$ 4403$^{3}$ (4881) 5000$^{2}$ 5337$^{2}$ 5512$^{4}$ (6554) >**72a 66f**<

**Jagger** 4 gr c Linamix (FR) -Sweetness Herself (Unfuwain (USA)) 3310$^{13}$ 4218$^{3}$ 4858$^{8}$ 5296$^{4}$ 5662a$^{11}$ >**89+a 110f**<

**Jahangir** 5 b g Zamindar (USA) -Imperial Jade (Lochnager) 787$^{3}$ 858$^{3}$ 930$^{9}$ 987$^{10}$ 999$^{7}$ >**50a 50 f**<

**Jahia (NZ)** 5 br m Jahafil-Lana (NZ) (Tristram s Heritage (NZ)) 1284$^{11}$ 4471$^{7}$ 4719$^{9}$ 5252$^{9}$ >**43f**<

**Jailbird** 3 b f Nicolotte-Grace Browning (Forzando) 2266$^{8}$ 2942$^{13}$ >**52f**<

**Jair Ohmsford (IRE)** 5 b g Hamas (IRE) -Harry s Irish Rose (USA) (Sir Harry Lewis (USA)) (406) 590$^{4}$ (734) (829) 1282$^{4}$ 2121$^{3}$ >**78+a 69f**<

**Jakarmi** 3 b g Merdon Melody-Lady Ploy (Deploy) (508) 696$^{6}$ (773) 909$^{3}$ 1214$^{2}$ 1422$^{2}$ 1688$^{2}$ 1997$^{3}$ 2665$^{2}$(3231) (3535) 3746$^{14}$ 5446$^{7}$ 5732$^{5}$ 5842$^{11}$ >**77a 76f**<

**Jakeal (IRE)** 5 b g Eagle Eyed (USA) -Karoi (IRE) (Kafu) 1098$^{10}$ 1451$^{4}$ 1620$^{11}$ 3167$^{11}$ 3471$^{2}$ 6548$^{13}$ >**43a 61 f**<

**Jake Black (IRE)** 4 b g Definite Article-Tirhala (IRE) (Chief Singer) 715$^{7}$ (940) (1079) 1093$^{5}$ 1527$^{3}$ (1715) 1856$^{5}$ 2216$^{15}$ 2584$^{4}$ 5129$^{4}$(5320) 5459$^{12}$ 5622$^{8}$ 6096$^{10}$ >**52a 68f**<

**Jalamid (IRE)** 2 b c Danehill (USA) -Vignelaure (IRE) (Royal Academy (USA)) (2890) 3672$^{11}$ >**78f**<

**Jalissa** 2 b f Mister Baileys-Julia Domna (Dominion) 5380$^{4}$ >**70a**<

**Jalons Star (IRE)** 6 b g Eagle Eyed (USA) -Regina St Cyr (IRE) (Doulab (USA)) 4029$^{10}$ 4262$^{7}$ 4398$^{13}$ >**38f**<

**Jalouhar** 4 b g Victory Note (USA) -Orient Way (IRE) (Danehill (USA)) 436$^{5}$ 670$^{4}$ 723$^{6}$ 884$^{5}$ 928$^{8}$ 1025$^{5}$ 1180$^{12}$1639$^{2}$ 2383$^{9}$ 2588$^{6}$ 2625$^{7}$ 2979$^{2}$ 3337$^{10}$ 3522$^{7}$ 3730$^{6}$4047$^{7}$ 4317$^{8}$ 4510$^{11}$ >**54a 75?f**<

**Jalousie Dream** 3 b f Easycall-Forest Maid (Thatching) 1619$^{7}$ 2145$^{5}$ 3015$^{3}$ 3837$^{12}$ 5365$^{8}$ >**36f**<

**Jalys (ITY)** 3 b f Sri Pekan (USA) -Villefranche (IRE) (Caerleon (USA)) 1778a$^{13}$ 6258a$^{5}$ >**94f**<

**Jamaaron** 2 ch c Bachir (IRE) -Kentmere (FR) (Galetto (FR)) 3664$^{3}$ 4480$^{7}$ (5114) 5885$^{14}$ >**76f**<

**Jamaican Flight (USA)** 11 b h Sunshine Forever (USA) -Kalamona (USA) (Hawaii) 461$^{3}$ 616$^{4}$ 1045$^{4}$ 1287$^{4}$ 1501$^{4}$ 2126$^{5}$ 5589$^{5}$ 6005$^{18}$ >**59a 59 f**<

**James Caird (IRE)** 4 ch g Catrail (USA) -Polish Saga (Polish Patriot (USA)) 2278$^{6}$ 2527$^{2}$ 2894$^{2}$ 3415$^{2}$ 3937$^{7}$ 4540$^{11}$ 5397$^{3}$ 5755$^{2}$ >**77a 94f**<

**Jamestown** 7 b g Merdon Melody-Thabeh (Shareef Dancer (USA)) 437$^{5}$ 516$^{9}$ 582$^{10}$ 627$^{7}$ 695$^{9}$ 878$^{8}$ 1373$^{13}$1511$^{4}$ 2943$^{11}$ 3880$^{4}$ 4925$^{8}$ 6057$^{13}$ >**52 a 52f**<

**Jamnica (ITY)** 4 b f Elmaamul (USA) -Kaberlaba (ITY) (Sikeston (USA)) 2607a$^{5}$ ><

**Jan Affrica (FR)** 3 b c True Brave (USA) -Sreca (FR) (Esprit Du Nord (USA)) 5433a$^{6}$ >**88f**<

**Jan Brueghel (USA)** 5 ch g Phone Trick (USA) -

Sunk (USA) (Polish Navy (USA)) *439[3] 565[4] 642[8]* **>52a 58f<**

**Jane Jubilee (IRE)** 2 b f Mister Baileys-Elsie Bamford (Tragic Role (USA)) 1990[3] 2550[5] 2972[2] 3406[2] (4012) (4278) 4835[5] 5149[10] 5939[11] 6174[13] **>92 f<**

**Jane s Park (IRE)** 2 ch c Central Park (IRE) -Janestra (IRE) (Steamer Duck (USA)) 6380a[6] **>86f<**

**Janes Valentine** 4 b f My Best Valentine-Jane Herring (Nishapour (FR)) *534[4] 660[8] 858[4] 1165[15] 1692[8]* 1986[17] *2056[6]* **>26a 26 f<**

**Jango Malfoy (IRE)** 3 ch g Russian Revival (USA) -Sialia (IRE) (Bluebird (USA)) *462[9] 741[11] 1422[10]* 4055[8] 4302[12] **>60a 29f<**

**Jaolins** 3 b f Groom Dancer (USA) -On The Top (High Top) *(744) 817[2] 885[10] 1047[10] 1086[5]* 1300[9] 1854[7] 2380[12]2766[14] 3229[7] *3707[6] 4093[5]* 5284[9] 6056[4] **>58a 40f<**

**Japigia (IRE)** 3 b f Singspiel (IRE) -Japan Exile (FR) (Arazi (USA)) 1805a[4] **><**

**Jarjoor** 4 b c Alhaarth (IRE) -Neptunalia (Slip Anchor) *830a[7]* **>13a 93f<**

**Jarraaf** 4 ch g Desert Story (IRE) -Bee Off (IRE) (Wolfhound (USA)) *824[5] 1138[5]* **>69a 63f<**

**Jarvo** 3 b g Pursuit Of Love-Pinkie Rose (FR) (Kenmare (FR)) 1532[2] *1679[5]* 3106[4] 3527[12] 3875[10] 4619[2] 5092[3] 5496[14]*6224[4]* **>62a 66f<**

**Jasmick (IRE)** 6 ch m Definite Article-Glass Minnow (IRE) (Alzao (USA)) 4297[5] 4441[7] 4647[9] 4777[6] 5073[7] 5152[2] **>91 f<**

**Jasmine Hill** 2 ch f Timeless Times (USA) -Coney Hills (Beverley Boy) 3950[10] 4212[6] 4607[7] 5241[8] **>44f<**

**Jasmine Pearl (IRE)** 3 b f King Of Kings (IRE) -Tumbleweed Pearl (Aragon) *514[3] 891[6] 983[11]* 1184[8] *1725[4]* 2380[16] 3260[2] 3991[5]4052[6] 4419[6] 4968[13] 5793[9] **>44a 43f<**

**Jath** 3 b f Bishop Of Cashel-Night Trader (USA) (Melyno) 1791[15] 2307[6] 2557[10] 4646[6] (5024) 5766[8] 6070[12] 6525[10] **>84f<**

**Java Dancer** 3 b g Danehill Dancer (IRE) -Evasive Step (Batshoof) 3447[7] 4306[6] *4880[6]* **>34a 50f<**

**Java Dawn (IRE)** 4 b f Fleetwood (IRE) -Krakatoa (Shirley Heights) 1858[10] *3087[10] 3303[3]* 3667[6] 4473[7] **>43a 43f<**

**Java Gold** 3 ch f The West (USA) -Another Jade (Beveled (USA)) 4617[12] 6079[14] *6577[10]* **>23a 24f<**

**Javelin** 8 ch g Generous (IRE) -Moss (Alzao (USA)) 3492[6] 4686[5] 5073[9] **>67f<**

**Jawwala (USA)** 5 b m Green Dancer (USA) -Fetch N Carry (USA) (Alleged (USA)) 4778[RR] 5205[16] **><**

**Jay (IRE)** 2 ch f Bluebird (USA) -Welsh Dawn (Zafonic (USA)) 2275[9] 2690[9] 3170[2] 4012[9] 4200[2] 4521[8] (4651) 5240[17] 5369[9] **>53f<**

**Jayanjay** 5 b g Piccolo-Morica (Moorestyle) *417[13] 607[4]* 2440[3] 2682[4] 3439[3] (3663) 4034[5] 4415[2] 4614[2]4847[5] 5181[8] (5933) *6496[6]* **>86a 93f<**

**Jayat** 2 b c Lujain (USA) -Finamai (IRE) (Royal Academy (USA)) 6380a[12] **>63f<**

**Jaycee Star (IRE)** 3 ch f Idris (IRE) -Shantung (IRE) (Anshan) *489[11] 5741[4] 5971[5]* **><**

**Jayer Gilles** 4 br g Busy Flight-Jadidh (Touching Wood (USA)) 3138[2] 3608[2] 4554[5] 6339[12] **>85f<**

**Jay Gee s Choice** 4 b g Barathea (IRE) -Llia (Shirley Heights) 1125[6] 1456[23] 1828[12] 2469[3] 2637[9] 2905[4] 3205[11] 4742[4]5177[6] (5590) 5886[3] 5937[4] *(6277)* **>98a 94f<**

**Jazil** 9 b g Nashwan (USA) -Gracious Beauty (USA) (Nijinsky (CAN)) *2127[6]* 2689[11] 3885[9] 4082[9] 6231[14] **>20a 36f<**

**Jazrawy** 2 b c Dansili-Dalila Di Mare (IRE) (Bob Back (USA)) 3014[4] 4335[4] *(6223)* **>70+a 64f<**

**Jazz D Allier (FR)** 7 b g Agent Bleu (FR) -Miss Akarad (FR) (Akarad (FR)) 1110a[2] 1435a[6] 4039a[7] **>105f<**

**Jazz Messenger (FR)** 4 b g Acatenango (GER) -In The Saltmine (FR) (Damister (USA)) 1623[6] 2044[15] 4742[9] 4887[10] 5401[6] **>68a 104f<**

**Jazz Princess (IRE)** 2 bb f Bahhare (USA) -Jazz Up (Cadeaux Genereux) (5961a) **>109f<**

**Jazz Scene (IRE)** 3 b c Danehill Dancer (IRE) -Dixie Jazz (Mtoto) 1459[9] 3001[8] 3295[2] 3542[2] 3959a[4] 5294[5] 5627[2] 5920[4]6116[2] 6193[15] **>101f<**

**Jazzy Millennium** 7 ch g Lion Cavern (USA) -Woodcrest (Niniski (USA)) 1268[8] 2707[3] 3174[6] 3558[3] 3828[3] 4085[7] 4336[4] (4548) 5039[2]5425[2] 5849[12] *6452[5]* **>64a 65f<**

**Jebal Suraaj (USA)** 4 b g Gone West (USA) -Trishyde (USA) (Nureyev (USA)) 633a[9] *688a[8] 832a[8]* **>70a 96f<**

**Jedburgh** 3 b c Selkirk (USA) -Conspiracy (Rudimentary (USA)) 1437[9] 1795[3] 2224[3] 3751[2] 4268[8] 4873[2] 5468[5] 5921[13] **>105f<**

**Jedeydd** 7 b g Shareef Dancer (USA) -Bilad (USA) (Riverman (USA)) 2172[10] 2459[8] 2776[4] 3167[7] 3321[6] 3579[4] 3895[10] 4199[7]4305[10] (4509) 5346[9] **>62f<**

**Jeepstar** 4 b g Muhtarram (USA) -Jungle Rose (Shirley Heights) 1539[16] 1928[10] 2471[6] 4005[2] 4343[2] (4777) 5318[8] (5517) 6335[2] 6573[4] **>85f<**

**Jefferson** 3 ch c The West (USA) -Musical Star (Music Boy) 4357a[11] **>95f<**

**Jeffslottery** 2 b g Rock City-Thieves Welcome (Most Welcome) 5098[11] 5831[6] 6207[7] 6464[2] **>55f<**

**Jelani (IRE)** 5 b h Darshaan-No Rehearsal (FR) (Baillamont (USA)) 1455[15] 1792[6] 2067[3] **>111f<**

**Jelly Baby** 3 b f Marju (IRE) -Daisy May (In The Wings) 1508[14] *(3087) (3305)* 3584[9] **>63a 13f<**

**Jemmy John (IRE)** 4 b g College Chapel-Moscow Tycoon (IRE) (Last Tycoon) 4371a[12] **>90f<**

**Jemmy s Brother (IRE)** 3 b g College Chapel-Gino Lady (IRE) (Perugino (USA)) 1256a[6] 5972a[12] **>95f<**

**Jem s Law** 5 b m Contract Law (USA) -Alnasr Jewel (USA) (Al Nasr (FR)) 1274[10] 2520[13] **><**

**Jenavive** 4 b f Danzig Connection (USA) -Promise Fulfilled (USA) (Bet Twice (USA)) *1081[9]* **>38a 58f<**

**Jenkins Lane (IRE)** 2 b c Revoque (IRE) -Suzy Street (IRE) (Dancing Dissident (USA)) 5322a[11] **>80f<**

**Jenna Stannis** 2 ch f Wolfhound (USA) -Darling Splodge (Elegant Air) 4753[11] 5247[8] 5846[10] **>66f<**

**Jennverse** 2 b f Opening Verse (USA) -Jennelle (Nomination) 6281[6] **>47f<**

**Jerome** 3 b g Nicolotte-Mim (Midyan (USA)) 1957[8] **>71f<**

**Jerry s Girl (IRE)** 2 ch f Danehill Dancer (IRE) -Lurgoe Lady (IRE) (Spectrum (IRE)) 2352[3] 2972[6] 4003[4] (4245) 4575[8] **>68f<**

**Jersey Bounce (IRE)** 3 b c Septieme Ciel (USA) -Marcotte (Nebos (GER)) 6170a[11] **>87f<**

**Jesse Samuel** 3 ch g First Trump-Miss Kellybell (Kirchner) 1300[14] 1594[4] 1908[8] **>29a 45 f<**

**Jessiaume** 2 gr f Mister Baileys-Jucinda (Midyan (USA)) 6454[4] **>68f<**

**Jessica s Style (IRE)** 2 b f Desert Style (IRE) -Mugello (Emarati (USA)) 2758[13] *4924[7]* 5125[9] **>33a 32f<**

**Jessie** 5 ch m Pivotal-Bold Gem (Never So Bold) *428[5] 474[6] 614[5] 737[2] 826[2] 934[2] 1021[4]*1992[7] *2811[5]* 3301[4] 3586[3] 5450[12] **>44a 46f<**

**Jessinca** 8 b m Minshaanshu Amad (USA) -Noble Soul (Sayf El Arab (USA)) *406[8] 503[10] 737[6] 2811[10]* 3264[3] 3423[2] 3670[9] 4045[5] 5502[11] **>27a 45f<**

**Je Suis Belle** 2 ch f Efisio-Blossom (Warning) 3588[7] 4776[3] 5115[2] (5606) 5938[13] **>72f<**

**Jeune Loup** 2 b g Loup Sauvage (USA) -Secret Waters (Pharly (FR)) 3758[8] 4131[4] 4861[7] **>69f<**

**Jeune Vigne (FR)** 5 b m Poliglote-Lady Hawke (FR) (General Holme (USA)) *5103a[0]* **><**

**Jewel In The Sand (IRE)** 2 b f Bluebird (USA) -Dancing Drop (Green Desert (USA)) (2535) (3031) (3599) 5325a[11] 5894[7] **>104 f<**

**Jewel Of India** 5 ch g Bijou D Inde-Low Hill (Rousillon (USA)) *677[7] 768[11]* 4613[6] **>94a 89 f<**

**Jezadil (IRE)** 6 b m Mujadil (USA) -Tender Time (Tender King) *1164[13] 1281[13]* 1580[3] 1721[9] 3165[6] **>63a 53f<**

**Jidiya (IRE)** 5 b g Lahib (USA) -Yaqatha (IRE) (Sadler s Wells (USA)) 2133[8] 4306[9] 4396[2] 4971[8] 5267[3] 5591[3] 6047[14] **>65f<**

**Jilly Why (IRE)** 3 b f Mujadil (USA) -Ruwy (Soviet Star (USA)) *906[8]* 5126[4] (5306) (5458) 5526[7] 5786[9] 5837[2] *6222[4]* 6267[11]*6482[5] 6538[6]* **>72a 80f<**

**Jim Lad** 4 b g Young Ern-Anne s Bank (IRE) (Burslem) 1580[5] **>42a 49?f<**

**Jimmy Byrne (IRE)** 4 ch g Red Sunset-Persian Sally (IRE) (Persian Bold) 1265[15] 1503[4] (1669) 2216[7] 2393[5] 3018[6] (3670) (3781) 3929[3] 5211[6] 5607[13] **>84f<**

**Jimmy Hay** 3 b g Bluegrass Prince (IRE) -Priory Bay (Petong) 3487[14] *5643[12]* 5843[15] 6055[12] **><**

**Jimmy Ryan (IRE)** 3 b c Orpen (USA) -Kaysama (FR) (Kenmare (FR)) 2082[7] 2589[7] (3273) 3723[2] (4289) **>110+f<**

**Jinksonthehouse** 3 b f Whittingham (IRE) -Aldwick Colonnade (Kind Of Hush) 1854[4] 2063[16] (2265) 2518[7] 2869[4] 3227[11] (3364) 4044[4] 4585[2] 4622[4]4854[11] **>7a 58f<**

**Jinx Johnson (IRE)** 3 b f Desert King (IRE) -Peace In The Park (IRE) (Ahonoora) 4251a[12] **>58f<**

**Joans Jewel** 3 ch f Wolfhound (USA) -Chatter s Princess (Cadeaux Genereux) *840[5] 963[5] 1096[6]* 2098[15] 2380[7] 4968[14] 5794[13] 6228[11] **>50a 41f<**

**Joe Charlie** 3 ch g Daggers Drawn (USA) -La Ballerine (Lafontaine (USA)) *731[10]* **>2a 44f<**

**Joe Jo Star** 2 b c Piccolo-Zagreb Flyer (Old Vic) 1462[6] 1961[6] 5233[9] 5617[16] **>62f<**

**Joely Green** 7 b g Binary Star (USA) -Comedy Lady (Comedy Star (USA)) *483[5] 740[10] 867[6] 919[6] 981[6]* 1441[10] 2171[2]2731[12] 2874[8] 3108[11] 3667[15] 4467[4] *5645[10]* **>58da 53f<**

**Joe Ninety (IRE)** 2 ch g Daggers Drawn (USA) -Sea Idol (IRE) (Astronef) *1060[5] 1117[6]* 1905[7] 2609[10] 2755[3] 2946[8] 4638[11] 5022[4]5218[11] **>57a 43f<**

**Joey Perhaps** 3 b g Danzig Connection (USA) -Realms Of Gold (USA) (Gulch (USA)) 1755[17] 2351[12] 3190[12] 3822[6] 3981[3] 4249[2] 4386[3] *4604[6]* **>51a 60f<**

**Joey The Schnoze** 6 ch g Zilzal (USA) -Linda s Design (Persian Bold) *676[7]* 3608[8] **>2a<**

**Johanino (FR)** 5 b g Cardoun (FR) -Johanina (FR) (Big John (FR)) *5103a[3]* **><**

**Johannian** 6 b g Hernando (FR) -Photo Call (Chief Singer) 1845[13] 2237[13] 2493[3] 2737[5] 2982[9] 3536[2] 3844[9] 4401[4]4672[6] 5017[3] 5176[2] (5496) 5574[2] 6358[11] **>78f<**

**Johayro** 11 ch g Clantime-Arroganza (Crofthall) 2342a[2] **>40f<**

**John Forbes** 2 b c High Estate-Mavourneen (USA) (Dynaformer (USA)) 3071[9] (3313) 3672[10] 4166[8] 5630[9] 6042[11] 6334[12] 6523[7] 6574[5] **>69f<**

**Johnny Alljays (IRE)** 3 b g Victory Note (USA) -It s Academic (Royal Academy (USA)) 1667[11] 2349[9] 2766[10] 2932[8] 3193[8] 3391[4] 4419[4] 4802[10] **>43f<**

**Johnny Chi (IRE)** 2 ch c Indian Lodge (IRE) -Bring Me Home (IRE) (Charnwood Forest (IRE)) 6476[19] **><**

**Johnny Jumpup (IRE)** 2 ch c Pivotal-Clarice Orsini (Common Grounds) (1853) (3748) 4949[7] (5457) 6340[2] **>98f<**

**Johnny Parkes** 3 b g Wolfhound (USA) -Lucky Parkes (Full Extent (USA)) (1209) 1883[11] 2131[3] 2552[7] **>89f<**

**Johnny Rook (IRE)** 3 ch g Woodman (USA) -Tani (USA) (Theatrical) *2486[7]* **>55a<**

**John O Groats (IRE)** 6 b g Distinctly North (USA) -Bannons Dream (IRE) (Thatching) 1454[7] 1774[16] 2130[11] 2261[14] 2421[8] 2734[10] 2936[11] 3010[16]3820[18] *4881[12]* 5452[12] 6059[13] (6469) **>32a 52f<**

**John Robie (USA)** 2 ch c Rahy (USA) -Diamond Flower (USA) (Fly So Free (USA)) 4124[6] 5319[3] *6394[4]* **>75+a 83f<**

**John s Champ (IRE)** 4 b g Mujadil (USA) -Big Buyer (USA) (Quest For Fame) 3238[8] **>57a 59f<**

**Johnston s Diamond (IRE)** 6 b g Tagula (IRE) -Toshair Flyer (Ballad Rock) *515[8] 680[12] (836) 1007[7]* 1391[4] 1923[6] 2391[2] 2857[8]3074[22] 3901[9] 4837[18] 5287[14] 5458[12] 5603[3] 5787[6] 5832[3]6070[8] 6517[3] **>82a 96f<**

**Joint Aspiration** 2 ch f Pivotal-Welcome Home (Most Welcome) (4682) (5272) 5779[6] **>104f<**

**Joint Destiny (IRE)** 3 b f Desert Prince (IRE) -Brogan s Well (IRE) (Caerleon (USA)) *566[5] 918[8] 1695[2] (2054)* 2595[7] 2974[4] 4201[8] 4264[6] **>51a 52f<**

**Jolie (IRE)** 2 b f Orpen (USA) -Arabian Dream (IRE) (Royal Academy (USA)) 5848[9] **>23f<**

**Jolizero** 3 br g Danzero (AUS) -Jolis Absent (Primo Dominie) 3154[4] 3746[9] 4346[3] 4630[2] 5159[5] 5584[9] *5914[6]* (6357) **>56a 68f<**

**Jomacomi** 3 b c Hector Protector (USA) -Stylish Rose (IRE) (Don t Forget Me) *(863)* 1672[3] 2070[6] 2683[7] 3584[6] **>60+a 87f<**

**Jomus** 3 b g Soviet Star (USA) -Oatey (Master Willie) *675[5] 802[2] (959) 1029[2]* 2378[9] 2847[10] 3589[10] 4127[4]4266[7] 5259[3] 5622[5] *6160[10] 6549[6]* **>72+a 60f<**

**Jonanaud** 5 b g Ballet Royal (USA) -Margaret Modes (Thatching) *5913[6]* 6082[7] **>65a 63f<**

**Jonny Ebeneezer** 5 b g Hurricane Sky (AUS) -Leap Of Faith (IRE) (Northiam (USA)) *1035[7]* 1185[13] 1361[18] 1533[2] 1877[9] 2209[2] (2322) 2703[9] *3024[3](3616)* 3742[7] 3810[2] 3841[2] (4034) (4090) *4188[4]* (4294) (4614) 4759[17] 5393[8] 5628[23](5787) 5921[3] (6071) 6190[6] **>72a 106+f<**

**Jonnyem** 3 b g Emarati (USA) -Deerlet (Darshaan) 5237[13] 5545[4] 5637[9] 6006[18] **>57f<**

**Jonny Fox S (IRE)** 2 ch g Foxhound (USA) -Lala Salama (IRE) (College Chapel) *2405[6]* 2773[8] 3526[6] 5003[13] 5746[8] **>49a 33f<**

**Jonquil (IRE)** 2 ch c Machiavellian (USA) -Jumilla (USA) (El Gran Senor (USA)) 3451[4] (4290) 5437[8] **>92f<**

**Jools** 6 b g Cadeaux Genereux-Madame Crecy (USA) (Al Nasr (FR)) *870[7] 1118[11]* (1273) 1623[5] 1938[3] 2278[8] 2537[14] 3159[4] 3347[4]3631[6] 3690[5] 4164[9] 4401[U] 4435[6] 4613[7] 5185[10] **>77a 87f<**

**Jordans Elect** 4 ch g Fleetwood (IRE) -Cal Norma s Lady (IRE) (Lyphard s Special (USA)) 1660[5] (2078) 2368[12] (2618) 2781[4] 2905[8] 3397[4] 4333[3] **>82f<**

**Jordans Spark** 3 ch g Opening Verse (USA) -Ribot s Pearl (Indian Ridge) 1662[5] 3015[7] 4492[12] 4829[6] (4985) 5344[6] 6097[14] *6556[6]* **>47a 63f<**

**Jorobaden (FR)** 4 gr g Poliglote-Mercalle (FR) (Kaldoun (FR)) *871[2]* (1224) 1401[6] (1832) 2047[8] 2684[6] 3310[18] 5288[15] **>50a 98f<**

**Josear** 2 b c Josr Algarhoud (IRE) -Real Popcorn (IRE) (Jareer (USA)) 1905[4] 2574[8] 2947[10] **>52f<**

**Joseph Henry** 2 b c Mujadil (USA) -Iris May (Brief Truce (USA)) (1340) (1751) 6068[4] 6212[4] 6348[3] 6459[5] **>99f<**

**Josephus (IRE)** 3 ch c King Of Kings (IRE) -Khulasah (USA) (Affirmed (USA)) 6474[11] **>101f<**

**Josh** 2 b c Josr Algarhoud (IRE) -Charlie Girl (Puissance) (3925) 4581[3] 5392[7] (5594) 5918[6] 6320a[3] **>106f<**

**Joshar** 2 b f Paris House-Penny Hasset (Lochnager) 1468[8] 1666[3] 1970[8] *2124[3]* 2248[3] 2364[4] 2858[13] **>30a 42f<**

**Joshuas Boy (IRE)** 4 ch g Bahhare (USA) -Broadway Rosie (Absalom) 1719[3] 2260[8] 4557[9] **>41f<**

**Joshua s Gold (IRE)** 3 b g Sesaro (USA) -Lady Of The Night (IRE) (Night Shift (USA)) *983[2]* 1869[3] 2251[6] 3155[13] 3636[9] 4151[8] (4259) 4425[4] 5063[2]5235[3] 5370[13] 5518[5] 5715[7] 5859[15] **>59a 62f<**

**Jostle** 2 b g Josr Algarhoud (IRE) -Russell Creek (Sandy Creek) 5718[10] **>36f<**

**Joursanvault (FR)** 3 gr c Verglas (IRE) -Jane Brust (FR) (Brustolon) 1218a[2] 1898a[4] 2072a[4] 3163a[2] 3791a[4] 5169a[6] **>110?f<**

**Joy And Pain** 3 b g Pursuit Of Love-Ice Chocolate (USA) (Icecapade (USA)) *597[14] 739[8] 766[6] 885[7] (983)* 1184[6] 2061[2] 2378[3]2915[8] 6131[7] 6445[16] **>59a 69f<**

**Joyce (GER)** 3 b f Chato (USA) -Juschika (Salse (USA)) 1983a[15] **>91f<**

**Joyce (IRE)** 2 b c Danehill Dancer (IRE) -Miss Kinabalu (Shirley Heights) 2314a[4] 2792a[2] 3352a[5] **>96f<**

**Joyce s Choice** 5 b g Mind Games-Madrina (Waajib) 1421[2] 1663[9] 1870[LFT] 2582[5] 2975[4] 3314[10] 3820[12] 3864[10]4247[2] 4422[6] (6059) **>42a 56f<**

**Joyeaux** 2 b f Mark Of Esteem (IRE) -Divine Secret (Hernando (FR)) *5375[8]* 5771[6] *6289[4]* **>65a 66f<**

**J R Stevenson (USA)** 8 ch g Lyphard (USA) -While It Lasts (USA) (Foolish Pleasure (USA)) *494[2] 577[12]* 1708[4] 2084[6] 3397[5] 4164[8] 6081[6] (6561) **>87a 79f<**

**Juantorena** 2 ch c Miswaki (USA) -Millyant (Primo Dominie) 2310[2] 2579[2] 2959[4] 4649[3] 5003[4] 5262[2] (5558) **>85f<**

**Jubilation** 5 b h Zamindar (USA) -Jubilee Trail (Shareef Dancer (USA)) *1954a[11] 5504a[7]* **>107f<**

**Jubilee Coin** 2 ch f Fumo Di Londra (IRE) -Money Supply (Brigadier Gerard) 5609[10] 5890[10] **>23f<**

**Jubilee Street (IRE)** 5 b g Dr Devious (IRE) -My Firebird (Rudimentary (USA)) *1595[9]* 1824[4] 2260[3] (2473) 3321[10] 3470[7] 4305[6] (4425) 5108[2] (5364)5713[8] 6094[7] 6210[16] **>43a 68f<**

**Jubilee Treat (USA)** 4 b f Seeking The Gold (USA) -Dance Treat (USA) (Nureyev (USA)) 1372[13] 2403[7] 3311[6] **>85f<**

**Judda** 3 b g Makbul-Pepeke (Mummy s Pet) 2236[15] 2505[11] *2815[12]* 6310[11] **>32f<**

**Judge Damuss (IRE)** 2 ch c Tagula (IRE) -Acicula (IRE) (Night Shift (USA)) 4761[18] 6197[12] **><**

**Jules Lee** 2 ch g Bluegrass Prince (IRE) -Jade s Girl (Emarati (USA)) 4638[13] 6127[13] **>5f<**

**Julie s Prize (USA)** 4 br f El Prado (IRE) -Julie Mis (USA) (Miswaki (USA)) *4735a[3]* **>104f<**

**Jumbo s Flyer** 7 ch g Jumbo Hirt (USA) -Fragrant Princess (Germont) 4257[10] **>49f<**

**Jumeirah Scarer** 3 b g Tagula (IRE) -Mountain Harvest (FR) (Shirley Heights) *447[2] 553[2]* **>73a<**

**Jummana (FR)** 4 ch f Cadeaux Genereux-Forty Belles (USA) (Forty Niner (USA)) 3969a[7] **>87a 97f<**

**Jun Fan (USA)** 2 br c Artax (USA) -Ringside Lady (NZ) (Clay Hero (AUS)) 2526[5] 2758[6] **>62f<**

**Jungle Lion** 6 ch g Lion Cavern (USA) -Star Ridge (USA) (Storm Bird (CAN)) *487[6] 545[2] 724[10] (937) 1042[13] (1238)* 1426[6] 1463[8]*2126[6]* **>57a 47f<**

**Juniper Banks** 3 ch g Night Shift (USA) -Beryl (Bering) 5342[6] 5803[6] 6114[10] 6200[12] *6274[3] 6538[12] 6578[6]* **>61a 63f<**

**Just A Fluke (IRE)** 3 b c Darshaan-Star Profile (IRE) (Sadler s Wells (USA)) 1224[4] 1712[7] 2934[2] 3238[3] 3872[13] 4258[5] 4987[2] (5478) 5835[4] **>82+f<**

**Just A Glimmer** 4 b f Bishop Of Cashel-Rockin Rosie (Song) *410[3] 544[7] (1013) 1139[2]* 1367[7] (1840) 2206[13] 5887[15] *6277[12]* **>93a 88f<**

**Justalord** 6 b g King s Signet (USA) -Just Lady (Emarati (USA)) *540[8] 586[2] (703) 841[2] 1061[3]* 1131[13] 3126[6] (4011) 4299[7](5062) **>96a 89f<**

**Justaquestion** 2 b f Pursuit Of Love-Queenbird (Warning) 1105[7] (1364) (2023) 3031[12] 3679[3] 4326[2] (4527) 5149[5] 5648[9] 6213[6] 6473[4] **>92f<**

**Just A Try (USA)** 2 ch c Lure (USA) -Boubasis (USA) (Diesis) 3939[8] 4681[6] 5256[7] **>65f<**

**Just Before (GER)** 3 br f Monsun (GER) -Just In Fun (GER) (In The Wings) 5822a[6] **>74f<**

**Just Beware** 2 b f Makbul-Bewails (IRE) (Caerleon (USA)) 2481[13] 3202[8] *6446[10]* **>34a<**

**Just Bonnie** 2 b c Lujain (USA) -Fairy Flight (IRE) (Fairy King (USA)) 2831[6] 4191[9] 4809[17] 5616[15] **>19f<**

**Just Cliff** 2 b c Handsome Ridge-Justforthecord (Forzando) *5911[11]* 6060[4] *6400[4]* **>54a 61f<**

**Just Dance Me (FR)** 3 gr f Linamix (FR) -Reine De La Ciel (USA) (Conquistador Cielo (USA)) 3222[2] 6130[6] **>67f<**

**Just Dashing** 5 b g Arrasas (USA) -Smitten (Run The Gantlet (USA)) 3245[12] 4337[9] 5999[16] **>16f<**

**Just Do It (UAE)** 2 b c Timber Country (USA) -Poised (USA) (Rahy (USA)) *4544[6]* 4913[2] 5173[5] 5636[14] 5995[9] **>55a 71df<**

**Just Elizabeth** 2 b f Aragon-Collison Lane (Reesh) 5771[13] 6211[8] 6569[21] **>15f<**

**Justenjoy Yourself** 2 b f Tipsy Creek (USA) -Habibi (Alhijaz) 1183[6] 2458[8] *3021[6]* 3526[4] 4700[8] 5022[3] 5556[15] **>29a 41f<**

**Juste Pour L Amour** 4 ch g Pharly (FR) -Fontaine Lady (Millfontaine) 2410[8] 2503[4] 2845[7] 3525[9] 3911[10] 4090[4] 4294[7] 4522[7](4802) 5017[5] 5403[2] 5614[6] 5821[4] **>87f<**

**Just Fly** 4 b g Efisio-Chrysalis (Soviet Star (USA)) *417[2] 544[2] 648[2]* 1708[17] 2206[3] 2575[12] 3698[13] 3910[8]4846[12] 5614[13] 5698[2] 5841[2] *6496[5]* **>94a 84f<**

**Justice Jones** 3 b g Emperor Jones (USA) -Rally For Justice (Dominion) *1012[9]* 1366[10] 1683[17] 2001[16] 2705[10] 3425[10] 3742[16] **>42f<**

**Just James** 5 b g Spectrum (IRE) -Fairy Flight (IRE) (Fairy King (USA)) 2021[15] 2957[13] 4745[11] **>119f<**

**Just Michael** 5 b h Bluegrass Prince (IRE) -Plucky Pet (Petong) *1953a[6]* **>88a 60f<**

**Just One Look** 3 b f Barathea (IRE) -Western Sal (Salse (USA)) *1229[7]* 1464[8] 1760[7] 2577[15] *2988[8]* 3700[6] 4871[10] 5260[5]6184[7] *6296[3] 6556[3]* **>59 a 57 f<**

**Just One Smile (IRE)** 4 b f Desert Prince (IRE) -Smile Awhile (USA) (Woodman (USA)) 1526[16] 1992[3] 2238[6] 2421[10] 3098[7] 3372[10] 3887[11] **>70a 66f<**

**Just Red** 6 ch g Meqdaam (USA) -Orchard Bay (Formidable (USA)) *484[10]* **>9a 45f<**

**Just Sing A Song** 5 b m Dolphin Street (FR) -Maniere D Amour (FR) (Baillamont (USA)) 2466a[6] **>83f<**

**Just Tim (IRE)** 3 ch c Inchinor-Simply Sooty (Absalom) *1064[4]* (1311) 1585[4] 2306[12] (2516) 2806[5] 3159[7] 4220[14] **>76a 83f<**

**Just Waz (USA)** 2 ch c Woodman (USA) -Just Tops (USA) (Topsider (USA)) 4625[8] (5186) 5819[5] 6334[10] **>68f<**

**Just Wiz** 8 b g Efisio-Jade Pet (Petong) *679[6] 759[3] 872[10] 972[2] 1037[3]* 1274[11] *1599[2]1629[5]* **>82a 47f<**

**Juwwi** **10** ch g Mujtahid (USA) -Nouvelle Star (AUS) (Luskin Star (AUS)) *417$^{10}$ 454$^{4}$ 526$^{11}$ 617$^{9}$ 799$^{4}$ 954$^{4}$* 1185$^{14}$ *1474$^{6}$* 2869$^{2}$ 3043$^{6}$ 3269$^{6}$ *3378$^{14}$* 3772$^{11}$ 3864$^{17}$ >**55a 55f**<

**K**

**Kabeer** **6** ch g Unfuwain (USA) -Ta Rib (USA) (Mr Prospector (USA)) 2596$^{4}$ 3106$^{3}$ 3487$^{11}$ 4293$^{8}$ *4602$^{5}$* 5841$^{6}$ 6152$^{12}$ *6452$^{6}$* >**63a 71f**<

**Kabis Amigos** **2** ch c Nashwan (USA) -River Saint (USA) (Irish River (FR)) 6148$^{9}$ 6351$^{9}$ >**60f**<

**Kabis Booie (IRE)** **3** ch c Night Shift (USA) -Perfect Welcome (Taufan (USA)) 5371$^{3}$ 6085$^{9}$ >**59a 66f**<

**Kabreet** **3** b c Night Shift (USA) -Red Rabbit (Suave Dancer (USA)) *493$^{3}$ (619)* 2082$^{9}$ 2309$^{15}$ 4051$^{8}$ 4688$^{8}$ >**86+a 68f**<

**Kafil (USA)** **10** bb g Housebuster (USA) -Alchaasibiyeh (USA) (Seattle Slew (USA)) *665$^{13}$ 1403$^{7}$ 2056$^{7}$* >**44a 39f**<

**Kaggamagic** **2** ch g Abou Zouz (USA) -Meadmore Magic (Mansingh (USA)) 2758$^{5}$ 3233$^{4}$ 3679$^{7}$ 5234$^{15}$ 5857$^{7}$ >**63f**<

**Kagoshima (IRE)** **9** b g Shirley Heights-Kashteh (IRE) (Green Desert (USA)) *432$^{2}$ 475$^{2}$ 568$^{3}$ 716$^{3}$ 839$^{6}$* >**47a 42f**<

**Kahira (IRE)** **2** ch f King s Best (USA) -Sine Labe (USA) (Vaguely Noble) 5592$^{8}$ 6118$^{2}$ >**75f**<

**Kahlua (GER)** **2** b f Dashing Blade-Karena (GER) (Midyan (USA)) 6377a$^{3}$ >**97f**<

**Kahn (GER)** **2** ch c Big Shuffle (USA) -Katah (Arazi (USA)) 6256a$^{2}$ ><

**Kahyasi Princess (IRE)** **4** b f Kahyasi-Dungeon Princess (IRE) (Danehill (USA)) 1744$^{5}$ >**89+f**<

**Kaid (IRE)** **9** b g Alzao (USA) -Very Charming (USA) (Vaguely Noble) *727$^{7}$* ><

**Kaieteur (USA)** **5** b h Marlin (USA) -Strong Embrace (USA) (Regal Embrace (CAN)) 2559$^{6}$ 2968$^{8}$ 3936$^{5}$ 5436$^{4}$ >**121f**<

**Kajul** **3** b f Emperor Jones (USA) -Andbell (Trojan Fen) 4683$^{10}$ *6017$^{10}$* >**28a 36f**<

**Kalabar** **4** b c Kahyasi-Imbabala (Zafonic (USA)) 1922a$^{6}$ 2924a$^{7}$ 4766a$^{7}$ >**115f**<

**Kalaman (IRE)** **4** b c Desert Prince (IRE) -Kalamba (IRE) (Green Dancer (USA)) 1397$^{2}$ (2398) 3540$^{3}$ (3978) 4834$^{6}$ >**123+f**<

**Kalamansi (IRE)** **3** b f Sadler s Wells (USA) -Musk Lime (USA) (Private Account (USA)) 2144$^{6}$ 2374$^{16}$ 2505$^{12}$ 2974$^{8}$ 4499$^{8}$ >**45f**<

**Kalanisha (IRE)** **4** ch g Ashkalani (IRE) -Camisha (IRE) (Shernazar) 1612$^{7}$ 1989$^{6}$ *2816$^{11}$ 3712$^{3}$ 5644$^{5}$* >**30a 45f**<

**Kalani Star (IRE)** **4** b c Ashkalani (IRE) -Bellissi (IRE) (Bluebird (USA)) *6553$^{7}$* >**61a 77f**<

**Kalatuna (FR)** **3** ch f Green Tune (USA) -Kalasinger (FR) (Chief Singer) 1320a$^{5}$ 2700a$^{2}$ 3566a$^{5}$ >**99f**<

**Kaldushka (FR)** **4** gr f Kaldounevees (FR) -Star System (FR) (Northern Treat (USA)) 3030a$^{10}$ >**99f**<

**Kali** **3** gr f Linamix (FR) -Alkarida (FR) (Akarad (FR)) 1189$^{3}$ 2182$^{3}$ 2577$^{2}$ (3106) 5652$^{6}$ *5912$^{4}$* 6350$^{6}$ *6579$^{2}$* >**83a 80f**<

**Kalifornia Blue (GER)** **3** b f Auenadler (GER) -Kanonade (GER) (Konigsstuhl (GER)) 1778a$^{7}$ >**86f**<

**Kalika (IRE)** **2** b f Bachir (IRE) -Ruwy (Soviet Star (USA)) *2453$^{6}$* 2730$^{12}$ *2985$^{8}$* 5946$^{13}$ >**18a 20f**<

**Kalimenta (USA)** **3** ch f Rahy (USA) -Toujours Elle (USA) (Lyphard (USA)) 3852$^{6}$ 4045$^{7}$ 4848$^{11}$ 5258$^{15}$ >**51+f**<

**Kalishka (IRE)** **3** b c Fasliyev (USA) -Andromaque (USA) (Woodman (USA)) 1557$^{6}$ 2259$^{5}$ 3921$^{14}$ 4138$^{11}$ 5715$^{8}$ 6120$^{13}$ >**63f**<

**Kallista s Pride** **4** b f Puissance-Clan Scotia (Clantime) 2209$^{9}$ 2843$^{2}$ 3227$^{9}$ (3747) 4194$^{12}$ 4299$^{6}$ 4923$^{11}$ 4970$^{5}$ 5253$^{12}$5849$^{13}$ *6273$^{7}$* >**48a 67f**<

**Kalmini (USA)** **2** bb f Rahy (USA) -Kilma (USA) (Silver Hawk (USA)) 3905$^{7}$ 4272$^{2}$ (4706) 5188$^{5}$ 5565$^{4}$ 5885$^{12}$ >**75f**<

**Kalou (GER)** **6** br g Law Society (USA) -Kompetenz (IRE) (Be My Guest (USA)) *966$^{3}$* 3917$^{7}$ 4086$^{3}$ 4616$^{9}$ 5658$^{7}$ >**54a 54f**<

**Kaluana Court** **8** b m Batshoof-Fairfields Cone (Celtic Cone) 5826$^{13}$ 6074$^{19}$ 6215$^{33}$ 6457$^{7}$ >**71f**<

**Kalush** **3** b g Makbul-The Lady Vanishes (Robin Des Pins (USA)) 1104$^{17}$ 1532$^{9}$ 2906$^{6}$ 4180$^{8}$ >**62f**<

**Kamakiri (IRE)** **2** b c Trans Island-Alpine Flair (IRE) (Tirol) 3749$^{7}$ (4078) (4645) >**98+f**<

**Kamala** **5** b m Priolo (USA) -Fleeting Vision (IRE) (Vision (USA)) *517$^{6}$* >**66a 68f**<

**Kamanda Laugh** **3** ch g Most Welcome-Kamada (USA) (Blushing Groom (FR)) *(1169)* 1841$^{2}$ (2239) (3230) (6193) 6475$^{5}$ >**76a 90f**<

**Kama s Wheel** **5** ch m Magic Ring (IRE) -Tea And Scandals (USA) (Key To The Kingdom (USA)) 3060$^{8}$ 4066$^{7}$ 4386$^{6}$ 4871$^{7}$ >**35a 50f**<

**Kamenka** **3** ch f Wolfhound (USA) -Aliuska (IRE) (Fijar Tango (FR)) 3267$^{4}$ 4320$^{4}$ 4608$^{4}$ 5193$^{17}$ 5674$^{11}$ 6009$^{3}$ 6200$^{3}$ *6275$^{6}$* >**47a 73f**<

**Kames Park (IRE)** **2** b g Desert Sun-Persian Sally (IRE) (Persian Bold) 5264$^{4}$ 5669$^{2}$ (6139) >**80f**<

**Kanad** **2** b g Bold Edge-Multi-Sofft (Northern State (USA)) 2095$^{3}$ 2382$^{2}$ 2904$^{7}$ 5376$^{2}$ 5720$^{5}$ (6207) >**74f**<

**Kandidate** **2** b c Kabool-Valleyrose (IRE) (Royal Academy (USA)) 3601$^{15}$ 3939$^{3}$ 4527$^{7}$ 5778$^{6}$ *6392$^{2}$* >**68a 99f**<

**Kaneko (TUR)** **3** b c Pivotal-Kalimat (Be My Guest (USA)) 5489a$^{6}$ ><

**Kangarilla Road** **5** b g Magic Ring (IRE) -Kangra Valley (Indian Ridge) 1113$^{18}$ 2130$^{7}$ 2423$^{2}$ 2490$^{13}$ 3010$^{14}$ 3407$^{14}$ >**50a 83f**<

**Kangrina** **2** b f Acatenango (GER) -Kirona (Robellino (USA)) *5741$^{5}$ 6020$^{4}$ (6479)* >**79+a**<

**Kanisfluh** **3** b f Pivotal-Kahina (GER) (Warning) 3959a$^{7}$ 4159a$^{6}$ >**91f**<

**Kanz Wood (USA)** **8** ch g Woodman (USA) -Kanz (USA) (The Minstrel (CAN)) *491$^{15}$ 932$^{5}$ 988$^{9}$* 1582$^{5}$ 1986$^{5}$ *2013$^{3}$ 2454$^{4}$2666$^{3}$ 2990$^{6}$ 3024$^{10}$* >**47a 27f**<

**Kapaje** **2** b f Lake Coniston (IRE) -Reina (Homeboy) 2786$^{18}$ 4081$^{5}$ 4966$^{3}$ 5792$^{8}$ >**67f**<

**Kaparolo (USA)** **5** ch g El Prado (IRE) -Parliament House (USA) (General Assembly (USA)) 1958$^{7}$ 6084$^{14}$ >**66f**<

**Kappelmann (FR)** **2** gr c Verglas (IRE) -Black Dalhia (FR) (Sanglamore (USA)) 3790a$^{2}$ 4963a$^{7}$ 6583a$^{7}$ >**92f**<

**Karakum** **5** b g Mtoto-Magongo (Be My Chief (USA)) 3492$^{4}$ 3774$^{10}$ 5751$^{9}$ >**33a 40f**<

**Karamea (SWI)** **3** gr f Rainbow Quest (USA) -Karapucha (IRE) (Kaldoun (FR)) 1440$^{3}$ (1770) 3528$^{5}$ 4915$^{11}$ 5266$^{8}$ >**81f**<

**Karaoke (IRE)** **4** b g Mujadil (USA) -Kayoko (IRE) (Shalford (IRE)) *650$^{14}$ 882$^{7}$ (964)* 1308$^{15}$ 1460$^{11}$ 1624$^{5}$ 1944$^{5}$ 2302$^{4}$2430$^{2}$ 2474$^{2}$ 2845$^{8}$ 3534$^{8}$ 3631$^{9}$ 3842$^{3}$ (3997) 4343$^{7}$ 4416$^{5}$ >**66a 75f**<

**Karaoke King** **6** ch h King s Signet (USA) -Brampton Grace (Tachypous) *503$^{6}$ 738$^{15}$ 896$^{11}$ 928$^{9}$* 1969$^{P}$ >**49 a 70 f**<

**Karashinko (IRE)** **3** b g Shinko Forest (IRE) -Kayoko (IRE) (Shalford (IRE)) 2311$^{13}$ 2675$^{14}$ ><

**Karathaena (IRE)** **4** b f Barathea (IRE) -Dabtara (IRE) (Kahyasi) *982$^{8}$ 1055$^{12}$* 1275$^{8}$ 1560$^{14}$ 1857$^{10}$ 5773$^{8}$ 5993$^{10}$ >**41a 55f**<

**Kareeb (FR)** **7** b g Green Desert (USA) -Braari (USA) (Gulch (USA)) *961$^{6}$* 1225$^{14}$ 1504$^{19}$ 2459$^{4}$ 3036$^{21}$ 3755$^{6}$ 4553$^{14}$ 4846$^{6}$5316$^{4}$ 5614$^{11}$ >**84a 84f**<

**Karelian** **3** gr g Linamix (FR) -Kalikala (Darshaan) 6115$^{3}$ 6535$^{6}$ >**71f**<

**Karen s Caper (USA)** **2** b f War Chant (USA) -Miss Caerleona (FR) (Caerleon (USA)) *6153$^{2}$ (6492)* >**85+a**<

**Karita** **2** ch f Inchinor-Ebba (Elmaamul (USA)) 1468$^{9}$ ><

**Karlsson (GER)** **5** b h Second Set (IRE) -Kalinikta (GER) (Konigsstuhl (GER)) 786a$^{9}$ >**97f**<

**Karlu (GER)** **2** ch c Big Shuffle (USA) -Krim (GER) (Lagunas) 3931$^{9}$ (5688) >**73f**<

**Karma Chamelian (USA)** **3** b f Diesis-Wild Rumour (IRE) (Sadler s Wells (USA)) 2479$^{12}$ 3106$^{5}$ 3338$^{7}$ >**43f**<

**Karminskey Park** **5** b m Sabrehill (USA) -Housefull (Habitat) 1525$^{6}$ 1872$^{2}$ 1956$^{6}$ 2252$^{5}$ 2734$^{3}$ 3010$^{2}$ (3225) 3399$^{7}$ 3744$^{7}$3920$^{7}$ 4452$^{9}$ 4828$^{8}$ 5126$^{5}$ 6117$^{10}$ *6559$^{6}$* >**67a 71f**<

**Karramalu (IRE)** **3** b f Entrepreneur-Bold Feather (Persian Bold) 4251a$^{13}$ >**65f**<

**Kartago (GER)** **2** ch c Big Shuffle (USA) -Katharina (GER) (Esclavo (FR)) 6256a$^{7}$ ><

**Karyon (IRE)** **4** b f Presidium-Stealthy (Kind Of Hush) 2408$^{5}$ *3803$^{9}$* 4261$^{10}$ >**46a 43f**<

**Kasai** **5** b g Brief Truce (USA) -Canna (Caerleon (USA)) 1655a$^{7}$ >**110f**<

**Kashimo (GER)** **5** b h Lomitas-Kardia (Mister Rock S (GER)) *887$^{5}$ 962$^{3}$* 1376$^{4}$ >**60a 60f**<

**Kashmar Flight** **2** b f Fraam-Evasive Step (Batshoof) 1839$^{8}$ 2213$^{7}$ 2961$^{6}$ 3406$^{5}$ 5753$^{11}$ >**56f**<

**Kashtanka (IRE)** **2** ch c Ashkalani (IRE) -Spark (IRE) (Flash Of Steel) 4446$^{17}$ 5098$^{6}$ 5301$^{6}$ >**47f**<

**Kaska (IRE)** **3** b f King Of Kings (IRE) -Antiguan Jane (Shirley Heights) 1395$^{7}$ 2085$^{6}$ >**70f**<

**Kastalia (GER)** **4** b f Spectrum (IRE) -Kalila (USA) (Gulch (USA)) (6255a) 6508a$^{7}$ >**101f**<

**Kasthari (IRE)** **5** gr g Vettori (IRE) -Karliyka (IRE) (Last Tycoon) (5415) 6218$^{11}$ >**117f**<

**Kastoria (GER)** **5** br m Dulcero (USA) -Kirsberry (GER) (Mulberry (FR)) 3504a$^{7}$ 3973a$^{6}$ 4980a$^{4}$ 6257a$^{6}$ >**95f**<

**Kasus (GER)** **6** br g Second Set (IRE) -Kettwig (GER) (Acatenango (GER)) 5254a$^{2}$ 5808a$^{4}$ 6512a$^{3}$ >**110f**<

**Katali** **7** ch m Clantime-Portvally (Import) *665$^{11}$* >**1a 42f**<

**Katana** **2** b f Spectrum (IRE) -Karlaska (Lashkari) 4851$^{14}$ 5114$^{12}$ *5735$^{5}$* 6072$^{5}$ >**58a 62f**<

**Katavi (USA)** **3** b f Stravinsky (USA) -Halholah (USA) (Secreto (USA)) *6397$^{5}$* >**58+a**<

**Katayeb (IRE)** **3** b f Machiavellian (USA) -Fair Of The Furze (Ela-Mana-Mou) 5445$^{8}$ >**11f**<

**Katdogawn** **4** b f Bahhare (USA) -Trempkate (USA) (Trempolino (USA)) 6488a$^{10}$ >**110f**<

**Kate Winslet (USA)** **3** b f Signal Tap (USA) -Frances Synatra (USA) (Eastern Echo (USA)) 1320a$^{6}$ 5033a$^{8}$ >**97f**<

**Kathology (IRE)** **7** b g College Chapel-Wicken Wonder (IRE) (Distant Relative) 2679$^{17}$ 2912$^{6}$ 3243$^{7}$ 3480$^{8}$ 4034$^{3}$ 4366$^{5}$ 6532$^{7}$ >**64a 91f**<

**Kathryn Janeway (IRE)** **2** b f In The Wings-Freak Out (FR) (Bering) 6123$^{12}$ 6336$^{6}$ >**58f**<

**Kathy Pekan (IRE)** **5** b m Sri Pekan (USA) -Katy Guest (IRE) (Be My Guest (USA)) 3816a$^{11}$ >**92f**<

**Kathys Job** **2** b f Silver Wizard (USA) -Kathy Fair (IRE) (Nicholas Bill) 1105$^{9}$ >**52f**<

**Katie Boo (IRE)** **2** br f Namid-Misty Peak (IRE) (Sri Pekan (USA)) 2173$^{3}$ 2458$^{2}$ (2933) 3224$^{3}$ 3704$^{5}$ 4150$^{2}$ 4348$^{2}$ (4876) >**85f**<

**Katie Can Dance (USA)** **2** b f Silic (FR) -Can Thou Dance (USA) (Seattle Dancer (USA)) 5330a$^{5}$ >**71f**<

**Katie Kai** **3** b f Cayman Kai (IRE) -Yemaail (IRE) (Shaadi (USA)) 6116$^{5}$ >**5f**<

**Katie Killane** **2** ch f Komaite (USA) -Efficacy (Efisio) 3531$^{7}$ 4243$^{12}$ 5865$^{13}$ *6023$^{12}$* >**39f**<

**Katie Mernagh (IRE)** **4** b f Danetime (IRE) -White Jasmin (Jalmood (USA)) 6438$^{5}$ >**23f**<

**Katie s Bath Time** **3** b f Lugana Beach-Eucharis (Tickled Pink) *731$^{11}$* 1196$^{12}$ >**26f**<

**Katie s Biscuit** **2** b f Cayman Kai (IRE) -Peppers (IRE) (Bluebird (USA)) 5633$^{6}$ 5946$^{10}$ 6514$^{6}$ >**53f**<

**Katie s Role** **3** b f Tragic Role (USA) -Mirkan Honey (Ballymore) *409$^{3}$ 587$^{4}$ 696$^{4}$ 1040$^{3}$* 1116$^{7}$ 1267$^{13}$ >**48a 50f**<

**Katiypour (IRE)** **7** ch g Be My Guest (USA) -Katiyfa (Auction Ring (USA)) *964$^{7}$ 1085$^{3}$ (1118) 1241$^{2}$* 1542$^{8}$ (2030) 2737$^{4}$ 3872$^{12}$ 4262$^{3}$4435$^{4}$ 4691$^{5}$ 5183$^{7}$ 5423$^{7}$ *5739$^{3}$* >**83a 83f**<

**Katy Jem** **2** b f Night Shift (USA) -Top Jem (Damister (USA)) 6471$^{15}$ >**17f**<

**Katy O Hara** **5** b m Komaite (USA) -Amy Leigh (IRE) (Imperial Frontier (USA)) *626$^{9}$ 728$^{2}$ 990$^{6}$* 5639$^{10}$ >**56a 59f**<

**Katz Pyjamas (IRE)** **3** b f Fasliyev (USA) -Allepolina (USA) (Trempolino (USA)) 4868$^{19}$ 5336$^{13}$ >**21a 46f**<

**Kauri Forest (USA)** **3** ch g Woodman (USA) -Kentucky Fall (FR) (Lead On Time (USA)) 1352$^{3}$ 3916$^{2}$ 4316$^{2}$ *6017$^{3}$ 6397$^{4}$* >**66a 89f**<

**Kavi (IRE)** **4** ch g Perugino (USA) -Premier Leap (IRE) (Salmon Leap (USA)) *650$^{7}$ 765$^{8}$ 867$^{11}$* >**62a 61f**<

**Kawaha (IRE)** **2** b f Danehill Dancer (IRE) -Kinn (FR) (Suave Dancer (USA)) 3436a$^{6}$ ><

**Kayak** **3** ch f Singspiel (IRE) -Kelang (Kris) 2341a$^{6}$ 4430a$^{9}$ >**94f**<

**Kayf Aramis** **2** b c Kayf Tara-Ara (Birthright) 2890$^{12}$ ><

**Kaymich Perfecto** **4** b g Sheikh Albadou-Manhattan Diamond (Primo Dominie) 5868$^{14}$ 6096$^{13}$ >**47f**<

**Kaypen (IRE)** **3** b c Orpen (USA) -Khaydariya (IRE) (Akarad (FR)) 2510a$^{7}$ 4965a$^{7}$ >**102f**<

**Kayseri (IRE)** **5** b h Alzao (USA) -Ms Calera (USA) (Diesis) 692a$^{2}$ 849a$^{2}$ 1003a$^{4}$ >**105f**<

**Kay Two (IRE)** **2** ch c Monashee Mountain (USA) -Tricky (Song) 2314a$^{2}$ 3352a$^{4}$ 3965a$^{5}$ (5971a) 6212$^{3}$ 6462a$^{8}$ >**103f**<

**Kedross (IRE)** **3** ch f King Of Kings (IRE) -Nom De Plume (USA) (Nodouble (USA)) *751$^{7}$ 1676$^{7}$ 2128$^{14}$* 2357$^{5}$ *2451$^{7}$* 2766$^{15}$ >**41a 33f**<

**Keelung (USA)** **3** b g Lear Fan (USA) -Miss Universal (IRE) (Lycius (USA)) *890$^{4}$ 1059$^{2}$* 1116$^{2}$ (1524) 1799$^{3}$ 2558$^{2}$ 2999$^{16}$ 5226$^{7}$ 5650$^{14}$5942$^{17}$ >**78a 94f**<

**Keeneland Swan (USA)** **5** b h Distant View (USA) -To Act (USA) (Roberto (USA)) 5982a$^{6}$ >**112f**<

**Keepasharplookout (IRE)** **2** b c Rossini (USA) -Zoyce (Zilzal (USA)) 1359$^{4}$ 1782$^{4}$ 2035$^{10}$ 2773$^{4}$ >**56f**<

**Keep Baccinkhit (IRE)** **2** b f Raise A Grand (IRE) -Taispeain (IRE) (Petorius) 3272$^{3}$ 3770$^{10}$ 3992$^{3}$ (4326) 4953$^{5}$ 5391$^{17}$ 5721$^{4}$ 6090$^{6}$ >**81f**<

**Keepers Knight (IRE)** **3** b c Sri Pekan (USA) -Keepers Dawn (IRE) (Alzao (USA)) *(490) 622$^{3}$ 822$^{5}$ 957$^{7}$* 1365$^{15}$ 3589$^{9}$ 4056$^{3}$ 4711$^{5}$6085$^{4}$ 6337$^{5}$ 6546$^{8}$ >**67a 66f**<

**Keeper s Lodge (IRE)** **3** ch f Grand Lodge (USA) -Gembira (USA) (Alysheba (USA)) 1904$^{4}$ 2284$^{16}$ 2905$^{7}$ (3478) 3926$^{8}$ 4318$^{3}$ 4906$^{5}$ 5145$^{2}$ 5293$^{15}$ >**78 f**<

**Keep Me Warm** **2** ch g Atraf-Little Greenbird (Ardkinglass) 6281$^{4}$ *6478$^{2}$* >**71a 64f**<

**Keep On Movin (IRE)** **3** b f Danehill Dancer (IRE) -Tormented (USA) (Alleged (USA)) 1222$^{5}$ 1394$^{8}$ 3528$^{2}$ 3873$^{7}$ 4642$^{4}$ 5300$^{13}$ >**71a 78f**<

**Keep The Peace (IRE)** **6** br g Petardia-Eiras Mood (Jalmood (USA)) 4080$^{17}$ >**10f**<

**Kehaar** **3** ch c Cadeaux Genereux-Lighthouse (Warning) (2808) (3671) 4273$^{11}$ (5781) >**107+f**<

**Kela (USA)** **6** b h Numerous (USA) -Bolshoi Comedy (USA) (Sovereign Dancer (USA)) *6487a$^{2}$* >**122a**<

**Kelbrook** **5** b g Unfuwain (USA) -Pidona (Baillamont (USA)) 1972$^{5}$ 2273$^{8}$ 3005$^{4}$ >**68f**<

**Kelseas Kolby (IRE)** **4** b g Perugino (USA) -Notre Dame (IRE) (Classic Music (USA)) 1225$^{13}$ 1971$^{13}$ (2209) 2362$^{4}$ 2928$^{3}$ 3247$^{4}$ 4386$^{4}$ 4568$^{2}$ 4818$^{2}$*5222$^{5}$* 5496$^{3}$ 5869$^{18}$ >**61a 63f**<

**Keltic Flute** **5** b g Piccolo-Nanny Doon (Dominion) *425$^{11}$ 527$^{4}$ 730$^{10}$ 809$^{6}$ 998$^{7}$ 1237$^{6}$ 1446$^{7}$* >**34a 34f**<

**Keltic Rainbow (IRE)** **3** b f Spectrum (IRE) -Secrets Of Honour (Belmez (USA)) *482$^{4}$* 1532$^{6}$ *2667$^{9}$* 3996$^{9}$ 4867$^{4}$ 5036$^{5}$ 5257$^{9}$ 6120$^{12}$ >**53a 42f**<

**Keltos (FR)** **6** gr h Kendor (FR) -Loxandra (Last Tycoon) 5169a$^{2}$ 5668a$^{3}$ 5967a$^{5}$ 6214$^{2}$ 6511a$^{3}$ >**96a 129f**<

**Kelucia (IRE)** **3** ch f Grand Lodge (USA) -Karachi (SPA) (Zino) 1123$^{5}$ 1791$^{11}$ 2476$^{5}$ 3033$^{6}$ 3541$^{6}$ 3978$^{6}$ 4322$^{6}$ 5474$^{7}$6044$^{16}$ >**94f**<

**Kempsey** **2** ch c Wolfhound (USA) -Mockingbird (Sharpo) 2376$^{10}$ 2947$^{6}$ *3418$^{4}$* 3930$^{4}$ 5078$^{4}$ 5490$^{6}$ 5839$^{13}$ 5996$^{8}$*6392$^{6}$* >**71a 64f**<

**Kenmore** **2** b c Compton Place-Watheeqah (USA) (Topsider (USA)) 5720$^{4}$ 6171$^{2}$ >**90+f**<

**Kennington** **4** ch g Compton Place-Mim (Midyan (USA)) *(541) 686$^{13}$ 897$^{4}$ 1032$^{9}$* 1268$^{3}$ *1477$^{4}$ 2123$^{9}$* 2473$^{7}$2823$^{2}$ *3277$^{7}$* 3593$^{7}$ 3864$^{4}$ 4105$^{12}$ *4881$^{2}$* 5157$^{4}$ 5597$^{5}$ >**61a 58f**<

**Kenny The Truth (IRE)** **5** b g Robellino (USA) -Just Blink (IRE) (Fairy King (USA)) *434$^{3}$ 567$^{2}$ 778$^{3}$ 824$^{3}$ 940$^{4}$ 989$^{5}$ (1024) 1093$^{4}$*1582$^{3}$ *2128$^{3}$* 2387$^{9}$ *2816$^{P}$ 3380$^{6}$ 3804$^{5}$* 3929$^{12}$ >**53a 48f**<

**Ken s Dream** **5** b g Bin Ajwaad (IRE) -Shoag (USA) (Affirmed (USA)) 1671$^{10}$ 2278$^{3}$ 2738$^{4}$ (3274) 3909$^{4}$ 4343$^{6}$ >**51a 87f**<

**Kensington (GER)** **3** br c Dashing Blade-Key To Win (Lead On Time (USA)) 1350a$^{7}$ 4284a$^{6}$ 5433a$^{5}$ 5965a$^{6}$ >**102f**<

**Kensington (IRE)** **3** b g Cape Cross (IRE) -March Star (IRE) (Mac s Imp (USA)) 1519$^{6}$ 1942$^{3}$ 2236$^{2}$ 2836$^{6}$ (5801) *6016$^{6}$ 6539$^{5}$* >**59a 72f**<

**Kentmere (IRE)** **3** b g Efisio-Addaya (IRE) (Persian Bold) 2519$^{6}$ *(3304)* >**72a 69f**<

**Kentucky Bankes** **2** b c Bluegrass Prince (IRE) -Countess Bankes (Son Pardo) *2125$^{11}$* 2515$^{6}$ 3824$^{8}$ >**21f**<

**Kentucky Blue (IRE)** **4** b g Revoque (IRE) -Delta Town (USA) (Sanglamore (USA)) 1604$^{3}$ 2022$^{12}$ 5211$^{13}$ >**92f**<

**Kentucky Bullet (USA)** **8** b g Housebuster (USA) -Exactly So (Caro) *456$^{3}$ 583$^{7}$ 1042$^{6}$ 1136$^{3}$ 1630$^{6}$ 2816$^{9}$ 3799$^{5}$4189$^{5}$* >**56a 46f**<

**Kentucky Express** **3** b c Air Express (IRE) -Hotel California (IRE) (Last Tycoon) 2367$^{7}$ 2621$^{2}$ 2984$^{3}$ >**76f**<

**Kentucky King (USA)** **4** b g Tale Of The Cat (USA) -Anna s Honor (USA) (Alleged (USA)) *669$^{6}$ 837$^{6}$ 915$^{8}$ (961) 1066$^{7}$* 1273$^{3}$ 1460$^{12}$ 1845$^{12}$2237$^{11}$ 3872$^{3}$ *4549$^{5}$* 4613$^{2}$ 4772$^{RR}$ 4852$^{4}$ 5006$^{RR}$ >**85 a 85f**<

**Kenwyn** **2** b g Efisio-Vilany (Never So Bold) 2058$^{9}$ 3808$^{15}$ >**42f**<

**Keon (IRE)** **2** b c Rossini (USA) -Lonely Brook (USA) (El Gran Senor (USA)) 6331$^{7}$ >**68f**<

**Kerashan (IRE)** **2** b c Sinndar (IRE) -Kerataka (IRE) (Doyoun) 5298$^{4}$ 5696$^{2}$ 6441$^{15}$ >**80+f**<

**Keresforth** **2** b g Mind Games-Bullion (Sabrehill (USA)) *1735$^{10}$* 1970$^{7}$ 2194$^{2}$ (2725) 3930$^{9}$ 4054$^{2}$ 4200$^{8}$ >**54f**<

**Kergolay (IRE)** **2** b c King s Theatre (IRE) -Trim Star (Terimon) *6020$^{6}$ 6393$^{10}$* >**54a**<

**Kerlis** **2** b c Singspiel (IRE) -King Park (IRE) (Marju (IRE)) 6259a$^{10}$ >**49f**<

**Kernel Dowery (IRE)** **4** b g Sri Pekan (USA) -Lady Dowery (USA) (Manila (USA)) 1308$^{8}$ 1611$^{8}$ 2324$^{2}$ (2594) (2930) 3459$^{7}$ 4436$^{7}$ 5038$^{4}$ 5374$^{5}$ 5869$^{13}$*6225$^{4}$ 6495$^{14}$* >**74a 71f**<

**Kerny (IRE)** **2** b c Rossini (USA) -Queen Of Sweden (IRE) (Solid Illusion (USA)) *2125$^{9}$* 4347$^{6}$ 4804$^{11}$ 5363$^{10}$ >**52f**<

**Kerristina** **3** b f So Factual (USA) -Arch Angel (IRE) (Archway (IRE)) 1842$^{13}$ 2425$^{11}$ 2911$^{10}$ *3303$^{7}$* 3990$^{12}$ 4476$^{10}$ >**27a 51f**<

**Kerry s Blade (IRE)** **2** ch g Daggers Drawn (USA) -Treasure (IRE) (Treasure Kay) 2096$^{11}$ 3444$^{5}$ 4824$^{6}$ 5477$^{2}$ 5596$^{6}$ *6021$^{8}$* >**58a 71f**<

**Keshya** **3** b f Mtoto-Liberatrice (FR) (Assert) 1309$^{3}$ 1688$^{4}$ *2005$^{2}$* 3700$^{4}$ >**67a 69f**<

**Kestrel Cross (IRE)** **2** b g Cape Cross (IRE) -Lady Rachel (IRE) (Priolo (USA)) (3286a) >**93f**<

**Kew The Music** **4** b g Botanic (USA) -Harmonia (Glint Of Gold) 1185$^{7}$ 1608$^{10}$ 2064$^{10}$ 4199$^{11}$ 4511$^{16}$ 4800 5081$^{15}$ 5261$^{8}$(5597) 5754$^{10}$ 6131$^{9}$ *6398$^{8}$* >**70a 69f**<

**Keyaki (IRE)** **3** b f Shinko Forest (IRE) -Woodie Dancer (USA) (Green Dancer (USA)) 1352$^{6}$ 1939$^{6}$ (2818) (3306) 4318$^{4}$ 5024$^{4}$ 5652$^{9}$ 6350$^{8}$ >**84f**<

**Keyalzao (IRE)** **2** b f Alzao (USA) -Key Partner (Law Society (USA)) 3233$^{15}$ 4559$^{8}$ 5543$^{9}$ 5946$^{12}$ >**30f**<

**Key Factor** **3** b f Defacto (USA) -Onemoretime (Timeless Times (USA)) 2530$^{4}$ 2777$^{10}$ 2962$^{11}$ *5000$^{14}$* >**2a 56f**<

**Key In** **3** ch f Unfuwain (USA) -Fleet Key (Afleet (CAN)) 1395$^{12}$ 5511$^{6}$ *5907$^{3}$* 6209$^{6}$ >**63a 51f**<

**Keynes (JPN)** **2** ch c Gold Fever (USA) -Eternal Reve (USA) (Diesis) *3377$^{3}$ 4022$^{11}$* 4335$^{2}$ >**51a 69f**<

**Key Of Gold (IRE)** **3** b g Key Of Luck (USA) -Damaslin (Camden Town) *3280$^{8}$* 3446$^{11}$ 4456$^{4}$ 4877$^{16}$ 5126$^{11}$ >**75a 59f**<

**Key Of Solomon (IRE)** **2** ch c Machiavellian (USA) -Minerva (IRE) (Caerleon (USA)) 6077$^{6}$ 6283$^{3}$ 6531$^{2}$ >**78f**<

**Key Partners (IRE)** **3** b g Key Of Luck (USA) -Teacher Preacher (IRE) (Taufan (USA)) (1370) 1640$^{7}$ 2019$^{2}$ 2207$^{8}$ 4490$^{11}$ >**86f**<

**Key Secret** **2** ch f Whittingham (IRE) -Foxkey (Foxhound (USA)) *(2003)* (2523) (3753) 4348$^{4}$ 4752$^{4}$ (5005) 5404a$^{6}$ 5602$^{7}$ 6202a$^{3}$ >**53a 90f**<

**Key To Pleasure (GER)** **4** b c Sharp Prod (USA) -Key To Love (FR) (Alzao (USA)) 2438a$^{9}$ 4596a$^{2}$ 5255a$^{2}$ 6379a$^{2}$ >**110f**<

**Khabfair** **3** b c Intikhab (USA) -Ruby Affair (IRE) (Night Shift (USA)) 3453$^{4}$ (4076) 4531$^{3}$ 4750$^{6}$ 5224$^{8}$ (5762) *6451$^{2}$* >**110a 106 f**<

**Khafayif (USA)** **3** b f Swain (IRE) -Copper Play (USA) (Fast Play (USA)) 1400$^{15}$ 2572$^{3}$ 3209$^{10}$ 4741$^{5}$ >**67f**<

**Khalidia (USA)** **3** b g Boundary (USA) -Maniches Slew (USA) (Slew O Gold (USA)) (2908) 3317$^{2}$ >**81f**<

**Khanjar (USA)** **4** ch g Kris S (USA) -Alyssum

(USA) (Storm Cat (USA)) 1318$^2$ 1746$^4$ 2210$^{13}$ *(4928)* 5210$^2$ 5631$^8$ 6069$^2$ **>81a 94f<**

**Kharish (IRE)** 2 b c Desert Prince (IRE) -Moy Water (IRE) (Tirol) 3726$^4$ 4169$^3$ 4689$^2$ (5268) 5417$^4$ **>87f<**

**Kheleyf (USA)** 3 bb c Green Desert (USA) -Society Lady (USA) (Mr Prospector (USA)) (2966) 3674$^{14}$ 4216$^3$ 4795a$^6$ 5888$^5$ **>117f<**

**Khuzdar (IRE)** 5 ch g Definite Article-Mariyda (IRE) (Vayrann) *432$^7$ 579$^3$ 594$^2$ 653$^{11}$ 661$^5$* (2344a) **>48a 48f<**

**Kiama** 2 b f Dansili-Catriona (Bustino) 5846$^8$ 6352$^6$ **>58f<**

**Kibryaa (USA)** 3 ch c Silver Hawk (USA) -Fleur De Nuit (USA) (Woodman (USA)) 2692$^6$ 3312$^2$ 3819$^2$ 4032$^4$ 4490$^5$ 4756$^7$ **>84+f<**

**Kicken Kris (USA)** 4 b c Kris S (USA) -Kicken Grass (USA) (Jade Hunter (USA)) (4768a) 5985a$^6$ **>123f<**

**Kid Z Play (IRE)** 8 b g Rudimentary (USA) -Saka Saka (Camden Town) 1103$^{16}$ 1661$^3$ 2039$^4$ 2619$^2$ (3005) 3265$^5$ 3796$^3$ 4830$^4$ 4990$^5$5584$^6$ 6535$^8$ **>23a 72f<**

**Kikis Girls (IRE)** 3 b f Spectrum (IRE) -Jane Heller (USA) (Halo (USA)) 4141$^7$ 5621$^{15}$ **><**

**Kilcullen Lass (IRE)** 3 ch f Fayruz-Foretell (Tirol) *890$^{10}$* 1309$^{10}$ **>45a 37f<**

**Kildare Chiller (IRE)** 10 ch g Shahrastani (USA) -Ballycuirke (Taufan (USA)) 1263$^6$ **>48f<**

**Kilindini** 3 gr g Silver Patriarch (IRE) -Newlands Corner (Forzando) 1911$^6$ 2729$^U$ 3994$^5$ 4693$^4$ 5340$^9$ **>70f<**

**Kilkenny Kitten (IRE)** 2 b f Blue Ocean (USA) -El Tina (Unfuwain (USA)) 1170$^6$ *1234$^7$* 2458$^{13}$ **>34a 39f<**

**Killaden (IRE)** 4 b g Barathea (IRE) -Kill The Crab (IRE) (Petorius) 4984a$^5$ **><**

**Killala (IRE)** 4 b g Among Men (USA) -Hat And Gloves (Wolver Hollow) 2172$^3$ 2492$^5$ 3365$^5$ 4132$^2$ 4276$^2$ 4568$^4$ 5459$^{16}$ *6024$^{13}$* **>73f<**

**Kill Cat (IRE)** 3 br c Catrail (USA) -Feather River (USA) (Strike The Gold (USA)) 1777a$^7$ **>93f<**

**Killena Boy (IRE)** 2 b g Imperial Ballet (IRE) -Habaza (IRE) (Shernazar) *4599$^8$* 4809$^8$ 5561$^4$ 6174$^{26}$ **>37a 64f<**

**Killerby Nicko** 3 ch g Pivotal-Bit Of A Tart (Distant Relative) *956$^6$* 1196$^7$ 2351$^6$ 2457$^9$ *2990$^5$* 3234$^U$ 3368$^3$ 3471$^9$3954$^5$ **>45a 55f<**

**Killing Joke** 4 b c Double Trigger (IRE) -Fleeting Vision (IRE) (Vision (USA)) 1287$^{11}$ 1615$^{15}$ **>81+a 68f<**

**Killing Me Softly** 3 b g Kingsinger (IRE) -Slims Lady (Theatrical Charmer) *508$^2$ 804$^8$* 5658$^4$ 6150$^{12}$ *6556$^{10}$* **>47a 55f<**

**Killington (IRE)** 2 ch g Kris-Miss Pickpocket (IRE) (Petorius) 4643$^2$ *5053$^9$* 5910$^{19}$ **>39a 72f<**

**Killmorey** 3 ch g Nashwan (USA) -Zarma (FR) (Machiavellian (USA)) 1794$^{16}$ 2479$^{10}$ 4180$^2$ 4749$^6$ (5191) **>76f<**

**Killoch Place (IRE)** 3 b g Compton Place-Hibernica (IRE) (Law Society (USA)) 1222$^{12}$ 1365$^{17}$ 1667$^7$ 2756$^{10}$ 2979$^3$ 3368$^4$ 3822$^8$ 5552$^9$ **>43f<**

**Kilmeena Lad** 8 b g Minshaanshu Amad (USA) -Kilmeena Glen (Beveled (USA)) *448$^2$ 526$^5$* **>75a 72f<**

**Kilmeena Star** 6 b g So Factual (USA) -Kilmeena Glen (Beveled (USA)) *465$^{10}$ 658$^9$ 858$^{12}$ 998$^4$ (1018) 1206$^2$* 1988$^8$ *2404$^7$*2869$^{10}$ **>57a 42f<**

**Kilminchy Lady (IRE)** 3 b f Cape Cross (IRE) -Lace Flower (Old Vic) 3392$^5$ 4018$^{13}$ 4460$^{10}$ **>42a 41f<**

**Kilmovee** 2 gr f Inchinor-Christmas Rose (Absalom) 2141$^5$ 2550$^9$ 3055$^5$ 3408$^5$ 5234$^{11}$ 5520$^{11}$ 5771$^8$ **>64f<**

**Kimberley Hall** 2 ch f Bachir (IRE) -Sedna (FR) (Bering) 2526$^7$ 5209$^{10}$ 5542$^{13}$ 5848$^{11}$ **>32f<**

**Kimoe Warrior** 6 ch g Royal Abjar (USA) -Thewaari (USA) (Eskimo (USA)) *1514$^5$ 3282$^{13}$* **>36a 47f<**

**Kinbrace** 3 b f Kirkwall-Cache (Bustino) 2536$^6$ 3589$^5$ 5510$^5$ *6399$^9$* **>25a 63f<**

**Kind (IRE)** 3 b f Danehill (USA) -Rainbow Lake (Rainbow Quest (USA)) 1400$^3$ (2301) (2576) (3203) (3914) (5671) **>92+f<**

**Kind Emperor** 7 br g Emperor Jones (USA) -Kind Lady (Kind Of Hush) 4199$^9$ 4655$^4$ 5158$^7$ 5554$^2$ 5853$^6$ 6566$^6$ **>73f<**

**Kindjhal (FR)** 4 b c Ashkalani (IRE) -En Public (FR) (Rainbow Quest (USA)) 1110a$^3$ (1435a) 1922a$^2$ 2924a$^4$ 5170a$^5$ 5968a$^8$ **>112f<**

**Kindlelight Debut** 4 b f Groom Dancer (USA) -Dancing Debut (Polar Falcon (USA)) 3086$^{13}$ 3910$^{17}$ 4148$^3$ 4551$^9$ 5275$^7$ 5419$^{16}$ 5614$^{21}$ *5740$^3$*5948$^{10}$ *6156$^6$ 6553$^{11}$* **>73a 81f<**

**Kindlelight Dream (IRE)** 2 b f Tagula (IRE) -Dioscorea (IRE) (Pharly (FR)) 1299$^8$ *5375$^6$ 5640$^{LFT}$* **>52a<**

**Kindling** 2 br f Dr Fong (USA) -Isle Of Flame (Shirley Heights) 5521$^5$ 5946$^4$ (6240) **>80+f<**

**Kindness** 4 ch f Indian Ridge-Kissing Gate (USA) (Easy Goer (USA)) *1244$^6$* 1875$^7$ 2597$^9$ 3117$^2$ 3264$^2$ 3827$^8$ 4264$^2$ 4771$^{11}$5285$^{14}$ 5830$^7$ 6132$^6$ *6364$^4$* **>51a 52f<**

**Kinfayre Boy** 2 b g Grey Eagle-Amber Gambler (ITY) (Nijin (USA)) 3100$^8$ **><**

**King After** 2 b g Bahamian Bounty-Child Star (FR) (Bellypha) *(1117)* 1383$^6$ 1878$^6$ 4439$^5$ 4907$^5$ 5119$^8$ 5421$^{12}$ 5839$^{14}$ **>68a 76f<**

**King At Last** 5 b g Zamindar (USA) -Louis Queen (IRE) (Tragic Role (USA)) *6015$^8$ 6397$^7$* **>56a 28f<**

**King Carnival (USA)** 3 ch c King Of Kings (IRE) -Miss Waki Club (USA) (Miswaki (USA)) 2224$^{12}$ 2534$^7$ 2891$^7$ 4742$^{15}$ **>97f<**

**Kingdom Of Dreams (IRE)** 2 b c Sadler s Wells (USA) -Regal Portrait (IRE) (Royal Academy (USA)) 6330$^7$ **>56f<**

**King Egbert (FR)** 3 b g Fasliyev (USA) -Exocet (USA) (Deposit Ticket (USA)) 4585$^4$ 4810$^7$ 5473$^3$ 5734$^8$ *6274$^6$* 6567$^5$ **>52a 58f<**

**King Eider** 5 bb g Mtoto-Hen Harrier (Polar Falcon (USA)) 5595$^{13}$ 5919$^9$ 6215$^{24}$ **>96f<**

**King Flyer (IRE)** 8 b g Ezzoud (IRE) -Al Guswa (Shernazar) *981$^8$* 1210$^2$ 1457$^3$ 2240$^{11}$ 2613$^2$ 2958$^{19}$ 3644$^9$ 4174$^7$5595$^8$ *5914$^3$ 6495$^6$* **>72a 87f<**

**King Forever** 2 b c King s Best (USA) -Elude (Slip Anchor) 3601$^6$ **>71f<**

**King Gabriel (IRE)** 2 b g Desert King (IRE) -Broken Spirit (IRE) (Slip Anchor) 5646$^{11}$ 6283$^6$ **>69f<**

**King Halling** 5 b h Halling (USA) -Flower Fairy (FR) (Fairy King (USA)) 2501$^8$ 3733$^6$ 4080$^{14}$ 5267$^4$ *6065$^5$* **>75a 49f<**

**Kingham** 4 ch g Desert Prince (IRE) -Marie De Flandre (FR) (Crystal Palace (FR)) *494$^{11}$ 556$^7$* **>50a 82f<**

**King Harson** 5 b g Greensmith-Safari Park (Absalom) 1772$^{10}$ 2366$^2$ 2469$^{11}$ 3036$^{26}$ 3409$^6$ 4134$^{11}$ (4908) 5077$^5$ 5631$^{18}$6070$^{17}$ 6525$^2$ **>90f<**

**King Henrik (USA)** 2 b g King Of Kings (IRE) -Ma Biche (USA) (Key To The Kingdom (USA)) 2961$^4$ 3406$^6$ 3974$^7$ 5636$^{18}$ **>57f<**

**King Jock (USA)** 3 b c Ghazi (USA) -Glen Kate (Glenstal (USA)) 3001$^{16}$ 4371a$^5$ **>97f<**

**King Kasyapa (IRE)** 2 b c Darshaan-Ezana (Ela-Mana-Mou) 5666a$^5$ **>99f<**

**Kingkohler (IRE)** 5 b g King s Theatre (IRE) -Legit (IRE) (Runnett) *1203$^6$* **>75a 76f<**

**King Marju (IRE)** 2 b c Marju (IRE) -Katoushka (IRE) (Hamas (IRE)) 4290$^6$ 5353$^2$ (5720) 6090$^2$ 6340$^3$ **>92f<**

**King Nicholas (USA)** 5 b g Nicholas (USA) -Lifetime Honour (USA) (Kingmambo (USA)) *952$^7$ (1025)* 1197$^{10}$ 1526$^4$ (1941) 3742$^9$ 4509$^6$ *4879$^8$* 5108$^6$*(6295) 6580$^4$* **>66a 62+f<**

**King Of Blues (IRE)** 2 ch c Bluebird (USA) -Highly Respected (IRE) (High Estate) 2904$^{10}$ 3259$^8$ *4023$^4$* (4365) 4953$^7$ 5719$^3$ **>65a 78f<**

**King Of Boxmeer (GER)** 5 b g Platini (GER) -Kitzmaid (GER) (Midyan (USA)) 1259a$^6$ 1802a$^{LFT}$ 2320a$^3$ 2508a$^9$ **>116?f<**

**King Of Cashel (IRE)** 3 b c King Of Kings (IRE) -Jaya (USA) (Ela-Mana-Mou) 2844$^3$ 3542$^9$ **>89f<**

**King Of Central (IRE)** 2 ch c Central Park (IRE) -Lady Mar (Generous (IRE)) 5388a$^5$ **><**

**King Of Cry (FR)** 3 ch c Freedom Cry-Queen s Mary (FR) (Marignan (USA)) 2073a$^5$ 2722a$^{14}$ 6170a$^7$ **>105f<**

**King Of Diamonds** 3 b c Mtoto-Capricious Lass (Corvaro (USA)) *1083$^2$ 1202$^6$ 1243$^2$* 3086$^{12}$ 4032$^7$ (4756) 5120$^{10}$ 5403$^4$5574$^{11}$ *6396$^2$ 6498$^2$* **>86a 83 f<**

**King Of Dreams (IRE)** 3 b c Sadler s Wells (USA) -Koniya (IRE) (Doyoun) (1116) 1414$^{11}$ (4173) 4540$^5$ 4831$^F$ **>103+f<**

**King Of Fire** 2 b g Magic Ring (IRE) -Alaskan Princess (IRE) (Prince Rupert (FR)) 2300$^9$ **>46f<**

**King Of Knight (IRE)** 3 gr g Orpen (USA) -Peace Melody (IRE) (Classic Music (USA)) 1371$^4$ 1613$^5$ 2097$^9$ 3050$^7$ 4655$^9$ 5156$^4$ *5914$^2$ 6495$^4$* **>64a 69f<**

**King Of Love** 2 b c King s Best (USA) -Fadaki Hawaki (USA) (Vice Regent (CAN)) (3197) **>66f<**

**King Of Meze (IRE)** 3 b g Croco Rouge (IRE) -Cossack Princess (IRE) (Lomond (USA)) *766$^8$ 840$^6$ 956$^{11}$ 3026$^9$* 6057$^9$ **>38a 34f<**

**King Of Music (USA)** 3 ch g Jade Hunter (USA) -Hail Roberta (USA) (Roberto (USA)) 2596$^8$ 4652$^7$ 5156$^6$ *6399$^2$* **>59a 67f<**

**King Priam (IRE)** 9 b g Priolo (USA) -Barinia (Corvaro (USA)) *430$^8$ 440$^4$ (471) 542$^4$ 570$^5$ 616$^9$ 682$^6$ 715$^6$781$^4$ 825$^5$ 880$^6$ 1026$^5$ 1028$^4$* 1103$^{20}$ *1448$^7$1698$^6$ 2851$^6$* **>39a 38f<**

**King Quantas (IRE)** 6 b h Danehill (USA) -Palacegate Episode (IRE) (Drumalis) 5505a$^{10}$ **><**

**King Revo (IRE)** 4 b g Revoque (IRE) -Tycoon Aly (IRE) (Last Tycoon) (1661) 2022$^{15}$ **>88a 90f<**

**King s Account (USA)** 2 ch c King Of Kings (IRE) -Fighting Countess (USA) (Ringside (USA)) 4606$^2$ 4900$^2$ 5256$^2$ (5561) (6140) **>87f<**

**King s Ballet (USA)** 6 b g Imperial Ballet (IRE) -Multimara (USA) (Arctic Tern (USA)) *453$^8$ 637$^8$ 796$^2$ 1033$^9$ 1180$^4$* 1368$^{11}$ 1537$^{11}$1872$^{13}$ 2178$^{16}$ **>50a 50f<**

**King s Boy (GER)** 7 ch h Platini (GER) -King s Blade (IRE) (Sure Blade (USA)) *1147a$^5$* **>97a 94f<**

**King s Caprice** 3 ch g Pursuit Of Love-Palace Street (USA) (Secreto (USA)) 1797$^7$ 2372$^3$ 2785$^4$ (3322) 3542$^7$ 3995$^4$ 4510$^4$ (4846) 5112$^5$ 5628$^{16}$6191$^2$ 6341$^7$ **>97f<**

**Kings College Boy** 4 b g College Chapel-The Kings Daughter (Indian King (USA)) 1974$^{17}$ 2261$^8$ 2784$^3$ 3016$^2$ 3399$^3$ 3509$^8$ 4013$^3$ 4133$^7$4452$^3$ 4828$^9$ (4935) 5107$^9$ 5458$^2$ 5579$^4$ 5605$^{12}$ 6046$^4$ 6518$^6$ **>76f<**

**King s County (IRE)** 6 b g Fairy King (USA) -Kardelle (Kalaglow) 1456$^3$ 2044$^{11}$ 2503$^3$ 2969$^{29}$ 3937$^{14}$ 5470$^2$ 5941$^{12}$ **>95f<**

**Kingscross** 6 ch g King s Signet (USA) -Calamanco (Clantime) 1185$^4$ 1608$^2$ (1825) 2477$^{15}$ 3663$^5$ 4759$^{19}$ 5075$^2$ 5263$^2$ 5730$^6$5874$^4$ 6070$^4$ 6477$^{20}$ **>90f<**

**Kingsdon (IRE)** 7 b g Brief Truce (USA) -Richly Deserved (IRE) (King s Lake (USA)) *653$^{10}$ (793) 947$^9$ 1277$^4$* 1527$^4$ (1722) *(2053) (3088)* (3265) 3510$^3$ **>62a 69f<**

**King s Drama (IRE)** 4 b g King s Theatre (IRE) -Last Drama (IRE) (Last Tycoon) 1163a$^8$ 1780a$^7$ 6384a$^5$ **>112f<**

**Kings Empire** 3 b g Second Empire (IRE) -Dancing Feather (Suave Dancer (USA)) 3152$^4$ 3706$^4$ 5768$^{19}$ 6332$^{14}$ **>78a 84f<**

**King s Envoy (USA)** 5 b g Royal Academy (USA) -Island Of Silver (USA) (Forty Niner (USA)) 1318$^4$ 1747$^3$ 2174$^5$ 2583$^9$ 5085$^{10}$ 5584$^{15}$ **>67f<**

**King s Gait** 2 b g Mujahid (USA) -Miller s Gait (Mill Reef (USA)) 1415$^6$ (1709) 2086$^4$ **>79f<**

**Kingsgate Bay (IRE)** 2 b g Desert Sun-Selkirk Flyer (Selkirk (USA)) 2761$^7$ *3418$^5$* 4643$^5$ (5234) **>59a 74f<**

**Kingsholm** 2 ch c Selkirk (USA) -Putuna (Generous (IRE)) 4030$^6$ 4689$^3$ 5302$^7$ **>73f<**

**King s Kama** 2 b c Giant s Causeway (USA) -Maid For The Hills (Indian Ridge) 4649$^4$ 5347$^4$ *6153$^3$* **>77a 77+f<**

**Kingsmaite** 3 b g Komaite (USA) -Antonias Melody (Rambo Dancer (CAN)) 1129$^{11}$ 1558$^4$ 2239$^9$ 2589$^5$ (3059) *4928$^3$* 5242$^{16}$ 5715$^5$ 6094$^{14}$*6482$^2$* **>87a 73f<**

**King s Majesty (IRE)** 2 b c King s Best (USA) -Tiavanita (USA) (J O Tobin (USA)) 5718$^7$ *6155$^2$ (6453)* **>84a 52+f<**

**King s Minstrel (IRE)** 3 b g Cape Cross (IRE) -Muwasim (USA) (Meadowlake (USA)) 2114$^{14}$ 2311$^7$ 5891$^{10}$ 6132$^7$ **>41f<**

**King s Mountain (USA)** 4 b g King Of Kings (IRE) -Statistic (USA) (Mr Prospector (USA)) 1369$^{18}$ 3099$^{10}$ **>13a 13f<**

**King Spinner (IRE)** 7 b g Mujadil (USA) -Money Spinner (USA) (Teenoso (USA)) 3743$^{12}$ **><**

**Kings Point (IRE)** 3 b c Fasliyev (USA) -Rahika Rose (Unfuwain (USA)) *1239$^5$* 1459$^{10}$ 2398$^5$ 2913$^3$ 3036$^{11}$ 3318$^4$ 3673$^{13}$ 4322$^3$5422$^7$ 5610$^8$ 5888$^7$ **>97a 106 f<**

**Kings Quay** 2 b c Montjeu (IRE) -Glen Rosie (IRE) (Mujtahid (USA)) (2627) 2954$^{12}$ 4088$^2$ (4716) 5895$^6$ **>101f<**

**Kings Rock** 3 ch g Kris-Both Sides Now (USA) (Topsider (USA)) *683$^2$ 835$^6$ 985$^9$* 1214$^7$ 2036$^6$ 2545$^3$ 3684$^{10}$ (4018) 4497$^2$(5141) 5370$^{18}$ 5541$^{12}$ 5992$^{14}$ **>61a 66f<**

**Kings Square** 4 b g Bal Harbour-Prime Property (IRE) (Tirol) 5229$^{12}$ **>31f<**

**King s Thought** 5 b h King s Theatre (IRE) -Lora s Guest (Be My Guest (USA)) 1124$^6$ 1328$^8$ 1540$^4$ 1762$^6$ 1902$^4$ 2672$^4$ 3119$^3$ **>90a 105f<**

**Kingston Town (USA)** 4 ch g King Of Kings (IRE) -Lady Ferial (FR) (Carwhite) *559$^9$ 590$^7$ 667$^4$ 735$^7$* 4262$^6$ 4458$^7$ *4925$^2$*5187$^5$ *5381$^{10}$* **>69a 60f<**

**Kings Topic (USA)** 4 ch g Kingmambo (USA) -Topicount (USA) (Private Account (USA)) *1404$^2$ (1545) (1691)* 2034$^7$ **>55a 53f<**

**King Summerland** 7 b g Minshaanshu Amad (USA) -Alaskan Princess (IRE) (Prince Rupert (FR)) 5673$^5$ 6142$^4$ **>57?f<**

**King s Welcome** 6 b g Most Welcome-Reine De Thebes (FR) (Darshaan) 6208$^6$ 6444$^{10}$ **>31f<**

**Kingsword (USA)** 3 bl c Dynaformer (USA) -Western Curtsey (USA) (Gone West (USA)) 2672$^5$ 3118$^2$ 4271$^{14}$ **>102f<**

**King Top** 3 b g Inchinor-Panorama (Shirley Heights) 3057$^4$ **>14f<**

**King Zafeen (IRE)** 2 b c Lend A Hand-Groom Dancing (Groom Dancer (USA)) 4523$^{13}$ 5302$^4$ 5592$^9$ 6515$^{16}$ **>72 f<**

**Kiniska** 3 b f Merdon Melody-Young Whip (Bold Owl) 2647$^9$ *6017$^{11}$* **>62a 57f<**

**Kinkozan** 3 ch c Peintre Celebre (USA) -Classic Design (Busted) 3447$^6$ *4128$^{12}$* **>51f<**

**Kinnaird (IRE)** 3 ch f Dr Devious (IRE) -Ribot s Guest (IRE) (Be My Guest (USA)) 2330a$^4$ 3033$^5$ 3699$^2$ 4430a$^2$ 5679a$^2$ **>110f<**

**Kinrande (IRE)** 2 b c Sri Pekan (USA) -Pipers Pool (IRE) (Mtoto) 5840$^3$ *6492$^3$* **>78a 68+f<**

**Kinsman (IRE)** 7 b g Distant Relative-Besito (Wassl) *469$^2$ (738) 815$^5$ 1121$^4$* 2803$^6$ 2886$^{10}$ 3174$^{11}$ 4546$^{11}$*6493$^5$* **>60a 69f<**

**Kintore** 3 ch c Inchinor-Souadah (USA) (General Holme (USA)) 2077$^6$ 3007$^4$ 3581$^{10}$ **>42f<**

**Kipsigis (IRE)** 3 b g Octagonal (NZ) -Kisumu (Damister (USA)) 4850$^7$ 5445$^4$ *5907$^4$* **>68+a 62f<**

**Kirat** 6 b g Darshaan-Kafsa (IRE) (Vayrann) *651$^{11}$ 818$^4$* **>50a 47f<**

**Kirkby s Treasure** 6 ro g Mind Games-Gem Of Gold (Jellaby) (1345) 2172$^2$ (2492) 2936$^3$ 3198$^9$ (3365) 3516$^2$ 4134$^{13}$ 4280$^2$ 4751$^2$ 4931$^6$5603$^{17}$ 5818$^3$ 6244$^5$ 6525$^3$ 6568$^2$ **>43a 82f<**

**Kirkham Abbey** 4 b g Selkirk (USA) -Totham (Shernazar) 2258$^7$ 2547$^3$ 2930$^2$ 3387$^6$ 3903$^5$ (4436) 5423$^{11}$ (5853) **>64a 76f<**

**Kirkhammerton (IRE)** 2 ch g Grand Lodge (USA) -Nawara (Welsh Pageant) 4611$^{14}$ 5015$^8$ 5494$^7$ 5616$^{14}$ **>36f<**

**Kirking (FR)** 2 ch c Kirkwall-Queen Of Kings (IRE) (King Of Clubs) 5389a$^8$ **><**

**Kirov King (IRE)** 4 b c Desert King (IRE) -Nymphs Echo (IRE) (Mujtahid (USA)) 1272$^9$ 1832$^7$ 2235$^7$ 2537$^{15}$ 3825$^6$ 5153$^{10}$ **>81f<**

**Kisses For Me (IRE)** 3 b f Sadler s Wells (USA) -Fanny Cerrito (USA) (Gulch (USA)) 1793$^5$ 2330a$^{10}$ 2640$^7$ 3969a$^3$ 4406a$^3$ 4884$^8$ 5162a$^3$ **>100f<**

**Kissing A Fool** 2 b g Tipsy Creek (USA) -Amathus Glory (Mummy s Pet) 1183$^5$ (1666) 1970$^{11}$ *2124$^5$* **>21a 45f<**

**Kissing Lights (IRE)** 2 b f Machiavellian (USA) -Nasaieb (IRE) (Fairy King (USA)) 2481$^5$ (2940) 3316$^6$ 4119$^3$ 4885$^8$ 5464$^3$ **>98f<**

**Kiss The Rain** 4 b f Forzando-Devils Dirge (Song) *510$^6$ 3381$^{12}$* 5364$^{16}$ 6007$^8$ **>58a 62f<**

**Kiswahili** 2 ch f Selkirk (USA) -Kiliniski (Niniski (USA)) 3870$^2$ (5831) **>86+f<**

**Kitara (GER)** 4 b f Camp David (GER) -Kantilene (GER) (Windwurf (GER)) 6107a$^9$ **>84f<**

**Kitcat (GER)** 3 b f Monsun (GER) -Kittiwake (Barathea (IRE)) 5823a$^3$ 6258a$^2$ **>100f<**

**Kitchen Sink (IRE)** 2 ch g Bold Fact (USA) -Voodoo Rocket (Lycius (USA)) 6126$^{10}$ 6281$^{10}$ **>46f<**

**Kitley** 3 b c Muhtarram (USA) -Salsita (Salse (USA)) 1508$^{13}$ 1997$^{16}$ 2377$^6$ 2915$^{14}$ *3304$^{10}$* **>48a 63f<**

**Kitten s Joy (USA)** 3 ch c El Prado (IRE) -Kitten s First (USA) (Lear Fan (USA)) (4769a) (5985a) 6490a$^2$ **>128f<**

**Kittylee** 5 b m Bal Harbour-Courtesy Call (Northfields (USA)) *430$^{12}$ 475$^6$* **>22a 14f<**

**Knead The Dough** 3 b g Wolfhound (USA) -Ridgewood Ruby (IRE) (Indian Ridge) *856$^2$* 5338$^6$ 5656$^7$ 6009$^2$ 6131$^{19}$ *6280$^5$* **>58a 54f<**

**Knickyknackienoo** 3 b g Bin Ajwaad (IRE) -Ring Fence (Polar Falcon (USA)) *1046$^4$* 1300$^2$ 1908$^2$ 2400$^{12}$ 2766$^3$ (3246) 3589$^7$ 4147$^2$ 4242$^5$*5222$^3$* 5496$^{11}$ **>63a 66+f<**

**Knight Of Hearts (IRE)** 3 gr g Idris (IRE) -Heart To Heart (IRE) (Double Schwartz) *1179$^5$ 1628$^5$* 2519$^{11}$ *3804$^{11}$* 4829$^4$ 5178$^8$ *6361$^2$* **>47a 43f<**

**Knight Of Silver** 7 gr g Presidium-Misty Rocket (Roan Rocket) 3776$^8$ **>45f<**

**Knight Onthe Tiles (IRE)** 3 ch g Primo Dominie-Blissful Night (Cadeaux Genereux) *462$^{11}$ 696$^9$* 3158$^9$ 3817$^{14}$ 4126$^8$ 4548$^{12}$ **>71da 72f<**

**Knightsbridge Hill (IRE)** 2 b c Raise A Grand (IRE) -Desert Gem (Green Desert (USA)) 4480$^5$ 4913$^6$ 5406$^4$ 5885$^{17}$ **>74f<**

**Knight To Remember (IRE)** 3 ch g Fayruz-Cheerful Knight (IRE) (Mac s Imp (USA)) *587$^3$ 751$^4$ 1040$^9$* 2040$^9$ 2346$^5$ 2657$^9$ *2986$^5$* 3513$^7$4102$^{13}$ **>50a 44f<**

**Knock Bridge (IRE)** 2 b f Rossini (USA) -Touraneena (Robellino (USA)) 2213$^4$ 2489$^2$ 2947$^8$ 5690$^3$ 6080$^{15}$ (6206) 6574$^{12}$ **>72f<**

**Knockdoo (IRE)** 11 ch g Be My Native (USA) -Ashken (Artaius (USA)) *594$^{10}$ 699$^3$* **>6a 40f<**

**Knocktopher Abbey** 7 ch g Pursuit Of Love-Kukri (Kris) *740$^{12}$* 5151$^7$ 5935$^{11}$ **>52a 52f<**

**Knot In Doubt (IRE)** 3 b g Woodborough (USA) -In The Mind (IRE) (Taufan (USA)) 2195$^9$ 2657$^{12}$ **>36f<**

**Knot In Wood (IRE)** 2 b c Shinko Forest (IRE) -Notley Park (Wolfhound (USA)) 5362$^{10}$ 5752$^6$ 6045$^3$ **>66f<**

**Known Maneuver (USA)** 6 b g Known Fact (USA) -Northernmaneuver (USA) (Al Nasr (FR)) *715$^4$ 829$^4$ 1023$^9$* **>41a 42f<**

**Kodiac** 3 b c Danehill (USA) -Rafha (Kris) (5378) 5776$^7$ 6477$^{17}$ **>83f<**

**Kolina (FR)** 3 b f Green Tune (USA) -Kalistina (FR) (Sillery (USA)) 3434a$^{10}$ **><**

**Kolyma (IRE)** 2 ch f Grand Lodge (USA) -Koniya (IRE) (Doyoun) 4143$^8$ 4706$^5$ 5368$^{12}$ **>61f<**

**Komac** 2 b c Komaite (USA) -Star Of Flanders (Puissance) 2024$^6$ 2502$^2$ 3196$^4$ 3531$^6$ *(4924)* 5418$^7$ 5947$^P$ **>65a 71f<**

**Komati River** 5 b g Wesaam (USA) -Christening (IRE) (Lahib (USA)) *583$^8$* 1858$^{16}$ 2305$^{12}$ **>57a 51f<**

**Komena** 6 b m Komaite (USA) -Mena (Blakeney) *519$^5$ 573$^9$ 654$^8$* 2823$^8$ 3151$^{10}$ 3533$^5$ 3828$^{16}$ 4708$^8$5283$^{14}$ **>37a 45f<**

**Komoto** 3 b g Mtoto-Imperial Scholar (IRE) (Royal Academy (USA)) *(3848)* 4242$^9$ 4618$^{10}$ 5037$^4$ 5826$^{17}$ **>70+a 56f<**

**Komreyev Star** 2 b c Komaite (USA) -L Ancressaan (Dalsaan) 5542$^9$ 5857$^{13}$ 6543$^8$ **>45f<**

**Kong (IRE)** 2 b c Sadler s Wells (USA) -Hill Of Snow (Reference Point) 5790$^4$ 6148$^3$ **>78f<**

**Konigstiger (GER)** 2 b c Tiger Hill (IRE) -Kittiwake (Barathea (IRE)) (6259a) **>105f<**

**Konker** 9 ch g Selkirk (USA) -Helens Dreamgirl (Caerleon (USA)) 1669$^3$ **>53f<**

**Koodoo** 3 gr g Fasliyev (USA) -Karsiyaka (IRE) (Kahyasi) 1972$^8$ 2367$^6$ 2760$^8$ 3581$^8$ 4259$^{13}$ 4989$^5$ 6467$^8$ **>60f<**

**Kool (IRE)** 5 b g Danehill Dancer (IRE) -New Rochelle (IRE) (Lafontaine (USA)) 1367$^3$ 1610$^7$ 1968$^5$ 2283$^5$ 2575$^3$ 3052$^5$ 3337$^4$ 4553$^9$4742$^2$ 5112$^3$ 5468$^6$ 5781$^2$ **>3a 99f<**

**Kool Acclaim** 3 b f Royal Applause-Carrie Kool (Prince Sabo) 4337$^2$ (4653) 5563$^{12}$ **>78+f<**

**Koolman (IRE)** 2 ch c King Of Kings (IRE) -Coolamon (USA) (Saratoga Six (USA)) 3352a$^6$ **>81f<**

**Kool Ovation** 2 b g Royal Applause-Carrie Kool (Prince Sabo) 4149$^5$ 4507$^3$ 5857$^3$ **>71f<**

**Koonunga Hill (GER)** 3 b f Big Shuffle (USA) -Karena (GER) (Midyan (USA)) 2335a$^6$ **>86f<**

**Kostar** 3 ch g Komaite (USA) -Black And Amber (Weldnaas (USA)) 3322$^4$ (4144) 4717$^{11}$ 5697$^4$ *6538$^2$*

>**83a 79f**<

**Krasivi s Boy (USA)** 2 bb c Swain (IRE) -Krasivi (USA) (Nijinsky (CAN)) 4544$^{9}$ 5114$^{2}$ 5735$^{4}$ 6129$^{12}$ >**67a 70f**<

**Krataios (FR)** 4 b c Sabrehill (USA) -Loxandra (Last Tycoon) 1780a$^{4}$ 2109$^{12}$ >**111f**<

**Krisman (IRE)** 5 ch h Kris-Corn Circle (IRE) (Thatching) 3816a$^{8}$ 6261a$^{2}$ 6513a$^{6}$ >**106f**<

**Kristalchen** 2 b f Singspiel (IRE) -Crystal Flite (IRE) (Darshaan) 4359$^{7}$ 4851$^{9}$ 5368$^{7}$ 6308$^{4}$ >**60f**<

**Kristal s Dream (IRE)** 3 b f Night Shift (USA) -Kristal s Paradise (IRE) (Bluebird (USA)) 1640$^{3}$ 2169$^{5}$ 2751$^{7}$ 3383$^{2}$ 4103$^{5}$ 4642$^{12}$ >**80f**<

**Kristensen** 5 ch g Kris S (USA) -Papaha (FR) (Green Desert (USA)) 1615$^{5}$ 1880$^{9}$ 2285$^{6}$ 2491$^{2}$ 3310$^{5}$ 3725$^{10}$ 4226$^{7}$ 4831$^{3}$5608$^{8}$ 5820$^{2}$ 6215$^{10}$ 6535$^{3}$ >**84 a 88f**<

**Kristiansand** 4 b g Halling (USA) -Zonda (Fabulous Dancer (USA)) 3738$^{8}$ 3903$^{6}$ 4333$^{4}$ 4826$^{10}$ >**73f**<

**Kristikhab (IRE)** 2 ch g Intikhab (USA) -Alajyal (IRE) (Kris) 1170$^{7}$ 1930$^{5}$ 2422$^{4}$ 2616$^{2}$ 2852$^{10}$ 3286a$^{12}$ 3893$^{7}$ 4329$^{5}$4675$^{8}$ 5234$^{19}$ 5670$^{8}$ 6544$^{15}$ >**49f**<

**Kristineau** 6 ch m Cadeaux Genereux-Kantikoy (Alzao (USA)) 2462$^{5}$ 2731$^{7}$ 2978$^{6}$ 3518$^{9}$ 3604$^{18}$ >**50f**<

**Kristinor (FR)** 2 ch g Inchinor-Kristina (Kris) 4292$^{6}$ 5871$^{9}$ >**72f**<

**Kristoffersen** 4 ch g Kris-Towaahi (IRE) (Caerleon (USA)) 887$^{9}$ 984$^{8}$ >**81a 77f**<

**Krugerrand (USA)** 5 ch g Gulch (USA) -Nasers Pride (USA) (Al Nasr (FR)) 872$^{9}$ 1114$^{13}$ 1273$^{10}$ 1708$^{13}$ (2894) 3347$^{3}$ 3842$^{6}$ 4214$^{11}$ 4319$^{5}$(5004) 5470$^{5}$ 5941$^{27}$ 6475$^{13}$ >**79a 94f**<

**Krullind (IRE)** 2 b g Rossini (USA) -Jemima Yorke (Be My Guest (USA)) 6171$^{21}$ 6476$^{6}$ 6563$^{6}$ >**64f**<

**Krumpet** 2 b f Mujahid (USA) -Dame Jude (Dilum (USA)) 4053$^{7}$ 4705$^{9}$ >**64f**<

**Krynica (USA)** 2 br f Danzig (USA) -Bionic (Zafonic (USA)) (3123) 3865$^{4}$ 5548$^{14}$ >**76f**<

**Kryssa** 3 ch f Kris-Alessandra (Generous (IRE)) 840$^{4}$ (963) 1086$^{3}$ 1312$^{3}$ 2063$^{5}$ (2577) 3180$^{3}$ (3700) 4264$^{3}$ (4580) 5566$^{11}$5739$^{6}$ >**71a 83f**<

**Kschessinka (USA)** 3 br f Nureyev (USA) -Gran Dama (USA) (Rahy (USA)) (2785) 3317$^{3}$ 3995$^{6}$ >**85f**<

**Kudbeme** 2 b f Forzando-Umbrian Gold (IRE) (Perugino (USA)) 2860$^{12}$ 6092$^{6}$ >**43f**<

**Kumakawa** 6 ch g Dancing Spree (USA) -Maria Cappuccini (Siberian Express (USA)) 491$^{13}$ 627$^{5}$ 659$^{8}$ 717$^{3}$ 894$^{7}$ 914$^{8}$ 952$^{2}$1019$^{6}$ 1233$^{7}$ 1274$^{9}$ 1863$^{8}$ 5929$^{5}$ 6551$^{10}$ >**57a 24f**<

**Kumala Ocean (IRE)** 2 ch f Blue Ocean (USA) -Kumala (IRE) (Simply Great (FR)) 4095$^{2}$ 4277$^{5}$ 4966$^{9}$ 5447$^{2}$ 5636$^{8}$ >**45a 56f**<

**Kumari (IRE)** 3 b f Desert Story (IRE) -Glow Tina (IRE) (Glow (USA)) 561$^{11}$ >**39a 42f**<

**Kunda (IRE)** 3 b f Intikhab (USA) -Ustka (Lomond (USA)) 2193a$^{6}$ 2641$^{2}$ 3105$^{3}$ 3541$^{7}$ 4077$^{7}$ 4773$^{10}$ >**99f**<

**Kundooz** 5 b g Sabrehill (USA) -Reem Albaraari (Sadler s Wells (USA)) 925a$^{2}$ 1006a$^{3}$ >**105f**<

**Kuringai** 3 b g Royal Applause-Talighta (USA) (Barathea (IRE)) 619$^{10}$ 819$^{4}$ 1209$^{3}$ 1333$^{8}$ 2063$^{17}$ 2444$^{10}$ 4052$^{10}$ 4299$^{10}$ >**65 a 73f**<

**Kurkova (IRE)** 2 b f Fasliyev (USA) -Bellissi (IRE) (Bluebird (USA)) 5971a$^{9}$ >**32f**<

**Kurm (IRE)** 3 b c Grand Lodge (USA) -Will Be Blue (IRE) (Darshaan) 1898a$^{3}$ >**103f**<

**Kussharro** 3 ch c Case Law-Risking (Risk Me (FR)) 5803$^{9}$ >**23f**<

**Kuster** 8 b g Indian Ridge-Ustka (Lomond (USA)) 2022$^{14}$ 2895$^{6}$ (3385) 3757$^{6}$ >**97f**<

**Kustom Kit For Her** 4 b f Overbury (IRE) -Antonias Melody (Rambo Dancer (CAN)) 541$^{6}$ 569$^{8}$ 625$^{10}$ 715$^{13}$ 729$^{2}$ 811$^{3}$ 877$^{2}$935$^{2}$ 997$^{4}$ 1022$^{8}$ 4093$^{8}$ 4925$^{10}$ >**43a 43f**<

**Kwaheri** 6 b m Efisio-Fleeting Affair (Hotfoot) 4686$^{9}$ >**53f**<

**Kwai Baby (USA)** 3 gr f Charnwood Forest (IRE) -Roses In The Snow (IRE) (Be My Guest (USA)) 5495$^{7}$ 5891$^{9}$ 6132$^{9}$ 6287$^{8}$ >**30f**<

**Kwame** 2 b f Kingsinger (IRE) -Admire (Last Tycoon) 2376$^{2}$ (2884) 3696$^{2}$ 4217$^{13}$ 4918$^{2}$ 5119$^{5}$ 5421$^{3}$ 5701$^{9}$ 6158$^{5}$ >**63a 79f**<

**Kyalami (IRE)** 5 b g Kylian (USA) -Nikkicola (USA) (Damascus (USA)) 432$^{3}$ 475$^{4}$ >**40a**<

**Kyber** 3 ch g First Trump-Mahbob Dancer (FR) (Groom Dancer (USA)) 3625$^{5}$ 4180$^{4}$ 4444$^{3}$ 4703$^{3}$ 5860$^{10}$ 6141$^{6}$ 6245$^{4}$ 6527$^{5}$ >**58?f**<

**Kykuit (IRE)** 2 b f Green Desert (USA) -Cromac (ITY) (Machiavellian (USA)) (5330a) >**96f**<

**Kyle Of Lochalsh** 4 gr g Vettori (IRE) -Shaieef (IRE) (Shareef Dancer (USA)) 525$^{3}$ 623$^{11}$ 2547$^{10}$ 2738$^{12}$ 3367$^{5}$ 4065$^{5}$ 4485$^{12}$ 6467$^{6}$ >**62a 49f**<

**Kylkenny** 9 b g Kylian (USA) -Fashion Flow (Balidar) 1030$^{3}$ 1272$^{11}$ 1460$^{13}$ 2591$^{6}$ 2895$^{5}$ 3274$^{3}$ 3752$^{4}$ 4086$^{4}$4641$^{4}$ 5229$^{14}$ 5764$^{10}$ 6152$^{8}$ >**98a 78f**<

**Kythia (IRE)** 3 b f Kahyasi-Another Rainbow (IRE) (Rainbows For Life (CAN)) 2169$^{4}$ 2848$^{3}$ 3557$^{2}$ 3989$^{7}$ 5203$^{6}$ 5560$^{9}$ 5869$^{14}$ >**77f**<

**L**

**Laabbij (USA)** 3 ch c Shuailaan (USA) -United Kingdom (USA) (Danzig (USA)) 1461$^{6}$ 2001$^{10}$ 2361$^{5}$ 4402$^{3}$ 4673$^{2}$ >**76f**<

**Laawaris (USA)** 3 b g Souvenir Copy (USA) -Seattle Kat (USA) (Seattle Song (USA)) 1588$^{8}$ 1831$^{12}$ 2244$^{9}$ >**73 f**<

**La Bella Grande (IRE)** 2 ch f Giant s Causeway (USA) -La Belle Otero (USA) (Nureyev (USA)) 6471$^{12}$ >**48f**<

**La Bella Rosa (IRE)** 2 b f Revoque (IRE) -Tempesta Rossa (IRE) (Persian Heights) 1961$^{10}$ 2140$^{8}$ 2904$^{17}$ ><

**Labelled With Love** 4 ch g Zilzal (USA) -Dream Baby (Master Willie) 2520$^{2}$ 2801$^{5}$ 3177$^{6}$ 3848$^{9}$ 5642$^{5}$ 5929$^{2}$ 6404$^{2}$ >**52a 56f**<

**Labrett** 7 b g Tragic Role (USA) -Play The Game (Mummy s Game) 494$^{3}$ 577$^{9}$ 677$^{5}$ 1066$^{2}$ 1139$^{3}$ 1475$^{7}$ >**90a 89f**<

**La Calera (GER)** 3 ch f Big Shuffle (USA) -La Luce (Niniski (USA)) 4265$^{5}$ 4387$^{3}$ 5036$^{3}$ 5282$^{12}$ 5702$^{9}$ 5843$^{5}$ 6056$^{11}$ 6228$^{4}$ >**51f**<

**La Concha (IRE)** 3 b g Kahyasi-Trojan Crown (IRE) (Trojan Fen) 553$^{8}$ 651$^{9}$ 739$^{11}$ 1508$^{8}$ 1947$^{8}$ 2822$^{8}$ >**47a 57f**<

**Laconia (IRE)** 3 b f Orpen (USA) -Mislead (IRE) (Distinctly North (USA)) 963$^{4}$ 1196$^{5}$ 1312$^{2}$ 1472$^{6}$ 1689$^{2}$ 2165$^{6}$ 2586$^{2}$ 2675$^{7}$3344$^{8}$ 6538$^{11}$ >**61a 75f**<

**Laconicos (IRE)** 2 ch c Foxhound (USA) -Thermopylae (Tenby) 1219$^{2}$ 2382$^{3}$ 3259$^{2}$ 4012$^{10}$ >**79f**<

**La Coruna** 3 b f Deploy-Valencia (Kenmare (FR)) 1829$^{4}$ >**91+f**<

**La Cucaracha** 3 b f Piccolo-Peggy Spencer (Formidable (USA)) 1685$^{2}$ 2080$^{6}$ 2373$^{3}$ >**103f**<

**La Cygne Blanche (IRE)** 2 gr f Saddlers Hall (IRE) -Ivory s Promise (Pursuit Of Love) 5847$^{11}$ 6153$^{14}$ 6294$^{6}$ >**45a 25f**<

**La Danseuse** 3 b f Groom Dancer (USA) -Alik (FR) (Targowice (USA)) 490$^{5}$ >**50a 47f**<

**Ladeena (IRE)** 2 bb f Dubai Millennium-Aqaarid (USA) (Nashwan (USA)) 6471$^{2}$ >**83f**<

**Ladies Knight** 4 b g Among Men (USA) -Lady Silk (Prince Sabo) 460$^{6}$ 560$^{3}$ 596$^{2}$ 638$^{5}$ 771$^{8}$ 896$^{6}$ 1027$^{3}$1082$^{7}$ 1262$^{5}$ 1625$^{8}$ >**63a 54f**<

**Ladruca** 2 bb f Dracula (AUS) -Promissory (Caerleon (USA)) 2275$^{8}$ 3444$^{7}$ 4521$^{5}$ (4638) 5240$^{19}$ >**54f**<

**Lady Alruna (IRE)** 5 ch m Alhaarth (IRE) -In Tranquility (IRE) (Shalford (IRE)) 423$^{8}$ >**14a 14 f**<

**Lady Ann Summers (USA)** 2 ch f Two Punch (USA) -Why Walk (USA) (Zilzal (USA)) 2970$^{10}$ 3413$^{3}$ 3693$^{4}$ 4752$^{10}$ 5052$^{14}$ >**41a 78f**<

**Lady Arnica** 5 b m Ezzoud (IRE) -Brand (Shareef Dancer (USA)) 781$^{7}$ 889$^{8}$ >**14f**<

**Lady At Leisure (IRE)** 4 ch f Dolphin Street (FR) -In A Hurry (FR) (In Fijar (USA)) 664$^{6}$ 787$^{11}$ 855$^{10}$ (1493) 1987$^{10}$ >**40a 34f**<

**Lady Bahia (IRE)** 3 b f Orpen (USA) -Do The Right Thing (Busted) 482$^{7}$ 522$^{6}$ (732) 747$^{7}$ (1008) >**64a 61f**<

**Lady Blade (IRE)** 3 b f Daggers Drawn (USA) -Singhana (IRE) (Mouktar) 2820$^{7}$ 3304$^{4}$ 3919$^{8}$ 4368$^{5}$ 4848$^{9}$ 5222$^{9}$ 6296$^{13}$ >**53a 62f**<

**Lady Chef** 2 ch f Double Trigger (IRE) -Dundeelin (Dunbeath (USA)) 1589$^{8}$ 2609$^{5}$ (3083) 4326$^{3}$ 5335$^{8}$ 5995$^{11}$ >**77f**<

**Lady Dan (IRE)** 2 b f Danzero (AUS) -Dubai Lady (Kris) 1961$^{4}$ 2458$^{3}$ 2860$^{2}$ 3164$^{9}$ 3753$^{6}$ 4575$^{7}$ 5233$^{3}$ 5800$^{P}$ >**65 f**<

**Lady Doris Watts** 2 b f Emarati (USA) -Wrong Bride (Reprimand) 5943$^{8}$ 6060$^{2}$ 6196$^{7}$ 6523$^{6}$ >**65f**<

**Lady Double U** 4 b f Sheikh Albadou-Bollin Victoria (Jalmood (USA)) 613$^{11}$ 760$^{7}$ 1711$^{9}$ 2350$^{15}$ 2556$^{7}$ >**37a 37f**<

**Lady Dulcet** 4 b f Thowra (FR) -Freedom Weekend (USA) (Shahrastani (USA)) 1582$^{10}$ >**3a 41f**<

**Lady Edge (IRE)** 2 ch f Bold Edge-Lady Sheriff (Taufan (USA)) 6002$^{11}$ >**1f**<

**Lady Ellendune** 3 b f Piccolo-Eileen s Lady (Mtoto) 530$^{13}$ >**22a 38f**<

**Lady Erica** 2 b f Komaite (USA) -Zamarra (Clantime) 1234$^{2}$ 1449$^{5}$ 2003$^{4}$ 2405$^{3}$ 5690$^{9}$ 6008$^{10}$ >**52a 54f**<

**Lady Fabiola (USA)** 2 ro f Open Forum (USA) -Sacre Look (FR) (Dom Pasquini (FR)) 5330a$^{8}$ ><

**Lady Filly** 2 ch f Atraf-Just Lady (Emarati (USA)) (1130) (1449) (1798) 2970$^{7}$ 3481$^{5}$ 6348$^{5}$ >**87f**<

**Lady Franpalm (IRE)** 4 b f Danehill Dancer (IRE) -Be Nimble (Wattlefield) 1352$^{15}$ 1519$^{7}$ 4125$^{9}$ 4926$^{13}$ 6089$^{10}$ >**49a 59f**<

**Lady Georgina** 3 gr f Linamix (FR) -Georgia Venture (Shirley Heights) 1613$^{3}$ 2119$^{6}$ (2377) 2694$^{2}$ (2838) 3457$^{5}$ >**85+f**<

**Lady Heccles** 5 b m Sayaarr (USA) -Rae Un Soleil (Rushmere) 948$^{10}$ ><

**Lady Hen** 2 b f Efisio-Royale Rose (FR) (Bering) 3675$^{8}$ 4243$^{6}$ 5847$^{8}$ >**61f**<

**Lady Hernanda** 2 ch f Hernando (FR) -Coquille (Grand Lodge (USA)) 5390a$^{11}$ ><

**Lady Hopeful (IRE)** 2 b f Lend A Hand-Treble Term (Lion Cavern (USA)) 1865$^{5}$ 2173$^{4}$ 2985$^{2}$ 3366$^{2}$ 3729$^{7}$ 3898$^{5}$ 5800$^{5}$ 6003$^{14}$6272$^{4}$ 6544$^{14}$ >**60a 60f**<

**Lady Indiana (IRE)** 2 b f King s Theatre (IRE) -Najeyba (Indian Ridge) 2140$^{9}$ 2904$^{16}$ 3100$^{7}$ 5142$^{11}$ ><

**Lady Jeannie** 7 b m Emarati (USA) -Cottonwood (Teenoso (USA)) 2737$^{7}$ 3264$^{10}$ 3670$^{11}$ 4129$^{8}$ >**56a 39f**<

**Lady Justice** 4 b f Compton Place-Zinzi (Song) 1750$^{13}$ 2586$^{4}$ 2875$^{14}$ 4025$^{8}$ 4484$^{6}$ >**44a 53f**<

**Lady Karr** 3 b f Mark Of Esteem (IRE) -Percy s Lass (Blakeney) 5239$^{7}$ 6095$^{3}$ (6524) >**69+f**<

**Lady Korrianda** 3 ch f Dr Fong (USA) -Prima Verde (Leading Counsel (USA)) 6089$^{9}$ 6493$^{9}$ >**58a 37f**<

**Lady Lakota (IRE)** 2 b f Indian Lodge (IRE) -Milady Lillie (IRE) (Distinctly North (USA)) 5569$^{14}$ >**31f**<

**Lady Lakshmi** 4 ch f Bahhare (USA) -Polish Honour (USA) (Danzig Connection (USA)) 1514$^{3}$ 1728$^{2}$ 5643$^{3}$ >**44a 51f**<

**Lady Le Quesne (IRE)** 2 ch f Alhaarth (IRE) -Lady Moranbon (USA) (Trempolino (USA)) 2786$^{6}$ 3176$^{2}$ (3659) (4041) 5648$^{13}$ 5938$^{7}$ >**81f**<

**Lady Lexie** 3 b f Cape Cross (IRE) -Lady Of The Land (Wollow) 2311$^{6}$ >**39f**<

**Lady Liesel** 4 b f Bin Ajwaad (IRE) -Griddle Cake (IRE) (Be My Guest (USA)) 659$^{10}$ 791$^{14}$ 860$^{3}$ 1095$^{7}$ 1165$^{11}$ 1494$^{4}$ 1723$^{7}$5285$^{12}$ 5644$^{9}$ 5927$^{12}$ >**34a 32f**<

**Lady Londra** 2 b f Fumo Di Londra (IRE) -Lady Phyl (Northiam (USA)) 4193$^{7}$ 4611$^{9}$ >**68f**<

**Lady Lucinda** 3 b f Muhtarram (USA) -Lady Phyl (Northiam (USA)) 5146$^{10}$ 5371$^{12}$ >**35f**<

**Lady Luisa (IRE)** 2 b f Lujain (USA) -Lady Of Dreams (IRE) (Prince Rupert (FR)) 3931$^{11}$ 4166$^{5}$ 5198$^{8}$ 5256$^{11}$ 5738$^{14}$ >**63f**<

**Lady McNair** 4 b f Sheikh Albadou-Bonita Bee (King Of Spain) 1272$^{4}$ 2084$^{11}$ 2403$^{2}$ 2537$^{4}$ >**60a 80 f**<

**Lady Misha** 2 b f Mister Baileys-Hakone (IRE) (Alzao (USA)) 1364$^{5}$ 2087$^{5}$ 2550$^{10}$ 3164$^{3}$ (4445) 5188$^{2}$ 6140$^{5}$ 6334$^{11}$ >**75f**<

**Lady Mo** 3 b f Young Ern-Just Run (IRE) (Runnett) 452$^{5}$ 521$^{3}$ 631$^{5}$ (736) (828) 965$^{12}$ (1478) 1627$^{2}$ 2061$^{3}$2577$^{13}$ 3689$^{6}$ (3871) 4127$^{2}$ 4265$^{2}$ 4414$^{3}$ 5155$^{5}$ 5425$^{5}$ >**75a 71f**<

**Lady Mytton** 4 ch f Lake Coniston (IRE) -The In-Laws (IRE) (Be My Guest (USA)) 1469$^{5}$ 5631$^{16}$ >**88 f**<

**Lady Natilda** 4 ch f First Trump-Ramajana (USA) (Shadeed (USA)) 480$^{4}$ 510$^{3}$ 626$^{11}$ 694$^{6}$ >**50a 50f**<

**Lady Netbetsports (IRE)** 5 b m In The Wings-Auntie Maureen (IRE) (Roi Danzig (USA)) 3008$^{7}$ 3221$^{3}$ 3300$^{7}$ 3508$^{2}$ 3782$^{8}$ 3928$^{10}$ >**67f**<

**Lady Of The Links (IRE)** 3 b f Desert Style (IRE) -Itkan (IRE) (Marju (IRE)) 1664$^{4}$ 1907$^{8}$ 2037$^{5}$ 2457$^{16}$ 6465$^{8}$ >**54f**<

**Lady Oriande** 3 b f Makbul-Lady Roxanne (Cyrano De Bergerac) 1169$^{6}$ 1293$^{8}$ >**22a 59f**<

**Lady Peaches** 3 ch f Bien Bien (USA) -Upper Club (IRE) (Taufan (USA)) 1793$^{7}$ 2001$^{3}$ 3091$^{8}$ 3421$^{4}$ 3825$^{5}$ >**72f**<

**Lady Pekan** 5 b m Sri Pekan (USA) -Cloudberry (Night Shift (USA)) 480$^{6}$ 578$^{3}$ 806$^{5}$ 904$^{6}$ 912$^{7}$ 1178$^{7}$ 1319$^{2}$1537$^{2}$ 1642$^{9}$ 1937$^{9}$ 2252$^{3}$ 2440$^{5}$ 2482$^{3}$ 2739$^{9}$ 2909$^{8}$3126$^{13}$ 3227$^{17}$ 6274$^{8}$ >**54a 54f**<

**Lady Pilot** 2 b f Dansili-Mighty Flyer (IRE) (Mujtahid (USA)) 4060$^{9}$ 5270$^{12}$ 5569$^{6}$ 5909$^{7}$ >**82f**<

**Lady Piste (IRE)** 3 b f Ali-Royal (IRE) -Alpine Lady (IRE) (Tirol) 420$^{12}$ 620$^{4}$ 678$^{2}$ 744$^{5}$ 817$^{3}$ (965) 1121$^{7}$ (2379)3271$^{4}$ >**57a 57 f**<

**Lady Portia (IRE)** 3 b f College Chapel-Nocturnal (FR) (Night Shift (USA)) 1893a$^{11}$ >**85f**<

**Lady Predominant** 3 b f Primo Dominie-Enlisted (IRE) (Sadler s Wells (USA)) 416$^{4}$ 451$^{4}$ 788$^{11}$ 927$^{6}$ 1086$^{11}$ (1195) 1467$^{12}$ 2005$^{5}$3193$^{13}$ 5072$^{14}$ 5793$^{16}$ 6361$^{10}$ >**45a 26f**<

**Lady Protector** 5 b m Sri Pekan (USA) -Scared (Royal Academy (USA)) 460$^{4}$ (499) 637$^{7}$ 721$^{3}$ 796$^{9}$ 1738$^{10}$ 1870$^{7}$ (2252) (2482)2909$^{3}$ 4232$^{3}$ 4622$^{3}$ 4854$^{8}$ 5862$^{7}$ >**58a 59f**<

**Lady Redera (IRE)** 3 b f Inzar (USA) -Era (Dalsaan) 2122$^{16}$ 2915$^{13}$ 4045$^{11}$ >**49f**<

**Ladystgeorge** 5 b m Mind Games-Indiahra (Indian Ridge) 421$^{11}$ ><

**Lady Stratagem** 5 gr m Mark Of Esteem (IRE) -Grey Angel (Kenmare (FR)) 3099$^{7}$ 3604$^{10}$ 4210$^{3}$ 4424$^{9}$ 5238$^{14}$ 5449$^{13}$ >**16f**<

**Lady Stripes** 3 gr f Alzao (USA) -Shamaya (IRE) (Doyoun) 675$^{8}$ 822$^{6}$ 1038$^{7}$ 2484$^{7}$ >**52a 53f**<

**Lady Suesanne (IRE)** 2 b f Cape Cross (IRE) -Lady At War (Warning) 2095$^{8}$ 2985$^{12}$ 5301$^{11}$ 5569$^{12}$ >**2a 44f**<

**Lady Sunset (IRE)** 3 b f Entrepreneur-Sunset Reigns (IRE) (Taufan (USA)) 1196$^{10}$ 1362$^{8}$ 2134$^{17}$ 2351$^{11}$ >**62f**<

**Lady s View (USA)** 3 b f Distant View (USA) -Karasavina (IRE) (Sadler s Wells (USA)) 5572$^{11}$ 6086$^{6}$ >**87f**<

**Lady Taverner** 3 b f Marju (IRE) -Prompting (Primo Dominie) 2182$^{15}$ 3630$^{10}$ 4168$^{5}$ 5425$^{9}$ 5748$^{8}$ >**57f**<

**Lady Tilly** 7 b m Puissance-Lady Of Itatiba (BEL) (King Of Macedon) 6465$^{9}$ >**14f**<

**Lady Vee (IRE)** 2 b f Rossini (USA) -Dama De Noche (Rusticaro (FR)) 4824$^{8}$ 5362$^{5}$ 5792$^{10}$ 6093$^{16}$ >**52f**<

**Lady Weasley (FR)** 2 b f Zieten (USA) -Top Speed (IRE) (Wolfhound (USA)) 3388a$^{4}$ 4382a$^{4}$ >**92f**<

**Ladywell Blaise (IRE)** 7 b m Turtle Island (IRE) -Duly Elected (Persian Bold) 468$^{7}$ 535$^{3}$ 662$^{6}$ >**51a 54f**<

**Lady West** 4 b f The West (USA) -Just Run (IRE) (Runnett) 3386$^{14}$ >**61a 28f**<

**Lady Xanthia** 3 ch f Bien Bien (USA) -Carmosa (USA) (Blushing John (USA)) 1076$^{8}$ 1493$^{4}$ 1728$^{8}$ >**30a 47f**<

**Laffah (USA)** 9 b g Silver Hawk (USA) -Sakiyah (USA) (Secretariat (USA)) 2613$^{12}$ >**59f**<

**Lafi (IRE)** 5 ch g Indian Ridge-Petal Girl (Caerleon (USA)) 2132$^{7}$ 2682$^{3}$ (3074) >**106f**<

**La Fonteyne** 3 b f Imperial Ballet (IRE) -Baliana (Midyan (USA)) 1991$^{5}$ 2688$^{17}$ 2986$^{2}$ 3229$^{12}$ 3711$^{5}$ 4489$^{16}$ 5086$^{3}$ 6228$^{19}$6465$^{4}$ >**42a 56f**<

**Laggan Bay (IRE)** 4 b g Alzao (USA) -Green Lucia (Green Dancer (USA)) 1801$^{7}$ 2110$^{6}$ 4831$^{7}$ 5093$^{7}$ 6215$^{19}$ 6460$^{2}$ >**80a 79f**<

**Laggan Minstrel (IRE)** 6 b g Mark Of Esteem (IRE) -Next Episode (USA) (Nijinsky (CAN)) 667$^{12}$ 2209$^{12}$ >**41a 41f**<

**Lago Di Como** 7 b g Piccolo-Farmer s Pet (Sharrood (USA)) (1914) 2381$^{9}$ >**63a 61f**<

**Lago D Orta (IRE)** 4 ch c Bahhare (USA) -Maelalong (IRE) (Maelstrom Lake) 1107$^{6}$ 1397$^{4}$ 1902$^{7}$ 2241$^{8}$ 2969$^{6}$ 3937$^{6}$ 4685$^{12}$ 5610$^{11}$6193$^{22}$ >**100f**<

**Lagosta (SAF)** 4 ch g Fort Wood (USA) -Rose Wine (Chilibang) 2133$^{13}$ >**54f**<

**La Hermana** 3 ch f Hernando (FR) -La Candela (GER) (Alzao (USA)) 1983a$^{5}$ 2723a$^{4}$ 4640$^{7}$ 6257a$^{2}$ >**94f**<

**Lahob** 4 ch c First Trump-Mystical Song (Mystiko (USA)) 3050$^{8}$ 3947$^{6}$ 4554$^{7}$ 4820$^{10}$ 5654$^{7}$ 6406$^{3}$ >**52a 37 f**<

**La Ina (GER)** 3 ch f Monsun (GER) -Limata (GER) (Big Shuffle (USA)) 1983a$^{2}$ 2723a$^{2}$ 4183a$^{6}$ >**100f**<

**Laird Dara Mac** 4 b c Presidium-Nishara (Nishapour (FR)) 937$^{7}$ >**33f**<

**Lakaam** 3 b f Danzero (AUS) -Langtry Lady (Pas De Seul) 916$^{14}$ 1050$^{8}$ 1221$^{3}$ >**49a 49f**<

**Lake Carezza (USA)** 2 b c Stravinsky (USA) -May Wedding (USA) (French Deputy (USA)) 6045$^{5}$ 6563$^{9}$ >**62f**<

**Lake Charlotte (USA)** 3 b f Danzig (USA) -Quinpool (USA) (Alydar (USA)) 3759$^{3}$ 4069$^{2}$ 4653$^{3}$ (5104) 5588$^{6}$ >**75f**<

**Lake Chini (IRE)** 2 b c Raise A Grand (IRE) -Where s The Money (Lochnager) 6010$^{11}$ 6145$^{7}$ 6454$^{2}$ >**52+a 80f**<

**Lake Diva** 3 ch f Docksider (USA) -Cutpurse Moll (Green Desert (USA)) 5345$^{3}$ 5836$^{4}$ 6271$^{10}$ (6556) >**58a 55f**<

**Lake Eyre (IRE)** 5 b m Bluebird (USA) -Pooh Wee (Music Boy) 438$^{5}$ 509$^{9}$ 584$^{8}$ 1913$^{5}$ 2227$^{5}$ >**49a 48f**<

**Lake Garda** 3 b c Komaite (USA) -Malcesine (IRE) (Auction Ring (USA)) 1323$^{5}$ 1602$^{3}$ (1881) (2115) 5393$^{22}$ >**96f**<

**Lakelands Lady (IRE)** 4 ch f Woodborough (USA) -Beautyofthepeace (IRE) (Exactly Sharp (USA)) 680$^{13}$ 801$^{7}$ 1033$^{11}$ 4557$^{17}$ 4782$^{9}$ 6059$^{14}$ 6229$^{4}$ 6558$^{4}$ >**55a 55f**<

**Lake Lover (ARG)** 4 b g Salt Lake (USA) -Love For Life (ARG) (Robin Des Bois (USA)) 2163a$^{4}$ ><

**Lake Of Dreams** 5 b g Polish Precedent (USA) -Rainbow Lake (Rainbow Quest (USA)) 1612$^{11}$ 2950$^{12}$ 3712$^{5}$ >**47a 40f**<

**Lake O Gold** 5 ch m Karinga Bay-Ginka (Petoski) 6005$^{8}$ >**55a 55f**<

**Lakesdale (IRE)** 2 b f Desert Style (IRE) -Option (IRE) (Red Ransom (USA)) 2396$^{11}$ 2515$^{2}$ 2819$^{2}$ 3532$^{9}$ 3987$^{4}$ 4089$^{9}$ 4521$^{2}$ 4699$^{3}$5054$^{6}$ (5218) 5548$^{10}$ 5593$^{13}$ 6093$^{8}$ >**62a 57f**<

**Lakeside Guy (IRE)** 3 b g Revoque (IRE) -Glen Of Imaal (IRE) (Common Grounds) 415$^{15}$ 840$^{8}$ 881$^{4}$ 1236$^{8}$ 3262$^{3}$ 3628$^{5}$ 4021$^{6}$ 4484$^{2}$4968$^{11}$ 6280$^{3}$ 6578$^{4}$ >**56a 63f**<

**Lake Verdi (IRE)** 5 ch g Lake Coniston (IRE) -Shore Lark (USA) (Storm Bird (CAN)) 2178$^{14}$ 2404$^{4}$ 3668$^{3}$ 4044$^{9}$ 4336$^{7}$ 4495$^{2}$ 4727$^{6}$ 5282$^{10}$ >**61a 57f**<

**Lake Wakatipu** 2 b f Lake Coniston (IRE) -Lady Broker (Petorius) 4243$^{7}$ 4824$^{4}$ 5455$^{3}$ 5789$^{6}$ 6139$^{6}$ >**56f**<

**Lakota Brave** 10 ch g Anshan-Pushkinia (FR) (Pharly (FR)) 485$^{2}$ 558$^{4}$ 641$^{7}$ 649$^{13}$ 837$^{10}$ 1011$^{6}$ 5540$^{4}$6081$^{10}$ 6561$^{2}$ >**98a 72f**<

**La Landonne** 3 b f Fraam-Le Pin (Persian Bold) 1303$^{4}$ 3139$^{3}$ 3530$^{6}$ 4024$^{6}$ 4338$^{11}$ 5156$^{13}$ 6295$^{2}$ >**64a 72f**<

**L Altro Mondo (IRE)** 2 b c Desert Prince (IRE) -Return Journey (IRE) (Pennine Walk) 2314a$^{2}$ 3352a$^{3}$ 5322a$^{6}$ 5680a$^{6}$ >**102f**<

**Lama Albarq (USA)** 2 ch c Nureyev (USA) -Nuts In May (USA) (A.P. Indy (USA)) 3588$^{14}$ 4481$^{6}$ 6010$^{10}$ >**50a 50f**<

**La Mago** 4 b f Wizard King-Dancing Dancer (Niniski (USA)) 5237$^{14}$ ><

**La Maitresse (IRE)** 2 b f Desert King (IRE) -Banariya (USA) (Lear Fan (USA)) 3286a$^{O}$ 3859a$^{3}$ 4158a$^{4}$ >**94f**<

**Lamantan (GER)** 5 b g Unfuwain (USA) -Lima (GER) (Surumu (GER)) (6509a) >**102f**<

**Lambriggan Lad** 2 b g Mazurek-Alfs Classic (FR) (Sanglamore (USA)) 5508$^{9}$ 6155$^{9}$ 6308$^{8}$ >**35a 17f**<

**Lamh Eile (IRE)** 2 b f Lend A Hand-Mothers Footprints (IRE) (Maelstrom Lake) (3080) (3834) 4527$^{3}$ 5391$^{13}$ >**87f**<

**Lampos (USA)** 4 bb g Southern Halo (USA) -Gone Private (USA) (Private Account (USA)) 446$^{3}$ (568) 616$^{2}$ 684$^{5}$ 1238$^{7}$ 1534$^{7}$ 1668$^{11}$ 6225$^{8}$6581$^{7}$ >**58 a 63f**<

**La Muette (IRE)** 4 b f Charnwood Forest (IRE) -Elton Grove (IRE) (Astronef) 666$^{7}$ 1245$^{10}$ 1332$^{8}$ 1369$^{16}$ >**57f**<

**La Musique** 2 b c Merdon Melody-Daleside Ladybird (Tolomeo) 5716$^{18}$ 6494$^{12}$ >**13a**<

**Lanas Turn** 2 b f Mister Baileys-Lana Turrel (USA) (Trempolino (USA)) 2458$^{14}$ 2985$^{5}$ 3164$^{8}$ 3532$^{16}$ 4304$^{4}$ 5097$^{6}$ 5556$^{9}$ >**25a 44f**<

**Land Army (IRE)** 3 b f Desert Style (IRE) -Family

At War (USA) (Explodent (USA)) 2182[13] >38f<
**Landerneau (IRE)** 3 b f Desert Prince (IRE) -Pont-Aven (Try My Best (USA)) 5255a[11] 6203a[0] >80f<
**Landescent (IRE)** 4 b g Grand Lodge (USA) -Traumerei (GER) (Surumu (GER)) 467[7] 551[4] 740[5] (855) (996) 1181[5] 2262[6] >55a 48f<
**Landing Strip (IRE)** 4 b g Dolphin Street (FR) -Funny Cut (IRE) (Sure Blade (USA)) 1354[20] 1504[20] 3195[5] 3558[11] 4291[25] 5016[11] 6026[7] >50a 50f<
**Landinium (ITY)** 5 b m Lando (GER) -Hollywood Girl (Cagliostro (GER)) 1355[4] 2042[4] (2607a) 3137a[3] 5970a[6] 6381a[5] >101f<
**Land n Stars** 4 b g Mtoto-Uncharted Waters (Celestial Storm (USA)) 1832[9] (2285) 2958[5] 3644[4] (5472) 5595[3] 6215[6] 6460[5] >91f<
**Land Of Fantasy** 5 ch g Hernando (FR) -Height Of Folly (Shirley Heights) (603) 684[2] 889[3] >66a 66df<
**Landofheartsdesire (IRE)** 5 b m Up And At Em-Ahonita (Ahonoora) 429[6] 474[7] 2387[16] >43a 43f<
**Land Of Nod (IRE)** 3 b f Barathea (IRE) -Rafif (USA) (Riverman (USA)) 1304[4] 3908[7] 4307[14] 5020[5] 5259[6] 5733[16] >54a 59f<
**Landslide (IRE)** 5 b g Bigstone (IRE) -Last Dream (IRE) (Alzao (USA)) 636a[4] 850a[4] 925a[11] >103f<
**Landucci** 3 b c Averti (IRE) -Divina Luna (Dowsing (USA)) 1476[2] 1997[7] 2371[6] (5020) 5399[3] 5737[4] 6094[10] 6537[2] >71a 72+f<
**Lane Marshal** 2 gr g Danzig Connection (USA) -Evening Falls (Beveled (USA)) 1523[6] 1709[5] 2141[15] 2570[7] 3506[7] 3883[6] 4699[5] 4997[11] 5192[5] >21a 44f<
**Lange Bleu (FR)** 5 ch g Beyssac (FR) -Dear Blue (FR) (Cyborg (FR)) 1786[8] 5514[11] >2f<
**Langford** 4 ch g Compton Place-Sharpening (Sharpo) 2237[2] (2410) 2969[12] 3597[15] (3879) 4543[4] 5470[11] 5650[11] 5813[5] 5941[19] >92f<
**Langston Boy** 2 b g Namid-Blinding Mission (IRE) (Marju (IRE)) 1219[4] 1607[2] 1960[3] 3677[9] 5052[2] 5453[4] 6176[8] >72a 63f<
**Lanos (POL)** 6 ch g Special Power-Lubeka (POL) (Milione (FR)) 513[5] 867[5] 1135[5] >65a 68f<
**Laona** 3 ch f Acatenango (GER) -Lanelly (GER) (Shining Steel) 1805a[8] ><
**Lapadar (IRE)** 5 bb m Woodborough (USA) -Indescent Blue (Bluebird (USA)) 461[6] 571[4] >42a 42f<
**Lapdancing** 3 ch f Pursuit Of Love-Petrikov (IRE) (In The Wings) 1318[9] 1784[8] >28f<
**La Peregrina** 3 bb f Zafonic (USA) -Flawless (Warning) 702[2] 766[5] >58a<
**La Persiana** 3 gr f Daylami (IRE) -La Papagena (Habitat) 1371[5] 2134[2] (2906) (3345) (4153) 5025[2] 5573[3] >105+f<
**La Petite Chinoise** 3 ch f Dr Fong (USA) -Susi Wong (IRE) (Selkirk (USA)) 816[6] 1086[8] 2419[4] 2977[2] 3421[2] 3837[5] (4518) >64a 79f<
**La Professoressa (IRE)** 3 b f Cadeaux Genereux-Fellwah (IRE) (Sadler s Wells (USA)) 2425[6] 2536[12] 2949[11] 4443[5] 4848[3] 5258[13] >64f<
**La Providence** 2 b f Takhlid (USA) -Petite Danseuse (Aragon) 4999[9] 5059[14] 6276[11] ><
**La Puce** 3 b f Danzero (AUS) -Verbena (IRE) (Don t Forget Me) 631[4] 704[8] (798) (970) 1036[4] 2820[6] 4020[8] 4340[7] 4483[8] 6290[2] (6461) >77a 67f<
**Lara Bay** 4 b f Polish Precedent (USA) -Way O Gold (USA) (Slew O Gold (USA)) 2216[11] 2381[12] 3327[9] >42a 68f<
**Larad (IRE)** 3 br g Desert Sun-Glenstal Priory (Glenstal (USA)) 662[3] 769[5] 873[9] 1019[7] 1102[5] 1278[5] (1405) 1495[3] 1600[3] 1844[4] 1908[6] (2348) 2649[7] 2760[6] 3190[7] 4713[6] 5750[5] 5863[9] 6230[4] (6361) >55a 52f<
**Lara Falana** 6 b m Tagula (IRE) -Victoria Mill (Free State) 960[7] 1053[2] 1097[5] 2403[4] 2705[2] 2881[6] 3264[4] (3933) 4230[8] >67a 72f<
**Lara s Girl** 2 b f Tipsy Creek (USA) -Joe s Dancer (Shareef Dancer (USA)) 2730[9] 3170[4] 3632[8] 4010[10] 4638[3] 5097[3] 5593[11] >47f<
**L Archonte (FR)** 4 b c Solon (GER) -Quelle Classe (FR) (Bikala) 1741a[12] >105?f<
**La Reine Mambo (USA)** 2 b f High Yield (USA) -Zappeuse (USA) (Kingmambo (USA)) 6297a[8] >83f<
**Largo (IRE)** 4 ch f Selkirk (USA) -Lady Of The Lake (Caerleon (USA)) 1768[10] 2062[5] >93f<
**Largs** 4 ch f Sheikh Albadou-Madam Zando (Forzando) 698[8] 805[3] 1032[3] 1092[2] 1516[6] 2123[3] 2451[2] >60a 45f<
**Larionov (IRE)** 3 ch c Machiavellian (USA) -Lunareva (USA) (Nureyev (USA)) 2072a[7] >86f<
**Larking About (USA)** 4 ch f Silver Hawk (USA) -Milly Ha Ha (Dancing Brave (USA)) 1962[11] 2262[9] 2501[13] 4033[6] 4820[7] 5027[2] 5243[13] >69 a 55f<
**Lark In The Park (IRE)** 4 ch f Grand Lodge (USA) -Jarrayan (Machiavellian (USA)) 1244[12] 1606[11] 3117[9] 3609[5] 4771[10] 5449[11] >9a 38f<
**Larkwing (IRE)** 3 b c Ela-Mana-Mou-The Dawn Trader (USA) (Naskra (USA)) 1271[2] 1926[3] (2312) 4229[2] 5226[5] 5699[S] 5919[7] >98f<
**Larky s Lob** 5 b g Lugana Beach-Eucharis (Tickled Pink) 422[2] (429) 503[4] 694[5] 782[3] 799[2] 807[4] 833[6] 941[3] (1696) 1913[2] 2123[2] (2663) 3025[6] 3820[2] 3864[3] 6066[5] 6246[9] 6554[8] >70a 55f<
**Larofino (GER)** 3 b c Laroche (GER) -L Orofina (GER) (Orofino (GER)) 2510a[15] >84f<
**La Rose** 4 b f Among Men (USA) -Marie La Rose (FR) (Night Shift (USA)) 478[6] >35a 41f<
**La Sabana (FR)** 4 b f Loup Solitaire (USA) -La Peregrina (FR) (Shirley Heights) 3973a[5] >98f<
**Lasanga** 5 ch g Zamindar (USA) -Shall We Run (Hotfoot) 5004[14] 5297[17] 6132[2] 6553[6] >63a 68f<
**Lashed (AUS)** 5 ch m Encosta De Lago (AUS) -Traffic Watch (AUS) (Salieri (USA)) 6528a[18] >105f<
**Lasika** 2 b f Pursuit Of Love-Lovina (ITY) (Love The Groom (USA)) 2668a[6] 5330a[4] 6108a[5] >91f<
**Laska (IRE)** 3 br f Fasliyev (USA) -Dacian (USA) (Diesis) 2211[4] 2450[4] 3105[11] >57f<
**Las Ramblas (IRE)** 7 b g Thatching-Raise A Warning (Warning) 5452[13] 5579[19] 5832[8] 6466[9] >37f<
**Lasser Light (IRE)** 4 bb g Inchinor-Light Ray (Rainbow Quest (USA)) 3245[10] 4615[7] 5079[5] 5751[11] 6364[12] >36a 56f<
**Last Appointment (USA)** 4 b c Elusive Quality (USA) -Motion In Limine (USA) (Temperence Hill (USA)) 2206[5] 2646[7] 4549[3] 5055[13] >84a 82f<
**Last Chapter (IRE)** 2 b g Desert Story (IRE) -Dutosky (Doulab (USA)) 6476[16] >18f<
**Last Empress (FR)** 4 b f Dernier Empereur (USA) -Such Is Life (FR) (Akarad (FR)) 1163a[12] 4039a[12] >100f<
**Lasting Delight** 3 b f Robellino (USA) -Last Result (Northern Park (USA)) 6221[0] >67 a 35f<
**Lasting Image** 2 br f Zilzal (USA) -Minsden s Image (Dancer s Image (USA)) 5569[15] >27f<
**Last Love (IRE)** 3 b f Danehill (USA) -Summerosa (USA) (Woodman (USA)) 2330a[9] >92f<
**Lastofthewhalleys** 6 b m Noble Patriarch-Pride Of Whalley (IRE) (Fayruz) 993[9] >13f<
**Last Pioneer (IRE)** 2 b g New Frontier (IRE) -Toordillon (IRE) (Contract Law (USA)) 3760[9] 5095[9] 5831[4] 6140[4] >64 f<
**Last Rebel (IRE)** 5 b g Danehill (USA) -La Curamalal (IRE) (Rainbow Quest (USA)) 1496[6] 2740[15] ><
**Last Song (USA)** 3 b f Unbridled s Song (USA) -Queen Of Spirit (USA) (Deputy Minister (CAN)) 9 >102a<
**La Sylphide** 7 ch m Rudimentary (USA) -Primitive Gift (Primitive Rising (USA)) 1604[2] 2022[5] 2624[6] 2982[10] 5211[2] (5788) 6173[3] 6570[4] >75a 95f<
**Latalomne (USA)** 10 ch g Zilzal (USA) -Sanctuary (Welsh Pageant) (3018) 3221[4] 4772[11] 5318[12] >80f<
**La Tard (FR)** 6 ch m Tot Ou Tard (IRE) -La Goetha (FR) (No Lute (FR)) 1741a[8] >97f<
**Late Arrival** 7 b g Emperor Jones (USA) -Try Vickers (USA) (Fuzzbuster (USA)) 1620[17] 2078[9] 2356[7] 2938[10] 3612[2] 3804[6] 4213[7] 4698[4] 5585[9] >46a 59f<
**Lateen Sails** 4 ch c Elmaamul (USA) -Felucca (Green Desert (USA)) 2559[7] 2957[15] 4539[5] >116 f<
**Late Opposition** 3 b c Unfuwain (USA) -Hawa (USA) (Woodman (USA)) 1222[4] 1509[2] 1672[2] 1998[2] 2197[11] 3231[9] 3746[3] (4829) 5190[2] 5608[2] 5944[11] >77f<
**Lateral Thinker (IRE)** 2 b f Desert Sun-Miss Margate (IRE) (Don t Forget Me) 1276[2] 1589[2] 1670[3] 2002[4] (3634) 3938[16] 4235[5] 4601[2] 5052[6] 5548[8] 5910[6] 6127[4] (6276) >68a 57f<
**Latice (IRE)** 3 ch f Inchinor-Laramie (USA) (Gulch (USA)) (1803a) (2925a) 5501a[8] 5981a[7] >121+f<
**Latif (USA)** 3 b c Red Ransom (USA) -Awaamir (Green Desert (USA)) 1461[16] 2286[4] >74f<
**Latin Express (IRE)** 2 b c Marju (IRE) -Sea Port (Averof) 5507[9] 6171[14] >49f<
**Latino Magic (IRE)** 4 ch c Lion Cavern (USA) -Tansy (Shareef Dancer (USA)) 1254a[5] 1849a[2] 2603a[4] 2793a[3] 3355a[3] 3967a[5] (4160a) 4587a[6] 4786a[4] >109f<
**Latin Queen (IRE)** 4 bb f Desert Prince (IRE) -Atlantic Dream (USA) (Muscovite (USA)) 2914[5] 3490[8] 3997[5] 4473[5] 4713[9] >57f<
**Latin Review (IRE)** 3 ch f Titus Livius (FR) -Law Review (IRE) (Case Law) 2897[19] >90f<
**Laugh n Cry** 3 b f In The Wings-The Kings Daughter (Indian King (USA)) 2632[10] 3044[5] >59f<
**Laura Lea** 4 b g Bishop Of Cashel-Kirriemuir (Lochnager) 811[P] 1820[12] >39f<
**Laurannah** 2 b f Diktat-Paris Babe (Teenoso (USA)) 6367a[4] >86f<
**Laurel Dawn** 6 gr g Paris House-Madrina (Waajib) 540[7] 1477[11] 1870[10] 2734[7] (3169) 3407[5] 3524[2] 3775[5] 3920[8] 4181[6] 4308[7] 4626[14] 4751[8] 4935[8] 5107[8] 5597[3] 6007[3] >68a 73f<
**Lauren Louise** 2 b f Tagula (IRE) -Movie Star (IRE) (Barathea (IRE)) 2045[11] 2985[9] 5227[11] >14a 16f<
**Laurens Girl (IRE)** 3 b f Imperial Ballet (IRE) -Tresor Vert (USA) (Storm Cat (USA)) 1226[9] 2729[6] 3529[4] >25a 56f<
**Lauro** 4 b f Mukaddamah (USA) -Lapu-Lapu (Prince Sabo) 1475[3] 1931[2] 2775[4] 3039[4] 5265[8] (5672) 6115[12] 6579[5] >77a 81f<
**Laurollie** 2 b f Makbul-Madonna Da Rossi (Mtoto) 4359[10] 4967[12] 5256[10] 6000[9] >39f<
**Laverock (IRE)** 2 b c Octagonal (NZ) -Sky Song (IRE) (Sadler s Wells (USA)) 6583a[3] >87f<
**La Vie Est Belle** 3 b f Makbul-La Belle Vie (Indian King (USA)) 1099[6] 1881[10] 2518[4] 3221[9] 4580[11] 4937[6] (5117) 5473[8] 5618[4] 6016[5] 6079[2] >68a 76f<
**La Vigna (IRE)** 3 ch g Woodborough (USA) -Bona Fide (Sharpo) 998[8] 1075[10] 1169[7] >30a 23f<
**La Viola** 2 b f Fraam-Arasong (Aragon) 6196[6] 6530[5] >60f<
**Lavish Times** 3 ch c Timeless Times (USA) -Lavernock Lady (Don t Forget Me) 524[7] 762[5] 865[3] 1196[11] 1236[6] 1689[3] 1788[6] 1934[8] 2353[6] 3364[5] 3801[7] 4391[11] >48a 52f<
**Lawaaheb (IRE)** 3 b g Alhaarth (IRE) -Ajayib (USA) (Riverman (USA)) 2578[8] 3231[14] 5381[13] 5936[7] >22a 65f<
**Law Breaker (IRE)** 6 ch g Case Law-Revelette (Runnett) 556[5] 703[5] 1106[2] 1126[9] 4837[16] 5224[12] 5704[8] 5874[16] 6496[11] >91a 97f<
**Lawgiver (IRE)** 3 b c Definite Article-Marylou Whitney (USA) (Fappiano (USA)) 1532[8] 2386[15] >11f<
**Law Maker** 4 b g Case Law-Bo Babbity (Strong Gale) 438[11] 499[9] 561[10] 930[13] 951[6] 1082[9] 1280[4] 1546[2] 2350[3] 2586[7] 2675[4] 2724[3] 3084[6] 3126[2] 4034[10] 4181[15] >45a 53f<
**Lawood (IRE)** 4 gr g Charnwood Forest (IRE) -La Susiane (Persepolis (FR)) 846[4] 1013[8] (1213) 1470[2] 2272[4] 2752[12] 2895[9] >73a 80f<
**Lawrence Of Arabia (IRE)** 4 b g Desert King (IRE) -Cumbres (FR) (Kahyasi) 3844[8] 4155[6] 4820[6] 5027[9] 5523[8] 6150[14] >35a 65+f<
**Lay Down Sally (IRE)** 6 ch m General Monash (USA) -Sally Fay (IRE) (Fayruz) 433[6] 791[7] >40a 40f<
**Layed Back Rocky** 2 ch c Lake Coniston (IRE) -Madam Taylor (Free State) 4239[6] 4930[9] 5455[2] 5790[6] 6543[6] >52f<
**Layman (USA)** 2 ch c Sunday Silence (USA) -Laiyl (IRE) (Nureyev (USA)) (4382a) 4981a[2] 5980a[3] >117f<
**Lazio (GER)** 3 b c Dashing Blade-Leontine (GER) (Selkirk (USA)) 2158a[2] 3335a[4] 4378a[4] 5809a[6] >108f<
**Lazzaz** 6 b g Muhtarram (USA) -Astern (USA) (Polish Navy (USA)) 455[4] 546[3] 592[5] 609[3] 645[3] 724[3] 777[7] 867[2] 2212[8] 3018[5] 3263[6] 3411[4] 3604[3] 3774[4] 4080[2] 4213[6] 4424[5] 5021[5] (5354) (5654) 5993[9] 6159[6] 6540[8] 6581[12] >68a 59f<
**League Of Nations (IRE)** 2 b c Indian Danehill (IRE) -Athens Belle (IRE) (Groom Dancer (USA)) 2111[8] 2453[5] 3124[2] >26a 70f<
**Leaping Brave (IRE)** 3 b g Indian Rocket-Island Heather (IRE) (Salmon Leap (USA)) 1841[4] 2516[2] 2834[4] 3527[9] 4031[8] 4479[9] >73a 78f<
**Learned Lad (FR)** 6 ch g Royal Academy (USA) -Blushing Storm (USA) (Blushing Groom (FR)) 705[2] 765[5] 820[9] 1935[11] 2537[12] 2643[12] 3631[15] 3844[15] 4220[18] 5733[14] >73a 41f<
**Learn The Lingo** 8 b g Teenoso (USA) -Charlotte Gray (Rolfe (USA)) 1138[11] ><
**Lebenstanz** 4 bb f Singspiel (IRE) -Reamur (Top Ville) 1059[6] 2060[6] 2950[6] 3919[6] 4448[9] 4820[8] >63a 60f<
**Le Boss (FR)** 3 b c Ski Chief (USA) -Angel Victory (IRE) (Exactly Sharp (USA)) 1289a[5] >84f<
**Le Carre (USA)** 6 gr g Miswaki (USA) -Dibs (USA) (Spectacular Bid (USA)) (1182a) 1578a[4] 2337a[4] 5503a[4] 5976a[3] 6382a[4] >114f<
**Le Chiffre (IRE)** 2 br c Celtic Swing-Implicit View (Persian Bold) 6092[3] >62f<
**Le Corvee (IRE)** 2 b c Rossini (USA) -Elupa (IRE) (Mtoto) (4315) 4807[3] 5395[4] 6063[2] >87a 91+f<
**Legacy (JPN)** 4 b g Carnegie (IRE) -Idraak (Kris) 636a[7] 754a[11] 6547[7] >33a 105f<
**Legal Approach** 5 b h Zafonic (USA) -Legaya (Shirley Heights) 1618[4] 2076[10] >99f<
**Legal Belle** 2 ch f Superpower-Legal Sound (Legal Eagle) 6566[3] >59f<
**Legalis (USA)** 6 ch g Gone West (USA) -Loyalize (USA) (Nureyev (USA)) 436[3] 584[2] 596[13] 670[3] (723) 834[3] 993[6] 1025[4] 1076[2] >59a 23f<
**Legality** 4 b f Polar Falcon (USA) -Lady Barrister (Law Society (USA)) 602[14] 4201[6] 4808[8] >65 a 65f<
**Legally Fast (USA)** 2 b c Deputy Minister (CAN) -Earthly Angel (USA) (Crafty Prospector (USA)) 4728[10] 6077[9] >48f<
**Legal Set (IRE)** 8 gr g Second Set (IRE) -Tiffany s Case (IRE) (Thatching) 884[4] 928[10] 987[5] 1082[12] 1279[2] 1787[12] 2260[15] 2292[9] 2581[10] 2784[9] 2976[4] 3038[2] (3226) 3298[4] 3446[7] 3606[2] 3754[4] 3901[10] 4130[11] 4179[2] 4577[12] 4635[4] 4904[5] 5126[7] 5242[8] 5364[2] 5518[4] 5713[9] 5757[11] 6097[5] 6210[2] 6273[5] 6452[7] 6499[8] >61a 67f<
**Legend Of Dance** 2 b f Dansili-Hard Task (Formidable (USA)) 4705[12] 5368[13] 5735[8] >40a 54f<
**Le Giare (IRE)** 2 b c Monashee Mountain (USA) -A La Longue (GER) (Mtoto) (6380a) >98f<
**Legion Of Honour (IRE)** 5 b h Danehill (USA) -Total Chic (USA) (Far North (CAN)) 2426[11] 4189[14] 5350[13] >27a 43f<
**Leg Spinner (IRE)** 3 b g Intikhab (USA) -Road Harbour (USA) (Rodrigo De Triano (USA)) 1371[3] 2934[3] (3194) 4274[7] (4572) (5300) >88f<
**Leicester Square (IRE)** 3 ch c Gone West (USA) -Stage Manner (In The Wings) 2476[2] 3000[7] >109f<
**Leiden (FR)** 4 br g Kaldounevees (FR) -Springtime Melody (USA) (Lomond (USA)) 5103a[5] ><
**Leighton (IRE)** 4 b g Desert Story (IRE) -Lady Fern (Old Vic) 1321[9] 2142[5] 2424[4] 3238[7] 3880[2] 4192[8] 4572[3] 5203[11] 5273[9] >88f<
**Leighton Buzzard** 2 b g Cyrano De Bergerac-Winsome Wooster (Primo Dominie) 5616[7] 5865[10] >56f<
**Leila (FR)** 3 ch f Lahint (USA) -Lespois (Sicyos (USA)) 1290a[7] >99f<
**Leitrim House** 3 ch c Cadeaux Genereux-Lonely Heart (Midyan (USA)) (1239) (1847a) 2315a[4] 2966[7] >106a 114f<
**Leitrim Rock (IRE)** 4 b g Barathea (IRE) -Kilshanny (Groom Dancer (USA)) 1369[15] 2426[8] 2801[4] 3697[6] 4460[8] >58a 61f<
**Lekka Ding (IRE)** 2 bb f Raise A Grand (IRE) -Non Dimenticar Me (IRE) (Don t Forget Me) 6153[9] 6331[8] >46a 65+f<
**Lemarate (USA)** 7 b g Gulch (USA) -Sayyedati (Shadeed (USA)) 441[3] 470[3] 567[8] 658[12] 778[5] >40a 25f<
**Le Meridien (IRE)** 6 ch m Magical Wonder (USA) -Dutch Queen (Ahonoora) 2909[5] 3169[17] 3314[7] 3680[7] 3820[6] 3864[5] (4104) 4181[8] 4548[3] 4779[10] >59f<
**Lennel** 6 b g Presidium-Ladykirk (Slip Anchor) 1369[5] 1539[7] 1660[4] 2120[11] 2424[7] 2753[4] 3731[13] 3781[6] 3929[4] (4005) 4363[3] 4416[2] 4493[3] 4911[3] 5182[7] 5607[5] 5632[6] 5935[2] >78f<
**Lenny The Lender (CAN)** 8 ch g Lac Ouimet (USA) -Nagger (USA) (Topsider (USA)) 6384a[10] >88f<
**Lenwade** 3 gr f Environment Friend-Branitska (Mummy s Pet) 1267[11] 1465[10] 1726[3] 2054[7] 3822[15] 4460[7] 4497[4] 4654[5] 4798[2] 5284[2] (5571) 5750[3] 5928[2] 6230[2] >40a 50f<
**Leoballero** 4 ch g Lion Cavern (USA) -Ball Gown (Jalmood (USA)) 2279[5] 3052[3] 3884[5] 5004[4] 5297[15] 5921[2] 6193[21] >67a 96f<
**Leonalto (IRE)** 2 ch g Raise A Grand (IRE) -Chrismas Carol (IRE) (Common Grounds) 1269[7] 1331[5] 1638[3] 3729[6] 4017[5] 4620[8] >58f<
**Leonora Truce (IRE)** 5 b m Brief Truce (USA) -Eleonora D Arborea (Prince Sabo) 425[8] 572[11] 809[8] >31a 31f<
**Leonor Fini (IRE)** 3 ch f Peintre Celebre (USA) -Friendly Finance (Auction Ring (USA)) 2711a[2] 2993a[5] 3969a[4] 4406a[4] 5162a[5] 5679a[8] >99f<
**Leopard Creek** 3 ch f Weldnaas (USA) -Indigo (Primo Dominie) 1200[9] 1750[12] 2353[2] 2556[10] 2778[2] 3201[8] 3820[16] 4132[15] 4391[7] 4881[5] >43a 60 f<
**Leopard Spot (IRE)** 6 b g Sadler s Wells (USA) -Savoureuse Lady (Caerleon (USA)) 4512[7] 4778[8] 4990[7] >45f<
**Leophin Dancer (USA)** 6 b g Green Dancer (USA) -Happy Gal (FR) (Habitat) 430[6] 446[7] (1402) 1543[2] 1690[2] 1728[3] 1862[4] >44a 45f<
**Leo s Lucky Star (USA)** 2 b c Forestry (USA) -Leo s Lucky Lady (USA) (Seattle Slew (USA)) (2422) (3373) 4949[8] 5437[10] >101+f<
**Leporello (IRE)** 4 b c Danehill (USA) -Why So Silent (Mill Reef (USA)) 1902[3] 2678[7] >119f<
**Le Reveur** 2 b c Machiavellian (USA) -Brooklyn s Dance (FR) (Shirley Heights) 5666a[6] >92f<
**Lerida** 2 ch g Groom Dancer (USA) -Catalonia (IRE) (Catrail (USA)) 1658[6] >18f<
**Le Royal (GER)** 4 b g Royal Solo (IRE) -Liebste (GER) (Nebos (GER)) 5808a[2] 6512a[7] >107f<
**Les Arcs (USA)** 4 br g Arch (USA) -La Sarto (USA) (Cormorant (USA)) 1284[10] 1821[12] 3166[2] (3397) 3470[3] 4319[6] 4831[16] 5590[6] 5835[10] 6244[3] >85f<
**L Escapade (IRE)** 2 ch c Grand Lodge (USA) -Brief Escapade (IRE) (Brief Truce (USA)) 3601[3] 4872[5] 5373[4] 5696[3] >79f<
**Leslingtaylor (IRE)** 2 b g Orpen (USA) -Rite Of Spring (Niniski (USA)) 4776[5] 5125[3] (5633) 6206[5] 6574[11] >74+f<
**L Etang Bleu (FR)** 6 gr g Graveron (FR) -Strawberry Jam (FR) (Fill My Hopes (FR)) 950[8] ><
**Le Tiss (IRE)** 3 b g Croco Rouge (IRE) -Manarah (Marju (IRE)) 1134[4] 2107[9] 2578[2] (2910) 2999[4] 4229[12] 4888[13] >98f<
**Let It Be** 3 ch f Entrepreneur-Noble Dane (IRE) (Danehill (USA)) 1617[2] 1946[5] 2347[7] 2760[5] (3371) (4015) 4307[5] 5130[2] 5546[10] 5860[5] >60f<
**Letitzia (GER)** 3 gr f Sternkoenig (IRE) -Lucky Love (GER) (Mondrian (GER)) 1983a[14] >73f<
**Let Me Try Again (IRE)** 4 b g Sadler s Wells (USA) -Dathiyna (IRE) (Kris) 1455[8] 1703[4] >81+a 111f<
**Lets Get It On (IRE)** 3 b f Perugino (USA) -Lets Clic Together (IRE) (Don t Forget Me) 1129[15] 1473[8] 1614[5] 2075[2] 2269[7] 3122[8] 3523[5] 3737[3] 5704[15] 6518[6] >85f<
**Let Slip** 2 b f Second Empire (IRE) -Loose Talk (Thatching) 6470[12] >57f<
**Let s Party (IRE)** 4 b f Victory Note (USA) -Mashoura (Shareef Dancer (USA)) 1557[11] 1710[11] 3701[7] >2a 2f<
**Let s Pretend** 3 b f Rainbow Quest (USA) -Imaginary (IRE) (Dancing Brave (USA)) 5339[4] >65f<
**Lets Roll** 3 b g Tamure (IRE) -Miss Petronella (Petoski) 1418[2] 1588[6] 2306[2] 2887[2] 3312[3] (3561) (3953) 4888[5] 5632[2] 6121[4] >92f<
**Let The Lion Roar** 3 b c Sadler s Wells (USA) -Ballerina (IRE) (Dancing Brave (USA)) (1439) 2043[3] 2680[3] 3353a[5] 4833[2] 5463[8] >121f<
**Levantine (IRE)** 7 b g Sadler s Wells (USA) -Spain Lane (USA) (Seeking The Gold (USA)) 725[3] 941[5] 1090[6] (5641) 5795[2] 5927[4] 6404[7] >47 a 53+f<
**Levelled** 10 b g Beveled (USA) -Baino Charm (USA) (Diesis) 638[8] 794[9] 813[7] 951[10] 1000[4] 1089[5] 1190[5] 1443[7] 1568[2] 1699[3] 1890[3] (2183) 3277[11] 3314[6] 3616[5] 3820[14] 3864[6] 4557[4] 4881[14] 6059[15] >49a 47f<
**Le Vernan (FR)** 4 b g Tot Ou Tard (IRE) -Tanbure (Law Society (USA)) 1435a[9] >97f<
**Le Vie Dei Colori** 4 b c Efisio-Mystic Tempo (USA) (El Gran Senor (USA)) 2155a[4] 4228[3] 5332a[8] 6076a[3] >121f<
**Levirat (GER)** 5 ch h Lomitas-Laurier D Or (Sassafras (FR)) 1259a[8] 1802a[6] 2320a[6] >108f<
**Levitator** 3 b c Sadler s Wells (USA) -Cantilever (Sanglamore (USA)) 1674[9] 2944[2] 3629[2] 4062[7] (4692) 5159[4] >80f<
**Lewis Island (IRE)** 5 b g Turtle Island (IRE) -

Phyllode (Pharly (FR)) 5607$^{14}$ 6043$^{13}$ *6450$^{4}$* **>75a 94f<**

**Lexicon** 4 ch f Weldnaas (USA) -Swift Move (Move Off) 5581$^{17}$ ><

**Leyaaly** 5 ch m Night Shift (USA) -Lower The Tone (IRE) (Phone Trick (USA)) *722$^{6}$ 1402$^{9}$* 1581$^{7}$ *(1885) 2811$^{2}$ 2990$^{4}$* 3412$^{20}$ **>42a<**

**Liability (IRE)** 2 b f Bluebird (USA) -Madaniyya (USA) (Shahrastani (USA)) 4606$^{11}$ 5227$^{6}$ 5855$^{6}$ **>43f<**

**Liakoura (GER)** 2 b g Royal Academy (USA) -Lady Member (FR) (Saint Estephe (FR)) (3749) 4295$^{8}$ (5246) **>96f<**

**Liameliss** 2 ch f Dr Fong (USA) -Ivory Palm (USA) (Sir Ivor (USA)) 2876$^{6}$ 3627$^{15}$ 4198$^{10}$ 5281$^{13}$ **>48f<**

**Libera** 3 b f Turtle Island (IRE) -Princess Louise (Efisio) 3209$^{9}$ **>65f<**

**Liberty Flag (USA)** 3 b f Kingmambo (USA) -Banner Dancer (USA) (Danzig (USA)) 3592$^{2}$ (4644) **>72f<**

**Liberty Royal** 5 b g Ali-Royal (IRE) -Hope Chest (Kris) *647$^{6}$* 1275$^{10}$ 1542$^{6}$ 2643$^{3}$ 3412$^{8}$ 4418$^{3}$ 4802$^{4}$ (5252) 5657$^{9}$*6156$^{9}$* **>75 a 75 f<**

**Liberty Run (IRE)** 2 ch c Grand Lodge (USA) -Bathe In Light (USA) (Sunshine Forever (USA)) 6187$^{17}$ *6448$^{3}$* **>67a 43f<**

**Liberty Seeker (FR)** 5 ch g Machiavellian (USA) -Samara (IRE) (Polish Patriot (USA)) 1503$^{8}$ 2235$^{8}$ 4007$^{2}$ **>62f<**

**Libras Child (IRE)** 5 b g Paris House-Butternut (IRE) (Alzao (USA)) 3961a$^{7}$ 4371a$^{13}$ 4956a$^{11}$ 5660a$^{15}$ **>90f<**

**Libre** 4 b g Bahamian Bounty-Premier Blues (FR) (Law Society (USA)) 1109$^{9}$ 1172$^{5}$ 1715$^{4}$ 2272$^{10}$ 2528$^{7}$ *2990$^{9}$* (3167) 3401$^{9}$ 3895$^{12}$4447$^{15}$ **>21a 65f<**

**Librettist (USA)** 2 b c Danzig (USA) -Mysterial (USA) (Alleged (USA)) (3913) (5395) 6217$^{5}$ **>115f<**

**Lieuday** 5 b g Atraf-Figment (Posse (USA)) *1515$^{5}$* 2122$^{14}$ 2658$^{3}$ 3148$^{10}$ **>36a 54 f<**

**Life (FR)** 3 gr f Anabaa (USA) -Igma (USA) (Grey Dawn (FR)) 4356a$^{4}$ **>101f<**

**Life Is Beautiful (IRE)** 5 b m Septieme Ciel (USA) -Palombella (FR) (Groom Dancer (USA)) 1560$^{6}$ (2347) 3008$^{5}$ (3165) 3472$^{6}$ 4561$^{2}$ 5238$^{4}$ 5714$^{2}$ **>24a 61f<**

**Lifted Way** 5 b h In The Wings-Stack Rock (Ballad Rock) *1118$^{9}$* (1624) *(1935)* 2534$^{14}$ 3205$^{6}$ 4164$^{5}$ 4690$^{4}$ 4920$^{10}$ 5444$^{14}$ **>83a 87f<**

**Light Brigade** 5 b g Kris-Mafatin (IRE) (Sadler s Wells (USA)) *1238$^{6}$ 1426$^{7}$ 2381$^{10}$ 3087$^{5}$* 3489$^{16}$ **>59a 62f<**

**Lighted Way** 2 b f Kris-Natchez Trace (Commanche Run) 4399$^{12}$ 4866$^{6}$ 5070$^{6}$ 5507$^{2}$ 5690$^{2}$ **>71f<**

**Lightening Fire (IRE)** 2 b g Woodborough (USA) -Glowlamp (IRE) (Glow (USA)) 3918$^{9}$ 4277$^{7}$ 5302$^{12}$ 6067$^{11}$ **>56f<**

**Lighthorne Lad** 2 ch c Hornbeam-Give Me A Day (Lucky Wednesday) 2502$^{9}$ 2947$^{11}$ 4809$^{13}$ **>26f<**

**Light Jig** 4 b f Danehill (USA) -Nashmeel (USA) (Blushing Groom (FR)) 6488a$^{7}$ **>111f<**

**Lightning Prospect** 2 ch f Zaha (CAN) -Lightning Blaze (Cosmonaut) 5209$^{12}$ **>17+f<**

**Lightning Star (USA)** 9 b g El Gran Senor (USA) -Cuz s Star (USA) (Galaxy Libra) 3996$^{7}$ **>60f<**

**Light Of Dubai (USA)** 2 b f Gone West (USA) -A. P. Assay (USA) (A.P. Indy (USA)) 5272$^{4}$ **>80+f<**

**Light Of Morn** 3 gr f Daylami (IRE) -My Emma (Marju (IRE)) 1521$^{2}$ 2460$^{3}$ (4028) 4367$^{4}$ 5394$^{6}$ 5916$^{4}$ **>99f<**

**Light The Dawn (IRE)** 4 ch f Indian Ridge-Flaming June (USA) (Storm Bird (CAN)) 1842$^{14}$ 2621$^{7}$ 3154$^{11}$ 6146$^{5}$ **>44a 50f<**

**Light Wind** 3 ch f Unfuwain (USA) -River Spey (Mill Reef (USA)) 1800$^{5}$ (3138) (3590) 4367$^{5}$ 5788$^{6}$ 6087$^{3}$ 6443$^{6}$ **>94+f<**

**Lightwood Lady (IRE)** 2 b f Anabaa (USA) -Lyrical Dance (USA) (Lear Fan (USA)) 6101a$^{6}$ **>82f<**

**Ligne D Eau** 3 ch c Cadeaux Genereux-Miss Waterline (Rock City) 1711$^{7}$ 2836$^{5}$ 3085$^{3}$ 4051$^{6}$ 4478$^{6}$ 4868$^{11}$ 5693$^{6}$ (6200) **>65f<**

**Lilian** 4 b f First Trump-Lillibella (Reprimand) *424$^{6}$ 473$^{5}$ 811$^{6}$ 3637$^{9}$* 3885$^{8}$ 4139$^{11}$ 4460$^{6}$ **>47a 49f<**

**Lilla Creek (USA)** 4 b f Quest For Fame-Alice Springs (USA) (Val De L Orne (FR)) 6437a$^{10}$ **>76f<**

**Lillas Forest** 2 b g Forestry (USA) -Lines Of Beauty (USA) (Line In The Sand (USA)) 5543$^{11}$ 6073$^{8}$ **>55f<**

**Lillebror (GER)** 6 b g Top Waltz (FR) -Lady Soliciti (GER) (Solicitor (FR)) 1326$^{12}$ 3683$^{7}$ 4033$^{3}$ 4647$^{11}$ **>59f<**

**Lillianna (IRE)** 3 ch f Barathea (IRE) -Machikane Akaiito (IRE) (Persian Bold) 1753$^{4}$ 2182$^{10}$ 3168$^{3}$ 3852$^{10}$ 5197$^{7}$ 5549$^{7}$ **>64f<**

**Lilli Marlane** 4 b f Sri Pekan (USA) -Fiveofive (IRE) (Fairy King (USA)) 1708$^{2}$ 1931$^{6}$ 2474$^{9}$ 2810$^{9}$ (3264) 3534$^{7}$ 3872$^{14}$ 4520$^{5}$ *5740$^{11}$6156$^{4}$ 6395$^{8}$* **>78+a 83f<**

**Lill s Star Lad** 6 ch g Kasakov-Lady Khadija (Nicholas Bill) *2229$^{10}$* 2386$^{13}$ **>16f<**

**Lilting Prose (IRE)** 2 ch f Indian Ridge-Kirkwood (Selkirk (USA)) 3992$^{5}$ 5943$^{11}$ **>63f<**

**Lily Lenat** 2 b f Josr Algarhoud (IRE) -Rushing River (USA) (Irish River (FR)) 2396$^{10}$ 2574$^{4}$ 2884$^{3}$ 3727$^{9}$ 5909$^{13}$ *6012$^{5}$* **>69a 67f<**

**Lily Of The Guild (IRE)** 5 ch m Lycius (USA) -Secreto Bold (Never So Bold) *599$^{10}$ 701$^{10}$ 918$^{2}$ 1098$^{4}$* 2428$^{4}$ 2886$^{5}$ 3747$^{8}$ 4083$^{13}$5282$^{13}$ *6405$^{2}$* **>55a 34 f<**

**Limehouse (USA)** 3 ch c Grand Slam (USA) -Dixieland Blues (USA) (Dixieland Band (USA)) *1781a$^{4}$* **>111a<**

**Limerick Boy (GER)** 6 b g Alwuhush (USA) -Limoges (GER) (Konigsstuhl (GER)) 1925$^{6}$ **>111f<**

**Limit (IRE)** 2 b f Barathea (IRE) -Orlena (USA) (Gone West (USA)) 5789$^{3}$ 6111$^{9}$ *6393$^{2}$ 6536$^{6}$* **>67a 67f<**

**Limit Down (IRE)** 3 b g Desert Story (IRE) -Princess Raisa (Indian King (USA)) *482$^{6}$ 561$^{5}$ 620$^{3}$ 678$^{6}$* **>50a 12f<**

**Limited Magician** 3 b f Wizard King-Pretty Scarce (Handsome Sailor) *569$^{13}$ 1423$^{9}$* ><

**Limonia (GER)** 2 b f Perugino (USA) -Limoges (GER) (Konigsstuhl (GER)) 1871$^{5}$ 2177$^{6}$ 2585$^{7}$ 5003$^{6}$ 5690$^{7}$ **>56f<**

**Linby Lad (IRE)** 4 ch g Dolphin Street (FR) -Classic Look (IRE) (Classic Music (USA)) *964$^{14}$ 1097$^{13}$* **>60a 75f<**

**Lincoln Dancer (IRE)** 7 b g Turtle Island (IRE) -Double Grange (IRE) (Double Schwartz) *544$^{10}$ 749$^{10}$* 1199$^{4}$ 1361$^{3}$ 1500$^{4}$ (1673) 1825$^{12}$ **>64a 87f<**

**Lincolneurocruiser** 2 b c Spectrum (IRE) -Rush Hour (IRE) (Night Shift (USA)) 1415$^{5}$ 1709$^{2}$ 2086$^{3}$ (2758) 3224$^{2}$ 3886$^{12}$ **>82f<**

**Linda Green** 3 b f Victory Note (USA) -Edge Of Darkness (Vaigly Great) (1196) 1742$^{4}$ **>53a 63f<**

**Linda s Colin (IRE)** 2 b c Xaar-Capable Kate (IRE) (Alzao (USA)) 5718$^{12}$ *6020$^{2}$ 6479$^{2}$* **>77a 21f<**

**Linden s Lady** 4 b f Compton Place-Jubilee Place (IRE) (Prince Sabo) 2143$^{10}$ 2407$^{6}$ 2735$^{11}$ 2963$^{5}$ 3101$^{6}$ 3923$^{5}$ 4133$^{12}$ 4425$^{5}$5235$^{4}$ 5575$^{3}$ 5639$^{8}$ *6363$^{11}$* **>23a 60f<**

**Lindholm (GER)** 5 b h Second Set (IRE) -Lindenblute (Surumu (GER)) 2608a$^{3}$ 5488a$^{4}$ 6379a$^{3}$ **>104f<**

**Line Ahead (IRE)** 2 b f Sadler s Wells (USA) -Alignment (IRE) (Alzao (USA)) 4851$^{16}$ **>33f<**

**Line Drawing** 3 b c Unfuwain (USA) -Fine Detail (IRE) (Shirley Heights) 1926$^{2}$ 2888$^{4}$ 3129$^{3}$ 5007$^{3}$ 5196$^{2}$ **>82f<**

**Linens Flame** 5 ch g Blushing Flame (USA) -Atlantic Air (Air Trooper) (1135) (1520) 1832$^{2}$ 2480$^{10}$ 2631$^{8}$ 5728$^{16}$ 6339$^{4}$ 6460$^{10}$ **>55a 74f<**

**Lin In Gold (IRE)** 3 b g Second Empire (IRE) -Wasmette (IRE) (Wassl) 1641$^{5}$ **>74f<**

**Linnet (GER)** 2 b f Dr Fong (USA) -Lauderdale (GER) (Nebos (GER)) 6471$^{6}$ **>74f<**

**Linngari (IRE)** 2 ch c Indian Ridge-Lidakiya (IRE) (Kahyasi) 4461$^{3}$ *(5051)* (5565) **>90a 92+f<**

**Linning Wine (IRE)** 8 b g Scenic-Zallaka (IRE) (Shardari) *558$^{13}$ 677$^{2}$* 1114$^{4}$ 1903$^{8}$ 2237$^{6}$ 2789$^{4}$ 4613$^{5}$ 4920$^{5}$5151$^{5}$ *5952$^{8}$ (6157)* **>104a 93f<**

**Linux (GER)** 5 b h Alwuhush (USA) -La Pena (IRE) (Be My Guest (USA)) 4377a$^{7}$ **>72f<**

**Linzis Lad** 2 ch g Magic Ring (IRE) -Come On Katie (Cadeaux Genereux) 5301$^{10}$ 6530$^{8}$ **>50f<**

**Lion Heart (USA)** 3 ch c Tale Of The Cat (USA) -Satin Sunrise (USA) (Mr. Leader (USA)) *1781a$^{2}$ 2139a$^{4}$* **>123a<**

**Lion Hunter (USA)** 5 b g Quest For Fame-Prodigious (FR) (Pharly (FR)) *768$^{13}$ 872$^{6}$* 1355$^{10}$ 1671$^{3}$ 2110$^{8}$ **>91a 94f<**

**Lion s Domane** 7 b g Lion Cavern (USA) -Vilany (Never So Bold) *422$^{9}$ 658$^{5}$ 813$^{6}$ 993$^{8}$* 1197$^{P}$ *1515$^{8}$* 1868$^{11}$3040$^{10}$ 3579$^{8}$ 4004$^{14}$ 4535$^{8}$ **>43a 41f<**

**Liquidate** 3 b g Hector Protector (USA) -Cut And Run (Slip Anchor) (1201) 1416$^{10}$ 2561$^{10}$ **>71f<**

**Liquid Form (IRE)** 4 br g Bahhare (USA) -Brogan s Well (IRE) (Caerleon (USA)) 1840$^{10}$ 2624$^{7}$ 3842$^{7}$ 4520$^{6}$ 5297$^{8}$ 5572$^{5}$ 5866$^{12}$ **>51a 79f<**

**Liquid Lover (IRE)** 2 b c Night Shift (USA) -New Tycoon (IRE) (Last Tycoon) 2804$^{10}$ 3438$^{11}$ 3931$^{13}$ 5373$^{12}$ **>56f<**

**Liquido (GER)** 5 br h Lomitas-Lolli Pop (GER) (Cagliostro (GER)) 1259a$^{9}$ (1779a) 2320a$^{4}$ 5254a$^{4}$ 5808a$^{3}$ (6512a) **>114?f<**

**Lirage** 2 b f Wizard King-Diamond Rouge (Puissance) 5771$^{12}$ **>18f<**

**Lisa Mona Lisa (IRE)** 2 b f Desert Style (IRE) -Amneris (IRE) (Alzao (USA)) (1115) 1449$^{4}$ (2819) 3677$^{10}$ *4094$^{4}$* (4482) 4909$^{8}$ 5477$^{6}$ **>55a 70f<**

**Liseberg (IRE)** 2 b c Gothenberg (IRE) -Read And Approved (IRE) (Husyan (USA)) 5097$^{14}$ ><

**Lisibila (GER)** 6 b m Acatenango (GER) -Like A Leaper (USA) (Lyphard s Wish (FR)) 5808a$^{7}$ **>77f<**

**Lisieux Orchid (IRE)** 3 b f Sadler s Wells (USA) -Clear Issue (USA) (Riverman (USA)) 2102a$^{6}$ 2993a$^{6}$ **>88f<**

**Lissahanelodge** 5 br g Grand Lodge (USA) -Lissahane Lass (Daring March) *(1164) 1281$^{2}$* 1644$^{7}$ 2375$^{6}$ 2787$^{6}$ 3429$^{6}$ **>49a 45 f<**

**Liss Ard (IRE)** 3 b c In The Wings-Beguine (USA) (Green Dancer (USA)) 2796a$^{7}$ 3862a$^{5}$ 4977a$^{11}$ **>91f<**

**Listen To Me** 2 gr g Petong-Time Clash (Timeless Times (USA)) 1607$^{5}$ 1853$^{12}$ 4638$^{5}$ 5218$^{14}$ **>43f<**

**Listen To Reason (IRE)** 3 b g Mukaddamah (USA) -Tenalist (IRE) (Tenby) (3839) 4438$^{11}$ 4817$^{8}$ 5063$^{12}$ **>67f<**

**Literatim** 4 b c Polish Precedent (USA) -Annie Albright (USA) (Verbatim (USA)) 1820$^{4}$ (4316) 4920$^{2}$ 5397$^{8}$ 6044$^{3}$ **>93+f<**

**Literator (FR)** 4 b g Danehill (USA) -Karamzin (USA) (Nureyev (USA)) *709a$^{3}$* ><

**Literature (USA)** 2 b f Notebook (USA) -Deputy s Mistress (USA) (Deputy Minister (CAN)) (5348) **>75f<**

**Lithos** 2 ch c Inchinor-Leisure (FR) (Fast Topaze (USA)) 4579$^{2}$ 5114$^{6}$ 5264$^{5}$ (5516) **>80f<**

**Litigado (ARG)** 8 br g Kitwood (USA) -Licitada (ARG) (Cinco Grande (USA)) *(688a)* **>87a 77f<**

**Little Biscuit (IRE)** 2 br f Indian Lodge (IRE) -Arjan (IRE) (Paris House) *(1137)* (1468) 1970$^{2}$ 2489$^{5}$ 2858$^{4}$ 3144$^{2}$ 3704$^{6}$ 3924$^{4}$ 6080$^{12}$ 6544$^{8}$ **>49a 59f<**

**Little Bob** 3 ch g Zilzal (USA) -Hunters Of Brora (IRE) (Sharpo) 1419$^{4}$ 1972$^{4}$ 2419$^{2}$ 3297$^{3}$ 3955$^{7}$ (4444) 5265$^{12}$ 5607$^{7}$ 6115$^{9}$ **>73f<**

**Little Dalham** 2 b c Diktat-Almost Amber (USA) (Mt. Livermore (USA)) 3406$^{4}$ 3748$^{2}$ (4149) 4953$^{6}$ 6356$^{4}$ **>80f<**

**Little Edward** 6 gr g King s Signet (USA) -Cedar Lady (Telsmoss) *1061$^{5}$* 1438$^{8}$ 2222$^{5}$ 2475$^{8}$ 2682$^{16}$ 2913$^{5}$ 3480$^{11}$ 4165$^{23}$4366$^{13}$ 4614$^{5}$ 4847$^{6}$ 5299$^{4}$ 5442$^{6}$ 5614$^{19}$ **>97a 88f<**

**Little Englander** 4 b g Piccolo-Anna Karietta (Precocious) 1715$^{5}$ 2212$^{9}$ 2547$^{8}$ 3154$^{5}$ (3536) 4238$^{7}$ 5496$^{10}$ 5868$^{4}$ 6124$^{4}$6311$^{5}$ **>65?f<**

**Little Eye (IRE)** 3 b g Groom Dancer (USA) -Beaming (Mtoto) *622$^{4}$ 704$^{9}$ 816$^{3}$* 2217$^{9}$ *2883$^{6}$* 3589$^{4}$ 3875$^{7}$ 4056$^{2}$(4443) **>66a 68f<**

**Little Flute** 3 b c Piccolo-Nordic Victory (USA) (Nordico (USA)) *496$^{4}$ 610$^{7}$ 732$^{7}$ 819$^{7}$ 918$^{10}$ (1571)* 2932$^{6}$ 5282$^{6}$6059$^{4}$ 6229$^{5}$ **>40a 51f<**

**Little Fox (IRE)** 9 br m Persian Bold-Dance Land (IRE) (Nordance (USA)) 3590$^{6}$ 4467$^{7}$ *4603$^{11}$* **>64a 57f<**

**Little Gannet** 3 ro f Bien Bien (USA) -Lady Kalliste (Another Realm) *3304$^{13}$* 4028$^{14}$ **>29a 41f<**

**Little Good Bay** 4 b c Danehill (USA) -Brave Kris (IRE) (Kris) *6451$^{11}$* **>96a 105f<**

**Little Indy** 2 ch c Forzando-Indian Nectar (Indian Ridge) 3805$^{11}$ 4169$^{11}$ 5347$^{10}$ 5687$^{6}$ *6294$^{9}$* **>33a 57f<**

**Little Jim (ARG)** 3 b c Roar (USA) -Clavija (ARG) (Cipayo (ARG)) *(691a) 975a$^{3}$ 1143a$^{3}$* **>109a<**

**Little Jimbob** 3 b g Desert Story (IRE) -Artistic Licence (High Top) (2934) 3230$^{2}$ 3507$^{4}$ 4140$^{3}$ 5399$^{5}$ 5990$^{2}$ 6266$^{4}$ *6498$^{6}$* **>69a 82f<**

**Little London** 3 b g Bahhare (USA) -North Kildare (USA) (Northjet) 5150$^{P}$ **>74f<**

**Little Matth Man (USA)** 3 br c Matty G (USA) -Lady s Legacy (USA) (Matchlite (USA)) *2139a$^{8}$* **>94a<**

**Little Miss Gracie** 2 gr f Efisio-Circled (USA) (Cozzene (USA)) 3202$^{3}$ 3560$^{3}$ 4584$^{2}$ 4963a$^{4}$ (5756) 6268$^{4}$ **>87+f<**

**Little Miss Lili** 3 b f Danzig Connection (USA) -Little Miss Rocker (Rock Hopper) 5749$^{8}$ 5867$^{13}$ ><

**Little Miss Tricky** 5 br m Magic Ring (IRE) -Mistook (USA) (Phone Trick (USA)) *793$^{8}$* **>24a 24f<**

**Little Richard (IRE)** 5 b g Alhaarth (IRE) -Intricacy (Formidable (USA)) *446$^{8}$ 568$^{9}$ 661$^{4}$ 727$^{3}$ (789) 857$^{4}$ 995$^{8}$ 1164$^{2}$1281$^{3}$ 1693$^{5}$ 1887$^{4}$* 6231$^{10}$ **>43a 23f<**

**Little Ridge (IRE)** 3 b g Charnwood Forest (IRE) -Princess Natalie (Rudimentary (USA)) 2549$^{10}$ 5263$^{10}$ *5912$^{12}$* (6518) *6538$^{3}$* **>76a 83f<**

**Little Sky** 7 gr m Terimon-Brown Coast (Oats) *1492$^{7}$* 2501$^{17}$ 3429$^{9}$ **>32a 58f<**

**Littlestar (FR)** 3 b g Robellino (USA) -Green Charter (Green Desert (USA)) 1224$^{14}$ 1509$^{10}$ 1998$^{13}$ 2402$^{12}$ 3556$^{2}$ 5320$^{11}$ **>59f<**

**Little Task** 6 b g Environment Friend-Lucky Thing (Green Desert (USA)) 2345$^{3}$ (2386) 3018$^{4}$ (3149) 3411$^{14}$ 3472$^{4}$ 3881$^{6}$ 4210$^{11}$ *6406$^{9}$* **>41a 44f<**

**Little Tobias (IRE)** 5 ch g Millkom-Barbara Frietchie (IRE) (Try My Best (USA)) 1534$^{6}$ 1754$^{13}$ (4261) 5343$^{3}$ 5638$^{3}$ 5991$^{14}$ 6110$^{4}$ **>62f<**

**Littleton Liberty** 3 b f Royal Applause-Lammastide (Martinmas) *927$^{8}$ 1568$^{7}$* **>19f<**

**Littleton Telchar (USA)** 4 ch c Atticus (USA) -Miss Waikiki (USA) (Miswaki (USA)) (2950) 3591$^{7}$ 4588a$^{10}$ 5074$^{9}$ **>72f<**

**Littleton Valar (IRE)** 4 ch g Definite Article-Fresh Look (IRE) (Alzao (USA)) *445$^{8}$* 1617$^{4}$ *2228$^{4}$* 2386$^{7}$ **>31a 43f<**

**Littleton Zephir (USA)** 5 b m Sandpit (BRZ) -Miss Gorgeous (IRE) (Damister (USA)) *503$^{7}$ 589$^{2}$ 604$^{8}$ 903$^{12}$ (1723) 1915$^{5}$ 3282$^{7}$* 3670$^{8}$4213$^{11}$ **>53a 56f<**

**Little Venice (IRE)** 4 b f Fumo Di Londra (IRE) -Petrine (IRE) (Petorius) 1354$^{16}$ 2064$^{5}$ 2788$^{3}$ (3320) 3597$^{11}$ 4178$^{9}$ 5004$^{7}$ (5574) **>95f<**

**Little Waltham** 2 ch f Tomba-Post Impressionist (IRE) (Ahonoora) 4243$^{14}$ *4544$^{10}$* 5154$^{8}$ ><

**Little Warning** 2 b f Piccolo-Iltimas (USA) (Dayjur (USA)) 4770$^{7}$ 5334$^{7}$ 5865$^{5}$ 6333$^{17}$ **>62f<**

**Little Whisper (IRE)** 3 bb f Be My Guest (USA) -Schust Madame (IRE) (Second Set (IRE)) 3328a$^{4}$ **>94f<**

**Little Wizzy** 2 b f Wizard King-Little Unknown (Known Fact (USA)) 1115$^{3}$ 1307$^{7}$ (1839) 1996$^{3}$ 2180$^{6}$ 6080$^{19}$ 6356$^{18}$ **>58f<**

**Litzinsky** 6 b g Muhtarram (USA) -Boulevard Girl (Nicholas Bill) *743$^{7}$* 1210$^{9}$ **>54a 62f<**

**Livadiya (IRE)** 8 b m Shernazar-Lilissa (IRE) (Doyoun) 1982a$^{7}$ 2102a$^{4}$ 2318a$^{2}$ 2329a$^{2}$ 2603a$^{7}$ 3331a$^{5}$ 5162a$^{11}$ 5484a$^{6}$5679a$^{7}$ **>108f<**

**Live And Learn (ITY)** 2 b f Love The Groom (USA) -Love Me Too (IRE) (Sesin) 2668a$^{5}$ **>68f<**

**Live In Hope** 2 b f High Estate-Movieland (USA) (Nureyev (USA)) 2213$^{13}$ 2730$^{10}$ 3918$^{14}$ **>24f<**

**Lively Felix** 7 b g Presidium-Full Of Life (Wolverlife) *572$^{4}$ 658$^{10}$ 1021$^{6}$ 1076$^{7}$ 1279$^{10}$* **>40a 29f<**

**Live Wire Lucy (USA)** 3 bb f King Of The Heap (USA) -Approach The Bench (USA) (Majestic Light (USA)) 2913$^{8}$ 3867$^{11}$ 4368$^{9}$ 4806$^{9}$ 5446$^{12}$ 5829$^{14}$ **>69f<**

**Livia (IRE)** 3 b f Titus Livius (FR) -Passing Beauty (Green Desert (USA)) *597$^{10}$ 739$^{6}$ 845$^{10}$ 983$^{4}$* 1184$^{12}$ 1300$^{6}$ 1908$^{9}$ 2061$^{12}$3193$^{7}$ 5863$^{14}$ 6056$^{2}$ *6402$^{4}$ 6541$^{11}$* **>53a 50f<**

**Living Symbol (USA)** 3 b c Nureyev (USA) -Journey Of Hope (USA) (Slew O Gold (USA)) 1777a$^{10}$ **>65f<**

**Livvies Lady (IRE)** 2 b f Opening Verse (USA) -Indian Wardance (ITY) (Indian Ridge) *6155$^{11}$ 6446$^{14}$* **>15a<**

**Liwa s Lake (USA)** 2 ch f Greenwood Lake (USA) -Champagne Sweep (USA) (End Sweep (USA)) 2535$^{3}$ 3382$^{7}$ 4607$^{11}$ **>69f<**

**Lizarazu (GER)** 5 b h Second Set (IRE) -Lilly (GER) (Motley (USA)) 3745$^{9}$ 4438$^{8}$ 4569$^{11}$ 5135$^{12}$ 6445$^{10}$ **>65f<**

**Lizhar (IRE)** 3 b f Danetime (IRE) -Amelesa (IRE) (Perugino (USA)) *547$^{4}$ 610$^{6}$ 617$^{4}$ 670$^{7}$ 678$^{4}$ 865$^{2}$ 1008$^{8}$1047$^{4}$ 1206$^{6}$* 1312$^{8}$ 3530$^{14}$ **>62a 48f<**

**Llamadas** 2 b g Josr Algarhoud (IRE) -Primulette (Mummy s Pet) 1865$^{3}$ 2860$^{9}$ 3080$^{3}$ *3611$^{4}$* 4131$^{10}$ 5060$^{3}$ 5233$^{6}$ 5475$^{6}$5636$^{15}$ *5954$^{2}$ 6294$^{7}$* **>56a 65f<**

**Loachapoka (GER)** 3 b f Monsun (GER) -La Curamalal (IRE) (Rainbow Quest (USA)) 5822a$^{8}$ **>66f<**

**Loaded Gun** 4 ch g Highest Honor (FR) -Woodwardia (USA) (El Gran Senor (USA)) *585$^{12}$* 4901$^{2}$ 5229$^{4}$ 5584$^{7}$ 6141$^{3}$ 6343$^{4}$ *6576$^{13}$* **>54a 60f<**

**Loaderfun (IRE)** 2 br c Danehill Dancer (IRE) -Sideloader Special (Song) 2522$^{4}$ 3808$^{2}$ (5536) 5802$^{2}$ **>90+f<**

**Lobengula (IRE)** 2 b g Spectrum (IRE) -Playwaki (USA) (Miswaki (USA)) 6045$^{10}$ 6514$^{5}$ **>61f<**

**Local Poet** 3 b c Robellino (USA) -Laugharne (Known Fact (USA)) (1127) 1384$^{5}$ 1883$^{8}$ 2294$^{5}$ 2897$^{17}$ 3598$^{18}$ 4538$^{14}$ **>90f<**

**Locator (IRE)** 3 b g Mujadil (USA) -Lifeboat (IRE) (Petorius) 1972$^{10}$ 2113$^{17}$ **>55a 48f<**

**Lochbuie (IRE)** 3 b c Definite Article-Uncertain Affair (IRE) (Darshaan) 1108$^{4}$ (1416) (1899) 3210$^{3}$ (4274) 4888$^{4}$ 5288$^{4}$ 5892$^{3}$ **>106f<**

**Loch Garman (IRE)** 3 ch g Spectrum (IRE) -Key To Coolcullen (IRE) (Royal Academy (USA)) 1487a$^{5}$ **>74f<**

**Loch Inch** 7 ch g Inchinor-Carrie Kool (Prince Sabo) 2246$^{12}$ 2440$^{9}$ 2724$^{12}$ 3126$^{4}$ 3558$^{9}$ 3810$^{4}$ 4085$^{2}$ 4308$^{3}$4400$^{3}$ 4774$^{P}$ **>59a 60f<**

**Loch Laird** 9 b g Beveled (USA) -Daisy Loch (Lochnager) *453$^{7}$ 573$^{8}$ (1020) 1098$^{9}$* 1909$^{5}$ 2703$^{10}$ 2886$^{13}$ 3828$^{5}$4912$^{4}$ 5039$^{3}$ 5260$^{10}$ *5642$^{7}$* **>53a 52f<**

**Loch Quest (IRE)** 2 ch g Giant s Causeway (USA) -Taibhseach (USA) (Secreto (USA)) 5467$^{5}$ 5729$^{8}$ 6077$^{8}$ **>73f<**

**Lochridge** 5 ch m Indian Ridge-Lochsong (Song) 2475$^{2}$ 2955$^{14}$ 3073$^{13}$ 3715$^{3}$ 4317$^{2}$ 4779$^{4}$ 5289$^{14}$ **>108f<**

**Lock And Key (IRE)** 2 b f Key Of Luck (USA) -Lock s Heath (CAN) (Topsider (USA)) 3286a$^{5}$ 4158a$^{2}$ 5322a$^{2}$ **>102f<**

**Lockstock (IRE)** 6 b g Inchinor-Risalah (Marju (IRE)) *667$^{7}$ 882$^{13}$* (1857) 2226$^{8}$ 2834$^{7}$ 5444$^{9}$ 5841$^{5}$ 6081$^{4}$ **>73a 74f<**

**Locombe Hill (IRE)** 8 b g Barathea (IRE) -Roberts Pride (Roberto (USA)) *491$^{11}$ 542$^{2}$* 1502$^{10}$ 2492$^{9}$ 2779$^{5}$ 3167$^{15}$ 3446$^{4}$ 3778$^{4}$3895$^{11}$ (4905) 5108$^{5}$ 5316$^{3}$ (5583) 5833$^{2}$ 6138$^{2}$ 6358$^{9}$ **>67a 75f<**

**Lodge Keeper** 4 ch g Grand Lodge (USA) -Aunt Tate (Tate Gallery (USA)) 633a$^{2}$ 853a$^{5}$ 976a$^{5}$ **>103f<**

**Lodger (FR)** 4 ch c Grand Lodge (USA) -Light River (USA) (Irish River (FR)) 3716$^{12}$ 4123$^{6}$ 4345$^{4}$ 5288$^{9}$ 5784$^{10}$ **>95f<**

**Lodgician (IRE)** 2 b c Grand Lodge (USA) -Dundel (IRE) (Machiavellian (USA)) 3313$^{4}$ 3718$^{3}$ 4208$^{9}$ 5477$^{4}$ 5636$^{11}$ 5989$^{13}$ **>67f<**

**Logger Rhythm (USA)** 4 b g Woodman (USA) -Formidable Dancer (USA) (Danzig (USA)) 1311$^{7}$ 1612$^{12}$ 1770$^{4}$ 2212$^{13}$ 5176$^{15}$ **>53f<**

**Logistical** 4 b c Grand Lodge (USA) -Magic Milly (Simply Great (FR)) 1877$^{13}$ 2483$^{10}$ 2834$^{5}$ 3321$^{11}$ 3841$^{15}$ 5260$^{9}$ 5411$^{14}$ *5642$^{9}$* **>32a 57f<**

**Loitokitok** 2 b g Piccolo-Bonita Bee (King Of Spain) *4544$^{8}$* 5269$^{10}$ 5696$^{8}$ **>29a 62f<**

**Lojo** 2 ch f Pivotal-Myhat (Factual (USA)) 2248$^{7}$ 2622$^{3}$ 2960$^{2}$ (3170) **>53f<**

**Lola Lola (IRE)** 3 b f Piccolo-French Gift (Cadeaux Genereux) 2842$^{10}$ *3710$^{8}$* 4674$^{18}$ **>29a 35f<**

**Lola Sapola (IRE)** 2 b f Benny The Dip (USA) -Cutpurse Moll (Green Desert (USA)) 4172$^{7}$ 4753$^{9}$ 5089$^{9}$ (5747) 6265$^{4}$ 6562$^{7}$ **>73f<**

**Lola s Destiny** 3 b f Mark Of Esteem (IRE) -Kristiana (Kris) *563$^{5}$ 683$^{6}$ 736$^{8}$* **>45a 43f<**

**Lomapamar** 3 b f Nashwan (USA) -Morina (USA) (Lyphard (USA)) 5079$^{3}$ 5732$^{12}$ *5913$^{13}$* (6310) **>73f<**

**Lommel (UAE)** 3 b c Lomitas-Idrica (Rainbow Quest (USA)) 1437$^{15}$ 1745$^{8}$ **>60a 77+f<**

**Londoner (USA)** 6 ch g Sky Classic (CAN) -Love And Affection (USA) (Exclusive Era (USA)) *419$^{7}$ 745$^{10}$ 882$^{8}$ 962$^{11}$ 1207$^{3}$* 2325$^{2}$ 2598$^{2}$(2803) 2943$^{7}$ 3103$^{5}$ 3174$^{3}$ 4127$^{5}$ 4418$^{2}$ 4435$^{12}$ 5017$^{7}$ *(5222)* 5496$^{6}$ **>70a 68f<**

**Londonnetdotcom (IRE)** 4 ch f Night Shift (USA) -Hopeful Sign (Warning) 690a$^{4}$ 831a$^{7}$ **>103f<**

**Lone Piper** 9 b g Warning-Shamisen (Diesis) *443$^{12}$ 460$^{8}$ 657$^{9}$ 876$^{6}$ 938$^{4}$ 944$^{3}$ 1089$^{6}$1180$^{6}$* 1584$^{11}$

1639[6] 2383[14] >38a 34f<

**Lone Plainsman** 3 b c Royal Applause-Suprematie (FR) (Gay Mecene (USA)) 3961a[4] 5660a[16] >84f<

**Loner** 6 b g Magic Ring (IRE) -Jolis Absent (Primo Dominie) 3559[15] 4246[2] 4425[9] >47a 61f<

**Lonesome Me (FR)** 2 br f Zafonic (USA) -Lone Spirit (IRE) (El Gran Senor (USA)) 5532a[4] 6320a[7] >90f<

**Longridge (GER)** 6 ch g Surumu (GER) -La Paz (GER) (Roi Dagobert) 5824a[7] 6378a[4] >106f<

**Long Road (USA)** 3 b g Diesis-Tuviah (USA) (Eastern Echo (USA)) 2114[2] 2311[2] 3268[2] (3603) >84f<

**Long Weekend (IRE)** 6 b g Flying Spur (AUS) -Friday Night (USA) (Trempolino (USA)) 530[7] 576[6] 658[6] 930[2] (951) (1000) 1018[4] 1087[6]1516[11] 2166[6] 2399[9] 2735[12] 2885[9] 4291[21] 6363[4] 6405[3] >59a 45f<

**Look Again** 3 ch g Zilzal (USA) -Last Look (Rainbow Quest (USA)) (4850) 5397[4] >91+f<

**Look At The Stars (IRE)** 2 b g Bachir (IRE) -Pizzazz (Unfuwain (USA)) 3808[9] (4488) 4958a[14] >84f<

**Look Here s Carol (IRE)** 4 ch f Safawan-Where s Carol (Anfield) 1825[3] 2117[3] 2685[6] 3337[3] (3755) 4553[7] 4889[5] 5249[2] 5416[7]5811[10] >98f<

**Look Honey (IRE)** 4 b c Sadler s Wells (USA) -Middle Prospect (USA) (Mr Prospector (USA)) 980a[9] 3030a[3] 4766a[5] 5727a[9] >115f<

**Looking Back (IRE)** 3 b f Stravinsky (USA) -Mustique Dream (Don t Forget Me) 1778a[8] >81f<

**Looking Down** 4 ch f Compton Place-High Stepping (IRE) (Taufan (USA)) 1358[13] 2528[12] >83a 83 f<

**Looking Great (USA)** 2 b g Gulch (USA) -Shoofha (IRE) (Bluebird (USA)) 3413[7] 3808[14] 4584[9] 5114[13] >59f<

**Lookouthereicome** 3 b f Rudimentary (USA) -Sylvatica (Thatching) 621[8] 890[12] 3348[9] 4583[10] 5352[8] >47a 47f<

**Looks Could Kill (USA)** 2 bb g Red Ransom (USA) -Mingling Glances (USA) (Woodman (USA)) 4290[2] (4633) 5292[4] 5630[3] 6338[2] >90f<

**Looks The Business (IRE)** 3 b g Marju (IRE) -Business Centre (IRE) (Digamist (USA)) 739[2] 835[4] 1064[5] 1271[9] 1392[14] 2168[8] >72a 64f<

**Lord Admiral (USA)** 3 b c El Prado (IRE) -Lady Ilsley (USA) (Trempolino (USA)) 1489a[3] 2333a[5] 2796a[6] 4784a[5] 5312a[2] 5481a[2] 6102a[11] >103f<

**Lord Arthur** 3 b g Mind Games-Flower O Cannie (IRE) (Mujadil (USA)) 3279[11] 3711[4] 4188[9] 5081[9] 5236[15] >50a 50f<

**Lord Baskerville** 3 br g Wolfhound (USA) -My Dear Watson (Chilibang) 462[13] 620[12] 1196[6] 1526[12] 1788[3] 2351[7] 3270[8] 3314[13]3407[13] 3624[2] 3877[2] 3954[4] 4259[8] 5141[4] 5346[4] 5859[16]5945[13] 6097[12] >46a 62f<

**Lord Chalfont (IRE)** 2 ch g Daggers Drawn (USA) -Byproxy (IRE) (Mujtahid (USA)) 1589[12] 1735[9] 2852[7] 3377[9] 4359[9] 4579[9] 5142[9] 5593[16] >13a 22f<

**Lord Chamberlain** 11 b g Be My Chief (USA) -Metaphysique (FR) (Law Society (USA)) 442[2] (504) 582[4] 695[4] 738[11] 834[2] 910[2] 953[9]2426[3] 2597[4] 2833[4] 2886[8] 3148[3] 3247[11] 3489[2] 3697[7](4479) 4546[4] 4871[11] 5260[2] 5493[5] 5575[9] >66a 65f<

**Lord Conyers (IRE)** 5 b m Inzar (USA) -Primelta (Primo Dominie) 1263[7] 1527[12] 1710[4] 2445[4] >44a 44f<

**Lord Darnley (IRE)** 3 b c Darshaan-Ghariba (Final Straw) 3359a[2] >106f<

**Lord Dundee (IRE)** 6 ch g Polish Precedent (USA) -Easy To Copy (USA) (Affirmed (USA)) 3078[9] 3474[9] 3892[4] >46 f<

**Lord Du Sud (FR)** 3 gr c Linamix (FR) -Marseillaise (FR) (Esprit Du Nord (USA)) (2073a) 2722a[6] 5500a[4] 5965a[2] >117+f<

**Lord Elrond** 2 b c Magic Ring (IRE) -Cactus Road (FR) (Iron Duke (FR)) 2370[8] >54f<

**Lord Eurolink (IRE)** 10 b g Danehill (USA) -Lady Eurolink (Kala Shikari) 5568[16] 6266[19] >80f<

**Lord Gizzmo** 7 ch g Democratic (USA) -Figrant (USA) (L Emigrant (USA)) 609[11] 693[6] 777[10] >24a 23f<

**Lord Greystoke (IRE)** 3 b g Petardia-Jungle Story (IRE) (Alzao (USA)) 490[9] 1997[17] 5259[13] 5654[12] 5863[11] >25a 34f<

**Lord John** 2 b c Piccolo-Mahbob Dancer (FR) (Groom Dancer (USA)) 1128[8] 1390[4] 2173[7] 3886[4] 4094[9] 4445[7] 4700[4] 5234[10]5363[2] 5520[3] >27a 59f<

**Lord Kintyre** 9 b g Makbul-Highland Rowena (Royben) 5071[8] >92a 92f<

**Lord Lahar** 5 b g Fraam-Brigadiers Bird (IRE) (Mujadil (USA)) 2257[6] 2525[8] 4202[12] 4473[13] 4624[5] 5175[7] 5340[4] 5638[17]6065[2] 6231[6] (6292) 6540[10] >58a 56f<

**Lord Lamb** 12 gr g Dunbeath (USA) -Caroline Lamb (Hotfoot) 2759[3] 3237[4] 3564[8] 3835[5] 4082[3] >56f<

**Lord Links (IRE)** 3 ch g Daggers Drawn (USA) -Lady From Limerick (IRE) (Rainbows For Life (CAN)) 2224[4] 3001[9] 3728[7] 4268[17] 4738[7] 5399[4] 5652[8] 5934[3](6086) >86f<

**Lord Mayfair (USA)** 2 b g Silic (FR) -Spring Wedding (USA) (Prized (USA)) 4824[2] 5543[5] 5772[6] >81f<

**Lord Mayor** 3 b g Machiavellian (USA) -Misleading Lady (Warning) 2018[3] (2676) 3000[5] 3927[5] 4965a[6] >80+a 103f<

**Lord Melbourne (IRE)** 5 b g Lycius (USA) -Adana (IRE) (Classic Music (USA)) 421[2] (536) 576[4] 698[3] 738[13] 858[5] (941) 972[6]3024[8] >56 a 50f<

**Lord Nellsson** 8 b g Arctic Lord-Miss Petronella (Petoski) 3194[4] 3885[7] 4028[10] 4870[5] 5340[8] 5826[7] >64?f<

**Lord Nelson (AUS)** 3 gr g Unbridled s Song (USA) -Kate s Choice (NZ) (Imposing (AUS)) 830a[2] 923a[6] >94a<

**Lord Normacote** 2 b g Loup Sauvage (USA) -Blessed Event (King s Lake (USA)) 2096[7] 3553[8] 4480[4] 5090[13] 5369[16] 5593[7] >60df<

**Lord Of Adventure (IRE)** 2 b c Inzar (USA) -Highly Fashionable (IRE) (Polish Precedent (USA)) 5281[8] >48f<

**Lord Of Dreams (IRE)** 2 ch c Barathea (IRE) -The Multiyorker (IRE) (Digamist (USA)) 4081[11] 5114[5] 5434[13] 5735[3] 5995[4] 6265[2] >71a 67f<

**Lord Of Flowers** 3 b c Lord Of Men-Battle Of Flowers (Shernazar) 1306a[13] ><

**Lord Of Methley** 5 gr g Zilzal (USA) -Paradise Waters (Celestial Storm (USA)) 1389[11] 1710[8] 2408[7] (4825) >46a 56f<

**Lord Of The East** 5 b g Emarati (USA) -Fairy Free (Rousillon (USA)) 1265[10] 1452[3] 1929[2] 2461[14] (2965) 3298[3] 3439[2] 3663[3] 3871[2](4047) 4152[10] 4291[17] 5419[20] >61a 85f<

**Lord Of The Fens** 4 b g Danzig Connection (USA) -Zizi (IRE) (Imp Society (USA)) 2236[17] 2517[17] 3019[6] >18f<

**Lord Of The Pines (AUS)** 9 u g Royal Academy (USA) -Glenview (NZ) (Sir Tristram (IRE)) 2156a[10] >94f<

**Lord Of The Sea (IRE)** 3 b g Perugino (USA) -Sea Mistress (Habitat) 644[3] 704[3] 959[4] 1064[10] 2244[7] 2648[9] 2842[4] 3089[13]5150[6] 5496[12] 6017[7] 6452[8] >74a 69f<

**Lord Wishingwell (IRE)** 3 b g Lake Coniston (IRE) -Spirito Libro (USA) (Lear Fan (USA)) 1617[8] 1985[3] 2556[3] 3234[10] 4101[4] 4440[6] 4968[7] 5451[14]5926[8] 6200[17] >42f<

**Lord Zinc** 3 b g Forzando-Zolica (Beveled (USA)) 2165[17] ><

**Loreo (GER)** 2 ch c Big Shuffle (USA) -Lorelei (GDR) (Cil (GER)) 6256a[10] ><

**Lores Joy (ARG)** 5 ch h Lode (USA) -Legion Joy (ARG) (Leap For Joy (USA)) 3552a[12] 5505a[8] ><

**Loriana (IRE)** 3 b f Dushyantor (USA) -Furibonda (IRE) (Danzig Connection (USA)) 2341a[3] 3137a[4] >98f<

**Lorien Hill (IRE)** 3 b f Danehill (USA) -Lothlorien (USA) (Woodman (USA)) 1507[6] 2122[5] (2572) 2788[7] 3306[2] 3949[8] 4646[3] 4938[7] 5698[5] >61a 77f<

**Lorna Dune** 2 b f Desert Story (IRE) -Autumn Affair (Lugana Beach) 2035[3] 2730[6] 3196[8] 3893[6] 4878[7] 5369[3] (5593) 5852[12] 6127[5] >51a 62f<

**Los Organos (IRE)** 2 br f Turtle Island (IRE) -Spicebird (IRE) (Ela-Mana-Mou) 6352[3] 6473[8] >87f<

**Lost Icon (IRE)** 3 ch f Intikhab (USA) -Luminosity (Sillery (USA)) 4899a[11] >86f<

**Lost Soldier Three (IRE)** 3 b g Barathea (IRE) -Donya (Mill Reef (USA)) 2114[6] (2611) 3345[5] 3915[4] 4715[2] (4888) (5435) 5892[4] >107f<

**Lost Spirit** 8 b g Strolling Along (USA) -Shoag (USA) (Affirmed (USA)) 2053[14] 2525[11] >51a 65f<

**Lotosmaid (GER)** 3 ch f Zinaad-Lotosschone (GDR) (Intervall (GER)) 6255a[2] >96f<

**Lotta (GER)** 3 b f Poliglote-Lorenza (GER) (Top Ville) 2341a[9] 3972a[6] >96f<

**Lottie** 3 b f Robellino (USA) -Montserrat (Aragon) 3759[7] 4068[5] 4316[4] 5547[17] 5702[14] >38f<

**Lottie Dundass** 2 ch f Polar Falcon (USA) -Sand Grouse (USA) (Arctic Tern (USA)) 3123[5] 3664[2] 5349[7] 5753[4] >73f<

**Loughlorien (IRE)** 5 b g Lake Coniston (IRE) -Fey Lady (IRE) (Fairy King (USA)) 2274[8] 2735[8] 3010[11] 3169[9] 3533[9] 3836[3] 4014[3] 4422[4]4557[7] (5452) 6007[2] 6526[3] >43a 58f<

**Louise Paris (IRE)** 2 b f Soviet Star (USA) -Avantage Service (IRE) (Exactly Sharp (USA)) 4544[11] ><

**Louise Rayner** 2 b f Vettori (IRE) -Showery (Rainbow Quest (USA)) 2819[5] 3164[4] 4016[9] 4601[9] (6308) >35a 67f<

**Louis Georgio** 5 b g Royal Applause-Swellegant (Midyan (USA)) 1642[12] 2123[12] 2383[12] >12a 34f<

**Louisiade (IRE)** 3 b g Tagula (IRE) -Titchwell Lass (Lead On Time (USA)) 1473[11] 2075[3] 2589[8] 3585[10] 4092[3] 4242[3] 4610[7] 5518[10] >69f<

**Louis Prima** 3 gr g Paris House-Chanson D Amour (IRE) (High Estate) 4247[8] 4391[8] 5342[11] 5674[15] >25f<

**Louphole** 2 ch g Loup Sauvage (USA) -Goodwood Lass (IRE) (Alzao (USA)) 3302[3] 3633[4] (3986) 4803[7] 5421[7] 5839[3] (5932) 6174[10] >85f<

**Louvain (IRE)** 2 b f Sinndar (IRE) -Flanders (IRE) (Common Grounds) 5313a[3] >93f<

**Love Affair (IRE)** 2 b f Tagula (IRE) -Changing Partners (Rainbow Quest (USA)) 4272[2] 5089[7] 5434[8] 5938[2] >75f<

**Love Always** 2 b f Piccolo-Lady Isabell (Rambo Dancer (CAN)) 5247[4] 5695[2] >76f<

**Love And Bubbles (USA)** 3 b f Loup Sauvage (USA) -Bubble Dream (FR) (Akarad (FR)) 2028a[2] 2925a[12] (3258a) 4430a[4] >106f<

**Love And Honour** 2 b f Silver Patriarch (IRE) -Fox Star (IRE) (Foxhound (USA)) 6441[20] ><

**Love And Laughter (IRE)** 2 b f Theatrical-Hoh Dear (IRE) (Sri Pekan (USA)) 3925[6] (4359) 5466[14] >72f<

**Love Angel (USA)** 2 bb c Woodman (USA) -Omnia (USA) (Green Dancer (USA)) 3643[4] 4003[3] >80f<

**Love Attack (IRE)** 2 b f Sri Pekan (USA) -Bradwell (IRE) (Taufan (USA)) 6221[6] 6400[6] 6569[18] >34a 35f<

**Love Beauty (USA)** 2 bb c Seeking The Gold (USA) -Heavenly Rhythm (USA) (Septieme Ciel (USA)) 2780[4] 3601[11] 5790[2] 6531[5] >78f<

**Love From Russia** 2 b g Xaar-Heart (Cadeaux Genereux) 5096[15] 5396[11] 5633[7] 6045[11] >32f<

**Love In Seattle (IRE)** 4 b c Seattle Slew (USA) -Tamise (USA) (Time For A Change (USA)) 1172[13] (1746) 2237[12] 2493[7] 2781[10] 6043[14] >86f<

**Love In The Mist (USA)** 3 b f Silver Hawk (USA) -Fast Nellie (USA) (Ack Ack (USA)) 420[10] >42a 59f<

**Loveisdangerous** 3 b f Pursuit Of Love-Brookhead Lady (Petong) 1236[5] 1934[10] 2411[8] >44a 48f<

**Lovelorn** 2 b g Mind Games-Love Letters (Pursuit Of Love) 2812[3] 4256[10] 4804[13] >50a 51f<

**Lovely Boy (SWI)** 10 b g Pennine Walk-La Diva (Orchestra) 786a[11] ><

**Love Me Tender** 2 b f Green Desert (USA) -Easy To Love (USA) (Diesis) 4560[7] 5088[5] 6454[8] >70f<

**Love Money (IRE)** 2 b f Intikhab (USA) -Love Money (IRE) (Intikhab (USA)) 4964a[7] >75f<

**Love Of Life** 3 b f Spectrum (IRE) -Night Over Day (Most Welcome) 1186[10] 1295[14] 3427[6] 3988[7] 4387[2] 5927[11] 6557[LFT] >53f<

**Love Of The Game (IRE)** 3 b f Croco Rouge (IRE) -Lovealoch (IRE) (Lomond (USA)) 3569a[4] ><

**Love Palace (IRE)** 2 b c King s Best (USA) -Vijaya (USA) (Lear Fan (USA)) 3505[2] 4633[2] 5228[4] (5669) 6189[5] >95f<

**Love s Design (IRE)** 7 bb g Pursuit Of Love-Cephista (Shirley Heights) 478[8] 531[6] 590[8] 642[10] 726[5] 810[5] 2209[4] >49a 52f<

**Loves Travelling (IRE)** 4 b g Blues Traveller (IRE) -Fast Love (IRE) (Second Set (IRE)) 2671[2] (3199) 3716[2] 5288[10] 5814[14] >62a 99 f<

**Love Thirty** 2 b f Mister Baileys-Polished Up (Polish Precedent (USA)) 4494[6] 5154[2] 5648[5] (5890) >92?f<

**Love Triangle (IRE)** 3 ch g Titus Livius (FR) -Kirsova (Absalom) 2536[3] 3203[7] 3542[11] 3750[9] 4145[4] 4648[5] 5739[7] >69a 84f<

**Love You Always (USA)** 4 ch g Woodman (USA) -Encorenous (USA) (Diesis) 1286[8] 5436[6] 5705[8] >85f<

**Loveyoulongtime** 3 gr f Compton Place-Sky Red (Night Shift (USA)) 2785[8] 3179[8] 3635[4] >38f<

**Low Cloud** 4 b g Danehill (USA) -Raincloud (Rainbow Quest (USA)) 1903[6] 2142[11] 2673[3] 2938[5] (3012) 3365[4] 3660[5] 3731[4] 4327[12]4988[10] 5607[17] >83f<

**Lowestoft Playboy** 2 ch g Pivotal-Red Typhoon (Belfort (FR)) 2502[8] 3051[6] 3413[5] 4124[7] 5947[21] 6158[4] 6359[5] 6562[20] >65a 69f<

**Loxias (FR)** 5 b h Saumarez-Loxandra (Last Tycoon) 2924a[6] >116f<

**Loyal Love (USA)** 2 bb f Danzig (USA) -Always Loyal (USA) (Zilzal (USA)) 5271[6] (5943) >88 f<

**Loyal Tycoon (IRE)** 6 br g Royal Abjar (USA) -Rosy Lydgate (Last Tycoon) 1106[17] 1500[7] 1825[2] 2477[5] 2682[15] 3036[8] (3439) 3691[8] 3901[5]4152[5] 4291[22] 4811[2] >90a 97f<

**Loyalty Lodge (IRE)** 2 ch g Grand Lodge (USA) -Gaily Grecian (IRE) (Ela-Mana-Mou) 2045[10] 3014[6] 3560[10] 5240[14] >55f<

**Lualua** 3 ch g Presidium-Tawny (Grey Ghost) 1760[4] 2131[2] 2589[3] 2877[14] 3077[4] 3777[3] 4289[14] 4608[13]5949[6] >82f<

**Luas Line (IRE)** 2 b f Danehill (USA) -Streetcar (IRE) (In The Wings) 3859a[7] 4592a[2] 5149[7] >96f<

**Lubeck** 2 b g Lujain (USA) -Milling (IRE) (In The Wings) 3760[5] (4172) 4836[9] >79f<

**Lubinas (IRE)** 5 b g Grand Lodge (USA) -Liebesgirl (Konigsstuhl (GER)) 1754[7] 2004[5] >45a 48f<

**Lucayan Belle** 3 b f Cadeaux Genereux-Floppie (FR) (Law Society (USA)) 1617[7] ><

**Lucayan Dancer** 4 b g Zieten (USA) -Tittle Tattle (IRE) (Soviet Lad (USA)) 1265[6] 1502[5] 3510[5] 4220[16] (5021) 5584[4] (5757) 6096[2] 6337[3] 6520[4] >68f<

**Lucayan Legend (IRE)** 3 b c Docksider (USA) -Capo Di Monte (Final Straw) 1827[6] 2204[3] (2392) 3001[2] 4271[15] >100f<

**Lucayan Monarch** 6 ch g Cadeaux Genereux-Flight Soundly (IRE) (Caerleon (USA)) 423[2] (439) (498) 565[2] 642[5] 695[13] 738[8] 888[2]895[3] 932[2] 1095[3] 1121[6] 1279[5] 1496[2] >61a 61 f<

**Luceball (IRE)** 4 b f Bluebird (USA) -Mysterious Plans (IRE) (Last Tycoon) 896[9] 917[11] >44a 50f<

**Lucefer (IRE)** 6 b g Lycius (USA) -Maharani (USA) (Red Ransom (USA)) 1207[9] 1373[8] 1910[3] 2034[4] 2387[4] 2573[8] 4802[3] (5017) 5176[8]5575[5] 5733[9] 6227[12] 6364[5] >49a 57f<

**Luchi** 3 ch f Mark Of Esteem (IRE) -Penmayne (Inchinor) 489[6] 673[10] >46a<

**Lucid Dreams (IRE)** 5 b g Sri Pekan (USA) -Scenaria (IRE) (Scenic) 469[5] 694[7] 738[4] (888) 933[2] 988[3] (1095) 1207[5] >64a 57f<

**Luciferous (USA)** 2 ch f Devil s Bag (USA) -Vital Laser (USA) (Seeking The Gold (USA)) 4143[5] 4936[6] >64f<

**Lucifer s Stone (USA)** 3 b f Horse Chestnut (SAF) -Ladue (USA) (Demons Begone (USA)) (5530a) ><

**Lucius Verrus (USA)** 4 b g Danzig (USA) -Magic Of Life (USA) (Seattle Slew (USA)) 479[3] 738[14] (1596) 1872[16] 2123[5] 2663[2] 3277[9] 3381[5]3616[6] 4542[15] 5000[3] >56a 47f<

**Lucky (IRE)** 3 b f Sadler s Wells (USA) -Zummerudd (Habitat) (1649a) 1980a[4] 2330a[15] 5679a[13] >104f<

**Lucky Again (IRE)** 3 br g Be My Guest (USA) -Persian Fantasia (Alzao (USA)) 1461[17] 1912[4] 2729[7] 3172[5] >48f<

**Lucky Archer** 11 b g North Briton-Preobrajenska (Double Form) 2547[7] 3103[11] 3489[11] 4042[7] 5585[6] >43a 36f<

**Lucky Arthur (IRE)** 3 ch f Grand Lodge (USA) -Soltura (IRE) (Sadler s Wells (USA)) 1967[8] 2168[5] 2374[8] 2977[3] 3572[2] 3695[3] 4307[15] 6006[8]6533[10] >67f<

**Lucky Emerald (IRE)** 2 b f Lend A Hand-Anita s Love (IRE) (Anita s Prince) 3531[2] 3805[7] (4474) 5351[14] 6080[5] 6394[9] >44a 69f<

**Lucky Judge** 7 b g Saddlers Hall (IRE) -Lady Lydia (Ela-Mana-Mou) 1245[4] 1661[12] (1973) 2987[5] (3236) (3564) 4934[6] 5100[5] >50a 76f<

**Lucky Largo (IRE)** 4 bb g Key Of Luck (USA) -Lingering Melody (IRE) (Nordico (USA)) 1172[10] 1389[5] 1660[14] 1783[8] 2487[4] 3002[7] 3082[2] 3369[6]3794[7] 4005[10] 4276[8] 4826[14] 4901[8] 5450[8] 5584[11] >42f<

**Lucky Leo** 4 b g Muhtarram (USA) -Wrong Bride (Reprimand) 1611[9] (2471) (3450) 3678[9] >56a 81+f<

**Lucky Owners (NZ)** 4 b g Danehill (USA) -Miss Priority (NZ) (Kaapstad (NZ)) 1657a[6] >122f<

**Lucky Pipit** 3 b f Key Of Luck (USA) -Meadow Pipit (CAN) (Meadowlake (USA)) 1398[5] 3105[2] (4068) 4286[8] 5416[14] 5811[4] 5948[8] >104f<

**Lucky Piscean** 3 b g River Falls-Celestine (Skyliner) 1174[5] 1557[8] 1820[19] 5110[15] 5860[11] >55f<

**Lucky Red Pepper** 2 b c Barathea (IRE) -Mutige (Warning) (4016) >73f<

**Lucky Romance** 5 b m Key Of Luck (USA) -In Love Again (IRE) (Prince Rupert (FR)) 445[5] 531[9] >43a 35f<

**Lucky Spin** 3 b f Pivotal-Perioscope (Legend Of France (USA)) 1441[2] (1939) (2548) (3105) 4286[12] 5610[3] >106f<

**Lucky Story (USA)** 3 b c Kris S (USA) -Spring Flight (USA) (Miswaki (USA)) 4685[2] 5332a[7] 5782[2] 6216[9] >127f<

**Lucky Strike** 6 br g Petong-Urania (Most Welcome) (2466a) (3552a) 4595a[6] 5255a[3] 5977a[13] >112f<

**Lucky Valentine** 4 b f My Best Valentine-Vera s First (IRE) (Exodal (USA)) 2800[2] 3175[4] 3575[3] 4025[3] 4469[6] >56a 55f<

**Lucretius** 5 b g Mind Games-Eastern Ember (Indian King (USA)) 520[9] 859[13] 946[14] 1407[4] 1591[4] >50a 47f<

**Lucy Parkes** 2 ch f Piccolo-Janette Parkes (Pursuit Of Love) 1449[8] 4507[4] 4776[11] 5555[10] 5797[14] >50f<

**Lugana Point** 2 b c Lugana Beach-Raisa Point (Raised Socially (USA)) 5555[7] 6478[9] >25a 32f<

**Luis Melendez (USA)** 2 ch c Horse Chestnut (SAF) -Egoli (USA) (Seeking The Gold (USA)) 5268[4] 5567[3] (6148) >82f<

**Lujain Rose** 2 b f Lujain (USA) -Rose Chime (IRE) (Tirol) 5846[9] >56f<

**Luke After Me (IRE)** 4 b g Victory Note (USA) -Summit Talk (Head For Heights) 717[7] 1197[2] 1342[3] 1748[10] 1971[2] 2260[12] 2292[4] 2660[3]2965[10] 3148[9] 4568[9] >50a 61f<

**Luke Sharp** 3 gr g Muhtarram (USA) -Heaven-Liegh-Grey (Grey Desire) 2621[15] 3368[8] 4097[8] >24f<

**Lumback (IRE)** 5 b g Desert Style (IRE) -Bellingham Jester (Jester) 3896[9] >2f<

**Luna Blu (IRE)** 2 b f Mujahid (USA) -Blu Tamantara (USA) (Miswaki (USA)) 4966[14] >18f<

**Lunar Exit (IRE)** 3 gr g Exit To Nowhere (USA) -Moon Magic (Polish Precedent (USA)) 2896[6] 3641[11] 5699[6] 5919[16] >93f<

**Lunar Leader (IRE)** 4 b f Mujadil (USA) -Moon River (FR) (Groom Dancer (USA)) 1213[10] 1535[12] 1539[19] 1783[12] 3050[10] 3489[17] 3662[U] >23a 23f<

**Lunar Lord** 8 b g Elmaamul (USA) -Cache (Bustino) 1109[7] 1687[8] 2590[7] 2835[8] 3437[4] 3743[2] 4139[2] 4473[8]5654[6] 5796[12] >50a 55f<

**Lunar Sky (USA)** 2 b f Lemon Drop Kid (USA) -Celestial Bliss (USA) (Relaunch (USA)) 3456[7] 4753[6] 5522[4] 5852[14] >70f<

**Lunar Sovereign (USA)** 5 br h Cobra King (USA) -January Moon (USA) (Apalachee (USA)) 976a[3] 1144a[11] 2968[10] 4121[11] >119f<

**Lundy s Lane (IRE)** 4 b g Darshaan-Lunda (IRE) (Soviet Star (USA)) 485[4] 1107[8] 1456[27] 3756[21] 5462[7] 5941[10] >98a 107f<

**Lundy s Liability (BRZ)** 3 b c Candy Stripes (USA) -Emerald Counter (USA) (Geiger Counter (USA)) 691a[4] 975a[2] (1143a) >112a<

**Lune D Or (FR)** 3 b f Green Tune (USA) -Luth D Or (FR) (Noir Et Or) (3566a) (4566a) 5501a[10] (6381a) >114f<

**Lupine (IRE)** 5 b m Lake Coniston (IRE) -Prosaic Star (IRE) (Common Grounds) 2903a[6] 3961a[17] 4956a[8] 5660a[11] 6104a[6] >94 f<

**Lupine Howl** 3 b c Wolfhound (USA) -Classic Fan (USA) (Lear Fan (USA)) 1760[9] 2207[12] 2351[9] 2756[13] 3582[6] 4241[10] >11a 42f<

**Luteur Des Pictons (FR)** 5 ch g Ragmar (FR) -Ezera (FR) (Chamberlin (FR)) 651[12] >24a<

**Luth High (FR)** 4 b c Luth Dancer (USA) -High Steppe (Petoski) 2163a[2] ><

**Luttis Champ (GER)** 3 b c Winged Love (IRE) -Lutte Marie (GER) (Frontal) 5974a[6] ><

**Luxi River (USA)** **4** b g Diesis-Mariella (USA) (Roberto (USA)) *484[5]* *517[5]* *630[4]* *722[4]* >**54a 54f**<

**Luxor (TUR)** **4** b c Distant Relative-Keep Shining (USA) (Stagedoor Johnny) (5488a) ><

**Luxor** **7** ch g Grand Lodge (USA) -Escrime (USA) (Sharpen Up) 2272[11] 3082[8] 3731[7] 4005[11] 4808[10] 5267[8] 5459[15] >**25 f**<

**Lyca Ballerina** **3** b f Marju (IRE) -Lovely Lyca (Night Shift (USA)) 1408[5] 1842[3] 2112[4] (2777) 3312[10] 3525[3] >**76f**<

**Lydgate (USA)** **4** b c Pulpit (USA) -Mariuka (USA) (Danzig (USA)) 2955[9] 5471[4] 6177[8] >**108f**<

**Lydia s Look (IRE)** **7** b m Distant View (USA) -Mrs Croesus (USA) (Key To The Mint (USA)) *576[12]* *792[5]* *917[5]* *1497[4]* 2350[5] (2778) 3169[6] 3820[13]4854[9] >**48a 54f**<

**Lyes Green** **3** gr g Bien Bien (USA) -Dissolve (Sharrood (USA)) 4673[4] *5907[12]* >**57a 48f**<

**Lyford Lass** **3** b f Bahamian Bounty-Ladykirk (Slip Anchor) 1250[2] (1528) 1931[8] 6115[14] 6520[12] >**66f**<

**Lygeton Lad** **6** b g Shaamit (IRE) -Smartie Lee (Dominion) *558[5]* *706[5]* *842[6]* *1065[5]* *(1242)* 1542[7] 1969[8] 2279[7]4122[8] 4462[4] 4652[6] *6451[5]* >**113a 71f**<

**Lyns Resolution** **4** b g Awesome-Our Resolution (Caerleon (USA)) 5408[14] 5851[4] >**60f**<

**Lyonels Glory** **3** b c Green Desert (USA) -La Virginia (GER) (Surumu (GER)) 3359a[3] 4215[6] (5168a) 5667a[3] >**108f**<

**Lyrical Girl (USA)** **3** b f Orpen (USA) -Lyric Theatre (USA) (Seeking The Gold (USA)) *(416)* *522[5]* 4045[10] 4241[6] 4479[14] 5257[12] >**56a 60f**<

**Lyrical Lady** **3** b f Merdon Melody-Gracious Imp (USA) (Imp Society (USA)) 2165[15] 2518[10] 2836[19] 5408[10] 5929[8] >**55 a 52f**<

**Lyrical Way** **5** b g Vettori (IRE) -Fortunate (Reference Point) *559[4]* *650[12]* *1085[5]* 2302[7] 2547[6] 2798[4] >**67a 62f**<

**Lyric Dances (FR)** **2** ch f Sendawar (IRE) -Romanche (FR) (Galetto (FR)) 4866[11] >**29f**<

**Lysander s Quest (IRE)** **6** br g King s Theatre (IRE) -Haramayda (FR) (Doyoun) 2324[15] 4513[8] *5217[5]* (5286) 5796[9] >**54a 51f**<

**Lysandra (IRE)** **2** b f Danehill (USA) -Oriane (Nashwan (USA)) 5348[2] 6471[4] >**79f**<

**Lysuna (GER)** **4** b f Monsun (GER) -La Lyra (Slip Anchor) 3434a[7] 4377a[4] 5683a[6] 6107a[6] >**104f**<

**Lytham (IRE)** **3** b g Spectrum (IRE) -Nousaiyra (IRE) (Be My Guest (USA)) *6549[2]* >**72a 69f**<

## M

**Ma Am (USA)** **2** ch f Royal Anthem (USA) -Hide The Bride (USA) (Runaway Groom (CAN)) *6494[8]* >**50a**<

**Mabella (IRE)** **2** b f Brave Act-Wee Merkin (IRE) (Thatching) 2761[8] 3382[5] 3840[7] 4621[4] 5202[10] 5738[12] >**69f**<

**Mabel Riley (IRE)** **4** b f Revoque (IRE) -Mystic Dispute (IRE) (Magical Strike (USA)) *425[5]* *487[7]* 1533[9] >**47a 51f**<

**Mac** **4** ch g Fleetwood (IRE) -Midnight Break (Night Shift (USA)) 5784[15] 6172[17] >**68a 96+f**<

**Macabre** **2** b c Machiavellian (USA) -Lady In Waiting (Kylian (USA)) 5765[2] >**81f**<

**Macaroni Gold (IRE)** **4** b g Rock Hopper-Strike It Rich (FR) (Rheingold) *603[9]* *827[4]* *981[4]* *1010[5]* 1316[7] 1754[3] *2126[3]*5274[6] 6198[6] >**73 a 69f**<

**Macaulay (IRE)** **2** ch c Zafonic (USA) -Wigging (Warning) *6453[3]* >**79a**<

**Macchiato** **3** br f Inchinor-Tereyna (Terimon) 1394[7] 3421[5] 3773[13] *4128[9]* 4499[9] *4883[8]* 5286[9] >**24a 40f**<

**Mac Cois Na Tine** **2** b g Cois Na Tine (IRE) -Berenice (ITY) (Marouble) 2024[7] 2256[2] 3009[3] 3677[7] >**66f**<

**Machinist (IRE)** **4** br g Machiavellian (USA) -Athene (IRE) (Rousillon (USA)) 2261[7] 3036[17] 3299[9] (3979) 4152[2] 4759[4] 5075[5] 5603[7] >**83+a 92+f**<

**Mac Leader (IRE)** **2** b c Sagamix (FR) -Tigava (USA) (Machiavellian (USA)) (5388a) ><

**Maclean** **3** b g Machiavellian (USA) -Celtic Cross (Selkirk (USA)) 1371[2] (1747) 2306[3] 2558[6] 4171[5] 4401[6] (4906) 5183[11] >**83f**<

**Mac Love** **3** b g Cape Cross (IRE) -My Lass (Elmaamul (USA)) 1223[5] 1706[4] 2080[2] 2913[2] 3598[6] 3940[6] (4317) 5289[13] (5422) 5780[9](5888) >**117f**<

**Mac Millennium** **2** b c Bachir (IRE) -Glittering Image (IRE) (Sadler s Wells (USA)) 3435a[3] ><

**Macpursie** **3** br f Botanic (USA) -Jeethgaya (USA) (Critique (USA)) *779[5]* *877[4]* >**27a 66f**<

**Mac Regal (IRE)** **3** b c King s Theatre (IRE) -Shine Silently (IRE) (Bering) 1439[3] 2068[2] 2510a[14] >**86f**<

**Mac Rhapsody** **2** b f Night Shift (USA) -Let Alone (Warning) 3436a[3] >**91f**<

**Mac s Elan** **4** b g Darshaan-Elabella (Ela-Mana-Mou) 1820[16] 4869[5] *5644[7]* 5999[6] 6130[2] 6524[2] >**28a 57f**<

**Mac s Talisman (IRE)** **4** ch c Hector Protector (USA) -Inherent Magic (IRE) (Magical Wonder (USA)) 2178[17] *2404[10]* 2948[12] *3376[2]* 3579[3] 3911[15] 5201[11] *(6493)* *(6580)* >**75a 72 f**<

**Mac The Knife (IRE)** **3** b g Daggers Drawn (USA) -Icefern (Moorestyle) 1388[17] 1797[10] 2379[8] 2762[8] 3391[8] 5702[13] >**27f**<

**Mad** **3** br f Pursuit Of Love-Emily-Mou (IRE) (Cadeaux Genereux) *5217[8]* 5537[10] *6015[9]* *6397[6]* >**55a**<

**Madaar (USA)** **5** b g Spinning World (USA) -Mur Taasha (USA) (Riverman (USA)) *3282[12]* 3607[8] >**30a 30 f**<

**Madaeh (USA)** **3** bb f Swain (IRE) -Tamgeed (USA) (Woodman (USA)) 2221[4] 2971[14] >**96f**<

**Madalyar (IRE)** **5** b g Darshaan-Madaniyya (USA) (Shahrastani (USA)) *837[12]* >**90f**<

**Madam Caversfield** **2** b f Pursuit Of Love-Madam Alison (Puissance) 2427[5] 2690[7] 2890[3] 3438[4] 4089[4] 4468[6] 5172[2] 6283[9] >**68f**<

**Madame Fatale (IRE)** **2** br f Daggers Drawn (USA) -Taajreh (IRE) (Mtoto) 6067[15] *6479[10]* >**40a 28f**<

**Madame Guillotine** **2** b f Sure Blade (USA) -Delicious (Dominion) 6196[13] *6478[13]* >**15f**<

**Madame Marie (IRE)** **4** b f Desert King (IRE) -Les Trois Lamas (IRE) (Machiavellian (USA)) 1298[11] 1939[7] 2122[2] 2943[15] 3412[6] 3670[7] *4339[7]* *4939[8]5221[8]* 5751[4] >**55a 61f**<

**Madame Roux** **6** b m Rudimentary (USA) -Foreign Mistress (Darshaan) *1890[6]* *2056[5]* >**8a**<

**Madame Topflight** **2** b f Komaite (USA) -Jamarj (Tyrnavos) 2749[8] 3577[2] (4003) 4358[5] 4962a[2] 5626[8] 6068[9] >**91f**<

**Madamoiselle Jones** **4** b f Emperor Jones (USA) -Tiriana (Common Grounds) 1821[10] 2119[4] 2282[5] (2521) 3048[6] 3660[4] 4812[6] 5135[11] 5403[10] >**51a 60 f**<

**Madcap Escapade (USA)** **3** b f Hennessy (USA) -Sassy Pants (USA) (Saratoga Six (USA)) *[3]* >**109a**<

**Mad Carew (USA)** **5** ch g Rahy (USA) -Poppy Carew (IRE) (Danehill (USA)) *618[5]* *(820)* *915[13]* *984[4]* 1540[11] 2226[5] 2845[5] 3048[4]4327[10] 5728[5] 6185[4] >**82a 82f**<

**Maddie s A Jem** **4** b f Emperor Jones (USA) -Royal Orchid (IRE) (Shalford (IRE)) (1185) (1518) 2091[3] 2506[5] 2670[6] 4194[4] 4740[2] (4855) 5157[6] 5588[2] >**73a 84f**<

**Madge** **2** b f Marju (IRE) -Aymara (Darshaan) 5946[6] >**64f**<

**Madhahir (IRE)** **4** b g Barathea (IRE) -Gharam (USA) (Green Dancer (USA)) *461[8]* *981[11]* (1188) 1376[3] 1754[10] 1958[8] 2212[10] 2584[6] >**69a 60f**<

**Madhavi** **2** gr f Diktat-Grey Galava (Generous (IRE)) 3675[7] 3904[3] 4231[5] 4612[9] 5648[20] 6174[17] >**76f**<

**Madhya (USA)** **3** b f Gone West (USA) -Khumba Mela (IRE) (Hero s Honor (USA)) 6203a[5] >**89f**<

**Madiba** **5** b g Emperor Jones (USA) -Priluki (Lycius (USA)) *(431)* *546[6]* *645[11]* *724[2]* *839[2]* *973[2]* 1457[12] 1973[2]*2126[2]* 2285[9] 2590[11] 3644[8] 3851[P] 5027[5] 5343[2] 6005[6]6084[2] *6450[6]* >**68a 63f**<

**Madid (IRE)** **3** br c Cape Cross (IRE) -Waffle On (Chief Singer) (2113) (2629) 2956[9] >**111+f**<

**Mad Marty Wildcard** **2** ch c Komaite (USA) -Done And Dusted (IRE) (Up And At Em) 6125[13] 6342[13] >**24f**<

**Mad Maurice** **3** ch g Grand Lodge (USA) -Amarella (FR) (Balleroy (USA)) 1820[17] 1939[12] 2298[10] 4499[13] 5286[13] >**32f**<

**Madra Rua (IRE)** **3** b g Foxhound (USA) -Fun Fashion (IRE) (Polish Patriot (USA)) 2075[9] 2353[7] 6114[11] >**64f**<

**Madrasee** **6** b m Beveled (USA) -Pendona (Blue Cashmere) *454[2]* *646[12]* *912[9]* *1057[4]* *1230[5]* 1537[7] 1937[5]2948[13] 3439[8] 4232[18] 4740[6] 5075[7] 5734[6] 6186[2] >**64a 64f**<

**Madresal (GER)** **5** gr h Lomitas-Midnight Society (USA) (Imp Society (USA)) 2336a[3] 3335a[9] 6106a[5] 6508a[2] >**107f**<

**Maeveen (IRE)** **4** b f Flying Spur (AUS) -Cool Gales (Lord Gayle (USA)) *5644[4]* >**32a 28f**<

**Mafaheem** **2** b c Mujahid (USA) -Legend Of Aragon (Aragon) (6045) >**84f**<

**Mafruz** **5** ch g Hamas (IRE) -Braari (USA) (Gulch (USA)) 3265[9] 3579[11] >**77f**<

**Maganda (IRE)** **3** b f Sadler s Wells (USA) -Minnie Habit (Habitat) (1619) 2107[6] 2692[13] 6069[18] >**82f**<

**Magari** **3** b f Royal Applause-Thatcher s Era (IRE) (Never So Bold) 4351[4] 4615[8] *5002[12]* 5448[5] 5830[3] 6227[4] >**11a 54f**<

**Magdelaine** **2** b f Sinndar (IRE) -Crystal Drop (Cadeaux Genereux) 4851[18] *6021[12]* *6291[12]* >**20a**<

**Magenta Rising (IRE)** **4** ch f College Chapel-Fashion Queen (Chilibang) *581[9]* 4605[17] ><

**Maggie Jordan (USA)** **2** b f Fusaichi Pegasus (USA) -Pharapache (USA) (Lyphard (USA)) (6455) >**82f**<

**Maggie Maquette** **4** ch f Atraf-Bronze Maquette (IRE) (Ahonoora) *574[5]* *963[6]* *1262[12]* >**49a**<

**Maggie s Pet** **7** b m Minshaanshu Amad (USA) -Run Fast For Gold (Deep Run) *425[2]* *552[5]* *614[2]* *652[2]* *787[4]* *939[5]* *(1681)* *2451[6]* >**56a 40f**<

**Maggie Tulliver (IRE)** **2** b f Spectrum (IRE) -Eliza Acton (Shirley Heights) 3588[12] 5247[7] 6118[15] *(6555)* >**67+a 67f**<

**Maghanim** **4** b c Nashwan (USA) -Azdihaar (USA) (Mr Prospector (USA)) 2200[5] 2588[3] 3036[2] 3673[10] 4273[9] 5470[10] >**106f**<

**Magical Mimi** **3** b f Magic Ring (IRE) -Naval Dispatch (Slip Anchor) 1418[11] 1795[17] 2587[8] 3117[4] 3897[5] 4138[13] 4318[5] 5544[15] >**74f**<

**Magical Quest** **4** b c Rainbow Quest (USA) -Apogee (Shirley Heights) 4028[8] (4513) 5472[11] >**89+f**<

**Magical Romance (IRE)** **2** b f Barathea (IRE) -Shouk (Shirley Heights) 3382[4] (3840) 4119[6] (5701) (5894) >**107f**<

**Magic Amigo** **3** ch g Zilzal (USA) -Emaline (FR) (Empery (USA)) *1597[2]* (1911) 2281[13] 2751[2] 2906[3] *3614[8]* 3981[4] 4170[3] 4582[6]4711[2] 5158[6] *5739[14]* >**66a 79f**<

**Magic Amour** **6** ch g Sanglamore (USA) -Rakli (Warning) 2459[2] 2806[6] 3426[7] 3884[4] 4122[18] 4577[16] (5201) 5425[15] 5798[7] >**66f**<

**Magic Box** **6** b g Magic Ring (IRE) -Princess Poquito (Hard Fought) *3804[15]* >**11a**<

**Magic Charm** **6** b m Magic Ring (IRE) -Loch Clair (IRE) (Lomond (USA)) *430[10]* *661[10]* *727[8]* 2287[4] 2501[15] 2659[6] 3018[13] 3369[8]4139[6] >**26a 45f**<

**Magic Combination (IRE)** **11** b g Scenic-Etage (Ile De Bourbon (USA)) 1173[2] 2935[5] 3120[2] 3564[2] (3782) (4512) 5318[11] >**89f**<

**Magic Eagle** **7** b g Magic Ring (IRE) -Shadow Bird (Martinmas) *421[5]* *572[7]* *813[10]* *1089[8]* 1197[12] *2229[7]* >**32 a 36f**<

**Magic Fact** **7** b g Factual (USA) -Miss Mirror (Magic Mirror) *5504a[6]* ><

**Magic Flo** **2** ch f Magic Ring (IRE) -Moore Stylish (Moorestyle) 5569[9] *6011[6]* 6471[10] >**48a 58f**<

**Magic Genie (IRE)** **2** b f Lujain (USA) -Haut Volee (Top Ville) 2858[5] 3444[8] 3980[7] >**41f**<

**Magic Glade** **5** b g Magic Ring (IRE) -Ash Glade (Nashwan (USA)) *511[8]* *(806)* *1205[2]* (1343) 2488[3] 2679[15] 2859[13] 5372[3] >**90a 96f**<

**Magic Mamma s Too** **4** b g Magic Ring (IRE) -Valona Valley (IRE) (Reprimand) *459[2]* *541[5]* *823[3]* *953[4]* 1748[9] 3247[5] 4386[16] >**63a 63f**<

**Magic Master (SAF)** **5** b g National Assembly (CAN) -Mystique (SAF) (Jungle Cove (USA)) *851a[5]* 1004a[3] >**98a 92f**<

**Magic Merlin** **3** b g Magic Ring (IRE) -St James s Antigua (IRE) (Law Society (USA)) 2267[3] (2517) 3230[4] >**81f**<

**Magic Music (IRE)** **5** b m Magic Ring (IRE) -Chiming Melody (Cure The Blues (USA)) 1825[9] 2670[10] 4104[13] >**81f**<

**Magico** **3** ch g Magic Ring (IRE) -Silken Dalliance (Rambo Dancer (CAN)) *521[7]* *620[7]* *3024[14]* 3391[3] 4018[2] 5336[9] 5926[15] >**36a 54f**<

**Magic Red** **4** ch g Magic Ring (IRE) -Jacquelina (USA) (Private Account (USA)) *(3712)* *(3803)* *4603[4]* *4883[2]* >**64+a 51 f**<

**Magic Spin** **4** b f Magic Ring (IRE) -Moon Spin (Night Shift (USA)) 4916[6] 5204[5] *6015[6]* >**49a 63f**<

**Magic Sting** **3** ch g Magic Ring (IRE) -Ground Game (Gildoran) 1271[5] *1476[5]* 1672[6] (1995) (2619) 3231[12] 3706[3] 4628[3] 5057[2] (5258)5672[2] 5998[5] >**43a 80+f**<

**Magic Stone** **4** br g Magic Ring (IRE) -Ridgewood Ruby (IRE) (Indian Ridge) *491[14]* *948[4]* >**43a 36f**<

**Magic Tree (UAE)** **2** ch f Timber Country (USA) -Moyesii (USA) (Diesis) 3627[13] >**55f**<

**Magic Verse** **3** ch f Opening Verse (USA) -Festival Sister (Belmez (USA)) 1794[18] 2374[15] *2853[4]* *3380[4]* *3710[4]* 4471[5] 5036[4] (5927)6184[8] 6561[10] >**56a 62f**<

**Magic Warrior** **4** b g Magic Ring (IRE) -Clarista (USA) (Riva Ridge (USA)) *525[3]* *623[4]* *765[6]* *3088[9]* 4479[13] 5795[10] >**62a 41f**<

**Magistretti (USA)** **4** b c Diesis-Ms Strike Zone (USA) (Deputy Minister (CAN)) 2639[6] 3642[4] 3936[4] 4768a[2] 5985a[2] 6490a[4] >**125f**<

**Magnetic Pole** **3** b c Machiavellian (USA) -Clear Attraction (USA) (Lear Fan (USA)) 1683[2] 2144[3] 3953[8] 5367[2] 5591[2] (6182) >**88+f**<

**Maharaat (USA)** **3** b c Bahri (USA) -Siyadah (USA) (Mr Prospector (USA)) 1395[5] 1967[5] 2729[2] >**77f**<

**Maharib (IRE)** **4** b c Alhaarth (IRE) -Diali (USA) (Dayjur (USA)) 3333a[7] 4977a[3] >**114f**<

**Mahfooth (USA)** **7** ch h Diesis-I Certainly Am (USA) (Affirmed (USA)) *689a[9]* 710a[10] 755a[10] >**60a 111f**<

**Mahlstick (IRE)** **6** b g Tagula (IRE) -Guv s Joy (IRE) (Thatching) *1167[6]* *1403[3]* *1544[4]* *1694[4]* 2836[20] 5929[9] >**46a 58f**<

**Mahmjra** **2** b c Josr Algarhoud (IRE) -Jamrat Samya (IRE) (Sadler s Wells (USA)) 6073[10] 6181[8] *6492[11]* >**40a 55f**<

**Mahmoom** **3** ch c Dr Fong (USA) -Rohita (IRE) (Waajib) 1408[17] 1795[14] 2115[6] 2981[8] (3317) 3598[2] 4268[6] 4750[2] >**100f**<

**Mahroos (USA)** **6** ch g Kingmambo (USA) -Mur Taasha (USA) (Riverman (USA)) 633a[10] *832a[9]* >**64a 101f**<

**Maia Eria (FR)** **4** b f Volochine (IRE) -Soldouna (FR) (Kaldoun (FR)) 911a[9] ><

**Maidaan** **8** b h Midyan (USA) -Panache Arabelle (Nashwan (USA)) 852a[3] 925a[6] >**98f**<

**Maidanni (USA)** **2** bb c Private Terms (USA) -Carley s Birthday (USA) (Marfa (USA)) 5716[4] (6067) 6334[8] >**82f**<

**Maid For Life (IRE)** **4** b f Entrepreneur-Arandora Star (USA) (Sagace (FR)) 4471[6] 5145[6] 5830[16] >**51a 63f**<

**Maids Causeway (IRE)** **2** ch f Giant s Causeway (USA) -Vallee Des Reves (USA) (Kingmambo (USA)) 2786[2] (3202) 4060[2] (4552) 5413[3] 5779[2] (6213) >**111f**<

**Maidstone Midas (IRE)** **3** b c Nashwan (USA) -Be Mine (Wolfhound (USA)) 1674[15] 1966[4] *2486[5]* 3107[6] >**60a 53f**<

**Maid The Cut** **3** ch f Silver Wizard (USA) -Third Dam (Slip Anchor) *683[4]* *955[8]* 4674[12] 5072[5] 5791[6] 6055[5] >**51a 40f**<

**Maid To Treasure (IRE)** **3** b f Rainbow Quest (USA) -Maid For The Hills (Indian Ridge) 2562[4] 3204[6] 6357[3] 6524[12] >**73f**<

**Mainly Mine (IRE)** **5** b m Lahib (USA) -Tasdik (Unfuwain (USA)) 4371a[4] >**93f**<

**Mainly Monroe (IRE)** **3** b f Dr Devious (IRE) -Nora Jeane (IRE) (Reprimand) 5969a[8] >**95f**<

**Majestical (IRE)** **2** b g Fayruz-Haraabah (USA) (Topsider (USA)) *1240[3]* 1638[4] 2376[12] 3930[10] 4413[4] 4620[2] 5509[4] 5839[7]6080[6] >**57a 60f**<

**Majestic Desert** **3** b f Fraam-Calcutta Queen (Night Shift (USA)) (1458) 1791[9] 2330a[7] 3033[2] 3547a[2] 4383a[2] 4795a[4] 5940[4] 6109a[2] >**113f**<

**Majestic Horizon** **4** b c Marju (IRE) -Jumairah Sunset (Be My Guest (USA)) *632a[5]* 690a[5] 853a[12] 924a[4] *977a[9]* >**67a 91f**<

**Majestic Missile (IRE)** **3** b c Royal Applause-Tshusick (Dancing Brave (USA)) 2955[5] 4269[8] 5647[6] >**118+f**<

**Majestic Movement (USA)** **2** ch c Diesis-Zarara (USA) (Manila (USA)) 4689[5] 4930[10] 5988[3] 6515[5] >**70f**<

**Majestic Star** **3** b f Fraam-Fun While It Lasts (Idiots Delight) 6357[7] ><

**Majestic Times (IRE)** **4** b g Bluebird (USA) -Simply Times (USA) (Dodge (USA)) 3961a[3] 4371a[3] >**57a 89f**<

**Majestic Vision** **3** ch g Desert King (IRE) -Triste Oeil (USA) (Raise A Cup (USA)) 1508[9] 3743[6] 4424[2] 5274[5] 5875[3] 6198[10] >**64a 74f**<

**Majhool** **5** b g Mark Of Esteem (IRE) -Be Peace (USA) (Septieme Ciel (USA)) *617[8]* *886[4]* *1121[5]* (3988) 4265[11] 5364[18] >**82a 54f**<

**Majik** **5** ch g Pivotal-Revoke (USA) (Riverman (USA)) *511[7]* *544[3]* *686[4]* 1361[15] 1504[4] 1665[10] 5541[4] 6131[5]6288[3] >**78a 63f**<

**Majlis (IRE)** **7** b g Caerleon (USA) -Ploy (Posse (USA)) *618[9]* *887[12]* *1054[5]* 1341[9] 2032[10] >**75a 73f**<

**Major Blade (GER)** **6** b g Dashing Blade-Misniniski (Niniski (USA)) 2084[14] 2302[15] 3997[10] >**6a 20f**<

**Majorca** **3** b c Green Desert (USA) -Majmu (USA) (Al Nasr (FR)) 1413[3] 2211[2] 2621[4] (2962) (3312) 3671[15] >**91f**<

**Major Effort (USA)** **3** b c Rahy (USA) -Tethkar (Machiavellian (USA)) 2135[4] 2557[12] >**78f**<

**Major Faux Pas (IRE)** **2** b g Barathea (IRE) -Edwina (IRE) (Caerleon (USA)) *(6291)* >**84a**<

**Major Project (IRE)** **3** ch g General Monash (USA) -Mini Project (IRE) (Project Manager) *808[9]* 2349[12] >**14a**<

**Majors Cast (IRE)** **3** b c Victory Note (USA) -Ziffany (Taufan (USA)) 3487[3] (4741) 5024[3] *(5220)* 5762[3] >**102+a 97+f**<

**Makarim (IRE)** **8** ch g Generous (IRE) -Emmaline (USA) (Affirmed (USA)) *467[10]* *603[11]* *839[3]* *973[5]* *1081[8]* 3488[4] 3776[14]4457[5] >**64a 46f**<

**Make It Happen Now** **2** bb f Octagonal (NZ) -Whittle Woods Girl (Emarati (USA)) 1853[7] 2164[4] 2970[17] 4637[9] *4924[13]* 5335[11] >**6a 31f**<

**Make It Snappy** **2** b f Mujadil (USA) -Snap Crackle Pop (IRE) (Statoblest) 5088[8] 6123[17] *6446[3]* >**60+a 58f**<

**Make My Hay** **5** b g Bluegrass Prince (IRE) -Shashi (IRE) (Shaadi (USA)) *431[3]* *676[6]* (1989) 2375[2] 3263[5] 3682[5] 3942[5] 4971[6] 5796[2]6183[4] >**49a 55f**<

**Makepeace (IRE)** **2** b c Xaar-Marillette (USA) (Diesis) 2736[11] 3081[4] 4930[7] 5377[18] >**62f**<

**Makes Perfect (IRE)** **2** b f Orpen (USA) -Practice (USA) (Diesis) 4040[8] 4413[6] >**48f**<

**Make Us Flush** **2** b f Mind Games-Pearls (Mon Tresor) 1601[4] 2296[7] 2617[4] 3123[9] (3444) (3924) 4358[7] 4508[2] (4676) 5212[7] 5670[12]5767[6] *6022[11]* >**22a 73f**<

**Makfool (FR)** **3** b c Spectrum (IRE) -Abeyr (Unfuwain (USA)) *1063[12]* 1123[3] 1384[4] 1900[9] 2295[2] (2642) 3001[21] 3673[8] 4273[12] >**78a 103f**<

**Makhlab (USA)** **4** b c Dixieland Band (USA) -Avasand (USA) (Avatar (USA)) 1107[5] 1610[5] 1758[4] 2623[2] 3730[2] 4745[13] >**108 f**<

**Maksad (IRE)** **4** b c Machiavellian (USA) -Balaabel (USA) (Sadler s Wells (USA)) 2283[15] >**74f**<

**Maktavish** **5** b g Makbul-La Belle Vie (Indian King (USA)) *(801)* (1113) 1343[2] (1454) 1923[3] 2293[14] 2679[14] 3293[8] 3795[4] 4538[6]5062[12] 5287[9] 5605[14] >**93a 93f**<

**Maktu** **2** ch g Bien Bien (USA) -Shalateeno (Teenoso (USA)) 4579[5] 5173[3] 5792[4] >**70f**<

**Maktub (ITY)** **5** b h Love The Groom (USA) -Carmen The Best (IRE) (Waajib) 1703[8] 2067[6] 3136a[2] 3540[11] 4380a[2] 5489a[2] 5985a[7] >**113f**<

**Makulu (IRE)** **4** b g Alzao (USA) -Karinski (USA) (Palace Music (USA)) 1272[15] 1457[18] 2856[2] 3291[7] >**80a 79f**<

**Makuti (IRE)** **2** b f Monashee Mountain (USA) -Lady Anna Livia (Ahonoora) 5681a[3] >**81f**<

**Makybe Diva** **7** b m Desert King (IRE) -Tugela (USA) (Riverman (USA)) (6528a) >**123f**<

**Malaah (IRE)** **8** gr g Pips Pride-Lingdale Lass (Petong) *788[8]* *859[14]* *946[4]* *1092[8]* *1165[10]* >**38a 38f**<

**Malahide Express (IRE)** **4** gr g Compton Place-Gracious Gretclo (Common Grounds) *540[4]* *680[5]* *904[9]* *954[2]* 1345[8] 1525[5] 1870[5] 2274[4](2784) 3407[9] 3524[9] 5562[3] *6274[13]* >**71a 67f**<

**Malaica (FR)** **3** gr f Roi Gironde (IRE) -Carmel (FR) (Highest Honor (FR)) 3769a[7] 6203a[6] >**98f**<

**Malaika** **2** b f Polar Prince (IRE) -Gold Belt (IRE) (Bellypha) 5213[5] 5865[4] 6281[3] >**64f**<

**Malak Al Moulouk (USA)** **4** ch g King Of Kings (IRE) -Honor To Her (USA) (Sir Ivor (USA)) 3387[4] 3997[2] 4616[11] 5252[11] >**65a 71f**<

**Malapropism** 4 ch g Compton Place-Mrs Malaprop (Night Shift (USA)) 2222$^{6}$ 2488$^{15}$ 2682$^{12}$ 3480$^{7}$ 3795$^{6}$ 4165$^{12}$ 4366$^{4}$ 4538$^{9}$4748$^{6}$ 5071$^{6}$ (5440) 5550$^{7}$ 5933$^{6}$ (6205) (6243) 6349$^{10}$ 6496$^{10}$ >**77a 98df**<

**Malarkey** 7 b g Mukaddamah (USA) -Malwiya (USA) (Shahrastani (USA)) 1101$^{5}$ (1210) 1302$^{2}$ (1457) 2480$^{5}$ 2613$^{3}$ 2958$^{25}$ >**74a 83f**<

**Malcheek (IRE)** 2 br c Lend A Hand-Russland (GER) (Surumu (GER)) 2898$^{4}$ >**68f**<

**Malevitch (IRE)** 3 b c Exit To Nowhere (USA) -Miss Tahiti (IRE) (Tirol) 1350a$^{6}$ 2073a$^{4}$ 3359a$^{5}$ >**103f**<

**Malibu (IRE)** 3 b g Second Empire (IRE) -Tootle (Main Reef) 1357$^{4}$ 2676$^{6}$ 3152$^{5}$ 3543$^{11}$ (3826) 4266$^{5}$ 4691$^{7}$ 5399$^{12}$ 5766$^{15}$ >**83f**<

**Malinas (GER)** 3 b c Lomitas-Majoritat (GER) (Konigsstuhl (GER)) (2926a) 3565a$^{2}$ 4794a$^{3}$ 5329a$^{6}$ >**111f**<

**Malinsa Blue (IRE)** 2 b f Desert Style (IRE) -Talina s Law (IRE) (Law Society (USA)) 2087$^{6}$ 2674$^{2}$ 3476$^{2}$ 4958a$^{6}$ 5307$^{2}$ (5466) 5938$^{12}$ >**83f**<

**Mallard (IRE)** 6 b g Tagula (IRE) -Frill (Henbit (USA)) 2580$^{3}$ 3167$^{12}$ 3419$^{2}$ 3520$^{6}$ 3734$^{8}$ 4447$^{7}$ 5055$^{11}$ 5379$^{4}$5952$^{3}$ >**84a 75f**<

**Mallia** 11 b g Statoblest-Pronetta (USA) (Mr Prospector (USA)) 1994$^{4}$ (2664) 3024$^{6}$ 3277$^{3}$ 3616$^{2}$ 4185$^{4}$ 4509$^{8}$ 4827$^{12}$ >**53a 52f**<

**Malmand (USA)** 5 ch g Distant View (USA) -Bidski (USA) (Explosive Bid (USA)) 427$^{8}$ (445) 537$^{10}$ 726$^{4}$ 989$^{7}$ >**42a 37f**<

**Maluti** 3 ch g Piccolo-Persian Blue (Persian Bold) 1689$^{8}$ 2380$^{6}$ 2932$^{3}$ (3175) 3562$^{4}$ 4043$^{2}$ 4800 5473$^{7}$ 6538$^{5}$ >**51a 61f**<

**Malvern Light** 3 b f Zieten (USA) -Michelle Hicks (Ballad Rock) 1398$^{4}$ 1964$^{8}$ 2685$^{8}$ 3602$^{3}$ >**101+f**<

**Mambazo** 2 b c Dansili-Kalindi (Efisio) 4172$^{8}$ 4866$^{17}$ 5570$^{12}$ 5838$^{9}$ 6289$^{2}$ >**74a 52f**<

**Mambembe (ARG)** 6 b h Gem Master (USA) -Matey (USA) (Strike Gold (USA)) 6378a$^{9}$ >**90f**<

**Mambina (USA)** 3 ch f Kingmambo (USA) -Sonata (Polish Precedent (USA)) 890$^{8}$ 1365$^{4}$ 1712$^{4}$ 1998$^{5}$ 2442$^{8}$ 4138$^{4}$ 4493$^{8}$ 4629$^{2}$4829$^{2}$ 5258$^{3}$ 5622$^{2}$ 5757$^{4}$ (5936) (6096) 6266$^{6}$ 6332$^{6}$ 6546$^{3}$ >**48a 74+f**<

**Mambo Slew (USA)** 3 br f Kingmambo (USA) -Slew Boyera (USA) (Seattle Slew (USA)) 5530a$^{5}$ 6254a$^{5}$ >**103f**<

**Mambo s Melody** 2 b f Kingmambo (USA) -Key Academy (Royal Academy (USA)) 6123$^{14}$ >**32f**<

**Mamcazma** 6 gr g Terimon-Merryhill Maid (IRE) (M Double M (USA)) 2691$^{7}$ 3310$^{15}$ 3757$^{4}$ 4218$^{11}$ 4550$^{11}$ 5093$^{11}$ 5619$^{10}$ 5784$^{2}$6460$^{11}$ >**69a 91f**<

**Mamela (GER)** 3 b f Protektor (GER) -My Rita (IRE) (Brief Truce (USA)) (4899a) >**103f**<

**Mamone (IRE)** 3 b c Titus Livius (FR) -Mamma Luigi (IRE) (Classic Music (USA)) 1306a$^{15}$ ><

**Mamool (IRE)** 5 b h In The Wings-Genovefa (USA) (Woodman (USA)) 4766a$^{3}$ (5296) 5981a$^{15}$ 6528a$^{7}$ >**119f**<

**Mamore Gap (IRE)** 6 b h General Monash (USA) -Ravensdale Rose (IRE) (Henbit (USA)) 494$^{8}$ 820$^{13}$ 1213$^{9}$ 3911$^{5}$ 4641$^{8}$ 5006$^{5}$ 5176$^{5}$ 5841$^{11}$ >**69a 71f**<

**Manaar (IRE)** 4 b g Titus Livius (FR) -Zurarah (Siberian Express (USA)) 1385$^{8}$ 2469$^{5}$ 3036$^{7}$ 3690$^{2}$ 4006$^{B}$ 5937$^{2}$ 6070$^{18}$ >**82a 91f**<

**Mana D Argent (IRE)** 7 b g Ela-Mana-Mou-Petite-D-Argent (Noalto) 1615$^{11}$ 1880$^{5}$ 2047$^{11}$ 2958$^{18}$ 3725$^{11}$ (4075) 4226$^{5}$ 5784$^{7}$ 6215$^{30}$6509a$^{5}$ >**93a 101f**<

**Manashin** 4 b f Whittingham (IRE) -Montagne (Midyan (USA)) 473$^{7}$ 991$^{4}$ >**25f**<

**Man At Arms (IRE)** 3 b c Daggers Drawn (USA) -Punta Gorda (IRE) (Roi Danzig (USA)) 2168$^{4}$ (2802) 3046$^{4}$ 3584$^{8}$ 3806$^{12}$ 4062$^{4}$ 4274$^{6}$ 5300$^{10}$ 5402$^{9}$5944$^{7}$ >**82f**<

**Manawa King (NZ)** 5 b g Zabeel (NZ) -Manawa Belle (NZ) (Zamazaan (FR)) 6582a$^{2}$ >**103f**<

**Man Crazy (IRE)** 3 b f Foxhound (USA) -Schonbein (IRE) (Persian Heights) 917$^{8}$ 1086$^{6}$ 1464$^{17}$ 2577$^{14}$ 3096$^{7}$ 3747$^{4}$ 3935$^{10}$ 4617$^{7}$5564$^{4}$ 6146$^{9}$ 6459$^{11}$ 6567$^{4}$ >**57a 61f**<

**Mandahar (IRE)** 5 b g Bluebird (USA) -Madiriya (Diesis) 846$^{9}$ 982$^{15}$ 1133$^{7}$ 1352$^{16}$ 2053$^{12}$ 3022$^{10}$ >**51a 9f**<

**Mandahush (GER)** 2 b f Alwuhush (USA) -Mandamou (GER) (Ela-Mana-Mou) 6377a$^{6}$ >**92f**<

**Mandarin Spirit (IRE)** 4 b g Primo Dominie-Lithe Spirit (IRE) (Dancing Dissident (USA)) 2094$^{11}$ 2441$^{5}$ 2727$^{5}$ 5124$^{10}$ 5364$^{5}$ (5425) 6066$^{4}$ 6445$^{3}$ >**71a 77 f**<

**Mandatum** 3 b g Mtoto-Reamur (Top Ville) 2983$^{2}$ 3922$^{2}$ (4554) 6335$^{4}$ >**82+f**<

**Mandinka** 4 b g Distinctly North (USA) -Primo Panache (Primo Dominie) 3060$^{13}$ 5110$^{4}$ 5350$^{8}$ 5757$^{10}$ >**32f**<

**Mandobi (IRE)** 3 ch c Mark Of Esteem (IRE) -Miss Queen (USA) (Miswaki (USA)) 2115$^{4}$ 2642$^{2}$ (3001) 4322$^{2}$ >**108f**<

**Mandoline (GER)** 3 br f Artan (IRE) -Manon Lescant (GER) (Experte (GER)) 2335a$^{11}$ >**18f**<

**Mandoob** 7 b g Zafonic (USA) -Thaidah (CAN) (Vice Regent (CAN)) 609$^{4}$ (759) (777) 971$^{10}$ 1135$^{12}$ 1677$^{2}$ 2032$^{12}$ 3087$^{4}$ 3303$^{4}$4603$^{6}$ >**70a 70f**<

**Mandrake El Mago (CHI)** 5 b h Golden Voyager (USA) -Manon Lescaut (CHI) (Musketeer (USA)) 1954a$^{2}$ (4984a) 5506a$^{3}$ >**111f**<

**Manduro (GER)** 2 br c Monsun (GER) -Mandellicht (IRE) (Be My Guest (USA)) (6256a) ><

**Mandy s Collection** 5 ch m Forzando-Instinction (Never So Bold) 1262$^{15}$ 1497$^{U}$ 2012$^{5}$ 2183$^{9}$ >**20a 20f**<

**Maneki Neko (IRE)** 2 b c Rudimentary (USA) -Ardbess (Balla Cove) 4172$^{4}$ 4797$^{2}$ 5516$^{2}$ 6090$^{15}$ >**73f**<

**Mango Mischief (IRE)** 3 ch f Desert King (IRE) -Eurolink Mischief (Be My Chief (USA)) (2764) 3327$^{2}$ 4640$^{4}$ 5401$^{2}$ 5761$^{10}$ (6571) >**97f**<

**Mangrove Cay (IRE)** 2 b c Danetime (IRE) -Art Duo (Artaius (USA)) 4966$^{8}$ 5476$^{4}$ 5953$^{5}$ 6294$^{5}$ >**66a 63f**<

**Mangus (IRE)** 10 b g Mac s Imp (USA) -Holly Bird (Runnett) 443$^{3}$ 792$^{7}$ 905$^{6}$ 1075$^{8}$ 1546$^{7}$ 1859$^{5}$ >**23a 23f**<

**Manhattan (ITY)** 2 b f Glen Jordan-Stenographer (IRE) (Royal Academy (USA)) 5390a$^{2}$ 5577a$^{3}$ ><

**Manhattan Jack** 3 ch g Forzando-Manhattan Diamond (Primo Dominie) 2145$^{8}$ 2412$^{5}$ 2783$^{2}$ 3561$^{9}$ >**71f**<

**Maniatis** 7 b g Slip Anchor-Tamassos (Dance In Time (CAN)) 1030$^{6}$ (1263) (1677) 2022$^{10}$ 3022$^{2}$ (3281) 3385$^{3}$ >**76a 75f**<

**Manic** 2 br f Polar Falcon (USA) -Gentle Irony (Mazilier (USA)) 4124$^{8}$ (5953) 6305$^{3}$ 6562$^{9}$ >**66a 58f**<

**Manikato (USA)** 10 b g Clever Trick (USA) -Pasampsi (USA) (Crow (FR)) 441$^{7}$ 532$^{7}$ 940$^{9}$ 2939$^{11}$ 4476$^{9}$ >**39a 39f**<

**Mannora** 4 b f Prince Sabo-Miss Bussell (Sabrehill (USA)) 2098$^{4}$ 2707$^{12}$ 2885$^{13}$ 3151$^{9}$ 3935$^{11}$ 4025$^{9}$ >**34a 40f**<

**Manny** 4 b g Emarati (USA) -Needwood Nymph (Bold Owl) 1514$^{8}$ 1668$^{12}$ 2015$^{5}$ >**33a 27f**<

**Mannyman (IRE)** 3 bb f Dr Devious (IRE) -Lithe Spirit (IRE) (Dancing Dissident (USA)) 5204$^{8}$ 5552$^{7}$ 6157$^{13}$ >**56f**<

**Man O Desert (FR)** 4 b c Green Desert (USA) -Miss Satamixa (IRE) (Linamix (FR)) 1741a$^{13}$ >**90f**<

**Man Of Aran** 4 b g Green Desert (USA) -Tahdid (Mtoto) 4588a$^{8}$ >**76f**<

**Man Of Letters (UAE)** 3 b c Belong To Me (USA) -Personal Business (USA) (Private Account (USA)) 1104$^{4}$ 1304$^{3}$ 1558$^{2}$ 1745$^{2}$ (1869) 2361$^{2}$ 2558$^{5}$ 3507$^{3}$ 3915$^{9}$ >**84f**<

**Manorshield Minx** 2 b f Pursuit Of Love-Polly s Teahouse (Shack (USA)) 4364$^{9}$ 5407$^{9}$ 5535$^{10}$ 5792$^{12}$ >**53f**<

**Manorson (IRE)** 5 ch g Desert King (IRE) -Familiar (USA) (Diesis) 2110$^{10}$ 2681$^{11}$ 5919$^{2}$ 6172$^{4}$ >**96f**<

**Man O World (IRE)** 2 b c Spinning World (USA) -Rihan (USA) (Dayjur (USA)) (2792a) 3352a$^{7}$ 5680a$^{5}$ >**97f**<

**Manrique (USA)** 2 ch c Rahy (USA) -Dance Trick (USA) (Diesis) 6569$^{20}$ >**15f**<

**Mansfield Park** 3 b f Green Desert (USA) -Park Appeal (Ahonoora) 5439$^{3}$ 5783$^{3}$ (6147) >**105f**<

**Mansiya** 2 ch f Vettori (IRE) -Bay Shade (USA) (Sharpen Up) 4480$^{2}$ 5846$^{6}$ >**63f**<

**Mantel Mini** 5 b m Reprimand-Foretell (Tirol) 948$^{9}$ 3661$^{6}$ 3932$^{12}$ 4337$^{10}$ >**25a 9f**<

**Man The Gate** 5 b g Elmaamul (USA) -Girl At The Gate (Formidable (USA)) 1188$^{2}$ 1611$^{5}$ 1801$^{11}$ 2212$^{3}$ 2501$^{6}$ 3450$^{2}$ (3658) 3873$^{5}$ 4616$^{8}$4736$^{8}$ 4971$^{7}$ >**70a 72f**<

**Mantilla** 7 b m Son Pardo-Well Tried (IRE) (Thatching) 1281$^{7}$ >**36a**<

**Mantles Pride** 9 br g Petong-State Romance (Free State) 1582$^{9}$ >**41a 62 f**<

**Mantles Prince** 10 ch g Emarati (USA) -Miami Mouse (Miami Springs) 973$^{6}$ ><

**Manyana (IRE)** 3 b c Alzao (USA) -Sometime (IRE) (Royal Academy (USA)) 1439$^{5}$ (2203) 2722a$^{11}$ 4215$^{8}$ >**108f**<

**Many Thanks** 4 b f Octagonal (NZ) -Answered Prayer (Green Desert (USA)) 797$^{5}$ 825$^{6}$ >**19a 75f**<

**Maple Syrple (CAN)** 3 br f American Chance (USA) -Sweet And Lowdown (USA) (Stalwart (USA)) 3105$^{8}$ >**90a 86f**<

**Maraahel (IRE)** 3 b c Alzao (USA) -Nasanice (IRE) (Nashwan (USA)) 2107$^{2}$ 2999$^{2}$ (4215) 5463$^{4}$ >**119f**<

**Maraakeb (FR)** 3 br c Linamix (FR) -Raheefa (USA) (Riverman (USA)) 3297$^{6}$ (5445) >**81f**<

**Marabar** 6 b m Sri Pekan (USA) -Erbaya (IRE) (El Gran Senor (USA)) 488$^{11}$ 685$^{6}$ 782$^{5}$ 1018$^{7}$ 1178$^{10}$ (1283) 1533$^{7}$ 1872$^{17}$1956$^{3}$ (2188) 2227$^{2}$ 2666$^{2}$ 2811$^{6}$ 2963$^{6}$ 3372$^{11}$ 5101$^{4}$6117$^{14}$ 6558$^{8}$ >**58a 64f**<

**Marajuana** 2 b f Robellino (USA) -Mara River (Efisio) (2947) >**78f**<

**Marakash (IRE)** 5 b g Ashkalani (IRE) -Marilaya (IRE) (Shernazar) 821$^{2}$ 873$^{8}$ 999$^{6}$ >**53a 71f**<

**Maralan (IRE)** 3 b c Priolo (USA) -Marilaya (IRE) (Shernazar) 2796a$^{9}$ >**87f**<

**Maramara** 3 gr f In The Wings-Midnight Society (USA) (Imp Society (USA)) 6255a$^{8}$ >**76f**<

**Maraud** 10 ch g Midyan (USA) -Peak Squaw (USA) (Icecapade (USA)) 432$^{5}$ 528$^{3}$ >**37a**<

**Maravedi (IRE)** 4 ch f Hector Protector (USA) -Manuetti (IRE) (Sadler s Wells (USA)) 1479$^{12}$ 1723$^{8}$ 2230$^{8}$ 6468$^{9}$ >**45a 44f**<

**Marble Arch** 8 b g Rock Hopper-Mayfair Minx (St Columbus) 6535$^{10}$ >**69+a 93f**<

**Marburyanna** 4 ch f Classic Cliche (IRE) -Lake Mistassiu (Tina s Pet) 5770$^{17}$ 6062$^{11}$ ><

**Marbush (IRE)** 3 ro c Linamix (FR) -Fig Tree Drive (USA) (Miswaki (USA)) 1395$^{3}$ 2144$^{2}$ (2487) 3728$^{5}$ 4754$^{3}$ >**89f**<

**Marbye (IRE)** 4 b f Marju (IRE) -Hambye (Distant Relative) 1776a$^{4}$ (2608a) 2967$^{5}$ (4383a) 6109a$^{6}$ 6381a$^{13}$ >**113f**<

**Marcela Zabala** 2 b f Zaha (CAN) -Bay Bianca (IRE) (Law Society (USA)) 1264$^{7}$ (3883) 4516$^{8}$ (5022) 5617$^{10}$ 6333$^{21}$ >**10a 55f**<

**Marchetta** 2 b f Mujadil (USA) -My Lewicia (IRE) (Taufan (USA)) 4706$^{6}$ 5272$^{5}$ 5653$^{3}$ >**71f**<

**Marching Song** 2 b c Royal Applause-Marl (Lycius (USA)) 1436$^{5}$ 2208$^{3}$ 2947$^{2}$ 3677$^{4}$ 4143$^{2}$ (4481) 5119$^{2}$ 5873$^{5}$ >**93f**<

**Marching West (USA)** 3 b f Gone West (USA) -Zaizafon (USA) (The Minstrel (CAN)) 6203a$^{0}$ >**91+f**<

**Marcus Eile (IRE)** 3 b g Daggers Drawn (USA) -Sherannda (USA) (Trempolino (USA)) 522$^{4}$ 595$^{4}$ 798$^{8}$ 6568$^{19}$ >**72 a 77f**<

**Mardonicdeclare** 3 b g Perpendicular-Daisy Girl (Main Reef) 4180$^{9}$ ><

**Maredsous (FR)** 4 b f Homme De Loi (IRE) -Tutti (FR) (Rahotep (FR)) 1922a$^{3}$ 2543a$^{5}$ 4982a$^{13}$ >**107f**<

**Maren (USA)** 3 b c Gulch (USA) -Fatina (Nashwan (USA)) 5444$^{7}$ 5698$^{18}$ 5934$^{12}$ >**86+f**<

**Marengo** 10 b g Never So Bold-Born To Dance (Dancing Brave (USA)) 430$^{11}$ 475$^{7}$ 783$^{6}$ 878$^{7}$ 945$^{7}$ 1715$^{6}$ 1861$^{4}$ 1918$^{7}$ 4808$^{13}$ 4925$^{9}$ 5184$^{11}$ >**28a 31f**<

**Marfinca (IRE)** 3 b c Marju (IRE) -Hamsaat (IRE) (Sadler s Wells (USA)) 4588a$^{14}$ >**89f**<

**Marfooq (USA)** 4 ch c Diesis-Fabulous Fairy (USA) (Alydar (USA)) 4371a$^{6}$ >**83f**<

**Margalita (IRE)** 4 b f Sesaro (USA) -Mamma Luigi (IRE) (Classic Music (USA)) 917$^{6}$ 1504$^{17}$ 2284$^{20}$ 2628$^{6}$ 2948$^{10}$ 3440$^{9}$ 4034$^{16}$ 5734$^{11}$6493$^{10}$ 6559$^{8}$ >**73a 65f**<

**Margaret s Dream (IRE)** 3 b f Muhtarram (USA) -Acidanthera (Alzao (USA)) 6567$^{3}$ >**62f**<

**Margarets Wish** 4 gr f Cloudings (IRE) -Gentle Gain (Final Straw) 567$^{11}$ 664$^{4}$ 793$^{7}$ 994$^{12}$ (1581) 1987$^{8}$ 2649$^{10}$ 2835$^{10}$3697$^{15}$ 4045$^{6}$ 4669$^{8}$ >**37a 43f**<

**Margery Daw (IRE)** 4 b f Sri Pekan (USA) -Suyayeb (USA) (The Minstrel (CAN)) 520$^{5}$ 1902$^{8}$ 1940$^{8}$ 2032$^{11}$ 2363$^{6}$ 2443$^{3}$ 2501$^{16}$ 2801$^{7}$2928$^{5}$ 5021$^{19}$ 5285$^{10}$ 5643$^{8}$ 5928$^{15}$ >**42a 42f**<

**Margold (IRE)** 4 ch f Goldmark (USA) -Arcevia (IRE) (Archway (IRE)) 459$^{7}$ 568$^{11}$ 2408$^{3}$ 3411$^{18}$ 4015$^{17}$ >**38a 64f**<

**Marhaba Million (IRE)** 2 gr c Linamix (FR) -Modelliste (Machiavellian (USA)) 5870$^{8}$ >**46f**<

**Marhoon (USA)** 2 ch c Lion Cavern (USA) -United Kingdom (USA) (Danzig (USA)) 6000$^{4}$ 6322$^{2}$ (6494) >**85a 73f**<

**Maria Bonita (IRE)** 3 b f Octagonal (NZ) -Nightitude (Night Shift (USA)) 1532$^{4}$ 2169$^{12}$ 3573$^{4}$ 4086$^{8}$ 4940$^{4}$ 5549$^{3}$ 6085$^{3}$ 6552$^{3}$ >**57a 71f**<

**Maria Delfina (IRE)** 2 ch f Giant s Causeway (USA) -Photographie (USA) (Trempolino (USA)) 6494$^{3}$ >**67+a**<

**Maria Maria (IRE)** 3 ch f Among Men (USA) -Yiayia s Girl (Smackover) 563$^{11}$ 1192$^{7}$ 1945$^{4}$ 2822$^{10}$ 3707$^{11}$ >**47f**<

**Marianis** 2 b f Lujain (USA) -Without Warning (IRE) (Warning) 2245$^{4}$ 2786$^{10}$ 3665$^{5}$ >**56f**<

**Marian s Gift** 2 ch f Bold Edge-Thimbalina (Salmon Leap (USA)) 2458$^{11}$ >**12f**<

**Marians Maid (IRE)** 2 b f Monashee Mountain (USA) -Speedy Action (Horage) 3157$^{13}$ 3632$^{6}$ 4198$^{13}$ >**47f**<

**Marias Magic** 3 b f Mtoto-Majoune (FR) (Take Risks (FR)) (6082) 6566$^{9}$ >**73f**<

**Mariday** 3 br g Trifolio-Classic Hand (Some Hand) 5495$^{6}$ 5913$^{9}$ 6182$^{6}$ >**55a 30f**<

**Mariella (GER)** 3 bb f Zinaad-Morgenrote (GER) (Aveiro) (3973a) 4980a$^{12}$ 5975a$^{9}$ >**83f**<

**Marinaite** 3 b f Komaite (USA) -Marina s Song (Savahra Sound) 585$^{2}$ (668) 1265$^{5}$ 1464$^{2}$ 1737$^{2}$ 2118$^{14}$ 2587$^{3}$ 5244$^{12}$6147$^{3}$ 6210$^{14}$ 6517$^{13}$ >**79a 77f**<

**Marine City (JPN)** 3 b f Carnegie (IRE) -Marienbad (FR) (Darshaan) (1521) 1899$^{6}$ 2529$^{6}$ 5191$^{3}$ 5595$^{4}$ 5850$^{3}$ 6339$^{5}$ >**77f**<

**Marinnette (IRE)** 3 ch f Be My Guest (USA) -Al Cairo (FR) (Vayrann) 3968a$^{5}$ 6102a$^{6}$ 6571$^{14}$ >**95?f**<

**Marino Mou (IRE)** 4 b c Darshaan-Lia s Dance (Lead On Time (USA)) 639$^{7}$ 697$^{7}$ 1235$^{6}$ 1520$^{3}$ 1866$^{10}$ 2249$^{9}$ >**46f**<

**Marita** 3 ch f Dancing Spree (USA) -Maria Cappuccini (Siberian Express (USA)) 508$^{5}$ 615$^{7}$ >**36a 26f**<

**Maritima** 2 b f Darshaan-Armeria (USA) (Northern Dancer) 6123$^{U}$ >**68+f**<

**Maritime Blues** 4 b g Fleetwood (IRE) -Dixie D Oats (Alhijaz) 1213$^{11}$ 1393$^{7}$ 1611$^{7}$ (2235) 2449$^{9}$ 2964$^{6}$ 3866$^{3}$ 4155$^{12}$ 4556$^{11}$(4901) 5129$^{7}$ 5344$^{5}$ 5584$^{8}$ 6025$^{8}$ 6520$^{2}$ >**64a 69f**<

**Marker** 4 ch g Pivotal-Palace Street (USA) (Secreto (USA)) 1132$^{6}$ 1354$^{8}$ 1765$^{13}$ 1968$^{4}$ 2477$^{9}$ 3205$^{4}$ 3455$^{10}$ 3698$^{10}$4677$^{4}$ (5075) 6517$^{10}$ >**89f**<

**Market Avenue** 5 b m Factual (USA) -The Lady Vanishes (Robin Des Pins (USA)) 2216$^{6}$ 3375$^{7}$ 3738$^{5}$ 4008$^{7}$ 4537$^{5}$ (5344) 5459$^{11}$ 5853$^{9}$ 6096$^{6}$6576$^{6}$ >**60a 76f**<

**Market Leader** 3 b f Marju (IRE) -I Will Lead (USA) (Seattle Slew (USA)) 4103$^{3}$ 5152$^{3}$ 5409$^{3}$ 6088$^{3}$ >**69f**<

**Market Trend** 2 b f Selkirk (USA) -Equity Princess (Warning) 5400$^{2}$ (5604) 6003$^{7}$ 6176$^{10}$ >**81f**<

**Marko Jadeo (IRE)** 6 b g Eagle Eyed (USA) -Fleeting Quest (Rainbow Quest (USA)) 2744a$^{7}$ 5920$^{10}$ >**96f**<

**Marksgold (IRE)** 3 b g Goldmark (USA) -Lady Of Shalott (King s Lake (USA)) 1366$^{3}$ 1597$^{6}$ 1854$^{6}$ 2061$^{10}$ 2485$^{5}$ 3229$^{9}$ >**55a 59f**<

**Mark Your Card** 2 ch f Mark Of Esteem (IRE) -Charolles (Ajdal (USA)) 4761$^{8}$ 5095$^{13}$ 5227$^{12}$ 5542$^{11}$ >**42f**<

**Mark Your Way** 4 b g Spectrum (IRE) -Titania s Way (Fairy King (USA)) 4641$^{11}$ 5175$^{13}$ 5350$^{10}$ >**33f**<

**Marlenes Girl (IRE)** 2 b f Foxhound (USA) -Premier Place (USA) (Out Of Place (USA)) 3818$^{15}$ 4507$^{6}$ 4776$^{16}$ >**48f**<

**Marmaduke (IRE)** 8 ch g Perugino (USA) -Sympathy (Precocious) 483$^{2}$ 603$^{5}$ 962$^{4}$ >**72a 66f**<

**Marne (IRE)** 2 b g Mtoto-Perfect Poppy (Shareef Dancer (USA)) 1137$^{4}$ ><

**Marnhac (FR)** 3 gr c Smadoun (FR) -One Way (FR) (Exit To Nowhere (USA)) 1350a$^{4}$ 2072a$^{5}$ >**107f**<

**Marnie** 7 ch m First Trump-Miss Aboyne (Lochnager) 888$^{9}$ (1019) 1102$^{3}$ 1244$^{9}$ 2426$^{2}$ 2871$^{2}$ 3191$^{5}$ 3771$^{5}$4264$^{5}$ 4771$^{8}$ 5795$^{6}$ >**52a 52f**<

**Maromito (IRE)** 7 b g Up And At Em-Amtico (Bairn (USA)) 721$^{11}$ 897$^{10}$ 1035$^{3}$ (1546) (1699) 2246$^{10}$ 2663$^{9}$ 4011$^{3}$4422$^{8}$ (5253) 5412$^{4}$ 5734$^{9}$ >**56a 68f**<

**Maron** 7 b g Puissance-Will Be Bold (Bold Lad (IRE)) 665$^{5}$ 944$^{2}$ 1406$^{4}$ >**36a 26f**<

**Maroochydore (IRE)** 3 b f Danehill (USA) -Biraya (Valiyar) 1649a$^{5}$ 1980a$^{8}$ 2744a$^{12}$ >**100+f**<

**Marrel** 6 b g Shareef Dancer (USA) -Upper Caen (High Top) 3851$^{5}$ 4473$^{6}$ >**46 a 50f**<

**Marsad (IRE)** 10 ch g Fayruz-Broad Haven (IRE) (Be My Guest (USA)) 1765$^{18}$ 2065$^{3}$ 2477$^{8}$ 2857$^{2}$ 3324$^{11}$ 4324$^{20}$ 4614$^{8}$ 5224$^{2}$5799$^{8}$ 6071$^{14}$ 6341$^{4}$ >**98f**<

**Marshal Bond** 6 b g Celtic Swing-Arminda (Blakeney) 652$^{9}$ >**22 a 22 f**<

**Marshall (FR)** 4 b c Anabaa (USA) -Monitrice (FR) (Groom Dancer (USA)) (911a) 1163a$^{11}$ 1780a$^{8}$ 3030a$^{7}$ 4039a$^{9}$ 5727a$^{2}$ 6170a$^{2}$ >**115f**<

**Marshallspark (IRE)** 5 b g Fayruz-Lindas Delight (Batshoof) 2079$^{7}$ 2461$^{15}$ 2735$^{9}$ 3226$^{5}$ (3887) 4179$^{8}$ (4534) 5440$^{6}$ 5730$^{2}$ >**57a 79f**<

**Marshman (IRE)** 5 ch g College Chapel-Gold Fly (IRE) (Be My Guest (USA)) 1114$^{17}$ 1385$^{3}$ 1968$^{7}$ 2503$^{8}$ 4120$^{18}$ 4553$^{12}$ 4742$^{10}$ 4908$^{3}$5177$^{3}$ 5631$^{5}$ (6070) 6191$^{5}$ 6451$^{6}$ >**98a 99f**<

**Marsh Orchid** 3 b g Lahib (USA) -Majalis (Mujadil (USA)) 1386$^{5}$ 4303$^{2}$ 4573$^{2}$ 5158$^{9}$ >**74f**<

**Martaline** 5 gr h Linamix (FR) -Coraline (Sadler s Wells (USA)) 1144a$^{12}$ 1792$^{5}$ 5170a$^{2}$ 5727a$^{7}$ 6263a$^{6}$ >**116f**<

**Martha Reilly (IRE)** 8 ch m Rainbows For Life (CAN) -Debach Delight (Great Nephew) 716$^{6}$ 789$^{9}$ >**32a 22f**<

**Martha Stewart (IRE)** 3 ch f Daggers Drawn (USA) -Sigonella (IRE) (Priolo (USA)) 1805a$^{5}$ 4383a$^{5}$ >**110f**<

**Martillo (GER)** 4 b c Anabaa (USA) -Maltage (USA) (Affirmed (USA)) 1146a$^{5}$ (1780a) 2957$^{9}$ (3792a) 5332a$^{9}$ >**118f**<

**Martin House (IRE)** 5 b g Mujadil (USA) -Dolcezza (FR) (Lichine (USA)) 3409$^{18}$ 3929$^{9}$ >**52f**<

**Marton Mere** 8 ch g Cadeaux Genereux-Hyatti (Habitat) 3835$^{8}$ 4423$^{14}$ >**31f**<

**Mary Carleton** 3 ch f Halling (USA) -Anne Bonny (Ajdal (USA)) 2505$^{13}$ 2818$^{6}$ 3251$^{13}$ 4798$^{10}$ 6360$^{10}$ >**31f**<

**Mary Ellen (IRE)** 6 b m Sri Pekan (USA) -Prickle (Sharpen Up) 5488a$^{11}$ ><

**Mary Gray** 2 gr f Mujahid (USA) -Ancestry (Persepolis (FR)) 4009$^{5}$ 4272$^{11}$ 6092$^{12}$ 6515$^{9}$ >**66f**<

**Mary Read** 2 ch f Bahamian Bounty-Hill Welcome (Most Welcome) 1498$^{3}$ (1743) 2568$^{3}$ (3346) 4217$^{2}$ 4744$^{9}$ 5602$^{2}$ 6174$^{7}$ >**100f**<

**Marysienka** 3 b f Primo Dominie-Polish Romance (USA) (Danzig (USA)) 4051$^{11}$ 4456$^{5}$ 4608$^{9}$ 4810$^{3}$ 5342$^{4}$ 5563$^{11}$ 6222$^{12}$ >**27a 72f**<

**Masa (USA)** 2 gr f Dixie Union (USA) -My Yellow Diamond (USA) (Housebuster (USA)) (2481) 3031$^{9}$ 3599$^{6}$ >**82f**<

**Masafi (IRE)** 3 b c Desert King (IRE) -Mrs Fisher (IRE) (Salmon Leap (USA)) 1019$^{2}$ (3804) (3897) (3990) (4056) (4096) (4249) (4258) 4435$^{5}$ 5755$^{7}$ >**80+a 97+f**<

**Masjoor** 4 ch g Unfuwain (USA) -Mihnah (IRE) (Lahib (USA)) 962$^{7}$ 1235$^{2}$ 1754$^{11}$ >**65a 66f**<

**Masked (IRE)** 3 b c Soviet Star (USA) -Moon Masquerade (IRE) (Darshaan) 1674$^{8}$ 1967$^{7}$ 2517$^{4}$ (2977) 3584$^{5}$ 3942$^{2}$ 4441$^{2}$ 5300$^{11}$ 5944$^{9}$ >**83f**<

**Mas O Menos (IRE)** 2 b g King s Theatre (IRE) -Promising Lady (Thunder Gulch (USA)) 1990$^{2}$ 2453$^{11}$ 3444$^{20}$ 5633$^{2}$ 5797$^{13}$ 6093$^{17}$ >**54f**<

**Masquerader (USA)** 2 ch c Unbridled (USA) -Guise (USA) (Believe It (USA)) 3718$^{7}$ >**48f**<

**Massey** 8 br g Machiavellian (USA) -Massaraat (USA) (Nureyev (USA)) (486) 607$^{12}$ (669) 3735$^{7}$ 4013$^{12}$ 4425$^{15}$ 4905$^{12}$ 5452$^{7}$ 6451$^{13}$ >**103a 32f**<

**Massif Centrale** 3 ch c Selkirk (USA) -Madame Dubois (Legend Of France (USA)) 1800$^{7}$ 2085$^{2}$ 2680$^{11}$ (3454) 4215$^{7}$ 5892$^{5}$ (6121) 6355$^{6}$ >**106f**<

**Master Cobbler (IRE)** 2 b c Alhaarth (IRE) -Lady Joshua (IRE) (Royal Academy (USA)) 3176$^{4}$ 4003$^{2}$ 5827$^{2}$ 6240$^{4}$ >**81f**<

**Master David (USA)** 3 ch c Grand Slam (USA) -Nadra (IRE) (Sadler s Wells (USA)) 1781a$^{12}$ 2701a$^{7}$ >**109?a 87f**<

**Master Joseph** 2 b c Komaite (USA) -Petit Peu (IRE) (King s Lake (USA)) 2263$^{4}$ 2804$^{7}$ 3083$^{8}$ 4445$^{11}$ 5090$^{2}$ 5240$^{5}$ >**62f**<

**Master Mahogany** 3 b g Bandmaster (USA) -Impropriety (Law Society (USA)) 744$^{9}$ 1301$^{4}$ 1683$^{9}$ 2169$^{8}$ 2400$^{6}$ 2809$^{5}$ 3231$^{4}$ 3773$^{6}$4147$^{10}$ 4619$^{3}$ 5259$^{10}$

(5510) 5829$^{6}$ >**26a 66f**<

**Masterman Ready** **3** b g Unfuwain (USA) -Maria Isabella (FR) (Young Generation) 2632$^{8}$ 3245$^{7}$ 3752$^{6}$ 4146$^{8}$ (4820) 5159$^{3}$ 5523$^{6}$ (5889) >**53a 74f**<

**Master Marvel (IRE)** **3** ch c Selkirk (USA) -Insijaam (USA) (Secretariat (USA)) 1104$^{2}$ (1318) (1795) 2676$^{8}$ 3001$^{19}$ 5443$^{6}$ 5942$^{9}$ >**96 f**<

**Master Nimbus** **4** b g Cloudings (IRE) -Miss Charlie (Pharly (FR)) 5450$^{10}$ >**39f**<

**Master Of The Race** **2** ch c Selkirk (USA) -Dust Dancer (Suave Dancer (USA)) 6476$^{2}$ >**93+f**<

**Master Rat** **3** b g Thowra (FR) -Race Against Time (Latest Model) 5204$^{13}$ 5564$^{12}$ 6079$^{17}$ >**16f**<

**Master Rattle** **5** b g Sabrehill (USA) -Miss Primula (Dominion) 491$^{10}$ 573$^{11}$ 698$^{11}$ 859$^{5}$ 895$^{2}$ 946$^{11}$ 1098$^{8}$1515$^{9}$ (2342a) 2384$^{2}$ >**52a 45f**<

**Master Robbie** **5** b g Piccolo-Victoria s Secret (IRE) (Law Society (USA)) 1132$^{12}$ 1385$^{19}$ 1765$^{24}$ 2283$^{8}$ (2503) 2750$^{6}$ 3036$^{19}$ 3673$^{9}$ 4120$^{12}$4371a$^{8}$ 4553$^{15}$ 4742$^{14}$ 5468$^{8}$ 5887$^{7}$ 5921$^{4}$ 6070$^{15}$ >**99 f**<

**Master Role (IRE)** **4** ch c Master Willie-Calaloo Sioux (USA) (Our Native (USA)) 697$^{2}$ 969$^{6}$ >**65a 81f**<

**Master T (USA)** **5** b g Trempolino (USA) -Our Little C (USA) (Marquetry (USA)) 602$^{12}$ 740$^{7}$ >**65a 65f**<

**Master Theo (USA)** **3** b g Southern Halo (USA) -Lilian Bayliss (IRE) (Sadler s Wells (USA)) 1794$^{7}$ 2519$^{3}$ 2777$^{3}$ 3268$^{3}$ 4738$^{3}$ 5244$^{8}$ 5706$^{3}$ 6017$^{4}$6086$^{2}$ >**75a 79f**<

**Master Wells (IRE)** **3** b g Sadler s Wells (USA) -Eljazzi (Artaius (USA)) (1713) 2070$^{8}$ 2683$^{8}$ 3292$^{2}$ 3584$^{7}$ 4062$^{11}$ 4934$^{2}$ (5100) 5608$^{4}$ 6143$^{8}$6575$^{7}$ >**87f**<

**Mastman (IRE)** **2** ch c Intikhab (USA) -Spanker (Suave Dancer (USA)) 3451$^{2}$ 3939$^{5}$ 4263$^{4}$ (4872) 5612$^{3}$ >**97f**<

**Match Ball (USA)** **2** bb f Grand Slam (USA) -Glitters (USA) (Glitterman (USA)) 3950$^{11}$ ><

**Material Witness (IRE)** **7** b g Barathea (IRE) -Dial Dream (Gay Mecene (USA)) 1354$^{13}$ 1968$^{11}$ 2206$^{2}$ 2467$^{8}$ (2646) (3337) (3673) 4273$^{2}$ 4324$^{9}$ 4889$^{4}$ (5112)5422$^{6}$ 5610$^{7}$ 5781$^{15}$ >**89a 110f**<

**Mathematician (IRE)** **2** br c Machiavellian (USA) -Zibilene (Rainbow Quest (USA)) 6320a$^{4}$ >**89f**<

**Mathmagician** **5** ch g Hector Protector (USA) -Inherent Magic (IRE) (Magical Wonder (USA)) 778$^{4}$ 823$^{5}$ 934$^{4}$ 953$^{8}$ 1026$^{4}$ 1091$^{6}$ 1193$^{6}$1535$^{10}$ 1697$^{3}$ 1918$^{5}$ >**39a 32f**<

**Matimoviestar (ITY)** **2** b f Roi Danzig (USA) -Forever Roses (Forzando) 5390a$^{13}$ ><

**Matin De Tempete (FR)** **4** b f Cardoun (FR) -Nuit Sans Fin (FR) (Lead On Time (USA)) 5169a$^{10}$ 6170a$^{10}$ >**92f**<

**Matipapi** **2** b f Spectrum (IRE) -Sarah Ransom (USA) (Red Ransom (USA)) 6108a$^{9}$ >**44f**<

**Matouraka (FR)** **3** bb f Great Palm (USA) -Madragoa (FR) (Kaldoun (FR)) 6343$^{16}$ ><

**Matriarchal** **4** ch f Presidium-Mayor (Laxton) 2528$^{13}$ 2979$^{5}$ 3376$^{8}$ 4105$^{11}$ 4509$^{9}$ >**12a 43f**<

**Matrice (ITY)** **2** br f Lend A Hand-Mamma Luigi (IRE) (Classic Music (USA)) 5390a$^{12}$ 5577a$^{13}$ ><

**Matrimony** **3** b c Groom Dancer (USA) -Zonda (Fabulous Dancer (USA)) 2250$^{P}$ ><

**Matrix (GER)** **3** b c Big Shuffle (USA) -Massena (GER) (Konigsstuhl (GER)) 2158a$^{7}$ 4596a$^{7}$ 5255a$^{7}$ >**100f**<

**Matsunosuke** **2** b c Magic Ring (IRE) -Lon Isa (Grey Desire) 5752$^{F}$ 6171$^{10}$ >**59f**<

**Matty Tun** **5** b g Lugana Beach-B Grade (Lucky Wednesday) 1391$^{9}$ 1763$^{5}$ 2041$^{5}$ 2293$^{7}$ 3074$^{29}$ 3266$^{10}$ 3480$^{5}$ 4538$^{10}$5440$^{10}$ 6267$^{10}$ (6349) >**81a 102f**<

**Maunby Raver** **3** ch g Pivotal-Colleen Liath (Another Realm) 462$^{7}$ 2389$^{4}$ 3624$^{13}$ >**66a 63f**<

**Maunby Rocker** **4** ch g Sheikh Albadou-Bullion (Sabrehill (USA)) 464$^{14}$ 627$^{9}$ 733$^{6}$ 937$^{5}$ >**40a 71f**<

**Maureen Ann** **4** b f Elmaamul (USA) -Running Glimpse (IRE) (Runnett) 3167$^{9}$ 3471$^{10}$ 4511$^{10}$ 5575$^{14}$ 5639$^{7}$ >**42a 64f**<

**Maureen s Lough (IRE)** **2** b f Bachir (IRE) -Tadjnama (USA) (Exceller (USA)) 1468$^{3}$ 1717$^{6}$ (2755) 3100$^{5}$ 3506$^{4}$ 4010$^{4}$ (4304) 4521$^{9}$ 5097$^{5}$ 5234$^{16}$5314$^{15}$ 5556$^{2}$ 5819$^{6}$ >**50f**<

**Mauro (IRE)** **2** b f Danehill Dancer (IRE) -Stop The Traffic (IRE) (College Chapel) 1607$^{4}$ 1751$^{2}$ 2177$^{4}$ 3659$^{6}$ 4803$^{11}$ >**57f**<

**Mawhoob (USA)** **6** gr g Dayjur (USA) -Asl (USA) (Caro) 471$^{9}$ >**43a 54f**<

**Mawwal** **4** b g Groom Dancer (USA) -Proudfoot (IRE) (Shareef Dancer (USA)) (709a) ><

**Maxamillion (IRE)** **2** b c Mujadil (USA) -Manazil (IRE) (Generous (IRE)) 5688$^{5}$ 6181$^{4}$ (6322) 6574$^{6}$ >**80f**<

**Maxilla (IRE)** **4** bb f Lahib (USA) -Lacinia (Groom Dancer (USA)) 1752$^{4}$ 2000$^{8}$ 2775$^{5}$ 3670$^{6}$ 4486$^{2}$ 5318$^{4}$ >**68a 80f**<

**Maximinus** **4** b g The West (USA) -Candarela (Damister (USA)) 1911$^{4}$ 2882$^{9}$ 3348$^{6}$ 4196$^{13}$ 5645$^{8}$ >**55a 61f**<

**Maxi s Princess (IRE)** **3** b f Revoque (IRE) -Harmer (IRE) (Alzao (USA)) 1689$^{6}$ 2033$^{9}$ 3344$^{11}$ >**46a 52f**<

**Maxwell (FR)** **4** b c Anabaa (USA) -Malaisie (USA) (Bering) 1163a$^{9}$ 1780a$^{3}$ 3791a$^{5}$ 5968a$^{12}$ 6511a$^{8}$ >**112f**<

**Mayadeen (IRE)** **2** b c King s Best (USA) -Inaaq (Lammtarra (USA)) 4747$^{3}$ (6077) >**79+f**<

**Ma Yahab** **3** ch c Dr Fong (USA) -Bay Shade (USA) (Sharpen Up) 2197$^{3}$ 2583$^{3}$ 3020$^{7}$ 4493$^{4}$ 5239$^{4}$ 5739$^{2}$ >**85a 81f**<

**Maybe Someday** **3** ch g Dr Fong (USA) -Shicklah (USA) (The Minstrel (CAN)) 450$^{3}$ 566$^{4}$ 675$^{6}$ 769$^{3}$ 845$^{3}$ 985$^{10}$ 1046$^{2}$2688$^{15}$ 2813$^{9}$ 3425$^{7}$ 4241$^{14}$ >**66a 54f**<

**Mayfair Maundy** **4** ch f The West (USA) -Mayfair Ballerina (King s Signet (USA)) 1860$^{4}$ 1988$^{10}$ >**25a**<

**May Morning (IRE)** **2** b f Danehill (USA) -Golden Digger (USA) (Mr Prospector (USA)) 5070$^{4}$ 5521$^{2}$ >**76f**<

**Maynooth Prince (IRE)** **2** b g Spectrum (IRE) -Muffle (Sadler s Wells (USA)) 5855$^{7}$ 6197$^{11}$ >**36f**<

**Mays Dream** **2** b f Josr Algarhoud (IRE) -Amber Mill (Doulab (USA)) 5604$^{8}$ >**25f**<

**Maystock** **4** ch f Magic Ring (IRE) -Stockline (Capricorn Line) (467) 887$^{10}$ 1053$^{3}$ 1684$^{8}$ 2062$^{10}$ 5423$^{3}$ 5728$^{11}$ 6128$^{7}$6286$^{11}$ >**83a 80+f**<

**Mayzin (IRE)** **4** b g Fayruz-Peep Of Day (USA) (Lypheor) 469$^{3}$ 491$^{2}$ 573$^{4}$ (702) 738$^{2}$ 847$^{3}$ 1057$^{3}$ (1082) 1230$^{4}$ 2166$^{10}$ 2483$^{8}$ 2628$^{7}$ 2885$^{14}$ 4336$^{14}$ 4403$^{7}$ 4546$^{10}$4923$^{3}$ 5282$^{5}$ >**75a 52f**<

**Mazepa (IRE)** **4** b c Indian Ridge-Please Believe Me (Try My Best (USA)) 1353$^{6}$ 1789$^{3}$ 2065$^{8}$ 2372$^{5}$ 5921$^{15}$ 6341$^{12}$ >**94a 102f**<

**Mazram** **5** b m Muhtarram (USA) -Royal Mazi (King s Lake (USA)) 4624$^{15}$ 5448$^{8}$ 5926$^{13}$ >**24f**<

**Mazuna (IRE)** **3** b f Cape Cross (IRE) -Keswa (King s Lake (USA)) (3421) 3908$^{2}$ 4167$^{3}$ 4749$^{2}$ 5394$^{2}$ (5763) 6381a$^{6}$ >**48a 107f**<

**Mbosi (USA)** **3** b g Kingmambo (USA) -April Starlight (USA) (Storm Bird (CAN)) 2420$^{3}$ 3660$^{3}$ 3869$^{8}$ 4136$^{2}$ 4319$^{14}$ 4533$^{3}$ 5135$^{13}$ 5403$^{13}$ >**68f**<

**Mccracken (IRE)** **8** b g Scenic-Sakanda (IRE) (Vayrann) 1501$^{6}$ >**32f**<

**Mceldowney** **2** b c Zafonic (USA) -Ayodhya (IRE) (Astronef) 2780$^{3}$ 3009$^{2}$ 3336$^{2}$ 3898$^{2}$ 4219$^{3}$ 4527$^{10}$ 5307$^{7}$ 5476$^{2}$5670$^{5}$ (6521) >**73 f**<

**Mcqueen (IRE)** **4** ch g Barathea (IRE) -Bibliotheque (USA) (Woodman (USA)) 618$^{15}$ 1522$^{6}$ 2120$^{8}$ 2375$^{12}$ 3023$^{6}$ 3614$^{9}$ 4808$^{2}$ (5080)(5175) 5459$^{8}$ 5768$^{5}$ (6343) (6520) 6546$^{2}$ >**85a 84f**<

**Meadaaf (IRE)** **3** b c Swain (IRE) -Virgin Hawk (USA) (Silver Hawk (USA)) (1640) 2146$^{2}$ 2732$^{3}$ 3561$^{6}$ 4715$^{3}$ >**89f**<

**Meadow** **3** b f Green Desert (USA) -Marl (Lycius (USA)) 4251a$^{10}$ >**67f**<

**Meadow Hawk (USA)** **4** ch g Spinning World (USA) -Sophonisbe (Wollow) 2090$^{10}$ >**73f**<

**Meath (IRE)** **3** b c Sadler s Wells (USA) -Twyla (Habitat) 1487a$^{2}$ 1982a$^{2}$ (2333a) 2680$^{14}$ >**106f**<

**Mecca s Mate** **3** gr f Paris House-Clancassie (Clantime) 3511$^{5}$ 3759$^{6}$ 4751$^{5}$ (5101) 5674$^{3}$ >**64f**<

**Medaglia D Oro (USA)** **5** br h El Prado (IRE) -Cappucino Bay (USA) (Bailjumper (USA)) 1147a$^{2}$ >**127a**<

**Medalla (FR)** **4** gr c Medaaly-Sharp Cracker (IRE) (Hamas (IRE)) 4781$^{3}$ 5146$^{5}$ 5345$^{7}$ 6096$^{7}$ >**76f**<

**Medallist** **5** b g Danehill (USA) -Obsessive (USA) (Seeking The Gold (USA)) 1624$^{6}$ 2039$^{6}$ >**75a 87f**<

**Media Hora (CHI)** **4** ch g Somersham (USA) -Membrana (CHI) (The Great Shark (USA)) 3552a$^{13}$ ><

**Media Puzzle (USA)** **7** ch g Theatrical-Market Slide (USA) (Gulch (USA)) 4587a$^{5}$ 5662a$^{7}$ 6528a$^{12}$ >**114f**<

**Medica Boba** **3** b f Dr Fong (USA) -Silly View (IRE) (Scenic) 2911$^{7}$ 3592$^{8}$ 4195$^{13}$ 4615$^{11}$ 5410$^{11}$ 5889$^{3}$ 6159$^{13}$ >**31a 59f**<

**Medici (GER)** **4** ch c Unfuwain (USA) -Mocambique (GER) (Frontal) 2336a$^{9}$ 3335a$^{10}$ >**101f**<

**Medicinal (IRE)** **3** gr c Linamix (FR) -Pharmacist (IRE) (Machiavellian (USA)) 1487a$^{4}$ 1979a$^{3}$ (2796a) 4160a$^{4}$ 4587a$^{3}$ 5481a$^{6}$ >**106f**<

**Medigating (FR)** **2** b c Dolphin Street (FR) -Self Made (FR) (Persepolis (FR)) 3790a$^{4}$ 4597a$^{5}$ 6169a$^{2}$ >**103f**<

**Meditation** **2** ch f Inchinor-Trojan Desert (Troy) 3456$^{9}$ 4023$^{7}$ 6010$^{7}$ (6155) 6574$^{20}$ >**65a 38f**<

**Medusa** **4** b f Emperor Jones (USA) -Diebiedale (Dominion) 1750$^{9}$ 2788$^{10}$ 3174$^{10}$ >**76f**<

**Meelup (IRE)** **4** ch g Night Shift (USA) -Centella (IRE) (Thatching) 624$^{11}$ 886$^{2}$ 926$^{2}$ (988) 1097$^{7}$ 1241$^{12}$ 1675$^{13}$ 2343a$^{2}$2078$^{2}$ 2560$^{10}$ 4083$^{16}$ 4511$^{12}$ 5260$^{8}$ 5733$^{15}$ 6295$^{11}$ >**64a 69f**<

**Megabond** **3** b g Danehill Dancer (IRE) -Apple Peeler (IRE) (Rainbows For Life (CAN)) 1047$^{5}$ 2989$^{10}$ 3708$^{4}$ 4309$^{11}$ 5346$^{10}$ (5448) 5748$^{11}$ 6290$^{5}$6452$^{9}$ >**62a 66f**<

**Megahertz** **5** ch m Pivotal-Heavenly Ray (USA) (Rahy (USA)) 6488a$^{11}$ >**116f**<

**Megan s Magic** **4** b f Blue Ocean (USA) -Hot Sunday Sport (Star Appeal) 1247$^{6}$ (1560) 1620$^{2}$ 1931$^{7}$ 2393$^{7}$ 2982$^{3}$ 3952$^{6}$ 4005$^{4}$ 5145$^{4}$5344$^{9}$ 5544$^{5}$ >**76+f**<

**Megec Blis (IRE)** **3** b f Soviet Star (USA) -Machaera (Machiavellian (USA)) 1649a$^{3}$ 5972a$^{6}$ >**104+f**<

**Megell (IRE)** **2** ch f Entrepreneur-Shalwell (IRE) (Shalford (IRE)) 1498$^{6}$ 2096$^{2}$ 3196$^{11}$ 4482$^{5}$ (4816) 5617$^{14}$ >**63f**<

**Mehmaas** **8** b g Distant Relative-Guest List (Be My Guest (USA)) 1783$^{10}$ 1993$^{18}$ 2368$^{18}$ 2459$^{16}$ 3058$^{4}$ 3559$^{13}$ 3612$^{8}$ (4132) 4447$^{13}$4577$^{11}$ 4825$^{5}$ 5187$^{7}$ >**65a 67df**<

**Meiner Select (JPN)** **5** ch h Forty Niner (USA) -Umeno Ascot (JPN) (Lucky Sovereign (USA)) 1145a$^{5}$ >**107a**<

**Meissen** **3** ch f Amfortas (IRE) -Musetta (IRE) (Cadeaux Genereux) 2888$^{2}$ 3417$^{2}$ (5913) >**75a 75f**<

**Mejhar (IRE)** **4** b c Desert Prince (IRE) -Factice (USA) (Known Fact (USA)) 2163a$^{7}$ >**86f**<

**Mekuria (JPN)** **3** b f Carnegie (IRE) -Noble Air (IRE) (Lycius (USA)) 2683$^{9}$ 3199$^{18}$ 3534$^{4}$ >**78 f**<

**Melaina** **3** b f Whittingham (IRE) -Oh I Say (Primo Dominie) 435$^{2}$ 561$^{7}$ 732$^{6}$ (1676) (1907) 2063$^{9}$ 2518$^{5}$ 3530$^{15}$ >**54a 64f**<

**Melalchrist** **2** b g Almaty (IRE) -Lawless Bridget (Alnasr Alwasheek) (1960) 2526$^{2}$ 3011$^{2}$ (3468) 4329$^{3}$ 4836$^{10}$ 6333$^{10}$ >**91f**<

**Melandre** **2** b f Lujain (USA) -Talighta (USA) (Barathea (IRE)) 1769$^{6}$ 2071$^{9}$ 2458$^{4}$ 2860$^{5}$ (5363) 5797$^{2}$ 5932$^{9}$ >**71f**<

**Melford Red (IRE)** **4** b g Sri Pekan (USA) -Sunflower (IRE) (Fairy King (USA)) 3380$^{15}$ >**6a 28f**<

**Meliksah (IRE)** **10** ch g Thatching-Lady Of Shalott (King s Lake (USA)) 2162a$^{9}$ 3162a$^{7}$ >**102f**<

**Melinda s Girl** **3** b f Intikhab (USA) -Polish Honour (USA) (Danzig Connection (USA)) 1844$^{9}$ 5750$^{6}$ 6184$^{9}$ >**41f**<

**Melkior (FR)** **7** b h Neverneyev (USA) -Mepa Discovery (USA) (Clever Trick (USA)) 2162a$^{8}$ 3162a$^{10}$ >**105f**<

**Melodian** **9** b h Grey Desire-Mere Melody (Dunphy) 671$^{5}$ 1172$^{4}$ 1393$^{5}$ (1503) 1962$^{2}$ 2039$^{3}$ 4449$^{2}$ (4493) 5085$^{6}$ 5144$^{9}$5344$^{10}$ 6047$^{15}$ 6520$^{10}$ >**44a 72f**<

**Melody King** **3** b g Merdon Melody-Retaliator (Rudimentary (USA)) 1270$^{15}$ 2266$^{3}$ 2610$^{2}$ 2754$^{5}$ 3195$^{4}$ 3628$^{3}$ 3702$^{6}$ 4043$^{5}$4299$^{U}$ 4617$^{8}$ 4874$^{6}$ 5473$^{9}$ 5702$^{4}$ 6079$^{12}$ 6567$^{10}$ >**70f**<

**Melody Que (IRE)** **2** b f Sadler s Wells (USA) -Bex (USA) (Explodent (USA)) 5109$^{6}$ >**57f**<

**Melograno (IRE)** **4** ch g Hector Protector (USA) -Just A Treat (IRE) (Glenstal (USA)) 1914$^{2}$ 2816$^{8}$ 3041$^{12}$ 3604$^{12}$ (6360) >**51a 51f**<

**Melon Rouge (IRE)** **3** b c Croco Rouge (IRE) -Rince Deas (IRE) (Alzao (USA)) 1777a$^{11}$ >**57f**<

**Melrose Avenue (USA)** **2** b c Kris S (USA) -Sham Street (USA) (Sham (USA)) 2890$^{5}$ (3483) 4959a$^{5}$ 5580$^{4}$ >**96f**<

**Mel s Moment (USA)** **2** b c Storm Creek (USA) -One Moment In Time (USA) (Magesterial (USA)) 5534$^{14}$ 5897$^{6}$ 6155$^{U}$ 6291$^{4}$ 6479$^{6}$ >**71a 79f**<

**Melvino** **2** b g Josr Algarhoud (IRE) -Safe Secret (Seclude (USA)) 2074$^{4}$ 2522$^{7}$ 2972$^{3}$ 3898$^{4}$ 5212$^{10}$ 5434$^{18}$ >**70f**<

**Membership (USA)** **4** ch c Belong To Me (USA) -Shamisen (Diesis) 689a$^{11}$ 850a$^{5}$ 978a$^{5}$ 1006a$^{2}$ 6345$^{8}$ >**104 a 105f**<

**Memory Man** **3** b g Primo Dominie-Surrealist (ITY) (Night Shift (USA)) 3085$^{11}$ 3487$^{4}$ 3848$^{3}$ 4236$^{7}$ 5448$^{9}$ >**17f**<

**Menai Straights** **3** ch g Alhaarth (IRE) -Kind Of Light (Primo Dominie) 1138$^{6}$ 1392$^{15}$ 2259$^{6}$ 2487$^{3}$ 2756$^{5}$ (3517) 3798$^{3}$ 3895$^{9}$ 5861$^{6}$6094$^{6}$ 6199$^{7}$ 6499$^{2}$ >**59a 65f**<

**Meneef (USA)** **3** b c Kingmambo (USA) -Black Penny (USA) (Private Account (USA)) 4069$^{3}$ 5621$^{2}$ 5994$^{3}$ >**80 f**<

**Menelaus** **3** b c Machiavellian (USA) -Mezzogiorno (Unfuwain (USA)) 4819$^{6}$ >**51f**<

**Menhoubah (USA)** **3** b f Dixieland Band (USA) -Private Seductress (USA) (Private Account (USA)) 711a$^{2}$ 1005a$^{3}$ 1143a$^{7}$ 1879$^{2}$ (2341a) 2925a$^{13}$ 4323$^{6}$ 4859$^{8}$5978a$^{8}$ >**105a 104f**<

**Menna** **2** b f Mark Of Esteem (IRE) -Pounelta (Tachypous) 2749$^{5}$ 3445$^{7}$ >**56f**<

**Menokee (USA)** **3** b c Cherokee Run (USA) -Meniatarra (USA) (Zilzal (USA)) 6458$^{2}$ >**108f**<

**Mensatiger (GER)** **3** b c Tiger Hill (IRE) -Mensa (GER) (Lagunas) 1656a$^{2}$ 3357a$^{7}$ >**101f**<

**Mephisto (IRE)** **5** b g Machiavellian (USA) -Cunning (Bustino) 1401$^{10}$ 2110$^{5}$ (2895) (3678) (4218) (4858) >**110f**<

**Mercari** **2** ch f Bahamian Bounty-Aonach Mor (Anabaa (USA)) 3014$^{9}$ 3741$^{12}$ 5521$^{8}$ 5865$^{6}$ 6093$^{4}$ >**60f**<

**Merchant (IRE)** **2** ch c Tagula (IRE) -Easy Pop (IRE) (Shernazar) 3664$^{5}$ 4048$^{3}$ 4256$^{2}$ (4824) (4890) (5090) (5612) 6259a$^{4}$ 6510a$^{7}$ >**102f**<

**Mercurious (IRE)** **4** ch f Grand Lodge (USA) -Rousinette (Rousillon (USA)) 1281$^{4}$ (1512) 1593$^{5}$ 2186$^{4}$ 3712$^{2}$ (4098) 4609$^{2}$ 4883$^{5}$(6005) >**55a 53f**<

**Merdiff** **5** b g Machiavellian (USA) -Balwa (USA) (Danzig (USA)) 1265$^{12}$ 2551$^{7}$ 3023$^{10}$ 3615$^{2}$ (3734) 3800$^{2}$ 4360$^{10}$ 4602$^{4}$4877$^{2}$ 5583$^{15}$ 5868$^{16}$ (6539) >**73a 68f**<

**Merger (USA)** **2** gr c Mr Greeley (USA) -Toledo Queen (IRE) (El Gran Senor (USA)) 6100a$^{2}$ >**105f**<

**Merlin s City** **4** b f Merdon Melody-Sharp Ego (USA) (Sharpen Up) 6200$^{19}$ 6516$^{10}$ ><

**Merlin s Dancer** **4** b g Magic Ring (IRE) -La Piaf (FR) (Fabulous Dancer (USA)) 1825$^{10}$ 2091$^{5}$ (2407) 3016$^{8}$ 3920$^{11}$ 4165$^{7}$ 4232$^{4}$ (4291) 5393$^{13}$ >**96f**<

**Merlins Profit** **4** b g Wizard King-Quick Profit (Formidable (USA)) 1720$^{5}$ 2214$^{4}$ 2348$^{2}$ 3041$^{7}$ 4825$^{U}$ 4985$^{4}$ 5449$^{3}$ 5928$^{6}$6142$^{8}$ >**42f**<

**Mermaid Island (IRE)** **2** b f Mujadil (USA) -Caumshinaun (IRE) (Indian Ridge) 6503a$^{9}$ >**82+f**<

**Mermaid s Cry** **2** b f Danzero (AUS) -Little Tramp (Trempolino (USA)) 2364$^{2}$ 2544$^{7}$ 2812$^{11}$ 3526$^{9}$ >**45f**<

**Merrymadcap (IRE)** **2** b g Lujain (USA) -Carina Clare (Slip Anchor) 2736$^{13}$ 3241$^{5}$ 3664$^{6}$ 4480$^{6}$ 5173$^{8}$ 5535$^{6}$ 5738$^{15}$ 5910$^{11}$ >**64f**<

**Merrymaker** **4** b g Machiavellian (USA) -Wild Pavane (Dancing Brave (USA)) 2032$^{4}$ 2235$^{6}$ 2595$^{4}$ 2964$^{P}$ (3042) 3474$^{2}$ (3942) 4155$^{11}$ 4486$^{8}$ 5144$^{3}$5517$^{5}$ 5632$^{5}$ (5956) 6286$^{5}$ >**83a 78f**<

**Mersey Sound (IRE)** **6** b g Ela-Mana-Mou-Coral Sound (IRE) (Glow (USA)) 1457$^{17}$ 1801$^{13}$ >**78a 76f**<

**Merwaha (IRE)** **3** b f Green Desert (USA) -Samheh (USA) (Private Account (USA)) 2647$^{4}$ 4168$^{3}$ 4644$^{4}$ >**70+f**<

**Mesayan (IRE)** **3** ch c Grand Lodge (USA) -Missish (Mummy s Pet) 2693$^{9}$ 3447$^{4}$ >**60f**<

**Meshaheer (USA)** **5** b h Nureyev (USA) -Race The Wild Wind (USA) (Sunny s Halo (CAN)) 1758$^{9}$ 5610$^{2}$ (6345) >**109f**<

**Meshty (IRE)** **9** b g Lahib (USA) -Merry Devil (IRE) (Sadler s Wells (USA)) 923a$^{7}$ ><

**Mesmerised** **4** b f Merdon Melody-Gracious Imp (USA) (Imp Society (USA)) 443$^{13}$ 530$^{9}$ 572$^{14}$ 608$^{13}$ 1568$^{6}$ 2017$^{7}$ 2369$^{10}$2520$^{12}$ >**19a 51f**<

**Messe De Minuit (IRE)** **3** ch c Grand Lodge (USA) -Scrimshaw (Selkirk (USA)) 1416$^{9}$ 3985$^{3}$ 4618$^{6}$ >**70a 78f**<

**Meteorite Sun (USA)** **6** b g Miesque s Son (USA) -Myth To Reality (FR) (Sadler s Wells (USA)) 1172$^{8}$ 1503$^{3}$ >**73f**<

**Methodical** **2** b f Lujain (USA) -Simple Logic (Aragon) 4048$^{4}$ 4936$^{9}$ 5609$^{5}$ 6356$^{19}$ >**61f**<

**Meticulous** **6** gr g Eagle Eyed (USA) -Careful (IRE) (Distinctly North (USA)) 439$^{7}$ 497$^{7}$ 583$^{9}$ 682$^{10}$ 713$^{12}$ 823$^{8}$ 1190$^{8}$1533$^{8}$ 1824$^{13}$ 2229$^{6}$ >**15a 17f**<

**Metolica** **2** b f Diktat-South Sea Bubble (IRE) (Bustino) 1735$^{11}$ 2141$^{11}$ 4625$^{11}$ >**16f**<

**Mexican (USA)** **5** b g Pine Bluff (USA) -Cuando Quiere (USA) (Affirmed (USA)) 1393$^{19}$ 1720$^{7}$ 2231$^{3}$ 3614$^{5}$ 3804$^{2}$ 6466$^{7}$ >**44a 58f**<

**Mexican Pete** **4** b g Atraf-Eskimo Nel (IRE) (Shy Groom (USA)) 1539$^{15}$ 1928$^{3}$ 2116$^{8}$ 2471$^{2}$ 2671$^{7}$ 3207$^{4}$ 3692$^{4}$ 4019$^{3}$4453$^{2}$ 4572$^{6}$ 5303$^{9}$ >**49a 85f**<

**Mezereon** **4** b f Alzao (USA) -Blown-Over (Ron s Victory (USA)) 602$^{7}$ 1479$^{7}$ >**55a 55f**<

**Mezuzah** **4** b g Barathea (IRE) -Mezzogiorno (Unfuwain (USA)) 1284$^{8}$ 2687$^{5}$ 3212$^{9}$ 6043$^{16}$ 6210$^{10}$ 6520$^{13}$ >**80f**<

**M For Magic** **5** ch g First Trump-Celestine (Skyliner) 4309$^{5}$ 5081$^{2}$ 5525$^{4}$ 5801$^{5}$ 6200$^{14}$ >**51f**<

**Michabo (IRE)** **3** b g Robellino (USA) -Mole Creek (Unfuwain (USA)) 2401$^{4}$ 2950$^{3}$ 3245$^{2}$ 3843$^{6}$ 4402$^{2}$ (4693) 5074$^{3}$ 5732$^{11}$ >**85f**<

**Michaels Dream (IRE)** **5** b g Spectrum (IRE) -Stormswept (USA) (Storm Bird (CAN)) 568$^{6}$ 2216$^{3}$ 2235$^{3}$ 2449$^{11}$ 2501$^{4}$ 3018$^{12}$ 5144$^{10}$ >**52 a 52 f**<

**Michaels Pride (IRE)** **2** b f Distant View (USA) -Ruacana Falls (USA) (Storm Bird (CAN)) 6545$^{10}$ >**31f**<

**Michelle Ma Belle (IRE)** **4** b f Shareef Dancer (USA) -April Magic (Magic Ring (IRE)) 960$^{8}$ 1229$^{2}$ 1294$^{2}$ 2064$^{8}$ 2284$^{14}$ 4067$^{7}$ (4403) 4614$^{13}$ 5075$^{12}$5730$^{16}$ >**79a 82f**<

**Michelucci (FR)** **2** b c Zieten (USA) -Terlana (Distant Relative) 4597a$^{6}$ >**79f**<

**Mickehaha** **2** b c Lake Coniston (IRE) -Minnehaha (Be My Chief (USA)) 3870$^{8}$ >**34f**<

**Mickey Boggitt** **2** b g Mind Games-Valldemosa (Music Boy) 2388$^{11}$ 2755$^{7}$ ><

**Mickey Pearce (IRE)** **2** b c Rossini (USA) -Lucky Coin (Hadeer) 3588$^{16}$ 4081$^{10}$ 4681$^{13}$ 4907$^{8}$ >**39f**<

**Mickledo** **2** b c Perryston View-Ever So Lonely (Headin Up) 3925$^{11}$ 4776$^{9}$ >**47f**<

**Mickledor (FR)** **4** ch f Lake Coniston (IRE) -Shamasiya (FR) (Vayrann) 2359$^{8}$ 2556$^{13}$ 2778$^{3}$ 3148$^{8}$ (3533) (3735) 4013$^{13}$ 4557$^{8}$ 5081$^{3}$ 5346$^{6}$5639$^{5}$ 5833$^{6}$ >**60f**<

**Micklegate** **3** b f Dracula (AUS) -Primulette (Mummy s Pet) 2937$^{4}$ 3517$^{4}$ 3817$^{12}$ 5448$^{P}$ >**60f**<

**Midas Eyes (USA)** **4** b c Touch Gold (USA) -Bayou Plans (USA) (Bayou Hebert (USA)) 6487a$^{10}$ >**118a**<

**Midas Way** **4** ch g Halling (USA) -Arietta s Way (IRE) (Darshaan) 4932$^{2}$ 5435$^{7}$ 5784$^{3}$ 6215$^{23}$ >**105f**<

**Midcap (IRE)** **2** b f Entrepreneur-Tis Juliet (USA) (Alydar (USA)) 3904$^{12}$ 4272$^{6}$ 4706$^{8}$ 5349$^{3}$ 5909$^{6}$ >**72f**<

**Middle Earth (USA)** **2** ch c Dixieland Band (USA) -Lite Twilight (USA) (Twilight Agenda (USA)) 4191$^{2}$ 4844$^{8}$ 6158$^{2}$ >**77a 74+f**<

**Middle Eastern** **2** b c Mujahid (USA) -Swissmatic (Petong) 3313$^{5}$ 4487$^{4}$ 5233$^{10}$ 5606$^{9}$ >**65f**<

**Middleham Park (IRE)** **4** b g Revoque (IRE) -Snap Crackle Pop (IRE) (Statoblest) 823$^{2}$ 2660$^{7}$ 3060$^{9}$ 4015$^{10}$ 6550$^{4}$ >**56a 57f**<

**Middleham Rose** **3** b f Dr Fong (USA) -Shallop (Salse (USA)) 532$^{6}$ 611$^{6}$ 2014$^{2}$ 2760$^{14}$ 4927$^{5}$ >**34a 34f**<

**Middlemarch (IRE)** **4** ch c Grand Lodge (USA) -Blanche Dubois (Nashwan (USA)) 1107$^{7}$ 1849a$^{4}$ 2066$^{13}$ 2894$^{5}$ 3355a$^{8}$ >**113f**<

**Middlemiss (IRE)** **4** b f Midhish-Teresa Deevey (Runnett) 1580$^{7}$ 1723$^{10}$ 1860$^{2}$ >**24a 22 f**<

**Middlethorpe** **7** b g Noble Patriarch-Prime Property (IRE) (Tirol) (1103) 1198$^{5}$ 1326$^{6}$ 5229$^{7}$ 6047$^{10}$ >**73f**<

**Middleton Grey** **6** gr g Ashkalani (IRE) -Petula (Petong) 507$^{7}$ 968$^{3}$ 1013$^{2}$ 1225$^{12}$ 2614$^{3}$ 3321$^{5}$ 3779$^{2}$ (4751) 6477$^{14}$ >**95a 74f**<

**Midges Pride** **4** b g Puissance-It s All Academic (IRE) (Mazaad) 824$^{10}$ >**51a 44f**<

**Midmaar (IRE)** **3** b c Cape Cross (IRE) -Khazinat El Dar (USA) (Slew O Gold (USA)) 3614$^{10}$ 4096$^{9}$ 4604$^{12}$ 5002$^{10}$ >**52a 70f**<

**Midnight Arrow** 6 b m Robellino (USA) -Princess Oberon (IRE) (Fairy King (USA)) 3734[15] 4260[8] >**45f**<

**Midnight Ballard (USA)** 3 bb g Mister Baileys-Shadow Music (USA) (Shadeed (USA)) 1413[6] 1975[4] 2207[2] 2378[15] (3261) 3884[8] 5299[19] *5912[9] 6222[11]* >**59a 71f**<

**Midnight Grace (IRE)** 2 b f Night Shift (USA) -Adamparis (Robellino (USA)) 3859a[12] >**88f**<

**Midnight In Moscow (IRE)** 2 b g Soviet Star (USA) -Solar Display (USA) (Diesis) 2447[6] 4761[14] 4861[9] >**38f**<

**Midnight Lace** 2 ch f Tomba-Royal Passion (Ahonoora) 3382[9] 3741[9] 5847[3] 6356[12] >**65f**<

**Midnight Mambo (USA)** 4 b f Kingmambo (USA) -Witching Hour (FR) (Fairy King (USA)) *760[5] 996[5] 1079[7]* 4818[12] 5175[14] 5285[2] >**46a 49f**<

**Midnight Parkes** 5 br g Polar Falcon (USA) -Summerhill Spruce (Windjammer (USA)) 1974[20] 2735[4] 3010[8] 3098[3] 3339[5] 3446[9] 3606[3] (3920) 4452[12]5242[9] 5440[3] 5562[13] 5754[7] 6144[3] >**78f**<

**Midnight Prince** 3 b g Dracula (AUS) -Phylian (Glint Of Gold) 3622[6] 4259[5] 4628[8] >**48f**<

**Midnight Promise** 3 b g Aragon-Uninvited (Be My Guest (USA)) *613[7] 816[13]* >**27a**<

**Midnight Tycoon** 2 b c Marju (IRE) -Midnight Allure (Aragon) (1930) 2570[3] 3224[4] 3924[9] >**86f**<

**Midshipman** 6 b h Executive Man-Midler (Comedy Star (USA)) *485[7] 600[16] 1030[9]* 1272[7] 1329[17] 1715[3] 2120[10] 2595[9]*3023[2] 3380[2] 3614[2] 4096[4]* 5175[10] 5733[6] *6225[5](6576)* >**69a 56f**<

**Midshipman Easy (USA)** 3 ch g Irish River (FR) -Winger (In The Wings) 1508[3] 2001[2] 2562[11] 3292[7] 3866[6] 4443[14] 6183[10] >**74f**<

**Mighty Empire (IRE)** 2 b c Second Empire (IRE) -Barnabas (ITY) (Slip Anchor) 2470[7] 3818[14] 4016[4] (4524) 5417[2] 5719[7] >**79f**<

**Mighty Max** 6 b g Well Beloved-Jokers High (USA) (Vaguely Noble) *483[10]* >**32a 45f**<

**Mighty Pip (IRE)** 8 b g Pips Pride-Hard To Stop (Hard Fought) 5658[12] 5928[5] >**53da 56f**<

**Migration** 8 b g Rainbow Quest (USA) -Armeria (USA) (Northern Dancer) 1754[9] *2126[10]* 3682[10] 3917[17] >**36a 36f**<

**Mijdaaf (FR)** 3 b c Mtoto-Zobaida (IRE) (Green Desert (USA)) 2888[6] 3607[2] >**84f**<

**Mikado** 3 b c Sadler s Wells (USA) -Free At Last (Shirley Heights) 3333a[4] 4215[4] 4858[3] 5463[5] (5962a) >**118f**<

**Mikao (IRE)** 3 b g Tagula (IRE) -Oumaladia (IRE) (Waajib) 1794[5] 2900[3] 3603[2] 4492[4] *5217[2]* (5999) >**55+a 76f**<

**Mikasa (IRE)** 4 b g Victory Note (USA) -Resiusa (ITY) (Niniski (USA)) *613[10] 1101[7]* 1263[8] 1867[3] 2214[8] *2454[10]* 3041[5] 3518[10]3835[11] 4007[9] 4421[6] >**26a 30f**<

**Mikes Mate** 3 b g Komaite (USA) -Pitcairn Princess (Capricorn Line) 1771[14] 2145[12] 2653[13] ><

**Milan All Stars (IRE)** 3 b c Red Ransom (USA) -Thakhayr (Sadler s Wells (USA)) 1306a[7] ><

**Military Two Step (IRE)** 3 b g General Monash (USA) -Con Dancer (Shareef Dancer (USA)) 1214[14] 1755[13] 2036[9] 2660[9] 5926[11] 6228[14] >**43a 44f**<

**Milk And Sultana** 4 b f Millkom-Premier Princess (Hard Fought) 1606[13] 2835[6] 3128[9] 3682[8] 3774[2] 4080[11] 4196[2] 4911[4](5267) (5459) 5622[4] 5869[15] *5956[3]* 6083[7] *6278[8]* >**73a 67f**<

**Milk It Mick** 3 b c Millkom-Lunar Music (Komaite (USA)) *1239[2]* 1459[5] 1764[8] 4317[3] 4873[3] 5439[2] >**106+a 118f**<

**Millafonic** 4 b c Zafonic (USA) -Milligram (Mill Reef (USA)) 2527[6] 3034[8] 3482[8] 6354[12] >**100f**<

**Millagros (IRE)** 4 b f Pennekamp (USA) -Grey Galava (Generous (IRE)) 1931[11] 2258[4] 2493[4] 3082[6] 3880[3] 4258[3] (4903) 5304[3] 5821[3]6115[4] *6579[9]* >**70a 77 f**<

**Millbag (IRE)** 3 b c Cape Cross (IRE) -Play With Fire (FR) (Priolo (USA)) (1706) 2294[7] 3350a[5] >**107f**<

**Mill By The Stream** 2 b g Lujain (USA) -Lonesome (Night Shift (USA)) 2300[14] 2860[10] 4149[12] 4498[6] 5989[18] 6272[9] >**49f**<

**Mill Emerald** 7 b m Old Vic-Milinetta (Milford) *568[12]* ><

**Millemix (FR)** 3 bl c Linamix (FR) -Milesime (USA) (Riverman (USA)) (1654a) 2159a[2] >**115f**<

**Millenary** 7 b h Rainbow Quest (USA) -Ballerina (IRE) (Dancing Brave (USA)) 1703[3] (2067) 4832[3] (5415) (6218) >**122f**<

**Mill End Chateau** 2 ch g Paris House-Mill End Quest (King s Signet (USA)) 2388[9] 2858[12] >**41f**<

**Mill End Teaser** 3 b f Mind Games-Mill End Quest (King s Signet (USA)) *657[10]* >**25a 38f**<

**Millenio (GER)** 4 ch c Big Shuffle (USA) -Molto In Forma (GER) (Surumu (GER)) *2883[2] 3023[15]* >**68a**<

**Millenium Mambo (FR)** 4 ch c Dernier Empereur (USA) -Blue Mary (FR) (Fabulous Dancer (USA)) 1435a[7] >**105f**<

**Millennium Force** 6 b g Bin Ajwaad (IRE) -Jumairah Sun (IRE) (Scenic) 1758[8] 2044[16] 2623[4] 3361a[2] 3730[3] 3967a[3] 4745[8] 5291[8]5668a[4] 5781[9] 5972a[5] 6345[2] 6572[2] >**111f**<

**Millennium Hall** 5 b g Saddlers Hall (IRE) -Millazure (USA) (Dayjur (USA)) 1660[13] 1783[6] 2038[3] 2615[3] (2782) (2978) 3199[12] 3474[6] 3740[6] 4826[13]4990[6] 5058[7] 5519[6] >**69f**<

**Miller Hill** 2 b g Prince Sabo-Atlantic Heiress (Thowra (FR)) 1960[12] *2124[2]* 2194[8] >**38a**<

**Millfields Dreams** 5 b g Dreams End-Millfields Lady (Sayf El Arab (USA)) (2836) 3043[11] 3698[12] 3941[11] 4154[7] 4617[6] 5261[10] 5408[8] 5736[7]6058[5] >**65f**<

**Millietom (IRE)** 3 b g General Monash (USA) -June Lady (Junius (USA)) *718[9]* >**22a**<

**Millinsky (USA)** 3 ch f Stravinsky (USA) -Millyant (Primo Dominie) 2675[6] 3179[3] 4440[2] 5253[3] 5845[2] >**66f**<

**Millionaia (IRE)** 3 b f Peintre Celebre (USA) -Moonlight Dance (USA) (Alysheba (USA)) 2925a[2] >**115f**<

**Million Percent** 5 b g Ashkalani (IRE) -Royal Jade (Last Tycoon) 1825[11] 2132[6] 2467[2] 3090[2] 3324[6] 3778[6] 5603[9] >**75a 91f**<

**Million Wishes** 2 b f Darshaan-Moonlight s Box (USA) (Nureyev (USA)) 4382a[6] 5922a[5] >**97f**<

**Millkom Elegance** 5 b m Millkom-Premier Princess (Hard Fought) 3411[8] 4605[3] 5587[11] >**51f**<

**Millquista D Or** 2 b f Millkom-Gild The Lily (Ile De Bourbon (USA)) 5792[17] *6223[7]* >**41a**<

**Millstreet** 5 ch g Polish Precedent (USA) -Mill Path (Mill Reef (USA)) 4285[8] 4834[5] 5483a[8] >**117f**<

**Millville** 4 ch g Millkom-Miss Topville (FR) (Top Ville) *(555) 770[9] (887) (1054)* 1401[8] 4345[5] 4831[4] 5288[5] 5919[13] 6346[2]6573[10] >**90+a 93f**<

**Millybaa (USA)** 4 b f Anabaa (USA) -Millyant (Primo Dominie) 1893a[2] 2117[4] 2719a[7] 4779[12] 5121[4] 5661a[8] 5893[8] 6104a[9]6572[10] >**104f**<

**Milly Golightly** 3 b f Mind Games-Milliscent (Primo Dominie) 1972[11] 2250[6] 2962[8] >**38f**<

**Milly s Lass** 6 b m Mind Games-Millie s Lady (IRE) (Common Grounds) *443[7]* >**40a 40 f**<

**Milly Waters** 3 b f Danzero (AUS) -Chilly Waters (Polar Falcon (USA)) 6147[5] *6497[5]* >**86a 83f**<

**Mimas Girl** 5 b m Samim (USA) -Cocked Hat Girl (Ballacashtal (CAN)) *502[5] 572[9] 656[5] 780[3] 824[7] 875[9] 998[13]1094[3] 1446[6]* >**40a 28f**<

**Mimic** 4 b f Royal Applause-Stripanoora (Ahonoora) 1974[13] 3195[8] 4090[10] 4522[9] (4687) 4854[5] 5526[11] 6131[11] *6293[3]* >**76a 76f**<

**Mimi Mouse** 2 br f Diktat-Shifty Mouse (Night Shift (USA)) 1449[6] 2234[4] 2860[3] (3370) (4150) 5392[14] 5602[8] >**86f**<

**Mina Alsalaam** 2 b f Lujain (USA) -Rain And Shine (FR) (Rainbow Quest (USA)) 3741[15] 4364[13] >**22f**<

**Mind Alert** 3 b g Mind Games-Bombay Sapphire (Be My Chief (USA)) 2269[11] 3122[2] 3523[15] 4340[8] 5674[9] 5862[9] 6199[5] *(6499) 6580[5]* >**66a 70f**<

**Mindful** 2 b c Mind Games-Blushing Victoria (Weldnaas (USA)) 1128[11] *1264[6] 2812[10]* 5209[13] >**33a 35f**<

**Mind Play** 3 b f Mind Games-Diplomatist (Dominion) *736[6] 804[9]* >**27a 21f**<

**Mindset (IRE)** 3 b f Vettori (IRE) -Eden (IRE) (Polish Precedent (USA)) 4683[8] >**71f**<

**Mind The Time** 3 b g Mind Games-Rare Indigo (Timeless Times (USA)) *569[9] 774[6] 1089[4]* 4021[9] >**32a**<

**Mine (IRE)** 6 b h Primo Dominie-Ellebanna (Tina s Pet) 1469[2] 2044[3] (2283) (2969) 3539[5] 4341[2] 4889[7] 5462[5] 5781[3] >**116f**<

**Mine Behind** 4 b g Sheikh Albadou-Arapi (IRE) (Arazi (USA)) (1504) 1663[6] 2132[2] 2261[2] 2488[8] 2682[7] 3324[12] (3775) 4152[12] 4614[16]5299[7] (5550) 5704[4] 6071[12] 6267[4] >**80a 96f**<

**Mineko** 2 b f Nashwan (USA) -Musetta (IRE) (Cadeaux Genereux) 6470[8] >**73f**<

**Mineral Star (IRE)** 2 b c Monashee Mountain (USA) -Summit Talk (Head For Heights) 5718[9] 6072[3] >**75f**<

**Minerwa (GER)** 4 b f Protektor (GER) -Marousskia (GER) (Feenpark (GER)) 3816a[13] ><

**Ming The Merciless** 4 b g Hector Protector (USA) -Sundae Girl (USA) (Green Dancer (USA)) *459[5] 545[6]* >**44a 69df**<

**Mingun (USA)** 4 bb c A.P. Indy (USA) -Miesque (USA) (Nureyev (USA)) 5962a[3] 6216[8] >**119f**<

**Ming Vase** 2 b c Vettori (IRE) -Minstrel s Dance (CAN) (Pleasant Colony (USA)) 1960[6] *3377[2] 3611[5]* 4676[6] 5188[8] 5989[5] 6272[3] >**54a 58f**<

**Minimum Bid** 3 b f First Trump-La Noisette (Rock Hopper) 2482[9] 3084[13] 3628[2] 3935[9] *4025[2]* 5219[10] 5425[10] >**62a 56f**<

**Minirina** 4 b f Mistertopogigo (IRE) -Fabulous Rina (FR) (Fabulous Dancer (USA)) *898[8] 1596[4] 1886[4] 2183[7]* 2620[8] >**25a 25f**<

**Minister Eric (USA)** 3 ch c Old Trieste (USA) -Musical Minister (USA) (Deputy Minister (CAN)) *1781a[16]* >**109a**<

**Minivet** 9 b g Midyan (USA) -Bronzewing (Beldale Flutter (USA)) *461[7]* 3149[5] 4990[4] (5479) 6533[9] >**16a 63f**<

**Mink Mitten** 2 b f Polish Precedent (USA) -Trefoil (FR) (Blakeney) 4292[10] 6091[8] >**51f**<

**Minnesinger** 2 b f Fraam-Rose Alto (Adonijah) 6336[7] >**29f**<

**Minnesota (USA)** 2 ch c Silver Hawk (USA) -Coco (USA) (Storm Bird (CAN)) 3192[2] (3931) 4639[3] 5565[3] >**83f**<

**Minnie s Mystery (FR)** 6 gr m Highest Honor (FR) -Madary (CAN) (Green Desert (USA)) 2343a[3] ><

**Minority Report** 4 b g Rainbow Quest (USA) -Queen Sceptre (IRE) (Fairy King (USA)) 2517[3] 3154[8] 4063[2] 4772[12] >**81f**<

**Minstrel Hall** 5 b m Saddlers Hall (IRE) -Mindomica (Dominion) 1867[4] 3796[5] 4005[7] >**58f**<

**Minstrel s Double** 3 ch g Jumbo Hirt (USA) -Hand On Heart (IRE) (Taufan (USA)) 3896[5] 5196[10] >**29f**<

**Mintlaw** 2 b f Mujahid (USA) -Rynavey (Rousillon (USA)) 4532[2] 6111[6] (6530) >**76+f**<

**Mi Odds** 8 b g Sure Blade (USA) -Vado Via (Ardross) *(641) 1009[5] 1062[14]* 1109[10] 2272[8] 3781[10] 5554[11] >**101a 62f**<

**Mirabilis (USA)** 2 b f Lear Fan (USA) -Media Nox (Lycius (USA)) 5979a[9] 6529a[2] >**102f**<

**Miracle Baby** 2 b f Atraf-Musica (Primo Dominie) 6543[7] >**46f**<

**Mirage Prince (IRE)** 2 ch g Desert Prince (IRE) -Belle Bijou (Midyan (USA)) 1390[6] 2234[10] 3336[6] 4208[5] 4872[4] 5200[13] >**71f**<

**Mirasol Princess** 3 ch f Ali-Royal (IRE) -Yanomami (USA) (Slew O Gold (USA)) 1673[8] 2181[7] 2264[4] 2889[6] 3628[6] *3849[6]* 4043[4] 4400[15](4585) 5117[7] 5563[3] 5949[9] >**74a 79f**<

**Mirjan (IRE)** 8 b g Tenby-Mirana (IRE) (Ela-Mana-Mou) 1316[3] (3310) 6215[7] >**99f**<

**Misaro (GER)** 3 b g Acambaro (GER) -Misniniski (Niniski (USA)) 1956[8] 2569[5] 3295[6] 4827[2] 5193[4] 5605[13] >**80f**<

**Misbehaviour** 5 b g Tragic Role (USA) -Exotic Forest (Dominion) *536[13] 860[7] 947[8]* >**34a**<

**Mis Chicaf (IRE)** 3 b f Prince Sabo-Champagne Season (USA) (Vaguely Noble) 1775[2] (2238) (2457) 2897[18] >**21a 94f**<

**Mischief** 8 ch g Generous (IRE) -Knight s Baroness (Rainbow Quest (USA)) 3018[14] 4457[P] >**49a 46f**<

**Mishap** 2 b f Mark Of Esteem (IRE) -Classic Colleen (IRE) (Sadler s Wells (USA)) 6226[14] ><

**Miskina** 3 b f Mark Of Esteem (IRE) -Najmat Alshemaal (IRE) (Dancing Brave (USA)) 1309[13] *1627[3]* 1932[7] *(2451)* 4902[5] 6097[15] *6537[4]* >**64+a 51f**<

**Miss Adelaide (IRE)** 3 b f Alzao (USA) -Sweet Adelaide (USA) (The Minstrel (CAN)) *1059[4]* 1250[4] 2257[2] 3139[7] >**65a 66f**<

**Missatacama (IRE)** 2 b f Desert Style (IRE) -Delta Town (USA) (Sanglamore (USA)) *6155[4] 6492[5]* >**71a**<

**Miss Bear (IRE)** 2 b f Orpen (USA) -The Poachers Lady (IRE) (Salmon Leap (USA)) 5307[10] 6067[9] >**43f**<

**Miss Cassia** 2 b f Compton Place-Miller s Melody (Chief Singer) 1399[3] 2884[2] 3770[S] 3986[3] (5078) 5648[17] 5839[6] >**74 f**<

**Miss Celerity** 4 b f Compton Place-Film Buff (Midyan (USA)) *520[11] 665[10] 873[4] 949[10]* 1274[13] *1403[10] 4925[11]* >**39a 26f**<

**Miss Ceylon** 4 b f Brief Truce (USA) -Five Islands (Bairn (USA)) *2227[10]* 3249[11] 3864[19] 4211[7] 4626[16] 5949[13] 6526[11] >**41a 41f**<

**Miss Champers (IRE)** 4 bb f Grand Lodge (USA) -Katherine Gorge (USA) (Hansel (USA)) *564[9] (627) (737) 763[4] 960[9]* >**75a 50 f**<

**Miss Chancelot** 3 b f Forzando-Suedoro (Hard Fought) 3410[12] 4351[8] 6004[8] *6280[11]* >**6a 1f**<

**Miss Chapman (IRE)** 3 b f Imperial Ballet (IRE) -Magnetic Point (USA) (Bering) 4251a[17] >**59f**<

**Miss Childrey (IRE)** 3 ch f Dr Fong (USA) -Blazing Glory (IRE) (Glow (USA)) 1256a[5] 1980a[3] 2330a[13] 2903a[9] 5162a[8] 5439[7] 5811[12] >**98f**<

**Miss Cotswold Lady** 2 b f Averti (IRE) -Celtic Bay (USA) (Green Dancer (USA)) 2544[5] 2940[4] 3272[2] 3583[8] 5351[8] 5738[20] *5954[11]* >**13a 67f**<

**Miss Cuisina** 2 b f Vettori (IRE) -Rewardia (IRE) (Petardia) 3083[16] *3377[8]* 4907[9] >**31f**<

**Miss Danbys** 9 b m Charmer-Dohty Baby (Hittite Glory) *2228[6]* >**5a**<

**Miss Dangerous** 9 b m Komaite (USA) -Khadine (Astec) *1178[11]* >**7a**<

**Miss De Bois** 7 ch m Elmaamul (USA) -Petite Melusine (IRE) (Fairy King (USA)) 4423[12] 5006[8] 5408[17] >**15f**<

**Miss Defying** 2 b f Shambo-Dugy (Risk Me (FR)) 5620[11] ><

**Miss Dinamite** 2 b f Polar Prince (IRE) -Over The Moon (Beveled (USA)) 5792[18] ><

**Missed A Beat** 2 b f Mister Baileys-Lonely Heart (Midyan (USA)) 2300[8] 2761[4] 4016[14] (5376) 5767[5] 6356[20] >**72f**<

**Missed Turn** 2 b f Mind Games-Miss Beverley (Beveled (USA)) *1735[5]* 1970[4] *2124[4]* 4017[6] 4797[9] 6003[12] >**29a 42f**<

**Missella (IRE)** 2 gr f Danehill (USA) -Delage (Bellypha) 6118[16] 6336[4] >**49f**<

**Miss Eloise** 3 b f Efisio-Zaima (IRE) (Green Desert (USA)) 1874[6] 2688[2] 3117[6] 3312[9] (3473) 3746[8] 3981[11] 4628[9] 5293[13] >**56f**<

**Miss Emma (IRE)** 4 b f Key Of Luck (USA) -Disregard That (IRE) (Don t Forget Me) 3769a[6] 4357a[2] 5333a[4] (6463a) >**116+f**<

**Miss Faye** 4 bb f Puissance-Bingo Bongo (Petong) 1583[7] 1860[3] 2384[10] >**27f**<

**Miss Fleurie** 4 b f Alzao (USA) -Miss Sancerre (Last Tycoon) *1044[9]* 1174[12] *1444[7] 1917[2]* 3578[6] 3919[7] 4015[18] 6516[2] >**36a 48f**<

**Miss France (FR)** 3 ch f Sabrehill (USA) -Tonic Stream (FR) (Bering) 1320a[3] 2028a[8] 3258a[5] 5969a[2] >**102f**<

**Miss George** 6 b m Pivotal-Brightside (IRE) (Last Tycoon) *(1056)* 1106[9] *1242[7]* 1673[3] 1964[9] 2373[6] 3324[8] 3645[12] 4194[3]4614[11] 4847[3] *5055[10]* 5299[15] *5379[3] 6277[2] (6497)* >**94a 85f**<

**Miss Glory Be** 6 b m Glory Of Dancer-Miss Blondie (USA) (Stop The Music (USA)) *464[11] 700[3] 737[5] 4190[2] 4339[3] 4604[3] 5002[7]*5285[6] 6230[3] >**40 a 47f**<

**Miss Good Time** 2 gr f Timeless Times (USA) -Fort Vally (Belfort (FR)) 1374[9] 1865[6] 2087[9] 3444[6] 3951[6] 4559[5] 5556[6] >**38f**<

**Miss Grace** 4 ch f Atticus (USA) -Jetbeeah (IRE) (Lomond (USA)) 1675[9] *1940[4]* 2284[11] 2573[3] >**76a 57f**<

**Miss Hanks (IRE)** 2 b f Fasliyev (USA) -Akamantis (Kris) (5577a) ><

**Miss Hermione** 2 ch f Bahamian Bounty-Try Vickers (USA) (Fuzzbuster (USA)) *5911[12]* 6226[10] 6563[5] >**58f**<

**Miss Hoofbeats** 3 b f Unfuwain (USA) -Oiselina (FR) (Linamix (FR)) 1465[14] *1740[8] 3305[15]* 4086[10] >**43f**<

**Missie** 4 ch f Compton Place-About Face (Midyan (USA)) 2367[9] 2620[12] >**42f**<

**Missie Baileys** 2 ch f Mister Baileys-Jilly Woo (Environment Friend) 4714[6] *5380[5]* 5695[8] (6127) >**66a 67f**<

**Miss Inkha** 3 b f Intikhab (USA) -Santi Sana (Formidable (USA)) 1400[16] 1794[12] 2842[6] 3246[6] 5038[2] 5293[11] 5773[3] 6083[5] >**66f**<

**Missin Margot** 2 b f Fraam-Abstone Queen (Presidium) 5633[5] *5953[7]* 6008[6] >**38a 35f**<

**Mission Affirmed (USA)** 3 ch g Stravinsky (USA) -Affirmed Legacy (USA) (Affirmed (USA)) *805[9] (955) 1029[5] (1427)* 1957[12] *2988[4]* 3780[10] 4249[5] *4882[2]*5364[3] 5868[8] >**76a 67f**<

**Mission Man** 3 b c Revoque (IRE) -Opopmil (IRE) (Pips Pride) 1111[4] 1386[2] (1942) 2378[4] 3317[7] 3728[4] 4032[5] 4780[7] 5120[11] >**85f**<

**Mission To Mars** 5 b g Muhtarram (USA) -Ideal Candidate (Celestial Storm (USA)) *(618) (844) 971[3]* >**105+a 69f**<

**Miss Issy (IRE)** 4 b f Victory Note (USA) -Shane s Girl (IRE) (Marktingo) *491[3]* >**63a 68f**<

**Miss Ivanhoe (IRE)** 4 b f Selkirk (USA) -Robellino Miss (USA) (Robellino (USA)) 1385[9] 1964[6] 6044[15] >**107f**<

**Miss Jellybean (IRE)** 2 b f Namid-Elfin Queen (IRE) (Fairy King (USA)) 2458[9] 5513[7] 6204[7] >**35f**<

**Miss Judged** 3 b f Case Law-Marie s Crusader (IRE) (Last Tycoon) *420[13] 508[7] 569[6] 728[9] 747[9]* >**46a 29f**<

**Miss Judgement (IRE)** 3 b f Revoque (IRE) -Mugello (Emarati (USA)) *1169[5]* 2380[3] 2942[2] (3151) 3530[3] *3849[8]* 4020[10] (4547) 5219[17]5337[13] 5618[18] 6079[7] >**56a 69f**<

**Miss Kiss** 2 b f Kingsinger (IRE) -Miss Bigwig (Distinctly North (USA)) (3436a) ><

**Miss Koen (IRE)** 5 b m Barathea (IRE) -Fanny Blankers (IRE) (Persian Heights) *773[6] 950[3] (984) 1053[8]* 1188[3] 1297[8] 1463[11] 2167[10] >**56a 60f**<

**Miss Ladybird (USA)** 3 bb f Labeeb-Bird Dance (USA) (Storm Bird (CAN)) 4680[8] >**56a 64f**<

**Miss Lalla S (IRE)** 2 b f Entrepreneur-Lalla s Rock (Ballad Rock) 5390a[10] ><

**Miss Langkawi** 3 gr f Daylami (IRE) -Miss Amanpuri (Alzao (USA)) 1357[10] 1672[9] 6457[3] 6571[12] >**76f**<

**Miss L Augeval** 2 b f Zilzal (USA) -Miss Sancerre (Last Tycoon) 3904[4] (4272) 5149[11] 5939[10] 6306[2] >**81f**<

**Miss Lehman** 6 ch m Beveled (USA) -Lehmans Lot (Oats) 2345[6] >**33f**<

**Miss Librate** 6 b m Librate-Hayley s Lass (Royal Boxer) 1310[8] *1476[8]* >**33f**<

**Miss Lyvennet** 3 ch f Then Again-Precious Girl (Precious Metal) 1197[17] >**49f**<

**Miss Madame (IRE)** 3 b f Cape Cross (IRE) -Cosmic Countess (IRE) (Lahib (USA)) *1678[3]* 2326[3] 2610[6] (4127) 4470[2] (4652) 5304[6] 5698[16] >**58a 76f**<

**Miss Malone (IRE)** 2 b f Daggers Drawn (USA) -Queen Molly (Emarati (USA)) 2786[7] 3286a[7] 3840[2] 4074[4] 4326[9] 5391[14] 5690[5] 5910[7] >**76df**<

**Miss Mambo (USA)** 3 b f Kingmambo (USA) -Troika (USA) (Strawberry Road (AUS)) 2160a[3] 2720a[2] 5940[5] >**108f**<

**Miss Me** 3 b f Marju (IRE) -Sandskip (Sanglamore (USA)) 2720a[9] >**100f**<

**Miss Meggy** 2 b f Pivotal-Selkirk Rose (IRE) (Pips Pride) (2129) (2568) 2970[9] 3599[6] 5143[5] 5391[6] 5626[4] >**95f**<

**Miss Merenda** 3 b f Sir Harry Lewis (USA) -Cool Merenda (IRE) (Glacial Storm (USA)) 1794[15] 2093[7] 2729[9] *6481[4]* >**51a 56f**<

**Miss Millietant** 3 b f Up And At Em-Annie Hall (Saddlers Hall (IRE)) *598[13] 998[6] 1094[8]* >**33a 8f**<

**Miss Monica (IRE)** 3 ch f Grand Lodge (USA) -Bea s Ruby (IRE) (Fairy King (USA)) 1842[6] 2243[4] 3392[3] 5265[14] 6152[11] >**74f**<

**Miss Monza** 3 b f Hazaaf (USA) -Monstrosa (Monsanto (FR)) 4144[8] 4718[10] 4916[3] 5338[12] 5845[8] >**69f**<

**Miss Mytton (USA)** 3 ch f Mt. Livermore (USA) -Sisterella (USA) (Diesis) 4877[15] >**39a 67f**<

**Miss Nashwan (IRE)** 4 b f Nashwan (USA) -Miss Carolina (IRE) (Danehill (USA)) (1776a) 2138a[5] >**105f**<

**Miss Noteriety** 4 b f Victory Note (USA) -Mystic Maid (IRE) (Mujtahid (USA)) *2813[11]* 2979[7] *3801[10]* >**6f**<

**Miss Ocean Monarch** 4 ch f Blue Ocean (USA) -Faraway Grey (Absalom) *1094[11] 1697[7] 1885[8] 2185[9]* 2345[2] 2757[9] 3008[8]3578[7] 4210[13] >**11a 42f**<

**Miss Particular (IRE)** 2 b f Sadler s Wells (USA) -Viz (USA) (Kris S (USA)) 5915[11] >**60f**<

**Miss Patricia** 2 b f Mister Baileys-Zoena (Emarati

(USA)) 3770$^7$ 4364$^7$ 4714$^4$ 5548$^3$ **>76f<**

**Miss Peaches** 6 b m Emperor Jones (USA) -Dear Person (Rainbow Quest (USA)) 533$^2$ 662$^8$ (787) 933$^3$ 1019$^5$ 1244$^4$ 1373$^6$ 2597$^5$3423$^{10}$ **>54a 56f<**

**Miss Pebbles (IRE)** 4 ch f Lake Coniston (IRE) -Sea Of Stone (USA) (Sanglamore (USA)) (1187) 1522$^4$ 2000$^7$ 2226$^7$ 2284$^5$ (3327) 3387$^2$ 4760$^5$ 4950$^{13}$ 5728$^{13}$ **>73 a 78f<**

**Missperon (IRE)** 2 b f Orpen (USA) -Secret Hideaway (USA) (Key To The Mint (USA)) 2213$^5$ 2550$^3$ (3116) 3753$^3$ 4358$^4$ 5434$^{12}$ 5606$^2$ **>79f<**

**Miss Polaris** 3 b f Polar Falcon (USA) -Sarabah (IRE) (Ela-Mana-Mou) 5621$^6$ (5994) 6279$^2$ **>81a 79+f<**

**Miss Poppets** 4 ch f Polar Falcon (USA) -Alifandango (IRE) (Alzao (USA)) 917$^9$ 1229$^{11}$ **>58a 62f<**

**Miss Porcia** 3 ch f Inchinor-Krista (Kris) (2660) 3004$^2$ 3246$^7$ **>20a 57f<**

**Miss Prim** 3 ch f Case Law-Calamanco (Clantime) 6009$^8$ 6275$^8$ **>16a 15f<**

**Miss Procurer (IRE)** 3 b f Entrepreneur-Kariyh (USA) (Shadeed (USA)) 3759$^5$ 4092$^{11}$ 4241$^4$ 4491$^5$ 5018$^3$ **>56 f<**

**Miss Rosie** 2 b f Xaar-Disallowed (IRE) (Distinctly North (USA)) 2470$^4$ 4208$^4$ 4606$^7$ **>67f<**

**Miss Sally (IRE)** 2 b f Danetime (IRE) -Evictress (IRE) (Sharp Victor (USA)) 5681a$^4$ **>77f<**

**Miss Serendipity (IRE)** 3 b f Key Of Luck (USA) -Disregard That (IRE) (Don t Forget Me) 1893a$^7$ 6104a$^{16}$ **>88f<**

**Miss Shangri La** 3 b f Rainbow Quest (USA) -Miss Rinjani (Shirley Heights) 1441$^{11}$ 2950$^9$ 3392$^6$ 4519$^{10}$ **>44f<**

**Miss Sharapova (IRE)** 2 b f Almutawakel-Dolcezza (FR) (Lichine (USA)) 4272$^4$ **>74f<**

**Miss St Albans** 3 b f Robellino (USA) -Alieria (IRE) (Lomond (USA)) 1466$^{12}$ 1912$^7$ 2505$^{15}$ 2729$^{10}$ 6228$^{20}$ **>26f<**

**Miss Sudbrook (IRE)** 2 ch f Daggers Drawn (USA) -Missed Opportunity (IRE) (Exhibitioner) 4621$^{11}$ 5688$^4$ 5953$^{10}$ **>5a 61f<**

**Miss The Boat** 2 b f Mtoto-Missed Again (High Top) 5247$^2$ **>79f<**

**Miss Tilly** 3 b f Nicolotte-Little White Lies (Runnett) 1796$^{14}$ 2766$^{17}$ **>34f<**

**Miss Tolerance (USA)** 2 ch f Mt. Livermore (USA) -Acquiesce (Generous (IRE)) 5694$^{12}$ 6126$^3$ 6394$^7$ **>61a 71f<**

**Miss Trendsetter (IRE)** 2 b f Desert Style (IRE) -Chummy s Friend (IRE) (Be My Guest (USA)) 3444$^{18}$ 4010$^8$ 4699$^{15}$ **>17f<**

**Miss Trial** 2 b f Zafonic (USA) -Perfect Alibi (Law Society (USA)) 4844$^6$ 5353$^3$ 5747$^3$ 6196$^3$ **>74f<**

**Miss Trinity** 4 b f Catrail (USA) -Rosy Sunset (IRE) (Red Sunset) 982$^{14}$ 1027$^{10}$ 1206$^9$ 1373$^{19}$ **>70a 63f<**

**Miss Trish (IRE)** 4 b f Danetime (IRE) -Fey Rouge (IRE) (Fayruz) 1634a$^4$ **>98f<**

**Miss Truant** 2 b f Zaha (CAN) -Miss Runaway (Runnett) 1374$^6$ 1670$^6$ **>64f<**

**Missturner (IRE)** 2 b f Danehill Dancer (IRE) -It s Academic (Royal Academy (USA)) 5322a$^{10}$ **>75f<**

**Missus Links (USA)** 3 b f Lure (USA) -Cozisaidso (USA) (Cozzene (USA)) 1464$^5$ 2082$^2$ 2536$^5$ 2875$^{13}$ 3211$^6$ 6001$^4$ 6117$^8$ **>68+a 75f<**

**Miss Wizz** 4 b f Wizard King-Fyas (Sayf El Arab (USA)) 434$^9$ 713$^4$ (780) 1171$^6$ 1699$^4$ 2582$^4$ 2778$^5$ (3269) 4425$^8$4557$^{11}$ 5000$^{13}$ 5639$^{11}$ 6469$^8$ **>34a 52f<**

**Miss Wong One (IRE)** 4 b f Eagle Eyed (USA) -Fakhira (IRE) (Jareer (USA)) 803$^{10}$ **>61a 49f<**

**Miss Woodpigeon** 8 b m Landyap (USA) -Pigeon Loft (IRE) (Bellypha) 3996$^3$ 4476$^7$ **>3a 47f<**

**Missy Cinofaz** 2 ch f Zafonic (USA) -Dancing Wolf (IRE) (Wolfhound (USA)) 5570$^{13}$ 6011$^4$ **>53a 27f<**

**Mistblack** 4 b f Wizard King-Dear Heart (Blakeney) 3801$^8$ **><**

**Mister Arjay (USA)** 4 b c Mister Baileys-Crystal Stepper (USA) (Fred Astaire (USA)) 1773$^9$ 2775$^6$ 6025$^{11}$ 6520$^{11}$ **>74a 84f<**

**Mister Aziz (IRE)** 2 b c Mister Baileys-Aziz Presenting (IRE) (Charnwood Forest (IRE)) 2300$^{10}$ 3611$^8$ 4058$^5$ 5351$^{11}$ **>37a 61f<**

**Mister Bell** 2 gr c Lujain (USA) -Zaragossa (Paris House) 1930$^3$ 2872$^6$ 4081$^{12}$ 5509$^8$ 6080$^{14}$ **>42f<**

**Mister Benji** 5 b g Catrail (USA) -Katy-Q (IRE) (Taufan (USA)) 604$^9$ 686$^5$ 6550$^7$ **>64a 67 f<**

**Mister Buzz** 2 b c Mind Games-Compact Disc (IRE) (Royal Academy (USA)) 2758$^{11}$ 3233$^{11}$ 3760$^8$ 4009$^4$ 5125$^4$ 5234$^{13}$ 6515$^{10}$ **>61f<**

**Mister Chalk** 3 gr c Silver Patriarch (IRE) -B B Glen (Hadeer) 5999$^{18}$ **><**

**Mister Clinton (IRE)** 7 ch g Lion Cavern (USA) -Thewaari (USA) (Eskimo (USA)) 469$^{11}$ 525$^{10}$ 602$^{11}$ 815$^{11}$ 918$^6$ 2803$^3$ 3174$^4$3423$^8$ (3555) 3828$^2$ 4127$^{10}$ (4418) 5020$^6$ 5425$^8$ 5841$^9$ 5868$^9$ **>48a 68f<**

**Mister Completely (IRE)** 3 b g Princely Heir (IRE) -Blue Goose (Belmez (USA)) 840$^2$ 885$^6$ 983$^5$ 1184$^7$ 2380$^{10}$ 2484$^9$ 2886$^{17}$ 3087$^7$(3193) 3612$^6$ 4302$^{10}$ (4941) 5021$^{14}$ 5791$^5$ 5863$^3$ 6438$^3$ **>59a 51f<**

**Mister Elegant** 2 b c Fraam-Risky Valentine (Risk Me (FR)) 3157$^{18}$ 5870$^4$ 6226$^6$ **>64f<**

**Mister Farmer (FR)** 3 ch c Trempolino (USA) -Planoise (FR) (Pampabird) 3359a$^4$ 4039a$^3$ 5500a$^6$ **>104f<**

**Mister Fasliyev (IRE)** 2 b c Fasliyev (USA) -Carisheba (USA) (Alysheba (USA)) 2669a$^6$ 6380a$^9$ **>82f<**

**Mister Genepi** 2 b c Mister Baileys-Ring Queen (USA) (Fairy King (USA)) 3749$^5$ 4315$^2$ 4730$^2$ 5179$^3$ 5437$^7$ 5895$^3$ (6072) **>103f<**

**Mister Graham** 9 b g Rock Hopper-Celestial Air (Rheingold) 1263$^9$ 1547$^4$ 1727$^6$ **>43a 26f<**

**Mister Hight (FR)** 2 bl c Take Risks (FR) -Miss High (FR) (Concorde (USA)) 6503a$^5$ **>88f<**

**Mister Links (IRE)** 4 b c Flying Spur (AUS) -Lady Anna Livia (Ahonoora) 1759$^3$ (2358) **>110f<**

**Mister Mal (IRE)** 8 b g Scenic-Fashion Parade (Mount Hagen (FR)) 866$^{10}$ 1197$^6$ (1526) 2656$^9$ 3836$^7$ 4782$^3$ (4926) 5107$^2$ 5579$^7$ **>65a 64f<**

**Mister Marmaduke** 3 b g Marju (IRE) -Lalique (IRE) (Lahib (USA)) 4280$^4$ 4874$^3$ 5062$^5$ 5474$^8$ 5818$^9$ 6222$^{13}$ **>14a 86f<**

**Mister Merlin (IRE)** 3 ch g Titus Livius (FR) -Official Secret (Polish Patriot (USA)) 5546$^{19}$ 5796$^{20}$ **>29f<**

**Mister Minty (IRE)** 2 b c Fasliyev (USA) -Sorb Apple (IRE) (Kris) 4488$^{13}$ **>12f<**

**Mister Monet (IRE)** 3 b c Peintre Celebre (USA) -Breyani (Commanche Run) 3671$^2$ (3878) (4118) (4539) (4965a) 6216$^P$ **>124+f<**

**Mister Muja (IRE)** 3 gr g Mujadil (USA) -Remiss (IRE) (Indian Ridge) 4683$^7$ 5204$^6$ (6397) **>69a 62f<**

**Misternando** 4 b c Hernando (FR) -Mistinguett (IRE) (Doyoun) 1703$^9$ 1880$^2$ 2533$^6$ 2998$^8$ 3538$^3$ 4270$^3$ **>112f<**

**Mister Putt (USA)** 6 bb g Mister Baileys-Theresita (GER) (Surumu (GER)) 1520$^2$ 6084$^{15}$ **>51a 64f<**

**Mister Quicksand (USA)** 5 ch h Sandpit (BRZ) -Get Friendly Quick (USA) (Perfect Parade (USA)) 2163a$^8$ **><**

**Mister Regent** 3 b g Mind Games-River Of Fortune (IRE) (Lahib (USA)) 1453$^3$ 1975$^8$ 2367$^{12}$ 3622$^{10}$ 5063$^{14}$ 5411$^8$ **>62f<**

**Mister Right (IRE)** 3 ch g Barathea (IRE) -Broken Spirit (IRE) (Slip Anchor) 6132$^3$ 6566$^{10}$ **>59f<**

**Mister Rushby** 4 b g Hamas (IRE) -Final Rush (Final Straw) 572$^{12}$ 1448$^9$ 1697$^9$ **>35a 57df<**

**Mister Sacha (FR)** 3 b c Tiger Hill (IRE) -Miss Sacha (IRE) (Last Tycoon) (2072a) 2721a$^5$ 5169a$^3$ 5967a$^3$ **>116f<**

**Mister Saif (USA)** 3 ch g Miswaki (USA) -Shawgatny (USA) (Danzig Connection (USA)) 1408$^7$ 1795$^U$ 2019$^5$ 2557$^9$ 2642$^4$ 2844$^2$ 3691$^{11}$ 4268$^{12}$ **>85a 92f<**

**Misters Sister** 2 b f Robellino (USA) -Baileys On Line (Shareef Dancer (USA)) 6067$^{14}$ 6309$^7$ 6565$^{13}$ **>41f<**

**Mister Sweets** 5 ch g Nashwan (USA) -Keyboogie (USA) (Lyphard (USA)) 1974$^6$ 2899$^{10}$ (3321) 3755$^5$ 4152$^{14}$ 4837$^{12}$ 4928$^6$ 5798$^{19}$ 5945$^{22}$6094$^9$ 6445$^{20}$ **>76 a 81f<**

**Mister Trickster (IRE)** 3 b c Woodborough (USA) -Tinos Island (IRE) (Alzao (USA)) 1222$^6$ 1365$^{13}$ 1998$^{11}$ (2614) 3180$^{11}$ 4242$^8$ 4871$^{13}$ 5748$^3$ **>68f<**

**Mister Troubridge** 2 ch c Mister Baileys-So True (So Blessed) 5535$^{13}$ 5872$^9$ 6322$^9$ **>45f<**

**Mist Opportunity (IRE)** 2 b g Danetime (IRE) -Lady Of The Mist (IRE) (Digamist (USA)) 2388$^{10}$ 2961$^{11}$ 4135$^8$ 5097$^{12}$ **>43f<**

**Mistral Sky** 5 b g Hurricane Sky (AUS) -Dusk In Daytona (Beveled (USA)) 742$^2$ 847$^{11}$ 968$^{13}$ 1225$^2$ 2064$^{11}$ 2358$^4$ 2483$^3$ 2834$^3$3086$^5$ 3525$^4$ 3841$^7$ (4244) 4459$^2$ 4547$^2$ (4727) 6293$^2$ 6482$^{12}$ **>82a 82f<**

**Mistress Hollie (IRE)** 3 b f Titus Livius (FR) -Soden (IRE) (Mujadil (USA)) 845$^8$ **>31a 2f<**

**Mistress Twister** 3 b f Pivotal-Foreign Mistress (Darshaan) 2962$^3$ 3096$^3$ 3622$^8$ 4260$^3$ 5223$^{11}$ (5945) **>78f<**

**Misty Bay** 2 b f Namaqualand (USA) -Paris Mist (Paris House) 3583$^9$ **><**

**Misty Heights** 3 b f Fasliyev (USA) -Mountains Of Mist (IRE) (Shirley Heights) 1485a$^3$ 1980a$^2$ 2330a$^8$ (2711a) 5162a$^{10}$ 5481a$^4$ **>103f<**

**Misty Man (USA)** 6 ch g El Gran Senor (USA) -Miasma (USA) (Lear Fan (USA)) 430$^3$ 532$^5$ (594) 1914$^4$ 1987$^5$ 2228$^5$ 6406$^8$ **>46a 46f<**

**Misty Miller** 2 b c Mind Games-Antonia s Folly (Music Boy) 1359$^5$ 2579$^8$ 2898$^6$ **>57f<**

**Misty Mountain (IRE)** 3 b f Namaqualand (USA) -Lightstorm (IRE) (Darshaan) 3969a$^6$ **>94f<**

**Misty Princess** 2 gr f Paris House-Miss Whittingham (IRE) (Fayruz) 1105$^{11}$ 1399$^5$ 1839$^6$ 2177$^{14}$ 2852$^9$ 3741$^{13}$ 4514$^8$ **>54a 48f<**

**Mitcham (IRE)** 8 br g Hamas (IRE) -Arab Scimetar (IRE) (Sure Blade (USA)) 1354$^{18}$ **>88a 100f<**

**Mitchelland** 2 b f Namaqualand (USA) -Precious Girl (Precious Metal) 1105$^4$ (1248) 1878$^9$ 2655$^6$ 3445$^6$ 3924$^3$ 4445$^5$ 4632$^5$ 4700$^5$5767$^{13}$ 5954$^5$ 6276$^2$ **>61a 72df<**

**Mith Hill** 3 b c Daylami (IRE) -Delirious Moment (IRE) (Kris) 4492$^7$ (4629) (6013) (6450) 6573$^{17}$ **>81+a 75f<**

**Mitraillette (USA)** 2 ch f Miswaki (USA) -Crockadore (USA) (Nijinsky (CAN)) 3296$^6$ 4137$^5$ 4706$^4$ (5377) **>79f<**

**Mitrash** 4 b g Darshaan-L Ideale (USA) (Alysheba (USA)) 5196$^8$ **>64f<**

**Mitsuki** 5 b m Puissance-Surrealist (ITY) (Night Shift (USA)) 3754$^9$ 4104$^5$ 4308$^8$ 5101$^9$ **>65f<**

**Mity Dancer (GER)** 4 br f Alzao (USA) -Molto In Gamba (GER) (Surumu (GER)) 2138a$^{10}$ 3504a$^4$ 4380a$^3$ 4980a$^3$ 5489a$^7$ 6107a$^2$ 6378a$^3$ **>96f<**

**Mitzi Caspar** 3 ch f Kirkwall-Petrovna (IRE) (Petardia) 1022$^7$ 1104$^{15}$ 1507$^{15}$ 1794$^{24}$ 2187$^3$ 2232$^2$ (2815) 3380$^9$4650$^{13}$ 5002$^{14}$ 5552$^{12}$ **>52a 4f<**

**Mix It Up** 3 gr f Linamix (FR) -Hawayah (IRE) (Shareef Dancer (USA)) 1310$^{10}$ **>40a 18f<**

**Mizhar (USA)** 8 bb g Dayjur (USA) -Futuh (USA) (Diesis) 503$^{11}$ 608$^5$ 642$^2$ 685$^5$ 799$^8$ 1283$^{11}$ (1680) 2006$^3$2013$^2$ 2383$^P$ **>63a 55f<**

**Mizz Tee (IRE)** 2 b f Orpen (USA) -D D s Jakette (USA) (Deputy Minister (CAN)) 2071$^2$ (2388) 2568$^5$ **>82+f<**

**Mkuzi** 5 ch h Halling (USA) -African Peace (USA) (Roberto (USA)) 712a$^6$ 849a$^6$ 976a$^8$ 1156a$^5$ (2498a) (3333a) 4784a$^3$ 4977a$^2$ 6218$^8$ **>113f<**

**Moaning Myrtle** 3 br f Desert King (IRE) -Grinning (IRE) (Bellypha) 5382$^4$ 5913$^{11}$ **>61a<**

**Moayed** 5 b g Selkirk (USA) -Song Of Years (IRE) (Shareef Dancer (USA)) (707) 768$^2$ 915$^6$ 1065$^3$ 1246$^3$ (1765) 2488$^{10}$ 2891$^4$ 6191$^{14}$(6496) **>100a 94f<**

**Mobane Flyer** 4 b g Groom Dancer (USA) -Enchant (Lion Cavern (USA)) 3755$^{12}$ 4134$^{10}$ 4624$^6$ 5085$^3$ 5320$^3$ (5518) 5859$^3$ 6311$^2$ 6337$^2$6546$^6$ **>73f<**

**Mobarhen (USA)** 2 bb c Red Ransom (USA) -Fit For A Queen (USA) (Fit To Fight (USA)) 4315$^5$ 4913$^5$ 5302$^2$ 5596$^3$ 6176$^9$ **>77 f<**

**Mobil (CAN)** 4 b c Langfuhr (CAN) -Kinetigal (USA) (Naskra (USA)) 4768a$^9$ **>109f<**

**Mobo-Baco** 7 ch g Bandmaster (USA) -Darakah (Doulab (USA)) 1687$^4$ 1857$^4$ 2170$^9$ 2426$^9$ 2833$^7$ 3103$^7$ (3489) 3697$^5$ 4122$^9$4546$^6$ 5080$^9$ 5260$^4$ 5408$^3$ 5733$^2$ 6550$^2$ **>61a 71f<**

**Mocca (IRE)** 3 b f Sri Pekan (USA) -Ewan (IRE) (Indian Ridge) 1414$^4$ 2107$^5$ (2848) 4367$^6$ 5397$^2$ 5761$^6$ 6257a$^3$ 6571$^5$ **>93f<**

**Mochaccino (IRE)** 2 b f Tagula (IRE) -Cafe Solo (Nomination) 4924$^{14}$ 5209$^8$ 5847$^{12}$ 6359$^{11}$ **>12a 32+f<**

**Mocham Glen (FR)** 7 br g Midyan (USA) -Marsoumeh (USA) (Green Dancer (USA)) 4039a$^5$ **>112f<**

**Model Figure (USA)** 3 b f Distant View (USA) -Sylph (USA) (Alleged (USA)) 4338$^{10}$ **>65f<**

**Modem (IRE)** 7 b g Midhish-Holy Water (Monseigneur (USA)) 715$^{10}$ 947$^B$ **>40a 40f<**

**Modesta (IRE)** 3 b f Sadler s Wells (USA) -Modena (USA) (Roberto (USA)) 1440$^4$ (2093) 2683$^2$ 2997$^8$ 4888$^6$ 5394$^5$ (6443) **>101f<**

**Modesty Blaise (SWE)** 4 br f Mango Express-Singoalla (IRE) (Alwuhush (USA)) (529) 614$^7$ 900$^5$ 6025$^{12}$ **>69a 57f<**

**Modraj** 2 b f Machiavellian (USA) -Saleela (USA) (Nureyev (USA)) 3904$^9$ 4714$^3$ **>75f<**

**Modulor (FR)** 12 gr g Less Ice-Chaumontaise (FR) (Armos) 5710$^{10}$ 6208$^{10}$ **><**

**Modus Vivendi** 4 b c Zafonic (USA) -Monroe (USA) (Sir Ivor) 925a$^8$ **>105f<**

**Mohandas (FR)** 3 b c Lomitas-Mille Espoir (FR) (Mille Balles (FR)) 3863a$^5$ 5329a$^8$ 6263a$^8$ **>105f<**

**Mojalid** 5 bb g Zafonic (USA) -Affair Of State (IRE) (Tate Gallery (USA)) 692a$^8$ **>104f<**

**Mokabra (IRE)** 3 b c Cape Cross (IRE) -Pacific Grove (Persian Bold) 1396$^6$ 1847a$^3$ 2158a$^8$ 3001$^{17}$ **>104f<**

**Mokaraba** 2 ch f Unfuwain (USA) -Muhaba (USA) (Mr Prospector (USA)) 4344$^4$ 4851$^4$ 5407$^2$ 6334$^2$ **>86f<**

**Molcon (IRE)** 3 b g Danetime (IRE) -Wicken Wonder (IRE) (Distant Relative) 1388$^5$ (1702) 1965$^5$ 2309$^3$ 2907$^4$ 3052$^4$ 3205$^{10}$ (4126) 4553$^8$ 4846$^7$5698$^{17}$ 6350$^{10}$ **>88f<**

**Molehill** 3 b f Salse (USA) -Mountain Lodge (Blakeney) 2653$^7$ 3121$^5$ 3608$^4$ 4778$^7$ 5116$^8$ **>63f<**

**Molem** 2 br c Green Desert (USA) -Injaad (Machiavellian (USA)) 5298$^6$ 6306$^4$ **>71f<**

**Molinia** 3 b f Nicolotte-Themeda (Sure Blade (USA)) 1997$^{11}$ 2587$^P$ 2790$^4$ 3155$^{11}$ 3949$^4$ 4338$^7$ 4817$^3$ 5552$^{14}$(6405) **>62a 59+f<**

**Molly Dancer** 2 b f Emarati (USA) -Perfect Partner (Be My Chief (USA)) 3840$^9$ 4099$^9$ 4797$^3$ 5174$^5$ 5558$^6$ **>63f<**

**Molly Marie (IRE)** 2 b f Fasliyev (USA) -Snoozeandyoulose (IRE) (Scenic) 2544$^2$ 3296$^4$ 3950$^6$ 4488$^2$ 4890$^7$ 5391$^{10}$ 5434$^9$ 5771$^2$ **>78f<**

**Molly Mello (GER)** 5 gr m Big Shuffle (USA) -Manitoba (GER) (Surumu (GER)) 784a$^3$ 786a$^6$ **>93f<**

**Molly Moon (IRE)** 3 gr f Primo Dominie-Snowing (Tate Gallery (USA)) 2131$^{14}$ 3702$^8$ 3995$^7$ **>79f<**

**Mollyputtheketelon (USA)** 3 b f Rainbow Quest (USA) -Nemea (USA) (The Minstrel (CAN)) 3969a$^8$ **>89f<**

**Molly s Secret** 6 b m Minshaanshu Amad (USA) -Secret Miss (Beveled (USA)) (549) 609$^8$ 777$^9$ 966$^{12}$ 3423$^3$ 4015$^7$ 4473$^3$ 5021$^6$5350$^3$ **>56a 56f<**

**Mollzam (IRE)** 2 b c Danehill (USA) -Matilda Bay (IRE) (Indian Ridge) 3241$^9$ 3749$^{12}$ **>48f<**

**Molotov** 4 b g Efisio-Mindomica (Dominion) (2350) 2663$^{10}$ 3151$^{17}$ 4181$^4$ (5016) 5282$^3$ 5452$^3$ 5597$^4$ (6246) **>46 a 63f<**

**Molto Bello (USA)** 2 b c Spinning World (USA) -Explore The Gold (USA) (Fast Gold (USA)) 4184a$^7$ 6320a$^8$ **>100f<**

**Mombassa (IRE)** 4 b g Mujadil (USA) -Twilight Tango (Groom Dancer (USA)) 3961a$^{18}$ 4371a$^{11}$ 6193$^8$ **>108f<**

**Moments I Treasure (USA)** 3 ch f Mt. Livermore (USA) -Munnaya (USA) (Nijinsky (CAN)) 1015$^6$ 1394$^9$ **>53a 64f<**

**Moments Of Joy** 4 b f Darshaan-My Emma (Marju (IRE)) 1792$^7$ **>110f<**

**Mommkin** 3 b f Royal Academy (USA) -Walimu (IRE) (Top Ville) 2244$^5$ 2751$^5$ 3213$^5$ 4056$^4$ 4618$^9$ **>78f<**

**Momou Sy (GER)** 3 b f Alkalde (GER) -Mauralee (GER) (King s Lake (USA)) 2335a$^5$ 6255a$^{13}$ **>81f<**

**Momtic (IRE)** 3 ch c Shinko Forest (IRE) -Uffizi (IRE) (Royal Academy (USA)) 1357$^3$ 1585$^3$ 2202$^9$ 2558$^4$ 3017$^4$ (3631) 4171$^2$ 4709$^5$ **>90f<**

**Monad (IRE)** 2 b f General Monash (USA) -Moon River (FR) (Groom Dancer (USA)) 4682$^{10}$ 5198$^{11}$ 5535$^8$ 5741$^8$ **>52a 54f<**

**Mona Lisa** 2 ch f Giant s Causeway (USA) -Colorsnap (Shirley Heights) 5779$^4$ 6485a$^{11}$ **>81a 112+f<**

**Mona Rose (CAN)** 4 b f Gold Legend (USA) -Royal Charmer (USA) (Lomond (USA)) 6383a$^5$ **>106f<**

**Monashee Miss** 2 ch f Monashee Mountain (USA) -Most Uppitty (Absalom) 1943$^4$ 2852$^8$ 3278$^3$ 3611$^{10}$ 4095$^P$ **>27a 27f<**

**Monashee Prince (IRE)** 2 ch g Monashee Mountain (USA) -Lodema (IRE) (Lycius (USA)) 1374$^2$ (1658) 1878$^5$ 2370$^3$ 2526$^4$ 4752$^{12}$ 5119$^{13}$ 5670$^9$ **>66f<**

**Monashee Rose (IRE)** 2 br f Monashee Mountain (USA) -Thorn Tree (Zafonic (USA)) 4058$^7$ (4388) (5060) 5509$^2$ 5797$^{10}$ 5839$^{10}$ 5971a$^6$ **>77f<**

**Monashee Star (IRE)** 2 b g Monashee Mountain (USA) -Dai E Dai (USA) (Seattle Dancer (USA)) 5322a$^4$ 5681a$^7$ **>93f<**

**Monash Girl (IRE)** 3 b f General Monash (USA) -Maricica (Ahonoora) 3391$^6$ 4195$^{11}$ 6184$^{11}$ **>28 f<**

**Monash Lad (IRE)** 2 ch g General Monash (USA) -Story Time (IRE) (Mansooj) 2522$^{12}$ 3051$^5$ 3633$^3$ 3876$^3$ 3975$^4$ 6523$^3$ **>73f<**

**Monduru** 7 b g Lion Cavern (USA) -Bint Albadou (IRE) (Green Desert (USA)) 537$^8$ (730) 793$^2$ 996$^2$ 1168$^3$ 1479$^2$ (1727) **>53+a 44f<**

**Monetary (GER)** 4 b f Winged Love (IRE) -Molto Forte (GER) (Surumu (GER)) 849a$^7$ 1002a$^9$ 5970a$^8$ **>106f<**

**Monica s Revenge (IRE)** 2 b f Josr Algarhoud (IRE) -Unimpeachable (IRE) (Namaqualand (USA)) 5353$^9$ 5687$^8$ 6020$^8$ **>36a 48f<**

**Monkey Madge** 2 br f Cape Cross (IRE) -Runelia (Runnett) 5542$^2$ 6272$^7$ **>68f<**

**Monkey Or Me (IRE)** 3 b g Sri Pekan (USA) -Ecco Mi (IRE) (Priolo (USA)) 506$^8$ 875$^{12}$ 1094$^4$ 1447$^2$ 1594$^3$ 2232$^3$ 2349$^4$5110$^{12}$ 5451$^{15}$ **>36a 36f<**

**Monkston Point (IRE)** 8 b g Fayruz-Doon Belle (Ardoon) 689a$^{13}$ **>26a 98 f<**

**Monolith** 6 b g Bigstone (IRE) -Ancara (Dancing Brave (USA)) 3078$^3$ 6215$^{16}$ **>85f<**

**Mon Plaisir** 2 br f Singspiel (IRE) -Mademoiselle Chloe (Night Shift (USA)) 6155$^{12}$ 6440$^{10}$ **>7a 34f<**

**Monsal Dale (IRE)** 5 ch g Desert King (IRE) -Zanella (IRE) (Nordico (USA)) 1136$^8$ 1193$^7$ 1463$^{14}$ 1547$^6$ **>65a 62f<**

**Mon Secret (IRE)** 6 b g General Monash (USA) -Ron s Secret (Efisio) 518$^4$ 1032$^7$ 1868$^{12}$ 2172$^6$ 2776$^{14}$ 4246$^6$ (5235) 5557$^{11}$ 6295$^9$6551$^6$ **>70a 63f<**

**Monsieur Bond (IRE)** 4 ch c Danehill Dancer (IRE) -Musical Essence (Song) 1126$^5$ (1254a) (2021) 3073$^{12}$ 3674$^6$ 4595a$^9$ 5289$^5$ 6076a$^4$ **>123f<**

**Monsieur Mirasol** 2 b g Mind Games-Nom Francais (First Trump) 1340$^3$ 1743$^3$ 2352$^5$ (3233) 3605$^8$ 4676$^2$ 5143$^4$ 5314$^7$ 5721$^5$5947$^{15}$ 6356$^{14}$ **>76f<**

**Monsignor Phil (IRE)** 4 bb g Definite Article-Kilboy Concorde (African Sky) 4588a$^{15}$ **>92f<**

**Monsoon Rain (USA)** 2 b c Old Trieste (USA) -Smokey Mirage (USA) (Holy Bull (USA)) 4523$^2$ (5396) **>84+f<**

**Montalegre (IRE)** 2 b c Montjeu (IRE) -Alma Alegre (IRE) (Lahib (USA)) 6380a$^5$ **>89f<**

**Montana** 4 b c Puissance-Mistral s Dancer (Shareef Dancer (USA)) 3810$^{10}$ 4801$^4$ 5597$^{18}$ **>54a 76f<**

**Montara (IRE)** 5 b h Perugino (USA) -Tatra (Niniski (USA)) (6406) 6551$^5$ **>55a 50f<**

**Montecito** 2 b f Montjeu (IRE) -Dancing Fire (USA) (Dayjur (USA)) 4714$^8$ 5248$^8$ 5873$^3$ 6171$^{22}$ **>78f<**

**Montecristo** 11 br g Warning-Sutosky (Great Nephew) 1768$^9$ 3199$^{15}$ 5997$^7$ 6286$^4$ 6527$^4$ **>80a 82f<**

**Monte Major (IRE)** 3 b g Docksider (USA) -Danalia (IRE) (Danehill (USA)) 415$^3$ 557$^4$ 628$^2$ (1052) 1266$^2$ 1775$^9$ **>70a 75f<**

**Monte Mayor Lad (IRE)** 4 b g Sesaro (USA) -Alcalali (USA) (Septieme Ciel (USA)) 2091$^{14}$ 2524$^7$ 2814$^{10}$ **>71a 76f<**

**Montgomery** 3 b g In Command (IRE) -Lightening Reef (Bon Sang (FR)) 4775$^6$ 5151$^6$ 5495$^5$ 5843$^8$ **>48f<**

**Montgomery s Arch (USA)** 2 bb c Arch (USA) -Inny River (USA) (Seattle Slew (USA)) (3664) (4288) 5980a$^4$ 6217$^3$ **>118f<**

**Montjeu Baby (IRE)** 2 b f Montjeu (IRE) -Catch The Lights (Deploy) 3741$^{11}$ 5247$^{14}$ 5406$^{12}$ 6078$^6$ **>56f<**

**Montmartre (IRE)** 4 br f Grand Lodge (USA) -French Quarter (Ile De Bourbon (USA)) 3757$^{13}$ 4349$^8$ **>98f<**

**Montosari** 5 ch g Persian Bold-Sartigila (Efisio) (661) 855$^6$ 995$^3$ (1492) 1691$^2$ 2375$^{13}$ 5221$^3$ 5796$^{10}$ 6159$^{12}$ **>62a 52f<**

**Mont Saint Michel (IRE)** 2 b c Montjeu (IRE) -Band Of Angels (IRE) (Alzao (USA)) 5570$^{14}$ 6148$^6$ **>65f<**

**Monturani (IRE)** 5 b m Indian Ridge-Mezzogiorno (Unfuwain (USA)) 1332[3] 2543a[6] 2967[2] 3600[4] 4383a[4] 4982a[5] (5679a) 6381a[11] **>111f<**
**Moon Bird** 2 b f Primo Dominie-Time For Tea (IRE) (Imperial Frontier (USA)) 4193[13] **>12f<**
**Moon Dazzle (USA)** 3 b f Kingmambo (USA) -June Moon (IRE) (Sadler s Wells (USA)) (2311) 3033[4] 3541[5] 4077[5] 4773[2] 5783[6] **>105f<**
**Moon Emperor** 7 b g Emperor Jones (USA) -Sir Hollow (USA) (Sir Ivor (USA)) 523[11] 606[5] 1329[9] 2047[4] 2631[6] 2893[6] 3851[8] 5274[13]6084[7] **>88a 88f<**
**Moonfleet (IRE)** 2 b f Entrepreneur-Lunasa (IRE) (Don t Forget Me) 3983[8] 5925[3] 6072[8] 6515[19] **>59f<**
**Moon Forest (IRE)** 2 br c Woodborough (USA) -Ma Bella Luna (Jalmood (USA)) 5198[2] 5578[4] (6060) (6338) **>81f<**
**Moonglade (USA)** 4 ch f Carson City (USA) -Moonshine Girl (USA) (Shadeed (USA)) 780[10] 951[13] 1591[8] 2384[5] 2886[15] 3175[6] 3991[12] **>11a 36f<**
**Moonjaz** 7 ch h Nashwan (USA) -Harayir (USA) (Gulch (USA)) (1655a) **>102f<**
**Moon Legend (USA)** 3 ch f Gulch (USA) -Highland Legend (USA) (Storm Bird (CAN)) 2505[7] 3457[3] 4020[9] (4351) 5737[9] 6064[6] **>61a 71f<**
**Moonlight Appeal (IRE)** 2 ch f Bahamian Bounty-Divine Appeal (El Gran Senor (USA)) 6045[13] **><**
**Moonlight Man** 3 ch c Night Shift (USA) -Fleeting Rainbow (Rainbow Quest (USA)) 1396[2] 1706[2] 2308[7] 3598[15] 3906[2] 4273[4] 4570[2] 5439[6]5948[9] **>105f<**
**Moonlight Song (IRE)** 7 b m Mujadil (USA) -Model Show (IRE) (Dominion) 1720[3] 1992[10] 2185[8] 2811[15] 3301[14] 3471[13] 3800[13] **>40a 48f<**
**Moonlight Tango (USA)** 3 br f Benny The Dip (USA) -Summer Dance (Sadler s Wells (USA)) 1683[5] 2059[5] 2514[4] **>78f<**
**Moonmaiden** 2 ch f Selkirk (USA) -Top Table (Shirley Heights) 4753[10] 5172[5] 5620[5] 5946[7] **>70f<**
**Moon Mischief (IRE)** 2 b f Desert Sun-Moonlight Path (IRE) (Fairy King (USA)) 2275[7] 3021[3] 3290[8] 3605[9] **>65a 53f<**
**Moon Over Miami (GER)** 3 br c Dashing Blade-Miss Esther (GER) (Alkalde (GER)) 3134a[6] 5809a[7] **>99f<**
**Moonrise (GER)** 3 br f Grand Lodge (USA) -Morning Queen (GER) (Konigsstuhl (GER)) 2028a[10] **>80f<**
**Moon Royale** 6 ch m Royal Abjar (USA) -Ragged Moon (Raga Navarro (ITY)) 470[8] 782[8] 1031[8] 4624[14] **>14a 26f<**
**Moon Shadow (AUS)** 6 br h Bellotto (USA) -Tafah (USA) (Danzig (USA)) 2156a[5] **>105f<**
**Moonshaft (USA)** 3 br c Capote (USA) -Moonshine Girl (USA) (Shadeed (USA)) 1224[17] 1382[7] 1713[4] 2567[8] 4987[4] 5955[5] 6397[13] **>70a 66f<**
**Moonshine Beach** 6 b g Lugana Beach-Monongelia (Welsh Pageant) 1302[4] 1501[7] 2116[6] 2409[3] 2613[6] 2874[5] 3108[4] 3488[P](3683) (3776) 4075[13] 4352[3] (4627) (5205) 5472[13] 5826[3] (5991) (6269) **>69a 84f<**
**Moonshine Bill** 5 ch g Master Willie-Monongelia (Welsh Pageant) 1305[3] 1503[7] **>60f<**
**Moon Shot** 8 gr g Pistolet Bleu (IRE) -La Luna (USA) (Lyphard (USA)) (908) 1045[2] 1203[4] 2000[15] **>75a 73f<**
**Moonside** 2 gr f Docksider (USA) -Moon Magic (Polish Precedent (USA)) 5825[12] 6123[15] 6470[14] **>32f<**
**Moon Spinner** 7 b m Elmaamul (USA) -Lunabelle (Idiots Delight) 5339[10] 5851[8] 5952[9] 6443[12] **>34a 44f<**
**Moonstruck** 2 ch c Fraam-Easter Moon (FR) (Easter Sun) 5735[7] **>49a<**
**Moon Unit (IRE)** 3 b f Intikhab (USA) -Chapka (IRE) (Green Desert (USA)) (1379a) 1893a[3] 3350a[2] 3961a[5] 4590a[9] 5327a[8] 5660a[2] **>107f<**
**Moors Myth** 3 b c Anabaa (USA) -West Devon (USA) (Gone West (USA)) 1386[3] 1771[6] 3487[5] 4813[6] (5525) 5912[7] **>57a 80f<**
**Moose Malloy** 7 ch g Formidable (USA) -Jolimo (Fortissimo) 1548[5] **><**
**Morag** 3 b f Aragon-Minnehaha (Be My Chief (USA)) 1613[4] 2169[10] 2371[8] 2703[11] 3780[6] 4066[6] 4817[2] 5020[7]5370[7] 5493[11] 6124[15] 6290[10] **>15a 64f<**
**Morahib** 6 ch h Nashwan (USA) -Irish Valley (USA) (Irish River (FR)) 4458[2] 5006[10] **>61f<**
**Morbidezza (GER)** 4 b f Lecroix (GER) -Miami Sun (GER) (Dashing Blade) 2138a[4] 3134a[3] 3972a[4] 5683a[3] 6107a[10] **>103f<**
**Morettina (GER)** 4 br f Law Society (USA) -Mirabella (GER) (Scenic) 5822a[7] **>74f<**
**Morgan Lewis (IRE)** 3 b g Orpen (USA) -Party Piece (Thatch (USA)) 4059[7] (4489) 4717[3] 4952[2] 5837[3] **>79+f<**
**Moritat (IRE)** 4 b g Night Shift (USA) -Aunty Eileen (Ahonoora) 3025[13] 4085[6] 4279[3] 4548[5] 5008[6] 5261[3] 5412[14] 6007[10] **>16a 67f<**
**Morning After** 4 b f Emperor Jones (USA) -Onefortheditch (USA) (With Approval (CAN)) 2237[8] 3419[6] 4067[6] 5740[4] **>73a 86+f<**
**Morning Eclipse** 4 b c Zafonic (USA) -Hunt The Sun (Rainbow Quest (USA)) 5968a[11] **>99f<**
**Morning Hawk (USA)** 3 b f Silver Hawk (USA) -Dawn Aurora (USA) (Night Shift (USA)) 580[7] 752[4] 1079[5] 1405[6] 3984[9] 4302[4] 4820[9] 5178[4]5928[11] **>43a 43f<**
**Morning Major (USA)** 2 b g Parade Ground (USA) -North Of Seattle (USA) (Northern Baby (CAN)) 3233[10] 4131[8] 5095[10] **>44f<**
**Morning Sun** 4 b f Starborough-Malham Tarn (Riverman (USA)) 445[9] **><**
**Morning World** 2 b c Bahamian Bounty-Snap Cracker (Inchinor) 1415[10] 1865[10] 2268[6] **>24f<**
**Mornin Reserves** 5 b g Atraf-Pusey Street Girl (Gildoran) 1763[13] 2955[15] 3537[11] **>111f<**
**Morozov (USA)** 5 b h Sadler s Wells (USA) -High Hawk (Shirley Heights) 1703[P] 2067[P] **>116f<**
**Morris Dancing (USA)** 5 b g Rahy (USA) -Summer Dance (Sadler s Wells (USA)) 500[9] 589[7] 727[9] 875[14] 947[5] 995[11] 1697[8]1885[7] 2228[3] 2851[5] 3492[10] **>39a 10 f<**
**Morse (IRE)** 3 b c Shinko Forest (IRE) -Auriga (Belmez (USA)) 1129[16] 1333[2] 1673[2] 1760[3] (1965) 2115[2] 2309[8] 3420[11] 3691[6]3941[14] 4874[13] 5265[15] (5656) 5786[8] 5952[2] 6350[5] **>90a 92f<**
**Morson Boy (USA)** 4 b g Lear Fan (USA) -Esprit D Escalier (USA) (Diesis) 2076[12] 2684[12] 3757[7] 4218[15] 4529[7] **>94 f<**
**Mortadelo (IRE)** 5 ch h Bigstone (IRE) -Poly Dancer (Suave Dancer (USA)) 2163a[11] **><**
**Morvern (IRE)** 4 ch g Titus Livius (FR) -Scotia Rose (Tap On Wood) 449[4] 1238[14] 2531[5] 3042[6] **>46a 65f<**
**Mosaahim (IRE)** 6 b h Nashwan (USA) -Azdihaar (USA) (Mr Prospector (USA)) (5103a) **>60f<**
**Moscow Ballet (IRE)** 3 b c Sadler s Wells (USA) -Fire The Groom (USA) (Blushing Groom (FR)) 2043[6] 2721a[6] (3000) 3353a[7] 4769a[3] **>109f<**
**Moscow Blue** 3 ch g Soviet Star (USA) -Aquamarine (Shardari) 1541[6] 2270[7] **>56f<**
**Moscow Burning (USA)** 4 b f Moscow Ballet (USA) -Burning Desire (USA) (Mr. Leader (USA)) 6488a[4] **>114f<**
**Moscow Mary** 3 b f Imperial Ballet (IRE) -Baileys Firecat (Catrail (USA)) 1474[8] 1676[10] 2942[12] 4414[10] 5282[7] 6056[13] **>24a 30f<**
**Moscow Music** 2 ch c Piccolo-Anna Karietta (Precocious) 1436[2] (1936) 2532[2] 3640[6] 4860[2] 5392[3] 5895[5] **>100f<**
**Moscow Times** 3 b g Soviet Star (USA) -Bargouzine (Hotfoot) 2063[6] 3180[5] 3689[7] (4147) 4438[3] 5275[11] 5912[5] **>70a 76f<**
**Moshkil (IRE)** 2 b c In The Wings-Brentsville (USA) (Arctic Tern (USA)) 2890[10] 4913[11] 5508[6] **>63f<**
**Mossmann Gorge** 2 b g Lujain (USA) -North Pine (Import) 2352[11] 5542[6] 5857[5] 6242[2] **>63f<**
**Moss Vale (IRE)** 3 b c Shinko Forest (IRE) -Wolf Cleugh (IRE) (Last Tycoon) 1388[4] (1883) (2294) (2913) 3674[20] 4886[9] 5661a[2] 6190[2] **>117f<**
**Mostanad** 2 b g Alhaarth (IRE) -Jeed (IRE) (Mujtahid (USA)) 3758[10] **>47f<**
**Mostarsil (USA)** 6 ch g Kingmambo (USA) -Naazeq (Nashwan (USA)) 1329[12] 1801[6] 2285[3] 2631[4] (2893) 3199[6] 3629[7] 4416[6] **>55a 77f<**
**Mostashaar (FR)** 2 b c Intikhab (USA) -Nasanice (IRE) (Nashwan (USA)) 4567[7] 6145[5] **>77f<**
**Most Definitely (IRE)** 4 b g Definite Article-Unbidden Melody (USA) (Chieftain) 2935[2] 3236[12] 3564[6] 4352[2] 5479[3] 5523[2] 5951[2] (6198) 6535[2] **>8a 85f<**
**Most-Saucy** 8 br m Most Welcome-So Saucy (Teenoso (USA)) 1535[6] 1684[6] 2032[5] 2212[7] 2363[3] 2767[4] 3128[5] 3181[7]3873[4] 4129[3] 4233[3] 4441[10] (5221) 5826[9] 6159[9] **>65a 65f<**
**Motarassed** 2 b c Green Desert (USA) -Sayedati Eljamilah (USA) (Mr Prospector (USA)) 3424[3] (4143) 5395[5] **>86+f<**
**Moth Ball** 2 b c Royal Applause-Chrysalis (Soviet Star (USA)) 4117[2] 4611[3] (4739) 5202[7] 5515[3] (5745) 5947[4] (6068) **>111f<**
**Mothecombe Dream (IRE)** 2 b c Foxhound (USA) -Another Shadow (IRE) (Topanoora) 4567[12] 5696[10] 6282[7] **>52f<**
**Motivator** 2 b c Montjeu (IRE) -Out West (USA) (Gone West (USA)) (4728) (6347) **>118+f<**
**Motive (FR)** 3 ch c Machiavellian (USA) -Mistle Song (Nashwan (USA)) 1830[5] (2374) 2896[2] 3641[8] 5942[8] 6121[9] **>97+f<**
**Motorway (IRE)** 3 b c Night Shift (USA) -Tadkiyra (IRE) (Darshaan) 1683[6] (3994) 4582[5] **>84f<**
**Motu (IRE)** 3 b g Desert Style (IRE) -Pink Cashmere (IRE) (Polar Falcon (USA)) 1333[7] 1702[11] 2306[8] 2790[7] 3745[7] 5108[9] 5657[3] 6271[6] **>74 f<**
**Mouftari (USA)** 3 b c Miswaki (USA) -Nature s Magic (USA) (Nijinsky (CAN)) 1419[5] 1926[4] 2298[5] 3574[2] 4939[3] 5867[5] **>73a 76f<**
**Mountain Breeze** 2 b f Monashee Mountain (USA) -Breezy Louise (Dilum (USA)) 5109[12] 6020[10] 6270[9] **>32a 9f<**
**Mountain Meadow** 3 ch g Deploy-Woodwardia (USA) (El Gran Senor (USA)) 1466[2] (3013) **>76+f<**
**Mount Arafat** 2 b g Erhaab (USA) -Cache (Bustino) 5173[9] 5508[8] 5827[11] **>17f<**
**Mount Benger** 4 ch g Selkirk (USA) -Vice Vixen (CAN) (Vice Regent (CAN)) 1213[6] 2835[11] 3662[4] (3929) 4849[9] 5129[3] 5584[10] 6083[2] **>75a 69f<**
**Mount Butler (IRE)** 2 b g Celtic Swing-Baylands Sunshine (IRE) (Classic Secret (USA)) 2898[7] 6072[13] 6309[6] **>46f<**
**Mountcharge (IRE)** 3 b g Intikhab (USA) -Zorilla (Belmez (USA)) 1795[19] 3089[10] 3426[5] 4806[10] 5657[13] **>78a 75f<**
**Mount Cottage** 3 b f Cape Cross (IRE) -Brecon Beacons (IRE) (Shirley Heights) 4180[6] 4679[4] 5146[6] 6230[14] **>43f<**
**Mount Eliza (IRE)** 2 b f Danehill (USA) -Siamoise (Caerleon (USA)) 5322a[5] 6101a[9] **>87f<**
**Mount Ephram (IRE)** 2 b g Entrepreneur-Happy Dancer (USA) (Seattle Dancer (USA)) 1248[4] 2035[5] 2248[6] 3100[4] (3366) 3834[4] 4010[2] 5819[7] 6242[8]6515[17] **>64f<**
**Mount Etna (IRE)** 2 ch g Mister Baileys-Taormina (IRE) (Ela-Mana-Mou) 6542a[12] **><**
**Mount Grace (IRE)** 3 b f Orpen (USA) -Go For Grace (IRE) (Shalford (IRE)) 5162a[6] 5357a[9] **>89f<**
**Mount Hillaby (IRE)** 4 b f Mujadil (USA) -Tetradonna (IRE) (Teenoso (USA)) (503) 588 [9] 4511[7] 4852[2] 5085[9] (5317) 5713[10] 6094[5] (6579) **>71a 71 f<**
**Mount Kellet (IRE)** 2 ch g Bluebird (USA) -Antinnaz (IRE) (Thatching) 5578[16] 5954[7] 6276[7] **>38a<**
**Mount Logan** 9 b h Shareef Dancer (USA) -Double Entendre (Dominion) 463[11] **>24a<**
**Mount Pekan (IRE)** 4 b g Sri Pekan (USA) -The Highlands (FR) (High Line) 1393[17] 2078[3] 2618[7] 3058[6] 3520[17] 4004[5] 4132[8] 4447[8]4825[7] **>52f<**
**Mount Royale (IRE)** 6 ch g Wolfhound (USA) -Mahabba (USA) (Elocutionist (USA)) 437[8] 512[7] 584[6] 686[3] (719) (833) 866[8] 1039[7]1268[6] 1424[2] 1595[2] 1748[2] 1971[3] 6539[12] **>69a 60f<**
**Mount Superior (USA)** 8 b g Conquistador Cielo (USA) -Zum Solitair (USA) (Vice Regent (CAN)) (470) 728[5] 860[10] 1191[7] **>45a 40f<**
**Mount Vettore** 3 br g Vettori (IRE) -Honeyspike (IRE) (Chief s Crown (USA)) (606) 1129[2] 1322[8] 1795[11] 2448[8] 2732[9] 3507[9] 3949[6] 4558[6]5370[3] 5945[2] **>73 a 77f<**
**Mouseman** 3 b g Young Ern-Scottish Royal (IRE) (Night Shift (USA)) 2326[5] 3338[9] 3838[12] **>27a 40f<**
**Movie King (IRE)** 5 ch g Catrail (USA) -Marilyn (IRE) (King s Lake (USA)) 1928[7] 2142[15] 2547[2] 2752[13] 3097[13] 4029[6] 4450[3] 5544[13] **>70a 70 f<**
**Moyne Pleasure (IRE)** 6 b g Exit To Nowhere (USA) -Ilanga (IRE) (Common Grounds) 483[8] 653[8] 875[11] 943[6] 1026[8] 1173[8] 1700[2]1862[7] 1885[2] 1917[3] (2184) 2345[4] 2583[6] 2816[7] 2990[8]3149[7] 3265[LFT] **>47a 49f<**
**Mozafin** 2 b c Zafonic (USA) -Bedara (Barathea (IRE)) 2579[6] 2904[2] 3925[4] 4420[3] 4953[2] 5186[8] 5543[2] (5790) **>82f<**
**Mpenzi** 2 b f Groom Dancer (USA) -Muschana (Deploy) 5915[7] 6351[14] **>65+f<**
**Mr Aitch (IRE)** 2 b c Soviet Star (USA) -Welsh Mist (Damister (USA)) 5838[2] 6492[4] **>78a 69f<**
**Mr Belvedere** 3 b g Royal Applause-Alarming Motown (Warning) 1214[11] 2207[9] 2545[10] 2762[3] 2928[2] 4242[10] 4941[4] 5750[8]6343[15] **>51a 58f<**
**Mr Bountiful (IRE)** 6 b g Mukaddamah (USA) -Nawadder (Kris) 624[8] 1971[9] 2260[4] 2965[8] 3409[10] 4013[6] 4257[4] 4425[13]6559[4] **>63+a 60f<**
**Mr Dinglawi (IRE)** 3 b g Danehill Dancer (IRE) -Princess Leona (IRE) (Naiyli (IRE)) 702[12] 821[10] 1050[5] 6182[7] **>62a<**
**Mr Dinos (IRE)** 5 b h Desert King (IRE) -Spear Dance (Gay Fandango (USA)) 2067[4] 2533[2] 2998[6] **>123f<**
**Mr Dip** 4 b g Reprimand-Scottish Lady (Dunbeath (USA)) 948[7] 1022[6] 1845[10] 3143[7] 3490[5] 3695[2] 3929[6] 4473[15] **>27a 65f<**
**Mr Ed (IRE)** 6 ch g In The Wings-Center Moriches (IRE) (Magical Wonder (USA)) 2893[2] 3485[2] (4441) 5619[2] 6215[2] **>89f<**
**Mr Fast (ARG)** 7 b h Numerous (USA) -Speediness (ARG) (Etienne Gerard) 2163a[13] **><**
**Mr Fleming** 5 bb g Bin Ajwaad (IRE) -Fabulous Night (FR) (Fabulous Dancer (USA)) 997[3] 2053[11] 3917[15] **>44a 39f<**
**Mr Fortywinks (IRE)** 10 ch g Fool s Holme (USA) -Dream On (Absalom) 1615[12] 1866[5] 2462[8] 3576[6] 4275[3] **>69f<**
**Mr Houdini (IRE)** 7 gr g Magical Wonder (USA) -Gravina (Godswalk (USA)) 2603a[6] **>103f<**
**Mr Hullabalou (IRE)** 3 b g Princely Heir (IRE) -Lomalou (IRE) (Lightning Dealer) 1083[10] 1293[15] 1796[4] 2301[5] 2576[7] 3086[9] 3384[8] 3874[7](4337) **>36a 75f<**
**Mr Independent (IRE)** 3 b g Cadeaux Genereux-Iris May (Brief Truce (USA)) 1755[9] 2361[8] 2400[13] **>56f<**
**Mr Jack Daniells (IRE)** 3 b g Mujadil (USA) -Neat Shilling (IRE) (Bob Back (USA)) 1841[3] 2306[6] 2692[3] 3230[8] 3452[4] (4032) 4648[4] 4749[13] 5265[3]5652[5] **>82f<**
**Mr Kalandi (IRE)** 2 gr c Grand Lodge (USA) -Singhana (IRE) (Mouktar) 2234[3] 2674[7] 4523[14] 5351[6] 5655[8] **>56 f<**
**Mr Lambros** 3 ch c Pivotal-Magical Veil (Majestic Light (USA)) (415) 770[2] 5762[7] 5937[7] 6341[11] **>91a 90+f<**
**Mr Lear (USA)** 5 b g Lear Fan (USA) -Majestic Mae (USA) (Crow (FR)) 1928[9] 2471[8] 6546[9] **>73a 80f<**
**Mr Lehman** 7 ch g Presidium-Lehmans Lot (Oats) 585[10] 630[7] **>21a<**
**Mr Lewin** 3 ch g Primo Dominie-Fighting Run (Runnett) 3004[7] 4680[9] 5957[5] 6184[10] 6401[8] **>52a 52f<**
**Mr Loverman (IRE)** 4 ch g Spectrum (IRE) -Soviet Artic (FR) (Bering) 1723[12] 2454[8] 2813[12] **>16a 16f<**
**Mr Malarkey (IRE)** 4 b g Pivotal-Girl Next Door (Local Suitor (USA)) 1608[4] 1765[10] 2094[4] 2467[6] 2899[3] 3416[3] 3645[8] 4130[6](4459) 4847[7] 5299[6] 5550[12] **>23a 87f<**
**Mr Marucci (USA)** 2 b c Miner s Mark (USA) -Appealing Style (USA) (Valid Appeal (USA)) 5098[5] 5301[9] 6020[5] **>60a 59f<**
**Mr Maxim** 2 ch g Lake Coniston (IRE) -White Hare (Indian Ridge) 2904[9] 3197[5] 3560[8] 5059[9] 5556[4] 5988[7] **>53f<**
**Mr Mayfair (IRE)** 2 ch g Entrepreneur-French Gift (Cadeaux Genereux) 5653[7] 6494[7] **>63a 58f<**
**Mr Midasman (IRE)** 3 b c Entrepreneur-Sifaara (IRE) (Caerleon (USA)) 1108[6] 1392[9] 1755[11] 1957[13] 2239[10] 4451[4] 4882[6] 5293[5]5459[3] 6560[3] **>55a 62f<**
**Mr Midaz** 5 ch g Danzig Connection (USA) -Marmy (Midyan (USA)) 3929[5] 4261[5] 5238[5] **>22a 65f<**
**Mr Mischief** 4 b g Millkom-Snow Huntress (Shirley Heights) 523[3] 600[12] (971) 4698[12] **>99a 72f<**
**Mr Mistral** 5 b g Zilzal (USA) -Miss Sancerre (Last Tycoon) 2596[2] (3268) 4122[25] **>81f<**
**Mr Moon** 3 b g Pursuit Of Love-Sound Of Sleat (Primo Dominie) 1425[6] 2176[6] 2356[12] 2760[10] 3042[7] 4102[6] 4387[10] 5110[5]5524[9] 6120[15] **>11a 29f<**
**Mr O Brien (IRE)** 5 ch g Mukaddamah (USA) -Laurel Delight (Presidium) 4768a[6] 6486a[9] **>121f<**
**Mr Perry (IRE)** 8 br g Perugino (USA) -Elegant Tune (USA) (Alysheba (USA)) 838[9] 940[5] 1090[10] **>33a<**
**Mr Pertemps** 6 b g Primo Dominie-Amber Mill (Doulab (USA)) 476[3] (510) 681[2] 721[5] 5261[14] 6066[8] 6246[6] **>67a 50f<**
**Mrs Boz** 4 b f Superpower-Bar None (Rabdan) 2056[4] 3261[9] 4419[12] **>17a 30f<**
**Mrs Brown** 3 b f Royal Applause-Shifting Mist (Night Shift (USA)) 550[3] 683[5] 760[6] 4055[10] 4339[5] 4604[8] 6061[4]6184[5] 6461[14] **>55a 41f<**
**Mrs Cee (IRE)** 3 b f Orpen (USA) -Cutleaf (Kris) 5147[7] **>30 f<**
**Mrs Chippy (IRE)** 2 ch f Docksider (USA) -Pile (USA) (Shadeed (USA)) 6470[16] **>10f<**
**Mrs Cube** 5 ch m Missed Flight-Norska (Northfields (USA)) (945) (994) 1024[3] 1079[3] 2053[4] 2324[10] 2594[14] **>50a 45f<**
**Mrs Kepple** 2 b f King s Best (USA) -Sabayik (IRE) (Unfuwain (USA)) 1930[4] 2208[8] 3164[7] **>35f<**
**Mrs Mason (IRE)** 3 b f Turtle Island (IRE) -Secretary Bird (IRE) (Kris) 2102a[5] **>90f<**
**Mr Smithers Jones** 4 br g Emperor Jones (USA) -Phylian (Glint Of Gold) 431[2] (501) 581[3] 1028[3] **>63a 48f<**
**Mrs Moh (IRE)** 3 b f Orpen (USA) -My Gray (FR) (Danehill (USA)) 1614[11] 2019[14] 2907[5] (3295) 4151[3] (4490) 5474[2] 5673[2] 6044[U] 6350[4] **>59a 91f<**
**Mrs Pankhurst** 3 b f Selkirk (USA) -Melodist (USA) (The Minstrel (CAN)) 1108[5] 1712[9] 2648[5] 3320[6] 5566[8] 6086[4] 6266[5] 6498[12] **>53a 71f<**
**Mrs Philip** 5 b m Puissance-Lightning Legacy (USA) (Super Concorde (USA)) 5339[7] 5828[8] 5999[11] 6082[9] **>55f<**
**Mr Spliffy (IRE)** 5 b g Fayruz-Johns Conquerer (IRE) (Conquering Hero (USA)) 411[7] 460[5] (538) 674[12] 893[7] 938[5] 1504[18] 2739[11]3016[11] 3169[11] 3407[10] 4011[11] 4105[8] 4308[10] 4422[2] **>53a 53f<**
**Mrs Shilling** 3 b f Dr Fong (USA) -Papaha (FR) (Green Desert (USA)) 4683[3] 5378[4] 5713[2] 5994[4] 6224[3] **>72a 72+f<**
**Mrs Spence** 3 b f Mind Games-Maid O Cannie (Efisio) 1473[13] 1602[6] 1992[14] 5849[19] 6114[15] **>58f<**
**Mrs St George (IRE)** 3 b f Orpen (USA) -Tamarzana (IRE) (Lear Fan (USA)) 4526[8] 5660a[13] **>89f<**
**Mr Strowger** 3 b c Dancing Spree (USA) -Matoaka (Be My Chief (USA)) 1844[6] 2395[3] 5072[15] 5692[11] **>43f<**
**Mr Stylish** 8 b g Mazilier (USA) -Moore Stylish (Moorestyle) 498[6] 725[6] **>44a 44 f<**
**Mrs Willy Nilly** 2 ch f Timeless Times (USA) -Laena (Roman Warrior) 1589[15] 1839[12] 3741[16] **>20f<**
**Mr Tambourine Man (IRE)** 3 b c Rainbow Quest (USA) -Girl From Ipanema (Salse (USA)) 1414[6] 1799[7] 2558[7] (2949) 3442[3] (4177) 5273[4] 5517[2] 5732[7] 5842[10] **>91f<**
**Mr Uppity** 5 b g Shareef Dancer (USA) -Queenfisher (Scottish Reel) 876[13] 1089[7] 1191[2] 1515[4] 1696[5] 2227[3] 2383[6]2823[5] 3277[4] 3991[2] 5283[8] 5793[5] **>47a 44f<**
**Mr Velocity (IRE)** 4 b g Tagula (IRE) -Miss Rusty (IRE) (Mukaddamah (USA)) 1624[3] 2119[2] (3101) 3755[11] 4569[6] 5185[3] (5403) (5821) 6358[2] 6568[6] **>69a 86+f<**
**Mr Whizz** 7 ch g Manhal-Panienka (POL) (Dom Racine (FR)) 495[9] (567) 604[4] 939[4] 1093[3] 1580[2] 1987[2] 2430[11]3667[5] (4433) 4778[11] 5257[4] 5928[7] **>44a 53f<**
**Mr Wolf** 3 b g Wolfhound (USA) -Madam Millie (Milford) 1196[2] 1362[2] (1664) (1775) 2131[6] 2981[6] 3446[13] 3702[9] 4837[13] 5094[5]5605[2] 5837[6] **>81f<**
**Ms Polly Garter** 2 b f Petong-Utopia (Primo Dominie) 1853[4] 2177[12] 2427[6] 3930[11] 4670[8] 6080[18] **>28f<**
**Ms Three** 2 b f Josr Algarhoud (IRE) -Swing Along (Alhijaz) 4488[12] 4999[6] 5558[5] 5816[6] 6093[10] 6359[12] **>11a 56f<**
**Mt Desert** 2 b c Rainbow Quest (USA) -Chief Bee (Chief s Crown (USA)) 5870[6] 6149[6] **>67+f<**
**Mtilly** 3 br f Mtoto-Corn Lily (Aragon) 5994[8] 6310[10] **>50f<**
**Mubeen (IRE)** 4 ch c Barathea (IRE) -Fernanda (Be My Chief (USA)) 688a[6] 757a[2] 922a[7] **>102a 102f<**
**Mubtaker (USA)** 7 ch h Silver Hawk (USA) -Gazayil (USA) (Irish River (FR)) (4746) 5329a[7]

6384a[4] >132f<

**Much Faster (IRE)** 3 b f Fasliyev (USA) -Interruption (Zafonic (USA)) 2162a[7] >111f<

**Mudawin (IRE)** 3 b g Intikhab (USA) -Fida (IRE) (Persian Heights) 1104[12] (1461) 1795[13] (2281) 2999[14] >101f<

**Muddy (IRE)** 2 ch g Monashee Mountain (USA) -Schonbein (IRE) (Persian Heights) 5154[5] 5353[8] 5570[11] 6305[8] >59f<

**Muestra (IRE)** 2 ch f Raise A Grand (IRE) -Iva s Flyer (IRE) (Imperial Frontier (USA)) 1589[11] 1853[10] 1984[8] 2427[7] 2946[5] 4095[3] 4638[9] 6195[10] >44a 35f<

**Mufreh (USA)** 6 br g Dayjur (USA) -Mathkurh (USA) (Riverman (USA)) (544) 749[5] 1007[2] 1265[4] 1531[12] >94+a 62f<

**Mugeba** 3 b f Primo Dominie-Ella Lamees (Statoblest) 506[5] 843[5] (3425) 4052[2] 4496[2] 4650[7] 6445[6] >57a 64+f<

**Mugharreb (USA)** 6 b h Gone West (USA) -Marling (IRE) (Lomond (USA)) 924a[5] 1006a[4] >73a 114f<

**Muhareb (USA)** 5 ch g Thunder Gulch (USA) -Queen Of Spirit (USA) (Deputy Minister (CAN)) 4123[5] 4530[9] 5401[11] 5761[5] 5919[17] 6172[19] >83a 100f<

**Muhaymin (USA)** 3 ch c A.P. Indy (USA) -Shadayid (USA) (Shadeed (USA)) 1414[8] 2306[9] 2841[4] 3230[7] >86f<

**Mujagem (IRE)** 8 br m Mujadil (USA) -Lili Bengam (Welsh Saint) 429[8] >30f<

**Mujalina (IRE)** 6 b g Mujadil (USA) -Talina s Law (IRE) (Law Society (USA)) 6215[27] >88f<

**Mujawer (USA)** 3 b g Gulch (USA) -Good Cents (USA) (Deputy Minister (CAN)) 3948[5] 4369[12] 5204[11] >65f<

**Mujazaf** 2 b c Grand Lodge (USA) -Decision Maid (USA) (Diesis) 5756[3] >74f<

**Mujkari (IRE)** 8 ch g Mujtahid (USA) -Hot Curry (USA) (Sharpen Up) 6551[12] >58a 54f<

**Mukafeh (USA)** 3 b c Danzig (USA) -Bint Salsabil (USA) (Nashwan (USA)) 1459[7] 2276[2] 2966[5] >107f<

**Mulan Princess (IRE)** 4 b f Mukaddamah (USA) -Notley Park (Wolfhound (USA)) 6461[3] >71a 66f<

**Mulberry Lad (IRE)** 2 b c Entrepreneur-Taisho (IRE) (Namaqualand (USA)) 3302[5] 3570[2] 3986[4] 4413[2] 5745[7] 6012[6] 6289[6] >64 a 69f<

**Mulberry Wine** 2 b f Benny The Dip (USA) -Top Berry (High Top) 3202[6] 3665[4] 4234[5] 4914[8] 5377[12] 5885[16] >71f<

**Mulsanne** 6 b g Clantime-Prim Lass (Reprimand) 5350[12] >12f<

**Multahab** 5 bb g Zafonic (USA) -Alumisiyah (USA) (Danzig (USA)) 560[2] 708[4] 963[2] 1228[4] 2118[12] 2675[10] 3428[10] 4522[8] 4800 4923[9] 5016[6] 6274[9] 6398[10] >48a 52f<

**Multazem (USA)** 4 b c Kingmambo (USA) -Spirit Of Tara (IRE) (Sadler s Wells (USA)) 1982a[6] 2603a[11] >107f<

**Multicolour** 4 ch f Rainbow Quest (USA) -Raymouna (IRE) (High Top) 1856[15] >59a 63f<

**Multidandy (AUS)** 5 b g Danehill (USA) -New Acquaintance (NZ) (Kings Island (IRE)) 1145a[11] >57a 110f<

**Multiple Choice (IRE)** 3 ch g Woodborough (USA) -Cosmona (Dominion) 1205[7] 1388[16] 1602[9] 3201[10] 3707[2] 4093[4] 4387[6] 4882[4] 5261[13] 6016[7] 6157[10] >64a 64f<

**Mumbling (IRE)** 6 ch g Dr Devious (IRE) -Valley Lights (IRE) (Dance Of Life (USA)) 5728[15] >67a 88df<

**Mummify (AUS)** 5 b g Jeune-Cleopatra s Girl (AUS) (At Talaq (USA)) 6528a[19] >121f<

**Munaahej (IRE)** 3 b c Soviet Star (USA) -Azyaa (Kris) 5702[15] >50f<

**Munaawashat (IRE)** 3 b f Marju (IRE) -Simaat (USA) (Mr Prospector (USA)) 2442[3] (2973) 3397[2] 4170[8] (4812) (5136) 5304[8] 6255a[6] >86f<

**Munaawesh (USA)** 3 b c Bahri (USA) -Istikbal (USA) (Kingmambo (USA)) 1015[9] 1266[3] 1422[9] 1531[14] 1874[9] 2259[13] 2814[9] 3231[13] 3379[7] 3561[4] 3581[2] 3981[8] 4249[4] 4562[2] 4820[2] 5245[9] 5365[4] 5546[5] 6005[10] >43a 62f<

**Munaddam (USA)** 2 ch c Aljabr (USA) -Etizaaz (USA) (Diesis) 4494[2] 5290[2] (5825) >94+f<

**Munfarid (IRE)** 4 ch g Alhaarth (IRE) -Meursault (IRE) (Salt Dome (USA)) 484[3] 645[7] 919[4] 1042[11] 1135[9] 1302[11] 4883[11] >64a 82f<

**Mungo Jerry (GER)** 3 b g Tannenkonig (IRE) -Mostly Sure (IRE) (Sure Blade (USA)) 1761[3] 2298[6] 3232[3] >74f<

**Munsef** 2 b c Zafonic (USA) -Mazaya (IRE) (Sadler s Wells (USA)) 6171[12] 6440[3] >70f<

**Muqarrar (IRE)** 5 ch h Alhaarth (IRE) -Narjis (USA) (Blushing Groom (FR)) 504[6] 582[6] 3380[16] 6227[16] (6466) >57a 59f<

**Muqbil (USA)** 4 ch c Swain (IRE) -Istiqlal (USA) (Diesis) 1622[8] (2672) (3936) 4539[2] 5492[4] 5812[5] >120f<

**Muqtadi (IRE)** 6 b g Marju (IRE) -Kadwah (USA) (Mr Prospector (USA)) 485[8] 519[3] 575[9] 674[6] 738[10] 821[4] (873) 894[5] 988[8] 1076[10] 1231[4] 1274[5] 1516[4] 1986[9] 2426[6] 3127[9] 3489[10] 3697[13] >50a 50f<

**Muraabet** 2 b c Dubai Millennium-Mahasin (USA) (Danzig (USA)) 6187[3] 6439[6] >81+f<

**Muraqeb** 4 ch g Grand Lodge (USA) -Oh So Well (IRE) (Sadler s Wells (USA)) 555[13] 874[13] 931[10] 1023[5] 1210[11] 1534[11] 6057[10] 6337[6] >43a 57f<

**Murashah (USA)** 4 ch c Storm Cat (USA) -Shadayid (USA) (Shadeed (USA)) 3299[13] >81+f<

**Murbaat (IRE)** 3 b c Deploy-Ozette (Dancing Brave (USA)) 2392[3] 3015[2] >80f<

**Murdinga** 5 br g Emperor Jones (USA) -Tintinara (Selkirk (USA)) 964[12] >66a 68f<

**Murzim** 5 b g Salse (USA) -Guilty Secret (IRE) (Kris) 919[12] >77da 77df<

**Musadif (USA)** 6 ch h Shadeed (USA) -Tadwin (Never So Bold) 3552a[11] 5505a[3] 6379a[7] >96f<

**Musahim (USA)** 2 bb c Dixieland Band (USA) -Tabheej (IRE) (Mujtahid (USA)) 5118[7] 5341[3] >75f<

**Musanid (USA)** 4 ch c Swain (IRE) -Siyadah (USA) (Mr Prospector (USA)) 1767[3] 3072[6] 3936[3] 4755[3] >111f<

**Musardiere** 2 b f Montjeu (IRE) -Majestic Image (Niniski (USA)) 5521[7] 5848[5] 5946[11] >56f<

**Muscle Man (NZ)** 5 ch g Rhythm (USA) -Togaris Pride (NZ) (Mcginty (NZ)) 2156a[15] ><

**Museeb (USA)** 2 b c Danzig (USA) -Elle Seule (USA) (Exclusive Native (USA)) 5290[4] 5646[2] >87f<

**Mushajer** 2 gr g Linamix (FR) -Luxurious (USA) (Lyphard (USA)) 2111[3] 3240[4] >86f<

**Musical Chimes (USA)** 4 bb f In Excess-Note Musicale (Sadler s Wells (USA)) 4767a[4] 6486a[6] >115f<

**Musical Day** 2 ch f Singspiel (IRE) -Dayville (USA) (Dayjur (USA)) 3905[11] 4198[7] 4706[10] 5109[2] 5648[12] 5938[4] 6020[3] (6393) >74 a 81f<

**Musical Fair** 4 b f Piccolo-Guarded Expression (Siberian Express (USA)) 1106[21] 1825[14] 2094[8] 2252[2] (2369) 2739[5] 3016[8] 3795[10] 4626[11] 5062[3] 5440[12] 5550[3] 6293[5] 6554[12] >79a 86f<

**Musical Gift** 4 ch g Cadeaux Genereux-Kazoo (Shareef Dancer (USA)) (639) 701[4] 862[4] 1118[5] 1275[7] 6480[7] >73a 40f<

**Musical Lyrics (USA)** 3 b f Quiet American (USA) -Foreign Courier (USA) (Sir Ivor (USA)) 1932[8] >60f<

**Musical Score** 5 b m Blushing Flame (USA) -Music In My Life (IRE) (Law Society (USA)) 2607a[3] 3137a[7] 5576a[5] >96f<

**Musical Top (USA)** 4 ch f Mt. Livermore (USA) -Brief Escapade (IRE) (Brief Truce (USA)) 4390[3] 5039[9] 5337[16] 5830[4] 6061[5] >55a 59f<

**Musicanna** 3 b f Cape Cross (IRE) -Upend (Main Reef) 2693[2] (5770) >71+f<

**Music Maid (IRE)** 6 b m Inzar (USA) -Richardstown Lass (IRE) (Muscatite) 2284[13] (2788) 3690[10] 4148[7] 5249[8] 5444[11] 5698[11] >81f<

**Music Mix (IRE)** 3 gr c Linamix (FR) -Baldemara (FR) (Sanglamore (USA)) 1997[12] 3231[11] (4604) 4710[4] 4853[4] 5197[8] 6006[9] >70a 58f<

**Musico (IRE)** 2 ch c Bold Fact (USA) -Scherzo Impromptu (Music Boy) 2609[4] 3157[6] 3588[4] 4365[2] 4671[3] 5434[16] 5995[12] >74+f<

**Music Teacher** 2 ch f Piccolo-Duena (Grand Lodge (USA)) 5271[12] >32f<

**Musiotal** 3 ch c Pivotal-Bemuse (Forzando) 1342[13] 1788[5] 1934[5] 2457[10] 3234[2] (3798) 4489[8] 4902[4] 6114[8] 6138[14] >57f<

**Muskatsturm (GER)** 5 b g Lecroix (GER) -Myrthe (GER) (Konigsstuhl (GER)) 1302[8] 1539[10] 3947[7] 5159[10] >72f<

**Musketier (GER)** 2 gr c Acatenango (GER) -Myth And Reality (Linamix (FR)) 5666a[2] (6262a) 6583a[5] >107f<

**Muslin** 3 ch f Bien Bien (USA) -Moidart (Electric) 1466[11] 1912[3] 2882[8] 3479[13] 4070[2] 5243[5] 5546[6] 6159[11] >54a 60f<

**Mustajed** 3 b g Alhaarth (IRE) -Jasarah (IRE) (Green Desert (USA)) 2200[6] 2476[8] >91f<

**Mustakhlas (USA)** 3 ch g Diesis-Katiba (USA) (Gulch (USA)) 1395[11] >56f<

**Mustanfar (USA)** 3 ch c Unbridled (USA) -Manwah (USA) (Lyphard (USA)) 6490a[5] >93a 114f<

**Mustang Ali (IRE)** 3 ch g Ali-Royal (IRE) -Classic Queen (IRE) (Classic Secret (USA)) 1466[6] 2179[7] 2578[3] 2840[5] 3387[5] 3572[3] 4027[5] 4518[6] 5410[6] 6083[13] 6183[8] >63a 76f<

**Must Be Magic** 7 b g Magic Ring (IRE) -Sequin Lady (Star Appeal) 705[4] 820[5] 1097[10] 2279[9] 2573[14] 3631[13] 4849[16] 5658[16] >65a 70f<

**Must Be So** 3 b f So Factual (USA) -Ovideo (Domynsky) 420[5] 521[8] 817[13] 891[11] 1725[6] 1985[8] 2800[4] 3175[10] 4338[13] 4469[5] 5473[12] >35a 45 f<

**Mutabari (USA)** 10 ch g Seeking The Gold (USA) -Cagey Exuberance (USA) (Exuberant (USA)) 1629[7] 1723[9] 1888[10] 2473[10] 2703[14] 2762[9] 4265[8] 5080[P] >25a 25f<

**Mutafanen** 3 gr c Linamix (FR) -Doomna (IRE) (Machiavellian (USA)) (1108) 1538[3] 2202[3] 3000[3] 3756[20] 4271[4] 4540[4] 5106[10] 5892[6] >112f<

**Mutahayya (IRE)** 3 b c Peintre Celebre (USA) -Winsa (USA) (Riverman (USA)) 1330[2] 2203[5] 3000[12] 6219[14] >107f<

**Mutajammel (FR)** 2 b c Kingmambo (USA) -Irtifa (Lahib (USA)) 5091[4] (5567) >86f<

**Mutamaasek (USA)** 2 bb c Swain (IRE) -Tamgeed (USA) (Woodman (USA)) 4169[5] 4728[7] 5620[4] 5988[5] >77f<

**Mutamared (USA)** 4 ch c Nureyev (USA) -Alydariel (USA) (Alydar (USA)) (2367) 5614[3] 6477[8] >90+f<

**Mutanabi (USA)** 2 b c Wild Rush (USA) -Freudenau (USA) (Meadowlake (USA)) 4599[2] 6010[3] >73a<

**Mutarafaa (USA)** 5 b g Red Ransom (USA) -Mashaarif (USA) (Mr Prospector (USA)) 477[4] 518[3] 562[2] 700[4] 765[7] 888[7] 932[8] 1043[2] 1098[13] 1233[9] 6548[16] >57 a 45f<

**Mutared (IRE)** 6 b g Marju (IRE) -Shahaada (USA) (Private Account (USA)) 589[12] 2643[14] 3282[11] 3604[16] 4386[10] 4818[19] >33a 38f<

**Mutasallil (USA)** 4 b c Gone West (USA) -Min Alhawa (USA) (Riverman (USA)) (2412) (3118) 4163[2] 4540[7] (5465) >110+f<

**Mutassem (FR)** 3 b c Fasliyev (USA) -Fee Eria (FR) (Always Fair (USA)) 1059[8] 1295[7] 3180[13] 4726[11] 4938[9] 5219[13] 5597[2] 6224[8] 6493[7] 6567[8] >60a 64f<

**Mutawaffer** 3 b c Marju (IRE) -Absaar (USA) (Alleged (USA)) 2043[7] 6345[4] >101f<

**Mutawaqed (IRE)** 6 ch g Zafonic (USA) -Waqood (USA) (Riverman (USA)) 2065[11] 2477[4] 2682[2] 3309[8] (4152) 4324[16] 4951[2] 5393[9] 5628[4] 6071[19] >91a 96f<

**Mutawassel (USA)** 3 b c Kingmambo (USA) -Danzig Darling (CAN) (Danzig (USA)) 1586[4] 1924[3] 4271[16] >98f<

**Mutayam** 4 b g Compton Place-Final Shot (Dalsaan) 3226[6] 3399[8] 3580[6] 4279[14] (5342) 5579[21] 5832[7] >52f<

**Muthaaber** 6 br h Machiavellian (USA) -Raheefa (USA) (Riverman (USA)) 688a[5] >79a 101f<

**Muwassi** 5 b h Grand Lodge (USA) -Sardonic (Kris) 690a[16] >96f<

**Muyassir (IRE)** 9 b g Brief Truce (USA) -Twine (Thatching) 464[8] (525) 2304[12] 2806[8] 3048[8] 3771[10] 6154[9] 6296[7] >57a 55f<

**Muy Bien** 3 ch c Daggers Drawn (USA) -Primula Bairn (Bairn (USA)) 458[2] 547[2] 669[10] 1008[3] (1270) 1303[2] 1702[3] 6350[9] >79a 82f<

**Muzio Scevola (IRE)** 3 ch g Titus Livius (FR) -Dancing Sunset (IRE) (Red Sunset) 1050[2] 1221[5] 1442[5] 1823[6] 3363[3] 5991[11] >67a 64f<

**My Ace** 6 b m Definite Article-Miss Springtime (Bluebird (USA)) 1318[6] >31f<

**Myannabanana (IRE)** 3 ch g Woodborough (USA) -Raging Storm (Horage) 450[5] 566[3] 746[4] 798[4] 1029[7] 1267[5] 1363[12] 1465[8] 5061[7] 5197[9] 5524[7] 5634[9] 5863[7] 6467[11] >63a 44+f<

**My Bayard** 5 ch g Efisio-Bay Bay (Bay Express) 775[6] 900[2] 967[5] 1103[19] (1595) 2215[15] 3226[4] 3515[3] 3894[7] 4827[3] >77a 70f<

**My Country Club** 7 b h Alzao (USA) -Merry Rous (Rousillon (USA)) 1533[6] 2209[6] 2454[7] 3742[18] 4476[6] >24a 47f<

**My Cousin Matt (USA)** 5 bb g Matty G (USA) -Conquistamiss (USA) (Conquistador Cielo (USA)) 6487a[3] >120a<

**My Dream (IRE)** 2 b f King s Theatre (IRE) -Dream Chaser (Record Token) 2868[4] >27f<

**My Dubai (IRE)** 2 ch f Dubai Millennium-Pastorale (Nureyev (USA)) 6470[3] >79f<

**My Gacho (IRE)** 2 b c Shinko Forest (IRE) -Floralia (Auction Ring (USA)) 4611[17] 5200[3] 5434[3] 6188[12] >80f<

**My Galliano (IRE)** 8 b g Muharib (USA) -Hogan Stand (Buckskin (FR)) 2000[13] 3239[3] 3662[6] 4262[5] >67a 72f<

**My Girl Pearl (IRE)** 4 b f Sri Pekan (USA) -Desert Bloom (FR) (Last Tycoon) 895[12] 1889[2] 2188[4] 2762[2] 2836[9] 3533[6] 3828[4] (3991)4548[7] 4708[3] 5261[6] (5411) 5575[4] 5691[8] >43a 55f<

**My Hope (IRE)** 3 b f Danehill (USA) -Lady Elgar (IRE) (Sadler s Wells (USA)) 1830[10] 2114[8] 3155[9] 3700[8] 4045[3] 4451[10] >50a 65f<

**My Last Bean (IRE)** 7 gr g Soviet Lad (USA) -Meanz Beanz (High Top) 5658[6] 5993[18] >81a 61f<

**My Legal Eagle (IRE)** 10 b g Law Society (USA) -Majestic Nurse (On Your Mark) (1887) 2004[4] 2186[2] (2462) (2590) (2787) 3449[2] >51a 66f<

**My Lilli (IRE)** 4 b f Marju (IRE) -Tamburello (IRE) (Roi Danzig (USA)) 463[3] 672[4] 767[7] 931[6] 1019[4] (1244) 1940[3] 2597[8] 3088[14] >61a 45f<

**My Line** 7 b g Perpendicular-My Desire (Grey Desire) 1287[10] >75df<

**My Little Sophia** 4 b f Wizard King-David James Girl (Faustus (USA)) 942[5] 1842[11] 2297[7] 3024[15] >18a 40f<

**My Maite (IRE)** 5 b g Komaite (USA) -Mena (Blakeney) 623[2] 765[4] 882[10] 1088[9] (2387) 2705[6] 3386[11] 3844[4] 4238[5] 4485[11] 4519[3] 5285[3] 5791[3] 6576[4] >64a 51f<

**My Michelle** 3 b f Ali-Royal (IRE) -April Magic (Magic Ring (IRE)) 1270[14] 2267[8] 4303[4] 4850[5] 5352[4] 5867[6] 6576[11] >38a 67f<

**Mynd** 4 b g Atraf-Prim Lass (Reprimand) (479) (638) 904[2] 1082[11] 1368[2] (1421) 1774[9] 1956[9] 2734[6] 3314[4] 3524[14] 4828[5] 5107[12] 5798[17] 6518[9] >71a 72f<

**My Paris** 3 b g Paris House-My Desire (Grey Desire) 506[3] 1425[2] 1771[2] 2145[2] 2448[5] 2906[2] 3610[2] (3955) (4570)(5120) >60a 98f<

**My Pension (IRE)** 3 b g Orpen (USA) -Woodenitbenice (USA) (Nasty And Bold (USA)) 1830[7] 1939[4] 2289[3] 2688[11] 5156[11] 5936[6] 6295[3] (6399) 6556[2] >66a 65f<

**My Portfolio (IRE)** 2 b g Montjeu (IRE) -Elaine s Honor (USA) (Chief s Crown (USA)) 4913[4] 5268[7] 6148[11] >69f<

**My Princess (IRE)** 2 b f Danehill Dancer (IRE) -Shanoora (IRE) (Don t Forget Me) 2736[3] 2972[5] 4296[3] (4432) 4836[7] 5090[5] 5417[5] 6003[2] 6206[14] >81 f<

**My Putra (USA)** 2 bb c Silver Hawk (USA) -Petite Triomphe (USA) (Wild Again (USA)) 4861[3] 5716[2] >81f<

**My Rascal (IRE)** 2 b c Imperial Ballet (IRE) -Derena (FR) (Crystal Palace (FR)) 4290[7] 4606[10] 5347[9] 6153[7] >54a 60f<

**My Renee (USA)** 4 bb f Kris S (USA) -Mayenne (USA) (Nureyev (USA)) 2416a[3] (4406a) 5763[2] >107f<

**My Risk (FR)** 5 b h Take Risks (FR) -Miss Pat (FR) (Vacarme (USA)) (1163a) 1780a[5] (2923a) 4795a[3] 5967a[8] >119f<

**Myrtus** 5 ch g Double Eclipse (IRE) -My Desire (Grey Desire) 1599[3] 2126[7] 4098[5] >33a 43f<

**My Sharp Grey** 5 gr m Tragic Role (USA) -Sharp Anne (Belfort (FR)) 705[8] >55a 62f<

**Mysterinch** 4 b g Inchinor-Hakone (IRE) (Alzao (USA)) 1469[3] 1762[7] 2637[8] 3337[2] 3477[7] 3717[7] 4553[17] 5099[4] >97a 97f<

**Mysterium** 10 gr g Mystiko (USA) -Way To Go (Troy) 551[3] 579[4] (992) 1512[5] 1693[6] >56a 56f<

**Mysterix (IRE)** 4 gr f Linamix (FR) -My Secret (GER) (Secreto (USA)) 3434a[8] 6258a[6] >90f<

**Mysterlover (IRE)** 4 b g Night Shift (USA) -Jacaranda City (IRE) (In The Wings) 555[12] 651[7] 919[7] 981[12] >55a<

**Mystery Giver (USA)** 6 b g Dynaformer (USA) -Ioya (USA) (Naskra (USA)) 4768a[10] >121f<

**Mystery Lot (IRE)** 2 b f Revoque (IRE) -Mystery Bid (Auction Ring (USA)) 4023[6] 4681[2] 5687[2] 6129[3] >58+a 75f<

**Mystery Maid (IRE)** 2 b f King s Theatre (IRE) -Duly Elected (Persian Bold) 1686[11] 2245[6] 2786[12] 3840[13] 5695[14] >46f<

**Mystery Mountain** 4 b g Mistertopogigo (IRE) -Don t Jump (IRE) (Entitled) 670[9] 807[5] 941[4] >36a<

**Mystery Pips** 4 b f Bin Ajwaad (IRE) -Le Shuttle (Presidium) 1870[11] 2252[10] 2369[7] 2778[11] 3147[4] 3524[15] 3820[8] 4105[4] 4422[3] 5579[14] 6059[12] 6403[12] >29a 57f<

**Mystery Solved (USA)** 4 b f Royal Academy (USA) -Golden Rhyme (Dom Racine (FR)) 1263[11] 2128[15] >57f<

**Mystical Girl (USA)** 3 ch f Rahy (USA) -Miss Twinkletoes (IRE) (Zafonic (USA)) 1309[3] 1957[3] (2134) 2244[2] (2557) 2676[3] 2971[12] 3641[6] 4287[8] 5025[5](5294) >101f<

**Mystical Land (IRE)** 2 b c Xaar-Samsung Spirit (Statoblest) 1324[2] (1819) 2996[2] 3640[3] 4288[2] 4981a[5] 5649[2] >108f<

**Mystic Lad** 3 gr g Magic Ring (IRE) -Jilly Woo (Environment Friend) 766[2] 1461[19] >66a 26f<

**Mystic Man (FR)** 6 b g Cadeaux Genereux-Shawanni (Shareef Dancer (USA)) 749[9] 1009[11] 1456[15] 1773[13] (2237) 2410[3] 3036[10] 3235[4] 5224[3] 5491[7] 5603[12] 6044[9] >81a 96f<

**Mystic Melody (USA)** 4 b f Seattle Slew (USA) -Munnaya (USA) (Nijinsky (CAN)) 1780a[9] >103f<

**Mystic Moon** 3 br f First Trump-Misty Moon (Polar Falcon (USA)) 597[9] 702[9] 1189[6] 1467[8] 1529[4] 1946[14] 2484[11] 4065[4] 4654[7] 4853[8] 5063[6] 5511[8] >43a 54f<

**Mystic Promise (IRE)** 3 gr g Among Men (USA) -Ivory s Promise (Pursuit Of Love) 591[11] 731[9] 802[8] 877[5] 1084[9] 1447[3] 1573[4] 1701[5] 2016[6] 2853[10] >31a 12f<

**My Sunshine (IRE)** 3 b f Alzao (USA) -Sunlit Ride (Ahonoora) 2562[10] 2900[7] 4619[8] 5222[8] 5510[11] 5830[14] >43a 61f<

**Mythe (FR)** 3 b c Sillery (USA) -Mythologie (FR) (Bering) 1654a[7] >103f<

**Mythical Charm** 5 b m Charnwood Forest (IRE) -Triple Tricks (IRE) (Royal Academy (USA)) 552[6] 705[13] 788[7] 855[9] 1166[6] 1404[3] 2052[3] 2284[7] 2573[11] 3386[7] 3593[3] 3626[5] 4220[15] 4740[7] 5080[2] 5496[2] 5795[9] 6343[12] >44a 62f<

**Mythical King (IRE)** 7 b g Fairy King (USA) -Whatcombe (USA) (Alleged (USA)) 2038[8] 2121[6] 6292[11] >16a 62 f<

**Mytori** 2 ch f Vettori (IRE) -Markievicz (IRE) (Doyoun) 4567[15] 4807[6] 5689[6] >21f<

**My True Love (IRE)** 5 b g Beneficial-Elfi (IRE) (Le Moss) 3341[5] 3912[9] 4513[4] 5354[10] >58f<

**Mytton s Bell (IRE)** 2 b f Bold Edge-Ionian Secret (Mystiko (USA)) 2296[2] 2453[3] 3925[10] 4358[3] 4488[7] 5059[5] 5578[15] 6242[3](6522) 6544[10] >55a 66f<

**Mytton s Dream** 2 br f Diktat-Courtisane (Persepolis (FR)) 1601[6] 1884[6] (2194) 3290[9] 3605[4] 4445[12] 5369[12] >53f<

**My Wild Rover** 4 b g Puissance-June Fayre (Sagaro) 1206[8] 1596[7] 2040[10] 2384[16] >15a 26f<

**N**

**Naaddey** 3 b c Seeking The Gold (USA) -Bahr (Generous (IRE)) 1411[7] 2276[6] 4140[4] >92f<

**Naahy** 4 ch c Bahamian Bounty-Daffodil Fields (Try My Best (USA)) (2200) (2793a) 3318[7] 3967a[4] 4216[4] 4596a[6] 5113[7] 5414[7] 5781[5] >83a 113f<

**Nabtat Saif** 3 b f Compton Place-Bahawir Pour (USA) (Green Dancer (USA)) 711a[7] 1005a[7] 3156[11] 3910[10] 4192[14] >81a 64f<

**Nadeszhda** 4 ch f Nashwan (USA) -Ninotchka (USA) (Nijinsky (CAN)) (3638) 3973a[10] >80+a 84+f<

**Nadir** 3 b c Pivotal-Amid The Stars (Midyan (USA)) 5123[9] 5345[6] 5999[10] >69f<

**Nafferton Girl (IRE)** 3 b f Orpen (USA) -Petomi (Presidium) 1293[4] 1600[7] 2484[8] 3190[10] >41a 43+f<

**Nafferton Heights (IRE)** 3 b c Peintre Celebre (USA) -Gold Mist (Darshaan) 1174[10] 1559[5] 2199[8] 2554[9] 3984[18] 4207[6] 4451[12] >47f<

**Naheef (IRE)** 5 b h Marju (IRE) -Golden Digger

(USA) (Mr Prospector (USA)) 979a[3] 2329a[5] 3642[8] (5133) 5731[5] 6216[10] >**110a 117f**<

**Naivety 2** ch f Machiavellian (USA) -Innocence (Unfuwain (USA)) 5089[2] 5559[7] >**77f**<

**Najaaba (USA) 4** b f Bahhare (USA) -Ashbilya (USA) (Nureyev (USA)) (457) (518) (552) (614) 892[5] (1036) 1332[5] 1790[6] 1931[5] 5886[10] 6497[7] >**85+a 84f**<

**Najeebon (FR) 5** ch g Cadeaux Genereux-Jumairah Sun (IRE) (Scenic) 1765[11] 2132[15] 2477[16] 2763[3] 3090[6] 3453[3] 3691[7] 3941[12]5124[9] 5299[2] 5730[3] 5874[10] >**90f**<

**Nakwa (IRE) 6** b g Namaqualand (USA) -Cajo (IRE) (Tirol) (446) 546[2] 609[2] 724[5] 1245[3] 1326[2] 1785[2] (2299) 2652[2]3449[6] 3644[10] 3902[10] 5584[16] 6215[22] >**64a 74 f**<

**Namat (IRE) 3** b f Daylami (IRE) -Masharik (IRE) (Caerleon (USA)) 5239[2] (5828) >**74f**<

**Named At Dinner 3** ch g Halling (USA) -Salanka (IRE) (Persian Heights) 1559[11] 2134[16] 2457[19] 5223[20] 5364[15] 5448[7] 5702[10] 5863[8] >**45f**<

**Namking 2** b g Namid-Kingdom Queen (IRE) (Night Shift (USA)) 1865[7] 2173[8] 3802[6] >**40a 52f**<

**Namroc (IRE) 3** b c Indian Ridge-Hesperia (Slip Anchor) (3094) 3750[4] 5590[2] 5942[4] 6354[7] >**93f**<

**Namroud (USA) 5** b g Irish River (FR) -Top Line (FR) (Top Ville) 1106[20] 1246[6] 2271[10] 3036[25] 3365[7] 4543[7] 4931[4] 5631[9]6244[6] 6445[9] >**84f**<

**Namura Big Time (JPN) 3** b c Sakura Bakushin O (JPN) -Taiki Mystery (USA) (Green Forest (USA)) 5982a[14] >**92f**<

**Nanabanana (IRE) 2** b f Anabaa (USA) -Tanabata (FR) (Shining Steel) 5149[2] 6456[2] >**102+f**<

**Nan Jan 2** b f Komaite (USA) -Dam Certain (IRE) (Damister (USA)) 3296[8] 5400[7] 5848[2] >**76f**<

**Nanna (IRE) 3** b f Danetime (IRE) -Pre Catelan (Polar Falcon (USA)) 514[5] 591[2] 732[9] 906[3] 1262[7] 1596[2] (2165) 2428[6]2850[2] (3562) (3838) 4320[6] 4608[7] 5949[3] 6538[8] >**58a 74f**<

**Nanton (USA) 2** rg c Spinning World (USA) -Grab The Green (USA) (Cozzene (USA)) 2058[7] 6492[6] >**75a 49f**<

**Nantucket Sound (USA) 3** b g Quiet American (USA) -Anna (Ela-Mana-Mou) 1613[9] 1997[4] (2430) 3152[8] 3806[8] >**66a 76f**<

**Napapijri (FR) 2** gr f Highest Honor (FR) -Les Marettes (FR) (Baillamont (USA)) 5089[5] 5789[7] 6077[4] >**58f**<

**Napoleon (IRE) 3** b c Sadler s Wells (USA) -Love For Ever (IRE) (Darshaan) 5662a[13] >**92f**<

**Napper Tandy (IRE) 4** ch g Spectrum (IRE) -La Meilleure (Lord Gayle (USA)) 1156a[2] 2329a[4] 2603a[2] 2796a[5] 3355a[4] 5481a[5] >**109f**<

**Narciso (GER) 4** ch g Acatenango (GER) -Notturna (Diu Star) 2654[10] 2777[8] 3279[9] 3896[10] 5243[6] 5320[13] 5638[6] >**22a 35f**<

**Narcisse Du Rheu (FR) 3** b f Saint Cyrien (FR) -Speed Du Rheu (FR) (Valanjou (FR)) 2028a[7] >**91f**<

**Narrative (IRE) 6** b h Sadler s Wells (USA) -Barger (USA) (Riverman (USA)) 1925[8] 2588[4] 3119[6] 3756[18] >**101f**<

**Nashaab (USA) 7** b g Zafonic (USA) -Tajannub (USA) (Dixieland Band (USA)) 558[12] 647[7] 1106[7] 1354[9] 1927[2] 2201[3] (4360) 4908[5] 5468[7]5813[8] 5941[14] (6044) 6193[14] >**82a 100f**<

**Nassau Street 4** gr g Bahamian Bounty-Milva (Jellaby) 814[3] 1077[8] 4669[11] 5283[3] >**43a 32f**<

**Nasseem Dubai (USA) 2** ch c Silver Hawk (USA) -Fleur De Nuit (USA) (Woodman (USA)) 4256[7] 4930[6] 5095[2] 5302[5] 5604[3] 6012[7] 6113[7] >**73a 77f**<

**Nassiria 3** b f Singspiel (IRE) -Naskhi (Nashwan (USA)) 1794[6] 2020[6] 2805[11] 3919[12] 4201[7] 4471[3] 5216[3] >**67a 69f**<

**Natalie Jane (IRE) 2** ch f Giant s Causeway (USA) -Kirk (Selkirk (USA)) 5846[7] 6078[3] (6309) 6472[3] >**82f**<

**Nataliya 3** b f Green Desert (USA) -Ninotchka (USA) (Nijinsky (CAN)) 1458[3] 1791[7] 3541[9] 4077[4] 4779[11] 5416[P] >**105f**<

**Nathan Brittles (USA) 4** ch g Cat s Career (USA) -Doc s Answer (USA) (Dr Schwartzman (USA)) (1199) >**83f**<

**Nathan Detroit 4** b g Entrepreneur-Mainly Sunset (Red Sunset) 4403[15] 4774[13] >**61a 45f**<

**Natikhab 2** b f Intikhab (USA) -Nappe Di Cardinale (IRE) (Distinctly North (USA)) 3436a[4] 5577a[2] ><

**National Currency (SAF) 5** b h National Assembly (CAN) -Enchanted Dollar (USA) (Spend A Buck (USA)) (689a) >**118a 126f**<

**National Icon (SAF) 4** ch c National Emblem (SAF) -Royal Fields (SAF) (Northfields (USA)) 632a[6] 755a[4] >**59a 78f**<

**National Swagger (IRE) 2** b f Giant s Causeway (USA) -Eva Luna (IRE) (Double Schwartz) 3859a[5] 4592a[4] 6101a[5] >**88f**<

**National Trust 2** b c Sadler s Wells (USA) -National Treasure (Shirley Heights) 6476[11] >**46f**<

**Native Title 6** b g Pivotal-Bermuda Lily (Dunbeath (USA)) 1923[4] 2461[8] (2682) 3074[18] 3309[16] 3754[3] 4324[19] 5603[10] 6349[8] >**97f**<

**Native Turk (USA) 3** b c Miswaki (USA) -Churn Dat Butter (USA) (Unbridled (USA)) 1371[14] 3666[11] 4880[2] 5424[5] >**69a 58f**<

**Natmsky (IRE) 5** b g Shadeed (USA) -Cockney Lass (Camden Town) 3411[19] 3835[9] 5305[15] >**13f**<

**Naughty Girl (IRE) 4** b f Dr Devious (IRE) -Mary Magdalene (Night Shift (USA)) 575[11] 681[8] 737[8] 1855[15] 2178[15] 2724[9] 2869[9] 3427[5]3807[4] 4004[4] 4066[12] 4477[2] 4771[12] (5336) 5587[10] 6146[8] >**32a 54f**<

**Naughty Nell 5** b m Danehill Dancer (IRE) -Hana Marie (Formidable (USA)) 831a[4] 921a[2] 1002a[6] >**90+a 84f**<

**Nautical 6** gr g Lion Cavern (USA) -Russian Royal (USA) (Nureyev (USA)) 1369[14] 1856[9] 3088[4] 3423[6] 3771[4] 3826[3] 4238[11] 4401[2]4751[7] (5260) (6024) 6154[8] 6220[2] >**75a 62f**<

**Nautical Star 9** b g Slip Anchor-Comic Talent (Pharly (FR)) 1721[5] >**44a 59f**<

**Naval Attache 2** b g Slip Anchor-Cayla (Tumble Wind) 6067[10] 6441[17] >**48f**<

**Naval Force 2** b c Forzando-Barsham (Be My Guest (USA)) 3588[9] 4022[4] 4256[3] 5119[16] 6338[13] >**71a 74f**<

**Navigation (IRE) 2** ch c Bahamian Bounty-Bridge Pool (First Trump) 5319[11] 5857[6] 6359[7] >**65+a 59f**<

**Nawaaem (USA) 2** bb f Swain (IRE) -Alattrah (USA) (Shadeed (USA)) 6470[5] >**76f**<

**Nawamees (IRE) 6** b g Darshaan-Truly Generous (IRE) (Generous (IRE)) 743[4] 844[2] 3325[2] 4218[10] 5814[12] >**90a 95f**<

**Nawow 4** b g Blushing Flame (USA) -Fair Test (Fair Season) 523[15] 1210[3] 1457[5] 2047[6] 5615[10] 5728[2] 5875[7] 5997[4] >**85a 86f**<

**Nayyir 6** ch g Indian Ridge-Pearl Kite (USA) (Silver Hawk (USA)) 1146a[3] 3674[16] 4228[2] 5113[2] 5782[4] 6076a[6] >**94a 126f**<

**Nazaaha (USA) 2** gr f Elnadim (USA) -Taatof (IRE) (Lahib (USA)) 4364[4] >**71f**<

**Nazzwah 3** ch f Rahy (USA) -Baaderah (IRE) (Cadeaux Genereux) 2808[6] 3044[6] 3554[9] >**63f**<

**Ndola 5** b g Emperor Jones (USA) -Lykoa (Shirley Heights) (427) 570[12] 996[12] 1277[3] >**45a 42f**<

**Neap Tide 3** br g Zafonic (USA) -Love The Rain (Rainbow Quest (USA)) 1688[13] 2790[19] >**73f**<

**Near Dock (GER) 3** b c Docksider (USA) -Night Year (IRE) (Jareer (USA)) 3134a[4] >**108f**<

**Near Honor (GER) 6** ro h Highest Honor (FR) -Night Year (IRE) (Jareer (USA)) 1259a[10] 3357a[5] 3972a[5] 5683a[4] 5975a[7] 6378a[6] >**107f**<

**Nearly A Fool 6** b g Komaite (USA) -Greenway Lady (Prince Daniel (USA)) (469) (573) 624[12] 928[2] (1032) 1204[8] (1265) 4142[3] 4301[4] 4602[8]4969[5] 5713[11] 6081[5] (6452) 6493[2] >**76a 76f**<

**Neath 3** b f Rainbow Quest (USA) -Welsh Autumn (Tenby) 5007[5] 5445[3] 6285[7] >**70f**<

**Nebraska City 3** b g Piccolo-Scarlet Veil (Tyrnavos) 1243[10] 2266[6] 3589[13] 4052[4] 4125[6] 4336[13] 4687[13] >**33a 65f**<

**Nebraska Lady (IRE) 2** b f Lujain (USA) -Montana Lady (IRE) (Be My Guest (USA)) 5971a[5] >**85 f**<

**Nebraska Tornado (USA) 4** bb f Storm Cat (USA) -Media Nox (Lycius (USA)) 2339a[5] 2957[4] 4383a[3] 5940[3] 6484a[8] >**97a 122f**<

**Neckar Valley (IRE) 5** b g Desert King (IRE) -Solar Attraction (IRE) (Salt Dome (USA)) 5607[12] >**85f**<

**Necklace 3** b f Darshaan-Spinning The Yarn (Barathea (IRE)) 1791[12] 2330a[6] 2640[4] 4767a[3] 5530a[4] >**115f**<

**Needles And Pins (IRE) 3** b f Fasliyev (USA) -Fairy Contessa (IRE) (Fairy King (USA)) 1417[4] 2117[7] 2685[5] 3976[7] 4862[12] >**100df**<

**Needwood Bucolic (IRE) 6** br g Charnwood Forest (IRE) -Greek Icon (Thatching) 2582[10] 2833[9] 2975[7] 3381[13] 3735[9] 4004[13] 4535[7] >**12a 41f**<

**Needwood Mystic 9** b m Rolfe (USA) -Enchanting Kate (Enchantment) 2798[2] >**55a 74f**<

**Needwood Spirit 9** b g Rolfe (USA) -Needwood Nymph (Bold Owl) 5238[15] 5638[16] >**23a 42f**<

**Nee Lemon Left 2** b f Puissance-Via Dolorosa (Chaddleworth (IRE)) 1340[2] 1782[6] 2980[3] 3408[7] 3577[6] 4986[4] 5060[12] >**60f**<

**Neferura 2** b f Mister Baileys-Boadicea s Chariot (Commanche Run) 5569[11] 5946[9] 6441[13] >**54f**<

**Negas (IRE) 2** b g Titus Livius (FR) -Alzeam (IRE) (Alzao (USA)) 2860[17] 3893[10] 4131[11] 4761[17] >**42f**<

**Negwa (IRE) 3** b f Bering-Ballet (Sharrood (USA)) 1116[5] 1640[8] 4726[10] >**70f**<

**Nella Fantasia (IRE) 2** ch f Giant s Causeway (USA) -Paper Moon (IRE) (Lake Coniston (IRE)) 2585[6] 3228[6] >**67f**<

**Nellie Gwyn 2** b f King s Best (USA) -On Tiptoes (Shareef Dancer (USA)) 6569[15] >**30f**<

**Nelson Creek (FR) 4** gr c Brier Creek (USA) -Slot Machine (FR) (Highest Honor (FR)) 1163a[10] >**93f**<

**Nelson s Luck 3** b g Young Ern-A Little Hot (Petong) 5378[15] >**12f**<

**Nemo Fugat (IRE) 5** b g Danehill Dancer (IRE) -Do The Right Thing (Busted) 1175[17] 2261[13] 2580[5] 2781[6] 3082[7] 4013[2] 4308[5] 4390[2]4702[15] 5020[13] 5317[3] 5518[8] >**68 f**<

**Neon Blue 3** bb g Atraf-Desert Lynx (IRE) (Green Desert (USA)) 1775[5] (2236) 2569[7] 2981[3] 3585[3] 3926[3] (4151) 4877[6] 5244[7] 5582[8]6199[11] >**76f**<

**Ne Oublie 2** b c Makbul-Parkside Prospect (Piccolo) 2686[6] 4124[4] 4607[3] 5060[10] >**65f**<

**Nepal (IRE) 2** ch f Monashee Mountain (USA) -Zetonic (Zafonic (USA)) 5521[6] 5856[2] 6092[4] >**63f**<

**Nephetriti Way (IRE) 3** b f Docksider (USA) -Velvet Appeal (IRE) (Petorius) 1704[7] 2548[5] 2844[5] 3826[5] >**84f**<

**Nepro (IRE) 2** b c Orpen (USA) -My Gray (FR) (Danehill (USA)) 3286a[3] >**85f**<

**Neptune 8** b g Dolphin Street (FR) -Seal Indigo (IRE) (Glenstal (USA)) 579[5] 857[11] 1101[9] 1402[2] 1543[4] 1989[5] 3087[3]3303[5] 3774[3] >**46a 42f**<

**Neqaawi 3** br f Alhaarth (IRE) -Jinsiyah (USA) (Housebuster (USA)) 2572[5] (2937) 3517[11] >**71f**<

**Nero s Return (IRE) 3** b g Mujadil (USA) -Snappy Dresser (Nishapour (FR)) 1330[6] 1459[8] 2294[6] 2897[15] 3482[7] 4076[5] 4531[7] >**100f**<

**Nesnaas (USA) 3** ch g Gulch (USA) -Sedrah (USA) (Dixieland Band (USA)) 2239[11] 3180[15] >**70f**<

**Nessen Dorma (IRE) 3** b g Entrepreneur-Goldilocks (IRE) (Caerleon (USA)) 450[4] 622[5] 1416[5] 1609[2] (1823) 2070[3] 2561[3] 3035[8] 3821[9]5632[7] >**76a 85f**<

**Neutral Night (IRE) 4** b f Night Shift (USA) -Neutrality (IRE) (Common Grounds) 422[3] 535[10] 654[7] 725[5] 934[3] 1021[2] 1080[4]1191[3] 1446[3] (1889) 2012[2] 2188[2] 2811[8] >**49a 37f**<

**Neutrino 2** b c Mtoto-Fair Seas (General Assembly (USA)) 6145[12] 6330[4] 6536[4] >**60a 72+f**<

**Nevada Desert (IRE) 4** b g Desert King (IRE) -Kayanga (Green Desert (USA)) 2142[4] 2410[5] 3952[2] 4155[7] (4988) 5194[8] 5607[18] 5835[8] 6525[6] >**81f**<

**Never Away 2** b f Royal Applause-Waypoint (Cadeaux Genereux) 3676[9] 3946[10] 4753[13] 5271[11] 5548[11] >**59f**<

**Never Cried Wolf 3** b g Wolfhound (USA) -Bold Difference (Bold Owl) 553[6] 621[10] 817[7] 873[6] 1019[12] >**54a**<

**Never Forget Bowie 8** b g Superpower-Heldigvis (Hot Grove) 4985[8] 6200[11] 6465[5] >**51f**<

**Neverletme Go (IRE) 2** b f Green Desert (USA) -Cassandra Go (IRE) (Indian Ridge) 4298[4] 5270[5] >**73+f**<

**Never Promise (FR) 6** b m Cadeaux Genereux-Yazeanhaa (USA) (Zilzal (USA)) 5449[6] 6466[8] >**3a 40f**<

**Never Will 3** b c Cadeaux Genereux-Answered Prayer (Green Desert (USA)) 1342[2] 1794[2] (2077) 2202[12] 3001[23] >**83f**<

**Never Without Me 4** ch g Mark Of Esteem (IRE) -Festival Sister (Belmez (USA)) 476[6] 626[4] 794[5] 1027[2] (1262) 1421[8] 1739[3] 1873[4](3025) (3277) 3887[2] 4179[4] 4452[2] 5157[2] 5704[6] 5798[12] >**75a 76f**<

**Nevinstown (IRE) 4** b c Lahib (USA) -Moon Tango (IRE) (Last Tycoon) 787[8] >**39a 39f**<

**Newclose 4** b g Barathea (IRE) -Wedgewood (USA) (Woodman (USA)) 425[3] 474[3] 570[3] 653[4] 1592[7] >**44a 60f**<

**Newcorp Lad 4** b g Komaite (USA) -Gleam Of Gold (Crested Lark) 1451[15] 1669[4] 2218[9] 2752[8] 3401[7] 3738[4] 3921[4] 4301[2]4511[4] 5236[14] 5518[3] (5859) 5945[4] 6097[7] >**76+f**<

**Newcorr (IRE) 5** b g Magical Wonder (USA) -Avionne (Derrylin) 1102[10] 1164[14] 1407[6] 1548[3] 1861[2] 2051[4] 4265[7]4669[7] >**37a 36f**<

**New Day Dawning 3** ch f First Trump-Tintinara (Selkirk (USA)) 1749[13] 2468[6] 2778[16] 4557[20] >**52f**<

**Newfoundland (USA) 4** ch c Storm Cat (USA) -Clear Mandate (USA) (Deputy Minister (CAN)) 6491a[12] >**111a 101f**<

**Newlands North (IRE) 3** ch c Goldmark (USA) -Park Cottage (IRE) (Thatching) 4588a[2] >**74f**<

**New Largue (USA) 2** b f Distant View (USA) -New Story (USA) (Dynaformer (USA)) 5979a[8] >**101f**<

**New Mexican 3** ch g Dr Fong (USA) -Apache Star (Arazi (USA)) 1123[4] 1411[5] >**103f**<

**New Morning (IRE) 3** b f Sadler s Wells (USA) -Hellenic (Darshaan) 2093[2] (2357) 2997[4] 3519[5] (4640) 5679a[6] >**109+f**<

**Newnham (IRE) 3** ch g Theatrical-Brief Escapade (IRE) (Brief Truce (USA)) 4615[2] 5007[4] 5409[2] 6245[3] >**76f**<

**New Options 7** b g Formidable (USA) -No Comebacks (Last Tycoon) 480[5] 612[4] 748[8] 799[5] 884[10] 1087[3] 1283[9]1496[3] 1665[17] 2120[14] 2666[7] 3277[5] >**63a 66 f**<

**New Order 3** b f Singspiel (IRE) -Eternal (Kris) 2046[3] (3448) (5148) 5766[6] 6332[17] >**83+f**<

**New Princess (GER) 5** br m Brief Truce (USA) -Nillfeedir (GER) (Fabulous Dancer (USA)) 3134a[10] 5823a[5] 6255a[5] >**93f**<

**New Prospective 6** b g Cadeaux Genereux-Amazing Bay (Mazilier (USA)) 474[12] >**48a 50f**<

**New Realm (USA) 2** b c Red Ransom (USA) -Mystery Rays (USA) (Nijinsky (CAN)) 6476[14] >**37f**<

**New Seeker 4** b g Green Desert (USA) -Ahbab (IRE) (Ajdal (USA)) 1705[2] 3036[4] 3724[8] 4120[6] 4956a[10] >**108+f**<

**New South Wales 4** b c In The Wings-Temora (IRE) (Ela-Mana-Mou) 2533[3] 2998[10] >**113f**<

**Newsround 2** ch c Cadeaux Genereux-Ring The Relatives (Bering) 5118[2] (5609) 6068[7] >**92f**<

**News Sky (USA) 3** b c Gone West (USA) -Dubian (High Line) 1461[15] 3447[2] 3994[2] 4396[3] 5936[3] 6082[8] >**83f**<

**Newton (IRE) 3** b c Danehill (USA) -Elite Guest (IRE) (Be My Guest (USA)) (1256a) 1847a[4] 2161a[6] 2315a[6] 2956[11] 5661a[10] 5972a[8] >**104f**<

**Newtonian (USA) 5** ch g Distant View (USA) -Polly Adler (USA) (Housebuster (USA)) 513[3] 651[8] 6208[4] >**73a 54f**<

**Newtown Chief 3** b g So Factual (USA) -Polish Descent (IRE) (Danehill (USA)) 3636[15] 4055[13] 4128[11] 4460[11] >**16a 51f**<

**New Wish (IRE) 4** b g Ali-Royal (IRE) -False Spring (IRE) (Petorius) 4301[5] 4577[9] 5316[12] 6097[11] >**63f**<

**New York (IRE) 3** b f Danzero (AUS) -Council Rock (General Assembly (USA)) 2097[13] 2377[10] 5366[3] 5748[5] 6200[8] >**49a 59f**<

**New York City (IRE) 3** b c Alzao (USA) -Eurolinka (IRE) (Tirol) 4850[8] >**26f**<

**Next Flight (IRE) 5** b g Woodborough (USA) -Sans Ceriph (IRE) (Thatching) 570[6] 781[2] 878[3] 1023[2] 1344[3] (1668) 2038[4] 2531[3]2987[2] 3236[3] 3576[4] 3803[6] 4424[8] >**55a 57f**<

**Next Gina (GER) 4** b f Perugino (USA) -Night Petticoat (GER) (Petoski) 3504a[2] 4385a[8] >**112f**<

**Next Society (GER) 3** b c Law Society (USA) -Night Petticoat (GER) (Petoski) 2541a[8] >**58f**<

**Next Time (IRE) 2** b f Danetime (IRE) -Muckross Park (Nomination) 1128[4] 1340[5] 2071[10] 2677[7] 3491[4] 4017[4] 4875[8] 5363[11] >**59f**<

**Next Time Around (IRE) 2** b c Namid-In Due Course (USA) (A.P. Indy (USA)) (1105) 1383[3] 2532[5] 2959[12] 5602[4] 6068[11] >**92f**<

**Niagara (IRE) 7** b g Rainbows For Life (CAN) -Highbrook (USA) (Alphabatim (USA)) 1282[12] 3459[6] 3917[16] >**65a 77f**<

**Nibbles (IRE) 2** b g Soviet Star (USA) -Tumbleweed Pearl (Aragon) 4997[13] ><

**Nice Tune 2** b f Diktat-Military Tune (IRE) (Nashwan (USA)) 5247[3] 5469[4] 6123[7] 6353[5] >**90f**<

**Nicholas Nickelby 4** gr g Fayruz-Alasib (Siberian Express (USA)) 1877[7] 2217[6] 2362[2] 2895[10] 3247[13] 3376[4] 3742[3] 4751[4]5104[4] 5448[2] 5803[5] 5830[11] >**56a 56f**<

**Niciara (IRE) 7** b g Soviet Lad (USA) -Verusa (IRE) (Petorius) 432[8] 716[9] >**12a**<

**Nickel Sungirl (IRE) 4** b f Petorius-Sharp Hint (Sharpo) 434[11] ><

**Nicki Hill (NOR) 8** ch g Basiluzzo (USA) -Nicki Line (NOR) (Sappeur) 5504a[4] ><

**Nick The Silver 3** gr c Nicolotte-Brillante (FR) (Green Dancer (USA)) 1222[14] 2179[6] 2787[10] 3752[U] 4146[11] 4346[12] >**61f**<

**Nicolaia (GER) 4** b f Alkalde (GER) -Nicol s Girl (Dunbeath (USA)) 3434a[5] 5823a[7] 6255a[14] >**86f**<

**Nietta 4** b f Zamindar (USA) -Kentfield (Busted) 3816a[15] ><

**Nietzsche (IRE) 3** b c Sadler s Wells (USA) -Wannabe (Shirley Heights) 1382[9] 1674[2] 2374[5] 6357[2] >**82+f**<

**Nifty Roy 4** b g Royal Applause-Nifty Fifty (IRE) (Runnett) 2216[16] 2356[13] 3616[13] 3735[11] >**8a 44f**<

**Night Air (IRE) 3** b g Night Shift (USA) -Pippas Song (Reference Point) (1771) 2207[5] 5244[2] 5652[2] >**83f**<

**Night Aurora 5** ch h Pennekamp (USA) -India Atlanta (Ahonoora) 921a[9] >**92f**<

**Night Bokbel (IRE) 5** b m Night Shift (USA) -Liu (IRE) (Top Ville) 911a[2] >**106f**<

**Night Cap (IRE) 5** ch g Night Shift (USA) -Classic Design (Busted) 453[6] 560[7] 930[11] 1280[2] 1497[7] 2885[3] 4403[17]4548[4] 5930[8] >**54a 54f**<

**Night Chapter 3** b c Night Shift (USA) -Context (Zafonic (USA)) 5171a[8] 5668a[7] (6075a) 6511a[4] >**106f**<

**Night Club Queen (IRE) 2** ch f Night Shift (USA) -Play The Queen (IRE) (King Of Clubs) 4399[13] 4712[9] 5270[14] >**35f**<

**Night Dance 12** ch g Weldnaas (USA) -Shift Over (USA) (Night Shift (USA)) 3911[18] >**5f**<

**Nightdance Forest (IRE) 3** b f Charnwood Forest (IRE) -Nightdance (GER) (Shareef Dancer (USA)) 3434a[2] ><

**Night Driver (IRE) 5** b g Night Shift (USA) -Highshaan (Pistolet Bleu (IRE)) 1857[13] 2226[14] 2560[12] 3423[11] 4485[13] 4600[10] >**45a 45f**<

**Nightfall (USA) 2** b c Rahy (USA) -Quality Gift (Last Tycoon) (4117) 4581[6] 5052[11] >**60a 82f**<

**Night Frolic 3** b f Night Shift (USA) -Miss D Ouilly (FR) (Bikala) (1830) 2355[3] 2848[7] 3478[6] 4580[6] 5156[9] 5693[4] 6097[2] 6461[5] >**68f**<

**Night Guest (IRE) 2** b c Danehill Dancer (IRE) -Meadow Grass (IRE) (Thatching) 4922[8] 5268[12] 5870[15] >**64f**<

**Night Hour (IRE) 2** b c Entrepreneur-Witching Hour (IRE) (Alzao (USA)) 5269[4] (5871) 6189[7] >**87+f**<

**Night Kiss (FR) 4** ch f Night Shift (USA) -Roxy (Rock City) 1828[13] 2064[9] 2284[10] >**67 a 55f**<

**Night Lagoon (GER) 3** b f Lagunas-Nenuphar (IRE) (Night Shift (USA)) 1983a[10] >**93f**<

**Night Mail 4** b g Shaamit (IRE) -Penlanfeigan (Abutammam) 456[6] 5449[8] >**42a 43f**<

**Night Market 6** ch g Inchinor-Night Transaction (Tina s Pet) 2128[11] (3103) 3375[9] 4386[7] 5021[18] 5450[6] >**53a 53f**<

**Night Of Joy (IRE) 2** b f King s Best (USA) -Gilah (IRE) (Saddlers Hall (IRE)) 2876[4] 3456[4] (4851) (5188) 5292[9] 6334[7] >**89f**<

**Night Out (FR) 2** b f Night Shift (USA) -My Lucky Day (FR) (Darshaan) 3950[9] 4399[6] 4770[10] >**65f**<

**Night Prayers (IRE) 2** ch c Night Shift (USA) -Eleanor Antoinette (IRE) (Double Schwartz) 6408a[5] >**91f**<

**Night Prospector 4** b c Night Shift (USA) -Pride Of My Heart (Lion Cavern (USA)) 2041[11] (2636) 3537[10] 4886[12] 5418[8] >**106df**<

**Nights Cross (IRE) 3** b c Cape Cross (IRE) -Cathy Garcia (IRE) (Be My Guest (USA)) 1323[4] 2080[3] 2955[8] 3073[10] 3940[7] 4165[17] 4362[3] 4590a[3]4750[3] 4862[8] 5171a[10] (5893) 6104a[14] >**109f**<

**Night Set (GER) 5** b g Second Set (IRE) -

Nenuphar (IRE) (Night Shift (USA)) 6379a[13] >**88f**<

**Night Sight (USA)** 7 b g Eagle Eyed (USA) -El Hamo (USA) (Search For Gold (USA)) 2235[9] 2449[2] 2671[3] 3300[4] 3866[4] (4450) 5229[5] (5303) 5764[4] 5950[5]6047[2] >**79 a 78f**<

**Night Spot** 3 ch g Night Shift (USA) -Rash Gift (Cadeaux Genereux) 2018[6] 3610[3] 4300[2] (4749) 5074[6] 5402[11] >**69a 90f**<

**Night Storm** 3 b f Night Shift (USA) -Monte Calvo (Shirley Heights) 492[5] 621[3] 741[3] 869[3] 959[6] 1939[15] (6557) >**70a 65f**<

**Night Warrior (IRE)** 4 b g Alhaarth (IRE) -Miniver (IRE) (Mujtahid (USA)) 559[10] 592[4] 618[4] 629[2] 679[7] >**73a 81f**<

**Night Wolf (IRE)** 4 gr g Indian Ridge-Nicer (IRE) (Pennine Walk) 1118[6] 1247[15] 2030[8] 2492[3] 3058[8] 3455[13] 3841[16] 4459[8]4495[5] 4877[14] 5305[11] >**41 a 41f**<

**Night Worker** 3 b c Dracula (AUS) -Crystal Magic (Mazilier (USA)) 1270[6] 1702[10] 1997[9] 2790[13] 3593[9] 3636[6] 4021[5] 4548[14]4674[10] 5072[9] 5691[7] >**54f**<

**Nikiforos** 3 b c Inchinor-Putout (Dowsing (USA)) 2286[8] 3094[6] 3448[8] 4024[4] 4478[4] 4868[7] 5219[12] >**64a 64f**<

**Nimbus Twothousand** 4 b f Cloudings (IRE) -Blueberry Parkes (Pursuit Of Love) 1233[5] >**45a 48f**<

**Nimello (USA)** 8 b g Kingmambo (USA) -Zakota (IRE) (Polish Precedent (USA)) 558[9] 1009[9] (1475) 1708[8] (3660) 4852[13] 6358[13] >**95a 86f**<

**Nina Fontenail (FR)** 3 gr f Kaldounevees (FR) -Ninon Fontenail (FR) (Turgeon (USA)) 1356[9] 1856[12] 2517[14] 2832[5] 4775[4] 4941[2] 6056[5] >**42a 43f**<

**Ninah** 3 b f First Trump-Alwal (Pharly (FR)) 1841[16] 2518[11] 3142[10] 5337[17] 5830[10] 6288[15] 6556[8] >**45a 45f**<

**Ninah s Intuition** 2 b c Piccolo-Gina Of Hithermoor (Reprimand) 1589[4] 1871[4] 3413[8] >**58f**<

**Nine Red** 3 b f Royal Applause-Sarcita (Primo Dominie) 2112[10] 2536[9] 2915[9] 3280[2] 5020[15] 5204[9] >**63a 57f**<

**Ninja Storm (IRE)** 2 b c Namid-Swan Lake (IRE) (Waajib) 3805[4] 4191[5] 4514[6] 4918[7] >**63a 71f**<

**Niobe s Way** 3 b f Singspiel (IRE) -Arietta s Way (IRE) (Darshaan) 3630[7] 4168[4] 4693[3] 6088[2] 6287[6] >**75f**<

**Nip Nip (IRE)** 2 b f Royal Applause-Rustic Bliss (Kris) 4682[9] 5068[8] >**39f**<

**Nipping (IRE)** 2 b f Night Shift (USA) -Zelda (IRE) (Caerleon (USA)) 4962a[7] 5922a[3] 6462a[6] >**99f**<

**Nippy Nipper** 3 b f Fraam-Elite Hope (USA) (Moment Of Hope (USA)) 5702[18] 6402[10] 6561[14] >**9a 2f**<

**Nisr** 7 b g Grand Lodge (USA) -Tharwa (IRE) (Last Tycoon) 5124[2] >**84a 86f**<

**Nisri Di San Jore (IRE)** 2 b c Sri Pekan (USA) -Ninna Nanna (IRE) (Green Desert (USA)) 3362a[8] >**47f**<

**Nistaki (USA)** 3 ch c Miswaki (USA) -Brandywine Belle (USA) (Trempolino (USA)) 1519[4] 2900[6] 3168[4] 4576[2] >**75f**<

**Niteowl Dream** 4 ch f Colonel Collins (USA) -Nite-Owl Dancer (Robellino (USA)) 2346[4] 2811[13] 2879[13] 3378[12] >**56a 60df**<

**Niteowl Express (IRE)** 3 b f Royal Applause-Nordan Raider (Domynsky) 956[8] 1038[6] 1447[5] 2187[4] 3742[10] 4132[9] >**38a 30f**<

**Nite-Owl Fizz** 6 b g Efisio-Nite-Owl Dancer (Robellino (USA)) 442[4] 531[2] 604[7] 773[4] >**54 a 31f**<

**Niteowl Lad (IRE)** 2 ch g Tagula (IRE) -Mareha (IRE) (Cadeaux Genereux) 1961[7] 3233[19] 3893[2] 4175[5] >**66f**<

**Nite Trippa (FR)** 3 b c Exit To Nowhere (USA) -Nativelee (FR) (Giboulee (CAN)) 1350a[8] >**90f**<

**Nivernais** 5 b g Forzando-Funny Wave (Lugana Beach) 1504[13] 2399[7] 2628[9] 2912[8] 3453[6] 3910[7] 4366[6] 4687[3](5008) 5299[5] >**81f**<

**Noahs Ark (IRE)** 3 b f Charnwood Forest (IRE) -Abstraction (Rainbow Quest (USA)) 1070a[4] 1847a[5] 3969a[2] 5530a[3] >**109f**<

**Nobbler** 2 br c Classic Cliche (IRE) -Nicely (IRE) (Bustino) 5407[7] 6072[11] 6565[6] >**62f**<

**Noble Calling (FR)** 7 b h Caller I.D. (USA) -Specificity (USA) (Alleged (USA)) 602[10] 2429[3] 2810[7] 2874[3] 3488[2] >**48a 63f**<

**Noble Cyrano** 9 ch g Generous (IRE) -Miss Bergerac (Bold Lad (IRE)) 455[6] 545[7] >**50 a 46 f**<

**Noble Desert (FR)** 3 b f Green Desert (USA) -Sporades (USA) (Vaguely Noble) 2046[7] 4653[5] 5000[10] 5451[12] 5929[7] 6056[12] >**34a 42f**<

**Noble Duty (USA)** 2 b c Dubai Millennium-Nijinsky s Lover (USA) (Nijinsky (CAN)) 5612[2] 6073[3] >**87f**<

**Noble Locks (IRE)** 6 ch g Night Shift (USA) -Imperial Graf (USA) (Blushing John (USA)) 476[8] 680[14] 866[11] 1477[12] 1625[4] 2455[13] >**81a 65f**<

**Noble Mind** 3 b g Mind Games-Lady Annabel (Alhijaz) 3161[2] 3487[7] 3994[9] 4880[3] 6549[11] >**49a 69f**<

**Noble Mount** 3 b g Muhtarram (USA) -Our Poppet (IRE) (Warning) 489[5] 606[7] 1906[11] 2620[3] 3708[7] 6493[12] >**56a 49f**<

**Noble Penny** 5 b m Pennekamp (USA) -Noble Form (Double Form) 1993[10] 2122[6] 2473[2] 2673[10] 3060[4] 3586[6] 4447[5] >**60a 56f**<

**Noble Philosopher** 4 ch g Faustus (USA) -Princess Lucy (Local Suitor (USA)) 1914[7] >**41a 30f**<

**Noble Pursuit** 7 b g Pursuit Of Love-Noble Peregrine (Lomond (USA)) 627[2] 717[2] 782[7] 903[7] 972[3] 1016[5] 1043[5]1090[7] 2965[12] 3247[2] 3471[4] 3604[13] 4132[3] 4386[12] 4605[9]5187[8] >**61da 61df**<

**Noble Stella (GER)** 3 b f Monsun (GER) -Noble Pearl (GER) (Dashing Blade) 5576a[3] ><

**Nobratinetta (FR)** 5 b m Celtic Swing-Bustinetta (Bustino) 1326[13] 1973[4] 2116[15] >**83f**<

**Nocatee (IRE)** 3 b g Vettori (IRE) -Rosy Sunset (IRE) (Red Sunset) 445[3] 746[3] 804[4] 1947[3] (2554) >**46a 58f**<

**No Chance To Dance (IRE)** 4 b g Revoque (IRE) -Song Of The Glens (Horage) 2121[14] 2597[10] 2879[4] 3401[3] 3911[6] 4485[6] 4826[7] 6230[9] >**61f**<

**Noches De Rosa (CHI)** 6 br m Stagecraft-Night Girl (CHI) (Noble Fighter (USA)) 4767a[11] >**103f**<

**No Commission (IRE)** 2 b g General Monash (USA) -Price Of Passion (Dolphin Street (FR)) 1170[9] 1782[5] 2256[4] 2651[7] 2852[5] 3398[4] 3514[8] 3793[2](3898) 4012[11] 4909[5] 5234[9] 5670[13] >**49a 73df**<

**No Dilemma (USA)** 3 ch g Rahy (USA) -Cascassi (USA) (Nijinsky (CAN)) 1271[13] >**51f**<

**Nodina** 2 br c Primo Dominie-Princess Tara (Prince Sabo) 5353[12] 5908[5] 6125[10] >**63f**<

**Nod N A Wink** 6 b g Factual (USA) -Singing Reply (USA) (The Minstrel (CAN)) 468[11] ><

**Nod s Nephew** 7 b g Efisio-Nordan Raider (Domynsky) 953[2] 1043[7] 1389[2] 1590[2] >**56a 67f**<

**Nod s Star** 3 ch f Starborough-Barsham (Be My Guest (USA)) 1528[5] 1820[9] 2392[9] 3026[7] 3473[7] 5130[3] 6005[7] >**29a 47f**<

**Nofa s Magic (IRE)** 4 b f Rainbow Quest (USA) -Garah (Ajdal (USA)) 1249[3] 1671[8] >**79f**<

**No Grouse** 4 b g Pursuit Of Love-Lady Joyce (FR) (Galetto (FR)) 544[11] 775[5] 1013[9] 1199[7] 1317[3] 2459[12] 2735[15] 3198[12]3409[7] 3623[7] 4360[5] 4577[14] 5316[5] 5713[4] 6094[2] 6210[5] >**73a 74f**<

**Nok Twice (IRE)** 3 b g Second Empire (IRE) -Bent Al Fala (IRE) (Green Desert (USA)) 4251a[3] >**72f**<

**Nonno Carlo (IRE)** 4 ch c Alhaarth (IRE) -Most Of People (Horage) 2155a[3] 3030a[5] >**110f**<

**Noodles** 2 b c Mind Games-Salacious (Sallust) 2651[8] 3197[2] 3918[8] 4348[10] 4761[16] >**62f**<

**Noora (IRE)** 3 ch f Bahhare (USA) -Esteraad (IRE) (Cadeaux Genereux) 1904[2] 2223[10] 3759[2] 4683[4] 4954[3] (6017) >**66a 82f**<

**Noorain** 2 ch f Kabool-Abeyr (Unfuwain (USA)) 3382[3] 3770[4] 4100[2] 4524[7] >**75f**<

**Nooshman (USA)** 7 ch g Woodman (USA) -Knoosh (USA) (Storm Bird (CAN)) 688a[2] 832a[5] >**88a 110f**<

**Nooska Tivoli (FR)** 3 b g Rajpoute (FR) -Passe Chesne (FR) (Rb Chesne) 4039a[8] >**94f**<

**Nopekan (IRE)** 4 b g Sri Pekan (USA) -Giadamar (IRE) (Be My Guest (USA)) 3075[13] 3475[7] 4363[8] 4808[7] >**69 f**<

**Nopleazinu** 4 ch f Sure Blade (USA) -Vado Via (Ardross) 5551[5] 5851[10] 6481[6] >**42a 42f**<

**Norcroft** 2 b g Fasliyev (USA) -Norcroft Joy (Rock Hopper) 1292[2] (1462) 1707[6] 2086[7] 3727[8] 4342[7] 4953[4] 5421[11] 5719[12]6276[3] 6472[9] >**66a 73f**<

**Nord (FR)** 4 ch g Kadounor (FR) -Lake Annecy (USA) (Capote (USA)) 5103a[0] ><

**Nordhal** 5 br g Halling (USA) -Nord s Lucy (IRE) (Nordico (USA)) 5970a[5] >**97f**<

**Nordhock (USA)** 2 gr f Luhuk (USA) -Starlight Dreams (USA) (Black Tie Affair) 3272[6] (3458) 3987[6] 4524[3] >**59f**<

**Nord s Cadeaux (IRE)** 2 b f Cadeaux Genereux-Nord s Lucy (IRE) (Nordico (USA)) 5577a[8] ><

**Nordwind (IRE)** 3 b c Acatenango (GER) -Narola (GER) (Nebos (GER)) 2270[3] 2654[4] (3846) (4300) 4648[2] (5402) (5732) 6121[12] >**78a 94+f**<

**No Refuge (IRE)** 4 ch g Hernando (FR) -Shamarra (FR) (Zayyani) 5254a[3] (5808a) 6215[18] >**91+a 109f**<

**Norina** 3 gr f Linamix (FR) -Nuit Indienne (Rainbow Quest (USA)) 6107a[5] >**88f**<

**Norma Speakman (IRE)** 4 ch f Among Men (USA) -Bride Bank (IRE) (Statoblest) 2659[11] 3008[6] 3411[20] 4423[10] >**31f**<

**Norse Dancer (IRE)** 4 b c Halling (USA) -River Patrol (Rousillon (USA)) 1621[4] 2109[3] 2957[14] 3540[4] 4228[4] (4685) 4834[2] 5483a[2] 5782[10]6216[4] >**125f**<

**Northanger Abbey (IRE)** 2 ch c In The Wings-Glenstal Priory (Glenstal (USA)) 3749[16] 4030[13] 5827[5] 5988[12] >**66f**<

**Northern Desert (IRE)** 5 b g Desert Style (IRE) -Rosie s Guest (IRE) (Be My Guest (USA)) 5769[10] 6044[18] 6568[12] >**104f**<

**Northern Games** 5 b g Mind Games-Northern Sal (Aragon) 2368[13] 2965[13] (4013) 4390[4] 5201[2] 5364[4] 5583[2] (6144) (6210) 6517[15] >**72a 85f**<

**Northern Nymph** 5 b g Makbul-Needwood Sprite (Joshua) 899[2] 1010[3] 1112[10] 1326[8] 1754[5] 1958[6] 2299[2] 2652[3]3449[4] 3782[7] 5456[5] 5826[5] 6074[2] >**86a 72f**<

**Northern Revoque (IRE)** 2 b f Revoque (IRE) -Delia (IRE) (Darshaan) 1819[5] 2141[13] 2904[13] 3709[5] 3951[7] 4010[7] 4699[4] 4907[7]6195[16] 6464[7] >**37f**<

**Northern Rock (JPN)** 6 ch g Northern Taste (CAN) -Special Jade (USA) (Cox s Ridge (USA)) 634a[2] 710a[7] >**102a 91f**<

**Northern Secret** 2 b f Sinndar (IRE) -Northern Goddess (Night Shift (USA)) 3601[7] 4705[3] 5095[7] 5909[15] >**70f**<

**Northern Shine (FR)** 7 b h Northern Crystal-Auction Rose (IRE) (Auction Ring (USA)) 911a[8] ><

**Northern Spirit** 3 b g Kadeed (IRE) -Elegant Spirit (Elegant Air) 1465[9] 1947[6] 2146[9] 2554[3] 3984[11] (4207) >**54f**<

**Northern Splendour (USA)** 2 ch c Giant s Causeway (USA) -Ribbonwood (USA) (Diesis) 3051[3] (3560) (4807) >**98+f**<

**Northern Summit (IRE)** 3 b g Danehill Dancer (IRE) -Book Choice (North Summit) 1201[12] 1740[6] 2014[6] >**11a 26f**<

**Northern Svengali (IRE)** 8 b g Distinctly North (USA) -Trilby s Dream (IRE) (Mansooj) 2423[16] 2784[13] 2975[8] 3399[5] 3580[5] 3735[6] >**17a 49f**<

**North Landing (IRE)** 4 b g Storm Bird (CAN) -Tirol Hope (IRE) (Tirol) 1915[7] 4449[9] >**7a 21 f**<

**North Light (IRE)** 3 b c Danehill (USA) -Sought Out (IRE) (Rainbow Quest (USA)) (2043) (2680) 3353a[2] 5981a[5] >**124+f**<

**North Point (IRE)** 6 b g Definite Article-Friendly Song (Song) 2032[13] 2429[8] 3393[4] >**67a 72df**<

**North Sea (IRE)** 3 b f Selkirk (USA) -Sea Spray (IRE) (Royal Academy (USA)) 1186[7] 3094[7] >**59f**<

**North Shore (IRE)** 2 b c Soviet Star (USA) -Escape Path (Wolver Hollow) 3451[6] 5396[5] 5996[9] >**73f**<

**Northside Lodge (IRE)** 6 b g Grand Lodge (USA) -Alongside (Slip Anchor) 577[2] 649[2] 768[12] 915[3] 1540[14] 1903[10] 2210[3] 2474[5]3046[2] 3678[11] 3953[7] 4416[11] 5303[5] 6266[9] >**97a 77 f**<

**North s Law (FR)** 4 gr f Northern Crystal-Law Law (FR) (Sky Lawyer (FR)) 5103a[6] ><

**Norton (IRE)** 7 ch g Barathea (IRE) -Primrose Valley (Mill Reef (USA)) 1125[21] 1456[5] 1540[7] 1828[4] 2969[7] 3212[8] 4690[3] (4920) 5813[14]6475[11] >**107a 105f**<

**Norton Rose** 2 ch f Dr Fong (USA) -Bonica (Rousillon (USA)) 3233[18] ><

**Norwegian** 3 b c Halling (USA) -Chicarica (USA) (The Minstrel (CAN)) 593[5] (628) 822[4] 959[3] 2134[15] >**69a 27f**<

**Nossenko (USA)** 3 b f Stravinsky (USA) -Humble Fifteen (USA) (Feather Ridge (USA)) 574[2] >**50a**<

**Nostradamus (USA)** 5 bb h Gone West (USA) -Madam North (CAN) (Halo (USA)) 4529[10] >**99 f**<

**Nostrana (GER)** 5 br m Lavirco (GER) -Niveole (IRE) (Soviet Star (USA)) 5823a[9] 6255a[4] >**89f**<

**Nota Bene** 2 b c Zafonic (USA) -Dodo (IRE) (Alzao (USA)) 4637[2] (6125) (6459) >**95f**<

**Notability (IRE)** 2 b c King s Best (USA) -Noble Rose (IRE) (Caerleon (USA)) 4728[8] 5570[2] (6078) >**80f**<

**Notable Guest (USA)** 3 b c Kingmambo (USA) -Yenda (Dancing Brave (USA)) 1508[5] 3915[3] (4332) >**95f**<

**Not Amused (UAE)** 4 ch g Indian Ridge-Amusing Time (IRE) (Sadler s Wells (USA)) 6286[13] >**84f**<

**Nothing Daunted** 7 ch g Selkirk (USA) -Khubza (Green Desert (USA)) 3269[12] >**48a 58f**<

**Nothing Matters** 3 b f Foxhound (USA) -Dawn Alarm (Warning) 451[6] 533[9] 587[10] >**33a 37f**<

**Nothing To Lose (USA)** 4 b c Sky Classic (CAN) -Cherlindrea (USA) (Clever Trick (USA)) 6486a[11] >**123f**<

**No Time (IRE)** 4 b c Danetime (IRE) -Muckross Park (Nomination) 417[6] 486[6] 648[6] 703[2] (841) (1061) 1113[11] 1343[10] 2132[19]5933[12] >**106a 84f**<

**Notjustaprettyface (USA)** 2 bb f Red Ransom (USA) -Maudie May (USA) (Gilded Time (USA)) (3413) 4744[4] 4885[4] 5602[10] >**95f**<

**Notnowcato** 2 ch c Inchinor-Rambling Rose (Cadeaux Genereux) 5347[2] 5872[3] >**81f**<

**Noul (USA)** 5 ch g Miswaki (USA) -Water Course (USA) (Irish River (FR)) 507[9] 548[2] 829[5] 1109[5] 1245[5] 1660[15] >**81a 75f**<

**Nounou** 3 b c Starborough-Watheeqah (USA) (Topsider (USA)) 1174[7] 1597[5] 2168[7] 2614[8] (4711) 4971[5] (5935) 6183[5] >**56a 75f**<

**Nouveau Riche (IRE)** 3 ch f Entrepreneur-Dime Bag (High Line) 2647[2] 2911[3] (4195) 4684[2] 5566[3] 5788[5] >**83f**<

**Nouvelle Noblesse (GER)** 2 b f Singspiel (IRE) -Nouvelle Perle (IRE) (Lando (GER)) (6108a) >**100f**<

**Novarra (IRE)** 2 b c Second Empire (IRE) -Nachtigall (GER) (Danehill (USA)) 6108a[4] 6529a[6] >**94f**<

**Nova Tor (IRE)** 2 b f Trans Island-Nordic Living (IRE) (Nordico (USA)) (1234) (1970) 2568[11] 3290[4] (3704) 3975[5] 4150[4] 4358[8] (4752) 4918[3] 5515[11]5681a[6] 5896[10] >**52a 91f**<

**Novelina (IRE)** 2 b f Fusaichi Pegasus (USA) -Novelette (Darshaan) 6555[3] >**56a**<

**Nowaday (GER)** 2 b g Dashing Blade-Notre Dame (GER) (Acatenango (GER)) 3313[7] 3983[6] 4625[6] 5098[8] >**62f**<

**Now And Again** 5 b g Shaamit (IRE) -Sweet Allegiance (Alleging (USA)) 459[3] 541[4] 639[3] 6401[3] >**50a**<

**Nowell House** 8 ch g Polar Falcon (USA) -Langtry Lady (Pas De Seul) 513[6] 2022[6] >**76a 89f**<

**Now Look Away (IRE)** 3 b g Dushyantor (USA) -Where s Carol (Anfield) 1761[8] >**15f**<

**Nufoos** 2 b f Zafonic (USA) -Desert Lynx (IRE) (Green Desert (USA)) 2071[3] (2360) 3031[11] 3599[8] (5143) 5626[2] 6068[2] >**102f**<

**Nuit Sombre (IRE)** 4 b g Night Shift (USA) -Belair Princess (USA) (Mr Prospector (USA)) 1623[13] 1845[5] 2687[4] 2905[6] >**33a 78f**<

**Nukhbah (USA)** 3 b f Bahri (USA) -El Nafis (USA) (Kingmambo (USA)) 1507[3] 1842[4] 2419[5] 3156[13] 3700[14] >**72f**<

**Numero Due** 2 b c Sinndar (IRE) -Kindle (Selkirk (USA)) 5988[6] 6306[3] >**63f**<

**Numitas (GER)** 4 b c Lomitas-Narola (GER) (Nebos (GER)) 1880[8] 2958[23] >**95f**<

**Numpty (IRE)** 3 b g Intikhab (USA) -Atsuko (IRE) (Mtoto) 435[5] 731[5] 871[11] 1465[12] 1667[10] 2232[6] >**33a 34f**<

**Nunki (USA)** 3 ch g Kingmambo (USA) -Aqua Galinte (USA) (Kris S (USA)) 1612[3] (2298) 2896[7] 5401[9] 5866[4] 6307[3] >**91f**<

**Nuts For You (IRE)** 3 b f Sri Pekan (USA) -Moon Festival (Be My Guest (USA)) (5410) 5956[11] >**60a 73f**<

**Nutty Times** 2 ch f Timeless Times (USA) -Nuthatch (IRE) (Thatching) 1137[2] 1234[3] 1307[3] 1670[13] 2124[7] 3571[8] >**45a 47f**<

**Nuzooa (USA)** 3 bb f A.P. Indy (USA) -Min Alhawa (USA) (Riverman (USA)) (2805) 3944[5] 5401[7] (6087) >**100f**<

**Nuzzle** 4 b f Salse (USA) -Lena (USA) (Woodman (USA)) 457[7] 552[12] 623[10] 1684[5] 1940[11] 2272[2] 2430[6] 2810[10]2871[3] 3191[7] 3609[3] 3731[11] 4045[9] 5791[9] 6404[5] >**50a 50f**<

**Nyramba** 3 b f Night Shift (USA) -Maramba (Rainbow Quest (USA)) 1458[2] 2160a[5] 2720a[5] 4286[2] 4779[5] 5416[5] >**107f**<

**Nysaean (IRE)** 5 b h Sadler s Wells (USA) -Irish Arms (FR) (Irish River (FR)) 980a[5] 1261a[4] 1355[5] 1622[2] (1849a) 2329a[3] 2559[4] 5134[5] 5502a[3]5611[6] >**114f**<

## O

**Oakboy (GER)** 3 b c Goofalik (USA) -Oakville (GER) (Alpenkonig (GER)) 3565a[15] 4377a[6] >**79f**<

**Oakley Absolute** 2 ch c Bluegrass Prince (IRE) -Susie Oakley Vii (Damsire Unregistered) 5687[11] 5870[7] 6351[10] >**53f**<

**Oakley Rambo** 5 br g Muhtarram (USA) -Westminster Waltz (Dance In Time (CAN)) 1225[5] 1623[14] 1708[6] 1968[2] 2206[14] 2516[6] 2838[7] 4672[7]4846[8] 6062[12] >**78a 88f**<

**Oases** 5 ch g Zilzal (USA) -Markievicz (IRE) (Doyoun) 1139[8] 1185[2] 1663[8] 1873[6] 1909[7] 2215[18] 3298[13] 3841[3]4083[5] 4425[6] 4702[10] 5108[4] 6124[9] 6558[5] >**43 a 61f**<

**Oasis Star (IRE)** 3 b f Desert King (IRE) -Sound Tap (IRE) (Warning) (1408) (1900) 2295[5] (2844) 3602[2] 4140[7] 5610[5] 5762[5] 6191[9] >**98f**<

**Oasis Way (GR)** 2 b f Wadood (USA) -Northern Moon (Ile De Bourbon (USA)) 4966[5] 5407[5] 5648[16] 5995[6] 6338[7] >**68f**<

**Oatcake** 2 ch f Selkirk (USA) -Humble Pie (Known Fact (USA)) 6569[3] >**61f**<

**Obay** 3 ch g Kingmambo (USA) -Parade Queen (USA) (A.P. Indy (USA)) 1271[4] (1450) 2244[4] 2809[2] 3590[3] 4636[2] 5619[13] >**92f**<

**Obe Bold (IRE)** 3 b f Orpen (USA) -Capable Kate (IRE) (Alzao (USA)) 1626[4] 1737[3] 2252[11] 2389[2] 2549[8] 2650[8] (2986) 3201[5]3314[11] 3737[4] 3838[3] 4320[8] (4576) 4874[7] 5193[14] 5588[4] 5674[12]6539[8] >**68a 71f**<

**Obed (IRE)** 3 b c Efisio-Charming Helene (Star Appeal (IRE)) 1777a[5] >**91f**<

**Obe Gold** 2 b c Namaqualand (USA) -Gagajulu (Al Hareb (USA)) 1961[3] (2057) 2677[4] 3362a[2] 3939[4] 4288[U] 4632[3] 5460[3] (5896) (5947) 6174[2]6462a[5] >**103f**<

**Obe One** 4 b g Puissance-Plum Bold (Be My Guest (USA)) 1343[9] 1765[16] 2132[11] 2391[6] 2490[4] 2754[8] 2859[2] 3010[3]3098[8] 3713[6] 3795[7] 3920[4] 4291[18] 5062[4] 5242[4] 5562[5]5603[11] 5754[5] 6066[7] >**62a 77f**<

**Obezyana (USA)** 2 ch c Rahy (USA) -Polish Treaty (USA) (Danzig (USA)) 6187[21] 6492[2] >**79a**<

**Oblique (IRE)** 2 b f Giant s Causeway (USA) -On Call (Alleged (USA)) 6153[12] 6447[11] 6543[4] >**63+a 48f**<

**Oboe** 3 ch f Piccolo-Bombay (Be My Chief (USA)) 574[9] 620[8] 1495[6] >**29a**<

**Obrigado (USA)** 4 b g Bahri (USA) -Glorious Diamond (USA) (His Majesty (USA)) 2237[10] 2503[2] 3036[27] (4006) 4558[9] 5055[2] 5379[10] >**89a 93f**<

**Observation** 3 ch f Polish Precedent (USA) -Search Party (Rainbow Quest (USA)) 1186[8] 1507[12] 5828[15] 6055[10] >**18f**<

**Observer (IRE)** 2 b c Distant View (USA) -Virgin Stanza (USA) (Opening Verse (USA)) (1292) 2831[3] 3727[7] >**81f**<

**Ocean Avenue (IRE)** 5 b g Dolphin Street (FR) -Trinity Hall (Hallgate) (2305) 3075[8] 4441[6] (5273) 5699[7] >**55a 91f**<

**Oceancookie (IRE)** 2 b f Dashing Blade-Sankaty Light (USA) (Summer Squall (USA)) 5319[5] 5640[5] 6333[6] >**59a 66f**<

**Ocean Gift** 2 b g Cadeaux Genereux-Sea Drift (FR) (Warning) 4219[6] 4743[4] 5649[8] 6187[8] >**87f**<

**Oceanico Dot Com (IRE)** 2 br f Hernando (FR) -Karen Blixen (Kris) 2749[7] 3532[12] 4607[2] (5209) 5363[3] (5515) 5797[6] 6042[8] >**74f**<

**Oceaninternational (USA)** 4 ch c Ghazi (USA) -Amakirtling (USA) (Kirtling) 2163a[3] ><

**Ocean Of Storms (IRE)** 9 bb h Arazi (USA) -Moon Cactus (Kris) 2637[10] 3075[12] 3442[4] 3909[5] 4327[2] 4737[7] >**84f**<

**Ocean Rock** 3 b c Perugino (USA) -Polistatic (Free State) 1050[7] 2085[15] 2562[13] 4055[14] 5654[11] >**59a 39f**<

**Ocean Tide** 7 b g Deploy-Dancing Tide (Pharly (FR)) 899[3] 1112[3] 1316[4] 1958[4] 2613[8] 3120[3] 3621[5] 3821[2]3928[5] >**63a 83f**<

**Ochil Hills Dancer (IRE)** 2 b f Bluebird (USA) -Classic Dilemma (Sandhurst Prince) 2458[7] 2617[5] 3514[7] 3868[4] 4330[5] 5060[6] 5363[14] 5670[11] >56 f<

**Ocotillo** 4 b g Mark Of Esteem (IRE) -Boojum (Mujtahid (USA)) 6141[12] >66a<

**Octennial** 5 gr g Octagonal (NZ) -Laune (AUS) (Kenmare (FR)) 3533[11] 3742[13] >57a 57f<

**October Mist (IRE)** 10 gr g Roselier (FR) -Bonny Joe (Derring Rose) (1249) >74f<

**October Moon (FR)** 3 b f Octagonal (NZ) -Glebe Place (FR) (Akarad (FR)) 5969a[6] >92f<

**Odabella (IRE)** 4 b f Selkirk (USA) -Circe s Isle (Be My Guest (USA)) 1372[3] 1931[9] 2446[8] 3042[4] >79a 74 f<

**Oddsmaker (IRE)** 3 b g Barathea (IRE) -Archipova (IRE) (Ela-Mana-Mou) 1322[3] 1712[2] 1899[5] (2069) 3001[20] (3299) 3477[5] 3943[3] 4151[7] 4271[13]5397[10] 5627[6] >95f<

**Odiham** 3 b g Deploy-Hug Me (Shareef Dancer (USA)) (2558) 2999[9] 4229[4] 5226[10] 6121[5] 6346[4] >74a 97f<

**Oeuf A La Neige** 4 b g Danehill (USA) -Reine De Neige (Kris) 1975[5] 2217[8] 2656[6] (4309) 4390[5] 4707[7] (5512) (6001) 6046[5] 6131[8] 6517[16] >60a 78+f<

**Ofaraby** 4 b g Sheikh Albadou-Maristax (Reprimand) 872[3] (1172) 1539[6] 1903[4] 2624[2] 3842[5] 4540[13] 5122[3] (6444) >88a 96f<

**Off Beat (USA)** 3 ch g Mister Baileys-Off Off (USA) (Theatrical) 493[6] 885[3] 1270[13] 2266[7] 2790[18] 3180[17] 5252[12] 5410[8]5748[6] 6160[7] 6533[8] >75a 61f<

**Off Colour** 2 b c Rainbow Quest (USA) -Air Of Distinction (IRE) (Distinctly North (USA)) 3483[4] 4030[10] 5269[6] >62f<

**Off Hire** 8 b g Clantime-Lady Pennington (Blue Cashmere) 638[2] 794[3] 1027[4] 1262[8] 2823[9] 3169[5] 3820[11] >51a 51f<

**Officer s Pink** 4 ch f Grand Lodge (USA) -Arethusa (Primo Dominie) 2238[10] 2670[8] 4194[10] >58a 76f<

**Ogilvy (USA)** 3 ch c Distant View (USA) -Shoogle (USA) (A.P. Indy (USA)) 1461[14] 3603[8] 4369[2] >74f<

**Oh Boy (IRE)** 4 b c Tagula (IRE) -Pretty Sally (IRE) (Polish Patriot (USA)) 1275[17] 2064[14] 2560[5] (2806) (3177) 3597[17] 3910[16] 4846[10] 5252[15] 5540[7] >79f<

**Oh Dara (USA)** 2 b f Aljabr (USA) -Sabaah Elfull (Kris) (3408) 3703[3] 4744[7] 5060[5] >81f<

**Oh Golly Gosh** 3 ch g Exit To Nowhere (USA) -Guerre De Troie (Risk Me (FR)) 1304[2] 1528[2] 1794[9] 2134[4] 2289[2] 2676[18] 4303[5] 4573[3](5001) 5316[9] 6064[10] >67a 62f<

**Oh So Hardy** 3 bb f Fleetwood (IRE) -Miss Hardy (Formidable (USA)) 1674[14] 2323[4] 2832[3] >53f<

**Oh So Rosie (IRE)** 4 b f Danehill Dancer (IRE) -Shinkoh Rose (FR) (Warning) 1225[4] 1275[3] 1606[3] 1969[9] 2521[3] 2757[2] 2871[5] 3412[11]3609[13] (4066) 4386[9] 4479[12] 4818[4] 4912[2] 5496[5] 6154[2] 6445[7]6550[9] >61a 65f<

**Ok Pal** 4 b g Primo Dominie-Sheila s Secret (IRE) (Bluebird (USA)) 841[U] 1007[3] 1391[13] 1673[7] 1937[6] 3243[12] 4855[6] (5564) 5704[2]5874[3] (6267) >93a 93df<

**Oktis Morilious (IRE)** 3 b g Octagonal (NZ) -Nottash (IRE) (Royal Academy (USA)) 587[8] 726[9] 999[4] (1166) 1405[2] 1579[3] 2054[4] 2395[2]2802[6] 3190[2] 3573[5] (3681) 3990[9] 4618[4] 4853[11] (5069) 5571[8] 5860[4]5991[6] >50a 65f<

**Olaso (GER)** 5 br g Law Society (USA) -Olaya (GER) (Acatenango (GER)) (1259a) (1802a) 2508a[4] >115f<

**Olaya (USA)** 2 b f Theatrical-Solaia (USA) (Miswaki (USA)) 6169a[3] >94f<

**Old Bailey (USA)** 4 gr g Lit De Justice (USA) -Olden Lek (USA) (Cozzene (USA)) 1526[6] 1665[9] 1868[5] 2260[9] (2666) 2936[9] 2989[11] 3615[9]3735[5] 3836[5] 4350[13] 4925[3] (5081) >63a 54f<

**Oldenway** 5 b g Most Welcome-Sickle Moon (Shirley Heights) 768[10] 964[9] 1109[2] 1213[2] 2174[4] 2258[2] (2775) 3097[4] 3521[7](3880) >67a 83f<

**Old Harry** 4 b g Case Law-Supreme Thought (Emarati (USA)) 2483[15] 4085[10] 4548[13] 5793[8] >36f<

**Oldstead Flyer (IRE)** 2 bb c Foxhound (USA) -Princess Tycoon (IRE) (Last Tycoon) 2268[10] 2852[6] 3319[14] 3611[9] >31a<

**Oligarch (IRE)** 2 b c Monashee Mountain (USA) -Courtier (Saddlers Hall (IRE)) 5015[2] 5392[10] 5592[3] (6181) 6574[7] >84f<

**Oligarchica (GER)** 3 b f Desert King (IRE) -Ostwahlerin (GER) (Waajib) 1805a[3] 2341a[10] >73f<

**Olimp (POL)** 8 ch g Saphir (GER) -Olgierda (POL) (Sentyment (POL)) 699[8] ><

**Olivander** 3 b g Danzero (AUS) -Mystic Goddess (USA) (Storm Bird (CAN)) 2046[8] 2704[3] 2887[9] 5749[2] >65+a 77f<

**Olivia Rose (IRE)** 5 b m Mujadil (USA) -Santana Lady (IRE) (Blakeney) 1560[7] (1752) 1944[3] (2216) 2446[2] 2775[3] (2982) 3327[4] (3952) 4136[3] 4343[10]5573[9] 5866[11] >68a 89f<

**Olivia Twist** 2 ch f Fraam-Tricata (Electric) 3665[9] >35f<

**Ollijay** 3 b g Wolfhound (USA) -Anthem Flight (USA) (Fly So Free (USA)) 4316[6] 4869[6] 5204[10] 6146[12] 6560[7] >17a 51f<

**O I Lucy Broon** 3 b f Royal Applause-Jay Gee Ell (Vaigly Great) 1742[9] 4489[14] 5452[15] 6114[7] 6363[5] >47a 49f<

**Olympias (IRE)** 3 b f Kahyasi-Premier Amour (Salmon Leap (USA)) 1189[5] 1521[8] 2243[7] 2840[6] 3919[4] 4870[14] 5340[3] 5826[16] >60f<

**Omachaun (IRE)** 2 ch c Soviet Star (USA) -Jilted (IRE) (Pursuit Of Love) 4958a[13] >67f<

**Omaha City (IRE)** 10 b g Night Shift (USA) -Be Discreet (Junius (USA)) 1241[10] 2201[10] 2406[2] (3048) 3597[12] 4220[10] 4287[13] 5444[10]5614[10] (5841) 6014[2] (6156) >79a 88df<

**Oman Gulf (USA)** 3 b g Diesis-Dabaweyaa (IRE) (Shareef Dancer (USA)) 2043[10] 2420[4] 6193[18] 6568[8] >78 f<

**Oman Sea (USA)** 3 b f Rahy (USA) -Ras Shaikh (USA) (Sheikh Albadou) 4873[5] >84f<

**Omasheriff (IRE)** 2 ch c Shinko Forest (IRE) -Lady Of Leisure (USA) (Diesis) 5392[4] >101f<

**Ometsz (IRE)** 3 br f Singspiel (IRE) -Jemifa (FR) (Fabulous Dancer (USA)) 2338a[5] 2925a[15] 6383a[7] >105f<

**Omikron (IRE)** 3 b c Germany (USA) -Ost Tycoon (GER) (Last Tycoon) 2158a[5] 2926a[2] 3565a[3] 4794a[5] 5329a[9] (5975a) >108f<

**On Action (USA)** 2 b c Miswaki (USA) -Dancing Action (USA) (Danzatore (CAN)) 5633[3] 5752[5] >54f<

**On A Jeune (AUS)** 4 b g Jeune-Chandada Rose (AUS) (King s High (AUS)) 6528a[11] >109f<

**Once (FR)** 4 gr g Hector Protector (USA) -Moon Magic (Polish Precedent (USA)) 2299[3] 2958[22] 4075[10] 4736[7] 5340[10] 5853[12] 6278[7] >70a 76f<

**Once Around (IRE)** 3 bb g Grand Lodge (USA) -Lady Lucre (IRE) (Last Tycoon) 492[7] 644[12] 1800[11] 2485[7] >53a 33f<

**On Cloud Nine** 3 ro f Cloudings (IRE) -Princess Moodyshoe (Jalmood (USA)) 1186[2] 2513[6] 3204[7] 3670[12] 4307[4] 4630[3] (5257) 5817[5] 6552[9] >29a 74 f<

**Onda Nova (USA)** 3 b f Keos (USA) -Northern Trick (USA) (Northern Dancer) (1290a) >98f<

**One Alone** 3 b f Atraf-Songsheet (Dominion) 482[8] 2378[12] 3301[11] 3386[10] 3637[4] 4600[3] >53da 40f<

**One Cool Cat (USA)** 3 b c Storm Cat (USA) -Tacha (USA) (Mr Prospector (USA)) 1764[13] 3959a[5] (4590a) 4886[3] 5289[6] >123 f<

**One For Me** 6 br m Tragic Role (USA) -Chantallee s Pride (Mansooj) 4226[17] >53a 45f<

**Onefortheboys (IRE)** 5 b g Distinctly North (USA) -Joyful Prospect (Hello Gorgeous (USA)) 434[7] 662[9] 720[6] 792[2] 856[4] 951[8] 987[9]1169[3] 1279[7] 1546[6] 1724[3] 3593[17] 3742[15] >45a 49f<

**One Good Thing (USA)** 2 b c Touch Gold (USA) -Once To Often (USA) (Raise A Native) 4611[10] 6149[5] 6441[12] >64f<

**One Great Idea (IRE)** 2 b g Night Shift (USA) -Scenaria (IRE) (Scenic) 4507[2] 5290[5] 5558[2] >75 f<

**Oneiro Way (IRE)** 2 b g King s Best (USA) -Koumiss (Unfuwain (USA)) 4922[9] 5871[10] >59f<

**One Last Time** 4 b g Primo Dominie-Leap Of Faith (IRE) (Northiam (USA)) 1265[14] 1620[19] 1783[9] 2219[2] 3126[14] 4181[13] >61a 67 f<

**One Little David (GER)** 4 b c Camp David (GER) -Open Heart (GER) (Sure Blade (USA)) 5970a[3] 6512a[9] >99f<

**One More Round (USA)** 6 b g Ghazi (USA) -Life Of The Party (USA) (Pleasant Colony (USA)) 710a[2] 852a[2] 977a[13] 1254a[10] 3967a[2] 4405a[2] 5972a[7] >95a 115f<

**One N Only (IRE)** 3 b f Desert Story (IRE) -Alpina (USA) (El Prado (IRE)) 1342[4] 1659[5] 1784[4] 2259[3] >60f<

**One Of Distinction** 3 b f Nashwan (USA) -Air Of Distinction (IRE) (Distinctly North (USA)) 4402[8] >22f<

**One Of Each (IRE)** 2 ch f Indian Lodge (IRE) -Indian City (Lahib (USA)) 4245[5] 4607[5] 4924[11] >15a 49f<

**One Off** 4 b g Barathea (IRE) -On Call (Alleged (USA)) 4977a[7] 5589[4] >66a 94f<

**One Of Them** 5 ch g Pharly (FR) -Hicklam Millie (Absalom) 2000[16] 2381[11] >35a 3f<

**One Putra (IRE)** 2 b c Indian Ridge-Triomphale (USA) (Nureyev (USA)) 4219[5] (4611) 4933[3] 5649[6] >93f<

**Oneshottwolions (IRE)** 2 b c Giant s Causeway (USA) -Fernanda (Be My Chief (USA)) 4169[12] >53f<

**One So Marvellous** 3 ch f Nashwan (USA) -Someone Special (Habitat) 3916[9] 4850[9] (5371) 5866[2] >84f<

**One To Win (IRE)** 2 b f Cape Cross (IRE) -Safe Exit (FR) (Exit To Nowhere (USA)) 5380[2] >75a<

**One Upmanship** 3 ch g Bahamian Bounty-Magnolia (Petong) 2063[11] 2444[8] 2790[11] 2833[6] 3338[3] 3839[2] 4127[6] (4491) 4940[2]5151[3] 5381[7] 6549[13] >64+a 69f<

**On Every Street** 3 b g Singspiel (IRE) -Nekhbet (Artaius (USA)) 2280[4] 2645[3] (3129) 4533[4] 5315[6] 5672[7] 6332[19] 6520[15] >81f<

**One Way Ticket** 4 ch c Pursuit Of Love-Prima Cominna (Unfuwain (USA)) 1675[16] 1877[12] 2215[13] 2477[3] 2524[2] 2779[9] 2873[3] (3141) 3381[8]3775[7] 3887[8] 4085[4] 4800 5016[5] 5253[11] 5734[2] >51a 78f<

**One Won One (USA)** 10 b g Naevus (USA) -Harvard s Bay (ARG) (Halpern Bay (USA)) 1893a[4] 1982a[8] 2316a[8] 2603a[5] 6104a[10] >54a 112f<

**On Guard** 6 b g Sabrehill (USA) -With Care (Warning) 855[3] 995[6] 1305[18] 1856[10] 2015[4] 2375[15] >48a 69f<

**Oniz Tiptoes (IRE)** 3 ch g Russian Revival (USA) -Edionda (IRE) (Magical Strike (USA)) 2908[14] 3121[6] 3582[4] 4207[2] 4710[10] >41f<

**Online Investor** 5 b g Puissance-Anytime Baby (Bairn (USA)) 1500[12] 1772[13] 1825[5] 2130[2] 2291[11] 2490[5] 2734[5] 2859[12]3314[14] 3894[17] 4232[11] 4291[10] 4828[2] 5016[4] 5562[4] 5754[8]6144[6] >79f<

**Only For Gold** 9 b g Presidium-Calvanne Miss (Martinmas) 944[5] 1094[7] >54a 53f<

**Only For Sue** 5 ch g Pivotal-Barbary Court (Grundy) 505[8] 609[9] 1463[3] (1858) 2590[8] >61a 62f<

**Only If I Laugh** 3 ch g Piccolo-Agony Aunt (Formidable (USA)) 1099[3] 1236[4] 1517[8] 2265[2] 2986[3] 3077[9] 3227[5] 3364[3]4320[12] 6538[4] >76a 68df<

**Only Make Believe** 2 ch c Selkirk (USA) -Land Of Dreams (Cadeaux Genereux) 5878a[4] >94f<

**Only One Legend (IRE)** 6 b g Eagle Eyed (USA) -Afifah (Nashwan (USA)) 417[9] 586[12] 680[11] 748[10] 987[7] 1171[3] 1787[9]2383[3] (2813) 3376[5] 3615[13] 3836[8] 4425[18] >71a 58f<

**Onlytime Will Tell** 6 ch g Efisio-Prejudice (Young Generation) 1066[8] 1125[20] 2625[5] 2750[4] 4076[2] 4349[7] (4811) 5224[4] 5628[6](6341) 6572[8] >75a 102f<

**Only Words (USA)** 7 ch g Shuailaan (USA) -Conversation Piece (USA) (Seeking The Gold (USA)) 3508[6] >30a 43f<

**On The Bright Side** 2 b f Cyrano De Bergerac-Jade Pet (Petong) 3514[3] >66+f<

**On The Horizon (IRE)** 4 b f Definite Article-Temporary Lull (USA) (Super Concorde (USA)) 4588a[13] >79f<

**On The Level** 5 ch m Beveled (USA) -Join The Clan (Clantime) 443[9] 792[10] 2823[12] >22a 48f<

**On The Trail** 7 ch g Catrail (USA) -From The Rooftops (IRE) (Thatching) 625[8] 654[11] 876[11] 936[10] (990) 1092[3] (1237) 1569[2](1739) 2664[3] 2813[4] 3820[3] 4185[3] (4452) (4782) 5107[4] 5346[5] 5526[2]5597[7] (6007) 6144[2] 6220[4] 6559[3] >65a 63f<

**On The Waterfront** 3 ch c Docksider (USA) -Film Buff (Midyan (USA)) 447[5] 598[5] 982[4] 1641[2] 2134[10] 2688[4] 2973[2] 4738[5] >66a 69f<

**On The Waterline (IRE)** 2 b f Compton Place-Miss Waterline (Rock City) 1462[2] 1884[3] 2208[9] 4231[4] 4803[2] 5119[11] 5391[20] (6000) 6158[6]6188[7] >59a 78f<

**On The Wing** 3 b f Pivotal-Come Fly With Me (Bluebird (USA)) 5992[12] >53a 75f<

**Ontos (GER)** 8 bb g Super Abound (USA) -Onestep (GER) (Konigsstuhl (GER)) 1287[12] ><

**Onward To Glory (USA)** 4 b c Zabeel (NZ) -Landaria (FR) (Sadler s Wells (USA)) 3752[9] 4033[11] 4819[4] 5773[6] 6083[10] (6527) >70f<

**Onya** 4 ch f Unfuwain (USA) -Reel Foyle (USA) (Irish River (FR)) 415[10] >34a 53f<

**Onyergo (IRE)** 2 b c Polish Precedent (USA) -Trick (IRE) (Shirley Heights) 5186[3] 6139[3] 6531[3] >70f<

**Onyx** 3 b g Bijou D Inde-Prime Surprise (Primo Dominie) 1127[6] 1942[8] 6280[7] >44a 34f<

**Oops (IRE)** 5 b g In The Wings-Atsuko (IRE) (Mtoto) 3099[8] (3508) 3928[6] 4202[2] 4609[3] 5214[2] 5354[4] 5638[4] 6005[9] >57f<

**Oos And Ahs** 4 b f Silver Wizard (USA) -Hot Feet (Marching On) 471[8] >27f<

**Open Book** 3 br f Mark Of Esteem (IRE) -Sweetness Herself (Unfuwain (USA)) 1800[10] 2168[11] 2374[10] 2645[8] 5286[3] 5645[7] 5796[3] >49a 54f<

**Open Handed (IRE)** 4 b g Cadeaux Genereux-Peralta (IRE) (Green Desert (USA)) 565[6] 861[10] 1197[11] (1389) 1620[13] 2473[5] 3471[5] 3869[7] 5080[8]6142[10] >38a 53f<

**Opening Ceremony (USA)** 5 br m Quest For Fame-Gleam Of Light (IRE) (Danehill (USA)) 2393[6] 3005[2] 3265[4] 3563[2] (3731) 3781[5] (4319) 4571[5] 5158[2] 5607[4]5739[8] >66a 80f<

**Open Mind** 3 b f Mind Games-Primum Tempus (Primo Dominie) 1788[4] 2351[3] 2468[7] 2942[6] 5193[13] 5547[16] >52f<

**Open Offer** 4 b f Cadeaux Genereux-Criquette (Shirley Heights) 5169a[4] 6508a[6] >97f<

**Open Verdict (IRE)** 2 b g Mujadil (USA) -Law Review (IRE) (Case Law) 2860[16] 3729[4] 5825[14] >56f<

**Opera Babe (IRE)** 3 b f Kahyasi-Fairybird (FR) (Pampabird) 1823[7] 4642[11] >70f<

**Opera Comique (FR)** 3 b f Singspiel (IRE) -Grace Note (FR) (Top Ville) 1793[6] 5394[8] 6443[10] >99f<

**Operashaan (IRE)** 4 b g Darshaan-Comic Opera (IRE) (Royal Academy (USA)) 463[8] >51a 44f<

**Opera Star (IRE)** 3 b f Sadler s Wells (USA) -Adjalisa (IRE) (Darshaan) 621[5] 1683[10] 3194[3] 3341[6] 4998[8] >54a 60f<

**Ophistrolie (IRE)** 2 b c Foxhound (USA) -Thoughtful Kate (Rock Hopper) 6352[10] ><

**Opportunist (IRE)** 5 b h Machiavellian (USA) -Fatefully (USA) (Private Account (USA)) 687a[7] 832a[6] >84a<

**Optimaite** 7 b g Komaite (USA) -Leprechaun Lady (Royal Blend) 2381[6] >67a 77f<

**Optimal (IRE)** 3 gr f Green Desert (USA) -On Call (Alleged (USA)) 3773[10] 4027[6] (4471) 5245[14] >43a 67f<

**Optimum (IRE)** 2 br g King s Best (USA) -Colour Dance (Rainbow Quest (USA)) 5373[14] 5756[5] 6011[10] >43a 64f<

**Optimum Night** 5 b g Superlative-Black Bess (Hasty Word) 1318[10] 1722[3] 1888[8] 2229[4] 2345[5] 3041[9] >22a 46f<

**Optimus (USA)** 2 ch c Elnadim (USA) -Ajfan (USA) (Woodman (USA)) 5054[5] 6010[2] 6453[4] >78a<

**Orange Touch (GER)** 4 b c Lando (GER) -Orange Bowl (General Assembly (USA)) 1767[6] (4755) (5111) 5662a[8] >114f<

**Orangino** 6 b g Primo Dominie-Sweet Jaffa (Never So Bold) 1929[10] 2556[2] 3060[7] 3735[2] 4309[8] 4827[15] 5945[21] >50f<

**Oranmore Castle (IRE)** 2 b c Giant s Causeway (USA) -Twice The Ease (Green Desert (USA)) 5609[2] 6455[6] >85+f<

**Oration** 3 b g Singspiel (IRE) -Blush Rambler (IRE) (Blushing Groom (FR)) 3843[13] ><

**Oratorio (IRE)** 2 b c Danehill (USA) -Mahrah (USA) (Vaguely Noble) 2954[7] (3965a) 4589a[2] (4959a) (5980a) 6217[2] >118f<

**Orcadian** 3 b g Kirkwall-Rosy Outlook (USA) (Trempolino (USA)) 2476[3] 3906[7] 5948[6] 6219[5] (6355) >108f<

**Orchestrated (AUS)** 7 b g Palace Music (USA) -Madam Zoffany (AUS) (Zoffany (USA)) 755a[8] 830a[5] 924a[9] 1004a[8] >61a 71f<

**Orchestration (IRE)** 3 ch g Stravinsky (USA) -Mora (IRE) (Second Set (IRE)) 673[4] 774[4] 2097[12] 3344[9] 4489[17] 6061[6] 6541[7] >52a 74df<

**Oregon** 5 b g Lorofino (NOR) -Oma s Pride (NOR) (Gonzales (USA)) 5504a[5] ><

**Orfisio** 5 b h Efisio-Thelma (Blakeney) 1259a[12] 1779a[4] >97f<

**Organizer (NOR)** 4 b c Zafonic (USA) -Orange Walk (IRE) (Alzao (USA)) 1954a[3] ><

**Oriental Moon (IRE)** 5 ch m Spectrum (IRE) -La Grande Cascade (USA) (Beaudelaire (USA)) 1402[8] >57a 51f<

**Oriental Warrior** 3 b c Alhaarth (IRE) -Oriental Fashion (IRE) (Marju (IRE)) 5439[5] >105f<

**Orientor** 6 b h Inchinor-Orient (Bay Express) 1126[2] 1254a[4] 1471[5] 2021[9] 2316a[5] 3350a[3] (3537) 4886[5] 5289[7]5977a[6] >118f<

**Original Sin (IRE)** 4 b g Bluebird (USA) -Majakerta (IRE) (Shernazar) 495[10] 575[12] 662[11] >41a 51f<

**Orinocovsky (IRE)** 5 ch g Grand Lodge (USA) -Brillantina (FR) (Crystal Glitters (USA)) (545) 609[7] 682[3] 743[10] 901[2] 1016[3] 1028[2] 1305[17](1599) 1677[3] 4416[12] >65a 65f<

**Orion Express** 3 b c Bahhare (USA) -Kaprisky (IRE) (Red Sunset) 1200[6] 1392[6] 1957[7] 2197[10] 2756[4] 3060[6] 3780[4] 3981[6]4449[6] 5223[13] 6576[10] >45a 63f<

**Orion s Belt** 4 ch g Compton Place-Follow The Stars (Sparkler) 1121[14] 1206[3] 1496[7] >51a 65f<

**Orlar (IRE)** 2 b f Green Desert (USA) -Soviet Maid (IRE) (Soviet Star (USA)) 5349[5] 5789[8] 6447[3] >69a 69f<

**Oro Street (IRE)** 8 b g Dolphin Street (FR) -Love Unlimited (Dominion) 693[5] 879[3] >46a<

**Oro Verde** 3 ch c Compton Place-Kastaway (Distant Relative) 1797[9] 1965[6] 2892[3] 3092[8] 6191[16] >83a 92f<

**Orpailleur** 3 gr g Mon Tresor-African Light (Kalaglow) 4588a[4] >82f<

**Orpen Annie (IRE)** 2 b f Orpen (USA) -Nisibis (In The Wings) 2177[18] 3116[3] 3665[6] 4094[8] 4521[4] 5369[8] 5593[2] >34a 58f<

**Orpenberry (IRE)** 3 b f Orpen (USA) -Forest Berries (IRE) (Thatching) 2269[13] 2589[11] 4451[8] 5364[14] 5702[12] >44f<

**Orpendonna (IRE)** 2 b f Orpen (USA) -Tetradonna (IRE) (Teenoso (USA)) 5578[11] 5846[3] 6072[6] >72f<

**Orpen Wide (IRE)** 2 b c Orpen (USA) -Melba (IRE) (Namaqualand (USA)) 4048[18] 5542[3] 5703[3] 5897[10] 6188[8] 6305[2] 6523[5] >69f<

**Orphan (IRE)** 2 b g Orpen (USA) -Ballinlee (IRE) (Skyliner) 3080[10] 3925[5] 5816[4] 6002[4] >63f<

**Orpington** 3 b c Hernando (FR) -Oops Pettie (Machiavellian (USA)) 5357a[2] 5965a[4] >108f<

**Oscar Pepper (USA)** 7 b g Brunswick (USA) -Princess Baja (USA) (Conquistador Cielo (USA)) 1757[5] 2368[10] 2551[6] 2618[3] 2982[4] 3097[5] 3559[2] 3903[4](4213) 4450[4] 4574[3] 5317[12] >99a 77f<

**Osidy (USA)** 2 b c Storm Cat (USA) -Que Belle (CAN) (Seattle Dancer (USA)) 4382a[5] 5432a[3] 6035a[5] >101f<

**Osla** 3 ch f Komaite (USA) -Orlaith (Final Straw) 2383[8] 2815[10] 3229[8] 3529[10] 3681[6] 4018[14] >35f<

**O So Neet** 6 bb g Teenoso (USA) -Unveiled (Sayf El Arab (USA)) 1692[7] 1987[9] >32a 11f<

**Osterhase (IRE)** 5 b g Flying Spur (AUS) -Ostrusa (AUT) (Rustan (HUN)) 2316a[6] (2744a) (3350a) (3961a) 4590a[4] 5327a[3] 5977a[4] >119f<

**Ostopet (IRE)** 3 b f Priolo (USA) -Ostrusa (AUT) (Rustan (HUN)) 4251a[18] >63?f<

**Otago (IRE)** 3 b g Desert Sun-Martino (Marju (IRE)) 2530[3] 2596[12] 3262[4] 3585[5] 3626[11] 4246[4] 5072[2] (5236) 5496[13](5748) 6271[12] 6549[5] >65a 71f<

**Otylia** 4 ch f Wolfhound (USA) -Soba (Most Secret) 805[5] 906[4] 5000[8] 5282[15] 5930[7] 6288[14] >45a 45f<

**Oublies Ca (FR)** 3 b c Starborough-Okocha (GER) (Platini (GER)) 5168a[7] >96f<

**Oude (USA)** 2 bb c Dubai Millennium-Chosen Lady (USA) (Secretariat (USA)) (4169) 4835[2] 5437[3] >106f<

**Ouija Board** 3 b f Cape Cross (IRE) -Selection Board (Welsh Pageant) (1793) (2640) (3968a) 5981a[3] (6488a) >124f<

**Ouimonamour (FR)** 3 b f Fasliyev (USA) -Moivouloirtoi (USA) (Bering) 1290a[6] >87f<

**Oulton Broad** 8 b g Midyan (USA) -Lady Quachita (USA) (Sovereign Dancer (USA)) 430[7] 750[5] 789[6] 2186[6] >42a 45f<

**Ouninpohja (IRE)** 3 b g Imperial Ballet (IRE) -Daziyra (IRE) (Doyoun) 3297[4] 3587[3] 3896[2] 5297[5] (6141) >78+f<

**Our Chelsea Blue (USA)** 6 ch m Distant View

(USA) -Eastern Connection (USA) (Danzig Connection (USA)) 480[7] 638[3] 794[6] 1087[13] 1262[9] 1497[8] >**49a 49f**<

**Our Choice (IRE)** 2 b c Indian Danehill (IRE) -Spring Daffodil (Pharly (FR)) 1383[8] 1658[4] 2310[7] 4601[6] 5090[7] 6197[6] >**56a 58f**<

**Our Destiny** 6 b g Mujadil (USA) -Superspring (Superlative) 562[3] 590[2] 693[4] 800[7] (1090) (1177) 1233[6] 1274[3](1629) 1687[2] 1856[4] 2031[3] (2324) 2594[9] 3173[4] (3423) 3682[7] 4192[5]4418[6] 4436[6] 5258[8] 5408[4] 5658[8] 6540[5] 6576[3] >**67a 63f**<

**Our Emmy Lou** 3 ch f Mark Of Esteem (IRE) -Regent s Folly (IRE) (Touching Wood (USA)) 3837[2] 3989[4] 4630[5] 4998[6] (5549) 5757[5] 5914[9] >**49a 66f**<

**Our Fred** 7 ch g Prince Sabo-Sheila s Secret (IRE) (Bluebird (USA)) 454[6] 578[7] 3227[13] >**76a 65f**<

**Our Fugitive (IRE)** 2 gr c Titus Livius (FR) -Mystical Jumbo (Mystiko (USA)) 1751[4] 3491[8] 4191[3] 4474[2] (5174) 6188[2] >**93f**<

**Our Gamble (IRE)** 3 b f Entrepreneur-Manilia (FR) (Kris) 1829[6] 2224[11] 2576[9] 3211[10] 4437[5] 5564[8] >**59f**<

**Our Glenard** 5 b g Royal Applause-Loucoum (FR) (Iron Duke (FR)) 455[2] 537[2] 715[11] 878[5] 1081[6] 1545[4] 1962[10]2053[7] 2348[4] >**53a 54f**<

**Our Imperial Bay (USA)** 5 b g Smart Strike (CAN) -Heat Lightning (USA) (Summer Squall (USA)) 981[10] 1135[10] (1194) 1426[8] 1547[3] 3103[12] 3281[3] 3712[6]3803[3] 4082[7] 5257[8] 5710[5] >**68a 46f**<

**Our Jaffa (IRE)** 3 br f Bin Ajwaad (IRE) -Griddle Cake (IRE) (Be My Guest (USA)) 1466[4] (2267) (2587) 3320[2] 5220[5] 5566[7] 5920[6] >**85a 86+f**<

**Our Kes (IRE)** 2 gr f Revoque (IRE) -Gracious Gretclo (Common Grounds) 2655[8] 5268[8] 5717[11] 5838[4] 6067[13] 6392[9] >**39a 58f**<

**Our Kid** 3 ch g Pursuit Of Love-Flower Princess (Slip Anchor) 1559[7] 2146[11] 2452[6] 4251a[14] >**57f**<

**Our Little Rosie** 3 b f Piccolo-Villella (Sadler s Wells (USA)) 447[7] 644[8] 739[5] (1179) 1365[19] 2665[P] 4493[14] 5914[15] >**62a**<

**Our Little Secret (IRE)** 2 ch f Rossini (USA) -Sports Post Lady (IRE) (M Double M (USA)) 5513[5] 5954[3] 6359[3] >**57a 38f**<

**Our Louis** 2 b f Abou Zouz (USA) -Ninfa Of Cisterna (Polish Patriot (USA)) 1468[6] 1556[8] 2194[5] 2980[4] (3144) 3468[5] 4046[7] 4348[8] 5143[10]5363[7] 5520[7] >**42f**<

**Our New Recruit (USA)** 5 ch h Alphabet Soup (USA) -Delta Danielle (USA) (Lord Avie (USA)) (1145a) 6487a[12] >**121a**<

**Our Nigel (IRE)** 2 gr g Namid-Mystical (Mystiko (USA)) 2627[8] 3570[7] 5132[7] 5825[15] >**33f**<

**Our Old Boy (IRE)** 4 br g Petorius-Minzal Legend (IRE) (Primo Dominie) 499[8] 718[8] 809[12] >**23a 35f**<

**Our Place (IRE)** 5 b g Distinctly North (USA) -Simplyhectic (IRE) (Simply Great (FR)) 973[10] >**40a 65f**<

**Our Sion** 4 b g Dreams End-Millfields Lady (Sayf El Arab (USA)) 1133[9] 2029[14] 2384[15] >**29f**<

**Our Teddy (IRE)** 4 ch g Grand Lodge (USA) -Lady Windley (Baillamont (USA)) 677[4] 1125[24] 2201[17] 2534[5] 2894[4] 3118[4] 3539[14] 4442[9] >**100 a 100f**<

**Our Wildest Dreams** 2 b f Benny The Dip (USA) -Imperial Scholar (IRE) (Royal Academy (USA)) 5858[10] >**30f**<

**Out After Dark** 3 b g Cadeaux Genereux-Midnight Shift (IRE) (Night Shift (USA)) 1702[5] (4456) (4952) 5263[3] 5563[2] 5762[6] >**91+f**<

**Outeast (IRE)** 4 b f Mujadil (USA) -Stifen (Burslem) 4701[4] >**43f**<

**Outer Hebrides** 3 b g Efisio-Reuval (Sharpen Up) 1408[14] 1795[15] 2239[4] 5912[2] 6445[2] >**83a 86f**<

**Out For A Stroll** 5 b g Zamindar (USA) -The Jotter (Night Shift (USA)) 1708[16] 1968[10] 4134[7] 4852[10] 6124[7] >**82 f**<

**Out Of My Way** 3 ch f Fraam-Ming Blue (Primo Dominie) 420[14] 817[14] 1167[8] 1726[4] 3421[11] >**26a 15f**<

**Out Of Tune** 4 ch g Elmaamul (USA) -Strawberry Song (Final Straw) 1279[9] 2175[9] >**45a 44f**<

**Outrageous Flirt (IRE)** 2 b f Indian Lodge (IRE) -Sofia Aurora (USA) (Chief Honcho (USA)) 2655[7] 3196[12] 3583[7] 5192[3] 5556[3] 6521[2] >**59f**<

**Outside Investor (IRE)** 4 bb g Cadeaux Genereux-Desert Ease (IRE) (Green Desert (USA)) 3850[12] 4192[16] 4971[12] >**26a 80f**<

**Outward (USA)** 4 b g Gone West (USA) -Seebe (USA) (Danzig (USA)) 1972[13] 2368[17] 3018[15] 3604[15] 4275[10] >**65?f**<

**Ovambo (IRE)** 6 b g Namaqualand (USA) -Razana (IRE) (Kahyasi) 5133[4] 5814[6] 5919[4] >**104f**<

**Overdrawn (IRE)** 3 b g Daggers Drawn (USA) -In Denial (IRE) (Maelstrom Lake) 1585[7] 1795[9] 2295[10] 2642[13] 2907[8] 5419[17] 5766[16] 6086[11]6557[5] >**73a 75f**<

**Overjoy Way** 2 b f Cadeaux Genereux-May Light (Midyan (USA)) 5348[7] 5838[8] 6153[5] >**60a 58+f**<

**Over Rating** 4 ch f Desert King (IRE) -Well Beyond (IRE) (Don t Forget Me) 406[7] 440[10] 601[6] >**67a 71f**<

**Override (IRE)** 4 b c Peintre Celebre (USA) -Catalonda (African Sky) (886) 3525[5] >**76a 85f**<

**Overstrand (IRE)** 5 b g In The Wings-Vaison La Romaine (Arctic Tern (USA)) 1316[5] >**59a 79f**<

**Over The Limit (IRE)** 2 b f Diktat-Premiere Cuvee (Formidable (USA)) 6569[9] >**48f**<

**Over The Rainbow (IRE)** 3 b c Rainbow Quest (USA) -Dimakya (USA) (Dayjur (USA)) (1064) 2676[10] 2999[15] 3543[10] 5183[6] 5998[7] 6286[10] >**80+a 86f**<

**Over The Years (USA)** 3 b g Silver Hawk (USA) -Sporting Green (USA) (Green Dancer (USA)) 1450[5] 1947[4] 3984[16] 5130[11] >**15a 35f**<

**Over Tipsy** 2 b c Tipsy Creek (USA) -Over Keen (Keen) 4866[9] 5376[10] 5646[13] 6282[9] >**46f**<

**Overtop Way (GR)** 2 b c Denebola Way (GR) -Dada (GR) (Ice Reef) 5200[15] 6021[7] >**61a 49f**<

**Over To You Bert** 5 b g Overbury (IRE) -Silvers Era (Balidar) 717[8] 791[6] 972[5] (999) 1274[4] 1582[7] 2387[13] 2833[14]3489[3] 3697[3] (3771) 4083[8] 4436[4] 4713[7] 5408[6] >**46a 51f**<

**Ovigo (GER)** 5 b g Monsagem (USA) -Ouvea (GER) (Konigsstuhl (GER)) (477) 544[4] 564[6] 589[3] 775[P] >**78a 61 f**<

**Owed** 2 b c Lujain (USA) -Nightingale (Night Shift (USA)) 4824[10] 5290[10] 5542[4] >**60f**<

**Own Line** 5 b g Classic Cliche (IRE) -Cold Line (Exdirectory) 6005[13] >**52a 52f**<

**Oxford Street Pete (IRE)** 2 b g Rossini (USA) -Thabeh (Shareef Dancer (USA)) 4359[3] 4930[13] 5455[7] >**68+f**<

**P**

**Paarl Rock** 9 ch g Common Grounds-Markievicz (IRE) (Doyoun) 973[8] 1077[10] 1512[7] >**16f**<

**Pablo** 5 b h Efisio-Winnebago (Kris) 1125[19] (1367) 1621[10] 2044[9] 3539[13] >**112f**<

**Pacific Dancer (NZ)** 4 br c Groom Dancer (USA) -Pacific Gem (NZ) (Kaapstad (NZ)) 6528a[21] >**76f**<

**Pacific Ocean (ARG)** 5 b h Fitzcarraldo (ARG) -Play Hard (ARG) (General (FR)) 639[2] 697[3] 797[3] 1310[6] 1522[8] 2943[4] 3490[3] 4192[6]4519[7] 4641[13] 5002[3] >**63a 59f**<

**Pacific Pirate (IRE)** 2 b c Mujadil (USA) -Jay And-A (IRE) (Elbio) 5118[10] 5720[6] 6091[9] >**65f**<

**Pacific Run (USA)** 3 b c Gone West (USA) -Miss Union Avenue (USA) (Steinlen) 5999[12] 6182[8] >**30f**<

**Pacific Star (IRE)** 2 b g Tagula (IRE) -Acidanthera (Alzao (USA)) 2096[10] 2890[6] 3259[5] 3553[6] >**64f**<

**Pacino** 7 b h Zafonic (USA) -June Moon (IRE) (Sadler s Wells (USA)) 690a[6] >**100a 88f**<

**Packin Em In** 6 b h Young Ern-Wendy s Way (Merdon Melody) 527[3] 665[2] 780[9] (1165) 1280[12] 1986[11] 4811[9] ><

**Paddy Boy (IRE)** 3 br g Overbury (IRE) -Arts Project (IRE) (Project Manager) 656[3] 1064[7] 3245[11] 3996[8] 4189[7] >**48a 30f**<

**Paddy Mul** 7 ch h Democratic (USA) -My Pretty Niece (Great Nephew) 430[2] (475) 716[4] 880[3] 1023[4] 1173[5] 3237[3] 3411[3](3576) 3803[4] 3902[4] 4352[P] >**47a 55f**<

**Paddy Oliver (IRE)** 2 b g Petorius-Creggan Vale Lass (Simply Great (FR)) 6060[11] >**25f**<

**Paddys Tern** 2 b c Fraam-Great Tern (Simply Great (FR)) 4193[12] >**19f**<

**Paddywack (IRE)** 7 b g Bigstone (IRE) -Millie s Return (IRE) (Ballad Rock) 1665[15] 1956[4] 2132[16] 2461[3] 2899[5] 3016[3] 3098[13] (3249) (3509) 3754[7]3920[3] 4047[6] 4626[3] 4855[3] 5440[8] 5605[4] 5704[5] 6518[5] >**88a 79 f**<

**Padrao (IRE)** 2 b c Cape Cross (IRE) -Dazilyn Lady (USA) (Zilzal (USA)) 5118[11] >**60f**<

**Pagan Ceremony (USA)** 3 ch g Rahy (USA) -Delightful Linda (USA) (Slew O Gold (USA)) 5196[11] 5538[10] 5907[14] >**46a 36f**<

**Pagan Dance (IRE)** 5 b g Revoque (IRE) -Ballade D Ainhoa (FR) (Al Nasr (FR)) 844[3] 1539[4] 1768[2] 3075[2] 3310[6] 3725[13] 4858[11] 5465[2]5814[4] >**96a 102f**<

**Pagan Magic (USA)** 3 b c Diesis-Great Lady Slew (USA) (Seattle Slew (USA)) 1967[3] 2202[11] (2578) 3543[13] 4915[5] 5402[4] 5728[7] 6396[3] >**81a 81f**<

**Pagan Prince** 7 br g Primo Dominie-Mory Kante (USA) (Icecapade (USA)) 4920[8] (5135) 5275[4] 5698[6] 6069[4] 6284[5] >**82a 87f**<

**Pagan Quest** 2 b c Lujain (USA) -Rohita (IRE) (Waajib) 5609[7] 6171[18] >**59f**<

**Pagan Sky (IRE)** 5 ch g Inchinor-Rosy Sunset (IRE) (Red Sunset) 1762[14] 2527[15] 5297[6] 5650[4] 5919[5] 6354[3] 6573[9] >**94f**<

**Pagan Storm (USA)** 4 ch g Tabasco Cat (USA) -Melodeon (USA) (Alydar (USA)) 847[15] 1121[11] 1317[7] 1787[8] 1974[5] 2219[10] 2291[10] 2656[14]3321[3] 3626[8] 4818[15] 5411[11] 6097[9] 6362[6] >**52a 64f**<

**Pagan Sword** 2 ch c Selkirk (USA) -Vanessa Bell (IRE) (Lahib (USA)) 6476[8] >**51f**<

**Pageant** 7 br m Inchinor-Positive Attitude (Red Sunset) 425[10] 441[6] 497[5] 533[4] 707[11] 730[9] 809[5]875[7] >**27a**<

**Paging The King (FR)** 4 ch g Spectrum (IRE) -Page Bleue (Sadler s Wells (USA)) 1110a[6] >**97f**<

**Pagnottella (IRE)** 2 b f Dansili-Pinfeather (Robellino (USA)) 3436a[2] 6108a[6] >**87f**<

**Paintbox** 3 b f Peintre Celebre (USA) -Photogenic (Midyan (USA)) 4168[6] 4615[3] 5424[2] 5828[6] 6160[12] >**53a 67f**<

**Paintbrush (IRE)** 4 b f Groom Dancer (USA) -Bristle (Thatch (USA)) 537[5] 947[4] >**43a 44f**<

**Painted Moon (USA)** 3 ch f Gone West (USA) -Crimson Conquest (USA) (Diesis) 3948[9] >**49f**<

**Paint The Lily (IRE)** 3 b f Barathea (IRE) -Chocolate Box (Most Welcome) 2632[12] 3204[11] 3294[4] 3919[10] 5638[13] >**57f**<

**Pairing (IRE)** 6 ch g Rudimentary (USA) -Splicing (Sharpo) 648[14] >**54a 52f**<

**Paita** 2 b f Intikhab (USA) -Prada (GER) (Lagunas) (6583a) ><

**Palabelle (IRE)** 3 b f Desert Prince (IRE) -Moviegoer (Pharly (FR)) 2182[9] 2425[7] 3142[7] 3448[5] 3852[9] >**61f**<

**Palace Star (IRE)** 3 b f Desert Style (IRE) -Feather Star (Soviet Star (USA)) 6104a[8] >**98f**<

**Palace Theatre (IRE)** 3 b g Imperial Ballet (IRE) -Luminary (Kalaglow) 1361[8] 1974[3] >**78f**<

**Palace Walk (FR)** 2 b c Sinndar (IRE) -Page Bleue (Sadler s Wells (USA)) 5870[9] 6073[6] 6351[15] >**57f**<

**Palala River** 11 ch m (FR) (FR) - (FR) (FR) (Simply Great (FR)) 2344a[3] ><

**Palanzo (IRE)** 6 b g Green Desert (USA) -Karpacka (IRE) (Rousillon (USA)) 1774[5] 1974[7] 2735[10] >**74 f**<

**Palatinate (FR)** 2 br c Desert Prince (IRE) -Dead Certain (Absalom) 4143[4] 5087[3] (5535) 5872[4] >**81f**<

**Palawan** 8 br g Polar Falcon (USA) -Krameria (Kris) 586[11] 703[7] 841[6] 1537[10] 1923[13] 2293[15] 2679[20] 5071[11]5440[18] 5734[12] >**57a 57 f**<

**Palmridge (GER)** 4 br g Law Society (USA) -Pariana (USA) (Bering) 1259a[15] 1802a[7] >**88f**<

**Palvic Moon** 3 ch f Cotation-Palvic Grey (Kampala) 1711[5] 1991[3] 3711[6] 3954[12] 4782[17] 6146[17] >**30a 59f**<

**Pamir (IRE)** 2 b g Namid-Mijouter (IRE) (Coquelin (USA)) 5720[9] 6000[3] (6478) >**75+a 71f**<

**Pancakehill** 5 ch m Sabrehill (USA) -Sawlah (Known Fact (USA)) 469[7] 525[11] 582[9] 707[10] 787[6] 859[7] 996[14]1043[10] >**42a 42f**<

**Pancake Role** 4 b g Tragic Role (USA) -My Foxy Lady (Jalmood (USA)) 3342[6] 3827[14] 4070[11] 4713[11] >**25a 32f**<

**Panfield Belle (IRE)** 3 b f Danetime (IRE) -Make Hay (Nomination) 3635[6] >**12f**<

**Pangloss (IRE)** 3 ch g Croco Rouge (IRE) -Kafayef (USA) (Secreto (USA)) 1509[3] 2648[7] 3210[5] 4346[9] 4915[4] 5116[5] 5538[6] 6085[6] >**50a 72f**<

**Pango** 5 ch g Bluegrass Prince (IRE) -Riverine (Risk Me (FR)) 2226[2] 2737[2] (3440) (3698) (4220) 4931[2] 5468[4] 5813[10] 6044[8] >**77a 91f**<

**Panjandrum** 6 b g Polar Falcon (USA) -Rengaine (FR) (Music Boy) 454[8] 617[3] 646[5] (748) 836[7] 893[6] 954[8] 1057[12]1642[4] 1872[15] 2246[8] (6577) >**73a 58f**<

**Panshir (FR)** 3 ch g Unfuwain (USA) -Jalcamin (IRE) (Jalmood (USA)) 1104[5] 1310[7] 1820[3] 2306[11] (2790) 3135a[6] 3949[2] 4236[6] >**86f**<

**Pantani (NZ)** 5 gr g Pentire-Dewamar (AUS) (Marscay (AUS)) 6582a[4] >**100f**<

**Pants** 5 b m Pivotal-Queenbird (Warning) 491[8] 599[7] 624[14] >**57a 49 f**<

**Panzer (GER)** 3 b g Vettori (IRE) -Prompt (Old Vic) 1224[6] >**57f**<

**Paolini (GER)** 7 ch h Lando (GER) -Prairie Darling (Stanford) (1146a) 1657a[13] 2156a[11] 5332a[6] >**120f**<

**Papality** 2 b f Giant s Causeway (USA) -Papabile (USA) (Chief s Crown (USA)) 3675[5] 5694[8] >**70f**<

**Paparaazi (IRE)** 2 b c Victory Note (USA) -Raazi (My Generation) 5561[5] 5856[9] 6400[3] >**60a 57f**<

**Papeete (GER)** 3 b f Alzao (USA) -Prairie Vela (Persian Bold) 2545[4] 2928[4] 4027[7] 4443[13] (5019) 5274[11] 6552[2] >**59a 59f**<

**Paper Talk (USA)** 2 br c Unbridled s Song (USA) -Journalist (IRE) (Night Shift (USA)) 3643[3] 5228[2] >**86f**<

**Papineau** 4 ch c Singspiel (IRE) -Early Rising (USA) (Grey Dawn Ii) (2220) (2533) (2998) >**124+f**<

**Papini (IRE)** 3 ch g Lomitas-Pariana (USA) (Bering) 2926a[7] >**87f**<

**Pappy (IRE)** 3 b f Petardia-Impressive Lady (Mr Fluorocarbon) 473[4] 3993[11] 4674[3] 5261[18] 5794[11] 6056[8] >**5a 46f**<

**Parachute** 5 ch g Hector Protector (USA) -Shortfall (Last Tycoon) 6286[12] >**84+a 87f**<

**Paradise Breeze** 3 b f Perugino (USA) -Paradise Forum (Prince Sabo) 3322[11] 3666[9] 4337[5] >**39f**<

**Paradise Garden (USA)** 7 b g Septieme Ciel (USA) -Water Course (USA) (Irish River (FR)) 1535[9] 1700[5] 1918[4] 2386[3] 2649[8] >**34a 37f**<

**Paradise Isle** 3 b f Bahamian Bounty-Merry Rous (Rousillon (USA)) 2131[10] 3092[4] 3744[2] (4531) 5454[7] (5898) 6175[3] >**108f**<

**Paradise Mill (USA)** 2 b f Horse Chestnut (SAF) -Eaton Place (IRE) (Zafonic (USA)) 6439[2] >**80f**<

**Paradise Time (USA)** 2 b f Count The Time (USA) -Paradise Won (USA) (Leo Castelli (USA)) 5388a[4] >**59f**<

**Paradise Valley** 4 b g Groom Dancer (USA) -Rose De Reve (IRE) (Persian Heights) (478) 908[6] 931[8] 966[5] 1041[7] 1231[2] 1305[14] 1858[5]2031[4] 2385[3] (2740) >**57a 57f**<

**Paragon Of Virtue** 7 ch g Cadeaux Genereux-Madame Dubois (Legend Of France (USA)) 577[3] 649[4] 872[7] 1066[3] 1232[6] 1935[5] >**87a 75f**<

**Parallel Lines (IRE)** 3 ch g Polish Precedent (USA) -Phone Booth (USA) (Phone Trick (USA)) 580[9] 731[8] 859[12] 930[4] 1000[8] 1300[10] 1725[3]2265[6] 2380[9] 2661[8] >**47a 35 f**<

**Parasol (IRE)** 5 br g Halling (USA) -Bunting (Shaadi (USA)) 1902[2] 2241[9] 2678[10] 5651[4] >**112+a 114 f**<

**Parchment (IRE)** 2 ch c Singspiel (IRE) -Hannalou (FR) (Shareef Dancer (USA)) 5084[4] >**30f**<

**Pardishar (IRE)** 6 b g Kahyasi-Parapa (IRE) (Akarad (FR)) 1671[11] >**71f**<

**Pardon Moi** 3 ch f First Trump-Mystical Song (Mystiko (USA)) 408[3] 452[4] 561[4] 744[7] 1517[7] 1913[4] (1985) 2098[13]2380[4] 2932[7] 3530[18] 4495[6] 4650[9] 4968[10] 5793[14] 6228[18] >**34 a 34f**<

**Par Indiana (IRE)** 3 b f Indian Rocket-Paryiana (IRE) (Shernazar) 1318[3] 1933[3] 2783[6] 5836[6] >**57a 61f**<

**Paris Bell** 2 bb c Paris House-Warning Bell (Bustino) 1359[3] 1961[5] 2352[8] 4012[7] 4676[4] 5520[8] (6113) (6356) (6523) >**82f**<

**Paris Dreamer** 3 b f Paris House-Stoproveritate (Scorpio (FR)) 422[8] 655[7] 746[8] >**28a 38f**<

**Paris Heights** 2 gr g Paris House-Petra Nova (First Trump) 2961[10] 3560[6] 5128[4] 5636[17] 5989[17] 6197[8] >**63f**<

**Parisian Playboy** 4 gr g Paris House-Exordium (Exorbitant) 1176[9] 1373[17] 1876[7] 2387[7] (3559) 4008[2] (4447) 4511[14] 5127[11] 6138[11] >**13a 59+f**<

**Parisi Princess** 3 ch f Shaddad (USA) -Crambella (IRE) (Red Sunset) 5146[9] 5634[7] 5867[9] >**43f**<

**Paris Latino (FR)** 5 b g Nikos-Tarbelissima (FR) (Tarbes (FR)) 963[10] 1059[12] >**29a**<

**Paris Tapis** 2 gr f Paris House-Time Of Night (USA) (Night Shift (USA)) 2960[7] 4095[4] 4559[2] 4675[2] (4999) 6023[7] 6442[6] >**55a 55f**<

**Par Jeu** 2 b f Montjeu (IRE) -Musical Twist (USA) (Woodman (USA)) 3627[10] >**59f**<

**Park Approach (IRE)** 2 gr f Indian Ridge-Abyat (USA) (Shadeed (USA)) 4712[4] 5003[3] 5441[2] >**75+f**<

**Park Ave Princess (IRE)** 3 b f Titus Livius (FR) -Satinette (Shirley Heights) 420[2] 521[2] 885[5] 983[3] 1086[2] 4929[9] 5223[18]5526[12] >**64a 58f**<

**Parker** 7 b g Magic Ring (IRE) -Miss Loving (Northfields (USA)) 448[4] 1013[3] 1039[6] 1204[11] 1595[6] 1857[12] 2455[5]2614[10] 4425[16] 5411[16] >**77a 70f**<

**Park Law (IRE)** 2 b f Fasliyev (USA) -Blanche Dubois (Nashwan (USA)) 3202[2] (3627) 4060[5] 5469[6] >**89f**<

**Park Romance (IRE)** 2 b f Dr Fong (USA) -Park Charger (Tirol) 2245[2] (2690) 3031[5] 4552[3] >**96f**<

**Parkside Pursuit** 6 b g Pursuit Of Love-Ivory Bride (Domynsky) 2118[9] (2246) (2423) 2490[9] 2763[4] (3125) 3195[3] (3395) 3920[15] 4291[14] 5704[11]6046[7] 6186[8] 6293[11] 6554[5] >**63a 83f**<

**Park Star** 4 b f Gothenberg (IRE) -Miriam (Forzando) 721[6] 803[3] 896[2] 917[10] 1421[10] 1608[U] 1750[4] 1992[4]3301[17] 6559[9] >**61a 59f**<

**Parkview Love (USA)** 3 bb c Mister Baileys-Jerre Jo Glanville (USA) (Skywalker (USA)) 1239[8] 1396[3] 2019[12] 2295[12] 2642[8] 3001[18] 4268[16] 4737[4]5474[5] 5755[3] 5942[11] 6350[11] >**91a 93f**<

**Parliament Act (IRE)** 3 b g Mujadil (USA) -Law Student (Precocious) 2236[13] 2586[8] 3338[8] >**43f**<

**Parliament Square (IRE)** 3 b c Sadler s Wells (USA) -Groom Order (Groom Dancer (USA)) 1382[3] 5445[5] 5907[2] >**68a 87f**<

**Parnassian** 4 ch g Sabrehill (USA) -Delphic Way (Warning) 1502[7] 1675[8] 1845[3] 1969[3] (2122) 2279[3] 2643[8] 3177[5] (3520) (3869) 4327[5]4569[4] 4920[3] 5185[7] 5540[3] (6081) 6358[8] >**81 f**<

**Parsley s Return** 2 b g Danzero (AUS) -The Frog Queen (Bin Ajwaad (IRE)) 2592[7] 2817[5] 3093[10] >**17f**<

**Partners In Jazz (USA)** 3 gr c Jambalaya Jazz (USA) -Just About Enough (USA) (Danzig (USA)) 2309[5] 4510[10] 4759[13] 4862[5] (5224) 5786[4] 6071[10] >**94f**<

**Part Time Love** 2 b c Royal Applause-Keen Melody (USA) (Sharpen Up) 2225[6] (2593) >**52f**<

**Party Boss** 2 gr c Silver Patriarch (IRE) -Third Party (Terimon) 5298[8] >**43f**<

**Party Ploy** 6 b g Deploy-Party Treat (IRE) (Millfontaine) 1754[18] 2116[7] 2531[2] (2615) (2964) 3199[7] (3794) 3953[2] (4019) 4416[7] 5158[4]5303[4] 6025[5] >**68a 78f**<

**Party Princess (IRE)** 3 b f Orpen (USA) -Summer Queen (Robellino (USA)) 1270[12] 2036[7] (2411) 2741[4] 3273[10] 3530[13] 4650[12] 5193[19] 5618[17](6398) >**68a 68f**<

**Pascali** 4 b f Compton Place-Pass The Rose (IRE) (Thatching) 2166[7] >**58f**<

**Pas De Surprise** 6 b g Dancing Spree (USA) -Supreme Rose (Frimley Park) 604[3] 695[12] 888[5] 926[5] 1095[4] 1681[10] 2459[10]2573[5] 3412[4] 3734[4] 3844[5] 4008[4] 4220[13] 4479[7] 5557[12]5581[10] 6404[6] 6551[11] >**60a 60f**<

**Paso Doble** 6 b g Dancing Spree (USA) -Delta Tempo (IRE) (Bluebird (USA)) 456[5] 589[8] 604[2] 861[6] 903[2] 2381[13] 2643[5]2762[4] 3282[2] 3412[14] 4086[9] 4398[10] >**69a 62f**<

**Passando** 4 b f Kris-Iota (Niniski (USA)) 555[11] >**34a 61f**<

**Pass Go** 3 b g Kris-Celt Song (IRE) (Unfuwain (USA)) 1342[8] 1906[13] 2610[7] 2932[10] 4128[14] >**68a 38f**<

**Passing Glance** 5 br h Polar Falcon (USA) -Spurned (USA) (Robellino (USA)) (2678) 4228[10] 4685[4] 5113[5] >**64a 120f**<

**Passionately Royal** 2 b c Royal Applause-Passionelle (Nashwan (USA)) 6002[8] 6543[10] >**36f**<

**Passion Fruit** 3 b f Pursuit Of Love-Reine De Thebes (FR) (Darshaan) 5223[17] 5639[12] 5992[7] 6184[6] (6465) >**57f**<

**Pass The Port** 3 ch g Docksider (USA) -One Of The Family (Alzao (USA)) 1827[5] (2853) 3728[6] 6284[9] >**72a 73f**<

**Pastoral Pursuits** 3 b c Bahamian Bounty-Star (Most Welcome) 2629[2] (3940) (5414) 6076a[5] >**118f**<

**Patandon Girl (IRE)** 4 b f Night Shift (USA) -Petite Jameel (IRE) (Ahonoora) 453[9] 576[11] >**43a 54 f**<

**Patapan (USA)** 2 b c Stravinsky (USA) -Pappa Reale (Indian Ridge) 2669a[3] 3362a[7] >**77f**<

**Patau** 2 ch c Inchinor-Haste (Halling (USA)) 4292[14]

>**35f**<

**Patavellian (IRE)** 6 bb g Machiavellian (USA) -Alessia (Caerleon (USA)) 2162a[3] 3674[10] 5289[3] 5977a[7] 6463a[3] >**51a 121f**<

**Patrician Dealer** 2 br g Millkom-Double Fault (IRE) (Zieten (USA)) 5687[9] *6223[11]* >**13a 34f**<

**Patrixprial** 3 gr c Linamix (FR) -Magnificent Star (USA) (Silver Hawk (USA)) 1926[5] 4087[5] (5159) 5595[8] 6143[4] 6460[6] >**81f**<

**Patrixtoo (FR)** 3 gr c Linamix (FR) -Maradadi (USA) (Shadeed (USA)) 1271[7] 1612[5] 3089[11] 4655[2] 5293[4] 5560[8] 6192[5] >**65f**<

**Patronage** 2 b c Royal Applause-Passionate Pursuit (Pursuit Of Love) 4730[5] 5179[5] 5716[3] >**79 f**<

**Patronofconfucius (IRE)** 2 b g Imperial Ballet (IRE) -Shefoog (Kefaah (USA)) 3726[9] 5534[12] >**41f**<

**Pat s Miracle (IRE)** 4 ch f College Chapel-Exemplaire (FR) (Polish Precedent (USA)) *539[8]* >**19a 40f**<

**Pat s Nemisis (IRE)** 3 b f Sri Pekan (USA) -Exemplaire (FR) (Polish Precedent (USA)) 1293[13] 1519[12] *2811[14]* >**40a 38f**<

**Patterdale** 3 b g Octagonal (NZ) -Baize (Efisio) 4683[2] (4801) 5399[7] 5992[2] 6128[6] 6358[6] >**78f**<

**Patternmaker (USA)** 2 bb g Elnadim (USA) -Attasliyah (IRE) (Marju (IRE)) 6000[6] >**60f**<

**Pattern Man** 3 b c Wizard King-Quick Profit (Formidable (USA)) 2090[8] 3984[P] *4883[16]* >**27a 46f**<

**Patterson (IRE)** 3 br f Turtle Island (IRE) -Richmond Lillie (Fairbairn) 4583[8] *4939[12]* 5409[6] >**32a 21f**<

**Patxaran (IRE)** 2 b f Revoque (IRE) -Stargard (Polish Precedent (USA)) 2730[8] 3876[5] 4560[4] 5188[6] 5753[3] 5852[6] 6515[18] >**63f**<

**Paula** 4 b f Compton Place-Be My Bird (Be My Chief (USA)) 1528[11] 1770[6] 2198[6] 2551[15] >**46f**<

**Paula Jo** 2 b f Factual (USA) -Superstream (Superpower) 3011[6] 3469[8] 3758[11] 4776[14] 5520[13] >**46f**<

**Paula Lane** 4 b f Factual (USA) -Colfax Classic (Jareer (USA)) *592[8] 666[5]* 1305[12] 1520[6] >**71a 62f**<

**Pauline s Prince** 2 b c Polar Prince (IRE) -Etma Rose (IRE) (Fairy King (USA)) 3104[6] *(3377) 4186[4]* 5989[9] 6206[8] >**65a 62f**<

**Pavilion** 2 b f Robellino (USA) -Chiltern Court (USA) (Topsider (USA)) 5694[14] ><

**Pawan (IRE)** 4 ch g Cadeaux Genereux-Born To Glamour (Ajdal (USA)) 1171[5] *1237[2]* 1361[2] *1477[8]* 1525[3] 1665[5] 2217[3] 2261[11]2492[2] 2623[10] (2941) 3127[6] 3198[6] 3365[3] 3409[11] (3563) 3714[9] 4136[5]4319[13] 4558[14] 6138[13] *6220[8] 6295[10] 6550[11]* >**48a 74f**<

**Pawn Broker** 7 ch g Selkirk (USA) -Dime Bag (High Line) *1062[10]* (4341) 5134[4] 5492[6] 5941[26] 6219[8] >**106a 116f**<

**Pawn In Life (IRE)** 6 b g Midhish-Lady-Mumtaz (Martin John) *488[9] 686[10] 719[9] 833[2] 866[7] 897[8]* >**68a 12f**<

**Pax** 7 ch g Brief Truce (USA) -Child s Play (USA) (Sharpen Up) 1113[6] 1454[6] 1774[8] (2461) 2682[8] 3606[9] 3901[8] 4165[10] 4291[16]5263[7] 5605[8] 6205[13] >**92f**<

**Pay Attention** 3 b f Revoque (IRE) -Catch Me (Rudimentary (USA)) 1363[4] 1529[8] 1946[2] 2355[7] 3981[2] (4449) 4630[4] 5145[5] >**70f**<

**Payola (USA)** 3 b f Red Ransom (USA) -Bevel (USA) (Mr Prospector (USA)) (4396) 4884[6] 5402[5] 6185[6] >**82f**<

**Payphone** 3 b f Anabaa (USA) -Phone West (USA) (Gone West (USA)) 5333a[7] >**99f**<

**Pays D Amour (IRE)** 7 b g Pursuit Of Love-Lady Of The Land (Wollow) *1027[9]* 1452[11] (1824) 2219[12] *2813[3] 3025[7]* 3269[5] 3409[13]4154[3] 4291[8] 4509[2] 4828[10] 4904[7] 5833[9] 6144[8] >**71a 73f**<

**Pay The Silver** 6 gr g Petong-Marjorie s Memory (IRE) (Fairy King (USA)) 1369[11] 1845[4] 2030[11] *2381[2]* 2643[10] 2798[3] 3873[3] *4129[9]*4416[P] >**74da 76f**<

**Pay Time** 5 ch m Timeless Times (USA) -Payvashooz (Ballacashtal (CAN)) 1991[6] 2350[20] 2620[9] 4351[5] 5801[6] 6200[15] 6526[8] >**13a 39f**<

**Peaceful Frontier** 2 b f Monashee Mountain (USA) -Edge Of Darkness (Vaigly Great) 3818[13] 4212[B] 4559[14] >**6f**<

**Peace Lily** 2 b f Dansili-Shall We Run (Hotfoot) 6125[5] 6471[9] >**65+f**<

**Peace Offering (IRE)** 4 b c Victory Note (USA) -Amnesty Bay (Thatching) 1379a[3] 1893a[10] 4405a[4] >**111f**<

**Peace Treaty (IRE)** 3 b f Turtle Island (IRE) -Beautyofthepeace (IRE) (Exactly Sharp (USA)) *472[10] 615[8] 726[8] 808[7]* 2349[11] 2661[6] 3229[10] >**21a 30 f**<

**Peak Of Perfection (IRE)** 3 b g Deploy-Nsx (Roi Danzig (USA)) 1466[5] *1679[3]* 2578[5] *(2882)* (3292) (4062) 4888[2] 5784[8] 6335[6] >**73a 100f**<

**Peak Park (USA)** 4 br g Dynaformer (USA) -Play Po (USA) (Play On (USA)) 2480[7] 3120[7] 3429[2] 3667[10] 5027[3] *5221[2] 6159[2] 6581[3]* >**54a 59f**<

**Peak To Creek** 3 b c Royal Applause-Rivers Rhapsody (Dominion) 1410[3] 2308[2] 2629[3] >**116f**<

**Pearl Farm** 3 b f Foxhound (USA) -Trinity Hall (Hallgate) 4845[9] *6397[3]* >**61a 11f**<

**Pearl Grey** 3 gr f Gone West (USA) -Zelanda (IRE) (Night Shift (USA)) 5454[3] 5811[2] 6175[14] >**99f**<

**Pearl Island (USA)** 3 b c Kingmambo (USA) -Mother Of Pearl (IRE) (Sadler s Wells (USA)) 5656[13] 5770[16] >**31f**<

**Pearl Of Love (IRE)** 3 b c Peintre Celebre (USA) -Aunt Pearl (USA) (Seattle Slew (USA)) 2721a[7] 2956[10] >**115 f**<

**Pearl Of York (DEN)** 3 b f Richard Of York-Laser Show (IRE) (Wassl) 1466[10] 2324[13] 2760[2] *3026[5]* (3581) 3897[3] 4449[5] >**50a 66f**<

**Pearl Pride (USA)** 3 ch f Theatrical-Spotlight Dance (USA) (Miswaki (USA)) 1995[10] 2390[12] 3982[8] 4630[10] >**67f**<

**Pearl s A Singer (IRE)** 2 ch f Spectrum (IRE) -Cultured Pearl (IRE) (Lammtarra (USA)) 4335[11] 4851[5] 5559[5] 5885[13] >**70f**<

**Pearnickity** 3 b f Bob s Return (IRE) -The Robe (Robellino (USA)) 2374[13] 2832[8] 4583[9] 5069[8] >**36f**<

**Pearson Glen (IRE)** 5 ch g Dolphin Street (FR) -Glendora (Glenstal (USA)) 5945[16] >**43a 65f**<

**Peartree House (IRE)** 10 b g Simply Majestic (USA) -Fashion Front (Habitat) *472[11] 588 [8] 730[7] 1573[7]* 1710[6] *1889[6]* 2387[6]2597[19] *2854[11]* 4818[8] 5587[16] >**24a 40f**<

**Pebble Mill (IRE)** 2 b c Cape Cross (IRE) -Mill Path (Mill Reef (USA)) 5857[10] 6149[12] >**44f**<

**Pedlar Of Dreams (IRE)** 2 b f Fayruz-Beautyofthepeace (IRE) (Exactly Sharp (USA)) 3950[3] 5475[5] 5847[9] >**67f**<

**Pedler s Profiles** 4 br g Topanoora-La Vie En Primrose (Henbit (USA)) *601[8] 659[9] 998[12]* >**32a 40f**<

**Pedrillo** 3 b g Singspiel (IRE) -Patria (USA) (Mr Prospector (USA)) 5294[3] (5673) 5941[22] >**108+f**<

**Pedro Jack (IRE)** 7 b g Mujadil (USA) -Festival Of Light (High Top) 1185[11] *(1569)* 1824[9] 2094[9] 2461[12] 3260[3] *4185[12]* >**64a 64f**<

**Pee Jay s Dream** 2 ch g Vettori (IRE) -Langtry Lady (Pas De Seul) *2125[6]* 3248[10] 5341[7] 5989[12] >**39a 52f**<

**Peeptoe (IRE)** 2 ch f Machiavellian (USA) -Alfaguara (USA) (Red Ransom (USA)) 3208[3] 3741[2] 5015[5] 5490[4] 5865[7] >**81+f**<

**Peeress** 3 ch f Pivotal-Noble One (Primo Dominie) (2425) (2963) (3602) 4268[3] *6497[4]* >**89+a 103+f**<

**Pella** 3 ch f Hector Protector (USA) -Norpella (Northfields (USA)) 1189[7] 1356[8] 2001[6] 2587[2] 3139[5] 3478[3] 3844[2] 4138[3]4580[8] (5156) 5252[7] (5715) 6271[4] *6498[5]* >**69a 72f**<

**Penalty Clause (IRE)** 4 b g Namaqualand (USA) -Lady Be Lucky (IRE) (Taufan (USA)) *501[5]* >**35a 52 f**<

**Penalty Kick (IRE)** 2 b c Montjeu (IRE) -Dafrah (USA) (Danzig (USA)) 3913[11] 4922[6] 5269[8] (5852) 5995[5] >**75+f**<

**Penang Sapphire** 2 b g Spectrum (IRE) -Penang Pearl (FR) (Bering) *4598[6]* 4866[16] 5376[15] (6544) >**60a 61f**<

**Pending (IRE)** 3 b g Pennekamp (USA) -Dolcezza (FR) (Lichine (USA)) 3154[3] 3745[8] 4238[6] 4726[8] 5038[3] 5554[15] >**73f**<

**Penel (IRE)** 3 b g Orpen (USA) -Jayess Elle (Sabrehill (USA)) *869[6]* 1214[8] 5656[2] 5844[5] *6295[13]* >**30a 57f**<

**Peninsular (FR)** 2 ch c Giant s Causeway (USA) -Blue Note (FR) (Habitat) 1436[7] >**59f**<

**Penkenna Princess (IRE)** 2 b f Pivotal-Tiriana (Common Grounds) 4739[8] (5271) 5721[3] (5939) 6213[2] >**106f**<

**Pennestamp (IRE)** 2 b c Pennekamp (USA) -Sopran Marida (IRE) (Darshaan) 1105[12] 2761[6] 3748[6] 4058[4] 4439[4] 5005[3] 5617[9] 5910[5]6127[8] >**55f**<

**Penny Cross** 4 b f Efisio-Addaya (IRE) (Persian Bold) 1132[11] 1773[14] 2201[11] 2469[7] 3200[3] >**95f**<

**Penny Island (IRE)** 2 b c Trans Island-Sparklingsovereign (Sparkler) 4016[7] 4567[6] 5114[3] 5719[5] 6090[10] >**71f**<

**Penny Pictures (IRE)** 5 b g Theatrical-Copper Creek (Habitat) 2958[3] 4529[5] 6215[20] >**94f**<

**Penny Pie (IRE)** 4 b f Spectrum (IRE) -Island Lover (IRE) (Turtle Island (IRE)) *464[13]* >**55a 69f**<

**Penny Stall** 3 b f Silver Patriarch (IRE) -Madiyla (Darshaan) 2361[9] 3479[4] 3928[2] 4778[6] 5875[4] >**69f**<

**Penny Valentine** 4 ch f My Best Valentine-Precision Finish (Safawan) *707[9] 793[6] 857[15]* >**19a 19f**<

**Penny Wedding (IRE)** 2 b f Pennekamp (USA) -Eilean Shona (Suave Dancer (USA)) 5716[9] 6067[6] >**53 f**<

**Penrith (FR)** 3 b c Singspiel (IRE) -Queen Mat (IRE) (Fairy King (USA)) (2448) 2764[3] 3415[11] 3977[3] 4178[5] 4540[20] 4988[2] 5474[3] 6044[4]6193[13] >**95 f**<

**Pension Fund** 10 b g Emperor Fountain-Navarino Bay (Averof) 1962[5] 2649[5] 3103[6] 3604[4] >**55f**<

**Pentecost** 5 ch g Tagula (IRE) -Boughtbyphone (Warning) 1125[10] 2044[6] 2969[25] (3539) 3724[4] 4287[9] (4528) 4685[9] 5462[9] (5651) 5917[8] >**114f**<

**Penwell Hill (USA)** 5 b g Distant View (USA) -Avie s Jill (USA) (Lord Avie (USA)) *(437) 643[7] 667[2] 775[2]* 1451[16] 3375[6] 3604[14] 3921[11]4246[3] (5450) 6201[11] >**80a 56f**<

**Penzance** 3 ch g Pennekamp (USA) -Kalinka (IRE) (Soviet Star (USA)) 1831[6] 2751[4] (3152) 3692[10] 5297[13] 5615[14] >**88+f**<

**Peopleton Brook** 2 b c Compton Place-Merch Rhyd-Y-Grug (Sabrehill (USA)) 2872[5] *3418[6]* 3938[18] 5617[15] 5909[17] 6270[10] >**56a 60f**<

**Pepe (IRE)** 3 b f Bahhare (USA) -Orange And Blue (Prince Sabo) *563[6] 746[6] 1235[3]* 1365[12] *(1740) 2452[4] 3026[11] 4927[8]*(5634) >**57a 57f**<

**Peppercorn (GER)** 7 b g Big Shuffle (USA) -Pasca (GER) (Lagunas) 3335a[5] 4378a[13] 5809a[4] (6106a) 6508a[10] >**113f**<

**Peppermint Tea (IRE)** 2 b f Intikhab (USA) -Karayb (IRE) (Last Tycoon) 3157[10] 3476[11] 5569[2] >**80f**<

**Pepper Road** 5 ch g Elmaamul (USA) -Floral Spark (Forzando) 1620[20] 1971[14] (2938) 3895[2] 4386[2] 5411[2] 5859[10] *6154[6] 6558[9]* >**60a 61f**<

**Peppershot (GER)** 5 bl h Big Shuffle (USA) -Pasca (GER) (Lagunas) 5215a[7] >**112f**<

**Pepperstorm (GER)** 3 br c Big Shuffle (USA) -Pasca (GER) (Lagunas) 2158a[4] 3335a[2] (4378a) (5215a) >**113f**<

**Peppone (ITY)** 2 ch c Earl Of Barking (IRE) -Precious Dame (Damister (USA)) 2669a[8] 6380a[10] >**75f**<

**Pequenita** 4 b f Rudimentary (USA) -Sierra Madrona (USA) (Woodman (USA)) 2000[6] 6343[5] >**57a 66f**<

**Percheron (IRE)** 2 ch g Perugino (USA) -Silvery Halo (USA) (Silver Ghost (USA)) 4824[9] 5098[9] 5475[3] >**66f**<

**Percussionist (IRE)** 3 b c Sadler s Wells (USA) -Magnificient Style (USA) (Silver Hawk (USA)) (1387) (1966) 2680[4] 3353a[10] 5629[2] 5965a[3] 6260a[6] 6382a[5] >**121f**<

**Percy Douglas** 4 b c Elmaamul (USA) -Qualitair Dream (Dreams To Reality (USA)) *638[11] 794[10]* 1268[9] 1872[11] 2423[13] 3039[8] 3118[6] 3299[11]3524[18] 3864[7] 4211[5] 4452[11] 4557[19] 4635[6] 4805[7] 5126[9] >**44a 31 f**<

**Percy-Verance (IRE)** 6 ch g Dolphin Street (FR) -Sinology (Rainbow Quest (USA)) 2214[5] 3518[4] >**41f**<

**Peregian (IRE)** 6 b g Eagle Eyed (USA) -Mo Pheata (Petorius) *1177[5] 1279[3]* 1748[11] 3828[15] >**58a 55f**<

**Perelandra (USA)** 4 ch f Cadeaux Genereux-Larentia (Salse (USA)) (5056) 5303[10] 5632[4] 5817[4] >**59a 77f**<

**Pererin** 3 b g Whittingham (IRE) -Antithesis (IRE) (Fairy King (USA)) 1530[13] (1864) 2766[9] 2803[8] 4241[8] 4497[3] 5336[8] 5927[6] 6057[11]6228[8] 6561[3] >**51f**<

**Perestroika (IRE)** 6 ch g Ashkalani (IRE) -Licentious (Reprimand) *899[10]* 1103[12] 2235[4] 2491[8] 3782[4] 4424[10] >**61f**<

**Perez (IRE)** 2 b c Mujadil (USA) -Kahla (Green Desert (USA)) 4809[10] 5118[13] 5373[6] 5507[8] >**73f**<

**Perfect Balance (IRE)** 3 bb g Shinko Forest (IRE) -Tumble (Mtoto) 1214[17] (1363) 1465[6] 1932[5] 1995[4] *2665[11]* 3102[7] 3479[17] >**63f**<

**Perfect Choice (IRE)** 2 gr c Daylami (IRE) -Fairy Contessa (IRE) (Fairy King (USA)) 2111[7] (2804) 3071[8] 4295[6] >**90f**<

**Perfect Drift (USA)** 5 b g Dynaformer (USA) -Nice Gal (USA) (Naskra (USA)) *6491a[4]* >**124a 115f**<

**Perfect Hindsight (IRE)** 3 b g Spectrum (IRE) -Vinicky (USA) (Kingmambo (USA)) 1270[7] 2207[15] 3486[8] 4336[16] >**62f**<

**Perfect Love** 4 b f Pursuit Of Love-Free Spirit (IRE) (Caerleon (USA)) 4260[12] 4877[12] 5244[13] 5316[15] 5862[14] >**84a 62f**<

**Perfect Memory (IRE)** 2 ch f Nashwan (USA) -Ghanaj (Caerleon (USA)) 5961a[5] >**78f**<

**Perfecto (IRE)** 3 b f Peintre Celebre (USA) -Tarascon (IRE) (Tirol) 3969a[10] >**84f**<

**Perfectperformance (USA)** 2 ch c Rahy (USA) -Balistroika (USA) (Nijinsky (CAN)) (3240) 4295[2] (4639) (5778) 6217[7] >**112 f**<

**Perfect Portrait** 4 ch g Selkirk (USA) -Flawless Image (USA) (The Minstrel (CAN)) 1294[3] 1531[7] 2206[7] 2553[4] >**77f**<

**Perfect Punch** 5 b g Reprimand-Aliuska (IRE) (Fijar Tango (FR)) 2121[2] 2591[7] 3232[7] 5554[7] 5875[2] 6074[16] >**71a 73f**<

**Perfect Setting** 4 b g Polish Precedent (USA) -Diamond Park (IRE) (Alzao (USA)) 2754[6] 3307[10] 3772[9] >**64f**<

**Perfect Solution (IRE)** 2 ch f Entrepreneur-Pearl Barley (IRE) (Polish Precedent (USA)) 5720[11] *6394[8]* >**58a 49f**<

**Perfect Storm** 5 b h Vettori (IRE) -Gorgeous Dancer (IRE) (Nordico (USA)) 1124[7] 1455[17] 1768[5] 2076[4] 3325[7] 6172[14] 6354[10] 6475[7] >**103f**<

**Perfect Tone (USA)** 2 ch f Silver Hawk (USA) -Copper Cachet (USA) (Sheikh Albadou) 6073[5] >**64f**<

**Perfidious (USA)** 6 b g Lear Fan (USA) -Perfolia (USA) (Nodouble (USA)) *419[3] 618[2] 679[5] 768[3]* 3872[15] >**79a 76f**<

**Performing Art** 2 b c Sadler s Wells (USA) -Charming Life (NZ) (Sir Tristram) 5396[10] >**31f**<

**Perianth (IRE)** 2 ch c Bluebird (USA) -Meandering Rose (USA) (Irish River (FR)) 1996[4] 2376[9] 2736[10] *4601[10]* 5509[3] 5910[8] 5989[10] >**28a 61f**<

**Pericles (GER)** 7 ch h Vettori (IRE) -Party Bloom (FR) (Baillamont (USA)) 784a[6] 786a[12] ><

**Perida (IRE)** 4 b f Perugino (USA) -Razida (IRE) (Last Tycoon) 3263[9] 3776[19] 4070[9] >**53f**<

**Perle D Or (IRE)** 3 b f Entrepreneur-Rose Society (Caerleon (USA)) (2217) (2820) (4318) 5304[5] >**87 f**<

**Perrywinkle** 2 b f Perryston View-Crab n Lobster (IRE) (Waajib) 4446[18] ><

**Perrywinkle Boy** 3 b g Piccolo-Flower Arrangement (Lomond (USA)) 4455[4] 4781[8] 5086[10] 6141[P] 6465[7] >**52f**<

**Persario** 5 b m Bishop Of Cashel-Barford Lady (Stanford) (1354) 1765[17] >**96f**<

**Persian Carpet** 2 b f Desert Style (IRE) -Kuwah (IRE) (Be My Guest (USA)) 3083[7] 3336[4] 3918[2] 4487[2] 5281[6] 5648[23] 6174[20] >**66f**<

**Persian Dagger (IRE)** 3 b g Daylami (IRE) -Persian Fantasy (Persian Bold) 1271[12] 1508[7] 1967[6] 2802[5] 3488[3] >**69+f**<

**Persian Genie (IRE)** 3 br f Grand Lodge (USA) -Persia (IRE) (Persian Bold) 3204[8] 3630[8] 3843[7] 4368[8] 4849[11] 5538[2] 5993[6] >**64f**<

**Persian Khanoom (IRE)** 2 b f Royal Applause-Kshessinskaya (Hadeer) *6393[6]* >**62+a**<

**Persian King (IRE)** 7 ch g Persian Bold-Queen s Share (Main Reef) 1272[12] 1539[14] 2305[9] 2631[7] 3181[6] 3437[3] 4518[4] >**69f**<

**Persian Lightning (IRE)** 5 b g Sri Pekan (USA) -Persian Fantasy (Persian Bold) 1767[4] 2220[4] (2638) 3034[4] 4285[6] >**113f**<

**Persian Majesty (IRE)** 4 b c Grand Lodge (USA) -Spa (Sadler s Wells (USA)) 1622[6] 2220[3] 3072[3] 3642[5] 4285[4] 5812[9] >**116f**<

**Persian Punch (IRE)** 11 ch g Persian Heights-Rum Cay (USA) (Our Native (USA)) 1703[P] >**121f**<

**Persian Rock (IRE)** 2 b c Namid-Cairo Lady (IRE) (Persian Bold) 1128[2] (4193) (4671) 5392[12] 5810[8] >**83f**<

**Personal Rush (USA)** 3 b c Wild Rush (USA) -Personally (USA) (Alydar (USA)) *6491a[6]* >**112a**<

**Personify** 2 ch c Zafonic (USA) -Dignify (IRE) (Rainbow Quest (USA)) (3424) 5457[4] 6188[9] >**80f**<

**Persuasivo Fitz (ARG)** 10 b h Fitzcarraldo (ARG) -Kalnipe (ARG) (Kaljerry (ARG)) *689a[2] 977a[6]* >**96a**<

**Pertemps Bianca** 4 b f Dancing Spree (USA) -Bay Bianca (IRE) (Law Society (USA)) *468[6] 594[12] 826[7]* >**18a 14f**<

**Pertemps Magus** 4 b f Silver Wizard (USA) -Brilliant Future (Welsh Saint) 3301[3] (4702) 4905[6] 5155[3] 5583[6] *6157[6] 6499[4]* >**59a 71f**<

**Pertemps Red** 3 ch c Dancing Spree (USA) -Lady Lullaby (IRE) (Ballad Rock) *1050[13]* 1370[12] ><

**Pertemps Sia** 4 b c Distinctly North (USA) -Shamrock Dancer (IRE) (Dance Of Life (USA)) 2874[13] 3776[5] 4139[3] >**27a 51f**<

**Pertemps Wizard** 4 br g Silver Wizard (USA) -Peristyle (Tolomeo) *823[9]* ><

**Pertino** 8 b g Terimon-Persian Fountain (IRE) (Persian Heights) 2525[9] >**35f**<

**Peruginos Flyer (IRE)** 5 br g Perugino (USA) -Kriva (Reference Point) 4380a[11] ><

**Peruvia (IRE)** 4 b f Perugino (USA) -Dane s Lane (IRE) (Danehill (USA)) 1752[7] *3022[5]* 3401[11] >**62a 82f**<

**Peruvian Breeze (IRE)** 3 b g Foxhound (USA) -Quietly Impressive (IRE) (Taufan (USA)) 1357[5] 1662[6] *(2485)* 2802[7] *3379[9]* 3996[2] >**66a 61f**<

**Peruvian Chief (IRE)** 7 b g Foxhound (USA) -John s Ballad (IRE) (Ballad Rock) *632a[9] 851a[6]* 921a[7] *977a[10] 1061[8]* 1438[2] 1763[9]2222[9] 2475[7] 4324[U] 5287[12] 5393[10] 5491[3] 5799[12] >**103a 98f**<

**Peruvian Prince (USA)** 2 b c Silver Hawk (USA) -Inca Dove (USA) (Mr Prospector (USA)) 5298[2] >**85f**<

**Peruvian Style (IRE)** 3 b g Desert Style (IRE) -Lady s Vision (IRE) (Vision (USA)) *(986) (1099)* 1388[10] 1760[5] 2082[10] 3777[7] 4043[6] 4267[5] 4434[2]4585[7] (5399) 5730[18] >**88a 79f**<

**Pesquera** 2 b f Green Desert (USA) -Rose Des Andes (IRE) (Royal Academy (USA)) 5569[10] 5996[3] >**67f**<

**Petana** 4 gr f Petong-Duxyana (IRE) (Cyrano De Bergerac) 1719[5] 2350[12] 2620[4] 2778[8] (3147) *4025[7]* 4422[10] 5452[10] >**39a 53f**<

**Petardias Magic (IRE)** 3 ch c Petardia-Alexander Confranc (IRE) (Magical Wonder (USA)) *913[4]* (1333) 1388[3] 1614[7] 1965[2] 2335a[4] 6190[14] 6349[11] >**83a 91f**<

**Peter Paul Rubens (USA)** 3 ch c Belong To Me (USA) -Skybox (USA) (Spend A Buck (USA)) 1830[9] 2046[4] (2286) 3036[5] (4031) (4268) (4873) 5422[2] >**113f**<

**Peter Roughley (IRE)** 2 b g Indian Lodge (IRE) -Dahabiah (Soviet Star (USA)) 5669[7] 6207[4] 6522[2] >**59f**<

**Peters Choice** 3 ch g Wolfhound (USA) -Dance Of The Swans (IRE) (Try My Best (USA)) 1343[13] 1473[12] 1742[5] 2423[12] 3077[7] 3894[2] 4279[8] >**84+a 75f**<

**Peters Delite** 2 b c Makbul-Steadfast Elite (IRE) (Glenstal (USA)) 3476[9] 4347[3] 5084[3] 5351[9] >**70f**<

**Peter s Imp (IRE)** 9 b g Imp Society (USA) -Catherine Clare (Sallust) (3835) 4275[5] 4423[3] 4578[4] 5638[8] 6208[3] >**51f**<

**Peters Ploy** 4 ch g Deploy-Alpi Dora (Valiyar) *3279[12]* 3882[10] *4939[14] 5216[8]* >**2f**<

**Petit Calva (FR)** 3 bb f Desert King (IRE) -Jimkana (FR) (Double Bed (FR)) 1290a[3] 1652a[2] 2720a[6] (4356a) >**106?f**<

**Petite Colleen (IRE)** 3 b f Desert Sun-Nishiki (USA) (Brogan (USA)) 1365[16] 2949[4] 3231[15] 3806[6] 4196[12] 4871[5] 5258[11] *6556[4]* >**67a 65f**<

**Petite Elle** 2 b f Wolfhound (USA) -Start Again (IRE) (Cyrano De Bergerac) *1137[3]* 2593[4] *3278[4]* 3458[3] >**32a 51f**<

**Petite Girl** 2 gr f Daylami (IRE) -Pagoda (FR) (Sadler s Wells (USA)) 5848[10] >**17f**<

**Petite Mac** 4 b f Timeless Times (USA) -Petite Elite (Anfield) 4782[15] 5101[7] >**55a 57f**<

**Petite Noire** 2 b f Lujain (USA) -Coffee Cream (Common Grounds) 1307[9] *3278[6] 4516[5]* >**25a**<

**Petite Rose (IRE)** 3 b f Turtle Island (IRE) -Double Grange (IRE) (Double Schwartz) (1293) 1417[2] 2117[8] >**96f**<

**Petite Speciale (USA)** 5 br m Atticus (USA) -Petite Sonnerie (Persian Bold) 4982a[8] 6437a[9] >**103f**<

**Petite Spectre** 2 ch f Spectrum (IRE) -Petite Epaulette (Night Shift (USA)) 6171[17] *6447[8]* >**61a 32f**<

**Petit Paris (CHI)** 3 ch c Hussonet (USA) -Petit

France (CHI) (Roy (USA)) 691a$^{5}$ (975a) 1143a$^{2}$ >111a<

**Petongski** 6 b g Petong-Madam Petoski (Petoski) 1421$^{19}$ 1525$^{8}$ 1994$^{7}$ >57a 51 f<

**Petrion** 3 b f Petong-Rion River (IRE) (Taufan (USA)) 2211$^{12}$ 2505$^{9}$ 2815$^{3}$ 3146$^{6}$ 6228$^{16}$ >41a 41f<

**Petrolero (ARG)** 5 gr g Perfect Parade (USA) -Louise (ARG) (Farnesio (ARG)) 4493$^{9}$ >46a 48f<

**Petrolina (IRE)** 3 b f Petardia-Arbitration (IRE) (Bigstone (IRE)) 1942$^{11}$ 2882$^{13}$ 3613$^{4}$ 4190$^{8}$ 5092$^{9}$ >53a 24f<

**Petrosa (IRE)** 4 ch f Grand Lodge (USA) -Top Brex (FR) (Top Ville) 4230$^{4}$ 4641$^{5}$ 5615$^{8}$ 5841$^{3}$ 5999$^{5}$ >76f<

**Petrovski (GER)** 3 ch c Night Shift (USA) -Panthere (GER) (Acatenango (GER)) 1306a$^{3}$ ><

**Petrula** 5 ch g Tagula (IRE) -Bouffant (High Top) 1903$^{2}$ 2142$^{6}$ 5303$^{14}$ 5607$^{16}$ 6043$^{7}$ >85 f<

**Petticoat Hill (UAE)** 2 b f Timber Country (USA) -Crinolette (IRE) (Sadler s Wells (USA)) 6153$^{13}$ >37a<

**Pevensey (IRE)** 2 b g Danehill (USA) -Champaka (IRE) (Caerleon (USA)) 2651$^{6}$ 4454$^{11}$ (5897) 6122$^{3}$ >89f<

**Phantom Flame (USA)** 4 b g Mt. Livermore (USA) -Phantom Creek (Mr Prospector (USA)) 503$^{5}$ 655$^{2}$ 725$^{11}$ 824$^{8}$ >42a 42f<

**Phantom Song (IRE)** 2 gr c Shinko Forest (IRE) -Natural Pearl (Petong) 4487$^{14}$ 4776$^{15}$ >21f<

**Phantom Stock** 4 b g Alzao (USA) -Strike Alight (USA) (Gulch (USA)) 461$^{2}$ (483) 645$^{4}$ 889$^{2}$ (981) 1010$^{7}$ 1112$^{4}$ >76 a 74f<

**Phantom Wind (USA)** 3 b f Storm Cat (USA) -Ryafan (USA) (Lear Fan (USA)) 1458$^{6}$ 3940$^{5}$ (4286) 5484a$^{3}$ 6254a$^{4}$ >111f<

**Pharaoh Hatshepsut (IRE)** 6 b m Definite Article-Maid Of Mourne (Fairy King (USA)) 1176$^{10}$ 1316$^{10}$ 1660$^{11}$ 1992$^{11}$ 3082$^{10}$ 3367$^{6}$ 4004$^{10}$ 4260$^{9}$4534$^{6}$ 4701$^{10}$ >36a 36f<

**Pharly Reef** 12 b g Pharly (FR) -Hay Reef (Mill Reef (USA)) 1581$^{4}$ ><

**Pharoah s Gold (IRE)** 6 b g Namaqualand (USA) -Queen Nefertiti (IRE) (Fairy King (USA)) 437$^{2}$ 564$^{10}$ 1139$^{5}$ 1225$^{7}$ 1427$^{3}$ 1598$^{7}$ (1660) 1875$^{9}$2078$^{7}$ 2881$^{9}$ 3082$^{4}$ 3321$^{16}$ 4702$^{11}$ 4826$^{17}$ 5127$^{8}$ 5236$^{13}$5691$^{10}$ 6024$^{11}$ >71a 67f<

**Pheckless** 5 ch g Be My Guest (USA) -Phlirty (Pharly (FR)) 544$^{15}$ 575$^{3}$ 646$^{4}$ 912$^{10}$ 1055$^{9}$ 1087$^{8}$ 1185$^{3}$2178$^{12}$ 6124$^{13}$ 6493$^{11}$ >74 a 70f<

**Phi (USA)** 2 bb c Rahy (USA) -Salchow (USA) (Nijinsky (CAN)) 5570$^{7}$ 5840$^{2}$ 6148$^{5}$ >77f<

**Philharmonic** 3 b g Victory Note (USA) -Lambast (Relkino) 3266$^{4}$ 3598$^{10}$ 5628$^{20}$ 5832$^{5}$ 6071$^{16}$ >107f<

**Philly Dee** 3 b f Bishop Of Cashel-Marbella Beach (IRE) (Bigstone (IRE)) 538$^{3}$ 620$^{10}$ 678$^{10}$ 1025$^{9}$ 1546$^{8}$ 2165$^{10}$ 2986$^{7}$4801$^{7}$ >45a 48f<

**Philosophic** 10 b g Be My Chief (USA) -Metaphysique (FR) (Law Society (USA)) 579$^{7}$ 661$^{14}$ 740$^{13}$ >21a<

**Phi Phi (IRE)** 2 b f Fasliyev (USA) -Council Rock (General Assembly (USA)) 2947$^{7}$ >55f<

**Phlaunt** 2 b f Faustus (USA) -Phlirty (Pharly (FR)) 3045$^{4}$ 3491$^{9}$ 4487$^{3}$ 5034$^{3}$ 5640$^{8}$ >30a 63f<

**Phluke** 3 b g Most Welcome-Phlirty (Pharly (FR)) 462$^{5}$ 668$^{3}$ 816$^{7}$ 1184$^{5}$ (1392) 1613$^{2}$ 1841$^{7}$ 2400$^{4}$ 3527$^{8}$4242$^{6}$ 5316$^{13}$ 5868$^{10}$ >74a 66f<

**Phoebe Woodstock (IRE)** 2 ch f Grand Lodge (USA) -Why So Silent (Mill Reef (USA)) 5694$^{3}$ >68+f<

**Phoenix Eye** 3 b c Tragic Role (USA) -Eye Sight (Roscoe Blake) 1926$^{8}$ 2298$^{8}$ 2777$^{9}$ 6405$^{12}$ >25a 52?f<

**Phoenix Nights (IRE)** 4 b g General Monash (USA) -Beauty Appeal (USA) (Shadeed (USA)) 412$^{10}$ 548$^{5}$ 641$^{10}$ 937$^{9}$ 3705$^{6}$ 4755$^{4}$ 5061$^{4}$ 5099$^{6}$5514$^{9}$ 5673$^{6}$ >33a 52f<

**Phoenix Reach (IRE)** 4 b c Alhaarth (IRE) -Carroll s Canyon (IRE) (Hatim (USA)) 2968$^{6}$ 3567a$^{6}$ 4121$^{10}$ >118f<

**Phone Tapping** 3 b g Robellino (USA) -Miss Party Line (USA) (Phone Trick (USA)) 2693$^{10}$ 3168$^{6}$ 3587$^{6}$ 4493$^{10}$ 6520$^{7}$ >56f<

**Photofit** 4 b g Polish Precedent (USA) -Photogenic (Midyan (USA)) 1295$^{6}$ 1708$^{14}$ >70f<

**Phred** 4 ch g Safawan-Phlirty (Pharly (FR)) 1275$^{6}$ 1757$^{4}$ 1969$^{6}$ 2170$^{5}$ 2614$^{4}$ 2945$^{2}$ 3177$^{9}$ 3412$^{10}$4719$^{5}$ 5259$^{19}$ 5493$^{9}$ 6024$^{9}$ >58a 69f<

**Phrenologist** 4 gr g Mind Games-Leading Princess (IRE) (Double Schwartz) 448$^{13}$ 2379$^{9}$ 6026$^{11}$ 6066$^{12}$ >71a 47f<

**Physical (IRE)** 2 b c Efisio-St Clair (Distant Relative) 6342$^{9}$ 6563$^{8}$ >56f<

**Physique (AUS)** 5 b g Zabeel (NZ) -Physique (NZ) (Foxbay (NZ)) 2156a$^{14}$ >90f<

**Pianoforte (USA)** 2 b g Grand Slam (USA) -Far Too Loud (CAN) (No Louder (CAN)) 3946$^{6}$ 4567$^{2}$ 5023$^{4}$ >83f<

**Piano Man** 2 b c Atraf-Pinup (Risk Me (FR)) 6503a$^{8}$ >78f<

**Piano Star** 4 b g Darshaan-De Stael (USA) (Nijinsky (CAN)) 1355$^{8}$ 1902$^{10}$ >105f<

**Piccled** 6 b g Piccolo-Creme De Menthe (IRE) (Green Desert (USA)) 1007$^{8}$ 1113$^{3}$ 1343$^{16}$ 1956$^{19}$ 2754$^{10}$ (2859) 3266$^{15}$ 3645$^{5}$ 4165$^{24}$4538$^{LFT}$ 5440$^{16}$ 5605$^{3}$ >107 a 90 f<

**Piccleyes** 3 b g Piccolo-Dark Eyed Lady (IRE) (Exhibitioner) 2377$^{8}$ 2790$^{12}$ 2836$^{8}$ (3085) 3593$^{11}$ 3871$^{9}$ 4320$^{3}$ 4585$^{6}$ 4811$^{8}$5737$^{3}$ 5849$^{2}$ >63a 65f<

**Piccola Giada (IRE)** 2 b f Dr Devious (IRE) -Sopran Dancer (IRE) (Fabulous Dancer (USA)) 3436a$^{10}$ ><

**Piccolomini** 2 b c Diktat-La Dama Bonita (USA) (El Gran Senor (USA)) 6530$^{3}$ >69f<

**Piccolo Prince** 3 ch g Piccolo-Aegean Flame (Anshan) 510$^{8}$ (610) 747$^{2}$ (958) 1047$^{2}$ (1266) 1602$^{2}$ 1881$^{9}$ 2411$^{2}$ 2981$^{12}$3523$^{14}$ 4320$^{5}$ 5193$^{8}$ 5674$^{5}$ >71a 71f<

**Pick A Berry** 3 b f Piccolo-Bonne De Berry (Habitat) 1052$^{15}$ 1288$^{9}$ 3486$^{6}$ 4127$^{9}$ 4653$^{7}$ >25a 56f<

**Pickapeppa** 2 ch f Piccolo-Cajole (IRE) (Barathea (IRE)) 5376$^{9}$ 5695$^{5}$ >69f<

**Pickle** 3 b f Piccolo-Crackle (Anshan) 574$^{3}$ 673$^{7}$ 1288$^{4}$ (1908) 2098$^{7}$ 2577$^{3}$ 3089$^{3}$ 3589$^{6}$ (3874) (4020)(4092) 4266$^{2}$ 5566$^{12}$ 5934$^{4}$ >48a 85f<

**Pick Of The Crop** 3 ch g Fraam-Fresh Fruit Daily (Reprimand) (569) 758$^{2}$ 885$^{8}$ 1357$^{11}$ 5652$^{22}$ 6124$^{18}$ >72a 65f<

**Pico Alto** 3 b f Lugana Beach-Noble Canonire (Gunner B) 5408$^{16}$ 5656$^{12}$ 6014$^{11}$ 6402$^{11}$ ><

**Picot De Say** 2 b g Largesse-Facsimile (Superlative) 3157$^{11}$ 4797$^{7}$ 5268$^{11}$ 6127$^{3}$ 6515$^{2}$ 6562$^{5}$ >63 f<

**Pictavia (IRE)** 2 ch f Sinndar (IRE) -Insijaam (USA) (Secretariat (USA)) 2745a$^{2}$ 5325a$^{2}$ 5961a$^{8}$ >104f<

**Pic Up Sticks** 5 gr g Piccolo-Between The Sticks (Pharly (FR)) 755a$^{3}$ (924a) 1004a$^{6}$ 1438$^{3}$ 3074$^{6}$ 4165$^{8}$ 4324$^{17}$ 5393$^{16}$ (5799) 6071$^{9}$6243$^{7}$ 6341$^{5}$ >106f<

**Piddies Pride (IRE)** 2 b f Indian Lodge (IRE) -Fairybird (FR) (Pampabird) 1769$^{5}$ 2234$^{6}$ 3045$^{6}$ 3444$^{4}$ (3824) (4054) 4235$^{3}$ 4342$^{2}$ 4552$^{11}$ 4836$^{4}$5351$^{12}$ 5490$^{5}$ 6022$^{9}$ 6333$^{7}$ 6442$^{2}$ 6544$^{12}$ >29a 75f<

**Pie Corner** 2 ch c Fumo Di Londra (IRE) -Ballystate (Ballacashtal (CAN)) 1853$^{11}$ 2058$^{10}$ 3259$^{13}$ 4040$^{13}$ >35f<

**Piergaudenzio (ITY)** 2 ch c Elmaamul (USA) -Dancer s Parade (ITY) (Midway Dancer (USA)) 6542a$^{7}$ ><

**Pieter Brueghel (USA)** 5 b g Citidancer (USA) -Smart Tally (USA) (Smarten (USA)) 2469$^{8}$ 2857$^{4}$ 3309$^{5}$ 3606$^{10}$ (3754) 3901$^{3}$ 4510$^{3}$ 4759$^{2}$ 5603$^{16}$5799$^{11}$ >94f<

**Pike Bishop (IRE)** 2 b c Namid-Pink Cashmere (IRE) (Polar Falcon (USA)) (2370) (2980) >99+f<

**Pilca (FR)** 4 ch g Pistolet Bleu (IRE) -Caricoe (Baillamont (USA)) 5867$^{11}$ >31f<

**Pilgrim Of Grace (FR)** 3 ch f Bering-Vagabond Chanteuse (Sanglamore (USA)) 5501a$^{13}$ ><

**Pilgrim Princess (IRE)** 6 b m Flying Spur (AUS) -Hasaid Lady (IRE) (Shaadi (USA)) 407$^{3}$ 530$^{5}$ 698$^{4}$ 803$^{6}$ 834$^{10}$ 1039$^{9}$ 1526$^{7}$ 2227$^{4}$ 4257$^{5}$ >49a 49f<

**Pilgrims Progress (IRE)** 4 b g Entrepreneur-Rose Bonbon (FR) (High Top) 4512$^{4}$ 4990$^{8}$ 5820$^{5}$ 6110$^{8}$ 6527$^{8}$ >86f<

**Pillars Of Wisdom** 2 ch c Desert Prince (IRE) -Eurolink Mischief (Be My Chief (USA)) 5298$^{7}$ 5718$^{3}$ >72f<

**Pinafore** 2 ch f Fleetwood (IRE) -Shi Shi (Alnasr Alwasheek) 4936$^{3}$ 5640$^{2}$ 5925$^{2}$ 6359$^{4}$ >63a 62f<

**Pinchbeck** 5 b g Petong-Veuve Hoornaert (IRE) (Standaan (FR)) 1608$^{16}$ 1825$^{4}$ (2094) 3298$^{17}$ (3778) 4130$^{4}$ 4510$^{6}$ 5224$^{10}$ >97f<

**Pinching (IRE)** 3 ch f Inchinor-Input (Primo Dominie) 1441$^{4}$ 1753$^{3}$ 2182$^{2}$ 3563$^{3}$ 3916$^{13}$ 5994$^{2}$ >75f<

**Pine Bay** 3 b f Sure Blade (USA) -Opuntia (Rousillon (USA)) 2286$^{6}$ 2647$^{7}$ 3304$^{14}$ 5652$^{23}$ (5844) >22a 64f<

**Pink Bay** 2 b f Forzando-Singer On The Roof (Chief Singer) 5281$^{4}$ 5953$^{2}$ >61a 57f<

**Pink Palace (IRE)** 3 b f Selkirk (USA) -Reef Squaw (Darshaan) 2028a$^{6}$ 2700a$^{6}$ 5033a$^{7}$ >97f<

**Pink Sapphire (IRE)** 3 ch f Bluebird (USA) -Highbrook (USA) (Alphabatim (USA)) 1333$^{15}$ 2284$^{2}$ 2536$^{4}$ 3694$^{6}$ 4148$^{4}$ 6117$^{12}$ >78f<

**Pink Supreme** 3 ch f Night Shift (USA) -Bright Spells (Salse (USA)) 1111$^{13}$ 2211$^{11}$ 2741$^{10}$ 3306$^{7}$ 3530$^{11}$ 3817$^{6}$ 4403$^{10}$ 4708$^{4}$4968$^{9}$ 5282$^{16}$ >30f<

**Pins n Needles (IRE)** 3 gr f Mark Of Esteem (IRE) -Khalisiyn (Shakapour) 1202$^{10}$ 2486$^{6}$ 5828$^{13}$ 6552$^{10}$ >53a 10f<

**Pintle** 4 b f Pivotal-Boozy (Absalom) 2873$^{4}$ (3457) (3884) 4220$^{6}$ 5444$^{4}$ (5861) >83+f<

**Piper** 4 ch g Atraf-Lady-H (Never So Bold) 4447$^{14}$ >41df<

**Piper General (IRE)** 2 br g General Monash (USA) -Pipewell (IRE) (Lake Coniston (IRE)) 6060$^{7}$ >41f<

**Piper Lily** 2 b f Piccolo-Polly Golightly (Weldnaas (USA)) 1884$^{5}$ (2686) 3346$^{6}$ 3704$^{8}$ 6042$^{12}$ 6442$^{8}$ >77f<

**Piper s Ash (USA)** 2 b f Royal Academy (USA) -Merida (Warning) 4364$^{6}$ (4643) >95+f<

**Pipoldchap (CHI)** 4 br g The Great Shark (USA) -Tiquitiquiti (CHI) (Cresta Rider (USA)) 5505a$^{6}$ ><

**Pippo Di Lucilla (IRE)** 3 gr c Orpen (USA) -To The Skies (USA) (Sky Classic (CAN)) 1777a$^{4}$ 3135a$^{5}$ >103f<

**Pips Pearl (IRE)** 2 b f Lil s Boy (USA) -Penka (IRE) (Don t Forget Me) 2300$^{18}$ 3588$^{18}$ 3748$^{8}$ 4584$^{10}$ 5218$^{5}$ 6195$^{17}$ >44f<

**Pipssalio (SPA)** 7 b g Pips Pride-Tesalia (SPA) (Finissimo (SPA)) 684$^{6}$ 812$^{2}$ 1754$^{6}$ 1989$^{2}$ 2816$^{13}$ 6084$^{11}$ >46a 47f<

**Pips Song (IRE)** 9 ch g Pips Pride-Friendly Song (Song) 421$^{7}$ 530$^{8}$ (608) 654$^{9}$ 694$^{9}$ 987$^{3}$ 1018$^{10}$ 1569$^{5}$1625$^{11}$ 2664$^{6}$ >42a 37f<

**Piquet** 6 br m Mind Games-Petonellajill (Petong) 537$^{3}$ (662) 701$^{6}$ 815$^{6}$ 874$^{9}$ 929$^{7}$ 2324$^{14}$ 2443$^{6}$3637$^{3}$ 4192$^{12}$ (4339) 4471$^{8}$ 4604$^{7}$ 5285$^{13}$ 5791$^{8}$ >34a 38f<

**Piran (IRE)** 2 b g Orpen (USA) -Dancing At Lunasa (IRE) (Dancing Dissident (USA)) 5406$^{8}$ 5646$^{9}$ 5838$^{5}$ 6181$^{12}$ >63f<

**Piri Piri (IRE)** 4 bb f Priolo (USA) -Hot Curry (USA) (Sharpen Up) 2210$^{6}$ 2595$^{2}$ 2782$^{3}$ 3274$^{8}$ 4297$^{3}$ 4556$^{2}$ 5297$^{7}$ 5554$^{9}$5853$^{10}$ >64a 75f<

**Pirlie Hill** 4 b f Sea Raven (IRE) -Panayr (Faraway Times (USA)) 1663$^{3}$ 1719$^{4}$ 2227$^{9}$ 2290$^{2}$ 2423$^{5}$ 2581$^{8}$ (2620) 2784$^{6}$ 3147$^{7}$3225$^{4}$ 3580$^{4}$ 3894$^{11}$ 4133$^{6}$ 4279$^{5}$ 4542$^{13}$ 4827$^{16}$ 5452$^{9}$ >9a 39f<

**Piroetta** 2 b f Averti (IRE) -Bint Albadou (IRE) (Green Desert (USA)) 5348$^{10}$ >47f<

**Pirouettes (IRE)** 4 b f Royal Applause-Dance Serenade (IRE) (Marju (IRE)) 469$^{9}$ 3911$^{20}$ 4336$^{11}$ 4604$^{9}$ 5642$^{4}$ 6227$^{9}$ >57a 57f<

**Piste Bleu (FR)** 4 b f Pistolet Bleu (IRE) -Thamissia (FR) (Riverman (USA)) 1042$^{15}$ 1282$^{13}$ 2174$^{9}$ (2408) 2525$^{6}$ 3165$^{4}$ 3774$^{13}$ 5791$^{16}$ >54a 39f<

**Pitcairn Island** 2 ch f Indian Ridge-Girl From Ipanema (Salse (USA)) 6330$^{10}$ 6569$^{12}$ >42f<

**Pitch Up (IRE)** 2 b c Cape Cross (IRE) -Uhud (IRE) (Mujtahid (USA)) 2627$^{7}$ 2846$^{3}$ 3588$^{6}$ (4058) (4514) 4752$^{5}$ 5464$^{7}$ 6174$^{9}$ 6212$^{11}$ >95a 88f<

**Pitton Mill** 4 b g Millkom-Sea Song (Prince Sabo) 2882$^{11}$ 3348$^{15}$ >37a 2f<

**Pittsburgh** 2 ch c Nashwan (USA) -Oatey (Master Willie) 5612$^{4}$ 6078$^{7}$ >83f<

**Pivotal Flame** 2 b c Pivotal-Reddening (Blushing Flame (USA)) (2045) 3672$^{5}$ 4949$^{4}$ (5703) 5947$^{6}$ (6333) >98f<

**Pivotal Point** 4 b g Pivotal-True Precision (Presidium) 2065$^{10}$ 3324$^{10}$ (3723) 4165$^{2}$ (4324) (5333a) 5647$^{5}$ (5780) >119f<

**Pivotal s Princess (IRE)** 2 ch f Pivotal-Art Princess (IRE) (Fairy King (USA)) 3868$^{3}$ 5800$^{3}$ 6045$^{2}$ >76f<

**Pizazz** 3 ch c Pivotal-Clare Celeste (Coquelin (USA)) 1413$^{5}$ 1827$^{2}$ 2114$^{5}$ 2536$^{2}$ 2808$^{2}$ 3001$^{24}$ 4126$^{3}$ (4236) 5468$^{16}$5610$^{13}$ >97f<

**Place Cowboy (IRE)** 3 b c Compton Place-Paris Joelle (IRE) (Fairy King (USA)) (1200) 2444$^{5}$ 3089$^{2}$ 3542$^{4}$ 3874$^{6}$ >69a 83f<

**Plain Chant** 7 b g Doyoun-Sing Softly (Luthier) 3108$^{8}$ >48f<

**Planet (IRE)** 2 b c Soviet Star (USA) -Laurentia (USA) (St Jovite (USA)) 5646$^{14}$ 6011$^{8}$ 6223$^{2}$ >66a 37f<

**Planet Tomato (IRE)** 2 b c Soviet Star (USA) -Via Splendida (IRE) (Project Manager) 1436$^{3}$ 1826$^{2}$ >86f<

**Planters Punch (IRE)** 3 b c Cape Cross (IRE) -Jamaican Punch (IRE) (Shareef Dancer (USA)) 1352$^{9}$ 1683$^{16}$ 2390$^{7}$ (2547) 3160$^{9}$ 3387$^{7}$ 3917$^{9}$ 5057$^{3}$ 5853$^{2}$6152$^{2}$ 6266$^{2}$ >79f<

**Plateau** 5 b g Zamindar (USA) -Painted Desert (Green Desert (USA)) 1106$^{6}$ 1765$^{28}$ 2679$^{2}$ 4165$^{21}$ 4291$^{20}$ 5181$^{3}$ 5605$^{9}$ >92f<

**Platinum Boy (IRE)** 4 b g Goldmark (USA) -Brown Foam (Horage) 505$^{10}$ 682$^{9}$ 812$^{10}$ 855$^{11}$ 947$^{3}$ 1167$^{7}$ 1277$^{7}$1691$^{5}$ 2386$^{11}$ >37a 13f<

**Platinum Charmer (IRE)** 4 b g Kahyasi-Mystic Charm (Nashwan (USA)) 517$^{2}$ (571) 962$^{10}$ 1041$^{2}$ (1867) 2127$^{4}$ 2214$^{2}$ 2354$^{4}$ 2584$^{8}$3149$^{3}$ 3461$^{2}$ 3892$^{5}$ (4423) 4698$^{7}$ 6110$^{6}$ 6209$^{5}$ >61a 61f<

**Platinum Chief** 3 b g Puissance-Miss Beverley (Beveled (USA)) 508$^{6}$ 615$^{6}$ 751$^{5}$ 939$^{9}$ 1570$^{5}$ 1701$^{3}$ 1916$^{4}$2016$^{4}$ 2349$^{10}$ >44a 52f<

**Platinum Pirate** 3 b g Merdon Melody-Woodland Steps (Bold Owl) 416$^{2}$ 622$^{9}$ 1084$^{2}$ (1360) 1529$^{3}$ 1559$^{6}$ 1995$^{5}$ 2783$^{4}$ 4940$^{7}$(5381) (5705) 6112$^{3}$ 6546$^{10}$ >67a 69f<

**Plattocrat** 4 b g Dancing Spree (USA) -No Comebacks (Last Tycoon) 1192$^{5}$ 2664$^{7}$ 3040$^{7}$ 4926$^{12}$ 5366$^{7}$ >26a 31f<

**Plausabelle** 3 b f Royal Applause-Sipsi Fach (Prince Sabo) 1363$^{7}$ 1710$^{2}$ 2038$^{9}$ 4307$^{12}$ 5110$^{3}$ 5524$^{2}$ >57f<

**Play Bouzouki** 3 b f Halling (USA) -Balalaika (Sadler s Wells (USA)) 4303$^{3}$ 5123$^{4}$ 5828$^{7}$ 6224$^{6}$ >68a 67f<

**Playful Act (IRE)** 2 b f Sadler s Wells (USA) -Magnificient Style (USA) (Silver Hawk (USA)) 4753$^{2}$ (5089) (5413) (5779) >113f<

**Playful Dane (IRE)** 7 b g Dolphin Street (FR) -Omicida (IRE) (Danehill (USA)) (2219) 2656$^{5}$ 3038$^{9}$ (4105) 5242$^{3}$ (5862) 5949$^{2}$ (6046) >48a 89+f<

**Playful Spirit** 5 b m Mind Games-Kalimat (Be My Guest (USA)) 407$^{7}$ 530$^{6}$ 584$^{3}$ 625$^{3}$ 721$^{7}$ 803$^{7}$ 1262$^{3}$2238$^{7}$ 2482$^{8}$ 2670$^{11}$ 3277$^{15}$ 6059$^{9}$ 6229$^{13}$ >55a 45f<

**Play Master (IRE)** 3 b g Second Empire (IRE) -Madam Waajib (IRE) (Waajib) 506$^{2}$ (593) 798$^{2}$ 1108$^{9}$ (1506) 2069$^{11}$ 2988$^{3}$ 4122$^{24}$ 5265$^{5}$ >76a 76f<

**Play That Tune** 4 ch f Zilzal (USA) -Military Tune (IRE) (Nashwan (USA)) 2044$^{7}$ 2630$^{5}$ 3223$^{4}$ 3717$^{3}$ 3867$^{3}$ 4889$^{9}$ >96f<

**Play The Melody (IRE)** 3 bb g Revoque (IRE) -Dumayla (Shernazar) 1911$^{3}$ (4972) >66+f<

**Playtime Blue** 4 b g Komaite (USA) -Miss Calculate (Mummy s Game) 480$^{2}$ 526$^{3}$ 578$^{6}$ (796) 836$^{2}$ (905) 1131$^{4}$ 1368$^{3}$ 1872$^{10}$2303$^{6}$ 2724$^{7}$ 2912$^{5}$ 3810$^{3}$ 3894$^{3}$ 4232$^{9}$ 4452$^{7}$ 4774$^{10}$6293$^{9}$ 6554$^{9}$ >76a 68f<

**Play Up Pompey** 2 b g Dansili-Search For Love (FR) (Groom Dancer (USA)) 3083$^{10}$ 3633$^{8}$ 4022$^{9}$ 4966$^{13}$ 5114$^{10}$ 5536$^{8}$ >55a 57f<

**Play With Fire (USA)** 2 bb f Boundary (USA) -Realm (USA) (Mr Prospector (USA)) 6485a$^{8}$ >99a<

**Plea Bargain** 2 b c Machiavellian (USA) -Time Saved (Green Desert (USA)) 5870$^{3}$ (6440) >90+f<

**Pleasant** 3 b f Topanoora-Devon Peasant (Deploy) 4402$^{4}$ 5007$^{2}$ 5828$^{12}$ 5999$^{8}$ >74f<

**Pleasantly Perfect (USA)** 6 b h Pleasant Colony (USA) -Regal State (USA) (Affirmed (USA)) (1147a) 6491a$^{3}$ >128a<

**Pleasure Seeker** 3 b f First Trump-Purse (Pursuit Of Love) 1796$^{7}$ 2267$^{9}$ 2820$^{9}$ 5092$^{10}$ 5692$^{6}$ >54f<

**Pleasure Time** 11 ch g Clantime-First Experience (Le Johnstan) 657$^{5}$ 876$^{7}$ 930$^{10}$ (1190) 1443$^{6}$ 2707$^{16}$ 6403$^{7}$ >47a 33f<

**Plenty Cried Wolf** 2 b g Wolfhound (USA) -Plentitude (FR) (Ela-Mana-Mou) 4048$^{17}$ 4446$^{14}$ 5307$^{4}$ 5447$^{7}$ 5855$^{3}$ 6021$^{6}$ 6521$^{3}$ >63a 70f<

**Plovers Lane (IRE)** 3 b g Dushyantor (USA) -Sweet Alma (Alzao (USA)) 2085$^{14}$ 2513$^{8}$ >25a 46f<

**Plum** 4 br f Pivotal-Rose Chime (IRE) (Tirol) (5039) 6210$^{7}$ >77+f<

**Plummet (USA)** 3 b f Silver Hawk (USA) -Fairy Heights (IRE) (Fairy King (USA)) 2374$^{4}$ 3843$^{2}$ 4583$^{3}$ >82f<

**Plumpie Mac (IRE)** 3 b f Key Of Luck (USA) -Petrine (IRE) (Petorius) 3252$^{6}$ 3817$^{11}$ 4259$^{16}$ >44f<

**Plungington Tavern (IRE)** 2 b c Josr Algarhoud (IRE) -Hever Golf Lady (Dominion) 5604$^{9}$ >20f<

**Plutocrat** 8 b g Polar Falcon (USA) -Choire Mhor (Dominion) 1316$^{2}$ 2174$^{10}$ >79f<

**Poacher s Paradise** 3 ch g Inchinor-Transylvania (Wolfhound (USA)) 561$^{12}$ 958$^{8}$ 1267$^{6}$ 1363$^{10}$ >37a 41f<

**Pocketwood** 2 b g Fleetwood (IRE) -Pocket Venus (IRE) (King s Theatre (IRE)) 2890$^{11}$ >49f<

**Poetical (IRE)** 3 ch f Croco Rouge (IRE) -Abyat (USA) (Shadeed (USA)) 5416$^{12}$ 5972a$^{3}$ >101f<

**Poetry n Passion** 3 b f Polish Precedent (USA) -Ghassanah (Pas De Seul) 4954$^{7}$ 6200$^{7}$ 6397$^{10}$ 6564$^{5}$ >33a 46f<

**Point Calimere (IRE)** 3 b g Fasliyev (USA) -Mountain Ash (Dominion) 1228$^{7}$ 1530$^{4}$ 1602$^{5}$ 2064$^{16}$ (3279) >65a 78f<

**Pointed (IRE)** 3 br f Selkirk (USA) -Tragic Point (IRE) (Tragic Role (USA)) 1820$^{15}$ 2198$^{10}$ 2555$^{3}$ 4883$^{13}$ >42f<

**Point Man (IRE)** 4 b g Pivotal-Pursuit Of Truth (USA) (Irish River (FR)) 1510$^{8}$ 1861$^{3}$ 2017$^{4}$ >18a 31f<

**Point Of Dispute** 9 b g Cyrano De Bergerac-Opuntia (Rousillon (USA)) 3455$^{5}$ 3910$^{2}$ 4690$^{8}$ 5055$^{4}$ 5379$^{9}$ 6062$^{3}$ >92a 92f<

**Poise (IRE)** 3 b f Rainbow Quest (USA) -Crepe Ginger (IRE) (Sadler s Wells (USA)) (4402) >87+f<

**Poker** 3 ch g Hector Protector (USA) -Clunie (Inchinor) (802) 1363$^{14}$ 5260$^{18}$ 5957$^{13}$ >51+a 49f<

**Poker Player (IRE)** 2 ch g Raise A Grand (IRE) -Look Nonchalant (IRE) (Fayruz) 6171$^{5}$ >76+f<

**Polanski Mill** 5 b g Polish Precedent (USA) -Mill On The Floss (Mill Reef (USA)) 1135$^{P}$ 2787$^{11}$ 3776$^{9}$ 4202$^{10}$ 4603$^{10}$ >15a 55df<

**Polar Bear** 4 ch g Polar Falcon (USA) -Aim For The Top (USA) (Irish River (FR)) 1968$^{3}$ 2969$^{24}$ (3235) (4889) 5967a$^{7}$ 6214$^{3}$ >66a 114f<

**Polar Ben** 5 b g Polar Falcon (USA) -Woodbeck (Terimon) 1610$^{2}$ 1758$^{2}$ 3318$^{8}$ (5917) 6214$^{9}$ >116f<

**Polar Dancer** 3 b f Polar Falcon (USA) -Petonica (IRE) (Petoski) 1998$^{18}$ 3852$^{3}$ 4346$^{11}$ 4710$^{11}$ 5495$^{3}$ 5891$^{3}$ 6085$^{8}$ >62a 63f<

**Polar Dawn** 2 b f Polar Falcon (USA) -Leave At Dawn (Slip Anchor) 2761$^{2}$ 4081$^{6}$ 4681$^{4}$ (5200) 6174$^{10}$ >72f<

**Polar Force** 4 ch g Polar Falcon (USA) -Irish Light (USA) (Irish River (FR)) 526$^{4}$ 771$^{9}$ 1051$^{7}$ 1082$^{3}$ 1421$^{16}$ 1639$^{3}$ 2823$^{10}$ >68a 68f<

**Polar Galaxy** 3 br f Polar Falcon (USA) -June Brilly (IRE) (Fayruz) 2658$^{9}$ 3146$^{5}$ 4259$^{12}$ 4509$^{4}$ 4879$^{10}$ >20a 50df<

**Polar Haze** 7 ch g Polar Falcon (USA) -Sky Music (Absalom) 465$^{4}$ 608$^{2}$ 626$^{6}$ (670) 748$^{5}$ 799$^{7}$ 1140$^{4}$ 1237$^{5}$1739$^{5}$ 2322$^{8}$ 2384$^{4}$ 2823$^{13}$ 6229$^{2}$ >44a 50f<

**Polar Impact** 5 br h Polar Falcon (USA) -Boozy (Absalom) 2206$^{12}$ 3043$^{5}$ (3326) 4034$^{4}$ 5008$^{5}$ 5075$^{9}$ >83f<

**Polar Jem** 4 b f Polar Falcon (USA) -Top Jem (Damister (USA)) 1752$^{3}$ 2000$^{4}$ (2393) (2474) (2630) (3091) 3756$^{6}$ 4173$^{3}$ 4367$^{2}$ (5573) 5763$^{6}$ >101f<

**Polar Kingdom** 6 b g Pivotal-Scarlet Lake (Reprimand) 511$^{3}$ (680) (749) 761$^{10}$ 1354$^{12}$ 1765$^{3}$ 3309$^{12}$ >90a 85f<

**Polar Magic** 3 ch c Polar Falcon (USA) -Enchant (Lion Cavern (USA)) (3251) 4938$^{2}$ (5912) >85+a 81+f<

**Polar Passion** 2 b f Polar Prince (IRE) -Priorite (IRE) (Kenmare (FR)) 5455$^{5}$ 5771$^{11}$ >36f<

**Polar Sun** 3 b g Polar Falcon (USA) -Barford Lady (Stanford) 2505$^{6}$ 3948$^{3}$ 4845$^{6}$ >67f<

**Polar Tryst** 5 ch m Polar Falcon (USA) -Lovers Tryst (Castle Keep) (5340) 5764$^{12}$ >76f<

**Polar Way** 5 ch g Polar Falcon (USA) -Fetish (Dancing Brave (USA)) 3073$^{14}$ 3906$^{3}$ 4120$^{2}$ 4745$^{9}$ (5199) 5888$^{3}$ 6214$^{4}$ >121f<

**Pole Star** 6 bb g Polar Falcon (USA) -Ellie Ardensky (Slip Anchor) 6218$^{10}$ >116f<

**Polesworth** 2 b f Wizard King-Nicholas Mistress

(Beveled (USA)) 4095$^{5}$ 4907$^{10}$ 5349$^{10}$ >**27a 44f**<

**Policy Maker (IRE)** 4 b c Sadler s Wells (USA) -Palmeraie (USA) (Lear Fan (USA)) 1261a$^{5}$ (2924a) 3567a$^{2}$ (5502a) 5981a$^{19}$ >**121f**<

**Polish Baron (IRE)** 7 b g Barathea (IRE) -Polish Mission (Polish Precedent (USA)) 471$^{6}$ ><

**Polish Eagle** 2 b c Polish Precedent (USA) -Tinashaan (IRE) (Darshaan) 6187$^{11}$ 6440$^{2}$ >**78f**<

**Polish Emperor (USA)** 4 ch g Polish Precedent (USA) -Empress Jackie (USA) (Mount Hagen (FR)) 417$^{4}$ 806$^{2}$ 912$^{2}$ 1131$^{5}$ 1313$^{16}$ 1642$^{3}$ (2130) 2682$^{13}$ 2739$^{8}$4232$^{10}$ 5094$^{6}$ 5550$^{10}$ (5949) 6554$^{7}$ >**83a 88f**<

**Polish Index** 2 b c Polish Precedent (USA) -Glossary (Reference Point) 5716$^{17}$ >**1f**<

**Polish Rhapsody (IRE)** 3 b f Charnwood Forest (IRE) -Polish Rhythm (IRE) (Polish Patriot (USA)) 644$^{11}$ 982$^{11}$ 1285$^{6}$ 1545$^{9}$ >**51a**<

**Polish Rose** 3 ch f Polish Precedent (USA) -Messila Rose (Darshaan) 5378$^{8}$ 5749$^{5}$ 6357$^{8}$ >**57df**<

**Polish Spirit** 9 b g Emarati (USA) -Gentle Star (Comedy Star (USA)) 3844$^{14}$ 4301$^{7}$ 4641$^{6}$ (5153) 6083$^{19}$ >**70f**<

**Polish Summer** 7 b h Polish Precedent (USA) -Hunt The Sun (Rainbow Quest (USA)) (980a) (1144a) 1804a$^{5}$ 3567a$^{7}$ 5502a$^{4}$ 5985a$^{5}$ >**118f**<

**Polka Princess** 4 b f Makbul-Liberatrice (FR) (Assert) 412$^{12}$ 570$^{13}$ 661$^{7}$ 789$^{3}$ 857$^{13}$ 995$^{10}$ 1164$^{9}$1402$^{12}$ 1887$^{5}$ >**38a 38f**<

**Pollard s Vision (USA)** 3 br c Carson City (USA) -Etats Unis (USA) (Dixieland Band (USA)) 1781a$^{17}$ >**53a**<

**Pollito (IRE)** 2 b g Rossini (USA) -Bezee (Belmez (USA)) 4193$^{5}$ 4797$^{6}$ 5179$^{4}$ 5741$^{3}$ >**73a 75+f**<

**Polly Alexander (IRE)** 2 ch f Foxhound (USA) -Fiveofive (IRE) (Fairy King (USA)) 1130$^{5}$ (1299) (1616) 2083$^{3}$ 2668a$^{2}$ (3242) 3599$^{9}$ 4597a$^{7}$ 6174$^{14}$ >**88f**<

**Polly Perkins (IRE)** 2 b f Pivotal-Prospering (Prince Sabo) (2173) (2532) 2970$^{11}$ 3316$^{8}$ (3481) >**101f**<

**Polonius** 3 b g Great Dane (IRE) -Bridge Pool (First Trump) 3751$^{6}$ >**91+f**<

**Polyfirst (FR)** 3 b f Poliglote-First Turn (USA) (Alleged (USA)) 1803a$^{4}$ 4356a$^{2}$ 5032a$^{3}$ >**103f**<

**Polygonal (FR)** 4 b g Octagonal (NZ) -Sectarine (FR) (Maelstrom Lake) 2894$^{6}$ 3756$^{19}$ 4118$^{5}$ (4520) 5461$^{8}$ >**100f**<

**Pomeranze (IRE)** 3 br f Polar Falcon (USA) -Petunia (GER) (Chief Singer) 711a$^{6}$ 1005a$^{5}$ >**90a 80f**<

**Pomfret Lad** 6 b g Cyrano De Bergerac-Lucky Flinders (Free State) 1113$^{19}$ 1923$^{14}$ 2065$^{12}$ 5393$^{14}$ 5628$^{22}$ 5921$^{12}$ 6071$^{17}$ 6267$^{18}$ >**92f**<

**Pompey Blue** 3 b f Abou Zouz (USA) -Habla Me (IRE) (Fairy King (USA)) 458$^{5}$ 619$^{5}$ 868$^{7}$ 2839$^{7}$ 3084$^{9}$ 3344$^{12}$ 3864$^{8}$ >**54a 54f**<

**Pompey Chimes** 4 b g Forzando-Silver Purse (Interrex (CAN)) 1133$^{4}$ 1295$^{13}$ 2166$^{15}$ >**42f**<

**Ponderon** 4 ch g Hector Protector (USA) -Blush Rambler (IRE) (Blushing Groom (FR)) 1329$^{8}$ 1880$^{6}$ 2684$^{11}$ >**81+a 98f**<

**Ponente** 2 b f Robellino (USA) -Polmara (IRE) (Polish Precedent (USA)) 4712$^{6}$ 5348$^{9}$ 6211$^{3}$ >**59 f**<

**Pongee** 4 b f Barathea (IRE) -Puce (Darshaan) 2062$^{3}$ (2297) (3519) 4321$^{2}$ 4859$^{2}$ >**83+a 109f**<

**Pon My Soul (IRE)** 2 b g Imperial Ballet (IRE) -Erin Anam Cara (IRE) (Exit To Nowhere (USA)) (3506) 4521$^{6}$ 5596$^{8}$ 6127$^{6}$ >**62f**<

**Pont Allaire (IRE)** 3 b f Rahy (USA) -Leonila (IRE) (Caerleon (USA)) (1753) 2081$^{7}$ 3320$^{5}$ >**79f**<

**Pont D Or (IRE)** 5 b h Exit To Nowhere (USA) -Pont Audemer (USA) (Chief s Crown (USA)) 4039a$^{4}$ 4766a$^{4}$ 6170a$^{4}$ >**106f**<

**Pont Neuf (IRE)** 4 b f Revoque (IRE) -Petite Maxine (Sharpo) 650$^{13}$ 767$^{8}$ 863$^{4}$ 3348$^{2}$ 3578$^{5}$ (3809) (4196) 4398$^{7}$ 4616$^{2}$4698$^{3}$ 6047$^{9}$ 6074$^{15}$ 6292$^{9}$ 6540$^{11}$ >**60da 74f**<

**Pooka s Daughter (IRE)** 4 b f Eagle Eyed (USA) -Gaelic s Fantasy (IRE) (Statoblest) 457$^{5}$ 565$^{7}$ 588$^{10}$ 665$^{7}$ 730$^{8}$ 809$^{2}$ 998$^{14}$1094$^{12}$ >**32a 21f**<

**Popee (FR)** 3 b f Take Risks (FR) -Pop Out (FR) (Ecossais (FR)) 2028a$^{4}$ >**106f**<

**Pope s Hill (IRE)** 3 b c Sadler s Wells (USA) -Ghost Tree (IRE) (Caerleon (USA)) 2273$^{4}$ 3138$^{4}$ 3417$^{6}$ 4027$^{3}$ 4647$^{4}$ 5100$^{4}$ 5472$^{6}$ >**78f**<

**Poppyfields** 2 b f Danzero (AUS) -Shalverton (IRE) (Shalford (IRE)) 5200$^{17}$ >**27f**<

**Poppyline** 4 b f Averti (IRE) -Shalverton (IRE) (Shalford (IRE)) 1229$^{9}$ 2226$^{11}$ 2356$^{U}$ 2597$^{3}$ 2879$^{6}$ 3555$^{3}$ 3828$^{10}$ 4418$^{7}$4708$^{6}$ 4801$^{5}$ 5282$^{4}$ >**63a 46f**<

**Poppys Footprint (IRE)** 3 ch f Titus Livius (FR) -Mica Male (ITY) (Law Society (USA)) 1129$^{21}$ 1408$^{11}$ 1614$^{10}$ 2069$^{5}$ 2239$^{3}$ 2569$^{4}$ 2907$^{9}$ 3478$^{P}$(5304) 5582$^{10}$ >**83f**<

**Pop Up Again** 4 ch f Bahamian Bounty-Bellair (Beveled (USA)) 2291$^{8}$ 2806$^{9}$ 3235$^{12}$ 3606$^{15}$ 6138$^{12}$ >**81 f**<

**Porlezza (FR)** 5 ch m Sicyos (USA) -Pupsi (FR) (Matahawk) 2719a$^{2}$ 3674$^{8}$ 4595a$^{14}$ >**117f**<

**Port D Argent (IRE)** 2 b f Docksider (USA) -Petite-D-Argent (Noalto) 6530$^{10}$ >**54+f**<

**Porthcawl** 3 b f Singspiel (IRE) -Dodo (IRE) (Alzao (USA)) (4954) (5566) 5783$^{10}$ >**84f**<

**Portichol Princess** 4 b f Bluegrass Prince (IRE) -Barbrallen (Rambo Dancer (CAN)) 997$^{6}$ >**33a**<

**Portmanteau** 3 b f Barathea (IRE) -Dayanata (Shirley Heights) 1507$^{13}$ (2198) 3415$^{8}$ (4368) 4582$^{2}$ >**93f**<

**Portmeirion** 3 b f Polish Precedent (USA) -India Atlanta (Ahonoora) 5621$^{10}$ >**57f**<

**Port Moreno (IRE)** 4 b g Turtle Island (IRE) -Infra Blue (IRE) (Bluebird (USA)) 716$^{5}$ 812$^{9}$ 3776$^{18}$ >**38a 38f**<

**Port Natal (IRE)** 6 b g Selkirk (USA) -Play Around (IRE) (Niniski (USA)) 504$^{7}$ 530$^{2}$ 861$^{U}$ 936$^{7}$ >**47a 47f**<

**Port n Starboard** 3 ch g Polar Falcon (USA) -Sally Slade (Dowsing (USA)) 2645$^{4}$ 3422$^{5}$ 4850$^{4}$ 5079$^{4}$ 5956$^{12}$ 6160$^{11}$ >**58a 67f**<

**Portrait Of A Lady (IRE)** 3 ch f Peintre Celebre (USA) -Starlight Smile (USA) (Green Dancer (USA)) 1521$^{3}$ (2133) 2514$^{3}$ (2809) (3528) 3944$^{3}$ 4321$^{6}$ >**99f**<

**Portrayal (USA)** 2 b f Saint Ballado (CAN) -True Glory (IRE) (In The Wings) 4184a$^{3}$ 4964a$^{4}$ 5532a$^{2}$ 5979a$^{5}$ >**106f**<

**Port Sodrick** 3 bb g Young Ern-Keepsake (IRE) (Distinctly North (USA)) 3848$^{6}$ 4303$^{6}$ 4545$^{4}$ 5571$^{5}$ 5843$^{9}$ 6055$^{7}$ 6287$^{2}$ >**61a 61f**<

**Port St Charles (IRE)** 7 bb g Night Shift (USA) -Safe Haven (Blakeney) 511$^{5}$ 607$^{11}$ 748$^{9}$ 968$^{12}$ 1177$^{4}$ 1313$^{4}$ 1504$^{15}$2178$^{8}$ 2440$^{4}$ 2628$^{3}$ 2739$^{7}$ 2912$^{7}$ 3227$^{14}$ 3836$^{4}$ 4181$^{7}$4415$^{6}$ 4626$^{12}$ 4879$^{2}$ 5201$^{7}$ >**82a 64f**<

**Posh Sheelagh** 3 b f Danzero (AUS) -Button Hole Flower (IRE) (Fairy King (USA)) 506$^{9}$ >**12a**<

**Posteritas (USA)** 3 b f Lear Fan (USA) -Imroz (USA) (Nureyev (USA)) 2647$^{3}$ 2911$^{2}$ (3374) 3915$^{5}$ (5025) 5397$^{6}$ 5699$^{11}$ >**93f**<

**Postgraduate (IRE)** 2 b c Almutawakel-Institutrice (IRE) (College Chapel) 6010$^{5}$ (6394) >**79a**<

**Potent Heir (USA)** 2 b c Forest Wildcat (USA) -Penniless Heiress (USA) (Pentelicus (USA)) (5341) >**86+f**<

**Potsdam** 6 ch g Rainbow Quest (USA) -Danilova (USA) (Lyphard (USA)) 695$^{7}$ 725$^{2}$ >**50a 67f**<

**Pouilly Fume** 3 b f Polish Precedent (USA) -Feather Bride (IRE) (Groom Dancer (USA)) 2001$^{18}$ >**2f**<

**Poule De Luxe (IRE)** 3 b f Cadeaux Genereux-Likely Story (IRE) (Night Shift (USA)) (1352) 5541$^{13}$ >**66f**<

**Poussin (IRE)** 6 b h Alzao (USA) -Paix Blanche (FR) (Fabulous Dancer (USA)) 980a$^{8}$ 3567a$^{10}$ >**108f**<

**Pout (IRE)** 2 b f Namid-Symphony (IRE) (Cyrano De Bergerac) 6101a$^{4}$ 6367a$^{8}$ >**80f**<

**Power And Demand** 7 b g Formidable (USA) -Mazurkanova (Song) 1513$^{4}$ 1573$^{8}$ >**9a**<

**Power Bird (IRE)** 4 b f Bluebird (USA) -Polynesian Goddess (IRE) (Salmon Leap (USA)) 575$^{2}$ 701$^{11}$ 745$^{9}$ 2483$^{13}$ 2813$^{8}$ 3260$^{5}$ 3489$^{12}$ >**58a 58f**<

**Powerful Parrish (USA)** 3 b f Quiet American (USA) -Parish Business (USA) (Phone Trick (USA)) 2479$^{11}$ 3142$^{2}$ 3574$^{4}$ 3908$^{12}$ 4368$^{7}$ 5339$^{8}$ >**74df**<

**Power Nap** 3 b f Acatenango (GER) -Dreams Are Free (IRE) (Caerleon (USA)) 3294$^{6}$ 3759$^{9}$ 4307$^{13}$ 4562$^{9}$ 5702$^{16}$ >**33f**<

**Powerscourt** 4 b c Sadler s Wells (USA) -Rainbow Lake (Rainbow Quest (USA)) (2329a) 2968$^{2}$ 3540$^{5}$ 4385a$^{2}$ 4768a$^{4}$ 5483a$^{3}$ 6490a$^{3}$ >**124f**<

**Power To Burn** 3 b g Superpower-Into The Fire (Dominion) 561$^{3}$ 732$^{5}$ 1293$^{9}$ 4868$^{17}$ >**53a 52f**<

**Prague** 6 b g Cyrano De Bergerac-Basenite (Mansingh (USA)) 555$^{14}$ >**60a 35f**<

**Prairie Falcon (IRE)** 10 b g Alzao (USA) -Sea Harrier (Grundy) 1401$^{3}$ 2277$^{7}$ 2684$^{9}$ 3095$^{P}$ >**91f**<

**Prairie Flower (IRE)** 3 b f Zieten (USA) -Prairie Runner (IRE) (Arazi (USA)) 2925a$^{17}$ 5433a$^{4}$ 5965a$^{5}$ 6437a$^{11}$ >**102f**<

**Prairie Law (GER)** 4 b g Law Society (USA) -Prairie Charm (IRE) (Thatching) 3917$^{6}$ 4485$^{4}$ 4713$^{3}$ 5354$^{9}$ 5546$^{13}$ >**46f**<

**Prairie Oyster** 3 b f Emperor Jones (USA) -Soba Up (Persian Heights) 2243$^{11}$ >**16f**<

**Prairie Sun (GER)** 3 b f Law Society (USA) -Prairie Flame (IRE) (Marju (IRE)) 1235$^{4}$ 1394$^{4}$ 1823$^{5}$ (2199) 2584$^{7}$ 3026$^{10}$ 3473$^{10}$ 4015$^{6}$ 4307$^{10}$4424$^{6}$ 5365$^{3}$ >**45a 58f**<

**Prairie Wolf** 8 ch g Wolfhound (USA) -Bay Queen (Damister (USA)) 1540$^{15}$ 1821$^{14}$ 2210$^{9}$ 2474$^{10}$ 3005$^{5}$ (3985) 4214$^{9}$ 4737$^{9}$ 5423$^{13}$6185$^{7}$ >**94f**<

**Prakara (IRE)** 2 ch f Indian Ridge-Prima Volta (Primo Dominie) 6470$^{15}$ >**17f**<

**Pralin Star (IRE)** 2 ch g Daggers Drawn (USA) -Polaregina (FR) (Rex Magna (FR)) 3931$^{15}$ 5034$^{4}$ 5467$^{12}$ >**52f**<

**Prayerful** 5 b m Syrtos-Pure Formality (Forzando) 1590$^{5}$ >**15a 45f**<

**Precious Freedom** 4 b g Ashkalani (IRE) -Prayers n Promises (USA) (Foolish Pleasure (USA)) 433$^{10}$ 572$^{15}$ 718$^{7}$ >**12a 44 f**<

**Precious Mystery (IRE)** 4 ch f Titus Livius (FR) -Ascoli (Skyliner) 4398$^{4}$ 5019$^{2}$ 6013$^{12}$ (6183) 6527$^{6}$ >**55a 70f**<

**Precious Sammi** 2 b g Mark Of Esteem (IRE) -Night Over Day (Most Welcome) 3665$^{8}$ 6011$^{5}$ 6226$^{11}$ 6453$^{9}$ >**53a 42f**<

**Pre Eminance (IRE)** 3 b c Peintre Celebre (USA) -Sorb Apple (IRE) (Kris) 2479$^{6}$ >**70f**<

**Pregnant Pause (IRE)** 3 b g General Monash (USA) -Dissidentia (IRE) (Dancing Dissident (USA)) 414$^{4}$ 462$^{10}$ 2706$^{4}$ 2915$^{5}$ 3171$^{4}$ >**69a 59f**<

**Prelude** 3 b f Danzero (AUS) -Dancing Debut (Polar Falcon (USA)) 1904$^{5}$ 2647$^{8}$ 3142$^{8}$ 3706$^{6}$ 4307$^{6}$ 4536$^{6}$ (5197) 5560$^{5}$ 6006$^{10}$ >**63f**<

**Premier Dane (IRE)** 2 b c Indian Danehill (IRE) -Crystal Blue (IRE) (Bluebird (USA)) 4589a$^{6}$ >**84f**<

**Premier Dream (USA)** 3 ch c Woodman (USA) -Marina Duff (Caerleon (USA)) 1301$^{6}$ 1419$^{6}$ 1557$^{3}$ (1874) 2251$^{14}$ 3586$^{4}$ 4672$^{11}$ 5410$^{14}$ >**73f**<

**Premier Fantasy** 2 b c Pivotal-Hemaca (Distinctly North (USA)) 5096$^{6}$ (5262) >**90f**<

**Premier Prospect (USA)** 3 b f Sahm (USA) -Tadwin (Never So Bold) 4251a$^{2}$ >**69f**<

**Premier Rouge** 3 b g Croco Rouge (IRE) -Petit Point (IRE) (Petorius) 2777$^{4}$ 3448$^{4}$ 4629$^{3}$ 5156$^{2}$ 5693$^{3}$ 6081$^{8}$ >**77f**<

**Premier Times** 2 ch g Timeless Times (USA) -Lady Magician (Lord Bud) 3577$^{5}$ (3951) 4278$^{6}$ 4559$^{7}$ 4699$^{8}$ >**52f**<

**Prends Ton Temps (FR)** 7 b h Exit To Nowhere (USA) -Sarooh s Love (USA) (Nureyev (USA)) 3030a$^{9}$ 4039a$^{11}$ 6170a$^{9}$ >**107f**<

**Prenup (IRE)** 3 ch f Diesis-Mutual Consent (IRE) (Reference Point) 1998$^{4}$ (2442) (2774) 3050$^{2}$ 3561$^{2}$ 4642$^{8}$ 5303$^{6}$ >**58a 82 f**<

**Present n Correct** 11 ch g Cadeaux Genereux-Emerald Eagle (Sandy Creek) 423$^{9}$ 441$^{8}$ 654$^{10}$ >**4a 2f**<

**Present Oriented (USA)** 3 ch c Southern Halo (USA) -Shy Beauty (CAN) (Great Gladiator (USA)) 2085$^{5}$ 2611$^{8}$ >**78f**<

**Preskani** 2 b g Sri Pekan (USA) -Lamarita (Emarati (USA)) 4567$^{16}$ 4924$^{12}$ 5616$^{13}$ 5953$^{9}$ >**25a 24f**<

**Press Express (IRE)** 2 ch c Entrepreneur-Nawaji (USA) (Trempolino (USA)) 4730$^{7}$ 5091$^{6}$ (5406) 5885$^{8}$ 6188$^{13}$ 6344$^{7}$ >**78f**<

**Preston Hall** 3 b g Accordion-Little Preston (IRE) (Pennine Walk) 739$^{7}$ 1064$^{8}$ 3666$^{6}$ 4057$^{5}$ 4710$^{12}$ >**55a 44f**<

**Presto Shinko (IRE)** 3 b g Shinko Forest (IRE) -Swift Chorus (Music Boy) (1083) 1881$^{6}$ 1965$^{3}$ 2589$^{2}$ (2839) 3995$^{3}$ 4614$^{4}$ 5874$^{12}$ >**67+a 89f**<

**Presto Vento** 4 b f Air Express (IRE) -Placement (Kris) 1789$^{7}$ 1964$^{11}$ >**96a 95f**<

**Presumptive (IRE)** 4 b g Danehill (USA) -Demure (Machiavellian (USA)) 1939$^{5}$ 3212$^{3}$ 3597$^{13}$ (4690) 5631$^{17}$ 6070$^{10}$ >**89+f**<

**Pretty Kool** 4 b f Inchinor-Carrie Kool (Prince Sabo) 3154$^{10}$ 4336$^{5}$ 4517$^{3}$ (4708) 5260$^{7}$ 5597$^{13}$ >**53a 57f**<

**Pretty Soon (FR)** 2 b f Zafonic (USA) -Bocanegra (FR) (Night Shift (USA)) 5532a$^{6}$ 6297a$^{4}$ >**96f**<

**Pretty Star (GER)** 4 b c Lando (GER) -Pretty Ballerina (Sadler s Wells (USA)) 4777$^{2}$ 4831$^{15}$ >**98f**<

**Pretty Woman (IRE)** 2 ch f Night Shift (USA) -Kind Of Cute (Prince Sabo) 5558$^{11}$ 5908$^{10}$ >**26f**<

**Pridaisy (IRE)** 2 b f Cape Cross (IRE) -Primisca (Double Form) 3436a$^{9}$ ><

**Pride (FR)** 4 b f Peintre Celebre (USA) -Specificity (USA) (Alleged (USA)) (1952a) 2543a$^{3}$ 3567a$^{5}$ 4982a$^{2}$ 5501a$^{3}$ 5981a$^{13}$ (6263a) >**67a 113f**<

**Pride Of Kinloch** 4 ch f Dr Devious (IRE) -Stormswept (USA) (Storm Bird (CAN)) 510$^{7}$ 613$^{6}$ 1452$^{9}$ 1620$^{4}$ 1875$^{13}$ 2215$^{3}$ 2459$^{7}$ 2899$^{9}$3098$^{17}$ 3954$^{3}$ 4309$^{2}$ 4557$^{6}$ 5526$^{15}$ 6548$^{15}$ >**43a 64f**<

**Pride Of London (IRE)** 2 b f Danetime (IRE) -Kavana (IRE) (Marju (IRE)) 3532$^{17}$ 4198$^{8}$ 4681$^{12}$ >**60f**<

**Pride Of Poona (IRE)** 2 b f Indian Ridge-Scandalous (Warning) 6158$^{8}$ 6446$^{8}$ >**35a**<

**Pridewood Dove** 5 b m Alderbrook-Flighty Dove (Cruise Missile) 2611$^{11}$ 3341$^{P}$ ><

**Prideyev (USA)** 4 ch g Nureyev (USA) -Pride Of Baino (USA) (Secretariat (USA)) 973$^{9}$ >**66f**<

**Prim (BRZ)** 3 ch c Ghadeer (USA) -Above Halo (ARG) (Southern Halo (USA)) 920a$^{7}$ 977a$^{11}$ >**94a**<

**Primarily** 2 b c Mind Games-Prim N Proper (Tragic Role (USA)) 5555$^{11}$ 5772$^{5}$ 6272$^{2}$ 6522$^{3}$ >**61f**<

**Prima Stella** 5 gr m Primo Dominie-Raffelina (USA) (Carson City (USA)) 407$^{4}$ (511) 648$^{10}$ 749$^{2}$ 836$^{6}$ 960$^{6}$ 1051$^{12}$ 3178$^{7}$3593$^{8}$ >**79a 71f**<

**Primatech (IRE)** 3 b f Priolo (USA) -Ida Lupino (IRE) (Statoblest) 4674$^{8}$ 5451$^{4}$ 6056$^{9}$ 6228$^{3}$ >**41f**<

**Primaxis (IRE)** 3 gr c Linamix (FR) -Ring Pink (USA) (Bering) 5500a$^{7}$ >**85f**<

**Prime Contender** 2 b c Efisio-Gecko Rouge (Rousillon (USA)) 6342$^{7}$ 6569$^{5}$ >**65+f**<

**Primed Up (IRE)** 2 b g Rainbow Quest (USA) -Cape Mist (USA) (Lure (USA)) 4290$^{12}$ ><

**Prime Offer** 8 b g Primo Dominie-Single Bid (Auction Ring (USA)) 1032$^{13}$ 1102$^{2}$ 1207$^{4}$ (2597) 2803$^{2}$ (3049) 3559$^{5}$ 4418$^{4}$ 5020$^{2}$5945$^{18}$ >**69a 73+f**<

**Prime Powered (IRE)** 3 b g Barathea (IRE) -Caribbean Quest (Rainbow Quest (USA)) 1414$^{5}$ 2676$^{5}$ 4229$^{8}$ 4737$^{2}$ 5183$^{8}$ 5732$^{4}$ 6354$^{14}$ >**92f**<

**Prime Recreation** 7 b g Primo Dominie-Night Transaction (Tina s Pet) 540$^{6}$ 586$^{16}$ 806$^{6}$ 905$^{8}$ 1131$^{9}$ 1368$^{15}$ 2118$^{3}$ 2303$^{9}$3227$^{12}$ 3945$^{4}$ 4299$^{11}$ 5094$^{12}$ (5157) 5550$^{8}$ 6518$^{3}$ >**68 a 77f**<

**Primeshade Promise** 3 ch f Opening Verse (USA) -Bonnie Lassie (Efisio) 3592$^{13}$ 3994$^{11}$ 4478$^{3}$ 5693$^{8}$ 6147$^{7}$ >**50f**<

**Primo Way** 3 b c Primo Dominie-Waypoint (Cadeaux Genereux) (1530) 2082$^{3}$ 2589$^{6}$ 2907$^{3}$ 3455$^{11}$ 5652$^{3}$ 6070$^{14}$ 6277$^{7}$ >**84a 93f**<

**Primus Inter Pares (IRE)** 3 b c Sadler s Wells (USA) -Life At The Top (Habitat) (3477) 3671$^{16}$ >**63+a 111+f**<

**Prince Aaron (IRE)** 4 b g Marju (IRE) -Spirito Libro (USA) (Lear Fan (USA)) (453) (576) 646$^{6}$ 771$^{2}$ (1051) 2407$^{3}$ (2477) 2682$^{5}$ (3691) (5121) 5628$^{24}$ >**89a 99+f**<

**Princeable Lady (IRE)** 2 b f Desert Prince (IRE) -Saucy Maid (IRE) (Sure Blade (USA)) 3123$^{7}$ 3741$^{10}$ 4099$^{12}$ 4507$^{9}$ >**58f**<

**Prince Albert** 6 ch g Rock City-Russell Creek (Sandy Creek) 1274$^{8}$ 1522$^{11}$ 1987$^{3}$ >**22f**<

**Prince Charming** 2 b c Royal Applause-Miss Primula (Dominion) (1331) (1707) 2532$^{8}$ 4962a$^{6}$ (5602) 5918$^{8}$ 6212$^{5}$ 6462a$^{4}$ >**105f**<

**Prince Cyrano** 5 b g Cyrano De Bergerac-Odilese (Mummy s Pet) 1106$^{22}$ 1354$^{15}$ 1765$^{14}$ 1968$^{6}$ 2503$^{11}$ 4090$^{3}$ 4522$^{5}$ 4923$^{2}$5094$^{9}$ 5704$^{13}$ 6046$^{8}$ >**79f**<

**Prince Dayjur (USA)** 5 bb g Dayjur (USA) -Distinct Beauty (USA) (Phone Trick (USA)) 2132$^{18}$ (3416) 3645$^{11}$ 3979$^{7}$ >**85f**<

**Prince Du Soleil (FR)** 8 b g Cardoun (FR) -Revelry (FR) (Blakeney) 860$^{6}$ 949$^{6}$ 1277$^{8}$ 2598$^{8}$ >**40a 58 f**<

**Prince Hector** 5 ch g Hector Protector (USA) -Ceanothus (IRE) (Bluebird (USA)) 1504$^{10}$ 2094$^{2}$ 2469$^{6}$ 2789$^{2}$ 4067$^{4}$ >**89f**<

**Prince Holing** 4 ch g Halling (USA) -Ella Mon Amour (Ela-Mana-Mou) 1286$^{5}$ 3078$^{7}$ 3474$^{8}$ 3866$^{8}$ 4424$^{7}$ >**69f**<

**Prince Ivor** 4 b g Polar Falcon (USA) -Mistook (USA) (Phone Trick (USA)) 663$^{9}$ 1231$^{7}$ 5644$^{8}$ 5928$^{19}$ >**37a 37f**<

**Prince Kirk (FR)** 4 b c Selkirk (USA) -Princess Manila (CAN) (Manila (USA)) (2339a) >**123f**<

**Princelet (IRE)** 2 b c Desert Prince (IRE) -Soeur Ti (FR) (Kaldoun (FR)) 6441$^{4}$ >**61f**<

**Princely Vale (IRE)** 2 b c Princely Heir (IRE) -Lomalou (IRE) (Lightning Dealer) 1589$^{7}$ 2515$^{4}$ (2960) (3100) (3390) 3886$^{3}$ 4278$^{4}$ 4676$^{5}$ 5174$^{2}$ >**70f**<

**Princelywallywogan** 2 b c Princely Heir (IRE) -Dublivia (Midyan (USA)) 4967$^{6}$ >**63f**<

**Prince Minata (IRE)** 9 b g Machiavellian (USA) -Aminata (Glenstal (USA)) 693$^{8}$ 966$^{13}$ 1090$^{3}$ 1233$^{10}$ 1263$^{4}$ 1681$^{11}$ 1723$^{6}$ >**54 a 46f**<

**Prince Monalulu (IRE)** 3 b c Intikhab (USA) -Lidanna (Nicholas (USA)) 1893a$^{5}$ 2744a$^{11}$ >**88+f**<

**Prince Namid** 2 b c Namid-Fen Princess (IRE) (Trojan Fen) 1415$^{4}$ 1709$^{3}$ (1990) >**71f**<

**Prince Nasseem (GER)** 7 b h Neshad (USA) -Penola (GER) (Acatenango (GER)) 973$^{7}$ >**8a**<

**Prince Nureyev (IRE)** 4 b g Desert King (IRE) -Annaletta (Belmez (USA)) 1328$^{9}$ 2066$^{9}$ 3075$^{9}$ 3482$^{2}$ >**103f**<

**Prince Of Aragon** 8 b g Aragon-Queens Welcome (Northfields (USA)) 3024$^{7}$ 3380$^{13}$ >**33a**<

**Prince Of Blues (IRE)** 6 b g Prince Of Birds (USA) -Reshift (Night Shift (USA)) 476$^{9}$ 578$^{2}$ 806$^{10}$ 836$^{13}$ 905$^{10}$ 1205$^{4}$ 1368$^{10}$1537$^{4}$ 1759$^{5}$ 2041$^{13}$ 2293$^{8}$ 2626$^{3}$ 2754$^{3}$ 3038$^{5}$ 3293$^{7}$3705$^{7}$ 4244$^{3}$ 4291$^{23}$ 4677$^{3}$ 4935$^{3}$ 5287$^{16}$ 5458$^{10}$ 5704$^{12}$ >**73 a 66 f**<

**Prince Of Denmark (IRE)** 3 b c Danetime (IRE) -Villa Nova (IRE) (Petardia) 691a$^{13}$ (848a) 920a$^{3}$ 975a$^{4}$ >**93a 91 f**<

**Prince Of Gold** 4 b c Polar Prince (IRE) -Gold Belt (IRE) (Bellypha) 1213$^{8}$ 1427$^{5}$ 1620$^{7}$ 2119$^{7}$ 2459$^{6}$ 2687$^{7}$ (2776) 3127$^{10}$ 3520$^{10}$3731$^{14}$ 4209$^{8}$ 4569$^{10}$ 5108$^{13}$ 5713$^{5}$ 5798$^{3}$ 6046$^{2}$ 6210$^{9}$(6273) 6539$^{2}$ >**73+a 74f**<

**Prince Of Perles** 3 b g Mind Games-Pearls (Mon Tresor) 802$^{10}$ 858$^{14}$ 958$^{3}$ 998$^{9}$ >**38a 32f**<

**Prince Of Thebes (IRE)** 3 b g Desert Prince (IRE) -Persian Walk (FR) (Persian Bold) (4164) 4709$^{3}$ >**97f**<

**Prince Of The Wood (IRE)** 4 ch g Woodborough (USA) -Ard Dauphine (IRE) (Forest Wind (USA)) 1693$^{2}$ (2186) 2462$^{4}$ 2613$^{7}$ 2731$^{5}$ 3564$^{9}$ 4007$^{4}$ >**57a 56f**<

**Prince Of War (AUS)** 6 b r Royal Academy (USA) -Scribbling (AUS) (Palace Music (USA)) (633a) 712a$^{2}$ 854a$^{3}$ 976a$^{2}$ >**103f**<

**Prince Prospect** 8 b g Lycius (USA) -Princess Dechtra (IRE) (Bellypha) 412$^{7}$ (655) 726$^{2}$ 838$^{2}$ 1136$^{9}$ 1479$^{8}$ 6142$^{7}$ >**55 a 55f**<

**Prince Pyramus** 6 b g Pyramus (USA) -Rekindled Flame (IRE) (King s Lake (USA)) 1956$^{10}$ 2350$^{18}$ >**47 f**<

**Prince Renesis** 3 b g Mind Games-Stoneydale (Tickled Pink) 1854$^{8}$ 2962$^{10}$ 3410$^{9}$ 5018$^{6}$ 5863$^{16}$ 6402$^{5}$ >**45a 45f**<

**Prince Samos (IRE)** 2 b c Mujadil (USA) -Sabaniya (FR) (Lashkari) 4117$^{4}$ 4611$^{7}$ 4844$^{5}$ 5054$^{3}$ 6188$^{3}$ >**78a 78f**<

**Prince Slayer** 8 b g Batshoof-Top Sovereign (High Top) 705$^{9}$ >**35a**<

**Princess Alina (IRE)** 3 b f Sadler s Wells (USA) -Eilanden (IRE) (Akarad (FR)) 492$^{8}$ 622$^{8}$ >**66a 28f**<

**Princess Bankes** 3 b f Vettori (IRE) -Lady Bankes (IRE) (Alzao (USA)) 1015$^{11}$ 1476$^{6}$ 2098$^{11}$ 2451$^{10}$ 3261$^{7}$ 5284$^{4}$ 5751$^{3}$ 6082$^{15}$6230$^{7}$ >**26a 39f**<

**Princesse Jasmine (FR)** 2 b f Gold Away (IRE) -Doucelisa (FR) (Cardoun (FR)) 5922a$^{6}$ 6202a$^{5}$ 6529a$^{5}$ >**95f**<

**Princess Erica** 4 b f Perpendicular-Birichino (Dilum (USA)) 1750$^{15}$ 1824$^{12}$ 2123$^{11}$ 2238$^{4}$ 2383$^{10}$ 2556$^{9}$ >**50a 50f**<

**Princess Galadriel** 3 b f Magic Ring (IRE) -Prim Lass (Reprimand) 1907$^{2}$ (2098) 2411$^{3}$ 2820$^{2}$ 3264$^{7}$ 3421$^{6}$ 4483$^{3}$ 4938$^{6}$ (5155) 5715$^{3}$6311$^{10}$ 6461$^{2}$ 6549$^{12}$ >**40a 71f**<

**Princess Ismene** 3 b f Sri Pekan (USA) -Be Practical (Tragic Role (USA)) (451) 521$^{5}$ 751$^{2}$ 828$^{2}$ 965$^{4}$ 1017$^{3}$ 1375$^{3}$ 1422$^{4}$1465$^{13}$ 2088$^{5}$ 2395$^{4}$ 2822$^{6}$ 4568$^{RR}$ 5145$^{9}$ 5408$^{LFT}$ 6560$^{P}$ >**55a 40f**<

**Princess Kai (IRE)** 3 b f Cayman Kai (IRE) -City Princess (Rock City) (414) 496$^{9}$ 619$^{8}$ 678$^{3}$ 1312$^{4}$ 1742$^{2}$ 2033$^{2}$ 2482$^{6}$2741$^{13}$ >**53a 58f**<

**Princess Kiotto** 3 b f Desert King (IRE) -Ferghana Ma (Mtoto) 1420$^{5}$ 1740$^{2}$ 3479$^{3}$ (3984) (5860) 6269$^{2}$ >**55a 75f**<

**Princess Links** 2 b f Bahamian Bounty-Miss Prism (Niniski (USA)) 6352$^{15}$ ><

**Princess Magdalena** 4 ch f Pennekamp (USA) -Reason To Dance (Damister (USA)) 1857$^{11}$ 2740$^{7}$ 3264$^{9}$ 3809$^{7}$ >**42f**<

**Prince Troy (GER)** 5 b h Acatenango (GER) -Princess Nana (Bellypha) 5970a$^{9}$ >**78f**<

**Prince Tum Tum (USA)** 4 b c Capote (USA) -La Grande Epoque (USA) (Lyphard (USA)) 2044$^{10}$ 3318$^{6}$ 3906$^{4}$ 5199$^{3}$ >**102+f**<

**Prince Valentine** 3 b g My Best Valentine-Affaire De Coeur (Imperial Fling (USA)) 598$^{10}$ 660$^{7}$ 1301$^{3}$ 1874$^{5}$ 2705$^{4}$ 2930$^{7}$ 3990$^{4}$ 4941$^{9}$5021$^{16}$ 5795$^{14}$ >**49a 49f**<

**Prince Vector** 2 b c Vettori (IRE) -The In-Laws (IRE) (Be My Guest (USA)) 6145$^{11}$ >**71+f**<

**Prince Vettori** 2 b c Vettori (IRE) -Bombalarina (IRE) (Barathea (IRE)) 4743$^{9}$ 5256$^{8}$ 5741$^{6}$ >**62a 55f**<

**Principal Witness (IRE)** 3 b g Definite Article-Double Eight (IRE) (Common Grounds) 1461$^{13}$ 2113$^{4}$ 2519$^{2}$ 3001$^{26}$ 3304$^{5}$ 3671$^{13}$ >**57a 83f**<

**Principessa** 3 b f Machiavellian (USA) -Party Doll (Be My Guest (USA)) 1507$^{5}$ 1683$^{11}$ 2169$^{9}$ 2848$^{10}$ 3231$^{2}$ 3473$^{2}$ 3908$^{9}$ 4618$^{2}$4910$^{4}$ 5511$^{3}$ 5828$^{2}$ 6006$^{16}$ 6396$^{10}$ >**75f**<

**Prins Willem (IRE)** 5 b g Alzao (USA) -American Gardens (USA) (Alleged (USA)) 1401$^{2}$ 1768$^{3}$ 2684$^{4}$ 3757$^{5}$ 4831$^{9}$ 5919$^{12}$ 6192$^{3}$ >**97f**<

**Printsmith (IRE)** 7 br m Petardia-Black And Blaze (Taufan (USA)) (434) 472$^{4}$ 725$^{4}$ 939$^{3}$ 1024$^{2}$ (1093) 1427$^{12}$ 1606$^{5}$1993$^{11}$ 2128$^{9}$ 6057$^{4}$ >**51a 48f**<

**Prinz Of Australia (GER)** 2 b c Big Shuffle (USA) -Pacaya (GER) (Acatenango (GER)) 6256a$^{4}$ ><

**Priors Dale** 4 b g Lahib (USA) -Mathaayl (USA) (Shadeed (USA)) 555$^{2}$ 644$^{6}$ 846$^{6}$ 2226$^{4}$ 5252$^{14}$ 6081$^{14}$ >**70a 73f**<

**Prithee** 2 b f Barathea (IRE) -Bina Ridge (Indian Ridge) 6471$^{7}$ >**70f**<

**Private Benjamin** 4 gr g Ridgewood Ben-Jilly Woo (Environment Friend) 740$^{9}$ (818) 887$^{7}$ 1122$^{6}$ 2032$^{3}$ 2324$^{9}$ (2767) 3046$^{9}$ 3393$^{5}$3752$^{10}$ 4616$^{12}$ 4736$^{5}$ 6159$^{3}$ >**65a 58f**<

**Private Charter** 4 b c Singspiel (IRE) -By Charter (Shirley Heights) 1062$^{13}$ 1767$^{2}$ 2220$^{10}$ 2329a$^{6}$ 5438$^{7}$ (5916) >**88a 114f**<

**Private Jessica** 3 ch f Cadeaux Genereux-Rose Bay (Shareef Dancer (USA)) 1441$^{10}$ 1749$^{9}$ 4069$^{4}$ 5002$^{15}$ 5733$^{17}$ >**52f**<

**Private Seal** 9 b g King s Signet (USA) -Slender (Aragon) 495$^{6}$ 663$^{3}$ 857$^{2}$ 947$^{2}$ 995$^{9}$ 1101$^{2}$ 1164$^{12}$1545$^{5}$ 2324$^{11}$ 2591$^{8}$ 2939$^{9}$ 3173$^{3}$ 3934$^{2}$ 4086$^{6}$ 4458$^{3}$5021$^{4}$ 5285$^{9}$ >**49a 49f**<

**Privy Seal (IRE)** 3 b g Cape Cross (IRE) -Lady Joshua (IRE) (Royal Academy (USA)) (1330) 1586$^{2}$ 1901$^{2}$ 2510a$^{3}$ 3000$^{9}$ 3360a$^{4}$ 5731$^{2}$ >**112f**<

**Prize Fighter (IRE)** 2 b g Desert Sun-Papal (Selkirk (USA)) 3083$^{2}$ (3611) 4186$^{2}$ >**85a 75f**<

**Prizeman (USA)** 6 b g Prized (USA) -Shuttle (USA) (Conquistador Cielo (USA)) 1456$^{24}$ 2687$^{2}$ >**105f**<

**Prize Ring** 5 ch g Bering-Spot Prize (USA) (Seattle Dancer (USA)) 3411$^{6}$ 3782$^{2}$ 4261$^{6}$ 4512$^{9}$ >**44a 58 f**<

**Proclamation (IRE)** 2 gr c King s Best (USA) -Shamarra (FR) (Zayyani) (6187) >**90+f**<

**Procrastinate (IRE)** 2 ch g Rossini (USA) -May Hinton (Main Reef) 1248$^{3}$ 1340$^{7}$ 2035$^{6}$ 2248$^{5}$ 2616$^{3}$ 2773$^{7}$ 2960$^{5}$ 3980$^{2}$5369$^{11}$ 5513$^{3}$ 5816$^{10}$ >**62f**<

**Procreate (IRE)** 4 b g Among Men (USA) -Woodbury Princess (Never So Bold) 2260$^{17}$ 4280$^{8}$ 6469$^{6}$ >**30a 47f**<

**Profit s Reality (IRE)** 2 br c Key Of Luck (USA) -Teacher Preacher (IRE) (Taufan (USA)) 2035$^{7}$ 2470$^{5}$ 4446$^{5}$ 4632$^{4}$ 4824$^{3}$ (5476) 5670$^{3}$ 6268$^{8}$ >**88f**<

**Promenade** 3 b f Primo Dominie-Hamsah (IRE) (Green Desert (USA)) 2115$^{5}$ 2552$^{10}$ 3092$^{9}$ >**83+f**<

**Promote** 8 gr g Linamix (FR) -Rive (USA) (Riverman (USA)) 855$^{14}$ 2385$^{6}$ 3108$^{6}$ 3851$^{10}$ 4202$^{11}$ >**14a 48f**<

**Promoted Deputy (USA)** 2 b f Deputy Minister (CAN) -Shouldnt Say Never (USA) (Meadowlake (USA)) (5375) >**76+a**<

**Promoter** 4 ch g Selkirk (USA) -Poplina (USA) (Roberto (USA)) 1457$^{10}$ 2047$^{9}$ 2958$^{2}$ 3310$^{9}$ 3725$^{4}$ 4226$^{18}$ 5093$^{2}$ >**64a 98f**<

**Promotion** 4 b g Sadler s Wells (USA) -Tempting Prospect (Shirley Heights) (1762) 3034$^{2}$ 3756$^{2}$ >**110f**<

**Propellor (IRE)** 2 ch c Pivotal-Clunie (Inchinor) 3233$^{3}$ (3876) 4330$^{3}$ 4757$^{4}$ 6113$^{4}$ >**85+f**<

**Prophet s Calling (IRE)** 2 b g Brave Act-Arbitration (IRE) (Bigstone (IRE)) 4198$^{14}$ 5592$^{10}$ 5953$^{8}$ >**41a 44f**<

**Propinquity** 2 b c Primo Dominie-Lydia Maria (Dancing Brave (USA)) (3241) 3726$^{3}$ 4949$^{3}$ 5246$^{5}$ >**101f**<

**Pro Prado (USA)** 3 gr c El Prado (IRE) -Mama s Pro (USA) (Proper Reality (USA)) 1781a$^{13}$ >**90a**<

**Proprioception (IRE)** 2 ch f Danehill Dancer (IRE) -Pepper And Salt (IRE) (Double Schwartz) 5114$^{11}$ >**39f**<

**Proprius** 4 b g Perpendicular-Pretty Pollyanna (General Assembly (USA)) 429$^{5}$ 567$^{16}$ >**32a 29f**<

**Prospect Court** 2 ch c Pivotal-Scierpan (USA) (Sharpen Up) 2024$^{8}$ 2579$^{3}$ 2959$^{13}$ (3605) 4342$^{9}$ 5119$^{12}$ 5721$^{7}$ 6042$^{13}$ >**75f**<

**Prospect Park** 3 b c Sadler s Wells (USA) -Brooklyn s Dance (FR) (Shirley Heights) 2073a$^{2}$ 2722a$^{2}$ (3359a) 5500a$^{2}$ 5981a$^{16}$ >**118f**<

**Prospect Point** 2 ch f Cayman Kai (IRE) -Sassy Lady (IRE) (Brief Truce (USA)) 6221$^{4}$ 6478$^{8}$ >**32a**<

**Protecting Heights (IRE)** 3 br g Hector Protector (USA) -Height Of Fantasy (IRE) (Shirley Heights) 1395$^{17}$ 1674$^{6}$ >**67f**<

**Protective** 3 ch c Hector Protector (USA) -You Make Me Real (USA) (Give Me Strength (USA)) 2144$^{4}$ 2298$^{7}$ (2653) 3927$^{4}$ 4229$^{16}$ 5226$^{9}$ 5834$^{3}$ 6346$^{9}$ 6573$^{16}$ >**92f**<

**Pro Tempore** 2 b f Fraam-Record Time (Clantime) 3370$^{4}$ (3893) 4348$^{6}$ 4803$^{6}$ 5234$^{3}$ 5636$^{9}$ 5989$^{8}$ 6195$^{6}$ >**66f**<

**Protocol (IRE)** 10 b g Taufan (USA) -Ukraine s Affair (USA) (The Minstrel (CAN)) 1282$^{7}$ 1501$^{9}$ 2851$^{7}$ >**41a 33f**<

**Proud Accolade (USA)** 2 bb c Yes It s True (USA) -Proud Ciel (USA) (Septieme Ciel (USA)) 6489a$^{6}$ >**110a**<

**Proud Boast** 6 b m Komaite (USA) -Red Rosein (Red Sunset) 1211$^{7}$ (1391) 1685$^{8}$ 2065$^{9}$ 3266$^{14}$ 3795$^{2}$ 3976$^{3}$ 4165$^{18}$ 4324$^{11}$4526$^{6}$ 5505a$^{5}$ 5893$^{11}$ >**106f**<

**Proud Native (IRE)** 10 b g Imp Society (USA) -Karamana (Habitat) 2041$^{19}$ 2461$^{17}$ 2582$^{8}$ 2843$^{3}$ 3249$^{10}$ >**96f**<

**Proud Scholar (USA)** 2 br f Royal Academy (USA) -Proud Fact (USA) (Known Fact (USA)) 3905$^{2}$ 5248$^{6}$ >**82f**<

**Proud Tradition (USA)** 3 b f Seeking The Gold (USA) -Family Tradition (IRE) (Sadler s Wells (USA)) 1879$^{9}$ 2807$^{6}$ >**70f**<

**Proud Victor (IRE)** 4 b g Victory Note (USA) -Alberjas (IRE) (Sure Blade (USA)) 425$^{4}$ 531$^{5}$ 567$^{6}$ 594$^{6}$ 720$^{5}$ >**48a 37f**<

**Proud Western (USA)** 6 bb g Gone West (USA) -Proud Lou (USA) (Proud Clarion) 1525$^{9}$ 1870$^{12}$ 2350$^{16}$ 3148$^{13}$ 3734$^{5}$ >**49a 56f**<

**Proven (USA)** 5 br h Benny The Dip (USA) -Night Fax (USA) (Known Fact (USA)) 692a$^{5}$ >**62a 103f**<

**Prunelle (GER)** 3 b f Waky Nao-Pelly (GER) (Acatenango (GER)) 1983a$^{13}$ 3434a$^{12}$ >**67f**<

**Psychiatrist** 3 ch g Dr Devious (IRE) -Zahwa (Cadeaux Genereux) 1330$^{3}$ 1411$^{2}$ 2276$^{4}$ 2966$^{10}$ 3906$^{6}$ 5813$^{13}$ >**105f**<

**Ptarmigan Ridge** 8 b h Sea Raven (IRE) -Panayr (Faraway Times (USA)) 1113$^{10}$ 1343$^{8}$ (1923) 2488$^{12}$ 2679$^{19}$ 3266$^{6}$ 3713$^{5}$ (3795) 4538$^{19}$ 5287$^{3}$5393$^{3}$ 5787$^{7}$ 6243$^{11}$ >**93f**<

**Pt s Grey Eagle (USA)** 3 rg g Pleasant Tap (USA) -Hemet Eagle (USA) (Swing Till Dawn (USA)) 6487a$^{8}$ >**114a**<

**Public Forum** 2 b c Rainbow Quest (USA) -Valentine Girl (Alzao (USA)) (6306) >**76+f**<

**Pugin (IRE)** 6 b h Darshaan-Gothic Dream (IRE) (Nashwan (USA)) 1062$^{5}$ 1455$^{5}$ 2220$^{8}$ 3076$^{9}$ >**108a 117f**<

**Pukka (IRE)** 3 b c Sadler s Wells (USA) -Puce (Darshaan) (2107) 2680$^{9}$ 3927$^{2}$ 4833$^{5}$ >**74 a 109f**<

**Pulse** 6 b g Salse (USA) -French Gift (Cadeaux Genereux) 1368$^{14}$ 1477$^{9}$ 1642$^{2}$ 1872$^{3}$ 2118$^{6}$ 2246$^{6}$ 2724$^{4}$ 3126$^{5}$3307$^{3}$ 3558$^{7}$ 3810$^{11}$ 4400$^{5}$ 4774$^{5}$ 4923$^{4}$ 5016$^{7}$ 5253$^{10}$5337$^{6}$ 5412$^{9}$ 5512$^{5}$ 5736$^{2}$ 6186$^{3}$ 6559$^{7}$ >**57a 66f**<

**Punctilious** 3 b f Danehill (USA) -Robertet (USA) (Roberto (USA)) (2020) 2640$^{3}$ (2997) 3968a$^{2}$ 4859$^{4}$ 6383a$^{2}$ >**114f**<

**Puppeteer** 4 b c Singspiel (IRE) -Pidona (Baillamont (USA)) 1163a$^{6}$ 1741a$^{2}$ (2438a) 2923a$^{4}$ 5171a$^{4}$ 5668a$^{2}$ >**113f**<

**Pup s Pride** 7 b g Efisio-Moogie (Young Generation) 548$^{6}$ 773$^{7}$ 4093$^{13}$ >**30a 42f**<

**Purdey** 4 ch f Double Trigger (IRE) -Euphorie (GER) (Feenpark (GER)) 1858$^{9}$ 2590$^{5}$ 2874$^{4}$ 3518$^{5}$ >**38a 52f**<

**Pure Emotion** 3 b f Primo Dominie-Yasalam (IRE) (Fairy King (USA)) 597$^{5}$ 673$^{8}$ 895$^{7}$ 1040$^{7}$ >**48a**<

**Pure Folly (IRE)** 3 b f Machiavellian (USA) -Spirit Willing (IRE) (Fairy King (USA)) 708$^{3}$ 764$^{4}$ 3849$^{4}$ 4390$^{8}$ 4929$^{7}$ >**61+a 9f**<

**Pure Imagination (IRE)** 3 ch g Royal Academy (USA) -Ivory Bride (Domynsky) 2301$^{6}$ 2765$^{3}$ 3487$^{12}$ 3954$^{6}$ 4309$^{20}$ 4868$^{4}$ 5219$^{8}$ 5512$^{13}$(5674) 6001$^{8}$ >**71+f**<

**Pure Mischief (IRE)** 5 b g Alhaarth (IRE) -Bellissi (IRE) (Bluebird (USA)) 1138$^{3}$ (1527) (1944) 2039$^{5}$ (3022) 3265$^{3}$ 3929$^{2}$ 4678$^{4}$ 4808$^{6}$ 5158$^{5}$6156$^{5}$ 6311$^{7}$ 6395$^{3}$ >**76a 79f**<

**Pure Speculation** 4 b f Salse (USA) -Just Speculation (IRE) (Ahonoora) 682$^{8}$ 964$^{10}$ 1187$^{6}$ 1502$^{4}$ 1876$^{8}$ >**66a 79f**<

**Pure Vintage (IRE)** 3 b g Fasliyev (USA) -Tootling (IRE) (Pennine Walk) 2367$^{8}$ 2654$^{6}$ 4101$^{8}$ 4449$^{8}$ 5063$^{6}$ >**57f**<

**Purge (USA)** 3 b c Pulpit (USA) -Copelan s Bid Girl (USA) (Copelan (USA)) 2701a$^{9}$ >**114a**<

**Puri** 5 b g Mujadil (USA) -Prosperous Lady (Prince Tenderfoot (USA)) 1476$^{4}$ 1820$^{7}$ 2666$^{10}$ 3490$^{P}$ 4535$^{4}$ 4818$^{18}$ >**50a 48f**<

**Purple Door** 2 b f Daggers Drawn (USA) -Carreamia (Weldnaas (USA)) 4621$^{6}$ 5059$^{10}$ 5376$^{6}$ 6174$^{23}$ >**55f**<

**Purple Rain (IRE)** 3 b f Celtic Swing-Calypso Grant (IRE) (Danehill (USA)) 1301$^{7}$ 1419$^{10}$ 1753$^{6}$ 2667$^{5}$ 3002$^{10}$ >**37a 57f**<

**Purr** 3 b g Pursuit Of Love-Catawba (Mill Reef (USA)) 2085$^{12}$ 2645$^{6}$ 3190$^{13}$ 4778$^{15}$ 4972$^{8}$ 5153$^{9}$ 5286$^{14}$ 6438$^{4}$ >**37f**<

**Purus (IRE)** 2 b c Night Shift (USA) -Pariana (USA) (Bering) 6256a$^{9}$ ><

**Pushkin (IRE)** 6 b h Caerleon (USA) -Palmeraie (USA) (Lear Fan (USA)) 5288$^{20}$ 5589$^{2}$ 5834$^{5}$ 6215$^{34}$ >**96f**<

**Pussy Cat** 2 b f Josr Algarhoud (IRE) -Swan Lake (FR) (Lyphard (USA)) 4637$^{8}$ 5131$^{6}$ 5248$^{13}$ 5747$^{5}$ 6282$^{10}$ >**49f**<

**Putra Kuantan** 4 b c Grand Lodge (USA) -Fade (Persepolis (FR)) 1328$^{6}$ 1762$^{3}$ (2534) 2969$^{15}$ 3717$^{6}$ 4287$^{11}$ 5941$^{13}$ 6193$^{12}$ >**109f**<

**Putra Pekan** 6 b h Grand Lodge (USA) -Mazarine Blue (Bellypha) (1705) (1999) 2923a$^{7}$ 5291$^{7}$ 5809a$^{2}$ 6106a$^{3}$ 6474$^{8}$ >**115f**<

**Putra Sandhurst (IRE)** 6 b h Royal Academy (USA) -Kharimata (IRE) (Kahyasi) (1618) 1767$^{9}$ 2681$^{7}$ 3912$^{7}$ 4118$^{8}$ >**107f**<

**Putra Sas (IRE)** 3 b c Sri Pekan (USA) -Puteri Wentworth (Sadler s Wells (USA)) 1587$^{2}$ 1924$^{2}$ 2510a$^{6}$ >**103f**<

**Puya** 2 b f Kris-Pervenche (Latest Model) 5996$^{2}$ 6455$^{2}$ >**76f**<

**Pyrrhic** 5 b g Salse (USA) -Bint Lariaaf (USA) (Diesis) 495$^{3}$ 537$^{7}$ 554$^{2}$ 651$^{10}$ 672$^{6}$ 855$^{5}$ 931$^{13}$996$^{6}$ 1166$^{8}$ 1231$^{6}$ 1404$^{6}$ >**35a 35 f**<

## Q

**Qabas (USA)** 4 b g Swain (IRE) -Classical Dance (CAN) (Regal Classic (CAN)) 2302$^{5}$ 2705$^{8}$ 2845$^{6}$ >**75f**<

**Qadar (IRE)** 2 b c Xaar-Iktidar (Green Desert (USA)) 2225$^{2}$ 2644$^{3}$ (6011) >**75+a 84+f**<

**Qasirah (IRE)** 3 b f Machiavellian (USA) -Altaweelah (IRE) (Fairy King (USA)) 1398$^{10}$ 1879$^{5}$ 2641$^{3}$ 2971$^{6}$ 3671$^{11}$ 5294$^{10}$ >**97f**<

**Qawaafil (USA)** 2 bb f Intidab (USA) -Indihash (USA) (Gulch (USA)) 2876$^{5}$ 5569$^{8}$ 5847$^{7}$ (6211) 6574$^{15}$ >**68f**<

**Qobtaan (USA)** 5 b g Capote (USA) -Queen s Gallery (USA) (Forty Niner (USA)) 406$^{6}$ (425) (512) 582$^{7}$ 1427$^{10}$ 1681$^{9}$ 4190$^{7}$ 4511$^{17}$6296$^{4}$ (6550) >**64a 49f**<

**Qualitair Wings** 5 b g Colonel Collins (USA) -Semperflorens (Don) 1772$^{3}$ 2271$^{11}$ 3198$^{17}$ 3409$^{8}$ 3660$^{2}$ 3982$^{9}$ 4293$^{2}$ 4558$^{8}$4988$^{6}$ 5127$^{3}$ 5607$^{8}$ 5835$^{5}$ 6210$^{8}$ >**75a 81f**<

**Quantica (IRE)** 5 b g Sri Pekan (USA) -Touche-A-Tout (IRE) (Royal Academy (USA)) 1361$^{6}$ 1774$^{15}$ 1974$^{15}$ 2899$^{15}$ 3298$^{15}$ 5346$^{16}$ 5597$^{6}$ >**38a 74f**<

**Quantum Leap** 7 b g Efisio-Prejudice (Young Generation) 559$^{11}$ 650$^{6}$ 677$^{3}$ 745$^{8}$ 1204$^{3}$ 2170$^{8}$ 2226$^{3}$(2483) 2575$^{6}$ 2838$^{6}$ 3086$^{4}$ 3440$^{2}$ 3663$^{4}$ 4122$^{22}$ 5614$^{20}$ 5887$^{6}$ >**70a 79 f**<

**Quarry Island (IRE)** 3 b f Turtle Island (IRE) -Last Quarry (Handsome Sailor) 416$^{5}$ 736$^{2}$ 802$^{9}$ 1046$^{7}$ 1084$^{7}$ 1579$^{2}$ 1856$^{8}$(2354) >**45a 51f**<

**Quarrymount** 3 b g Polar Falcon (USA) -Quilt (Terimon) 2029$^{12}$ 3875$^{2}$ (4128) 4536$^{2}$ (5037) 5191$^{2}$ 5842$^{2}$ (5944) 5997$^{2}$ 6335$^{5}$ >**67+a 88f**<

**Quarter To** 5 gr m Chocolat De Meguro (USA) -Miss Lakeland (Pongee) 998$^{15}$ >**17f**<

**Quartier Latin (USA)** 3 b c Woodman (USA) -Qui Bid (USA) (Spectacular Bid (USA)) 5974a$^{4}$ 6512a$^{4}$ >**106f**<

**Quartino** 3 b c Dynaformer (USA) -Qirmazi (USA) (Riverman (USA)) 3641$^{10}$ 4915$^{9}$ 5732$^{8}$ 5850$^{7}$ 6185$^{2}$ >**85+f**<

**Quatre Saisons** 2 ch c Bering-Inseparable (Insan (USA)) 6455$^{7}$ >**39f**<

**Quay Walloper** 3 b g In Command (IRE) -Myrrh (Salse (USA)) 2144$^{7}$ 2554$^{12}$ 3026$^{8}$ 3479$^{14}$ 4015$^{12}$ 5110$^{17}$ >**40f**<

**Qudraat (IRE)** 3 b c In The Wings-Urgent Liaison (IRE) (High Estate) 2632$^{5}$ 3417$^{8}$ (5196) 5732$^{2}$ 6121$^{7}$ 6346$^{12}$ >**93f**<

**Qudrah (IRE)** 4 b f Darshaan-Alwiyda (USA) (Trempolino (USA)) 915$^{7}$ 1030$^{8}$ 1053$^{5}$ 1212$^{4}$ 3944$^{8}$ 4176$^{5}$ 5025$^{12}$ 5619$^{16}$ >**91a 91f**<

**Quebo (GER)** 6 br g Elsurimo (GER) -Queba (FR) (Orofino (GER)) 1779a$^{2}$ >**97f**<

**Quedex** 8 b g Deploy-Alwal (Pharly (FR)) (2480) 2613$^{5}$ 3236$^{2}$ (3485) (3928) 4226$^{9}$ 5956$^{10}$ 6215$^{4}$ >**55a 88f**<

**Queen (IRE)** 3 gr f Sadler s Wells (USA) -Infamy (Shirley Heights) 6102a$^{12}$ >**80f**<

**Queen Astrid (IRE)** 4 b f Revoque (IRE) -Talina s Law (IRE) (Law Society (USA)) 1634a$^{2}$ 5162a$^{2}$ 5966a$^{9}$ >**103f**<

**Queen Charlotte (IRE)** 5 ch m Tagula (IRE) -Tisima (FR) (Selkirk (USA)) 1315$^{2}$ 2215$^{11}$ 2410$^{9}$ 3049$^{7}$ 5317$^{5}$ 5544$^{6}$ 6094$^{11}$ >**60a 69f**<

**Queen Excalibur** 5 ch m Sabrehill (USA) -Blue Room (Gorytus (USA)) 415$^{8}$ 442$^{9}$ 535$^{7}$ 949$^{9}$ 1103$^{7}$ 1369$^{6}$ 1590$^{3}$ 1917$^{5}$ >**43a 50 f**<

**Queen Louisa** 4 b f Piccolo-Queen Of Scotland (IRE) (Mujadil (USA)) 941$^{10}$ 6516$^{11}$ >**20a**<

**Queen Lucia (IRE)** 3 b f Pursuit Of Love-Inquirendo (USA) (Roberto (USA)) 1420$^{4}$ 1747$^{4}$ 2289$^{4}$ 3156$^{5}$ 3473$^{4}$ 4128$^{7}$ 4848$^{2}$ 5072$^{3}$6061$^{7}$ >**43a 62f**<

**Queen Nefitari** 2 b f Celtic Swing-Opalette (Sharrood (USA)) 6072$^{10}$ >**58f**<

**Queen Of Bulgaria (IRE)** 3 b f Imperial Ballet (IRE) -Sofia Aurora (USA) (Chief Honcho (USA)) 905$^{9}$ 1220$^{7}$ 1750$^{10}$ 2359$^{13}$ 2942$^{9}$ 4052$^{11}$ 5930$^{13}$ 6229$^{19}$ >**48a 55f**<

**Queen Of Iceni** 2 b f Erhaab (USA) -Princess Genista (Ile De Bourbon (USA)) 5915$^{19}$ 6123$^{2}$ 6470$^{10}$ >**74f**<

**Queen Of Night** 4 b f Piccolo-Cardinal Press (Sharrood (USA)) 436$^{7}$ 1423$^{4}$ 1956$^{18}$ 2006$^{4}$ 2979$^{LFT}$ 3269$^{10}$ (3378) (3801) 4014$^{2}$4279$^{12}$ 4452$^{5}$ 4854$^{6}$ 5101$^{6}$ >**66a 61f**<

**Queen Of Palms (IRE)** 3 ch f Desert Prince (IRE) -Tapolite (Tap On Wood) 2330a$^{14}$ (4893a) 5972a$^{11}$ >**104f**<

**Queen Of Poland** 2 b f Halling (USA) -Polska (USA) (Danzig (USA)) (3456) (4060) 5413$^{2}$ 5979a$^{6}$ >**108f**<

**Queensberry** 5 b g Up And At Em-Princess Poquito (Hard Fought) 5221$^{13}$ 6065$^{10}$ >**67a 47f**<

**Queen s Dancer** 2 b f Groom Dancer (USA) -Special Beat (Bustino) 5717$^{15}$ 6352$^{5}$ 6545$^{2}$ >**65f**<

**Queen s Echo** 3 b f Wizard King-Sunday News N Echo (USA) (Trempolino (USA)) 5086$^{2}$ 5345$^{5}$ 6141$^{8}$ 6541$^{9}$ >**41a 57f**<

**Queen s Fantasy** 3 ch f Grand Lodge (USA) -Alcalali (USA) (Septieme Ciel (USA)) 563$^{10}$ 1221$^{4}$ 1465$^{16}$ 1643$^{2}$ (2665) 2987$^{6}$ 4138$^{6}$ >**68a 64f**<

**Queen s Glory (IRE)** 2 b f Mujadil (USA) -Karenaragon (Aragon) 1984$^{6}$ 2321$^{2}$ 2702$^{6}$ 2927$^{5}$ 3634$^{5}$ 3886$^{7}$ 4094$^{11}$ 4516$^{6}$4671$^{6}$ 5746$^{3}$ >**23a 63f**<

**Queens Hand (IRE)** 2 b f Lend A Hand-Winchester Queen (IRE) (Persian Bold) 6195$^{11}$ 6478$^{7}$ >**37a 26f**<

**Queenslander (IRE)** 3 b f Inchinor-Royal Subject (USA) (Kingmambo (USA)) 1318$^{11}$ >**13f**<

**Queens Rhapsody** 4 bb g Baryshnikov (AUS) -Digamist Girl (IRE) (Digamist (USA)) 556$^{2}$ 648$^{9}$ 761$^{2}$ 1011$^{4}$ 1065$^{7}$ 1367$^{4}$ 1773$^{10}$1927$^{9}$ 5419$^{7}$ 5603$^{5}$ 6477$^{3}$ 6568$^{3}$ >**95a 86f**<

**Queens Square** 3 b f Forzando-Queens Check (Komaite (USA)) 1362$^{9}$ 1737$^{7}$ 2349$^{7}$ 2556$^{17}$ >**7a 37f**<

**Queenstown (IRE)** 3 b g Desert Style (IRE) -Fanciful (IRE) (Mujtahid (USA)) 3689$^{10}$ 3932$^{3}$ 4145$^{5}$ 4451$^{7}$ 4817$^{11}$ 5656$^{4}$ >**71a 71f**<

**Queen Titi (IRE)** 2 b f Sadler s Wells (USA) -Litani River (USA) (Irish River (FR)) 6367a$^{5}$ >**84f**<

**Queen Tomyra (IRE)** 2 b f Montjeu (IRE) -Kama Tashoof (Mtoto) 5717$^{13}$ 6118$^{11}$ 6291$^{3}$ >**70a 48f**<

**Quel Del Giaz (IRE)** 5 b h Flying Spur (AUS) -Velate (USA) (Spend A Buck (USA)) 2155a$^{6}$ >**109f**<

**Querido (USA)** 2 b c Spectrum (IRE) -Polent (Polish Precedent (USA)) 3760$^{4}$ (4480) >**82+f**<

**Quero Quero (USA)** 4 b f Royal Academy (USA) -Big Dreams (USA) (Great Above (USA)) 4767a$^{10}$ >**104f**<

**Quest On Air** 5 b g Star Quest-Stormy Heights (Golden Heights) 1492$^{2}$ 2385$^{11}$ 2595$^{6}$ >**41a 50f**<

**Quetena (GER)** 4 br f Acatenango (GER) -Quebrada (IRE) (Devil s Bag (USA)) 3973a$^{9}$ 4980a$^{7}$ 6381a$^{12}$ >**86f**<

**Queue Up** 2 b g Royal Applause-Faraway Lass (Distant Relative) 2904$^{3}$ 4454$^{12}$ 5616$^{11}$ >**78f**<

**Quick** 4 b g Kahyasi-Prompt (Old Vic) 3108$^{P}$ 3488$^{9}$ >**64a 53f**<

**Quickfire** 2 b f Dubai Millennium-Daring Miss (Sadler s Wells (USA)) 3904$^{2}$ (5695) >**79+f**<

**Quick Grand (IRE)** 2 br f Raise A Grand (IRE) -Rose n Reason (IRE) (Reasonable (FR)) 4003$^{6}$ 4245$^{6}$ 4532$^{6}$ >**44f**<

**Quicks The Word** 4 b g Sri Pekan (USA) -Fast Tempo (IRE) (Statoblest) 1175$^{8}$ 1361$^{12}$ 1872$^{4}$ 2274$^{9}$ 2936$^{12}$ 3247$^{7}$ 3579$^{2}$ 3911$^{2}$4511$^{6}$ 4905$^{2}$ >**74f**<

**Quickstyx** 3 b f Night Shift (USA) -Red Bouquet (Reference Point) (644) 1214$^{4}$ 1392$^{5}$ 5197$^{4}$ 5410$^{4}$ 5560$^{6}$ 5860$^{7}$ 6006$^{6}$ 6087$^{6}$ >**70a 74f**<

**Qui Es Tu (IRE)** 4 b f Desert King (IRE) -Voliere (USA) (Arctic Tern (USA)) 911a$^{6}$ 980a$^{6}$ >**81f**<

**Quiet Reading (USA)** 7 b g Northern Flagship (USA) -Forlis Key (USA) (Forli (ARG)) 437$^{3}$ 564$^{4}$ 604$^{6}$ 967$^{3}$ 1427$^{2}$ 1598$^{2}$ 1875$^{8}$2406$^{11}$ 3023$^{4}$ 3282$^{9}$ >**76a 41f**<

**Quiet Storm (IRE)** 4 b f Desert Prince (IRE) -Hertford Castle (Reference Point) 1767$^{7}$ 2201$^{16}$ 2733$^{3}$ 4273$^{6}$ >**91 a 100f**<

**Quiet Times (IRE)** 5 ch g Dolphin Street (FR) -Super Times (Sayf El Arab (USA)) (515) 586$^{4}$ 607$^{9}$ 669$^{4}$ (1007) 1361$^{5}$ 1526$^{5}$ 1929$^{8}$ 1974$^{18}$6496$^{2}$ >**99a 66f**<

**Quiff** 3 b f Sadler s Wells (USA) -Wince (Selkirk (USA)) (2059) 2997$^{3}$ (4859) 5463$^{2}$ >**122f**<

**Quilanga (GER)** 3 b f Lomitas-Quebrada (IRE) (Devil s Bag (USA)) (1805a) (4430a) 5168a$^{3}$ >**107f**<

**Quincannon (USA)** 3 b g Kayrawan (USA) -Sulalat (Hamas (IRE)) 438$^{6}$ >**54a**<

**Quinn** 4 ch g First Trump-Celestine (Skyliner) 1193$^{10}$ 2347$^{10}$ >**42f**<

**Quintillion** 3 gr g Petong-Lady Quinta (IRE) (Gallic League) 1169$^{8}$ 2236$^{12}$ 3146$^{7}$ 6004$^{10}$ >**15a 33f**<

**Quintons Gold Rush (USA)** 3 ch c Wild Rush (USA) -Hollywood Gold (USA) (Mr Prospector (USA)) 1781a$^{18}$ >**115a**<

**Quintoto** 4 b g Mtoto-Ballet (Sharrood (USA)) 5061$^{6}$ 5320$^{14}$ 5374$^{9}$ 5657$^{15}$ 6483$^{12}$ 6551$^{13}$ >**45a 61 f**<

**Quirinale (USA)** 4 gr g Kris S (USA) -Quest For Ladies (Rainbow Quest (USA)) 2163a$^{18}$ ><

**Quite Lovely (USA)** 4 ch f Not For Love (USA) -

Quite Amazing (USA) (Bear Hunt (USA)) 1002a[5] >**80f**<

**Quito (IRE)** **7** b r Machiavellian (USA) -Qirmazi (USA) (Riverman (USA)) (761) 1009[10] 1065[6] 1125[2] 1242[5] 1367[5] 1758[6] (2065) 2109[10]2623[6] 3308[5] (3522) 4745[6] 5628[5] 6190[3] 6345[3] 6474[5] (6572) >**112a 112f**<

**Quizzene (USA)** **2** gr c Cozzene (USA) -Company Binness (USA) (Seattle Dancer (USA)) 6441[5] (6565) >**71f**<

**R**

**Raakaan** **3** b c Halling (USA) -Glimpse (Night Shift (USA)) 3161[3] (3882) >**76+f**<

**Rabbit** **3** b f Muhtarram (USA) -Ninia (USA) (Affirmed (USA)) 4615[12] 5851[9] 6089[5] >**48f**<

**Rabitatit (IRE)** **3** b f Robellino (USA) -Coupled (Wolfhound (USA)) 1309[2] 2355[4] 2571[9] 2974[2] 3223[5] 3670[5] 4145[6] 4921[2]5410[7] 5672[4] 5757[12] >**69?f**<

**Raccoon (IRE)** **4** b g Raphane (USA) -Kunucu (IRE) (Bluebird (USA)) 2130[4] (2293) (2488) 2679[16] 4324[8] 4538[7] 5393[19] 5628[11] >**100f**<

**Race The Ace** **3** b g First Trump-Princess Genista (Ile De Bourbon (USA)) 1612[4] 2280[5] 3121[2] 3743[3] 4647[3] (5116) 5850[2] (6460) >**101+f**<

**Rachel s Verdict** **3** b f Royal Applause-Shady Street (USA) (Shadeed (USA)) 3085[4] 4555[5] (4916) >**75+f**<

**Racing Night (USA)** **4** b g Lear Fan (USA) -Broom Dance (USA) (Dance Spell (USA)) 1066[11] 1624[9] >**59a 83f**<

**Radiant Bride** **4** ch f Groom Dancer (USA) -Radiancy (IRE) (Mujtahid (USA)) 467[11] 579[2] 661[6] (716) 879[2] 919[8] (950) 992[4] >**53a 43f**<

**Radish (IRE)** **3** b f Alhaarth (IRE) -Nichodoula (Doulab (USA)) 3916[12] (6285) >**65+f**<

**Radlett Lady** **3** ch f Wolfhound (USA) -Royal Dream (Ardkinglass) 1243[8] 1906[10] 2236[14] 3322[9] 6059[11] >**46a 37f**<

**Radmore Spirit** **4** b f Whittingham (IRE) -Ruda (FR) (Free Round (USA)) 811[8] 2586[10] 6578[10] >**5a 35f**<

**Raetihi** **3** b f Wizard King-Foreno (Formidable (USA)) 2236[11] 4758[4] 5342[10] 6275[9] >**13a 29f**<

**Raffelberger (GER)** **3** b g Auenadler (GER) -Royal Cat (Royal Academy (USA)) 3552a[7] 4357a[4] (5255a) 5977a[11] (6261a) >**111f**<

**Rafferty (IRE)** **5** ch g Lion Cavern (USA) -Badawi (USA) (Diesis) 3597[7] 4067[5] 4401[3] 4613[4] 5574[7] 5813[9] >**73a 88f**<

**Raffish** **2** ch g Atraf-Valadon (High Line) 4480[8] 5200[4] (5741) 6174[28] >**71a 79f**<

**Rafters Music (IRE)** **9** b g Thatching-Princess Dixieland (USA) (Dixieland Band (USA)) 480[3] 968[8] 1140[2] 1265[16] 1824[5] 2118[5] 2664[4] >**65a 65f**<

**Ragamuffin** **6** ch g Prince Sabo-Valldemosa (Music Boy) 1825[7] 2132[13] 2407[5] 2581[11] >**73 f**<

**Ragasah** **6** b m Glory Of Dancer-Slight Risk (Risk Me (FR)) 3934[7] 5641[4] >**36a 33f**<

**Ragazzi (IRE)** **3** ch g Raphane (USA) -Zalotti (IRE) (Polish Patriot (USA)) 1453[10] 2908[9] 3229[17] 4097[3] 4880[5] 5448[11] >**66?a 36f**<

**Ragged Glory (IRE)** **2** br c Foxhound (USA) -Resurgence (Polar Falcon (USA)) 2205[4] 2396[6] 3931[2] 4913[13] 5741[2] 6063[6] >**74a 72f**<

**Ragged Jack (IRE)** **3** b g Cape Cross (IRE) -Isticanna (USA) (Far North (CAN)) 3085[2] 3486[3] (3739) 4024[5] 4515[6] 4814[6] 5092[12] >**71a 75f**<

**Raggtime Toon (IRE)** **4** bb f Dolphin Street (FR) -Silent Melody (IRE) (Last Tycoon) 2498a[6] >**84f**<

**Raging Creek (USA)** **5** b h Storm Creek (USA) -Yardstick (USA) (Sunny Clime (USA)) 851a[4] >**91a**<

**Raheed (IRE)** **3** b g Daggers Drawn (USA) -In Due Course (USA) (A.P. Indy (USA)) 1227[6] 1559[10] 2390[15] 5370[8] 5551[4] >**55a 61f**<

**Raheel (IRE)** **4** ch g Barathea (IRE) -Tajawuz (Kris) 467[5] 601[4] 815[7] 887[6] (914) 966[4] 1097[3] 2883[7]2945[8] 4713[12] 5222[7] 5914[11] 6013[11] 6230[12] >**66a 52f**<

**Raheibb (IRE)** **6** ch g Lion Cavern (USA) -Abeyr (Unfuwain (USA)) 632a[7] 830a[3] >**83a 98f**<

**Rahjel Sultan** **6** b g Puissance-Dalby Dancer (Bustiki) 729[3] 1080[6] (1310) 1502[6] 5945[26] >**38a 57f**<

**Rahn** **5** ch h Elmaamul (USA) -Taghareed (USA) (Shadeed (USA)) 692a[12] >**95f**<

**Rahwaan (IRE)** **5** b g Darshaan-Fawaakeh (USA) (Lyphard (USA)) (1112) 1880[17] >**94f**<

**Rainbow Colours (IRE)** **3** gr f Linamix (FR) -Mill Rainbow (FR) (Rainbow Quest (USA)) 2198[7] 3154[9] >**46f**<

**Rainbow Iris** **2** bb f Mister Baileys-Kastaway (Distant Relative) 4212[4] 4824[5] 5096[2] 5434[14] 5670[6] 6042[5] 6294[8] 6523[4] >**44a 70f**<

**Rainbow Majestic (IRE)** **2** ch c Alhaarth (IRE) -Rainbow Magic (IRE) (Fairy King (USA)) 6542a[13] ><

**Rainbow Queen** **4** b f Rainbow Quest (USA) -Dazzle (Gone West (USA)) 4153[3] 4856[11] 5573[11] >**96+f**<

**Rainbow Rising (IRE)** **2** bb c Desert King (IRE) -Fantastic Bid (USA) (Auction Ring (USA)) 4256[4] 4757[2] 5392[9] >**91f**<

**Rainbow Sky** **2** b f Rainbow Quest (USA) -Safayn (USA) (Lyphard (USA)) 5915[20] >**37f**<

**Rainbow Treasure (IRE)** **2** ch f Rainbow Quest (USA) -Gaily Royal (IRE) (Royal Academy (USA)) 5228[7] 5604[6] 6196[12] >**57f**<

**Rainbow World (IRE)** **4** b c Rainbow Quest (USA) -Far Fetched (IRE) (Distant Relative) 837[11] 984[3] 1122[8] 1272[18] 2740[3] 3046[10] 3591[3] 3844[7]3997[7] 4192[9] >**64a 64f**<

**Raining** **6** b m Mukaddamah (USA) -Piney River (Pharly (FR)) 3961a[16] 4956a[12] >**86f**<

**Rain Lily (IRE)** **4** b f Red Ransom (USA) -Charlock (IRE) (Nureyev (USA)) 785a[10] >**90f**<

**Rainsborough Hill** **3** b g Groom Dancer (USA) -Ellebanna (Tina s Pet) 1911[8] 4473[17] >**37a 38f**<

**Rain Stops Play (IRE)** **2** b c Desert Prince (IRE) -Pinta (IRE) (Ahonoora) 5298[3] 5646[8] 6078[2] (6283) >**81+f**<

**Rainstorm** **9** b g Rainbow Quest (USA) -Katsina (USA) (Cox s Ridge (USA)) 1681[6] 2262[5] 2643[6] 2753[7] 3412[7] 3604[11] 4122[23] 4213[2]4386[8] 4479[5] >**39a 47f**<

**Raise A Tune (IRE)** **2** ch c Raise A Grand (IRE) -Magic Melody (Petong) 5467[9] (5735) >**74a 51f**<

**Raison Detre** **2** b c Mtoto-Kelimutu (Top Ville) 6476[12] >**45f**<

**Raisoot (USA)** **3** b c Honor Grades (USA) -Granny Kelly (USA) (Irish River (FR)) 920a[6] ><

**Rajam** **6** b g Sadler s Wells (USA) -Rafif (USA) (Riverman (USA)) 1103[8] 1198[6] 1287[7] (2174) 2287[3] 2491[7] 2753[6] 3199[5] 3873[2]4155[2] 4453[4] 4772[8] 4934[9] 5182[9] >**82f**<

**Rajayoga** **3** ch g Kris-Optimistic (Reprimand) 1422[11] 2371[7] 3852[4] 4556[7] 6566[7] >**20a 59f**<

**Rajpute (GER)** **4** b c Deploy-Rosonora (GER) (Highest Honor (FR)) 1259a[14] 3134a[7] 4378a[8] 5975a[5] >**101f**<

**Rajwa (USA)** **2** ch c Dubai Millennium-Zelanda (IRE) (Night Shift (USA)) 4219[2] 4861[2] 5460[2] >**93f**<

**Rakti** **5** b h Polish Precedent (USA) -Ragera (IRE) (Rainbow Quest (USA)) (2968) 3540[8] 5483a[5] (5782) >**129+f**<

**Ralpha (FR)** **2** b f Septieme Ciel (USA) -Icicle (FR) (Alzao (USA)) 3388a[6] >**81f**<

**Rambo Blue** **4** b g Elmaamul (USA) -Copper Trader (Faustus (USA)) 5867[12] 6082[6] 6481[10] >**42a 64f**<

**Rampage** **3** ch f Pivotal-Noor El Houdah (IRE) (Fayruz) (3267) >**73f**<

**Ramsgill (USA)** **2** b c Prized (USA) -Crazee Mental (Magic Ring (IRE)) 6555[8] >**47a**<

**Rancho Cucamonga (IRE)** **2** ch f Raphane (USA) -Kunucu (IRE) (Bluebird (USA)) 2860[7] 3196[7] (3532) 3975[8] 4325[7] 4803[5] 5363[5] 5617[18] 5989[2] >**71f**<

**Randalls Touch** **2** b c Mind Games-L A Touch (Tina s Pet) 5262[11] 5953[12] 6221[8] ><

**Random Quest** **6** b g Rainbow Quest (USA) -Anne Bonny (Ajdal (USA)) 1457[7] 1880[7] 2684[8] 3725[2] 4550[9] >**95f**<

**Rangoon (USA)** **3** ch c Distant View (USA) -Rustic (IRE) (Grand Lodge (USA)) 1133[2] 1295[2] 1519[5] 4741[2] (5352) >**78f**<

**Rani Two** **5** b m Wolfhound (USA) -Donya (Mill Reef (USA)) 2752[11] 3091[9] 3327[6] 3731[5] 4153[4] 4760[4] 5183[10] 5374[2]5869[2] 6266[11] >**60a 78f**<

**Ranny** **4** b f Emperor Jones (USA) -Defined Feature (IRE) (Nabeel Dancer (USA)) 815[4] 960[2] 1098[2] 1373[15] 2098[6] 3321[4] 4066[4] 4517[5]4802[6] >**56a 56f**<

**Ransacker** **2** b g Bahamian Bounty-Hazy Heights (Shirley Heights) 2439[5] 2674[3] >**63+f**<

**Ranville** **6** ch g Deploy-Kibitka (FR) (Baby Turk) 3325[9] 3757[10] 4777[5] 5093[8] >**92f**<

**Raphael (IRE)** **5** b m Perugino (USA) -Danny s Miracle (Superlative) 1199[11] (1772) 1927[11] 2963[3] 3235[15] 3409[4] 3755[8] 3867[2] 4134[2]4349[2] 4558[16] >**87f**<

**Rapid Flow** **2** b c Fasliyev (USA) -Fleet River (USA) (Riverman (USA)) 4747[8] 5118[8] >**67f**<

**Rapid River** **2** b f Lahib (USA) -Cast A Spell (Magic Ring (IRE)) 5319[8] >**61f**<

**Rapid Romance (USA)** **2** b f Theatrical-Fast Nellie (USA) (Ack Ack (USA)) 3741[5] 4137[6] 5689[4] >**61f**<

**Rare Coincidence** **3** ch g Atraf-Green Seed (IRE) (Lead On Time (USA)) (615) (700) 1029[3] 1141[6] 1427[8] 1932[4] 2251[4] 2618[4] 2814[11]3738[9] 4680[3] 5063[4] 5583[10] 6138[9] >**76a 68f**<

**Rare Cross (IRE)** **2** b f Cape Cross (IRE) -Hebrides (Gone West (USA)) 3965a[8] 5971a[4] 6101a[8] >**87f**<

**Rarefied (IRE)** **3** b g Danehill (USA) -Tenuous (Generous (IRE)) 1224[8] (1672) 1899[7] 3210[7] 4780[8] 5127[7] 5821[9] 5950[4] 6266[10] >**86f**<

**Rare Presence (IRE)** **5** b g Sadler s Wells (USA) -Celebrity Style (USA) (Seeking The Gold (USA)) 2740[11] >**41f**<

**Rasa Sayang (USA)** **2** bb c Salt Lake (USA) -Annie Ruth (USA) (Gulch (USA)) 1462[9] 3469[2] 4009[2] 4575[6] >**67f**<

**Ras Hafa (USA)** **3** ch c Parade Ground (USA) -Copperama (AUS) (Comeram (FR)) 691a[7] 848a[3] >**90a**<

**Rashbag** **5** b h Reprimand-Pleasuring (Good Times (ITY)) 911a[5] >**111f**<

**Rashida** **2** b f King s Best (USA) -Nimble Lady (AUS) (Fairy King (USA)) 4541[3] 5349[8] >**67f**<

**Rasid (USA)** **6** b g Bahri (USA) -Makadir (USA) (Woodman (USA)) (559) 618[16] 1203[2] 1470[3] (1669) 1768[13] 2474[13] 2881[5] 3274[3](3534) 5211[12] 5615[11] 6043[20] 6450[12] 6546[11] >**75a 83f**<

**Rasseem (IRE)** **2** b f Fasliyev (USA) -Yorba Linda (IRE) (Night Shift (USA)) 4298[2] 5070[7] 5521[3] 5848[6] >**76f**<

**Rathmullan** **5** ch g Bluegrass Prince (IRE) -National Time (USA) (Lord Avie (USA)) 465[12] 1090[8] 1237[3] 1639[4] 1889[3] (2012) 2051[3] 2185[5]2473[9] 3277[13] 3988[10] 4469[4] 5641[10] 5929[3] >**42a 42f**<

**Ratio** **6** ch g Pivotal-Owdbetts (IRE) (High Estate) (4357a) 5289[10] 5780[11] 5977a[12] 6463a[7] >**114f**<

**Ratukidul (FR)** **2** b f Danehill (USA) -Whakilyric (USA) (Miswaki (USA)) (4705) 5753[5] 6090[9] >**80+f**<

**Ravel (IRE)** **3** b g Fasliyev (USA) -Lili Cup (FR) (Fabulous Dancer (USA)) 1771[12] 2211[13] 2760[11] >**38f**<

**Raven (IRE)** **2** b f Alzao (USA) -Eman s Joy (Lion Cavern (USA)) 6127[9] 6569[6] >**59f**<

**Ravenglass (USA)** **5** b h Miswaki (USA) -Urus (USA) (Kris S (USA)) 1124[8] 1457[6] 2277[5] 2613[P] >**86f**<

**Rave Reviews (IRE)** **3** b f Sadler s Wells (USA) -Pieds De Plume (FR) (Seattle Slew (USA)) 1793[3] (2081) 2997[9] 4566a[9] >**105f**<

**Rawaabet (IRE)** **2** b c Bahhare (USA) -Haddeyah (USA) (Dayjur (USA)) 3241[8] 4030[11] >**59f**<

**Rawalpindi** **3** ch g Intikhab (USA) -Just A Treat (IRE) (Glenstal (USA)) 1519[8] 2505[10] 3094[9] 4927[2] 5340[5] 5991[9] >**68a 56f**<

**Rawdon (IRE)** **3** b c Singspiel (IRE) -Rebecca Sharp (Machiavellian (USA)) 1395[9] 2888[5] >**70f**<

**Rawhide (GER)** **3** br f Monsun (GER) -Royal Army (GER) (Pirate Army (USA)) 2723a[P] ><

**Rawyaan** **5** b h Machiavellian (USA) -Raheefa (USA) (Riverman (USA)) (849a) 976a[6] 1144a[8] 1925[7] 2220[13] >**115f**<

**Raybers Magic** **3** b f Magic Ring (IRE) -Kirkadian (Norwick (USA)) 3015[8] 3513[8] 3817[13] 4332[7] >**7f**<

**Raymond s Pride** **4** b g Mind Games-Northern Sal (Aragon) 681[9] 801[11] 1175[5] (1525) (1665) 1774[4] 1956[5] 5799[13] 6525[9] >**67a 89f**<

**Rayshan (IRE)** **4** b g Darshaan-Rayseka (IRE) (Dancing Brave (USA)) 1880[14] 2895[7] 3310[16] 4858[19] >**103df**<

**Raysoot (IRE)** **3** b c Cape Cross (IRE) -Mashkorah (USA) (Miswaki (USA)) 1453[8] 2667[2] 3155[5] 3874[9] (4619) >**68a 68f**<

**Rayware Boy (IRE)** **8** b g Scenic-Amata (USA) (Nodouble (USA)) 950[9] >**27a 27f**<

**Raza Cab (IRE)** **2** b g Intikhab (USA) -Laraissa (Machiavellian (USA)) 3093[3] (4022) 4835[6] 5051[2] 5417[9] >**93a 87f**<

**Raze** **2** ch f Halling (USA) -Rive (USA) (Riverman (USA)) 5089[8] >**53f**<

**Razkalla (USA)** **6** b g Caerleon (USA) -Larrocha (IRE) (Sadler s Wells (USA)) (712a) 976a[4] 1144a[4] 5916[5] 6528a[9] >**100a 119+f**<

**Reaching Out (IRE)** **2** b g Desert Prince (IRE) -Alwiyda (USA) (Trempolino (USA)) 3377[10] 6145[15] >**60f**<

**Read Federica** **2** ch f Fusaichi Pegasus (USA) -Reading Habit (USA) (Half A Year (USA)) (6470) >**82f**<

**Read The Footnotes (USA)** **3** b c Smoke Glacken (USA) -Baydon Belle (USA) (Al Nasr (FR)) 1781a[7] >**99a**<

**Ready Teddy Go** **2** b g Danzig Connection (USA) -Mariette (Blushing Scribe (USA)) 6448[7] >**30a**<

**Real Cool Cat (USA)** **2** gr f Storm Cat (USA) -Hail Kris (USA) (Kris S (USA)) 6045[4] 6331[10] >**60f**<

**Real Estate** **10** b g High Estate-Haitienne (FR) (Green Dancer (USA)) 2740[10] 3488[7] 3667[8] 3776[12] >**44f**<

**Realism (FR)** **4** b g Machiavellian (USA) -Kissing Cousin (IRE) (Danehill (USA)) 588 [4] 760[4] (824) 909[8] 1275[5] 1427[7] 1757[3] 2170[6](2591) 2835[2] (3143) (3375) 3942[7] (4240) 4450[5] 5423[6] 5866[8] >**73a 87f**<

**Real Quality (USA)** **2** br g Elusive Quality (USA) -Pleasant Prize (USA) (Pleasant Colony (USA)) 5578[2] (6092) >**86+f**<

**Real Ting** **8** br g Forzando-St Helena (Monsanto (FR)) 1510[9] ><

**Reap** **6** b g Emperor Jones (USA) -Corn Futures (Nomination) 705[7] 1247[3] 1757[8] 2218[6] 6152[17] 6566[4] >**74a 75f**<

**Rebate** **4** b g Pursuit Of Love-Aigua Blava (USA) (Solford (USA)) 872[8] 1088[5] 1298[12] 1624[12] 2226[12] 2406[3] 2930[3] 3143[6]3573[3] 4029[5] 4220[9] 4556[5] 4736[6] 5381[5] 5705[7] >**76a 80f**<

**Rebel Leader** **7** br g Ezzoud (IRE) -Haitienne (FR) (Green Dancer (USA)) 3937[12] >**77f**<

**Rebel Raider (IRE)** **5** b g Mujadil (USA) -Emily s Pride (Shirley Heights) (6061) 6296[9] 6540[2] >**64a 67f**<

**Rebel Rebel (IRE)** **2** b c Revoque (IRE) -French Quarter (Ile De Bourbon (USA)) 3946[7] 4169[8] 4728[5] 5377[4] (5596) (5738) 5810[2] >**94+f**<

**Rebel Rouser** **3** b g Kris-Nanouche (Dayjur (USA)) 1304[5] 1600[5] 1740[7] >**36a 34f**<

**Rebuttal (USA)** **2** b c Mr Greeley (USA) -Reboot (USA) (Rubiano (USA)) 4611[2] (4844) 5649[3] 5918[2] >**119f**<

**Reckless Fred** **5** ch g So Factual (USA) -Winnie Reckless (Local Suitor (USA)) 574[7] 644[10] 894[10] >**41a**<

**Reckless Moment** **3** b f Victory Note (USA) -Blue Indigo (FR) (Pistolet Bleu (IRE)) 6056[16] >**33a**<

**Recognise (IRE)** **3** ch g Groom Dancer (USA) -Broken Romance (IRE) (Ela-Mana-Mou) 1786[2] 1933[4] 3013[2] 3341[2] >**71f**<

**Recount (FR)** **4** b g Sillery (USA) -Dear Countess (FR) (Fabulous Dancer (USA)) 1540[9] 2491[11] 2727[6] 3048[5] 3419[12] 3844[11] 4029[2] 4192[3]4233[4] 5158[3] 5568[9] >**60a 83f**<

**Rectangle (IRE)** **4** ch g Fayruz-Moona (USA) (Lear Fan (USA)) 1113[20] 1454[8] 2859[11] 3509[13] 3923[2] 4181[11] 4279[7] 5458[11]5579[18] >**88f**<

**Red Acer (IRE)** **3** ch g Shinko Forest (IRE) -Another Baileys (Deploy) 416[9] 945[9] 2740[14] ><

**Red Admiral (USA)** **2** b c Red Ransom (USA) -Ausherra (USA) (Diesis) 4922[14] (5592) >**89+f**<

**Red Affleck (USA)** **2** b g Nicholas (USA) -Lucie Mon Amour (USA) (Meadowlake (USA)) 1374[3] 5087[2] (5653) 6176[7] 6344[4] 6574[8] >**83f**<

**Red Apache (IRE)** **2** b c Namid-Special Dissident (Dancing Dissident (USA)) 5373[13] 6563[13] >**45f**<

**Redbank (IRE)** **3** b g Night Shift (USA) -Bush Rose (Rainbow Quest (USA)) 451[2] 675[9] 816[8] 890[7] >**53 a 62f**<

**Red Birr (IRE)** **3** b g Bahhare (USA) -Cappella (IRE) (College Chapel) 1129[9] 2197[4] (3213) 3543[7] 4274[8] >**82f**<

**Red Bloom** **3** b f Selkirk (USA) -Red Camellia (Polar Falcon (USA)) 1791[4] 3033[3] (5225) 5679a[4] >**118+f**<

**Red-Bull (SPA)** **8** b h Sherman (SPA) -Steady Lady (Lord Gayle (USA)) 2163a[5] ><

**Red Chairman** **2** br c Red Ransom (USA) -Chine (Inchinor) 3319[9] 3601[5] 4088[4] 4342[6] >**78f**<

**Red Contact (USA)** **3** b g Sahm (USA) -Basma (USA) (Grey Dawn Ii) 2377[14] >**72a 39f**<

**Red Crescent (SAF)** **6** b g Northern Guest (USA) -Salaadims Pride (SAF) (Salaadim (USA)) 690a[13] 853a[10] 922a[5] >**73f**<

**Red Crystal** **6** b m Presidium-Crystallography (Primitive Rising (USA)) 431[6] ><

**Red Damson (IRE)** **3** b g Croco Rouge (IRE) -Damascene (IRE) (Scenic) 4513[2] (4939) 5300[2] >**83a 94f**<

**Red Delirium** **8** b g Robellino (USA) -Made Of Pearl (USA) (Nureyev (USA)) 442[6] 570[4] 714[5] 939[2] 1024[5] 1090[5] 1194[2]1426[5] 1660[12] >**53a 43f**<

**Red Duchess** **2** ch f Halling (USA) -Red Empress (Nashwan (USA)) 5247[9] 5717[9] >**65f**<

**Red Feather (IRE)** **3** b f Marju (IRE) -Galyph (USA) (Lyphard (USA)) 3547a[3] (3959a) 5484a[4] 5917[9] >**109f**<

**Red Finesse** **2** b f Soviet Star (USA) -Jouet (Reprimand) 4399[8] 6171[9] >**64f**<

**Red Flyer (IRE)** **5** br g Catrail (USA) -Marostica (ITY) (Stone) (1446) >**49a 44f**<

**Red Forest (IRE)** **5** b g Charnwood Forest (IRE) -High Atlas (Shirley Heights) 1426[3] (1630) 1858[6] (2449) (2659) 2810[5] 3199[9] 3614[3] 3902[3] 4424[3](5058) 5144[6] (5951) 6335[7] >**65a 76f**<

**Red Fort (IRE)** **4** b g Green Desert (USA) -Red Bouquet (Reference Point) (1604) 2110[3] (3034) 3756[4] 5436[2] >**118f**<

**Red Galaxy (IRE)** **4** b f Tagula (IRE) -Dancing Season (Warrshan (USA)) 1225[15] 1708[P] 6117[17] 6579[13] >**15a 90f**<

**Red Hot Ruby** **3** ch f Komaite (USA) -Gleam Of Gold (Crested Lark) 2621[14] 3511[3] 3739[3] 5547[11] >**35f**<

**Redi (ITY)** **3** b c Danehill Dancer (IRE) -Rossella (Shareef Dancer (USA)) 1241[7] 2390[4] 2915[6] 4398[3] (4673) 5619[9] 6013[2] >**78+a 74f**<

**Red Lancer** **3** ch g Deploy-Miss Bussell (Sabrehill (USA)) 695[6] (746) (864) 957[2] 1134[2] 1322[2] 1437[2] 1588[2] (1901) 2203[3]3035[6] 3310[14] 3927[6] 4229[7] 4833[6] >**83a 111 f**<

**Red Lantern** **3** ch g Young Ern-Croft Sally (Crofthall) 6397[11] >**22a**<

**Red Leicester** **4** b f Magic Ring (IRE) -Tonic Chord (La Grange Music) 1824[3] 2098[12] 2359[5] (2586) 2663[6] 3010[10] 3680[5] 3864[16] 4854[10]6059[6] 6403[3] >**48a 62f**<

**Redmarley (IRE)** **3** b g Croco Rouge (IRE) -Dazzling Fire (IRE) (Bluebird (USA)) 2145[6] 2567[7] >**49f**<

**Red Marteeney** **2** ch c Indian Lodge (IRE) -Miss Rossi (Artaius (USA)) 4809[11] 5353[6] 5910[13] >**56f**<

**Red Melodica (USA)** **4** b f Red Ransom (USA) -Melodica (Machiavellian (USA)) 2451[8] 2811[16] >**31a 45f**<

**Red Mo (USA)** **3** b c Red Ransom (USA) -Moiava (FR) (Bering) 1289a[2] >**95f**<

**Red Monarch (IRE)** **3** ch g Woodborough (USA) -Sans Ceriph (IRE) (Thatching) 956[9] 1975[10] 2165[7] 2392[6] 2932[2] (3954) (4828) 5126[10] >**30a 71f**<

**Red Moor (IRE)** **4** gr g Eagle Eyed (USA) -Faakirah (Dragonara Palace (USA)) 878[2] 1079[6] (1426) 1572[2] 2004[3] 2816[10] >**53a 54?f**<

**Red Mountain** **3** b c Unfuwain (USA) -Red Cascade (IRE) (Danehill (USA)) 3475[9] 4444[7] 6524[11] >**46f**<

**Red Opera** **2** ch g Nashwan (USA) -La Papagena (Habitat) 5756[7] 5858[9] 6010[12] 6155[8] >**41a 53f**<

**Redoubtable (USA)** **13** b h Grey Dawn Ii-Seattle Rockette (USA) (Seattle Slew (USA)) 502[6] (665) 780[4] (946) 1020[13] 1526[9] (1719) 1941[7] 2260[11] 3151[2](3471) 3734[6] 3895[8] 4350[4] 4425[11] 4827[11] 5081[4] 5346[13] 6058[9] >**49a 57f**<

**Red Pearl (FR)** **3** b f Zieten (USA) -River Pearl (GER) (Turfkonig (GER)) 1983a[7] >**89f**<

**Red Peony** **2** b f Montjeu (IRE) -Red Azalea (Shirley Heights) (4263) 5149[3] 5413[6] 6151[2] >**94f**<

**Red Racketeer (USA)** **2** b c Red Ransom (USA) -Furajet (USA) (The Minstrel (CAN)) 6439[4] >**78f**<

**Red Rackham (IRE)** **4** b g Groom Dancer (USA) -Manarah (Marju (IRE)) 5907[7] 6450[16] >**65a**<

**Red Riot (USA)** **2** b c Red Ransom (USA) -Musical Treat (IRE) (Royal Academy (USA)) 4625[5] 5398[3] 5827[9] >**67f**<

**Red River Rebel** **6** b g Inchinor-Bidweaya (USA) (Lear Fan (USA)) 2212[12] 2449[4] 3128[8] 3472[2] 3682[2] 4210[4] >**24a 74 f**<

**Red River Rock (IRE)** **2** b c Spectrum (IRE) -Ann s Annie (IRE) (Alzao (USA)) 4967$^{3}$ 5620$^{9}$ 6078$^{9}$ 6479$^{4}$ >**79a 79f**<

**Red Rocky** **3** b f Danzero (AUS) -Post Mistress (IRE) (Cyrano De Bergerac) 452$^{7}$ 2351$^{10}$ 2545$^{5}$ 2942$^{8}$ 3229$^{2}$ 3530$^{16}$ 4018$^{3}$ 4241$^{5}$5702$^{3}$ 6120$^{3}$ 6361$^{8}$ >**52a 49f**<

**Red Romeo** **3** ch g Case Law-Enchanting Eve (Risk Me (FR)) 1614$^{2}$ 2269$^{4}$ 2839$^{4}$ (3122) (3384) (3845) 4051$^{2}$ 5121$^{3}$ >**97f**<

**Red Rudy** **2** ch c Pivotal-Piroshka (Soviet Star (USA)) 4193$^{6}$ 5095$^{3}$ 5561$^{7}$ 6356$^{7}$ >**71f**<

**Red Sahara (IRE)** **3** ch f Desert Sun-Red Reema (IRE) (Red Sunset) (2112) 2521$^{6}$ 2694$^{6}$ 3807$^{2}$ 4684$^{4}$ 5136$^{11}$ 5574$^{8}$ 5861$^{10}$ >**71a 87f**<

**Red Sail** **3** ch f Dr Fong (USA) -Manhattan Sunset (USA) (El Gran Senor (USA)) 2693$^{3}$ 4369$^{3}$ 5445$^{9}$ 6095$^{5}$ >**69+f**<

**Red Scorpion (USA)** **5** ch g Nureyev (USA) -Pricket (USA) (Diesis) (413) 603$^{6}$ 743$^{5}$ 1973$^{8}$ 2759$^{2}$ 3095$^{3}$ 3449$^{8}$ 4075$^{6}$ 4550$^{5}$5274$^{12}$ >**81a 73 f**<

**Red Silk** **3** b f Polish Precedent (USA) -Red Tulle (USA) (A.P. Indy (USA)) 492$^{14}$ 1271$^{14}$ ><

**Red Skelton (IRE)** **3** ch g Croco Rouge (IRE) -Newala (Royal Academy (USA)) 1712$^{10}$ 2841$^{8}$ 3232$^{10}$ 4065$^{10}$ 5381$^{3}$ 5635$^{8}$ 5773$^{12}$ 6005$^{11}$6495$^{16}$ 6552$^{11}$ >**69a 55f**<

**Red Sovereign** **3** b f Danzig Connection (USA) -Ruby Princess (IRE) (Mac s Imp (USA)) 1702$^{12}$ 2063$^{15}$ (3628) 5563$^{7}$ 5893$^{5}$ 6079$^{8}$ 6577$^{7}$ >**72a 89?f**<

**Red Spell (IRE)** **3** ch c Soviet Star (USA) -A-To-Z (IRE) (Ahonoora) 1273$^{12}$ 1437$^{5}$ (2306) 2692$^{2}$ 3212$^{6}$ 3452$^{3}$ >**76a 88+f**<

**Redspin (IRE)** **4** ch g Spectrum (IRE) -Trendy Indian (IRE) (Indian Ridge) 413$^{3}$ 1109$^{12}$ 1457$^{15}$ 2958$^{4}$ 3244$^{4}$ 3485$^{4}$ 3644$^{12}$ 4226$^{12}$4457$^{8}$ 5058$^{3}$ 5456$^{8}$ 6084$^{10}$ >**74a 74f**<

**Red Storm** **5** ch m Dancing Spree (USA) -Dam Certain (IRE) (Damister (USA)) 406$^{13}$ 505$^{6}$ (652) 763$^{5}$ 874$^{14}$ 1181$^{6}$ >**55a 57f**<

**Red Sun** **7** b g Foxhound (USA) -Superetta (Superlative) (2249) 2409$^{2}$ 2731$^{6}$ 3236$^{10}$ 4686$^{6}$ 5456$^{3}$ 5826$^{12}$ >**56a 67 f**<

**Redswan** **9** ch g Risk Me (FR) -Bocas Rose (Jalmood (USA)) 5259$^{2}$ >**63 a 73f**<

**Red Top (IRE)** **3** b f Fasliyev (USA) -Petite Epaulette (Night Shift (USA)) 1400$^{2}$ 1704$^{3}$ 2286$^{2}$ 2971$^{7}$ 3209$^{2}$ (3701) >**91f**<

**Red Tune (FR)** **3** ch c Green Tune (USA) -Born Gold (USA) (Blushing Groom (FR)) 2072a$^{2}$ >**105f**<

**Red Wine** **5** b g Hamas (IRE) -Red Bouquet (Reference Point) 971$^{5}$ 1329$^{7}$ >**92 a 102f**<

**Redwood Rocks (IRE)** **3** b g Blush Rambler (USA) -Crisp And Cool (USA) (Ogygian (USA)) 1129$^{20}$ (1745) 2019$^{13}$ 5474$^{6}$ 5818$^{11}$ >**85f**<

**Redwood Star** **4** b f Piccolo-Thewaari (USA) (Eskimo (USA)) 2246$^{4}$ 2482$^{12}$ 2875$^{10}$ 3175$^{3}$ 4232$^{17}$ 4415$^{4}$ 4800 5016$^{3}$5412$^{2}$ >**60a 63f**<

**Reedsman (IRE)** **3** ch g Fayruz-The Way She Moves (North Stoke) 620$^{2}$ 1363$^{13}$ 2251$^{12}$ 2556$^{15}$ 3371$^{11}$ >**51a 15f**<

**Reefscape** **3** gr c Linamix (FR) -Coraline (Sadler s Wells (USA)) 2722a$^{7}$ 5433a$^{2}$ (5965a) >**118f**<

**Reem One (IRE)** **3** b f Rainbow Quest (USA) -Felona (Caerleon (USA)) (5836) 6115$^{2}$ 6457$^{2}$ >**80f**<

**Reem Two** **3** b f Mtoto-Jamrat Samya (IRE) (Sadler s Wells (USA)) 3701$^{6}$ 4332$^{3}$ 4910$^{2}$ 5237$^{7}$ >**47f**<

**Reference (IRE)** **2** b c Almutawakel-Uffizi (IRE) (Royal Academy (USA)) 4016$^{18}$ 4611$^{16}$ 6077$^{12}$ >**31f**<

**Reflex Blue** **7** b g Ezzoud (IRE) -Briggsmaid (Elegant Air) (699) 750$^{4}$ >**48a 57f**<

**Refuse To Bend (IRE)** **4** b c Sadler s Wells (USA) -Market Slide (USA) (Gulch (USA)) 1146a$^{8}$ 2109$^{8}$ (2957) (3540) 4228$^{11}$ 5782$^{3}$ 6216$^{5}$ >**126f**<

**Regal Ali (IRE)** **5** ch g Ali-Royal (IRE) -Depeche (FR) (King s Lake (USA)) 1138$^{12}$ >**3a 48f**<

**Regal Attire (USA)** **2** ch c Kingmambo (USA) -Style Setter (USA) (Manila (USA)) 4078$^{6}$ >**63f**<

**Regal Dream (IRE)** **2** b c Namid-Lovely Me (IRE) (Vision (USA)) 4191$^{7}$ 5400$^{3}$ 5825$^{3}$ >**78f**<

**Regal Fantasy (IRE)** **4** b f King s Theatre (IRE) -Threesome (USA) (Seattle Dancer (USA)) 2939$^{12}$ 3411$^{10}$ (4275) 4609$^{5}$ >**52f**<

**Regal Flight (IRE)** **3** b g King s Theatre (IRE) -Green Belt (FR) (Tirol) 2658$^{6}$ 2949$^{14}$ 3554$^{6}$ 4338$^{9}$ 5261$^{16}$ >**53f**<

**Regal Gallery (IRE)** **6** b m Royal Academy (USA) -Polistatic (Free State) (602) (767) 892$^{3}$ 964$^{4}$ 3638$^{2}$ 6013$^{4}$ 6278$^{6}$ 6450$^{13}$ >**78a 57f**<

**Regal Lustre** **2** b f Averti (IRE) -Noble Lustre (USA) (Lyphard s Wish (FR)) 2247$^{3}$ 3080$^{5}$ 3736$^{2}$ 4012$^{6}$ 4330$^{6}$ >**54f**<

**Regal Performer (IRE)** **3** b g Ali-Royal (IRE) -Khatiynza (Nishapour (FR)) 1508$^{10}$ 1683$^{19}$ 2402$^{2}$ 3107$^{2}$ 3172$^{3}$ 3669$^{4}$ 4055$^{5}$ 4433$^{6}$4867$^{6}$ >**59f**<

**Regal Repose** **4** b f Classic Cliche (IRE) -Ideal Candidate (Celestial Storm (USA)) 1547$^{7}$ 2228$^{7}$ 2662$^{6}$ 4082$^{14}$ >**15a 15f**<

**Regal Setting (IRE)** **3** br g King s Theatre (IRE) -Cartier Bijoux (Ahonoora) 5273$^{6}$ (5619) (5785) >**71+a 93+f**<

**Regal Song (IRE)** **8** b g Anita s Prince-Song Beam (Song) 573$^{13}$ 896$^{10}$ 1131$^{17}$ 2079$^{8}$ 5107$^{19}$ 5579$^{20}$ 6246$^{13}$ (6363) >**64a 79f**<

**Regal Vintage (USA)** **4** ch g Kingmambo (USA) -Grapevine (IRE) (Sadler s Wells (USA)) 1245$^{8}$ 1501$^{5}$ >**74f**<

**Regency Malaya** **3** b f Sri Pekan (USA) -Paola (FR) (Fabulous Dancer (USA)) 472$^{8}$ 746$^{5}$ 999$^{2}$ 1080$^{7}$ 1278$^{7}$ 1405$^{3}$ 1495$^{2}$2016$^{5}$ 2054$^{6}$ >**48a 36 f**<

**Regency Red (IRE)** **6** ch g Dolphin Street (FR) -Future Romance (Distant Relative) 5243$^{4}$ 5456$^{11}$ (5710) 5796$^{15}$ 6005$^{12}$ 6231$^{4}$ >**27a 56f**<

**Regent Bluff (JPN)** **8** b h Park Regent (CAN) -Sally Belle (JPN) (Goodly (FR)) 1147a$^{9}$ >**92a**<

**Regent s Secret (USA)** **4** br g Cryptoclearance (USA) -Misty Regent (CAN) (Vice Regent (CAN)) 1315$^{4}$ 1868$^{7}$ 2292$^{7}$ 3060$^{2}$ 3401$^{4}$ 4008$^{11}$ 4280$^{3}$ 4511$^{3}$4826$^{12}$ 5317$^{6}$ 5518$^{11}$ 5945$^{3}$ 6097$^{3}$ (6483) >**69a 65f**<

**Regina** **2** b f Green Desert (USA) -Dazzle (Gone West (USA)) 4298$^{3}$ (4815) 5250$^{6}$ (6204) >**89f**<

**Regina Saura** **6** ch m Wolfhound (USA) -Reine Maid (USA) (Mr Prospector (USA)) 3816a$^{2}$ 6261a$^{3}$ >**102f**<

**Regis Flight** **2** b c Piccolo-Anthem Flight (USA) (Fly So Free (USA)) 3248$^{8}$ 3758$^{6}$ >**67f**<

**Registrar** **2** ch c Machiavellian (USA) -Confidante (USA) (Dayjur (USA)) 5718$^{5}$ 6149$^{2}$ 6492$^{7}$ >**71a 70f**<

**Regulated (IRE)** **3** b g Alzao (USA) -Royal Hostess (IRE) (Be My Guest (USA)) 613$^{2}$ 835$^{11}$ (1084) 1422$^{5}$ 2092$^{5}$ (2520) 2740$^{6}$ 3173$^{9}$ 3637$^{5}$4600$^{12}$ 5069$^{7}$ 5493$^{10}$ 5843$^{11}$ >**63a 63f**<

**Rehearsal** **3** b g Singspiel (IRE) -Daralaka (IRE) (The Minstrel (CAN)) 1461$^{2}$ (1794) 2307$^{5}$ 3671$^{6}$ 5226$^{8}$ >**94f**<

**Rehia** **3** b f Desert Style (IRE) -Goes A Treat (IRE) (Common Grounds) 496$^{7}$ 620$^{6}$ 678$^{5}$ 744$^{4}$ 865$^{4}$ 1689$^{11}$ 2033$^{3}$2265$^{5}$ 2800$^{10}$ 4043$^{3}$ (4393) 5736$^{17}$ 6363$^{10}$ >**48a 57f**<

**Reidies Choice** **3** b g Royal Applause-Fairy Ring (IRE) (Fairy King (USA)) 1614$^{12}$ 2239$^{2}$ 2448$^{7}$ 3101$^{4}$ 3622$^{2}$ 4151$^{9}$ 5244$^{3}$ 5656$^{5}$5861$^{2}$ >**81+f**<

**Reign Of Fire (IRE)** **3** b f Perugino (USA) -White Heat (Last Tycoon) 1507$^{14}$ 2169$^{13}$ 5222$^{11}$ 5585$^{12}$ 5863$^{13}$ >**60a 60f**<

**Reine De Vati (FR)** **5** gr m Take Risks (FR) -Vatipan (FR) (Trepan (FR)) 6075a$^{4}$ 6511a$^{10}$ >**86f**<

**Reine D Opale (FR)** **2** ch f Lord Of Men-Round Sister (FR) (Romildo) 4962a$^{9}$ >**71f**<

**Rejoyce (IRE)** **3** ch f Dancing Spree (USA) -Zoyce (Zilzal (USA)) 508$^{8}$ ><

**Rekindled Applause** **3** b f Royal Applause-Rekindled Affair (IRE) (Rainbow Quest (USA)) 1778a$^{6}$ 6203a$^{9}$ 6513a$^{12}$ >**92f**<

**Relative Hero (IRE)** **4** ch g Entrepreneur-Aunty (FR) (Riverman (USA)) 2362$^{9}$ 2520$^{8}$ 3885$^{2}$ 4476$^{3}$ 4630$^{6}$ 5069$^{4}$ >**45a 45f**<

**Relaxed (USA)** **3** b f Royal Academy (USA) -Sleep Easy (USA) (Seattle Slew (USA)) (1400) 3033$^{8}$ >**90f**<

**Relaxed Gesture (IRE)** **3** ch c Indian Ridge-Token Gesture (IRE) (Alzao (USA)) 1979a$^{2}$ >**79a 108f**<

**Released (USA)** **2** b f Red Ransom (USA) -Ispirata (IRE) (Lure (USA)) 5368$^{11}$ >**51f**<

**Rellim** **5** b m Rudimentary (USA) -Tycoon Girl (IRE) (Last Tycoon) 560$^{5}$ 721$^{8}$ 1075$^{11}$ 6059$^{16}$ 6403$^{13}$ >**57 a 56f**<

**Remaadd (USA)** **3** rg c Daylami (IRE) -Bint Albaadiya (USA) (Woodman (USA)) (2085) 4215$^{3}$ 4755$^{2}$ >**111f**<

**Remembrance** **4** b g Sabrehill (USA) -Perfect Poppy (Shareef Dancer (USA)) 705$^{12}$ >**65a 65f**<

**Reminiscent (IRE)** **5** b g Kahyasi-Eliza Orzeszkowa (IRE) (Polish Patriot (USA)) 666$^{4}$ 2212$^{2}$ 2381$^{4}$ 2767$^{5}$ 3181$^{8}$ 3774$^{14}$ >**76a 68f**<

**Remonstrate (IRE)** **3** b g Alhaarth (IRE) -Truffa (IRE) (Selkirk (USA)) 2195$^{6}$ 2654$^{9}$ >**59f**<

**Rendezvous Point (USA)** **3** ch f Kingmambo (USA) -Reggie V (USA) (Vanlandingham (USA)) 1793$^{8}$ 2472$^{8}$ >**71+a 63f**<

**Rene Barbier (IRE)** **3** b g Desert Style (IRE) -Sweet Decision (IRE) (Common Grounds) 1749$^{10}$ 1942$^{4}$ (2675) 3122$^{5}$ 3201$^{6}$ 3585$^{8}$ 5364$^{12}$ 5849$^{9}$ 6199$^{9}$ >**64f**<

**Reno s Magic** **3** b f Hello Mister-Mountain Magic (Magic Ring (IRE)) 1472$^{8}$ >**35a 38f**<

**Ren s Magic** **6** gr g Petong-Bath (Runnett) 6231$^{12}$ >**55 a 53f**<

**Repeat (IRE)** **4** ch g Night Shift (USA) -Identical (IRE) (Machiavellian (USA)) (423) 481$^{2}$ 504$^{10}$ 627$^{4}$ 720$^{4}$ 972$^{8}$ 993$^{7}$ 3227$^{10}$3489$^{6}$ 3742$^{14}$ 3988$^{11}$ >**50a 50f**<

**Repent At Leisure** **4** b g Bishop Of Cashel-Sutosky (Great Nephew) 4819$^{8}$ 5159$^{8}$ 5286$^{11}$ >**41f**<

**Repertory** **11** b g Anshan-Susie s Baby (Balidar) 1438$^{9}$ 1763$^{11}$ 2222$^{10}$ 2636$^{7}$ 2913$^{6}$ 3480$^{9}$ >**86 f**<

**Repetoire (FR)** **4** ch f Zafonic (USA) -Lady Kate (USA) (Trempolino (USA)) 427$^{10}$ 528$^{6}$ >**55f**<

**Repulse Bay (IRE)** **6** b g Barathea (IRE) -Bourbon Topsy (Ile De Bourbon (USA)) 1315$^{6}$ 1785$^{8}$ 2171$^{3}$ 2299$^{7}$ 2671$^{5}$ 3041$^{14}$ 3369$^{9}$ 4005$^{12}$4275$^{7}$ 4901$^{7}$ 5058$^{8}$ 5584$^{17}$ >**53a 60f**<

**Reqqa** **2** b c Royal Applause-Kangra Valley (Indian Ridge) 3760$^{6}$ (4454) 5195$^{4}$ 5460$^{4}$ >**96+f**<

**Request For Parole (USA)** **5** bb h Judge T C (USA) -Madison s Quest (USA) (Deputy Minister (CAN)) 5985a$^{4}$ 6490a$^{6}$ >**105a 120f**<

**Rescind (IRE)** **4** b f Revoque (IRE) -Sunlit Ride (Ahonoora) 6406$^{10}$ >**36a 48 f**<

**Reservoir (IRE)** **3** b g Green Desert (USA) -Spout (Salse (USA)) 2077$^{2}$ (2645) 3345$^{7}$ 4729$^{5}$ 4888$^{11}$ 5266$^{2}$ >**85f**<

**Residential** **3** ch g Zilzal (USA) -House Hunting (Zafonic (USA)) 4125$^{4}$ 5123$^{6}$ 5999$^{4}$ >**68f**<

**Resistance Heroine** **2** b f Dr Fong (USA) -Odette (Pursuit Of Love) 3741$^{7}$ 4053$^{12}$ 4560$^{3}$ 5172$^{7}$ 5738$^{4}$ >**71+f**<

**Resonance** **3** b f Slip Anchor-Music In My Life (IRE) (Law Society (USA)) 818$^{2}$ 916$^{8}$ 1297$^{3}$ 4686$^{7}$ >**65a 72f**<

**Resonate (IRE)** **6** b h Erin s Isle-Petronelli (USA) (Sir Ivor) 2064$^{4}$ 3631$^{10}$ (5423) 5956$^{2}$ >**71a 86f**<

**Resplendent Cee (IRE)** **5** ch h Polar Falcon (USA) -Western Friend (USA) (Gone West (USA)) 4759$^{18}$ >**109f**<

**Resplendent King (USA)** **3** b g King Of Kings (IRE) -Sister Fromseattle (USA) (Seattle Slew (USA)) 462$^{3}$ 580$^{3}$ 741$^{5}$ 869$^{5}$ 1541$^{3}$ 2401$^{2}$ 2802$^{3}$ 3556$^{3}$3875$^{13}$ >**75a 75df**<

**Resplendent One (IRE)** **3** b c Marju (IRE) -Licentious (Reprimand) 2476$^{6}$ 3001$^{27}$ 3671$^{4}$ 4322$^{4}$ 5769$^{8}$ >**104f**<

**Resplendent Prince** **2** ch c Primo Dominie-Last Result (Northern Park (USA)) 4023$^{8}$ >**58a**<

**Ressource (FR)** **5** b g Broadway Flyer (USA) -Rayonne (Sadler s Wells (USA)) 1281$^{5}$ >**41a**<

**Restart (IRE)** **3** b g Revoque (IRE) -Stargard (Polish Precedent (USA)) 2251$^{10}$ 3479$^{8}$ (5130) 5243$^{8}$ 5860$^{2}$ 5991$^{12}$ >**56a 67f**<

**Restoration (FR)** **2** gr c Zafonic (USA) -Restless Mixa (IRE) (Linamix (FR)) 6514$^{2}$ >**68f**<

**Retail Therapy (IRE)** **4** b f Bahhare (USA) -Elect (USA) (Vaguely Noble) 484$^{2}$ 549$^{6}$ 1463$^{12}$ 5286$^{15}$ >**55a 35f**<

**Retirement** **5** b g Zilzal (USA) -Adeptation (USA) (Exceller (USA)) (1708) 1927$^{3}$ 3299$^{10}$ 3714$^{10}$ 4920$^{7}$ 5194$^{11}$ 6568$^{11}$ >**81a 91f**<

**Reveillez** **5** gr g First Trump-Amalancher (USA) (Alleged (USA)) 1329$^{6}$ 2240$^{5}$ >**99f**<

**Revelino (IRE)** **5** b g Revoque (IRE) -Forelino (USA) (Trempolino (USA)) 4911$^{6}$ >**90f**<

**Revenir (IRE)** **3** ch g Spectrum (IRE) -Petite Liqueurelle (IRE) (Shernazar) 2808$^{7}$ 3448$^{2}$ 3846$^{2}$ 5366$^{2}$ 5936$^{4}$ (6160) 6337$^{10}$ >**76a 78f**<

**Revenue (IRE)** **4** ch c Cadeaux Genereux-Bareilly (USA) (Lyphard (USA)) 1379a$^{4}$ 1893a$^{13}$ >**105f**<

**Reverie Solitaire (IRE)** **3** b f Nashwan (USA) -Cloud Castle (In The Wings) 2700a$^{3}$ 3566a$^{4}$ 5033a$^{2}$ 5966a$^{5}$ 6437a$^{5}$ >**107f**<

**Reversionary** **3** b g Poyle George-Harold s Girl (FR) (Northfields (USA)) 1196$^{8}$ 1467$^{10}$ 2036$^{5}$ 2411$^{10}$ 2457$^{15}$ 3234$^{7}$ (3513) 3822$^{9}$ 4190$^{3}$6142$^{2}$ 6467$^{2}$ >**54a 52f**<

**Revien (IRE)** **2** b c Rossini (USA) -Kazimiera (IRE) (Polish Patriot (USA)) 6008$^{3}$ 6289$^{3}$ >**72a 54f**<

**Reviewer (IRE)** **6** b g Sadler s Wells (USA) -Clandestina (USA) (Secretariat (USA)) 679$^{15}$ 2501$^{7}$ 2787$^{12}$ 3207$^{5}$ 3752$^{5}$ >**19a 79f**<

**Revivalist** **2** b f Benny The Dip (USA) -Brave Revival (Dancing Brave (USA)) 3259$^{9}$ >**31f**<

**Rewayaat** **3** b f Bahhare (USA) -Alumisiyah (USA) (Danzig (USA)) 2369$^{9}$ >**75 f**<

**Rex (IRE)** **7** b g Lake Coniston (IRE) -Surfing (Grundy) 1953a$^{5}$ 5505a$^{9}$ >**75a**<

**Rex Romelio (IRE)** **5** ch g Priolo (USA) -Romelia (USA) (Woodman (USA)) 512$^{10}$ 630$^{2}$ 672$^{12}$ >**51a**<

**Rhapsody In Silver (FR)** **2** gr c Medaaly-Concert (Polar Falcon (USA)) 3664$^{9}$ >**43f**<

**Rhetoric (IRE)** **5** b g Desert King (IRE) -Squaw Talk (USA) (Gulch (USA)) 1193$^{8}$ 1514$^{4}$ (1700) 1987$^{12}$ 2230$^{6}$ >**42a 63f**<

**Rhetorical** **3** b g Unfuwain (USA) -Miswaki Belle (USA) (Miswaki (USA)) 4562$^{5}$ 5057$^{12}$ 5479$^{6}$ 5638$^{10}$ 5796$^{11}$ >**48a 45f**<

**Rhinefield Boy** **3** ch g Wolfhound (USA) -Rhinefield Beauty (IRE) (Shalford (IRE)) 2175$^{8}$ 2620$^{11}$ >**42 f**<

**Rhoslan (IRE)** **2** b c Trans Island-Flimmering (Dancing Brave (USA)) 3913$^{10}$ 4335$^{13}$ 4966$^{10}$ >**57f**<

**Rhum** **4** ch g Bahamian Bounty-Rynavey (Rousillon (USA)) 4781$^{P}$ 5189$^{5}$ 6141$^{10}$ >**47f**<

**Ribbons And Bows (IRE)** **4** gr f Dr Devious (IRE) -Nichodoula (Doulab (USA)) 1272$^{13}$ 2062$^{6}$ 2381$^{8}$ 2914$^{4}$ 3919$^{13}$ 4603$^{9}$ 5175$^{4}$ 5658$^{5}$6231$^{5}$ (6551) 6576$^{8}$ >**64a 58f**<

**Ribbons Of Gold** **2** b f Primo Dominie-In Love Again (IRE) (Prince Rupert (FR)) 1299$^{6}$ 4621$^{10}$ >**44f**<

**Ribella (IRE)** **5** b m Revoque (IRE) -Tajarib (IRE) (Last Tycoon) 5488a$^{3}$ ><

**Rich Albi** **2** b g Mind Games-Bollin Sophie (Efisio) 2388$^{6}$ 2860$^{14}$ 3248$^{4}$ 4836$^{12}$ 6265$^{18}$ >**69f**<

**Rich Chic (IRE)** **3** bb f Sri Pekan (USA) -Ring Side (IRE) (Alzao (USA)) 2654$^{12}$ 3268$^{4}$ 3587$^{8}$ >**39f**<

**Richemaur (IRE)** **4** b f Alhaarth (IRE) -Lady President (IRE) (Dominion) 1372$^{4}$ 1623$^{16}$ 1931$^{12}$ 2671$^{4}$ 3046$^{11}$ 3450$^{9}$ >**71a 81f**<

**Richie Boy** **3** b c Dr Fong (USA) -Alathezal (USA) (Zilzal (USA)) 2808$^{9}$ 4195$^{6}$ 4940$^{10}$ 5176$^{12}$ (6055) 6120$^{8}$ (6311) (6516) >**53a 71f**<

**Richmond Lodge (IRE)** **4** br g Sesaro (USA) -Richmond Lillie (Fairbairn) 4641$^{14}$ 5038$^{5}$ >**62f**<

**Richon (IRE)** **3** b c Croco Rouge (IRE) -Spring Haven (USA) (Lear Fan (USA)) 1218a$^{4}$ ><

**Rich Sense (USA)** **3** ch f Mt. Livermore (USA) -Seasonal Style (IRE) (Generous (IRE)) 4406a$^{5}$ >**88f**<

**Richtee (IRE)** **3** ch f Desert Sun-Santarene (IRE) (Scenic) (2760) 3102$^{2}$ 3561$^{5}$ (4307) 4536$^{3}$ (4636) 5191$^{4}$ 5850$^{6}$ >**78f**<

**Ricky Martan** **3** ch c Foxhound (USA) -Cyrillic (Rock City) 580$^{10}$ 741$^{9}$ 891$^{8}$ 983$^{9}$ 1854$^{10}$ 2931$^{6}$ 4259$^{11}$ 5643$^{6}$5796$^{13}$ 6360$^{9}$ >**44a 44f**<

**Ridapour (IRE)** **5** b g Kahyasi-Ridiyara (IRE) (Persian Bold) 1112$^{12}$ >**8a 15f**<

**Ridder** **2** b c Dr Fong (USA) -Frond (Alzao (USA)) 2300$^{4}$ 3192$^{5}$ 3748$^{7}$ 4235$^{2}$ 4914$^{2}$ (5319) 5878a$^{3}$ >**95f**<

**Ride Safari** **2** b g Fraam-Vocation (IRE) (Royal Academy (USA)) 2376$^{6}$ 2927$^{3}$ 3259$^{4}$ >**66f**<

**Ridgeback** **4** ch g Indian Ridge-Valbra (Dancing Brave (USA)) 1106$^{16}$ >**76f**<

**Ridge Boy (IRE)** **3** b c Indian Ridge-Bold Tina (IRE) (Persian Bold) 2204$^{5}$ 2517$^{6}$ 3322$^{7}$ (3589) 3844$^{12}$ 4814$^{3}$ 5252$^{2}$ (5934) 6358$^{10}$ >**81f**<

**Ridicule** **5** b g Piccolo-Mockingbird (Sharpo) 681$^{10}$ 1313$^{8}$ 1608$^{12}$ 1873$^{7}$ 2166$^{11}$ 2843$^{7}$ 3533$^{17}$ 4617$^{11}$ >**57a 57f**<

**Rifleman (IRE)** **4** ch g Starborough-En Garde (USA) (Irish River (FR)) 1199$^{15}$ 2142$^{17}$ 2618$^{8}$ 3563$^{7}$ >**82a 89df**<

**Right Answer** **2** b f Lujain (USA) -Quiz Show (Primo Dominie) 2884$^{4}$ (3208) 3346$^{2}$ 3753$^{2}$ 4119$^{5}$ 4744$^{3}$ 5392$^{20}$ 6212$^{10}$ >**95f**<

**Right Approach** **5** b h Machiavellian (USA) -Abbey Strand (USA) (Shadeed (USA)) (853a) (1146a) 1657a$^{5}$ >**120f**<

**Rightful Ruler** **2** b c Montjoy (USA) -Lady Of The Realm (Prince Daniel (USA)) 5508$^{4}$ 6078$^{4}$ 6441$^{14}$ >**77f**<

**Right Key (IRE)** **2** b f Key Of Luck (USA) -Sarifa (IRE) (Kahyasi) 4592a$^{6}$ 5325a$^{10}$ >**94f**<

**Rightprice Premier (IRE)** **2** b f Cape Cross (IRE) -Machudi (Bluebird (USA)) 1314$^{3}$ 1601$^{2}$ (2002) 2933$^{5}$ >**74a 64f**<

**Right To Roam (IRE)** **2** b c Namid-Lloc (Absalom) 2817$^{4}$ 5376$^{7}$ 5911$^{5}$ >**51+a 56f**<

**Righty Ho** **10** b g Reprimand-Challanging (Mill Reef (USA)) (1721) 2214$^{3}$ 2348$^{3}$ 3411$^{7}$ 3835$^{6}$ (4561) 5243$^{10}$ 5710$^{3}$ >**50f**<

**Rigonza** **3** ch g Vettori (IRE) -Desert Nomad (Green Desert (USA)) 1392$^{11}$ 1712$^{8}$ 3102$^{5}$ 3561$^{13}$ 3955$^{3}$ 4444$^{4}$ 4703$^{2}$ >**68f**<

**Rihla (IRE)** **3** ch f Soviet Star (USA) -Ridaiyma (IRE) (Kahyasi) 1980a$^{6}$ 2711a$^{7}$ >**89f**<

**Riley Boys (IRE)** **3** ch g Most Welcome-Scarlett Holly (Red Sunset) (1078) 1392$^{2}$ (1755) 1957$^{2}$ (2571) 2880$^{2}$ 3012$^{2}$ 3507$^{2}$ 3745$^{2}$ 4780$^{6}$ >**61a 85f**<

**Rileys Dream** **5** b m Rudimentary (USA) -Dorazine (Kalaglow) 1283$^{8}$ 1533$^{5}$ 1855$^{10}$ 2178$^{9}$ (2359) 2833$^{13}$ 3533$^{12}$ 3988$^{5}$ (4469) 5035$^{2}$5261$^{17}$ >**68f**<

**Rileys Rocket** **5** b m Makbul-Star Of Flanders (Puissance) 945$^{11}$ 2348$^{10}$ 2547$^{11}$ 2854$^{12}$ >**17a 17 f**<

**Rill** **2** ch f Unfuwain (USA) -River Cara (USA) (Irish River (FR)) 5846$^{4}$ >**68f**<

**Rince Donn (IRE)** **2** b g Imperial Ballet (IRE) -Arrow Field (USA) (Sunshine Forever (USA)) 4958a$^{16}$ >**56f**<

**Ringarooma** **2** b f Erhaab (USA) -Tatouma (USA) (The Minstrel (CAN)) 3676$^{5}$ 4198$^{9}$ 4966$^{4}$ 5362$^{2}$ 5701$^{13}$ >**68f**<

**Ringmoor Down** **5** b m Pivotal-Floppie (FR) (Law Society (USA)) 1438$^{6}$ (1685) 2316a$^{3}$ 2955$^{4}$ 3537$^{2}$ 3715$^{4}$ (4269) (5327a) 5780$^{7}$ 5977a$^{8}$ 6175$^{2}$ >**112f**<

**Ring Of Destiny** **5** b g Magic Ring (IRE) -Canna (Caerleon (USA)) 1401$^{14}$ 2022$^{11}$ 2681$^{8}$ >**89f**<

**Ringside Jack** **8** b g Batshoof-Celestine (Skyliner) 1287$^{3}$ 1326$^{7}$ 1958$^{9}$ >**6a 57f**<

**Ringsider (IRE)** **3** ch g Docksider (USA) -Red Comes Up (USA) (Blushing Groom (FR)) 1900$^{11}$ 2676$^{17}$ 4220$^{2}$ (4327) 5106$^{9}$ (5842) >**93+f**<

**Rinjani (USA)** **3** b c Gone West (USA) -Ringshaan (FR) (Darshaan) 3345$^{9}$ 4709$^{7}$ >**88f**<

**Rinneen (IRE)** **3** b f Bien Bien (USA) -Sparky s Song (Electric) 1688$^{9}$ 1998$^{9}$ 2402$^{5}$ 3669$^{3}$ 4055$^{4}$ 5178$^{5}$ >**44a 60f**<

**Rio Branco** **3** b f Efisio-Los Alamos (Keen) (550) >**68a 53f**<

**Rio De Janeiro (IRE)** **3** b c Sadler s Wells (USA) -Alleged Devotion (USA) (Alleged (USA)) 4833$^{7}$ >**89f**<

**Rio De Jumeirah** **3** b f Seeking The Gold (USA) -Tegwen (USA) (Nijinsky (CAN)) 1963$^{3}$ 2281$^{6}$ 2558$^{11}$ 3230$^{5}$ (4049) 4395$^{2}$ >**91f**<

**Rio Real (FR)** **7** b g Neverneyev (USA) -Alhucema (IRE) (Tirol) 5103a$^{4}$ ><

**Rio Riva** **2** b c Pivotal-Dixie Favor (USA) (Dixieland Band (USA)) 5772$^{2}$ >**84+f**<

**Ripcord (IRE)** **6** b g Diesis-Native Twine (Be My Native (USA)) 539$^{5}$ 2055$^{6}$ 3263$^{8}$ >**26a 32f**<

**Ripley (GER)** **4** b f Platini (GER) -Royal Army (GER) (Pirate Army (USA)) 3434a$^{4}$ 5823a$^{8}$ 6255a$^{9}$ >**81f**<

**Ripple Effect** **4** ch f Elmaamul (USA) -Sharp Chief (Chief Singer) 519$^{2}$ (575) 599$^{2}$ 646$^{10}$ 886$^{5}$ (960) 1057$^{5}$ 1139$^{6}$1824$^{7}$ >**85a 77 f**<

**Riquewihr** **4** ch f Compton Place-Juvenilia (IRE) (Masterclass (USA)) 4937$^{4}$ 5618$^{3}$ 6117$^{4}$ >**65f**<

**Risata** **2** b f Distinctly North (USA) -Rosa Bianca (Rock City) 5577a$^{5}$ ><

**Rise** **3** b f Polar Falcon (USA) -Splice (Sharpo) 619$^{9}$ 1504$^{16}$ 1907$^{6}$ 2378$^{7}$ 2741$^{7}$ (3211) 3530$^{2}$ 3926$^{7}$ (4650) 5219$^{2}$5454$^{8}$ >**65a 75f**<

**Rising Shadow (IRE)** **3** b g Efisio-Jouet (Reprimand) 3317$^{6}$ 3926$^{2}$ 4151$^{4}$ 4570$^{6}$ 4874$^{10}$ 5603$^{15}$ >**81a 86f**<

**Riska King** **4** b g Forzando-Artistic Licence (High

Top) *437[7] 900[7]* 1927[12] 2215[19] 2492[8] 3012[4] 3397[3] 3516[3]3982[6] (5108) 5236[5] 5706[4] *(5955) 6156[7]* **>75a 81f<**

**Riskaverse (USA)** 5 bb m Dynaformer (USA) -The Bink (USA) (Seeking The Gold (USA)) 4767a[2] 6488a[8] **>116f<**

**Risk Free** 7 ch g Risk Me (FR) -Princess Lily (Blakeney) 3734[10] 4014[6] 4280[7] 4702[13] 4877[13] *6062[8]* **>74a 71f<**

**Risk Seeker** 4 b c Elmaamul (USA) -Robertet (USA) (Roberto (USA)) 1182a[2] (1703) 2533[4] 3963a[4] **>121f<**

**Risky Way** 8 b g Risk Me (FR) -Hot Sunday Sport (Star Appeal) *937[8]* **><**

**Risque De Verglas (FR)** 3 gr f Verglas (IRE) -Frundin (Anshan) 2700a[5] 4356a[9] 6203a[4] **>96f<**

**Ritter (ITY)** 2 b c Dashing Blade-Morvan Marida (ITY) (Love The Groom (USA)) 5388a[2] **><**

**Rival (IRE)** 5 b g Desert Style (IRE) -Arab Scimetar (IRE) (Sure Blade (USA)) *838[10] 972[9]* **><**

**Riva Royale** 4 b f Royal Applause-Regatta (Mtoto) 1610[8] 1964[10] 2143[14] 2788[4] 3047[6] 4067[9] **>71a 88f<**

**Rivelli (IRE)** 5 b m Lure (USA) -Kama Tashoof (Mtoto) *940[11]* **>41a 75f<**

**Rivendell** 8 b m Saddlers Hall (IRE) -Fairy Kingdom (Prince Sabo) *422[6] 713[9] 810[8]* **>23a 9f<**

**River Alhaarth (IRE)** 2 b c Alhaarth (IRE) -Sudden Interest (FR) (Highest Honor (FR)) 5347[5] (6149) **>72f<**

**River Belle** 3 ch f Lahib (USA) -Dixie Favor (USA) (Dixieland Band (USA)) 6254a[3] **>109f<**

**River Biscuit (USA)** 2 ch c Diesis-Elle Est Revenue (IRE) (Night Shift (USA)) 3601[8] 4078[5] 4913[14] 6090[5] **>69f<**

**Riverbride (USA)** 2 br f Kingmambo (USA) -Anklet (USA) (Wild Again (USA)) 3790a[8] 5313a[2] 6169a[4] **>94f<**

**River Canyon (IRE)** 8 b g College Chapel-Na-Ammah (IRE) (Ela-Mana-Mou) *782[9]* **>54f<**

**River Card** 2 ch f Zaha (CAN) -Light Hand (Star Appeal) 5592[7] 6242[10] **>58f<**

**River Dancer (IRE)** 5 b g Sadler s Wells (USA) -Darara (Top Ville) (1657a) **>118f<**

**River Days (IRE)** 6 b m Tagula (USA) -Straw Boater (Thatch (USA)) *646[9] 762[2] 904[10] 941[6] 1018[5] 1178[2] 1474[4]* **>52a 52f<**

**River Dominie (IRE)** 3 ch f Primo Dominie-Key To The River (USA) (Irish River (FR)) 1306a[14] **><**

**River Falcon** 4 b g Pivotal-Pearly River (Elegant Air) 1113[5] 1343[7] (2041) 2488[11] 2857[7] 3309[3] 4152[11] (4510) 5287[11] 5628[18]5787[4] 6071[5] 6243[10] 6517[14] **>96f<**

**River Gypsy** 3 b c In The Wings-River Erne (USA) (Irish River (FR)) 1800[2] **>69a 73f<**

**River Lark (USA)** 5 b m Miswaki (USA) -Gold Blossom (USA) (Blushing John (USA)) *612[6] 801[4] 1033[4] 1262[6]* 1368[8] 1824[6] 1988[5] 2778[13]*3378[3]* 3742[17] **>53a 51f<**

**River Liffey** 2 b c Forzando-Rion River (IRE) (Taufan (USA)) 4446[8] 4907[2] 5142[2] **>83f<**

**River Line (USA)** 3 b g Keos (USA) -Portio (USA) (Riva Ridge (USA)) 2555[4] 3581[7] 3981[12] 4448[10] 5243[9] **>49f<**

**River Nurey (IRE)** 3 gr c Fasliyev (USA) -Dundel (IRE) (Machiavellian (USA)) 2596[3] 3106[2] 3554[5] 4306[2] 4679[2] 5345[4] **>72f<**

**River Of Babylon** 3 b f Marju (IRE) -Isle Of Flame (Shirley Heights) 1370[2] 2097[6] 5123[5] (5366) *(5740)* 6203a[7] **>77a 86f<**

**River Of Diamonds** 3 b g Muhtarram (USA) -City Gambler (Rock City) 5123[8] 5999[7] 6182[2] (6564) **>63f<**

**River Of Fire** 6 ch g Dilum (USA) -Bracey Brook (Gay Fandango (USA)) 1593[7] *1887[3] 2126[9]* 2386[4] 2595[8] 2874[9] 3263[11] (3667) 4007[5]4202[6] **>37a 46f<**

**River Royale** 2 b c Royal Applause-Trundley Wood (Wassl) 5118[3] 6171[3] 6476[3] **>88+f<**

**River Treat (FR)** 3 ch g Irish River (FR) -Dance Treat (USA) (Nureyev (USA)) (1366) 1745[6] 2981[5] 3384[9] 4236[4] 5572[2] 5950[9] **>85f<**

**Riverweld** 2 ch g Weldnaas (USA) -Riverain (Bustino) 2140[6] 2755[4] 3100[2] 3506[5] 5556[12] 6195[12] **>55f<**

**Riviera Red (IRE)** 4 b g Rainbow Quest (USA) -Banquise (IRE) (Last Tycoon) 4554[11] *5913[8]* **>56a<**

**Riyadh** 6 ch g Caerleon (USA) -Ausherra (USA) (Diesis) 1112[9] 1316[8] 1457[9] 1615[10] 1973[3] 2491[9] 2731[3] 2958[7]3508[7] 4075[2] 4226[16] 4448[2] 5027[6] 5274[7] 5472[4] 5826[6]5991[4] 6269[3] **>76f<**

**Riyma (IRE)** 2 b f Dr Fong (USA) -Riyafa (IRE) (Kahyasi) 3456[10] 5109[9] **>54f<**

**Road Rage (IRE)** 2 b f Giant s Causeway (USA) -Endorsement (Warning) 3913[3] (4344) 5413[8] **>75 f<**

**Road To Heaven (USA)** 2 ch c Southern Halo (USA) -Glory Way (USA) (Woodman (USA)) 3483[3] 4030[8] 5373[11] 6265[13] **>62f<**

**Roaming Vagabond (IRE)** 3 ch g Spectrum (IRE) -Fiveofive (IRE) (Fairy King (USA)) 1933[6] 2375[18] 3391[7] **>42f<**

**Roan Raider (USA)** 4 rg g El Prado (IRE) -Flirtacious Wonder (USA) (Wolf Power (SAF)) *415[11] 805[11]* 1371[8] 1870[3] 2175[4] 2359[10] 2383[5] 2675[3]2908[5] 3151[12] 3512[2] 3810[12] 3864[2] 5306[5] 5754[9] 5862[8]6007[7] **>42a 61f<**

**Robbie Can Can** 5 b g Robellino (USA) -Can Can Lady (Anshan) *(693) 777[3] (867)* 1103[2] **>67a 73f<**

**Robbo** 10 b g Robellino (USA) -Basha (USA) (Chief s Crown (USA)) 6269[8] **>59f<**

**Robeson** 2 br g Primo Dominie-Montserrat (Aragon) 3093[9] 5716[5] **>72f<**

**Robin Sharp** 6 ch h First Trump-Mo Stopher (Sharpo) *582[2] 667[6] 918[11] 1020[5] 1176[12] 1515[7] 1723[4]*1986[12] *2052[2]* **>9a 9f<**

**Robinzal** 2 b g Zilzal (USA) -Sulitelma (USA) (The Minstrel (CAN)) 4315[9] 4606[3] 5098[2] 5307[6] 6140[7] **>69f<**

**Robmantra** 2 b c Prince Sabo-Eliza Jane (Mistertopogigo (IRE)) 3124[6] 3343[5] 3696[3] 5005[6] 5406[15] 5690[4] 6080[8] 6544[7] **>57 f<**

**Rob Roy (USA)** 2 bb c Lear Fan (USA) -Camanoe (USA) (Gone West (USA)) (5915) **>86+f<**

**Robury** 2 b g Robellino (USA) -Youdontsay (Most Welcome) 1709[7] 2470[9] 3514[11] **>19f<**

**Robwillcall** 4 b f Timeless Times (USA) -Lavernock Lady (Don t Forget Me) 1870[14] 2175[5] (2975) 3147[5] 4331[5] 4782[10] 5452[5] 5579[15] 6144[13]6246[7] 6526[2] **>50a 50f<**

**Roca Azul (IRE)** 2 br f Cape Cross (IRE) -Rumba Azul (FR) (Fabulous Dancer (USA)) (5390a) **><**

**Rocamadour** 2 b c Celtic Swing-Watch Me (IRE) (Green Desert (USA)) 4716[5] (5142) 5580[2] 5931[2] **>86f<**

**Rocinante (IRE)** 4 b g Desert Story (IRE) -Antapoura (IRE) (Bustino) *800[9] 926[8] 1043[8] 1176[3]* 1305[11] (1710) (1993) *2456[8]* 2879[14]*4190[6]* 6201[13] 6548[9] **>63a 63f<**

**Rockburst** 2 b f Xaar-Topwinder (USA) (Topsider (USA)) 1498[5] 2234[2] (2617) 3445[3] 4890[8] (5864) 6174[15] **>93f<**

**Rock Chick** 2 ch f Halling (USA) -Band (USA) (Northern Dancer) 2481[9] **>49f<**

**Rock Concert** 6 b m Bishop Of Cashel-Summer Pageant (Chief s Crown (USA)) *(412) 477[2] 590[3] 6580[8]* **>72a 61 f<**

**Rock Dove (IRE)** 2 b f Danehill (USA) -Littlefeather (IRE) (Indian Ridge) (5865) **>75+f<**

**Rockerfella Lad (IRE)** 4 b g Danetime (IRE) -Soucaro (Rusticaro (FR)) 1393[10] 1620[18] **>70f<**

**Rocket (IRE)** 3 ch g Cadeaux Genereux-Prends Ca (IRE) (Reprimand) 1370[9] *1496[4]* 1854[3] 2061[11] 4811[3] **>47a 57f<**

**Rocket Force (USA)** 4 ch g Spinning World (USA) -Pat Us (USA) (Caucasus (USA)) 1355[11] 1767[10] 2638[11] **>87f<**

**Rockets n Rollers (IRE)** 4 b c Victory Note (USA) -Holly Bird (Runnett) *1011[3]* 1107[3] 1254a[3] 1367[2] 1610[3] (1758) 1999[4] 2438a[5] 2793a[4]4889[8] 5488a[7] 5888[10] **>94a 109f<**

**Rock Fever (IRE)** 2 ch f Desert Sun-Icefern (Moorestyle) 3123[8] 5943[10] 6322[7] 6563[14] **>58f<**

**Rock Hard Ten (USA)** 3 br c Kris S (USA) -Tersa (USA) (Mr Prospector (USA)) *2139a[2] 2701a[5]* **>117a<**

**Rock Haven (IRE)** 2 b c Danehill Dancer (IRE) -Mahabba (USA) (Elocutionist (USA)) 4454[10] **>30f<**

**Rockley Bay (IRE)** 3 b c Mujadil (USA) -Kilkee Bay (IRE) (Case Law) 1796[8] 2790[15] 3158[7] 3684[9] 4968[2] 5261[19] *6014[7]* **>58a 61f<**

**Rock Lobster** 3 b g Desert Sun-Distant Music (Darshaan) 1360[7] 1609[5] 1995[6] *2665[3] 3379[6]* (4138) 4449[4] 4806[6] **>73a 71f<**

**Rock Of Angels (IRE)** 3 ch f Bahamian Bounty-Rock Of Gold (Rainbow Quest (USA)) 3569a[4] **><**

**Rockpiler** 2 b g Halling (USA) -Emma Peel (Emarati (USA)) 4392[4] 5302[14] **><**

**Rocky Rambo** 3 b g Sayaarr (USA) -Kingston Girl (Formidable (USA)) 1770[8] *2853[12]* **><**

**Rocky Reppin** 4 b g Rock City-Tino Reppin (Neltino) 1213[13] 1451[13] 2122[15] 2473[17] *2854[3] 3804[4] 4190[10]* 6057[8]6227[11] **>48a 67f<**

**Rockys Girl** 2 b f Piccolo-Lady Rockstar (Rock Hopper) 3840[11] *5375[7]* 5694[15] 6440[13] 6563[15] **>46a 35f<**

**Rodiak** 5 b g Distant Relative-Misty Silks (Scottish Reel) *568[10] 663[13]* **>53f<**

**Rodin (IRE)** 8 b g Be My Guest (USA) -Marseillaise (Artaius (USA)) *5103a[0]* **><**

**Roehampton** 3 b c Machiavellian (USA) -Come On Rosi (Valiyar) 1411[6] 1901[5] 5461[3] 5814[13] 6307[8] **>103f<**

**Ro Eridani** 4 b f Binary Star (USA) -Hat Hill (Roan Rocket) *533[7] 663[11] 793[12]* **>32a 51f<**

**Rojabaa** 5 b g Anabaa (USA) -Slava (USA) (Diesis) 2594[6] 3056[5] 3173[5] 4042[5] 5791[11] **>46f<**

**Roko** 2 b g Komaite (USA) -Robert s Daughter (Robellino (USA)) *2125[7]* 2858[9] 3444[11] 3818[4] 3980[3] 4675[3] *(4997)* 5314[12] 5690[8]6544[13] **>51a 54f<**

**Rolex Free (ARG)** 6 ch g Friul (ARG) -Karolera (ARG) (Kaljerry (ARG)) *679[12] 899[6]* 3591[8] *3934[8]* 4042[3] *(4189)* 4433[4] *(4600)* 4934[11]5056[4] 5257[3] 5826[20] **>64a 57f<**

**Rollerbird** 2 b f Sinndar (IRE) -Speedybird (IRE) (Danehill (USA)) *6494[2]* **>73a<**

**Rollswood (USA)** 4 ch g Diesis-Spit Curl (USA) (Northern Dancer) *871[5]* 4492[6] *4939[6]* 5869[8] *6013[7]* **>64a 64f<**

**Roman Arch (AUS)** 5 b g Archway (IRE) -Celestial Option (AUS) (Clear Choice (USA)) 6528a[14] **>111f<**

**Roman Army (IRE)** 2 b c Trans Island-Contravene (IRE) (Contract Law (USA)) 6545[5] **>58f<**

**Roman Empire** 4 b g Efisio-Gena Ivor (USA) (Sir Ivor (USA)) *873[7] 987[4] (2123) 2989[3] 3025[3] 3800[5]* 4702[4] 4827[10](5346) *6273[8]* **>64a 60f<**

**Roman Forum** 3 b c Selkirk (USA) -Flit (USA) (Lyphard (USA)) 2412[6] 3417[5] **>70f<**

**Roman King (IRE)** 9 b g Sadler s Wells (USA) -Romantic Feeling (Shirley Heights) 1263[10] **>58 f<**

**Roman Love (IRE)** 3 ch f Perugino (USA) -Bordighera (USA) (Alysheba (USA)) *5001[4]* **>38a<**

**Roman Maze** 4 ch g Lycius (USA) -Maze Garden (USA) (Riverman (USA)) 2172[12] 2421[5] 3086[7] 3755[7] 3884[7] 4305[4] 4360[2] 5020[4]5316[2] 5583[12] *6539[3]* **>73a 71f<**

**Roman Mistress (IRE)** 4 ch f Titus Livius (FR) -Repique (USA) (Sharpen Up) 1974[11] 2252[4] 2369[6] 2670[3] 3249[8] 3744[5] 4104[7] 4331[4](4854) 5107[10] 5579[22] 6046[9] **>76f<**

**Romanova (IRE)** 2 b f Grand Lodge (USA) -Millitrix (Doyoun) 4712[8] 5348[4] 6118[13] **>69f<**

**Roman Quintet (IRE)** 4 ch g Titus Livius (FR) -Quintellina (Robellino (USA)) *806[9] 1051[10]* 1131[14] 4748[3] 5512[2] 6001[2] 6131[2] *6452[2]* **>73a 71f<**

**Roman Ruler (USA)** 2 bb c Fusaichi Pegasus (USA) -Silvery Swan (USA) (Silver Deputy (CAN)) *6489a[5]* **>112a<**

**Roman The Park (IRE)** 3 b f Titus Livius (FR) -Missfortuna (Priolo (USA)) *1195[3] (1447) 1701[2] 1916[3]* (2349) 3146[3] 3581[4] 4259[3] 5451[2]6056[10] **>42a 45f<**

**Romantic Drama (IRE)** 3 b f Primo Dominie-Antonia s Choice (Music Boy) 5201[13] 5510[13] 6058[13] **>53a 58f<**

**Romantic Gift** 2 b f Cadeaux Genereux-Last Romance (IRE) (Last Tycoon) 2177[10] 2481[8] 4053[8] 4753[12] 6113[13] **>64f<**

**Romany Nights (IRE)** 4 b g Night Shift (USA) -Gipsy Moth (Efisio) *836[5] 968[11] 1139[4]* 1608[3] 2391[4] 2461[2] 2626[2] 2754[2]3243[4] 3293[6] 3606[16] 3775[2] 4011[7] 4291[5] 4394[3] 6572[12] **>78a 88f<**

**Romany Prince** 5 b g Robellino (USA) -Vicki Romara (Old Vic) 2240[3] 3076[3] 3538[2] 4270[5] 4832[5] 5415[7] **>110f<**

**Romaric (USA)** 3 b g Red Ransom (USA) -Eternal Reve (USA) (Diesis) 5199[4] 5992[10] 6568[15] **>64a 87f<**

**Roma Valley (FR)** 2 gr f Sagamix (FR) -Lois (IRE) (Be My Guest (USA)) 5695[13] 6118[19] **>28f<**

**Rome (IRE)** 5 br g Singspiel (IRE) -Ela Romara (Ela-Mana-Mou) *818[3]* 1832[12] 2631[3] 2893[5] 3437[5] 4033[4] 5274[14] 5764[11] **>73a 71f<**

**Romeo s Day** 3 ch g Pursuit Of Love-Daarat Alayaam (IRE) (Reference Point) 1946[11] 2092[2] 2146[4] 2402[3] 2554[11] 3984[7] 4302[8] 4710[8]5069[5] 5571[4] 5843[10] (5928) *(6065)* **>59a 48f<**

**Romil Star (GER)** 7 b g Chief s Crown (USA) -Romelia (USA) (Woodman (USA)) 1463[7] 1534[8] 1866[2] *(2228)* 2443[4] *(2662) (2851) 3022[3]* 3237[5] *3281[2]*(4698) 5058[11] 5229[6] **>68 a 68f<**

**Rondelet (IRE)** 3 b g Bering-Triomphale (USA) (Nureyev (USA)) 1506[2] 2069[9] 2517[2] 2887[3] 3294[2] (3872) 4319[7] 5183[4] 5446[5]6069[5] **>87+f<**

**Ronnie From Donny (IRE)** 4 b g Eagle Eyed (USA) -New Rochelle (IRE) (Lafontaine (USA)) *410[4] 511[11] 862[7]* 1175[10] 1199[5] 1358[5] 1526[11] 2219[11]2459[5] 2776[5] 3409[5] 3606[17] 4013[10] 5242[14] *6026[12] 6062[10]* **>79a 73f<**

**Ronnies Lad** 2 b g Lake Coniston (IRE) -Lycius Touch (Lycius (USA)) *1264[5] 1735[8]* (2248) 2799[2] 3390[2] 3987[8] 5745[4] **>34a 53f<**

**Rood Boy (IRE)** 3 b c Great Commotion (USA) -Cnocma (IRE) (Tender King) *955[4]* 1311[5] 1506[5] 2517[12] 6130[5] 6343[10] **>57a 57f<**

**Roodeye** 2 b f Inchinor-Roo (Rudimentary (USA)) 2427[2] (3382) 4217[5] 4744[6] 5250[3] 5594[4] 5947[13] **>94f<**

**Rooftop Protest (IRE)** 7 b g Thatching-Seattle Siren (USA) (Seattle Slew (USA)) (5456) **>77+f<**

**Rooks Bridge (IRE)** 2 ch g General Monash (USA) -Lisa s Pride (IRE) (Pips Pride) 5353[14] *5640[13] 6221[7] 6359[9]* **>36a 26f<**

**Roppongi Dancer** 5 b m Mtoto-Ice Chocolate (USA) (Icecapade (USA)) *426[5] 471[3] 579[8] 699[5]* 3461[7] **>11a 33f<**

**Rosablanca (IRE)** 2 b f Sinndar (IRE) -Elegant Bloom (IRE) (Be My Guest (USA)) *6447[14]* **>39a<**

**Rosacara** 3 b f Green Desert (USA) -Rambling Rose (Cadeaux Genereux) 3006[2] 3589[2] 3875[15] 5637[7] **>71f<**

**Rosapenna (IRE)** 2 b f Spectrum (IRE) -Blaine (USA) (Lyphard s Wish (FR)) 3272[5] 3741[14] *4598[5]* 5694[6] 6176[11] **>58a 58f<**

**Roseanna (FR)** 3 b f Anabaa (USA) -Dancing Rose (FR) (Dancing Spree (USA)) 1398[3] 1778a[10] **>96f<**

**Rose Bien** 2 bb f Bien Bien (USA) -Madame Bovary (Ile De Bourbon (USA)) 6226[9] **>36f<**

**Rosecliff** 2 b c Montjeu (IRE) -Dance Clear (IRE) (Marju (IRE)) 4728[4] 6565[4] **>68f<**

**Rosein** 2 b f Komaite (USA) -Red Rosein (Red Sunset) *(2125)* 2568[7] 5212[6] **>71a 73f<**

**Rosencrans (USA)** 3 b c Forest Wildcat (USA) -General s Mistress (USA) (General Meeting (USA)) *691a[3] (920a) (1063) 1239[4]* 2629[6] **>106a 37f<**

**Rose Of York (IRE)** 4 b f Emarati (USA) -True Ring (High Top) 5803[4] 6200[10] **>52f<**

**Rose Shift (IRE)** 4 b f Night Shift (USA) -Santa Rosa (IRE) (Lahib (USA)) 6258a[4] 6513a[10] **>95f<**

**Roses In May (USA)** 4 bb c Devil His Due (USA) -Tell A Secret (USA) (Speak John) *6491a[2]* **>128a<**

**Roses Of Spring** 6 gr m Shareef Dancer (USA) -Couleur De Rose (Kalaglow) 1937[7] 2222[3] 2488[17] 2909[10] 3945[10] 4232[6] 4415[7] 4740[11] **>88a 79f<**

**Rose Tea (IRE)** 5 ro m Alhaarth (IRE) -Shakamiyn (Nishapour (FR)) 1593[8] **>41a 55f<**

**Rosiella** 2 b f Tagula (IRE) -Queen Of Silk (IRE) (Brief Truce (USA)) 2481[12] 3157[5] (4621) 5068[3] 5363[4] 5617[6] 5839[16] **>70f<**

**Rosie Mac** 3 ch f First Trump-Carol Again (Kind Of Hush) 2962[6] 3251[3] 3759[4] 4101[6] 4395[6] 5223[10] 6095[4] **>58f<**

**Rosie Maloney (IRE)** 3 b f Docksider (USA) -Magic Lady (IRE) (Bigstone (IRE)) 1370[11] **>23a<**

**Rosie Muir** 2 br f Mind Games-Step On Degas (Superpower) 5507[10] 6126[7] **>45f<**

**Rosie s Result** 4 ch g Case Law-Precious Girl (Precious Metal) 1525[10] 2784[10] 3820[10] (3864) 4105[9] 4422[11] 4782[6] 5081[13] 5452[11] **>47f<**

**Rosings** 3 ch f Grand Lodge (USA) -Hajat (Mujtahid (USA)) 3592[14] 5239[9] **>48f<**

**Roskilde (IRE)** 4 b g Danehill (USA) -Melisendra (FR) (Highest Honor (FR)) 4178[8] 5462[14] **>102f<**

**Rossall Point** 3 b g Fleetwood (IRE) -Loch Clair (IRE) (Lomond (USA)) 2611[4] 3348[5] 3994[8] 4820[4] 5205[12] 6084[3] 6287[3] **>69f<**

**Rossbeigh (IRE)** 2 b c Alhaarth (IRE) -Ring Of Kerry (IRE) (Kenmare (FR)) 5087[10] **>61f<**

**Rosselli (USA)** 8 b g Puissance-Miss Rossi (Artaius (USA)) 1787[13] 1955[7] 2625[11] 3039[10] 3337[8] 3522[8] 4006[F] **>20a 67?f<**

**Rossin Gold (IRE)** 2 b g Rossini (USA) -Sacred Heart (IRE) (Catrail (USA)) *6478[6]* **>43a<**

**Ross Is Boss** 2 gr g Paris House-Billie Grey (Chilibang) 5341[10] 5947[23] **><**

**Ross Moor** 2 b c Dansili-Snipe Hall (Crofthall) 5716[14] **>36f<**

**Rosti** 4 b g Whittingham (IRE) -Uaeflame (IRE) (Polish Precedent (USA)) *(428) (472) 533[3] 667[8] 939[6]* 1720[8] **>53a 56f<**

**Rotteck (GER)** 4 br c Law Society (USA) -Rofania (GER) (Orfano (GER)) 2508a[2] (3357a) 4183a[3] 4794a[7] **>115f<**

**Rotulo (ARG)** 6 b h Roy (USA) -Romana-Red (ARG) (Turkoman (USA)) *632a[2] 689a[7] 830a[4]* 921a[3] *974a[7] 1954a[4] 5504a[8]* **>91a<**

**Rotuma (IRE)** 5 b g Tagula (IRE) -Cross Question (USA) (Alleged (USA)) 1172[9] 1503[5] 1660[8] 2272[3] (2583) 2752[6] (3166) 3534[2] 3952[5] (4571) 5211[9]5607[9] 6115[7] 6520[8] **>24a 82f<**

**Rouge Blanc (USA)** 4 b f King Of Kings (IRE) -Style N Elegance (USA) (Alysheba (USA)) 1866[9] 2409[7] 2462[13] **>44a 61f<**

**Rouge Et Noir** 6 b g Hernando (FR) -Bayrouge (IRE) (Gorytus (USA)) 3587[14] 3899[7] 4396[4] 5243[3] 5638[9] **>56f<**

**Rousing Thunder** 7 b g Theatrical-Moss (USA) (Woodman (USA)) *432[10] 570[16]* **>3a 54?f<**

**Route Sixty Six (IRE)** 8 b m Brief Truce (USA) -Lyphards Goddess (IRE) (Lyphard s Special (USA)) *412[8]* 1875[6] 3200[2] 3301[16] 4511[8] 4760[6] **>37a 55f<**

**Rovella** 3 b f Robellino (USA) -Spring Flyer (IRE) (Waajib) 1521[7] 1946[12] *2185[7]* 2347[8] **>14a 33f<**

**Roving Vixen (IRE)** 3 b f Foxhound (USA) -Rend Rover (FR) (Monseigneur (USA)) *965[13]* 1370[8] *1889[4]* 1987[13] *2185[3] 2545[3]* 3193[4]3427[7] 4460[9] 5926[5] 6056[6] 6228[5] **>43a 43f<**

**Rowan Lodge (IRE)** 2 ch c Indian Lodge (IRE) -Tirol Hope (IRE) (Tirol) 2736[14] 3248[3] (3823) 4482[2] (4700) 5119[9] 5453[2] 5721[9] 6042[4] **>83 f<**

**Rowan Pursuit** 3 b f Pursuit Of Love-Golden Seattle (IRE) (Seattle Dancer (USA)) *(420) 557[3] 599[5] 845[7]* 4619[11] 5020[16] **>74a 56f<**

**Rowan Tree** 2 b c Singspiel (IRE) -Dashing Water (Dashing Blade) 3672[8] 4227[7] 5678a[7] **>97f<**

**Rowan Warning** 2 b c Diktat-Golden Seattle (IRE) (Seattle Dancer (USA)) 3150[5] **>31f<**

**Roxagu (GER)** 3 gr c Oxalagu (GER) -Rosobolda (GER) (Never So Bold) 3134a[5] 6513a[4] **>102f<**

**Roxanne Mill** 6 b m Cyrano De Bergerac-It Must Be Millie (Reprimand) 1518[3] 1937[2] 2079[6] 2490[3] 2912[2] 3147[3] 3307[5] 3744[6](4014) 4331[2] 4701[9] 4970[2] 5062[16] **>57a 77 f<**

**Royal Abigail (IRE)** 2 b f Inchinor-Lady Abigail (IRE) (Royal Academy (USA)) 3532[15] 4292[13] **>45f<**

**Royal Accolade** 2 b f Royal Applause-Zafaaf (Kris) 1839[9] 2177[16] 3302[7] **>42f<**

**Royal Advocate** 4 b g Royal Applause-Kept Waiting (Tanfirion) *2406[4] 2883[5]* 3593[6] 3596[8] **>65a 60f<**

**Royal Alchemist** 2 b f Kingsinger (IRE) -Pure Gold (Dilum (USA)) (2087) 3316[2] 4552[7] 5149[8] 5649[5] 5939[13] **>92f<**

**Royal Approach** 3 b f Royal Applause-Passionelle (Nashwan (USA)) 1761[5] *3379[11]* 5622[9] **>57f<**

**Royal Assault (USA)** 3 ch c Kris S (USA) -Fit For A Queen (USA) (Fit To Fight (USA)) *2701a[3]* **>112a<**

**Royal Atalza (FR)** 7 gr g Saint Preuil (FR) -Crystalza (FR) (Crystal Palace (FR)) *(797) 899[8]* **>68a<**

**Royal Awakening (IRE)** 3 b g Ali-Royal (IRE) -Morning Surprise (Tragic Role (USA)) *744[8]* 3562[11] 3839[4] 4391[5] 4576[7] 5366[4] **>27a 50f<**

**Royal Axminster** 9 b g Alzao (USA) -Number One Spot (Reference Point) *455[7] 1543[5]* 2501[2] 3018[7] 3450[U] (4473) **>44a 50f<**

**Royal Bathwick (IRE)** 4 b f King s Theatre (IRE) -Ring Of Light (Auction Ring (USA)) 4240[3] 4642[3] 5074[4] 5997[6] 6286[8] **>87f<**

**Royal Beacon** 4 b c Royal Applause-Tenderetta (Tender King) 850a[9] 921a[6] 1001a[6] **>37a 107f<**

**Royal Castle (IRE)** 10 b g Caerleon (USA) -Sun Princess (English Prince) 2249[6] 2759[6] **><**

**Royal Cavalier** **7** b g Prince Of Birds (USA) -Gold Belt (IRE) (Bellypha) 418$^{12}$ (1124) 1925$^{4}$ 3521$^{5}$ 3757$^{9}$ 4858$^{17}$ >**74a 107f**<

**Royal Challenge** **3** b c Royal Applause-Anotheranniversary (Emarati (USA)) 3179$^{2}$ (3511) (4059) 4289$^{6}$ 5071$^{3}$ 5442$^{2}$ 5697$^{8}$ >**89+f**<

**Royal Claudette (ITY)** **2** b f Android (USA) -Rosa Di Renaccio (ITY) (Marouble) 5577a$^{9}$ ><

**Royal Copenhagen (FR)** **2** b f Inchinor-Amnesia (USA) (Septieme Ciel (USA)) 4964a$^{2}$ >**104f**<

**Royal Cozyfire (IRE)** **2** b g Revoque (IRE) -Mystic Thoughts (IRE) (Shernazar) 2515$^{5}$ (3140) >**57f**<

**Royal Devotion (IRE)** **4** b f Sadler s Wells (USA) -Alleged Devotion (USA) (Alleged (USA)) 2498a$^{4}$ 2993a$^{7}$ 4977a$^{8}$ (5357a) 6102a$^{10}$ >**98f**<

**Royal Dignitary (USA)** **4** bb g Saint Ballado (CAN) -Star Actress (USA) (Star De Naskra (USA)) 634a$^{3}$ 754a$^{6}$ 852a$^{5}$ 1065$^{15}$ >**90a 108f**<

**Royal Distant (USA)** **3** ch f Distant View (USA) -Encorenous (USA) (Diesis) 1322$^{6}$ 1558$^{7}$ 2070$^{7}$ 2472$^{9}$ 2732$^{8}$ 3102$^{9}$ 3473$^{8}$ 4177$^{2}$4307$^{7}$ 5223$^{14}$ 5560$^{7}$ 6074$^{9}$ 6520$^{9}$ >**70f**<

**Royale Pearl** **4** gr f Cloudings (IRE) -Ivy Edith (Blakeney) 788$^{10}$ 855$^{13}$ 1164$^{4}$ (1728) 2385$^{4}$ 3638$^{5}$ 4202$^{5}$ 4603$^{13}$ >**47a 54f**<

**Royal Experiment (USA)** **5** gr h Royal Academy (USA) -Morning Games (USA) (Grey Dawn Ii) 4380a$^{10}$ 4984a$^{7}$ 5506a$^{6}$ 6378a$^{7}$ >**102f**<

**Royal Exposure (IRE)** **7** b g Emperor Jones (USA) -Blue Garter (Targowice (USA)) 2184$^{4}$ >**10a**<

**Royal Fantasy (GER)** **4** ch f Monsun (GER) -Rudolfina (CAN) (Pleasant Colony (USA)) 3963a$^{2}$ 4566a$^{5}$ 5501a$^{2}$ 5966a$^{7}$ 6381a$^{4}$ >**111f**<

**Royal Fashion (IRE)** **4** b f Ali-Royal (IRE) -Fun Fashion (IRE) (Polish Patriot (USA)) 705$^{6}$ 821$^{9}$ >**63a 68f**<

**Royal Fire (GER)** **5** b h Bin Ajwaad (IRE) -Royal Future (GER) ( (IRE)) 3357a$^{9}$ ><

**Royal Flight** **3** b c Royal Applause-Duende (High Top) 1352$^{13}$ 5621$^{14}$ 5830$^{13}$ >**52f**<

**Royal Flynn** **2** b g Royal Applause-Shamriyna (IRE) (Darshaan) 2422$^{6}$ 3009$^{4}$ 3918$^{10}$ 5059$^{6}$ 5477$^{5}$ >**59f**<

**Royal Game** **2** b g Vettori (IRE) -Ground Game (Gildoran) 5741$^{10}$ >**42a**<

**Royal Grand** **4** ch c Prince Sabo-Hemline (Sharpo) 515$^{3}$ 681$^{11}$ 900$^{8}$ 1199$^{13}$ >**72a 78f**<

**Royal Indulgence** **4** b g Royal Applause-Silent Indulgence (USA) (Woodman (USA)) (4537) 5285$^{4}$ 5585$^{4}$ >**55f**<

**Royal Island (IRE)** **2** b c Trans Island-Royal House (FR) (Royal Academy (USA)) (1961) (2247) 2677$^{2}$ 2959$^{9}$ 4217$^{11}$ 4857$^{10}$ >**101f**<

**Royal Jelly** **2** b f King s Best (USA) -Baked Alaska (Green Desert (USA)) 5694$^{11}$ 6123$^{8}$ (6446) >**74+a 67f**<

**Royal Jet** **2** b g Royal Applause-Red Bouquet (Reference Point) 5467$^{3}$ 5716$^{6}$ 5988$^{2}$ 6308$^{5}$ >**80 f**<

**Royal Logic** **3** b f Royal Applause-Lucie Edward (Puissance) 2785$^{10}$ 3044$^{7}$ 5749$^{6}$ 5926$^{14}$ >**35f**<

**Royal Lustre** **3** b c Deputy Minister (CAN) -Snow Bride (USA) (Blushing Groom (FR)) 3916$^{11}$ 4455$^{3}$ 5007$^{9}$ 5495$^{2}$ 5891$^{5}$ >**72+f**<

**Royal Melbourne (IRE)** **4** ch g Among Men (USA) -Calachuchi (Martinmas) (2038) 2394$^{6}$ 3041$^{10}$ 3472$^{9}$ >**25a 61f**<

**Royal Millennium (IRE)** **6** b g Royal Academy (USA) -Galatrix (Be My Guest (USA)) (3308) 4595a$^{12}$ 5289$^{4}$ (5661a) 5977a$^{3}$ (6190) >**121f**<

**Royal Mistress** **2** b f Fasliyev (USA) -Regal Peace (Known Fact (USA)) 3790a$^{3}$ 4597a$^{8}$ 6320a$^{6}$ >**88f**<

**Royal Mougins** **2** br c Daylami (IRE) -Miss Riviera Golf (Hernando (FR)) 3946$^{12}$ 5653$^{5}$ 5870$^{5}$ 6265$^{3}$ 6330$^{5}$ >**69+f**<

**Royal Nite Owl** **3** b g Royal Applause-Nite-Owl Dancer (Robellino (USA)) 1012$^{8}$ 1325$^{11}$ 1701$^{4}$ 2556$^{4}$ 4391$^{3}$ 6229$^{11}$ >**23a 45f**<

**Royal Orissa** **2** b c Royal Applause-Ling Lane (Slip Anchor) 2804$^{4}$ 3240$^{5}$ 3808$^{3}$ 4235$^{8}$ 5434$^{2}$ 5896$^{5}$ 6574$^{2}$ >**84f**<

**Royal Ovation** **5** b g Royal Applause-Thevetia (Mummy s Pet) 442$^{10}$ >**62f**<

**Royal Pardon** **2** b f Royal Applause-Miss Mercy (IRE) (Law Society (USA)) 2758$^{7}$ 3741$^{8}$ 4481$^{4}$ 5234$^{4}$ 5738$^{5}$ >**56f**<

**Royal Pavillion (IRE)** **3** b g Cape Cross (IRE) -Regal Scintilla (King Of Spain) 489$^{3}$ (774) 1270$^{4}$ 1333$^{10}$ >**65a 57f**<

**Royal Prince** **3** gr c Royal Applause-Onefortheditch (USA) (With Approval (CAN)) 1295$^{4}$ (2596) (2880) 4570$^{3}$ 5443$^{3}$ 5813$^{4}$ (5920) >**70a 103f**<

**Royal Prodigy (USA)** **5** ch g Royal Academy (USA) -Prospector s Queen (USA) (Mr Prospector (USA)) 467$^{9}$ 740$^{4}$ 759$^{2}$ 5826$^{19}$ >**74a 74f**<

**Royal Racer (FR)** **6** b g Danehill (USA) -Green Rosy (USA) (Green Dancer (USA)) (1298) 1522$^{3}$ 1910$^{6}$ 2886$^{7}$ 3911$^{9}$ (4485) 5714$^{6}$ 6201$^{15}$ >**66a 66f**<

**Royal Rebel** **8** b g Robellino (USA) -Greenvera (USA) (Riverman (USA)) 1703$^{5}$ 2533$^{7}$ 2998$^{4}$ 3538$^{4}$ 4270$^{2}$ 4832$^{7}$ >**116f**<

**Royal Sailor (IRE)** **2** b c Bahhare (USA) -Old Tradition (IRE) (Royal Academy (USA)) 5716$^{11}$ 6072$^{7}$ 6453$^{7}$ 6545$^{11}$ >**56a 66f**<

**Royal Sapphire (USA)** **2** b c Kingmambo (USA) -Amethyst (IRE) (Sadler s Wells (USA)) 6331$^{9}$ >**65f**<

**Royal Shepley** **3** b f Royal Applause-Dekelsmary (Komaite (USA)) 805$^{13}$ 956$^{15}$ 1025$^{10}$ ><

**Royal Starlet** **3** b f Royal Applause-Legend (Belmez (USA)) 2842$^{8}$ 3572$^{8}$ 4499$^{4}$ 4710$^{5}$ 4798$^{9}$ 5116$^{12}$ 5549$^{8}$ >**53f**<

**Royal Storm (IRE)** **5** b h Royal Applause-Wakayi (Persian Bold) 1385$^{15}$ (1789) 3074$^{4}$ 3673$^{6}$ 4120$^{9}$ 4324$^{14}$ 4553$^{2}$ 5422$^{8}$ 5468$^{9}$(5610) 5781$^{14}$ 5888$^{9}$ 6572$^{4}$ >**87a 108f**<

**Royal Supremacy (IRE)** **3** ch f Desert Prince (IRE) -Saucy Maid (IRE) (Sure Blade (USA)) 1855$^{16}$ 2166$^{18}$ 4622$^{11}$ >**51f**<

**Royaltea** **3** ch f Desert King (IRE) -Come To Tea (IRE) (Be My Guest (USA)) 409$^{6}$ 506$^{6}$ 593$^{4}$ 1012$^{7}$ 2456$^{7}$ 5237$^{8}$ 5794$^{10}$ >**45a 36f**<

**Royal Tigress (USA)** **3** b f Storm Cat (USA) -Warm Mood (USA) (Alydar (USA)) 1070a$^{3}$ (1485a) 2160a$^{13}$ 3033$^{7}$ 3547a$^{5}$ 3968a$^{7}$ 4859$^{7}$ >**101f**<

**Royal Trigger** **4** b g Double Trigger (IRE) -Jeronime (USA) (Sauce Boat (USA)) 1272$^{20}$ 2084$^{19}$ 3181$^{11}$ 3776$^{15}$ 4473$^{16}$ 5073$^{14}$ >**50 a 50f**<

**Royal Upstart** **3** b g Up And At Em-Tycoon Tina (Tina s Pet) 1267$^{12}$ 1570$^{3}$ 2016$^{2}$ 2554$^{6}$ 2822$^{5}$ 3371$^{7}$ 4207$^{8}$ >**42a 44f**<

**Royal Warrant** **3** b c Royal Applause-Brand (Shareef Dancer (USA)) 466$^{3}$ 557$^{6}$ (843) 913$^{3}$ 2202$^{4}$ 2676$^{2}$ 3345$^{2}$ 3641$^{2}$4271$^{6}$ >**86a 102f**<

**Royal Wedding** **2** b g King s Best (USA) -Liaison (USA) (Blushing Groom (FR)) 4494$^{7}$ 4861$^{8}$ 5543$^{8}$ >**64f**<

**Royal Windmill (IRE)** **5** b g Ali-Royal (IRE) -Salarya (FR) (Darshaan) 1197$^{8}$ 1389$^{13}$ 1718$^{5}$ 3040$^{2}$ 3148$^{7}$ 3247$^{6}$ 3579$^{6}$ 4557$^{3}$5452$^{14}$ >**53 a 52f**<

**Royal Zephyr (USA)** **3** b f Royal Academy (USA) -Cassation (USA) (Lear Fan (USA)) 5510$^{10}$ >**55f**<

**Roy McAvoy (IRE)** **6** b g Danehill (USA) -Decadence (Vaigly Great) 967$^{10}$ 1082$^{14}$ 1207$^{10}$ 1691$^{4}$ 2209$^{10}$ >**79a 68f**<

**Rozanee** **4** ch f Nashwan (USA) -Belle Genius (USA) (Beau Genius (CAN)) 767$^{6}$ 1369$^{13}$ 5153$^{12}$ >**65a 68f**<

**Rubaiyat (IRE)** **3** b g Desert Story (IRE) -Lovers Parlour (Beldale Flutter (USA)) 1827$^{12}$ 2597$^{17}$ 3026$^{4}$ 3305$^{3}$ 4128$^{2}$ 4941$^{5}$ 5352$^{3}$5957$^{3}$ 6017$^{2}$ >**68a 62f**<

**Rubies** **2** ch f Inchinor-Fur Will Fly (Petong) 5070$^{2}$ 5441$^{6}$ 5825$^{2}$ 6123$^{4}$ >**74f**<

**Rubyanne (IRE)** **2** b f Fasliyev (USA) -Phyliel (USA) (Lyphard (USA)) 2370$^{6}$ (4064) 4744$^{8}$ >**84+f**<

**Ruby Muja** **2** b f Mujahid (USA) -Ruby Julie (Clantime) 3208$^{10}$ 3805$^{8}$ 4620$^{3}$ (5132) 5910$^{15}$ >**58f**<

**Ruby Murray** **2** b f Zafonic (USA) -Poppadam (Salse (USA)) 4611$^{13}$ 5270$^{9}$ 5943$^{13}$ 6118$^{10}$ >**61f**<

**Ruby Queen (GER)** **6** b m Dashing Blade-Ruby Fire (Big Shuffle (USA)) 784a$^{7}$ ><

**Ruby Rebel** **2** ch f Tomba-Miss Chiquita (IRE) (Waajib) 1390$^{15}$ 2194$^{10}$ 2364$^{10}$ 2960$^{9}$ ><

**Ruby Rocket (IRE)** **3** b f Indian Rocket-Geht Schnell (Fairy King (USA)) 1458$^{5}$ 2685$^{2}$ 3308$^{3}$ 3715$^{2}$ 4159a$^{3}$ 5471$^{2}$ 5661a$^{7}$ (6175) 6572$^{3}$ >**110f**<

**Ruby s Dream** **2** b f Tipsy Creek (USA) -Sure Flyer (IRE) (Sure Blade (USA)) 1839$^{4}$ 1984$^{2}$ 2177$^{3}$ 2382$^{4}$ 2702$^{3}$ 3770$^{5}$ 3950$^{4}$ 4243$^{8}$5839$^{12}$ 6080$^{13}$ 6294$^{12}$ >**11a 67f**<

**Ruby Wine** **2** b f Kayf Tara-Cribella (USA) (Robellino (USA)) 4712$^{2}$ >**73f**<

**Rudaki** **2** ch g Opening Verse (USA) -Persian Fountain (IRE) (Persian Heights) 3319$^{13}$ 5154$^{4}$ 5856$^{3}$ 6174$^{24}$ >**60f**<

**Rudood (USA)** **4** b g Theatrical-Kardashina (FR) (Darshaan) 647$^{5}$ 2493$^{9}$ >**82a 82f**<

**Rue D Alsace** **2** b f Danehill Dancer (IRE) -Dim Ofan (Petong) 5280a$^{5}$ >**92f**<

**Rue De Paris** **4** br g Paris House-Innocent Abroad (DEN) (Viking (USA)) 3954$^{11}$ 4568$^{5}$ 4926$^{7}$ 5283$^{15}$ >**35a 41f**<

**Rue La Fayette (SWE)** **4** b f Flying Spur (AUS) -Rue Pigalle (IRE) (Bluebird (USA)) 2162a$^{5}$ 3162a$^{2}$ 3552a$^{10}$ 4357a$^{9}$ >**106f**<

**Ruggtah** **3** gr f Daylami (IRE) -Raneen Alwatar (Sadler s Wells (USA)) 2243$^{10}$ 5339$^{3}$ 5913$^{5}$ 6088$^{10}$ >**62a 65f**<

**Rule Of Law (USA)** **3** b c Kingmambo (USA) -Crystal Crossing (IRE) (Royal Academy (USA)) 2043$^{2}$ 2680$^{2}$ 3353a$^{4}$ (4833) (5463) >**122f**<

**Rules For Jokers (IRE)** **3** b g Mujadil (USA) -Exciting (Mill Reef (USA)) 1129$^{22}$ 1478$^{6}$ >**43a 77f**<

**Ruman (IRE)** **2** b g Fayruz-Starway To Heaven (ITY) (Nordance (USA)) 5772$^{11}$ 6045$^{7}$ >**53f**<

**Rumbalara** **2** b f Intikhab (USA) -Bint Zamayem (IRE) (Rainbow Quest (USA)) 4272$^{7}$ 5179$^{2}$ (5508) >**82f**<

**Rumba Loca (IRE)** **3** b f Sri Pekan (USA) -Rumba Azul (FR) (Fabulous Dancer (USA)) (1778a) 2160a$^{10}$ 2341a$^{4}$ 4383a$^{8}$ >**103f**<

**Rumbling Bridge** **3** ch g Air Express (IRE) -Rushing River (USA) (Irish River (FR)) 4147$^{9}$ 4641$^{9}$ 5037$^{2}$ 6183$^{3}$ >**56f**<

**Rum Creek** **2** ch c Tipsy Creek (USA) -Carnbrea Belle (IRE) (Kefaah (USA)) 3749$^{15}$ 4193$^{8}$ 5534$^{11}$ 5825$^{16}$ >**65f**<

**Rum Destiny (IRE)** **5** b g Mujadil (USA) -Ruby River (Red God) 2656$^{12}$ 3169$^{18}$ 3820$^{20}$ 3864$^{13}$ 4422$^{13}$ >**32f**<

**Rumour** **4** b f Lion Cavern (USA) -Thea (USA) (Marju (IRE)) (3613) >**75+a 68+f**<

**Rumour Mill (IRE)** **3** b c Entrepreneur-Pursuit Of Truth (USA) (Irish River (FR)) 482$^{5}$ 1465$^{15}$ 2168$^{10}$ 2667$^{11}$ 3348$^{17}$ 4018$^{8}$ 4476$^{8}$ 5080$^{10}$5284$^{12}$ 5336$^{12}$ 5408$^{15}$ >**24a 24f**<

**Rum Shot** **3** b c Efisio-Glass (Bering) 2080$^{4}$ 2294$^{9}$ (4362) 4745$^{3}$ 5171a$^{6}$ 5610$^{14}$ >**113f**<

**Run On** **6** b h Runnett-Polar Storm (IRE) (Law Society (USA)) 1941$^{15}$ 2166$^{12}$ 2707$^{13}$ 2885$^{16}$ 3772$^{5}$ 4472$^{5}$ 5930$^{15}$ 6403$^{10}$ >**33a 49f**<

**Runway Model (USA)** **2** bb f Petionville (USA) -Ticket To Houston (USA) (Houston (USA)) 6485a$^{3}$ >**109a**<

**Rusky Dusky (USA)** **2** b c Stravinsky (USA) -Celtic Shade (Lomond (USA)) 2111$^{11}$ 3192$^{3}$ 3588$^{2}$ 4637$^{5}$ 4918$^{5}$ 5434$^{6}$ 5825$^{6}$ 5908$^{4}$ >**77f**<

**Russalka** **3** b f Opening Verse (USA) -Philarmonique (FR) (Trempolino (USA)) 492$^{10}$ 1309$^{15}$ 1627$^{5}$ 1843$^{8}$ 3394$^{2}$ 3827$^{6}$ 3990$^{7}$ 4654$^{6}$4853$^{13}$ 5524$^{10}$ 5702$^{5}$ 5795$^{11}$ >**63a 47 f**<

**Russian Applause** **4** b g Royal Applause-Zeffirella (Known Fact (USA)) 4615$^{9}$ 4972$^{11}$ 5204$^{4}$ 6132$^{5}$ >**68f**<

**Russian Blue (IRE)** **2** b c Danehill (USA) -Soviet Artic (FR) (Bering) (2314a) 3352a$^{2}$ 4589a$^{3}$ 4981a$^{3}$ 5678a$^{3}$ 5918$^{5}$ >**113f**<

**Russian Cafe (IRE)** **3** b f Stravinsky (USA) -Bistro (USA) (Strawberry Road (AUS)) 6089$^{3}$ 6200$^{2}$ >**64+f**<

**Russian Comrade (IRE)** **8** b g Polish Patriot (USA) -Tikarna (FR) (Targowice (USA)) 4672$^{P}$ >**69+f**<

**Russian Consort (IRE)** **2** ch c Groom Dancer (USA) -Ukraine Venture (Slip Anchor) 4022$^{2}$ (4544) 6340$^{11}$ >**83+a 68f**<

**Russian Dance (USA)** **3** br f Nureyev (USA) -Population (General Assembly (USA)) 3119$^{8}$ >**98 f**<

**Russian General (IRE)** **2** b c Soviet Star (USA) -Azra (IRE) (Danehill (USA)) (2164) >**51+f**<

**Russian Hill** **4** ch f Indian Ridge-Dievotchka (Dancing Brave (USA)) 1952a$^{2}$ 2543a$^{10}$ 4982a$^{7}$ 5966a$^{2}$ 6437a$^{4}$ >**111f**<

**Russian Icon** **3** b f Wace (USA) -Lady Millennium (IRE) (Prince Rupert (FR)) 3934$^{12}$ 4513$^{10}$ ><

**Russiannightingale** **2** b g Fraam-Nightingale Song (Tina s Pet) 6045$^{12}$ 6211$^{9}$ ><

**Russian Relation (USA)** **4** b g Kris S (USA) -Tereshkova (USA) (Mr Prospector (USA)) 709a$^{2}$ >**80f**<

**Russian Revolution** **2** b f Dubai Millennium-Russian Snows (IRE) (Sadler s Wells (USA)) 5717$^{3}$ (6111) >**80f**<

**Russian Rhythm (USA)** **4** ch f Kingmambo (USA) -Balistroika (USA) (Nijinsky (CAN)) (2109) >**123 f**<

**Russian Rio (IRE)** **2** b g Imperial Ballet (IRE) -L Harmonie (USA) (Bering) 4924$^{9}$ 5233$^{5}$ 5555$^{5}$ >**31a 66f**<

**Russian Rocket (IRE)** **2** b g Indian Rocket-Soviet Girl (IRE) (Soviet Star (USA)) 1984$^{7}$ 2376$^{5}$ 2702$^{2}$ (3418) 3930$^{2}$ 4514$^{5}$ 5947$^{17}$ (6442) >**77a 81f**<

**Russian Ruby (FR)** **3** b f Vettori (IRE) -Pink Sovietstaia (FR) (Soviet Star (USA)) 4551$^{5}$ >**79f**<

**Russian Samba (IRE)** **5** ch m Laroche (GER) -Russland (GER) (Surumu (GER)) 1259a$^{7}$ 3357a$^{8}$ 6257a$^{4}$ >**93f**<

**Russian Servana (IRE)** **2** b f Rossini (USA) -Ring Of Light (Auction Ring (USA)) 3192$^{9}$ 3526$^{2}$ 4212$^{5}$ 4651$^{5}$ >**47f**<

**Russian Symphony (USA)** **3** ch g Stravinsky (USA) -Backwoods Teacher (USA) (Woodman (USA)) 1295$^{10}$ 5541$^{6}$ 5737$^{7}$ 5801$^{8}$ 6064$^{2}$ >**73a 70f**<

**Russian Valour (IRE)** **3** b c Fasliyev (USA) -Vert Val (USA) (Septieme Ciel (USA)) 1396$^{10}$ 1706$^{6}$ 5372$^{7}$ 5553$^{7}$ >**108f**<

**Russian Waltz (IRE)** **2** b f Spectrum (IRE) -Russian Countess (USA) (Nureyev (USA)) 6101a$^{10}$ >**81f**<

**Rust En Vrede** **5** b g Royal Applause-Souveniers (Relko) (939) (1233) >**67a 53f**<

**Rustic Charm (IRE)** **4** b f Charnwood Forest (IRE) -Kabayil (Dancing Brave (USA)) 5705$^{P}$ >**73f**<

**Rustler** **2** b c Green Desert (USA) -Borgia (Machiavellian (USA)) 6555$^{7}$ >**57a**<

**Rusty Boy** **3** b g Defacto (USA) -Berl s Gift (Prince Sabo) 3839$^{7}$ 3892$^{7}$ 4393$^{9}$ >**28f**<

**Rutland Chantry (USA)** **10** b g Dixieland Band (USA) -Christchurch (FR) (So Blessed) 1305$^{5}$ 1463$^{10}$ >**67df**<

**Rutters Rebel (IRE)** **3** b g Entrepreneur-No Quest (IRE) (Rainbow Quest (USA)) 1470$^{5}$ 1899$^{9}$ 2529$^{4}$ 2782$^{7}$ 3232$^{2}$ 3584$^{4}$ 3953$^{9}$ (4536) 5303$^{11}$5517$^{6}$ 5842$^{9}$ >**77f**<

**Ryan s Bliss (IRE)** **4** b f Danetime (IRE) -Raja Moulana (Raja Baba (USA)) 821$^{8}$ 948$^{8}$ 1166$^{2}$ 1277$^{5}$ 1545$^{3}$ 2053$^{2}$ 2939$^{8}$3490$^{9}$ 4339$^{10}$ 4519$^{5}$ 4972$^{6}$ (5643) 6154$^{3}$ >**62a 48 f**<

**Ryan s Future (IRE)** **4** b c Danetime (IRE) -Era (Dalsaan) 577$^{5}$ 649$^{8}$ 3872$^{9}$ 4237$^{5}$ 4691$^{2}$ 4950$^{7}$ 5423$^{4}$ 5866$^{5}$6043$^{8}$ (6546) >**87 a 87f**<

**Ryans Lil Ol Gal** **2** b f Namaqualand (USA) -Kirby s Princess (Indian King (USA)) 1589$^{14}$ 1735$^{12}$ 2140$^{11}$ >**8f**<

**Ryan s Quest (IRE)** **5** b m Mukaddamah (USA) -Preponderance (IRE) (Cyrano De Bergerac) 1228$^{8}$ 2482$^{15}$ 3175$^{8}$ 4440$^{3}$ >**49a 55f**<

**Rydal (USA)** **3** ch g Gilded Time (USA) -Tennis Partner (USA) (Northern Dancer) 1063$^{13}$ 1745$^{4}$ 2897$^{11}$ 3092$^{6}$ 3777$^{2}$ 3926$^{4}$ 4289$^{7}$ (4688) 4952$^{4}$5660a$^{5}$ 5762$^{8}$ 6243$^{8}$ >**76+a 90f**<

**Rye (IRE)** **3** b f Charnwood Forest (IRE) -Silver Hut (USA) (Silver Hawk (USA)) (948) 1100$^{6}$ 1297$^{7}$ 1579$^{4}$ >**64a 64f**<

**Ryedane (IRE)** **2** b c Danetime (IRE) -Miss Valediction (IRE) (Petardia) 2035$^{9}$ 2526$^{3}$ 3196$^{9}$ 3605$^{5}$ 4046$^{3}$ 4508$^{7}$ 5234$^{12}$ >**63f**<

**Rymer s Rascal** **12** b g Rymer-City Sound (On Your Mark) 1710$^{3}$ 2368$^{2}$ 2938$^{8}$ 3247$^{8}$ 3520$^{2}$ 4511$^{15}$ 4605$^{6}$ (5305) 5587$^{2}$6142$^{3}$ >**9a 56f**<

**Ryono (USA)** **5** ch h Mountain Cat (USA) -Racing Blue (Reference Point) (3791a) 5169a$^{5}$ 5809a$^{5}$ 6109a$^{7}$ >**118?f**<

## S

**Saadigg (IRE)** **2** b c Indian Danehill (IRE) -White Cap S (Shirley Heights) 4023$^{3}$ 4544$^{4}$ (5264) 6122$^{6}$ >**65a 88f**<

**Saameq (IRE)** **3** b g Bahhare (USA) -Tajawuz (Kris) 1116$^{6}$ 1285$^{7}$ 3007$^{7}$ 3369$^{3}$ 3881$^{4}$ 4536$^{4}$ >**53f**<

**Sabalara (IRE)** **4** b f Mujadil (USA) -Sabaniya (FR) (Lashkari) 1265$^{8}$ 1606$^{7}$ 1992$^{15}$ 2597$^{13}$ >**66f**<

**Sabana (IRE)** **6** b g Sri Pekan (USA) -Atyaaf (USA) (Irish River (FR)) 422$^{4}$ 530$^{3}$ 573$^{5}$ 725$^{9}$ (799) 936$^{3}$ 1018$^{11}$ 1477$^{6}$1516$^{13}$ 1994$^{8}$ 2178$^{11}$ 3533$^{14}$ (3742) 3935$^{6}$ 4350$^{9}$ >**59a 58f**<

**Sabander Bay (USA)** **3** b f Lear Fan (USA) -Sambac (USA) (Mr Prospector (USA)) 4916$^{8}$ 5537$^{8}$ >**55f**<

**Sabbaag (USA)** **3** ch c Mark Of Esteem (IRE) -Saabga (USA) (Woodman (USA)) 550$^{2}$ (585) 704$^{10}$ >**75a**<

**Sabbeeh (USA)** **3** b c Red Ransom (USA) -Capistrano Day (USA) (Diesis) 5610$^{9}$ (6116) >**107 f**<

**Sabbiosa (IRE)** **2** b f Desert Prince (IRE) -Alla Marcia (IRE) (Marju (IRE)) 3272$^{7}$ 4053$^{10}$ 4705$^{8}$ 5114$^{7}$ >**63+f**<

**Sabiango (GER)** **6** ch h Acatenango (GER) -Spirit Of Eagles (USA) (Beau s Eagle (USA)) 4768a$^{11}$ 6384a$^{9}$ >**116f**<

**Sabirli (TUR)** **3** b c Strike The Gold (USA) -Free Trade (TUR) (Shareef Dancer (USA)) 5488a$^{2}$ ><

**Sable n Silk** **3** b f Prince Sabo-Sibilant (Selkirk (USA)) 640$^{7}$ 758$^{6}$ >**51a**<

**Sabo Prince** **2** ch g Atraf-Moving Princess (Prince Sabo) 2140$^{7}$ 2321$^{5}$ 2702$^{9}$ 3140$^{8}$ >**24f**<

**Sabreline** **5** ch m Sabrehill (USA) -Story Line (In The Wings) 655$^{9}$ ><

**Sabrina Brown** **3** br f Polar Falcon (USA) -So True (So Blessed) 3211$^{2}$ 3700$^{2}$ 3910$^{14}$ 4680$^{6}$ (4868) 5148$^{2}$ 5887$^{14}$ >**52a 77f**<

**Saccharine** **3** b f Whittingham (IRE) -Sweet And Lucky (Lucky Wednesday) 3271$^{10}$ 4484$^{3}$ 4801$^{6}$ 5001$^{7}$ >**19a 47f**<

**Sachin** **3** b g Bijou D Inde-Dark Kristal (IRE) (Gorytus (USA)) 891$^{7}$ 1119$^{6}$ 4126$^{9}$ 5424$^{4}$ (5829) 6271$^{3}$ 6461$^{8}$ 6549$^{7}$ >**59a 70f**<

**Sacho (GER)** **6** br g Dashing Blade-She s His Guest (IRE) (Be My Guest (USA)) 2466a$^{3}$ 3552a$^{8}$ 5255a$^{8}$ >**100f**<

**Sachsenwalzer (GER)** **6** ch g Top Waltz (FR) -Stairway To Heaven (GER) (Nebos (GER)) 2547$^{9}$ >**36f**<

**Sacranun** **2** ch c Pivotal-Spanish Craft (IRE) (Jareer (USA)) 3568a$^{2}$ 3925$^{3}$ 5290$^{7}$ 5772$^{4}$ >**80f**<

**Sacred Nuts (IRE)** **2** b c Sri Pekan (USA) -Sagrada (GER) (Primo Dominie) 2674$^{5}$ (2972) (3727) 4166$^{3}$ 4342$^{5}$ 4857$^{4}$ >**100f**<

**Sacsayhuaman** **5** b m Halling (USA) -La Dolce Vita (Mazilier (USA)) 734$^{7}$ >**51a 70f**<

**Saddad (USA)** **5** ch h Gone West (USA) -Lite Light (USA) (Majestic Light (USA)) (923a) >**92a 112f**<

**Saddler s Quest** **7** b g Saddlers Hall (IRE) -Seren Quest (Rainbow Quest (USA)) 3929$^{13}$ 4398$^{9}$ 4911$^{8}$ 5238$^{13}$ >**40a 45f**<

**Sadie s Star (IRE)** **2** b f Indian Lodge (IRE) -Nishiki (USA) (Brogan (USA)) 5307$^{8}$ 5856$^{5}$ 6479$^{12}$ >**20a 47f**<

**Sadie Thompson (IRE)** **2** b f King s Best (USA) -Femme Fatale (Fairy King (USA)) 3905$^{8}$ (5349) >**77f**<

**Sadler s Pride (IRE)** **4** b g Sadler s Wells (USA) -Gentle Thoughts (Darshaan) 1662$^{2}$ 2090$^{2}$ 2652$^{4}$ 4210$^{12}$ 4870$^{15}$ 5229$^{8}$ 5635$^{5}$ >**73f**<

**Sadler s Rock (IRE)** **6** b g Sadler s Wells (USA) -Triple Couronne (USA) (Riverman (USA)) 4939$^{9}$ 5133$^{7}$ >**58a 70f**<

**Sadlers Swing (USA)** **8** b g Red Ransom (USA) -Noblissima (IRE) (Sadler s Wells (USA)) 940$^{2}$ 989$^{4}$ 1592$^{9}$ >**45a 25f**<

**Sa Erola (ITY)** **4** b f Muhtarram (USA) -Bella Domani (Cadeaux Genereux) 1776a$^{5}$ >**99f**<

**Safa Park** **3** ch g Machiavellian (USA) -Ozone Friendly (USA) (Green Forest (USA)) 2401$^{8}$ 3843$^{9}$ >**65f**<

**Safari Sunset (IRE)** **2** b g Fayruz-Umlani (IRE) (Great Commotion (USA)) (2522) 2959$^{3}$ 3696$^{4}$ 4217$^{3}$ 5295$^{8}$ 5464$^{9}$ >**94f**<

**Sa Fem Zifulum (IRE)** **3** ch c Desert King (IRE) -Velate (USA) (Spend A Buck (USA)) 2510a$^{9}$ 3136a$^{5}$ >**107f**<

**Safendonseabiscuit** **2** b c Danzig Connection (USA) -The Fugative (Nicholas (USA)) 2225$^{5}$ 2470$^{3}$ 3259$^{3}$ 3553$^{4}$ 3886$^{2}$ 4342$^{10}$ 5202$^{12}$ 5745$^{3}$(5989) 6174$^{18}$ >**81f**<

**Saffa Garden (IRE)** **2** b f King s Best (USA) -Allegheny River (USA) (Lear Fan (USA)) 2388$^{8}$ 3676$^{10}$ 5250$^{11}$ >**58f**<

**Saffron Fox** **3** ch f Safawan-Fox Oa (FR) (French Friend (USA)) 1322$^{4}$ 1588$^{7}$ 2557$^{4}$ 3728$^{2}$ 4368$^{10}$ 4760$^{7}$ 5990$^{5}$ 6332$^{18}$ >**85f**<

**Saffron River** **3** b c Polar Prince (IRE) -Cloudy

Reef (Cragador) *6275$^5$* **>54a<**
**Safin (GER)** 4 b c Pennekamp (USA) -Sankt Johanna (GER) (High Game) 785a$^7$ 1655a$^{DSQ}$ ><
**Safirah** 3 b f Singspiel (IRE) -Princess Haifa (USA) (Mr Prospector (USA)) 3422$^3$ 3843$^5$ 4583$^5$ 5768$^{10}$ 6082$^2$ (6519) **>70f<**
**Safranine (IRE)** 7 b m Dolphin Street (FR) -Webbiana (African Sky) *4531$^{11}$ 6371$^{10}$ 8761$^{12}$* 2143$^9$ 2366$^9$ 2506$^{10}$ 2909$^9$ 3098$^{16}$3126$^8$ 3223$^6$ 3339$^9$ 3407$^{17}$ 4104$^{14}$ 4317$^6$ **>35a 81f<**
**Safsoof (USA)** 2 b c Gilded Time (USA) -Halcyon Bird (IRE) (Storm Bird (CAN)) 2574$^2$ 2959$^{10}$ *(4187)* 5711$^3$ **>83a 88f<**
**Sahaat** 6 bb g Machiavellian (USA) -Tawaaded (IRE) (Nashwan (USA)) *1009$^7$* 1114$^{22}$ 1272$^{14}$ 2116$^{14}$ 3143$^5$ 3536$^{10}$ *4093$^2$* 4616$^5$4852$^8$ 5006$^4$ 5257$^6$ 5853$^7$ 6096$^4$ (6266) **>84a 75f<**
**Sahara Mist (IRE)** 2 b f Desert Style (IRE) -Tereed Elhawa (Cadeaux Genereux) 1105$^{14}$ *1234$^6$* 1751$^5$ 4804$^{12}$ 5753$^{10}$ **>34a 41f<**
**Saharan Song (IRE)** 3 ch f Singspiel (IRE) -Sahara Baladee (USA) (Shadeed (USA)) 1461$^{12}$ 2145$^9$ 3156$^9$ 5622$^{12}$ *6061$^{12}$* **>57a 60f<**
**Sahara Prince (IRE)** 4 b g Desert King (IRE) -Chehana (Posse (USA)) (4677) **>89f<**
**Sahara Scirocco (IRE)** 3 b g Spectrum (IRE) -St Bride s Bay (Caerleon (USA)) *6157$^{14}$ 6224$^{11}$* **>53f<**
**Sahara Silk (IRE)** 3 b f Desert Style (IRE) -Buddy And Soda (IRE) (Imperial Frontier (USA)) *5431$^0$ 6101$^4$ 731$^6$ (747) 819$^3$ 868$^4$ (1047) 1626$^2$1737$^8$ 2850$^3$* 3077$^{12}$ 3273$^9$ 3624$^7$ **>74a 59f<**
**Sahara Sonnet (USA)** 3 b f Stravinsky (USA) -Sahara Sun (USA) (Alysheba (USA)) 1634a$^S$ **>86f<**
**Sahara Storm (IRE)** 3 b f Desert Prince (IRE) -Deluge (Rainbow Quest (USA)) *1229$^{10}$* 2577$^{10}$ **>65a 71f<**
**Sahem (IRE)** 7 b g Sadler s Wells (USA) -Sumava (IRE) (Sure Blade (USA)) 1112$^5$ 1661$^7$ 1785$^4$ 2047$^7$ (2935) 3078$^2$ 3725$^{17}$ 4453$^3$ 4777$^3$(4990) 5288$^{12}$ 5517$^3$ 5834$^6$ **>89f<**
**Sahool** 3 b f Unfuwain (USA) -Mathaayl (USA) (Shadeed (USA)) 1793$^2$ 2081$^2$ 2997$^2$ 3519$^2$ (4367) 4859$^5$ **>109f<**
**Saida Lenasera (FR)** 3 b f Fasliyev (USA) -Lanasara (Generous (IRE)) 2070$^9$ 2472$^6$ 3050$^6$ 4628$^{10}$ 5410$^5$ 6006$^5$ *6495$^7$* **>59a 74f<**
**Saif Sareea** 4 b g Atraf-Slipperose (Persepolis (FR)) 2779$^{11}$ 3226$^8$ 3559$^{14}$ **>21a 54f<**
**Sailing Through** 4 b g Bahhare (USA) -Hopesay (Warning) 5761$^{13}$ **>76a 101+f<**
**Sailmaker (IRE)** 3 ch g Peintre Celebre (USA) -Princess Amalie (USA) (Rahy (USA)) 1311$^2$ 1827$^3$ 2169$^7$ 2841$^3$ 3213$^4$ **>78+f<**
**Sailorman** 3 b g Alzao (USA) -Sweet Pea (Persian Bold) *2486$^9$* **>52a<**
**Sail With The Tide (IRE)** 4 b f Charnwood Forest (IRE) -Good Relations (Be My Guest (USA)) 831a$^{10}$ 1002a$^8$ **>53a 78f<**
**Saint Clements (USA)** 2 b g Lemon Drop Kid (USA) -Sophisticated Lynn (USA) (Clever Trick (USA)) 2234$^9$ 2674$^{10}$ 5082$^4$ **>40f<**
**Saint Etienne (IRE)** 3 b f Robellino (USA) -Stop Out (Rudimentary (USA)) *(816)* 2308$^5$ 4286$^{10}$ **>55+a 86f<**
**Saint Lazare (IRE)** 3 b c Peintre Celebre (USA) -Height Of Passion (Shirley Heights) 1224$^{16}$ **>55f<**
**Saintly Place** 3 ch g Compton Place-Always On A Sunday (Star Appeal) 3747$^{12}$ 4717$^{13}$ 4868$^{15}$ 5336$^5$ 5552$^2$ 6058$^8$ *6401$^9$* **>26a 57f<**
**Saintly Rachel (IRE)** 6 b m Religiously (USA) -Ursha (IRE) (Shardari) 4588a$^6$ **>81f<**
**Saintly Scholar (USA)** 3 b f Danzig (USA) -Tres Facile (USA) (Easy Goer (USA)) *982$^{10}$ 1052$^9$ 1202$^5$* **>58a<**
**Saintly Thoughts (USA)** 9 bb g St Jovite (USA) -Free Thinker (USA) (Shadeed (USA)) 1754$^{15}$ **>62da 62df<**
**Saint Zita (IRE)** 3 b f Desert Sun-Chatelsong (USA) (Seattle Song (USA)) *766$^7$ 9161$^0$* 3681$^7$ **>47a<**
**Sake (IRE)** 2 b g Shinko Forest (IRE) -Drosera (IRE) (Thatching) 5858$^{12}$ 6067$^{12}$ **>41f<**
**Salagama (IRE)** 4 br f Alzao (USA) -Waffle On (Chief Singer) 1931$^4$ 2630$^3$ 3320$^9$ 3597$^{20}$ **>87f<**
**Salamanca** 2 ch f Pivotal-Salanka (IRE) (Persian Heights) (4714) (5648) 5939$^6$ **>95f<**
**Salamba** 3 ch g Indian Ridge-Towaahi (IRE) (Caerleon (USA)) 1747$^5$ 4062$^{10}$ 4512$^8$ 6074$^5$ 6198$^7$ 6269$^7$ **>73f<**
**Saldentigerin (GER)** 3 b f Tiger Hill (IRE) -Salde (GER) (Alkalde (GER)) 2157a$^2$ 2723a$^3$ 3565a$^4$ 5168a$^2$ 5824a$^2$ 6381a$^8$ **>108f<**
**Saleen (IRE)** 4 b f Kahyasi-Sabrata (IRE) (Zino) *5201$^0$* **>18a<**
**Salerno** 5 ch g Mark Of Esteem (IRE) -Shamwari (USA) (Shahrastani (USA)) *411$^8$ 460$^9$* **>61 a 60df<**
**Salford City (IRE)** 3 b c Desert Sun-Summer Fashion (Moorestyle) (1459) 1764$^6$ 2680$^5$ 3540$^9$ **>119 f<**
**Salford Flyer** 8 b g Pharly (FR) -Edge Of Darkness (Vaigly Great) *1054$^{12}$ 1101$^6$* 1308$^7$ 1687$^3$ 1858$^3$ 2375$^{16}$ **>44a 50f<**
**Salford Rocket** 4 b g Slip Anchor-Mysterious Maid (USA) (L Emigrant (USA)) *1628$^8$* 1911$^9$ 2323$^6$ 2978$^9$ *4883$^6$* 5159$^9$ **>13a 21f<**
**Salinja (USA)** 2 b c Boundary (USA) -Lasha (USA) (Rahy (USA)) 4172$^3$ 5535$^3$ 5897$^2$ **>89f<**
**Salinor** 4 ch g Inchinor-Salanka (IRE) (Persian Heights) (1675) (2304) 3198$^{16}$ 5574$^6$ 5886$^{12}$ **>47a 89+f<**
**Salisbury Plain** 3 b c Mark Of Esteem (IRE) -Wild Pavane (Dancing Brave (USA)) 1831$^{10}$ 2202$^{18}$ **>70f<**
**Sally Traffic** 5 b m River Falls-Yankeedoodledancer (Mashhor Dancer (USA)) *502$^7$* **>22a 41f<**
**Salonhonor (GER)** 3 b c Highest Honor (FR) -Salonrolle (IRE) (Tirol) 3565a$^7$ 5168a$^5$ 5975a$^2$ **>107f<**
**Salonika Sky** 3 ch f Pursuit Of Love-Willisa (Polar Falcon (USA)) *5301$^2$ 718$^6$ 7801$^2$* 3364$^6$ 3836$^{14}$ **>15a 37f<**
**Salon Prive** 4 b g Green Desert (USA) -Shot At Love (IRE) (Last Tycoon) *1087$^9$* 2030$^{15}$ *4026$^2$* 4522$^6$ 5261$^2$ 5597$^{11}$ **>72a 60f<**
**Salon Turtle (GER)** 5 b h Turtle Island (IRE) -Salonrolle (IRE) (Tirol) 6508a$^4$ **>90f<**
**Salsa Brava (IRE)** 2 b f Almutawakel-Ridotto (Salse (USA)) (2177) 3031$^3$ 3599$^2$ 4885$^2$ 5649$^4$ **>103 f<**
**Salsalino** 4 ch g Salse (USA) -Alicedale (USA) (Trempolino (USA)) 1455$^6$ 2067$^8$ 2220$^{12}$ 4858$^{15}$ 5435$^{15}$ **>88a 111f<**
**Salsaneyev (FR)** 4 b f Stepneyev (IRE) -Salsola (USA) (Storm Bird (CAN)) *5103a$^9$* ><
**Salse Bravo** 3 b f Salse (USA) -Amapola (IRE) (Shirley Heights) 1805a$^6$ (3569a) ><
**Salselon** 5 b h Salse (USA) -Heady (Rousillon (USA)) 1621$^9$ 2109$^2$ 2957$^3$ 3724$^7$ 4795a$^5$ 5225$^2$ 5492$^3$ 5917$^2$6216$^6$ **>120f<**
**Saltango (GER)** 5 b g Acatenango (GER) -Salde (GER) (Alkalde (GER)) *2881$^8$* 3199$^3$ 4033$^5$ **>66a 79f<**
**Salutare (IRE)** 4 b f Sadler s Wells (USA) -Contare (Shirley Heights) 1182a$^7$ 2320a$^7$ **>94f<**
**Salut Saint Cloud** 3 b g Primo Dominie-Tiriana (Common Grounds) 1363$^6$ 2657$^8$ *2854$^5$* (3056) 3393$^3$ *4189$^3$* 4467$^3$ *(4883) 4927$^4$*(5178) 5354$^8$ **>67a 72+f<**
**Salut Thomas (FR)** 2 ch c Adnaan (IRE) -Salut Bebs (FR) (Kendor (FR)) 3388a$^3$ 4184a$^5$ 4382a$^3$ 4981a$^6$ 5404a$^3$ 5922a$^4$ 6202a$^2$ 6462a$^2$ **>112f<**
**Salviati (USA)** 7 b g Lahib (USA) -Mother Courage (Busted) 2041$^{20}$ 2293$^{12}$ 2488$^{16}$ 3074$^{23}$ 3266$^{12}$ 3645$^{15}$ 3775$^8$ 3920$^{12}$4011$^4$ 4232$^5$ (4366) 4538$^{18}$ 4748$^{10}$ 5071$^{10}$ 5550$^9$ **>96f<**
**Salydora (FR)** 4 ch f Peintre Celebre (USA) -Silwana (FR) (Nashwan (USA)) 1952a$^9$ **>99f<**
**Samalan** 2 b g Grey Desire-Shalari (IRE) (Shalford (IRE)) 2248$^9$ 3469$^{11}$ **>17f<**
**Samando (FR)** 4 ch f Hernando (FR) -Samshu (Nashwan (USA)) 980a$^3$ 1261a$^6$ 1952a$^3$ 2543a$^7$ 4039a$^6$ 4982a$^6$ (5966a) 6383a$^4$ **>111f<**
**Samara Sound** 3 b c Savahra Sound-Hosting (Thatching) *7321$^0$ 1243$^6$* 1689$^{13}$ **>54?a 41f<**
**Samaria (GER)** 3 bb f Acatenango (GER) -Suanita (GER) (Big Shuffle (USA)) 3348$^{13}$ 4583$^4$ 4819$^2$ 5196$^4$ *5913$^3$* 6443$^7$ **>69a 73f<**
**Samar Qand** 5 b m Selkirk (USA) -Sit Alkul (USA) (Mr Prospector (USA)) *427$^5$ 783$^3$ 1026$^3$ 1091$^4$* 1263$^{13}$ **>41a 35f<**
**Samba Beat** 5 ch m Efisio-Special Beat (Bustino) *939$^{11}$ 952$^9$ 1091$^9$ 2229$^8$* **>42a 20f<**
**Sambaprinz (GER)** 5 br h Big Shuffle (USA) -Samambaia (GER) (Ti Amo (GER)) 2336a$^5$ (3335a) 3792a$^5$ 4378a$^{12}$ **>111f<**
**Sambarina (IRE)** 2 b f Victory Note (USA) -Brazilia (Forzando) 3476$^3$ 4243$^5$ **>66f<**
**Sammagefromtenesse (IRE)** 7 b g Petardia-Canoora (Ahonoora) *5644$^2$* **>38a 51f<**
**Sammiyo (IRE)** 4 b c Revoque (IRE) -Sigonella (IRE) (Priolo (USA)) 2340a$^4$ **>102f<**
**Sammy s Shuffle** 9 b g Touch Of Grey-Cabinet Shuffle (Thatching) *765$^9$ 874$^4$ 966$^7$* 1644$^9$ 2034$^{11}$ 2594$^4$ *3088$^8$* 3459$^5$ **>54a 49f<**
**Samson Quest** 2 b c Cyrano De Bergerac-Zenita (IRE) (Zieten (USA)) *4023$^5$* 5534$^9$ **>54a 51f<**
**Sam s Secret** 2 b f Josr Algarhoud (IRE) -Twilight Time (Aragon) 5319$^2$ 5586$^3$ 5864$^2$ 6344$^{12}$ **>85f<**
**Sam The Sorcerer** 3 b g Wizard King-Awham (USA) (Lear Fan (USA)) 1942$^9$ *(2187) 2232$^9$* 3234$^3$ 5081$^{11}$ 6567$^{16}$ **>43a 40f<**
**Samuel Charles** 6 b g Green Desert (USA) -Hejraan (USA) (Alydar (USA)) *(1207) 1475$^2$* 2030$^3$ (2218) 2291$^2$ 2553$^2$ 2838$^3$ 3039$^3$ 3079$^4$3525$^2$ 4067$^{11}$ (4437) 5244$^6$ 5818$^{10}$ *(5952) 6062$^4$ 6480$^3$* **>83a 83f<**
**San Antonio** 4 b g Efisio-Winnebago (Kris) 1840$^8$ 4061$^6$ 4569$^{12}$ **>32a 91f<**
**Sanbonah (USA)** 3 b f King Of Kings (IRE) -Oh Nellie (USA) (Tilt The Stars (CAN)) 2306$^{14}$ **>70f<**
**Sanchi (IRE)** 2 b c Darshaan-Samara (IRE) (Polish Patriot (USA)) 5396$^3$ **>84+f<**
**Sand And Stars (IRE)** 3 ch f Dr Devious (IRE) -Charm The Stars (Roi Danzig (USA)) 2529$^3$ 2848$^5$ 3250$^2$ (3584) 3919$^2$ 4888$^8$ 5402$^3$ 6087$^2$ **>87f<**
**San Dany (IRE)** 4 b c Danetime (IRE) -Pharmacy (Mtoto) 3816a$^9$ **>79f<**
**Sandbox (IRE)** 3 ch f Grand Lodge (USA) -Seralia (FR) (Royal Academy (USA)) 5969a$^5$ **>96f<**
**San Deng** 2 gr c Averti (IRE) -Miss Mirror (Magic Mirror) 4117$^8$ 4481$^3$ 4866$^{13}$ 5376$^{14}$ *6012$^8$* **>44a 61f<**
**Sandgate Cygnet** 4 ch f Fleetwood (IRE) -Dance Of The Swans (IRE) (Try My Best (USA)) *(407)* **>75a 66f<**
**San Dimas (USA)** 7 gr g Distant View (USA) -Chrystophard (USA) (Lypheor) 4275$^9$ **>43a 16f<**
**Sand Iron (IRE)** 2 b f Desert Style (IRE) -Mettlesome (Lomond (USA)) *5380$^6$* 5771$^4$ *6291$^8$* **>62a 67f<**
**Sand N Sea (IRE)** 3 b f Desert Story (IRE) -Poscimur (IRE) (Prince Rupert (FR)) 2711a$^3$ 2971$^{16}$ 5162a$^{12}$ **>86f<**
**Sandokan (GER)** 3 b g Tiger Hill (IRE) -Suivez (FR) (Fioravanti (USA)) 4972$^7$ 6130$^{11}$ 6310$^7$ 6524$^8$ **>59f<**
**Sandorra** 6 b m Emperor Jones (USA) -Oribi (Top Ville) *429$^3$ (474) 588$^6$ 7001$^1$ 9391$^0$ (1915)* 1992$^6$ *2811$^{12}$3800$^8$* 4905$^5$ **>53a 49f<**
**Sand Repeal (IRE)** 2 b g Revoque (IRE) -Columbian Sand (IRE) (Salmon Leap (USA)) 4169$^7$ 5023$^3$ 6308$^2$ **>70f<**
**Sandy Bay (IRE)** 5 b g Spectrum (IRE) -Karinski (USA) (Palace Music (USA)) *1077$^{12}$* 1318$^8$ 4004$^8$ 4423$^{11}$ 4631$^4$ 5344$^{12}$ 5817$^3$ 6245$^5$ **>43?f<**
**Sandy s Legend (USA)** 2 ch c Tale Of The Cat (USA) -Avasand (USA) (Avatar (USA)) 5897$^{11}$ *6223$^5$ 6555$^2$* **>62a 48f<**
**Sanfrancullinan (IRE)** 2 b f Bluebird (USA) -Harir (Kris) 5681a$^9$ **>73f<**
**Sangiovese** 5 b g Piccolo-Kaprisky (IRE) (Red Sunset) *5771$^0$ 749$^3$ 837$^3$* 1132$^5$ 1757$^2$ 2170$^3$ (2810) (3207) 3678$^7$4772$^5$ 5297$^{14}$ 6128$^5$ (6358) **>91a 84f<**
**San Hernando** 4 b g Hernando (FR) -Sandrella (IRE) (Darshaan) 1135$^6$ 1457$^4$ 1801$^{10}$ 2285$^7$ 2787$^4$ 3244$^9$ 3851$^4$ 4146$^2$4647$^8$ 5274$^8$ 5875$^{19}$ (6084) 6460$^3$ **>79f<**
**San Lorenzo (UAE)** 3 ch f Machiavellian (USA) -Sanchez (Wolfhound (USA)) 2223$^8$ 2621$^3$ 2984$^2$ **>70f<**
**San Marco (IRE)** 6 b g Brief Truce (USA) -Nuit Des Temps (Sadler s Wells (USA)) *7241$^1$ 812$^7$* **>20 a 20 f<**
**San Rachele (USA)** 3 b f Stravinsky (USA) -Viridis (USA) (Green Dancer (USA)) 3816a$^{14}$ ><
**San Salvador (USA)** 7 bb g Dayjur (USA) -Sheer Gold (USA) (Cutlass (USA)) *(632a) 689a$^3$ 977a$^3$* **>102a<**
**Sanserif (IRE)** 2 b f Fasliyev (USA) -Certain Charm (USA) (Thunder Gulch (USA)) 5325a$^8$ **>94f<**
**Santa Catalina (IRE)** 5 br m Tagula (IRE) -Bui-Doi (IRE) (Dance Of Life (USA)) *472$^7$ 7871$^0$ 953$^5$ 1024$^4$ 1136$^{10}$ 1277$^{13}$* **>46a 46f<**
**Santa Caterina (IRE)** 3 b f Daylami (IRE) -Samara (IRE) (Polish Patriot (USA)) 2059$^4$ 3232$^5$ 3746$^2$ 4493$^{11}$ 5293$^7$ 5770$^3$ 6285$^2$ 6546$^7$ **>76f<**
**Santa Fe (IRE)** 2 b c Green Desert (USA) -Shimna (Mr Prospector (USA)) 4494$^5$ (5373) 5895$^4$ **>102f<**
**Santando** 4 b g Hernando (FR) -Santarem (USA) (El Gran Senor (USA)) *418$^5$ 558$^3$ 688a$^{10}$* 849a$^5$ 3521$^{14}$ 3757$^8$ 4218$^4$ 4529$^9$4858$^{12}$ 5435$^{10}$ 6346$^8$ **>103a 99f<**
**Santiago Matias (CHI)** 5 b h Golden Voyager (USA) -Costa Azul (USA) (Semenenko) 4380a$^8$ 5506a$^5$ 6378a$^{11}$ **>74f<**
**Santiburi Lad (IRE)** 7 b g Namaqualand (USA) -Suggia (Alzao (USA)) 1962$^3$ 2394$^2$ (2649) (3510) 3781$^2$ 4213$^{17}$ 5317$^8$ 5768$^7$ 6096$^{14}$ **>61a 75f<**
**Sant Jordi** 2 b c Cape Cross (IRE) -Foresta Verde (USA) (Green Forest (USA)) *3847$^3$* (4809) 5872$^2$ 6100a$^3$ **>71a 95f<**
**Saoire** 2 ch f Pivotal-Polish Descent (IRE) (Danehill (USA)) 5325a$^3$ 5961a$^2$ **>102f<**
**Saorsie** 6 b g Emperor Jones (USA) -Exclusive Lottery (Presidium) *4603$^7$* ><
**Saposcat (IRE)** 4 b g Groom Dancer (USA) -Dance Of Joy (Shareef Dancer (USA)) 4042$^8$ **>19f<**
**Sapphire Dream** 2 b f Mind Games-Bombay Sapphire (Be My Chief (USA)) 1498$^2$ 1878$^2$ (2296) 2568$^6$ 3031$^{17}$ 4541$^4$ 4875$^4$ 5434$^{11}$ **>77f<**
**Sapphire Princess** 2 b f Namaqualand (USA) -Breakfast Creek (Hallgate) 2725$^4$ 3140$^5$ 3571$^5$ 4200$^6$ *(4516)* 4620$^5$ 4816$^7$ 5369$^{19}$ **>54a 43f<**
**Sapphire Sky** 3 bb f Compton Place-Jewel (IRE) (Cyrano De Bergerac) *1243$^{12}$* 1906$^{12}$ 2586$^{15}$ ><
**Sarafan (USA)** 7 b g Lear Fan (USA) -Saraa Ree (USA) (Caro) 1146a$^{10}$ 1657a$^{12}$ **>120f<**
**Sarah Brown (IRE)** 2 b f Benny The Dip (USA) -Lalique (IRE) (Lahib (USA)) 2263$^7$ 3259$^{10}$ 4913$^{10}$ 5172$^{10}$ **>48f<**
**Saratan (IRE)** 7 gr g Tirol-Sarafia (Dalsaan) 1780a$^{11}$ 2438a$^2$ 2923a$^8$ 3361a$^6$ **>113f<**
**Saratoga Splendour (USA)** 3 b f Diesis-Saratoga One (USA) (Saratoga Six (USA)) 1250$^6$ 2411$^{11}$ 3581$^9$ **>42f<**
**Saratoga Sugar (USA)** 3 b f Gone West (USA) -Connecting Link (USA) (Linkage (USA)) 5530a$^7$ ><
**Sarayat** 4 br c Polar Falcon (USA) -Montserrat (Aragon) *634a$^9$* 755a$^{13}$ *923a$^8$* **>69a 104f<**
**Sarem (USA)** 2 bb c Kingmambo (USA) -Storm Beauty (USA) (Storm Cat (USA)) 4747$^7$ 5915$^4$ **>77+f<**
**Sarenne** 3 b f Desert Sun-Fabulous Pet (Somethingfabulous (USA)) 4987$^6$ 5237$^6$ 6182$^5$ **>45f<**
**Sargents Dream** 4 b f Regal Embers (IRE) -Dance Lady (Cosmonaut) *5021$^0$* **>5a<**
**Sariba** 5 b m Persian Bold-En Vacances (IRE) (Old Vic) *839$^7$ 1281$^6$ (1547)* 2429$^5$ 2874$^6$ **>42a 48f<**
**Saristar** 3 b f Starborough-Sari (Faustus (USA)) (1388) 2309$^{18}$ 4126$^7$ 5148$^5$ (5588) 5762$^{13}$ 5898$^6$ 6341$^9$ **>77a 97+f<**
**Sarn** 5 b g Atraf-Covent Garden Girl (Sizzling Melody) *1080$^9$ 1697$^4$* 1971$^{15}$ 2462$^7$ 2649$^4$ 2753$^8$ 3018$^3$ 3221$^2$3449$^7$ 3733$^4$ 4080$^7$ 4275$^4$ **>48f<**
**Saros (IRE)** 3 bb c Desert Sun-Fight Right (FR) (Crystal Glitters (USA)) 1363$^{15}$ *(1701) (1916) 2128$^6$ 2854$^{14}$* 3368$^2$ 3622$^7$ 4305$^3$ 4390$^7$(5063) 5364$^9$ *6220$^{11}$ 6549$^3$* **>63a 68f<**
**Sarraaf (IRE)** 8 ch g Perugino (USA) -Blue Vista (IRE) (Pennine Walk) *1013$^4$* 1199$^2$ 1315$^3$ 1345$^2$ 1451$^5$ 1746$^7$ 2078$^5$ 2459$^3$2905$^3$ 3079$^3$ 3235$^5$ 3977$^9$ 4276$^5$ 4535$^2$ 4826$^9$ 5061$^3$5317$^4$ 5514$^6$ 5581$^9$ 5859$^4$ 6210$^{11}$ *6483$^9$ 6580$^6$* **>75a 71f<**
**Sarrasin (FR)** 5 b g Bering-Sevilliana (General Holme (USA)) 980a$^4$ 2156a$^7$ **>103f<**
**Sarre (FR)** 4 b f Freedom Cry-Stenoree (FR) (Garde Royale) 1163a$^3$ 1780a$^2$ **>111f<**
**Sartaena (IRE)** 2 b f Imperial Ballet (IRE) -Joza (Marju (IRE)) 4474$^8$ 4670$^7$ 5746$^7$ **>35f<**
**Sasanuma (USA)** 4 b f Kingmambo (USA) -Sassy Bird (USA) (Storm Bird (CAN)) 4982a$^4$ **>108f<**
**Sashay** 6 b m Bishop Of Cashel-St James s Antigua (IRE) (Law Society (USA)) *839$^5$ 981$^2$* 1534$^{10}$ 2167$^3$ 2429$^6$ 5205$^{11}$ **>71a 61df<**
**Saspys Lad** 7 b g Faustus (USA) -Legendary Lady (Reprimand) 1470$^6$ 2619$^5$ 4616$^{15}$ **>59f<**
**Sastre (IRE)** 2 b f Bluebird (USA) -No Rehearsal (FR) (Baillamont (USA)) 2522$^{17}$ 3659$^4$ *4023$^{12}$* 4914$^9$ **>61f<**
**Satan s Sister** 3 ch f Tout Ensemble-Winter Greeting (Hello Gorgeous (USA)) 2647$^{10}$ ><
**Satchem (IRE)** 2 br c Inchinor-Mohican Princess (Shirley Heights) 2360$^2$ (2817) (3677) (5295) 5918$^4$ **>110f<**
**Satin Finish (IRE)** 2 b f Kingmambo (USA) -Shimaal (Sadler s Wells (USA)) 3675$^4$ (3950) 4119$^4$ 4744$^{10}$ 5195$^6$ **>93f<**
**Satin Kiss (USA)** 2 b f Seeking The Gold (USA) -Satin Flower (USA) (Shadeed (USA)) (2876) 3599$^{10}$ (4541) 5250$^4$ **>93f<**
**Satin Rose** 2 b f Lujain (USA) -Shamwari (USA) (Shahrastani (USA)) 2234$^5$ *2985$^6$* 5098$^{13}$ 5561$^6$ 6093$^{15}$ **>31a 53f<**
**Sat Nam (IRE)** 3 b f Fayruz-Shocker (IRE) (Sabrehill (USA)) 4588a$^{16}$ **>71+f<**
**Satsu (IRE)** 3 ch f Shinko Forest (IRE) -Cap And Gown (IRE) (Royal Academy (USA)) 1214$^9$ 1360$^8$ 1667$^6$ *2451$^{12}$* **>7a 53f<**
**Sattam** 5 b g Danehill (USA) -Mayaasa (USA) (Lyphard (USA)) 5444$^2$ 5698$^3$ 5886$^8$ **>86f<**
**Saturday s Child (FR)** 2 ch f Hamas (IRE) -Pleasant Whisper (FR) (Marignan (USA)) 5507$^{11}$ ><
**Saturn (IRE)** 4 b g Marju (IRE) -Delphinus (Soviet Star (USA)) 1657a$^7$ **>112f<**
**Saucepot** 2 ch f Bold Edge-Apple Sauce (Prince Sabo) 2884$^9$ 3382$^6$ 4124$^2$ 4508$^{11}$ 4770$^3$ 5334$^6$ 5509$^9$ **>65f<**
**Saucy** 3 b f Muhtarram (USA) -So Saucy (Teenoso (USA)) 1186$^6$ 1304$^6$ 2402$^9$ *2484$^5$* 3190$^3$ 3581$^5$ 4669$^{13}$ **>48a 48f<**
**Saucy Pickle** 3 b f Makbul-Bewails (IRE) (Caerleon (USA)) *5531$^0$ 6601$^0$* **>40a<**
**Savannah Bay** 5 ch g In The Wings-High Savannah (Rousillon (USA)) 1703$^7$ 2108$^4$ 2533$^8$ 3076$^7$ **>116f<**
**Savannah River (IRE)** 3 b f Desert King (IRE) -Hayward (Indian Ridge) 1288$^8$ 1465$^3$ 1843$^2$ 2554$^5$ 2774$^4$ 3837$^3$ 3984$^6$ 4346$^{16}$5130$^4$ 5197$^{10}$ **>48f<**
**Savannah Sue** 3 b f Emarati (USA) -Bidweaya (USA) (Lear Fan (USA)) 1991$^7$ *2815$^9$ 3279$^{10}$* 3562$^{14}$ **>9a 19f<**
**Savernake Brave (IRE)** 3 b g Charnwood Forest (IRE) -Jordinda (IRE) (Indian Ridge) *408$^5$ 1676$^2$* 2033$^8$ 2932$^4$ 3175$^7$ 3991$^{10}$ *4881$^7$* (5283)5794$^{12}$ *6362$^4$* **>48a 48 f<**
**Savile s Delight (IRE)** 5 b g Cadeaux Genereux-Across The Ice (USA) (General Holme (USA)) *453$^3$ 509$^2$ 637$^4$* 1504$^3$ (1873) 2118$^2$ 2477$^7$ (3446) (3779) 4084$^4$5077$^3$ 5299$^{13}$ *6554$^4$* **>73a 86f<**
**Saville Row (USA)** 3 b g Gone West (USA) -Style Setter (USA) (Manila (USA)) 1654a$^8$ **>102f<**
**Saviours Spirit** 3 ch g Komaite (USA) -Greenway Lady (Prince Daniel (USA)) *489$^2$ 673$^2$ (840)* 5399$^9$ 5652$^{10}$ *6016$^2$ 6222$^5$* **>77a 71f<**
**Savoie** 2 ch f Grand Lodge (USA) -Spry (Suave Dancer (USA)) 6470$^{13}$ **>54f<**
**Savoy Chapel** 2 br c Xaar-Royal Gift (Cadeaux Genereux) *5054$^9$* 5347$^{12}$ 5653$^{13}$ 5840$^8$ **>48a 53f<**
**Sawah** 4 gr g Linamix (FR) -Tarhhib (Danzig (USA)) *422$^5$ 1094$^{10}$* **>26a<**
**Sawwaah (IRE)** 7 b g Marju (IRE) -Just A Mirage (Green Desert (USA)) 1114$^{24}$ 1746$^8$ (2215) 2366$^3$ 2637$^4$ 3036$^{16}$ 3235$^{13}$ 3440$^8$ 4122$^3$4287$^{15}$ 4543$^2$ (4742) 4931$^{13}$ 5419$^4$ 5937$^{10}$ **>91f<**
**Saxe-Coburg (IRE)** 7 b g Warning-Saxon Maid (Sadler s Wells (USA)) *1681$^5$* (1856) 2120$^9$ 2262$^3$ 2590$^3$ 2767$^{10}$ 3342$^3$ 3492$^5$ 3629$^3$3942$^4$ 4630$^9$ 4849$^4$ 5073$^6$ 5875$^{13}$ *5914$^P$* **>65 a 66f<**
**Saxon Lil (IRE)** 2 b f Second Empire (IRE) -Salva (Grand Lodge (USA)) 5198$^{13}$ **>25f<**
**Sayadaw (FR)** 4 b c Darshaan-Vingt Et Une (FR) (Sadler s Wells (USA)) 1455$^4$ **>113f<**
**Sayrianna** 3 br f Sayaarr (USA) -Arianna Aldini (Habitat) 3161$^{13}$ 3630$^{11}$ 4057$^4$ 4710$^7$ **>53f<**
**Sayuri (IRE)** 4 ch f Zafonic (USA) -Sagar Pride (IRE) (Jareer (USA)) 1776a$^2$ **>103f<**
**Saywaan (USA)** 2 ch f Fusaichi Pegasus (USA) -Sharp Cat (USA) (Storm Cat (USA)) (6123) **>83+f<**
**Say What You See (IRE)** 4 b c Charnwood Forest (IRE) -Aster Aweke (IRE) (Alzao (USA)) *643$^9$ 820$^4$ 964$^2$ (1085)* 1308$^5$ 2210$^4$ 2591$^2$ 2845$^2$3097$^9$ 3842$^4$ 4327$^8$ **>81a 80f<**
**Scabiun (IRE)** 6 b h Dolphin Street (FR) -Glenross

(IRE) (Warning) 6109a[4] >**114f**<

**Scale The Heights (IRE)** **2** b g Spectrum (IRE) -Decrescendo (IRE) (Polish Precedent (USA)) 3451[9] 3679[8] 5173[7] 5407[13] >**66f**<

**Scalloway (IRE)** **4** b g Marju (IRE) -Zany (Junius (USA)) 5657[16] 6450[14] >**51a 73f**<

**Scandinavia (USA)** **2** b c Fusaichi Pegasus (USA) -Party Cited (USA) (Alleged (USA)) 5778[2] 6489a[8] >**87a 109f**<

**Scarborough Flyer** **2** b c Almaty (IRE) -Calamanco (Clantime) 6270[12] 6478[10] >**7a**<

**Scarlet Empress** **3** b f Second Empire (IRE) -Daltak (Night Shift (USA)) 4717[15] 5588[9] >**76a 68f**<

**Scarlet Invader (IRE)** **2** b g Indian Ridge-Scarlet Plume (Warning) 3228[4] 4016[8] 4682[2] 5539[6] 6176[12] >**78f**<

**Scarlett Breeze** **3** b f Shinko Forest (IRE) -La Suquet (Puissance) 2098[17] 2380[13] 2932[12] 3179[5] 3628[8] 4440[4] 4881[11] 4968[4]5338[7] 5930[14] 6229[15] >**49a 49f**<

**Scarlett Rose** **3** b f Royal Applause-Billie Blue (Ballad Rock) 1530[6] 2694[10] 4020[3] 4340[3] 5148[7] 5370[15] 6499[13] >**58a 69f**<

**Scarp (USA)** **2** bb c Gulch (USA) -Rhetorical Lass (USA) (Capote (USA)) 4730[9] 5091[11] 5716[7] >**64f**<

**Scarpia** **4** ch g Rudimentary (USA) -Floria Tosca (Petong) 3487[9] 4083[17] 4604[5] >**37a 55f**<

**Scarrabus (IRE)** **3** b g Charnwood Forest (IRE) -Errazuriz (IRE) (Classic Music (USA)) 1356[4] 2070[10] 2648[6] 4057[3] 4346[4] 5217 [3] 5382[5] 5889[7] >**58a 68f**<

**Scarrottoo** **6** ch g Zilzal (USA) -Bold And Beautiful (Bold Lad (IRE)) 469[8] 674[3] 698[5] 738[16] 895[11] 918[5] 1185[5](1373) 1971[4] 2703[12] 2886[3] (4265) 4546[5] 4818[14] 5425[3] 5575[16] 6364[9]6405[5] >**55a 65f**<

**Scary Night (IRE)** **4** b g Night Shift (USA) -Private Bucks (USA) (Spend A Buck (USA)) 681[12] 748[11] (954) 1027[6] 1423[7] 1625[10] 2123[6] 2663[13]3378[2] 3864[18] 4881[10] 6363[9] >**56a 47 f**<

**Scenic Flight** **3** b f Distant View (USA) -Bird Of Time (IRE) (Persian Bold) 1300[13] 1496[8] 1985[9] >**18a 42 f**<

**Scenic Lady (IRE)** **8** b m Scenic-Tu Tu Maori (IRE) (King s Lake (USA)) 3264[5] 3437[7] >**17a 68 f**<

**Scent** **2** b f Groom Dancer (USA) -Sweet Pea (Persian Bold) 4712[5] 5248[12] 5687[3] 6265[5] >**62f**<

**Schapiro (USA)** **3** b g Nureyev (USA) -Konvincha (USA) (Cormorant (USA)) 1831[11] 2179[3] 2578[4] (3121) >**79f**<

**Schinken Otto (IRE)** **3** ch c Shinko Forest (IRE) -Athassel Rose (IRE) (Reasonable (FR)) 2688[14] 3368[6] 3822[7] 5237[5] 5547[12] >**48f**<

**Scholarship (IRE)** **3** b g College Chapel-Royal Bracelet (IRE) (Night Shift (USA)) 3180[20] 3846[3] >**69a 58f**<

**Science Academy (USA)** **3** ch f Silver Hawk (USA) -Dance Design (IRE) (Sadler s Wells (USA)) 1998[10] 2363[5] 3572[6] 4055[2] (4499) (4710) 5019[6] 6498[7] >**67a 70+f**<

**Scientist** **3** ch g Dr Fong (USA) -Green Bonnet (IRE) (Green Desert (USA)) 1386[10] 1975[13] 2790[3] 3452[9] 4266[6] 5868[12] (6199) 6547[8] >**77f**<

**Scissors (IRE)** **2** ch f Desert King (IRE) -Clipping (Kris) 3123[10] 3664[8] >**56f**<

**Scooby Dooby Do** **3** b f Atraf-Redgrave Design (Nebbiolo) 1362[5] 3267[6] 3954[15] 4393[6] 5193[18] 5702[17] >**57f**<

**Scorch** **3** b g Mark Of Esteem (IRE) -Red Hot Dancer (USA) (Seattle Dancer (USA)) 550[4] 644[9] 1375[2] >**39a 57df**<

**Scorchio (IRE)** **3** b g Desert Sun-White-Wash (Final Straw) 1600[6] 1726[2] 2014[5] 3107[4] 3371[6] >**47a 46f**<

**Scorpio Sally (IRE)** **2** b f Mujadil (USA) -Clear Procedure (USA) (The Minstrel (CAN)) 2730[14] 3398[5] 4131[6] 5109[5] 5476[5] 5852[16] >**58f**<

**Scotland The Brave** **4** ch f Zilzal (USA) -Hunters Of Brora (IRE) (Sharpo) 1931[14] 2421[3] 2733[5] 2963[8] 3623[4] (3867) 4551[4] 4903[2] 5583[9]6138[7] >**76f**<

**Scott** **3** gr g Polar Falcon (USA) -Circled (USA) (Cozzene (USA)) 2777[7] 3168[10] 3422[6] 4055[12] 4499[3] (4927) 5914[4] (6047) 6183[2]6527[3] >**69a 69f**<

**Scottish Exile (IRE)** **3** b f Ashkalani (IRE) -Royal Jade (Last Tycoon) 458[6] 610[4] 1209[4] 1626[3] (1788) 2181[10] 2610[8] 3147[2] (3344)3838[11] 4331[3] 4472[4] 4727[7] 5949[10] >**62 a 74f**<

**Scottish River (USA)** **5** b g Thunder Gulch (USA) -Overbrook (Storm Cat (USA)) 412[3] 464[10] (590) 705[5] (861) (903) 970[7] 1141[5] 1540[6](2000) 2304[4] 2612[6] 3159[6] (3662) 3872[2] 4136[4] 4540[17] 5182[4] 5423[10]5764[6] >**76a 88f**<

**Scott s View** **5** b g Selkirk (USA) -Milly Of The Vally (Caerleon (USA)) 712a[4] (854a) 976a[11] (1003a) 1144a[3] (1355) 1657a[3] 2508a[3] 2639[7] 2968[5]3978[5] 4385a[4] >**70a 118f**<

**Scotty s Future (IRE)** **6** b g Namaqualand (USA) -Persian Empress (IRE) (Persian Bold) 577[7] (664) 775[11] (894) 1088[8] 5006[6] 5315[5] 5514[4] 5581[8] >**86a 78f**<

**Scramble (USA)** **6** ch g Gulch (USA) -Syzygy (ARG) (Big Play (USA)) 1971[6] 2368[14] 4246[11] 4276[6] >**65da 58f**<

**Screaming Shamal (USA)** **3** gr f Tabasco Cat (USA) -Carefree Cheetah (USA) (Trempolino (USA)) 711a[8] 1005a[4] >**83a 43f**<

**Scream To Scream (IRE)** **4** b c Dr Devious (IRE) -My Firebird (Rudimentary (USA)) 5489a[9] ><

**Screenplay** **3** ch g In The Wings-Erudite (Generous (IRE)) 1414[10] >**68f**<

**Screwdriver** **2** b c Entrepreneur-Lust (Pursuit Of Love) 2111[2] (2677) >**99f**<

**Scripted** **2** b g Diktat-Krameria (Kris) 5911[4] 6091[4] >**66a 67f**<

**Scriptorium** **3** b g Singspiel (IRE) -Annie Albright (USA) (Verbatim (USA)) 1064[6] 1271[10] 2551[2] 2930[4] 4138[2] 4655[8] 5829[10] 6119[7] >**59a 70f**<

**Scriptwriter (IRE)** **2** b c Sadler s Wells (USA) -Dayanata (Shirley Heights) 6139[5] 6441[2] >**74f**<

**Scrooby Baby** **2** b f Mind Games-Lunar Music (Komaite (USA)) 3770[2] 4137[7] 4598[2] 4797[4] 5052[12] 5434[15] >**73a 69f**<

**Scrunch** **3** b f Royal Applause-Antonia s Folly (Music Boy) 1133[6] 2223[9] 3209[4] 3711[3] >**52a 70f**<

**Scurra** **5** b g Spectrum (IRE) -Tamnia (Green Desert (USA)) 1245[6] 1527[13] 1718[3] (3041) 3265[2] 3740[4] 4493[6] 4901[5] 5238[2]6209[4] 6533[7] >**45a 69f**<

**Sea Cove** **4** b f Terimon-Regal Pursuit (IRE) (Roi Danzig (USA)) 1426[4] 2171[5] 2816[5] 3250[5] 3712[4] >**50a 45f**<

**Sea Dart (USA)** **4** ch c Diesis-Wedding Of The Sea (USA) (Blushing Groom (FR)) 1254a[9] 3967a[7] >**108f**<

**Sea Fern** **3** b g Petong-Duxyana (IRE) (Cyrano De Bergerac) 1664[5] 2423[11] 3838[7] 4279[10] 5547[6] 5803[10] >**43f**<

**Seafield Towers** **4** ch g Compton Place-Midnight Spell (Night Shift (USA)) 1343[15] 2132[10] 2293[3] 2488[14] 2679[12] 3098[12] 3795[9] 3901[7]3979[8] 4152[13] >**81f**<

**Seagold** **3** b f Shahrastani (USA) -Raeleen (Jupiter Island) 1674[16] 2267[10] 2882[14] 5643[14] >**2a 42f**<

**Sea Hunter** **2** b c Lend A Hand-Ocean Grove (IRE) (Fairy King (USA)) 1462[7] (1782) 2180[4] 3677[2] 4089[3] 4890[5] 5417[10] 6176[4] >**90f**<

**Sea Jade (IRE)** **5** b m Mujadil (USA) -Mirabiliary (USA) (Crow (FR)) 1592[4] 1863[2] 2051[2] 2428[8] >**40a 44f**<

**Sea Lark** **2** b g Green Horizon-Fiora (IRE) (Sri Pekan (USA)) 6536[9] >**36a**<

**Seal Of Office** **5** ch g Mark Of Esteem (IRE) -Minskip (USA) (The Minstrel (CAN)) 1675[17] 2302[P] ><

**Sea Map** **2** ch c Fraam-Shehana (USA) (The Minstrel (CAN)) 3336[9] 4016[10] 4579[U] 6078[10] 6545[6] >**53f**<

**Sea Mark** **8** ro g Warning-Mettlesome (Lomond (USA)) 1265[3] 2172[5] 2410[11] >**64f**<

**Seamless** **2** b c Gold Away (IRE) -Fallara (FR) (Tropular) 3476[5] 6478[5] >**64a 64f**<

**Seamus Shindig** **2** b g Aragon-Sheesha (USA) (Shadeed (USA)) (5586) 6333[4] >**87+f**<

**Sean Nos (IRE)** **3** b c Sri Pekan (USA) -Coolaba Princess (IRE) (Danehill (USA)) 4251a[7] >**68f**<

**Sean s Memory (USA)** **4** b g Theatrical-Memories (IRE) (Don t Forget Me) 484[8] 722[2] 889[6] 1238[P] >**55a**<

**Sea Nymph (IRE)** **3** b f Spectrum (IRE) -Sea Picture (IRE) (Royal Academy (USA)) 3916[5] 4195[2] (4615) 5136[2] 5566[13] >**83f**<

**Sea Of Gold** **3** b f Docksider (USA) -Shadow Bird (Martinmas) 1400[14] 2182[6] 3392[2] 3993[6] 5381[4] 5829[15] 6015[11] >**62a 73f**<

**Sea Of Happiness** **4** b g Pivotal-Ella Lamees (Statoblest) 2347[13] 2759[9] 3411[15] >**35f**<

**Sea Plume** **5** b m Slip Anchor-Fine Quill (Unfuwain (USA)) 1521[5] 2491[10] 3244[8] 4033[9] >**66a 82f**<

**Search Mission (USA)** **3** b f Red Ransom (USA) -Skimble (USA) (Lyphard (USA)) 3457[2] 4148[9] >**86f**<

**Seasons Estates** **2** b f Mark Of Esteem (IRE) -La Fazenda (Warning) 1299[4] 1686[10] 4682[4] 5377[3] (5909) >**67f**<

**Season Ticket (GER)** **2** b f Kornado-Second Game (GER) (Second Set (IRE)) 4804[15] 4936[8] 5319[17] 5856[10] >**46f**<

**Sea Storm (IRE)** **6** b g Dolphin Street (FR) -Prime Interest (IRE) (King s Lake (USA)) 1199[16] 1345[5] 1773[8] 2291[3] 2421[7] (2493) 2894[10] 3119[7] 3977[6]4134[5] 4349[6] 4577[4] 4931[3] 5419[19] 5631[2] (5818) 6244[8] >**90a 87f**<

**Sea Tern** **4** b f Emarati (USA) -Great Tern (Simply Great (FR)) 2229[9] 2386[14] >**29f**<

**Sea The World (IRE)** **4** b g Inzar (USA) -Annie s Travels (IRE) (Mac s Imp (USA)) 540[5] (721) 801[3] 1033[2] 1205[6] 1738[9] 1909[11] >**69a 46f**<

**Seattle Art (USA)** **10** b g Seattle Slew (USA) -Artiste (Artaius (USA)) 2810[12] ><

**Seattle Prince (USA)** **6** gr g Cozzene (USA) -Chicken Slew (USA) (Seattle Slew (USA)) 5027[8] 6005[17] >**63f**<

**Seattle Robber** **2** b g Robellino (USA) -Seattle Ribbon (USA) (Seattle Dancer (USA)) 6145[14] >**62f**<

**Sea Ya Maite** **10** b g Komaite (USA) -Marina Plata (Julio Mariner) 430[14] 471[5] 497[2] 630[3] 655[5] 714[4] 781[5]1026[10] 1090[2] 1444[4] 2345[7] 3380[8] 3612[7] >**43a 25f**<

**Secam (POL)** **5** gr g Alywar (USA) -Scytia (POL) (Euro Star) 867[13] 1233[3] 3747[9] 4127[11] 4190[11] >**47a 47f**<

**Secluded** **4** b g Compton Place-Secret Dance (Sadler s Wells (USA)) 2738[5] 3387[8] 3911[14] (5038) 5459[5] 6266[15] >**71a 73f**<

**Second Generation (IRE)** **7** ch g Cadeaux Genereux-Title Roll (IRE) (Tate Gallery (USA)) 718[5] 1546[5] 1694[3] 1890[4] 2184[5] >**36a 27f**<

**Second Minister** **5** ch g Lion Cavern (USA) -Crime Of Passion (Dragonara Palace (USA)) 963[3] 1044[8] 1140[6] 2885[18] 3043[10] 4026[11] 4185[13] >**61a 34f**<

**Second Of May** **4** ch f Lion Cavern (USA) -Giant Nipper (Nashwan (USA)) 4436[8] >**70a 70f**<

**Second Paige (IRE)** **7** b g Nicolotte-My First Paige (IRE) (Runnett) 789[4] >**42a 42 f**<

**Second Reef** **2** b c Second Empire (IRE) -Vax Lady (Millfontaine) 4924[3] 5947[19] >**57a 45f**<

**Second User** **3** b g Zilzal (USA) -Glossary (Reference Point) 553[11] 739[13] 2001[20] 2374[18] >**10a 1f**<

**Second Venture (IRE)** **6** b g Petardia-Hilton Gateway (Hello Gorgeous (USA)) 531[8] 567[3] 658[8] >**41a 63f**<

**Second Warning** **3** ch c Piccolo-St Helena (Monsanto (FR)) 1541[5] 2883[8] 4615[5] 4850[6] >**56a 59f**<

**Second Wind** **9** ch g Kris-Rimosa s Pet (Petingo) 5832[9] 6466[12] >**30a 30f**<

**Secret Affair** **2** b c Piccolo-Secret Circle (Magic Ring (IRE)) 5054[8] 5373[8] 6283[10] >**52a 71f**<

**Secretary General (IRE)** **3** b c Fasliyev (USA) -Katie McLain (USA) (Java Gold (USA)) 1795[7] 2089[2] 2295[8] 2692[5] 3671[9] (4140) 4709[2] 5226[2] 5699[8]6121[11] >**99f**<

**Secret Bloom** **3** b g My Best Valentine-Rose Elegance (Bairn (USA)) 408[4] 508[4] 696[11] 804[5] 1040[4] 1195[2] 1447[4](1570) 2016[3] 6361[7] >**48a**<

**Secret Cavern (USA)** **2** b c Lion Cavern (USA) -River Dyna (USA) (Dynaformer (USA)) 4488[6] 5301[7] 6322[4] >**78 f**<

**Secret Charm (IRE)** **3** b f Green Desert (USA) -Viz (USA) (Kris S (USA)) 1791[5] 2330a[5] 3033[11] (5439) 5917[5] >**108 f**<

**Secret Connection** **4** b f Danzig Connection (USA) -Red Secret (IRE) (Valiyar) 811[7] ><

**Secret Crypt (USA)** **2** gr f Honour And Glory (USA) -Cryptocari (USA) (Cryptoclearance (USA)) 6367a[12] >**56f**<

**Secret De Famille (FR)** **5** b g Octagonal (NZ) -Belle Du Bresil (FR) (Akarad (FR)) 6170a[12] >**76f**<

**Secret Diva (IRE)** **2** ch f Dr Devious (IRE) -Deerussa (IRE) (Jareer (USA)) 2396[9] 2761[12] 4474[10] 4638[7] 5218[9] 5735[11] >**17a 31f**<

**Secret Flame** **3** b f Machiavellian (USA) -Secret Obsession (USA) (Secretariat (USA)) 2113[3] 2805[3] (3222) 4032[9] 5446[6] 5739[5] >**71a 77f**<

**Secret Formula** **4** b f So Factual (USA) -Ancient Secret (Warrshan (USA)) 1385[20] 2064[18] >**89f**<

**Secret History (USA)** **2** b f Bahri (USA) -Ravnina (USA) (Nureyev (USA)) 3123[2] 3398[3] 4074[5] (5098) 5466[7] 5995[2] 6338[3] >**79f**<

**Secret Jewel (FR)** **4** b f Hernando (FR) -Opalette (Sharrood (USA)) 2562[6] 3348[8] 3866[5] 4849[17] 5869[12] 6150[2] 6438[2] >**62f**<

**Secret Melody (FR)** **3** b f Inchinor-Secret Music (USA) (Dixieland Band (USA)) 2193a[3] 4356a[3] 4899a[4] (5823a) 6258a[3] >**102f**<

**Secret Of Secrets** **3** b g Timeless Times (USA) -Sophisticated Baby (Bairn (USA)) 5342[13] 5801[10] ><

**Secret Pact (IRE)** **2** br c Lend A Hand-Schust Madame (IRE) (Second Set (IRE)) 1743[4] 2035[2] 3870[3] 4700[7] (5447) (5636) 5885[2] 6334[3] >**89f**<

**Secret Place** **3** ch g Compton Place-Secret Circle (Magic Ring (IRE)) (409) (557) 843[3] 1408[9] (2224) 2642[16] 3690[13] >**88 a 96f**<

**Sedge (USA)** **4** b g Lure (USA) -First Flyer (USA) (Riverman (USA)) (2528) 3559[12] 3921[16] 4209[7] 5557[7] 6201[4] >**62f**<

**Seejay** **4** b f Bahamian Bounty-Grand Splendour (Shirley Heights) 1244[3] 1856[17] 2387[8] 2835[9] >**55a 38f**<

**Seeking An Alibi (USA)** **2** ch c Storm Cat (USA) -Seeking Regina (USA) (Seeking The Gold (USA)) 6148[10] 6492[8] >**68a 56f**<

**Seeking A Way (USA)** **3** b f Seeking The Gold (USA) -Seattle Way (USA) (Seattle Slew (USA)) 3194[2] 4141[3] 4692[7] 5340[6] 5913[2] 6182[3] >**74a 81+f**<

**Seeking Bellissimo (IRE)** **4** b c Rainbow Quest (USA) -Priory Belle (IRE) (Priolo (USA)) 5312a[3] >**89f**<

**Seeking The Dia (USA)** **3** b c Storm Cat (USA) -Seeking The Pearl (USA) (Seeking The Gold (USA)) 3674[12] 4595a[15] >**108f**<

**Seel** **2** b f Spectrum (IRE) -Charming Helene (Star Appeal (IRE)) 2668a[7] >**49f**<

**Seel Of Approval** **5** b g Polar Falcon (USA) -Petit Point (IRE) (Petorius) 1789[2] >**112f**<

**Seeyaaj** **4** b g Darshaan-Subya (Night Shift (USA)) 4572[5] 5615[9] 6339[10] >**84f**<

**Seguidilla (IRE)** **3** b f Mujadil (USA) -Alzeam (IRE) (Alzao (USA)) 1293[14] 1664[6] >**75 f**<

**Seihali (IRE)** **5** b h Alzao (USA) -Edwina (IRE) (Caerleon (USA)) (690a) 853a[8] >**105f**<

**Sekwana (POL)** **5** b m Duke Valentino-Surmia (POL) (Demon Club (POL)) 602[13] 645[10] 2803[11] >**27a 12f**<

**Selebela** **3** ch f Grand Lodge (USA) -Risarshana (FR) (Darshaan) 1755[7] (2363) (2546) (2914) 3210[2] 3944[2] 4367[3] 4884[2] 5394[10] >**101 f**<

**Selective** **5** b g Selkirk (USA) -Portelet (Night Shift (USA)) 1469[4] 2283[13] 3036[24] 3850[4] 4528[10] 5112[4] 5755[6] 6044[5]6193[5] >**97a 106f**<

**Self Belief** **3** b f Easycall-Princess Of Spain (King Of Spain) 2131[11] 5342[12] 5862[15] >**67f**<

**Self Defense** **7** b g Warning-Dansara (Dancing Brave (USA)) 3310[8] 3725[6] 4218[5] 4858[5] 5812[2] 6355[3] >**114f**<

**Self Evident (USA)** **4** bb c Known Fact (USA) -Palisade (USA) (Gone West (USA)) 754a[3] 925a[12] >**86a 102f**<

**Self Respect (USA)** **2** b c Lear Fan (USA) -Cap Of Dignity (Shirley Heights) 6565[7] >**60f**<

**Selika (IRE)** **2** ch c Daggers Drawn (USA) -Hint-Of-Romance (IRE) (Treasure Kay) 5118[12] 5570[9] 6067[4] 6265[8] >**73f**<

**Selkirk Grace** **4** b g Selkirk (USA) -Polina (Polish Precedent (USA)) 5705[5] 6524[4] >**70 f**<

**Selkirk Storm (IRE)** **2** b c Trans Island-Force Divine (FR) (L Emigrant (USA)) (2035) 2655[2] 3224[5] 4150[7] 4836[11] 5314[14] 5767[10] 6113[3] 6333[14] >**66f**<

**Semarang** **2** b c Hernando (FR) -Obscura (USA) (Mr Prospector (USA)) 6202a[4] >**95f**<

**Semelle De Vent (USA)** **3** b f Sadler s Wells (USA) -Heeremandi (IRE) (Royal Academy (USA)) 1179[3] 1394[3] 1998[20] 3305[9] 4339[2] 4798[7] 6061[3](6560) >**61a 59f**<

**Semenovskii** **4** b g Fraam-Country Spirit (Sayf El Arab (USA)) 646[3] 3645[6] 4090[11] (4522) 4837[15] 5299[16] 5730[15] 6210[13] 6445[5] >**71 a 80f**<

**Semper Paratus (USA)** **5** b g Foxhound (USA) -Bletcha Lass (AUS) (Bletchingly (AUS)) 584[4] 719[8] 1451[12] 1941[2] 2814[12] 3381[3] 4403[14]4877[11] 5261[12] (5691) >**66a 65f**<

**Senator s Alibi** **6** b h Caerleon (USA) -Salul (Soviet Star (USA)) 4371a[2] >**68a 98f**<

**Sendeed (USA)** **2** bb c Gulch (USA) -Aghsaan (USA) (Wild Again (USA)) 4030[14] 4730[16] >**55f**<

**Sendintank** **4** ch g Halling (USA) -Colleville (Pharly (FR)) (505) (546) (583) (592) 1282[3] (5027) (5093) (5190) (5266) 5288[3] (6535) (6575) >**78+a 104f**<

**Seneschal** **3** b g Polar Falcon (USA) -Broughton Singer (IRE) (Common Grounds) 1437[10] 1799[8] 4271[12] 4906[10] 5120[9] 5399[14] 5652[5] (6094) 6138[6]6199[2] 6210[6] (6350) >**90f**<

**Senex (GER)** **4** b c Pelder (IRE) -Septima (GER) (Touching Wood (USA)) 1802a[3] 2508a[5] (3136a) 4183a[7] (5489a) >**117f**<

**Senhor Vencedor (BRZ)** **3** b c Spring Halo (ARG) -Up And Winning (USA) (Alysheba (USA)) 975a[6] >**41a**<

**Senior Minister** **6** b g Lion Cavern (USA) -Crime Ofthecentury (Pharly (FR)) 2262[8] (2928) 3167[10] 3555[8] 3997[12] 4238[12] 5259[15] 5370[19] 6024[12] >**65f**<

**Senior Whim** **2** b c Lahib (USA) -Euphorie (GER) (Feenpark (GER)) 6309[8] >**3f**<

**Senna (IRE)** **4** b g Petardia-Saborinie (Prince Sabo) 525[12] >**61a 40f**<

**Sennen Cove** **5** ch g Bering-Dame Laura (IRE) (Royal Academy (USA)) 438[10] 527[7] 1094[6] 1493[3] 1548[6] 1718[6] (2345) (3148) 4818[9]5450[7] >**32a 52f**<

**Senor Benny (USA)** **5** br h Benny The Dip (USA) -Senora Tippy (USA) (El Gran Senor (USA)) 6104a[3] >**108f**<

**Senor Bond (USA)** **3** ch g Hennessy (USA) -Troppa Freska (USA) (Silver Hawk (USA)) 1029[6] 1303[3] 1392[12] 3122[6] 3615[10] 4926[10] >**61a 73 f**<

**Senor Eduardo** **7** gr g Terimon-Jasmin Path (Warpath) 1174[9] 1373[11] 3247[3] 3489[5] (4065) 4458[6] 4985[2] 5229[3] 5557[15]5714[3] 5993[7] 6201[12] >**37a 63f**<

**Senor Miro** **6** b g Be My Guest (USA) -Classic Moonlight (IRE) (Machiavellian (USA)) 481[P] >**63a 56 f**<

**Senor Set (GER)** **3** b g Second Set (IRE) -Shine Share (IRE) (El Gran Senor (USA)) 2853[2] >**60a**<

**Senor Swinger (USA)** **4** gr c El Prado (IRE) -Smooth Swinger (USA) (Kris S (USA)) 4768a[7] 6384a[6] >**113f**<

**Senor Toran (USA)** **4** b g Barathea (IRE) -Applaud (USA) (Rahy (USA)) 664[3] 894[4] 1231[3] 1393[16] 1727[2] 2031[5] >**50a 45f**<

**Sense Of Style (USA)** **2** b f Thunder Gulch (USA) -Save Me The Waltz (King s Lake (USA)) 6485a[9] >**93a**<

**Sentiero Rosso (USA)** **2** b c Intidab (USA) -Kheyrah (USA) (Dayjur (USA)) 2579[4] 4776[2] (5084) 5195[3] 5602[9] 5947[9] 6068[8] 6344[13] >**96f**<

**Sentry (IRE)** **4** b g In Command (IRE) -Keep Bobbin Up (IRE) (Bob Back (USA)) (1401) 1661[4] 1801[3] 2684[3] 2958[21] 3725[7] >**73a 94f**<

**Senza Scrupoli** **4** ch g Inchinor-Gravette (Kris) 1617[3] >**49f**<

**Sept Clefs** **4** b c Deploy-Clef De Sol (USA) (Diesis) 6512a[11] >**69f**<

**Seraph** **4** ch g Vettori (IRE) -Dahlawise (IRE) (Caerleon (USA)) 427[3] (500) 715[8] 943[3] 1042[3] 1448[2] (1690) 1728[9]2230[3] 2408[9] 4189[11] >**46a 49f**<

**Seraphine (GER)** **4** ch f Dashing Blade-Sovereign Touch (IRE) (Pennine Walk) 1952a[8] 3504a[6] 4039a[10] 6106a[8] >**99f**<

**Serbelloni** **4** b g Spectrum (IRE) -Rose Vibert (Caerleon (USA)) 4814[5] >**75f**<

**Serene Pearl (IRE)** **2** b f Night Shift (USA) -Shanjah (Darshaan) 1415[11] 2129[8] 2933[6] 3408[6] 4187[4] 4878[13] 6002[10] >**44a 52f**<

**Serengeti Sky (USA)** **3** br c Southern Halo (USA) -Genovefa (USA) (Woodman (USA)) 1285[8] 1561[4] 1912[6] >**15f**<

**Serenus (GER)** **6** br g Acatenango (GER) -Serenissima (GER) (Le Glorieux) 4385a[7] 5970a[2] >**105f**<

**Sergeant Cecil** **5** ch g King s Signet (USA) -Jadidh (Touching Wood (USA)) 1539[20] 3046[3] 3485[5] (3692) 4218[2] 5288[2] 5435[2] 5814[3] >**67a 102f**<

**Sergeant Lewis** **2** gr c Mind Games-Silver Blessings (Statoblest) 5747[6] 5910[18] >**21f**<

**Sergeant Shinko (IRE)** 2 ch g Shinko Forest (IRE) -Sea Modena (IRE) (Mac s Imp (USA)) $5855^{11}$ $6021^{11}$ $6308^{9}$ >33a<

**Sergeant s Inn** 7 b g Sabrehill (USA) -Pink Brief (IRE) (Ela-Mana-Mou) $880^{7}$ >48f<

**Sergeant Slipper** 7 ch g Never So Bold-Pretty Scarce (Handsome Sailor) $625^{13}$ $657^{3}$ $728^{10}$ $796^{3}$ (876) $936^{2}$ $1011^{7}$ (1423) $1994^{5}$ $2707^{14}$ $3151^{14}$ >58?a 48f<

**Sergeant Small (IRE)** 2 b g Dr Devious (IRE) -Yavarro (Raga Navarro (ITY)) $4936^{17}$ $5319^{20}$ >17f<

**Serieux** 5 b h Cadeaux Genereux-Seranda (IRE) (Petoski) $677^{10}$ $1125^{11}$ $1328^{14}$ $1456^{2}$ $3937^{18}$ $4287^{21}$ $4442^{8}$ $5004^{12}$ $5419^{9}$ $5614^{4}$ $5813^{12}$ $5886^{5}$ >87a 87f<

**Serov (IRE)** 6 ch g Mujtahid (USA) -Title Roll (IRE) (Tate Gallery (USA)) $3961a^{14}$ >86f<

**Serpenta (GER)** 5 br m Protektor (GER) -Semplice (IRE) (Common Grounds) $785a^{5}$ >101f<

**Serramanna** 3 ch f Grand Lodge (USA) -Spry (Suave Dancer (USA)) $1440^{6}$ $4049^{5}$ $4806^{3}$ $5196^{3}$ $5619^{8}$ >80f<

**Serraval (FR)** 6 ch m Sanglamore (USA) -Saone (USA) (Bering) $4485^{2}$ $4736^{3}$ $5019^{5}$ $5153^{3}$ >66f<

**Serre Chevalier (IRE)** 3 b g Marju (IRE) -Ski Lodge (IRE) (Persian Bold) $2479^{2}$ (4063) $5444^{8}$ $6477^{15}$ >81f<

**Sesamoid (IRE)** 3 b c Grand Lodge (USA) -Shergaara (FR) (Doyoun) $1306a^{11}$ ><

**Sessay** 3 b g Cyrano De Bergerac-Green Supreme (Primo Dominie) $1771^{4}$ $1881^{3}$ $2217^{5}$ $4289^{18}$ $5193^{6}$ $5316^{8}$ $5579^{6}$ (6004) $6114^{9}$ >71f<

**Ses Seline** 3 b f Salse (USA) -Absentee (Slip Anchor) $1822^{4}$ $1945^{5}$ $2357^{8}$ $5130^{13}$ $6120^{16}$ >37f<

**Set Alight** 3 b f Forzando-Me Spede (Valiyar) $1441^{9}$ $2818^{4}$ $3261^{3}$ $4926^{8}$ $5155^{8}$ >42a 52f<

**Settlement Craic (IRE)** 3 b c Ela-Mana-Mou-Medway (IRE) (Shernazar) (1050) $1416^{4}$ $2558^{3}$ $2999^{11}$ (3806) $4229^{13}$ $6121^{15}$ >69a 95+f<

**Seulement (USA)** 2 ch c Rahy (USA) -Only Seule (USA) (Lyphard (USA)) $4963a^{5}$ $5313a^{6}$ >86f<

**Seven Magicians (USA)** 2 bb f Silver Hawk (USA) -Mambo Jambo (USA) (Kingmambo (USA)) $5695^{4}$ >70f<

**Seven No Trumps** 7 ch g Pips Pride-Classic Ring (IRE) (Auction Ring (USA)) $1131^{2}$ $1354^{5}$ $1504^{12}$ $1774^{11}$ $1937^{11}$ $2303^{3}$ $2477^{6}$ $2739^{10}$ $2912^{4}$ $3243^{8}$ $3307^{8}$ $3713^{2}$ $4034^{8}$ $4626^{10}$ $4748^{4}$ $5071^{7}$ $6554^{P}$ >83f<

**Seven Shirt** 3 b g Great Dane (IRE) -Bride s Answer (Anshan) $4871^{8}$ $5176^{14}$ $5424^{7}$ $5691^{6}$ $6056^{17}$ >59f<

**Seven Year Itch (IRE)** 4 b g Danehill (USA) -Itching (IRE) (Thatching) $1967^{2}$ $2412^{2}$ >73a 81f<

**Severely (FR)** 2 b f Cape Cross (IRE) -Sevres (USA) (Lyphard s Wish (FR)) $3992^{7}$ >55f<

**Sevillano** 3 b g Nicolotte-Nashville Blues (IRE) (Try My Best (USA)) (1223) (1659) $2080^{7}$ >72a 109+f<

**Sewmore Character** 4 b c Hector Protector (USA) -Kyle Rhea (In The Wings) $494^{4}$ $555^{6}$ $846^{2}$ $1226^{5}$ $4852^{15}$ $5108^{14}$ $5381^{2}$ $6013^{9}$ $6450^{15}$ >79a 73f<

**Sewmuch Character** 5 b g Magic Ring (IRE) -Diplomatist (Dominion) $1603^{4}$ $2091^{15}$ $2673^{6}$ $3141^{4}$ $3593^{2}$ $3923^{7}$ (4707) $5008^{17}$ $5512^{6}$ $6066^{3}$ $6480^{10}$ >73a 73f<

**Sew N So Character (IRE)** 3 b c Imperial Ballet (IRE) -Hope And Glory (USA) (Well Decorated (USA)) $1900^{4}$ $2202^{10}$ $2896^{3}$ $3477^{4}$ $3943^{4}$ $4273^{7}$ $4709^{4}$ $5106^{6}$ $5443^{7}$ $5768^{2}$ $6307^{4}$ >100 f<

**Seyaadi** 2 b g Intikhab (USA) -Sioux Chef (Be My Chief (USA)) $3319^{5}$ $3718^{2}$ $4022^{5}$ >69a 77f<

**Seyed (IRE)** 4 b g Desert Prince (IRE) -Royal Bounty (IRE) (Generous (IRE)) $2346^{3}$ >57f<

**Sfilzatore (ITY)** 3 b c Glen Jordan-Sfilza (Indian Ridge) $3135a^{B}$ ><

**Sforzando** 3 b f Robellino (USA) -Mory Kante (USA) (Icecapade (USA)) (2097) $2694^{5}$ $3180^{7}$ $3807^{7}$ >74f<

**Sgt Pepper (IRE)** 3 b c Fasliyev (USA) -Amandine (IRE) (Darshaan) $2308^{8}$ $2966^{11}$ $3751^{4}$ $5294^{6}$ $5651^{5}$ $5942^{15}$ >94f<

**Shaaban (IRE)** 3 b g Woodman (USA) -Ashbilya (USA) (Nureyev (USA)) $2113^{13}$ $2479^{7}$ $2842^{7}$ $3294^{5}$ $4726^{9}$ >69f<

**Shaamit s All Over** 5 br m Shaamit (IRE) -First Time Over (Derrylin) $449^{7}$ $1277^{14}$ $1918^{3}$ $5926^{6}$ $6130^{8}$ >51a 35f<

**Shaconage (USA)** 4 rg f El Prado (IRE) -Carita Tostada (USA) (Gallantsky (USA)) $4767a^{8}$ $6488a^{6}$ >109f<

**Shades Of Green** 2 b f Loup Sauvage (USA) -Green Light (FR) (Green Dancer (USA)) $5717^{10}$ $6446^{6}$ >52a 44f<

**Shadowfax** 4 b g Anabaa (USA) -Prends Ca (IRE) (Reprimand) $438^{4}$ $510^{11}$ $805^{8}$ $910^{7}$ $1044^{2}$ $2006^{8}$ >59a 42f<

**Shady Deal** 8 b g No Big Deal-Taskalady (Touching Wood (USA)) $938^{11}$ $944^{9}$ $1368^{13}$ $1516^{8}$ $1994^{3}$ $2166^{14}$ $2383^{7}$ $3533^{3}$ $3575^{15}$ $3742^{8}$ >20a 54f<

**Shady Reflection (USA)** 3 b f Sultry Song (USA) -Woodland Melody (USA) (Woodman (USA)) (1704) $2221^{5}$ >93f<

**Shahama (IRE)** 2 gr c Daylami (IRE) -Albertville (USA) (Polish Precedent (USA)) $4030^{12}$ $4913^{12}$ >57f<

**Shaheer (IRE)** 2 b g Shahrastani (USA) -Atmospheric Blues (IRE) (Double Schwartz) $2111^{6}$ $2300^{2}$ $2609^{12}$ $5377^{6}$ $5852^{13}$ >75f<

**Shahm (IRE)** 5 b g Marju (IRE) -Istibshar (USA) (Mr Prospector (USA)) $626^{8}$ $988^{7}$ >60a 57f<

**Shahzan House (IRE)** 5 b h Sri Pekan (USA) -Nsx (Roi Danzig (USA)) $1540^{3}$ $2066^{2}$ $2638^{3}$ $3482^{3}$ $4540^{3}$ $4856^{3}$ $6354^{6}$ >106f<

**Shakis (IRE)** 4 b c Machiavellian (USA) -Tawaaded (IRE) (Nashwan (USA)) $5968a^{5}$ >108f<

**Shalati Princess** 3 b f Bluegrass Prince (IRE) -Shalati (FR) (High Line) $621^{7}$ $766^{11}$ $948^{6}$ $1096^{7}$ $1405^{4}$ $1800^{9}$ $2054^{3}$ $3305^{7}$ $4545^{5}$ >50a 47f<

**Shalaya (IRE)** 3 b f Marju (IRE) -Shalama (IRE) (Kahyasi) $2281^{5}$ $2887^{11}$ >89f<

**Shalbeblue (IRE)** 7 b g Shalford (IRE) -Alberjas (IRE) (Sure Blade (USA)) $2501^{11}$ $2753^{9}$ $3149^{8}$ $4213^{8}$ $4698^{11}$ >50a 55f<

**Shalimar (ITY)** 2 b f College Chapel-Picadora (ITY) (Primo Dominie) $2668a^{3}$ >85f<

**Shaman** 7 b g Fraam-Magic Maggie (Beveled (USA)) $672^{5}$ $931^{12}$ $1910^{4}$ >49a 49f<

**Shamara (IRE)** 4 b f Spectrum (IRE) -Hamara (FR) (Akarad (FR)) $2142^{2}$ $2630^{2}$ $3311^{4}$ $3699^{7}$ $5573^{2}$ $6173^{6}$ >97f<

**Shamardal (USA)** 2 b c Giant s Causeway (USA) -Helsinki (Machiavellian (USA)) (3793) (4227) (6217) >125f<

**Shambar (IRE)** 5 gr g Linamix (FR) -Shamawna (IRE) (Darshaan) $2562^{3}$ $2950^{5}$ $3661^{3}$ >98?f<

**Shamdian (IRE)** 4 b g Indian Ridge-Shamadara (IRE) (Kahyasi) $1460^{9}$ $6397^{9}$ >47a 81f<

**Shameless** 7 ch g Prince Daniel (USA) -Level Edge (Beveled (USA)) $2851^{9}$ $5146^{8}$ $5710^{9}$ $6208^{9}$ >15f<

**Shami** 5 ch h Rainbow Quest (USA) -Bosra Sham (USA) (Woodman (USA)) $633a^{4}$ $692a^{4}$ $849a^{4}$ ><

**Shamrock Bay** 2 b f Celtic Swing-Kabayil (Dancing Brave (USA)) $4137^{9}$ $5559^{4}$ $6118^{8}$ >63f<

**Shamrock City (IRE)** 7 b g Rock City-Actualite (Polish Precedent (USA)) $2672^{6}$ $2969^{31}$ $3415^{12}$ >79f<

**Shamrock Tea** 3 b g Imperial Ballet (IRE) -Yellow Ribbon (IRE) (Hamas (IRE)) $2269^{12}$ $2661^{5}$ (3234) $3585^{4}$ $4489^{13}$ $5849^{14}$ $6124^{20}$ >13a 62f<

**Shamsada (IRE)** 4 b f Kahyasi-Shamawna (IRE) (Darshaan) $5312a^{4}$ >62f<

**Shamwari Fire (IRE)** 4 ch g Idris (IRE) -Bobby s Dream (Reference Point) $424^{4}$ $536^{6}$ $1165^{13}$ $2122^{7}$ (2346) $2776^{6}$ $2943^{8}$ $3103^{10}$ $3471^{3}$ $3921^{3}$ $4246^{8}$ $4605^{13}$ (5285) $5450^{3}$ $5571^{6}$ $5714^{9}$ $5927^{3}$ >40a 54f<

**Shanghai Lily (IRE)** 2 b f King s Best (USA) -Marlene-D (Selkirk (USA)) (4712) (5613) >100+f<

**Shanghai Surprise** 3 b g Komaite (USA) -Shanghai Lil (Petong) $1736^{5}$ $2088^{8}$ $2468^{8}$ $2661^{7}$ $3801^{9}$ >45f<

**Shankly Bond (IRE)** 2 ch g Danehill Dancer (IRE) -Fanellan (Try My Best (USA)) $5095^{8}$ $5290^{9}$ $5543^{6}$ >61f<

**Shannkara s Quest (USA)** 3 bb c Coronado s Quest (USA) -Shannkara (IRE) (Akarad (FR)) $766^{12}$ $845^{11}$ $4845^{12}$ >12a<

**Shannon s Dream** 8 gr m Anshan-Jenny s Call (Petong) $3138^{7}$ $4799^{4}$ >30f<

**Shannon Springs (IRE)** 2 b c Darshaan-Our Queen Of Kings (Arazi (USA)) $4169^{2}$ $4835^{3}$ $5396^{2}$ $6259a^{7}$ >94f<

**Shanty Star (IRE)** 4 gr g Hector Protector (USA) -Shawanni (Shareef Dancer (USA)) $2067^{9}$ $2533^{P}$ $5916^{3}$ $6218^{9}$ >108f<

**Shape Up (IRE)** 4 b g Octagonal (NZ) -Bint Kaldoun (IRE) (Kaldoun (FR)) $1630^{3}$ $1910^{2}$ $2375^{4}$ (2501) (2753) (6533) >70a 71f<

**Shapira (GER)** 3 ch f Kornado-Semplice (IRE) (Common Grounds) (1983a) $5978a^{7}$ >106+f<

**Sharaab (USA)** 3 b c Erhaab (USA) -Ghashtah (USA) (Nijinsky (CAN)) $1382^{6}$ $2197^{8}$ $2505^{5}$ $2900^{2}$ $3922^{9}$ $4443^{7}$ $5544^{16}$ >75f<

**Sharabad (FR)** 6 b g Ela-Mana-Mou-Sharbada (FR) (Kahyasi) $2257^{5}$ $3607^{7}$ $4276^{10}$ $5238^{10}$ >46f<

**Sharaby (IRE)** 2 b f Cadeaux Genereux-Shawanni (Shareef Dancer (USA)) $3627^{3}$ $4272^{12}$ $5109^{11}$ $6470^{2}$ >81f<

**Sharadi (IRE)** 3 b g Desert Sun-Sharadiya (IRE) (Akarad (FR)) $2645^{7}$ $3561^{10}$ $4346^{8}$ $4692^{2}$ $5116^{2}$ $5479^{2}$ (5519) $5944^{3}$ (6287) >79+f<

**Sharaiji Blossom (USA)** 2 b f Saint Ballado (CAN) -Lilac Garden (USA) (Roberto (USA)) $5559^{3}$ (5846) >76f<

**Shardda** 4 b f Barathea (IRE) -Kronengold (USA) (Golden Act (USA)) $1250^{3}$ $1931^{15}$ $5085^{12}$ $5345^{11}$ $6097^{10}$ $6516^{5}$ >69f<

**Shareb (USA)** 2 b c El Prado (IRE) -My Hansel (USA) (Hansel (USA)) $6171^{11}$ >57f<

**Shared Dreams** 2 b f Seeking The Gold (USA) -Coretta (IRE) (Caerleon (USA)) $6471^{3}$ >80f<

**Shares (IRE)** 4 b g Turtle Island (IRE) -Glendora (Glenstal (USA)) $1172^{2}$ $6141^{4}$ >50a 65f<

**Sharmy (IRE)** 8 b g Caerleon (USA) -Petticoat Lane (Ela-Mana-Mou) $5761^{11}$ $6172^{11}$ >90f<

**Sharoura** 8 ch m Inchinor-Kinkajoo (Precocious) $2369^{5}$ $2875^{8}$ (3372) $3606^{13}$ $3735^{3}$ $3979^{4}$ $4104^{2}$ $4260^{4}$ $4877^{8}$ $5242^{12}$ $5583^{3}$ $6117^{11}$ $6499^{12}$ >57a 74f<

**Sharp As A Tack (IRE)** 2 b f Zafonic (USA) -Pretty Sharp (Interrex (CAN)) $3992^{8}$ $4137^{2}$ (4681) $5149^{12}$ $5613^{2}$ $6353^{6}$ >88f<

**Sharp Diversion (USA)** 2 ch f Diesis-Jamie De Vil (USA) (Digression (USA)) $5241^{6}$ >47f<

**Sharp Hat** 10 b g Shavian-Madam Trilby (Grundy) $411^{5}$ $436^{2}$ $681^{3}$ $748^{7}$ $897^{5}$ $954^{5}$ $1027^{8}$ $1230^{12}$ $1956^{7}$ $2976^{7}$ $3309^{7}$ $3407^{3}$ $3524^{7}$ $4011^{2}$ $4828^{4}$ $5579^{5}$ $5798^{16}$ $6046^{14}$ $6144^{9}$ $6274^{4}$ >73a 74f<

**Sharpinch** 6 b g Beveled (USA) -Giant Nipper (Nashwan (USA)) $448^{16}$ >82a 67f<

**Sharplaw Destiny (IRE)** 3 b f Petardia-Coolrain Lady (IRE) (Common Grounds) $1678^{5}$ $2484^{10}$ $2766^{12}$ $3391^{9}$ >45a 42f<

**Sharplaw Star** 2 b f Xaar-Hamsah (IRE) (Green Desert (USA)) (2544) $2970^{3}$ (5711) $6449^{3}$ >73a 95f<

**Sharplaw Venture** 4 b f Polar Falcon (USA) -Breakaway (Song) $3223^{3}$ $3850^{8}$ $4442^{7}$ >76a 82f<

**Sharp Lisa (USA)** 2 ch f Dixieland Band (USA) -Winter s Gone (USA) (Dynaformer (USA)) $6485a^{6}$ >104a<

**Sharp Needle** 3 b f Mark Of Esteem (IRE) -Blushing Sunrise (USA) (Cox s Ridge (USA)) $1400^{9}$ $1747^{2}$ $2182^{5}$ (2974) (4574) $5304^{4}$ (6395) >84+a 75 f<

**Sharp N Frosty** 2 b g Somayda (IRE) -Wily Miss (Teenoso (USA)) $1462^{4}$ $1884^{7}$ $3124^{4}$ $4012^{4}$ $5188^{U}$ $5596^{9}$ $6309^{5}$ >55f<

**Sharp Prince (FR)** 8 b h Caerwent-Sharpmiss (FR) (Sharpman) $786a^{10}$ ><

**Sharp Reply (USA)** 2 b c Diesis-Questonia (Rainbow Quest (USA)) $6331^{4}$ >76+f<

**Sharp Rigging (IRE)** 4 b g Son Of Sharp Shot (IRE) -In The Rigging (USA) (Topsider (USA)) $6152^{16}$ >71f<

**Sharp Secret (IRE)** 6 b m College Chapel-State Treasure (USA) (Secretariat (USA)) $2521^{5}$ (3117) $3609^{8}$ $5304^{7}$ $6024^{7}$ >49a 63f<

**Sharp Spice** 8 b m Lugana Beach-Ewar Empress (IRE) (Persian Bold) $1402^{6}$ >52a 41f<

**Sharvie** 7 b g Rock Hopper-Heresheis (Free State) $789^{7}$ $992^{5}$ ><

**Shastye (IRE)** 3 b f Danehill (USA) -Saganeca (USA) (Sagace (FR)) $2374^{7}$ $3454^{3}$ $3922^{4}$ (5907) $6443^{9}$ >73+a 69f<

**Shatin Leader** 2 b f Atraf-Star Dancer (Groom Dancer (USA)) $2489^{P}$ $3144^{6}$ $3893^{3}$ $4388^{4}$ $5060^{11}$ $5578^{18}$ $6093^{18}$ >60f<

**Shatin Special** 4 ch f Titus Livius (FR) -Lawn Order (Efisio) $455^{5}$ $571^{2}$ $671^{F}$ $759^{4}$ (812) $902^{6}$ $937^{6}$ $2092^{6}$ $2375^{9}$ $2408^{8}$ $2816^{3}$ $3281^{8}$ >47a 47f<

**Shatin Star** 2 bb c Killer Instinct-Anetta (Aragon) $5718^{13}$ >20f<

**Shawdon** 9 b h Inchinor-Play With Me (IRE) (Alzao (USA)) $5505a^{4}$ >95f<

**Shayadi (IRE)** 7 b g Kahyasi-Shayrdia (IRE) (Storm Bird (CAN)) $1903^{5}$ >67a 86f<

**Shaykhan (IRE)** 6 ch h Polar Falcon (USA) -Shayraz (Darshaan) $4588a^{7}$ >69f<

**Shaymee s Girl** 3 b f Wizard King-Mouchez Le Nez (IRE) (Cyrano De Bergerac) $774^{5}$ $956^{3}$ $1038^{3}$ $1788^{8}$ $6004^{3}$ $6274^{10}$ $6578^{2}$ >61a 45f<

**Shazana** 3 gr f Key Of Luck (USA) -Shawanni (Shareef Dancer (USA)) $1441^{6}$ $2632^{7}$ $3304^{6}$ >52a 61f<

**Sheapys Lass** 3 b f Perugino (USA) -Nilu (IRE) (Ballad Rock) $543^{11}$ $569^{11}$ $683^{12}$ $876^{14}$ >30a 38f<

**Shebaan** 3 b f Compton Place-Chairmans Daughter (Unfuwain (USA)) $1400^{17}$ $2251^{13}$ $3158^{8}$ $4496^{11}$ $5092^{11}$ $6228^{17}$ >43f<

**Sheboygan (IRE)** 2 ch f Grand Lodge (USA) -White Satin (IRE) (Fairy King (USA)) $5271^{3}$ (5946) $6353^{3}$ >82f<

**She Breeze** 4 b f Selkirk (USA) -She Bat (Batshoof) $1776a^{6}$ $5668a^{12}$ >94f<

**Sheer Focus (IRE)** 6 b g Eagle Eyed (USA) -Persian Danser (IRE) (Persian Bold) $5714^{18}$ $5927^{13}$ $6406^{12}$ >66a 64f<

**Sheer Tenby (IRE)** 7 b h Tenby-Take My Pledge (IRE) (Ahonoora) $2744a^{4}$ $3074^{19}$ $4371a^{7}$ >99f<

**She Is Tosho (JPN)** 4 b f Sakura Bakushin O (JPN) -Jane Tosho (JPN) (Tosho Fleet (JPN)) $5982a^{7}$ >107f<

**Shekan Star** 2 b f Sri Pekan (USA) -Celestial Welcome (Most Welcome) $4048^{15}$ $4446^{12}$ $4761^{10}$ $6196^{8}$ >50f<

**Sherbourne** 2 b f Tipsy Creek (USA) -Margarets First (Puissance) $1984^{10}$ $2382^{10}$ $4197^{6}$ $4523^{12}$ $5088^{10}$ $5369^{15}$ $5593^{14}$ $6063^{7}$ >27a 44f<

**Sheriff s Deputy** 4 b g Atraf-Forest Fantasy (Rambo Dancer (CAN)) $2271^{8}$ $3536^{8}$ $3771^{3}$ $3929^{15}$ $4569^{9}$ >83a 78f<

**Shersha (IRE)** 5 b m Priolo (USA) -Sheriya (USA) (Green Dancer (USA)) $4159a^{2}$ $4405a^{3}$ $4956a^{6}$ >98f<

**Sherwood Forest** 4 ch g Fleetwood (IRE) -Jay Gee Ell (Vaigly Great) $3040^{8}$ $3367^{3}$ $3794^{6}$ $3881^{8}$ $4005^{5}$ $4275^{2}$ $5058^{6}$ $5229^{13}$ $5238^{8}$ >58 f<

**Sherzabad (IRE)** 7 bb g Doyoun-Sheriya (USA) (Green Dancer (USA)) $2525^{10}$ >47a 49f<

**She s A Diamond** 7 b m Mystiko (USA) -Fairy Kingdom (Prince Sabo) $567^{14}$ >41a 15f<

**She s A Fox** 3 b f Wizard King-Foxie Lady (Wolfhound (USA)) $5537^{7}$ $5851^{11}$ >38f<

**She s Archie (AUS)** 5 br m Archway (IRE) -A Little Timid (AUS) (Almaarad) $6528a^{24}$ >111f<

**Sheshalan (IRE)** 3 ch c Indian Ridge-Sheshara (IRE) (Kahyasi) $6357^{4}$ >35f<

**She s My Dream (IRE)** 2 ch f General Monash (USA) -She s My Love (Most Welcome) $1276^{10}$ $1374^{8}$ $2405^{10}$ $2515^{7}$ >34a 20f<

**She s My Outsider** 2 b f Docksider (USA) -Solar Flare (IRE) (Danehill (USA)) $3627^{11}$ $4234^{3}$ (5407) $6213^{7}$ >79f<

**She s Our Lass (IRE)** 3 b f Orpen (USA) -Sharadja (IRE) (Doyoun) $983^{12}$ $1111^{10}$ (1300) $1467^{3}$ (2292) (3004) (4242) (4610) $4902^{2}$ $5582^{7}$ >51a 85+f<

**Shibumi** 3 ch f Cigar-Hurricane Rose (Windjammer (USA)) $2675^{5}$ $3085^{5}$ $3636^{4}$ $4259^{4}$ >55f<

**Shielaligh** 3 ch f Aragon-Sheesha (USA) (Shadeed (USA)) $986^{8}$ $1388^{7}$ $2264^{3}$ $2589^{10}$ $3158^{6}$ $4701^{6}$ $5101^{5}$ $6079^{5}$ >64a 70f<

**Shifting Place** 2 ch f Compton Place-Shifting Mist (Night Shift (USA)) (3362a) $4184a^{2}$ $4981a^{9}$ $5404a^{9}$ >100f<

**Shifty** 5 b g Night Shift (USA) -Crodelle (IRE) (Formidable (USA)) $546^{5}$ $874^{12}$ $1247^{13}$ $1502^{9}$ $1748^{4}$ $1868^{8}$ $1993^{5}$ $2356^{2}$ $2854^{4}$ $3167^{4}$ $3516^{9}$ $3586^{9}$ $4246^{13}$ >62a 62 f<

**Shifty Night (IRE)** 3 b f Night Shift (USA) -Bean Island (USA) (Afleet (CAN)) $2211^{15}$ $2675^{9}$ $3381^{4}$ (3708) $4104^{10}$ $4338^{6}$ $4650^{10}$ $4817^{9}$ $4926^{4}$ $6567^{12}$ >54a 46f<

**Shingle Street (IRE)** 2 b g Bahhare (USA) -Sandystones (Selkirk (USA)) $2234^{7}$ $2674^{9}$ $5227^{8}$ $6181^{2}$ $6322^{5}$ >70f<

**Shinko Femme (IRE)** 3 b f Shinko Forest (IRE) -Kilshanny (Groom Dancer (USA)) $2046^{10}$ $2351^{13}$ $2457^{13}$ $3002^{5}$ (3368) $3622^{9}$ $4241^{9}$ (4568) $5141^{3}$ $5552^{8}$ >59f<

**Shinko s Best (IRE)** 3 ch g Shinko Forest (IRE) -Sail Away (GER) (Platini (GER)) $6379a^{8}$ >87f<

**Shiny Thing (USA)** 2 br f Lear Fan (USA) -Juliet s Jewel (USA) (Houston (USA)) $5694^{5}$ $6078^{8}$ >60f<

**Shirley Not** 8 gr g Paris House-Hollia (Touch Boy) $1421^{20}$ $1533^{12}$ >59a 41 f<

**Shirley Oaks (IRE)** 6 b m Sri Pekan (USA) -Duly Elected (Persian Bold) $536^{12}$ $791^{5}$ $858^{10}$ $951^{2}$ $1165^{3}$ (1280) $1986^{6}$ $2188^{3}$ (2762) $2886^{2}$ $3103^{9}$ $3828^{11}$ $4148^{6}$ $4546^{7}$ >51a 58f<

**Shirocco (GER)** 3 b c Monsun (GER) -So Sedulous (USA) (The Minstrel (CAN)) $2926a^{3}$ (3565a) $5329a^{3}$ (6260a) >120f<

**Shish (IRE)** 2 b f Rossini (USA) -Kebabs (IRE) (Catrail (USA)) $2003^{6}$ $2124^{6}$ $2405^{4}$ $2725^{3}$ $2946^{7}$ >45a 32f<

**Shivaree** 2 ch f Rahy (USA) -Shmoose (IRE) (Caerleon (USA)) $2245^{3}$ (3398) $3599^{4}$ $4060^{7}$ $4757^{3}$ $5719^{10}$ $6206^{13}$ >87f<

**Shohrah (IRE)** 2 ch f Giant s Causeway (USA) -Taqreem (IRE) (Nashwan (USA)) (4074) $5779^{5}$ >105f<

**Shoko** 3 b f Efisio-Gold Florenly (FR) (Goldneyev (USA)) $1778a^{4}$ $2341a^{8}$ $4430a^{12}$ $6258a^{7}$ >91f<

**Sholay (IRE)** 5 b g Bluebird (USA) -Splicing (Sharpo) $740^{8}$ $821^{7}$ $1016^{9}$ $2034^{12}$ $3695^{4}$ $4736^{10}$ >42a 42f<

**Sholto** 6 b g Tragic Role (USA) -Rose Mill (Puissance) $1872^{7}$ $2734^{2}$ $3126^{15}$ $6539^{11}$ >43a 65f<

**Shongweni (IRE)** 3 gr g Desert King (IRE) -Spend A Rubble (USA) (Spend A Buck (USA)) $2093^{4}$ $2882^{3}$ $3348^{3}$ $4062^{8}$ $4448^{5}$ >69a 77f<

**Shooting Lodge (IRE)** 3 b f Grand Lodge (USA) -Sidama (FR) (Top Ville) $2562^{5}$ >66f<

**Shortbread** 2 ch c Selkirk (USA) -Breadcrumb (Final Straw) $6145^{13}$ $6351^{8}$ >63f<

**Short Change (IRE)** 5 b g Revoque (IRE) -Maafi Esm (Polish Precedent (USA)) $1644^{8}$ $1858^{4}$ $2705^{5}$ (2939) >54f<

**Short Chorus** 3 ch f Inchinor-Strawberry Song (Final Straw) $1209^{8}$ $1517^{4}$ $1676^{9}$ (2910) $3562^{2}$ $3838^{4}$ $4320^{2}$ $4688^{4}$ $5473^{13}$ $6114^{3}$ >29a 60f<

**Short Pause** 5 b h Sadler s Wells (USA) -Interval (Habitat) $1261a^{3}$ (1922a) $2924a^{3}$ $3567a^{4}$ $5502a^{2}$ >116f<

**Shoshana (IRE)** 3 b f Perugino (USA) -Nishan (Nashwan (USA)) $3328a^{3}$ >81f<

**Shosolosa (IRE)** 2 br f Dansili-Hajat (Mujtahid (USA)) $2786^{11}$ $3045^{2}$ $3532^{2}$ $4621^{3}$ $5648^{10}$ $5938^{5}$ $6574^{16}$ >74f<

**Shotley Dancer** 5 ch m Danehill Dancer (IRE) -Hayhurst (Sandhurst Prince) $823^{4}$ $934^{10}$ $1389^{12}$ $2811^{4}$ $3060^{3}$ $3612^{5}$ $3919^{3}$ (4210) $4397^{4}$ $4627^{2}$ (5145) $5638^{11}$ >35a 56f<

**Shot To Fame (USA)** 5 b g Quest For Fame-Exocet (USA) (Deposit Ticket (USA)) $1284^{5}$ $1456^{18}$ (1828) (2588) $3323^{2}$ (3724) $4685^{5}$ $5291^{5}$ $5917^{12}$ >114f<

**Showbiz (IRE)** 2 b f Sadler s Wells (USA) -Movie Legend (USA) (Affirmed (USA)) $6367a^{9}$ >81+f<

**Show Me Heaven** 7 b m Rock City-Tufty Lady (Riboboy (USA)) $4631^{2}$ >7a<

**Show No Fear** 3 b c Groom Dancer (USA) -La Piaf (FR) (Fabulous Dancer (USA)) (1357) $1831^{8}$ $2134^{11}$ $2361^{6}$ >54a 74f<

**Showtime Annie** 3 b f Wizard King-Rebel County (IRE) (Maelstrom Lake) $907^{6}$ (1038) $1464^{16}$ $1678^{4}$ (2259) $4877^{5}$ $5063^{8}$ $5370^{9}$ $5582^{2}$ $5859^{12}$ $6138^{16}$ >62a 72f<

**Showtime Faye** 2 b f Overbury (IRE) -Rebel County (IRE) (Maelstrom Lake) $5855^{9}$ $6139^{8}$ $6400^{8}$ >3a 21f<

**Shredded (USA)** 4 b c Diesis-Shiitake (USA) (Green Dancer (USA)) $2000^{9}$ $2084^{2}$ (2631) $3325^{8}$ $4715^{6}$ $6143^{3}$ $6573^{14}$ >84f<

**Shrine Mountain (USA)** 2 b c Distorted Humor (USA) -Fancy Ruler (USA) (Half A Year (USA)) $3946^{9}$ $4461^{2}$ $4835^{7}$ $5417^{16}$ >81f<

**Shrink** 3 b f Mind Games-Miss Mercy (IRE) (Law Society (USA)) $881^{2}$ (1228) $1775^{4}$ $2444^{4}$ $2741^{16}$ $4299^{9}$ $4650^{3}$ >69a 69f<

**Shuchbaa** 2 b f Zaha (CAN) -Little Miss Rocker (Rock Hopper) $2364^{3}$ $2858^{11}$ $3506^{12}$ $5192^{7}$ >38f<

**Shuheb 3** ch f Nashwan (USA) -Shimna (Mr Prospector (USA)) 2401$^5$ 2807$^4$ **>96f<**

**Shujune Al Hawaa (IRE) 2** ch f Grand Lodge (USA) -Bank On Her (USA) (Rahy (USA)) 2205$^5$ 3476$^6$ 3974$^3$ 4365$^9$ 4907$^{11}$ 5738$^{18}$ 5885$^6$ 6140$^{10}$ **>63f<**

**Shush 6** b g Shambo-Abuzz (Absalom) 5875$^{15}$ 6183$^7$ **>65a 66f<**

**Shyshiyra (IRE) 3** b f Kahyasi-Shiyra (Darshaan) 3607$^{10}$ **>16f<**

**Sian Thomas 3** ch f Magic Ring (IRE) -Midnight Break (Night Shift (USA)) 5424$^3$ 5621$^{12}$ 5828$^5$ **>62+f<**

**Siberian Highness (FR) 3** b f Highest Honor (FR) -Emblem (FR) (Siberian Express (USA)) 2028a$^9$ **>91f<**

**Siberion (GER) 3** br c Acambaro (GER) -Siberian s Image (Siberian Express (USA)) 1656a$^3$ 2541a$^6$ **>98f<**

**Sideshow 2** ch f In The Wings-Sheer Harmony (USA) (Woodman (USA)) 4851$^{11}$ 5789$^4$ **>58f<**

**Siegfrieds Night (IRE) 3** ch g Night Shift (USA) -Shelbiana (USA) (Chieftain) *(435) 610$^4$ 732$^3$ 804$^2$ 957$^3$* 1108$^3$ 1201$^3$ 1509$^6$1823$^2$ (2146) 2546$^3$ 2821$^3$ 3020$^5$ *3379$^5$* 3584$^3$ 3837$^7$ 4346$^7$4457$^2$ 5365$^5$ 5860$^9$ **>68a 68f<**

**Siena Gold 2** bb f Key Of Luck (USA) -Corn Futures (Nomination) (1399) (2083) 2970$^8$ (3938) 4217$^8$ 4962a$^4$ 5404a$^7$ 6456$^3$ **>93f<**

**Siena Star (IRE) 6** b g Brief Truce (USA) -Gooseberry Pie (Green Desert (USA)) *1085$^2$* **>85a 84f<**

**Sienna Sunset (IRE) 5** ch m Spectrum (IRE) -Wasabi (IRE) (Polar Falcon (USA)) 1606$^{10}$ 1752$^6$ 3264$^6$ 4045$^2$ 4471$^4$ (4760) 5145$^3$ 5374$^{12}$ 5622$^7$6343$^{11}$ *6551$^3$* **>58a 69f<**

**Siera Spirit (IRE) 3** b f Desert Sun-Jay And-A (IRE) (Elbio) *489$^4$ 673$^3$ 1052$^8$* 1184$^2$ 1300$^3$ **>52a 61+f<**

**Sierra 3** ch f Dr Fong (USA) -Warning Belle (Warning) 3374$^5$ 3922$^6$ 4451$^6$ 5223$^5$ 5410$^{12}$ **>60f<**

**Sierra Vista 4** ch f Atraf-Park Vista (Taufan (USA)) 1113$^{14}$ 1343$^3$ 1774$^{10}$ 2041$^9$ 2143$^5$ (3309) 3754$^6$ 4134$^9$ 4759$^{15}$5263$^5$ 5603$^8$ 6205$^9$ **>90f<**

**Sights On Gold (IRE) 5** ch h Indian Ridge-Summer Trysting (USA) (Alleged (USA)) (5180) (5611) 5968a$^7$ 6219$^2$ **>117+f<**

**Sign Of Luck (IRE) 2** ch f Daylami (IRE) -Ascot Cyclone (USA) (Rahy (USA)) 5695$^9$ *6447$^4$* **>68a 57f<**

**Sign Of Promise 2** b f Groom Dancer (USA) -Happy Omen (Warning) 6226$^{12}$ **><**

**Sign Of The Wolf 4** b c Loup Solitaire (USA) -Sign Of The Vine (FR) (Kendor (FR)) 853a$^{11}$ 978a$^{11}$ **>107f<**

**Signora Panettiera (FR) 3** ch f Lord Of Men-Karaferya (USA) (Green Dancer (USA)) 1394$^6$ 1499$^8$ *2485$^6$* 2822$^{11}$ 3572$^9$ 5538$^7$ 5634$^4$ 6438$^6$ **>25a 33f<**

**Signor Panettiere 3** b c Night Shift (USA) -Christmas Kiss (Taufan (USA)) 2063$^8$ 2266$^2$ 3273$^6$ 3344$^7$ 4044$^2$ **>75f<**

**Sign Writer (USA) 2** b c Quiet American (USA) -Mata Cara (Storm Bird (CAN)) 3643$^6$ 3946$^2$ *4334$^4$* 5154$^3$ 6129$^8$ **>54a 83f<**

**Silber Mond 2** gr c Monsun (GER) -Salinova (FR) (Linamix (FR)) 6441$^{11}$ 6565$^{10}$ **>51f<**

**Silca s Gift 3** b f Cadeaux Genereux-Odette (Pursuit Of Love) (1398) 1791$^8$ 2117$^5$ 2966$^9$ 3715$^9$ **>106f<**

**Silence Is Golden 5** ch m Danehill Dancer (IRE) -Silent Girl (Krayyan) (1328) 1790$^2$ 2543a$^9$ 3484$^2$ 4323$^2$ **>115f<**

**Silencio (IRE) 3** b g Sillery (USA) -Flabbergasted (IRE) (Sadler s Wells (USA)) 1674$^7$ 2001$^{13}$ 2374$^{14}$ 2611$^7$ 3342$^5$ 3572$^7$ **>65 f<**

**Silent Angel 4** b f Petong-Valls D Andorra (Free State) *718$^{11}$ 944$^{10}$* **>18f<**

**Silent Deal (JPN) 4** b c Sunday Silence (USA) -Fairy Doll (USA) (Nureyev (USA)) *1147a$^{12}$* **>113a 108f<**

**Silent Flight (FR) 3** ch f Sicyos (USA) -Flying Past (FR) (Kendor (FR)) 6203a$^0$ **><**

**Silent Hawk (IRE) 3** b c Halling (USA) -Nightbird (IRE) (Night Shift (USA)) 1794$^4$ (2280) 2676$^{12}$ 3641$^4$ 4950$^{10}$ 5397$^{11}$ 6444$^5$ **>89f<**

**Silent Jo (JPN) 2** b c Sunday Silence (USA) -Jo Knows (USA) (The Minstrel (CAN)) 4290$^3$ 5373$^2$ 6151$^3$ **>87+f<**

**Silent Name (JPN) 2** b c Sunday Silence (USA) -Danzigaway (USA) (Danehill (USA)) 6320a$^2$ **>98f<**

**Silent Sighs (USA) 3** br f Benchmark (USA) -Quiet Romance (USA) (Bertrando (USA)) $^{10}$ **>111a<**

**Silent Spring (USA) 2** b f Honour And Glory (USA) -Polar Bird (Thatching) 3676$^8$ **>60f<**

**Silent Storm 4** ch c Zafonic (USA) -Nanda (Nashwan (USA)) *3279$^3$* 4063$^3$ 4511$^{13}$ *4602$^{10}$ 4926$^2$ 6026$^3$ (6066)* **>78a 79f<**

**Silistra 5** gr g Sadler s Wells (USA) -Dundel (IRE) (Machiavellian (USA)) *818$^8$ 914$^{14}$* 2728$^{11}$ 3828$^{14}$ 4485$^5$ 4802$^7$ 5283$^6$ **>43f<**

**Silk And Scarlet 2** b f Sadler s Wells (USA) -Danilova (USA) (Lyphard (USA)) (3859a) (4592a) 5325a$^7$ **>102f<**

**Silk Cravat (IRE) 3** ch g Dr Devious (IRE) -Dances With Dreams (Be My Chief (USA)) 3094$^8$ **>48f<**

**Silken Brief (IRE) 5** gr m Ali-Royal (IRE) -Tiffany s Case (IRE) (Thatching) *577$^6$ 870$^{11}$* **>81a 81f<**

**Silken John (IRE) 3** ch g Grand Lodge (USA) -Lady Ela (IRE) (Ela-Mana-Mou) 2168$^{13}$ 5538$^5$ 6088$^{11}$ **>50f<**

**Silk Fan (IRE) 3** b f Unfuwain (USA) -Alikhlas (Lahib (USA)) (3542) 4286$^6$ 4948$^4$ 5249$^4$ 5573$^4$ 6147$^4$ **>101f<**

**Silky Lagoon (JPN) 4** br f Brian s Time (USA) -Sea Venus (JPN) (Dayjur (USA)) 5982a$^5$ **>108f<**

**Silloth Spirit 4** b g Atraf-Gaelic Air (Ballad Rock) 5345$^{12}$ 5591$^4$ 5851$^{13}$ **>11f<**

**Silsong (USA) 2** ch f Stephen Got Even (USA) -Silver Trainor (USA) (Silver Hawk (USA)) 4682$^5$ 5198$^{15}$ 5620$^8$ 5852$^{11}$ **>61f<**

**Silvaline 5** gr g Linamix (FR) -Upend (Main Reef) *820$^6$ 964$^{11}$ 1085$^4$* 1460$^5$ 1540$^5$ 2142$^{14}$ 2474$^6$ 2687$^8$*(2881)* (3482) 3692$^8$ 4343$^3$ 4540$^{10}$ 4950$^2$ 5122$^6$ *5739$^{10}$* **>73a 92f<**

**Silver Bark 2** b f Royal Applause-Argent Du Bois (USA) (Silver Hawk (USA)) 5720$^8$ 5890$^5$ **>56f<**

**Silver Cache (USA) 3** b f Silver Hawk (USA) -Nina Ashley (USA) (Criminal Type (USA)) *447$^{10}$ 563$^9$ 846$^5$* 1643$^4$ **>55a 55f<**

**Silver Chime 4** gr f Robellino (USA) -Silver Charm (Dashing Blade) *1051$^9$* 1750$^{11}$ 2219$^4$ (2506) 2875$^5$ 3326$^6$ 3439$^6$ 4522$^{11}$ 4751$^9$5242$^{11}$ 5425$^{14}$ 5618$^{10}$ *6273$^{12}$* **>70a 79f<**

**Silver City 4** ro g Unfuwain (USA) -Madiyla (Darshaan) 3442$^2$ 3909$^7$ 4737$^{10}$ 5423$^{12}$ 5728$^{10}$ 6150$^4$ **>85f<**

**Silver Court 2** b c Silver Patriarch (IRE) -Double Stake (USA) (Kokand (USA)) 5703$^6$ 6078$^{14}$ 6309$^9$ **><**

**Silver Creek 2** gr c Tipsy Creek (USA) -Silver Wedding (Warning) 4770$^{11}$ 4966$^{12}$ 5200$^{16}$ *5640$^{10}$* **>18a 46f<**

**Silver Crystal (IRE) 4** b f Among Men (USA) -Silver Moon (Environment Friend) *456$^9$ 518$^8$ 997$^8$* **><**

**Silver Dreamer (IRE) 2** b f Brave Act-Heads We Called (IRE) (Bluebird (USA)) 5172$^{11}$ 5348$^{11}$ **>39f<**

**Silver Emperor (IRE) 3** gr g Lil s Boy (USA) -Just Possible (Kalaglow) *409$^7$ 585$^7$* **>36a<**

**Silver Gilt 4** b g Silver Hawk (USA) -Memory s Gold (USA) (Java Gold (USA)) 1618$^3$ 2672$^3$ (3538) 4270$^6$ 4832$^9$ 5415$^8$ **>110f<**

**Silver Harbour (USA) 3** b f Silver Hawk (USA) -Bristol Channel (Generous (IRE)) 4251a$^5$ **>42f<**

**Silverhay 3** b g Inchinor-Moon Spin (Night Shift (USA)) 1957$^4$ 2529$^2$ 2977$^4$ (3780) (4451) 4780$^4$ 5582$^3$ **>77f<**

**Silver Highlight (CAN) 2** rg f Silver Charm (USA) -Rare Opportunity (USA) (Danzig Connection (USA)) 3905$^9$ 4498$^2$ 5508$^2$ **>84f<**

**Silver Island 3** ch g Silver Patriarch (IRE) -Island Maid (Forzando) *2853$^7$ 3279$^7$* 4669$^{12}$ 5794$^6$ 6228$^{15}$ **>33a 41f<**

**Silverleaf 2** b c Lujain (USA) -Lovely Millie (IRE) (Bluebird (USA)) 3319$^6$ 4290$^5$ 4922$^5$ 5269$^7$ 5596$^{20}$ **>69f<**

**Silver Louie (IRE) 4** gr f Titus Livius (FR) -Shakamiyn (Nishapour (FR)) *914$^{12}$ 1278$^{11}$* 2573$^{RR}$ **><**

**Silver Mascot 5** gr g Mukaddamah (USA) -Always Lucky (Absalom) *530$^4$ 573$^7$ 658$^2$ 807$^2$ 934$^5$ (993) 1176$^4$ 1423$^2$*1533$^3$ 2260$^{10}$ 2656$^{11}$ (2936) 3226$^2$ *3615$^{12}$* 4011$^{10}$ 4751$^{12}$ 5572$^{26}$ **>59a 64f<**

**Silver Mistress 5** gr m Syrtos-Galava (CAN) (Graustark) 1989$^7$ **>57f<**

**Silver Phantom (IRE) 2** b g Spectrum (IRE) -Beat It (USA) (Diesis) 1390$^{11}$ **><**

**Silver Prelude 3** gr g Prince Sabo-Silver Blessings (Statoblest) 2115$^7$ 2552$^8$ 2877$^{11}$ 3273$^3$ (3645) 3777$^8$ 4289$^{16}$ 4810$^9$ 5440$^{17}$5563$^{10}$ 5893$^{14}$ **>91f<**

**Silver Prophet (IRE) 5** gr g Idris (IRE) -Silver Heart (Yankee Gold) 1460$^{18}$ 2000$^5$ 2305$^5$ 2787$^5$ 3244$^7$ 4080$^{16}$ (4849) 5203$^5$ 5875$^6$6286$^3$ **>74a 76f<**

**Silver Rain (FR) 4** ch f Rainbow Quest (USA) -Riviere D Argent (USA) (Nijinsky (CAN)) 4982a$^{10}$ **>101f<**

**Silver Reign 3** gr g Prince Sabo-Primo Donna Magna (Primo Dominie) 1133$^5$ 1293$^6$ 5147$^9$ 6288$^{18}$ **>40f<**

**Silver Rhythm 3** ch f Silver Patriarch (IRE) -Party Treat (IRE) (Millfontaine) 1524$^3$ 1933$^5$ 2977$^7$ 4307$^8$ *4927$^7$* 6208$^5$ **>13a 51f<**

**Silver Sash (GER) 3** gr f Mark Of Esteem (IRE) -Salinova (FR) (Linamix (FR)) 2805$^6$ 3204$^3$ (3625) 4884$^5$ 5300$^8$ 5822a$^{11}$ **>89f<**

**Silver Seeker (USA) 4** gr g Seeking The Gold (USA) -Zelanda (IRE) (Night Shift (USA)) *1011$^5$* 1246$^{13}$ 2366$^{10}$ 2528$^2$ 3365$^8$ 3895$^6$ 4280$^9$ 4827$^7$5346$^{15}$ 5821$^{11}$ **>61a 61f<**

**Silver Silence (JPN) 3** bb c Sunday Silence (USA) -Island Of Silver (USA) (Forty Niner (USA)) 5357a$^8$ **>89f<**

**Silverskaya (USA) 3** bb f Silver Hawk (USA) -Boubskaia (Niniski (USA)) (2700a) 3566a$^7$ (5033a) 5501a$^6$ 5981a$^8$ **>115f<**

**Silver Song 2** gr c Silver Patriarch (IRE) -Singing The Blues (Bonny Scot (IRE)) 5269$^{12}$ 5870$^{11}$ 6565$^{11}$ **>50f<**

**Silverstein (USA) 3** bb c Seeking The Gold (USA) -Salchow (USA) (Nijinsky (CAN)) 2114$^3$ **>78f<**

**Silver Swan (USA) 4** br f Silver Hawk (USA) -Shy Swan (USA) (Nureyev (USA)) 6107a$^8$ **>85f<**

**Silver Swing 2** gr c Celtic Swing-Poetry In Motion (IRE) (Ballad Rock) *5911$^9$* 6000$^{10}$ 6272$^6$ **>32a 32f<**

**Silvertown 9** b g Danehill (USA) -Docklands (USA) (Theatrical) 1172$^{12}$ 2583$^7$ 3199$^{16}$ 6096$^{17}$ 6198$^4$ **>79f<**

**Silver Tree (USA) 4** ch c Hennessy (USA) -Blue Begum (USA) (With Approval (CAN)) 6486a$^5$ **>116f<**

**Silver Visage (IRE) 2** b g Lujain (USA) -About Face (Midyan (USA)) 1374$^5$ 2095$^5$ 3083$^5$ 5596$^{16}$ *6393$^5$* **>64a 59f<**

**Silver Wraith (IRE) 2** b c Danehill Dancer (IRE) -Alpine Lady (IRE) (Tirol) 2225$^4$ 2439$^2$ (2702) (2868) 3677$^3$ (4089) 4288$^3$ 4949$^5$ **>102f<**

**Silver Zetto (IRE) 3** ch c Foxhound (USA) -Krayyalei (IRE) (Krayyan) 5982a$^{10}$ **>101f<**

**Simeon 5** b h Lammtarra (USA) -Noble Lily (USA) (Vaguely Noble) 712a$^7$ 850a$^7$ 978a$^{12}$ 1003a$^2$ **>114f<**

**Simianna 5** b m Bluegrass Prince (IRE) -Lowrianna (IRE) (Cyrano De Bergerac) 1391$^5$ 1685$^5$ 1923$^2$ 2143$^8$ 2488$^6$ 2685$^7$ 2903a$^2$ 3074$^7$3308$^7$ 3901$^4$ 4152$^6$ 4324$^5$ 4590a$^7$ 4779$^3$ 5105$^2$ (5454) 5671$^5$5780$^8$ 5948$^7$ **>86a 103f<**

**Simlet 9** b g Forzando-Besito (Wassl) 6005$^5$ **>45f<**

**Simonas (IRE) 5** gr h Sternkoenig (IRE) -Sistadari (Shardari) 3136a$^6$ 4794a$^4$ 5329a$^4$ 6384a$^2$ **>122f<**

**Simonda 3** ch f Singspiel (IRE) -Jetbeeah (IRE) (Lomond (USA)) 4813$^2$ (5339) **>79f<**

**Simonovski (USA) 3** b c Miswaki (USA) -Earthra (USA) (Rahy (USA)) *1052$^7$* 1688$^8$ 3529$^3$ 4082$^2$ 5274$^{15}$ 5875$^{17}$ **>66a 66f<**

**Simon s Seat (USA) 5** ch g Woodman (USA) -Spire (USA) (Topsider (USA)) 1210$^6$ 3095$^6$ 4554$^6$ 5027$^{10}$ *5907$^8$ 6581$^6$* **>63a 75f<**

**Simple Exchange (IRE) 3** b c Danehill (USA) -Summer Trysting (USA) (Alleged (USA)) 3000$^4$ 4769a$^4$ 5968a$^6$ **>110f<**

**Simple Ideals (USA) 10** bb g Woodman (USA) -Comfort And Style (Be My Guest (USA)) 3236$^5$ 3564$^4$ *3803$^8$* 4448$^6$ 4609$^7$ 5214$^5$ **>40a 48?f<**

**Simplex (FR) 3** b c Rainbow Quest (USA) -Russyskia (USA) (Green Dancer (USA)) 6263a$^2$ **>111f<**

**Simplify 2** b c Fasliyev (USA) -Simplicity (Polish Precedent (USA)) 1436$^4$ 2592$^5$ 3124$^3$ 3634$^2$ 3886$^5$ 4365$^7$ (5202) 5421$^8$ 6091$^{13}$ **>79f<**

**Simply Honest (IRE) 9** ch g Simply Great (FR) -Susans Glory (Billion (USA)) 2285$^{11}$ **>60 f<**

**Simply Red 3** ch g Vettori (IRE) -Amidst (Midyan (USA)) 1111$^9$ 1304$^8$ *1571$^7$* 2359$^{12}$ **>38f<**

**Simply St Lucia 2** b f Charnwood Forest (IRE) -Mubadara (IRE) (Lahib (USA)) *(2985)* 4919$^3$ 5082$^3$ 5292$^6$ **>64a 70f<**

**Simply The Guest (IRE) 5** b g Mujadil (USA) -Ned s Contessa (IRE) (Persian Heights) *434$^2$ 472$^2$ (582) (667) 1032$^4$ 1427$^{11}$* 5526$^{13}$ 6124$^{16}$ **>67a 43f<**

**Simpsons Mount (IRE) 3** ch g Tagula (IRE) -Brunswick (Warning) *764$^6$ 1083$^5$ 1228$^3$* 2063$^7$ 2165$^5$ 2399$^{10}$ (2726) 2889$^5$5473$^{16}$ 5737$^{10}$ *(6016)* **>75+a 70f<**

**Sinaada (GER) 3** br f Zinaad-Seta Pura (FR) (Konigsstuhl (GER)) 5822a$^5$ **>75f<**

**Sinamay (USA) 3** b f Saint Ballado (CAN) -Chenille (IRE) (Tenby) 4781$^{10}$ **><**

**Singhalese 2** ch f Singspiel (IRE) -Baize (Efisio) 4315$^4$ 4851$^3$ 5088$^3$ (5417) **>88f<**

**Singhalongtasveer 2** b g Namaqualand (USA) -Felinwen (White Mill) 2140$^{10}$ 2755$^5$ 3951$^3$ 4304$^7$ 5097$^9$ 5447$^5$ 6093$^9$ 6195$^9$ **>54f<**

**Singitta 3** b f Singspiel (IRE) -Ferber s Follies (USA) (Saratoga Six (USA)) 1508$^{11}$ 2832$^7$ 6285$^9$ **>41f<**

**Singlet 3** ch c Singspiel (IRE) -Ball Gown (Jalmood (USA)) 3297$^7$ 3843$^8$ **>65f<**

**Singletary (USA) 4** b c Sultry Song (USA) -Joiski s Star (USA) (Star De Naskra (USA)) (6486a) **>123f<**

**Single Track Mind 6** b g Mind Games-Compact Disc (IRE) (Royal Academy (USA)) *527$^{10}$ 858$^2$ 999$^5$ 1020$^4$ 1165$^5$ 1204$^9$ 1278$^2$1692$^3$ 1723$^5$* 1986$^8$ 2441$^7$ 2886$^6$ 3049$^4$ 3423$^7$ 3441$^7$*6404$^{13}$* **>50a 48f<**

**Singularity 4** b g Rudimentary (USA) -Lyrical Bid (USA) (Lyphard (USA)) *1077$^{11}$ 1723$^{11}$ 3932$^{11}$ 5641$^{LFT}$* **>26 a 26f<**

**Sinistra 3** br f Dracula (AUS) -Sardegna (Pharly (FR)) 2085$^{10}$ **>38f<**

**Sinjaree 6** b g Mark Of Esteem (IRE) -Forthwith (Midyan (USA)) *437$^{10}$ 903$^5$ (989) 1181$^7$* 1503$^6$ 3917$^{12}$ 4493$^7$ 4852$^{14}$6057$^7$ *6406$^4$* 6561$^6$ **>53a 53f<**

**Sink Or Swim (IRE) 6** b m Big Sink Hope (USA) -Cragreagh VII (Damsire Unregistered) *984$^{10}$ 1055$^{11}$ 1727$^5$* 1989$^8$ **>30a<**

**Sion Hill (IRE) 3** b g Desert Prince (IRE) -Mobilia (Last Tycoon) 3920$^{13}$ 4059$^{10}$ 5244$^{11}$ 5715$^{10}$ 6271$^9$ *6537$^7$* **>57a 70f<**

**Siraj 5** b g Piccolo-Masuri Kabisa (USA) (Ascot Knight (CAN)) *1595$^8$ (4879)* 5094$^{10}$ 6001$^9$ *6220$^7$ 6273$^4$ 6499$^9$* **>72a 73f<**

**Sir Alfred 5** b g Royal Academy (USA) -Magnificent Star (USA) (Silver Hawk (USA)) 3873$^8$ 4146$^4$ 4616$^{10}$ *6296$^{11}$* **>48a 59f<**

**Sir Anthony (IRE) 2** b c Danehill Dancer (IRE) -Brief Fairy (IRE) (Brief Truce (USA)) (3248) 3865$^3$ 4445$^2$ 4890$^6$ 5128$^2$ 5417$^3$ **>88+f<**

**Sir Bluebird (IRE) 2** ch c Bluebird (USA) -Persian Tapestry (Tap On Wood) 5003$^{11}$ 5118$^9$ 5609$^6$ *6012$^{10}$* **>30a 64f<**

**Sir Bond (IRE) 3** ch g Desert Sun-In Tranquility (IRE) (Shalford (IRE)) 1116$^9$ 1450$^4$ 1722$^5$ **>33f<**

**Sirce (IRE) 2** b f Josr Algarhoud (IRE) -Trading Aces (Be My Chief (USA)) 2786$^{17}$ 3343$^6$ 3770$^8$ 5335$^{12}$ 6226$^4$ **>49f<**

**Sir Desmond 6** gr g Petong-I m Your Lady (Risk Me (FR)) *417$^3$ 607$^8$* 3309$^{18}$ 3723$^3$ 3945$^5$ 4751$^6$ 5075$^4$ 5603$^{20}$6205$^4$ (6517) **>86a 88f<**

**Sir Don (IRE) 5** b g Lake Coniston (IRE) -New Sensitive (Wattlefield) 1199$^9$ 1452$^{10}$ 1825$^{17}$ 2899$^{20}$ (2976) 3298$^{16}$ 3623$^3$ 3979$^5$ 4013$^8$4291$^{24}$ 5008$^{14}$ 5020$^{14}$ 5458$^9$ 5583$^{16}$ **>62 a 73f<**

**Sir Edward Burrow (IRE) 6** b g Distinctly North (USA) -Alalja (IRE) (Entitled) 6209$^8$ 6468$^2$ **>41a 54f<**

**Sir Edwin Landseer (USA) 4** gr c Lit De Justice (USA) -Wildcat Blue (USA) (Cure The Blues (USA)) 3036$^{20}$ 3941$^{13}$ 4232$^{20}$ 4366$^{11}$ 4748$^7$ **>82f<**

**Sir Ernest (IRE) 3** b g Daggers Drawn (USA) -Kyra Crown (IRE) (Astronef) 1788$^7$ 1883$^6$ 2552$^{11}$ 2650$^2$ 3077$^{11}$ 3338$^4$ 3702$^2$ 3920$^{17}$4862$^{14}$ 5181$^{14}$ 5458$^6$ **>66a 79f<**

**Sir Francis (IRE) 6** b g Common Grounds-Red Note (Rusticaro (FR)) *647$^9$ 742$^{10}$ 847$^8$ 1204$^{10}$* 1877$^5$ **>78a 79f<**

**Sir Frank Gibson 3** b g Primo Dominie-Serotina (IRE) (Mtoto) *531$^7$ 611$^4$ 752$^2$ 804$^3$ 957$^8$ 2054$^5$ 2452$^5$*3809$^5$ *3934$^9$* **>44a 50f<**

**Sir Galahad 3** ch g Hector Protector (USA) -Sharpening (Sharpo) *956$^7$ 1044$^7$* 1360$^5$ 1667$^3$ 2037$^4$ **>40a 56f<**

**Sir George Turner 5** ch g Nashwan (USA) -Ingozi (Warning) 1622$^{10}$ 2066$^{14}$ 2527$^8$ 2638$^{10}$ 3034$^{13}$ 4214$^7$ 4530$^8$ 5468$^{11}$5627$^3$ **>101f<**

**Sir Haydn 4** ch g Definite Article-Snowscape (Niniski (USA)) 1213$^3$ 1611$^6$ 2000$^{10}$ 2277$^6$ 3276$^7$ 3534$^5$ 3997$^3$ 4196$^{11}$4950$^{11}$ 5492$^7$ 5853$^8$ **>75 f<**

**Sir Jasper (IRE) 3** b g Sri Pekan (USA) -Ashover Amber (Green Desert (USA)) *(514) 561$^9$ 595$^3$ 758$^4$ 955$^{10}$* **>62a<**

**Sir Laughalot 4** b g Alzao (USA) -Funny Hilarious (USA) (Sir Ivor (USA)) *415$^2$ 448$^7$ 742$^3$ 870$^2$ 1118$^3$* 1624$^2$ 5615$^{15}$ **>80a 77f<**

**Sir Loin 3** ch g Compton Place-Charnwood Queen (Cadeaux Genereux) 2650$^{10}$ 3270$^7$ 3562$^5$ 3838$^2$ 4309$^6$ 4608$^8$ 5104$^2$ 5473$^2$6114$^2$ **>67f<**

**Sir Monty (USA) 2** ch g Cat s Career (USA) -Lady Of Meadowlane (USA) (Pancho Jay (USA)) 4335$^5$ 4682$^6$ 5114$^4$ 5539$^9$ **>68f<**

**Sir Night (IRE) 4** b g Night Shift (USA) -Highly Respected (IRE) (High Estate) 2216$^4$ 2272$^7$ 2964$^8$ **>54a 54f<**

**Sir Ninja (IRE) 7** b g Turtle Island (IRE) -The Poachers Lady (IRE) (Salmon Leap (USA)) 1263$^2$ 1535$^4$ 2120$^7$ **>65a 65f<**

**Sir Sandrovitch (IRE) 8** b g Polish Patriot (USA) -Old Downie (Be My Guest (USA)) 1956$^{14}$ 2130$^{14}$ 3010$^6$ 3227$^7$ **>69a 71f<**

**Sir Shackleton (USA) 3** ch c Miswaki (USA) -Naskra Colors (USA) (Star De Naskra (USA)) *2139a$^6$* **>105a<**

**Sis City (USA) 2** b f Slew City Slew (USA) -Smart Sis (USA) (Beau Genius (CAN)) *6485a$^4$* **>107a<**

**Si Si Amiga (IRE) 3** b f Desert Style (IRE) -No Hard Feelings (IRE) (Alzao (USA)) 1879$^4$ 2307$^4$ 2807$^5$ 3519$^8$ 4888$^{12}$ **>95f<**

**Si Si Si 2** b f Lomitas-Nottuma (Diu Star) 4420$^7$ **>39f<**

**Sissy Slew (USA) 4** b f Unbridled s Song (USA) -Missy Slew (USA) (Seattle Slew (USA)) 1634a$^5$ 2711a$^6$ **>92f<**

**Sister Gee (IRE) 2** b f Desert Story (IRE) -My Gloria (IRE) (Saint Estephe (FR)) *2985$^4$ 3802$^3$ 4187$^2$* 5671$^{13}$ **>54a 40+f<**

**Sister Moonshine (FR) 3** ch f Piccolo-Cootamundra (FR) (Double Bed (FR)) 3162a$^5$ 4357a$^{10}$ 5333a$^6$ 5671$^{10}$ **>99f<**

**Sister Sophia (USA) 4** bb f Deputy Commander (USA) -Sophiaschoice (USA) (Clev-Er-Tell (USA)) 1372$^{14}$ 3841$^{14}$ 4199$^3$ 4551$^6$ 5155$^7$ 5657$^{17}$ *6154$^7$* **>78a 70f<**

**Six Pack (IRE) 6** ch g Royal Abjar (USA) -Regal Entrance (Be My Guest (USA)) *1080$^2$ 1545$^2$ 1888$^4$ 2053$^{10}$* **>48a 44f<**

**Six Perfections (FR) 4** b f Celtic Swing-Yogya (USA) (Riverman (USA)) 2339a$^2$ 2957$^6$ 4795a$^2$ 6486a$^3$ **>123f<**

**Sixtilsix (IRE) 3** ch g Night Shift (USA) -Assafiyah (IRE) (Kris) 3666$^8$ 3994$^{12}$ *4941$^3$* 5585$^{11}$ *6361$^6$* **>42a 35f<**

**Skater Boy 3** b g Wizard King-Makalu (Godswalk (USA)) 3173$^8$ **>38f<**

**Skelligs Rock (IRE) 4** b c Key Of Luck (USA) -Drew (IRE) (Double Schwartz) 1272$^5$ 1832$^8$ **>72f<**

**Skelthwaite 3** b g Desert Story (IRE) -Skip To Somerfield (Shavian) 3817$^9$ *5001$^9$* 5284$^3$ 5549$^{11}$ *5644$^U$* **>30a 30f<**

**Skibereen (IRE) 4** b g Ashkalani (IRE) -Your Village (IRE) (Be My Guest (USA)) *601$^5$ 651$^6$* 1213$^4$ 1318$^5$ *1475$^8$* 2119$^3$ 2368$^5$ 2752$^{10}$4852$^{12}$ 5317$^{17}$ 5571$^2$ 5867$^2$ 5935$^8$ **>56a 72?f<**

**Skiddaw Jones 4** b g Emperor Jones (USA) -Woodrising (Nomination) 1783$^{11}$ 2424$^5$ 2583$^8$ 2618$^6$ 4537$^2$ 4901$^6$ 5450$^{14}$ **>56f<**

**Skiddaw Wolf 2** ch f Wolfhound (USA) -Stealthy (Kind Of Hush) 2860$^8$ 3197$^3$ 3514$^6$ 4046$^5$ 5797$^4$ 6270$^2$ 6544$^9$ **>62f<**

**Skidmark 3** b c Pennekamp (USA) -Flourishing (IRE) (Trojan Fen) *466$^2$ (704) (883) 1239$^3$* 1538$^4$ 2043$^9$ 5731$^6$ **>103+a 103f<**

**Skidrow 2** b c Bachir (IRE) -Flourishing (IRE) (Trojan Fen) 3336$^7$ (4131) 4872$^2$ 5082$^2$ 6189$^3$ **>85f<**

**Ski Jump (USA) 4** gr g El Prado (IRE) -Skiable (IRE) (Niniski (USA)) (2612) 3207$^6$ 4540$^9$ 4831$^6$ 5288$^7$ 5517$^7$ 5619$^{12}$ 6043$^4$ 6535$^4$ **>87f<**

**Skip Of Colour 4** b g Rainbow Quest (USA) -Minskip (USA) (The Minstrel (CAN)) *520$^4$ 639$^5$ (805)*

897$^{2}$ 1057$^{10}$ 3098$^{6}$ 3293$^{5}$ 5603$^{22}$ >**73a 73f**<

**Skippit John** **2** b g Abou Zouz (USA) -Lady Quinta (IRE) (Gallic League) 1961$^{2}$ 2173$^{6}$ 2904$^{6}$ 4445$^{8}$ 4700$^{9}$ 4997$^{7}$ >**49a 59f**<

**Skoozi (NZ)** **9** b g Prince Of Praise (NZ) -Tweed View (NZ) (Imposing (AUS)) 710a$^{8}$ 925a$^{3}$ 1006a$^{5}$ >**116a 103f**<

**Sky Cove** **3** b g Spectrum (IRE) -Aurora Bay (IRE) (Night Shift (USA)) 567$^{13}$ >**23a 33f**<

**Sky Crusader** **2** b c Mujahid (USA) -Red Cloud (IRE) (Taufan (USA)) (3259) 3726$^{6}$ 4601$^{5}$ 5810$^{3}$ >**77+a 83f**<

**Sky Dome (IRE)** **11** ch g Bluebird (USA) -God Speed Her (Pas De Seul) 1373$^{5}$ >**75a 70f**<

**Skye s Folly (USA)** **4** b g Kris S (USA) -Bittersweet Hour (USA) (Seattle Slew (USA)) 1973$^{7}$ 2285$^{14}$ 2684$^{13}$ 4174$^{3}$ 4578$^{3}$ 5318$^{3}$ 5619$^{4}$ 6074$^{4}$6278$^{2}$ >**84a 79f**<

**Sky Galaxy (USA)** **3** ch f Sky Classic (CAN) -Fly To The Moon (USA) (Blushing Groom (FR)) 2239$^{7}$ 2587$^{10}$ 3826$^{6}$ >**82df**<

**Skyharbor** **3** b g Cyrano De Bergerac-Pea Green (Try My Best (USA)) 1900$^{15}$ 3090$^{5}$ 3523$^{11}$ 4289$^{5}$ 4810$^{2}$ 4952$^{3}$ 5563$^{4}$ 5697$^{13}$5730$^{9}$ 6538$^{7}$ >**59a 87 f**<

**Skylark** **7** ch m Polar Falcon (USA) -Boozy (Absalom) 2813$^{7}$ 3409$^{12}$ 3804$^{14}$ >**30a 66f**<

**Skylarker (USA)** **6** b g Sky Classic (CAN) -O My Darling (USA) (Mr Prospector (USA)) 507$^{2}$ 643$^{3}$ 775$^{3}$ 915$^{12}$ 1624$^{11}$ 2000$^{14}$ 2430$^{4}$ 2835$^{4}$(3492) 4398$^{5}$ 5182$^{5}$ (5764) 6286$^{2}$ >**86a 86f**<

**Sky Quest (IRE)** **6** b g Spectrum (IRE) -Rose Vibert (Caerleon (USA)) (4061) (4737) 5650$^{12}$ >**74a 97+f**<

**Skyscape** **2** b f Zafonic (USA) -Aquarelle (Kenmare (FR)) 6077$^{3}$ >**59f**<

**Skythe (GER)** **4** b c Spectrum (IRE) -Slawa (GER) (Polish Precedent (USA)) 3134a$^{11}$ >**89f**<

**Skywards** **2** b c Machiavellian (USA) -Nawaiet (USA) (Zilzal (USA)) 2024$^{5}$ (2502) 2996$^{3}$ 4217$^{7}$ 5464$^{10}$ >**101f**<

**Slalom (IRE)** **4** b g Royal Applause-Skisette (Malinowski (USA)) (1138) 1460$^{19}$ 3419$^{7}$ 3745$^{5}$ 3911$^{8}$ 4678$^{5}$ 6266$^{13}$ 6395$^{2}$ >**77a 74f**<

**Slamy (USA)** **2** b f Grand Slam (USA) -Accountable Lady (USA) (The Minstrel (CAN)) 5313a$^{10}$ >**56f**<

**Slane Hill (USA)** **3** b c Indian Charlie (USA) -Token Of Esteem (USA) (Fappiano (USA)) 753a$^{2}$ 920a$^{4}$ ><

**Slate Grey** **2** gr c Paris House-Slipperose (Persepolis (FR)) 2674$^{13}$ 2904$^{11}$ 3893$^{8}$ 4507$^{8}$ 5578$^{12}$ 6333$^{20}$ >**51f**<

**Slavonic (USA)** **3** ch g Royal Academy (USA) -Cyrillic (USA) (Irish River (FR)) 1134$^{5}$ 1311$^{4}$ 1640$^{4}$ 2169$^{6}$ 2648$^{4}$ 5994$^{7}$ 6332$^{9}$ 6533$^{11}$ >**72f**<

**Sleeping Indian** **3** b c Indian Ridge-Las Flores (IRE) (Sadler s Wells (USA)) (6132) (6474) >**112+f**<

**Sleeping Weapon (USA)** **5** b h Gulch (USA) -Beating The Buzz (IRE) (Bluebird (USA)) 923a$^{2}$ 977a$^{2}$ >**101a**<

**Slip Catch (IRE)** **2** b f Intikhab (USA) -Buckle (IRE) (Common Grounds) 4936$^{14}$ 5348$^{6}$ >**58f**<

**Slip Dance (IRE)** **2** br f Celtic Swing-Hawala (IRE) (Warning) 2745a$^{4}$ (3316) 3965a$^{6}$ 4552$^{2}$ 5325a$^{6}$ (5681a) 5894$^{5}$ >**103f**<

**Slite** **2** gr f Mind Games-Sapphire Mill (Petong) 4040$^{12}$ 4638$^{2}$ 5132$^{5}$ 5369$^{5}$ 6226$^{5}$ >**52f**<

**Smala Tica (FR)** **4** ch f Loup Solitaire (USA) -Smala (FR) (Antheus (USA)) 2543a$^{8}$ >**91f**<

**Small Promises (CAN)** **6** gr m Carson City (USA) -Promiseville (CAN) (Alwasmi (USA)) 4735a$^{5}$ ><

**Small Stakes (IRE)** **2** b c Pennekamp (USA) -Poker Chip (Bluebird (USA)) 5441$^{7}$ 6289$^{5}$ >**66a 62f**<

**Small Time Blues (IRE)** **2** b f Danetime (IRE) -Barinia (Corvaro (USA)) 5864$^{10}$ ><

**Smart Boy Prince (IRE)** **3** b g Princely Heir (IRE) -Miss Mulaz (FR) (Luthier) (587) (611) 959$^{7}$ 1046$^{5}$ 1365$^{9}$ 1422$^{3}$ 2928$^{8}$ 5197$^{11}$ 5267$^{6}$5733$^{13}$ 5863$^{2}$ 6120$^{2}$ >**38a 59f**<

**Smart Danny** **3** gr g Danzero (AUS) -She s Smart (Absalom) 956$^{13}$ 1209$^{5}$ 1676$^{5}$ 2350$^{7}$ 3234$^{8}$ 3562$^{8}$ 3877$^{5}$ 4489$^{12}$ >**38a 45f**<

**Smart Dawn** **2** ch f Cadeaux Genereux-Blugem (FR) (Bluebird (USA)) 2300$^{19}$ 5694$^{13}$ 5870$^{14}$ >**48f**<

**Smarter Charter** **11** br g Master Willie-Irene s Charter (Persian Bold) 1402$^{5}$ 1543$^{7}$ 1722$^{2}$ 1987$^{7}$ 2462$^{6}$ 2525$^{5}$ 3041$^{11}$ 3149$^{4}$3429$^{5}$ 3658$^{6}$ 4250$^{4}$ 5644$^{3}$ 6231$^{7}$ 6468$^{5}$ >**42a 47f**<

**Smart Hostess** **5** gr m Most Welcome-She s Smart (Absalom) 1113$^{15}$ 5224$^{9}$ 5671$^{9}$ 5799$^{3}$ 6071$^{18}$ 6349$^{13}$ >**86a 102f**<

**Smart John** **4** b g Bin Ajwaad (IRE) -Katy-Q (IRE) (Taufan (USA)) 1944$^{4}$ (2272) 3143$^{4}$ 3375$^{2}$ (3474) 3782$^{3}$ 4486$^{5}$ 4729$^{4}$ (5203) 5303$^{3}$ 5764$^{9}$6047$^{6}$ >**80f**<

**Smart Minister** **4** gr g Muhtarram (USA) -She s Smart (Absalom) 1681$^{12}$ 1993$^{13}$ 2346$^{7}$ (3019) 3409$^{15}$ 3923$^{6}$ >**49a 63f**<

**Smart Scot** **5** ch g Selkirk (USA) -Amazing Bay (Mazilier (USA)) (497) (713) (934) (1021) 1093$^{2}$ 1427$^{14}$ 6296$^{5}$ 6558$^{11}$ >**57a 31f**<

**Smart Starprincess (IRE)** **3** b f Soviet Star (USA) -Takeshi (IRE) (Cadeaux Genereux) (496) (524) 610$^{2}$ 747$^{3}$ 868$^{5}$ 3530$^{17}$ 3887$^{12}$ 4320$^{10}$ 6186$^{4}$6246$^{12}$ >**68a 55f**<

**Smarty Jones (USA)** **3** ch c Elusive Quality (USA) -I Ll Get Along (USA) (Smile (USA)) (1781a) (2139a) 2701a$^{2}$ >**131a**<

**Smeorach** **3** ch f My Generation-Mohican (Great Nephew) 1718$^{7}$ 2783$^{8}$ 4421$^{7}$ >**36f**<

**Smiddy Hill** **2** b f Factual (USA) -Hello Hobson S (IRE) (Fayruz) 1415$^{3}$ 1717$^{2}$ 2071$^{4}$ (2458) 2655$^{4}$ 3930$^{5}$ (4197) 5060$^{9}$ 5515$^{2}$ 5932$^{3}$6241$^{6}$ >**86f**<

**Smiling Starduster (IRE)** **2** b c Danehill Dancer (IRE) -Evriza (IRE) (Kahyasi) 4606$^{13}$ 4997$^{12}$ 5476$^{7}$ >**20a 20f**<

**Smirfys Dance Hall (IRE)** **4** b f Halling (USA) -Bigger Dances (USA) (Moscow Ballet (USA)) 4306$^{4}$ 5635$^{9}$ 6061$^{11}$ >**11a 52+f**<

**Smirfys Night** **5** b g Tina s Pet-Nightmare Lady (Celestial Storm (USA)) 2118$^{17}$ 2734$^{11}$ 3820$^{19}$ 4542$^{5}$ 4782$^{4}$ 5949$^{12}$ >**55f**<

**Smirfys Party** **6** ch g Clantime-Party Scenes (Most Welcome) 1787$^{14}$ 2735$^{13}$ 3446$^{8}$ 4542$^{3}$ 4782$^{5}$ 5008$^{9}$ 5949$^{8}$ >**66a 56 f**<

**Smirfys Systems** **5** b g Safawan-Saint Systems (Uncle Pokey) 1471$^{7}$ 1927$^{17}$ 2467$^{5}$ 3778$^{8}$ 4047$^{9}$ 4308$^{2}$ 5631$^{10}$ 6482$^{8}$ >**67a 86f**<

**Smith N Allan Oils** **5** b g Bahamian Bounty-Grand Splendour (Shirley Heights) (448) 624$^{10}$ 1868$^{9}$ 2172$^{7}$ 2368$^{8}$ 2776$^{10}$ 2938$^{11}$ 2965$^{7}$ 3167$^{5}$3409$^{2}$ 3623$^{2}$ 3895$^{4}$ 4199$^{6}$ 4425$^{7}$ 6062$^{5}$ >**70a 68f**<

**Smokin Beau** **7** b g Cigar-Beau Dada (IRE) (Pine Circle (USA)) 1126$^{6}$ 1353$^{2}$ 1763$^{7}$ 1923$^{10}$ 2955$^{17}$ 3324$^{4}$ 4165$^{14}$ 4324$^{15}$(4538) (4759) (4951) >**116f**<

**Smokincanon** **2** ch c Fumo Di Londra (IRE) -Secret Miss (Beveled (USA)) 1183$^{3}$ (1276) 1769$^{6}$ 2405$^{5}$ >**62a 62f**<

**Smokin Joe** **3** b g Cigar-Beau Dada (IRE) (Pine Circle (USA)) 619$^{4}$ 747$^{10}$ 891$^{5}$ 1702$^{14}$ 3231$^{18}$ 4052$^{12}$ 4515$^{8}$5219$^{14}$ 5736$^{16}$ 6220$^{5}$ 6493$^{3}$ >**70a 62f**<

**Smoothie (IRE)** **6** gr g Definite Article-Limpopo (Green Desert (USA)) 4196$^{7}$ 4486$^{6}$ 4971$^{13}$ (5374) 5869$^{9}$ 6495$^{3}$ >**72a 69f**<

**Smoothly Does It** **3** b g Efisio-Exotic Forest (Dominion) 1688$^{11}$ 1997$^{2}$ 2400$^{9}$ 2949$^{6}$ 3386$^{9}$ 4479$^{4}$ 4802$^{8}$ (5176) 5693$^{2}$5998$^{6}$ 6081$^{9}$ >**24a 73f**<

**Snap** **3** ch g Dr Fong (USA) -Reactress (USA) (Sharpen Up) 1749$^{2}$ (1975) 2569$^{3}$ (3252) 4134$^{3}$ >**85f**<

**Sninfia (IRE)** **4** b f Hector Protector (USA) -Christmas Kiss (Taufan (USA)) 1308$^{10}$ 1684$^{7}$ 1857$^{7}$ 2590$^{4}$ 3776$^{7}$ 4146$^{9}$ 4261$^{8}$ 4883$^{14}$5069$^{10}$ >**38f**<

**Snookered Again** **2** b g Lujain (USA) -Highest Bid (FR) (Highest Honor (FR)) 1970$^{5}$ (2812) 3605$^{7}$ 4186$^{3}$ 4890$^{10}$ 5240$^{8}$ >**69a 56f**<

**Snow Bunting** **6** ch g Polar Falcon (USA) -Marl (Lycius (USA)) 1225$^{8}$ 1373$^{14}$ 2261$^{3}$ 2423$^{15}$ 2581$^{2}$ 2673$^{8}$ 3098$^{5}$ 4130$^{3}$4294$^{3}$ 4522$^{4}$ 5242$^{7}$ 5526$^{6}$ (6124) >**53a 70f**<

**Snow Cap (FR)** **5** b h Bering-Girl Of France (Legend Of France (USA)) 1435a$^{5}$ >**105f**<

**Snow Chance (IRE)** **3** ch f Compton Place-Snowscape (Niniski (USA)) 2760$^{13}$ 3707$^{8}$ 4302$^{13}$ >**23a 33f**<

**Snowdrift** **2** b f Desert Prince (IRE) -Snowing (Tate Gallery (USA)) 5847$^{13}$ 6449$^{5}$ >**41a**<

**Snowed Under** **3** gr g Most Welcome-Snowy Mantle (Siberian Express (USA)) 1557$^{5}$ 2144$^{5}$ 2774$^{5}$ 3746$^{12}$ 4138$^{7}$ (5110) 5374$^{6}$ 5757$^{3}$ 6337$^{9}$ >**64f**<

**Snow Goose** **3** b f Polar Falcon (USA) -Bronzewing (Beldale Flutter (USA)) 1398$^{11}$ 3105$^{4}$ 3541$^{2}$ 4077$^{3}$ 4640$^{3}$ 5823a$^{2}$ (6258a) >**104f**<

**Snow Joke (IRE)** **3** b f Desert Sun-Snowcap (IRE) (Snow Chief (USA)) 1366$^{7}$ 2301$^{4}$ 2577$^{8}$ 3156$^{14}$ 3684$^{11}$ 3993$^{10}$ 4683$^{5}$ 5260$^{17}$ >**57f**<

**Snow Lynx (USA)** **2** ch f Lemon Drop Kid (USA) -Snow Forest (USA) (Woodman (USA)) 6471$^{16}$ >**15f**<

**Snow Ridge (IRE)** **3** b c Indian Ridge-Snow Princess (IRE) (Ela-Mana-Mou) 1764$^{2}$ 2680$^{7}$ >**122f**<

**Snow s Ride** **4** gr g Hernando (FR) -Crodelle (IRE) (Formidable (USA)) 1112$^{14}$ 1329$^{16}$ 2047$^{15}$ 2480$^{9}$ 2893$^{7}$ 3153$^{6}$ 5205$^{4}$ 5875$^{14}$6084$^{4}$ 6209$^{2}$ >**96+a 81f**<

**Snow Tempest (USA)** **2** b g Theatrical-January s Storm (USA) (Hennessy (USA)) 3241$^{7}$ 3749$^{9}$ 3931$^{14}$ 5567$^{6}$ >**62f**<

**Snow Wolf** **3** ch g Wolfhound (USA) -Christmas Rose (Absalom) 2303$^{7}$ (2530) 2726$^{2}$ 2981$^{9}$ 3845$^{9}$ 4810$^{4}$ 5563$^{14}$ 6205$^{14}$ 6538$^{9}$ >**45a 85 f**<

**Snuki** **5** b g Pivotal-Kennedys Prima (Primo Dominie) 650$^{9}$ 765$^{10}$ 882$^{9}$ >**53a 53 f**<

**Soaked** **11** b g Dowsing (USA) -Water Well (Sadler s Wells (USA)) 460$^{2}$ 560$^{6}$ 576$^{7}$ 637$^{9}$ 762$^{4}$ 941$^{7}$ 1075$^{2}$1180$^{3}$ 1262$^{4}$ 1956$^{15}$ 2423$^{4}$ (2582) 2975$^{2}$ (3314) 3894$^{5}$ 4105$^{2}$4247$^{3}$ 4452$^{14}$ 4701$^{3}$ 5107$^{18}$ 5562$^{9}$ >**53a 71f**<

**Soap Watcher (IRE)** **3** b g Revoque (IRE) -Princess Of Zurich (IRE) (Law Society (USA)) (4379a) >**53f**<

**Soar** **2** b f Danzero (AUS) -Splice (Sharpo) (2574) 2970$^{2}$ (4119) (4885) 5894$^{6}$ >**110 f**<

**Soaring Free (CAN)** **5** bb g Smart Strike (CAN) -Dancing With Wings (CAN) (Danzig (USA)) 6486a$^{4}$ >**120f**<

**Soba Jones** **7** b g Emperor Jones (USA) -Soba (Most Secret) (480) 511$^{2}$ 543$^{4}$ 607$^{3}$ 669$^{2}$ 761$^{5}$ 1175$^{6}$ 3298$^{5}$3515$^{4}$ 3920$^{2}$ 4047$^{5}$ 4626$^{9}$ 4855$^{5}$ >**85a 83f**<

**Social Contract** **7** b g Emarati (USA) -Just Buy Baileys (Formidable (USA)) 469$^{13}$ 686$^{7}$ 719$^{7}$ 821$^{6}$ 858$^{8}$ 886$^{6}$ 946$^{2}$1020$^{10}$ 1121$^{12}$ 1176$^{7}$ 3663$^{8}$ 3828$^{8}$ 3871$^{8}$ 5035$^{8}$ 5184$^{6}$ >**44a 49f**<

**Society Music (IRE)** **2** b f Almutawakel-Society Fair (FR) (Always Fair (USA)) (1498) 2447$^{3}$ (3145) 3834$^{3}$ 4445$^{6}$ 5119$^{7}$ 5314$^{5}$ 5738$^{8}$ 6113$^{9}$ >**76f**<

**Society Pet** **5** b m Runnett-Polar Storm (IRE) (Law Society (USA)) 4916$^{9}$ 5793$^{19}$ >**33a 40f**<

**Society Selection (USA)** **3** b f Coronado s Quest (USA) -Love That Jazz (USA) (Dixieland Band (USA)) 6484a$^{9}$ >**117a**<

**Society Times (USA)** **11** b g Imp Society (USA) -Mauna Loa (USA) (Hawaii) 4276$^{7}$ 4537$^{10}$ 4985$^{7}$ 5061$^{8}$ 5629$^{5}$ >**36?f**<

**Socks For Glenn** **4** ch g Factual (USA) -Payvashooz (Ballacashtal (CAN)) 2719a$^{8}$ >**86f**<

**So Determined (IRE)** **3** b g Soviet Star (USA) -Memory Green (USA) (Green Forest (USA)) 2808$^{12}$ 4417$^{2}$ 4939$^{11}$ >**53a 57+f**<

**So Elegant (IRE)** **2** b f Bahhare (USA) -Soignee (Night Shift (USA)) 6060$^{10}$ 6400$^{5}$ >**35a 29f**<

**Sofia s Stream (ITY)** **2** ch f Shantou (USA) -Snug Dinner (IRE) (Jareer (USA)) 6108a$^{7}$ >**67f**<

**Sofistication (IRE)** **3** b f Dayjur (USA) -Cieladeed (USA) (Shadeed (USA)) 415$^{9}$ (597) >**70a**<

**Soft Focus (IRE)** **2** b f Spectrum (IRE) -Creme Caramel (USA) (Septieme Ciel (USA)) 5741$^{7}$ 6020$^{7}$ 6392$^{11}$ 6543$^{12}$ >**53a 12f**<

**Soft Mist (IRE)** **4** gr f Up And At Em-Morgiana (Godswalk (USA)) 457$^{6}$ 590$^{11}$ 1620$^{14}$ 1962$^{8}$ 2368$^{11}$ 2943$^{17}$ >**45a 47f**<

**Sogna Di Me** **3** b f Danehill (USA) -Vanille (USA) (Diesis) 3135a$^{3}$ 3569a$^{3}$ 4356a$^{5}$ 4899a$^{10}$ >**97f**<

**Soignee (GER)** **2** b f Dashing Blade-Suivez (FR) (Fioravanti (USA)) 6297a$^{2}$ >**101f**<

**So Independent** **2** b f Tipsy Creek (USA) -So Bold (Never So Bold) 4009$^{8}$ 4256$^{11}$ >**33f**<

**Sokoke** **3** ch g Compton Place-Sally Green (IRE) (Common Grounds) 3635$^{2}$ 4021$^{3}$ 5147$^{8}$ 5338$^{8}$ 6275$^{7}$ >**22a 68f**<

**Solar Falcon** **2** ch f Polar Falcon (USA) -Beryl (Bering) 5838$^{10}$ 6078$^{15}$ >**23f**<

**Solarias Quest** **2** b g Pursuit Of Love-Persuasion (Batshoof) 5407$^{3}$ 5790$^{3}$ 6309$^{2}$ >**77f**<

**Solar Power (IRE)** **3** b f Marju (IRE) -Next Round (IRE) (Common Grounds) 1372$^{2}$ 1704$^{4}$ 2306$^{4}$ 3602$^{4}$ 4731$^{3}$ (5263) 5786$^{2}$ 5898$^{2}$ >**101f**<

**Solar Prince (IRE)** **3** b g Desert Prince (IRE) -Quiche (Formidable (USA)) 4422$^{17}$ 5674$^{14}$ >**46df**<

**Soldera (USA)** **4** b f Polish Numbers (USA) -La Pepite (USA) (Mr Prospector (USA)) 2967$^{3}$ 3331a$^{4}$ 4982a$^{9}$ 5783$^{4}$ 6219$^{12}$ >**106f**<

**Soldier Hollow** **4** b c In The Wings-Island Race (Common Grounds) 1259a$^{4}$ 2508a$^{7}$ 3030a$^{2}$ (3972a) (5683a) >**113f**<

**Soldier s Tale (USA)** **3** ch c Stravinsky (USA) -Myrtle (Batshoof) 1413$^{2}$ (2046) >**102f**<

**Sole (BRZ)** **6** b h Bright Again (USA) -La Revolucion (BRZ) (St Chad) 633a$^{7}$ 690a$^{7}$ 853a$^{9}$ >**85f**<

**Sole Agent (IRE)** **2** b g Trans Island-Seattle Siren (USA) (Seattle Slew (USA)) 5467$^{11}$ 6181$^{3}$ 6322$^{10}$ >**63f**<

**Soleil D Hiver** **3** b f Bahamian Bounty-Catriona (Bustino) 427$^{7}$ 615$^{5}$ 2346$^{9}$ >**23a 29f**<

**Solent (IRE)** **2** b c Montjeu (IRE) -Stylish (Anshan) (3319) 4227$^{9}$ 5246$^{3}$ >**93f**<

**Soliniki** **3** b g Danzero (AUS) -Pride Of My Heart (Lion Cavern (USA)) 1225$^{17}$ 4051$^{7}$ 5652$^{24}$ 6222$^{8}$ >**49a 72+f**<

**Solipsist (IRE)** **3** ch c Grand Lodge (USA) -Mijouter (IRE) (Coquelin (USA)) 2113$^{14}$ 2765$^{10}$ >**51f**<

**Solista** **4** b g Singspiel (IRE) -Ginevra Di Camelot (FR) (Alzao (USA)) 5970a$^{4}$ >**97f**<

**Soliza (IRE)** **3** b f Intikhab (USA) -Razana (IRE) (Kahyasi) (4588a) >**85f**<

**Soller Bay** **7** b g Contract Law (USA) -Bichette (Lidhame) 1275$^{2}$ 1927$^{16}$ 4543$^{8}$ 4903$^{4}$ 5127$^{12}$ 5581$^{11}$ 5997$^{11}$ >**80da 86f**<

**Solmorin** **6** b m Fraam-Reclusive (Sunley Builds) 534$^{5}$ >**37a**<

**Solo Flight** **7** gr g Mtoto-Silver Singer (Pharly (FR)) 2278$^{2}$ 2671$^{6}$ 4319$^{15}$ 4754$^{2}$ 5122$^{9}$ (5615) 5919$^{3}$ 6172$^{7}$ >**95f**<

**Solor** **3** b c Spectrum (IRE) -Bayadere (USA) (Green Dancer (USA)) 1227$^{4}$ (1683) 6354$^{11}$ >**67a 81f**<

**Solo Sole (ITY)** **3** b g Grand Lodge (USA) -Storm Flash (Green Desert (USA)) 1688$^{14}$ 1997$^{13}$ 3155$^{10}$ >**62a 49f**<

**Sol Rojo** **2** b g Efisio-Shining Cloud (Indian Ridge) 6126$^{12}$ 6291$^{9}$ 6393$^{7}$ 6479$^{5}$ >**74a 42f**<

**Solskjaer (IRE)** **4** b c Danehill (USA) -Lyndonville (IRE) (Top Ville) 3355a$^{2}$ 4160a$^{2}$ (4587a) 4834$^{8}$ >**106f**<

**Solved (USA)** **3** b f Hennessy (USA) -Claradane (IRE) (Danehill (USA)) 2264$^{8}$ >**77f**<

**Somayda (IRE)** **9** b g Last Tycoon-Flame Of Tara (Artaius (USA)) 2643$^{11}$ 2810$^{11}$ 3412$^{15}$ 3747$^{3}$ 4080$^{15}$ 4398$^{6}$ 5080$^{5}$ >**32a 47f**<

**Some Night (IRE)** **2** b f Night Shift (USA) -Some Merit (Midyan (USA)) 2245$^{5}$ 5070$^{11}$ 6196$^{10}$ >**54f**<

**Someone s Angel (USA)** **3** gr f Runaway Groom (CAN) -Yazeenhaa (USA) (Zilzal (USA)) 1711$^{10}$ >**52f**<

**Somerset West (IRE)** **4** b g Catrail (USA) -Pizzazz (Unfuwain (USA)) 617$^{6}$ 674$^{8}$ 987$^{13}$ (1279) (1969) 2598$^{9}$ 3043$^{7}$ (3227) 3747$^{7}$ 3775$^{9}$ >**58a 78f**<

**Something (IRE)** **2** b c Trans Island-Persian Polly (Persian Bold) 4809$^{2}$ 5873$^{6}$ >**85f**<

**Somethingabouther** **4** b f Whittingham (IRE) -Paula s Joy (Danehill (USA)) 444$^{4}$ 479$^{5}$ 762$^{8}$ 792$^{3}$ 856$^{7}$ 1000$^{5}$ 2165$^{13}$2620$^{2}$ 2800$^{9}$ 3169$^{19}$ 3575$^{14}$ >**42a 50f**<

**Something Exciting** **2** ch f Halling (USA) -Faraway Waters (Pharly (FR)) 3905$^{4}$ 4272$^{10}$ 5247$^{13}$ (5539) (5885) (6189) 6473$^{2}$ >**106f**<

**Somethingforsunday (IRE)** **4** b f Desert Style (IRE) -Lough N Uisce (IRE) (Boyne Valley) 4406a$^{7}$ >**89f**<

**Somewhere My Love** **3** br f Pursuit Of Love-Grand Coronet (Grand Lodge (USA)) (621) 885$^{11}$ 959$^{10}$ 2005$^{3}$ 6117$^{16}$ >**67a 57f**<

**Somewin (IRE)** **4** b f Goldmark (USA) -Janet Oliphant (Red Sunset) 4082$^{11}$ >**26f**<

**Somnus** **4** b g Pivotal-Midnight s Reward (Night Shift (USA)) 2021$^{7}$ 3308$^{2}$ 3674$^{5}$ (4595a) 5289$^{2}$ (6076a) >**125f**<

**Son And Heir (IRE)** **3** b c Princely Heir (IRE) -Margarets Memory (IRE) (Imperial Frontier (USA)) 6015$^{12}$ >**9a**<

**Sonderborg** **3** b f Great Dane (IRE) -Nordico Princess (Nordico (USA)) 420$^{6}$ 521$^{4}$ 660$^{5}$ 808$^{3}$ 942$^{2}$ 965$^{2}$ 1020$^{2}$1086$^{10}$ 1611$^{11}$ 2176$^{2}$ 2660$^{6}$ 3380$^{14}$ 3827$^{16}$ 4580$^{9}$ 4848$^{6}$4941$^{6}$ 5382$^{6}$ 5795$^{3}$ 6227$^{13}$ >**57a 52f**<

**Sonearsofar (IRE)** **4** b g General Monash (USA) -Not Too Near (IRE) (Nashamaa) 2777$^{11}$ 3896$^{6}$ 4781$^{7}$ 5110$^{13}$ 6362$^{11}$ >**38f**<

**Songerie** **2** b f Hernando (FR) -Summer Night (Nashwan (USA)) (5687) 5961a$^{9}$ (6297a) >**102f**<

**Songgaria** **2** b f Kingsinger (IRE) -Paula s Joy (Danehill (USA)) 2725$^{2}$ 2946$^{3}$ 3144$^{7}$ 3506$^{2}$ >**52f**<

**Song Koi** **3** b f Sri Pekan (USA) -Eastern Lyric (Petong) 1200$^{10}$ 5342$^{2}$ 5736$^{18}$ 6280$^{4}$ >**44a 58f**<

**Songlark** **4** br c Singspiel (IRE) -Negligent (Ahonoora) 1767$^{5}$ 2220$^{2}$ 3072$^{4}$ >**115a 111f**<

**Song Of Night (GER)** **3** b f Tiger Hill (IRE) -Song Of Georgia (FR) (Lashkari) 2157a$^{10}$ 2723a$^{15}$ >**65f**<

**Song Of The Sea** **3** ch f Bering-Calypso Run (Lycius (USA)) 2562$^{8}$ 3204$^{9}$ 3454$^{4}$ 4647$^{12}$ 4870$^{13}$ 5216$^{7}$ >**47a 60f**<

**Song Of The Sword (USA)** **3** b c Unbridled s Song (USA) -Appealing Ms Sword (USA) (Crusader Sword (USA)) 1781a$^{11}$ 2139a$^{9}$ >**94a**<

**Song Of Vala** **3** ch g Peintre Celebre (USA) -Yanka (USA) (Blushing John (USA)) 1134$^{9}$ 2513$^{5}$ 3152$^{7}$ 4032$^{6}$ 4756$^{3}$ 6015$^{4}$ >**58a 80+f**<

**Songoku (IRE)** **2** b c Bahhare (USA) -Khardoun (Doyoun) 4597a$^{3}$ 6169a$^{7}$ >**89f**<

**Song Sparrow** **2** b f Vettori (IRE) -Fanfare (Deploy) 6011$^{12}$ 6155$^{6}$ >**40a**<

**Song Thrush (USA)** **2** rg f Unbridled s Song (USA) -Virgin Michael (USA) (Green Dancer (USA)) (6471) >**89+f**<

**Sonic Anthem (USA)** **2** b g Royal Anthem (USA) -Whisperifyoudare (USA) (Red Ransom (USA)) 5578$^{17}$ ><

**Sonntag Blue (IRE)** **2** b g Bluebird (USA) -Laura Margaret (Persian Bold) 4193$^{11}$ 4487$^{10}$ 4598$^{9}$ 5616$^{10}$ >**32a 57f**<

**Sono** **7** b g Robellino (USA) -Sweet Holland (USA) (Alydar (USA)) 1316$^{9}$ 1973$^{5}$ 2409$^{4}$ >**77f**<

**Son Of Rembrandt (IRE)** **3** b g Titus Livius (FR) -Avidal Park (Horage) 489$^{9}$ 610$^{13}$ 881$^{5}$ 1046$^{3}$ 1220$^{6}$ 1478$^{3}$ 2029$^{11}$2667$^{12}$ 2766$^{18}$ >**50a 30f**<

**Son Of Thunder (IRE)** **3** ch g Dr Fong (USA) -Sakura Queen (IRE) (Woodman (USA)) 1869$^{6}$ (2176) 3007$^{6}$ 3146$^{2}$ 3684$^{8}$ (4246) 5063$^{9}$ 6549$^{10}$ >**44a 70f**<

**Sonoma (IRE)** **4** ch f Dr Devious (IRE) -Mazarine Blue (USA) (Chief s Crown (USA)) 1210$^{5}$ 1457$^{8}$ 1832$^{6}$ 2116$^{9}$ 2590$^{12}$ (3153) 3743$^{4}$ 4352$^{4}$ 5027$^{4}$5519$^{3}$ >**68f**<

**Sooyou Sir (IRE)** **2** bb g Orpen (USA) -Naivement (IRE) (Doyoun) 5543$^{10}$ 5988$^{13}$ 6521$^{8}$ >**29f**<

**Sophomore** **10** b g Sanglamore (USA) -Livry (USA) (Lyphard (USA)) 425$^{9}$ 714$^{6}$ 945$^{3}$ 1026$^{14}$ >**34a 38f**<

**Sophrano (IRE)** **4** b g Spectrum (IRE) -Sophrana (IRE) (Polar Falcon (USA)) 2588$^{5}$ 2941$^{3}$ 4510$^{9}$ 4635$^{3}$ 4825$^{3}$ 5177$^{7}$ 5448$^{4}$ 6058$^{12}$ >**48a 48f**<

**Sopran Foldan (IRE)** **6** b g Danehill (USA) -Foolish Heart (IRE) (Fool s Holme (USA)) 6261a$^{6}$ >**108f**<

**Sorbiesharry (IRE)** **5** gr g Sorbie Tower (IRE) -Silver Moon (Environment Friend) 412$^{5}$ 512$^{2}$ 588 $^{3}$ 590$^{5}$ (695) 902$^{5}$ 953$^{10}$ (1181) 1233$^{4}$ 1479$^{11}$ 2128$^{5}$ 5002$^{8}$ 6364$^{11}$ >**55a 53f**<

**Sorceress** **2** b f Wizard King-Aonia (Mummy s Pet) 5521$^{9}$ 6125$^{11}$ >**37f**<

**Soreze (FR)** **6** b g Saumarez-Asania (FR) (Ace Of Aces (USA)) 6137a$^{7}$ >**107f**<

**So Royal (GER)** **5** ch m Royal Solo (IRE) -Seta Pura (FR) (Konigsstuhl (GER)) 6508a$^{3}$ >**88f**<

**Sorrent (GER)** **2** br f Monsun (GER) -Salka (GER) (Doyoun) (6377a) >**106+f**<

**Sorrento King** **7** ch g First Trump-Star Face (African Sky) 2230$^{7}$ >**8a 8f**<

**So Sober (IRE)** **6** b g Common Grounds-Femme Savante (Glenstal (USA)) (443) 637$^{5}$ 794$^{4}$ 884$^{8}$ 938$^{8}$ 1075$^{4}$ 1859$^{3}$ 2350$^{8}$3864$^{12}$ 4085$^{9}$ 4701$^{5}$ 4881$^{6}$ >**44a 48f**<

**So Sure (IRE)** **4** b g Definite Article-Zorilla (Belmez (USA)) 902$^{4}$ 914$^{6}$ 3773$^{9}$ >**48a 65f**<

**Soterio (GER)** **4** b c Lavirco (GER) -So Rarely (USA) (Arctic Tern (USA)) (5254a) 5824a$^{8}$ >**114f**<

**Sotonian (HOL)** **11** br g Statoblest-Visage (Vision (USA)) 499$^{5}$ 637$^{3}$ 813$^{3}$ 904$^{7}$ 951$^{5}$ 1000$^{3}$ 1406$^{3}$1724$^{4}$ 2183$^{5}$ (2384) 3616$^{11}$ 5793$^{18}$ 6229$^{20}$ >**43a 39f**<

**Soulacroix** **3** b c Kylian (USA) -California Dreamin (Slip Anchor) 4167$^{2}$ (4715) 4888$^{7}$ 6172$^{3}$ 6346$^{10}$ >**98f**<

**Soul Dance** **3** b f Imperial Ballet (IRE) -Piccante (Wolfhound (USA)) 5844$^{2}$ >**63f**<

**Soul Of Magic (IRE)** **5** b m Definite Article-Blazing Soul (IRE) (Common Grounds) 1655a$^{12}$ >**93f**<

**Soul Provider (IRE)** 3 ch f Danehill Dancer (IRE) -Wing And A Prayer (IRE) (Shalford (IRE)) 606[5] 774[3] 956[4] 1015[3] 1220[2] 1366[4] 3193[9] 3425[5]3817[8] 4517[12] 5092[7] 5642[12] >**17a 17 f**<

**Soumillon** 2 br f Benny The Dip (USA) -Kembla (Known Fact (USA)) 6223[12] ><

**Sound And Vision (IRE)** 2 b g Fayruz-Lyrical Vision (IRE) (Vision (USA)) 2256[5] 2674[6] 3009[5] 3233[6] 5542[5] 5989[14] >**58f**<

**Sound Blaster (IRE)** 3 ch g Zafonic (USA) -Blasted Heath (Thatching) 1640[5] 2847[9] >**74f**<

**Sound Breeze** 2 ch c Giant s Causeway (USA) -Madame Est Sortie (FR) (Longleat (USA)) 6455[4] >**67f**<

**Sound Of Fleet (USA)** 3 ch c Cozzene (USA) -Tempo (USA) (Gone West (USA)) 1674[4] 2113[6] (2361) 2896[5] 3345[8] 3902[2] 4888[10] 5300[12] 5619[15] >**95f**<

**Sounds Lucky** 8 b g Savahra Sound-Sweet And Lucky (Lucky Wednesday) 526[10] 596[5] 771[12] (893) 987[2] 1051[6] 1082[8] 1206[4]1738[12] 3277[16] 3533[15] 6363[13] >**60a 52f**<

**Sound That Alarm** 2 b g Groom Dancer (USA) -Warning Star (Warning) 3729[2] 4058[6] >**74f**<

**Sound The Drum (USA)** 2 b c Stravinsky (USA) -Uhavethebeat (USA) (Unbridled (USA)) 4637[3] 5616[2] >**80f**<

**Southampton Joe (USA)** 4 ch g Just A Cat (USA) -Maple Hill Jill (USA) (Executive Pride) 3697[12] 4042[6] >**31a 31f**<

**Southburgh (IRE)** 3 b g Spectrum (IRE) -College Night (IRE) (Night Shift (USA)) 3916[20] >**11f**<

**Southern Africa (USA)** 2 bb c Cape Town (USA) -Al Fahda (Be My Chief (USA)) (3176) 3481[2] (4166) >**89f**<

**Southern Bazaar (USA)** 3 ch c Southern Halo (USA) -Sunday Bazaar (USA) (Nureyev (USA)) 2706[2] (5749) >**86f**<

**Southern Bound (IRE)** 3 b f Fasliyev (USA) -Headrest (Habitat) 6104a[12] >**91f**<

**Southern Queen** 3 b f Anabaa (USA) -Due South (Darshaan) 1290a[4] >**97f**<

**Southern Star (GER)** 4 gr g Sternkoenig (IRE) -Sun Mate (IRE) (Miller s Mate) 1249[4] >**52f**<

**Southern Tide (USA)** 2 b c Southern Halo (USA) -My Own Lovely Lee (USA) (Bucksplasher (USA)) 4016[17] 4611[11] 5688[10] 5897[13] >**58f**<

**South Face** 3 ch g Hector Protector (USA) -Crystal Cavern (USA) (Be My Guest (USA)) 1111[2] >**77f**<

**South O The Border** 2 b c Wolfhound (USA) -Abbey s Gal (Efisio) 2890[9] 4523[11] 4922[10] 5871[13] >**56f**<

**So Vain (ITY)** 2 b c Ski Chief (USA) -Escondida (USA) (Alysheba (USA)) 2669a[5] 3362a[U] >**60f**<

**Sovereign Dreamer (USA)** 4 b c Kingmambo (USA) -Spend A Dream (USA) (Spend A Buck (USA)) 2022[18] 2365[6] 2671[11] 3095[7] 4518[7] 5635[11] 6074[11] >**77f**<

**Sovereign Girl** 3 b f Sovereign Water (FR) -The Quaker (Oats) 2168[15] 2357[6] >**16f**<

**Sovereign Spirit (IRE)** 2 b g Desert Prince (IRE) -Sheer Spirit (IRE) (Caerleon (USA)) 4922[11] 5406[7] 5756[6] >**59f**<

**Sovereign State (IRE)** 7 b g Soviet Lad (USA) -Portree (Slip Anchor) (3411) 3682[4] 4015[5] 4250[2] 4609[8] 5243[2] 5546[8] >**39a 55f**<

**Sovereignty (JPN)** 2 b g King s Best (USA) -Calando (USA) (Storm Cat (USA)) 3424[2] 3808[4] >**79f**<

**Soviet Belle (IRE)** 3 b f Soviet Star (USA) -Ingabelle (Taufan (USA)) 4893a[11] >**87f**<

**Soviet Sceptre (IRE)** 3 ch c Soviet Star (USA) -Princess Sceptre (Cadeaux Genereux) 1749[3] 2236[10] 4491[4] 4817[6] 5092[8] 5571[9] (5843) 6085[5] 6279[12] >**55a 74f**<

**Soviet Song (IRE)** 4 b f Marju (IRE) -Kalinka (IRE) (Soviet Star (USA)) 1332[2] 1621[3] (2318a) 2957[2] (3600) (4228) (5484a) 5782[6] >**124f**<

**Soviet Spirit** 3 ch f Soviet Star (USA) -Kristina (Kris) 1753[5] 2001[19] 2777[5] 3427[3] 3993[5] 4241[13] 4654[4] 5036[7]5571[7] 6014[10] >**60f**<

**Sovietta (IRE)** 3 b f Soviet Star (USA) -La Riveraine (USA) (Riverman (USA)) 4141[4] 4775[3] 5339[9] (6150) >**66f**<

**Soviet Treat (IRE)** 3 b f Ashkalani (IRE) -Mystery Treat (Plugged Nickle (USA)) 2392[5] >**89f**<

**So Vital** 4 b c Pivotal-Sumoto (Mtoto) (651) 827[7] 1122[3] 1768[14] 2305[11] 2731[13] >**75a 58f**<

**Sowerby** 2 b c Grey Desire-Brief Star (IRE) (Brief Truce (USA)) 2045[9] 2858[6] 3469[4] 3753[10] 5143[9] >**60f**<

**So Will I** 3 ch c Inchinor-Fur Will Fly (Petong) 1459[3] (2080) 3308[8] 3940[4] 4216[7] 4745[5] 5471[3] 5888[4] >**112f**<

**Soyuz (IRE)** 4 ch g Cadeaux Genereux-Welsh Mist (Damister (USA)) 1273[2] 1623[3] (1938) 2575[5] 3235[9] 3698[19] 6070[7] 6277[5] (6568) >**89a 96f**<

**Space Cowboy (IRE)** 4 b c Anabaa (USA) -Lady Moranbon (USA) (Trempolino (USA)) 6128[14] >**55a 78f**<

**Spaced (IRE)** 2 b c Indian Rocket-Tolomena (Tolomeo) 2300[12] 3083[6] (3665) 4890[3] (5292) >**85f**<

**Space Maker** 2 b c Almutawakel-Into Orbit (Safawan) 2736[4] 3003[8] (5555) >**85f**<

**Space Shuttle** 2 b c Makbul-Sky Music (Absalom) 1819[3] 2268[2] (2674) 3011[3] 4342[3] 4575[3] (4836) (5195) 6333[12] >**98f**<

**Spainkris** 5 b g Kris-Pennycairn (Last Tycoon) 592[9] >**7a 90f**<

**Spainnash (IRE)** 4 b g Nashwan (USA) -Agreed (Green Desert (USA)) 911a[4] >**97f**<

**Spanish Ace** 3 b g First Trump-Spanish Heart (King Of Spain) 1063[14] 1396[8] 2295[18] 2642[10] 3598[5] 3941[5] 4289[15] 4847[4](5071) 5393[18] >**60a 99f**<

**Spanish Cove (IRE)** 3 b c Key Of Luck (USA) -Lovely Ali (IRE) (Dunbeath (USA)) 4251a[11] >**65f**<

**Spanish Don** 6 b g Zafonic (USA) -Spanish Wells (IRE) (Sadler s Wells (USA)) 1456[14] 2201[13] 2789[5] (3415) (3842) 4214[5] 5650[9] (5941) (6458) >**109f**<

**Spanish Gold** 4 b f Vettori (IRE) -Spanish Heart (King Of Spain) 507[12] >**85a 70f**<

**Spanish Law** 2 b g Zaha (CAN) -Misty Moon (Polar Falcon (USA)) 3081[7] >**36f**<

**Spanish Ridge (IRE)** 2 b c Indian Ridge-Spanish Lady (IRE) (Bering) 4747[5] 5718[4] 6145[18] >**74f**<

**Spanish Star** 7 b g Hernando (FR) -Desert Girl (Green Desert (USA)) 456[4] 583[6] (682) 714[3] 901[3] 1042[8] 1426[11] 3799[7]4189[10] 6360[4] >**56a 46f**<

**Sparkford (USA)** 2 b c Red Ransom (USA) -Arsaan (USA) (Nureyev (USA)) 5897[12] >**48f**<

**Sparkling Clear** 3 b f Efisio-Shoot Clear (Bay Express) 1047[9] 1184[10] 1571[6] 1864[7] >**42a 16f**<

**Sparkling Jewel** 4 b f Bijou D Inde-Jobiska (Dunbeath (USA)) 2506[8] 2763[6] 3195[2] 3416[8] >**85a 74f**<

**Sparkling Water (USA)** 5 b h Woodman (USA) -Shirley Valentine (Shirley Heights) 1457[11] >**65f**<

**Spark Up** 4 b f Lahib (USA) -Catch The Flame (USA) (Storm Bird (CAN)) 488[7] 588 [7] 772[6] 1036[2] 1141[4] 1475[4] (1598) 1752[8]2284[6] 2473[16] 3301[7] 3609[6] >**66a 62f**<

**Sparkwell** 2 b c Dansili-West Devon (USA) (Gone West (USA)) 5646[5] >**80f**<

**Spartan Odyssey** 3 b g Overbury (IRE) -Spartan Native (Native Bazaar) 1078[7] ><

**Spartan Principle** 4 b f Spartan Monarch-Altar Point (Persian Bold) 1138[8] >**12a 29f**<

**Spartan Spear** 3 b g Sure Blade (USA) -Confection (Formidable (USA)) 1749[11] 2217[11] 4050[9] >**71f**<

**Spatzolita (GER)** 5 br m Goofalik (USA) -Santa Clara (Star Appeal) (6257a) >**93f**<

**Speagle (IRE)** 2 ch c Desert Sun-Pohutakawa (FR) (Affirmed (USA)) 2758[12] 3081[5] 3870[6] 5477[12] >**58f**<

**Spear (IRE)** 2 b c Almutawakel-Les Hurlants (IRE) (Barathea (IRE)) 4292[2] 4900[3] (5522) >**80f**<

**Spearious (IRE)** 3 b g Tagula (IRE) -Gloria Crown (IRE) (Waajib) 2165[4] >**62a 70f**<

**Spear Thistle** 2 ch c Selkirk (USA) -Ardisia (USA) (Affirmed (USA)) 5396[4] 5729[4] (6351) >**85f**<

**Special Branch** 4 ch g Woodborough (USA) -Sixslip (USA) (Diesis) 4778[16] 5238[16] >**43a 53f**<

**Special Delivery (IRE)** 4 b f Danehill (USA) -Seconde Bleue (Glint Of Gold) 1790[3] >**102f**<

**Speciale (USA)** 2 b f War Chant (USA) -Spenderella (FR) (Common Grounds) 5404a[5] 5922a[7] >**94f**<

**Special Envoy** 4 b c Barathea (IRE) -Wosaita (Generous (IRE)) 786a[5] >**51a 70+f**<

**Special Gold** 2 b c Josr Algarhoud (IRE) -Inya Lake (Whittingham (IRE)) 1324[5] 1769[4] >**68f**<

**Specialise** 2 b f Atraf-Summerhill Special (IRE) (Roi Danzig (USA)) 4010[11] 4304[P] 5447[10] >**28f**<

**Special Kaldoun (IRE)** 5 b h Alzao (USA) -Special Lady (FR) (Kaldoun (FR)) 1163a[7] 1780a[10] 3791a[3] (4766a) 5727a[3] 5968a[3] >**121f**<

**Special Parade (SAF)** 6 b m Elliodor (FR) -Triumphal Parade (SAF) (Foveros) 690a[14] 1002a[3] >**96f**<

**Special Ring (USA)** 7 b g Nureyev (USA) -Ring Beaune (USA) (Bering) 6486a[13] >**118f**<

**Spectacular Hope** 4 b f Marju (IRE) -Distant Music (Darshaan) 839[8] >**53f**<

**Spectait** 2 b g Spectrum (IRE) -Shanghai Girl (Distant Relative) 5688[2] 5953[11] 6223[3] >**62a 72f**<

**Spectested (IRE)** 3 ch g Spectrum (IRE) -Nisibis (In The Wings) 1365[7] 1947[9] 2452[2] 3340[5] 3806[9] 4806[4] 5178[2] >**59a 59f**<

**Spector (IRE)** 4 gr g Spectrum (IRE) -Safkana (IRE) (Doyoun) 1371[7] 1939[13] 2517[16] >**52f**<

**Spectrometer** 7 ch g Rainbow Quest (USA) -Selection Board (Welsh Pageant) 1661[14] 3310[19] 4831[19] >**94f**<

**Spectrum Of Light** 2 b f Spectrum (IRE) -Empress Of Light (Emperor Jones (USA)) 2550[12] 2980[5] >**51f**<

**Spectrum Star** 4 b g Spectrum (IRE) -Persia (IRE) (Persian Bold) 6141[9] 6468[7] >**35a 19f**<

**Speedbird (USA)** 3 ch f Sky Classic (CAN) -Egoli (USA) (Seeking The Gold (USA)) 1400[12] 2097[2] 2587[7] >**76f**<

**Speed Cop** 4 ch f Cadeaux Genereux-Blue Siren (Bluebird (USA)) 1061[2] 1685[3] 2636[9] 2955[18] 4526[4] 4951[6] 5181[9] 5372[8] >**94a 105f**<

**Speed Dial Harry (IRE)** 2 b g General Monash (USA) -Jacobina (Magic Ring (IRE)) 1276[5] 1359[2] 1717[3] (2124) 2592[3] 3290[2] (3736) 3975[7] 4329[4] >**62+a 75f**<

**Speedfit Free (IRE)** 7 b g Night Shift (USA) -Dedicated Lady (IRE) (Pennine Walk) 433[2] 510[5] 799[6] 1025[2] 1171[4] 1197[9] 1283[10] 1569[3]1738[7] 1783[14] 2123[4] 2291[9] 2421[9] 2524[6] 2625[10] 3125[7]3151[20] 3337[11] 3616[14] 3735[13] 6144[19] >**40a 49f**<

**Speedie Rossini (IRE)** 2 b g Rossini (USA) -Skatt (Caerleon (USA)) 4335[12] 4480[9] 4967[14] 5716[12] >**46f**<

**Speed Of Sound** 2 ch f Zafonic (USA) -Blue Siren (Bluebird (USA)) 1798[3] 2180[3] 2585[4] >**62f**<

**Speed On** 11 b g Sharpo-Pretty Poppy (Song) 1941[8] 2663[7] >**29a 29f**<

**Speed Racer** 3 b f Zieten (USA) -Sharenara (USA) (Vaguely Noble) 2756[14] 3267[5] 3624[14] 4180[3] 5086[6] 5525[3] 5851[7] 6056[7] >**54f**<

**Speedy James (IRE)** 8 ch g Fayruz-Haraabah (USA) (Topsider (USA)) 572[8] 626[14] 1171[2] 1283[16] >**28a 78f**<

**Speedy Spirit** 2 ch f Wolfhound (USA) -Ansellady (Absalom) 5609[9] 6078[16] 6342[11] >**35f**<

**Speightstown (USA)** 6 ch h Gone West (USA) -Silken Cat (USA) (Storm Cat (USA)) (6487a) >**126a**<

**Speightstown** 2 gr c Grand Lodge (USA) -Farfala (FR) (Linamix (FR)) 4922[7] 5620[3] (5838) 6129[7] >**77f**<

**Spence Appeal (IRE)** 2 b g Nicolotte-It s All Academic (IRE) (Mazaad) 3758[9] 4498[8] 6331[11] >**59f**<

**Sperrin Valley (IRE)** 2 ch f Rossini (USA) -Astra (IRE) (Glenstal (USA)) 5640[12] ><

**Spes Bona (USA)** 3 b c Rakeen (USA) -Novelette (Darshaan) 3094[10] 3587[4] 4615[13] 5715[15] 6065[7] >**34a 51+f**<

**Sphynx (GER)** 2 b f Chato (USA) -Suguta (GER) (Lagunas) 5577a[4] ><

**Spiders Web** 4 gr g Linamix (FR) -Cattermole (USA) (Roberto (USA)) 415[14] 520[12] 818[9] 871[10] 947[B] 994[2] 1091[3]1167[11] 1493[7] 1697[10] 3997[11] >**33a**<

**Spill A Little** 2 b c Zafonic (USA) -Lypharitissima (FR) (Lightning (FR)) 3483[6] 5508[5] 5729[9] >**76f**<

**Spindor (USA)** 5 ch g Spinning World (USA) -Doree (USA) (Stop The Music (USA)) 503[2] 584[5] 694[3] 834[4] 1082[2] (1204) 1477[7] 1595[3]1783[3] 2030[6] 2170[12] 2406[9] 3615[4] >**68a 70f**<

**Spinetail Rufous (IRE)** 6 b g Prince Of Birds (USA) -Miss Kinabalu (Shirley Heights) 5642[11] (5793) (5930) 6186[7] 6288[7] >**29a 60f**<

**Spin King (IRE)** 3 b g Intikhab (USA) -Special Dissident (Dancing Dissident (USA)) 1414[7] 1795[4] 2207[11] 2880[3] 3527[4] 3949[7] 4340[6] 5092[13] >**84f**<

**Spinnakers Girl** 2 b f Bluegrass Prince (IRE) -Brac Princess (IRE) (Nicolotte) 2617[9] 3145[3] 4135[2] 4445[4] 4878[8] 6242[11] 6464[4] 6522[8] >**53a 66f**<

**Spinning Coin** 2 b f Mujahid (USA) -Cointosser (IRE) (Nordico (USA)) 2786[19] 3627[6] 4234[7] 5114[8] 5335[9] >**65f**<

**Spinning Dove** 4 ch f Vettori (IRE) -Northern Bird (Interrex (CAN)) 448[3] 644[2] 846[LFT] 1241[5] 2346[LFT] >**70a 69f**<

**Spinning Jenni** 4 b f Mind Games-Giddy (Polar Falcon (USA)) 674[13] >**55a 51 f**<

**Spirit Of Chester (IRE)** 2 b f Lend A Hand-It Takes Two (IRE) (Alzao (USA)) 2083[4] 3031[2] 3286a[9] 4885[3] >**98f**<

**Spirit Of Desert (IRE)** 3 b c Desert Prince (IRE) -Nomothetis (IRE) (Law Society (USA)) (1777a) >**111f**<

**Spirit Of France (IRE)** 2 b c Anabaa (USA) -Les Planches (Tropular) 1523[2] 2627[2] (3014) 3605[2] 4527[5] 5719[6] >**93f**<

**Spiriton (GER)** 2 b c Areion (GER) -Sadlerella (IRE) (King s Theatre (IRE)) 5280a[6] >**69f**<

**Spirit s Awakening** 5 b g Danzig Connection (USA) -Mo Stopher (Sharpo) 1675[10] 2226[6] 2560[3] 2806[2] 4122[4] 4690[2] 4920[6] 5496[9](5868) 6311[8] 6445[14] >**69f**<

**Spitfire Bob (USA)** 5 b g Mister Baileys-Gulf Cyclone (USA) (Sheikh Albadou) 590[10] 5635[12] >**77a 68f**<

**Spitting Image (IRE)** 4 ch f Spectrum (IRE) -Decrescendo (IRE) (Polish Precedent (USA)) 1198[8] 1341[3] 1785[7] 2354[2] 2531[4] (2759) 3153[2] 3564[3] (4578) 5214[6]5951[7] >**49a 68f**<

**Splendid Touch** 4 b f Distinctly North (USA) -Soft Touch (GER) (Horst-Herbert) 500[10] 5056[8] >**44a**<

**Spliff** 3 b c Royal Applause-Snipe Hall (Crofthall) (1797) 2309[7] 3598[12] 3945[11] 4750[11] 5491[5] 5786[11] >**97f**<

**Splodger Mac (IRE)** 5 b g Lahib (USA) -Little Love (Warrshan (USA)) 3471[14] 3586[10] (4209) 4577[2] 4852[6] 5127[10] 5305[2] 5557[4] 5945[19] >**60f**<

**Sporting Gesture** 7 ch g Safawan-Polly Packer (Reform) 2022[8] 2365[5] 2895[4] 3199[4] 3953[4] 4155[3] 4363[6] 4831[U]5303[2] 5619[5] >**84f**<

**Sportsman (IRE)** 5 b g Sri Pekan (USA) -Ardent Range (IRE) (Archway (IRE)) 839[4] 2126[4] 2408[11] >**33a 30f**<

**Spot In Time** 4 b f Mtoto-Kelimutu (Top Ville) 969[7] 2060[8] 3297[8] 3896[7] 5019[8] >**55f**<

**Spotlight** 3 ch f Dr Fong (USA) -Dust Dancer (Suave Dancer (USA)) 1458[4] 1791[16] 2221[2] >**104f**<

**Spree (IRE)** 2 gr f Dansili-Ibiza (GER) (Linamix (FR)) 1798[6] (2846) 2996[9] 4217[12] 5864[7] >**93 f**<

**Spree Vision** 8 b g Suave Dancer (USA) -Regent s Folly (IRE) (Touching Wood (USA)) 1527[6] 1661[8] 3474[4] 3794[2] 3892[2] 4328[4] 4830[5] 5581[6]6467[4] >**59f**<

**Spring Adieu** 3 b f Green Desert (USA) -Nanda (Nashwan (USA)) 3044[4] 3473[9] 4443[11] 5019[4] 5340[7] >**59f**<

**Springalong (USA)** 4 ch g Gone West (USA) -Seven Springs (USA) (Irish River (FR)) 555[7] 871[4] 964[5] 1308[13] 2122[10] 2705[7] 3087[8] 4065[6] >**72a 58f**<

**Spring Breeze** 3 ch g Dr Fong (USA) -Trading Aces (Be My Chief (USA)) 1360[6] 2199[9] 2554[2] 3984[3] 4302[2] 5130[5] 5519[2] (5638) 5860[6]6110[3] >**63+f**<

**Spring Dancer** 3 b f Imperial Ballet (IRE) -Roxy Music (IRE) (Song) 1086[13] 1270[8] 2061[13] 2395[5] 2667[3] 4260[6] 4605[12] 5639[6]6362[7] >**40a 50f**<

**Spring Gift** 7 b m Slip Anchor-Belmez Melody (Belmez (USA)) 630[8] >**40a**<

**Spring Goddess (IRE)** 3 b f Daggers Drawn (USA) -Easter Girl (Efisio) 2281[3] 2676[9] 2896[4] 3694[3] 4230[3] >**87f**<

**Spring Jim** 3 b g First Trump-Spring Sixpence (Dowsing (USA)) 2727[4] (3155) 3631[2] 4300[4] 5446[2] >**87 f**<

**Spring Pursuit** 8 b g Rudimentary (USA) -Pursuit Of Truth (USA) (Irish River (FR)) 5073[4] >**62 a 58 f**<

**Spring Surprise** 3 b f Hector Protector (USA) -Tender Moment (IRE) (Caerleon (USA)) 1327[6] >**70f**<

**Spring Time Girl** 2 b f Timeless Times (USA) -Daira (Daring March) 5558[10] >**22f**<

**Springtime Romance (USA)** 3 br f Kris S (USA) -Khamsin (USA) (Mr Prospector (USA)) 1271[3] 1387[6] (2243) 2841[6] 3206[4] 3807[8] >**82f**<

**Spring Whisper (IRE)** 3 b f Halling (USA) -Light Fresh Air (USA) (Rahy (USA)) 490[7] 5642[13] 5796[17] 5928[18] >**47a 9f**<

**Spuradich (IRE)** 4 b c Barathea (IRE) -Svanzega (USA) (Sharpen Up) 2196[10] 3118[3] 4118[6] (5650) >**60a 102+f**<

**Spy Gun (USA)** 4 ch g Mt. Livermore (USA) -Takeover Target (USA) (Nodouble (USA)) 477[3] 518[5] 700[8] 772[8] 910[5] 953[7] 1039[4]1305[15] 1531[6] 2128[2] 2459[13] 3177[13] >**62a 55f**<

**Spy King (USA)** 2 ch c Distant View (USA) -Regal Princess (USA) (Royal And Regal (USA)) 3876[2] (4446) (4632) 5119[3] >**91f**<

**Spy Master** 6 b g Green Desert (USA) -Obsessive (USA) (Seeking The Gold (USA)) 718[3] 780[2] 936[5] 1025[7] 1190[6] 1510[5] 3381[10]3742[11] 4185[8] 5579[23] >**34a 34f**<

**Square Dancer** 8 b g Then Again-Cubist (IRE) (Tate Gallery (USA)) 1719[8] 1929[12] 2260[16] >**8 f**<

**Squaw Dance** 2 ch f Indian Ridge-Likely Story (IRE) (Night Shift (USA)) 4809[6] 5771[3] 6111[2] (6473) >**102f**<

**Squeaky** 7 ch m Infantry-Steady Saunter Vii (Damsire Unregistered) 575[13] >**42a 71f**<

**Squirtle Turtle** 4 ch g Peintre Celebre (USA) -Hatton Gardens (Auction Ring (USA)) (456) 693[9] 2305[13] 2689[4] 2798[5] 3153[4] >**74a 77f**<

**Sri Diamond** 4 b g Sri Pekan (USA) -Hana Marie (Formidable (USA)) 1828[10] 2201[8] 2560[6] 3177[2] >**88a 82 f**<

**Sri Lipis** 2 ch c Cadeaux Genereux-Katrina (IRE) (Ela-Mana-Mou) 3093[4] 3601[4] >**75f**<

**Staff Nurse (IRE)** 4 b f Night Shift (USA) -Akebia (USA) (Trempolino (USA)) 1245[12] 1426[9] 2230[4] 2987[8] 3919[5] 4883[3] 4998[3]5710[2] 6468[4] >**42a 51f**<

**Stafford King (IRE)** 7 b h Nicolotte-Opening Day (Day Is Done) 4473[14] 4669[9] 4870[10] >**36a 36f**<

**Stagbury Hill (USA)** 2 ch c Woodman (USA) -Shalabia (Fast Topaze (USA)) (3051) 4227[6] 4872[3] 5295[6] >**99f**<

**Stagecoach Ruby** 3 b f Bijou D Inde-Forum Girl (USA) (Sheikh Albadou) 822[10] 1278[9] 1405[5] 1495[4] 1695[3] 1864[3] 4414[7]4469[7] 5283[5] (5644) 5794[8] >**41a 41f**<

**Stage Direction (USA)** 7 b g Theatrical-Carya (USA) (Northern Dancer) 3695[12] >**51f**<

**Stage Left** 3 ch f Nashwan (USA) -Interval (Habitat) 6310[2] >**72+f**<

**Stagelight (IRE)** 2 b c Montjeu (IRE) -Zivania (IRE) (Shernazar) 4158a[6] >**93f**<

**Stage Right** 3 b c In The Wings-Spot Prize (USA) (Seattle Dancer (USA)) 597[4] 3161[6] (3417) 4229[5] 4715[4] 4915[6] 5111[3] >**55a 95f**<

**Stage School (USA)** 2 bb f Sunday Silence (USA) -Danseur Fabuleux (USA) (Northern Dancer) 6563[2] >**65f**<

**Stage Secret (IRE)** 3 ch c Zilzal (USA) -Tuxford Hideaway (Cawston s Clown) 4402[7] >**60f**<

**Stage Two (IRE)** 3 b g Sadler s Wells (USA) -Meteor Stage (USA) (Stage Door Johnny (USA)) 1050[12] 1179[6] 1344[4] 1843[7] 1989[9] 2347[2] 2554[8] >**17a 50f**<

**Stagnite** 4 ch g Compton Place-Superspring (Superlative) 2836[17] 3428[6] 3935[2] (4085) 4232[8] 4415[8] 5253[6] 5337[5] 5512[11]5754[11] 6559[11] >**60 a 65f**<

**Stai Su** 3 ch f Dr Fong (USA) -Mystic Tempo (USA) (El Gran Senor (USA)) 1778a[12] >**79f**<

**Stakhanov** 2 b g Dr Fong (USA) -Russian Grace (IRE) (Soviet Star (USA)) 4730[15] >**47f**<

**Stakhanovite (IRE)** 4 b c Darshaan-Homage (Ajdal (USA)) 1311[9] >**71f**<

**Stallone** 7 ch g Brief Truce (USA) -Bering Honneur (USA) (Bering) 1821[13] 2142[3] 2393[4] 2895[3] 3953[6] 4155[8] 5303[8] 5635[6]5950[6] 6047[3] 6533[5] >**46a 79 f**<

**Stamford Blue** 3 b g Bluegrass Prince (IRE) -Fayre Holly (IRE) (Fayruz) 452[2] 524[4] 619[6] 744[2] 817[8] 868[6] 965[11](1220) 1270[2] 6398[9] >**54a 69f**<

**Stanbury (USA)** 2 ch c Zamindar (USA) -Staffin (Salse (USA)) 1170[2] >**78f**<

**Stance** 5 b g Salse (USA) -De Stael (USA) (Nijinsky (CAN)) 2958[9] 4226[2] 5784[14] 6215[26] >**85f**<

**Stancomb Wills (IRE)** 2 b c Trans Island-First Nadia (Auction Ring (USA)) 4730[13] 5087[7] 5561[2] 6140[2] >**80f**<

**Standby Dancer (GER)** 8 b g Fabulous Dancer (USA) -Stand By Me (GER) (Acatenango (GER)) 1655a[5] 6378a[8] >**93f**<

**St Andrews (IRE)** 4 b c Celtic Swing-Viola Royale (IRE) (Royal Academy (USA)) 2358[2] 3036[6] 3539[2] 4120[5] 4528[7] (5769) 5941[18] (6547) >**110f**<

**St Andrews Storm (USA)** 2 b c Storm Creek (USA) -L Amour Toujours (USA) (Blushing Groom (FR)) (3051) 3640$^4$ 3907$^4$ 6340$^8$ **>99f<**

**Stanhope Forbes (IRE)** 3 b c Danehill Dancer (IRE) -Hinari Disk Deck (Indian King (USA)) *452$^3$ 620$^5$* **>50a 63df<**

**Stanley Arthur** 2 b g Mind Games-Midnight Orchid (IRE) (Petardia) 5578$^{13}$ 6092$^{13}$ **>18f<**

**Stanley Crane (USA)** 3 br g Bahri (USA) -Grey Starling (Pharly (FR)) 2281$^{12}$ 2596$^5$ 2934$^4$ *3848$^5$* 4242$^4$ 4562$^3$ 4853$^{10}$ **>70a 70f<**

**Stan s Girl** 2 b f Fraam-Gigetta (IRE) (Brief Truce (USA)) 1364$^8$ 1601$^3$ 2140$^2$ 6000$^{12}$ 6305$^9$ **>55f<**

**Star Applause** 4 b f Royal Applause-Cominna (Dominion) *4431$^{11}$ 5301$^{10}$* 3147$^6$ 3524$^{16}$ 4105$^{13}$ 4279$^{15}$ 4534$^4$ **>52a 52f<**

**Starbeck (IRE)** 6 b m Spectrum (IRE) -Tide Of Fortune (Soviet Star (USA)) 1610$^9$ 1964$^7$ 2242$^5$ 2282$^4$ 2967$^{10}$ 3477$^{12}$ 3691$^5$ 3867$^4$4294$^8$ 4553$^{11}$ 4731$^4$ 5416$^{13}$ *5740$^8$* 5811$^9$ 6191$^8$ **>68a 87f<**

**Starbright** 3 b g Polar Falcon (USA) -Treasure Hunt (Hadeer) 5237$^{12}$ **>13f<**

**Starchy** 2 b f Cadeaux Genereux-Sahara Star (Green Desert (USA)) (6543) **>79+f<**

**Starcross Venture** 3 b f Orpen (USA) -Maculatus (USA) (Sharpen Up) *438$^8$ 574$^8$* **>60a<**

**Starduster** 2 gr f Paris House-To The Stars (IRE) (Zieten (USA)) 4474$^9$ 4804$^2$ 5334$^{10}$ 5839$^2$ 5932$^2$ 6080$^2$ **>70f<**

**Star Fern** 3 br g Young Ern-Christening (IRE) (Lahib (USA)) *553$^5$ 927$^5$ 1204$^{13}$* 1939$^{11}$ 2377$^{15}$ 5597$^{12}$ *6275$^4$* **>60a 31f<**

**Stargate (GER)** 5 b h Acatenango (GER) -Sennica (GER) (Fabulous Dancer (USA)) 6509a$^4$ **>81f<**

**Stargem** 3 b f Compton Place-Holy Smoke (Statoblest) 3322$^2$ *4097$^2$* 4459$^9$ 5147$^2$ 5551$^2$ **>66a 75f<**

**Starjestic** 3 b f Bijou D Inde-Risalah (Marju (IRE)) 6285$^{13}$ **><**

**Starla (GER)** 4 b f Lando (GER) -Saquiace (USA) (Sagace (FR)) 6255a$^{11}$ **>72f<**

**Star Lad (IRE)** 4 ch g Lake Coniston (IRE) -Simply Special (IRE) (Petit Loup (USA)) *423$^3$ (481) 565$^9$ 728$^7$ (936) 990$^4$ 1474$^5$* 1941$^{10}$*2663$^3$* 2885$^{15}$ *3277$^8$* **>56a 49f<**

**Starlight River (IRE)** 2 b f Spectrum (IRE) -Prosaic Star (IRE) (Common Grounds) 3531$^8$ 4231$^7$ 4670$^3$ 5363$^9$ 5909$^4$ *6392$^8$* **>43a 63f<**

**Starling (IRE)** 2 ch f Cadeaux Genereux-Warrior Wings (Indian Ridge) 4958a$^7$ **>71 f<**

**Star Magnitude (USA)** 3 ch c Distant View (USA) -Stellaria (USA) (Roberto (USA)) 1371$^{11}$ 1820$^2$ 2195$^2$ 6082$^5$ **>77f<**

**Star Member (IRE)** 5 b g Hernando (FR) -Constellation (IRE) (Kaldoun (FR)) 1832$^5$ (2047) 2285$^4$ (2855) 3757$^2$ 4858$^6$ 5435$^6$ 6172$^{15}$ **>83a 105f<**

**Starmix** 3 br g Linamix (FR) -Danlu (USA) (Danzig (USA)) *1050$^9$* 1967$^9$ 2204$^4$ 3806$^{11}$ 4147$^7$ 4654$^8$ **>42a 67f<**

**Star Of Kildare (IRE)** 2 b f Raphane (USA) -Lady Fleetsin (IRE) (Double Schwartz) 2860$^{15}$ 3469$^{10}$ 4212$^8$ 4607$^{12}$ *4999$^7$* **>9a 36f<**

**Star Of Light** 3 b g Mtoto-Star Entry (In The Wings) 3910$^3$ 5446$^4$ **>73a 81f<**

**Star Of Normandie (USA)** 5 b m Gulch (USA) -Depaze (USA) (Deputy Minister (CAN)) *558$^8$ 6491$^2$* 5866$^9$ 6173$^9$ *6497$^8$* 6571$^2$ **>92a 89f<**

**Star Ovation (IRE)** 7 ch g Fourstars Allstar (USA) -Standing Ovation (Godswalk (USA)) 4425$^{14}$ **>62f<**

**Star Over The Bay (USA)** 6 rg g Cozzene (USA) -Lituya Bay (USA) (Empery (USA)) 6490a$^8$ **>122f<**

**Star Pupil** 3 ch g Selkirk (USA) -Lochangel (Night Shift (USA)) 1386$^4$ 1797$^2$ 1965$^7$ 2295$^{14}$ 3347$^5$ 4917$^5$ 5177$^5$ 5652$^4$(6119) **>86f<**

**Star Quest (DEN)** 3 b c Richard Of York-Isabella Cannes (IRE) (Ahonoora) 4379a$^6$ **><**

**Starry Lodge (IRE)** 4 b c Grand Lodge (USA) -Stara (Star Appeal) (2681) 3756$^3$ 4530$^5$ 5438$^5$ **>60a 105f<**

**Starry Mary** 6 b m Deploy-Darling Splodge (Elegant Air) 1297$^2$ 1534$^2$ 1754$^{16}$ 3153$^5$ 5258$^{10}$ **>48a 64f<**

**Starrystarrynight (IRE)** 3 b f Sadler s Wells (USA) -Upper Circle (Shirley Heights) 2711a$^{11}$ 6102a$^2$ **>100f<**

**Starry Wings (IRE)** 2 b f In The Wings-Stara (Star Appeal) 5390a$^8$ **><**

**Starsailor (GER)** 4 br g Pennekamp (USA) -Sephala (USA) (Mr Prospector (USA)) *709a$^5$* **><**

**Stars At Midnight** 4 b f Magic Ring (IRE) -Boughtbyphone (Warning) 2594$^{16}$ 4871$^{14}$ 5260$^6$ **>48a 55+f<**

**Star Sensation (IRE)** 4 bb f Sri Pekan (USA) -Dancing Sensation (USA) (Faliraki) 1456$^6$ 2196$^5$ 2789$^6$ 3212$^{13}$ 4067$^{10}$ 5017$^4$ 5574$^9$ 5887$^{11}$ **>97f<**

**Star Seventeen** 6 ch m Rock City-Westminster Waltz (Dance In Time (CAN)) *901$^5$ 984$^9$ 1238$^{15}$* **>34a<**

**Star Side (IRE)** 2 b c Ashkalani (IRE) -Rachel Pringle (IRE) (Doulab (USA)) 4966$^6$ **>63f<**

**Startled** 5 ch m Zilzal (USA) -Zelda (USA) (Sharpen Up) *4741$^1$* **>43a 39f<**

**Start Of Authority** 3 ch g Muhtarram (USA) -Heiden s Delight (USA) (Shadeed (USA)) 3994$^{15}$ 4679$^5$ 5352$^9$ **>45f<**

**Star Valley (FR)** 4 b c Starborough-Valleyrose (IRE) (Royal Academy (USA)) 1741a$^4$ 2923a$^3$ (5171a) 6463a$^9$ **>114f<**

**Star Welcome** 3 ch f Most Welcome-My Greatest Star (Great Nephew) *779$^7$ 948$^3$* **>50a 40f<**

**Star Wonder** 4 b f Syrtos-Galava (CAN) (Graustark) *809$^9$* **>6a 18f<**

**State City (USA)** 5 ch h Carson City (USA) -Wajna (USA) (Nureyev (USA)) *1145a$^7$* 2200$^4$ **>121a 100f<**

**State Dilemma (IRE)** 3 b c Green Desert (USA) -Nuriva (USA) (Woodman (USA)) 1795$^5$ (2019) 3001$^{12}$ 3671$^8$ 4887$^{14}$ 5294$^4$ 5920$^7$ **>97f<**

**State Of Balance** 6 ch m Mizoram (USA) -Equilibrium (Statoblest) *650$^8$ 1628$^4$ (1940) 5222$^6$ 5914$^8$* **>67a<**

**Stateroom (USA)** 6 ch g Affirmed (USA) -Sleet (USA) (Summer Squall (USA)) *768$^5$* 2393$^3$ 3631$^{11}$ **>76a 87df<**

**State Shinto (USA)** 8 br h Pleasant Colony (USA) -Sha Tha (USA) (Mr Prospector (USA)) *(635a) 756a$^6$ 979a$^5$ 1147a$^{11}$* **>115a<**

**Statoyork** 11 b g Statoblest-Ultimate Dream (Kafu) *657$^4$ 728$^{11}$* **>43a 43f<**

**St Austell** 4 b g Compton Place-Paris Joelle (IRE) (Fairy King (USA)) 4727$^8$ 5094$^{11}$ 5337$^{11}$ 5849$^{16}$ *6559$^5$* **>60a 78f<**

**Stavros (IRE)** 4 b g General Monash (USA) -Rivers Rainbow (Primo Dominie) 1453$^9$ 1870$^{13}$ 2040$^5$ 2350$^{19}$ **>48f<**

**St Barchan (IRE)** 3 ch g Grand Lodge (USA) -Moon Tango (IRE) (Last Tycoon) 3422$^4$ 4444$^2$ 5146$^3$ (6085) **>72+f<**

**Stealing Beauty (IRE)** 4 b f Sadler s Wells (USA) -Imitation (Darshaan) 2277$^4$ 2514$^7$ 3557$^5$ **>81f<**

**Steal The Thunder** 2 br g Timeless Times (USA) -Lavernock Lady (Don t Forget Me) 1314$^8$ 1658$^5$ 2140$^5$ 2489$^8$ 2773$^{12}$ 5213$^7$ 6241$^5$ 6521$^6$ **>50f<**

**Stedfast McStaunch (IRE)** 2 gr g Desert Style (IRE) -Aneydia (IRE) (Kenmare (FR)) 1826$^4$ 2086$^2$ 2439$^3$ (2961) **>76f<**

**Steel Blue** 4 b g Atraf-Something Blue (Petong) (1106) 1354$^{17}$ 1765$^{25}$ (2391) 2625$^2$ 2857$^5$ 3266$^3$ **>78a 102f<**

**Steel Princess (IRE)** 3 b f Danehill (USA) -Champaka (IRE) (Caerleon (USA)) (2028a) 2925a$^{10}$ **>101f<**

**Steely Dan** 5 b g Danzig Connection (USA) -No Comebacks (Last Tycoon) *596$^9$ 701$^9$ 738$^{12}$ 815$^2$ 874$^2$ (895) 929$^3$ (966) (1088) 1122$^2$ (1203) (1241)* 1376$^6$ 1624$^{10}$ 2218$^4$ 2304$^{10}$ 2483$^9$ **>89a 73f<**

**Steenberg (IRE)** 5 ch g Flying Spur (AUS) -Kip s Sister (Cawston s Clown) 1254a$^2$ (1759) 2021$^2$ 3073$^9$ 3674$^{18}$ 5780$^{12}$ **>118f<**

**Stella Blue (FR)** 2 b f Anabaa (USA) -Libanoor (FR) (Highest Honor (FR)) (6529a) **>106f<**

**Stella Marais (IRE)** 3 b f Second Empire (IRE) -Karakapa (FR) (Subotica (FR)) 2871$^6$ **>56f<**

**Stellar Jayne (USA)** 3 rg f Wild Rush (USA) -To The Hunt (USA) (Relaunch (USA)) *$^7$ 6484a$^3$* **>118a<**

**Stellite** 4 ch g Pivotal-Donation (Generous (IRE)) 1527$^7$ (1720) 1993$^7$ 4447$^{10}$ 4905$^7$ 6469$^2$ **>52f<**

**Stepastray** 7 gr g Alhijaz-Wandering Stranger (Petong) 2216$^5$ 2551$^{13}$ 3411$^9$ 3604$^7$ 3880$^5$ 4423$^9$ 4624$^{11}$ 5129$^8$5449$^7$ **>39a 39f<**

**Step Back (IRE)** 11 ch g Salt Dome (USA) -Hazy Lady (Habitat) 3961a$^6$ 5660a$^9$ **>47a 89f<**

**Step Danzer (IRE)** 3 b f Desert Prince (IRE) -Salsa Sound (ITY) (Law Society (USA)) 2341a$^2$ 3258a$^6$ 6381a$^9$ **>100f<**

**Stephanie s Mind** 2 b f Mind Games-Adorable Cherub (USA) (Halo (USA)) 2177$^8$ 2481$^3$ 2786$^4$ 4815$^4$ 5070$^8$ **>78f<**

**Stephano** 3 ch g Efisio-Polo (Warning) 1111$^7$ 3168$^5$ 4680$^{10}$ (5245) (5293) 5410$^2$ 6152$^{13}$ **>79 f<**

**Steppenwolf** 3 gr g Sesaro (USA) -Lozzie (Siberian Express (USA)) *845$^6$ 871$^7$ 1166$^7$* 1644$^{13}$ 1946$^7$ 2168$^{12}$ *3304$^8$* 3771$^9$4561$^5$ 4578$^6$ **>48?a 31f<**

**Sterling Guarantee (USA)** 6 b g Silver Hawk (USA) -Sterling Pound (USA) (Seeking The Gold (USA)) *495$^2$ 867$^4$ 931$^7$ 1016$^4$* **>59a 76?f<**

**Sterling Supporter** 2 b f Josr Algarhoud (IRE) -Riyoom (USA) (Vaguely Noble) 5521$^{12}$ **><**

**Stetchworth Prince** 2 b c Cadeaux Genereux-Elfin Laughter (Alzao (USA)) (3643) 4288$^4$ 4857$^6$ **>98f<**

**Stevedore (IRE)** 3 ch c Docksider (USA) -La Belle Katherine (USA) (Lyphard (USA)) 2134$^{14}$ 2557$^7$ 3089$^7$ *3707$^4$* (4241) 4619$^5$ (4938) 5150$^5$ 5652$^{13}$ 5887$^5$*6557$^6$* **>62a 80f<**

**Steve s Champ (CHI)** 4 br c Foxhound (USA) -Emigracion (CHI) (Semenenko (USA)) *1953a$^{10}$* 3732$^8$ (5505a) 5893$^2$ **>110f<**

**Stevmarie Star** 2 b f Muhtarram (USA) -Cabaret Artiste (Shareef Dancer (USA)) 5771$^9$ 6207$^6$ *6478$^{12}$* **>42f<**

**St Expedit** 7 b h Sadler s Wells (USA) -Miss Rinjani (Shirley Heights) 690a$^{12}$ 710a$^4$ *756a$^8$ 832a$^{10}$* 853a$^3$ 925a$^9$ 976a$^{12}$ 1001a$^9$ **>80a 118f<**

**St Francis Wood (USA)** 3 ch f Irish River (FR) -Francisco Road (USA) (Strawberry Road (AUS)) 1398$^{13}$ *2486$^2$* (2706) 2971$^{18}$ **>71a 93f<**

**St George s Girl** 3 b f Muthahb (IRE) -Nickelodeon (Nickel King) 1507$^{17}$ 1985$^7$ *2849$^8$* 3425$^{11}$ **>20f<**

**Stick At Nothing (IRE)** 2 b c Tagula (IRE) -Statokips (IRE) (Statoblest) 6380a$^4$ **>89f<**

**Stiletto Lady (IRE)** 3 b f Daggers Drawn (USA) -Nordic Pride (Horage) *2005$^4$* 2371$^{14}$ 2688$^{12}$ 3581$^{11}$ **>61a 59f<**

**Sting Like A Bee (IRE)** 5 b g Ali-Royal (IRE) -Hidden Agenda (FR) (Machiavellian (USA)) *(589) 700$^7$ 902$^2$ 967$^4$* 1109$^4$ 1660$^6$ 2424$^6$ (3082) 3794$^5$ **>64a 59f<**

**St Ivian** 4 b g Inchinor-Lamarita (Emarati (USA)) *476$^4$ 543$^6$ 596$^{11}$ 680$^2$ 806$^7$ 897$^7$ 1039$^2$*1265$^9$ 1368$^{19}$ *2455$^9$* 2965$^{14}$ 3227$^8$ *3800$^7$ 4188$^7$* 4336$^{10}$*6577$^3$* **>75a 72f<**

**St Jerome** 4 ch g Danzig Connection (USA) -Indigo Dawn (Rainbow Quest (USA)) 1754$^{17}$ 2212$^{15}$ 2590$^{17}$ **>64df<**

**St Jude** 4 b c Deploy-Little Nutmeg (Gabitat) 4306$^7$ 5146$^7$ 6057$^{12}$ **>35f<**

**Stocking Island** 3 ch f Desert King (IRE) -Rawya (USA) (Woodman (USA)) 1400$^{13}$ 1619$^2$ 2273$^3$ 2805$^8$ 3743$^7$ 4910$^3$ *5382$^P$* **>76f<**

**Stoic Leader (IRE)** 4 b g Danehill Dancer (IRE) -Starlust (Sallust) *905$^4$ 1032$^8$ (1035) (1098)* 1175$^4$ 1265$^{13}$ (1757) (1868) (1929) 2206$^9$ 2226$^{18}$3039$^2$ 3198$^4$ 3365$^2$ 3516$^6$ 3705$^5$ 3797$^2$ 3977$^5$ 4908$^6$5265$^4$ 5419$^{11}$ 5590$^4$ 5673$^4$ 5818$^7$ **>74a 79 f<**

**Stokesies Wish** 4 ch f Fumo Di Londra (IRE) -Jess Rebec (Kala Shikari) 1368$^{12}$ 1504$^{11}$ 2399$^{15}$ 3043$^2$ 3298$^{12}$ 3593$^5$ 3887$^4$ 4104$^8$4194$^6$ 4547$^3$ 4937$^3$ 5020$^{11}$ 5412$^7$ (5618) 6001$^5$ **>36a 69f<**

**Stolen** 2 b c Groom Dancer (USA) -Jezyah (USA) (Chief s Crown (USA)) 5198$^{12}$ 5407$^{12}$ *6021$^9$* 6282$^8$ **>36a 52f<**

**Stolen Hours (USA)** 4 bb c Silver Deputy (CAN) -Fasta (USA) (Seattle Song (USA)) 1539$^{18}$ 1801$^{16}$ 2305$^8$ 2738$^9$ 3181$^2$ 3437$^2$ 3658$^3$ (4297) 4729$^3$5258$^7$ **>74f<**

**Stolen Song** 4 b g Sheikh Albadou-Sparky s Song (Electric) *4644 (616) 734$^6$* 1457$^{16}$ 3743$^{11}$ 3997$^6$ 4196$^3$ 4398$^2$ 4616$^6$ **>65a 73 f<**

**Stoneacre** 4 ch f Gothenberg (IRE) -Musical Star (Music Boy) 1200$^{11}$ **><**

**Stone Crest (IRE)** 6 b m Bigstone (IRE) -Hillcrest (IRE) (Thatching) 2473$^{11}$ *2990$^{12}$* 3247$^{14}$ **>38f<**

**Stonor Lady (USA)** 3 bb f French Deputy (USA) -Blush With Love (USA) (Mt. Livermore (USA)) *7411$^0$ 8171$^1$ 9831$^0$ (1040)* 1267$^8$ 4497$^9$ **>48a 14f<**

**Stoop To Conquer** 4 b g Polar Falcon (USA) -Princess Genista (Ile De Bourbon (USA)) 1801$^8$ 2285$^{10}$ (2731) 3120$^4$ (5152) 5472$^9$ (6339) **>84+f<**

**Stop Making Sense** 2 b c Lujain (USA) -Freeway (FR) (Exit To Nowhere (USA)) 5432a$^2$ 6035a$^3$ 6510a$^5$ **>104f<**

**Stop The Nonsense (IRE)** 3 b g Orpen (USA) -Skip The Nonsense (IRE) (Astronef) *1227$^5$* 1466$^{14}$ 2122$^{18}$ 2658$^8$ **>37 a 37f<**

**Stopwatch (IRE)** 9 b g Lead On Time (USA) -Rose Bonbon (FR) (High Top) *793$^{11}$ 857$^9$ 889$^5$* 3667$^{13}$ **>31a<**

**Storm Chase (USA)** 2 bb g Awad (USA) -Night Duja (USA) (Dayjur (USA)) *5053$^{12}$* 5558$^7$ **>21a 34f<**

**Storm Clear (IRE)** 5 b h Mujadil (USA) -Escape Path (Wolver Hollow) *9661$^0$* **>45a 63 f<**

**Storm Clouds** 3 gr g Cloudings (IRE) -Khalsheva (Shirley Heights) 1771$^9$ 2390$^{13}$ **>47f<**

**Storm Flag Flying (USA)** 4 bb f Storm Cat (USA) -My Flag (USA) (Easy Goer (USA)) *6484a$^2$* **>117a<**

**Storm Fury (USA)** 2 b g Storm Creek (USA) -Danseuse Du Nord (IRE) (Kahyasi) 3749$^{13}$ 4239$^3$ 4743$^7$ 5202$^9$ 5421$^{10}$ 5909$^{11}$ **>65f<**

**Storm Of Tara (USA)** 3 b c Scatmandu (USA) -Aire Mystique (USA) (Sportin Life (USA)) *691a$^{11}$ 848a$^5$ 920a$^2$ 975a$^5$* **>87a<**

**Stormont (IRE)** 4 gr c Marju (IRE) -Legal Steps (IRE) (Law Society (USA)) *923a$^4$* 1004a$^{10}$ 2373$^7$ 2955$^{12}$ 3537$^7$ 3906$^8$ 4324$^{26}$ **>98a 112f<**

**Storm Racer (AUS)** 7 b g Racer s Edge (AUS) -Storm Street (NZ) (Red Anchor (NZ)) 755a$^7$ 924a$^6$ 1004a$^5$ **>86f<**

**Storm Shower (IRE)** 6 b g Catrail (USA) -Crimson Shower (Dowsing (USA)) *428$^4$* **>44 a 44df<**

**Storm Silk (CAN)** 2 bb c Stormin Fever (USA) -Carpenter s Lace (USA) (Woodman (USA)) 4739$^4$ (5298) **>97+f<**

**Storm Trooper (GER)** 4 ch c Monsun (GER) -So Sedulous (USA) (The Minstrel (CAN)) 1802a$^4$ 3357a$^2$ 4766a$^6$ **>112f<**

**Stormville (IRE)** 7 b g Catrail (USA) -Haut Volee (Top Ville) 1175$^{13}$ 4132$^{11}$ 4447$^2$ 4905$^9$ 5235$^{13}$ **>53a 71f<**

**Stormy Day** 4 b f Rainbow Quest (USA) -Broken Peace (USA) (Devil s Bag (USA)) 5339$^6$ *(6495)* **>66a 59f<**

**Stormy Larissa (IRE)** 4 b f Royal Applause-Sabayik (IRE) (Unfuwain (USA)) 4588a$^5$ **>81f<**

**Stormy Nature (IRE)** 3 bb f Mujadil (USA) -Ossana (USA) (Tejano (USA)) 1333$^3$ 1702$^9$ 2269$^{10}$ 5124$^8$ 5618$^{11}$ *(6064) 6480$^2$* **>78a 80f<**

**Story Of One (IRE)** 2 b g Desert Story (IRE) -One O One (IRE) (Wolfhound (USA)) 1556$^2$ 1960$^9$ *(2405)* 2593$^3$ 2799$^5$ 3526$^5$ **>59a 50 f<**

**Storyville** 2 br c Lujain (USA) -Slow Jazz (USA) (Chief s Crown (USA)) 5376$^{13}$ **>43f<**

**St Pancras (IRE)** 4 b c Danehill Dancer (IRE) -Lauretta Blue (IRE) (Bluebird (USA)) 1385$^{14}$ 1762$^8$ 2066$^8$ 2504$^2$ 2638$^8$ (3191) 3597$^5$ 3884$^3$ 4917$^2$5122$^8$ 6568$^7$ **>93f<**

**St Paul House** 6 ch h Machiavellian (USA) -Mamaluna (USA) (Roberto (USA)) 2162a$^{12}$ 3816a$^7$ **>109f<**

**St Petersburg** 4 ch g Polar Falcon (USA) -First Law (Primo Dominie) 1114$^2$ (1284) 1456$^{21}$ 1828$^2$ (3717) 4887$^3$ 5291$^6$ **>83a 106f<**

**Straffan (IRE)** 2 bb f Shinko Forest (IRE) -Katherine Gorge (USA) (Hansel (USA)) 1364$^6$ 1556$^3$ *2003$^3$* 2248$^2$ 2616$^5$ 2799$^4$ (3571) 3883$^2$ 4017$^2$4508$^{12}$ **>50a 60f<**

**Strangely Brown (IRE)** 3 b g Second Empire (IRE) -Damerela (IRE) (Alzao (USA)) *835$^7$* 1200$^8$ 1946$^3$ 2390$^9$ *3026$^{14}$* 3984$^2$ (4302) (4647) (5608) 5820$^3$5944$^5$ 6287$^4$ **>29a 82+f<**

**Strasbourg (AUS)** 5 ch g Umatilla (NZ) -Bella Ragazza (AUS) (Myocard (NZ)) 6528a$^{10}$ **>115f<**

**Strasbourg (USA)** 7 ch g Dehere (USA) -Pixie Erin (Golden Fleece (USA)) *2163a$^{10}$* **>26a 59f<**

**Strategy** 4 br f Machiavellian (USA) -Island Story (Shirley Heights) 2284$^{12}$ 3091$^6$ 3327$^8$ **>86 f<**

**Strathclyde (IRE)** 5 b g Petong-It s Academic (Royal Academy (USA)) *7031$^0$* 4034$^{17}$ 4522$^{12}$ 4855$^7$ **>82a 85f<**

**Strathspey** 5 ch m Dancing Spree (USA) -Diebiedale (Dominion) *6013$^5$* 6185$^5$ 6561$^4$ **>74a 76f<**

**Strathtay** 2 ch f Pivotal-Cressida (Polish Precedent (USA)) 2388$^3$ 2617$^8$ 3014$^5$ 4700$^6$ 5059$^8$ 5636$^{13}$ 6093$^2$ (6242) 6515$^4$ **>59f<**

**Stravmour** 8 ch h Seymour Hicks (FR) -La Stravaganza (Slip Anchor) *546$^7$ 629$^5$ 937$^3$ 992$^3$ (1023) (1193) (1448)* **>57+a 54f<**

**Stravonian** 4 b g Luso-In The Evening (IRE) (Distinctly North (USA)) 1344$^7$ 4987$^7$ 6141$^5$ 6245$^6$ **>44f<**

**Straw Bear (USA)** 3 ch c Diesis-Highland Ceilidh (IRE) (Scottish Reel) 4032$^2$ 4691$^3$ 4988$^5$ (5607) (5768) 5866$^3$ **>79+a 106+f<**

**Strawberry Dale (IRE)** 2 b f Bering-Manchaca (FR) (Highest Honor (FR)) (3514) (4100) 4552$^9$ 5391$^9$ **>90+f<**

**Strawberry Fair** 3 b f Kingmambo (USA) -Storm Song (USA) (Summer Squall (USA)) 3142$^4$ 3592$^7$ 4032$^{10}$ 5637$^6$ **>74f<**

**Strawberry Patch (IRE)** 5 b g Woodborough (USA) -Okino (USA) (Strawberry Road (AUS)) 3038$^{11}$ 3580$^{10}$ 4133$^5$ 4279$^{11}$ 4534$^2$ (4748) 5094$^7$ 5242$^6$ 5579$^2$5754$^{13}$ 6144$^{17}$ **>65f<**

**Streamix (FR)** 4 gr c Linamix (FR) -Slipstream Queen (USA) (Conquistador Cielo (USA)) 1163a$^5$ **>107f<**

**Stream Of Gold (IRE)** 3 b c Rainbow Quest (USA) -River Dancer (Irish River (FR)) 3603$^5$ (4781) 5443$^4$ (6191) **>106+f<**

**Street Ballad (IRE)** 2 b f Fasliyev (USA) -Nancy Maloney (IRE) (Persian Bold) 4454$^4$ 5109$^7$ 5362$^3$ 5753$^7$ 6003$^{11}$ 6242$^7$ **>62f<**

**Street Cred** 2 ch g Bold Edge-Trump Street (First Trump) (3588) 3907$^8$ 4527$^9$ 4914$^{12}$ **>79f<**

**Street Dancer (IRE)** 2 b g Imperial Ballet (IRE) -Life On The Street (Statoblest) 4761$^{15}$ 5307$^{11}$ 5542$^8$ 6543$^5$ **>52f<**

**Street Games** 5 b g Mind Games-Pusey Street (Native Bazaar) 4669$^5$ *5644$^6$* **>30a 34f<**

**Street Life (IRE)** 6 ch g Dolphin Street (FR) -Wolf Cleugh (IRE) (Last Tycoon) *516$^2$ 589$^5$* 1460$^2$ 1611$^3$ 2000$^3$ 2474$^4$ 2845$^3$ 3274$^5$3678$^4$ 5297$^4$ 6128$^4$ (6566) **>79a 83f<**

**Strensall** 7 b g Beveled (USA) -Payvashooz (Ballacashtal (CAN)) 2130$^{17}$ 2490$^2$ 2859$^7$ 3016$^7$ 3249$^3$ 3399$^4$ 3580$^7$ 4011$^5$4133$^{11}$ 4805$^5$ 4935$^5$ 5062$^2$ 5458$^8$ 5712$^9$ 6518$^{11}$ 6532$^{10}$ **>67a 85f<**

**Stretford End (IRE)** 2 b g Zieten (USA) -Creese (USA) (Diesis) 3793$^F$ 4446$^2$ 5096$^4$ **>86+f<**

**Stretton (IRE)** 6 br g Doyoun-Awayil (USA) (Woodman (USA)) 1903$^7$ 2196$^6$ 2527$^9$ 2894$^9$ 3097$^3$ 3482$^4$ 4061$^4$ 4343$^8$(5211) 5572$^7$ 6043$^3$ **>89f<**

**Strezkov** 3 b c Zafonic (USA) -Schezerade (USA) (Tom Rolfe) 1777a$^9$ **>81f<**

**Strider** 3 ch c Pivotal-Sahara Belle (USA) (Sanglamore (USA)) *1628$^2$* 2472$^4$ 3952$^4$ (4691) 5211$^{14}$ **>80a 86f<**

**Strides Of Fire (IRE)** 3 b c General Monash (USA) -Lagrion (USA) (Diesis) 1796$^{16}$ 1942$^{10}$ **>18f<**

**Strike** 3 b c Silver Hawk (USA) -Shemozzle (IRE) (Shirley Heights) 1442$^2$ 1800$^6$ (2273) 3035$^5$ **>88f<**

**Strike Gold** 2 b c Mujahid (USA) -Gracious Beauty (USA) (Nijinsky (CAN)) 4922$^{13}$ 5406$^3$ 5687$^7$ **>74f<**

**Strike Lucky** 4 ch g Millkom-Lucky Flinders (Free State) *(444) 3381$^{15}$* 3935$^8$ *6363$^{12}$* **>56a 50f<**

**Striking Ambition** 4 b c Makbul-Lady Roxanne (Cyrano De Bergerac) *1061$^9$* 1126$^{13}$ 5171a$^3$ (6104a) 6463a$^2$ **>94a 115f<**

**Striking Endeavour** 2 b c Makbul-Nineteenth Of May (Homing) (1905) 2592$^6$ 5434$^{20}$ 6113$^{14}$ **>79f<**

**String Serenade (IRE)** 3 b f Key Of Luck (USA) -Bubbly Dancer (USA) (Crafty Prospector (USA)) 4251a$^4$ **>53f<**

**Strong Cat (IRE)** 3 b g Catrail (USA) -Mary Strong (FR) (Taufan (USA)) 1306a$^6$ **><**

**Strong Hand** 4 b f First Trump-Better Still (IRE) (Glenstal (USA)) 1114$^6$ 1284$^3$ 3867$^9$ 4931$^9$ 5194$^{12}$ 5607$^6$ 5835$^2$ 6210$^4$ **>98 a 83f<**

**Strut The Stage (USA)** 6 ch h Theatrical-Ruby Ransom (CAN) (Red Ransom (USA)) 6490a$^7$ **>114f<**

**St Savarin (FR)** 3 ch g Highest Honor (FR) -Sacara (GER) (Monsagem (USA)) *493$^2$ 580$^5$ 619$^3$ (675)* 1900$^7$ 2378$^{13}$ 3819$^3$ 3982$^3$(4280) *4549$^{10}$ 5220$^{11}$* 5399$^{11}$ 5706$^5$ 5950$^2$ *6279$^5$* **>78a 81f<**

**St Tropez (IRE)** 3 b f Revoque (IRE) -Kaziranga (USA) (Lear Fan (USA)) 1507$^9$ 2001$^{15}$ 3368$^9$ 5795$^{18}$ **>24a 49f<**

**Stunning Magic** 4 b g Magic Ring (IRE) -Absolutelystunning (Aragon) 419$^{8}$ 539$^{9}$ **>31a 29f<**
**Stunning Spark** 2 b f Fraam-Lady Jo (Phountzi (USA)) 5840$^{9}$ 6127$^{12}$ **>18f<**
**Stylish Dancer** 3 b f Muhtarram (USA) -Iltimas (USA) (Dayjur (USA)) 2374$^{11}$ 2645$^{5}$ 3608$^{7}$ 4128$^{6}$ 4939$^{15}$ 5692$^{9}$ **>36a 51f<**
**Stylish Prince** 4 b g Polar Prince (IRE) -Simply Style (Bairn (USA)) 714$^{8}$ **><**
**Stylish Sunrise (IRE)** 3 b g Desert Style (IRE) -Anita At Dawn (IRE) (Anita s Prince) 1120$^{8}$ 2092$^{4}$ 2520$^{3}$ 2783$^{5}$ 3342$^{7}$ 3934$^{3}$ 4853$^{14}$ 5221$^{5}$ **>52a 66f<**
**Sualda (IRE)** 5 b g Idris (IRE) -Winning Heart (Horage) 2753$^{5}$ 3018$^{2}$ (3472) 3740$^{2}$ 3881$^{3}$ (4363) 4550$^{4}$ (4831) 5318$^{10}$ **>85f<**
**Suave Quartet (USA)** 3 b g Slew City Slew (USA) -Leallah M (USA) (Big Spruce (USA)) 3171$^{5}$ **>77a 58f<**
**Subadar Major** 7 b g Komaite (USA) -Rather Gorgeous (Billion (USA)) 5214$^{9}$ 5456$^{15}$ 5638$^{18}$ **>11a 17f<**
**Sublimity (FR)** 4 b g Selkirk (USA) -Fig Tree Drive (USA) (Miswaki (USA)) (1107) 1621$^{7}$ 2241$^{4}$ 2678$^{11}$ 4341$^{3}$ 4685$^{11}$ **>114 f<**
**Submissive** 3 ch c Young Ern-Sublime (Conquering Hero (USA)) 1386$^{8}$ (1679) 5135$^{10}$ **>70a 72f<**
**Subpoena** 2 b c Diktat-Trefoil (Kris) (5228) 5895$^{7}$ **>91f<**
**Subtle Affair (IRE)** 2 b f Barathea (IRE) -Uncertain Affair (IRE) (Darshaan) 5396$^{7}$ 6565$^{3}$ **>65f<**
**Subtle Breeze (USA)** 3 ch f Storm Cat (USA) -Morning Devotion (USA) (Affirmed (USA)) 5378$^{3}$ 5621$^{7}$ 6017$^{6}$ **>52a 71+f<**
**Subtle Move (USA)** 4 b f Known Fact (USA) -Substance (USA) (Diesis) 499$^{14}$ **>21a 65f<**
**Subyan Dreams** 2 b f Spectrum (IRE) -Subya (Night Shift (USA)) 3693$^{5}$ 4243$^{3}$ 4716$^{3}$ 5149$^{9}$ 5871$^{5}$ **>94df<**
**Succession** 2 ch f Groom Dancer (USA) -Pitcroy (Unfuwain (USA)) 4243$^{9}$ 4446$^{10}$ 4730$^{10}$ 5142$^{6}$ (5477) (5548) (5819) 5885$^{3}$ **>86f<**
**Successor** 4 ch g Entrepreneur-Petralona (USA) (Alleged (USA)) 2654$^{11}$ 3154$^{6}$ **>62f<**
**Suchwot (IRE)** 3 b g Intikhab (USA) -Fairy Water (Warning) 1214$^{10}$ 1365$^{6}$ 1874$^{2}$ 5693$^{9}$ 6006$^{19}$ **>62f<**
**Sudden** 9 ch g Positive Statement (USA) -Tala a Ranee (Layal) 1168$^{6}$ **><**
**Sudden Dismissal (IRE)** 2 b c Inchinor-Suddenly (Puissance) 4611$^{4}$ (4936) 5295$^{7}$ (5872) 6340$^{7}$ **>93f<**
**Sudden Flight (IRE)** 7 b g In The Wings-Ma Petite Cherie (USA) (Caro) 418$^{9}$ 618$^{13}$ 679$^{8}$ 1045$^{3}$ 1928$^{11}$ 2000$^{11}$ 2480$^{4}$ 3449$^{3}$(3733) 3851$^{6}$ 4233$^{5}$ 4441$^{8}$ 4849$^{3}$ 5773$^{9}$ **>79a 76+f<**
**Sudden Impulse** 3 b f Silver Patriarch (IRE) -Sanshang (FR) (Astronef) 2911$^{6}$ 3304$^{7}$ **>43a 64f<**
**Sudden Silence (IRE)** 3 b f Kris-Suddenly (Puissance) 1980a$^{7}$ 3328a$^{14}$ 4893a$^{6}$ 5162a$^{7}$ **>88f<**
**Sudra** 7 b g Indian Ridge-Bunting (Shaadi (USA)) 442$^{3}$ 487$^{3}$ 498$^{4}$ 642$^{4}$ 685$^{3}$ (782) 810$^{4}$ 3380$^{3}$ 5002$^{9}$ **>63a 58f<**
**Suerte** 4 b f Halling (USA) -Play With Me (IRE) (Alzao (USA)) 552$^{10}$ 2122$^{13}$ 2456$^{12}$ 3264$^{8}$ 3710$^{13}$ **>55a 63f<**
**Suez** 2 b f Green Desert (USA) -Repeat Warning (Warning) (4231) (5250) 5894$^{2}$ **>106 f<**
**Sufian** 5 b h Marju (IRE) -Mazarine Blue (Bellypha) 5504a$^{10}$ **><**
**Sugar Cube Treat** 8 b m Lugana Beach-Fair Eleanor (Saritamer (USA)) 422$^{10}$ 936$^{13}$ 1283$^{14}$ 1603$^{5}$ 1750$^{8}$ 2734$^{9}$ 3225$^{6}$ 4360$^{12}$ 4509$^{U}$ **>14a 38 f<**
**Sugarhoneybaby (IRE)** 3 b f Docksider (USA) -Royal House (FR) (Royal Academy (USA)) (3328a) **>96f<**
**Sugar Snap** 4 b f Sesaro (USA) -Cuddle Bunny (IRE) (Statoblest) 583$^{11}$ 3025$^{14}$ **>22a 59f<**
**Suggestive** 6 b g Reprimand-Pleasuring (Good Times (ITY)) 1107$^{4}$ 1409$^{5}$ 2200$^{2}$ (2623) 3361a$^{4}$ 3724$^{10}$ 4216$^{2}$ 4745$^{2}$ 5414$^{6}$ 5610$^{6}$ 5888$^{8}$ **>115f<**
**Sugitani (USA)** 2 b c Kingmambo (USA) -Lady Reiko (IRE) (Sadler s Wells (USA)) 5228$^{8}$ 5915$^{16}$ **>50f<**
**Suitcase Murphy (IRE)** 3 b g Petardia-Noble Rocket (Reprimand) 561$^{10}$ 5452$^{6}$ 5547$^{3}$ 5793$^{10}$ 6056$^{15}$ **>47f<**
**Suivez Moi (IRE)** 2 ch c Daggers Drawn (USA) -Pamiers (Huntercombe) 6563$^{12}$ **>45f<**
**Sujimoto (USA)** 3 ch c Woodman (USA) -Slew Of Comfort (USA) (Seattle Slew (USA)) 3163a$^{4}$ **><**
**Sujosise** 3 b c Prince Sabo-Statuette (Statoblest) 1975$^{12}$ 3201$^{9}$ 3624$^{11}$ 3954$^{13}$ **>44f<**
**Sukuma (IRE)** 2 ch f Highest Honor (FR) -Selva (IRE) (Darshaan) 2296$^{8}$ 2985$^{7}$ 4364$^{11}$ **>22a 46f<**
**Sulamani (IRE)** 5 b h Hernando (FR) -Soul Dream (USA) (Alleged (USA)) 2968$^{4}$ 3642$^{2}$ 4121$^{3}$ (4834) (6384a) **>128f<**
**Summer Bounty** 8 b g Lugana Beach-Tender Moment (IRE) (Caerleon (USA)) 1369$^{12}$ (1875) (2121) 2474$^{11}$ 2752$^{3}$ 3238$^{2}$ 3731$^{10}$ 4240$^{5}$ **>59a 84f<**
**Summer Charm** 2 b f Dansili-Regent s Folly (IRE) (Touching Wood (USA)) 4936$^{11}$ 5200$^{12}$ 5353$^{11}$ 5640$^{17}$ **>9a 48 f<**
**Summer Cherry (USA)** 7 b g Summer Squall (USA) -Cherryrob (USA) (Roberto (USA)) 2032$^{15}$ 2728$^{2}$ 3050$^{5}$ 3263$^{7}$ 3393$^{7}$ 3827$^{13}$ **>58a 47f<**
**Summerise** 3 b f Atraf-Summerhill Special (IRE) (Roi Danzig (USA)) 1244$^{7}$ 1529$^{6}$ 1844$^{3}$ 1946$^{8}$ 6147$^{6}$ **>48a 53f<**
**Summer Joy** 3 b f Myfontaine-Marycee (IRE) (King s Ride) 1304$^{9}$ 2765$^{14}$ **><**
**Summer Recluse (USA)** 5 gr g Cozzene (USA) -Summer Retreat (USA) (Gone West (USA)) 647$^{8}$ 770$^{7}$ 961$^{5}$ 1066$^{4}$ **>86a 85f<**
**Summer Serenade** 3 b f Sadler s Wells (USA) -Summer Sonnet (Baillamont (USA)) 2950$^{2}$ 3630$^{3}$ **>79f<**
**Summer Shades** 6 b m Green Desert (USA) -Sally Slade (Dowsing (USA)) 1598$^{6}$ 2304$^{5}$ 2521$^{2}$ 2757$^{4}$ 2963$^{4}$ 3320$^{3}$ 3563$^{5}$ 4142$^{6}$(4301) 4551$^{2}$ 4812$^{5}$ 5821$^{2}$ 5955$^{11}$ 6579$^{11}$ **>68 a 79f<**
**Summer Silks** 2 ch f Bahamian Bounty-Sadler s Song (Saddlers Hall (IRE)) 3818$^{8}$ 4135$^{4}$ 4606$^{12}$ 5240$^{15}$ 6003$^{17}$ **>57f<**
**Summer Special** 4 b g Mind Games-Summerhill Special (IRE) (Roi Danzig (USA)) 1268$^{5}$ 1527$^{5}$ 1660$^{3}$ 2038$^{12}$ 2375$^{5}$ 2753$^{11}$ 3002$^{3}$ 3040$^{3}$ 3579$^{7}$ 4132$^{13}$ 4605$^{7}$ 5187$^{4}$ 5587$^{13}$ **>34a 46f<**
**Summer Stock (USA)** 6 b g Theatrical-Lake Placid (IRE) (Royal Academy (USA)) 554$^{11}$ 6406$^{7}$ **>62a 67f<**
**Summer Sunset (IRE)** 3 ch f Grand Lodge (USA) -Elegant Bloom (IRE) (Be My Guest (USA)) 1980a$^{5}$ 2793a$^{5}$ 2971$^{19}$ 3328a$^{10}$ 3547a$^{7}$ 4893a$^{9}$ **>93f<**
**Summer Wine** 5 b m Desert King (IRE) -Generous Lady (Generous (IRE)) 1752$^{9}$ **>76a 83f<**
**Summitville** 4 b f Grand Lodge (USA) -Tina Heights (Shirley Heights) 2042$^{3}$ 2993a$^{2}$ 3519$^{6}$ 4321$^{3}$ 4980a$^{6}$ 5763$^{4}$ **>113f<**
**Sumora (IRE)** 2 b f Danehill (USA) -Rain Flower (IRE) (Indian Ridge) (4334) (4744) 5464$^{6}$ 6212$^{8}$ **>82+a 102f<**
**Sun And Showers (IRE)** 2 b c Rainbow Quest (USA) -Las Flores (IRE) (Sadler s Wells (USA)) 6441$^{9}$ **>51f<**
**Sun Bird (IRE)** 6 ch g Prince Of Birds (USA) -Summer Fashion (Moorestyle) 2076$^{5}$ **>107f<**
**Suncliff** 2 b g Most Welcome-Marjorie s Orchid (Petong) 6479$^{13}$ **><**
**Sundance (IRE)** 2 ch c Namid-Titchwell Lass (Lead On Time (USA)) (3805) 4514$^{2}$ (5213) 5602$^{6}$ 6068$^{10}$ **>90a 95f<**
**Sunday City (JPN)** 3 ch c Sunday Silence (USA) -Diamond City (USA) (Mr Prospector (USA)) 2133$^{3}$ 3121$^{3}$ 3574$^{5}$ 4820$^{5}$ 5340$^{2}$ 5860$^{13}$ **>77f<**
**Sunday Doubt (USA)** 3 br c Sunday Silence (USA) -Pas De Reponse (USA) (Danzig (USA)) 2161a$^{7}$ 3361a$^{3}$ 5668a$^{11}$ **>111f<**
**Sunday Joy (AUS)** 5 b m Sunday Silence (USA) -Joie Denise (AUS) (Danehill (USA)) 3862a$^{9}$ **>98f<**
**Sunday Symphony** 2 br c Sunday Silence (USA) -Darrery (Darshaan) 4728$^{2}$ (5302) (6122) 6472$^{5}$ **>89f<**
**Sundried Tomato** 5 b g Lugana Beach-Little Scarlett (Mazilier (USA)) 486$^{10}$ 544$^{6}$ 607$^{4}$ 761$^{6}$ 836$^{10}$ 968$^{6}$ 1313$^{9}$ 5541$^{8}$ 5833$^{5}$ 6001$^{10}$ 6131$^{10}$ **>81a 93f<**
**Sundrop (JPN)** 3 b f Sunday Silence (USA) -Oenothera (IRE) (Night Shift (USA)) 1791$^{2}$ 2640$^{6}$ (6173) **>82+a 114 f<**
**Sungio** 6 b g Halling (USA) -Time Or Never (FR) (Dowsing (USA)) (579) 740$^{3}$ (838) 950$^{2}$ 1041$^{3}$ 1081$^{3}$ 1547$^{5}$ 6084$^{8}$(6581) **>59a 55f<**
**Sun Hill** 4 b g Robellino (USA) -Manhattan Sunset (USA) (El Gran Senor (USA)) (724) (973) (1010) 1112$^{13}$ 1302$^{10}$ 1801$^{5}$ 2116$^{12}$ 5773$^{14}$ 6084$^{12}$ 6339$^{13}$ **>86+a 76f<**
**Sunisa (IRE)** 3 b f Daggers Drawn (USA) -Winged Victory (IRE) (Dancing Brave (USA)) 1227$^{2}$ (1476) 2472$^{3}$ 2887$^{8}$ 3206$^{2}$ 5297$^{19}$ 6263$^{5}$ **>73a 86f<**
**Sun King (USA)** 2 bb c Charismatic (USA) -Clever But Costly (USA) (Clever Trick (USA)) 6489a$^{3}$ **>118a<**
**Sun Kissed (JPN)** 2 ch c Sunday Silence (USA) -Flying Kiss (IRE) (Sadler s Wells (USA)) (4296) 5246$^{2}$ 6189$^{9}$ **>94f<**
**Sunley Sense** 8 b g Komaite (USA) -Brown Velvet (Mansingh (USA)) 2739$^{3}$ 3016$^{9}$ 3243$^{10}$ 3713$^{12}$ 4211$^{6}$ **>81f<**
**Sunningdale (JPN)** 5 br h Warning-Kadizadeh (IRE) (Darshaan) 5982a$^{9}$ **>105f<**
**Sunny Glenn** 6 ch h Rock Hopper-La Ballerine (Lafontaine (USA)) 2639$^{11}$ 3046$^{6}$ 3315$^{7}$ 5768$^{16}$ **>48a 101f<**
**Sunny Lady (FR)** 3 ch f Nashwan (USA) -Like The Sun (USA) (Woodman (USA)) 1356$^{2}$ 2133$^{2}$ 2323$^{2}$ 2840$^{2}$ (3172) 3557$^{4}$ 5842$^{4}$ 6396$^{6}$ **>76a 82f<**
**Sunny Nature** 2 b f Sadler s Wells (USA) -Bright Spells (USA) (Alleged (USA)) 6470$^{19}$ **><**
**Sunnyside Royale (IRE)** 5 b g Ali-Royal (IRE) -Kuwah (IRE) (Be My Guest (USA)) 1463$^{13}$ (1698) 1914$^{3}$ 2126$^{8}$ **>52a 52f<**
**Sunny Sky (FR)** 2 ch c Septieme Ciel (USA) -Silicon Run (FR) (Commanche Run) 4184a$^{6}$ **>89f<**
**Sunny Times (IRE)** 2 b f Raise A Grand (IRE) -Dragon Star (Rudimentary (USA)) 3633$^{5}$ 4212$^{7}$ 5281$^{10}$ 5792$^{5}$ 6226$^{2}$ 6562$^{8}$ **>59f<**
**Sun On The Sea (IRE)** 4 ch f Bering-Shimmer (FR) (Green Dancer (USA)) 2042$^{6}$ **>105f<**
**Sunridge Fairy (IRE)** 5 b m Definite Article-Foxy Fairy (IRE) (Fairy King (USA)) 1233$^{14}$ 2348$^{6}$ **>67a 40f<**
**Sunset Blues (FR)** 4 ch g Green Tune (USA) -Sunset Reef (Mill Reef (USA)) 907$^{5}$ 1059$^{10}$ 1138$^{10}$ 1407$^{3}$ 2231$^{8}$ **>41a<**
**Sunset Dreamer (USA)** 3 ch f Boundary (USA) -Quaff (USA) (Raise A Cup (USA)) 447$^{6}$ 597$^{11}$ 1352$^{11}$ 2484$^{14}$ 5791$^{13}$ 6227$^{18}$ **>51a 38f<**
**Sunset King (USA)** 4 b c King Of Kings (IRE) -Sunset River (USA) (Northern Flagship (USA)) 1207$^{12}$ **>23a 62f<**
**Sunset Mirage (USA)** 3 br f Swain (IRE) -Yafill (USA) (Nureyev (USA)) 1612$^{2}$ 2093$^{6}$ (2355) 2847$^{11}$ 3139$^{6}$ 3670$^{10}$ 4201$^{4}$ 4471$^{2}$ 4711$^{3}$ 4989$^{2}$ **>73f<**
**Sunset Strip** 2 b c Josr Algarhoud (IRE) -Shady Street (USA) (Shadeed (USA)) 2422$^{2}$ 3665$^{2}$ 4143$^{3}$ 4446$^{6}$ **>75f<**
**Sunshine On Me** 3 ch f Kris-Degannwy (Caerleon (USA)) 4369$^{9}$ 4939$^{5}$ 5907$^{9}$ 6495$^{12}$ **>58+a 56f<**
**Sun Slash (IRE)** 4 b f Entrepreneur-Charmed Lady (Rainbow Quest (USA)) 1379a$^{8}$ 1893a$^{12}$ 2316a$^{10}$ 2903a$^{5}$ **>103f<**
**Sunstrach (IRE)** 6 b h Polar Falcon (USA) -Lorne Lady (Local Suitor (USA)) 1622$^{3}$ 2339a$^{4}$ 2559$^{3}$ 3484$^{3}$ **>118f<**
**Supamach (IRE)** 3 b f Machiavellian (USA) -Supamova (USA) (Seattle Slew (USA)) 2486$^{3}$ 2900$^{4}$ 3592$^{4}$ 4092$^{10}$ 5293$^{16}$ 5537$^{9}$ 6224$^{9}$ **>66a 69f<**
**Super Bobbina (IRE)** 3 b f Daggers Drawn (USA) -Lucky Coin (Hadeer) 1778a$^{2}$ 2720a$^{4}$ 4356a$^{6}$ 6381a$^{3}$ **>109f<**
**Super Boston** 4 b g Saddlers Hall (IRE) -Nasowas (IRE) (Cardinal Flower) 3154$^{12}$ 5189$^{6}$ **>38f<**
**Super Brand (SAF)** 5 b m Royal Chalice (SAF) -Popular (SAF) (Elliodor (FR)) 924a$^{2}$ 6488a$^{9}$ **>104f<**
**Super Canyon** 6 ch g Gulch (USA) -Marina Park (Local Suitor (USA)) 836$^{4}$ 1035$^{2}$ 1204$^{14}$ 2473$^{13}$ 3151$^{19}$ 3800$^{9}$ **>74 a 64f<**
**Superchief** 9 b g Precocious-Rome Express (Siberian Express (USA)) 448$^{14}$ 575$^{6}$ 596$^{4}$ 624$^{3}$ 742$^{5}$ 771$^{5}$ 847$^{2}$ 870$^{5}$ 1935$^{10}$ 5282$^{11}$ 6157$^{12}$ 6499$^{10}$ **>72a 33f<**
**Superclean** 4 ch f Environment Friend-Star Mover (Move Off) 1167$^{9}$ 1402$^{10}$ 1581$^{6}$ 2055$^{9}$ **>38a 20f<**
**Super Dominion** 7 ch g Superpower-Smartie Lee (Dominion) 1888$^{5}$ (2185) 2456$^{4}$ 2666$^{9}$ (3282) 3804$^{10}$ 4190$^{12}$ 4605$^{8}$ 4925$^{5}$ 5587$^{4}$ **>51a 51f<**
**Supereva (IRE)** 4 b f Sadler s Wells (USA) -Final Farewell (USA) (Proud Truth (USA)) 2138a$^{12}$ 3137a$^{8}$ 5576a$^{7}$ **>86f<**
**Super Fellow (IRE)** 10 b g Shy Groom (USA) -Killough (Lord Gayle (USA)) 4202$^{3}$ (4609) (4778) 5638$^{5}$ 5991$^{5}$ **>56f<**
**Superfling** 3 ch g Superpower-Jobiska (Dunbeath (USA)) 4683$^{9}$ 5338$^{4}$ 5844$^{9}$ 6452$^{12}$ **>34a 56f<**
**Superior Star (AUS)** 4 b f Nothin Leica Dane (AUS) -Musters (AUS) (Pasakos (USA)) 2156a$^{8}$ **>99f<**
**Super King** 3 b g Kingsinger (IRE) -Super Sisters (AUS) (Call Report (USA)) 2519$^{9}$ 2900$^{12}$ 3613$^{7}$ 3819$^{8}$ 3981$^{5}$ 4628$^{2}$ 5189$^{3}$ 5773$^{19}$ 6096$^{9}$ **>48a 67f<**
**Super Lina (FR)** 3 gr f Linamix (FR) -Supergirl (USA) (Woodman (USA)) 1320a$^{2}$ 2338a$^{4}$ 2700a$^{4}$ 3566a$^{6}$ **>105f<**
**Superman (FR)** 5 ch g Bigstone (IRE) -Supergirl (USA) (Woodman (USA)) 6137a$^{2}$ **><**
**Superpridetwo** 4 b g Superpower-Lindrake s Pride (Mandrake Major) 1403$^{9}$ **>11a 42f<**
**Super Song** 4 b g Desert Prince (IRE) -Highland Rhapsody (IRE) (Kris) 1066$^{12}$ 1275$^{9}$ 1451$^{10}$ 2524$^{10}$ 2948$^{16}$ 3593$^{13}$ 3841$^{6}$ 4232$^{22}$ 5411$^{19}$ 5691$^{13}$ **>48 a 58f<**
**Superstitious (IRE)** 2 b c Bluebird (USA) -Stellar Empress (USA) (Star De Naskra (USA)) 3760$^{7}$ 4219$^{10}$ 4743$^{6}$ 5434$^{21}$ 6574$^{18}$ **>67f<**
**Supertramp (GER)** 8 br h General Assembly (USA) -Sinope (GER) (Tauchsport (GER)) (784a) **><**
**Supremacy** 5 ch g Vettori (IRE) -High Tern (High Line) 1703$^{10}$ 3912$^{4}$ 4270$^{7}$ 5111$^{4}$ 5435$^{9}$ 5815$^{3}$ **>110f<**
**Supreme Salutation** 8 ch g Most Welcome-Cardinal Press (Sharrood (USA)) 686$^{12}$ (1043) (1121) 1675$^{11}$ (1876) 1935$^{4}$ (2120) 5004$^{11}$ 5135$^{4}$ 5568$^{15}$ 5698$^{14}$ **>80a 92f<**
**Surbiton (USA)** 4 ch c El Prado (IRE) -Mastina (USA) (Gulch (USA)) 687a$^{5}$ 922a$^{9}$ 978a$^{9}$ **>86a 110f<**
**Surdoue** 4 b g Bishop Of Cashel-Chatter s Princess (Cadeaux Genereux) 440$^{8}$ 671$^{2}$ 734$^{4}$ 829$^{2}$ 903$^{8}$ 1502$^{11}$ 1675$^{18}$ 6013$^{13}$ 6483$^{10}$ **>70a<**
**Sure Future** 8 b g Kylian (USA) -Lady Ever-So-Sure (Malicious) 1989$^{3}$ **>29f<**
**Surface To Air** 3 b g Samraan (USA) -Travelling Lady (Almoojid) 2486$^{12}$ 2950$^{7}$ 3994$^{10}$ 5371$^{7}$ 6159$^{5}$ **>56a 49f<**
**Surf The Net** 3 b f Cape Cross (IRE) -On The Tide (Slip Anchor) 2548$^{3}$ 2971$^{15}$ 3867$^{10}$ 4068$^{3}$ 4812$^{4}$ 5294$^{9}$ 5652$^{19}$ 6477$^{11}$ **>88f<**
**Sur Ma Vie (USA)** 2 br f Fusaichi Pegasus (USA) -Boubskaia (Niniski (USA)) 4964a$^{5}$ **>91f<**
**Surreptitious** 3 ch f Machiavellian (USA) -Nadma (USA) (Northern Dancer) (3948) 4726$^{3}$ 5148$^{8}$ **>67f<**
**Surrey Downs Girl** 2 ch f Lake Coniston (IRE) -Kingston Girl (Formidable (USA)) 3021$^{7}$ **><**
**Surveyor (SAF)** 4 ch g Western Winter (USA) -Crescent Fields (SAF) (Northfields (USA)) 710a$^{3}$ 853a$^{2}$ (978a) 1146a$^{11}$ 2156a$^{2}$ **>116f<**
**Surwaki (USA)** 2 b c Miswaki (USA) -Quinella (Generous (IRE)) 4030$^{3}$ 4922$^{2}$ 5437$^{9}$ **>84f<**
**Susiedil (IRE)** 3 b f Mujadil (USA) -Don t Take Me (IRE) (Don t Forget Me) 1613$^{10}$ 1997$^{10}$ 2587$^{6}$ 2929$^{6}$ 3828$^{13}$ 5639$^{15}$ 5927$^{7}$ 6404$^{12}$ **>62f<**
**Suspicious Minds** 3 b f Anabaa (USA) -Paloma Bay (IRE) (Alzao (USA)) 1059$^{7}$ 1794$^{14}$ 2311$^{11}$ 3204$^{13}$ **>57a 50f<**
**Sussex Style (IRE)** 3 b g Desert Style (IRE) -Anita s Love (IRE) (Anita s Prince) 489$^{10}$ 766$^{9}$ 1083$^{6}$ 1243$^{7}$ 2326$^{6}$ 2380$^{15}$ 2726$^{8}$ 2932$^{5}$ **>52a 44f<**
**Sustainable Style (FR)** 3 gr f Formal Gold (CAN) -Spectacular Face (USA) (Spectacular Bid (USA)) 6132$^{8}$ 6561$^{16}$ **>31f<**
**Sutter s Fort (IRE)** 3 b c Seeking The Gold (USA) -Mayenne (USA) (Nureyev (USA)) 691a$^{10}$ **>55a 98f<**
**Suturia** 2 b f Cadeaux Genereux-Cream Tease (Pursuit Of Love) 6447$^{12}$ **>48a<**
**Suvari** 3 b f Indian Ridge-Falconera (IRE) (Tirol) 1052$^{6}$ 1371$^{13}$ **>44a 34f<**
**Svedov (FR)** 3 ch c Exit To Nowhere (USA) -Carla (FR) (Cardoun (FR)) 1218a$^{5}$ 6511a$^{2}$ **>108f<**
**Svenson** 3 ch c Dancing Spree (USA) -Bella Bambola (IRE) (Tate Gallery (USA)) 438$^{12}$ 529$^{10}$ 3607$^{11}$ 4102$^{11}$ 5345$^{9}$ 5451$^{13}$ 6004$^{6}$ 6200$^{13}$ **>14a 43?f<**
**Swagger Stick (USA)** 3 gr c Cozzene (USA) -Regal State (USA) (Affirmed (USA)) (1222) (1609) 2999$^{6}$ 3521$^{8}$ 3915$^{10}$ 4906$^{6}$ 5397$^{9}$ 5650$^{7}$ 6172$^{5}$ **>92f<**
**Swahili Dancer (USA)** 3 b c Swain (IRE) -Bella Ballerina (Sadler s Wells (USA)) 2555$^{5}$ **>39f<**
**Swain Davis** 4 b f Swain (IRE) -Exclusive Davis (USA) (Our Native (USA)) 2987$^{13}$ **>69a 59f<**
**Swainson (USA)** 3 br c Swain (IRE) -Lyphard s Delta (USA) (Lyphard (USA)) 916$^{3}$ 1967$^{4}$ (2486) 2841$^{2}$ 3543$^{16}$ 4167$^{5}$ 4229$^{14}$ **>77a 86f<**
**Swainsworld (USA)** 3 bb g Swain (IRE) -Highest Dream (IRE) (Highest Honor (FR)) 2367$^{4}$ 2962$^{4}$ (3168) 3507$^{8}$ **>75f<**
**Swallow Falls (IRE)** 2 b f Lake Coniston (IRE) -Common Cause (Polish Patriot (USA)) 3729$^{8}$ 4359$^{5}$ 5771$^{10}$ **>62f<**
**Swallow Senora (IRE)** 2 b f Entrepreneur-Sangra (USA) (El Gran Senor (USA)) 6470$^{11}$ **>63f<**
**Swan Nebula (USA)** 2 bb f Seeking The Gold (USA) -Bright Tiara (USA) (Chief s Crown (USA)) 3296$^{3}$ 3905$^{5}$ (4364) (5391) 5626$^{7}$ **>89f<**
**Swedish Shave (FR)** 6 ch h Midyan (USA) -Shavya (Shavian) 2162a$^{11}$ 3769a$^{2}$ 4357a$^{8}$ 5171a$^{2}$ 6463a$^{5}$ **>113f<**
**Sweeney Todd (IRE)** 2 ch g Raise A Grand (IRE) -Optional (Prince Sabo) 4432$^{6}$ 4638$^{8}$ **>48f<**
**Sweep The Board (IRE)** 3 b g Fasliyev (USA) -Fun Board (FR) (Saumarez) 4369$^{13}$ 4615$^{6}$ 5560$^{11}$ **>59f<**
**Sweet At Heart (IRE)** 3 b f Catrail (USA) -Lost Shadow (First Trump) 2853$^{9}$ 5196$^{7}$ 5367$^{5}$ **>31f<**
**Sweet Az** 4 b f Averti (IRE) -Yen Haven (USA) (Lear Fan (USA)) 2517$^{13}$ 2836$^{13}$ 3773$^{8}$ **>20a 45f<**
**Sweet Cando (IRE)** 3 bb f Royal Applause-Fizzygig (Efisio) 2075$^{6}$ 2756$^{9}$ 3077$^{2}$ 3201$^{7}$ 3270$^{5}$ 3877$^{8}$ 4748$^{11}$ 5094$^{3}$ 5557$^{10}$ 5674$^{8}$ 6114$^{6}$ **>46a 69f<**
**Sweet Catomine (USA)** 2 b f Storm Cat (USA) -Sweet Life (USA) (Kris S (USA)) (6485a) **>119+a<**
**Sweet Celtic** 2 b f Celtic Swing-Simil (USA) (Apalachee (USA)) 5390a$^{9}$ **><**
**Sweet Coincidence** 2 b f Mujahid (USA) -Sibilant (Selkirk (USA)) 3045$^{3}$ 3532$^{8}$ (4081) **>66f<**
**Sweet Coral (FR)** 4 b f Pennekamp (USA) -Sweet Contralto (Danehill (USA)) 541$^{7}$ 567$^{4}$ 627$^{8}$ 813$^{8}$ 934$^{7}$ **>41a 35f<**
**Sweetest Revenge (IRE)** 3 ch f Daggers Drawn (USA) -Joza (Marju (IRE)) 2741$^{11}$ 3420$^{6}$ 3628$^{9}$ 4024$^{3}$ 4515$^{3}$ 4774$^{7}$ **>77a 67f<**
**Sweet Gypsy Rose (IRE)** 2 b f Darshaan-Kincara Palace (IRE) (Fairy King (USA)) 4592a$^{7}$ 6367a$^{6}$ 6503a$^{7}$ **>83f<**
**Sweet Indulgence (IRE)** 3 ch c Inchinor-Silent Indulgence (USA) (Woodman (USA)) 2306$^{7}$ 3671$^{10}$ 3943$^{5}$ 4237$^{3}$ 4756$^{4}$ 5106$^{7}$ **>87f<**
**Sweet Lorraine** 2 b f Dashing Blade-Royal Future (IRE) (Royal Academy (USA)) 4053$^{2}$ 4705$^{7}$ **>69f<**
**Sweet Marguerite** 2 b f Diktat-Margaret s Gift (Beveled (USA)) 2296$^{5}$ 2730$^{4}$ 3003$^{4}$ 3532$^{6}$ 5240$^{18}$ 5578$^{8}$ 5800$^{7}$ 6093$^{7}$ **>49f<**
**Sweet Mistress (IRE)** 4 ch f Desert Story (IRE) -Kidston Lass (IRE) (Alzao (USA)) 5489a$^{10}$ **><**
**Sweet Namibia (IRE)** 2 ch f Namid-Almond Flower (IRE) (Alzao (USA)) 6294$^{3}$ 6478$^{3}$ **>62a<**
**Sweet Pickle** 3 b f Piccolo-Sweet Wilhelmina (Indian Ridge) 2444$^{2}$ 3125$^{4}$ 4547$^{6}$ 5219$^{20}$ 5656$^{8}$ 5849$^{6}$ **>72f<**
**Sweet Potato (IRE)** 2 b f Monashee Mountain (USA) -Villafranca (IRE) (In The Wings) 5125$^{5}$ 5946$^{8}$ 6195$^{8}$ **>57f<**
**Sweet Reflection (IRE)** 4 b f Victory Note (USA) -Shining Creek (CAN) (Bering) 996$^{9}$ 1277$^{9}$ 1690$^{5}$ 2643$^{13}$ **>38a 40f<**
**Sweet Reply** 3 ch f Opening Verse (USA) -Sweet Revival (Claude Monet (USA)) 1408$^{16}$ 2135$^{5}$ (2704) 3105$^{9}$ 3819$^{10}$ 4938$^{5}$ 5399$^{13}$ 6199$^{10}$ 6498$^{11}$ **>51a 84f<**
**Sweet Repose (USA)** 3 b f Gulch (USA) -Bint Baladee (Nashwan (USA)) 1420$^{7}$ 2198$^{8}$ **>42f<**
**Sweet Return** 4 ch c Elmaamul (USA) -Sweet Revival (Claude Monet (USA)) 4768a$^{8}$ **>121f<**
**Sweet Royale** 2 b f Royal Applause-Sorara (Aragon) 2173$^{2}$ (3003) 3736$^{5}$ 4744$^{11}$ **>75f<**
**Sweet Salsa (FR)** 3 b f Highest Honor (FR) -Sweet Contralto (Danehill (USA)) 2162a$^{10}$ **>97f<**
**Sweet Sioux** 2 ch f Halling (USA) -Mohican Girl (Dancing Brave (USA)) 6536$^{10}$ **>14a<**
**Sweet Stream (ITY)** 4 b f Shantou (USA) -Snug Dinner (IRE) (Jareer (USA)) 1952a$^{11}$ 4566a$^{3}$ (5501a) 6260a$^{3}$ **>112f<**
**Sweet Talking Girl** 4 b f Bin Ajwaad (IRE) -Arabellajill (Aragon) 1591$^{9}$ 1750$^{16}$ 4309$^{18}$ 4708$^{12}$

5016$^{12}$ >38f<

**Sweet Wake (GER) 3** ch c Waky Nao-Sweet Royale (GER) (Garde Royale) 3565a$^{17}$ 5168a$^{4}$ 5975a$^{6}$ >102f<

**Sweetwater (GER) 4** b f Goofalik (USA) -Safrane (GER) (Mister Rock S (GER)) 6025$^{6}$ 6192$^{7}$ 6581$^{8}$ >68a 32f<

**Swell Lad 2** b g Sadler s Wells (USA) -Lydara (USA) (Alydar (USA)) 3071$^{11}$ 4030$^{15}$ 4747$^{6}$ 5335$^{2}$ 5719$^{9}$ 5995$^{13}$ >70f<

**Swellmova 5** b g Sadler s Wells (USA) -Supamova (USA) (Seattle Slew (USA)) 2302$^{2}$ (3050) 3678$^{6}$ >70f<

**Swift Alchemist 4** b f Fleetwood (IRE) -Pure Gold (Dilum (USA)) 1624$^{8}$ 1757$^{10}$ 1877$^{3}$ 2883$^{10}$ 3841$^{12}$ 4319$^{11}$ 4616$^{7}$ 4849$^{7}$(5129) 5374$^{18}$ 6083$^{14}$ >58a 61f<

**Swift Dame (IRE) 2** b f Montjeu (IRE) -Velvet Appeal (IRE) (Petorius) 5248$^{15}$ 5375$^{5}$ 5848$^{12}$ 6281$^{7}$ >54a 46f<

**Swift Oscar 2** b c Mark Of Esteem (IRE) -Surf Bird (Shareef Dancer (USA)) 4149$^{6}$ 4681$^{7}$ >65f<

**Swift Sailing (USA) 3** b c Storm Cat (USA) -Saytarra (USA) (Seeking The Gold (USA)) 2069$^{13}$ 2378$^{11}$ 2790$^{10}$ 3152$^{2}$ 3394$^{4}$ >73+f<

**Swift Sailor 3** gr c Slip Anchor-New Wind (GER) (Windwurf (GER)) 6082$^{3}$ (6245) >75f<

**Swift Tango (IRE) 4** b g Desert Prince (IRE) -Ballet Society (FR) (Sadler s Wells (USA)) (577) 757a$^{11}$ 922a$^{2}$ 1114$^{3}$ 1286$^{4}$ (2110) 2681$^{2}$ 3075$^{3}$ 3521$^{6}$4118$^{4}$ 4530$^{3}$ (4932) 5111$^{2}$ 5438$^{3}$ 5815$^{2}$ >93a 116f<

**Swinbrook (USA) 3** ch g Stravinsky (USA) -Dance Diane (USA) (Affirmed (USA)) 1413$^{9}$ 2309$^{12}$ 2576$^{2}$ (3262) 5730$^{14}$ 5874$^{15}$ >84 f<

**Swing West (USA) 10** b g Gone West (USA) -Danlu (USA) (Danzig (USA)) 1041$^{4}$ 1238$^{9}$ >19a 35f<

**Swing Wing 5** b g In The Wings-Swift Spring (FR) (Bluebird (USA)) 1578a$^{5}$ 1880$^{16}$ (2340a) 3310$^{2}$ 4832$^{4}$ 5170a$^{4}$ >78a 113f<

**Swinton 3** gr c Grey Desire-Portite Sophie (Doulab (USA)) 5086$^{7}$ 5345$^{8}$ >34f<

**Sword Roche (GER) 3** br f Laroche (GER) -Sappho (GER) (Windwurf (GER)) 2157a$^{4}$ 2723a$^{11}$ 5974a$^{2}$ >86f<

**Swords 2** b c Vettori (IRE) -Pomorie (IRE) (Be My Guest (USA)) 5716$^{13}$ 5897$^{8}$ 6122$^{5}$ 6562$^{15}$ >72f<

**Swords At Dawn (IRE) 3** ch f Daggers Drawn (USA) -Caraway (Shadeed (USA)) 4987$^{10}$ ><

**Sworn To Secrecy 3** ch f Prince Sabo-Polly s Teahouse (Shack (USA)) 1083$^{8}$ 1464$^{9}$ 1627$^{7}$ 2371$^{10}$ 2536$^{11}$ 2741$^{6}$ 3628$^{11}$ 4241$^{11}$4568$^{7}$ >37a 65f<

**Swynford Pleasure 8** b m Reprimand-Pleasuring (Good Times (ITY)) 2235$^{2}$ 2449$^{5}$ 2659$^{4}$ 3443$^{3}$ >59f<

**Sybill 4** b f Danzig Connection (USA) -Stock Pile (Galveston) 1078$^{5}$ 1425$^{7}$ ><

**Sydneyroughdiamond 2** b g Whittingham (IRE) -November Song (Scorpio (FR)) 3925$^{9}$ 4900$^{5}$ 5290$^{8}$ 5767$^{8}$ 6113$^{10}$ >68f<

**Sydney Star 3** b f Machiavellian (USA) -Sena Desert (Green Desert (USA)) (1904) 2692$^{9}$ 6477$^{7}$ >87f<

**Sylvan Twister 5** br g First Trump-Storm Party (IRE) (Bluebird (USA)) 1404$^{5}$ 1493$^{5}$ 1728$^{5}$ 2055$^{3}$ >39a 39f<

**Sylva Royal (IRE) 3** gr f Royal Applause-Trim Star (Terimon) 1202$^{4}$ 4337$^{4}$ 4653$^{6}$ 5000$^{9}$ (5642) 6184$^{4}$ 6399$^{3}$ >64a 42f<

**Sylvaticus (IRE) 3** b c Shinko Forest (IRE) -Calamity Kate (IRE) (Fairy King (USA)) 2301$^{8}$ 4195$^{17}$ ><

**Symboli West (USA) 4** br c Gone West (USA) -Kenbu (FR) (Kenmare (FR)) 2744a$^{10}$ 5660a$^{8}$ >85f<

**Symphony Of Psalms (USA) 3** b f Stravinsky (USA) -Merion Miss (USA) (Halo (USA)) 2925a$^{16}$ >79f<

**Syndaco (IRE) 5** b h Surumu (GER) -Sintenis (GER) (Polish Precedent (USA)) 786a$^{3}$ 1655a$^{3}$ ><

**Syracruz (GER) 4** b c Law Society (USA) -She s His Guest (IRE) (Be My Guest (USA)) 1259a$^{13}$ >86f<

**Systematic 5** b h Rainbow Quest (USA) -Sensation (Soviet Star (USA)) 1124$^{3}$ 1792$^{2}$ (1925) 2639$^{10}$ 3072$^{5}$ 3642$^{6}$ >118f<

**Szeroki Bor (POL) 5** b g In Camera (IRE) -Szuana (POL) (Five Star Camp (USA)) 1010$^{8}$ >17a<

T

**Taakeed 2** b c Mark Of Esteem (IRE) -Walimu (IRE) (Top Ville) 6476$^{13}$ >44f<

**Taaqaah 3** ch g Grand Lodge (USA) -Belle Ile (USA) (Diesis) 2962$^{2}$ 3452$^{2}$ 3845$^{10}$ 4478$^{2}$ >88+f<

**Tabarka (GER) 3** b f Big Shuffle (USA) -Tirana (GER) (Esclavo (FR)) 898$^{5}$ 958$^{11}$ >32a 51f<

**Tableau (USA) 3** ch c Marquetry (USA) -Model Bride (USA) (Blushing Groom (FR)) 1111$^{3}$ (2519) (4171) 4906$^{9}$ 5194$^{7}$ >89f<

**Taboor (IRE) 6** b g Mujadil (USA) -Christoph s Girl (Efisio) 454$^{9}$ 526$^{8}$ 578$^{8}$ 801$^{5}$ 904$^{11}$ 1368$^{7}$ 1642$^{5}$1872$^{12}$ 2628$^{2}$ 2912$^{9}$ 3558$^{6}$ 4034$^{11}$ (4415) 4800 5094$^{2}$ 5512$^{9}$6186$^{5}$ 6398$^{2}$ >66a 65f<

**Tabor King (IRE) 2** b c Mujadil (USA) -Tiffany Sharp (USA) (Diesis) 6542a$^{10}$ ><

**Taca D Oli (FR) 5** br m Octagonal (NZ) -Marie De Fontenoy (FR) (Lightning (FR)) 914$^{13}$ >59f<

**Tacitus (IRE) 4** ch c Titus Livius (FR) -Idara (Top Ville) 1849a$^{6}$ >105 f<

**Tadawul (USA) 3** b f Diesis-Barakat (Bustino) 3916$^{10}$ (5424) 5706$^{6}$ 6185$^{8}$ >70+f<

**Tafaahum (USA) 3** b g Erhaab (USA) -Makadir (USA) (Woodman (USA)) 1795$^{18}$ 3017$^{6}$ >85+f<

**Taffrail 6** b g Slip Anchor-Tizona (Pharly (FR)) 1212$^{5}$ 4572$^{7}$ >90f<

**Tag Team (IRE) 3** ch c Tagula (IRE) -Okay Baby (IRE) (Treasure Kay) (708) (891) 986$^{3}$ 1388$^{14}$ 2181$^{5}$ (2266) 2726$^{3}$ 3420$^{2}$ 6205$^{12}$ >83a 81f<

**Tagula Bay (IRE) 2** b f Tagula (IRE) -Nezool Almatar (IRE) (Last Tycoon) 1960$^{2}$ 2213$^{3}$ 2458$^{5}$ >61f<

**Tagula Blue (IRE) 4** b g Tagula (IRE) -Palace Blue (IRE) (Dara Monarch) 1247$^{U}$ 1840$^{9}$ 2410$^{LFT}$ 3475$^{3}$ 3921$^{6}$ 4142$^{5}$ 5085$^{4}$ 5317$^{13}$(5657) 6081$^{3}$ 6546$^{5}$ >76f<

**Tagula Sunrise (IRE) 2** ch f Tagula (IRE) -Lady From Limerick (IRE) (Rainbows For Life (CAN)) 2352$^{2}$ 2568$^{2}$ 3370$^{2}$ 3938$^{15}$ 4446$^{3}$ 5241$^{2}$ (5434) (5767) >83f<

**Tahirah 4** b f Green Desert (USA) -Kismah (Machiavellian (USA)) 2763$^{11}$ 3052$^{7}$ 4120$^{8}$ 4553$^{20}$ 4773$^{8}$ 5416$^{8}$ 5811$^{3}$ 6214$^{12}$6497$^{2}$ >90a 94?f<

**Tahlal (IRE) 2** b c Dr Fong (USA) -Chatterberry (Aragon) 3893$^{5}$ 5096$^{11}$ 5200$^{8}$ 5856$^{4}$ 6393$^{11}$ >22a 60+f<

**Tahreeb (FR) 3** ch c Indian Ridge-Native Twine (Be My Native (USA)) 1396$^{4}$ 1766$^{2}$ (2476) (3134a) 3539$^{4}$ 4378a$^{3}$ >115f<

**Tahrir (IRE) 2** gr f Linamix (FR) -Miss Sacha (IRE) (Last Tycoon) 5272$^{2}$ 5613$^{3}$ >86f<

**Tahtheeb (IRE) 3** b f Muhtarram (USA) -Mihnah (IRE) (Lahib (USA)) (4369) 4640$^{2}$ 6173$^{4}$ >106+f<

**Taili 3** b f Taipan (IRE) -Doubtfire (Jalmood (USA)) 2487$^{7}$ 5367$^{6}$ 6245$^{9}$ ><

**Taipan Tommy (IRE) 2** ch g Shinko Forest (IRE) -Adieu Cherie (IRE) (Bustino) 1905$^{6}$ 2360$^{6}$ 3228$^{8}$ 3413$^{6}$ 3823$^{6}$ >59f<

**Taiyo 4** b f Tagula (IRE) -Tharwa (IRE) (Last Tycoon) 469$^{6}$ 525$^{6}$ 697$^{4}$ 800$^{4}$ 910$^{9}$ 1244$^{11}$ 2387$^{P}$2597$^{18}$ (4460) 4818$^{5}$ 5575$^{6}$ 5642$^{8}$ >45a 46f<

**Tajaathub (USA) 2** ch f Aljabr (USA) -Tajannub (USA) (Dixieland Band (USA)) 6118$^{4}$ >74+f<

**Taj India (USA) 2** bb c Gone West (USA) -Circle Of Gold (IRE) (Royal Academy (USA)) 4117$^{5}$ 5347$^{8}$ >70f<

**Take A Bow 3** b c Royal Applause-Giant Nipper (Nashwan (USA)) (3161) (3750) 4268$^{4}$ (4646) 4887$^{2}$ 5443$^{2}$ 5941$^{2}$ 6474$^{3}$ >110f<

**Take A Tangle (IRE) 2** b c Tagula (IRE) -Receptionist (Reference Point) 4958a$^{15}$ >67f<

**Take Good Time (IRE) 4** ch g Among Men (USA) -Bold Motion (Anshan) 2040$^{4}$ >39f<

**Take It There 2** ch f Cadeaux Genereux-Feel Free (IRE) (Generous (IRE)) 3627$^{9}$ 3905$^{10}$ >63f<

**Takemetoyourheart 2** ch f Zaha (CAN) -Mother Molly (USA) (Irish River (FR)) 5054$^{12}$ 5838$^{11}$ >18a<

**Takes Tutu (USA) 5** b g Afternoon Deelites (USA) -Lady Affirmed (USA) (Affirmed (USA)) 1367$^{9}$ 1773$^{15}$ 2142$^{7}$ 2493$^{2}$ 2618$^{2}$ 2781$^{5}$ 3198$^{5}$ 3409$^{17}$3884$^{2}$ 4122$^{20}$ 4287$^{20}$ 4435$^{3}$ 5061$^{5}$ 5403$^{7}$ 6157$^{4}$ >80a 85f<

**Takhleed (USA) 2** b c Stravinsky (USA) -Bold Threat (CAN) (Bold Ruckus (USA)) 5051$^{5}$ 5612$^{5}$ >71a 77f<

**Takhmin (IRE) 2** b c Almutawakel-Magdalene (FR) (College Chapel) 2758$^{9}$ 3248$^{2}$ 4078$^{3}$ 5630$^{6}$ >81f<

**Takrice 3** b f Cadeaux Genereux-Hasanat (Night Shift (USA)) 1070a$^{8}$ 1485a$^{2}$ 2330a$^{11}$ 4893a$^{7}$ >101f<

**Tak s Girl 2** ch f Takhlid (USA) -Sans Rivale (Elmaamul (USA)) 2773$^{13}$ 3055$^{7}$ 3444$^{19}$ 4010$^{9}$ >13f<

**Tala Ya (USA) 6** ch h Storm Bird (CAN) -Fly To The Moon (USA) (Blushing Groom (FR)) 689a$^{5}$ 851a$^{7}$ >84a<

**Talbot Avenue 6** b g Puissance-Dancing Daughter (Dance In Time (CAN)) 1923$^{8}$ 2293$^{5}$ 2461$^{5}$ 2679$^{8}$ 3480$^{2}$ 3732$^{2}$ 4152$^{7}$ 4362$^{2}$4886$^{8}$ 5372$^{2}$ 5418$^{2}$ 5647$^{7}$ 6071$^{2}$ >108f<

**Talcen Gwyn (IRE) 2** b g Fayruz-Cheerful Knight (IRE) (Mac s Imp (USA)) 2702$^{4}$ (2927) 3704$^{4}$ 3930$^{7}$ 4325$^{4}$ 5078$^{5}$ 5421$^{9}$ 5515$^{4}$ (5797) 5932$^{10}$6241$^{4}$ 6442$^{7}$ >79f<

**Tale Of Dubai (USA) 2** ch f Tale Of The Cat (USA) -Jamaican Me Smile (USA) (Sovereign Dancer (USA)) 5717$^{14}$ >31f<

**Tale Of The Tiger 3** ch g Bijou D Inde-La Belle Dominique (Dominion) 4891$^{2}$ 6285$^{5}$ >9f<

**Talk To Mojo 7** ch g Deploy-Balnaha (Lomond (USA)) 1103$^{18}$ >79f<

**Talldark N Andsome 5** b g Efisio-Fleur Du Val (Valiyar) 6043$^{12}$ 6573$^{15}$ >86a 87f<

**Tally (IRE) 4** ch g Tagula (IRE) -Sally Chase (Sallust) 410$^{8}$ 526$^{13}$ 748$^{12}$ 1308$^{12}$ 1876$^{6}$ 2172$^{11}$ 2423$^{3}$ (2581)2656$^{2}$ 2899$^{19}$ 3010$^{12}$ 3249$^{2}$ 3293$^{4}$ 3509$^{4}$ 3713$^{3}$ 3894$^{16}$4130$^{7}$ (4188) 4299$^{4}$ 4614$^{10}$ 4837$^{11}$ 4926$^{6}$ 5562$^{8}$ 5798$^{13}$ 6026$^{10}$6046$^{17}$ >69a 72f<

**Talwandi (IRE) 3** b c Alhaarth (IRE) -Talwara (USA) (Diesis) 1612$^{6}$ 2093$^{3}$ (2323) >84f<

**Tamalain (USA) 2** b f Royal Academy (USA) -Woodland Orchid (IRE) (Woodman (USA)) 5248$^{5}$ 5717$^{4}$ >77f<

**Tamamo Hot Play (JPN) 3** b c Fuji Kiseki (JPN) -Hot Play (JPN) (Northern Taste (CAN)) 5982a$^{8}$ >103f<

**Tamarella (IRE) 4** b f Tamarisk (IRE) -Miss Siham (IRE) (Green Forest (USA)) 576$^{9}$ 896$^{7}$ 930$^{8}$ 1319$^{5}$ 2252$^{12}$ 2482$^{7}$ 2875$^{11}$ 3151$^{8}$3575$^{5}$ 4415$^{9}$ 5282$^{14}$ 6229$^{17}$ 6403$^{11}$ >49a 49f<

**Tamarillo 3** gr f Daylami (IRE) -Up And About (Barathea (IRE)) 711a$^{5}$ 848a$^{2}$ (1005a) 1143a$^{6}$ 2341a$^{5}$ 3035$^{9}$ 3699$^{10}$ >105a 95f<

**Tamarina (IRE) 3** ch f Foxhound (USA) -Tamasriya (IRE) (Doyoun) 563$^{7}$ 587$^{15}$ 651$^{14}$ 3008$^{10}$ 4018$^{12}$ 4476$^{5}$ 5018$^{5}$ 5408$^{11}$ >51a 44f<

**Tamatave (IRE) 2** b c Darshaan-Manuetti (IRE) (Sadler s Wells (USA)) 4728$^{6}$ 5467$^{4}$ 5858$^{2}$ 6283$^{4}$ >88f<

**Taminoula (IRE) 3** b f Tagula (IRE) -Taormina (IRE) (Ela-Mana-Mou) 4230$^{7}$ 5150$^{7}$ 5566$^{6}$ 5766$^{13}$ 6128$^{12}$ 6279$^{8}$ >73a 78f<

**Tamora 2** ch f Dr Fong (USA) -Tahara (IRE) (Caerleon (USA)) 3693$^{6}$ 4364$^{14}$ 5559$^{8}$ 6021$^{3}$ 6265$^{14}$ >64a 58f<

**Tamweel (USA) 4** ch f Gulch (USA) -Naazeq (Nashwan (USA)) (4735a) 6484a$^{4}$ >110a 86f<

**Tamworth (IRE) 2** b c Perugino (USA) -Faiblesse (Welsh Saint) 5971a$^{7}$ >68f<

**Tanaffus 4** ch g Cadeaux Genereux-El Rabab (USA) (Roberto (USA)) 574$^{12}$ 823$^{10}$ 1032$^{12}$ 1268$^{13}$ 3954$^{17}$ >19a 19f<

**Tanaji 5** b m Marju (IRE) -Hamsaat (IRE) (Sadler s Wells (USA)) 577$^{14}$ >55a 78f<

**Tancred Arms 8** b m Clantime-Mischievous Miss (Niniski (USA)) 1197$^{13}$ 1720$^{4}$ 3006$^{9}$ 4132$^{12}$ 4447$^{4}$ 5587$^{8}$ >44a 51f<

**Tancred Imp 3** b f Atraf-Tancred Mischief (Northern State (USA)) 1363$^{8}$ 1667$^{5}$ 1784$^{3}$ 2146$^{12}$ 4207$^{10}$ 5197$^{3}$ 5350$^{9}$ >44f<

**Tancred Miss 5** b m Presidium-Mischievous Miss (Niniski (USA)) (2854) 3006$^{8}$ 3612$^{3}$ 4447$^{11}$ 5187$^{9}$ >43a 32f<

**Tancred Times 9** ch m Clantime-Mischievous Miss (Niniski (USA)) 1262$^{11}$ 1663$^{4}$ 1787$^{4}$ 2252$^{8}$ 2976$^{3}$ 3225$^{3}$ (3836) 4013$^{4}$ (4154) 4459$^{3}$5008$^{2}$ 5618$^{8}$ >67 a 71f<

**Tandava (IRE) 6** ch g Indian Ridge-Kashka (USA) (The Minstrel (CAN)) (1341) 1785$^{10}$ 2491$^{5}$ 2615$^{4}$ 3236$^{9}$ 3902$^{5}$ >80f<

**Tangible 2** b f Hernando (FR) -Trinity Reef (Bustino) 6181$^{7}$ 6446$^{5}$ 6555$^{10}$ >64+a 50f<

**Tania Di Sceptre (ITY) 4** b f King s Theatre (IRE) -Timarete (ITY) (Green Dancer (USA)) 6581$^{13}$ >42f<

**Tank (IRE) 3** ch g Woodborough (USA) -Fiddes (IRE) (Alzao (USA)) 5891$^{7}$ >23f<

**Tanmeya 3** gr f Linamix (FR) -Ta Awun (USA) (Housebuster (USA)) 3204$^{12}$ >42f<

**Tanne Blixen 3** b f Great Dane (IRE) -Night Transaction (Tina s Pet) 4097$^{9}$ 5204$^{12}$ 5845$^{11}$ 6280$^{9}$ >30a 17f<

**Tanning 2** b f Atraf-Gerundive (USA) (Twilight Agenda (USA)) 4474$^{6}$ 4770$^{2}$ 5281$^{3}$ 5909$^{14}$ >62f<

**Tannoor (USA) 3** b c Miswaki (USA) -Iolani (Alzao (USA)) 1356$^{3}$ (2257) 2732$^{5}$ 3415$^{10}$ 4056$^{6}$ 4726$^{4}$ >79 f<

**Tante Rose (IRE) 4** b f Barathea (IRE) -My Branch (Distant Relative) (2685) (3715) (5289) >121f<

**Tantien 2** b f Diktat-Tahilla (Moorestyle) 1601$^{5}$ 2035$^{4}$ 2568$^{9}$ 3373$^{5}$ 5240$^{20}$ 5548$^{13}$ >64f<

**Tantric 5** br g Greensmith-Petunia (GER) (Chief Singer) 866$^{9}$ 1039$^{10}$ 2528$^{3}$ 3516$^{8}$ 3623$^{9}$ 3923$^{3}$ 4181$^{3}$ 4626$^{4}$4828$^{3}$ >55 a 76 f<

**Tanzani (USA) 2** b c Giant s Causeway (USA) -Aunt Pearl (USA) (Seattle Slew (USA)) 3424$^{4}$ 3907$^{7}$ >81f<

**Tanzanite (IRE) 2** b f Revoque (IRE) -Resume (IRE) (Lahib (USA)) 4712$^{11}$ 5864$^{6}$ 6351$^{3}$ >72f<

**Tap 7** b g Emarati (USA) -Pubby (Doctor Wall) (1748) (1971) 3623$^{5}$ 5108$^{11}$ >58a 65f<

**Tapa 2** b f Tagula (IRE) -Tweed Mill (Selkirk (USA)) 5890$^{6}$ 6174$^{21}$ >55f<

**Tapau (IRE) 6** b m Nicolotte-Urtica (IRE) (Cyrano De Bergerac) 1518$^{5}$ 2238$^{9}$ 2656$^{10}$ 2948$^{14}$ 3301$^{13}$ 3457$^{8}$ 3698$^{20}$ >71a 71df<

**Tap Dance City (USA) 7** b h Pleasant Tap (USA) -All Dance (USA) (Northern Dancer) 5981a$^{17}$ >121f<

**Tap Dancer (USA) 3** ch c Sword Dance-Heaven s Gate (USA) (Septieme Ciel (USA)) 2701a$^{6}$ >86a<

**Tap Dancer (IRE) 6** b g Sadler s Wells (USA) -Watch Out (USA) (Mr Prospector (USA)) 5641$^{9}$ 5928$^{9}$ >28a 16f<

**Tapioka City (USA) 3** b f Danehill (USA) -Taroob (IRE) (Roberto (USA)) 3569a$^{7}$ ><

**Tapit (USA) 3** gr c Pulpit (USA) -Tap Your Heels (USA) (Unbridled (USA)) 1781a$^{9}$ >110?a<

**Tapleon 3** br f Danzig Connection (USA) -Reem El Fala (FR) (Fabulous Dancer (USA)) 1362$^{6}$ 1719$^{9}$ 2232$^{10}$ >27f<

**Tappit (IRE) 5** b g Mujadil (USA) -Green Life (Green Desert (USA)) 1185$^{15}$ 1313$^{15}$ 1642$^{11}$ 1877$^{11}$ 2359$^{3}$ 2582$^{9}$ 2869$^{5}$ 3575$^{16}$4336$^{12}$ 4548$^{15}$ 4687$^{6}$ 5412$^{13}$ 5930$^{5}$ (6229) 6288$^{5}$ 6363$^{6}$ >56a 56f<

**Tarabut 2** b f Green Desert (USA) -Nabadhaat (USA) (Mr Prospector (USA)) 5348$^{8}$ 6118$^{7}$ >56f<

**Taragan 2** b f Kayf Tara-Morgannwg (IRE) (Simply Great (FR)) 5771$^{7}$ 6522$^{9}$ >44f<

**Tarakala (IRE) 3** ch f Dr Fong (USA) -Tarakana (USA) (Shahrastani (USA)) 2498a$^{3}$ 2993a$^{3}$ 4406a$^{2}$ (4884) 5394$^{4}$ 6102a$^{3}$ >105f<

**Taranai (IRE) 3** ch f Russian Revival (USA) -Miss Flite (IRE) (Law Society (USA)) 420$^{4}$ 622$^{11}$ 885$^{12}$ 926$^{7}$ 1300$^{12}$ 1864$^{4}$ 1985$^{6}$ >51a 42f<

**Taranaki 6** b h Delta Dancer-Miss Ticklepenny (Distant Relative) 417$^{8}$ 1132$^{4}$ (1225) 1354$^{4}$ 1968$^{8}$ (2206) 2503$^{5}$ 3690$^{8}$ 4120$^{15}$ 4549$^{12}$4742$^{3}$ 5112$^{6}$ 5379$^{5}$ 5874$^{19}$ 5887$^{4}$ 6191$^{10}$ >75a 94f<

**Tarandot (IRE) 3** b f Singspiel (IRE) -Rifada (Ela-Mana-Mou) 2198$^{2}$ (2460) 3035$^{7}$ 3641$^{9}$ >81f<

**Taras Treasure (IRE) 2** b f Desert King (IRE) -Oklahoma (Shareef Dancer (USA)) 2213$^{2}$ 2550$^{6}$ 3123$^{4}$ 3406$^{3}$ 4575$^{5}$ (5542) 6344$^{5}$ >71f<

**Tara Tara (IRE) 2** b f Fayruz-Gobolino (Don) (1170) 1878$^{8}$ 2970$^{15}$ 4803$^{10}$ >81 f<

**Tarawan 8** ch g Nashwan (USA) -Soluce (Junius (USA)) 5584$^{14}$ 5869$^{17}$ >70a 79f<

**Tardis 3** ch f Vettori (IRE) -Time Lapse (The Noble Player (USA)) 2442$^{7}$ 2820$^{8}$ 3529$^{8}$ 4066$^{11}$ 4497$^{6}$ 5552$^{10}$ 6228$^{7}$ >59f<

**Tarfaa Bint Swain (USA) 4** b f Swain (IRE) -Escape To Victory (Salse (USA)) 831a$^{12}$ >46f<

**Tarfah (USA) 3** b f Kingmambo (USA) -Fickle (Danehill (USA)) (4168) (4613) 4906$^{2}$ (5783) >102+f<

**Tarjman 4** b c Cadeaux Genereux-Dodo (IRE) (Alzao (USA)) 3323$^{7}$ 4341$^{5}$ >115f<

**Tarkeez (USA) 3** b g Lear Fan (USA) -Mt Morna (USA) (Mt. Livermore (USA)) 4880$^{8}$ >27a 79f<

**Tarkwa 5** gr m Doyoun-Shining Fire (Kalaglow) 445$^{6}$ 537$^{13}$ (2052) 2348$^{7}$ 2643$^{7}$ 2929$^{5}$ >49a 37f<

**Tarot Card 3** b f Fasliyev (USA) -Well Beyond (IRE) (Don t Forget Me) 5439$^{9}$ >100f<

**Tarraman (USA) 2** b c Fusaichi Pegasus (USA) -Gerri N Jo Go (USA) (Top Command (USA)) 6073$^{2}$ >80+f<

**Tartan Special 2** b c Fasliyev (USA) -Colchica (Machiavellian (USA)) 3793$^{4}$ 4861$^{6}$ 5353$^{5}$ >62f<

**Tartatartufata 2** b f Tagula (IRE) -It s So Easy (Shaadi (USA)) 1390$^{13}$ 1709$^{4}$ 4514$^{9}$ 4803$^{8}$ 4924$^{2}$ 5143$^{8}$ 6333$^{18}$ >57a 55f<

**Tartiruga (IRE) 3** b g Turtle Island (IRE) -Palio Flyer (Slip Anchor) 2765$^{13}$ 3245$^{13}$ 3695$^{11}$ 4195$^{8}$ 4674$^{5}$ 5352$^{6}$ 5692$^{2}$ 5928$^{4}$ >50f<

**Tartouche 3** b f Pursuit Of Love-Megan s Flight (Welsh Pageant) (3204) (3694) (5397) 5788$^{2}$ >99f<

**Tartuffo (GER) 4** br c Big Shuffle (USA) -Tamacana (Windwurf (GER)) 4378a$^{7}$ >98f<

**Taruskin (IRE) 3** b g Danehill Dancer (IRE) -Jungle Jezebel (Thatching) 1408$^{3}$ (1641) 1797$^{3}$ 2642$^{11}$ 3671$^{12}$ 5886$^{11}$ >91f<

**Tasdeed 2** ch c Cadeaux Genereux-Miss Universe (IRE) (Warning) (6331) >85f<

**Tashkil (IRE) 3** b g Royal Applause-Surprise Visitor (IRE) (Be My Guest (USA)) 2966$^{14}$ 4317$^{5}$ 4908$^{7}$ >103 f<

**Tashreefat (IRE) 3** b f Danehill (USA) -Aigue (High Top) 3054$^{3}$ 3843$^{4}$ 5339$^{2}$ 6088$^{4}$ >69f<

**Tashyra (IRE) 2** b f Tagula (IRE) -Shiyra (Darshaan) 4040$^{4}$ 4670$^{4}$ 5277$^{11}$ 5509$^{11}$ >60f<

**Task s Muppet (IRE) 2** ch f Raise A Grand (IRE) -Highland Crumpet (First Trump) 4040$^{5}$ 4670$^{5}$ 5281$^{5}$ 5509$^{10}$ 6544$^{4}$ >57f<

**Tasneef (USA) 5** b g Gulch (USA) -Min Alhawa (USA) (Riverman (USA)) 2449$^{8}$ 3128$^{6}$ 3450$^{6}$ 4196$^{8}$ 5654$^{4}$ 5796$^{4}$ 6230$^{5}$ >55f<

**Tass Heel (IRE) 5** b g Danehill (USA) -Mamouna (USA) (Vaguely Noble) 5935$^{13}$ >72a 62f<

**Tatamagouche (IRE) 2** b f Sadler s Wells (USA) -Imitation (Darshaan) 6408a$^{6}$ >45f<

**Tata Naka 4** ch f Nashwan (USA) -Overcast (IRE) (Caerleon (USA)) 914$^{9}$ 1820$^{18}$ 2099$^{5}$ 2506$^{11}$ 3380$^{10}$ 4065$^{2}$ 4499$^{2}$ 5019$^{3}$5286$^{4}$ (5572) 5757$^{7}$ 6173$^{10}$ 6566$^{8}$ >52a 73f<

**Tatweer (IRE) 4** b g Among Men (USA) -Sandystones (Selkirk (USA)) 1516$^{5}$ (2040) 2734$^{12}$ 3314$^{9}$ 3663$^{10}$ 4301$^{8}$ 4473$^{18}$ 4825$^{2}$ 5002$^{5}$ >59a 58f<

**Tavalu (USA) 2** b c Kingmambo (USA) -Larrocha (IRE) (Sadler s Wells (USA)) 5455$^{6}$ 5871$^{11}$ >40f<

**Tawny Way 4** b f Polar Falcon (USA) -Ma Petite Anglaise (Reprimand) 1321$^{5}$ (1671) 2062$^{2}$ 3078$^{6}$ 3944$^{7}$ (4345) (4729) 5814$^{11}$ 6172$^{9}$ >98f<

**Tawoos (FR) 5** b m Rainbow Quest (USA) -Queen Of Dance (IRE) (Sadler s Wells (USA)) 6571$^{13}$ >92f<

**Tawqeet (USA) 2** ch c Kingmambo (USA) -Caerless (IRE) (Caerleon (USA)) 6187$^{14}$ (6545) >72f<

**Taxman (IRE) 2** ch c Singspiel (IRE) -Love Of Silver (USA) (Arctic Tern (USA)) 6439$^{12}$ 6555$^{4}$ >61a 46f<

**Tayif 8** gr g Taufan (USA) -Rich Lass (Broxted) 453$^{2}$ (465) (526) 573$^{2}$ 771$^{6}$ 847$^{7}$ 1087$^{2}$ 1230$^{14}$1504$^{5}$ 1909$^{3}$ (2656) 6539$^{7}$ >74a 74f<

**Taylors Tree Rock (IRE) 3** b f Bahhare (USA) -Pamina (Brigadier Gerard) 4251a$^{15}$ >57f<

**Tbm Can 5** b g Rock City-Fire Sprite (Mummy s Game) 1341$^{6}$ 1785$^{5}$ 2174$^{6}$ >41a 76f<

**Tcherina (IRE) 2** b f Danehill Dancer (IRE) -Forget Paris (IRE) (Broken Hearted) 3014$^{7}$ 3296$^{7}$ 4420$^{2}$ 5142$^{3}$ 5417$^{11}$ (5789) >76f<

**Tea For Texas 7** ch m Weldnaas (USA) -Polly s Teahouse (Shack (USA)) 1510$^{11}$ >13a 48f<

**Team-Mate (IRE) 6** b g Nashwan (USA) -Ustka (Lomond (USA)) 706$^{8}$ 3276$^{5}$ 3678$^{5}$ >71a 88f<

**Team Player 3** b c Mark Of Esteem (IRE) -Colorspin (FR) (High Top) 2900$^{8}$ >63f<

**Team Tactics (IRE) 3** b f Son Of Sharp Shot (IRE) -Sportin Notion (USA) (Sportin Life (USA)) 4027$^{10}$ 4517$^{11}$ >31a 57df<

**Te Anau 7** b m Reprimand-Neenah (Bold Lad (IRE)) 778$^{7}$ 823$^{6}$ 1493$^{6}$ 2228$^{8}$ >23a<

**Technician (IRE) 9** ch g Archway (IRE) -How It Works (Commanche Run) 1406$^{5}$ >67da 72f<

**Tedburrow 12** b g Dowsing (USA) -Gwiffina (Welsh Saint) 1955$^{5}$ 2625$^{3}$ 4317$^{4}$ >96f<

**Tedo (GER) 2** gr c Sternkoenig (IRE) -Tirajana (GER) (Riboprince) 6380a$^{2}$ >92f<

**Tedsdale Mac 5** ch g Presidium-Stilvella (Camden

Town) 2473[8] 2936[4] 3167[2] 3470[5] 3714[2] 3952[3] 4209[2] 4319[2]5144[5] 5317[2] 5635[10] 5945[11] (6097) 6266[8] 6337[4] >**68f**<

**Tedstale (USA) 6** ch g Irish River (FR) -Carefree Kate (USA) (Lyphard (USA)) 1385[16] 1773[12] 2237[5] 2894[15] 3198[3] 3470[6] 3879[4] 4209[5]4558[3] 4852[9] 5211[4] 5514[8] 6069[12] >**90f**<

**Tedzar (IRE) 4** b g Inzar (USA) -Chesham Lady (IRE) (Fayruz) 533[8] >**29a 40f**<

**Teeba (USA) 2** ch f Seeking The Gold (USA) -Shadayid (USA) (Shadeed (USA)) 6171[4] >**84+f**<

**Teehee (IRE) 6** b g Anita s Prince-Regal Charmer (Royal And Regal (USA)) 772[4] 1424[6] 2455[11] 2814[7] 2989[2] 3615[3] 3800[4]5259[12] >**75a 75f**<

**Tee Jay Kassidy 4** b g Petong-Priceless Fantasy (Dunbeath (USA)) (1094) 1513[2] 1583[5] 1915[2] 1986[13] 2231[4] 2703[2] 2803[5]3174[7] >**41a 44f**<

**Tefi 6** ch g Efisio-Masuri Kabisa (USA) (Ascot Knight (CAN)) 429[9] 481[3] 498[5] >**41a 9 f**<

**T E Lawrence (USA) 4** b c Charnwood Forest (IRE) -Only Gossip (USA) (Trempolino (USA)) (3816a) >**82f**<

**Telefonica (USA) 3** b f Distant View (USA) -Call Account (USA) (Private Account (USA)) 2311[4] 2694[11] 3613[2] >**65a 73 f**<

**Telegram Sam (IRE) 2** b c Soviet Star (USA) -She s The Tops (Shernazar) 6045[9] 6514[11] >**49f**<

**Telemachus 4** b g Bishop Of Cashel-Indian Imp (Indian Ridge) 1604[6] (1821) 2066[10] 2527[10] 3097[8] 3716[8] 4214[14] 4540[14] (4950) 5211[5]5650[8] >**78a 96f**<

**Telepathic (IRE) 4** b g Mind Games-Madrina (Waajib) 476[10] 905[7] 1474[7] 1787[6] 1929[7] 2274[10] 2625[9] 2941[4]3039[6] 3337[9] 3730[5] 3797[6] 3879[5] 4006[4] 4047[11] 4317[7]4510[8] 4635[5] 4782[13] 6246[8] >**46a 63 f**<

**Tell The Trees 3** br f Tamure (IRE) -Bluebell Copse (Formidable (USA)) 2401[7] 3190[5] 3984[5] (4421) >**55+f**<

**Tempelwachter (GER) 10** b h Acatenango (GER) -Tempelwache (GER) (Konigsstuhl (GER)) 4377a[5] >**85f**<

**Temper Tantrum 6** b g Pursuit Of Love-Queenbird (Warning) 448[5] 624[5] 646[2] 847[13] 2325[4] 3205[12] 3440[5] 3826[4]5039[6] 5411[5] 5575[8] 6024[3] (6296) 6580[3] >**70a 68f**<

**Tempestad (IRE) 2** b f Giant s Causeway (USA) -Arutua (USA) (Riverman (USA)) 6118[3] 6473[5] >**89f**<

**Temple Belle Xpres 2** b f Overbury (IRE) -Kustom Kit Xpres (Absalom) 5616[12] 5847[10] >**34f**<

**Temple Place (IRE) 3** b c Sadler s Wells (USA) -Puzzled Look (USA) (Gulch (USA)) 1411[3] 1901[3] >**103f**<

**Templet (USA) 4** b g Souvenir Copy (USA) -Two Step Trudy (USA) (Capote (USA)) 1249[2] 1662[3] 2619[4] 3297[5] 3794[3] 4005[13] 4486[10] 4631[2](4987) 5236[4] 5768[11] 6480[4] >**72a 73f**<

**Tempsford (USA) 4** b c Bering-Nadra (IRE) (Sadler s Wells (USA)) 1030[5] 2047[17] 5784[5] 6215[31] (6346) 6573[13] >**97a 96f**<

**Temptation Island (IRE) 5** b m Spectrum (IRE) -Kiya (USA) (Dominion) 910[10] 939[13] >**18a 49f**<

**Ten Carat 4** ch c Grand Lodge (USA) -Emerald (USA) (El Gran Senor (USA)) 3644[3] 4226[13] 5093[9] >**100f**<

**Ten-Cents 2** b f Dansili-Daylight Dreams (Indian Ridge) 5131[4] 5271[4] 5569[4] >**72f**<

**Tender (IRE) 4** b f Zieten (USA) -Jayess Elle (Sabrehill (USA)) 1319[3] 2178[5] 2282[7] 2440[8] 2707[5] 2885[8] 3151[7] 3593[15]3680[4] (4025) 4400[13] 4622[7] 4854[3] 4970[6] 5564[6] >**58a 58 f**<

**Tender Cove (IRE) 6** b g Balla Cove-Fair Tender (Tender King) 1254a[12] >**106f**<

**Tender Falcon 4** br g Polar Falcon (USA) -Tendresse (IRE) (Tender King) 2537[5] (3232) 3692[9] 4019[2] (4772) (5182) 5764[3] 6573[8] >**89f**<

**Tenderlit (USA) 2** b f Lit De Justice (USA) -Tender Moment (USA) (Copy Chief) (2668a) 3362a[3] >**94f**<

**Tennessee Master (GER) 3** ch g Big Shuffle (USA) -Traummaid (GER) (Riboprince (USA)) 2335a[9] >**82f**<

**Tenny s Gold (IRE) 3** b f Marju (IRE) -Itatinga (USA) (Riverman (USA)) 2182[4] 2842[3] 5511[5] 5770[4] 6119[3] (6537) 6579[7] >**68a 70f**<

**Ten Past Six 12** ch g Kris-Tashinsky (USA) (Nijinsky (CAN)) 430[13] ><

**Tentative (USA) 3** ch f Distant View (USA) -Danzante (USA) (Danzig (USA)) 1685[11] 3275[6] >**88f**<

**Teorban (POL) 5** b g Don Corleone-Tabaka (POL) (Pyjama Hunt) 1010[6] (4082) 4647[7] 5205[7] 5456[9] 5826[2] >**80a 65f**<

**Te Quiero 6** gr g Bering-Ma Lumiere (FR) (Niniski (USA)) 544[9] 600[8] 649[11] 837[2] 1009[2] 1273[7] 1954a[7]2278[7] 3177[7] 3690[12] 4751[11] 6451[12] >**108a 76f**<

**Tequila Sheila (IRE) 2** ch f Raise A Grand (IRE) -Hever Rosina (Efisio) 2730[7] (3224) 3898[6] (4612) 4876[6] 5670[7] 6003[4] >**81f**<

**Terdad (USA) 11** ch g Lomond (USA) -Istiska (FR) (Irish River (FR)) 616[10] >**12a**<

**Terenure Girl 3** br f Averti (IRE) -Royal Fontaine (IRE) (Royal Academy (USA)) 5551[6] 5844[10] 6397[14] >**11a 21f**<

**Terenzium (IRE) 2** b c Cape Cross (IRE) -Tatanka (ITY) (Luge) 6542a[11] ><

**Teresa 4** b f Darshaan-Morina (USA) (Lyphard (USA)) 1329[2] 1779a[6] 2958[6] 3644[7] 4226[11] 4934[7] 5619[17] 6339[2]6460[9] >**85f**<

**Termac (CZE) 9** b h Dictator s Song (USA) -Tempelherrin (GER) (Homing) (785a) ><

**Terminate (GER) 2** ch g Acatenango (GER) -Taghareed (USA) (Shadeed (USA)) 4208[11] 4544[7] 5023[5] 5596[14] >**44a 63f**<

**Termonfeckin 6** b g Runnett-Crimson Sol (Crimson Beau) 1210[10] 1463[15] 1590[7] >**6a 55f**<

**Tern Intern (IRE) 5** bb g Dr Devious (IRE) -Arctic Bird (USA) (Storm Bird (CAN)) 940[10] 998[11] 1090[11] 1233[15] >**28a 62f**<

**Terraquin (IRE) 4** b g Turtle Island (IRE) -Play The Queen (IRE) (King Of Clubs) 494[10] 647[4] 1132[13] 1354[19] 1708[5] 2575[13] 2838[5] 3205[5]3455[7] 3631[7] 4220[19] 4912[9] 4969[3] 5252[6] 5541[14] >**74a 79f**<

**Terrazzo (USA) 9** br g Nureyev (USA) -Diese (USA) (Diesis) 1182a[6] >**112f**<

**Tesary 2** b f Danehill (USA) -Baldemara (FR) (Sanglamore (USA)) 2071[6] 2481[2] (3302) 3634[4] 3930[3] 5202[3] 5421[13] 5617[2] >**76f**<

**Tesorero (SWE) 8** b h Funambule (IRE) -Factually (Known Fact (USA)) 4984a[8] ><

**Tetchy 4** b f Robellino (USA) -Putout (Dowsing (USA)) 1842[12] 2654[14] >**38f**<

**Tetcott (IRE) 3** ch f Definite Article-Charlene Lacy (IRE) (Pips Pride) 3209[5] 4718[3] 4916[4] 5656[3] 6498[10] >**57a 69f**<

**Tetou (IRE) 4** ch f Peintre Celebre (USA) -Place Of Honour (Be My Guest (USA)) 1940[9] 2210[11] >**69a 60f**<

**Tetra Sing (IRE) 2** b f Sinndar (IRE) -Tetralogy (USA) (Mt. Livermore (USA)) 5186[7] 5559[9] 5858[11] >**57f**<

**Tewitfield Lass 2** b f Bluegrass Prince (IRE) -Madam Marash (IRE) (Astronef) 3506[13] 4010[5] 4304[9] 4699[11] >**32f**<

**Texas Gold 6** ch g Cadeaux Genereux-Star Tulip (Night Shift (USA)) 2222[2] 2679[4] 3074[26] 3723[6] 3945[6] 4324[12] 5181[2] 5393[2](5491) 5647[4] 5893[4] 6572[11] >**99+a 108f**<

**Text 3** b g Atraf-Idle Chat (USA) (Assert) 3684[7] 4125[2] 4741[3] 5147[5] 5378[6] 5829[9] 5955[10] >**58a 68f**<

**Teyaar 8** b g Polar Falcon (USA) -Music In My Life (IRE) (Law Society (USA)) 526[14] 578[9] 681[6] 771[7] 897[13] 1087[5] 1268[12]1474[2] 1569[4] >**60a 68f**<

**Thadea (IRE) 3** bb f Grand Lodge (USA) -Kama Tashoof (Mtoto) 1214[12] 1841[13] 2207[P] >**61f**<

**Thai Dancer (IRE) 2** b c Midyan (USA) -Double Line (FR) (What A Guest) 5280a[7] >**61f**<

**Thai Express (DEN) 3** b f Cajun Cadet-Habibi (DEN) (Jammed Red (CAN)) 4379a[3] ><

**Thajja (IRE) 3** b c Daylami (IRE) -Jawlaat (USA) (Dayjur (USA)) (1587) 5439[8] 5813[2] 6193[17] >**105f**<

**Thakafaat (IRE) 2** b f Unfuwain (USA) -Frappe (IRE) (Inchinor) 4344[5] (5088) 6176[6] >**84f**<

**Thaminah (USA) 3** b f Danzig (USA) -Bashayer (USA) (Mr Prospector (USA)) 5811[5] 6175[12] >**89f**<

**Thanksgiving (GER) 3** ch f Lomitas-Tawinja (GER) (Windwurf (GER)) 5974a[5] ><

**Thara A (IRE) 3** b f Desert Prince (IRE) -Tycoon s Drama (IRE) (Last Tycoon) 1419[2] 1753[7] 2577[5] 4024[9] >**39a 69f**<

**Tharua (IRE) 2** b f Indian Danehill (IRE) -Peig Sayers (IRE) (Royal Academy (USA)) 5915[3] 6226[3] >**74 f**<

**Thats All Jazz 6** b m Prince Sabo-Gate Of Heaven (Starry Night (USA)) 498[8] 536[10] 663[7] 947[B] 996[10] >**43a 43f**<

**That s Racing 4** ch g Classic Cliche (IRE) -All On (Dunbeath (USA)) 1091[2] 1282[6] 1501[12] 4883[9] 5129[9] >**40a 58f**<

**The Abbess 2** gr f Bishop Of Cashel-Nisha (Nishapour (FR)) (5616) >**80+f**<

**Theas Dance 2** b f Danzig (USA) -Teggiano (IRE) (Mujtahid (USA)) 3456[5] 3693[8] 5115[3] 5548[9] >**71f**<

**Theatre (USA) 5** b g Theatrical-Fasta (USA) (Seattle Song (USA)) 1801[15] 2240[S] 2480[2] 3095[2] 3485[3] 3725[15] 5093[13] 5472[7]5784[12] 6215[13] >**88a 92f**<

**Theatre Belle 3** b f King s Theatre (IRE) -Cumbrian Rhapsody (Sharrood (USA)) 1419[8] 1771[13] 3026[13] 3250[6] 3371[5] 5243[11] 5638[7] >**26a 52f**<

**Theatre Lady (IRE) 6** b m King s Theatre (IRE) -Littlepace (Indian King (USA)) (663) 860[2] 929[8] 949[3] 966[6] 1166[3] 1244[8] 1305[4]1723[3] 2324[5] 2356[6] 2939[6] 3461[11] (3774) 3827[5] (4080) 4213[10] 4457[6](5796) >**48a 57f**<

**Theatre Of Dreams 2** b c Averti (IRE) -Loch Fyne (Ardkinglass) 1128[5] 1884[4] (2489) 4217[10] 5213[6] 5602[12] >**83f**<

**Theatre Time (USA) 4** b g Theatrical-Kyka (USA) (Blushing John (USA)) 4571[6] 5266[7] >**81f**<

**Theatre Tinka (IRE) 5** b g King s Theatre (IRE) -Orange Grouse (IRE) (Taufan (USA)) 516[5] 609[5] 682[5] 825[2] 1198[4] 1535[11] 1677[5]3128[2] 3488[8] 4424[4] 5546[3] 6083[16] >**62a 65f**<

**The Baroness (IRE) 4** b f Blues Traveller (IRE) -Wicken Wonder (IRE) (Distant Relative) 4026[8] 4881[9] 5736[19] >**60a 66f**<

**The Beduth Navi 4** b g Forzando-Sweets (IRE) (Persian Heights) 653[2] 789[2] (991) 1026[2] 1238[3] 1534[4] 2004[8] >**60+a 50f**<

**The Best Yet 6** ch h King s Signet (USA) -Miss Klew (Never So Bold) 648[4] 1241[8] 2763[12] >**84a 77f**<

**The Block Monster (IRE) 5** b m Petorius-Balgren (IRE) (Ballad Rock) 433[9] 627[10] 730[12] >**1a 60 f**<

**The Bonus King 4** b g Royal Applause-Selvi (Mummy s Pet) 837[4] 1056[5] 1284[2] 1321[8] 1671[13] 1845[11] 2196[7] 2421[2]2516[4] 3079[10] 3884[11] 4928[5] 5706[7] 5955[6] >**87a 96 f**<

**The Butterfly Boy 3** ch c Inchinor-Crime Of Passion (Dragonara Palace (USA)) 1370[10] 1596[3] 2836[14] 3628[12] >**40a 65f**<

**The Cat s Whiskers (NZ) 4** b f Tale Of The Cat (USA) -Good Faith (NZ) (Straight Strike (USA)) 5416[9] 5893[6] >**88f**<

**The Chequered Lady 2** b f Benny The Dip (USA) -Hymne D Amour (USA) (Dixieland Band (USA)) 4706[12] >**32f**<

**The Cliff s Edge (USA) 3** br c Gulch (USA) -Zigember (USA) (Danzig (USA)) 1781a[5] >**121a**<

**The Coires (IRE) 2** b c Green Desert (USA) -Purple Heather (USA) (Rahy (USA)) 3913[8] 4523[7] (5091) 5417[6] 5810[11] >**87f**<

**The Composer 2** b c Royal Applause-Superspring (Superlative) 5696[4] (5870) >**81f**<

**The Copt 5** b g Charmer-Coptic Dancer (Sayf El Arab (USA)) 3282[14] 3616[15] >**14a**<

**The Count (FR) 5** b g Sillery (USA) -Dear Countess (FR) (Fabulous Dancer (USA)) 6466[5] >**55a 45f**<

**The Crooked Ring 2** b g Magic Ring (IRE) -My Bonus (Cyrano De Bergerac) 1412[5] 1686[2] 1882[3] 2087[2] (3104) 3414[3] 3703[4] (3975) (4235) 4439[2] 4836[3]6068[6] 6333[5] >**97f**<

**The Duke Of Dixie (USA) 2** b c Dixieland Band (USA) -Money Madam (USA) (A.P. Indy (USA)) 2898[3] 5091[3] 5827[6] >**79f**<

**The Fairy Flag (IRE) 6** ch m Inchinor-Good Reference (IRE) (Reference Point) 1962[4] 2121[11] 5584[12] 6527[7] >**64f**<

**The Fisio 4** b g Efisio-Misellina (FR) (Polish Precedent (USA)) (454) (540) 578[5] 801[6] 912[3] 1051[8] 1131[7] 1313[2] 1421[14]1518[4] (2079) 2628[8] 3326[2] 4034[14] 4211[9] 4935[9] 5704[16] >**83a 83f**<

**Theflyingscottie 2** gr g Paris House-Miss Flossa (FR) (Big John (FR)) 4040[10] 4474[12] >**33f**<

**The Footballresult 3** b f The West (USA) -Bunny Gee (Last Tycoon) 660[11] 766[10] 2061[5] 2762[11] 3190[9] >**19a 31f**<

**The Fox s Head (IRE) 3** b f Imperial Ballet (IRE) -Lovely Leitrim (IRE) (Erin s Hope) 1784[5] 2783[7] >**41f**<

**The Fun Merchant 3** b g Mind Games-Sinking (Midyan (USA)) 1370[7] (3002) (3271) 4092[2] 4242[7] 5829[5] 6160[9] 6279[7] 6461[3] >**69a 74+f**<

**The Gaikwar (IRE) 5** b h Indian Ridge-Broadmara (IRE) (Thatching) 448[6] 575[4] 707[2] 847[5] 964[8] (1055) 1542[2] 1875[U]2170[11] 3412[17] 3698[17] 4083[4] 4238[3] 4438[2] 4672[3] 4912[6] >**73a 73f**<

**The Gambler 4** ch g First Trump-Future Options (Lomond (USA)) 1345[9] 1527[14] 1665[11] 1868[2] 2123[8] 3103[16] 3148[12] 4350[12]5081[6] 5305[5] >**56da 45 f**<

**The Gay Fox 10** gr g Never So Bold-School Concert (Music Boy) 536[2] 728[4] 791[2] 859[3] 886[8] 946[9] 993[3]1020[11] 1121[8] 1165[6] >**52a 48f**<

**The Geezer 2** ch c Halling (USA) -Polygueza (FR) (Be My Guest (USA)) 6494[4] >**71a**<

**The Great Gatsby (IRE) 4** b c Sadler s Wells (USA) -Ionian Sea (Slip Anchor) 3136a[3] 3642[7] 4746[4] 4983a[8] >**121f**<

**The Job 3** ch c Dancing Spree (USA) -Bay Bianca (IRE) (Law Society (USA)) 462[6] 1119[2] 1214[5] 1997[15] 6537[5] >**61a 60f**<

**The Jobber (IRE) 3** b g Foxhound (USA) -Clairification (IRE) (Shernazar) 3203[4] 3645[10] 3845[6] 4515[2] 4717[2] 4874[14] 5697[5] >**85a 85f**<

**The Keep 2** ch f Shinko Forest (IRE) -Poyle Amber (Sharrood (USA)) 3633[7] 4364[10] 5200[9] 5353[4] 5701[11] 6063[8] >**22a 56f**<

**The Kelt (IRE) 7** b g Leading Counsel (USA) -Casheral (Le Soleil) (3518) 3712[P] >**48f**<

**The Khamsin (DEN) 5** b h Kateb (IRE) -Medinova (Mas Media) 4380a[5] 5812[7] >**101f**<

**The Kiddykid (IRE) 4** b g Danetime (IRE) -Mezzanine (Sadler s Wells (USA)) 1126[3] 1409[7] (2316a) 3308[4] 3537[6] 3940[8] 4590a[2] 5171a[7] >**114f**<

**The King Of Rock 3** b c Nicolotte-Lv Girl (IRE) (Mukaddamah (USA)) 561[8] 1365[5] 1559[4] 2146[8] 3026[2] 3572[4] 4055[6] 4853[5] >**53a 62f**<

**The King s Bishop 3** b g Bishop Of Cashel-Kennedys Prima (Primo Dominie) 644[4] 982[13] 1295[3] >**65a 74f**<

**The Lady Would (IRE) 5** ch m Woodborough (USA) -Kealbra Lady (Petong) 1089[10] 1280[8] 1510[7] >**39a 39 f**<

**The Last Cast 5** ch g Prince Of Birds (USA) -Atan s Gem (USA) (Sharpen Up) (1801) 6215[11] >**55a 83f**<

**The Last Mohican 5** b g Common Grounds-Arndilly (Robellino (USA)) 426[4] 528[2] 661[3] 699[2] 727[4] 950[4] 1164[7]1281[8] 1543[3] 1887[2] (1917) 2055[10] 2851[8] 4883[7] >**43a 38f**<

**The Laverton Lad 3** ch g Keen-Wyse Folly (Colmore Row) 427[11] >**27f**<

**The Leather Wedge (IRE) 5** b h Hamas (IRE) -Wallflower (Polar Falcon (USA)) 411[6] 637[11] 876[4] 938[10] 1075[5] 1180[2] 1738[5]3378[5] 4014[9] 4881[3] 6403[9] 6526[4] >**54a 46 f**<

**The Loose Screw (IRE) 6** b g Bigstone (IRE) -Princess Of Dance (IRE) (Dancing Dissident (USA)) 1305[10] 1527[9] 2216[13] 2462[12] 3520[12] 4444[5] 5770[5] 6057[6]6465[2] >**4a 53?f**<

**The Lord 4** b g Averti (IRE) -Lady Longmead (Crimson Beau) 4076[3] 4366[7] 4677[6] 4748[13] 4935[6] >**100df**<

**Theme Park 4** b g Classic Cliche (IRE) -Arcady (Slip Anchor) 501[7] 722[7] >**56a 71f**<

**Themesofgreen 3** ch g Botanic (USA) -Harmonia (Glint Of Gold) 2586[9] 2785[7] 3085[8] 3368[5] >**52f**<

**Theme Song (IRE) 5** b h Singspiel (IRE) -Glatisant (Rainbow Quest (USA)) 3757[11] >**94f**<

**The Mog 5** b g Atraf-Safe Secret (Seclude (USA)) 1024[7] >**54a 49f**<

**The Nibbler 3** b g General Monash (USA) -Spoilt Again (Mummy s Pet) 3427[4] 3846[6] 4545[7] 5545[6] 6184[12] >**38a 56f**<

**The Number 3** gr g Silver Wizard (USA) -Elite Number (USA) (Elmaamul (USA)) 4306[3] 4902[3] 5063[5] 5478[2] 5859[6] 6224[7] >**54a 70f**<

**The Old Soldier 6** b g Magic Ring (IRE) -Grecian Belle (Ilium) 1268[7] 1526[13] 3148[2] 5346[12] 6058[2] 6246[5] 6401[2] >**58a 65f**<

**The Palletman 4** ch g Lion Cavern (USA) -Aquarela (Shirley Heights) 3846[9] >**16a**<

**The Pen 2** ch f Lake Coniston (IRE) -Come To The Point (Pursuit Of Love) 4099[7] (4559) 5240[2] (6515) >**64f**<

**The Persuader (IRE) 4** b g Sadler s Wells (USA) -Sister Dot (USA) (Secretariat (USA)) 1198[13] 1401[19] 1958[10] 2787[13] >**55a 87 f**<

**The Pheasant Flyer 2** ch g Prince Sabo-Don t Jump (IRE) (Entitled) 5015[3] (5353) (5721) 6340[12] >**92f**<

**The Plainsman 2** b g Atraf-Mylania (Midyan (USA)) 3373[6] >**23f**<

**The Player 5** b g Octagonal (NZ) -Patria (USA) (Mr Prospector (USA)) 5185[12] >**70+a 66f**<

**The Prince 10** b g Machiavellian (USA) -Mohican Girl (Dancing Brave (USA)) (3427) (4631) 5103a[2] (5151) (5514) (5581) (6069) 6475[3] >**95a 97f**<

**The Quiet Woman (IRE) 2** b f Barathea (IRE) -Tajawuz (Kris) 3286a[4] 3938[14] >**77f**<

**The Recruiter 4** gr g Danzig Connection (USA) -Tabeeba (Diesis) 500[8] >**47a 40f**<

**The Ring (IRE) 4** b g Definite Article-Renata s Ring (IRE) (Auction Ring (USA)) 1210[7] 1615[2] 1958[3] 3236[13] 3644[5] 3902[9] 4174[5] 5479[5] >**75a 79f**<

**The Rip 3** ch g Definite Article-Polgwynne (Forzando) 2934[7] 5545[3] 6006[12] >**64f**<

**The Rort (USA) 7** b h Diesis-Free Thinker (USA) (Shadeed (USA)) 784a[2] ><

**The Roundsills 10** ch g Handsome Sailor-Eye Sight (Roscoe Blake) 3929[11] 4453[6] >**15f**<

**The Spook 4** b g Bin Ajwaad (IRE) -Rose Mill (Puissance) 3367[10] 4386[15] 4535[9] 6142[5] 6516[7] >**47f**<

**The Stick 3** b f Singspiel (IRE) -Fatah Flare (USA) (Alydar (USA)) 1086[7] 1201[10] 1874[11] 2259[7] 2760[12] 3700[9] >**60a 53f**<

**The Tatling (IRE) 7** bb g Perugino (USA) -Aunty Eileen (Ahonoora) 2162a[2] 2475[3] 2719a[4] (2955) 3537[9] 4269[3] 4886[2] 5333a[2] (5647) 5780[3]5977a[2] >**120f**<

**The Terminator (IRE) 2** b g Night Shift (USA) -Surmise (USA) (Alleged (USA)) 1882[7] 2651[10] 3233[20] 4532[7] 5209[9] 5455[4] 6240[7] >**49f**<

**The Trader (IRE) 6** ch g Selkirk (USA) -Snowing (Tate Gallery (USA)) (2162a) 2719a[3] 2955[10] (3769a) 4595a[5] 5289[19] 5977a[14] >**118f**<

**The Varlet 4** b g Groom Dancer (USA) -Valagalore (Generous (IRE)) 2631[10] 3050[3] 3437[6] (4146) 4550[10] 5073[13] 5274[16] >**58a 82 f**<

**Thevenis 3** ch c Dr Fong (USA) -Pigeon Hole (Green Desert (USA)) 957[9] >**53a 56f**<

**The Violin Player (USA) 3** b g King Of Kings (IRE) -Silk Masque (USA) (Woodman (USA)) 1322[9] 2134[8] 2692[8] 3535[7] 4518[5] 5402[7] 6160[2] (6498) >**79a 67f**<

**The Warley Warrior 3** b g Primo Dominie-Brief Glimpse (IRE) (Taufan (USA)) 1711[6] 1975[11] 2411[13] >**45f**<

**The Way We Were 3** ch c Vettori (IRE) -Pandrop (Sharrood (USA)) 1506[6] 2400[5] 2847[12] 4147[3] 5829[13] >**72+a 74f**<

**Thewhirlingdervish (IRE) 6** ch g Definite Article-Nomadic Dancer (IRE) (Nabeel Dancer (USA)) 1326[3] 1615[4] 1973[10] 2855[3] (3120) 3725[3] 4361[2] 4550[6] 5595[9]5784[11] >**92f**<

**The Whistling Teal 8** b g Rudimentary (USA) -Lonely Shore (Blakeney) 1455[7] 1925[2] (2108) 3333a[5] 6355[4] >**118f**<

**The Wise Lady (FR) 4** b f Ganges (USA) -Miller s Lily (FR) (Miller s Mate) 1741a[5] 2438a[7] 3769a[4] >**99f**<

**The Wizard Mul 4** br g Wizard King-Longden Pride (Superpower) 1175[14] 1620[10] 4447[12] 4827[8] 5235[8] 5346[14] 6201[3] 6467[5] >**70f**<

**Thihn (IRE) 9** ch g Machiavellian (USA) -Hasana (USA) (Private Account (USA)) 1114[10] (1385) 1456[11] 5941[28] >**101f**<

**Thingmebob 4** b f Bob Back (USA) -Kip s Sister (Cawston s Clown) 2042[5] 2297[5] >**108df**<

**Think It Over (IRE) 5** ch m Bijou D Inde-Good News (IRE) (Ajraas (USA)) 415[13] 519[9] 821[12] >**15a**<

**Think Quick (IRE) 4** b f Goldmark (USA) -Crimson Ring (Persian Bold) 570[14] 653[5] 726[6] 812[6] 838[3] 901[4] 943[7]991[3] 1026[12] 1091[7] 1194[6] 3799[2] 4139[7] 4423[4]4883[12] >**43a 41f**<

**Third Empire 3** b g Second Empire (IRE) -Tahnee (Cadeaux Genereux) 1360[3] 1995[9] 3312[5] 3897[2] 4177[4] 5085[8] >**68f**<

**Thirteen Tricks (USA) 3** b f Grand Slam (USA) -Talltalelady (USA) (Naskra (USA)) 1831[13] 3206[3] 3908[4] (4417) 5057[11] >**66a 78f**<

**This Is My Song 2** b f Polish Precedent (USA) -Narva (Nashwan (USA)) 4712[7] 5089[3] >**73f**<

**Thistle 3** ch c Selkirk (USA) -Ardisia (USA) (Affirmed (USA)) 4781[9] 5123[2] 5345[2] 5851[2] (6130)

>76f<
**This Way That Way** 3 b g Dr Devious (IRE) -Ellway Dancer (IRE) (Mujadil (USA)) 683[10] >19a<
**Thomas Lawrence (USA)** 3 ch g Horse Chestnut (SAF) -Olatha (USA) (Miswaki (USA)) 4337[6] 4845[3] 5306[7] >70df<
**Thornaby Green** 3 b g Whittingham (IRE) -Dona Filipa (Precocious) 2353[4] 3624[4] (3877) 4305[11] 4489[5] 4827[4] 5063[7] 5674[2] 6144[18] >70f<
**Thornber Court (IRE)** 2 b f Desert Sun-Goldfinch (Zilzal (USA)) 4009[7] 5192[4] 5475[8] 5800[2] 6002[3] 6204[5] >64f<
**Thorntoun Piccolo** 2 ch f Groom Dancer (USA) -Massorah (FR) (Habitat) 4900[8] 5604[5] >66f<
**Thorny Mandate** 2 b c Diktat-Rosa Canina (Bustino) 4682[11] 5535[12] >49f<
**Threat** 8 br g Zafonic (USA) -Prophecy (IRE) (Warning) 421[9] 470[4] 499[7] 565[10] 665[3] 1584[4] 1859[4]1988[6] 2178[7] 2322[5] 2383[4] >36a 50f<
**Three Aces (IRE)** 2 ch f Raise A Grand (IRE) -Fallacy (Selkirk (USA)) 3208[9] 3531[5] 3986[6] 5377[19] 5738[7] 6140[11] 6515[7] >56f<
**Three Boars** 2 ch g Most Welcome-Precious Poppy (Polish Precedent (USA)) 4649[7] 5716[10] 5988[9] >51f<
**Three Degrees (IRE)** 2 gr f Singspiel (IRE) -Miss University (USA) (Beau Genius (CAN)) 5616[3] 6092[2] >77+f<
**Three Deuces (USA)** 2 rg f Two Punch (USA) -Too Fast To Catch (USA) (Nice Catch (USA)) 5003[5] 6153[4] 6394[6] >65a 61f<
**Three Eagles (USA)** 7 ch g Eagle Eyed (USA) -Tertiary (USA) (Vaguely Noble) 3683[6] >19f<
**Three Graces (GER)** 4 ch g Peintre Celebre (USA) -Trefoil (Kris) (852a) 1004a[7] 2623[3] >110f<
**Three Pennies** 2 b f Pennekamp (USA) -Triple Zee (USA) (Zilzal (USA)) 2213[10] (3164) 3505[3] 4365[11] 5466[12] 5701[10] 6063[5] >63a 69f<
**Three Points** 7 b h Bering-Trazl (IRE) (Zalazl (USA)) 689a[8] 923a[9] 1006a[7] >80a 119f<
**Three Secrets (IRE)** 3 b f Danehill (USA) -Castilian Queen (USA) (Diesis) 1413[7] (3487) 4068[2] 4948[3] 5783[11] >97+f<
**Three Ships** 3 ch g Dr Fong (USA) -River Lullaby (USA) (Riverman (USA)) 2114[10] 2962[5] 6064[9] >56a 65f<
**Three Strikes (IRE)** 2 b f Selkirk (USA) -Special Oasis (Green Desert (USA)) 2522[10] 6281[5] >54f<
**Three Valleys (USA)** 3 ch c Diesis-Skiable (IRE) (Niniski (USA)) 1410[2] 1764[11] >117f<
**Three Welshmen** 3 b g Muhtarram (USA) -Merch Rhyd-Y-Grug (Sabrehill (USA)) 816[14] 1040[8] 1467[5] (1844) 1908[3] 2546[13] 2915[7] 3556[8] 3684[2] >48 a 59f<
**Three Wrens (IRE)** 2 b f Second Empire (IRE) -Three Terns (USA) (Arctic Tern (USA)) 6197[3] (6464) >58f<
**Threezedzz** 6 ch g Emarati (USA) -Exotic Forest (Dominion) 2064[12] 2614[7] 3043[9] (4083) 4403[11] (4462) 4602[7] (4672) 4852[3] 4871[3](5177) 5419[14] 6069[20] 6128[15] 6284[13] >59a 90f<
**Through The Slips (USA)** 3 ch f Boundary (USA) -Fast Selection (USA) (Talinum (USA)) 3882[7] 4303[8] 5001[3] 5639[16] >47a 39f<
**Throwmeupsomething (IRE)** 3 b g Cape Cross (IRE) -Hawksbill Special (IRE) (Taufan (USA)) 6245[10] ><
**Throw The Dice** 2 b c Lujain (USA) -Euridice (IRE) (Woodman (USA)) 3925[2] (4487) 5767[4] >84+f<
**Thumamah (IRE)** 5 b m Charnwood Forest (IRE) -Anam (Persian Bold) 926[9] 988[11] 1606[14] 2362[6] 2811[11] 4605[15] >33a 33f<
**Thunder Calling (USA)** 2 b f Thunder Gulch (USA) -Glorious Calling (USA) (Nijinsky (CAN)) 2275[4] >67f<
**Thunderclap** 5 bb g Royal Applause-Gloriana (Formidable (USA)) (952) 967[2] 1102[8] 1598[10] 1993[16] 4702[9] >69da 68f<
**Thundering Surf** 7 b g Lugana Beach-Thunder Bug (USA) (Secreto (USA)) 2110[13] 2691[9] >67f<
**Thunderwing (IRE)** 2 bb c Indian Danehill (IRE) -Scandisk (IRE) (Kenmare (FR)) 4100[3] (4606) (5082) (5580) 6169a[5] >93+f<
**Thurlestone Rock** 4 ch g Sheikh Albadou-Don t Smile (Sizzling Melody) 2477[11] 2763[5] 2948[17] (5299) 5730[11] >87a 84f<
**Thwaab** 12 b g Dominion-Velvet Habit (Habitat) 3040[9] 4386[13] 4574[8] 5929[10] >39f<
**Thyolo (IRE)** 3 ch g Bering-Topline (GER) (Acatenango (GER)) 1795[2] 2018[10] 3001[3] 3539[11] 4322[7] 5650[15] 6121[8] >105f<
**Ti Adora (IRE)** 2 b f Montjeu (IRE) -Wavy Up (IRE) (Brustolon) 5694[9] 6118[14] 6565[8] >54+f<
**Tiamo** 2 ch c Vettori (IRE) -Speed To Lead (IRE) (Darshaan) 4730[12] 5467[6] 6073[7] >67f<
**Tiber (IRE)** 4 b c Titus Livius (FR) -Exciting (Mill Reef (USA)) 1657a[14] >122f<
**Tiberius Caesar (FR)** 4 b c Zieten (USA) -Thekla (GER) (Prince Ippi (GER)) (6508a) >111f<
**Tiber Tiger (IRE)** 4 b g Titus Livius (FR) -Genetta (Green Desert (USA)) 1275[4] (2279) 2504[7] 3127[2] 3198[13] 3597[19] 4293[5] 4558[5] 4577[5]5017[6] 5185[13] 5574[10] 5841[13] 6566[11] >28a 89f<
**Ticero** 3 ch g First Trump-Lucky Flinders (Free State) 1104[13] 1881[14] 2880[8] 3849[11] 5370[4] 5829[12] 6014[12] >44a 74f<
**Ticina (GER)** 4 b f Royal Solo (IRE) -Tannenprima (GER) (Sure Blade (USA)) 6255a[10] >73f<
**Ticker Tape** 3 b f Royal Applause-Argent Du Bois (USA) (Silver Hawk (USA)) (6254a) >111f<
**Ticki Tori (IRE)** 2 b f Vettori (IRE) -Lamees (USA) (Lomond (USA)) 6067[3] 6439[3] >80f<
**Tickle** 6 b m Primo Dominie-Funny Choice (IRE) (Commanche Run) 538[4] 646[8] 791[3] 1283[6] 1518[6] 2178[13] 3378[10] >53a 53f<
**Ticklepenny Lock (IRE)** 3 b c Mujadil (USA) -Barncogue (Monseigneur (USA)) 587[12] 611[9] 804[10] >22a 36 f<
**Tictactoe** 3 b f Komaite (USA) -White Valley (IRE) (Tirol) 514[6] 1517[6] 4414[9] 6058[7] >57a 51f<
**Tidal** 5 br m Bin Ajwaad (IRE) -So Saucy (Teenoso (USA)) 1856[6] (2514) (2835) 3046[7] 3699[3] 3872[4] 4367[7] (5297) 5573[10] >18a 93f<
**Tidal Fury (IRE)** 2 b c Night Shift (USA) -Tidal Reach (USA) (Kris S (USA)) 3918[12] 5098[4] >66f<
**Tides** 3 b f Bahamian Bounty-Petriece (Mummy s Pet) 3948[8] 4555[6] 4653[8] >43f<
**Tidy (IRE)** 4 b c Mujadil (USA) -Neat Shilling (IRE) (Bob Back (USA)) 836[11] (1246) 1500[5] 1608[U] 3079[8] 3235[3] 3516[7] 3755[15] 4134[4]6358[4] 6477[5] 6568[16] >54a 85f<
**Tiegs (IRE)** 2 ch f Desert Prince (IRE) -Helianthus (Groom Dancer (USA)) 5348[12] ><
**Tiffin Brown** 2 br g Erhaab (USA) -Cockatrice (Petong) 3760[10] >52f<
**Tiffin Deano (IRE)** 2 b g Mujadil (USA) -Xania (Mujtahid (USA)) 1390[5] 1743[8] 3476[10] 5466[13] 6008[4] >53f<
**Tiganello (GER)** 3 br c Acatenango (GER) -Tiyi (FR) (Fairy King (USA)) 3863a[6] 5169a[11] 6075a[2] 6511a[5] >109f<
**Tiger Bond** 2 br g Diktat-Blackpool Belle (The Brianstan) 3818[10] 5241[5] >53f<
**Tiger Dawn (IRE)** 2 b g Anabaa (USA) -Armorique (IRE) (Top Ville) 6078[13] (6221) >64+a 27f<
**Tiger Frog (USA)** 5 b g French Deputy (USA) -Woodyoubelieveit (USA) (Woodman (USA)) (3881) 4019[5] 4397[3] >59a 70f<
**Tiger Hunter** 2 b g Lake Coniston (IRE) -Daynabee (Common Grounds) 3458[8] 5218[10] 5792[15] 6221[3] >43a 34f<
**Tiger Royal (IRE)** 8 gr g Royal Academy (USA) -Lady Redford (Bold Lad (IRE)) 1379a[5] 1893a[6] 2744a[8] 3350a[6] 5660a[7] >110f<
**Tiger Tiger (FR)** 3 b c Tiger Hill (IRE) -Adorable Emilie (FR) (Iron Duke (FR)) (846) 1120[3] (1542) 1799[2] 2202[7] 2676[7] 3210[4] 4379a[2] (6354) 6444[4] >74a 99f<
**Tiger Tops** 5 ch g Sabrehill (USA) -Rose Chime (IRE) (Tirol) 701[5] 870[9] >70a 70df<
**Tiggers Touch** 2 b f Fraam-Beacon Silver (Belmez (USA)) 4637[4] 5248[9] 5534[6] 6125[7] >66f<
**Tight Circle** 2 b f Danzero (AUS) -Tight Spin (High Top) 2396[7] 2884[5] 3290[6] (4040) >71f<
**Tight Squeeze** 7 br m Petoski-Snowline (Bay Express) 418[6] 523[5] 600[3] 649[7] 768[8] (892) 1054[8] (1232) 2062[7] 2210[8] 2403[6] 3166[3] >89a 86f<
**Tigim (IRE)** 5 b g Fayruz-Rousalong (Rousillon (USA)) 3961a[10] 5660a[3] >96f<
**Tigress (IRE)** 5 b m Desert Style (IRE) -Ervedya (IRE) (Doyoun) 407[6] 509[5] 637[2] 796[6] 905[2] 954[7] 1178[9] >64a 54f<
**Tikitano (IRE)** 3 b f Dr Fong (USA) -Asterita (Rainbow Quest (USA)) 2236[18] 2505[14] 3344[13] 4025[10] >55f<
**Tilla** 4 b f Bin Ajwaad (IRE) -Tosca (Be My Guest (USA)) 2631[5] 3120[6] 4033[10] 4512[2] 4686[2] 5093[6] 5318[5] 5875[9] >42a 78f<
**Tillerman** 8 b h In The Wings-Autumn Tint (USA) (Roberto (USA)) 2957[5] 4228[6] 5414[8] >123f<
**Tillingborn Dancer (IRE)** 2 b g Imperial Ballet (IRE) -Exhibit Air (IRE) (Exhibitioner) 2352[10] 3080[11] 3406[9] 4135[10] 4761[9] >49f<
**Till There Was You** 3 b f Vettori (IRE) -Fleur Rouge (Pharly (FR)) 553[12] 3666[10] 4044[11] 5926[12] >5a 30f<
**Tilt** 2 b c Daylami (IRE) -Tromond (Lomond (USA)) 6148[8] >61f<
**Timaviet (IRE)** 2 ch c Soviet Star (USA) -Tima (IRE) (Machiavellian (USA)) 6259a[9] >67f<
**Timber Ice (USA)** 4 bb f Woodman (USA) -Salchow (USA) (Nijinsky (CAN)) 4155[10] 4819[5] 5371[5] >68f<
**Timber Scorpion (UAE)** 2 b c Timber Country (USA) -Aqraba (Polish Precedent (USA)) 5522[5] 5827[7] >66f<
**Timbuktu** 3 b g Efisio-Sirene Bleu Marine (USA) (Secreto (USA)) 445[7] 1267[9] 1465[7] 1721[2] 1862[8] 3479[12] >35a 47f<
**Time Flyer** 4 b g My Best Valentine-Sally s Trust (IRE) (Classic Secret (USA)) 702[7] 846[10] 1164[10] 1277[12] 1371[16] 1591[6] >45a 39f<
**Time For Mee** 2 ch f Timeless Times (USA) -Heemee (On Your Mark) 5800[9] 6270[11] >19f<
**Time For You** 2 b f Vettori (IRE) -La Fija (USA) (Dixieland Band (USA)) 2275[10] 3083[4] (3632) 4089[11] 4671[4] 5052[8] 6174[27] >47a 60f<
**Timely Twist** 3 b f Kirkwall-Timely Raise (USA) (Raise A Man (USA)) 416[7] >27a 40f<
**Time Marches On** 6 b g Timeless Times (USA) -Tees Gazette Girl (Kalaglow) 814[4] 943[9] (5585) 5757[8] >33a 48f<
**Time N Time Again** 6 b g Timeless Times (USA) -Primum Tempus (Primo Dominie) 476[5] (543) 586[8] (681) 761[3] 806[3] 836[3] (968) 1007[5]1126[16] 1927[7] 2091[6] 2391[3] 2407[7] 3293[3] 3446[2] 3515[2]3778[3] 4179[6] >89a 78f<
**Times Review (USA)** 3 b c Crafty Prospector (USA) -Previewed (USA) (Ogygian (USA)) 1760[2] 2239[5] (2549) 2897[14] 3523[8] 4394[7] 4874[11] >64a 86f<
**Time s The Master (IRE)** 3 b g Danetime (IRE) -Travel Tricks (IRE) (Presidium) 958[13] >14a 38f<
**Time To Regret** 4 b g Presidium-Scoffera (Scottish Reel) 1888[6] 2346[2] 2528[4] 2938[13] (3921) 3982[7] 4246[10] 5236[12] 5557[2]5714[5] (6201) 6364[6] 6548[4] >50a 64+f<
**Time To Relax (IRE)** 3 b f Orpen (USA) -Lassalia (Sallust) 956[2] 1044[4] (1309) 1559[8] 1932[2] 2251[3] >58a 69f<
**Time To Remember (IRE)** 6 b g Pennekamp (USA) -Bequeath (USA) (Lyphard (USA)) 1772[14] 1974[14] 2130[16] 2292[6] 2656[17] 3298[14] 3895[7] 4232[2]4291[15] 4425[12] 5544[10] 6007[12] 6550[6] >49a 60f<
**Time To Succeed** 2 b g Pennekamp (USA) -Ivory League (Last Tycoon) 5142[12] 5319[19] >13f<
**Time Traveller** 2 b g Timeless Times (USA) -Belltina (Belfort (FR)) 4598[10] 5218[17] ><
**Timmy** 2 b c Timeless Times (USA) -Ohnonotagain (Kind Of Hush) 1960[8] 2141[12] 2773[10] 3506[11] 3951[5] 4559[15] 4997[14] >36f<
**Tinian** 6 b g Mtoto-Housefull (Habitat) 468[5] 542[3] 604[10] 720[3] 939[12] 1197[4] 1389[9]1718[4] 2006[5] 2013[4] 2362[3] 2594[2] 3040[4] 3265[8] 3799[3] >57a 59f<
**Tinker s First** 2 b f First Trump-Tinker Osmaston (Dunbeath (USA)) 4620[9] 5218[15] 5375[10] >6a 16f<
**Tinta** 4 b f Robellino (USA) -Albahaca (USA) (Green Dancer (USA)) 2126[12] ><
**Tintawn Gold (IRE)** 4 b f Rudimentary (USA) -Clear Ahead (Primo Dominie) 874[11] 2643[9] 3263[4] 3490[2] 4485[10] 5286[2] 5796[19] >37a 53f<
**Tiny Tim (IRE)** 6 b g Brief Truce (USA) -Nonnita (Welsh Saint) 665[4] 949[4] 998[2] 1167[3] 1403[5] 1548[2] 1694[2](1860) 1890[5] 2056[2] 2229[2] 5283[11] >44a 28f<
**Tioga Gold (IRE)** 5 b g Goldmark (USA) -Coffee Bean (Doulab (USA)) 1914[5] 2531[9] 4883[10] 6209[11] >54a 60f<
**Tipperary All Star (FR)** 4 b g Highest Honor (FR) -Moucha (FR) (Fabulous Dancer (USA)) 1156a[6] 5962a[8] (6102a) >107f<
**Tipsy Lady** 3 b f Intikhab (USA) -Creme De Menthe (IRE) (Green Desert (USA)) 1796[15] 2223[7] 2911[9] 4369[8] 4644[5] 4954[5] 5541[15] >61f<
**Tipsy Lillie** 2 ch f Tipsy Creek (USA) -Belle De Nuit (IRE) (Statoblest) 1984[5] 2439[7] 2674[11] 2812[8] (3526) 3883[4] (4200) 4816[4] 6305[4] >21a 56f<
**Tip The Dip (USA)** 4 ch c Benny The Dip (USA) -Senora Tippy (USA) (El Gran Senor (USA)) 5615[2] 5919[10] 6444[3] 6573[23] >93f<
**Tip Toes (IRE)** 2 b f Bianconi (USA) -Tip Tap Toe (USA) (Pleasant Tap (USA)) 2208[10] 3571[6] 3824[7] 3951[4] 4200[5] 4521[12] 4699[6] 5593[4]6228[8] >43f<
**Tit For Tat** 2 b f Diktat-Wenda (IRE) (Priolo (USA)) 2522[14] 2961[5] 5095[4] 5596[19] 6093[12] >57f<
**Titian Flame (IRE)** 4 ch f Titus Livius (FR) -Golden Choice (Midyan (USA)) 3412[19] 4093[9] >30a 67f<
**Titian Lass** 5 ch m Bijou D Inde-Liebsidelass (IRE) (Be My Guest (USA)) 412[4] (535) 895[5] 1207[2] 1244[5] 2597[16] >56a 65df<
**Titian Time (USA)** 2 b f Red Ransom (USA) -Timely (King s Lake (USA)) 4747[2] 5272[3] (5717) 5979a[2] >107f<
**Tito Gofirst** 2 b c Gone West (USA) -Torgau (IRE) (Zieten (USA)) 6455[9] >37f<
**Titus Rock (IRE)** 2 b f Titus Livius (FR) -Cossack Princess (IRE) (Lomond (USA)) 3514[12] ><
**Titus Salt (USA)** 3 ch g Gentlemen (ARG) -Farewell Partner (USA) (Northern Dancer) 955[3] 1129[13] >80a 58f<
**Tiviski (IRE)** 2 b f Desert Style (IRE) -Mummys Best (Bustino) 1128[3] 1340[4] (1884) 2568[8] 3373[4] 3703[5] 4358[9] 4958a[9] 5314[9]5767[14] >64 f<
**Tiyango (GER)** 4 br c Acatenango (GER) -Tiyi (FR) (Fairy King (USA)) 1110a[9] >100f<
**Tiyoun (IRE)** 6 b g Kahyasi-Taysala (IRE) (Akarad (FR)) 1198[2] 1785[6] (2409) 2855[7] 3621[2] 4226[10] >69a 88f<
**Tizdubai (USA)** 3 b f Cee s Tizzy (USA) -Cee s Song (USA) (Seattle Song (USA)) 2641[6] 3600[7] >89f<
**Tizi Ouzou (IRE)** 3 ch f Desert Prince (IRE) -Tresor (USA) (Pleasant Tap (USA)) 5445[6] 5843[2] >52f<
**Tiz Molly (IRE)** 3 ch f Definite Article-Almadaniyah (Dunbeath (USA)) 4057[P] >45f<
**Tiz Wiz** 3 b f Wizard King-Dannistar (Puissance) 1363[9] 1719[2] 4391[10] 5141[10] 6466[13] >39f<
**Tizzy May (FR)** 4 ch c Highest Honor (FR) -Forentia (Formidable (USA)) 1328[13] 1762[2] 2220[5] 2681[10] 3315[4] 3538[8] 4285[7] 4525[5]5133[5] 5699[9] 6354[9] >85a 105f<
**Tizzy s Law** 3 b f Case Law-Bo Babbity (Strong Gale) (1472) 1775[6] 2411[4] 2650[5] 3273[8] 4608[11] (4970) 5117[5] 5473[5] >69f<
**T K O Gym** 5 b g Atraf-Pearl Pet (Mummy s Pet) 428[7] 477[5] >52a 49f<
**Toberoe Commotion (IRE)** 6 b g Great Commotion (USA) -Fionn Varragh (IRE) (Tender King) 594[11] 2426[14] ><
**Toby s Dream (IRE)** 2 b c Mujadil (USA) -Islandagore (IRE) (Indian Ridge) 3228[10] (4256) 4836[8] 5421[6] 5896[11] >77f<
**Toccata Aria** 6 b m Unfuwain (USA) -Distant Music (Darshaan) (3490) (3670) 3919[9] 4477[7] >59f<
**Toddeano** 8 b g Perpendicular-Phisus (Henbit (USA)) 1076[9] 2209[13] ><
**Todlea (IRE)** 4 b g Desert Prince (IRE) -Imelda (USA) (Manila (USA)) 419[6] 1624[4] 2084[4] 2474[3] 2738[6] 3412[2] 3573[2] 3844[3](4238) 4435[13] 5210[3] 5514[3] 5698[13] >72a 82f<
**Tofastforyou** 7 b h Mtoto-Pure Formality (Forzando) 5975a[8] >92f<
**Toffee Vodka (IRE)** 2 b f Danehill Dancer (IRE) -Vieux Carre (Pas De Seul) 3840[6] 4231[3] (5053) 5434[7] 5938[9] >69a 72f<
**Together (FR)** 4 b f Valanour (IRE) -Toomixa (FR) (Linamix (FR)) 3162a[9] 4357a[7] 5171a[9] >103f<
**Tohama** 2 b f In The Wings-Tanouma (USA) (Miswaki (USA)) 4344[6] 5109[8] 5534[5] 5885[10] >72+f<
**Toile** 3 ch f Zafonic (USA) -Princess Sadie (Shavian) 5251[6] ><
**Tojoneski** 5 b g Emperor Jones (USA) -Sampower Lady (Rock City) 857[10] 949[7] 998[3] 1167[4] 1511[2] 1592[2] 1986[2]2387[3] 2943[3] 3148[4] 3441[2] 3520[7] 4276[3] 4546[9] 5039[7] >41a 59f<
**Tokewanna** 4 b f Danehill (USA) -High Atlas (Shirley Heights) 2666[11] 3301[18] 3701[3] 4248[7] 4517[4] 4771[5] 5450[4] 5639[3]5795[5] 6227[10] (6362) (6404) 6580[10] >61a 54f<
**Tolaga Bay** 6 ch m Dr Devious (IRE) -Swordlestown Miss (USA) (Apalachee (USA)) 1599[4] >48a<
**Toldo (IRE)** 2 gr g Tagula (IRE) -Mystic Belle (IRE) (Thatching) 2686[7] 3197[9] 3514[9] 3736[4] 4256[12] 4699[2] (5059) (5083) (6265) 6344[11] >72f<
**Toledo Sun** 4 b g Zamindar (USA) -Shafir (IRE) (Shaadi (USA)) 735[3] 1376[5] (2004) 2385[2] >62a 59f<
**Tolpuddle (IRE)** 4 b g College Chapel-Tabdea (USA) (Topsider (USA)) 1982a[3] 5962a[11] >109f<
**Tolzey (USA)** 3 ch f Rahy (USA) -Legal Opinion (IRE) (Polish Precedent (USA)) 2193a[5] 4356a[8] >96f<
**Tomasino** 6 br g Celtic Swing-Bustinetta (Bustino) 2856[4] 3237[6] 3796[7] (3892) 4155[9] 5100[3] 5632[8] >76f<
**Tom Bell (IRE)** 4 b g King s Theatre (IRE) -Nordic Display (IRE) (Nordico (USA)) 1282[2] 1463[9] 2525[4] 2978[4] 3518[2] 3667[4] 4473[12] (5751) >22a 59+f<
**Tombola (FR)** 2 b g Trempolino (USA) -Green Charter (Green Desert (USA)) 3241[4] 4292[12] 5347[13] >68f<
**Tom Forest** 2 b c Forest Wildcat (USA) -Silk Masque (USA) (Woodman (USA)) 2470[6] 3014[2] 3373[2] 3974[5] 4890[11] 6338[11] >78f<
**Tom From Bounty** 4 ch g Opera Ghost-Tempus Fugit (Timeless Times (USA)) 6229[10] >55 f<
**Tomina** 4 b g Deploy-Cavina (Ardross) 1457[2] 6339[11] >63a 82f<
**Tommy Carson** 9 b g Last Tycoon-Ivory Palm (USA) (Sir Ivor (USA)) 684[3] 3461[10] (4603) 6084[6] >46a 51f<
**Tommy Smith** 6 ch g Timeless Times (USA) -Superstream (Superpower) 1454[9] 1774[20] 2130[8] 2274[11] (2734) 2859[8] 3920[16] 4211[8] 5107[15]5562[14] >75 f<
**Tomobel** 2 b f Josr Algarhoud (IRE) -Eileen s Lady (Mtoto) 2458[10] 4706[9] 5198[5] 5596[2] >64f<
**Tomokim (IRE)** 3 b c Mujadil (USA) -Snowtop (Thatching) 949[11] >7a<
**Tomoohat (USA)** 2 b f Danzig (USA) -Crystal Downs (USA) (Alleged (USA)) (6171) >89+f<
**Tomorrow s Party (NZ)** 5 b g Yamanin Vital (NZ) -Lal s Gift (NZ) (Noble Bijou (USA)) 6582a[7] >94f<
**Tomsk (IRE)** 4 b g Definite Article-Merry Twinkle (Martinmas) 2185[6] 4669[3] 5644[10] >31a 39f<
**Tomthevic** 6 ch g Emarati (USA) -Madame Bovary (Ile De Bourbon (USA)) 2303[14] 2724[11] 3084[8] 3575[7] 4014[4] 5107[11] 5253[5] 5412[11]5597[16] 6246[10] >47a 53f<
**Tom Tun** 9 b g Bold Arrangement-B Grade (Lucky Wednesday) 1759[7] 2065[2] 2625[8] 3522[4] 3901[2] 4759[16] 4837[3] 5224[5]5628[10] 6071[8] 6349[3] 6572[7] >93a 106f<
**Ton-Chee** 5 b g Vettori (IRE) -Najariya (Northfields (USA)) 992[6] 2186[7] 3518[6] 3576[10] >45?f<
**Tong Ice** 5 gr g Petong-Efficacious (IRE) (Efisio) 1407[8] 1694[6] 1724[5] >49a 21f<
**Toni Alcala** 5 b g Ezzoud (IRE) -Etourdie (USA) (Arctic Tern (USA)) 908[3] 1041[5] 1173[4] 1245[7] 1341[2] 1501[3] (1744) 1973[6] (2287)2491[3] 2615[5] 2731[2] 2935[4] 3120[5] (3363) (4448) 4578[5] 4934[5] 5190[6]5608[7] 5820[4] 5991[13] 6269[10] >66a 81f<
**Tonight (IRE)** 2 b g Imperial Ballet (IRE) -No Tomorrow (IRE) (Night Shift (USA)) 2288[3] 2622[4] 2819[3] 4010[6] 5083[7] 5369[10] 5593[8] >51f<
**Tonto (FR)** 3 gr g Second Empire (IRE) -Malabarista (FR) (Assert) 489[7] 613[4] 683[3] 802[7] 913[6] 1017[10] 3684[F] >63a 66 f<
**Tony James (IRE)** 2 b c Xaar-Sunset Ridge (FR) (Green Tune (USA)) (2447) 2954[4] 3640[5] (4857) 5980a[6] 6462a[9] >107f<
**Tony The Tap** 3 b g Most Welcome-Laleston (Junius (USA)) (881) 2877[2] 3092[2] 3273[2] 3874[5] 4090[2] (4267) 4294[9] 4837[7] 5124[5]5550[2] 5762[12] >65+a 89f<
**Tony Tie** 8 b g Ardkinglass-Queen Of The Quorn (Governor General) 1172[6] 1393[2] 1746[2] 2258[5] 2474[15] 2781[2] (3039) 3235[6] (3797) 4558[11]4634[6] 4988[9] 5627[5] 5835[7] 6069[17] 6244[10] >88f<
**Too Keen** 3 ch f Keen-Janie-O (Hittite Glory) 2815[5] 3251[11] 3613[8] >19a<
**Top Achiever (IRE)** 3 ch g Intikhab (USA) -Nancy Maloney (IRE) (Persian Bold) 1325[7] 1557[7] 2122[11] 3002[6] 4710[2] >62f<
**Toparudi** 3 b g Rudimentary (USA) -Topatori (IRE)

(Topanoora) 1418[9] (1613) 2692[11] 3689[3] >**75f**<

**Topatoo** **2** ch f Bahamian Bounty-Topatori (IRE) (Topanoora) 6455[3] >**67f**<

**Top Call (GER)** **3** b f Lando (GER) -Tatra (GER) (Windwurf (GER)) 2157a[6] 3973a[2] 5822a[4] 6257a[9] >**80f**<

**Top Dirham** **6** ch g Night Shift (USA) -Miller s Melody (Chief Singer) 1247[2] 1451[3] 2580[2] 2894[11] 3198[8] (3977) 4134[6] 5821[6] >**84f**<

**Top Form (IRE)** **2** b f Almutawakel-Top Of The Form (IRE) (Masterclass (USA)) 2690[8] 3823[5] (4099) 5351[5] 5648[21] 5932[11] >**80f**<

**Top Gear** **2** b c Robellino (USA) -Bundle (Cadeaux Genereux) 5871[2] >**84f**<

**Topkamp** **4** b f Pennekamp (USA) -Victoria Regia (IRE) (Lomond (USA)) 2466a[2] 2903a[3] 3275[3] 3715[6] >**108f**<

**Topkat (IRE)** **3** b g Simply Great (FR) -Kitty s Sister (Bustino) 3245[8] 4057[2] 4369[5] (4915) 5300[7] >**84 f**<

**Top Line Dancer (IRE)** **3** b c Fasliyev (USA) -Twafeaj (USA) (Topsider (USA)) 1200[4] 1358[12] 2756[8] 5545[9] >**67f**<

**Top Mark** **2** b c Mark Of Esteem (IRE) -Red White And Blue (Zafonic (USA)) 6352[11] ><

**Top Of The Bill (USA)** **3** b c Lear Fan (USA) -Note Musicale (Sadler s Wells (USA)) 2722a[9] >**111f**<

**Top Of The Class (IRE)** **7** b m Rudimentary (USA) -School Mum (Reprimand) 406[10] 590[6] 693[3] 763[3] 767[4] 867[8] 892[7]931[14] 996[3] 1042[5] 1077[7] 1369[4] 1535[7] 2262[7] 2381[7]2514[8] >**51a 63f**<

**Top Place** **3** b f Compton Place-Double Top (IRE) (Thatching) 678[7] 791[8] 1083[9] 1280[5] 1591[5] 1859[10] 3106[6] 6089[8] >**38a 38f**<

**Topple** **3** b f Master Willie-Top Cover (High Top) 2243[9] >**38f**<

**Toppling** **6** b g Cadeaux Genereux-Topicality (USA) (Topsider (USA)) 453[12] 2524[8] 2656[8] 3043[8] 3151[4] 3935[13] 4013[11] 4305[9]4546[14] 5260[11] >**39a 55f**<

**Top Pursuit** **2** b g Pursuit Of Love-Top Of The Parkes (Mistertopogigo (IRE)) 3553[7] >**48f**<

**Top Romance (IRE)** **3** ch f Entrepreneur-Heart s Harmony (Blushing Groom (FR)) 1398[8] 2641[4] 4640[8] >**103f**<

**Top Seed (IRE)** **3** b c Cadeaux Genereux-Midnight Heights (Persian Heights) 1439[2] 2043[4] 2722a[13] 3035[3] 3639[2] 4858[16] 5814[8] 6355[P]6570[P] >**112f**<

**Top Spec (IRE)** **3** b g Spectrum (IRE) -Pearl Marine (IRE) (Bluebird (USA)) 2018[8] 2281[11] 2612[5] 3543[12] 4145[2] 4749[7] (4921) 5297[2] (5446) 5761[9]6192[4] 6332[7] >**88f**<

**Top Style (IRE)** **6** ch g Topanoora-Kept In Style (Castle Keep) 783[7] 1403[2] 1493[2] (6467) >**40a 52f**<

**Top Tenor (IRE)** **4** b g Sadler s Wells (USA) -Posta Vecchia (USA) (Rainbow Quest (USA)) 603[12] 679[11] 984[6] 1101[3] >**56a 78f**<

**Top The Charts** **2** b c Singspiel (IRE) -On The Tide (Slip Anchor) 5087[4] 5646[4] 5871[3] 6344[2] >**88f**<

**Topton (IRE)** **10** b g Royal Academy (USA) -Circo (High Top) 419[4] 667[3] (870) 1273[13] 1708[15] 2237[9] 2504[4] 3299[6] 3426[2]3597[6] 3869[5] 4293[4] 4569[7] 4672[5] 6445[13] >**81a 83f**<

**Top Trees** **6** b g Charnwood Forest (IRE) -Low Line (High Line) 2767[9] 3776[6] (4033) 4647[5] 5073[8] 5654[5] >**64a 56f**<

**Top World (FR)** **5** b h Lost World (IRE) -Topkar (FR) (Arokar (FR)) 6137a[3] >**91f**<

**Toque** **2** ch f King s Best (USA) -Barboukh (Night Shift (USA)) 6118[9] 6494[9] >**48a 53f**<

**Torbato** **4** b c Machiavellian (USA) -True Joy (IRE) (Zilzal (USA)) 5103a[0] ><

**Torcello (IRE)** **6** b g Royal Academy (USA) -Vanya (Busted) 5755[5] 6354[4] >**106f**<

**Torchlight (USA)** **4** bb f Seeking The Gold (USA) -Cap Beino (USA) (Lyphard (USA)) 2182[11] 3154[13] >**62f**<

**Torinmoor (USA)** **3** ch g Intikhab (USA) -Tochar Ban (USA) (Assert) 1799[5] 3345[3] 3641[3] 4831[5] 5122[4] >**98f**<

**Tornado Bay (IRE)** **3** b f Desert Style (IRE) -Dromoland (Cadeaux Genereux) 2144[11] 2452[7] >**22f**<

**Toro Bravo (IRE)** **4** b g Alhaarth (IRE) -Set Trail (IRE) (Second Set (IRE)) 487[5] 548[3] >**69a 70f**<

**Toronto Heights (USA)** **3** ch g King Of Kings (IRE) -Revoltosa (IRE) (Catrail (USA)) 606[2] (673) (819) 885[9] 1408[19] 4515[7] 5124[12] >**81a 78f**<

**Torquemada (IRE)** **3** ch c Desert Sun-Gaelic s Fantasy (IRE) (Statoblest) 1083[3] 1270[11] 1702[16] 2790[8] 3420[3] 4026[7] 4687[9] (5370)5737[5] 6452[3] >**69a 68f**<

**Torrens (IRE)** **2** b c Royal Anthem (USA) -Azure Lake (USA) (Lac Ouimet (USA)) 4922[4] (5173) 5539[7] 6265[10] 6515[3] 6574[14] >**74+f**<

**Torrent** **9** ch g Prince Sabo-Maiden Pool (Sharpen Up) 443[2] 573[6] 626[3] (657) 796[5] 876[3] 936[8] 1033[7](1075) 1180[9] 1421[9] 1870[9] (3016) 3227[2] 3820[7] 4350[8] 4422[7]5562[2] 5798[20] 6526[7] >**55a 61f**<

**Torrestrella (IRE)** **3** b f Orpen (USA) -Sea Ring (FR) (Bering) (2160a) 2925a[11] 5530a[6] >**115f**<

**Torrid Kentavr (USA)** **7** b g Trempolino (USA) -Torrid Tango (USA) (Green Dancer (USA)) 1247[7] (1502) 3470[2] >**75f**<

**Tortuette** **3** b f Turtle Island (IRE) -Allmosa (Alleging (USA)) 482[9] 533[10] 736[9] >**20a 34f**<

**Torzal** **4** br g Hector Protector (USA) -Alathezal (USA) (Zilzal (USA)) 6150[15] >**32a 43f**<

**Toshi (USA)** **2** b c Kingmambo (USA) -Majestic Role (FR) (Theatrical) 4219[7] 4930[8] >**56f**<

**Toss The Caber (IRE)** **2** ch g Dr Devious (IRE) -Celtic Fling (Lion Cavern (USA)) 2256[7] 2898[8] >**40f**<

**Total Force (IRE)** **3** b c Night Shift (USA) -Capegulch (USA) (Gulch (USA)) 2517[11] 3180[16] >**54f**<

**Totally Scottish** **8** b g Mtoto-Glenfinlass (Lomond (USA)) 1534[3] 6005[3] >**53f**<

**Totally Yours (IRE)** **3** b f Desert Sun-Total Aloof (Groom Dancer (USA)) 1398[9] 2548[4] 2971[17] 3867[5] 4230[11] 5263[8] 5697[9] 5874[2]6341[10] 6459[9] >**88f**<

**Total Turtle (IRE)** **5** b g Turtle Island (IRE) -Chagrin D Amour (IRE) (Last Tycoon) 5465[6] 5815[5] >**72a 108f**<

**Touch Of Ebony (IRE)** **5** b g Darshaan-Cormorant Wood (Home Guard (USA)) 5450[15] 5935[10] 6231[2] 6468[3] >**53f**<

**Touch Of Land (FR)** **4** b c Lando (GER) -Touch Of Class (GER) (Be My Guest (USA)) 1435a[2] 1804a[6] (2508a) 3567a[8] 5489a[3] (5968a) >**122f**<

**Touch Of Silk (IRE)** **2** ch f Night Shift (USA) -Blew Her Top (USA) (Blushing John (USA)) 2177[5] 2535[2] 3031[15] 5290[11] >**77f**<

**Touch Of Spice** **2** ch g Lake Coniston (IRE) -Soft Touch (GER) (Horst-Herbert) 4809[16] 5640[9] 5792[16] >**26a**<

**Touch Of Spirit** **5** b m Dancing Spree (USA) -Soft Touch (GER) (Horst-Herbert) 497[9] >**41a 26f**<

**Tough Enough (IRE)** **2** ch c Raise A Grand (IRE) -Hostess (Be My Guest (USA)) 2792a[4] >**68f**<

**Tough Love** **5** ch g Pursuit Of Love-Food Of Love (Music Boy) 1125[22] 1246[7] 1385[7] 1773[16] 4178[10] 4543[5] 4931[10] 5419[15] >**84f**<

**Toujours Amour (IRE)** **3** b f Croco Rouge (IRE) -Blueprint (USA) (Shadeed (USA)) 2700a[7] >**93f**<

**Toupie** **2** ch f Intikhab (USA) -Turpitude (Caerleon (USA)) 4597a[2] 4962a[5] (5404a) 6261a[4] >**101f**<

**Tournedos (IRE)** **2** b c Rossini (USA) -Don t Care (IRE) (Nordico (USA)) (1436) 2570[2] 2959[2] 3938[8] (4217) 4981a[7] 5280a[3] 5464[2] 5681a[5] 5971a[2]6212[6] >**105f**<

**Tour Of The Cat (USA)** **6** b g Tour D Or (USA) -Tune In To The Cat (USA) (Tunerup (USA)) 1145a[8] >**84a**<

**Tout Les Sous** **3** ch g Tout Ensemble-Suzie Sue (IRE) (Ore) 2357[7] 3417[9] >**10f**<

**Tout Seul (IRE)** **4** b c Ali-Royal (IRE) -Total Aloof (Groom Dancer (USA)) (1610) 2109[15] 2623[11] 3967a[6] 4685[10] 5917[4] 6474[4] >**111f**<

**To Wit To Woo** **4** b g Efisio-Sioux (Kris) 643[2] 800[8] 1298[9] 1876[5] >**65a 56f**<

**Town End Tom** **2** b g Entrepreneur-Prima Silk (Primo Dominie) 2502[5] 3150[6] 3491[6] 5240[16] 6080[16] >**56f**<

**Town House** **2** gr f Paris House-Avondale Girl (IRE) (Case Law) 1208[5] 1364[7] 1882[2] (2382) 3290[7] 3924[7] 4348[9] 6023[10] >**5a 72f**<

**Toylsome** **5** ch h Cadeaux Genereux-Treasure Trove (USA) (The Minstrel (CAN)) 4596a[9] 6379a[11] >**105f**<

**Trackattack** **2** ch g Atraf-Verbena (IRE) (Don t Forget Me) 3632[3] 3802[5] 4040[7] 4365[10] 5218[12] >**57a 68f**<

**Tractor Boy** **2** b c Mind Games-Day Star (Dayjur (USA)) 5003[12] (6126) >**80f**<

**Trade Fair** **4** b c Zafonic (USA) -Danefair (Danehill (USA)) 2021[14] 3318[3] (3967a) 4216[6] >**126f**<

**Trademark (SAF)** **7** b g Goldmark (USA) -Popular (SAF) (Elliodor (FR)) 853a[7] 978a[4] 1001a[2] >**113f**<

**Trafalgar Square** **2** b c King s Best (USA) -Pat Or Else (Alzao (USA)) 5718[8] >**43f**<

**Tragedian (USA)** **2** ch c Theatrical-Foreign Courier (USA) (Sir Ivor (USA)) 6145[3] >**80f**<

**Tragic Dancer** **8** b g Tragic Role (USA) -Chantallee s Pride (Mansooj) 1188[8] >**25a 61f**<

**Traianos (USA)** **2** bb c Mt. Livermore (USA) -Shiitake (USA) (Green Dancer (USA)) 2804[5] 3913[6] 4292[5] 5292[7] >**73f**<

**Trance (IRE)** **4** ch g Bahhare (USA) -Lady Of Dreams (IRE) (Prince Rupert (FR)) 2216[9] 2583[4] (2671) (3078) 4777[9] 5288[11] 5619[7] 5785[3] 6215[9] 6575[5] >**65a 93f**<

**Tranquilizer** **2** b f Dr Fong (USA) -Tranquillity (Night Shift (USA)) 4584[6] 5114[U] 5792[7] 6077[2] 6479[3] >**69+a 62f**<

**Tranquil Sky** **3** b f Intikhab (USA) -Tranquillity (Night Shift (USA)) 1408[18] 1795[16] 2202[5] 2448[2] 2692[7] 3689[4] 5294[7] 5818[5]6086[5] >**89f**<

**Transaction (IRE)** **2** ch g Trans Island-Meranie Girl (IRE) (Mujadil (USA)) 1117[3] 3228[2] (3760) (4342) 4836[6] 5392[8] 5767[15] >**71a 91f**<

**Transcendantale (FR)** **6** bb m Apple Tree (FR) -Kataba (FR) (Shardari) 1376[2] 1560[3] 1752[5] 2297[6] 2446[9] 2733[7] 3008[4] 3117[8]3443[4] 3807[5] 4486[9] 5305[7] 5587[15] >**35a 43f**<

**Transgress (IRE)** **2** b c Trans Island-Ned s Contessa (IRE) (Persian Heights) 3451[3] 3749[8] 4739[6] 5420[5] >**77df**<

**Transit** **5** b g Lion Cavern (USA) -Black Fighter (USA) (Secretariat (USA)) 1249[5] >**49a 67f**<

**Transkei** **3** b f Sesaro (USA) -In The Sky (IRE) (Imp Society (USA)) 3587[13] 4703[4] 5237[10] 6465[12] >**20f**<

**Transvestite (IRE)** **2** b c Trans Island-Christoph s Girl (Efisio) 2574[5] 3157[4] 3531[3] 5453[6] 5738[11] 6012[3] >**71a 77f**<

**Trappeto (IRE)** **2** b c Barathea (IRE) -Campiglia (IRE) (Fairy King (USA)) 5200[11] >**59f**<

**Travellers Joy** **4** b f The West (USA) -Persian Fortune (Forzando) 1280[9] 1584[8] 1886[3] 2183[8] 2384[6] 2836[9] 3227[6] 3680[8] >**27a 53f**<

**Traveller s Tale** **5** b g Selkirk (USA) -Chere Amie (USA) (Mr Prospector (USA)) 559[13] 1213[7] 1308[6] 2084[12] 2767[7] 3232[6] 3573[7] 4196[6]4736[2] 4849[2] 5073[11] 6292[3] 6540[4] >**70a 69f**<

**Travelling Band (IRE)** **6** b g Blues Traveller (IRE) -Kind Of Cute (Prince Sabo) 577[13] 3477[13] 3872[6] 4950[9] 5151[2] 5581[12] 6081[13] >**68a 91f**<

**Travelling Times** **5** ch g Timeless Times (USA) -Bollin Sophie (Efisio) 433[5] 436[6] 2383[11] 2936[15] 3169[4] 3735[12] 4185[2] 5000[6]6403[6] >**59a 47f**<

**Travel Tardia (IRE)** **6** br h Petardia-Annie s Travels (IRE) (Mac s Imp (USA)) 554[13] 949[8] 993[4] (1076) 1194[7] 1197[15] >**64a 40f**<

**Travel Tip (USA)** **2** ch c Gone West (USA) -Cap Beino (USA) (Lyphard (USA)) 5756[4] 6148[P] >**69+f**<

**Traytonic** **3** b c Botanic (USA) -Lady Parker (IRE) (Nordico (USA)) 2131[5] 2309[14] (2625) 2897[3] 3598[8] 4750[7] 5781[4] 6345[6] >**107f**<

**Treason Trial** **3** b g Peintre Celebre (USA) -Pampabella (IRE) (High Estate) 3447[11] 3875[6] 4018[4] 4491[3] (4654) 4921[3] 5037[3] 5274[4] (6074) >**69+f**<

**Treasure Cay** **3** ch c Bahamian Bounty-Madame Sisu (Emarati (USA)) 1099[5] 1775[3] 2269[5] 2889[3] (3201) 3777[9] 4059[3] 4289[2] 4688[6] >**74a 87f**<

**Treasure House (IRE)** **3** b g Grand Lodge (USA) -Royal Wolff (Prince Tenderfoot (USA)) 1063[8] 1437[12] 1706[5] 2224[8] 5299[14] 5704[14] 6267[13] >**92a 77 f**<

**Treasure The Lady (IRE)** **3** b f Indian Ridge-Kasora (IRE) (Darshaan) 1485a[4] 3969a[5] 5162a[4] 5783[9] >**95f**<

**Treasure Trail** **5** b g Millkom-Forever Shineing (Glint Of Gold) 413[5] 1832[10] 2116[11] (2429) 2480[6] >**63a 76f**<

**Treasury (IRE)** **2** b f King s Best (USA) -Copious (IRE) (Generous (IRE)) 5846[17] >**33f**<

**Treat Me Wild (IRE)** **2** ch f Loup Sauvage (USA) -Goes A Treat (IRE) (Common Grounds) (1307) 3679[6] 3987[5] (4439) 4914[4] 5466[9] 6174[16] >**69f**<

**Trebello** **3** b c Robellino (USA) -Trempkate (USA) (Trempolino (USA)) 5836[8] >**32f**<

**Treble Seven (USA)** **2** bb f Fusaichi Pegasus (USA) -Nemea (USA) (The Minstrel (CAN)) 5570[6] 5943[12] >**59f**<

**Tre Colline** **5** b g Efisio-Triple Joy (Most Welcome) 1175[12] 1358[11] 1665[16] 2215[9] 2459[15] (2814) 2989[5] (3023) 3419[4]3745[6] (3932) 4132[7] 4549[6] 5055[8] 5952[4] >**82a 70f**<

**Tree Chopper (USA)** **3** ch f Woodman (USA) -Gazayil (USA) (Irish River (FR)) 3936[7] >**68+f**<

**Tree Roofer** **5** b g King s Signet (USA) -Armaiti (Sayf El Arab (USA)) 918[12] 963[9] 987[8] 1018[2] >**55a 51f**<

**Tree Tops** **3** b f Grand Lodge (USA) -The Faraway Tree (Suave Dancer (USA)) 1441[5] 1753[2] 2198[3] 3908[3] 4368[6] 5446[11] 5999[15] 6285[11] >**75f**<

**Treetops Hotel (IRE)** **5** ch g Grand Lodge (USA) -Rousinette (Rousillon (USA)) 650[2] 2030[9] 2483[11] 2886[9] 2943[2] 3825[4] 4122[2] 4736[11]5008[12] 5222[4] >**64a 64f**<

**Trefflich (GER)** **3** ch c Polish Precedent (USA) -Trefula (IRE) (Rainbow Quest (USA)) 3959a[2] 4587a[4] 5481a[3] 5962a[6] >**106f**<

**Tregarron** **3** br c Efisio-Language Of Love (Rock City) (3179) 4059[4] 4267[2] 4952[7] 5193[3] 5563[15] 5697[10] 6477[16] >**39a 77f**<

**Tregenna** **3** b f Forzando-Nineteenth Of May (Homing) 4068[4] 4316[5] 5123[14] 5791[18] >**39f**<

**Tremar** **2** b c Royal Applause-Sabina (Prince Sabo) 1130[4] 1269[3] 4844[2] (5054) 5295[4] (5922a) 6217[6] >**85a 108 f**<

**Trempjane** **2** b f Lujain (USA) -Trempkate (USA) (Trempolino (USA)) (2837) 3346[5] 3643[5] 4326[8] 5490[8] >**75f**<

**Trench Coat (USA)** **3** ch c Gulch (USA) -Glamor Queen (USA) (Prized (USA)) 982[2] 1869[7] 2207[10] 3023[13] >**68a 62f**<

**Tresor Secret (FR)** **4** b g Green Desert (USA) -Tresor (USA) (Pleasant Tap (USA)) 1762[16] 2278[5] 2516[7] 3087[2] 3303[2] >**53a 76f**<

**Trevian** **3** ch g Atraf-Ascend (IRE) (Glint Of Gold) 462[14] (580) 622[6] 741[6] 959[5] 5496[8] >**75 a 65f**<

**Trew Class** **3** ch f Inchinor-Inimitable (Polish Precedent (USA)) 1842[7] 2001[17] (2888) (3610) 4049[3] 5572[8] 5842[6] >**80f**<

**Trew Flight (USA)** **2** b c Rahy (USA) -Magdala (IRE) (Sadler s Wells (USA)) 6187[19] 6521[5] >**48f**<

**Trew Style** **2** ch c Desert King (IRE) -Southern Psychic (USA) (Alwasmi (USA)) 6187[15] 6476[4] >**76f**<

**Triage (IRE)** **3** b f Mujadil (USA) -Trebles (IRE) (Kenmare (FR)) 1133[8] ><

**Tribute (IRE)** **3** b g Green Desert (USA) -Zooming (IRE) (Indian Ridge) 1883[10] 2131[7] 2726[5] 3273[5] 4874[5] 5614[24] 6532[11] >**78f**<

**Trick Cyclist** **3** b g Mind Games-Sabonis (USA) (The Minstrel (CAN)) 986[2] 1099[4] 1504[7] 2264[6] 3384[7] 4211[2] (4472) 4617[3] 4952[5]5440[15] 6079[4] 6532[8] >**86a 81f**<

**Trickshot** **2** ch f Mister Baileys-Zizi (IRE) (Imp Society (USA)) 2074[2] 2730[16] 4135[7] >**59f**<

**Trickstep** **3** b g Imperial Ballet (IRE) -Trick Of Ace (USA) (Clever Trick (USA)) (6112) 6552[5] >**49a 65f**<

**Tricky Venture** **4** gr g Linamix (FR) -Ukraine Venture (Slip Anchor) 5146[2] 5705[4] >**60a 69f**<

**Trifti** **3** b g Vettori (IRE) -Time For Tea (IRE) (Imperial Frontier (USA)) 1226[4] 1382[11] 3085[10] 3420[8] 3848[4] 4483[2] 4738[9] 5748[12] >**68a 56f**<

**Trigger Mead** **4** b f Double Trigger (IRE) -Normead Lass (Norwick (USA)) 5643[11] >**57+f**<

**Triggers Double** **3** ch c Double Trigger (IRE) -Princess Alaska (Northern State (USA)) 2882[15] ><

**Trigony (IRE)** **2** b g Brave Act-Lulu Island (Zafonic (USA)) 4131[12] 5095[12] 5522[6] >**60f**<

**Trilemma** **3** b f Slip Anchor-Thracian (Green Desert (USA)) 2039[9] 3746[11] 4346[6] (5214) (5343) (5850) 6339[7] >**91+f**<

**Trim Image** **2** br f Averti (IRE) -Altizaf (Zafonic (USA)) 3055[3] 3577[3] (4670) 5515[12] >**69f**<

**Trinaree (IRE)** **3** b g Revoque (IRE) -Ball Cat (FR) (Cricket Ball (USA)) 2675[11] 2908[12] 3229[15] 4102[16] >**23f**<

**Trinculo (IRE)** **7** b g Anita s Prince-Fandangerina (USA) (Grey Dawn Ii) 486[7] 586[10] 703[8] 841[U] 1113[2] 1211[5] 1391[11] 1438[11]1759[6] 2041[15] 5157[9] 5287[10] 5605[5] (6526) >**76a 91+f**<

**Trinity (IRE)** **8** b h College Chapel-Kaskazi (Dancing Brave (USA)) 1665[8] 1971[10] 4133[10] 4542[19] >**46a 62f**<

**Trinity Fair** **3** b f Polish Precedent (USA) -Chita Rivera (Chief Singer) 2900[11] 3630[13] 4306[10] 4819[10] >**47f**<

**Trinity Joy** **3** b f Vettori (IRE) -Triple Joy (Most Welcome) 1320a[4] 1803a[6] 5032a[2] 5667a[8] 6437a[13] >**90f**<

**Triphenia (IRE)** **6** b g Ashkalani (IRE) -Atsuko (IRE) (Mtoto) 2471[9] >**85a 89f**<

**Triple Jump** **3** ch g Inchinor-Meteoric (High Line) 3587[2] (4306) 4906[3] 5768[15] >**80f**<

**Triple Zero (IRE)** **2** b f Raise A Grand (IRE) -Locorotondo (IRE) (Broken Hearted) 3045[8] 3627[14] (4335) >**65f**<

**Tripti (IRE)** **4** b f Sesaro (USA) -Chatelsong (USA) (Seattle Song (USA)) 465[2] 576[10] 859[10] 884[2] 1018[8] 1051[13] 1280[10]1642[13] 4400[12] 4970[4] 5184[5] >**55a 63f**<

**Trishay** **3** gr f Petong-Marjorie s Memory (IRE) (Fairy King (USA)) 675[10] 769[7] >**53a 51f**<

**Triton Dance (IRE)** **4** b f Hector Protector (USA) -Dancing Drop (Green Desert (USA)) 1649a[6] 3328a[15] >**92f**<

**Tritonville Lodge (IRE)** **2** b g Grand Lodge (USA) -Olean (Sadler s Wells (USA)) 6351[7] >**54f**<

**Trivial Pursuit** **3** b c Mind Games-Chushan Venture (Pursuit Of Love) 3425[9] >**19f**<

**Trofana Falcon** **4** b g Polar Falcon (USA) -Silk St James (Pas De Seul) 2653[11] 3297[16] >**25a 32f**<

**Trois Etoiles (IRE)** **3** ch f Grand Lodge (USA) -Stardance (USA) (Rahy (USA)) 2621[5] 3180[9] 3527[5] 3852[5] 4477[3] 5510[6] 5957[10] 6541[6] >**51a 63f**<

**Trojan Flight** **3** ch g Hector Protector (USA) -Fairywings (Kris) 1453[4] 1957[5] 2036[4] 2569[6] 3155[8] 3897[6] 4309[4] 4489[3]4608[2] (4626) 5193[2] (5242) 5579[9] 5674[4] 5754[2] 6114[4] 6144[7] >**81+f**<

**Trojan Wolf** **9** ch g Wolfhound (USA) -Trojan Lady (USA) (Irish River (FR)) 714[7] 880[4] 1026[16] 1091[5] >**40a 24f**<

**Tromp** **3** ch c Zilzal (USA) -Sulitelma (USA) (The Minstrel (CAN)) 2765[5] 3261[6] 6481[2] >**69a 53f**<

**Trompe L Oeil (IRE)** **3** b f Distant View (USA) -Milly Ha Ha (Dancing Brave (USA)) 490[8] 822[7] 1017[6] 1086[9] 1309[8] 1844[13] >**55a 53f**<

**Troodos Jet** **3** b g Atraf-Costa Verde (King Of Spain) 2984[4] 3486[4] 4097[4] (4758) 5126[12] 5674[13] 6114[14] >**64a 64f**<

**Tropical Coral (IRE)** **4** ch f Pennekamp (USA) -Tropical Dance (USA) (Thorn Dance (USA)) 507[6] >**80a 82f**<

**Tropical Lady (IRE)** **4** b f Sri Pekan (USA) -Tropical Lake (IRE) (Lomond (USA)) (3547a) (3969a) 4587a[2] 4786a[5] 5679a[5] 5962a[10] >**115f**<

**Tropical Son** **5** b g Distant Relative-Douce Maison (IRE) (Fool s Holme (USA)) 427[2] 472[5] (537) 589[9] 740[2] 795[5] 874[7] 931[5]6540[9] >**52a 37f**<

**Tropical Star (IRE)** **4** ch g Machiavellian (USA) -Tropical (Green Desert (USA)) 635a[2] 756a[3] 974a[2] 1142a[2] >**111a**<

**Tropical Storm (IRE)** **3** ch g Alhaarth (IRE) -Rainstone (Rainbow Quest (USA)) 2301[3] 3251[9] 4555[4] 4707[2] (5086) >**77f**<

**Trotters Bottom** **3** b g Mind Games-Fleeting Affair (Hotfoot) 1099[7] 2576[5] >**78a 78f**<

**Troubadour (IRE)** **3** b c Danehill (USA) -Taking Liberties (IRE) (Royal Academy (USA)) 5291[2] 5917[11] >**113f**<

**Troubleinparadise (IRE)** **3** b f Pursuit Of Love-Sweet Holland (USA) (Alydar (USA)) 1222[17] 1365[18] 3305[13] >**9a 49f**<

**Trouble Mountain (USA)** **7** br g Mt. Livermore (USA) -Trouble Free (USA) (Nodouble (USA)) 516[3] 1393[3] 1535[3] 1928[5] 2216[2] 2394[4] 2752[4] 2982[7]4493[2] (4678) 5194[4] 5607[2] 5768[3] 6115[5] >**83a 83f**<

**Trouble Next Door (IRE)** **6** b g Persian Bold-Adjacent (IRE) (Doulab (USA)) 449[3] 539[2] >**46a 46f**<

**Troublesome Gerri** **2** b f Thowra (FR) -Sid s Pretence (Southern Music) 1853[6] 2164[3] 2831[5] >**39f**<

**Trousers** **5** b g Pivotal-Palo Blanco (Precocious) 1118[7] (1247) 3536[3] 3869[4] >**80a 69f**<

**Trouville (IRE)** **5** b m Mukaddamah (USA) -Trouville Lass (IRE) (Be My Native (USA)) 4588a[12] >**65f**<

**Truckle** 2 b c Vettori (IRE) -Proud Titania (IRE) (Fairy King (USA)) 2087[8] 5302[6] 6072[4] **>69f<**

**True (IRE)** 3 ch f Barathea (IRE) -Bibliotheque (USA) (Woodman (USA)) 1507[7] 2112[11] 2657[2] 3301[12] 3622[3] 3819[4] 4020[12] 4781[6] 5108[8] 5545[2] 5715[14] 5994[5] 6461[9] **>66f<**

**True Companion** 5 b g Brief Truce (USA) -Comanche Companion (Commanche Run) *559[8] (650) 820[3] 870[8] 1088[3]* (1369) 1928[4] 2537[2] *2881[13]* **>73a 78f<**

**True Holly** 4 b f Bishop Of Cashel-Polly s Teahouse (Shack (USA)) *884[9] 951[7] 1021[5]* **>38a 47f<**

**True Lover (GER)** 7 b g Winged Love (IRE) -Truneba (GER) (Nebos (GER)) 6218[3] **>110f<**

**True Magic** 3 b f Magic Ring (IRE) -True Precision (Presidium) 1472[5] 2236[6] 2552[2] 3201[2] (4021) (4608) 5062[8] 5440[13] 6267[7] **>79f<**

**True Night** 7 b g Night Shift (USA) -Dead Certain (Absalom) 1345[13] 1608[14] 1772[10] 2132[12] 2291[4] 2477[2] 2750[3] 3036[3] 3198[11] 3597[3] (3690) (4134) 4360[3] 4558[12] 4931[12] 5315[2] 5631[12] 5937[8] **>93f<**

**Trueno (IRE)** 5 b g Desert King (IRE) -Stitching (IRE) (High Estate) (2278) 2612[2] 3097[11] 4343[5] 4754[5] 5273[7] 6043[6] **>89f<**

**True Patriot** 3 b g Rainbow Quest (USA) -High Standard (Kris) 2085[17] 2395[8] **>37f<**

**True To Yourself (USA)** 3 b g Royal Academy (USA) -Romilly (Machiavellian (USA)) 1325[10] *1570[2] (2014)* 2546[8] *3026[6]* **>49a 43f<**

**Trullitti (IRE)** 3 b f Bahri (USA) -Penza (Soviet Star (USA)) 1619[3] 3535[5] 4486[P] (5079) 5822a[3] 6443[11] **>78f<**

**Trull s Trump (ITY)** 2 b c Spectrum (IRE) -Trull (Lomond (USA)) 3435a[5] **><**

**Truman** 3 b c Entrepreneur-Sabria (USA) (Miswaki (USA)) 2236[7] 2785[3] 3261[5] 5652[11] *6224[2]* **>72a 72f<**

**Trusted Instinct (IRE)** 4 b c Polish Precedent (USA) -Trust In Luck (IRE) (Nashwan (USA)) *679[14] 870[10]* 1275[16] 2501[18] 2928[9] 5026[5] 5451[17] **>10a 10f<**

**Trusted Mole (IRE)** 6 b g Eagle Eyed (USA) -Orient Air (Prince Sabo) 2212[5] (2525) 2615[6] 2939[2] (3342) 3492[8] 4397[10] 5635[7] *6225[7]* **>57a 65f<**

**Trust Rule** 4 b c Selkirk (USA) -Hagwah (USA) (Dancing Brave (USA)) 1328[12] 1768[6] 2681[5] 3075[10] 3521[11] 4858[14] 5288[16] 5435[4] 5814[7] **>68 a 96f<**

**Try And Fly (FR)** 7 b h Le Balafre (FR) -Tres Speciale (Lyphard s Special (USA)) *5103a[8]* **><**

**Trylko (USA)** 2 ch f Diesis-Gossamer (USA) (Seattle Slew (USA)) 3296[2] **>67f<**

**Trysting Grove (IRE)** 3 b f Cape Cross (IRE) -Elton Grove (IRE) (Astronef) 1419[9] 1771[8] 2962[9] 3817[5] 4259[15] (4867) **>51f<**

**Try The Air (IRE)** 3 ch f Foxhound (USA) -Try To Catch Me (USA) (Shareef Dancer (USA)) *5211[1]* **>14a 56df<**

**Tsarbuck** 3 b g Perugino (USA) -Form At Last (Formidable (USA)) 1371[15] 1541[7] 1827[8] *(2232)* 2349[5] *2854[2]* 3252[5] *3708[2] 3800[3] 4188[3]* 4968[12] 5547[9] 6228[6] *6398[4] 6537[10]* **>64a 47f<**

**Tsaroxy (IRE)** 2 b c Xaar-Belsay (Belmez (USA)) 3313[3] 3793[3] (5125) 6113[5] 6523[10] **>77f<**

**Tshukudu** 3 ch f Fleetwood (IRE) -Pab s Choice (Telsmoss) *1678[7] 3305[12] 3932[9]* 4018[10] 4654[3] *4941[11]* 5018[2] 5284[7] *5644[11]* 5928[14] **>33a 43f<**

**Tsigane (FR)** 5 b h Anabaa (USA) -Trevillari (USA) (Riverman (USA)) *1145a[6]* **>106a 99f<**

**Tubbertown Rose (IRE)** 6 b m Elbio-Super Dream (Tumble Wind) 3961a[9] **>80f<**

**Tucker** 2 b c Inchinor-Tender Moment (IRE) (Caerleon (USA)) 6171[8] (6454) **>85+f<**

**Tudor Bell (IRE)** 3 b c Definite Article-Late Night Lady (IRE) (Mujadil (USA)) 1104[8] 1285[2] 1466[3] (1933) (2179) 2782[6] 2910[2] (3244) 3621[3] 5595[11] 5850[4] 6534[5] **>89f<**

**Tudor Wood** 5 b h Royal Applause-Silent Indulgence (USA) (Woodman (USA)) *634a[6]* 852a[7] 924a[8] **>73a 106f<**

**Tulipe Royale (FR)** 3 ch f Java Gold (USA) -Nigrita (GER) (Lichine (USA)) 2160a[11] 4356a[7] 4899a[3] **>104f<**

**Tumbaga (USA)** 3 b c Seeking The Gold (USA) -Didina (Nashwan (USA)) 1395[13] 2085[13] 2479[5] **>71f<**

**Tumblebrutus (USA)** 3 br c Storm Cat (USA) -Mariah s Storm (USA) (Rahy (USA)) 1764[9] **>104f<**

**Tumbleweed Galore (IRE)** 2 b g Bluebird (USA) -Mary Hinge (Dowsing (USA)) 3483[7] 4016[3] 4208[3] 4728[3] 5090[6] 5738[2] *6063[3]* 6338[5] **>74a 74f<**

**Tunduru (IRE)** 3 ch c Croco Rouge (IRE) -Spring Daffodil (Pharly (FR)) 6170a[3] **>108f<**

**Tungsten Strike (USA)** 3 ch g Smart Strike (CAN) -Bathilde (IRE) (Generous (IRE)) 3160[11] (3629) (3851) 4274[3] 4550[2] (5892) 6215[28] **>110f<**

**Tuning Fork** 4 b g Alzao (USA) -Tuning (Rainbow Quest (USA)) 1355[12] 2220[7] 2508a[10] 3034[14] 3539[15] 4287[3] 4742[12] 5134[8] 5470[9] 5813[11] **>101 f<**

**Turbo (IRE)** 5 b g Piccolo-By Arrangement (IRE) (Bold Arrangement) *915[14]* 1328[10] 2110[4] 3521[13] 4831[12] 5465[7] 5650[13] 6354[2] 6573[12] **>84a 104f<**

**Turf Princess** 3 b f Wizard King-Turf Moor (IRE) (Mac s Imp (USA)) *(408) 514[2] 640[4] 696[5]* 2036[3] 2657[7] 3817[4] *4882[9]* 5081[14] 5346[17] **>57a 59f<**

**Turftanzer (GER)** 5 b g Lomitas-Tower Bridge (GER) (Big Shuffle (USA)) *430[5] 568[7] 878[4] 1024[6]* 1282[16] 1715[8] 2214[9] 2408[12] 3056[4] 3165[5] 4397[7] 5187[10] 5585[5] 5757[9] 6516[6] **>52a 45f<**

**Turibius** 5 b g Puissance-Compact Disc (IRE) (Royal Academy (USA)) *703[6] (912) 1205[3]* 2222[8] 2477[18] 3645[9] 4034[12] 4291[26] 5704[10] 5730[4] **>84a 85f<**

**Turkana Girl** 2 ch f Hernando (FR) -Miss Penton (Primo Dominie) 5847[6] **>52f<**

**Turkish Delight** 3 b f Prince Sabo-Delicious (Dominion) *1737[5]* 2457[6] 2741[12] 3530[8] 3877[3] 4489[10] 4650[14] 5219[15] 5547[13] 5736[15] **>50a 63f<**

**Turks And Caicos (IRE)** 3 bb g Turtle Island (IRE) -Need You Badly (Robellino (USA)) *473[2] 656[2] (804)* 3881[7] *5957[6] 6552[6]* **>56a 51f<**

**Turks Wood (IRE)** 2 b c Charnwood Forest (IRE) -Nairasha (IRE) (Niniski (USA)) 2376[4] 4487[5] 4649[5] 5292[10] 5630[8] 6270[8] **>75f<**

**Turnaround (GER)** 2 gr g Highest Honor (FR) -Tamacana (Windwurf (GER)) 2686[3] 3313[2] (4347) 4836[13] 5466[2] 5896[8] **>84 f<**

**Turn Around** 4 b g Pivotal-Bemuse (Forzando) *476[7]* 1275[14] *1629[2] (2006) 2666[5] (3024) 3277[14]* **>72a 87 f<**

**Turn Back Time (IRE)** 4 ch f Erin s Isle-Miss Margaux (IRE) (Royal Academy (USA)) 2102a[8] **>100f<**

**Turnberry (IRE)** 3 b c Petardia-Sunrise (IRE) (Sri Pekan (USA)) *493[4] 640[3] 802[6]* 1844[2] 2766[2] 2931[5] **>55a 60f<**

**Turner** 3 gr g El Prado (IRE) -Gaily Royal (IRE) (Royal Academy (USA)) 2273[6] 2751[3] 3294[3] 4079[8] 5245[10] 5293[17] **>63a 66f<**

**Turnkey** 2 br c Pivotal-Persian Air (Persian Bold) 1412[2] (1826) 2954[5] 3965a[4] 4857[7] **>101f<**

**Turn n Burn** 3 b g Unfuwain (USA) -Seasonal Splendour (IRE) (Prince Rupert (FR)) 1387[7] 3922[3] 4775[2] *5216[4]* **>72a 75f<**

**Turn Of Phrase (IRE)** 5 b g Cadeaux Genereux-Token Gesture (IRE) (Alzao (USA)) *743[8]* 4210[8] 5058[2] (5238) 5479[4] **>63a 70f<**

**Turn On The Style** 2 ch g Pivotal-Elegant Rose (Noalto) 4488[9] 5362[7] 5816[2] (6008) **>69f<**

**Turnover** 2 ch f Gold Away (IRE) -Turn To Vodka (FR) (Polish Precedent (USA)) 5687[5] 6149[13] **>49f<**

**Turnstile** 3 gr c Linamix (FR) -Kissing Gate (USA) (Easy Goer (USA)) 1442[4] 2312[2] 2561[9] 3752[3] 4554[2] 4915[8] 5300[6] (6088) **>80f<**

**Turtle Bay** 2 ch f Dr Fong (USA) -My Valentina (Royal Academy (USA)) *5051[8]* **>45a<**

**Turtle Dancer (IRE)** 6 b g Turtle Island (IRE) -Love Me Please (IRE) (Darshaan) 2039[2] *2987[11]* **>73f<**

**Turtle Magic (IRE)** 2 b f Turtle Island (IRE) -Theda (Mummy s Pet) *1117[8]* 1390[2] 1589[3] 1686[8] *2002[6]* 2248[4] 3444[9] 3883[3] *4516[4]* 4770[6] 5132[4] 5281[11] **>32a 50f<**

**Turtle Patriarch (IRE)** 3 b c Turtle Island (IRE) -La Doyenne (IRE) (Masterclass (USA)) 1293[10] 3875[16] 4147[8] 4711[4] 4971[2] 5293[6] *5914[12]* 6519[2] **>42a 67f<**

**Turtle Valley (IRE)** 8 b g Turtle Island (IRE) -Primrose Valley (Mill Reef (USA)) *919[5] 981[9]* 1135[3] (1302) 1326[9] 1801[12] **>63 a 82 f<**

**Turturilla (IRE)** 5 b m Charnwood Forest (IRE) -Talikota (ITY) (Fire Of Life (USA)) *2163a[9]* **>55f<**

**Tuscan Dream** 9 b g Clantime-Excavator Lady (Most Secret) *499[11] 638[9] 657[7] 944[7] 1089[2] 1190[2] 1443[5](1568) 1699[5] 1886[5] 2183[11]* **>41a 18 f<**

**Tuscan Flyer** 6 b g Clantime-Excavator Lady (Most Secret) 1929[9] 2219[13] 2598[3] 2899[12] 3227[4] 3509[11] 3894[4] 4534[7] 5157[7] 5562[11] 5754[3] **>57a 71f<**

**Tuscan Treaty** 4 b f Brief Truce (USA) -Fiorenz (USA) (Chromite (USA)) *469[14]* 1857[8] 2099[4] 2707[7] 2875[6] 3151[13] 3911[13] 5930[4] **>44a 49f<**

**Tuscarora (IRE)** 5 b m Revoque (IRE) -Fresh Look (IRE) (Alzao (USA)) 1750[7] 2284[9] 2943[5] 3555[2] 3698[6] (3807) 3910[9] 4230[5] (4477) 4877[3] 5136[3] 5252[4] 5849[8] **>63 a 67+f<**

**Tuvalu (GER)** 2 ch c Dashing Blade-Tepana (GER) (Polish Precedent (USA)) 2890[8] 3438[5] 5198[6] 6129[4] **>69f<**

**Tweed** 7 ch g Barathea (IRE) -In Perpetuity (Great Nephew) 5257[10] **>70a 53f<**

**Twelve Bar Blues** 3 ch f Nashwan (USA) -Throw Away Line (USA) (Assert) 1674[11] 2060[7] 2323[5] 5410[10] **>62f<**

**Twentytwoandchange (IRE)** 5 b g Lure (USA) -Plouray (IRE) (Caerleon (USA)) 1254a[6] **>101f<**

**Twentytwosilver (IRE)** 4 rg g Emarati (USA) -St Louis Lady (Absalom) *554[10]* **>81a 73f<**

**Twice Nightly** 2 b g Wolfhound (USA) -Dusty s Darling (Doyoun) 1769[3] 2141[3] 3196[6] 4012[5] 4445[9] 5059[7] 5617[8] **>64f<**

**Twice Royal (IRE)** 3 br f Imperial Ballet (IRE) -Royal Rumpus (Prince Tenderfoot (USA)) 2335a[10] **>77f<**

**Twice Unbridled (USA)** 2 bb c Unbridled s Song (USA) -Lady Millicent (USA) (Chief s Crown (USA)) *6489a[7]* **>89a<**

**Twice Upon A Time** 5 ch m Primo Dominie-Opuntia (Rousillon (USA)) 2079[4] 2143[4] 2490[14] 3098[15] 3339[8] 3744[4] 3920[14] 4299[8] 5062[6] 5562[7] **>80f<**

**Twiggy s Sister (IRE)** 6 ch m Flying Spur (AUS) -Winsome Girl (Music Boy) 1070a[6] 1649a[4] 1982a[5] 2603a[8] **>102f<**

**Twilight Blues (IRE)** 5 ch h Bluebird (USA) -Pretty Sharp (Interrex (CAN)) 2373[5] 3073[11] 3537[5] 5948[2] 6190[8] **>118f<**

**Twilight Years** 3 b g Silver Patriarch (IRE) -Adjusting (IRE) (Busted) 2298[9] 3013[7] 3625[4] 4302[6] 5130[10] **>44f<**

**Twofan (USA)** 3 b c Lear Fan (USA) -Double Wedge (USA) (Northern Baby (CAN)) 1524[2] 1761[2] (2090) 3485[6] 4174[4] 4274[5] **>84f<**

**Twogoodreasons (IRE)** 4 ch c College Chapel-Khafaya (Unfuwain (USA)) 4371a[14] **>89f<**

**Two Miles West (IRE)** 3 b c Sadler s Wells (USA) -User Friendly (Slip Anchor) 3035[2] 3862a[2] 4784a[4] 5662a[6] **>114f<**

**Two Of A Kind (IRE)** 4 ch g Ashkalani (IRE) -Dulcinea (Selkirk (USA)) *(449)* **>58a 66f<**

**Two Of Clubs** 3 b g First Trump-Sulaka (Owington) *529[3] 631[3] (942)* 5141[5] *(6290)* **>73a 67f<**

**Two Step Kid (USA)** 3 ch c Gone West (USA) -Marsha s Dancer (USA) (Northern Dancer) 1384[6] 2131[4] (2897) 3598[3] 4152[4] 4324[4] 5491[4] **>87+a 106+f<**

**Two Steps To Go (USA)** 5 b g Rhythm (USA) -Lyonushka (CAN) (Private Account (USA)) *430[4] 500[4] 605[5]* **>43 a 43f<**

**Twyla Tharp (IRE)** 2 b f Sadler s Wells (USA) -Sumoto (Mtoto) 4851[10] 6336[2] **>66+f<**

**Tybalt** 2 b c Polar Falcon (USA) -Once Removed (Distant Relative) 3632[2] 4048[5] 4454[8] 5240[12] 5738[3] 6562[17] **>63f<**

**Tycheros** 2 b g Polar Falcon (USA) -Marie De Flandre (FR) (Crystal Palace (FR)) 6126[11] **>43f<**

**Tychy** 5 ch m Suave Dancer (USA) -Touch Of White (Song) 1765[5] 2679[3] 3074[27] 4165[11] 4269[5] (4526) 4779[8] 5181[4] 5289[15] 5454[9] 6175[7] **>103f<**

**Tycoon** 3 b c Sadler s Wells (USA) -Fleeting Glimpse (Rainbow Quest (USA)) 3353a[3] 4121[6] 4834[9] 5463[3] 5985a[3] **>123f<**

**Tycoon Hall (IRE)** 4 ch g Halling (USA) -Tycooness (IRE) (Last Tycoon) 1328[16] **>100f<**

**Tyne** 3 b g Komaite (USA) -High Typha (Dowsing (USA)) 1473[7] 2552[6] 3059[4] 3580[9] **>80 f<**

**Tyneham** 4 b c Robellino (USA) -Diamond Wedding (USA) (Diamond Shoal) *(6402)* 6561[11] **>61a 66f<**

**Type One (IRE)** 6 b g Bigstone (IRE) -Isca (Caerleon (USA)) *417[11] (617) 761[13] 841[7]* 1106[18] 1361[17] 1824[2] 2219[14] 2626[7] 3269[4] **>84a 72f<**

**Typhoon Ginger (IRE)** 9 ch m Archway (IRE) -Pallas Viking (Viking (USA)) 6345[9] **>18f<**

**Typhoon Tilly** 7 b g Hernando (FR) -Meavy (Kalaglow) *523[6] 603[4] 743[3] 844[6]* 1135[4] 1329[10] 4686[3] 5073[2](5274) 5559[6] 6535[7] **>83a 83f<**

**Tyrone Sam** 2 b g Mind Games-Crystal Sand (GER) (Forzando) 4175[7] 5241[9] 6530[14] **>49f<**

**Tyrrellspass (IRE)** 7 b g Alzao (USA) -Alpine Chime (IRE) (Tirol) *809[10]* 1581[5] **>6a 21f<**

**Tyson Returns** 2 b g Mujahid (USA) -Mabrookah (Deploy) 2087[11] *2812[9]* **>23a 43f<**

**Tytheknot** 3 b g Pursuit Of Love-Bundled Up (USA) (Sharpen Up) 1325[2] 1712[3] 3312[6] 3535[4] 4177[3] (5189) 5582[5] 6115[13] 6332[15] **>77f<**

**Tytherley** 3 b f Man Among Men (IRE) -Sharp Thistle (Sharpo) 2182[P] **><**

**Tyup Pompey (IRE)** 3 ch g Docksider (USA) -Cindys Baby (Bairn (USA)) 5495[4] 6082[14] 6357[5] **>53f<**

**Tyzack (IRE)** 3 b g Fasliyev (USA) -Rabea (USA) (Devil s Bag (USA)) 1303[5] 2217[7] 4050[8] 4817[10] 5558[5] **>64f<**

**Tzatziki (DEN)** 3 b f Richard Of York-Ta-Ta-Ta (DEN) (Miami Springs) 4379a[4] **><**

**U**

**Ugly Sister (USA)** 2 gr f Aljabr (USA) -Cinderella Ball (USA) (Nureyev (USA)) 2096[9] *3377[7]* 5034[6] 5369[20] **>18a 41f<**

**Ugo Capeto** 2 ch c Cadeaux Genereux-Ginevra Di Camelot (FR) (Alzao (USA)) 6542a[5] **><**

**Uhoomagoo** 6 b g Namaqualand (USA) -Point Of Law (Law Society (USA)) *(900)* 1456[7] 1773[7] 2271[7] (2469) (2637) 2969[11] 3036[13] 4120[3] 4287[7] 5468[14] 5781[12] *6451[9]* **>88a 101f<**

**Uhuru Peak** 3 ch c Bal Harbour-Catherines Well (Junius (USA)) *898[3] 1044[10]* 1200[5] 2457[11] 2756[7] 3624[3] 3954[2] 4309[13] 4610[6] 5547[8] 6199[3] **>42a 62f<**

**Uig** 3 ch f Bien Bien (USA) -Madam Zando (Forzando) 1683[8] 2059[8] 2374[3] 4583[2] 4884[9] 5136[4] 5511[2] 5788[7] 5936[2] **>78f<**

**Ulfah (USA)** 3 b f Danzig (USA) -Sayedat Alhadh (USA) (Mr Prospector (USA)) 1980a[9] 2744a[6] (4159a) 4590a[5] (4956a) 5327a[5] 5661a[6] 6104a[7] **>107f<**

**Ulisse (IRE)** 2 b c Fasliyev (USA) -L Ereditiera (Alzao (USA)) 6542a[8] **><**

**Ulshaw** 7 ch g Salse (USA) -Kintail (Kris) 1501[11] 3108[10] 3776[16] 4082[10] **>58a 64f<**

**Ultimata** 4 ch f Unfuwain (USA) -Last Look (Rainbow Quest (USA)) 2278[9] 3159[2] 4812[2] 5025[9] 6069[15] (6194) 6444[6] **>88f<**

**Ultramar (TUR)** 5 b h Mujtahid (USA) -Fiorella (TUR) (Karayel (USA)) 5489a[5] **><**

**Ultra Marine (IRE)** 4 b c Blues Traveller (IRE) -The Aspecto Girl (IRE) (Alzao (USA)) 3056[7] 3411[17] 3682[13] **>53 f<**

**Ulundi** 9 b g Rainbow Quest (USA) -Flit (USA) (Lyphard (USA)) *558[10]* 2220[11] 2527[12] 3034[12] **>97a 97f<**

**Ulysees (IRE)** 5 b g Turtle Island (IRE) -Tamasriya (IRE) (Doyoun) (1663) 1787[7] 2581[3] (3038) 3235[8] 3515[5] 4130[14] 4635[7] 4904[4] 5631[7] 5833[11] 6144[5] 6525[8] **>63a 76f<**

**Umniya (IRE)** 2 b f Bluebird (USA) -Sparky s Song (Electric) 1839[3] 2023[2] (2213) 2478[3] 2745a[3] 3031[4] 3316[5] 4885[6] 5149[6] 5325a[4] 5648[3] 5939[5] 6108a[3] 6259a[6] 6510a[8] **>102f<**

**Un Autre Espere** 5 b g Golden Heights-Drummer s Dream (IRE) (Drumalis) *945[12] 994[6] 1080[10] 1138[9] 1403[8] 1573[5]* (1583) *1697[5]* 1858[14] **>26a 41f<**

**Unbridled s Dream (USA)** 3 rg c Unbridled s Song (USA) -Diamond Dream (FR) (Diamond Prospect (USA)) 1794[19] **>44f<**

**Uncle Batty** 4 b g Bob Back (USA) -Aunt Sadie (Pursuit Of Love) 2520[4] 3138[5] **>50f<**

**Uncle Bulgaria (IRE)** 2 b c Alhaarth (IRE) -Istibshar (USA) (Mr Prospector (USA)) *3611[3]* 4967[7] 5268[10] 5596[5] 6562[6] **>51a 62f<**

**Uncle John** 3 b g Atraf-Bit O May (Mummy s Pet) 2400[7] 2841[7] 3556[4] 3825[2] 4167[4] 5057[9] 5410[9] 5692[12] *6225[3] 6495[2]* **>67a 67f<**

**Undergraduate (IRE)** 2 b g Unfuwain (USA) -Starlet (Teenoso (USA)) 6283[5] **>70f<**

**Under My Skin (IRE)** 3 ch f Mark Of Esteem (IRE) -Convenience (IRE) (Ela-Mana-Mou) 3630[12] 4718[7] **>49f<**

**Under My Spell** 3 b f Wizard King-Gagajulu (Al Hareb (USA)) 1129[17] 1464[10] 2091[2] 2518[2] 2741[5] (2875) 3523[10] 3979[9] 4194[8] 4672[10] **>82 f<**

**Underthemistletoe (IRE)** 2 b f Lujain (USA) -Christmas Kiss (Taufan (USA)) 2213[6] 3736[3] 4149[10] 6002[6] **>49f<**

**Undeterred** 8 ch g Zafonic (USA) -Mint Crisp (IRE) (Green Desert (USA)) 1361[11] 2261[5] 2391[7] 2682[10] 2899[4] 3098[4] 3606[4] (4179) 4291[12] 5730[13] **>83f<**

**Unfurled (IRE)** 2 ch c Unfuwain (USA) -Peony (Lion Cavern (USA)) 5696[6] 6187[2] **>83f<**

**Unicorn Reward (IRE)** 4 b c Turtle Island (IRE) -Kingdom Pearl (Statoblest) 1114[23] 1284[4] 2410[12] **>72a 89f<**

**Unintentional** 3 b f Dr Devious (IRE) -Tamnia (Green Desert (USA)) *593[6] 1627[8]* 1946[6] 2402[14] 4673[P] 5692[10] *6401[10]* **>59a 46f<**

**Union Jack Jackson (IRE)** 2 b c Daggers Drawn (USA) -Beechwood Quest (IRE) (River Falls) 3080[4] 3476[7] 4446[7] *4878[6]* 5596[4] 5662[4] **>62a 66f<**

**United Nations** 3 ch c Halling (USA) -Congress (IRE) (Dancing Brave (USA)) (1395) 1587[3] 5474[4] 5920[8] **>94f<**

**United Spirit (IRE)** 3 b f Fasliyev (USA) -Atlantic Desire (IRE) (Ela-Mana-Mou) 2577[7] 3004[6] 3636[3] (4336) *(4517)* 4938[4] 5219[5] 5618[14] **>72a 68f<**

**United Union (IRE)** 3 bb g Imperial Ballet (IRE) -Madagascar (Puissance) 1220[4] 1312[9] **>53a 64f<**

**Unleaded** 4 ch f Danzig Connection (USA) -Mo Stopher (Sharpo) *426[2] (528) 716[2] 789[5]* 1135[8] *1512[4] 2186[5]* **>48a 29f<**

**Unlimited** 2 b g Bold Edge-Cabcharge Blue (Midyan (USA)) *1264[2] (1735)* 2247[2] 2655[5] *4186[7]* 4392[3] 5202[5] 5606[10] **>69a 70f<**

**Uno Mente** 5 b m Mind Games-One Half Silver (CAN) (Plugged Nickle (USA)) 1560[10] 1931[10] 2216[8] 2757[6] 3117[3] 3609[7] 3921[9] 4213[9] 4852[11] 5714[19] **>60a 59f<**

**Unprecedented (IRE)** 3 br g Primo Dominie-Misellina (FR) (Polish Precedent (USA)) *802[11]* 1386[12] 2145[4] 2392[7] 5545[7] 6132[11] **>8a 51f<**

**Unreal** 2 b f Dansili-Illusory (King s Lake (USA)) 2083[6] 3675[2] 4231[6] 5202[2] (5441) **>82f<**

**Unscrupulous** 5 ch g Machiavellian (USA) -Footlight Fantasy (USA) (Nureyev (USA)) 2504[3] (3036) **>103f<**

**Unshakable (IRE)** 5 b g Eagle Eyed (USA) -Pepper And Salt (IRE) (Double Schwartz) 1125[8] 1328[11] (1623) 3539[3] 4287[10] 4528[5] 4887[4] 5941[5] 6193[7] 6475[12] **>108f<**

**Unshaken** 10 b h Environment Friend-Reel Foyle (USA) (Irish River (FR)) 2779[13] 3039[12] **>62a 66f<**

**Unshooda** 3 ch f Machiavellian (USA) -Rawaabe (USA) (Nureyev (USA)) 1458[7] 2685[9] **>95f<**

**Unsuited** 5 b m Revoque (IRE) -Nagnagnag (IRE) (Red Sunset) *463[10] 652[3] 814[2] 989[6]* 1582[4] (1987) (2573) (3206) 3909[3] 5568[8] 5869[16] **>44a 75f<**

**Untidy Daughter** 5 b m Sabrehill (USA) -Branitska (Mummy s Pet) 1560[5] 2174[7] 2446[3] 3265[7] **>57f<**

**Unveil** 6 b m Rudimentary (USA) -Magical Veil (Majestic Light (USA)) 2342a[3] **>36f<**

**Up Anchor (USA)** 3 br c Polish Navy (USA) -All Mine Again (USA) (Seattle Song (USA)) 4769a[7] **>89f<**

**Up And Away (GER)** 10 b g Le Glorieux-Ultima Ratio (GER) (Vice Regal (CAN)) 2336a[4] 3335a[11] 5215a[6] **>115f<**

**Upsetthym (NZ)** 5 br m Rhythm (USA) -Set Up (NZ) (Zabeel (NZ)) 6528a[15] **>101f<**

**Up Tempo (IRE)** 6 b g Flying Spur (AUS) -Musical Essence (Song) *504[2] (584) 833[3] (897)* (1175) (1358) 1452[4] 1603[2] 2215[10] 2459[11] 2750[5] 2899[8] *(6480)* **>84a 82f<**

**Up The Aisle** 7 b g Rambo Dancer (CAN) -Mardessa (Ardross) 5371[11] 5591[5] **><**

**Upthedale (IRE)** 3 b g General Monash (USA) -Pimpinella (IRE) (Reprimand) 1300[7] *1570[4]* 1932[3] 1995[U] 2347[5] 2554[10] 3013[6] **>32a 41?f<**

**Urabande** 2 b f Tipsy Creek (USA) -La Belle Mystere (Lycius (USA)) 1415[12] *1735[2] 2125[10]* 2773[6] 2960[4] 3458[7] **>56a 28f<**

**Urban Calm** 3 b f Cadeaux Genereux-Silver Sun (Green Desert (USA)) 1472[4] 1906[2] 2675[2] 3096[9] 3668[4] **>63f<**

**Urban Rose** 3 b f Piccolo-Blue Lamp (USA) (Shadeed (USA)) 1464[7] 1841[14] 2518[3] 2741[8] 4650[4] 4740[9] 5473[4] 5734[13] **>59f<**

**Uredale (IRE)** 2 b c Bahhare (USA) -Baileys First

(IRE) (Alzao (USA)) 1523[5] 2125[8] 2526[6] 3834[5] (4010) 4445[13] 5477[14] >**35a 62f**<

**Urgente** 2 b c Halling (USA) -Persian Filly (IRE) (Persian Bold) 6380a[11] >**71f**<

**Urowells (IRE)** 4 b g Sadler s Wells (USA) -Highest Accolade (Shirley Heights) 2691[8] 3716[9] 4777[7] 5607[11] 5835[9] >**89f**<

**Ursa Major** 10 b g Warning-Double Entendre (Dominion) 2210[12] 2594[7] 3629[6] 3917[8] 4485[7] >**89a 63f**<

**Ushindi (IRE)** 2 b f Montjeu (IRE) -Fern (Shirley Heights) 3905[13] 4851[12] 5349[4] 6003[3] >**71f**<

**Ussaro (IRE)** 2 b c Primo Dominie-Urmia (Persian Bold) 5389a[2] ><

**Ustad (IRE)** 2 br c Giant s Causeway (USA) -Winsa (USA) (Riverman (USA)) 5087[8] 5567[7] >**62f**<

**Ustilla (GER)** 3 b f Lomitas-Ustina (GER) (Star Appeal) 2157a[9] >**70f**<

**Utah Flats (IRE)** 3 ch g Bluebird (USA) -Desert Rose (Green Desert (USA)) 668[7] 805[10] >**32a**<

## V

**Vademecum** 3 br g Shinko Forest (IRE) -Sunshine Coast (Posse (USA)) 1558[6] 2075[10] 4151[10] 5244[10] 5674[10] 6094[13] 6537[11] >**34a 74f**<

**Vague Star (ITY)** 2 b c Soviet Star (USA) -Simova (USA) (Vaguely Noble) 5353[13] 5865[3] 6158[3] 6453[8] >**73a 72f**<

**Vahana (FR)** 7 b m Sicyos (USA) -Vouivre (FR) (Matahawk) 5103a[10] ><

**Valance (IRE)** 4 br g Bahhare (USA) -Glowlamp (IRE) (Glow (USA)) 2277[3] 3244[5] (3644) 4075[4] 4226[8] 5318[2] 5784[13] >**74a 88f**<

**Valazar (USA)** 5 b g Nicholas (USA) -Valor s Minion (USA) (Turkey Shoot (USA)) 721[10] 938[9] 1075[7] 1443[2] 1696[3] 2383[2] 3227[3]3378[4] 4422[16] >**49a 51f**<

**Valdasho** 5 b m Classic Cliche (IRE) -Ma Rivale (Last Tycoon) 894[9] >**17a 35f**<

**Val De Fleurie (GER)** 9 b m Mondrian (GER) -Valbonne (Master Willie) 1188[6] >**62f**<

**Val De Maal (IRE)** 4 ch g Eagle Eyed (USA) -Miss Bojangles (Gay Fandango (USA)) 1625[3] 1968[14] 2407[4] 2750[7] 5008[4] 5201[6] 5798[11] 6026[9]6539[6] >**76a 80f**<

**Valdesco (IRE)** 6 ch g Bluebird (USA) -Allegheny River (USA) (Lear Fan (USA)) 3199[11] 3781[7] 4778[13] >**66f**<

**Val D Isere** 2 ch c Tomba-Dancing Diana (Raga Navarro (ITY)) 6022[12] >**24a**<

**Vale De Lobo** 2 b f Loup Sauvage (USA) -Frog (Akarad (FR)) 3847[5] (4095) 5090[3] >**65+a 71f**<

**Vale Mantovani** 4 ch f Wolfhound (USA) -Cue The Groom (USA) (Blushing Groom (FR)) 2138a[3] (3137a) >**101f**<

**Valentia (IRE)** 3 b f Perugino (USA) -Teide (Sabrehill (USA)) 963[8] >**40a 56f**<

**Valentin (IRE)** 2 ch f King Of Kings (IRE) -Slip Ashore (IRE) (Slip Anchor) (3693) 4119[2] 4552[8] 5250[8] >**99f**<

**Valentina Guest (IRE)** 3 b f Be My Guest (USA) -Karamiyna (IRE) (Shernazar) 3862a[3] 4406a[6] 4784a[7] >**93f**<

**Valentino (FR)** 5 b g Valanour (IRE) -Rotina (FR) (Crystal Glitters (USA)) 5968a[4] (6170a) (6511a) >**113f**<

**Valet** 2 b c Kayf Tara-Val De Fleurie (GER) (Mondrian (GER)) 6145[19] 6531[9] >**17f**<

**Valeureux** 6 ch g Cadeaux Genereux-La Strada (Niniski (USA)) 3375[3] 3604[2] 3658[4] 4015[8] >**64 f**<

**Valhalling** 2 ch f Halling-Warranty Applied (USA) (Monteverdi) 5577a[11] ><

**Valiant Act (IRE)** 2 b f Brave Act-Jungle Story (IRE) (Alzao (USA)) 5688[6] 6060[3] >**65f**<

**Valiant Air (IRE)** 3 b g Spectrum (IRE) -Shining Desert (IRE) (Green Desert (USA)) 1179[4] 1344[5] 1499[2] 1740[4] 1947[10] 2554[7] 3371[4] 5863[5]6120[11] 6208[7] 6360[3] >**41a 54f**<

**Valiant Effort** 5 bb g In The Wings-Viz (USA) (Kris S (USA)) 2110[16] >**81f**<

**Valiant Romeo** 4 b g Primo Dominie-Desert Lynx (IRE) (Green Desert (USA)) 1421[5] 1870[2] 2274[2] 3010[4] 3407[11] 3820[5] 4279[2] 4452[15]5157[3] 5736[3] 6246[3] 6559[12] >**35a 61f**<

**Valios (IRE)** 2 b c Royal Applause-Swing And Brave (IRE) (Arctic Tern (USA)) 3808[11] 4481[7] >**51f**<

**Valixir (IRE)** 3 b c Trempolino (USA) -Vadlamixa (FR) (Linamix (FR)) 2159a[3] 2722a[3] (3863a) (5500a) 5981a[10] >**118f**<

**Valjarv (IRE)** 3 b f Bluebird (USA) -Iktidar (Green Desert (USA)) 1063[9] 1398[7] 1791[13] 2309[10] 3105[7] 3275[4] 3598[4] 3914[2]4531[9] 4750[9] 5898[5] 6071[13] 6175[4] 6459[4] 6497[12] >**81a 96f**<

**Valkiria (IRE)** 2 b f Xaar-Martine Bellis (ITY) (Darshaan) 5390a[4] ><

**Vallee Blanche (IRE)** 2 b f Zafonic (USA) -Grail (USA) (Quest For Fame) 6503a[6] >**84f**<

**Vallee Enchantee (IRE)** 4 b f Peintre Celebre (USA) -Verveine (USA) (Lear Fan (USA)) 1804a[4] 2639[3] 4121[5] 5981a[6] >**120+f**<

**Vallera (GER)** 3 b f Monsun (GER) -Val D Etoile (GER) (Big Shuffle (USA)) 2157a[3] 2723a[7] (3504a) (4980a) 5501a[4] 5978a[10] >**110f**<

**Valtar (FR)** 4 b f Tot Ou Tard (IRE) -Valiance (FR) (Akarad (FR)) 980a[7] >**88f**<

**Valuable Gift** 7 ch g Cadeaux Genereux-Valbra (Dancing Brave (USA)) 433[8] 670[8] 1191[8] 1283[13] 2556[8] >**38a 38f**<

**Value Plus (IRE)** 2 b f Mujadil (USA) -Brittas Blues (IRE) (Blues Traveller (IRE)) 3398[2] 3770[B] >**72f**<

**Vamose (IRE)** 3 ro g Victory Note (USA) -Narrow Band (IRE) (Standaan (FR)) 1641[4] 2093[8] 3955[4] >**67f**<

**Vamp** 3 b f Dracula (AUS) -Circe (Main Reef) 1441[7] 2267[2] 2729[3] (3574) 4079[5] 5297[11] 5572[4] 5842[3] 6194[2] >**80f**<

**Vampire Queen (IRE)** 3 b f General Monash (USA) -Taniokey (Grundy) (561) 731[4] 958[7] 983[8] >**56a 43f**<

**Vanbrugh (FR)** 4 ch g Starborough-Renovate (Generous (IRE)) (461) 743[9] 827[6] 1973[11] 2116[13] 2299[10] 2590[13] 2731[9]2874[7] 2987[9] 4202[8] 5027[7] 5159[7] 5354[6] 6231[11] 6278[12]6581[11] >**41a 51f**<

**Vancouver Gold (IRE)** 2 b f Monashee Mountain (USA) -Forest Berries (IRE) (Thatching) 5307[3] 5855[5] >**69f**<

**Vandenberghe** 5 b g Millkom-Child Star (FR) (Bellypha) (2007) 2034[5] 2456[3] 2728[4] 2939[3] 3423[5] 3774[6] 4080[3] 4261[3]4603[3] 5221[4] 5286[7] 5796[7] (6159) >**61a 52 f**<

**Vanderlin** 5 ch g Halling (USA) -Massorah (FR) (Habitat) 1242[3] 2398[3] 2678[5] 3323[3] (3730) 4216[8] 4889[3] 5422[3] 5888[2]6214[7] >**112a 112f**<

**Vangelis (USA)** 5 gr h Highest Honor (FR) -Capades Dancer (USA) (Gate Dancer (USA)) (1261a) 1804a[7] 4768a[5] >**119f**<

**Vanilla Moon** 4 b f Emperor Jones (USA) -Daarat Alayaam (IRE) (Reference Point) 449[5] 534[2] 676[4] 2375[3] 3383[6] 4070[4] 4499[6] 5645[4] >**50a 55f**<

**Vanished (IRE)** 4 b f Fayruz-Where s The Money (Lochnager) 721[12] 806[8] 954[9] >**61a 61 f**<

**Vantage (IRE)** 3 b g Marju (IRE) -Anna Comnena (IRE) (Shareef Dancer (USA)) 985[2] 1064[2] 1387[3] (1561) 1609[4] 2179[5] 2676[13] 5076[4] 5572[6]5842[7] >**84a 82f**<

**Var (USA)** 5 bb h Forest Wildcat (USA) -Loma Preata (USA) (Zilzal (USA)) (5471) 5647[2] (5977a) >**121f**<

**Varenka (IRE)** 2 b f Fasliyev (USA) -Castara Beach (IRE) (Danehill (USA)) 4420[5] (4625) 5330a[2] >**91f**<

**Variety Club** 3 b g Royal Applause-Starfida (Soviet Star (USA)) 2833[16] 3697[14] 4497[10] >**58f**<

**Varnay** 3 b f Machiavellian (USA) -Valleria (Sadler s Wells (USA)) 2019[11] >**89+f**<

**Varuni (IRE)** 3 b f Ali-Royal (IRE) -Sauvignon (IRE) (Alzao (USA)) (769) 985[7] 1394[2] 1998[15] 2848[9] 3669[5] 5538[4] >**62a 65f**<

**Vassilievsky (IRE)** 3 ch c Peintre Celebre (USA) -Verveine (USA) (Lear Fan (USA)) 1654a[3] 5727a[6] >**107f**<

**Vas Y Carla (USA)** 3 ch f Gone West (USA) -Lady Carla (Caerleon (USA)) 1372[12] 2572[2] 3139[10] >**70f**<

**Vasywait (FR)** 5 b h Valanour (IRE) -Wait And See One (FR) (The Wonder (FR)) (1741a) 3162a[4] 3769a[3] 4595a[16] >**114f**<

**Vatori (FR)** 2 ch c Vettori (IRE) -High Mecene (FR) (Highest Honor (FR)) 5666a[3] (6035a) >**106f**<

**Vaudevire** 3 b g Dancing Spree (USA) -Approved Quality (IRE) (Persian Heights) 1078[6] 1192[9] 1568[3] 1890[7] 3037[4] 3364[4] 4393[7] >**19a 42?f**<

**Vaughan** 3 b c Machiavellian (USA) -Labibeh (USA) (Lyphard (USA)) 5470[8] 5699[4] 5919[8] >**94f**<

**Vegas Queen (IRE)** 2 br f Celtic Swing-Dwingeloo (IRE) (Dancing Dissident (USA)) 5330a[3] >**84f**<

**Velocitas** 3 b g Magic Ring (IRE) -Folly Finnesse (Joligeneration) 1127[4] 1530[10] 2377[12] 2688[9] 5352[5] 5957[2] 6560[2] >**63a 53f**<

**Velocitys Image (IRE)** 4 b f Tagula (IRE) -Pike Creek (USA) (Alwasmi (USA)) 479[7] 713[7] >**7a 33f**<

**Velveteen Rabbit** 2 b f Singspiel (IRE) -Velvet Lady (Nashwan (USA)) 3675[9] 4053[3] 4706[2] 5548[7] 6140[8] >**70f**<

**Velvet Heights (IRE)** 2 b c Barathea (IRE) -Height Of Fantasy (IRE) (Shirley Heights) 3319[10] 4030[7] (4689) 5188[7] 5719[11] >**81f**<

**Velvet Jones** 11 gr g Sharrood (USA) -Cradle Of Love (USA) (Roberto (USA)) 4869[7] >**33f**<

**Velvet Rhythm** 4 b f Forzando-Bold Gayle (Never So Bold) 439[8] 613[8] 783[12] >**17a**<

**Velvet Touch** 3 b f Danzig Connection (USA) -Soft Touch (GER) (Horst-Herbert) 561[2] 673[6] 1184[9] 1737[6] 1906[5] 2850[11] 2986[8]6280[12] 6567[14] >**56a 65f**<

**Velvet Waters** 3 b f Unfuwain (USA) -Gleaming Water (Kalaglow) 2168[3] 2442[6] 2821[4] (3572) 4027[2] 4307[2] (4618) 4915[3] 5300[3] 5728[9] >**77f**<

**Venables (USA)** 3 ch c Stravinsky (USA) -Hope For A Breeze (CAN) (Briartic (CAN)) 1063[5] 1396[11] 2080[11] >**102a 102f**<

**Vendors Mistake (IRE)** 3 b f Danehill (USA) -Sunspangled (IRE) (Caerleon (USA)) 420[8] 561[6] 2098[3] 2661[3] 2800[6] 6567[6] >**41a 53f**<

**Veneer (IRE)** 2 b g Woodborough (USA) -Sweet Lass (Belmez (USA)) 1183[4] 1324[8] 2609[15] 6242[5] >**53f**<

**Venerdi Tredici (IRE)** 3 b f Desert Style (IRE) -Stifen (Burslem) 3102[11] 3368[12] 5018[7] >**19a 52f**<

**Venetian King (USA)** 2 b g King Of Kings (IRE) -Vena (IRE) (Danehill (USA)) 2898[5] 3974[2] >**72f**<

**Venetian Romance (IRE)** 3 ch f Desert Story (IRE) -Cipriani (Habitat) 1478[5] 1844[10] 2324[18] 2915[10] 3700[7] 4055[7] 4710[3] 5130[12]6120[9] 6231[8] >**10a 53f**<

**Veneziana** 3 ch f Vettori (IRE) -Fairy Story (IRE) (Persian Bold) 4196[15] 4491[8] >**60a 50f**<

**Vengeance** 4 b g Fleetwood (IRE) -Lady Isabell (Rambo Dancer (CAN)) 1328[7] 1539[3] (3325) 3716[5] 4163[5] >**104f**<

**Vengerov** 3 b g Piccolo-Shining Cloud (Indian Ridge) (683) 798[6] 2870[3] 3535[10] >**72 a 68f**<

**Ventalle (SPA)** 4 u c Zieten (USA) -Molinera (SPA) (( (USA)) (USA)) 5668a[9] >**89f**<

**Verasi** 3 b g Kahyasi-Fair Verona (USA) (Alleged (USA)) 1830[4] 2546[10] 3107[7] 5913[7] 6088[9] >**60+a 60f**<

**Verbier (USA)** 2 bb f Fusaichi Pegasus (USA) -Oh Nellie (USA) (Tilt The Stars (CAN)) 5270[6] (5559) 5885[5] >**75f**<

**Veritable** 2 br f So Factual (USA) -Madam Trilby (Grundy) 2058[4] 4399[11] 5270[10] >**66f**<

**Verkhotina** 3 b f Barathea (IRE) -Alusha (Soviet Star (USA)) 1366[6] (2518) 2741[9] 3306[3] 3728[8] >**85f**<

**Vermilion Creek** 5 b m Makbul-Cloudy Reef (Cragador) 441[5] 570[8] 653[6] 814[6] 1389[6] 1606[2] 2879[9] 3536[6]4511[11] (5587) >**41a 63f**<

**Vermilliann (IRE)** 3 b f Mujadil (USA) -Refined (IRE) (Statoblest) 1685[10] 2117[9] 2877[16] >**88 f**<

**Verstone (IRE)** 2 b f Brave Act-Golden Charm (IRE) (Common Grounds) 1170[8] 1264[8] 1498[8] >**3a 7f**<

**Vertedanz (IRE)** 4 b f Sesaro (USA) -Blade Of Grass (Kris) 4083[18] 4818[20] 5283[12] >**60a 12f**<

**Very Wise** 2 b c Pursuit Of Love-With Care (Warning) (6441) >**74f**<

**Vespone (IRE)** 4 ch c Llandaff (USA) -Vanishing Prairie (USA) (Alysheba (USA)) 978a[2] 1804a[2] 2155a[2] 2678[8] 3936[2] 4768a[12] 5492[5] >**119f**<

**Vesta Flame** 3 b f Vettori (IRE) -Ciel De Feu (USA) (Blushing John (USA)) 532[3] 730[3] 1201[11] >**37a 14f**<

**Vettori Loose (IRE)** 3 b f Vettori (IRE) -Dan Loose (IRE) (Danehill (USA)) 1778a[14] >**64f**<

**Vettorious** 2 ch c Vettori (IRE) -Sleepless (Night Shift (USA)) 6331[12] >**40f**<

**Viable** 2 b g Vettori (IRE) -Danseuse Davis (FR) (Glow (USA)) 4625[9] >**41f**<

**Viagrah (IRE)** 3 b g Danetime (IRE) -Classic Choice (Patch) 835[10] ><

**Via Milano (FR)** 3 b f Singspiel (IRE) -Salvinaxia (FR) (Linamix (FR)) 1652a[4] 2160a[4] 4430a[7] 6203a[8] >**107f**<

**Vibe** 3 gr g Danzero (AUS) -Courting (Pursuit Of Love) 1420[U] 1528[7] 1820[13] 2195[4] 2732[11] 3166[6] >**69f**<

**Vicario** 3 gr g Vettori (IRE) -Arantxa (Sharpo) 1911[5] (2402) 2567[3] 3020[3] 3669[2] 3837[6] 4692[5] 5214[4] 5860[3] >**65f**<

**Vicars Destiny** 6 b m Sir Harry Lewis (USA) -Church Leap (Pollerton) 1112[2] 1287[2] 1615[13] 2299[8] 2731[10] 3621[6] 3821[4] 4627[3]4778[3] 5100[2] 5589[3] 5991[3] 6269[9] >**72f**<

**Vicat Cole** 3 ch g Hector Protector (USA) -Dancing Spirit (IRE) (Ahonoora) 1794[23] 2882[5] 3417[7] 4262[8] >**68a 68f**<

**Vicchio** 6 ch g Cadeaux Genereux-Centaine (Royal Academy (USA)) 784a[4] >**74f**<

**Vicious Knight** 6 b g Night Shift (USA) -Myth (Troy) 2894[14] 2969[21] 3673[12] 4120[13] 4273[10] 4887[5] 5099[3] 6044[13]6358[7] >**88f**<

**Vicious Prince (IRE)** 5 b g Sadler s Wells (USA) -Sunny Flower (FR) (Dom Racine (FR)) 1470[4] 2624[8] 3199[8] 3564[5] >**79f**<

**Vicious Warrior** 5 b g Elmaamul (USA) -Ling Lane (Slip Anchor) 1773[2] 2196[8] 2527[5] 2894[3] 3756[7] 3977[2] 4178[2] 5194[3]5941[15] 6044[6] >**56a 95f**<

**Vicomte (GER)** 3 b c Lagunas-Vivora (Risk Me (FR)) 2158a[9] >**64f**<

**Victimised (IRE)** 2 b g Victory Note (USA) -Eurolink Virago (Charmer) 1390[9] 3083[14] 3824[5] >**45f**<

**Victor Buckwell** 2 br c Pivotal-Lonely Shore (Blakeney) 5604[11] 6092[9] 6352[8] >**41f**<

**Victoriana** 3 b f Wolfhound (USA) -Silk St James (Pas De Seul) 1942[6] 4845[4] 5104[5] 5849[15] 6089[11] >**58f**<

**Victorian Dancer (IRE)** 3 b f Groom Dancer (USA) -Victoria Regia (IRE) (Lomond (USA)) 2036[10] >**15a 58f**<

**Victoria Page (FR)** 2 br f Anabaa (USA) -Valley Springs (Saratoga Six (USA)) 5532a[5] >**89f**<

**Victoria Peek (IRE)** 2 b f Cape Cross (IRE) -Night Spirit (IRE) (Night Shift (USA)) 1882[4] 2677[8] 3003[7] >**63f**<

**Victory Design (IRE)** 2 b c Danehill (USA) -Sun Silk (USA) (Gone West (USA)) 5118[6] >**69f**<

**Victory Flip (IRE)** 4 b f Victory Note (USA) -Two Magpies (Doulab (USA)) 509[13] 700[6] 826[5] 952[3] >**42a 53 f**<

**Victory Hymn (IRE)** 2 b f Victory Note (USA) -Nordic Union (IRE) (Nordico (USA)) 3045[7] 3366[5] 4234[13] >**47f**<

**Victory Lap (GER)** 3 ch f Grand Lodge (USA) -Vicenca (USA) (Sky Classic (CAN)) 1800[8] 2133[6] 2567[5] 3341[7] >**59a 65f**<

**Victory Moon (SAF)** 5 b h Al Mufti (USA) -Dancing Flower (SAF) (Dancing Champ (USA)) 635a[3] (756a) (979a) 1147a[3] >**120+a 117+f**<

**Victory Quest (IRE)** 4 b g Victory Note (USA) -Marade (USA) (Dahar (USA)) 523[16] 629[7] (827) (899) 1010[4] >**91a 68f**<

**Victory Taita (FR)** 4 br c Solid Illusion (USA) -Mlle Saumarez (FR) (Saumarez) 1578a[6] >**98f**<

**Victory U.S.A. (USA)** 3 ch f Victory Gallop (CAN) -Fordyce (USA) (Cox s Ridge (USA)) [4] >**110a**<

**Victory Vee** 4 ch g Vettori (IRE) -Aldevonie (Green Desert (USA)) 834[9] 967[6] 1136[11] 1595[10] >**61a 56f**<

**Victory Venture (IRE)** 4 b g Victory Note (USA) -Shirley Venture (Be My Chief (USA)) 2738[14] 3909[9] 4192[13] 4616[16] >**80f**<

**Victram (IRE)** 4 b c Victory Note (USA) -Lady Tristram (Miami Springs) 4588a[3] >**91f**<

**Vienna s Boy (IRE)** 3 b c Victory Note (USA) -Shinkoh Rose (FR) (Warning) 1223[4] 1965[4] 2309[6] 2549[4] 2739[6] 2877[13] 3203[5] 3384[2]3845[5] 4237[4] 4917[4] (5092) 6477[19] >**87f**<

**Viewforth** 6 b g Emarati (USA) -Miriam (Forzando) 1343[4] 1525[4] 1765[12] 2132[9] 2461[7] 2899[14] 3314[12] 3524[4]3580[3] 3795[8] 3894[15] 4133[8] 4542[12] 5126[8] 5579[24] 5833[3] >**82f**<

**View The Facts** 5 br m So Factual (USA) -Scenic View (IRE) (Scenic) 657[8] 793[10] >**29a 57f**<

**Vigorous (IRE)** 4 b f Danetime (IRE) -Merrily (Sharrood (USA)) 1825[15] 2079[5] 2369[8] 3407[16] 4452[6] 5798[2] 5862[5] >**80 f**<

**Vijay (IRE)** 5 ch g Eagle Eyed (USA) -Foolish Fun (Fool s Holme (USA)) 796[10] 904[3] 968[10] 1421[6] 1787[15] 2175[2] 2423[9] 2784[7]2975[6] 3735[14] 4014[8] 4257[2] 4535[6] >**60a 59f**<

**Viking Spirit** 2 b c Mind Games-Dane Dancing (IRE) (Danehill (USA)) 3808[8] 4149[2] 4866[2] (5351) (5617) 5896[7] >**94+f**<

**Villa Chigi (IRE)** 2 ch g Pistolet Bleu (IRE) -Musical Refrain (IRE) (Dancing Dissident (USA)) 6091[10] >**32f**<

**Villadolide (FR)** 3 bl f Anabaa (USA) -Vassia (USA) (Machiavellian (USA)) 4357a[6] 5333a[8] >**106f**<

**Villarosi (IRE)** 2 b f Rossini (USA) -Trinida (Jaazeiro (USA)) 6471[5] >**74f**<

**Villarrica (USA)** 2 ch f Selkirk (USA) -Melikah (IRE) (Lammtarra (USA)) 5534[4] 5946[3] >**75f**<

**Vinando** 3 ch c Hernando (FR) -Sirena (GER) (Tejano (USA)) (1508) 2107[7] (4167) 5699[5] (5919) >**105f**<

**Vincent** 9 b g Anshan-Top-Anna (IRE) (Ela-Mana-Mou) 461[4] 483[3] (551) 616[6] 750[3] >**56a 41f**<

**Vindication** 4 ch g Compton Place-Prince s Feather (IRE) (Cadeaux Genereux) 2283[12] 2503[6] 3052[6] 3337[7] 5468[10] 5921[9] 6277[9] 6568[20] >**83a 101 f**<

**Vin Du Pays** 4 b g Alzao (USA) -Royale Rose (FR) (Bering) 1302[9] 3909[11] 4686[10] 4971[10] 5205[14] 6025[10] 6278[11] >**79a 50f**<

**Vinnie Roe (IRE)** 6 bb h Definite Article-Kayu (Tap On Wood) 2416a[2] 4784a[2] (5662a) 6528a[2] >**126f**<

**Vino Venus** 2 b f Tipsy Creek (USA) -Galaxy Glow (Kalaglow) 4797[8] 5925[5] >**43f**<

**Vintage Premium** 7 b g Forzando-Julia Domna (Dominion) 842[7] 1009[6] 1062[8] (2066) 2076[2] >**104a 113f**<

**Vintage Style** 5 ch g Piccolo-Gibaltarik (IRE) (Jareer (USA)) 3151[15] 3533[19] >**72a 59f**<

**Viola Da Braccio (IRE)** 3 ch f Vettori (IRE) -Push A Button (Bold Lad (IRE)) 1842[10] 2311[5] 2977[5] 3613[6] >**44a 57f**<

**Violet Avenue** 3 ch f Muhtarram (USA) -Ivoronica (Targowice (USA)) 2259[10] 3155[6] 3478[4] 4127[7] 4817[5] 5156[7] 5658[13] >**59f**<

**Violet Moon (FR)** 5 b m Kendor (FR) -Violet Dancer (FR) (Fabulous Dancer (USA)) 6137a[8] ><

**Violet Park** 3 b f Pivotal-Petonellajill (Petong) 3666[2] 3948[2] 4195[3] (4478) (4731) 5652[12] >**78f**<

**Vip** 2 ch c Dubai Millennium-Danish (IRE) (Danehill (USA)) 6440[4] >**67f**<

**Virginia Waters (USA)** 2 b f Kingmambo (USA) -Legend Maker (IRE) (Sadler s Wells (USA)) 5322a[8] 5961a[3] 6101a[2] >**98f**<

**Virgin s Tears** 2 b f Bishop Of Cashel-Lola Mora (Nearly A Hand) 6067[7] 6342[10] >**48f**<

**Visionist (IRE)** 2 b c Orpen (USA) -Lady Taufan (IRE) (Taufan (USA)) (3758) 4295[4] 4958a[3] 5295[3] >**101f**<

**Vision Victory (GER)** 2 b g Dashing Blade-Val D Isere (GER) (Surumu (GER)) 1523[4] 1960[10] 2758[10] 5466[11] 6515[13] >**53f**<

**Visorama (IRE)** 4 bb f Linamix (FR) -Visor (USA) (Mr Prospector (USA)) 1952a[5] 2543a[2] 3567a[3] 4566a[7] 5501a[7] >**113f**<

**Visorhill (FR)** 6 b g Danehill (USA) -Visor (USA) (Mr Prospector (USA)) 1657a[8] >**114f**<

**Vita Spericolata (IRE)** 7 b m Prince Sabo-Ahonita (Ahonoora) 1391[8] 1923[9] 1955[3] 2488[5] 2682[17] 3509[12] 3715[8] 4091[5]4362[5] 4779[6] 5105[9] >**95?f**<

**Vitelucy** 5 b m Vettori (IRE) -Classic Line (Last Tycoon) 812[5] 1077[5] 1193[3] 1572[5] 6360[5] >**41a 40f**<

**Vittorioso (IRE)** 3 b g Victory Note (USA) -Miss Anita (IRE) (Anita s Prince) 409[5] 496[3] 764[3] 898[2] 963[7] 4021[8] 4484[5]5547[10] 5702[7] 5843[6] 6120[5] >**56a 52f**<

**Viva Atlas Espana** 4 b f Piccolo-Bay Risk (Risk Me (FR)) 415[16] 1910[8] >**49f**<

**Viva La Diva (IRE)** 4 b f Danetime (IRE) -Almasa (Faustus (USA)) 4893a[5] >**88f**<

**Vivre Sa Vie** 3 ch f Nashwan (USA) -La Strada (Niniski (USA)) 563[4] 628[3] 797[2] 863[5] 6209[7] >**63a 2f**<

**Vizulize** 5 b m Robellino (USA) -Euridice (IRE) (Woodman (USA)) 469[12] 525[6] 613[5] 895[9] 933 [9] 1165[4] 1244[10]5929[11] 6057[3] >**37a 54f**<

**Vlasta Weiner** 4 b g Magic Ring (IRE) -Armaiti (Sayf El Arab (USA)) 422[7] 441[2] 533[5] 567[10] 658[4] 824[6] 860[4]932[6] 2384[12] 2836[16] >**44a 40 f**<

**Vocative (GER)** 2 gr f Acatenango (GER) -Vadinaxa (FR) (Linamix (FR)) 5858[7] >**60f**<

**Voice Mail** 5 b g So Factual (USA) -Wizardry (Shirley Heights) 1187[7] 1542[9] (2170) (2262) 2430[3] 2637[11] 3191[2] 3415[7] 3705[3] 4327[4]4435[8] 4772[3] 5297[12] 6156[8] >**79a 82f**<

**Voice Of An Angel (IRE)** **2** b f Desert Style (IRE) -Madame Curie (Polish Precedent (USA)) 1234[5] 1865[8] 2003[5] 2248[12] 3144[5] >**46a 35f**<

**Voile (IRE)** **3** b f Barathea (IRE) -Samriah (IRE) (Wassl) 5811[7] 6175[8] 6497[9] >**81a 100f**<

**Voir Dire** **2** b c Vettori (IRE) -Bobbie Dee (Blakeney) 3451[13] 3939[7] 4913[8] 5871[8] 6309[3] >**63f**<

**Voix Du Nord (FR)** **3** b c Valanour (IRE) -Dame Edith (FR) (Top Ville) (1350a) (2159a) >**115f**<

**Volaticus (IRE)** **3** b c Desert Story (IRE) -Haysel (IRE) (Petorius) 1127[2] 1453[14] 2457[4] 3270[4] 3624[12] >**65f**<

**Volitio** **2** b c Mind Games-Millie s Lady (IRE) (Common Grounds) 4681[16] 4967[13] 5407[11] 6077[7] 6562[10] >**53f**<

**Vonadaisy** **3** b f Averti (IRE) -Vavona (Ballad Rock) (5204) 5652[21] 5740[5] 5955[9] 6290[4] >**73a 70f**<

**Vondova** **2** b f Efisio-Well Proud (IRE) (Sadler s Wells (USA)) 2940[3] 3202[7] (3676) 4060[8] 4876[2] 5250[9] >**86f**<

**Von Dutch (IRE)** **2** ch c Namid-Vasilopoula (IRE) (Kenmare (FR)) 5280a[8] >**19f**<

**Von Wessex** **2** b g Wizard King-Gay Da Cheen (IRE) (Tenby) 1128[6] 1240[5] (1374) 1556[6] 1970[3] 2523[3] (2773) 3980[4] 4675[6] 5132[6]5746[2] >**24a 58f**<

**Voom** **2** b f Fraam-Natalie Jay (Ballacashtal (CAN)) 3192[8] 3458[4] 3571[3] >**47f**<

**Vortex** **5** b g Danehill (USA) -Roupala (USA) (Vaguely Noble) (564) (647) (775) (862) (1009) 1062[12] 1456[17] (1954a) 2283[3] 2969[10] 3937[2]4120[4] 4528[2] (5504a) 5948[4] >**104a 112f**<

**Vrisaki (IRE)** **3** b g Docksider (USA) -Kingdom Queen (IRE) (Night Shift (USA)) 409[2] 640[8] 1908[4] 2251[9] 2402[7] 2822[3] 3190[6] 3461[3]4055[11] 4346[17] 4499[14] >**55a 54f**<

**Vrubel (IRE)** **5** ch g Entrepreneur-Renzola (Dragonara Palace (USA)) 6406[2] >**61a 57f**<

**Vulnerable** **3** ch f Hector Protector (USA) -Beleaguer (Rainbow Quest (USA)) 2193a[8] >**91f**<

## W

**Waaedah (USA)** **3** ch f Halling (USA) -Agama (USA) (Nureyev (USA)) 2112[19] >**75f**<

**Waatheb (IRE)** **2** b c Barathea (IRE) -Bally Souza (IRE) (Alzao (USA)) 2804[11] 6171[7] 6393[8] >**64a 75f**<

**Wafani** **5** b g Mtoto-Wafa (IRE) (Kefaah (USA)) 2520[11] >**2a 7f**<

**Waggledance (IRE)** **2** b g Mujadil (USA) -Assertive Lass (USA) (Assert) 2570[5] 3818[9] 4175[8] 5233[7] 5555[2] 5816[9] >**64f**<

**Wahchi (IRE)** **5** ch g Nashwan (USA) -Nafhaat (USA) (Roberto (USA)) 1286[7] 1768[19] 2022[16] 2583[10] 3097[6] >**62f**<

**Wahoo Sam (USA)** **4** ch g Sandpit (BRZ) -Good Reputation (USA) (Gran Zar (MEX)) 1452[12] 2580[8] 2938[3] (3401) (3738) 4005[8] (4333) 4634[2] 4826[11] >**78 a 80+f**<

**Wahsheeq** **4** b c Green Desert (USA) -Moss (USA) (Woodman (USA)) 925a[10] >**98f**<

**Wainwright (IRE)** **4** b g Victory Note (USA) -Double Opus (IRE) (Petorius) (476) 526[9] 1175[9] 2118[11] 2391[11] 2528[6] >**73a 77df**<

**Wait For Spring (USA)** **3** b f Seeking The Gold (USA) -Polish Spring (IRE) (Polish Precedent (USA)) 3630[5] 4693[2] 5123[16] 5828[9] >**75f**<

**Wait For The Will (USA)** **8** ch g Seeking The Gold (USA) -You d Be Surprised (USA) (Blushing Groom (FR)) 1401[16] 1768[16] 2240[10] (3046) (3276) 4345[2] 5111[5] 5699[10] >**96a 96 f**<

**Wake (USA)** **4** b c Storm Cat (USA) -Ladies Cruise (USA) (Fappiano (USA)) (1059) 1397[6] 2241[10] 6475[6] >**81a 88f**<

**Wake Up Henry** **3** ch g Nashwan (USA) -River Saint (USA) (Irish River (FR)) 1874[8] 2361[3] 2802[4] 5585[13] >**50a 61f**<

**Wakired (USA)** **3** b f Red Ransom (USA) -Waki Decree (USA) (Miswaki (USA)) 2193a[11] >**83f**<

**Waldblume (GER)** **2** ch f Halling (USA) -Wurftaube (GER) (Acatenango (GER)) 6367a[10] >**84+f**<

**Walerie (GER)** **3** br f Law Society (USA) -Warwara (GER) (Nebos (GER)) 6257a[5] >**72f**<

**Walkamia (FR)** **4** gr f Linamix (FR) -Walk On Air (IRE) (Cure The Blues (USA)) 1922a[5] 2924a[5] 4566a[4] 5978a[3] 6381a[2] >**112f**<

**Walker Bay (IRE)** **6** ch m Efisio-Lalandria (FR) (Highest Honor (FR)) 495[5] 661[9] >**36a 51f**<

**Walk In The Park (IRE)** **2** b c Montjeu (IRE) -Classic Park (Robellino (USA)) 6510a[3] >**109f**<

**Walkonthewildside** **2** b c Giant s Causeway (USA) -Wannabe Grand (IRE) (Danehill (USA)) 4296[5] 4567[4] (5347) 5895[9] >**78+f**<

**Wall Street Runner** **3** ch f Kirkwall-Running Tycoon (IRE) (Last Tycoon) 5618[20] 6157[8] 6295[7] 6452[10] 6537[8] >**62a 57 f**<

**Walmooh** **8** b h In The Wings-Walimu (IRE) (Top Ville) 635a[9] 754a[2] 925a[4] (1006a) >**91a 110f**<

**Waltzing Beau** **3** ch g Dancing Spree (USA) -Blushing Belle (Local Suitor (USA)) 563[2] 598[9] 2546[12] 2840[9] 3190[8] 3681[2] 3990[3] 4798[6]5221[6] 5751[8] >**57a 53f**<

**Waltzing Wizard** **5** b g Magic Ring (IRE) -Legendary Dancer (Shareef Dancer (USA)) 504[3] 588[5] 694[4] 833[5] 1663[5] 1748[5] 1971[7] 2260[5]2421[4] 2938[9] 3148[6] 3409[3] 3516[4] 3895[13] 4390[6] 5235[11] >**54a 61f**<

**Waluck (ITY)** **3** b c Alkalde (GER) -Cotton Bowl (IRE) (Mtoto) 1306a[9] ><

**Wanchai Lad** **3** b c Danzero (AUS) -Frisson (Slip Anchor) 1883[3] 2897[7] 3092[5] 3293[9] 5440[11] 5605[15] 5631[11] >**89f**<

**Wandering Act (IRE)** **2** b c Brave Act-Cwm Deri (IRE) (Alzao (USA)) 4432[7] 5023[7] >**47f**<

**Wanna Shout** **6** b m Missed Flight-Lulu (Polar Falcon (USA)) 662[2] (788) 855[2] (1102) 1244[2] 1940[7] 2430[5] 3177[8] 3638[6]3933[3] 4517[6] >**66 a 53f**<

**Wansdyke Lass** **2** b f Josr Algarhoud (IRE) -Silankka (Slip Anchor) 3451[5] >**64f**<

**Want (USA)** **3** ch c Miswaki (USA) -Substance (USA) (Diesis) 1794[10] 2113[10] >**63f**<

**Waquaas** **8** b g Green Desert (USA) -Hamaya (USA) (Mr Prospector (USA)) 1953a[4] 5505a[2] >**94a 97f**<

**Waraqa (USA)** **5** b m Red Ransom (USA) -Jafn (Sharpo) 453[14] >**20a 48f**<

**War At Sea (IRE)** **2** b c Bering-Naval Affair (IRE) (Last Tycoon) 5087[5] >**72f**<

**Warbreck** **3** ch g Selkirk (USA) -Wigging (Warning) 1771[15] 3448[7] 5770[8] 6015[5] >**56a 54f**<

**Warden Complex** **3** b g Compton Place-Miss Rimex (IRE) (Ezzoud (IRE)) 1096[3] 1293[2] (2207) (2907) 3690[7] 4031[5] 5379[2] >**93a 96f**<

**Warden Warren** **6** b g Petong-Silver Spell (Aragon) 488[3] 719[4] 749[6] (866) 1013[7] 1139[9] (1424) 1927[18]2094[12] 2473[4] (2553) 2673[9] 3052[9] 4652[2] 6445[12] 6568[18] >**83a 81f**<

**Wares Home (IRE)** **3** b g Indian Rocket-Pepilin (Coquelin (USA)) 557[7] 631[6] 1506[8] 2389[3] 2657[4] 3037[3] 3425[3] 3836[2]4004[3] 4276[11] 4495[3] 5081[7] >**56a 56f**<

**Warif (USA)** **3** ch c Diesis-Alshoowg (USA) (Riverman (USA)) 1959[5] 2092[7] 2485[8] 6361[11] >**39a 39f**<

**Warlingham (IRE)** **6** b g Catrail (USA) -Tadjnama (USA) (Exceller (USA)) 509[10] 575[8] (642) (698) 772[5] 834[7] (2099) 2325[10] 2703[5]2948[7] 3174[5] 3428[8] 4199[8] 4403[9] 5597[17] 6220[12] 6398[7]6499[7] >**67a 65f**<

**Warningcamp (GER)** **3** b g Lando (GER) -Wilette (GER) (Top Ville) 2632[4] 3245[6] 3882[3] 4852[16] >**76f**<

**War Owl (USA)** **7** gr g Linamix (FR) -Ganasheba (USA) (Alysheba (USA)) 518[2] 820[8] (882) (1308) 1369[3] 1604[5] 2000[12] (2738) 3731[9] 4319[8]4634[4] 5568[14] >**69a 79f**<

**War Pennant** **2** b g Selkirk (USA) -Bunting (Shaadi (USA)) 5840[6] 6223[9] >**28a 48f**<

**Warrad (USA)** **3** b c Kingmambo (USA) -Shalimar Garden (IRE) (Caerleon (USA)) 1587[4] 3850[3] 4271[5] 5076[3] >**96+a 97f**<

**Warren Place** **4** ch g Presidium-Coney Hills (Beverley Boy) 4190[13] 4557[18] 5104[8] 5342[9] >**20a 51f**<

**Warrsan (IRE)** **6** b h Caerleon (USA) -Lucayan Princess (High Line) 1144a[5] 1792[3] (2639) 3540[2] 4121[9] (5329a) 5981a[9] >**126f**<

**Wasalat (USA)** **2** b f Bahri (USA) -Saabga (USA) (Woodman (USA)) 2296[4] 2651[2] 3014[3] 3987[2] 4263[9] 4909[6] >**76f**<

**Washbrook** **3** b g Royal Applause-Alacrity (Alzao (USA)) 1755[16] 2371[11] 2756[3] 5364[8] 5859[17] 6138[15] >**60f**<

**Washington Pink (IRE)** **5** b g Tagula (IRE) -Little Red Rose (Precocious) 1282[15] 1393[13] 1668[4] 1867[8] 2462[10] 3576[11] >**59f**<

**Wasted Talent (IRE)** **4** b f Sesaro (USA) -Miss Garuda (Persian Bold) (1684) 2514[2] 2958[11] 5182[10] 5728[4] >**63a 82f**<

**Watamu (IRE)** **3** b c Groom Dancer (USA) -Miss Golden Sands (Kris) 1437[13] 1831[9] (2244) 2397[2] 3210[6] 4271[3] 4737[5] >**97+f**<

**Watchful Witness** **4** ch c In The Wings-Eternal (Kris) 2090[3] 2460[4] 3348[16] 4129[11] >**33a 63f**<

**Watching** **7** ch g Indian Ridge-Sweeping (Indian King (USA)) 1199[3] 1765[22] 2041[2] 2679[5] 2859[5] 3324[7] 3509[10] 3713[11]4553[13] 4837[2] 5075[3] 5631[3] 6070[11] >**76a 92f**<

**Watchmyeyes (IRE)** **2** ch g Bold Fact (USA) -Shadow Smile (IRE) (Slip Anchor) 4040[6] 4359[4] 4866[4] 5377[2] 5735[2] (6020) (6063) >**82a 78f**<

**Water Cannon (USA)** **3** gr g Waquoit (USA) -Crying In The Rain (USA) (Baederwood (USA)) 2139a[10] >**84a**<

**Waterfront Dancer** **2** b g Groom Dancer (USA) -Azula (Bluebird (USA)) 5865[15] 5908[9] 6023[11] 6126[13] >**8a 34f**<

**Waterline Blue (IRE)** **3** b g Mujadil (USA) -Blues Queen (Lahib (USA)) 2209[5] 2404[11] >**35a 73f**<

**Waterline Dancer (IRE)** **4** bb f Danehill Dancer (IRE) -Thrill Seeker (IRE) (Treasure Kay) 664[8] 707[8] 858[9] 940[7] 1076[4] 1986[14] >**34a 34f**<

**Waterline Lover** **2** ch f Efisio-Food Of Love (Music Boy) 1399[6] 1670[10] 1839[11] 2644[4] 4048[7] 4475[6] 5005[4] 6080[17] >**52f**<

**Waterline Spirit** **4** b g Piccolo-Gina Of Hithermoor (Reprimand) 3774[16] 4275[11] >**46a 48f**<

**Waterloo Corner** **2** b g Cayman Kai (IRE) -Rasin Luck (Primitive Rising (USA)) 6207[9] ><

**Water Of Life (IRE)** **5** b m Dr Devious (IRE) -Simulcast (Generous (IRE)) 554[7] 623[12] >**51a 50 f**<

**Waterpark** **6** b m Namaqualand (USA) -Willisa (Polar Falcon (USA)) 1941[13] (1992) 2128[13] 2963[2] >**46a 65f**<

**Water Pistol** **2** b g Double Trigger (IRE) -Water Flower (Environment Friend) 4967[8] 5256[9] 5729[6] 6338[9] >**69f**<

**Watership Crystal (IRE)** **3** b f Sadler s Wells (USA) -Crystal Spray (Beldale Flutter (USA)) 2805[10] >**50f**<

**Watership Down (IRE)** **7** b g Dolphin Street (FR) -Persian Myth (Persian Bold) 2385[9] 3263[16] >**40f**<

**Waterside (IRE)** **5** ch g Lake Coniston (IRE) -Classic Ring (IRE) (Auction Ring (USA)) 1185[10] 1313[12] 1873[3] 2091[11] 2404[3] (2727) (2891) 3205[2] 3439[4] 4360[6]4553[16] 4917[3] (5077) 5444[12] 5887[13] >**89a 92f**<

**Water Taxi** **3** ch c Zafonic (USA) -Trellis Bay (Sadler s Wells (USA)) 1800[4] 2312[3] 2944[3] >**73f**<

**Wathab (IRE)** **3** b c Cadeaux Genereux-Bally Souza (IRE) (Alzao (USA)) 1256a[4] 3959a[3] 4956a[4] 5661a[12] >**115f**<

**Waverley Road** **7** ch g Pelder (IRE) -Lillicara (FR) (Caracolero (USA)) 962[13] 1693[4] >**56a 56f**<

**Wavertree Girl (IRE)** **3** b f Marju (IRE) -Lust (Pursuit Of Love) 927[3] 1015[8] 1558[5] 2112[7] 2290[4] 3211[3] 4024[10] 4650[11] >**63a 68f**<

**Wavertree Spirit** **3** ch g Hector Protector (USA) -Miss Clarinet (Pharly (FR)) 2280[6] >**58f**<

**Wavertree Warrior (IRE)** **2** br c Indian Lodge (IRE) -Karamana (Habitat) 2804[9] 3758[3] 4649[2] 5681a[10] 6090[3] 6334[9] >**78f**<

**Wavet** **4** b f Pursuit Of Love-Ballerina Bay (Myjinski (USA)) 3088[7] 3710[2] >**52a 61f**<

**Way Out** **3** b f Robellino (USA) -Exit (Exbourne (USA)) 3142[11] 3448[10] >**8f**<

**Wayward Melody** **4** b f Merdon Melody-Dubitable (Formidable (USA)) 1690[4] >**32a 44f**<

**Wayward Shot (IRE)** **2** b g Desert Prince (IRE) -Style Parade (USA) (Diesis) 3469[5] 4347[7] 4776[12] 5636[5] 6206[4] >**62f**<

**Wazir (USA)** **2** bb c Pulpit (USA) -Top Order (USA) (Dayjur (USA)) 3847[2] (5494) >**86+a 81f**<

**Waziri (IRE)** **3** b g Mtoto-Euphorie (GER) (Feenpark (GER)) (2648) 3872[7] 4274[9] 4719[3] 5057[10] 5693[7] 6152[15] >**74a 76f**<

**Weakest Link** **3** b g Mind Games-Sky Music (Absalom) 529[2] 569[3] 779[3] 983[7] 4489[15] 5557[14] 6004[4] >**59a 44f**<

**Weaver Of Dreams (IRE)** **4** b g Victory Note (USA) -Daziyra (IRE) (Doyoun) 1245[11] >**50?f**<

**Weaver Spell** **3** b g Wizard King-Impy Fox (IRE) (Imp Society (USA)) 1571[5] 1701[6] 2088[4] 3371[9] 5634[10] 6120[17] >**14a 33f**<

**Webbington Lass (IRE)** **3** b f Petardia-Richardstown Lass (IRE) (Muscatite) 1405[8] 4674[11] 4868[14] >**46f**<

**Webbswood Lad (IRE)** **3** b g Robellino (USA) -Poleaxe (Selkirk (USA)) 447[3] 621[2] >**68a**<

**Web Racer (IRE)** **2** b f Bold Fact (USA) -Sky Lover (Ela-Mana-Mou) 2422[5] 2961[9] 4095[8] >**17a 35f**<

**Wedding Cake (IRE)** **3** ch f Groom Dancer (USA) -Greektown (Ela-Mana-Mou) 3161[8] 3574[3] 4028[4] (5216) 5732[10] >**73+a 70f**<

**Wedding Party** **2** ch f Groom Dancer (USA) -Ceanothus (IRE) (Bluebird (USA)) 3840[3] (4599) 5052[4] (5938) 6353[2] >**83 a 86f**<

**Wedlock** **2** b c Pursuit Of Love-Promise Fulfilled (USA) (Bet Twice (USA)) 2651[4] 3014[8] 3248[12] >**61f**<

**Wedowannagiveuthat (IRE)** **3** b f Desert Prince (IRE) -Mimansa (USA) (El Gran Senor (USA)) 1419[7] 1820[14] 2572[6] 3473[12] 3710[12] 4102[12] >**10a 56f**<

**Weecandoo (IRE)** **6** b m Turtle Island (IRE) -Romantic Air (He Loves Me) 3484[7] 4118[9] 5461[5] 5573[7] 5814[9] 6173[8] 6458[6] >**71a 95?f**<

**Wee Dinns (IRE)** **3** b f Marju (IRE) -Tir-An-Oir (IRE) (Law Society (USA)) 1440[7] 1755[5] 2442[2] 2848[2] (3908) 4230[2] 4737[6] 5025[6] >**94 f**<

**Weet A Head (IRE)** **3** b c Foxhound (USA) -Morale (Bluebird (USA)) 864[5] 1321[3] 1712[5] 2018[6] 2237[3] 2448[4] 2751[6] 4490[8]5706[8] 6150[3] >**77a 83f**<

**Weet An Haul** **3** b g Danzero (AUS) -Island Ruler (Ile De Bourbon (USA)) 2411[7] 2667[8] 4102[3] 6541[12] >**53a 52f**<

**Weet An Store (IRE)** **3** gr c Spectrum (IRE) -Karmisymixa (FR) (Linamix (FR)) 3013[8] ><

**Weet For Me** **8** b g Warning-Naswara (USA) (Al Nasr (FR)) 2047[18] 2409[9] 3733[2] 4174[6] 4512[5] 5318[6] 5619[14] 6198[12] >**78f**<

**Weet N Measures** **2** b c Weet-A-Minute (IRE) -Weet Ees Girl (IRE) (Common Grounds) 4675[5] 4997[5] >**50a 54f**<

**Weet Watchers** **4** b g Polar Prince (IRE) -Weet Ees Girl (IRE) (Common Grounds) (685) 719[6] 900[4] 1389[3] 2215[16] 2528[5] (2979) 3167[P] 5364[13]6539[13] >**68a 68f**<

**Weet Yer Tern (IRE)** **2** b c Brave Act-Maxime (IRE) (Mac s Imp (USA)) 1208[4] 1638[2] 2852[4] >**52a 65f**<

**Weightless** **4** ch g In The Wings-Orford Ness (Selkirk (USA)) 1261a[8] 5968a[9] 6170a[5] >**118f**<

**Weir s Annie** **3** b f Puissance-Hyde Princess (Touch Paper) 1942[7] 2165[16] 2586[13] >**32f**<

**Wekiwa Springs (FR)** **7** gr g Kendor (FR) -Ti Mamaille (FR) (Dom Racine (FR)) 562[6] >**64a**<

**Welcome Archie** **4** ch g Most Welcome-Indefinite Article (IRE) (Indian Ridge) 1718[9] 1994[9] 2346[10] 3579[12] >**31f**<

**Welcome Back** **7** ch g Most Welcome-Villavina (Top Ville) 426[3] >**40a 41f**<

**Welcome Dream** **2** ch f Most Welcome-Sweet Dreams (Selkirk (USA)) 1390[7] 3611[11] >**37f**<

**Welcome Signal** **4** ch g Most Welcome-Glenfinlass (Lomond (USA)) 2881[12] 3049[5] 3917[5] 4556[8] 5020[3] 5370[2] 6081[2] >**66a 77f**<

**Welcome Stranger** **4** b g Most Welcome-Just Julia (Natroun (FR)) 1273[8] 2201[9] 2537[9] 3086[2] (3426) 4164[2] (4237) 4442[2] 5462[8] (5813) 6044[14] >**74a 103f**<

**Welkino s Boy** **3** ch g Most Welcome-Khadino (Relkino) 3297[13] 3608[5] 3882[6] 4820[3] 5190[3] 6074[12] >**69f**<

**Well Connected (IRE)** **4** b g Among Men (USA) -Wire To Wire (Welsh Saint) 5237[11] 5450[11] >**16f**<

**Well Established (IRE)** **2** b c Sadler s Wells (USA) -Riveryev (USA) (Irish River (FR)) 6187[6] >**70f**<

**Wellington Hall (GER)** **6** b g Halling (USA) -Wells Whisper (FR) (Sadler s Wells (USA)) (1376) 2032[9] (4556) 5203[3] 5554[5] (6337) >**64a 72f**<

**Well Knit** **3** b f Robellino (USA) -Wydah (Suave Dancer (USA)) 913[7] 1063[15] 1123[7] 1384[7] 1946[13] 2402[13] >**56a 51f**<

**Well Known** **3** b f Sadler s Wells (USA) -Danefair (Danehill (USA)) (2060) 4367[8] 4640[9] >**81+f**<

**Well Made (GER)** **7** br h Mondrian (GER) -Well Known (GER) (Konigsstuhl (GER)) 1259a[11] 1802a[2] 3357a[4] 4794a[6] 5329a[10] 5824a[6] >**122f**<

**We ll Meet Again** **4** ch g Bin Ajwaad (IRE) -Tantalizing Song (CAN) (The Minstrel (CAN)) 2356[3] 2776[12] 3103[4] 3375[5] >**61f**<

**Wellvita (GER)** **3** b f Vettori (IRE) -Wellanca (GER) (Acatenango (GER)) 2157a[11] >**85f**<

**Welsh And Wylde (IRE)** **4** b g Anita s Prince-Waikiki (GER) (Zampano (GER)) 1426[10] 4098[6] >**52a 61f**<

**Welsh Dream** **7** b g Mtoto-Morgannwg (IRE) (Simply Great (FR)) 3363[6] 4275[6] >**56a 66f**<

**Welsh Emperor (IRE)** **5** b g Emperor Jones (USA) -Simply Times (USA) (Dodge (USA)) (1471) 2021[4] 3308[6] 3552a[5] 4889[2] 5289[8] (5832) 6463a[8] >**89a 111f**<

**Welsh Empress** **3** b f Bahamian Bounty-Azola (IRE) (Alzao (USA)) 1467[7] 2176[3] 2820[10] 5072[10] 5260[12] 5794[15] >**34f**<

**Welsh Galaxy (IRE)** **2** b f Pennekamp (USA) -Jamaiel (IRE) (Polish Precedent (USA)) 4023[10] 4851[17] 5227[13] 5407[10] 5721[10] >**10a 48f**<

**Welsh Main** **7** br g Zafonic (USA) -Welsh Daylight (Welsh Pageant) 3743[9] >**66f**<

**Welsh Whisper** **5** b m Overbury (IRE) -Grugiar (Red Sunset) 442[7] 562[7] 730[4] 945[8] 994[7] 1076[5] 1510[6]1573[6] (1890) 2017[3] 2359[9] 2664[9] >**45a 32f**<

**Welsh Wind (IRE)** **8** b g Tenby-Bavaria (Top Ville) 464[3] 602[2] 700[12] 765[3] (926) 962[9] 1097[4] 2121[9] >**65a 65f**<

**Wembury Point (IRE)** **2** gr c Monashee Mountain (USA) -Lady Celina (FR) (Crystal Palace (FR)) 4219[9] 4747[10] 5347[11] 5447[6] 5738[13] 6181[9] 6392[5] >**58a 54f**<

**Wendy s Girl (IRE)** **3** b f Ashkalani (IRE) -Mrs Evans (IRE) (College Chapel) 1008[7] 1119[8] 1266[5] 1478[2] 1676[P] 1934[4] 2620[7] (2942)3234[12] (3624) 3838[6] 4247[5] 4608[5] 4929[3] 5040[3] >**63a 64f**<

**Wensum Dancer** **7** b m Shareef Dancer (USA) -Burning Ambition (Troy) 2102a[9] >**89f**<

**We Re Stonybroke (IRE)** **5** b g College Chapel-Mokaite (Komaite (USA)) 3911[19] >**50a 78df**<

**Wessex (USA)** **4** ch g Gone West (USA) -Satin Velvet (USA) (El Gran Senor (USA)) 1772[15] 2366[6] 2781[8] 3079[7] 4008[5] 4258[9] 5544[11] 5798[8] >**89f**<

**Westborough (IRE)** **3** ch g Woodborough (USA) -Filey Brigg (Weldnaas (USA)) 2040[2] 2353[5] 2815[8] 3234[5] 3739[2] 4021[7] 4929[8] 5104[6]5342[7] 5547[2] 5845[9] (6009) (6114) >**38a 68f**<

**Westbrook Blue** **2** b c Kingsinger (IRE) -Gold And Blue (IRE) (Bluebird (USA)) 1105[3] (1264) 4041[3] 4514[4] 4875[6] >**71a 78f**<

**West Country (UAE)** **3** br c Gone West (USA) -Crystal Gazing (USA) (El Gran Senor (USA)) 709a[4] 753a[3] 1129[18] 1760[8] 2870[4] >**82f**<

**Westcourt Dream** **4** ch f Bal Harbour-Katie s Kitty (Noble Patriarch) 2757[3] (3008) 3250[8] 5320[6] 5546[14] 6201[8] >**53f**<

**West End Wonder (IRE)** **5** b g Idris (IRE) -Miss Plum (Ardross) 3297[15] 4417[4] 4819[7] >**43f**<

**Wester Lodge (IRE)** **2** ch c Fraam-Reamzafonic (Grand Lodge (USA)) 5373[9] 6091[2] 6440[8] >**75f**<

**Western (IRE)** **4** ch g Gone West (USA) -Madame Est Sortie (FR) (Longleat (USA)) 413[2] 523[14] 899[9] 3752[11] 4441[11] 4849[12] 5875[12] 6083[18]6450[10] >**81a 78f**<

**Western Bluebird (IRE)** **6** b g Bluebird (USA) -Arrastra (Bustino) 1866[6] 2171[4] 2462[11] 3363[2] 3576[7] >**46f**<

**Western Command (GER)** **8** b g Saddlers Hall (IRE) -Western Friend (USA) (Gone West (USA)) 434[10] 455[8] 497[4] 581[5] 589[6] 727[6] 783[8]945[5] 1026[11] 1042[9] 1193[5] 1238[5] 1448[3] 1572[3]1630[5] 1888[9] 2230[5] 2851[2] 3281[6] 3712[7] 3799[8]4189[6] >**45a**<

**Western Devil (IRE)** **4** b c Dr Devious (IRE) -Western Sal (Salse (USA)) 1779a[5] 2320a[5] >**100f**<

**Western Diplomat (USA)** **4** bb c Gone West (USA) -Dabaweyaa (IRE) (Shareef Dancer (USA)) 850a[2] >**105f**<

**Westerner** **5** b h Danehill (USA) -Walensee (Troy) (1578a) 2337a[2] 2998[2] 3567a[9] (5503a) (5976a) (6382a) >**123f**<

**Westernmost** **6** b g Most Welcome-Dakota Girl (Northern State (USA)) 3518[12] >**20f**<

**Western Ridge (FR)** **7** b g Darshaan-Helvellyn (USA) (Gone West (USA)) 1858[8] 3488[P] >**64a 50f**<

**Western Roots** **3** ch g Dr Fong (USA) -Chrysalis (Soviet Star (USA)) 557[2] 843[4] 985[8] 1322[7] 2239[6] (2545) 3039[5] 3271[5] 4142[9]5381[11] 5955[12] 6157[2] 6461[16] >**85a 81f**<

**Westfalenkrone (GER)** **3** b f Mondrian (GER) -

Westindia (GER) (Dashing Blade) 6509a$^{7}$ ><

**Westfield Boy 2** b c Unfuwain (USA) -Pick Of The Pops (High Top) 6187$^{20}$ 6565$^{12}$ >**46f**<

**West Highland Way (IRE) 3** b g Foxhound (USA) -Gilding The Lily (IRE) (High Estate) (2289) 3017$^{5}$ 5582$^{9}$ *6480$^{5}$* >**71a 80f**<

**Westlake Bond (IRE) 2** b f Josr Algarhoud (IRE) -Rania (Aragon) 6196$^{5}$ 6569$^{2}$ >**63f**<

**Westland (USA) 2** gr c Cozzene (USA) -Cherie Yvonne (USA) (Vice Regent (CAN)) 6342$^{2}$ (6563) >**79+f**<

**Westmead Etoile 4** b f Unfuwain (USA) -Glossary (Reference Point) *535$^{9}$ 737$^{3}$ 1278$^{10}$ 1889$^{7}$* 1986$^{10}$ *2229$^{3}$* >**39a 43f**<

**Westmead Tango 4** b f Pursuit Of Love-Tango Teaser (Shareef Dancer (USA)) *519$^{6}$ 538$^{6}$ 859$^{11}$ 1280$^{7}$* >**52a 54f**<

**Westmoreland Road (USA) 4** b g Diesis-Tia Gigi (USA) (Assert) 3315$^{2}$ 3912$^{2}$ 5251$^{4}$ 5611$^{7}$ >**112f**<

**West Order (USA) 6** ch h Gone West (USA) -Irish Order (USA) (Irish River (FR)) *688a$^{12}$ 974a$^{8}$* >**76a 72f**<

**Wethaab (USA) 7** b g Pleasant Colony (USA) -Binntastic (USA) (Lyphard s Wish (FR)) *1091$^{8}$ 1194$^{8}$ 1511$^{5}$ 1572$^{6}$* 1593$^{9}$ >**43a 29f**<

**Wet Lips (AUS) 6** ch g Grand Lodge (USA) -Kissing (AUS) (Somalia (AUS)) 4831$^{13}$ >**58f**<

**Whaleef 6** br g Darshaan-Wilayif (USA) (Danzig (USA)) 5006$^{2}$ >**78a 83f**<

**What-A-Dancer (IRE) 7** b g Dancing Dissident (USA) -Cool Gales (Lord Gayle (USA)) *770$^{4}$ 1056$^{3}$ (1065)* 1317$^{4}$ 2366$^{8}$ 2469$^{4}$ 2838$^{4}$ 3409$^{9}$ 4122$^{6}$4220$^{5}$ 4553$^{4}$ 4577$^{6}$ >**94a 86 f**<

**Whatatodo 2** b f Compton Place-Emerald Dream (IRE) (Vision (USA)) 2300$^{7}$ 2730$^{3}$ 3080$^{8}$ (3987) 4089$^{2}$ 5119$^{14}$ 5548$^{4}$ 6174$^{12}$ >**70f**<

**Whatsheworth 2** b g Pyramus (USA) -Princess Aurora (Prince Sabo) 2502$^{10}$ 2725$^{6}$ ><

**What s Up Doc (IRE) 3** b c Dr Massini (IRE) -Surprise Treat (IRE) (Shalford (IRE)) (2250) 2578$^{6}$ >**85 f**<

**Whazzat 2** b f Daylami (IRE) -Wosaita (Generous (IRE)) (2786) (3071) >**103f**<

**Whenwillitwin 3** b g Bluegrass Prince (IRE) -Madam Marash (IRE) (Astronef) 3574$^{6}$ 3809$^{6}$ 4065$^{7}$ >**53f**<

**Where With All (IRE) 2** b c Montjeu (IRE) -Zelding (IRE) (Warning) (2651) 3071$^{7}$ (3983) >**94+f**<

**Whilly (IRE) 3** b c Sri Pekan (USA) -Santa Rosa (IRE) (Lahib (USA)) 1777a$^{6}$ 2510a$^{8}$ >**106f**<

**Whinhill House 4** ch g Paris House-Darussalam (Tina s Pet) 2936$^{16}$ 3010$^{19}$ 4782$^{18}$ 6059$^{3}$ 6229$^{12}$ >**61a 55f**<

**Whiplash (IRE) 3** b g Orpen (USA) -La Colombari (ITY) (Lomond (USA)) 1274$^{12}$ 1296$^{4}$ 1997$^{18}$ (2061) 3180$^{18}$ *3932$^{6}$ 4128$^{10}$* 4546$^{12}$ 4674$^{6}$5072$^{13}$ 5794$^{9}$ >**25a 39f**<

**Whippasnapper 4** b g Cayman Kai (IRE) -Give Us A Treat (Cree Song) *488$^{10}$ (596) 617$^{2}$ (646) 701$^{3}$ 742$^{9}$* 1504$^{2}$ (1608) 1642$^{8}$1929$^{3}$ 2215$^{2}$ 2292$^{2}$ 2492$^{7}$ 4280$^{10}$ *4602$^{11}$* 4877$^{4}$ 5425$^{13}$6001$^{13}$ *6026$^{6}$* >**73a 73f**<

**Whipper (USA) 3** b c Miesque s Son (USA) -Myth To Reality (FR) (Sadler s Wells (USA)) (1289a) 1764$^{5}$ 4595a$^{2}$ (4795a) 5332a$^{5}$ 6486a$^{10}$ >**124f**<

**Whirling 2** ch f Groom Dancer (USA) -Supersonic (Shirley Heights) 6111$^{8}$ *6479$^{11}$* >**27a 36f**<

**Whirly Bird 3** b f Nashwan (USA) -Inchyre (Shirley Heights) 6285$^{3}$ *(6481)* >**68+a 53f**<

**Whispered Promises (USA) 3** b g Real Quiet (USA) -Anna s Honor (USA) (Alleged (USA)) 2018$^{12}$ 3207$^{3}$ 3678$^{8}$ 4177$^{5}$ >**87f**<

**Whispering Death 2** br c Pivotal-Lucky Arrow (Indian Ridge) 6171$^{23}$ 6330$^{11}$ 6440$^{11}$ >**37f**<

**Whispering Valley 4** ch f The West (USA) -Taciturn (USA) (Tasso (USA)) 4028$^{12}$ 4513$^{9}$ 4972$^{9}$ 5658$^{15}$ 5830$^{15}$ >**51f**<

**Whist Drive 4** ch g First Trump-Fine Quill (Unfuwain (USA)) 1302$^{6}$ >**65f**<

**Whistful (IRE) 3** b f First Trump-Atmospheric Blues (IRE) (Double Schwartz) 1464$^{3}$ 1907$^{9}$ 2741$^{3}$ 3158$^{5}$ 3680$^{11}$ 4707$^{4}$ 5737$^{8}$ 6009$^{4}$ >**73f**<

**Whistler 7** ch g Selkirk (USA) -French Gift (Cadeaux Genereux) 1131$^{12}$ 1774$^{17}$ 2130$^{9}$ 2274$^{3}$ 2490$^{7}$ (2628) 2754$^{7}$ 2912$^{3}$ (3243) 3339$^{7}$(3480) 3723$^{4}$ 4165$^{15}$ 4366$^{3}$ 4538$^{4}$ 5287$^{15}$ 5393$^{4}$ 5787$^{2}$ 6177$^{6}$6243$^{5}$ >**97f**<

**Whistling Along 2** b c Atraf-Forest Song (Forzando) 1505$^{8}$ 1751$^{6}$ 2141$^{10}$ 4191$^{8}$ >**36f**<

**Whitbarrow (IRE) 5** b g Royal Abjar (USA) -Danccini (IRE) (Dancing Dissident (USA)) 1438$^{5}$ 1923$^{12}$ 2041$^{12}$ (2222) 2488$^{7}$ 2679$^{7}$ 3074$^{14}$ 3266$^{9}$ 3723$^{8}$4165$^{9}$ 4324$^{21}$ 5181$^{13}$ 5287$^{7}$ 5393$^{5}$ 5553$^{4}$ 5787$^{9}$ 5933$^{9}$6243$^{3}$ 6349$^{2}$ >**71a 99f**<

**Whitcomb (USA) 4** br c Skip Away (USA) -Whitebread (USA) (Grand Zar (MEX)) *2163a$^{14}$* ><

**White Hawk 3** b c Silver Hawk (USA) -Polska (USA) (Danzig (USA)) 1439$^{4}$ 1900$^{12}$ 2295$^{16}$ >**96 a 80f**<

**White Ledger (IRE) 5** ch g Ali-Royal (IRE) -Boranwood (IRE) (Exhibitioner) *3025$^{12}$ 3615$^{11}$* 4509$^{3}$ (4701) (4923) 5157$^{8}$ 6186$^{6}$ *6274$^{2}$* >**75a 63+f**<

**White O Morn 5** gr m Petong-I m Your Lady (Risk Me (FR)) *541$^{11}$ 638$^{4}$ 718$^{2}$ 898$^{4}$ (944) 1075$^{9}$ 1886$^{2}$ 2183$^{12}$*2350$^{4}$ 2778$^{10}$ 4854$^{7}$ >**37a 44f**<

**White Park Bay (IRE) 4** b f Blues Traveller (IRE) -Valiant Friend (USA) (Shahrastani (USA)) *431$^{5}$* 3809$^{2}$ *4189$^{12}$* 5056$^{6}$ >**62a 58f**<

**White Sail 3** b f Polar Falcon (USA) -Felucca (Green Desert (USA)) 2596$^{11}$ >**32f**<

**White Star Magic 2** ch c Bluegrass Prince (IRE) -Bless (Beveled (USA)) 4900$^{7}$ 5083$^{9}$ 5341$^{6}$ *6276$^{4}$* >**55a 63f**<

**Whitgift Rock 3** b c Piccolo-Fly South (Polar Falcon (USA)) *(466) 1120$^{2}$* 1392$^{13}$ 2536$^{7}$ 2847$^{7}$ 3230$^{3}$ 3535$^{2}$ 3872$^{10}$ *5220$^{7}$*5403$^{12}$ *5739$^{12}$* >**77a 73f**<

**Whitkirk Star (IRE) 3** b g Alhaarth (IRE) -Three Stars (Star Appeal) 4679$^{6}$ 6519$^{8}$ ><

**Whitland 2** b g Namaqualand (USA) -Whittle Rock (Rock City) 4681$^{14}$ 5534$^{8}$ 5792$^{9}$ >**55f**<

**Whitsbury Cross 3** b c Cape Cross (IRE) -Vallauris (Faustus (USA)) 1461$^{5}$ 2113$^{5}$ (2729) 3000$^{11}$ 3543$^{4}$ 4061$^{3}$ 4749$^{5}$ >**90+f**<

**Whittinghamvillage 3** b f Whittingham (IRE) -Shaa Spin (Shaadi (USA)) *408$^{6}$* >**35a 54f**<

**Whittle Warrior 4** b g Averti (IRE) -Polish Descent (IRE) (Danehill (USA)) 5526$^{14}$ >**43a 74f**<

**Who Cares Wins 8** ch g Kris-Anne Bonny (Ajdal (USA)) 6231$^{9}$ >**13f**<

**Whole Grain 3** b f Polish Precedent (USA) -Mill Line (Mill Reef (USA)) 3204$^{4}$ >**72f**<

**Whoopsie 2** b f Unfuwain (USA) -Oops Pettie (Machiavellian (USA)) 5396$^{9}$ 5846$^{16}$ 6336$^{11}$ >**35f**<

**Whortleberry (FR) 4** ch f Starborough-Rotina (FR) (Crystal Glitters (USA)) 1922a$^{4}$ 2543a$^{4}$ 4566a$^{6}$ (4982a) 5501a$^{9}$ 5978a$^{6}$ >**115f**<

**Who s Winning (IRE) 3** ch g Docksider (USA) -Quintellina (Robellino (USA)) 1388$^{18}$ 2131$^{8}$ 2726$^{6}$ 3089$^{8}$ 3338$^{2}$ (4434) 5253$^{2}$ (5473) (5697) *6496$^{7}$* >**77a 88f**<

**Why Dubai (USA) 3** br f Kris S (USA) -Highest Goal (USA) (Slew O Gold (USA)) 1327$^{8}$ 4230$^{6}$ 4773$^{6}$ 5416$^{10}$ >**91f**<

**Why Harry 2** b g Cyrano De Bergerac-Golden Ciel (USA) (Septieme Ciel (USA)) *1264$^{3}$* 1415$^{7}$ (1556) 1970$^{6}$ 2194$^{6}$ >**65a 58f**<

**Wicked Uncle 5** b g Distant Relative-The Kings Daughter (Indian King (USA)) 2628$^{10}$ 2754$^{9}$ (3407) >**87f**<

**Wiggy Smith 5** ch g Master Willie-Monsoon (Royal Palace) 1671$^{5}$ 2110$^{17}$ (5183) 6444$^{2}$ >**57a 91f**<

**Wigman (USA) 4** b f Rahy (USA) -Urjwan (USA) (Seattle Slew (USA)) 2138a$^{13}$ 3137a$^{6}$ >**87f**<

**Wigmo Princess 5** ch m Factual (USA) -Queen Of Shannon (IRE) (Nordico (USA)) *777$^{11}$* >**41a 41f**<

**Wigwam Willie (IRE) 2** b g Indian Rocket-Sweet Nature (IRE) (Classic Secret (USA)) 4149$^{4}$ 4804$^{5}$ 5125$^{2}$ 5434$^{19}$ >**75f**<

**Wild Angel (IRE) 3** br f Acatenango (GER) -World s Vision (GER) (Platini (GER)) 4980a$^{8}$ >**89f**<

**Wild Daughter 2** ch f Bachir (IRE) -Wild Woman (Polar Falcon (USA)) 5330a$^{6}$ >**48f**<

**Wildest Dream (IRE) 5** br h Zafonic (USA) -Bedside Story (Mtoto) 6512a$^{10}$ >**101f**<

**Wild Pitch 3** ch g Piccolo-Western Horizon (USA) (Gone West (USA)) *598$^{7}$* 2001$^{12}$ 2400$^{3}$ 3160$^{12}$ 3556$^{6}$ >**57a 66f**<

**Wild Power (GER) 6** b g Turtle Island (IRE) -White On Red (GER) (Konigsstuhl (GER)) 5258$^{4}$ 5546$^{2}$ 5714$^{4}$ >**63f**<

**Wild Tide 5** b m Runnett-Polly Two (Reesh) 3587$^{16}$ 4257$^{7}$ 4509$^{7}$ 4825$^{9}$ 5305$^{10}$ >**33f**<

**Wild Wild Wes 4** ch g The West (USA) -Dam Certain (IRE) (Damister (USA)) *651$^{15}$ 871$^{13}$* ><

**Wilford Maverick (IRE) 2** b c Fasliyev (USA) -Lioness (Lion Cavern (USA)) 3051$^{7}$ *3802$^{9}$* 4048$^{13}$ *5954$^{10}$* >**32a 60f**<

**Wilfred (IRE) 3** b g Desert King (IRE) -Kharaliya (FR) (Doyoun) 1509$^{7}$ 2179$^{8}$ >**67f**<

**Wilful 4** ch c Bering-Prickwillow (USA) (Nureyev (USA)) 633a$^{8}$ 690a$^{11}$ *754a$^{8}$* >**68a 105f**<

**Wilheheckaslike 3** b g Wizard King-La Ciotat (IRE) (Gallic League) *1024$^{8}$* 1171$^{8}$ *1699$^{9}$* 2389$^{6}$ 4350$^{17}$ 4561$^{6}$ >**4a 45f**<

**Wilko (USA) 2** ch c Awesome Again (CAN) -Native Roots (IRE) (Indian Ridge) 1826$^{3}$ 2045$^{7}$ (2592) 3071$^{3}$ 3672$^{3}$ 4227$^{2}$ (4461) 4716$^{2}$ 5437$^{4}$ 5778$^{3}$*(6489a)* >**120a 112 f**<

**Willheconquertoo 4** ch g Primo Dominie-Sure Care (Caerleon (USA)) *1935$^{8}$* 2703$^{15}$ 3043$^{3}$ 3439$^{5}$ (3593) 3810$^{9}$ 4614$^{14}$ 4811$^{5}$ 5337$^{4}$*6026$^{4}$ 6066$^{13}$ 6539$^{4}$ 6577$^{2}$* >**72a 78f**<

**Willhego 3** ch g Pivotal-Woodrising (Nomination) 1906$^{9}$ 2356$^{8}$ *2484$^{2}$ 4128$^{3}$* (5057) *5914$^{5}$* 6271$^{13}$ *6495$^{8}$* >**62a 66f**<

**Will He Wish 8** b g Winning Gallery-More To Life (Northern Tempest (USA)) 1126$^{12}$ *1242$^{8}$* 1353$^{5}$ 1610$^{6}$ 1758$^{7}$ 2283$^{18}$ 2857$^{10}$ 3036$^{12}$3755$^{13}$ (4067) 4442$^{3}$ 4690$^{6}$ 5194$^{2}$ 5462$^{11}$ 5769$^{7}$ >**87a 97f**<

**Willhewiz 4** b c Wizard King-Leave It To Lib (Tender King) 1113$^{13}$ 1454$^{5}$ 2094$^{6}$ 2467$^{7}$ (2843) (3090) 3324$^{13}$ 3453$^{8}$ 4232$^{16}$ 4742$^{13}$5071$^{4}$ 5299$^{17}$ 5564$^{10}$ *6066$^{2}$ 6482$^{9}$* >**79a 80f**<

**William Conqueror (ITY) 2** br c Reckless William (IRE) -Diffidente (USA) (Al Nasr (FR)) 5389a$^{9}$ ><

**William James 2** b g Mujahid (USA) -Pain Perdu (IRE) (Waajib) 4815$^{5}$ 5179$^{11}$ *5954$^{6}$* >**39a 50f**<

**William s Well 10** ch g Superpower-Catherines Well (Junius (USA)) 1526$^{10}$ 1974$^{12}$ 2581$^{9}$ 3446$^{5}$ 4130$^{13}$ 4542$^{6}$ 5126$^{3}$ 5346$^{3}$5579$^{16}$ 6007$^{5}$ >**70df**<

**William Tell (IRE) 2** b c Rossini (USA) -Livry (USA) (Lyphard (USA)) 3939$^{6}$ 4689$^{4}$ 5256$^{5}$ 5539$^{2}$ 6072$^{2}$ 6197$^{2}$ >**79f**<

**Willingly (GER) 5** b h Second Set (IRE) -Winara (GER) (Konigsstuhl (GER)) 3134a$^{8}$ 3972a$^{7}$ >**101f**<

**Willjojo 3** b f Mind Games-Millie s Lady (IRE) (Common Grounds) 1196$^{3}$ 2351$^{5}$ *2849$^{4}$* (3229) (3622) 3798$^{5}$ >**49a 61f**<

**Willofcourse 3** b g Aragon-Willyet (Nicholas Bill) 2211$^{9}$ >**72+f**<

**Will The Till 2** b g Fraam-Prim Ajwaad (Bin Ajwaad (IRE)) 4474$^{11}$ 5825$^{9}$ 6145$^{17}$ >**52f**<

**Willyever 10** b g Merdon Melody-Stonebroker (Morston (FR)) *807$^{9}$* >**61f**<

**Wilom (GER) 6** ch g Lomitas-Whispering Willows (Mansingh (USA)) *468$^{2}$ 535$^{5}$ 662$^{4}$ 787$^{5}$ 855$^{8}$ 1166$^{9}$ 1278$^{12}$*1863$^{6}$ >**46a 19 f**<

**Wilson Bluebottle (IRE) 5** ch g Priolo (USA) -Mauras Pride (IRE) (Cadeaux Genereux) *425$^{6}$ (814) 939$^{8}$ 1079$^{2}$ 1233$^{2}$ 1479$^{10}$ 2128$^{8}$* 2551$^{12}$4005$^{9}$ *4185$^{6}$ 4925$^{6}$* >**53a 53f**<

**Wiltshire (IRE) 2** br c Spectrum (IRE) -Mary Magdalene (Night Shift (USA)) 4922$^{12}$ 5059$^{13}$ 5302$^{10}$ 5567$^{8}$ (5746) 5910$^{14}$ 6093$^{3}$ >**58f**<

**Win Alot 6** b g Aragon-Having Fun (Hard Fought) 6527$^{10}$ >**54 a 56f**<

**Wind Chime (IRE) 7** ch h Arazi (USA) -Shamisen (Diesis) *623$^{7}$ 929$^{2}$ 1019$^{11}$* (3127) 3626$^{3}$ 4327$^{11}$ 5493$^{7}$ *6580$^{7}$* >**55a 76f**<

**Windermere (IRE) 5** b h Lear Fan (USA) -Madame L Enjoleur (USA) (L Enjoleur (CAN)) (2416a) 3076$^{12}$ >**113f**<

**Windermere Island 2** b f Cadeaux Genereux-Corndavon (USA) (Sheikh Albadou) 4494$^{4}$ >**66f**<

**Windscreamer 2** b f Josr Algarhoud (IRE) -St James s Antigua (IRE) (Law Society (USA)) (3905) 4552$^{6}$ 5413$^{7}$ >**90f**<

**Winds Of March (IRE) 3** b f Sadler s Wells (USA) -Alidiva (Chief Singer) (1440) 2081$^{4}$ >**95f**<

**Winds Of Time (IRE) 2** b f Danehill (USA) -Windmill (Ezzoud (IRE)) (3675) >**81f**<

**Windsor Beauty (IRE) 6** bb g Woods Of Windsor (USA) -Tumble Dale (Tumble Wind) 1520$^{7}$ >**75f**<

**Windsor Knot (IRE) 2** ch c Pivotal-Triple Tie (USA) (The Minstrel (CAN)) 4030$^{4}$ (4523) (4949) >**108f**<

**Windwood (IRE) 2** b c Piccolo-Presently (Cadeaux Genereux) 5441$^{8}$ 5825$^{7}$ *6022$^{5}$* >**53a 58f**<

**Windy Britain 5** b m Mark Of Esteem (IRE) -For My Love (Kahyasi) 2474$^{12}$ 3091$^{4}$ 3694$^{2}$ 4214$^{6}$ 4540$^{8}$ 5025$^{7}$ (5576a) 6381a$^{7}$ >**96a 98f**<

**Windy Prospect 2** ch c Intikhab (USA) -Yellow Ribbon (IRE) (Hamas (IRE)) *1060$^{3}$* 1105$^{5}$ 1865$^{2}$ *(2453)* 2996$^{7}$ 4278$^{3}$ 4330$^{2}$ 4575$^{2}$ *(4878)* (5670) >**89a 99f**<

**Wing Collar 3** b g In The Wings-Riyoom (USA) (Vaguely Noble) 1416$^{11}$ 1995$^{3}$ 2390$^{3}$ 2774$^{2}$ 3561$^{8}$ 4627$^{4}$ 5245$^{3}$ (5560) 6198$^{2}$ >**78+f**<

**Wing Commander 5** b g Royal Applause-Southern Psychic (USA) (Alwasmi (USA)) 1125$^{4}$ 1286$^{3}$ 2503$^{9}$ 2969$^{14}$ 3756$^{8}$ (4178) 4287$^{16}$ 4528$^{3}$ 4856$^{7}$5401$^{5}$ 5627$^{7}$ 5941$^{21}$ >**102f**<

**Winged D Argent (IRE) 3** b c In The Wings-Petite-D-Argent (Noalto) (1285) 1588$^{5}$ (6143) (6335) 6534$^{2}$ >**102+f**<

**Wingman (IRE) 2** b c In The Wings-Precedence (IRE) (Polish Precedent (USA)) 4523$^{10}$ 5228$^{5}$ (5729) 6262a$^{3}$ >**92f**<

**Wings Of Glory (GER) 2** br f Monsun (GER) -Wishing Joy (IRE) (Alzao (USA)) 6377a$^{4}$ >**93f**<

**Wings Of Morning (IRE) 3** ch g Fumo Di Londra (IRE) -Hay Knot (Main Reef) *(613) 758$^{5}$ 900$^{6}$* 1392$^{3}$ 2448$^{11}$ *3280$^{7}$* 4631$^{3}$ *4879$^{4}$*5552$^{11}$ *6537$^{12}$* >**76a 69f**<

**Wingspeed (IRE) 2** b g Bluebird (USA) -Aneeda (Rainbow Quest (USA)) 4743$^{5}$ 5420$^{2}$ 5747$^{4}$ >**77f**<

**Winisk River (IRE) 4** b c Barathea (IRE) -Brisighella (IRE) (Al Hareb (USA)) *(830a)* (1001a) >**100+a 109f**<

**Winners Delight 3** ch g First Trump-Real Popcorn (IRE) (Jareer (USA)) 1134$^{8}$ 1357$^{9}$ 2557$^{5}$ 3046$^{5}$ 3543$^{3}$ 3915$^{7}$ 4749$^{8}$ 5572$^{3}$5944$^{6}$ *(6396)* >**88a 86f**<

**Winning Belle (NZ) 4** b f Zabeel (NZ) -Kirin Belle (NZ) (Mcginty (NZ)) 6528a$^{17}$ >**103f**<

**Winning Dash (GER) 4** b c Dashing Blade-Wonderful Lady (GER) (Surumu (GER)) 1259a$^{3}$ 2508a$^{6}$ 3972a$^{3}$ >**110f**<

**Winning Pleasure (IRE) 6** b g Ashkalani (IRE) -Karamana (Habitat) *515$^{6}$* >**89da 68 f**<

**Winning Venture 7** b g Owington-Push A Button (Bold Lad (IRE)) 1354$^{6}$ 1765$^{21}$ 3299$^{3}$ 4006$^{2}$ 4220$^{7}$ 4931$^{7}$ 5177$^{2}$ 5614$^{8}$*6277$^{10}$* 6477$^{18}$ >**72a 97 f**<

**Win Radius (JPN) 6** b h Sunday Silence (USA) -Jono Matiere (JPN) (Maruzensky (JPN)) 5982a$^{4}$ >**112f**<

**Winslow Boy (USA) 3** bb g Expelled (USA) -Acusteal (USA) (Acaroid (USA)) 1466$^{8}$ 2199$^{4}$ 2402$^{6}$ (2822) 3479$^{2}$ 4146$^{6}$ 4692$^{3}$ 5159$^{6}$ 5817$^{6}$6110$^{2}$ >**19a 65f**<

**Winslow Homer (FR) 3** b c Peintre Celebre (USA) -Armorique (IRE) (Top Ville) 5007$^{10}$ >**14f**<

**Winter Mist 2** gr f Tomba-Misty Goddess (IRE) (Godswalk (USA)) 3444$^{17}$ *4599$^{9}$* 5349$^{11}$ 6565$^{15}$ >**14a 9f**<

**Winter Moon 2** b f Mujadil (USA) -Crofters Ceilidh (Scottish Reel) 3992$^{9}$ >**46f**<

**Winthorpe (IRE) 4** b g Tagula (IRE) -Zazu (Cure The Blues (USA)) *515$^{10}$ 607$^{10}$* 1106$^{12}$ 1361$^{10}$ 1825$^{16}$ 2461$^{4}$ 2899$^{17}$ 3314$^{3}$3509$^{2}$ 3645$^{16}$ 3920$^{5}$ 4133$^{4}$ 4211$^{4}$ 5526$^{3}$ 5798$^{15}$ 6046$^{6}$ >**68a 81+f**<

**Wise Dennis 2** b g Polar Falcon (USA) -Bowden Rose (Dashing Blade) 2225$^{7}$ 3438$^{10}$ 4494$^{3}$ *5052$^{3}$* 5292$^{3}$ (5810) 6268$^{2}$ >**77a 96f**<

**Wise Owl 2** b c Danehill (USA) -Mistle Thrush (USA) (Storm Bird (CAN)) 2898$^{2}$ 5118$^{4}$ (5752) 6042$^{14}$ >**82+f**<

**Wise Wager (IRE) 2** b f Titus Livius (FR) -Londubh (Tumble Wind) *2002$^{2}$* 2933$^{3}$ 3583$^{3}$ 4150$^{3}$ (4348) 4752$^{2}$ 4875$^{2}$ 5515$^{7}$ >**72a 81f**<

**Wistman (UAE) 3** br c Woodman (USA) -Saik (USA) (Riverman (USA)) (1295) 1558$^{3}$ >**86f**<

**Witches Broom 3** b f Fraam-Carte Blanche (Cadeaux Genereux) *1227$^{8}$* 4125$^{3}$ 4644$^{6}$ 5219$^{16}$ >**14a 59f**<

**Witching 3** b f Hector Protector (USA) -Charming Life (Habitat) 4057$^{6}$ >**22f**<

**Witchry 2** b g Green Desert (USA) -Indian Skimmer (USA) (Storm Bird (CAN)) 2111$^{4}$ 2502$^{3}$ (4175) 4752$^{7}$ >**84+f**<

**Witchy Vibes 2** ch f Tomba-Risk The Witch (Risk Me (FR)) 5771$^{14}$ 6060$^{13}$ ><

**Withering Lady (IRE) 2** b f Tagula (IRE) -Princess Oberon (IRE) (Fairy King (USA)) 1364$^{3}$ 1686$^{4}$ 2205$^{6}$ 3208$^{2}$ 3938$^{7}$ (4212) 4612$^{8}$ 5068$^{5}$ 5839$^{4}$ >**77f**<

**With Honours 2** b f Bien Bien (USA) -Fair Test (Fair Season) 6521$^{7}$ >**8f**<

**Withorwithoutyou (IRE) 3** b f Danehill (USA) -Morningsurprice (USA) (Future Storm (USA)) 1211$^{6}$ 1417$^{5}$ 1685$^{14}$ 3105$^{10}$ 3602$^{8}$ >**89f**<

**Without Connexion (IRE) 5** b h Rainbow Quest (USA) -Flabbergasted (IRE) (Sadler s Wells (USA)) 3030a$^{8}$ (5970a) 6260a$^{7}$ >**113f**<

**Without Notice (USA) 4** br c Judge T C (USA) -Shaa Wing (USA) (Shadeed (USA)) *1953a$^{8}$* ><

**With Reason (USA) 6** ch g Nashwan (USA) -Just Cause (Law Society (USA)) 2109$^{13}$ (5291) >**93a 116f**<

**Witten (USA) 2** b f Fusaichi Pegasus (USA) -Word O Ransom (USA) (Red Ransom (USA)) (6169a) >**104f**<

**Wittily 4** ch f Whittingham (IRE) -Lucky Dip (Tirol) *499$^{13}$* >**35 a 52f**<

**Witty Girl 2** b f Whittingham (IRE) -Zando s Charm (Forzando) 3140$^{3}$ 3390$^{4}$ 4099$^{11}$ >**46f**<

**Witwatersrand (IRE) 2** b f Unfuwain (USA) -Valley Of Gold (FR) (Shirley Heights) 5694$^{4}$ >**69+f**<

**Wizard Looking 3** b g Wizard King-High Stepping (IRE) (Taufan (USA)) 2304$^{6}$ 2536$^{10}$ 2790$^{16}$ 3271$^{6}$ *3932$^{7}$* 4018$^{7}$ >**41a 41f**<

**Wizardmicktee (IRE) 2** b c Monashee Mountain (USA) -Epsilon (Environment Friend) 3925$^{8}$ 4359$^{2}$ 4761$^{2}$ 4933$^{4}$ 5060$^{8}$ 6544$^{16}$ >**73f**<

**Wizard Of Edge 4** b g Wizard King-Forever Shineing (Glint Of Gold) *463$^{6}$* 4080$^{8}$ 4719$^{4}$ >**71a 69f**<

**Wizard Of Noz 4** b g Inchinor-Winning Girl (Green Desert (USA)) 690a$^{2}$ 852a$^{6}$ 2969$^{22}$ 3717$^{5}$ 4273$^{5}$ 4553$^{5}$ 5099$^{5}$ (5921) 6191$^{11}$ >**107f**<

**Wizard Of The West 4** b g Wizard King-Rose Burton (Lucky Wednesday) 2501$^{9}$ 3263$^{13}$ 3667$^{9}$ >**63a 49f**<

**Wizard Of Us 4** b g Wizard King-Sian s Girl (Mystiko (USA)) (6138) *6364$^{13}$* 6548$^{2}$ >**43a 67f**<

**Wizards Princess 4** b f Wizard King-Chalice (Governor General) 4703$^{5}$ 5239$^{8}$ >**25f**<

**Wiz In 2** gr g Wizard King-Great Intent (Aragon) *5911$^{8}$ 6494$^{11}$* >**44a**<

**Wizzskilad 2** b c Wizard King-Sure Babe (Sure Blade (USA)) *1117$^{7}$* 1269$^{4}$ 1589$^{6}$ 1984$^{3}$ 2382$^{8}$ 3140$^{4}$ 4804$^{10}$ 5132$^{3}$ >**39a 52f**<

**Wodhill Be 4** b f Danzig Connection (USA) -Muarij (Star Appeal) *550$^{5}$ 982$^{6}$ 1095$^{5}$* 1373$^{9}$ 1710$^{10}$ 2209$^{3}$ 3457$^{11}$ 4066$^{13}$4568$^{8}$ 4818$^{7}$ 5408$^{7}$ 5926$^{2}$ 6229$^{8}$ >**49a 49f**<

**Wodhill Folly 7** ch m Faustus (USA) -Muarij (Star Appeal) *552$^{4}$ 655$^{6}$ 763$^{8}$* >**51a 51 f**<

**Wodhill Gold 3** ch g Dancing Spree (USA) -Golden Filigree (Faustus (USA)) 2113$^{15}$ >**38f**<

**Wodhill Hope 4** b f Distinctly North (USA) -Golden Filigree (Faustus (USA)) 2090$^{4}$ 3460$^{3}$ 4554$^{8}$ 4820$^{11}$ 5654$^{10}$ 6150$^{9}$ >**51f**<

**Wolds Dancer 2** b f Fraam-Dancing Em (Rambo Dancer (CAN)) 2141$^{6}$ 2550$^{7}$ 3009$^{7}$ >**61f**<

**Wolf Cub 3** ch g Wolfhound (USA) -Ansellady (Absalom) 1939$^{16}$ ><

**Wolf Hammer (USA) 2** ch g Diesis-Polly s Link (USA) (Phone Trick (USA)) 3560$^{7}$ 4392$^{2}$ 5084$^{2}$ >**75f**<

**Woman In White (FR) 3** gr f Daylami (IRE) -Nicer (IRE) (Pennine Walk) 1441$^{8}$ 3044$^{2}$ 3630$^{6}$ 4028$^{3}$ 4642$^{6}$ >**72f**<

**Wonder Again (USA) 5** b m Silver Hawk (USA) -Ameriflora (USA) (Danzig (USA)) 6488a$^{3}$ >**117f**<

**Wonderful Day (GER) 2** b f Kahyasi-Wonderful Dreams (GER) (Dashing Blade) 6377a$^{10}$ >**72f**<

**Wonderful Mind 2** b c Mind Games-Signs And Wonders (Danehill (USA)) 1415$^{8}$ 2686$^{5}$ 3055$^{2}$ (3469) 3753$^{5}$ 4150$^{6}$ 4875$^{3}$ 5060$^{2}$ 5515$^{13}$5797$^{5}$ 5932$^{7}$ >**73f**<

**Wonder Seattle (JPN) 5** b h Seattle Dancer (USA) -Wonder Resist (JPN) (Tosho Boy (JPN)) 5982a$^{12}$ >**100f**<

**Wonder Wolf 3** b f Wolfhound (USA) -Wrangbrook (Shirley Heights) 2908$^{7}$ 4573$^{5}$ 5587$^{9}$ >**36f**<

**Wonky Donkey 3** b g Piccolo-Salinas (Bay Express) *907$^{3}$ 1012$^{4}$ 1676$^{3}$* 2524$^{12}$ *2850$^{5}$* 3636$^{16}$ >**54a 10f**<

**Won Of A Few 4** b g Danzig Connection (USA) -Wonderful Day (Niniski (USA)) *6481$^{9}$ 6578$^{7}$* >**43a**<

**Woodbury 5** b m Woodborough (USA) -Jeewan

(Touching Wood (USA)) 917$^{7}$ 1087$^{4}$ (4026) 4403$^{16}$ 4740$^{4}$ (5337) 5512$^{7}$ 5618$^{6}$ 6273$^{2}$ 6398$^{5}$ >66a 67f<

**Woodbury Lane (USA)** 2 br f Wild Wonder (USA) -Maximum Blue (USA) (Blue Ensign (USA)) 6197$^{5}$ >55f<

**Woodcote (IRE)** 2 b c Monashee Mountain (USA) -Tootle (Main Reef) (5003) 6068$^{3}$ >100f<

**Woodcracker** 3 ch g Docksider (USA) -Hen Harrier (Polar Falcon (USA)) (1466) 2018$^{2}$ 2999$^{13}$ (3641) >104f<

**Wood Dalling (USA)** 6 b g Woodman (USA) -Cloelia (USA) (Lyphard (USA)) 2291$^{7}$ 2938$^{7}$ 3401$^{6}$ (3895) 4008$^{6}$ 4537$^{6}$ 4905$^{10}$ 5235$^{6}$ 5518$^{13}$ >54a 63f<

**Wood Fern (UAE)** 4 b g Green Desert (USA) -Woodsia (Woodman (USA)) 624$^{13}$ 1132$^{10}$ 1275$^{12}$ 1876$^{11}$ 2762$^{5}$ 3086$^{11}$ 3555$^{9}$ 3910$^{15}$ 4546$^{13}$ 4825$^{6}$ (5035) 5260$^{20}$ 5575$^{13}$ 5691$^{4}$ 5795$^{8}$ 5927$^{10}$ 6227$^{3}$ >50a 50 f<

**Woodford Consult** 2 b f Benny The Dip (USA) -Chicodove (In The Wings) 6067$^{8}$ 6291$^{10}$ 6464$^{3}$ >45a 45f<

**Woodford Wonder (IRE)** 2 b f Xaar-Unscathed (Warning) 5319$^{18}$ 5800$^{14}$ 6092$^{10}$ >27f<

**Woodland Glade** 3 b f Mark Of Esteem (IRE) -Incendio (Siberian Express (USA)) 4718$^{2}$ 5537$^{2}$ 6119$^{5}$ >76f<

**Woodsley House (IRE)** 2 b c Orpen (USA) -Flame And Shadow (IRE) (Turtle Island (IRE)) 3749$^{2}$ 4030$^{2}$ 5227$^{2}$ 6340$^{5}$ >86f<

**Wood Spirit (IRE)** 2 b f Woodborough (USA) -Windomen (IRE) (Forest Wind (USA)) 2057$^{6}$ 5536$^{6}$ 6197$^{4}$ >58f<

**Wood Sprite** 2 b f Mister Baileys-Woodbeck (Terimon) 6336$^{9}$ >22f<

**Woodstock Express** 4 b g Alflora (IRE) -Young Tess (Teenoso (USA)) 2874$^{11}$ >19f<

**Wood Street (IRE)** 5 b g Eagle Eyed (USA) -San-Catrinia (IRE) (Knesset (USA)) 2430$^{9}$ >70a 67f<

**Woodwind Down** 7 b m Piccolo-Bint El Oumara (Al Nasr (FR)) (3578) 4007$^{8}$ 5546$^{18}$ >52f<

**Woody Valentine (USA)** 3 ch g Woodman (USA) -Mudslinger (USA) (El Gran Senor (USA)) 1201$^{4}$ 1360$^{2}$ (1712) 2202$^{6}$ 2887$^{6}$ (3442) 3879$^{2}$ 4271$^{7}$ 4558$^{7}$ 5423$^{5}$ 5886$^{2}$ 6332$^{4}$ >87f<

**Woolfall Joanna** 2 gr f Petong-Real Princess (Aragon) 6171$^{19}$ 6471$^{14}$ >30f<

**Woolly Back (IRE)** 3 b g Alzao (USA) -Hopping Higgins (IRE) (Brief Truce (USA)) 1605$^{2}$ 2273$^{2}$ 2653$^{6}$ 6192$^{10}$ >81f<

**Woolsack (USA)** 2 ch c Spinning World (USA) -Rich And Famous (FR) (Deep Roots) 6331$^{5}$ 6530$^{6}$ >74f<

**Woolstone Boy (USA)** 3 ch g Will s Way (USA) -My Pleasure (USA) (Marfa (USA)) 6082$^{13}$ 6310$^{5}$ >68?f<

**Worcester Lodge** 3 ch g Grand Lodge (USA) -Borgia (Machiavellian (USA)) (4346) 4849$^{13}$ >62a 78+f<

**Word Perfect** 2 b f Diktat-Better Still (IRE) (Glenstal (USA)) 1170$^{3}$ (1415) (3868) 4757$^{5}$ 5212$^{8}$ 5606$^{5}$ 5947$^{7}$ 6042$^{3}$ 6459$^{2}$ >89f<

**Wor Kid** 2 br f Charnwood Forest (IRE) -Patience Please (King Of Spain) 3197$^{8}$ 3560$^{9}$ >35f<

**Worlaby Dale** 8 b g Terimon-Restandbethankful (Random Shot) 432$^{4}$ 568$^{4}$ 616$^{7}$ 750$^{6}$ >44a 51f<

**World At My Feet** 2 b f Wolfhound (USA) -Rehaab (Mtoto) 1449$^{2}$ (1769) 2129$^{3}$ 3753$^{9}$ 5213$^{4}$ 5626$^{9}$ 5947$^{14}$ 6204$^{4}$ 6333$^{16}$ >82f<

**World Music (USA)** 2 b f Dixieland Band (USA) -Headline (Machiavellian (USA)) 5070$^{3}$ 5911$^{6}$ >45a 67+f<

**World Report (USA)** 2 bb c Spinning World (USA) -Miss Woodchuck (USA) (Woodman (USA)) 4861$^{4}$ 5406$^{6}$ 6145$^{4}$ 6342$^{5}$ >80f<

**Worth Abbey** 2 b g Mujadil (USA) -Housefull (Habitat) 3451$^{8}$ 3588$^{10}$ 4809$^{14}$ 5609$^{8}$ >66f<

**Worth A Gamble** 6 ch g So Factual (USA) -The Strid (IRE) (Persian Bold) 3022$^{8}$ >26a 55f<

**Worth A Grand (IRE)** 2 br g Raise A Grand (IRE) -Ballykett Pride (IRE) (Indian Ridge) 3240$^{7}$ 3748$^{5}$ 4413$^{5}$ 5539$^{11}$ 5690$^{6}$ 6276$^{5}$ >42a 66f<

**Wotchalike (IRE)** 2 ch c Spectrum (IRE) -Juno Madonna (IRE) (Sadler s Wells (USA)) 4523$^{5}$ 5376$^{8}$ 5535$^{2}$ 5870$^{2}$ (6282) 6472$^{6}$ >80f<

**Wou Oodd** 3 ch f Barathea (IRE) -Abyaan (IRE) (Ela-Mana-Mou) 2060$^{4}$ 2412$^{3}$ 2841$^{5}$ 3292$^{4}$ 3746$^{13}$ >78f<

**Wrenlane** 3 ch g Fraam-Hi Hoh (IRE) (Fayruz) 2450$^{2}$ 3059$^{6}$ 3819$^{5}$ 4209$^{9}$ 4610$^{4}$ 5223$^{8}$ 5622$^{3}$ 6097$^{4}$(6271) 6483$^{3}$ (6549) >71a 70f<

**Wub Cub** 4 b f Averti (IRE) -Ray Of Hope (Rainbow Quest (USA)) 936$^{6}$ 1092$^{10}$ 1699$^{10}$ >28a 51?f<

**Wujood** 2 b c Alzao (USA) -Rahayeb (Arazi (USA)) 3913$^{7}$ 4567$^{10}$ 5347$^{7}$ 6282$^{2}$ >74f<

**Wunderbra (IRE)** 3 b f Second Empire (IRE) -Supportive (IRE) (Nashamaa) 1293$^{3}$ 2815$^{4}$ 3279$^{5}$ (4194) 4585$^{3}$ (4810) (4929) (5040) 5117$^{2}$ 5837$^{5}$ >68a 80+f<

**Wunderwood (USA)** 5 b g Faltaat (USA) -Jasoorah (IRE) (Sadler s Wells (USA)) 1401$^{9}$ 2110$^{9}$ (2691) (3075) (4163) 5465$^{3}$ 6170a$^{8}$ >74a 111+f<

**Wurfklinge (GER)** 4 br f Acatenango (GER) -Wurfbahn (GER) (Frontal) 4980a$^{9}$ >86f<

**Wuxi Venture** 9 b g Wolfhound (USA) -Push A Button (Bold Lad (IRE)) 1962$^{7}$ 2078$^{6}$ 3470$^{9}$ 4213$^{18}$ 5320$^{12}$ >67f<

**Wyatt Earp (IRE)** 3 b g Piccolo-Tribal Lady (Absalom) 1388$^{12}$ (2082) 3775$^{10}$ 5124$^{7}$ 5299$^{9}$ 5697$^{2}$ 5912$^{3}$ >81a 84f<

**Wychbury (USA)** 3 ch g Swain (IRE) -Garden Rose (IRE) (Caerleon (USA)) 2029$^{5}$ 2367$^{2}$ 2704$^{2}$ 2847$^{8}$ (4101) 4338$^{5}$ 5446$^{8}$ 5934$^{9}$ >78f<

**Wyoming** 3 ch f Inchinor-Shoshone (Be My Chief (USA)) 1939$^{3}$ 2848$^{8}$ 3231$^{8}$ 3669$^{7}$ 4971$^{3}$ 5116$^{7}$ 5993$^{3}$ >9a 62f<

**Wyvern (GER)** 3 b c Unfuwain (USA) -Wladinova (GER) (Aspros (GER)) 5371$^{8}$ >44f<

X

**Xaara Doon (IRE)** 2 b f Xaar-Hill Of Doon (IRE) (Fairy King (USA)) 6446$^{9}$ >35a<

**Xaarist (IRE)** 2 b c Xaar-Can Can Lady (Anshan) 3233$^{12}$ 4135$^{11}$ >30f<

**Xaloc Bay (IRE)** 6 br g Charnwood Forest (IRE) -Royal Jade (Last Tycoon) 439$^{2}$ 565$^{8}$ 625$^{12}$ (717) (821) 873$^{2}$ 932$^{3}$ 1032$^{6}$ 1197$^{7}$ 1629$^{3}$ 2128$^{7}$ 2454$^{6}$ 2625$^{12}$ >62a 60f<

**Xanadu** 8 ch g Casteddu-Bellatrix (Persian Bold) 1748$^{13}$ 1787$^{2}$ 2172$^{13}$ 2261$^{9}$ 2423$^{10}$ 2779$^{6}$ 2936$^{2}$ 3010$^{15}$ 3735$^{10}$ 3894$^{6}$ 4557$^{5}$ 5346$^{7}$ >61f<

**Xebec (IRE)** 2 b c Xaar-Via Camp (Kris) 6045$^{8}$ 6282$^{11}$ >53f<

**Xeeran** 2 b f Xaar-Cyclone Flyer (College Chapel) 2535$^{5}$ 2940$^{5}$ 5271$^{5}$ 5701$^{4}$ 5989$^{3}$ 6543$^{13}$ >60f<

**Xeight Express (IRE)** 2 b f Ashkalani (IRE) -Believing (Belmez (USA)) 2960$^{8}$ 3444$^{13}$ 3729$^{9}$ 5097$^{10}$ >26f<

**Xellance (IRE)** 7 b g Be My Guest (USA) -Excellent Alibi (USA) (Exceller (USA)) 2958$^{29}$ >94a 82f<

**Xixita** 4 ch f Fleetwood (IRE) -Conquista (Aragon) 446$^{6}$ 501$^{4}$ 716$^{8}$ >39a<

**Xpres Digital** 3 b c Komaite (USA) -Kustom Kit Xpres (Absalom) 1531$^{13}$ 1614$^{4}$ 1841$^{8}$ 2455$^{3}$ 3585$^{11}$ 4926$^{11}$ >75a 72f<

**Xpressions** 3 b g Turtle Island (IRE) -Make Ready (Beveled (USA)) 2199$^{6}$ 2567$^{6}$ >48f<

**Xsynna** 8 b g Cyrano De Bergerac-Rose Ciel (IRE) (Red Sunset) 465$^{3}$ 536$^{14}$ 859$^{6}$ 1021$^{7}$ 1591$^{3}$ 3575$^{10}$ 4244$^{7}$ >41a 46?f<

**Xtra Torrential (USA)** 2 b c Torrential (USA) -Offering (USA) (Majestic Light (USA)) (5227) 6189$^{4}$ >87f<

Y

**Yaahomm** 3 ch c Unfuwain (USA) -Walesiana (GER) (Star Appeal) 1442$^{3}$ (2145) 2751$^{8}$ 3610$^{7}$ >80f<

**Yaheska (IRE)** 7 b m Prince Of Birds (USA) -How Ya Been (IRE) (Last Tycoon) 6231$^{13}$ >45f<

**Yajbill (IRE)** 2 b c Royal Applause-Tee Cee (Lion Cavern (USA)) 3758$^{2}$ 4088$^{3}$ 4454$^{2}$ 4739$^{2}$ (5015) (5421) (5873) 6068$^{5}$ >99f<

**Yakimov (USA)** 5 ch g Affirmed (USA) -Ballet Troupe (USA) (Nureyev (USA)) 1065$^{11}$ 1456$^{26}$ 1828$^{14}$ 2575$^{10}$ >77 a 77 f<

**Yallambie** 5 b m Revoque (IRE) -Tahnee (Cadeaux Genereux) 1590$^{6}$ 2013$^{6}$ >38a 63f<

**Yamato Pink** 3 ch f Bijou D Inde-Time Or Never (FR) (Dowsing (USA)) 1086$^{15}$ (1725) 2380$^{2}$ 2766$^{5}$ 2942$^{3}$ 5261$^{11}$ 5581$^{4}$ 5930$^{6}$ >51a 55f<

**Yankeedoodledandy (IRE)** 3 b g Orpen (USA) -Laura Margaret (Persian Bold) (482) 535$^{2}$ (631) 746$^{2}$ (957) 1201$^{2}$ 3474$^{3}$ 4086$^{2}$ 4512$^{3}$ 4762$^{2}$ 4990$^{2}$ >75a 86f<

**Yankey** 2 b c Amfortas (IRE) -Key (Midyan (USA)) 5114$^{14}$ 5398$^{5}$ 5561$^{10}$ 6226$^{13}$ >10f<

**Yardstick** 2 ch c Inchinor-Fair Verona (USA) (Alleged (USA)) 3870$^{7}$ 5407$^{6}$ 5741$^{9}$ 5988$^{11}$ 6562$^{19}$ >57a 60f<

**Yaria (IRE)** 2 b f Danehill (USA) -Yara (IRE) (Sri Pekan (USA)) 2745a$^{6}$ >73f<

**Yashin (IRE)** 3 b g Soviet Star (USA) -My Mariam (Salse (USA)) 2377$^{13}$ 3025$^{10}$ 3271$^{3}$ 3874$^{2}$ 4199$^{10}$ 4483$^{4}$ 5092$^{14}$ 5552$^{3}$(6120) 6292$^{4}$ 6557$^{2}$ >72+a 69+f<

**Yawmi** 4 ch c Zafonic (USA) -Reine Wells (IRE) (Sadler s Wells (USA)) 1622$^{11}$ 2108$^{8}$ >105f<

**Ydravlis** 6 ch m Alflora (IRE) -Levantine Rose (Levanter) 3087$^{11}$ ><

**Year Two Thousand** 6 b h Darshaan-Vingt Et Une (FR) (Sadler s Wells (USA)) 4984a$^{11}$ 5506a$^{8}$ >108f<

**Yeats (IRE)** 3 b c Sadler s Wells (USA) -Lyndonville (IRE) (Top Ville) (1489a) (1979a) >117+f<

**Yehudi (IRE)** 2 b c Sadler s Wells (USA) -Bella Vitessa (IRE) (Thatching) (6503a) 6583a$^{2}$ >101f<

**Yeldham Lady** 2 b f Mujahid (USA) -Future Options (Lomond (USA)) 3676$^{7}$ 4016$^{13}$ 4516$^{2}$ 5022$^{7}$ 5281$^{7}$ 5593$^{3}$ >48a 48f<

**Yellow River (IRE)** 4 b g Sesaro (USA) -Amtico (Bairn (USA)) 589$^{4}$ 643$^{10}$ 834$^{8}$ 1969$^{12}$ 2384$^{14}$ >25a 25f<

**Yenaled** 7 gr g Rambo Dancer (CAN) -Fancy Flight (FR) (Arctic Tern (USA)) 582$^{3}$ 686$^{8}$ 719$^{5}$ 903$^{9}$ 1109$^{11}$ 1427$^{4}$ 1783$^{5}$(1962) (2128) 2753$^{2}$ 3731$^{2}$ 4213$^{4}$ 4826$^{2}$ (5061) 5514$^{7}$ 5581$^{4}$ (5817) (6208) >76a 82f<

**Yeoman Lad** 4 b g Groom Dancer (USA) -First Amendment (IRE) (Caerleon (USA)) 2206$^{15}$ 2738$^{11}$ 2945$^{4}$ 3239$^{5}$ 3637$^{8}$ >10a 77f<

**Yesterday (IRE)** 4 b f Sadler s Wells (USA) -Jude (Darshaan) 5484a$^{5}$ 5978a$^{4}$ 6488a$^{5}$ >117f<

**Ylang Ylang (IRE)** 3 ch f Hennessy (USA) -Princess Alydar (USA) (Alydar (USA)) 585$^{4}$ (835) 957$^{6}$ >64a 69f<

**Ynys** 3 b g Turtle Island (IRE) -Kiss Me Goodknight (First Trump) 567$^{12}$ 814$^{11}$ >30a 9f<

**Yomalo (IRE)** 4 ch f Woodborough (USA) -Alkariyh (USA) (Alydar (USA)) 1421$^{11}$ 1855$^{8}$ 2428$^{5}$ 2948$^{6}$ 3428$^{2}$ 4130$^{5}$ 4459$^{6}$ 5618$^{2}$(6131) >55a 81f<

**Yorik** 3 b c Danehill (USA) -Silver Fun (FR) (Saumarez) 2722a$^{15}$ >50f<

**York Cliff** 6 b g Marju (IRE) -Azm (Unfuwain (USA)) 544$^{12}$ 649$^{5}$ 795$^{4}$ 844$^{5}$ 5581$^{7}$ 6115$^{8}$ 6311$^{12}$ >80a 88f<

**Yorker (USA)** 6 b g Boundary (USA) -Shallows (USA) (Cox s Ridge (USA)) 488$^{2}$ 564$^{5}$ 719$^{3}$ 775$^{4}$ 866$^{2}$ 908$^{2}$ 967$^{7}$ 1013$^{10}$ 1757$^{7}$ 2814$^{3}$ 2989$^{6}$ 5108$^{12}$ (5833) 6094$^{3}$ 6220$^{10}$ 6483$^{11}$ 6548$^{14}$ >75a 73f<

**Yorke s Folly (USA)** 3 b f Stravinsky (USA) -Tommelise (USA) (Dayjur (USA)) 2984$^{7}$ 3517$^{8}$ 3877$^{10}$ 4391$^{12}$ 5306$^{3}$ 5547$^{5}$ 6200$^{16}$ >35a 47f<

**Yorkie** 5 b g Aragon-Light The Way (Nicholas Bill) (987) 1033$^{10}$ 1051$^{11}$ 1642$^{7}$ 2440$^{2}$ 3175$^{2}$ 3407$^{7}$ 4774$^{4}$ 4800 5016$^{8}$ >65a 69f<

**Yorkies Boy** 9 gr g Clantime-Slipperose (Persepolis (FR)) 2303$^{5}$ 2739$^{4}$ 2885$^{7}$ 3126$^{9}$ 3935$^{12}$ 4085$^{8}$ 4400$^{4}$ 4522$^{10}$ 4751$^{3}$ (5261) (5282) 5411$^{12}$ 5597$^{10}$ 5736$^{5}$ 6007$^{6}$ 6288$^{10}$ >59+f<

**Yorkshire Blue** 5 b g Atraf-Something Blue (Petong) 1748$^{7}$ 2260$^{7}$ (2421) (2673) 2965$^{9}$ 3910$^{5}$ (4577) 5316$^{10}$ 5583$^{13}$ >57a 67 f<

**Yorkshire Lad (IRE)** 2 b c Second Empire (IRE) -Villaminta (IRE) (Grand Lodge (USA)) 1105$^{8}$ 4454$^{6}$ 4761$^{5}$ >63+f<

**Yorkshire Spirit** 3 b g Imperial Ballet (IRE) -Barnacla (IRE) (Bluebird (USA)) 1528$^{9}$ ><

**Yoshka** 3 ch c Grand Lodge (USA) -Greenvera (USA) (Riverman (USA)) 1609$^{3}$ (3020) (3621) 4274$^{2}$ 5435$^{11}$ >100+f<

**You Found Me** 2 b f Robellino (USA) -Hana Marie (Formidable (USA)) 2786$^{8}$ 3259$^{6}$ 5172$^{3}$ 5852$^{9}$ 6265$^{6}$ >65f<

**Young Alex (IRE)** 6 ch g Midhish-Snipe Hunt (IRE) (Stalker) 5252$^{5}$ 5541$^{2}$ 6124$^{19}$ >89a 83f<

**Young Boldric** 2 b g Faustus (USA) -Bold Byzantium (Bold Arrangement) 3808$^{13}$ 4809$^{9}$ 5687$^{10}$ >37f<

**Young Dynasty** 4 ch g Young Ern-Miss Michelle (Jalmood (USA)) 644$^{7}$ 948$^{5}$ 997$^{5}$ 1939$^{10}$ 2188$^{5}$ 2643$^{16}$ 3697$^{17}$ >36a 38f<

**Young Kate** 3 b f Desert King (IRE) -Stardyn (Star Appeal) 6200$^{6}$ 6397$^{12}$ 6578$^{8}$ >26a 55f<

**Young Love** 3 ch f Pursuit Of Love-Polar Fair (Polar Falcon (USA)) 2001$^{8}$ 2401$^{6}$ 3139$^{4}$ 3636$^{14}$ 4477$^{6}$ 5035$^{4}$ 5336$^{4}$ 5643$^{4}$ >51a 55f<

**Young Mick** 2 br g King s Theatre (IRE) -Just Warning (Warning) 3601$^{13}$ 4335$^{3}$ 5142$^{4}$ 5596$^{13}$ >69f<

**Young Mr Grace (IRE)** 4 b c Danetime (IRE) -Maid Of Mourne (Fairy King (USA)) 1106$^{15}$ 1358$^{3}$ 1772$^{4}$ 2271$^{2}$ 2493$^{5}$ (3516) 3869$^{6}$ 3982$^{2}$ (4543) 4988$^{3}$ 5194$^{9}$ (5627) 5769$^{5}$ 6070$^{16}$ 6525$^{5}$ >51a 91f<

**Young Owen** 6 b g Balnibarbi-Polly Potter (Pollerton) 478$^{5}$ 484$^{9}$ ><

**Young Patriarch** 3 b g Silver Patriarch (IRE) -Mortify (Prince Sabo) 1382$^{10}$ 2032$^{16}$ 2688$^{13}$ >54f<

**Young Rooney** 4 b g Danzig Connection (USA) -Lady Broker (Petorius) 4240$^{4}$ 4486$^{11}$ 4901$^{3}$ 5237$^{2}$ 5459$^{2}$ 5769$^{6}$ 5950$^{3}$ 6141$^{2}$ 6520$^{6}$ 6570$^{3}$ >70a 77f<

**Youngs Forth** 4 b f Most Welcome-Pegs (Mandrake Major) 694$^{10}$ 859$^{8}$ 946$^{5}$ 1080$^{5}$ 1407$^{P}$ >38a 52f<

**Young Thomas (IRE)** 2 ch g Inchinor-Splicing (Sharpo) 2300$^{13}$ 3366$^{4}$ 3679$^{4}$ 4909$^{3}$ 5188$^{3}$ 5630$^{5}$ 6265$^{19}$ >68f<

**Young Tiger (FR)** 3 b c Tiger Hill (IRE) -Youngolina (IRE) (Trempolino (USA)) 1350a$^{4}$ 1898a$^{2}$ >107f<

**Young Valentino** 2 ch g Komaite (USA) -Caprice (Mystiko (USA)) 6342$^{12}$ >20f<

**Young Warrior (IRE)** 3 b g Desert Style (IRE) -Arctic Splendour (USA) (Arctic Tern (USA)) 1174$^{16}$ 2487$^{5}$ 2934$^{6}$ >53f<

**Your Just Lovely (IRE)** 3 b f Second Empire (IRE) -Nawaji (USA) (Trempolino (USA)) 983$^{14}$ 1220$^{9}$ >38a 56f<

**Yours Sincerely (IRE)** 2 ch c Mark Of Esteem (IRE) -Evrobi (IRE) (Grand Lodge (USA)) 2360$^{4}$ >37f<

**Youthopia (IRE)** 3 b f Titus Livius (FR) -Lykoa (Shirley Heights) 1805a$^{7}$ ><

**Ysoldina (FR)** 2 gr f Kendor (FR) -Rotina (FR) (Crystal Glitters (USA)) 6297a$^{3}$ >100f<

Z

**Zaajel (IRE)** 5 b h Nashwan (USA) -Mehthaaf (USA) (Nureyev (USA)) (692a) 854a$^{5}$ 1003a$^{6}$ >98f<

**Zabadani** 2 ch f Zafonic (USA) -Blou Dan (USA) (Damascus (USA)) 6492$^{9}$ >62a<

**Zabadou** 3 b g Abou Zouz (USA) -Strapped (Reprimand) 1325$^{9}$ 1617$^{6}$ 1913$^{7}$ >30a 31f<

**Zabeel Palace** 2 b c Grand Lodge (USA) -Applecross (Glint Of Gold) 3726$^{7}$ 4100$^{5}$ 4461$^{4}$ >71f<

**Zachela (IRE)** 2 b f Mujadil (USA) -Sarazade (Saumarez) 5577a$^{10}$ ><

**Zachy Boy** 2 b g Inchinor-Ellway Dancer (IRE) (Mujadil (USA)) 1276$^{6}$ 1374$^{7}$ 1589$^{5}$ 1984$^{11}$ 2609$^{17}$ 2946$^{6}$ 3140$^{6}$ 3458$^{5}$ 3571$^{4}$ 4620$^{6}$ >38a 50f<

**Zadalrakib** 2 ch c Machiavellian (USA) -Party Doll (Be My Guest (USA)) 6476$^{5}$ >72f<

**Zafarshah (IRE)** 5 b g Danehill (USA) -Zafarana (FR) (Shernazar) (491) 624$^{4}$ (701) 847$^{4}$ 1204$^{6}$ 2170$^{2}$ 2406$^{8}$ 2646$^{3}$ 3127$^{8}$ 3698$^{11}$ 4238$^{4}$ 4301$^{10}$ (5259) 5868$^{5}$ >68a 72f<

**Zaffeu** 3 ch g Zafonic (USA) -Leaping Flame (USA) (Trempolino (USA)) 739$^{10}$ 916$^{6}$ 1050$^{6}$ 1365$^{2}$ 1714$^{4}$ 2472$^{5}$ (2870) 3210$^{8}$ 4300$^{6}$ 4618$^{11}$ 5293$^{12}$ 5549$^{9}$ 6083$^{11}$ 6564$^{2}$ >63a 62f<

**Zagala** 4 b f Polar Falcon (USA) -Whittle Woods Girl (Emarati (USA)) 407$^{2}$ 803$^{9}$ 1477$^{2}$ 2989$^{7}$ 3615$^{8}$ 4026$^{9}$ 6273$^{6}$ >72a<

**Zagreus (GER)** 2 gr g Fasliyev (USA) -Zephyrine (IRE) (Highest Honor (FR)) 5561$^{3}$ >70f<

**Zahunda (IRE)** 5 b m Spectrum (IRE) -Gift Of Glory (FR) (Niniski (USA)) 533$^{6}$ 658$^{7}$ 700$^{2}$ 763$^{7}$ 861$^{4}$ 940$^{6}$ 1036$^{3}$ 1080$^{3}$ 1592$^{6}$ 1606$^{4}$ 3697$^{9}$ 4004$^{2}$ 4248$^{4}$ 4535$^{5}$ 4905$^{14}$ 6466$^{10}$ >49a 48f<

**Zak Attack** 3 ch g Young Ern-Premiere Moon (Bold Owl) 3916$^{19}$ >48f<

**Zak Facta (IRE)** 4 b g Danetime (IRE) -Alexander Goddess (IRE) (Alzao (USA)) 569$^{5}$ 738$^{5}$ 805$^{2}$ 918$^{4}$ 1044$^{6}$ 1423$^{8}$ 1941$^{11}$ 1971$^{11}$ 2209$^{7}$ 2456$^{11}$ 2664$^{11}$ >11a 11f<

**Zakfree (IRE)** 3 b g Danetime (IRE) -Clipper Queen (Balidar) 769$^{2}$ 5189$^{2}$ 5999$^{2}$ 6112$^{6}$ >63a 67f<

**Zalaal (USA)** 2 b c A.P. Indy (USA) -Scoot Yer Boots (USA) (Seeking The Gold (USA)) 3931$^{6}$ 4544$^{2}$ 5023$^{9}$ >76a 67f<

**Zalam (IRE)** 4 b g Alzao (USA) -Zarlana (IRE) (Darshaan) 5866$^{15}$ >75f<

**Zalda** 3 ch f Zilzal (USA) -Gold Luck (USA) (Slew O Gold (USA)) (2567) 3020$^{6}$ 3479$^{5}$ 4146$^{13}$ (4686) >47a 73f<

**Zalebe** 3 b f Bahamian Bounty-Alo Ez (Alzao (USA)) 2519$^{12}$ 5204$^{7}$ (5552) 6146$^{11}$ >56f<

**Zalkani (IRE)** 4 ch g Cadeaux Genereux-Zallaka (IRE) (Shardari) 555$^{3}$ 601$^{3}$ 745$^{12}$ 1298$^{13}$ 2122$^{9}$ 2594$^{5}$ 3490$^{10}$ 3697$^{11}$ 4669$^{4}$ 4940$^{11}$ 5175$^{8}$ 5643$^{2}$ >56a 40f<

**Zalongo** 2 ch c Zafonic (USA) -Tamassos (Dance In Time (CAN)) (6439) >86f<

**Zambezi River** 5 ch g Zamindar (USA) -Double River (USA) (Irish River (FR)) 1311$^{11}$ 1476$^{7}$ 1939$^{17}$ 2359$^{6}$ 2836$^{12}$ 4869$^{8}$ 5412$^{15}$ 5793$^{11}$ >26a 22f<

**Zamboozle (IRE)** 2 ch c Halling (USA) -Blue Sirocco (Bluebird (USA)) 4290$^{4}$ 4913$^{7}$ >72f<

**Zameel (IRE)** 3 b g Marju (IRE) -Impatiente (USA) (Vaguely Noble) 2133$^{12}$ >40f<

**Zameyla (IRE)** 3 b f Cape Cross (IRE) -Angelic Sounds (IRE) (The Noble Player (USA)) 2211$^{8}$ 2505$^{2}$ 2818$^{2}$ (5537) (5706) 5835$^{11}$ 6284$^{10}$ >84+f<

**Zamir** 5 ch g Zamindar (USA) -Fairy Flax (IRE) (Dancing Brave (USA)) 6208$^{11}$ >37f<

**Zamyatina (IRE)** 5 br m Danehill Dancer (IRE) -Miss Pickpocket (IRE) (Petorius) 1531$^{11}$ 1971$^{12}$ 2879$^{7}$ 2943$^{13}$ 3301$^{5}$ 3734$^{9}$ 4350$^{10}$ 5305$^{12}$ >26 a 26f<

**Zandeed (IRE)** 6 b g Inchinor-Persian Song (Persian Bold) 4537$^{11}$ 4905$^{3}$ (5127) 5344$^{4}$ 5518$^{12}$ 5584$^{5}$ 6337$^{7}$ >66f<

**Zanderido** 2 b g Forzando-Triple Concerto (Grand Lodge (USA)) 3468$^{4}$ 3760$^{12}$ 4009$^{6}$ 5556$^{16}$ >52?f<

**Zando** 2 b g Forzando-Rockin Rosie (Song) 2453$^{8}$ 2860$^{11}$ 4135$^{6}$ 5240$^{10}$ >14a 56f<

**Zangeal** 3 ch c Selkirk (USA) -Generous Lady (Generous (IRE)) 916$^{4}$ 2632$^{3}$ 3121$^{4}$ 3994$^{4}$ 4738$^{4}$ >66a 79f<

**Zanjeer** 4 b g Averti (IRE) -Cloudslea (USA) (Chief s Crown (USA)) 541$^{8}$ (3060) 3559$^{6}$ 3895$^{3}$ (3982) 4360$^{7}$ 4903$^{5}$ 6480$^{12}$ >23a 77+f<

**Zan Lo (IRE)** 4 ch f Grand Lodge (USA) -Zanella (IRE) (Nordico (USA)) 1470$^{7}$ 2039$^{8}$ 2446$^{6}$ 2659$^{10}$ 3866$^{7}$ 4210$^{7}$ 4397$^{9}$ 5058$^{4}$(5243) 5638$^{15}$ 5993$^{11}$ 6074$^{14}$ 6198$^{11}$ >55f<

**Zantero** 2 b c Danzero (AUS) -Cruinn A Bhord (Inchinor) 2453$^{4}$ 4359$^{6}$ 4924$^{4}$ 5234$^{6}$ 5477$^{8}$ 5636$^{6}$ 6207$^{5}$ >40a 64f<

**Zap Attack** 4 b g Zafonic (USA) -Rappa Tap Tap (FR) (Tap On Wood) 2219$^{16}$ 4305$^{7}$ 4574$^{4}$ 5316$^{16}$ 5849$^{17}$ >44a 61f<

**Zaqrah (USA)** 3 b f Silver Hawk (USA) -Istiqlal (USA) (Diesis) 1400$^{10}$ >79+f<

**Zarafsha (IRE)** 3 ro f Alzao (USA) -Zarabaya (IRE) (Doyoun) 2102a$^{7}$ 6102a$^{5}$ >98f<

**Zara Louise** 4 b f Mistertopogigo (IRE) -Petonica (IRE) (Petoski) 502$^{4}$ 713$^{10}$ 780$^{8}$ >29a 29f<

**Zarazienne (FR)** 3 b f Zieten (USA) -Arazienne (Arazi (USA)) 6255a$^{15}$ >59f<

**Zargus** 5 b g Zamindar (USA) -My First Romance (Danehill (USA)) 1205$^{5}$ 1313$^{10}$ 1642$^{10}$ 3243$^{11}$ 3524$^{13}$ >59a 86f<

**Zariano** 4 b g Emperor Jones (USA) -Douce Maison (IRE) (Fool s Holme (USA)) 3932$^{2}$ 4549$^{8}$ 4814$^{9}$ 5252$^{8}$ 5841$^{12}$ 6480$^{9}$ >76a 102f<

**Zarin (IRE)** 6 b g Inzar (USA) -Non Dimenticar Me (IRE) (Don t Forget Me) 667$^{9}$ 900$^{3}$ 2814$^{13}$ 3247$^{9}$ 3615$^{7}$ 4004$^{6}$ 4605$^{2}$ (4925) 5127$^{5}$ 5236$^{8}$ 5945$^{20}$ 6551$^{8}$ >67a 55f<

**Zarneeta** 3 b f Tragic Role (USA) -Compton Amber (Puissance) 3306$^{8}$ 3773$^{12}$ 4562$^{7}$ 5257$^{7}$ 5511$^{7}$ 5928$^{8}$ 5999$^{3}$ 6230$^{15}$ 6560$^{6}$ >14a 52 f<

**Zarova (IRE)** 2 gr c Zafonic (USA) -Estarova (FR) (Saint Estephe (FR)) 2234$^{11}$ 3469$^{6}$ 3918$^{15}$ 5234$^{14}$ >53f<

**Zarzu** 5 b g Magic Ring (IRE) -Rivers Rhapsody (Dominion) 486$^{3}$ 586$^{5}$ 703$^{4}$ 841$^{3}$ 1113$^{4}$ 1313$^{3}$ 2477$^{12}$ 2859$^{9}$ 3266$^{13}$ (3580) 3920$^{6}$ 4538$^{5}$ 4748$^{12}$ 4847$^{8}$ 5440$^{5}$ 5730$^{19}$ 5893$^{13}$ >93a 88+f<

**Zathonia** 3 b f Zafonic (USA) -Danthonia (USA) (Northern Dancer) 3154$^{2}$ 3592$^{3}$ 4455$^{2}$ >72f<

**Zaville** 2 gr f Zafonic (USA) -Colleville (Pharly (FR)) 5694$^{10}$ 6149$^{10}$ >51f<

**Zawrak (IRE)** 5 ch g Zafonic (USA) -Gharam (USA)

(Green Dancer (USA)) 467$^{6}$ 602$^{3}$ 650$^{11}$ (2356) 3520$^{15}$ 3773$^{5}$ 3921$^{2}$ 4333$^{8}$ 5554$^{16}$5713$^{13}$ 6483$^{4}$ 6576$^{7}$ >**66a 69+f**<

**Zayn Zen 2** ch f Singspiel (IRE) -Roshani (IRE) (Kris) 5088$^{6}$ 5368$^{4}$ 5846$^{2}$ 6111$^{5}$ >**73f**<

**Zazous 3** b c Zafonic (USA) -Confidentiality (USA) (Lyphard (USA)) 3322$^{6}$ 4316$^{3}$ 4478$^{9}$ 5829$^{11}$ 6150$^{11}$ >**67+f**<

**Zazzman (AUS) 6** b g Distinctly North (USA) -Glen Iris (AUS) (Marscay (AUS)) 6528a$^{3}$ >**111f**<

**Zeena 2** b f Unfuwain (USA) -Forest Fire (SWE) (Never So Bold) 5115$^{5}$ 5535$^{4}$ 5840$^{5}$ >**60f**<

**Zeis (IRE) 4** ch g Bahhare (USA) -Zoom Lens (IRE) (Caerleon (USA)) 961$^{9}$ 1118$^{10}$ 2120$^{12}$ (3173) (3885) 4240$^{7}$ 5554$^{10}$ 5956$^{9}$ 6025$^{7}$6278$^{9}$ >**66a 67f**<

**Zeitgeist (IRE) 3** b c Singspiel (IRE) -Diamond Quest (Rainbow Quest (USA)) 1672$^{4}$ (2529) 2782$^{2}$ 3692$^{5}$ 4229$^{9}$ (5834) 6121$^{2}$ 6512a$^{8}$ >**98+f**<

**Zeitlos 5** b g Timeless Times (USA) -Petitesse (Petong) 519$^{12}$ >**50a 50f**<

**Zelea (IRE) 5** br m Be My Guest (USA) -Ebony And Ivory (IRE) (Bob Back (USA)) 1448$^{5}$ 1700$^{4}$ 1917$^{4}$ >**49a 47f**<

**Zelkova (IRE) 2** b c Barathea (IRE) -Answer (Warning) 4158a$^{5}$ 5878a$^{2}$ >**95f**<

**Zeloso 6** b g Alzao (USA) -Silk Petal (Petorius) 3934$^{6}$ 4604$^{2}$ >**47a 47f**<

**Zendaro 2** b g Danzero (AUS) -Countess Maud (Mtoto) 1735$^{4}$ 2300$^{6}$ 3080$^{9}$ 5234$^{18}$ 6270$^{6}$ >**41a 54f**<

**Zerlina (USA) 3** b f Singspiel (IRE) -Tass (Soviet Star (USA)) 1327$^{7}$ 2089$^{7}$ 4731$^{8}$ 5220$^{4}$ 5566$^{2}$ (5990) 6497$^{11}$ >**87a 87f**<

**Zero Tolerance (IRE) 4** ch g Nashwan (USA) -Place De L Opera (Sadler s Wells (USA)) (1321) 2527$^{4}$ 2969$^{17}$ 3756$^{12}$ 4173$^{7}$ 4856$^{2}$ 5122$^{2}$ (6475) >**80+a 103f**<

**Zhitomir 6** ch g Lion Cavern (USA) -Treasure Trove (USA) (The Minstrel (CAN)) (1197) 1993$^{6}$ 2260$^{6}$ (4004) 4702$^{6}$ 4905$^{4}$ 5235$^{10}$ 5691$^{2}$ (6058) 6220$^{6}$6558$^{2}$ >**60a 67f**<

**Zibeline (IRE) 7** b g Cadeaux Genereux-Zia (USA) (Shareef Dancer (USA)) 2681$^{3}$ 3310$^{10}$ 5435$^{14}$ >**98f**<

**Ziet D Alsace (FR) 4** b f Zieten (USA) -Providenc Mill (FR) (French Stress (USA)) 2030$^{14}$ 2322$^{2}$ 2426$^{12}$ 2597$^{12}$ 3174$^{2}$ 3626$^{10}$ (3828) 4067$^{8}$ 4414$^{4}$4437$^{6}$ 5849$^{7}$ 6024$^{2}$ 6154$^{11}$ 6295$^{5}$ 6550$^{3}$ >**64a 64f**<

**Zietory 4** b f Zieten (USA) -Fairy Story (IRE) (Persian Bold) 1790$^{5}$ 2242$^{8}$ 4773$^{3}$ (4948) 5249$^{11}$ 6497$^{3}$ >**99a 104f**<

**Zietzig (IRE) 7** b g Zieten (USA) -Missing You (Ahonoora) 1824$^{14}$ 1971$^{8}$ 3024$^{11}$ 3169$^{13}$ 3533$^{8}$ 3742$^{5}$ 3836$^{6}$ (4350) 4557$^{10}$ >**43a 55f**<

**Ziggy Dan 4** b g Slip Anchor-Nikatino (Bustino) 991$^{5}$ >**20a**<

**Zilch 6** ch g Zilzal (USA) -Bunty Boo (Noalto) (1132) 1246$^{2}$ 1354$^{2}$ (1500) 1789$^{4}$ 3235$^{10}$ (3324) 3673$^{11}$ 4614$^{7}$ 5628$^{8}$ 6071$^{20}$ >**81a 106f**<

**Zilmy (IRE) 3** ch g Zilzal (USA) -My Lewicia (IRE) (Taufan (USA)) 2204$^{7}$ >**58f**<

**Zimbali 2** ch f Lahib (USA) -Dawn (Owington) 1307$^{5}$ 1364$^{4}$ (1589) 1751$^{3}$ 2321$^{4}$ 2593$^{2}$ 3458$^{2}$ >**64f**<

**Zinging 5** b g Fraam-Hi Hoh (IRE) (Fayruz) 453$^{5}$ 672$^{7}$ 738$^{6}$ 888$^{4}$ 933$^{7}$ 1098$^{7}$ 1583$^{6}$1863$^{5}$ 2325$^{5}$ 2703$^{6}$ 3174$^{9}$ 3932$^{10}$ 5039$^{4}$ 5283$^{7}$ 5793$^{6}$5929$^{4}$ >**42a 43f**<

**Zirna (NZ) 5** b m Deputy Governor (USA) -Riverly Lass (NZ) (Gleam Machine (USA)) 853a$^{6}$ 1001a$^{5}$ >**101f**<

**Ziyar (FR) 4** ch g Valanour (IRE) -Zariya (USA) (Blushing Groom (FR)) 5103a$^{0}$ ><

**Zohar (USA) 2** b c Aljabr (USA) -Dafnah (USA) (Housebuster (USA)) (5290) 6340$^{13}$ >**82+f**<

**Zolash (IRE) 2** b c General Monash (USA) -Zolba (IRE) (Classic Secret (USA)) 2382$^{5}$ 2761$^{9}$ 3633$^{6}$ 4263$^{7}$ 4498$^{4}$ 4638$^{4}$ 5059$^{3}$ 5335$^{6}$5593$^{9}$ 6555$^{9}$ >**43a 67f**<

**Zoltano (GER) 6** b g In The Wings-Zarella (GER) (Anatas) 1173$^{3}$ (1316) 1615$^{17}$ >**76f**<

**Zolushka (IRE) 3** ch f Russian Revival (USA) -Persian Myth (Persian Bold) 451$^{3}$ 662$^{10}$ 946$^{12}$ 965$^{10}$ >**36a 40f**<

**Zomerlust 2** b g Josr Algarhoud (IRE) -Passiflora (Night Shift (USA)) 4175$^{3}$ (4761) 5212$^{2}$ 5466$^{4}$ 5896$^{4}$ 6113$^{2}$ 6574$^{3}$ >**85f**<

**Zona (ITY) 3** b f Mr Greeley (USA) -Miss Gally (USA) (Dayjur (USA)) 1778a$^{9}$ 2720a$^{8}$ >**93f**<

**Zonergem 6** ch g Zafonic (USA) -Anasazi (IRE) (Sadler s Wells (USA)) 558$^{7}$ 706$^{6}$ 2969$^{3}$ 5401$^{3}$ 5941$^{25}$ >**100a 101f**<

**Zonic 2** b f Zafonic (USA) -Ferber s Follies (USA) (Saratoga Six (USA)) 4399$^{7}$ 5380$^{7}$ 5752$^{3}$ >**62a 64f**<

**Zonic Boom (FR) 4** bb g Zafonic (USA) -Rosi Zambotti (IRE) (Law Society (USA)) 1310$^{5}$ 1675$^{3}$ 5657$^{8}$ 5867$^{3}$ 6152$^{9}$ 6225$^{6}$ >**61a 71f**<

**Zonnebeke 3** b f Orpen (USA) -Canlubang (Mujtahid (USA)) 409$^{4}$ 587$^{5}$ 659$^{2}$ 736$^{7}$ 946$^{3}$ 1086$^{14}$ 2942$^{10}$3229$^{3}$ 3425$^{4}$ (4102) 4460$^{2}$ 4818$^{10}$ 5036$^{6}$ 5575$^{12}$ 6228$^{10}$ 6567$^{15}$ >**43a 53f**<

**Zonus 3** b c Pivotal-Jade Mistress (Damister (USA)) (1111) 1437$^{4}$ 1900$^{2}$ 2295$^{3}$ 3001$^{11}$ 3542$^{3}$ 3943$^{7}$ (4931) 5610$^{10}$ >**107f**<

**Zoomiezando 3** b g Forzando-Zarah (Rudimentary (USA)) 4303$^{7}$ 4573$^{7}$ 5141$^{14}$ >**53f**<

**Zoom Zoom 4** b c Abou Zouz (USA) -Iltimas (USA) (Dayjur (USA)) (1603) 2261$^{10}$ 2628$^{5}$ 5603$^{13}$ 5861$^{4}$ 6144$^{14}$ (6553) >**79a 80f**<

**Zoripp (IRE) 2** b g Spectrum (IRE) -Allspice (Alzao (USA)) 3718$^{6}$ 4315$^{10}$ 5653$^{12}$ >**49f**<

**Zorn 5** br h Dilum (USA) -Very Good (Noalto) 5999$^{17}$ 6130$^{10}$ >**52a 9f**<

**Zosima (USA) 3** bb f Capote (USA) -Grafin (USA) (Miswaki (USA)) 2971$^{3}$ 4323$^{4}$ 5416$^{11}$ >**84a 114+f**<

**Zouave (IRE) 3** b g Spectrum (IRE) -Lady Windley (Baillamont (USA)) 2203$^{7}$ 2683$^{12}$ 2910$^{5}$ 3035$^{10}$ >**86f**<

**Zouche 4** b g Zamindar (USA) -Al Corniche (IRE) (Bluebird (USA)) 2356$^{11}$ 3247$^{10}$ 3490$^{13}$ >**49a 49 f**<

**Zucchero 8** br g Dilum (USA) -Legal Sound (Legal Eagle) 3212$^{12}$ 3745$^{3}$ 3937$^{10}$ >**78 f**<

**Zuhair 11** ch g Mujtahid (USA) -Ghzaalh (USA) (Northern Dancer) 1774$^{13}$ 1974$^{10}$ 2219$^{7}$ 2461$^{11}$ 3407$^{15}$ 3778$^{9}$ >**83f**<

**Zuleta 3** ch f Vettori (IRE) -Victoria (Old Vic) 3143$^{8}$ 4519$^{9}$ 4710$^{6}$ 4867$^{2}$ 5069$^{2}$ 5634$^{2}$ 5863$^{4}$ 6055$^{2}$ >**49a 51f**<

**Zuloago (USA) 3** b f Stravinsky (USA) -Attitre (FR) (Mtoto) 668$^{5}$ 835$^{3}$ 1012$^{2}$ 1422$^{12}$ 1627$^{11}$ 3707$^{9}$ >**57a**<

**Zuma (IRE) 3** b c Grand Lodge (USA) -Paradise Waters (Celestial Storm (USA)) 2114$^{7}$ 2479$^{3}$ 2888$^{7}$ 3245$^{5}$ 3706$^{5}$ 4087$^{4}$ 5217$^{4}$ 6085$^{2}$6192$^{6}$ >**53a 78f**<

**Zurbaran (IND) 5** b h Peaks And Valleys (USA) -Cut Of The Cloth (USA) (Dauphin Fabuleux (CAN)) 757a$^{10}$ 854a$^{7}$ 1003a$^{7}$ >**50a 84f**<

**Zuri (IRE) 3** b f Kris S (USA) -Amizette (USA) (Forty Niner (USA)) 2693$^{6}$ 3054$^{4}$ 3592$^{9}$ 4307$^{9}$ 4641$^{7}$ 5510$^{9}$ 6017$^{8}$ >**40a 63f**<

**Zwadi (IRE) 3** b f Docksider (USA) -Local Custom (IRE) (Be My Native (USA)) 2479$^{4}$ 2911$^{8}$ 3306$^{5}$ 4194$^{7}$ 4496$^{3}$ 4916$^{2}$ 5306$^{4}$ 5637$^{3}$6130$^{4}$ >**62a 74f**<

**Zweibrucken (IRE) 3** b f Alhaarth (IRE) -Solar Attraction (IRE) (Salt Dome (USA)) 2202$^{17}$ 2887$^{10}$ (4684) 5265$^{11}$ 5766$^{11}$ 6284$^{7}$ >**86+f**<

# Leading Flat Trainers - 2004

| NAME | WINS-RUNS | 2nd | 3rd | 4th | WIN £ | TOTAL £ | £1 STAKE |
|---|---|---|---|---|---|---|---|
| Saeed Bin Suroor | 115-455 (25%) | 75 | 42 | 39 | 3,057,921.70 | 4,324,101.32 | +11.88 |
| Sir Michael Stoute | 85-398 (21%) | 49 | 46 | 50 | 2,309,110.74 | 2,934,406.02 | +27.40 |
| M Johnston | 119-783 (15%) | 110 | 76 | 71 | 1,726,936.59 | 2,435,553.90 | -140.74 |
| M R Channon | 91-995 (9%) | 121 | 97 | 95 | 878,686.44 | 1,711,091.08 | -369.78 |
| B W Hills | 78-628 (12%) | 76 | 60 | 55 | 1,086,481.03 | 1,543,153.60 | -167.51 |
| R Hannon | 110-1168 (9%) | 120 | 123 | 115 | 782,525.89 | 1,444,163.13 | -238.82 |
| M A Jarvis | 64-365 (18%) | 49 | 44 | 35 | 939,081.15 | 1,306,376.65 | -62.91 |
| J H M Gosden | 65-436 (15%) | 62 | 56 | 31 | 723,968.45 | 1,256,829.33 | -70.70 |
| J R Fanshawe | 44-284 (15%) | 37 | 32 | 34 | 860,348.40 | 1,182,197.91 | -65.08 |
| J L Dunlop | 55-510 (11%) | 51 | 63 | 53 | 636,040.59 | 1,171,667.41 | -116.65 |
| L M Cumani | 40-277 (14%) | 42 | 34 | 30 | 630,082.12 | 1,046,458.96 | -65.84 |
| T D Easterby | 60-731 (8%) | 85 | 71 | 62 | 552,264.40 | 908,700.91 | -287.04 |
| D Nicholls | 55-676 (8%) | 50 | 54 | 50 | 614,422.77 | 874,519.19 | -212.48 |
| B J Meehan | 55-464 (12%) | 41 | 48 | 41 | 535,834.97 | 826,578.10 | -9.54 |
| A P O'Brien | 4-60 (7%) | 8 | 7 | 5 | 246,894.67 | 804,447.17 | -38.50 |
| D R C Elsworth | 36-297 (12%) | 21 | 30 | 37 | 447,890.03 | 790,991.63 | +129.48 |
| E A L Dunlop | 44-379 (12%) | 45 | 43 | 42 | 553,705.70 | 790,869.55 | -124.17 |
| R A Fahey | 75-612 (12%) | 57 | 69 | 51 | 497,225.02 | 728,123.01 | -34.16 |
| Mrs A J Perrett | 47-376 (13%) | 46 | 42 | 35 | 415,334.70 | 726,197.29 | -54.30 |
| C E Brittain | 25-306 (8%) | 28 | 19 | 24 | 385,921.15 | 694,487.20 | -27.92 |
| A M Balding | 47-522 (9%) | 58 | 53 | 47 | 388,255.22 | 675,665.82 | -158.78 |
| P F I Cole | 38-351 (11%) | 36 | 33 | 40 | 299,300.40 | 625,715.14 | -104.83 |
| M L W Bell | 55-417 (13%) | 48 | 47 | 44 | 421,571.87 | 622,226.07 | -107.55 |
| M P Tregoning | 26-187 (14%) | 27 | 22 | 23 | 323,476.25 | 615,132.23 | -30.07 |
| W J Haggas | 45-289 (16%) | 27 | 24 | 27 | 318,045.27 | 595,813.02 | +39.93 |
| R Charlton | 35-211 (17%) | 22 | 25 | 21 | 447,938.78 | 594,938.78 | +13.85 |
| K A Ryan | 60-441 (14%) | 48 | 51 | 34 | 336,222.42 | 590,612.07 | +17.77 |
| P W Harris | 42-335 (13%) | 36 | 37 | 20 | 370,290.04 | 534,192.59 | -20.53 |
| J M Bradley | 38-674 (6%) | 54 | 50 | 72 | 292,798.38 | 531,666.00 | -214.35 |
| Sir Mark Prescott | 66-228 (29%) | 28 | 15 | 14 | 426,235.35 | 526,633.70 | -21.07 |
| N P Littmoden | 42-477 (9%) | 56 | 44 | 39 | 332,906.32 | 516,095.84 | -73.03 |
| H Morrison | 33-313 (11%) | 37 | 37 | 26 | 329,623.70 | 509,292.54 | -88.40 |
| J Noseda | 33-207 (16%) | 32 | 28 | 21 | 269,373.14 | 491,724.14 | -7.80 |
| H Candy | 23-189 (12%) | 21 | 21 | 21 | 317,281.95 | 484,776.06 | -47.38 |
| M H Tompkins | 33-299 (11%) | 32 | 33 | 33 | 277,398.00 | 484,665.14 | -61.85 |
| T D Barron | 53-414 (13%) | 36 | 51 | 49 | 316,340.45 | 459,301.73 | -20.75 |
| D R Loder | 44-338 (13%) | 36 | 36 | 38 | 268,625.65 | 455,032.86 | -131.06 |
| G A Butler | 27-270 (10%) | 32 | 33 | 36 | 163,830.00 | 439,547.88 | -91.82 |
| G Wragg | 22-169 (13%) | 18 | 19 | 17 | 241,627.69 | 433,030.59 | -21.52 |
| S Kirk | 30-345 (9%) | 43 | 23 | 26 | 304,094.10 | 423,158.45 | -78.05 |
| P D Evans | 61-631 (10%) | 56 | 64 | 77 | 257,159.72 | 403,808.45 | -92.57 |
| P Chapple-Hyam | 29-148 (20%) | 17 | 17 | 7 | 278,882.87 | 387,188.22 | -12.45 |
| K R Burke | 58-437 (13%) | 49 | 42 | 48 | 246,980.32 | 362,399.87 | +3.05 |
| B A McMahon | 27-224 (12%) | 18 | 19 | 19 | 223,689.20 | 332,165.92 | +51.97 |
| W R Muir | 18-275 (7%) | 35 | 21 | 26 | 177,552.74 | 329,312.04 | -96.87 |
| J J Quinn | 30-320 (9%) | 27 | 22 | 31 | 188,225.66 | 328,184.45 | -123.13 |
| N A Callaghan | 32-270 (12%) | 23 | 21 | 19 | 192,432.80 | 328,088.19 | -99.75 |
| A Berry | 35-545 (6%) | 39 | 45 | 54 | 192,411.87 | 323,249.42 | -148.80 |
| G L Moore | 40-436 (9%) | 44 | 36 | 55 | 182,334.69 | 310,277.97 | -126.99 |
| J A Osborne | 36-390 (9%) | 36 | 45 | 40 | 190,484.05 | 307,427.88 | -142.39 |
| B Smart | 27-363 (7%) | 28 | 32 | 37 | 189,126.70 | 306,808.03 | -80.17 |
| J G Given | 29-472 (6%) | 29 | 44 | 52 | 136,166.65 | 300,064.94 | -145.92 |
| M W Easterby | 31-459 (7%) | 28 | 40 | 42 | 165,884.80 | 293,005.15 | -183.55 |
| C F Wall | 18-207 (9%) | 21 | 26 | 23 | 137,156.03 | 292,203.22 | -44.25 |
| John M Oxx | 3-11 (27%) | 0 | 4 | 1 | 165,684.75 | 289,379.90 | +2.50 |
| J D Bethell | 19-189 (10%) | 16 | 24 | 23 | 195,854.29 | 277,563.66 | -10.90 |
| W M Brisbourne | 48-577 (8%) | 45 | 45 | 65 | 166,384.95 | 274,268.98 | -211.48 |

# Leading Flat Jockeys

## (turf season 25th March - 6th November 2004)

| NAME | WIN £ | 1st | 2nd | 3rd | 4th | MOUNTS | % | £1 STAKE |
|---|---|---|---|---|---|---|---|---|
| L Dettori | 3381591 | 173 | 120 | 78 | 404 | 775 | 22.3 | + 65.66 |
| K Fallon | 3313895 | 159 | 135 | 115 | 521 | 930 | 17.0 | - 162.70 |
| S Sanders | 1271972 | 143 | 107 | 72 | 539 | 861 | 16.6 | + 98.01 |
| R L Moore | 824586 | 114 | 113 | 87 | 569 | 883 | 12.9 | + 126.80 |
| D Holland | 1161289 | 107 | 102 | 106 | 609 | 924 | 11.5 | - 291.41 |
| R Winston | 722913 | 87 | 80 | 87 | 521 | 775 | 11.2 | - 63.99 |
| P Hanagan | 710221 | 83 | 56 | 73 | 413 | 625 | 13.2 | + 120.51 |
| K Darley | 1184229 | 81 | 96 | 86 | 534 | 797 | 10.1 | - 236.70 |
| S Drowne | 687588 | 72 | 69 | 73 | 567 | 781 | 9.2 | - 114.16 |
| J P Murtagh | 1208563 | 71 | 50 | 54 | 355 | 530 | 13.3 | - 75.85 |
| J Fanning | 637541 | 70 | 53 | 48 | 367 | 538 | 13.0 | - 39.49 |
| P Robinson | 984556 | 66 | 57 | 63 | 347 | 533 | 12.3 | - 138.10 |
| N Callan | 394782 | 65 | 64 | 55 | 389 | 573 | 11.3 | - 13.00 |
| R Hills | 1096852 | 62 | 46 | 64 | 261 | 433 | 14.3 | - 80.89 |
| E Ahern | 504061 | 61 | 64 | 64 | 489 | 678 | 8.9 | - 159.79 |
| T Quinn | 691779 | 60 | 62 | 64 | 353 | 539 | 11.1 | - 9.55 |
| A Culhane | 415340 | 60 | 63 | 64 | 426 | 613 | 9.7 | - 119.57 |
| M Hills | 524985 | 55 | 55 | 36 | 306 | 452 | 12.1 | - 101.49 |
| R Hughes | 568154 | 55 | 58 | 63 | 380 | 556 | 9.8 | - 246.92 |
| J Fortune | 731996 | 55 | 71 | 61 | 308 | 495 | 11.1 | - 177.89 |
| Martin Dwyer | 561252 | 54 | 60 | 49 | 436 | 599 | 9.0 | - 125.69 |
| Dane O Neill | 489045 | 53 | 55 | 66 | 508 | 682 | 7.7 | - 229.81 |
| T P Queally | 303014 | 50 | 47 | 44 | 421 | 562 | 8.8 | - 231.18 |
| F Norton | 297221 | 49 | 50 | 47 | 304 | 450 | 10.8 | - 13.04 |
| W Supple | 489292 | 48 | 69 | 64 | 414 | 595 | 8.0 | - 190.71 |
| J F Egan | 333224 | 47 | 48 | 40 | 400 | 535 | 8.7 | - 32.47 |
| N Mackay | 416214 | 44 | 35 | 29 | 211 | 319 | 13.7 | + 79.82 |
| K McEvoy | 645239 | 43 | 30 | 30 | 214 | 317 | 13.5 | - 42.74 |
| R Ffrench | 268098 | 40 | 48 | 36 | 352 | 476 | 8.4 | - 138.84 |
| J Quinn | 309987 | 39 | 46 | 55 | 446 | 586 | 6.6 | - 164.03 |
| D Allan | 253173 | 38 | 53 | 50 | 334 | 475 | 8.0 | - 134.97 |
| T E Durcan | 311974 | 38 | 54 | 40 | 433 | 565 | 6.7 | - 248.51 |
| F Lynch | 261500 | 37 | 24 | 38 | 240 | 339 | 10.9 | + 47.55 |
| S W Kelly | 218550 | 34 | 42 | 46 | 354 | 476 | 7.1 | - 269.49 |
| C Catlin | 289288 | 33 | 47 | 31 | 464 | 575 | 5.7 | - 199.18 |
| T Eaves | 170647 | 32 | 25 | 28 | 376 | 461 | 6.9 | - 142.26 |
| M Fenton | 221736 | 32 | 38 | 44 | 360 | 474 | 6.7 | - 148.18 |
| I Mongan | 154951 | 31 | 38 | 32 | 296 | 397 | 7.8 | - 112.44 |
| W Ryan | 181879 | 30 | 15 | 26 | 196 | 267 | 11.2 | - 57.89 |
| Darren Williams | 140530 | 30 | 32 | 24 | 234 | 320 | 9.3 | + 29.49 |
| P Makin | 125722 | 27 | 15 | 20 | 187 | 249 | 10.8 | + 19.50 |
| Hayley Turner | 160353 | 27 | 25 | 25 | 192 | 269 | 10.0 | + 83.80 |
| R Thomas | 156161 | 26 | 16 | 25 | 182 | 249 | 10.4 | - 30.68 |
| F P Ferris | 123209 | 26 | 17 | 18 | 199 | 260 | 10.0 | - 0.00 |
| J F McDonald | 244196 | 26 | 20 | 25 | 246 | 317 | 8.2 | - 78.38 |
| Dale Gibson | 128252 | 26 | 29 | 34 | 315 | 404 | 6.4 | - 34.80 |
| Lisa Jones | 141552 | 25 | 16 | 22 | 296 | 359 | 6.9 | - 45.75 |
| P Mulrennan | 152227 | 25 | 17 | 31 | 288 | 361 | 6.9 | - 122.25 |
| D Sweeney | 129315 | 25 | 31 | 22 | 259 | 337 | 7.4 | - 90.03 |
| J Mackay | 147531 | 24 | 23 | 16 | 258 | 321 | 7.4 | - 98.88 |
| G Gibbons | 174349 | 22 | 13 | 15 | 156 | 206 | 10.6 | + 57.46 |
| R Miles | 162716 | 22 | 17 | 22 | 185 | 246 | 8.9 | - 40.93 |
| O Urbina | 135100 | 22 | 20 | 16 | 106 | 164 | 13.4 | + 14.76 |

# Leading Flat Owners - 2004

| NAME | WINS-RUNS | 2nd | 3rd | 4th | WIN £ | TOTAL £ | £1 STAKE |
|---|---|---|---|---|---|---|---|
| Godolphin | 115-455 (25%) | 75 | 42 | 39 | 3,057,921.70 | 4,324,101.32 | +11.88 |
| Hamdan Al Maktoum | 73-463 (16%) | 46 | 66 | 57 | 1,179,555.44 | 1,753,034.57 | -60.25 |
| Cheveley Park Stud | 55-215 (26%) | 29 | 29 | 16 | 703,836.05 | 1,134,359.26 | -21.37 |
| Ballymacoll Stud | 7-27 (26%) | 3 | 2 | 3 | 921,091.29 | 929,401.04 | +2.07 |
| K Abdulla | 54-328 (16%) | 45 | 38 | 28 | 523,383.35 | 923,911.88 | -54.72 |
| Maktoum Al Maktoum | 32-234 (14%) | 32 | 29 | 29 | 563,969.68 | 771,597.65 | -59.44 |
| Sheikh Mohamm'd | 52-308 (17%) | 42 | 37 | 32 | 403,317.30 | 684,651.07 | -61.90 |
| Elite Racing Club | 16-64 (25%) | 7 | 6 | 7 | 409,126.55 | 560,885.55 | +23.78 |
| Duke Of Roxburghe | 3-5 (60%) | 1 | 0 | 0 | 443,018.49 | 487,018.49 | +7.75 |
| Sh. Ahmed Al Maktoum | 36-265 (14%) | 49 | 26 | 31 | 225,088.35 | 463,645.04 | -81.52 |
| H H Aga Khan | 10-41 (24%) | 6 | 6 | 5 | 272,394.55 | 460,828.95 | -9.24 |
| L Neil Jones | 4-13 (31%) | 1 | 5 | 1 | 166,187.00 | 382,154.10 | +4.00 |
| Gary A Tanaka | 3-11 (27%) | 0 | 1 | 1 | 356,932.00 | 368,282.00 | +4.00 |
| Saeed Manana | 7-85 (8%) | 11 | 6 | 6 | 196,431.50 | 360,541.25 | -16.00 |
| J C Smith | 6-103 (6%) | 8 | 15 | 19 | 94,525.00 | 357,250.90 | -23.50 |
| Mrs J Magnier & M Tabor | 2-22 (9%) | 3 | 4 | 1 | 123,938.67 | 328,838.67 | -11.75 |
| Sangster Family | 8-30 (27%) | 8 | 1 | 3 | 210,089.00 | 322,324.30 | +7.15 |
| Lucayan Stud | 20-164 (12%) | 21 | 14 | 18 | 215,015.25 | 307,680.40 | -42.29 |
| Mrs John Magnier | 1-14 (7%) | 1 | 1 | 1 | 110,606.00 | 278,361.00 | -8.50 |
| H R H Sultan Ahmad Shah | 11-66 (17%) | 8 | 10 | 4 | 170,135.04 | 259,152.44 | -20.67 |
| P D Savill | 15-109 (14%) | 11 | 10 | 8 | 141,772.30 | 241,707.40 | -4.58 |
| Abdulla Buhaleeba | 11-67 (16%) | 9 | 5 | 8 | 122,859.00 | 229,592.75 | -18.50 |
| Lord Derby | 2-2 (100%) | 0 | 0 | 0 | 220,400.00 | 220,400.00 | +5.50 |
| Nigel Shields | 29-163 (18%) | 18 | 26 | 17 | 155,514.55 | 216,548.10 | +70.23 |
| The Queen | 15-82 (18%) | 18 | 11 | 6 | 98,131.10 | 212,182.66 | +23.92 |
| Jaber Abdullah | 6-77 (8%) | 11 | 7 | 6 | 51,354.50 | 207,457.25 | -53.65 |
| Hesmonds Stud | 13-70 (19%) | 5 | 9 | 11 | 146,322.90 | 197,795.20 | -7.98 |
| Mrs J Hopper/ Mrs E Grundy | 2-5 (40%) | 1 | 1 | 0 | 174,000.00 | 196,000.00 | +12.63 |
| Fittocks Stud | 6-33 (18%) | 9 | 2 | 3 | 104,465.45 | 194,946.80 | -8.33 |
| B E Nielsen | 4-13 (31%) | 2 | 1 | 3 | 185,312.32 | 190,524.82 | +10.00 |
| Dab Hand Racing | 4-26 (15%) | 3 | 7 | 1 | 118,331.00 | 190,410.00 | +11.99 |
| Mollers Racing | 13-52 (25%) | 3 | 6 | 8 | 134,209.39 | 188,974.34 | +27.36 |
| M Tabor & Mrs J Magnier | 2-19 (11%) | 3 | 2 | 1 | 27,327.50 | 185,534.50 | +5.00 |
| Mrs Angie Silver | 4-6 (67%) | 0 | 0 | 0 | 183,778.00 | 184,528.00 | +19.50 |
| Mill House Partnership | 3-3 (100%) | 0 | 0 | 0 | 184,017.75 | 184,017.75 | +6.23 |
| BDR Partnership | 2-26 (8%) | 3 | 3 | 6 | 142,218.00 | 182,882.95 | +3.50 |
| Mrs P W Harris | 13-98 (13%) | 13 | 16 | 9 | 133,823.15 | 181,354.57 | -16.80 |
| Paul J Dixon | 21-279 (8%) | 29 | 24 | 30 | 109,004.25 | 179,138.40 | -148.35 |
| M J Dawson | 5-65 (8%) | 8 | 9 | 6 | 111,419.50 | 176,054.52 | -8.50 |
| Franconson Partners | 6-33 (18%) | 1 | 5 | 1 | 136,102.72 | 168,684.72 | -6.35 |
| J C Fretwell | 13-102 (13%) | 8 | 11 | 7 | 123,626.85 | 166,203.22 | -21.53 |
| Team Victory | 0-1 | 1 | 0 | 0 | 0.00 | 165,000.00 | -1.00 |
| Andrea & Graham Wylie | 6-38 (16%) | 6 | 4 | 4 | 117,946.50 | 160,138.50 | +5.55 |
| Raymond Tooth | 9-126 (7%) | 12 | 15 | 14 | 93,630.20 | 158,681.45 | -52.68 |
| Ridgeway Downs Racing | 7-40 (18%) | 9 | 8 | 3 | 75,777.20 | 157,847.60 | +16.75 |
| Saeed Suhail | 5-57 (9%) | 7 | 5 | 9 | 104,149.50 | 156,577.18 | -33.38 |
| Gainsborough Stud | 1-9 (11%) | 0 | 3 | 0 | 152,772.00 | 154,497.00 | -3.50 |
| Mrs Susan Roy | 14-94 (15%) | 11 | 15 | 11 | 65,296.39 | 152,646.84 | -20.67 |
| Wood Street Syndicate | 2-5 (40%) | 0 | 0 | 1 | 151,766.00 | 152,577.00 | +9.50 |
| F C T Wilson | 6-20 (30%) | 2 | 1 | 1 | 133,463.25 | 151,758.00 | +48.50 |
| S'kh Rashid Bin Mohamm'd | 12-56 (21%) | 12 | 4 | 10 | 71,327.26 | 147,475.46 | -15.78 |
| W H Ponsonby | 5-50 (10%) | 2 | 2 | 4 | 134,060.00 | 147,422.37 | -18.25 |
| Ecurie Wildenstein | 1-7 (14%) | 1 | 2 | 2 | 29,000.00 | 146,264.00 | -0.50 |
| M Tabor | 9-61 (15%) | 4 | 10 | 8 | 65,520.50 | 145,143.65 | -20.43 |
| Jonathan Gill | 1-4 (25%) | 0 | 0 | 0 | 145,000.00 | 145,000.00 | +9.00 |

# Addenda to previous annuals

## Races that took place in 2003

616 Absolute Utopia (USA) disqualified: prohibited substance in urine race awarded to Hidden Surprise.
5270 LOBOS disqualified: prohibited substance in urine, race awarded to Cooden Beach
5933 LOBOS unplaced disqualified: prohibited substance in urine.
AYR races run as 1m1f20y, in previous seasons were actually 40y short at 1m200y.

## Races that took place in 2002

5772 Paula Lane disqualified: prohibited substance in urine.
5791 Pawn In Life (IRE) disqualified: prohibited substance in urine.
5819 Valazar (USA) disqualified: prohibited substance in urine.
5861 Escalade disqualified: prohibited substance in urine.
5907 Perfidious (USA) disqualified: prohibited substance in urine.
5915 Red Storm disqualified: prohibited substance in urine, race awarded to Champain Sands (IRE).
5932 Red Storm (USA) disqualified: prohibited substance in urine.
5821 Zagala disqualified: prohibited substance in urine.
5823 Supreme Salutation disqualified: prohibited substance in urine.
5826 Beauvrai disqualified: prohibited substance in urine, race awarded to Percy Douglas.
5828 Massey disqualified: prohibited substance in urine.
5843 Benny The Vice (USA) disqualified: prohibited substance in urine.
5845 Crusoe (IRE) disqualified: prohibited substance in urine.
5854 Faraway Look (USA) disqualified: prohibited substance in urine.
5870 Valazar (USA) disqualified: prohibited substance in urine, race awarded to Festive Affair.
5983 Takrir (IRE) disqualified: prohibited substance in urine.

NB: The prohibited substance, traces of which were found in the samples of all of the above, was morphine. The source of which was determined as being a batch of Connolly's Red Mills 14% Racehorse Cubes. No fines were imposed on the trainers involved.

# Raceform median times 2004

### ASCOT
5f ... 1m 1.93
6f ... 1m 15.99
7f ... 1m 29.67
1m Rnd ... 1m 43.04
1m Str ... 1m 41.92
1m 2f ... 2m 8.73
1m 4f ... 2m 33.56
2m 45y ... 3m 34.84
2m 4f ... 4m 24.53
2m 6f 34y ... 4m 56.57

### AYR
5f ... 1m 0.43
6f ... 1m 13.72
7f 50y ... 1m 32.47
1m ... 1m 43.12
1m 1f 20y ... 1m 54.21
1m 2f ... 2m 12.19
1m 2f 192y ... 2m 23.32
1m 5f 13y ... 2m 55.85
1m 7f ... 3m 22.47
2m 1f 105y ... 3m 54.77

### BATH
5f 11y ... 1m 2.50
5f 161y ... 1m 11.14
1m 5y ... 1m 41.00
1m 2f 46y ... 2m 11.00
1m 3f 144y ... 2m 30.30
1m 5f 22y ... 2m 51.30
2m 1f 34y ... 3m 49.60

### BEVERLEY
5f ... 1m 4.00
7f 100y ... 1m 34.30
1m 100y ... 1m 47.30
1m 1f 207y ... 2m 7.20
1m 4f 16y ... 2m 39.30
2m 35y ... 3m 39.40

### BRIGHTON
5f 59y ... 1m 2.27
5f 213y ... 1m 10.10
6f 209y ... 1m 22.60
7f 214y ... 1m 35.00
1m 1f 209y ... 2m 2.54
1m 3f 196y ... 2m 32.10

### CARLISLE
5f ... 1m 1.50
5f 193y ... 1m 14.20
6f 192y ... 1m 27.10
7f 200y ... 1m 40.00
1m 1f 61y ... 1m 58.03
1m 3f 206y ... 2m 32.40
1m 6f 32y ... 3m 7.30
2m 1f 52y ... 3m 49.90

### CATTERICK
5f ... 1m 0.60
5f 212y ... 1m 14.00
7f ... 1m 27.50
1m 3f 214y ... 2m 39.00
1m 5f 175y ... 3m 4.50
1m 7f 177y ... 3m 31.40

### CHEPSTOW
5f 16y ... 59.50
6f 16y ... 1m 12.20
7f 16y ... 1m 23.20
1m 14y ... 1m 35.90
1m 2f 36y ... 2m 9.60
1m 4f 23y ... 2m 38.50
2m 49y ... 3m 39.10
2m 2f ... 4m 0.20

### CHESTER
5f 16y ... 1m 1.98
6f 18y ... 1m 15.88
7f 2y ... 1m 28.29
7f 122y ... 1m 34.75
1m 2f 75y ... 2m 12.55
1m 3f 79y ... 2m 25.49
1m 4f 66y ... 2m 40.52
1m 5f 89y ... 2m 55.39
1m 7f 195y ... 3m 33.78
2m 2f 147y ... 4m 5.38

### DONCASTER
5f ... 1m 1.42
5f 140y ... 1m 8.09
6f ... 1m 14.28
6f 110y ... 1m 20.48
7f ... 1m 27.81
1m Rnd ... 1m 40.55
1m Str ... 1m 41.60
1m 2f 60y ... 2m 11.76
1m 4f ... 2m 35.70
1m 6f 132y ... 3m 9.74
2m 110y ... 3m 41.96
2m 2f ... 3m 57.93

### EPSOM
5f ... 55.68
6f ... 1m 10.63
7f ... 1m 23.95
1m 114y ... 1m 45.74
1m 2f 18y ... 2m 8.70
1m 4f 10y ... 2m 38.72

### FOLKESTONE
5f ... 1m 0.70
6f ... 1m 13.60
6f 189y ... 1m 25.70
7f ... 1m 27.80
1m 1f 149y ... 2m 5.16
1m 4f ... 2m 40.40
1m 7f 92y ... 3m 27.20
2m 93y ... 3m 40.60

### GOODWOOD
5f ... 59.05
6f ... 1m 12.84
7f ... 1m 28.03
1m ... 1m 40.27
1m 1f ... 1m 56.86
1m 1f 192y ... 2m 7.68
1m 3f ... 2m 26.11
1m 4f ... 2m 38.93
1m 6f ... 3m 3.75
2m ... 3m 30.66
2m 4f ... 4m 20.89

### HAMILTON
5f 4y ... 1m 1.26
6f 5y ... 1m 13.10
1m 65y ... 1m 49.30
1m 1f 36y ... 1m 59.60
1m 3f 16y ... 2m 26.50
1m 4f 17y ... 2m 39.20
1m 5f 9y ... 2m 53.40

### HAYDOCK
5f ... 1m 2.07
6f ... 1m 14.89
7f 30y ... 1m 32.16
1m 30y ... 1m 45.55
1m 2f 120y ... 2m 17.73
1m 3f 200y ... 2m 35.16
1m 6f ... 3m 6.15
2m 45y ... 3m 37.90

### KEMPTON
5f ... 1m 1.21
6f ... 1m 13.07
7f Jub ... 1m 27.27
7f Rnd ... 1m 26.61
1m Jub ... 1m 40.47
1m Rnd ... 1m 39.62
1m 1f ... 1m 54.33
1m 2f ... 2m 6.14
1m 3f 30y ... 2m 23.05
1m 4f ... 2m 35.00
1m 6f 92y ... 3m 10.66
2m ... 3m 30.36

### LEICESTER
5f 2y ... 1m 0.93
5f 218y ... 1m 13.40
7f 9y ... 1m 26.10
1m 9y ... 1m 42.60
1m 1f 218y ... 2m 8.40
1m 3f 183y ... 2m 34.68

### LINGFIELD (TURF)
5f ... 58.87
6f ... 1m 11.65
7f ... 1m 24.21
7f 140y ... 1m 31.46
1m 1f ... 1m 55.29
1m 2f ... 2m 9.60
1m 3f 106y ... 2m 29.52
1m 6f ... 3m 6.92
2m ... 3m 33.19

### LINGFIELD (A.W)
5f ... 59.78
6f ... 1m 12.92
7f ... 1m 25.94
1m ... 1m 39.55
1m 2f ... 2m 7.58
1m 4f ... 2m 34.08
1m 5f ... 2m 48.08
2m ... 3m 28.58

### MUSSELBURGH
5f ... 1m 0.40
7f 30y ... 1m 29.53
1m ... 1m 42.70
1m 1f ... 1m 53.20
1m 4f ... 2m 38.02
1m 6f ... 3m 5.60
2m ... 3m 33.70

### NEWBURY
5f 34y ... 1m 2.65
6f 8y ... 1m 14.37
7f ... 1m 27.22
7f 64y ... 1m 31.26
1m Str ... 1m 40.83
1m 7y ... 1m 38.73
1m 1f ... 1m 54.35
1m 2f 6y ... 2m 8.71
1m 3f 5y ... 2m 22.81
1m 4f 5y ... 2m 36.29
1m 5f 61y ... 2m 50.99
2m ... 3m 35.43

### NEWCASTLE
5f ... 1m 1.53
6f ... 1m 15.04
7f ... 1m 28.02
1m ... 1m 43.48
1m 3y Str ... 1m 41.20
1m 1f 9y ... 1m 57.80
1m 2f 32y ... 2m 11.60
1m 4f 93y ... 2m 43.30
1m 6f 97y ... 3m 9.90
2m 19y ... 3m 35.03

### NEWMARKET (ROWLEY)
5f ... 1m 0.41
6f ... 1m 13.09
7f ... 1m 26.47
1m ... 1m39.40
1m 1f ... 1m 51.91
1m 2f ... 2m 5.69
1m 4f ... 2m 33.46
1m 6f ... 3m 0.32
2m ... 3m 26.52
2m 2f ... 3m 52.62

### NEWMARKET (JULY)
5f ... 59.65
6f ... 1m 13.32
7f ... 1m 26.77
1m ... 1m 40.48
1m 2f ... 2m 6.46
1m 4f ... 2m 32.96
1m 6f 175y ... 3m 10.76
2m 24y ... 3m 26.99

### NOTTINGHAM
5f 13y ... 1m 1.80
6f 15y ... 1m 14.80
1m 54y ... 1m 46.40
1m 1f 213y ... 2m 9.50
1m 6f 15y ... 3m 7.20
2m 9y ... 3m 33.50

### PONTEFRACT
5f ... 1m 3.80
6f ... 1m 17.30
1m 4y ... 1m 45.60
1m 2f 6y ... 2m 13.91
1m 4f 8y ... 2m 40.05
2m 1f 22y ... 3m 50.50
2m 1f 216y ... 4m 3.00
2m 5f 122y ... 4m 57.60

### REDCAR
5f ... 58.70
6f ... 1m 11.70
7f ... 1m 24.90
1m ... 1m 37.70
1m 1f ... 1m 53.40
1m 2f ... 2m 6.80
1m 3f ... 2m 21.00
1m 6f 19y ... 3m 5.00
2m 4y ... 3m 31.50

### RIPON
5f ... 1m 0.20
6f ... 1m 12.90
1m ... 1m 41.10
1m 1f ... 1m 53.85
1m 2f ... 2m 8.00
1m 4f 60y ... 2m 39.90
2m ... 3m 33.50

### SALISBURY
5f ... 1m 1.57
6f ... 1m 14.94
6f 212y ... 1m 29.00
1m ... 1m 42.97
1m 1f 198y ... 2m 8.32
1m 4f ... 2m 36.35
1m 6f 15y ... 3m 6.00

### SANDOWN
5f 6y ... 1m 2.19
7f 16y ... 1m 31.09
1m 14y ... 1m 43.92
1m 1f ... 1m 56.11
1m 2f 7y ... 2m 10.18
1m 3f 91y ... 2m 28.07
1m 6f ... 3m 4.37
2m 78y ... 3m 38.23

### SOUTHWELL (TURF)
6f ... 1m 15.80
7f ... 1m 29.20
1m 2f ... 2m 13.90
1m 4f ... 2m 40.30
2m ... 3m 37.20

### SOUTHWELL(A.W)
5f ... 1m 0.40
6f ... 1m 16.90
7f ... 1m 30.80
1m ... 1m 44.60
1m 3f ... 2m 28.90
1m 4f ... 2m 42.10
1m 6f ... 3m 9.70
2m ... 3m 52.40

### THIRSK
5f ... 59.90
6f ... 1m 12.50
7f ... 1m 27.10
1m ... 1m 39.70
1m 4f ... 2m 35.20
2m ... 3m 31.20

### WARWICK
5f ... 1m 0.20
6f 21y ... 1m 12.30
7f 26y ... 1m 24.90
1m 22y ... 1m 39.30
1m 2f 188y ... 2m 19.40
1m 4f 134y ... 2m 43.30
1m 6f 213y ... 3m 15.20
2m 39y ... 3m 31.81

### WINDSOR
5f 10y ... 1m 1.20
6f ... 1m 13.84
1m 67y ... 1m 45.60
1m 2f 7y ... 2m 8.30
1m 3f 135y ... 2m 30.10

### WOLVERHAMPTON
5f ... 1m 2.80
6f ... 1m 15.80
7f ... 1m 30.32
1m 100y ... 1m 51.09
1m 1f 79y ... 2m 3.00
1m 4f ... 2m 41.80
1m 6f 166y ... 3m 21.50
2m 46y ... 3m 42.30

### YARMOUTH
5f 43y ... 1m 2.70
6f 3y ... 1m 13.60
7f 3y ... 1m 26.50
1m 3y ... 1m 39.70
1m 2f 21y ... 2m 7.97
1m 3f 101y ... 2m 27.40
1m 6f 17y ... 3m 5.20
2m ... 3m 33.00
2m 2f 51y ... 4m 6.90

### YORK
5f 3y ... 58.74
6f 3y ... 1m 11.07
6f 217y ... 1m 23.31
7f 205y ... 1m 37.74
1m 208y ... 1m 49.96
1m 2f 88y ... 2m 9.44
1m 3f 198y ... 2m 28.86
1m 5f 197y ... 2m 56.40
1m 7f 198y ... 3m 23.25

# Raceform Flat speed figures 2004

(Best time performances achieved 9th November 2003 - 6th November 2004 (min. rating 110, two-year-olds 105)

## THREE YEAR-OLDS AND UPWARDS - Turf

A One 114 (8f,Wdr,GF,Jun 27)
Abunawwas 113 (6f,Naa,Y,May 5)
Ace 115 (8f,Leo,GF,Aug 15)
Ace Of Hearts 111 (8f,Pon,GF,Jun 20)
Acropolis 119 (12f,Lon,G,Oct 3)
Actrice 115 (10 1/2f,Sai,GS,May 31)
Agata 110 (10 1/2f,Cha,GS,Jun 13)
Aintnecessarilyso 110 (6f,Don,G,Jun 26)
Airwave 113 (5f,Yor,S,Aug 19)
Al Eile 113 (16f,Leo,SH,Oct 31)
Albinus 110 (11f,Nby,G,Sep 17)
Alcazar 110 (14f,Not,G,Mar 31)
Alexander Goldrun 114 (10f,Lon,G,Oct 3)
Alkaadhem 114 (10f,Goo,GF,Sep 12)
Alkaased 113 (12f,Hay,G,Jly 3)
All Too Beautiful 114(10f,Cur,G,Sep 19)
Almond Mousse 115 (8f,Sai,VS,May 1)
Almuraad 114 (8f,Nmk,GF,May 21)
Always First 111 (12f,Goo,G,Jly 28)
Always Waining 110 (12f,Asc,GF,Jly 24)
Amarula Ridge 110 (8f,Leo,S,Apr 18)
Amathia 111 (10f,Cha,S,May 7)
American Post 111 (8f,Lon,GS,Apr 25)
Ancient World 114 (10f,Wdr,GS,Aug 28)
Andean 110 (8f,Yar,GF,Apr 12)
Ange Gardien 114 (12f,Cha,GS,Jun 6)
Ansar 111 (16f,Leo,G,Jun 2)
Antediluvian 110 (8f,Ham,G,Jun 24)
Antonius Pius 117 (8f,Asc,GF,Jun 15)
Apeiron 110 (10f,Dea,HY,Aug 21)
Aperitif 111 (8f,Nmk,GS,Jly 8)
Appalachian Trail 110 (8f,Hay,GF,May 22)
Apsara 114 (10f,Pon,GF,Jly 6)
Apsis 111 (10f,Lon,GS,Sep 18)
Arakan 114 (7f,Nmk,GF,Jun 26)
Arcalis 111 (10 1/2f,Yor,G,Jly 10)
Arch Rebel 113 (10f,Cur,GF,Aug 21)
Arkholme 111 (8f,Asc,G,Jly 9)
Art Master 116 (8f,Cha,GS,Jun 21)
Art Moderne 113 (8f,Sai,S,Mar 28)
Ashdown Express 115 (6f,Nmk,GS,Jly 8)
Ask For The Moon 115 (10 1/2f,Sai,GS,Apr 9)
Assigh Lady 111 (5f,Cur,HY,Mar 21)
Athlumney Lad 111 (10f,Naa,Y,May 5)
Atlantic Viking 110 (5f,Ncs,S,Jun 25)
Attraction 120 (8f,Leo,GF,Sep 11)
Attune 110 (7f,Don,GF,Sep 9)
Aubonne 113 (10f,Lon,GS,Jun 17)
Audience 114 (8f,Yor,S,Aug 19)
Autumn Glory 119 (8f,Yor,GS,May 12)
Autumn Pearl 110 (5f,Ham,S,Sep 19)
Avonbridge 115 (5f,Cha,GS,Jun 6)
Awake 114 (5f,Nmk,GF,Jly 7)
Azamour 119 (8f,Asc,GF,Jun 15)
Azarole 110 (8f,Kem,GF,May 29)

Babodana 113 (8f,Wdr,GF,Jun 26)
Bachelor Duke 114 (8f,Asc,GF,Jun 15)
Bago 122 (12f,Lon,G,Oct 3)
Bahamian Pirate 117 (5f,Yor,S,Aug 19)
Bahiano 112 (7f,Asc,GF,Jun 16)
Bailador 110 (10f,Lon,G,Jun 17)
Bailamos 110 (16f,Yor,G,Aug 17)
Balkan Knight 110 (12f,Yor,GS,May 11)
Balmont 112 (6f,Nmk,GS,Jly 8)
Baltic King 110 (5f,Bev,GS,Aug 28)
Bandari 115 (10f,San,GS,Jun 1)
Bandit Queen 111 (7f,Chs,GF,Jun 8)
Baqah 115 (8f,Cha,GS,Jun 6)
Barancella 111 (10 1/2f,Sai,S,May 11)
Barella 110 (7f,Cur,S,Apr 25)
Barking Mad 111 (10f,Ayr,GF,Aug 7)
Barolo 112 (14f,Leo,GY,Jly 14)
Battle Chant 112 (10f,Goo,GF,Sep 12)
Battle Games 111 (12f,Leo,GY,May 9)
Bayhirr 112 (8f,Wdr,GF,Jun 27)
Beauchamp Pilot 114 (8f,Wdr,GF,Jun 26)
Behkara 112 (15f,Dea,VS,Aug 22)
Benbaun 112 (5f,Cur,GF,Sep 5)
Beneventa 110 (12f,Nmk,G,Jly 17)
Bessemer 112 (10f,Ayr,GF,Aug 7)
Big Bad Bob 111 (10f,Lon,GS,Jun 17)
Big Moment 110 (14f,Hay,S,Sep 25)
Binary Vision 112 (8f,Yor,GF,Jun 12)
Blessyourpinksox 110 (10f,Naa,GF,Jun 7)
Blue Away 113 (16f,Leo,G,Jun 2)
Blue Canari 117 (12f,Cha,GS,Jun 6)
Blue Spinnaker 116 (8f,Yor,GS,May 12)
Bocaccio 114 (8f,Cur,Y,Sep 18)
Boogie Street 112 (5f,Goo,GF,Jly 29)
Boston Lodge 114 (7f,Goo,GF,Sep 11)
Bourgeois 112 (12f,Ham,GS,May 14)
Bowman s Crossing 110 (8f,Asc,G,Jly 10)
Brian Boru 116 (15f,Dea,VS,Aug 22)
Briareus 111 (10f,Don,GS,May 3)
Bricks And Porter 112 (8f,Leo,GY,May 9)
Brief Goodbye 110 (10f,Don,GS,May 3)
Bright Abundance 112 (8f,Cha,GS,Jun 6)
Bright Sky 115 (10f,Sai,GS,Mar 6)
Brunel 116 (8f,Asc,GF,Jun 15)
Byron 115 (7f,Goo,G,Jly 27)

Cache Creek 111 (10f,Leo,GF,Jly 24)
Cacique 112 (8f,Lon,G,Oct 2)
Caesarion 110 (8f,Cha,GS,Jun 13)
Cairdeas 113 (10f,Naa,Y,May 5)
Cairns 110 (8f,Lon,GF,May 16)
Calcutta 111 (8f,Don,F,Sep 11)
Callow Lake 110 (16f,Leo,G,Jun 2)
Cape Of Good Hope 113 (6f,Asc,F,Jun 19)
Caradak 110 (8f,Cur,G,Sep 19)
Caribbean Coral 115 (5f,Ncs,S,Jun 25)
Carini 110 (10f,Nmk,GF,Aug 6)
Cartography 112 (7f,Asc,GF,Jun 16)
Castleton 116 (8f,Asc,GF,Jun 15)
Cattiva Generosa 112 (8f,Dea,G,Aug 1)
Caustic Wit 111 (6f,Nby,GF,Jly 1)
Celtic Heroine 112 (8f,Asc,GF,Jly 23)
Celtic Mill 112 (5f,Don,GF,Sep 9)
Chancellor 111 (10 1/2f,Lon,VS,May 2)
Chappel Cresent 110 (7 1/2f,Chs,GS,May 7)
Charming Groom 114 (8f,Cha,GS,Jun 13)
Charmo 112 (8f,Cha,GS,Jun 21)
Chateau Nicol 111 (7f,Kem,G,Jun 23)
Checkit 114 (10f,Ayr,GF,Jly 19)
Cherry Mix 121 (12f,Lon,G,Oct 3)
Chic 114 (7f,Nby,G,Aug 14)
Chineur 110 (5f,Cha,GS,Jun 6)
Chookie Heiton 113 (5f,Bev,GS,Aug 28)
Chorist 114 (10f,Cur,G,Jun 26)
Christavelli 115 (8f,Leo,GY,May 9)
Ciel 110 (12f,Leo,S,Apr 18)
Circuit Dancer 110 (6f,Yor,GF,Jun 11)
Clety 113 (15f,Dea,VS,Aug 22)
Collier Hill 114 (12f,Ham,GS,May 14)
Colour Wheel 111 (7f,Nmk,GF,Jun 18)
Comete 113 (7f,Lon,GS,Sep 18)
Comfy 110 (10f,Asc,GF,Jun 16)
Compton Bolter 111 (11f,Nby,G,Sep 17)
Compton s Eleven 111 (7f,Goo,GF,Jly 29)
Coquette Rouge 111 (16f,Leo,SH,Oct 31)
Coroner 110 (10f,Lon,GS,Apr 4)
Corrib Eclipse 112 (16f,Yor,G,Aug 17)
Corridor Creeper 113 (5f,Ncs,S,Jun 25)
Corriolanus 112 (10f,Nmk,GF,Aug 6)
Country Reel 112 (6f,Asc,F,Jun 19)
Court Masterpiece 118 (7f,Asc,GF,Jly 24)
Coy 113 (8f,Asc,GF,Jly 23)
Craig s Falcon 112 (12f,Lon,HO,May 6)
Crimson Palace 110 (10 1/2f,Yor,GS,May 12)
Crocodile Dundee113(10f,San,GS,Jly 2)
Crow Wood 110 (12f,Hay,G,Jly 3)
Crystal Castle 113 (6f,Asc,F,Jun 19)
Currency 114 (5f,Nmk,GF,Jly 7)
Cut Quartz 116 (15f,Dea,VS,Aug 22)
Cutting Crew 112 (12f,Goo,G,Jly 28)

Dalicia 110 (10f,Lon,GS,Sep 18)
Dalna 111 (6f,Msn,VS,Oct 29)
Dancing Bay 116 (16f,Yor,G,Aug 17)
Danelissima 110 (12f,Hay,G,Jly 3)
Dawn Invasion 111 (10f,Leo,Y,Mar 28)
Day Flight 116 (12f,Cha,GS,Jun 6)
Day Or Night 113 (12f,Cha,GS,Jun 6)
Day Ticket 112 (10f,Cur,GF,Aug 21)
Delfos 113 (10f,Sai,GS,May 5)
Demon Dancer 112 (10f,Dea,HO,Aug 14)
Denebola 116 (7f,Lon,S,Oct 9)
Desert Destiny 113 (7f,Nmk,GF,Jun 26)
Desert Fantasy 113 (6f,Cur,GF,Aug 21)
Desert Quest 111 (10f,Eps,G,Jun 4)
Desert Star 110 (8f,Don,F,Sep 11)
Devise 113 (5f,Nmk,GF,Jly 7)
Dexterity 110 (6 1/2f,Dea,GS,Aug 8)
Diamond Green 118 (8f,Asc,GF,Jun 15)
Diamond Tango 114 (12f,Lon,S,Sep 12)
Dobby Road 111 (5f,Cha,GS,Jun 6)
Dolma 115 (6 1/2f,Dea,GS,Aug 8)
Domirati 111 (5f,Nmk,GF,Jly 7)
Double Obsession 115 (15f,Dea,VS,Aug 22)
Doyen 120 (12f,Asc,F,Jun 19)
Dragon Flyer 110 (5f,Lei,GF,Sep 7)
Dubai Success 114 (12f,Nby,G,Apr 17)
Duck Row 117 (8f,Yor,GS,May 12)
Duke Of Venice 110 (16f,Asc,F,Jun 18)
Dumaran 110 (10f,Nby,GS,Sep 18)
Dunaskin 116 (10 1/2f,Yor,S,Aug 18)

Ecomium 111 (10f,Cur,YS,Oct 2)
Eisteddfod 111 (7f,Sal,GS,Aug 20)
Eklim 114 (8f,Cur,S,Apr 25)
El Coto 116 (8f,Yor,GS,May 12)
El Hurano 110 (12f,Lon,HY,Oct 17)
Elshadi 110 (10f,Nmk,GF,Aug 6)
Elusive Dream 110 (12f,Asc,GF,Sep 26)
Enchanted 110 (7f,Asc,GF,May 22)
Enchantment 111 (5f,Yor,S,Aug 18)
Ephesus 110 (7f,San,GF,Jun 12)
Essex 113 (16f,Cur,GY,Oct 10)
Ettrick Water 116 (7f,Goo,GF,Sep 11)
Europaea 111 (6f,Cur,GF,May 23)
Everest 110 (8f,Nby,G,Jly 17)
Execute 117 (10 1/2f,Lon,VS,May 2)
Exterior 111 (9f,Goo,GS,Aug 27)

Fair Mix 115 (10 1/2f,Lon,VS,May 2)
Fandango Dancer 112 (8f,Leo,GY,Jly 14)
Fantasy Believer 115 (6f,Nby,GF,Jly 1)
Fast And Furious 110 (11f,Lon,GS,Apr 11)
Fayr Jag 114 (6f,Asc,F,Jun 19)
Fearn Royal 112 (8f,Leo,G,Jun 2)
Fire Up The Band 112 (5f,Chs,G,Jly 10)
Firebreak 116 (7f,Nmk,S,Oct 16)
First Charter 117 (16f,Yor,G,Aug 17)
Fit The Cove 111 (8f,Leo,SH,Oct 31)
Five Dynasties 113 (12f,Cha,GS,Jun 6)
Flamboyant Lad 111(12f,Nmk,S,Oct 14)
Flighty Fellow 110 (8f,Don,F,Sep 11)
Flying Bantam 110 (6f,Red,S,Nov 1)
Fokine 113 (7f,Asc,GF,Jun 16)
Fong s Thong 113 (7f,Nby,G,Jly 16)
Forever Phoenix 113 (5f,Lin,S,May 7)
Fort 112 (12f,Asc,GF,Sep 26)
Frizzante 116 (6f,Nmk,GS,Jly 8)
Fromsong 111 (5f,Not,G,Mar 31)
Fruhlingssturm 113 (10f,Eps,GS,Jly 8)
Fruit Of Glory 112 (5f,Not,G,Jly 10)
Funfair 110 (8f,Don,F,Sep 11)
Funfair Wane 111 (6f,Ayr,S,Sep 18)

Gamut 119 (12f,Sai,GS,Jly 4)
Gateman 116 (8f,Wdr,GF,Jun 26)
Gatwick 112 (8f,Hay,GF,May 22)
Gemini Guest 112 (16f,Cur,GF,Jun 27)
Geordieland 111 (12f,Lon,HY,Oct 17)
Glocca Morra 112 (5f,Cur,GF,Sep 5)
Go For Gold 110 (12f,Goo,G,Jly 27)
Gold Medallist 117 (15f,Dea,VS,Aug 22)
Golden Nun 110 (6 1/2f,Dea,GS,Aug 8)
Golden Sahara 113 (7f,Goo,GF,Sep 11)
Golden Triangle 110 (14f,Leo,GY,Jly 3)
Goldeva 112 (6f,Pon,GS,Aug 15)
Gonfilia 111 (7f,Lin,S,May 8)
Goodbye Mr Bond 110 (9f,Crl,GF,Jly 29)
Grampian 110 (12f,Hay,G,Jly 3)
Grand Passion 112 (8f,Cur,GF,Jun 27)
Grand Reward 112 (6f,Cur,GF,Aug 21)
Granston 110 (8f,Asc,GF,Sep 24)
Greenslades 111 (7f,Asc,GF,May 22)
Grey Cossack 111 (6f,Red,S,Apr 12)
Grey Lilas 113 (8f,Lon,GF,May 16)
Grey Swallow 115 (10f,Leo,GF,Sep 11)

H Harrison 114 (7f,Chs,GF,Jun 8)
Haafhd 117 (8f,Asc,GF,Jun 15)
Halmahera 111 (5f,Ncs,S,Jun 25)
Hamairi 113 (7f,Leo,GF,Jun 9)
Hanabad 110 (6f,Cur,GF,Aug 21)
Harry Potter 110 (8f,Not,GF,Jly 24)
Hasik 110 (16f,Cur,GF,Jun 27)
Hatch 110 (7f,Mus,G,Apr 30)
Hathrah 111 (8f,Nmk,G,May 2)
Hazarista 115 (12f,Cur,GF,Jly 18)
Hidden Hope 111 (12f,Asc,GF,Sep 24)
High Accolade 116 (12f,Asc,F,Jun 19)
High Flash 110 (8f,Dea,VS,Aug 10)
Hills Spitfire 110 (10f,Pon,GF,Jly 6)
Hurricane Alan 115 (8f,San,GS,Apr 24)

Icklingham 113 (12f,Leo,GY,May 9)
Ikhtyar 115 (10f,Asc,GF,Jun 16)
Illustrious Miss 114 (7f,Lin,S,May 8)
Imperial Dancer 116 (12f,Lon,G,Oct 3)
Imperialistic 110 (7 1/2f,Bev,GS,Apr 22)
Imtiyaz 112 (10f,Eps,GS,Jly 8)
Indian Haven 111 (8f,San,GS,Apr 24)
Into The Dark 112 (11f,Ayr,S,Sep 18)
Intricate Web 110 (10f,Red,G,Jun 19)
Islero Noir 110 (10f,Dea,HY,Aug 21)
Ivowen 110 (14f,Leo,GY,Jly 14)

Jabaar 112 (10f,Nby,GS,Sep 18)
Jacks Estate 114 (5f,Cur,G,Jly 17)
Jedburgh 111 (7f,Goo,GF,Sep 11)
Jimmy Ryan 112 (5f,Nmk,GF,Jun 25)
Johannian 110 (8f,Not,GS,Jly 3)
Johnston s Diamond 110 (5f,Chs,GS,May 7)
Jonny Ebeneezer 112 (5f,Hay,S,Sep 25)
Joursanvault 113 (8f,Cha,GS,Jun 21)

Kalabar 115 (12f,Lon,HO,May 6)
Kalaman 117 (10f,Ayr,GF,Jly 19)
Kalatuna 110 (10 1/2f,Sai,G,Apr 9)
Kehaar 113 (8f,Nmk,GS,Jly 8)
Keltos 114 (7f,Nmk,S,Oct 16)
Khabfair 111 (6f,Nby,GF,Jly 1)
Kheleyf 115 (7f,Asc,GF,Jun 16)
Kid Z Play 111 (10f,Ayr,G,Jun 17)
Killmorey 110 (12 1/2f,Ncs,S,Aug 30)
Kind 111 (5f,Ham,S,Sep 19)
Kindjhal 117 (12f,Lon,HO,May 6)
King Harson 110 (7f,Chs,S,Aug 20)
King Jock 114 (8f,Leo,GF,May 26)
King Of Cry 110 (12f,Lon,VS,May 13)
King s Drama 115 (8f,Sai,VS,May 1)
Kings College Boy 111 (5f,Pon,GF,Aug 4)
Kings Point 110 (7f,Nmk,GF,Jun 26)
Kinnaird 114 (10f,Cur,G,Sep 19)
Kisses For Me 114 (9f,Cur,GF,Jly 18)
Kool 110 (7f,War,GS,Apr 12)
Krataios 115 (8f,Sai,VS,May 1)

Lady Portia 110 (6f,Cur,S,Apr 4)
Larkwing 111 (12f,Goo,G,Jly 28)
Latice 119 (12f,Lon,G,Oct 3)
Latino Magic 115 (10f,Leo,GF,Jly 24)
Le Leopard 110 (16f,Cur,GF,Jun 27)
Le Vie Dei Colori 115 (8f,Goo,G,Jly 28)
Leeside Music 113 (8f,Cur,Y,Sep 18)
Legend Has It 111 (12f,Leo,GY,May 9)
Leicester Square 113 (8f,Kem,GF,May 29)
Leitrim House 114 (7f,Cur,G,May 3)
Lennel 110 (10f,Ayr,GF,Jly 20)
Leoballero 111 (7f,Nmk,GF,Jun 18)
Leonor Fini 113 (9f,Cur,GF,Jly 18)
Leos Shuil 111 (12f,Leo,S,Apr 18)

Let The Lion Roar 111(12f,Eps,G,Jun 5)
Lets Roll 111 (12f,Rip,S,Jly 17)
Life 111 (8f,Dea,GS,Jly 31)
Life Class 110 (7f,Cur,HY,Mar 21)
Little Englander 112 (8f,Not,GS,Jly 3)
Lochridge 110 (6f,Yor,GS,Jly 9)
Lone Plainsman 110 (5f,Cur,G,Jly 17)
Look Honey 111 (10f,Lon,GS,Jun 17)
Lord Darnley 113 (12f,Lon,GS,Jun 27)
Lord Du Sud 117 (12f,Lon,VS,May 13)
Lorikeet 111 (16f,Cur,GF,Jun 27)
Love And Bubbles 111 (10 1/2f,Sai,S,May 11)
Love In Seattle 111 (8f,Mus,G,Apr 30)
Loyal Tycoon 116 (6f,Eps,GF,Jly 1)
Lucky Spin 113 (7f,War,GF,Jun 19)
Lucky Story 119 (8f,Asc,GF,Sep 25)
Lucky Strike 111 (6 1/2f,Dea,GS,Aug 8)
Lune D Or 111 (12 1/2f,Dea,GS,Aug 7)
Lyonels Glory 112 (12f,Lon,GS,Jun 27)

Mac Love 112 (6f,Sal,F,Jun 13)
Madid 113 (7f,San,G,Jun 3)
Magic Glade 111 (5f,Mus,GF,Apr 11)
Majestic Desert 115 (8f,Asc,F,Jun 18)
Majestic Times 113 (6f,Cur,S,Apr 4)
Major Title 112 (8f,Cur,GF,May 22)
Makfool 110 (8f,Hay,GF,May 22)
Makhlab 110 (7f,Hay,GF,Jun 3)
Maktavish 113 (5f,Chs,GS,May 7)
Malevitch 113 (12f,Lon,VS,May 13)
Mamool 116 (12f,Lon,G,Oct 3)
Man At Arms 110 (12f,Bri,F,Jun 10)
Man Of Letters 110 (7f,Mus,G,Apr 30)
Mango Mischief 110 (10f,Sal,GF,Jun 8)
Manyana 111 (12f,Cha,GS,Jun 6)
Maraahel 111 (12f,Goo,G,Jly 27)
Maralan 111 (10f,Leo,GF,May 26)
Marbye 114 (8f,Dea,G,Aug 1)
Maredsous 117 (12f,Lon,HO,May 6)
Marinnette 110 (12f,Cur,GY,Oct 10)
Maritime Blues 110 (10f,Ayr,S,Aug 20)
Marnhac 110 (11f,Lon,GS,Apr 11)
Marshall 112 (8f,Sai,VS,May 1)
Martaline 110 (12 1/2f,Dea,HY,Aug 29)
Martha Stewart 112 (8f,Dea,G,Aug 1)
Martillo 118 (8f,Sai,VS,May 1)
Masafi 113 (9f,Crl,GF,Jly 29)
Master Robbie 110 (7f,Goo,GF,Sep 11)
Material Witness 110(7f,War,GF,Jun 27)
Matin De Tempete 110 (8f,Dea,GS,Aug 8)
Matty Tun 113 (5f,Don,S,Oct 23)
Maxwell 116 (8f,Sai,VS,May 1)
Mazuna 113 (12f,Asc,GF,Sep 24)
Meath 113 (8f,Leo,S,Apr 18)
Medicinal 110 (10f,Leo,GF,Jly 24)
Mighty Mist 112 (16f,Leo,G,Jun 2)
Mijdaaf 111 (10f,Pon,GF,Jly 6)
Mikado 113 (10f,Cur,YS,Oct 2)
Millagros 110 (9f,Crl,GF,Jly 29)
Millenary 115 (16f,Yor,G,Aug 17)
Millennium Force 110 (7f,Lon,GS,Jun 27)
Millionaia 112 (10 1/2f,Cha,GS,Jun 13)
Millybaa 112 (6f,Naa,Y,May 5)
Mine 116 (8f,Yor,GS,May 12)
Mingun 110 (10f,Cur,YS,Oct 2)
Miss Emma 116 (6f,Msn,VS,Oct 29)
Miss France 113 (10 1/2f,Sai,G,Apr 9)
Miss Mambo 114 (8f,Cha,GS,Jun 6)
Mister Farmer 111 (12f,Lon,GS,Jun 27)
Mister Monet 115 (10f,Dea,HY,Aug 21)
Mister Sacha 114 (9f,Lon,VS,May 13)
Misty Mountain 111 (9f,Cur,GF,Jly 18)
Moayed 110 (6f,Nmk,G,May 1)
Mombassa 112 (8f,Cur,Y,Sep 18)
Monsieur Bond 116 (7f,Cur,YS,Apr 4)
Monsignor Phil 114 (12f,Leo,GY,May 9)
Monturani 115 (10f,Cur,G,Sep 19)
Moon Dazzle 111 (8f,Asc,F,Jun 18)
Moon Unit 112 (6f,Naa,Y,May 5)
Moss Vale 113 (6f,Sal,F,Jun 13)
Mount Hillaby 113 (8f,Yor,GF,Sep 5)
Mr Houdini 110 (8f,Leo,G,Jun 2)
Mr Malarkey 110 (5f,Nmk,GF,Jly 7)
Mukafeh 113 (8f,Nmk,GF,May 21)
Muqbil 115 (10f,Nby,G,Jly 17)
Mutasallil 115 (12f,Don,GF,Sep 11)
My Renee 112 (12f,Asc,GF,Sep 24)
My Risk 115 (8f,Sai,VS,May 1)
Mystic Melody 111 (8f,Sai,VS,May 1)

Naahil 110 (16f,Cur,GF,Jun 27)
Naahy 114 (7f,Leo,GF,Jun 9)
Najeebon 111 (6f,Nby,GF,Jly 1)
Napoletano 110 (8f,Dea,VS,Aug 10)
Napper Tandy 113 (10f,Leo,Y,Mar 28)
Nashaab 110 (7f,Goo,GF,Sep 11)
Nataliya 110 (8f,Asc,GF,Jly 23)
Native Title 112 (5f,Chs,GS,May 7)
Nayyir 117 (8f,Goo,G,Jly 28)
Nebraska Tornado 112(8f,Dea,G,Aug 1)
Nemo Fugat 111 (8f,Yor,GF,Sep 5)
Never Without Me 111 (5f,Pon,GF,Aug 4)
New Morning 114 (10f,Sal,GF,Aug 11)
New Seeker 115 (8f,Asc,GS,Apr 28)
Nights Cross 112 (6f,Chs,GF,Aug 1)
Noahs Ark 114 (9f,Cur,GF,Jly 18)
Nonno Carlo 110 (10f,Lon,GS,Jun 17)
Nopekan 112 (12f,Leo,GY,May 9)
Norse Dancer 116 (10f,Leo,GF,Sep 11)
North Light 119 (12f,Lon,G,Oct 3)
Nyramba 113 (8f,Cha,GS,Jun 6)
Nysaean 112 (10f,Lon,GS,Apr 4)

Odiham 110 (12f,Goo,G,Jly 28)
On The Trail 112 (5f,Pon,GF,Aug 4)
One Cool Cat 114 (5f,Yor,S,Aug 19)
One More Round 111 (8f,Cur,S,Apr 25)
One Won One 112 (6f,Naa,Y,May 5)
Oops 111 (16f,Rip,GS,Aug 31)
Orange Touch 112 (14f,Goo,GS,Aug 28)
Orcadian 110 (8f,Kem,GF,May 29)
Orientor 114 (5f,Yor,S,Aug 19)
Orpailleur 110 (10f,Cur,GF,Aug 21)
Osterhase 117 (5f,Cur,G,Jly 17)
Ouija Board 121 (12f,Lon,G,Oct 3)
Out After Dark 110 (6f,Pon,GF,Aug 4)

Pablo 112 (7f,War,GS,Apr 12)
Pagan Dance 114 (12f,Don,GF,Sep 11)
Pagan Sky 111 (10f,Nby,GS,Sep 18)
Pango 112 (7f,Goo,GF,Sep 11)
Paolini 110 (8f,Lon,GS,Sep 5)
Papineau 114 (12f,Goo,GF,May 19)
Paradise Isle 111 (5f,Not,G,Jly 10)
Parkside Pursuit 110 (6f,War,F,Jun 20)
Passing Glance 111 (8 1/2f,Eps,G,Jun 5)
Pastoral Pursuits 114(7f,Don,GF,Sep 9)
Patavellian 114 (6f,Msn,VS,Oct 29)
Pawan 110 (6f,Red,S,Apr 12)
Peconic 112 (16f,Leo,G,Jun 2)
Peeress 110 (7f,Nmk,GF,Jly 6)
Peineve 110 (8f,Leo,SH,Oct 31)
Pentecost 113 (8f,Asc,G,Aug 7)
Pepperwood 110 (8f,Cur,S,Apr 25)
Percussionist 112 (11 1/2f,Lin,S,May 8)
Perfect Storm 111 (12f,Ham,GS,May 14)
Persian Lightning 112(10f,Eps,G,Jun 4)
Persian Majesty 115 (12f,Asc,F,Jun 19)
Peter Paul Rubens 113 (7f,Goo,GF,Jly 29)
Petit Calva 113 (8f,Dea,GS,Jly 31)
Petite Rose 112 (6f,Fol,GS,Apr 7)
Phantom Wind 115 (8f,Leo,GF,Sep 11)
Philharmonic 111 (5f,Ncs,S,Jun 25)
Phoenix Reach 115 (12f,Sai,GS,Jly 4)
Piccled 112 (5f,Nmk,GF,Jly 7)
Pink Palace 110 (10 1/2f,Sai,S,May 11)
Pivotal Point 114 (5f,Lon,GS,Sep 5)
Polar Bear 114 (7f,Nmk,S,Oct 16)
Polar Ben 110 (8f,Nmk,G,Oct 1)
Polar Way 117 (7f,Asc,GF,Jly 24)

Policy Maker 117 (12f,Sai,GS,Jly 4)
Polish Summer 116 (10f,Sai,GS,Mar 6)
Polyfirst 112 (8f,Dea,GS,Jly 31)
Polygonal 110 (10f,Nmk,GF,Aug 6)
Pongee 111 (12f,Hay,G,Jly 3)
Pont D Or 110 (10f,Dea,HO,Aug 14)
Popee 110 (10 1/2f,Sai,S,May 11)
Porlezza 114 (5f,Cha,GS,Jun 6)
Powerscourt 116 (10f,Leo,GF,Sep 11)
Pride 116 (12f,Sai,GS,Jly 4)
Primus Inter Pares 111 (8f,Hay,G,Jly 2)
Prince Kirk 113 (9f,Lon,G,May 23)
Promotion 110 (10 1/2f,Yor,G,Jly 10)
Prospect Park 116 (12f,Lon,VS,May 13)
Ptarmigan Ridge 115 (5f,Chs,GS,May 7)
Punctilious 116 (12f,Cur,GF,Jly 18)
Puppeteer 113 (7f,Lon,GS,May 27)
Pure Mischief 110 (10f,Not,G,May 7)
Putra Pekan 119 (8f,Asc,S,Apr 28)

Quarrymount 110 (14f,Nmk,G,Oct 2)
Queen Charlotte 110 (8f,Yor,GF,Sep 5)
Quest For A Star 112 (12f,Leo,GY,May 9)
Quiff 111 (12f,Asc,GF,Jun 17)
Quilanga 110 (10f,Dea,GS,Aug 3)
Quito 111 (6f,Ncs,S,Jun 26)

Raccoon 111 (5f,Mus,GF,May 29)
Raggtime Toon 113 (12f,Leo,GY,May 9)
Rakti 120 (8f,Asc,GF,Sep 25)
Red Bloom 115 (8f,Asc,F,Jun 18)
Red Feather 112 (7f,Leo,GY,Jly 3)
Red Fort 114 (10f,Asc,F,Jun 18)
Red Sun 111 (16f,Rip,GF,May 26)
Red Tune 112 (9f,Lon,VS,May 13)
Redwood Rocks 111 (7f,Mus,G,Apr 30)
Reefscape 114 (12f,Cha,GS,Jun 6)
Refuse To Bend 117 (8f,Asc,GF,Sep 25)
Regal Setting 111 (14f,Hay,S,Sep 25)
Revenue 110 (7f,Leo,GF,Jun 9)
Ringmoor Down 113 (5f,Goo,GF,Jly 29)
Risque De Verglas 110 (8f,Dea,GS,Jly 31)
Rockets n Rollers 111 (7f,War,GS,Apr 12)
Romany Prince 113 (16f,Yor,G,Aug 17)
Royal Challenge 112 (5f,Bev,GS,Jly 3)
Royal Fantasy 114 (12f,Lon,S,Sep 12)
Royal Fortune 110 (8f,Cur,Y,Sep 18)
Royal Millennium 115 (6f,Ncs,S,Jun 26)
Royal Rebel 111 (16f,Yor,G,Aug 17)
Royal Storm 110 (7f,Nby,G,Sep 17)
Royal Tigress 110 (7f,Leo,S,Apr 18)
Ruby Rocket 113 (6f,Ncs,S,Jun 26)
Rule Of Law 112 (12f,Eps,G,Jun 5)
Rum Shot 115 (6f,Chs,GF,Aug 1)
Russian Hill 113 (10f,Cha,S,May 7)
Russian Rhythm 115 (8f,Nby,G,May 15)
Ryono 113 (8f,Dea,GS,Jly 11)

Sahool 112 (12f,Asc,GF,Jun 17)
Salford City 111 (8f,Nmk,G,May 1)
Salselon 114 (8f,Nby,G,May 15)
Salydora 111 (10f,Cha,S,May 7)
Samando 115 (10f,Sai,GS,Mar 6)
Santiburi Lad 113 (10f,Bev,GS,Jly 3)
Saratan 112 (7f,Lon,GS,May 27)
Sarraaf 111 (8f,Yor,GF,Sep 5)
Sarrasin 113 (10f,Sai,GS,Mar 6)
Sarre 117 (8f,Sai,VS,May 1)
Sayadaw 111 (12f,Nby,G,Apr 17)
Scott s View 113 (10f,Asc,GF,Jun 16)
Sea Storm 110 (8f,Mus,GF,May 29)
Secret Melody 112 (8f,Dea,GS,Jly 31)
Semenovskii 111 (5f,Nmk,GF,Jly 7)
Sendintank 110 (15f,Nmk,S,Aug 27)
Seraphine 111 (10f,Cha,S,May 7)
Shahzan House 110 (10f,Eps,G,Jun 4)
Shakis 113 (10f,Lon,G,Oct 2)
Shersha 110 (6f,Cur,GF,Aug 21)
Short Pause 118 (12f,Lon,HO,May 6)
Shot To Fame 115 (8f,Wdr,GF,Jun 26)
Sights On Gold 113 (11f,Nby,G,Sep 17)
Sigourney 110 (8f,Leo,GY,May 9)
Silence Is Golden 112 (10f,San,GS,Jly 2)
Silver Prelude 115 (5f,Nmk,GF,Jly 7)
Silverskaya 117 (12f,Lon,G,Oct 3)
Simianna 114 (5f,Chs,GS,May 7)
Simple Exchange 111 (10f,Lon,G,Oct 2)
Simplex 111 (12f,Lon,HY,Oct 17)

Sir Desmond 111 (6f,Red,S,Nov 1)
Six Perfections 117 (8f,Dea,S,Aug 15)
Sleeping Indian 110 (8f,Nmk,GS,Oct 30)
Smokin Beau 110 (6f,Rip,S,Aug 14)
Snow Goose 112 (8f,Asc,GF,Jly 23)
Snow Ridge 114 (8f,Nmk,G,May 1)
So Will I 110 (7f,Goo,G,Jly 27)
Sogna Di Me 111 (8f,Dea,GS,Jly 31)
Soldier Hollow 111 (10f,Lon,GS,Jun 17)
Solerina 110 (16f,Cur,GY,Oct 10)
Solskjaer 114 (10f,Leo,GF,Jly 24)
Somnus 117 (7f,Lon,S,Oct 9)
Songlark 114 (12f,Asc,F,Jun 19)
Soviet Song 121 (8f,Leo,GF,Sep 11)
Spanish Ace 111 (5f,Bat,GS,Aug 27)
Spanish Don 110 (9f,Kem,GF,Jun 30)
Special Kaldoun 115 (10f,Lon,G,Oct 2)
Spuradich 113 (10f,Nby,GS,Sep 18)
St Andrews 111 (8f,San,GS,Jly 3)
St Pancras 110 (7f,Sal,GS,Aug 20)
St Petersburg 113 (8f,Yor,S,Aug 19)
Star Valley 113 (6f,Dea,HY,Aug 29)
Starrystarrynight 112 (12f,Cur,GY,Oct 10)
Steel Blue 112 (5f,Ncs,S,Jun 25)
Steel Princess 112 (10 1/2f,Sai,S,May 11)
Steenberg 114 (6f,Yor,GS,May 11)
Stormy Larissa 112 (8f,Cur,Y,Sep 18)
Streamix 111 (8f,Sai,S,Mar 28)
Striking Ambition 115 (6f,Cur,YS,Oct 10)
Sualda 110 (12f,Yor,G,Aug 17)
Sublimity 112 (8f,Don,G,Mar 25)
Sudden Flight 111 (16f,Chs,G,Jly 10)
Suggestive 114 (7f,Goo,G,Jly 27)
Sujimoto 112 (8f,Cha,GS,Jun 21)
Sulamani 114 (10 1/2f,Yor,G,Aug 17)
Summitville 110 (12f,Asc,GF,Sep 24)
Sunday Doubt 110 (7f,Lon,GS,Jun 27)
Sundrop 111 (8f,Nmk,G,May 2)
Sunstrach 110 (10f,San,GS,Jly 2)
Super Bobbina 113 (8f,Cha,GS,Jun 6)
Super Lina 113 (10 1/2f,Sai,G,Apr 9)
Swedish Shave 111 (5 1/2f,Cha,G,Oct 1)
Sweet Stream 115 (12f,Lon,S,Sep 12)
Swift Tango 110 (12f,Asc,F,Jun 19)
Swing Wing 114 (16f,Yor,G,Aug 17)
Systematic 114 (13 1/2f,Chs,GS,May 7)

Tacitus 113 (8f,Cur,S,Apr 25)
Tahreeb 114 (8f,Kem,GF,May 29)
Tahtheeb 112 (10f,Sal,GF,Aug 11)
Take A Bow 113 (8f,Yor,S,Aug 19)
Talbot Avenue 114 (6f,Chs,GF,Aug 1)
Tante Rose 116 (6f,Yor,GS,Jly 9)
Tap Dance City 110 (12f,Lon,G,Oct 3)
Tarakala 112 (12f,Cur,GY,Oct 10)
Tarfah 113 (8f,Wdr,GS,Aug 9)
Tedsdale Mac 112 (8f,Yor,GF,Sep 5)
Telemachus 112 (10f,Don,GS,May 3)
Texas Gold 111 (6f,Goo,GF,Sep 12)
Thajja 112 (8f,Asc,GF,Sep 26)
The Fun Merchant 110 (8f,Nmk,GF,Jun 25)
The Kiddykid 112 (6f,Ncs,S,Jun 26)
The Tatling 116 (5f,Yor,S,Aug 19)
The Trader 113 (5f,Lon,GF,May 16)
The Whistling Teal 112 (13 1/2f,Chs,GS,May 7)
Theme Song 110 (12f,Cur,GF,Jun 27)
Three Graces 110 (7f,Hay,GF,Jun 3)
Tiganello 113 (8f,Dea,VS,Aug 10)
Tiger Tiger 110 (10f,Nby,HY,Oct 23)
Tillerman 113 (8f,Goo,G,Jly 28)
Tipperary All Star 113 (8f,Cur,S,Apr 25)
Tiyoun 112 (16f,Rip,GF,May 26)
Tolpuddle 115 (8f,Cur,S,Apr 25)
Tolzey 110 (8f,Dea,GS,Jly 31)
Tony The Tap 110 (5f,Nmk,GF,Jun 25)
Tony Tie 110 (8f,Mus,G,Apr 30)
Top Of The Bill 113 (12f,Cha,GS,Jun 6)
Torrestrella 115 (8f,Lon,GF,May 16)
Touch Of Land 117 (10f,Lon,G,Oct 2)
Trade Fair 113 (7f,Cur,GF,Jly 18)
Treasure The Lady 111 (9f,Cur,GF,Jly 18)
Treculiar 110 (16f,Cur,GF,Jun 27)
Trilemma 112 (16f,Rip,GS,Aug 31)
Trinity Joy 112 (10 1/2f,Sai,G,Apr 9)
Tropical Lady 116 (9f,Cur,GF,Jly 18)
Troubadour 112 (8f,Cur,G,Sep 19)
Trousers 110 (8f,Not,GS,Jly 3)
True Night 110 (7f,Chs,GF,Jun 8)

Tulipe Royale 110 (8f,Dea,GS,Jly 31)
Tungsten Strike 111 (14f,Nmk,G,Sep 30)
Turibius 110 (5f,Nmk,GF,Jly 7)
Turnstile 110 (14f,Goo,GS,Oct 10)
Two Miles West 111 (14f,Leo,GY,Jly 14)
Tycoon 112 (12f,Cur,GF,Jun 27)

Uhoomagoo 116 (7f,Asc,GF,Jly 24)
Ulfah 114 (6f,Cur,GF,Aug 21)
Unshakable 111 (8f,Yor,S,Aug 19)

Valentina Guest 112 (10f,Leo,GF,May 26)
Valentino 115 (10f,Lon,G,Oct 2)
Valixir 117 (12f,Lon,G,Oct 3)
Vallee Enchantee 119 (12f,Lon,G,Oct 3)
Vallera 114 (12f,Lon,S,Sep 12)
Vanderlin 114 (8f,Wdr,GF,Jun 26)
Vangelis 115 (10f,Lon,GS,Apr 4)
Var 117 (5f,Lon,G,Oct 3)
Vasywait 113 (7f,Lon,S,Apr 29)
Vespone 115 (10 1/2f,Lon,VS,May 2)
Via Milano 111 (8f,Lon,GF,May 16)
Vicious Knight 111 (8f,Yor,S,Aug 19)
Vinnie Roe 111 (14f,Leo,GF,May 26)
Vintage Premium 113 (12f,Ham,GS,May 14)

Visorama 116 (12f,Sai,GS,Jly 4)
Voix Du Nord 113 (11f,Lon,GS,Apr 11)
Vortex 114 (7f,Asc,GF,Jly 24)

Wait For The Will 110 (12f,Goo,GF,Jun 18)
Walkamia 116 (12f,Lon,HO,May 6)
Warrsan 117 (12f,Lon,G,Oct 3)
Waterside 112 (7f,Goo,GS,Aug 27)
Wathab 111 (6f,Cur,GF,Aug 21)
Welcome Stranger 114 (8f,Asc,GF,Sep 26)
Welsh Emperor 111 (6f,Yor,GS,May 11)
Wendy s Girl 110 (6f,War,F,Jun 14)
Westerner 114 (12f,Sai,GS,Jly 4)
Whipper 118 (8f,Dea,S,Aug 15)
Whitbarrow 111 (5f,Don,S,Oct 23)
Whortleberry 116 (12f,Lon,HO,May 6)
Windermere 114 (14f,Leo,GF,May 26)
Wing Commander 110 (8f,Asc,G,Aug 7)
Wunderwood 113 (12f,Asc,F,Jun 19)

Yeats 115 (10f,Leo,S,Apr 18)
Yesterday 110 (10f,Lon,G,Oct 3)
Young Tiger 111 (10f,Sai,GS,May 5)

Zarafsha 111 (12f,Cur,GY,Oct 10)
Zero Tolerance 110 (10 1/2f,Yor,S,Aug 18)
Zonus 110 (8f,Hay,GF,May 22)

## THREE YEAR-OLDS AND UPWARDS - Sand

Another Glimpse 110(6f,Lin,SD,Mar 19)

Bella Pavlina 114 (12f,Sth,SS,Mar 16)
Bid For Fame 113 (14f,Sth,SD,Dec 9)
Blakeshall Quest 111 (5f,Wol,SS,Mar 29)
Bond Boy 111 (6f,Wol,SD,Jan 9)

Cardinal Venture 110 (8 1/2f,Wol,SD,Nov 10)
Chateau Nicol 112 (7f,Lin,SD,Nov 29)
Cold Turkey 110 (12f,Lin,SD,Jan 24)
Consonant 110 (8 1/2f,Wol,SW,Feb 20)

Dancing Mystery 110 (5f,Lin,SD,Feb 7)
Del Mar Sunset 110 (9 1/2f,Wol,SW,Dec 31)

Dragon Flyer 114 (5f,Lin,SD,Mar 20)

Dusty Dazzler 113 (6f,Lin,SD,Jan 17)

Eastern Breeze 110 (10f,Lin,SD,Feb 21)

Fall In Line 114 (11f,Sth,SD,Feb 3)
Fire Up The Band 112(5f,Lin,SD,Mar 20)
Flint River 112 (6f,Wol,SD,Jan 9)
Fokine 110 (7f,Lin,SD,Mar 20)

General 113 (12f,Sth,SS,Mar 16)
George Stubbs 110 (12f,Sth,SD,Dec 19)
Global Achiever 110 (6f,Wol,SW,Feb 27)
Glory Quest 110 (12f,Wol,SW,Mar 5)
Grand Passion 111 (10f,Lin,SD,Feb 21)
Grey Pearl 111 (7f,Lin,SD,Jan 31)

Hip Hop Harry 110 (10f,Lin,SD,Feb 24)
Hurricane Coast 111 (6f,Lin,SD,Jan 14)

Intricate Web 111 (9 1/2f,Wol,SD,Nov 29)

Jair Ohmsford 111 (12f,Sth,SS,Feb 10)
Justalord 115 (5f,Lin,SD,Mar 20)

Labrett 110 (8f,Lin,SD,Dec 30)
Law Breaker 114 (6f,Lin,SD,Dec 20)
Linning Wine 111 (8f,Lin,SD,Dec 20)
Little Edward 113 (5f,Lin,SD,Mar 20)
Lygeton Lad 110 (6f,Lin,SD,Dec 20)

Masafi 111 (8f,Sth,SD,Jly 23)
Massey 114 (6f,Wol,SD,Jan 9)
Mi Odds 113 (9 1/2f,Wol,SD,Nov 29)
Mission To Mars 110 (12f,Wol,SW,Mar 5)
Mr Mischief 112 (12f,Wol,SW,Mar 5)

Nimello 115 (9 1/2f,Wol,SW,Dec 31)
No Time 117 (5f,Lin,SD,Mar 20)

Ofaraby 110 (9 1/2f,Wol,SD,Nov 29)

Peruvian Chief 110 (5f,Lin,SD,Mar 20)
Polar Kingdom 113 (7f,Sth,SD,Feb 12)
Prima Stella 110 (7f,Sth,SD,Feb 12)
Prince Aaron 113 (6f,Lin,SD,Mar 19)

Queens Rhapsody 111 (6f,Lin,SD,Jan 17)
Quito 111 (6f,Wol,SS,Feb 13)

Rosencrans 111 (7f,Lin,SD,Mar 20)

Sangiovese 113 (8f,Sth,SW,Dec 13)
Sea Holly 105 (12f,Lin,SD,Nov 29)
Speed Cop 116 (5f,Lin,SD,Mar 20)
Striking Ambition 110 (5f,Lin,SD,Mar 20)
Strong Hand 114 (9 1/2f,Wol,SD,Nov 29)

Te Quiero 114 (8 1/2f,Wol,SS,Mar 13)
Texas Gold 112 (6f,Lin,SD,Dec 20)

Victory Quest 110 (14f,Sth,SD,Dec 9)
Vortex 115 (8 1/2f,Wol,SS,Mar 13)

Waterside 111 (6f,Lin,SD,Dec 20)
What-A-Dancer 110 (7f,Lin,SD,Dec 10)

Zarzu 112 (6f,Wol,SD,Jan 9)

## TWO YEAR-OLDS - Turf

Ad Valorem 106 (6f,Nmk,G,Oct 1)
Albert Hall 110 (8f,Don,S,Oct 23)
Alexander Queen 105 (5f,Cur,Y,Sep 18)
All Woman 108 (7f,Leo,SH,Oct 31)

Amsterdam 108 (7f,Leo,GF,Jly 24)
Annatalia 106 (5f,Bat,F,Jly 5)

Beaver Patrol 106 (6f,Cur,GF,Aug 21)
Beckermet 106 (5f,Chs,G,Jly 9)
Bective Ranger 105 (7f,Leo,SH,Oct 31)
Berenson 112 (7f,Cur,Y,Sep 19)
Bogside Dancer 106 (7f,Leo,SH,Oct 31)
Bonita Rock 105 (7f,Cur,YS,Oct 10)
Brecon Beacon 109 (7f,Nmk,GF,Jly 30)
Bunny Rabbit 105 (7f,Nmk,GF,Jly 30)

Caesar Beware 106 (6f,Chp,G,Jun 3)
Campo Bueno 114 (6f,Msn,VS,Oct 29)
Capable Guest 108 (8f,Lon,GS,Sep 18)
Captain Hurricane 110 (6f,Nmk,GF,Jly 7)
Castelletto 109 (5f,Nmk,S,Oct 16)
Centaurus 106 (7f,Nmk,GS,Oct 30)
Centifolia 117 (6f,Msn,VS,Oct 29)
Chelsea Rose 107 (7f,Cur,GF,Sep 5)
Cherokee 107 (6f,Cur,GF,Sep 5)
Clonard 105 (7f,Leo,SH,Oct 31)
Comic Strip 106 (8f,Pon,G,Oct 18)
Cornus 107 (5f,Nmk,S,Oct 16)
Council Member 109 (6f,Nmk,GF,Jly 7)
Crossover 105 (6f,Dea,G,Aug 1)
Cupid s Glory 109 (7f,Nby,S,Oct 22)

Damson 109 (6f,Cur,GF,Aug 8)
Dance Away 105 (5f,Yor,GS,May 13)
Dash To The Top 106 (8f,Asc,GF,Sep 25)
Defi 105 (7f,Leo,SH,Oct 31)
Democratic Deficit 107 (7f,Cur,Y,Sep 19)
Diktatorial 109 (7f,San,GS,Aug 20)
Dipterous 106 (7f,Leo,SH,Oct 31)
Divine Proportions 115 (8f,Lon,G,Oct 3)
Don t Tell Mum 107 (5f,Bat,F,May 27)
Dream Tonic 106 (8f,Mus,GS,Nov 3)
Dubai Surprise 105 (8f,Sai,VS,Oct 31)
Dubawi 116 (7f,Cur,Y,Sep 19)

Early March 110 (7f,Lon,G,Oct 3)
Elliots World 105 (8f,Asc,GF,Sep 25)
Elusive Double 110 (7f,Leo,GF,Jly 24)
Embossed 110 (7f,San,S,Aug 21)
Etlaala 110 (7f,Don,GF,Sep 10)

Favourita 105 (7f,Nmk,S,Oct 16)
Firmount 105 (7f,Leo,SH,Oct 31)
Fontanally Springs 105 (7f,Leo,SH,Oct 31)
Footstepsinthesand 115 (7f,Leo,S,Oct 25)
Fraloga 112 (8f,Lon,G,Oct 3)
Fuerta Ventura 105 (7f,Leo,SH,Oct 31)
Full Moon Tonight 110 (7f,Leo,S,Oct 25)

Gaff 112 (7f,Leo,S,Oct 25)
Galeota 107 (6f,Nby,GS,Sep 18)
Gloved Hand 106 (5f,Not,GF,Jun 2)
Golden Legacy 105 (6f,Chs,GF,Aug 1)
Gorella 111 (8f,Lon,G,Oct 3)
Grand Central 108 (7f,Leo,S,Oct 25)
Gypsy King 108 (7f,Leo,SH,Oct 31)

Haatmey 106 (10f,Bat,G,Sep 27)
Hallucinate 105 (8f,Yor,G,Sep 1)
Helios Quercus 109 (8f,Lon,GS,Sep 18)
Henrik 109 (8f,Don,S,Oct 23)

Iceman 113 (7f,Nmk,S,Oct 16)
In The Fan 106 (7f,Nmk,GF,Jly 30)
Ingleton 106 (6f,Nmk,S,Oct 15)
Intrigued 112 (8f,Lon,G,Oct 3)
Istan 105 (6f,Msn,VS,Oct 29)

Jazz Princess 108 (7f,Cur,YS,Oct 2)
Jewel In The Sand 105 (6f,Nmk,GF,Jly 6)
Jolie Etoile 105 (6f,Dea,G,Aug 1)
Joseph Henry 108 (5f,Not,S,Apr 30)

Kay Two 105 (5f,Nmk,S,Oct 16)

Kenmore 106 (6f,Nmk,S,Oct 14)
Kharaline 105 (7f,Leo,SH,Oct 31)

King Kasyapa 105 (8f,Lon,GS,Sep 18)
Kissing Lights 105 (6f,Asc,GF,Jly 24)

La Maitresse 108 (7f,Leo,GF,Jly 24)
Lady Filly 106 (5f,Sal,S,May 2)
Layman 110 (7f,Lon,G,Oct 3)
Leventina 106 (9f,Lon,HY,Oct 24)
Librettist 112 (7f,Nmk,S,Oct 16)
Lock And Key 108 (7f,Leo,GF,Jly 24)
Looks Could Kill 105 (8f,Ham,S,Aug 11)
Lough Gem 109 (7f,Leo,SH,Oct 31)
Luas Line 108 (7f,Cur,GF,Aug 8)

Magical Romance 107 (6f,Lei,GS,Sep 20)
Maids Causeway 107 (8f,Asc,GF,Sep 25)
Makuti 105 (7f,Leo,SH,Oct 31)
Merger 107 (8f,Cur,YS,Oct 10)
Mirabilis 107 (8f,Lon,G,Oct 3)
Miss Sundance 105 (7f,Leo,SH,Oct 31)
Mona Lisa 106 (8f,Asc,GF,Sep 25)
Montgomery s Arch 113 (7f,Nmk,S,Oct 16)
Moth Ball 105 (6f,Bri,F,Sep 23)
Motivator 113 (8f,Don,S,Oct 23)
Musketier 108 (8f,Lon,GS,Sep 18)
Mystical Land 108 (6f,Nmk,GF,Jly 7)

National Swagger 105 (7f,Cur,GF,Aug 8)
Nebraska Lady 105 (7f,Leo,SH,Oct 31)
New Largue 110 (8f,Lon,G,Oct 3)
Nipping 108 (6f,Msn,VS,Oct 29)
Nova Tor 106 (5f,Nmk,GS,Aug 14)

Obe Gold 109 (6f,Msn,VS,Oct 29)
Optimise 105 (7f,Leo,SH,Oct 31)
Oratorio 114 (7f,Nmk,S,Oct 16)
Oude 106 (7f,Don,GF,Sep 10)
Our Fugitive 105 (6f,Nmk,S,Oct 15)

Penkenna Princess 105 (7f,Nmk,S,Oct 16)
Perfectperformance 109 (8f,Asc,GF,Sep 25)
Pictavia 106 (7f,Cur,GF,Sep 5)
Pivotal Flame 106 (7f,San,S,Aug 21)
Playful Act 108 (8f,Asc,GF,Sep 25)
Portrayal 112 (8f,Lon,G,Oct 3)
Pout 105 (7f,Leo,SH,Oct 31)
Premier Dane 105 (7f,Leo,SH,Oct 31)
Prince Charming 110 (6f,Msn,VS,Oct 29)
Propinquity 109 (7f,San,S,Aug 21)
Public Forum 105 (8f,Not,HY,Oct 20)

Queen Of Poland 112 (8f,Lon,G,Oct 3)

Rebuttal 105 (6f,Nby,GS,Sep 18)
Red Peony 105 (7f,Eps,GF,Jly 29)
Reggae 105 (7f,Leo,S,Oct 25)
River Royale 105 (6f,Nmk,S,Oct 14)
Roodeye 106 (5f,Bat,F,May 27)
Russian Blue 110 (7f,Cur,Y,Sep 19)

Sailor King 106 (6f,Dea,G,Aug 1)
Salut Thomas 114 (6f,Msn,VS,Oct 29)
Saoire 105 (7f,Cur,GF,Sep 5)
Satchem 106 (7f,Nmk,GS,Jly 8)
Scandinavia 107 (8f,Asc,GF,Sep 25)
Sea Hunter 105 (7f,Nmk,GS,Jly 8)
Shamardal 117 (7f,Nmk,S,Oct 16)
Silk And Scarlet 109 (7f,Cur,GF,Aug 8)
Sina Cova 107 (7f,Leo,S,Oct 25)
Soar 108 (6f,Asc,GF,Jly 24)
Speciale 109 (6f,Dea,G,Aug 1)
St Andrews Storm 106 (6f,Nmk,GF,Jly 7)
Stagelight 106 (7f,Leo,GF,Jly 24)
Stetchworth Prince 105 (6f,Nmk,GF,Jly 7)

Succession 105 (8f,Mus,GF,Sep 26)
Suez 105 (6f,Sal,G,Sep 2)
Sumora 107 (5f,Nby,G,Aug 14)

Titian Time 113 (8f,Lon,G,Oct 3)
Tomoohat 108 (6f,Nmk,S,Oct 14)
Tony James 106 (6f,Nmk,GF,Jly 7)
Toupie 106 (5 1/2f,Cha,G,Sep 8)
Turnkey 106 (5f,Kem,HY,May 3)

Umniya 105 (7f,Cur,GF,Sep 5)

Valentin 105 (6f,Asc,GF,Jly 24)
Vatori 108 (8f,Lon,GS,Sep 18)
Visionist 106 (7f,Nmk,GF,Jly 30)

Walk In The Park 105 (8f,Sai,VS,Oct 31)
Wilko 106 (8f,Asc,GF,Sep 25)
Windsor Knot 113 (7f,San,S,Aug 21)
Woodsley House 106 (8f,Yor,G,Sep 1)

Xtra Torrential 107 (8f,Yor,G,Sep 1)

Yajbill 109 (6f,Eps,GF,Sep 9)
Yehudi 105 (9f,Leo,SH,Oct 31)

Zelkova 106 (7f,Leo,GF,Jly 24)

## TWO YEAR-OLDS - Sand

Afrashad 108 (6f,Lin,SD,Jly 14)

Canton 106 (5f,Lin,SD,Aug 6)
Countrywide Flyer 108 (8f,Sth,SD,Nov 24)

Fadeela 106 (7f,Wol,SD,Nov 28)

Petardias Magic 105 (6f,Lin,SD,Nov 22)
Peters Choice 111 (5f,Wol,SD,Nov 14)
Pitch Up 110 (5f,Lin,SD,Aug 6)

Queenstown 107 (8f,Sth,SD,Nov 24)

Sundance 107 (5f,Lin,SD,Aug 6)

Weet A Head 105 (8f,Sth,SD,Nov 24)

# Raceform Flat record times

## ASCOT

| Distance | Time | Age | Weight | Going | Horse | Date |
|---|---|---|---|---|---|---|
| 5f | 59.7 secs | 2 | 8-8 | Gd to Firm | Lyric Fantasy | Jun 17 1992 |
| 5f | 59.1 secs | 3 | 8-8 | Firm | Orient | Jun 12 1986 |
| 6f | 1m 13.6 | 2 | 8-12 | Gd to Firm | Three Valleys | Jun 17 2003 |
| 6f | 1m 12.1 | 5 | 9-3 | Firm | Ratio | Jun 21 2003 |
| 6f | 1m 12.1 | 4 | 9-6 | Firm | Fayr Jag (IRE) | Jun 21 2003 |
| 7f | 1m 27.2 | 2 | 8-11 | Gd to Firm | Celtic Swing | Oct 8 1994 |
| 7f | 1m 25.8 | 4 | 8-2 | Gd to Firm | Master Robbie | Sep 27 2003 |
| 1m | 1m 40.8 | 2 | 8-10 | Gd to Firm | Red Bloom | Sep 27 2003 |
| 1m | 1m 38.0 | 4 | 7-8 | Gd to Firm | Colour Sergeant | Jun 17 1992 |
| 1m | 1m 38.5 | 3 | 9-0 | Gd to Firm | Russian Rhythm | Jun 20 2003 |
| 1m 2f | 2m 2.7 | 4 | 9-3 | Gd to Firm | First Island (IRE) | Jun 18 1996 |
| 1m 4f | 2m 26.5 | 4 | 8-9 | Firm | Doyen (IRE) | Jun 19 2004 |
| 2m 45y | 3m 25.2 | 3 | 8-11 | Gd to Firm | Landowner | Jun 17 1992 |
| 2m 4f | 4m 15.3 | 5 | 9-0 | Gd to Firm | Royal Gait (disq) | Jun 16 1988 |
| 2m 6f 34y | 4m 47.8 | 6 | 9-3 | Firm | Cover Up (IRE) | Jun 21 2003 |

## AYR

| Distance | Time | Age | Weight | Going | Horse | Date |
|---|---|---|---|---|---|---|
| 5f | 56.9 secs | 2 | 8-11 | Good | Boogie Street | Sep 18 2003 |
| 5f | 57.2 secs | 4 | 9-5 | Gd to Firm | Sir Joey | Sep 16 1993 |
| 6f | 69.7 secs | 2 | 7-10 | Good | Sir Bert | Sep 17 1969 |
| 6f | 68.9 secs | 7 | 8-8 | Gd to Firm | Sobering Thoughts | Sep 18 1993 |
| 7f | 1m 25.7 | 2 | 9-0 | Gd to Firm | Jazeel | Sep 16 1993 |
| 7f | 1m 24.9 | 5 | 7-11 | Firm | Sir Arthur Hobbs | Jun 19 1992 |
| 7f 50y | 1m 28.9 | 2 | 9-0 | Good | Tafaahum (USA) | Sep 19 2003 |
| 7f 50y | 1m 28.2 | 4 | 9-2 | Gd to Firm | Flur Na H Alba | Jun 21 2003 |
| 1m | 1m 39.2 | 2 | 9-0 | Gd to Firm | Kribensis | Sep 17 1986 |
| 1m | 1m 36.0 | 4 | 7-13 | Firm | Sufi | Sep 16 1959 |
| 1m 1f 20y | 1m 50.3 | 4 | 9-3 | Good | Retirement | Sep 19 2003 |
| 1m 2f | 2m 4.0 | 4 | 9-9 | Gd to Firm | Endless Hall | Jly 17 2000 |
| 1m 2f192y | 2m 13.3 | 4 | 9-0 | Gd to Firm | Azzaam | Sep 18 1991 |
| 1m 5f 13y | 2m 45.8 | 4 | 9-7 | Gd to Firm | Eden s Close | Sep 18 1993 |
| 1m 7f | 3m 13.1 | 3 | 9-4 | Good | Romany Rye | Sep 19 1991 |
| 2m 1f105y | 3m 45.0 | 4 | 6-13 | Good | Curry | Sep 16 1955 |

## BATH

| Distance | Time | Age | Weight | Going | Horse | Date |
|---|---|---|---|---|---|---|
| 5f 11y | 60.1 secs | 2 | 8-11 | Firm | Double Fantasy | Aug 25 2000 |
| 5f 11y | 59.9 secs | 6 | 9-2 | Firm | Cauda Equina | Aug 25 2000 |
| 5f 161y | 69.1 secs | 2 | 8-7 | Firm | Sibla | Aug 25 2000 |
| 5f 161y | 68.1 secs | 6 | 9-0 | Firm | Madraco | May 22 1989 |
| 1m 5y | 1m 39.7 | 2 | 8-9 | Firm | Casual Look | Sep 16 2002 |
| 1m 5y | 1m 37.2 | 5 | 8-12 | Gd to Firm | Adobe | Jun 17 2000 |
| 1m 5y | 1m 37.2 | 3 | 8-7 | Firm | Alasha (IRE) | Aug 18 2002 |
| 1m 2f 46y | 2m 5.8 | 3 | 9-0 | Gd to Firm | Connoisseur Bay(USA) | May 29 1998 |
| 1m 3f144y | 2m 26.1 | 3 | 8-12 | Firm | Anticipate | Sep 10 2001 |
| 1m 5f 22y | 2m 47.2 | 4 | 10-0 | Firm | Flown | Aug 13 1991 |
| 2m 1f 34y | 3m 43.4 | 6 | 7-9 | Firm | Yaheska (IRE) | Jun 14 2003 |

## BEVERLEY

| Distance | Time | Age | Weight | Going | Horse | Date |
|---|---|---|---|---|---|---|
| 5f | 61.0 secs | 2 | 8-2 | Gd to Firm | Addo (IRE) | Jly 17 2001 |
| 5f | 60.1 secs | 4 | 9-5 | Firm | Pic Up Sticks | Apr 16 2003 |
| 7f 100y | 1m 31.1 | 2 | 9-7 | Gd to Firm | Champagne Prince | Aug 10 1995 |
| 7f 100y | 1m 31.1 | 2 | 9-0 | Firm | Majal (IRE) | Jly 30 1991 |
| 7f 100y | 1m 29.5 | 3 | 7-8 | Firm | Who s Tef | Jly 30 1991 |
| 1m 100y | 1m 43.3 | 2 | 9-0 | Firm | Arden | Sep 24 1986 |
| 1m 100y | 1m 42.2 | 3 | 8-4 | Firm | Legal Case | Jun 14 1989 |
| 1m 1f 207y | 2m 1.8 | 3 | 9-7 | Firm | Rose Alto | Jly 5 1991 |
| 1m 3f 216y | 2m 30.8 | 3 | 8-1 | Hard | Coinage | Jun 18 1986 |
| 1m 4f 16y | 2m 35.8 | 4 | 9-3 | Gd to Firm | Red River Rebel | Aug 25 2002 |
| 2m 35y | 3m 29.5 | 4 | 9-2 | Gd to Firm | Rushen Raider | Aug 14 1996 |

## BRIGHTON

| Distance | Time | Age | Weight | Going | Horse | Date |
|---|---|---|---|---|---|---|
| 5f 59y | 60.1 secs | 2 | 9-0 | Firm | Bid for Blue | May 6 1993 |
| 5f 59y | 59.3 secs | 3 | 8-9 | Firm | Play Hever Golf | May 26 1993 |
| 5f 213y | 68.1 secs | 2 | 8-9 | Firm | Song Mist (IRE) | Jly 16 1996 |
| 5f 213y | 67.3 secs | 3 | 8-9 | Firm | Third Party | Jun 3 1997 |
| 5f 213y | 67.3 secs | 5 | 9-1 | Gd to Firm | Blundell Lane | May 4 2000 |
| 6f 209y | 1m 19.9 | 2 | 8-11 | Hard | Rain Burst | Sep 15 1988 |
| 6f 209y | 1m 19.4 | 4 | 9-3 | Gd to Firm | Sawaki | Sep 3 1991 |
| 7f 214y | 1m 32.8 | 2 | 9-7 | Firm | Asian Pete | Oct 3 1989 |
| 7f 214y | 1m 30.5 | 5 | 8-11 | Firm | Mystic Ridge | May 27 1999 |
| 1m 1f 209y | 2m 4.7 | 2 | 9-0 | Gd to Soft | Esteemed Master | Nov 2 2001 |
| 1m 1f 209y | 1m 57.2 | 3 | 9-0 | Firm | Get The Message | Apr 30 1984 |
| 1m 3f 196y | 2m 25.8 | 4 | 8-2 | Firm | New Zealand | Jly 4 1985 |

## CARLISLE

| Distance | Time | Age | Weight | Going | Horse | Date |
|---|---|---|---|---|---|---|
| 5f | 60.1 secs | 2 | 8-5 | Firm | La Tortuga | Aug 2 1999 |
| 5f | 58.8 secs | 3 | 9-8 | Gd to Firm | Esatto | Aug 21 2002 |
| 5f 193y | 1m 11.7 | 5 | 8-6 | Gd to Firm | Chairman Bobby | Jun 15 2003 |
| 5f 207y | 1m 12.8 | 2 | 8-9 | Hard | Parfait Armour | Sep 10 1991 |
| 5f 207y | 1m 11.8 | 6 | 8-13 | Firm | Night Patrol | Aug 27 1970 |
| 6f 192y | 1m 24.3 | 3 | 8-9 | Gd to Firm | Marjurita (IRE) | Aug 21 2002 |
| 6f 206y | 1m 26.5 | 2 | 9-4 | Hard | Sense of Priority | Sep 10 1991 |
| 6f 206y | 1m 25.3 | 4 | 9-1 | Firm | Move With Edes | Jly 6 1996 |
| 7f 200y | 1m 37.4 | 4 | 9-8 | Gd to Firm | Gifted Flame | Jun 15 2003 |
| 7f 214y | 1m 44.6 | 2 | 8-8 | Firm | Blue Garter | Sep 9 1980 |
| 7f 214y | 1m 37.3 | 5 | 7-12 | Hard | Thatched (IRE) | Aug 21 1995 |
| 1m 1f 61y | 1m 53.8 | 3 | 9-0 | Firm | Little Jimbob | Jun 14 2004 |
| 1m 3f 206y | 2m 29.4 | 8 | 8-13 | Firm | Silvertown | Jun 26 2003 |
| 1m 4f | 2m 28.8 | 3 | 8-5 | Firm | Desert Frolic (IRE) | Jun 27 1996 |
| 1m 6f 32y | 3m 2.2 | 6 | 8-10 | Firm | Explosive Speed | May 26 1994 |
| 2m 1f 52y | 3m 46.2 | 3 | 7-10 | Gd to Firm | Warring Kingdom | Aug 25 1999 |

## CATTERICK

| Distance | Time | Age | Weight | Going | Horse | Date |
|---|---|---|---|---|---|---|
| 5f | 57.6 secs | 2 | 9-0 | Firm | H Harrison | Oct 8 2002 |
| 5f | 57.1 secs | 4 | 8-7 | Fast | Kabcast | Jly 7 1989 |
| 5f 212y | 1m 11.4 | 2 | 9-4 | Firm | Captain Nick | Jly 11 1978 |
| 5f 212y | 69.8 secs | 9 | 8-13 | Gd to Firm | Sharp Hat | May 30 2003 |
| 7f | 1m 24.1 | 2 | 8-11 | Firm | Lindas Fantasy | Sep 18 1982 |
| 7f | 1m 22.5 | 6 | 8-7 | Firm | Differential (USA) | May 31 2003 |
| 1m 3f 214y | 2m 30.5 | 3 | 8-8 | Gd to Firm | Rahaf | May 30 2003 |
| 1m 5f 175y | 2m 54.8 | 3 | 8-5 | Firm | Geryon | May 31 1984 |
| 1m 7f 177y | 3m 20.8 | 4 | 7-11 | Firm | Bean Boy | Jly 8 1982 |

## CHEPSTOW

| Distance | Time | Age | Weight | Going | Horse | Date |
|---|---|---|---|---|---|---|
| 5f 16y | 57.6 secs | 2 | 8-11 | Firm | Micro Love | Jly 8 1986 |
| 5f 16y | 56.8 secs | 3 | 8-4 | Firm | Torbay Express | Sep 15 1979 |
| 6f 16y | 69.4 secs | 2 | 9-0 | Fast | Royal Fifi | Sep 9 1989 |
| 6f 16y | 68.1 secs | 3 | 9-7 | Firm | America Calling (USA) | Sep 18 2001 |
| 7f 16y | 1m 20.8 | 2 | 9-0 | Gd to Firm | Royal Amaretto (IRE) | Sep 12 1996 |
| 7f 16y | 1m 19.3 | 3 | 9-0 | Firm | Taranaki | Sep 18 2001 |
| 1m 14y | 1m 33.1 | 2 | 8-11 | Gd to Firm | Ski Academy (IRE) | Aug 28 1995 |
| 1m 14y | 1m 31.6 | 3 | 8-13 | Firm | Stoli (IRE) | Sep 18 2001 |
| 1m 2f 36y | 2m 4.1 | 5 | 8-9 | Hard | Leonidas | Jly 5 1983 |
| 1m 2f 36y | 2m 4.1 | 5 | 7-8 | Gd to Firm | It s Varadan | Sep 9 1989 |
| 1m 2f 36y | 2m 4.1 | 3 | 8-5 | Gd to Firm | Ela Athena | Jly 23 1999 |
| 1m 4f 23y | 2m 31.0 | 3 | 8-9 | Gd to Firm | Spritsail | Jly 13 1989 |
| 1m 4f 23y | 2m 31.0 | 7 | 9-6 | Hard | Maintop | Aug 27 1984 |
| 2m 49y | 3m 27.7 | 4 | 9-0 | Gd to Firm | Wizzard Artist | Jly 1 1989 |
| 2m 2f | 3m 56.4 | 5 | 8-7 | Gd to Firm | Laffah | Jly 8 2000 |

## CHESTER

| Distance | Time | Age | Weight | Going | Horse | Date |
|---|---|---|---|---|---|---|
| 5f 16y | 60.2 secs | 2 | 9-0 | Gd to Firm | Majestic Missile (IRE) | Jly 11 2003 |
| 5f 16y | 59.2 secs | 3 | 10-0 | Firm | Althrey Don | Jly 10 1964 |
| 6f 18y | 1m 12.8 | 2 | 8-10 | Gd to Firm | Flying Express | Aug 31 2002 |
| 6f 18y | 1m 12.7 | 3 | 8-3 | Gd to Firm | Play Hever Golf | May 4 1993 |
| 6f 18y | 1m 12.7 | 6 | 9-2 | Good | Stack Rock | Jun 23 1993 |
| 7f 2y | 1m 25.2 | 2 | 9-0 | Gd to Firm | Due Respect (IRE) | Sep 25 2002 |
| 7f 2y | 1m 24.3 | 5 | 8-13 | Gd to Firm | Grey Eminence (FR) | Jly 13 2002 |
| 7f 122y | 1m 32.2 | 2 | 9-0 | Gd to Firm | Big Bad Bob (IRE) | Sep 25 2002 |
| 7f 122y | 1m 30.9 | 6 | 8-5 | Gd to Firm | Hormuz (IRE) | May 9 2002 |
| 1m 2f 75y | 2m 7.7 | 3 | 8-9 | Gd to Firm | Fragrant View | May 7 2002 |
| 1m 3f 79y | 2m 22.5 | 3 | 8-9 | Gd to Firm | Rockerlong | May 9 2001 |
| 1m 4f 66y | 2m 33.7 | 3 | 8-10 | Gd to Firm | Fight Your Corner | May 7 2002 |
| 1m 5f 89y | 2m 45.4 | 5 | 8-11 | Firm | Rakaposhi King | May 7 1987 |
| 1m 7f 195y | 3m 20.3 | 4 | 9-0 | Gd to Firm | Grand Fromage (IRE) | Jly 13 2002 |
| 2m 2f 147y | 4m 0.2 | 6 | 8-9 | Gd to Firm | Fantasy Hill (IRE) | May 8 2002 |

## DONCASTER

| Distance | Time | Age | Weight | Going | Horse | Date |
|---|---|---|---|---|---|---|
| 5f | 58.4 secs | 2 | 9-5 | Firm | Sing Sing | Sep 11 1959 |
| 5f | 58.4 secs | 2 | 9-0 | Good | D Urberville | Sep 13 1967 |
| 5f | 57.2 secs | 6 | 9-12 | Gd to Firm | Celtic Mill | Sep 9 2004 |
| 5f 140y | 67.2 secs | 2 | 9-0 | Gd to Firm | Cartography (IRE) | Jun 29 2003 |
| 5f 140y | 65.6 secs | 9 | 9-10 | Good | Halmahera (IRE) | Sep 8 2004 |
| 6f | 69.6 secs | 2 | 8-11 | Good | Caesar Beware (IRE) | Sep 8 2004 |
| 6f | 69.7 secs | 3 | 8-9 | Gd to Firm | Iltimas (USA) | Jly 26 1995 |
| 6f 110y | 1m 17.9 | 2 | 8-13 | Good | Swan Nebula (USA) | Sep 8 2004 |
| 7f | 1m 22.6 | 2 | 9-1 | Good | Librettist (USA) | Sep 8 2004 |
| 7f | 1m 21.6 | 3 | 8-10 | Gd to Firm | Pastoral Pursuits | Sep 9 2004 |
| 1m | 1m 36.5 | 2 | 8-6 | Gd to Firm | Singhalese | Sep 9 2004 |
| 1m (R) | 1m 37.4 | 2 | 9-0 | Gd to Firm | Midnight Line (USA) | Sep 11 1997 |
| 1m | 1m 35.3 | 3 | 9-0 | Gd to Firm | Gneiss | May 2 1994 |
| 1m (R) | 1m 36.6 | 7 | 9-9 | Gd to Firm | Invader | Jun 29 2003 |
| 1m 2f 60y | 2m 13.4 | 2 | 8-8 | Good | Yard Bird | Nov 6 1981 |
| 1m 2f 60y | 2m 5.4 | 3 | 8-8 | Gd to Firm | Carlito Brigante | Jly 26 1995 |
| 1m 4f | 2m 27.7 | 3 | 8-12 | Gd to Firm | Takwin (IRE) | Sep 9 2000 |
| 1m 6f 132y | 3m 2.2 | 3 | 8-3 | Gd to Firm | Brier Creek | Sep 10 1992 |
| 2m 110y | 3m 34.4 | 4 | 9-12 | Gd to Firm | Farsi | Jun 12 1992 |
| 2m 2f | 3m 50.2 | 7 | 9-1 | Gd to Firm | Boreas | Sep 12 2002 |

## EPSOM

| Distance | Time | Age | Weight | Going | Horse | Date |
|---|---|---|---|---|---|---|
| 5f | 55.0 secs | 2 | 8-9 | Gd to Firm | Prince Aslia | Jun 9 1995 |
| 5f | 53.6 secs | 4 | 9-5 | Firm | Indigenous | Jun 2 1960 |
| 6f | 67.8 secs | 2 | 8-11 | Gd to Firm | Showbrook | Jun 5 1991 |
| 6f | 67.3 secs | 5 | 8-12 | Good | Loyal Tycoon (IRE) | Jun 7 2003 |
| 7f | 1m 21.3 | 2 | 8-9 | Gd to Firm | Red Peony | Jul 29 2004 |
| 7f | 1m 20.1 | 4 | 8-7 | Firm | Capistrano | Jun 7 1972 |

| | | | | | | |
|---|---|---|---|---|---|---|
| 1m 114y | 1m 42.8 | 2 | 8-5 | Gd to Firm | Nightstalker | Aug 30 1988 |
| 1m 114y | 1m 40.7 | 3 | 8-6 | Gd to Firm | Sylva Honda | Jun 5 1991 |
| 1m 2f 18y | 2m 3.5 | 5 | 7-13 | Good | Crossbow | Jun 7 1967 |
| 1m 4f 10y | 2m 32.3 | 3 | 9-0 | Gd to Firm | Lammtarra | Jun 10 1995 |

## FOLKESTONE

| Distance | Time | Age | Weight | Going | Horse | Date |
|---|---|---|---|---|---|---|
| 5f | 58.4 secs | 2 | 9-2 | Gd to Firm | Pivotal | Nov 6 1995 |
| 5f | 58.6 secs | 3 | 9-0 | Gd to Firm | Zarzu | Jun 28 2002 |
| 6f | 1m 10.8 | 2 | 8-9 | Good | Boomerang Blade | Jly 16 1998 |
| 6f | 69.5 secs | 4 | 8-12 | Gd to Firm | Double Oscar (IRE) | Jly 14 1997 |
| 6f 189y | 1m 23.7 | 2 | 8-11 | Good | Hen Harrier | Jly 3 1996 |
| 6f 189y | 1m 22.0 | 4 | 10-0 | Firm | Neuwest | Jun 28 1996 |
| 7f | 1m 25.2 | 2 | 8-11 | Gd to Firm | Persian Jasmine | Aug 12 2002 |
| 7f | 1m 21.4 | 3 | 8-9 | Firm | Cielamour (USA) | Aug 9 1988 |
| 1m 1f 149y | 1m 59.7 | 3 | 8-6 | Gd to Firm | Dizzy | Jly 23 1991 |
| 1m 4f | 2m 33.2 | 4 | 8-8 | Hard | Snow Blizzard | Jun 30 1992 |
| 1m 7f 92y | 3m 23.1 | 3 | 9-11 | Firm | Mata Askari | Sep 12 1991 |
| 2m 93y | 3m 34.9 | 3 | 8-12 | Gd to Firm | Candle Smoke (USA) | Aug 20 1996 |

## GOODWOOD

| Distance | Time | Age | Weight | Going | Horse | Date |
|---|---|---|---|---|---|---|
| 5f | 57.5 secs | 2 | 8-12 | Gd to Firm | Poets Cove | Aug 3 1990 |
| 5f | 56.0 secs | 5 | 9-0 | Gd to Firm | Rudi s Pet | Jly 27 1999 |
| 6f | 69.8 secs | 2 | 8-11 | Gd to Firm | Bachir (IRE) | Jly 28 1999 |
| 6f | 69.5 secs | 4 | 8-3 | Firm | For The Present | Jly 30 1994 |
| 7f | 1m 24.9 | 2 | 8-11 | Gd to Firm | Ekraar | Jly 29 1999 |
| 7f | 1m 23.8 | 3 | 8-7 | Firm | Brief Glimpse (IRE) | Jly 25 1995 |
| 1m | 1m 38.1 | 2 | 8-11 | Good | Rimrod (USA) | Sep 13 2002 |
| 1m | 1m 35.6 | 3 | 8-13 | Gd to Firm | Aljabr (USA) | Jly 28 1999 |
| 1m 1f | 1m 52.8 | 3 | 9-6 | Good | Vena (IRE) | Jly 27 1995 |
| 1m 1f 192y | 2m 3.4 | 3 | 8-12 | Good | Moon Ballad (IRE) | Sep 14 2002 |
| 1m 3f | 2m 23.0 | 3 | 8-8 | Gd to Firm | Asian Heights | May 22 2001 |
| 1m 4f | 2m 31.5 | 3 | 8-10 | Firm | Presenting | Jly 25 1995 |
| 1m 6f | 2m 58.5 | 4 | 9-2 | Gd to Firm | Mowbray | Jly 27 1999 |
| 2m | 3m 21.6 | 5 | 9-2 | Gd to Firm | Jardine s Lookout | Aug 1 2002 |
| 2m 4f | 4m 11.7 | 3 | 7-10 | Firm | Lucky Moon | Aug 2 1990 |

## HAMILTON

| Distance | Time | Age | Weight | Going | Horse | Date |
|---|---|---|---|---|---|---|
| 5f 4y | 58.0 secs | 3 | 7-8 | Firm | Fair Dandy | Sep 25 1972 |
| 5f 4y | 58.0 secs | 5 | 8-6 | Firm | Golden Sleigh | Sep 6 1972 |
| 6f 5y | 1m 10.0 | 2 | 8-12 | Gd to Firm | Break The Code | Aug 24 1999 |
| 6f 5y | 69.3 secs | 4 | 8-7 | Firm | Marcus Game | Jly 11 1974 |
| 1m 65y | 1m 45.8 | 2 | 8-11 | Firm | Hopeful Subject | Sep 24 1973 |
| 1m 65y | 1m 42.7 | 6 | 7-7 | Firm | Cranley | Sep 25 1972 |
| 1m 1f 36y | 1m 54.1 | 5 | 9-4 | Gd to Firm | Jedi Knight | Aug 24 1999 |
| 1m 3f 16y | 2m 20.7 | 8 | 9-9 | Firm | Desert Fighter | Jly 9 1999 |
| 1m 3f 16y | 2m 20.7 | 5 | 9-8 | Gd to Firm | Wadi | Jly 20 2000 |
| 1m 4f 17y | 2m 32.0 | 4 | 10-0 | Firm | Hold Tight | Aug 22 1983 |
| 1m 4f 17y | 2m 32.0 | 4 | 7-4 | Firm | Fine Point | Aug 24 1981 |
| 1m 5f 9y | 2m 45.1 | 6 | 9-6 | Firm | Mentalasanythin | Jun 14 1995 |

## HAYDOCK

| Distance | Time | Age | Weight | Going | Horse | Date |
|---|---|---|---|---|---|---|
| 5f | 59.2 secs | 2 | 9-4 | Firm | Money For Nothing | Aug 21 1964 |
| 5f | 58.5 secs | 6 | 8-9 | Gd to Firm | Whistler | Aug 9 2003 |
| 6f | 1m 10.9 | 4 | 9-9 | Gd to Firm | Wolfhound (USA) | Sep 4 1993 |
| 6f | 69.9 secs | 4 | 9-0 | Gd to Firm | Iktamal (USA) | Sep 7 1996 |
| 7f 30y | 1m 29.4 | 2 | 9-0 | Gd to Firm | Apprehension | Sep 7 1996 |
| 7f 30y | 1m 26.8 | 3 | 8-7 | Gd to Firm | Lady Zonda | Sep 28 2002 |
| 1m 30y | 1m 40.6 | 2 | 8-12 | Gd to Firm | Besiege | Sep 7 1996 |
| 1m 30y | 1m 40.1 | 3 | 9-2 | Firm | Untold Riches (USA) | Jly 11 1999 |
| 1m 2f 120y | 2m 22.2 | 2 | 8-11 | Soft | Persian Haze | Oct 9 1994 |
| 1m 2f 120y | 2m 8.5 | 3 | 8-7 | Gd to Firm | Fahal (USA) | Aug 5 1995 |
| 1m 3f 200y | 2m 26.4 | 5 | 8-2 | Firm | New Member | Jly 4 1970 |
| 1m 6f | 2m 59.5 | 3 | 8-3 | Gd to Firm | Castle Secret | Sep 30 1989 |
| 2m 45y | 3m 27.0 | 4 | 8-13 | Firm | Prince of Peace | May 26 1984 |
| 2m 1f 130y | 3m 55.0 | 3 | 8-12 | Good | Crystal Spirit | Sep 8 1990 |

## KEMPTON

| Distance | Time | Age | Weight | Going | Horse | Date |
|---|---|---|---|---|---|---|
| 5f | 58.3 secs | 2 | 9-0 | Firm | Schweppeshire Lad | Jun 3 1978 |
| 5f | 57.4 secs | 4 | 9-3 | Gd to Firm | Almaty (IRE) | May 31 1997 |
| 6f | 1m 10.6 | 2 | 8-10 | Gd to Firm | Don Puccini | May 29 1999 |
| 6f | 69.7 secs | 4 | 9-1 | Gd to Firm | Magic Rainbow | May 29 1999 |
| 7f | 1m 26.7 | 2 | 8-8 | Good | Exclusive | Sep 10 1997 |
| 7f | 1m 24.7 | 2 | 9-0 | Gd to Firm | Canons Park | Jun 28 1995 |
| 7f | 1m 23.5 | 3 | 9-2 | Gd to Firm | Wild Rice | Aug 2 1995 |
| 7f | 1m 23.6 | 3 | 9-0 | Gd to Firm | Shaheen (USA) | May 31 1997 |
| 1m | 1m 43.4 | 2 | 7-0 | Good | Fascinating | Nov 3 1956 |
| 1m | 1m 38.7 | 2 | 9-0 | Gd to Firm | Taverner Society (IRE) | Sep 22 1997 |
| 1m | 1m 35.8 | 4 | 9-1 | Firm | County Broker | May 23 1984 |
| 1m | 1m 35.3 | 3 | 8-12 | Gd to Firm | Private Line | Jun 28 1995 |
| 1m 1f | 1m 50.0 | 4 | 9-11 | Gd to Firm | Bahrqueen (USA) | Jun 25 2003 |
| 1m 2f | 1m 59.5 | 4 | 9-6 | Firm | Batshoof | Apr 6 1990 |
| 1m 3f 30y | 2m 16.2 | 4 | 9-2 | Firm | Shernazar | Sep 6 1985 |
| 1m 4f | 2m 30.1 | 6 | 8-5 | Firm | Going Going | Sep 7 1985 |
| 1m 6f 92y | 3m 6.5 | 4 | 9-8 | Gd to Firm | Renzo (IRE) | Sep 21 1997 |
| 2m | 3m 24.3 | 4 | 8-9 | Gd to Firm | Eminence Grise (IRE) | May 29 1999 |

## LEICESTER

| Distance | Time | Age | Weight | Going | Horse | Date |
|---|---|---|---|---|---|---|
| 5f 2y | 58.4 secs | 2 | 9-0 | Firm | Cutting Blade | Jun 9 1986 |
| 5f 2y | 58.0 secs | 3 | 7-13 | Gd to Firm | Emerald Peace (IRE) | Sep 5 2000 |
| 5f 218y | 1m 10.1 | 2 | 9-0 | Firm | Thordis (IRE) | Oct 24 1995 |
| 5f 218y | 69.4 secs | 3 | 8-12 | Gd to Firm | Lakeland Beauty | May 29 1990 |
| 7f 9y | 1m 22.8 | 2 | 8-6 | Good | Miss Dragonfly (IRE) | Sep 22 1997 |
| 7f 9y | 1m 20.8 | 3 | 8-7 | Firm | Flower Bowl | Jun 9 1986 |
| 1m 8y | 1m 34.5 | 2 | 8-9 | Firm | Lady Carla | Oct 24 1995 |
| 1m 8y | 1m 33.6 | 5 | 7-13 | Gd to Firm | Derryquinn | Aug 13 2000 |
| 1m 9y | 1m 39.2 | 4 | 8-11 | Firm | Nashaab (USA) | May 28 2001 |
| 1m 1f 218y | 2m 5.3 | 2 | 9-1 | Gd to Firm | Windsor Castle | Oct 14 1996 |
| 1m 1f 218y | 2m 2.4 | 3 | 8-11 | Firm | Effigy | Nov 4 1985 |
| 1m 1f 218y | 2m 2.4 | 4 | 9-6 | Gd to Firm | Lady Angharad (IRE) | Jun 18 2000 |
| 1m 3f 183y | 2m 27.1 | 5 | 8-12 | Gd to Firm | Murghem (IRE) | Jun 18 2000 |

## LINGFIELD (TURF)

| Distance | Time | Age | Weight | Going | Horse | Date |
|---|---|---|---|---|---|---|
| 5f | 57.1 secs | 2 | 8-9 | Good | Emerald Peace | Aug 6 1999 |
| 5f | 56.2 secs | 3 | 9-1 | Gd to Firm | Eveningperformance | Jly 25 1994 |
| 6f | 68.6 secs | 2 | 9-3 | Firm | The Ritz | Jun 11 1965 |
| 6f | 68.2 secs | 6 | 9-10 | Firm | Al Amead | Jly 2 1986 |
| 7f | 1m 21.3 | 2 | 7-6 | Firm | Mandav | Oct 3 1980 |
| 7f | 1m 20.1 | 3 | 8-7 | Gd to Firm | Zelah (IRE) | May 13 1998 |
| 7f 140y | 1m 29.9 | 2 | 8-12 | Firm | Rather Warm | Nov 7 1978 |
| 7f 140y | 1m 26.7 | 3 | 8-6 | Fast | Hiaam | Nov 7 1978 |
| 1m 1f | 1m 52.4 | 4 | 9-2 | Gd to Firm | Quandary (USA) | Jly 15 1995 |
| 1m 2f | 2m 4.6 | 3 | 9-3 | Firm | Usran | Jly 15 1989 |
| 1m 3f 106y | 2m 23.9 | 3 | 8-5 | Firm | Night-Shirt | Jly 14 1990 |
| 1m 6f | 2m 59.1 | 5 | 9-5 | Firm | Ibn Bey | Jly 1 1989 |
| 2m | 3m 23.7 | 3 | 9-5 | Gd to Firm | Lauries Crusader | Aug 13 1988 |

## LINGFIELD (A.W)

| Distance | Time | Age | Weight | Going | Horse | Date |
|---|---|---|---|---|---|---|
| 5f | 58.6 secs | 2 | 9-7 | Standard | Classy Cleo (IRE) | Nov 28 1997 |
| 5f | 57.3 secs | 4 | 9-5 | Standard | No Time (IRE) | Mar 20 2004 |
| 6f | 1m 11.5 | 2 | 8-8 | Standard | Two Step Kid (USA) | Oct 27 2003 |
| 6f | 1m 10.5 | 4 | 9-4 | Standard | J Cheever Loophole | Nov 23 1989 |
| 7f | 1m 24.0 | 2 | 8-12 | Standard | Scottish Castle | Nov 2 1990 |
| 7f | 1m 22.9 | 3 | 9-3 | Standard | Confronter | Jly 18 1992 |
| 1m | 1m 36.5 | 2 | 9-5 | Standard | San Pier Niceto | Nov 30 1989 |
| 1m | 1m 36.3 | 5 | 9-5 | Standard | Vanroy | Nov 30 1989 |
| 1m 2f | 2m 2.6 | 3 | 8-10 | Standard | Compton Bolter | Nov 18 2000 |
| 1m 4f | 2m 29.2 | 6 | 8-13 | Standard | Ursa Major | Dec 28 2000 |
| 1m 5f | 2m 42.9 | 3 | 9-7 | Standard | Global Dancer | Dec 7 1994 |
| 2m | 3m 20.0 | 3 | 9-0 | Standard | Yenoora | Aug 8 1992 |

## MUSSELBURGH

| Distance | Time | Age | Weight | Going | Horse | Date |
|---|---|---|---|---|---|---|
| 5f | 57.7 secs | 2 | 8-2 | Firm | Arasong | May 16 1994 |
| 5f | 57.3 secs | 3 | 8-12 | Firm | Corunna | Jun 3 2000 |
| 7f 30y | 1m 28.4 | 2 | 8-8 | Firm | Sand Bankes | Jun 26 2000 |
| 7f 30y | 1m 26.3 | 3 | 9-5 | Firm | Waltzing Wizard | Aug 22 2002 |
| 1m | 1m 40.3 | 2 | 8-12 | Gd to Firm | Succession | Sep 26 2004 |
| 1m | 1m 38.8 | 6 | 9-4 | Gd to Firm | Sea Storm (IRE) | May 29 2004 |
| 1m 1f | 1m 50.8 | 3 | 9-2 | Firm | Short Respite | Aug 22 2002 |
| 1m 4f | 2m 33.7 | 3 | 9-11 | Firm | Alexandrine | Jun 26 2000 |
| 1m 5f | 2m 51.1 | 9 | 8-6 | Gd to Firm | Cosmic Case | July 28 2004 |
| 1m 6f | 2m 59.2 | 3 | 9-7 | Firm | Forum Chris | Jly 3 2000 |
| 2m | 3m 26.6 | 5 | 9-6 | Gd to Firm | Jack Dawson (IRE) | Jun 1 2002 |

## NEWBURY

| Distance | Time | Age | Weight | Going | Horse | Date |
|---|---|---|---|---|---|---|
| 5f 34y | 59.1 secs | 2 | 8-6 | Gd to Firm | Superstar Leo | Jly 22 2000 |
| 5f 34y | 59.2 secs | 3 | 9-5 | Gd to Firm | The Trader (IRE) | Aug 18 2001 |
| 6f 8y | 1m 11.4 | 2 | 8-6 | Gd to Firm | Ascension | Jly 22 2000 |
| 6f 8y | 69.8 secs | 3 | 8-12 | Gd to Firm | Auenklang (GER) | Jly 22 2000 |
| 7f | 1m 23.0 | 2 | 8-11 | Gd to Firm | Haafhd | Aug 15 2003 |
| 7f | 1m 21.5 | 3 | 8-4 | Gd to Firm | Three Points | Jly 21 2000 |
| 1m | 1m 37.7 | 2 | 8-10 | Good | Ethmaar (USA) | Sep 17 1999 |
| 1m | 1m 35.1 | 3 | 8-11 | Gd to Firm | Dancing Tribute (USA) | Sep 23 1989 |
| 1m 1f | 1m 49.6 | 3 | 8-0 | Gd to Firm | Holtye | May 21 1995 |
| 1m 2f 6y | 2m 1.2 | 3 | 8-7 | Gd to Firm | Wall Street (USA) | Jly 20 1996 |
| 1m 3f 5y | 2m 16.5 | 3 | 8-9 | Gd to Firm | Grandera (IRE) | Sep 22 2001 |
| 1m 4f 5y | 2m 29.2 | 4 | 8-9 | Hard | Vidi Vic | Jun 21 1951 |
| 1m 5f 61y | 2m 44.9 | 5 | 10-0 | Gd to Firm | Mystic Hill | Jly 20 1996 |
| 2m | 3m 25.4 | 8 | 9-12 | Gd to Firm | Moonlight Quest | Jly 19 1996 |

## NEWCASTLE

| Distance | Time | Age | Weight | Going | Horse | Date |
|---|---|---|---|---|---|---|
| 5f | 58.8 secs | 2 | 9-0 | Firm | Atlantic Viking (IRE) | Jun 4 1997 |
| 5f | 58.0 secs | 4 | 9-2 | Firm | Princess Oberon | Jly 23 1994 |
| 6f | 1m 12.3 | 2 | 9-0 | Gd to Firm | Crosspeace (IRE) | Sep 29 2004 |
| 6f | 1m 10.6 | 8 | 9-5 | Firm | Tedburrow | Jly 1 2000 |
| 7f | 1m 24.2 | 2 | 9-0 | Gd to Firm | Iscan (IRE) | Aug 31 1998 |
| 7f | 1m 23.3 | 4 | 9-2 | Gd to Firm | Quiet Venture | Aug 31 1998 |
| 1m | 1m 38.9 | 2 | 9-0 | Gd to Firm | Stowaway | Oct 2 1996 |
| 1m | 1m 38.9 | 3 | 8-12 | Firm | Jacamar | Jly 22 1989 |
| 1m 3y | 1m 37.1 | 2 | 8-3 | Gd to Firm | Hoh Steamer (IRE) | Aug 31 1998 |
| 1m 3y | 1m 37.3 | 3 | 8-8 | Gd to Firm | Its Magic | May 27 1999 |
| 1m 1f 9y | 2m 3.2 | 2 | 8-13 | Soft | Response | Oct 30 1993 |
| 1m 1f 9y | 1m 52.3 | 3 | 6-3 | Good | Ferniehurst | Jun 23 1936 |
| 1m 2f 32y | 2m 6.5 | 4 | 8-9 | Fast | Missionary Ridge | Jly 29 1990 |

| Distance | Time | Age | Weight | Going | Horse | Date |
|---|---|---|---|---|---|---|
| 1m 4f 93y | 2m 37.3 | 5 | 8-12 | Firm | Retender | Jun 25 1994 |
| 1m 6f 97y | 3m 6.4 | 3 | 9-6 | Gd to Firm | One Off | Aug 6 2003 |
| 2m 19y | 3m 24.3 | 4 | 8-10 | Good | Far Cry (IRE) | Jun 26 1999 |

## NEWMARKET (ROWLEY)

| Distance | Time | Age | Weight | Going | Horse | Date |
|---|---|---|---|---|---|---|
| 5f | 58.7 secs | 2 | 8-5 | Gd to Firm | Valiant Romeo | Oct 3 2002 |
| 5f | 56.8 secs | 6 | 9-2 | Gd to Firm | Lochsong | Apr 30 1994 |
| 6f | 69.6 secs | 2 | 8-11 | Gd to Firm | Oasis Dream | Oct 3 2002 |
| 6f | 1m 10.2 | 4 | 9-8 | Gd to Firm | Lake Coniston | Apr 18 1995 |
| 7f | 1m 22.9 | 2 | 8-11 | Gd to Firm | Grosvenor Square(IRE) | Sep 21 2004 |
| 7f | 1m 22.2 | 4 | 9-5 | Gd to Firm | Perfolia | Oct 17 1991 |
| 1m | 1m 35.7 | 2 | 9-0 | Gd to Firm | Forward Move (IRE) | Sep 21 2004 |
| 1m | 1m 34.5 | 4 | 9-0 | Gd to Firm | Desert Deer | Oct 3 2002 |
| 1m 1f | 1m 47.2 | 4 | 9-5 | Firm | Beauchamp Pilot | Oct 5 2002 |
| 1m 2f | 2m 4.6 | 2 | 9-4 | Good | Highland Chieftain | Nov 2 1985 |
| 1m 2f | 2m 1.0 | 3 | 8-10 | Good | Palace Music | Oct 20 1984 |
| 1m 4f | 2m 27.1 | 5 | 8-12 | Gd to Firm | Eastern Breeze | Oct 3 2003 |
| 1m 6f | 2m 54.3 | 5 | 8-6 | Gd to Firm | Tudor Island | Sep 30 1994 |
| 2m | 3m 19.5 | 5 | 9-5 | Gd to Firm | Grey Shot | Oct 4 1997 |
| 2m 2f | 3m 47.5 | 3 | 7-12 | Hard | Whiteway | Oct 15 1947 |

## NEWMARKET (JULY)

| Distance | Time | Age | Weight | Going | Horse | Date |
|---|---|---|---|---|---|---|
| 5f | 58.5 secs | 2 | 8-10 | Good | Seductress | Jly 10 1990 |
| 5f | 57.3 secs | 6 | 8-12 | Gd to Firm | Rambling Bear | Jan 1 1999 |
| 6f | 1m 10.6 | 2 | 8-10 | Gd to Firm | Mujtahid | Jly 11 1990 |
| 6f | 69.5 secs | 3 | 8-13 | Gd to Firm | Stravinsky (USA) | Jly 8 1999 |
| 7f | 1m 24.1 | 2 | 8-11 | Good | My Hansel | Aug 27 1999 |
| 7f | 1m 22.5 | 3 | 9-7 | Firm | Ho Leng (IRE) | Jly 9 1998 |
| 1m | 1m 39.0 | 2 | 8-11 | Good | Traceability | Aug 25 1995 |
| 1m | 1m 35.5 | 3 | 8-6 | Gd to Firm | Lovers Knot | Jly 8 1998 |
| 1m 110y | 1m 44.1 | 3 | 8-11 | Good | Golden Snake | Apr 15 1999 |
| 1m 2f | 2m 0.9 | 4 | 9-3 | Gd to Firm | Elhayq (IRE) | May 1 1999 |
| 1m 4f | 2m 25.2 | 4 | 9-2 | Good | Craigsteel | Jly 6 1999 |
| 1m 6f 175y | 3m 4.2 | 3 | 8-5 | Good | Arrive | Jly 11 2001 |
| 2m 24y | 3m 20.2 | 7 | 9-10 | Good | Yorkshire | Jly 11 2001 |

## NOTTINGHAM

| Distance | Time | Age | Weight | Going | Horse | Date |
|---|---|---|---|---|---|---|
| 5f 13y | 57.9 secs | 2 | 8-9 | Firm | Hoh Magic | May 13 1994 |
| 5f 13y | 57.9 secs | 9 | 9-1 | Good | Bahamian Pirate (USA) | Mar 31 2004 |
| 6f 15y | 1m 11.4 | 2 | 811 | Firm | Jameelapi | Aug 8 1983 |
| 6f 15y | 1m 10.0 | 4 | 9-2 | Firm | Ajanac | Aug 8 1988 |
| 1m 54y | 1m 40.8 | 2 | 9-0 | Gd to Firm | King s Loch | Sep 2 1991 |
| 1m 54y | 1m 39.6 | 4 | 8-2 | Gd to Firm | Blake s Treasure | Sep 2 1991 |
| 1m 1f 213y | 2m 5.6 | 2 | 9-0 | Firm | Al Salite | Oct 28 1985 |
| 1m 1f 213y | 2m 2.3 | 2 | 9-0 | Firm | Ayaabi | Jly 21 1984 |
| 1m 6f 15y | 2m 57.8 | 3 | 8-10 | Firm | Buster Jo | Oct 1 1985 |
| 2m 9y | 3m 24.0 | 5 | 7-7 | Firm | Fet | Oct 5 2036 |
| 2m 2f 18y | 3m 55.1 | 9 | 9-10 | Gd to Firm | Pearl Run | May 1 1990 |

## PONTEFRACT

| Distance | Time | Age | Weight | Going | Horse | Date |
|---|---|---|---|---|---|---|
| 5f | 61.1 secs | 2 | 9-0 | Firm | Golden Bounty | Sep 20 2001 |
| 5f | 60.8 secs | 4 | 8-9 | Firm | Blue Maeve | Sep 29 2004 |
| 6f | 1m 14.0 | 2 | 9-3 | Firm | Fawzi | Sep 6 1983 |
| 6f | 1m 12.6 | 3 | 7-13 | Firm | Merry One | Aug 29 1970 |
| 1m 4y | 1m 42.8 | 2 | 9-13 | | Star Spray | Sep 6 1970 |
| 1m 4y | 1m 42.8 | 2 | 9-0 | Firm | Alasil (USA) | Sep 26 2002 |
| 1m 4y | 1m 40.6 | 4 | 9-10 | Gd to Firm | Island Light | Apr 13 2002 |
| 1m 2f 6y | 2m 10.1 | 2 | 9-0 | Firm | Shanty Star | Oct 7 2002 |
| 1m 2f 6y | 2m 8.2 | 4 | 7-8 | Hard | Happy Hector | Jly 9 1979 |
| 1m 2f 6y | 2m 8.2 | 3 | 7-13 | Hard | Tom Noddy | Aug 21 1972 |
| 1m 4f 8y | 2m 34.1 | 3 | 9-5 | Gd to Firm | High Action | Aug 6 2003 |
| 2m 1f 22y | 3m 42.1 | 3 | 9-2 | Firm | Night Eye | Sep 6 1983 |
| 2m 1f 216y | 3m 51.1 | 3 | 8-8 | Firm | Kudz | Sep 9 1986 |
| 2m 5f 122y | 4m 47.8 | 4 | 8-4 | Firm | Physical | May 14 1984 |

## REDCAR

| Distance | Time | Age | Weight | Going | Horse | Date |
|---|---|---|---|---|---|---|
| 5f | 56.9 secs | 2 | 9-0 | Firm | Mister Joel | Oct 24 1995 |
| 5f | 56.1 secs | 5 | 9-10 | Firm | Salviati (USA) | Jun 4 2002 |
| 6f | 68.8 secs | 2 | 8-3 | Gd to Firm | Obe Gold | Oct 2 2004 |
| 6f | 68.6 secs | 3 | 9-2 | Gd to Firm | Sizzling Saga | Jun 21 1991 |
| 7f | 1m 21.9 | 2 | 8-11 | Firm | Nagwa | Sep 27 1975 |
| 7f | 1m 21.0 | 3 | 9-1 | Firm | Empty Quarter | Oct 3 1995 |
| 1m | 1m 36.1 | 2 | 7-11 | Gd to Soft | Master Soden | Nov 1 1999 |
| 1m | 1m 33.1 | 3 | 9-5 | Firm | Night Wink (USA) | Oct 24 1995 |
| 1m 1f | 1m 52.4 | 2 | 9-0 | Firm | Spear (IRE) | Sep 13 2004 |
| 1m 1f | 1m 48.5 | 5 | 8-12 | Firm | Mellottie | Jly 25 1990 |
| 1m 2f | 2m 10.1 | 2 | 8-11 | Good | Adding | Nov 10 1989 |
| 1m 2f | 2m 1.4 | 5 | 9-2 | Firm | Eradicate | May 28 1990 |
| 1m 3f | 2m 17.2 | 3 | 8-9 | Firm | Photo Call | Aug 7 1990 |
| 1m 5f 135y | 2m 54.7 | 6 | 9-10 | Firm | Brodessa | Jun 20 1992 |
| 1m 6f 19y | 2m 59.9 | 3 | 8-7 | Firm | Trainglot | Jly 25 1990 |
| 2m 4y | 3m 24.9 | 3 | 9-3 | Gd to Firm | Subsonic | Oct 8 1991 |
| 2m 3f | 4m 10.1 | 5 | 7-4 | Gd to Firm | Seldom In | Aug 9 1991 |

## RIPON

| Distance | Time | Age | Weight | Going | Horse | Date |
|---|---|---|---|---|---|---|
| 5f | 57.8 secs | 2 | 8-8 | Firm | Super Rocky | Jly 5 1991 |
| 5f | 57.6 secs | 5 | 8-5 | Good | Broadstairs Beauty | May 21 1995 |
| 6f | 1m 10.4 | 2 | 9-2 | Good | Cumbrian Venture | Aug 17 2002 |
| 6f | 69.8 secs | 4 | 9-8 | Gd to Firm | Tadeo | Aug 16 1997 |
| 6f | 69.8 secs | 5 | 7-10 | Firm | Quoit | Jly 23 1966 |
| 1m | 1m 40.1 | 2 | 8-4 | Gd to Firm | Whittle Warrior | Aug 31 2002 |
| 1m | 1m 37.0 | 4 | 7-10 | Firm | Crown Witness | Aug 25 1980 |
| 1m 1f | 1m 50.4 | 3 | 9-2 | Gd to Firm | Bold Words (CAN) | Apr 9 1997 |
| 1m 2f | 2m 2.6 | 3 | 9-4 | Firm | Swift Sword | Jly 20 1990 |
| 1m 4f 60y | 2m 32.2 | 7 | 8-3 | Hard | Crusaders Horn | Aug 8 1950 |
| 1m 4f 60y | 2m 32.2 | 6 | 8-7 | Firm | Cholo | Sep 27 1941 |
| 2m | 3m 27.8 | 6 | 9-0 | Gd to Firm | Samain | Aug 31 1993 |

## SALISBURY

| Distance | Time | Age | Weight | Going | Horse | Date |
|---|---|---|---|---|---|---|
| 5f | 59.8 secs | 2 | 8-5 | Gd to Firm | Tarf (USA) | Aug 17 1995 |
| 5f | 59.4 secs | 3 | 8-11 | Firm | Bellsabanging | May 5 1993 |
| 6f | 1m 12.1 | 2 | 8-0 | Gd to Firm | Parisian Lady (IRE) | Jun 10 1997 |
| 6f | 1m 11.5 | 4 | 8-7 | Gd to Firm | Prince Sky | Jun 25 1986 |
| 6f 212y | 1m 25.9 | 2 | 9-0 | Firm | More Royal (USA) | Jun 29 1995 |
| 6f 212y | 1m 24.9 | 3 | 9-7 | Firm | High Summer (USA) | Sep 5 1996 |
| 1m | 1m 40.4 | 2 | 8-13 | Firm | Choir Master (USA) | Sep 17 2002 |
| 1m | 1m 38.6 | 4 | 8-8 | Firm | Take Heart | Jly 14 1990 |
| 1m 1f 198y | 2m 4.9 | 3 | 8-6 | Gd to Firm | Zante | Aug 12 1998 |
| 1m 4f | 2m 31.6 | 3 | 9-5 | Gd to Firm | Arrive | Jun 27 2001 |
| 1m 6f 15y | 2m 59.4 | 3 | 8-6 | Gd to Firm | Tabareeh | Sep 2 1999 |

## SANDOWN

| Distance | Time | Age | Weight | Going | Horse | Date |
|---|---|---|---|---|---|---|
| 5f 6y | 59.4 secs | 2 | 9-3 | Firm | Times Time | Jly 22 1982 |
| 5f 6y | 58.8 secs | 6 | 8-9 | Gd to Firm | Palacegate Touch | Sep 17 1996 |
| 7f 16y | 1m 27.8 | 2 | 8-12 | Gd to Firm | Red Camellia | Jly 25 1996 |
| 7f 16y | 1m 26.3 | 3 | 9-0 | Firm | Mawsuff | Jun 14 1983 |
| 1m 14y | 1m 41.1 | 2 | 8-11 | Fast | Reference Point | Sep 23 1986 |
| 1m 14y | 1m 39.0 | 3 | 8-8 | Firm | Linda s Fantasy | Aug 19 1983 |
| 1m 1f | 1m 54.6 | 2 | 8-8 | Gd to Firm | French Pretender | Sep 20 1988 |
| 1m 1f | 1m 52.6 | 3 | 8-9 | Gd to Firm | Darnelle | Aug 19 1988 |
| 1m 2f 7y | 2m 2.1 | 4 | 8-11 | Firm | Kalaglow | May 31 1982 |
| 1m 3f 91y | 2m 21.6 | 4 | 8-3 | Fast | Aylesfield | Jly 7 1984 |
| 1m 6f | 2m 56.9 | 4 | 8-7 | Gd to Firm | Lady Rosanna | Jly 19 1989 |
| 2m 78y | 3m 29.9 | 6 | 9-2 | Firm | Sadeem | May 29 1989 |

## SOUTHWELL (TURF)

| Distance | Time | Age | Weight | Going | Horse | Date |
|---|---|---|---|---|---|---|
| 6f | 1m 15.6 | 2 | 8-11 | Gd to Firm | Yaselda | Jly 4 2001 |
| 6f | 1m 14.1 | 4 | 9-12 | Gd to Firm | Miss Haggis | Jly 26 1993 |
| 7f | 1m 29.1 | 2 | 9-0 | Gd to Firm | Dulcet Spear | Jly 4 2001 |
| 7f | 1m 26.5 | 3 | 9-5 | Gd to Firm | Sea Storm (IRE) | Jly 5 2001 |
| 1m 2f | 2m 10.0 | 3 | 9-4 | Good | Bronze Maquette (IRE) | Jly 26 1993 |
| 1m 3f | 2m 21.9 | 3 | 8-5 | Gd to Firm | Pims Gunner (IRE) | Aug 15 1991 |
| 1m 4f | 2m 34.4 | 5 | 9-3 | Gd to Firm | Corn Lily | Aug 10 1991 |
| 2m | 3m 34.1 | 5 | 9-1 | Gd to Firm | Triplicate | Sep 20 1991 |

## SOUTHWELL (A.W)

| Distance | Time | Age | Weight | Going | Horse | Date |
|---|---|---|---|---|---|---|
| 5f | 58.5 secs | 2 | 8-1 | Standard | Primrose and Rose | Apr 4 2001 |
| 5f | 57.4 secs | 4 | 9-4 | Standard | Woodland Blaze | May 8 2003 |
| 6f | 1m 14.0 | 2 | 8-5 | Standard | Panalo | Nov 8 1989 |
| 6f | 1m 13.3 | 3 | 9-2 | Standard | Rambo Express | Dec 18 1990 |
| 7f | 1m 27.1 | 2 | 8-2 | Standard | Mystic Crystal | Nov 20 1990 |
| 7f | 1m 26.8 | 5 | 8-4 | Standard | Amenable | Dec 13 1990 |
| 1m | 1m 38.0 | 2 | 8-9 | Standard | Alpha Rascal | Nov 13 1990 |
| 1m | 1m 38.0 | 2 | 8-10 | Standard | Andrew s First | Dec 30 1989 |
| 1m | 1m 37.2 | 3 | 8-6 | Standard | Valira | Nov 3 1990 |
| 1m 3f | 2m 21.5 | 4 | 9-7 | Standard | Tempering | Dec 5 1990 |
| 1m 4f | 2m 33.9 | 4 | 9-12 | Standard | Fast Chick | Nov 8 1989 |
| 1m 6f | 3m 1.6 | 3 | 7-7 | Standard | Qualitair Aviator | Dec 1 1989 |
| 1m 6f | 3m 1.6 | 3 | 7-8 | Standard | Erevnon | Dec 29 1990 |
| 2m | 3m 37.6 | 9 | 8-12 | Standard | Old Hubert | Dec 5 1990 |

## THIRSK

| Distance | Time | Age | Weight | Going | Horse | Date |
|---|---|---|---|---|---|---|
| 5f | 57.2 secs | 2 | 9-7 | Gd to Firm | Proud Boast | Aug 5 2000 |
| 5f | 56.9 secs | 5 | 9-6 | Firm | Charlie Parkes | April 11 2003 |
| 6f | 69.2 secs | 2 | 9-6 | Gd to Firm | Westcourt Magic | Aug 25 1995 |
| 6f | 68.8 secs | 6 | 9-4 | Firm | Johayro | Jly 23 1999 |
| 7f | 1m 23.7 | 2 | 8-9 | Firm | Courting | Jly 23 1999 |
| 7f | 1m 22.8 | 4 | 8-5 | Firm | Silver Haze | May 21 1988 |
| 1m | 1m 37.9 | 2 | 9-0 | Firm | Sunday Symphony | Sep 4 2004 |
| 1m | 1m 34.8 | 4 | 8-13 | Firm | Yearsley | May 5 1990 |
| 1m 4f | 2m 29.9 | 5 | 9-12 | Firm | Gallery God | Jun 4 2001 |
| 2m | 3m 22.3 | | - | | Tomaschek | Aug 1 1964 |

## WARWICK

| Distance | Time | Age | Weight | Going | Horse | Date |
|---|---|---|---|---|---|---|
| 5f | 58.4 secs | 2 | 9-7 | Gd to Firm | Prenonamoss | Oct 9 1990 |
| 5f | 57.7 secs | 4 | 9-6 | Gd to Firm | Little Edward | Jly 7 2002 |
| 5f 110y | 63.6 secs | 5 | 8-6 | Gd to Firm | Dizzy In The Head | Jun 27 2004 |
| 6f 21y | 1m 10.6 | 2 | 9-0 | Gd to Firm | Viking Spirit | Sep 6 2004 |
| 6f 21y | 69.6 secs | 6 | 9-2 | Firm | Parkside Pursuit | Jun 20 2004 |
| 7f 26y | 1m 22.9 | 2 | 9-0 | Firm | Country Rambler(USA) | Jun 20 2004 |
| 7f 26y | 1m 21.2 | 3 | 8-11 | Gd to Firm | Lucky Spin | Jun 19 2004 |
| 1m 22y | 1m 37.1 | 3 | 8-11 | Firm | Orinocovsky (IRE) | Jun 26 2002 |
| 1m 2f 188y | 2m 16.2 | 6 | 7-12 | Gd to Firm | Scented Air | Apr 21 2003 |
| 1m 4f 134y | 2m 39.5 | 3 | 8-13 | Gd to Firm | Maimana (IRE) | Jun 22 2002 |
| 1m 6f 135y | 3m 7.5 | 3 | 9-7 | Gd to Firm | Burma Baby (USA) | Jly 2 1999 |
| 2m 39y | 3m 27.9 | 3 | 8-1 | Firm | Decoy | Jun 26 2002 |

## WINDSOR

| Distance | Time | Age | Weight | Going | Horse | Date |
|---|---|---|---|---|---|---|
| 5f 10y | 58.9 secs | 2 | 9-0 | Firm | Strictly Private | Jly 22 1974 |
| 5f 10y | 58.9 secs | 2 | 9-0 | Gd to Firm | Bad As I Wannabe | Jly 31 2000 |
| 5f 10y | 58.3 secs | 5 | 7-10 | Gd to Firm | Beyond The Clouds | Jun 2 2001 |
| 5f 217y | 69.0 secs | 2 | 8-7 | Gd to Firm | Options Open | Jly 25 1994 |
| 5f 217y | 1m 10.1 | 3 | 8-4 | Firm | Sweet Relief | Sep 11 1978 |
| 6f | 1m 10.5 | 2 | 9-5 | Gd to Firm | Cubism (USA) | Aug 17 1998 |
| 6f | 1m 10.3 | 4 | 8-12 | Gd to Firm | Carlton (IRE) | Jun 22 1998 |
| 1m 67y | 1m 44.4 | 2 | 9-0 | Gd to Firm | Temple Place | Sep 29 2003 |
| 1m 67y | 1m 40.6 | 7 | 9-8 | Gd to Firm | Gateman | Jun 26 2004 |
| 1m 2f 7y | 2m 3.0 | 2 | 9-1 | Firm | Moomba Masquerade | May 19 1990 |
| 1m 3f 135y | 2m 21.5 | 3 | 9-2 | Firm | Double Florin | May 19 1980 |

## WOLVERHAMPTON (Fibresand A.W.)

| Distance | Time | Age | Weight | Going | Horse | Date |
|---|---|---|---|---|---|---|
| 5f | 61.4 secs | 2 | 9-0 | Standard | Danehurst | Oct 3 2000 |
| 5f | 60.1 secs | 7 | 8-7 | Standard | Sir Tasker | Jan 4 1995 |
| 6f | 1m 13.8 | 2 | 9-0 | Standard | Shouf Al Badou (USA) | Oct 2 1999 |
| 6f | 1m 13.8 | 2 | 8-9 | Standard | Nozomi (IRE) | Oct 3 1998 |
| 6f | 1m 13.8 | 2 | 8-7 | Standard | Reactive (IRE) | Oct 17 1998 |
| 6f | 1m 13.8 | 2 | 8-3 | Standard | Thurlestone Rock | Oct 21 2002 |
| 6f | 1m 13.0 | 3 | 9-0 | Standard | Magic Glade | Jly 26 2002 |
| 7f | 1m 28.0 | 2 | 8-1 | Standard | Aswhatilldois (IRE) | Oct 17 2000 |
| 7f | 1m 26.8 | 4 | 9-11 | Standard | Musafi (USA) | Jan 10 1998 |
| 1m 100y | 1m 48.2 | 2 | 9-0 | Standard | Gralmano (IRE) | Dec 29 1997 |
| 1m 100y | 1m 45.7 | 5 | 9-0 | Standard | Cashmere Lady | Jun 21 1997 |
| 1m 1f 79y | 2m 0.2 | 2 | 8-11 | Standard | Bound | Oct 20 2000 |
| 1m 1f 79y | 1m 57.5 | 3 | 9-7 | Standard | Hal s Pal | Aug 17 1996 |
| 1m 4f | 2m 35.0 | 4 | 9-7 | Standard | State Approval | Jun 21 1997 |
| 1m 6f 166y | 3m 11.4 | 4 | 8-11 | Standard | Noufari | Jan 4 1995 |
| 2m 46y | 3m 36.6 | 7 | 9-10 | Standard | Harik | Dec 5 2001 |

## YARMOUTH

| Distance | Time | Age | Weight | Going | Horse | Date |
|---|---|---|---|---|---|---|
| 5f 43y | 60.4 secs | 2 | 8-6 | Gd to Firm | Ebba | Jly 26 1999 |
| 5f 43y | 59.8 secs | 4 | 8-13 | Gd to Firm | Roxanne Mill | Aug 25 2002 |
| 6f 3y | 1m 10.4 | 2 | 9-0 | Fast | Lanchester | Aug 15 1988 |
| 6f 3y | 69.9 secs | 4 | 8-9 | Firm | Malhub (USA) | Jun 13 2002 |
| 7f 3y | 1m 22.2 | 2 | 9-0 | Gd to Firm | Warrshan | Sep 14 1988 |
| 7f 3y | 1m 22.2 | 3 | 8-7 | Firm | Cielamour | Sep 15 1988 |
| 1m 3y | 1m 36.3 | 2 | 8-2 | Gd to Firm | Outrun | Sep 15 1988 |
| 1m 3y | 1m 33.9 | 3 | 8-8 | Firm | Bonne Etoile | Jun 27 1995 |
| 1m 2f 21y | 2m 3.1 | 4 | 8-9 | Gd to Firm | Supreme Sound | Aug 9 1998 |
| 1m 3f 101y | 2m 23.1 | 3 | 8-9 | Firm | Rahil | Jly 1 1993 |
| 1m 6f 17y | 2m 57.8 | 3 | 8-2 | Gd to Firm | Barakat | Jly 24 1990 |
| 2m | 3m 26.7 | 4 | 8-2 | Gd to Firm | Alhesn (USA) | Jly 26 1999 |
| 2m 2f 51y | 3m 56.8 | 4 | 9-10 | Firm | Provence | Sep 19 1991 |

## YORK

| Distance | Time | Age | Weight | Going | Horse | Date |
|---|---|---|---|---|---|---|
| 5f | 57.3 secs | 2 | 7-8 | Gd to Firm | Lyric Fantasy | Aug 20 1992 |
| 5f | 56.1 secs | 3 | 9-3 | Gd to Firm | Dayjur | Aug 23 1990 |
| 5f 3y | 58.4 secs | 2 | 8-11 | Gd to Firm | Howick Falls (USA) | Aug 20 2003 |
| 5f 3y | 56.2 secs | 3 | 9-9 | Gd to Firm | Oasis Dream | Aug 21 2003 |
| 6f | 69.5 secs | 2 | 9-0 | Gd to Firm | Indiscreet (CAN) | Aug 22 1996 |
| 6f | 68.8 secs | 4 | 9-4 | Gd to Firm | Shalford | May 14 1992 |
| 6f 3y | 1m 10.6 | 2 | 8-11 | Gd to Firm | Carry on Katie (USA) | Aug 21 2003 |
| 6f 3y | 69.4 secs | 3 | 8-2 | Gd to Firm | Dazzling Bay | Jun 14 2003 |
| 6f 214y | 1m 22.9 | 2 | 8-10 | Gd to Firm | Options Open | Aug 16 1994 |
| 6f 214y | 1m 21.3 | 3 | 9-0 | Firm | Bold Fact (USA) | Aug 20 1998 |
| 6f 217y | 1m 22.6 | 2 | 9-0 | Gd to Firm | Moonlight Man | Oct 9 2003 |
| 6f 217y | 1m 22.0 | 4 | 9-0 | Gd to Firm | Vanderlin | Aug 21 2003 |
| 7f 202y | 1m 37.2 | 2 | 9-4 | Gd to Firm | The Wife | Sep 2 1999 |
| 7f 202y | 1m 34.8 | 4 | 8-10 | Gd to Firm | Concer Un | Aug 22 1996 |
| 7f 205y | 1m 36.0 | 5 | 8-7 | Gd to Firm | Faithful Warrior (USA) | Jly 11 2003 |
| 1m 205y | 1m 52.4 | 2 | 8-1 | Gd to Firm | Oral Evidence | Oct 6 1988 |
| 1m 205y | 1m 47.0 | 3 | 8-10 | Gd to Firm | Gold Academy | Sep 2 1999 |
| 1m 208y | 1m 48.9 | 4 | 8-5 | Gd to Firm | Krugerrand (USA) | Jun 14 2003 |
| 1m 2f 85y | 2m 6.1 | 3 | 9-0 | Firm | Erhaab | May 11 1994 |
| 1m 2f 88y | 2m 6.5 | 4 | 9-4 | Gd to Firm | Far Lane (USA) | Jly 12 2003 |
| 1m 3f 195y | 2m 25.1 | 3 | 8-9 | Gd to Firm | Sea Wave (IRE) | Aug 18 1998 |
| 1m 3f 198y | 2m 27.4 | 4 | 9-4 | Gd to Firm | Islington (IRE) | Aug 20 2003 |
| 1m 5f 194y | 2m 51.8 | 3 | 8-7 | Gd to Firm | Tuning | Aug 19 1998 |
| 1m 5f 197y | 2m 52.5 | 4 | 8-9 | Gd to Firm | Mamool (IRE) | May 15 2003 |
| 1m 7f 195y | 3m 18.4 | 3 | 8-0 | Gd to Firm | Dam Busters | Aug 16 1988 |

# Racing Post top rated 2004

(Best performance figures recorded between 9th November 2003 and 6th November 2004)

Ghostzapper (USA)............................133
Doyen (IRE)......................................131
Smarty Jones (USA)..........................131
Silent Witness (AUS)........................130
Falbrav (IRE)......................................129
Congaree (USA)................................129
Rakti....................................................129
Haafhd.................................................129
Bago (FR)...........................................129
Pleasantly Perfect (USA)..................128
Pico Central (BRZ)............................128
Cherry Mix (FR)................................128
Roses In May (USA).........................128
Sulamani (IRE)..................................127
Medaglia D Oro (USA)......................127
Lucky Story (USA)............................127
Vinnie Roe (IRE)...............................126
Calstone Light O (JPN).....................126
Warrsan (IRE)....................................126
Nayyir..................................................126
Refuse To Bend (IRE).......................126
Grey Swallow (IRE)...........................126
Azamour (IRE)...................................126
Kitten s Joy (USA).............................126
Speightstown (USA)..........................126
Norse Dancer (IRE)...........................125
North Light (IRE)...............................125
Birdstone (USA).................................125
Shamardal (USA)...............................125
Azeri (USA)........................................124
Perfect Drift (USA).............................124
Somnus...............................................124
Symboli Kris S (USA).........................124
Soviet Song (IRE)...............................124
Powerscourt........................................124
Mister Monet (IRE)..............................124
Whipper (USA)....................................124
Ouija Board..........................................124
Champali (USA)..................................124
Better Talk Now (USA).......................124
Firebreak..............................................123
Bandari (IRE).......................................123
Total Impact (CHI)...............................123
Kalaman (IRE)......................................123
Chic.......................................................123
Snow Ridge (IRE)................................123
Sightseek (USA)..................................123
Hard Buck (BRZ).................................123
Attraction..............................................123
National Currency (SAF)....................123
Acropolis (IRE).....................................123
Kicken Kris (USA)................................123
Singletary (USA)..................................123
Cajun Beat (USA).................................123
Makybe Diva.........................................123
Egerton (GER)......................................123
Lion Heart (USA)..................................123
Nothing To Lose (USA)........................123
Lonhro (AUS)........................................122
Ikhtyar (IRE)..........................................122
Telegnosis (JPN)...................................122
Tsurumaru Boy (JPN)...........................122
Tiber (IRE)..............................................122
Shirocco (GER)......................................122
Kela (USA)..............................................122
Touch Of Land (FR)...............................122
Funny Cide (USA)..................................122
Tycoon.....................................................122
Zenno Rob Roy (JPN)...........................122
Rule Of Law (USA).................................122
During (USA)...........................................122
Quiff.........................................................122
Simonas (IRE).........................................122
Cheerful Fortune (NZ)............................122
Southern Image (USA)...........................122
Dubawi (IRE)...........................................122
Star Over The Bay (USA).......................122
Cape Of Good Hope................................121
Millenary...................................................121
Mubtaker (USA).......................................121
Electronic Unicorn (USA).......................121
Gamut (IRE).............................................121
Royal Millennium (IRE)...........................121
Patavellian (IRE)......................................121
Ashdown Express (IRE)..........................121
Chorist......................................................121
Policy Maker (IRE)...................................121
Risk Seeker..............................................121
Tap Dance City (USA).............................121
Mr O Brien (IRE).......................................121
Westerner..................................................121
Newfoundland (USA)...............................121
Polar Way..................................................121
Le Vie Dei Colori.......................................121
High Accolade...........................................121
Vallee Enchantee (IRE)............................121
Tante Rose (IRE)......................................121
Super Kid (NZ)..........................................121

Papineau ..... 121
Let The Lion Roar ..... 121
Figures (NZ) ..... 121
Stay Young (IRE) ..... 121
Bluesthestandard (USA) ..... 121
Saint Liam (USA) ..... 121
Grand Armee (AUS) ..... 121
One Cool Cat (USA) ..... 121
Prince Kirk (FR) ..... 121
Antonius Pius (USA) ..... 121
Diamond Green (FR) ..... 121
Percussionist (IRE) ..... 121
Latice (IRE) ..... 121
Lucky Owners (NZ) ..... 121
Mustanfar (USA) ..... 121
Reset (AUS) ..... 121
Our New Recruit (USA) ..... 121
The Cliff s Edge (USA) ..... 121
Ad Valorem (USA) ..... 121
Var (USA) ..... 121
Passing Glance ..... 120
Sarafan (USA) ..... 120
Paolini (GER) ..... 120
Right Approach ..... 120
Balto Star (USA) ..... 120
Salselon ..... 120
Request For Parole (USA) ..... 120
Magistretti (USA) ..... 120
Epalo (GER) ..... 120
Perfect Soul (IRE) ..... 120
My Cousin Matt (USA) ..... 120
Victory Moon (SAF) ..... 120
Peace Rules (USA) ..... 120
Ingrandire (JPN) ..... 120
Ancient World (USA) ..... 120
Bachelor Duke (USA) ..... 120
Soaring Free (CAN) ..... 120
Spark Of Life (AUS) ..... 120
Alinghi (AUS) ..... 120
Fire Slam (USA) ..... 120
Pohave (USA) ..... 120
Grand Zulu (AUS) ..... 120
Dance Hero (AUS) ..... 120
Electrocutionist (USA) ..... 120
Savabeel (AUS) ..... 120
Wilko (USA) ..... 120
Purge (USA) ..... 120
Afleet Alex (USA) ..... 120
Proud Accolade (USA) ..... 120
Gin And Sin (USA) ..... 120
Scintillation (AUS) ..... 120
Plastered (AUS) ..... 120
Frizzante ..... 119
The Tatling (IRE) ..... 119
Imperial Dancer ..... 119
Bowman s Crossing (IRE) ..... 119
Osterhase (IRE) ..... 119
Mr Dinos (IRE) ..... 119
Mamool (IRE) ..... 119
Fair Mix (IRE) ..... 119
Balance Of Game (JPN) ..... 119
Muqbil (USA) ..... 119
Pivotal Point ..... 119
Elegant Fashion (AUS) ..... 119
Monsieur Bond (IRE) ..... 119
Six Perfections (FR) ..... 119
Brian Boru ..... 119
Avonbridge ..... 119
Vangelis (USA) ..... 119
Fields Of Omagh (AUS) ..... 119
Cat Genius (USA) ..... 119
Vespone (IRE) ..... 119
Domestic Dispute (USA) ..... 119
Super Elegant (AUS) ..... 119
My Risk (FR) ..... 119
That s The Plenty (JPN) ..... 119
Senex (GER) ..... 119
Nebraska Tornado (USA) ..... 119
Utopia (JPN) ..... 119
Denebola (USA) ..... 119
Maraahel (IRE) ..... 119
Elvstroem (AUS) ..... 119
Beau s Town (USA) ..... 119
A Huevo (USA) ..... 119
Sweep Tosho (JPN) ..... 119
House Of Fortune (USA) ..... 119
Surveyor (SAF) ..... 119
Starcraft (NZ) ..... 119
Alke (USA) ..... 119
Oratorio (IRE) ..... 119
Charge Forward (AUS) ..... 119
King Kamehameha (JPN) ..... 119
Rebuttal (USA) ..... 119
Sweet Catomine (USA) ..... 119
Barolo ..... 118
Bahamian Pirate (USA) ..... 118
Dancing Bay ..... 118
Polish Summer ..... 118
Firebolt (IRE) ..... 118
The Trader (IRE) ..... 118
Evening Attire (USA) ..... 118
Orientor ..... 118
Sights On Gold (IRE) ..... 118
Systematic ..... 118
Fayr Jag (IRE) ..... 118
Ho Choi ..... 118
River Dancer (IRE) ..... 118
First Charter ..... 118